Prayer to the Holy Spirit

Come, Holy Spirit, and fill the hearts of the faithful, and kindle in them the fire of divine love.

V. Send forth your Spirit and they shall be created.

R. And you shall renew the face of the earth.

Let us pray: O God, who have instructed the hearts of the faithful by the light of the Holy Spirit; grant that by the gift of the same Spirit, we may be ever truly wise and rejoice in His consolation, through Christ our Lord. Amen.

THE CATHOLIC BIBLE

CONCORDANCE

Revised Standard Version, Catholic Edition

THE CATHOLIC BIBLE

CONCORDANCE

Revised Standard Version, Catholic Edition

C.W. LYONS
WITH THOMAS DELIDUKA

STEUBENVILLE, OHIO

Emmaus Road Publishing
827 North Fourth Street
Steubenville, Ohio 43952

13 12 11 10 2 3 4 5 6

Library of Congress Control Number: 2008940776
ISBN: 978-1-931018-49-4

Printed in China by Graphics TwoFortyFour, Inc.

Cover design and layout by
Catherine Ryland and
Theresa Westling

Table of Contents

To my mom and dad
from whose example
I have learned much
about sacrifice and commitment.

Foreword

SAINT Anthony of Padua is surely among the best loved of the saints in glory. He is the patron of those who search for lost objects. Artists portray him in his Franciscan habit, holding the baby Jesus.

We all call upon Saint Anthony when we're looking for something. But I invoke him today for a different reason. I recall him to you because he was a biblical scholar *par excellence*, with so prodigious a memory that he has been called "The Concordance."

Saint Anthony was a bit like the book you're holding in your hands. He was able to retrieve passages from the Bible at a moment's notice. Name a theme, and he could draw relevant Scriptures from many points in the biblical canon.

In fact, he was himself fond of the word "concordance" (in all its Latin equivalents), though he didn't use it to describe a book. He used it to describe a reality: the unity of the two testaments, the unity of the whole Bible.

> The God of the New Testament is one and the same as the God of the Old, and is indeed Jesus Christ the Son of God. We may apply to him the words of Isaiah: *I myself that spoke, behold, I am here* (Is 52:6). I spoke to the fathers in the prophets; I am here in the truth of the Incarnation. That is the justification for seeking *to concord* the scriptures of both Testaments.[1]

Saint Anthony was on to something important here, a truth we assume whenever we pick up one of these books we call a "biblical concordance." If the Bible were not a single book, then this book—and all the work that went into its making—would be in vain. If the Bible were not the work of a single principal author, God Himself, then why should we care to compare the Hebrew verbs of the Book of Genesis with their Greek equivalents in Revelation?

Our medieval Paduan was merely passing on a timeless truth of the faith. Almost a millennium before, the Fathers of the Egyptian desert had applied themselves to the same task, and for all the same reasons. They would chant all the Psalms every day; and, in those centuries when few people could own books, they would gather for daily and weekly *synaxes* to hear the Word of God and commit it to memory. In fourth-century Egypt, Saint Sisoes the Great was asked the secret to his wisdom and holiness. He said: "What shall I say to you? I read the New Testament, and I turn to the Old?"[2]

What those saints meant by *concordance* is "the juxtaposition and correlation of Scriptural passages, so that they illuminate and interpret one another." [3]

And that's what books like *The Catholic Bible Concordance* are up to. Saints Anthony and Sisoes would have loved to hold the book you're holding. In their day, there were no such comprehensive lexical indices to the Bible. To my knowledge, the first book that fits the bill appeared in the thirteenth century, produced by a team of five hundred monks!

Yet here we are. We live in a day when great books and search engines can power through the Bible in seconds—doing the work of many monks, and even many monasteries. We live in a day when Catholic Bible-study curricula are available free online (see *SalvationHistory.com*), along with scriptural homily helps and audio lectures on biblical studies. We live in a day when—for the first time in decades—a Catholic publisher has brought out an exhaustive concordance.

This book is an invaluable tool for Christians in all walks of life. It will speed the research of scholars in fields as diverse as biblical studies, theology, literary criticism, and the history of ideas. It will be a grace to lay people as they pray and ponder the Scriptures. It will empower preachers—priests and deacons—as they prepare their homilies.

This book is a sign of the times, and these are great times indeed for Catholic biblical studies. But, unlike former periods of renewal, ours is not confined by the walls of the abbeys or by the towers of the universities. Books like *The Catholic Bible Concordance* give us a kind of spiritual technology—interpretive elevators, to borrow a metaphor from Saint Therese of Lisieux.

May we all rise to the occasion, using tools like *The Catholic Bible Concordance* to become "concordances" ourselves, like Saint Anthony and so many of our ancestors in the faith.

Scott Hahn, Ph.D
Steubenville, Ohio

[1] S.R.P. Spilsbury, *The Concordance of Scripture: The Homiletic and Exigetical Methods of St. Anthony of Padua*, doctoral dissertation, University of Bristol, 1999. Posted online at *http://www.franciscan-archive.org/antonius/spils-d0.html*

[2] Quoted in Douglas Burton-Christie, *The Word in the Desert* (New York: Oxford University Press, 1993), 112

[3] Spilsbury, *op. cit.*

Introduction

In his opening speech to the Second Vatican Council, Pope John XXIII clearly set forth the mission of the Council; namely, to transmit the doctrine of the Catholic Church, "pure and integral, without any attenuation or distortion."[1] He reaffirmed that the teaching of the Catholic Church is already clearly defined, but acknowledged that the deposit of faith needed to be presented in a manner that would engage a rapidly changing world. With this in mind, the Council produced one of its most splendid documents, *Dei Verbum.* With clarity and brevity, this document set forth the Church's teaching on divine revelation and how it is preserved and handed on in Sacred Tradition and Sacred Scripture.

Recalling the words of Saint Jerome, the Council reminds all Christians that biblical literacy is of utmost importance—that ignorance of Scripture is ignorance of Christ.[2] This understanding inspired the Fathers of the early Church to truthful and fruitful interpretation of Sacred Scripture through the eyes of the Church.

Of course, the Fathers of the Church did not interpret Scripture in isolation, but in the context of Apostolic tradition. When one reads Scripture, one is not simply reading the words of a highly regarded author, but the very "word of God."[3] For "all scripture is inspired by God and profitable for teaching, for reproof, for correction, and for training in righteousness" (2 Tim 3:16). In other words, the content of Scripture is not arbitrary, but has been divinely deposited for the sake of our salvation and must be understood within the tradition through which it was received. The Church invites all the Christian faithful, from laymen to bishops, to listen carefully to the Word of God in Sacred Scripture and to understand it within the Sacred Tradition of the Mystical Body of Christ (Eph 4:4-13).

Since there is great reverence for Scripture among Protestants as well as Catholics, the Second Vatican Council encouraged collaboration on Bible translations with our separated brethren—knowing that such ventures would benefit all Christians. The Revised Standard Version (RSV) of the Bible is a venerable Protestant translation, which sought to "embody the best results of modern scholarship as to the meaning of the Scriptures."[4] In 1952, the RSV translation was complete and published. Then in 1966, in accordance with *Dei Verbum* and with ecclesial approval, the Catholic Biblical Association of Great Britain produced and published a Catholic edition of the Revised Standard Version (RSV-CE).

Ever since its original publication, the RSV-CE has become the translation of choice for Scripture scholars and beginners alike. In fact, the RSV-CE is exclusively used in the English edition of the *Catechism of the Catholic Church* and as the basis for Scripture quotes used in English translations of Magisterial documents. The RSV-CE is also the preferred English translation for the Congregation of the Clergy's Scripture study and resource site, *www.clerus.org*. The volume you now hold in your hands, the exhaustive concordance of the Revised Standard Version-Catholic Edition, is an effort to help continue the Church's mission to make Scripture accessible and understandable for all Christians.

The Catholic Bible Concordance indexes the text of both the original and second editions of the RSV-CE. The second edition, published in 2006, aligns the translation more closely with traditional Catholic renderings of particular verses. For instance, in the original RSV-CE, the Hebrew word *almah* in Isaiah 7:14 is translated as "young woman", instead of the traditional translation of "virgin". While "young woman" is a viable translation, the Church has always used "virgin" because of the indisputable support from the early Church, which recognized "virgin" to be more accurate in light of the Church's inspired interpretive tradition. This is illustrated by the fact that both the Greek Septuagint and Matthew 1:23 use *parthenos*, which specifically means virgin, when translating Isaiah 7:14. Therefore, the second Catholic edition of the RSV restores the use of "virgin" to the text of Isaiah 7:14. While the majority of the revisions are minor and do not involve this level of significance, the desire to make this volume a truly comprehensive and valuable resource motivated the inclusion of a complete list of these second edition revisions as an appendix at the end of this volume.

How to Use This Concordance

The Catholic Bible Concordance is exhaustive, which means that every word in the entire Bible has been indexed for quick and easy reference. Words are listed alphabetically, and to the right of each indexed word is a number in parenthesis that indicates how many times the word appears in the Bible. Each instance of the word is listed by book, chapter, and verse and is placed in its immediate context by including a brief phrase in which the word is used. Below is a sample for the name of *Abel*, Adam and Eve's second child. Note that the word *Abel* is represented only by a single capital letter A in the contextual listings.

ABEL (15)

Gen	4:2	And again, she bore his brother A
	4:2	Now A was a keeper of sheep, and Cain
	4:4	of the ground, and A brought of the firstlings
	4:4	LORD had regard for A and his offering,
	4:8	Cain said to A his brother, "Let us go
	4:8	up against his brother A, and killed him.
	4:9	to Cain, "Where is A your brother?" He said,
	4:25	another child instead of A, for Cain slew him."
2Sam	20:14	tribes of Israel to A of Beth-maacah; and all
	20:15	and besieged him in A of Beth-maacah; they cast
	20:18	but ask counsel at A; and so they settled
Mt	23:34	the blood of innocent A to the blood of
Lk	11:51	from the blood of A to the blood of
Heb	11:4	By faith A offered to God a more acceptable
	12:24	that speaks more graciously than the blood of A

One can use this work for abundant purposes. First, the *Concordance* is essential for finding and comparing multiple verses that contain the same or similar key words. For example, if you desire to pursue a systematic study on "sacrifice", you could effortlessly find all the references to "sacrifice" and begin reading the passages in context to gain a broad understanding of the topic at hand. You could then easily expand your search to include the word "sacrificial", and other variations, to make sure you are not overlooking important texts.

Second, the *Concordance* is very effective for preparing a Bible study or catechesis on a particular topic. While the *Catechism* makes extensive use of Scripture, it cannot reference all relevant passages. With a concordance, you can assemble a catechesis on Baptism by quickly locating verses that refer to "baptism", "baptize", "washing", "regeneration", "forgiveness", "sin" and more.

Third, the *Concordance* is tremendously helpful for finding a verse that one can only partially recall. If you can remember only a word or two from a verse, simply look up that word in the concordance and you will see the list of verses that contain that word. You can then scan the references and promptly find the verse you need.

This book will prove an indispensable tool for scholars studying particular topics, catechists and apologists preparing to explain the Faith to others, and the incalculable number of faithful who simply desire to become more familiar with Sacred Scripture. Use this resource as a key to unlock the awesome treasures contained in the Scriptures, and may it help you to "let the word of Christ dwell in you richly" (Col 3:16).

Like a wise shepherd who knows the needs of his flock, Pope John XXIII convened the Second Vatican Council and set in motion a renewal in the Church that has only just begun. The Council touched on every aspect of Catholic life and made it clear that Scripture is to be a cornerstone for all who profess the Christian faith. This renewal is for bishops, priests, religious, and all the lay faithful. The Council hoped in confidence that "just as the life of the Church is strengthened through more frequent celebration of the Eucharistic mystery, similarly we may hope for a new stimulus for the life of the Spirit from a growing reverence for the word of God, which 'lasts forever'" (Is. 40:8; see 1 Pet 1:23-25).[5]

With special gratitude we thank the author of this volume, Christopher Lyons, and his talented colleague, Thomas Deliduka, for the invaluable work of providing the Church with *The Catholic Bible Concordance*. He undertook this daunting task to help Catholics more fully learn and understand the Word of God. May his work bear abundant fruit in all who make use of this unique resource.

Mike Sullivan
Publisher,
Emmaus Road Publishing

[1] John XXIII
[2] *DV* 25
[3] *DV* 24
[4] RSV-CE Introduction
[5] *DV* 26

Abbreviations

OLD TESTAMENT
Gen/Genesis
Ex/Exodus
Lev/Leviticus
Num/Numbers
Deut/Deuteronomy
Josh/Joshua
Judg/Judges
Ruth/Ruth
1Sam/1 Samuel
2Sam/2 Samuel
1Kgs/1 Kings
2Kgs/2 Kings
1Chr/1 Chronicles
2Chr/2 Chroncles
Ezra/Ezra
Neh/Nehemiah
Tob/Tobit
Jud/Judith
Esth/Esther
Job/Job
Ps/Psalms
Prov/Proverbs
Eccl/Ecclesiastes
Song/Song of Solomon
Wis/Wisdom
Sir/Sirach
Is/Isaiah
Jer/Jeremiah
Lam/Lamentations
Bar/Baruch
Ezek/Ezekiel
Dan/Daniel
Hos/Hosea
Joel/Joel
Amos/Amos
Obad/Obadiah
Jon/Jonah
Mic/Micah
Nah/Nahum
Hab/Habakkuk
Zeph/Zephaniah
Hag/Haggai
Zech/Zechariah
Mal/Malachi
1Mac/1 Maccabees
2Mac/2 Maccabees

NEW TESTAMENT
Mt/Matthew
Mk/Mark
Lk/Luke
Jn/John
Acts/Acts of the Apostles
Rom/Romans
1Cor/1 Corinthians
2Cor/2 Corinthians
Gal/Galatians
Eph/Ephesians
Phil/Phillipians
Col/Colossians
1Thes/1 Thessalonians
2Thes/2 Thessalonians
1Tim/1 Timothy
2Tim/2 Timothy
Tit/Titus
Philem/Philemon
Heb/Hebrews
Jas/James
1Pet/1 Peter
2Pet/2 Peter
1Jn/1 John
2Jn/2 John
3Jn/3 John
Jude/Jude
Rev/Revelation

MAIN CONCORDANCE

A

AARON (358)

Ex 4:14 said, "Is there not A, your brother, the Levite?
4:27 The LORD said to A, "Go into the wilderness
4:28 And Moses told A all the words of the
4:29 Then Moses and A went and gathered together all
4:30 And A spoke all the words which the LORD
5:1 Afterward Moses and A went to Pharaoh and said,
5:4 to them, "Moses and A, why do you take
5:20 They met Moses and A, who were waiting for
6:13 spoke to Moses and A, and gave them a
6:20 and she bore him A and Moses, the years
6:23 A took to wife Elisheba, the daughter of Amminadab
6:25 Eleazar, A's son, took to wife one of the
6:26 These are the A and Moses to whom the
6:27 of Israel from Egypt, this Moses and this A
7:1 God to Pharaoh; and A your brother shall be
7:2 I command you; and A your brother shall tell
7:6 And Moses and A did so; they did as
7:7 eighty years old, and A eighty-three years old, when
7:8 said to Moses and A,
7:9 you shall say to A, 'Take your rod and
7:10 So Moses and A went to Pharaoh and did
7:10 as the LORD commanded; A cast down his rod
7:12 But A's rod swallowed up their rods.
7:19 to Moses, "Say to A, 'Take your rod and
7:20 Moses and A did as the LORD commanded; in
8:5 to Moses, "Say to A, 'Stretch out your hand
8:6 So A stretched out his hand over the waters
8:8 Pharaoh called Moses and A, and said, "Entreat the
8:12 So Moses and A went out from Pharaoh; and
8:16 to Moses, "Say to A, 'Stretch out your rod
8:17 And they did so; A stretched out his hand
8:25 Pharaoh called Moses and A, and said, "Go, sacrifice
9:8 said to Moses and A, "Take handfuls of ashes
9:27 and called Moses and A, and said to them,
10:3 So Moses and A went in to Pharaoh, and
10:8 So Moses and A were brought back to Pharaoh;
10:16 Pharaoh called Moses and A in haste, and said,
11:10 Moses and A did all these wonders before Pharaoh;
12:1 said to Moses and A in the land of
12:28 had commanded Moses and A, so they did.
12:31 he summoned Moses and A by night, and said,
12:43 said to Moses and A, "This is the ordinance
12:50 LORD commanded Moses and A, so they did.
15:20 prophetess, the sister of A, took a timbrel in
16:2 murmured against Moses and A in the wilderness,
16:6 So Moses and A said to all the people
16:9 And Moses said to A, "Say to the whole
16:10 And as A spoke to the whole congregation of
16:33 And Moses said to A, "Take a jar, and
16:34 LORD commanded Moses, so A placed it before the
17:10 with Amalek; and Moses, A, and Hur went up
17:12 sat upon it, and A and Hur held up
18:12 sacrifices to God; and A came with all the
19:24 and come up bringing A with you; but do
24:1 the LORD, you and A, Nadab, and Abihu, and
24:9 Then Moses and A, Nadab, and Abihu, and seventy
24:14 you again; and, behold, A and Hur are with
27:21 is before the testimony, A and his sons shall
28:1 bring near to you A your brother, and his
28:1 serve me as priests– A and Aaron's sons, Nadab
28:1 as priests–Aaron and A's sons, Nadab and Abihu,
28:2 make holy garments for A your brother, for glory
28:3 mind, that they make A's garments to consecrate him
28:4 make holy garments for A your brother and his
28:12 sons of Israel; and A shall bear their names
28:29 So A shall bear the names of the sons
28:30 they shall be upon A's heart, when he goes
28:30 before the LORD; thus A shall bear the judgment
28:35 it shall be upon A when he ministers, and
28:38 It shall be upon A's forehead, and Aaron shall
28:38 upon Aaron's forehead, and A shall take upon himself
28:40 "And for A's sons you shall make coats and
28:41 shall put them upon A your brother, and upon
28:43 they shall be upon A, and upon his sons,
29:4 You shall bring A and his sons to the
29:5 garments, and put on A the coat and the
29:9 Thus you shall ordain A and his sons.
29:10 A and his sons shall lay their hands upon
29:15 of the rams, and A and his sons shall
29:19 the other ram; and A and his sons shall
29:20 the right ear of A and upon the tips
29:21 and sprinkle it upon A and his garments, and
29:24 in the hands of A and in the hands
29:26 of the ram of A's ordination and wave it
29:27 since it is for A and for his sons.
29:28 It shall be for A and his sons as
29:29 "The holy garments of A shall be for his
29:32 a holy place; and A and his sons shall
29:35 you shall do to A and to his sons,
29:44 meeting and the altar; A also and his sons
30:7 And A shall burn fragrant incense on it; every
30:8 burn it, and when A sets up the lamps
30:10 A shall make atonement upon its horns once a
30:19 in it, with which A and his sons shall
30:30 And you shall anoint A and his sons, and
31:10 the holy garments for A the priest and the
32:1 gathered themselves together to A, and said to him,
32:2 And A said to them, "Take off the rings
32:3 were in their ears, and brought them to A
32:5 When A saw this, he built an altar before
32:5 altar before it; and A made proclamation and said,
32:21 And Moses said to A, "What did this people
32:22 And A said, "Let not the anger of my
32:25 had broken loose (for A had let them break
32:35 made the calf which A made.
34:30 And when A and all the people of Israel
34:31 called to them; and A and all the leaders
35:19 the holy garments for A the priest, and the
38:21 Ithamar the son of A the priest.
39:1 the holy garments for A; as the LORD had
39:27 of fine linen, for A and his sons,
39:41 the holy garments for A the priest, and the

Lev 1:5 before the LORD; and A's sons the priests shall
1:7 and the sons of A the priest shall put
1:8 upon the fire; and A's sons the priests shall
1:11 before the LORD, and A's sons the priests shall
2:2 and bring it to A's sons the priests.
2:3 offering shall be for A and his sons; it
2:10 offering shall be for A and his sons; it
3:2 tent of meeting; and A's sons the priests shall
3:5 Then A's sons shall burn it on the altar
3:8 tent of meeting; and A's sons shall throw its
3:13 and the sons of A shall throw its blood
6:9 said to Moses, "Command A and his sons, saying,
6:14 The sons of A shall offer it before the
6:16 the rest of it A and his sons shall
6:18 among the children of A may eat of it,
6:20 is the offering which A and his sons shall
6:22 The priest from among A's sons, who is anointed
6:25 to Moses, "Say to A and his sons, This
7:10 all the sons of A, one as well as
7:31 breast shall be for A and his sons.
7:33 among the sons of A who offers the blood
7:34 have given them to A the priest and to
7:35 is the portion of A and of his sons
8:2 said to Moses, "Take A and his sons with
8:6 And Moses brought A and his sons, and washed
8:12 the anointing oil on A's head, and anointed him,
8:13 And Moses brought A's sons, and clothed them with
8:14 the sin offering; and A and his sons laid
8:18 the burnt offering; and A and his sons laid
8:22 ram of ordination; and A and his sons laid
8:23 on the tip of A's right ear and on
8:24 And A's sons were brought, and Moses put some
8:27 in the hands of A and in the hands
8:30 and sprinkled it upon A and his garments, and
8:30 garments; so he consecrated A and his garments, and
8:31 And Moses said to A and his sons, "Boil
8:31 as I commanded, saying, A and his sons shall
8:36 And A and his sons did all the things
9:1 eighth day Moses called A and his sons and
9:2 and he said to A, "Take a bull calf
9:7 Then Moses said to A, "Draw near to the
9:8 So A drew near to the altar, and killed
9:9 And the sons of A presented the blood to
9:12 the burnt offering; and A's sons delivered to him
9:18 for the people; and A's sons delivered to him
9:21 and the right thigh A waved for a wave
9:22 Then A lifted up his hands toward the people
9:23 And Moses and A went into the tent of
10:1 Abihu, the sons of A, each took his censer,
10:3 Then Moses said to A, "This is what the
10:3 And A held his peace.
10:4 Uzziel the uncle of A, and said to them,

A

10:6 And Moses said to A and to Eleazar and
10:8 the LORD spoke to A, saying,
10:12 And Moses said to A and to Eleazar and
10:16 Ithamar, the sons of A who were left, saying,
10:19 And A said to Moses, "Behold, today they have
11:1 said to Moses and A,
13:1 said to Moses and A,
13:2 shall be brought to A the priest or to
14:33 said to Moses and A,
15:1 said to Moses and A,
16:1 the two sons of A, when they drew near
16:2 said to Moses, "Tell A your brother not to
16:3 But thus shall A come into the holy place:
16:6 "And A shall offer the bull as a sin
16:8 tent of meeting; and A shall cast lots upon
16:9 And A shall present the goat on which the
16:11 A shall present the bull as a sin offering
16:21 the live goat; and A shall lay both his
16:23 "Then A shall come into the tent of meeting,
17:2 to Moses, "Say to A and his sons, and
21:1 priests, the sons of A, and say to them
21:17 to Moses, "Say to A, None of your descendants
21:21 of the descendants of A the priest who has
21:24 So Moses spoke to A and to his sons
22:2 said to Moses, "Tell A and his sons to
22:4 of the line of A who is a leper
22:18 to Moses, "Say to A and his sons and
24:3 the tent of meeting, A shall keep it in
24:8 Every sabbath day A shall set it in order
24:9 it shall be for A and his sons, and
Num 1:3 to war, you and A shall number them, company
1:17 Moses and A took these men who have been
1:44 numbered, whom Moses and A numbered with the
2:1 said to Moses and A,
3:1 are the generations of A and Moses at the
3:2 of the sons of A: Nadab the first-born, and
3:3 of the sons of A, the anointed priests, whom
3:4 in the lifetime of A their father.
3:6 and set them before A the priest, that they
3:9 give the Levites to A and his sons; they
3:10 And you shall appoint A and his sons, and
3:32 Eleazar the son of A the priest was to
3:38 sunrise, were Moses and A and his sons, having
3:39 whom Moses and A numbered at the commandment
3:48 them is redeemed to A and his sons."
3:51 the redemption money to A and his sons, according
4:1 said to Moses and A,
4:5 is to set out, A and his sons shall
4:15 And when A and his sons have finished covering
4:16 Eleazar the son of A the priest shall have
4:17 said to Moses and A,
4:19 the most holy things: A and his sons shall
4:27 at the command of A and his sons, in
4:28 Ithamar the son of A the priest.
4:33 Ithamar the son of A the priest."
4:34 And Moses and A and the leaders of the
4:37 meeting, whom Moses and A numbered according to
4:41 meeting, whom Moses and A numbered according to
4:45 Merari, whom Moses and A numbered according to
4:46 Levites, whom Moses and A and the leaders of
6:23 to Moses, "Say to A and his sons, Thus
7:8 Ithamar the son of A the priest.
8:2 to Moses, "Say to A, When you set up
8:3 And A did so; he set up its lamps
8:11 upon the Levites, and A shall offer the Levites
8:13 the Levites to attend A and his sons, and
8:19 as a gift to A and his sons from
8:20 Thus did Moses and A and all the congregation
8:21 washed their clothes; and A offered them as a
8:21 before the LORD, and A made atonement for them
8:22 meeting in attendance upon A and his sons; as
9:6 came before Moses and A on that day;
10:8 And the sons of A, the priests, shall blow
12:1 Miriam and A spoke against Moses because of the
12:4 to Moses and to A and Miriam, "Come out,
12:5 the tent, and called A and Miriam; and they
12:10 And A turned towards Miriam, and behold, she was
12:11 And A said to Moses, "Oh, my lord, do
13:26 came to Moses and A and to all the
14:2 against Moses and A; the whole congregation said
14:5 Then Moses and A fell on their faces before
14:26 to Moses and to A,
15:33 him to Moses and A, and to all the
16:3 against Moses and against A, and said to them,
16:11 gathered together; what is A that you murmur
16:16 you and they, and A, tomorrow;
16:17 censers; you also, and A, each his censer."
16:18 of the tent of meeting with Moses and A
16:20 to Moses and to A,
16:37 Eleazar the son of A the priest to take
16:40 of the descendants of A, should draw near to
16:41 against Moses and against A, saying, "You have killed
16:42 against Moses and against A, they turned toward the
16:43 And Moses and A came to the front of
16:46 And Moses said to A, "Take your censer, and
16:47 So A took it as Moses said, and ran
16:50 And A returned to Moses at the entrance of
17:3 his rod, and write A's name upon the rod
17:6 and the rod of A was among their rods.
17:8 behold, the rod of A for the house of
17:10 back the rod of A before the testimony, to
18:1 the LORD said to A, "You and your sons
18:8 the LORD said to A, "And behold, I have
18:20 the LORD said to A, "You shall have no
18:28 the LORD's offering to A the priest.
19:1 to Moses and to A,
20:2 themselves together against Moses and against A
20:6 Then Moses and A went from the presence of
20:8 the congregation, you and A your brother, and tell
20:10 And Moses and A gathered the assembly together
20:12 said to Moses and A, "Because you did not
20:23 said to Moses and A at Mount Hor, on
20:24 the land of Edom, A shall be gathered to
20:25 Take A and Eleazar his son, and bring them
20:26 Mount Hor; and strip A of his garments, and
20:26 Eleazar his son; and A shall be gathered to
20:28 And Moses stripped A of his garments, and put
20:28 Eleazar his son; and A died there on the
20:29 the congregation saw that A was dead, all the
20:29 of Israel wept for A thirty days.
25:7 of Eleazar, son of A the priest, saw it,
25:11 of Eleazar, son of A the priest, has turned
26:1 Eleazar the son of A, the priest,
26:9 contended against Moses and A in the company of
26:59 she bore to Amram A and Moses and Miriam
26:60 And to A were born Nadab, Abihu, Eleazar and
26:64 numbered by Moses and A the priest, who had
27:13 people, as your brother A was gathered,
33:1 their hosts under the leadership of Moses and A
33:38 And A the priest went up Mount Hor at
33:39 And A was a hundred and twenty-three years old
Deut 9:20 was so angry with A that he was ready
9:20 and I prayed for A also at the same
10:6 There A died, and there he was buried; and
32:50 to your people, as A your brother died in
Josh 21:4 who were descendants of A the priest received by
21:10 to the descendants of A, one of the families
21:13 to the descendants of A the priest they gave
21:19 of the descendants of A, the priests, were in
24:5 I sent Moses and A, and I plagued Egypt
24:33 Eleazar the son of A died; and they buried
Judg 20:28 of Eleazar, son of A, ministered before it in
1Sam 12:6 appointed Moses and A and brought your fathers
12:8 LORD sent Moses and A, who brought forth your
1Chr 6:3 The children of Amram: A, Moses, and Miriam.
6:3 The sons of A: Nadab, Abihu, Eleazar, and Ithamar.
6:49 But A and his sons made offerings upon the
6:50 are the sons of A: Eleazar his son, Phinehas
6:54 to the sons of A of the families of
6:57 To the sons of A they gave the cities
12:27 of the house of A, and with him three
15:4 together the sons of A and the Levites:
23:13 The sons of Amram: A and Moses.
23:13 A was set apart to consecrate the most holy
23:28 assist the sons of A for the service of
23:32 attend the sons of A, their brethren, for the
24:1 of the sons of A were these.
24:1 The sons of A: Nadab, Abihu, Eleazar, and Ithamar.
24:19 established for them by A their father, as the
24:31 brethren the sons of A, in the presence of
27:17 son of Kemuel; for A, Zadok;
2Chr 13:9 LORD, the sons of A, and the Levites, and
13:10 who are sons of A, and Levites for their
26:18 priests the sons of A, who are consecrated to
29:21 priests the sons of A to offer them on
31:19 for the sons of A, the priests, who were
35:14 priests the sons of A were busied in offering
35:14 themselves and for the priests the sons of A
Ezra 7:5 of Eleazar, son of A the chief priest--
Neh 10:38 priest, the son of A, shall be with the
12:47 apart that which was for the sons of A
Tob 1:6 priests, the sons of A, at the altar.

Ps 77:20 a flock by the hand of Moses and A
99:6 Moses and A were among his priests, Samuel also
105:26 Moses his servant, and A whom he had chosen.
106:16 jealous of Moses and A, the holy one of
115:10 O house of A, put your trust in the
115:12 bless the house of A;
118:3 Let the house of A say, "His steadfast love
133:2 upon the beard of A, running down on the
135:19 O house of A, bless the LORD!
Sir 36:17 to the blessing of A for thy people, and
45:6 He exalted A, the brother of Moses, a holy
45:20 He added glory to A and gave him a
45:25 so the heritage of A is for his descendants.
50:13 all the sons of A in their splendor with
50:16 Then the sons of A shouted, they sounded the
Mic 6:4 sent before you Moses, A, and Miriam.
1Mac 7:14 of the line of A has come with the
Lk 1:5 of the daughters of A, and her name was
Acts 7:40 to Egypt, saying to A, 'Make for us gods
Heb 5:4 by God, just as A was.
7:11 rather than one named after the order of A
9:4 holding the manna, and A's rod that budded, and

ABADDON (7)

Job 26:6 naked before God, and A has no covering.
28:22 A and Death say, 'We have heard a rumor
31:12 fire which consumes unto A, and it would burn
Ps 88:11 declared in the grave, or thy faithfulness in A
Prov 15:11 Sheol and A lie open before the LORD, how
27:20 Sheol and A are never satisfied, and never satisfied
Rev 9:11 name in Hebrew is A, and in Greek he

ABAGTHA

Esth 1:10 Biztha, Harbona, Bigtha and A, Zethar and Carkas,

ABANA

2Kgs 5:12 Are not A and Pharpar, the rivers of Damascus,

ABANDON (9)

Num 32:15 him, he will again A them in the wilderness;
Neh 9:28 thee, and thou didst A them to the hand
Ps 37:33 The LORD will not A him to his power,
94:14 people; he will not A his heritage;
Sir 23:1 my life, do not A me to their counsel,
29:17 not feel grateful will A his rescuer.
Bar 6:42 cannot perceive this and A them, for they have
Acts 2:27 For thou wilt not A my soul to Hades,
Jude 1:11 way of Cain, and A themselves for the sake

ABANDONED (9)

2Chr 12:5 says the LORD, 'You A me, so I have
12:5 me, so I have A you to the hand
Job 20:19 he has crushed and A the poor, he has
Jer 12:7 my house, I have A my heritage; I have
1Mac 1:15 marks of circumcision, and A the holy covenant.
2Mac 10:13 because he had A Cyprus, which Philometor had
Acts 2:31 that he was not A to Hades, nor did
27:20 hope of our being saved was at last A
Rev 2:4 you, that you have A the love you had

ABARIM (5)

Num 27:12 into this mountain of A, and see the land
33:47 in the mountains of A, before Nebo.
33:48 from the mountains of A, and encamped in the
Deut 32:49 this mountain of the A, Mount Nebo, which is
Jer 22:20 in Bashan; cry from A, for all your lovers

ABASE (3)

Job 40:11 that is proud, and A him.
Ezek 21:26 which is low, and A that which is high.
Dan 4:37 who walk in pride he is able to A

ABASED (4)

2Sam 6:22 and I will be A in your eyes; but
Ps 44:9 cast us off and A us, and hast not
Mal 2:9 make you despised and A before all the people,
Phil 4:12 know how to be A, and I know how

ABASES (2)

Job 22:29 For God A the proud, but he saves the
Sir 7:11 there is One who A and exalts.

ABASING

2Cor 11:7 commit a sin in A myself so that you

ABATE (2)

Gen 8:5 the waters continued to A until the tenth month;
2Mac 9:18 not in any way A, for the judgment of

ABATED (6)

Gen 8:3 days the waters had A;
Num 11:2 Moses prayed to the LORD, and the fire A
Deut 34:7 eye was not dim, nor his natural force A
Judg 8:3 anger against him was A, when he had said
Esth 2:1 of King Ahasuerus had A, he remembered Vashti and
7:10 Then the anger of the king A

ABBA (3)

Mk 14:36 And he said, A, Father, all things are possible
Rom 8:15 When we cry, A
Gal 4:6 Spirit of his Son into our hearts, crying, A

ABBREVIATING

2Mac 2:26 undertaken the toil of A, it is no light

ABDA (2)

1Kgs 4:6 Adoniram the son of A was in charge of
Neh 11:17 among his brethren; and A the son of Shammua,

ABDEEL

Jer 36:26 Shelemiah the son of A to seize Baruch the

ABDI (3)

1Chr 6:44 of Kishi, son of A, son of Malluch,
2Chr 29:12 Kish the son of A, and Azariah the son
Ezra 10:26 Zechariah, Jehiel, A, Jeremoth, and Elijah.

ABDI-EL

1Chr 5:15 Ahi the son of A, son of Guni, was

ABDON (8)

Josh 21:30 with its pasture lands, A with its pasture lands,
Judg 12:13 After him A the son of Hillel the Pirathonite
12:15 Then A the son of Hillel the Pirathonite died,
1Chr 6:74 with its pasture lands, A with its pasture lands,
8:23 Ishpan, Eber, Eliel, A, Zichri, Hanan,
8:30 His first-born son: A, then Zur, Kish, Baal, Nadab,
9:36 and his first-born son A, then Zur, Kish, Baal,
2Chr 34:20 the son of Shaphan, A the son of Micah,

ABEDNEGO (15)

Dan 1:7 Mishael he called Meshach, and Azariah he called A
2:49 appointed Shadrach, Meshach, and A over the affairs
3:12 the province of Babylon: Shadrach, Meshach, and A
3:13 that Shadrach, Meshach, and A be brought.
3:14 O Shadrach, Meshach, and A, that you do not
3:16 Shadrach, Meshach, and A answered the king, "O
3:19 face was changed against Shadrach, Meshach, and A
3:20 bind Shadrach, Meshach, and A, and to cast them
3:22 those men who took up Shadrach, Meshach, and A
3:23 men, Shadrach, Meshach, and A, fell bound into the
3:94 said, "Shadrach, Meshach, and A, servants of the
3:94 Then Shadrach, Meshach, and A came out from the
3:96 of Shadrach, Meshach, and A, who has sent his
3:97 of Shadrach, Meshach, and A shall be torn limb
3:98 promoted Shadrach, Meshach, and A in the province

ABEL (15)

Gen 4:2 And again, she bore his brother A
4:2 Now A was a keeper of sheep, and Cain
4:4 of the ground, and A brought of the firstlings
4:4 LORD had regard for A and his offering,
4:8 Cain said to A his brother, "Let us go
4:8 up against his brother A, and killed him.
4:9 to Cain, "Where is A your brother?" He said,
4:25 another child instead of A, for Cain slew him."
2Sam 20:14 tribes of Israel to A of Beth-maacah; and all
20:15 and besieged him in A of Beth-maacah; they cast
20:18 but ask counsel at A; and so they settled
Mt 23:34 the blood of innocent A to the blood of
Lk 11:51 from the blood of A to the blood of
Heb 11:4 By faith A offered to God a more acceptable
12:24 that speaks more graciously than the blood of A

ABEL-BETH-MAACAH (2)

1Kgs 15:20 and conquered Ijon, Dan, A, and all Chinneroth, with
2Kgs 15:29 and captured Ijon, A, Jan-oah, Kedesh, Hazor, Gilead,

ABEL-KERAMIM

Judg 11:33 and as far as A, with a very great

ABEL-MAIM

2Chr 16:4 they conquered Ijon, Dan, A, and all the store-cities

ABEL-MEHOLAH (3)

Judg 7:22 as the border of A, by Tabbath.
1Kgs 4:12 and from Beth-shean to A, as far as the
19:16 son of Shaphat of A you shall anoint to

ABEL-MIZRAIM

Gen 50:11 the place was named A; it is beyond the

ABEL-SHITTIM

Num 33:49 Beth-jeshimoth as far as A in the plains of

ABHOR (17)

Lev 26:11 my soul shall not A you.
26:30 and my soul will A you.
26:44 them, neither will I A them so as to
Deut 7:26 shall utterly detest and A it; for it is
23:7 "You shall not A an Edomite, for he is
23:7 brother; you shall not A an Egyptian, because you
Esth 14:15 of the wicked and A the bed of the
14:16 necessity _ that I A the sign of my
14:16 I A it like a menstruous rag, and I
Job 9:31 my own clothes will A me.
19:19 All my intimate friends A me, and those whom
30:10 They A me, they keep aloof from me; they
Ps 119:163 I hate and A falsehood, but I love thy
Amos 5:10 the gate, and they A him who speaks the
6:8 God of hosts): "I A the pride of Jacob,
Mic 3:9 house of Israel, who A justice and pervert all
Rom 2:22 You who A idols, do you rob temples?

ABHORRED (11)

Lev 20:23 things, and therefore I A them.
26:43 ordinances, and their soul A my statutes.
1Sam 27:12 has made himself utterly A by his people Israel;
1Kgs 11:25 Hadad did; and he A Israel, and reigned over
Jud 9:4 zealous for thee, and A the pollution of their
Ps 22:24 has not despised or A the affliction of the
106:40 his people, and he A his heritage;
Prov 24:24 be cursed by peoples, A by nations;
Is 49:7 to one deeply despised, A by the nations, the
Ezek 16:5 field, for you were A, on the day that
2Mac 5:8 against the laws, and A as the executioner of

ABHORRENCE

Is 66:24 they shall be an A to all flesh."

ABHORRENT

1Chr 21:6 the king's command was A to Joab.

ABHORS (2)

Lev 26:15 and if your soul A my ordinances, so that
Ps 5:6 lies; the LORD A bloodthirsty and deceitful men.

ABI

2Kgs 18:2 His mother's name was A the daughter of Zechariah.

ABI-ALBON

2Sam 23:31 the brooks of Gaash, A the Arbathite, Azmaveth of

ABI-EZER (6)

Josh 17:2 by their families, A, Helek, Asriel, Shechem, Hepher,
Judg 8:2 grapes of Ephraim better than the vintage of A
2Sam 23:27 of Ikkesh of Tekoa, A, of Anathoth, Mebunnai the
1Chr 7:18 sister Hammolecheth bore Ishhod, A, and Mahlah.
11:28 of Ikkesh of Tekoa, A of Anathoth,
27:12 the ninth month, was A of Anathoth, a Benjaminite;

ABIASAPH

Ex 6:24 Korah: Assir, Elkanah, and A; these are the families

ABIATHAR (32)

1Sam 22:20 son of Ahitub, named A, escaped and fled after
22:21 And A told David that Saul had killed the
22:22 And David said to A, "I knew on that
23:6 When A the son of Ahimelech fled to David
23:9 and he said to A the priest, "Bring the
30:7 And David said to A the priest, the son
30:7 So A brought the ephod to David.
2Sam 8:17 Ahimelech the son of A were priests; and Seraiah
15:24 And A came up, and lo, Zadok came also,
15:27 in peace, you and A, with your two sons,
15:27 Ahima-az your son, and Jonathan the son of A
15:29 So Zadok and A carried the ark of God
15:35 Are not Zadok and A the priests with you
15:35 it to Zadok and A the priests.
15:36 Zadok's son, and Jonathan, A's son; and by them
17:15 said to Zadok and A the priests, "Thus and
19:11 message to Zadok and A the priests, "Say to
20:25 secretary; and Zadok and A were priests;
1Kgs 1:7 of Zeruiah and with A the priest; and they
1:19 sons of the king, A the priest, and Joab
1:25 of the army, and A the priest; and behold,
1:42 Jonathan the son of A the priest came; and
2:22 on his side are A the priest and Joab
2:26 And to A the priest the king said, "Go
2:27 So Solomon expelled A from being priest to the
2:35 put Zadok the priest in the place of A
4:4 the army; Zadok and A were priests;
1Chr 15:11 the priests Zadok and A, and the Levites Uriel,
18:16 Ahimelech the son of A were priests; and Shavsha
24:6 Ahimelech the son of A, and the heads of
27:34 succeeded by Jehoiada the son of Benaiah, and A
Mk 2:26 house of God, when A was high priest, and

ABIB (6)

Ex 13:4 are to go forth, in the month of A
23:15 in the month of A, for in it you
34:18 appointed in the month A; for in the month
34:18 for in the month A you came out from
Deut 16:1 "Observe the month of A, and keep the passover
16:1 in the month of A the LORD your God

ABIDA (2)

Gen 25:4 were Ephah, Epher, Hanoch, A, and Eldaah.
1Chr 1:33 Midian: Ephah, Epher, Hanoch, A, and Eldaah.

ABIDAN (5)

Num 1:11 of Pedahzur; from Benjamin, A the son of Gideoni;
2:22 people of Benjamin being A the son of Gideoni,
7:60 On the ninth day A the son of Gideoni,
7:65 was the offering of A the son of Gideoni.
10:24 men of Benjamin was A the son of Gideoni.

ABIDE (34)

Gen 6:3 "My spirit shall not A in man for ever,
Judg 5:17 Dan, why did he A with the ships?
1Sam 1:22 of the LORD, and A there for ever."
Ps 25:13 He himself shall A in prosperity, and his children
37:18 and their heritage will A for ever;
37:27 good; so shall you A for ever.
49:12 Man cannot A in his pomp, he is like
49:20 Man cannot A in his pomp, he is like
89:21 my hand shall ever A with him, my arm
Prov 15:31 heeds wholesome admonition will A among the wise.
Wis 3:9 and the faithful will A with him in love,
Is 32:16 wilderness, and righteousness A in the fruitful field.
32:18 My people will A in a peaceful habitation, in
Hab 2:5 wine is treacherous; the arrogant man shall not A
Zech 5:4 name; and it shall A in his house and
Jn 15:4 A in me, and I in you.
15:4 can you, unless you A in me.
15:6 a man does not A in me, he is
15:7 If you A in me, and my words abide
15:7 me, and my words A in you, ask whatever
15:9 have I loved you; A in my love.
15:10 my commandments, you will A in my love, just
15:10 my Father's commandments and A in his love.
15:16 that your fruit should A; so that whatever you
1Cor 13:13 So faith, hope, love A, these three; but the
Gal 3:10 one who does not A by all things written
1Jn 2:24 heard from the beginning A in you.
2:24 you, then you will A in the Son and
2:27 it has taught you, A in him.
2:28 And now, little children, A in him, so that
3:17 how does God's love A in him?
3:24 who keep his commandments A in him, and he
4:13 we know that we A in him and he
2Jn 1:9 ahead and does not A in the doctrine of

ABIDES (27)

Lev 16:16 tent of meeting, which A with them in the
Job 41:22 In his neck A strength, and terror dances before
Ps 91:1 the Most High, who A in the shadow of
125:1 cannot be moved, but A for ever.
Prov 14:33 Wisdom A in the mind of a man of
Hag 2:5 My Spirit A among you; fear not.
Jn 6:56 and drinks my blood A in me, and I
15:4 by itself, unless it A in the vine, neither
15:5 He who A in me, and I in him,

1Pet 1:25 word of the Lord A for ever." That word
1Jn 2:6 he who says he A in him ought to
2:10 who loves his brother A in the light, and
2:14 the word of God A in you, and you
2:17 the will of God A for ever.
2:24 heard from the beginning A in you, then you
2:27 you received from him A in you, and you
3:6 No one who A in him sins; no one
3:9 sin; for God's nature A in him, and he
3:14 who does not love A in death.
3:24 we know that he A in us, by the
4:12 love one another, God A in us and his
4:15 Son of God, God A in him, and he
4:16 love, and he who A in love abides in
4:16 who abides in love A in God, and God
4:16 in God, and God A in him.
2Jn 1:2 of the truth which A in us and will
1:9 have God; he who A in the doctrine has

ABIDING (6)

Num 9:22 continued over the tabernacle, A there, the people of
1Chr 29:15 are like a shadow, and there is no A
Jn 5:37 not have his word A in you, for you
Heb 10:34 better possession and an A one.
1Pet 1:23 through the living and A word of God;
1Jn 3:15 murderer has eternal life A in him.

ABIEL (3)

1Sam 9:1 Kish, the son of A, son of Zeror, son
14:51 the father of Abner was the son of A
1Chr 11:32 the brooks of Gaash, A the Arbathite,

ABIEZRITE

Judg 6:11 belonged to Joash the A, as his son Gideon

ABIEZRITES (3)

Judg 6:24 still stands at Ophrah, which belongs to the A
6:34 the trumpet, and the A were called out to
8:32 of Joash his father, at Ophrah of the A

ABIGAIL (16)

1Sam 25:3 was Nabal, and the name of his wife A
25:14 the young men told A, Nabal's wife, "Behold, David
25:18 Then A made haste, and took two hundred loaves,
25:23 When A saw David, she made haste, and alighted
25:32 And David said to A, "Blessed be the LORD,
25:36 And A came to Nabal; and, lo, he was
25:39 David sent and wooed A, to make her his
25:40 of David came to A at Carmel, they said
25:42 And A made haste and rose and mounted on
27:3 Ahino-am of Jezreel, and A of Carmel, Nabal's
30:5 Ahino-am of Jezreel, and A the widow of Nabal
2Sam 2:2 Ahino-am of Jezreel, and A the widow of Nabal
3:3 his second, Chile-ab, of A the widow of Nabal
1Chr 2:16 the seventh; and their sisters were Zeruiah and A
2:17 A bore Amasa, and the father of Amasa was
3:1 the second Daniel, by A the Carmelitess,

ABIGAL

2Sam 17:25 who had married A the daughter of Nahash,

ABIHAIL (6)

Num 3:35 Zuriel the son of A; they were to encamp
1Chr 2:29 of Abishur's wife was A, and she bore him
5:14 were the sons of A the son of Huri,
2Chr 11:18 of David, and of A the daughter of Eliab
Esth 2:15 Esther the daughter of A the uncle of Mordecai,
9:29 Esther, the daughter of A, and Mordecai the Jew

ABIHU (12)

Ex 6:23 she bore him Nadab, A, Eleazar, and Ithamar.
24:1 and Aaron, Nadab, and A, and seventy of the
24:9 and Aaron, Nadab, and A, and seventy of the
28:1 Aaron's sons, Nadab and A, Eleazar and Ithamar.
Lev 10:1 Now Nadab and A, the sons of Aaron, each
Num 3:2 Nadab the first-born, and A, Eleazar, and Ithamar;
3:4 But Nadab and A died before the LORD when
26:60 Aaron were born Nadab, A, Eleazar and Ithamar.
26:61 But Nadab and A died when they offered unholy
1Chr 6:3 sons of Aaron: Nadab, A, Eleazar, and Ithamar.
24:1 sons of Aaron: Nadab, A, Eleazar, and Ithamar.
24:2 But Nadab and A died before their father, and

ABIHUD

1Chr 8:3 had sons: Addar, Gera, A,

ABIJAH (27)

1Sam 8:2 name of his second, A; they were judges in
1Kgs 14:1 At that time A the son of Jeroboam fell
1Chr 3:10 descendants of Solomon: Rehoboam, A his son, Asa
6:28 sons of Samuel: Joel his first-born, the second A
7:8 Eliezer, Eli-o-enai, Omri, Jeremoth, A, Anathoth, and
24:10 Hakkoz, the eighth to A,
2Chr 11:20 Absalom, who bore him A, Attai, Ziza, and
11:22 daughters); and Rehoboam appointed A the son of
12:16 city of David; and A his son reigned in
13:1 year of King Jeroboam A began to reign over
13:2 there was war between A and Jeroboam.
13:3 A went out to battle having an army of
13:4 Then A stood up on Mount Zemaraim which is
13:15 and all Israel before A and Judah.
13:17 A and his people slew them with a great
13:19 And A pursued Jeroboam, and took cities from him,
13:20 in the days of A; and the LORD smote
13:21 But A grew mighty.
13:22 of the acts of A, his ways and his
14:1 So A slept with his fathers, and they buried
29:1 His mother's name was A the daughter of Zechariah.
Neh 10:7 Daniel, Ginnethon, Baruch, Meshullam, A, Mijamin,
12:4 Rehum, Meremoth, Iddo, Ginnethoi, A,
12:17 of Ginnethon, Meshullam; of A, Zichri; of Miniamin,
Mt 1:7 Rehoboam the father of A, and Abijah the father
1:7 father of Abijah, and A the father of Asa,
Lk 1:5 of the division of A; and he had a

ABIJAM (5)

1Kgs 14:31 And A his son reigned in his stead.
15:1 the son of Nebat, A began to reign over
15:7 of the acts of A, and all that he
15:7 there was war between A and Jeroboam.
15:8 And A slept with his fathers; and they buried

ABILENE

Lk 3:1 and Lysani-as tetrarch of A,

ABILITY (19)

Ex 28:3 to all who have A, whom I have endowed
31:3 Spirit of God, with A and intelligence, with
31:6 to all able men A, that they may make
35:25 all women who had A spun with their hands,
35:26 hearts were moved with A spun the goats' hair.
35:31 Spirit of God, with A, with intelligence, with
35:35 has filled them with A to do every sort
36:1 the LORD has put A and intelligence to know
36:2 the LORD had put A, every one whose heart
Lev 27:8 him; according to the A of him who vowed
1Chr 26:6 fathers' houses, for they were men of great A
26:30 seven hundred men of A, had the oversight of
26:31 and men of great A among them were found
26:32 seven hundred men of A, heads of fathers' houses,
Ezra 2:69 site; according to their A they gave to the
Sir 29:20 neighbor according to your A, but take heed to
Mt 25:15 to another one, to each according to his A
Acts 11:29 one according to his A, to send relief to
1Cor 12:10 prophecy, to another the A to distinguish between

ABIMA-EL (2)

Gen 10:28 Hadoram, Uzal, Diklah, Obal, A, Sheba,
1Chr 1:22 Hadoram, Uzal, Diklah, Ebal, A, Sheba,

ABIMELECH (65)

Gen 20:2 And A king of Gerar sent and took Sarah.
20:3 But God came to A in a dream by
20:4 Now A had not approached her; so he said,
20:8 So A rose early in the morning, and called
20:9 Then A called Abraham, and said to him, "What
20:10 And A said to Abraham, "What were you thinking
20:14 Then A took sheep and oxen, and male and
20:15 And A said, "Behold, my land is before you;
20:17 God; and God healed A, and also healed his
20:18 of the house of A because of Sarah, Abraham's
21:22 At that time A and Phicol the commander of
21:25 When Abraham complained to A about a well of
21:25 well of water which A's servants had seized,
21:26 Abimelech's servants had seized, A said, "I do not
21:27 and gave them to A, and the two men
21:29 And A said to Abraham, "What is the meaning
21:32 Then A and Phicol the commander of his army
26:1 went to Gerar, to A king of the Philistines.
26:8 there a long time, A king of the Philistines
26:9 So A called Isaac, and said, "Behold, she is
26:10 A said, "What is this you have done to

26:11 So A warned all the people, saying, "Whoever
26:16 Abraham his father.) And A said to Isaac, "Go
26:26 Then A went to him from Gerar with Ahuzzath
Judg 8:31 him a son, and he called his name A
9:1 Now A the son of Jerubbaal went to Shechem
9:3 hearts inclined to follow A, for they said, "He
9:4 of Baal-berith with which A hired worthless and
9:6 they went and made A king, by the oak
9:16 honor when you made A king, and if you
9:18 stone, and have made A, the son of his
9:19 day, then rejoice in A, and let him also
9:20 fire come out from A, and devour the citizens
9:20 of Shechem, and from Beth-millo, and devour A
9:21 there, for fear of A his brother.
9:22 A ruled over Israel three years.
9:23 an evil spirit between A and the men of
9:23 Shechem dealt treacherously with A;
9:24 blood be laid upon A their brother, who slew
9:25 them along that way; and it was told A
9:27 their god, and ate and drank and reviled A
9:28 Ebed said, "Who is A, and who are we
9:29 then I would remove A
9:29 I would say to A, 'Increase your army, and
9:31 he sent messengers to A at Arumah, saying, "Behold,
9:34 And A and all the men that were with
9:35 of the city; and A and the men that
9:38 who said, 'Who is A, that we should serve
9:39 of the men of Shechem, and fought with A
9:40 And A chased him, and he fled before him;
9:41 And A dwelt at Arumah; and Zebul drove out
9:42 And A was told.
9:44 A and the company that was with him rushed
9:45 And A fought against the city all that day;
9:47 A was told that all the people of the
9:48 And A went up to Mount Zalmon, he and
9:48 were with him; and A took an axe in
9:49 his bundle and following A put it against the
9:50 Then A went to Thebez, and encamped against
9:52 And A came to the tower, and fought against
9:53 an upper millstone upon A's head, and crushed his
9:55 of Israel saw that A was dead, they departed
9:56 requited the crime of A, which he committed against
10:1 After A there arose to deliver Israel Tola the
2Sam 11:21 Who killed A the son of Jerubbesheth?

ABINADAB (11)
1Sam 7:1 to the house of A on the hill; and
16:8 Then Jesse called A, and made him pass before
17:13 and next to him A, and the third Shammah.
31:2 Philistines slew Jonathan and A and Malchishua, the
2Sam 6:3 of the house of A which was on the
6:3 Ahio, the sons of A, were driving the new
1Chr 2:13 of Eliab his first-born, A the second, Shimea the
8:33 Saul of Jonathan, Malchishua, A, and Eshbaal;
9:39 Saul of Jonathan, Malchishua, A, and Eshbaal;
10:2 Philistines slew Jonathan and A and Malchishua, the
13:7 from the house of A, and Uzzah and Ahio

ABINO-AM (4)
Judg 4:6 Barak the son of A from Kedesh in Naphtali,
4:12 Barak the son of A had gone up to
5:1 Barak the son of A on that day:
5:12 Barak, lead away your captives, O son of A

ABIRAM (12)
Num 16:1 Levi, and Dathan and A the sons of Eliab,
16:12 to call Dathan and A the sons of Eliab;
16:24 from about the dwelling of Korah, Dathan, and A
16:25 went to Dathan and A; and the elders of
16:27 of Korah, Dathan, and A; and Dathan and Abiram
16:27 Abiram; and Dathan and A came out and stood
26:9 The sons of Eliab: Nemuel, Dathan, and A
26:9 are the Dathan and A, chosen from the congregation,
Deut 11:6 did to Dathan and A the sons of Eliab,
1Kgs 16:34 at the cost of A his first-born, and set
Ps 106:17 swallowed up Dathan, and covered the company of A
Sir 45:18 the wilderness, Dathan and A and their men and

ABISHAG (5)
1Kgs 1:3 of Israel, and found A the Shunammite, and brought
1:15 was very old, and A the Shunammite was ministering
2:17 you—to give me A the Shunammite as my
2:21 She said, "Let A the Shunammite be given to
2:22 why do you ask A the Shunammite for Adonijah?

ABISHAI (26)
1Sam 26:6 and to Joab's brother A the son of Zeruiah,
26:6 And A said, "I will go down with you."
26:7 So David and A went to the army by
26:8 Then said A to David, "God has given your
26:9 But David said to A, "Do not destroy him;
2Sam 2:18 Zeruiah were there, Joab, A, and Asahel.
2:24 But Joab and A pursued Abner; and as the
3:30 So Joab and A his brother slew Abner, because
10:10 in the charge of A his brother, and he
10:14 they likewise fled before A, and entered the city.
16:9 Then A the son of Zeruiah said to the
16:11 And David said to A and to all his
18:2 under the command of A the son of Zeruiah,
18:5 king ordered Joab and A and Ittai, "Deal gently
18:12 king commanded you and A and Ittai, 'For my
19:21 A the son of Zeruiah answered, "Shall not Shimei
20:6 And David said to A, "Now Sheba the son
20:7 there went out after A, Joab and the Cherethites
20:10 Then Joab and A his brother pursued Sheba the
21:17 But A the son of Zeruiah came to his
23:18 Now A, the brother of Joab, the son of
1Chr 2:16 The sons of Zeruiah: A, Joab, and Asahel, three.
11:20 Now A, the brother of Joab, was chief of
18:12 And A, the son of Zeruiah, slew eighteen thousand
19:11 in the charge of A his brother, and they
19:15 they likewise fled before A, Joab's brother, and

ABISHALOM (2)
1Kgs 15:2 His mother's name was Maacah the daughter of A
15:10 His mother's name was Maacah the daughter of A

ABISHUA (5)
1Chr 6:4 of Phinehas, Phinehas of A,
6:5 Phinehas, Phinehas of Abishua, A of Bukki, Bukki of
6:50 son, Phinehas his son, A his son,
8:4 sons: Addar, Gera, Abihud, A, Naaman, Ahoah,
Ezra 7:5 of Bukki, son of A, son of Phinehas, son

ABISHUR (2)
1Chr 2:28 The sons of Shammai: Nadab and A
2:29 The name of A's wife was Abihail, and she

ABITAL (2)
2Sam 3:4 Shephatiah the son of A;
1Chr 3:3 the fifth Shephatiah, by A; the sixth Ithream, by

ABITUB
1Chr 8:11 had sons by Hushim: A and Elpaal.

ABIUD (2)
Mt 1:13 Zerubbabel the father of A, and Abiud the father
1:13 father of Abiud, and A the father of Eliakim,

ABLAZE (4)
Ps 58:9 thorns, whether green or A, may he sweep them
83:14 flame sets the mountains A,
1Mac 6:39 brass, the hills were A with them and gleamed
Jas 3:5 a forest is set A by a small fire!

ABLE (170)
Gen 15:5 stars, if you are A to number them." Then
47:6 if you know any A men among them, put
Ex 18:18 you; you are not A to perform it alone.
18:21 Moreover choose A men from all the people, such
18:23 then you will be A to endure, and all
18:25 Moses chose A men out of all Israel, and
28:3 have endowed with an A mind, that they make
31:6 have given to all A men ability, that they
35:10 "And let every A man among you come and
36:1 and Oholiab and every A man in whom the
36:2 and Oholiab and every A man in whose mind
36:4 so that all the A men who were doing
36:8 And all the A men among the workmen made
Num 1:3 in Israel who are A to go forth to
1:20 upward, all who were A to go forth to
1:22 upward, all who were A to go forth to
1:24 upward, all who were A to go forth to
1:26 and upward, every man A to go forth to
1:28 and upward, every man A to go forth to
1:30 and upward, every man A to go forth to
1:32 and upward, every man A to go forth to
1:34 and upward, every man A to go forth to
1:36 and upward, every man A to go forth to
1:38 and upward, every man A to go forth to
1:40 and upward, every man A to go forth to

1:42 and upward, every man A to go forth to
1:45 and upward, every man A to go forth to
11:14 eat.' I am not A to carry all this
13:30 for we are well A to overcome it."
13:31 said, "We are not A to go up against
14:16 the LORD was not A to bring this people
22:6 perhaps I shall be A to defeat them and
22:11 perhaps I shall be A to fight against them
22:37 Am I not A to honor you?"
24:13 I would not be A to go beyond the
26:2 in Israel who are A to go forth to
Deut 1:9 you, 'I am not A alone to bear you;
7:24 a man shall be A to stand against you,
9:28 the LORD was not A to bring them into
11:25 No man shall be A to stand against you;
14:24 that you are not A to bring the tithe,
16:17 give as he is A, according to the blessing
31:2 I am no longer A to go out and
Josh 1:5 No man shall be A to stand before you
23:9 no man has been A to withstand you to
Judg 8:3 what have I been A to do in comparison
18:2 the Danites sent five A men from the whole
1Sam 6:20 Beth-shemesh said, "Who is A to stand before the
17:9 If he is A to fight with me and
17:33 David, "You are not A to go against this
1Kgs 3:9 evil; for who is A to govern this thy
11:28 man Jeroboam was very A, and when Solomon saw
2Kgs 3:21 them, all who were A to put on armor,
18:23 horses, if you are A on your part to
18:29 he will not be A to deliver you out
1Chr 9:13 hundred and sixty, very A men for the work
26:7 Elzabad, whose brethren were A men, Elihu and
26:8 their sons and brethren, A men qualified for the
26:9 had sons and brethren, A men, eighteen.
29:2 far as I was A, the gold for the
29:14 that we should be A thus to offer willingly?
2Chr 2:6 But who is A to build him a house,
20:6 so that none is A to withstand thee.
20:37 wrecked and were not A to go to Tarshish.
22:9 Ahaziah had no one A to rule the kingdom.
25:5 men, fit for war, A to handle spear and
25:9 answered, "The LORD is A to give you much
32:13 those lands at all A to deliver their lands
32:14 fathers utterly destroyed was A to deliver his people
32:14 your God should be A to deliver you from
32:15 or kingdom has been A to deliver his people
Neh 4:10 rubbish; we are not A to work on the
5:8 far as we are A, have bought back our
Jud 10:19 go they will be A to ensnare the whole
Ps 18:38 that they were not A to rise; they fell
Eccl 6:10 that he is not A to dispute with one
Wis 17:5 power of fire was A to give light, nor
Sir 8:17 he will not be A to keep a secret.
Is 36:8 horses, if you are A on your part to
36:14 he will not be A to deliver you.
47:11 you will not be A to expiate; and ruin
47:12 perhaps you may be A to succeed, perhaps you
Jer 49:10 and he is not A to conceal himself.
Bar 6:34 they will not be A to repay it.
6:35 Likewise they are not A to give either wealth
6:41 as though Bel were A to understand.
6:57 and gold are not A to save themselves from
6:58 they will not be A to help themselves.
6:64 for they are not A either to decide a
Ezek 7:19 and gold are not A to deliver them in
33:12 righteous shall not be A to live by his
46:5 much as he is A, together with a hin
46:7 much as he is A, together with a hin
46:11 much as one is A to give, together with
Dan 2:26 was Belteshazzar, "Are you A to make known to
2:47 for you have been A to reveal this mystery."
3:17 whom we serve is A to deliver us from
3:97 other god who is A to deliver in this
4:18 my kingdom are not A to make known to
4:18 interpretation, but you are A, for the spirit of
4:37 in pride he is A to abase.
6:20 you serve continually, been A to deliver you from
Hos 5:13 But he is not A to cure you or
Amos 7:10 the land is not A to bear all his
Zeph 1:18 their gold shall be A to deliver them on
1Mac 3:53 How will we be A to withstand them, if
5:40 we will not be A to resist him, for
6:27 you will not be A to stop them."
9:8 We may be A to fight them."
9:9 tried to dissuade him, saying, "We are not A
10:73 you will not be A to withstand my cavalry
2Mac 8:18 Almighty God, who is A with a single nod
9:10 stench no one was A to carry the man
Mt 3:9 tell you, God is A from these stones to
9:28 believe that I am A to do this?" They
19:12 He who is A to receive this, let him
20:22 Are you A to drink the cup that I
20:22 They said to him, "We are A
22:46 And no one was A to answer him a
26:61 fellow said, 'I am A to destroy the temple
Mk 3:25 house will not be A to stand.
4:33 them, as they were A to hear it;
9:18 to cast it out, and they were not A
9:39 my name will be A soon after to speak
10:38 Are you A to drink the cup that I
10:39 And they said to him, "We are A
Lk 3:8 tell you, God is A from these stones to
12:26 then you are not A to do as small
13:24 will seek to enter and will not be A
14:29 foundation, and is not A to finish, all who
14:30 build, and was not A to finish.'
14:31 counsel whether he is A with ten thousand to
16:26 you may not be A, and none may cross
20:26 And they were not A in the presence of
21:15 your adversaries will be A to withstand or contradict.
Jn 10:29 and no one is A to snatch them out
21:6 now they were not A to haul it in,
Acts 5:39 you will not be A to overthrow them.
15:10 nor we have been A to bear?
20:32 his grace, which is A to build you up
24:7 yourself you will be A to learn from him
Rom 4:21 convinced that God was A to do what he
8:39 all creation, will be A to separate us from
14:4 for the Master is A to make him stand.
15:14 with all knowledge, and A to instruct one another.
16:24 to him who is A to strengthen you according
1Cor 2:14 and he is not A to understand them because
10:13 that you may be A to endure it.
2Cor 1:4 that we may be A to comfort those who
5:12 that you may be A to answer those who
9:8 And God is A to provide you with every
Eph 3:20 work within us is A to do far more
4:28 that he may be A to give to those
6:11 that you may be A to stand against the
6:13 that you may be A to withstand in the
2Tim 1:12 sure that he is A to guard until that
2:2 men who will be A to teach others also.
3:15 sacred writings which are A to instruct you for
Tit 1:8 that he may be A to give instruction in
Heb 2:18 been tempted, he is A to help those who
5:7 to him who was A to save him from
7:25 Consequently he is A for all time to save
11:19 considered that God was A to raise men even
Jas 1:20 implanted word, which is A to save your souls.
3:2 is a perfect man, A to bridle the whole
4:12 judge, he who is A to save and to
2Pet 1:15 departure you may be A at any time to
Jude 1:24 to him who is A to keep you from
Rev 3:8 which no one is A to shut; I know
5:3 under the earth was A to open the scroll

ABLE-BODIED

Judg 3:29 the Moabites, all strong, A men; not a man

ABLUTIONS (2)

Heb 6:2 God, with instruction about A, the laying on of
9:10 and drink and various A, regulations for the body

ABNER (63)

1Sam 14:50 of his army was A the son of Ner,
14:51 Ner the father of A was the son of
17:55 Philistine, he said to A, the commander of the
17:55 commander of the army, A, whose son is this
17:55 And A said, "As your soul lives, O king,
17:57 slaughter of the Philistine, A took him, and brought
20:25 Jonathan sat opposite, and A sat by Saul's side,
26:5 where Saul lay, with A the son of Ner,
26:7 at his head; and A and the army lay
26:14 the army, and to A the son of Ner,
26:14 son of Ner, saying, "Will you not answer, A
26:14 Then A answered, "Who are you that calls to
26:15 And David said to A, "Are you not a
2Sam 2:8 Now A the son of Ner, commander of Saul's
2:12 A the son of Ner, and the servants of
2:14 And A said to Joab, "Let the young men
2:17 fierce that day; and A and the men of
2:19 gazelle; and Asahel pursued A, and as he went

A

2:19 right hand nor to the left from following A
2:20 Then A looked behind him and said, "Is it
2:21 A said to him, "Turn aside to your right
2:22 And A said again to Asahel, "Turn aside from
2:23 to turn aside; therefore A smote him in the
2:24 Joab and Abishai pursued A; and as the sun
2:25 themselves together behind A, and became one band,
2:26 Then A called to Joab, "Shall the sword devour
2:29 And A and his men went all that night
2:30 from the pursuit of A; and when he had
2:31 hundred and sixty of A's men.
3:6 the house of David, A was making himself strong
3:7 and Ish-bosheth said to A, "Why have you gone
3:8 Then A was very angry over the words of
3:9 God do so to A, and more also, if
3:11 Ish-bosheth could not answer A another word,
3:12 And A sent messengers to David at Hebron, saying,
3:16 Then A said to him, "Go, return"; and he
3:17 And A conferred with the elders of Israel, saying,
3:19 A also spoke to Benjamin; and then Abner went
3:19 to Benjamin; and then A went to tell David
3:20 When A came with twenty men to David at
3:20 made a feast for A and the men who
3:21 And A said to David, "I will arise and
3:21 So David sent A away; and he went in
3:22 But A was not with David at Hebron, for
3:23 it was told Joab, A the son of Ner
3:24 Behold, A came to you; why is it that
3:25 You know that A the son of Ner came
3:26 he sent messengers after A, and they brought him
3:27 And when A returned to Hebron, Joab took him
3:28 for the blood of A the son of Ner.
3:30 Abishai his brother slew A, because he had killed
3:31 clothes, and gird on sackcloth, and mourn before A
3:32 They buried A at Hebron; and the king lifted
3:32 at the grave of A; and all the people
3:33 the king lamented for A, saying, "Should Abner die
3:33 for Abner, saying, "Should A die as a fool
3:37 king's will to slay A the son of Ner.
4:1 Saul's son, heard that A had died at Hebron,
4:12 in the tomb of A at Hebron.
1Kgs 2:5 the armies of Israel, A the son of Ner,
2:32 and better than himself, A the son of Ner,
1Chr 26:28 son of Kish, and A the son of Ner,
27:21 Jaasiel the son of A;

ABOARD (3)

Jn 21:11 So Simon Peter went A and hauled the net
Acts 20:13 intending to take Paul A there; for so he
21:2 to Phoenicia, we went A, and set sail.

ABODE (10)

Ex 15:13 guided them by thy strength to thy holy A
15:17 hast made for thy A, the sanctuary, O LORD,
Lev 26:11 I will make my A among you, and my
Judg 20:47 rock of Rimmon, and A at the rock of
Tob 3:6 go to the eternal A; do not turn thy
Ps 68:16 God desired for his A, yea, where the LORD
76:2 His A has been established in Salem, his dwelling
104:13 From thy lofty A thou waterest the mountains; the
Prov 3:33 but he blesses the A of the righteous.
Is 34:13 haunt of jackals, an A for ostriches.

ABOLISH (4)

Esth 14:9 with their idols to A what thy mouth has
Hos 2:18 ground; and I will A the bow, the sword,
Mt 5:17 I have come to A the law and the
5:17 have come not to A them but to fulfil

ABOLISHED (3)

1Mac 6:59 their laws which we A that they became angry
2Mac 2:22 were about to be A, while the Lord with
2Tim 1:10 Savior Christ Jesus, who A death and brought life

ABOLISHES

Heb 10:9 He A the first in order to establish the

ABOLISHING (2)

1Mac 3:29 in the land by A the laws that had
Eph 2:15 wall of hostility, by A in his flesh the

ABOMINABLE (39)

Ex 8:26 LORD our God offerings A to the Egyptians.
8:26 If we sacrifice offerings A to the Egyptians before
Lev 11:43 shall not make yourselves A with any swarming thing
18:30 practice any of these A customs which were
20:25 shall not make yourselves A by beast or by
Deut 7:26 shall not bring an A thing into your house,
12:31 your God; for every A thing which the LORD
13:14 certain that such an A thing has been done
14:3 shall not eat any A thing.
17:4 certain that such an A thing has been done
18:9 learn to follow the A practices of those nations.
18:12 and because of these A practices the LORD your
20:18 according to all their A practices which they have
32:16 with strange gods; with A practices they provoked
1Kgs 15:13 because she had an A image made for Asherah;
2Kgs 16:3 offering, according to the A practices of the nations
21:2 LORD, according to the A practices of the nations
2Chr 15:8 and put away the A idols from all the
15:16 she had made an A image for Asherah.
28:3 offering, according to the A practices of the nations
33:2 LORD, according to the A practices of the nations
Job 15:16 less one who is A and corrupt, a man
Ps 14:1 are corrupt, they do A deeds, there is none
53:1 They are corrupt, doing A iniquity; there is none
Sir 19:20 a cleverness which is A, but there is a
41:5 children of sinners are A children, and they frequent
Is 65:4 flesh, and broth of A things is in their
Jer 44:4 do not do this A thing that I hate!'
Ezek 7:20 and they made their A images and their detestable
16:50 were haughty, and did A things before me; therefore
18:13 has done all these A things; he shall surely
18:24 and does the same A things that the wicked
22:2 to her all her A deeds.
23:36 declare to them their A deeds.
36:31 your iniquities and your A deeds.
1Mac 1:48 were to make themselves A by everything unclean
2Mac 6:5 altar was covered with A offerings which were
9:13 Then the A fellow made a vow to the
15:5 in carrying out his A design.

ABOMINABLY (2)

1Kgs 21:26 He did very A in going after idols, as
Ezek 16:52 which you acted more A than they, they are

ABOMINATION (72)

Gen 43:32 for that is an A to the Egyptians.
46:34 every shepherd is an A to the Egyptians."
Lev 7:18 it shall be an A, and he who eats
7:21 beast or any unclean A, and then eats of
11:10 the waters, is an A to you.
11:11 They shall remain an A to you; of their
11:11 eat, and their carcasses you shall have in A
11:12 and scales is an A to you.
11:13 you shall have in A among the birds, they
11:13 eaten, they are an A: the eagle, the vulture,
11:20 all fours are an A to you.
11:23 four feet are an A to you.
11:41 the earth is an A; it shall not be
11:42 you shall not eat; for they are an A
18:22 male as with a woman; it is an A
19:7 day, it is an A; it will not be
20:13 them have committed an A; they shall be put
Deut 7:25 for it is an A to the LORD your
17:1 for that is an A to the LORD your
18:12 these things is an A to the LORD; and
22:5 these things is an A to the LORD your
23:18 of these are an A to the LORD your
24:4 for that is an A before the LORD, and
25:16 act dishonestly, are an A to the LORD your
27:15 or molten image, an A to the LORD, a
Judg 20:6 for they have committed A and wantonness in Israel.
1Kgs 11:5 and after Milcom the A of the Ammonites.
11:7 place for Chemosh the A of Moab, and for
11:7 and for Molech the A of the Ammonites, on
2Kgs 23:13 built for Ashtoreth the A of the Sidonians, and
23:13 and for Chemosh the A of Moab, and for
23:13 and for Milcom the A of the Ammonites.
Prov 3:32 perverse man is an A to the LORD, but
6:16 seven which are an A to him:
8:7 truth; wickedness is an A to my lips.
11:1 false balance is an A to the LORD, but
11:20 perverse mind are an A to the LORD, but
12:22 Lying lips are an A to the LORD, but
13:19 from evil is an A to fools.
15:8 the wicked is an A to the LORD, but
15:9 the wicked is an A to the LORD, but
15:26 the wicked are an A to the LORD, the
16:5 is arrogant is an A to the LORD; be
16:12 It is an A to kings to do evil,
17:15 are both alike an A to the LORD.

20:10 are both alike an A to the LORD.
20:23 Diverse weights are an A to the LORD, and
21:27 the wicked is an A; how much more when
24:9 the scoffer is an A to men.
28:9 hearing the law, even his prayer is an A
29:27 unjust man is an A to the righteous, but
29:27 is straight is an A to the wicked.
Wis 14:11 created, they became an A, and became traps for
Sir 1:22 but godliness is an A to a sinner.
13:19 Humility is an A to a proud man; likewise
13:19 poor man is an A to a rich one.
Is 1:13 offerings; incense is an A to me.
41:24 work is nought; an A is he who chooses
44:19 shall I make the residue of it an A
66:17 swine's flesh and the A and mice, shall come
Jer 2:7 defiled my land, and made my heritage an A
6:15 Were they ashamed when they committed A
8:12 Were they ashamed when they committed A
32:35 they should do this A, to cause Judah to
Ezek 18:12 to the idols, commits A,
22:11 One commits A with his neighbor's wife; another
Dan 11:31 shall set up the A that makes desolate.
12:11 taken away, and the A that makes desolate is
Mal 2:11 has been faithless, and A has been committed in
1Mac 6:7 had torn down the A which he had erected
Lk 16:15 among men is an A in the sight of
Rev 21:27 any one who practices A or falsehood, but only

ABOMINATIONS (64)

Lev 18:26 do none of these A, either the native or
18:27 (for all of these A the men of the
18:29 do any of these A, the persons that do
1Kgs 14:24 according to all the A of the nations which
2Kgs 21:11 Judah has committed these A, and has done things
23:24 idols and all the A that were seen in
2Chr 34:33 took away all the A from all the territory
36:8 of Jehoiakim, and the A which he did, and
36:14 unfaithful, following all the A of the nations; and
Ezra 9:1 the lands with their A, from the Canaanites, the
9:11 the lands, with their A which have filled it
9:14 intermarry with the peoples who practice these A
Prov 26:25 for there are seven A in his heart;
Wis 12:23 unrighteously thou didst torment through their own A
Sir 10:13 the man who clings to it pours out A
15:13 The Lord hates all A, and they are not
17:21 from iniquity, and hate A intensely.
27:30 wrath, these also are A, and the sinful man
49:2 and took away the A of iniquity.
Is 66:3 soul delights in their A;
Jer 4:1 If you remove your A from my presence, and
7:10 delivered!'—only to go on doing all these A
7:30 they have set their A in the house which
13:27 I have seen your A, your adulteries and neighings,
16:18 idols, and have filled my inheritance with their A
32:34 They set up their A in the house which
44:22 your evil-doings and the A which you committed;
Ezek 5:9 because of all your A I will do with
5:11 and with all your A, therefore I will cut
6:9 evils which they have committed, for all their A
6:11 of all the evil A of the house of
7:3 and I will punish you for all your A
7:4 your ways, while your A are in your midst.
7:8 and I will punish you for all your A
7:9 your ways, while your A are in your midst.
8:6 are doing, the great A that the house of
8:6 But you will see still greater A
8:9 and see the vile A that they are committing
8:13 will see still greater A which they commit."
8:15 will see still greater A than these."
8:17 Judah to commit the A which they commit here,
9:4 groan over all the A that are committed in
11:18 it all its detestable things and all its A
11:21 detestable things and their A, I will requite their
12:16 may confess all their A among the nations where
14:6 and turn away your faces from all your A
16:2 known to Jerusalem her A,
16:22 And in all your A and your harlotries you
16:43 not committed lewdness in addition to all your A
16:47 do according to their A; within a very little
16:51 you have committed more A than they, and have
16:51 righteous by all the A which you have committed.
16:58 your lewdness and your A, says the LORD.
20:4 let them know the A of their fathers,
33:26 the sword, you commit A and each of you
33:29 because of all their A which they have committed.
43:8 holy name by their A which they have committed,
44:6 end to all your A,
44:7 broken my covenant, in addition to all your A
44:13 shame, because of the A which they have committed.
Dan 9:27 upon the wing of A shall come one who
Zech 9:7 its mouth, and its A from between its teeth;
Rev 17:4 golden cup full of A and the impurities of
17:5 the great, mother of harlots and of earth's A

ABOUND (11)

Deut 28:11 LORD will make you A in prosperity, in the
Ps 4:7 than they have when their grain and wine A
72:7 righteousness flourish, and peace A, till the moon be
Prov 28:20 A faithful man will A with blessings, but he
Sir 23:3 my sins may not A; then I will not
Rom 6:1 we to continue in sin that grace may A
15:13 Holy Spirit you may A in hope.
Phil 1:9 that your love may A more and more, with
4:12 I know how to A; in any and all
1Thes 3:12 make you increase and A in love to one
2Pet 1:8 things are yours and A, they keep you from

ABOUNDED (2)

Rom 5:15 one man Jesus Christ A for many.
5:20 where sin increased, grace A all the more,

ABOUNDING (12)

Ex 34:6 slow to anger, and A in steadfast love and
Num 14:18 slow to anger, and A in steadfast love, forgiving
Neh 9:17 slow to anger and A in steadfast love, and
Ps 86:5 art good and forgiving, A in steadfast love to
86:15 slow to anger and A in steadfast love and
103:8 slow to anger and A in steadfast love.
145:8 slow to anger and A in steadfast love.
Prov 8:24 there were no springs A with water.
Joel 2:13 slow to anger, and A in steadfast love, and
Jon 4:2 slow to anger, and A in steadfast love, and
1Cor 15:58 be steadfast, immovable, always A in the work of
Col 2:7 as you were taught, A in thanksgiving.

ABOUNDS (2)

Sir 11:12 who lacks strength and A in poverty; but the
Rom 3:7 my falsehood God's truthfulness A to his glory, why

ABRAHAM (262)

Gen 17:5 your name shall be A; for I have made
17:9 And God said to A, "As for you, you
17:15 And God said to A, "As for Sarai your
17:17 Then A fell on his face and laughed, and
17:18 And A said to God, "O that Ishmael might
17:22 finished talking with him, God went up from A
17:23 Then A took Ishmael his son and all the
17:23 among the men of A's house, and he circumcised
17:24 A was ninety-nine years old when he was
17:26 That very day A and his son Ishmael were
18:6 And A hastened into the tent to Sarah, and
18:7 And A ran to the herd, and took a
18:11 Now A and Sarah were old, advanced in age;
18:13 The LORD said to A, "Why did Sarah laugh,
18:16 looked toward Sodom; and A went with them to
18:17 "Shall I hide from A what I am about
18:18 to do, seeing that A shall become a great
18:19 LORD may bring to A what he has promised
18:22 went toward Sodom; but A still stood before the
18:23 Then A drew near, and said, "Wilt thou indeed
18:27 A answered, "Behold, I have taken upon myself to
18:33 had finished speaking to A; and Abraham returned to
18:33 speaking to Abraham; and A returned to his place.
19:27 And A went early in the morning to the
19:29 the valley, God remembered A, and sent Lot out
20:1 From there A journeyed toward the territory of the
20:2 And A said of Sarah his wife, "She is
20:9 Then Abimelech called A, and said to him, "What
20:10 And Abimelech said to A, "What were you thinking
20:11 A said, "I did it because I thought, There
20:14 and gave them to A, and restored Sarah his
20:17 Then A prayed to God; and God healed Abimelech,
20:18 Abimelech because of Sarah, A's wife.
21:2 Sarah conceived, and bore A a son in his
21:3 A called the name of his son who was
21:4 And A circumcised his son Isaac when he was
21:5 A was a hundred years old when his son
21:7 would have said to A that Sarah would suckle
21:8 and was weaned; and A made a great feast
21:9 she had borne to A, playing with her son
21:10 So she said to A, "Cast out this slave
21:11 was very displeasing to A on account of his

21:12 But God said to A, "Be not displeased because
21:14 So A rose early in the morning, and took
21:22 his army said to A, "God is with you
21:24 And A said, "I will swear."
21:25 When A complained to Abimelech about a well of
21:27 So A took sheep and oxen and gave them
21:28 A set seven ewe lambs of the flock apart.
21:29 And Abimelech said to A, "What is the meaning
21:33 A planted a tamarisk tree in Beer-sheba, and called
21:34 And A sojourned many days in the land of
22:1 these things God tested A, and said to him,
22:1 things God tested Abraham, and said to him, A
22:3 So A rose early in the morning, saddled his
22:4 On the third day A lifted up his eyes
22:5 Then A said to his young men, "Stay here
22:6 And A took the wood of the burnt offering,
22:7 said to his father A, "My father!" And he
22:8 A said, "God will provide himself the lamb for
22:9 God had told him, A built an altar there,
22:10 Then A put forth his hand, and took the
22:11 from heaven, and said, A, Abraham!" And he said,
22:11 called to him from heaven, and said, "Abraham, A
22:13 And A lifted up his eyes and looked, and
22:13 by his horns; and A went and took the
22:14 So A called the name of that place The
22:15 the LORD called to A a second time from
22:19 So A returned to his young men, and they
22:19 together to Beer-sheba; and A dwelt at Beer-sheba.
22:20 things it was told A, "Behold, Milcah also has
22:23 Milcah bore to Nahor, A's brother.
23:2 land of Canaan; and A went in to mourn
23:3 And A rose up from before his dead, and
23:5 The Hittites answered A,
23:7 A rose and bowed to the Hittites, the people
23:10 Ephron the Hittite answered A in the hearing of
23:12 Then A bowed down before the people of the
23:14 Ephron answered A,
23:16 A agreed with Ephron; and Abraham weighed out
23:16 agreed with Ephron; and A weighed out for Ephron
23:18 was made over to A as a possession in
23:19 After this, A buried Sarah his wife in the
23:20 were made over to A as a possession for
24:1 Now A was old, well advanced in years; and
24:1 the LORD had blessed A in all things.
24:2 And A said to his servant, the oldest of
24:6 A said to him, "See to it that you
24:9 under the thigh of A his master, and swore
24:12 God of my master A, grant me success today,
24:12 thee, and show steadfast love to my master A
24:15 the wife of Nahor, A's brother, came out with
24:27 God of my master A, who has not forsaken
24:34 he said, "I am A's servant.
24:42 God of my master A, if now thou wilt
24:48 God of my master A, who had led me
24:52 When A's servant heard their words, he bowed
24:59 and her nurse, and A's servant and his men.
25:1 A took another wife, whose name was Keturah.
25:5 A gave all he had to Isaac.
25:6 sons of his concubines A gave gifts, and while
25:7 of the years of A's life, a hundred and
25:8 A breathed his last and died in a good
25:10 Mamre, the field which A purchased from the.
25:10 There A was buried, with Sarah his wife.
25:11 After the death of A God blessed Isaac his
25:12 the descendants of Ishmael, A's son, whom Hagar
25:12 whom Hagar the Egyptian, Sarah's maid, bore to A
25:19 the descendants of Isaac, A's son: Abraham was the
25:19 of Isaac, Abraham's son: A was the father of
26:1 former famine that was in the days of A
26:3 which I swore to A your father.
26:5 shall bless themselves: because A obeyed my voice
26:15 in the days of A his father.)
26:18 in the days of A his father; for the
26:18 after the death of A; and he gave them
26:24 am the God of A your father; fear not,
26:24 descendants for my servant A's sake."
28:4 give the blessing of A to you and to
28:4 land of your sojournings which God gave to A
28:9 the daughter of Ishmael A's son, the sister of
28:13 LORD, the God of A your father and the
31:42 father, the God of A and the Fear of
31:53 The God of A and the God of Nahor,
32:9 God of my father A and God of my
35:12 which I gave to A and Isaac I will
35:27 (that is, Hebron), where A and Isaac had sojourned.
48:15 before whom my fathers A and Isaac walked, the
48:16 name of my fathers A and Isaac; and let
49:30 land of Canaan, which A bought with the field
49:31 There they buried A and Sarah his wife; there
50:13 east of Mamre, which A bought with the field
50:24 which he swore to A, to Isaac, and to
Ex 2:24 remembered his covenant with A, with Isaac, and
3:6 father, the God of A, the God of Isaac,
3:15 fathers, the God of A, the God of Isaac,
3:16 fathers, the God of A, of Isaac, and of
4:5 fathers, the God of A, the God of Isaac,
6:3 I appeared to A, to Isaac, and to Jacob,
6:8 swore to give to A, to Isaac, and to
32:13 Remember A, Isaac, and Israel, thy servants, to
33:1 which I swore to A, Isaac, and Jacob, saying,
Lev 26:42 and my covenant with A, and I will remember
Num 32:11 swore to give to A, to Isaac, and to
Deut 1:8 to your fathers, to A, to Isaac, and to
6:10 to your fathers, to A, to Isaac, and to
9:5 to your fathers, to A, to Isaac, and to
9:27 Remember thy servants, A, Isaac, and Jacob; do not
29:13 to your fathers, to A, to Isaac, and to
30:20 to your fathers, to A, to Isaac, and to
34:4 which I swore to A, to Isaac, and to
Josh 24:2 Terah, the father of A and of Nahor; and
24:3 I took your father A from beyond the River
1Kgs 18:36 "O LORD, God of A, Isaac, and Israel, let
2Kgs 13:23 of his covenant with A, Isaac, and Jacob, and
1Chr 1:27 Serug, Nahor, Terah; Abram, that is, A
1:28 The sons of A: Isaac and Ishmael.
1:32 The sons of Keturah, A's concubine: she bore Zimran,
1:34 A was the father of Isaac.
16:13 uttered, O offspring of A his servant, sons of
16:16 which he made with A, his sworn promise to
29:18 LORD, the God of A, Isaac, and Israel, our
2Chr 20:7 to the descendants of A thy friend?
30:6 LORD, the God of A, Isaac, and Israel, that
Neh 9:7 give him the name A;
Tob 4:12 my son, that Noah, A, Isaac, and Jacob, our
Jud 8:26 what he did with A, and how he tested
Esth 13:15 and King, God of A, spare thy people; for
14:18 now, except in thee, O Lord God of A
Ps 47:9 gather as the people of the God of A
105:6 uttered, O offspring of A his servant, sons of
105:9 which he made with A, his sworn promise to
105:42 his holy promise, and A his servant.
Sir 44:20 A was the great father of a multitude of
44:23 for the sake of A his father.
Is 29:22 the LORD, who redeemed A, concerning the house of
41:8 chosen, the offspring of A, my friend;
51:2 Look to A your father and to Sarah who
63:16 art our Father, though A does not know us
Jer 33:26 over the seed of A, Isaac, and Jacob.
Bar 2:34 to their fathers, to A and to Isaac and
Ezek 33:24 of Israel keep saying, A was only one man,
Dan 3:35 for the sake of A thy beloved and for
Mic 7:20 and steadfast love to A, as thou hast sworn
1Mac 2:52 Was not A found faithful when tested, and it
12:21 are brethren and are of the family of A
2Mac 1:2 remember his covenant with A and Isaac and Jacob,
Mt 1:1 Christ, the son of David, the son of A
1:2 A was the father of Isaac, and Isaac the
1:17 all the generations from A to David were fourteen
3:9 to yourselves, 'We have A as our father'; for
3:9 from these stones to raise up children to A
8:11 sit at table with A, Isaac, and Jacob in
22:32 am the God of A, and the God of
Mk 12:26 am the God of A, and the God of
Lk 1:55 to our fathers, to A and to his posterity
1:73 swore to our father A,
3:8 to yourselves, 'We have A as our father'; for
3:8 from these stones to raise up children to A
3:34 Isaac, the son of A, the son of Terah,
13:16 woman, a daughter of A whom Satan bound for
13:28 teeth, when you see A and Isaac and Jacob
16:22 by the angels to A's bosom.
16:23 his eyes, and saw A far-off and Lazarus in
16:24 he called out, 'Father A, have mercy upon me,
16:25 in this flame.' But A said, 'Son, remember that
16:29 place of torment.' But A said, 'They have Moses
16:30 he said, 'No, father A; but if some one
19:9 house, since he also is a son of A
20:37 Lord the God of A and the God of
Jn 8:33 "We are descendants of A, and have never been
8:37 you are descendants of A; yet you seek to
8:39 They answered him, A is our father." Jesus said
8:39 them, "If you were A's children, you would do

8:39 you would do what A did,
8:40 this is not what A did.
8:52 A died, as did the prophets; and you say,
8:53 greater than our father A, who died?
8:56 Your father A rejoiced that he was to see
8:57 yet fifty years old, and have you seen A
8:58 say to you, before A was, I am."
Acts 3:13 The God of A and of Isaac and of
3:25 your fathers, saying to A, 'And in your posterity
7:2 appeared to our father A, when he was in
7:8 And so A became the father of Isaac, and
7:16 in the tomb that A had bought for a
7:17 God had granted to A, the people grew and
7:32 fathers, the God of A and of Isaac and
13:26 of the family of A, and those among you
Rom 4:1 shall we say about A, our forefather according to
4:2 For if A was justified by works, he has
4:3 A believed God, and it was reckoned to him
4:9 faith was reckoned to A as righteousness.
4:12 faith which our father A had before he was
4:13 The promise to A and his descendants, that they
4:16 share the faith of A, for he is the
9:7 all are children of A because they are his
11:1 Israelite, a descendant of A, a member of the
2Cor 11:22 Are they descendants of A
Gal 3:6 Thus A "believed God, and it was reckoned to
3:7 men of faith who are the sons of A
3:8 the gospel beforehand to A, saying, "In you shall
3:9 faith are blessed with A who had faith.
3:14 Jesus the blessing of A might come upon the
3:16 promises were made to A and to his offspring.
3:18 God gave it to A by a promise.
3:29 Christs, then you are A's offspring, heirs according to
4:22 it is written that A had two sons, one
Heb 2:16 he is concerned but with the descendants of A
6:13 made a promise to A, since he had no
6:15 And thus A, having patiently endured, obtained the.
7:1 Most High God, met A returning from the slaughter
7:2 him; and to him A apportioned a tenth part
7:4 A the patriarch gave him a tithe of the
7:5 brethren, though these also are descended from A
7:6 genealogy received tithes from A and blessed him
7:9 tithes, paid tithes through A,
11:8 By faith A obeyed when he was called to
11:17 By faith A, when he was tested, offered up
Jas 2:21 Was not A our father justified by works, when
2:23 was fulfilled which says, A believed God, and it
1Pet 3:6 husbands, as Sarah obeyed A, calling him lord.

ABRAM (62)

Gen 11:26 became the father of A, Nahor, and Haran.
11:27 was the father of A, Nahor, and Haran; and
11:29 And A and Nahor took wives; the name of
11:29 wives; the name of A's wife was Sarai, and
11:31 Terah took A his son and Lot the son
11:31 his daughter-in-law, his son A's wife, and they went
12:1 the LORD said to A, "Go from your country
12:4 So A went, as the LORD had told him;
12:4 A was seventy-five years old when he departed from
12:5 And A took Sarai his wife, and Lot his
12:6 the land of Canaan, A passed through the land
12:7 the LORD appeared to A, and said, "To your
12:9 And A journeyed on, still going toward the Negeb.
12:10 So A went down to Egypt to sojourn there,
12:14 When A entered Egypt the Egyptians saw that the
12:16 he dealt well with A; and he had sheep,
12:17 plagues because of Sarai, A's wife.
12:18 So Pharaoh called A, and said, "What is this
13:1 So A went up from Egypt, he and his
13:2 Now A was very rich in cattle, in silver,
13:4 the first; and there A called on the name
13:5 Lot, who went with A, also had flocks and
13:7 between the herdsmen of A's cattle and the
13:8 Then A said to Lot, "Let there be no
13:12 A dwelt in the land of Canaan, while Lot
13:14 The LORD said to A, after Lot had separated
13:18 So A moved his tent, and came and dwelt
14:12 Lot, the son of A's brother, who dwelt in
14:13 escaped came, and told A the Hebrew, who was
14:13 Eshcol and of Aner; these were allies of A
14:14 When A heard that his kinsman had been taken
14:19 and said, "Blessed be A by God Most High,
14:20 And A gave him a tenth of everything.
14:21 of Sodom said to A, "Give me the persons,
14:22 But A said to the king of Sodom, "I
14:23 say, 'I have made A rich.'
15:1 the LORD came to A in a vision, "Fear
15:1 a vision, "Fear not, A, I am your shield;
15:2 But A said, "O Lord GOD, what wilt thou
15:3 And A said, "Behold, thou hast given me no
15:11 down upon the carcasses, A drove them away.
15:12 deep sleep fell on A; and lo, a dread
15:13 the LORD said to A, "Know of a surety
15:18 made a covenant with A, saying, "To your
16:1 Now Sarai, A's wife, bore him no children.
16:2 and Sarai said to A, "Behold now, the LORD
16:2 And A hearkened to the voice of Sarai.
16:3 So, after A had dwelt ten years in the
16:3 land of Canaan, Sarai, A's wife, took Hagar the
16:3 and gave her to A her husband as a
16:5 And Sarai said to A, "May the wrong done
16:6 But A said to Sarai, "Behold, your maid is
16:15 And Hagar bore A a son; and Abram called
16:15 Abram a son; and A called the name of
16:16 A was eighty-six years old when Hagar bore Ishmael
16:16 eighty-six years old when Hagar bore Ishmael to A
17:1 When A was ninety-nine years old the LORD
17:1 the LORD appeared to A, and said to him,
17:3 Then A fell on his face; and God said
17:5 shall your name be A, but your name shall
1Chr 1:27 Serug, Nahor, Terah; A, that is, Abraham.
Neh 9:7 God who didst choose A and bring him forth

ABROAD (34)

Gen 10:18 Afterward the families of the Canaanites spread A
10:32 these the nations spread A on the earth after
11:4 lest we be scattered A upon the face of
11:8 the LORD scattered them A from there over the
11:9 the LORD scattered them A over the face of
28:14 and you shall spread A to the west and
Ex 1:11 more they multiplied and the more they spread A
5:12 the people were scattered A throughout all the land
21:19 rises again and walks A with his staff, he
Lev 18:9 your mother, whether born at home or born A
25:9 Then you shall send A the loud trumpet on
25:9 atonement you shall send A the trumpet throughout
1Sam 2:24 I hear the people of the LORD spreading A
30:16 behold, they were spread A over all the land,
1Chr 13:2 God, let us send A to our brethren who
2Chr 31:5 the command was spread A, the people of Israel
Esth 3:8 a certain people scattered A and dispersed among
Job 15:23 He wanders A for bread, saying, 'Where is it?'
Ps 41:6 mischief; when he goes out, he tells it A
68:9 God, thou didst shed A; thou didst restore thy
Prov 5:16 your springs be scattered A, streams of water in
Song 4:16 upon my garden, let its fragrance be wafted A
Wis 18:10 their piteous lament for their children was spread A
Is 16:8 desert; its shoots spread A and passed over the
54:3 For you will spread A to the right and
Ezek 34:12 sheep have been scattered A, so will I seek
34:21 you have scattered them A,
Zech 2:6 I have spread you A as the four winds
2Mac 4:39 of them had spread A, the populace gathered against
Lk 5:15 more the report went A concerning him; and great
Jn 11:52 one the children of God who are scattered A
21:23 The saying spread A among the brethren that this
2Cor 9:9 is written, "He scatters A, he gives to the
Rev 16:14 performing signs, who go A to the kings of

ABRON

Jud 2:24 cities along the brook A, as far as the

ABRONAH (2)

Num 33:34 they set out from Jotbathah, and encamped at A
33:35 they set out from A, and encamped at Ezion-geber.

ABSALOM (111)

2Sam 3:3 Carmel; and the third, A the son of Maacah
13:1 Now A, David's son, had a beautiful sister, whose
13:4 love Tamar, my brother A's sister."
13:20 And her brother A said to her, "Has Amnon
13:20 woman, in her brother A's house.
13:22 But A spoke to Amnon neither good nor bad;
13:22 good nor bad; for A hated Amnon, because he
13:23 two full years A had sheepshearers at Baal-hazor,
13:23 is near Ephraim, and A invited all the king's
13:24 And A came to the king, and said, "Behold,
13:25 the king said to A, "No, my son, let
13:26 Then A said, "If not, pray let my brother
13:27 But A pressed him until he let Amnon and
13:28 Then A commanded his servants, "Mark when
13:29 So the servants of A did to Amnon as

A

13:29 did to Amnon as A had commanded.
13:30 tidings came to David, A has slain all the
13:32 by the command of A this has been determined
13:34 But A fled.
13:37 But A fled, and went to Talmai the son
13:38 So A fled, and went to Geshur, and was
13:39 to go forth to A; for he was comforted
14:1 perceived that the king's heart went out to A
14:21 grant this; go, bring back the young man A
14:23 to Geshur, and brought A to Jerusalem.
14:24 So A dwelt apart in his own house, and
14:25 for his beauty as A; from the sole of
14:27 There were born to A three sons, and one
14:28 So A dwelt two full years in Jerusalem, without
14:29 Then A sent for Joab, to send him to
14:30 So A's servants set the field on fire.
14:31 arose and went to A at his house, and
14:32 A answered Joab, "Behold, I sent word to you,
14:33 the king, and told him; and he summoned A
14:33 ground before the king; and the king kissed A
15:1 After this A got himself a chariot and horses,
15:2 And A used to rise early and stand beside
15:2 the king for judgment, A would call to him,
15:3 A would say to him, "See, your claims are
15:4 A said moreover, "Oh that I were judge in
15:6 Thus A did to all of Israel who came
15:6 king for judgment; so A stole the hearts of
15:7 end of four years A said to the king,
15:10 But A sent secret messengers throughout all the
15:10 the trumpet, then say, A is king at Hebron!'"
15:11 With A went two hundred men from Jerusalem who
15:12 And while A was offering the sacrifices, he sent
15:12 and the people with A kept increasing.
15:13 of the men of Israel have gone after A
15:14 escape for us from A; go in haste, lest
15:31 David, "Ahithophel is among the conspirators with A
15:34 city, and say to A, 'I will be your
15:37 the city, just as A was entering Jerusalem.
16:8 the kingdom into the hand of your son A
16:15 Now A and all the people, the men of
16:16 David's friend, came to A, Hushai said to A,
16:17 And A said to Hushai, "Is this your loyalty
16:18 And Hushai said to A, "No; for whom the
16:20 Then A said to Ahithophel, "Give your counsel; what
16:21 Ahithophel said to A, "Go in to your father's
16:22 pitched a tent for A upon the roof; and
16:22 upon the roof; and A went in to his
16:23 of Ahithophel esteemed, both by David and by A
17:1 Moreover Ahithophel said to A, "Let me choose
17:4 And the advice pleased A and all the elders
17:5 Then A said, "Call Hushai the Archite also, and
17:6 when Hushai came to A, Absalom said to him,
17:6 Hushai came to Absalom, A said to him, "Thus
17:7 Then Hushai said to A, "This time the counsel
17:9 the people who follow A
17:14 And A and all the men of Israel said,
17:14 so that the LORD might bring evil upon A
17:15 so did Ahithophel counsel A and the elders of
17:18 saw them, and told A; so both of them
17:20 When A's servants came to the woman at the
17:24 And A crossed the Jordan with all the men
17:25 Now A had set Amasa over the army instead
17:26 And Israel and A encamped in the land of
18:5 gently for my sake with the young man A
18:5 king gave orders to all the commanders about A
18:9 And A chanced to meet the servants of David.
18:9 A was riding upon his mule, and the mule
18:10 Joab, "Behold, I saw A hanging in an oak."
18:12 protect the young man A
18:14 into the heart of A, while he was still
18:15 Joab's armor-bearers, surrounded A and struck him,
18:17 And they took A, and threw him into a
18:18 Now A in his lifetime had taken and set
18:18 and it is called A's monument to this day.
18:29 said, "Is it well with the young man A
18:32 Cushite, "Is it well with the young man A
18:33 "O my son A, my son, my son A
18:33 instead of you, O A, my son, my son!"
19:1 "Behold, the king is weeping and mourning for A
19:4 voice, "O my son A, O Absalom, my son,
19:4 my son Absalom, O A, my son, my son!"
19:6 I perceive that if A were alive and all
19:9 he has fled out of the land from A
19:10 But A, whom we anointed over us, is dead
20:6 us more harm than A; take your lord's servants
1Kgs 1:6 handsome man; and he was born next after A
2:7 when I fled from A your brother.
2:28 he had not supported A – Joab fled to
1Chr 3:2 the Carmelitess, the third A, whose mother was
2Chr 11:20 Maacah the daughter of A, who bore him Abijah,
11:21 Maacah the daughter of A above all his wives
1Mac 11:70 Mattathias the son of A and Judas the son
13:11 Jonathan the son of A to Joppa, and with
2Mac 11:17 John and A, who were sent by you, have

ABSENCE (3)

Lk 22:6 to them in the A of the multitude.
1Cor 16:17 made up for your A;
Phil 2:12 much more in my A, work out your own

ABSENT (9)

Gen 31:49 me, when we are A one from the other.
Wis 11:11 Whether A or present, they were equally distressed,
14:17 they might flatter the A one as though present.
1Mac 4:4 the division was still A from the camp.
1Cor 5:3 For though A in body I am present in
2Cor 10:11 say by letter when A, we do when present.
13:2 warn them now while A, as I did when
Phil 1:27 see you or am A, I may hear of
Col 2:5 For though I am A in body, yet I

ABSTAIN (6)

Acts 15:20 write to them to A from the pollutions of
15:29 necessary things: that you A from what has been
21:25 judgment that they should A from what has been
1Thes 4:3 your sanctification: that you A from unchastity;
5:22 fast what is good, A from every form of
1Pet 2:11 aliens and exiles to A from the passions of

ABSTAINS (4)

Rom 14:3 eats despise him who A, and let not him
14:3 let not him who A pass judgment on him
14:6 God; while he who A, abstains in honor of
14:6 while he who abstains, A in honor of the

ABSTINENCE

1Tim 4:3 forbid marriage and enjoin A from foods which God

ABUBUS (2)

1Mac 16:11 Ptolemy the son of A had been appointed governor
16:15 The son of A received them treacherously in the

ABUNDANCE (72)

Gen 41:49 up grain in great A, like the sand of
Deut 28:47 by reason of the A of all things,
33:15 ancient mountains, and the A of the everlasting hills,
1Kgs 1:19 fatlings, and sheep in A, and has invited all
1:25 fatlings, and sheep in A, and has invited all
10:10 again came such an A of spices as these
1Chr 22:15 You have an A of workmen: stonecutters, masons,
29:16 our God, all this A that we have provided
29:21 offerings, and sacrifices in A for all Israel;
2Chr 2:9 timber for me in A, for the house I
14:15 carried away sheep in A and camels.
18:2 And Ahab killed an A of sheep and oxen
24:11 did day after day, and collected money in A
31:5 of Israel gave in A the first fruits of
32:5 He also made weapons and shields in A
32:29 flocks and herds in A; for God had given
Neh 5:18 skins of wine in A; yet with all this
9:25 and fruit trees in A; so they ate, and
Tob 2:2 Upon seeing the A of food I said to
Job 36:31 these he judges peoples; he gives food in A
Ps 5:7 But I through the A of thy steadfast love
36:8 They feast on the A of thy house, and
37:16 righteous has than the A of many wicked.
37:19 times, in the days of famine they have A
49:6 and boast of the A of their riches?
52:7 but trusted in the A of his riches, and
68:9 Rain in A, O God, thou didst shed abroad;
69:13 O God, in the A of thy steadfast love
72:16 May there be A of grain in the land;
78:25 of the angels; he sent them food in A
105:40 quails, and gave them bread from heaven in A
106:7 did not remember the A of thy steadfast love,
106:45 relented according to the A of his steadfast love.
Prov 11:14 falls; but in an A of counselors there is
20:15 There is gold, and A of costly stones; but
21:5 diligent lead surely to A, but every one who
24:6 your war, and in A of counselors there is
Sir 10:26 works and has an A of everything, than one
13:11 equal, nor trust his A of words; for he

	18:11	be evil; therefore he grants them forgiveness in A
	45:20	of first fruits in A;
Is	7:22	and because of the A of milk which they
	15:7	Therefore the A they have gained and what they
	30:33	fire and wood in A; the breath of the
	33:6	stability of your times, A of salvation, wisdom, and
	33:23	prey and spoil in A will be divided; even
	60:5	and rejoice; because the A of the sea shall
	63:7	mercy, according to the A of his steadfast love.
	66:11	with delight from the A of her glory."
Jer	31:14	of the priests with A, and my people shall
	33:6	and reveal to them A of prosperity and security.
	40:12	they gathered wine and summer fruits in great A
Lam	3:32	compassion according to the A of his steadfast love;
Ezek	7:11	shall remain, nor their A, nor their wealth; neither
	28:16	In the A of your trade you were filled
Zech	14:14	be collected, gold, silver, and garments in great A
1Mac	10:21	recruited troops and equipped them with arms in A
Mt	12:34	For out of the A of the heart the
	13:12	and he will have A; but from him who
	25:29	and he will have A; but from him who
Mk	12:44	contributed out of their A; but she out of
Lk	6:45	for out of the A of the heart his
	12:15	not consist in the A of his possessions."
	21:4	contributed out of their A, but she out of
Rom	5:17	those who receive the A of grace and the
2Cor	8:2	test of affliction, their A of joy and their
	8:14	matter of equality your A at the present time
	8:14	want, so that their A may supply your want,
	9:8	with every blessing in A, so that you may
	9:8	and may provide in A for every good work.
	12:7	too elated by the A of revelations, a thorn
Phil	4:12	facing plenty and hunger, A and want.

ABUNDANT (34)

1Chr	12:40	mules and on oxen, A provisions of meal, cakes
2Chr	11:23	and he gave them A provisions, and procured wives
Esth	10:6	and the sun and A water _ the river
	11:10	a great river, with A water;
Job	37:23	power and justice, and A righteousness he will not
Ps	31:19	O how A is thy goodness, which thou hast
	37:11	and delight themselves in A prosperity.
	51:1	love; according to thy A mercy blot out my
	69:16	good; according to thy A mercy, turn to me.
	145:7	the fame of thy A goodness, and shall sing
	147:5	is our LORD, and A in power; his understanding
Prov	3:2	years of life and A welfare will they give
	14:4	is no grain; but A crops come by the
Wis	11:7	infants, thou gavest them A water unexpectedly,
Sir	24:17	blossoms became glorious and A fruit.
	24:27	her thought is more A than the sea, and
Is	23:18	her merchandise will supply A food and fine clothing
Ezek	17:5	he placed it beside A waters.
	17:8	to good soil by A waters, that it might
	19:10	branches by reason of A water.
	27:16	you because of your A goods; they exchanged for
	27:18	with you for your A goods, because of your
	27:33	many peoples; with your A wealth and merchandise
	31:5	its branches long, from A water in its shoots.
	31:7	roots went down to A waters.
	36:29	grain and make it A and lay no famine
	36:30	increase of the field A, that you may never
Dan	3:42	forbearance and in thy A mercy.
	4:12	fair and its fruit A, and in it was
	4:21	fair and its fruit A, and in which was
	11:13	a great army and A supplies.
Joel	2:23	poured down for you A rain, the early and
1Mac	6:6	the arms, supplies, and A spoils which they had
2Cor	2:4	let you know the A love that I have

ABUNDANTLY (20)

Gen	8:17	that they may breed A on the earth, and
	9:7	and multiply, bring forth A on the earth and
	30:30	and it has increased A; and the LORD has
	41:47	the earth brought forth A,
Num	20:11	and water came forth A, and the congregation drank,
Deut	30:9	God will make you A prosperous in all the
2Chr	31:5	and they brought in A the tithe of everything.
Job	36:28	the skies pour down, and drop upon man A
Ps	31:23	preserves the faithful, but A requites him who acts
	65:10	Thou waterest its furrows A, settling its ridges,
	78:15	and gave them drink A as from the deep.
	104:16	the LORD are watered A, the cedars of Lebanon
	132:15	I will A bless her provisions; I will satisfy
Is	35:2	crocus it shall blossom A, and rejoice with joy
	55:7	God, for he will A pardon.
Jn	10:10	that they may have life, and have it A
2Cor	1:5	For as we share A in Christ's sufferings, so
	1:5	through Christ we share A in comfort too.
Eph	3:20	to do far more A than all that we
2Thes	1:3	your faith is growing A, and the love of

ABUSE (12)

Prov	9:7	a scoffer gets himself A, and he who reproves
	22:10	out, and quarreling and A will cease.
Sir	7:20	Do not A a servant who performs his work
	27:15	to bloodshed, and their A is grievous to hear.
	27:21	there is reconciliation after A, but whoever has
	27:28	Mockery and A issue from the proud man, but
Jer	38:19	to them and they A me."
Lk	6:28	pray for those who A you.
Heb	10:33	being publicly exposed to A and affliction, and
	11:26	He considered A suffered for the Christ greater
	13:13	camp and bear the A he endured.
1Pet	4:4	wild profligacy, and they A you;

ABUSED (2)

Judg	19:25	they knew her, and A her all night until
1Pet	3:16	that, when you are A, those who revile your

ABUSIVE (3)

Sir	18:17	fool is ungracious and A, and the gift of
	41:22	approach her bed; of A words, before friends–
2Tim	3:2	of money, proud, arrogant, A, disobedient to their

ABYSS (7)

Sir	1:3	of the earth, the A, and wisdom–who can
	16:16	the highest heaven, the A and the earth, will
	24:5	and have walked in the depths of the A
	24:27	sea, and her counsel deeper than the great A
	42:18	He searches out the A, and the hearts of
Lk	8:31	not to command them to depart into the A
Rom	10:7	Christ down) or "Who will descend into the A

ACACIA (28)

Ex	25:5	tanned rams' skins, goatskins, A wood,
	25:10	make an ark of A wood; two cubits and
	25:13	shall make poles of A wood, and overlay them
	25:23	make a table of A wood; two cubits shall
	25:28	make the poles of A wood, and overlay them
	26:15	for the tabernacle of A wood.
	26:26	shall make bars of A wood, five for the
	26:32	upon four pillars of A overlaid with gold, with
	26:37	screen five pillars of A, and overlay them with
	27:1	make the altar of A wood, five cubits long
	27:6	the altar, poles of A wood, and overlay them
	30:1	burn incense upon; of A wood shall you make
	30:5	make the poles of A wood, and overlay them
	35:7	rams' skins, and goatskins; A wood,
	35:24	with whom was found A wood of any use
	36:20	for the tabernacle of A wood.
	36:31	he made bars of A wood, five for the
	36:36	made four pillars of A, and overlaid them with
	37:1	made the ark of A wood; two cubits and
	37:4	he made poles of A wood, and overlaid them
	37:10	made the table of A wood; two cubits was
	37:15	made the poles of A wood to carry the
	37:25	altar of incense of A wood; its length was
	37:28	made the poles of A wood, and overlaid them
	38:1	burnt offering also of A wood; five cubits was
	38:6	made the poles of A wood, and overlaid them
Deut	10:3	made an ark of A wood, and hewed two
Is	41:19	wilderness the cedar, the A, the myrtle, and the

ACCAD

Gen	10:10	was Babel, Erech, and A, all of them in

ACCENT

Mt	26:73	of them, for your A betrays you."

ACCEPT (61)

Gen	23:13	price of the field; A it from me, that
	32:20	face; perhaps he will A me."
	33:10	in your sight, then A my present from my
	33:11	A, I pray you, my gift that is brought
Ex	22:11	and the owner shall A the oath, and he
Num	7:5	LORD said to Moses, A these from them, that
	35:31	Moreover you shall A no ransom for the life
	35:32	And you shall A no ransom for him who
Deut	33:11	LORD, his substance, and A the work of his
1Sam	2:15	for he will not A boiled meat from you,
	10:4	bread, which you shall A from their hand.

	26:19	against me, may he A an offering; but if
2Sam	24:23	"The LORD your God A you."
2Kgs	5:15	but in Israel; so A now a present from
	5:23	said, "Be pleased to A two talents." And he
	5:26	it a time to A money and garments, olive
Tob	13:6	knows if he will A you and have mercy
Jud	11:5	Judith replied to him, A the words of your
Esth	4:4	but he would not A them.
Job	21:29	and do you not A their testimony
	42:8	you, for I will A his prayer not to
Ps	50:9	I will A no bull from your house, nor
	119:108	A my offerings of praise, O LORD, and teach
Prov	4:11	Hear, my son, and A my words, that the
	6:35	He will A no compensation, nor be appeased though
	19:20	Listen to advice and A instruction, that you may
Eccl	5:19	enjoy them, and to A his lot and find
Sir	2:4	A whatever is brought upon you, and in changes
	6:23	Listen, my son, and A my judgment; do not
	7:9	High God he will A it."
	18:13	compassion on those who A his discipline and who
	32:14	fears the Lord will A his discipline, and those
	35:12	for he will not A it; and do not
	36:21	A woman will A any man, but one daughter
Is	29:24	those who murmur will A instruction."
Jer	7:28	God, and did not A discipline; truth has perished;
	14:10	the LORD does not A them, now he will
	14:12	offering, I will not A them; but I will
	25:28	if they refuse to A the cup from your
Ezek	20:40	land; there I will A them, and there I
	20:41	pleasing odor I will A you, when I bring
	43:27	offerings; and I will A you, says the Lord
Hos	14:2	"Take away all iniquity; A that which is good
Amos	5:22	offerings, I will not A them, and the peace
Zeph	3:7	fear me, she will A correction; she will not
Mal	1:10	and I will not A an offering from your
	1:13	Shall I A that from your hand?
1Mac	10:46	did not believe or A them, because they remembered
	15:20	good to us to A the shield from them.
2Mac	1:26	fathers and consecrate them, A this sacrifice on
	7:29	A death, so that in God's mercy I may
Mt	11:14	you are willing to A it, he is Elijah
Mk	4:20	hear the word and A it and bear fruit,
Acts	16:21	for us Romans to A or practice."
	22:18	because they will not A your testimony about me.'
	24:3	way and everywhere we A this with all gratitude.
	24:14	God which these themselves A, that there will be
2Cor	6:1	entreat you not to A the grace of God
	11:4	received, or if you A a different gospel from
	11:16	even if you do, A me as a fool,
Heb	11:35	were tortured, refusing to A release, that they might

ACCEPTABLE (32)

Lev	10:19	would it have been A in the sight of
	22:20	it will not be A for you.
	22:27	on it shall be A as an offering by
Ps	19:14	of my heart be A in thy sight, O
	51:17	The sacrifice A to God is a broken spirit;
	69:13	At an A time, O God, in the abundance
Prov	10:32	righteous know what is A, but the mouth of
	21:3	and justice is more A to the LORD than
Wis	9:12	my works will be A, and I shall judge
Sir	2:5	in the fire, and A men in the furnace
	34:18	blemished; the gifts of the lawless are not A
	35:7	a righteous man is A, and the memory of
Is	58:5	fast, and a day A to the LORD?
Jer	6:20	burnt offerings are not A, nor your sacrifices pleasing
Dan	4:27	let my counsel be A to you; break off
Lk	4:19	oppressed, to proclaim the A year of the Lord."
	4:24	you, no prophet is A in his own country.
Acts	10:35	what is right is A to him.
Rom	12:1	living sacrifice, holy and A to God, which is
	12:2	what is good and A and perfect.
	14:18	thus serves Christ is A to God and approved
	15:16	the Gentiles may be A, sanctified by the Holy
	15:31	for Jerusalem may be A to the saints,
2Cor	6:2	he says, "At the A time I have listened
	6:2	Behold, now is the A time; behold, now is
	8:12	is there, it is A according to what a
Phil	4:18	fragrant offering, a sacrifice A and pleasing to God.
1Tim	2:3	good, and it is A in the sight of
	5:4	parents; for this is A in the sight of
Heb	11:4	to God a more A sacrifice than Cain, through
	12:28	us offer to God A worship, with reverence and
1Pet	2:5	to offer spiritual sacrifices A to God through Jesus

ACCEPTANCE (5)

Lev	23:11	that you may find A; on the morrow after
Is	60:7	shall come up with A on my altar, and
Rom	11:15	world, what will their A mean but life from
1Tim	1:15	and worthy of full A, that Christ Jesus came
	4:9	The saying is sure and worthy of full A

ACCEPTED (29)

Gen	4:7	If you do well, will you not be A
Ex	28:38	that they may be A before the LORD.
Lev	1:3	that he may be A before the LORD;
	1:4	and it shall be A for him to make
	7:18	it shall not be A, neither shall it be
	19:5	shall offer it so that you may be A
	19:7	it will not be A,
	22:19	burnt offering, to be A you shall offer a
	22:21	the flock, to be A it must be perfect;
	22:23	but for a votive offering it cannot be A
	22:25	they will not be A for you."
	22:29	shall sacrifice it so that you may be A
Judg	13:23	he would not have A a burnt offering and
Job	42:9	them; and the LORD A Job's prayer.
Wis	3:6	sacrificial burnt offering he A them.
Sir	35:16	the Lord will be A, and his prayer will
Is	56:7	their sacrifices will be A on my altar; for
Dan	3:39	spirit may we be A, as though it were
1Mac	1:43	All the Gentiles A the command of the king.
	6:60	of peace, and they A it.
	9:31	Jonathan at that time A the leadership and took
	14:47	So Simon A and agreed to be high priest,
2Mac	12:4	And when they A, because they wished to live
2Cor	8:17	For he not only A our appeal, but being
	10:18	commends himself that is A, but the man whom
	11:4	from the one you A, you submit to it
1Thes	2:13	heard from us, you A it not as the
Heb	10:34	prisoners, and you joyfully A the plundering of your
3 Jn	1:7	his sake and have A nothing from the heathen.

ACCEPTING (4)

2Kgs	5:20	the Syrian, in not A from his hand what
Wis	12:24	the paths of error, A as gods those animals
2Cor	11:8	robbed other churches by A support from them in
Heb	11:4	God bearing witness by A his gifts; he died,

ACCEPTS (6)

Job	33:26	to God, and he A him, he comes into
Ps	6:9	my supplication; the LORD A my prayer.
Prov	17:23	A wicked man A a bribe from the bosom
Sir	3:17	you will be loved by those whom God A
Zeph	3:2	to no voice, she A no correction.
Mal	2:13	regards the offering or A it with favor at

ACCESS (6)

Zech	3:7	you the right of A among those who are
2Mac	12:21	besiege and difficult of A because of the narrowness
	14:3	safe or to have A again to the holy
Rom	5:2	him we have obtained A to this grace in
Eph	2:18	him we both have A in one Spirit to
	3:12	boldness and confidence of A through our faith in

ACCESSORIES (2)

Num	3:36	bases, and all their A; all the service pertaining
	4:32	equipment and all their A; and you shall assign

ACCO

Judg	1:31	out the inhabitants of A, or the inhabitants of

ACCOMPANIED (10)

2Chr	29:27	also, and the trumpets, A by the instruments of
Tob	12:8	Prayer is good when A by fasting, almsgiving, and
1Mac	12:47	Galilee, while a thousand A him.
Lk	14:25	Now great multitudes A him; and he turned and
Acts	1:21	the men who have A us during all the
	10:23	the brethren from Joppa A him.
	11:12	These six brethren also A me, and we entered
	20:4	the son of Pyrrhus, A him; and of the
	27:2	we put to sea, A by Aristarchus, a Macedonian
1Cor	9:5	the right to be A by a wife, as

ACCOMPANY (6)

Jud	10:17	a hundred men to A her and her maid,
2Mac	3:24	so bold as to A him were astounded by
Mk	16:17	And these signs will A those who believe: in
Acts	10:20	and go down, and A them without hesitation; for
	16:3	Paul wanted Timothy to A him; and he took
1Cor	16:4	go also, they will A me.

ACCOMPLISH (14)

2Sam	3:9	if I do not A for David what the
Jud	10:9	will go out and A the things about which
	11:6	your maidservant, God will A something through you,
	11:16	has sent me to A with you things that
Job	35:6	sinned, what do you A against him?
	37:12	by his guidance, to A all that he commands
Is	37:32	LORD of hosts will A this.
	46:10	stand, and I will A all my purpose,'
	55:11	empty, but it shall A that which I purpose,
2Mac	14:29	for an opportunity to A this by a stratagem.
Lk	9:31	which he was to A at Jerusalem.
Jn	4:34	sent me, and to A his work.
	5:35	has granted me to A, these very works which
Acts	20:24	if only I may A my course and the

ACCOMPLISHED (21)

2Chr	7:11	LORD and in his own house he successfully A
	8:16	Thus was A all the work of Solomon from
	36:22	of Jeremiah might be A, the LORD stirred up
Ezra	1:1	of Jeremiah might be A, the LORD stirred up
Neh	6:16	this work had been A with the help of
Esth	13:3	how this might be A, Haman who excels among
	16:7	"What has been wickedly A through the pestilent
Jer	23:20	he has executed and A the intents of his
	30:24	he has executed and A the intents of his
	39:16	and they shall be A before you on that
Lam	4:22	daughter of Zion, is A, he will keep you
Dan	11:36	till the indignation is A; for what is determined
	12:7	to an end all these things would be A
2Mac	10:38	When they had A these things, with hymns and
Mt	5:18	will pass from the law until all is A
Mk	13:4	sign when these things are all to be A
Lk	1:1	things which have been A among us,
	12:50	and how I am constrained until it is A
	18:31	Son of man by the prophets will be A
Jn	17:4	thee on earth, having A the work which thou
Eph	1:20	great might which he A in Christ when he

ACCOMPLISHES (2)

Tob	14:11	children, consider what almsgiving A and how
Eph	1:11	purpose of him who A all things according to

ACCOMPLISHING

2Mac	12:18	from the region without A anything, though in one

ACCORD (30)

Num	16:28	that it has not been of my own A
Josh	9:2	gathered together with one A to fight Joshua and
1Kgs	22:13	the prophets with one A are favorable to the
2Chr	18:12	the prophets with one A are favorable to the
Jud	13:17	and said with one A, "Blessed art thou, our
	15:5	heard it, with one A they fell upon the
	15:9	blessed her with one A and said to her,
Ps	83:5	they conspire with one A; against thee they make
Wis	10:20	and praised with one A thy defending hand,
	18:9	sacrifices, and with one A agreed to the divine
Sir	37:12	whose soul is in A with your soul, and
Jer	9:13	voice, or walked in A with it,
Zeph	3:9	of the LORD and serve him with one A
1Mac	14:46	right to act in A with these decisions.
2Mac	6:19	rack of his own A, spitting out the flesh,
Jn	5:18	nothing of his own A, but only what he
	7:28	come of my own A; he who sent me
	8:42	not of my own A, but he sent me.
	10:18	but I lay it down of my own A
	11:51	this of his own A, but being high priest
	18:34	this of your own A, or did others say
Acts	1:14	All these with one A devoted themselves to prayer,
	8:6	the multitudes with one A gave heed to what
	12:10	them of its own A, and they went out
	15:25	having come to one A, to choose men and
Rom	15:5	with one another, in A with Christ Jesus,
2Cor	6:15	What A has Christ with Belial?
	8:17	he is going to you of his own A
Phil	2:2	love, being in full A and of one mind.
2Thes	3:6	idleness and not in A with the tradition that

ACCORDANCE (29)

Ex	24:8	made with you in A with all these words."
	34:27	"Write these words; in A with these words I
	36:1	sanctuary shall work in A with all that the
Num	6:21	he can afford; in A with the vow which
	35:24	avenger of blood, in A with these ordinances;
Deut	29:21	Israel for calamity, in A with all the curses
2Sam	7:17	In A with all these words, and in accordance
	7:17	these words, and in A with all this vision,
2Kgs	6:18	them with blindness in A with the prayer of
	9:26	plot of ground, in A with the word of
	16:11	built the altar; in A with all that King
	17:13	and my statutes, in A with all the law
1Chr	17:15	In A with all these words, and in accordance
	17:15	these words, and in A with all this vision,
2Chr	31:21	of God and in A with the law and
Tob	7:12	her right now, in A with the law.
Sir	16:14	one will receive in A with his deeds.
	46:1	He became, in A with his name, a great
Jer	32:8	of the guard, in A with the word of
Bar	2:2	done in Jerusalem, in A with what is written
Ezek	36:19	through the countries; in A with their conduct and
Dan	3:43	Deliver us in A with thy marvelous works, and
	13:62	their neighbor; acting in A with the law of
1Mac	7:16	in one day, in A with the word which
	10:64	was paid him, in A with the proclamation, and
1Cor	15:3	for our sins in A with the scriptures,
	15:4	the third day in A with the scriptures,
1Tim	1:11	to sound doctrine, in A with the glorious gospel
	1:18	Timothy, my son, in A with the prophetic utterances

ACCORDING (667)

Gen	1:11	is their seed, each A to its kind, upon
	1:12	vegetation, plants yielding seed A to their own kinds,
	1:12	is their seed, each A to its kind.
	1:21	which the waters swarm, A to their kinds, and
	1:21	and every winged bird A to its kind.
	1:24	bring forth living creatures A to their kinds: cattle
	1:24	beasts of the earth A to their kinds." And
	1:25	beasts of the earth A to their kinds and
	1:25	kinds and the cattle A to their kinds, and
	1:25	creeps upon the ground A to its kind.
	6:20	Of the birds A to their kinds, and of
	6:20	and of the animals A to their kinds, of
	6:20	thing of the ground A to its kind, two
	7:14	they and every beast A to its kind, and
	7:14	and all the cattle A to their kinds, and
	7:14	creeps on the earth A to its kind, and
	7:14	kind, and every bird A to its kind, every
	10:32	the sons of Noah, A to their genealogies, in
	18:21	they have done altogether A to the outcry which
	23:16	hundred shekels of silver, A to the weights current
	25:16	their encampments, twelve princes A to their tribes.
	33:14	will lead on slowly, A to the pace of
	33:14	are before me and A to the pace of
	34:12	and I will give A as you say to
	36:30	chiefs of the Horites, A to their clans in
	36:40	the chiefs of Esau, A to their families and
	36:43	the father of Edom), A to their dwelling places
	41:12	interpretation to each man A to his dream.
	43:33	before him, the first-born A to his birthright and
	43:33	birthright and the youngest A to his youth; and
	45:21	Joseph gave them wagons, A to the command of
	47:12	father's household with food, A to the number of
Ex	6:16	the sons of Levi A to their generations: Gershon,
	6:19	families of the Levites A to their generations.
	8:13	And the LORD did A to the word of
	12:3	every man a lamb A to their fathers' houses,
	12:4	his house shall take A to the number of
	12:4	the number of persons; A to what each can
	12:21	"Select lambs for yourselves A to your families, and
	16:16	take an omer apiece, A to the number of
	16:18	no lack; each gathered A to what he could
	17:1	of Sin by stages, A to the commandment of
	21:22	her shall be fined, A as the woman's husband
	21:31	shall be dealt with A to this same rule.
	23:24	serve them, nor do A to their works, but
	24:4	mountain, and twelve pillars, A to the twelve tribes
	25:9	A to all that I show you concerning the
	26:30	shall erect the tabernacle A to the plan for
	28:21	stones with their names A to the names of
	29:35	and to his sons, A to all that I
	30:13	this: half a shekel A to the shekel of
	30:24	of cassia five hundred, A to the shekel of
	30:37	which you shall make A to its composition, you
	31:11	A to all that I have commanded you they
	32:28	sons of Levi did A to the word of
	39:6	engravings of a signet, A to the names of
	39:14	stones with their names A to the names of
	39:32	of Israel had done A to all that the
	39:42	A to all that the LORD had commanded Moses,
Lev	5:10	for a burnt offering A to the ordinance; and
	5:15	in shekels of silver, A to the shekel of
	9:16	offering, and offered it A to the ordinance.

A

10:7 And they did A to the word of Moses.
11:14 the kite, the falcon A to its kind,
11:15 its kind, every raven A to its kind,
11:16 sea gull, the hawk A to its kind,
11:19 the stork, the heron A to its kind, the
11:22 may eat: the locust A to its kind, the
11:22 kind, the bald locust A to its kind, the
11:22 its kind, the cricket A to its kind, and
11:22 kind, and the grasshopper A to its kind.
11:29 mouse, the great lizard A to its kind,
25:15 A to the number of years after the jubilee,
25:15 from your neighbor, and A to the number of
25:50 his release shall be A to the number of
25:51 are still many years, A to them he shall
25:52 a reckoning with him; A to the years of
27:3 fifty shekels of silver, A to the shekel of
27:8 priest shall value him; A to the ability of
27:16 your valuation shall be A to the seed for
27:18 the money-value for it A to the years that
27:25 Every valuation shall be A to the shekel of
Num 1:2 families, by fathers' houses, A to the number of
1:18 families, by fathers' houses, A to the number of
1:20 by their fathers' houses, A to the number of
1:22 them that were numbered, A to the number of
1:24 by their fathers' houses, A to the number of
1:26 by their fathers' houses, A to the number of
1:28 by their fathers' houses, A to the number of
1:30 by their fathers' houses, A to the number of
1:32 by their fathers' houses, A to the number of
1:34 by their fathers' houses, A to the number of
1:36 by their fathers' houses, A to the number of
1:38 by their fathers' houses, A to the number of
1:40 by their fathers' houses, A to the number of
1:42 by their fathers' houses, A to the number of
1:54 of Israel; they did A to all that the
2:34 A to all that the LORD commanded Moses, so
2:34 one in his family, A to his fathers' house.
3:16 So Moses numbered them A to the word of
3:22 Their number A to the number of all the
3:28 A to the number of all the males, from
3:34 Their number A to the number of all the
3:43 all the first-born males, A to the number of
3:51 Aaron and his sons, A to the word of
4:37 Moses and Aaron numbered A to the commandment
4:41 Moses and Aaron numbered A to the commandment
4:45 Moses and Aaron numbered A to the commandment
4:49 A to the commandment of the LORD through Moses
6:21 the LORD shall be A to his vow as
6:21 so shall he do A to the law for
7:5 Levites, to each man A to his service."
7:7 the sons of Gershon, A to their service;
7:8 the sons of Merari, A to their service, under
7:13 basin of seventy shekels, A to the shekel of
7:19 basin of seventy shekels, A to the shekel of
7:25 basin of seventy shekels, A to the shekel of
7:31 basin of seventy shekels, A to the shekel of
7:37 basin of seventy shekels, A to the shekel of
7:43 basin of seventy shekels, A to the shekel of
7:49 basin of seventy shekels, A to the shekel of
7:55 basin of seventy shekels, A to the shekel of
7:61 basin of seventy shekels, A to the shekel of
7:67 basin of seventy shekels, A to the shekel of
7:73 basin of seventy shekels, A to the shekel of
7:79 basin of seventy shekels, A to the shekel of
7:85 thousand four hundred shekels A to the shekel of
7:86 weighing ten shekels apiece A to the shekel of
8:4 it was hammered work; A to the pattern which
8:20 Israel to the Levites; A to all that the
9:3 at its appointed time; A to all its statutes
9:5 the wilderness of Sinai; A to all that the
9:12 a bone of it; A to all the statute
9:14 passover to the LORD, A to the statute of
9:14 of the passover and A to its ordinance, so
9:20 over the tabernacle, and A to the command of
9:20 remained in camp; then A to the command of
10:28 the people of Israel A to their hosts, when
13:3 the wilderness of Paran, A to the command of
14:19 people, I pray thee, A to the greatness of
14:19 thy steadfast love, and A as thou hast forgiven
14:20 said, "I have pardoned, A to your word;
14:34 A to the number of the days in which
15:12 A to the number that you prepare, so shall
15:12 do with every one A to their number.
15:24 and its drink offering, A to the ordinance, and
17:2 from all their leaders A to their fathers' houses,
17:6 one for each leader, A to their fathers' houses,
18:16 five shekels in silver, A to the shekel of
26:12 The sons of Simeon A to their families: of
26:15 The sons of Gad A to their families: of
26:18 the sons of Gad A to their number, forty
26:20 the sons of Judah A to their families were:
26:22 the families of Judah A to their number, seventy-six
26:23 The sons of Issachar A to their families: of
26:25 the families of Issachar A to their number, sixty-four
26:26 The sons of Zebulun, A to their families: of
26:27 families of the Zebulunites A to their number, sixty
26:28 The sons of Joseph A to their families: Manasseh
26:35 the sons of Ephraim A to their families: of
26:37 the sons of Ephraim A to their number, thirty-two
26:37 the sons of Joseph A to their families.
26:38 The sons of Benjamin A to their families: of
26:41 the sons of Benjamin A to their families; and
26:42 the sons of Dan A to their families: of
26:42 the families of Dan A to their families.
26:43 families of the Shuhamites, A to their number, were
26:44 The sons of Asher A to their families: of
26:47 the sons of Asher A to their number, fifty-three
26:48 The sons of Naphtali A to their families: of
26:50 the families of Naphtali A to their families; and
26:53 be divided for inheritance A to the number of
26:54 be given its inheritance A to its numbers.
26:55 be divided by lot; A to the names of
26:56 inheritance shall be divided A to lot between the
26:57 the Levites as numbered A to their families: of
29:6 and their drink offering, A to the ordinance for
29:18 the lambs, by number, A to the ordinance;
29:21 the lambs, by number, A to the ordinance;
29:24 the lambs, by number, A to the ordinance;
29:27 the lambs, by number, A to the ordinance;
29:30 the lambs, by number, A to the ordinance;
29:33 the lambs, by number, A to the ordinance;
29:37 the lambs, by number, A to the ordinance;
30:2 word; he shall do A to all that proceeds
33:2 these are their stages A to their starting places.
33:54 the land by lot A to your families; to
33:54 that shall be his; A to the tribes of
36:5 the people of Israel A to the word of
Deut 1:3 the people of Israel A to all that the
1:13 and experienced men, A to your tribes, and
3:11 four cubits its breadth, A to the common cubit.
4:34 and by great terrors, A to all that the
12:8 You shall not do A to all that we
12:15 much as you desire, A to the blessing of
16:17 as he is able, A to the blessing of
16:18 your God gives you, A to your tribes; and
17:10 Then you shall do A to what they declare
17:10 be careful to do A to all that they
17:11 that they direct you; A to the instructions which
17:11 they give you, and A to the decision which
20:18 teach you to do A to all their abominable
24:8 very careful to do A to all that the
26:13 fatherless, and the widow, A to all thy commandment
26:14 God, I have done A to all that thou
31:5 shall do to them A to all the commandment
32:8 bounds of the peoples A to the number of
34:5 the land of Moab, A to the word of
Josh 1:7 being careful to do A to all the law
1:8 be careful to do A to all that is
2:21 And she said, A to your words, so be
4:5 stone upon his shoulder, A to the number of
4:8 midst of the Jordan, A to the number of
4:10 to tell the people, A to all that Moses
8:27 took as their booty, A to the word of
8:34 blessing and the curse, A to all that is
11:23 took the whole land, A to all that the
11:23 an inheritance to Israel A to their tribal allotments.
12:7 Israel as a possession A to their allotments,
13:15 tribe of the Reubenites A to their families.
13:23 inheritance of the Reubenites, A to their families
13:24 tribe of the Gadites, A to their families.
13:28 inheritance of the Gadites A to their families, with
13:29 half-tribe of the Manassites A to their families.
13:31 half of the Machirites A to their families.
15:1 the people of Judah A to their families reached
15:12 the people of Judah A to their families.
15:13 A to the commandment of the LORD to Joshua,
15:20 the people of Judah A to their families.
17:4 So A to the commandment of the LORD he
18:11 the tribe of Benjamin A to its families came
18:20 the tribe of Benjamin, A to its families, boundary
18:21 the tribe of Benjamin A to their families were
18:28 the tribe of Benjamin A to its families.

19:1 the tribe of Simeon, A to its families; and
19:8 the tribe of Simeon A to its families.
19:10 the tribe of Zebulun, A to its families.
19:16 the tribe of Zebulun, A to its families–these
19:17 the tribe of Issachar, A to its families.
19:23 the tribe of Issachar, A to its families–the
19:24 the tribe of Asher A to its families.
19:31 the tribe of Asher A to its families–these
19:32 the tribe of Naphtali, A to its families.
19:39 the tribe of Naphtali A to its families–the
19:40 the tribe of Dan, A to its families.
19:48 the tribe of Dan, A to their families–these
21:7 The Merarites A to their families received from the
Judg 11:36 LORD, do to me A to what has gone
11:39 who did with her A to his vow which
21:23 and took their wives, A to their number, from
1Sam 2:35 priest, who shall do A to what is in
6:4 and five golden mice, A to the number of
6:18 also the golden mice, A to the number of
8:8 A to all the deeds which they have done
23:20 come down, O king, A to all your heart's
25:30 done to my lord A to all the good
2Sam 3:39 LORD requite the evildoer A to his wickedness!"
7:21 of thy promise, and A to thy own heart,
7:22 no God besides thee, A to all that we
9:11 said to the king, A to all that my
22:21 "The LORD rewarded me A to my righteousness;
22:21 according to my righteousness; A to the cleanness of
22:25 LORD has recompensed me A to my righteousness,
22:25 according to my righteousness, A to my cleanness in
1Kgs 2:6 Act therefore A to your wisdom, but do not
3:12 behold, I now do A to your word.
4:28 it was required, each A to his charge.
6:38 all its parts, and A to all its specifications.
7:9 of costly stones, hewn A to measure, sawed with
7:11 were costly stones, hewn A to measurement, and
7:36 lions, and palm trees, A to the space of
8:32 righteous by rewarding him A to his righteousness.
8:39 whose heart thou knowest, A to all his ways
8:43 dwelling place, and do A to all for which
8:56 to his people Israel, A to all that he
9:4 heart and uprightness, doing A to all that I
12:14 he spoke to them A to the counsel of
12:24 and went home again, A to the word of
13:5 out from the altar, A to the sign which
13:26 him and slain him, A to the word which
14:18 and mourned for him, A to the word of
14:24 They did A to all the abominations of the
15:29 he had destroyed it, A to the word of
16:12 the house of Baasha, A to the word of
16:34 his youngest son Segub, A to the word of
17:5 he went and did A to the word of
17:16 cruse of oil fail, A to the word of
18:31 Elijah took twelve stones, A to the number of
22:38 washed themselves in it, A to the word of
2Kgs 1:17 So he died A to the word of the
2:22 wholesome to this day, A to the word which
4:44 and had some left, A to the word of
5:14 times in the Jordan, A to the word of
7:16 barley for a shekel, A to the word of
8:2 woman arose, and did A to the word of
10:17 had wiped them out, A to the word of
10:30 the house of Ahab A to all that was
11:9 The captains did A to all that Jehoiada the
11:14 standing by the pillar, A to the custom, and
14:6 children of the murderers; A to what is written
14:25 Sea of the Arabah, A to the word of
15:3 eyes of the LORD, A to all that his
15:34 eyes of the LORD, A to all that his
16:3 son as an offering, A to the abominable practices
17:34 this day they do A to the former manner.
17:40 listen, but they did A to their former manner.
18:3 eyes of the LORD, A to all that David
21:2 sight of the LORD, A to the abominable practices
21:8 be careful to do A to all that I
21:8 have commanded them, and A to all the law
22:13 this book, to do A to all that is
23:16 altar, and defiled it, A to the word of
23:19 he did to them A to all that he
23:25 with all his might, A to all the law
23:32 sight of the LORD, A to all that his
23:35 to give the money A to the command of
23:35 land, from every one A to his assessment, to
23:37 sight of the LORD, A to all that his
24:2 Judah to destroy it, A to the word of
24:3 the sins of Manasseh, A to all that he
24:9 sight of the LORD, A to all that his
24:19 sight of the LORD, A to all that Jehoiakim
1Chr 5:1 enrolled in the genealogy A to the birthright;
5:13 their kinsmen A to their fathers' houses: Michael,
6:19 families of the Levites A to their fathers.
6:49 make atonement for Israel, A to all that Moses
6:54 are their dwelling places A to their settlements
6:62 To the Gershomites A to their families were allotted
6:63 To the Merarites A to their families were allotted
7:4 them, by their generations, A to their fathers' houses,
7:9 enrollment by genealogies, A to their generations, as
7:11 the sons of Jedia-el A to the heads of
8:28 heads of fathers' houses, A to their generations, chief
9:9 Ibnijah; and their kinsmen A to their generations,
9:9 heads of fathers' houses A to their fathers' houses.
9:34 houses of the Levites, A to their generations, leaders,
11:3 David king over Israel, A to the word of
11:10 to make him king, A to the word of
12:23 Saul over to him, A to the word of
15:15 as Moses had commanded A to the word of
15:20 were to play harps A to Alamoth;
15:21 to lead with lyres A to the Sheminith.
16:40 continually morning and evening, A to all that is
17:19 sake, O LORD, and A to thy own heart,
17:20 no God besides thee, A to all that we
23:24 as they were registered A to the number of
23:31 moons, and feast days, A to the number required
24:3 Ithamar, David organized them A to the appointed
24:19 house of the LORD A to the procedure established
24:30 sons of the Levites A to their fathers' houses.
25:5 Heman the king's seer, A to the promise of
28:15 lampstand and its lamps, A to the use of
28:19 work to be done A to the plan.
2Chr 6:23 righteous by rewarding him A to his righteousness.
6:30 whose heart thou knowest, A to all his ways
6:33 dwelling place, and do A to all for which
7:17 your father walked, doing A to all that I
8:13 each day required, offering A to the commandment
8:14 A to the ordinance of David his father, he
10:14 Rehoboam spoke to them A to the counsel of
17:4 his commandments, and not A to the ways of
23:8 and all Judah did A to all that Jehoiada
23:18 rejoicing and with singing, A to the order of
25:4 their children to death, A to what is written
26:4 eyes of the LORD, A to all that his
26:11 for war, in divisions A to the numbers in
27:2 eyes of the LORD A to all that his
28:3 sons as an offering, A to the abominable practices
29:2 eyes of the LORD, A to all that David
29:25 cymbals, harps, and lyres, A to the commandment of
30:16 took their accustomed posts A to the law of
30:19 fathers, even though not A to the sanctuary's rules
31:2 division by division, each A to his service, the
31:16 required, for their service A to their offices, by
31:17 of the priests was A to their fathers' houses;
31:17 old and upwards was A to their offices, by
32:25 did not make return A to the benefit done
33:2 sight of the LORD, A to the abominable practices
34:21 the LORD, to do A to all that is
34:32 inhabitants of Jerusalem did A to the covenant of
35:4 Prepare yourselves A to your fathers' houses by your
35:5 in the holy place A to the groupings of
35:6 your brethren, to do A to the word of
35:10 Levites in their divisions A to the king's command.
35:12 they might distribute them A to the groupings of
35:13 passover lamb with fire A to the ordinance; and
35:15 were in their place A to the command of
35:16 altar of the LORD, A to the command of
35:26 and his good deeds A to what is written
Ezra 2:69 it on its site; A to their ability they
3:4 burnt offerings by number A to the ordinance, as
3:7 the sea, to Joppa, A to the grant which
3:10 to praise the LORD, A to the directions of
6:13 Then, A to the word sent by Darius the
6:17 all Israel twelve he-goats, A to the number of
7:14 about Judah and Jerusalem A to the law of
7:18 gold, you may do, A to the will of
7:25 "And you, Ezra, A to the wisdom of your
10:3 wives and their children, A to the counsel of
10:3 let it be done A to the law.
10:16 heads of fathers' houses, A to their fathers' houses,
Neh 4:13 I stationed the people A to their families, with
6:6 to become their king, A to this report.
6:7 reported to the king A to these words.
6:14 Sanballat, O my God, A to these things that
8:18 was a solemn assembly, A to the ordinance.

9:27 them from heaven; and A to thy great mercies
9:28 thou didst deliver them A to thy mercies.
10:34 house of our God, A to our fathers' houses,
12:24 and to give thanks, A to the commandment of
12:44 and for the Levites A to the fields of
12:45 singers and the gatekeepers, A to the command of
13:22 God, and spare me A to the greatness of
Tob 3:6 now deal with me A to thy pleasure; command
4:8 be afraid to give A to the little you
4:19 all good things, and A to his will he
6:12 I know that Raguel, A to the law of
7:13 she is; take her A to the law of
8:16 thou hast treated us A to thy great mercy.
Jud 7:29 fathers, who punishes us A to our sins and
Esth 1:7 royal wine was lavished A to the bounty of
1:8 And drinking was A to the law, no one
1:15 in the kingdom--: A to the law, what
1:22 own house and speak A to the language of
3:12 month, and an edict, A to all that Haman
8:9 an edict was written A to all that Mordecai
9:13 tomorrow also to do A to this day's edict.
9:27 keep these two days A to what was written
Job 1:5 and offer burnt offerings A to the number of
34:11 For A to the work of a man he
34:11 will requite him, and A to his ways he
42:8 to deal with you A to your folly; for
Ps 7:8 judge me, O LORD, A to my righteousness and
7:8 to my righteousness and A to the integrity that
18:20 The LORD rewarded me A to my righteousness;
18:20 according to my righteousness; A to the cleanness of
18:24 LORD has recompensed me A to my righteousness,
18:24 according to my righteousness, A to the cleanness of
25:7 youth, or my transgressions; A to thy steadfast love
28:4 Requite them A to their work, and according to
28:4 to their work, and A to the evil of
28:4 their deeds; requite them A to the work of
35:24 O LORD, my God, A to thy righteousness; and
51:1 on me, O God, A to thy steadfast love;
51:1 to thy steadfast love; A to thy abundant mercy
62:12 dost requite a man A to his work.
69:16 steadfast love is good; A to thy abundant mercy,
78:10 but refused to walk A to his law.
79:11 prisoners come before thee; A to thy great power
89:30 and do not walk A to my ordinances,
90:11 anger, and thy wrath A to the fear of
103:10 not deal with us A to our sins, nor
103:10 sins, nor requite us A to our iniquities.
106:45 his covenant, and relented A to the abundance of
109:26 Save me A to thy steadfast love!
119:9 By guarding it A to thy word.
119:25 the dust; revive me A to thy word!
119:28 for sorrow; strengthen me A to thy word!
119:41 O LORD, thy salvation A to thy promise;
119:58 be gracious to me A to thy promise.
119:65 thy servant, O LORD, A to thy word.
119:76 ready to comfort me A to thy promise to
119:107 me life, O LORD, A to thy word!
119:116 Uphold me A to thy promise, that I may
119:124 Deal with thy servant A to thy steadfast love,
119:133 Keep steady my steps A to thy promise, and
119:154 me; give me life A to thy promise!
119:156 LORD; give me life A to thy justice.
119:159 Preserve my life A to thy steadfast love.
119:169 LORD; give me understanding A to thy word!
119:170 before thee; deliver me A to thy word.
150:2 deeds; praise him A to his exceeding greatness!
Prov 12:8 A man is commended A to his good sense,
24:12 he not requite man A to his work?
26:4 Answer not a fool A to his folly, lest
26:5 Answer a fool A to his folly, lest he
Eccl 8:14 to whom it happens A to the deeds of
8:14 to whom it happens A to the deeds of
Wis 2:20 a shameful death, for, A to what he says,
6:4 the law, nor walk A to the purpose of
9:9 and what is right A to thy commandments.
16:25 served thy all-nourishing bounty, A to the desire of
Sir 1:8 dwells with all flesh A to his gift, and
5:2 inclination and strength, walking A to the desires of
10:27 ascribe to yourself honor A to your worth.
11:24 the day of death A to his conduct.
14:11 son, treat yourself well, A to your means, and
16:12 he judges a man A to his deeds.
29:11 Lay up your treasure A to the commandments of
29:20 Assist your neighbor A to your ability, but take
32:17 will find a decision A to his liking.
35:19 he repays the man A to his deeds, and
35:19 the works of men A to their devices; till
36:17 prayer of thy servants, A to the blessing of
38:1 the honor due him, A to your need of
38:17 fervent; observe the mourning A to his merit, for
45:11 reminder, in engraved letters, A to the number of
49:6 made her streets desolate, A to the word of
50:22 and deals with us A to his mercy.
51:18 I resolved to live A to wisdom, and I
Is 21:16 me, "Within a year, A to the years of
59:18 A to their deeds, so will he repay, wrath
63:7 praises of the LORD, A to all that the
63:7 he has granted them A to his mercy, according
63:7 according to his mercy, A to the abundance of
Jer 13:2 I bought a waistcloth A to the word of
17:10 give to every man A to his ways, according
17:10 according to his ways, A to the fruit of
18:12 will every one act A to the stubbornness of
21:2 will deal with us A to all his wonderful
21:14 I will punish you A to the fruit of
25:14 I will recompense them A to their deeds and
32:19 men, rewarding every man A to his ways and
32:19 to his ways and A to the fruit of
34:16 you had set free A to their desire, and
42:4 the LORD your God A to your request, and
42:5 we do not act A to all the word
50:29 Requite her A to her deeds, do to her
50:29 deeds, do to her A to all that she
52:2 sight of the LORD, A to all that Jehoiakim
Lam 3:32 he will have compassion A to the abundance of
3:64 requite them, O LORD, A to the work of
Ezek 5:7 ordinances, but have acted A to the ordinances of
7:3 and will judge you A to your ways; and
7:8 you, and judge you A to your ways; and
7:9 I will punish you A to your ways, while
7:27 A to their way I will do to them,
7:27 do to them, and A to their own judgments
11:12 ordinances, but have acted A to the ordinances of
16:47 their ways, or do A to their abominations; within
18:30 of Israel, every one A to his ways, says
20:44 my name's sake, not A to your evil ways,
20:44 your evil ways, nor A to your corrupt doings,
22:6 in you, every one A to his power, have
23:24 they shall judge you A to their judgments.
24:14 I will not repent; A to your ways and
24:24 to you a sign; A to all that he
25:14 shall do in Edom A to my anger and
25:14 to my anger and A to my wrath; and
33:20 judge each of you A to his ways."
35:11 will deal with you A to the anger and
39:24 I dealt with them A to their uncleanness and
44:24 they shall judge it A to my judgments.
45:8 Israel have the land A to their tribes.
47:21 this land among you A to the tribes of
Dan 1:13 observed by you, and A to what you see
4:35 nothing; and he does A to his will in
6:8 it cannot be changed, A to the law of
6:12 "The thing stands fast, A to the law of
9:2 number of years which, A to the word of
9:16 O Lord, A to all thy righteous acts, let
10:15 had spoken to me A to these words, I
11:3 great dominion and do A to his will.
11:4 to his posterity, nor A to the dominion with
11:16 against him shall do A to his own will,
11:36 the king shall do A to his will; he
13:3 had taught their daughter A to the law of
Hos 12:2 and will punish Jacob A to his ways, and
12:2 ways, and requite him A to his deeds.
Jon 3:3 and went to Nineveh, A to the word of
Hab 3:1 of Habakkuk the prophet, A to Shigionoth.
Hag 2:5 the LORD of hosts, A to the promise that
Zech 5:3 be cut off henceforth A to it, and every
5:3 be cut off henceforth A to it.
1Mac 1:14 a gymnasium in Jerusalem, A to Gentile custom,
1:60 A to the decree, they put to death the
2:23 the altar in Modein, A to the king's command.
3:56 return to his home, A to the law.
7:42 sanctuary, and judge him A to this wickedness."
13:46 "Do not treat us A to our wicked acts
13:46 our wicked acts but A to your mercy."
15:21 he may punish them A to their law."
2Mac 6:23 childhood, and moreover A to the holy God-given
11:25 and that they live A to the customs of
12:38 on, they purified themselves A to the custom, and
Mt 2:16 years old or under, A to the time which
9:29 touched their eyes, saying, A to your faith be
25:15 another one, to each A to his ability.

Mk 7:5 your disciples not live A to the tradition of
Lk 1:9 division was on duty, A to the custom of
1:38 it be to me A to your word." And
2:22 came for their purification A to the law of
2:24 to offer a sacrifice A to what is said
2:27 to do for him A to the custom of
2:29 servant depart in peace, A to thy word;
2:39 they had performed everything A to the law of
2:42 old, they went up A to custom;
12:47 make ready or act A to his will, shall
23:55 the sabbath they rested A to the commandment.
Jn 8:15 You judge A to the flesh, I judge no
8:44 he lies, he speaks A to his own nature,
Acts 2:23 this Jesus, delivered up A to the definite plan
7:44 him to make it, A to the pattern that
11:29 disciples determined, every one A to his ability, to
15:1 "Unless you are circumcised A to the custom of
22:3 feet of Gamali-el, educated A to the strict manner
22:12 Ananias, a devout man A to the law, well
23:3 sitting to judge me A to the law, and
23:31 So the soldiers, A to their instructions, took Paul
24:13 admit to you, that A to the Way, which
26:5 willing to testify, that A to the strictest party
Rom 1:3 was descended from David A to the flesh
1:4 of God in power A to the Spirit of
2:6 render to every man A to his works:
2:16 on that day when, A to my gospel, God
4:1 about Abraham, our forefather A to the flesh?
8:4 us, who walk not A to the flesh but
8:4 to the flesh but A to the Spirit.
8:5 For those who live A to the flesh set
8:5 but those who live A to the Spirit set
8:12 the flesh, to live A to the flesh--
8:13 for if you live A to the flesh you
8:27 intercedes for the saints A to the will of
8:28 him, who are called A to his purpose.
9:5 and of their race, A to the flesh, is
12:3 with sober judgment, each A to the measure of
12:6 Having gifts that differ A to the grace given
16:24 able to strengthen you A to my gospel and
16:24 preaching of Jesus Christ, A to the revelation of
16:25 known to all nations, A to the command of
1Cor 1:26 of you were wise A to worldly standards, not
3:8 shall receive his wages A to his labor.
3:10 A to the grace of God given to me,
12:8 the utterance of knowledge A to the same Spirit,
2Cor 5:10 receive good or evil, A to what he has
8:3 For they gave A to their means, as I
8:12 there, it is acceptable A to what a man
8:12 a man has, not A to what he has
Gal 1:4 the present evil age, A to the will of
3:29 are Abraham's offspring, heirs A to promise.
4:23 the slave was born A to the flesh, the
4:29 he who was born A to the flesh persecuted
4:29 him who was born A to the Spirit, so
Eph 1:5 sons through Jesus Christ, A to the purpose of
1:7 forgiveness of our trespasses, A to the riches of
1:9 mystery of his will, A to his purpose which
1:11 In him, A to the purpose of him who
1:11 who accomplishes all things A to the counsel of
1:19 in us who believe, A to the working of
3:7 was made a minister A to the gift of
3:11 This was A to the eternal purpose which he
3:16 earth is named, that A to the riches of
4:7 to each of us A to the measure of
Phil 4:19 every need of yours A to his riches in
Col 1:11 strengthened with all power, A to his glorious might,
1:25 I became a minister A to the divine office
2:8 philosophy and empty deceit, A to human tradition, A
2:8 the universe, and not A to Christ.
2:22 as they are used), A to human precepts and
2Thes 1:12 and you in him, A to the grace of
2Tim 1:1 the will of God A to the promise of
2:5 crowned unless he competes A to the rules.
Heb 2:4 the Holy Spirit distributed A to his own will.
7:16 become a priest, not A to a legal requirement
8:4 priests who offer gifts A to the law.
8:5 that you make everything A to the pattern which
9:9 A to this arrangement, gifts and sacrifices are
10:8 (these are offered A to the law),
Jas 2:8 fulfil the royal law, A to the scripture, "You
1Pet 1:17 judges each one impartially A to his deeds, conduct
4:19 let those who suffer A to God's will do
2Pet 2:22 has happened to them A to the true proverb,
3:13 But A to his promise we wait for new
3:15 Paul wrote to you A to the wisdom given
1Jn 1:6 and do not live A to the truth;
5:14 if we ask anything A to his will he

ACCORDINGLY (7)

Esth 16:24 which does not act A, shall be destroyed in
Sir 3:1 O children; and act A, that you may be
1Mac 12:23 therefore command that our envoys report to you A
2Mac 11:25 A, since we choose that this nation also be
Rom 7:3 A, she will be called an adulteress if she
2Cor 8:6 A we have urged Titus that as he had
Philem 1:8 A, though I am bold enough in Christ to

ACCORDS (2)

1Tim 6:3 and the teaching which A with godliness,
Tit 1:1 of the truth which A with godliness,

ACCOS

1Mac 8:17 of John, son of A, and Jason the son

ACCOUNT (80)

Gen 12:13 that my life may be spared on your A
21:11 displeasing to Abraham on A of his son.
Lev 7:24 use, but on no A shall you eat it.
19:28 in your flesh on A of the dead or
Num 25:18 of the plague on A of Peor."
Deut 1:37 me also on your A, and said, 'You also
3:26 with me on your A, and would not hearken
4:21 with me on your A, and he swore that
28:20 and perish quickly, on A of the evil of
31:18 in that day on A of all the evil
Judg 6:7 to the LORD on A of the Midianites,
18:12 On this A that place is called Mahaneh-dan to
1Sam 23:10 to Keilah, to destroy the city on my A
1Kgs 9:15 And this is the A of the forced labor
1Chr 11:11 This is an A of David's mighty men: Jashobe-am,
16:19 number, and of little A, and sojourners in it,
16:21 rebuked kings on their A,
Neh 13:26 of Israel sin on A of such women?
Tob 6:14 mother to the grave in sorrow on my A
Esth 10:2 might, and the full A of the high honor
12:4 and Mordecai wrote an A of them.
Job 31:37 would give him an A of all my steps;
40:4 I am of small A; what shall I answer
Ps 10:13 in his heart, "Thou wilt not call to A
65:3 all flesh come on A of sins.
105:12 in number, of little A, and sojourners in it,
105:14 rebuked kings on their A,
106:32 with Moses on their A;
Wis 3:17 be held of no A, and finally their old
6:15 is vigilant on her A will soon be free
Sir 10:8 nation to nation on A of injustice and insolence
16:8 whom he loathed on A of their insolence.
23:14 deemed a fool on A of your habits; then
32:2 be merry on their A and receive a wreath
40:10 wicked, and on their A the flood came.
Is 2:22 breath, for of what A is he?
Ezek 12:19 all it contains, on A of the violence of
16:61 daughters, but not on A of the covenant with
Dan 6:2 these satraps should give A, so that the king
Joel 3:2 with them there, on A of my people and
Amos 8:8 land tremble on this A, and every one mourn
Jon 1:7 may know on whose A this evil has come
1:8 "Tell us, on whose A this evil has come
1Mac 6:59 for it was on A of their laws which
2Mac 2:14 had been lost on A of the war which
3:6 not belong to the A of the sacrifices, but
4:28 by the king on A of this issue.
6:22 be treated kindly on A of his old friendship
7:18 things on our own A, because of our sins
8:35 as of the least A, took off his splendid
11:4 He took no A whatever of the power of
12:43 well and honorably, taking A of the resurrection.
Mt 5:11 kinds of evil against you falsely on my A
12:36 judgment men will render A for every careless word
13:21 or persecution arises on A of the word, immediately
Mk 4:17 or persecution arises on A of the word, immediately
Lk 1:3 to write an orderly A for you, most excellent
6:22 name as evil, on A of the Son of
16:2 Turn in the A of your stewardship, for you
19:3 but could not, on A of the crowd, because
Jn 11:42 have said this on A of the people standing
12:9 came, not only on A of Jesus but also
12:11 to death, because on A of him many of
15:21 to you on my A, because they do not
Acts 20:24 But I do not A my life of any
Rom 14:12 of us shall give A of himself to God.

1Cor 14:24 he is called to A by all,
2Cor 7:12 it was not on A of the one who
7:12 the wrong, nor on A of the one who
10:10 presence is weak, and his speech of no A
Phil 1:24 in the flesh is more necessary on your A
Col 3:6 On A of these the wrath of God is
4:3 mystery of Christ, on A of which I am
Philem 1:18 or owes you anything, charge that to my A
Heb 6:6 God on their own A and hold him up
13:17 souls, as men who will have to give A
1Pet 3:15 who calls you to A for the hope that
4:5 but they will give A to him who is
Rev 1:7 earth will wail on A of him.
1:9 island called Patmos on A of the word of

ACCOUNTABLE

Rom 3:19 world may be held A to God.

ACCOUNTED (10)

Ps 44:22 the day long, and A as sheep for the
Wis 7:8 and thrones, and I A wealth as nothing in
7:9 and silver will be A as clay before her.
15:2 know that we are A thine.
Sir 40:19 a blameless wife is A better than both.
Is 40:15 a bucket, and are A as the dust on
40:17 before him, they are A by him as less
53:11 make many to be A righteous; and he shall
Dan 4:35 of the earth are A as nothing; and he
Lk 20:35 but those who are A worthy to attain to

ACCOUNTING (2)

2Kgs 12:15 did not ask an A from the men into
22:7 But no A shall be asked from them for

ACCOUNTS (7)

1Chr 29:30 Gad the seer, with A of all his rule
2Chr 24:27 A of his sons, and of the many oracles
Tob 1:21 Anael, over all the A of his kingdom and
1:22 of administration of the A, for Esarhaddon had
Sir 42:3 the ungodly; of keeping A with a partner or
Mt 18:22 who wished to settle A with his servants.
25:19 servants came and settled A with them.

ACCREDIT

1Cor 16:3 send those whom you A by letter to carry

ACCUMULATE

2Tim 4:3 itching ears they will A for themselves teachers to

ACCUMULATES (3)

Sir 14:4 Whoever A by depriving himself, accumulates for
14:4 accumulates by depriving himself, A for others; and
31:3 toils as his wealth A, and when he rests

ACCURACY

Sir 42:4 inheritance of friends; of A with scales and weights,

ACCURATE (3)

Sir 31:24 food, and their testimony to his niggardliness is A
32:3 you should, but with A knowledge, and do not
Acts 24:21 Felix, having a rather A knowledge of the Way,

ACCURATELY (3)

Sir 16:23 instruction by weight, and declare knowledge A
Acts 18:25 he spoke and taught A the things concerning Jesus,
18:26 expounded to him the way of God more A

ACCURSED (18)

Deut 7:26 your house, and become A like it; you shall
7:26 for it is an A thing.
21:23 a hanged man is A by God; you shall
Ps 119:21 dost rebuke the insolent, A ones, who wander from
Wis 3:13 foolish, and their children evil; their offspring are A
12:11 For they were an A race from the beginning,
14:8 made with hands is A, and so is he
Is 65:20 the sinner a hundred years old shall be A
Mic 6:10 the wicked, and the scant measure that is A
2Mac 7:9 breath, he said, "You A wretch, you dismiss us
12:35 wishing to take the A man alive, when one
Jn 7:49 crowd, who do not know the law, are A
Rom 9:3 that I myself were A and cut off from
1Cor 16:22 no love for the Lord, let him be A
Gal 1:8 which we preached to you, let him be A
1:9 to that which you received, let him be A
2Pet 2:14 A children!
Rev 22:3 no more be anything A, but the throne of

ACCUSATION (7)

Ezra 4:6 reign, they wrote an A against the inhabitants of
Sir 26:5 a mob, and false A —all these are worse
1Mac 7:6 to the king this A against the people: "Judas
Lk 3:14 violence or by false A, and be content with
6:7 they might find an A against him.
Jn 18:29 them and said, "What A do you bring against
Acts 24:18 and to make an A, if they have anything

ACCUSATIONS (2)

2Mac 14:27 provoked by the false A of that depraved man,
Acts 26:2 today against all the A of the Jews,

ACCUSE (14)

Deut 19:16 against any man to A him of wrongdoing,
Ps 109:4 for my love they A me, even as I
Wis 12:12 Who will A thee for the destruction of nations
Hos 4:4 contend, and let none A, for with you is
Zech 3:1 his right hand to A him.
1Mac 10:61 together against him to A him; but the king
Mt 12:10 so that they might A him.
Mk 3:2 so that they might A him.
Lk 23:2 And they began to A him, saying, "We found
Jn 5:44 think that I shall A you to the Father;
Acts 24:2 Tertullus began to A him, saying: "Since through
24:7 everything of which we A him."
25:5 the man, let them A him."
Rom 2:15 and their conflicting thoughts A or perhaps excuse

ACCUSED (16)

Deut 19:18 false witness and has A his brother falsely,
Wis 10:14 Those who A him she showed to be false,
Sir 46:19 And no man A him.
Dan 3:8 came forward and maliciously A the Jews.
6:24 those men who had A Daniel were brought and
2Mac 5:8 A before Aretas the ruler of the Arabs, fleeing
10:13 a result he was A before Eupator by the
10:21 of the people, and A these men of having
14:38 Gentiles, he had been A of Judaism, and for
Mt 27:12 But when he was A by the chief priests
Mk 15:3 And the chief priests A him of many things.
Acts 22:30 reason why the Jews A him, he unbound him,
23:28 charge on which they A him, I brought him
23:29 found that he was A about questions of their
25:16 any one before the A met the accusers face
26:7 this hope I am A by Jews, O king!

ACCUSER (6)

Job 9:15 him; I must appeal for mercy to my A
Ps 109:6 against him; let an A bring him to trial.
Mt 5:25 friends quickly with your A, while you are going
5:25 to court, lest your A hand you over to
Lk 12:58 you go with your A before the magistrate, make
Rev 12:10 have come, for the A of our brethren has

ACCUSERS (9)

Ps 71:13 May my A be put to shame and consumed;
109:20 the reward of my A from the LORD, of
109:25 of scorn to my A; when they see me,
109:29 May my A be clothed with dishonor; may they
1Mac 10:64 And when his A saw the honor that was
Acts 23:30 at once, ordering his A also to state before
23:35 hear you when your A arrive." And he commanded
25:16 the accused met the A face to face, and
25:18 When the A stood up, they brought no charge

ACCUSES (3)

Wis 2:12 against the law, and A us of sins against
Jn 5:44 it is Moses who A you, on whom you
Rev 12:10 been thrown down, who A them day and night

ACCUSING (2)

2Mac 4:5 to the king, not A his fellow citizens but
Lk 23:10 scribes stood by, vehemently A him.

ACCUSTOM (2)

Sir 23:9 Do not A your mouth to oaths, and do
23:13 Do not A your mouth to lewd vulgarity, for

ACCUSTOMED (12)

Ex 21:29 the ox has been A to gore in the
21:36 the ox has been A to gore in the
Num 22:30 Was I ever A to do so to you?"
2Chr 30:16 They took their A posts according to the law
Jud 13:10 together, as they were A to go for prayer;
Sir 23:15 A man A to use insulting words will never

Jer 13:23 do good who are A to do evil.
Dan 14:15 children, as they were A to do, and ate
14:21 through which they were A to enter and devour
1Mac 6:30 horsemen, and thirty-two elephants A to war.
Mt 27:15 feast the governor was A to release for the
1Cor 8:7 some, through being hitherto A to idols, eat food

ACHAIA (10)
Acts 18:12 Gallio was proconsul of A, the Jews made a
18:27 wished to cross to A, the brethren encouraged him,
19:21 pass through Macedonia and A and go to Jerusalem,
Rom 15:26 For Macedonia and A have been pleased to make
1Cor 16:15 the first converts in A, and they have devoted
2Cor 1:1 in the whole of A:
9:2 of Macedonia, saying that A has been ready since
11:10 shall not be silenced in the regions of A
1Thes 1:7 to all the believers in Macedonia and in A
1:8 you in Macedonia and A, but your faith in

ACHAICUS
1Cor 16:17 Stephanas and Fortunatus and A, because they have

ACHAN (6)
Josh 7:1 the devoted things; for A the son of Carmi,
7:18 man by man, and A the son of Carmi,
7:19 Then Joshua said to A, "My son, give glory
7:20 And A answered Joshua, "Of a truth I have
7:24 Israel with him took A the son of Zerah,
22:20 Did not A the son of Zerah break faith

ACHAR
1Chr 2:7 The sons of Carmi: A, the troubler of Israel,

ACHBOR (7)
Gen 36:38 Baal-hanan the son of A reigned in his stead.
36:39 Baal-hanan the son of A died, and Hadar reigned
2Kgs 22:12 son of Shaphan, and A the son of Micaiah,
22:14 priest, and Ahikam, and A, and Shaphan, and Asaiah
1Chr 1:49 Baal-hanan, the son of A, reigned in his stead.
Jer 26:22 Elnathan the son of A and others with him,
36:12 Elnathan the son of A, Gemariah the son of

ACHIEVE (2)
Jud 11:6 will not fail to A his purposes.
Job 5:12 so that their hands A no success.

ACHIEVEMENTS
1Mac 16:23 he built, and his A,

ACHIM (2)
Mt 1:14 Zadok the father of A, and Achim the father
1:14 father of Achim, and A the father of Eliud,

ACHIOR (13)
Jud 5:5 Then A, the leader of all the Ammonites, said
5:22 When A had finished saying this, all the men
6:1 Assyrian army, said to A and all the Moabites
6:2 "And who are you, A, and you hirelings of
6:5 "But you, A, you Ammonite hireling, who have said
6:10 his tent, to seize A and take him to
6:13 hill and they bound A and left him lying
6:16 assembly; and they set A in the midst of
6:20 Then they consoled A, and praised him greatly.
11:9 as for the things A said in your council,
14:5 do all this, bring A the Ammonite to me,
14:6 So they summoned A from the house of Uzziah.
14:10 And when A saw all that the God of

ACHISH (21)
1Sam 21:10 Saul, and went to A the king of Gath.
21:11 And the servants of A said to him, "Is
21:12 was much afraid of A the king of Gath.
21:14 Then said A to his servants, "Lo, you see
27:2 were with him, to A the son of Maoch,
27:3 And David dwelt with A at Gath, he and
27:5 Then David said to A, "If I have found
27:6 So that day A gave him Ziklag; therefore Ziklag
27:9 camels, and the garments, and came back to A
27:10 When A asked, "Against whom have you made a
27:12 And A trusted David, thinking, "He has made himself
28:1 And A said to David, "Understand that you and
28:2 David said to A, "Very well, you shall know
28:2 And A said to David, "Very well, I will
29:2 in the rear with A,
29:3 And A said to the commanders of the Philistines,
29:6 Then A called David and said to him, "As
29:8 And David said to A, "But what have I
29:9 And A made answer to David, "I know that
1Kgs 2:39 slaves ran away to A, son of Maacah, king
2:40 went to Gath to A, to seek his slaves;

ACHOR (5)
Josh 7:24 they brought them up to the Valley of A
7:26 of that place is called the Valley of A
15:7 from the Valley of A, and so northward, turning
Is 65:10 and the Valley of A a place for herds
Hos 2:15 make the Valley of A a door of hope.

ACHSAH (5)
Josh 15:16 him will I give A my daughter as wife."
15:17 and he gave him A his daughter as wife.
Judg 1:12 I will give him A my daughter as wife."
1:13 and he gave him A his daughter as wife.
1Chr 2:49 of Gibe-a; and the daughter of Caleb was A

ACHSHAPH (3)
Josh 11:1 to the king of A,
12:20 one; the king of A, one;
19:25 included Helkath, Hali, Beten, A,

ACHZIB (4)
Josh 15:44 Iphtah, Ashnah, Nezib, Keilah, A, and Mareshah: nine
19:29 at the sea; Mahalab, A,
Judg 1:31 of Ahlab, or of A, or of Helbah, or
Mic 1:14 Moresheth-gath; the houses of A shall be a deceitful

ACKNOWLEDGE (24)
Deut 21:17 first-born, but he shall A the first-born, the son
1Kgs 8:33 again to thee, and A thy name, and pray
8:35 toward this place, and A thy name, and turn
2Chr 6:24 they turn again and A thy name, and pray
6:26 toward this place, and A thy name, and turn
Tob 13:3 A him before the nations, O sons of Israel;
Job 40:14 Then will I also A to you, that your
Prov 3:6 In all your ways A him, and he will
Is 26:13 ruled over us, but thy name alone we A
33:13 you who are near, A my might.
61:9 who see them shall A them, that they are
63:16 and Israel does not A us; thou, O LORD,
Jer 3:13 Only A your guilt, that you rebelled against the
14:20 We A our wickedness, O LORD, and the iniquity
Dan 11:39 foreign god; those who A him he shall magnify
Hos 5:15 my place, until they A their guilt and seek
Mt 10:32 men, I also will A before my Father who
Lk 12:8 of man also will A before the angels of
Acts 23:8 spirit; but the Pharisees A them all.
Rom 1:28 not see fit to A God, God gave them
1Cor 14:37 or spiritual, he should A that what I am
Heb 13:15 fruit of lips that A his name.
2Jn 1:7 men who will not A the coming of Jesus
3 Jn 1:9 himself first, does not A my authority.

ACKNOWLEDGED (6)
Gen 38:26 Then Judah A them and said, "She is more
Tob 12:22 works of God, and A that the angel of
Ps 32:5 [Selah] I A my sin to thee, and I
Wis 18:13 first-born were destroyed, they A thy people to be
Sir 44:24 head of Jacob; he A him with his blessings,
Heb 11:13 from afar, and having A that they were strangers

ACKNOWLEDGES (2)
Mt 10:32 So every one who A me before men, I
Lk 12:8 you, every one who A me before men, the

ACKNOWLEDGING
2Cor 9:13 by your obedience in A the gospel of Christ,

ACQUAINTANCE (2)
2Kgs 12:5 take, each from his A; and let them repair
2Mac 6:21 because of their long A with him, and privately

ACQUAINTANCES (6)
2Kgs 12:7 more money from your A, but hand it over
Job 19:13 from me, and my A are wholly estranged from
Ps 31:11 of dread to my A; those who see me
Sir 30:2 by him, and will boast of him among A
Lk 2:44 among their kinsfolk and A;
23:48 And all his A and the women who had

ACQUAINTED (6)
Tob 5:5 Are you A with that region?"
Job 24:13 light, who are not A with its ways, and

A

Ps 139:3 lying down, and art A with all my ways.
Is 53:3 man of sorrows, and A with grief; and as
2Mac 14:9 Since you are A, O king, with the details
2Tim 3:15 childhood you have been A with the sacred writings

ACQUIRE (7)

Jud 8:22 eyes of those who A us.
Prov 1:5 the man of understanding A skill,
14:18 The simple A folly, but the prudent are crowned
23:4 Do not toil to A wealth; be wise enough
Sir 15:6 of rejoicing, and will A an everlasting name.
16:22 me, my son, and A knowledge, and pay close
Eph 1:14 our inheritance until we A possession of it, to

ACQUIRED (5)

Gen 31:18 possession which he had A in Paddan-aram, to go
36:6 property which he had A in the land of
Neh 5:16 on this wall, and A no land; and all
Eccl 1:16 to myself, "I have A great wisdom, surpassing all
Sir 14:15 another, and what you A by toil to be

ACQUIRES (3)

Prov 18:15 An intelligent mind A knowledge, and the ear of
Sir 34:10 he that has traveled A much cleverness.
36:24 He who A a wife gets his best possession,

ACQUIRING

Sir 42:4 and weights, and of A much or little;

ACQUIT (7)

Ex 23:7 for I will not A the wicked.
1Sam 4:9 Take courage, and A yourselves like men, O
4:9 have been to you; A yourselves like men and
Job 10:14 me, and dost not A me of my iniquity.
Sir 42:2 of rendering judgment to A the ungodly;
Is 5:23 mixing strong drink, who A the guilty for a
Mic 6:11 Shall I A the man with wicked scales and

ACQUITTAL (2)

Ps 69:27 may they have no A from thee.
Rom 5:18 of righteousness leads to A and life for all

ACQUITTED (3)

Job 23:7 and I should be A for ever by my
2Mac 4:47 all the evil, he A of the charges against
1Cor 4:4 anything against myself, but I am not thereby A

ACQUITTING

Deut 25:1 judges decide between them, A the innocent and

ACRABA

Jud 7:18 and the east, toward A, which is near Chusi

ACRE

1Sam 14:14 furrow's length in an A of land.

ACRES

Is 5:10 For ten A of vineyard shall yield but one

ACROSS (19)

Gen 1:20 fly above the earth A the firmament of the
32:23 them and sent them A the stream, and likewise
Num 32:5 do not take us A the Jordan."
1Kgs 6:21 drew chains of gold A, in front of the
Jud 15:2 fled by every path A the plain and through
Job 1:19 a great wind came A the wilderness, and struck
Jer 25:22 kings of the coastland A the sea;
Dan 8:5 came from the west A the face of the
1Mac 5:39 and they are encamped A the stream, ready to
9:48 the Jordan and swam A to the other side,
2Mac 8:35 like a runaway slave A the country till he
Mt 4:15 Naphtali, toward the sea, A the Jordan, Galilee of
Mk 4:35 them, "Let us go A to the other side."
Lk 8:22 them, "Let us go A to the other side
Jn 6:17 a boat, and started A the sea to Caperna-um.
10:40 He went away again A the Jordan to the
18:1 forth with his disciples A the Kidron valley, where
Acts 27:5 when we had sailed A the sea which is
27:27 as we were drifting A the sea of Adria,

ACT (60)

Gen 19:7 my brothers, do not A so wickedly.
Num 5:13 not taken in the A;
31:16 of Balaam, to A treacherously against the LORD
Deut 4:16 fire, beware lest you A corruptly by making a
4:25 the land, if you A corruptly by making a
17:13 and fear, and not A presumptuously again.
25:16 such things, all who A dishonestly, are an
31:29 death you will surely A corruptly, and turn aside
Judg 19:23 my brethren, do not A so wickedly; seeing that
1Kgs 2:6 A therefore according to your wisdom, but do not
8:32 thou in heaven, and A, and judge thy servants,
8:39 place, and forgive, and A, and render to each
2Chr 6:23 thou from heaven, and A, and judge thy servants,
Neh 6:13 should be afraid and A in this way and
13:18 Did not your fathers A in this way, and
13:27 this great evil and A treacherously against our God
Jud 13:16 yet he committed no A of sin with me,
Esth 16:24 exception, which does not A accordingly, shall be
Ps 14:2 there are any that A wisely, that seek after
36:3 he has ceased to A wisely and do good.
37:5 the LORD; trust in him, and he will A
119:126 for the LORD to A, for thy law has
Prov 12:22 LORD, but those who A faithfully are his delight.
Wis 12:18 thou hast power to A whenever thou dost choose.
18:21 man was quick to A as their champion; he
Sir 3:1 father, O children; and A accordingly, that you may
5:15 small matters do not A amiss, and do not
8:15 you; for he will A as he pleases, and
15:15 the commandments, and to A faithfully is a matter
16:14 make room for every A of mercy; every one
32:9 the great do not A as their equal; and
32:23 Guard yourself in every A, for this is the
33:29 Do not A immoderately toward anybody, and do
Jer 6:28 iron, all of them A corruptly.
14:7 iniquities testify against us, A, O LORD, for thy
18:12 and will every one A according to the stubbornness
42:5 if we do not A according to all the
Ezek 36:22 I am about to A, but for the sake
36:32 sake that I will A, says the Lord GOD;
44:24 a controversy they shall A as judges, and they
Dan 9:19 LORD, give heed and A; delay not, for thy
11:23 with him he shall A deceitfully; and he shall
Mal 3:17 the day when I A, and I will spare
4:3 the day when I A, says the LORD of
1Mac 7:3 But when this A became known to him, he
8:25 of the Jews shall A as their allies wholeheartedly,
8:27 the Romans shall willingly A as their allies, as
10:4 he said, "Let us A first to make peace
14:46 Simon the right to A in accord with these
16:17 So he committed an A of great treachery and
2Mac 4:31 of high rank, to A as his deputy.
5:18 back from his rash A as soon as he
Lk 12:47 not make ready or A according to his will,
Jn 8:4 been caught in the A of adultery.
Rom 5:18 men, so one man's A of righteousness leads to
14:23 because he does not A from faith; for whatever
2Cor 12:18 Did we not A in the same spirit?
Heb 5:1 men is appointed to A on behalf of men
13:18 clear conscience, desiring to A honorably in all
Jas 2:12 So speak and so A as those who are

ACTED (33)

Num 5:27 defiled herself and has A unfaithfully against her
Deut 9:12 brought from Egypt have A corruptly; they have
Josh 9:4 they on their part A with cunning, and went
Judg 9:16 "Now therefore, if you A in good faith and
9:19 if you then have A in good faith and
1Kgs 8:47 have sinned, and have A perversely and wickedly';
2Chr 6:37 have sinned, and have A perversely and wickedly';
Neh 1:7 We have A very corruptly against thee, and have
9:10 thou knewest that they A insolently against our
9:16 they and our fathers A presumptuously and stiffened
9:29 Yet they A presumptuously and did not obey thy
9:33 faithfully and we have A wickedly;
Ps 78:57 but turned away and A treacherously like their
Sir 32:19 and when you have A, do not regret it.
Ezek 5:7 my ordinances, but have A according to the
11:12 my ordinances, but have A according to the
15:8 because they have A faithlessly, says the Lord
16:52 sins in which you A more abominably than they,
20:9 But I A for the sake of my name,
20:14 But I A for the sake of my name,
20:22 withheld my hand, and A for the sake of
25:12 Lord GOD: Because Edom A revengefully against
25:15 GOD: Because the Philistines A revengefully and
Dan 8:12 ground, and the horn A and prospered.
9:5 and done wrong and A wickedly and rebelled,
Hos 2:5 that conceived them has A shamefully.
2Mac 3:30 the Lord who had A marvelously for his own
6:29 a little before had A toward him with good
12:43 In doing this he A very well and honorably,

Acts 3:17 I know that you A in ignorance, as did
Gal 2:13 rest of the Jews A insincerely, so that even
1Tim 1:13 mercy because I had A ignorantly in unbelief,
Jude 1:7 surrounding cities, which likewise A immorally and

ACTING (8)

Num 10:25 the men of Dan, A as the rear guard
Esth 13:2 of authority but always A reasonably and with
Ezek 14:13 sins against me by A faithlessly, and I stretch
24:19 us, that you are A thus?"
Dan 13:62 do to their neighbor; A in accordance with the
2Mac 7:2 One of them, A as their spokesman, said, "What
Acts 17:7 and they are all A against the decrees of
2Cor 10:2 who suspect us of A in worldly fashion.

ACTION (4)

Dan 11:30 be enraged and take A against the holy covenant.
11:32 know their God shall stand firm and take A
1Mac 4:34 of Lysias five thousand men; they fell in A
2Mac 15:28 When the A was over and they were returning

ACTIONS (6)

1Sam 2:3 knowledge, and by him A are weighed.
Wis 2:12 us and opposes our A; he reproaches us for
9:11 me wisely in my A and guard me with
19:1 advance even their future A,
Sir 11:29 evil, and to worthy A he will attach blame.
Rom 7:15 I do not understand my own A

ACTIVE (3)

Wis 15:11 inspired him with an A soul and breathed into
Heb 4:12 God is living and A, sharper than any two-edged
Jas 2:22 see that faith was A along with his works,

ACTIVITIES

Sir 11:10 matters; if you multiply A you will not go

ACTIVITY (2)

Wis 7:17 the world and the A of the elements;
2Thes 2:9 lawless one by the A of Satan will be

ACTS (87)

Ex 6:6 arm and with great A of judgment,
7:4 of Egypt by great A of judgment.
Num 5:12 wife goes astray and A unfaithfully against him,
Deut 3:24 such works and mighty A as thine?
17:12 The man who A presumptuously, by not obeying the
1Kgs 11:41 the rest of the A of Solomon, and all
11:41 the book of the A of Solomon?
14:19 the rest of the A of Jeroboam, how he
14:29 the rest of the A of Rehoboam, and all
15:7 The rest of the A of Abijam, and all
15:23 rest of all the A of Asa, all his
15:31 the rest of the A of Nadab, and all
16:5 the rest of the A of Baasha, and what
16:14 the rest of the A of Elah, and all
16:20 the rest of the A of Zimri, and the
16:27 the rest of the A of Omri which he
22:39 the rest of the A of Ahab, and all
22:45 the rest of the A of Jehoshaphat, and his
2Kgs 1:18 the rest of the A of Ahaziah which he
8:23 the rest of the A of Joram, and all
10:34 the rest of the A of Jehu, and all
12:19 the rest of the A of Joash, and all
13:8 the rest of the A of Jehoahaz and all
13:12 the rest of the A of Joash, and all
14:15 the rest of the A of Jehoash which he
14:28 the rest of the A of Jeroboam, and all
15:6 the rest of the A of Azariah, and all
15:31 the rest of the A of Pekah, and all
15:36 the rest of the A of Jotham, and all
16:19 the rest of the A of Ahaz which he
21:17 the rest of the A of Manasseh, and all
21:25 the rest of the A of Amon which he
23:28 the rest of the A of Josiah, and all
1Chr 29:29 Now the A of King David, from first to
2Chr 9:29 the rest of the A of Solomon, from first
12:15 Now the A of Rehoboam, from first to last,
13:22 The rest of the A of Abijah, his ways
16:11 The A of Asa, from first to last, are
20:34 the rest of the A of Jehoshaphat, from first
26:22 the rest of the A of Uzziah, from first
27:7 the rest of the A of Jotham, and all
28:26 the rest of his A and all his ways,
32:1 these things and these A of faithfulness Sennacherib
32:32 the rest of the A of Hezekiah, and his
33:18 the rest of the A of Manasseh, and his
35:26 the rest of the A of Josiah, and his
35:27 the LORD, and his A, first and last, behold,
36:8 the rest of the A of Jehoiakim, and the
Tob 1:1 The book of the A of Tobit the son
1:3 and I performed many A of charity to my
1:16 Shalmaneser I performed many A of charity to my
Esth 10:2 And all the A of his power and might,
Ps 31:23 abundantly requites him who A haughtily.
71:15 tell of thy righteous A, of thy deeds of
103:7 ways to Moses, his A to the people of
106:39 became unclean by their A, and played the harlot
145:4 works to another, and shall declare thy mighty A
145:6 might of thy terrible A, and I will declare
Prov 8:22 the first of his A of old.
13:5 but a wicked man A shamefully and disgracefully.
13:16 everything a prudent man A with knowledge, but a
14:17 man of quick temper A foolishly, but a man
14:35 falls on one who A shamefully.
17:2 over a son who A shamefully, and will share
20:11 himself known by his A, whether what he does
21:24 proud, haughty man who A with arrogant pride.
Wis 19:13 because of their wicked A; for they practiced a
Sir 10:6 not attempt anything by A of insolence.
16:20 Who will announce his A of justice?
22:4 husband, but one who A shamefully brings grief to
31:11 assembly will relate his A of charity.
Ezek 14:21 Jerusalem my four sore A of judgment, sword,
30:14 Zoan, and will execute A of judgment upon Thebes.
30:19 Thus I will execute A of judgment upon Egypt.
Dan 9:16 to all thy righteous A, let thy anger and
Mic 6:5 may know the saving A of the LORD."
1Mac 9:22 the rest of the A of Judas, and his
13:46 according to our wicked A but according to your
14:45 Whoever A contrary to these decisions or nullifies
16:23 The rest of the A of John and his
2Mac 4:33 fully aware of these A he publicly exposed them,
4:39 When many A of sacrilege had been committed in
8:18 trust to arms and A of daring," he said,
Acts 9:36 of good works and A of charity.
Rom 1:27 another, men committing shameless A with men and
12:8 zeal; he who does A of mercy, with cheerfulness.
Jas 1:24 but a doer that A, he shall be blessed

ACTUALLY (2)

Acts 21:35 the steps, he was A carried by the soldiers
1Cor 5:1 It is A reported that there is immorality among

ADADAH

Josh 15:22 Eder, Jagur, Kinah, Dimonah, A,

ADAH (8)

Gen 4:19 of the one was A, and the name of
4:20 A bore Jabal; he was the father of those
4:23 said to his wives: A and Zillah, hear my
36:2 wives from the Canaanites: A the daughter of Elon
36:4 And A bore to Esau, Eliphaz; Basemath bore Reuel;
36:10 Eliphaz the son of A the wife of Esau,
36:12 are the sons of A, Esau's wife.
36:16 land of Edom; they are the sons of A

ADAIAH (9)

2Kgs 22:1 Jedidah the daughter of A of Bozkath.
1Chr 6:41 of Zerah, son of A,
8:21 Eli-enai, Zillethai, Eliel, A, Beraiah, and Shimrath
9:12 house of God; and A the son of Jeroham,
2Chr 23:1 Ma-aseiah the son of A, and Elishaphat the son
Ezra 10:29 Meshullum, Malluch, A, Jashub, Sheal, and Jeremoth
10:39 Binnui: Shimei, Shelemiah, Nathan, A,
Neh 11:5 of Hazaiah, son of A, son of Joiarib, son
11:12 hundred and twenty-two; and A the son of Jeroham,

ADALIA

Esth 9:8 Aspatha and Poratha and A and Aridatha

ADAM (25)

Gen 3:17 And to A he said, "Because you have listened
3:21 LORD God made for A and for his wife
4:1 Now A knew Eve his wife, and she conceived
4:25 And A knew his wife again, and she bore
5:1 This is the book of the generations of A
5:3 When A had lived a hundred and thirty years,
5:4 The days of A after he became the father
5:5 all the days that A lived were nine hundred
Josh 3:16 a heap far-off, at A, the city that is
1Chr 1:1 A, Seth, Enosh;

A

	1:1	Adam, Seth, Enosh; A, Seth, Enosh;
Tob	8:6	Thou madest A and gavest him Eve his wife
Sir	33:10	from the ground, and A was created of the
	40:1	upon the sons of A, from the day they
	49:16	honored among men, and A above every living being
Hos	6:7	But at A they transgressed the covenant; there they
Lk	3:38	Seth, the son of A, the son of God.
Rom	5:14	Yet death reigned from A to Moses, even over
	5:14	like the transgression of A, who was a type
1Cor	15:22	For as in A all die, so also in
	15:45	written, "The first man A became a living being";
	15:45	living being"; the last A became a life-giving spirit.
1Tim	2:13	For A was formed first, then Eve;
	2:14	first, then Eve; and A was not deceived, but
Jude	1:14	generation from A prophesied, saying, "Behold, the

ADAMAH

Josh	19:36	Zer, Hammath, Rakkath, Chinnereth, A, Ramah,

ADAMANT (2)

Ezek	3:9	Like A harder than flint have I made your
Zech	7:12	made their hearts like A lest they should hear

ADAMI-NEKEB

Josh	19:33	oak in Za-anannim, and A, and Jabneel, as far

ADAR (15)

Ezra	6:15	of the month of A, in the sixth year
Esth	3:7	the twelfth month, which is the month of A
	3:13	is the month of A, and to plunder their
	8:12	the twelfth month, which is the month of A
	9:1	is the month of A, on the thirteenth day
	9:15	of the month of A and they slew three
	9:17	of the month of A, and on the fourteenth
	9:19	of the month of A as a day for
	9:21	day of the month A and also the fifteenth
	10:13	in the month of A, on the fourteenth and
	13:6	of the twelfth month, A, of this present year,
	16:20	of the twelfth month, A, on that very day
1Mac	7:43	on the thirteenth day of the month of A
	7:49	celebrated each year on the thirteenth day of A
2Mac	15:36	which is called A in the Syrian language

ADASA (2)

1Mac	7:40	And Judas encamped in A with three thousand men.
	7:45	a day's journey, from A as far as Gazara,

ADBEEL (2)

Gen	25:13	of Ishmael; and Kedar, A, Mibsam,
1Chr	1:29	Ishmael, Nebaioth; and Kedar, A, Mibsam,

ADD (39)

Gen	30:24	saying, "May the LORD A to me another son!"
Lev	5:16	holy thing, and shall A a fifth to it
	6:5	in full, and shall A a fifth to it,
	22:14	thing unwittingly, he shall A the fifth of its
	27:13	redeem it, he shall A a fifth to the
	27:15	his house, he shall A a fifth of the
	27:19	it, then he shall A a fifth of the
	27:27	at your valuation, and A a fifth to it;
	27:31	his tithe, he shall A a fifth to it.
Deut	4:2	You shall not A to the word which I
	12:32	do; you shall not A to it or take
	19:9	ways—then you shall A three other cities to
2Sam	12:8	too little, I would A to you as much
	24:3	the LORD your God A to the people a
1Kgs	12:11	heavy yoke, I will A to your yoke.
	12:14	heavy, but I will A to your yoke; my
2Kgs	20:6	And I will A fifteen years to your life.
1Chr	21:3	said, "May the LORD A to his people a
	22:14	To these you must A
2Chr	10:11	heavy yoke, I will A to your yoke.
	10:14	heavy, but I will A to it; my father
Tob	5:15	And besides, I will A to your wages if
	5:18	Do not A money to money, but consider it
Ps	69:27	A to them punishment upon punishment; may they
Prov	30:6	Do not A to his words, lest he rebuke
Sir	4:3	Do not A to the troubles of an angry
	5:5	of atonement that you A sin to sin.
	13:3	wrong, and he must A apologies.
	21:15	will praise it and A to it; when a
Is	5:8	house to house, who A field to field, until
	29:1	A year to year; let the feasts run their
	30:1	spirit, that they may A sin to sin;
	38:5	tears; behold, I will A fifteen years to your
Jer	7:21	the God of Israel: A your burnt offerings to
1Mac	8:30	parties shall determine to A or delete anything, they
	11:1	kingdom by trickery and A it to his own
Mt	6:27	by being anxious can A one cubit to his
Lk	12:25	by being anxious can A a cubit to his
Rev	22:18	to them, God will A to him the plagues

ADDAN

Ezra	2:59	Tel-melah, Tel-harsha, Cherub, A, and Immer, though

ADDAR (2)

Josh	15:3	by Hezron, up to A, turns about to Karka,
1Chr	8:3	And Bela had sons: A, Gera, Abihud,

ADDED (27)

Gen	24:25	She A, "We have both straw and provender enough,
Num	19:17	running water shall be A in a vessel;
	36:3	of our fathers, and A to the inheritance of
	36:4	their inheritance will be A to the inheritance of
Deut	5:22	loud voice; and he A no more.
1Sam	12:19	die; for we have A to all our sins
2Sam	19:35	your servant be an A burden to my lord
Esth	5:12	And Haman A, "Even Queen Esther let no one
Prov	9:11	and years will be A to your life.
Eccl	3:14	ever; nothing can be A to it, nor anything
Sir	42:21	Nothing can be A or taken away, and he
	45:20	He A glory to Aaron and gave him a
Jer	36:32	many similar words were A to them.
	45:3	for the LORD has A sorrow to my pain;
Dan	4:36	still more greatness was A to me.
1Mac	10:30	from the three districts A to it from Samaria
	10:38	districts that have been A to Judea from the
	11:34	region bordering them, were A to Judea from
	14:15	the sanctuary glorious, and A to the vessels of
Lk	3:20	that Herod had done, A this to them all,
Acts	2:41	baptized, and there were A that day about three
	2:47	And the Lord A to their number day by
	5:14	than ever believers were A to the Lord, multitudes
	11:24	a large company was A to the Lord.
Gal	2:6	who were of repute A nothing to me;
	3:19	It was A because of transgressions, till the offspring
Heb	10:9	the law), then he A, "Lo, I have come

ADDER (5)

Ps	58:4	serpent, like the deaf A that stops its ear,
	91:13	the lion and the A, the young lion and
Prov	23:32	bites like a serpent, and stings like an A
Is	11:8	his hand on the A's den.
	14:29	will come forth an A, and its fruit will

ADDERS (2)

Is	59:5	They hatch A eggs, they weave the spider's web;
Jer	8:17	sending among you serpents, A which cannot be

ADDI

Lk	3:28	Melchi, the son of A, the son of Cosam,

ADDICTED

1Tim	3:8	serious, not double-tongued, not A to much wine, not

ADDING (4)

Num	5:7	restitution for his wrong, A a fifth to it,
Eccl	7:27	found, says the Preacher, A one thing to another
Sir	31:30	reducing his strength and A wounds.
2Mac	2:32	us begin our narrative, A only so much to

ADDITION (13)

Ex	29:25	on the altar in A to the burnt offering,
Num	5:8	for the priest, in A to the ram of
	29:39	your appointed feasts, in A to your votive offerings
	35:6	to flee, and in A to them you shall
1Chr	29:3	Moreover, in A to all that I have provided
2Chr	28:13	against the LORD in A to our present sins
Tob	2:14	as a gift in A to my wages." But
Ezek	16:43	committed lewdness in A to all your abominations?
	44:7	broken my covenant, in A to all your abominations.
1Mac	8:30	their discretion, and any A or deletion that they
2Mac	4:9	In A to this he promised to pay one
	9:17	own revenues; and in A to all this he
	12:2	and Demophon, and in A to these Nicanor the

ADDITIONAL

1Mac	10:41	And all the A funds which the government officials

ADDON

Neh	7:61	from Tel-melah, Tel-harsha, Cherub, A, and Immer,

ADDRESS (3)
Ps 45:1 a goodly theme; I A my verses to the
Wis 13:17 is not ashamed to A a lifeless thing.
1Cor 3:1 I, brethren, could not A you as spiritual men,

ADDRESSED (9)
Ezra 10:2 the sons of Elam, A Ezra: "We have broken
1Mac 14:40 that the Jews were A by the Romans as
2Mac 15:15 he gave it he A him thus:
Lk 23:19 Pilate A them once more, desiring to release Jesus;
Acts 2:14 up his voice and A them, "Men of Judea
3:12 Peter saw it he A the people, "Men of
22:2 they heard that he A them in the Hebrew
Heb 7:21 but this one was A with an oath, "The
Rev 7:13 one of the elders A me, saying, "Who are

ADDRESSES
Heb 12:5 forgotten the exhortation which A you as sons?--

ADDRESSING
Eph 5:19 filled with the Spirit, A one another in psalms

ADDS (8)
Job 34:37 For he A rebellion to his sin; he claps
Prov 10:22 makes rich, and he A no sorrow with it.
16:23 his speech judicious, and A persuasiveness to his lips.
Sir 13:3 wrong, and he even A reproaches; a poor man
26:15 A modest wife A charm to charm, and no
Gal 3:15 a man's will, or A to it, once it
Heb 10:17 then he A, "I will remember their sins and
Rev 22:18 book: if any one A to them, God will

ADHERED
1Mac 1:57 or if any one A to the law, the

ADHERENTS (3)
Rom 4:14 If it is the A of the law who
4:16 not only to the A of the law but
Heb 13:9 not by foods, which have not benefited their A

ADI-EL (3)
1Chr 4:36 Eli-o-enai, Ja-akobah, Jeshohaiah, Asaiah, A,
9:12 Maasai the son of A, son of Jahzerah, son
27:25 Azmaveth the son of A; and over the treasuries

ADIDA (2)
1Mac 12:38 And Simon built A in the Shephelah; he fortified
13:13 And Simon encamped in A, facing the plain.

ADIN (4)
Ezra 2:15 The sons of A, four hundred and fifty-four.
8:6 Of the sons of A, Ebed the son of
Neh 7:20 The sons of A, six hundred and fifty-five.
10:16 Azgad, Bebai, Adonijah, Bigvai, A,

ADINA
1Chr 11:42 the son of Ahlai, A the son of Shiza

ADITHAIM
Josh 15:36 Adullam, Socoh, Azekah, Shaaraim, A, Gederah,

ADJOINING (17)
Ezek 42:3 A the twenty cubits which belonged to the inner
48:2 A the territory of Dan, from the east side
48:3 A the territory of Asher, from the east side
48:4 A the territory of Naphtali, from the east side
48:5 A the territory of Manasseh, from the east side
48:6 A the territory of Ephraim, from the east side
48:7 A the territory of Reuben, from the east side
48:8 A the territory of Judah, from the east side
48:12 a most holy place, A the territory of the
48:24 A the territory of Benjamin, from the east side
48:25 A the territory of Simeon, from the east side
48:26 A the territory of Issachar, from the east side
48:27 A the territory of Zebulun, from the east side
48:28 And A the territory of Gad to the south,
Dan 13:4 had a spacious garden A his house; and the
1Mac 10:39 Ptolemais and the land A it I have given
2Mac 12:16 numbers, so that the A lake, a quarter of

ADJURATION
Lev 5:1 he hears a public A to testify and though

ADJURE (11)
1Kgs 22:16 many times shall I A you that you speak
2Chr 18:15 many times shall I A you that you speak
Song 2:7 I A you, O daughters of Jerusalem, by the
3:5 I A you, O daughters of Jerusalem, by the
5:8 I A you, O daughters of Jerusalem, if you
5:9 beloved, that you thus A us?
8:4 I A you, O daughters of Jerusalem, that you
Mt 26:63 said to him, "I A you by the living
Mk 5:7 I A you by God, do not torment me."
Acts 19:13 evil spirits, saying, "I A you by the Jesus
1Thes 5:27 I A you by the Lord that this letter

ADJURED
2Sam 21:17 Then David's men A him, "You shall no more

ADLAI
1Chr 27:29 in the valleys was Shaphat the son of A

ADMAH (5)
Gen 10:19 direction of Sodom, Gomorrah, A, and Zeboiim, as
14:2 Gomorrah, Shinab king of A, Shemeber king of
14:8 Gomorrah, the king of A, the king of Zeboiim,
Deut 29:23 of Sodom and Gomorrah, A and Zeboiim, which the
Hos 11:8 How can I make you like A

ADMATHA
Esth 1:14 Carshena, Shethar, A, Tarshish, Meres, Marsena

ADMIN
Lk 3:33 Amminadab, the son of A, the son of Arni,

ADMINISTERED (3)
1Sam 7:17 and there also he A justice to Israel.
2Sam 8:15 all Israel; and David A justice and equity to
1Chr 18:14 all Israel; and he A justice and equity to

ADMINISTERING
2Cor 8:20 gift which we are A,

ADMINISTRATION (4)
Tob 1:21 accounts of his kingdom and over the entire A
1:22 and in charge of A of the accounts, for
Esth 16:5 been entrusted with the A of public affairs,
2Mac 3:4 high priest about the A of the city market;

ADMINISTRATORS
1Cor 12:28 miracles, then healers, helpers, A, speakers in various

ADMIRABLE
2Mac 7:20 The mother was especially A and worthy of

ADMIRED (5)
Jud 10:7 clothing changed, they greatly A her beauty, and said
10:19 at her beauty, and A the Israelites, judging them
Wis 8:11 in the sight of rulers I shall be A
Sir 38:3 in the presence of great men he is A
2Mac 4:16 ways of living they A and wished to imitate

ADMIRES
Sir 27:23 all sweetness, and he A your words; but later

ADMISSION
Jude 1:4 For A has been secretly gained by some who

ADMIT (3)
Bar 6:56 then must any one A or think that they
Acts 24:13 But this I A to you, that according to
1Tim 5:19 Never A any charge against an elder except on

ADMITTED (2)
Jud 13:13 opened the gate and A them, and they kindled
Ezek 44:5 those who may be A to the temple and

ADMITTING
Ezek 44:7 abominations, in A foreigners, uncircumcised in heart

ADMONISH (8)
1Kgs 2:42 the LORD, and solemnly A you, saying, 'Know for
Jud 8:27 him, in order to A them."
Ps 81:8 my people, while I A you!
Acts 20:31 night or day to A every one with tears.
1Cor 4:14 you ashamed, but to A you as my beloved
Col 3:16 you richly, teach and A one another in all
1Thes 5:12 in the Lord and A you,
5:14 we exhort you, brethren, A the idlers, encourage the

ADMONISHING
Tit 3:10 who is factious, after A him once or twice,

ADMONITION (4)
Prov 15:5 but he who heeds A is prudent.
15:31 whose ear heeds wholesome A will abide among the
15:32 but he who heeds A gains understanding.
22:20 you thirty sayings of A and knowledge,

ADNA (2)
Ezra 10:30 sons of Pahath-moab: A, Chelal, Benaiah, Ma-aseiah,
Neh 12:15 Shebaniah, Joseph; of Harim, A; of Meraioth,

ADNAH (2)
1Chr 12:20 deserted to him: A, Jozabad, Jedia-el, Michael,
2Chr 17:14 the commanders of thousands: A the commander,

ADONI-BEZEK (3)
Judg 1:5 They came upon A at Bezek, and fought against
1:6 A fled; but they pursued him, and caught him,
1:7 And A said, "Seventy kings with their thumbs and

ADONI-ZEDEK (2)
Josh 10:1 When A king of Jerusalem heard how Joshua had
10:3 So A king of Jerusalem sent to Hoham king

ADONIJAH (26)
2Sam 3:4 Geshur; and the fourth, A the son of Haggith;
1Kgs 1:5 Now A the son of Haggith exalted himself, saying,
1:7 priest; and they followed A and helped him.
1:8 Rei, and David's mighty men were not with A
1:9 A sacrificed sheep, oxen, and fatlings by the
1:11 you not heard that A the son of Haggith
1:13 Why then is A king?'
1:18 throne.' And now, behold, A is king, although you,
1:24 king, have you said, A shall reign after me,
1:25 saying, 'Long live King A
1:41 A and all the guests who were with him
1:42 the priest came; and A said, "Come in, for
1:43 Jonathan answered A, "No, for our lord King David
1:49 all the guests of A trembled, and rose, and
1:50 And A feared Solomon; and he arose, and went,
1:51 was told Solomon, "Behold, A fears King Solomon;,
2:13 Then A the son of Haggith came to Bathsheba
2:19 Solomon, to speak to him on behalf of A
2:21 Shunammite be given to A your brother as his
2:22 why do you ask Abishag the Shunammite for A
2:23 word does not cost A his life!
2:24 house, as he promised, A shall be put to
2:28 for Joab had supported A although he had not
1Chr 3:2 of Geshur; the fourth A, whose mother was Haggith;
2Chr 17:8 Zebadiah, Asahel, Shemiramoth, Jehonathan, A, ,
Neh 10:16 Bunni, Azgad, Bebai, A, Bigvai, Adin,

ADONIKAM (3)
Ezra 2:13 The sons of A, six hundred and sixty-six.
8:13 Of the sons of A, those who came later,
Neh 7:18 The sons of A, six hundred and sixty-seven.

ADONIRAM (2)
1Kgs 4:6 of the palace; and A the son of Abda
5:14 two months at home; A was in charge of

ADOPT
2Mac 6:8 cities, that they should A the same policy toward

ADOPTED (4)
Esth 2:7 her mother died, Mordecai A her as his own
2:15 of Mordecai, who had A her as his own
1Mac 1:43 even from Israel gladly A his religion; they sacrificed
Acts 7:21 was exposed, Pharaoh's daughter A him and brought

ADOPTION (3)
2Mac 4:13 and increase in the A of foreign ways because
Rom 8:23 as we wait for A as sons, the redemption
Gal 4:5 that we might receive A as sons.

ADORA
1Mac 13:20 and he circled around by the way to A

ADORAIM
2Chr 11:9 Gath, Mareshah, Ziph, A, Lachish, Azekah,

ADORAM (2)
2Sam 20:24 and the Pelethites; and A was in charge of
1Kgs 12:18 Then King Rehoboam sent A, who was taskmaster

ADORN (7)
Esth 14:2 that she loved to A she covered with her
Jer 31:4 Again you shall A yourself with timbrels, and shall
2Mac 9:16 formerly plundered, he would A with the finest
Mt 23:28 of the prophets and A the monuments of the
1Tim 2:9 also that women should A themselves modestly and
Tit 2:10 in everything they may A the doctrine of God
1Pet 3:5 in God used to A themselves and were submissive

ADORNED (9)
2Kgs 9:30 painted her eyes, and A her head, and looked
2Chr 3:6 He A the house with settings of precious stones.
Esth 15:2 Then, majestically A, after invoking the aid of the
Sir 45:12 an expert, the delight of the eyes, richly A
48:11 those who have been A in love; for we
50:9 vessel of hammered gold A with all kinds of
Lk 21:5 temple, how it was A with noble stones and
Rev 21:2 prepared as a bride A for her husband;
21:19 of the city were A with every jewel; the

ADORNING
1Pet 3:3 yours be the outward A with braiding of hair,

ADORNMENT (4)
Prov 3:22 for your soul and A for your neck.
1Mac 2:11 All her A has been taken away; no longer
2Mac 2:2 seeing the gold and silver statues and their A
2:29 is suitable for its A, such in my judgment

ADORNS (2)
Ps 149:4 in his people; he A the humble with victory.
Is 61:10 and as a bride A herself with her jewels.

ADRAMMELECH (3)
2Kgs 17:31 in the fire to A and Anammelech, the gods
19:37 of Nisroch his god, A and Sharezer, his sons,
Is 37:38 of Nisroch his god, A and Sharezer, his sons,

ADRAMYTTIUM
Acts 27:2 in a ship of A, which was about to

ADRIA
Acts 27:27 across the sea of A, about midnight the sailors

ADRIEL (2)
1Sam 18:19 she was given to A the Meholathite for a
2Sam 21:8 whom she bore to A the son of Barzillai

ADRIFT
2Cor 11:25 day I have been A at sea;

ADUEL
Tob 1:1 of Ananiel, son of A, son of Gabael, of

ADULLAM (9)
Josh 12:15 one; the king of A, one;
15:35 En-gannim, Tappuah, Enam, Jarmuth, A, Socoh,
1Sam 22:1 to the cave of A; and when his brothers
2Sam 23:13 at the cave of A, when a band of
1Chr 11:15 at the cave of A, when the army of
2Chr 11:7 Etam, Tekoa, Bethzur, Soco, A,
Neh 11:30 Zorah, in Jarmuth, Zanoah, A, and their villages,
Mic 1:15 Mareshah; the glory of Israel shall come to A
2Mac 12:38 his army and went to the city of A

ADULLAMITE (3)
Gen 38:1 in to a certain A, whose name was Hirah.
38:12 his sheepshearers, he and his friend Hirah the A
38:20 by his friend the A, to receive the pledge

ADULTERER (3)
Lev 20:10 his neighbor, both the A and the adulteress shall
Job 24:15 The eye of the A also waits for the
Is 57:3 sorceress, offspring of the A and the harlot.

ADULTERERS (8)
Ps 50:18 friend of his; and you keep company with A
Wis 3:16 But children of A will not come to maturity,
Jer 9:2 For they are all A, a company of treacherous
23:10 land is full of A; because of the curse
Hos 7:5 They are all A; they are like a heated
Mal 3:5 the sorcerers, against the A, against those who swear
Lk 18:11 other men, extortioners, unjust, A, or even like this
1Cor 6:9 immoral, nor idolaters, nor A, nor homosexuals,

ADULTERESS (7)
Lev 20:10 the adulterer and the A shall be put to
Prov 6:26 of bread, but an A stalks a man's very

30:20 the way of an A: she eats, and wipes
Hos 3:1 paramour and is an A; even as the LORD
Mt 5:32 unchastity, makes her an A; and whoever marries a
Rom 7:3 will be called an A if she lives with
7:3 she marries another man she is not an A

ADULTERESSES (2)

Ezek 23:45 with the sentence of A, and with the sentence
23:45 blood; because they are A, and blood is upon

ADULTERIES (2)

Jer 3:8 that for all the A of that faithless one,
13:27 seen your abominations, your A and neighings, your

ADULTEROUS (6)

Sir 25:2 a liar, and an A old man who lacks
Ezek 16:32 A wife, who receives strangers instead of her
Mt 12:39 them, "An evil and A generation seeks for a
16:4 An evil and A generation seeks for a sign,
Mk 8:38 my words in this A and sinful generation, of
Heb 13:4 undefiled; for God will judge the immoral and A

ADULTERY (42)

Ex 20:14 "You shall not commit A
Lev 20:10 "If a man commits A with the wife of
Deut 5:18 "'Neither shall you commit A
Prov 6:32 He who commits A has no sense; he who
Wis 14:24 grieve one another by A,
14:26 perversion, disorder in marriage, A, and debauchery.
Sir 23:23 third, she has committed A through harlotry and
Jer 3:9 polluted the land, committing A with stone and tree.
5:7 the full, they committed A and trooped to the
7:9 you steal, murder, commit A, swear falsely, burn
23:14 horrible thing: they commit A and walk in lies;
29:23 Israel, they have committed A with their neighbors'
Ezek 23:37 For they have committed A, and blood is upon
23:37 idols they have committed A; and they have even
23:43 not men now commit A when they practice harlotry
Hos 2:2 her face, and her A from between her breasts;
4:2 killing, stealing, and committing A; they break all
4:13 daughters play the harlot, and your brides commit A
4:14 brides when they commit A; for the men themselves
Mt 5:27 'You shall not commit A
5:28 lustfully has already committed A with her in his
5:32 and whoever marries a divorced woman commits A
15:19 come evil thoughts, murder, A, fornication, theft, false
19:9 and marries another, commits A; and he who marries
19:9 and he who marries a divorced woman, commits A
19:18 You shall not commit A, You shall not steal,
Mk 7:20 thoughts, fornication, theft, murder, A,
10:11 and marries another, commits A against her;
10:12 her husband and marries another, she commits A
10:19 kill, Do not commit A, Do not steal, Do
Lk 16:18 and marries another commits A, and he who marries
16:18 a woman divorced from her husband commits A
18:20 commandments: 'Do not commit A, Do not kill, Do
Jn 8:3 had been caught in A, and placing her in
8:4 woman has been caught in the act of A
Rom 2:22 one must not commit A, do you commit adultery?
2:22 one must not commit adultery, do you commit A
13:9 "You shall not commit A, You shall not kill,
Jas 2:11 For he who said, "Do not commit A
2:11 you do not commit A but do kill, you
2Pet 2:14 have eyes full of A, insatiable for sin.
Rev 2:22 and those who commit A with her I will

ADUMMIM (2)

Josh 15:7 opposite the ascent of A, which is on the
18:17 opposite the ascent of A; then it goes down

ADVANCE (11)

Jud 2:10 and seize all their territory for me in A
9:6 ways are prepared in A, and thy judgment is
Wis 19:1 for God knew in A even their future actions,
Sir 20:26 who speaks wisely will A himself, and a sensible
Jer 46:3 buckler and shield, and A for battle!
46:9 A, O horses, and rage, O chariots!
49:28 the LORD: "Rise up, A against Kedar!
49:31 "Rise up, A against a nation at ease, that
Ezek 38:9 You will A, coming on like a storm, you
2Cor 9:5 me, and arrange in A for this gift you
Phil 1:12 has really served to A the gospel,

ADVANCED (27)

Gen 18:11 and Sarah were old, A in age; it had
24:1 Abraham was old, well A in years; and the
Josh 13:1 Joshua was old and A in years; and the
13:1 "You are old and A in years, and there
23:1 was old and well A in years,
23:2 now old and well A in years;
1Sam 17:12 was already old and A in years.
1Kgs 1:1 David was old and A in years, and although
Esth 2:9 the king's palace, and A her and her maids
3:1 son of Hammedatha, and A him and set his
5:11 and how he had A him above the princes
10:2 to which the king A him, are they not
1Mac 1:3 He A to the ends of the earth, and
6:40 the plain, and they A steadily and in good
6:42 Judas and his army A to the battle, and
9:12 two companies, the phalanx A to the sound of
10:77 the same time he A into the plain, for
2Mac 4:40 certain Auranus, a man A in years and no
4:40 years and no less A in folly.
6:18 position, a man now A in age and of
10:27 up their arms and A a considerable distance from
11:10 They A in battle order, having their heavenly ally,
13:19 He A against Bethzur, a strong fortress of the
15:25 Nicanor and his men A with trumpets and battle
Lk 1:7 barren, and both were A in years.
1:18 and my wife is A in years."
Gal 1:14 destroy it; and I A in Judaism beyond many

ADVANTAGE (24)

2Sam 11:23 "The men gained an A over us, and came
Jud 5:11 to them; he took A of them and set
Job 35:3 that you ask, 'What A have I?
Eccl 3:19 and man has no A over the beasts; for
5:9 a king is an A to a land with
6:8 For what A has the wise man over the
7:11 with an inheritance, an A to those who see
7:12 of money; and the A of knowledge is that
10:11 charmed, there is no A in a charmer.
Sir 20:29 and unseen treasure, what A is there in either
37:22 wise to his own A, and the fruits of
41:14 and unseen treasure, what A is there in either
Dan 11:17 it shall not stand or be to his A
Jn 16:7 it is to your A that I go away,
Rom 3:1 Then what A has the Jew?
1Cor 10:33 not seeking my own A, but that of many,
2Cor 2:11 Satan from gaining the A over us; for we
7:2 one, we have taken A of no one.
11:20 upon you, or takes A of you, or puts
12:17 Did I take A of you through any of
12:18 Did Titus take A of you?
Gal 5:2 will be of no A to you.
Heb 13:17 would be of no A to you.
Jude 1:16 loud-mouthed boasters, flattering people to gain A

ADVANTAGEOUS

2Mac 8:7 found the nights most A for such attacks.

ADVANTAGES

Bar 4:3 to another, or your A to an alien people.

ADVENTURES

Prov 23:27 a deep pit; an A is a narrow well.

ADVENTURESS (4)

Prov 2:16 loose woman, from the A with her smooth words,
5:20 loose woman and embrace the bosom of an A
6:24 evil woman, from the smooth tongue of the A
7:5 loose woman, from the A with her smooth words.

ADVERSARIES (47)

Ex 15:7 majesty thou overthrowest thy A; thou sendest forth
23:22 to your enemies and an adversary to your A
Num 24:8 up the nations his A, and shall break their
Deut 32:27 the enemy, lest their A should judge amiss, lest
32:41 take vengeance on my A, and will requite those
32:43 takes vengeance on his A, and makes expiation for
33:7 for him, and be a help against his A
33:11 the loins of his A, of those that hate
Josh 5:13 him, "Are you for us, or for our A
Judg 2:3 them out before you; but they shall become A
1Sam 2:10 The A of the LORD shall be broken to
2Sam 22:49 exalt me above my A, thou didst deliver me
1Chr 12:17 betray me to my A, although there is no
Ezra 4:1 Now when the A of Judah and Benjamin heard
Job 22:20 scorn, saying, 'Surely our A are cut off, and
Ps 17:7 seek refuge from their A at thy right hand.
18:48 exalt me above my A; thou didst deliver me
27:2 slanders against me, my A and foes, they shall

27:12 the will of my A; for false witnesses have
31:11 scorn of all my A, a horror to my
38:20 for good are my A because I follow after
42:10 in my body, my A taunt me, while they
74:23 the uproar of thy A which goes up continually!
78:66 And he put his A to rout; he put
97:3 and burns up his A round about.
106:11 the waters covered their A; not one of them
112:8 afraid, until he sees his desire on his A
119:157 my persecutors and my A, but I do not
143:12 and destroy all my A, for I am thy
Wis 2:18 will deliver him from the hand of his A
Sir 23:3 not fall before my A, and my enemy will
47:7 side, and annihilated his A the Philistines; he crushed
Is 9:11 So the LORD raises A against them, and stirs
26:11 the fire for thy A consume them.
59:18 repay, wrath to his A, requital to his enemies;
63:18 a little while; our A have trodden it down.
64:2 name known to thy A, and that the nations
Ezek 39:23 the hand of their A, and they all fell
Mic 5:9 lifted up over your A, and all your enemies
Nah 1:2 takes vengeance on his A and keeps wrath for
1:8 full end of his A, and will pursue his
2Mac 10:26 an adversary to their A, as the law declares.
15:16 God, with which you will strike down your A
Lk 13:17 said this, all his A were put to shame;
21:15 which none of your A will be able to
1Cor 16:9 has opened to me, and there are many A
Heb 10:27 a fury of fire which will consume the A

ADVERSARY (22)

Ex 23:22 your enemies and an A to your adversaries.
Num 10:9 your land against the A who oppresses you, then
22:22 took his stand in the way as his A
1Sam 29:4 battle he become an A to us.
2Sam 19:22 day be as an A to me?
1Kgs 5:4 side; there is neither A nor misfortune.
11:14 LORD raised up an A against Solomon, Hadad the
11:23 raised up as an A to him, Rezon the
11:25 He was an A of Israel all the days
Job 6:23 'Deliver me from the A's hand?
16:9 teeth at me; my A sharpens his eyes against
19:11 wrath against me, and counts me as his A
31:35 that I had the indictment written by my A
Ps 55:12 it is not an A who deals insolently with
Sir 21:27 ungodly man curses his A, he curses his own
36:7 thy wrath; destroy the A and wipe out the
Is 50:8 Who is my A
Amos 3:11 the Lord GOD: "An A shall surround the land,
1Mac 1:36 the sanctuary, an evil A of Israel continually.
2Mac 10:26 their enemies and an A to their adversaries, as
Lk 18:3 'Vindicate me against my A
1Pet 5:8 Your A the devil prowls around like a roaring

ADVERSITIES

Ps 31:7 taken heed of my A,

ADVERSITY (14)

Num 20:14 You know all the A that has befallen us:
2Sam 4:9 life out of every A,
1Kgs 1:29 soul out of every A,
Job 36:15 by their affliction, and opens their ear by A
Ps 10:6 moved; throughout all generations I shall not meet A
Prov 17:17 all times, and a brother is born for A
24:10 in the day of A, your strength is small.
Eccl 7:14 in the day of A consider; God has made
Sir 11:23 the day of prosperity, A is forgotten, and in
11:23 in the day of A, prosperity is not remembered.
12:8 prosperity, nor will an enemy be hidden in A
12:9 prospers, and in his A even his friend will
20:8 for a man in A, and a windfall may
Is 30:20 you the bread of A and the water of

ADVICE (10)

Judg 20:7 of you, give your A and counsel here."
2Sam 17:4 And the A pleased Absalom and all the elders
Tob 4:18 Seek A from every wise man, and do not
Esth 1:21 This A pleased the king and the princes, and
Prov 12:15 own eyes, but a wise man listens to A
13:10 with those who take A is wisdom.
19:20 Listen to A and accept instruction, that you may
Eccl 4:13 will no longer take A,
Acts 5:40 So they took his A, and when they had
2Cor 8:10 matter I give my A: it is best for

ADVISABLE

1Cor 16:4 If it seems A that I should go also,

ADVISE (5)

1Kgs 12:6 saying, "How do you A me to answer this
12:9 them, "What do you A that we answer this
2Chr 10:6 saying, "How do you A me to answer this
10:9 them, "What do you A that we answer this
2Mac 7:25 and urged her to A the youth to save

ADVISED (3)

Esth 2:15 king's eunuch, who had charge of the women, A
Acts 27:9 already gone by, Paul A them,
27:12 winter in, the majority A to put to sea

ADVISER

Gen 26:26 Gerar with Ahuzzath his A and Phicol the

ADVISERS (2)

Prov 15:22 wrong, but with many A they succeed.
Sir 6:6 many, but let your A be one in a

ADVISES

2Sam 17:6 has Ahithophel spoken; shall we do as he A

ADVOCATE (3)

Wis 12:12 to plead as an A for unrighteous men?
Acts 16:21 They A customs which it is not lawful for
1Jn 2:1 sin, we have an A with the Father, Jesus

AENEAS (2)

Acts 9:33 found a man named A, who had been bedridden
9:34 Peter said to him, A, Jesus Christ heals you;

AENON

Jn 3:23 also was baptizing at A near Salim, because there

AESORA

Jud 4:4 and to Choba and A and the valley of

AFAR (51)

Gen 22:4 and saw the place A off.
37:18 They saw him A off, and before he came
Ex 20:18 trembled; and they stood A off,
20:21 And the people stood A off, while Moses drew
24:1 of Israel, and worship A off.
Num 9:10 dead body, or is A off on a journey,
24:6 Like valleys that stretch A, like gardens beside a
Deut 28:49 nation against you from A, from the end of
32:26 "I will scatter them A, I will make the
1Sam 26:13 other side, and stood A off on the top
Ezra 3:13 a great shout, and the sound was heard A
Neh 12:43 of Jerusalem was heard A off.
Tob 13:11 nations will come from A to the name of
Jud 13:11 Judith called out from A to the watchmen at
Job 2:12 they saw him from A, they did not recognize
28:4 by travelers, they hang A from men, they swing
36:3 my knowledge from A, and ascribe righteousness to
36:25 have looked on it; man beholds it from A
39:25 smells the battle from A, the thunder of the
39:29 his eyes behold it A off.
Ps 10:1 Why dost thou stand A off, O LORD?
38:11 and my kinsmen stand A off.
55:7 yea, I would wander A, I would lodge in
138:6 the lowly; but the haughty he knows from A
139:2 I rise up; thou discernest my thoughts from A
Prov 31:14 of the merchant, she brings her food from A
Sir 21:7 speech is known from A; but the sensible man,
24:30 will make it shine A;
Is 5:26 signal for a nation A off, and whistle for
10:3 punishment, in the storm which will come from A
23:7 of old, whose feet carried her to settle A
33:17 beauty; they will behold a land that stretches A
43:6 bring my sons from A and my daughters from
49:1 me, O coastlands, and hearken, you peoples from A
49:12 these shall come from A, and lo, these from
59:14 back, and righteousness stands A off; for truth has
66:19 Javan, to the coastlands A off, that have not
Jer 5:15 you a nation from A, O house of Israel,
23:23 and not a God A off?
30:10 will save you from A, and your offspring from
31:3 for rest, the LORD appeared to him from A
31:10 it in the coastlands A off; say, 'He who
46:27 will save you from A, and your offspring from
51:50 Remember the LORD from A, and let Jerusalem
Bar 4:15 them a nation from A, a shameless nation, of

Mic 4:3 decide for strong nations A off; and they shall
Hab 1:8 their horsemen come from A; they fly like an
Mt 27:55 there, looking on from A, who had followed Jesus
Mk 5:6 he saw Jesus from A, he ran and worshiped
15:39 women looking on from A, among whom were Mary
Heb 11:13 and greeted it from A, and having acknowledged that

AFFAIR (3)

Num 16:49 who died in the A of Korah.
Esth 2:23 When the A was investigated and found to be
2Mac 8:20 all went into the A, with four thousand Macedonians;

AFFAIRS (30)

2Sam 14:20 change the course of A your servant Joab did
19:29 to him, "Why speak any more of your A
1Kgs 10:6 own land of your A and of your wisdom,
12:15 was a turn of A brought about by the
1Chr 26:32 God and for the A of the king.
2Chr 9:5 own land of your A and of your wisdom,
10:15 was a turn of A brought about by God
Jud 12:11 charge of his personal A, "Go now and persuade
14:13 of all his personal A, "Wake up our lord,
Esth 13:6 is in charge of A and is our second
16:5 the administration of public A,
Ps 112:5 lends, who conducts his A with justice.
Dan 2:49 and Abednego over the A of the province of
3:12 have appointed over the A of the province of
1Mac 3:32 charge of the king's A from the river Euphrates
6:57 is strong, and the A of the kingdom press
2Mac 3:7 in charge of his A, and sent him with
4:6 the king's attention public A could not again reach
4:30 was the state of A, it happened that the
7:24 for his friend and entrust him with public A
9:20 are well and your A are as you wish,
11:23 kingdom be undisturbed in caring for their own A
11:26 on happily in the conduct of their own A
11:29 to return home and look after your own A
1Cor 7:32 is anxious about the A of the Lord, how
7:33 is anxious about worldly A, how to please his
7:34 is anxious about the A of the Lord, how
7:34 is anxious about worldly A, how to please her
Col 4:7 you all about my A; he is a beloved
1Thes 4:11 to mind your own A, and to work with

AFFECTION (7)

Prov 5:19 Let her A fill you at all times with
2Mac 9:21 heaven, I remember with A your esteem and good
Rom 12:10 one another with brotherly A; outdo one another in
Phil 1:8 you all with the A of Christ Jesus.
2:1 in the Spirit, any A and sympathy,
2Pet 1:7 godliness with brotherly A, and brotherly affection
1:7 brotherly affection, and brotherly A with love.

AFFECTIONATELY

1Thes 2:8 So, being A desirous of you, we were ready

AFFECTIONS

2Cor 6:12 us, but you are restricted in your own A

AFFIRM

Eph 4:17 Now this I A and testify in the Lord,

AFFIRMING

Acts 24:8 joined in the charge, A that all this was

AFFLICT (31)

Ex 1:10 taskmasters over them to A them with heavy
22:22 You shall not A any widow or orphan.
22:23 If you do A them, and they cry out
Lev 16:29 the month, you shall A yourselves, and shall do
16:31 you, and you shall A yourselves; it is a
23:27 convocation, and you shall A yourselves and present
23:32 rest, and you shall A yourselves; on the ninth
Num 24:24 from Kittim and shall A Asshur and Eber; and
29:7 a holy convocation, and A yourselves; you shall do
30:13 any binding oath to A herself, her husband may
2Sam 7:10 and violent men shall A them no more, as
1Kgs 8:35 sin, when thou dost A them,
11:39 I will for this A the descendants of David,
2Chr 6:26 sin, when thou dost A them,
Tob 13:5 He will A us for our iniquities; and again
13:9 holy city, he will A you for the deeds
Ps 44:2 didst plant; thou didst A the peoples, but them
69:26 thou hast wounded, they A still more.
94:5 people, O LORD, and A thy heritage.
Sir 30:21 sorrow, and do not A yourself deliberately.
31:31 him, and do not A him by making demands
49:7 to pluck up and A and destroy, and likewise
Is 64:12 thou keep silent, and A us sorely?
Jer 19:9 who seek their life A them.'
Lam 3:33 he does not willingly A or grieve the sons
Amos 5:12 your sins--you who A the righteous, who take
Nah 1:12 afflicted you, I will A you no more.
2Mac 1:28 A those who oppress and are insolent with pride.
5:22 he left governors to A the people: at Jerusalem,
Phil 1:17 sincerely but thinking to A me in my imprisonment.
2Thes 1:6 with affliction those who A you,

AFFLICTED (69)

Gen 12:17 But the LORD A Pharaoh and his house with
Lev 13:9 "When a man is A with leprosy, he shall
23:29 For whoever is not A on this same day
Deut 26:6 treated us harshly, and A us, and laid upon
Judg 2:18 because of those who A and oppressed them.
Ruth 1:21 when the LORD has A me and the Almighty
1Sam 5:6 and he terrified and A them with tumors, both
5:9 great panic, and he A the men of the
2Kgs 17:20 descendants of Israel, and A them, and gave them
2Chr 15:5 in, for great disturbances A all the inhabitants of
28:20 against him, and A him instead of strengthening
Tob 11:15 For thou hast A me, but thou hast had
Jud 5:12 their God, and he A the whole land of
Job 2:7 of the LORD, and A Job with loathsome sores
34:28 the cry of the A –
36:6 alive, but gives the A their right.
36:15 He delivers the A by their affliction, and opens
Ps 9:12 he does not forget the cry of the A
10:12 God, lift up thy hand; forget not the A
22:21 of the lion, my A soul from the horns
22:24 the affliction of the A; and he has not
22:26 The A shall eat and be satisfied; those who
25:16 gracious to me; for I am lonely and A
34:2 the LORD; let the A hear and be glad.
35:13 I wore sackcloth, I A myself with fasting.
69:29 But I am A and in pain; let thy
82:3 the right of the A and the destitute.
88:15 A and close to death from my youth up,
90:15 days as thou hast A us, and as many
116:10 said, "I am greatly A;
119:67 Before I was A I went astray; but now
119:71 me that I was A, that I might learn
119:75 in faithfulness thou hast A me.
119:107 I am sorely A; give me life, O LORD,
129:1 "Sorely have they A me from my youth," let
129:2 "Sorely have they A me from my youth,
140:12 the cause of the A, and executes justice for
Prov 15:15 the days of the A are evil, but a
22:22 poor, or crush the A at the gate;
31:5 decreed, and pervert the rights of all the A
Wis 5:1 of those who have A him, and those who
19:16 with festal celebrations, A with terrible sufferings
Sir 3:24 stubborn mind will be A at the end, and
4:4 Do not reject an A suppliant, nor turn your
30:14 man who is severely A in body.
30:19 is he who is A by the Lord;
49:7 For they had A him; yet he had been
Is 14:32 and in her the A of his people find
49:13 his people, and will have compassion on his A
51:21 this, you who are A, who are drunk, but
53:4 we esteemed him stricken, smitten by God, and A
53:7 oppressed, and he was A, yet he opened not
54:11 "O A one, storm-tossed, and not comforted, behold, I
58:10 the desire of the A, then shall your light
61:1 good tidings to the A; he has sent me
63:9 their affliction he was A, and the angel of
Bar 4:31 will be those who A you and rejoiced at
Amos 2:7 the way of the A; a man and his
Mic 4:6 those whom I have A;
Nah 1:12 Though I have A you, I will afflict you
Zech 10:2 like sheep; they are A for want of a
Mt 4:24 all the sick, those A with various diseases and
Acts 5:16 the sick and those A with unclean spirits, and
2Cor 1:6 If we are A, it is for your comfort
4:8 We are A in every way, but not crushed;
7:5 rest but we were A at every turn--fighting
2Thes 1:7 to you who are A, when the Lord Jesus
1Tim 5:10 the saints, relieved the A, and devoted herself to
Heb 11:37 sheep and goats, destitute, A, ill-treated--

AFFLICTION (78)

Gen 16:11 because the LORD has given heed to your A
29:32 has looked upon my A; surely now my husband

31:42 God saw my A and the labor of my
41:52 made me fruitful in the land of my A
Ex 3:7 "I have seen the A of my people who
3:17 up out of the A of Egypt, to the
4:31 he had seen their A, they bowed their heads
Deut 16:3 bread, the bread of A --for you came out
26:7 voice, and saw our A, our toil, and our
28:61 sickness also, and every A which is not recorded
1Sam 1:11 indeed look on the A of thy maidservant, and
9:16 I have seen the A of my people, because
2Sam 16:12 will look upon my A, and that the LORD
1Kgs 2:26 shared in all the A of my father."
8:38 Israel, each knowing the A of his own heart
2Kgs 14:26 LORD saw that the A of Israel was very
2Chr 6:29 each knowing his own A, and his own sorrow
20:9 to thee in our A, and thou wilt hear
Neh 9:9 thou didst see the A of our fathers in
Jud 4:13 and looked upon their A; for the people fasted
Esth 7:4 my peace; for our A is not to be
11:8 gloom, tribulation and distress, A and great tumult
14:12 this time of our A, and give me courage,
16:20 who attach them at the time of their A
Job 5:6 For A does not come from the dust, nor
10:15 am filled with disgrace and look upon my A
30:16 within me; days of A have taken hold of
30:27 never still; days of A come to meet me.
36:8 in the cords of A,
36:15 the afflicted by their A, and opens their ear
36:21 iniquity, for this you have chosen rather than A
Ps 22:24 despised or abhorred the A of the afflicted; and
25:18 Consider my A and my trouble, and forgive all
31:7 thou hast seen my A, thou hast taken heed
44:24 dost thou forget our A and oppression?
66:11 net; thou didst lay A on our loins;
107:10 in gloom, prisoners in A and in irons,
107:17 of their iniquities suffered A;
107:41 the needy out of A, and makes their families
119:50 my comfort in my A that thy promise gives
119:92 my delight, I should have perished in my A
119:153 Look on my A and deliver me, for I
Eccl 6:2 them; this is vanity; it is a sore A
Wis 3:2 thought to be an A,
Sir 2:11 he forgives sins and saves in time of A
3:15 the day of your A it will be remembered
3:26 The A of the proud has no healing, for
22:21 him in time of A, that you may share
29:12 rescue you from all A;
40:9 sword, calamities, famine and A and plague.
51:10 in the days of A, at the time when
Is 30:20 and the water of A, yet your Teacher will
48:10 I have tried you in the furnace of A
63:9 In all their A he was afflicted, and the
66:4 I also will choose A for them, and bring
Jer 10:19 "Truly this is an A, and I must bear
48:16 at hand and his A hastens apace.
Lam 1:3 into exile because of A and hard servitude; she
1:7 the days of her A and bitterness all the
1:9 "O LORD, behold my A, for the enemy has
3:1 man who has seen A under the rod of
3:19 Remember my A and my bitterness, the wormwood
Bar 5:1 of your sorrow and A, O Jerusalem, and put
Hab 3:7 tents of Cushan in A; the curtains of the
Acts 7:11 and Canaan, and great A, and our fathers could
2Cor 1:4 us in all our A, so that we may
1:4 who are in any A, with the comfort with
1:8 ignorant, brethren, of the A we experienced in Asia;
2:4 you out of much A and anguish of heart
4:17 For this slight momentary A is preparing for us
7:4 With all our A, I am overjoyed.
8:2 a severe test of A, their abundance of joy
1Thes 1:6 the word in much A, with joy inspired by
3:4 we were to suffer A; just as it has
3:7 all our distress and A we have been comforted
2Thes 1:6 just to repay with A those who afflict you,
Heb 10:33 exposed to abuse and A, and sometimes being
Jas 1:26 and widows in their A, and to keep oneself

AFFLICTIONS (15)

Deut 28:59 and your offspring extraordinary A, afflictions severe
28:59 your offspring extraordinary afflictions, A severe and
29:22 when they see the A of that land and
Tob 13:14 grieved over all your A; for they will rejoice
Ps 34:19 Many are the A of the righteous; but the
Sir 10:13 brought upon them extraordinary A, and destroyed
51:3 life, from the many A that I endured,
1Mac 12:13 as for ourselves, many A and many wars have
2Mac 7:37 our nation and by A and plagues to make
Acts 7:10 out of all his A, and gave him favor
20:23 city that imprisonment and A await me.
2Cor 6:4 through great endurance, in A, hardships, calamities,
Col 1:24 is lacking in Christ's A for the sake of
1Thes 3:3 you, that no one be moved by these A
2Thes 1:4 persecutions and in the A which you are enduring.

AFFLICTS (3)

Tob 13:2 For he A, and he shows mercy; he leads
Sir 35:20 as welcome when he A them as clouds of
Zech 14:18 with which the LORD A the nations that do

AFFLUENCE

Deut 33:19 for they suck the A of the seas and

AFFORD (9)

Lev 5:7 "But if he cannot A a lamb, then he
5:11 "But if he cannot A two turtledoves or two
12:8 And if she cannot A a lamb, then she
14:21 is poor and cannot A so much, then he
14:22 such as he can A; the one shall be
14:30 such as he can A,
14:32 leprous disease, who cannot A the offerings for his
Num 6:21 what else he can A; in accordance with the
Sir 38:11 on your offering, as much as you can A

AFLAME (4)

Prov 29:8 Scoffers set a city A, but wise men turn
Is 13:8 aghast at one another; their faces will be A
2Mac 14:45 Still alive and A with anger, he rose, and
1Cor 7:9 marry than to be A with passion.

AFORESAID (2)

2Mac 3:7 the removal of the A money.
3:28 had just entered the A treasury with a great

AFRAID (180)

Gen 3:10 garden, and I was A, because I was naked;
18:15 saying, "I did not laugh"; for she was A
19:30 daughters, for he was A to dwell in Zoar;
20:8 these things; and the men were very much A
28:17 And he was A, and said, "How awesome is
31:31 Laban, "Because I was A, for I thought that
32:7 Then Jacob was greatly A and distressed; and he
43:18 And the men were A because they were brought
43:23 assured, do not be A; your God and the
46:3 father; do not be A to go down to
Ex 2:14 Then Moses was A, and thought, "Surely the thing
3:6 face, for he was A to look at God.
20:18 smoking, the people were A and trembled; and they
34:30 shone, and they were A to come near him.
Lev 26:6 none shall make you A; and I will remove
Num 12:8 then were you not A to speak against my
Deut 1:17 you shall not be A of the face of
1:29 be in dread or A of them.
2:4 and they will be A of you.
5:5 LORD; for you were A because of the fire,
7:18 you shall not be A of them, but you
7:19 to all the peoples of whom you are A
9:19 For I was A of the anger and hot
18:22 you need not be A of him.
20:1 you shall not be A of them; for the
28:10 and they shall be A of you.
28:60 Egypt, which you were A of; and they shall
Josh 10:25 them, "Do not be A or dismayed; be strong
11:6 Joshua, "Do not be A of them, for tomorrow
Judg 6:27 because he was too A of his family and
8:20 sword; for he was A, because he was still
1Sam 3:15 And Samuel was A to tell the vision to
4:7 camp, the Philistines were A; for they said, "A
7:7 of it they were A of the Philistines.
17:11 of the Philistine, they were dismayed and greatly A
17:24 the man, fled from him, and were much A
18:12 Saul was A of David, because the LORD was
18:29 Saul was still more A of David.
21:12 heart, and was much A of Achish the king
23:3 him, "Behold, we are A here in Judah; how
23:15 And David was A because Saul had come out
28:5 the Philistines, he was A, and his heart trembled
2Sam 1:14 it you were not A to put forth your
6:9 And David was A of the LORD that day;
14:15 people have made me A; and your handmaid thought,
1Kgs 19:3 Then he was A, and he arose and went
2Kgs 1:15 him; do not be A of him." So he
10:4 But they were exceedingly A, and said, "Behold, the

	19:6	LORD: Do not be A because of the words
	25:24	saying, "Do not be A because of the Chaldean
	25:26	Egypt; for they were A of the Chaldeans.
1Chr	13:12	And David was A of God that day; and
	21:30	God, for he was A of the sword of
2Chr	32:7	Do not be A or dismayed before the king
Ezra	4:4	Judah, and made them A to build,
Neh	2:2	Then I was very much A
	4:14	people, "Do not be A of them.
	6:13	that I should be A and act in this
	6:14	of the prophets who wanted to make me A
	6:16	round about us were A and fell greatly in
	6:19	And Tobiah sent letters to make me A
Tob	2:8	"He is no longer A that he will be
	4:8	few, do not be A to give according to
	4:21	Do not be A, my son, because we have
	6:14	has, and I am A that if I go
	6:17	Do not be A, for she was destined for
	12:16	they fell upon their faces, for they were A
	12:17	them, "Do not be A; you will be safe.
Jud	1:11	for they were not A of him, but looked
	5:23	"we will not be A of the Israelites; they
	10:16	him, do not be A in your heart, but
	11:1	and do not be A in your heart, for
Job	6:21	to me; you see my calamity, and are A
	9:28	good cheer,' I become A of all my suffering,
	11:19	none will make you A; many will entreat your
	19:29	found in him'; be A of the sword, for
	32:6	I was timid and A to declare my opinion
	41:25	up the mighty are A; at the crashing they
Ps	3:6	I am not A of ten thousands of people
	27:1	of my life; of whom shall I be A
	49:16	[Selah] Be not A when one becomes rich, when
	56:3	When I am A, I put my trust in
	65:8	earth's farthest bounds are A at thy signs; thou
	77:16	saw thee, they were A, yea, the deep trembled.
	78:53	that they were not A; but the sea overwhelmed
	112:7	He is not A of evil tidings; his heart
	112:8	he will not be A, until he sees his
	119:120	thee, and I am A of thy judgments.
Prov	3:24	you will not be A; when you lie down,
	3:25	Neighbor Do not be A of sudden panic, or
	31:21	She is not A of snow for her household,
Eccl	12:5	brought low; they are A also of what is
Wis	8:15	dread monarchs will be A of me when they
Sir	22:14	counsel will not be A in a crisis.
	26:5	things my heart is A, and of a fourth
	29:7	lend; they have been A of being defrauded
Is	10:24	in Zion, be not A of the Assyrians when
	12:2	and will not be A; for the LORD GOD
	17:2	will lie down, and none will make them A
	33:14	sinners in Zion are A; trembling has seized the
	37:6	LORD: Do not be A because of the words
	41:5	have seen and are A, the ends of the
	44:8	Fear not, nor be A; have I not told
	51:12	you that you are A of man who dies,
Jer	1:8	Be not A of them, for I am with
	10:5	Be not A of them, for they cannot do
	22:25	of whom you are A, even into the hand
	26:21	of it, he was A and fled and escaped
	30:10	quiet and ease, and none shall make him A
	36:24	all these words, was A, nor did they rend
	38:19	to Jeremiah, "I am A of the Jews who
	39:17	hand of the men of whom you are A
	40:9	saying, "Do not be A to serve the Chaldeans.
	41:18	Chaldeans; for they were A of them, because
	42:11	of whom you are A; do not fear him,
	42:16	of which you are A shall follow hard after
	46:27	quiet and ease, and none shall make him A
Ezek	2:6	of man, be not A of them, nor be
	2:6	of them, nor be A of their words, though
	2:6	upon scorpions; be not A of their words, nor
	27:35	their kings are horribly A, their faces are convulsed.
	34:28	shall dwell securely, and none shall make them A
	39:26	none to make them A,
Dan	4:5	dream which made me A; as I lay in
	11:30	and he shall be A and withdraw, and shall
Amos	3:6	in a city, and the people are not A
Jon	1:5	Then the mariners were A, and each cried to
	1:10	the men were exceedingly A, and said to him,
Mic	4:4	none shall make them A; for the mouth of
Zeph	3:13	and lie down, and none shall make them A
Zech	9:5	see it, and be A; Gaza too, and shall
1Mac	3:22	you, do not be A of them."
	4:8	their numbers or be A when they charge.
	7:30	intent, and he was A of him and would
	10:76	of the city became A and opened the gates,
	12:28	for battle, they were A and were terrified at
	12:42	large army, he was A to raise his hand
	14:12	tree, and there was none to make them A
	16:6	that the soldiers were A to cross the stream,
Mt	2:22	father Herod, he was A to go there, and
	8:26	them, "Why are you A, O men of little
	9:8	saw it, they were A, and they glorified God,
	14:30	the wind, he was A, and beginning to sink
	21:26	'From men,' we are A of the multitude; for
	25:25	winnow; so I was A, and I went and
	28:5	women, "Do not be A; for I know that
	28:10	them, "Do not be A; go and tell my
Mk	4:40	He said to them, "Why are you A
	5:15	who had had the legion; and they were A
	9:6	know what to say, for they were exceedingly A
	9:32	saying, and they were A to ask him.
	10:32	they were amazed, and those who followed were A
	11:31	'From men'?"--they were A of the people, for
	16:8	said nothing to any one, for they were A
Lk	1:13	him, "Do not be A, Zechariah, for your prayer
	1:30	her, "Do not be A, Mary, for you have
	2:10	to them, "Be not A; for behold, I bring
	5:10	Simon, "Do not be A; henceforth you will be
	8:25	And they were A, and they marveled, saying to
	8:35	and in his right mind; and they were A
	9:34	them; and they were A as they entered the
	9:45	it; and they were A to ask him about
	19:21	napkin; for I was A of you, because you
Jn	6:20	to them, "It is I; do not be A
	14:27	your hearts be troubled, neither let them be A
	19:8	he was the more A;
Acts	5:26	violence, for they were A of being stoned by
	9:26	and they were all A of him, for they
	16:38	magistrates, and they were A when they heard that
	18:9	vision, "Do not be A, but speak and do
	22:29	the tribune also was A, for he realized that
	23:10	became violent, the tribune, A that Paul would be
	27:24	said, 'Do not be A, Paul; you must stand
Rom	13:4	you do wrong, be A, for he does not
2Cor	11:3	But I am A that as the serpent deceived
Gal	4:11	I am A I have labored over you in
Heb	11:23	and they were not A of the king's edict.
	11:27	left Egypt, not being A of the anger of
	13:6	I will not be A; what can man do
2Pet	2:10	wilful, they are not A to revile the glorious

AFRESH

Job	7:5	and dirt; my skin hardens, then breaks out A

AFTERBIRTH

Deut	28:57	to her daughter, her A that comes out from

AFTERNOON (2)

2Sam	11:2	It happened, late one A, when David arose from
1Mac	10:80	at his men from early morning till late A

AFTERWARD (72)

Gen	6:4	those days, and also A, when the sons of
	10:18	A the families of the Canaanites spread abroad.
	15:14	which they serve, and A they shall come out
	25:26	A his brother came forth, and his hand had
	38:30	A his brother came out with the scarlet thread
Ex	5:1	A Moses and Aaron went to Pharaoh and said,
	34:32	And A all the people of Israel came near,
Lev	14:19	And A he shall kill the burnt offering;
	14:36	be declared unclean; and A the priest shall go
	16:26	body in water, and A he may come into
	16:28	body in water, and A he may come into
	22:7	shall be clean; and A he may eat of
Num	5:26	upon the altar, and A shall make the woman
	31:2	Israel on the Midianites; A you shall be gathered
	31:24	shall be clean; and A you shall come into
Deut	17:7	him to death, and A the hand of all
	24:21	shall not glean it A; it shall be for
Josh	2:16	pursuers have returned; then A you may go your
	8:34	And A he read all the words of the
	10:26	And A Joshua smote them and put them to
	23:1	A long time A, when the LORD had given
Judg	1:9	And A the men of Judah went down to
	7:11	what they say, and A your hands shall be
1Sam	9:13	must bless the sacrifice; A those eat who are
	24:5	And A David's heart smote him, because he had
	24:8	A David also arose, and went out of the
2Sam	3:28	A, when David heard of it, he said, "I
1Kgs	17:13	it to me, and A make for yourself and

A

2Kgs 6:24 A Ben-hadad king of Syria mustered his entire army,
1Chr 2:21 A Hezron went in to the daughter of Machir
2Chr 35:14 And A they prepared for themselves and for the
Ps 73:24 with thy counsel, and A thou wilt receive me
Prov 20:17 to a man, but A his mouth will be
28:23 rebukes a man will A find more favor than
Wis 5:11 of its wings, and A no sign of its
14:22 A it was not enough for them to err
19:11 A they saw also a new kind of birds,
Sir 17:18 A he will arise and requite them, and he
40:6 or no rest, and A in his sleep, as
Is 1:26 A you shall be called the city of righteousness,
Jer 21:7 A, says the LORD, I will give Zedekiah king
34:11 But A they turned around and took back the
46:26 A Egypt shall be inhabited as in the days
49:6 But A I will restore the fortunes of the
51:46 in one year and A a report in another
Bar 3:37 A she appeared upon earth and lived among men.
6:50 and silver, it will A be known that they
Ezek 43:1 A he brought me to the gate, the gate
Dan 11:18 A he shall turn his face to the coastlands,
Hos 3:5 A the children of Israel shall return and seek
Joel 2:28 shall come to pass A, that I will pour
1Mac 4:18 and fight them, and A seize the plunder boldly."
2Mac 5:20 befell the nation and A participated in its benefits;
6:15 take vengeance on us A when our sins have
Mt 4:2 and forty nights, and A he was hungry.
21:29 'I will not'; but A he repented and went.
21:32 it, you did not A repent and believe him.
21:37 A he sent his son to them, saying, 'They
25:11 A the other maidens came also, saying, 'Lord, lord,
Mk 16:14 A he appeared to the eleven themselves as they
Lk 7:11 Soon A he went to a city called Nain,
8:1 Soon A he went on through cities and villages,
17:8 eat and drink; and A you shall eat and
18:4 while he refused; but A he said to himself,
20:32 A the woman also died.
Jn 5:13 A, Jesus found him in the temple, and said
13:7 not know now, but A you will understand."
13:36 cannot follow me now; but you shall follow A
Gal 3:17 hundred and thirty years A, does not annul a
Heb 4:7 through David so long A, in the words already
12:17 For you know that A, when he desired to
Jude 1:5 the land of Egypt, A destroyed those who did

AFTERWARDS (10)

Gen 30:21 A she bore a daughter, and called her name
32:20 goes before me, and A I shall see his
Ex 11:1 Pharaoh and upon Egypt; A he will let you
Num 19:7 body in water, and A he shall come into
Deut 13:9 him to death, and A the hand of all
Josh 24:5 midst of it; and A I brought you out.
2Chr 33:14 A he built an outer wall for the city
Sir 13:7 Should he see you A, he will forsake you,
Jer 16:16 shall catch them; and A I will send for
Acts 3:24 and those who came A, also proclaimed these days.

AGABUS (2)

Acts 11:28 one of them named A stood up and foretold
21:10 days, a prophet named A came down from Judea.

AGAG (8)

Num 24:7 shall be higher than A, and his kingdom shall
1Sam 15:8 And he took A the king of the Amalekites
15:9 and the people spared A, and the best of
15:20 me, I have brought A the king of Amalek,
15:32 "Bring here to me A the king of the
15:32 And A came to him cheerfully.
15:32 A said, "Surely the bitterness of death is past."
15:33 And Samuel hewed A in pieces before the LORD

AGAGITE (5)

Esth 3:1 Ahasuerus promoted Haman the A, the son of
3:10 it to Haman the A, the son of Hammedatha,
8:3 design of Haman the A and the plot which
8:5 devised by Haman the A, the son of Hammedatha,
9:24 For Haman the A, the son of Hammedatha, the

AGATE (5)

Ex 28:19 row a jacinth, an A, and an amethyst;
39:12 row, a jacinth, an A, and an amethyst;
Is 54:12 make your pinnacles of A, your gates of carbuncles,
Ezek 27:16 purple, embroidered work, fine linen, coral, and A
Rev 21:19 second sapphire, the third A, the fourth emerald,

AGE (74)

Gen 15:15 you shall be buried in a good old A
18:11 were old, advanced in A; it had ceased to
21:2 son in his old A at the time of
21:7 have borne him a son in his old A
25:8 in a good old A, an old man and
37:3 son of his old A; and he made him
44:20 child of his old A; and his brother is
48:10 Israel were dim with A, so that he could
Num 8:25 meeting; and from the A of fifty years they
Judg 2:8 LORD, died at the A of one hundred and
8:32 in a good old A, and was buried in
Ruth 4:15 nourisher of your old A; for your daughter-in-law who
1Kgs 14:4 for his eyes were dim because of his A
15:23 But in his old A he was diseased in
1Chr 27:23 below twenty years of A, for the LORD had
29:28 in a good old A, full of days, riches,
Tob 3:10 shall bring his old A down in sorrow to
14:5 the times of the A are completed.
14:14 of Media at the A of a hundred and
Job 5:26 grave in ripe old A, as a shock of
21:7 wicked live, reach old A, and grow mighty in
Ps 71:9 the time of old A; forsake me not when
71:18 So even to old A and gray hairs, O
92:14 forth fruit in old A, they are ever full
Wis 3:17 and finally their old A will be without honor.
4:8 For old A is not honored for length of
4:9 men, and a blameless life is ripe old A
4:16 condemn the prolonged old A of the unrighteous
Sir 3:12 father in his old A, and do not grieve
25:3 then can you find anything in your old A
30:24 anxiety brings on old A too soon.
42:18 and he looks into the signs of the A
46:9 with him to old A, so that he went
Is 46:4 even to your old A I am He, and
60:15 ever, a joy from A to age.
60:15 majestic for ever, a joy from age to A
Ezek 16:8 you were at the A for love; and I
Dan 1:10 than the youths who are of your own A
Zech 8:4 Jerusalem, each with staff in hand for very A
2Mac 6:18 man now advanced in A and of noble presence,
6:23 dignity of his old A and the gray hairs
6:25 me, while I defile and disgrace my old A
6:27 worthy of my old A
Mt 12:32 forgiven, either in this A or in the age
12:32 age or in the A to come.
13:39 the close of the A, and the reapers are
13:40 will it be at the close of the A
13:49 it will be at the close of the A
24:3 your coming and of the close of the A
28:20 with you always, to the close of the A
Mk 5:42 was twelve years of A, and they were immediately
10:30 persecutions, and in the A to come eternal life.
Lk 1:36 Elizabeth in her old A has also conceived a
2:36 was of a great A, having lived with her
3:23 about thirty years of A, being the son (as
8:42 about twelve years of A, and she was dying.
18:30 time, and in the A to come eternal life."
20:34 "The sons of this A marry and are given
20:35 to attain to that A and to the resurrection
Jn 9:21 him; he is of A, he will speak for
9:23 said, "He is of A, ask him."
1Cor 1:20 Where is the debater of this A
2:6 a wisdom of this A or of the rulers
2:6 the rulers of this A, who are doomed to
2:8 the rulers of this A understood this; for if
3:18 is wise in this A, let him become a
Gal 1:4 from the present evil A, according to the will
1:14 many of my own A among my people, so
Eph 1:21 not only in this A but also in that
1Tim 5:9 than sixty years of A, having been the wife
Heb 6:5 the powers of the A to come,
9:9 still standing (which is symbolic for the present A
9:26 the end of the A to put away sin
11:11 she was past the A, since she considered him

AGED (21)

2Sam 19:32 Barzillai was a very A man, eighty years old;
2Chr 36:17 virgin, old man or A; he gave them all
Job 12:12 Wisdom is with the A, and understanding in length
15:10 the gray-haired and the A are among us, older
29:8 and withdrew, and the A rose and stood;
32:6 years, and you are A; therefore I was timid
32:9 are wise, nor the A that understand what is
Ps 119:100 understand more than the A, for I keep thy
Prov 17:6 the crown of the A, and the glory of

Wis	2:10	widow nor regard the gray hairs of the A
Sir	8:9	the discourse of the A, for they themselves learned
	9:10	wine; when it has A you will drink it
	25:4	men, and for the A to possess good counsel!
	25:5	is wisdom in the A, and understanding and counsel
	25:6	the crown of the A, and their boast is
	25:19	the feet of the A – such is a
	42:8	or foolish or the A man who quarrels with
Is	47:6	no mercy; on the A you made your yoke
Jer	6:11	be taken, the old folk and the very A
Joel	1:2	Pethuel: Hear this, you A men, give ear, all
2Mac	8:30	and also to the A, shares equal to their

AGEE

2Sam	23:11	Shammah, the son of A the Hararite.

AGENT

Gal	2:17	is Christ then an A of sin?

AGENTS

2Mac	4:3	one of Simon's approved A,

AGES (17)

Tob	13:6	of righteousness, and exalt the King of the A
	13:10	the King of the A, that his tent may
Job	8:8	pray you, of bygone A, and consider what the
Ps	135:13	for ever, thy renown, O LORD, throughout all A
Prov	8:23	A ago I was set up, at the first,
Eccl	1:10	been already, in the A before us.
Sir	36:17	thou art the Lord, the God of the A
Rom	16:24	kept secret for long A
1Cor	2:7	God decreed before the A for our glorification.
	10:11	the end of the A has come.
Eph	2:7	that in the coming A he might show the
	3:9	the mystery hidden for A in God who created
Col	1:26	the mystery hidden for A and generations but now
1Tim	1:17	To the King of A, immortal, invisible, the only
2Tim	1:9	us in Christ Jesus A ago,
Tit	1:2	who never lies, promised A ago
Rev	15:3	true are thy ways, O King of the A

AGHAST

Is	13:8	They will look A at one another; their faces

AGILE

Gen	49:24	his arms were made A by the hands of

AGITATED

Esth	15:16	And the king was A, and all his servants

AGITATOR

Acts	24:5	a pestilent fellow, an A among all the Jews

AGLOW

Rom	12:11	flag in zeal, be A with the Spirit, serve

AGO (23)

1Sam	9:20	were lost three days A, do not set your
	30:13	me behind because I fell sick three days A
2Kgs	19:25	you not heard that I determined it long A
Ezra	5:11	was built many years A, which a great king
Ps	77:5	days of old, I remember the years long A
Prov	8:23	Ages A I was set up, at the first,
Is	22:11	have regard for him who planned it long A
	37:26	you not heard that I determined it long A
	45:21	Who told this long A
	48:7	created now, not long A; before today you have
	51:9	in days of old, the generations of long A
Jer	2:20	"For long A you broke your yoke and burst
Lam	2:17	as he ordained long A, he has demolished without
	3:6	dwell in darkness like the dead of long A
Mt	11:21	would have repented long A in sackcloth and ashes.
Lk	10:13	would have repented long A, sitting in sackcloth and
Acts	10:30	Cornelius said, "Four days A, about this hour, I
2Cor	8:10	complete what a year A you began not only
	12:2	Christ who fourteen years A was caught up to
2Tim	1:9	in Christ Jesus ages A,
Tit	1:2	never lies, promised ages A
2Pet	3:5	God heavens existed long A, and an earth formed
Jude	1:4	by some who long A were designated for this

AGONY (4)

2Chr	21:19	of the disease, and he died in great A
Is	13:8	Pangs and A will seize them; they will be
Ezek	30:16	shall be in great A; Thebes shall be breached,
1Mac	9:56	And Alcimus died at that time in great A

AGREE (16)

Gen	34:22	condition will the men A to dwell with us,
	34:23	Only let us A with them, and they will
Esth	14:13	him and those who A with him.
Job	22:21	the fire has consumed.' A with God, and be
1Mac	6:59	all their nation, and A to let them live
Mt	18:18	if two of you A on earth about anything
	20:13	wrong; did you not A with me for a
Mk	14:56	witness against him, and their witness did not A
	14:59	Yet not even so did their testimony A
Acts	15:15	words of the prophets A, as it is written,
Rom	7:16	do not want, I A that the law is
1Cor	1:10	that all of you A and that there be
2Cor	13:11	ways, heed my appeal, A with one another, live
Phil	4:2	I entreat Syntyche to A in the Lord.
1Tim	6:3	otherwise and does not A with the sound words
1Jn	5:8	the water, and the blood; and these three A

AGREED (20)

Gen	23:16	Abraham A with Ephron; and Abraham weighed out
Ex	8:12	frogs, as he had A with Pharaoh.
2Kgs	12:8	So the priests A that they should take no
1Chr	13:4	All the assembly A to do so, for the
2Chr	30:23	Then the whole assembly A together to keep the
Tob	5:15	So they A to these terms.
Wis	18:9	and with one accord A to the divine law,
Dan	2:9	You have A to speak lying and corrupt words
	6:7	and the governors are A that the king should
1Mac	9:71	He A, and did as he said; and he
	14:46	And all the people A to grant Simon the
	14:47	So Simon accepted and A to be high priest,
2Mac	11:15	for the common good, A to all that Lysias
	11:18	him, and he has A to what was possible.
	12:12	useful in many ways, A to make peace with
	14:20	of one mind, they A to the covenant.
Lk	22:6	So he A, and sought an opportunity to betray
Jn	9:22	the Jews had already A that if any one
Acts	5:9	it that you have A together to tempt the
	23:20	said, "The Jews have A to ask you to

AGREEING

Mt	20:2	After A with the laborers for a denarius a

AGREEMENT (15)

Tob	7:11	you make a binding A with me."
Wis	10:5	the nations in wicked A had been confounded,
Sir	25:1	Lord and of men; A between brothers, friendship
Is	28:15	Sheol we have an A; when the overwhelming
	28:18	be annulled, and your A with Sheol will not
Dan	6:6	and satraps came by A to the king and
	6:11	these men came by A and found Daniel making
	6:15	these men came by A to the king, and
1Mac	7:18	they have violated the A and the oath which
	10:26	you have kept your A with us and have
	13:47	So Simon reached an A with them and stopped
2Mac	12:1	When this A had been reached, Lysias returned to
	14:28	had to annul their A when the man had
1Cor	7:5	another except perhaps by A for a season, that
2Cor	6:16	What A has the temple of God with idols?

AGREEMENTS

1Mac	15:27	he broke all the A he formerly had made

AGRIPPA (11)

Acts	25:13	some days had passed, A the king and Bernice
	25:22	And A said to Festus, "I should like to
	25:23	So on the morrow A and Bernice came with
	25:24	And Festus said, "King A and all who are
	25:26	especially before you, King A, that, after we have
	26:1	A said to Paul, "You have permission to speak
	26:2	is before you, King A, I am to make
	26:19	me.' "Wherefore, O King A, I was not disobedient
	26:27	King A, do you believe the prophets?
	26:28	And A said to Paul, "In a short time
	26:32	And A said to Festus, "This man could have

AGROUND

Acts	27:41	they ran the vessel A; the bow stuck and

AGUR

Prov	30:1	The words of A son of Jakeh of Massa.

AH (24)

Is	1:4	A, sinful nation, a people laden with iniquity,
	1:24	Mighty One of Israel: A, I will vent my
	10:5	A, Assyria, the rod of my anger, the staff

	17:12	A, the thunder of many peoples, they thunder like
	17:12	A, the roar of nations, they roar like the
	18:1	A, land of whirring wings which is beyond the
Jer	1:6	Then I said, A, Lord GOD!
	4:10	Then I said, A, Lord GOD, surely thou hast
	14:13	Then I said: A, Lord GOD, behold, the prophets
	22:18	lament for him, saying, A my brother!' or 'Ah
	22:18	'Ah my brother!' or A sister!' They shall not
	22:18	lament for him, saying, A lord!' or 'Ah his
	22:18	saying, 'Ah lord!' or A his majesty!'
	32:17	to the LORD, saying: A Lord GOD!
	47:6	A, sword of the LORD!
Lam	2:16	A, this is the day we longed for; now
Ezek	4:14	Then I said, A Lord GOD!
	9:8	my face, and cried, A Lord GOD!
	11:13	loud voice, and said, A Lord GOD!
	20:49	Then I said, A Lord GOD!
	21:15	I have given the glittering sword; A
Hos	12:8	Ephraim has said, A, but I am rich, I
Lk	4:34	and he cried out with a loud voice, A
Jn	16:29	His disciples said, A, now you are speaking plainly,

AHA (13)

Job	39:25	trumpet sounds, he says A He smells the battle
Ps	35:21	against me; they say, A, Aha!
	35:21	wide their mouths against me; they say, "Aha, A
	35:25	not say to themselves, A, we have our heart's
	40:15	who say to me, A, Aha!"
	40:15	of their shame who say to me, "Aha, A
	70:3	their shame who say, A, Aha!"
	70:3	appalled because of their shame who say, "Aha, A
Is	44:16	warms himself and says, A, I am warm, I
Ezek	25:3	GOD, Because you said, A over my sanctuary when
	26:2	Tyre said concerning Jerusalem, A, the gate of the
	36:2	enemy said of you, A and, 'The ancient heights
Mk	15:28	by derided him, wagging their heads, and saying, A

AHAB (94)

1Kgs	16:28	buried in Samaria; and A his son reigned in
	16:29	Asa king of Judah, A the son of Omri
	16:29	reign over Israel, and A the son of Omri
	16:30	And A the son of Omri did evil in
	16:33	And A made an Asherah.
	16:33	A did more to provoke the LORD, the God
	17:1	in Gilead, said to A, "As the LORD the
	18:1	"Go, show yourself to A; and I will send
	18:2	So Elijah went to show himself to A
	18:3	And A called Obadiah, who was over the household.
	18:5	bread and water.) And A said to Obadiah, "Go
	18:6	to pass through it; A went in one direction
	18:9	into the hand of A, to kill me?
	18:12	I come and tell A and he cannot find
	18:16	Obadiah went to meet A, and told him; and
	18:16	and told him; and A went to meet Elijah.
	18:17	When A saw Elijah, Ahab said to him, "Is
	18:17	When Ahab saw Elijah, A said to him, "Is
	18:20	So A sent to all the people of Israel,
	18:41	And Elijah said to A, "Go up, eat and
	18:42	So A went up to eat and to drink.
	18:44	"Go up, say to A, 'Prepare your chariot and
	18:45	And A rode and went to Jezreel.
	18:46	loins and ran before A to the entrance of
	19:1	A told Jezebel all that Elijah had done, and
	20:2	into the city to A king of Israel, and
	20:13	prophet came near to A king of Israel and
	20:14	And A said, "By whom?" He said, "Thus says
	20:34	And A said, "I will let you go on
	21:1	beside the palace of A king of Samaria.
	21:2	And after this A said to Naboth, "Give me
	21:3	But Naboth said to A, "The LORD forbid that
	21:4	And A went into his house vexed and sullen
	21:8	she wrote letters in A's name and sealed them
	21:15	dead, Jezebel said to A, "Arise, take possession of
	21:16	And as soon as A heard that Naboth was
	21:16	that Naboth was dead, A arose to go down
	21:18	go down to meet A king of Israel, who
	21:20	A said to Elijah, "Have you found me, O
	21:21	will cut off from A every male, bond or
	21:24	Any one belonging to A who dies in the
	21:25	of the LORD like A, whom Jezebel his wife
	21:27	of Israel.) And when A heard those words, he
	21:29	"Have you seen how A has humbled himself before
	22:20	said, 'Who will entice A, that he may go
	22:39	of the acts of A, and all that he
	22:40	So A slept with his fathers; and Ahaziah his
	22:41	the fourth year of A king of Israel.
	22:49	Ahaziah the son of A said to Jehoshaphat, "Let
	22:51	Ahaziah the son of A began to reign over
2Kgs	1:1	After the death of A, Moab rebelled against Israel.
	3:1	Jehoram the son of A became king over Israel
	3:5	But when A died, the king of Moab rebelled
	8:16	Joram the son of A, king of Israel, Jehoram
	8:18	as the house of A had done, for the
	8:18	for the daughter of A was his wife.
	8:25	Joram the son of A, king of Israel, Ahaziah
	8:27	of the house of A, and did what was
	8:27	as the house of A had done, for he
	8:27	for he was son-in-law to the house of A
	8:28	Joram the son of A to make war against
	8:29	Joram the son of A in Jezreel, because he
	9:7	down the house of A your master, that I
	9:8	the whole house of A shall perish; and I
	9:8	will cut off from A every male, bond or
	9:9	make the house of A like the house of
	9:25	side by side behind A his father, how the
	9:29	Joram the son of A, Ahaziah began to reign
	10:1	Now A had seventy sons in Samaria.
	10:1	of the sons of A, saying,
	10:10	concerning the house of A; for the LORD has
	10:11	of the house of A in Jezreel, all his
	10:17	all that remained to A in Samaria, till he
	10:18	and said to them, A served Baal a little;
	10:30	to the house of A according to all that
	21:3	made an Asherah, as A king of Israel had
	21:13	of the house of A; and I will wipe
2Chr	18:1	honor; and he made a marriage alliance with A
	18:2	he went down to A in Samaria.
	18:2	And A killed an abundance of sheep and oxen
	18:3	A king of Israel said to Jehoshaphat king of
	18:19	said, 'Who will entice A the king of Israel,
	21:6	as the house of A had done; for the
	21:6	for the daughter of A was his wife.
	21:13	as the house of A led Israel into unfaithfulness,
	22:3	of the house of A, for his mother was
	22:4	as the house of A had done; for after
	22:5	Jehoram the son of A king of Israel to
	22:6	Joram the son of A in Jezreel, because he
	22:7	LORD had anointed to destroy the house of A
	22:8	upon the house of A, he met the princes
Jer	29:21	God of Israel, concerning A the son of Kolaiah
	29:22	you like Zedekiah and A, whom the king of
Mic	6:16	of the house of A; and you have walked

AHARAH

1Chr	8:1	first-born, Ashbel the second, A the third,

AHARHEL

1Chr	4:8	and the families of A the son of Harum.

AHASBAI

2Sam	23:34	Eliphelet the son of A of Maacah, Eliam the

AHASUERUS (32)

Ezra	4:6	in the reign of A, in the beginning of
Tob	14:15	Nineveh, which Nebuchadnezzar and A had
Esth	1:1	In the days of A, the Ahasuerus who reigned
	1:1	days of Ahasuerus, the A who reigned from India
	1:2	those days when King A sat on his royal
	1:9	women in the palace which belonged to King A
	1:10	eunuchs who served King A as chamberlains,
	1:15	the command of King A conveyed by the eunuchs?"
	1:16	who are in all the provinces of King A
	1:17	they will say, 'King A commanded Queen Vashti to
	1:19	no more before King A; and let the king
	2:1	the anger of King A had abated, he remembered
	2:12	go in to King A, after being twelve months
	2:16	was taken to King A into his royal palace
	2:21	angry and sought to lay hands on King A
	3:1	After these things King A promoted Haman the
	3:6	of Mordecai, throughout the whole kingdom of A
	3:7	twelfth year of King A, they cast Pur, that
	3:8	Haman said to King A, "There is a certain
	3:12	the name of King A and sealed with the
	6:2	who had sought to lay hands upon King A
	7:5	Then King A said to Queen Esther, "Who is
	8:1	On that day King A gave to Queen Esther
	8:7	Then King A said to Queen Esther and to
	8:10	the name of King A and sealed with the
	8:12	the provinces of King A, on the thirteenth day
	9:2	the provinces of King A to lay hands on
	9:20	the provinces of King A, both near and far,
	9:30	of the kingdom of A, in words of peace

10:1 King A laid tribute on the land and on
10:3 in rank to King A, and he was great
Dan 9:1 Darius the son of A, by birth a Mede,

AHAVA (3)

Ezra 8:15 river that runs to A, and there we encamped
8:21 there, at the river A, that we might humble
8:31 departed from the river A on the twelfth day

AHAZ (44)

2Kgs 15:38 David his father; and A his son reigned in
16:1 the son of Remaliah, A the son of Jotham,
16:2 A was twenty years old when he began to
16:5 Jerusalem, and they besieged A but could not
16:7 So A sent messengers to Tiglath-pileser king of
16:8 A also took the silver and gold that was
16:10 King A went to Damascus to meet Tiglath-pileser
16:10 And King A sent to Uriah the priest a
16:11 with all that King A had sent from Damascus,
16:11 made it, before King A arrived from Damascus.
16:15 King A commanded Uriah the priest, saying, "Upon
16:16 all this, as King A commanded.
16:17 And King A cut off the frames of the
16:19 of the acts of A which he did, are
16:20 And A slept with his fathers, and was buried
17:1 the twelfth year of A king of Judah Hoshea
18:1 Hezekiah the son of A, king of Judah, began
20:11 the sun had declined on the dial of A
23:12 the upper chamber of A, which the kings of
1Chr 3:13 son, Jotham his son, A his son, Hezekiah his
8:35 The sons of Micah: Pithon, Melech, Tarea, and A
8:36 A was the father of Jehoaddah; and Jehoaddah was
9:41 Pithon, Melech, Tahre-a, and A;
9:42 Tahre-a, and Ahaz; and A was the father of
2Chr 27:9 city of David; and A his son reigned in
28:1 A was twenty years old when he began to
28:16 At that time King A sent to the king
28:19 Judah low because of A king of Israel, for
28:21 For A took from the house of the LORD
28:22 more faithless to the LORD—this same King A
28:24 And A gathered together the vessels of the house
28:27 And A slept with his fathers, and they buried
29:19 the utensils which King A discarded in his reign
Is 1:1 days of Uzziah, Jotham, A, and Hezekiah, kings of
7:1 In the days of A the son of Jotham,
7:3 "Go forth to meet A, you and Shear-jashub your
7:10 the LORD spoke to A,
7:12 But A said, "I will not ask, and I
14:28 the year that King A died came this oracle:
38:8 on the dial of A turn back ten steps."
Hos 1:1 days of Uzziah, Jotham, A, and Hezekiah, kings of
Mic 1:1 the days of Jotham, A, and Hezekiah, kings of
Mt 1:9 Jotham the father of A, and Ahaz the father
1:9 father of Ahaz, and A the father of Hezekiah,

AHAZIAH (40)

1Kgs 22:40 with his fathers; and A his son reigned in
22:49 Then A the son of Ahab said to Jehoshaphat,
22:51 A the son of Ahab began to reign over
2Kgs 1:2 Now A fell through the lattice in his upper
1:17 king of Judah, because A had no son.
1:18 of the acts of A which he did, are
8:24 city of David; and A his son reigned in
8:25 Ahab, king of Israel, A the son of Jehoram,
8:26 A was twenty-two years old when he began to
8:29 And A the son of Jehoram king of Judah
9:16 And A king of Judah had come down to
9:21 king of Israel and A king of Judah set
9:23 and fled, saying to A, "Treachery, O Ahaziah!"
9:23 about and fled, saying to Ahaziah, "Treachery, O A
9:27 When A the king of Judah saw this, he
9:29 the son of Ahab, A began to reign over
10:13 met the kinsmen of A king of Judah, and
10:13 are the kinsmen of A, and we came down
11:1 Athaliah the mother of A saw that her son
11:2 King Joram, sister of A, took Joash the son
11:2 Joash the son of A, and stole him away
12:18 Jehoshaphat and Jehoram and A, his fathers, the
13:1 Joash the son of A, king of Judah, Jehoahaz
14:13 of Jehoash, son of A, at Beth-shemesh, and came
1Chr 3:11 son, Joram his son, A his son, Joash his
2Chr 20:35 of Judah joined with A king of Israel, who
20:37 you have joined with A, the LORD will destroy
22:1 of Jerusalem made A his youngest son king
22:1 So A the son of Jehoram king of Judah
22:2 A was forty-two years old when he began to
22:6 And A the son of Jehoram king of Judah
22:7 that the downfall of A should come about through
22:8 and the sons of A's brothers, who attended Ahaziah,
22:8 Ahaziah's brothers, who attended A, and he killed
22:9 He searched for A, and he was captured while
22:9 And the house of A had no one able
22:10 Athaliah the mother of A saw that her son
22:11 Joash the son of A, and stole him away
22:11 was a sister of A, hid him from Athaliah,
25:23 of Joash, son of A, at Beth-shemesh, and brought

AHBAN

1Chr 2:29 and she bore him A and Molid.

AHEAD (23)

Num 22:26 of the LORD went A, and stood in a
1Sam 9:12 behold, he is just A of you.
23:24 and went to Ziph A of Saul.
2Kgs 4:31 Gehazi went on A and laid the staff upon
Tob 11:3 Let us run A of your wife and prepare
Jud 2:19 whole army, to go A of King Nebuchadnezzar and
Ps 105:17 had sent a man A of them, Joseph, who
Sir 12:17 will find him there A of you; and while
Ezek 46:9 he entered, but each shall go out straight A
1Mac 9:11 and the archers went A of the army, as
10:23 Alexander has gotten A of us in forming a
16:21 But some one ran A and reported to John
2Mac 8:8 that he was pushing A with more frequent successes,
Mk 6:33 towns, and got there A of them.
10:32 and Jesus was walking A of them; and they
Lk 9:52 And he sent messengers A of him, who went
10:1 and sent them on A of him, two by
19:4 So he ran on A and climbed up into
19:28 this, he went on A, going up to Jerusalem.
Acts 20:13 But going A to the ship, we set sail
1Cor 11:21 eating, each one goes A with his own meal,
Phil 3:13 forward to what lies A,
2Jn 1:9 Any one who goes A and does not abide

AHER

1Chr 7:12 the sons of Ir, Hushim the sons of A

AHI

1Chr 5:15 Jahdo, son of Buz; A the son of Abdi-el,

AHIAH

Neh 10:26 Rehum, Hashabnah, Ma-aseiah, A, Hanan, Anan,

AHIAM (2)

2Sam 23:33 Jonathan, Shammah the Hararite, A the son of
1Chr 11:35 of Shagee the Hararite, A the son of Sachar

AHIAN

1Chr 7:19 sons of Shemida were A, Shechem, Likhi, and

AHIEZER (6)

Num 1:12 of Gideoni; from Dan, A the son of Ammishaddai;
2:25 people of Dan being A the son of Ammishaddai,
7:66 On the tenth day A the son of Ammishaddai,
7:71 was the offering of A the son of Ammishaddai.
10:25 over their host was A the son of Ammishaddai.
1Chr 12:3 The chief was A, then Joash, both sons of

AHIHUD (2)

Num 34:27 of Asher a leader, A the son of Shelomi.
1Chr 8:7 Heglam, who was the father of Uzza and A

AHIJAH (24)

1Sam 14:3 six hundred men, and A the son of Ahitub,
14:18 And Saul said to A, "Bring hither the ark
1Kgs 4:3 the priest; Elihoreph and A the sons of Shisha
11:29 of Jerusalem, the prophet A the Shilonite found him
11:29 Now A had clad himself with a new garment;
11:30 Then A laid hold of the new garment that
12:15 the LORD spoke by A the Shilonite to Jeroboam
14:2 go to Shiloh; behold, A the prophet is there,
14:4 to Shiloh, and came to the house of A
14:4 Now A could not see, for his eyes were
14:5 the LORD said to A, "Behold, the wife of
14:6 But when A heard the sound of her feet,
14:18 spoke by his servant A the prophet.
15:27 Baasha the son of A, of the house of
15:29 spoke by his servant A the Shilonite;
15:33 Baasha the son of A began to reign over
21:22 Baasha the son of A, for the anger to
2Kgs 9:9 like the house of Baasha the son of A

1Chr 2:25 Ram, his first-born, Bunah, Oren, Ozem, and A
8:7 exile to Manahath): Naaman, A, and Gera, that is,
11:36 Ur, Hepher the Mecherathite, A the Pelonite,
26:20 And of the Levites, A had charge of the
2Chr 9:29 in the prophecy of A the Shilonite, and in
10:15 which he spoke by A the Shilonite to Jeroboam

AHIKAM (20)

2Kgs 22:12 Hilkiah the priest, and A the son of Shaphan,
22:14 Hilkiah the priest, and A, and Achbor, and Shaphan,
25:22 Gedaliah the son of A, son of Shaphan, governor.
2Chr 34:20 the king commanded Hilkiah, A the son of Shaphan,
Jer 26:24 But the hand of A the son of Shaphan
39:14 Gedaliah the son of A, son of Shaphan, that
40:5 Gedaliah the son of A, son of Shaphan, whom
40:6 Gedaliah the son of A, at Mizpah, and dwelt
40:7 Gedaliah the son of A governor in the land,
40:9 Gedaliah the son of A, son of Shaphan, swore
40:11 Gedaliah the son of A, son of Shaphan, as
40:14 Gedaliah the son of A would not believe them.
40:16 Gedaliah the son of A said to Johanan the
41:1 Gedaliah the son of A, at Mizpah.
41:2 Gedaliah the son of A, son of Shaphan, with
41:6 them, "Come in to Gedaliah the son of A
41:10 guard, had committed to Gedaliah the son of A
41:16 Gedaliah the son of A –soldiers, women, children,
41:18 Gedaliah the son of A, whom the king of
43:6 Gedaliah the son of A, son of Shaphan; also

AHIKAR (8)

Tob 1:21 place; and he appointed A, the son of my
1:22 A interceded for me, and I returned to Nineveh.
1:22 Now A was cupbearer, keeper of the signet, and
2:10 A, however, took care of me until he went
11:18 A and his nephew Nadab came,
14:10 what Nadab did to A who had reared him,
14:10 But A was saved, and the other received repayment
14:10 A gave alms and escaped the deathtrap which Nadab

AHILUD (5)

2Sam 8:16 Jehoshaphat the son of A was recorder;
20:24 Jehoshaphat the son of A was the recorder;
1Kgs 4:3 Jehoshaphat the son of A was recorder;
4:12 Baana the son of A, in Taanach, Megiddo, and
1Chr 18:15 Jehoshaphat the son of A was recorder;

AHIMA-AZ (15)

1Sam 14:50 of Saul's wife was Ahino-am the daughter of A
2Sam 15:27 with your two sons, A your son, and Jonathan
15:36 are with them there, A, Zadok's son, and Jonathan,
17:17 Now Jonathan and A were waiting at En-rogel; a
17:20 they said, "Where are A and Jonathan?" And the
18:19 Then said A the son of Zadok, "Let me
18:22 Then A the son of Zadok said again to
18:23 Then A ran by the way of the plain,
18:27 like the running of A the son of Zadok."
18:28 Then A cried out to the king, "All is
18:29 A answered, "When Joab sent your servant, I saw
1Kgs 4:15 of Iddo, in Mahanaim; A, in Naphtali (he had
1Chr 6:8 of Zadok, Zadok of A,
6:9 Zadok, Zadok of Ahima-az, A of Azariah, Azariah of
6:53 son, Zadok his son, A his son.

AHIMAN (4)

Num 13:22 came to Hebron; and A, Sheshai, and Talmai, the
Josh 15:14 of Anak, Sheshai and A and Talmai, the descendants
Judg 1:10 they defeated Sheshai and A and Talmai.
1Chr 9:17 were: Shallum, Akkub, Talmon, A, and their kinsmen

AHIMELECH (17)

1Sam 21:1 David to Nob to A the priest; and Ahimelech
21:1 Ahimelech the priest; and A came to meet David
21:2 And David said to A the priest, "The king
21:8 And David said to A, "And have you not
22:9 coming to Nob, to A the son of Ahitub,
22:11 king sent to summon A the priest, the son
22:14 Then A answered the king, "And who among all
22:16 "You shall surely die, A, you and all your
22:20 of the sons of A the son of Ahitub,
23:6 Abiathar the son of A fled to David to
26:6 Then David said to A the Hittite, and to
30:7 priest, the son of A, "Bring me the ephod."
2Sam 8:17 son of Ahitub and A the son of Abiathar
1Chr 18:16 son of Ahitub and A the son of Abiathar
24:3 sons of Eleazar, and A of the sons of
24:6 Zadok the priest, and A the son of Abiathar,
24:31 of King David, Zadok, A, and the heads of

AHIMOTH

1Chr 6:25 of Elkanah: Amasai and A,

AHINADAB

1Kgs 4:14 walls and bronze bars); A the son of Iddo,

AHINO-AM (7)

1Sam 14:50 of Saul's wife was A the daughter of Ahima-az.
25:43 David also took A of Jezreel; and both of
27:3 with his two wives, A of Jezreel, and Abigail
30:5 had been taken captive, A of Jezreel, and Abigail
2Sam 2:2 his two wives also, A of Jezreel, and Abigail
3:2 first-born was Amnon, of A of Jezreel;
1Chr 3:1 the first-born Amnon, by A the Jezreelitess; the

AHIO (6)

2Sam 6:3 hill; and Uzzah and A, the sons of Abinadab,
6:4 ark of God; and A went before the ark.
1Chr 8:14 inhabitants of Gath); and A, Shashak, and Jeremoth.
8:31 Kish, Baal, Nadab, Gedor, A, Zecher,
9:37 Baal, Ner, Nadab, Gedor, A, Zechariah and Mikloth;
13:7 Abinadab, and Uzzah and A were driving the cart.

AHIRA (5)

Num 1:15 of Deuel; from Naphtali, A the son of Enan."
2:29 people of Naphtali being A the son of Enan,
7:78 On the twelfth day A the son of Enan,
7:83 was the offering of A the son of Enan.
10:27 men of Naphtali was A the son of Enan.

AHIRAM

Num 26:38 of the Ashbelites; of A, the family of the

AHIRAMITES

Num 26:38 the family of the A;

AHISAMACH (3)

Ex 31:6 Oholiab, the son of A, of the tribe of
35:34 Oholiab the son of A of the tribe of
38:23 Oholiab the son of A, of the tribe of

AHISHAHAR

1Chr 7:10 Bilhan: Jeush, Benjamin, Ehud, Chenaanah, Zethan,

AHISHAR

1Kgs 4:6 priest and king's friend; A was in charge of

AHITHOPHEL (20)

2Sam 15:12 sacrifices, he sent for A the Gilonite, David's
15:31 it was told David, A is among the conspirators
15:31 turn the counsel of A into foolishness."
15:34 you will defeat for me the counsel of A
16:15 came to Jerusalem, and A with him.
16:20 Then Absalom said to A, "Give your counsel; what
16:21 A said to Absalom, "Go in to your father's
16:23 days the counsel which A gave was as if
16:23 all the counsel of A esteemed, both by David
17:1 Moreover A said to Absalom, "Let me choose twelve
17:6 to him, "Thus has A spoken; shall we do
17:7 time the counsel which A has given is not
17:14 the Archite is better than the counsel of A
17:14 the good counsel of A, so that the LORD
17:15 "Thus and so did A counsel Absalom and the
17:21 thus and so has A counseled against you."
17:23 When A saw that his counsel was not followed,
23:34 Eliam the son of A of Gilo,
1Chr 27:33 A was the king's counselor, and Hushai the Archite
27:34 A was succeeded by Jehoiada the son of Benaiah,

AHITUB (16)

1Sam 14:3 Ahijah the son of A, Ichabod's brother, son of
22:9 Ahimelech the son of A,
22:11 priest, the son of A, and all his father's
22:12 And Saul said, "Hear now, son of A
22:20 Ahimelech the son of A, named Abiathar, escaped
2Sam 8:17 Zadok the son of A and Ahimelech the son
1Chr 6:7 of Amariah, Amariah of A,
6:8 Amariah, Amariah of Ahitub, A of Zadok, Zadok of
6:11 of Amariah, Amariah of A,
6:12 Amariah, Amariah of Ahitub, A of Zadok, Zadok of
6:52 son, Amariah his son, A his son,
9:11 of Meraioth, son of A, the chief officer of
18:16 Zadok the son of A and Ahimelech the son
Ezra 7:2 of Zadok, son of A,

Neh 11:11 of Meraioth, son of A, ruler of the house
Jud 8:1 of Raphaim, son of A, son of Elijah, son

AHLAB
Judg 1:31 of Sidon, or of A, or of Achzib, or

AHLAI (2)
1Chr 2:31 The sons of Sheshan: A
11:41 Zabad the son of A,

AHOAH
1Chr 8:4 Gera, Abihud, Abishua, Naaman, A,

AHOHI
2Sam 23:9 was Eleazar the son of Dodo, son of A

AHOHITE (4)
2Sam 23:28 the Hushathite, Zalmon the A, Maharai of Netophah,
1Chr 11:12 men was Eleazar the son of Dodo, the A
11:29 the Hushathite, Ilai the A,
27:4 Dodai the A was in charge of the division

AHUMAI
1Chr 4:2 was the father of A and Lahad.

AHUZZAM
1Chr 4:6 Naarah; Naarah bore him A, Hepher, Temeni,

AHUZZATH
Gen 26:26 him from Gerar with A his adviser and Phicol

AHZAI
Neh 11:13 of Azarel, son of A, son of Meshillemoth, son

AI (37)
Gen 12:8 on the west and A on the east; and
13:3 beginning, between Bethel and A,
Josh 7:2 men from Jericho to A, which is near Beth-aven,
7:2 And the men went up and spied out A
7:3 go up and attack A; do not make the
7:4 before the men of A,
7:5 and the men of A killed about thirty-six men
8:1 arise, go up to A; see, I have given
8:1 hand the king of A, and his people, his
8:2 you shall do to A and its king as
8:3 to go up to A; and Joshua chose thirty
8:9 lay between Bethel and A, to the west of
8:9 to the west of A; but Joshua spent that
8:10 the elders of Israel, before the people to A
8:11 the north side of A, with a ravine between
8:11 of Ai, with a ravine between them and A
8:12 ambush between Bethel and A, to the west of
8:14 when the king of A saw this he and
8:17 a man left in A or Bethel, who did
8:18 in your hand toward A; for I will give
8:20 when the men of A looked back, behold, the
8:21 they turned back and smote the men of A
8:23 But the king of A they took alive, and
8:24 all the inhabitants of A in the open wilderness
8:24 all Israel returned to A, and smote it with
8:25 women, were twelve thousand, all the people of A
8:26 he had utterly destroyed all the inhabitants of A
8:28 So Joshua burned A, and made it for ever
8:29 hanged the king of A on a tree until
9:3 to Jericho and to A,
10:1 how Joshua had taken A, and had utterly destroyed
10:1 destroyed it, doing to A and its king as
10:2 it was greater than A, and all its men
12:9 one; the king of A, which is beside Bethel,
Ezra 2:28 men of Bethel and A, two hundred and twenty-three.
Neh 7:32 men of Bethel and A, a hundred and twenty-three.
Jer 49:3 "Wail, O Heshbon, for A is laid waste!

AIAH (6)
Gen 36:24 the sons of Zibeon: A and Anah; he is
2Sam 3:7 Rizpah, the daughter of A; and Ish-bosheth said to
21:8 Rizpah the daughter of A, whom she bore to
21:10 Rizpah the daughter of A took sackcloth, and spread
21:11 Rizpah the daughter of A, the concubine of Saul,
1Chr 1:40 The sons of Zibeon: A and Anah.

AIATH
Is 10:28 he has come to A; he has passed through

AID (14)
2Sam 21:17 Zeruiah came to his A, and attacked the Philistine
Esth 15:2 adorned, after invoking the A of the all-seeing God
Ps 22:19 O thou my help, hasten to my A
Wis 13:18 that is dead; for A he entreats a thing
Ezek 16:49 ease, but did not A the poor and needy.
29:16 their iniquity, when they turn to them for A
1Mac 11:47 the Jews to his A, and they all rallied
12:15 from Heaven for our A; and we were delivered
16:18 to send troops to A him and to turn
2Mac 3:39 himself and brings it A, and he strikes and
8:8 Coelesyria and Phoenicia, for A to the king's
11:7 lives with him to A their brethren.
Rom 12:8 liberality; he who gives A, with zeal; he who
15:25 going to Jerusalem with A for the saints.

AIDE
2Kgs 9:25 said to Bidkar his A, "Take him up, and

AIDED (3)
Ezra 1:6 who were about them A them with vessels of
6:22 them, so that he A them in the work
8:36 the River; and they A the people and the

AIJA
Neh 11:31 Geba onward, at Michmash, A, Bethel and its

AIJALON (10)
Josh 10:12 Gibeon, and thou Moon in the valley of A
19:42 Zorah, Eshtaol, Ir-shemesh, Sha-alabbin, A, Ithlah,
21:24 with its pasture lands, A with its pasture lands,
Judg 1:35 dwelling in Har-heres, in A, and in Sha-albim, but
12:12 and was buried at A in the land of
1Sam 14:31 down the Philistines that day from Michmash to A
1Chr 6:69 with its pasture lands, A with its pasture lands,
8:13 of the inhabitants of A, who put to flight
2Chr 11:10 Adoraim, Lachish, Azekah, Zorah, A, and Hebron,
28:18 had taken Beth-shemesh, A, Gederoth, Soco with its

AILMENT
Gal 4:13 because of a bodily A that I preached the

AILMENTS
1Tim 5:23 the sake of your stomach and your frequent A

AILS (4)
Judg 18:23 said to Micah, "What A you that you come
18:24 you ask me, 'What A you?"
1Sam 11:5 and Saul said, "What A the people, that they
Ps 114:5 What A you, O sea, that you flee?

AIM (13)
Ps 21:12 to flight; you will A at their faces with
64:3 tongues like swords, who A bitter words like arrows,
Wis 5:21 will fly with true A, and will leap to
Sir 9:14 much as you can, A to know your neighbors,
31:25 Do not A to be valiant over wine, for
1Cor 14:1 Make love your A, and earnestly desire the spiritual
2Cor 5:9 we make it our A to please him.
8:21 are administering, for we A at what is honorable
1Tim 1:5 in faith; whereas the A of our charge is
6:11 God, shun all this; A at righteousness, godliness, faith,
2Tim 2:4 civilian pursuits, since his A is to satisfy the
2:22 shun youthful passions and A at righteousness, faith,
3:10 teaching, my conduct, my A in life, my faith,

AIMED
2Mac 2:25 of material, we have A to please those who

AIMLESSLY
1Cor 9:26 I do not run A, I do not box

AIN (4)
Num 34:11 the east side of A; and the boundary shall
Josh 15:32 Sansannah, Lebaoth, Shilhim, A, and Rimmon: in
21:16 with its pasture lands, A with its pasture lands,
1Chr 4:32 their villages were Etam, A, Rimmon, Tochen, and

AIR (74)
Gen 1:26 the birds of the A, and over the cattle,
1:28 the birds of the A and over every living
1:30 every bird of the A, and to everything that
2:19 every bird of the A, and brought them to
2:20 the birds of the A, and to every beast
6:7 and birds of the A, for I am sorry
7:3 the birds of the A also, male and female,
7:23 and birds of the A; they were blotted out
9:2 every bird of the A, upon everything that creeps

Deut	4:17	that flies in the A,
	28:26	all birds of the A, and for the beasts
1Sam	17:44	the birds of the A and to the beasts
	17:46	the birds of the A and to the wild
2Sam	21:10	the birds of the A to come upon them
1Kgs	14:11	the birds of the A shall eat; for the
	16:4	the birds of the A shall eat."
	21:24	the birds of the A shall eat."
Jud	11:7	the birds of the A will live by your
Job	12:7	the birds of the A, and they will tell
	28:21	living, and concealed from the birds of the A
	35:11	the birds of the A
	41:16	to another that no A can come between them.
Ps	8:8	the birds of the A, and the fish of
	50:11	the birds of the A, and all that moves
	79:2	the birds of the A for food, the flesh
	104:12	the birds of the A have their habitation; they
Eccl	10:20	a bird of the A will carry your voice,
Wis	2:3	ashes, and the spirit will dissolve like empty A
	5:11	bird flies through the A, no evidence of its
	5:11	is found; the light A, lashed by the beat
	5:12	at a target, the A, thus divided, comes together
	7:3	to breathe the common A, and fell upon the
	13:2	or wind or swift A, or the circle of
	17:10	look even at the A, though it nowhere could
Jer	4:25	the birds of the A had fled.
	7:33	the birds of the A, and for the beasts
	9:10	the birds of the A and the beasts have
	14:6	heights, they pant for A like jackals; their eyes
	15:3	the birds of the A and the beasts of
	16:4	the birds of the A and for the beasts
	19:7	the birds of the A and to the beasts
	34:20	the birds of the A and the beasts of
Bar	3:17	the birds of the A, and who hoard up
Ezek	29:5	the birds of the A I have given you
	31:6	the birds of the A made their nests in
	31:13	the birds of the A, and upon its branches
	32:4	the birds of the A to settle on you,
	38:20	the birds of the A, and the beasts of
Dan	2:38	the birds of the A, making you rule over
	3:81	all birds of the A, sing praise to him
	4:12	the birds of the A dwelt in its branches,
	4:21	the birds of the A dwelt--
Hos	2:18	the birds of the A, and the creeping things
	4:3	the birds of the A; and even the fish
	7:13	like birds of the A; I will chastise them
Zeph	1:3	the birds of the A and the fish of
2Mac	4:24	extolled him with an A of authority, and secured
	5:2	horsemen charging through the A, in companies fully
Mt	6:26	the birds of the A: they neither sow nor
	8:20	and birds of the A have nests; but the
	13:32	the birds of the A come and make nests
Mk	4:32	the birds of the A can make nests in
Lk	8:5	the birds of the A devoured it.
	9:58	and birds of the A have nests; but the
	13:19	the birds of the A made nests in its
Acts	10:12	of animals and reptiles and birds of the A
	11:6	of prey and reptiles and birds of the A
	22:23	threw dust into the A,
1Cor	9:26	as one beating the A;
	14:9	For you will be speaking into the A
Eph	2:2	the power of the A, the spirit that is
1Thes	4:17	the Lord in the A; and so we shall
Rev	9:2	the sun and the A were darkened with the
	16:17	his bowl into the A, and a loud voice

AIRS

2Cor	11:20	you, or puts on A, or strikes you in

AKAN

Gen	36:27	are the sons of Ezer: Bilhan, Zaavan, and A

AKELDAMA

Acts	1:19	called in their language A, that is, Field of

AKKUB (8)

1Chr	3:24	Eli-o-enai: Hodaviah, Eliashib, Pelaiah, A, Johanan,
	9:17	gatekeepers were: Shallum, A, Talmon, Ahiman, and
Ezra	2:42	Talmon, the sons of A, the sons of Hatita,
	2:45	Hagabah, the sons of A,
Neh	7:45	Talmon, the sons of A, the sons of Hatita,
	8:7	Sherebiah, Jamin, A, Shabbethai, Hodiah, Ma-aseiah,
	11:19	The gatekeepers, A, Talmon and their brethren, who
	12:25	Meshullam, Talmon, and A were gatekeepers

AKRABATTENE

1Mac	5:3	Esau in Idumea, at A, because they kept lying

AKRABBIM (3)

Num	34:4	of the ascent of A, and cross to Zin,
Josh	15:3	of the ascent of A, passes along to Zin,
Judg	1:36	from the ascent of A, from Sela and upward.

ALABASTER (4)

Song	5:15	His legs are A columns, set upon bases of
Mt	26:7	to him with an A flask of very expensive
Mk	14:3	woman came with an A flask of ointment of
Lk	7:37	Pharisee's house, brought an A flask of ointment,

ALACRITY

2Mac	4:12	For with A he founded a gymnasium right under

ALAMOTH

1Chr	15:20	play harps according to A;

ALARM (17)

Num	10:5	When you blow an A, the camps that are
	10:6	when you blow an A the second time, the
	10:6	An A is to be blown whenever they are
	10:7	shall blow, but you shall not sound an A
	10:9	you shall sound an A with the trumpets, that
	31:6	the trumpets for the A in his hand.
Esth	15:8	to gentleness, and in A he sprang from his
Ps	31:22	had said in my A, "I am driven far
Jer	4:19	of the trumpet, the A of war.
	20:16	the morning and an A at noon,
Ezek	19:4	The nations sounded an A against him; he was
Dan	4:19	dream or the interpretation A you." Belteshazzar
	5:10	Let not your thoughts A you or your color
	11:44	and the north shall A him, and he shall
Hos	5:8	Sound the A at Beth-aven; tremble, O Benjamin!
Joel	2:1	in Zion; sound the A on my holy mountain!
2Cor	7:11	what indignation, what A, what longing, what zeal,

ALARMED (15)

Tob	12:16	They were both A; and they fell upon their
Jud	4:2	his approach, and were A both for Jerusalem and
	14:7	nation those who hear your name will be A
Wis	17:3	they were scattered, terribly A, and appalled by
Dan	4:5	visions of my head A me.
	4:19	moment, and his thoughts A him.
	5:6	changed, and his thoughts A him; his limbs gave
	5:9	King Belshazzar was greatly A, and his color
	7:15	visions of my head A me.
	7:28	Daniel, my thoughts greatly A me, and my color
1Mac	10:8	They were greatly A when they heard that the
Mt	24:6	that you are not A; for this must take
Mk	13:7	wars, do not be A; this must take place,
Acts	20:10	said, "Do not be A, for his life is
	24:24	future judgment, Felix was A and said, "Go away

ALARMS

Song	3:8	at his thigh, against A by night.

ALAS (27)

Ex	32:31	the LORD and said, A, this people have sinned
Num	24:23	his discourse, and said, A, who shall live when
Josh	7:7	And Joshua said, A, O Lord GOD, why hast
Judg	6:22	LORD; and Gideon said, A, O Lord GOD!
	11:35	his clothes, and said, A, my daughter!
2Sam	14:5	She answered, A, I am a widow; my husband
1Kgs	13:30	mourned over him, saying, A, my brother!"
2Kgs	3:10	Then the king of Israel said, A
	6:5	and he cried out, A, my master!
	6:15	And the servant said, A, my master!
Jer	30:7	A! That day is so great there is none like it
	34:5	lament for you, saying, A, lord!'" For I have
Ezek	6:11	your hands, and stamp your foot, and say, A
	30:2	the Lord GOD: "Wail, A for the day!'
Joel	1:14	A for the day!
Amos	5:16	and in all the streets they shall say, A
	5:16	A They shall call the farmers to mourning and
1Mac	2:7	committed in Judah and Jerusalem, and said, A
Mt	24:19	And A for those who are with child and
Mk	13:17	And A for those who are with child and
Lk	21:23	A for those who are with child and for
Rev	18:10	far-off, in fear of her torment, and say, A
	18:10	A, A thou great city, thou mighty city, Babylon
	18:16	weeping and mourning aloud, A, A, for the great
	18:19	mourned, crying out, "A, A, for the great city

ALCIMUS (15)
1Mac 7:5 they were led by A, who wanted to be
7:9 with him the ungodly A, whom he made high
7:12 in a body before A and Bacchides to ask
7:20 He placed A in charge of the country and
7:21 A strove for the high-priesthood,
7:23 all the evil that A and those with him
7:25 When A saw that Judas and those with him
9:1 he sent Bacchides and A into the land of
9:54 in the second month, A gave orders to tear
9:55 for at that time A was stricken and his
9:56 And A died at that time in great agony.
9:57 When Bacchides saw that A was dead, he returned
2Mac 14:3 Now a certain A, who had formerly been high
14:13 and to set up A as high priest of
14:26 But when A noticed their good will for one

ALEMA (2)
1Mac 5:26 Bozrah and Bosor, in A and Chaspho, Maked and
5:35 he turned aside to A, and fought against it

ALEMETH (4)
1Chr 6:60 with its pasture lands, A with its pasture lands,
7:8 Eli-o-enai, Omri, Jeremoth, Abijah, Anathoth, and A
8:36 was the father of A, Azmaveth, and Zimri; Zimri
9:42 Jarah, and Jarah of A, Azmaveth, and Zimri; and

ALERT (3)
1Mac 12:27 his men to be A and to keep their
Acts 20:31 Therefore be A, remembering that for three years I
Eph 6:18 To that end keep A with all perseverance, making

ALEXANDER (35)
1Mac 1:1 After A son of Philip, the
1:7 And after A had reigned twelve years, he died.
6:2 weapons left there by A, the son of Philip,
10:1 hundred and sixtieth year A Epiphanes, the son of
10:4 he makes peace with A against us,
10:15 Now A the king heard of all the promises
10:18 following words: "King A to his brother Jonathan,
10:23 A has gotten ahead of us in forming a
10:47 They favored A, because he had been the first
10:48 Now A the king assembled large forces and
10:49 of Demetrius fled, and A pursued him and defeated
10:51 Then A sent ambassadors to Ptolemy king of Egypt
10:58 A the king met him, and Ptolemy gave him
10:59 Then A the king wrote to Jonathan to come
10:68 When A the king heard of it, he was
10:88 When A the king heard of these things, he
11:1 to get possession of A's kingdom by trickery and
11:2 to meet him, for A the king had commanded
11:2 him, since he was A's father-in-law.
11:8 sea, and he kept devising evil designs against A
11:9 my daughter who was A's wife, and you shall
11:11 He threw blame on A because he coveted his
11:12 He was estranged from A, and their enmity became
11:14 Now A the king was in Cilicia at that
11:15 And A heard of it and came against him
11:16 So A fled into Arabia to find protection there,
11:17 off the head of A and sent it to
11:39 formerly been one of A's supporters.
11:39 the young son of A,
Mk 15:21 country, the father of A and Rufus, to carry
Acts 4:6 Caiaphas and John and A, and all who were
19:33 of the crowd prompted A, whom the Jews had
19:33 And A motioned with his hand, wishing to make
1Tim 1:20 among them Hymenaeus and A, whom I have
2Tim 4:14 A the coppersmith did me great harm; the Lord

ALEXANDRIA (3)
Acts 18:24 Apollos, a native of A, came to Ephesus.
27:6 found a ship of A sailing for Italy, and
28:11 island, a ship of A, with the Twin Brothers

ALEXANDRIANS
Acts 6:9 Cyrenians, and of the A, and of those from

ALGUM (3)
2Chr 2:8 also cedar, cypress, and A timber from Lebanon, for
9:10 gold from Ophir, brought A wood and precious
9:11 king made of the A wood steps for the

ALIAH
1Chr 1:51 Edom were: chiefs Timna, A, Jetheth,

ALIAN
1Chr 1:40 The sons of Shobal: A, Manahath, Ebal, Shephi, and

ALIEN (19)
Ex 23:12 your bondmaid, and the A, may be refreshed.
Deut 1:16 his brother or the A that is with him.
14:21 give it to the A who is within your
Jud 4:10 cattle and every resident A and hired laborer and
Esth 14:15 the bed of the uncircumcised and of any A
16:10 a Macedonian (really an A to the Persian blood,
Job 19:15 I have become an A in their eyes.
Ps 69:8 to my brethren, an A to my mother's sons.
Prov 5:10 the house of an A;
Wis 12:15 things righteously, deeming it A to thy power to
Is 17:10 out slips of an A god,
28:11 lips and with an A tongue the LORD will
28:21 work his work-- A is his work!
Jer 7:6 do not oppress the A, the fatherless or the
22:3 or violence to the A, the fatherless, and the
Bar 4:3 your advantages to an A people.
Ezek 47:23 In whatever tribe the A resides, there you shall
Hos 5:7 for they have borne A children.
2Mac 6:24 gone over to an A religion,

ALIENATE
Ezek 48:14 it; they shall not A this choice portion of

ALIENATED (3)
Jer 6:8 Jerusalem, lest I be A from you; lest I
Eph 2:12 separated from Christ, A from the commonwealth of
4:18 darkened in their understanding, A from the life of

ALIENATES
Prov 17:9 who repeats a matter A a friend.

ALIENS (21)
1Chr 22:2 to gather together the A who were in the
2Chr 2:17 census of all the A who were in the
Ps 144:7 from the hand of A,
144:11 from the hand of A, whose mouths speak lies,
Wis 19:15 hostile reception of the A;
Is 1:7 in your very presence A devour your land; it
1:7 your land; it is desolate, as overthrown by A
14:1 their own land, and A will join them and
25:2 ruin; the palace of A is a city no
25:5 the noise of the A; as heat by the
61:5 A shall stand and feed your flocks, foreigners shall
Jer 51:51 covered our face, for A have come into the
Lam 5:2 been turned over to strangers, our homes to A
Ezek 47:22 yourselves and for the A who reside among you
Hos 7:10 A devour his strength, and he knows it not;
8:7 it were to yield, A would devour it.
1Mac 2:7 to the enemy, the sanctuary given over to A
3:36 from the place, settle A in all their territory,
3:45 and the sons of A held the citadel; it
Acts 7:6 his posterity would be A in a land belonging
1Pet 2:11 I beseech you as A and exiles to abstain

ALIGHT (3)
Prov 26:2 flying, a curse that is causeless does not A
Is 34:14 shall the night hag A, and find for herself
50:11 you who kindle a fire, who set brands A

ALIGHTED (6)
Gen 24:64 she saw Isaac, she A from the camel,
Josh 15:18 a field; and she A from her ass, and
Judg 1:14 a field; and she A from her ass, and
4:15 the sword; and Sisera A from his chariot and
1Sam 25:23 she made haste, and A from the ass, and
2Kgs 5:21 running after him, he A from the chariot to

ALIGHTING (2)
Sir 43:17 flying down, and its descent is like locusts A
Mt 3:16 like a dove, and A on him;

ALIKE (29)
Deut 1:17 small and the great A; you shall not be
12:22 unclean and the clean A may eat of it.
15:22 unclean and the clean A may eat it, as
29:19 to the sweeping away of moist and dry A
1Sam 30:24 who stays by the baggage; they shall share A
1Kgs 7:37 of them were cast A, of the same measure
1Chr 24:5 them by lot, all A, for there were officers
24:31 and his younger brother A, cast lots, just as
25:8 their duties, small and great, teacher and pupil A
26:13 houses, small and great A, for their gates.

2Chr 31:15 brethren, old and young A, by divisions,
Esth 4:11 but one law; all A are to be put
Job 21:26 They lie down A in the dust, and the
Ps 14:3 astray, they are all A corrupt; there is none
49:10 fool and the stupid A must perish and leave
53:3 away; they are all A depraved; there is none
87:7 [Selah] Singers and dancers A say, "All my springs
Prov 17:15 the righteous are both A an abomination to the
20:10 diverse measures are both A an abomination to the
27:15 a contentious woman are A;
Eccl 11:6 that, or whether both A will be good.
Wis 6:7 and great, and he takes thought for all A
18:9 the saints would share A the same things, both
Is 46:5 equal, and compare me, that we may be A
Jer 5:5 But they all A had broken the yoke, they
Ezek 14:10 the inquirer shall be A –
Lk 14:18 ready.' But they all A began to make excuses.
Rom 14:5 than another, while another man esteems all days A
1Cor 15:39 not all flesh is A, but there is one

ALIVE (120)

Gen 6:19 ark, to keep them A with you; they shall
6:20 shall come in to you, to keep them A
7:3 to keep their kind A upon the face of
16:13 seen God and remained A after seeing him?"
43:7 and our kindred, saying, 'Is your father still A
43:27 Is he still A
43:28 servant our father is well, he is still A
45:3 brothers, "I am Joseph; is my father still A
45:7 earth, and to keep A for you many survivors.
45:26 him, "Joseph is still A, and he is ruler
45:28 my son is still A; I will go and
46:30 your face and know that you are still A
50:20 people should be kept A, as they are today.
Ex 4:18 in Egypt and see whether they are still A
22:2 stolen beast is found A in his possession, whether
Lev 16:10 Azazel shall be presented A before the LORD to
18:18 uncovering her nakedness while her sister is yet A
Num 14:38 son of Jephunneh remained A, of those men who
16:30 and they go down A into Sheol, then you
16:33 to them went down A into Sheol; and the
31:18 lying with him, keep A for yourselves.
Deut 4:4 your God are all A this day.
5:3 all of us here A this day.
6:24 he might preserve us A, as at this day.
20:16 inheritance, you shall save A nothing that breathes,
31:27 while I am yet A with you, today you
32:39 kill and I make A; I wound and I
Josh 2:13 sure sign, and save A my father and mother,
6:25 to her, Joshua saved A; and she dwelt in
8:23 of Ai they took A, and brought him to
14:10 LORD has kept me A, as he said, these
Judg 8:19 you had saved them A, I would not slay
21:14 whom they had saved A of the women of
1Sam 15:8 king of the Amalekites A, and utterly destroyed all
20:14 If I am still A, show me the loyal
27:9 neither man nor woman A, but took away the
27:11 neither man nor woman A, to bring tidings to
2Sam 12:18 the child was yet A, we spoke to him,
12:21 child while it was A; but when the child
12:22 the child was still A, I fasted and wept;
18:14 while he was still A in the oak.
19:6 that if Absalom were A and all of us
1Kgs 3:23 my son that is A, and your son is
3:26 woman whose son was A said to the king,
12:6 while he was yet A, saying, "How do you
18:5 the horses and mules A, and not lose some
20:18 for peace, take them A; or if they have
20:18 they have come out for war, take them A
21:15 for Naboth is not A, but dead."
2Kgs 5:7 kill and to make A, that this man sends
7:12 we shall take them A and get into the
10:14 He said, "Take them A
10:14 And they took them A, and slew them at
1Chr 5:21 two thousand asses, and a hundred thousand men A
2Chr 10:6 while he was yet A, saying, "How do you
14:13 fell until none remained A; for they were broken
25:12 captured another ten thousand A, and took them to
Neh 5:2 get grain, that we may eat and keep A
Tob 7:5 They replied, "He is A and in good health."
8:12 see whether he is A; and if he is
8:14 came out and told them that he was A
Jud 10:19 had better be left A, for if we let
Job 36:6 not keep the wicked A, but gives the afflicted
Ps 22:29 the dust, and he who cannot keep himself A
33:19 death, and keep them A in famine.
41:2 him and keeps him A; he is called blessed
55:15 go down to Sheol A; let them go away
124:3 have swallowed us up A, when their anger was
Prov 1:12 let us swallow them A and whole, like those
Eccl 4:2 living who are still A;
Sir 17:22 do those who are A and give thanks?
17:23 ceased; he who is A and well sings the
30:5 one like himself; while A he saw and rejoiced,
33:20 While you are still A and have breath in
Is 7:21 a man will keep A a young cow and
Jer 49:11 I will keep them A; and let your widows
Lam 3:53 cause; they flung me A into the pit and
Ezek 6:8 "Yet I will leave some of you A
13:18 and keep other souls A for your profit?
13:19 not die and keeping A persons who should not
Dan 5:19 he would he kept A; whom he would he
Zech 13:8 and perish, and one third shall be left A
1Mac 1:6 his kingdom among them while he was still A
8:7 them; they took him A and decreed that he
10:85 sword, with those burned A, came to eight thousand
14:2 sent one of his commanders to take him A
2Mac 5:27 himself and his companions A in the mountains as
7:24 youngest brother being still A, Antiochus not only
10:36 they kindled fires and burned the blasphemers A
12:35 take the accursed man A, when one of the
14:45 Still A and aflame with anger, he rose, and
Mt 6:30 field, which today is A and tomorrow is thrown
27:63 while he was still A, 'After three days I
Mk 16:11 heard that he was A and had been seen
Lk 12:28 the grass which is A in the field today
15:24 was dead, and is A again; he was lost,
15:32 was dead, and is A; he was lost, and
24:23 vision of angels, who said that he was A
Acts 1:3 them he presented himself A after his passion by
7:19 their infants, that they might not be kept A
9:41 calling the saints and widows he presented her A
20:12 took the lad away A, and were not a
25:19 was dead, but whom Paul asserted to be A
Rom 6:11 dead to sin and A to God in Christ
7:3 lives with another man while her husband is A
7:9 I was once A apart from the law, but
8:10 sin, your spirits are A because of righteousness.
1Cor 15:6 of whom are still A, though some have fallen
15:22 so also in Christ shall all be made A
Gal 3:21 given which could make A, then righteousness would
Eph 2:1 And you he made A, when you were dead
2:5 our trespasses, made us A together with Christ (by
Col 2:13 your flesh, God made A together with him, having
1Thes 4:15 that we who are A, who are left until
4:17 then we who are A, who are left, shall
Heb 9:17 long as the one who made it is A
1Pet 3:18 the flesh but made A in the spirit;
Rev 1:18 and behold I am A for evermore, and I
3:1 the name of being A, and you are dead.
19:20 These two were thrown A into the lake of

ALL-NOURISHING

Wis 16:25 forms, it served thy A bounty, according to the

ALL-POWERFUL (3)

Wis 7:23 sure, free from anxiety, A, overseeing all, and
11:17 For thy A hand, which created the world out
18:15 now half gone, thy A word leaped from heaven,

ALL-SEEING (3)

Esth 15:2 the aid of the A God and Savior, she
2Mac 7:35 judgment of the almighty, A God.
9:5 But the A Lord, the God of Israel, struck

ALLAMMELECH

Josh 19:26 Hali, Beten, Achshaph, A, Amad, and Mishal; on

ALLEGIANCE (3)

1Chr 12:29 had hitherto kept their A to the house of
29:24 King David, pledged their A to King Solomon.
Is 19:18 of Canaan and swear A to the LORD of

ALLEGORICALLY

Rev 11:8 great city which is A called Sodom and Egypt,

ALLEGORIES

Ezek 20:49 of me, 'Is he not a maker of A

ALLEGORY (3)

Ezek 17:2 riddle, and speak an A to the house of
24:3 And utter an A to the rebellious house and

Gal	4:24	Now this is an A: these women are two

ALLIANCE (16)

1Kgs	3:1	Solomon made a marriage A with Pharaoh king of
2Chr	18:1	he made a marriage A with Ahab.
Dan	11:6	they shall make an A, and the daughter of
	11:23	the time that an A is made with him
1Mac	8:1	all who made an A with them, that they
	8:17	to establish friendship and A,
	8:20	to you to establish A and peace with you,
	8:22	memorial of peace and A:
	12:3	the former friendship and A with them."
	12:8	a clear declaration of A and friendship.
	12:16	our former friendship and A with them.
	14:18	him the friendship and A which they had established
	14:24	minas, to confirm the A with the Romans.
	15:17	and allies to renew our ancient friendship and A
	15:19	their country, or make A with those who war
2Mac	4:11	to establish friendship and A with the Romans; and

ALLIED

Ps	94:20	Can wicked rulers be A with thee, who frame

ALLIES (17)

Gen	14:13	of Aner; these were A of Abram.
Jud	3:6	and took picked men from them as his A
	7:1	army, and all the A who had joined him,
Hos	8:10	Though they hire A among the nations, I will
Obad	1:7	All your A have deceived you, they have driven
1Mac	8:20	be enrolled as your A and friends."
	8:24	to any of their A in all their dominion,
	8:25	shall act as their A wholeheartedly, as the occasion
	8:27	willingly act as their A, as the occasion may
	8:28	And to the enemy A shall be given no
	8:31	upon our friends and A the Jews?
	9:60	letters to all his A in Judea, telling them
	10:47	and they remained his A all his days.
	11:60	the army of Syria gathered to him as A
	12:14	you and our other A and friends with these
	14:40	Romans as friends and A and brethren, and that
	15:17	as our friends and A to renew our ancient

ALLON

1Chr	4:37	of Shiphi, son of A, son of Jedaiah, son

ALLON-BACUTH

Gen	35:8	Bethel; so the name of it was called A

ALLOT (5)

Josh	13:6	people of Israel; only A the land to Israel
Neh	9:22	and peoples, and didst A to them every corner;
Ezek	45:1	"When you A the land as a possession, you
	47:22	You shall A it as an inheritance for yourselves
	48:29	land which you shall A as an inheritance among

ALLOTMENT (4)

Josh	16:1	The A of the descendants of Joseph went from
	17:1	Then A was made to the tribe of Manasseh,
Ezek	48:10	shall have an A measuring twenty-five thousand
	48:13	Levites shall have an A twenty-five thousand cubits in

ALLOTMENTS (4)

Josh	11:23	an inheritance to Israel according to their tribal A
	12:7	possession according to their A,
	17:2	And A were made to the rest of the
Ezek	48:10	These shall be the A of the holy portion:

ALLOTTED (30)

Deut	4:19	LORD your God has A to all the peoples
	29:26	whom he had not A to them;
	32:9	his people, Jacob his A heritage.
Josh	13:29	of Manasseh; it was A to the half-tribe of
	13:31	in Bashan; these were A to the people of
	14:5	LORD commanded Moses; they A the land.
	17:1	father of Gilead, were A Gilead and Bashan, because
	17:6	land of Gilead was A to the rest of
	18:11	up, and the territory A to it fell between
	21:20	the Levites, the cities A to them were out
	21:40	of the Levites, those A to them were in
	23:4	Behold, I have A to you as an inheritance
Judg	1:3	me into the territory A to me, that we
	1:3	you into the territory A to you." So Simeon
1Chr	6:62	to their families were A thirteen cities out of
	6:63	to their families were A twelve cities out of
	6:77	of the Merarites were A out of the tribe
	26:15	to his sons was A the storehouse.
Job	7:3	wages, so I am A months of emptiness, and
Ps	125:3	rest upon the land A to the righteous, lest
Wis	2:5	For our A time is the passing of a
Sir	11:16	this is the reward A to him:
	17:9	knowledge upon them, and A to them the law
	45:20	him a heritage; he A to him the first
Ezek	16:27	you, and diminished your A portion, and delivered
	47:22	you they shall be A an inheritance among the
Dan	12:13	shall stand in your A place at the end
2Mac	8:27	for that day and A it to them as
Acts	1:17	among us, and was A his share in this
	17:26	the earth, having determined A periods and the

ALLOW (15)

Gen	30:27	him, "If you will A me to say so,
Ex	12:23	door, and will not A the destroyer to enter
Num	21:23	But Sihon would not A Israel to pass through
Judg	1:34	for they did not A them to come down
	15:1	her father would not A him to go in.
2Sam	21:10	and she did not A the birds of the
Sir	18:30	If you A your soul to take pleasure in
	25:24	A no outlet to water, and no boldness of
	27:19	And as you A a bird to escape from
Dan	1:8	of the eunuchs to A him not to defile
Mt	23:13	neither enter yourselves, nor A those who would
Mk	11:16	and he would not A any one to carry
Lk	4:41	them, and would not A them to speak, because
Acts	16:7	of Jesus did not A them;
	27:7	the wind did not A us to go on,

ALLOWANCE (10)

Gen	47:22	priests had a fixed A from Pharaoh, and lived
	47:22	and lived on the A which Pharaoh gave them;
1Kgs	11:18	and assigned him an A of food, and gave
2Kgs	25:30	table; and for his A, a regular allowance was
	25:30	his allowance, a regular A was given him by
Neh	5:14	brethren ate the food A of the governor.
	5:18	not demand the food A of the governor, because
Jer	40:5	guard gave him an A of food and a
	52:34	table; as for his A, a regular allowance was
	52:34	his allowance, a regular A was given him by

ALLOWED (21)

Deut	18:14	your God has not A you so to do.
Judg	3:28	against the Moabites, and A not a man to
1Chr	16:21	to another people, he A no one to oppress
Esth	8:11	By these the king A the Jews who were
	9:13	are in Susa be A tomorrow also to do
Ps	105:14	to another people, he A no one to oppress
2Mac	2:31	the narrative should be A to strive for brevity
	11:24	their own customs be A them.
Mt	19:8	hardness of heart Moses A you to divorce your
	20:15	Am I not A to do what I choose
Mk	5:37	And he A no one to follow him except
	10:4	They said, "Moses A a man to write a
Acts	14:16	In past generations he A all the nations to
	28:4	sea, justice has not A him to live."
	28:16	into Rome, Paul was A to stay by himself,
Rev	9:5	their foreheads; they were A to torture them for
	13:5	words, and it was A to exercise authority for
	13:7	Also it was A to make war on the
	13:14	signs which it is A to work in the
	13:15	lived; and it was A to give breath to
	16:8	sun, and it was A to scorch men with

ALLOWS

2Kgs	10:24	said, "The man who A any of those whom

ALLOY

Is	1:25	dross as with lye and remove all your A

ALLURE

Hos	2:14	"Therefore, behold, I will A her, and bring her

ALLURED

Job	36:16	He also A you out of distress into a

ALLY (5)

1Mac	10:6	and to become his A; and he commanded that
	10:16	now, we will make him our friend and A
2Mac	8:24	the Almighty as their A, they slew more than
	11:10	order, having their heavenly A, for the Lord had
	12:36	to show himself their A and leader in the

ALMIGHTY (81)

Gen	17:1	him, "I am God A; walk before me, and

28:3 God A bless you and make you fruitful and
35:11 him, "I am God A: be fruitful and multiply;
43:14 the man; may God A grant you mercy before
48:3 said to Joseph, "God A appeared to me at
49:25 help you, by God A who will bless you
Ex 6:3 to Jacob, as God A, but by my name
Num 24:4 the vision of the A, falling down, but having
24:16 the vision of the A, falling down, but having
Ruth 1:20 me Mara, for the A has dealt very bitterly
1:21 afflicted me and the A has brought calamity upon
Jud 4:13 in Jerusalem before the sanctuary of the Lord A
8:13 are putting the Lord A to the test--but
15:10 May the A Lord bless you for ever!" And
16:6 But the Lord A has foiled them by the
16:17 The Lord A will take vengeance on them in
Job 5:17 therefore despise not the chastening of the A
6:4 the arrows of the A are in me; my
6:14 from a friend forsakes the fear of the A
8:3 Or does the A pervert the right?
8:5 make supplication to the A,
11:7 Can you find out the limit of the A
13:3 would speak to the A, and I desire to
15:25 bids defiance to the A,
21:15 What is the A, that we should serve him?
21:20 let them drink of the wrath of the A
22:3 any pleasure to the A if you are righteous,
22:17 and 'What can the A do to us?'
22:23 you return to the A and humble yourself, if
22:25 torrent-bed, and if the A is your gold, and
22:26 delight yourself in the A, and lift up your
23:16 my heart faint; the A has terrified me;
24:1 judgment kept by the A, and why do those
27:2 my right, and the A, who has made my
27:10 Will he take delight in the A
27:11 what is with the A I will not conceal.
27:13 oppressors receive from the A:
29:5 my tent; when the A was yet with me,
31:2 my heritage from the A on high?
31:35 let the A answer me!) Oh, that I had
32:8 the breath of the A, that makes him understand.
33:4 the breath of the A gives me life.
34:10 wickedness, and from the A that he should do
34:12 do wickedly, and the A will not pervert justice.
35:13 cry, nor does the A regard it.
37:23 The A --we cannot find him; he is great
40:2 to Job: "Shall a faultfinder contend with the A
Ps 68:14 When the A scattered kings there, snow fell on
91:1 the shadow of the A,
Wis 7:25 the glory of the A; therefore nothing defiled gains
Sir 42:17 which the Lord the A has established that the
50:14 the Most High, the A,
50:17 worship their Lord, the A, God Most High.
Is 13:6 as destruction from the A it will come!
Bar 3:1 "O Lord A, God of Israel, the soul in
3:4 O Lord A, God of Israel, hear now the
Ezek 1:24 the thunder of the A, a sound of tumult
10:5 the voice of God A when he speaks.
Joel 1:14 as destruction from the A it comes.
2Mac 1:25 alone art just and A and eternal, who dost
3:22 were calling upon the A Lord that he would
3:30 gladness, now that the A Lord had appeared.
5:20 the wrath of the A was restored again in
6:26 I shall not escape the hands of the A
7:35 the judgment of the A, all-seeing God.
7:38 the wrath of the A which has justly fallen
8:11 the judgment from the A that was about to
8:18 we trust in the A God, who is able
8:24 With the A as their ally, they slew more
15:8 the victory which the A would give them.
15:32 holy house of the A;
2Cor 6:18 be my sons and daughters, says the Lord A
Rev 1:8 who was and who is to come, the A
4:8 is the Lord God A, who was and is
11:17 to thee, Lord God A, who art and who
15:3 wonderful are thy deeds, O Lord God the A
16:7 "Yea, Lord God the A, true and just are
16:14 battle on the great day of God the A
19:6 Lord our God the A reigns.
19:15 the fury of the wrath of God the A
21:22 the Lord God the A and the Lamb.

ALMODAD (2)
Gen 10:26 became the father of A, Sheleph, Hazarmaveth,
1Chr 1:20 was the father of A, Sheleph, Hazarmaveth, Jerah,

ALMON
Josh 21:18 its pasture lands, and A with its pasture lands--

ALMON-DIBLATHAIM (2)
Num 33:46 they set out from Dibon-gad, and encamped at A
33:47 they set out from A, and encamped in the

ALMOND (3)
Gen 30:37 rods of poplar and A and plane, and peeled
Eccl 12:5 in the way; the A tree blossoms, the grasshopper
Jer 1:11 And I said, "I see a rod of A

ALMONDS (8)
Gen 43:11 a little honey, gum, myrrh, pistachio nuts, and A
Ex 25:33 three cups made like A, each with capital and
25:33 three cups made like A, each with capital and
25:34 four cups made like A, with their capitals and
37:19 three cups made like A, each with capital and
37:19 three cups made like A, each with capital and
37:20 four cups made like A, with their capitals and
Num 17:8 buds, and produced blossoms, and it bore ripe A

ALMOST (9)
Ex 17:4 They are A ready to stone me."
Jud 11:12 and their water has A given out, they have
Ps 73:2 me, my feet had A stumbled, my steps had
119:87 They have A made an end of me on
2Mac 5:2 all the city, for A forty days, there appeared
Acts 13:44 The next sabbath A the whole city gathered together
19:26 only at Ephesus but A throughout all Asia this
21:27 the seven days were A completed, the Jews from
Heb 9:22 Indeed, under the law A everything is purified with

ALMS (20)
Tob 4:7 Give A from your possessions to all who live
12:8 is better to give A than to treasure up
14:2 He gave A, and he continued to fear the
14:10 Ahikar gave A and escaped the deathtrap which
Sir 7:10 fainthearted in your prayer, nor neglect to give A
12:3 evil or to him who does not give A
29:8 and do not make him wait for your A
35:2 and he who gives A sacrifices a thank offering.
Mt 6:2 "Thus, when you give A, sound no trumpet before
6:3 But when you give A, do not let your
6:4 doing, so that your A may be in secret;
Lk 11:41 But give for A those things which are within;
12:33 your possessions, and give A; provide yourselves with
Acts 3:2 called Beautiful to ask A of those who entered
3:3 to go into the temple, he asked for A
3:10 one who sat for A at the Beautiful Gate
10:2 all his household, gave A liberally to the people,
10:4 "Your prayers and your A have ascended as a
10:31 been heard and your A have been remembered
24:16 bring to my nation A and offerings.

ALMSGIVING (8)
Tob 12:8 when accompanied by fasting, A, and righteousness.
12:9 For A delivers from death, and it will purge
14:11 my children, consider what A accomplishes and how
Sir 3:28 a blazing fire: so A atones for sin.
17:17 A man's A is like a signet with the
29:12 Store up A in your treasury, and it will
40:17 garden of blessings, and A endures for ever.
40:24 time of trouble, but A rescues better than both.

ALMUG (3)
1Kgs 10:11 very great amount of A wood and precious stones.
10:12 king made of the A wood supports for the
10:12 the singers; no such A wood has come or

ALOES (5)
Num 24:6 beside a river, like A that the LORD has
Ps 45:8 fragrant with myrrh and A and cassia.
Prov 7:17 my bed with myrrh, A, and cinnamon.
Song 4:14 of frankincense, myrrh and A, with all chief spices--
Jn 19:39 mixture of myrrh and A, about a hundred pounds'

ALOFT (3)
Ezek 19:11 ruler's scepter; it towered A among the thick boughs;
Obad 1:4 Though you soar A like the eagle, though your
Zech 14:10 But Jerusalem shall remain A upon its site from

ALONE (155)
Gen 2:18 the man should be A; I will make him
32:24 And Jacob was left A; and a man wrestled
44:20 is dead, and he A is left of his

47:26 land of the priests A did not become Pharaohs.
Ex 4:26 So he let him A
14:12 in Egypt, 'Let us A and let us serve
18:14 Why do you sit A, and all the people
18:18 you; you are not able to perform it A
21:4 be her master's and he shall go out A
24:2 Moses A shall come near to the LORD; but
32:10 now therefore let me A, that my wrath may
Lev 13:46 unclean; he shall dwell A in a habitation outside
Num 11:14 carry all this people A, the burden is too
11:17 you, that you may not bear it yourself A
23:9 lo, a people dwelling A, and not reckoning itself
Deut 1:9 'I am not able A to bear you;
1:12 How can I bear A the weight and burden
8:3 not live by bread A, but that man lives
9:14 stubborn people; let me A, that I may destroy
32:12 its pinions, the LORD A did lead him, and
33:28 the fountain of Jacob A, in a land of
Josh 13:12 and in Edre-i (he A was left of the
13:14 the tribe of Levi A Moses gave no inheritance;
22:20 he did not perish A for his iniquity.'"
Judg 3:20 as he was sitting A in his cool roof
6:37 dew on the fleece A, and it is dry
11:37 for me; let me A two months, that I
1Sam 21:1 him, "Why are you A, and no one with
25:24 and said, "Upon me A, my lord, be the
2Sam 13:32 king's sons, for Amnon A is dead, for by
13:33 are dead; for Amnon A is dead."
16:11 Let him A, and let him curse; for the
18:24 eyes and looked, he saw a man running A
18:25 said, "If he is A, there are tidings in
18:26 the gate and said, "See, another man running A
20:21 David; give up him A, and I will withdraw
1Kgs 3:18 birth; and we were A; there was no one
11:29 two of them were A in the open country.
2Kgs 4:27 God said, "Let her A, for she is in
19:15 art the God, thou A, of all the kingdoms
19:19 may know that thou, O LORD, art God A
23:18 they let his bones A, with the bones of
1Chr 29:1 "Solomon my son, whom A God has chosen, is
Ezra 4:3 our God; but we A will build to the
6:7 this house of God A; let the governor of
Neh 9:6 art the LORD, thou A; thou hast made heaven,
Tob 1:6 But I A went often to Jerusalem for the
8:4 and the two were A, Tobias got up from
8:6 the man should be A; let us make a
Jud 5:4 And why have they A, of all who live
9:14 who protects the people of Israel but thou A
13:2 So Judith was left A in the tent,
Esth 3:6 But he disdained to lay hands on Mordecai A
13:5 this people, and it A, stands constantly in opposition
14:3 help me, who am A and have no helper
14:14 help me, who am A and have no helper
Job 1:15 the sword; and I A have escaped to tell
1:16 consumed them; and I A have escaped to tell
1:17 the sword; and I A have escaped to tell
1:19 are dead; and I A have escaped to tell
7:16 Let me A, for my days are a breath.
7:19 me, nor let me A till I swallow my
9:8 up the stars; who A stretched out the heavens,
10:20 Let me A, that I may find a little
15:19 not hidden, to whom A the land was given,
31:17 have eaten my morsel A, and the fatherless has
Ps 4:8 and sleep; for thou A, O LORD, makest me
62:1 For God A my soul waits in silence; from
62:5 [Selah] For God A my soul waits in silence,
71:16 will come, I will praise thy righteousness, thine A
72:18 God of Israel, who A does wondrous things.
83:18 them know that thou A, whose name is the
86:10 doest wondrous things, thou A art God.
136:4 ever; to him who A does great wonders, for
148:13 LORD, for his name A is exalted; his glory
Prov 5:17 them be for yourself A, and not for strangers
9:12 if you scoff, you A will bear it.
Eccl 4:10 to him who is A when he falls and
4:11 are warm; but how can one be warm A
4:12 against one who is A, two will withstand him.
7:29 Behold, this A I found, that God made man
Wis 10:1 the world, when he A had been created; she
17:21 while over those men A heavy night was spread,
Sir 18:2 whole universe; the Lord A will be declared
24:5 A I have made the circuit of the vault
24:32 not labored for myself A, but for all who
33:17 not labored for myself A, but for all who
46:8 And these two A were preserved out of six
Is 2:11 humbled; and the LORD A will be exalted in
2:17 low; and the LORD A will be exalted in
5:8 are made to dwell A in the midst of
26:13 us, but thy name A we acknowledge.
37:16 art the God, thou A, of all the kingdoms
37:20 may know that thou A art the LORD."
44:24 stretched out the heavens A, who spread out the
49:21 Behold, I was left A; whence then have these
63:3 trodden the wine press A, and from the peoples
Jer 15:17 I rejoice; I sat A, because thy hand was
49:31 that has no gates or bars, that dwells A
Lam 3:28 Let him sit A in silence when he has
Ezek 9:8 and I was left A, I fell upon my
14:16 sons nor daughters; they A would be delivered, but
14:18 nor daughters, but they A would be delivered.
40:46 sons of Zadok, who A among the sons of
Dan 10:7 And I, Daniel, A saw the vision, for the
10:8 So I was left A and saw this great
13:14 for a time when they could find her A
13:36 walking in the garden A, this woman came in
14:14 whole temple in the presence of the king A
Hos 4:17 Ephraim is joined to idols, let him A
8:9 a wild ass wandering A; Ephraim has hired lovers.
Mic 7:14 thy inheritance, who dwell A in a forest in
1Mac 6:25 And not against us A have they stretched out
13:4 of Israel, and I A am left.
2Mac 1:24 just and merciful, who A art King and art
1:25 and art kind, who A art bountiful, who alone
1:25 alone art bountiful, who A art just and almighty
6:13 to let the impious A for long, but to
7:37 you confess that he A is God,
8:35 and made his way A like a runaway slave
15:39 harmful to drink wine A, or, again, to drink
15:39 again, to drink water A, while wine mixed with
Mt 4:4 not live by bread A, but by every word
14:23 came, he was there A,
15:14 Let them A; they are blind guides.
18:14 tell him his fault, between you and him A
Mk 2:7 Who can forgive sins but God A
4:10 And when he was A, those who were about
6:47 sea, and he was A on the land.
10:18 No one is good but God A
14:6 Jesus said, "Let her A; why do you trouble
Lk 4:4 is written, 'Man shall not live by bread A
9:18 as he was praying A the disciples were with
9:36 when the voice had spoken, Jesus was found A
10:40 that my sister has left me to serve A
13:8 answered him, 'Let it A, sir, this year also,
18:19 No one is good but God A
Jn 6:22 disciples, but that his disciples had gone away A
8:9 and Jesus was left A with the woman standing
8:16 it is not I A that judge, but I
8:29 has not left me A, for I always do
12:7 Jesus said, "Let her A, let her keep it
12:24 and dies, it remains A; but if it dies,
16:32 and will leave me A; yet I am not
16:32 yet I am not A, for the Father is
Acts 5:38 men and let them A; for if this plan
Rom 4:23 not for his sake A,
11:3 thy altars, and I A am left, and they
Gal 6:4 will be in himself A and not in his
1Thes 3:1 left behind at Athens A,
1Tim 5:5 and is left all A, has set her hope
6:16 Lord of lords, who A has immortality and dwells
2Tim 4:11 Luke A is with me.
Jas 2:24 is justified by works and not by faith A
Rev 15:4 For thou A art holy.

ALONGSIDE (6)

Ezek 45:6 A the portion set apart as the holy district
45:7 property of the city, A the holy district and
48:13 And A the territory of the priests, the Levites
48:18 remainder of the length A the holy portion shall
48:18 and it shall be A the holy portion.
1Mac 13:52 of the temple hill A the citadel, and he

ALOOF (6)

2Sam 18:13 the king), then you yourself would have stood A
Job 30:10 abhor me, they keep A from me; they do
Ps 38:11 friends and companions stand A from my plague, and
Prov 20:3 a man to keep A from strife; but every
Sir 37:9 and then stand A to see what will happen
Obad 1:11 day that you stood A, on the day that

ALOUD (49)

Gen 29:11 Then Jacob kissed Rachel, and wept A
45:2 And he wept A, so that the Egyptians heard

Judg 9:7 Mount Gerizim, and cried A and said to them,
1Sam 11:4 of the people; and all the people wept A
2Sam 13:19 and went away, crying A as she went.
15:23 all the country wept A as all the people
1Kgs 18:27 mocked them, saying, "Cry A, for he is a
18:28 And they cried A, and cut themselves after their
Ezra 3:12 laid, though many shouted A for joy;
Job 19:7 not answered; I call A, but there is no
Ps 3:4 I cry A to the LORD, and he answers
26:7 altar, O LORD, singing A a song of thanksgiving,
27:7 LORD, when I cry A, be gracious to me
51:14 my tongue will sing A of thy deliverance.
59:16 might; I will sing A of thy steadfast love
66:17 I cried A to him, and he was extolled
77:1 I cry A to God, aloud to God, that
77:1 cry aloud to God, A to God, that he
81:1 Sing A to God our strength; shout for joy
145:7 goodness, and shall sing A of thy righteousness.
Prov 1:20 Wisdom's Warning Wisdom cries A in the street; in
8:3 the portals she cries A:
Is 10:30 Cry A, O daughter of Gallim!
13:2 raise a signal, cry A to them; wave the
15:4 men of Moab cry A; his soul trembles.
42:13 cries out, he shouts A, he shows himself mighty
54:1 into singing and cry A, you who have not
58:1 "Cry A, spare not, lift up your voice like
Jer 4:5 through the land; cry A and say, 'Assemble, and
31:7 says the LORD: "Sing A with gladness for Jacob,
31:12 shall come and sing A on the height of
Lam 2:18 Cry A to the Lord!
Ezek 24:17 Sigh, but not A; make no mourning for the
27:30 the shore and wail A over you, and cry
Dan 3:4 And the herald proclaimed A, "You are commanded,
4:14 He cried A and said thus, 'Hew down the
5:7 The king cried A to bring in the enchanters,
Mic 4:9 Now why do you cry A
Zeph 1:14 the mighty man cries A there.
3:14 Sing A, O daughter of Zion; shout, O Israel!
Zech 9:9 Shout A, O daughter of Jerusalem!
1Mac 3:50 days; and they cried A to Heaven, saying, "What
5:33 their trumpets and cried A in prayer.
2Mac 6:30 the blows, he groaned A and said: "It is
8:23 appointed Eleazar to read A from the holy book,
Mt 9:27 men followed him, crying A, "Have mercy on us,
12:19 not wrangle or cry A, nor will any one
Rev 1:3 is he who reads A the words of the
18:15 torment, weeping and mourning A,

ALPHA (3)

Rev 1:8 "I am the A and the Omega," says the
21:6 I am the A and the Omega, the beginning
22:13 I am the A and the Omega, the first

ALPHAEUS (5)

Mt 10:3 James the son of A, and Thaddaeus;
Mk 2:14 Levi the son of A sitting at the tax
3:18 James the son of A, and Thaddaeus, and Simon
Lk 6:15 James the son of A, and Simon who was
Acts 1:13 James the son of A and Simon the Zealot

ALREADY (68)

Ex 1:4 seventy persons; Joseph was A in Egypt.
Num 16:47 behold, the plague had A begun among the people;
Deut 31:21 purposes which they are A forming, before I have
Josh 23:4 nations that I have A cut off, from the
Judg 8:6 "Are Zebah and Zalmunna A in your hand, that
8:15 'Are Zebah and Zalmunna A in your hand, that
1Sam 17:12 Saul the man was A old and advanced in
2Kgs 7:13 of Israel that have A perished; let us send
2Chr 28:13 For our guilt is A great, and there is
Neh 5:5 of our daughters have A been enslaved; but it
Tob 3:8 You A have had seven and have had no
3:15 A seven husbands of mine are dead.
Eccl 1:10 It has been A, in the ages before us.
2:12 Only what he has A done.
3:15 That which is, A has been; that which is
3:15 which is to be, A has been; and God
4:2 the dead who are A dead more fortunate than
6:10 come to be has A been named, and it
9:6 and their envy have A perished, and they have
9:7 heart; for God has A approved what you do.
Wis 18:9 blessings and dangers; and A they were singing the
18:23 when the dead had A fallen on one another
19:16 sufferings those who had A shared the same rights.
Is 56:8 to him besides those A gathered."
Hos 8:8 Israel is swallowed up; A they are among the
Mal 2:2 blessings; indeed I have A cursed them, because you
1Mac 12:7 A in time past a letter was sent to
2Mac 2:32 much to what has A been said; for it
4:39 the gold vessels had A been stolen.
4:45 But Menelaus, A as good as beaten, promised a
15:20 and the enemy was A close at hand with
Mt 5:28 a woman lustfully has A committed adultery with her
17:12 you that Elijah has A come, and they did
Mk 4:37 that the boat was A filling.
11:11 everything, as it was A late, he went out
15:43 wondered if he were A dead; and summoning the
15:43 him whether he was A dead.
Lk 12:49 would that it were A kindled!
21:30 that the summer is A near.
Jn 3:18 not believe is condemned A, because he has not
4:35 how the fields are A white for harvest.
9:22 for the Jews had A agreed that if any
9:27 "I have told you A, and you would not
11:17 found that Lazarus had A been in the tomb
13:2 when the devil had A put it into the
15:3 You are A made clean by the word which
19:33 saw that he was A dead, they did not
Acts 4:3 morrow, for it was A evening.
27:9 and the voyage was A dangerous because the fast
27:9 because the fast had A gone by, Paul advised
Rom 3:9 all; for I have A charged that all men,
15:20 not where Christ has A been named, lest I
1Cor 4:8 A you are filled!
4:8 A you have become rich!
5:3 if present, I have A pronounced judgment
7:18 time of his call A circumcised?
2Cor 8:6 that as he had A made a beginning, he
10:16 without boasting of work A done in another's field.
Phil 3:12 Not that I have A obtained this or am
3:12 obtained this or am A perfect; but I press
1Thes 2:2 but though we had A suffered and been shamefully
2Thes 2:7 mystery of lawlessness is A at work; only he
1Tim 5:15 For some have A strayed after Satan.
2Tim 2:18 truth by holding that the resurrection is past A
4:6 For I am A on the point of being
Heb 4:7 afterward, in the words A quoted, "Today, when you
1Jn 2:8 the true light is A shining.
4:3 coming, and now it is in the world A

ALTAR (415)

Gen 8:20 Then Noah built an A to the LORD, and
8:20 clean bird, and offered burnt offerings on the A
12:7 he built there an A to the LORD, who
12:8 there he built an A to the LORD and
13:4 he had made an A at the first; and
13:18 there he built an A to the LORD.
22:9 him, Abraham built an A there, and laid the
22:9 laid him on the A, upon the wood.
26:25 So he built an A there and called upon
33:20 There he erected an A and called it El-Elohe-Israel.
35:1 and make there an A to the God who
35:3 may make there an A to the God who
35:7 there he built an A, and called the place
Ex 17:15 And Moses built an A and called the name
20:24 An A of earth you shall make for me
20:25 you make me an A of stone, you shall
20:26 by steps to my A, that your nakedness be
21:14 take him from my A, that he may die.
24:4 morning, and built an A at the foot of
24:6 half of the blood he threw against the A
27:1 "You shall make the A of acacia wood, five
27:1 five cubits broad; the A shall be square, and
27:5 the ledge of the A so that the net
27:5 that the net shall extend halfway down the A
27:6 make poles for the A, poles of acacia wood,
27:7 two sides of the A, when it is carried.
28:43 they come near the A to minister in the
29:12 the horns of the A with your finger, and
29:12 shall pour out at the base of the A
29:13 is on them, and burn them upon the A
29:16 throw it against the A round about.
29:18 whole ram upon the A; it is a burnt
29:20 the blood against the A round about.
29:21 that is on the A, and of the anointing
29:25 burn them on the A in addition to the
29:36 sin offering for the A, when you make atonement
29:37 make atonement for the A, and consecrate it, and
29:37 consecrate it, and the A shall be most holy;
29:37 holy; whatever touches the A shall become holy.
29:38 shall offer upon the A: two lambs a year
29:44 of meeting and the A; Aaron also and his

ALTAR

	30:1	"You shall make an A to burn incense upon;
	30:18	of meeting and the A, and you shall put
	30:20	they come near the A to minister, to burn
	30:27	its utensils, and the A of incense,
	30:28	of incense, and the A of burnt offering with
	31:8	its utensils, and the A of incense,
	31:9	of incense, and the A of burnt offering with
	32:5	this, he built an A before it; and Aaron
	35:15	the light; and the A of incense, with its
	35:16	of the tabernacle; the A of burnt offering, with
	37:25	He made the A of incense of acacia wood;
	38:1	He made the A of burnt offering also of
	38:3	the utensils of the A, the pots, the shovels,
	38:4	he made for the A a grating, a network
	38:7	the sides of the A, to carry it with
	38:30	of meeting, the bronze A and the bronze grating
	38:30	the utensils of the A,
	39:38	the light; the golden A, the anointing oil and
	39:39	the tent; the bronze A, and its grating of
Lev	1:5	round about against the A that is at the
	1:7	put fire on the A, and lay wood in
	1:8	the fire upon the A;
	1:9	the whole on the A, as a burnt offering,
	1:11	north side of the A before the LORD, and
	1:11	its blood against the A round about.
	1:12	the fire upon the A;
	1:13	burn it on the A; it is a burnt
	1:15	bring it to the A and wring off its
	1:15	burn it on the A; and its blood shall
	1:15	the side of the A;
	1:16	cast it beside the A on the east side,
	1:17	burn it on the A, upon the wood that
	2:2	memorial portion upon the A, an offering by fire,
	2:8	the priest, he shall bring it to the A
	2:9	burn this on the A, an offering by fire,
	2:12	be offered on the A for a pleasing odor.
	3:2	the blood against the A round about.
	3:5	burn it on the A upon the burnt offering,
	3:8	its blood against the A round about.
	3:11	burn it on the A as food offered by
	3:13	its blood against the A round about.
	3:16	burn them on the A as food offered by
	4:7	the horns of the A of fragrant incense before
	4:7	the base of the A of burnt offering which
	4:10	burn them upon the A of burnt offering.
	4:18	the horns of the A which is in the
	4:18	the base of the A of burnt offering which
	4:19	shall take from it and burn upon the A
	4:25	the horns of the A of burnt offering, and
	4:25	the base of the A of burnt offering.
	4:26	shall burn on the A, like the fat of
	4:30	the horns of the A of burnt offering, and
	4:30	of its blood at the base of the A
	4:31	burn it upon the A for a pleasing odor
	4:34	the horns of the A of burnt offering, and
	4:34	of its blood at the base of the A
	4:35	burn it on the A, upon the offerings by
	5:9	the side of the A, while the rest of
	5:9	the base of the A; it is a sin
	5:12	burn this on the A, upon the offerings by
	6:9	the hearth upon the A all night until the
	6:9	the fire of the A shall be kept burning
	6:10	burnt offering on the A, and put them beside
	6:10	on the altar, and put them beside the A
	6:12	The fire on the A shall be kept burning
	6:13	kept burning upon the A continually; it shall not
	6:14	it before the LORD, in front of the A
	6:15	memorial portion on the A, a pleasing odor to
	7:2	be thrown on the A round about.
	7:5	burn them on the A as an offering by
	7:31	the fat on the A, but the breast shall
	8:11	of it on the A seven times, and anointed
	8:11	times, and anointed the A and all its utensils,
	8:15	the horns of the A round about, and purified
	8:15	about, and purified the A, and poured out the
	8:15	the base of the A, and consecrated it, to
	8:16	their fat, and Moses burned them on the A
	8:19	the blood upon the A round about.
	8:21	whole ram on the A, as a burnt offering,
	8:24	the blood upon the A round about.
	8:28	burned them on the A with the burnt offering,
	8:30	which was on the A, and sprinkled it upon
	9:7	"Draw near to the A, and offer your sin
	9:8	drew near to the A, and killed the calf
	9:9	the horns of the A, and poured out the
	9:9	the base of the A;
	9:10	he burned upon the A, as the LORD commanded
	9:12	threw it on the A round about.
	9:13	the head; and he burned them upon the A
	9:14	burned them with the burnt offering on the A
	9:17	burned it upon the A, besides the burnt offering
	9:18	he threw upon the A round about,
	9:20	the fat upon the A,
	9:24	the fat upon the A; and when all the
	10:12	it unleavened beside the A, for it is most
	14:20	burnt offering and the cereal offering on the A
	16:12	of fire from the A before the LORD, and
	16:18	go out to the A which is before the
	16:18	the horns of the A round about.
	16:20	of meeting and the A, he shall present the
	16:25	the sin offering he shall burn upon the A
	16:33	meeting and for the A, and he shall make
	17:6	the blood on the A of the LORD at
	17:11	for you upon the A to make atonement for
	21:23	veil or approach the A, because he has a
	22:22	by fire upon the A to the LORD.
Num	3:26	the tabernacle and the A, and its cords; all
	4:11	And over the golden A they shall spread a purple
	4:13	the ashes from the A, and spread a purple
	4:14	the utensils of the A, which are used for
	4:14	the utensils of the A; and they shall spread
	4:26	the tabernacle and the A, and their cords, and
	5:25	bring it to the A;
	5:26	burn it upon the A, and afterward shall make
	7:1	anointed and consecrated the A with all its utensils,
	7:10	the dedication of the A on the day it
	7:10	and the leaders offered their offering before the A
	7:11	leader each day, for the dedication of the A
	7:84	dedication offering for the A, on the day when
	7:88	dedication offering for the A, after it was anointed.
	16:38	a covering for the A, for they offered them
	16:39	a covering for the A,
	16:46	therein from off the A, and lay incense on
	18:3	sanctuary or to the A, lest they, and you,
	18:5	the duties of the A, that there be wrath
	18:7	all that concerns the A and that is within
	18:17	their blood upon the A, and shall burn their
	23:2	Balaam offered on each A a bull and a
	23:4	have offered upon each A a bull and a
	23:14	offered a bull and a ram on each A
	23:30	offered a bull and a ram on each A
Deut	12:27	the blood, on the A of the LORD your
	12:27	poured out on the A of the LORD your
	16:21	an Asherah beside the A of the LORD your
	26:4	it down before the A of the LORD your
	27:5	you shall build an A to the LORD your
	27:5	LORD your God, an A of stones; you shall
	27:6	You shall build an A to the LORD your
	33:10	before thee, and whole burnt offering upon thy A
Josh	8:30	Then Joshua built an A in Mount Ebal to
	8:31	law of Moses, "an A of unhewn stones, upon
	9:27	congregation and for the A of the LORD, to
	22:10	Manasseh built there an A by the Jordan, an
	22:10	by the Jordan, an A of great size.
	22:11	Manasseh have built an A at the frontier of
	22:16	by building yourselves an A this day in rebellion
	22:19	by building yourselves an A other than the altar
	22:19	altar other than the A of the LORD our
	22:23	today for building an A to turn away from
	22:26	us now build an A, not for burnt offering,
	22:28	the copy of the A of the LORD, which
	22:29	LORD by building an A for burnt offering, cereal
	22:29	sacrifice, other than the A of the LORD our
	22:34	the Gadites called the A Witness; "For," said they,
Judg	6:24	Then Gideon built an A there to the LORD,
	6:25	and pull down the A of Baal which your
	6:26	it; and build an A to the LORD your
	6:28	the morning, behold, the A of Baal was broken
	6:28	was offered upon the A which had been built.
	6:30	has pulled down the A of Baal and cut
	6:31	for himself, because his A has been pulled down."
	6:32	because he pulled down his A
	13:20	toward heaven from the A, the angel of the
	13:20	the flame of the A while Manoah and his
	21:4	and built there an A, and offered burnt offerings
1Sam	2:28	go up to my A, to burn incense, to
	2:33	cut off from my A shall be spared to
	7:17	he built there an A to the LORD.
	14:35	And Saul built an A to the LORD; it
	14:35	it was the first A that he built to
2Sam	24:18	"Go up, rear an A to the LORD on
	24:21	order to build an A to the LORD, that

Book	Ref	Context
	24:25	David built there an A to the LORD, and
1Kgs	1:50	and caught hold of the horns of the A
	1:51	the horns of the A, saying, 'Let King Solomon
	1:53	sent, and they brought him down from the A
	2:28	and caught hold of the horns of the A
	2:29	the LORD, and behold, he is beside the A
	3:4	to offer a thousand burnt offerings upon that A
	6:20	He also made an A of cedar.
	6:22	Also the whole A that belonged to the inner
	7:48	the LORD: the golden A, the golden table for
	8:22	Solomon stood before the A of the LORD in
	8:31	his oath before thine A in this house,
	8:54	arose from before the A of the LORD, where
	8:64	offerings, because the bronze A that was before the
	9:25	peace offerings upon the A which he built to
	12:32	offered sacrifices upon the A; so he did in
	12:33	went up to the A which he had made
	12:33	went up to the A to burn incense.
	13:1	was standing by the A to burn incense.
	13:2	man cried against the A by the word of
	13:2	LORD, and said, "O A, altar, thus says the
	13:2	and said, "O altar, A, thus says the LORD:
	13:3	has spoken: 'Behold, the A shall be torn down,
	13:4	he cried against the A at Bethel, Jeroboam stretched
	13:4	his hand from the A, saying, "Lay hold of
	13:5	The A also was torn down, and the ashes
	13:5	poured out from the A, according to the sign
	13:32	the LORD against the A in Bethel, and against
	16:32	He erected an A for Baal in the house
	18:26	they limped about the A which they had made.
	18:30	And he repaired the A of the LORD that
	18:32	stones he built an A in the name of
	18:32	a trench about the A, as great as would
	18:35	ran round about the A, and filled the trench
2Kgs	11:11	the house, around the A and the house.
	12:9	set it beside the A on the right side
	16:10	Assyria, he saw the A that was at Damascus.
	16:10	a model of the A, and its pattern, exact
	16:11	the priest built the A; in accordance with all
	16:12	king came from Damascus, the king viewed the A
	16:12	drew near to the A, and went up on
	16:13	the blood of his peace offerings upon the A
	16:14	And the bronze A which was before the LORD
	16:14	the place between his A and the house of
	16:14	put it on the north side of his A
	16:15	saying, "Upon the great A burn the morning burnt
	16:15	sacrifice; but the bronze A shall be for me
	18:22	shall worship before this A in Jerusalem"?
	23:9	come up to the A of the LORD in
	23:15	Moreover the A at Bethel, the high place erected
	23:15	Israel to sin, that A with the high place
	23:16	burned them upon the A, and defiled it, according
	23:17	have done against the A at Bethel."
1Chr	6:49	made offerings upon the A of burnt offering and
	6:49	offering and upon the A of incense for all
	16:40	the LORD upon the A of burnt offering continually
	21:18	up and rear an A to the LORD on
	21:22	build on it an A to the LORD--give
	21:26	David built there an A to the LORD and
	21:26	from heaven upon the A of burnt offering.
	21:29	the wilderness, and the A of burnt offering were
	22:1	God and here the A of burnt offering for
	28:18	of each; for the A of incense made of
2Chr	1:5	Jerusalem.) Moreover the bronze A that Bezalel the
	1:6	there to the bronze A before the LORD, which
	4:1	He made an A of bronze, twenty cubits long,
	4:19	of God: the golden A, the tables for the
	5:12	stood east of the A with a hundred and
	6:12	Solomon stood before the A of the LORD in
	6:22	his oath before thy A in this house,
	7:7	offerings, because the bronze A Solomon had made
	7:9	the dedication of the A seven days and the
	8:12	the LORD upon the A of the LORD which
	15:8	and he repaired the A of the LORD that
	23:10	the house, around the A and the house.
	26:16	burn incense on the A of incense.
	26:19	the LORD, by the A of incense.
	29:18	of the LORD, the A of burnt offering and
	29:19	they are before the A of the LORD."
	29:21	offer them on the A of the LORD.
	29:22	threw it against the A; and they killed the
	29:22	was thrown against the A; and they killed the
	29:22	lambs and their blood was thrown against the A
	29:24	their blood on the A, to make atonement for
	29:27	that the burnt offering be offered on the A
	32:12	and Jerusalem, "Before one A you shall worship, and
	33:16	He also restored the A of the LORD and
	35:16	burnt offerings on the A of the LORD, according
Ezra	3:2	and they built the A of the God of
	3:3	They set the A in its place, for fear
	7:17	offer them upon the A of the house of
Neh	10:34	to burn upon the A of the LORD our
Tob	1:6	the priests, the sons of Aaron, at the A
Jud	4:3	sacred vessels and the A and the temple had
	4:12	They even surrounded the A with sackcloth and cried
	8:24	the temple and the A rest upon us.
	9:8	the horn of thy A with the sword.
Esth	14:9	and to quench thy A and the glory of
Ps	26:6	and go about thy A, O LORD,
	43:4	will go to the A of God, to God
	51:19	offerings; then bulls will be offered on thy A
	118:27	with branches, up to the horns of the A
Wis	9:8	holy mountain, and an A in the city of
Sir	35:6	righteous man anoints the A, and its pleasing odor
	47:9	placed singers before the A, to make sweet melody
	50:11	up to the holy A, he made the court
	50:12	the hearth of the A with a garland of
	50:15	the foot of the A, a pleasing odor to
Is	6:6	which he had taken with tongs from the A
	19:19	there will be an A to the LORD in
	36:7	and to Jerusalem, "You shall worship before this A
	56:7	be accepted on my A; for my house shall
	60:7	with acceptance on my A, and I will glorify
Lam	2:7	Lord has scorned his A, disowned his sanctuary; he
Bar	1:10	offer them upon the A of the Lord our
Ezek	8:5	behold, north of the A gate, in the entrance,
	8:16	the porch and the A, were about twenty-five men,
	9:2	they went in and stood beside the bronze A
	40:46	have charge of the A; these are the sons
	40:47	broad, foursquare; and the A was in front of
	41:22	was something resembling an A of wood, three
	43:13	the dimensions of the A by cubits (the cubit
	43:13	the height of the A:
	43:15	one cubit; and the A hearth, four cubits; and
	43:15	cubits; and from the A hearth projecting upward,
	43:16	The A hearth shall be square, twelve cubits long
	43:17	The steps of the A shall face east."
	43:18	the ordinances for the A: On the day when
	43:20	four horns of the A, and on the four
	43:20	you shall cleanse the A and make atonement for
	43:22	sin offering; and the A shall be cleansed, as
	43:26	make atonement for the A and purify it, and
	43:27	shall offer upon the A your burnt offerings and
	45:19	the ledge of the A, and the posts of
	47:1	the threshold of the temple, south of the A
Joel	1:12	lament, O priests, wail, O ministers of the A
	2:17	the vestibule and the A let the priests, the
Amos	2:8	themselves down beside every A upon garments
	3:14	the horns of the A shall be cut off
	9:1	LORD standing beside the A, and he said: "Smite
Zech	9:15	a bowl, drenched like the corners of the A
	14:20	the bowls before the A;
Mal	1:7	thy name?' By offering polluted food upon my A
	1:10	kindle fire upon my A in vain!
	2:13	You cover the LORD's A with tears, with weeping
1Mac	1:21	and took the golden A, the lampstand for the
	1:54	desolating sacrilege upon the A of burnt offering.
	1:59	offered sacrifice on the A which was upon the
	1:59	which was upon the A of burnt offering.
	2:23	offer sacrifice upon the A in Modein, according to
	2:24	anger; he ran and killed him upon the A
	2:25	them to sacrifice, and he tore down the A
	4:38	the sanctuary desolate, the A profaned, and the gates
	4:44	to do about the A of burnt offering, which
	4:45	they tore down the A,
	4:47	and built a new A like the former one.
	4:49	brought the lampstand, the A of incense, and the
	4:50	burned incense on the A and lighted the lamps
	4:53	directs, on the new A of burnt offering which
	4:56	the dedication of the A for eight days, and
	4:59	of dedication of the A should be observed with
	5:1	about heard that the A had been built and
	6:7	had erected upon the A in Jerusalem; and that
	7:36	and stood before the A and the temple, and
2Mac	1:18	the temple and the A, offered sacrifices.
	1:19	the fire of the A and secretly hid it
	1:32	the light from the A shone back, it went
	2:5	the ark and the A of incense, and he
	2:19	the dedication of the A,
	3:15	prostrated themselves before the A in their priestly
	4:14	no longer intent upon their service at the A
	6:5	The A was covered with abominable offerings which

10:3 sanctuary, and made another A of sacrifice; then,
10:26 the steps before the A, they besought him to
13:8 many sins against the A whose fire and ashes
14:3 again to the holy A,
14:33 and tear down the A, and I will build
15:31 the priests before the A, he sent for those
Mt 5:23 your gift at the A, and there remember that
5:24 gift there before the A and go; first be
23:17 one swears by the A, it is nothing; but
23:17 that is on the A, he is bound by
23:18 the gift or the A that makes the gift
23:19 who swears by the A, swears by it and
23:34 you murdered between the sanctuary and the A
Lk 1:11 right side of the A of incense.
11:51 who perished between the A and the sanctuary.
Acts 17:23 I found also an A with this inscription, 'To
1Cor 9:13 who serve at the A share in the sacrificial
10:18 those who eat the sacrifices partners in the A
Heb 7:13 which no one has ever served at the A
9:4 Holies, having the golden A of incense and the
13:10 We have an A from which those who serve
Jas 2:21 when he offered his son Isaac upon the A
Rev 6:9 I saw under the A the souls of those
8:3 and stood at the A with a golden censer;
8:3 saints upon the golden A before the throne;
8:5 with fire from the A and threw it on
9:13 horns of the golden A before God,
11:1 of God and the A and those who worship
14:18 came out from the A, the angel who has
16:7 And I heard the A cry, "Yea, Lord God

ALTARS (70)

Ex 34:13 shall tear down their A, and break their pillars,
Lev 26:30 cut down your incense A, and cast your dead
Num 3:31 table, the lampstand, the A, the vessels of the
23:1 for me here seven A, and provide for me
23:4 have prepared the seven A, and I have offered
23:14 Pisgah, and built seven A, and offered a bull
23:29 for me here seven A, and provide for me
Deut 7:5 shall break down their A, and dash in pieces
12:3 shall tear down their A, and dash in pieces
Judg 2:2 shall break down their A But you have not
1Kgs 19:10 covenant, thrown down thy A, and slain thy prophets
19:14 covenant, thrown down thy A, and slain thy prophets
2Kgs 11:18 tore it down; his A and his images they
11:18 slew Mattan the priest of Baal before the A
18:22 whose high places and A Hezekiah has removed,
21:3 destroyed; and he erected A for Baal, and made
21:4 And he built A in the house of the
21:5 And he built A for all the host of
23:12 And the A on the roof of the upper
23:12 had made, and the A which Manasseh had made
23:20 were there, upon the A, and burned the bones
2Chr 14:3 took away the foreign A and the high places,
14:5 of Judah the high places and the incense A
23:17 tore it down; his A and his images they
23:17 slew Mattan the priest of Baal before the A
28:24 and he made himself A in every corner of
30:14 work and removed the A that were in Jerusalem,
30:14 Jerusalem, and all the A for burning incense they
31:1 high places and the A throughout all Judah and
32:12 high places and his A and commanded Judah and
33:3 broken down, and erected A to the Baals, and
33:4 And he built A in the house of the
33:5 And he built A for all the host of
33:15 LORD, and all the A that he had built
34:4 they broke down the A of the Baals in
34:4 hewed down the incense A which stood above them;
34:5 the priests on their A, and purged Judah and
34:7 he broke down the A, and beat the Asherim
34:7 down all the incense A throughout all the land
Ps 84:3 her young, at thy A, O LORD of hosts,
Sir 50:14 the service at the A, and arranging the offering
Is 17:8 have regard for the A, the work of their
17:8 the Asherim or the A of incense.
27:9 the stones of the A like chalkstones crushed to
27:9 no Asherim or incense A will remain standing.
36:7 whose high places and A Hezekiah has removed,
Jer 11:13 of Jerusalem are the A you have set up
11:13 set up to shame, A to burn incense to
17:1 the horns of their A,
17:2 their children remember their A and their Asherim,
Ezek 6:4 Your A shall become desolate, and your incense
6:4 desolate, and your incense A shall be broken; and
6:5 I will scatter your bones round about your A
6:6 ruined, so that your A will be waste and
6:6 and destroyed, your incense A cut down, and your
6:13 idols round about their A, upon every high hill,
Hos 4:19 and they shall be ashamed because of their A
8:11 Because Ephraim has multiplied A for sinning, they
8:11 have become to him A for sinning.
10:1 fruit increased the more A he built; as his
10:2 will break down their A, and destroy their pillars.
10:8 grow up on their A; and they shall say
12:11 they sacrifice bulls, their A also shall be like
Amos 3:14 I will punish the A of Bethel, and the
1Mac 1:47 the priests, to build A and sacred precincts and
1:54 They also built A in the surrounding cities of
2:45 and tore down the A;
5:68 he tore down their A, and the graven images
2Mac 10:2 they tore down the A which had been built
Rom 11:3 they have demolished thy A, and I alone am

ALTER (2)

Ezra 6:12 forth a hand to A this, or to destroy
Ps 89:34 violate my covenant, or A the word that went

ALTERED (3)

Jud 10:7 how her face was A and her clothing changed,
Esth 1:19 it may not be A, that Vashti is to
Lk 9:29 of his countenance was A, and his raiment became

ALTERNATIONS

Wis 7:18 middle of times, the A of the solstices and

ALTERS

Ezra 6:11 that if any one A this edict, a beam

ALTHOUGH (41)

Gen 31:37 A you have felt through all my goods, what
31:50 wives besides my daughters, A no man is with
39:10 And A she spoke to Joseph day after day,
Ex 13:17 land of the Philistines, A that was near; for
34:9 the midst of us, A it is a stiff-necked
Num 14:44 of the hill country, A neither the ark of
Josh 17:14 portion as an inheritance, A I am a numerous
1Sam 1:5 sons and daughters; and, A he loved Hannah, he
2Sam 21:2 remnant of the Amorites; A the people of Israel
1Kgs 1:1 advanced in years, and A they covered him with
1:18 behold, Adonijah is king, A you, my lord the
2:28 Joab had supported Adonijah A he had not supported
3:7 of David my father, A I am but a
18:12 he will kill me, A I your servant have
1Chr 12:17 me to my adversaries, A there is no wrong
Neh 6:1 breach left in it A up to that time
Jud 11:13 our God at Jerusalem— A it is not lawful
Job 2:3 holds fast his integrity, A you moved me against
10:7 search for my sin, A thou knowest that I
16:17 eyelids is deep darkness; A there is no violence
32:3 had found no answer, A they had declared Job
Eccl 8:6 its time and way, A man's trouble lies heavy
Is 53:9 man in his death, A he had done no
Jer 14:15 prophesy in my name A I did not send
25:4 your ears to hear, A the LORD persistently sent
Ezek 13:7 said, 'Says the LORD,' A I have not spoken?"
13:22 disheartened the righteous falsely, A I have not
35:10 take possession of them,— A the LORD was there—
Hos 7:16 A I trained and strengthened their arms, yet they
1Mac 11:25 A certain lawless men of his nation kept making
Jn 4:2 more disciples than John A Jesus himself did not
21:11 fifty-three of them; and A there were so many,
Acts 15:24 words, unsettling your minds, A we gave them no
Rom 1:21 are without excuse; for A they knew God they
3:21 manifested apart from law, A the law and the
8:10 Christ is in you, A your bodies are dead
1Cor 2:6 we do impart wisdom, A it is not a
8:5 For A there may be so-called gods in heaven
2Cor 7:12 So A I wrote to you, it was not
Heb 4:3 A his works were finished from the foundation of
5:8 A he was a Son, he learned obedience through

ALTOGETHER (10)

Gen 18:21 whether they have done A according to the outcry
46:15 with his daughter Dinah; A his sons and his
Deut 16:15 that you will be A joyful.
Job 27:12 then have you become A vain?
Ps 19:9 ordinances of the LORD are true, and righteous A
35:26 to shame and confusion A who rejoice at my
37:38 But transgressors shall be A destroyed; the posterity
40:14 to shame and confusion A who seek to snatch
139:4 my tongue, lo, O LORD, thou knowest it A
Song 5:16 sweet, and he is A desirable.

ALUSH (2)

Num 33:13 they set out from Dophkah, and encamped at A
33:14 they set out from A, and encamped at Rephidim,

ALVAH

Gen 36:40 names: the chiefs Timna, A, Jetheth,

ALVAN

Gen 36:23 the sons of Shobal: A, Manahath, Ebal, Shepho, and

ALWAYS (94)

Ex 25:30 of the Presence on the table before me A
28:38 holy gifts; it shall A be upon his forehead,
Deut 5:29 a mind as this A, to fear me and
6:24 God, for our good A, that he might preserve
11:1 statutes, his ordinances, and his commandments A
11:12 LORD your God are A upon it, from the
14:23 may learn to fear the LORD your God A
Josh 9:23 some of you shall A be slaves, hewers of
1Sam 21:5 kept from us as A when I go on
27:12 people Israel; therefore he shall be my servant A
2Sam 9:7 father; and you shall eat at my table A
9:10 your master's son shall A eat at my table."
9:13 Jerusalem; for he ate A at the king's table.
1Kgs 5:1 his father; for Hiram A loved David.
11:36 David my servant may A have a lamp before
2Kgs 17:37 for you, you shall A be careful to do.
2Chr 18:7 good concerning me, but A evil." And Jehoshaphat
Esth 13:2 presumption of authority but A acting reasonably and
16:4 justice of God, who A sees everything.
16:9 changing our methods and A judging what comes
Ps 9:18 the needy shall not A be forgotten, and the
16:8 I keep the LORD A before me; because he
73:12 these are the wicked; A at ease, they increase
103:9 He will not A chide, nor will he keep
Prov 5:19 with delight, be infatuated A with her love.
6:21 them upon your heart A; tie them about your
8:30 delight, rejoicing before him A,
28:14 who fears the LORD A; but he who hardens
Eccl 9:8 Let your garments be A white; let not oil
Wis 11:21 For it is A in thy power to show
14:31 those who sin, that A pursues the transgression of
17:11 by conscience, it has A exaggerated the difficulties.
Sir 17:13 Their ways are A before him, they will not
23:10 also the man who A swears and utters the
27:11 the godly man is A wise, but the fool
38:29 his feet; he is A deeply concerned over his
Is 57:16 ever, nor will I A be angry; for from
1Mac 2:65 is wise in counsel; A listen to him; he
2Mac 14:15 people for ever and A upholds his own heritage
14:24 And he kept Judas A in his presence; he
Mt 18:10 in heaven their angels A behold the face of
26:11 For you A have the poor with you, but
26:11 but you will not A have me.
28:20 I am with you A, to the close of
Mk 5:5 the mountains he was A crying out, and bruising
14:7 For you A have the poor with you, and
14:7 but you will not A have me.
Lk 15:31 him, 'Son, you are A with me, and all
18:1 effect that they ought A to pray and not
Jn 6:34 said to him, "Lord, give us this bread A
7:6 but your time is A here.
8:29 me alone, for I A do what is pleasing
11:42 that thou hearest me A, but I have said
12:8 The poor you A have with you, but you
12:8 but you do not A have me."
18:20 the world; I have A taught in synagogues and
Acts 2:25 'I saw the Lord A before me, for he
7:51 heart and ears, you A resist the Holy Spirit.
24:15 So I A take pains to have a clear
Rom 1:9 ceasing I mention you A in my prayers,
1Cor 1:4 give thanks to God A for you because of
15:58 be steadfast, immovable, A abounding in the work
2Cor 1:19 in him it is A Yes.
2:14 God, who in Christ A leads us in triumph,
4:10 down, but not destroyed; A carrying in the body
4:11 we live we are A being given up to
5:6 So we are A of good courage; we know
6:10 killed; as sorrowful, yet A rejoicing; as poor, yet
9:8 so that you may A have enough of everything
Gal 4:18 good purpose it is A good to be made
Eph 5:20 with all your heart, A and for everything giving
Phil 1:4 my remembrance of you, A in every prayer of
1:20 full courage now as A Christ will be honored
2:12 beloved, as you have A obeyed, so now, not
4:4 Rejoice in the Lord A; again I will say,
Col 1:3 We A thank God, the Father of our Lord
4:6 Let your speech A be gracious, seasoned with salt,
4:12 Christ Jesus, greets you, A remembering you
1Thes 1:2 give thanks to God A for you all, constantly
2:16 be saved--so as A to fill up the
3:6 and reported that you A remember us kindly and
4:17 and so we shall A be with the Lord.
5:15 evil for evil, but A seek to do good
5:16 Rejoice A,
2Thes 1:3 give thanks to God A for you, brethren, as
1:11 To this end we A pray for you, that
2:13 give thanks to God A for you, brethren beloved
2Tim 4:5 As for you, A be steady, endure suffering, do
Tit 1:11 own, said, "Cretans are A liars, evil beasts, lazy
Philem 1:4 I thank my God A when I remember you
Heb 3:10 generation, and said, 'They A go astray in their
7:25 through him, since he A lives to make intercession
1Pet 3:15 A be prepared to make a defense to any
2Pet 1:12 Therefore I intend A to remind you of these

AMAD

Josh 19:26 Hali, Beten, Achshaph, Allammelech, A, and Mishal;

AMAL

1Chr 7:35 of Helem his brother: Zophah, Imna, Shelesh, and A

AMALEK (22)

Gen 36:12 Esau's son; she bore A to Eliphaz.) These are
36:16 Kenaz, Korah, Gatam, and A; these are the chiefs
Ex 17:8 Then came A and fought with Israel at Rephidim.
17:9 go out, fight with A; tomorrow I will stand
17:10 him, and fought with A; and Moses, Aaron, and
17:11 he lowered his hand, A prevailed.
17:13 And Joshua mowed down A and his people with
17:14 out the remembrance of A from under heaven."
17:16 will have war with A from generation to generation."
Num 24:20 Then he looked on A, and took up his
24:20 his discourse, and said, A was the first of
Deut 25:17 "Remember what A did to you on the way
25:19 out the remembrance of A from under heaven; you
1Sam 15:2 'I will punish what A did to Israel in
15:3 Now go and smite A, and utterly destroy all
15:5 to the city of A, and lay in wait
15:20 Agag the king of A, and I have utterly
28:18 his fierce wrath against A, therefore the LORD has
2Sam 8:12 the Ammonites, the Philistines, A, and from the spoil
1Chr 1:36 Teman, Omar, Zephi, Gatam, Kenaz, Timna, and A
18:11 Edom, Moab, the Ammonites, the Philistines, and A
Ps 83:7 Gebal and Ammon and A, Philistia with the

AMALEKITE (3)

1Sam 30:13 Egypt, servant to an A; and my master left
2Sam 1:8 him, 'I am an A
1:13 "I am the son of a sojourner, an A

AMALEKITES (25)

Gen 14:7 the country of the A, and also the Amorites
Num 13:29 The A dwell in the land of the Negeb;
14:25 Now, since the A and the Canaanites dwell in
14:43 For there the A and the Canaanites are before
14:45 Then the A and the Canaanites who dwelt in
Judg 3:13 the Ammonites and the A, and went and defeated
6:3 the Midianites and the A and the people of
6:33 the Midianites and the A and the people of
7:12 the Midianites and the A and all the people
10:12 Sidonians also, and the A, and the Maonites,
12:15 of Ephraim, in the hill country of the A
1Sam 14:48 valiantly, and smote the A, and delivered Israel out
15:6 down from among the A, lest I destroy you
15:6 So the Kenites departed from among the A
15:7 And Saul defeated the A, from Havilah as far
15:8 the king of the A alive, and utterly destroyed
15:15 brought them from the A; for the people spared
15:18 destroy the sinners, the A, and fight against them
15:20 of Amalek, and I have utterly destroyed the A
15:32 here to me Agag the king of the A
27:8 the Girzites, and the A; for these were the
30:1 the third day, the A had made a raid
30:18 recovered all that the A had taken; and David
2Sam 1:1 the slaughter of the A, David remained two days
1Chr 4:43 the remnant of the A that had escaped, and

AMAM

Josh 15:26 Kerioth-hezron (that is, Hazor), A, Shema, Moladah,

AMANA

Song 4:8 from the peak of A, from the peak of

AMARIAH (16)

1Chr 6:7 of Meraioth, Meraioth of A, Amariah of Ahitub,
6:7 Meraioth, Meraioth of Amariah, A of Ahitub,
6:11 was the father of A, Amariah of Ahitub,
6:11 the father of Amariah, A of Ahitub,
6:52 son, Meraioth his son, A his son, Ahitub his
23:19 Hebron: Jeriah the chief, A the second, Jahaziel the
24:23 Hebron: Jeriah the chief, A the second, Jahaziel the
2Chr 19:11 And behold, A the chief priest is over you
31:15 Jeshua, Shemaiah, A, and Shecaniah were faithful
Ezra 7:3 of Ahitub, son of A, son of Azariah, son
10:42 Azarel, Shelemiah, Shemariah, Shallum, A, and
Neh 10:3 Seraiah, Azariah, Jeremiah, Pashhur, A, Malchijah,
11:4 of Zechariah, son of A, son of Shephatiah, son
12:2 Jeshua: Seraiah, Jeremiah, Ezra, A, Malluch,
12:13 of Ezra, Meshullam; of A, Jehohanan;
Zeph 1:1 of Gedaliah, son of A, son of Hezekiah, in

AMASA (17)

2Sam 17:25 Now Absalom had set A over the army instead
17:25 A was the son of a man named Ithra
19:13 king?' And say to A, 'Are you not my
20:4 the king said to A, "Call the men of
20:5 So A went to summon Judah; but he delayed
20:8 which is in Gibeon, A came to meet them.
20:9 And Joab said to A, "Is it well with
20:9 And Joab took A by the beard with his
20:10 But A did not observe the sword which was
20:11 took his stand by A, and said, "Whoever favors
20:12 And A lay wallowing in his blood in the
20:12 people stopped, he carried A out of the highway
1Kgs 2:5 son of Ner, and A the son of Jether,
2:32 army of Israel, and A the son of Jether,
1Chr 2:17 Abigail bore A, and the father of Amasa was
2:17 and the father of A was Jether the Ishmaelite.
2Chr 28:12 son of Shallum, and A the son of Hadlai,

AMASAI (5)

1Chr 6:25 The sons of Elkanah: A and Ahimoth,
6:35 of Mahath, son of A,
12:18 the Spirit came upon A, chief of the thirty,
15:24 Joshaphat, Nethanel, A, Zechariah, Benaiah, and
2Chr 29:12 Mahath the son of A, and Joel the son

AMASHSAI

Neh 11:13 hundred and forty-two; and A, the son of Azarel,

AMASIAH

2Chr 17:16 and next to him A the son of Zichri,

AMASSED

Sir 47:18 gold like tin and A silver like lead.

AMASSES

Sir 43:15 In his majesty he A the clouds, and the

AMAW

Num 22:5 in the land of A to call him, saying,

AMAZED (29)

Tob 11:16 as he went were A because he could see.
Jud 15:1 heard it, they were A at what had happened.
Eccl 5:8 away, do not be A at the matter; for
Wis 5:2 and they will be A at his unexpected salvation.
13:4 And if men were A at their power and
Sir 11:13 so that many are A at him.
43:18 and the mind is A at its falling.
1Mac 15:32 silver plate, and his great magnificence, he was A
Mt 12:23 all the people were A, and said, "Can this
Mk 1:27 And they were all A, so that they questioned
2:12 that they were all A and glorified God, saying,
9:15 saw him, were greatly A, and ran up to
10:24 And the disciples were A at his words.
10:32 them; and they were A, and those who followed
12:17 And they were A at him.
16:5 dressed in a white robe; and they were A
16:6 them, "Do not be A; you seek Jesus of
Lk 2:47 who heard him were A at his understanding and
4:36 And they were all A and said to one
8:56 And her parents were A; but he charged them
24:22 women of our company A us.
Acts 2:7 And they were A and wondered, saying, "Are not
2:12 And all were A and perplexed, saying to one
8:9 in the city and A the nation of Samaria,
8:11 long time he had A them with his magic.
8:13 seeing signs and great miracles performed, he was A
9:21 who heard him were A, and said, "Is not
10:45 came with Peter were A, because the gift of
12:16 when they opened, they saw him and were A

AMAZEMENT (4)

Gen 43:33 and the men looked at one another in A
Mk 5:42 of age), and they were immediately overcome with A
Lk 5:26 And A seized them all, and they glorified God
Acts 3:10 filled with wonder and A at what had happened

AMAZIAH (39)

2Kgs 12:21 city of David, and A his son reigned in
13:12 which he fought against A king of Judah, are
14:1 Joahaz, king of Israel, A the son of Joash,
14:8 Then A sent messengers to Jehoash the son of
14:9 Israel sent word to A king of Judah, "A
14:11 But A would not listen.
14:11 up, and he and A king of Judah faced
14:13 king of Israel captured A king of Judah, the
14:15 how he fought with A king of Judah, are
14:17 A the son of Joash, king of Judah, lived
14:18 of the deeds of A, are they not written
14:21 and made him king instead of his father A
14:23 the fifteenth year of A the son of Joash,
15:1 Azariah the son of A, king of Judah, began
15:3 all that his father A had done.
1Chr 3:12 son, Joash his son, A his son, Azariah his
4:34 Joshah the son of A,
6:45 of Hashabiah, son of A, son of Hilkiah,
2Chr 24:27 And A his son reigned in his stead.
25:1 A was twenty-five years old when he began to
25:5 Then A assembled the men of Judah, and set
25:9 And A said to the man of God, "But
25:10 Then A discharged the army that had come to
25:11 But A took courage, and led out his people,
25:13 of the army whom A sent back, not letting
25:14 After A came from the slaughter of the Edomites,
25:15 LORD was angry with A and sent to him
25:17 Then A king of Judah took counsel and sent
25:18 Israel sent word to A king of Judah, "A
25:20 But A would not listen; for it was of
25:21 up; and he and A king of Judah faced
25:23 king of Israel captured A king of Judah, the
25:25 A the son of Joash king of Judah lived
25:26 of the deeds of A, from first to last,
26:1 and made him king instead of his father A
26:4 all that his father A had done.
Amos 7:10 Then A the priest of Bethel sent to Jeroboam
7:12 And A said to Amos, "O seer, go, flee
7:14 Then Amos answered A, "I am no prophet, nor

AMBASSADOR (2)

Eph 6:20 which I am an A in chains; that I
Philem 1:9 you—I, Paul, an A and now a prisoner

AMBASSADORS (5)

Is 18:2 of Ethiopia; which sends A by the Nile, in
Ezek 17:15 against him by sending A to Egypt, that they
1Mac 9:70 of this, he sent A to him to make
10:51 Then Alexander sent A to Ptolemy king of Egypt
2Cor 5:20 So we are A for Christ, God making his

AMBITION (4)

Wis 14:18 Then the A of the craftsman impelled even those
Rom 15:20 thus making it my A to preach the gospel,
Jas 3:14 bitter jealousy and selfish A in your hearts, do
3:16 where jealousy and selfish A exist, there will be

AMBUSH (35)

Josh 8:2 for yourselves; lay an A against the city, behind
8:4 you shall lie in A against the city, behind
8:7 rise up from the A, and seize the city;
8:9 to the place of A, and lay between Bethel
8:12 and set them in A between Bethel and Ai,
8:14 that there was an A against him behind the
8:19 And the A rose quickly out of their place,
8:21 Israel saw that the A had taken the city,
Judg 9:25 Shechem put men in A against him on the
9:35 men that were with him rose from the A
20:29 Israel set men in A round about Gibe-ah.
20:33 Israel who were in A rushed out of their
20:36 to the men in A whom they had set
20:37 And the men in A made haste and rushed

20:37 Gibe-ah; the men in A moved out and smote
20:38 and the men in A was that when they
2Chr 13:13 Jeroboam had sent an A around to come on
13:13 of Judah, and the A was behind them.
20:22 the LORD set an A against the men of
Ps 10:8 He sits in A in the villages; in hiding
17:12 to tear, as a young lion lurking in A
64:4 like arrows, shooting from A at the blameless,
Prov 1:11 blood, let us wantonly A the innocent;
1:18 blood, they set an A for their own lives.
Sir 5:14 do not lie in A with your tongue; for
8:11 lest he lie in A against your words.
Jer 9:8 heart he plans an A for him.
1Mac 1:36 It became an A against the sanctuary, an evil
9:40 upon them from the A and began killing them.
10:80 that there was an A behind him, for they
11:68 they had set an A against him in the
11:69 Then the men in A emerged from their places
Acts 23:16 sister heard of their A; so he went and
23:21 their men lie in A for him, having bound
25:3 to Jerusalem, planning an A to kill him on

AMBUSHED

1Mac 5:4 to the people and A them on the highways.

AMBUSHES (2)

Ezra 8:31 the enemy and from A by the way.
Jer 51:12 up watchmen; prepare the A; for the LORD has

AMEN (59)

Num 5:22 the woman shall say, A, Amen.'
5:22 woman shall say, 'Amen, A
Deut 27:15 shall answer and say, A
27:16 the people shall say, A
27:17 the people shall say, A
27:18 the people shall say, A
27:19 the people shall say, A
27:20 the people shall say, A
27:21 the people shall say, A
27:22 the people shall say, A
27:23 the people shall say, A
27:24 the people shall say, A
27:25 the people shall say, A
27:26 the people shall say, A
1Kgs 1:36 Benaiah the son of Jehoiada answered the king, A
1Chr 16:36 Then all the people said A
Neh 5:13 And all the assembly said A
8:6 all the people answered, A, Amen," lifting up their
8:6 great God; and all the people answered, "Amen, A
Tob 8:8 And she said with him, A
Ps 41:13 A and Amen.
41:13 Amen and A
72:19 A and Amen!
72:19 Amen and A
89:52 A and Amen.
89:52 Amen and A
106:48 And let all the people say, A
Jer 28:6 of the LORD; and the prophet Jeremiah said, A
Mk 16:20 by the signs that attended it. A
Rom 1:25 rather than the Creator, who is blessed forever. A
9:5 who is God over all, blessed forever. A
11:36 To him be glory for ever. A
15:33 The God of peace be with you all. A
16:27 be glory for evermore through Jesus Christ. A
1Cor 14:16 in the position of an outsider say the A
16:24 My love be with you all in Jesus Christ. A
2Cor 1:20 why we utter the A through him, to the
Gal 1:5 for ever and ever. A
6:18 be with your spirit, brethren. A
Eph 3:21 to all generations, for ever and ever. A
Phil 4:20 To our God and Father be glory for ever and ever. A
1Tim 1:17 for ever and ever. A
6:16 To him be honor and eternal dominion. A
2Tim 4:18 for ever and ever A
Heb 13:21 for ever and ever A
13:25 Grace be with all of you. A
1Pet 4:11 for ever and ever A
5:11 for ever and ever A
2Pet 3:18 both now and to the day of eternity. A
Jude 1:25 before all time and now and for ever. A
Rev 1:6 for ever and ever A
1:7 Even so. A
3:14 'The words of the A, the faithful and true
5:14 And the four living creatures said, A
7:12 faces before the throne and worshiped God, saying, A
7:12 for ever and ever! A
19:4 God who is seated on the throne, saying, A
22:20 A Come Lord Jesus!
22:21 with all the saints. A

AMEND (6)

Jer 7:3 the God of Israel, A your ways and your
7:5 "For if you truly A your ways and your
18:11 his evil way, and A your ways and your
26:13 Now therefore A your ways and your doings, and
35:15 his evil way, and A your doings, and do
Tit 1:4 Crete, that you might A what was defective, and

AMENDS (3)

Lev 26:41 humbled and they make A for their iniquity;
26:43 and they shall make A for their iniquity, because
Eccl 10:4 for deference will make A for great offenses.

AMETHYST (3)

Ex 28:19 an agate, and an A;
39:12 an agate, and an A;
Rev 21:20 tenth chrysoprase, the eleventh jacinth, the twelfth A

AMI

Ezra 2:57 the sons of Pochereth-hazzebaim, and the sons of A

AMID (8)

Job 4:13 A thoughts from visions of the night, when deep
30:14 wide breach they come; A the crash they roll
Is 44:4 spring up like grass A waters, like willows by
Ezek 32:20 uncircumcised.' They shall fall A those who are slain
Dan 4:15 of iron and bronze, A the tender grass of
Amos 2:2 and Moab shall die A uproar, amid shouting and
2:2 shall die amid uproar, A shouting and the sound
Zech 4:7 forward the top stone A shouts of 'Grace, grace

AMISS (4)

Lev 5:16 what he has done A in the holy thing,
Deut 32:27 their adversaries should judge A, lest they should say,
Sir 5:15 matters do not act A, and do not become
40:23 companion never meets one A, but a wife with

AMITTAI (2)

2Kgs 14:25 Jonah the son of A, the prophet, who was
Jon 1:1 Jonah the son of A, saying,

AMMAH

2Sam 2:24 to the hill of A, which lies before Giah

AMMIEL (6)

Num 13:12 the tribe of Dan, A the son of Gemalli;
2Sam 9:4 Machir the son of A, at Lo-debar."
9:5 Machir the son of A, at Lo-debar.
17:27 Machir the son of A from Lo-debar, and Barzillai
1Chr 3:5 Bath-shua, the daughter of A;
26:5 fourth, Nethanel the fifth, A the sixth, Issachar the

AMMIHUD (10)

Num 1:10 Elishama the son of A, and from Manasseh, Gamaliel
2:18 Elishama the son of A,
7:48 Elishama the son of A, the leader of the
7:53 was the offering of Elishama the son of A
10:22 over their host was Elishama the son of A
34:20 the sons of Simeon, Shemuel the son of A
34:28 of Naphtali a leader, Pedahel the son of A
2Sam 13:37 Talmai the son of A, king of Geshur.
1Chr 7:26 son, Ladan his son, A his son, Elishama his
9:4 Uthai the son of A, son of Omri, son

AMMINADAB (16)

Ex 6:23 Elisheba, the daughter of A and the sister of
Num 1:7 Nahshon the son of A;
2:3 Nahshon the son of A,
7:12 Nahshon the son of A, of the tribe of
7:17 was the offering of Nahshon the son of A
10:14 over their host was Nahshon the son of A
Ruth 4:19 of Ram, Ram of A,
4:20 Ram, Ram of Amminadab, A of Nahshon, Nahshon of
1Chr 2:10 was the father of A, and Amminadab was the
2:10 father of Amminadab, and A was the father of
6:22 The sons of Kohath: A his son, Korah his
15:10 the sons of Uzziel, A the chief, with a
15:11 Joel, Shemaiah, Eliel, and A,
Mt 1:4 Ram the father of A, and Amminadab the father
1:4 father of Amminadab, and A the father of Nahshon,
Lk 3:33 Nahshon, the son of A, the son of Admin,

AMMISHADDAI (5)

Num	1:12	Ahiezer the son of A;
	2:25	Ahiezer the son of A,
	7:66	Ahiezer the son of A, the leader of the
	7:71	was the offering of Ahiezer the son of A
	10:25	over their host was Ahiezer the son of A

AMMIZABAD

1Chr	27:6	command of the thirty; A his son was in

AMMON (16)

Deut	2:19	of the sons of A, do not harass them
	2:19	of the sons of A as a possession, because
	2:37	of the sons of A you did not draw
Judg	11:27	the people of Israel and the people of A
2Chr	20:10	behold, the men of A and Moab and Mount
	20:22	against the men of A, Moab, and Mount Seir,
	20:23	For the men of A and Moab rose against
Neh	13:23	married women of Ashdod, A, and Moab;
Jud	1:12	and the people of A, and all Judea, and
	5:2	and the commanders of A and all the governors
	7:18	and the sons of A went up and encamped
Ps	83:7	the Hagrites, Gebal and A and Amalek, Philistia with
Jer	9:26	Edom, the sons of A, Moab, and all who
	25:21	and the sons of A;
	27:3	of the sons of A, the king of Tyre,
2Mac	4:26	driven as a fugitive into the land of A

AMMONITE (12)

Deut	23:3	"No A or Moabite shall enter the assembly of
1Sam	11:1	Nahash the A went up and besieged Jabesh-gilead;
	11:2	But Nahash the A said to them, "On this
2Sam	23:37	the Gadite, Zelek the A, Naharai of Be-eroth, the
1Kgs	11:1	of Pharaoh, and Moabite, A, Edomite, Sidonian, and
1Chr	11:39	of Hagri, Zelek the A, Naharai of Be-eroth, the
Neh	2:10	Tobiah the servant, the A, heard this, it displeased
	2:19	Tobiah the servant, the A, and Geshem the Arab
	4:3	Tobiah the A was by him, and he said,
	13:1	found written that no A or Moabite should ever
Jud	6:5	"But you, Achior, you A hireling, who have said
	14:5	this, bring Achior the A to me, and let

AMMONITES (103)

Gen	19:38	the father of the A to this day.
Num	21:24	far as to the A; for Jazer was the
	21:24	Ammonites; for Jazer was the boundary of the A
Deut	2:20	lived there, but the A call them Zamzummim,
	3:11	iron; is it not in Rabbah of the A
	3:16	the boundary of the A;
Josh	12:2	the boundary of the A, that is, half of
	13:10	the boundary of the A;
	13:25	the land of the A, to Aroer, which is
Judg	3:13	gathered to himself the A and the Amalekites, and
	10:6	the gods of the A, and the gods of
	10:7	the hand of the A,
	10:9	And the A crossed the Jordan to fight also
	10:11	the Amorites, from the A and from the Philistines?
	10:17	Then the A were called to arms, and they
	10:18	man that will begin to fight against the A
	11:4	After a time the A made war against Israel.
	11:5	And when the A made war against Israel, the
	11:6	our leader, that we may fight with the A
	11:8	and fight with the A, and be our head
	11:9	to fight with the A, and the LORD gives
	11:12	the king of the A and said, "What have
	11:13	the king of the A answered the messengers of
	11:14	the king of the A
	11:15	the land of the A,
	11:28	the king of the A did not heed the
	11:29	Mizpah of Gilead he passed on to the A
	11:30	thou wilt give the A into my hand,
	11:31	return victorious from the A, shall be the LORDs,
	11:32	crossed over to the A to fight against them;
	11:33	So the A were subdued before the people of
	11:36	has avenged you on your enemies, on the A
	12:1	to fight against the A, and did not call
	12:2	great feud with the A; and when I called
	12:3	crossed over against the A, and the LORD gave
1Sam	11:11	and cut down the A until the heat of
	12:12	the king of the A came against you, you
	14:47	against Moab, against the A, against Edom, against
2Sam	8:12	from Edom, Moab, the A, the Philistines, Amalek,
	10:1	the king of the A died, and Hanun his
	10:2	David's servants came into the land of the A
	10:3	the princes of the A said to Hanun their
	10:6	When the A saw that they had become odious
	10:6	odious to David, the A sent and hired the
	10:8	And the A came out and drew up in
	10:10	his brother, and he arrayed them against the A
	10:11	me; but if the A are too strong for
	10:14	And when the A saw that the Syrians fled,
	10:14	from fighting against the A, and came to Jerusalem.
	10:19	feared to help the A any more.
	11:1	and they ravaged the A, and besieged Rabbah.
	12:9	have slain him with the sword of the A
	12:26	against Rabbah of the A, and took the royal
	12:31	he did to all the cities of the A
	17:27	from Rabbah of the A, and Machir the son
1Kgs	11:5	and after Milcom the abomination of the A
	11:7	the abomination of the A, on the mountain east
	11:33	the god of the A, and has not walked
2Kgs	23:13	Moab, and for Milcom the abomination of the A
	24:2	and bands of the A, and sent them against
1Chr	18:11	Edom, Moab, the A, the Philistines, and Amalek.
	19:1	the king of the A died, and his son
	19:2	the land of the A, to console him.
	19:3	the princes of the A said to Hanun, "Do
	19:6	When the A saw that they had made themselves
	19:6	David, Hanun and the A sent a thousand talents
	19:7	And the A were mustered from their cities and
	19:9	And the A came out and drew up in
	19:11	his brother, and they were arrayed against the A
	19:12	me; but if the A are too strong for
	19:15	And when the A saw that the Syrians fled,
	19:19	willing to help the A any more.
	20:1	the country of the A, and came and besieged
	20:3	David did to all the cities of the A
2Chr	20:1	this the Moabites and A, and with them some
	26:8	The A paid tribute to Uzziah, and his fame
	27:5	the king of the A and prevailed against them.
	27:5	And the A gave him that year a hundred
	27:5	The A paid him the same amount in the
Ezra	9:1	Perizzites, the Jebusites, the A, the Moabites, the
Neh	4:7	the Arabs and the A and the Ashdodites heard
Jud	5:5	leader of all the A, said to him, "Let
	7:17	the army of the A moved forward, together with
Is	11:14	and Moab, and the A shall obey them.
Jer	40:11	Moab and among the A and in Edom and
	40:14	the king of the A has sent Ishmael the
	41:10	and set out to cross over to the A
	41:15	Johanan with eight men, and went to the A
	49:1	Concerning the A
	49:2	against Rabbah of the A; it shall become a
	49:6	the fortunes of the A, says the LORD."
Ezek	21:20	to Rabbah of the A and to Judah and
	21:28	Lord GOD concerning the A, and concerning their
	25:2	your face toward the A, and prophesy against them.
	25:3	Say to the A, Hear the word of the
	25:5	the cities of the A a fold for flocks.
	25:10	it along with the A to the people of
Dan	11:41	and Moab and the main part of the A
Amos	1:13	three transgressions of the A, and for four, I
Zeph	2:8	the revilings of the A, how they have taunted
	2:9	like Sodom, and the A like Gomorrah, a land
1Mac	5:6	over to attack the A, where he found a
2Mac	5:7	and fled again into the country of the A

AMMONITESS (4)

1Kgs	14:21	His mother's name was Naamah the A
	14:31	His mother's name was Naamah the A
2Chr	12:13	His mother's name was Naamah the A
	24:26	son of Shimeath the A, and Jehozabad the son

AMNON (28)

2Sam	3:2	Hebron: his first-born was A, of Ahino-am of Jezreel;
	13:1	and after a time A, David's son, loved her.
	13:2	And A was so tormented that he made himself
	13:2	it seemed impossible to A to do anything to
	13:3	But A had a friend, whose name was Jonadab,
	13:4	A said to him, "I love Tamar, my brother
	13:6	So A lay down, and pretended to be ill;
	13:6	came to see him, A said to the king,
	13:7	"Go to your brother A's house, and prepare food
	13:8	went to her brother A's house, where he was
	13:9	And A said, "Send out every one from me."
	13:10	Then A said to Tamar, "Bring the food into
	13:10	into the chamber to A her brother.
	13:15	Then A hated her with very great hatred; so
	13:15	And A said to her, "Arise, be gone."
	13:20	said to her, "Has A your brother been with
	13:22	But Absalom spoke to A neither good nor bad;
	13:22	bad; for Absalom hated A, because he had forced

13:26 pray let my brother A go with us." And
13:27 him until he let A and all the king's
13:28 his servants, "Mark when A's heart is merry with
13:28 say to you, 'Strike A then kill him.
13:29 of Absalom did to A as Absalom had commanded.
13:32 the king's sons, for A alone is dead, for
13:33 sons are dead; for A alone is dead."
13:39 he was comforted about A, seeing he was dead.
1Chr 3:1 the first-born A, by Ahino-am the Jezreelitess;
4:20 The sons of Shimon: A, Rinnah, Ben-hanan, and

AMOK (2)

Neh 12:7 Shemaiah, Joiarib, Jedaiah, Sallu, A, Hilkiah,
12:20 of Sallai, Kallai; of A, Eber;

AMON (18)

1Kgs 22:26 take him back to A the governor of the
2Kgs 21:18 garden of Uzza; and A his son reigned in
21:19 A was twenty-two years old when he began to
21:23 And the servants of A conspired against him, and
21:24 had conspired against King A, and the people of
21:25 of the acts of A which he did, are
1Chr 3:14 son, Manasseh his son, A his son, Josiah his
2Chr 18:25 take him back to A the governor of the
33:20 in his house; and A his son reigned in
33:21 A was twenty-two years old when he began to
33:22 A sacrificed to all the images that Manasseh his
33:23 humbled himself, but this A incurred guilt more and
33:25 had conspired against King A; and the people of
Neh 7:59 the sons of Pochereth-hazzebaim, the sons of A
Jer 1:2 Josiah the son of A, king of Judah, in
25:3 Josiah the son of A, king of Judah, to
46:25 bringing punishment upon A of Thebes, and Pharaoh,
Zeph 1:1 Josiah the son of A, king of Judah.

AMORITE (8)

Gen 14:13 oaks of Mamre the A, brother of Eshcol and
Num 21:29 daughters captives, to an A king, Sihon.
Deut 2:24 your hand Sihon the A, king of Heshbon, and
Neh 9:8 Canaanite, the Hittite, the A, the Perizzite, the
Ezek 16:3 your father was an A, and your mother a
16:45 mother was a Hittite and your father an A
Amos 2:9 "Yet I destroyed the A before them, whose height
2:10 the wilderness, to possess the land of the A

AMORITES (81)

Gen 10:16 and the Jebusites, the A, the Girgashites,
14:7 and also the A who dwelt in Hazazon-tamar.
15:16 the iniquity of the A is not yet complete."
15:21 Perizzites, the Rephaim, the A, the Canaanites, the
48:22 the hand of the A with my sword and
Ex 3:8 Canaanites, the Hittites, the A, the Perizzites, the
3:17 Canaanites, the Hittites, the A, the Perizzites, the
13:5 Canaanites, the Hittites, the A, the Hivites, and the
23:23 you in to the A, and the Hittites, and
33:2 out the Canaanites, the A, the Hittites, the Perizzites,
34:11 out before you the A, the Canaanites, the Hittites,
Num 13:29 the Jebusites, and the A dwell in the hill
21:13 the boundary of the A; for the Arnon is
21:13 the boundary of Moab, between Moab and the A
21:21 Sihon king of the A, saying,
21:25 the cities of the A, in Heshbon, and in
21:26 the king of the A, who had fought against
21:31 Thus Israel dwelt in the land of the A
21:32 villages, and dispossessed the A that were there.
21:34 Sihon king of the A, who dwelt at Heshbon."
22:2 saw all that Israel had done to the A
32:33 Sihon king of the A and the kingdom of
32:39 it, and dispossessed the A who were in it.
Deut 1:4 the king of the A, who lived in Heshbon,
1:7 hill country of the A, and to all their
1:19 hill country of the A, as the LORD our
1:20 hill country of the A, which the LORD our
1:27 the hand of the A, to destroy us.
1:44 Then the A who lived in that hill country
3:2 the king of the A, who dwelt at Heshbon.'
3:8 two kings of the A who were beyond the
3:9 Hermon Sirion, while the A call it Senir),
4:46 the king of the A, who lived at Heshbon,
4:47 two kings of the A, who lived to the
7:1 Hittites, the Girgashites, the A, the Canaanites, the
20:17 the Hittites and the A, the Canaanites and the
31:4 the kings of the A, and to their land,
Josh 2:10 two kings of the A that were beyond the
3:10 Perizzites, the Girgashites, the A, and the Jebusites.
5:1 the kings of the A that were beyond the
7:7 the hands of the A, to destroy us?
9:1 Lebanon, the Hittites, the A, the Canaanites, the
9:10 two kings of the A who were beyond the
10:5 five kings of the A, the king of Jerusalem,
10:6 the kings of the A that dwell in the
10:12 the LORD gave the A over to the men
11:3 and the west, the A, the Hittites, the Perizzites,
12:2 Sihon king of the A who dwelt at Heshbon,
12:8 of the Hittites, the A, the Canaanites, the Perizzites,
13:4 the boundary of the A,
13:10 Sihon king of the A, who reigned in Heshbon,
13:21 Sihon king of the A, who reigned in Heshbon,
24:8 the land of the A, who lived on the
24:11 you, and also the A, the Perizzites, the Canaanites,
24:12 two kings of the A; it was not by
24:15 the gods of the A in whose land you
24:18 all the peoples, the A who lived in the
Judg 1:34 The A pressed the Danites back into the hill
1:35 to the plain; the A persisted in dwelling in
1:36 the border of the A ran from the ascent
3:5 Canaanites, the Hittites, the A, the Perizzites, the
6:10 the gods of the A, in whose land you
10:8 the land of the A, which is in Gilead.
10:11 Egyptians and from the A, from the Ammonites and
11:19 Sihon king of the A, king of Heshbon; and
11:21 the land of the A, who inhabited that country.
11:22 the territory of the A from the Arnon to
11:23 of Israel, dispossessed the A from before his people
1Sam 7:14 There was peace also between Israel and the A
2Sam 21:2 the remnant of the A; although the people of
1Kgs 4:19 Sihon king of the A and of Og king
9:20 were left of the A, the Hittites, the Perizzites,
21:26 after idols, as the A had done, whom the
2Kgs 21:11 than all that the A did, who were before
1Chr 1:14 and the Jebusites, the A, the Girgashites,
2Chr 8:7 of the Hittites, the A, the Perizzites, the Hivites,
Ezra 9:1 Ammonites, the Moabites, the Egyptians, and the A
Jud 5:15 the land of the A, and by their might
Ps 135:11 Sihon, king of the A, and Og, king of
136:19 Sihon, king of the A, for his steadfast love
Is 17:9 the Hivites and the A, which they deserted because

AMOS (11)

Tob 2:6 remembered the prophecy of A, how he said, "Your
Amos 1:1 The words of A, who was among the
7:8 LORD said to me, A, what do you see?"
7:10 king of Israel, saying, A has conspired against you
7:11 For thus A has said, 'Jeroboam shall die by
7:12 And Amaziah said to A, "O seer, go, flee
7:14 Then A answered Amaziah, "I am no prophet, nor
8:2 And he said, A, what do you see?" And
Mt 1:10 Manasseh the father of A, and Amos the father
1:10 father of Amos, and A the father of Josiah,
Lk 3:25 Mattathias, the son of A, the son of Nah,

AMOUNT (12)

Lev 27:23 man shall give the A of the valuation on
2Sam 12:30 the spoil of the city, a very great A
1Kgs 9:28 there gold, to the A of four hundred and
10:11 Ophir a very great A of almug wood and
2Kgs 22:4 he may reckon the A of the money which
1Chr 20:2 the spoil of the city, a very great A
2Chr 27:5 paid him the same A in the second and
Jud 2:18 man, and a huge A of gold and silver
15:7 plain got a great A of booty, for there
1Mac 9:35 with them the great A of baggage which they
2Mac 3:6 money, so that the A of the funds could
12:43 by man, to the A of two thousand drachmas

AMOUNTS

1Mac 3:41 and gold in immense A, and fetters, and went

AMOZ (13)

2Kgs 19:2 sackcloth, to the prophet Isaiah the son of A
19:20 Isaiah the son of A sent to Hezekiah, saying,
20:1 prophet the son of A came to him, and
2Chr 26:22 prophet the son of A wrote.
32:20 prophet, the son of A, prayed because of this
32:32 prophet the son of A, in the Book of
Is 1:1 Isaiah the son of A, which he saw concerning
2:1 Isaiah the son of A saw concerning Judah and
13:1 Isaiah the son of A saw.
20:2 Isaiah the son of A, saying, "Go, and loose
37:2 sackcloth, to the prophet Isaiah the son of A
37:21 Isaiah the son of A sent to Hezekiah, saying,
38:1 prophet the son of A came to him, and

AMPHIPOLIS
Acts 17:1 they had passed through A and Apollonia, they came

AMPLE (4)
Sir 31:19 How A a little is for a well-disciplined man!
47:23 one of his sons, A in folly and lacking
Lk 12:19 soul, Soul, you have A goods laid up for
Phil 1:26 me you may have A cause to glory in

AMPLIATUS
Rom 16:8 Greet A, my beloved in the Lord.

AMPLY
Sir 47:12 wise son who fared A because of him;

AMRAM (14)
Ex 6:18 The sons of Kohath: A, Izhar, Hebron, and Uzziel,
6:20 A took to wife Jochebed his father's sister and
6:20 of the life of A being one hundred and
Num 3:19 Kohath by their families: A, Izhar, Hebron, and
26:58 And Kohath was the father of A
26:59 The name of A's wife was Jochebed the daughter
26:59 and she bore to A Aaron and Moses and
1Chr 6:2 The sons of Kohath: A, Izhar, Hebron, and Uzziel.
6:3 The children of A: Aaron, Moses, and Miriam.
6:18 The sons of Kohath: A, Izhar, Hebron, and Uzziel.
23:12 The sons of Kohath: A, Izhar, Hebron, and Uzziel,
23:13 The sons of A: Aaron and Moses.
24:20 of the sons of A, Shuba-el; of the sons
Ezra 10:34 sons of Bani: Ma-adai, A, Uel,

AMRAMITES (2)
Num 3:27 the family of the A, and the family of
1Chr 26:23 Of the A, the Izharites, the Hebronites, and the

AMRAPHEL (2)
Gen 14:1 In the days of A king of Shinar, Arioch
14:9 Tidal king of Goiim, A king of Shinar, and

AMULETS
Is 3:20 perfume boxes, and the A;

AMUSE
Sir 32:12 A yourself there, and do what you have in

AMZI (2)
1Chr 6:46 of Hilkiah, son of A, son of Bani, son
Neh 11:12 of Pelaliah, son of A, son of Zechariah, son

ANAB (2)
Josh 11:21 Hebron, from Debir, from A, and from all the
15:50 Kiriath-sannah (that is, Debir), A, Eshtemoh, Anim,

ANAEL
Tob 1:21 son of my brother A, over all the accounts

ANAH (12)
Gen 36:2 Oholibamah the daughter of A the son of Zibeon
36:14 Oholibamah the daughter of A the son of Zibeon,
36:18 Oholibamah the daughter of A, Esau's wife.
36:20 land: Lotan, Shobal, Zibeon, A,
36:24 of Zibeon: Aiah and A; he is the Anah
36:24 Anah; he is the A who found the hot
36:25 are the children of A: Dishon and Oholibamah the
36:25 of Anah: Dishon and Oholibamah the daughter of A
36:29 chiefs Lotan, Shobal, Zibeon, A,
1Chr 1:38 Seir: Lotan, Shobal, Zibeon, A, Dishon, Ezer, and
1:40 The sons of Zibeon: Aiah and A
1:41 The sons of A: Dishon.

ANAHARATH
Josh 19:19 Chesulloth, Shunem, Haphara-im, Shion, A,

ANAIAH (2)
Neh 8:4 him stood Mattithiah, Shema, A, Uriah, Hilkiah, and
10:22 Zadok, Jaddu-a, Pelatiah, Hanan, A,

ANAK (9)
Num 13:22 Talmai, the descendants of A, were there.
13:28 saw the descendants of A there.
13:33 Nephilim (the sons of A, who come from the
Deut 9:2 before the sons of A
Josh 15:13 that is, Hebron (Arba was the father of A
15:14 the three sons of A, Sheshai and Ahiman and
15:14 and Ahiman and Talmai, the descendants of A
21:11 being the father of A, that is Hebron, in
Judg 1:20 drove out from it the three sons of A

ANAKIM (10)
Deut 1:28 the sons of the A there.'"
2:10 and tall as the A;
2:11 the Anakim; like the A they are also known
2:21 and tall as the A; but the LORD destroyed
9:2 the sons of the A, whom you know, and
Josh 11:21 and wiped out the A from the hill country,
11:22 was none of the A left in the land
14:12 that day how the A were there, with great
14:15 this Arba was the greatest man among the A
Jer 47:5 O remnant of the A, how long will you

ANAMIM (2)
Gen 10:13 the father of Ludim, A, Lehabim, Naph-tuhim,
1Chr 1:11 the father of Ludim, A, Lehabim, Naph-tuhim,

ANAMMELECH
2Kgs 17:31 fire to Adrammelech and A, the gods of Sepharvaim.

ANAN
Neh 10:26 Hashabnah, Ma-aseiah, Ahiah, Hanan, A,

ANANI
1Chr 3:24 Akkub, Johanan, Delaiah, and A, seven.

ANANIAH (2)
Neh 3:23 of Ma-aseiah, son of A repaired beside his own
11:32 its villages, Anathoth, Nob, A,

ANANIAS (14)
Tob 5:12 son of the great A, one of your relatives."
5:13 I used to know A and Jathan, the sons
Jud 8:1 of Elkiah, son of A, son of Gideon, son
Acts 5:1 But a man named A with his wife Sapphira
5:3 But Peter said, A, why has Satan filled your
5:5 When A heard these words, he fell down and
9:10 Now there was a disciple at Damascus named A
9:10 The Lord said to him in a vision, A
9:12 seen a man named A come in and lay
9:13 But A answered, "Lord, I have heard from many
9:17 So A departed and entered the house.
22:12 "And one A, a devout man according to the
23:2 And the high priest A commanded those who stood
24:1 days the high priest A came down with some

ANANIEL
Tob 1:1 of Tobiel, son of A, son of Aduel, son

ANATH (2)
Judg 3:31 Shamgar the son of A, who killed six hundred
5:6 of Shamgar, son of A, in the days of

ANATHOTH (20)
Josh 21:18 with its pasture lands, A with its pasture lands,
2Sam 23:27 of Tekoa, Abi-ezer, of A, Mebunnai the Hushathite,
1Kgs 2:26 king said, "Go to A, to your estate; for
1Chr 6:60 its pasture lands, and A with its pasture lands.
7:8 Eli-o-enai, Omri, Jeremoth, Abijah, A, and Alemeth.
11:28 of Tekoa, Abi-ezer of A,
12:3 Azmaveth; Beracah, Jehu of A,
27:12 month, was Abi-ezer of A, a Benjaminite; in his
Ezra 2:23 The men of A, one hundred and twenty-eight.
Neh 7:27 The men of A, a hundred and twenty-eight.
10:19 Hodiah, Hashum, Bezai, Hariph, A, Nebai,
11:32 Bethel and its villages, A, Nob, Ananiah,
Is 10:30 Answer her, O A
Jer 1:1 priests who were in A in the land of
11:21 concerning the men of A, who seek your life,
11:23 upon the men of A, the year of their
29:27 not rebuked Jeremiah of A who is prophesying to
32:7 field which is at A, for the right of
32:8 field which is at A in the land of
32:9 bought the field at A from Hanamel my cousin,

ANCESTOR (3)
Josh 19:47 Leshem, Dan, after the name of Dan their A
Judg 18:29 name of Dan their A, who was born to
Heb 7:10 the loins of his A when Melchizedek met him.

ANCESTORS (5)
Jud 5:8 the ways of their A, and they worshiped the
Esth 14:5 from among all their A, for an everlasting
Sir 8:4 ill-bred person, lest your A be disgraced.
2Mac 8:19 help came to their A; both the time of

11:25 they live according to the customs of their A

ANCESTRAL (4)
Num 1:16 the leaders of their A tribes, the heads of
1:47 not numbered by their A tribe along with them.
2Mac 8:17 the overthrow of their A way of life.
14:7 have laid aside my A glory – I

ANCHOR (2)
Acts 27:13 their purpose, they weighed A and sailed along Crete,
Heb 6:19 a sure and steadfast A of the soul, a

ANCHORS (3)
Acts 27:29 they let out four A from the stern, and
27:30 pretense of laying out A from the bow,
27:40 they cast off the A and left them in

ANCIENT (28)
Deut 33:15 finest produce of the A mountains, and the
1Chr 4:22 and returned to Lehem (now the records are A
Esth 16:7 much from the more A records which we hand
Ps 24:7 be lifted up, O A doors!
24:9 be lifted up, O A doors!
68:33 in the heavens, the A heavens; lo, he sends
Prov 22:28 Remove not the A landmark which your fathers have
23:10 Do not remove an A landmark or enter the
Wis 13:10 the work of an A hand.
Sir 2:10 Consider the A generations and see: who ever
16:7 not propitiated for the A giants who revolted in
Is 19:11 wise, a son of A kings"?
46:10 the beginning and from A times things not yet
58:12 And your A ruins shall be rebuilt; you shall
61:4 shall build up the A ruins, they shall raise
Jer 5:15 nation, it is an A nation, a nation whose
6:16 and ask for the A paths, where the good
18:15 their ways, in the A roads, and have gone
28:8 you and me from A times prophesied war, famine,
Ezek 36:2 you, 'Aha!' and, 'The A heights have become our
Dan 7:9 and one that was A of days took his
7:13 he came to the A of Days and was
7:22 over them, until the A of Days came, and
Mic 5:2 from of old, from A days.
1Mac 15:17 allies to renew our A friendship and alliance.
2Pet 2:5 did not spare the A world, but preserved Noah,
Rev 12:9 was thrown down, that A serpent, who is called
20:2 seized the dragon, that A serpent, who is the

ANCIENTS (2)
1Sam 24:13 the proverb of the A says, 'Out of the
Sir 39:1 wisdom of all the A, and will be concerned

ANDREW (13)
Mt 4:18 is called Peter and A his brother, casting a
10:2 is called Peter, and A his brother; James the
Mk 1:16 he saw Simon and A the brother of Simon
1:29 house of Simon and A, with James and John.
3:18 is, sons of thunder; A, and Philip, and Bartholomew,
13:3 James and John and A asked him privately,
Lk 6:14 he named Peter, and A his brother, and James
Jn 1:40 and followed him, was A, Simon Peter's brother.
1:44 Beth-saida, the city of A and Peter.
6:8 One of his disciples, A, Simon Peter's brother, said
12:22 Philip went and told A; Andrew went with Philip
12:22 went and told Andrew; A went with Philip and
Acts 1:13 John and James and A, Philip and Thomas,

ANDRONICUS (7)
2Mac 4:31 settle the trouble, leaving A, a man of high
4:32 and gave them to A; other vessels, as it
4:34 Therefore Menelaus, taking A aside, urged him to
4:34 A came to Onias, and resorting to treachery offered
4:38 the purple robe from A, tore off his garments,
5:23 him; and at Gerizim, A; and besides these Menelaus,
Rom 16:7 Greet A and Junias, my kinsmen and my fellow

ANEM
1Chr 6:73 its pasture lands, and A with its pasture lands;

ANER (3)
Gen 14:13 of Eshcol and of A; these were allies of
14:24 went with me; let A, Eshcol, and Mamre take
1Chr 6:70 the half-tribe of Manasseh, A with its pasture lands,

ANEW (7)
Wis 19:6 its nature was fashioned A, complying with thy
Sir 36:6 Show signs A, and work further wonders; make thy
1Mac 15:25 the king besieged Dor A, continually throwing his
Jn 3:3 unless one is born A, he cannot see the
3:7 'You must be born A
1Pet 1:3 we have been born A to a living hope
1:23 You have been born A, not of perishable seed

ANGEL (230)
Gen 16:7 The A of the LORD found her by a
16:9 The A of the LORD said to her, "Return
16:10 The A of the LORD also said to her,
16:11 And the A of the LORD said to her,
21:17 the lad; and the A of God called to
22:11 But the A of the LORD called to him
22:15 And the A of the LORD called to Abraham
24:7 he will send his A before you, and you
24:40 walk, will send his A with you and prosper
31:11 Then the A of God said to me in
48:16 to this day, the A who has redeemed me
Ex 3:2 And the A of the LORD appeared to him
14:19 Then the A of God who went before the
23:20 "Behold, I send an A before you, to guard
23:23 "When my A goes before you, and brings you
32:34 to you; behold, my A shall go before you.
33:2 I will send an A before you, and I
Num 20:16 voice, and sent an A and brought us forth
22:22 he went; and the A of the LORD took
22:23 the ass saw the A of the LORD standing
22:24 Then the A of the LORD stood in a
22:25 the ass saw the A of the LORD, she
22:26 Then the A of the LORD went ahead, and
22:27 the ass saw the A of the LORD, she
22:31 and he saw the A of the LORD standing
22:32 And the A of the LORD said to him,
22:34 Balaam said to the A of the LORD, "I
22:35 And the A of the LORD said to Balaam,
Judg 2:1 Now the A of the LORD went up from
2:4 When the A of the LORD spoke these words
5:23 "Curse Meroz, says the A of the LORD, curse
6:11 Now the A of the LORD came and sat
6:12 And the A of the LORD appeared to him
6:20 And the A of God said to him, "Take
6:21 Then the A of the LORD reached out the
6:21 unleavened cakes; and the A of the LORD vanished
6:22 that he was the A of the LORD; and
6:22 I have seen the A of the LORD face
13:3 And the A of the LORD appeared to the
13:6 the countenance of the A of God, very terrible;
13:9 of Manoah, and the A of God came again
13:13 And the A of the LORD said to Manoah,
13:15 Manoah said to the A of the LORD, "Pray,
13:16 And the A of the LORD said to Manoah,
13:16 that he was the A of the LORD.)
13:17 Manoah said to the A of the LORD, "What
13:18 And the A of the LORD said to him,
13:20 from the altar, the A of the LORD ascended
13:21 The A of the LORD appeared no more to
13:21 that he was the A of the LORD.
1Sam 29:9 my sight as an A of God; nevertheless the
2Sam 14:17 king is like the A of God to discern
14:20 the wisdom of the A of God to know
19:27 king is like the A of God; do therefore
24:16 And when the A stretched forth his hand toward
24:16 and said to the A who was working destruction
24:16 And the A of the LORD was by the
24:17 when he saw the A who was smiting the
1Kgs 13:18 you are, and an A spoke to me by
19:5 tree; and behold, an A touched him, and said
19:7 And the A of the LORD came again a
2Kgs 1:3 But the A of the LORD said to Elijah
1:15 Then the A of the LORD said to Elijah,
19:35 And that night the A of the LORD went
1Chr 21:12 the land, and the A of the LORD destroying
21:15 And God sent the A to Jerusalem to destroy
21:15 said to the destroying A, "It is enough; now
21:15 And the A of the LORD was standing by
21:16 eyes and saw the A of the LORD standing
21:18 Then the A of the LORD commanded Gad to
21:20 turned and saw the A, and his four sons
21:27 the LORD commanded the A; and he put his
21:30 the sword of the A of the LORD.
2Chr 32:21 the LORD sent an A, who cut off all
Tob 5:4 Raphael, who was an A,
5:6 The A replied, "I will go with you; I
5:16 way, and may his A attend you." So they
5:21 For a good A will go with him; his
6:3 young man; and the A said to him, "Catch

6:4 Then the A said to him, "Cut open the
6:5 man did as the A told him; and they
6:6 man said to the A, "Brother Azarias, of what
6:10 they approached Ecbatana, the A said to the young
6:13 man said to the A, "Brother Azarias, I have
6:15 But the A said to him, "Do you not
8:3 of Egypt, and the A bound him.
12:5 So he called the A and said to him,
12:6 Then the A called the two of them privately
12:22 and acknowledged that the A of the Lord had
Esth 15:13 my lord, like an A of God, and my
Job 33:23 be for him an A, a mediator, one of
Ps 34:7 The A of the LORD encamps around those who
35:5 the wind, with the A of the LORD driving
35:6 and slippery, with the A of the LORD pursuing
Sir 48:21 the Assyrians, and his A wiped them out.
Is 37:36 And the A of the LORD went forth, and
63:9 was afflicted, and the A of his presence saved
Bar 6:7 For my A is with you, and he is
Dan 3:49 But the A of the Lord came down into
3:96 who has sent his A and delivered his servants,
6:22 My God sent his A and shut the lions'
13:55 own head, for the A of God has received
13:59 own head, for the A of God is waiting
14:34 But the A of the Lord said to Habakkuk,
14:36 Then the A of the Lord took him by
14:39 And the A of God immediately returned Habakkuk
Hos 12:4 He strove with the A and prevailed, he wept
Zech 1:9 these, my lord?' The A who talked with me
1:11 And they answered the A of the LORD who
1:12 at rest.' Then the A of the LORD said,
1:13 comforting words to the A who talked with me.
1:14 So the A who talked with me said to
1:19 I said to the A who talked with me,
2:3 And behold, the A who talked with me came
2:3 came forward, and another A came forward to meet
3:1 priest standing before the A of the LORD, and
3:3 was standing before the A, clothed with filthy
3:4 And the A said to those who were standing
3:5 with garments; and the A of the LORD was
3:6 And the A of the LORD enjoined Joshua,
4:1 And the A who talked with me came again,
4:4 I said to the A who talked with me,
4:5 Then the A who talked with me answered me,
5:5 Then the A who talked with me came forward
5:10 I said to the A who talked with me,
6:4 I said to the A who talked with me,
6:5 And the A answered me, "These are going forth
12:8 like God, like the A of the LORD, at
1Mac 7:41 king spoke blasphemy, thy A went forth and struck
2Mac 11:6 to send a good A to save Israel.
15:22 thou didst send thy A in the time of
15:23 heavens, send a good A to carry terror and
Mt 1:20 considered this, behold, an A of the Lord appeared
1:24 he did as the A of the Lord commanded
2:13 had departed, behold, an A of the Lord appeared
2:19 Herod died, behold, an A of the Lord appeared
28:2 great earthquake; for an A of the Lord descended
28:5 But the A said to the women, "Do not
Lk 1:11 appeared to him an A of the Lord standing
1:13 But the A said to him, "Do not be
1:18 Zechariah said to the A, "How shall I know
1:19 And the A answered him, "I am Gabriel, who
1:26 the sixth month the A Gabriel was sent from
1:30 And the A said to her, "Do not be
1:34 Mary said to the A, "How shall this be,
1:35 And the A said to her, "The Holy Spirit
1:38 And the A departed from her.
2:9 And an A of the Lord appeared to them,
2:10 And the A said to them, "Be not afraid;
2:13 there was with the A a multitude of the
2:21 name given by the A before he was conceived
Jn 12:29 Others said, "An A has spoken to him."
Acts 5:19 But at night an A of the Lord opened
6:15 his face was like the face of an A
7:30 years had passed, an A appeared to him in
7:35 the hand of the A that appeared to him
7:38 the wilderness with the A who spoke to him
8:26 But an A of the Lord said to Philip,
10:3 in a vision an A of God coming in
10:7 When the A who spoke to him had departed,
10:22 directed by a holy A to send for you
11:13 he had seen the A standing in his house
12:7 prison; and behold, an A of the Lord appeared,
12:8 And the A said to him, "Dress yourself and
12:9 was done by the A was real, but thought
12:10 street; and immediately the A left him.
12:11 Lord has sent his A and rescued me from
12:15 They said, "It is his A
12:23 Immediately an A of the Lord smote him, because
23:8 is no resurrection, nor A, nor spirit; but the
23:9 a spirit or an A spoke to him?"
27:23 stood by me an A of the God to
2Cor 11:14 disguises himself as an A of light.
Gal 1:8 if we, or an A from heaven, should preach
4:14 received me as an A of God, as Christ
Heb 1:5 For to what A did God ever say, "Thou
1:13 But to what A has he ever said, "Sit
Rev 1:1 known by sending his A to his servant John,
2:1 "To the A of the church in Ephesus write:
2:8 God.' "And to the A of the church in
2:12 death.' "And to the A of the church in
2:18 it.' "And to the A of the church in
3:1 "And to the A of the church in Sardis
3:7 "And to the A of the church in Philadelphia
3:14 churches.' "And to the A of the church in
5:2 I saw a strong A proclaiming with a loud
7:2 Then I saw another A ascend from the rising
8:3 And another A came and stood at the altar
8:4 the hand of the A before God.
8:5 Then the A took the censer and filled it
8:7 The first A blew his trumpet, and there followed
8:8 The second A blew his trumpet, and something like
8:10 The third A blew his trumpet, and a great
8:12 The fourth A blew his trumpet, and a third
9:1 And the fifth A blew his trumpet, and I
9:11 king over them the A of the bottomless pit;
9:13 Then the sixth A blew his trumpet, and I
9:14 saying to the sixth A who had the trumpet,
10:1 I saw another mighty A coming down from heaven,
10:5 And the A whom I saw standing on sea
10:7 sounded by the seventh A, the mystery of God,
10:8 the hand of the A who is standing on
10:9 I went to the A and told him to
10:10 the hand of the A and ate it; it
11:15 Then the seventh A blew his trumpet, and there
14:6 Then I saw another A flying in midheaven, with
14:8 Another A, a second, followed, saying, "Fallen, fallen
14:9 And another A, a third, followed them, saying with
14:15 And another A came out of the temple, calling
14:17 And another A came out of the temple in
14:18 Then another A came out from the altar, the
14:18 from the altar, the A who has power over
14:19 So the A swung his sickle on the earth
16:2 So the first A went and poured his bowl
16:3 The second A poured his bowl into the sea,
16:4 The third A poured his bowl into the rivers
16:5 And I heard the A of water say, "Just
16:8 The fourth A poured his bowl on the sun,
16:10 The fifth A poured his bowl on the throne
16:12 The sixth A poured his bowl on the great
16:17 The seventh A poured his bowl into the air,
17:7 But the A said to me, "Why marvel?
18:1 this I saw another A coming down from heaven,
18:21 Then a mighty A took up a stone like
19:9 And the A said to me, "Write this: Blessed
19:17 Then I saw an A standing in the sun,
20:1 Then I saw an A coming down from heaven,
22:6 prophets, has sent his A to show his servants
22:8 the feet of the A who showed them to
22:16 Jesus have sent my A to you with this

ANGELS (96)

Gen 19:1 The two A came to Sodom in the evening;
19:15 morning dawned, the A urged Lot, saying, "Arise,
28:12 heaven; and behold, the A of God were ascending
32:1 his way and the A of God met him;
Tob 8:15 thee; let all thy A and thy chosen people
11:14 for ever, and blessed are all thy holy A
12:15 of the seven holy A who present the prayers
Job 4:18 no trust, and his A he charges with error;
Ps 78:25 the bread of the A; he sent them food
78:49 indignation, and distress, a company of destroying A
91:11 he will give his A charge of you to
103:20 LORD, O you his A, you mighty ones who
148:2 Praise him, all his A, praise him, all his
Wis 10:10 gave him knowledge of A; she prospered him in
16:20 thy people food of A, and without their toil
Dan 3:60 Bless the Lord, you A of the Lord, sing
Mt 4:6 'He will give his A charge of you,' and
4:11 left him, and behold, A came and ministered to
13:39 close of the age, and the reapers are A

ANGER (305)

	9:8	their power in thy A; for they intend to
	11:11	provoke their God to A when they do what
Esth	1:12	was enraged, and his A burned within him.
	2:1	these things, when the A of King Ahasuerus had
	7:10	Then the A of the king abated.
	15:7	with splendor, he looked at her in fierce A
Job	4:9	the blast of his A they are consumed.
	9:5	overturns them in his A;
	9:13	not turn back his A; beneath him bowed the
	18:4	tear yourself in your A, shall the earth be
	20:23	will send his fierce A into him, and rain
	21:17	That God distributes pains in his A
	35:15	And now, because his A does not punish, and
	36:13	godless in heart cherish A; they do not cry
	36:33	who is jealous with A against iniquity.
	40:11	the overflowings of your A, and look on every
Ps	6:1	me not in thy A, nor chasten me in
	7:6	O LORD, in thy A, lift thyself up against
	27:9	thy servant away in A, thou who hast been
	30:5	For his A is but for a moment, and
	37:8	Refrain from A, and forsake wrath!
	38:1	me not in thy A, nor chasten me in
	55:3	upon me, and in A they cherish enmity against
	69:24	and let thy burning A overtake them.
	74:1	Why does thy A smoke against the sheep of
	76:7	thee when once thy A is roused?
	77:9	Has he in A shut up his compassion?" [Selah]
	78:21	kindled against Jacob, his A mounted against Israel;
	78:31	in their mouths, the A of God rose against
	78:38	them; he restrained his A often, and did not
	78:49	on them his fierce A, wrath, indignation, and distress,
	78:50	a path for his A; he did not spare
	78:58	they provoked him to A with their high places;
	79:6	Pour out thy A on the nations that do
	85:3	thy wrath; thou didst turn from thy hot A
	85:5	Wilt thou prolong thy A to all generations?
	86:15	and gracious, slow to A and abounding in steadfast
	90:7	are consumed by thy A; by thy wrath we
	90:11	the power of thy A, and thy wrath according
	95:11	I swore in my A that they should not
	102:10	of thy indignation and A; for thou hast taken
	103:8	and gracious, slow to A and abounding in steadfast
	103:9	will he keep his A for ever.
	106:29	provoked the LORD to A with their doings, and
	106:40	Then the A of the LORD was kindled against
	124:3	up alive, when their A was kindled against us;
	145:8	and merciful, slow to A and abounding in steadfast
Prov	14:29	who is slow to A has great understanding, but
	15:1	away wrath, but a harsh word stirs up A
	15:18	who is slow to A quiets contention.
	16:32	who is slow to A is better than the
	19:11	a man slow to A, and it is his
	20:2	who provokes him to A forfeits his life.
	21:14	gift in secret averts A; and a bribe in
	22:24	a man given to A, nor go with a
	24:18	and turn away his A from him.
	27:4	Wrath is cruel, A is overwhelming; but who can
	29:11	full vent to his A, but a wise man
	29:22	a man given to A causes much transgression.
	30:33	produces blood, and pressing A produces strife.
Eccl	7:9	Be not quick to A, for anger lodges in
	7:9	quick to anger, for A lodges in the bosom
	10:4	If the A of the ruler rises against you,
Wis	10:3	from her in his A, he perished because in
	18:21	incense; he withstood the A and put an end
	19:1	the end by pitiless A, for God knew in
Sir	1:19	Unrighteous A cannot be justified, for a man's anger
	1:19	justified, for a man's A tips the scale to
	4:2	who is hungry, nor A a man in want.
	5:4	for the Lord is slow to A
	5:6	with him, and his A rests on sinners.
	10:18	for men, nor fierce A for those born of
	26:8	There is great A when a wife is drunken;
	26:19	because of a third A comes over me: a
	27:30	A and wrath, these also are abominations, and the
	28:3	Does a man harbor A against another, and yet
	28:8	a man given to A will kindle strife,
	28:10	man will be his A, and in proportion to
	28:19	been exposed to its A, who has not borne
	30:24	Jealousy and A shorten life, and anxiety brings on
	31:30	Drunkenness increases the A of a fool to his
	36:7	Rouse thy A and pour out thy wrath; destroy
	39:28	vengeance, and in their A they scourge heavily; in
	39:28	strength and calm the A of their Maker.
	40:5	in burlap; there is A and envy and trouble
	45:18	and the company of Korah, in wrath and A

	45:19	the wrath of his A they were destroyed; he
Is	5:25	Therefore the A of the LORD was kindled against
	5:25	For all this his A is not turned away
	7:4	firebrands, at the fierce A of Rezin and Syria
	9:12	For all this his A is not turned away
	9:17	For all this his A is not turned away
	9:21	For all this his A is not turned away
	10:4	For all this his A is not turned away
	10:5	the rod of my A, the staff of my
	10:25	an end, and my A will be directed to
	12:1	angry with me, thy A turned away, and thou
	13:3	men to execute my A, my proudly exulting ones.
	13:9	with wrath and fierce A, to make the earth
	13:13	of hosts in the day of his fierce A
	14:6	ruled the nations in A with unrelenting persecution.
	30:27	far, burning with his A, and in thick rising
	30:30	be seen, in furious A and a flame of
	42:25	the heat of his A and the might of
	48:9	sake I defer my A, for the sake of
	63:3	trod them in my A and trampled them in
	63:6	the peoples in my A, I made them drunk
	66:15	stormwind, to render his A in fury, and his
Jer	2:35	am innocent; surely his A has turned from me.'
	3:12	look on you in A, for I am merciful,
	4:8	wail; for the fierce A of the LORD has
	4:26	in ruins before the LORD, before his fierce A
	7:18	offerings to other gods, to provoke me to A
	7:20	Lord GOD: Behold, my A and my wrath will
	8:19	they provoked me to A with their graven images,
	10:24	measure; not in thy A, lest thou bring me
	11:17	done, provoking me to A by burning incense to
	12:13	because of the fierce A of the LORD."
	15:14	know, for in my A a fire is kindled
	17:4	know, for in my A a fire is kindled
	18:23	deal with them in the time of thine A
	21:5	and strong arm, in A, and in fury, and
	23:20	The A of the LORD will not turn back
	25:6	or provoke me to A with the work of
	25:7	might provoke me to A with the work of
	25:37	because of the fierce A of the LORD.
	25:38	of the oppressor, and because of his fierce A
	30:24	The fierce A of the LORD will not turn
	32:29	out to other gods, to provoke me to A
	32:30	but provoke me to A by the work of
	32:31	city has aroused my A and wrath, from the
	32:32	to provoke me to A --their kings and their
	32:37	drove them in my A and my wrath and
	33:5	shall smite in my A and my wrath, for
	36:7	for great is the A and wrath that the
	42:18	of Israel: As my A and my wrath were
	44:3	committed, provoking me to A, in that they went
	44:6	my wrath and my A were poured forth and
	44:8	you provoke me to A with the works of
	49:37	upon them, my fierce A, says the LORD.
	51:45	life from the fierce A of the LORD!
	52:3	Surely because of the A of the LORD things
Lam	1:12	LORD inflicted on the day of his fierce A
	2:1	the Lord in his A has set the daughter
	2:1	remembered his footstool in the day of his A
	2:3	cut down in fierce A all the might of
	2:21	the day of thy A thou hast slain them,
	2:22	the day of the A of the LORD none
	3:43	hast wrapped thyself with A and pursued us, slaying
	3:66	wilt pursue them in A and destroy them from
	4:11	poured out his hot A; and he kindled a
Bar	1:13	to this day the A of the Lord and
	2:13	Let thy A turn away from us, for we
	2:20	thou hast sent thy A and thy wrath upon
Ezek	5:13	"Thus shall my A spend itself, and I will
	5:15	judgments on you in A and fury, and with
	7:3	will let loose my A upon you, and will
	7:8	you, and spend my A against you, and judge
	8:17	land with violence, and provoke me further to A
	13:13	of rain in my A, and great hailstones in
	16:26	multiplying your harlotry, to provoke me to A
	20:8	them and spend my A against them in the
	20:21	them and spend my A against them in the
	22:20	gather you in my A and in my wrath,
	25:14	Edom according to my A and according to my
	35:11	you according to the A and envy which you
	43:8	committed, so I have consumed them in my A
Dan	9:16	righteous acts, let thy A and thy wrath turn
	11:11	the south, moved with A, shall come out and
	11:20	be broken, neither in A nor in battle.
Hos	7:7	intrigue; all night their A smolders; in the morning
	8:5	My A burns against them.

A

11:9 not execute my fierce A, I will not again
13:11 you kings in my A, and I have taken
14:4 them freely, for my A has turned from them.
Joel 2:13 and merciful, slow to A, and abounding in steadfast
Amos 1:11 all pity, and his A tore perpetually, and he
Jon 3:9 turn from his fierce A, so that we perish
4:2 and merciful, slow to A, and abounding in steadfast
Mic 5:15 And in A and wrath I will execute vengeance
7:18 does not retain his A for ever because he
Nah 1:3 LORD is slow to A and of great might,
1:6 Who can endure the heat of his A
Hab 3:8 Was thy A against the rivers, or thy indignation
3:12 in fury, thou didst trample the nations in A
Zeph 2:2 upon you the fierce A of the LORD, before
3:8 the heat of my A; for in the fire
Zech 10:3 "My A is hot against the shepherds, and I
1Mac 2:24 gave vent to righteous A; he ran and killed
2:44 down sinners in their A and lawless men in
2:49 it is a time of ruin and furious A
7:35 spoke arrogantly, and in A he swore this oath,
7:35 And he went out in great A
2Mac 4:38 and inflamed with A, he immediately stripped off
4:40 aroused and filled with A, Lysimachus armed about
10:35 of Maccabeus, fired with A because of the
13:4 of kings aroused the A of Antiochus against the
14:45 alive and aflame with A, he rose, and though
Mt 18:33 on you?' And in A his lord delivered him
Mk 3:5 around at them with A, grieved at their hardness
Lk 14:21 Then the householder in A said to his servant,
2Cor 12:20 may be quarreling, jealousy, A, selfishness, slander,
Gal 5:20 sorcery, enmity, strife, jealousy, A, selfishness,
Eph 4:26 go down on your A,
4:31 bitterness and wrath and A and clamor and slander
6:4 provoke your children to A, but bring them up
Col 3:8 put them all away: A, wrath, malice, slander, and
1Tim 2:8 lifting holy hands without A or quarreling;
Heb 11:27 being afraid of the A of the king; for
Jas 1:18 to speak, slow to A,
1:19 to anger, for the A of man does not
Rev 14:10 the cup of his A, and he shall be

ANGERED (7)

Deut 1:34 your words, and was A, and he swore,
Ezra 5:12 because our fathers had A the God of heaven,
Ps 106:32 They A him at the waters of Meribah, and
Bar 4:6 your enemies because you A God.
1Mac 3:27 reports, he was greatly A; and he sent and
15:36 And the king was greatly A
2Mac 5:17 that the Lord was A for a little while

ANGERS

Sir 3:16 a blasphemer, and whoever A his mother is cursed

ANGLE (5)

2Chr 26:9 Gate and at the A, and fortified them.
Neh 3:19 opposite the ascent to the armory at the A
3:20 another section from the A to the door of
3:24 of Azariah to the A
3:25 Uzai repaired opposite the A and the tower

ANGRY (110)

Gen 4:5 So Cain was very A, and his countenance fell.
4:6 Cain, "Why are you A, and why has your
18:30 not the Lord be A, and I will speak.
18:32 not the Lord be A, and I will speak
31:35 not my lord be A that I cannot rise
31:36 Then Jacob became A, and upbraided Laban; Jacob
34:7 were indignant and very A, because he had wrought
40:2 And Pharaoh was A with his two officers, the
41:10 When Pharaoh was A with his servants, and put
45:5 not be distressed, or A with yourselves, because you
Ex 16:20 foul; and Moses was A with them.
Lev 10:16 And he was A with Eleazar and Ithamar, the
Num 16:15 And Moses was very A, and said to the
16:22 and wilt thou be A with all the congregation?"
31:14 And Moses was A with the officers of the
Deut 1:37 LORD!' The LORD was A with me also on
3:26 But the LORD was A with me on your
4:21 Furthermore the LORD was A with me on your
9:8 the LORD was so A with you that he
9:20 the LORD was so A with Aaron that he
Josh 22:18 today he will be A with the whole congregation
Judg 18:25 heard among us, lest A fellows fall upon you,
19:2 And his concubine became A with him, and she
1Sam 15:11 And Samuel was A; and he cried to the
18:8 And Saul was very A, and this saying displeased
20:7 but if he is A, then know that evil
29:4 of the Philistines were A with him; and the
2Sam 3:8 Then Abner was very A over the words of
6:8 And David was A because the LORD had broken
13:21 heard of all these things, he was very A
19:42 Why then are you A over this matter?
22:8 the heavens trembled and quaked, because he was A
1Kgs 8:46 sin--and thou art A with them, and dost
11:9 And the LORD was A with Solomon, because his
2Kgs 5:11 But Naaman was A, and went away, saying, "Behold,
13:19 man of God was A with him, and said,
17:18 the LORD was very A with Israel, and removed
1Chr 13:11 And David was A because the LORD had broken
2Chr 6:36 sin--and thou art A with them, and dost
16:10 Then Asa was A with the seer, and put
25:10 And they became very A with Judah, and returned
25:15 Therefore the LORD was A with Amaziah and sent
26:19 Then Uzziah was A
26:19 and when he became A with the priests leprosy
28:9 of your fathers, was A with Judah, he gave
Ezra 9:14 Wouldst thou not be A with us till thou
Neh 4:1 the wall, he was A and greatly enraged, and
4:7 closed, they were very A;
5:6 I was very A when I heard their outcry
13:8 And I was very A, and I threw all
Tob 5:13 Do not be A with me because I tried
Jud 1:12 Then Nebuchadnezzar was very A with this whole
5:2 up barricades in the plains, he was very A
Esth 2:21 guarded the threshold, became A and sought to lay
Job 32:2 the Buzite, of the family of Ram, became A
32:2 He was A at Job because he justified himself
32:3 than God; he was A also at Job's three
32:5 the mouth of these three men, he became A
Ps 2:12 feet, lest he be A, and you perish in
4:4 Be A, but sin not; commune with your own
18:7 mountains trembled and quaked, because he was A
60:1 defenses; thou hast been A; oh, restore us.
79:5 Wilt thou be A for ever?
80:4 long wilt thou be A with thy people's prayers?
85:5 Wilt thou be A with us for ever?
112:10 sees it and is A; he gnashes his teeth
Prov 22:14 whom the LORD is A will fall into it.
25:23 and a backbiting tongue, A looks.
Eccl 5:6 why should God be A at your voice, and
Song 1:6 My mother's sons were A with me, they made
Sir 4:3 the troubles of an A mind, nor delay your
10:6 Do not be A with your neighbor for any
20:2 better it is to reprove than to stay A
28:7 and do not be A with your neighbor; remember
Is 12:1 for though thou wast A with me, thy anger
47:6 I was A with my people, I profaned my
54:9 I will not be A with you and will
57:16 will I always be A; for from me proceeds
57:17 his covetousness I was A, I smote him, I
57:17 my face and was A; but he went on
64:5 Behold, thou wast A, and we sinned; in our
64:9 Be not exceedingly A, O LORD, and remember not
Jer 3:5 will he be A for ever, will he
3:12 I will not be A for ever.
Lam 5:22 Art thou exceedingly A with us?
Ezek 16:42 will be calm, and will no more be A
Dan 2:12 this the king was A and very furious, and
14:8 Then the king was A, and he called his
Jon 4:1 But it displeased Jonah exceedingly, and he was A
4:4 LORD said, "Do you do well to be A
4:9 do well to be A for the plant?" And
4:9 do well to be A, angry enough to die."
4:9 well to be angry, A enough to die."
Zech 1:2 "The LORD was very A with your fathers.
1:15 And I am very A with the nations that
1:15 for while I was A but a little they
Mal 1:4 whom the LORD is A for ever."
1Mac 5:1 before, they became very A,
6:59 abolished that they became A and did all these
11:22 heard this he was A, and as soon as
2Mac 7:33 our living Lord is A for a little while,
13:25 fact they were so A that they wanted to
Mt 5:22 every one who is A with his brother shall
22:7 The king was A, and he sent his troops
Lk 15:28 sound.' But he was A and refused to go
Jn 7:23 be broken, are you A with me because on
Acts 12:20 Now Herod was A with the people of Tyre
Rom 10:19 with a foolish nation I will make you A
Eph 4:26 Be A but do not sin; do not let
Rev 12:17 Then the dragon was A with the woman, and

ANGUISH (47)

Deut 2:25 tremble and be in A because of you.'
2Sam 1:9 and slay me; for A has seized me, and
Tob 3:1 and I prayed in A, saying,
Job 7:11 will speak in the A of my spirit; I
15:24 his hand; distress and A terrify him; they prevail
Ps 48:6 hold of them there, A as of a woman
55:4 My heart is in A within me, the terrors
116:3 laid hold on me; I suffered distress and A
119:143 Trouble and A have come upon me, but thy
Prov 1:27 whirlwind, when distress and A come upon you.
Wis 4:19 and they will suffer A, and the memory of
5:3 in repentance, and in A of spirit they will
Sir 48:19 and they were in A, like women in travail.
Is 8:22 darkness, the gloom of A; and they will be
9:1 be no gloom for her that was in A
13:8 they will be in A like a woman in
21:3 loins are filled with A; pangs have seized me,
23:5 they will be in A over the report about
30:6 land of trouble and A, from where come the
65:14 and shall wail for A of spirit.
Jer 4:19 My A, my anguish!
4:19 My anguish, my A
4:31 a woman in travail, A as of one bringing
5:3 but they felt no A; thou hast consumed them,
6:24 our hands fall helpless; A has taken hold of
15:8 noonday; I have made A and terror fall upon
49:24 and panic seized her; A and sorrows have taken
50:43 his hands fell helpless; A seized him, pain as
Bar 3:1 Israel, the soul in A and the wearied spirit
Ezek 7:25 When A comes, they will seek peace, but there
30:4 come upon Egypt, and A shall be in Ethiopia,
30:9 the unsuspecting Ethiopians; and A shall come upon
Dan 6:20 in a tone of A and said to Daniel,
Joel 2:6 them peoples are in A, all faces grow pale.
Nah 2:10 faint and knees tremble, A is on all loins,
Zeph 1:15 day of distress and A, a day of ruin
Zech 9:5 and shall writhe in A; Ekron also, because its
2Mac 3:16 his color disclosed the A of his soul.
3:21 anxiety of the high priest in his great A
9:9 was still living in A and pain, his flesh
Lk 16:24 for I am in A in this flame.'
16:25 he is comforted here, and you are in A
Jn 16:21 no longer remembers the A, for joy that a
Rom 9:2 great sorrow and unceasing A in my heart.
2Cor 2:4 of much affliction and A of heart and with
Rev 12:2 pangs of birth, in A for delivery.
16:10 gnawed their tongues in A

ANIAM

1Chr 7:19 sons of Shemida were Ahian, Shechem, Likhi, and A

ANIM

Josh 15:50 is, Debir), Anab, Eshtemoh, A,

ANIMAL (17)

Gen 8:20 took of every clean A and of every clean
43:16 house, and slaughter an A and make ready, for
Lev 3:1 if he offers an A from the herd, male
3:6 the LORD is an A from the flock, male
7:24 The fat of an A that dies of itself,
7:25 the fat of an A of which an offering
7:26 of fowl or of A, in any of your
11:26 Every A which parts the hoof but is not
11:39 "And if any A of which you may eat
22:24 Any A which has its testicles bruised or crushed
27:9 "If it is an A such as men offer
27:11 it is an unclean A such as is not
27:11 man shall bring the A before the priest,
27:27 it is an unclean A, then he shall buy
27:32 and flocks, every tenth A of all that pass
Deut 14:6 Every A that parts the hoof and has the
Wis 13:14 it like some worthless A, giving it a coat

ANIMALS (39)

Gen 3:14 and above all wild A; upon your belly you
6:20 kinds, and of the A according to their kinds,
7:2 pairs of all clean A, the male and his
7:2 a pair of the A that are not clean,
7:8 Of clean A, and of animals that are not
7:8 clean animals, and of A that are not clean,
7:23 the ground, man and A and creeping things and
8:17 all flesh--birds and A and every creeping thing
29:7 not time for the A to be gathered together;
Lev 11:3 the cud, among the A, you may eat.
11:27 their paws, among the A that go on all
22:22 A blind or disabled or mutilated or having a
22:25 your God any such A gotten from a foreigner.
27:26 "But a firstling of A, which as a firstling
Deut 14:4 These are the A you may eat: the ox,
14:6 the cud, among the A, you may eat.
1Kgs 18:5 mules alive, and not lose some of the A
Wis 7:20 stars, the natures of A and the tempers of
11:15 irrational serpents and worthless A, thou didst send
12:24 accepting as gods those A which even their enemies
13:10 skill, and likenesses of A, or a useless stone,
15:18 even the most hateful A, which are worse than
15:19 intelligence; and even as A they are not so
16:1 creatures, and were tormented by a multitude of A
17:19 unseen running of leaping A, or the sound of
19:10 how instead of producing A the earth brought forth
19:19 For land A were transformed into water creatures,
Jer 27:5 with the men and A that are on the
Mal 1:8 When you offer blind A in sacrifice, is that
1Mac 1:47 sacrifice swine and unclean A,
2Mac 5:27 the mountains as wild A do; they continued to
10:6 wandering in the mountains and caves like wild A
Acts 10:12 were all kinds of A and reptiles and birds
11:6 it closely I observed A and beasts of prey
Rom 1:23 man or birds or A or reptiles.
1Cor 15:39 for men, another for A, another for birds, and
Heb 13:11 the bodies of those A whose blood is brought
2Pet 2:12 But these, like irrational A, creatures of instinct, born
Jude 1:10 by instinct as irrational A do, they are destroyed.

ANKLE-DEEP

Ezek 47:3 led me through the water; and it was A

ANKLES

Acts 3:7 immediately his feet and A were made strong.

ANKLETS (2)

Jud 10:4 and put on her A and bracelets and rings,
Is 3:18 the finery of the A, the headbands, and the

ANNA (9)

Tob 1:9 a man I married A, a member of our
1:20 me except my wife A and my son Tobias.
2:1 home and my wife A and my son Tobias
2:11 Then my wife A earned money at women's work.
5:17 But A, his mother, began to weep, and said
11:5 Now A sat looking intently down the road for
11:9 Then A ran to meet them, and embraced her
14:12 And when A died he buried her with his
Lk 2:36 there was a prophetess, A, the daughter of Phanu-el,

ANNAS (4)

Lk 3:2 in the high-priesthood of A and Caiaphas, the word
Jn 18:13 they led him to A; for he was the
18:24 A then sent him bound to Caiaphas the high
Acts 4:6 together in Jerusalem, with A the high priest and

ANNEXED

1Mac 10:38 let them be so A to Judea that they

ANNIHILATE (4)

Esth 3:13 to slay, and to A all Jews, young and
8:11 to slay, and to A any armed force of
13:15 are upon us to A us, and they desire
1Mac 5:15 of the Gentiles, "to A us."

ANNIHILATED (2)

Esth 7:4 be destroyed, to be slain, and to be A
Sir 47:7 on every side, and A his adversaries the Philistines;

ANNIHILATION

Esth 16:15 who were consigned to A by this thrice-accursed

ANNOUNCE (4)

Sir 16:20 Who will A his acts of justice?
Is 21:6 a watchman, let him A what he sees.
21:10 God of Israel, I A to you.
Jer 4:16 that he is coming; A to Jerusalem, "Besiegers come

ANNOUNCED (8)

Judg 13:23 these things, or now A to us such things
Jud 11:19 my foreknowledge; it was A to me, and I
Is 44:7 Who has A from of old the things to
48:5 came to pass I A them to you, lest
Lam 1:21 the day thou hast A, and let them be
Acts 7:52 they killed those who A beforehand the coming of
1Pet 1:12 which have now been A to you by those

Rev 10:7 of God, as he A to his servants the

ANNOUNCING

Is 63:1 "It is I, A vindication, mighty to save."

ANNOY (3)

1Mac 10:35 anything from them or A any of them about
10:63 and let no one A him for any reason."
12:14 We were unwilling to A you and our other

ANNOYED (2)

Acts 4:2 Sadducees came upon them, A because they were
16:18 But Paul was A, and turned and said to

ANNOYING

2Mac 9:21 Persia I suffered an A illness, and I have

ANNUAL

2Chr 8:13 moons, and the three A feasts--the feast of

ANNUALLY

2Kgs 3:4 he had to deliver A to the king of

ANNUL (4)

Is 14:27 purposed, and who will A it?
2Mac 13:25 that they wanted to A its terms.
14:28 that he had to A their agreement when the
Gal 3:17 years afterward, does not A a covenant previously

ANNULLED (2)

Is 28:18 with death will be A, and your agreement with
Zech 11:11 So it was A on that day, and the

ANNULLING (2)

Zech 11:10 and I broke it, A the covenant which I
11:14 my second staff Union, A the brotherhood between

ANNULS

Gal 3:15 example, brethren: no one A even a man's will,

ANOINT (32)

Ex 28:41 with him, and shall A them and ordain them
29:7 on his head and A him.
29:36 for it, and shall A it, to consecrate it.
30:26 And you shall A with it the tent of
30:30 And you shall A Aaron and his sons, and
Deut 28:40 but you shall not A yourself with the oil;
Judg 9:8 once went forth to A a king over them;
Ruth 3:3 Wash therefore and A yourself, and put on your
1Sam 9:16 Benjamin, and you shall A him to be prince
15:1 LORD sent me to A you king over his
16:3 do; and you shall A for me him whom
16:12 the LORD said, "Arise, A him; for this is
2Sam 14:2 mourning garments; do not A yourself with oil, but
1Kgs 1:34 Nathan the prophet there A him king over Israel;
19:15 you arrive, you shall A Hazael to be king
19:16 of Nimshi you shall A to be king over
19:16 of Abel-meholah you shall A to be prophet in
2Kgs 9:3 says the LORD, I A you king over Israel.'
9:6 God of Israel, I A you king over the
9:12 says the LORD, I A you king over Israel.'"
Tob 6:8 as for the gall, A with it a man
11:8 You therefore must A his eyes with the gall;
Ps 141:5 of the wicked never A my head; for my
Dan 9:24 and prophet, and to A a most holy place.
10:3 mouth, nor did I A myself at all, for
Amos 6:6 wine in bowls, and A themselves with the finest
Mic 6:15 tread olives, but not A yourselves with oil; you
Mt 6:17 But when you fast, A your head and wash
Mk 16:1 they might go and A him.
Lk 7:46 You did not A my head with oil, but
Acts 4:27 Jesus, whom thou didst A, both Herod and Pontius
Rev 3:18 seen, and salve to A your eyes, that you

ANOINTED (103)

Gen 31:13 of Bethel, where you A a pillar and made
Ex 29:29 after him, to be A in them and ordained
Lev 4:3 if it is the A priest who sins, thus
4:5 And the A priest shall take some of the
4:16 Then the A priest shall bring some of the
6:20 day when he is A: a tenth of an
6:22 Aaron's sons, who is A to succeed him, shall
7:36 day that they were A; it is a perpetual
8:10 the anointing oil, and A the tabernacle and all
8:11 altar seven times, and A the altar and all
8:12 on Aaron's head, and A him, to consecrate him.
16:32 the priest who is A and consecrated as priest
Num 3:3 sons of Aaron, the A priests, whom he ordained
7:1 the tabernacle, and had A and consecrated it with
7:1 its furnishings, and had A and consecrated the altar
7:10 the day it was A; and the leaders offered
7:84 day when it was A, from the leaders of
7:88 dedication offering for the altar, after it was A
35:25 high priest who was A with the holy oil.
1Sam 2:10 his king, and exalt the power of his A
2:35 and out before my A for ever.
10:1 "Has not the LORD A you to be prince
10:1 that the LORD has A you to be prince
12:3 against me before the LORD and before his A
12:5 against you, and his A is witness this day,
15:17 The LORD A you king over Israel.
16:6 thought, "Surely the LORD's A is before him."
16:13 horn of oil, and A him in the midst
24:6 my lord, the LORD's A, to put forth my
24:6 hand against him, seeing he is the LORD's A
24:10 he is the LORD's A
26:9 hand against the LORD's A, and be guiltless?"
26:11 hand against the LORD's A; but take now the
26:16 not kept watch over your lord, the LORD's A
26:23 not put forth my hand against the LORD's A
2Sam 1:14 put forth your hand to destroy the LORD's A
1:16 against you, saying, 'I have slain the LORD's A
1:21 shield of Saul, not A with oil.
2:4 came, and there they A David king over the
2:7 house of Judah has A me king over them."
3:39 this day weak, though A king; these men the
5:3 the LORD, and they A David king over Israel.
5:17 that David had been A king over Israel, all
12:7 God of Israel, 'I A you king over Israel,
12:20 earth, and washed, and A himself, and changed his
19:10 But Absalom, whom we A over us, is dead
19:21 death for this, because he cursed the LORD's A
22:51 steadfast love to his A, to David, and his
23:1 raised on high, the A of the God of
1Kgs 1:39 from the tent, and A Solomon.
1:45 Nathan the prophet have A him king at Gihon;
5:1 heard that they had A him king in place
2Kgs 11:12 proclaimed him king, and A him; and they clapped
23:30 son of Josiah, and A him, and made him
1Chr 11:3 the LORD, and they A David king over Israel,
14:8 that David had been A king over all Israel,
16:22 saying, "Touch not my A ones, do my prophets
29:22 second time, and they A him as prince for
2Chr 6:42 the face of thy A one!
22:7 whom the LORD had A to destroy the house
23:11 Jehoiada and his sons A him, and they said,
28:15 food and drink, and A them; and carrying all
Jud 10:3 body with water, and A herself with precious
16:8 She A her face with ointment and fastened her
Ps 2:2 the LORD and his A, saying,
18:50 steadfast love to his A, to David and his
20:6 LORD will help his A; he will answer him
28:8 people, he is the saving refuge of his A
45:7 God, your God, has A you with the oil
84:9 O God; look upon the face of thine A
89:20 holy oil I have A him;
89:38 rejected, thou art full of wrath against thy A
89:51 with which they mock the footsteps of thy A
105:15 saying, "Touch not my A ones, do my prophets
132:10 the face of thy A one.
132:17 David; I have prepared a lamp for my A
Sir 45:15 Moses ordained him, and A him with holy oil;
46:13 established the kingdom and A rulers over his people.
46:19 the Lord and his A: "I have not taken
48:8 vengeance at Horeb; who A kings to inflict
Is 45:1 the LORD to his A, to Cyrus, whose right
61:1 because the LORD has A me to bring good
Lam 4:20 our nostrils, the LORD's A, was taken in their
Ezek 16:9 blood from you, and A you with oil.
28:14 With an A guardian cherub I placed you; you
Dan 9:25 the coming of an A one, a prince, there
9:26 the sixty-two weeks, an A one shall be cut
Hab 3:13 of thy people, for the salvation of thy A
Zech 4:14 "These are the two A who stand by the
2Mac 1:10 the family of the A priests, teacher of Ptolemy
Mk 6:13 out many demons, and A with oil many that
14:8 she could; she has A my body beforehand for
Lk 4:18 me, because he has A me to preach good
7:38 kissed his feet, and A them with the ointment.
7:46 oil, but she has A my feet with ointment.
Jn 9:6 of the spittle and A the man's eyes with
9:11 Jesus made clay and A my eyes and said

11:2 It was Mary who A the Lord with ointment
12:3 of pure nard and A the feet of Jesus
Acts 4:26 Lord and against his A –
10:38 John preached: how God A Jesus of Nazareth with
Heb 1:9 God, thy God, has A thee with the oil
1Jn 2:20 But you have been A by the Holy One,

ANOINTEST
Ps 23:5 of my enemies; thou A my head with oil,

ANOINTING (26)
Ex 25:6 lamps, spices for the A oil and for the
29:7 you shall take the A oil, and pour it
29:21 altar, and of the A oil, and sprinkle it
30:25 of these a sacred A oil blended as by
30:25 the perfumer; a holy A oil it shall be.
30:31 shall be my holy A oil throughout your generations.
31:11 as priests, and the A oil and the fragrant
35:8 light, spices for the A oil and for the
35:15 its poles, and the A oil and the fragrant
35:28 light, and for the A oil, and for the
37:29 He made the holy A oil also, and the
39:38 the golden altar, the A oil and the fragrant
Lev 8:2 the garments, and the A oil, and the bull
8:10 Then Moses took the A oil, and anointed the
8:12 poured some of the A oil on Aaron's head,
8:30 took some of the A oil and of the
10:7 you die; for the A oil of the LORD
21:10 upon whose head the A oil is poured, and
21:12 the consecration of the A oil of his God
Num 4:16 cereal offering, and the A oil, with the oversight
Judg 9:15 good faith you are A me king over you,
Song 1:3 better than wine, your A oils are fragrant, your
Hos 8:10 a little while from A king and princes.
Jas 5:14 them pray over him, A him with oil in
1Jn 2:27 deceive you; but the A which you received from
2:27 teach you; as his A teaches you about everything,

ANOINTS
Sir 35:6 of a righteous man A the altar, and its

ANOTHER (508)
Gen 4:25 has appointed for me A child instead of Abel,
8:10 He waited A seven days, and again he sent
8:12 Then he waited A seven days, and sent forth
11:3 they said to one A, "Come, let us make
11:7 may not understand one A's speech."
25:1 Abraham took A wife, whose name was Keturah.
26:21 Then they dug A well, and they quarreled over
26:22 from there and dug A well, and over that
26:31 took oath with one A; and Isaac set them
29:27 return for serving me A seven years."
29:30 and served Laban for A seven years.
30:24 LORD add to me A son!"
35:17 now you will have A son."
37:9 Then he dreamed A dream, and told it to
37:9 "Behold, I have dreamed A dream; and behold, the
37:19 They said to one A, "Here comes this dreamer.
42:1 his sons, "Why do you look at one A
42:21 they said to one A, "In truth we are
42:28 turned trembling to one A, saying, "What is this
43:6 man that you had A brother?"
43:7 Have you A brother?' What we told him was
43:33 men looked at one A in amazement.
Ex 10:23 did not see one A, nor did any rise
16:15 they said to one A, "What is it?" For
21:10 If he takes A wife to himself, he shall
21:14 a man willfully attacks A to kill him treacherously,
22:5 and it feeds in A man's field, he shall
25:20 their faces one to A; toward the mercy seat
26:3 be coupled to one A; and the other five
26:3 other five curtains shall be coupled to one A
26:5 second set; the loops shall be opposite one A
26:19 and two bases under A frame for its two
26:21 and two bases under A frame;
26:25 and two bases under A frame.
36:10 five curtains to one A, and the other five
36:10 the other five curtains he coupled to one A
36:12 the second set; the loops were opposite one A
36:24 and two bases under A frame for its two
36:26 and two bases under A frame.
37:9 their faces one to A; toward the mercy seat
Lev 7:10 the sons of Aaron, one as well as A
19:11 steal, nor deal falsely, nor lie to one A
19:20 a slave, betrothed to A man and not yet
25:14 from your neighbor, you shall not wrong one A
25:17 shall not wrong one A, but you shall fear
25:46 not rule, one over A, with harshness.
26:37 shall stumble over one A, as if to escape
27:20 sold the field to A man, it shall not
Num 8:8 and you shall take A young bull for a
14:4 they said to one A, "Let us choose a
23:13 "Come with me to A place, from which you
23:27 will take you to A place; perhaps it will
36:7 from one tribe to A; for every one of
36:9 from one tribe to A; for each of the
Deut 4:34 from the midst of A nation, by trials, by
17:8 kind of homicide and A, one kind of legal
17:8 of legal right and A, or one kind of
17:8 kind of assault and A, any case within your
20:5 in the battle and A man dedicate it.
20:6 in the battle and A man enjoy its fruit.
20:7 in the battle and A man take her.'
22:22 with the wife of A man, both of them
24:2 she goes and becomes A man's wife,
25:11 men fight with one A, and the wife of
28:30 betroth a wife, and A man shall lie with
28:32 shall be given to A people, while your eyes
29:28 and cast them into A land, as at this
Josh 18:14 the boundary goes in A direction, turning on the
Judg 2:10 fathers; and there arose A generation after them,
6:29 they said to one A, "Who has done this
10:18 Gilead, said one to A, "Who is the man
11:2 are the son of A woman."
Ruth 2:8 go to glean in A field or leave this
2:22 his maidens, lest in A field you be molested."
3:14 before one could recognize A; and he said, "Let
1Sam 10:3 one carrying three kids, A carrying three loaves of
10:3 loaves of bread, and A carrying a skin of
10:6 and be turned into A man.
10:9 Samuel, God gave him A heart; and all these
10:11 people said to one A, "What has come over
13:18 land of Shual, A company turned toward Beth-horon,
13:18 toward Beth-horon, and A company turned toward
17:30 away from him toward A, and spoke in the
18:7 women sang to one A as they made merry,
20:41 and they kissed one A, and wept with one
20:41 and wept with one A, until David recovered himself.
21:11 not sing to one A of him in dances,
29:5 they sing to one A in dances, 'Saul has
2Sam 3:11 could not answer Abner A word, because he feared
11:25 now one and now A; strengthen your attack upon
14:6 they quarreled with one A in the field; there
18:20 you may carry tidings A day, but today you
18:26 And the watchman saw A man running; and the
18:26 gate and said, "See, A man running alone!" The
1Kgs 13:10 So he went A way, and did not return
14:5 she pretended to be A woman.
14:6 of Jeroboam; why do you pretend to be A
18:6 and Obadiah went in A direction by himself.
20:29 they encamped opposite one A seven days.
20:37 Then he found A man, and said, "Strike me,
21:6 I will give you A vineyard for it'; and
22:7 "Is there not here A prophet of the LORD
22:20 said one thing, and A said another.
22:20 And one said one thing, and another said A
2Kgs 1:11 king sent to him A captain of fifty men
3:23 kings have surely fought together, and slain one A
4:6 her son, "Bring me A vessel." And he said
4:6 And he said to her, "There is not A
7:3 they said to one A, "Why do we sit
7:6 they said to one A, "Behold, the king of
7:8 came back, and entered A tent, and carried off
7:9 they said to one A, "We are not doing
11:6 guard the king's house A third being at the
14:8 let us look one A in the face."
14:11 of Judah faced one A in battle at Beth-shemesh,
21:16 from one end to A, besides the sin which
1Chr 2:26 Jerahmeel also had A wife, whose name was Atarah;
16:20 from one kingdom to A people,
2Chr 18:6 "Is there not here A prophet of the LORD
18:19 said one thing, and A said another.
18:19 And one said one thing, and another said A
20:23 of Seir, they all helped to destroy one A
25:12 men of Judah captured A ten thousand alive, and
25:17 let us look one A in the face."
25:21 of Judah faced one A in battle at Beth-shemesh,
30:23 keep the feast for A seven days; so they
30:23 they kept it for A seven days with gladness.
32:5 outside it he built A wall; and he strengthened
Neh 3:11 son of Pahath-moab repaired A section and the
3:19 ruler of Mizpah, repaired A section opposite the

3:20 son of Zabbai repaired A section from the Angle
3:21 son of Hakkoz repaired A section from the door
3:24 son of Henadad repaired A section, from the house
3:27 him the Tekoites repaired A section opposite the
3:30 son of Zalaph repaired A section.
4:19 are separated on the wall, far from one A
9:3 of the day; for A fourth of it they
Tob 6:12 cannot give her to A man without incurring the
Jud 15:2 not wait for one A, but with one impulse
Esth 1:19 her royal position to A who is better than
4:14 for the Jews from A quarter, but you and
9:19 on which they send choice portions to one A
9:22 choice portions to one A and gifts to the
Job 1:16 yet speaking, there came A, and said, "The fire
1:17 yet speaking, there came A, and said, "The
1:18 yet speaking, there came A, and said, "Your sons
19:27 side, and my eyes shall behold, and not A
21:25 A dies in bitterness of soul, never having tasted
31:8 let me sow, and A eat; and let what
31:10 my wife grind for A, and let others bow
41:16 is so near to A that no air can
41:17 are joined one to A; they clasp each other
Ps 16:4 Those who choose A god multiply their sorrows;
75:7 executes judgment, putting down one and lifting up A
105:13 from one kingdom to A people,
109:8 days be few; may A seize his goods!
145:4 laud thy works to A, and shall declare thy
Prov 11:24 grows all the richer; A withholds what he should
13:7 rich, yet has nothing; A pretends to be poor,
23:35 I will seek A drink."
25:9 and do not disclose A's secret;
27:2 Let A praise you, and not your own mouth;
27:17 Iron sharpens iron, and one man sharpens A
28:17 with the blood of A, let him be a
Eccl 4:10 falls and has not A to lift him up.
7:27 adding one thing to A to find the sum,
Song 5:9 your beloved more than A beloved, O fairest among
5:9 your beloved more than A beloved, that you thus
Wis 5:3 will speak to one A in repentance, and in
14:24 either treacherously kill one A, or grieve one another
14:24 another, or grieve one A by adultery,
16:14 in his wickedness kills A, but he cannot bring
16:19 of God; and at A time even in the
18:18 and one here and A there, hurled down half
18:23 already fallen on one A in heaps, he intervened
19:3 their dead, they reached A foolish decision, and
19:18 changed places with one A, as on a harp
Sir 9:8 at beauty belonging to A; many have been misled
9:9 Never dine with A man's wife, nor revel with
11:12 There is A who is slow and needs help,
14:15 of your labors to A, and what you acquired
14:18 blood: one dies and A is born.
16:26 do not crowd one A aside, and they will
20:4 is found wise, while A is detested for being
20:5 has no answer, while A keeps silent because he
23:23 brought forth children by A man.
28:3 man harbor anger against A, and yet seek for
29:5 A man will kiss A's hands until he gets
29:22 than sumptuous food in A man's house.
32:9 their equal; and when A is speaking, do not
33:7 any day better than A, when all the daylight
33:19 give your property to A, lest you change your
34:23 When one builds and A tears down, what do
34:24 When one prays and A curses, to whose voice
36:18 any food, yet one food is better than A
36:21 any man, but one daughter is better than A
40:29 to the table of A, his existence cannot be
40:29 He pollutes himself with A man's food, but a
41:21 and of gazing at A man's wife;
Is 3:5 people will oppress one A, every man his fellow
6:3 And one called to A and said: "Holy, holy,
13:8 look aghast at one A; their faces will be
44:5 'I am the LORDs,' A will call himself by
44:5 name of Jacob, and A will write on his
48:11 My glory I will not give to A
65:22 shall not build and A inhabit; they shall not
65:22 shall not plant and A eat; for like the
Jer 3:1 from him and becomes A man's wife, will he
7:5 execute justice one with A,
13:14 dash them one against A, fathers and sons together,
18:4 he reworked it into A vessel, as it seemed
22:26 who bore you into A country, where you were
23:27 which they tell one A, even as their fathers
23:30 the LORD, who steal my words from one A
25:26 and near, one after A, and all the kingdoms
26:20 There was A man who prophesied in the name
36:16 they turned one to A in fear; and they
36:28 came to Jeremiah: "Take A scroll and write on
36:32 Then Jeremiah took A scroll and gave it to
46:16 they said one to A, 'Arise, and let us
51:31 runner runs to meet A, and one messenger to
51:31 one messenger to meet A, to tell the king
51:46 afterward a report in A year, and violence is
Bar 2:3 of his son and A the flesh of his
4:3 give your glory to A, or your advantages to
Ezek 1:9 their wings touched one A; they went every one
1:11 touched the wing of A, while two covered their
1:23 out straight, one toward A; and each creature had
3:13 as they touched one A, and the sound of
4:17 and look at one A in dismay, and waste
12:3 from your place to A place in their sight.
17:7 "But there was A great eagle with great wings
19:5 was lost, she took A of her whelps and
22:11 neighbor's wife; A lewdly defiles his daughter-in-law;
22:11 lewdly defiles his daughter-in-law; A in you defiles
24:23 away in your iniquities and groan to one A
33:30 houses, say to one A, each to his brother,
37:16 with him'; then take A stick and write upon
41:6 three stories, one over A, thirty in each story.
41:11 toward the north, and A door toward the south;
45:5 A section, twenty-five thousand cubits long and ten
Dan 2:39 After you shall arise A kingdom inferior to you,
2:43 will mix with one A in marriage, but they
2:44 sovereignty be left to A people.
5:17 give your rewards to A; nevertheless I will read
7:3 up out of the sea, different from one A
7:5 And behold, A beast, a second one, like a
7:6 I looked, and lo, A, like a leopard, with
7:8 came up among them A horn, a little one,
7:24 kings shall arise, and A shall arise after them;
8:13 holy one speaking; and A holy one said to
Hos 3:3 harlot, or belong to A man; so will I
Joel 1:3 children, and their children A generation.
2:8 do not jostle one A, each marches in his
Amos 4:7 send no rain upon A city; one field would
Jon 1:7 they said to one A, "Come, let us cast
Zech 2:3 me came forward, and A angel came forward to
8:16 the truth to one A, render in your gates
8:17 your hearts against one A, and love no false
8:21 city shall go to A, saying, 'Let us go
11:9 that are left devour the flesh of one A
Mal 2:10 we faithless to one A, profaning the covenant of
3:16 LORD spoke with one A; the LORD heeded and
1Mac 3:43 they said to one A, "Let us repair the
5:37 these things Timothy gathered A army and encamped
7:29 and they greeted one A peaceably.
10:16 said, "Shall we find A such man?
10:54 establish friendship with one A; give me now your
10:56 we may see one A, and I will become
11:6 and they greeted one A and spent the night
12:50 and they encouraged one A and kept marching in
13:28 seven pyramids, opposite one A, for his father and
2Mac 3:37 suitable to send on A mission to Jerusalem, he
4:8 of silver and, from A source of revenue, eighty
4:19 to expend it for A purpose.
4:26 brother was supplanted by A man, was driven as
7:5 their mother encouraged one A to die nobly, saying,
10:3 the sanctuary, and made A altar of sacrifice; then,
14:26 good will for one A, he took the covenant
Mt 2:12 their own country by A way.
8:9 he goes, and to A, 'Come,' and he comes,
8:21 A of the disciples said to him, "Lord, let
11:3 is to come, or shall we look for A
13:23 case a hundredfold, in A sixty, and in another
13:23 another sixty, and in A thirty."
13:24 A parable he put before them, saying, "The kingdom
13:31 A parable he put before them, saying, "The kingdom
13:33 He told them A parable.
19:9 for unchastity, and marries A, commits adultery; and
21:25 they argued with one A, "If we say, 'From
21:33 "Hear A parable.
21:33 tenants, and went into A country.
21:35 and beat one, killed A, and stoned another.
21:35 servants and beat one, killed another, and stoned A
22:5 one to his farm, A to his business,
24:2 here one stone upon A, that will not be
24:10 away, and betray one A, and hate one another.
24:10 away, and betray one another, and hate one A
25:15 gave five talents, to A two, to another one,
25:15 to another two, to A one, to each according
25:32 separate them one from A as a shepherd separates
26:22 to him one after A, "Is it I, Lord?"

	26:71	out to the porch, A maid saw him, and
Mk	4:41	and said to one A, "Who then is this,
	8:16	discussed it with one A, saying, "We have no
	9:34	had discussed with one A who was the greatest.
	9:48	in yourselves, and be at peace with one A
	10:11	his wife and marries A, commits adultery against
	10:12	her husband and marries A, she commits adultery."
	11:30	they argued with one A, "If we say, 'From
	12:1	tenants, and went into A country.
	12:4	he sent to them A servant, and they wounded
	12:5	And he sent A, and him they killed; and
	12:7	tenants said to one A, 'This is the heir;
	12:28	them disputing with one A, and seeing that he
	13:2	here one stone upon A, that will not be
	14:19	to him one after A, "Is it I?"
	14:58	days I will build A, not made with hands.'"
	15:30	mocked him to one A with the scribes, saying,
	16:3	were saying to one A, "Who will roll away
	16:12	this he appeared in A form to two of
Lk	2:15	shepherds said to one A, "Let us go over
	4:36	and said to one A, "What is this word?
	6:6	On A sabbath, when he entered the synagogue and
	6:11	and discussed with one A what they might do
	7:8	he goes; and to A, 'Come,' and he comes;
	7:19	is to come, or shall we look for A
	7:20	is to come, or shall we look for A
	7:32	and calling to one A, 'We piped to you,
	8:25	marveled, saying to one A, "Who then is this,
	9:56	they went on to A village.
	9:59	To A he said, "Follow me." But he said,
	9:61	A said, "I will follow you, Lord; but let
	12:1	they trod upon one A, he began to say
	14:19	have me excused.' And A said, 'I have bought
	14:20	have me excused.' And A said, 'I have married
	14:31	king, going to encounter A king in war, will
	16:7	Then he said to A, 'And how much do
	16:18	his wife and marries A commits adultery, and he
	19:20	over five cities.' Then A came, saying, 'Lord, here
	19:44	leave one stone upon A in you; because you
	20:5	discussed it with one A, saying, "If we say,
	20:9	tenants, and went into A country for a long
	20:11	And he sent A servant; him also they beat
	21:6	here one stone upon A that will not be
	22:23	began to question one A, which of them it
	22:57	about an hour still A insisted, saying, "Certainly this
Jn	4:33	disciples said to one A, "Has any one brought
	4:37	true, 'One sows and A reaps.'
	5:6	while I am going A steps down before me."
	5:31	not true; there is A who bears witness to
	5:42	not receive me; if A comes in his own
	5:43	receive glory from one A and do not seek
	7:35	Jews said to one A, "Where does this man
	10:1	but climbs in by A way, that man is
	11:56	and saying to one A as they stood in
	12:19	then said to one A, "You see that you
	13:14	ought to wash one A's feet.
	13:22	disciples looked at one A, uncertain of whom he
	13:34	that you love one A; even as I have
	13:34	have loved you, that you also love one A
	13:35	my disciples, if you have love for one A
	14:16	he will give you A Counselor, to be with
	15:12	that you love one A as I have loved
	15:17	This I command you, to love one A
	16:17	disciples said to one A, "What is this that
	18:15	Jesus, and so did A disciple.
	19:24	they said to one A, "Let us not tear
	19:37	And again A scripture says, "They shall look on
	21:18	out your hands, and A will gird you and
Acts	1:20	and 'His office let A take.'
	2:12	perplexed, saying to one A, "What does this mean?"
	4:15	they conferred with one A,
	7:18	there arose over Egypt A king who had not
	10:28	visit any one of A nation; but God has
	12:17	departed and went to A place.
	13:35	he says also in A psalm, 'Thou wilt not
	17:7	saying that there is A king, Jesus."
	19:32	cried one thing, some A; for the assembly was
	19:38	are proconsuls; let them bring charges against one A
	21:5	prayed and bade one A farewell.
	21:34	shouted one thing, some A; and as he could
	26:31	they said to one A, "This man is doing
	28:4	they said to one A, "No doubt this man
Rom	1:27	with passion for one A, men committing shameless
	2:1	are, when you judge A; for in passing judgment
	7:3	if she lives with A man while her husband
	7:3	and if she marries A man she is not
	7:4	you may belong to A, to him who has
	7:23	see in my members A law at war with
	9:21	vessel for beauty and A for menial use?
	12:5	body in Christ, and individually members one of A
	12:10	is good; love one A with brotherly affection; outdo
	12:10	brotherly affection; outdo one A in showing honor.
	12:16	in harmony with one A; do not be haughty,
	13:8	except to love one A; for he who loves
	14:4	you to pass judgment on the servant of A
	14:5	day as better than A, while another man esteems
	14:5	better than another, while A man esteems all days
	14:13	pass judgment on one A, but rather decide never
	15:5	such harmony with one A, in accord with Christ
	15:7	Welcome one A, therefore, as Christ has welcomed
	15:14	with all knowledge, and able to instruct one A
	15:20	lest I build on A man's foundation,
	16:16	Greet one A with a holy kiss.
1Cor	3:4	and A, "I belong to Apollos," are you not
	3:10	laid a foundation, and A man is building upon
	4:6	be puffed up in favor of one against A
	6:7	at all with one A is defeat for you.
	7:5	Do not refuse one A except perhaps by agreement
	7:7	God, one of one kind and one of A
	10:29	liberty be determined by A man's scruples?
	11:21	one is hungry and A is drunk.
	11:33	eat, wait for one A --
	12:8	of wisdom, and to A the utterance of knowledge
	12:9	the same Spirit, to A faith by the same
	12:9	the same Spirit, to A gifts of healing by
	12:10	the one Spirit, to A the working of miracles,
	12:10	working of miracles, to A prophecy, to another the
	12:10	to another prophecy, to A the ability to distinguish
	12:10	distinguish between spirits, to A various kinds of
	12:10	kinds of tongues, to A the interpretation of tongues.
	12:25	members may have the same care for one A
	14:30	revelation is made to A sitting by, let the
	15:39	one kind for men, A for animals, another for
	15:39	men, another for animals, A for birds, and another
	15:39	another for birds, and A for fish.
	15:40	one, and the glory of the terrestrial is A
	15:41	of the sun, and A glory of the moon,
	15:41	of the moon, and A glory of the stars;
	16:20	Greet one A with a holy kiss.
2Cor	2:1	not to make you A painful visit.
	3:18	degree of glory to A; for this comes from
	10:12	measure themselves by one A, and compare
	10:12	compare themselves with one A, they are without
	10:16	work already done in A's field.
	11:4	one comes and preaches A Jesus than the one
	13:11	appeal, agree with one A, live in peace, and
	13:12	Greet one A with a holy kiss.
Gal	1:7	not that there is A gospel, but there are
	5:13	flesh, but through love be servants of one A
	5:15	bite and devour one A take heed that you
	5:15	heed that you are not consumed by one A
	5:26	no provoking of one A, no envy of one
	5:26	provoking of one another, no envy of one A
	6:2	Bear one A's burdens, and so fulfil the law
Eph	4:2	with patience, forbearing one A in love,
	4:25	his neighbor, for we are members one of A
	4:32	be kind to one A, tenderhearted, forgiving one
	4:32	another, tenderhearted, forgiving one A, as God in
	5:19	the Spirit, addressing one A in psalms and hymns
	5:21	Be subject to one A out of reverence for
Col	3:9	not lie to one A, seeing that you have
	3:13	and patience, forbearing one A and, if one has
	3:13	has a complaint against A, forgiving each other; as
	3:16	teach and admonish one A in all wisdom, and
1Thes	3:12	in love to one A and to all men,
	4:9	God to love one A;
	4:18	Therefore comfort one A with these words.
	5:11	Therefore encourage one A and build one another
	5:11	another and build one A up, just as you
	5:15	do good to one A and to all.
2Thes	1:3	of you for one A is increasing.
1Tim	5:22	hands, nor participate in A man's sins; keep yourself
Tit	3:3	men and hating one A;
Heb	3:13	But exhort one A every day, as long as
	4:8	not speak later of A day.
	5:6	he says also in A place, "Thou art a
	7:11	there have been for A priest to arise after
	7:13	are spoken belonged to A tribe, from which no
	7:15	even more evident when A priest arises in the
	10:24	to stir up one A to love and good
	10:25	some, but encouraging one A, and all the more
Jas	2:25	and sent them out A way?

A

4:11 speak evil against one A, brethren.
5:9 grumble, brethren, against one A, that you may not
5:16 your sins to one A, and pray for one
5:16 and pray for one A, that you may be
1Pet 1:22 the brethren, love one A earnestly from the heart.
4:8 your love for one A, since love covers a
4:9 Practice hospitality ungrudgingly to one A
4:10 employ it for one A, as good stewards of
5:5 with humility toward one A, for "God opposes the
5:14 Greet one A with the kiss of love.
1Jn 1:7 have fellowship with one A, and the blood of
3:11 we should love one A,
3:23 Christ and love one A, just as he has
4:7 let us love one A; for love is of
4:11 loved us, we also ought to love one A
4:12 if we love one A, God abides in us
2Jn 1:5 had from the beginning, that we love one A
Rev 6:4 And out came A horse, bright red; its rider
6:4 men should slay one A; and he was given
7:2 Then I saw A angel ascend from the rising
8:3 And A angel came and stood at the altar
10:1 Then I saw A mighty angel coming down from
12:3 And A portent appeared in heaven; behold, a great
13:11 Then I saw A beast which rose out of
14:6 Then I saw A angel flying in midheaven, with
14:8 A angel, a second, followed, saying, "Fallen, fallen is
14:9 And A angel, a third, followed them, saying with
14:15 And A angel came out of the temple, calling
14:17 And A angel came out of the temple in
14:18 Then A angel came out from the altar, the
15:1 Then I saw A portent in heaven, great and
18:1 After this I saw A angel coming down from
18:4 Then I heard A voice from heaven saying, "Come
20:12 Also A book was opened, which is the book

ANOTHERS (2)

Ex 21:35 one man's ox hurts A, so that it dies,
Lk 16:12 in that which is A, who will give you

ANSWER (183)

Gen 30:33 So my honesty will A for me later, when
41:16 in me; God will give Pharaoh a favorable A
43:7 told him was in A to these questions; could
45:3 his brothers could not A him, for they were
Deut 20:11 And if its A to you is peace and
25:9 face; and she shall A and say, 'So shall
27:15 all the people shall A and say, 'Amen.'
Josh 22:21 of Manasseh said in A to the heads of
Judg 5:29 Her wisest ladies make A, nay, she gives answer
5:29 answer, nay, she gives A to herself,
19:28 But there was no A
1Sam 4:20 But she did not A or give heed.
8:18 the LORD will not A you in that day."
14:37 But he did not A him that day.
26:14 saying, "Will you not A, Abner?" Then Abner
26:22 And David made A, "Here is the spear, O
28:6 the LORD did not A him, either by dreams,
29:9 And Achish made A to David, "I know that
2Sam 3:11 And Ish-bosheth could not A Abner another word,
22:42 but he did not A them.
24:13 consider, and decide what A I shall return to
1Kgs 12:6 you advise me to A this people?"
12:7 to them when you A them, then they will
12:9 you advise that we A this people who have
18:21 the people did not A him a word.
18:26 noon, saying, "O Baal, A us!" But there was
18:37 A me, O LORD, answer me, that this people
18:37 Answer me, O LORD, A me, that this people
2Kgs 18:36 command was, "Do not A him."
1Chr 21:12 Israel.' Now decide what A I shall return to
2Chr 10:6 you advise me to A this people?"
10:9 you advise that we A this people who have
Ezra 4:17 The king sent an A: "To Rehum the commander
5:5 reach Darius and then A be returned by letter
Esth 4:13 told them to return A to Esther, "Think not
Job 5:1 any one who will A you?
9:3 him, one could not A him once in a
9:14 How then can I A him, choosing my words
9:15 am innocent, I cannot A him; I must appeal
9:32 am, that I might A him, that we should
13:22 call, and I will A; or let me speak,
14:15 call, and I would A thee; thou wouldest long
15:2 "Should a wise man A with windy knowledge, and
16:3 Or what provokes you that you A
19:16 he gives me no A; I must beseech him
20:2 answered: "Therefore my thoughts A me, because of
23:5 learn what he would A me, and understand what
30:20 and thou dost not A me; I stand, and
31:14 inquiry, what shall I A him?
31:35 let the Almighty A me!) Oh, that I had
32:1 three men ceased to A Job, because he was
32:3 they had found no A, although they had declared
32:5 that there was no A in the mouth of
32:14 and I will not A him with your speeches.
32:15 "They are discomfited, they A no more; they have
32:16 they stand there, and A no more?
32:17 also will give my A; I also will declare
32:20 find relief; I must open my lips and A
33:5 A me, if you can; set your words in
33:12 I will A you.
33:13 him, saying, 'He will A none of my words'?
33:32 have anything to say, A me; speak, for I
35:4 had sinned?' I will A you and your friends
35:12 but he does not A, because of the pride
40:2 with God, let him A it."
40:4 account; what shall I A thee?
40:5 and I will not A; twice, but I will
Ps 4:1 [Selah] A me when I call, O God of
13:3 Consider and A me, O LORD my God; lighten
17:6 thee, for thou wilt A me, O God; incline
18:41 but he did not A them.
20:1 The LORD A you in the day of trouble!
20:6 his anointed; he will A him from his holy
20:9 the king, O LORD; A us when we call.
22:2 but thou dost not A; and by night, but
27:7 gracious to me and A me!
38:15 is thou, O LORD my God, who wilt A
55:2 Attend to me, and A me; I am overcome
60:5 thy right hand and A us!
65:5 dread deeds thou dost A us with deliverance, O
69:13 of thy steadfast love A me.
69:16 A me, O LORD, for thy steadfast love is
69:17 distress, make haste to A me.
86:1 ear, O LORD, and A me, for I am
86:7 thee, for thou dost A me.
91:15 to me, I will A him; I will be
99:8 our God, thou didst A them; thou wast a
102:2 thy ear to me; A me speedily in the
108:6 thy right hand, and A me!
119:26 my ways, thou didst A me; teach me thy
119:42 shall I have an A for those who taunt
119:145 whole heart I cry; A me, O LORD!
120:1 LORD, that he may A me:
138:3 I called, thou didst A me, my strength of
143:1 In thy faithfulness A me, in thy righteousness!
143:7 [Selah] Make haste to A me, O LORD!
Prov 1:28 but I will not A; they will seek me
15:1 A soft A turns away wrath, but a harsh
15:23 To make an apt A is a joy to
15:28 righteous ponders how to A, but the mouth of
16:1 to man, but the A of the tongue is
18:13 If one gives A before he hears, it is
18:23 entreaties, but the rich A roughly.
22:21 may give a true A to those who sent
24:26 who gives a right A kisses the lips.
26:4 A not a fool according to his folly, lest
26:5 A a fool according to his folly, lest he
26:16 seven men who can A discreetly.
27:11 glad, that I may A him who reproaches me.
Song 3:1 not; I called him, but he gave no A
5:6 not; I called him, but he gave no A
Sir 4:8 to the poor, and A him peaceably and gently.
5:12 If you have understanding, A your neighbor; but if
8:9 how to give an A in time of need.
11:8 Do not A before you have heard, nor interrupt
20:5 because he has no A, while another keeps silent
33:4 bind together your instruction, and make your A
Is 10:30 A her, O Anathoth!
14:32 What will one A the messengers of the nation?
30:19 hears it, he will A you.
36:21 command was, "Do not A him."
41:17 I the LORD will A them, I the God
41:28 no counselor who, when I ask, gives an A
46:7 it, it does not A or save him from
50:2 When I called, was there no one to A
58:9 and the LORD will A; you shall cry, and
65:12 called, you did not A, when I spoke, you
65:24 they call I will A, while they are yet
Jer 7:13 you, you did not A,
7:27 but they will not A you.
22:9 And they will A, "Because they forsook the covenant
33:3 me and I will A you, and will tell

44:20 had given him this A:
Ezek 14:4 I the LORD will A him myself because of
14:7 I the LORD will A him myself;
Dan 3:16 have no need to A you in this matter.
Hos 2:15 And there she shall A as in the days
2:21 the LORD, I will A the heavens and they
2:21 heavens and they shall A the earth;
2:22 and the earth shall A the grain, the wine,
2:22 oil, and they shall A Jezreel;
14:8 It is I who A and look after you.
Mic 3:4 but he will not A them; he will hide
3:7 for there is no A from God.
6:3 A me!
Hab 2:1 and what I will A concerning my complaint.
Zech 10:6 God and I will A them.
13:9 name, and I will A them.
Mal 2:12 any to witness or A, or to bring an
1Mac 2:36 But they did not A them or hurl a
15:35 Athenobius did not A him a word,
Mt 15:23 But he did not A her a word.
21:24 you tell me the A, then I also will
22:46 one was able to A him a word, nor
25:37 Then the righteous will A him, 'Lord, when did
25:40 And the King will A them, 'Truly, I say
25:44 Then they also will A, 'Lord, when did we
25:45 thee?' Then he will A them, 'Truly, I say
26:62 said, "Have you no A to make?
27:12 the chief priests and elders, he made no A
27:14 he gave him no A, not even to a
Mk 11:28 ask you a question; A me, and I will
11:29 A me."
14:40 not know what to A him.
14:60 Jesus, "Have you no A to make?
14:61 But he was silent and made no A
15:4 him, "Have you no A to make?
15:5 Jesus made no further A, so that Pilate wondered.
Lk 11:7 him'; and he will A from within, 'Do not
12:11 what you are to A or what you are
13:25 to us.' He will A you, 'I do not
20:26 but marveling at his A they were silent.
21:14 meditate beforehand how to A;
22:66 and if I ask you, you will not A
23:9 him at some length; but he made no A
Jn 1:22 Let us have an A for those who sent
18:22 "Is that how you A the high priest?"
19:9 But Jesus gave no A
Acts 12:13 the gateway, a maid named Rhoda came to A
Rom 9:20 you, a man, to A back to God?
2Cor 1:11 blessing granted us in A to many prayers.
5:12 may be able to A those who pride themselves
Col 4:6 how you ought to A every one.

ANSWERED (417)

Gen 18:27 Abraham A, "Behold, I have taken upon myself to
18:29 He A, "For the sake of forty I will
18:30 He A, "I will not do it, if I
18:31 He A, "For the sake of twenty I will
18:32 He A, "For the sake of ten I will
23:5 The Hittites A Abraham,
23:10 and Ephron the Hittite A Abraham in the hearing
23:14 Ephron A Abraham,
24:50 Then Laban and Bethuel A, "The thing comes from
27:1 "My son"; and he A, "Here I am."
27:20 He A, "Because the LORD your God granted me
27:24 He A, "I am."
27:32 He A, "I am your son, your first-born, Esau."
27:37 Isaac A Esau, "Behold, I have made him your
27:39 Then Isaac his father A him: "Behold, away from
31:14 Then Rachel and Leah A him, "Is there any
31:31 Jacob A Laban, "Because I was afraid, for I
31:43 Then Laban A and said to Jacob, "The daughters
33:8 Jacob A, "To find favor in the sight of
34:13 The sons of Jacob A Shechem and his father
35:3 to the God who A me in the day
38:17 He A, "I will send you a kid from
40:18 And Joseph A, "This is its interpretation: the three
41:16 Joseph A Pharaoh, "It is not in me; God
42:22 And Reuben A them, "Did I not tell you
47:16 And Joseph A, "Give your cattle, and I will
47:30 He A, "I will do as you have said."
50:6 And Pharaoh A, "Go up, and bury your father,
Ex 2:14 He A, "Who made you a prince and a
4:1 Then Moses A, "But behold, they will not believe
19:8 And all the people A together and said, "All
19:19 Moses spoke, and God A him in thunder.
24:3 and all the people A with one voice, and
Num 22:18 But Balaam A and said to the servants of
23:12 And he A, "Must I not take heed to
23:26 But Balaam A Balak, "Did I not tell you,
32:31 the sons of Reuben A, "As the LORD has
Deut 1:14 your heads.' And you A me, 'The thing that
1:41 Red Sea.' "Then you A me, 'We have sinned
Josh 1:16 And they A Joshua, "All that you have commanded
7:20 And Achan A Joshua, "Of a truth I have
9:24 They A Joshua, "Because it was told to your
24:16 Then the people A, "Far be it from us
Judg 7:14 And his comrade A, "This is no other than
8:8 the men of Penuel A him as the men
8:8 answered him as the men of Succoth had A
8:18 They A, "As you are, so were they, every
8:25 were Ishmaelites.) And they A, "We will willingly
11:13 king of the Ammonites A the messengers of
20:4 woman who was murdered, A and said, "I came
Ruth 2:4 And they A, "The LORD bless you."
2:6 charge of the reapers A, "It is the Moabite
2:11 But Boaz A her, "All that you have done
3:9 And she A, "I am Ruth, your maidservant; spread
1Sam 1:15 But Hannah A, "No, my lord, I am a
1:17 Then Eli A, "Go in peace, and the God
4:17 who brought the tidings A and said, "Israel has
5:8 They A, "Let the ark of the God of
6:4 They A, "Five golden tumors and five golden mice,
7:9 Israel, and the LORD A him.
9:8 The servant A Saul again, "Here, I have with
9:12 They A, "He is; behold, he is just ahead
9:19 Samuel A Saul, "I am the seer; go up
9:21 Saul A, "Am I not a Benjaminite, from the
10:12 man of the place A, "And who is their
14:39 all the people that A him.
14:41 why hast thou not A thy servant this day?
16:18 of the young men A, "Behold, I have seen
17:27 And the people A him in the same way,
17:30 way; and the people A him again as before.
17:58 And David A, "I am the son of your
19:17 And Michal A Saul, "He said to me, 'Let
20:28 Jonathan A Saul, "David earnestly asked leave of me
20:32 Then Jonathan A Saul his father, "Why should he
21:4 And the priest A David, "I have no common
21:5 And David A the priest, "Of a truth women
22:9 Then A Doeg the Edomite, who stood by the
22:12 And he A, "Here I am, my lord."
22:14 Then Ahimelech A the king, "And who among all
23:4 And the LORD A him, "Arise, go down to
25:10 And Nabal A David's servants, "Who is David?
26:14 Then Abner A, "Who are you that calls to
28:15 Saul A, "I am in great distress; for the
30:8 He A him, "Pursue; for you shall surely overtake
2Sam 1:4 And he A, "The people have fled from the
1:7 And I A, 'Here I am.'
1:8 'Who are you?' I A him, 'I am an
1:13 And he A, "I am the son of a
2:20 And he A, "It is I."
4:9 But David A Rechab and Baanah his brother, the
9:6 And he A, "Behold, your servant."
13:12 She A him, "No, my brother, do not force
14:5 She A, "Alas, I am a widow; my husband
14:18 Then the king A the woman, "Do not hide
14:19 The woman A and said, "As surely as you
14:32 Absalom A Joab, "Behold, I sent word to you,
15:21 But Ittai A the king, "As the LORD lives,
16:2 Ziba A, "The asses are for the king's household
18:29 Ahima-az A, "When Joab sent your servant, I saw
18:32 And the Cushite A, "May the enemies of my
19:21 the son of Zeruiah A, "Shall not Shimei be
19:26 He A, "My lord, O king, my servant deceived
19:38 And the king A, "Chimham shall go over with
19:42 the men of Judah A the men of Israel,
19:43 the men of Israel A the men of Judah,
20:17 He A, "I am." Then she said to him,
20:17 And he A, "I am listening."
20:20 Joab A, "Far be it from me, far be
1Kgs 1:28 Then King David A, "Call Bathsheba to me." So
1:36 the son of Jehoiada A the king, "Amen!
1:43 Jonathan A Adonijah, "No, for our lord King David
2:22 King Solomon A his mother, "And why do you
2:30 Joab, and thus he A me."
3:27 Then the king A and said, "Give the living
10:3 And Solomon A all her questions; there was nothing
12:13 And the king A the people harshly, and forsaking
12:16 to them, the people A the king, "What portion
18:8 And he A him, "It is I.
18:18 And he A, "I have not troubled Israel; but

18:24 And all the people A, "It is well spoken."
18:26 But there was no voice, and no one A
18:29 no voice; no one A, no one heeded.
20:4 the king of Israel A, "As you say, my
20:11 the king of Israel A, "Tell him, 'Let not
20:14 He A, "You."
21:6 for it'; and he A, 'I will not give
21:20 He A, "I have found you, because you have
22:15 And he A him, "Go up and triumph; the
2Kgs 1:8 They A him, "He wore a garment of haircloth,
1:10 But Elijah A the captain of fifty, "If I
1:12 But Elijah A them, "If I am a man
2:5 And he A, "Yes, I know it; hold your
3:8 Jehoram A, "By the way of the wilderness of
3:11 king of Israel's servants A, "Elisha the son of
4:13 She A, "I dwell among my own people."
4:14 Gehazi A, "Well, she has no son, and her
4:26 And she A, "It is well."
6:2 And he A, "Go."
6:3 And he A, "I will go."
6:22 He A, "You shall not slay them.
6:28 She A, "This woman said to me, 'Give your
7:19 the captain had A the man of God, "If
8:12 He A, "Because I know the evil that you
8:13 Elisha A, "The LORD has shown me that you
8:14 And he A, "He told me that you would
9:19 And Jehu A, "What have you to do with
9:22 He A, "What peace can there be, so long
10:13 And they A, "We are the kinsmen of Ahaziah,
10:15 And Jehonadab A, "It is." Jehu said, "If it
18:36 people were silent and A him not a word,
20:10 And Hezekiah A, "It is an easy thing for
20:15 And Hezekiah A, "They have seen all that is
1Chr 21:26 the LORD, and he A him with fire from
21:28 that the LORD had A him at the threshing
2Chr 1:11 God A Solomon, "Because this was in your heart,
2:11 the king of Tyre A in a letter which
9:2 And Solomon A all her questions; there was nothing
10:13 And the king A them harshly, and forsaking the
10:16 to them, the people A the king, "What portion
18:3 He A him, "I am as you are, my
18:14 And he A, "Go up and triumph; they will
25:9 The man of God A, "The LORD is able
31:10 the house of Zadok, A him, "Since they began
32:24 the LORD; and he A him and gave him
Ezra 10:12 Then all the assembly A with a loud voice,
Neh 6:4 this way and I A them in the same
8:6 and all the people A, "Amen, Amen," lifting up
Tob 5:1 Then Tobias A him, "Father, I will do everything
5:11 But he A, "Are you looking for a tribe
7:3 They A him, "We belong to the sons of
10:7 And she A him, "Be still and stop deceiving
Jud 6:17 He A and told them what had taken place
14:15 But when no one A, he opened it and
Esth 7:3 Then Queen Esther A, "If I have found favor
Job 1:7 Satan A the LORD, "From going to and fro
1:9 Then Satan A the LORD, "Does Job fear God
2:2 Satan A the LORD, "From going to and fro
2:4 Then Satan A the LORD, "Skin for skin!
4:1 Then Eliphaz the Temanite A:
6:1 Then Job A:
8:1 Then Bildad the Shuhite A:
9:1 Then Job A:
9:16 summoned him and he A me, I would not
11:1 Then Zophar the Naamathite A:
12:1 Then Job A:
12:4 upon God and he A me, a just and
15:1 Then Eliphaz the Temanite A:
16:1 Then Job A:
18:1 Then Bildad the Shuhite A:
19:1 Then Job A:
19:7 but I am not A; I call aloud, but
20:1 Then Zophar the Naamathite A:
21:1 Then Job A:
22:1 Then Eliphaz the Temanite A:
23:1 Then Job A:
25:1 Then Bildad the Shuhite A:
26:1 Then Job A:
32:6 of Barachel the Buzite A: "I am young in
32:12 confuted Job, or that A his words, among you.
38:1 Then the LORD A Job out of the whirlwind:
40:3 Then Job A the LORD:
40:6 Then the LORD A Job out of the whirlwind:
42:1 Then Job A the LORD:
Ps 34:4 the LORD, and he A me, and delivered me
81:7 I delivered you; I A you in the secret
99:6 the LORD, and he A them.
118:5 the LORD; the LORD A me and set me
118:21 thee that thou hast A me and hast become
Sir 46:6 and the great Lord A him with hailstones of
Is 21:9 And he A, "Fallen, fallen is Babylon; and all
36:21 they were silent and A him not a word,
39:4 Hezekiah A, "They have seen all that is in
49:8 of favor I have A you, in a day
66:4 I called, no one A, when I spoke they
Jer 11:5 Then I A, "So be it, LORD."
23:35 'What has the LORD A or 'What has the
23:37 'What has the LORD A you?' or 'What has
35:6 But they A, "We will drink no wine, for
35:17 have called to them and they have not A
36:18 Baruch A them, "He dictated all these words to
38:27 asked him, and he A them as the king
44:15 the land of Egypt, A Jeremiah:
Ezek 37:3 And I A, "O Lord GOD, thou knowest."
Dan 2:5 The king A the Chaldeans, "The word from me
2:7 They A a second time, "Let the king tell
2:8 The king A, "I know with certainty that you
2:10 The Chaldeans A the king, "There is not a
2:27 Daniel A the king, "No wise men, enchanters,
3:16 Shadrach, Meshach, and Abednego A the king, "O
3:92 They A the king, "True, O king."
3:93 He A, "But I see four men loose, walking
4:19 Belteshazzar A, "My lord, may the dream be for
5:17 Then Daniel A before the king, "Let your gifts
6:12 The king A, "The thing stands fast, according to
6:13 Then they A before the king, "That Daniel, who
13:54 He A, "Under a mastic tree."
13:58 He A, "Under an evergreen oak."
14:5 He A, "Because I do not revere man-made idols,
14:17 He A, "They are unbroken, O king."
Joel 2:19 The LORD A and said to his people, "Behold,
Amos 7:14 Then Amos A Amaziah, "I am no prophet, nor
Jon 2:2 my distress, and he A me; out of the
Mic 6:5 the son of Beor A him, and what happened
Hab 2:2 And the LORD A me: "Write the vision; make
Hag 2:12 The priests A, "No."
2:13 The priests A, "It does become unclean."
Zech 1:10 among the myrtle trees A, 'These are they whom
1:11 the earth.' And they A the angel of the
1:13 years?' And the LORD A gracious and comforting
1:19 And he A me, "These are the horns which
1:21 He A, "These are the horns which scattered Judah,
4:5 who talked with me A me, "Do you not
5:2 I A, "I see a flying scroll; its length
6:5 And the angel A me, "These are going forth
1Mac 2:19 But Mattathias A and said in a loud voice:
13:8 these words, and they A in a loud voice,
2Mac 14:5 He A:
Mt 3:15 But Jesus A him, "Let it be so now;
4:4 But he A, "It is written, 'Man shall not
8:8 But the centurion A him, "Lord, I am not
11:4 And Jesus A them, "Go and tell John what
12:39 But he A them, "An evil and adulterous generation
13:11 And he A them, "To you it has been
13:37 He A, "He who sows the good seed is
14:28 And Peter A him, "Lord, if it is you,
15:3 He A them, "And why do you transgress the
15:13 He A, "Every plant which my heavenly Father has
15:24 He A, "I was sent only to the lost
15:26 And he A, "It is not fair to take
15:28 Then Jesus A her, "O woman, great is your
16:2 He A them, "When it is evening, you say,
16:17 And Jesus A him, "Blessed are you, Simon Bar-Jona!
17:17 And Jesus A, "O faithless and perverse generation,
19:4 He A, "Have you not read that he who
20:22 But Jesus A, "You do not know what you
21:21 And Jesus A them, "Truly, I say to you,
21:24 Jesus A them, "I also will ask you a
21:27 So they A Jesus, "We do not know." And
21:29 vineyard today.' And he A, 'I will not'; but
21:30 the same; and he A, 'I go, sir,' but
22:29 But Jesus A them, "You are wrong, because you
24:2 But he A them, "You see all these, do
24:4 And Jesus A them, "Take heed that no one
25:26 yours.' But his master A him, 'You wicked and
26:23 He A, "He who has dipped his hand in
26:66 They A, "He deserves death."
27:25 And all the people A, "His blood be on
Mk 6:37 But he A them, "You give them something to
7:27 But she A him, "Yes, Lord; yet even the
8:4 And his disciples A him, "How can one feed
8:29 Peter A him, "You are the Christ."

	9:17	one of the crowd A him, "Teacher, I brought
	9:19	And he A them, "O faithless generation, how long
	10:3	He A them, "What did Moses command you?"
	11:22	And Jesus A them, "Have faith in God.
	11:32	So they A Jesus, "We do not know." And
	12:28	and seeing that he A them well, asked him,
	12:29	Jesus A, "The first is, 'Hear, O Israel: The
	12:34	Jesus saw that he A wisely, he said to
	15:2	And he A him, "You have said so."
	15:9	And he A them, "Do you want me to
Lk	1:19	And the angel A him, "I am Gabriel, who
	3:11	And he A them, "He who has two coats,
	3:16	were the Christ, John A them all, "I baptize
	4:4	And Jesus A him, "It is written, 'Man shall
	4:8	And Jesus A him, "It is written, 'You shall
	4:12	And Jesus A him, "It is said, 'You shall
	5:5	And Simon A, "Master, we toiled all night and
	5:22	perceived their questionings, he A them, "Why do
	5:31	And Jesus A them, "Those who are well have
	6:3	And Jesus A, "Have you not read what David
	7:22	And he A them, "Go and tell John what
	7:40	And he A, "What is it, Teacher?"
	7:43	Simon A, "The one, I suppose, to whom he
	8:50	Jesus on hearing this A him, "Do not fear;
	9:19	And they A, "John the Baptist; but others say,
	9:20	And Peter A, "The Christ of God."
	9:41	Jesus A, "O faithless and perverse generation, how
	9:49	John A, "Master, we saw a man casting out
	10:27	And he A, "You shall love the Lord your
	10:28	to him, "You have A right; do this, and
	10:41	But the Lord A her, "Martha, Martha, you are
	11:45	One of the lawyers A him, "Teacher, in saying
	13:2	And he A them, "Do you think that these
	13:8	the ground?' And he A him, 'Let it alone,
	13:15	Then the Lord A him, "You hypocrites!
	15:29	entreated him, but he A his father, 'Lo, these
	17:20	God was coming, he A them, "The kingdom of
	19:40	He A, "I tell you, if these were silent,
	20:3	He A them, "I also will ask you a
	20:7	So they A that they did not know whence
	20:39	some of the scribes A, "Teacher, you have spoken
	23:3	And he A him, "You have said so."
	24:18	of them, named Cleopas, A him, "Are you the
Jn	1:21	And he A, "No."
	1:26	John A them, "I baptize with water; but among
	1:48	Jesus A him, "Before Philip called you, when you
	1:49	Nathanael A him, "Rabbi, you are the Son of
	1:50	Jesus A him, "Because I said to you, I
	2:19	Jesus A them, "Destroy this temple, and in three
	3:3	Jesus A him, "Truly, truly, I say to you,
	3:5	Jesus A, "Truly, truly, I say to you, unless
	3:10	Jesus A him, "Are you a teacher of Israel,
	3:27	John A, "No one can receive anything except what
	4:10	Jesus A her, "If you knew the gift of
	4:17	The woman A him, "I have no husband." Jesus
	5:6	The sick man A him, "Sir, I have no
	5:10	But he A them, "The man who healed me
	5:16	But Jesus A them, "My Father is working still,
	6:7	Philip A him, "Two hundred denarii would not buy
	6:26	Jesus A them, "Truly, truly, I say to you,
	6:29	Jesus A them, "This is the work of God,
	6:43	Jesus A them, "Do not murmur among yourselves.
	6:68	Simon Peter A him, "Lord, to whom shall we
	6:70	Jesus A them, "Did I not choose you, the
	7:16	So Jesus A them, "My teaching is not mine,
	7:20	The people A, "You have a demon!
	7:21	Jesus A them, "I did one deed, and you
	7:46	The officers A, "No man ever spoke like this
	7:47	The Pharisees A them, "Are you led astray, you
	8:14	Jesus A, "Even if I do bear witness to
	8:19	Jesus A, "You know neither me nor my Father;
	8:33	They A him, "We are descendants of Abraham, and
	8:34	Jesus A them, "Truly, truly, I say to you,
	8:39	They A him, "Abraham is our father." Jesus said
	8:48	The Jews A him, "Are we not right in
	8:49	Jesus A, "I have not a demon; but I
	8:54	Jesus A, "If I glorify myself, my glory is
	9:3	Jesus A, "It was not that this man sinned,
	9:11	He A, "The man called Jesus made clay and
	9:20	His parents A, "We know that this is our
	9:25	He A, "Whether he is a sinner, I do
	9:27	He A them, "I have told you already, and
	9:30	The man A, "Why, this is a marvel!
	9:34	They A him, "You were born in utter sin,
	9:36	He A, "And who is he, sir, that I
	10:25	Jesus A them, "I told you, and you do
	10:32	Jesus A them, "I have shown you many good
	10:33	The Jews A him, "It is not for a
	10:34	Jesus A them, "Is it not written in your
	11:9	Jesus A, "Are there not twelve hours in the
	12:23	And Jesus A them, "The hour has come for
	12:30	Jesus A, "This voice has come for your sake,
	12:34	The crowd A him, "We have heard from the
	13:7	Jesus A him, "What I am doing you do
	13:8	Jesus A him, "If I do not wash you,
	13:26	Jesus A, "It is he to whom I shall
	13:36	Jesus A, "Where I am going you cannot follow
	13:38	Jesus A, "Will you lay down your life for
	14:23	Jesus A him, "If a man loves me, he
	16:31	Jesus A them, "Do you now believe?
	18:5	They A him, "Jesus of Nazareth." Jesus said to
	18:8	Jesus A, "I told you that I am he;
	18:20	Jesus A him, "I have spoken openly to the
	18:23	Jesus A him, "If I have spoken wrongly, bear
	18:30	They A him, "If this man were not an
	18:34	Jesus A, "Do you say this of your own
	18:35	Pilate A, "Am I a Jew?
	18:36	Jesus A, "My kingship is not of this world;
	18:37	Jesus A, "You say that I am a king.
	19:7	The Jews A him, "We have a law, and
	19:11	Jesus A him, "You would have no power over
	19:15	The chief priests A, "We have no king but
	19:22	Pilate A, "What I have written I have written."
	20:28	Thomas A him, "My Lord and my God!"
	21:5	They A him, "No."
Acts	4:19	But Peter and John A them, "Whether it is
	5:29	Peter and the apostles A, "We must obey God
	8:24	And Simon A, "Pray for me to the Lord,
	9:13	But Ananias A, "Lord, I have heard from many
	11:9	mouth.' But the voice A a second time from
	19:15	But the evil spirit A them, "Jesus I know,
	21:13	Then Paul A, "What are you doing, weeping and
	22:8	persecute me?' And I A, 'Who are you, Lord?'
	22:28	The tribune A, "I bought this citizenship for a
	25:12	conferred with his council, A, "You have appealed to
	25:16	I A them that it was not the custom

ANSWERING (2)

Sir	5:11	Be quick to hear, and be deliberate in A
Lk	7:40	And Jesus A said to him, "Simon, I have

ANSWERS (11)

1Sam	20:10	me if your father A you roughly?"
	28:15	away from me and A me no more, either
1Kgs	18:24	and the God who A by fire, he is
Job	20:3	my understanding a spirit A me.
	21:34	nothing left of your A but falsehood."
	34:36	the end, because he A like wicked men.
Ps	3:4	the LORD, and he A me from his holy
Prov	27:19	As in water face A to face, so the
Eccl	10:19	gladdens life, and money A everything.
Jer	42:4	and whatever the LORD A you I will tell
Lk	2:47	him were amazed at his understanding and his A

ANT

Prov	6:6	Go to the A, O sluggard; consider her ways,

ANTELOPE (2)

Deut	14:5	goat, the ibex, the A, and the mountain-sheep.
Is	51:20	every street like an A in a net; they

ANTHOTHIJAH

1Chr	8:24	Zichri, Hanan, Hananiah, Elam, A,

ANTICHRIST (4)

1Jn	2:18	you have heard that A is coming, so now
	2:22	This is the A, he who denies the Father
	4:3	is the spirit of A, of which you heard
2Jn	1:7	such a one is the deceiver and the A

ANTICHRISTS

1Jn	2:18	coming, so now many A have come; therefore we

ANTILEBANON

Jud	1:7	Damascus and Lebanon and A and all who lived

ANTIMONY (2)

1Chr	29:2	and stones for setting, A, colored stones, all sorts
Is	54:11	set your stones in A, and lay your foundations

ANTIOCH (34)

1Mac	3:37	troops and departed from A his capital in the

A

4:35 nobly, he departed to A and enlisted mercenaries, to
6:63 Then he departed with haste and returned to A
10:68 it, he was greatly grieved and returned to A
11:13 Then Ptolemy entered A and put on the crown
11:44 men to him at A, and when they came
11:56 captured the elephants and gained control of A
2Mac 4:9 enrol the men of Jerusalem as citizens of A
4:33 to a place of sanctuary at Daphne near A
5:21 and hurried away to A, thinking in his arrogance
8:35 country till he reached A, having succeeded chiefly in
11:36 For we are on our way to A
13:23 government, had revolted in A; he was dismayed,
13:26 gained their good will, and set out for A
14:27 to send Maccabeus to A as a prisoner without
Acts 6:5 Timon, and Parmenas, and Nicolaus, a proselyte of A
11:19 Phoenicia and Cyprus and A, speaking the word to
11:20 who on coming to A spoke to the Greeks
11:22 church in Jerusalem, and they sent Barnabas to A
11:26 he had found him, he brought him to A
11:26 of people; and in A the disciples were for
11:27 these days prophets came down from Jerusalem to A
13:1 in the church at A there were prophets and
13:14 Perga and came to A of Pisidia.
14:19 Jews came there from A and Iconium; and having
14:21 to Iconium and to A,
14:26 there they sailed to A, where they had been
15:22 and send them to A with Paul and Barnabas.
15:23 of the Gentiles in A and Syria and Cilicia,
15:30 they went down to A; and having gathered the
15:34 and Barnabas remained in A, teaching and preaching
18:22 greeted the church, and then went down to A
Gal 2:11 when Cephas came to A I opposed him to
2Tim 3:11 what befell me at A, at Iconium, and at

ANTIOCHIAN

2Mac 4:19 envoys, chosen as being A citizens from Jerusalem,

ANTIOCHIS

2Mac 4:30 as a present to A, the king's concubine.

ANTIOCHUS (59)

1Mac 1:10 forth a sinful root, A Epiphanes, son of Antiochus
1:10 Antiochus Epiphanes, son of A the king; he had
1:16 When A saw that his kingdom was established, he
1:20 After subduing Egypt, A returned in the one hundred
3:27 When king A heard these reports, he was greatly
3:33 to take care of A his son until he
6:1 King A was going through the upper provinces when
6:15 that he might guide A his son and bring
6:16 Thus A the king died there in the one
6:17 dead, he set up A the king's son to
6:55 that Philip, whom King A while still living had
6:55 appointed to bring up A his son to be
7:2 fathers, the army seized A and Lysias to bring
8:6 They also defeated A the Great, king of Asia,
10:1 Epiphanes, the son of A, landed and occupied
11:39 who was bringing up A, the young son of
11:40 urged him to hand A over to him, to
11:54 him the young boy A who began to reign
11:57 Then the young A wrote to Jonathan, saying, "I
12:16 Numenius the son of A and Antipater the son
12:39 raise his hand against A the king.
13:31 with the young king A; he killed him
14:22 'Numenius the son of A and Antipater the son
15:1 A, the son of Demetrius the king, sent a
15:2 were as follows: "King A to Simon the high
15:10 hundred and seventy-fourth year A set out and
15:11 A pursued him, and he came in his flight
15:13 So A encamped against Dor, and with him were
15:25 A the king besieged Dor anew, continually throwing
15:26 And Simon sent to A two thousand picked men,
2Mac 1:14 intending to marry her, A came to the place
1:15 out the treasures and A had come with a
2:20 further the wars against A Epiphanes and his son
4:7 When Seleucus died and A who was called
4:21 of Philometor as king, A learned that Philometor
4:37 Therefore A was grieved at heart and filled with
5:1 About this time A made his second invasion of
5:5 false rumor arose that A was dead, Jason took
5:15 Not content with this, A dared to enter the
5:17 A was elated in spirit, and did not perceive
5:21 So A carried off eighteen hundred talents from the
5:24 toward the Jewish citizens, A sent Apollonius, the
7:24 A felt that he was being treated with contempt,
7:24 brother being still alive, A not only appealed to
9:1 time, as it happened, A had retreated in disorder
9:2 rescue with arms, and A and his men were
9:2 with the result that A was put to flight
9:19 his worthy Jewish citizens, A their king and general
9:25 have appointed my son A to be king, whom
9:29 fearing the son of A, he betook himself to
10:9 was the end of A, who was called Epiphanes.
10:10 what took place under A Eupator, who was the
10:13 had gone over to A Epiphanes.
11:22 letter ran thus: "King A to his brother Lysias,
11:27 was as follows: "King A to the senate of
13:1 and his men that A Eupator was coming with
13:3 with utter hypocrisy urged A on, not for the
13:4 aroused the anger of A against the scoundrel; and
14:2 having made away with A and his guardian Lysias.

ANTIPAS

Rev 2:13 in the days of A my witness, my faithful

ANTIPATER (2)

1Mac 12:16 son of Antiochus and A the son of Jason,
14:22 son of Antiochus and A the son of Jason,

ANTIPATRIS

Acts 23:31 took Paul and brought him by night to A

ANTS

Prov 30:25 are exceedingly wise: the A are a people not

ANUB

1Chr 4:8 was the father of A, Zobebah, and the families

ANVIL (2)

Sir 38:28 smith sitting by the A, intent upon his handiwork
Is 41:7 him who strikes the A, saying of the soldering,

ANXIETIES (2)

1Cor 7:32 I want you to be free from A
1Pet 5:7 Cast all your A on him, for he cares

ANXIETY (11)

1Sam 1:16 out of my great A and vexation."
Esth 14:1 queen, seized with deathly A, fled to the Lord;
Prov 12:25 A in a man's heart weighs him down, but
Wis 7:23 sure, free from A, all-powerful, overseeing all, and
Sir 30:24 anger shorten life, and A brings on old age
31:1 away one's flesh, and A about it removes sleep.
31:2 Wakeful A prevents slumber, and a severe illness
2Mac 3:21 whole populace and the A of the high priest
2Cor 5:4 tent, we sigh with A; not that we would
11:28 upon me of my A for all the churches.
Phil 4:6 Have no A about anything, but in everything by

ANXIOUS (28)

1Sam 9:5 the asses and become A about us."
10:2 the asses and is A about you, saying, "What
Ps 127:2 eating the bread of A toil; for he gives
Sir 40:2 of heart– their A thought is the day
Jer 17:8 green, and is not A in the year of
Bar 3:18 get silver, and are A, whose labors are beyond
Dan 7:15 spirit within me was A and the visions of
2Mac 15:19 no little distress, being A over the encounter in
Mt 6:25 you, do not be A about your life, what
6:27 of you by being A can add one cubit
6:28 And why are you A about clothing?
6:31 Therefore do not be A, saying, 'What shall we
6:34 "Therefore do not be A about tomorrow, for
6:34 for tomorrow will be A for itself.
10:19 up, do not be A how you are to
Mk 13:11 up, do not be A beforehand what you are
Lk 10:41 "Martha, Martha, you are A and troubled about
12:11 authorities, do not be A how or what you
12:22 you, do not be A about your life, what
12:25 of you by being A can add a cubit
12:26 that, why are you A about the rest?
12:29 drink, nor be of A mind.
1Cor 7:32 The unmarried man is A about the affairs of
7:33 the married man is A about worldly affairs, how
7:34 woman or girl is A about the affairs of
7:34 the married woman is A about worldly affairs, how
Phil 2:20 who will be genuinely A for your welfare.
2:28 him again, and that I may be less A

ANXIOUSLY (2)

Mic 1:12 inhabitants of Maroth wait A for good, because evil
Lk 2:48 father and I have been looking for you A

ANYBODY (2)

Sir 33:29 not act immoderately toward A, and do nothing
2Tim 3:7 who will listen to A and can never arrive

ANYONE

Lk 8:43 not be healed by A

ANYTHING (171)

Gen 14:23 or a sandal-thong or A that is yours, lest
18:14 I am old?' Is A too hard for the
22:12 the lad or do A to him; for now
30:31 shall not give me A; if you will do
39:6 had no concern for A but the food which
39:8 has no concern about A in the house, and
39:9 has he kept back A from me except yourself,
39:23 paid no heed to A that was in Joseph's
Ex 12:10 remain until the morning, A that remains until the
20:4 or any likeness of A that is in heaven
20:17 or his ass, or A that is your neighbors."
22:14 "If a man borrows A of his neighbor, and
35:29 moved them to bring A for the work which
36:6 man nor woman do A more for the offering
Lev 6:5 which he found, or A about which he has
11:10 But A in the seas or the rivers that
11:32 And A upon which any of them falls when
13:48 a skin or in A made of skin,
13:49 in skin or in A made of skin, it
13:52 woolen or linen, or A of skin, for it
13:53 or woof or in A of skin,
13:57 or woof, or in A of skin, it is
13:58 warp or woof, or A of skin from which
13:59 or woof, or in A of skin, to decide
15:6 And whoever sits on A on which he who
15:10 And whoever touches A that was under him shall
15:22 And whoever touches A upon which she sits shall
15:23 is the bed or A upon which she sits,
19:6 on the morrow; and A left over until the
20:25 by bird or by A with which the ground
22:4 Whoever touches A that is unclean through contact
22:20 You shall not offer A that has a blemish,
27:10 He shall not substitute A for it or exchange
27:28 to the LORD, of A that he has, whether
Num 15:29 for him who does A unwittingly, for him who
15:30 the person who does A with a high hand,
22:38 I now any power at all to speak A
30:9 of a divorced woman, A by which she has
35:22 without enmity, or hurled A on him without lying
Deut 4:18 air, the likeness of A that creeps on the
4:23 in the form of A which the LORD your
4:25 in the form of A, and by doing what
5:8 or any likeness of A that is in heaven
5:21 or his ass, or A that is your neighbors.'
14:21 "You shall not eat A that dies of itself;
22:5 woman shall not wear A that pertains to a
23:14 he may not see A indecent among you, and
23:19 on victuals, interest on A that is lent for
Judg 13:14 may not eat of A that comes from the
18:10 is no lack of A that is in the
19:19 with your servants; there is no lack of A
1Sam 3:17 also, if you hide A from me of all
10:16 Samuel had spoken, he did not tell him A
12:4 oppressed us or taken A from any man's hand."
12:5 you have not found A in my hand." And
19:3 and if I learn A I will tell you."
20:26 Saul did not say A that day; for he
21:2 'Let no one know A of the matter about
22:15 not the king impute A to his servant or
25:15 we did not miss A when we were in
30:19 or daughters, spoil or A that had been taken;
2Sam 3:35 I taste bread or A else till the sun
13:2 to Amnon to do A to her.
14:10 "If any one says A to you, bring him
14:18 not hide from me A I ask you." And
14:19 to the left from A that my lord the
1Kgs 10:21 was not considered as A in the days of
15:5 not turn aside from A that he commanded him
2Chr 9:20 was not considered as A in the days of
Tob 2:4 So before I tasted A I sprang up and
12:11 "I will not conceal A from you.
Jud 8:13 to the test—but you will never know A
Job 20:20 he will not save A in which he delights.
31:16 "If I have withheld A that the poor desired,
33:32 If you have A to say, answer me; speak,
Ps 101:3 set before my eyes A that is base.
Eccl 3:14 added to it, nor A taken from it; God
6:5 the sun or known A; yet it finds rest
7:14 may not find out A that will be after
12:12 My son, beware of A beyond these.
Wis 10:12 might learn that godliness is more powerful than A
11:24 wouldst not have made A if thou hadst hated
11:25 How would A have endured if thou hadst not
11:25 Or how would A not called forth by thee
Sir 8:12 if you do lend A, be as one who
10:6 and do not attempt A by acts of insolence.
19:13 but if he did A, so that he may
25:3 then can you find A in your old age?
29:26 and if you have A at hand, let me
Jer 32:27 of all flesh; is A too hard for me?
42:21 LORD your God in A that he sent me
Ezek 15:3 Is wood taken from it to make A
15:4 of it is charred, is it useful for A
15:5 is charred, can it ever be used for A
29:18 nor his army got A from Tyre to pay
44:18 not gird themselves with A that causes sweat.
44:31 shall not eat of A, whether bird or beast,
Dan 3:97 or language that speaks A against the God of
14:7 brass outside, and it never ate or drank A
Jon 3:7 herd nor flock, taste A; let them not feed,
1Mac 8:30 to add or delete A, they shall do so
10:35 have authority to exact A from them or annoy
2Mac 9:24 successor, so that, if A unexpected happened or any
12:18 the region without accomplishing A, though in one
Mt 5:13 no longer good for A except to be thrown
5:37 simply 'Yes' or 'No'; A more than this comes
9:33 marveled, saying, "Never was A like this seen in
18:18 agree on earth about A they ask, it will
21:3 If any one says A to you, you shall
Mk 2:12 saying, "We never saw A like this!"
4:22 made manifest; nor is A secret, except to come
7:12 permit him to do A for his father or
8:23 upon him, he asked him, "Do you see A
9:22 if you can do A, have pity on us
9:29 be driven out by A but prayer and fasting."
11:13 if he could find A on it.
11:16 any one to carry A through the temple.
11:25 forgive, if you have A against any one; so
13:15 his house, to take A away;
Lk 8:17 be made manifest, nor A secret that shall not
9:36 one in those days A of what they had
11:7 bed; I cannot get up and give you A
11:8 up and give him A because he is his
15:16 the swine ate; and no one gave him A
19:8 defrauded any one of A, I restore it fourfold."
19:48 they did not find A they could do, for
22:35 purse or bag or sandals, did you lack A
24:41 to them, "Have you A here to eat?"
Jn 1:3 without him was not A made that was made.
1:46 said to him, "Can A good come out of
3:27 "No one can receive A except what is given
14:14 Son; if you ask A in my name, I
16:23 you, if you ask A of the Father, he
Acts 10:14 I have never eaten A that is common or
17:25 as though he needed A, since he himself gives
19:39 But if you seek A further, it shall be
20:20 from declaring to you A that was profitable, and
24:18 accusation, if they have A against me.
25:5 and if there is A wrong about the man,
25:11 wrongdoer, and have committed A for which I
Rom 8:39 height, nor depth, nor A else in all creation,
13:8 Owe no one A, except to love one another;
14:2 believes he may eat A, while the weak man
14:21 drink wine or do A that makes your brother
15:18 venture to speak of A except what Christ has
1Cor 3:7 he who waters is A, but only God who
4:4 am not aware of A against myself, but I
4:7 For who sees A different in you?
6:12 but I will not be enslaved by A
7:19 circumcision counts for A nor uncircumcision, but
9:12 right, but we endure A rather than put an
10:19 offered to idols is A, or that an idol
10:19 idols is anything, or that an idol is A
14:35 If there is A they desire to know, let
2Cor 2:10 if I have forgiven A, has been for your
3:5 of ourselves to claim A as coming from us;
13:8 For we cannot do A against the truth, but
Gal 6:15 circumcision counts for A, nor uncircumcision, but a
Eph 5:13 in secret; but when A is exposed by the
5:13 it becomes visible, for A that becomes visible is
Phil 1:28 and not frightened in A by your opponents.
3:15 minded; and if in A you are otherwise minded,
4:6 Have no anxiety about A, but in everything by
4:8 excellence, if there is A worthy of praise, think

1Thes 1:8 forth everywhere, so that we need not say A
5:1 no need to have A written to you.
1Tim 6:7 and we cannot take A out of the world;
Philem 1:18 all, or owes you A, charge that to my
Jas 1:7 his ways, will receive A from the Lord.
1Jn 5:14 that if we ask A according to his will
Rev 22:3 shall no more be A accursed, but the throne

ANYWHERE

Gen 19:17 look back or stop A in the valley; flee

APACE (2)

2Sam 18:25 And he came A, and drew near.
Jer 48:16 is near at hand and his affliction hastens A

APART (54)

Gen 21:28 Abraham set seven ewe lambs of the flock A
21:29 these seven ewe lambs which you have set A
30:40 put his own droves A, and did not put
Ex 8:22 day I will set A the land of Goshen,
13:12 you, you shall set A to the LORD all
Lev 20:25 which I have set A for you to hold
Num 6:21 vow as a Nazirite, A from what else he
Deut 4:41 Then Moses set A three cities in the east
10:8 time the LORD set A the tribe of Levi
19:2 houses, you shall set A three cities for you
19:7 you, You shall set A three cities.
Josh 16:9 towns which were set A for the Ephraimites within
20:7 So they set A Kedesh in Galilee in the
Judg 20:17 the men of Israel, A from Benjamin, mustered four
2Sam 14:24 said, "Let him dwell A in his own house;
14:24 So Absalom dwelt A in his own house, and
1Chr 23:13 Aaron was set A to consecrate the most holy
25:1 the service also set A for the service certain
Ezra 8:20 his officials had set A to attend the Levites.
8:24 Then I set A twelve of the leading priests:
Neh 12:47 gatekeepers; and they set A that which was for
12:47 and the Levites set A that which was for
Ps 4:3 the LORD has set A the godly for himself;
16:2 I have no good A from thee."
Eccl 2:25 hand of God; for A from him who can
Wis 11:20 Even A from these, men could fall at a
Is 65:5 for I am set A from you." These are
Jer 12:3 slaughter, and set them A for the day of
Ezek 39:14 They will set A men to pass through the
45:1 possession, you shall set A for the LORD a
45:6 "Alongside the portion set A as the holy district
48:8 which you shall set A, twenty-five thousand cubits in
48:9 which you shall set A for the LORD shall
48:20 which you shall set A shall be twenty-five thousand
Mt 14:13 there in a boat to a lonely place A
17:1 brother, and led them up a high mountain A
Mk 5:4 the chains he wrenched A, and the fetters he
9:2 up a high mountain A by themselves; and he
Lk 9:10 took them and withdrew A to a city called
Jn 15:5 bears much fruit, for A from me you can
Acts 13:2 Holy Spirit said, "Set A for me Barnabas and
Rom 1:1 be an apostle, set A for the gospel of
3:21 God has been manifested A from law, although the
3:28 is justified by faith A from works of law.
4:6 whom God reckons righteousness A from works:
7:8 A from the law sin lies dead.
7:9 I was once alive A from the law, but
2Cor 11:28 And, A from other things, there is the daily
Gal 1:15 who had set me A before I was born,
Heb 11:40 better for us, that A from us they should
Jas 2:18 Show me your faith A from your works, and
2:20 shallow man, that faith A from works is barren?
2:26 For as the body A from the spirit is
2:26 is dead, so faith A from works is dead.

APELLES

Rom 16:10 Greet A, who is approved in Christ.

APES (2)

1Kgs 10:22 bringing gold, silver, ivory, A, and peacocks.
2Chr 9:21 bringing gold, silver, ivory, A, and peacocks.

APHAIREMA

1Mac 11:34 the three districts of A and Lydda and Rathamin;

APHEK (8)

Josh 12:18 one; the king of A, one; the king of
13:4 to the Sidonians, to A, to the boundary of
19:30 Mahalab, Achzib, Ummah, A and Rehob--twenty-two
1Sam 4:1 at Ebenezer, and the Philistines encamped at A
29:1 all their forces at A; and the Israelites were
1Kgs 20:26 and went up to A, to fight against Israel.
20:30 into the city of A; and the wall fell
2Kgs 13:17 fight the Syrians in A until you have made

APHEKAH

Josh 15:53 Dumah, Eshan, Janim, Beth-tappuah, A,

APHIAH

1Sam 9:1 of Becorath, son of A, a Benjaminite, a man

APHIK

Judg 1:31 of Helbah, or of A, or of Rehob;

APIECE (5)

Ex 16:16 shall take an omer A, according to the number
16:22 much bread, two omers A; and when all the
Num 3:47 shall take five shekels A; reckoning by the shekel
7:86 incense, weighing ten shekels A according to the
Ezek 41:24 doors had two leaves A, two swinging leaves for

APIS

Jer 46:15 about you.' Why has A fled?

APOLLONIA

Acts 17:1 passed through Amphipolis and A, they came to

APOLLONIUS (13)

1Mac 3:10 But A gathered together Gentiles and a large force
3:12 took the sword of A, and used it in
10:69 Demetrius appointed A the governor of Coelesyria,
10:74 heard the words of A, his spirit was aroused.
10:75 closed its gates, for A had a garrison in
10:77 When A heard of it, he mustered three thousand
10:79 Now A had secretly left a thousand cavalry behind
2Mac 3:5 Onias he went to A of Tarsus, who at
3:7 When A met the king, he told him of
4:4 was serious and that A, the son of Menestheus
4:21 When A the son of Menestheus was sent to
5:24 Jewish citizens, Antiochus sent A, the captain of the
12:2 various places, Timothy and A the son of Gennaeus,

APOLLOPHANES

2Mac 10:37 in a cistern, and his brother Chaereas, and A

APOLLOS (10)

Acts 18:24 Now a Jew named A, a native of Alexandria,
19:1 While A was at Corinth, Paul passed through the
1Cor 1:12 or "I belong to A
3:4 and another, "I belong to A
3:5 What then is A
3:6 I planted, A watered, but God gave the growth.
3:22 yours, whether Paul or A or Cephas or the
4:6 this to myself and A for your benefit, brethren,
16:12 As for our brother A, I strongly urged him
Tit 3:13 Zenas the lawyer and A on their way; see

APOLLYON

Rev 9:11 is Abaddon, and in Greek he is called A

APOLOGIES

Sir 13:3 poor man suffers wrong, and he must add A

APOLOGIZED

Acts 16:39 so they came and A to them.

APOSTASIES

Jer 5:6 transgressions are many, their A are great.

APOSTASY (4)

Tob 1:5 tribes that joined in A used to sacrifice to
Jer 2:19 chasten you, and your A will reprove you.
1Mac 2:15 who were enforcing the A came to the city
Heb 6:6 if they then commit A, since they crucify the

APOSTLE (19)

Rom 1:1 called to be an A, set apart for the
11:13 as I am an A to the Gentiles, I
1Cor 1:1 God to be an A of Christ Jesus, and
9:1 Am I not an A
9:2 I am not an A, at least I am
15:9 to be called an A, because I persecuted the
2Cor 1:1 Paul, an A of Christ Jesus by
12:12 signs of a true A were performed among you
Gal 1:1 Paul an A --not from men nor
Eph 1:1 Paul, an A of Christ Jesus by

Col	1:1	Paul, an A of Christ Jesus by
1Tim	1:1	Paul, an A of Christ Jesus by
	2:7	appointed a preacher and A (I am telling the
2Tim	1:1	Paul, an A of Christ Jesus by
	1:11	appointed a preacher and A and teacher,
Tit	1:1	of God and an A of Jesus Christ, to
Heb	3:1	call, consider Jesus, the A and high priest of
1Pet	1:1	Peter, an A of Jesus Christ, to
2Pet	1:1	Peter, a servant and A of Jesus Christ, To

APOSTLES (58)

Mt	10:2	names of the twelve A are these: first, Simon,
Mk	6:30	The A returned to Jesus, and told him all
Lk	6:13	twelve, whom he named A;
	9:10	On their return the A told him what they
	11:49	send them prophets and A, some of whom they
	17:5	The A said to the Lord, "Increase our faith!"
	22:14	at table, and the A with him.
	24:10	told this to the A;
Acts	1:2	Holy Spirit to the A whom he had chosen.
	1:26	Matthias; and he was enrolled with the eleven A
	2:37	the rest of the A, "Brethren, what shall we
	2:42	devoted themselves to the A teaching and fellowship,
	2:43	many wonders and signs were done through the A
	4:33	with great power the A gave their testimony to
	4:35	laid it at the A feet; and distribution was
	4:36	was surnamed by the A Barnabas (which means, Son
	4:37	laid it at the A feet.
	5:2	laid it at the A feet.
	5:12	among the people by the hands of the A
	5:18	jealousy they arrested the A and put them in
	5:29	But Peter and the A answered, "We must obey
	5:40	had called in the A, they beat them and
	6:6	they set before the A, and they prayed and
	8:1	the region of Judea and Samaria, except the A
	8:14	Now when the A at Jerusalem heard that Samaria
	8:18	laying on of the A hands, he offered them
	9:27	brought him to the A, and declared to them
	11:1	Now the A and the brethren who were in
	14:4	sided with the Jews, and some with the A
	14:14	But when the A Barnabas and Paul heard of
	15:2	to Jerusalem to the A and the elders about
	15:4	the church and the A and the elders, and
	15:6	The A and the elders were gathered together to
	15:22	seemed good to the A and the elders, with
	15:23	"The brethren, both the A and the elders, to
	16:4	been reached by the A and elders who were
Rom	16:7	of note among the A, and they were in
1Cor	4:9	God has exhibited us A as last of all,
	9:5	wife, as the other A and the brothers of
	12:28	in the church first A, second prophets, third teachers,
	12:29	Are all A
	15:7	he appeared to James, then to all the A
	15:9	the least of the A, unfit to be called
2Cor	11:5	not in the least inferior to these superlative A
	11:13	such men are false A, deceitful workmen, disguising
	11:13	workmen, disguising themselves as A of Christ.
	12:11	inferior to these superlative A, even though I am
Gal	1:17	to those who were A before me, but I
	1:19	none of the other A except James the Lord's
Eph	2:20	the foundation of the A and prophets, Christ Jesus
	3:5	revealed to his holy A and prophets by the
	4:11	that some should be A, some prophets, some
1Thes	2:6	have made demands as A of Christ.
2Pet	3:2	of the Lord and Savior through your A
Jude	1:17	the predictions of the A of our Lord Jesus
Rev	2:2	those who call themselves A but are not, and
	18:20	heaven, O saints and A and prophets, for God
	21:14	names of the twelve A of the Lamb.

APOSTLESHIP (3)

Acts	1:25	in this ministry and A from which Judas turned
Rom	1:5	have received grace and A to bring about the
1Cor	9:2	the seal of my A in the Lord.

APPA-IM (2)

1Chr	2:30	of Nadab: Seled and A; and Seled died childless.
	2:31	The sons of A: Ishi.

APPALLED (22)

Ezra	9:3	hair from my head and beard, and sat A
	9:4	me while I sat A until the evening sacrifice.
Job	17:8	Upright men are A at this, and the innocent
	18:20	of the west are A at his day, and
	21:5	at me, and be A, and lay your hand
Ps	40:15	Let them be A because of their shame who
	70:3	Let them be A because of their shame who
	143:4	faints within me; my heart within me is A
Wis	17:3	scattered, terribly alarmed, and A by specters.
Is	21:4	mind reels, horror has A me; the twilight I
	63:5	to help; I was A, but there was no
Jer	2:12	Be A, O heavens, at this, be shocked, be
	4:9	the priests shall be A and the prophets astounded."
	49:20	their fold shall be A at their fate.
	50:13	by Babylon shall be A, and hiss because of
	50:45	their fold shall be A at their fate.
Ezek	19:7	and the land was A and all who were
	26:16	every moment, and be A at you.
	27:35	of the coastlands are A at you; and their
	28:19	among the peoples are A at you; you have
	32:10	will make many peoples A at you, and their
Dan	8:27	business; but I was A by the vision and

APPALLING

Jer	5:30	An A and horrible thing has happened in the

APPAREL (12)

Judg	17:10	and a suit of A, and your living."
2Sam	1:24	scarlet, who put ornaments of gold upon your A
Jud	10:3	herself in her gayest A, which she used to
Esth	14:2	took off her splendid A and put on the
Is	63:1	is glorious in his A, marching in the greatness
	63:2	Why is thy A red, and thy garments like
Zech	3:4	you, and I will clothe you with rich A
Lk	23:11	arraying him in gorgeous A, he sent him back
	24:4	by them in dazzling A;
Acts	10:30	before me in bright A,
	20:33	I coveted no one's silver or gold or A
1Tim	2:9	and sensibly in seemly A, not with braided hair

APPARELED

Lk	7:25	those who are gorgeously A and live in luxury

APPARITION

2Mac	5:4	men prayed that the A might prove to have

APPARITIONS

Wis	18:17	Then at once A in dreadful dreams greatly troubled

APPEAL (19)

2Kgs	8:3	she went forth to A to the king for
Job	9:15	answer him; I must A for mercy to my
Sir	41:21	and of rejecting the A of a kinsman; of
1Mac	8:32	If now they A again for help against you,
Mt	26:53	think that I cannot A to my Father, and
Acts	25:11	I A to Caesar."
	28:19	I was compelled to A to Caesar--though I
Rom	12:1	I A to you therefore, brethren, by the mercies
	15:30	I A to you, brethren, by our Lord Jesus
	16:17	I A to you, brethren, to take note of
1Cor	1:10	I A to you, brethren, by the name of
2Cor	5:20	Christ, God making his A through us.
	8:17	not only accepted our A, but being himself very
	13:11	your ways, heed my A, agree with one another,
1Thes	2:3	For our A does not spring from error or
Philem	1:9	sake I prefer to A to you--I, Paul,
	1:10	Christ Jesus-- I A to you for my
Heb	13:22	I A to you, brethren, bear with my word
1Pet	3:21	body but as an A to God for a

APPEALED (10)

2Kgs	8:5	had restored to life A to the king for
Wis	8:21	was-- so I A to the Lord and
Sir	47:5	For he A to the Lord, the Most High,
	51:10	I A to the Lord, the Father of my
2Mac	4:36	Jews in the city A to him with regard
	7:24	alive, Antiochus not only A to him in words,
Acts	25:12	council, answered, "You have A to Caesar; to Caesar
	25:21	But when Paul had A to be kept in
	25:25	and as he himself A to the emperor, I
	26:32	if he had not A to Caesar."

APPEALING (3)

Wis	18:22	he subdued the punisher, A to the oaths and
2Mac	7:37	laws of our fathers, A to God to show
Jude	1:3	it necessary to write A to you to contend

APPEALS

Wis	13:18	For health he A to a thing that is

APPEAR (48)

Gen	1:9	into one place, and let the dry land A

46:28 him to Joseph, to A before him in Goshen;
Ex 4:1 'The LORD did not A to you.'"
23:15 None shall A before me empty-handed.
23:17 shall all your males A before the Lord GOD.
34:20 And none shall A before me empty.
34:23 shall all your males A before the LORD God,
34:24 you go up to A before the LORD your
Lev 9:4 today the LORD will A to you.'"
9:6 of the LORD will A to you."
13:7 his cleansing, he shall A again before the priest;
16:2 die; for I will A in the cloud upon
Deut 16:16 all your males shall A before the LORD your
16:16 They shall not A before the LORD empty-handed;
19:17 to the dispute shall A before the LORD, before
31:11 all Israel comes to A before the LORD your
1Sam 1:22 him, that he may A in the presence of
Esth 14:16 the days when I A in public.
Ps 21:9 make them as a blazing oven when you A
102:16 up Zion, he will A in his glory;
Song 2:12 The flowers A on the earth, the time of
Sir 35:4 Do not A before the Lord empty-handed,
37:18 four turns of fortune A, good and evil, life
39:4 among great men and A before rulers; he will
Is 1:12 "When you come to A before me, who requires
49:9 who are in darkness, A They shall feed along
Ezek 16:51 have made your sisters A righteous by all the
16:52 have made your sisters A righteous.
21:24 your doings your sins A –because you have come
Dan 11:31 Forces from him shall A and profane the temple
Hag 1:8 and that I may A in my glory, says
Zech 9:14 Then the LORD will A over them, and his
1Mac 9:27 that prophets ceased to A among them.
2Mac 2:8 and the cloud will A, as they were shown
Mt 23:26 tombs, which outwardly A beautiful, but within the
23:27 So you also outwardly A righteous to men, but
24:30 be shaken; then will A the sign of the
Lk 19:11 of God was to A immediately.
Acts 26:16 in which I will A to you,
2Cor 5:10 For we must all A before the judgment seat
13:7 not that we may A to have met the
Col 3:4 then you also will A with him in glory.
1Tim 5:24 the sins of others A later.
Heb 9:24 heaven itself, now to A in the presence of
9:28 sins of many, will A a second time, not
11:3 was made out of things which do not A
1Pet 4:18 scarcely saved, where will the impious and sinner A
1Jn 3:2 it does not yet A what we shall be,

APPEARANCE (61)

Ex 24:17 Now the A of the glory of the LORD
Lev 13:43 bald forehead, like the A of leprosy in the
Num 9:15 the tabernacle like the A of fire until morning.
9:16 by day, and the A of fire by night.
11:7 coriander seed, and its A like that of bdellium.
1Sam 16:7 not look on his A or on the height
16:7 looks on the outward A, but the LORD looks
17:42 was but a youth, ruddy and comely in A
28:14 He said to her, "What is his A
Tob 1:13 me favor and good A in the sight of
Jud 8:7 She was beautiful in A, and had a very
11:23 not only beautiful in A, but wise in speech;
Job 4:16 stood still, but I could not discern its A
Song 5:15 His A is like Lebanon, choice as the cedars.
Wis 14:17 distance, they imagined their A far away, and made
15:5 with varied colors, whose A arouses yearning in fools,
15:19 not so beautiful in A that one would desire
17:6 they saw to be worse than that unseen A
Sir 11:2 looks, nor loathe a man because of his A
19:26 is known by his A, and a sensible man
25:16 a wife changes her A, and darkens her face
43:1 the clear firmament, the A of heaven in a
Is 52:14 at him– his A was so marred, beyond
Bar 6:63 compared with them in A or power.
Ezek 1:5 And this was their A: they had the form
1:16 As for the A of the wheels and their
1:16 and their construction: their A was like the gleaming
1:26 of a throne, in A like sapphire; and seated
1:27 from what had the A of his loins I
1:27 gleaming bronze, like the A of fire enclosed round
1:27 from what had the A of his loins I
1:27 as it were the A of fire, and there
1:28 Like the A of the bow that is in
1:28 rain, so was the A of the brightness round
1:28 Such was the A of the likeness of the
8:2 form that had the A of a man; below
8:2 it was like the A of brightness, like gleaming
10:9 each cherub; and the A of the wheels was
10:10 And as for their A, the four had the
10:22 the very faces whose A I had seen by
40:3 was a man, whose A was like bronze, with
43:10 the temple and its A and plan, that they
Dan 1:13 Then let our A and the appearance of the
1:13 our appearance and the A of the youths who
1:15 they were better in A and fatter in flesh
2:31 before you, and its A was frightening.
3:93 not hurt; and the A of the fourth is
8:15 me one having the A of a man.
10:6 his face like the A of lightning, his eyes
10:8 in me; my radiant A was fearfully changed, and
10:18 Again one having the A of a man touched
13:31 a woman of great refinement, and beautiful in A
Joel 2:4 Their A is like the appearance of horses, and
2:4 appearance is like the A of horses, and like
2Mac 3:16 To see the A of the high priest was
Mt 16:3 how to interpret the A of the sky, but
28:3 His A was like lightning, and his raiment white
Lk 9:29 he was praying, the A of his countenance was
12:56 how to interpret the A of earth and sky;
Col 2:23 These have indeed an A of wisdom in promoting
Rev 9:7 In A the locusts were like horses arrayed for

APPEARANCES (2)

2Mac 2:21 son Eupator, and the A which came from heaven
Jn 7:24 Do not judge by A, but judge with right

APPEARED (104)

Gen 12:7 Then the LORD A to Abram, and said, "To
12:7 the LORD, who had A to him.
17:1 years old the LORD A to Abram, and said
18:1 And the LORD A to him by the oaks
26:2 And the LORD A to him, and said, "Do
26:24 And the LORD A to him the same night
35:1 to the God who A to you when you
35:9 God A to Jacob again, when he came from
48:3 to Joseph, "God Almighty A to me at Luz
Ex 3:2 angel of the LORD A to him in a
3:16 and of Jacob, has A to me, saying, "I
4:5 God of Jacob, has A to you."
6:3 I A to Abraham, to Isaac, and to Jacob,
14:27 flow when the morning A; and the Egyptians fled
16:10 glory of the LORD A in the cloud.
Lev 9:23 glory of the LORD A to all the people.
Num 14:10 glory of the LORD A at the tent of
16:19 glory of the LORD A to all the congregation.
16:42 covered it, and the glory of the LORD A
20:6 glory of the LORD A to them,
Deut 31:15 And the LORD A in the tent in a
Judg 6:12 angel of the LORD A to him and said
13:3 angel of the LORD A to the woman and
13:10 the other day has A to me."
13:21 angel of the LORD A no more to Manoah
19:26 And as morning A, the woman came and fell
1Sam 3:21 And the LORD A again at Shiloh, for the
1Kgs 3:5 At Gibeon the LORD A to Solomon in a
9:2 to build, the LORD A to Solomon a second
9:2 time, as he had A to him at Gibeon.
11:9 of Israel, who had A to him twice,
2Chr 1:7 In that night God A to Solomon, and said
3:1 where the LORD had A to David his father,
7:12 Then the LORD A to Solomon in the night
Tob 12:19 these days I merely A to you and did
12:22 of the Lord had A to them.
Wis 17:4 them, and dismal phantoms with gloomy faces A
Jer 31:3 for rest, the LORD A to him from afar.
Bar 3:37 Afterward she A upon earth and lived among men.
Ezek 8:2 a man; below what A to be his loins
10:1 of the cherubim there A above them something like
10:8 The cherubim A to have the form of a
Dan 5:5 of a man's hand A and wrote on the
8:1 King Belshazzar a vision A to me, Daniel, after
8:1 Daniel, after that which A to me at the
1Mac 4:6 At daybreak Judas A in the plain with three
4:19 this speech, a detachment A, coming out of the
7:12 a group of scribes A in a body before
9:23 parts of Israel; all the doers of injustice A
2Mac 1:33 fire, the liquid had A with which Nehemiah and
3:25 For there A to them a magnificently caparisoned
3:26 Two young men also A to him, remarkably strong,
3:30 and gladness, now that the Almighty Lord had A
3:33 the same young men A again to Heliodorus dressed
5:2 forty days, there A golden-clad horsemen charging
10:29 battle became fierce, there A to the enemy from

11:8 near Jerusalem, a horseman A at their head, clothed
12:16 of a mile wide, A to be running over
12:22 when Judas' first division A, terror and fear came
14:20 people, and it had A that they were of
15:13 Then likewise a man A, distinguished by his gray
Mt 1:20 angel of the Lord A to him in a
2:7 what time the star A;
2:13 angel of the Lord A to Joseph in a
2:19 angel of the Lord A in a dream to
13:26 grain, then the weeds A also.
17:3 And behold, there A to them Moses and Elijah,
27:53 the holy city and A to many.
Mk 1:4 John the baptizer A in the wilderness, preaching a
9:4 And there A to them Elijah with Moses; and
16:9 of the week, he A first to Mary Magdalene,
16:12 After this he A in another form to two
16:14 Afterward he A to the eleven themselves as they
Lk 1:11 And there A to him an angel of the
2:9 angel of the Lord A to them, and the
9:8 some that Elijah had A, and by others that
9:31 Moses and Elijah, who A in glory and spoke
24:28 He A to be going further,
24:34 risen indeed, and has A to Simon!"
Acts 2:3 And there A to them tongues as of fire,
7:2 The God of glory A to our father Abraham,
7:26 the following day he A to them as they
7:30 had passed, an angel A to him in the
7:35 of the angel that A to him in the
9:17 the Lord Jesus who A to you on the
12:7 angel of the Lord A, and a light shone
13:31 for many days he A to those who came
16:9 And a vision A to Paul in the night:
26:16 feet; for I have A to you for this
27:20 neither sun nor stars A for many a day,
1Cor 15:5 scriptures, and that he A to Cephas, then to
15:6 Then he A to more than five hundred brethren
15:7 Then he A to James, then to all the
15:8 one untimely born, he A also to me.
Tit 2:11 grace of God has A for the salvation of
3:4 of God our Savior A,
Heb 9:11 But when Christ A as a high priest of
9:26 it is, he has A once for all at
1Jn 3:5 You know that he A to take away sins,
3:8 the Son of God A was to destroy the
Rev 4:3 he who sat there A like jasper and carnelian,
12:1 And a great portent A in heaven, a woman
12:3 And another portent A in heaven; behold, a great
15:2 And I saw what A to be a sea

APPEARING (8)

Sir 43:16 At his A the mountains are shaken; at his
Acts 1:3 passion by many proofs, A to them during forty
2Thes 2:8 destroy him by his A and his coming.
1Tim 6:14 from reproach until the A of our Lord Jesus
2Tim 1:10 has manifested through the A of our Savior Christ
4:1 dead, and by his A and his kingdom:
4:8 but also to all who have loved his A
Tit 2:13 our blessed hope, the A of the glory of

APPEARS (23)

Lev 13:3 white and the disease A to be deeper than
13:4 of his body, and A no deeper than the
13:14 But when raw flesh A on him, he shall
13:20 examination, and if it A deeper than the skin
13:25 turned white and it A deeper than the skin,
13:30 disease; and if it A deeper than the skin,
13:31 itching disease, and it A no deeper than the
13:32 hair, and the itch A to be no deeper
13:34 the skin and it A to be no deeper
13:57 woof; then if it A again in the garment,
14:37 spots, and if it A to be deeper than
Prov 27:25 and the new growth A, and the herbage of
Wis 6:16 her, and she graciously A to them in their
Sir 43:2 The sun, when it A, making proclamation as it
43:22 things; when the dew A, it refreshes from the
Zech 13:3 if any one again A as a prophet, his
Mal 3:2 his coming, and who can stand when he A
Jn 7:27 and when the Christ A, no one will know
7:31 said, "When the Christ A, will he do more
Col 3:4 who is our life A, then you also will
Jas 4:14 are a mist that A for a little time
1Jn 2:28 so that when he A we may have confidence
3:2 know that when he A we shall be like

APPEASE (2)

Gen 32:20 he thought, "I may A him with the present
Prov 16:14 a wise man will A it.

APPEASED (3)

Prov 6:35 no compensation, nor be A though you multiply gifts.
Is 57:6 Shall I be A for these things?
2Mac 13:26 defense, convinced them, A them, gained their

APPENDAGE (11)

Ex 29:13 the entrails, and the A of the liver, and
29:22 the entrails, and the A of the liver, and
Lev 3:4 the loins, and the A of the liver which
3:10 the loins, and the A of the liver which
3:15 the loins, and the A of the liver which
4:9 the loins, and the A of the liver which
7:4 the loins, and the A of the liver which
8:16 the entrails, and the A of the liver, and
8:25 the entrails, and the A of the liver, and
9:10 the kidneys and the A of the liver from
9:19 the kidneys, and the A of the liver;

APPENDED

1Mac 12:7 our brethren, as the A copy shows.

APPETITE (14)

Deut 14:26 strong drink, whatever your A craves; and you shall
Job 6:7 My A refuses to touch them; they are as
33:20 loathes bread, and his A dainty food.
38:39 lion, or satisfy the A of the young lions,
Prov 6:30 steals to satisfy his A when he is hungry?
13:25 enough to satisfy his A, but the belly of
16:26 A worker's A works for him; his mouth urges
23:2 throat if you are a man given to A
Eccl 6:7 his mouth, yet his A is not satisfied.
Wis 16:2 satisfy the desire of A;
16:3 the least remnant of A because of the odious
Sir 37:29 not have an insatiable A for any luxury, and
Is 5:14 Sheol has enlarged its A and opened its mouth
56:11 dogs have a mighty A; they never have enough.

APPETITES (2)

Sir 18:29 not follow your base desires, but restrain your A
Rom 16:18 Christ, but their own A, and by fair and

APPHIA

Philem 1:2 beloved fellow worker and A our sister and

APPHUS

1Mac 2:5 Eleazar called Avaran, and Jonathan called A

APPIUS

Acts 28:15 as the Forum of A and Three Taverns to

APPLE (8)

Deut 32:10 kept him as the A of his eye.
Ps 17:8 Keep me as the A of the eye; hide
Prov 7:2 my teachings as the A of your eye;
Song 2:3 As an A tree among the trees of the
8:5 Under the A tree I awakened you.
Sir 17:17 person's kindness like the A of his eye.
Joel 1:11 Pomegranate, palm, and A, all the trees of the
Zech 2:8 touches you touches the A of his eye:

APPLES (3)

Prov 25:11 fitly spoken is like A of gold in a
Song 2:5 raisins, refresh me with A; for I am sick
7:8 of your breath like A,

APPLIED (6)

1Kgs 6:35 them with gold evenly A upon the carved work.
Eccl 1:13 And I A my mind to seek and to
1:17 And I A my mind to know wisdom and
8:16 When I A my mind to know wisdom, and
2Mac 4:20 its carriers it was A to the construction of
1Cor 4:6 I have A all this to myself and Apollos

APPLIES

Esth 15:10 die, for our law A only to the people.

APPLY (6)

Prov 22:17 of the wise, and A your mind to my
23:12 A your mind to instruction and your ear to
Sir 6:32 taught, and if you A yourself you will become
Is 38:21 cake of figs, and A it to the boil,
Tit 3:8 may be careful to A themselves to good deeds;
3:14 our people learn to A themselves to good deeds,

APPLYING

Eccl	8:9	this I observed while A my mind to all

APPOINT (36)

Gen	41:34	Let Pharaoh proceed to A overseers over the land,
Ex	21:13	hand, then I will A for you a place
	30:16	of Israel, and shall A it for the service
Lev	26:16	to you: I will A over you sudden terror,
Num	1:50	people of Israel; but A the Levites over the
	3:10	And you shall A Aaron and his sons, and
	4:19	shall go in and A them each to his
	27:16	spirits of all flesh, A a man over the
Deut	1:13	tribes, and I will A them as your heads.'
	16:18	"You shall A judges and officers in all your
Josh	20:2	the people of Israel, A the cities of refuge,
1Sam	8:5	in your ways; now A for us a king
	8:11	take your sons and A them to his chariots
	8:12	chariots; and he will A for himself commanders of
2Sam	6:21	all his house, to A me as prince over
	7:10	And I will A a place for my people
1Chr	15:16	of the Levites to A their brethren as the
	17:9	And I will A a place for my people
Ezra	7:25	is in your hand, A magistrates and judges who
Neh	7:3	A guards from among the inhabitants of Jerusalem,
Esth	2:3	And let the king A officers in all the
Job	14:13	past, that thou wouldest A me a set time,
Ps	75:2	set time which I A I will judge with
	104:8	place which thou didst A for them.
	109:6	A a wicked man against him; let an accuser
Jer	15:3	to captivity."' "I will A over them four kinds
	49:19	her; and I will A over her whomever I
	50:44	her; and I will A over her whomever I
	51:27	Ararat, Minni, and Ashkenaz; A a marshal against
Ezek	44:14	Yet I will A them to keep charge of
Dan	2:16	besought the king to A him a time, that
Hos	1:11	together, and they shall A for themselves one head;
1Mac	14:42	of the sanctuary and A men over its tasks
Acts	6:3	wisdom, whom we may A to this duty.
	26:16	for this purpose, to A you to serve and
Tit	1:4	what was defective, and A elders in every town

APPOINTED (184)

Gen	4:25	she said, "God has A for me another child
	18:14	At the A time I will return to you,
	24:14	one whom thou hast A for thy servant Isaac.
	24:44	whom the LORD has A for my master's son.'
Ex	13:10	this ordinance at its A time from year to
	23:15	seven days at the A time in the month
	31:6	And behold, I have A with him Oholiab, the
	34:18	you, at the time A in the month Abib;
Lev	23:2	people of Israel, The A feasts of the LORD
	23:2	as holy convocations, my A feasts, are these.
	23:4	"These are the A feasts of the LORD, the
	23:4	proclaim at the time A for them.
	23:37	"These are the A feasts of the LORD, which
	23:44	people of Israel the A feasts of the LORD.
Num	3:36	And the A charge of the sons of Merari
	4:49	through Moses they were A, each to his task
	9:2	the passover at its A time.
	9:3	keep it at its A time; according to all
	9:7	LORD's offering at its A time among the people
	9:13	LORD's offering at its A time; that man shall
	10:10	also, and at your A feasts, and at the
	15:3	offering or at your A feasts, to make a
	29:39	the LORD at your A feasts, in addition to
Deut	20:9	then commanders shall be A at the head of
Josh	4:4	Israel, whom he had A, a man from each
	20:8	east of Jericho, they A Bezer in the wilderness
Judg	20:38	Now the A signal between the men of Israel
1Sam	9:24	you until the hour A, that you might eat
	12:6	LORD is witness, who A Moses and Aaron and
	13:8	seven days, the time A by Samuel; but Samuel
	13:11	come within the days A, and that the Philistines
	13:14	and the LORD has A him to be prince
	25:30	concerning you, and has A you prince over Israel,
2Sam	7:11	the time that I A judges over my people
	20:5	time which had been A him.
	24:15	the morning until the A time; and there died
1Kgs	1:35	stead; and I have A him to be ruler
	12:31	on high places, and A priests from among all
	12:32	And Jeroboam A a feast on the fifteenth day
2Kgs	7:17	Now the king had A the captain on whose
	8:6	So the king A an official for her, saying,
	17:32	feared the LORD, and A from among themselves all
	25:22	Babylon had left, he A Gedaliah the son of
	25:23	king of Babylon had A Gedaliah governor, they came
1Chr	6:48	brethren the Levites were A for all the service
	9:29	Others of them were A over the furniture, and
	15:17	So the Levites A Heman the son of Joel;
	16:4	Moreover he A certain of the Levites as ministers
	16:7	that day David first A that thanksgiving be sung
	16:42	sons of Jeduthun were A to the gate.
	17:10	the time that I A judges over my people
	24:3	them according to the A duties in their service.
	24:19	These had as their A duty in their service
	26:29	and his sons were A to outside duties for
	26:32	in Gilead.) King David A him and his brethren,
2Chr	2:4	new moons and the A feasts of the LORD
	3:1	place that David had A, on the threshing floor
	8:14	David his father, he A the divisions of the
	11:15	the LORD, and he A his own priests for
	11:22	sixty daughters); and Rehoboam A Abijah the son of
	19:5	He A judges in the land in all the
	19:8	in Jerusalem Jehoshaphat A certain Levites and
	20:21	with the people, he A those who were to
	31:2	And Hezekiah A the divisions of the priests and
	31:3	new moons, and the A feasts, as it is
	33:8	the land which I A for your fathers, if
	35:2	He A the priests to their offices and encouraged
Ezra	3:5	and at all the A feasts of the LORD,
	3:8	They A the Levites, from twenty years old and
	10:14	foreign wives come at A times, and with them
Neh	5:14	time that I was A to be their governor
	7:1	the Levites had been A,
	9:17	stiffened their neck and A a leader to return
	10:33	the new moons, the A feasts, the holy things,
	10:34	fathers' houses, at times A, year by year, to
	12:31	upon the wall, and A two great companies which
	12:44	that day men were A over the chambers for
	13:4	the priest, who was A over the chambers of
	13:13	And I A as treasurers over the storehouses
	13:31	the wood offering, at A times, and for the
Tob	1:21	his place; and he A Ahikar, the son of
	1:22	accounts, for Esarhaddon had A him second to
Jud	5:18	way which he had A for them, they were
Esth	4:5	eunuchs, who had been A to attend her, and
	9:27	and at the time A every year,
	9:31	be observed at their A seasons, as Mordecai the
Job	14:5	thee, and thou hast A his bounds that he
	30:23	and to the house A for all living.
	34:23	For he has not A a time for any
Ps	7:6	my God; thou hast A a judgment.
	49:14	Like sheep they are A for Sheol; Death shall
	78:5	testimony in Jacob, and A a law in Israel,
	102:13	to favor her; the A time has come.
	119:138	Thou hast A thy testimonies in righteousness and in
Eccl	3:17	wicked, for he has A a time for every
Sir	17:14	He A a ruler for every nation, but Israel
	33:8	were distinguished, and he A the different seasons
	33:11	Lord distinguished them and A their different ways;
	36:8	day, and remember the A time, and let people
	48:10	are ready at the A time, it is written,
	51:30	your work before the A time, and in God's
Is	1:14	new moons and your A feasts my soul hates;
	33:20	the city of our A feasts!
Jer	1:5	I consecrated you; I A you a prophet to
	5:24	for us the weeks A for the harvest.'
	33:20	not come at their A time,
	40:5	the king of Babylon A governor of the cities
	40:7	king of Babylon had A Gedaliah the son of
	40:11	in Judah and had A Gedaliah the son of
	41:2	king of Babylon had A governor in the land.
	47:7	the seashore he has A it."
Lam	1:4	none come to the A feasts; all her gates
	2:6	the place of his A feasts; the LORD has
	2:6	an end in Zion A feast and sabbath, and
	2:7	the day of an A feast.
	2:22	the day of an A feast my terrors on
Bar	1:14	the feasts and at A seasons.
Ezek	22:4	your day near, the A time of your years
	36:38	at Jerusalem during her A feasts, so shall the
	43:21	be burnt in the A place belonging to the
	44:24	statutes in all my A feasts, and they shall
	45:17	the sabbaths, all the A feasts of the house
	46:9	the LORD at the A feasts, he who enters
	46:11	the feasts and the A seasons the cereal offering
Dan	1:10	lord the king, who A your food and your
	1:11	of the eunuchs had A over Daniel, Hananiah,
	2:24	whom the king had A to destroy the wise
	2:49	the king, and he A Shadrach, Meshach, and
	3:12	Jews whom you have A over the affairs of
	8:19	it pertains to the A time of the end.

11:27 end is yet to be at the time A
11:29 "At the time A he shall return and come
11:35 end, for it is yet for the time A
13:5 from the people were A as judges.
Hos 2:11 sabbaths, and all her A feasts.
6:11 For you also, O Judah, a harvest is A
9:5 on the day of A festival, and on the
11:7 me; so they are A to the yoke, and
12:9 the days of the A feast.
Jon 1:17 And the LORD A a great fish to swallow
4:6 And the LORD God A a plant, and made
4:7 the next day, God A a worm which attacked
4:8 the sun rose, God A a sultry east wind,
1Mac 1:51 And he A inspectors over all the people and
3:55 After this Judas A leaders of the people, in
6:55 while still living had A to bring up Antiochus
10:20 And so we have A you today to be
10:34 and new moons and A days, and the three
10:69 Demetrius A Apollonius the governor of Coelesyria,
16:11 of Abubus had been A governor over the plain
2Mac 5:22 than the man who A him;
8:9 And Ptolemy promptly A Nicanor the son of
8:22 He A his brothers also, Simon and Joseph and
8:23 Besides, he A Eleazar to read aloud from the
9:23 into the upper country, A his successor,
9:25 So I have A my son Antiochus to be
10:11 succeeded to the kingdom, A one Lysias to have
14:12 command of the elephants, A him governor of Judea,
14:26 government, for he had A that conspirator against
Mk 3:14 And he A twelve, to be with him, and
Lk 3:13 no more than is A you."
10:1 After this the Lord A seventy others, and sent
Jn 15:16 I chose you and A you that you should
Acts 3:20 may send the Christ A for you, Jesus,
12:21 On an A day Herod put on his royal
14:23 And when they had A elders for them in
15:2 of the others were A to go up to
17:31 man whom he has A, and of this he
22:10 told all that is A for you to do.'
22:14 God of our fathers A you to know his
28:23 When they had A a day for him, they
Rom 13:2 resists what God has A, and those who resist
1Cor 7:29 I mean, brethren, the A time has grown very
12:28 And God has A in the church first apostles,
2Cor 8:19 but he has been A by the churches to
Eph 1:12 have been destined and A to live for the
1Tim 2:7 For this I was A a preacher and apostle
2Tim 1:11 this gospel I was A a preacher and apostle
Heb 1:2 a Son, whom he A the heir of all
3:2 faithful to him who A him, just as Moses
5:1 from among men is A to act on behalf
5:5 high priest, but was A by him who said
8:3 every high priest is A to offer gifts and
9:27 just as it is A for men to die

APPOINTING

1Tim 1:12 judged me faithful by A me to his service,

APPOINTMENT (6)

1Sam 20:35 the field to the A with David, and with
21:2 I have made an A with the young men
2Chr 31:13 his brother, by the A of Hezekiah the king
Job 2:11 They made an A together to come to condole
Ps 119:91 By thy A they stand this day; for all
Amos 3:3 two walk together, unless they have made an A

APPOINTS (3)

Job 23:14 will complete what he A for me; and many
Heb 7:28 Indeed, the law A men in their weakness as
7:28 later than the law, A a Son who has

APPORTION (2)

2Chr 31:14 offerings to God, to A the contribution reserved for
Is 49:8 establish the land, to A the desolate heritages;

APPORTIONED (9)

Josh 18:2 seven tribes whose inheritance had not yet been A
18:10 LORD; and there Joshua A the land to the
Job 7:3 nights of misery are A to me.
Ps 78:55 nations before them; he A them for a possession
Sir 1:7 he saw her and A her, he poured her
1:17 He saw her and A her; he rained down
44:2 The Lord A to them great glory, his majesty
2Cor 10:13 the limits God has A us, to reach even
Heb 7:2 and to him Abraham A a tenth part of

APPORTIONS

1Cor 12:11 the same Spirit, who A to each one individually

APPRECIATE

Sir 31:22 the end you will A my words.

APPROACH (27)

Lev 18:6 "None of you shall A any one near of
18:14 is, you shall not A his wife; she is
18:19 "You shall not A a woman to uncover her
21:17 has a blemish may A to offer the bread
21:23 near the veil or A the altar, because he
Deut 2:19 Ar; and when you A the frontier of the
31:14 Moses, "Behold, the days A when you must die;
Josh 8:5 are with me, will A the city.
Tob 6:14 one except those who A her.
6:17 And when you A her, rise up, both of
Jud 4:2 greatly terrified at his A, and were alarmed both
4:7 to enter, for the A was narrow, only wide
Job 31:37 a prince I would A him.
Wis 1:5 be ashamed at the A of unrighteousness.
Sir 1:25 the Lord; do not A him with a divided
9:13 But if you A him, make no misstep, lest
21:2 snake; for if you A sin, it will bite
41:22 and do not A her bed; of abusive
Is 41:1 their strength; let them A, then let them speak;
Jer 30:21 near, and he shall A me, for who would
30:21 dare of himself to A me?
37:11 from Jerusalem at the A of Pharaoh's army,
Ezek 18:6 his neighbor's wife or A a woman in her
42:13 where the priests who A the LORD shall eat
44:16 sanctuary, and they shall A my table, to minister
45:4 in the sanctuary and A the LORD to minister
2Mac 12:21 Timothy learned of the A of Judas, he sent

APPROACHED (14)

Gen 20:4 Now Abimelech had not A her; so he said,
1Sam 9:18 Then Saul A Samuel in the gate, and said,
Ezra 4:2 God of Israel, they A Zerubbabel and the heads
9:1 been done, the officials A me and said, "The
Tob 6:9 When they A Ecbatana,
Jud 12:13 presence of Holofernes, and A her and said, "This
Esth 5:2 Then Esther A and touched the top of the
Dan 7:16 I A one of those who stood there and
1Mac 3:16 When he A the ascent of Beth-horon, Judas went
5:42 When Judas A the stream of water, he stationed
11:4 When he A Azotus, they showed him the temple
13:23 When he A Baskama, he killed Jonathan, and he
2Mac 11:5 Invading Judea, he A Bethzur, which was a fortified
Acts 9:3 as he journeyed he A Damascus, and suddenly a

APPROACHES (6)

Lev 20:16 If a woman A any beast and lies with
22:3 throughout your generations A the holy things, which
2Kgs 11:8 his hand; and whoever A the ranks is to
Jud 7:7 Bethulia, and examined the A to the city, and
2Mac 12:21 access because of the narrowness of all the A
Lk 12:33 fail, where no thief A and no moth destroys.

APPROACHING

Gen 27:41 for my father are A; then I will kill

APPROPRIATE (3)

1Mac 10:40 the king's revenues from A places.
12:11 feasts and on other A days, at the sacrifices
2Mac 11:36 we may make proposals A for you.

APPROVAL (7)

Sir 2:16 Lord will seek his A, and those who love
32:10 before the thunder, and A precedes a modest man.
Jer 44:19 it without our husbands' A that we made cakes
Rom 13:3 you will receive his A,
Heb 11:2 by it the men of old received divine A
11:4 through which he received A as righteous, God
1Pet 2:20 it you take it patiently, you have God's A

APPROVE (5)

1Sam 29:6 the lords do not A of you.
Lam 3:36 man in his cause, the Lord does not A
Rom 1:32 only do them but A those who practice them.
2:18 know his will and A what is excellent, because
Phil 1:10 so that you may A what is excellent, and

APPROVED (10)

1Chr 7:40 heads of fathers' houses, A, mighty warriors, chief of
Job 29:11 the eye saw, it A;

A

Eccl 9:7 for God has already A what you do.
Sir 42:8 instructed, and will be A before all men.
2Mac 4:3 by one of Simon's A agents,
Rom 14:18 acceptable to God and A by men.
16:10 Greet Apelles, who is A in Christ.
1Thes 2:4 as we have been A by God to be
2Tim 2:15 to God as one A, a workman who has
1Pet 2:19 For one is A if, mindful of God, he

APPROVES (2)

Sir 11:15 godly, and what he A will have lasting success.
Rom 14:22 no reason to judge himself for what he A

APPROVING

Acts 22:20 was standing by and A, and keeping the garments

APRONS (2)

Gen 3:7 sewed fig leaves together and made themselves A
Acts 19:12 so that handkerchiefs or A were carried away from

APT (4)

Prov 15:23 To make an A answer is a joy to
Sir 18:28 themselves, and pour forth A proverbs.
1Tim 3:2 sensible, dignified, hospitable, an A teacher,
2Tim 2:24 to every one, an A teacher, forbearing,

AQUILA (6)

Acts 18:2 found a Jew named A, a native of Pontus,
18:18 sailed for Syria, and with him Priscilla and A
18:26 but when Priscilla and A heard him, they took
Rom 16:3 Greet Prisca and A, my fellow workers in Christ
1Cor 16:19 A and Prisca, together with the church in their
2Tim 4:19 Greet Prisca and A, and the household of

AR (6)

Num 21:15 to the seat of A, and leans to the
21:28 It devoured A of Moab, the lords of the
Deut 2:9 because I have given A to the sons of
2:18 boundary of Moab at A;
2:29 Moabites who live in A did for me, until
Is 15:1 Because A is laid waste in a night Moab

ARA

1Chr 7:38 The sons of Jether: Jephunneh, Pispa, and A

ARAB (7)

Josh 15:52 A, Dumah, Eshan,
Neh 2:19 Ammonite, and Geshem the A heard of it, they
6:1 and to Geshem the A and to the rest
Is 13:20 for all generations; no A will pitch his tent
Jer 3:2 awaiting lovers like an A in the wilderness.
1Mac 11:17 And Zabdiel the A cut off the head of
11:39 went to Imalkue the A, who was bringing up

ARABAH (26)

Deut 1:1 the wilderness, in the A over against Suph, between
1:7 their neighbors in the A, in the hill country
2:8 Seir, away from the A road from Elath and
3:17 of the Ammonites; the A also, with the Jordan
3:17 the sea of the A, the Salt Sea, under
4:49 together with all the A on the east side
4:49 the Sea of the A, under the slopes of
11:30 who live in the A, over against Gilgal, beside
Josh 3:16 the sea of the A, the Salt Sea, were
8:14 the descent toward the A to meet Israel in
11:2 country, and in the A south of Chinneroth, and
11:16 the lowland and the A and the hill country
12:1 Hermon, with all the A eastward:
12:3 of Gilead, and the A to the Sea of
12:3 the sea of the A, the Salt Sea, southward
12:8 the lowland, in the A, in the slopes, in
18:18 goes down to the A;
1Sam 23:24 of Maon, in the A to the south of
2Sam 2:29 that night through the A; they crossed the Jordan,
4:7 the way of the A all night,
2Kgs 14:25 the Sea of the A, according to the word
25:4 And they went in the direction of the A
Jer 39:4 the two walls; and they went toward the A
52:7 And they went in the direction of the A
Ezek 47:8 goes down into the A; and when it enters
Amos 6:14 entrance of Hamath to the Brook of the A

ARABIA (11)

1Kgs 10:15 all the kings of A and from the governors
2Chr 9:14 all the kings of A and the governors of
Jud 2:25 the southern borders of Japheth, fronting toward A
Is 21:13 The oracle concerning A
21:13 In the thickets in A you will lodge, O
Jer 25:24 all the kings of A and all the kings
Ezek 27:21 A and all the princes of Kedar were your
30:5 and Lud, and all A, and Libya, and the
1Mac 11:16 So Alexander fled into A to find protection there,
Gal 1:17 I went away into A; and again I returned
4:25 is Mount Sinai in A; she corresponds to the

ARABIANS

Acts 2:11 and proselytes, Cretans and A, we hear them telling

ARABS (9)

2Chr 17:11 for tribute; and the A also brought him seven
21:16 Philistines and of the A who are near the
22:1 that came with the A to the camp had
26:7 Philistines, and against the A that dwelt in Gurbaal,
Neh 4:7 and Tobiah and the A and the Ammonites and
1Mac 5:39 They also have hired A to help them, and
12:31 turned aside against the A who are called
2Mac 5:8 the ruler of the A, fleeing from city to
12:10 less than five thousand A with five hundred horsemen

ARAD (5)

Num 21:1 Canaanite, the king of A, who dwelt in the
33:40 Canaanite, the king of A, who dwelt in the
Josh 12:14 one; the king of A, one;
Judg 1:16 in the Negeb near A; and they went and
1Chr 8:15 Zebadiah, A, Eder,

ARADUS

1Mac 15:23 to Side, and to A and Gortyna and Cnidus

ARAH (4)

1Chr 7:39 The sons of Ulla: A, Hanniel, and Rizia.
Ezra 2:5 The sons of A, seven hundred and seventy-five.
Neh 6:18 Shecaniah the son of A: and his son Jehohanan
7:10 The sons of A, six hundred and fifty-two.

ARAM (11)

Gen 10:22 sons of Shem: Elam, Asshur, Arpachshad, Lud, and A
10:23 The sons of A: Uz, Hul, Gether, and Mash.
22:21 Kemuel the father of A,
Num 23:7 discourse, and said, "From A Balak has brought me,
2Sam 8:6 David put garrisons in A of Damascus; and the
15:8 dwelt at Geshur in A, saying, 'If the LORD
1Chr 1:17 Elam, Asshur, Arpachshad, Lud, A, Uz, Hul, Gether,
2:23 But Geshur and A took from them Havvoth-jair,
7:34 of Shemer his brother: Rohgah, Jehubbah, and A
Hos 12:12 to the land of A, there Israel did service
Zech 9:1 belong the cities of A, even as all the

ARAM-MAACAH

1Chr 19:6 horsemen from Mesopotamia, from A, and from

ARAMAIC (3)

2Kgs 18:26 your servants in the A language, for we understand
Ezra 4:7 letter was written in A and translated.
Is 36:11 to your servants in A, for we understand it;

ARAMEAN (7)

Gen 25:20 daughter of Bethuel the A of Paddan-aram, the
25:20 Aramean of Paddan-aram, the sister of Laban the A
28:5 son of Bethuel the A, the brother of Rebekah,
31:20 Jacob outwitted Laban the A, in that he did
31:24 came to Laban the A in a dream by
Deut 26:5 your God, 'A wandering A was my father; and
1Chr 7:14 Manasseh: Asriel, whom his A concubine bore; she

ARAN (2)

Gen 36:28 These are the sons of Dishan: Uz and A
1Chr 1:42 The sons of Dishan: Uz and A

ARARAT (5)

Gen 8:4 ark came to rest upon the mountains of A
2Kgs 19:37 the sword, and escaped into the land of A
Tob 1:21 him, and they fled to the mountains of A
Is 37:38 the sword, and escaped into the land of A
Jer 51:27 against her the kingdoms, A, Minni, and Ashkenaz;

ARAUNAH (9)

2Sam 24:16 the threshing floor of A the Jebusite.
24:18 the threshing floor of A the Jebusite."
24:20 And when A looked down, he saw the king
24:20 on toward him; and A went forth, and did
24:21 And A said, "Why has my lord the king

24:22 Then A said to David, "Let my lord the
24:23 All this, O king, A gives to the king."
24:23 And A said to the king, "The LORD your
24:24 the king said to A, "No, but I will

ARBA (3)

Josh 14:15 formerly was Kiriath-arba; this A was the greatest
15:13 Kiriath-arba, that is, Hebron A was the father of
21:11 They gave them Kiriath-arba A being the father of

ARBATHITE (2)

2Sam 23:31 of Gaash, Abi-albon the A, Azmaveth of Bahurim,
1Chr 11:32 of Gaash, Abiel the A,

ARBATTA

1Mac 5:23 Jews of Galilee and A, with their wives and

ARBELA

1Mac 9:2 encamped against Mesaloth in A, and they took it

ARBITE

2Sam 23:35 of Carmel, Paarai the A,

ARC

Sir 43:12 heaven with its glorious A; the hands of the

ARCHANGEL (2)

1Thes 4:16 of command, with the A's call, and with the
Jude 1:9 But when the A Michael, contending with the devil,

ARCHELAUS

Mt 2:22 when he heard that A reigned over Judea in

ARCHER (3)

Prov 26:10 Like an A who wounds everybody is he who
Jer 4:29 noise of horseman and A every city takes to
51:3 Let not the A bend his bow, and let

ARCHERS (12)

Gen 49:23 The A fiercely attacked him, shot at him, and
1Sam 31:3 upon Saul, and the A found him; and he
31:3 him; and he was badly wounded by the A
2Sam 11:24 Then the A shot at your servants from the
1Chr 10:3 upon Saul, and the A found him; and he
10:3 found him; and he was wounded by the A
2Chr 35:23 And the A shot King Josiah; and the king
Jud 2:15 together with twelve thousand A on horseback,
Job 16:13 as his target, his A surround me.
Is 21:17 the remainder of the A of the mighty men
Jer 50:29 "Summon A against Babylon, all those who bend the
1Mac 9:11 the slingers and the A went ahead of the

ARCHIPPUS (2)

Col 4:17 And say to A, "See that you fulfil the
Philem 1:2 Apphia our sister and A our fellow soldier, and

ARCHITE (5)

2Sam 15:32 worshiped, behold, Hushai the A came to meet him
16:16 And when Hushai the A, David's friend, came to
17:5 said, "Call Hushai the A also, and let us
17:14 counsel of Hushai the A is better than the
1Chr 27:33 counselor, and Hushai the A was the king's friend.

ARCHITES

Josh 16:2 the territory of the A;

ARCHIVES (3)

Ezra 5:17 made in the royal A there in Babylon, to
6:1 the house of the A where the documents were
1Mac 14:23 words in the public A, so that the people

ARD (3)

Gen 46:21 Rosh, Muppim, Huppim, and A
Num 26:40 sons of Bela were A and Naaman: of Ard,
26:40 Ard and Naaman: of A, the family of the

ARDITES

Num 26:40 the family of the A; of Naaman, the family

ARDON

1Chr 2:18 and these were her sons: Jesher, Shobab, and A

ARDUOUS

Wis 10:12 for him; in his A contest she gave him

ARE-OPAGITE

Acts 17:34 among them Dionysius the A and a woman named

ARE-OPAGUS (2)

Acts 17:19 brought him to the A, saying, "May we know
17:22 the middle of the A, said: "Men of Athens,

AREA (7)

Gen 23:17 field, throughout its whole A, was made over
Deut 19:3 into three parts the A of the land which
Ezek 40:5 outside of the temple A, and the length of
42:15 interior of the temple A, he led me out
42:15 and measured the temple A round about.
43:21 place belonging to the temple, outside the sacred A
45:6 of the city an A five thousand cubits broad,

ARELI (2)

Gen 46:16 Gad: Ziphion, Haggi, Shuni, Ezbon, Eri, Arodi, and A
Num 26:17 of the Arodites; of A, the family of the

ARELITES

Num 26:17 the Arodites; of Areli, the family of the A

ARENA

2Mac 4:14 proceedings in the wrestling A after the call to

ARETAS (2)

2Mac 5:8 Accused before A the ruler of the Arabs, fleeing
2Cor 11:32 the governor under King A guarded the city of

ARGOB (4)

Deut 3:4 the whole region of A, the kingdom of Og
3:13 all the region of A, I gave to the
3:14 all the region of A, that is, Bashan, as
1Kgs 4:13 had the region of A, which is in Bashan,

ARGUE (7)

Job 13:3 and I desire to A my case with God.
15:3 Should he A in unprofitable talk, or in words
Prov 25:9 A your case with your neighbor himself, and do
Sir 8:3 Do not A with a chatterer, nor heap wood
11:9 Do not A about a matter which does not
Is 43:26 in remembrance, let us A together; set forth your
Mk 8:11 came and began to A with him, seeking from

ARGUED (8)

Mt 21:25 And they A with one another, "If we say,
Mk 11:30 And they A with one another, "If we say,
Acts 17:2 for three weeks he A with them from the
17:17 So he A in the synagogue with the Jews
18:4 And he A in the synagogue every sabbath, and
18:19 into the synagogue and A with the Jews.
19:9 disciples with him, and A daily in the hall
24:24 And as he A about justice and self-control and

ARGUES

Job 40:2 He who A with God, let him answer it."

ARGUING (2)

Mk 9:14 about them, and scribes A with them.
Acts 19:8 three months spoke boldly, A and pleading about the

ARGUMENT (3)

Job 19:5 make my humiliation an A against me,
Prov 29:9 wise man has an A with a fool, the
Lk 9:46 And an A arose among them as to which

ARGUMENTS (2)

Job 23:4 case before him and fill my mouth with A
2Cor 10:5 We destroy A and every proud obstacle to the

ARIARATHES

1Mac 15:22 and to Attalus and A and Arsaces,

ARIDAI

Esth 9:9 Parmashta and Arisai and A and Vaizatha,

ARIDATHA

Esth 9:8 Poratha and Adalia and A

ARIEL (6)

Ezra 8:16 I sent for Eliezer, A, Shemaiah, Elnathan, Jarib, Elnathan,
Is 29:1 Ho A, Ariel, the city where David encamped!
29:1 Ho Ariel, A, the city where David encamped!
29:2 Yet I will distress A, and there shall be

29:2 and she shall be to me like an A
29:7 nations that fight against A, all that fight against

ARIELS (2)

2Sam 23:20 deeds; he smote two A of Moab.
1Chr 11:22 deeds; he smote two A of Moab.

ARIGHT (10)

Job 11:13 you set your heart A, you will stretch out
Ps 50:23 who orders his way A I will show the
Prov 15:21 no sense, but a man of understanding walks A
Sir 6:17 Lord directs his friendship A, for as he is,
38:10 and direct your hands A, and cleanse your heart
39:7 his counsel and knowledge A, and meditate on his
49:2 He was led A in converting the people, and
49:9 did good to those who directed their ways A
Is 28:26 For he is instructed A; his God teaches him.
Jer 8:6 they have not spoken A; no man repents of

ARIMATHEA (4)

Mt 27:57 a rich man from A, named Joseph, who also
Mk 15:42 the sabbath, Joseph of A, a respected member of
Lk 23:49 man named Joseph from the Jewish town of A
Jn 19:38 After this Joseph of A, who was a disciple

ARIOCH (8)

Gen 14:1 king of Shinar, A king of Ellasar, Ched-or-laomer
14:9 king of Shinar, and A king of Ellasar, four
Jud 1:6 in the plain where A ruled the Elymaeans.
Dan 2:14 prudence and discretion to A, the captain of the
2:15 Babylon; he said to A, the king's captain, "Why
2:15 Then A made the matter known to Daniel.
2:24 Daniel went in to A, whom the king had
2:25 Then A brought in Daniel before the king in

ARISAI

Esth 9:9 and Parmashta and A and Aridai and Vaizatha,

ARISE (130)

Gen 13:17 A, walk through the length and the breadth of
19:15 angels urged Lot, saying, A, take your wife and
21:18 A, lift up the lad, and hold him fast
27:31 father, "Let my father A, and eat of his
27:43 son, obey my voice; A, flee to Laban my
28:2 A, go to Paddan-aram to the house of Bethuel
31:13 Now A, go forth from this land, and return
35:1 God said to Jacob, A, go up to Bethel,
35:3 garments; then let us A and go up to
41:30 after them there will A seven years of famine,
43:8 me, and we will A and go, that we
43:13 also your brother, and A, go again to the
Num 10:35 set out, Moses said, A, O LORD, and let
Deut 9:12 LORD said to me, A, go down quickly from
10:11 LORD said to me, A, go on your journey
17:8 you, then you shall A and go up to
Josh 1:2 is dead; now therefore A, go over this Jordan,
7:10 LORD said to Joshua, A, why have you thus
8:1 men with you, and A, go up to Ai;
Judg 5:12 A, Barak, lead away your captives, O son of
7:9 LORD said to him, A, go down against the
7:15 of Israel, and said, A; for the LORD has
18:9 They said, A, and let us go up against
19:9 and tomorrow you shall A early in the morning
1Sam 9:3 servants with you, and A, go and look for
16:12 And the LORD said, A, anoint him; for this
23:4 the LORD answered him, A, go down to Keilah;
2Sam 2:14 "Let the young men A and play before us."
2:14 And Joab said, "Let them A
3:21 to David, "I will A and go, and will
13:15 Amnon said to her, A, be gone."
15:14 with him at Jerusalem, A, and let us flee;
17:21 They said to David, A, and go quickly over
19:7 Now therefore A, go out and speak kindly to
1Kgs 3:12 none like you shall A after you.
14:2 said to his wife, A, and disguise yourself, that
14:12 LORD has spoken it.'" A therefore, go to your
17:9 LORD came to him, A, go to Zarephath, which
19:5 and said to him, A and eat."
19:7 touched him, and said, A and eat, else the
21:7 A, and eat bread, and let your heart be
21:15 Jezebel said to Ahab, A, take possession of the
21:18 Elijah the Tishbite, saying, A, go down to meet
2Kgs 1:3 to Elijah the Tishbite, A, go up to meet
8:1 had restored to life, A, and depart with your
23:25 did any like him A after him.
1Chr 22:16 A and be doing!
22:19 A and build the sanctuary of the LORD God,
2Chr 6:41 "And now A, O LORD God, and go to
Ezra 10:4 A, for it is your task, and we are
Neh 2:20 we his servants will A and build; but you
7:65 until a priest with Urim and Thummim should A
Job 7:4 say, 'When shall I A But the night is
25:3 Upon whom does his light not A
Ps 3:7 A, O LORD!
7:6 [Selah] A, O LORD, in thy anger, lift thyself
9:19 A, O LORD!
10:12 A, O LORD; O God, lift up thy hand;
12:5 despoiled, because the needy groan, I will now A
17:13 A, O LORD!
27:3 not fear; though war A against me, yet I
68:1 Let God A, let his enemies be scattered; let
74:22 A, O God, plead thy cause; remember how the
78:6 children yet unborn, and A and tell them to
82:8 A, O God, judge the earth; for to thee
102:13 Thou wilt A and have pity on Zion; it
132:8 A, O LORD, and go to thy resting place,
Prov 6:9 When will you A from your sleep?
Song 2:10 and says to me: A, my love, my fair
2:13 A, my love, my fair one, and come away.
Sir 17:18 Afterward he will A and requite them, and he
Is 21:5 A, O princes, oil the shield!
23:12 virgin daughter of Sidon; A, pass over to Cyprus,
26:14 shades, they will not A; to that end thou
31:2 his words, but will A against the house of
33:10 "Now I will A
49:7 "Kings shall see and A; princes, and they shall
52:2 yourself from the dust, A, O captive Jerusalem; loose
60:1 A, shine; for your light has come, and the
60:2 but the LORD will A upon you, and his
Jer 1:17 gird up your loins; A, and say to them
2:27 their trouble they say, A and save us!'
2:28 Let them A, if they can save you, in
13:4 upon your loins, and A, go to the Euphrates,
13:6 LORD said to me, A, go to the Euphrates,
18:2 Jeremiah from the LORD: A, and go down to
31:6 hill country of Ephraim: A, and let us go
46:16 said one to another, A, and let us go
Lam 2:19 A, cry out in the night, at the beginning
Bar 5:5 A, O Jerusalem, stand upon the height and look
Ezek 3:22 he said to me, A, go forth into the
Dan 2:39 After you shall A another kingdom inferior to you,
7:5 and it was told, A, devour much flesh.'
7:17 four kings who shall A out of the earth.
7:24 kingdom ten kings shall A, and another shall arise
7:24 arise, and another shall A after them; he shall
8:22 arose, four kingdoms shall A from his nation, but
8:23 countenance, one who understands riddles, shall A
11:2 three more kings shall A in Persia; and a
11:3 a mighty king shall A, who shall rule with
11:7 from her roots shall A in his place; he
11:20 "Then shall A in his place one who shall
11:21 In his place shall A a contemptible person to
12:1 "At that time shall A Michael, the great prince
Hos 10:14 tumult of war shall A among your people, and
Jon 1:2 son of Amittai, saying, A, go to Nineveh, that
1:6 A, call upon your god!
3:2 the second time, saying, A, go to Nineveh, that
Mic 2:10 A and go, for this is no place to
4:13 A and thresh, O daughter of Zion, for I
6:1 what the LORD says: A, plead your case before
Hab 1:3 and violence are before me; strife and contention A
2:7 not your debtors suddenly A, and those awake who
2:19 a wooden thing, Awake; to a dumb stone, A
Zeph 3:8 the day when I A as a witness.
1Mac 14:41 a trustworthy prophet should A,
Mt 12:41 men of Nineveh will A at the judgment with
12:42 of the South will A at the judgment with
24:11 many false prophets will A and lead many astray.
24:24 and false prophets will A and show great signs
Mk 5:41 which means, "Little girl, I say to you, A
13:22 and false prophets will A and show signs and
Lk 7:14 he said, "Young man, I say to you, A
8:54 her by the hand he called, saying, "Child, A
11:31 of the South will A at the judgment with
11:32 men of Nineveh will A at the judgment with
15:18 I will A and go to my father, and
Acts 20:30 your own selves will A men speaking perverse things,
Eph 5:14 "Awake, O sleeper, and A from the dead, and
Heb 7:11 for another priest to A after the order of

ARISEN (5)

Deut 34:10 And there has not A a prophet since in

1Sam 14:38 how this sin has A today.
Bar 3:19 Hades, and others have A in their place.
Dan 11:4 And when he has A, his kingdom shall be
Lk 7:16 "A great prophet has A among us!" and "God

ARISES (5)

Deut 13:1 "If a prophet A among you, or a dreamer
17:8 "If any case A requiring decision between one kind
Mt 13:21 when tribulation or persecution A on account of the
Mk 4:17 when tribulation or persecution A on account of the
Heb 7:15 evident when another priest A in the likeness of

ARISTARCHUS (5)

Acts 19:29 with them Gaius and A, Macedonians who were
20:4 and of the Thessalonians, A and Secundus; and Gaius
27:2 to sea, accompanied by A, a Macedonian from
Col 4:10 A my fellow prisoner greets you, and Mark the
Philem 1:24 and so do Mark, A, Demas, and Luke, my

ARISTOBULUS (2)

2Mac 1:10 senate and Judas, To A, who is of the
Rom 16:10 Greet those who belong to the family of A

ARIUS (2)

1Mac 12:7 the high priest from A, who was king among
12:20 they sent to Onias: A, king of the Spartans,

ARK (221)

Gen 6:14 Make yourself an A of gopher wood; make rooms
6:14 make rooms in the A, and cover it inside
6:15 the length of the A three hundred cubits, its
6:16 a roof for the A, and finish it to
6:16 the door of the A in its side; make
6:18 shall come into the A, you, your sons, your
6:19 every sort into the A, to keep them alive
7:1 Noah, "Go into the A, you and all your
7:7 him went into the A, to escape the waters
7:9 female, went into the A with Noah, as God
7:13 with them entered the A,
7:15 They went into the A with Noah, two and
7:17 and bore up the A, and it rose high
7:18 the earth; and the A floated on the face
7:23 and those that were with him in the A
8:1 the cattle that were with him in the A
8:4 of the month, the A came to rest upon
8:6 the window of the A which he had made,
8:9 to him to the A, for the waters were
8:9 brought her into the A with him.
8:10 dove out of the A;
8:13 the covering of the A, and looked, and behold,
8:16 "Go forth from the A, you and your wife,
8:19 earth, went forth by families out of the A
9:10 you, as many as came out of the A
9:18 went forth from the A were Shem, Ham, and
Ex 25:10 "They shall make an A of acacia wood; two
25:14 the sides of the A, to carry the A
25:15 the rings of the A; they shall not be
25:16 shall put into the A the testimony which I
25:21 the top of the A; and in the A
25:22 that are upon the A of the testimony, I
26:33 clasps, and bring the A of the testimony in
26:34 mercy seat upon the A of the testimony in
30:6 that is by the A of the testimony, before
30:26 of meeting and the A of the testimony,
31:7 of meeting, and the A of the testimony, and
35:12 and its bases; the A with its poles, the
37:1 Bezalel made the A of acacia wood; two cubits
37:5 the sides of the A, to carry the ark.
37:5 the sides of the ark, to carry the A
39:35 of the screen; the A of the testimony with
Lev 16:2 which is upon the A, lest he die; for
Num 3:31 was to be the A, the table, the lampstand,
4:5 screen, and cover the A of the testimony with
7:89 that was upon the A of the testimony, from
10:33 days' journey; and the A of the covenant of
10:35 And whenever the A set out, Moses said, "Arise,
14:44 country, although neither the A of the covenant of
Deut 10:1 mountain, and make an A of wood.
10:2 put them in the A
10:3 So I made an A of acacia wood, and
10:5 the tables in the A which I had made;
10:8 Levi to carry the A of the covenant of
31:9 Levi, who carried the A of the covenant of
31:25 Levites who carried the A of the covenant of
31:26 the side of the A of the covenant of
Josh 3:3 "When you see the A of the covenant of
3:6 priests, "Take up the A of the covenant, and
3:6 they took up the A of the covenant, and
3:8 priests who bear the A of the covenant, 'When
3:11 Behold, the A of the covenant of the Lord
3:13 priests who bear the A of the LORD, the
3:14 the priests bearing the A of the covenant before
3:15 those who bore the A had come to the
3:15 the priests bearing the A were dipped in the
3:17 priests who bore the A of the covenant of
4:5 "Pass on before the A of the LORD your
4:7 cut off before the A of the covenant of
4:9 the priests bearing the A of the covenant had
4:10 priests who bore the A stood in the midst
4:11 finished passing over, the A of the LORD and
4:16 priests who bear the A of the testimony to
4:18 the priests bearing the A of the covenant of
6:4 rams' horns before the A; and on the seventh
6:6 them, "Take up the A of the covenant, and
6:6 rams' horns before the A of the LORD."
6:7 pass on before the A of the LORD."
6:8 the trumpets, with the A of the covenant of
6:9 guard came after the A, while the trumpets blew
6:11 So he caused the A of the LORD to
6:12 priests took up the A of the LORD.
6:13 rams' horns before the A of the LORD passed
6:13 guard came after the A of the LORD, while
7:6 his face before the A of the LORD until
8:33 opposite sides of the A before the Levitical priests
8:33 priests who carried the A of the covenant of
Judg 20:27 the LORD (for the A of the covenant of
1Sam 3:3 the LORD, where the A of God was.
4:3 Let us bring the A of the covenant of
4:4 brought from there the A of the covenant of
4:4 were there with the A of the covenant of
4:5 When the A of the covenant of the LORD
4:6 they learned that the A of the LORD had
4:11 And the A of God was captured; and the
4:13 heart trembled for the A of God.
4:17 are dead, and the A of God has been
4:18 When he mentioned the A of God, Eli fell
4:19 the tidings that the A of God was captured,
4:21 because the A of God had been captured and
4:22 from Israel, for the A of God has been
5:1 the Philistines captured the A of God, they carried
5:2 the Philistines took the A of God and brought
5:3 the ground before the A of the LORD.
5:4 the ground before the A of the LORD, and
5:7 were, they said, "The A of the God of
5:8 we do with the A of the God of
5:8 They answered, "Let the A of the God of
5:8 So they brought the A of the God of
5:10 So they sent the A of God to Ekron.
5:10 But when the A of God came to Ekron,
5:10 around to us the A of the God of
5:11 said, "Send away the A of the God of
6:1 The A of the LORD was in the country
6:2 we do with the A of the LORD?
6:3 you send away the A of the God of
6:8 And take the A of the LORD and place
6:11 And they put the A of the LORD on
6:13 eyes and saw the A, they rejoiced to see
6:15 Levites took down the A of the LORD and
6:18 they set down the A of the LORD, is
6:19 they looked into the A of the LORD; he
6:21 Philistines have returned the A of the LORD.
7:1 and took up the A of the LORD, and
7:1 have charge of the A of the LORD.
7:2 the day that the A was lodged at Kiriath-jearim,
14:18 Ahijah, "Bring hither the A of God." For the
14:18 For the A of God went at that time
2Sam 6:2 up from there the A of God, which is
6:3 And they carried the A of God upon a
6:4 new cart with the A of God; and Ahio
6:4 ark of God; and Ahio went before the A
6:6 his hand to the A of God and took
6:7 his hand to the A; and he died there
6:7 died there beside the A of God.
6:9 said, "How can the A of the LORD come
6:10 willing to take the A of the LORD into
6:11 And the A of the LORD remained in the
6:12 him, because of the A of God." So David
6:12 and brought up the A of God from the
6:13 those who bore the A of the LORD had
6:15 Israel brought up the A of the LORD with
6:16 As the A of the LORD came into the
6:17 they brought in the A of the LORD, and

A

7:2 of cedar, but the A of God dwells in
11:11 said to David, "The A and Israel and Judah
15:24 the Levites, bearing the A of the covenant of
15:24 they set down the A of God, until the
15:25 to Zadok, "Carry the A of God back into
15:29 and Abiathar carried the A of God back to
1Kgs 2:26 because you bore the A of the Lord GOD
3:15 and stood before the A of the covenant of
6:19 to set there the A of the covenant of
8:1 to bring up the A of the covenant of
8:3 Israel came, and the priests took up the A
8:4 they brought up the A of the LORD, the
8:5 with him before the A, sacrificing so many sheep
8:6 the priests brought the A of the covenant of
8:7 the place of the A, so that the cherubim
8:7 a covering above the A and its poles.
8:9 was nothing in the A except the two tables
8:21 a place for the A, in which is the
1Chr 6:31 the LORD, after the A rested there.
13:3 us bring again the A of our God to
13:5 Hamath, to bring the A of God from Kiriath-jearim.
13:6 up from there the A of God, which is
13:7 And they carried the A of God upon a
13:9 hand to hold the A, for the oxen stumbled.
13:10 his hand to the A; and he died there
13:12 can I bring the A of God home to
13:13 did not take the A home into the city
13:14 And the A of God remained with the household
15:1 a place for the A of God, and pitched
15:2 Levites may carry the A of God, for the
15:2 them to carry the A of the LORD and
15:3 to bring up the A of the LORD to
15:12 may bring up the A of the LORD, the
15:14 to bring up the A of the LORD, the
15:15 the Levites carried the A of God upon their
15:23 and Elkanah were to be gatekeepers for the A
15:24 the trumpets before the A of God.
15:24 Jehiah also were to be gatekeepers for the A
15:25 to bring up the A of the covenant of
15:26 who were carrying the A of the covenant of
15:27 who were carrying the A, and the singers, and
15:28 Israel brought up the A of the covenant of
15:29 And as the A of the covenant of the
16:1 And they brought the A of God, and set
16:4 as ministers before the A of the LORD, to
16:6 trumpets continually, before the A of the covenant of
16:37 brethren there before the A of the covenant of
16:37 minister continually before the A as each day
17:1 of cedar, but the A of the covenant of
22:19 God, so that the A of the covenant of
28:2 of rest for the A of the covenant of
28:18 wings and covered the A of the covenant of
2Chr 1:4 had brought up the A of God from Kiriath-jearim
5:2 to bring up the A of the covenant of
5:4 Israel came, and the Levites took up the A
5:5 they brought up the A, the tent of meeting,
5:6 him, were before the A, sacrificing so many sheep
5:7 the priests brought the A of the covenant of
5:8 the place of the A, so that the cherubim
5:8 a covering above the A and its poles.
5:10 was nothing in the A except the two tables
6:11 I have set the A, in which is the
6:41 place, thou and the A of thy might.
8:11 places to which the A of the LORD has
35:3 LORD, "Put the holy A in the house which
Ps 132:8 place, thou and the A of thy might.
Jer 3:16 no more say, "The A of the covenant of
2Mac 2:4 the tent and the A should follow with him,
2:5 the tent and the A and the altar of
Mt 24:38 when Noah entered the A,
Lk 17:27 when Noah entered the A, and the flood came
Heb 9:4 of incense and the A of the covenant covered
11:7 heed and constructed an A for the saving of
1Pet 3:20 the building of the A, in which a few,
Rev 11:19 was opened, and the A of his covenant was

ARKITES (2)

Gen 10:17 Girgashites, the Hivites, the A, the Sinites,
1Chr 1:15 Girgashites, the Hivites, the A, the Sinites,

ARM (82)

Ex 6:6 you with an outstretched A and with great acts
15:16 the greatness of thy A, they are as still
Num 31:3 said to the people, A men from among you
Deut 4:34 hand and an outstretched A, and by great terrors,
5:15 hand and an outstretched A; therefore the LORD
7:19 hand, and the outstretched A, by which the LORD
9:29 and by thy outstretched A
11:2 hand and his outstretched A,
26:8 hand and an outstretched A, with great terror, with
33:20 lion, he tears the A, and the crown of
2Sam 1:10 which was on his A, and I have brought
1Kgs 8:42 and of thy outstretched A, when he comes and
10:19 of the seat were A rests and two lions
10:19 lions standing beside the A rests,
2Kgs 5:18 there, leaning on my A, and I bow myself
17:36 and with an outstretched A; you shall bow yourselves
2Chr 6:32 hand, and thy outstretched A, when he comes and
9:18 of the seat were A rests and two lions
9:18 lions standing beside the A rests,
32:8 With him is an A of flesh; but with
Job 26:2 you have saved the A that has no strength!
31:22 shoulder, and let my A be broken from its
35:9 help because of the A of the mighty.
38:15 withheld, and their uplifted A is broken.
40:9 Have you an A like God, and can you
Ps 10:15 Break thou the A of the wicked and evildoer;
44:3 nor did their own A give them victory; but
44:3 right hand, and thy A, and the light of
77:15 Thou didst with thy A redeem thy people, the
83:8 they are the strong A of the children of
89:10 thou didst scatter thy enemies with thy mighty A
89:13 Thou hast a mighty A; strong is thy hand,
89:21 abide with him, my A also shall strengthen him.
98:1 hand and his holy A have gotten him victory.
136:12 hand and an outstretched A, for his steadfast love
Song 8:6 a seal upon your A; for love is strong
Wis 5:16 them, and with his A he will shield them.
5:17 whole armor, and will A all creation to repel
11:21 and who can withstand the might of thy A
16:16 the strength of thy A, pursued by unusual rains
Sir 21:21 ornament, and like a bracelet on the right A
36:6 hand and thy right A glorious.
38:30 the clay with his A and makes it pliable
Is 17:5 standing grain and his A harvests the ears, and
30:30 descending blow of his A to be seen, in
30:32 lyres; battling with brandished A he will fight with
33:2 Be our A every morning, our salvation in the
40:10 with might, and his A rules for him; behold,
44:12 it with his strong A; he becomes hungry and
48:14 on Babylon, and his A shall be against the
51:5 me, and for my A they hope.
51:9 put on strength, O A of the LORD; awake,
52:10 has bared his holy A before the eyes of
53:1 to whom has the A of the LORD been
59:16 intervene; then his own A brought him victory, and
62:8 and by his mighty A: "I will not again
63:5 uphold; so my own A brought me victory, and
63:12 who caused his glorious A to go at the
Jer 17:5 and makes flesh his A, whose heart turns away
21:5 outstretched hand and strong A, in anger, and in
27:5 power and my outstretched A have made the earth,
32:17 by thy great power and by thy outstretched A
32:21 strong hand and outstretched A, and with great
48:25 cut off, and his A is broken, says the
Bar 2:11 great power and outstretched A, and hast made thee
Ezek 4:7 of Jerusalem, with your A bared; and you shall
17:9 not take a strong A or many people to
20:33 hand and an outstretched A, and with wrath poured
20:34 hand and an outstretched A, and with wrath poured
30:21 I have broken the A of Pharaoh king of
30:22 arms, both the strong A and the one that
Dan 11:6 the strength of her A, and he and his
Zech 11:17 the sword smite his A and his right eye!
11:17 Let his A be wholly withered, his right eye
2Mac 12:35 and cut off his A; so Gorgias escaped and
15:24 the might of thy A may these blasphemers who
15:30 off Nicanor's head and A and carry them to
15:32 and that profane man's A, which had been boastfully
Lk 1:51 shown strength with his A, he has scattered the
Jn 12:38 to whom has the A of the Lord been
Acts 13:17 Egypt, and with uplifted A he led them out
1Pet 4:1 suffered in the flesh, A yourselves with the same

ARMAGEDDON

Rev 16:16 at the place which is called in Hebrew A

ARMAMENT

Sir 46:6 nations might know his A, that he was fighting

ARMED (41)

Num 31:5 each tribe, twelve thousand A for war.

	32:21	the war, and every A man of you will
	32:27	every man who is A for war, before the
	32:29	every man who is A to battle before the
	32:30	pass over with you A, they shall have possessions
	32:32	We will pass over A before the LORD into
Deut	3:18	valor shall pass over A before your brethren the
Josh	1:14	you shall pass over A before your brethren and
	4:12	of Manasseh passed over A before the people of
	4:13	about forty thousand ready A for war passed over
	6:7	city, and let the A men pass on before
	6:9	And the A men went before the priests who
	6:13	trumpets continually; and the A men went before
Judg	7:11	the outposts of the A men that were in
	18:11	the tribe of Dan, A with weapons of war,
	18:16	men of the Danites, A with their weapons of
	18:17	the six hundred men A with weapons of war.
1Sam	17:5	head, and he was A with a coat of
1Chr	12:23	the divisions of the A troops, who came to
	12:24	six thousand eight hundred A troops.
	12:34	were thirty-seven thousand men A with shield and
	12:37	and twenty thousand men A with all the weapons
2Chr	14:8	hundred thousand from Judah, A with bucklers and
	17:17	two hundred thousand men A with bow and shield,
	17:18	hundred and eighty thousand A for war.
	28:14	So the A men left the captives and the
Esth	8:11	and to annihilate any A force of any people
Ps	78:9	The Ephraimites, A with the bow, turned back on
Prov	6:11	and want like an A man.
	24:34	and want like an A man.
Is	15:4	as Jahaz; therefore the A men of Moab cry
1Mac	6:35	stationed a thousand men A with coats of mail,
	6:37	upon each were four A men who fought from
	14:32	his own money; he A the men of his
2Mac	4:40	filled with anger, Lysimachus A about three thousand
	5:2	air, in companies fully A with lances and drawn
	5:26	the city with his A men and killed great
	13:2	and three hundred chariots A with scythes.
	14:22	in place; Judas posted A men in readiness at
	15:11	He A each of them not so much with
Lk	11:21	a strong man, fully A, guards his own palace,

ARMIES (29)

Josh	10:5	up with all their A and encamped against Gibeon,
1Sam	17:1	the Philistines gathered their A for battle; and they
	17:26	he should defy the A of the living God?"
	17:36	he has defied the A of the living God."
	17:45	the God of the A of Israel, whom you
	23:3	to Keilah against the A of the Philistines?"
1Kgs	2:5	two commanders of the A of Israel, Abner the
	15:20	the commanders of his A against the cities of
1Chr	11:26	mighty men of the A were Asahel the brother
2Chr	16:4	the commanders of his A against the cities of
Jud	1:4	wide, so that his A could march out in
	2:7	the feet of my A, and will hand them
Job	25:3	Is there any number to his A
Ps	44:9	us, and hast not gone out with our A
	60:10	dost not go forth, O God, with our A
	68:12	"The kings of the A, they flee, they flee!"
	108:11	dost not go forth, O God, with our A
Song	6:13	the Shulammite, as upon a dance before two A
Dan	11:22	A shall be utterly swept away before him and
1Mac	6:5	and reported that the A which had gone into
	6:6	had taken from the A they had cut down;
	7:43	So the A met in battle on the thirteenth
	9:13	the noise of the A, and the battle raged
	10:78	to Azotus, and the A engaged in battle.
2Mac	10:28	was breaking, the two A joined battle, the one
Lk	21:20	see Jerusalem surrounded by A, then know that its
Heb	11:34	in war, put foreign A to flight.
Rev	19:14	And the A of heaven, arrayed in fine linen,
	19:19	the earth with their A gathered to make war

ARMLET

2Sam	1:10	his head and the A which was on his

ARMLETS (3)

Ex	35:22	and signet rings and A, all sorts of gold
Num	31:50	found, articles of gold, A and bracelets, signet rings,
Is	3:20	scarfs; the headdresses, the A, the sashes, the

ARMONI

2Sam	21:8	she bore to Saul, A and Mephibosheth; and the

ARMOR (31)

1Sam	14:1	man who bore his A, "Come, let us go
	14:6	man who bore his A, "Come, let us go
	17:38	clothed David with his A; he put a helmet
	17:39	his sword over his A, and he tried in
	17:54	but he put his A in his tent.
	18:4	to David, and his A, and even his sword
	31:9	and stripped off his A, and sent messengers
	31:10	They put his A in the temple of Ashtaroth;
1Kgs	20:11	that girds on his A boast himself as he
	22:34	Israel between the scale A and the breastplate;
2Kgs	3:21	able to put on A, from the youngest to
1Chr	10:9	his head and his A, and sent messengers throughout
	10:10	And they put his A in the temple of
2Chr	18:33	Israel between the scale A and the breastplate;
Wis	5:17	zeal as his whole A, and will arm all
Ezek	23:12	warriors clothed in full A, horsemen riding on horses,
	38:4	them clothed in full A, a great company, all
1Mac	3:3	he girded on his A of war and waged
	4:6	they did not have A and swords such as
	4:30	Saul, and of the man who carried his A
	6:43	one of the beasts was equipped with royal A
	13:29	he put suits of A for a permanent memorial,
	13:29	beside the suits of A carved ships, so that
2Mac	3:25	was seen to have A and weapons of gold.
	5:3	of golden trappings, and A of all sorts.
	10:30	him with their own A and weapons, they kept
	15:28	joy, they recognized Nicanor, lying dead, in full A
Lk	11:22	he takes away his A in which he trusted,
Rom	13:12	and put on the A of light;
Eph	6:11	Put on the whole A of God, that you
	6:13	Therefore take the whole A of God, that you

ARMOR-BEARER (18)

Judg	9:54	the young man his A, and said to him,
1Sam	14:7	And his A said to him, "Do all that
	14:12	hailed Jonathan and his A, and said, "Come up
	14:12	Jonathan said to his A, "Come up after me;
	14:13	and feet, and his A after him.
	14:13	before Jonathan, and his A killed them after him;
	14:14	which Jonathan and his A made, was of about
	14:17	behold, Jonathan and his A were not there.
	16:21	Saul loved him greatly, and he became his A
	31:4	Saul said to his A, "Draw your sword, and
	31:4	But his A would not; for he feared greatly.
	31:5	And when his A saw that Saul was dead,
	31:6	three sons, and his A, and all his men,
2Sam	23:37	Naharai of Be-eroth, the A of Joab the son
1Chr	10:4	Saul said to his A, "Draw your sword, and
	10:4	But his A would not; for he feared greatly.
	10:5	And when his A saw that Saul was dead,
	11:39	Naharai of Be-eroth, the A of Joab the son

ARMOR-BEARERS

2Sam	18:15	ten young men, Joab's A, surrounded Absalom and

ARMORY (4)

2Kgs	20:13	the precious oil, his A, all that was found
Neh	3:19	the ascent to the A at the Angle.
Is	39:2	precious oil, his whole A, all that was found
Jer	50:25	LORD has opened his A, and brought out the

ARMPITS

Jer	38:12	and clothes between your A and the ropes."

ARMS (62)

Gen	24:22	two bracelets for her A weighing ten gold shekels,
	24:30	bracelets on his sister's A, and when he heard
	24:47	on her nose, and the bracelets on her A
	49:24	bow remained unmoved, his A were made agile by
Num	32:17	we will take up A, ready to go before
	32:20	you will take up A to go before the
Deut	33:27	dwelling place, and underneath are the everlasting A
Judg	10:17	Ammonites were called to A, and they encamped in
	12:1	Ephraim were called to A, and they crossed to
	15:14	which were on his A became as flax that
	16:12	the ropes off his A like a thread.
2Sam	22:35	war, so that my A can bend a bow
	23:7	man who touches them A himself with iron and
Jud	14:3	they will seize their A and go into the
	15:13	Israel followed, bearing their A and wearing garlands
Esth	15:8	took her in his A until she came to
Job	22:9	away empty, and the A of the fatherless were
Ps	18:34	war, so that my A can bend a bow
	37:17	For the A of the wicked shall be broken;
Prov	31:17	strength and makes her A strong.
Song	5:14	His A are rounded gold, set with jewels.
Wis	18:22	not by force of A, but by his word
Is	40:11	the lambs in his A, he will carry them

51:5 gone forth, and my A will rule the peoples;
60:4 and your daughters shall be carried in the A
Ezek 13:20 tear them from your A; and I will let
16:11 put bracelets on your A, and a chain on
30:22 and will break his A, both the strong arm
30:24 I will strengthen the A of the king of
30:24 I will break the A of Pharaoh, and he
30:25 I will strengthen the A of the king of
30:25 of Babylon, but the A of Pharaoh shall fall;
Dan 2:32 gold, its breast and A of silver, its belly
10:6 like flaming torches, his A and legs like the
Hos 7:16 trained and strengthened their A, yet they devise evil
11:3 them up in my A; but they did not
1Mac 1:35 position; they stored up A and food, and collecting
5:43 they threw away their A and fled into the
6:6 grown strong from the A, supplies, and abundant
6:41 the clanking of their A, trembled, for the army
7:44 they threw down their A and fled.
8:26 give or supply grain, A, money, or ships, as
8:28 be given no grain, A, money, or ships, as
10:6 to equip them with A, and to become his
10:21 and equipped them with A in abundance.
11:51 they threw down their A and made peace.
12:27 and to keep their A at hand so as
14:33 Judea, where formerly the A of the enemy had
2Mac 5:25 work, he ordered his men to parade under A
8:18 "For they trust to A and acts of daring,"
8:27 they had collected the A of the enemy and
8:31 Collecting the A of the enemy, they stored them
9:2 to the rescue with A, and Antiochus and his
10:23 Having success at A in everything he undertook, he
10:27 they took up their A and advanced a considerable
11:7 first to take up A, and he urged the
15:5 you to take up A and finish the king's
15:21 the varied supply of A and the savagery of
15:21 it is not by A, but as the Lord
Mk 9:36 taking him in his A, he said to them,
10:16 took them in his A and blessed them, laying
Lk 2:28 him up in his A and blessed God and

ARMY (292)

Gen 21:22 the commander of his A said to Abraham, "God
21:32 the commander of his A rose up and returned
26:26 his adviser and Phicol the commander of his A
32:2 Jacob saw them he said, "This is God's A
Ex 14:6 chariot and took his A with him,
14:9 his horsemen and his A, and overtook them
Num 31:14 the officers of the A, the commanders of thousands
31:48 the thousands of the A, the captains of thousands
Deut 11:4 he did to the A of Egypt, to their
20:1 and chariots and an A larger than your own,
24:5 go out with the A or be charged with
Josh 5:14 as commander of the A of the LORD I
5:15 commander of the LORD's A said to Joshua, "Put
Judg 4:2 the commander of his A was Sisera, who dwelt
4:7 the general of Jabin's A, to meet you by
4:15 chariots and all his A before Barak at the
4:16 the chariots and the A to Harosheth-ha-goiim, and all
4:16 Harosheth-ha-goiim, and all the A of Sisera fell by
7:21 camp, and all the A ran; they cried out
7:22 and against all the A; and the army fled
7:22 the army; and the A fled as far as
8:6 hand, that we should give bread to your A
8:10 in Karkor with their A, about fifteen thousand men,
8:10 left of all the A of the people of
8:11 Jogbehah, and attacked the A; for the army was
8:11 the army; for the A was off its guard.
8:12 he threw all the A into a panic.
9:29 to Abimelech, 'Increase your A, and come out.'"
20:26 of Israel, the whole A, went up and came
1Sam 12:9 Sisera, commander of the A of Jabin king of
14:50 the commander of his A was Abner the son
17:21 drew up for battle, A against army.
17:21 the Philistines drew up for battle, army against A
17:55 the commander of the A, "Abner, whose son is
26:5 the commander of his A; Saul was lying within
26:5 the encampment, while the A was encamped around
26:7 Abishai went to the A by night; and there
26:7 and Abner and the A lay around him.
26:14 David called to the A, and to Abner the
28:1 are to go out with me in the A
28:5 When Saul saw the A of the Philistines, he
28:19 LORD will give the A of Israel also into
2Sam 2:8 Ner, commander of Saul's A, had taken Ish-bosheth
3:23 Joab and all the A that was with him
5:24 you to smite the A of the Philistines."
8:9 had defeated the whole A of Hadadezer,
8:16 Zeruiah was over the A; and Jehoshaphat the son
10:16 the commander of the A of Hadadezer at their
10:18 the commander of their A, so that he died
17:25 set Amasa over the A instead of Joab.
18:2 David sent forth the A, one third under the
18:4 gate, while all the A marched out by hundreds
18:6 So the A went out into the field against
19:13 not commander of my A henceforth in place of
20:23 command of all the A of Israel; and Benaiah
24:2 the commanders of the A, who were with him,
24:4 prevailed against Joab and the commanders of the A
24:4 the commanders of the A went out from the
1Kgs 1:19 the commander of the A; but Solomon your servant
1:25 the commander of the A, and Abiathar the priest;
2:32 Ner, commander of the A of Israel, and Amasa
2:32 Jether, commander of the A of Judah.
2:35 of Jehoiada over the A in place of Joab,
4:4 in command of the A; Zadok and Abiathar were
11:15 the commander of the A went up to bury
11:21 the commander of the A was dead, Hadad said
16:16 the commander of the A, king over Israel that
20:1 Syria gathered all his A together; thirty-two kings
20:19 the districts, and the A which followed them.
20:25 places; and muster an A like the army that
20:25 an army like the A that you have lost,
22:36 cry went through the A, "Every man to his
2Kgs 3:9 no water for the A or for the beasts
4:13 the king or to the commander of the A
5:1 Naaman, commander of the A of the king of
6:14 chariots and a great A; and they came by
6:15 went out, behold, an A with horses and chariots
6:24 Syria mustered his entire A, and went up, and
7:6 Lord had made the A of the Syrians hear
7:6 sound of a great A, so that they said
7:14 sent them after the A of the Syrians, saying,
8:21 surrounded him; but his A fled home.
9:5 the commanders of the A were in council; and
11:15 were set over the A, "Bring her out between
13:7 left to Jehoahaz an A of more than fifty
18:17 Rabshakeh with a great A from Lachish to King
25:1 came with all his A against Jerusalem, and laid
25:5 But the A of the Chaldeans pursued the king,
25:5 Jericho; and all his A was scattered from him.
25:10 And all the A of the Chaldeans, who were
25:19 the commander of the A who mustered the people
1Chr 7:4 were units of the A for war, thirty-six thousand,
10:7 valley saw that the A had fled and that
11:15 of Adullam, when the A of Philistines was encamped
12:14 were officers of the A, the lesser over a
12:21 men of valor, and were commanders in the A
12:22 there was a great A, like an army of
12:22 great army, like an A of God.
14:15 you to smite the A of the Philistines."
14:16 they smote the Philistine A from Gibeon to Gezer.
18:9 had defeated the whole A of Hadadezer, king of
18:15 Zeruiah was over the A; and Jehoshaphat the son
19:7 of Maacah with his A, who came and encamped
19:8 Joab and all the A of the mighty men.
19:16 the commander of the A of Hadadezer at their
19:18 and killed also Shophach the commander of their A
20:1 Joab led out the A, and ravaged the country
21:2 the commanders of the A, "Go, number Israel, from
26:26 the commanders of the A, had dedicated.
27:3 the commanders of the A for the first month.
27:34 Joab was commander of the king's A
2Chr 13:3 to battle having an A of valiant men of
14:8 And Asa had an A of three hundred thousand
14:9 against them with an A of a million men
14:13 they were broken before the LORD and his A
16:7 LORD your God, the A of the king of
16:8 the Libyans a huge A with exceedingly many chariots
20:21 they went before the A, and say, "Give thanks
23:14 were set over the A, saying to them, "Bring
24:23 of the year the A of the Syrians came
24:24 Though the A of the Syrians had come with
24:24 hand a very great A, because they had forsaken
25:7 do not let the A of Israel go with
25:9 have given to the A of Israel?" The man
25:10 Then Amaziah discharged the A that had come to
25:13 the men of the A whom Amaziah sent back,
26:11 Moreover Uzziah had an A of soldiers, fit for
26:13 their command was an A of three hundred and
26:14 prepared for all the A shields, spears, helmets, coats
28:9 out to meet the A that came to Samaria,
33:11 the commanders of the A of the king of

33:14 put commanders of the A in all the fortified
Neh 2:9 me officers of the A and horsemen.
4:2 brethren and of the A of Samaria, "What are
Jud 1:13 and overthrew the whole A of Arphaxad, and all
2:4 chief general of his A, second only to himself,
2:14 officers of the Assyrian A,
2:16 them as a great A is marshaled for a
2:19 out with his whole A, to go ahead of
2:22 Holofernes took his whole A, his infantry, cavalry,
3:6 the seacoast with his A and stationed garrisons in
3:10 order to assemble all the supplies for his A
5:1 general of the Assyrian A, heard that the people
5:3 How large is their A, and in what does
5:3 Who rules over them as king, leading their A
5:24 and they will be devoured by your vast A
6:1 commander of the Assyrian A, said to Achior and
6:6 the sword of my A and the spear of
7:1 Holofernes ordered his whole A, and all the allies
7:7 soldiers over them, and then returned to his A
7:9 a word, lest his A be defeated.
7:11 a man of your A will fall.
7:17 So the A of the Ammonites moved forward, together
7:18 rest of the Assyrian A encamped in the plain,
7:20 The whole Assyrian A, their infantry, chariots, and
7:27 whole city to the A of Holofernes and to
10:13 the commander of your A, to give him a
11:18 out with your whole A, and not one of
13:15 commander of the Assyrian A, and here is the
14:3 officers of the Assyrian A; and they will rush
14:19 leaders of the Assyrian A heard this, they rent
16:12 they perished before the A of my Lord.
Esth 1:3 princes and servants, the A chiefs of Persia and
Ps 33:16 saved by his great A; a warrior is not
Song 6:4 Jerusalem, terrible as an A with banners.
6:10 sun, terrible as an A with banners?"
Wis 12:8 as forerunners of thy A, to destroy them little
Is 36:2 to King Hezekiah at Jerusalem, with a great A
43:17 forth chariot and horse, A and warrior; they lie
Jer 32:2 At that time the A of the king of
34:1 Babylon and all his A and all the kingdoms
34:7 in Jerusalem, when the A of the king of
34:21 the hand of the A of the king of
35:11 for fear of the A of the Chaldeans and
35:11 the Chaldeans and the A of the Syrians.' So
37:5 The A of Pharaoh had come out of Egypt;
37:7 of me, 'Behold, Pharaoh's A which came to help
37:10 should defeat the whole A of Chaldeans who are
37:11 Now when the Chaldean A had withdrawn from
37:11 the approach of Pharaoh's A,
38:3 the hand of the A of the king of
39:1 Babylon and all his A came against Jerusalem and
39:5 But the A of the Chaldeans pursued them, and
46:2 Concerning the A of Pharaoh Neco, king of Egypt,
52:4 came with all his A against Jerusalem, and they
52:8 But the A of the Chaldeans pursued the king,
52:8 Jericho; and all his A was scattered from him.
52:14 And all the A of the Chaldeans, who were
52:25 the commander of the A who mustered the people
Ezek 17:15 they might give him horses and a large A
17:17 Pharaoh with his mighty A and great company will
27:10 Put were in your A as your men of
29:18 of Babylon made his A labor hard against Tyre;
29:18 neither he nor his A got anything from Tyre
29:19 and it shall be the wages for his A
32:31 Pharaoh and all his A, slain by the sword,
38:4 forth, and all your A, horses and horsemen, all
38:15 great host, a mighty A;
Dan 3:20 mighty men of his A to bind Shadrach, Meshach,
11:7 shall come against the A and enter the fortress
11:13 on with a great A and abundant supplies.
11:25 south with a great A; and the king of
11:25 exceedingly great and mighty A; but he shall not
11:26 be his undoing; his A shall be swept away,
Joel 2:5 stubble, like a powerful A drawn up for battle.
2:11 his voice before his A, for his host is
2:25 the cutter, my great A, which I sent among
1Mac 1:4 gathered a very strong A and ruled over countries,
2:44 They organized an A, and struck down sinners in
2:66 he shall command the A for you and fight
3:13 commander of the Syrian A, heard that Judas had
3:15 And again a strong A of ungodly men went
3:17 when they saw the A coming to meet them,
3:19 the size of the A that victory in battle
3:23 against Seron and his A, and they were crushed
3:27 the forces of his kingdom, a very strong A
3:57 Then the A marched out and encamped to the
4:10 fathers and crush this A before us today.
4:20 They saw that their A had been put to
4:21 they also saw the A of Judas drawn up
4:30 he saw that the A was strong, he prayed,
4:31 thou hem in this A by the hand of
4:34 there fell of the A of Lysias five thousand
4:35 to invade Judea again with an even larger A
4:37 So all the A assembled and they went up
5:28 Then Judas and his A quickly turned back by
5:34 And when the A of Timothy realized that it
5:37 Timothy gathered another A and encamped opposite
5:40 as Judas and his A drew near to the
5:43 first, and the whole A followed him.
5:49 be made to the A that each should encamp
6:33 rose and took his A by a forced march
6:38 two flanks of the A, to harass the enemy
6:40 part of the king's A was spread out on
6:41 arms, trembled, for the A was very large and
6:42 But Judas and his A advanced to the battle,
6:42 men of the king's A fell.
6:48 soldiers of the king's A went up to Jerusalem
7:2 of his fathers, the A seized Antiochus and Lysias
7:4 So the A killed them, and Demetrius took his
7:14 has come with the A, and he will not
7:32 hundred men of the A of Nicanor fell, and
7:35 "Unless Judas and his A are delivered into my
7:38 man and on his A, and let them fall
7:39 Beth-horon, and the Syrian A joined him.
7:42 So also crush this A before us today; let
7:43 The A of Nicanor was crushed, and he himself
7:44 When his A saw that Nicanor had fallen, they
8:6 with cavalry and chariots and a very large A
9:1 that Nicanor and his A had fallen in battle,
9:1 and with them the right wing of the A
9:7 Judas saw that his A had slipped away and
9:11 Then the A of Bacchides marched out from the
9:11 went ahead of the A, as did all the
9:14 the strength of his A were on the right;
9:34 he with all his A crossed the Jordan.
10:2 assembled a very large A and marched out to
10:49 in battle, and the A of Demetrius fled, and
10:53 and he and his A were crushed by us,
10:73 cavalry and such an A in the plain, where
10:77 cavalry and a large A, and went to Azotus
10:80 for they surrounded his A and shot arrows at
11:60 cities, and all the A of Syria gathered to
11:63 Galilee with a large A, intending to remove him
11:67 Jonathan and his A encamped by the waters of
11:68 Hazor, and behold, the A of the foreigners met
11:70 of Chalphi, commanders of the forces of the A
12:42 come with a large A, he was afraid to
13:1 had assembled a large A to invade the land
13:11 with him a considerable A; he drove out its
13:12 Ptolemais with a large A to invade the land
13:20 But Simon and his A kept marching along opposite
14:3 went and defeated the A of Demetrius, and seized
16:6 Then he and his A lined up against them.
16:7 Then he divided the A and placed the horsemen
16:8 and Cendebeus and his A were put to flight,
2Mac 5:24 the Mysians, with an A of twenty-two thousand, and
8:5 as Maccabeus got his A organized, the Gentiles could
8:12 the arrival of the A,
8:21 then he divided his A into four parts.
8:24 disabled most of Nicanor's A, and forced them all
8:35 succeeded chiefly in the destruction of his own A
9:9 his stench the whole A felt revulsion at his
10:35 young men in the A of Maccabeus, fired with
12:20 But Maccabeus arranged his A in divisions, set men
12:38 Then Judas assembled his A and went to the
13:1 coming with a great A against Judea,
13:13 God before the king's A could enter Judea and
14:1 Tripolis with a strong A and a fleet,
14:21 came forward from each A; seats of honor were
15:20 at hand with their A drawn up for battle,
Rev 19:19 who sits upon the horse and against his A

ARNAN

1Chr 3:21 son Rephaiah, his son A, his son Obadiah, his

ARNI

Lk 3:33 Admin, the son of A, the son of Hezron,

ARNON (25)

Num 21:13 other side of the A, which is in the
21:13 the Amorites; for the A is the boundary of
21:14 the valleys of the A,

21:24 his land from the A to the Jabbok, as
21:26 out of his hand, as far as the A
21:28 Moab, the lords of the heights of the A
22:36 boundary formed by the A, at the extremity of
Deut 2:24 the valley of the A; behold, I have given
2:36 the valley of the A, and from the city
3:8 the valley of the A to Mount Hermon
3:12 the valley of the A, and half the hill
3:16 the valley of the A, with the middle of
4:48 the valley of the A, as far as Mount
Josh 12:1 the valley of the A to Mount Hermon, with
12:2 the valley of the A, and from the middle
13:9 the valley of the A, and the city that
13:16 the valley of the A, and the city that
Judg 11:13 my land, from the A to the Jabbok and
11:18 other side of the A; but they did not
11:18 of Moab, for the A was the boundary of
11:22 the Amorites from the A to the Jabbok and
11:26 the banks of the A, three hundred years, why
2Kgs 10:33 the valley of the A, that is, Gilead and
Is 16:2 daughters of Moab at the fords of the A
Jer 48:20 Tell it by the A, that Moab is laid

AROD

Num 26:17 of the Erites; of A, the family of the

ARODI

Gen 46:16 Haggi, Shuni, Ezbon, Eri, A, and Areli.

ARODITES

Num 26:17 the family of the A; of Areli, the family

AROER (15)

Num 32:34 Gad built Dibon, Ataroth, A,
Deut 2:36 From A, which is on the edge of the
3:12 the territory beginning at A, which is on the
4:48 beyond the Jordan; from A, which is on the
Josh 12:2 Heshbon, and ruled from A, which is on the
13:9 LORD gave them: from A, which is on the
13:16 their territory was from A, which is on the
13:25 of the Ammonites, to A, which is east of
Judg 11:26 its villages, and in A and its villages, and
11:33 he smote them from A to the neighborhood of
1Sam 30:28 Negeb, in Jattir, in A, in Siphmoth, in Eshtemoa,
2Sam 24:5 Jordan, and began from A, and from the city
2Kgs 10:33 and the Manassites, from A, which is by the
1Chr 5:8 Joel, who dwelt in A, as far as Nebo
Jer 48:19 by the way and watch, O inhabitant of A

AROERITE

1Chr 11:44 sons of Hotham the A,

AROMA (2)

Sir 24:15 I gave forth the A of spices, and like
2Cor 2:15 For we are the A of Christ to God

AROMATIC

Ex 30:23 and fifty, and of A cane two hundred and

AROSE (144)

Gen 19:33 know when she lay down or when she A
19:35 also; and the younger A, and lay with him;
19:35 know when she lay down or when she A
22:3 the burnt offering, and A and went to the
22:19 young men, and they A and went together to
24:10 his master; and he A, and went to Mesopotamia,
24:54 When they A in the morning, he said, "Send
24:61 Rebekah and her maids A, and rode upon the
31:17 So Jacob A, and set his sons and his
31:21 that he had, and A and crossed the Euphrates,
31:55 in the morning Laban A, and kissed his grandchildren
32:22 The same night he A and took his two
37:7 and lo, my sheaf A and stood upright; and
38:19 Then she A and went away, and taking off
43:15 and Benjamin; and they A and went down to
Ex 1:7 Now there A a new king over Egypt, who
Josh 8:3 So Joshua A, and all the fighting men, to
8:10 And Joshua A early in the morning and mustered
24:9 Zippor, king of Moab, A and fought against Israel;
Judg 2:10 their fathers; and there A another generation after
3:20 And he A from his seat.
4:9 Then Deborah A, and went with Barak to Kedesh.
5:7 they ceased until you A, Deborah, arose as a
5:7 until you arose, Deborah, A as a mother in
8:21 And Gideon A and slew Zebah and Zalmunna; and
10:1 After Abimelech there A to deliver Israel Tola the
10:3 After him A Jair the Gileadite, who judged Israel
13:11 And Manoah A and went after his wife, and
16:3 and at midnight he A and took hold of
19:3 Then her husband A and went after her, to
19:5 the fourth day they A early in the morning,
19:8 the fifth day he A early in the morning
20:8 And all the people A as one man, saying,
20:18 The people of Israel A and went up to
Ruth 3:14 until the morning, but A before one could recognize
1Sam 3:6 And Samuel A and went to Eli, and said,
3:8 And he A and went to Eli, and said,
9:26 So Saul A, and both he and Samuel went
13:15 And Samuel A, and went up from Gilgal to
17:35 mouth; and if he A against me, I caught
17:48 When the Philistine A and came and drew near
18:27 time had expired, David A and went, along with
23:13 were about six hundred, A and departed from Keilah,
23:24 And they A, and went to Ziph ahead of
24:4 Then David A and stealthily cut off the skirt
24:8 Afterward David also A, and went out of the
26:2 So Saul A and went down to the wilderness
27:2 So David A and went over, he and the
28:23 So he A from the earth, and sat upon
31:12 all the valiant men A, and went all night,
2Sam 2:15 Then they A and passed over by number, twelve
6:2 And David A and went with all the people
11:2 one afternoon, when David A from his couch and
12:20 Then David A from the earth, and washed, and
12:21 the child died, you A and ate food."
13:29 all the king's sons A, and each mounted his
13:31 Then the king A, and rent his garments, and
14:23 So Joab A and went to Geshur, and brought
14:31 Then Joab A and went to Absalom at his
15:9 So he A, and went to Hebron.
17:22 Then David A, and all the people who were
19:8 Then the king A, and took his seat in
24:11 And when David A in the morning, the word
1Kgs 1:50 feared Solomon; and he A, and went, and caught
2:40 Shimei A and saddled an ass, and went to
3:20 And she A at midnight, and took my son
8:54 to the LORD, he A from before the altar
11:40 kill Jeroboam; but Jeroboam A, and fled into Egypt,
14:4 wife did so; she A, and went to Shiloh,
14:17 Then Jeroboam's wife A, and departed, and came to
17:10 So he A and went to Zarephath; and when
19:3 was afraid, and he A and went for his
19:8 And he A, and ate and drank, and went
19:21 Then he A and went after Elijah, and ministered
21:16 Naboth was dead, Ahab A to go down to
2Kgs 1:15 So he A and went down with him to
4:30 So he A and followed her.
7:5 So they A at twilight to go to the
8:2 So the woman A, and did according to the
9:6 So he A, and went into the house; and
11:1 son was dead, she A and destroyed all the
12:20 His servants A and made a conspiracy, and slew
19:35 Assyrians; and when men A early in the morning,
25:26 captains of the forces A, and went to Egypt;
1Chr 10:12 all the valiant men A, and took away the
20:4 And after this there A a war with the Philistines
2Chr 22:10 son was dead, she A and destroyed all the
29:12 Then the Levites A, Mahath the son of Amasai,
30:27 priests and the Levites A and blessed the people,
Ezra 3:2 Then A Jeshua the son of Jozadak, with his
5:2 the son of Jozadak A and began to rebuild
10:5 Then Ezra A and made the leading priests and
Neh 2:12 Then I A in the night, I and a
4:14 And I looked, and A, and said to the
5:1 Now there A a great outcry of the people
Tob 8:9 But Raguel A and went and dug a grave,
10:10 So Raguel A and gave him his wife Sarah
Jud 7:30 and general lamentation A throughout the assembly,
12:5 the morning watch she A
14:19 loud cries and shouts A in the midst of
Job 1:20 Then Job A, and rent his robe, and shaved
Ps 76:9 was still, when God A to establish judgment to
Song 5:5 I A to open to my beloved, and my
Sir 47:21 and a disobedient kingdom A out of Ephraim.
48:1 Then the prophet Elijah A like a fire, and
Is 37:36 Assyrians; and when men A early in the morning,
Jer 26:17 elders of the land A and spoke to all
Ezek 3:12 glory of the LORD A from its place, I
3:23 So I A and went forth into the plain;
Dan 6:19 of day, the king A and went in haste
8:22 of which four others A, four kingdoms shall arise
14:39 So Daniel A and ate.

Jon 3:3 So Jonah A and went to Nineveh, according to
3:6 of Nineveh, and he A from his throne, removed
1Mac 13:44 and a great tumult A in the city.
16:5 in the morning they A and marched into the
2Mac 5:5 When a false rumor A that Antiochus was dead,
Mt 8:24 And behold, there A a great storm on the
9:25 took her by the hand, and the girl A
Mk 4:37 great storm of wind A, and the waves beat
7:23 And from there he A and went away to
9:27 the hand and lifted him up, and he A
Lk 1:39 In those days Mary A and went with haste
4:38 And he A and left the synagogue, and entered
6:48 and when a flood A, the stream broke against
9:46 And an argument A among them as to which
15:14 everything, a great famine A in that country, and
15:20 hired servants.'" And he A and came to his
22:24 A dispute also A among them, which of them
23:1 whole company of them A, and brought him before
Jn 3:25 Now a discussion A between John's disciples and a
Acts 5:36 before these days Theudas A, giving himself out to
5:37 him Judas the Galilean A in the days of
6:9 from Cilicia and Asia, A and disputed with Stephen.
7:18 in Egypt till there A over Egypt another king
8:1 day a great persecution A against the church in
9:8 Saul A from the ground; and when his eyes
11:19 of the persecution that A over Stephen traveled as
15:38 And there A a sharp contention, so that they
19:23 About that time there A no little stir concerning
23:7 said this, a dissension A between the Pharisees and
23:9 Then a great clamor A; and some of the
2Pet 2:1 But false prophets also A among the people, just
Rev 12:7 Now war A in heaven, Michael and his angels

AROUSE (3)

1Mac 6:34 grapes and mulberries, to A them for battle.
13:17 the sons, lest he A great hostility among the
2Pet 1:13 in this body, to A you by way of

AROUSED (10)

Is 45:13 I have A him in righteousness, and I will
Jer 32:31 This city has A my anger and wrath, from
Dan 13:45 put to death, God A the holy spirit of
1Mac 10:74 heard the words of Apollonius, his spirit was A
2Mac 4:40 the crowds were becoming A and filled with anger,
13:4 the King of kings A the anger of Antiochus
15:10 And when he had A their courage, he gave
Acts 21:30 all the city was A, and the people ran
Rom 7:5 flesh, our sinful passions, A by the law, were
2Pet 3:1 of them I have A your sincere mind by

AROUSES

Wis 15:5 varied colors, whose appearance A yearning in fools,

AROUSING

2Mac 15:17 and so effective in A valor and awaking manliness

ARPACHSHAD (9)

Gen 10:22 of Shem: Elam, Asshur, A, Lud, and Aram.
10:24 A became the father of Shelah; and Shelah became
11:10 became the father of A two years after the
11:11 after the birth of A five hundred years, and
11:12 When A had lived thirty-five years, he became the
11:13 father of Shelah; and A lived after the birth
1Chr 1:17 of Shem: Elam, Asshur, A, Lud, Aram, Uz, Hul,
1:18 A was the father of Shelah; and Shelah was
1:24 Shem, A, Shelah;

ARPAD (6)

2Kgs 18:34 Where are the gods of Hamath and A
19:13 Hamath, the king of A, the king of the
Is 10:9 Is not Hamath like A
36:19 Where are the gods of Hamath and A
37:13 Hamath, the king of A, the king of the
Jer 49:23 "Hamath and A are confounded, for they have heard

ARPHAXAD (6)

Jud 1:1 in the days of A, who ruled over the
1:5 made war against King A in the great plain
1:13 his forces against King A, and defeated him in
1:13 the whole army of A, and all his cavalry
1:15 He captured A in the mountains of Ragae and
Lk 3:36 Ca-inan, the son of A, the son of Shem,

ARRANGE

2Cor 9:5 you before me, and A in advance for this

ARRANGED (7)

Wis 11:20 But thou hast A all things by measure and
Sir 16:25 He A his works in an eternal order, and
47:10 to the feasts, and A their times throughout the
Dan 13:14 And then together they A for a time when
2Mac 12:20 But Maccabeus A his army in divisions, set men
Acts 20:13 for so he had A, intending himself to go
1Cor 12:18 as it is, God A the organs in the

ARRANGEMENT (2)

Ezek 43:11 portray the temple, its A, its exits and its
Heb 9:9 According to this A, gifts and sacrifices are offered

ARRANGEMENTS

Ezek 42:11 the same exits and A and doors.

ARRANGING (2)

Eccl 12:9 weighing and studying and A proverbs with great
Sir 50:14 at the altars, and A the offering to the

ARRAY (19)

Judg 20:30 and set themselves in A against Gibe-ah, as at
20:33 and set themselves in A at Baal-tamar; and the
2Sam 10:8 drew up in battle A at the entrance of
1Chr 16:29 the LORD in holy A;
19:9 drew up in battle A at the entrance of
19:17 set the battle in A against the Syrians, they
2Chr 20:21 praise him in holy A, as they went before
Jud 7:11 against them in battle A, and not a man
Esth 6:9 noble princes; let him A the man whom the
15:6 clothed in the full A of his majesty, all
Ps 29:2 of his name; worship the LORD in holy A
96:9 the LORD in holy A; tremble before him, all
Sir 43:9 of heaven, a gleaming A in the heights of
Jer 6:23 upon horses, set in A as a man for
50:9 country; and they shall A themselves against her;
50:14 Set yourselves in A against Babylon round about, all
Nah 2:3 flame when mustered in A; the chargers prance.
Zeph 1:8 sons and all who A themselves in foreign attire.
Acts 4:26 earth set themselves in A, and the rulers were

ARRAYED (24)

Gen 41:42 on Joseph's hand, and A him in garments of
Judg 6:31 to all who were A against him, "Will you
2Sam 10:9 men of Israel, and A them against the Syrians;
10:10 his brother, and he A them against the Ammonites.
10:17 And the Syrians A themselves against David, and
1Kgs 22:10 sitting on their thrones, A in their robes, at
1Chr 12:38 these, men of war, A in battle order, came
19:10 men of Israel, and A them against the Syrians;
19:11 brother, and they were A against the Ammonites.
2Chr 5:12 their sons and kinsmen, A in fine linen, with
18:9 sitting on their thrones, A in their robes; and
Jud 10:3 on a tiara, and A herself in her gayest
12:15 she got up and A herself in all her
Esth 6:11 the horse, and he A Mordecai and made him
15:1 she had worshipped, and A herself in splendid attire.
Job 6:4 terrors of God are A against me.
Ps 55:18 wage, for many are A against me.
Jer 50:42 they ride upon horses, A as a man for
Mt 6:29 his glory was not A like one of these.
Lk 12:27 his glory was not A like one of these.
Jn 19:2 on his head, and A him in a purple
Rev 9:7 locusts were like horses A for battle; on their
17:4 The woman was A in purple and scarlet, and
19:14 the armies of heaven, A in fine linen, white

ARRAYING

Lk 23:11 and mocked him; then, A him in gorgeous apparel,

ARREST (11)

2Mac 14:39 five hundred soldiers to A him;
Mt 21:46 when they tried to A him, they feared the
26:4 together in order to A Jesus by stealth and
Mk 12:12 And they tried to A him, but feared the
14:1 were seeking how to A him by stealth, and
Jn 7:30 So they sought to A him; but no one
7:32 Pharisees sent officers to A him.
7:44 of them wanted to A him, but no one
10:39 Again they tried to A him, but he escaped
11:57 so that they might A him.
Acts 12:3 Jews, he proceeded to A Peter also.

ARRESTED (8)

2Mac 7:1 and their mother were A and were being compelled
Mt 4:12 that John had been A, he withdrew into Galilee;

Mk 1:14 Now after John was A, Jesus came into Galilee,
Jn 8:20 temple; but no one A him, because his hour
Acts 1:16 guide to those who A Jesus.
4:3 And they A them and put them in custody
5:18 filled with jealousy they A the apostles and put
21:33 tribune came up and A him, and ordered him

ARRESTING

2Mac 14:40 he thought that by A him he would do

ARRIVAL (4)

Num 10:21 and the tabernacle was set up before their A
Jud 10:18 whole camp, for her A was reported from tent
1Mac 11:44 to the king, the king rejoiced at their A
2Mac 8:12 his companions of the A of the army,

ARRIVE (8)

Gen 19:22 do nothing till you A there." Therefore the name
Ex 10:26 the LORD until we A there."
1Kgs 19:15 Damascus; and when you A, you shall anoint Hazael
2Kgs 9:2 And when you A, look there for Jehu the
Tob 10:1 and they did not A,
Acts 23:35 said, "I will hear you when your accusers A
1Cor 16:3 And when I A, I will send those whom
2Tim 3:7 anybody and can never A at a knowledge of

ARRIVED (37)

Judg 3:27 When he A, he sounded the trumpet in the
11:18 land of Moab, and A on the east side
19:10 up and departed, and A opposite Jebus (that is,
1Sam 4:13 When he A, Eli was sitting upon his seat
2Sam 3:22 the servants of David A with Joab from a
16:14 who were with him, A weary at the Jordan;
2Kgs 6:32 but before the messenger A Elisha said to the
16:11 it, before King Ahaz A from Damascus.
18:17 When they A, they came and stood by the
Tob 2:1 When I A home and my wife Anna and
7:1 they reached Ecbatana and A at the house of
Jud 16:18 When they A at Jerusalem they worshiped God.
Esth 6:14 him, the king's eunuchs A and brought Haman in
Jer 41:5 of it, eighty men A from Shechem and Shiloh
43:7 And they A at Tahpanhes.
Ezek 16:7 and became tall and A at full maidenhood; your
Zech 6:10 and Jedaiah, who have A from Babylon; and go
1Mac 3:40 and when they A they encamped near Emmaus
15:15 Numenius and his companions A from Rome, with
2Mac 3:9 When he had A at Jerusalem and had been
3:24 But when he A at the treasury with his
5:25 When this man A in Jerusalem, he pretended to
15:31 And when he A there and had called his
Lk 8:26 Then they A at the country of the Gerasenes,
11:6 friend of mine has A on a journey, and
Acts 11:11 very moment three men A at the house in
13:5 When they A at Salamis, they proclaimed the word
14:27 And when they A, they gathered the church together
17:10 Beroea; and when they A they went into the
18:5 When Silas and Timothy A from Macedonia, Paul
18:27 When he A, he greatly helped those who through
21:7 voyage from Tyre, we A at Ptolemais; and we
25:13 the king and Bernice A at Caesarea to welcome
27:7 number of days, and A with difficulty off Cnidus,
28:13 made a circuit and A at Rhegium; and after
2Tim 1:17 chains, but when he A in Rome he searched
3 Jn 1:3 some of the brethren A and testified to the

ARRIVING (2)

2Mac 2:28 devoting our effort to A at the outlines of
4:21 Therefore upon A at Joppa he proceeded to

ARROGANCE (27)

1Sam 2:3 very proudly, let not A come from your mouth;
2Kgs 19:28 against me and your A has come into my
Jud 6:19 of heaven, behold their A, and have pity on
9:10 his servant; crush their A by the hand of
Esth 16:12 unable to restrain his A, he undertook to deprive
Ps 10:2 In A the wicked hotly pursue the poor; let
36:11 not the foot of A come upon me, nor
Prov 8:13 Pride and A and the way of evil and
Wis 5:8 What has our A profited us?
Sir 10:7 A is hateful before the Lord and before men,
22:20 but as for reviling, A, disclosure of secrets, or
48:18 against Zion and made great boasts in his A
Is 9:9 in pride and in A of heart:
16:6 he was; of his A, his pride, and his
37:29 against me and your A has come to my
Jer 48:29 his pride, and his A, and the haughtiness of
1Mac 1:24 committed deeds of murder, and spoke with great A
2:49 said to his sons: A and reproach have now
2Mac 5:21 Antioch, thinking in his A that he could sail
7:36 of God, will receive just punishment for your A
9:4 For in his A he said, "When I get
9:7 even more filled with A, breathing fire in his
9:8 sea, in his superhuman A, and imagining that he
9:11 lose much of his A and to come to
13:9 The king with barbarous A was coming to show
15:6 his utter boastfulness and A had determined to erect
Jas 4:16 As it is, you boast in your A

ARROGANT (20)

Ps 73:3 was envious of the A, when I saw the
94:4 They pour out their A words, they boast, all
101:5 of haughty looks and A heart I will not
140:5 A men have hidden a trap for me, and
Prov 16:5 Every one who is A is an abomination to
21:24 man who acts with A pride.
Wis 14:6 in the beginning, when A giants were perishing, the
Sir 23:8 the reviler and the A are tripped by them.
Is 10:12 he will punish the A boasting of the king
13:11 the pride of the A, and lay low the
Hab 2:5 wine is treacherous; the A man shall not abide.
Mal 3:15 Henceforth we deem the A blessed; evildoers not
4:1 oven, when all the A and all evildoers will
1Mac 2:47 They hunted down the A men, and the work
1Cor 4:18 Some are A, as though I were not coming
4:19 the talk of these A people but their power.
5:2 And you are A
13:5 boastful; it is not A or rude.
2Tim 3:2 lovers of money, proud, A, abusive, disobedient to
Tit 1:6 he must not be A or quick-tempered or a

ARROGANTLY (6)

Ex 18:11 Egyptians, when they dealt A with them."
Job 36:9 work and their transgressions, that they are behaving A
Ps 17:10 hearts to pity; with their mouths they speak A
1Mac 1:21 He A entered the sanctuary and took the golden
7:34 defiled them and spoke A,
7:47 hand which he so A stretched out, and brought

ARROW (23)

1Sam 20:36 ran, he shot an A beyond him.
20:37 the place of the A which Jonathan had shot,
20:37 said, "Is not the A beyond you?"
2Kgs 9:24 shoulders, so that the A pierced his heart, and
13:17 he said, "The LORD's A of victory, the arrow
13:17 arrow of victory, the A of victory over Syria!
19:32 city or shoot an A there, or come before
Job 20:24 iron weapon; a bronze A will strike him through.
41:28 The A cannot make him flee; for him slingstones
Ps 11:2 they have fitted their A to the string, to
64:7 God will shoot his A at them; they will
91:5 the night, nor the A that flies by day,
Prov 7:23 caught fast till an A pierces its entrails; as
25:18 war club, or a sword, or a sharp A
Wis 5:12 or as, when an A is shot at a
Sir 19:12 Like an A stuck in the flesh of the
26:12 every post and open her quiver to the A
Is 37:33 city, or shoot an A there, or come before
49:2 made me a polished A, in his quiver he
Jer 9:8 tongue is a deadly A; it speaks deceitfully; with
Lam 3:12 and set me as a mark for his A
Zech 9:13 as my bow; I have made Ephraim its A
9:14 over them, and his A go forth like lightning;

ARROWS (44)

Num 24:8 in pieces, and pierce them through with his A
Deut 32:23 I will spend my A upon them;
32:42 I will make my A drunk with blood, and
1Sam 20:20 I will shoot three A to the side of
20:21 saying, 'Go, find the A If I say to
20:21 the lad, 'Look, the A are on this side
20:22 the youth, 'Look, the A are beyond you,' then
20:36 "Run and find the A which I shoot." As
20:38 lad gathered up the A, and came to his
2Sam 22:15 And he sent out A, and scattered them; lightning,
2Kgs 13:15 "Take a bow and A; so he took a
13:15 and arrows"; so he took a bow and A
13:18 he said, "Take the A; and he took them.
1Chr 12:2 bowmen, and could shoot A and sling stones with
2Chr 26:15 the corners, to shoot A and great stones.
Job 6:4 For the A of the Almighty are in me;
Ps 7:13 deadly weapons, making his A fiery shafts.

18:14 he sent out his A, and scattered them; he
38:2 For thy A have sunk into me, and thy
45:5 Your A are sharp in the heart of the
57:4 teeth are spears and A, their tongues sharp swords.
64:3 aim bitter words like A,
76:3 he broke the flashing A, the shield, the sword,
77:17 gave forth thunder; thy A flashed on every side.
120:4 A warrior's sharp A, with glowing coals of the
127:4 Like A in the hand of a warrior are
144:6 them, send out thy A and rout them!
Prov 26:18 madman who throws firebrands, A, and death,
Is 5:28 a sandal-thong broken; their A are sharp, all their
7:24 With bow and A men will come there, for
Jer 50:9 Their A are like a skilled warrior who does
50:14 at her, spare no A, for she has sinned
51:11 "Sharpen the A
Lam 3:13 into my heart the A of his quiver;
Ezek 5:16 against you my deadly A of famine, arrows for
5:16 deadly arrows of famine, A for destruction, which I
21:21 divination; he shakes the A, he consults the teraphim,
39:3 and will make your A drop out of your
39:9 and bucklers, bows and A, handpikes and spears, and
Hab 3:9 bow, and put the A to the string.
3:11 the light of thine A as they sped, at
1Mac 6:51 stones, machines to shoot A, and catapults.
10:80 his army and shot A at his men from
2Mac 10:30 And they showered A and thunderbolts upon the

ARSACES (3)

1Mac 14:2 When A the king of Persia and Media heard
14:3 and took him to A, who put him under
15:22 Attalus and Ariarathes and A,

ARSENAL

Song 4:4 David, built for an A, whereon hang a thousand

ART (184)

Gen 16:13 spoke to her, "Thou A a God of seeing";
Num 14:14 that thou, O LORD, A in the midst of
14:14 for thou, O LORD, A seen face to face,
2Sam 7:22 Therefore thou A great, O LORD God; for there
7:28 O Lord GOD, thou A God, and thy words
22:29 Yea, thou A my lamp, O LORD, and my
1Kgs 8:46 not sin–and thou A angry with them, and
18:36 this day that thou A God in Israel, and
18:37 that thou, O LORD, A God, and that thou
2Kgs 19:15 God of Israel, who A enthroned above the cherubim,
19:15 above the cherubim, thou A the God, thou alone,
19:19 that thou, O LORD, A God alone."
1Chr 17:26 now, O LORD, thou A God, and thou hast
29:10 and David said: "Blessed A thou, O LORD, the
29:11 O LORD, and thou A exalted as head above
2Chr 6:36 not sin–and thou A angry with them, and
14:11 O LORD, thou A our God; let not man
16:14 prepared by the perfumer's A; and they made a
20:6 God of our fathers, A thou not God in
Ezra 9:15 God of Israel, thou A just, for we are
Neh 9:6 And Ezra said: "Thou A the LORD, thou alone;
9:7 Thou A the LORD, the God who didst choose
9:8 thy promise, for thou A righteous.
9:17 But thou A a God ready to forgive, gracious
9:31 forsake them; for thou A a gracious and merciful
Tob 3:2 in anguish, saying, "Righteous A thou, O Lord; all
3:11 window and said, "Blessed A thou, O Lord my
8:5 began to pray, "Blessed A thou, O God of
8:15 God and said, "Blessed A thou, O God, with
8:16 Blessed A thou, because thou hast made me glad.
8:17 Blessed A thou, because thou hast had compassion
11:14 wept and said, "Blessed A thou, O God, and
Jud 9:7 know not that thou A the Lord who crushest
9:11 of strength; for thou A God of the lowly,
9:14 and understand that thou A God, the God of
13:17 with one accord, "Blessed A thou, our God, who
Esth 13:11 under heaven, and thou A Lord of all, and
13:11 can resist thee, who A the Lord.
13:14 but to thee, who A my Lord; and I
14:3 my Lord, thou only A our King; help me,
14:7 Thou A righteous, O Lord!
Ps 3:3 But thou, O LORD, A a shield about me,
5:4 For thou A not a God who delights in
8:4 is man that thou A mindful of him, and
16:2 to the LORD, "Thou A my Lord; I have
22:1 Why A thou so far from helping me, from
22:3 Yet thou A holy, enthroned on the praises of
22:9 Yet thou A he who took me from the
23:4 no evil; for thou A with me; thy rod
25:5 teach me, for thou A the God of my
31:3 Yea, thou A my rock and my fortress; for
31:4 for me, for thou A my refuge.
31:14 LORD, I say, "Thou A my God."
32:7 Thou A a hiding place for me, thou preservest
40:17 Thou A my help and my deliverer; do not
41:11 I know that thou A pleased with me, in
43:2 For thou A the God in whom I take
44:4 Thou A my King and my God, who ordainest
51:4 sight, so that thou A justified in thy sentence
59:5 LORD God of hosts, A God of Israel.
59:9 for thou, O God, A my fortress.
59:17 for thou, O God, A my fortress, the God
61:3 than I; for thou A my refuge, a strong
63:1 O God, thou A my God, I seek thee,
65:5 of our salvation, who A the hope of all
70:5 Thou A my help and my deliverer; O LORD,
71:3 save me, for thou A my rock and my
71:5 For thou, O Lord, A my hope, my trust,
71:6 from my birth; thou A he who took me
71:7 to many; but thou A my strong refuge.
76:4 [Selah] Glorious A thou, more majestic than the
76:7 But thou, terrible A thou!
77:14 Thou A the God who workest wonders, who hast
80:1 Thou who A enthroned upon the cherubim, shine
83:18 name is the LORD, A the Most High over
86:2 Thou A my God;
86:5 For thou, O Lord, A good and forgiving, abounding
86:10 For thou A great and doest wondrous things, thou
86:10 wondrous things, thou alone A God.
86:15 But thou, O Lord, A a God merciful and
89:8 is mighty as thou A, O LORD, with thy
89:17 For thou A the glory of their strength; by
89:26 cry to me, 'Thou A my Father, my God,
89:38 off and rejected, thou A full of wrath against
90:2 everlasting to everlasting thou A God.
92:8 but thou, O LORD, A on high for ever.
93:2 from of old; thou A from everlasting.
97:9 For thou, O LORD, A most high over all
97:9 all the earth; thou A exalted far above all
102:12 But thou, O LORD, A enthroned for ever; thy
102:27 pass away; but thou A the same, and thy
104:1 LORD my God, thou A very great!
104:1 Thou A clothed with honor and majesty,
118:28 Thou A my God, and I will give thanks
118:28 thanks to thee; thou A my God, I will
119:68 Thou A good and doest good; teach me thy
119:114 Thou A my hiding place and my shield; I
119:137 Righteous A thou, O LORD, and right are thy
119:151 But thou A near, O LORD, and all thy
123:1 eyes, O thou who A enthroned in the heavens!
139:3 my lying down, and A acquainted with all my
139:8 ascend to heaven, thou A there!
139:8 bed in Sheol, thou A there!
139:14 praise thee, for thou A fearful and wonderful.
140:6 to the LORD, Thou A my God; give ear
142:5 LORD; I say, Thou A my refuge, my portion
143:10 thy will, for thou A my God!
Wis 11:23 But thou A merciful to all, for thou canst
12:15 Thou A righteous and rulest all things righteously,
12:18 Thou who A sovereign in strength dost judge with
15:1 But thou, our God, A kind and true, patient,
15:4 evil intent of human A misled us, nor the
17:7 delusions of their magic A lay humbled, and their
Sir 36:17 will know that thou A the Lord, the God
49:1 incense prepared by the A of the perfumer; it
Is 25:1 O LORD, thou A my God; I will exalt
26:15 increased the nation; thou A glorified; thou hast
37:16 God of Israel, who A enthroned above the cherubim,
37:16 above the cherubim, thou A the God, thou alone,
37:20 know that thou alone A the LORD."
44:17 "Deliver me, for thou A my god!"
45:15 Truly, thou A a God who hidest thyself, O
63:16 For thou A our Father, though Abraham does not
63:16 us; thou, O LORD, A our Father, our Redeemer
64:8 Yet, O LORD, thou A our Father; we are
64:8 the clay, and thou A our potter; we are
Jer 3:4 me, 'My father, thou A the friend of my
3:22 to thee; for thou A the LORD our God.
10:6 thee, O LORD; thou A great, and thy name
12:1 Righteous A thou, O LORD, when I complain to
12:2 bring forth fruit; thou A near in their mouth
14:9 Yet thou, O LORD, A in the midst of
14:22 A thou not he, O LORD our God?
17:14 be saved; for thou A my praise.
17:17 terror to me; thou A my refuge in the

15:16 Maacah, his mother, King A removed from being
15:16 A cut down her image, crushed it, and burned
15:17 Nevertheless the heart of A was blameless all his
15:19 until the thirty-fifth year of the reign of A
16:1 of the reign of A, Baasha king of Israel
16:1 or come in to A king of Judah.
16:2 Then A took silver and gold from the treasures
16:4 Ben-hadad hearkened to King A, and sent the
16:6 Then King A took all Judah, and they carried
16:7 the seer came to A king of Judah, and
16:10 Then A was angry with the seer, and put
16:10 And A inflicted cruelties upon some of the people
16:11 The acts of A, from first to last, are
16:12 year of his reign A was diseased in his
16:13 And A slept with his fathers, dying in the
17:2 cities of Ephraim which A his father had taken.
20:32 in the way of A his father and did
21:12 in the ways of A king of Judah,
Jer 41:9 large cistern which King A had made for defense
Mt 1:7 Abijah the father of A,
1:8 father of Asa, and A the father of Jehoshaphat,

ASAHEL (18)

2Sam 2:18 sons of Zeruiah were there, Joab, Abishai, and A
2:18 Now A was as swift of foot as a
2:19 a wild gazelle; and A pursued Abner, and as
2:20 looked behind him and said, "Is it you, A
2:21 But A would not turn aside from following him.
2:22 Abner said again to A, "Turn aside from following
2:23 to the place where A had fallen and died,
2:30 missing of David's servants nineteen men besides A
2:32 And they took up A, and buried him in
3:27 for the blood of A his brother.
3:30 had killed their brother A in the battle at
23:24 A the brother of Joab was one of the
1Chr 2:16 Zeruiah: Abishai, Joab, and A, three.
11:26 of the armies were A the brother of Joab,
27:7 A the brother of Joab was fourth, for the
2Chr 17:8 Levites, Shemaiah, Nethaniah, Zebadiah, A,
31:13 while Jehiel, Azaziah, Nahath, A, Jerimoth, Jozabad,
Ezra 10:15 Jonathan the son of A and Jahzeiah the son

ASAIAH (8)

2Kgs 22:12 Shaphan the secretary, and A the king's servant,
22:14 Achbor, and Shaphan, and A went to Huldah the
1Chr 4:36 Asiel, Eli-o-enai, Ja-akobah, Jeshohaiah, A, Adi-el,
6:30 Haggiah his son, and A his son.
9:5 And of the Shilonites: A the first-born, and his
15:6 the sons of Merari, A the chief, with two
15:11 and the Levites Uriel, A, Joel, Shemaiah, Eliel, and
2Chr 34:20 Shaphan the secretary, and A the king's servant,

ASAPH (34)

2Kgs 18:18 Joah the son of A, the recorder.
18:37 Joah the son of A, the recorder, came to
1Chr 6:39 Israel; and his brother A, who stood on his
6:39 his right hand, namely, A the son of Berechiah,
9:15 of Zichri, son of A;
15:17 and of his brethren A the son of Berechiah;
15:19 The singers, Heman, A, and Ethan, were to sound
16:5 A was the chief, and second to him were
16:5 play harps and lyres; A was to sound the
16:7 to the LORD by A and his brethren.
16:37 So David left A and his brethren there before
25:1 of the sons of A, and of Heman, and
25:2 Of the sons of A: Zaccur, Joseph, Nethaniah, and
25:2 and Asharelah, sons of A, under the direction of
25:2 under the direction of A, who prophesied under the
25:6 A, Jeduthun, and Heman were under the order of
25:9 first lot fell for A to Joseph; the second
26:1 the son of Kore, of the sons of A
2Chr 5:12 all the Levitical singers, A, Heman, and Jeduthun,
20:14 of the sons of A, in the midst of
29:13 of the sons of A, Zechariah and Mattaniah;
29:30 of David and of A the seer.
35:15 singers, the sons of A, were in their place
35:15 command of David, and A, and Heman, and Jeduthun
Ezra 2:41 singers: the sons of A, one hundred and twenty-eight.
3:10 Levites, the sons of A, with cymbals, to praise
Neh 2:8 and a letter to A, the keeper of the
7:44 singers: the sons of A, a hundred and forty-eight.
11:17 of Zabdi, son of A, who was the leader
11:22 of the sons of A, the singers, over the
12:35 of Zaccur, son of A;
12:46 days of David and A of old there was
Is 36:3 Joah the son of A, the recorder.
36:22 Joah the son of A, the recorder, came to

ASARAMEL

1Mac 14:28 great high priest, in A, in the great assembly

ASAREL

1Chr 4:16 The sons of Jehallelel: Ziph, Ziphah, Tiri-a, and A

ASCALON

Jud 2:28 lived in Azotus and A feared him exceedingly.

ASCEND (11)

Deut 32:49 Moses that very day, A this mountain of the
32:50 the mountain which you A, and be gathered to
Ps 24:3 Who shall A the hill of the LORD?
68:18 Thou didst A the high mount, leading captives in
139:8 If I A to heaven, thou art there!
Is 14:13 your heart, 'I will A to heaven; above the
14:14 far north; I will A above the heights of
Acts 2:34 For David did not A into the heavens; but
Rom 10:6 your heart, "Who will A into heaven?" (that is,
Rev 7:2 I saw another angel A from the rising of
17:8 not, and is to A from the bottomless pit

ASCENDED (9)

Judg 13:20 angel of the LORD A in the flame of
2Chr 21:4 When Jehoram had A the throne of his father
Prov 30:4 Who has A to heaven and come down?
Jn 3:13 No one has A into heaven but he who
20:17 I have not yet A to the Father; but
Acts 10:4 and your alms have A as a memorial before
Eph 4:8 is said, "When he A on high he led
4:9 (In saying, "He A
4:10 is he who also A far above all the

ASCENDING (5)

Gen 28:12 angels of God were A and descending on it!
Tob 12:20 God, for I am A to him who sent
Jn 1:51 the angels of God A and descending upon the
6:62 the Son of man A where he was before?
20:17 to them, I am A to my Father and

ASCENDS

Rev 11:7 testimony, the beast that A from the bottomless pit

ASCENT (18)

Num 34:4 turn south of the A of Akrabbim, and cross
Josh 10:10 the way of the A of Beth-horon, and smote
10:11 were going down the A of Beth-horon, the LORD
15:3 out southward of the A of Akrabbim, passes along
15:7 which is opposite the A of Adummim, which is
18:17 which is opposite the A of Adummim; then it
Judg 1:36 Amorites ran from the A of Akrabbim, from Sela
8:13 the battle by the A of Heres.
2Sam 15:30 David went up the A of the Mount of
2Kgs 9:27 the chariot at the A of Gur, which is
2Chr 20:16 come up by the A of Ziz; you will
32:33 buried him in the A of the tombs of
Neh 3:19 another section opposite the A to the armory at
12:37 of David, at the A of the wall, above
Sir 25:19 A sandy A for the feet of the aged—
Is 15:5 For at the A of Luhith they go up
Jer 48:5 For at the A of Luhith they go up
1Mac 3:16 When he approached the A of Beth-horon, Judas

ASCERTAIN

Acts 24:10 As you may A, it is not more than

ASCERTAINED (3)

2Chr 4:18 that the weight of the bronze was not A
Mt 2:7 wise men secretly and A from them what time
2:16 time which he had A from the wise men.

ASCRIBE (16)

Deut 32:3 A greatness to our God!
1Chr 16:28 A to the LORD, O families of the peoples,
16:28 families of the peoples, A to the LORD glory
16:29 A to the LORD the glory due his name;
Job 36:3 knowledge from afar, and A righteousness to my
Ps 29:1 A to the LORD, O heavenly beings, ascribe to
29:1 LORD, O heavenly beings, A to the LORD glory
29:2 A to the LORD the glory of his name;
68:34 A power to God, whose majesty is over Israel,
96:7 A to the LORD, O families of the peoples,
96:7 families of the peoples, A to the LORD glory
96:8 A to the LORD the glory due his name;

A

Sir 10:27 yourself with humility, and A to yourself honor
39:15 for all his works; A majesty to his name
Bar 2:17 their bodies, will not A glory or justice to
2:18 person that hungers, will A to thee glory and

ASCRIBED (2)

1Sam 18:8 he said, "They have A to David ten thousands,
18:8 to me they have A thousands; and what more

ASCRIPTIONS

Sir 47:8 the Most High, with A of glory; he sang

ASENATH (3)

Gen 41:45 gave him in marriage A, the daughter of Potiphera
41:50 had two sons, whom A, the daughter of Potiphera
46:20 Manasseh and Ephraim, whom A, the daughter of

ASH (3)

1Sam 2:8 the needy from the A heap, to make them
Ps 113:7 the needy from the A heap,
Lam 4:5 in purple lie on A heaps.

ASHAMED (73)

Gen 2:25 his wife were both naked, and were not A
2Sam 10:5 to meet them, for the men were greatly A
19:3 steal in who are A when they flee in
2Kgs 2:17 him till he was A, he said, "Send." They
8:11 gaze and stared at him, until he was A
1Chr 19:5 to meet them, for the men were greatly A
Ezra 8:22 For I was A to ask the king for
9:6 my God, I am A and blush to lift
Jud 9:3 their bed, which was A of the deceit they
Job 19:3 me; are you not A to wrong me?
Ps 6:10 my enemies shall be A and sorely troubled; they
25:3 shame; let them be A who are wantonly treacherous.
34:5 be radiant; so your faces shall never be A
Wis 1:5 thoughts, and will be A at the approach of
13:17 children, he is not A to address a lifeless
Sir 4:26 Do not be A to confess your sins, and
22:23 I will not be A to protect a friend,
41:17 Be A of immorality, before your father or mother;
41:19 Be A before the truth of God and his
41:19 Be A of selfish behavior at meals, of surliness
42:1 things do not be A, and do not let
42:8 Do not be A to instruct the stupid or
Is 1:29 For you shall be A of the oaks in
23:4 Be A, O Sidon, for the sea has spoken,
24:23 confounded, and the sun A; for the LORD of
26:11 see thy zeal for thy people, and be A
29:22 shall no more be A, no more shall his
45:24 shall come and be A, all who were incensed
54:4 you will not be A; be not confounded, for
Jer 3:3 have a harlot's brow, you refuse to be A
6:15 Were they A when they committed abomination?
6:15 were not at all A; they did not know
8:12 Were they A when they committed abomination?
8:12 were not at all A; they did not know
12:13 They shall be A of their harvests because of
14:3 vessels empty; they are A and confounded and cover
14:4 land, the farmers are A, they cover their heads.
22:22 then you will be A and confounded because of
31:19 my thigh; I was A, and I was confounded,
48:13 Then Moab shall be A of Chemosh, as the
48:13 house of Israel was A of Bethel, their confidence.
Bar 6:27 who serve them are A because through them these
Ezek 16:27 the Philistines, who were A of your lewd behavior.
16:52 So be A, you also, and bear your disgrace,
16:54 your disgrace and be A of all that you
16:61 your ways, and be A when I take your
36:32 Be A and confounded for your ways, O house
43:10 that they may be A of their iniquities.
43:11 And if they are A of all that they
Dan 13:11 distress, for they were A to disclose their lustful
13:27 the servants were greatly A, for nothing like this
Hos 4:19 and they shall be A because of their altars.
10:6 and Israel shall be A of his idol.
Mic 7:16 shall see and be A of all their might;
Zech 13:4 every prophet will be A of his vision when
1Mac 4:31 and let them be A of their troops and
Mk 8:38 For whoever is A of me and of my
8:38 of man also be A, when he comes in
Lk 9:26 For whoever is A of me and of my
9:26 Son of man be A when he comes in
16:3 dig, and I am A to beg.
Rom 1:16 For I am not A of the gospel: it
6:21 from the things of which you are now A
1Cor 4:14 this to make you A, but to admonish you
Phil 1:20 not be at all A, but that with full
2Thes 3:14 to do with him, that he may be A
2Tim 1:8 Do not be A then of testifying to our
1:12 But I am not A, for I know whom
1:16 me; he was not A of my chains,
2:15 no need to be A, rightly handling the word
Heb 2:11 why he is not A to call them brethren,
11:16 Therefore God is not A to be called their
1Pet 4:16 let him not be A, but under that name

ASHAN (4)

Josh 15:42 Libnah, Ether, A,
19:7 villages; En-rimmon, Ether, and A --four cities with
1Chr 4:32 Ain, Rimmon, Tochen, and A, five cities,
6:59 with its pasture lands, A with its pasture lands,

ASHARELAH

1Chr 25:2 Zaccur, Joseph, Nethaniah, and A, sons of Asaph,

ASHBEL (3)

Gen 46:21 of Benjamin: Bela, Becher, A, Gera, Naaman, Ehi,
Num 26:38 of the Bela-ites; of A, the family of the
1Chr 8:1 of Bela his first-born, A the second, Aharah the

ASHBELITES

Num 26:38 the family of the A; of Ahiram, the family

ASHDOD (20)

Josh 11:22 in Gath, and in A, did some remain.
13:3 Philistines, those of Gaza, A, Ashkelon, Gath, and
15:46 by the side of A, with their villages.
15:47 A, its towns and its villages; Gaza, its towns
1Sam 5:1 it from Ebenezer to A;
5:3 when the people of A rose early the next
5:5 threshold of Dagon in A to this day.
5:6 upon the people of A, and he terrified and
5:6 them with tumors, both A and its territory.
5:7 when the men of A saw how things were,
6:17 the LORD: one for A, one for Gaza, one
2Chr 26:6 and the wall of A; and he built cities
26:6 in the territory of A and elsewhere among the
Neh 13:23 had married women of A, Ammon, and Moab;
13:24 spoke the language of A, and they could not
Is 20:1 of Assyria, came to A and fought against it
Jer 25:20 and the remnant of A;
Amos 1:8 off the inhabitants from A, and him that holds
Zeph 2:4 shall become a desolation; A's people shall be driven
Zech 9:6 people shall dwell in A; and I will make

ASHDODITES

Neh 4:7 the Ammonites and the A heard that the repairing

ASHER (46)

Gen 30:13 call me happy"; so she called his name A
35:26 The sons of Zilpah, Leah's maid: Gad and A
46:17 The sons of A: Imnah, Ishvah, Ishvi, Beriah, with
49:20 A's food shall be rich, and he shall yield
Ex 1:3 and Benjamin, Dan and Naphtali, Gad and A
Num 1:13 son of Ammishaddai; from A, Pagiel the son of
1:40 Of the people of A, their generations, by their
1:41 of the tribe of A was forty-one thousand five
2:27 be the tribe of A, the leader of the
2:27 of the people of A being Pagiel the son
7:72 of the men of A:
10:26 of the men of A was Pagiel the son
13:13 from the tribe of A, Sethur the son of
26:44 The sons of A according to their families: of
26:46 of the daughter of A was Serah.
26:47 of the sons of A according to their number,
34:27 of the sons of A a leader, Ahihud the
Deut 27:13 curse: Reuben, Gad, A, Zebulun, Dan, and Naphtali.
33:24 And of A he said, "Blessed above sons be
33:24 "Blessed above sons be A; let him be the
Josh 17:7 Manasseh reached from A to Mich-methath, which is
17:10 boundary; on the north A is reached, and on
17:11 in Issachar and in A Manasseh had Beth-shean and
19:24 for the tribe of A according to its families.
19:31 of the tribe of A according to its families--
19:34 at the south, and A on the west, and
21:6 from the tribe of A, from the tribe of
21:30 of the tribe of A, Mishal with its pasture
Judg 1:31 A did not drive out the inhabitants of Acco,
5:17 A sat still at the coast of the sea,
6:35 he sent messengers to A, Zebulun, and Naphtali; and
7:23 from Naphtali and from A and from all Manasseh,

1Kgs 4:16 son of Hushai, in A and Bealoth;
1Chr 2:2 Dan, Joseph, Benjamin, Naphtali, Gad, and A
6:62 the tribes of Issachar, A, Naphtali, and Manasseh in
6:74 of the tribe of A: Mashal with its pasture
7:30 The sons of A: Imnah, Ishvah, Ishvi, Beriah, and
7:40 these were men of A, heads of fathers' houses,
12:36 Of A forty thousand seasoned troops ready for battle.
2Chr 30:11 a few men of A, of Manasseh, and of
Tob 1:2 the south of Kedesh Naphtali in Galilee above A
Ezek 48:2 side to the west, A, one portion.
48:3 Adjoining the territory of A, from the east side
48:34 Gad, the gate of A, and the gate of
Lk 2:36 of the tribe of A; she was of a
Rev 7:6 of the tribe of A, twelve thousand of the

ASHERAH (18)

Deut 16:21 any tree as an A beside the altar of
Judg 6:25 and cut down the A that is beside it;
6:26 the wood of the A which you shall cut
6:28 broken down, and the A beside it was cut
6:30 and cut down the A beside it."
1Kgs 15:13 abominable image made for A; and Asa cut down
16:33 And Ahab made an A
18:19 four hundred prophets of A, who eat at Jezebel's
2Kgs 13:6 in them; and the A also remained in Samaria.)
17:16 and they made an A, and worshiped all the
18:4 and broke the pillars, and cut down the A
21:3 Baal, and made an A, as Ahab king of
21:7 the graven image of A that he had made
23:4 made for Baal, for A, and for all the
23:6 he brought out the A from the house of
23:7 LORD, where the women wove hangings for the A
23:15 crushing them to dust; also he burned the A
2Chr 15:16 because she had made an abominable image for A

ASHERAHS (2)

2Chr 19:3 for you destroyed the A out of the land,
33:3 the Baals, and made A, and worshiped all the

ASHERIM (19)

Ex 34:13 and cut down their A
Deut 7:5 and hew down their A, and burn their graven
12:3 pillars, and burn their A with fire; you shall
1Kgs 14:15 they have made their A, provoking the LORD to
14:23 places, and pillars, and A on every high hill
2Kgs 17:10 for themselves pillars and A on every high hill
23:14 and cut down the A, and filled their places
2Chr 14:3 and hewed down the A,
17:6 high places and the A out of Judah.
24:18 fathers, and served the A and the idols.
31:1 and hewed down the A and broke down the
33:19 and set up the A and the images, before
34:3 the high places, the A, and the graven and
34:4 broke in pieces the A and the graven and
34:7 altars, and beat the A and the images into
Is 17:8 have made, either the A or the altars of
27:9 crushed to pieces, no A or incense altars will
Jer 17:2 their altars and their A, beside every green tree,
Mic 5:14 will root out your A from among you and

ASHERITES

Judg 1:32 of Rehob; but the A dwelt among the Canaanites,

ASHEROTH

Judg 3:7 their God, and serving the Baals and the A

ASHES (60)

Gen 18:27 the Lord, I who am but dust and A
Ex 9:8 Aaron, "Take handfuls of A from the kiln, and
9:10 So they took A from the kiln, and stood
27:3 it to receive its A, and shovels and basins
Lev 1:16 in the place for A;
4:12 clean place, where the A are poured out, and
4:12 of wood; where the A are poured out it
6:10 shall take up the A to which the fire
6:11 and carry forth the A outside the camp to
Num 4:13 shall take away the A from the altar, and
19:9 shall gather up the A of the heifer, and
19:10 he who gathers the A of the heifer shall
19:17 they shall take some A of the burnt sin
2Sam 13:19 And Tamar put A on her head, and rent
1Kgs 13:3 torn down, and the A that are upon it
13:5 torn down, and the A poured out from the
2Kgs 23:4 Kidron, and carried their A to Bethel.
Tob 6:16 you shall take live A of incense and lay
8:2 he took the live A of incense and put
Jud 4:11 the temple and put A on their heads and
4:15 With A upon their turbans, they cried out to
9:1 her face, and put A on her head, and
Esth 4:1 put on sackcloth and A, and went out into
4:3 and most of them lay in sackcloth and A
14:2 covered her head with A and dung, and she
Job 2:8 which to scrape himself, and sat among the A
13:12 maxims are proverbs of A, your defenses are
30:19 mire, and I have become like dust and A
42:6 I despise myself, and repent in dust and A
Ps 102:9 For I eat A like bread, and mingle tears
147:16 gives snow like wool; he scatters hoarfrost like A
Wis 2:3 body will turn to A, and the spirit will
15:10 His heart is A, his hope is cheaper than
Sir 10:9 who is dust and A be proud?
17:27 of heaven; but all men are dust and A
40:3 humbled in dust and A,
Is 44:20 He feeds on A; a deluded mind has led
58:5 to spread sackcloth and A under him?
61:3 a garland instead of A, the oil of gladness
Jer 6:26 sackcloth, and roll in A; make mourning as for
25:34 cry, and roll in A, you lords of the
31:40 dead bodies and the A, and all the fields
Lam 3:16 made me cower in A;
Ezek 27:30 heads and wallow in A;
28:18 I turned you to A upon the earth in
Dan 9:3 and supplications with fasting and sackcloth and A
14:14 his servants to bring A and they sifted them
Jon 3:6 and covered himself with sackcloth, and sat in A
Mal 4:3 for they will be A under the soles of
1Mac 3:47 on sackcloth and sprinkled A on their heads, and
4:39 great lamentation, and sprinkled themselves with A
2Mac 4:41 took handfuls of the A that were lying about,
13:5 cubits high, full of A, and it has a
13:5 which on all sides inclines precipitously into the A
13:8 altar whose fire and A were holy, he met
13:8 ashes were holy, he met his death in A
Mt 11:21 would have repented long ago in sackcloth and A
Lk 10:13 have repented long ago, sitting in sackcloth and A
Heb 9:13 bulls and with the A of a heifer sanctifies
2Pet 2:6 Sodom and Gomorrah to A he condemned them to

ASHHUR (2)

1Chr 2:24 and she bore him A, the father of Tekoa.
4:5 A, the father of Tekoa, had two wives, Helah

ASHIMA

2Kgs 17:30 men of Hamath made A,

ASHIMAH

Amos 8:14 Those who swear by A of Samaria, and say,

ASHKELON (13)

Josh 13:3 those of Gaza, Ashdod, A, Gath, and Ekron), and
Judg 1:18 with its territory, and A with its territory, and
14:19 he went down to A and killed thirty men
1Sam 6:17 for Gaza, one for A, one for Gath, one
2Sam 1:20 in the streets of A; lest the daughters of
Jer 25:20 land of the Philistines A, Gaza, Ekron, and the
47:5 has come upon Gaza, A has perished.
47:7 Against A and against the seashore he has appointed
Amos 1:8 holds the scepter from A; I will turn my
Zeph 2:4 shall be deserted, and A shall become a desolation;
2:7 in the houses of A they shall lie down
Zech 9:5 A shall see it, and be afraid; Gaza too,
9:5 shall perish from Gaza; A shall be uninhabited;

ASHKENAZ (3)

Gen 10:3 The sons of Gomer: A, Riphath, and Togarmah.
1Chr 1:6 The sons of Gomer: A, Diphath, and Togarmah.
Jer 51:27 kingdoms, Ararat, Minni, and A; appoint a marshal

ASHNAH (2)

Josh 15:33 the lowland, Eshtaol, Zorah, A,
15:43 Libnah, Ether, Ashan, Iphtah, A, Nezib,

ASHORE (6)

2Mac 5:8 citizens, he was cast A in Egypt;
Mt 13:48 full, men drew it A and sat down and
14:14 As he went A he saw a great throng;
Mk 6:34 As he went A he saw a great throng,
Jn 21:11 and hauled the net A, full of large fish,
Acts 27:39 they planned if possible to bring the ship A

ASHPENAZ

Dan 1:3 Then the king commanded A, his chief eunuch, to

ASHTAROTH (12)
Deut 1:4 Bashan, who lived in A and in Edre-i.
Josh 9:10 and Og king of Bashan, who dwelt in A
12:4 Rephaim, who dwelt at A and at Edre-i
13:12 Bashan, who reigned in A and in Edre-i (he
13:31 and half Gilead, and A, and Edre-i, the cities
Judg 2:13 the LORD, and served the Baals and the A
10:6 the Baals and the A, the gods of Syria,
1Sam 7:3 foreign gods and the A from among you, and
7:4 the Baals and the A, and they served the
12:10 the Baals and the A; but now deliver us
31:10 in the temple of A; and they fastened his
1Chr 6:71 its pasture lands and A with its pasture lands;

ASHTERATHITE
1Chr 11:44 the Mithnite, Uzzia the A, Shama and Je-iel the

ASHTEROTH-KARNAIM
Gen 14:5 subdued the Rephaim in A, the Zuzim in Ham,

ASHTORETH (3)
1Kgs 11:5 For Solomon went after A the goddess of the
11:33 forsaken me, and worshiped A the goddess of the
2Kgs 23:13 Israel had built for A the abomination of the

ASHURITES
2Sam 2:9 over Gilead and the A and Jezreel and Ephraim

ASHVATH
1Chr 7:33 The sons of Japhlet: Pasach, Bimhal, and A

ASI-ARCHS
Acts 19:31 him; some of the A also, who were friends

ASIA (25)
1Mac 8:6 the Great, king of A, who went to fight
11:13 entered Antioch and put on the crown of A
11:13 head, the crown of Egypt and that of A
12:39 to become king in A and put on the
13:32 on the crown of A; and he brought great
2Mac 3:3 Seleucus, the king of A, defrayed from his own
10:24 collected the cavalry from A in no small number.
Acts 2:9 and Cappadocia, Pontus and A,
6:9 those from Cilicia and A, arose and disputed with
16:6 the Holy Spirit to speak the word in A
19:10 all the residents of A heard the word of
19:22 he himself stayed in A for a while.
19:26 but almost throughout all A this Paul has persuaded
19:27 magnificence, she whom all A and the world
20:16 to spend time in A; for he was hastening
20:18 I set foot in A,
21:27 completed, the Jews from A, who had seen him
24:17 But some Jews from A --
27:2 along the coast of A, we put to sea,
Rom 16:5 the first convert in A for Christ.
1Cor 16:19 The churches of A send greetings.
2Cor 1:8 affliction we experienced in A; for we were so
2Tim 1:15 all who are in A turned away from me,
1Pet 1:1 in Pontus, Galatia, Cappadocia, A, and Bithynia,
Rev 1:4 churches that are in A: Grace to you and

ASIANS
Acts 20:4 and Timothy; and the A, Tychicus and Trophimus.

ASIDE (114)
Gen 19:2 said, "My lords, turn A, I pray you, to
19:3 strongly; so they turned A to him and entered
Ex 3:3 said, "I will turn A and see this great
3:4 saw that he turned A to see, God called
23:2 in a suit, turning A after a multitude, so
32:8 themselves; they have turned A quickly out of the
Num 5:19 you have not turned A to uncleanness, while you
20:17 we will not turn A to the right hand
21:22 we will not turn A into field or vineyard;
22:23 and the ass turned A out of the road,
22:33 saw me, and turned A before me these three
22:33 she had not turned A from me, surely just
Deut 2:27 road, I will turn A neither to the right
5:32 you shall not turn A to the right hand
9:12 corruptly; they have turned A quickly out of the
9:16 calf; you had turned A quickly from the way
11:16 deceived, and you turn A and serve other gods
11:28 your God, but turn A from the way which
17:11 you shall not turn A from the verdict which
17:20 he may not turn A from the commandment, either
28:14 you do not turn A from any of the
31:29 act corruptly, and turn A from the way which
Josh 23:6 law of Moses, turning A from it neither to
Judg 2:17 them; they soon turned A from the way in
4:18 said to him, "Turn A, my lord, turn aside
4:18 aside, my lord, turn A to me; have no
4:18 So he turned A to her into the tent,
14:8 her; and he turned A to see the carcass
18:3 Levite; and they turned A and said to him,
18:15 And they turned A thither, and came to the
19:11 now, let us turn A to this city of
19:12 "We will not turn A into the city of
19:15 Benjamin, and they turned A there, to go in
Ruth 4:1 So Boaz said, "Turn A, friend; sit down here";
4:1 here"; and he turned A and sat down.
1Sam 8:3 his ways, but turned A after gain; they took
9:23 of which I said to you, 'Put it A
12:20 yet do not turn A from following the LORD,
12:21 and do not turn A after vain things which
2Sam 2:21 said to him, "Turn A to your right hand
2:21 Asahel would not turn A from following him.
2:22 again to Asahel, "Turn A from following me; why
2:23 he refused to turn A; therefore Abner smote him
3:27 Hebron, Joab took him A into the midst of
6:10 but David took it A to the house of
18:30 the king said, "Turn A, and stand here." So
18:30 So he turned A, and stood still.
22:23 and from his statutes I did not turn A
1Kgs 9:6 But if you turn A from following me, you
15:5 and did not turn A from anything that he
18:27 or he has gone A, or he is on
22:43 he did not turn A from it, doing what
2Kgs 4:4 vessels; and when one is full, set it A
10:29 Jehu did not turn A from the sins of
22:2 he did not turn A to the right hand
1Chr 13:13 David, but took it A to the house of
2Chr 7:19 "But if you turn A and forsake my statutes
8:15 they did not turn A from what the king
20:32 and did not turn A from it; he did
34:2 he did not turn A to the right or
35:12 And they set A the burnt offerings that they
Jud 11:13 had consecrated and set A for the priests who
Job 6:18 The caravans turn A from their course; they go
23:11 have kept his way and have not turned A
31:7 my step has turned A from the way, and
33:17 he may turn man A from his deed, and
34:27 men, because they turned A from following him, and
36:18 not the greatness of the ransom turn you A
Ps 119:102 I do not turn A from thy ordinances, for
125:5 But those who turn A upon their crooked ways
Prov 7:25 not your heart turn A to her ways, do
16:17 of the upright turns A from evil; he who
Sir 2:7 mercy; and turn not A, lest you fall.
9:9 lest your heart turn A to her, and in
16:26 not crowd one another A, and they will never
Is 10:2 writing oppression, to turn A the needy from justice
29:21 an empty plea turn A him who is in
30:11 leave the way, turn A from the path, let
Jer 5:23 heart; they have turned A and gone away.
14:8 a wayfarer who turns A to tarry for a
15:5 Who will turn A to ask about your welfare?
Lam 3:35 the earth, to turn A the right of a
Dan 9:5 wickedly and rebelled, turning A from thy
9:11 thy law and turned A, refusing to obey thy
13:56 Then he put him A, and commanded them to
Hos 4:14 the men themselves go A with harlots, and sacrifice
Amos 2:7 the earth, and turn A the way of the
5:12 a bribe, and turn A the needy in the
Mal 2:8 But you have turned A from the way; you
3:5 against those who thrust A the sojourner, and do
3:7 fathers you have turned A from my statutes and
1Mac 2:22 king's words by turning A from our religion to
5:35 Next he turned A to Alema, and fought against
5:68 But Judas turned A to Azotus in the land
12:31 So Jonathan turned A against the Arabs who are
12:33 He turned A to Joppa and took it by
2Mac 4:11 He set A the existing royal concessions to the
4:34 Menelaus, taking Andronicus A, urged him to kill
4:46 Ptolemy, taking the king A into a colonnade as
6:21 sacrifice took the man A, because of their long
14:7 Therefore I have laid A my ancestral glory --
Mt 20:17 took the twelve disciples A, and on the way
Mk 7:32 And taking him A from the multitude privately, he
Jn 13:4 rose from supper, laid A his garments, and girded
Acts 1:25 from which Judas turned A, to go to his
4:15 commanded them to go A out of the council,
7:27 his neighbor thrust him A, saying, 'Who made you

7:39 him, but thrust him A, and in their hearts
23:19 the hand, and going A asked him privately, "What
Rom 3:12 All have turned A, together they have gone wrong;
1Cor 16:2 is to put something A and store it up,
Col 2:14 demands; this he set A, nailing it to the
Heb 7:18 former commandment is set A because of its
12:1 let us also lay A every weight, and sin

ASIEL (2)
1Chr 4:35 of Seraiah, son of A,
Tob 1:1 of the descendants of A and the tribe of

ASKALON (3)
1Mac 10:86 there and encamped against A, and the men of
11:60 When he came to A, the people of the
12:33 country as far as A and the neighboring strongholds.

ASLEEP (28)
Gen 41:5 And he fell A and dreamed a second time;
Judg 4:21 he was lying fast A from weariness.
1Sam 26:12 for they were all A, because a deep sleep
1Kgs 18:27 or perhaps he is A and must be awakened."
Tob 8:13 door and went in, and found them both A
Sir 46:20 after he had fallen A he prophesied and revealed
Jon 1:5 ship and had lain down, and was fast A
Nah 3:18 Your shepherds are A, O king of Assyria; your
2Mac 12:45 for those who fall A in godliness, it was
Mt 8:24 being swamped by the waves; but he was A
27:52 saints who had fallen A were raised,
28:13 away while we were A
Mk 4:38 was in the stern, A on the cushion; and
13:36 lest he come suddenly and find you A
14:37 and he said to Peter, "Simon, are you A
Lk 8:23 set out, and as they sailed he fell A
Jn 11:11 friend Lazarus has fallen A, but I go to
11:12 if he has fallen A, he will recover."
Acts 7:60 And when he had said this, he fell A
13:36 his own generation, fell A, and was laid with
1Cor 15:6 whom are still alive, though some have fallen A
15:18 also who have fallen A in Christ have perished.
15:20 the first fruits of those who have fallen A
1Thes 4:13 concerning those who are A, that you may not
4:14 will bring with him those who have fallen A
4:15 Lord, shall not precede those who have fallen A
2Pet 2:3 been idle, and their destruction has not been A
3:4 since the fathers fell A, all things have continued

ASMODEUS (2)
Tob 3:8 and the evil demon A had slain each of
3:17 Tobit, and to bind A the evil demon, because

ASNAH
Ezra 2:50 Besai, the sons of A, the sons of Me-unim,

ASP
Is 11:8 the hole of the A, and the weaned child

ASPATHA
Esth 9:7 Par-shan-datha and Dalphon and A

ASPHAR
1Mac 9:33 camped by the water of the pool of A

ASPIRE
1Thes 4:11 more and more, to A to live quietly, to

ASPIRES
1Tim 3:1 sure: If any one A to the office of

ASPS (4)
Deut 32:33 poison of serpents, and the cruel venom of A
Job 20:14 is the gall of A within him.
20:16 suck the poison of A; the tongue of a
Rom 3:13 "The venom of A is under their lips."

ASRIEL (3)
Num 26:31 the Helekites; and of A, the family of the
Josh 17:2 families, Abi-ezer, Helek, A, Shechem, Hepher, and
1Chr 7:14 The sons of Manasseh: A, whom his Aramean

ASRIELITES
Num 26:31 the family of the A; and of Shechem, the

ASS (89)
Gen 16:12 shall be a wild A of a man, his
22:3 the morning, saddled his A, and took two of
22:5 "Stay here with the A; I and the lad
42:27 sack to give his A provender at the lodging
44:13 every man loaded his A, and they returned to
49:11 the vine and his A's colt to the choice
49:14 Issachar is a strong A, crouching between the
Ex 4:20 set them on an A, and went back to
13:13 Every firstling of an A you shall redeem with
20:17 his ox, or his A, or anything that is
21:33 an ox or an A falls into it,
22:2 an ox or an A or a sheep, he
22:9 is for ox, for A, for sheep, for clothing,
22:10 to his neighbor an A or an ox or
23:4 enemy's ox or his A going astray, you shall
23:5 If you see the A of one who hates
23:12 your ox and your A may have rest, and
34:20 The firstling of an A you shall redeem with
Num 16:15 have not taken one A from them, and I
22:21 morning, and saddled his A, and went with the
22:22 was riding on the A, and his two servants
22:23 And the A saw the angel of the LORD
22:23 his hand; and the A turned aside out of
22:23 and Balaam struck the A, to turn her into
22:25 And when the A saw the angel of the
22:27 When the A saw the angel of the LORD,
22:27 and he struck the A with his staff.
22:28 the mouth of the A, and she said to
22:29 Balaam said to the A, "Because you have made
22:30 And the A said to Balaam, "Am I not
22:30 "Am I not your A, upon which you have
22:32 have you struck your A these three times?
22:33 before me; and the A saw me, and turned
Deut 5:14 your ox, or your A, or any of your
5:21 his ox, or his A, or anything that is
22:3 shall do with his A; so you shall do
22:4 not see your brother's A or his ox fallen
22:10 an ox and an A together.
28:31 eat of it; your A shall be violently taken
Josh 15:18 she alighted from her A, and Caleb said to
Judg 1:14 she alighted from her A, and Caleb said to
6:4 in Israel, and no sheep or ox or A
15:15 fresh jawbone of an A, and put out his
15:16 the jawbone of an A, heaps upon heaps, with
15:16 the jawbone of an A have I slain a
19:28 put her upon the A; and the man rose
1Sam 12:3 Or whose A have I taken?
15:3 infant and suckling, ox and sheep, camel and A
16:20 And Jesse took an A laden with bread, and
25:20 she rode on the A, and came down under
25:23 and alighted from the A, and fell before David
25:42 and mounted on an A, and her five maidens
2Sam 17:23 followed, he saddled his A, and went off home
19:26 to him, 'Saddle an A for me, that I
1Kgs 2:40 arose and saddled an A, and went to Gath
13:13 his sons, "Saddle the A for me." So they
13:13 So they saddled the A for him and he
13:23 drunk, he saddled the A for the prophet whom
13:24 the road, and the A stood beside it; the
13:27 his sons, "Saddle the A for me." And they
13:28 the road, and the A and the lion standing
13:28 had not eaten the body or torn the A
13:29 laid it upon the A, and brought it back
2Kgs 4:24 Then she saddled the A, and she said to
6:25 besieged it, until an A's head was sold for
Job 6:5 Does the wild A bray when he has grass,
11:12 understanding, when a wild A's colt is born a
24:3 They drive away the A of the fatherless; they
39:5 has let the wild A go free?
39:5 bonds of the swift A,
Prov 26:3 a bridle for the A, and a rod for
Sir 33:24 and burdens for an A; bread and discipline and
Is 1:3 its owner, and the A its master's crib; but
32:20 the ox and the A range free.
Jer 2:24 her tracks, a wild A used to the wilderness,
22:19 the burial of an A he shall be buried,
48:6 Be like a wild A in the desert!
Hos 8:9 to Assyria, a wild A wandering alone; Ephraim has
Zech 9:9 and riding on an A, on a colt the
9:9 ass, on a colt the foal of an A
Mt 21:2 you will find an A tied, and a colt
21:5 and mounted on an A, and on a colt,
21:5 and on a colt, the foal of an A
21:7 them; they brought the A and the colt, and
Lk 13:15 his ox or his A from the manger, and
14:5 of you, having an A or an ox that
Jn 12:14 Jesus found a young A and sat upon it;
12:15 coming, sitting on an A's colt!"

2Pet 2:16 own transgression; a dumb A spoke with human

ASSAIL (3)

Ps 27:2 When evildoers A me, uttering slanders against me,
Ezek 38:12 carry off plunder; to A the waste places which
2Mac 11:9 in heart, ready to A not only men but

ASSAILANTS (6)

2Sam 22:40 thou didst make my A sink under me.
Ps 18:39 thou didst make my A sink under me.
44:5 foes; through thy name we tread down our A
92:11 ears have heard the doom of my evil A
109:28 Let my A be put to shame; may thy
Lam 3:62 and thoughts of my A are against me all

ASSAILED (4)

2Sam 22:5 the torrents of perdition A me;
Ps 18:4 the torrents of perdition A me;
Wis 18:17 them, and unexpected fears A them;
19:1 But the ungodly were A to the end by

ASSAILS

Lk 11:22 one stronger than he A him and overcomes him,

ASSASSINS

Acts 21:38 thousand men of the A out into the wilderness?"

ASSAULT (4)

Deut 17:8 or one kind of A and another, any case
21:5 every dispute and every A shall be settled.
Esth 7:8 said, "Will he even A the queen in my
2Mac 5:5 and suddenly made an A upon the city.

ASSAULTED (4)

Josh 10:31 siege to it, and A it:
10:34 siege to it, and A it;
10:36 to Hebron; and they A it,
10:38 back to Debir and A it,

ASSAULTS

Ps 88:16 over me; thy dread A destroy me.

ASSAY

Jer 6:27 you may know and A their ways.

ASSAYER

Jer 6:27 have made you an A and tester among my

ASSEMBLE (27)

Gen 49:2 A and hear, O sons of Jacob, and hearken
Lev 8:3 of unleavened bread; and A all the congregation at
Num 8:9 tent of meeting, and A the whole congregation of
20:8 "Take the rod, and A the congregation, you and
Deut 31:12 A the people, men, women, and little ones, and
31:28 A to me all the elders of your tribes,
Ezra 10:7 exiles that they should A at Jerusalem,
Neh 7:5 into my mind to A the nobles and the
Jud 3:10 month in order to A all the supplies for
Is 11:12 the nations, and will A the outcasts of Israel,
43:9 the nations gather together, and let the peoples A
44:11 men; let them all A, let them stand forth,
45:20 A yourselves and come, draw near together, you
48:14 A, all of you, and hear!
Jer 4:5 cry aloud and say, A, and let us go
12:9 Go, A all the wild beasts; bring them to
Ezek 11:17 from the peoples, and A you out of the
39:17 beasts of the field, A and come, gather from
Dan 3:2 King Nebuchadnezzar sent to A the satraps, the
11:10 shall wage war and A a multitude of great
Joel 2:16 Sanctify the congregation; A the elders; gather the
Amos 3:9 of Egypt, and say, A yourselves upon the mountains
Mic 4:6 the LORD, I will A the lame and gather
Zeph 3:8 to gather nations, to A kingdoms, to pour out
1Mac 9:7 had no time to A them.
1Cor 11:18 first place, when you A as a church, I
Rev 16:14 the whole world, to A them for battle on

ASSEMBLED (65)

Ex 35:1 Moses A all the congregation of the people of
Lev 8:4 and the congregation was A at the door of
Num 1:18 the second month, they A the whole congregation
16:3 well-known men; and they A themselves together
16:19 Then Korah A all the congregation against them at
16:42 when the congregation had A against Moses and
20:2 the congregation; and they A themselves together
Josh 18:1 the people of Israel A at Shiloh, and set
Judg 20:1 Gilead, and the congregation A as one man to
1Sam 25:1 died; and all Israel A and mourned for him,
28:4 Philistines A, and came and encamped at Shunem;
2Sam 20:14 and all the Bichrites A, and followed him in.
1Kgs 8:1 Then Solomon A the elders of Israel and all
8:2 the men of Israel A to King Solomon at
8:5 of Israel, who had A before him, were with
12:21 came to Jerusalem, he A all the house of
2Kgs 10:18 Then Jehu A all the people, and said to
1Chr 13:5 So David A all Israel from the Shihor of
15:3 And David A all Israel at Jerusalem, to bring
23:2 David A all the leaders of Israel and the
28:1 David A at Jerusalem all the officials of Israel,
2Chr 5:2 Then Solomon A the elders of Israel and all
5:3 the men of Israel A before the king at
5:6 of Israel, who had A before him, were before
11:1 came to Jerusalem, he A the house of Judah,
20:4 And Judah A to seek help from the LORD;
20:26 the fourth day they A in the Valley of
25:5 Then Amaziah A the men of Judah, and set
29:4 and the Levites, and A them in the square
30:3 nor had the people A in Jerusalem--
Ezra 10:9 of Judah and Benjamin A at Jerusalem within the
Neh 9:1 people of Israel were A with fasting and in
Ps 48:4 For lo, the kings A, they came on together.
Prov 5:14 utter ruin in the A congregation."
Sir 16:10 on foot, who rebelliously A in their stubbornness.
Jer 26:17 spoke to all the A people, saying,
Ezek 38:7 the hosts that are A about you, and be
38:13 Have you A your hosts to carry off plunder,
Dan 3:3 of the provinces, were A for the dedication of
Mic 4:11 Now many nations are A against you, saying, "Let
1Mac 2:16 to them; and Mattathias and his sons were A
3:44 And the congregation A to be ready for battle,
3:46 So they A and went to Mizpah, opposite Jerusalem,
3:52 behold, the Gentiles are A against us to destroy
3:58 these Gentiles who have A against us to destroy
4:37 So all the army A and they went up
6:19 to destroy them, and A all the people to
6:28 He A all his friends, the commanders of his
9:28 the friends of Judas A and said to Jonathan,
9:63 learned of this, he A all his forces, and
10:2 heard of it, he A a very large army
10:48 Now Alexander the king A large forces and
10:69 of Coelesyria, and he A a large force and
11:20 In those days Jonathan A the men of Judea
11:45 men of the city A within the city, to
13:1 heard that Trypho had A a large army to
13:10 So he A all the warriors and hastened to
14:1 year Demetrius the king A his forces and marched
2Mac 6:11 Others who had A in the caves near by,
12:38 Then Judas A his army and went to the
Mt 28:12 And when they had A with the elders and
Mk 14:53 priests and the elders and the scribes were A
Lk 23:47 all the multitudes who A to see the sight,
1Cor 5:4 When you are A, and my spirit is present,
Rev 16:16 seen exposed!") And they A them at the place

ASSEMBLES

1Cor 14:23 therefore, the whole church A and all speak in

ASSEMBLIES (3)

Is 1:13 and the calling of A -- I cannot endure
4:5 Zion and over her A a cloud by day,
Amos 5:21 and I take no delight in your solemn A

ASSEMBLING (2)

Mt 2:4 Jerusalem with him; and A all the chief priests
2Thes 2:1 Jesus Christ and our A to meet him, we

ASSEMBLY (138)

Ex 12:6 month, when the whole A of the congregation of
12:16 shall hold a holy A, and on the seventh
12:16 seventh day a holy A; no work shall be
16:3 to kill this whole A with hunger."
Lev 4:13 the eyes of the A, and they do any
4:14 committed becomes known, the A shall offer a young
4:21 bull; it is the sin offering for the A
16:17 and for all the A of Israel.
16:33 priests and for all the people of the A
23:36 it is a solemn A; you shall do no
Num 10:7 But when the A is to be gathered together,
14:5 faces before all the A of the congregation of
15:15 For the A, there shall be one statute for
16:2 congregation, chosen from the A, well-known men;
16:3 exalt yourselves above the A of the LORD?"

16:33 and they perished from the midst of the A
16:47 the midst of the A; and behold, the plague
19:20 the midst of the A, since he has defiled
20:4 have you brought the A of the LORD into
20:6 the presence of the A to the door of
20:10 and Aaron gathered the A together before the rock,
20:12 shall not bring this A into the land which
29:35 shall have a solemn A: you shall do no
Deut 5:22 spoke to all your A at the mountain out
9:10 of the fire on the day of the A
10:4 the day of the A; and the LORD gave
16:8 shall be a solemn A to the LORD your
18:16 the day of the A, when you said, 'Let
23:1 shall not enter the A of the LORD.
23:2 bastard shall enter the A of the LORD; even
23:2 descendants shall enter the A of the LORD.
23:3 Moabite shall enter the A of the LORD; even
23:3 them shall enter the A of the LORD for
23:8 them may enter the A of the LORD.
31:30 ears of all the A of Israel."
33:4 a possession for the A of Jacob.
Josh 8:35 read before all the A of Israel, and the
22:12 of it, the whole A of the people of
Judg 20:2 presented themselves in the A of the people of
21:5 come up in the A to the LORD?" For
21:8 come to the camp from Jabesh-gilead, to the A
1Sam 17:47 and that all this A may know that the
1Kgs 8:14 and blessed all the A of Israel, while all
8:14 Israel, while all the A of Israel stood.
8:22 presence of all the A of Israel, and spread
8:55 and blessed all the A of Israel with a
8:65 with him, a great A, from the entrance of
12:3 Jeroboam and all the A of Israel came and
12:20 called him to the A and made him king
2Kgs 10:20 ordered, "Sanctify a solemn A for Baal." So they
1Chr 13:2 said to all the A of Israel, "If it
13:4 All the A agreed to do so, for the
28:8 of all Israel, the A of the LORD, and
29:1 said to all the A, "Solomon my son, whom
29:10 presence of all the A; and David said: "Blessed
29:20 said to all the A, "Bless the LORD your
29:20 And all the A blessed the LORD, the God
2Chr 1:3 Solomon, and all the A with him, went to
1:5 And Solomon and the A sought the LORD.
6:3 and blessed all the A of Israel, while all
6:3 Israel, while all the A of Israel stood.
6:12 presence of all the A of Israel, and spread
6:13 presence of all the A of Israel, and spread
7:9 they held a solemn A; for they had kept
20:5 Jehoshaphat stood in the A of Judah and Jerusalem,
20:14 sons of Asaph, in the midst of the A
23:3 And all the A made a covenant with the
28:14 the spoil before the princes and all the A
29:23 the king and the A, and they laid their
29:28 The whole A worshiped, and the singers sang, and
29:31 And the A brought sacrifices and thank offerings; and
29:32 burnt offerings which the A brought was seventy
30:2 princes and all the A in Jerusalem had taken
30:4 seemed right to the king and all the A
30:13 bread in the second month, a very great A
30:17 were many in the A who had not sanctified
30:23 Then the whole A agreed together to keep the
30:24 of Judah gave the A a thousand bulls and
30:24 the princes gave the A a thousand bulls and
30:25 The whole A of Judah, and the priests and
30:25 Levites, and the whole A that came out of
Ezra 2:64 The whole A together was forty-two thousand three
10:1 God, a very great A of men, women, and
10:12 Then all the A answered with a loud voice,
10:14 stand for the whole A; let all in our
Neh 5:7 I held a great A against them,
5:13 And all the A said "Amen" and praised the
7:66 The whole A together was forty-two thousand three
8:2 the law before the A, both men and women
8:17 And all the A of those who had returned
8:18 there was a solemn A, according to the ordinance.
13:1 should ever enter the A of God;
Jud 6:16 women ran to the A; and they set Achior
6:21 took him from the A to his own house
7:30 lamentation arose throughout the A, and they cried
Esth 10:13 that month, with an A and joy and gladness
Job 30:28 stand up in the A, and cry for help.
Ps 7:7 Let the A of the peoples be gathered about
89:5 thy faithfulness in the A of the holy ones!
107:32 praise him in the A of the elders.
149:1 his praise in the A of the faithful!
Prov 21:16 will rest in the A of the dead.
26:26 guile, his wickedness will be exposed in the A
Sir 6:34 Stand in the A of the elders.
7:14 not prattle in the A of the elders, nor
15:5 open his mouth in the midst of the A
16:6 In an A of sinners a fire will be
21:9 An A of the wicked is like tow gathered
21:17 be sought in the A, and they will ponder
23:24 be brought before the A, and punishment will fall
24:2 In the A of the Most High she will
31:11 be established, and the A will relate his acts
38:33 nor do they attain eminence in the public A
Is 1:13 assemblies-- I cannot endure iniquity and solemn A
14:13 on the mount of A in the far north;
Jer 44:15 stood by, a great A, all the people who
Lam 1:15 me; he summoned an A against me to crush
Dan 13:41 The A believed them, because they were elders of
13:60 Then all the A shouted loudly and blessed God,
Joel 1:13 Sanctify a fast, call a solemn A
2:15 fast; call a solemn A;
Mic 2:5 by lot in the A of the LORD.
6:9 "Hear, O tribe and A of the city!
Zeph 2:1 Come together and hold A, O shameless nation,
1Mac 2:56 he testified in the A, received an inheritance in
4:59 brothers and all the A of Israel determined that
5:16 these messages, a great A was called to determine
14:19 were read before the A in Jerusalem.
14:28 Asaramel, in the great A of the priests and
14:44 or to convene an A in the country without
Lk 22:64 When day came, the A of the elders of
Acts 15:12 And all the A kept silence; and they listened
19:32 some another; for the A was in confusion, and
19:39 further, it shall be settled in the regular A
19:41 when he had said this, he dismissed the A
23:7 the Sadducees; and the A was divided.
Heb 12:23 gathering, and to the A of the first-born who
Jas 2:2 clothing comes into your A, and a poor man

ASSENTED

2Mac 4:10 When the king A and Jason came to office,

ASSERT

Sir 7:5 Do not A your righteousness before the Lord, nor

ASSERTED

Acts 25:19 dead, but whom Paul A to be alive.

ASSERTIONS

1Tim 1:7 saying or the things about which they make A

ASSES (63)

Gen 24:35 gold, menservants and maidservants, camels and A
30:43 maidservants and menservants, and camels and A
32:5 and I have oxen, A, flocks, menservants, and
34:28 and their herds, their A, and whatever was in
36:24 as he pastured the A of Zibeon his father.
42:26 Then they loaded their A with their grain, and
43:18 to make slaves of us and seize our A
43:24 he had given their A provender,
44:3 light, the men were sent awy with their A
45:23 sent as follows: ten A loaded with the good
47:17 the herds, and the A: and he supplied them
Ex 9:3 field, the horses, the A, the camels, the herds,
Num 31:28 oxen and of the A and of the flocks;
31:30 the oxen, of the A, and of the flocks,
31:34 thousand cattle, sixty-one thousand A,
31:39 The A were thirty thousand five hundred, of which
31:45 thirty thousand five hundred A,
Josh 6:21 old, oxen, sheep, and A, with the edge of
7:24 and his oxen and A and sheep, and his
9:4 sacks upon their A, and wineskins, worn-out and
Judg 5:10 who ride on tawny A, you who sit on
10:4 who rode on thirty A; and they had thirty
12:14 who rode on seventy A; and he judged Israel
19:3 with him his servant and a couple of A
19:10 a couple of saddled A, and his concubine was
19:19 and provender for our A, with bread and wine
19:21 house, and gave the A provender; and they washed
1Sam 8:16 your cattle and your A, and put them to
9:3 Now the A of Kish, Saul's father, were lost.
9:3 you, and arise, go and look for the A
9:5 to care about the A and become anxious about
9:20 As for your A that were lost three days
10:2 say to you, 'The A which you went to
10:2 to care about the A and is anxious about
10:14 said, "To seek the A; and when we saw

A

	10:16	us plainly that the A had been found." But
	22:19	children and sucklings, oxen, A and sheep, he put
	25:18	hundred cakes of figs, and laid them on A
	27:9	sheep, the oxen, the A, the camels, and the
2Sam	16:1	with a couple of A saddled, bearing two hundred
	16:2	Ziba answered, "The A are for the king's household
2Kgs	4:22	and one of the A, that I may quickly
	7:7	their horses, and their A, leaving the camp as
	7:10	horses tied, and the A tied, and the tents
1Chr	5:21	thousand sheep, two thousand A, and a hundred
	12:40	came bringing food on A and on camels and
2Chr	28:15	feeble among them on A, they brought them to
Ezra	2:67	and thirty-five, and their A were six thousand seven
Neh	7:69	and thirty-five, and their A six thousand seven
	13:15	and loading them on A; and also wine, grapes,
Jud	2:17	number of camels and A and mules for transport,
Job	1:14	were plowing and the A feeding beside them;
	24:5	Behold, like wild A in the desert they go
Ps	104:11	the field; the wild A quench their thirst.
Sir	13:18	Wild A in the wilderness are the prey of
Is	21:7	in pairs, riders on A, riders on camels, let
	30:6	on the backs of A, and their treasures on
	30:24	the oxen and the A that till the ground
	32:14	a joy of wild A, a pasture of flocks;
Jer	14:6	The wild A stand on the bare heights, they
Ezek	23:20	were like those of A, and whose issue was
Dan	5:21	was with the wild A; he was fed grass
Zech	14:15	mules, the camels, the A, and whatever beasts may

ASSESSED

2Kgs	12:4	which each man is A --the money from the

ASSESSMENT (2)

2Kgs	12:4	the money from the A of persons--and the
	23:35	one according to his A, to give it to

ASSHUR (5)

Gen	10:22	sons of Shem: Elam, A, Arpachshad, Lud, and Aram.
Num	24:22	How long shall A take you away captive?"
	24:24	Kittim and shall afflict A and Eber; and he
1Chr	1:17	sons of Shem: Elam, A, Arpachshad, Lud, Aram, Uz,
Ezek	27:23	Haran, Canneh, Eden, A, and Chilmad traded with

ASSHURIM

Gen	25:3	sons of Dedan were A, Letushim, and Le-ummim.

ASSIGN (7)

Num	4:27	do; and you shall A to their charge all
	4:32	accessories; and you shall A by name the objects
Ezek	4:5	For I A to you a number of days,
	4:6	Judah; forty days I A you, a day for
	45:6	holy district you shall A for the possession of
	47:23	resides, there you shall A him his inheritance, says
Lk	22:29	my trials; and I A to you, as my

ASSIGNED (16)

1Sam	29:4	to which you have A him; he shall not
2Sam	11:16	besieging the city, he A Uriah to the place
1Kgs	11:18	him a house, and A him an allowance of
2Chr	2:2	And Solomon A seventy thousand men to bear
	2:14	design that may be A him, with your craftsmen,
	2:18	thousand of them he A to bear burdens, eighty
Prov	8:29	the deep, when he A to the sea its
Sir	3:21	upon what has been A to you, for you
	24:8	one who created me A a place for my
Dan	1:5	The king A them a daily portion of the
1Mac	5:20	three thousand men were A to Simon to go
	6:35	hundred picked horsemen were A to each beast.
Lk	22:29	you, as my Father A to me, a kingdom,
Rom	12:3	faith which God has A him.
1Cor	3:5	believed, as the Lord A to each.
	7:17	which the Lord has A to him, and in

ASSIGNING

Num	8:26	to the Levites in A their duties."

ASSIGNS

Deut	21:16	the day when he A his possessions as an

ASSIR (4)

Ex	6:24	The sons of Korah: A, Elkanah, and Abiasaph; these
1Chr	6:22	son, Korah his son, A his son,
	6:23	son, Ebiasaph his son, A his son,
	6:37	of Tahath, son of A, son of Ebiasaph, son

ASSIST (6)

1Chr	23:28	duty shall be to A the sons of Aaron
	23:29	house of God; to A also with the showbread,
Sir	29:20	A your neighbor according to your ability, but take
Acts	13:5	they had John to A them.
1Tim	5:16	are widows, let her A them; let the church
	5:16	so that it may A those who are real

ASSISTANCE

Sir	51:7	I looked for the A of men, and there

ASSISTANT

Neh	13:13	Levites, and as their A Hanan the son of

ASSISTED

Ezra	1:4	place he sojourns, be A by the men of

ASSISTING (2)

2Chr	31:13	and Benaiah were overseers A Conaniah and Shimei
	31:15	and Shecaniah were faithfully A him in the cities

ASSOCIATE (12)

Prov	20:19	secrets; therefore do not A with one who speaks
Wis	6:23	for envy does not A with wisdom.
	8:4	of God, and an A in his works.
Sir	9:4	Do not A with a woman singer, lest you
	13:2	beyond your strength, nor A with a man mightier
	13:2	can the clay pot A with the iron kettle?
	13:15	neighbor; all living beings A by species, and a
Acts	10:28	for a Jew to A with or to visit
Rom	12:16	not be haughty, but A with the lowly; never
1Cor	5:9	my letter not to A with immoral men;
	5:11	to you not to A with any one who
Eph	5:7	Therefore do not A with them,

ASSOCIATED (4)

Ezek	37:16	the children of Israel A with him'; then take
	37:16	the house of Israel A with him';
	37:19	the tribes of Israel A with him; and I
2Mac	8:9	He A with him Gorgias, a general and a

ASSOCIATES (12)

Ezra	4:7	the rest of their A wrote to Artaxerxes king
	4:9	the rest of their A, the judges, the governors,
	4:17	the rest of their A who live in Samaria
	4:23	the scribe and their A, they went in haste
	5:3	and Shethar-bozenai and their A came to them and
	5:6	and Shethar-bozenai and his A the governors who
	6:6	Shethar-bozenai, and your A the governors who are
	6:13	River, Shethar-bozenai, and their A did with all
Sir	12:14	pity a man who A with a sinner and
	13:1	be defiled, and whoever A with a proud man
2Mac	1:33	which Nehemiah and his A had burned the materials
	1:36	Nehemiah and his A called this "nephthar," which

ASSOS (2)

Acts	20:13	we set sail for A, intending to take Paul
	20:14	he met us at A, we took him on

ASSUAGE (2)

Job	16:5	of my lips would A your pain.
Sir	18:15	Does not the dew A the scorching heat?

ASSUAGED

Job	16:6	my pain is not A, and if I forbear,

ASSUAGING

Nah	3:19	There is no A your hurt, your wound is

ASSUME

1Mac	10:70	Why do you A authority against us in the

ASSUMED

Wis	13:3	of these things men A them to be gods,

ASSUMING (2)

Eph	3:2	of you Gentiles-- A that you have heard
	4:21	so learn Christ!-- A that you have heard

ASSURANCE (7)

Deut	28:66	dread, and have no A of your life.
Wis	6:18	to her laws is A of immortality,
Sir	44:23	he gave the same A for the sake of
Acts	17:31	this he has given A to all men by
Heb	6:11	in realizing the full A of hope until the
	10:22	true heart in full A of faith, with our

11:1 Now faith is the A of things hoped for,

ASSURED (7)

Gen 43:23 He replied, "Rest A, do not be afraid; your
Prov 11:21 Be A, an evil man will not go unpunished,
16:5 to the LORD; be A, he will not go
Sir 44:22 Therefore the Lord A him by an oath that
Jer 14:13 I will give you A peace in this place.'"
Col 2:2 all the riches of A understanding and the knowledge
4:12 stand mature and fully A in all the will

ASSUREDLY (2)

Josh 23:13 and they yours, know A that the LORD your
Acts 2:36 of Israel therefore know A that God has made

ASSYRIA (131)

Gen 2:14 third river is Tigris, which flows east of A
10:11 land he went into A, and built Nineveh, Rehoboth-Ir,
25:18 in the direction of A; he settled over against
2Kgs 15:19 Pul the king of A came against the land;
15:20 every man, to give to the king of A
15:20 So the king of A turned back, and did
15:29 Israel Tiglath-pileser king of A came and captured
15:29 Naphtali; and he carried the people captive to A
16:7 to Tiglath-pileser king of A, saying, "I am your
16:8 and sent a present to the king of A
16:9 And the king of A hearkened to him; the
16:9 him; the king of A marched up against Damascus,
16:10 meet Tiglath-pileser king of A, he saw the altar
16:18 of the LORD, because of the king of A
17:3 up Shalmaneser king of A; and Hoshea became his
17:4 But the king of A found treachery in Hoshea;
17:4 to the king of A, as he had done
17:4 therefore the king of A shut him up, and
17:5 Then the king of A invaded all the land
17:6 Hoshea the king of A captured Samaria, and he
17:6 the Israelites away to A, and placed them in
17:23 their own land to A until this day.
17:24 And the king of A brought people from Babylon,
17:26 So the king of A was told, "The nations
17:27 Then the king of A commanded, "Send there one
18:7 against the king of A, and would not serve
18:9 Israel, Shalmaneser king of A came up against
18:11 The king of A carried the Israelites away to
18:11 the Israelites away to A, and put them in
18:13 Hezekiah Sennacherib king of A came up against all
18:14 to the king of A at Lachish, saying, "I
18:14 And the king of A required of Hezekiah king
18:16 overlaid and gave it to the king of A
18:17 And the king of A sent the Tartan, the
18:19 king, the king of A: On what do you
18:23 master the king of A: I will give you
18:28 word of the great king, the king of A
18:30 of the king of A
18:31 says the king of A: 'Make your peace with
18:33 out of the hand of the king of A
19:4 master the king of A has sent to mock
19:6 of the king of A have reviled me.
19:8 found the king of A fighting against Libnah; for
19:10 given into the hand of the king of A
19:11 what the kings of A have done to all
19:17 LORD, the kings of A have laid waste the
19:20 about Sennacherib king of A I have heard.
19:32 concerning the king of A, He shall not come
19:36 Then Sennacherib king of A departed, and went
20:6 of the king of A, and I will defend
23:29 to the king of A to the river Euphrates.
1Chr 5:6 whom Tilgath-pilneser king of A carried away into
5:26 of Pul king of A, the spirit of Tilgath-pilneser
5:26 of Tilgath-pilneser king of A, and he carried them
2Chr 28:16 to the king of A for help.
28:20 So Tilgath-pilneser king of A came against him, and
28:21 to the king of A; but it did not
30:6 escaped from the hand of the kings of A
32:1 faithfulness Sennacherib king of A came and invaded
32:4 should the kings of A come and find much
32:7 before the king of A and all the horde
32:9 this Sennacherib king of A, who was besieging
32:10 says Sennacherib king of A, 'On what are you
32:11 us from the hand of the king of A
32:21 officers in the camp of the king of A
32:22 of Sennacherib king of A and from the hand
33:11 of the king of A, who took Manasseh with
Ezra 4:2 of Esarhaddon king of A who brought us here."
6:22 of the king of A to them, so that
Neh 9:32 of the kings of A until this day.
Ps 83:8 the inhabitants of Tyre; A also has joined them;
Is 7:17 Ephraim departed from Judah-- the king of A
7:18 the bee which is in the land of A
7:20 with the king of A -- the head and
8:4 will be carried away before the king of A
8:7 many, the king of A and all his glory;
10:5 Ah, A, the rod of my anger, the staff
10:12 of the king of A and his haughty pride.
11:11 of his people, from A, from Egypt, from Pathros,
11:16 be a highway from A for the remnant which
19:23 highway from Egypt to A, and the Assyrian will
19:23 and the Egyptian into A, and the Egyptians will
19:24 third with Egypt and A, a blessing in the
19:25 Egypt my people, and A the work of my
20:1 Sargon the king of A, came to Ashdod and
20:4 shall the king of A lead away the Egyptians
20:6 help to be delivered from the king of A
23:13 This is the people; it was not A
27:13 in the land of A and those who were
36:1 Hezekiah, Sennacherib king of A came up against all
36:2 And the king of A sent the Rabshakeh from
36:4 king, the king of A: On what do you
36:8 master the king of A: I will give you
36:13 words of the great king, the king of A
36:15 given into the hand of the king of A
36:16 says the king of A: Make your peace with
36:18 out of the hand of the king of A
37:4 master the king of A has sent to mock
37:6 of the king of A have reviled me.
37:8 found the king of A fighting against Libnah; for
37:10 given into the hand of the king of A
37:11 what the kings of A have done to all
37:18 LORD, the kings of A have laid waste all
37:21 concerning Sennacherib king of A,
37:33 concerning the king of A: He shall not come
37:37 Then Sennacherib king of A departed, and went
38:6 of the king of A, and defend this city.
Jer 2:18 gain by going to A, to drink the waters
2:36 Egypt as you were put to shame by A
50:17 First the king of A devoured him, and now
50:18 his land, as I punished the king of A
Lam 5:6 to Egypt, and to A, to get bread enough.
Ezek 23:7 the choicest men of A all of them; and
32:22 slain by the sword.' A is there, and all
Hos 5:13 then Ephraim went to A, and sent to the
7:12 and without sense, calling to Egypt, going to A
8:9 have gone up to A, a wild ass wandering
9:3 Egypt, and they shall eat unclean food in A
9:6 they are going to A; Egypt shall gather them,
10:6 shall be carried to A, as tribute to the
11:5 land of Egypt, and A shall be their king,
11:11 from the land of A; and I will return
12:1 make a bargain with A, and oil is carried
14:3 A shall not save us, we will not ride
Amos 3:9 to the strongholds in A, and to the strongholds
Mic 5:6 rule the land of A with the sword, and
7:12 come to you, from A to Egypt, and from
Nah 3:18 asleep, O king of A; your nobles slumber.
Zeph 2:13 the north, and destroy A; and he will make
Zech 10:10 and gather them from A; and I will bring
10:11 The pride of A shall be laid low, and

ASSYRIAN (19)

Jud 2:14 and officers of the A army,
5:1 the general of the A army, heard that the
6:1 the commander of the A army, said to Achior
6:17 the presence of the A leaders, and all that
7:18 The rest of the A army encamped in the
7:20 The whole A army, their infantry, chariots, and
10:11 the valley; and an A patrol met her
13:15 the commander of the A army, and here is
14:2 the plain against the A outpost; only do not
14:3 the officers of the A army; and they will
14:19 the leaders of the A army heard this, they
15:6 Bethulia fell upon the A camp and plundered it,
16:4 The A came down from the mountains of the
Is 14:25 I will break the A in my land, and
19:23 to Assyria, and the A will come into Egypt,
31:8 "And the A shall fall by a sword, not
52:4 sojourn there, and the A oppressed them for nothing.
Mic 5:5 be peace, when the A comes into our land
5:6 deliver us from the A when he comes into

ASSYRIANS (26)

2Kgs 19:35 the camp of the A; and when men arose
Tob 1:2 Shalmaneser, king of the A, was taken into captivity

A

1:3 the land of the A, to Nineveh.
Jud 1:1 who ruled over the A in the great city
1:7 Nebuchadnezzar king of the A sent to all who
1:11 Nebuchadnezzar king of the A, and refused to join
2:1 Nebuchadnezzar king of the A about carrying out his
2:4 Nebuchadnezzar king of the A called Holofernes, the
4:1 the king of the A, had done to the
7:17 together with five thousand A, and they encamped in
7:25 great injury in not making peace with the A
8:9 the city to the A after five days,
9:7 "Behold now, the A are increased in their might;
12:13 the daughters of the A who serve in the
14:12 And when the A saw them they sent word
Sir 48:21 the camp of the A, and his angel wiped
Is 10:24 not afraid of the A when they smite with
19:23 Assyria, and the Egyptians will worship with the A
30:31 The A will be terror-stricken at the voice of
37:36 the camp of the A; and when men arose
Ezek 16:28 harlot also with the A, because you were insatiable;
23:5 on her lovers the A,
23:9 the hands of the A, upon whom she doted.
23:12 She doted upon the A, governors and commanders,
23:23 Koa, and all the A with them, desirable young
1Mac 7:41 down one hundred and eighty-five thousand of the A

ASTONISH

Jud 11:16 you things that will A the whole world, as

ASTONISHED (23)

Lev 26:32 in it shall be A at it.
1Kgs 9:8 by it will be A, and will hiss; and
2Chr 7:21 passing by will be A, and say, 'Why has
Jud 13:17 the people were greatly A, and bowed down and
Is 52:14 As many were A at him– his appearance
Dan 3:92 Then King Nebuchadnezzar was A and rose up in
2Mac 7:12 those with him were A at the young man's
Mt 7:28 sayings, the crowds were A at his teaching,
13:54 so that they were A, and said, "Where did
19:25 this they were greatly A, saying, "Who then can
22:33 heard it, they were A at his teaching.
Mk 1:22 And they were A at his teaching, for he
6:2 who heard him were A, saying, "Where did this
7:36 And they were A beyond measure, saying, "He has
10:26 And they were exceedingly A, and said to him,
11:18 all the multitude was A at his teaching.
Lk 2:48 saw him they were A; and his mother said
4:32 sabbath; and they were A at his teaching, for
5:9 For he was A, and all that were with
9:43 And all were A at the majesty of God.
11:38 The Pharisee was A to see that he did
Acts 13:12 occurred, for he was A at the teaching of
Gal 1:6 I am A that you are so quickly deserting

ASTONISHING

Dan 11:36 god, and shall speak A things against the God

ASTONISHMENT (2)

2Chr 29:8 object of horror, of A, and of hissing, as
Mk 16:8 tomb; for trembling and A had come upon them;

ASTOUNDED (8)

Job 26:11 heaven tremble, and are A at his rebuke.
Ps 48:5 saw it, they were A, they were in panic,
Jer 4:9 the priests shall be appalled and the prophets A
Hab 1:5 among the nations, and see; wonder and be A
1Mac 6:8 this news, he was A and badly shaken.
2Mac 3:24 to accompany him were A by the power of
Mk 6:51 And they were utterly A,
Acts 3:11 together to them in the portico called Solomons, A

ASTOUNDING

2Mac 7:18 Therefore A things have happened.

ASTRAY (68)

Ex 23:4 or his ass going A, you shall bring it
Num 5:12 any man's wife goes A and acts unfaithfully against
5:20 if you have gone A, though you are under
5:29 her husband's authority, goes A and defiles herself,
Deut 22:1 or his sheep go A, and withhold your help
2Chr 21:11 Jerusalem into unfaithfulness, and made Judah go A
Tob 5:13 They did not go A in the error of
Ps 14:3 They have all gone A, they are all alike
40:4 to those who go A after false gods!
58:3 The wicked go A from the womb, they err
119:67 was afflicted I went A; but now I keep
119:118 spurn all who go A from thy statutes; yea,
119:176 I have gone A like a lost sheep; seek
Prov 10:17 to life, but he who rejects reproof goes A
12:26 but the way of the wicked leads them A
20:1 and whoever is led A by it is not
Wis 2:21 but they were led A, for their wickedness blinded
11:15 thoughts, which led them A to worship irrational
12:24 For they went far A on the paths of
13:6 for perhaps they go A while seeking God and
17:1 to describe; therefore unintructed souls have gone A
Sir 3:23 judgment has led many A, and wrong opinion has
4:19 If he goes A she will forsake him, and
13:8 not to be led A, and not to be
15:12 he who led me A; for he had no
19:2 women lead intelligent men A, and the man who
31:5 money will be led A by it.
Is 9:16 this people lead them A, and those who are
19:13 the cornerstones of her tribes have led Egypt A
30:28 jaws of the peoples a bridle that leads A
44:20 mind has led him A, and he cannot deliver
47:10 your knowledge led you A, and you said in
53:6 like sheep have gone A; we have turned every
Jer 23:13 prophesied by Baal and led my people Israel A
23:32 and lead my people A by their lies and
42:20 that you have gone A at the cost of
50:6 shepherds have led them A, turning them away on
Bar 4:28 you purposed to go A from God, return with
Ezek 14:11 may go no more A from me, nor defile
20:30 your fathers and go A after their detestable things?
44:10 far from me, going A from me after their
44:10 idols when Israel went A, shall bear their
44:15 people of Israel went A from me, shall come
48:11 who did not go A when the people of
48:11 people of Israel went A, as the Levites did.
Hos 4:12 harlotry has led them A, and they have left
Amos 2:4 lies have led them A, after which their fathers
Mic 3:5 who lead my people A, who cry "Peace" when
2Mac 2:2 nor to be led A in their thoughts upon
6:25 they should be led A because of me, while
Mt 18:11 of them has gone A, does he not leave
18:11 go in search of the one that went A
18:12 more than over the ninety-nine that never went A
24:4 them, "Take heed that no one leads you A
24:5 am the Christ,' and they will lead many A
24:11 many false prophets will arise and lead many A
24:24 so as to lead A, if possible, even the
Mk 13:5 them, "Take heed that no one leads you A
13:6 'I am he!' and they will lead many A
13:22 and wonders, to lead A, if possible, the elect.
Lk 21:8 you are not led A; for many will come
Jn 7:12 others said, "No, he is leading the people A
7:47 them, "Are you led A, you also?
1Cor 12:2 heathen, you were led A to dumb idols, however
2Cor 11:3 thoughts will be led A from a sincere and
Tit 3:3 once foolish, disobedient, led A, slaves to various
Heb 3:10 said, 'They always go A in their hearts; they
2Pet 2:15 way they have gone A; they have followed the

ASTROLOGERS (4)

Dan 2:27 men, enchanters, magicians, or A can show to the
4:7 the Chaldeans, and the A came in; and I
5:7 bring in the enchanters, the Chaldeans, and the A
5:11 magicians, enchanters, Chaldeans, and A,

ASTYAGES

Dan 14:1 When King A was laid with his fathers, Cyrus

ASUNDER (12)

Lev 1:17 by its wings, but shall not divide it A
Num 16:31 ground under them split A;
Judg 14:6 he tore the lion A as one tears a
Job 16:12 and he broke me A; he seized me by
Ps 2:3 us burst their bonds A, and cast their cords
107:14 of darkness and gloom, and broke their bonds A
Is 24:19 the earth is rent A, the earth is violently
45:2 of bronze and cut A the bars of iron,
Nah 1:6 the rocks are broken A by him.
1:13 from off you and will burst your bonds A
Mt 19:6 God has joined together, let not man put A
Mk 10:9 God has joined together, let not man put A

ASYNCRITUS

Rom 16:14 Greet A, Phlegon, Hermes, Patrobas, Hermas, and

ATAD (2)

Gen 50:10 the threshing floor of A, which is beyond the
50:11 the threshing floor of A, they said, "This is

ATARAH

1Chr	2:26	wife, whose name was A; she was the mother

ATARGATIS

2Mac	12:26	and the temple of A, and slaughtered twenty-five

ATAROTH (4)

Num	32:3	leaders of the congregation, A, Dibon, Jazer, Nimrah,
	32:34	of Gad built Dibon, A, Aroer,
Josh	16:2	it passes along to A, the territory of the
	16:7	down from Jan-oah to A and to Naarah, and

ATAROTH-ADDAR (2)

Josh	16:5	on the east was A as far as Upper
	18:13	boundary goes down to A, upon the mountain that

ATE (125)

Gen	3:6	of its fruit and A; and she also gave
	3:6	also gave some to her husband, and he A
	3:12	gave me fruit of the tree, and I A
	3:13	woman said, "The serpent beguiled me, and I A
	18:8	stood by them under the tree while they A
	19:3	a feast, and baked unleavened bread, and they A
	24:54	who were with him A and drank, and they
	25:28	loved Esau, because he A of his game; but
	25:34	of lentils, and he A and drank, and rose
	26:30	a feast, and they A and drank.
	27:25	to him, and he A; and he brought him
	27:33	to me, and I A it all before you
	31:46	a heap; and they A there by the heap.
	31:54	eat bread; and they A bread and tarried all
	39:6	concern for anything but the food which he A
	41:4	gaunt and thin cows A up the seven sleek
	41:20	thin and gaunt cows A up the first seven
	43:32	and the Egyptians who A with him by themselves,
Ex	10:15	was darkened, and they A all the plants in
	16:3	by the fleshpots and A bread to the full;
	16:35	the people of Israel A the manna forty years,
	16:35	a habitable land; they A the manna, till they
	24:11	they beheld God, and A and drank.
	34:28	forty nights; he neither A bread nor drank water.
Num	11:5	remember the fish we A in Egypt for nothing,
	25:2	gods, and the people A, and bowed down to
Deut	9:9	forty nights; I neither A bread nor drank water.
	9:18	forty nights; I neither A bread nor drank water,
	32:13	the earth, and he A the produce of the
	32:38	they took refuge, who A the fat of their
Josh	5:11	that very day, they A of the produce of
	5:12	the morrow, when they A of the produce of
	5:12	manna no more, but A of the fruit of
Judg	9:27	of their god, and A and drank and reviled
	14:9	mother, and gave some to them, and they A
	19:4	three days; so they A and drank, and lodged
	19:6	two men sat and A and drank together; and
	19:8	So they A, both of them.
	19:21	washed their feet, and A and drank.
Ruth	2:14	parched grain; and she A until she was satisfied,
1Sam	1:18	went her way and A, and her countenance was
	9:24	So Saul A with Samuel that day.
	14:32	ground; and the people A them with the blood.
	20:34	in fierce anger and A no food the second
	28:25	it before Saul and his servants; and they A
	30:11	him bread and he A, they gave him water
2Sam	9:11	So Mephibosheth A at David's table, like one of
	9:13	in Jerusalem; for he A always at the king's
	11:13	invited him, and he A in his presence and
	12:20	asked, they set food before him, and he A
	12:21	died, you arose and A food."
1Kgs	4:20	by the sea; they A and drank and were
	13:19	back with him, and A bread in his house,
	17:15	he, and her household A for many days.
	19:6	And he A and drank, and lay down again.
	19:8	And he arose, and A and drank, and went
	19:21	and gave it to the people, and they A
2Kgs	4:44	And they A, and had some left, according to
	6:29	boiled my son, and A him.
	7:8	into a tent, and A and drank, and they
	9:34	he went in and A and drank; and he
	23:9	in Jerusalem, but they A unleavened bread among
1Chr	29:22	all Israel; and they A and drank before the
2Chr	30:18	cleansed themselves, yet they A the passover
	30:22	So the people A the food of the festival
Neh	5:14	I nor my brethren A the food allowance of
	9:25	in abundance; so they A, and were filled and
Tob	1:10	brethren and my relatives A the food of the
	2:5	I washed myself and A my food in sorrow.
	6:5	and they roasted and A the fish.
	10:7	they had left; she A nothing in the daytime,
Jud	12:9	the tent until she A her food toward evening.
	12:15	that she might recline on them when she A
	12:19	Then she took and A and drank before him
Job	42:11	known him before, and A bread with him in
Ps	41:9	whom I trusted, who A of my bread, has
	78:25	Man A of the bread of the angels; he
	78:29	And they A and were well filled, for he
	105:35	in their land, and A up the fruit of
	106:28	Baal of Peor, and A sacrifices offered to the
Jer	2:3	All who A of it became guilty; evil came
	15:16	were found, and I A them, and thy words
	41:1	As they A bread together there at Mizpah,
Ezek	3:3	Then I A it; and it was in my
	16:13	and embroidered cloth; you A fine flour and honey
Dan	1:5	food which the king A, and of the wine
	1:15	all the youths who A the king's rich food.
	4:33	from among men, and A grass like an ox,
	10:3	I A no delicacies, no meat or wine entered
	14:7	outside, and it never A or drank anything."
	14:15	accustomed to do, and A and drank everything.
	14:27	The dragon A them, and burst open.
	14:39	So Daniel arose and A
Mt	12:4	house of God and A the bread of the
	14:20	And they all A and were satisfied.
	14:21	And those who A were about five thousand men,
	15:37	And they all A and were satisfied; and they
	15:38	Those who A were four thousand men, besides
Mk	1:6	around his waist, and A locusts and wild honey.
	2:26	was high priest, and A the bread of the
	6:42	And they all A and were satisfied.
	6:44	And those who A the loaves were five thousand
	7:2	some of his disciples A with hands defiled, that
	8:8	And they A, and were satisfied; and they took
Lk	4:2	And he A nothing in those days; and when
	6:1	his disciples plucked and A some heads of grain,
	6:4	God, and took and A the bread of the
	9:17	And all A and were satisfied.
	13:26	begin to say, 'We A and drank in your
	15:16	pods that the swine A; and no one gave
	17:27	They A, they drank, they married, they were given
	17:28	days of Lot—they A, they drank, they bought,
	24:43	he took it and A before them.
Jn	6:23	the place where they A the bread after the
	6:26	signs, but because you A your fill of the
	6:31	Our fathers A the manna in the wilderness; as
	6:49	Your fathers A the manna in the wilderness, and
	6:58	such as the fathers A and died; he who
	13:18	be fulfilled, 'He who A my bread has lifted
Acts	9:9	without sight, and neither A nor drank.
	10:41	God as witnesses, who A and drank with him
	27:36	all were encouraged and A some food themselves.
1Cor	10:3	the sea, and all A the same supernatural food
Gal	2:12	came from James, he A with the Gentiles; but
Rev	10:10	of the angel and A it; it was sweet

ATER (5)

Ezra	2:16	The sons of A, namely of Hezekiah, ninety-eight.
	2:42	Shallum, the sons of A, the sons of Talmon,
Neh	7:21	The sons of A, namely of Hezekiah, ninety-eight.
	7:45	Shallum, the sons of A, the sons of Talmon,
	10:17	Adonijah, Bigvai, Adin, A, Hezekiah, Azzur,

ATHACH

1Sam	30:30	Hormah, in Borashan, in A,

ATHAIAH

Neh	11:4	the sons of Judah: A the son of Uzziah,

ATHALIAH (17)

2Kgs	8:26	His mother's name was A; she was a granddaughter
	11:1	Now when A the mother of Ahaziah saw that
	11:2	she hid him from A, so that he was
	11:3	of the LORD, while A reigned over the land.
	11:13	When A heard the noise of the guard and
	11:14	And A rent her clothes, and cried, "Treason!
	11:20	city was quiet after A had been slain with
1Chr	8:26	Shamsherai, Shehariah, A,
2Chr	22:2	His mother's name was A, the granddaughter of
	22:10	Now when A the mother of Ahaziah saw that
	22:11	Ahaziah, hid him from A, so that she did
	22:12	house of God, while A reigned over the land.
	23:12	When A heard the noise of the people running
	23:13	And A rent her clothes, and cried, "Treason!
	23:21	city was quiet, after A had been slain with

24:7 For the sons of A, that wicked woman, had
Ezra 8:7 Jeshaiah the son of A, and with him seventy

ATHARIM
Num 21:1 by the way of A, he fought against Israel,

ATHENIAN
2Mac 6:1 the king sent an A senator to compel the

ATHENIANS
Acts 17:21 Now all the A and the foreigners who lived

ATHENOBIUS (3)
1Mac 15:28 He sent to him A, one of his friends,
15:32 So A the friend of the king came to
15:35 A did not answer him a word,

ATHENS (6)
2Mac 9:15 equal to citizens of A;
Acts 17:15 him as far as A; and receiving a command
17:16 waiting for them at A, his spirit was provoked
17:22 Are-opagus, said: "Men of A, I perceive that in
18:1 After this he left A and went to Corinth.
1Thes 3:1 be left behind at A alone,

ATHLAI
Ezra 10:28 of Bebai were Jehohanan, Hananiah, Zabbai, and A

ATHLETE (2)
1Cor 9:25 Every A exercises self-control in all things.
2Tim 2:5 An A is not crowned unless he competes according

ATONE (3)
Sir 20:27 pleases great men will A for injustice.
Is 47:11 for which you cannot A; disaster shall fall upon
Dan 9:24 to sin, and to A for iniquity, to bring

ATONED
Prov 16:6 and faithfulness iniquity is A for, and by the

ATONEMENT (93)
Ex 29:33 those things with which A was made, to ordain
29:36 offer a bull as a sin offering for A
29:36 altar, when you make A for it, and shall
29:37 days you shall make A for the altar, and
30:10 Aaron shall make A upon its horns once a
30:10 the sin offering of A he shall make atonement
30:10 atonement he shall make A for it once in
30:15 LORD's offering to make A for yourselves.
30:16 you shall take the A money from the people
30:16 so as to make A for yourselves."
32:30 perhaps I can make A for your sin."
Lev 1:4 for him to make A for him.
4:20 the priest shall make A for them, and they
4:26 the priest shall make A for him for his
4:31 the priest shall make A for him, and he
4:35 the priest shall make A for him for the
5:6 the priest shall make A for him for his
5:10 the priest shall make A for him for the
5:13 the priest shall make A for him for the
5:16 the priest shall make A for him with the
5:18 the priest shall make A for him for the
6:7 the priest shall make A for him before the
6:30 of meeting to make A in the holy place;
7:7 the priest who makes A with it shall have
8:15 consecrated it, to make A for it.
8:34 be done to make A for you.
9:7 burnt offering, and make A for yourself and for
9:7 the people, and make A for them; as the
10:17 the congregation, to make A for them before the
12:7 the LORD, and make A for her; then she
12:8 the priest shall make A for her, and she
14:18 the priest shall make A for him before the
14:19 sin offering, to make A for him who is
14:20 the priest shall make A for him, and he
14:21 be waved, to make A for him, and a
14:29 be cleansed, to make A for him before the
14:31 the priest shall make A before the LORD for
14:53 so he shall make A for the house, and
15:15 the priest shall make A for him before the
15:30 the priest shall make A for her before the
16:6 himself, and shall make A for himself and for
16:10 the LORD to make A over it, that it
16:11 himself, and shall make A for himself and for
16:16 thus he shall make A for the holy place,
16:17 he enters to make A in the holy place
16:17 out and has made A for himself and for
16:18 the LORD and make A for it, and shall
16:24 the people, and make A for himself and for
16:27 brought in to make A in the holy place,
16:30 on this day shall A be made for you,
16:32 father's place shall make A, wearing the holy linen
16:33 garments; he shall make A for the sanctuary, and
16:33 and he shall make A for the tent of
16:33 and he shall make A for the priests and
16:34 statute for you, that A may be made for
17:11 the altar to make A for your souls; for
17:11 the blood that makes A, by reason of the
19:22 the priest shall make A for him with the
23:27 is the day of A; it shall be for
23:28 is a day of A, to make A for
25:9 on the day of A you shall send abroad
Num 5:8 to the ram of A with which atonement is
5:8 of atonement with which A is made for him.
6:11 burnt offering, and make A for him, because he
8:12 the LORD, to make A for the Levites.
8:19 meeting, and to make A for the people of
8:21 LORD, and Aaron made A for them to cleanse
15:25 the priest shall make A for all the congregation
15:28 the priest shall make A before the LORD for
15:28 sins unwittingly, to make A for him; and he
16:46 the congregation, and make A for them; for wrath
16:47 the incense, and made A for the people.
25:13 his God, and made A for the people of
28:22 sin offering, to make A for you.
28:30 male goat, to make A for you.
29:5 sin offering, to make A for you;
29:11 the sin offering of A, and the continual burnt
31:50 and beads, to make A for ourselves before the
1Chr 6:49 place, and to make A for Israel, according to
2Chr 29:24 the altar, to make A for all Israel.
Neh 10:33 sin offerings to make A for Israel, and for
Sir 5:5 be so confident of A that you add sin
35:3 to the Lord, and to forsake unrighteousness is A
45:16 memorial portion, to make A for the people.
45:23 his soul, and made A for Israel.
Ezek 43:20 the altar and make A for it.
43:26 days shall they make A for the altar and
45:15 peace offerings, to make A for them, says the
45:17 peace offerings, to make A for the house of
45:20 so you shall make A for the temple.
2Mac 3:33 making the offering of A, the same young men
12:45 Therefore he made A for the dead, that they

ATONES (2)
Sir 3:3 Whoever honors his father A for sins,
3:28 blazing fire: so almsgiving A for sin.

ATONING
Lev 16:20 made an end of A for the holy place

ATROTH-BETH-JOAB
1Chr 2:54 Salma: Bethlehem, the Netophathites, A, and half of

ATROTH-SHOPHAN
Num 32:35 built Dibon, Ataroth, Aroer, A, Jazer, Jogbehah,

ATTACH (6)
Ex 28:14 cords; and you shall A the corded chains to
28:25 two cords you shall A to the two settings
28:25 of filigree, and so A it in front to
28:27 rings of gold, and A them in front to
Esth 16:20 themselves against those who A them at the time
Sir 11:29 worthy actions he will A blame.

ATTACHED (8)
Ex 28:7 shall have two shoulder-pieces A to its two edges,
39:18 two cords they had A to the two settings
39:18 of filigree; thus they A it in front to
39:20 rings of gold, and A them in front to
1Sam 14:52 any valiant man, he A him to himself.
2Chr 9:18 of gold, which were A to the throne, and
Ps 106:28 Then they A themselves to the Baal of Peor,
2Mac 14:24 presence; he was warmly A to the man.

ATTACK (40)
Gen 34:30 themselves against me and A me, I shall be
Deut 24:8 "Take heed, in an A of leprosy, to be
Josh 7:3 men go up and A Ai; do not make
Judg 6:3 would come up and A them;
1Sam 7:10 Philistines drew near to A Israel; but the LORD
23:2 "Shall I go and A these Philistines?" And the

23:2 to David, "Go and A the Philistines and save
24:7 not permit them to A Saul.
2Sam 5:8 the water shaft to A the lame and the
11:25 now another; strengthen your A upon the city, and
17:9 fall at the first A, whoever hears it will
Jud 2:6 Go and A the whole west country, because they
Esth 8:11 or province that might A them, with their children
Ps 69:4 destroy me, those who A me with lies.
109:3 words of hate, and A me without cause.
Sir 25:13 Any A, but not an attack from those who
25:13 attack, but not an A from those who hate!
Jer 6:4 up, and let us A at noon!" "Woe to
6:5 "Up, and let us A by night, and destroy
Dan 11:40 of the south shall A him; but the king
1Mac 2:35 the enemy hastened to A them.
2:41 man who comes to A us on the sabbath
4:2 of the Jews and A them suddenly.
4:3 men moved out to A the king's force in
4:30 who didst crush the A of the mighty warrior
5:6 he crossed over to A the Ammonites, where he
5:27 are getting ready to A the strongholds tomorrow and
6:47 might and the fierce A of the forces, they
9:48 cross the Jordan to A them.
9:67 Then he began to A and went into battle
11:20 men of Judea to A the citadel in Jerusalem,
2Mac 4:40 and launched an unjust A, under the leadership of
4:41 became aware of Lysimachus' A, some picked up
13:26 is how the king's A and withdrawal turned out.
15:1 he made plans to A them with complete safety
15:8 not to fear the A of the Gentiles, but
15:17 a campaign but to A bravely, and to decide
Mt 7:6 foot and turn to A you.
Acts 18:10 and no man shall A you to harm you;
18:12 Jews made a united A upon Paul and brought

ATTACKED (20)
Gen 49:23 The archers fiercely A him, shot at him, and
Deut 25:18 of Egypt, how he A you on the way,
Judg 8:11 Nobah and Jogbehah, and A the army; for the
2Sam 21:17 to his aid, and A the Philistine and killed
1Kgs 2:32 my father David, he A and slew with the
2Kgs 3:24 the Israelites rose and A the Moabites, till they
25:25 with ten men, and A and killed Gedaliah and
Jon 4:7 appointed a worm which A the plant, so that
1Mac 2:38 So they A them on the sabbath, and they
4:34 Then both sides A, and there fell of the
5:16 distress and were being A by enemies.
8:10 against the Greeks and A them.
2Mac 12:6 God the righteous Judge, A the murderers of his
12:9 living among them, he A the people of Jamnia
12:10 with five hundred horsemen A them.
12:13 He also A a certain city which was strongly
13:15 bravest young men, he A the king's pavilion at
13:19 Jews, was turned back, A again, and was defeated.
13:22 pledges, received theirs, withdrew, A Judas and his
Acts 17:5 in an uproar, and A the house of Jason,

ATTACKING (7)
Deut 22:26 that of a man A and murdering his neighbor;
2Kgs 16:7 of Israel, who are A me."
Dan 11:8 he shall refrain from A the king of the
1Mac 5:30 capture the stronghold, and A the Jews within.
2Mac 10:17 A them vigorously, they gained possession of the
13:18 Jews, tried strategy in A their positions.
Acts 16:22 The crowd joined in A them; and the magistrates

ATTACKS (5)
Ex 21:14 if a man willfully A another to kill him
Deut 19:11 wait for him, and A him, and wounds him
Judg 1:12 Caleb said, "He who A Kiriath-sepher and takes it,
2Mac 5:3 of horsemen drawn up, A and counterattacks made
8:7 He found the nights most advantageous for such A

ATTAI (4)
1Chr 2:35 to Jarha his slave; and she bore him A
2:36 A was the father of Nathan and Nathan of
12:11 Mishmannah fourth, Jeremiah fifth, A sixth, Eliel
2Chr 11:20 who bore him Abijah, A, Ziza, and Shelomith.

ATTAIN (13)
2Sam 23:19 but he did not A to the three.
23:23 but he did not A to the three.
1Chr 11:21 but he did not A to the three.
11:25 but he did not A to the three.
Esth 13:5 our kingdom may not A stability.
Ps 139:6 is high, I cannot A it.
Sir 27:8 pursue justice, you will A it and wear it
38:33 people, nor do they A eminence in the public
2Mac 14:6 not let the kingdom A tranquillity.
Lk 20:35 are accounted worthy to A to that age and
Acts 26:7 twelve tribes hope to A, as they earnestly worship
Eph 4:13 Christ, until we all A to the unity of
Phil 3:11 if possible I may A the resurrection from the

ATTAINABLE
Heb 7:11 if perfection had been A through the Levitical

ATTAINED (5)
Gen 47:9 and they have not A to the days of
Esth 13:3 steadfast fidelity, and has A the second place in
Sir 22:9 dead, for he has A rest; but the life
Rom 9:30 not pursue righteousness have A it, that is,
Phil 3:16 let us hold true to what we have A

ATTALIA
Acts 14:25 they went down to A;

ATTALUS
1Mac 15:22 the king and to A and Ariarathes and Arsaces,

ATTEMPT (3)
Sir 10:6 injury, and do not A anything by acts of
2Mac 2:23 five volumes, we shall A to condense into a
Acts 14:5 When an A was made by both Gentiles and

ATTEMPTED (8)
Deut 4:34 has any god ever A to go and take
Dan 14:42 the men who had A his destruction, and they
1Mac 12:39 Then Trypho A to become king in Asia and
2Mac 9:2 city called Persepolis, and A to rob the temples
10:12 done to them, and A to maintain peaceful relations
Acts 9:26 come to Jerusalem he A to join the disciples;
16:7 come opposite Mysia, they A to go into Bithynia,
Heb 11:29 the Egyptians, when they A to do the same,

ATTEND (21)
Num 1:5 the men who shall A you.
3:8 tent of meeting, and A to the duties for
3:10 sons, and they shall A to their priesthood; but
8:13 cause the Levites to A Aaron and his sons,
18:3 They shall A you and attend to all duties
18:3 shall attend you and A to all duties of
18:4 shall join you, and A to the tent of
18:5 And you shall A to the duties of the
18:7 sons with you shall A to your priesthood for
1Chr 23:32 the sanctuary, and shall A the sons of Aaron,
Ezra 8:20 had set apart to A the Levites.
Tob 5:16 and may his angel A you." So they both
Esth 4:5 had been appointed to A her, and ordered him
Ps 17:1 just cause, O LORD; A to my cry!
55:2 A to me, and answer me; I am overcome
Sir 11:18 by your covenant and A to it, and grow
Is 42:23 ear to this, will A and listen for the
Jer 23:2 Behold, I will A to you for your evil-doings,
Ezek 44:11 people, and they shall A on the people, to
44:15 me; and they shall A on me to offer
1Tim 4:13 Till I come, A to the public reading of

ATTENDANCE (4)
Num 8:22 tent of meeting in A upon Aaron and his
1Kgs 10:5 his officials, and the A of his servants, their
2Chr 9:4 his officials, and the A of his servants, and
Esth 7:9 of the eunuchs in A on the king, "Moreover,

ATTENDANT
Lk 4:20 it back to the A, and sat down; and

ATTENDANTS (4)
Judg 3:19 And all his A went out from his presence.
Jud 13:1 and shut out the A from his master's presence;
Dan 11:6 given up, and her A, her child, and he
Mt 22:13 king said to the A, 'Bind him hand and

ATTENDED (9)
Gen 39:4 in his sight and A him, and he made
1Sam 25:42 and her five maidens A her; she went after
1Chr 27:32 the son of Hachmoni A the king's sons.
2Chr 22:8 of Ahaziah's brothers, who A Ahaziah, and he killed
Esth 2:2 the king's servants who A him said, "Let beautiful
6:3 The king's servants who A him said, "Nothing has
Jer 23:2 and you have not A to them.
Mk 16:20 by the signs that A it.

A

2Cor 3:8 of the Spirit be A with greater splendor?

ATTENDING (6)

Num 3:28 eight thousand six hundred, A to the duties of
1Sam 4:20 her death the women A her said to her,
1Mac 16:14 of the country and A to their needs, and
Acts 2:46 And day by day, A the temple together and
24:22 should be prevented from A to his needs.
Rom 13:6 are ministers of God, A to this very thing.

ATTENTION (17)

Job 24:12 yet God pays no A to their prayer.
32:12 I gave you my A, and, behold, there was
Prov 8:5 simple ones, learn prudence; O foolish men, pay A
27:23 your flocks, and give A to your herds;
Sir 13:21 reproach him; he speaks sensibly, and receives no A
16:22 knowledge, and pay close A to my words.
37:11 task– pay no A to these in any
Jer 27:22 day when I give A to them, says the
1Mac 7:11 But they paid no A to their words, for
10:61 the king paid no A to them.
2Mac 4:6 that without the king's A public affairs could not
Acts 3:5 And he fixed his A upon them, expecting to
18:17 But Gallio paid no A to this.
27:11 the centurion paid more A to the captain and
Heb 2:1 must pay the closer A to what we have
Jas 2:3 in, and you pay A to the one who
2Pet 1:19 do well to pay A to this as to

ATTENTIVE (13)

2Chr 6:40 open and thy ears A to a prayer of
7:15 open and my ears A to the prayer that
Neh 1:6 let thy ear be A, and thy eyes open,
1:11 let thy ear be A to the prayer of
8:3 all the people were A to the book of
Ps 130:2 Let thy ears be A to the voice of
Prov 2:2 you, making your ear A to wisdom and inclining
4:2 father's instruction, and be A, that you may gain
4:21 My son, be A to my words; incline your
5:1 My son, be A to my wisdom, incline your
7:24 to me, and be A to the words of
Sir 3:27 a parable, and an A ear is the wise
25:9 he who speaks to A listeners.

ATTENTIVELY

Ex 23:22 "But if you hearken A to his voice and

ATTEST

Is 8:2 son of Jeberechiah, to A for me.

ATTESTED (5)

Acts 2:22 of Nazareth, a man A to you by God
1Tim 5:10 she must be well A for her good deeds,
Heb 2:3 Lord, and it was A to us by those
11:5 was taken he was A as having pleased God.
11:39 all these, though well A by their faith, did

ATTESTING

Ruth 4:7 was the manner of A in Israel.

ATTIRE (5)

Esth 15:1 had worshipped, and arrayed herself in splendid A
Sir 19:27 A man's A and open-mouthed laughter, and a man's
Jer 2:32 maiden forget her ornaments, or a bride her A
Zeph 1:8 sons and all who array themselves in foreign A
1Tim 2:9 or pearls or costly A

ATTRACTED

Wis 14:20 form, and the multitude, A by the charm of

ATTRACTIVE (3)

Sir 25:4 What an A thing is judgment in gray-haired men,
25:5 How A is wisdom in the aged, and understanding
Bar 6:43 she was not as A as herself and her

AUDIENCE

Acts 25:23 and they entered the A hall with the military

AUGMENTS

Prov 28:8 He who A his wealth by interest and increase

AUGUR

Deut 18:10 a soothsayer, or an A, or a sorcerer,

AUGURY (3)

Lev 19:26 You shall not practice A or witchcraft.
2Kgs 21:6 and practiced soothsaying and A, and dealt with
2Chr 33:6 and practiced soothsaying and A and sorcery, and

AUGUSTAN

Acts 27:1 a centurion of the A Cohort, named Julius.

AUGUSTUS

Lk 2:1 went out from Caesar A that all the world

AUNT

Lev 18:14 shall not approach his wife; she is your A

AURANUS

2Mac 4:40 leadership of a certain A, a man advanced in

AUSTERE

2Mac 14:30 that Nicanor was more A in his dealings with

AUSTERITY

2Mac 14:30 custom, concluded that this A did not spring from

AUTHENTIC

Wis 18:16 sharp sword of thy A command, and stood and

AUTHOR (2)

Wis 13:3 their Lord, for the A of beauty created them.
Acts 3:15 you, and killed the A of life, whom God

AUTHORITIES (12)

Lk 12:11 the rulers and the A, do not be anxious
Jn 7:26 it be that the A really know that this
7:48 Have any of the A or of the Pharisees
12:42 many even of the A believed in him, but
Acts 17:6 brethren before the city A, crying, "These men who
17:8 people and the city A were disturbed when they
Rom 13:1 Let every person be subject to the governing A
13:2 he who resists the A resists what God has
13:6 pay taxes, for the A are ministers of God,
Col 1:16 dominions or principalities or A –all things were
Tit 3:1 submissive to rulers and A, to be obedient, to
1Pet 3:22 of God, with angels, A, and powers subject to

AUTHORITY (103)

Gen 41:35 up grain under the A of Pharaoh for food
Num 5:19 were under your husband's A, be free from this
5:20 are under your husband's A, and if you have
5:29 though under her husband's A, goes astray and defiles
27:20 with some of your A, that all the congregation
2Chr 8:10 and fifty, who exercised A over the people.
28:7 Elkanah the next in A to the king.
Esth 9:29 Jew gave full written A, confirming this second letter
13:2 elated with presumption of A but always acting
16:5 set in places of A have been made in
16:7 of those who exercise A unworthily, can be seen
Prov 29:2 the righteous are in A, the people rejoice; but
29:16 the wicked are in A, transgression increases; but the
Eccl 8:8 retain the spirit, or A over the day of
Wis 10:14 of a kingdom and A over his masters.
14:21 misfortune or to royal A, bestowed on objects of
Sir 17:2 time, but granted them A over the things upon
30:11 Give him no A in his youth, and do
45:8 with the symbols of A, the linen breeches, the
45:17 commandments he gave him A and statutes and,
Is 22:21 and will commit your A to his hand; and
1Mac 6:28 the commanders of his forces and those in A
10:6 So Demetrius gave him A to recruit troops, to
10:8 king had given him A to recruit troops.
10:35 No one shall have A to exact anything from
10:38 and obey no other A but the high priest.
10:70 Why do you assume A against us in the
2Mac 3:24 spirits and of all A caused so great a
4:9 to establish by his A a gymnasium and a
4:24 with an air of A, and secured the high-priesthood
7:16 said, "Because you have A among men, mortal
15:13 hair and dignity, and of marvelous majesty and A
Mt 7:29 as one who had A, and not as their
8:9 am a man under A, with soldiers under me;
9:6 Son of man has A on earth to forgive
9:8 who had given such A to men.
10:1 disciples and gave them A over unclean spirits, to
20:25 their great men exercise A over them.
21:23 and said, "By what A are you doing these
21:23 doing these things, and who gave you this A
21:24 tell you by what A I do these things.
21:27 tell you by what A I do these things.
28:18 said to them, "All A in heaven and on

Mk 1:22 as one who had A, and not as the
1:27 With A he commands even the unclean spirits, and
2:10 Son of man has A on earth to forgive
3:15 to preach and have A to cast out demons:
6:7 two, and gave them A over the unclean spirits.
10:42 their great men exercise A over them.
11:27 to him, "By what A are you doing these
11:27 who gave you this A to do them?"
11:28 tell you by what A I do these things.
11:32 tell you by what A I do these things."
Lk 4:6 will give all this A and their glory; for
4:32 at his teaching, for his word was with A
4:36 For with A and power he commands the unclean
5:24 Son of man has A on earth to forgive
7:8 a man set under A, with soldiers under me:
9:1 gave them power and A over all demons and
10:19 I have given you A to tread upon serpents
19:17 little, you shall have A over ten cities.'
20:2 "Tell us by what A you do these things,
20:2 or who it is that gave you this A
20:8 tell you by what A I do these things."
20:20 him up to the A and jurisdiction of the
22:25 them; and those in A over them are called
Jn 5:26 and has given him A to execute judgment, because
5:29 nothing on my own A; as I hear, I
7:17 or whether I am speaking on my own A
7:18 speaks on his own A seeks his own glory;
8:28 nothing on my own A but speak thus as
12:49 spoken on my own A; the Father who sent
14:10 speak on my own A; but the Father who
16:13 speak on his own A, but whatever he hears
Acts 1:7 which the Father has fixed by his own A
9:14 and here he has A from the chief priests
25:5 "let the men of A among you go down
26:10 saints in prison, by A from the chief priests,
26:12 to Damascus with the A and commission of the
Rom 13:1 For there is no A except from God, and
13:3 have no fear of him who is in A
1Cor 9:8 Do I say this on human A
15:24 every rule and every A and power.
2Cor 10:8 too much of our A, which the Lord gave
11:17 not with the Lord's A but as a fool,
13:10 my use of the A which the Lord has
Eph 1:21 above all rule and A and power and dominion,
Col 2:10 who is the head of all rule and A
1Tim 2:12 teach or to have A over men; she is
Tit 2:15 Declare these things; exhort and reprove with all A
2Pet 2:10 in the lust of defiling passion and despise A
3 Jn 1:9 to put himself first, does not acknowledge my A
Jude 1:8 defile the flesh, reject A, and revile the glorious
1:25 glory, majesty, dominion, and A, before all time and
Rev 12:10 our God and the A of his Christ have
13:2 gave his power and his throne and great A
13:4 he had given his A to the beast, and
13:5 was allowed to exercise A for forty-two months;
13:7 And A was given it over every tribe and
13:12 It exercises all the A of the first beast
17:12 they are to receive A as kings for one
17:13 over their power and A to the beast;
18:1 from heaven, having great A; and the earth was

AUTHORIZED

1Mac 1:13 He A them to observe the ordinances of the

AUTUMN (4)

Job 29:4 I was in my A days, when the friendship
Prov 20:4 not plow in the A; he will seek at
Jer 5:24 in its season, the A rain and the spring
Jude 1:12 fruitless trees in late A, twice dead, uprooted;

AVAIL (11)

Esth 3:4 whether Mordecai's words would A; for he had told
Job 36:19 Will your cry A to keep you from distress,
41:26 him, it does not A; nor the spear, the
Ps 39:2 my peace to no A; my distress grew worse,
Prov 21:30 understanding, no counsel, can A against the LORD.
Wis 17:5 flames of the stars A to illumine that hateful
Jer 7:8 "Behold, you trust in deceptive words to no A
Dan 11:27 table, but to no A; for the end is
Jn 6:63 flesh is of no A; the words that I
1Cor 7:21 can gain your freedom, A yourself of the opportunity.
Gal 5:6 uncircumcision is of any A, but faith working through

AVARAN (2)

1Mac 2:5 Maccabeus, Eleazar called A, and Jonathan called
6:43 And Eleazar, called A, saw that one of the

AVEN (2)

Hos 10:8 The high places of A, the sin of Israel,
Amos 1:5 from the Valley of A, and him that holds

AVENGE (16)

Num 31:2 LORD said to Moses, A the people of Israel
1Sam 24:12 you, may the LORD A me upon you; but
2Kgs 9:7 master, that I may A on Jezebel the blood
2Chr 24:22 dying, he said, "May the LORD see and A
Esth 8:13 on that day to A themselves upon their enemies.
Is 1:24 on my enemies, and A myself on my foes.
Jer 5:9 and shall I not A myself on a nation
5:29 and shall I not A myself on a nation
9:9 and shall I not A myself on a nation
46:10 day of vengeance, to A himself on his foes.
Joel 3:21 I will A their blood, and I will not
1Mac 2:67 observe the law, and A the wrong done to
6:22 do justice and to A our brethren?
13:6 But I will A my nation and the sanctuary
Rom 12:19 Beloved, never A yourselves, but leave it to the
Rev 6:10 thou wilt judge and A our blood on those

AVENGED (13)

Gen 4:24 Cain is A sevenfold, truly Lamech seventy-sevenfold."
Judg 11:36 that the LORD has A you on your enemies,
15:7 swear I will be A upon you, and after
16:28 that I may be A upon the Philistines for
1Sam 14:24 evening and I am A on my enemies." So
18:25 that he may be A of the king's enemies."'
25:39 the LORD who has A the insult I received
2Sam 4:8 life; the LORD has A my lord the king
16:8 The LORD has A upon you all the blood
Jud 13:20 brought low, but have A our ruin, walking in
1Mac 9:42 when they had fully A the blood of their
Acts 7:24 the oppressed man and A him by striking the
Rev 19:2 fornication, and he has A on her the blood

AVENGER (18)

Num 35:12 a refuge from the A, that the manslayer may
35:19 The A of blood shall himself put the murderer
35:21 is a murderer; the A of blood shall put
35:24 the manslayer and the A of blood, in accordance
35:25 the hand of the A of blood, and the
35:27 he fled, and the A of blood finds him
35:27 of refuge, and the A of blood slays the
Deut 19:6 his life; lest the A of blood in hot
19:12 him over to the A of blood, so that
Josh 20:3 a refuge from the A of blood.
20:5 And if the A of blood pursues him, they
20:9 the hand of the A of blood, till he
2Sam 14:11 your God, that the A of blood slay no
Ps 8:2 thy foes, to still the enemy and the A
44:16 at the sight of the enemy and the A
99:8 to them, but an A of their wrongdoings.
Sir 30:6 left behind him an A against his enemies, and
1Thes 4:6 the Lord is an A in all these things,

AVENGES (2)

Deut 32:43 you nations; for he A the blood of his
Ps 9:12 For he who A blood is mindful of them;

AVENGING (5)

1Sam 25:33 from bloodguilt and from A myself with my own
1Kgs 2:5 Jether, whom he murdered, A in time of peace
Ps 79:10 Let the A of the outpoured blood of thy
Nah 1:2 a jealous God and A, the LORD is avenging
1:2 avenging, the LORD is A and wrathful; the LORD

AVERT (5)

Esth 8:3 him with tears to A the evil design of
Sir 4:5 Do not A your eye from the needy, nor
20:28 on the mouth they A reproofs.
27:1 to get rich will A his eyes.
Jer 11:15 vows and sacrificial flesh A your doom?

AVERTED (4)

2Sam 24:21 the plague may be A from the people."
24:25 and the plague was A from Israel.
1Chr 21:22 the plague may be A from the people."
Ezra 10:14 over this matter be A from us."

AVERTS (2)

Prov 21:14 A gift in secret A anger; and a bribe
Sir 14:8 a grudging eye; he A his face and disregards

AVITH (2)
Gen 36:35 his stead, the name of his city being A
1Chr 1:46 stead; and the name of his city was A

AVOID (16)
Prov 4:16 A it; do not go on it; turn away
13:14 life, that one may A the snares of death.
14:27 life, that one may A the snares of death.
15:24 life, that he may A Sheol beneath.
Sir 22:11 he shakes himself off; A him and you will
37:31 who is careful to A it prolongs his life.
38:17 day, or two, to A criticism; then be comforted
2Mac 6:26 the present I should A the punishment of men,
Rom 13:5 subject, not only to A God's wrath but also
16:17 you have been taught; A them.
1Tim 6:20 A the godless chatter and contradictions of what is
2Tim 2:14 before the Lord to A disputing about words, which
2:16 A such godless chatter, for it will lead people
3:5 A such people.
Tit 3:2 of no one, to A quarreling, to be gentle,
3:9 But A stupid controversies, genealogies, dissensions,

AVOIDED (3)
2Chr 20:10 Egypt, and whom they A and did not destroy—
Ps 17:4 thy lips I have A the ways of the
Wis 17:10 at the air, though it nowhere could be A

AVOIDS (2)
Prov 16:6 the LORD a man A evil.
Wis 2:16 something base, and he A our ways as unclean;

AVVA
2Kgs 17:24 people from Babylon, Cuthah, A, Hamath, and

AVVIM (3)
Deut 2:23 As for the A, who lived in villages as
Josh 13:3 and those of the A,
18:23 Beth-arabah, Zemaraim, Bethel, A, Parah, Ophrah,

AVVITES
2Kgs 17:31 made Ashima, and the A made Nibhaz and Tartak;

AWAIT (3)
Sir 16:20 Or who will A them?
Acts 20:23 that imprisonment and afflictions A me.
Phil 3:20 and from it we A a Savior, the Lord

AWAITING (2)
Jer 3:2 waysides you have sat A lovers like an Arab
Tit 2:13 lives in this world, A our blessed hope, the

AWAITS
Hab 2:3 For still the vision A its time; it hastens

AWAKE (44)
Judg 5:12 A, awake, Deborah!
5:12 "Awake, A, Deborah!
5:12 A, awake, utter a song!
5:12 Awake, A, utter a song!
1Sam 26:12 it, nor did any A; for they were all
Job 14:12 more he will not A, or be roused out
Ps 7:6 fury of my enemies; A, O my God; thou
17:15 in righteousness; when I A, I shall be satisfied
35:23 Bestir thyself, and A for my right, for my
44:23 A! Do not cast us off forever!
57:8 A, my soul!
57:8 A, O harp and lyre!
57:8 I will A the dawn!
59:5 A to punish all the nations; spare none of
102:7 waste places; I lie A, I am like a
108:1 A, my soul!
108:2 A, O harp and lyre!
108:2 I will A the dawn!
119:148 My eyes are A before the watches of the
127:1 city, the watchman stays A in vain.
139:18 When I A, I am still with thee.
Prov 6:22 you; and when you A, they will talk with
23:35 When shall I A
Song 4:16 A, O north wind, and come, O south wind!
5:2 I slept, but my heart was A
Is 26:19 dwellers in the dust, A and sing for joy!
51:9 A, awake, put on strength, O arm of the
51:9 Awake, A, put on strength, O arm of the
51:9 arm of the LORD; A, as in days of
52:1 A, awake, put on your strength, O Zion; put
52:1 Awake, A, put on your strength, O Zion; put
Dan 12:2 of the earth shall A, some to everlasting life,
Joel 1:5 A, you drunkards, and weep; and wail, all you
Hab 2:7 suddenly arise, and those A who will make you
2:19 to a wooden thing, A; to a dumb stone,
Zech 13:7 A, O sword, against my shepherd, against the man
Lk 12:37 whom the master finds A when he comes; truly,
12:39 he would have been A and would not have
Jn 11:11 but I go to A him out of sleep."
Eph 5:14 Therefore it is said, A, O sleeper, and arise
1Thes 5:6 but let us keep A and be sober.
Rev 3:2 A, and strengthen what remains and is on the
3:3 If you will not A, I will come like
16:15 is he who is A, keeping his garments that

AWAKED
2Kgs 4:31 him, and told him, "The child has not A

AWAKEN (3)
Song 2:7 stir not up nor A love until it please.
3:5 stir not up nor A love until it please.
8:4 stir not up nor A love until it please.

AWAKENED (3)
1Kgs 18:27 or perhaps he is asleep and must be A
Song 8:5 the apple tree I A you.
Ezek 7:6 has come; it has A against you.

AWAKES (3)
Ps 73:20 a dream when one A, on awaking you despise
Is 29:8 he is eating and A with his hunger not
29:8 he is drinking and A faint, with his thirst

AWAKING (2)
Ps 73:20 when one awakes, on A you despise their phantoms.
2Mac 15:17 in arousing valor and A manliness in the souls

AWARD
2Tim 4:8 the righteous judge, will A to me on that

AWARE (14)
Tob 11:2 Tobias, "Are you not A, brother, of how you
Song 6:12 Before I was A, my fancy set me in
Sir 21:7 when he slips, is A of it.
Dan 13:42 is secret, who art A of all things before
2Mac 4:33 When Onias became fully A of these acts he
4:41 when the Jews became A of Lysimachus' attack,
14:31 When the latter became A that he had been
Mt 12:15 Jesus, A of this, withdrew from there.
16:8 But Jesus, A of this, said, "O men of
22:18 But Jesus, A of their malice, said, "Why put
26:10 But Jesus, A of this, said to them, "Why
Mk 8:17 And being A of it, Jesus said to them,
1Cor 4:4 I am not A of anything against myself, but
2Tim 1:15 You are A that all who are in Asia

AWAY (933)
Gen 4:14 driven me this day A from the ground; and
4:16 Then Cain went A from the presence of the
9:23 their faces were turned A, and they did not
15:11 came down upon the carcasses, Abram drove them A
21:14 shoulder, along with the child, and sent her A
24:59 So they sent A Rebekah their sister and her
25:6 living he sent them A from his son Isaac,
26:16 said to Isaac, "Go A from us; for you
26:27 and have sent me A from you?"
26:29 and have sent you A in peace.
27:35 and he has taken A your blessing."
27:36 He took A my birthright; and behold, now he
27:36 now he has taken A my blessing." Then he
27:39 father answered him: "Behold, A from the fatness of
27:39 your dwelling be, and A from the dew of
27:44 your brother's fury turns A;
27:45 your brother's anger turns A, and he forgets what
28:5 Thus Isaac sent Jacob A; and he went to
28:6 Jacob and sent him A to Paddan-aram to take
30:15 that you have taken A my husband?
30:15 Would you take A my son's mandrakes also?" Rachel
30:23 said, "God has taken A my reproach";
30:25 to Laban, "Send me A, that I may go
31:9 Thus God has taken A the cattle of your
31:16 which God has taken A from our father belongs
31:18 camels; and he drove A all his cattle, all
31:26 cheated me, and carried A my daughters like
31:27 might have sent you A with mirth and songs,
31:30 now you have gone A because you longed greatly
31:42 would have sent me A empty-handed.

	34:26	took Dinah out of Shechem's house, and went A
	35:2	were with him, "Put A the foreign gods that
	36:6	went into a land A from his brother Jacob.
	37:17	said, "They have gone A, for I heard them
	38:19	she arose and went A, and taking off her
	42:24	Then he turned A from them and wept; and
	45:24	he sent his brothers A, and as they departed,
Ex	2:9	her, "Take this child A, and nurse him for
	2:17	came and drove them A; but Moses stood up
	5:4	you take the people A from their work?
	8:8	the LORD to take A the frogs from me
	8:28	wilderness; only you shall not go very far A
	10:28	said to him, "Get A from me; take heed
	11:1	he will drive you A completely.
	12:15	day you shall put A leaven out of your
	14:11	you have taken us A to die in the
	15:15	them; all the inhabitants of Canaan have melted A
	18:2	he had sent her A,
	22:10	hurt or is driven A, without any one seeing
	23:25	I will take sickness A from the midst of
	33:23	then I will take A my hand, and you
Lev	1:16	and he shall take A its crop with the
	3:4	which he shall take A with the kidneys.
	3:9	tail entire, taking it A close by the backbone,
	3:10	which he shall take A with the kidneys.
	3:15	which he shall take A with the kidneys.
	4:9	which he shall take A with the kidneys
	7:4	which he shall take A with the kidneys;
	16:10	it may be sent A into the wilderness to
	16:21	goat, and send him A into the wilderness by
	22:2	his sons to keep A from the holy things
	26:16	waste the eyes and cause life to pine A
	26:39	are left shall pine A in your enemies' lands
	26:39	fathers they shall pine A like them.
Num	4:13	And they shall take A the ashes from the
	5:21	makes your thigh fall A and your body swell;
	5:22	and your thigh fall A And the woman shall
	5:27	her thigh shall fall A, and the woman shall
	16:24	to the congregation, Get A from about the dwelling
	16:26	lest you be swept A with all their sins."
	16:27	So they got A from about the dwelling of
	16:45	said to Moses, "Get A from the midst of
	20:21	territory; so Israel turned A from him.
	21:7	LORD, that he take A the serpents from us."
	24:22	shall Asshur take you A captive?"
	25:4	the LORD may turn A from Israel."
	27:4	our father be taken A from his family, because
	32:15	For if you turn A from following him, he
	36:3	it will be taken A from the lot of
Deut	2:8	So we went on, A from our brethren the
	2:8	who live in Seir, A from the Arabah road
	4:19	heaven, you be drawn A and worship them and
	7:1	of it, and clears A many nations before you,
	7:4	For they would turn A your sons from following
	7:15	the LORD will take A from you all sickness;
	7:22	your God will clear A these nations before you
	13:10	sought to draw you A from the LORD your
	13:13	you and have drawn A the inhabitants of the
	17:17	lest his heart turn A; nor shall he greatly
	22:19	may not put her A all his days.
	22:29	may not put her A all his days.
	23:14	among you, and turn A from you.
	24:4	husband, who sent her A, may not take her
	28:26	there shall be no one to frighten them A
	28:31	shall be violently taken A before your face, and
	28:37	the peoples where the LORD will lead you A
	29:18	tribe, whose heart turns A this day from the
	29:19	lead to the sweeping A of moist and dry
	30:17	if your heart turns A, and you will not
	30:17	hear, but are drawn A to worship other gods
Josh	2:9	of the land melt A before you.
	2:21	Then she sent them A, and they departed; and
	5:9	day I have rolled A the reproach of Egypt
	7:13	enemies, until you take A the devoted things from
	8:6	we have drawn them A from the city; for
	8:16	Joshua they were drawn A from the city.
	22:6	them, and sent them A; and they went to
	22:7	when Joshua sent them A to their homes and
	22:16	of Israel in turning A this day from following
	22:18	that you must turn A this day from following
	22:23	an altar to turn A from following the LORD;
	22:29	the LORD, and turn A this day from following
	24:14	and in faithfulness; put A the gods which your
	24:23	He said, "Then put A the foreign gods which
	24:28	Joshua sent the people A, every man to his
Judg	3:18	the tribute, he sent A the people that carried
	4:11	his tent as far A as the oak in
	4:15	his chariot and fled A on foot.
	4:17	But Sisera fled A on foot to the tent
	5:12	Arise, Barak, lead A your captives, O son of
	5:21	torrent Kishon swept them A, the onrushing torrent,
	9:21	And Jotham ran A and fled, and went to
	10:16	So they put A the foreign gods from among
	11:13	coming from Egypt took A my land, from the
	11:15	Israel did not take A the land of Moab
	11:38	And he sent her A for two months; and
	15:17	finished speaking, he threw A the jawbone out of
	16:14	his sleep, and pulled A the pin, the loom,
	18:24	the priest, and go A, and what have I
	19:2	him, and she went A from him to her
	19:28	rose up and went A to his home.
	20:13	to death, and put A evil from Israel." But
	20:31	people, and were drawn A from the city; and
	20:32	flee, and draw them A from the city to
Ruth	1:21	I went A full, and the LORD has brought
1Sam	1:14	Put A your wine from you."
	5:11	Philistines, and said, "Send A the ark of the
	6:3	said, "If you send A the ark of the
	6:3	hand does not turn A from you."
	6:7	take their calves home, A from them.
	6:20	shall he go up A from us?"
	7:3	your heart, then put A the foreign gods and
	7:4	So Israel put A the Baals and the Ashtaroth,
	10:25	sent all the people A, each one to his
	12:22	LORD will not cast A his people, for his
	12:25	you shall be swept A, both you and your
	15:27	Samuel turned to go A, Saul laid hold upon
	17:26	this Philistine, and takes A the reproach from Israel?
	17:30	And he turned A from him toward another, and
	19:12	window; and he fled A and escaped.
	20:13	you, and send you A, that you may go
	20:22	then go; for the LORD has sent you A
	20:29	eyes, let me get A, and see my brothers.'
	21:6	hot bread on the day it is taken A
	23:5	the Philistines, and brought A their cattle, and made
	23:26	making haste to get A from Saul, as Saul
	24:19	he let him go A safe?
	25:10	nowadays who are breaking A from their masters.
	25:12	David's young men turned A, and came back and
	26:12	of water from Saul's head; and they went A
	26:20	fall to the earth A from the presence of
	27:9	woman alive, but took A the sheep, the oxen,
	28:15	and God has turned A from me and answers
	28:25	they rose and went A that night.
	30:22	each man may lead A his wife and children,
2Sam	3:21	So David sent Abner A; and he went in
	3:22	he had sent him A, and he had gone
	3:24	you have sent him A, so that he is
	5:21	there, and David and his men carried them A
	7:15	Saul, whom I put A from before you.
	10:4	the middle, at their hips, and sent them A
	12:13	LORD also has put A your sin; you shall
	13:16	wrong in sending me A is greater than the
	13:19	her head, and went A, crying aloud as she
	14:14	God will not take A the life of him
	17:18	both of them went A quickly, and came to
	19:41	of Judah stolen you A, and brought the king
	23:6	thorns that are thrown A; for they cannot be
	24:10	I pray thee, take A the iniquity of thy
1Kgs	2:31	him; and thus take A from me and from
	2:39	of Shimei's slaves ran A to Achish, son of
	8:46	that they are carried A captive to the land
	8:66	he sent the people A; and they blessed the
	11:2	surely they will turn A your heart after their
	11:3	and his wives turned A his heart.
	11:4	old his wives turned A his heart after other
	11:9	his heart had turned A from the LORD, the
	11:13	I will not tear A all the kingdom; but
	12:5	So the people went A
	13:24	And as he went A a lion met him
	14:8	and tore the kingdom A from the house of
	14:26	against Jerusalem; he took A the treasures of the
	14:26	king's house; he took A everything.
	14:26	He also took A all the shields of gold
	15:12	He put A the male cult prostitutes out of
	15:14	But the high places were not taken A
	15:22	exempt, and they carried A the stones of Ramah
	16:3	I will utterly sweep A Baasha and his house,
	19:4	now, O LORD, take A my life; for I
	19:10	and they seek my life, to take it A
	19:14	and they seek my life, to take it A
	20:6	hands on whatever pleases them, and take it A

A

20:41 to take the bandage A from his eyes; and
21:4 his bed, and turned A his face, and would
21:21 will utterly sweep you A, and will cut off
22:43 places were not taken A, and the people still
2Kgs 2:3 the LORD will take A your master from over
2:5 the LORD will take A your master from over
3:2 mother, for he put A the pillar of Baal
4:27 And Gehazi came to thrust her A
5:11 was angry, and went A, saying, "Behold, I thought
5:12 he turned and went A in a rage.
5:24 he sent the men A, and they departed.
6:23 drunk, he sent them A, and they went to
7:7 So they fled A in the twilight and forsook
7:15 the Syrians had thrown A in their haste.
11:2 Ahaziah, and stole him A from among the king's
12:3 places were not taken A; the people continued to
12:18 Then Hazael went A from Jerusalem.
15:4 places were not taken A; the people still sacrificed
15:24 he did not turn A from the sins of
17:6 he carried the Israelites A to Assyria, and placed
17:11 whom the LORD carried A before them.
17:26 which you have carried A and placed in the
17:27 priests whom you carried A thence; and let him
17:28 whom they had carried A from Samaria came and
17:33 nations from among whom they had been carried A
18:11 Assyria carried the Israelites A to Assyria, and put
18:32 come and take you A to a land like
20:18 you, shall be taken A; and they shall be
23:24 Moreover Josiah put A the mediums and the wizards
23:34 But he took Jehoahaz A; and he came to
24:14 He carried A all Jerusalem, and all the princes,
24:15 And he carried A Jehoiachin to Babylon; the king's
25:14 And they took A the pots, and the shovels,
25:15 of the guard took A as gold, and what
1Chr 5:6 king of Assyria carried A into exile; he was
5:26 and he carried them A, namely, the Reubenites, the
8:8 after he had sent A Hushim and Baara his
10:12 men arose, and took A the body of Saul
12:19 counsel and sent him A, saying, "At peril to
19:4 hips, and sent them A;
21:8 I pray thee, take A the iniquity of thy
2Chr 6:36 that they are carried A captive to a land
6:42 God, do not turn A the face of thy
7:10 he sent the people A to their homes, joyful
10:5 So the people went A
12:9 against Jerusalem; he took A the treasures of the
12:9 king's house; he took A everything.
12:9 He also took A the shields of gold which
14:3 He took A the foreign altars and the high
14:13 men of Judah carried A very much booty.
14:15 had cattle, and carried A sheep in abundance and
15:8 took courage, and put A the abominable idols from
16:6 Judah, and they carried A the stones of Ramah
18:31 God drew them A from him,
20:33 however, were not taken A; the people had not
21:17 invaded it, and carried A all the possessions they
22:11 Ahaziah, and stole him A from among the king's
25:27 time when he turned A from the LORD they
28:17 defeated Judah, and carried A captives.
29:6 him, and have turned A their faces from the
29:10 fierce anger may turn A from us.
30:8 fierce anger may turn A from you.
30:9 and will not turn A his face from you,
30:14 burning incense they took A and threw into the
32:12 this same Hezekiah taken A his high places and
33:15 And he took A the foreign gods and the
34:33 And Josiah took A all the abominations from all
34:33 they did not turn A from following the LORD
35:22 Josiah would not turn A from him, but disguised
35:23 his servants, "Take me A, for I am badly
Ezra 1:7 Nebuchadnezzar had carried A from Jerusalem and
5:12 this house and carried A the people to Babylonia.
6:6 Beyond the River, keep A;
10:3 our God to put A all these wives and
10:19 pledged themselves to put A their wives, and their
10:44 and they put them A with their children.
Tob 1:10 when I was carried A captive to Nineveh, all
2:8 this; he once ran A, and here he is
3:6 not turn thy face A from me."
3:17 of them: to scale A the white films of
4:7 not turn your face A from any poor man,
4:7 will not be turned A from you.
5:17 to Tobit, "Why have you sent our child A
6:4 gall and put them A safely."
6:17 smell it and flee A, and will never again
10:11 them he sent them A, saying, "The God of
11:8 white films to fall A, and he will see
12:9 and it will purge A every sin.
Jud 2:9 I will lead them A captive to the ends
5:18 battles and were led A captive to a foreign
7:14 and children will waste A with famine, and before
Esth 2:6 who had been carried A from Jerusalem among the
2:6 among the captives carried A with Jeconiah king of
2:6 Nebuchadnezzar king of Babylon had carried A
4:17 Mordecai then went A and did everything as Esther
16:4 They not only take A thankfulness from among men,
16:4 among men, but, carried A by the boasts of
Job 1:1 feared God, and turned A from evil.
1:8 fears God and turns A from evil?"
1:21 the LORD has taken A; blessed be the name
2:3 fears God and turns A from evil?
6:15 as freshets that pass A,
7:19 wilt thou not look A from me, nor let
7:21 my transgression and take A my iniquity?
9:12 Behold, he snatches A; who can hinder him?
9:25 a runner; they flee A, they see no good.
9:34 him take his rod A from me, and let
11:14 hand, put it far A, and let not wickedness
11:16 will remember it as waters that have passed A
12:17 He leads counselors A stripped, and judges he makes
12:19 He leads priests A stripped, and overthrows the
12:20 are trusted, and takes A the discernment of the
12:23 destroys them: he enlarges nations, and leads them A
12:24 He takes A understanding from the chiefs of the
13:28 Man wastes A like a rotten thing, like a
14:6 he cannot pass, look A from him, and desist,
14:11 and a river wastes A and dries up,
14:18 mountain falls and crumbles A, and the rock is
14:19 place; the waters wear A the stones; the torrents
14:19 stones; the torrents wash A the soil of the
14:20 thou changest his countenance, and sendest him A
15:4 But you are doing A with the fear of
15:12 your heart carry you A, and why do your
15:30 blossom will be swept A by the wind.
20:8 he?' He will fly A like a dream, and
20:8 he will be chased A like a vision of
20:28 house will be carried A, dragged off in the
21:18 wind, and like chaff that the storm carries A
22:9 You have sent widows A empty, and the arms
22:16 They were snatched A before their time; their
22:16 before their time; their foundation was washed A
24:3 They drive A the ass of the fatherless; they
24:18 "They are swiftly carried A upon the face of
24:19 Drought and heat snatch A the snow waters; so
27:2 lives, who has taken A my right, and the
27:5 I will not put A my integrity from me.
27:8 off, when God takes A his life?
28:4 shafts in a valley A from where men live;
30:15 my prosperity has passed A like a cloud.
33:21 flesh is so wasted A that it cannot be
34:5 and God has taken A my right;
34:20 are shaken and pass A, and the mighty are
34:20 the mighty are taken A by no human hand.
Ps 1:4 but are like chaff which the wind drives A
6:7 My eye wastes A because of grief, it grows
7:2 rend me, dragging me A, with none to rescue.
18:22 I did not put A from me.
26:9 Sweep me not A with sinners, nor my life
27:9 Turn not thy servant A in anger, thou who
31:10 because of my misery, and my bones waste A
32:3 sin, my body wasted A through my groaning all
36:11 nor the hand of the wicked drive me A
37:20 the pastures, they vanish—like smoke they vanish A
39:13 Look A from me, that I may know gladness,
40:14 who seek to snatch A my life; let them
49:14 their form shall waste A; Sheol shall be their
49:17 he will carry nothing A; his glory will not
51:11 Cast me not A from thy presence, and take
53:3 They have all fallen A; they are all alike
55:6 I would fly A and be at rest;
55:15 alive; let them go A in terror into their
58:7 like water that runs A; like grass let them
58:9 whether green or ablaze, may he sweep them A
68:2 As smoke is driven A, so drive them away;
68:2 away, so drive them A; as wax melts before
73:19 in a moment, swept A utterly by terrors!
78:57 his testimonies, but turned A and acted treacherously
85:4 our salvation, and put A thy indignation toward us!
90:5 Thou dost sweep men A; they are like a
90:9 all our days pass A under thy wrath, our
90:10 trouble; they are soon gone, and we fly A
101:3 of those who fall A; it shall not cleave

AWAY

102:3 For my days pass A like smoke, and my
102:10 thou hast taken me up and thrown me A
102:11 evening shadow; I wither A like grass.
102:26 raiment, and they pass A;
104:22 rises, they get them A and lie down in
104:29 dismayed; when thou takest A their breath, they die
106:23 before him, to turn A his wrath from destroying
107:26 depths; their courage melted A in their evil plight;
112:10 his teeth and melts A; the desire of the
119:22 from thy commandments; take A from me their
119:28 My soul melts A for sorrow; strengthen me according
119:39 Turn A the reproach which I dread; for thy
119:51 I do not turn A from thy law.
124:4 would have swept us A, the torrent would have
125:5 the LORD will lead A with evildoers!
132:10 sake do not turn A the face of thy
Prov 1:19 by violence; it takes A the life of its
1:32 killed by their turning A, and the complacence of
3:7 the LORD, and turn A from evil.
4:6 and do not turn A from the words of
4:16 go on it; turn A from it and pass
4:25 Put A from you crooked speech, and put devious
4:28 left; turn your foot A from evil.
6:33 get, and his disgrace will not be wiped A
11:30 life, but lawlessness takes A lives.
12:26 A righteous man turns A from evil, but the
13:19 soul; but to turn A from evil is an
13:23 but it is swept A through injustice.
14:16 is cautious and turns A from evil, but a
15:1 A soft answer turns A wrath, but a harsh
19:26 his father and chases A his mother is a
20:14 but when he goes A, then he boasts.
20:30 Blows that wound cleanse A evil; strokes make clean
21:7 wicked will sweep them A, because they refuse to
24:11 who are being taken A to death; hold back
24:18 be displeased, and turn A his anger from him.
25:4 Take A the dross from the silver, and the
25:5 for a vessel; take A the wicked from the
27:10 is near than a brother who is far A
28:9 If one turns A his ear from hearing the
29:8 but wise men turn A wrath.
Eccl 3:5 a time to cast A stones, and a time
3:6 a time to cast A;
3:15 been; and God seeks what has been driven A
5:8 and right violently taken A, do not be amazed
5:15 which he may carry A in his hand.
11:10 your mind, and put A pain from your body;
Song 2:10 fair one, and come A;
2:13 Arise, my love, my fair one, and come A
5:7 wounded me, they took A my mantle, those
6:5 Turn A your eyes from me, for they disturb
Wis 1:16 a friend, they pined A, and they made a
2:4 our life will pass A like the traces of
5:14 a light hoarfrost driven A by a storm; it
5:23 and like a tempest it will winnow them A
14:17 imagined their appearance far A, and made a visible
16:29 wintry frost, and flow A like waste water.
18:5 didst in punishment take A a multitude of their
Sir 3:15 frost in fair weather, your sins will melt A
4:4 nor turn your face A from the poor.
7:2 Stay A from wrong, and it will turn away
7:2 and it will turn A from you.
8:5 man who is turning A from sin; remember that
8:19 one, lest you drive A your good luck.
9:8 Turn A your eyes from a shapely woman, and
13:20 he is even pushed A by friends.
14:19 made it will pass A with it.
17:21 Most High and turn A from iniquity, and hate
18:23 vengeance when he turns A his face.
19:3 him, and the reckless soul will be snatched A
22:18 at birds scares them A, and one who reviles
28:15 Slander has driven A courageous women, and
29:9 do not send him A empty.
31:1 Wakefulness over wealth wastes A one's flesh, and
33:31 he leaves and runs A, which way will you
34:22 To take A a neighbor's living is to murder
35:18 nations; till he takes A the multitude of the
38:7 he heals and takes A pain;
38:20 to sorrow; drive it A, remembering the end of
38:28 flesh, and he wastes A in the heat of
41:21 a kinsman; of taking A some one's portion or
42:21 be added or taken A, and he needs no
45:23 when the people turned A, in the ready goodness
46:11 who did not turn A from the Lord--
47:4 a giant, and take A reproach from the people,
47:11 The Lord took A his sins, and exalted his

48:15 till they were carried A captive from their land
49:2 the people, and took A the abominations of iniquity.
Is 1:25 you and will smelt A your dross as with
2:18 And the idols shall utterly pass A
2:22 Turn A from man in whose nostrils is breath,
3:1 of hosts, is taking A from Jerusalem and from
3:18 the Lord will take A the finery of the
4:1 by your name; take A our reproach."
4:4 Lord shall have washed A the filth of the
5:25 anger is not turned A and his hand is
6:7 your guilt is taken A, and your sin forgiven."
6:12 LORD removes men far A, and the forsaken places
7:20 and it will sweep A the beard also.
8:4 Samaria will be carried A before the king of
9:12 anger is not turned A and his hand is
9:17 anger is not turned A and his hand is
9:21 anger is not turned A and his hand is
10:4 anger is not turned A and his hand is
10:18 will be as when a sick man wastes A
12:1 me, thy anger turned A, and thou didst comfort
14:19 you are cast out, A from your sepulchre, like
15:7 laid up they carry A over the Brook of
16:10 and gladness are taken A from the fruitful field;
17:11 the harvest will flee A in a day of
17:13 they will flee far A, chased like chaff on
18:5 hooks, and the spreading branches he will hew A
19:6 and dry up, reeds and rushes will rot A
19:7 dry up, be driven A, and be no more.
20:4 king of Assyria lead A the Egyptians captives and
22:3 found were captured, though they had fled far A
22:4 Therefore I said: "Look A from me, let me
22:8 He has taken A the covering of Judah.
22:17 LORD will hurl you A violently, O you strong
24:16 I say, "I pine A, I pine away.
24:16 But I say, "I pine away, I pine A
25:8 Lord GOD will wipe A tears from all faces,
25:8 people he will take A from all the earth;
28:17 and hail will sweep A the refuge of lies,
30:16 therefore you shall speed A; and, "We will ride
31:7 every one shall cast A his idols of silver
31:9 His rock shall pass A in terror, and his
33:9 is confounded and withers A; Sharon is like a
34:4 of heaven shall rot A, and the skies roll
35:10 and gladness, and sorrow and sighing shall flee A
36:17 come and take you A to a land like
39:7 you, shall be taken A; and they shall be
41:16 wind shall carry them A, and the tempest shall
44:22 I have swept A your transgressions like a cloud,
49:2 polished arrow, in his quiver he hid me A
49:19 those who swallowed you up will be far A
49:21 barren, exiled and put A, but who has brought
50:1 bill of divorce, with which I put her A
50:1 and for your transgressions your mother was put A
51:11 and gladness, and sorrow and sighing shall flee A
52:5 my people are taken A for nothing?
53:8 judgment he was taken A; and as for his
57:1 devout men are taken A, while no one understands.
57:1 righteous man is taken A from calamity,
57:13 carry them off, a breath will take them A
58:9 "If you take A from the midst of you
59:13 the LORD, and turning A from following our God,
64:6 and our iniquities, like the wind, take us A
Jer 1:13 a boiling pot, facing A from the north."
2:37 too you will come A with your hands upon
3:8 I had sent her A with a decree of
5:10 a full end; strip A her branches, for they
5:23 rebellious heart; they have turned aside and gone A
5:25 iniquities have turned these A, and your sins have
7:29 hair and cast it A; raise a lamentation on
7:33 of the earth; and none will frighten them A
8:4 If one turns A, does he not return?
8:5 has this people turned A in perpetual backsliding?
8:13 gave them has passed A from them."
9:2 my people and go A from them!
12:4 the birds are swept A, because men said, "He
15:9 languished; she has swooned A; her sun went down
15:15 forbearance take me not A; know that for thy
16:5 for I have taken A my peace from this
17:5 arm, whose heart turns A from the LORD.
17:13 shame; those who turn A from thee shall be
18:20 for them, to turn A thy wrath from them.
22:10 for him who goes A, for he shall return
22:11 father, and who went A from this place: "He
23:2 and have driven them A, and you have not
23:39 up and cast you A from my presence, you
24:5 whom I have sent A from this place to

A

27:20 Babylon did not take A, when he took into
28:3 king of Babylon took A from this place and
29:20 exiles whom I sent A from Jerusalem to Babylon:
31:19 after I had turned A I repented; and after
32:40 I will not turn A from doing good to
37:9 Chaldeans will surely stay A from us," for they
37:9 for they will not stay A
38:22 the mire, they turn A from you.'
41:14 whom Ishmael had carried A captive from Mizpah
41:16 of Nethaniah had carried A captive from Mizpah
43:12 them and carry them A captive; and he shall
43:12 and he shall go A from there in peace.
46:6 The swift cannot flee A, nor the warrior escape;
46:22 like a serpent gliding A; for her enemies march
48:9 for she would fly A; her cities shall become
48:33 joy have been taken A from the fruitful land
49:19 suddenly make them run A from her; and I
49:20 flock shall be dragged A; surely their fold shall
49:29 camels shall be borne A from them, and men
49:30 side!' Flee, wander far A, dwell in the depths,
50:3 in it; both man and beast shall flee A
50:6 them astray, turning them A on the mountains; from
50:17 a hunted sheep driven A by lions.
50:44 suddenly make them run A from her; and I
50:45 flock shall be dragged A; surely their fold shall
51:39 drunk, till they swoon A and sleep a perpetual
52:15 of the guard carried A captive some of the
52:18 And they took A the pots, and the shovels,
52:19 of the guard took A as gold, and what
52:28 Nebuchadrezzar carried A captive: in the seventh
52:29 he carried A captive from Jerusalem
52:30 of the guard carried A captive of the Jews
Lam 1:4 maidens have been dragged A, and she herself
1:5 her children have gone A, captives before the foe.
1:8 yea, she herself groans, and turns her face A
3:4 and my skin waste A, and broken my bones;
4:9 of hunger, who pined A, stricken by want of
4:15 A! Unclean
4:15 men cried at them; A! A! touch them not.
Bar 1:8 which had been carried A from the temple, to
1:9 of Babylon had carried A from Jerusalem Jeconiah
1:13 wrath have not turned A from us.
2:8 the Lord by turning A, each of us, from
2:13 Let thy anger turn A from us, for we
3:7 for we have put A from our hearts all
4:11 but I sent them A with weeping and sorrow.
4:12 children, because they turned A from the law of
4:16 They led A the widow's beloved sons, and bereaved
4:26 roads; they were taken A like a flock carried
4:34 And I will take A her pride in her
4:37 coming, whom you sent A; they are coming, gathered
5:6 you on foot, led A by their enemies; but
6:3 I will bring you A from there in peace.
Ezek 3:14 up and took me A, and I went in
4:17 in dismay, and waste A under their punishment.
14:6 GOD: Repent and turn A from your idols; and
14:6 your idols; and turn A your faces from all
17:10 wind strikes it--wither A on the bed where
17:13 land he had taken A,
18:21 a wicked man turns A from all his sins
18:24 a righteous man turns A from his righteousness and
18:26 a righteous man turns A from his righteousness and
18:27 a wicked man turns A from the wickedness he
18:28 he considered and turned A from all the
18:31 Cast A from you all the transgressions which you
20:7 said to them, Cast A the detestable things your
20:8 not every man cast A the detestable things their
23:26 your clothes and take A your fine jewels.
23:29 in hatred, and take A all the fruit of
24:16 delight of your eyes A from you at a
24:23 but you shall pine A in your iniquities and
30:4 her wealth is carried A, and her foundations are
33:4 comes and takes him A, his blood shall be
33:6 that man is taken A in his iniquity, but
33:10 us, and we waste A because of them; how
38:13 off plunder, to carry A silver and gold, to
38:13 and gold, to take A cattle and goods, to
42:5 the galleries took more A from them than from
43:9 Now let them put A their idolatry and the
45:9 Put A violence and oppression, and execute justice
Dan 1:16 So the steward took A their rich food and
2:35 the wind carried them A, so that not a
7:12 their dominion was taken A, but their lives were
7:14 which shall not pass A, and his kingdom one
7:26 dominion shall be taken A, to be consumed and
8:11 burnt offering was taken A from him, and the
9:7 those that are far A, in all the lands
9:16 and thy wrath turn A from thy city Jerusalem,
11:22 shall be utterly swept A before him and broken,
11:26 army shall be swept A, and many shall fall
11:31 fortress, and shall take A the continual burnt
12:11 burnt offering is taken A, and the abomination that
13:9 their minds and turned A their eyes from looking
13:21 and this was why you sent your maids A
13:45 she was being led A to be put to
Hos 2:2 husband--that she put A her harlotry from her
2:9 and I will take A my wool and my
4:3 even the fish of the sea are taken A
4:11 and new wine take A the understanding.
5:14 will rend and go A, I will carry off,
6:4 morning cloud, like the dew that goes early A
9:11 Ephraim's glory shall fly A like a bird--no
11:7 are bent on turning A from me; so they
13:3 dew that goes early A, like the chaff that
13:11 I have taken them A in my wrath.
14:2 say to him, "Take A all iniquity; accept that
Amos 2:16 the mighty shall flee A naked in that day,"
4:2 they shall take you A with hooks, even the
4:10 the sword; I carried A your horses; and I
5:23 Take A from me the noise of your songs;
6:3 you who put far A the evil day, and
6:7 revelry of those who stretch themselves shall pass A
7:11 must go into exile A from his land.'"
7:12 "O seer, go, flee A to the land of
7:17 surely go into exile A from its land.'"
9:1 of them shall flee A, not one of them
Jon 1:3 with them to Tarshish, A from the presence of
Mic 1:11 of Beth-ezel shall take A from you its standing
2:2 houses, and take them A; they oppress a man
2:9 young children you take A my glory for ever.
4:6 who have been driven A, and those whom I
6:14 parts; you shall put A, but not save, and
Nah 1:12 many, they will be cut off and pass A
2:8 Nineveh is like a pool whose waters run A
3:10 Yet she was carried A, she went into captivity;
3:16 The locust spreads its wings and flies A
3:17 sun rises, they fly A; no one knows where
Zeph 1:2 "I will utterly sweep A everything from the face
1:3 "I will sweep A man and beast; I will
1:3 beast; I will sweep A the birds of the
2:2 before you are driven A like the drifting chaff,
3:15 The LORD has taken A the judgments against you,
Hag 1:9 when you brought it home, I blew it A
Zech 3:4 have taken your iniquity A from you, and I
9:7 I will take A its blood from its mouth,
1Mac 2:11 adornment has been taken A; no longer free, she
3:8 land; thus he turned A wrath from Israel.
5:43 him, and they threw A their arms and fled
6:32 Then Judas marched A from the citadel and
6:47 the forces, they turned A in flight.
7:10 So they marched A and came with a large
9:6 frightened, and many slipped A from the camp, until
9:7 his army had slipped A and the battle was
11:12 he took his daughter A from him and gave
12:25 So he marched A from Jerusalem and met them
12:46 he said; he sent A the troops, and they
14:14 the law, and did A with every lawless and
14:16 Rome, and as far A as Sparta, that Jonathan
16:13 his sons, to do A with them.
16:19 to Gazara to do A with John; he sent
2Mac 3:28 stretcher and carried him A, this man who had
5:16 polluted hands, and swept A with profane hands the
5:21 the temple, and hurried A to Antioch, thinking in
5:27 about nine others, got A to the wilderness, and
8:13 distrustful of God's justice ran off and got A
9:9 pain, his flesh rotted A, and because of his
10:20 seventy thousand drachmas let some of them slip A
11:12 Most of them got A stripped and wounded, and
14:2 the country, having made A with Antiochus and his
14:34 Having said this, he went A
Mt 1:19 put her to shame, resolved to send her A
5:18 heaven and earth pass A, not an iota, not
5:29 out and throw it A; it is better that
5:30 off and throw it A; it is better that
8:31 us out, send us A into the herd of
9:15 the bridegroom is taken A from them, and then
9:16 for the patch tears A from the garment, and
9:31 But they went A and spread his fame through
9:32 As they were going A, behold, a dumb demoniac
11:7 As they went A, Jesus began to speak to
13:6 and since they had no root they withered A
13:12 not, even what he has will be taken A

13:19 one comes and snatches A what is sown in
13:21 on account of the word, immediately he falls A
13:25 and sowed weeds among the wheat, and went A
13:48 into vessels but threw A the bad.
13:53 these parables, he went A from there,
14:15 over; send the crowds A to go into the
14:16 "They need not go A; you give them something
15:21 And Jesus went A from there and withdrew to
15:23 him, saying, "Send her A, for she is crying
15:32 unwilling to send them A hungry, lest they faint
15:39 And sending A the crowds, he got into the
18:8 off and throw it A; it is better for
18:9 out and throw it A; it is better for
19:1 these sayings, he went A from Galilee and entered
19:7 a certificate of divorce, and to put her A
19:15 he laid his hands on them and went A
19:22 heard this he went A sorrowful; for he had
21:43 God will be taken A from you and given
22:22 they marveled; and they left him and went A
24:1 temple and was going A, when his disciples came
24:10 then many will fall A, and betray one another,
24:34 generation will not pass A till all these things
24:35 and earth will pass A, but my words will
24:35 pass away, but my words will not pass A
24:39 and swept them all A, so will be the
25:15 Then he went A
25:29 not, even what he has will be taken A
25:46 And they will go A into eternal punishment, but
26:31 "You will all fall A because of me this
26:33 "Though they all fall A because of you, I
26:33 away because of you, I will never fall A
26:42 second time, he went A and prayed, "My Father,
26:44 them again, he went A and prayed for the
27:2 him and led him A and delivered him to
27:31 him, and led him A to crucify him.
27:64 go and steal him A, and tell the people,
28:13 night and stole him A while we were asleep.'

Mk 1:43 him, and sent him A at once,
2:20 the bridegroom is taken A from them, and then
2:21 does, the patch tears A from it, the new
4:6 and since it had no root it withered A
4:15 immediately comes and takes A the word which is
4:17 on account of the word, immediately they fall A
4:25 not, even what he has will be taken A
5:20 And he went A and began to proclaim in
6:1 He went A from there and came to his
6:31 said to them, "Come A by yourselves to a
6:32 And they went A in the boat to a
6:36 now late; send them A, to go into the
7:23 he arose and went A to the region of
8:3 if I send them A hungry to their homes,
8:10 And he sent them A; and immediately he got
8:26 And he sent him A to his home, saying,
10:4 a certificate of divorce, and to put her A
10:22 fell, and he went A sorrowful; for he had
11:4 And they went A, and found a colt tied
11:20 the fig tree withered A to its roots.
12:3 him, and sent him A empty-handed.
12:12 against them; so they left him and went A
13:15 house, to take anything A;
13:30 generation will not pass A before all these things
13:31 and earth will pass A, but my words will
13:31 pass away, but my words will not pass A
14:27 "You will all fall A; for it is written,
14:29 though they all fall A, I will not."
14:39 And again he went A and prayed, saying the
14:44 him and lead him A under guard."
14:52 linen cloth and ran A naked.
15:1 Jesus and led him A and delivered him to
15:16 the soldiers led him A inside the palace (that
16:3 another, "Who will roll A the stone for us

Lk 1:25 on me, to take A my reproach among men."
1:53 things, and the rich he has sent empty A
2:15 When the angels went A from them into heaven,
4:30 passing through the midst of them he went A
5:35 the bridegroom is taken A from them, and then
6:29 from him who takes A your coat do not
6:30 of him who takes A your goods do not
8:6 grew up, it withered A, because it had no
8:12 devil comes and takes A the word from their
8:13 a while and in time of temptation fall A
8:18 he thinks that he has will be taken A
8:38 but he sent him A, saying,
8:39 And he went A, proclaiming throughout the whole
9:12 day began to wear A; and the twelve came
9:12 him, "Send the crowd A, to go into the
10:42 shall not be taken A from her."
11:22 overcomes him, he takes A his armor in which
11:52 for you have taken A the key of knowledge;
11:53 As he went A from there, the scribes and
13:15 manger, and lead it A to water it?
13:31 said to him, "Get A from here, for Herod
13:33 a prophet should perish A from Jerusalem.'
14:35 land nor for the dunghill; men throw it A
16:3 is taking the stewardship A from me?
16:17 and earth to pass A, than for one dot
17:31 down to take them A; and likewise let him
19:20 which I kept laid A in a napkin;
19:26 not, even what he has will be taken A
19:32 who were sent went A and found it as
20:10 him, and sent him A empty-handed.
20:11 shamefully, and sent him A empty-handed.
21:32 generation will not pass A till all has taken
21:33 and earth will pass A, but my words will
21:33 pass away, but my words will not pass A
22:4 the twelve; he went A and conferred with the
22:52 him and led him A, bringing him into the
22:64 and they led him A to their council, and
23:17 all cried out together, A with this man, and
23:25 as they led him A, they seized one Simon
23:31 were criminals, were led A to be put to
24:2 found the stone rolled A from the tomb,

Jn 1:29 of God, who takes A the sin of the
2:16 pigeons, "Take these things A; you shall not make
4:8 his disciples had gone A into the city to
4:28 water jar, and went A into the city, and
5:14 The man went A and told the Jews that
6:22 his disciples had gone A alone.
6:67 the twelve, "Do you also wish to go A
8:9 heard it, they went A, one by one, beginning
8:21 to them, "I go A, and you will seek
10:40 He went A again across the Jordan to the
11:39 Jesus said, "Take A the stone." Martha, the sister
11:41 So they took A the stone.
12:11 the Jews were going A and believing in Jesus.
14:28 to you, 'I go A, and I will come
15:2 no fruit, he takes A, and every branch that
16:1 this to you to keep you from falling A
16:7 advantage that I go A, for if I do
16:7 I do not go A, the Counselor will not
19:15 They cried out, A with him, away with him,
19:15 out, "Away with him, A with him, crucify him!"
19:31 be broken, and that they might be taken A
19:38 that he might take A the body of Jesus,
19:38 he came and took A his body.
20:1 stone had been taken A from the tomb.
20:13 "Because they have taken A my Lord, and I
20:15 you have carried him A, tell me where you
20:15 have laid him, and I will take him A

Acts 1:12 a sabbath day's journey A;
5:37 the census and drew A some of the people
5:38 I tell you, keep A from these men and
13:8 them, seeking to turn A the proconsul from the
15:38 with him and sailed A to Cyprus,
17:10 sent Paul and Silas A by night to Beroea;
19:12 or aprons were carried A from his body to
19:26 has persuaded and turned A a considerable company
20:6 Troas, but we sailed A from Philippi after the
20:12 they took the lad A alive, and were not
20:30 perverse things, to draw A the disciples after them.
21:36 the people followed, crying, A with him!"
22:16 be baptized, and wash A your sins, calling on
22:21 will send you far A to the Gentiles.'"
22:22 their voices and said, A with such a fellow
24:24 alarmed and said, "Go A for the present; when
27:32 Then the soldiers cut A the ropes of the
27:42 lest any should swim A and escape;

Rom 11:27 them when I take A their sins."

1Cor 2:6 of this age, who are doomed to pass A
7:31 For the form of this world is passing A
13:3 If I give A all I have, and if
13:8 prophecies, they will pass A; as for tongues, they
13:8 will cease; as for knowledge, it will pass A
13:10 when the perfect comes, the imperfect will pass A

2Cor 3:11 For if what faded A came with splendor, what
3:14 unlifted, because only through Christ is it taken A
4:16 outer nature is wasting A, our inner nature is
5:6 the body we are A from the Lord,
5:8 we would rather be A from the body and
5:9 are at home or A, we make it our
5:17 the old has passed A, behold, the new has
10:1 you when I am A --

13:10 this while I am A from you, in order
Gal 1:17 me, but I went A into Arabia; and again
2:13 even Barnabas was carried A by their insincerity.
5:4 law; you have fallen A from grace.
Eph 4:25 Therefore, putting A falsehood, let every one speak
4:31 and slander be put A from you, with all
Col 3:8 now put them all A: anger, wrath, malice, slander,
2Thes 3:6 Christ, that you keep A from any brother who
1Tim 1:6 from these have wandered A into vain discussion,
6:10 that some have wandered A from the faith and
2Tim 1:15 are in Asia turned A from me, and among
4:4 likings, and will turn A from listening to the
Heb 2:1 heard, lest we drift A from it.
3:12 leading you to fall A from the living God.
8:13 obsolete and growing old is ready to vanish A
9:26 the age to put A sin by the sacrifice
10:4 and goats should take A sins.
10:11 which can never take A sins.
10:35 Therefore do not throw A your confidence, which has
13:9 Do not be led A by diverse and strange
Jas 1:9 the flower of the grass he will pass A
1:10 the rich man fade A in the midst of
1:20 Therefore put A all filthiness and rank growth of
1:23 observes himself and goes A and at once forgets
1Pet 2:1 So put A all malice and all guile and
3:11 guile; let him turn A from evil and do
2Pet 3:10 the heavens will pass A with a loud noise,
3:17 lest you be carried A with the error of
1Jn 2:8 the darkness is passing A and the true light
2:17 And the world passes A, and the lust of
3:5 he appeared to take A sins, and in him
Rev 7:17 and God will wipe A every tear from their
12:15 woman, to sweep her A with the flood.
16:20 And every island fled A, and no mountains were
17:3 And he carried me A in the Spirit into
20:11 earth and sky fled A, and no place was
21:1 first earth had passed A, and the sea was
21:4 them; he will wipe A every tear from their
21:4 any more, for the former things have passed A
21:10 Spirit he carried me A to a great, high
22:19 if any one takes A from the words of
22:19 prophecy, God will take A his share in the

AWE (17)

Josh 4:14 and they stood in A of him, as they
4:14 they had stood in A of Moses, all the
1Sam 18:15 success, he stood in A of him.
1Kgs 3:28 and they stood in A of the king, because
1Chr 16:25 to be held in A above all gods.
Ps 22:23 him, and stand in A of him, all you
33:8 the world stand in A of him!
119:161 my heart stands in A of thy words.
Wis 6:7 will not stand in A of any one, nor
Is 29:23 and will stand in A of the God of
Mal 2:5 me, he stood in A of my name.
Mt 17:6 fell on their faces, and were filled with A
27:54 they were filled with A, and said, "Truly this
Mk 4:41 they were filled with A, and said to one
Lk 5:26 and were filled with A, saying, "We have seen
Rom 11:20 So do not become proud, but stand in A
Heb 12:28 worship, with reverence and A;

AWE-INSPIRING

2Mac 1:24 all things, who art A and strong and just

AWESOME

Gen 28:17 afraid, and said, "How A is this place!

AWFUL

Deut 28:58 fear this glorious and A name, the LORD your

AWL (2)

Ex 21:6 ear through with an A; and he shall serve
Deut 15:17 you shall take an A, and thrust it through

AWNING

Ezek 27:7 purple from the coasts of Elishah was your A

AWOKE (13)

Gen 9:24 When Noah A from his wine and knew what
28:16 Then Jacob A from his sleep and said, "Surely
41:4 And Pharaoh A
41:7 And Pharaoh A, and behold, it was a dream.
41:21 Then I A
Judg 16:14 But he A from his sleep, and pulled away
16:20 And he A from his sleep, and said, "I
1Kgs 3:15 And Solomon A, and behold, it was a dream.
Esth 11:12 do, and after he A he had it on
Ps 78:65 Then the Lord A as from sleep, like a
Jer 31:26 Thereupon I A and looked, and my sleep was
Mk 4:39 And he A and rebuked the wind, and said
Lk 8:24 And he A and rebuked the wind and the

AWY

Gen 44:3 the men were sent A with their asses.

AXE (12)

Deut 19:5 his hand swings the A to cut down a
20:19 trees by wielding an A against them; for you
Judg 9:48 and Abimelech took an A in his hand, and
1Sam 13:20 plowshare, his mattock, his A, or his sickle;
1Kgs 6:7 that neither hammer nor A nor any tool of
2Kgs 6:5 felling a log, his A head fell into the
Is 10:15 Shall the A vaunt itself over him who hews
10:34 the forest with an A, and Lebanon with its
Jer 10:3 and worked with an A by the hands of
Bar 6:15 hand, and has an A; but it cannot save
Mt 3:10 Even now the A is laid to the root
Lk 3:9 Even now the A is laid to the root

AXES (6)

1Sam 13:21 shekel for sharpening the A and for setting the
2Sam 12:31 iron picks and iron A, and made them toil
1Chr 20:3 and iron picks and A; and thus David did
Ps 74:5 entrance they hacked the wooden trellis with A
Jer 46:22 come against her with A, like those who fell
Ezek 26:9 walls, and with his A he will break down

AXLE

Sir 33:5 cart wheel, and his thoughts like a turning A

AXLES (3)

1Kgs 7:30 four bronze wheels and A of bronze; and at
7:32 underneath the panels; the A of the wheels were
7:33 a chariot wheel; their A, their rims, their spokes,

AYYAH

1Chr 7:28 and its towns, and A and its towns;

AZALIAH (2)

2Kgs 22:3 Shaphan the son of A, son of Meshullam, the
2Chr 34:8 Shaphan the son of A, and Ma-aseiah the governor

AZANIAH

Neh 10:9 Jeshua the son of A, Binnui of the sons

AZAREL (6)

1Chr 12:6 Elkanah, Isshiah, A, Jo-ezer, and Jashobe-a
25:18 twelve; the eleventh to A, his sons and his
27:22 of Abner; for Dan, A the son of Jeroham.
Ezra 10:41 Machnadebai, Shashai, Sharai, A, Shelemiah,
Neh 11:13 Amashsai, the son of A, son of Ahzai, son
12:36 and his kinsmen, Shemaiah, A, Milalai, Gilalai, Maai,

AZARIAH (57)

1Kgs 4:2 were his high officials: A the son of Zadok
4:5 and Abiathar were priests; A the son of Nathan
2Kgs 14:21 people of Judah took A, who was sixteen years
15:1 Jeroboam king of Israel A the son of Amaziah,
15:6 of the acts of A, and all that he
15:7 And A slept with his fathers, and they buried
15:8 the thirty-eighth year of A king of Judah Zechariah
15:17 the thirty-ninth year of A king of Judah Menahem
15:23 the fiftieth year of A king of Judah Pekahiah
15:27 the fifty-second year of A king of Judah Pekah
1Chr 2:8 of the devoted thing; and Ethan's son was A
2:38 was the father of Jehu, and Jehu of A
2:39 A was the father of Helez, and Helez of
3:12 son, Amaziah his son, A his son, Jotham his
6:9 of Ahima-az, Ahima-az of A, Azariah of Johanan,
6:9 Ahima-az, Ahima-az of Azariah, A of Johanan,
6:10 Johanan, and Johanan of A (it was he who
6:11 A was the father of Amariah, Amariah of Ahitub,
6:13 of Hilkiah, Hilkiah of A,
6:14 Hilkiah, Hilkiah of Azariah, A of Seraiah, Seraiah of
6:36 of Joel, son of A, son of Zephaniah,
9:11 Jedaiah, Jehoiarib, Jachin, and A the son of Hilkiah,
2Chr 15:1 of God came upon A the son of Oded,
15:8 words, the prophecy of A the son of Oded,
21:2 sons of Jehoshaphat: A, Jehiel, Zechariah, A,
23:1 the commanders of hundreds, A the son of Jeroham,
23:1 the son of Jehohanan, A the son of Obed,

26:17 But A the priest went in after him, with
26:20 And A the chief priest, and all the priests,
28:12 the men of Ephraim, A the son of Johanan,
29:12 Joel the son of A, of the sons of
29:12 son of Abdi, and A the son of Jehallelel;
31:10 A the chief priest, who was of the house
31:13 Hezekiah the king and A the chief officer of
Ezra 7:1 of Seraiah, son of A, son of Hilkiah,
7:3 of Amariah, son of A, son of Meraioth,
Neh 3:23 After them A the son of Ma-aseiah, son of
3:24 from the house of A to the Angle
7:7 with Zerubbabel, Jeshua, Nehemiah, A, Raamiah,
8:7 Hodiah, Ma-aseiah, Kelita, A, Jozabad, Hanan,
10:2 of Hacaliah, Zedekiah, Seraiah, A, Jeremiah,
12:33 princes of Judah, and A, Ezra, Meshullam,
Jer 42:1 son of Kareah and A the son of Hoshaiah,
43:2 sent him to them, A the son of Hoshaiah
Dan 1:6 Daniel, Hananiah, Mishael, and A of the tribe of
1:7 he called Meshach, and A he called Abednego.
1:11 Daniel, Hananiah, Mishael, and A;
1:19 Daniel, Hananiah, Mishael, and A; therefore they
2:17 to Hananiah, Mishael, and A, his companions,
3:25 Then A stood and offered this prayer; in the
3:49 furnace to be with A and his companions, and
3:89 Bless the Lord, Hananiah, A, and Mishael, sing
1Mac 2:59 Hannaniah, A, and Mishael believed and were saved
5:18 son of Zechariah, and A, a leader of the
5:56 son of Zechariah, and A, the commanders of the
5:60 Then Joseph and A were routed, and were pursued

AZARIAS (5)

Tob 5:12 He replied, "I am A the son of the
6:6 to the angel, "Brother A, of what use is
6:13 to the angel, "Brother A, I have heard that
7:8 said to Raphael, "Brother A, speak of those things
9:2 said to him, "Brother A, take a servant and

AZAZ

1Chr 5:8 Bela the son of A, son of Shema, son

AZAZEL (4)

Lev 16:8 for the LORD and the other lot for A
16:10 the lot fell for A shall be presented alive
16:10 may be sent away into the wilderness to A
16:26 the goat go to A shall wash his clothes

AZAZIAH (3)

1Chr 15:21 Mikneiah, Obed-edom, Je-iel, and A were to lead
27:20 Hoshea the son of A; for the half-tribe of
2Chr 31:13 as second; while Jehiel, A, Nahath, Asahel, Jerimoth,

AZBUK

Neh 3:16 Nehemiah the son of A, ruler of half the

AZEKAH (7)

Josh 10:10 them as far as A and Makkedah.
10:11 them as far as A, and they died; there
15:35 Enam, Jarmuth, Adullam, Socoh, A,
1Sam 17:1 encamped between Socoh and A, in Ephes-dammim.
2Chr 11:9 Mareshah, Ziph, Adoraim, Lachish, A,
Neh 11:30 and its fields, and A and its villages.
Jer 34:7 were left, Lachish and A; for these were the

AZEL (6)

1Chr 8:37 son, Ele-asah his son, A his son.
8:38 A had six sons, and these are their names:
8:38 All these were the sons of A
9:43 son, Ele-asah his son, A his son.
9:44 A had six sons and these are their names:
9:44 Obadiah, and Hanan; these were the sons of A

AZGAD (4)

Ezra 2:12 The sons of A, one thousand two hundred and
8:12 Of the sons of A, Johanan the son of
Neh 7:17 The sons of A, two thousand three hundred and
10:15 Elam, Zattu, Bani, Bunni, A, Bebai,

AZI-EL

1Chr 15:20 sound bronze cymbals; Zechariah, A, Shemiramoth,

AZIZA

Ezra 10:27 of Zattu: Eli-o-enai, Eliashib, Mattaniah, Jeremoth,

AZMAVETH (8)

2Sam 23:31 Gaash, Abi-albon the Arbathite, A of Bahurim,
1Chr 8:36 the father of Alemeth, A, and Zimri; Zimri was
9:42 and Jarah of Alemeth, A, and Zimri; and Zimri
11:33 Gaash, Abiel the Arbathite, A of Baharum, Eliahba of
12:3 Pelet the sons of A; Beracah, Jehu of Anathoth,
27:25 the king's treasuries was A the son of Adi-el;
Ezra 2:24 The sons of A, forty-two.
Neh 12:29 region of Geba and A; for the singers had

AZMON (3)

Num 34:4 and pass along to A;
34:5 boundary shall turn from A to the Brook of
Josh 15:4 Karka, passes along to A, goes out by the

AZNOTH-TABOR

Josh 19:34 boundary turns westward to A, and goes from there

AZOR (2)

Mt 1:13 Eliakim the father of A,
1:14 father of Azor, and A the father of Zadok,

AZOTUS (13)

Jud 2:28 Those who lived in A and Ascalon feared him
1Mac 4:15 of Idumea, and to A and Jamnia; and three
5:68 Judas turned aside to A in the land of
9:15 and he pursued them as far as Mount A
10:77 army, and went to A as though he were
10:78 Jonathan pursued him to A, and the armies engaged
10:83 They fled to A and entered Beth-dagon, the temple
10:84 But Jonathan burned A and the surrounding towns
11:4 When he approached A, they showed him the temple
11:4 Dagon burned down, and A and its suburbs destroyed,
14:34 on the borders of A, where the enemy formerly
16:10 in the fields of A, and John burned it
Acts 8:39 Philip was found at A, and passing on he

AZRIEL (3)

1Chr 5:24 houses: Epher, Ishi, Eliel, A, Jeremiah, Hodaviah, and
27:19 Jeremoth the son of A;
Jer 36:26 Seraiah the son of A and Shelemiah the son

AZRIKAM (6)

1Chr 3:23 Neariah: Eli-o-enai, Hizkiah, and A, three.
8:38 are their names: A, Bocheru, Ishmael, She-ariah,
9:14 of Hasshub, son of A, son of Hashabiah, of
9:44 are their names: A, Bocheru, Ishmael, She-ariah,
2Chr 28:7 the king's son and A the commander of the
Neh 11:15 of Hasshub, son of A, son of Hashabiah, son

AZUBAH (4)

1Kgs 22:42 His mother's name was A the daughter of Shilhi.
1Chr 2:18 children by his wife A, and by Jerioth; and
2:19 When A died, Caleb married Ephrath, who bore him
2Chr 20:31 His mother's name was A the daughter of Shilhi.

AZZAN

Num 34:26 of Issachar a leader, Paltiel the son of A

AZZUR (3)

Neh 10:17 Bigvai, Adin, Ater, Hezekiah, A,
Jer 28:1 Hananiah the son of A, the prophet from Gibeon,
Ezek 11:1 Ja-azaniah the son of A, and Pelatiah the son

B

BA-ASEIAH

1Chr 6:40 of Michael, son of B, son of Malchijah,

BAAL (70)

Num 25:3 Israel yoked himself to B of Peor.
25:5 have yoked themselves to B of Peor."
Deut 4:3 men who followed the B of Peor;
Judg 6:25 down the altar of B which your father has,
6:28 behold, the altar of B was broken down, and
6:30 down the altar of B and cut down the
6:31 were arrayed against him, "Will you contend for B
6:32 is to say, "Let B contend against him," because
1Kgs 16:31 and went and served B, and worshiped him.
16:32 erected an altar for B in the house of
16:32 in the house of B, which he built in
18:19 and fifty prophets of B and the four hundred
18:21 follow him; but if B, then follow him." And
18:22 of the LORD; but B's prophets are four hundred
18:25 to the prophets of B, "Choose for yourselves one
18:26 on the name of B from morning until noon,
18:26 until noon, saying, "O B, answer us!" But there

18:40 "Seize the prophets of B; let not one of
19:18 have not bowed to B, and every mouth that
22:53 He served B and worshiped him, and provoked the
2Kgs 3:2 away the pillar of B which his father had
10:18 to them, "Ahab served B a little; but Jehu
10:19 all the prophets of B, all his worshipers and
10:19 sacrifice to offer to B; whoever is missing shall
10:19 cunning in order to destroy the worshipers of B
10:20 Jehu ordered, "Sanctify a solemn assembly for B
10:21 all the worshipers of B came, so that there
10:21 entered the house of B, and the house of B was
10:22 out the vestments for all the worshipers of B
10:23 into the house of B with Jehonadab the son
10:23 to the worshipers of B, "Search, and see that
10:23 here among you, but only the worshipers of B
10:25 of the house of B
10:26 in the house of B, and burned it.
10:27 the pillar of B, and demolished the house of B
10:28 Thus Jehu wiped out B from Israel.
11:18 to the house of B, and tore it down;
11:18 Mattan the priest of B before the altars.
17:16 worshiped all the host of heaven, and served B
21:3 he erected altars for B, and made an Asherah,
23:4 the vessels made for B, for Asherah, and for
23:5 who burned incense to B, to the sun, and
1Chr 4:33 were round about these cities as far as B
5:5 son, Re-aiah his son, B his son,
8:30 Abdon, then Zur, Kish, B, Nadab,
9:36 Abdon, then Zur, Kish, B, Ner, Nadab,
2Chr 23:17 to the house of B, and tore it down;
23:17 Mattan the priest of B before the altars.
Tob 1:5 sacrifice to the calf B, and so did the
Ps 106:28 attached themselves to the B of Peor, and ate
Jer 2:8 the prophets prophesied by B, and went after things
7:9 falsely, burn incense to B, and go after other
11:13 up to shame, altars to burn incense to B
11:17 provoking me to anger by burning incense to B
12:16 people to swear by B, then they shall be
19:5 the high places of B to burn their sons
19:5 as burnt offerings to B, which I did not
23:13 thing: they prophesied by B and led my people
23:27 even as their fathers forgot my name for B
32:29 has been offered to B and drink offerings have
32:35 the high places of B in the valley of
Hos 2:8 her silver and gold which they used for B
2:16 you call me, 'My B
7:17 They turn to B; they are like a treacherous
9:10 consecrated themselves to B, and became detestable
13:1 he incurred guilt through B and died.
Zeph 1:4 place the remnant of B and the name of
Rom 11:4 men who have not bowed the knee to B

BAAL-BERITH (2)

Judg 8:33 the Baals, and made B their god.
9:4 of the house of B with which Abimelech hired

BAAL-GAD (3)

Josh 11:17 Seir, as far as B in the valley of
12:7 of the Jordan, from B in the valley of
13:5 toward the sunrising, from B below Mount Hermon

BAAL-HAMON

Song 8:11 had a vineyard at B; he let out the

BAAL-HANAN (5)

Gen 36:38 Shaul died, and B the son of Achbor reigned
36:39 B the son of Achbor died, and Hadar reigned
1Chr 1:49 When Shaul died, B, the son of Achbor, reigned
1:50 When B died, Hadad reigned in his stead; and
27:28 in the Shephelah was B the Gederite; and over

BAAL-HAZOR

2Sam 13:23 Absalom had sheepshearers at B, which is near

BAAL-HERMON (2)

Judg 3:3 Mount Lebanon, from Mount B as far as the
1Chr 5:23 numerous from Bashan to B, Senir, and Mount

BAAL-MEON (3)

Num 32:38 Elealeh, Kiriathaim, Nebo, and B (their names to be
1Chr 5:8 dwelt in Aroer, as far as Nebo and B
Ezek 25:9 of the country, Beth-jeshimoth, B, and Kiriathaim.

BAAL-PEOR (2)

Deut 4:3 the LORD did at B; for the LORD your
Hos 9:10 But they came to B, and consecrated themselves to

BAAL-PERAZIM (4)

2Sam 5:20 And David came to B, and David defeated them
5:20 Therefore the name of that place is called B
1Chr 14:11 he went up to B, and David defeated them
14:11 Therefore the name of that place is called B

BAAL-SHALISHAH

2Kgs 4:42 A man came from B, bringing the man of

BAAL-TAMAR

Judg 20:33 themselves in array at B; and the men of

BAAL-ZEBUB (4)

2Kgs 1:2 them, "Go, inquire of B, the god of Ekron,
1:3 going to inquire of B, the god of Ekron?'
1:6 sending to inquire of B, the god of Ekron?
1:16 messengers to inquire of B, the god of Ekron,–

BAAL-ZEPHON (3)

Ex 14:2 sea, in front of B; you shall encamp over
14:9 at the sea, by Pi-ha-hiroth, in front of B
Num 33:7 which is east of B; and they encamped before

BAALAH (5)

Josh 15:9 boundary bends round to B (that is, Kiriath-jearim);
15:10 boundary circles west of B to Mount Seir, passes
15:11 passes along to Mount B, and goes out to
15:29 Hazar-shual, Beer-sheba, Biziothiah, B, Iim, Ezem,
1Chr 13:6 Israel went up to B, that is, to Kiriath-jearim

BAALATH (3)

Josh 19:44 Timnah, Ekron, Eltekeh, Gibbethon, B,
1Kgs 9:18 and Lower Beth-horon and B and Tamar in the
2Chr 8:6 gates, and bars, and B, and all the store-cities

BAALATH-BEER

Josh 19:8 cities as far as B, Ramah of the Negeb.

BAALE-JUDAH

2Sam 6:2 were with him from B, to bring up from

BAALIS

Jer 40:14 "Do you know that B the king of the

BAALS (19)

Judg 2:11 LORD and served the B;
2:13 LORD, and served the B and the Ashtaroth.
3:7 God, and serving the B and the Asheroth.
8:33 the harlot after the B, and made Baal-berith their
10:6 LORD, and served the B and the Ashtaroth, the
10:10 have forsaken our God and have served the B
1Sam 7:4 Israel put away the B and the Ashtaroth, and
12:10 and have served the B and the Ashtaroth; but
1Kgs 18:18 the commandments of the LORD and followed the B
2Chr 17:3 did not seek the B,
24:7 of the house of the LORD for the B
28:2 molten images for the B;
33:3 erected altars to the B, and made Asherahs, and
34:4 the altars of the B in his presence; and
Jer 2:23 not defiled, I have not gone after the B
9:14 have gone after the B, as their fathers taught
Hos 2:13 feast days of the B when she burned incense
2:17 the names of the B from her mouth, and
11:2 kept sacrificing to the B, and burning incense to

BAANA (3)

1Kgs 4:12 Solomon as his wife); B the son of Ahilud,
4:16 Solomon as his wife); B the son of Hushai,
Neh 3:4 Zadok the son of B repaired.

BAANAH (9)

2Sam 4:2 of the one was B, and the name of
4:5 the Be-erothite, Rechab and B, set out, and about
4:6 slept; so Rechab and B his brother slipped in.
4:9 David answered Rechab and B his brother, the sons
23:29 Heleb the son of B of Netophah, Ittai the
1Chr 11:30 Heled the son of B of Netophah,
Ezra 2:2 Re-el-aiah, Mordecai, Bilshan, Mispar, Bigvai,
Neh 7:7 Azariah, Raamiah, Nahamani, Mordecai, Bilshan,
10:27 Ahiah, Hanan, Anan, Malluch, Harim, B

BAARA

1Chr 8:8 sent away Hushim and B his wives.

BAASHA (28)

1Kgs 15:16 war between Asa and B king of Israel

15:17 B king of Israel went up against Judah, and
15:19 break your league with B king of Israel, that
15:21 And when B heard of it, he stopped building
15:22 its timber, with which B had been building; and
15:27 B the son of Ahijah, of the house of
15:27 conspired against him; and B struck him down at
15:28 So B killed him in the third year of
15:32 war between Asa and B king of Israel all
15:33 Asa king of Judah, B the son of Ahijah
16:1 son of Hanani against B, saying,
16:3 will utterly sweep away B and his house, and
16:4 Any one belonging to B who dies in the
16:5 of the acts of B, and what he did,
16:6 And B slept with his fathers, and was buried
16:7 son of Hanani against B and his house, both
16:8 Elah the son of B began to reign over
16:11 all the house of B; he did not leave
16:12 all the house of B, according to the word
16:12 which he spoke against B by Jehu the prophet,
16:13 all the sins of B and the sins of
21:22 like the house of B the son of Ahijah,
2Kgs 9:9 like the house of B the son of Ahijah.
2Chr 16:1 the reign of Asa, B king of Israel went
16:3 break your league with B king of Israel, that
16:5 And when B heard of it, he stopped building
16:6 its timber, with which B had been building, and
Jer 41:9 made for defense against B king of Israel; Ishmael

BABBLE (2)
Job 11:3 Should your B silence men, and when you mock,
Sir 32:9 equal; and when another is speaking, do not B

BABBLER (2)
Sir 9:18 A B is feared in his city, and the
Acts 17:18 said, "What would this B say?" Others said, "He

BABBLING
Prov 10:14 up knowledge, but the B of a fool brings

BABE (5)
Ex 2:6 child; and lo, the B was crying.
Lk 1:41 greeting of Mary, the B leaped in her womb;
1:44 to my ears, the B in my womb leaped
2:12 you will find a B wrapped in swaddling cloths
2:16 and Joseph, and the B lying in a manger.

BABEL (2)
Gen 10:10 of his kingdom was B, Erech, and Accad, all
11:9 its name was called B, because there the LORD

BABES (15)
Jud 7:28 the death of our B before our eyes, or
Ps 8:2 by the mouth of B and infants, thou hast
17:14 enough; may they leave something over to their B
Wis 10:21 made the tongues of B speak clearly.
12:24 enemies despised; they were deceived like foolish B
18:5 resolved to kill the B of thy holy ones,
Is 3:4 boys their princes, and B shall rule over them.
Lam 2:11 people, because infants and B faint in the streets
1Mac 2:9 Her B have been killed in her streets, her
Mt 11:25 and revealed them to B;
21:16 of the mouth of B and sucklings thou hast
Lk 10:21 and revealed them to B; yea, Father, for such
1Cor 3:1 of the flesh, as B in Christ.
14:20 in your thinking; be B in evil, but in
1Pet 2:2 Like newborn B, long for the pure spiritual milk,

BABIES (2)
2Mac 6:10 the city, with their B hung at their breasts,
8:4 destruction of the innocent B and the blasphemies

BABYLON (308)
2Kgs 17:24 Assyria brought people from B, Cuthah, Avva,
17:30 dwelt; the men of B made Succoth-benoth, the men
20:12 of Baladan, king of B, sent envoys with letters
20:14 "They have come from a far country, from B
20:17 shall be carried to B; nothing shall be left,
20:18 eunuchs in the palace of the king of B
24:1 days Nebuchadnezzar king of B came up, and
24:7 for the king of B had taken all that
24:10 of Nebuchadnezzar king of B came up to Jerusalem,
24:11 And Nebuchadnezzar king of B came to the city,
24:12 to the king of B, himself, and his mother,
24:12 The king of B took him prisoner in the
24:15 carried away Jehoiachin to B; the king's mother, the
24:15 land, he took into captivity from Jerusalem to B
24:16 And the king of B brought captive to Babylon
24:16 Babylon brought captive to B all the men of
24:17 And the king of B made Mattaniah, Jehoiachin's
24:20 And Zedekiah rebelled against the king of B
25:1 month, Nebuchadnezzar king of B came with all his
25:6 to the king of B at Riblah, who passed
25:7 bound him in fetters, and took him to B
25:8 King Nebuchadnezzar, king of B –Nebuzaradan, the
25:8 of the king of B, came to Jerusalem.
25:11 to the king of B, together with the rest
25:13 broke in pieces, and carried the bronze to B
25:20 to the king of B at Riblah.
25:21 And the king of B smote them, and put
25:22 whom Nebuchadnezzar king of B had left, he
25:23 that the king of B had appointed Gedaliah governor,
25:24 serve the king of B, and it shall be
25:27 month, Evil-merodach king of B, in the year that
25:28 of the kings who were with him in B
1Chr 9:1 taken into exile in B because of their unfaithfulness.
2Chr 32:31 of the princes of B, who had been sent
33:11 with fetters of bronze and brought him to B
36:6 up Nebuchadnezzar king of B, and bound him in
36:6 bound him in fetters to take him to B
36:7 of the LORD to B and put them in
36:7 Babylon and put them in his palace in B
36:10 and brought him to B, with the precious vessels
36:18 of his princes, all these he brought to B
36:20 took into exile in B those who had escaped
Ezra 2:1 Nebuchadnezzar the king of B had carried captive to
5:12 of Nebuchadnezzar king of B, the Chaldean, who
5:13 of Cyrus king of B, Cyrus the king made
5:14 into the temple of B, these Cyrus the king
5:14 of the temple of B, and they were delivered
5:17 royal archives there in B, to see whether a
6:5 Jerusalem and brought to B, be restored and brought
Neh 7:6 Nebuchadnezzar the king of B had carried into exile;
13:6 of Artaxerxes king of B I went to the
Esth 2:6 whom Nebuchadnezzar king of B had carried away.
11:4 whom Nebuchadnezzar king of B had brought from
Ps 87:4 I mention Rahab and B; behold, Philistia and Tyre,
137:1 By the waters of B, there we sat down
137:8 O daughter of B, you devastator!
Is 13:1 The oracle concerning B which Isaiah the son of
13:19 And B, the glory of kingdoms, the splendor and
14:4 against the king of B: "How the oppressor has
14:22 will cut off from B name and remnant, offspring
21:9 answered, "Fallen, fallen is B; and all the images
39:1 of Baladan, king of B, sent envoys with letters
39:3 come to me from a far country, from B
39:6 shall be carried to B; nothing shall be left,
39:7 eunuchs in the palace of the king of B
43:14 I will send to B and break down all
47:1 O virgin daughter of B; sit on the ground
48:14 perform his purpose on B, and his arm shall
48:20 Go forth from B, flee from Chaldea, declare this
Jer 20:4 of the king of B; he shall carry them
20:4 carry them captive to B, and shall slay them
20:5 them, and seize them, and carry them to B
20:6 go into captivity; to B you shall go; and
21:2 for Nebuchadrezzar king of B is making war against
21:4 against the king of B and against the Chaldeans
21:7 of Nebuchadrezzar king of B and into the hand
21:10 of the king of B, and he shall burn
22:25 of Nebuchadrezzar king of B and into the hand
24:1 After Nebuchadrezzar king of B had taken into exile
24:1 had brought them to B, the LORD showed me
25:1 of Nebuchadrezzar king of B,
25:9 Nebuchadrezzar the king of B, my servant, and I
25:11 serve the king of B seventy years.
25:12 punish the king of B and that nation, the
25:26 them the king of B shall drink.
27:6 Nebuchadnezzar, the king of B, my servant, and I
27:8 this Nebuchadnezzar king of B, and put its neck
27:8 of the king of B, I will punish that
27:9 serve the king of B
27:11 of the king of B and serve him, I
27:12 of the king of B, and serve him and
27:13 nation which will not serve the king of B
27:14 serve the king of B for it is a
27:16 be brought back from B for it is a
27:17 serve the king of B and live.
27:18 Judah, and in Jerusalem may not go to B
27:20 which Nebuchadnezzar king of B did not take away,
27:20 exile from Jerusalem to B Jeconiah the son of
27:22 shall be carried to B and remain there until
28:2 have broken the yoke of the king of B

B

2:14 the wise men of B;
2:18 with the rest of the wise men of B
2:24 the wise men of B; he went and said
2:24 the wise men of B; bring me in before
2:48 the whole province of B, and chief prefect over
2:48 chief prefect over all the wise men of B
2:49 of the province of B; but Daniel remained at
3:1 the plain of Dura, in the province of B
3:12 province of B: Shadrach, Meshach, and Abednego.
3:98 Meshach, and Abednego in the province of B
4:6 the wise men of B should be brought before
4:29 the royal palace of B,
4:30 "Is not this great B, which I have built
5:7 the wise men of B, "Whoever reads this writing,
7:1 of Belshazzar king of B, Daniel had a dream
13:1 a man living in B whose name was Joakim.
13:5 "Iniquity came forth from B, from elders who were
14:34 which you have to B, to Daniel, in the
14:35 I have never seen B, and I know nothing
14:36 set him down in B, right over the den,
Mic 4:10 in the open country; you shall go to B
Zech 2:7 Zion, you who dwell with the daughter of B
6:10 who have arrived from B; and go the same
1Mac 6:4 great grief departed from there to return to B
Mt 1:11 brothers, at the time of the deportation to B
1:12 after the deportation to B: Jechoniah was the father
1:17 to the deportation to B fourteen generations, and
1:17 from the deportation to B to the Christ fourteen
Acts 7:43 will remove you beyond B
1Pet 5:13 She who is at B, who is likewise chosen,
Rev 14:8 saying, "Fallen, fallen is B the great, she who
16:19 and God remembered great B, to make her drain
17:5 a name of mystery: B the great, mother of
18:2 voice, "Fallen, fallen is B the great!
18:10 thou great city, thou mighty city, B
18:21 sea, saying, "So shall B the great city be

BABYLONIA (9)

Ezra 1:11 were brought up from B to Jerusalem.
2:1 had carried captive to B; they returned to Jerusalem
5:12 this house and carried away the people to B
6:1 search was made in B, in the house of
7:6 chief priest-- this Ezra went up from B
7:9 to go up from B, and on the first
7:16 the whole province of B, and with the freewill
8:1 up with me from B, in the reign of
2Mac 8:20 that took place in B, when eight thousand in

BABYLONIANS (9)

Ezra 4:9 men of Erech, the B, the men of Susa,
Bar 6:1 the king of the B, to give them the
6:2 as captives by Nebuchadnezzar, king of the B
Ezek 23:15 officers, a picture of B whose native land was
23:17 And the B came to her into the bed
23:23 from every side: the B and all the Chaldeans,
Dan 14:3 Now the B had an idol called Bel, and
14:23 great dragon, which the B revered.
14:28 When the B heard it, they were very indignant

BACA

Ps 84:6 through the valley of B they make it a

BACCHIDES (23)

1Mac 7:8 So the king chose B, one of the king's
7:12 body before Alcimus and B to ask for just
7:19 Then B departed from Jerusalem and encamped in
7:20 to help him; then B went back to the
9:1 in battle, he sent B and Alcimus into the
9:11 Then the army of B marched out from the
9:12 B was on the right wing.
9:14 Judas saw that B and the strength of his
9:25 And B chose the ungodly and put them in
9:26 and brought them to B, and he took vengeance
9:29 against our enemies and B, and to deal with
9:32 When B learned of this, he tried to kill
9:34 B found this out on the sabbath day, and
9:43 When B heard of this, he came with a
9:47 his hand to strike B, but he eluded him
9:49 about one thousand of B men fell that day.
9:50 B then returned to Jerusalem and built strong cities
9:57 When B saw that Alcimus was dead, he returned
9:58 now let us bring B back, and he will
9:63 When B learned of this, he assembled all his
9:68 They fought with B, and he was crushed by
10:12 in the strongholds that B had built fled;
2Mac 8:30 forces of Timothy and B they killed more than

BACENOR

2Mac 12:35 certain Dositheus, one of B's men, who was on

BACK (448)

Gen 8:11 and the dove came B to him in the
14:7 wilderness; then they turned B and came to
14:16 Then he brought B all the goods, and also
14:16 goods, and also brought B his kinsman Lot with
15:16 And they shall come B here in the fourth
19:9 But they said, "Stand B
19:17 life; do not look B or stop anywhere in
19:26 wife behind him looked B, and she became a
24:5 then take your son B to the land from
24:6 not take my son B there.
24:8 not take my son B there."
24:54 he said, "Send me B to my master."
28:15 and will bring you B to this land; for
29:3 and put the stone B in its place upon
38:29 But as he drew B his hand, behold, his
39:9 nor has he kept B anything from me except
42:28 money has been put B; here it is in
42:37 do not bring him B to you; put him
42:37 I will bring him B to you."
43:9 do not bring him B to you and set
43:12 money with you; carry B with you the money
43:14 that he may send B your other brother and
44:8 our sacks, we brought B to you from the
44:24 more.' When we went B to your servant my
44:32 do not bring him B to you, then I
44:33 let the lad go B with his brothers.
44:34 how can I go B to my father if
45:17 your beasts and go B to the land of
50:15 us and pay us B for all the evil
Ex 4:7 said, "Put your hand B into your bosom." So
4:7 he put his hand B into his bosom; and
4:18 Moses went B to Jethro his father-in-law and said
4:18 him, "Let me go B, I pray, to my
4:19 Moses in Midian, "Go B to Egypt; for all
4:20 an ass, and went B to the land of
4:21 Moses, "When you go B to Egypt, see that
10:8 and Aaron were brought B to Pharaoh; and he
14:2 of Israel to turn B and encam in front
14:21 LORD drove the sea B by a strong east
14:26 the water may come B upon the Egyptians, upon
15:19 sea, the LORD brought B the waters of the
23:4 you shall bring it B to him.
26:12 shall hang over the B of the tabernacle.
33:23 you shall see my B; but my face shall
Lev 13:55 spot is on the B or on the front.
25:27 sold it and pay B the overpayment to the
25:28 means to get it B for himself, then what
25:41 with him, and go B to his own family,
27:27 he shall buy it B at your valuation, and
Num 13:26 at Kadesh; they brought B word to them and
14:3 for us to go B to Egypt?"
14:4 a captain, and go B to Egypt."
14:43 because you have turned B from following the LORD,
17:10 said to Moses, "Put B the rod of Aaron
22:8 and I will bring B word to you, as
22:34 sight, I will go B again."
24:11 LORD has held you B from honor."
24:25 Balaam rose, and went B to his place; and
25:11 the priest, has turned B my wrath from the
33:7 from Etham, and turned B to Pi-hahiroth, which is
Deut 20:5 Let him go B to his house, lest he
20:6 Let him go B to his house, lest he
20:7 Let him go B to his house, lest he
20:8 Let him go B to his house, lest the
22:1 you shall take them B to your brother.
23:13 with it, and turn B and cover up your
24:19 you shall not go B to get it; it
28:68 LORD will bring you B in ships to Egypt,
Josh 8:20 men of Ai looked B, behold, the smoke of
8:20 to the wilderness turned B upon the pursuers.
8:21 up, then they turned B and smote the men
8:26 Joshua did not draw B his hand, with which
10:38 with all Israel, turned B to Debir and assaulted
11:10 And Joshua turned B at that time, and took
22:8 said to them, "Go B to your homes with
22:32 of Israel, and brought B word to them.
23:5 God will push them B before you, and drive
23:12 For if you turn B, and join the remnant
Judg 1:34 Amorites pressed the Danites B into the hill country,
2:19 judge died, they turned B and behaved worse than
3:19 But he himself turned B at the sculptured stones
9:57 men of Shechem fall B upon their heads, and

B

11:35 and I cannot take B my vow."
14:19 hot anger he went B to his father's house.
18:26 he turned and went B to his home.
19:3 to speak kindly to her and bring her B
20:48 men of Israel turned B against the Benjaminites, and
Ruth 1:11 But Naomi said, "Turn B, my daughters, why will
1:12 Turn B, my daughters, go your way, for I
1:15 your sister-in-law has gone B to her people and
1:21 LORD has brought me B empty.
2:6 Moabite maiden, who came B with Naomi from the
3:17 must not go B empty-handed to your mother-in-law.'"
4:3 "Naomi, who has come B from the country of
1Sam 1:19 LORD; then they went B to their house at
5:3 Dagon and put him B in his place.
7:17 Then he would come B to Ramah, for his
9:5 "Come, let us go B, lest my father cease
10:9 When he turned his B to leave Samuel, God
15:11 for he has turned B from following me, and
15:31 So Samuel turned B after Saul; and Saul worshiped
17:15 Saul, but David went B and forth from Saul
17:53 the Israelites came B from chasing the Philistines,
23:23 he hides, and come B to me with sure
25:12 turned away, and came B and told him all
25:39 Nabal, and has kept B his servant from evil;
27:9 the garments, and came B to Achish.
29:4 him, "Send the man B, that he may return
29:7 So go B now; and go peaceably, that you
30:19 been taken; David brought B all.
2Sam 1:22 of Jonathan turned not B, and the sword of
2:23 came out at his B; and he fell there,
3:26 and they brought him B from the cistern of
11:15 fighting, and then draw B from him, that he
11:23 but we drove them B to the entrance of
12:23 Can I bring him B again?
14:21 grant this; go, bring B the young man Absalom."
15:8 will indeed bring me B to Jerusalem, then I
15:19 Go B, and stay with the king; for you
15:20 Go B, and take your brethren with you; and
15:25 the ark of God B into the city.
15:25 he will bring me B and let me see
15:27 the priest, "Look, go B to the city in
15:29 the ark of God B to Jerusalem; and they
16:3 Israel will give me B the kingdom of my
17:3 bring all the people B to you as a
18:16 and the troops came B from pursuing Israel; for
19:10 do you say nothing about bringing the king B
19:11 to bring the king B to his house, when
19:12 the last to bring B the king?'
19:15 So the king came B to the Jordan; and
19:24 the day he came B in safety.
19:43 to speak of bringing B our king?" But the
22:38 and did not turn B until they were consumed.
1Kgs 2:32 The LORD will bring B his bloody deeds upon
2:33 shall their blood come B upon the head of
2:44 the LORD will bring B your evil upon your
7:8 in the other court B of the hall, was
7:9 measure, sawed with saws, B and front, even from
10:13 she turned and went B to her own land,
10:19 steps, and at the B of the throne was
12:26 the kingdom will turn B to the house of
13:4 could not draw it B to himself.
13:18 LORD, saying, 'Bring him B with you into your
13:19 So he went B with him, and ate bread
13:20 who had brought him B;
13:22 you, but have come B, and have eaten bread
13:23 ass for the prophet whom he had brought B
13:26 who had brought him B from the way heard
13:29 ass, and brought it B to the city, to
14:9 cast me behind your B;
14:28 them and brought them B to the guardroom.
18:37 God, and that thou hast turned their hearts B
19:20 said to him, "Go B again; for what have
22:26 Micaiah, and take him B to Amon the governor
22:33 of Israel, they turned B from pursuing him.
2Kgs 1:6 said to us, 'Go B to the king who
2:13 from him, and went B and stood on the
2:18 And they came B to him, while he tarried
4:22 of God, and come B again."
7:8 them; then they came B, and entered another tent,
9:18 messenger reached them, but he is not coming B
9:20 "He reached them, but he is not coming B
9:36 When they came B and told him, he said,
15:20 king of Assyria turned B, and did not stay
19:28 I will turn you B on the way by
20:5 came to him: "Turn B, and say to Hezekiah
20:9 ten steps, or go B ten steps?"
20:10 let the shadow go B ten steps."
20:11 he brought the shadow B ten steps, by which
22:20 And they brought B word to the king.
1Chr 21:4 all Israel, and came B to Jerusalem.
21:27 he put his sword B into its sheath.
2Chr 9:12 she turned and went B to her own land,
12:11 them, and brought them B to the guardroom.
18:25 Micaiah, and take him B to Amon the governor
18:32 of Israel, they turned B from pursuing him.
19:4 Ephraim, and brought them B to the LORD, the
24:19 them to bring them B to the LORD; these
25:13 army whom Amaziah sent B, not letting them go
28:11 hear me, and send B the captives from your
34:28 And they brought B word to the king.
Ezra 6:5 be restored and brought B to the temple which
Neh 2:15 wall; and I turned B and entered by the
4:4 we are despised; turn B their taunt upon their
5:8 are able, have bought B our Jewish brethren who
9:26 thy law behind their B and killed thy prophets,
9:26 order to turn them B to thee, and they
9:29 order to turn them B to thy law.
13:9 chambers; and I brought B thither the vessels of
Tob 2:3 But he came B and said, "Father, one of
5:21 and he will come B safe and sound." So
10:7 to Raguel, "Send me B, for my father and
10:9 replied, "No, send me B to my father."
10:12 of heaven bring you B safely, dear brother, and
12:2 give him half of what I have brought B
12:3 he has led me B to you safely, he
12:5 half of all that you two have brought B
13:6 Turn B, you sinners, and do right before him;
14:5 them, and bring them B into their land; and
Jud 1:11 man, and they sent B his messengers empty-handed
5:19 God, and have come B from the places to
6:7 going to take you B into the hill country
7:15 you will pay them B with evil, because they
11:14 doing this, to bring B to them permission from
16:11 up their voices, and the enemy were turned B
Esth 2:14 the morning she came B to the second harem
Job 9:13 "God will not turn B his anger; beneath him
20:10 his hands will give B his wealth.
20:18 He will give B the fruit of his toil,
33:18 from man; he keeps B his soul from the
33:30 a man, to bring B his soul from the
34:14 If he should take B his spirit to himself,
39:22 he does not turn B from the sword.
41:15 His B is made of rows of shields, shut
Ps 6:10 troubled; they shall turn B, and be put to
9:3 When my enemies turned B, they stumbled and
18:37 and did not turn B till they were consumed.
19:13 Keep B thy servant also from presumptuous sins; let
35:4 Let them be turned B and confounded who devise
37:21 borrows, and cannot pay B, but the righteous is
40:14 let them be turned B and brought to dishonor
44:10 hast made us turn B from the foe; and
44:18 heart has not turned B, nor have our steps
56:9 enemies will be turned B in the day when
59:6 Each evening they come B, howling like dogs and
59:14 Each evening they come B, howling like dogs and
68:22 "I will bring them B from Bashan, I will
68:22 I will bring them B from the depths of
70:2 Let them be turned B and brought to dishonor
74:11 Why dost thou hold B thy hand, why dost
78:9 with the bow, turned B on the day of
80:18 we will never turn B from thee; give us
89:43 Yea, thou hast turned B the edge of his
90:3 Thou turnest man B to the dust, and sayest,
90:3 dust, and sayest, "Turn B, O children of men!"
94:23 He will bring B on them their iniquity and
114:3 The sea looked and fled, Jordan turned B
114:5 O Jordan, that you turn B
119:101 I hold B my feet from every evil way,
129:3 plowers plowed upon my B; they made long their
132:11 he will not turn B: "One of the sons
Prov 1:15 way with them, hold B your foot from their
2:19 go to her come B nor do they regain
10:13 rod is for the B of him who lacks
11:26 curse him who holds B grain, but a blessing
12:14 a man's hand comes B to him.
14:3 a rod for his B, but the lips of
19:24 not even bring it B to his mouth.
21:26 but the righteous gives and does not hold B
24:11 away to death; hold B those who are stumbling
24:29 will pay the man B for what he has
26:3 a rod for the B of fools.
26:15 out to bring it B to his mouth.

Acts 5:2 wife's knowledge he kept B some of the proceeds,
5:3 Spirit and to keep B part of the proceeds
7:16 and they were carried B to Shechem and laid
Rom 8:15 of slavery to fall B into fear, but you
9:20 a man, to answer B to God?
11:24 natural branches be grafted B into their own olive
2Cor 1:16 Macedonia, and to come B to you from Macedonia
Gal 2:12 they came he drew B and separated himself, fearing
4:9 how can you turn B again to the weak
Col 3:25 wrongdoer will be paid B for the wrong he
Philem 1:12 I am sending him B to you, sending my
1:15 you might have him B for ever,
Heb 10:38 and if he shrinks B, my soul has no
10:39 of those who shrink B and are destroyed, but
11:19 hence, figuratively speaking, he did receive him B
Jas 5:4 fields, which you kept B by fraud, cry out;
5:19 some one brings him B,
5:20 know that whoever brings B a sinner from the
2Pet 2:21 knowing it to turn B from the holy commandment
2:22 proverb, The dog turns B to his own vomit,
Rev 5:1 within and on the B, sealed with seven seals;
7:1 of the earth, holding B the four winds of

BACKBITING

Prov 25:23 forth rain; and a B tongue, angry looks.

BACKBONE

Lev 3:9 away close by the B, and the fat that

BACKS (11)

Ex 23:27 your enemies turn their B to you.
Josh 7:8 Israel has turned their B before their enemies!
7:12 enemies; they turn their B before their enemies,
Judg 20:42 Therefore they turned their B before the men of
2Sam 22:41 my enemies turn their B to me, those who
2Chr 29:6 the habitation of the LORD, and turned their B
Ps 18:40 my enemies turn their B to me, and those
Prov 19:29 and flogging for the B of fools.
Is 30:6 their riches on the B of asses, and their
Ezek 8:16 twenty-five men, with their B to the temple of
Rom 11:10 see, and bend their B for ever."

BACKSLIDING (2)

Is 57:17 but he went on B in the way of
Jer 8:5 then has this people turned away in perpetual B

BACKSLIDINGS (2)

Jer 14:7 name's sake; for our B are many, we have
Ezek 37:23 them from all the B in which they have

BACKWARD (11)

Gen 9:23 their shoulders, and walked B and covered the
49:17 the horse's heels so that his rider falls B
1Sam 4:18 God, Eli fell over B from his seat by
Job 23:8 is not there; and B, but I cannot perceive
Ps 129:5 hate Zion be put to shame and turned B
Sir 48:23 days the sun went B, and he lengthened the
Is 28:13 may go, and fall B, and be broken, and
50:5 and I was not rebellious, I turned not B
Jer 7:24 evil hearts, and went B and not forward.
15:6 LORD, you keep going B; so I have stretched
46:5 They are dismayed and have turned B

BAD (41)

Gen 24:50 cannot speak to you B or good.
31:24 not a word to Jacob, either good or B
31:29 Jacob neither good nor B
Lev 27:10 a good for a B, or a bad for
27:10 a bad, or a B for a good; and
27:12 as either good or B; as you, the priest,
27:14 as either good or B; as the priest values
27:33 it is good or B, neither shall he exchange
Num 13:19 in is good or B, and whether the cities
24:13 do either good or B of my own will;
2Sam 13:22 Amnon neither good nor B; for Absalom hated
2Kgs 2:19 but the water is B, and the land is
Prov 13:17 A B messenger plunges men into trouble, but a
20:14 "It is B, it is bad," says the buyer;
20:14 "It is bad, it is B
25:19 trouble is like a B tooth or a foot
Eccl 5:14 were lost in a B venture; and he is
Sir 6:1 for a B name incurs shame and reproach: so
11:14 Good things and B, life and death, poverty and
31:13 greedy eye is a B thing.
37:27 live; see what is B for it and do
Jer 24:2 other basket had very B figs, so bad that
24:2 very bad figs, so B that they could not
24:3 very good, and the B figs very bad, so
24:3 the bad figs very B, so bad that they
24:3 figs very bad, so B that they cannot be
24:8 the LORD: Like the B figs which are so
24:8 figs which are so B they cannot be eaten,
29:17 figs which are so B they cannot be eaten.
Mt 7:17 good fruit, but the B tree bears evil fruit.
7:18 fruit, nor can a B tree bear good fruit.
12:33 or make the tree B, and its fruit bad;
12:33 bad, and its fruit B; for the tree is
13:48 the good into vessels but threw away the B
22:10 whom they found, both B and good; so the
Lk 6:43 no good tree bears B fruit, nor again does
6:43 nor again does a B tree bear good fruit;
Rom 9:11 nothing either good or B, in order that God's
13:3 not a terror to good conduct, but to B
1Cor 15:33 Do not be deceived: B company ruins good morals."
2Tim 3:13 will go on from B to worse, deceivers and

BADE (6)

Gen 43:17 man did as Joseph B him, and brought the
Ex 16:24 the morning, as Moses B them; and it did
Josh 11:9 them as the LORD B him; he hamstrung their
1Sam 24:10 the cave; and some B me kill you, but
2Sam 14:19 your servant Joab who B me; it was he
Acts 21:5 beach we prayed and B one another farewell.

BADGER (2)

Lev 11:5 And the rock B, because it chews the cud
Deut 14:7 hare, and the rock B, because they chew the

BADGERS (2)

Ps 104:18 goats; the rocks are a refuge for the B
Prov 30:26 in the summer; the B are a people not

BADLY (3)

1Sam 31:3 him; and he was B wounded by the archers.
2Chr 35:23 away, for I am B wounded."
1Mac 6:8 he was astounded and B shaken.

BAEAN

1Mac 5:4 of the sons of B, who were a trap

BAFFLED

Ezek 19:5 saw that she was B, that her hope was

BAFFLES

Sir 10:10 A long illness B the physician; the king of

BAG (18)

Deut 25:13 not have in your B two kinds of weights,
1Sam 17:40 them in his shepherd's B or wallet; his sling
17:49 his hand in his B and took out a
Jud 10:5 oil, and filled a B with parched grain and
13:10 her maid, who placed it in her food B
13:15 head out of the B and showed it to
Job 14:17 sealed up in a B, and thou wouldest cover
Prov 7:20 journey; he took a B of money with him;
16:11 the weights in the B are his work.
Song 1:13 is to me a B of myrrh, that lies
Mic 6:11 scales and with a B of deceitful weights?
Hag 1:6 put them into a B with holes.
Mt 10:10 in your belts, no B for your journey, nor
Mk 6:8 staff; no bread, no B, no money in their
Lk 9:3 journey, no staff, nor B, nor bread, nor money;
10:4 Carry no purse, no B, no sandals; and salute
22:35 with no purse or B or sandals, did you
22:36 has a purse take it, and likewise a B

BAGGAGE (17)

1Sam 10:22 said, "Behold, he has hidden himself among the B
17:22 the keeper of the B, and ran to the
25:13 after David, while two hundred remained with the B
30:24 who stays by the B; they shall share alike."
Jud 7:2 cavalry, together with the B and the foot soldiers
Is 10:28 Michmash he stores his B;
Jer 46:19 Prepare yourselves B for exile, O inhabitants of
Ezek 12:3 for yourself an exile's B, and go into exile
12:4 shall bring out your B by day in their
12:4 in their sight, as B for exile; and you
12:6 you shall lift the B upon your shoulder, and
12:7 I brought out my B by day, as baggage
12:7 baggage by day, as B for exile, and in
12:12 them shall lift his B upon his shoulder in
1Mac 9:35 the great amount of B which they had.

9:39 procession with much B; and the bridegroom came
2Mac 12:21 children and also the B to a place called

BAGOAS (6)

Jud 12:11 And he said to B, the eunuch who had
12:13 So B went out from the presence of Holofernes,
12:15 she had received from B for her daily use,
13:1 slaves quickly withdrew, and B closed the tent from
13:3 And she had said the same thing to B
14:14 So B went in and knocked at the door

BAGPIPE (4)

Dan 3:5 pipe, lyre, trigon, harp, B, and every kind of
3:7 pipe, lyre, trigon, harp, B, and every kind of
3:10 pipe, lyre, trigon, harp, B, and every kind of
3:15 pipe, lyre, trigon, harp, B, and every kind of

BAGS (5)

Gen 42:25 orders to fill their B with grain, and to
43:11 the land in your B, and carry down to
2Kgs 5:23 of silver in two B, with two festal garments,
12:10 and tied up in B the money that was
Tob 9:5 brought out the money B with their seals intact

BAHARUM

1Chr 11:33 the Arbathite, Azmaveth of B, Eliahba of Sha-albon,

BAHURIM (6)

2Sam 3:16 her, weeping after her all the way to B
16:5 King David came to B, there came out a
17:18 of a man at B, who had a well
19:16 Gera, the Benjaminite, from B, made haste to come
23:31 the Arbathite, Azmaveth of B,
1Kgs 2:8 Gera, the Benjaminite from B, who cursed me with

BAKBAKKAR

1Chr 9:15 sons of Merari; and B, Heresh, Galal, and Mattaniah

BAKBUK (2)

Ezra 2:51 Nephisim, the sons of B, the sons of Hakupha,
Neh 7:53 Nephushesim, the sons of B, the sons of Hakupha,

BAKBUKIAH (3)

Neh 11:17 thanksgiving in prayer, and B, the second among his
12:9 And B and Unno their brethren stood opposite them
12:25 Mattaniah, B, Obadiah, Meshullam, Talmon, and

BAKE (5)

Ex 16:23 sabbath to the LORD; B what you will bake
16:23 bake what you will B and boil what you
Lev 24:5 take fine flour, and B twelve cakes of it;
26:26 bread, ten women shall B your bread in one
Ezek 46:20 and where they shall B the cereal offering, in

BAKED (16)

Gen 19:3 them a feast, and B unleavened bread, and they
40:17 were all sorts of B food for Pharaoh, but
Ex 12:39 And they B unleavened cakes of the dough which
Lev 2:4 bring a cereal offering B in the oven as
2:5 is a cereal offering B on a griddle, it
6:17 It shall not be B with leaven.
6:21 it well mixed, in B pieces like a cereal
7:9 And every cereal offering B in the oven and
23:17 flour, they shall be B with leaven, as first
Num 11:8 the taste of cakes B with oil.
1Sam 28:24 and kneaded it and B unleavened bread of it,
2Sam 13:8 in his sight, and B the cakes.
1Kgs 17:12 lives, I have nothing B, only a handful of
19:6 his head a cake B on hot stones and
1Chr 23:29 of unleavened bread, the B offering, the offering
Is 44:19 the fire, I also B bread on its coals,

BAKER (9)

Gen 40:1 of Egypt and his B offended their lord the
40:2 butler and the chief B,
40:5 the butler and the B of the king of
40:16 When the chief B saw that the interpretation was
40:20 head of the chief B among his servants.
40:22 he hanged the chief B, as Joseph had interpreted
41:10 me and the chief B in custody in the
41:13 my office, and the B was hanged."
Hos 7:5 a heated oven, whose B ceases to stir the

BAKERS (2)

1Sam 8:13 your daughters to be perfumers and cooks and B
Jer 37:21 him daily from the B street, until all the

BAKES

Is 44:15 kindles a fire and B bread; also he makes

BAKING

Ezek 4:12 as a barley cake, B it in their sight

BALAAM (67)

Num 22:5 time, sent messengers to B the son of Beor
22:7 and they came to B, and gave him Balak's
22:8 me"; so the princes of Moab stayed with B
22:9 And God came to B and said, "Who are
22:10 And B said to God, "Balak the son of
22:12 God said to B, "You shall not go with
22:13 So B rose in the morning, and said to
22:14 to Balak, and said, B refuses to come with
22:16 And they came to B and said to him,
22:18 But B answered and said to the servants of
22:20 And God came to B at night and said
22:21 So B rose in the morning, and saddled his
22:23 into the field; and B struck the ass, to
22:25 the wall, and pressed B's foot against the wall;
22:27 she lay down under B; and Balaam's anger was
22:27 down under Balaam; and B's anger was kindled, and
22:28 and she said to B, "What have I done
22:29 And B said to the ass, "Because you have
22:30 the ass said to B, "Am I not your
22:31 opened the eyes of B, and he saw the
22:34 Then B said to the angel of the LORD,
22:35 the LORD said to B, "Go with the men;
22:35 So B went on with the princes of Balak.
22:36 When Balak heard that B had come, he went
22:37 And Balak said to B, "Did I not send
22:38 B said to Balak, "Lo, I have come to
22:39 Then B went with Balak, and they came to
22:40 sheep, and sent to B and to the princes
22:41 the morrow Balak took B and brought him up
23:1 And B said to Balak, "Build for me here
23:2 Balak did as B had said; and Balak and
23:2 said; and Balak and B offered on each altar
23:3 And B said to Balak, "Stand beside your burnt
23:4 And God met B; and Balaam said to him,
23:4 God met Balaam; and B said to him, "I
23:5 put a word in B's mouth, and said, "Return
23:7 And B took up his discourse, and said, "From
23:11 And Balak said to B, "What have you done
23:15 B said to Balak, "Stand here beside your burnt
23:16 And the LORD met B, and put a word
23:18 And B took up his discourse, and said, "Rise,
23:25 And Balak said to B, "Neither curse them at
23:26 But B answered Balak, "Did I not tell you,
23:27 And Balak said to B, "Come now, I will
23:28 So Balak took B to the top of Peor,
23:29 And B said to Balak, "Build for me here
23:30 And Balak did as B had said, and offered
24:1 When B saw that it pleased the LORD to
24:2 And B lifted up his eyes, and saw Israel
24:3 said, "The oracle of B the son of Beor,
24:10 anger was kindled against B, and he struck his
24:10 and Balak said to B, "I called you to
24:12 And B said to Balak, "Did I not tell
24:15 said, "The oracle of B the son of Beor,
24:25 Then B rose, and went back to his place;
31:8 and they also slew B the son of Beor
31:16 by the counsel of B, to act treacherously against
Deut 23:4 they hired against you B the son of Beor
23:5 would not hearken to B; but the LORD your
Josh 13:22 B also, the son of Beor, the soothsayer, the
24:9 he sent and invited B the son of Beor
24:10 would not listen to B; therefore he blessed you;
Neh 13:2 and water, but hired B against them to curse
Mic 6:5 Moab devised, and what B the son of Beor
2Pet 2:15 followed the way of B, the son of Beor,
Jude 1:11 sake of gain to B's error, and perish in
Rev 2:14 hold the teaching of B, who taught Balak to

BALADAN (2)

2Kgs 20:12 Merodach-baladan the son of B, king of Babylon,
Is 39:1 Merodach-baladan the son of B, king of Babylon,

BALAH

Josh 19:3 Beer-sheba, Sheba, Moladah, Hazar-shual, B, Ezem,

BALAK (44)

Num 22:2 And B the son of Zippor saw all that
22:4 So B the son of Zippor, who was king
22:7 Balaam, and gave him B's message.

22:10 Balaam said to God, B the son of Zippor,
22:13 to the princes of B, "Go to your own
22:14 rose and went to B, and said, "Balaam refuses
22:15 Once again B sent princes, more in number and
22:16 to him, "Thus says B the son of Zippor:
22:18 to the servants of B, "Though Balak were to
22:18 servants of Balak, "Though B were to give me
22:35 So Balaam went on with the princes of B
22:36 When B heard that Balaam had come, he went
22:37 And B said to Balaam, "Did I not send
22:38 Balaam said to B, "Lo, I have come to
22:39 Then Balaam went with B, and they came to
22:40 And B sacrificed oxen and sheep, and sent to
22:41 And on the morrow B took Balaam and brought
23:1 And Balaam said to B, "Build for me here
23:2 B did as Balaam had said; and Balak and
23:2 Balaam had said; and B and Balaam offered on
23:3 And Balaam said to B, "Stand beside your burnt
23:5 and said, "Return to B, and thus you shall
23:7 and said, "From Aram B has brought me, the
23:11 And B said to Balaam, "What have you done
23:13 And B said to him, "Come with me to
23:15 Balaam said to B, "Stand here beside your burnt
23:16 and said, "Return to B, and thus shall you
23:17 And B said to him, "What has the LORD
23:18 discourse, and said, "Rise, B, and hear; hearken to
23:25 And B said to Balaam, "Neither curse them at
23:26 But Balaam answered B, "Did I not tell you,
23:27 And B said to Balaam, "Come now, I will
23:28 So B took Balaam to the top of Peor,
23:29 And Balaam said to B, "Build for me here
23:30 And B did as Balaam had said, and offered
24:10 And B's anger was kindled against Balaam, and he
24:10 his hands together; and B said to Balaam, "I
24:12 And Balaam said to B, "Did I not tell
24:13 sent to me, 'If B should give me his
24:25 to his place; and B also went his way.
Josh 24:9 Then B the son of Zippor, king of Moab,
Judg 11:25 you any better than B the son of Zippor,
Mic 6:5 my people, remember what B king of Moab devised,
Rev 2:14 of Balaam, who taught B to put a stumbling

BALAMON

Jud 8:3 his fathers in the field between Dothan and B

BALANCE (8)

Job 31:6 weighed in a just B, and let God know
Prov 11:1 A false B is an abomination to the LORD,
16:11 A just B and scales are the LORDs; all
Sir 21:25 of the prudent will be weighed in the B
26:15 to charm, and no B can weigh the value
Is 40:12 mountains in scales and the hills in a B
2Mac 9:8 high mountains in a B, was brought down to
Rev 6:5 its rider had a B in his hand;

BALANCES (9)

Lev 19:36 You shall have just B, just weights, a just
Job 6:2 weighed, and all my calamity laid in the B
Ps 62:9 a delusion; in the B they go up; they
Sir 28:25 silver and gold, make B and scales for your
Ezek 5:1 your beard; then take B for weighing, and divide
45:10 "You shall have just B, a just ephah, and
Dan 5:27 been weighed in the B and found wanting;
Hos 12:7 whose hands are false B, he loves to oppress.
Amos 8:5 deal deceitfully with false B,

BALANCINGS

Job 37:16 Do you know the B of the clouds, the

BALBAIM

Jud 7:3 Dothan as far as B and in length from

BALD (13)

Lev 11:22 to its kind, the B locust according to its
13:40 his head, he is B but he is clean.
13:42 there is on the B head or the bald
13:42 bald head or the B forehead a reddish-white
13:42 breaking out on his B head or his bald
13:42 bald head or his B forehead.
13:43 is reddish-white on his B head or on his
13:43 head or on his B forehead, like the appearance
Jer 16:6 himself or make himself B for them.
Ezek 27:31 ashes; they make themselves B for you, and gird
29:18 every head was made B and every shoulder was
Mic 1:16 Make yourselves B and cut off your hair, for
1:16 delight; make yourselves as B as the eagle, for

BALDHEAD (2)

2Kgs 2:23 and jeered at him, saying, "Go up, you B
2:23 Go up, you B

BALDNESS (8)

Lev 13:41 and temples, he has B of the forehead but
Deut 14:1 yourselves or make any B on your foreheads for
Is 3:24 instead of well-set hair, B; and instead of a
15:2 On every head is B, every beard is shorn;
22:12 weeping and mourning, to B and girding with
Jer 47:5 B has come upon Gaza, Ashkelon has perished.
Ezek 7:18 upon all faces, and B on all their heads.
Amos 8:10 upon all loins, and B on every head; I

BALL

Is 22:18 throw you like a B into a wide land;

BALLAD

Num 21:27 Therefore the B singers say, "Come to Heshbon, let

BALM (6)

Gen 37:25 their camels bearing gum, B, and myrrh, on their
43:11 a present, a little B and a little honey,
Jer 8:22 Is there no B in Gilead?
46:11 to Gilead, and take B, O virgin daughter of
51:8 Take B for her pain; perhaps she may be
Ezek 27:17 wheat, olives and early figs, honey, oil, and B

BALSAM (4)

2Sam 5:23 upon them opposite the B trees.
5:24 the tops of the B trees, then bestir yourself;
1Chr 14:14 upon them opposite the B trees.
14:15 the tops of the B trees, then go out

BAMAH

Ezek 20:29 its name is called B to this day.)

BAMOTH (2)

Num 21:19 and from Nahaliel to B,
21:20 to Bamoth, and from B to the valley lying

BAMOTH-BAAL (2)

Num 22:41 brought him up to B; and from there he
Josh 13:17 the tableland; Dibon, and B, and Beth-baal-meon,

BAND (36)

Ex 28:8 And the skilfully woven B upon it, to gird
28:27 above the skilfully woven B of the ephod.
28:28 upon the skilfully woven B of the ephod, and
29:5 with the skilfully woven B of the ephod;
39:5 And the skilfully woven B upon it, to gird
39:20 above the skilfully woven B of the ephod.
39:21 upon the skilfully woven B of the ephod, and
Lev 8:7 with the skilfully woven B of the ephod, binding
1Sam 10:5 you will meet a B of prophets coming down
10:10 to Gibe-ah, behold, a B of prophets met him;
30:8 of the LORD, "Shall I pursue after this B
30:15 him, "Will you take me down to this B
30:15 and I will take you down to this B
30:23 into our hand the B that came against us.
2Sam 2:25 Abner, and became one B, and took their stand
23:13 of Adullam, when a B of Philistines was encamped
1Kgs 7:35 there was a round B half a cubit high;
11:24 leader of a marauding B, after the slaughter by
2Kgs 13:21 buried, lo, a marauding B was seen and the
19:31 of Mount Zion a B of survivors.
1Chr 12:21 helped David against the B of raiders; for they
2Chr 22:1 his stead; for the B of men that came
Ezra 8:22 the king for a B of soldiers and horsemen
Job 38:9 thick darkness its swaddling B,
Ps 56:6 They B themselves together, they lurk, they watch
59:3 my life; fierce men B themselves against me.
86:14 up against me; a B of ruthless men seek
94:21 They B together against the life of the righteous,
Is 31:4 prey, and when a B of shepherds is called
37:32 of Mount Zion a B of survivors.
Dan 4:15 earth, bound with a B of iron and bronze,
4:23 earth, bound with a B of iron and bronze,
Hos 4:18 A B of drunkards, they give themselves to harlotry;
1Mac 5:6 he found a strong B and many people with
Jn 18:3 So Judas, procuring a B of soldiers and some
18:12 So the B of soldiers and their captain and

BANDAGE (3)

1Kgs 20:38 disguising himself with a B over his eyes.
20:41 haste to take the B away from his eyes;

Ezek 30:21 binding it with a B, so that it may

BANDAGED

Sir 27:21 a wound may be B, and there is reconciliation

BANDAGES

Jn 11:44 and feet bound with B, and his face wrapped

BANDED

Hos 6:9 so the priests are B together; they murder on

BANDITS

Hos 7:2 breaks in, and the B raid without.

BANDS (10)

2Sam 4:2 were captains of raiding B; the name of the
2Kgs 13:20 Now B of Moabites used to invade the land
24:2 LORD sent against him B of the Chaldeans, and
24:2 of the Chaldeans, and B of the Syrians, and
24:2 of the Syrians, and B of the Moabites, and
24:2 of the Moabites, and B of the Ammonites, and
Ezek 13:18 women who sew magic B upon all wrists, and
13:20 am against your magic B with which you hunt
16:4 you, nor rubbed with salt, nor swathed with B
Hos 11:4 of compassion, with the B of love, and I

BANI (15)

2Sam 23:36 of Nathan of Zobah, B the Gadite,
1Chr 6:46 of Amzi, son of B, son of Shemer,
9:4 of Imri, son of B, from the sons of
Ezra 2:10 The sons of B, six hundred and forty-two.
8:10 Of the sons of B, Shelomith the son of
10:29 Of the sons of B were Meshullum, Malluch, Adaiah,
10:34 Of the sons of B: Ma-adai, Amram, Uel,
Neh 3:17 Rehum the son of B; next to him Hashabiah,
8:7 Also Jeshua, B, Sherebiah, Jamin, Akkub,
9:4 the Levites stood Jeshua, B, Kadmi-el, Shebaniah,
9:4 Shebaniah, Bunni, Sherebiah, B, and Chenani; and
9:5 the Levites, Jeshua, Kadmi-el, B, Hashabneiah,
10:13 Zaccur, Sherebiah, Shebaniah, Hodiah, B, Beninu.
10:14 Parosh, Pahath-moab, Elam, Zattu, B,
11:22 Uzzi the son of B, son of Hashabiah, son

BANISH (4)

Jer 25:10 Moreover, I will B from them the voice of
Ezek 34:25 covenant of peace and B wild beasts from the
1Mac 3:35 Jerusalem; he was to B the memory of them
Rom 11:26 from Zion, he will B ungodliness from Jacob";

BANISHED (4)

2Sam 14:13 does not bring his B one home again.
14:14 not to keep his B one an outcast.
Is 24:11 its eventide; the gladness of the earth is B
2Mac 10:15 received those who were B from Jerusalem, and

BANISHMENT

Ezra 7:26 for death or for B or for confiscation of

BANK (15)

Gen 41:3 other cows on the B of the Nile.
2Kgs 2:13 and stood on the B of the Jordan.
Sir 40:16 any water or river B will be plucked up
Ezek 47:6 me back along the B of the river.
47:7 I saw upon the B of the river very
Dan 8:3 ram standing on the B of the river.
8:6 seen standing on the B of the river, and
10:4 was standing on the B of the great river,
12:5 stood, one on this B of the stream and
12:5 and one on that B of the stream.
Mt 8:32 rushed down the steep B into the sea, and
Mk 5:13 rushed down the steep B into the sea, and
Lk 8:33 rushed down the steep B into the lake and
19:23 my money into the B, and at my coming
19:43 will cast up a B about you and surround

BANKERS

Mt 25:27 my money with the B, and at my coming

BANKS (10)

Gen 41:17 was standing on the B of the Nile;
Deut 2:37 is, to all the B of the river Jabbok
Josh 3:15 Jordan overflows all its B throughout the time of
4:18 and overflowed all its B, as before.
Judg 11:26 that are on the B of the Arnon, three
1Chr 12:15 was overflowing all its B, and put to flight
Is 8:7 go over all its B;

Ezek 47:12 And on the B, on both sides of the
Dan 8:16 man's voice between the B of the Ulai, and
1Mac 9:43 sabbath day to the B of the Jordan.

BANNED

Ezra 10:8 forfeited, and he himself B from the congregation of

BANNER (5)

Ex 17:15 The LORD is my B,
17:16 "A hand upon the B of the LORD!
Ps 60:4 hast set up a B for those who fear
Song 2:4 banqueting house, and his B over me was love.
Jer 50:2 proclaim, set up a B and proclaim, conceal it

BANNERS (3)

Ps 20:5 the name of our God set up our B
Song 6:4 comely as Jerusalem, terrible as an army with B
6:10 as the sun, terrible as an army with B

BANQUET (21)

Jud 6:21 house and gave a B for the elders; and
12:10 day Holofernes held a B for his slave only,
13:1 were weary because the B had lasted long.
Esth 1:3 reign he gave a B for all his princes
1:5 great and small, a B lasting for seven days,
1:9 Vashti also gave a B for the women in
2:18 king gave a great B to all his princes
2:18 all his princes and servants; it was Esther's B
5:12 the king to the B she prepared but myself.
6:14 in haste to the B that Esther had prepared.
Sir 31:31 your neighbor at a B of wine, and do
32:5 of music at a B of wine.
49:1 like music at a B of wine.
1Mac 16:15 gave them a great B, and hid men there.
16:16 against Simon in the B hall, and they killed
2Mac 2:27 one who prepares a B and seeks the benefit
Mk 6:21 his birthday gave a B for his courtiers and
Lk 14:12 a dinner or a B, do not invite your
14:16 once gave a great B, and invited many;
14:17 the time for the B he sent his servant
14:24 those men who were invited shall taste my B

BANQUETING (2)

Song 2:4 brought me to the B house, and his banner
Dan 5:10 lords, came into the B hall; and the queen

BAPTISM (20)

Mt 3:7 and Sadducees coming for B, he said to them,
21:25 The B of John, whence was it?
Mk 1:4 the wilderness, preaching a B of repentance for the
10:38 be baptized with the B with which I am
10:39 drink; and with the B with which I am
11:29 Was the B of John from heaven or from
Lk 3:3 the Jordan, preaching a B of repentance for the
7:29 been baptized with the B of John;
12:50 I have a B to be baptized with; and
20:4 tell me, Was the B of John from heaven
Acts 1:22 us, beginning from the B of John until the
10:37 from Galilee after the B which John preached:
13:24 John had preached a B of repentance to all
18:25 he knew only the B of John.
19:3 They said, "Into John's B
19:4 "John baptized with the B of repentance, telling the
Rom 6:4 therefore with him by B into death, so that
Eph 4:5 Lord, one faith, one B,
Col 2:12 buried with him in B, in which you were
1Pet 3:21 B, which corresponds to this, now saves you, not

BAPTIST (12)

Mt 3:1 days came John the B, preaching in the wilderness
11:11 greater than John the B; yet he who is
11:12 days of John the B until now the kingdom
14:2 "This is John the B, he has been raised
14:8 head of John the B here on a platter."
16:14 "Some say John the B, others say Elijah, and
17:13 he was speaking to them of John the B
Mk 6:25 head of John the B on a platter."
8:28 told him, "John the B; and others say, Elijah;
Lk 7:20 they said, "John the B has sent us to
7:33 weep.' For John the B has come eating no
9:19 they answered, "John the B; but others say, Elijah;

BAPTIZE (10)

Mt 3:11 "I B you with water for repentance, but he
3:11 to carry; he will B you with the Holy
Mk 1:8 water; but he will B you with the Holy

Lk 3:16 answered them all, "I B you with water; but
3:16 to untie; he will B you with the Holy
Jn 1:26 John answered them, "I B with water; but among
1:33 who sent me to B with water said to
4:2 Jesus himself did not B, but only his disciples),
1Cor 1:16 (I did B also the household of Stephanas.
1:17 not send me to B but to preach the

BAPTIZED (53)

Mt 3:6 Jordan, and they were B by him in the
3:13 to John, to be B by him.
3:14 "I need to be B by you, and do
3:16 And when Jesus was B, he went up immediately
Mk 1:5 Jerusalem; and they were B by him in the
1:8 I have B you with water; but he will
1:9 of Galilee and was B by John in the
10:38 drink, or to be B with the baptism with
10:38 baptized with the baptism with which I am B
10:39 with which I am B, you will be baptized;
10:39 baptized, you will be B;
16:16 who believes and is B will be saved; but
Lk 3:7 came out to be B by him, "You brood
3:12 also came to be B, and said to him,
3:21 all the people were B, and when Jesus also
3:21 Jesus also had been B and was praying, the
7:29 justified God, having been B with the baptism of
7:30 themselves, not having been B by him.)
12:50 a baptism to be B with; and how I
Jn 3:22 of Judea; there he remained with them and B
3:23 much water there; and people came and were B
10:40 where John at first B, and there he remained.
Acts 1:5 from me, for John B with water, but before
1:5 days you shall be B with the Holy Spirit."
2:38 them, "Repent, and be B every one of you
2:41 received his word were B, and there were added
8:12 Jesus Christ, they were B, both men and women.
8:13 believed, and after being B he continued with Philip.
8:16 they had only been B in the name of
8:36 What is to prevent my being B
8:37 the eunuch, and he B him.
9:18 he rose and was B,
10:48 commanded them to be B in the name of
11:16 how he said, 'John B with water, but you
11:16 but you shall be B with the Holy Spirit.'
16:15 And when she was B, with her household, she
16:33 wounds, and he was B at once, with all
18:8 of the Corinthians hearing Paul believed and were B
19:3 And he said, "Into what then were you B
19:4 And Paul said, "John B with the baptism of
19:5 hearing this, they were B in the name of
22:16 Rise and be B, and wash away your sins,
Rom 6:3 us who have been B into Christ Jesus were
6:3 into Christ Jesus were B into his death?
1Cor 1:13 Or were you B in the name of Paul?
1:14 am thankful that I B none of you except
1:15 say that you were B in my name.
1:16 not know whether I B any one else.)
10:2 sea, and all were B into Moses in the
12:13 Spirit we were all B into one body--Jews
15:29 people mean by being B on behalf of the
15:29 all, why are people B on their behalf?
Gal 3:27 of you as were B into Christ have put

BAPTIZER (3)

Mk 1:4 John the B appeared in the wilderness, preaching a
6:14 Some said, "John the B has been raised from
6:24 And she said, "The head of John the B

BAPTIZES

Jn 1:33 this is he who B with the Holy Spirit.'

BAPTIZING (8)

Mt 28:19 disciples of all nations, B them in the name
Jn 1:25 "Then why are you B, if you are neither
1:28 in Bethany beyond the Jordan, where John was B
1:31 for this I came B with water, that he
3:23 John also was B at Aenon near Salim, because
3:26 witness, here he is, B, and all are going
4:1 Jesus was making and B more disciples than John
Acts 10:47 one forbid water for B these people who have

BAR (7)

Ex 26:28 The middle B, halfway up the frames, shall pass
36:33 he made the middle B to pass through from
Josh 7:21 of silver, and a B of gold weighing fifty
7:24 the mantle and the B of gold, and his
Judg 16:3 and pulled them up, B and all, and put
Neh 7:3 let them shut and B the doors.
Amos 1:5 I will break the B of Damascus, and cut

BAR-JESUS

Acts 13:6 a certain magician, a Jewish false prophet, named B

BAR-JONA

Mt 16:17 And Jesus answered him, "Blessed are you, Simon B

BARABBAS (11)

Mt 27:16 And they had then a notorious prisoner, called B
27:17 to release for you, B or Jesus who is
27:20 people to ask for B and destroy Jesus.
27:21 And they said, B
27:26 he released for them B, and having scourged Jesus,
Mk 15:7 in the insurrection, there was a man called B
15:11 him release for them B instead.
15:15 released for them B; and having scourged Jesus,
Lk 23:17 and release to us B --
Jn 18:40 They cried out again, "Not this man, but B
18:40 Now B was a robber.

BARACHEL (2)

Job 32:2 Elihu the son of B the Buzite, of the
32:6 Elihu the son of B the Buzite answered: "I

BARACHIAH

Mt 23:34 Zechariah the son of B, whom you murdered

BARAK (15)

Judg 4:6 She sent and summoned B the son of Abino-am
4:8 B said to her, "If you will go with
4:9 arose, and went with B to Kedesh.
4:10 And B summoned Zebulun and Naphtali to Kedesh;
4:12 Sisera was told that B the son of Abino-am
4:14 And Deborah said to B, "Up!
4:14 So B went down from Mount Tabor with ten
4:15 all his army before B at the edge of
4:16 And B pursued the chariots and the army to
4:22 And behold, as B pursued Sisera, Jael went out
5:1 Then sang Deborah and B the son of Abino-am
5:12 Arise, B, lead away your captives, O son of
5:15 and Issachar faithful to B; into the valley they
1Sam 12:11 LORD sent Jerubbaal and B, and Jephthah, and
Heb 11:32 to tell of Gideon, B, Samson, Jephthah, of David

BARBARIAN (2)

2Mac 2:21 land and pursued the B hordes,
Col 3:11 and uncircumcised, B, Scythian, slave, free man,

BARBARIANS

Rom 1:14 to Greeks and to B, both to the wise

BARBAROUS (3)

2Mac 5:22 and in character more B than the man who
10:4 over to blasphemous and B nations.
13:9 The king with B arrogance was coming to show

BARBAROUSLY

2Mac 15:2 destroy so savagely and B, but show respect for

BARBER

Ezek 5:1 use it as a B's razor and pass it

BARE (35)

Lev 19:10 not strip your vineyard B, neither shall you gather
Num 23:3 he went to a B height.
2Sam 22:16 the world were laid B, at the rebuke of
2Kgs 9:13 under him on the B steps, and they blew
Ps 18:15 the world were laid B, at thy rebuke, O
29:9 and strips the forests B; and in his temple
Is 3:17 the LORD will lay B their secret parts.
13:2 On a B hill raise a signal, cry aloud
19:7 There will be B places by the Nile, on
32:11 strip, and make yourselves B, and gird sackcloth
41:18 open rivers on the B heights, and fountains in
49:9 the ways, on all B heights shall be their
Jer 3:2 your eyes to the B heights, and see!
3:21 A voice on the B heights is heard, the
4:11 hot wind from the B heights in the desert
7:29 a lamentation on the B heights, for the LORD
12:12 Upon all the B heights in the desert destroyers
14:6 asses stand on the B heights, they pant for
49:10 I have stripped Esau B, I have uncovered his
Lam 4:21 pass; you shall become drunk and strip yourself B

Ezek 13:14 foundation will be laid B; when it falls, you
16:7 hair had grown; yet you were naked and B
16:22 you were naked and B, weltering in your blood.
16:36 your shame was laid B and your nakedness
16:39 your fair jewels, and leave you naked and B
23:29 leave you naked and B, and the nakedness of
24:7 put it on the B rock, she did not
24:8 have set on the B rock the blood she
26:4 and make her a B rock.
26:14 will make you a B rock; you shall be
29:18 every shoulder was rubbed B; yet neither he nor
Hab 3:13 the wicked, laying him B from thigh to neck.
Zeph 2:14 threshold; for her cedar work will be laid B
1Cor 15:37 to be, but a B kernel, perhaps of wheat
Heb 4:13 are open and laid B to the eyes of

BARED (2)

Is 52:10 The LORD has B his holy arm before the
Ezek 4:7 Jerusalem, with your arm B; and you shall prophesy

BAREFOOT (4)

2Sam 15:30 weeping as he went, B and with his head
Is 20:2 so, walking naked and B --
20:3 has walked naked and B for three years as
20:4 the old, naked and B, with buttocks uncovered, to

BARELY

2Pet 2:18 flesh men who have B escaped from those who

BARGAIN (4)

Job 6:27 over the fatherless, and B over your friend.
41:6 Will traders B over him?
Is 57:8 you have made a B for yourself with them,
Hos 12:1 violence; they make a B with Assyria, and oil

BARIAH

1Chr 3:22 of Shemaiah: Hattush, Igal, B, Neariah, and Shaphat,

BARK (3)

Wis 13:11 strip off all its B, and then with pleasing
Is 56:10 dumb dogs, they cannot B; dreaming, lying down,
Joel 1:7 has stripped off their B and thrown it down;

BARKOS (2)

Ezra 2:53 Harsha, the sons of B, the sons of Sisera,
Neh 7:55 Harsha, the sons of B, the sons of Sisera,

BARLEY (37)

Ex 9:31 (The flax and the B were ruined, for the
9:31 were ruined, for the B was in the ear
Lev 27:16 of a homer of B shall be valued at
Num 5:15 of an ephah of B meal; he shall pour
Deut 8:8 land of wheat and B, of vines and fig
Judg 7:13 lo, a cake of B bread tumbled into the
Ruth 1:22 at the beginning of B harvest.
2:17 gleaned, and it was about an ephah of B
2:23 the end of the B and wheat harvests; and
3:2 See, he is winnowing B tonight at the threshing
3:15 out six measures of B, and laid it upon
3:17 "These six measures of B he gave to me,
2Sam 14:30 mine, and he has B there; go and set
17:28 and earthen vessels, wheat, B, meal, parched grain,
21:9 at the beginning of B harvest.
1Kgs 4:28 B also and straw for the horses and swift
2Kgs 4:42 fruits, twenty loaves of B, and fresh ears of
7:1 and two measures of B for a shekel, at
7:16 and two measures of B for a shekel, according
7:18 king, "Two measures of B shall be sold for
1Chr 11:13 of ground full of B, and the men fled
2Chr 2:10 twenty thousand cors of B, twenty thousand baths of
2:15 therefore the wheat and B, oil and wine, of
27:5 thousand cors of wheat and ten thousand of B
Jud 8:2 had died during the B harvest.
Job 31:40 instead of wheat, and foul weeds instead of B
Is 28:25 wheat in rows and B in its proper place,
Jer 41:8 have stores of wheat, B, oil, and honey hidden
Ezek 4:9 you, take wheat and B, beans and lentils, millet
4:12 eat it as a B cake, baking it in
13:19 people for handfuls of B and for pieces of
45:13 from each homer of B,
Hos 3:2 silver and a homer and a lethech of B
Joel 1:10 the wheat and the B; because the harvest of
Jn 6:9 here who has five B loaves and two fish;
6:13 fragments from the five B loaves, left by those
Rev 6:6 and three quarts of B for a denarius; but

BARN (3)

Hag 2:19 laid, consider: Is the seed yet in the B
Mt 13:30 be burned, but gather the wheat into my B
Lk 12:24 have neither storehouse nor B, and yet God feeds

BARNABAS (29)

Acts 4:36 surnamed by the apostles B (which means, Son of
9:27 But B took him, and brought him to the
11:22 Jerusalem, and they sent B to Antioch.
11:25 So B went to Tarsus to look for Saul;
11:30 by the hand of B and Saul.
12:25 And B and Saul returned from Jerusalem when they
13:1 were prophets and teachers, B, Simeon who was
13:2 "Set apart for me B and Saul for the
13:7 of intelligence, who summoned B and Saul and
13:43 Judaism followed Paul and B, who spoke to them
13:46 And Paul and B spoke out boldly, saying, "It
13:50 persecution against Paul and B, and drove them out
14:12 B they called Zeus, and Paul, because he was
14:14 But when the apostles B and Paul heard of
14:20 he went on with B to Derbe.
15:2 And when Paul and B had no small dissension
15:2 with them, Paul and B and some of the
15:12 and they listened to B and Paul as they
15:22 and send them to Antioch with Paul and B
15:25 you with our beloved B and Paul,
15:34 But Paul and B remained in Antioch, teaching and
15:35 days Paul said to B, "Come, let us return
15:36 And B wanted to take with them John called
15:38 separated from each other; B took Mark with him
1Cor 9:6 Or is it only B and I who have
Gal 2:1 again to Jerusalem with B, taking Titus along with
2:9 gave to me and B the right hand of
2:13 insincerely, so that even B was carried away by
Col 4:10 Mark the cousin of B (concerning whom you have

BARNS (4)

Deut 28:8 upon you in your B, and in all that
Prov 3:10 your produce; then your B will be filled with
Mt 6:26 reap nor gather into B, and yet your heavenly
Lk 12:18 will pull down my B, and build larger ones;

BARRACKS (6)

Acts 21:34 he ordered him to be brought into the B
21:37 be brought into the B, he said to the
22:24 be brought into the B, and ordered him to
23:10 from among them and bring him into the B
23:16 went and entered the B and told Paul.
23:32 they returned to the B, leaving the horsemen to

BARREN (23)

Gen 11:30 Now Sarai was B; she had no child.
25:21 wife, because she was B; and the LORD granted
29:31 hated, he opened her womb; but Rachel was B
Ex 23:26 her young or be B in your land; I
Deut 7:14 be male or female B among you, or among
Judg 13:2 and his wife was B and had no children.
13:3 her, "Behold, you are B and have no children;
1Sam 2:5 The B has borne seven, but she who has
Job 3:7 let that night be B; let no joyful cry
15:34 of the godless is B, and fire consumes the
24:21 "They feed on the B childless woman, and do
Ps 113:9 He gives the B woman a home, making her
Prov 30:16 say, "Enough": Sheol, the B womb, the earth ever
Wis 3:13 For blessed is the B woman who is undefiled,
4:19 left utterly dry and B, and they will suffer
Sir 42:10 prove unfaithful, or, though married, lest she be B
Is 49:21 I was bereaved and B, exiled and put away,
54:1 "Sing, O B one, who did not bear; break
Lk 1:7 child, because Elizabeth was B, and both were
1:36 the sixth month with her who was called B
23:28 say, 'Blessed are the B, and the wombs that
Gal 4:27 is written, "Rejoice, O B one who does not
Jas 2:20 shallow man, that faith apart from works is B

BARRENNESS

Rom 4:19 when he considered the B of Sarah's womb.

BARRICADES

Jud 5:1 hilltops and set up B in the plains,

BARRIER (3)

Jer 5:22 the sea, a perpetual B which it cannot pass;
Ezek 40:12 There was a B before the side rooms, one
1Mac 12:36 to erect a high B between the citadel and

BARS (47)

Ex 26:26 "And you shall make B of acacia wood, five
26:27 the tabernacle, and five B for the frames of
26:27 the tabernacle, and five B for the frames of
26:29 for holders for the B; and you shall overlay
26:29 you shall overlay the B with gold.
35:11 and its frames, its B, its pillars, and its
36:31 And he made B of acacia wood, five for
36:32 the tabernacle, and five B for the frames of
36:32 the tabernacle, and five B for the frames of
36:34 for holders for the B, and overlaid the bars
36:34 bars, and overlaid the B with gold.
39:33 hooks, its frames, its B, its pillars, and its
Lev 26:13 I have broken the B of your yoke and
Num 3:36 of the tabernacle, the B, the pillars, the bases,
4:31 the tabernacle, with its B, pillars, and bases,
Deut 3:5 high walls, gates, and B, besides very many unwalled
33:25 Your B shall be iron and bronze; and as
1Sam 23:7 by entering a town that has gates and B
1Kgs 4:13 with walls and bronze B;
2Chr 8:5 with walls, gates, and B,
14:7 and towers, gates and B; the land is still
Neh 3:3 and set its doors, its bolts, and its B
3:6 and set its doors, its bolts, and its B
3:13 its bolts, and its B, and repaired a thousand
3:14 and set its doors, its bolts, and its B
3:15 its bolts, and its B; and he built the
Job 17:16 go down to the B of Sheol?
38:10 for it, and set B and doors,
40:18 bronze, his limbs like B of iron.
Ps 107:16 cuts in two the B of iron.
147:13 For he strengthens the B of your gates; he
Prov 18:19 quarreling is like the B of a castle.
Sir 49:13 up the gates and B and rebuilt our ruined
Is 43:14 break down all the B, and the shouting of
45:2 and cut asunder the B of iron,
Jer 28:13 You have broken wooden B, but I will make
28:13 make in their place B of iron.
49:31 has no gates or B, that dwells alone.
51:30 are on fire, her B are broken.
Lam 2:9 ruined and broken her B; her king and princes
Bar 6:18 doors and locks and B, in order that they
Ezek 34:27 when I break the B of their yoke, and
38:11 walls, and having no B or gates';
Hos 11:6 their cities, consume the B of their gates, and
Jon 2:6 to the land whose B closed upon me for
Nah 3:13 open to your foes; fire has devoured your B
1Mac 9:50 and Tephon, with high walls and gates and B

BARSABBAS (2)

Acts 1:23 forward two, Joseph called B, who was surnamed
15:22 They sent Judas called B, and Silas, leading men

BARTER (2)

Sir 37:11 with a merchant about B or with a buyer
Ezek 27:9 were in you, to B for your wares.

BARTERED

Ezek 27:19 cassia, and calamus were B for your merchandise.

BARTHOLOMEW (4)

Mt 10:3 his brother; Philip and B; Thomas and Matthew the
Mk 3:18 Andrew, and Philip, and B, and Matthew, and
Lk 6:14 John, and Philip, and B,
Acts 1:13 Andrew, Philip and Thomas, B and Matthew, James

BARTIMAEUS

Mk 10:46 and a great multitude, B, a blind beggar, the

BARUCH (29)

Neh 3:20 After him B the son of Zabbai repaired another
10:6 Meremoth, Obadiah, Daniel, Ginnethon, B,
11:5 Ma-aseiah the son of B, son of Colhozeh, son
Jer 32:12 deed of purchase to B the son of Neriah
32:13 I charged B in their presence, saying,
32:16 deed of purchase to B the son of Neriah,
36:4 Then Jeremiah called B the son of Neriah, and
36:4 son of Neriah, and B wrote upon a scroll
36:5 And Jeremiah ordered B, saying, "I am debarred
36:8 And B the son of Neriah did all that
36:10 of all the people, B read the words of
36:13 he had heard, when B read the scroll in
36:14 Cushi, to say to B, "Take in your hand
36:14 So B the son of Neriah took the scroll
36:15 So B read it to them.
36:16 and they said to B, "We must report all
36:17 Then they asked B, "Tell us, how did you
36:18 B answered them, "He dictated all these words to
36:19 the princes said to B, "Go and hide, you
36:26 of Abdeel to seize B the secretary and Jeremiah
36:27 with the words which B wrote at Jeremiah's
36:32 and gave it to B the scribe, the son
43:3 to live there'; but B the son of Neriah
43:6 Jeremiah the prophet and B the son of Neriah.
45:1 the prophet spoke to B the son of Neriah,
45:2 Israel, to you, O B:
Bar 1:1 of the book which B the son of Neraiah,
1:3 And B read the words of this book in
1:8 tenth day of Sivan, B took the vessels of

BARZILLAI (12)

2Sam 17:27 Ammiel from Lo-debar, and B the Gileadite from
19:31 Now B the Gileadite had come down from Rogelim;
19:32 B was a very aged man, eighty years old;
19:33 the king said to B, "Come over with me,
19:34 But B said to the king, "How many years
19:39 and the king kissed B and blessed him, and
21:8 Adriel the son of B the Meholathite;
1Kgs 2:7 with the sons of B the Gileadite, and let
Ezra 2:61 and the sons of B (who had taken a
2:61 from the daughters of B the Gileadite, and was
Neh 7:63 Hakkoz, the sons of B (who had taken a
7:63 of the daughters of B the Gileadite and was

BASE (44)

Ex 25:31 The B and the shaft of the lampstand shall
29:12 pour out at the B of the altar.
30:18 of bronze, with its B of bronze, for washing.
30:28 the laver and its B;
31:9 the laver and its B;
35:16 the laver and its B;
37:17 The B and the shaft of the lampstand were
38:8 of bronze and its B of bronze, from the
38:27 for the hundred talents, a talent for a B
39:39 the laver and its B;
Lev 4:7 pour out at the B of the altar of
4:18 pour out at the B of the altar of
4:25 its blood at the B of the altar of
4:30 its blood at the B of the altar.
4:34 its blood at the B of the altar.
5:9 drained out at the B of the altar; it
8:11 the laver and its B, to consecrate them.
8:15 the blood at the B of the altar, and
9:9 the blood at the B of the altar;
Num 8:4 of gold; from its B to its flowers, it
Deut 13:13 dwell there, that certain B fellows have gone out
15:9 lest there be a B thought in your heart,
Judg 19:22 men of the city, B fellows, beset the house
20:13 up the men, the B fellows in Gibe-ah, that
1Sam 1:16 your maidservant as a B woman, for all along
30:22 all the wicked and B fellows among the men
1Kgs 21:10 people; and set two B fellows opposite him, and
21:13 And the two B fellows came in and sat
21:13 opposite him; and the B fellows brought a charge
Ps 101:3 not set before my eyes anything that is B
Wis 2:16 by him as something B, and he avoids our
15:12 one can, even by B means.
Sir 18:29 Do not follow your B desires, but restrain your
18:30 to take pleasure in B desire, it will make
26:18 of gold on a B of silver, so are
Is 3:5 the elder, and the B fellow to the honorable.
Ezek 41:22 broad; its corners, its B, and its walls were
43:13 and a handbreadth): its B shall be one cubit
43:14 the altar: from the B on the ground to
43:17 cubit broad, and its B one cubit round about.
Zech 5:11 will set the ephah down there on its B
Rom 1:28 them up to a B mind and to improper
1Tim 6:4 produce envy, dissension, slander, B suspicions,
Tit 1:10 families by teaching for B gain what they have

BASED (5)

Rom 9:31 the righteousness which is B on law did not
9:32 as if it were B on works.
10:5 the righteousness which is B on the law shall
10:6 But the righteousness B on faith says, Do not
Phil 3:9 righteousness of my own, B on law, but that

BASEMATH (7)

Gen 26:34 Be-eri the Hittite, and B the daughter of Elon
36:3 Zibeon the Hivite, and B, Ishmael's daughter, the
36:4 bore to Esau, Eliphaz; B bore Reuel;
36:10 Reuel the son of B the wife of Esau.

36:13 are the sons of B, Esau's wife.
36:17 are the sons of B, Esau's wife.
1Kgs 4:15 Naphtali (he had taken B the daughter of Solomon

BASENESS (2)

Sir 14:6 the retribution for his B;
14:7 unintentionally, and betrays his B in the end.

BASES (53)

Ex 26:19 south side; and forty B of silver you shall
26:19 the twenty frames, two B under one frame for
26:19 two tenons, and two B under another frame for
26:21 frames, and their forty B of silver, two bases
26:21 bases of silver, two B under one frame, and
26:21 one frame, and two B under another frame;
26:25 eight frames, with their B of silver, sixteen bases;
26:25 bases of silver, sixteen B; two bases under one
26:25 silver, sixteen bases; two B under one frame, and
26:25 one frame, and two B under another frame.
26:32 of gold, upon four B of silver.
26:37 you shall cast five B of bronze for them.
27:10 be twenty and their B twenty, of bronze, but
27:11 pillars twenty and their B twenty, of bronze, but
27:12 for fifty cubits, with ten pillars and ten B
27:14 be fifteen cubits, with three pillars and three B
27:15 be fifteen cubits, with three pillars and three B
27:16 shall have four pillars and with them four B
27:17 of silver, and their B of bronze.
27:18 fine twined linen and B of bronze.
35:11 its pillars, and its B;
35:17 its pillars and its B, and the screen for
36:24 and he made forty B of silver under the
36:24 the twenty frames, two B under one frame for
36:24 two tenons, and two B under another frame for
36:26 frames and their forty B of silver, two bases
36:26 bases of silver, two B under one frame and
36:26 one frame and two B under another frame.
36:30 eight frames with their B of silver: sixteen bases,
36:30 bases of silver: sixteen B, under every frame two
36:30 of silver: sixteen bases, under every frame two B
36:36 cast for them four B of silver.
36:38 gold, but their five B were of bronze.
38:10 were twenty and their B twenty, of bronze, but
38:11 their pillars twenty, their B twenty, of bronze, but
38:14 were fifteen cubits, with three pillars and three B
38:15 of fifteen cubits, with three pillars and three B
38:17 And the B for the pillars were of bronze,
38:19 were four; their four B were of bronze, their
38:27 were for casting the B of the sanctuary, and
38:27 the sanctuary, and the B of the veil; a
38:27 the veil; a hundred B for the hundred talents,
38:30 it he made the B for the door of
38:31 of the altar, the B round about the court,
38:31 the court, and the B of the gate of
39:33 its pillars, and its B;
39:40 its pillars, and its B, and the screen for
Num 3:36 bars, the pillars, the B, and all their accessories;
3:37 round about, with their B and pegs and cords.
4:31 its bars, pillars, and B,
4:32 round about with their B, pegs, and cords, with
Job 38:6 On what were its B sunk, or who laid
Song 5:15 alabaster columns, set upon B of gold.

BASHAN (60)

Num 21:33 by the way to B; and Og the king
21:33 Og the king of B came out against them,
32:33 of Og king of B, the land and its
Deut 1:4 Og the king of B, who lived in Ashtaroth
3:1 up the way to B; and Og the king
3:1 Og the king of B came out against us,
3:3 also, the king of B, and all his people;
3:4 region of Argob, the kingdom of Og in B
3:10 all Gilead and all B, as far as Salecah
3:10 Edre-i, cities of the kingdom of Og in B
3:11 Og the king of B was left of the
3:13 of Gilead, and all B, the kingdom of Og,
3:13 (The whole of that B is called the land
3:14 of Argob, that is, B, as far as the
4:43 Gadites, and Golan in B for the Manassites.
4:47 Og the king of B, the two kings of
29:7 Og the king of B came out against us
32:14 and rams, herds of B and goats, with the
33:22 is a lion's whelp, that leaps forth from B
Josh 9:10 and Og king of B, who dwelt in Ashtaroth.
12:4 and Og king of B, one of the remnant
12:5 and Salecah and all B to the boundary of
13:11 Mount Hermon, and all B to Salecah;
13:12 kingdom of Og in B, who reigned in Ashtaroth
13:30 from Mahanaim, through all B, the whole kingdom
13:30 of Og king of B, and all the towns
13:30 Jair, which are in B, sixty cities,
13:31 kingdom of Og in B; these were allotted to
17:1 were allotted Gilead and B, because he was a
17:5 land of Gilead and B, which is on the
20:8 Gad, and Golan in B, from the tribe of
21:6 half-tribe of Manasseh in B, thirteen cities.
21:27 of Manasseh, Golan in B with its pasture lands,
22:7 given a possession in B; but to the other
1Kgs 4:13 Argob, which is in B, sixty great cities with
4:19 of the Amorites and of Og king of B
2Kgs 10:33 valley of the Arnon, that is, Gilead and B
1Chr 5:11 in the land of B as far as Salecah:
5:12 chief, Shapham the second, Janai, and Shaphat in B
5:16 dwelt in Gilead, in B and in its towns,
5:23 were very numerous from B to Baal-hermon, Senir,
6:62 of Issachar, Asher, Naphtali, and Manasseh in B
6:71 of Manasseh: Golan in B with its pasture lands
Neh 9:22 Heshbon and the land of Og king of B
Ps 22:12 me, strong bulls of B surround me;
68:15 mountain, mountain of B; O many-peaked mountain,
68:15 of Bashan; O many-peaked mountain, mountain of B
68:22 bring them back from B, I will bring them
135:11 and Og, king of B, and all the kingdoms
136:20 and Og, king of B, for his steadfast love
Is 2:13 all the oaks of B;
33:9 like a desert; and B and Carmel shake off
Jer 22:20 up your voice in B; cry from Abarim, for
50:19 on Carmel and in B, and his desire shall
Ezek 27:6 Of oaks of B they made your oars; they
39:18 goats, of bulls, all of them fatlings of B
Amos 4:1 word, you cows of B, who are in the
Mic 7:14 let them feed in B and Gilead as in
Nah 1:4 up all the rivers; B and Carmel wither, the
Zech 11:2 Wail, oaks of B, for the thick forest has

BASIC

Sir 39:26 B to all the needs of man's life are

BASIN (16)

Ex 12:22 which is in the B, and touch the lintel
12:22 which is in the B; and none of you
Num 7:13 thirty shekels, one silver B of seventy shekels,
7:19 thirty shekels, one silver B of seventy shekels,
7:25 thirty shekels, one silver B of seventy shekels,
7:31 thirty shekels, one silver B of seventy shekels,
7:37 thirty shekels, one silver B of seventy shekels,
7:43 thirty shekels, one silver B of seventy shekels,
7:49 thirty shekels, one silver B of seventy shekels,
7:55 thirty shekels, one silver B of seventy shekels,
7:61 thirty shekels, one silver B of seventy shekels,
7:67 thirty shekels, one silver B of seventy shekels,
7:73 thirty shekels, one silver B of seventy shekels,
7:79 thirty shekels, one silver B of seventy shekels,
7:85 thirty shekels and each B seventy, all the silver
Jn 13:5 poured water into a B, and began to wash

BASINS (19)

Ex 24:6 and put it in B, and half of the
27:3 ashes, and shovels and B and forks and firepans;
38:3 pots, the shovels, the B, the forks, and the
Num 4:14 the shovels, and the B, all the utensils of
7:84 silver plates, twelve silver B, twelve golden dishes,
2Sam 17:28 from Rogelim, brought beds, B, and earthen vessels,
1Kgs 7:40 also made the pots, the shovels, and the B
7:45 the shovels, and the B, all these vessels in
7:50 gold; the cups, snuffers, B, dishes for incense, and
2Kgs 12:13 house of the LORD B of silver, snuffers, bowls,
1Chr 28:17 for the forks, the B, and the cups; for
2Chr 4:8 he made a hundred B of gold.
4:11 also made the pots, the shovels, and the B
4:22 purest gold; the snuffers, B, dishes for incense, and
Ezra 1:9 of them: a thousand B of gold, a thousand
1:9 of gold, a thousand B of silver, twenty-nine censers,
Neh 7:70 darics of gold, fifty B, five hundred and thirty
Jer 52:18 the snuffers, and the B, and the dishes for
52:19 the firepans, and the B, and the pots, and

BASIS

Rom 11:6 no longer on the B of works; otherwise grace

BASKAMA

1Mac 13:23 When he approached B, he killed Jonathan, and he

B

BASKET (27)

Gen 40:17 and in the uppermost B there were all sorts
40:17 it out of the B on my head."
Ex 2:3 took for him a B made of bulrushes, and
2:5 river; she saw the B among the reeds and
29:3 put them in one B and bring them in
29:3 bring them in the B, and bring the bull
29:23 wafer, out of the B of unleavened bread that
29:32 that is in the B, at the door of
Lev 8:2 two rams, and the B of unleavened bread;
8:26 and out of the B of unleavened bread which
8:31 that is in the B of ordination offerings, as
Num 6:15 peace offering, and a B of unleavened bread, cakes
6:17 the LORD, with the B of unleavened bread; the
6:19 cake out of the B, and one unleavened wafer,
Deut 26:2 put it in a B, and you shall go
26:4 priest shall take the B from your hand, and
28:5 Blessed shall be your B and your kneading-trough.
28:17 Cursed shall be your B and your kneading-trough.
Judg 6:19 he put in a B, and the broth he
Ps 81:6 the burden; your hands were freed from the B
Jer 5:27 Like a B full of birds, their houses are
24:2 One B had very good figs, like first-ripe figs,
24:2 figs, but the other B had very bad figs,
Amos 8:1 showed me: behold, a B of summer fruit.
8:2 And I said, "A B of summer fruit." Then
Acts 9:25 down over the wall, lowering him in a B
2Cor 11:33 let down in a B through a window in

BASKETS (14)

Gen 40:16 there were three cake B on my head,
40:18 its interpretation: the three B are three days;
2Kgs 10:7 put their heads in B, and sent them to
Jer 24:1 this vision: Behold, two B of figs placed before
Mt 14:20 they took up twelve B full of the broken
15:37 they took up seven B full of the broken
16:9 thousand, and how many B you gathered?
16:10 thousand, and how many B you gathered?
Mk 6:43 they took up twelve B full of broken pieces
8:8 pieces left over, seven B full.
8:19 five thousand, how many B full of broken pieces
8:20 four thousand, how many B full of broken pieces
Lk 9:17 was left over, twelve B of broken pieces.
Jn 6:13 up and filled twelve B with fragments from the

BASTARD

Deut 23:2 "No B shall enter the assembly of the LORD;

BAT (2)

Lev 11:19 according to its kind, the hoopoe, and the B
Deut 14:18 heron, after their kinds; the hoopoe and the B

BATH (5)

Is 5:10 shall yield but one B, and a homer of
Ezek 45:10 just balances, a just ephah, and a just B
45:11 The ephah and the B shall be of the
45:11 the same measure, the B containing one tenth of
45:14 one tenth of a B from each cor (the

BATH-RABBIM

Song 7:4 are pools in Heshbon, by the gate of B

BATH-SHUA (2)

1Chr 2:3 and Shelah; these three B the Canaanitess bore to
3:5 and Solomon, four by B, the daughter of Ammiel;

BATHE (29)

Ex 2:5 Pharaoh came down to B at the river, and
Lev 14:8 all his hair, and B himself in water, and
14:9 wash his clothes, and B his body in water,
15:5 wash his clothes, and B himself in water, and
15:6 wash his clothes, and B himself in water, and
15:7 wash his clothes, and B himself in water, and
15:8 wash his clothes, and B himself in water, and
15:10 wash his clothes, and B himself in water, and
15:11 wash his clothes, and B himself in water, and
15:13 clothes; and he shall B his body in running
15:16 of semen, he shall B his whole body in
15:18 both of them shall B themselves in water, and
15:21 wash his clothes, and B himself in water, and
15:22 wash his clothes, and B himself in water, and
15:27 wash his clothes, and B himself in water, and
16:4 He shall B his body in water, and then
16:24 there; and he shall B his body in water
16:26 wash his clothes and B his body in water,
16:28 wash his clothes and B his body in water,
17:15 wash his clothes, and B himself in water, and
17:16 not wash them or B his flesh, he shall
Num 19:7 wash his clothes and B his body in water,
19:8 clothes in water and B his body in water,
19:19 wash his clothes and B himself in water, and
Deut 23:11 comes on, he shall B himself in water, and
Ps 58:10 the vengeance; he will B his feet in the
68:23 sea, that you may B your feet in blood,
Dan 13:15 maids, and wished to B in the garden, for
13:17 shut the garden doors so that I may B

BATHED (8)

Lev 22:6 things unless he has B his body in water.
Jud 10:3 her widow's garments, and B her body with water,
12:7 valley of Bethulia, and B at the spring in
Song 5:3 I had B my feet, how could I soil
5:12 beside springs of water, B in milk, fitly set.
Ezek 16:9 Then I B you with water and washed off
23:40 For them you B yourself, painted your eyes, and
Jn 13:10 him, "He who has B does not need to

BATHING

2Sam 11:2 the roof a woman B; and the woman was

BATHS (8)

1Kgs 7:26 flower of a lily; it held two thousand B
7:38 each laver held forty B, each laver measured four
2Chr 2:10 of barley, twenty thousand B of wine, and twenty
2:10 wine, and twenty thousand B of oil."
4:5 of a lily; it held over three thousand B
Ezra 7:22 of wheat, a hundred B of wine, a hundred
7:22 of wine, a hundred B of oil, and salt
Ezek 45:14 the homer, contains ten B;

BATHSHEBA (10)

2Sam 11:3 said, "Is not this B, the daughter of Eliam,
12:24 David comforted his wife, B, and went in to
1Kgs 1:11 Then Nathan said to B the mother of Solomon,
1:15 So B went to the king into his chamber
1:16 B bowed and did obeisance to the king, and
1:28 King David answered, "Call B to me." So she
1:31 Then B bowed with her face to the ground,
2:13 of Haggith came to B the mother of Solomon.
2:18 B said, "Very well; I will speak for you
2:19 So B went to King Solomon, to speak to

BATS (2)

Is 2:20 moles and to the B,
Bar 6:22 B, swallows, and birds light on their bodies and

BATTALION (2)

Mt 27:27 they gathered the whole B before him.
Mk 15:16 praetorium); and they called together the whole B

BATTERED (2)

Is 24:12 city, the gates are B into ruins.
1Mac 13:43 to the city, and B and captured one tower.

BATTERING (2)

2Sam 20:15 rampart; and they were B the wall, to throw
Is 22:5 valley of vision, a B down of walls and

BATTERING-RAMS (4)

Ezek 4:2 against it, and plant B against it round about.
21:22 with shouting, to set B against the gates, to
26:9 the shock of his B against your walls, and
2Mac 12:15 the world, who without B or engines of war

BATTLE (243)

Gen 14:8 out, and they joined B in the Valley of
Ex 13:18 out of the land of Egypt equipped for B
Num 21:33 all his people, to B at Edre-i.
31:21 who had gone to B: "This is the statute
31:27 who went out to B and all the congregation.
31:28 who went out to B, one out of five
32:27 before the LORD to B, as my lord orders."
32:29 who is armed to B before the LORD, will
Deut 2:9 contend with them in B, for I will not
2:24 to take possession, and contend with him in B
2:32 all his people, to B at Jahaz.
3:1 all his people, to B at Edre-i.
20:2 draw near to the B, the priest shall come
20:3 near this day to B against your enemies: let
20:5 he die in the B and another man dedicate
20:6 he die in the B and another man enjoy
20:7 he die in the B and another man take

BATTLE

29:7 out against us to B, but we defeated them;
Josh 4:13 before the LORD for B, to the plains of
8:14 to meet Israel in B; but he did not
11:19 the inhabitants of Gibeon; they took all in B
11:20 come against Israel in B, in order that they
Judg 8:13 Joash returned from the B by the ascent of
20:14 to go out to B against the people of
20:18 go up first to B against the Benjaminites?" And
20:20 Israel went out to B against Benjamin; and the
20:20 Israel drew up the B line against them at
20:22 and again formed the B line in the same
20:23 again draw near to B against our brethren the
20:28 again go out to B against our brethren the
20:34 all Israel, and the B was hard; but the
20:39 city the men of Israel should turn in B
20:39 smitten down before us, as in the first B
20:42 the wilderness; but the B overtook them, and those
21:22 them his wife in B, neither did you give
1Sam 4:1 Israel went out to B against the Philistines; they
4:2 Israel, and when the B spread, Israel was defeated
4:2 about four thousand men on the field of B
4:12 Benjamin ran from the B line, and came to
4:16 has come from the B; I fled from the
4:16 I fled from the B today." And he said,
13:22 the day of the B there was neither sword
14:20 and went into the B; and behold, every man's
14:22 they too followed hard after them in the B
14:23 that day; and the B passed beyond Beth-aven.
17:1 gathered their armies for B; and they were gathered
17:2 up in line of B against the Philistines.
17:8 have you come out to draw up for B
17:13 followed Saul to the B; and the names of
17:13 who went to the B were Eliab the first-born,
17:20 going forth to the B line, shouting the war
17:21 Philistines drew up for B, army against army.
17:28 for you have come down to see the B
17:47 and spear; for the B is the LORD's and
17:48 ran quickly toward the B line to meet the
18:30 Philistines came out to B, and as often as
26:10 shall go down into B and perish.
29:4 down with us to B, lest in the battle
29:4 battle, lest in the B he become an adversary
29:9 with us to the B
30:24 goes down into the B, so shall his share
31:3 The B pressed hard upon Saul, and the archers
2Sam 1:4 have fled from the B, and many of the
1:25 the mighty fallen in the midst of the B
2:17 And the B was very fierce that day; and
3:30 brother Asahel in the B at Gibeon.
10:8 and drew up in B array at the entrance
10:9 Joab saw that the B was set against him
10:13 him drew near to B against the Syrians; and
11:1 kings go forth to B, David sent Joab, and
17:11 that you go to B in person.
18:6 against Israel; and the B was fought in the
18:8 The B spread over the face of all the
19:3 in who are ashamed when they flee in B
19:10 whom we anointed over us, is dead in B
21:17 out with us to B, lest you quench the
22:40 with strength for the B; thou didst make my
23:9 were gathered there for B, and the men of
1Kgs 8:44 people go out to B against their enemy, by
20:14 Then he said, "Who shall begin the B
20:29 the seventh day the B was joined; and the
20:39 the midst of the B; and behold, a soldier
22:4 with me to B at Ramoth-gilead?" And Jehoshaphat
22:6 "Shall I go to B against Ramoth-gilead, or shall
22:15 go to Ramoth-gilead to B, or shall we forbear?"
22:30 myself and go into B, but you wear your
22:30 king of Israel disguised himself and went into B
22:34 me out of the B, for I am wounded."
22:35 And the B grew hot that day, and the
2Kgs 3:7 go with me to B against Moab?" And he
3:26 Moab saw that the B was going against him,
14:11 faced one another in B at Beth-shemesh, which
1Chr 5:20 to God in the B, and he granted their
10:3 The B pressed hard upon Saul, and the archers
11:13 when the Philistines were gathered there for B
12:19 the Philistines for the B against Saul.
12:33 seasoned troops, equipped for B with all the weapons
12:35 thousand six hundred men equipped for B
12:36 Of Asher forty thousand seasoned troops ready for B
12:38 of war, arrayed in B order, came to Hebron
14:15 then go out to B; for God has gone
19:7 were mustered from their cities and came to B
19:9 and drew up in B array at the entrance
19:10 Joab saw that the B was set against him
19:14 before the Syrians for B; and they fled before
19:17 when David set the B in array against the
20:1 kings go forth to B, Joab led out the
2Chr 6:34 people go out to B against their enemies, by
13:3 Abijah went out to B having an army of
13:3 up his line of B against him with eight
13:12 his priests with their B trumpets to sound the
13:12 sound the call to B against you.
13:14 Judah looked, behold, the B was before and behind
13:15 of Judah raised the B shout.
14:10 up their lines of B in the valley of
18:5 "Shall we go to B against Ramoth-gilead, or shall
18:14 go to Ramoth-gilead to B, or shall I forbear?"
18:29 myself and go into B, but you wear your
18:29 of Israel disguised himself; and they went into B
18:33 me out of the B, for I am wounded."
18:34 And the B grew hot that day, and the
20:1 of the Me-unites, came against Jehoshaphat for B
20:15 great multitude; for the B is not yours but
20:17 to fight in this B; take your position, stand
25:13 go with him to B, fell upon the cities
25:21 faced one another in B at Beth-shemesh, which
35:22 of God, but joined B in the plain of
Jud 1:13 and defeated him in B, and overthrew the whole
7:11 fight against them in B array, and not a
14:13 against us to give B, in order to be
Job 15:24 prevail against him, like a king prepared for B
38:23 for the day of B and war?
39:25 'Aha!' He smells the B from afar, the thunder
41:8 him; think of the B; you will not do
Ps 18:39 with strength for the B; thou didst make my
24:8 LORD, strong and mighty, the LORD, mighty in B
55:18 in safety from the B that I wage, for
78:9 the bow, turned back on the day of B
89:43 and thou hast not made him stand in B
140:7 hast covered my head in the day of B
144:1 and my fingers for B;
Prov 21:31 for the day of B, but the victory belongs
Eccl 9:11 the swift, nor the B to the strong, nor
Wis 12:9 of the righteous in B, or to destroy them
Sir 37:5 in the face of B take up the shield.
Is 3:25 by the sword and your mighty men in B
9:5 the tramping warrior in B tumult and every garment
13:4 LORD of hosts is mustering a host for B
16:9 and your harvest the B shout has fallen.
21:15 the bent bow, and from the press of B
22:2 not slain with the sword or dead in B
27:4 Would that I had thorns and briers to B
28:6 who turn back the B at the gate.
42:25 and the might of B; it set him on
Jer 6:23 as a man for B, against you, O daughter
8:6 own course, like a horse plunging headlong into B
18:21 their youths be slain by the sword in B
46:3 "Prepare buckler and shield, and advance for B
49:2 I will cause the B cry to be heard
49:14 and come against her, and rise up for B
50:22 The noise of B is in the land, and
50:42 as a man for B against you, O daughter
Ezek 7:14 but none goes to B, for my wrath is
13:5 it might stand in B in the day of
Dan 11:20 shall be broken, neither in anger nor in B
Hos 10:14 on the day of B; mothers were dashed in
Joel 2:5 stubble, like a powerful army drawn up for B
Amos 1:14 in the day of B, with a tempest in
Obad 1:1 let us rise against her for B
Zeph 1:16 of trumpet blast and B cry against the fortified
Zech 9:10 from Jerusalem; and the B bow shall be cut
10:3 will make them like his proud steed in B
10:4 out of them the B bow, out of them
10:5 like mighty men in B, trampling the foe in
14:2 nations against Jerusalem to B, and the city shall
14:3 as when he fights on a day of B
1Mac 1:18 king of Egypt in B, and Ptolemy turned and
2:32 them and prepared for B against them on the
2:66 you and fight the B against the peoples.
3:12 and used it in B the rest of his
3:13 and went out to B,
3:19 army that victory in B depends, but strength comes
3:44 to be ready for B, and to pray and
3:59 us to die in B than to see the
4:13 them, they went forth from their camp to B
4:14 with Judas blew their trumpets and engaged in B
4:17 for there is a B before us;
4:21 in the plain for B,
5:19 do not engage in B with the Gentiles until

5:31 Judas saw that the B had begun and that
5:42 to encamp, but make them all enter the B
5:59 out of the city to meet them in B
5:67 brave deed, fell in B, for they went out
5:67 they went out to B unwisely.
6:4 of the city and they withstood him in B
6:33 troops made ready for B and sounded their trumpets.
6:34 of grapes and mulberries, to arouse them for B
6:42 army advanced to the B, and six hundred men
7:31 to meet Judas in B near Caphar-salama.
7:43 the armies met in B on the thirteenth day
7:43 himself was the first to fall in the B
7:45 followed kept sounding the B call on the trumpets.
8:5 them, they crushed in B and conquered.
9:1 army had fallen in B, he sent Bacchides and
9:7 slipped away and the B was imminent, he was
9:13 the armies, and the B raged from morning till
9:17 The B became desperate, and many on both sides
9:30 as our ruler and leader, to fight our B
9:45 the B is in front of us and behind
9:47 So the B began, and Jonathan stretched out his
9:67 attack and went into B with his forces; and
10:2 army and marched out to meet him in B
10:49 two kings met in B, and the army of
10:50 He pressed the B strongly until the sun set,
10:53 I met him in B, and he and his
10:78 him to Azotus, and the armies engaged in B
10:82 engaged the phalanx in B (for the cavalry was
11:15 heard of it and came against him in B
11:69 in ambush emerged from their places and joined B
11:72 turned back to the B against the enemy and
12:27 ready all night for B, and he stationed outposts
12:28 men were prepared for B, they were afraid and
12:50 and kept marching in close formation, ready for B
13:14 was about to join B with him, so he
15:14 and the ships joined B from the sea; he
2Mac 8:20 the time of the B with the Galatians that
8:23 division himself, he joined B with Nicanor.
10:28 the two armies joined B, the one having as
10:29 When the B became fierce, there appeared to the
11:10 They advanced in B order, having their heavenly ally,
12:34 When they joined B, it happened that a few
12:36 show himself their ally and leader in the B
12:37 fathers he raised the B cry, with hymns; then
14:16 and engaged them in B at a village called
14:18 and their courage in B for their country, shrank
15:20 army drawn up for B, the elephants strategically
15:25 advanced with trumpets and B songs;
15:26 met the enemy in B with invocation to God
1Cor 14:8 an indistinct sound, who will get ready for B
Rev 9:7 like horses arrayed for B; on their heads were
9:9 noise of many chariots with horses rushing into B
16:14 to assemble them for B on the great day
20:8 to gather them for B; their number is like

BATTLE-FRONT
Sir 40:6 has escaped from the B;

BATTLEMENT
Song 8:9 build upon her a B of silver; but if

BATTLEMENTS (4)
Tob 13:16 and her towers and B with pure gold.
Sir 9:13 that you are going about on the city B
Zeph 1:16 against the fortified cities and against the lofty B
3:6 cut off nations; their B are in ruins; I

BATTLES (13)
1Sam 8:20 and go out before us and fight our B
18:17 be valiant for me and fight the LORD's B
25:28 lord is fighting the B of the LORD; and
1Chr 26:27 From spoil won in B they dedicated gifts for
2Chr 32:8 God, to help us and to fight our B
Jud 5:18 utterly defeated in many B and were led away
1Mac 1:2 Greece.) He fought many B, conquered strongholds,
3:3 of war and waged B, protecting the host by
3:26 Gentiles talked of the B of Judas.
5:7 He engaged in many B with them and they
5:21 Galilee and fought many B against the Gentiles, and
10:15 told him of the B that Jonathan and his
13:9 Fight our B, and all that you say to

BATTLING
Is 30:32 of timbrels and lyres; B with brandished arm he

BAVVAI
Neh 3:18 him their brethren repaired: B the son of Henadad,

BAY (4)
Josh 15:2 Salt Sea, from the B that faces southward;
15:5 side runs from the B of the sea at
18:19 ends at the northern B of the Salt Sea,
Acts 27:39 but they noticed a B with a beach, on

BAZAARS
1Kgs 20:34 and you may establish B for yourself in Damascus,

BAZLITH
Neh 7:54 Harhur, the sons of B, the sons of Mehida,

BAZLUTH
Ezra 2:52 Harhur, the sons of B, the sons of Mehida,

BDELLIUM (2)
Gen 2:12 that land is good; B and onyx stone are
Num 11:7 coriander seed, and its appearance like that of B

BE-ELZEBUL (7)
Mt 10:25 master of the house B, how much more will
12:24 "It is only by B, the prince of demons,
12:27 cast out demons by B, by whom do your
Mk 3:22 "He is possessed by B, and by the prince
Lk 11:15 casts out demons by B, the prince of demons";
11:18 you say that I cast out demons by B
11:19 cast out demons by B, by whom do your

BE-ERA
1Chr 7:37 Imrah, Bezer, Hod, Shamma, Shilshah, Ithran, and B

BE-ERAH
1Chr 5:6 son, Baal his son, B his son, whom Tilgath-pilneser

BE-ERI (2)
Gen 26:34 Judith the daughter of B the Hittite, and Basemath
Hos 1:1 Hosea the son of B, in the days of

BE-EROTH (9)
Deut 10:6 of Israel journeyed from B Bene-jaakan to Moserah.
Josh 9:17 cities were Gibeon, Chephirah, B, and Kiriath-jearim.
18:25 their villages: Gibeon, Ramah, B,
2Sam 4:2 man of Benjamin from B (for Be-eroth also is
4:2 Benjamin from Be-eroth (for B also is reckoned to
23:37 Ammonite, Naharai of B, the armor-bearer of Joab
1Chr 11:39 Ammonite, Naharai of B, the armor-bearer of Joab
Ezra 2:25 of Kiriatharim, Chephirah, and B, seven hundred and
Neh 7:29 of Kiriath-jearim, Chephirah, and B, seven hundred

BE-EROTHITE (2)
2Sam 4:5 sons of Rimmon the B, Rechab and Baanah, set
4:9 sons of Rimmon the B, "As the LORD lives,

BE-EROTHITES
2Sam 4:3 reckoned to Benjamin; the B fled to Gittaim, and

BEACH (5)
Mt 13:2 there; and the whole crowd stood on the B
Jn 21:4 Jesus stood on the B; yet the disciples did
Acts 21:5 kneeling down on the B we prayed and bade
27:39 a bay with a B, on which they planned
27:40 foresail to the wind they made for the B

BEADS
Num 31:50 signet rings, earrings, and B, to make atonement for

BEALIAH
1Chr 12:5 of Gederah, Eluzai, Jerimoth, B, Shemariah,

BEALOTH (2)
Josh 15:24 Hazor, Ithnan, Ziph, Telem, B,
1Kgs 4:16 Hushai, in Asher and B;

BEAM (8)
1Sam 17:7 was like a weaver's B, and his spear's head
2Sam 21:19 shaft of whose spear was like a weaver's B
1Chr 11:23 spear like a weaver's B; but Benaiah went down
20:5 shaft of whose spear was like a weaver's B
Ezra 6:11 alters this edict, a B shall be pulled out
Sir 22:14 A wooden B firmly bonded into a building will
Bar 6:20 are just like a B of the temple, but
Hab 2:11 the wall, and the B from the woodwork respond.

BEAMS (14)

1Kgs 6:6 order that the supporting B should not be inserted
6:9 of the house of B and planks of cedar.
6:36 of hewn stone and one course of cedar B
7:2 cedar pillars, with cedar B upon the pillars.
7:12 a course of cedar B; so had the inner
2Chr 3:7 house with gold--its B, its thresholds, its walls,
34:11 timber for binders and B for the buildings which
Neh 2:8 me timber to make B for the gates of
3:3 Gate; they laid its B and set its doors,
3:6 Gate; they laid its B and set its doors,
Ps 104:3 who hast laid the B of thy chambers on
Song 1:17 couch is green; the B of our house are
Sir 43:4 vapors, and with bright B it blinds the eyes.
Bar 6:55 the gods will be burnt in two like B

BEANS (2)

2Sam 17:28 barley, meal, parched grain, B and lentils,
Ezek 4:9 take wheat and barley, B and lentils, millet and

BEAR (220)

Gen 4:13 LORD, "My punishment is greater than I can B
16:11 with child, and shall B a son; you shall
17:17 is ninety years old, B a child?"
17:19 Sarah your wife shall B you a son, and
17:21 Isaac, whom Sarah shall B to you at this
18:13 say, 'Shall I indeed B a child, now that
30:3 her, that she may B upon my knees, and
43:9 you, then let me B the blame for ever;
44:32 you, then I shall B the blame in the
49:15 bowed his shoulder to B, and became a slave
Ex 18:22 you, and they will B the burden with you.
20:16 "You shall not B false witness against your neighbor.
23:2 evil; nor shall you B witness in a suit,
28:12 Israel; and Aaron shall B their names before the
28:29 So Aaron shall B the names of the sons
28:30 LORD; thus Aaron shall B the judgment of the
Lev 5:1 not speak, he shall B his iniquity.
5:17 is guilty and shall B his iniquity.
7:18 eats of it shall B his iniquity.
10:17 you that you may B the iniquity of the
16:22 The goat shall B all their iniquities upon him
17:16 his flesh, he shall B his iniquity."
19:8 who eats it shall B his iniquity, because he
19:17 your neighbor, lest you B sin because of him.
19:18 not take vengeance or B any grudge against the
20:17 sister's nakedness, he shall B his iniquity.
20:19 near kin; they shall B their iniquity.
20:20 uncle's nakedness; they shall B their sin, they shall
22:9 my charge, lest they B sin for it and
22:16 so cause them to B iniquity and guilt, by
24:15 curses his God shall B his sin.
Num 5:31 but the woman shall B her iniquity."
9:13 time; that man shall B his sin.
11:17 them; and they shall B the burden of the
11:17 that you may not B it yourself alone.
14:34 a year, you shall B your iniquity, forty years,
18:1 house with you shall B iniquity in connection with
18:1 sons with you shall B iniquity in connection with
18:22 of meeting, lest they B sin and die.
18:23 meeting, and they shall B their iniquity; it shall
18:32 And you shall B no sin by reason of
30:15 them, then he shall B her iniquity."
Deut 1:9 not able alone to B you;
1:12 How can I B alone the weight and burden
5:20 "'Neither shall you B false witness against your
Josh 3:8 command the priests who B the ark of the
3:13 of the priests who B the ark of the
4:16 "Command the priests who B the ark of the
6:4 And seven priests shall B seven trumpets of rams'
6:6 and let seven priests B seven trumpets of rams'
Judg 5:14 from Zebulun those who B the marshal's staff;
13:3 you shall conceive and B a son.
13:5 you shall conceive and B a son.
13:7 you shall conceive and B a son; so then
Ruth 1:12 this night and should B sons,
1Sam 17:34 a lion, or a B, and took a lamb
17:37 the paw of the B, will deliver me from
2Sam 17:8 are enraged, like a B robbed of her cubs
19:19 let not the king B it in mind.
2Kgs 18:14 me; whatever you impose on me I will B
19:30 take root downward, and B fruit upward;
2Chr 2:2 seventy thousand men to B burdens and eighty
2:18 them he assigned to B burdens, eighty thousand to
Neh 9:30 Many years thou didst B with them, and didst
Jud 7:4 nor the hills will B their weight."
Job 9:9 sea; who made the B and Orion, the Pleiades
21:3 B with me, and I will speak, and after
36:2 Elihu continued, and said: B with me a little,
38:32 can you guide the B with its children?
Ps 5:10 Make them B their guilt, O God; let them
13:2 How long must I B pain in my soul,
55:12 then I could B it; it is not
68:29 temple at Jerusalem kings B gifts to thee.
72:3 Let the mountains B prosperity for the people, and
89:50 is scorned; how I B in my bosom the
91:12 their hands they will B you up, lest you
Prov 9:12 scoff, you alone will B it.
18:14 endure sickness; but a broken spirit who can B
28:15 lion or a charging B is a wicked ruler
30:21 under four it cannot B up:
Song 4:2 washing, all of which B twins, and not one
6:6 washing, all of them B twins, not one among
Sir 22:13 iron are easier to B than a stupid man.
23:25 her branches will not B fruit.
25:16 and darkens her face like that of a B
29:28 things are hard to B for a man who
36:15 B witness to those whom thou didst create in
Is 7:14 woman shall conceive and B a son, and shall
11:7 The cow and the B shall feed; their young
37:31 take root downward, and B fruit upward;
46:4 made, and I will B; I will carry and
52:11 purify yourselves, you who B the vessels of the
53:11 righteous; and he shall B their iniquities.
54:1 one, who did not B; break forth into singing
65:23 labor in vain, or B children for calamity; for
Jer 10:19 affliction, and I must B it."
15:15 for thy sake I B reproach.
17:8 does not cease to B fruit."
17:21 lives, and do not B a burden on the
17:27 holy, and not to B a burden and enter
29:6 marriage, that they may B sons and daughters;
30:6 see, can a man B a child?
44:22 LORD could no longer B your evil-doings and the
Lam 3:10 to me like a B lying in wait, like
3:27 a man that he B the yoke in his
5:7 no more; and we B their iniquities.
Ezek 4:4 upon it, you shall B their punishment.
4:5 so long shall you B the punishment of the
4:6 your right side, and B the punishment of the
14:10 And they shall B their punishment--the punishment
16:52 B your disgrace, you also, for you have made
16:52 ashamed, you also, and B your disgrace, for you
16:54 them, that you may B your disgrace and be
16:58 You B the penalty of your lewdness and your
17:8 bring forth branches, and B fruit, and become a
17:23 bring forth boughs and B fruit, and become a
23:35 behind your back, therefore B the consequences of
23:49 you, and you shall B the penalty for your
32:24 the living, and they B their shame with those
32:25 the living, and they B their shame with those
32:30 by the sword, and B their shame with those
36:15 you shall no longer B the disgrace of the
44:10 Israel went astray, shall B their punishment.
44:12 GOD, that they shall B their punishment.
44:13 sacred; but they shall B their shame, because of
47:12 fail, but they will B fresh fruit every month,
Dan 7:5 behold, another beast, a second one, like a B
Hos 9:16 dried up, they shall B no fruit.
10:2 false; now they must B their guilt.
13:8 upon them like a B robbed of her cubs,
13:16 Samaria shall B her guilt, because she has rebelled
Amos 5:19 a lion, and a B met him; or went
7:10 is not able to B all his words.
Mic 6:16 hissing; so you shall B the scorn of the
7:9 I will B the indignation of the LORD because
Zeph 3:18 that you will not B reproach for it.
Zech 6:13 the LORD, and shall B royal honor, and shall
Mal 3:11 shall not fail to B, says the LORD of
Mt 1:21 Holy Spirit; she will B a son, and you
1:23 virgin shall conceive and B a son, and his
3:8 B fruit that befits repentance,
3:10 therefore that does not B good fruit is cut
4:6 their hands they will B you up, lest you
7:18 A sound tree cannot B evil fruit, nor can
7:18 can a bad tree B good fruit.
7:19 tree that does not B good fruit is cut
10:18 for my sake, to B testimony before them and
17:17 long am I to B with you?
19:18 steal, You shall not B false witness,
23:4 heavy burdens, hard to B, and lay them on
Mk 4:20 and accept it and B fruit, thirtyfold and sixtyfold

B

9:19 long am I to B with you?
9:41 to drink because you B the name of Christ,
10:19 not steal, Do not B false witness, Do not
13:9 for my sake, to B testimony before them.
Lk 1:13 your wife Elizabeth will B you a son, and
1:31 in your womb and B a son, and you
3:8 B fruits that befit repentance, and do not begin
3:9 therefore that does not B good fruit is cut
4:11 their hands they will B you up, lest you
6:43 does a bad tree B good fruit;
9:41 be with you and B with you?
11:46 with burdens hard to B, and you yourselves do
14:27 Whoever does not B his own cross and come
18:20 not steal, Do not B false witness, Honor your
21:13 time for you to B testimony.
Jn 1:7 came for testimony, to B witness to the light,
1:8 light, but came to B witness to the light.
2:25 needed no one to B witness of man; for
3:11 what we know, and B witness to what we
3:28 You yourselves B me witness, that I said, I
5:30 If I B witness to myself, my testimony is
5:35 which I am doing, B me witness that the
5:38 it is they that B witness to me;
8:14 "Even if I do B witness to myself, my
8:18 men is true; I B witness to myself, and
8:43 is because you cannot B to hear my word.
10:25 my Father's name, they B witness to me;
15:2 every branch that does B fruit he prunes, that
15:2 prunes, that it may B more fruit.
15:4 As the branch cannot B fruit by itself, unless
15:8 is glorified, that you B much fruit, and so
15:16 you should go and B fruit and that your
15:26 the Father, he will B witness to me;
16:12 you, but you cannot B them now.
18:23 I have spoken wrongly, B witness to the wrong;
18:37 into the world, to B witness to the truth.
Acts 10:43 him all the prophets B witness that every one
15:10 our fathers nor we have been able to B
18:14 should have reason to B with you, O Jews;
22:5 whole council of elders B me witness.
23:11 Jerusalem, so you must B witness also at Rome."
26:16 you to serve and B witness to the things
Rom 3:21 law and the prophets B witness to it,
7:4 order that we may B fruit for God.
7:5 in our members to B fruit for death.
10:2 I B them witness that they have a zeal
13:4 for he does not B the sword in vain;
15:1 are strong ought to B with the failings of
1Cor 15:49 dust, we shall also B the image of the
2Cor 11:1 I wish you would B with me in a
11:1 Do B with me!
11:19 boast.) For you gladly B with fools, being wise
11:20 For you B it if a man makes slaves
Gal 4:15 For I B you witness that, if possible, you
4:27 one who does not B; break forth and shout,
5:10 is troubling you will B his judgment, whoever he
6:2 B one another's burdens, and so fulfil the law
6:5 man will have to B his own load.
6:17 trouble me; for I B on my body the
Col 4:13 For I B him witness that he has worked
1Thes 3:1 Therefore when we could B it no longer, we
3:5 reason, when I could B it no longer, I
1Tim 5:14 have younger widows marry, B children, rule their
Heb 9:28 been offered once to B the sins of many,
13:13 outside the camp and B the abuse he endured.
13:22 appeal to you, brethren, B with my word of
Rev 2:2 and how you cannot B evil men but have
12:4 who was about to B a child, that he
12:17 commandments of God and B testimony to Jesus.

BEARD (17)

Lev 13:29 the head or the B,
13:30 itch, a leprosy of the head or the B
14:9 shall shave off his B and his eyebrows, all
19:27 your temples or mar the edges of your B
1Sam 17:35 caught him by his B, and smote him and
21:13 gate, and let his spittle run down his B
2Sam 10:4 shaved off half the B of each, and cut
19:24 feet, nor trimmed his B, nor washed his clothes,
20:9 took Amasa by the B with his right hand
Ezra 9:3 from my head and B, and sat appalled.
Ps 133:2 running down upon the B, upon the beard of
133:2 the beard, upon the B of Aaron, running down
Is 7:20 will sweep away the B also.
15:2 head is baldness, every B is shorn;
50:6 who pulled out the B; I hid not my
Jer 48:37 is shaved and every B cut off; upon all
Ezek 5:1 your head and your B; then take balances for

BEARDS (5)

Lev 21:5 the edges of their B, nor make any cuttings
2Sam 10:5 at Jericho until your B have grown, and then
1Chr 19:5 at Jericho until your B have grown, and then
Jer 41:5 and Samaria, with their B shaved and their clothes
Bar 6:31 rent, their heads and B shaved, and their heads

BEARERS

Lk 7:14 the bier, and the B stood still.

BEARING (42)

Gen 1:11 seed, and fruit trees B fruit in which is
1:12 own kinds, and trees B fruit in which is
16:2 has prevented me from B children; go in to
29:35 she called his name Judah; then she ceased B
30:9 that she had ceased B children, she took her
37:25 Gilead, with their camels B gum, balm, and myrrh,
Num 4:24 Gershonites, in serving and B burdens:
4:47 and the work of B burdens in the tent
Deut 29:18 among you a root B poisonous and bitter fruit,
32:11 its wings, catching them, B them on its pinions,
Josh 3:14 Jordan with the priests B the ark of the
3:15 feet of the priests B the ark were dipped
4:9 feet of the priests B the ark of the
4:18 And when the priests B the ark of the
6:8 people, the seven priests B the seven trumpets of
6:13 And the seven priests B the seven trumpets of
2Sam 15:24 with all the Levites, B the ark of the
16:1 couple of asses saddled, B two hundred loaves of
1Kgs 10:2 great retinue, with camels B spices, and very much
1Chr 12:24 The men of Judah B shield and spear were
2Chr 9:1 great retinue and camels B spices and very much
Tob 13:11 of the Lord God, B gifts in their hands,
Jud 15:13 men of Israel followed, B their arms and wearing
Ps 126:6 that goes forth weeping, B the seed for sowing,
144:14 mischance or failure in B; may there be no
Wis 10:7 smoking wasteland, plants B fruit that does not
Is 1:14 I am weary of B them.
Jer 44:19 made cakes for her B her image and poured
Dan 13:61 had convicted them of B false witness;
2Mac 10:7 Therefore B ivy-wreathed wands and beautiful
15:12 good man, of modest B and gentle manner, one
Jn 8:13 to him, "You are B witness to yourself; your
19:17 and he went out, B his own cross, to
21:24 the disciple who is B witness to these things,
Rom 8:16 is the Spirit himself B witness with our spirit
Gal 4:24 is from Mount Sinai, B children for slavery; she
Col 1:6 whole world it is B fruit and growing--so
1:10 fully pleasing to him, B fruit in every good
1Tim 2:15 will be saved through B children, if she continues
2Tim 2:19 God's firm foundation stands, B this seal: "The Lord
Heb 11:4 approval as righteous, God B witness by accepting
Rev 2:3 are enduring patiently and B up for my name's

BEARS (35)

Gen 49:21 hind let loose, that B comely fawns.
Ex 21:4 a wife and she B him sons or daughters,
Lev 12:2 a woman conceives, and B a male child, then
12:5 But if she B a female child, then she
12:7 law for her who B a child, either male
Deut 1:31 you, as a man B his son, in all
25:6 first son whom she B shall succeed to the
28:57 her children whom she B, because she will eat
1Sam 17:36 both lions and B; and this uncircumcised Philistine
Ps 68:19 the Lord, who daily B us up; God is
Prov 25:18 A man who B false witness against his neighbor
Wis 11:17 them a multitude of B, or bold lions,
Sir 47:3 young goats, and with B as with lambs of
Is 59:11 We all growl like B, we moan and moan
Joel 2:22 are green; the tree B its fruit, the fig
Mt 7:17 So, every sound tree B good fruit, but the
7:17 but the bad tree B evil fruit.
13:23 understands it; he indeed B fruit, and yields, in
Lk 6:43 "For no good tree B bad fruit, nor again
13:9 And if it B fruit next year, well and
Jn 3:32 He B witness to what he has seen and
5:31 there is another who B witness to me, and
5:31 the testimony which he B to me is true.
8:18 Father who sent me B witness to me."
12:24 if it dies, it B much fruit.
15:2 branch of mine that B no fruit, he takes
15:5 he it is that B much fruit, for apart
Rom 2:15 while their conscience also B witness and their

9:1 not lying; my conscience B me witness in the
1Cor 5:11 with any one who B the name of brother
13:7 Love B all things, believes all things, hopes all
Heb 1:3 glory of God and B the very stamp of
6:8 But if it B thorns and thistles, it is
10:15 the Holy Spirit also B witness to us; for
Rev 13:2 feet were like a B, and its mouth was

BEAST (147)

Gen 1:30 And to every B of the earth, and to
2:19 LORD God formed every B of the field and
2:20 air, and to every B of the field; but
6:7 the ground, man and B and creeping things and
7:14 ark, they and every B according to its kind,
8:19 And every B, every creeping thing, and every bird,
9:2 shall be upon every B of the earth, and
9:5 a reckoning; of every B I will require it
9:10 the cattle, and every B of the earth with
37:20 say that a wild B has devoured him, and
37:33 son's robe; a wild B has devoured him; Joseph
Ex 8:17 gnats on man and B; all the dust of
8:18 So there were gnats on man and B
9:9 sores on man and B throughout all the land
9:10 boils breaking out in sores on man and B
9:19 upon every man and B that is in the
9:22 Egypt, upon man and B and every plant of
9:25 Egypt, both man and B; and the hail struck
11:7 Israel, either man or B, not a dog shall
12:12 Egypt, both man and B; and on all the
13:2 of man and of B, is mine."
19:13 stoned or shot; whether B or man, he shall
21:34 owner, and the dead B shall be his.
21:35 it; and the dead B also they shall divide.
21:36 ox, and the dead B shall be his.
22:2 If the stolen B is found alive in his
22:5 over, or lets his B loose and it feeds
22:10 a sheep or any B to keep, and it
22:19 "Whoever lies with a B shall be put to
Lev 5:2 carcass of an unclean B or a carcass of
7:21 man or an unclean B or any unclean abomination,
11:46 the law pertaining to B and bird and every
17:13 takes in hunting any B or bird that may
18:23 not lie with any B and defile yourself with
18:23 give herself to a B to lie with it:
20:15 man lies with a B, he shall be put
20:15 put to death; and you shall kill the B
20:16 a woman approaches any B and lies with it,
20:16 the woman and the B; they shall be put
20:25 distinction between the clean B and the unclean, and
20:25 make yourselves abominable by B or by bird or
24:18 He who kills a B shall make it good,
24:21 He who kills a B shall make it good;
27:10 makes any exchange of B for beast, then both
27:10 exchange of beast for B, then both it and
27:28 whether of man or B, or of his inherited
Num 3:13 of man and of B; they shall be mine:
8:17 of man and of B; on the day that
18:15 flesh, whether man or B, which they offer to
31:11 all the booty, both of man and of B
31:26 of man and of B, you and Eleazar the
Deut 4:17 the likeness of any B that is on the
27:21 with any kind of B And all the people
2Kgs 4:24 her servant, "Urge the B on; do not slacken
14:9 wife'; and a wild B of Lebanon passed by
2Chr 25:18 wife'; and a wild B of Lebanon passed by
Neh 2:12 There was no B with me but the beast
2:12 with me but the B on which I rode.
2:14 no place for the B that was under me
Job 39:15 and that the wild B may trample them.
Ps 36:6 great deep; man and B thou savest, O LORD.
50:10 For every B of the forest is mine, the
73:22 I was like a B toward thee.
104:11 give drink to every B of the field; the
135:8 of man and of B;
Prov 12:10 the life of his B, but the mercy of
Eccl 3:21 the spirit of the B goes down to the
Sir 40:8 flesh, both man and B, and upon sinners seven
Is 35:9 nor shall any ravenous B come up on it;
Jer 7:20 place, upon man and B, upon the trees of
21:6 city, both man and B; they shall die of
31:27 the seed of man and the seed of B
32:43 desolation, without man or B; it is given into
33:10 waste without man or B in the cities of
33:10 man or inhabitant or B, there shall be heard
33:12 waste, without man or B, and in all of
36:29 and will cut off from it man and B
50:3 it; both man and B shall flee away.
51:62 it, neither man nor B, and it shall be
Ezek 14:13 from it man and B,
14:17 from it man and B;
14:19 from it man and B;
14:21 pestilence, to cut off from it man and B
25:13 from it man and B; and I will make
29:8 from you man and B;
29:11 and no foot of B shall pass through it;
36:11 upon you man and B; and they shall increase
44:31 anything, whether bird or B, that has died of
Dan 4:16 mans, and let a B's mind be given to
5:21 like that of a B, and his dwelling was
7:5 And behold, another B, a second one, like a
7:6 its back; and the B had four heads; and
7:7 and behold, a fourth B, terrible and dreadful and
7:11 as I looked, the B was slain, and its
7:19 truth concerning the fourth B, which was different
7:23 'As for the fourth B, there shall be a
8:4 northward and southward; no B could stand before
Hos 13:8 lion, as a wild B would rend them.
Jon 3:7 Let neither man nor B, herd nor flock, taste
3:8 but let man and B be covered with sackcloth,
Zeph 1:3 sweep away man and B; I will sweep away
Zech 8:10 or any wage for B, neither was there any
1Mac 6:35 hundred picked horsemen were assigned to each B
6:36 position beforehand wherever the B was; wherever it
6:37 were fastened upon each B by special harness, and
2Mac 4:25 tyrant and the rage of a savage wild B
Lk 10:34 him on his own B and brought him to
Heb 12:20 given, "If even a B touches the mountain, it
Jas 3:7 For every kind of B and bird, of reptile
Rev 11:7 finished their testimony, the B that ascends from the
13:1 And I saw a B rising out of the
13:2 And the B that I saw was like a
13:3 whole earth followed the B with wonder.
13:4 his authority to the B, and they worshiped the
13:4 and they worshiped the B, saying, "Who is like
13:4 "Who is like the B, and who can fight
13:5 And the B was given a mouth uttering haughty
13:11 Then I saw another B which rose out of
13:12 authority of the first B in its presence, and
13:12 inhabitants worship the first B, whose mortal wound
13:14 the presence of the B, it deceives those who
13:14 an image for the B which was wounded by
13:15 the image of the B so that the image
13:15 the image of the B should even speak, and
13:15 the image of the B to be slain.
13:17 the name of the B or the number of
13:18 the number of the B, for it is a
14:9 any one worships the B and its image, and
14:11 these worshipers of the B and its image, and
15:2 who had conquered the B and its image and
16:2 the mark of the B and worshiped its image.
16:10 the throne of the B, and its kingdom was
16:13 the mouth of the B and from the mouth
17:3 sitting on a scarlet B which was full of
17:7 woman, and of the B with seven heads and
17:8 The B that you saw was, and is not,
17:8 marvel to behold the B, because it was and
17:11 As for the B that was and is not,
17:12 as kings for one hour, together with the B
17:13 and authority to the B;
17:16 saw, they and the B will hate the harlot;
17:17 royal power to the B, until the words of
19:19 And I saw the B and the kings of
19:20 And the B was captured, and with it the
19:20 the mark of the B and those who worshiped
20:4 had not worshipped the B or its image and
20:10 and sulphur where the B and the false prophet

BEASTS (150)

Gen 1:24 and creeping things and B of the earth according
1:25 And God made the B of the earth according
7:21 the earth, birds, cattle, B, all swarming creatures
8:1 Noah and all the B and all the cattle
31:39 was torn by wild B I did not bring
34:23 property and all their B be ours?
36:6 his cattle, all his B, and all his property
45:17 'Do this: load your B and go back to
Ex 22:13 it is torn by B, let him bring it
22:31 that is torn by B in the field; you
23:11 they leave the wild B may eat.
23:29 desolate and the wild B multiply against you.
Lev 7:24 that is torn by B, may be put to
11:2 eat among all the B that are on the

17:15 what is torn by B, whether he is a
22:8 or is torn by B he shall not eat,
25:7 also and for the B that are in your
26:6 I will remove evil B from the land, and
26:22 let loose the wild B among you, which shall
Num 18:15 the firstling of unclean B you shall redeem.
31:47 of persons and of B, and gave them to
35:3 and for their livestock and for all their B
Deut 7:22 once, lest the wild B grow too numerous for
28:4 the fruit of your B, the increase of your
28:26 air, and for the B of the earth; and
32:24 send the teeth of B against them, with venom
Judg 20:48 the sword, men and B and all that they
1Sam 17:44 air and to the B of the field."
17:46 and to the wild B of the earth; that
2Sam 21:10 by day, or the B of the field by
1Kgs 4:33 he spoke also of B, and of birds, and
2Kgs 3:9 army or for the B which followed them.
3:17 your cattle, and your B
Ezra 1:4 with goods and with B, besides freewill offerings for
1:6 gold, with goods, with B, and with costly wares,
Jud 11:7 you, but also the B of the field and
Esth 16:24 for all time to B and birds."
Job 5:22 shall not fear the B of the earth.
5:23 the field, and the B of the field shall
12:7 "But ask the B, and they will teach you;
28:8 The proud B have not trodden it; the lion
35:11 us more than the B of the earth, and
37:8 Then the B go into their lairs, and remain
40:20 where all the wild B play.
Ps 8:7 oxen, and also the B of the field,
49:12 he is like the B that perish.
49:20 he is like the B that perish.
68:30 Rebuke the B that dwell among the reeds, the
74:19 dove to the wild B; do not forget the
79:2 thy saints to the B of the earth.
104:20 night, when all the B of the forest creep
147:9 He gives to the B their food, and to
148:10 B and all cattle, creeping things and flying birds!
Prov 9:2 She has slaughtered her B, she has mixed her
30:30 which is mightiest among B and does not turn
Eccl 3:18 them to show them that they are but B
3:19 and the fate of B is the same; as
3:19 no advantage over the B; for all is vanity.
Wis 7:20 the tempers of wild B, the powers of spirits
11:18 or newly created unknown B full of rage, or
12:9 blow by dread wild B or thy stern word.
16:5 terrible rage of wild B came upon thy people
17:9 by the passing of B and the hissing of
17:19 the most savage roaring B, or an echo thrown
Sir 10:11 creeping things, and wild B, and worms.
12:13 a serpent, or any who go near wild B
17:4 granted them dominion over B and birds.
39:30 the teeth of wild B, and scorpions and vipers,
Is 1:11 the fat of fed B; I do not delight
13:21 But wild B will lie down there, and its
18:6 mountains and to the B of the earth.
18:6 them, and all the B of the earth will
23:13 They destined Tyre for wild B
30:6 An oracle on the B of the Negeb.
34:14 And wild B shall meet with hyenas, the satyr
40:16 fuel, nor are its B enough for a burnt
43:20 The wild B will honor me, the jackals and
46:1 their idols are on B and cattle; these things
46:1 you carry are loaded as burdens on weary B
56:9 All you B of the field, come to devour–
56:9 devour– all you B in the forest.
Jer 7:33 air, and for the B of the earth; and
9:10 the air and the B have fled and are
12:4 dwell in it the B and the birds are
12:9 assemble all the wild B; bring them to devour.
15:3 the air and the B of the earth to
16:4 air and for the B of the earth.
19:7 air and to the B of the earth.
27:6 given him also the B of the field to
28:14 to him even the B of the field.'"
34:20 the air and the B of the earth.
50:39 "Therefore wild B shall dwell with hyenas in
Bar 3:16 who rule over the B on earth;
6:68 The wild B are better than they are, for
Ezek 4:14 or was torn by B, nor has foul flesh
5:17 send famine and wild B against you, and they
8:10 creeping things, and loathsome B, and all the idols
14:15 If I cause wild B to pass through the
14:15 through because of the B;
14:21 judgment, sword, famine, evil B, and pestilence, to
17:23 dwell all kinds of B; in the shade of
29:5 To the B of the earth and to the
31:6 its branches all the B of the field brought
31:13 will be all the B of the field.
32:4 I will gorge the B of the whole earth
32:13 will destroy all its B from beside many waters;
32:13 shall the hoofs of B trouble them.
33:27 will give to the B to be devoured; and
34:5 and they became food for all the wild B
34:8 for all the wild B, since there was no
34:25 peace and banish wild B from the land, so
34:28 nations, nor shall the B of the land devour
38:20 the air, and the B of the field, and
39:4 and to the wild B to be devoured.
39:17 sort and to all B of the field, 'Assemble
Dan 2:38 sons of men, the B of the field, and
3:82 Bless the Lord, all B and cattle, sing praise
4:12 The B of the field found shade under it,
4:14 its fruit; let the B flee from under it
4:15 lot be with the B in the grass of
4:21 for all; under which B of the field found
4:23 lot be with the B of the field, till
4:25 shall be with the B of the field; you
4:32 shall be with the B of the field; and
7:3 And four great B came up out of the
7:7 different from all the B that were before it;
7:12 the rest of the B, their dominion was taken
7:17 'These four great B are four kings who shall
Hos 2:12 a forest, and the B of the field shall
2:18 that day with the B of the field, the
4:3 languish, and also the B of the field, and
Joel 1:17 How the B groan!
1:19 Even the wild B cry to thee because the
2:22 Fear not, you B of the field, for the
Amos 5:22 offerings of your fatted B I will not look
Mic 5:8 a lion among the B of the forest, like
Hab 2:17 the destruction of the B will terrify you, for
Zeph 2:14 of her, all the B of the field; the
2:15 desolation she has become, a lair for wild B
Zech 14:15 the asses, and whatever B may be in those
1Mac 6:35 And they distributed the B among the phalanxes;
6:43 that one of the B was equipped with royal
2Mac 9:15 their children to the B, for the birds to
11:9 men but the wildest B or walls of iron.
Mk 1:13 was with the wild B; and the angels ministered
Acts 7:42 offer to me slain B and sacrifices, forty years
11:6 I observed animals and B of prey and reptiles
1Cor 15:32 speaking, I fought with B at Ephesus?
Tit 1:11 are always liars, evil B, lazy gluttons."
Rev 6:8 pestilence and by wild B of the earth.

BEAT (46)

Ex 30:36 holy; and you shall B some of it very
Num 11:8 it in mills or B it in mortars, and
Deut 1:44 as bees do and B you down in Seir
24:20 When you B your olive trees, you shall not
25:3 should go on to B him with more stripes
Judg 5:22 "Then loud B the horses' hoofs with the galloping,
Ruth 2:17 until evening; then she B out what she had
2Sam 22:43 I B them fine as the dust of the
2Kgs 23:6 the brook Kidron, and B it to dust and
2Chr 34:7 down the altars, and B the Asherim and the
Neh 13:25 and cursed them and B some of them and
Tob 3:9 Why do you B us?
Ps 18:42 I B them fine as dust before the wind;
Prov 23:13 a child; if you B him with a rod,
23:14 If you B him with the rod you will
23:35 was not hurt; they B me, but I did
Song 5:7 in the city; they B me, they wounded me,
Wis 5:11 air, lashed by the B of its pinions and
Sir 30:12 in his youth, and B his sides while he
Is 2:4 and they shall B their swords into plowshares,
32:12 B upon your breasts for the pleasant fields, for
Jer 20:2 Then Pashhur B Jeremiah the prophet, and put him
37:15 at Jeremiah, and they B him and imprisoned him
Joel 3:10 B your plowshares into swords, and your pruning
Jon 4:8 wind, and the sun B upon the head of
Mic 4:3 off; and they shall B their swords into plowshares,
4:13 hoofs bronze; you shall B in pieces many peoples,
2Mac 9:2 by the inhabitants and B a shameful retreat.
10:17 of the places, and B off all who fought
Mt 7:25 the winds blew and B upon that house, but
7:27 the winds blew and B against that house, and
21:35 took his servants and B one, killed another, and
24:49 delayed,' and begins to B his fellow servants, and
Mk 4:37 arose, and the waves B into the boat, so

12:3 they took him and B him, and sent him
12:5 many others, some they B and some they killed.
Lk 10:30 who stripped him and B him, and departed, leaving
12:45 coming,' and begins to B the menservants and the
18:13 eyes to heaven, but B his breast, saying, 'God,
20:10 vineyard; but the tenants B him, and sent him
20:11 servant; him also they B and treated shamefully, and
22:61 Jesus mocked him and B him;
Acts 5:40 in the apostles, they B them and charged them
16:22 and gave orders to B them with rods.
18:17 of the synagogue, and B him in front of
22:19 synagogue I imprisoned and B those who believed in

BEATEN (30)

Ex 5:14 set over them, were B, and were asked, "Why
5:16 behold, your servants are B; but the fault is
27:20 bring to you pure B olive oil for the
29:40 of a hin of B oil, and a fourth
Lev 16:12 handfuls of sweet incense B small; and he shall
24:2 you pure oil from B olives for the lamp,
Num 28:5 of a hin of B oil.
Deut 25:2 man deserves to be B, the judge shall cause
25:2 lie down and be B in his presence with
Josh 8:15 a pretense of being B before them, and fled
2Sam 2:17 men of Israel were B before the servants of
1Kgs 5:11 twenty thousand cors of B oil.
10:16 hundred large shields of B gold; six hundred shekels
10:17 three hundred shields of B gold; three minas of
2Chr 9:15 hundred large shields of B gold; six hundred shekels
9:15 six hundred shekels of B gold went into each
9:16 three hundred shields of B gold; three hundred
Is 17:6 an olive tree is B – two or three
24:13 an olive tree is B, as at the gleaning
28:18 through you will be B down by it.
28:27 cummin; but dill is B out with a stick,
Jer 10:9 B silver is brought from Tarshish, and gold from
46:5 Their warriors are B down, and have fled in
Mic 1:7 her images shall be B to pieces, all her
2Mac 4:45 already as good as B, promised a substantial bribe
Mt 14:24 distant from the land, B by the waves; for
Mk 13:9 and you will be B in synagogues; and you
Acts 16:37 to them, "They have B us publicly, uncondemned,
2Cor 11:25 times I have been B with rods; once I
1Pet 2:20 do wrong and are B for it you take

BEATING (15)

Ex 2:11 he saw an Egyptian B a Hebrew, one of
Deut 25:11 of him who is B him, and puts out
Judg 6:11 his son Gideon was B out wheat in the
19:22 the house round about, B on the door; and
Prov 28:3 the poor is a B rain that leaves no
Wis 2:2 spark kindled by the B of our hearts.
Jer 4:19 My heart is B wildly; I cannot keep silent;
Nah 2:7 moaning like doves, and B their breasts.
2Mac 6:30 my body under this B, but in my soul
Lk 12:47 according to his will, shall receive a severe B
12:48 did what deserved a B, shall receive a light
12:48 what deserved a beating, shall receive a light B
23:47 taken place, returned home B their breasts.
Acts 21:32 the soldiers, they stopped B Paul.
1Cor 9:26 not box as one B the air;

BEATINGS (2)

2Cor 6:5 in afflictions, hardships, calamities, B, imprisonments,
11:23 more imprisonments, with countless B, and often

BEAUTEOUS

Jer 3:19 land, a heritage most B of all nations.

BEAUTIFUL (70)

Gen 12:11 you are a woman B to behold;
12:14 the Egyptians saw that the woman was very B
29:17 weak, but Rachel was B and lovely.
Deut 21:11 among the captives a B woman, and you have
Josh 7:21 among the spoil a B mantle from Shinar, and
1Sam 16:12 was ruddy, and had B eyes, and was handsome.
25:3 of good understanding and B, but the man was
2Sam 11:2 a woman bathing; and the woman was very B
13:1 David's son, had a B sister, whose name was
14:27 Tamar; she was a B woman.
1Kgs 1:3 they sought for a B maiden throughout all the
1:4 The maiden was very B; and she became the
Tob 6:12 The girl is also B and sensible.
Jud 8:7 She was B in appearance, and had a very
10:4 and made herself very B, to entice the eyes
10:14 in their eyes marvelously B –they said to her,
11:23 You are not only B in appearance, but wise
12:13 her and said, "This B maidservant will please come
Esth 2:2 attended him said, "Let B young virgins be sought
2:3 to gather all the B young virgins to the
2:7 mother; the maiden was B and lovely, and when
Ps 48:2 His holy mountain, B in elevation, is the joy
Prov 4:10 bestow on you a B crown." Good and Evil
11:22 swine's snout is a B woman without discretion.
Eccl 3:11 He has made everything B in its time; also
Song 1:15 Behold, you are B, my love; behold, you are
1:15 love; behold, you are B; your eyes are doves.
1:16 Behold, you are B, my beloved, truly lovely.
4:1 Behold, you are B, my love, behold, you are
4:1 you are beautiful, my love, behold, you are B
6:4 You are B as Tirzah, my love, comely as
Wis 5:16 glorious crown and a B diadem from the hand
7:29 For she is more B than the sun, and
13:7 see, because the things that are seen are B
14:19 likeness to take more B form,
15:19 they are not so B in appearance that one
Sir 24:14 in Jericho; like a B olive tree in the
25:1 things, and they are B in the sight of
26:17 lampstand, so is a B face on a stately
26:18 of silver, so are B feet with a steadfast
43:11 who made it, exceedingly B in its brightness.
45:13 there never were such B things.
Is 2:16 and against all the B craft.
4:2 the LORD shall be B and glorious, and the
5:9 be desolate, large and B houses, without inhabitant.
52:1 Zion; put on your B garments, O Jerusalem, the
52:7 How B upon the mountains are the feet of
64:11 Our holy and B house, where our fathers praised
Jer 13:18 lowly seat, for your B crown has come down
13:20 was given you, your B flock?
46:20 "A B heifer is Egypt, but a gadfly from
Ezek 7:20 Their B ornament they used for vainglory, and they
16:12 your ears, and a B crown upon your head.
16:13 You grew exceedingly B, and came to regal estate.
23:42 of the women, and B crowns upon their heads.
31:7 It was B in its greatness, in the length
31:9 I made it B in the mass of its
33:32 love songs with a B voice and plays well
Dan 13:2 of Hilkiah, a very B woman and one who
13:31 of great refinement, and B in appearance.
2Mac 3:26 strong, gloriously B and splendidly dressed,
10:7 ivy-wreathed wands and B branches and also fronds
Mt 23:26 tombs, which outwardly appear B, but within they
26:10 she has done a B thing to me.
Mk 14:6 She has done a B thing to me.
Acts 3:2 temple which is called B to ask alms of
3:10 for alms at the B Gate of the temple;
7:20 was born, and was B before God.
Rom 10:15 it is written, "How B are the feet of
Heb 11:23 that the child was B; and they were not

BEAUTIFY (3)

Ezra 7:27 of the king, to B the house of the
Is 60:13 and the pine, to B the place of my
Jer 4:30 In vain you B yourself.

BEAUTIFYING

Esth 2:12 regular period of their B, six months with oil

BEAUTY (65)

Ex 28:2 for Aaron your brother, for glory and for B
28:40 caps; you shall make them for glory and B
2Sam 14:25 be praised for his B as Absalom; from the
Jud 1:14 markets, and turned its B into shame.
10:7 they greatly admired her B, and said to her,
10:19 they marveled at her B, and admired the Israelites,
10:23 all marveled at the B of her face; and
11:21 the other, either for B of face or wisdom
16:7 undid him with the B of her countenance.
16:9 ravished his eyes, her B captivated his mind, and
Esth 1:11 and the princes her B; for she was fair
15:5 was radiant with perfect B, and she looked happy,
Ps 27:4 life, to behold the B of the LORD, and
45:11 father's house; and the king will desire your B
50:2 Zion, the perfection of B, God shines forth.
96:6 before him; strength and B are in his sanctuary.
Prov 6:25 Do not desire her B in your heart, and
20:29 their strength, but the B of old men is
31:30 Charm is deceitful, and B is vain, but a
Wis 7:10 more than health and B, and I chose to
8:2 my bride, and I became enamored of her B
13:3 through delight in the B of these things men

B

11:9 And David B greater and greater, for the LORD
11:21 of the thirty, and B their commander; but he
18:2 Moab, and the Moabites B servants to David and
18:6 Damascus; and the Syrians B servants to David, and
18:13 and all the Edomites B David's servants.
19:19 peace with David, and B subject to him.
23:11 many sons, therefore they B a father's house in
24:2 so Eleazar and Ithamar B the priests.
2Chr 16:12 feet, and his disease B severe; yet even in
21:5 years old when he B king, and he reigned
25:10 And they B very angry with Judah, and returned
26:8 of Egypt, for he B very strong.
26:19 incense, and when he B angry with the priests
27:6 So Jotham B mighty, because he ordered his ways
28:22 of his distress he B yet more faithless to
32:24 In those days Hezekiah B sick and was at
36:20 the sword, and they B servants to him and
Neh 9:25 and were filled and B fat, and delighted themselves
Tob 1:9 When I B a man I married Anna, a
1:9 and by her I B the father of Tobias.
Jud 5:10 food; and there they B a great multitude--
5:11 the king of Egypt B hostile to them; he
16:23 She B more and more famous, and grew old
Esth 2:21 who guarded the threshold, B angry and sought to
10:6 The tiny spring which B a river, and there
Job 32:2 the family of Ram, B angry.
32:5 these three men, he B angry.
Ps 39:3 grew worse, my heart B hot within me.
69:10 soul with fasting, it B my reproach.
69:11 sackcloth my clothing, I B a byword to them.
83:10 destroyed at Endor, who B dung for the ground.
106:9 Red Sea, and it B dry; and he led
106:36 served their idols, which B a snare to them.
106:39 Thus they B unclean by their acts, and played
114:2 of strange language, Judah B his sanctuary, Israel his
Eccl 2:9 So I B great and surpassed all who were
Wis 2:14 He B to us a reproof of our thoughts;
8:2 my bride, and I B enamored of her beauty.
10:17 a marvelous way, and B a shelter to them
12:27 in their suffering they B incensed at those creatures
14:11 what God created, they B an abomination, and
14:11 became an abomination, and B traps for the souls
14:21 And this B a hidden trap for mankind, because
Sir 24:17 bud, and my blossoms B glorious and abundant fruit.
24:29 and lo, my canal B a river, and my
24:29 river, and my river B a sea.
46:1 He B, in accordance with his name, a great
46:15 by his words he B known as a trustworthy
47:14 How wise you B in your youth!
47:24 Their sins B exceedingly many, so as to remove
Is 38:1 In those days Hezekiah B sick and was at
63:8 deal falsely; and he B their Savior.
Jer 2:3 who ate of it B guilty; evil came upon
2:5 went after worthlessness, and B worthless?
15:16 them, and thy words B to me a joy
44:6 of Jerusalem; and they B a waste and a
52:1 years old when he B king; and he reigned
52:31 the year that he B king, lifted up the
Lam 1:8 sinned grievously, therefore she B filthy; all who
4:10 their own children; they B their food in the
4:15 So they B fugitives and wanderers; men said among
Ezek 16:7 you grew up and B tall and arrived at
16:8 Lord GOD, and you B mine.
17:6 and it sprouted and B a low spreading vine,
17:6 So it B a vine, and brought forth branches
19:3 of her whelps; he B a young lion, and
19:6 among the lions; he B a young lion, and
19:11 Its strongest stem B a ruler's scepter; it towered
23:4 They B mine, and they bore sons and daughters.
23:10 the sword; and she B a byword among women,
34:5 no shepherd; and they B food for all the
36:3 sides, so that you B the possession of the
36:3 the nations, and you B the talk and evil
41:7 And the side chambers B broader as they rose
44:12 before their idols and B a stumbling block of
Dan 2:35 broken in pieces, and B like the chaff of
2:35 that struck the image B a great mountain and
4:11 The tree grew and B strong, and its top
4:20 saw, which grew and B strong, so that its
6:3 Then this Daniel B distinguished above all the other
9:1 birth a Mede, who B king over the realm
Hos 7:6 our king the princes B sick with the heat
9:10 themselves to Baal, and B detestable like the thing
11:4 of love, and I B to them as one,
Joel 2:18 Then the LORD B jealous for his land, and
Zech 11:7 So I B the shepherd of the flock doomed
11:8 But I B impatient with them, and they also
1Mac 1:3 When the earth B quiet before him, he was
1:4 and princes, and they B tributary to him.
1:26 maidens and young men B faint, the beauty of
1:33 strong towers, and it B their citadel.
1:35 stored them there, and B a great snare.
1:36 It B an ambush against the sanctuary, an evil
1:38 of Jerusalem fled; she B a dwelling of strangers;
1:38 dwelling of strangers; she B strange to her offspring,
1:39 Her sanctuary B desolate as a desert; her feasts
2:43 And all who B fugitives to escape their troubles
2:53 kept the commandment, and B lord of Egypt.
2:55 he fulfilled the command, B a judge in Israel.
5:1 it was before, they B very angry,
6:3 not, because his plan B known to the men
6:8 to his bed and B sick from grief, because
6:24 besieged the citadel and B hostile to us; moreover,
6:59 we abolished that they B angry and did all
7:3 But when this act B known to him, he
7:30 It B known to Judas that Nicanor had come
8:10 destroy them, but this B known to them, and
9:8 He B faint, but he said to those who
9:17 The battle B desperate, and many on both sides
9:60 it, because their plan B known.
10:76 men of the city B afraid and opened the
11:12 Alexander, and their enmity B manifest.
11:19 So Demetrius B king in the one hundred and
11:53 had promised; and he B estranged from Jonathan
13:32 he killed him and B king in his place,
14:30 rallied the nation, and B their high priest, and
15:27 made with Simon, and B estranged from him.
16:24 the time that he B high priest after his
2Mac 1:33 When this matter B known, and it was reported
2:22 Lord with great kindness B gracious to them--
3:24 power of God, and B faint with terror.
4:16 wished to imitate completely B their enemies and
4:33 When Onias B fully aware of these acts he
4:41 But when the Jews B aware of Lysimachus' attack,
5:20 when the great Lord B reconciled.
10:14 When Gorgias B governor of the region, he
10:29 When the battle B fierce, there appeared to the
12:40 And it B clear to all that this was
14:27 The king B excited and, provoked by the false
14:31 When the latter B aware that he had been
Mt 17:2 sun, and his garments B white as light.
28:4 the guards trembled and B like dead men.
Mk 9:3 them, and his garments B glistening, intensely white,
Lk 1:80 the child grew and B strong in spirit, and
2:40 the child grew and B strong, filled with wisdom;
6:16 and Judas Iscariot, who B a traitor.
9:29 altered, and his raiment B dazzling white.
11:30 For as Jonah B a sign to the men
13:19 and it grew and B a tree, and the
18:23 he heard this he B sad, for he was
23:12 And Herod and Pilate B friends with each other
Jn 1:14 And the Word B flesh and dwelt among us,
Acts 1:19 And it B known to all the inhabitants of
7:8 And so Abraham B the father of Isaac, and
7:8 eighth day; and Isaac B the father of Jacob,
7:13 brothers, and Joseph's family B known to Pharaoh.
7:29 retort Moses fled, and B an exile in the
7:29 of Midian, where he B the father of two
9:24 him, but their plot B known to Saul.
9:42 And it B known throughout all Joppa, and many
10:10 And he B hungry and desired something to eat;
19:17 And this B known to all residents of Ephesus,
23:10 And when the dissension B violent, the tribune,
Rom 1:21 to him, but they B futile in their thinking
1:22 to be wise, they B fools,
15:8 tell you that Christ B a servant to the
1Cor 4:15 For I B your father in Christ Jesus through
9:20 To the Jews I B as a Jew, in
9:20 under the law I B as one under the
9:21 outside the law I B as one outside the
9:22 To the weak I B weak, that I might
13:11 a child; when I B a man, I gave
15:45 "The first man Adam B a living being"; the
15:45 being"; the last Adam B a life-giving spirit.
2Cor 8:9 for your sake he B poor, so that by
Phil 2:8 he humbled himself and B obedient unto death, even
Col 1:23 of which I, Paul, B a minister.
1:25 church, of which I B a minister according to
1Thes 1:6 And you B imitators of us and of the
1:7 Spirit; so that you B an example to all
2:14 For you, brethren, B imitators of the churches of
1Tim 2:14 woman was deceived and B a transgressor.

Heb 5:9 being made perfect he B the source of eternal
7:21 Those who formerly B priests took their office
11:7 condemned the world and B an heir of the
11:34 strength out of weakness, B mighty in war, put
Rev 6:12 earthquake; and the sun B black as sackcloth, the
6:12 sackcloth, the full moon B like blood,
8:9 third of the sea B blood, a third of
8:11 third of the waters B wormwood, and many men
16:3 the sea, and it B like the blood of
16:4 of water, and they B blood.

BECHER (5)

Gen 46:21 sons of Benjamin: Bela, B, Ashbel, Gera, Naaman,
Num 26:35 of the Shuthelahites; of B, the family of the
1Chr 7:6 sons of Benjamin: Bela, B, and Jedia-el, three.
7:8 The sons of B: Zemirah, Joash, Eliezer, Eli-o-enai,
7:8 were the sons of B;

BECHERITES

Num 26:35 the family of the B; of Tahan, the family

BECKONED (2)

Lk 5:7 nets were breaking, they B to their partners in
Jn 13:24 Jesus; so Simon Peter B to him and said,

BECOME (370)

Gen 2:24 his wife, and they B one flesh.
3:22 "Behold, the man has B like one of us,
9:15 waters shall never again B a flood to destroy
18:18 seeing that Abraham shall B a great and mighty
19:13 against its people has B great before the LORD,
24:35 master, and he has B great; he has given
28:3 you, that you may B a company of peoples.
32:10 and now I have B two companies.
34:15 you: that you will B as we are and
34:16 dwell with you and B one people.
34:22 dwell with us, to B one people: that every
37:20 shall see what will B of his dreams."
47:26 priests alone did not B Pharaohs.
48:19 know; he also shall B a people, and he
48:19 and his descendants shall B a multitude of nations."
49:13 the sea; he shall B a haven for ships,
Ex 4:9 from the Nile will B blood upon the dry
7:9 Pharaoh, that it may B a serpent.'"
7:18 and the Nile shall B foul, and the Egyptians
7:19 water, that they may B blood; and there shall
8:16 earth, that it may B gnats throughout all the
9:9 And it shall B fine dust over all the
9:9 land of Egypt, and B boils breaking out in
15:2 song, and he has B my salvation; this is
16:24 and it did not B foul, and there were
22:24 and your wives shall B widows and your children
23:29 year, lest the land B desolate and the wild
29:37 touches the altar shall B holy.
30:29 whatever touches them will B holy.
32:1 not know what has B of him."
32:23 not know what has B of him.'
34:12 you go, lest it B a snare in the
Lev 5:2 him, and he has B unclean, he shall be
6:4 one has sinned and B guilty, he shall restore
6:7 may do and thereby B guilty."
6:18 whoever touches them shall B holy."
11:24 by these you shall B unclean; whoever touches their
11:43 with them, lest you B unclean.
19:29 harlotry and the land B full of wickedness.
26:22 that your ways shall B desolate.
Num 5:27 and the woman shall B an execration among her
14:3 our little ones will B a prey; would it
14:31 who you said would B a prey, I will
16:40 the LORD, lest he B as Korah and as
19:12 day, he will not B clean.
Deut 1:39 who you said would B a prey, and your
7:26 into your house, and B accursed like it; you
27:9 this day you have B the people of the
28:37 And you shall B a horror, a proverb, and
Josh 7:12 enemies, because they have B a thing for destruction.
16:10 this day but have B slaves to do forced
Judg 2:3 you; but they shall B adversaries." to you, and
11:35 low, and you have B the cause of great
16:7 dried, then I shall B weak, and be like
16:11 used, then I shall B weak, and be like
16:13 pin, then I shall B weak, and be like
16:17 me, and I shall B weak, and be like
18:4 me, and I have B his priest."
Ruth 1:11 womb that they may B your husbands?
1Sam 4:9 O Philistines, lest you B slaves to the Hebrews
9:5 about the asses and B anxious about us."
13:4 also that Israel had B odious to the Philistines.
14:29 how my eyes have B bright, because I tasted
18:22 love you; now then B the king's son-in-law.'"
18:23 a little thing to B the king's son-in-law, seeing
18:27 king, that he might B the king's son-in-law.
28:16 turned from you and B your enemy?
29:4 in the battle he B an adversary to us.
2Sam 7:24 thou, O LORD, didst B their God.
10:6 saw that they had B odious to David, the
1Kgs 1:11 son of Haggith has B king and David our
2:15 has turned about and B my brothers, for it
9:7 sight; and Israel will B a proverb and a
9:8 And this house will B a heap of ruins;
2Kgs 19:26 and confounded, and have B like plants of the
21:14 enemies, and they shall B a prey and a
22:19 inhabitants, that they should B a desolation and a
1Chr 17:22 thou, O LORD, didst B their God.
Neh 6:6 and you wish to B their king, according to
Tob 3:6 I may depart and B dust.
4:21 son, because we have B poor.
6:15 brother, for she will B your wife; and do
Jud 12:13 merry with us, and B today like one of
Esth 13:2 them, writes thus: "Having B ruler of many nations
16:2 their benefactors, the more proud do many men B
16:10 of our kindliness), having B our guest,
Job 6:21 Such you have now B to me; you see
7:20 Why have I B a burden to thee?
9:28 of good cheer,' I B afraid of all my
15:28 which were destined to B heaps of ruins;
19:15 a stranger; I have B an alien in their
27:12 why then have you B altogether vain?
30:9 "And now I have B their song, I am
30:19 mire, and I have B like dust and ashes.
33:25 ransom; let his flesh B fresh with youth; let
38:30 The waters B hard like stone, and the face
39:4 Their young ones B strong, they grow up in
Ps 28:1 silent to me, I B like those who go
31:12 is dead; I have B like a broken vessel.
37:26 lending, and his children B a blessing.
69:8 I have B a stranger to my brethren, an
69:22 own table before them B a snare; let their
79:4 We have B a taunt to our neighbors, mocked
89:41 despoil him; he has B the scorn of his
94:22 But the LORD has B my stronghold, and my
109:24 fasting; my body has B gaunt.
118:14 my song; he has B my salvation.
118:21 answered me and hast B my salvation.
118:22 the builders rejected has B the head of the
119:83 For I have B like a wineskin in the
Prov 6:1 son, if you have B surety for your neighbor,
22:26 who give pledges, who B surety for debts.
25:17 neighbor's house, lest he B weary of you and
Wis 4:18 After this they will B dishonored corpses, and an
16:11 into deep forgetfulness and B unresponsive to thy
Sir 5:15 amiss, and do not B an enemy instead of
6:27 seek, and she will B known to you; and
6:29 Then her fetters will B for you a strong
6:32 apply yourself you will B clever.
6:33 your ear you will B wise.
7:6 Do not seek to B a judge, lest you
13:1 a proud man will B like him.
14:17 All living beings B old like a garment, for
18:28 who understand sayings B skilled themselves, and
18:31 great luxury, lest you B impoverished by its expense.
18:32 Do not B a beggar by feasting with borrowed
19:1 a drunkard will not B rich; he who despises
23:15 insulting words will never B disciplined all his days.
30:12 is young, lest he B stubborn and disobey you,
38:24 has little business may B wise.
38:25 How can he B wise who handles the plow,
42:10 she be defiled or B pregnant in her father's
44:10 not lived; they have B as though they had
46:4 did not one day B as long as two?
50:28 them to heart will B wise.
Is 1:9 been like Sodom, and B like Gomorrah.
1:14 soul hates; they have B a burden to me,
1:18 like crimson, they shall B like wool.
1:21 the faithful city has B a harlot, she that
1:22 Your silver has B dross, your wine mixed with
1:31 And the strong shall B tow, and his work
7:23 shekels of silver, will B briers and thorns.
7:25 thorns; but they will B a place where cattle
8:14 And he will B a sanctuary, and a stone
10:17 light of Israel will B a fire, and his
12:2 song, and he has B my salvation."

14:10 you: 'You too have B as weak as we!
14:10 You have B like us!'
17:1 a city, and will B a heap of ruins.
19:6 and its canals will B foul, and the branches
19:13 princes of Zoan have B fools, and the princes
19:17 land of Judah will B a terror to the
22:23 place, and he will B a throne of honor
29:11 of all this has B to you like the
32:14 and the watchtower will B dens for ever, a
34:9 brimstone; her land shall B burning pitch.
35:7 the burning sand shall B a pool, and the
35:7 haunt of jackals shall B a swamp, the grass
35:7 swamp, the grass shall B reeds and rushes.
37:27 and confounded, and have B like plants of the
40:4 the uneven ground shall B level, and the rough
42:22 in prisons; they have B a prey with none
49:5 and my God has B my strength–
60:22 The least one shall B a clan, and the
63:19 We have B like those over whom thou hast
64:6 We have all B like one who is unclean,
64:10 Thy holy cities have B a wilderness, Zion has
64:10 a wilderness, Zion has B a wilderness, Jerusalem a
64:11 our pleasant places have B ruins.
65:10 Sharon shall B a pasture for flocks, and the
Jer 2:14 Why then has he B a prey?
2:21 you turned degenerate and B a wild vine?
5:13 The prophets will B wind; the word is not
5:27 treachery; therefore they have B great and rich,
7:11 called by my name, B a den of robbers
7:34 for the land shall B a waste.
11:13 For your gods have B as many as your
12:8 My heritage has B to me like a lion
18:21 sword, let their wives B childless and widowed.
20:7 I have B a laughingstock all the day; every
20:8 of the LORD has B for me a reproach
22:5 that this house shall B a desolation.
23:14 all of them have B like Sodom to me,
25:11 This whole land shall B a ruin and a
25:38 for their land has B a waste because of
26:18 a field; Jerusalem shall B a heap of ruins,
27:17 Why should this city B a desolation?
30:16 who despoil you shall B a spoil, and all
42:18 You shall B an execration, a horror, a curse,
44:8 be cut off and B a curse and a
44:12 famine; and they shall B an execration, a horror,
44:22 therefore your land has B a desolation and a
46:19 For Memphis shall B a waste, a ruin, without
47:2 the north, and shall B an overflowing torrent; they
48:9 away; her cities shall B a desolation, with no
48:34 of Nimrim also have B desolate.
48:39 So Moab has B a derision and a horror
49:2 the Ammonites; it shall B a desolate mound, and
49:13 LORD, that Bozrah shall B a horror, a taunt,
49:17 "Edom shall B a horror; every one who passes
49:24 Damascus has B feeble, she turned to flee, and
49:32 Their camels shall B booty, their herds of cattle
49:33 Hazor shall B a haunt of jackals, an everlasting
50:23 How Babylon has B a horror among the nations!
50:36 diviners, that they may B fools!
50:37 midst, that they may B women!
51:30 has failed, they have B women; her dwellings are
51:37 dry; and Babylon shall B a heap of ruins,
51:41 How Babylon has B a horror among the nations!
51:43 Her cities have B a horror, a land of
Lam 1:1 a widow has she B, she that was great
1:1 among the cities has B a vassal.
1:2 with her, they have B her enemies.
1:5 Her foes have B the head, her enemies prosper,
1:6 Her princes have B like harts that find no
1:17 his foes; Jerusalem has B a filthy thing among
2:5 The Lord has B like an enemy, he has
3:14 his quiver; I have B the laughingstock of all
4:3 of my people has B cruel, like the ostriches
4:8 their bones, it has B as dry as wood.
4:21 shall pass; you shall B drunk and strip yourself
5:3 We have B orphans, fatherless; our mothers are like
5:17 this our heart has B sick, for these things
Bar 6:5 take care not to B at all like the
Ezek 6:4 Your altars shall B desolate, and your incense altars
12:20 and the land shall B a desolation; and you
16:57 Now you have B like her an object of
17:8 and bear fruit, and B a noble vine.
17:23 and bear fruit, and B a noble cedar; and
19:14 a lamentation, and has B a lamentation.
22:4 You have B guilty by the blood which you
22:18 house of Israel has B dross to me; all
22:18 in the furnace, have B dross.
22:19 Because you have all B dross, therefore, behold, I
24:11 coals, that it may B hot, and its copper
26:5 GOD; and she shall B a spoil to the
28:5 and your heart has B proud in your wealth–
30:21 so that it may B strong to wield the
34:8 because my sheep have B a prey, and my
34:8 and my sheep have B food for all the
35:4 waste, and you shall B a desolation; and you
36:2 'The ancient heights have B our possession,'
36:4 deserted cities, which have B a prey and derision
36:35 that was desolate has B like the garden of
37:17 stick, that they may B one in your hand.
47:8 sea, the water will B fresh.
47:9 of the sea may B fresh; so everything will
47:11 and marshes will not B fresh; they are to
Dan 3:37 we, O Lord, have B fewer than any nation,
4:22 who have grown and B strong.
9:16 and thy people have B a byword among all
11:2 and when he has B strong through his riches,
11:23 deceitfully; and he shall B strong with a small
11:43 He shall B ruler of the treasures of gold
14:28 saying, "The king has B a Jew; he has
Hos 4:15 Israel, let not Judah B guilty.
5:9 Ephraim shall B a desolation in the day of
5:10 princes of Judah have B like those who remove
8:11 for sinning, they have B to him altars for
Joel 3:19 "Egypt shall B a desolation and Edom a desolate
Amos 8:3 of the temple shall B wailings in that day,"
Jon 4:5 should see what would B of the city.
Mic 3:12 a field; Jerusalem shall B a heap of ruins,
7:1 For I have B as when the summer fruit
Zeph 2:4 deserted, and Ashkelon shall B a desolation; Ashdod's
2:7 The seacoast shall B the possession of the remnant
2:9 of Israel, "Moab shall B like Sodom, and the
2:15 a desolation she has B, a lair for wild
Hag 2:12 of food, does it B holy?" The priests answered,
2:13 of these, does it B unclean?" The priests answered,
2:13 priests answered, "It does B unclean."
Zech 2:9 them, and they shall B plunder for those who
4:7 Before Zerubbabel you shall B a plain; and he
10:7 Then Ephraim shall B like a mighty warrior, and
11:4 the LORD my God: B shepherd of the flock
11:5 the LORD, I have B rich'; and their own
14:9 And the LORD will B king over all the
1Mac 1:1 (He had previously B king of Greece.)
1:16 established, he determined to B king of the land
2:8 Her temple has B like a man without honor;
2:11 longer free, she has B a slave.
2:49 and reproach have now B strong; it is a
10:6 with arms, and to B his ally; and he
10:54 wife, and I will B your son-in-law, and will
10:56 another, and I will B your father-in-law, as you
10:70 us, and I have B a laughingstock and reproach
11:40 over to him, to B king in place of
12:10 that we may not B estranged from you, for
12:39 Then Trypho attempted to B king in Asia and
14:17 Simon his brother had B high priest in his
15:9 that your glory will B manifest in all the
2Mac 4:21 that Philometor had B hostile to his government,
4:50 growing in wickedness, having B the chief plotter
5:15 by Menelaus, who had B a traitor both to
9:17 this he also would B a Jew and would
12:39 that time it had B necessary, Judas and his
Mt 4:3 command these stones to B loaves of bread."
18:3 unless you turn and B like children, you will
19:5 and the two shall B one'?
21:42 the builders rejected has B the head of the
Mk 1:17 I will make you B fishers of men."
6:14 for Jesus' name had B known.
10:8 and the two shall B one.' So they are
12:10 the builders rejected has B the head of the
Lk 4:3 command this stone to B bread."
16:17 of the law to B void.
20:17 the builders rejected has B the head of the
22:26 the greatest among you B as the youngest, and
Jn 1:12 he gave power to B children of God;
2:9 tasted the water now B wine, and did not
4:14 shall give him will B in him a spring
9:27 you too want to B his disciples?"
9:39 those who see may B blind."
12:36 light, that you may B sons of light." When
17:23 me, that they may B perfectly one, so that
Acts 1:20 Psalms, 'Let his habitation B desolate, and let there
1:22 of these men must B with us a witness
4:11 builders, but which has B the head of the

	7:40	not know what has B of him.'
	12:18	soldiers over what had B of Peter.
	26:29	me this day might B such as I am–
Rom	4:18	hope, that he should B the father of many
	6:17	slaves of sin have B obedient from the heart
	6:18	free from sin, have B slaves of righteousness.
	6:22	from sin and have B slaves of God, the
	7:13	the commandment might B sinful beyond measure.
	11:9	says, "Let their table B a snare and a
	11:20	So do not B proud, but stand in awe.
1Cor	3:13	each man's work will B manifest; for the Day
	3:18	this age, let him B a fool that he
	3:18	fool that he may B wise.
	4:8	Already you have B rich!
	4:8	Without us you have B kings!
	4:9	death; because we have B a spectacle to the
	4:13	to conciliate; we have B, and are now, as
	6:16	written, "The two shall B one."
	7:23	a price; do not B slaves of men.
	8:9	liberty of yours somehow B a stumbling block to
	9:22	I have B all things to all men, that
2Cor	5:21	in him we might B the righteousness of God.
	8:9	his poverty you might B rich.
Gal	3:13	of the law, having B a curse for us–
	4:12	Brethren, I beseech you, B as I am, for
	4:12	for I also have B as you are.
	4:15	What has B of the satisfaction you felt?
	4:16	Have I then B your enemy by telling you
Eph	4:19	of heart; they have B callous and have given
	5:31	and the two shall B one flesh."
Phil	1:13	so that it has B known throughout the whole
Col	3:21	your children, lest they B discouraged.
1Thes	2:8	selves, because you had B very dear to us.
Tit	3:7	by his grace and B heirs in hope of
Philem	1:10	whose father I have B in my imprisonment.
Heb	1:4	Majesty on high, having B as much superior to
	2:17	so that he might B a merciful and faithful
	5:11	explain, since you have B dull of hearing.
	6:4	heavenly gift, and have B partakers of the Holy
	6:20	on our behalf, having B a high priest for
	7:16	of Melchizedek, who has B a priest, not according
	12:15	by it the many B defiled;
Jas	2:4	distinctions among yourselves, and B judges with evil
	2:10	in one point has B guilty of all of
	2:11	do kill, you have B a transgressor of the
	3:1	not many of you B teachers, my brethren, for
1Pet	2:7	the builders rejected has B the head of the
2Pet	1:4	because of passion, and B partakers of the divine
	2:20	the last state has B worse for them than
Rev	11:15	of the world has B the kingdom of our
	17:2	dwellers on earth have B drunk."
	18:2	It has B a dwelling place of demons, a

BECOMES (40)

Lev	4:14	which they have committed B known, the assembly
	5:3	be with which one B unclean, and it is
	13:24	flesh of the burn B a spot, reddish-white or
	25:25	"If your brother B poor, and sells part of
	25:26	it, and then himself B prosperous and finds sufficient
	25:35	"And if your brother B poor, and cannot maintain
	25:39	"And if your brother B poor beside you, and
	25:47	or sojourner with you B rich, and your brother
	25:47	your brother beside him B poor and sells himself
Num	11:20	at your nostrils and B loathsome to you, because
Deut	24:2	if she goes and B another man's wife,
2Chr	13:9	bull or seven rams B a priest of what
Ps	49:16	not afraid when one B rich, when the glory
Prov	13:20	walks with wise men B wise, but the companion
	17:18	gives a pledge, and B surety in the presence
	21:11	is punished, the simple B wise; when a wise
	30:22	a slave when he B king, and a fool
Sir	12:14	with a sinner and B involved in his sins.
	31:4	when he rests he B needy.
	43:19	when it freezes, it B pointed thorns.
Is	18:5	over, and the flower B a ripening grape, he
	32:15	high, and the wilderness B a fruitful field, and
	44:12	his strong arm; he B hungry and his strength
	44:15	Then it B fuel for a man; he takes
Jer	3:1	goes from him and B another man's wife, will
Mt	12:45	state of that man B worse than the first.
	13:32	greatest of shrubs and B a tree, so that
	23:14	proselyte, and when he B a proselyte, you make
	24:32	soon as its branch B tender and puts forth
Mk	4:32	it grows up and B the greatest of all
	9:18	grinds his teeth and B rigid; and I asked
	13:28	soon as its branch B tender and puts forth
Lk	11:26	state of that man B worse than the first."
Rom	2:25	the law, your circumcision B uncircumcision.
	3:27	Then what B of our boasting?
1Cor	6:16	himself to a prostitute B one body with her?
	6:17	united to the Lord B one spirit with him.
Eph	5:13	by the light it B visible, for anything that
	5:13	visible, for anything that B visible is light.
Heb	7:15	This B even more evident when another priest arises

BECOMING (6)

Lev	15:32	an emission of semen, B unclean thereby;
Prov	17:7	Fine speech is not B to a fool; still
Ezek	16:54	that you have done, B a consolation to them.
2Mac	4:40	since the crowds were B aroused and filled with
Phil	3:10	may share his sufferings, B like him in his
Heb	8:13	And what is B obsolete and growing old is

BECOMINGLY

Rom	13:13	let us conduct ourselves B as in the day,

BECORATH

1Sam	9:1	of Zeror, son of B, son of Aphiah, a

BECTILETH (2)

Jud	2:21	to the plain of B, and camped opposite Bectileth
	2:21	Bectileth, and camped opposite B near the mountain

BED (88)

Gen	47:31	Israel bowed himself upon the head of his B
	48:2	Israel summoned his strength, and sat up in B
	49:4	up to your father's B; then you defiled it–
	49:33	his feet into the B, and breathed his last,
Ex	8:3	bedchamber and on your B, and into the houses
	21:18	die but keeps his B,
Lev	15:4	Every B on which he who has the discharge
	15:5	one who touches his B shall wash his clothes,
	15:21	And whoever touches her B shall wash his clothes,
	15:23	whether it is the B or anything upon which
	15:24	seven days; and every B on which he lies
	15:26	Every B on which she lies, all the days
	15:26	to her as the B of her impurity; and
1Sam	9:25	into the city, a B was spread for Saul
	19:13	laid it on the B and put a pillow
	19:15	to me in the B, that I may kill
	19:16	image was in the B, with the pillow of
	28:23	arose from the earth, and sat upon the B
2Sam	4:7	he lay on his B in his bedchamber, they
	4:11	own house upon his B, shall I not now
	13:5	"Lie down on your B, and pretend to be
1Kgs	1:47	throne.' And the king bowed himself upon the B
	17:19	he lodged, and laid him upon his own B
	21:4	lay down on his B, and turned away his
2Kgs	1:4	come down from the B to which you have
	1:6	come down from the B to which you have
	1:16	come down from the B to which you have
	4:10	there for him a B, a table, a chair,
	4:21	laid him on the B of the man of
	4:32	he saw the child lying dead on his B
2Chr	24:25	Jehoiada the priest, and slew him on his B
Tob	8:4	got up from the B and said, "Sister, get
	14:11	As he said this he died in his B
Jud	8:3	and took to his B and died in Bethulia
	9:3	be slain, and their B, which was ashamed of
	10:21	was resting on his B, under a canopy which
	13:1	and they went to B, for they all were
	13:2	stretched out on his B, for he was overcome
	13:4	Judith, standing beside his B, said in her heart,
	13:6	the end of the B, above Holofernes' head, and
	13:7	came close to his B and took hold of
	13:9	his body off the B and pulled down the
Esth	14:15	wicked and abhor the B of the uncircumcised and
Job	7:13	When I say, 'My B will comfort me, my
	27:19	He goes to B rich, but will do so
	33:19	with pain upon his B, and with continual strife
Ps	6:6	night I flood my B with tears; I drench
	36:4	mischief while on his B; he sets himself in
	63:6	of thee upon my B, and meditate on thee
	132:3	or get into my B;
	139:8	If I make my B in Sheol, thou art
Prov	7:17	I have perfumed my B with myrrh, aloes, and
	22:27	pay, why should your B be taken from under
	26:14	its hinges, so does a sluggard on his B
Song	3:1	Upon my B by night I sought him whom
Sir	31:19	He does not breathe heavily upon his B
	40:5	one rests upon his B, his sleep at night
	41:22	do not approach her B; of abusive words, before

Is 14:11 harps; maggots are the B beneath you, and worms
28:20 For the B is too short to stretch oneself
57:7 you have set your B, and thither you went
57:8 you have uncovered your B, you have gone up
57:8 you have loved their B, you have looked on
Bar 6:70 scarecrow in a cucumber B, that guards nothing, so
Ezek 17:7 From the B where it was planted
17:10 wither away on the B where it grew?"
23:17 to her into the B of love, and they
32:25 have made her a B among the slain with
Dan 2:28 as you lay in B are these:
2:29 as you lay in B came thoughts of what
4:5 as I lay in B the fancies and the
4:10 as I lay in B were these: I saw,
4:13 as I lay in B, and behold, a watcher,
7:1 of his head as he lay in his B
Amos 3:12 corner of a couch and part of a B
1Mac 6:8 He took to his B and became sick from
Mt 9:2 paralytic, lying on his B; and when Jesus saw
9:6 "Rise, take up your B and go home."
Mk 4:21 bushel, or under a B, and not on a
7:29 the child lying in B, and the demon gone.
Lk 5:18 were bringing on a B a man who was
5:19 him down with his B through the tiles into
5:24 rise, take up your B and go home."
8:16 puts it under a B, but puts it on
11:7 are with me in B; I cannot get up
17:34 be two in one B; one will be taken
Acts 9:34 Jesus Christ heals you; rise and make your B
Heb 13:4 and let the marriage B be undefiled; for God

BEDAD (2)

Gen 36:35 Hadad the son of B, who defeated Midian in
1Chr 1:46 Hadad the son of B, who defeated Midian in

BEDAN

1Chr 7:17 The sons of Ulam: B

BEDCHAMBER (10)

Ex 8:3 house, and into your B and on your bed,
2Sam 4:7 his bed in his B, they smote him, and
2Kgs 6:12 Israel the words that you speak in your B
11:2 she put him and his nurse in a B
2Chr 22:11 she put him and his nurse in a B
Jud 13:3 to stand outside the B and to wait for
13:4 either small or great, was left in the B
14:15 and went into the B and found him thrown
16:19 for herself from his B she gave as a
Eccl 10:20 king, nor in your B curse the rich; for

BEDECKED (2)

Rev 17:4 purple and scarlet, and B with gold and jewels
18:16 in purple and scarlet, B with gold, with jewels,

BEDEIAH

Ezra 10:35 Ma-adai, Amram, Uel, Benaiah, B, Cheluhi,

BEDRIDDEN

Acts 9:33 Aeneas, who had been B for eight years and

BEDS (13)

2Sam 17:28 from Rogelim, brought B, basins, and earthen
Jud 15:11 silver dishes and his B and his bowls and
Job 33:15 they slumber on their B,
Ps 4:4 own hearts on your B, and be silent.
Song 5:13 His cheeks are like B of spices, yielding fragrance.
6:2 his garden, to the B of spices, to pasture
Sir 48:6 famous men from their B;
Is 57:2 they rest in their B who walk in their
Hos 7:15 they wail upon their B; for grain and wine
Joel 3:18 and all the stream B of Judah shall flow
Amos 6:4 those who lie upon B of ivory, and stretch
Mic 2:1 who devise wickedness and work evil upon their B
Acts 5:15 and laid them on B and pallets, that as

BEDSTEAD (2)

Deut 3:11 the Rephaim; behold, his B was a bedstead of
3:11 his bedstead was a B of iron; is it

BEE (2)

Sir 11:3 The B is small among flying creatures, but her
Is 7:18 Egypt, and for the B which is in the

BEELIADA

1Chr 14:7 Nogah, Nepheg, Japhia, Elishama, B, and Eliphelet.

BEER (2)

Num 21:16 there they continued to B; that is the well
Judg 9:21 fled, and went to B and dwelt there, for

BEER-ELIM

Is 15:8 wailing reaches to Eglaim, the wailing reaches to B

BEER-LAHAI-ROI (3)

Gen 16:14 the well was called B; it lies between Kadesh
24:62 Isaac had come from B, and was dwelling in
25:11 And Isaac dwelt at B

BEER-SHEBA (34)

Gen 21:14 she departed, and wandered in the wilderness of B
21:31 that place was called B; because there both of
21:32 So they made a covenant at B
21:33 a tamarisk tree in B, and called there on
22:19 and went together to B; and Abraham dwelt at
22:19 together to Beer-sheba; and Abraham dwelt at B
26:23 From there he went up to B
26:33 of the city is B to this day.
28:10 Jacob left B, and went toward Haran.
46:1 had, and came to B, and offered sacrifices to
46:5 Jacob set out from B; and the sons of
Josh 15:28 Hazar-gaddah, Heshmon, Beth-pelet, Hazar-shual, B,
19:2 had for its inheritance B, Sheba, Moladah,
Judg 20:1 out, from Dan to B, including the land of
1Sam 3:20 Israel from Dan to B knew that Samuel was
8:2 of his second, Abijah; they were judges in B
2Sam 3:10 over Israel and over Judah, from Dan to B
17:11 you, from Dan to B, as the sand by
24:2 Israel, from Dan to B, and number the people,
24:7 went out to the Negeb of Judah at B
24:15 people from Dan to B seventy thousand men.
1Kgs 4:25 from Dan even to B, every man under his
19:3 life, and came to B, which belongs to Judah,
2Kgs 12:1 His mother's name was Zibiah of B
23:8 incense, from Geba to B; and he broke down
1Chr 4:28 They dwelt in B, Moladah, Hazar-shual,
21:2 "Go, number Israel, from B to Dan, and bring
2Chr 19:4 among the people, from B to the hill country
24:1 in Jerusalem; his mother's name was Zibiah of B
30:5 throughout all Israel, from B to Dan, that the
Neh 11:27 Beth-pelet, in Hazar-shual, in B and its villages,
11:30 So they encamped from B to the valley of
Amos 5:5 or cross over to B; for Gilgal shall surely
8:14 'As the way of B lives,' they shall fall,

BEES (3)

Deut 1:44 and chased you as B do and beat you
Judg 14:8 was a swarm of B in the body of
Ps 118:12 They surrounded me like B, they blazed like a

BEESHTERAH

Josh 21:27 for the slayer, and B with its pasture lands--

BEFALL (20)

Gen 41:36 famine which are to B the land of Egypt,
42:4 feared that harm might B him.
42:38 If harm should B him on the journey that
49:1 tell you what shall B you in days to
Ex 1:9 multiply, and, if war B us, they join our
Deut 31:29 to come evil will B you, because you will
1Sam 2:34 And this which shall B your two sons, Hophni
Job 31:3 Does not calamity B the unrighteous, and disaster
34:11 he will make it B him.
Ps 91:10 habitation, no evil shall B you, no scourge come
Eccl 2:15 befalls the fool will B me also; why then
Sir 7:1 and evil will never B you.
25:18 may a sinner's lot B her!
33:1 No evil will B the man who fears the
Is 47:13 moons predict what shall B you.
Dan 10:14 understand what is to B your people in the
Amos 3:6 Does evil B a city, unless the LORD has
Jn 5:13 more, that nothing worse B you."
18:4 all that was to B him, came forward and
Acts 20:22 not knowing what shall B me there;

BEFALLEN (14)

Gen 42:29 him all that had B them, saying,
Lev 10:19 things as these have B me!
Num 20:14 the adversity that has B us:
Josh 2:23 him all that had B them.
Judg 6:13 then has all this B us?
1Sam 20:26 he thought, "Something has B him; he is not
1Chr 7:23 Beriah, because evil had B his house.

Esth 6:13 friends everything that had B him.
9:26 and of what had B them,
Is 51:19 These two things have B you-- who will
Jer 44:23 that this evil has B you, as at this
Lam 5:1 O LORD, what has B us; behold, and see
Dan 3:33 shame and disgrace have B thy servants and
2Mac 11:13 the defeat which had B him, and realized that

BEFALLS (6)

Gen 44:29 from me, and harm B him, you will bring
Job 3:25 and what I dread B me.
Prov 12:21 No ill B the righteous, but the wicked are
15:6 much treasure, but trouble B the income of the
Eccl 2:15 said to myself, "What B the fool will befall
Sir 12:17 If calamity B you, you will find him there

BEFELL (3)

2Mac 5:20 in the misfortunes that B the nation and afterward
Acts 20:19 and with trials which B me through the plots
2Tim 3:11 persecutions, my sufferings, what B me at Antioch, at

BEFIT

Lk 3:8 Bear fruits that B repentance, and do not begin

BEFITS (8)

Ps 33:1 Praise B the upright.
93:5 are very sure; holiness B thy house, O LORD,
Wis 13:15 it a niche that B it, and sets it
Mt 3:8 Bear fruit that B repentance,
Rom 16:2 in the Lord as B the saints, and help
1Tim 2:10 by good deeds, as B women who profess religion.
Tit 2:1 for you, teach what B sound doctrine.
3Jn 1:6 on their journey as B God's service.

BEFOREHAND (15)

Wis 18:6 night was made known B to our fathers, so
1Mac 6:36 These took their position B wherever the beast was;
Mt 24:25 Lo, I have told you B
Mk 13:11 do not be anxious B what you are to
13:23 take heed; I have told you all things B
14:8 has anointed my body B for burying.
Lk 21:14 minds, not to meditate B how to answer;
Acts 1:16 the Holy Spirit spoke B by the mouth of
7:52 killed those who announced B the coming of the
Rom 1:2 which he promised B through his prophets in the
9:23 which he has prepared B for glory,
Gal 3:8 faith, preached the gospel B to Abraham, saying, "In
Eph 2:10 works, which God prepared B, that we should walk
1Thes 3:4 you, we told you B that we were to
2Pet 3:17 therefore, beloved, knowing this B, beware lest you

BEFORETIME

Is 41:26 we might know, and B, that we might say,

BEG (18)

Gen 19:7 him, and said, "I B you, my brothers, do
Esth 7:7 but Haman stayed to B his life from Queen
Ps 109:10 children wander about and B; may they be driven
Sir 40:28 beggar; it is better to die than to B
Lam 4:4 for thirst; the children B for food, but no
Mk 5:17 And they began to B Jesus to depart from
Lk 9:38 crowd cried, "Teacher, I B you to look upon
16:3 enough to dig, and I am ashamed to B
16:27 he said, 'Then I B you, father, to send
Jn 9:8 this the man who used to sit and B
Acts 21:39 no mean city; I B you, let me speak
24:4 you no further, I B you in your kindness
26:3 the Jews; therefore I B you to listen to
2Cor 2:8 So I B you to reaffirm your love for
10:2 am away!-- I B of you that when
Eph 4:1 prisoner for the Lord, B you to lead a
2Thes 2:1 to meet him, we B you, brethren,
2Jn 1:5 And now I B you, lady, not as though

BEGAN (198)

Gen 4:26 At that time men B to call upon the
6:1 When men B to multiply on the face of
41:54 seven years of famine B to come, as Joseph
Num 25:1 in Shittim the people B to play the harlot
Josh 18:12 north side their boundary B at the Jordan; then
Judg 13:25 Spirit of the LORD B to stir him in
16:19 Then she B to torment him, and his strength
16:22 hair of his head B to grow again after
19:25 And as the dawn B to break, they let
20:31 at other times they B to smite and kill
20:40 But when the signal B to rise out of
1Sam 13:1 years old when he B to reign; and he
2Sam 2:10 years old when he B to reign over Israel,
5:4 years old when he B to reign, and he
24:5 crossed the Jordan, and B from Aroer, and from
1Kgs 6:1 the second month, he B to build the house
14:21 years old when he B to reign, and he
15:1 son of Nebat, Abijam B to reign over Judah.
15:9 king of Israel Asa B to reign over Judah,
15:25 the son of Jeroboam B to reign over Israel
15:33 the son of Ahijah B to reign over all
16:8 the son of Baasha B to reign over Israel
16:11 When he B to reign, as soon as he
16:23 king of Judah, Omri B to reign over Israel,
16:29 the son of Omri B to reign over Israel,
22:41 the son of Asa B to reign over Judah
22:42 years old when he B to reign, and he
22:51 the son of Ahab B to reign over Israel
2Kgs 8:16 Jehoshaphat, king of Judah, B to reign.
8:25 Jehoram, king of Judah, B to reign.
8:26 years old when he B to reign, and he
9:29 son of Ahab, Ahaziah B to reign over Judah.
10:32 those days the LORD B to cut off parts
11:21 years old when he B to reign.
12:1 year of Jehu Jehoash B to reign, and he
13:1 the son of Jehu B to reign over Israel
13:10 the son of Jehoahaz B to reign over Israel
14:1 Joash, king of Judah, B to reign.
14:2 years old when he B to reign, and he
14:23 Joash, king of Israel, B to reign in Samaria,
15:1 Amaziah, king of Judah, B to reign.
15:2 years old when he B to reign, and he
15:13 the son of Jabesh B to reign in the
15:17 the son of Gadi B to reign over Israel,
15:23 the son of Menahem B to reign over Israel
15:27 the son of Remaliah B to reign over Israel
15:32 Uzziah, king of Judah, B to reign.
15:33 years old when he B to reign, and he
15:37 those days the LORD B to send Rezin the
16:1 Jotham, king of Judah, B to reign.
16:2 years old when he B to reign, and he
17:1 the son of Elah B to reign in Samaria
18:1 Ahaz, king of Judah, B to reign.
18:2 years old when he B to reign, and he
21:1 years old when he B to reign, and he
21:19 years old when he B to reign, and he
22:1 years old when he B to reign, and he
23:31 years old when he B to reign, and he
23:36 years old when he B to reign, and he
25:27 the year that he B to reign, graciously freed
1Chr 1:10 father of Nimrod; he B to be a mighty
27:24 the son of Zeruiah B to number, but did
2Chr 3:1 Then Solomon B to build the house of the
3:2 He B to build in the second month of
12:13 years old when he B to reign, and he
13:1 of King Jeroboam Abijah B to reign over Judah.
20:22 And when they B to sing and praise, the
20:31 years old when he B to reign, and he
21:20 years old when he B to reign, and he
22:2 years old when he B to reign, and he
24:1 years old when he B to reign, and he
25:1 years old when he B to reign, and he
26:3 years old when he B to reign, and he
27:1 years old when he B to reign, and he
27:8 years old when he B to reign, and he
28:1 years old when he B to reign, and he
29:1 Hezekiah B to reign when he was twenty-five years
29:17 They B to sanctify on the first day of
29:27 when the burnt offering B, the song to the
29:27 song to the LORD B also, and the trumpets,
31:7 the third month they B to pile up the
31:10 answered him, "Since they B to bring the
33:1 years old when he B to reign, and he
33:21 years old when he B to reign, and he
34:1 years old when he B to reign, and he
34:3 yet a boy, he B to seek the God
34:3 the twelfth year he B to purge Judah and
36:2 years old when he B to reign; and he
36:5 years old when he B to reign, and he
36:9 years old when he B to reign, and he
36:11 years old when he B to reign, and he
Ezra 3:6 the seventh month they B to offer burnt offerings
5:2 of Jozadak arose and B to rebuild the house
7:9 the first month he B to go up from
Neh 13:19 When it B to be dark at the gates
Tob 2:13 returned to me it B to bleat.
5:17 But Anna, his mother, B to weep, and said

	7:15	Then they B to eat.
	7:17	there; and the girl B to weep.
	8:5	And Tobias B to pray, "Blessed art thou, O
	10:4	Then she B to mourn for him, and said,
	11:12	And when his eyes B to smart he rubbed
Jud	5:22	standing around the tent B to complain; Holofernes'
	16:1	Then Judith B this thanksgiving before all Israel, and
Esth	14:11	of the man who B this against us.
Job	38:12	morning since your days B, and caused the dawn
Wis	7:3	I was born, I B to breathe the common
Ezek	9:6	So they B with the elders who were before
Dan	13:8	walking about, and they B to desire her.
Hos	9:15	in Gilgal; there I B to hate them.
Jon	3:4	Jonah B to go into the city, going a
1Mac	1:8	Then his officers B to rule, each in his
	1:10	He B to reign in the one hundred and
	3:25	Judas and his brothers B to be feared, and
	5:2	So they B to kill and destroy among the
	7:1	the sea, and there B to reign.
	9:40	from the ambush and B killing them.
	9:47	So the battle B, and Jonathan stretched out his
	9:55	But he only B to tear it down, for
	9:67	Then he B to attack and went into battle
	9:73	And Jonathan B to judge the people, and he
	10:1	him, and there he B to reign.
	10:10	dwelt in Jerusalem and B to rebuild and restore
	11:46	of the city and B to fight.
	11:54	young boy Antiochus who B to reign and put
	13:42	Israel, and the people B to write in their
	15:40	came to Jamnia and B to provoke the people
2Mac	9:11	broken in spirit, he B to lose much of
Mt	4:17	From that time Jesus B to preach, saying, "Repent,
	11:7	they went away, Jesus B to speak to the
	11:20	Then he B to upbraid the cities where most
	12:1	were hungry, and they B to pluck heads of
	16:21	From that time Jesus B to show his disciples
	16:22	Peter took him and B to rebuke him, saying,
	18:23	When he B the reckoning, one was brought to
	26:22	were very sorrowful, and B to say to him
	26:37	sons of Zebedee, he B to be sorrowful and
	26:74	Then he B to invoke a curse on himself
Mk	1:45	he went out and B to talk freely about
	2:23	their way his disciples B to pluck heads of
	4:1	Again he B to teach beside the sea.
	5:17	And they B to beg Jesus to depart from
	5:20	he went away and B to proclaim in the
	6:2	on the sabbath he B to teach in the
	6:7	him the twelve, and B to send them out
	6:34	a shepherd; and he B to teach them many
	6:55	the whole neighborhood and B to bring sick people
	8:11	The Pharisees came and B to argue with him,
	8:31	And he B to teach them that the Son
	8:32	Peter took him, and B to rebuke him.
	10:28	Peter B to say to him, "Lo, we have
	10:32	the twelve again, he B to tell them what
	10:41	ten heard it, they B to be indignant at
	10:47	Jesus of Nazareth, he B to cry out and
	11:15	entered the temple and B to drive out those
	12:1	And he B to speak to them in parables.
	13:5	And Jesus B to say to them, "Take heed
	14:19	They B to be sorrowful, and to say to
	14:33	James and John, and B to be greatly distressed
	14:65	And some B to spit on him, and to
	14:69	maid saw him, and B again to say to
	14:71	But he B to invoke a curse on himself
	15:8	crowd came up and B to ask Pilate to
	15:18	And they B to salute him, "Hail, King of
Lk	3:23	Jesus, when he B his ministry, was about thirty
	4:21	And he B to say to them, "Today this
	5:7	boats, so that they B to sink.
	5:21	and the Pharisees B to question, saying, "Who
	7:15	man sat up, and B to speak.
	7:24	John had gone, he B to speak to the
	7:38	his feet, weeping, she B to wet his feet
	7:49	at table with him B to say among themselves,
	9:12	Now the day B to wear away; and the
	11:29	crowds were increasing, he B to say, "This
	11:53	scribes and the Pharisees B to press him hard,
	12:1	upon one another, he B to say to his
	14:18	But they all alike B to make excuses.
	14:30	him, saying, 'This man B to build, and was
	15:14	that country, and he B to be in want.
	15:24	is found.' And they B to make merry.
	19:37	multitude of the disciples B to rejoice and praise
	19:45	entered the temple and B to drive out those
	20:9	And he B to tell the people this parable:
	22:23	And they B to question one another, which of
	23:2	And they B to accuse him, saying, "We found
Jn	4:52	the hour when he B to mend, and they
	9:32	Never since the world B has it been heard
	13:5	into a basin, and B to wash the disciples'
Acts	1:1	with all that Jesus B to do and teach,
	2:4	the Holy Spirit and B to speak in other
	11:4	But Peter B and explained to them in order:
	11:15	your household.' As I B to speak, the Holy
	18:26	He B to speak boldly in the synagogue; but
	24:2	he was called, Tertullus B to accuse him, saying:
	27:18	were violently storm-tossed, they B next day to
	27:35	he broke it and B to eat.
2Cor	8:10	a year ago you B not only to do
Phil	1:6	sure that he who B a good work in

BEGET (2)

Deut	4:25	"When you B children and children's children, and
	28:41	You shall B sons and daughters, but they shall

BEGETS (4)

Prov	23:24	greatly rejoice; he who B a wise son will
Eccl	6:3	If a man B a hundred children, and lives
Ezek	18:10	"If he B a son who is a robber,
	18:14	"But if this man B a son who sees

BEGETTING

Is	45:10	father, 'What are you B or to a woman,

BEGGAR (6)

Sir	4:3	angry mind, nor delay your gift to a B
	18:32	Do not become a B by feasting with borrowed
	25:2	at their life: a B who is proud, a
	40:28	the life of a B; it is better to
Mk	10:46	multitude, Bartimaeus, a blind B, the son of Timaeus,
Jn	9:8	him before as a B, said, "Is not this

BEGGARLY

Gal	4:9	to the weak and B elemental spirits, whose slaves

BEGGED (19)

Wis	18:2	no injury; and they B their pardon for having
	19:3	those whom they had B and compelled to depart.
1Mac	9:35	of the multitude and B the Nabateans, who were
Mt	8:31	And the demons B him, "If you cast us
	8:34	they saw him, they B him to leave their
	15:23	his disciples came and B him, saying, "Send her
Mk	5:10	And he B him eagerly not to send them
	5:12	the hillside; and they B him, "Send us to
	5:18	been possessed with demons B him that he might
	7:25	And she B him to cast the demon out
	8:22	a blind man, and B him to touch him.
Lk	8:31	And they B him not to command them to
	8:32	the hillside; and they B him to let them
	8:38	the demons had gone B that he might be
	9:40	And I B your disciples to cast it out,
Jn	4:47	Galilee, he went and B him to come down
Acts	13:42	went out, the people B that these things might
	19:31	sent to him and B him not to venture
	21:12	and the people there B him not to go

BEGGING (4)

Ps	37:25	forsaken or his children B bread.
Sir	40:30	mouth of the shameless B is sweet, but in
Lk	18:35	sitting by the roadside B
2Cor	8:4	their own free will, B us earnestly for the

BEGIN (23)

Deut	2:24	Heshbon, and his land; B to take possession, and
	2:25	This day I will B to put the dread
	2:31	land over to you; B to take possession, that
	16:9	shall count seven weeks; B to count the seven
Josh	3:7	"This day I will B to exalt you in
Judg	10:18	the man that will B to fight against the
	13:5	birth; and he shall B to deliver Israel from
1Kgs	20:14	he said, "Who shall B the battle?" He answered,
Neh	11:17	was the leader to B the thanksgiving in prayer,
Jud	16:2	And Judith said, B a song to my God
Sir	38:16	who is suffering grievously B the lament.
Jer	25:29	For behold, I B to work evil at the
Ezek	9:6	And B at my sanctuary." So they began with
2Mac	2:32	point therefore let us B our narrative, adding only
Lk	3:8	repentance, and do not B to say to yourselves,
	13:25	the door, you will B to stand outside and
	13:26	from.' Then you will B to say, 'We ate
	14:9	and then you will B with shame to take

B

14:29 all who see it B to mock him,
21:28 Now when these things B to take place, look
23:29 suck!' Then they will B to say to the
Rom 3:2 To B with, the Jews are entrusted with the
1Pet 4:17 come for judgment to B with the household of

BEGINNING (126)

Gen 1:1 IN the B God created the heavens
10:10 The B of his kingdom was Babel, Erech, and
11:6 this is only the B of what they will
13:3 had been at the B, between Bethel and Ai,
41:21 they were still as gaunt as at the B
44:12 And he searched, B with the eldest and ending
Ex 12:2 be for you the B of months; it shall
Lev 23:32 day of the month B at evening, from evening
Deut 3:12 the Gadites the territory B at Aroer, which is
11:12 upon it, from the B of the year to
Judg 7:19 the camp at the B of the middle watch,
Ruth 1:22 to Bethlehem at the B of barley harvest.
1Sam 3:12 concerning his house, from B to end.
2Sam 21:9 of harvest, at the B of barley harvest.
21:10 the rock, from the B of harvest until rain
2Kgs 17:25 And at the B of their dwelling there, they
Ezra 3:8 of Jozadak made a B, together with the rest
4:6 of Ahasuerus, in the B of his reign, they
Neh 4:7 that the breaches were B to be closed, they
Jud 8:29 shown, but from the B of your life all
Esth 13:15 the inheritance that has been thine from the B
Job 8:7 And though your B was small, your latter days
42:12 Job more than his B; and he had fourteen
Ps 111:10 the LORD is the B of wisdom; a good
Prov 1:7 the LORD is the B of knowledge; fools despise
4:8 The B of wisdom is this: Get wisdom, and
8:22 created me at the B of his work, the
8:23 the first, before the B of the earth.
9:10 the LORD is the B of wisdom, and the
17:14 The B of strife is like letting out water;
20:21 gotten hastily in the B will in the end
Eccl 3:11 has done from the B to the end.
7:8 a thing than its B; and the patient in
10:13 The B of the words of his mouth is
Wis 6:17 The B of wisdom is the most sincere desire
6:22 her course from the B of creation, and make
7:5 has had a different B of existence;
7:18 of the elements; the B and end and middle
9:8 holy tent which thou didst prepare from the B
12:11 accursed race from the B, and it was not
14:6 For even in the B, when arrogant giants were
14:12 making idols was the B of fornication, and the
14:13 they existed from the B nor will they exist
14:27 be named is the B and cause and end
Sir 1:12 the Lord is the B of wisdom she is
10:12 The B of man's pride is to depart from
10:13 For the B of pride is sin, and the
15:14 created man in the B, and he left him
16:24 have existed from the B by his creation, and
18:6 finished, he is just B, and when he stops,
24:9 From eternity, in the B, he created me, and
25:23 woman sin had its B, and because of her
36:11 and give them their inheritance, as at the B
36:15 didst create in the B, and fulfil the prophecies
37:16 Reason is the B of every work, and counsel
39:25 From the B good things were created for good
39:32 Therefore from the B I have been convinced, and
44:2 to them great glory, his majesty from the B
Is 1:26 the first, and your counselors as at the B
40:21 Has it not been told you from the B
41:4 and done this, calling the generations from the B
41:26 declared it from the B, that we might know,
46:10 the end from the B and from ancient times
48:16 hear this: from the B I have not spoken
Jer 17:12 on high from the B is the place of
26:1 In the B of the reign of Jehoiakim the
27:1 In the B of the reign of Zedekiah the
28:1 same year, at the B of the reign of
49:34 concerning Elam, in the B of the reign of
Lam 2:19 the night, at the B of the watches!
Ezek 40:1 our exile, at the B of the year, on
48:1 names of the tribes: B at the northern border,
Dan 9:23 At the B of your supplications a word went
Amos 7:1 forming locusts in the B of the shooting up
Mic 1:13 Lachish; you were the B of sin to the
1Mac 4:59 joy for eight days, B with the twenty-fifth day
2Mac 7:23 world, who shaped the B of man and devised
8:27 to them as the B of mercy.
Mt 14:30 he was afraid, and B to sink he cried
19:4 made them from the B made them male and
19:8 wives, but from the B it was not so.
20:8 pay them their wages, B with the last, up
24:8 this is but the B of the birth-pangs.
24:21 not been from the B of the world until
27:24 that a riot was B, he took water and
Mk 1:1 The B of the gospel of
10:6 But from the B of creation, 'God made them
13:8 this is but the B of the birth-pangs.
13:19 not been from the B of the creation which
Lk 1:2 those who from the B were eyewitnesses and
23:53 the day of Preparation, and the sabbath was B
24:27 And B with Moses and all the prophets, he
24:47 name to all nations, B from Jerusalem.
Jn 1:1 In the B was the Word, and
1:2 He was in the B with God;
8:9 away, one by one, B with the eldest, and
8:25 "Even what I have told you from the B
8:44 a murderer from the B, and has nothing to
15:27 because you have been with me from the B
16:4 to you from the B, because I was with
Acts 1:22 and out among us, B from the baptism of
8:35 opened his mouth, and B with this scripture he
10:37 proclaimed throughout all Judea, B from Galilee
11:15 on them just as on us at the B
26:4 youth, spent from the B among my own nation
2Cor 3:1 Are we B to commend ourselves again?
8:6 had already made a B, he should also complete
Phil 4:15 know that in the B of the gospel, when
Col 1:18 church; he is the B, the first-born from the
2Thes 2:13 chose you from the B to be saved, through
Heb 1:10 the earth in the B, and the heavens are
7:3 genealogy, and has neither B of days nor end
2Pet 3:4 they were from the B of creation."
1Jn 1:1 which was from the B, which we have heard,
2:7 you had from the B; the old commandment is
2:13 because you know him who is from the B
2:14 because you know him who is from the B
2:24 you heard from the B abide in you.
2:24 you heard from the B abides in you, then
3:8 devil; for the devil has sinned from the B
3:11 have heard from the B, that we should love
2Jn 1:5 have had from the B, that we love one
1:6 have heard from the B, that you follow love.
Rev 3:14 and true witness, the B of God's creation.
21:6 and the Omega, the B and the end.
22:13 and the last, the B and the end."

BEGINNINGS (2)

Num 10:10 feasts, and at the B of your months, you
28:11 "At the B of your months you shall offer

BEGINS (5)

Josh 18:15 And the southern side B at the outskirts of
Ezek 42:10 from the outer court, where the outside wall B
Mt 24:49 master is delayed,' and B to beat his fellow
Lk 12:45 delayed in coming,' and B to beat the menservants
1Pet 4:17 God; and if it B with us, what will

BEGONE (4)

2Sam 16:7 said as he cursed, B, begone, you man of
16:7 as he cursed, "Begone, B, you man of blood,
Is 30:22 as unclean things; you will say to them, B
Mt 4:10 Jesus said to him, B, Satan!

BEGOT (4)

Deut 32:18 of the Rock that B you, and you forgot
1Chr 14:3 in Jerusalem, and David B more sons and daughters.
Prov 23:22 to your father who B you, and do not
Jer 16:3 and the fathers who B them in this land:

BEGOTTEN (7)

Lev 18:11 your father's wife's daughter, B by your father, since
Job 38:28 father, or who has B the drops of dew?
Ps 2:7 son, today I have B you.
Ezek 47:22 among you and have B children among you.
Acts 13:33 Son, today I have B thee.'
Heb 1:5 Son, today I have B thee"?
5:5 Son, today I have B thee";

BEGRUDGE (3)

Tob 4:7 not let your eye B the gift when you
4:16 not let your eye B the gift when you
Mt 20:15 Or do you B my generosity?'

BEGRUDGES
Sir 14:10 A stingy man's eye B bread, and it is

BEGS (2)
Mt 5:42 Give to him who B from you, and do
Lk 6:30 to every one who B from you; and of

BEGUILE (2)
Esth 16:6 of their evil natures B the sincere good will
Sir 14:16 Give, and take, and B yourself, because in Hades

BEGUILED (2)
Gen 3:13 woman said, "The serpent B me, and I ate."
Num 25:18 wiles, with which they B you in the matter

BEGUILING (2)
Col 2:4 may delude you with B speech.
Rev 2:20 and is teaching and B my servants to practice

BEGUN (14)
Num 16:46 gone forth from the LORD, the plague has B
16:47 the plague had already B among the people; and
Deut 2:31 me, 'Behold, I have B to give Sihon and
3:24 GOD, thou hast only B to show thy servant
Judg 20:39 Now Benjamin had B to smite and kill about
1Sam 3:2 Eli, whose eyesight had B to grow dim, so
Esth 6:13 before whom you have B to fall, is of
9:23 do as they had B, and as Mordecai had
Mic 6:13 Therefore I have B to smite you, making you
1Mac 5:31 that the battle had B and that the cry
2Mac 13:11 people who had just B to revive fall into
Acts 28:2 all, because it had B to rain and was
Gal 3:3 Having B with the Spirit, are you now ending
Rev 11:17 thy great power and B to reign.

BEHALF (32)
Lev 24:8 the LORD continually on B of the people of
Judg 9:3 these words on his B in the ears of
1Kgs 2:19 speak to him on B of Adonijah.
2Kgs 4:13 word spoken on your B to the king or
2Chr 16:9 show his might in B of those whose heart
20:17 the LORD on your B, O Judah and Jerusalem.'
Esth 4:16 a fast on my B, and neither eat nor
Job 36:2 I have yet something to say on God's B
Ps 109:21 Lord, deal on my B for thy name's sake;
Wis 16:24 in kindness relaxes on B of those who trust
Sir 29:13 will fight on your B against your enemy.
Is 8:19 consult the dead on B of the living?
Jer 11:14 or prayer on their B, for I will not
15:11 pleaded with thee on B of the enemy in
29:7 the LORD on its B, for in its welfare
2Mac 1:26 accept this sacrifice on B of all thy people
2:21 who strove zealously on B of Judaism, so that
11:15 granted every request in B of the Jews which
Acts 24:2 reforms are introduced on B of this nation,
Rom 15:30 to God on my B,
1Cor 15:29 by being baptized on B of the dead?
15:29 at all, why are people baptized on their B
2Cor 1:11 give thanks on our B for the blessing granted
5:20 We beseech you on B of Christ, be reconciled
12:5 On B of this man I will boast, but
12:5 but on my own B I will not boast,
Eph 3:1 for Christ Jesus on B of you Gentiles--
Col 1:7 of Christ on our B
Philem 1:13 serve me on your B during my imprisonment for
Heb 5:1 appointed to act on B of men in relation
6:20 a forerunner on our B, having become a high
9:24 appear in the presence of God on our B

BEHAVE (2)
2Sam 14:2 yourself with oil, but B like a woman who
1Tim 3:15 how one ought to B in the household of

BEHAVED (4)
Judg 2:19 they turned back and B worse than their fathers,
2Mac 1:17 upon those who have B impiously.
12:14 supply of provisions, B most insolently toward Judas
2Cor 1:12 conscience that we have B in the world, and

BEHAVING (3)
Job 36:9 transgressions, that they are B arrogantly.
1Cor 3:3 of the flesh, and B like ordinary men?
7:36 that he is not B properly toward his betrothed,

BEHAVIOR (10)
1Sam 21:13 So he changed his B before them, and feigned
Esth 1:18 heard of the queen's B will be telling it
16:7 accomplished through the pestilent B of those who
Sir 41:19 Be ashamed of selfish B at meals, of surliness
Ezek 16:27 the Philistines, who were ashamed of your lewd B
1Thes 2:10 and blameless was our B to you believers;
Tit 2:3 to be reverent in B, not to be slanderers
1Pet 3:1 a word by the B of their wives,
3:2 wives, when they see your reverent and chaste B
3:16 who revile your good B in Christ may be

BEHEADED (6)
2Sam 4:7 and slew him, and B him.
Mt 14:10 sent and had John B in the prison,
Mk 6:16 said, "John, whom I B, has been raised."
6:27 He went and B him in the prison,
Lk 9:9 Herod said, "John I B; but who is this
Rev 20:4 those who had been B for their testimony to

BEHELD (7)
Gen 19:28 of the valley, and B, and lo, the smoke
Ex 24:11 people of Israel; they B God, and ate and
Num 23:21 He has not B misfortune in Jacob; nor has
Ps 139:16 Thy eyes B my unformed substance; in thy book
Ezek 8:2 Then I B, and, lo, a form that had
Mk 3:11 whenever the unclean spirits B him, they fell down
Jn 1:14 and truth; we have B his glory, glory as

BEHEMOTH
Job 40:15 "Behold, B, which I made as I made you;

BEHIND (84)
Gen 18:10 at the tent door B him.
19:26 But Lot's wife B him looked back, and she
22:13 and looked, and behold, B him was a ram,
32:18 and moreover he is B us.'"
32:20 your servant Jacob is B us.'" For he thought,
Ex 10:24 only let your flocks and your herds remain B
10:26 hoof shall be left B, for we must take
11:5 the maidservant who is B the mill; and all
14:19 Israel moved and went B them; and the pillar
14:19 before them and stood B them,
Num 3:23 Gershonites were to encamp B the tabernacle on the
Deut 25:18 rear all who lagged B you; and he did
Josh 8:2 ambush against the city, B it."
8:4 ambush against the city, B it; do not go
8:14 an ambush against him B the city.
Judg 20:40 smoke, the Benjaminites looked B them; and behold,
1Sam 11:5 coming from the field B the oxen; and Saul
21:9 wrapped in a cloth B the ephod; if you
24:8 And when Saul looked B him, David bowed with
30:9 brook Besor, where those stayed who were left B
30:10 men; two hundred stayed B, who were too exhausted
30:13 my master left me B because I fell sick
2Sam 1:7 And when he looked B him, he saw me,
2:20 Then Abner looked B him and said, "Is it
2:25 gathered themselves together B Abner, and became
1Kgs 14:9 and have cast me B your back;
2Kgs 6:32 of his master's feet B him?"
9:18 Turn round and ride B me." And the watchman
9:19 Turn round and ride B me."
9:25 rode side by side B Ahab his father, how
11:6 third at the gate B the guards), shall guard
19:21 she wags her head B you--the daughter of
2Chr 13:13 come on them from B; thus his troops were
13:13 and the ambush was B them.
13:14 battle was before and B them; and they cried
Neh 4:13 parts of the space B the wall, in open
4:16 and the leaders stood B all the house of
9:26 and cast thy law B their back and killed
Tob 1:17 dead and thrown out B the wall of Nineveh,
11:4 the dog went along B them.
Job 41:32 B him he leaves a shining wake; one would
Ps 50:17 you cast my words B you.
139:5 Thou dost beset me B and before, and layest
Song 2:9 Behold, there he stands B our wall, gazing in
4:1 Your eyes are doves B your veil.
4:3 halves of a pomegranate B your veil.
6:7 halves of a pomegranate B your veil.
Wis 17:3 sins they were unobserved B a dark curtain of
Sir 21:15 it and casts it B his back.
30:4 for he has left B him one like himself;
30:6 grieved; he has left B him an avenger against
47:23 his fathers, and left B him one of his
Is 26:20 and shut your doors B you; hide yourselves for
30:21 shall hear a word B you, saying, "This is
37:22 she wags her head B you-- the daughter

38:17 cast all my sins B thy back.
57:8 B the door and the doorpost you have set
Bar 6:5 the multitude before and B them worshiping them.
Ezek 3:12 its place, I heard B me the sound of
23:35 me and cast me B your back, therefore bear
24:21 daughters whom you left B shall fall by the
Joel 2:3 devours before them, and B them a flame burns.
2:14 and leave a blessing B him, a cereal offering
Hab 3:5 him went pestilence, and plague followed close B
Zech 1:8 in the glen; and B him were red, sorrel,
1Mac 5:33 Then he came up B them in three companies,
9:16 turned and followed close B Judas and his men.
9:45 front of us and B us; the water of
10:79 left a thousand cavalry B them.
10:80 there was an ambush B him, for they surrounded
Mt 9:20 twelve years came up B him and touched the
16:23 said to Peter, "Get B me, Satan!
Mk 5:27 Jesus, and came up B him in the crowd
8:33 Peter, and said, "Get B me, Satan!
Lk 2:43 the boy Jesus stayed B in Jerusalem.
7:38 of ointment, and standing B him at his feet,
8:44 by anyone came up B him, and touched the
23:25 cross, to carry it B Jesus.
Phil 3:13 do, forgetting what lies B and straining forward to
1Thes 3:1 willing to be left B at Athens alone,
Heb 6:19 into the inner shrine B the curtain,
9:3 B the second curtain stood a tent called the
Rev 1:10 day, and I heard B me a loud voice
4:6 eyes in front and B:

BEHOLD (1,045)

Gen 1:29 And God said, B, I have given you every
1:31 he had made, and B, it was very good.
3:22 the LORD God said, B, the man has become
4:14 B, thou hast driven me this day away from
6:12 saw the earth, and B, it was corrupt; for
6:13 with violence through them; B, I will destroy them
6:17 For B, I will bring a flood of waters
8:13 ark, and looked, and B, the face of the
9:9 his sons with him, B, I establish my covenant
11:6 And the LORD said, B, they are one people,
12:11 a woman beautiful to B;
15:3 And Abram said, B, thou hast given me no
15:4 And B, the word of the LORD came to
15:17 and it was dark, B, a smoking fire pot
16:2 Sarai said to Abram, B now, the LORD has
16:6 Abram said to Sarai, B, your maid is in
16:11 LORD said to her, B, you are with child,
17:4 God said to him, B, my covenant is with
17:20 I have heard you; B, I will bless him
18:2 eyes and looked, and B, three men stood in
18:27 Abraham answered, B, I have taken upon myself to
18:31 He said, B, I have taken upon myself to
19:8 B, I have two daughters who have not known
19:19 "Oh, no, my lords; B, your servant has found
19:20 B, yonder city is near enough to flee to,
19:21 He said to him, B, I grant you this
19:34 said to the younger, B, I lay last night
20:3 and said to him, B, you are a dead
20:15 And Abimelech said, B, my land is before you;
20:16 To Sarah he said, B, I have given your
22:7 He said, B, the fire and the wood; but
22:13 eyes and looked, and B, behind him was a
22:20 it was told Abraham, B, Milcah also has borne
24:13 B, I am standing by the spring of water,
24:15 he had done speaking, B, Rebekah, who was born
24:30 to the man; and B, he was standing by
24:43 way which I go, B, I am standing by
24:45 speaking in my heart, B, Rebekah came out with
24:51 B, Rebekah is before you, take her and go,
24:63 eyes and looked, and B, there were camels coming.
25:24 be delivered were fulfilled, B, there were twins in
26:9 called Isaac, and said, B, she is your wife;
27:2 He said, B, I am old; I do not
27:11 to Rebekah his mother, B, my brother Esau is
27:36 away my birthright; and B, now he has taken
27:37 Isaac answered Esau, B, I have made him your
27:39 his father answered him: B, away from the fatness
27:42 and said to him, B, your brother Esau comforts
28:12 reached to heaven; and B, the angels of God
28:13 And B, the LORD stood above it and said,
28:15 B, I am with you and will keep you
29:7 He said, B, it is still high day, it
29:25 And in the morning, B, it was Leah; and
33:1 eyes and looked, and B, Esau was coming, and
34:21 trade in it, for B, the land is large
37:7 which I have dreamed: B, we were binding sheaves
37:7 and stood upright; and B, your sheaves gathered
37:9 his brothers, and said, B, I have dreamed another
37:9 dreamed another dream; and B, the sun, the moon,
38:29 drew back his hand, B, his brother came out;
41:2 by the Nile, and B, there came up out
41:3 And B, seven other cows, gaunt and thin, came
41:5 a second time; and B, seven ears of grain,
41:6 And B, after them sprouted seven ears, thin and
41:7 And Pharaoh awoke, and B, it was a dream.
41:17 Pharaoh said to Joseph, B, in my dream I
41:41 Pharaoh said to Joseph, B, I have set you
42:2 And he said, B, I have heard that there
42:13 land of Canaan; and B, the youngest is this
42:35 they emptied their sacks, B, every man's bundle of
44:8 B, the money which we found in the mouth
44:16 guilt of your servants; B, we are my lord's
47:23 said to the people, B, I have this day
48:1 this Joseph was told, B, your father is ill";
48:4 and said to me, B, I will make you
48:21 Israel said to Joseph, B, I am about to
50:18 before him, and said, B, we are your servants."
Ex 1:8 said to his people, B, the people of Israel
2:13 out the next day, B, two Hebrews were struggling
3:9 And now, B, the cry of the people of
4:1 Then Moses answered, "But B, they will not believe
4:6 he took it out, B, his hand was leprous,
4:7 he took it out, B, it was restored like
4:14 can speak well; and B, he is coming out
4:23 to let him go, B, I will slay your
5:5 And Pharaoh said, B, the people of the land
5:16 us, 'Make bricks!' And B, your servants are beaten;
6:12 said to the LORD, B, the people of Israel
6:30 said to the LORD, B, I am of uncircumcised
7:16 in the wilderness; and B, you have not yet
7:17 I am the LORD: B, I will strike the
8:2 to let them go, B, I will plague all
8:21 let my people go, B, I will send swarms
8:29 Then Moses said, B, I am going out from
9:3 and still hold them, B, the hand of the
9:7 And Pharaoh sent, and B, not one of the
9:18 B, tomorrow about this time I will cause very
10:4 let my people go, B, tomorrow I will bring
14:10 up their eyes, and B, the Egyptians were marching
16:4 LORD said to Moses, B, I will rain bread
16:10 toward the wilderness, and B, the glory of the
17:6 B, I will stand before you there on the
23:20 B, I send an angel before you, to guard
24:8 the people, and said, B the blood of the
24:14 to you again; and, B, Aaron and Hur are
31:6 And B, I have appointed with him Oholiab, the
32:9 seen this people, and B, it is a stiff-necked
32:34 have spoken to you; B, my angel shall go
33:21 And the LORD said, B, there is a place
34:10 And he said, B, I make a covenant.
34:11 B, I will drive out before you the Amorites,
34:30 of Israel saw Moses, B, the skin of his
39:43 all the work, and B, they had done it;
Lev 10:16 the sin offering, and B, it was burned!
10:18 B, its blood was not brought into the inner
10:19 Aaron said to Moses, B, today they have offered
Num 3:12 LORD said to Moses, B, I have taken the
12:10 from over the tent, B, Miriam was leprous, as
12:10 turned towards Miriam, and B, she was leprous.
16:42 tent of meeting; and B, the cloud covered it,
16:47 of the assembly; and B, the plague had already
17:8 of the testimony; and B, the rod of Aaron
17:12 Israel said to Moses, B, we perish, we are
18:6 And B, I have taken your brethren the Levites
18:8 said to Aaron, "And B, I have given you
22:5 to call him, saying, B, a people has come
22:11 sent to me, saying, B, a people has come
22:32 B, I have come forth to withstand you, because
23:9 from the hills I B him; lo, a people
23:11 curse my enemies, and B, you have done nothing
23:20 B, I received a command to bless: he has
23:24 'What has God wrought!' B, a people!
24:10 curse my enemies, and B, you have blessed them
24:14 And now, B, I am going to my people;
24:17 but not now; I B him, but not nigh:
25:6 And B, one of the people of Israel came
25:12 Therefore say, B, I give to him my covenant
31:16 B, these caused the people of Israel, by the
32:1 land of Gilead, and B, the place was a
32:14 And B, you have risen in your fathers' stead,
32:23 will not do so, B, you have sinned against

Deut 1:8 B, I have set the land before you; go
1:10 has multiplied you, and B, you are this day
1:21 B, the LORD your God has set the land
2:24 valley of the Arnon; B, I have given into
2:31 LORD said to me, B, I have begun to
3:11 remnant of the Rephaim; B, his bedstead was a
3:27 southward and eastward, and B it with your eyes;
4:5 B, I have taught you statutes and ordinances, as
5:24 elders; and you said, B, the LORD our God
9:13 seen this people, and B, it is a stubborn
9:16 And I looked, and B, you had sinned against
10:14 B, to the LORD your God belong heaven and
11:26 B, I set before you this day a blessing
13:14 and ask diligently; and B, if it be true
26:10 And B, now I bring the first of the
31:14 LORD said to Moses, B, the days approach when
31:16 LORD said to Moses, B, you are about to
31:27 and stubborn you are; B, while I am yet
Josh 2:2 the king of Jericho, B, certain men of Israel
2:18 B, when we come into the land, you shall
3:11 B, the ark of the covenant of the Lord
5:13 eyes and looked, and B, a man stood before
7:21 and took them; and B, they are hidden in
7:22 to the tent; and B, it was hidden in
8:4 And he commanded them, B, you shall lie in
8:20 of Ai looked back, B, the smoke of the
9:12 to you, but now, B, it is dry and
9:13 we filled them, and B, they are burst; and
9:25 And now, B, we are in your hand: do
14:10 my God.' And now, B, the LORD has kept
22:11 of Israel heard say, B, the Reubenites and the
22:28 come, we should say, B the copy of the
23:4 B, I have allotted to you as an inheritance
24:27 to all the people, B, this stone shall be
Judg 1:2 "Judah shall go up; B, I have given the
4:22 And B, as Barak pursued Sisera, Jael went out
6:15 B, my clan is the weakest in Manasseh, and
6:28 early in the morning, B, the altar of Baal
6:37 as thou hast said, B, I am laying a
7:13 When Gideon came, B, a man was telling a
7:13 comrade; and he said, B, I dreamed a dream;
8:15 of Succoth, and said, B Zebah and Zalmunna, about
9:31 Abimelech at Arumah, saying, B, Gaal the son of
11:34 home at Mizpah; and B, his daughter came out
13:3 and said to her, B, you are barren and
13:7 he said to me, B, you shall conceive and
13:10 and told her husband, B, the man who came
14:5 And B, a young lion roared against him;
14:8 of the lion, and B, there was a swarm
14:16 he said to her, B, I have not told
16:10 Delilah said to Samson, B, you have mocked me,
17:2 it in my ears, B, the silver is with
18:9 seen the land, and B, it is very fertile.
18:12 Mahaneh-dan to this day; B, it is west of
19:9 father, said to him, B, now the day has
19:9 B, the day draws to its close; lodge here
19:16 And B, an old man was coming from his
19:22 making their hearts merry, B, the men of the
19:24 B, here are my virgin daughter and his concubine;
19:27 go on his way, B, there was his concubine
20:7 B, you people of Israel, all of you, give
20:40 looked behind them; and B, the whole of the
21:8 And B, no one had come to the camp
21:9 the people were mustered, B, not one of the
21:19 So they said, B, there is the yearly feast
Ruth 2:4 And B, Boaz came from Bethlehem; and he said
3:8 and turned over, and B, a woman lay at
4:1 sat down there; and B, the next of kin,
1Sam 2:31 B, the days are coming, when I will cut
3:11 LORD said to Samuel, B, I am about to
5:3 early the next day, B, Dagon had fallen face
5:4 on the next morning, B, Dagon had fallen face
8:5 and said to him, B, you are old and
9:6 he said to him, B, there is a man
9:12 They answered, "He is; B, he is just ahead
10:8 me to Gilgal; and B, I am coming to
10:10 they came to Gibe-ah, B, a band of prophets
10:22 and the LORD said, B, he has hidden himself
12:1 said to all Israel, B, I have hearkened to
12:2 And now, B, the king walks before you; and
12:2 old and gray, and B, my sons are with
12:13 And now B the king whom you have chosen,
12:13 whom you have asked; B, the LORD has set
13:10 the burnt offering, B, Samuel came; and Saul
14:7 your mind inclines to; B, I am with you,
14:8 Then said Jonathan, B, we will cross over to
14:16 of Benjamin looked; and B, the multitude was
14:17 had numbered, B, Jonathan and his armor-bearer
14:20 into the battle; and B, every man's sword was
14:26 people entered the forest, B, the honey was
14:33 Then they told Saul, B, the people are sinning
15:12 came to Carmel, and B, he set up a
15:22 B, to obey is better than sacrifice, and to
16:11 yet the youngest, but B, he is keeping the
16:15 servants said to him, B now, an evil spirit
16:18 the young men answered, B, I have seen a
17:23 he talked with them, B, the champion, the Philistine
18:22 in private and say, B, the king has delight
19:16 the messengers came in, B, the image was in
19:19 it was told Saul, B, David is at Naioth
19:22 And one said, B, they are at Naioth in
20:2 B, my father does nothing either great or small
20:5 David said to Jonathan, B, tomorrow is the new
20:12 or the third day, B, if he is well-disposed
20:21 And B, I will send the lad, saying, 'Go,
20:23 and I have spoken, B, the LORD is between
21:9 the valley of Elah, B, it is here wrapped
23:1 Now they told David, B, the Philistines are fighting
23:3 men said to him, B, we are afraid here
24:1 Philistines, he was told, B, David is in the
24:4 LORD said to you, B, I will give your
24:9 of men who say, B, David seeks your hurt?
24:20 And now, B, I know that you shall surely
25:14 told Abigail, Nabal's wife, B, David sent messengers
25:19 "Go on before me; B, I come after you."
25:20 cover of the mountain, B, David and his men
25:41 the ground, and said, B, your handmaid is a
26:21 your eyes this day; B, I have played the
26:24 B, as your life was precious this day in
28:7 servants said to him, B, there is a medium
28:21 she said to him, B, your handmaid has hearkened
30:16 had taken him down, B, they were spread abroad
2Sam 1:2 on the third day, B, a man came from
1:18 the people of Judah; B, it is written in
3:12 covenant with me, and B, my hand shall be
3:24 B, Abner came to you; why is it that
4:6 And B, the doorkeeper of the house had been
4:10 when one told me, B, Saul is dead,' and
5:1 at Hebron, and said, B, we are your bone
9:6 And he answered, B, your servant."
12:11 Thus says the LORD, B, I will raise up
12:18 dead; for they said, B, while the child was
13:24 the king, and said, B, your servant has sheepshearers;
13:34 eyes, and looked, and B, many people were coming
13:35 said to the king, B, the king's sons have
13:36 he had finished speaking, B, the king's sons came,
14:21 king said to Joab, B now, I grant this;
14:32 Absalom answered Joab, B, I sent word to you,
15:15 said to the king, B, your servants are ready
15:26 no pleasure in you,' B, here I am, let
15:32 where God was worshiped, B, Hushai the Archite
15:36 B, their two sons are with them there, Ahima-az,
16:3 said to the king, B, he remains in Jerusalem;
16:4 king said to Ziba, B, all that belonged to
16:11 to all his servants, B, my own son seeks
17:9 B, even now he has hidden himself in one
18:10 it, and told Joab, B, I saw Absalom hanging
18:31 And B, the Cushite came; and the Cushite said,
19:1 It was told Joab, B, the king is weeping
19:8 people were all told, B, the king is sitting
19:20 I have sinned; therefore, B, I have come this
20:21 woman said to Joab, B, his head shall be
1Kgs 1:18 my throne.' And now, B, Adonijah is king, although
1:25 Abiathar the priest; and B, they are eating and
1:42 he was still speaking, B, Jonathan the son of
1:51 was told Solomon, B, Adonijah fears King Solomon;
2:29 of the LORD, and B, he is beside the
2:39 it was told Shimei, B, your slaves are in
3:12 discern what is right, B, I now do according
3:12 B, I give you a wise and discerning mind,
3:15 And Solomon awoke, and B, it was a dream.
3:21 to nurse my child, B, it was dead; but
3:21 closely in the morning, B, it was not the
8:27 B, heaven and the highest heaven cannot contain
10:7 had seen it; and, B, the half was not
11:31 the God of Israel, B, I am about to
12:28 B your gods, O Israel, who brought you up
13:1 And B, a man of God came out of
13:2 thus says the LORD: B, a son shall be
13:3 the LORD has spoken: B, the altar shall be
13:25 And B, men passed by, and saw the body
14:2 and go to Shiloh; B, Ahijah the prophet is

B

	14:5	LORD said to Ahijah, B, the wife of Jeroboam
	14:10	behind your back; therefore B, I will bring evil
	14:19	and how he reigned, B, they are written in
	15:19	father and your father: B, I am sending to
	16:3	anger with their sins, B, I will utterly sweep
	17:9	B, I have commanded a widow there to feed
	17:10	gate of the city, B, a widow was there
	18:7	was on the way, B, Elijah met him; and
	18:8	Go, tell your lord, B, Elijah is here.'"
	18:11	'Go, tell your lord, B, Elijah is here."'
	18:14	'Go, tell your lord, B, Elijah is here"'; and
	18:44	seventh time he said, B, a little cloud like
	19:5	a broom tree; and B, an angel touched him,
	19:6	And he looked, and B, there was at his
	19:9	and lodged there; and B, the word of the
	19:11	And B, the LORD passed by, and a great
	19:13	And B, there came a voice to him, and
	20:13	And B, a prophet came near to Ahab king
	20:13	B, I will give it into your hand this
	20:31	servants said to him, B now, we have heard
	20:36	voice of the LORD, B, as soon as you
	20:39	of the battle; and B, a soldier turned and
	21:18	who is in Samaria; B, he is in the
	21:21	B, I will bring evil upon you; I will
	22:13	Micaiah said to him, B, the words of the
	22:23	do so.' Now therefore B, the LORD has put
	22:25	And Micaiah said, B, you shall see on that
2Kgs	2:11	went on and talked, B, a chariot of fire
	2:16	they said to him, B now, there are with
	2:19	city said to Elisha, B, the situation of this
	3:20	of offering the sacrifice, B, water came from the
	4:9	said to her husband, B now, I perceive that
	5:11	and went away, saying, B, I thought that he
	5:15	him; and he said, B, I know that there
	6:13	It was told him, B, he is in Dothan."
	6:15	morning and went out, B, an army with horses
	6:17	and he saw; and B, the mountain was full
	6:30	the people looked, and B, he had sackcloth beneath
	7:5	camp of the Syrians, B, there was no one
	7:6	said to one another, B, the king of Israel
	7:10	of the Syrians, and B, there was no one
	8:5	the dead to life, B, the woman whose son
	9:5	And when he came, B, the commanders of the
	10:4	exceedingly afraid, and said, B, the two kings could
	15:11	the deeds of Zechariah, B, they are written in
	15:15	conspiracy which he made, B, they are written in
	15:26	all that he did, B, they are written in
	15:31	all that he did, B, they are written in
	17:26	lions among them, and B, they are killing them,
	18:21	B, you are relying now on Egypt, that broken
	19:7	B, I will put a spirit in him, so
	19:9	Tirhakah king of Ethiopia, B, he has set out
	19:11	B, you have heard what the kings of Assyria
	19:35	early in the morning, B, these were all dead
	20:5	have seen your tears; B, I will heal you;
	20:17	word of the LORD: B, the days are coming,
	21:12	the God of Israel, B, I am bringing upon
	22:16	Thus says the LORD, B, I will bring evil
	22:20	Therefore, B, I will gather you to your fathers,
1Chr	11:1	at Hebron, and said, B, we are your bone
	17:1	to Nathan the prophet, B, I dwell in a
	22:9	B, a son shall be born to you; he
	28:21	And B the divisions of the priests and the
2Chr	2:4	B, I am about to build a house for
	6:18	B, heaven and the highest heaven cannot contain
	9:6	had seen it; and B, half the greatness of
	13:12	B, God is with us at our head, and
	13:14	And when Judah looked, B, the battle was before
	16:3	father and your father; B, I am sending to
	18:12	Micaiah said to him, B, the words of the
	18:22	do so.' Now therefore B, the LORD has put
	18:24	And Micaiah said, B, you shall see on that
	19:11	And B, Amariah the chief priest is over you
	20:2	beyond the sea; and, B, they are in Hazazon-tamar"
	20:10	and save.' And now B, the men of Ammon
	20:11	did not destroy-- B, they reward us by
	20:16	go down against them; B, they will come up
	20:24	toward the multitude; and B, they were dead bodies
	21:14	were better than yourself; B, the LORD will bring
	23:3	Jehoiada said to them, B, the king's son!
	26:20	looked at him, and B, he was leprous in
	27:7	wars, and his ways, B, they are written in
	28:9	and said to them, B, because the LORD, the
	28:26	from first to last, B, they are written in
	29:19	ready and sanctified; and B, they are before the
	32:32	and his good deeds, B, they are written in
	33:18	the God of Israel, B, they are in the
	33:19	before he humbled himself, B, they are written in
	34:24	Thus says the LORD, B, I will bring evil
	34:28	B, I will gather you to your fathers, and
	35:25	an ordinance in Israel; B, they are written in
	35:27	acts, first and last, B, they are written in
	36:8	was found against him, B, they are written in
Ezra	9:15	B, we are before thee in our guilt, for
Neh	9:36	B, we are slaves this day; in the land
	9:36	and its good gifts, B, we are slaves.
Tob	11:6	said to his father, B, your son is coming,
	14:3	son, take your sons; B, I have grown old
Jud	3:2	for peace, and said, B, we the servants of
	3:3	B, our buildings, and all our land, and all
	6:19	Lord God of heaven, B their arrogance, and have
	9:7	B now, the Assyrians are increased in their might;
	9:9	B their pride, and send thy wrath upon their
Esth	1:11	princes her beauty; for she was fair to B
	8:7	to Mordecai the Jew, B, I have given Esther
	11:5	this was his dream: B, noise and confusion, thunders
	11:6	And B, two great dragons came forward, both ready
	11:8	And B, a day of darkness and gloom, tribulation
Job	1:12	LORD said to Satan, B, all that he has
	1:19	eldest brother's house; and B, a great wind came
	2:6	LORD said to Satan, B, he is in your
	4:3	B, you have instructed many, and you have
	5:17	B, happy is the man whom God reproves; therefore
	7:8	who sees me will B me no more; while
	8:19	have never seen you.' B, this is the joy
	8:20	B, God will not reject a blameless man, nor
	9:12	B, he snatches away; who can hinder him?
	9:19	a contest of strength, B him!
	13:15	B, he will slay me; I have no hope;
	13:18	B, I have prepared my case; I know that
	15:15	B, God puts no trust in his holy ones,
	16:19	Even now, B, my witness is in heaven, and
	19:7	B, I cry out, 'Violence!' but I am not
	19:27	and my eyes shall B, and not another.
	20:9	his place any more B him.
	21:16	we pray to him?' B, is not their prosperity
	21:27	B, I know your thoughts, and your schemes to
	23:8	B, I go forward, but he is not there;
	23:9	him, but I cannot B him; I turn to
	24:5	B, like wild asses in the desert they go
	25:5	B, even the moon is not bright and the
	27:12	B, all of you have seen it yourselves; why
	28:28	he said to man, B, the fear of the
	32:11	also declare my opinion.' B, I waited for your
	32:12	you my attention, and, B, there was none that
	32:19	B, my heart is like wine that has no
	33:2	B, I open my mouth; the tongue in my
	33:6	B, I am toward God as you are; I
	33:7	B, no fear of me need terrify you; my
	33:10	B, he finds occasions against me, he counts me
	33:12	watches all my paths.' B, in this you are
	33:29	shall see the light.' B, God does all these
	34:29	his face, who can B him, whether it be
	35:5	heavens, and see; and B the clouds, which are
	36:5	B, God is mighty, and does not despise any;
	36:22	B, God is exalted in his power; who is
	36:26	B, God is great, and we know him not;
	36:30	B, he scatters his lightning about him, and covers
	39:29	the prey; his eyes B it afar off.
	40:4	Job answered the LORD: B, I am of small
	40:15	B, Behemoth, which I made as I made you;
	40:16	B, his strength in his loins, and his power
	40:23	B, if the river is turbulent he is not
	41:9	B, the hope of a man is disappointed; he
Ps	7:14	B, the wicked man conceives evil, and is pregnant
	9:13	B what I suffer from those who hate me,
	11:4	in heaven; his eyes B, his eyelids test, the
	11:7	deeds; the upright shall B his face.
	17:15	for me, I shall B thy face in righteousness;
	27:4	of my life, to B the beauty of the
	33:18	B, the eye of the LORD is on those
	37:37	the blameless man, and B the upright, for there
	39:5	B, thou hast made my days a few handbreadths,
	42:2	shall I come and B the face of God?
	46:8	[Selah] Come, B the works of the LORD, how
	51:5	B, I was brought forth in iniquity, and in
	51:6	B, thou desirest truth in the inward being; therefore
	54:4	[Selah] B, God is my helper; the Lord is
	73:12	B, these are the wicked; always at ease, they
	84:9	[Selah] B our shield, O God; look upon the
	87:4	mention Rahab and Babylon; B, Philistia and Tyre,
	97:6	and all the peoples B his glory.

119:18 eyes, that I may B wondrous things out of
119:40 B, I long for thy precepts; in thy righteousness
121:4 B, he who keeps Israel will neither slumber nor
123:2 B, as the eyes of servants look to the
133:1 B, how good and pleasant it is when brothers
Prov 1:23 heed to my reproof; B, I will pour out
24:12 If you say, B, we did not know this,"
Eccl 1:14 under the sun; and B, all is vanity and
2:1 But B, this also was vanity.
2:11 in doing it, and B, all was vanity and
4:1 And B, the tears of the oppressed, and they
5:18 B, what I have seen to be good and
7:27 B, this is what I found, says the Preacher,
7:29 B, this alone I found, that God made man
11:7 for the eyes to B the sun.
Song 1:15 B, you are beautiful, my love; behold, you are
1:15 are beautiful, my love; B, you are beautiful; your
1:16 B, you are beautiful, my beloved, truly lovely.
2:8 B, he comes, leaping upon the mountains, bounding
2:9 B, there he stands behind our wall, gazing in
3:7 B, it is the litter of Solomon!
3:11 daughters of Zion, and B King Solomon, with the
4:1 B, you are beautiful, my love, behold, you are
4:1 are beautiful, my love, B, you are beautiful!
Sir 16:16 B, heaven and the highest heaven, the abyss and
Is 3:1 For, B, the Lord, the LORD of hosts, is
5:7 for justice, but B, bloodshed; for righteousness, but
5:7 bloodshed; for righteousness, but B, a cry!
5:30 look to the land, B, darkness and distress; and
6:7 my mouth, and said: B, this has touched your
7:14 B, a young woman shall conceive and bear a
8:7 son of Remaliah; therefore, B, the Lord is bringing
8:18 B, I and the children whom the LORD has
8:22 to the earth, but B, distress and darkness, the
10:33 B, the Lord, the LORD of hosts will lop
12:2 B, God is my salvation; I will trust, and
13:9 B, the day of the LORD comes, cruel, with
13:17 B, I am stirring up the Medes against them,
17:1 B, Damascus will cease to be a city, and
17:14 At evening time, B, terror!
19:1 B, the LORD is riding on a swift cloud
20:6 say in that day, B, this is what has
21:9 And, B, here come riders, horsemen in pairs!" And
22:13 girding with sackcloth; and B, joy and gladness,
22:17 B, the LORD will hurl you away violently, O
23:13 B the land of the Chaldeans!
24:1 B, the LORD will lay waste the earth and
26:21 For B, the LORD is coming forth out of
28:2 B, the Lord has one who is mighty and
28:16 says the Lord GOD, B, I am laying in
29:14 learned by rote; therefore, B, I will again do
30:27 B, the name of the LORD comes from far,
32:1 B, a king will reign in righteousness, and princes
33:7 B, the valiant ones cry without; the envoys of
33:17 his beauty; they will B a land that stretches
34:5 fill in the heavens; B, it descends for judgment
35:4 B, your God will come with vengeance, with the
36:6 B, you are relying on Egypt, that broken reed
37:7 B, I will put a spirit in him, so
37:11 B, you have heard what the kings of Assyria
37:36 early in the morning, B, these were all dead
38:5 have seen your tears; B, I will add fifteen
38:8 that he has promised: B, I will make the
39:6 the LORD of hosts: B, the days are coming,
40:9 the cities of Judah, B your God!"
40:10 B, the Lord GOD comes with might, and his
40:10 arm rules for him; B, his reward is with
40:15 B, the nations are like a drop from a
40:15 dust on the scales; B, he takes up the
41:11 B, all who are incensed against you shall be
41:15 B, I will make of you a threshing sledge,
41:24 B, you are nothing, and your work is nought;
41:29 B, they are all a delusion; their works are
42:1 B my servant, whom I uphold, my chosen, in
42:9 B, the former things have come to pass, and
43:19 B, I am doing a new thing; now it
44:11 B, all his fellows shall be put to shame,
47:14 B, they are like stubble, the fire consumes them;
48:7 lest you should say, B, I knew them.'
48:10 B, I have refined you, but not like silver;
49:16 B, I have graven you on the palms of
49:21 B, I was left alone; whence then have these
49:22 says the Lord GOD: B, I will lift up
50:1 B, for your iniquities you were sold, and for
50:2 B, by my rebuke I dry up the sea,
50:9 B, the Lord GOD helps me; who will declare
50:9 B, all of them will wear out like a
50:11 B, all you who kindle a fire, who set
51:22 cause of his people: B, I have taken from
52:13 B, my servant shall prosper, he shall be exalted
54:11 storm-tossed, and not comforted, B, I will set your
54:16 B, I have created the smith who blows the
55:4 B, I made him a witness to the peoples,
55:5 B, you shall call nations that you know not,
56:3 not the eunuch say, B, I am a dry
58:3 no knowledge of it?' B, in the day of
58:4 B, you fast only to quarrel and to fight
59:1 B, the LORD's hand is not shortened, that it
59:9 look for light, and B, darkness, and for brightness,
60:2 For B, darkness shall cover the earth, and thick
62:11 B, the LORD has proclaimed to the end of
62:11 the daughter of Zion, B, your salvation comes;
62:11 "Behold, your salvation comes; B, his reward is with
64:5 B, thou wast angry, and we sinned; in our
64:9 B, consider, we are all thy people.
65:6 B, it is written before me: "I will not
65:13 says the Lord GOD: B, my servants shall eat,
65:13 you shall be hungry; B, my servants shall drink,
65:13 you shall be thirsty; B, my servants shall rejoice,
65:14 be put to shame; B, my servants shall sing
65:17 "For B, I create new heavens and a new
65:18 which I create; for B, I create Jerusalem a
66:12 thus says the LORD: B, I will extend prosperity
66:15 "For B, the LORD will come in fire, and
Jer 1:6 B, I do not know how to speak, for
1:9 LORD said to me, B, I have put my
1:18 And I, B, I make you this day a
2:35 has turned from me.' B, I will bring you
3:5 indignant to the end?' B, you have spoken, but
3:22 B, we come to thee; for thou art the
4:13 B, he comes up like clouds, his chariots like
5:14 have spoken this word, B, I am making my
5:15 B, I am bringing upon you a nation from
6:10 B, their ears are closed, they cannot listen; behold,
6:10 closed, they cannot listen; B, the word of the
6:19 Hear, O earth; B, I am bringing evil upon
6:21 thus says the LORD: B, I will lay before
6:22 Thus says the LORD: B, a people is coming
7:8 B, you trust in deceptive words to no avail.
7:11 B, I myself have seen it, says the LORD.
7:20 says the Lord GOD: B, my anger and my
7:32 Therefore, B, the days are coming, says the LORD,
8:8 But, B, the false pen of the scribes has
8:15 time of healing, but B, terror.
8:17 For B, I am sending among you serpents, adders
9:7 the LORD of hosts: B, I will refine them
9:15 the God of Israel: B, I will feed this
9:25 B, the days are coming, says the LORD, when
10:18 thus says the LORD: B, I am slinging out
10:22 B, it comes!--a great commotion out of the
11:11 thus says the LORD, B, I am bringing evil
11:22 the LORD of hosts: B, I will punish them;
12:14 people Israel to inherit: B, I will pluck them
13:7 And B, the waistcloth was spoiled; it was good
13:13 'Thus says the LORD: B, I will fill with
14:13 said: "Ah, Lord GOD, B, the prophets say to
14:18 out into the field, B, those slain by the
14:18 I enter the city, B, the diseases of famine!
14:19 time of healing, but B, terror.
16:9 the God of Israel: B, I will make to
16:12 than your fathers, for B, every one of you
16:14 you no favor.' "Therefore, B, the days are coming,
16:16 B, I am sending for many fishers, says the
16:21 "Therefore, B, I will make them know, this once
17:15 B, they say to me, "Where is the word
18:6 B, like the clay in the potter's hand, so
18:11 'Thus says the LORD, B, I am shaping evil
19:3 the God of Israel, B, I am bringing such
19:6 into my mind; therefore, B, days are coming, says
19:15 the God of Israel, B, I am bringing upon
20:4 thus says the LORD: B, I will make you
21:4 the God of Israel: B, I will turn back
21:8 'Thus says the LORD: B, I set before you
21:13 B, I am against you, O inhabitant of the
23:2 B, I will attend to you for your evil-doings,
23:5 B, the days are coming, says the LORD, when
23:7 is our righteousness.' "Therefore, B, the days are
23:15 hosts concerning the prophets: B, I will feed them
23:19 B, the storm of the LORD!
23:30 Therefore, B, I am against the prophets, says the
23:31 B, I am against the prophets, says the LORD,
23:32 say, 'Says the LORD.' B, I am against those

B

23:39 therefore, B, I will surely lift you up and
24:1 showed me this vision: B, two baskets of figs
25:9 not obeyed my words, B, I will send for
25:29 For B, I begin to work evil at the
25:32 the LORD of hosts: B, evil is going forth
26:14 But as for me, B, I am in your
27:16 prophesying to you, saying, B, the vessels of the
28:16 thus says the LORD: B, I will remove you
29:17 the LORD of hosts, B, I am sending on
29:21 you in my name: B, I will deliver them
29:32 thus says the LORD: B, I will punish Shemaiah
30:3 For B, days are coming, says the LORD, when
30:18 "Thus says the LORD: B, I will restore the
30:23 B the storm of the LORD!
31:8 the remnant of Israel.' B, I will bring them
31:27 B, the days are coming, says the LORD, when
31:31 B, the days are coming, says the LORD, when
31:38 B, the days are coming, says the LORD, when
32:3 'Thus says the LORD: B, I am giving this
32:7 LORD came to me: B, Hanamel the son of
32:24 B, the siege mounds have come up to the
32:24 come to pass, and B, thou seest it.
32:27 LORD came to Jeremiah: B, I am the LORD,
32:28 thus says the LORD: B, I am giving this
32:37 famine, and by pestilence: B, I will gather them
33:6 B, I will bring to it health and healing,
33:14 B, the days are coming, says the LORD, when
34:2 'Thus says the LORD: B, I am giving this
34:17 and to his neighbor; B, I proclaim to you
34:22 B, I will command, says the LORD, and will
35:17 the God of Israel: B, I am bringing on
37:7 to inquire of me, B, Pharaoh's army which came
38:5 King Zedekiah said, B, he is in your hands;
38:22 has shown to me: B, all the women left
39:16 the God of Israel: B, I will fulfil my
40:4 Now, B, I release you today from the chains
42:4 "I have heard you; B, I will pray to
43:10 the God of Israel: B, I will send and
44:2 B, this day they are a desolation, and no
44:11 the God of Israel: B, I will set my
44:26 the land of Egypt: B, I have sworn by
44:27 the Lord GOD lives.' B, I am watching over
44:30 Thus says the LORD, B, I will give Pharaoh
45:4 Thus says the LORD: B, what I have built
45:5 Seek them not; for, B, I am bringing evil
46:25 God of Israel, said: B, I am bringing punishment
47:2 "Thus says the LORD: B, waters are rising out
48:12 "Therefore, B, the days are coming, says the LORD,
48:40 thus says the LORD: B, one shall fly swiftly
49:2 Therefore, B, the days are coming, says the LORD,
49:5 will come against me?' B, I will bring terror
49:15 For B, I will make you small among the
49:19 B, like a lion coming up from the jungle
49:22 B, one shall mount up and fly swiftly like
49:35 the LORD of hosts: B, I will break the
50:9 For B, I am stirring up and bringing against
50:18 the God of Israel: B, I am bringing punishment
50:31 B, I am against you, O proud one, says
50:41 B, a people comes from the north; a mighty
50:44 B, like a lion coming up from the jungle
51:1 Thus says the LORD: B, I will stir up
51:25 B, I am against you, O destroying mountain, says
51:36 thus says the LORD: B, I will plead your
51:47 "Therefore, B, the days are coming when I will
51:52 the LORD's house.' "Therefore, B, the days are
Lam 1:9 "O LORD, B my affliction, for the enemy has
1:11 "Look, O LORD, and B, for I am despised."
1:18 all you peoples, and B my suffering; my maidens
1:20 B, O LORD, for I am in distress, my
3:63 B their sitting and their rising; I am the
5:1 what has befallen us; B, and see our disgrace!
Bar 2:25 of their graves; and B, they have been cast
3:8 B, we are today in our exile where thou
4:37 B, your sons are coming, whom you sent away;
Ezek 1:4 As I looked, B, a stormy wind came out
2:9 And when I looked, B, a hand was stretched
3:8 B, I have made your face hard against their
3:25 O son of man, B, cords will be placed
4:8 And, B, I will put cords upon you, so
4:14 B, I have never defiled myself; from my youth
4:16 me, "Son of man, B, I will break the
5:8 says the Lord GOD: B, I, even I, am
6:3 ravines and the valleys: B, I, even I, will
7:5 B, it comes.
7:6 B, it comes.
7:10 B, the day!
7:10 B, it comes!
8:4 And B, the glory of the God of Israel
8:5 toward the north, and B, north of the altar
8:7 and when I looked, B, there was a hole
8:14 of the LORD; and B, there sat women weeping
8:16 of the LORD; and B, at the door of
10:1 Then I looked, and B, on the firmament that
10:9 And I looked, and B, there were four wheels
11:1 And B, at the door of the gateway there
12:27 me: "Son of man, B, they of the house
13:8 and seen lies, therefore B, I am against you,
13:20 says the Lord GOD: B, I am against your
15:5 B, when it was whole, it was used for
16:8 and looked upon you, B, you were at the
16:27 B, therefore, I stretched out my hand against you,
16:37 gave to them, therefore, B, I will gather all
16:43 all these things; therefore, B, I will requite your
16:44 B, every one who uses proverbs will use this
16:49 B, this was the guilt of your sister Sodom:
17:7 and much plumage; and B, this vine bent its
17:10 B, when it is transplanted, will it thrive?
17:12 Tell them, B, the king of Babylon came to
18:4 B, all souls are mine; the soul of the
18:18 good among his people, B, he shall die for
20:47 says the Lord GOD, B, I will kindle a
21:3 Thus says the LORD: B, I am against you,
21:7 B, it comes and it will be fulfilled," says
22:6 B, the princes of Israel in you, every one
22:13 B, therefore, I strike my hands together at the
22:19 all become dross, therefore, B, I will gather you
23:22 says the Lord GOD: B, I will rouse against
23:28 says the Lord GOD: B, I will deliver you
24:16 me: "Son of man, B, I am about to
24:21 says the Lord GOD: B, I will profane my
25:7 land of Israel, therefore, B, I have stretched out
25:8 GOD: Because Moab said, B, the house of Judah
25:16 says the Lord GOD, B, I will stretch out
26:3 says the Lord GOD: B, I am against you,
26:7 says the Lord GOD: B, I will bring upon
28:7 as a god, therefore, B, I will bring strangers
28:22 says the Lord GOD: B, I am against you,
29:3 says the Lord GOD: B, I am against you,
29:8 says the Lord GOD: B, I will bring a
29:10 I made it,' therefore, B, I am against you,
29:19 says the Lord GOD: B, I will give the
30:22 says the Lord GOD: B, I am against Pharaoh
31:3 B, I will liken you to a cedar in
34:10 says the Lord GOD, B, I am against the
34:11 says the Lord GOD: B, I, I myself will
34:17 says the Lord GOD: B, I judge between sheep
34:20 Lord GOD to them: B, I, I myself will
35:3 says the Lord GOD: B, I am against you,
36:6 says the Lord GOD: B, I speak in my
36:9 For, B, I am for you, and I will
37:2 round among them; and B, there were very many
37:5 GOD to these bones: B, I will cause breath
37:7 was a noise, and B, a rattling; and the
37:11 B, they say, 'Our bones are dried up, and
37:12 says the Lord GOD: B, I will open your
37:19 says the Lord GOD: B, I am about to
37:21 says the Lord GOD: B, I will take the
38:3 says the Lord GOD: B, I am against you,
39:1 says the Lord GOD: B, I am against you,
39:8 B, it is coming and it will be brought
40:3 he brought me there, B, there was a man,
40:5 And B, there was a wall all around the
40:17 the outer court; and B, there were chambers and
40:20 to the north, and B, there was a gate
40:24 toward the south, and B, there was a gate
40:44 the inner court, and B, there were two chambers
43:2 And B, the glory of the God of Israel
43:5 the inner court; and B, the glory of the
43:12 B, this is the law of the temple.
44:4 and I looked, and B, the glory of the
47:1 of the temple; and B, water was issuing from
Dan 2:31 saw, O king, and B, a great image.
4:10 these: I saw, and B, a tree in the
4:13 lay in bed, and B, a watcher, a holy
7:2 vision by night, and B, the four winds of
7:5 And B, another beast, a second one, like a
7:7 the night visions, and B, a fourth beast, terrible
7:8 considered the horns, and B, there came up among
7:8 by the roots; and B, in this horn were
7:13 the night visions, and B, with the clouds of
8:3 eyes and saw, and B, a ram standing on
8:5 As I was considering, B, a he-goat came from

8:15 to understand it; and B, there stood before me
8:19 He said, B, I will make known to you
9:18 open thy eyes and B our desolations, and the
10:5 eyes and looked, and B, a man clothed in
10:10 And B, a hand touched me and set me
10:16 And B, one in the likeness of the sons
11:2 B, three more kings shall arise in Persia; and
12:5 I Daniel looked, and B, two others stood, one
14:11 priests of Bel said, B, we are going outside;
Hos 2:14 "Therefore, B, I will allure her, and bring her
9:6 For B, they are going to Assyria; Egypt shall
Joel 2:19 said to his people, B, I am sending to
3:1 "For B, in those days and at that time,
Amos 2:13 'You shall not prophesy.' B, I will press you
4:2 by his holiness that, B, the days are coming
6:11 For B, the LORD commands, and the great house
6:14 "For B, I will raise up against you a
7:1 Lord GOD showed me: B, he was forming locusts
7:4 Lord GOD showed me: B, the Lord GOD was
7:7 He showed me: B, the Lord was standing beside
7:8 Then the Lord said, B, I am setting a
8:1 Lord GOD showed me: B, a basket of summer
8:11 B, the days are coming," says the Lord GOD,
9:8 B, the eyes of the Lord GOD are upon
9:13 B, the days are coming," says the LORD, "when
Obad 1:2 B, I will make you small among the nations,
Mic 1:3 For B, the LORD is coming forth out of
2:3 thus says the LORD: B, against this family I
7:9 the light; I shall B his deliverance.
Nah 1:15 B, on the mountains the feet of him who
2:13 B, I am against you, says the LORD of
3:5 B, I am against you, says the LORD of
3:13 B, your troops are women in your midst.
Hab 1:13 purer eyes than to B evil and canst not
2:4 B, he whose soul is not upright in him
2:13 B, is it not from the LORD of hosts
2:19 B, it is overlaid with gold and silver, and
Zeph 3:19 B, at that time I will deal with all
Zech 1:8 in the night, and B, a man riding upon
1:11 patrolled the earth, and B, all the earth remains
1:18 eyes and saw, and B, four horns!
2:1 eyes and saw, and B, a man with a
2:3 And B, the angel who talked with me came
2:9 apple of his eye: B, I will shake my
3:4 to him he said, B, I have taken your
3:8 men of good omen: B, I will bring my
3:9 For B, upon the stone which I have set
4:2 said, "I see, and B, a lampstand all of
5:1 eyes and saw, and B, a flying scroll!
5:7 And B, the leaden cover was lifted, and there
5:9 eyes and saw, and B, two women coming forward!
6:1 eyes and saw, and B, four chariots came out
6:8 he cried to me, B, those who go toward
6:12 the LORD of hosts, B, the man whose name
8:7 the LORD of hosts: B, I will save my
14:1 B, a day of the LORD is coming, when
Mal 2:3 B, I will rebuke your offspring, and spread dung
3:1 B, I send my messenger to prepare the way
3:1 in whom you delight, B, he is coming, says
4:1 "For B, the day comes, burning like an oven,
4:5 B, I will send you Elijah the prophet before
1Mac 2:12 And B, our holy place, our beauty, and our
2:65 "Now B, I know that Simeon your brother is
3:52 And B, the Gentiles are assembled against us to
4:36 Judas and his brothers, B, our enemies are crushed;
5:14 was still being read, B, other messengers, with their
5:30 they looked up, and B, a large company, that
6:13 come upon me; and B, I am perishing of
6:26 And B, today they have encamped against the citadel
11:68 plain of Hazor, and B, the army of the
16:5 into the plain, and B, a large force of
16:24 built, and his achievements, B, they are written in
Mt 1:20 as he considered this, B, an angel of the
1:23 spoken by the prophet: B, a virgin shall conceive
2:1 of Herod the king, B, wise men from the
2:13 when they had departed, B, an angel of the
2:19 But when Herod died, B, an angel of the
3:16 from the water, and B, the heavens were opened
4:11 devil left him, and B, angels came and ministered
8:2 crowds followed him; and B, a leper came to
8:24 And B, there arose a great storm on the
8:29 And B, they cried out, "What have you to
8:32 into the swine; and B, the whole herd rushed
8:34 And B, all the city came out to meet
9:2 And B, they brought to him a paralytic, lying
9:3 And B, some of the scribes said to themselves,
9:10 table in the house, B, many tax collectors and
9:18 thus speaking to them, B, a ruler came in
9:20 And B, a woman who had suffered from a
9:32 they were going away, B, a dumb demoniac was
10:16 B, I send you out as sheep in the
11:7 did you go out into the wilderness to B
11:8 B, those who wear soft raiment are in kings'
11:10 whom it is written, B, I send my messenger
11:19 drinking, and they say, B, a glutton and a
12:10 And B, there was a man with a withered
12:18 by the prophet Isaiah: B, my servant whom I
12:41 preaching of Jonah, and B, something greater than
12:42 wisdom of Solomon, and B, something greater than
12:46 speaking to the people, B, his mother and his
15:22 And B, a Canaanite woman from that region came
17:3 And B, there appeared to them Moses and Elijah,
18:10 heaven their angels always B the face of my
19:16 And B, one came up to him, saying, "Teacher,
20:18 he said to them, B, we are going up
20:30 And B, two blind men sitting by the roadside,
21:5 the daughter of Zion, B, your king is coming
22:4 those who are invited, B, I have made ready
23:37 B, your house is forsaken and desolate.
25:6 there was a cry, B, the bridegroom!
26:45 B, the hour is at hand, and the Son
26:51 And B, one of those who were with Jesus
27:51 And B, the curtain of the temple was torn
28:2 And B, there was a great earthquake; for an
28:7 from the dead, and B, he is going before
28:9 And B, Jesus met them and said, "Hail!" And
28:11 While they were going, B, some of the guard
Mk 1:2 in Isaiah the prophet, B, I send my messenger
10:33 happen to him, saying, B, we are going up
15:34 bystanders hearing it said, B, he is calling Elijah."
Lk 1:20 And B, you will be silent and unable to
1:31 And B, you will conceive in your womb and
1:36 And B, your kinswoman Elizabeth in her old age
1:38 And Mary said, B, I am the handmaid of
1:44 For B, when the voice of your greeting came
1:48 For B, henceforth all generations will call me
2:10 "Be not afraid; for B, I bring you good
2:34 to Mary his mother, B, this child is set
2:48 B, your father and I have been looking for
5:18 And B, men were bringing on a bed a
6:23 leap for joy, for B, your reward is great
7:12 gate of the city, B, a man who had
7:24 did you go out into the wilderness to B
7:25 B, those who are gorgeously appareled and live in
7:27 whom it is written, B, I send my messenger
7:34 drinking; and you say, B, a glutton and a
7:37 And B, a woman of the city, who was
9:30 And B, two men talked with him, Moses and
9:38 And B, a man from the crowd cried, "Teacher,
9:39 my only child; and B, a spirit seizes him,
10:3 Go your way; B, I send you out as
10:19 B, I have given you authority to tread upon
10:25 And B, a lawyer stood up to put him
11:31 wisdom of Solomon, and B, something greater than
11:32 preaching of Jonah, and B, something greater than
11:41 which are within; and B, everything is clean for
13:30 And B, some are last who will be first,
13:32 and tell that fox, B, I cast out demons
13:35 B, your house is forsaken.
14:2 And B, there was a man before him who
17:21 is!' or 'There!' for B, the kingdom of God
18:31 he said to them, B, we are going up
19:8 said to the Lord, B, Lord, the half of
22:10 He said to them, B, when you have entered
22:21 But B the hand of him who betrays me
22:31 "Simon, Simon, B, Satan demanded to have you,
23:14 examining him before you, B, I did not find
23:15 B, nothing deserving death has been done by him;
23:28 For B, the days are coming when they will
24:4 were perplexed about this, B, two men stood by
24:49 And B, I send the promise of my Father
Jn 1:29 toward him, and said, B, the Lamb of God,
1:36 he walked, and said, B, the Lamb of God!"
1:47 and said of him, B, an Israelite indeed, in
12:15 not, daughter of Zion; B, your king is coming,
17:24 where I am, to B my glory which thou
19:5 Pilate said to them, B the man!"
19:14 said to the Jews, B your King!"
19:26 to his mother, "Woman, B, your son!"
19:27 said to the disciple, B, your mother!" And from
Acts 1:10 heaven as he went, B, two men stood by
7:56 God; and he said, B, I see the heavens

B

8:27 And B, an Ethiopian, a eunuch, a minister of
9:11 Tarsus named Saul; for B, he is praying,
10:17 had seen might mean, B, the men that were
10:19 Spirit said to him, B, three men are looking
10:30 in my house; and B, a man stood before
12:7 guarding the prison; and B, an angel of the
13:11 And now, B, the hand of the Lord is
13:41 said in the prophets: B, you scoffers, and wonder,
13:46 unworthy of eternal life, B, we turn to the
20:22 And now, B, I am going to Jerusalem, bound
20:25 And now, B, I know that all you among
Rom 9:33 as it is written, B, I am laying in
2Cor 5:17 old has passed away, B, the new has come.
6:2 B, now is the acceptable time; behold, now is
6:2 is the acceptable time; B, now is the day
6:9 well-known; as dying, and B we live; as punished,
Jas 5:4 B, the wages of the laborers who mowed your
5:7 B, the farmer waits for the precious fruit of
5:9 may not be judged; B, the Judge is standing
5:11 B, we call those happy who were steadfast.
1Pet 2:6 it stands in scripture: B, I am laying in
Jude 1:14 from Adam prophesied, saying, B, the Lord came
Rev 1:7 B, he is coming with the clouds, and every
1:18 one; I died, and B I am alive for
2:10 B, the devil is about to throw some of
2:22 B, I will throw her on a sickbed, and
3:8 B, I have set before you an open door,
3:9 B, I will make those of the synagogue of
3:9 are not, but lie-- B, I will make them
3:20 B, I stand at the door and knock; if
6:2 And I saw, and B, a white horse, and
6:5 And I saw, and B, a black horse, and
6:8 And I saw, and B, a pale horse, and
6:12 seal, I looked, and B, there was a great
7:9 this I looked, and B, a great multitude which
9:12 first woe has passed; B, two woes are still
11:14 second woe has passed; B, the third woe is
12:3 portent appeared in heaven; B, a great red dragon,
17:8 world, will marvel to B the beast, because it
19:11 saw heaven opened, and B, a white horse!
21:3 from the throne saying, B, the dwelling of God
21:5 upon the throne said, B, I make all things
22:7 And B, I am coming soon." Blessed is he
22:12 B, I am coming soon, bringing my recompense, to

BEHOLDING (4)

Ps 17:15 shall be satisfied with B thy form.
63:2 thee in the sanctuary, B thy power and glory.
Sir 42:25 can have enough of B his glory?
2Cor 3:18 all, with unveiled face, B the glory of the

BEHOLDS (4)

Num 12:8 dark speech; and he B the form of the
Job 36:25 looked on it; man B it from afar.
41:34 He B everything that is high; he is king
Sir 39:20 everlasting to everlasting he B them, and nothing is

BEING (266)

Gen 2:7 breath of life; and man became a living B
19:16 the hand, the LORD B merciful to him, and
36:32 name of his city B Dinhabah.
36:35 name of his city B Avith.
36:39 name of his city B Pau; his wife's name
37:2 Joseph, B seventeen years old, was shepherding the
38:25 As she was B brought out, she sent word
50:26 So Joseph died, B a hundred and ten years
Ex 6:16 the life of Levi B a hundred and thirty-seven
6:18 the life of Kohath B a hundred and thirty-three
6:20 the life of Amram B one hundred and thirty-seven
12:34 leavened, their kneading bowls B bound up in their
14:22 dry ground, the waters B a wall to them
14:29 the sea, the waters B a wall to them
22:14 dies, the owner not B with it, he shall
25:40 for them, which is B shown you on the
Lev 14:31 for him who is B cleansed.
Num 1:4 each tribe, each man B the head of the
2:3 the people of Judah B Nahshon the son of
2:4 his host as numbered B seventy-four thousand six
2:5 the people of Issachar B Nethanel the son of
2:6 his host as numbered B fifty-four thousand four
2:7 the people of Zebulun B Eliab the son of
2:8 his host as numbered B fifty-seven thousand four
2:10 the people of Reuben B Elizur the son of
2:11 his host as numbered B forty-six thousand five
2:12 the people of Simeon B Shelumi-el the son of
2:13 his host as numbered B fifty-nine thousand three
2:14 the people of Gad B Eliasaph the son of
2:15 his host as numbered B forty-five thousand six
2:18 the people of Ephraim B Elishama the son of
2:19 his host as numbered B forty thousand five hundred.
2:20 the people of Manasseh B Gamaliel the son of
2:21 his host as numbered B thirty-two thousand two
2:22 the people of Benjamin B Abidan the son of
2:23 his host as numbered B thirty-five thousand four
2:25 the people of Dan B Ahiezer the son of
2:26 his host as numbered B sixty-two thousand seven
2:27 the people of Asher B Pagiel the son of
2:28 his host as numbered B forty-one thousand five
2:29 the people of Naphtali B Ahira the son of
2:30 his host as numbered B fifty-three thousand four
7:86 gold of the dishes B a hundred and twenty
35:5 thousand cubits, the city B in the middle; this
Deut 4:42 neighbor unintentionally, without B at enmity with
15:5 the LORD your God, B careful to do all
28:1 the LORD your God, B careful to do all
28:13 command you this day, B careful to do them,
32:31 even our enemies themselves B judges.
Josh 1:7 strong and very courageous, B careful to do
3:3 the LORD your God B carried by the Levitical
8:15 made a pretense of B beaten before them, and
17:10 land to the south B Ephraim's and that to
17:10 that to the north B Manassehs, with the sea
21:11 gave them Kiriath-arba (Arba B the father of Anak),
24:29 of the LORD, died, B a hundred and ten
Ruth 2:18 had left over after B satisfied.
1Sam 8:7 have rejected me from B king over them.
15:23 also rejected you from B king."
15:26 has rejected you from B king over Israel."
16:1 have rejected him from B king over Israel?
2Sam 13:14 listen to her; and B stronger than she, he
1Kgs 2:27 expelled Abiathar from B priest to the LORD,
6:7 temple, while it was B built.
11:17 his father's servants, Hadad B yet a little child.
15:13 Maacah his mother from B queen mother because
16:7 of his hands, in B like the house of
2Kgs 2:10 me as I am B taken from you, it
11:6 king's house (another third B at the gate Sur
13:21 as a man was B buried, lo, a marauding
1Chr 7:2 the days of David B twenty-two thousand six
9:17 and their kinsmen (Shallum B the chief),
24:6 Levites; one father's house B chosen for Eleazar and
27:32 uncle, was a counselor, B a man of understanding
2Chr 15:16 King Asa removed from B queen mother because she
26:21 of his death, and B a leper dwelt in
Ezra 3:12 foundation of this house B laid, though many shouted
5:8 It is B built with huge stones, and timber
8:13 later, their names B Eliphelet, Jeuel, and Shemaiah,
Tob 1:19 learned that I was B searched for, to be
Jud 8:16 nor like a human B, to be won over
9:1 that evening's incense was B offered in the house
Esth 1:3 governors of the provinces B before him,
1:14 next to him B Carshena, Shethar, Admatha, Tarshish,
2:12 to King Ahasuerus, after B twelve months under the
4:11 the inner court without B called, there is but
14:11 to what has no B; and do not let
Job 21:23 dies in full prosperity, B wholly at ease and
Ps 51:6 truth in the inward B; therefore teach me wisdom
65:6 hast established the mountains, B girded with might;
78:38 Yet he, B compassionate, forgave their iniquity, and
104:33 sing praise to my God while I have B
139:15 thee, when I was B made in secret, intricately
146:2 sing praises to my God while I have B
Prov 1:22 ones, will you love B simple?
3:26 keep your foot from B caught.
24:11 Rescue those who are B taken away to death;
Eccl 12:9 Besides B wise, the Preacher also taught the people
Wis 4:13 B perfected in a short time, he fulfilled long
8:20 my lot; or rather, B good, I entered an
11:9 tried, though they were B disciplined in mercy, they
12:27 thought to be gods, B punished by means of
14:15 once a dead human B, and handed on to
16:4 how their enemies were B tormented.
16:5 people and they were B destroyed by the bites
16:18 know that they were B pursued by the judgment
16:22 of their enemies were B destroyed by the fire
17:13 inner expectation of help, B weak, prefers ignorance
Sir 20:4 another is detested for B too talkative.
28:5 If he himself, B flesh, maintains wrath, who will
29:7 have been afraid of B defrauded needlessly.
29:18 B surety has ruined many men who were prosperous,
29:25 and provide drink without B thanked, and besides
31:16 Eat like a human B what is set before

49:16 Adam above every living B in the creation.
Jer 31:36 of Israel cease from B a nation before me
38:22 king of Judah were B led out to the
40:1 and Judah who were B exiled to Babylon.
48:2 cut her off from B a nation!' You also,
Lam 4:6 a moment, no hand B laid on it.
Bar 6:24 even when they were B cast, they had no
Ezek 1:16 same likeness, their construction B as it were a
3:14 hand of the LORD B strong upon me;
36:34 be tilled, instead of B the desolation that it
40:5 six long cubits, each B a cubit and a
43:13 by cubits (the cubit B a cubit and a
48:31 gates of the city B named after the tribes
Dan 5:31 Mede received the kingdom, B about sixty-two years
13:45 And as she was B led away to be
13:54 did you see them B intimate with each other?"
13:58 did you catch them B intimate with each other?"
Hos 4:6 I reject you from B a priest to me.
Jon 4:10 grow, which came into B in a night, and
1Mac 2:6 He saw the blasphemies B committed in Judah and
5:14 the letter was still B read, behold, other messengers,
5:16 in distress and were B attacked by enemies.
6:38 harass the enemy while B themselves protected by
7:33 burnt offering that was B offered for the king.
12:26 that the enemy were B drawn up in formation
2Mac 1:19 when our fathers were B led captive to Persia,
1:23 while the sacrifice was B consumed, the priests
2:1 ordered those who were B deported to take some
2:2 instructed those who were B deported not to forget
2:9 made clear that B possessed of wisdom Solomon
4:18 the quadrennial games were B held at Tyre and
4:19 sent envoys, chosen as B Antiochian citizens from
5:5 last the city was B taken, Menelaus took refuge
6:18 of noble presence, was B forced to open his
7:1 were arrested and were B compelled by the king,
7:14 that God gives of B raised again by him.
7:22 how you came into B in my womb.
7:24 felt that he was B treated with contempt, and
7:24 The youngest brother B still alive, Antiochus not only
7:28 Thus also mankind comes into B
7:39 worse than the others, B exasperated at his scorn.
8:3 the city which was B destroyed and about to
10:30 they kept him from B wounded.
11:1 charge of the government, B vexed at what had
13:10 on the point of B deprived of the law
14:41 B surrounded, Razis fell upon his own sword,
15:19 in no little distress, B anxious over the encounter
Mt 1:19 and her husband Joseph, B a just man and
2:12 And B warned in a dream not to return
2:22 to go there, and B warned in a dream
6:27 which of you by B anxious can add one
8:24 that the boat was B swamped by the waves;
23:7 the market places, and B called rabbi by men.
23:32 are you to escape B sentenced to hell?
24:22 been shortened, no human B would be saved; but
Mk 8:17 And B aware of it, Jesus said to them,
12:26 as for the dead B raised, have you not
13:20 the days, no human B would be saved; but
Lk 1:74 grant us that we, B delivered from the hand
3:1 Tiberi-us Caesar, Pontius Pilate B governor of Judea,
3:1 of Judea, and Herod B tetrarch of Galilee, and
3:23 thirty years of age, B the son (as was
4:15 taught in their synagogues, B glorified by all.
7:12 who had died was B carried out, the only
12:25 which of you by B anxious can add a
16:23 buried; and in Hades, B in torment, he lifted
17:20 B asked by the Pharisees when the kingdom of
20:36 are sons of God, B sons of the resurrection.
Jn 10:33 for blasphemy; because you, B a man, make yourself
11:51 his own accord, but B high priest that year
20:19 the week, the doors B shut where the disciples
Acts 2:30 B therefore a prophet, and knowing that God had
2:33 B therefore exalted at the right hand of God,
2:47 day those who were B saved.
3:2 lame from birth was B carried, whom they laid
4:9 elders, if we are B examined today concerning a
5:26 they were afraid of B stoned by the people.
7:24 seeing one of them B wronged, he defended the
8:13 himself believed, and after B baptized he continued
8:36 is to prevent my B baptized?"
13:4 So, B sent out by the Holy Spirit, they
15:3 So, B sent on their way by the church,
15:39 chose Silas and departed, B commended by the
17:24 and everything in it, B Lord of heaven and
17:28 move and have our B; as even some of
17:29 are indeed his offspring.' B then God's offspring, we
18:25 of the Lord; and B fervent in spirit, he
19:40 are in danger of B charged with rioting today,
19:40 with rioting today, there B no cause that we
20:9 talked still longer; and B overcome by sleep, he
22:3 law of our fathers, B zealous for God as
25:4 replied that Paul was B kept at Caesarea, and
25:20 B at a loss how to investigate these questions,
26:23 suffer, and that, by B the first to rise
27:20 all hope of our B saved was at last
Rom 2:9 distress for every human B who does evil, the
3:7 why am I still B condemned as a sinner?
3:20 For no human B will be justified in his
4:11 all who believe without B circumcised and who thus
6:9 we know that Christ B raised from the dead
8:36 thy sake we are B killed all the day
10:3 For, B ignorant of the righteousness that comes from
14:15 If your brother is B injured by what you
1Cor 1:18 to us who are B saved it is the
1:29 so that no human B might boast in the
7:37 established in his heart, B under no necessity but
8:7 But some, through B hitherto accustomed to idols,
8:7 idol; and their conscience, B weak, is defiled.
9:20 the law--though not B myself under the law--
9:21 outside the law--not B without law toward God
15:29 do people mean by B baptized on behalf of
15:45 Adam became a living B; the last Adam became
2Cor 2:15 among those who are B saved and among those
3:18 of the Lord, are B changed into his likeness
4:11 live we are always B given up to death
4:16 our inner nature is B renewed every day.
8:17 accepted our appeal, but B himself very earnest he
9:4 nothing of you--for B so confident.
10:6 captive to obey Christ, B ready to punish every
11:19 gladly bear with fools, B wise yourselves!
12:7 to keep me from B too elated by the
12:7 to keep me from B too elated.
Eph 2:20 prophets, Christ Jesus himself B the cornerstone,
3:17 through faith; that you, B rooted and grounded in
Phil 2:2 complete my joy by B of the same mind,
2:2 having the same love, B in full accord and
2:7 form of a servant, B born in the likeness
2:8 And B found in human form he humbled himself
Col 3:10 new nature, which is B renewed in knowledge after
4:2 Continue steadfastly in prayer, B watchful in it with
1Thes 2:8 So, B affectionately desirous of you, we were ready
2Tim 2:26 of the devil, after B captured by him to
4:6 on the point of B sacrificed; the time of
Tit 1:5 to the charge of B profligate or insubordinate.
Heb 5:9 what he suffered; and B made perfect he became
5:10 all who obey him, B designated by God a
6:8 worthless and near to B cursed; its end is
10:33 with sufferings, sometimes B publicly exposed to
10:33 and affliction, and sometimes B partners with those
11:7 By faith Noah, B warned by God concerning events
11:27 he left Egypt, not B afraid of the anger
Jas 1:24 of liberty, and perseveres, B no hearer that forgets
3:8 humankind, but no human B can tame the tongue--
5:7 fruit of the earth, B patient over it until
1Pet 3:18 bring us to God, B put to death in
5:3 in your charge but B examples to the flock.
2Pet 1:8 they keep you from B ineffective or unfruitful in
3:7 stored up for fire, B kept until the day
Jude 1:3 Beloved, B very eager to write to you of
Rev 3:1 have the name of B alive, and you are
3:18 of your nakedness from B seen, and salve to
17:17 out his purpose by B of one mind and

BEINGS (8)

Ps 29:1 the LORD, O heavenly B, ascribe to the LORD
89:6 Who among the heavenly B is like the LORD,
Sir 13:15 his neighbor; all living B associate by species, and
14:17 All living B become old like a garment, for
16:28 all kinds of living B he covered its surface,
17:4 them in all living B, and granted them dominion
18:12 compassion of the Lord is for all living B
Gal 4:8 were in bondage to B that by nature are

BEKA

Ex 38:26 of the sanctuary: a B a head (that is,

BEL (18)

Is 46:1 B bows down, Nebo stoops, their idols are on
Jer 50:2 say: 'Babylon is taken, B is put to shame,
51:44 And I will punish B in Babylon, and take
Bar 6:41 bring him and pray B that the man may
6:41 may speak, as though B were able to understand.

B

Dan 14:3 had an idol called B, and every day they
14:5 said to him, "Why do you not worship B
14:6 you not think that B is a living God?
14:9 if you prove that B is eating them, Daniel
14:9 Daniel shall die, because he blasphemed against B
14:10 were seventy priests of B, besides their wives and
14:10 king went with Daniel into the temple of B
14:11 And the priests of B said, "Behold, we are
14:12 do not find that B has eaten it all,
14:14 out, the king set forth the food for B
14:18 "You are great, O B; and with you there
14:22 to death, and gave B over to Daniel, who
14:28 Jew; he has destroyed B, and slain the dragon,

BELA (14)
Gen 14:2 and the king of B (that is, Zoar).
14:8 and the king of B (that is, Zoar) went
36:32 B the son of Beor reigned in Edom, the
36:33 B died, and Jobab the son of Zerah of
46:21 sons of Benjamin: B, Becher, Ashbel, Gera, Naaman,
Num 26:38 to their families: of B, the family of the
26:40 And the sons of B were Ard and Naaman:
1Chr 1:43 reigned over the Israelites: B the son of Beor,
1:44 When B died, Jobab the son of Zerah of
5:8 Je-iel, and Zechariah, and B the son of Azaz,
7:6 The sons of Benjamin: B, Becher, and Jedia-el, three.
7:7 The sons of B: Ezbon, Uzzi, Uzziel, Jerimoth, and
8:1 was the father of B his first-born, Ashbel the
8:3 And B had sons: Addar, Gera, Abihud,

BELA-ITES
Num 26:38 the family of the B; of Ashbel, the family

BELCH
Wis 11:18 out fiery breath, or B forth a thick pall

BELIAL
2Cor 6:15 What accord has Christ with B

BELIEF (2)
2Mac 15:11 a sort of vision, which was worthy of B
2Thes 2:13 by the Spirit and B in the truth.

BELIEVE (155)
Gen 45:26 for he did not B them.
Ex 4:1 behold, they will not B me or listen to
4:5 "that they may B that the LORD, the
4:8 "If they will not B you," God said, "or
4:8 first sign, they may B the latter sign.
4:9 If they will not B even these two signs
19:9 you, and may also B you for ever." Then
Num 14:11 long will they not B in me, in spite
20:12 "Because you did not B in me, to sanctify
Deut 1:32 word you did not B the LORD your God,
9:23 God, and did not B him or obey his
1Kgs 10:7 but I did not B the reports until I
2Kgs 17:14 been, who did not B in the LORD their
2Chr 9:6 but I did not B the reports until I
20:20 B in the LORD your God, and you will
20:20 you will be established; B his prophets, and you
32:15 fashion, and do not B him, for no god
Tob 2:14 But I did not B her, and told her
14:4 son, for I fully B what Jonah the prophet
Job 9:16 me, I would not B that he was listening
15:22 He does not B that he will return out
Ps 27:13 I B that I shall see the goodness of
78:32 still sinned; despite his wonders they did not B
119:66 and knowledge, for I B in thy commandments.
Prov 26:25 when he speaks graciously, B him not, for there
Sir 19:15 slander; so do not B everything you hear.
Is 7:9 If you will not B, surely you shall not
43:10 you may know and B me and understand that
Jer 12:6 full cry after you; B them not, though they
40:14 of Ahikam would not B them.
Lam 4:12 the earth did not B, or any of the
Hab 1:5 that you would not B if told.
1Mac 10:46 words, they did not B or accept them, because
Mt 9:28 to them, "Do you B that I am able
18:6 these little ones who B in me to sin,
21:25 then did you not B him?'
21:32 and you did not B him, but the tax
21:32 not afterward repent and B him.
24:23 he is!' do not B it.
24:26 inner rooms,' do not B it.
27:42 cross, and we will B in him.
Mk 1:15 at hand; repent, and B in the gospel."
5:36 ruler of the synagogue, "Do not fear, only B
9:24 out and said, "I B; help my unbelief!"
9:42 these little ones who B in me to sin,
11:24 you ask in prayer, B that you have received
11:30 then did you not B him?'
13:21 he is!' do not B it.
15:31 from the cross, that we may see and B
16:11 her, they would not B it.
16:13 but they did not B them.
16:16 he who does not B will be condemned.
16:17 will accompany those who B: in my name they
Lk 1:20 because you did not B my words, which will
8:12 that they may not B and be saved.
8:13 have no root, they B for a while and
8:50 "Do not fear; only B, and she shall be
20:5 'Why did you not B him?'
22:65 you, you will not B;
24:11 and they did not B them.
24:25 slow of heart to B all that the prophets
Jn 1:7 light, that all might B through him.
1:50 saw you under the fig tree, do you B
3:12 and you do not B, how can you believe
3:12 believe, how can you B if I tell you
3:18 he who does not B is condemned already, because
4:21 said to her, "Woman, B me, the hour is
4:42 your words that we B, for we have heard
4:48 you see signs and wonders you will not B
5:37 for you do not B him whom he has
5:43 How can you B, who receive glory from one
5:45 believed Moses, you would B me, for he wrote
5:46 if you do not B his writings, how will
5:46 writings, how will you B my words?"
6:29 of God, that you B in him whom he
6:30 we may see, and B you?
6:36 you have seen me and yet do not B
6:64 there are some of you that do not B
6:64 were that did not B, and who it was
7:5 his brothers did not B in him.
8:24 your sins unless you B that I am he."
8:45 truth, you do not B me.
8:46 why do you not B me?
9:18 The Jews did not B that he had been
9:35 he said, "Do you B in the Son of
9:36 sir, that I may B in him?"
9:38 He said, "Lord, I B; and he worshipped him.
10:25 them, "I told you, and you do not B
10:26 but you do not B, because you do not
10:37 Father, then do not B me;
10:38 though you do not B me, believe the works,
10:38 do not believe me, B the works, that you
11:15 I was not there, so that you may B
11:26 Do you B this?"
11:27 him, "Yes, Lord; I B that you are the
11:40 that if you would B you would see the
11:42 by, that they may B that thou didst send
11:48 thus, every one will B in him, and the
12:36 you have the light, B in the light, that
12:37 yet they did not B in him;
12:39 Therefore they could not B
13:19 take place you may B that I am he.
14:1 your hearts be troubled; B in God, believe also
14:1 troubled; believe in God, B also in me.
14:10 Do you not B that I am in the
14:11 B me that I am in the Father and
14:11 in me; or else B me for the sake
14:29 that when it does take place, you may B
16:9 because they do not B in me;
16:30 you; by this we B that you came from
16:31 Jesus answered them, "Do you now B
17:20 also for those who B in me through their
17:21 that the world may B that thou hast sent
19:35 he tells the truth--that you also may B
20:25 my hand in his side, I will not B
20:29 are those who have not seen and yet B
20:31 written that you may B that Jesus is the
Acts 9:26 for they did not B that he was a
13:41 deed you will never B, if one declares it
15:7 should hear the word of the gospel and B
15:11 But we B that we shall be saved through
16:31 And they said, B in the Lord Jesus, and
19:4 telling the people to B in the one who
26:27 King Agrippa, do you B the prophets?
26:27 I know that you B
Rom 3:22 through faith in Jesus Christ for all who B
4:11 father of all who B without being circumcised and
4:24 reckoned to us who B in him that raised

6:8 died with Christ, we B that we shall also
10:9 Jesus is Lord and B in your heart that
10:14 how are they to B in him of whom
1Cor 1:21 of what we preach to save those who B
11:18 you; and I partly B it,
2Cor 4:13 we too B, and so we speak,
Gal 3:22 Jesus Christ might be given to those who B
Eph 1:19 power in us who B, according to the working
Phil 1:29 you should not only B in him but also
1Thes 4:14 For since we B that Jesus died and rose
2Thes 2:11 delusion, to make them B what is false,
2:12 condemned who did not B the truth but had
1Tim 1:16 those who were to B in him for eternal
4:3 thanksgiving by those who B and know the truth.
4:10 Savior of all men, especially of those who B
Heb 11:6 near to God must B that he exists and
Jas 2:19 You B that God is one; you do well.
2:19 Even the demons B—and shudder.
1Pet 1:8 now see him you B in him and rejoice
2:7 To you therefore who B, he is precious, but
2:7 those who do not B, "The very stone which
1Jn 3:23 commandment, that we should B in the name of
4:1 Beloved, do not B every spirit, but test the
4:16 So we know and B the love God has
5:10 He who does not B God has made him
5:13 this to you who B in the name of
Jude 1:5 of Egypt, afterward destroyed those who did not B

BELIEVED (82)

Gen 15:6 And he B the LORD; and he reckoned it
Ex 4:31 And the people B; and when they heard that
14:31 the LORD; and they B in the LORD and
Jud 14:10 Israel had done, he B firmly in God, and
Ps 106:12 Then they B his words; they sang his praise.
Is 53:1 Who has B what we have heard?
Dan 13:41 The assembly B them, because they were elders of
Jon 3:5 the people of Nineveh B God; they proclaimed a
1Mac 1:30 to them, and they B him; but he suddenly
2:59 Hannaniah, Azariah, and Mishael B and were saved
Mt 8:13 be it done for you as you have B
21:32 collectors and the harlots B him; and even when
Mk 16:14 because they had not B those who saw him
Lk 1:45 blessed is she who B that there would be
Jn 1:12 who received him, who B in his name, he
2:11 glory; and his disciples B in him.
2:22 said this; and they B the scripture and the
2:23 the Passover feast, many B in his name when
3:18 because he has not B in the name of
4:39 Samaritans from that city B in him because of
4:41 And many more B because of his word.
4:50 The man B the word that Jesus spoke to
4:53 live"; and he himself B, and all his household.
5:45 If you B Moses, you would believe me, for
6:69 life; and we have B, and have come to
7:31 many of the people B in him; they said,
7:39 Spirit, which those who B in him were to
7:48 or of the Pharisees B in him?
8:30 he spoke thus, many B in him.
8:31 the Jews who had B in him, "If you
10:42 And many B in him there.
11:45 seen what he did, B in him;
12:38 fulfilled: "Lord, who has B our report, and to
12:42 even of the authorities B in him, but for
16:27 loved me and have B that I came from
17:8 thee; and they have B that thou didst send
20:8 and he saw and B;
20:29 to him, "Have you B because you have seen
Acts 2:44 And all who B were together and had all
4:4 who heard the word B; and the number of
4:32 company of those who B were of one heart
8:12 But when they B Philip as he preached good
8:13 Even Simon himself B, and after being baptized he
9:42 all Joppa, and many B in the Lord.
11:17 to us when we B in the Lord Jesus
11:21 a great number that B turned to the Lord.
13:12 Then the proconsul B, when he saw what had
13:48 as many as were ordained to eternal life B
14:1 that a great company B, both of Jews and
14:23 committed them to the Lord in whom they B
16:34 household that he had B in God.
17:12 Many of them therefore B, with not a few
17:34 men joined him and B, among them Dionysius the
18:8 ruler of the synagogue, B in the Lord, together
18:8 the Corinthians hearing Paul B and were baptized.
18:27 who through grace had B,
19:2 "Did you receive the Holy Spirit when you B
21:20 of those who have B; they are all zealous
21:25 the Gentiles who have B, we have sent a
22:19 and beat those who B in thee.
Rom 4:3 "Abraham B God, and it was reckoned to him
4:17 God in whom he B, who gives life to
4:18 In hope he B against hope, that he should
10:14 call upon him in whom they have not B
10:16 says, "Lord, who has B what he has heard
13:11 than when we first B;
1Cor 3:5 Servants through whom you B, as the Lord assigned
15:2 it fast—unless you B in vain.
15:11 or they, so we preach and so you B
2Cor 4:13 had who wrote, "I B, and so I spoke,"
Gal 2:16 Christ, even we have B in Christ Jesus, in
3:6 Thus Abraham B God, and it was reckoned to
Eph 1:13 your salvation, and have B in him, were sealed
2Thes 1:10 in all who have B, because our testimony to
1:10 have believed, because our testimony to you was B
1Tim 3:16 preached among the nations, B on in the world,
2Tim 1:12 know whom I have B, and I am sure
3:14 learned and have firmly B, knowing from whom you
Tit 3:8 that those who have B in God may be
Heb 4:3 For we who have B enter that rest, as
Jas 2:23 fulfilled which says, "Abraham B God, and it was
1Jn 5:10 because he has not B in the testimony that

BELIEVER (2)

Acts 16:1 woman who was a B; but his father was
2Cor 6:15 Or what has a B in common with an

BELIEVERS (12)

Acts 5:14 And more than ever B were added to the
10:45 And the B from among the circumcised who came
15:5 But some B who belonged to the party of
19:18 who were now B came, confessing and divulging
1Cor 14:22 a sign not for B but for unbelievers, while
14:22 while prophecy is not for unbelievers but for B
1Thes 1:7 example to all the B in Macedonia and in
2:10 our behavior to you B;
2:13 of God, which is at work in you B
1Tim 4:12 youth, but set the B an example in speech
6:2 by their service are B and beloved.
Tit 1:5 and his children are B and not open to

BELIEVES (32)

Prov 14:15 The simple B everything, but the prudent looks
Sir 32:24 He who B the law gives heed to the
Is 28:16 sure foundation: 'He who B will not be in
Mk 9:23 All things are possible to him who B
11:23 in his heart, but B that what he says
16:16 He who B and is baptized will be saved;
Jn 3:15 lifted up, that whoever B in him may have
3:16 only Son, that whoever B in him should not
3:18 He who B in him is not condemned; he
3:36 He who B in the Son has eternal life;
5:23 hears my word and B him who sent me,
6:35 hunger, and he who B in me shall never
6:40 sees the Son and B in him should have
6:47 to you, he who B has eternal life.
7:38 He who B in me, as the scripture has
11:25 the life; he who B in me, though he
11:26 and whoever lives and B in me shall never
12:44 and said, "He who B in me, believes not
12:44 who believes in me, B not in me but
12:46 the world, that whoever B in me may not
14:12 to you, he who B in me will also
Acts 10:43 that every one who B in him receives forgiveness
13:39 him every one that B is freed from everything
Rom 9:33 fall; and he who B in him will not
10:10 For man B with his heart and so is
10:11 says, "No one who B in him will be
14:2 One B he may eat anything, while the weak
1Cor 13:7 Love bears all things, B all things, hopes all
1Pet 2:6 precious, and he who B in him will not
1Jn 5:1 Every one who B that Jesus is the Christ
5:5 world but he who B that Jesus is the
5:10 He who B in the Son of God has

BELIEVING (7)

Jn 12:11 were going away and B in Jesus.
20:27 in my side; do not be faithless, but B
20:31 of God, and that B you may have life
Acts 24:13 God of our fathers, B everything laid down by
Rom 15:13 joy and peace in B, so that by the
1Tim 5:16 If any B woman has relatives who are widows,
6:2 Those who have B masters must not be disrespectful

B

BELITTLES

Prov 11:12 He who B his neighbor lacks sense, but a

BELL (4)

Ex 28:34 between them, a golden B and a pomegranate, a
28:34 a pomegranate, a golden B and a pomegranate,
39:26 between the pomegranates; a B and a pomegranate,
39:26 and a pomegranate, a B and a pomegranate round

BELLOWING

Ps 59:7 There they are, B with their mouths, and snarling

BELLOWS

Jer 6:29 The B blow fiercely, the lead is consumed by

BELLS (5)

Ex 28:33 around its skirts, with B of gold between them,
39:25 They also made B of pure gold, and put
39:25 gold, and put the B between the pomegranates upon
Sir 45:9 with very many golden B round about, to send
Zech 14:20 be inscribed on the B of the horses, "Holy

BELLY (20)

Gen 3:14 wild animals; upon your B you shall go, and
Lev 11:42 Whatever goes on its B, and whatever goes on
Judg 3:21 thrust it into his B;
3:22 sword out of his B; and the dirt came
2Sam 2:23 smote him in the B with the butt of
3:27 smote him in the B, so that he died,
Job 20:15 up again; God casts them out of his B
20:23 To fill his B to the full God will
40:16 and his power in the muscles of his B
Ps 17:14 May their B be filled with what thou hast
Prov 13:25 his appetite, but the B of the wicked suffers
Song 7:2 Your B is a heap of wheat, encircled with
Sir 51:5 the depths of the B of Hades, from an
Jer 51:34 he has filled his B with my delicacies, he
Dan 2:32 arms of silver, its B and thighs of bronze,
Jon 1:17 Jonah was in the B of the fish three
2:1 his God from the B of the fish,
2:2 me; out of the B of Sheol I cried,
Mt 12:40 three nights in the B of the whale, so
Phil 3:19 their god is the B, and they glory in

BELMAIN

Jud 4:4 Kona and Beth-horon and B and Jericho and to

BELONG (66)

Gen 32:17 you, and asks you, 'To whom do you B
32:18 you shall say, 'They B to your servant Jacob;
38:25 man to whom these B, I am with child."
40:8 them, "Do not interpretations B to God?
Lev 7:9 or a griddle shall B to the priest who
7:14 the LORD; it shall B to the priest who
Num 35:5 the middle; this shall B to them as pasture
36:3 tribe to which they B; so it will be
36:4 tribe to which they B; and their inheritance will
Deut 10:14 the LORD your God B heaven and the heaven
29:29 day.' "The secret things B to the LORD our
29:29 things that are revealed B to us and to
Josh 2:13 sisters, and all who B to them, and deliver
6:22 woman, and all who B to her, as you
17:9 the cities of Manasseh, B to Ephraim.
Judg 19:12 foreigners, who do not B to the people of
1Sam 25:22 male of all who B to him."
30:13 David said to him, "To whom do you B
2Sam 3:12 at Hebron, saying, "To whom does the land B
Tob 5:10 brother, to what tribe and family do you B
7:3 They answered him, "We B to the sons of
Jud 10:12 what people do you B, and where are you
Ps 47:9 shields of the earth B to God; he is
82:8 earth; for to thee B all the nations!
Prov 16:1 plans of the mind B to man, but the
Wis 1:16 they are fit to B to his party.
2:24 world, and those who B to his party experience
Ezek 44:30 all your offerings, shall B to the priests; you
45:6 cubits long; it shall B to the whole house
45:7 to the prince shall B the land on both
46:16 his inheritance, it shall B to his sons, it
48:12 And it shall B to them as a special
48:21 of the city shall B to the prince.
48:21 tribal portions, it shall B to the prince.
Dan 2:20 to whom B wisdom and might.
9:9 the Lord our God B mercy and forgiveness; because
Hos 3:3 play the harlot, or B to another man; so
Zech 9:1 For to the LORD B the cities of Aram,
1Mac 5:62 But they did not B to the family of
12:23 cattle and your property B to us, and ours
12:23 to us, and ours B to you.
2Mac 3:6 that they did not B to the account of
Jn 10:26 because you do not B to my sheep.
Acts 27:23 God to whom I B and whom I worship,
Rom 1:6 who are called to B to Jesus Christ;
7:4 so that you may B to another, to him
8:9 of Christ does not B to him.
9:4 Israelites, and to them B the sonship, the glory,
9:5 the promises; to them B the patriarchs, and of
9:6 are descended from Israel B to Israel,
16:10 Greet those who B to the family of Aristobulus.
16:11 in the Lord who B to the family of
1Cor 1:12 of you says, "I B to Paul," or "I
1:12 or "I B to Apollos," or "I belong to
1:12 or "I B to Cephas," or "I belong to
1:12 or "I B to Christ."
3:4 when one says, "I B to Paul," and another,
3:4 and another, "I B to Apollos," are you not
12:15 hand, I do not B to the body," that
12:16 eye, I do not B to the body," that
15:23 his coming those who B to Christ.
Gal 5:24 And those who B to Christ Jesus have crucified
1Thes 5:8 But, since we B to the day, let us
Heb 6:9 of better things that B to salvation.
1Pet 4:11 To him B glory and dominion for ever and
Rev 19:1 and glory and power B to our God,

BELONGED (43)

Num 16:32 all the men that B to Korah and all
16:33 they and all that B to them went down
Josh 6:23 brothers and all who B to her; and they
6:25 household, and all who B to her, Joshua saved
17:8 The land of Tappuah B to Manasseh, but the
17:8 the boundary of Manasseh B to the sons of
21:10 of the Kohathites who B to the Levites; since
Judg 6:11 oak at Ophrah, which B to Joash the Abiezrite,
18:27 and the priest who B to him, the Danites
Ruth 4:3 parcel of land which B to our kinsman Elimelech.
4:9 of Naomi all that B to Elimelech and all
4:9 Elimelech and all that B to Chilion and to
1Sam 25:21 missed of all that B to him; and he
27:6 Ziklag; therefore Ziklag has B to the kings of
2Sam 9:9 to him, "All that B to Saul and to
16:4 Ziba, "Behold, all that B to Mephibosheth is now
1Kgs 4:10 in Arubboth (to him B Socoh and all the
6:22 the whole altar that B to the inner sanctuary
15:27 down at Gibbethon, which B to the Philistines; for
16:15 encamped against Gibbethon, which B to the
2Kgs 12:16 of the LORD; it B to the priests.
14:28 and Hamath, which had B to Judah, are they
24:7 had taken all that B to the king of
1Chr 4:40 the former inhabitants there B to Ham.
5:2 him, yet the birthright B to Joseph),
2Chr 21:17 possessions they found that B to the king's house,
26:23 the burial field which B to the kings, for
34:33 all the territory that B to the people of
Ezra 2:59 their descent, whether they B to Israel:
Neh 7:61 their descent, whether they B to Israel:
Jud 8:2 Her husband Manasseh, who B to her tribe and
Esth 1:9 in the palace which B to King Ahasuerus.
Ezek 42:3 the twenty cubits which B to the inner court,
42:3 facing the pavement which B to the outer court,
Lk 14:1 of a ruler who B to the Pharisees, they
23:7 he learned that he B to Herod's jurisdiction, he
Acts 4:37 sold a field which B to him, and brought
6:9 some of those who B to the synagogue of
12:1 hands upon some who B to the church.
15:5 But some believers who B to the party of
23:34 the letter, he asked to what province he B
Col 2:20 as if you still B to the world?
Heb 7:13 these things are spoken B to another tribe, from

BELONGING (29)

Gen 46:26 All the persons B to Jacob who came into
Lev 25:34 fields of common land B to their cities may
25:49 or a near kinsman B to his family may
Num 25:14 of a fathers' house B to the Simeonites.
Deut 23:3 the tenth generation none B to them shall enter
Josh 15:21 The cities B to the tribe of the people
18:14 is, Kiriath-jearim), a city B to the tribe of
21:20 rest of the Kohathites B to the Kohathite families
Ruth 2:3 part of the field B to Boaz, who was
1Sam 6:18 cities of the Philistines B to the five lords,
1Kgs 14:11 Any one B to Jeroboam who dies in the

16:4 Any one B to Baasha who dies in the
21:24 of Jezreel.' Any one B to Ahab who dies
2Kgs 9:25 the plot of ground B to Naboth the Jezreelite;
1Chr 7:5 Their kinsmen B to all the families of Issachar
26:21 sons of the Gershonites B to Ladan, the heads
26:21 of the fathers' houses B to Ladan the Gershonite:
2Chr 31:19 fields of common land B to their cities, there
Jud 7:20 the vessels of water B to every inhabitant of
Sir 9:8 look intently at beauty B to another; many have
Is 8:1 in common characters, B to Maher-shalal-hash-baz.'"
Ezek 13:18 you hunt down souls B to my people, and
40:20 faced toward the north, B to the outer court.
43:21 in the appointed place B to the temple, outside
2Mac 3:10 there were some deposits B to widows and orphans,
Acts 2:10 the parts of Libya B to Cyrene, and visitors
7:6 aliens in a land B to others, who would
9:2 if he found any B to the Way, men
28:7 that place were lands B to the chief man

BELONGINGS

Jer 20:5 gains, all its prized B, and all the treasures

BELONGS (52)

Gen 31:16 away from our father B to us and to
49:10 comes to whom it B; and to him shall
Ex 9:4 die of all that B to the people of
Lev 6:5 him to whom it B, on the day of
14:13 like the sin offering, B to the priest; it
27:24 to whom the land B as a possession by
27:26 which as a firstling B to the LORD, no
Num 1:50 and over all that B to it; they are
16:30 up, with all that B to them, and they
Josh 13:4 Canaanites, and Mearah which B to the Sidonians, to
22:11 on the side that B to the people of
Judg 6:24 stands at Ophrah, which B to the Abiezrites.
18:28 in the valley which B to Beth-rehob.
19:14 them near Gibe-ah, which B to Benjamin,
20:4 came to Gibe-ah that B to Benjamin, I and
1Sam 17:1 gathered at Socoh, which B to Judah, and encamped
30:14 and upon that which B to Judah and upon
2Sam 6:12 Obed-edom and all that B to him, because of
1Kgs 17:9 go to Zarephath, which B to Sidon, and dwell
19:3 came to Beer-sheba, which B to Judah, and left
22:3 you know that Ramoth-gilead B to us, and we
2Kgs 14:11 battle at Beth-shemesh, which B to Judah.
1Chr 13:6 is, to Kiriath-jearim which B to Judah, to bring
2Chr 25:21 battle at Beth-shemesh, which B to Judah.
Tob 5:8 to what tribe he B, and whether he is
Ps 3:8 Deliverance B to the LORD; thy blessing be upon
22:28 For dominion B to the LORD, and he rules
62:11 heard this: that power B to God;
62:12 to thee, O Lord, B steadfast love.
68:20 to GOD, the Lord, B escape from death.
89:18 For our shield B to the LORD, our king
Prov 21:31 battle, but the victory B to the LORD.
Bar 1:15 you shall say: 'Righteousness B to the Lord our
2:6 "'Righteousness B to the Lord our God, but
Ezek 48:22 midst of that which B to the prince.
Dan 9:7 To thee, O Lord, B righteousness, but to us
9:8 To us, O Lord, B confusion of face, to
Jon 2:9 Deliverance B to the LORD!"
1Mac 10:42 is canceled, because it B to the priests who
2Mac 15:12 childhood in all that B to excellence, was praying
Mt 19:14 them; for to such B the kingdom of heaven."
20:14 Take what B to you, and go; I choose
20:15 I choose with what B to me?
Mk 10:14 them; for to such B the kingdom of God.
Lk 18:16 them; for to such B the kingdom of God.
Jn 3:31 is of the earth B to the earth, and
2Cor 4:7 that the transcendent power B to God and not
Eph 4:4 the one hope that B to your call,
4:22 your old nature which B to your former manner
Col 2:17 come; but the substance B to Christ.
Rev 7:10 a loud voice, "Salvation B to our God who
17:11 an eighth but it B to the seven, and

BELOVED (125)

Deut 33:12 Benjamin he said, "The B of the LORD, he
2Sam 1:23 "Saul and Jonathan, B and lovely!
Neh 13:26 him, and he was B by his God, and
Jud 9:4 be divided among thy B sons, who were zealous
Esth 15:5 looked happy, as if B, but her heart was
Ps 60:5 [Selah] That thy B may be delivered, give victory
108:6 That thy B may be delivered, give help by
127:2 he gives to his B sleep.
Song 1:13 My B is to me a bag of myrrh,
1:14 My B is to me a cluster of henna
1:16 you are beautiful, my B, truly lovely.
2:3 wood, so is my B among young men.
2:8 The voice of my B
2:9 My B is like a gazelle, or a young
2:10 My B speaks and says to me: "Arise, my
2:16 My B is mine and I am his, he
2:17 shadows flee, turn, my B, be like a gazelle,
4:16 Let my B come to his garden, and eat
5:2 my B is knocking.
5:4 My B put his hand to the latch, and
5:5 to open to my B, and my hands dripped
5:6 I opened to my B, but my beloved had
5:6 my beloved, but my B had turned and gone.
5:8 if you find my B, that you tell him
5:9 What is your B more than another beloved, O
5:9 beloved more than another B, O fairest among
5:9 What is your B more than another beloved, that
5:9 beloved more than another B, that you thus adjure
5:10 My B is all radiant and ruddy, distinguished among
5:16 This is my B and this is my friend,
6:1 Whither has your B gone, O fairest among women?
6:1 Whither has your B turned, that we may seek
6:2 My B has gone down to his garden, to
6:3 I am my B's and my beloved is mine;
6:3 my beloved's and my B is mine; he pastures
7:11 Come, my B, let us go forth into the
7:13 I have laid up for you, O my B
8:5 coming up from the wilderness, leaning upon her B
8:14 Make haste, my B, and be like a gazelle
Sir 4:7 Make yourself B in the congregation; bow your head
20:12 wise man makes himself B through his words, but
24:11 In the B city likewise he gave me a
45:1 all flesh and was B by God and man,
46:13 Samuel, B by his Lord, a prophet of the
Is 5:1 me sing for my B a love song concerning
5:1 concerning his vineyard: My B had a vineyard on
Jer 11:15 What right has my B in my house, when
12:7 I have given the B of my soul into
Bar 4:16 led away the widow's B sons, and bereaved the
Dan 3:35 sake of Abraham thy B and for the sake
9:23 for you are greatly B; therefore consider the word
10:11 "O Daniel, man greatly B, give heed to the
10:19 said, "O man greatly B, fear not, peace be
11:37 or to the one B by women; he shall
Hos 3:1 a woman who is B of a paramour and
9:16 I will slay their B children.
1Mac 6:11 I was kind and B in my power.'
Mt 3:17 saying, "This is my B Son, with whom I
12:18 I have chosen, my B with whom my soul
17:5 said, "This is my B Son, with whom I
Mk 1:11 heaven, "Thou art my B Son; with thee I
9:7 cloud, "This is my B Son; listen to him."
12:6 still one other, a B son; finally he sent
Lk 3:22 heaven, "Thou art my B Son; with thee I
20:13 I will send my B son; it may be
Acts 15:25 to you with our B Barnabas and Paul,
Rom 1:7 Christ; To all God's B in Rome, who are
9:25 her who was not B I will call 'my
9:25 who was not beloved I will call 'my B
11:28 regards election they are B for the sake of
12:19 B, never avenge yourselves, but leave it to the
16:5 Greet my B Epaenetus, who was the first convert
16:8 Greet Ampliatus, my B in the Lord.
16:9 in Christ, and my B Stachys.
16:12 Greet the B Persis, who has worked hard in
1Cor 4:14 admonish you as my B children.
4:17 to you Timothy, my B and faithful child in
10:14 Therefore, my B, shun the worship of idols.
15:58 my B brethren, be steadfast, immovable, always
2Cor 7:1 we have these promises, B, let us cleanse ourselves
12:19 speaking in Christ, and all for your upbuilding, B
Eph 1:6 which he freely bestowed on us in the B
5:1 imitators of God, as B children.
6:21 doing, Tychicus the B brother and faithful minister
Phil 2:12 Therefore, my B, as you have always obeyed, so
4:1 crown, stand firm thus in the Lord, my B
Col 1:7 it from Epaphras our B fellow servant.
1:13 the kingdom of his B Son,
3:12 ones, holy and B, compassion, kindness, lowliness,
4:7 affairs; he is a B brother and faithful minister
4:9 Onesimus, the faithful and B brother, who is one
4:14 Luke the B physician and Demas greet you.
1Thes 1:4 For we know, brethren B by God, that he
2Thes 2:13 always for you, brethren B by the Lord, because
1Tim 6:2 who benefit by their service are believers and B

B

B

2Tim 1:2 Jesus, To Timothy, my B child: Grace, mercy, and
Philem 1:1 brother, To Philemon our B fellow worker
1:16 a slave, as a B brother, especially to me
Heb 6:9 yet in your case, B, we feel sure of
Jas 1:15 not be deceived, my B brethren.
1:18 Know this, my B brethren.
2:5 Listen, my B brethren.
1Pet 2:11 B, I beseech you as aliens and exiles to
4:12 B, do not be surprised at the fiery ordeal
2Pet 1:17 Glory, "This is my B Son, with whom I
3:1 have written to you, B, and in both of
3:8 ignore this one fact, B, that with the Lord
3:14 Therefore, B, since you wait for these, be zealous
3:15 So also our B brother Paul wrote to you
3:17 therefore, B, knowing this beforehand, beware lest
1Jn 2:7 B, I am writing you no new commandment, but
3:2 B, we are God's children now; it does not
3:21 B, if our hearts do not condemn us, we
4:1 B, do not believe every spirit, but test the
4:7 B, let us love one another; for love is
4:11 B, if God so loved us, we also ought
3Jn 1:1 The elder to the B Gaius, whom I love
1:2 B, I pray that all may go well with
1:5 B, it is a loyal thing you do when
1:11 B, do not imitate evil but imitate good.
Jude 1:1 those who are called, B in God the Father
1:3 B, being very eager to write to you of
1:17 But you must remember, B, the predictions of the
1:20 But you, B, build yourselves up on your most
Rev 20:9 the saints and the B city; but fire came

BELOVEDS
Song 7:10 I am my B, and his desire is for

BELOW (19)
Gen 35:8 buried under an oak B Bethel; so the name
Josh 11:17 the valley of Lebanon B Mount Hermon.
13:5 the sunrising, from Baal-gad B Mount Hermon to
Judg 7:8 camp of Midian was B him in the valley.
1Sam 7:11 them, as far as B Beth-car.
1Kgs 4:12 is beside Zarethan B Jezreel, and from Beth-shean
7:29 frames, both above and B the lions and oxen,
1Chr 27:23 did not number those B twenty years of age,
Jud 6:11 came to the springs B Bethulia.
Job 26:5 The shades B tremble, the waters and their
40:13 dust together; bind their faces in the world B
Jer 31:37 foundations of the earth B can be explored, then
Ezek 8:2 appearance of a man; B what appeared to be
42:9 B these chambers was an entrance on the east
42:12 And B the south chambers was an entrance on
47:1 water was issuing from B the threshold of the
47:1 was flowing down from B the south end of
Mk 14:66 And as Peter was B in the courtyard, one
Jn 8:23 them, "You are from B, I am from above;

BELSHAZZAR (10)
Bar 1:11 for the life of B his son, that their
1:12 under the protection of B his son, and we
Dan 5:1 King B made a great feast for a thousand
5:2 B, when he tasted the wine, commanded that the
5:9 Then King B was greatly alarmed, and his color
5:22 And you his son, B, have not humbled your
5:29 Then B commanded, and Daniel was clothed with
5:30 That very night B the Chaldean king was slain.
7:1 the first year of B king of Babylon, Daniel
8:1 the reign of King B a vision appeared to

BELT (2)
Job 12:21 princes, and looses the B of the strong.
Ps 109:19 round him, like a B with which he daily

BELTESHAZZAR (10)
Dan 1:7 names: Daniel he called B, Hananiah he called
2:26 Daniel, whose name was B, "Are you able to
4:8 he who was named B after the name of
4:9 the dream, saying, "O B, chief of the magicians,
4:18 And you, O B, declare the interpretation, because all
4:19 Daniel, whose name was B, was dismayed for a
4:19 The king said, B, let not the dream or
4:19 B answered, "My lord, may the dream be for
5:12 found in this Daniel, whom the king named B
10:1 word was revealed to Daniel, who was named B

BELTS (3)
Ezek 23:15 in vermilion, girded with B on their loins, with
Mt 10:9 nor copper in your B,
Mk 6:8 no money in their B;

BEMOAN (5)
Jer 15:5 Jerusalem, or who will B you?
16:5 go to lament, or B them; for I have
22:10 who is dead, nor B him; but weep bitterly
48:17 B him, all you who are round about him,
Nah 3:7 is Nineveh; who will B her?

BEMOANING
Jer 31:18 I have heard Ephraim B, 'Thou hast chastened me,

BEN-ABINADAB
1Kgs 4:11 the land of Hepher); B, in all Naphath-dor (he

BEN-AMMI
Gen 19:38 and called his name B; he is the father

BEN-DEKER
1Kgs 4:9 hill country of Ephraim; B, in Makaz, Sha-albim,

BEN-GEBER
1Kgs 4:13 other side of Jokmeam; B, in Ramoth-gilead (he had

BEN-HADAD (27)
1Kgs 15:18 Asa sent them to B the son of Tabrimmon,
15:20 And B hearkened to King Asa, and sent the
20:1 B the king of Syria gathered all his army
20:2 to him, "Thus says B:
20:5 and said, "Thus says B: 'I sent to you,
20:9 to the messengers of B, "Tell my lord the
20:10 B sent to him and said, "The gods do
20:12 When B heard this message as he was drinking
20:16 out at noon, while B was drinking himself drunk
20:17 And B sent out scouts, and they reported to
20:20 Israel pursued them, but B king of Syria escaped
20:26 In the spring B mustered the Syrians, and went
20:30 B also fled, and entered an inner chamber in
20:32 and said, "Your servant B says, 'Pray, let me
20:33 up from him and said, "Yes, your brother B
20:33 Then B came forth to him; and he caused
20:34 And B said to him, "The cities which my
2Kgs 6:24 Afterward B king of Syria mustered his entire army,
8:7 B the king of Syria was sick; and when
8:9 he said, "Your son B king of Syria has
13:3 into the hand of B the son of Hazael.
13:24 king of Syria died, B his son became king
13:25 Jehoahaz took again from B the son of Hazael
2Chr 16:2 and sent them to B king of Syria, who
16:4 And B hearkened to King Asa, and sent the
Jer 49:27 Damascus, and it shall devour the strongholds of B
Amos 1:4 Hazael, and it shall devour the strongholds of B

BEN-HAIL
2Chr 17:7 he sent his princes, B, Obadiah, Zechariah, Nethanel,

BEN-HANAN
1Chr 4:20 of Shimon: Amnon, Rinnah, B, and Tilon.

BEN-HESED
1Kgs 4:10 Sha-albim, Beth-shemesh, and Elonbeth-hanan; B, in

BEN-HUR
1Kgs 4:8 These were their names: B, in the hill country

BEN-ONI
Gen 35:18 she called his name B; but his father called

BEN-ZOHETH
1Chr 4:20 The sons of Ishi: Zoheth and B

BENAIAH (44)
2Sam 8:18 Seraiah was secretary; and B the son of Jehoiada
20:23 army of Israel; and B the son of Jehoiada
23:20 And B the son of Jehoiada was a valiant
23:21 in his hand; but B went down to him
23:22 These things did B the son of Jehoiada, and
23:30 Gibe-ah of the Benjaminites, B of Pirathon, Hiddai
1Kgs 1:8 Zadok the priest, and B the son of Jehoiada,
1:10 Nathan the prophet or B or the mighty men
1:26 Zadok the priest, and B the son of Jehoiada,
1:32 Nathan the prophet, and B the son of Jehoiada."
1:36 And B the son of Jehoiada answered the king,
1:38 Nathan the prophet, and B the son of Jehoiada,
1:44 Nathan the prophet, and B the son of Jehoiada,
2:25 So King Solomon sent B the son of Jehoiada;

2:29 Solomon sent B the son of Jehoiada, saying, "Go,
2:30 So B came to the tent of the LORD,
2:30 Then B brought the king word again, saying, "Thus
2:34 Then B the son of Jehoiada went up, and
2:35 The king put B the son of Jehoiada over
2:46 Then the king commanded B the son of Jehoiada;
4:4 of Ahilud was recorder; B the son of Jehoiada
1Chr 4:36 Jeshohaiah, Asaiah, Adi-el, Jesimiel, B,
11:22 And B the son of Jehoiada was a valiant
11:23 a weaver's beam; but B went down to him
11:24 These things did B the son of Jehoiada, and
11:31 Gibe-ah of the Benjaminites, B of Pirathon,
15:18 Jehiel, Unni, Eliab, B, Ma-aseiah, Mattithiah, Eliph
15:20 Unni, Eliab, Ma-aseiah, and B were to play harps
15:24 Joshaphat, Nethanel, Amasai, Zechariah, B, and
16:5 Jehiel, Mattithiah, Eliab, B, Obed-edom, and Je-iel,
16:6 sound the cymbals, and B and Jahaziel the priests
18:17 Shavsha was secretary; and B the son of Jehoiada
27:5 the third month, was B, the son of Jehoiada
27:6 This is the B who was a mighty man
27:14 the eleventh month, was B of Pirathon, of the
27:34 Jehoiada the son of B, and Abiathar.
2Chr 20:14 of Zechariah, son of B, son of Je-iel, son
31:13 Eliel, Ismachiah, Mahath, and B were overseers
Ezra 10:25 Parosh: Ramiah, Izziah, Malchijah, Mijamin,
10:30 Adna, Chelal, B, Ma-aseiah, Mattaniah, Bezalel, B
10:35 Bani: Ma-adai, Amram, Uel, B, Bedeiah, Cheluhi,
10:43 Mattithiah, Zabad, Zebina, Jaddai, Joel, and B
Ezek 11:1 Pelatiah the son of B, princes of the people.
11:13 Pelatiah the son of B died.

BEND (10)
2Sam 22:35 that my arms can B a bow of bronze.
Ps 11:2 for lo, the wicked B the bow, they have
18:34 that my arms can B a bow of bronze.
37:14 draw the sword and B their bows, to bring
Jer 9:3 They B their tongue like a bow; falsehood and
50:14 about, all you that B the bow; shoot at
50:29 Babylon, all those who B the bow.
51:3 Let not the archer B his bow, and let
Bar 2:21 "Thus says the Lord: B your shoulders and serve
Rom 11:10 they cannot see, and B their backs for ever."

BENDING
Is 60:14 oppressed you shall come B low to you; and

BENDS (4)
Josh 15:9 Ephron; then the boundary B round to Baalah (that
15:11 Ekron, then the boundary B round to Shikkeron, and
18:17 to En-rogel; then it B in a northerly direction
19:13 on to Rimmon it B toward Neah;

BENE-BERAK
Josh 19:45 Eltekeh, Gibbethon, Baalath, Jehud, B, Gath-rimmon,

BENE-JAAKAN (3)
Num 33:31 they set out from Moseroth, and encamped at B
33:32 set out from B, and encamped at Hor-haggidgad.
Deut 10:6 Israel journeyed from Be-eroth B to Moserah.

BENEATH (25)
Gen 49:25 the deep that couches B, blessings of the breasts
Ex 20:4 is in the earth B, or that is in
26:24 they shall be separate B, but joined at the
36:29 And they were separate B, but joined at the
Deut 4:39 and on the earth B; there is no other.
5:8 is on the earth B, or that is in
33:13 the deep that couches B,
Josh 2:11 is God in heaven above and on earth B
1Kgs 8:23 above or on earth B, keeping covenant and showing
2Kgs 6:30 behold, he had sackcloth B upon his body—
Jud 13:15 here is the canopy B which he lay in
Job 9:13 turn back his anger; B him bowed the helpers
18:16 His roots dry up B, and his branches wither
Prov 15:24 upward to life, that he may avoid Sheol B
Eccl 2:22 with which he toils B the sun?
Sir 51:6 and my life was very near to Hades B
Is 14:9 up against us.' Sheol B is stirred up to
14:11 maggots are the bed B you, and worms are
51:6 look at the earth B; for the heavens will
Dan 14:13 They were unconcerned, for B the table they had
Hos 14:7 shall return and dwell B my shadow, they shall
Amos 2:9 I destroyed his fruit above, and his roots B
Hab 3:16 bones, my steps totter B me.
1Mac 6:46 elephant, stabbed it from B, and killed it; but
Acts 2:19 signs on the earth B, blood, and fire, and

BENEFACTOR (2)
Esth 16:13 our savior and perpetual B, and of Esther, the
2Mac 4:2 man who was the B of the city, the

BENEFACTORS (4)
Esth 16:2 great kindness of their B, the more proud do
16:3 they even undertake to scheme against their own B
Wis 19:14 these made slaves of guests who were their B
Lk 22:25 and those in authority over them are called B

BENEFICENT
Wis 7:23 good, keen, irresistible, B, humane, steadfast, sure,

BENEFIT (12)
2Chr 32:25 return according to the B done to him, for
Tob 3:8 and have had no B from any of them.
Wis 11:5 punished, they themselves received B in their need.
11:13 the righteous had received B, they perceived it was
Sir 5:8 for it will not B you in the day
2Mac 2:27 banquet and seeks the B of others.
1Cor 4:6 and Apollos for your B, brethren, that you may
7:35 this for your own B, not to lay any
14:6 tongues, how shall I B you unless I bring
1Tim 6:2 better since those who B by their service are
Philem 1:20 brother, I want some B from you in the
Heb 4:2 they heard did not B them, because it did

BENEFITED
Heb 13:9 foods, which have not B their adherents.

BENEFITS (4)
Ps 103:2 forget not all his B,
Prov 11:17 man who is kind B himself, but a cruel
2Mac 5:20 afterward participated in its B; and what was
1Cor 9:11 it too much if we reap your material B

BENINU
Neh 10:13 Zaccur, Sherebiah, Shebaniah, Hodiah, Bani, B

BENJAMIN (148)
Gen 35:18 name Ben-oni; but his father called his name B
35:24 The sons of Rachel: Joseph and B
42:4 Jacob did not send B, Joseph's brother, with his
42:36 now you would take B; all this has come
43:14 he may send back your other brother and B
43:15 money with them, and B; and they arose and
43:16 When Joseph saw B with them, he said to
43:29 and saw his brother B, his mother's son, and
43:34 from Joseph's table, but B's portion was five times
44:12 cup was found in B's sack.
45:12 eyes of my brother B see, that it is
45:14 fell upon his brother B's neck and wept; and
45:14 neck and wept; and B wept upon his neck.
45:22 festal garments; but to B he gave three hundred
46:19 The sons of Rachel, Jacob's wife: Joseph and B
46:21 And the sons of B: Bela, Becher, Ashbel, Gera,
49:27 B is a ravenous wolf, in the morning devouring
Ex 1:3 Judah, Issachar, Zebulun, and B, Dan and Naphtali,
Num 1:11 son of Pedahzur; from B, Abidan the son of
1:36 Of the people of B, their generations, by their
1:37 of the tribe of B was thirty-five thousand four
2:22 Then the tribe of B, the leader of the
2:22 of the people of B being Abidan the son
7:60 of the men of B:
10:24 of the men of B was Abidan the son
13:9 from the tribe of B, Palti the son of
26:38 The sons of B according to their families: of
26:41 are the sons of B according to their families;
34:21 Of the tribe of B, Elidad the son of
Deut 27:12 people: Simeon, Levi, Judah, Issachar, Joseph, and B
33:12 Of B he said, "The beloved of the LORD,
Josh 18:11 of the tribe of B according to its families
18:20 of the tribe of B, according to its families,
18:21 of the tribe of B according to their families
18:28 of the tribe of B according to its families.
21:4 of Judah, Simeon, and B, thirteen cities.
21:17 of the tribe of B, Gibeon with its pasture
Judg 1:21 But the people of B did not drive out
1:21 with the people of B in Jerusalem to this
5:14 the valley, following you, B, with your kinsmen; from
10:9 against Judah and against B and against the house
19:14 Gibe-ah, which belongs to B,
20:4 Gibe-ah that belongs to B, I and my concubine,
20:10 may requite Gibe-ah of B, for all the wanton
20:12 all the tribe of B, saying, "What wickedness is
20:17 of Israel, apart from B, mustered four hundred

B

B

20:20 out to battle against B; and the men of
20:25 And B went against them out of Gibe-ah the
20:35 And the LORD defeated B before Israel; and the
20:35 one hundred men of B that day; all these
20:36 Israel gave ground to B, because they trusted to
20:39 Now B had begun to smite and kill about
20:41 and the men of B were dismayed, for they
20:44 Eighteen thousand men of B fell, all of them
20:46 fell that day of B were twenty-five thousand men
21:1 us shall give his daughter in marriage to B
21:6 Israel had compassion for B their brother, and said,
21:14 And B returned at that time; and they gave
21:15 people had compassion on B because the LORD had
21:16 left, since the women are destroyed out of B
21:17 for the survivors of B, that a tribe be
21:18 "Cursed be he who gives a wife to B
21:21 of Shiloh, and go to the land of B
1Sam 4:12 A man of B ran from the battle line,
9:1 was a man of B whose name was Kish,
9:4 through the land of B, but did not find
9:16 from the land of B, and you shall anoint
9:21 of all the families of the tribe of B
10:2 in the territory of B at Zelzah, and they
10:20 and the tribe of B was taken by lot.
10:21 brought the tribe of B near by its families,
13:2 Jonathan in Gibe-ah of B; the rest of the
13:15 and went up from Gilgal to Gibe-ah of B
13:16 stayed in Geba of B; but the Philistines encamped
14:16 Saul in Gibe-ah of B looked; and behold, the
2Sam 2:9 Jezreel and Ephraim and B and all Israel.
2:15 by number, twelve for B and Ish-bosheth the son
2:31 David had slain of B three hundred and sixty
3:19 Abner also spoke to B; and then Abner went
3:19 the whole house of B thought good to do.
4:2 Rimmon a man of B from Be-eroth (for Be-eroth
4:2 also is reckoned to B;
19:17 and with him were a thousand men from B
21:14 in the land of B in Zela, in the
1Kgs 4:18 son of Ela, in B;
12:21 and the tribe of B, a hundred and eighty
12:23 house of Judah and B, and to the rest
15:22 Asa built Geba of B and Mizpah.
1Chr 2:2 Issachar, Zebulun, Dan, Joseph, B, Naphtali, Gad, and
6:60 from the tribe of B, Geba with its pasture
6:65 of Judah, Simeon, and B these cities which are
7:6 The sons of B: Bela, Becher, and Jedia-el, three.
7:10 sons of Bilhan: Jeush, B, Ehud, Chenaanah, Zethan,
8:1 B was the father of Bela his first-born, Ashbel
9:3 the people of Judah, B, Ephraim, and Manasseh
12:16 of the men of B and Judah came to
21:6 not include Levi and B in the numbering, for
27:21 son of Zechariah; for B, Jaasiel the son of
2Chr 11:1 house of Judah, and B, a hundred and eighty
11:3 Israel in Judah and B,
11:10 fortified cities which are in Judah and in B
11:12 So he held Judah and B
11:23 districts of Judah and B, in all the fortified
14:8 eighty thousand men from B, that carried shields and
15:2 and all Judah and B: The LORD is with
15:8 land of Judah and B and from the cities
15:9 gathered all Judah and B, and those from Ephraim,
17:17 Of B: Eliada, a mighty man of valor, with
25:5 thousands and of hundreds for all Judah and B
31:1 throughout all Judah and B, and in Ephraim and
34:9 from all Judah and B and from the inhabitants
34:32 in Jerusalem and in B stand to it.
Ezra 1:5 houses of Judah and B, and the priests and
4:1 adversaries of Judah and B heard that the returned
10:9 men of Judah and B assembled at Jerusalem within
10:32 Malchijah, Shemaiah, Shime-on, B, Malluch, and
Neh 3:23 After them B and Hasshub repaired opposite their
11:4 sons of Judah and of the sons of B
11:7 are the sons of B: Sallu the son of
11:31 The people of B also lived from Geba onward,
11:36 of the Levites in Judah were joined to B
12:34 Azariah, Ezra, Meshullam, Judah, B, Shemaiah, and
Esth 11:2 of the tribe of B, had a dream.
Ps 68:27 There is B, the least of them, in the
80:2 forth before Ephraim and B and Manasseh!
Jer 1:1 in the land of B,
6:1 safety, O people of B, from the midst of
17:19 and stand in the B Gate, by which the
17:26 from the land of B, from the Shephelah, from
20:2 were in the upper B Gate of the house
32:8 in the land of B, for the right of
32:44 in the land of B, in the places about
33:13 in the land of B, the places about Jerusalem,
37:12 to the land of B to receive his portion
37:13 he was at the B Gate, a sentry there
38:7 was sitting in the B Gate--
Ezek 48:22 the territory of Judah and the territory of B
48:23 side to the west, B, one portion.
48:24 Adjoining the territory of B, from the east side
48:32 Joseph, the gate of B, and the gate of
Hos 5:8 Sound the alarm at Beth-aven; tremble, O B
Obad 1:19 land of Samaria and B shall possess Gilead.
Zech 14:10 from the Gate of B to the place of
2Mac 3:4 of the tribe of B, who had been made
Acts 13:21 of the tribe of B, for forty years.
Rom 11:1 of Abraham, a member of the tribe of B
Phil 3:5 of the tribe of B, a Hebrew born of
Rev 7:8 twelve thousand sealed out of the tribe of B

BENJAMINITE (9)

Judg 3:15 son of Gera, the B, a left-handed man.
1Sam 9:1 son of Aphiah, a B, a man of wealth;
9:21 "Am I not a B, from the least of
2Sam 16:11 my life; how much more now may this B
19:16 son of Gera, the B, from Bahurim, made haste
20:1 son of Bichri, a B; and he blew the
1Kgs 2:8 son of Gera, the B from Bahurim, who cursed
1Chr 27:12 Abi-ezer of Anathoth, a B; in his division were
Esth 2:5 son of Kish, a B,

BENJAMINITES (29)

Judg 19:16 in Gibe-ah; the men of the place were B
20:3 (Now the B heard that the people of Israel
20:13 But the B would not listen to the voice
20:14 And the B came together out of the cities
20:15 And the B mustered out of their cities on
20:18 shall go up first to battle against the B
20:21 The B came out of Gibe-ah, and felled to
20:23 draw near to battle against our brethren the B
20:24 came near against the B the second day.
20:28 against our brethren the B, or shall we cease?"
20:30 went up against the B on the third day,
20:31 And the B went out against the people, and
20:32 And the B said, "They are routed before us,
20:34 was hard; but the B did not know that
20:36 So the B saw that they were defeated.
20:40 column of smoke, the B looked behind them; and
20:43 Cutting down the B, they pursued them and trod
20:48 turned back against the B, and smote them with
21:13 sent word to the B who were at the
21:20 And they commanded the B, saying, "Go and lie
21:23 And the B did so, and took their wives,
1Sam 22:7 him, "Hear now, you B; will the son of
2Sam 2:25 the B gathered themselves together behind Abner,
23:29 of Gibe-ah of the B,
1Chr 8:40 All these were B
9:7 Of the B: Sallu the son of Meshullam, son
11:31 of Gibe-ah of the B, Benaiah of Pirathon,
12:2 left hand; they were B, Saul's kinsmen.
12:29 Of the B, the kinsmen of Saul, three thousand,

BENO (2)

1Chr 24:26 The sons of Ja-aziah: B
24:27 of Merari: of Ja-aziah, B, Shoham, Zaccur, and Ibri.

BENT (17)

Ps 7:12 his sword; he has B and strung his bow;
Eccl 12:3 the strong men are B, and the grinders cease
Is 5:28 sharp, all their bows B, their horses' hoofs seem
21:15 drawn sword, from the B bow, and from the
Lam 2:4 He has B his bow like an enemy, with
3:12 made me desolate; he B his bow and set
Bar 2:18 distressed, that goes about B over and feeble, and
Ezek 17:7 and behold, this vine B its roots toward him,
22:6 his power, have been B on shedding blood.
Dan 11:27 their minds shall be B on mischief; they shall
Hos 11:4 their jaws, and I B down to them and
11:7 My people are B on turning away from me;
Zech 9:13 For I have B Judah as my bow; I
Lk 13:11 eighteen years; she was B over and could not
Jn 8:6 Jesus B down and wrote with his finger on
8:8 And once more he B down and wrote with
Acts 20:10 Paul went down and B over him, and embracing

BEON

Num 32:3 Elealeh, Sebam, Nebo, and B,

B

BEOR (11)
Gen 36:32 Bela the son of B reigned in Edom, the
Num 22:5 Balaam the son of B at Pethor, which is
24:3 Balaam the son of B, the oracle of the
24:15 Balaam the son of B, the oracle of the
31:8 Balaam the son of B with the sword.
Deut 23:4 Balaam the son of B from Pethor of Mesopotamia,
Josh 13:22 also, the son of B, the soothsayer, the people
24:9 Balaam the son of B to curse you,
1Chr 1:43 Bela the son of B, the name of whose
Mic 6:5 Balaam the son of B answered him, and what
2Pet 2:15 Balaam, the son of B, who loved gain from

BEQUEATH
Lev 25:46 You may B them to your sons after you,

BERA
Gen 14:2 kings made war with B king of Sodom, Birsha

BERACAH (3)
1Chr 12:3 the sons of Azmaveth; B, Jehu of Anathoth,
2Chr 20:26 in the Valley of B, for there they blessed
20:26 called the Valley of B to this day.

BERAIAH
1Chr 8:21 Eli-enai, Zillethai, Eliel, Adaiah, B, and Shimrath

BEREA
1Mac 9:4 off and went to B with twenty thousand foot

BEREAVE (5)
Deut 32:25 open the sword shall B, and in the chambers
Ezek 36:12 you shall no longer B them of children.
36:13 devour men, and you B your nation of children,'
36:14 men and no longer B your nation of children,
Hos 9:12 up children, I will B them till none is

BEREAVED (9)
Gen 42:36 to them, "You have B me of my children:
43:14 If I am B of my children, I am
43:14 I am bereaved of my children, I am B
Song 4:2 bear twins, and not one among them is B
6:6 them bear twins, not one among them is B
Is 49:21 I was B and barren, exiled and put away,
Jer 15:7 the land; I have B them, I have destroyed
Bar 4:12 me, a widow and B of many; I was
4:16 widow's beloved sons, and B the lonely woman of

BEREAVEMENT (2)
Wis 14:15 grief at an untimely B, made an image of
Is 49:20 the time of your B will yet say in

BEREAVES
Lam 1:20 the street the sword B; in the house it

BERECHIAH (11)
1Chr 3:20 and Hashubah, Ohel, B, Hasadiah, and Jushab-hesed,
6:39 Asaph the son of B, son of Shimea,
9:16 son of Jeduthun, and B the son of Asa,
15:17 Asaph the son of B; and of the sons
15:23 B and Elkanah were to be gatekeepers for the
2Chr 28:12 the son of Johanan, B the son of Meshillemoth,
Neh 3:4 Meshullam the son of B, son of Meshezabel
3:30 Meshullam the son of B repaired opposite his
6:18 Meshullam the son of B as his wife.
Zech 1:1 Zechariah the son of B, son of Iddo, the
1:7 Zechariah the son of B, son of Iddo, the

BERED (2)
Gen 16:14 called Beer-lahai-roi; it lies between Kadesh and B
1Chr 7:20 of Ephraim: Shuthelah, and B his son, Tahath his

BEREFT (5)
Gen 27:45 Why should I be B of you both in
Ruth 1:5 that the woman was B of her two sons
Lam 3:17 ashes; my soul is B of peace, I have
1Thes 2:17 But since we were B of you, brethren, for
1Tim 6:5 depraved in mind and B of the truth, imagining

BERI
1Chr 7:36 Zophah: Suah, Harnepher, Shual, B, Imrah,

BERIAH (11)
Gen 46:17 Asher: Imnah, Ishvah, Ishvi, B, with Serah their
46:17 And the sons of B: Heber and Malchi-el
Num 26:44 of the Ishvites; of B, the family of the
26:45 Of the sons of B: of Heber, the family
1Chr 7:23 he called his name B, because evil had befallen
7:30 Asher: Imnah, Ishvah, Ishvi, B, and their sister
7:31 The sons of B: Heber and Malchi-el, who was
8:13 with its towns, and B and Shema (they were
8:16 Eder, Michael, Ishpah, and Joha were sons of B
23:10 sons of Shimei: Jahath, Zina, and Jeush, and B
23:11 second; but Jeush and B had not many sons,

BERIITES
Num 26:44 the Ishvites; of Beriah, the family of the B

BERNICE (3)
Acts 25:13 Agrippa the king and B arrived at Caesarea to
25:23 the morrow Agrippa and B came with great pomp,
26:30 and the governor and B and those who were

BEROEA (4)
2Mac 13:4 to take him to B and to put him
Acts 17:10 away by night to B; and when they arrived
17:13 proclaimed by Paul at B also, they came there
20:4 Sopater of B, the son of Pyrrhus, accompanied him;

BEROTHAH
Ezek 47:16 and on to Zedad, B, Sibraim (which lies on

BEROTHAI
2Sam 8:8 from Betah and from B, cities of Hadadezer, King

BERRIES
Is 17:6 two or three B in the top of

BERYL (6)
Ex 28:20 the fourth row a B, an onyx, and a
39:13 the fourth row, a B, an onyx, and a
Tob 13:17 will be paved with B and ruby and stones
Ezek 28:13 topaz, and jasper, chrysolite, B, and onyx, sapphire,
Dan 10:6 His body was like B, his face like the
Rev 21:20 seventh chrysolite, the eighth B, the ninth topaz, the

BESAI (2)
Ezra 2:49 Paseah, the sons of B,
Neh 7:52 Paseah, the sons of B, the sons of Me-unim,

BESEECH (22)
Num 12:13 her, O God, I B thee."
1Sam 23:11 God of Israel, I B thee, tell thy servant."
2Kgs 19:19 God, save us, I B thee, from his hand,
20:3 now, O LORD, I B thee, how I have
Esth 4:8 B the Lord and speak to the king concerning
Job 19:16 no answer; I must B him with my mouth.
Ps 116:4 LORD: "O LORD, I B thee, save my life!"
118:25 Save us, we B thee, O LORD!
118:25 O LORD, we B thee, give us success!
Is 38:3 now, O LORD, I B thee, how I have
Amos 7:2 Lord GOD, forgive, I B thee!
7:5 Lord GOD, cease, I B thee!
Jon 1:14 to the LORD, "We B thee, O LORD, let
4:3 life from me, I B thee, for it is
2Mac 7:28 I B you, my child, to look at the
9:26 I therefore urge and B you to remember the
Lk 8:28 I B you, do not torment me."
2Cor 5:20 We B you on behalf of Christ, be reconciled
Gal 4:12 Brethren, I B you, become as I am, for
1Thes 4:1 Finally, brethren, we B and exhort you in the
5:12 But we B you, brethren, to respect those who
1Pet 2:11 Beloved, I B you as aliens and exiles to

BESEECHING (5)
2Mac 10:16 making solemn supplication and B God to fight on
12:42 they turned to prayer, B that the sin which
Mt 8:5 came forward to him, B him
Mk 1:40 leper came to him B him, and kneeling said
Acts 16:9 of Macedonia was standing B him and saying,

BESEIGED
1Mac 11:61 So he B it and burned its suburbs with

BESET (7)
Judg 19:22 the city, base fellows, B the house round about,
20:5 rose against me, and B the house round about
Ps 31:21 me when I was B as in a besieged
109:3 They B me with words of hate, and attack
139:5 Thou dost B me behind and before, and layest
Wis 17:14 really powerless, and which B them from the
Heb 5:2 since he himself is B with weakness.

BESIEGE (10)
Deut 20:12 you, then you shall B it;
20:19 "When you B a city for a long time,
28:52 They shall B you in all your towns, until
28:52 land; and they shall B you in all your
1Sam 23:8 down to Keilah, to B David and his men.
2Chr 6:28 caterpillar; if their enemies B them in any of
Is 29:3 round about, and will B you with towers and
1Mac 6:19 all the people to B them.
2Mac 10:19 a force sufficient to B them; and he himself
12:21 place was hard to B and difficult of access

BESIEGED (25)
Deut 20:19 that they should be B by you?
1Sam 11:1 Ammonite went up and B Jabesh-gilead; and all the
2Sam 11:1 ravaged the Ammonites, and B Rabbah.
20:15 with Joab came and B him in Abel of
1Kgs 16:17 with him, and they B Tirzah.
20:1 he went up and B Samaria, and fought against
2Kgs 6:24 and went up, and B Samaria.
6:25 in Samaria, as they B it, until an ass's
16:5 on Jerusalem, and they B Ahaz but could not
17:5 for three years he B it.
18:9 up against Samaria and B it
24:10 came up to Jerusalem, and the city was B
25:2 So the city was B till the eleventh year
1Chr 20:1 Ammonites, and came and B Rabbah.
Ps 31:21 beset as in a B city.
Eccl 9:14 came against it and B it, building great siegeworks
Is 1:8 cucumber field, like a B city.
Jer 39:1 came against Jerusalem and B it;
52:5 So the city was B till the eleventh year
Lam 3:5 my bones; he has B and enveloped me with
Dan 1:1 came to Jerusalem and B it.
1Mac 6:20 They gathered together and B the citadel in the
6:24 sons of our people B the citadel and became
15:25 Antiochus the king B Dor anew, continually throwing
2Mac 10:33 were glad, and they B the fort for four

BESIEGERS
Jer 4:16 coming; announce to Jerusalem, B come from a

BESIEGES
1Kgs 8:37 caterpillar; if their enemy B them in any of

BESIEGING (9)
2Sam 11:16 And as Joab was B the city, he assigned
2Kgs 24:11 while his servants were B it;
2Chr 32:9 of Assyria, who was B Lachish with all his
Jer 21:4 the Chaldeans who are B you outside the walls;
21:9 the Chaldeans who are B you shall live and
32:2 king of Babylon was B Jerusalem, and Jeremiah the
37:5 the Chaldeans who were B Jerusalem heard news of
1Mac 11:21 him that Jonathan was B the citadel.
2Mac 11:6 word that Lysias was B the strongholds, they and

BESMEAR
Ps 119:69 The godless B me with lies, but with my

BESODEIAH
Neh 3:6 Meshullam the son of B repaired the Old Gate;

BESOR (3)
1Sam 30:9 came to the brook B, where those stayed who
30:10 who were too exhausted to cross the brook B
30:21 left at the brook B; and they went out

BESOUGHT (33)
Gen 42:21 his soul, when he B us and we would
Ex 32:11 But Moses B the LORD his God, and said,
Deut 3:23 for you.' "And I B the LORD at that
2Sam 12:16 David therefore B God for the child; and David
2Kgs 13:4 Then Jehoahaz B the LORD, and the LORD
Ezra 8:23 So we fasted and B our God for this,
Esth 8:3 at his feet and B him with tears to
Wis 8:21 to the Lord and B him, and with my
Sir 50:19 And the people B the Lord Most High in
Dan 2:16 Daniel went in and B the king to appoint
2Mac 1:8 We B the Lord and we were heard, and
8:2 They B the Lord to look upon the people
8:14 at the same time B the Lord to rescue
8:29 made common supplication and B the merciful Lord
10:4 they fell prostrate and B the Lord that they
10:26 before the altar, they B him to be gracious
11:6 with lamentations and tears, B the Lord to send
12:11 The defeated nomads B Judas to grant them pledges
12:24 With great guile he B them to let him
13:12 same petition and had B the merciful Lord with
Mt 14:36 that were sick, and B him that they might
18:28 servant fell down and B him, 'Have patience with
18:31 that debt because you B me;
Mk 5:23 at his feet, and B him, saying, "My little
6:56 the market places, and B him that they might
7:31 his speech; and they B him to lay his
Lk 4:38 high fever, and they B him for her.
5:12 on his face and B him, "Lord, if you
7:4 came to Jesus, they B him earnestly, saying, "He
8:41 at Jesus' feet he B him to come to
Jn 4:31 Meanwhile the disciples B him, saying, "Rabbi, eat."
Acts 16:15 with her household, she B us, saying, "If you
2Cor 12:8 Three times I B the Lord about this, that

BEST (51)
Gen 27:15 Then Rebekah took the B garments of Esau her
45:18 will give you the B of the land of
45:20 your goods, for the B of all the land
47:6 your brothers in the B of the land; let
47:11 of Egypt, in the B of the land, in
Ex 22:5 make restitution from the B in his own field
Num 18:12 All the B of the oil, and all the
18:12 oil, and all the B of the wine and
18:29 LORD, from all the B of them, giving the
18:30 offered from it the B of it, then the
18:32 you have offered the B of it.
36:6 marry whom they think B; only, they shall marry
Deut 23:16 where it pleases him B; you shall not oppress
33:16 everlasting hills, with the B gifts of the earth
33:21 He chose the B of the land for himself,
Judg 14:20 who had been his B man.
Ruth 3:3 and put on your B clothes and go down
1Sam 1:23 her, "Do what seems B to you, wait until
8:14 He will take the B of your fields and
8:16 and maidservants, and the B of your cattle and
15:9 spared Agag, and the B of the sheep and
15:15 the people spared the B of the sheep and
15:21 sheep and oxen, the B of the things devoted
2Sam 18:4 to them, "Whatever seems B to you I will
2Kgs 10:3 and weapons, select the B and fittest of your
Tob 7:12 merciful God will guide you both for the B
Esth 2:9 her maids to the B place in the harem.
Song 7:9 your kisses like the B wine that goes down
Sir 11:3 her product is the B of sweet things.
36:24 a wife gets his B possession, a helper fit
Ezek 27:22 for your wares the B of all kinds of
31:16 Eden, the choice and B of Lebanon, all that
Mic 7:4 The B of them is like a brier, the
1Mac 4:45 And they thought it B to tear it down,
8:7 surrender some of their B provinces,
2Mac 4:19 the money, however, thought B not to use it
13:26 public platform, made the B possible defense,
14:30 not spring from the B motives.
15:38 mediocre, that was the B I could do.
Mt 23:6 at feasts and the B seats in the synagogues,
Mk 12:39 market places and the B seats in the synagogues
Lk 11:43 for you love the B seat in the synagogues
15:22 servants, 'Bring quickly the B robe, and put it
20:46 market places and the B seats in the synagogues
Acts 15:37 But Paul thought B not to take with them
2Cor 8:10 my advice: it is B for you now to
2Tim 2:15 Do your B to present yourself to God as
4:9 Do your B to come to me soon.
4:21 Do your B to come before winter.
Tit 3:12 to you, do your B to come to me
3:13 Do your B to speed Zenas the lawyer and

BESTIR (4)
2Sam 5:24 the balsam trees, then B yourself; for then the
Ps 35:23 B thyself, and awake for my right, for my
Ezek 38:14 dwelling securely, you will B yourself
Joel 3:12 Let the nations B themselves, and come up to

BESTIRS
Is 64:7 upon thy name, that B himself to take hold

BESTOW (4)
Ex 32:29 brother, that he may B a blessing upon you
Ps 21:5 and majesty thou dost B upon him.
Prov 4:10 fair garland; she will B on you a beautiful
1Mac 15:9 our kingdom, we will B great honor upon you

BESTOWED (12)
1Sam 2:32 prosperity which shall be B upon Israel; and there

1Chr 29:25 of all Israel, and B upon him such royal
Esth 6:3 or dignity has been B on Mordecai for this?"
Wis 14:21 or to royal authority, B on objects of stone
Sir 17:9 He B knowledge upon them, and allotted to them
47:6 the glorious diadem was B upon him.
Ezek 16:14 splendor which I had B upon you, says the
23:7 She B her harlotries upon them, the choicest men
Lk 7:21 that were blind he B sight.
1Cor 2:12 might understand the gifts B on us by God.
Eph 1:6 grace which he freely B on us in the
Phil 2:9 highly exalted him and B on him the name

BESTOWER
Is 23:8 this against Tyre, the B of crowns, whose merchants

BESTOWING
1Pet 3:7 considerately with your wives, B honor on the

BESTOWS (2)
Ps 84:11 sun and shield; he B favor and honor.
Rom 10:12 Lord of all and B his riches upon all

BESTRIDE
Hab 3:12 Thou didst B the earth in fury, thou didst

BETAH
2Sam 8:8 And from B and from Berothai, cities of Hadadezer,

BETEN
Josh 19:25 territory included Helkath, Hali, B, Achshaph,

BETH-ANATH (3)
Josh 19:38 En-hazor, Yiron, Migdal-el, Horem, B, and
Judg 1:33 or the inhabitants of B, but dwelt among the
1:33 of Beth-shemesh and of B became subject to forced

BETH-ANOTH
Josh 15:59 Halhul, Bethzur, Gedor, Maarath, B, and Eltekon: six

BETH-ARABAH (4)
Josh 15:6 passes along north of B; and the boundary goes
15:61 In the wilderness, B, Middin, Secacah,
18:18 of the shoulder of B it goes down to
18:22 Jericho, Beth-hoglah, Emek-keziz, B, Zemaraim,

BETH-ARBEL
Hos 10:14 destroyed, as Shalman destroyed B on the day of

BETH-ASHBEA
1Chr 4:21 of linen workers at B;

BETH-AVEN (7)
Josh 7:2 Ai, which is near B, east of Bethel, and
18:12 westward; and it ends at the wilderness of B
1Sam 13:5 and encamped in Michmash, to the east of B
14:23 Israel that day; and the battle passed beyond B
Hos 4:15 nor go up to B, and swear not, "As
5:8 Sound the alarm at B; tremble, O Benjamin!
10:5 inhabitants of Samaria tremble for the calf of B

BETH-AZMAVETH
Neh 7:28 The men of B, forty-two.

BETH-BAAL-MEON
Josh 13:17 Dibon, and Bamoth-baal, and B,

BETH-BARAH (2)
Judg 7:24 them, as far as B, and also the Jordan."
7:24 waters as far as B, and also the Jordan.

BETH-BIRI
1Chr 4:31 Hormah, Ziklag, Beth-marcaboth, Hazar-susim, B,

BETH-CAR
1Sam 7:11 Philistines, and smote them, as far as below B

BETH-DAGON (3)
Josh 15:41 Cabbon, Lahmam, Chitlish, Gederoth, B, Naamah,
19:27 eastward, it goes to B, and touches Zebulun and
1Mac 10:83 to Azotus and entered B, the temple of their

BETH-DIBLATHAIM
Jer 48:22 Dibon, and Nebo, and B,

BETH-EDEN
Amos 1:5 holds the scepter from B; and the people of

BETH-EKED (2)
2Kgs 10:12 when he was at B of the Shepherds,
10:14 at the pit of B, forty-two persons, and he

BETH-EMEK
Josh 19:27 of Iphtahel northward to B and Neiel; then it

BETH-EZEL
Mic 1:11 forth; the wailing of B shall take away from

BETH-GADER
1Chr 2:51 father of Bethelem, and Hareph the father of B

BETH-GAMUL
Jer 48:23 Beth-diblathaim, and Kiriathaim, and B, and

BETH-GILGAL
Neh 12:29 the Netophathites; also from B and from the region

BETH-HACCHEREM (2)
Neh 3:14 of the district of B, repaired the Dung Gate;
Jer 6:1 raise a signal on B; for evil looms out

BETH-HAGGAN
2Kgs 9:27 saw this, he fled in the direction of B

BETH-HARAM
Josh 13:27 and in the valley B, Beth-nimrah, Succoth, and

BETH-HARAN
Num 32:36 Jazer, Jogbehah, Beth-nimrah and B, fortified cities,

BETH-HOGLAH (3)
Josh 15:6 boundary goes up to B, and passes along north
18:19 of the shoulder of B; and the boundary ends
18:21 their families were Jericho, B, Emek-keziz,

BETH-HORON (20)
Josh 10:10 of the ascent of B, and smote them as
10:11 down the ascent of B, the LORD threw down
16:3 the territory of Lower B, then to Gezer, and
16:5 as far as Upper B,
18:13 upon the mountain that lies south of Lower B
18:14 to the south, opposite B, and it ends at
21:22 with its pasture lands, B with its pasture lands--
1Sam 13:18 another company turned toward B, and another
1Kgs 9:17 rebuilt Gezer) and Lower B
1Chr 6:68 with its pasture lands, B with its pasture lands,
7:24 both Lower and Upper B, and Uzzen-sheerah.
2Chr 8:5 He also built Upper B and Lower Beth-horon,
8:5 Upper Beth-horon and Lower B, fortified cities with,
25:13 Judah, from Samaria to B, and killed three thousand
Jud 4:4 and to Kona and B and Belmain and Jericho
Sir 46:6 at the descent of B he destroyed those who
1Mac 3:16 approached the ascent of B, Judas went out to
3:24 down the descent of B to the plain; eight
7:39 Jerusalem and encamped in B, and the Syrian army
9:50 Jericho, and Emmaus, and B, and Bethel, and

BETH-JESHIMOTH (4)
Num 33:49 by the Jordan from B as far as Abel-shittim
Josh 12:3 in the direction of B, to the sea of
13:20 slopes of Pisgah, and B,
Ezek 25:9 glory of the country, B, Baal-meon, and Kiriathaim.

BETH-LE-APHRAH
Mic 1:10 not at all; in B roll yourselves in the

BETH-LEBAOTH
Josh 19:6 Ziklag, Beth-marcaboth, Hazar-susah, B, and

BETH-MAACAH (2)
2Sam 20:14 Israel to Abel of B; and all the Bichrites
20:15 him in Abel of B; they cast up a

BETH-MARCABOTH (2)
Josh 19:5 Eltolad, Bethul, Hormah, Ziklag, B, Hazar-susah,
1Chr 4:31 Bethuel, Hormah, Ziklag, B, Hazar-susim, Beth-biri,

BETH-MEON
Jer 48:23 Kiriathaim, and Beth-gamul, and B,

BETH-MILLO (3)
Judg 9:6 came together, and all B, and they went and
9:20 citizens of Shechem, and B; and let fire come
9:20 of Shechem, and from B, and devour Abimelech."

B

BETH-NIMRAH (2)
Num 32:36 Atroth-shophan, Jazer, Jogbehah, B and Beth-haran,
Josh 13:27 in the valley Beth-haram, B, Succoth, and Zaphon,

BETH-PAZZEZ
Josh 19:21 Ebez, Remeth, En-gannim, En-haddah, B;

BETH-PELET (2)
Josh 15:27 Shema, Moladah, Hazar-gaddah, Heshmon, B,
Neh 11:26 and in Moladah and B,

BETH-PEOR (4)
Deut 3:29 see.' So we remained in the valley opposite B
4:46 in the valley opposite B, in the land of
34:6 land of Moab opposite B; but no man knows
Josh 13:20 of the valley, and B, and the slopes of

BETH-REHOB (2)
Judg 18:28 It was in the valley which belongs to B
2Sam 10:6 hired the Syrians of B, and the Syrians of

BETH-SAIDA (7)
Mt 11:21 woe to you, B
Mk 6:45 the other side, to B, while he dismissed the
8:22 And they came to B
Lk 9:10 them and withdrew apart to a city called B
10:13 woe to you, B
Jn 1:44 Now Philip was from B, the city of Andrew
12:21 Philip, who was from B in Galilee, and said

BETH-SHAN (6)
1Sam 31:10 they fastened his body to the wall of B
31:12 from the wall of B; and they came to
2Sam 21:12 the public square of B, where the Philistines had
1Mac 5:52 crossed the Jordan into the large plain before B
12:40 him, and he marched forth and came to B
12:41 thousand picked fighting men, and he came to B

BETH-SHEAN (6)
Josh 17:11 in Asher Manasseh had B and its villages, and
17:16 iron, both those in B and its villages and
Judg 1:27 out the inhabitants of B and its villages, or
1Kgs 4:12 Taanach, Megiddo, and all B which is beside
4:12 below Jezreel, and from B to Abel-meholah, as far
1Chr 7:29 borders of the Manassites, B and its towns, Taanach

BETH-SHEMESH (22)
Josh 15:10 and goes down to B, and passes along by
19:22 touches Tabor, Shahazumah, and B, and its boundary
19:38 Migdal-el, Horem, Beth-anath, and B -- nineteen
21:16 with its pasture lands, B with its pasture lands--
Judg 1:33 out the inhabitants of B, or the inhabitants of
1:33 nevertheless the inhabitants of B and of Beth-anath
1Sam 6:9 its own land, to B, then it is he
6:12 in the direction of B along one highway, lowing
6:12 after them as far as the border of B
6:13 Now the people of B were reaping their wheat
6:14 field of Joshua of B, and stopped there.
6:15 and the men of B offered burnt offerings and
6:18 this day in the field of Joshua of B
6:19 of the men of B, because they looked into
6:20 Then the men of B said, "Who is able
1Kgs 4:9 Ben-deker, in Makaz, Sha-albim, B, and
2Kgs 14:11 another in battle at B, which belongs to Judah.
14:13 son of Ahaziah, at B, and came to Jerusalem,
1Chr 6:59 its pasture lands, and B with its pasture lands;
2Chr 25:21 another in battle at B, which belongs to Judah.
25:23 son of Ahaziah, at B, and brought him to
28:18 Judah, and had taken B, Aijalon, Gederoth, Soco

BETH-SHITTAH
Judg 7:22 fled as far as B toward Zererah, as far

BETH-TAPPUAH
Josh 15:53 Arab, Dumah, Eshan, Janim, B, Aphekah,

BETH-TOGARMAH (2)
Ezek 27:14 B exchanged for your wares horses, war horses, and
38:6 and all his hordes; B from the uttermost parts

BETH-ZAITH
1Mac 7:19 departed from Jerusalem and encamped in B

BETH-ZATHA
Jn 5:2 pool, in Hebrew called B, which has five porticoes.

BETH-ZECHARIAH (2)
1Mac 6:32 citadel and encamped at B, opposite the camp of
6:33 along the road to B, and his troops made

BETHANY (13)
Jud 1:9 far as Jerusalem and B and Chelous and Kadesh
Mt 21:17 of the city to B and lodged there.
26:6 when Jesus was at B in the house of
Mk 11:1 Jerusalem, to Bethphage and B, at the Mount of
11:11 he went out to B with the twelve.
11:12 when they came from B, he was hungry.
14:3 while he was at B in the house of
Lk 19:29 near to Bethphage and B, at the mount that
24:50 out as far as B, and lifting up his
Jn 1:28 This took place in B beyond the Jordan, where
11:1 was ill, Lazarus of B, the village of Mary
11:18 B was near Jerusalem, about two miles off,
12:1 Passover, Jesus came to B, where Lazarus was,

BETHBASI (2)
1Mac 9:62 and Simon, withdrew to B in the wilderness; he
9:64 came and encamped against B; he fought against it

BETHEL (73)
Gen 12:8 on the east of B, and pitched his tent,
12:8 pitched his tent, with B on the west and
13:3 Negeb as far as B, to the place where
13:3 at the beginning, between B and Ai,
28:19 name of that place B; but the name of
31:13 am the God of B, where you anointed a
35:1 "Arise, go up to B, and dwell there; and
35:3 and go up to B, that I may make
35:6 to Luz (that is, B, which is in the
35:8 under an oak below B; so the name of
35:15 the place where God had spoken with him, B
35:16 Then they journeyed from B; and when they were
Josh 7:2 near Beth-aven, east of B, and said to them,
8:9 ambush, and lay between B and Ai, to the
8:12 them in ambush between B and Ai, to the
8:17 left in Ai or B, who did not go
12:9 Ai, which is beside B, one;
12:16 one; the king of B, one;
16:1 the hill country to B;
16:2 Bethel; then going from B to Luz, it passes
18:13 Luz (the same is B, then the boundary goes
18:22 Emek-keziz, Beth-arabah, Zemaraim, B,
Judg 1:22 also went up against B; and the LORD was
1:23 the house of Joseph sent to spy out B
4:5 Deborah between Ramah and B in the hill country
20:18 and went up to B, and inquired of God,
20:26 up and came to B and wept; they sat
20:31 which goes up to B and the other to
21:2 the people came to B, and sat there till
21:19 which is north of B, on the east of
21:19 that goes up from B to Shechem, and south
1Sam 7:16 year by year to B, Gilgal, and Mizpah; and
10:3 up to God at B will meet you there,
13:2 the hill country of B, and a thousand were
30:27 was for those in B, in Ramoth of the
1Kgs 12:29 he set one in B, and the other he
12:30 to the one at B and to the other
12:32 so he did in B, sacrificing to the calves
12:32 And he placed in B the priests of the
12:33 he had made in B on the fifteenth day
13:1 Judah by the word of the LORD to B
13:4 against the altar at B, Jeroboam stretched out his
13:10 return by the way that he came to B
13:11 Now there dwelt an old prophet in B
13:11 done that day in B; the words also which
13:32 against the altar in B, and against all the
16:34 his days Hiel of B built Jericho; he laid
2Kgs 2:2 the LORD has sent me as far as B
2:2 So they went down to B
2:3 prophets who were in B came out to Elisha,
2:23 up from there to B; and while he was
10:29 calves that were in B, and in Dan.
17:28 came and dwelt in B, and taught them how
23:4 of the Kidron, and carried their ashes to B
23:15 Moreover the altar at B, the high place erected
23:17 which you have done against the altar at B
23:19 according to all that he had done at B
1Chr 7:28 possessions and settlements were B and its towns,
2Chr 13:19 took cities from him, B with its villages and
Ezra 2:28 The men of B and Ai, two hundred and
Neh 7:32 The men of B and Ai, a hundred and
11:31 onward, at Michmash, Aija, B and its villages,

Jer	48:13	Israel was ashamed of B, their confidence.
Hos	12:4	He met God at B, and there God spoke
Amos	3:14	punish the altars of B, and the horns of
	4:4	"Come to B, and transgress; to Gilgal, and multiply
	5:5	but do not seek B, and do not enter
	5:5	go into exile, and B shall come to nought."
	5:6	to quench it for B,
	7:10	Amaziah the priest of B sent to Jeroboam king
	7:13	never again prophesy at B, for it is the
Zech	7:2	Now the people of B had sent Sharezer and
1Mac	9:50	Emmaus, and Beth-horon, and B, and Timnath, and

BETHELEM

1Chr	2:51	Salma, the father of B, and Hareph the father

BETHLEHEM (48)

Gen	35:19	to Ephrath (that is, B,
	48:7	there on the way to Ephrath (that is, B
Josh	19:15	Nahalal, Shimron, Idalah, and B --twelve cities with
Judg	12:8	After him Ibzan of B judged Israel.
	12:10	Then Ibzan died, and was buried at B
	17:7	a young man of B in Judah, of the
	17:8	from the town of B in Judah, to live
	17:9	am a Levite of B in Judah, and I
	19:1	himself a concubine from B in Judah.
	19:2	her father's house at B in Judah, and was
	19:18	"We are passing from B in Judah to the
	19:18	I went to B in Judah; and I am
Ruth	1:1	a certain man of B in Judah went to
	1:2	they were Ephrathites from B in Judah.
	1:19	of them went on until they came to B
	1:19	when they came to B, the whole town was
	1:22	And they came to B at the beginning of
	2:4	behold, Boaz came from B; and he said to
	4:11	and be renowned in B;
1Sam	16:4	did what the LORD commanded, and came to B
	17:12	of an Ephrathite of B in Judah, named Jesse,
	17:15	from Saul to feed his father's sheep at B
	20:6	me to run to B his city; for there
	20:28	me to go to B;
2Sam	2:32	the tomb of his father, which was at B
	23:14	the garrison of the Philistines was then at B
	23:15	from the well of B which is by the
	23:16	of the well of B which was by the
	23:24	son of Dodo of B,
1Chr	2:54	The sons of Salma: B, the Netophathites,
	4:4	Hur, the first-born of Ephrathah, the father of B
	11:16	the garrison of the Philistines was then at B
	11:17	from the well of B which is by the
	11:18	of the well of B which was by the
	11:26	son of Dodo of B,
2Chr	11:6	He built B, Etam, Tekoa,
Ezra	2:21	The sons of B, one hundred and twenty-three.
Neh	7:26	The men of B and Netophah, a hundred and
Jer	41:17	at Geruth Chimham near B, intending to go to
Mic	5:2	But you, O B Ephrathah, who are little to
Mt	2:1	Jesus was born in B of Judea in the
	2:5	They told him, "In B of Judea; for so
	2:6	prophet: 'And you, O B, in the land of
	2:8	he sent them to B, saying, "Go and search
	2:16	the male children in B and in all that
Lk	2:4	David, which is called B, because he was of
	2:15	us go over to B and see this thing
Jn	7:42	David, and comes from B, the village where David

BETHLEHEMITE (4)

1Sam	16:1	you to Jesse the B, for I have provided
	16:18	son of Jesse the B, who is skilful in
	17:58	am the son of your servant Jesse the B
2Sam	21:19	son of Jaareoregim, the B, slew Goliath the Gittite,

BETHPHAGE (3)

Mt	21:1	Jerusalem and came to B, to the Mount of
Mk	11:1	near to Jerusalem, to B and Bethany, at the
Lk	19:29	he drew near to B and Bethany, at the

BETHRAPHA

1Chr	4:12	was the father of B, Paseah, and Tehinnah the

BETHUEL (10)

Gen	22:22	of Aram, Chesed, Hazo, Pildash, Jidlaph, and B
	22:23	B became the father of Rebekah.
	24:15	who was born to B the son of Milcah,
	24:24	am the daughter of B the son of Milcah,
	24:47	said, The daughter of B, Nahor's son, whom Milcah
	24:50	Then Laban and B answered, "The thing comes from
	25:20	Rebekah, the daughter of B the Aramean of,
	28:2	to the house of B your mother's father; and
	28:5	Laban, the son of B the Aramean, the brother
1Chr	4:30	Bilhah, Ezem, Tolad, B, Hormah, Ziklag,

BETHUL

Josh	19:4	Hazar-shual, Balah, Ezem, Eltolad, B, Hormah,

BETHULIA (20)

Jud	4:6	to the people of B and Betomesthaim, which faces
	6:10	and take him to B and hand him over
	6:11	hill country and came to the springs below B
	6:14	and brought him into B and placed him before
	7:1	camp and move against B, and to seize the
	7:3	in the valley near B, beside the spring, and
	7:3	and in length from B to Cyamon, which faces
	7:6	of the Israelites in B,
	7:13	all the people of B get their water.
	7:20	to every inhabitant of B were empty;
	8:3	bed and died in B his city.
	8:11	"Listen to me, rulers of the people of B
	10:6	the city gate of B, and found Uzziah standing
	11:9	for the men of B spared him and he
	12:7	to the valley of B, and bathed at the
	13:10	up the mountain to B and came to its
	15:3	in the hills around B also took to flight.
	15:6	of the people of B fell upon the Assyrian
	16:21	and Judith went to B, and remained on her
	16:23	She died in B, and they buried her in

BETHZUR (19)

Josh	15:58	Halhul, B, Gedor,
1Chr	2:45	Shammai: Maon; and Maon was the father of B
2Chr	11:7	built Bethlehem, Etam, Tekoa, B, Soco, Adullam,
Neh	3:16	half the district of B, repaired to a point
1Mac	4:29	Idumea and encamped at B, and Judas met them
	4:61	He also fortified B, so that the people might
	6:7	as before, and also B, his city.
	6:26	both the sanctuary and B;
	6:31	Idumea and encamped against B, and for many days
	6:49	with the men of B, and they evacuated the
	6:50	So the king took B and stationed a guard
	9:52	fortified the city of B, and Gazara, and the
	10:14	Only in B did some remain who had forsaken
	11:65	Simon encamped before B and fought against it for
	14:7	ruled over Gazara and B and the citadel, and
	14:33	cities of Judea, and B on the borders of
2Mac	11:5	Invading Judea, he approached B, which was a
	13:19	He advanced against B, a strong fortress of the
	13:22	with the people in B, gave pledges, received theirs,

BETOMASTHAIM

Jud	15:4	Uzziah sent men to B and Bebai and Choba

BETOMESTHAIM

Jud	4:6	people of Bethulia and B, which faces Esdraelon

BETONIM

Josh	13:26	Heshbon to Ramath-mizpeh and B, and from

BETOOK (2)

2Mac	4:5	So he B himself to the king, not accusing
	9:29	son of Antiochus, he B himself to Ptolemy

BETRAY (20)

1Chr	12:17	you; but if to B me to my adversaries,
Sir	27:17	him; but if you B his secrets, do not
Is	16:3	noon; hide the outcasts, B not the fugitive;
Mt	24:10	will fall away, and B one another, and hate
	26:16	sought an opportunity to B him.
	26:21	one of you will B me."
	26:23	dish with me, will B me.
Mk	14:10	priests in order to B him to them.
	14:11	sought an opportunity to B him.
	14:18	one of you will B me, one who is
Lk	22:4	officers how he might B him to them.
	22:6	sought an opportunity to B him to them in
	22:46	him, "Judas, would you B the Son of man
Jn	6:64	it was that would B him.
	6:71	the twelve, was to B him.
	12:4	(he who was to B him), said,
	13:2	Iscariot, Simon's son, to B him,
	13:11	knew who was to B him; that was why
	13:21	one of you will B me."
	21:20	that is going to B you?"

BETRAYED (14)

Sir 27:21 abuse, but whoever has B secrets is without hope.
2Mac 6:11 seventh day secretly, were B to Philip and were
Mt 10:4 and Judas Iscariot, who B him.
26:24 man by whom the Son of man is B
26:25 Judas, who B him, said, "Is it I, Master?"
26:45 Son of man is B into the hands of
Mk 3:19 and Judas Iscariot, who B him.
14:21 man by whom the Son of man is B
14:41 Son of man is B into the hands of
Lk 22:22 woe to that man by whom he is B
Jn 18:2 Now Judas, who B him, also knew the place;
18:5 Judas, who B him, was standing with them.
Acts 7:52 whom you have now B and murdered,
1Cor 11:23 night when he was B took bread,

BETRAYER (6)

Prov 14:25 lives, but one who utters lies is a B
Mt 26:46 be going; see, my B is at hand."
26:48 Now the B had given them a sign, saying,
27:3 When Judas, his B, saw that he was condemned,
Mk 14:42 be going; see, my B is at hand."
14:44 Now the B had given them a sign, saying,

BETRAYING

Mt 27:4 "I have sinned in B innocent blood." They said,

BETRAYS (5)

Sir 14:7 does it unintentionally, and B his baseness in the
27:16 Whoever B secrets destroys confidence, and he will
Nah 3:4 of deadly charms, who B nations with her harlotries,
Mt 26:73 them, for your accent B you."
Lk 22:21 hand of him who B me is with me

BETROTH (4)

Deut 28:30 You shall B a wife, and another man shall
Hos 2:19 And I will B you to me for ever;
2:19 for ever; I will B you to me in
2:20 I will B you to me in faithfulness; and

BETROTHED (16)

Ex 22:16 virgin who is not B, and lies with her,
Lev 19:20 who is a slave, B to another man and
Deut 20:7 is there that has B a wife and has
22:23 "If there is a B virgin, and a man
22:25 young woman who is B, and the man seizes
22:27 country, and though the B young woman cried for
22:28 virgin who is not B, and seizes her and
2Sam 3:14 wife Michal, whom I B at the price of
1Mac 3:56 building houses, or were B, or were planting
Mt 1:18 mother Mary had been B to Joseph, before they
Lk 1:27 Nazareth, to a virgin B to a man whose
2:5 enrolled with Mary, his B, who was with child.
1Cor 7:36 behaving properly toward his B, if his passions are
7:37 keep her as his B, he will do well.
7:38 he who marries his B does well; and he
2Cor 11:2 for you, for I B you to Christ to

BETTER (165)

Gen 29:19 Laban said, "It is B that I give her
Ex 14:12 it would have been B for us to serve
Num 14:3 would it not be B for us to go
Judg 8:2 the grapes of Ephraim B than the vintage of
9:2 of Shechem, 'Which is B for you, that all
11:25 Now are you any B than Balak the son
18:19 Is it B for you to be priest to
1Sam 14:30 How much B if the people had eaten freely
15:22 Behold, to obey is B than sacrifice, and to
15:28 of yours, who is B than you.
27:1 Saul; there is nothing B for me than that
2Sam 14:32 It would be B for me to be there
17:14 Hushai the Archite is B than the counsel of
18:3 us; therefore it is B that you send us
1Kgs 2:32 men more righteous and B than himself, Abner the
19:4 for I am no B than my fathers."
21:2 will give you a B vineyard for it; or,
2Kgs 5:12 the rivers of Damascus, B than all the waters
2Chr 21:13 father's house, who were B than yourself;
Tob 3:6 For it is B for me to die than
12:8 little with righteousness is B than much with
12:8 It is B to give alms than to treasure
Jud 7:28 For it would be B for us to be
10:19 man of them had B be left alive, for
Esth 1:19 to another who is B than she.
Job 35:3 How am I B off than if I had
Ps 37:16 B is a little that the righteous has than
63:3 thy steadfast love is B than life, my lips
84:10 in thy courts is B than a thousand elsewhere.
118:8 It is B to take refuge in the LORD
118:9 It is B to take refuge in the LORD
119:72 of thy mouth is B to me than thousands
Prov 3:14 gain from it is B than gain from silver
3:14 silver and its profit B than gold.
8:11 gold; for wisdom is B than jewels, and all
8:19 My fruit is B than gold, even fine gold,
12:9 B is a man of humble standing who works
15:16 B is a little with the fear of the
15:17 B is a dinner of herbs where love is
16:8 B is a little with righteousness than great revenues
16:16 To get wisdom is B than gold; to get
16:19 It is B to be of a lowly spirit
16:32 slow to anger is B than the mighty, and
17:1 B is a dry morsel with quiet than a
19:1 B is a poor man who walks in his
19:22 a poor man is B than a liar.
21:9 It is B to live in a corner of
21:19 It is B to live in a desert land
22:1 riches, and favor is B than silver or gold.
25:7 great; for it is B to be told, "Come
25:24 It is B to live in a corner of
27:5 B is open rebuke than hidden love.
27:10 B is a neighbor who is near than a
28:6 B is a poor man who walks in his
Eccl 2:24 There is nothing B for a man than that
3:12 that there is nothing B for them than to
3:22 that there is nothing B than that a man
4:3 are still alive; but B than both is he
4:6 B is a handful of quietness than two hands
4:9 Two are B than one, because they have a
4:13 B is a poor and wise youth than an
5:1 near to listen is B than to offer the
5:5 It is B that you should not vow than
6:3 an untimely birth is B off than he.
6:9 B is the sight of the eyes than the
6:11 the more vanity, and what is man the B
7:1 A good name is B than precious ointment; and
7:2 It is B to go to the house of
7:3 Sorrow is B than laughter, for by sadness of
7:5 It is B for a man to hear the
7:8 B is the end of a thing than its
7:8 patient in spirit is B than the proud in
7:10 were the former days B than these?" For it
9:4 a living dog is B than a dead lion.
9:16 say that wisdom is B than might, though the
9:17 heard in quiet are B than the shouting of
9:18 Wisdom is B than weapons of war, but one
Song 1:2 For your love is B than wine,
4:10 how much B is your love than wine, and
Wis 4:1 B than this is childlessness with virtue, for in
13:3 them know how much B than these is their
15:17 dead, for he is B than the objects he
Sir 10:26 B is a man who works and has an
16:3 multitude; for one is B than a thousand, and
16:3 to die childless is B than to have ungodly
18:15 So a word is B than a gift.
19:21 B is the God-fearing man who lacks intelligence,
20:2 How much B it is to reprove than to
20:17 on the pavement is B than a slip of
20:30 B is the man who hides his folly than
23:27 recognize that nothing is B than the fear of
29:22 B is the life of a poor man under
30:14 B off is a poor man who is well
30:15 Health and soundness are B than all gold, and
30:16 There is no wealth B than health of body,
30:17 Death is B than a miserable life, and eternal
33:7 Why is any day B than another, when all
33:21 For it is B that your children should ask
36:18 yet one food is B than another.
36:21 but one daughter is B than another.
37:14 soul sometimes keeps him B informed than seven
40:18 who finds treasure is B off than both.
40:19 blameless wife is accounted B than both.
40:20 love of wisdom is B than both.
40:21 a pleasant voice is B than both.
40:23 with her husband is B than both.
40:24 trouble, but almsgiving rescues B than both.
40:26 of the Lord is B than both.
40:27 and covers a man B than any glory.
40:28 a beggar; it is B to die than to
41:15 B is the man who hides his folly than
42:14 B is the wickedness of a man than a
Is 56:5 monument and a name B than sons and daughters;

Bar 6:59 So it is B to be a king who
6:59 be these false gods; B even the door of
6:59 than these false gods; B also a wooden pillar
6:68 The wild beasts are B than they are, for
6:73 B therefore is a just man who has no
Dan 1:15 seen that they were B in appearance and fatter
1:20 found them ten times B than all the magicians
Hos 2:7 husband, for it was B with me then than
Amos 6:2 Are they B than these kingdoms?
Jon 4:3 thee, for it is B for me to die
4:8 and said, "It is B for me to die
Nah 3:8 Are you B than Thebes that sat by the
1Mac 3:59 It is B for us to die in battle
10:11 with squared stones, for B fortification; and they did
13:5 for I am not B than my brothers.
Mt 5:29 it away; it is B that you lose one
5:30 it away; it is B that you lose one
18:6 sin, it would be B for him to have
18:8 it away; it is B for you to enter
18:9 it away; it is B for you to enter
26:24 It would have been B for that man if
Mk 5:26 had, and was no B but rather grew worse.
9:42 sin, it would be B for him if a
9:43 it off; it is B for you to enter
9:44 it off; it is B for you to enter
9:45 it out; it is B for you to enter
14:21 It would have been B for that man if
Lk 17:2 It would be B for him if a millstone
Rom 3:9 Are we Jews any B off?
14:5 esteems one day as B than another, while another
1Cor 7:9 For it is B to marry than to be
7:38 and he who refrains from marriage will do B
8:8 not eat, and no B off if we do.
11:17 is not for the B but for the worse.
2Cor 11:23 I am a B one--I am talking like
12:16 say, and got the B of you by guile.
Gal 4:1 a child, is no B than a slave, though
Phil 1:23 and be with Christ, for that is far B
2:3 in humility count others B than yourselves.
1Tim 6:2 must serve all the B since those who benefit
Heb 6:9 we feel sure of B things that belong to
7:19 the other hand, a B hope is introduced, through
7:22 the surety of a B covenant.
8:6 covenant he mediates is B, since it is enacted
8:6 it is enacted on B promises.
9:23 heavenly things themselves with B sacrifices than
10:34 you yourselves had a B possession and an abiding
11:16 is, they desire a B country, that is, a
11:35 rise again to a B life.
11:40 God had foreseen something B for us, that apart
1Pet 3:17 For it is B to suffer for doing right,
2Pet 2:21 it would have been B for them never to

BETWEEN (245)

Gen 3:15 I will put enmity B you and the woman,
3:15 and the woman, and B your seed and her
9:12 covenant which I make B me and you and
9:13 sign of the covenant B me and the earth.
9:15 my covenant which is B me and you and
9:16 remember the everlasting covenant B God and every
9:17 which I have established B me and all flesh
10:12 Rehoboth-Ir, Calah, and Resen B Nineveh and Calah;
13:3 been at the beginning, B Bethel and Ai,
13:7 and there was strife B the herdsmen of Abram's
13:8 there be no strife B you and me, and
13:8 you and me, and B your herdsmen and my
15:17 a flaming torch passed B these pieces.
16:5 May the LORD judge B you and me!"
16:14 called Beer-lahai-roi; it lies B Kadesh and Bered.
17:2 will make my covenant B me and you, and
17:7 will establish my covenant B me and you and
17:10 which you shall keep, B me and you and
17:11 sign of the covenant B me and you.
20:1 the Negeb, and dwelt B Kadesh and Shur; and
23:15 silver, what is that B you and me?
26:28 there be an oath B you and us, and
30:36 of three days' journey B himself and Jacob; and
31:37 that they may decide B us two.
31:44 it be a witness B you and me."
31:48 heap is a witness B you and me today."
31:49 said, "The LORD watch B you and me, when
31:50 remember, God is witness B you and me."
31:51 which I have set B you and me.
31:53 of their father, judge B us." So Jacob swore
32:16 and put a space B drove and drove."
42:23 there was an interpreter B them.
49:10 the ruler's staff from B his feet, until he
49:14 a strong ass, crouching B the sheepfolds;
Ex 8:23 will put a division B my people and your
9:4 will make a distinction B the cattle of Israel
11:7 LORD makes a distinction B the Egyptians and
13:9 and as a memorial B your eyes, that the
13:16 your hand or frontlets B your eyes; for by
14:2 in front of Pi-ha-hiroth, B Migdol and the sea,
14:20 stood behind them, coming B the host of Egypt
16:1 of Sin, which is B Elim and Sinai, on
18:16 me and I decide B a man and his
22:11 the LORD shall be B them both to see
25:22 the mercy seat, from B the two cherubim that
28:33 with bells of gold B them,
30:18 you shall put it B the tent of meeting
31:13 this is a sign B me and you throughout
31:17 a sign for ever B me and the people
39:25 and put the bells B the pomegranates upon the
39:25 the robe round about, B the pomegranates;
Lev 10:10 You are to distinguish B the holy and the
10:10 and the common, and B the unclean and the
11:47 to make a distinction B the unclean and the
11:47 and the clean and B the living creature that
20:25 therefore make a distinction B the clean beast and
20:25 and the unclean, and B the unclean bird and
26:46 which the LORD made B him and the people
Num 7:89 of the testimony, from B the two cherubim; and
11:33 the meat was yet B their teeth, before it
13:23 it on a pole B two of them; they
16:48 And he stood B the dead and the living;
21:13 the boundary of Moab, B Moab and the Amorites.
22:24 in a narrow path B the vineyards, with a
26:56 divided according to lot B the larger and the
30:16 LORD commanded Moses, as B a man and his
30:16 and his wife, and B a father and his
31:27 booty into two parts, B the warriors who went
35:24 the congregation shall judge B the manslayer and
Deut 1:1 Arabah over against Suph, B Paran and Tophel,
1:16 time, 'Hear the cases B your brethren, and judge
1:16 brethren, and judge righteously B a man and his
5:5 fire, while I stood B the LORD and you
6:8 shall be as frontlets B your eyes.
11:18 shall be as frontlets B your eyes.
17:8 case arises requiring decision B one kind of homicide
25:1 there is a dispute B men, and they come
25:1 and the judges decide B them, acquitting the
28:57 that comes out from B her feet and her
33:12 and makes his dwelling B his shoulders."
Josh 3:4 shall be a space B you and it, a
8:9 of ambush, and lay B Bethel and Ai, to
8:11 Ai, with a ravine B them and Ai.
8:12 set them in ambush B Bethel and Ai, to
18:11 allotted to it fell B the tribe of Judah
22:25 the Jordan a boundary B us and you, you
22:27 to be a witness B us and you, and
22:27 us and you, and B the generations after us,
22:28 to be a witness B us and you.'
22:34 "it is a witness B us that the LORD
24:7 LORD, he put darkness B you and the Egyptians,
Judg 4:5 the palm of Deborah B Ramah and Bethel in
4:17 for there was peace B Jabin the king of
9:23 sent an evil spirit B Abimelech and the men
11:10 LORD will be witness B us; we will surely
11:27 Judge, decide this day B the people of Israel
13:25 stir him in Mahaneh-dan, B Zorah and Eshtaol.
15:4 and put a torch B each pair of tails.
16:25 They made him stand B the pillars;
16:31 up and buried him B Zorah and Eshtaol in
20:38 Now the appointed signal B the men of Israel
1Sam 7:12 and set it up B Mizpah and Jeshanah, and
7:14 There was peace also B Israel and the Amorites.
14:42 said, "Cast the lot B me and my son
17:1 to Judah, and encamped B Socoh and Azekah, in
17:3 side, with a valley B them.
17:6 javelin of bronze slung B his shoulders.
20:3 is but a step B me and death."
20:23 behold, the LORD is B you and me for
20:42 'The LORD shall be B me and you, and
20:42 me and you, and B my descendants and your
24:12 May the LORD judge B me and you, may
24:15 judge, and give sentence B me and you, and
26:13 with a great space B them;
2Sam 3:1 was a long war B the house of Saul
3:6 While there was war B the house of Saul
18:9 he was left hanging B heaven and earth, while
18:24 Now David was sitting B the two gates; and

B

21:4 of silver or gold B us and Saul or
21:7 the LORD which was B them, between David and
21:7 which was between them, B David and Jonathan the
1Kgs 3:9 that I may discern B good and evil; for
5:12 and there was peace B Hiram and Solomon; and
7:46 in the clay ground B Succoth and Zarethan.
14:30 And there was war B Rehoboam and Jeroboam
15:6 Now there was war B Rehoboam and Jeroboam all
15:7 And there was war B Abijam and Jeroboam.
15:16 And there was war B Asa and Baasha king
15:19 there be a league B me and you, as
15:19 me and you, as B my father and your
15:32 And there was war B Asa and Baasha king
18:6 they divided the land B them to pass through
18:42 and put his face B his knees.
22:34 the king of Israel B the scale armor and
2Kgs 9:24 strength, and shot Joram B the shoulders, so that
11:15 army, "Bring her out B the ranks; and slay
11:17 Jehoiada made a covenant B the LORD and the
11:17 LORD's people; and also B the king and the
16:14 house, from the place B his altar and the
25:4 way of the gate B the two walls, by
1Chr 21:16 of the LORD standing B earth and heaven, and
2Chr 4:17 in the clay ground B Succoth and Zeredah.
12:15 were continual wars B Rehoboam and Jeroboam.
13:2 Now there was war B Abijah and Jeroboam.
14:11 like thee to help, B the mighty and the
16:3 there be a league B me and you, as
16:3 me and you, as B my father and your
18:33 the king of Israel B the scale armor and
23:14 them, "Bring her out B the ranks; any one
23:16 Jehoiada made a covenant B himself and all the
Neh 3:32 And B the upper chamber of the corner and
Jud 3:10 Judea; here he camped B Geba and Scythopolis, and
7:25 elders, "God be judge B you and us!
8:3 fathers in the field B Dothan and Balamon.
8:11 and pronounced this oath B God and you, promising
Job 4:20 B morning and evening they are destroyed; they
9:33 There is no umpire B us, who might lay
26:10 waters at the boundary B light and darkness.
41:16 no air can come B them.
Ps 68:25 the minstrels last, B them maidens playing timbrels:
104:10 the valleys; they flow B the hills,
Prov 18:18 to disputes and decides B powerful contenders.
Song 1:13 of myrrh, that lies B my breasts.
Sir 13:17 What peace is there B a hyena and a
13:17 And what peace B a rich man and a
25:1 of men; agreement B brothers, friendship between
25:1 between brothers, friendship B neighbors, and a wife
27:2 firmly into a fissure B stones, so sin is
27:2 sin is wedged in B selling and buying.
Is 2:4 He shall judge B the nations, and shall decide
5:3 judge, I pray you, B me and my vineyard.
22:11 You made a reservoir B the two walls for
59:2 have made a separation B you and your God,
Jer 34:18 in two and passed B its parts--
34:19 the land who passed B the parts of the
38:12 the rags and clothes B your armpits and the
39:4 garden through the gate B the two walls; and
52:7 way of a gate B the two walls, by
Bar 6:54 they are like crows B heaven and earth.
Ezek 4:3 as an iron wall B you and the city;
8:3 Spirit lifted me up B earth and heaven, and
8:16 temple of the LORD, B the porch and the
10:2 with burning coals from B the cherubim, and scatter
10:6 linen, "Take fire from B the whirling wheels, from
10:6 the whirling wheels, from B the cherubim," he went
10:7 forth his hand from B the cherubim to the
10:7 the fire that was B the cherubim, and took
18:8 iniquity, executes true justice B man and man,
20:12 sabbaths, as a sign B me and them, that
20:20 may be a sign B me and you, that
22:26 have made no distinction B the holy and the
22:26 they taught the difference B the unclean and the
34:17 GOD: Behold, I judge B sheep and sheep, rams
34:20 I myself will judge B the fat sheep and
34:22 and I will judge B sheep and sheep.
40:7 broad; and the space B the side rooms, five
41:9 B the platform of the temple and the
41:18 trees, a palm tree B cherub and cherub.
42:20 to make a separation B the holy and the
43:8 with only a wall B me and them.
44:23 my people the difference B the holy and the
44:23 them how to distinguish B the unclean and the
47:16 lies on the border B Damascus and Hamath), as
47:18 shall run from Hazar-enon B Hauran and Damascus;
47:18 Damascus; along the Jordan B Gilead and the land
48:22 the prince shall lie B the territory of Judah
Dan 7:5 ribs in its mouth B its teeth; and it
8:5 had a conspicuous horn B his eyes.
8:16 heard a man's voice B the banks of the
8:21 and the great horn B his eyes is the
11:45 pitch his palatial tents B the sea and the
Hos 2:2 and her adultery from B her breasts;
Joel 2:17 B the vestibule and the altar let the priests,
Mic 4:3 He shall judge B many peoples, and shall decide
Zech 5:9 lifted up the ephah B earth and heaven.
6:1 chariots came out from B two mountains; and the
6:13 peaceful understanding shall be B them both."'
9:7 and its abominations from B its teeth; it too
11:14 Union, annulling the brotherhood B Judah and Israel.
Mal 2:14 witness to the covenant B you and the wife
3:18 more you shall distinguish B the righteous and the
3:18 righteous and the wicked, B one who serves God
1Mac 3:18 there is no difference B saving by many or
7:28 there be no fighting B me and you; I
12:36 erect a high barrier B the citadel and the
13:40 let there be peace B us."
16:5 and a stream lay B them.
Mt 18:14 tell him his fault, B you and him alone.
23:34 Barachiah, whom you murdered B the sanctuary and
Lk 11:51 of Zechariah, who perished B the altar and the
15:12 he divided his living B them.
16:26 And besides all this, B us and you a
17:11 he was passing along B Samaria and Galilee.
Jn 3:25 Now a discussion arose B John's disciples and a
19:18 either side, and Jesus B them.
Acts 12:6 out, Peter was sleeping B two soldiers, bound with
15:9 he made no distinction B us and them, but
23:7 this, a dissension arose B the Pharisees and the
Rom 10:12 there is no distinction B Jew and Greek; the
14:22 that you have, keep B yourself and God; happy
1Cor 6:5 enough to decide B members of the brotherhood,
12:10 the ability to distinguish B spirits, to another various
Phil 1:23 I am hard-pressed B the two.
1Tim 2:5 there is one mediator B God and men, the
Rev 5:6 And B the throne and the four living creatures

BEVELED

1Kgs 7:29 there were wreaths of B work.

BEWAIL (3)

Lev 10:6 house of Israel, may B the burning which the
Deut 21:13 in your house and B her father and her
Judg 11:37 on the mountains, and B my virginity, I and

BEWAILED (3)

Judg 11:38 and her companions, and B her virginity upon the
1Mac 13:26 All Israel B him with great lamentation, and
Lk 23:26 and of women who B and lamented him.

BEWAILING

Lk 8:52 all were weeping and B her; but he said,

BEWARE (34)

Deut 4:16 midst of the fire, B lest you act corruptly
4:19 And B lest you lift up your eyes to
8:17 B lest you say in your heart, 'My power
29:18 B lest there be among you a man or
Judg 13:4 Therefore B, and drink no wine or strong drink,
13:13 that I said to the woman let her B
2Kgs 6:9 the king of Israel, B that you do not
Tob 4:12 B, my son, of all immorality.
Job 32:13 B lest you say, 'We have found wisdom; God
36:18 B lest wrath entice you into scoffing; and let
Prov 1:7 B of the Path of Greed and Violence
Eccl 12:12 My son, B of anything beyond these.
Wis 1:11 B then of useless murmuring, and keep your tongue
Sir 4:20 the right time, and B of evil; and do
11:31 B of a scoundrel, for he devises evil, lest
17:12 he said to them, B of all unrighteousness." And
22:24 hears of it will B of him.
28:26 B lest you err with your tongue, lest you
Is 36:18 B lest Hezekiah mislead you by saying, "The LORD
Jer 9:4 Let every one B of his neighbor, and put
Mt 6:1 B of practicing your piety before men in order
7:15 B of false prophets, who come to you in
10:17 B of men; for they will deliver you up
16:6 them, "Take heed and B of the leaven of
16:11 B of the leaven of the Pharisees and Sadducees."
16:12 not tell them to B of the leaven of
Mk 8:15 them, saying, "Take heed, B of the leaven of

12:38 his teaching he said, B of the scribes, who
Lk 12:1 to his disciples first, B of the leaven of
12:15 them, "Take heed, and B of all covetousness; for
20:46 said to his disciples, B of the scribes, who
Acts 13:40 B, therefore, lest there come upon you what is
2Tim 4:15 B of him yourself, for he strongly opposed our
2Pet 3:17 beloved, knowing this beforehand, B lest you be

BEWILDERED

Acts 2:6 together, and they were B, because each one heard

BEWITCHED

Gal 3:1 Who has B you, before whose eyes Jesus Christ

BEYOND (131)

Gen 35:21 and pitched his tent B the tower of Eder.
49:26 your father are mighty B the blessings of the
50:10 of Atad, which is B the Jordan, they lamented
50:11 named Abel-mizraim; it is B the Jordan.
Lev 15:25 she has a discharge B the time of her
Num 22:1 the plains of Moab B the Jordan at Jericho.
22:18 I could not go B the command of the
24:13 be able to go B the word of the
32:19 of the Jordan and B; because our inheritance has
32:32 shall remain with us B the Jordan."
34:15 received their inheritance B the Jordan at Jericho
35:14 shall give three cities B the Jordan, and three
35:26 at any time go B the bounds of his
Deut 1:1 spoke to all Israel B the Jordan in the
1:5 B the Jordan, in the land of Moab, Moses
3:8 the Amorites who were B the Jordan, from the
3:20 your God gives them B the Jordan; then you
3:25 see the good land B the Jordan, that goodly
4:41 cities in the east B the Jordan,
4:46 came out of Egypt, B the Jordan in the
4:47 lived to the east B the Jordan;
11:30 Are they not B the Jordan, west of the
30:13 it?' Neither is it B the sea, that you
Josh 1:14 which Moses gave you B the Jordan; but all
1:15 the LORD gave you B the Jordan toward the
2:10 the Amorites that were B the Jordan, to Sihon
5:1 the Amorites that were B the Jordan to the
7:7 been content to dwell B the Jordan!
9:1 the kings who were B the Jordan in the
9:10 the Amorites who were B the Jordan, Sihon the
12:1 possession of their land B the Jordan toward the
13:8 which Moses gave them, B the Jordan eastward, as
13:27 Sea of Chinnereth, eastward B the Jordan.
13:32 the plains of Moab, B the Jordan east of
14:3 two and one-half tribes B the Jordan; but to
16:6 Taanath-shiloh, and passes along B it on the east
18:7 received their inheritance B the Jordan eastward,
20:8 And B the Jordan east of Jericho, they appointed
24:2 fathers lived of old B the Euphrates, Terah, the
24:3 your father Abraham from B the River and led
24:14 which your fathers served B the River, and in
24:15 served in the region B the River, or the
Judg 3:26 they delayed, and passed B the sculptured stones,
5:17 Gilead stayed B the Jordan; and Dan, why did
7:25 and Zeeb to Gideon B the Jordan.
10:8 of Israel that were B the Jordan in the
1Sam 14:23 and the battle passed B Beth-aven.
20:22 'Look, the arrows are B you,' then go; for
20:36 he shot an arrow B him.
20:37 "Is not the arrow B you?"
31:7 the valley and those B the Jordan saw that
2Sam 10:16 the Syrians who were B the Euphrates; and they
16:1 had passed a little B the summit, Ziba the
20:5 Judah; but he delayed B the set time which
1Kgs 4:29 Solomon wisdom and understanding B measure, and
14:15 fathers, and scatter them B the Euphrates, because
2Kgs 25:16 all these vessels was B weight.
1Chr 6:78 its pasture lands, and B the Jordan at Jericho,
12:37 half-tribe of Manasseh from B the Jordan, one
19:16 the Syrians who were B the Euphrates, with
22:3 as bronze in quantities B weighing,
22:14 and bronze and iron B weighing, for there is
2Chr 20:2 you from Edom, from B the sea; and, behold,
Ezra 4:10 rest of the province B the River, and now
4:11 men of the province B the River, send greeting.
4:16 possession in the province B the River."
4:17 rest of the province B the River, greeting.
4:20 over the whole province B the River, to whom
5:3 of the province B the River and Shethar-bozenai
5:6 of the province B the River and Shethar-bozenai
5:6 were in the province B the River sent to
6:6 of the province B the River, Shethar-bozenai, and
6:6 are in the province B the River, keep away;
6:8 of the province from B the River.
6:13 of the province B the River, Shethar-bozenai, and
7:21 treasurers in the province B the River: Whatever
7:25 people in the province B the River, all such
8:36 governors of the province B the River; and they
Neh 2:7 governors of the province B the River, that they
2:9 governors of the province B the River, and gave
3:7 governor of the province B the River.
Jud 1:9 its surrounding towns, and B the Jordan as far
1:10 land of Goshen, even B Tanis and Memphis, and
15:5 with great slaughter, even B Damascus and its.
Job 9:10 does great things B understanding, and marvelous
Ps 147:5 power; his understanding is B measure.
Prov 6:15 he will be broken B healing.
29:1 will suddenly be broken B healing.
Eccl 12:12 son, beware of anything B these.
Sir 3:20 nor investigate what is B your power.
3:22 meddle in what is B your tasks, for matters
8:13 Do not give surety B your means, but if
13:2 not lift a weight B your strength, nor associate
20:6 braggart and fool goes B the right moment.
Is 5:14 and opened its mouth B measure, and the nobility
7:20 razor which is hired B the River-- with
9:1 the sea, the land B the Jordan, Galilee of
18:1 whirring wings which is B the rivers of Ethiopia;
52:14 appearance was so marred, B human semblance, and
52:14 semblance, and his form B that of the sons
56:12 like this day, great B measure."
Jer 8:18 My grief is B healing, my heart is sick
22:19 dragged and cast forth B the gates of Jerusalem."
52:20 all these things was B weight.
Bar 3:18 anxious, whose labors are B measure?
Ezek 41:4 its breadth, twenty cubits, B the nave.
Amos 5:27 take you into exile B Damascus," says the LORD,
Zeph 3:10 From B the rivers of Ethiopia my suppliants, the
Mal 1:5 "Great is the LORD, B the border of Israel!"
1Mac 7:8 governor of the province B the River; he was
11:60 set forth and traveled B the river and among
Mt 4:25 and Judea and from B the Jordan.
19:1 the region of Judea B the Jordan;
Mk 3:8 and Idumea and from B the Jordan and from
7:36 And they were astonished B measure, saying, "He
10:1 region of Judea and B the Jordan, and crowds
Jn 1:28 took place in Bethany B the Jordan, where John
3:26 who was with you B the Jordan, to whom
Acts 7:43 I will remove you B Babylon.'
Rom 7:13 commandment might become sinful B measure.
1Cor 1:16 B that, I do not know whether I baptized
4:6 us not to go B what is written, that
10:13 let you be tempted B your strength, but with
2Cor 4:17 eternal weight of glory B all comparison,
8:3 I can testify, and B their means, of their
10:13 we will not boast B limit, but will keep
10:15 We do not boast B limit, in other men's
10:16 the gospel in lands B you, without boasting of
Gal 1:14 I advanced in Judaism B many of my own
Heb 1:9 the oil of gladness B thy comrades."
7:7 It is B dispute that the inferior is blessed

BEZAI (3)

Ezra 2:17 The sons of B, three hundred and twenty-three.
Neh 7:23 The sons of B, three hundred and twenty-four.
10:18 Hezekiah, Azzur, Hodiah, Hashum, B,

BEZALEL (9)

Ex 31:2 have called by name B the son of Uri,
35:30 has called by name B the son of Uri,
36:1 B and Oholiab and every able man in whom
36:2 And Moses called B and Oholiab and every able
37:1 B made the ark of acacia wood; two cubits
38:22 B the son of Uri, son of Hur, of
1Chr 2:20 of Uri, and Uri was the father of B
2Chr 1:5 the bronze altar that B the son of Uri,
Ezra 10:30 Benaiah, Ma-aseiah, Mattaniah, B, Binnui, and

BEZEK (3)

Judg 1:4 and they defeated ten thousand of them at B
1:5 came upon Adoni-bezek at B, and fought against him,
1Sam 11:8 he mustered them at B, the men of Israel

BEZER (5)

Deut 4:43 might save his life: B in the wilderness on
Josh 20:8 of Jericho, they appointed B in the wilderness on
21:36 the tribe of Reuben, B with its pasture lands,

1Chr 6:78 the tribe of Reuben: B in the steppe with
7:37 Shual, Beri, Imrah, B, Hod, Shamma, Shilshah,

BICHRI (8)
2Sam 20:1 Sheba, the son of B, a Benjaminite; and he
20:2 Sheba the son of B; but the men of
20:6 Sheba the son of B will do us more
20:7 from Jerusalem to pursue Sheba the son of B
20:10 Abishai his brother pursued Sheba the son of B
20:13 after Joab to pursue Sheba the son of B
20:21 Sheba the son of B, has lifted up his
20:22 Sheba the son of B, and threw it out

BICHRITES
2Sam 20:14 Beth-maacah; and all the B assembled, and followed

BID (17)
Num 15:38 people of Israel, and B them to make tassels
22:20 but only what I B you, that shall you
22:35 the word which I B you, that shall you
Josh 5:14 "What does my lord B his servant?"
6:10 until the day I B you shout; then you
2Sam 2:26 it be before you B your people turn from
2Kgs 9:2 and go in and B him rise from among
10:5 do all that you B us.
Ps 61:7 for ever before God; B steadfast love and faithfulness
Mt 14:28 if it is you, B me come to you
Lk 9:54 you want us to B fire come down from
12:13 said to him, "Teacher, B my brother divide the
Acts 27:22 I now B you take heart; for there will
Rom 12:3 given to me I B every one among you
Tit 2:2 B the older men be temperate, serious, sensible,
2:3 B the older women likewise to be reverent in
2:9 B slaves to be submissive to their masters and

BIDDEN (5)
Josh 4:12 Israel, as Moses had B them;
8:8 as the LORD has B; see, I have commanded
2Sam 16:11 for the LORD has B him.
2Mac 3:35 his life, and having B Onias farewell, he marched
Jn 12:50 as the Father has B me."

BIDDING
Rev 13:14 who dwell on earth, B them make an image

BIDKAR
2Kgs 9:25 Jehu said to B his aide, "Take him up,

BIDS
Job 15:25 hand against God, and B defiance to the Almighty,

BIER (3)
2Sam 3:31 And King David followed the B
2Chr 16:14 laid him on a B which had been filled
Lk 7:14 came and touched the B, and the bearers stood

BIG
Sir 37:11 lazy servant about a B task-- pay no

BIGTHA
Esth 1:10 commanded Mehuman, Biztha, Harbona, B and

BIGTHAN
Esth 2:21 at the king's gate, B and Teresh, two of

BIGTHANA
Esth 6:2 Mordecai had told about B and Teresh, two of

BIGVAI (6)
Ezra 2:2 Re-el-aiah, Mordecai, Bilshan, Mispar, B, Rehum,
2:14 The sons of B, two thousand and fifty-six.
8:14 Of the sons of B, Uthai and Zaccur, and
Neh 7:7 Nahamani, Mordecai, Bilshan, Mispereth, B, Nehum,
7:19 The sons of B, two thousand and sixty-seven.
10:16 Bunni, Azgad, Bebai, Adonijah, B, Adin,

BILDAD (5)
Job 2:11 place, Eliphaz the Temanite, B the Shuhite, and
8:1 Then B the Shuhite answered:
18:1 Then B the Shuhite answered:
25:1 Then B the Shuhite answered:
42:9 Eliphaz the Temanite and B the Shuhite and Zophar

BILE-AM
1Chr 6:70 its pasture lands, and B with its pasture lands,

BILGAH (3)
1Chr 24:14 Jeshebe-ab, the fifteenth to B, the sixteenth to
Neh 12:5 Ginnethoi, Abijah, Mijamin, Ma-adiah, B,
12:18 of Moadiah, Piltai; of B, Shammua; of Shemaiah,

BILGAI
Neh 10:8 Abijah, Mijamin, Ma-aziah, B, Shemaiah; these

BILHAH (11)
Gen 29:29 (Laban gave his maid B to his daughter Rachel
30:3 "Here is my maid B; go in to her,
30:4 gave him her maid B as a wife; and
30:5 And B conceived and bore Jacob a son.
30:7 Rachel's maid B conceived again and bore Jacob a
35:22 went and lay with B his father's concubine; and
35:25 The sons of B, Rachel's maid: Dan and Naphtali.
37:2 with the sons of B and Zilpah, his father's
46:25 are the sons of B, whom Laban gave to
1Chr 4:29 in Beer-sheba, Moladah, Hazar-shual, B, Ezem,
7:13 Jahzi-el, Guni, Jezer, and Shallum, the offspring of B

BILHAN (4)
Gen 36:27 the sons of Ezer: B, Zaavan, and Akan.
1Chr 1:42 The sons of Ezer: B, Zaavan, and Jaakan.
7:10 The sons of Jedia-el: B
7:10 And the sons of B: Jeush, Benjamin, Ehud,

BILL (5)
Deut 24:1 he writes her a B of divorce and puts
24:3 and writes her a B of divorce and puts
Is 50:1 "Where is your mother's B of divorce, with which
Lk 16:6 to him, 'Take your B, and sit down quickly
16:7 to him, 'Take your B, and write eighty.'

BILLOWS (3)
Ps 42:7 thy waves and thy B have gone over me.
Wis 14:5 and passing through the B on a raft they
Jon 2:3 thy waves and thy B passed over me.

BILLOWY
Wis 5:10 that sails through the B water, and when it

BILSHAN (2)
Ezra 2:2 Nehemiah, Seraiah, Re-el-aiah, Mordecai, B, Mispar,
Neh 7:7 Raamiah, Nahamani, Mordecai, B, Mispereth,

BIMHAL
1Chr 7:33 sons of Japhlet: Pasach, B, and Ashvath.

BIND (44)
Ex 28:28 And they shall B the breastpiece by its rings
29:9 them with girdles and B caps on them; and
Num 30:2 swears an oath to B himself by a pledge,
Deut 6:8 And you shall B them as a sign upon
11:18 soul; and you shall B them as a sign
14:25 it into money, and B up the money in
Josh 2:18 the land, you shall B this scarlet cord in
Judg 15:10 have come up to B Samson, to do to
15:12 have come down to B you, that we may
15:13 "No; we will only B you and give you
16:5 him, that we may B him to subdue him;
16:7 to her, "If they B me with seven fresh
16:11 to her, "If they B me with new ropes
Tob 3:17 of Tobit, and to B Asmodeus the evil demon,
Jud 8:16 Do not try to B the purposes of the
Job 31:36 my shoulder; I would B it on me as
38:31 "Can you B the chains of the Pleiades, or
39:10 Can you B him in the furrow with ropes,
40:13 in the dust together; B their faces in the
Ps 118:27 B the festal procession with branches, up to the
149:8 on the peoples, to B their kings with chains
Prov 3:3 and faithfulness forsake you; B them about your
6:21 B them upon your heart always; tie them about
7:3 apple of your eye; B them on your fingers,
Sir 30:7 spoils his son will B up his wounds, and
33:4 you will be heard; B together your instruction, and
Is 8:16 B up the testimony, seal the teaching among my
22:21 your robe, and will B your girdle on him,
49:18 an ornament, you shall B them on as a
61:1 has sent me to B up the brokenhearted, to
Jer 51:63 finish reading this book, B a stone to it,
Ezek 5:3 a small number, and B them in the skirts
24:17 B on your turban, and put your shoes on
34:16 strayed, and I will B up the crippled, and
Dan 3:20 of his army to B Shadrach, Meshach, and Abednego,
Hos 6:1 stricken, and he will B us up.

Mt 13:30 the weeds first and B them in bundles to
16:19 heaven, and whatever you B on earth shall be
18:17 to you, whatever you B on earth shall be
22:13 said to the attendants, B him hand and foot,
23:4 They B heavy burdens, hard to bear, and lay
Mk 5:3 and no one could B him any more, even
Acts 9:14 the chief priests to B all who call upon
21:11 the Jews at Jerusalem B the man who owns

BINDER

Ps 129:7 his hand or the B of sheaves his bosom,

BINDERS

2Chr 34:11 stone, and timber for B and beams for the

BINDING (11)

Gen 37:7 dreamed: behold, we were B sheaves in the field,
49:11 B his foal to the vine and his ass's
Ex 28:32 head, with a woven B around the opening, like
39:23 a garment, with a B around the opening, that
Lev 8:7 band of the ephod, B it to him therewith.
Num 30:13 Any vow and any B oath to afflict herself,
Tob 7:11 until you make a B agreement with me."
Jud 8:3 the men who were B sheaves in the field,
Ezek 30:21 to heal it by B it with a bandage,
Acts 22:4 Way to the death, B and delivering to prison
Rom 7:1 that the law is B on a person only

BINDS (13)

Num 30:3 to the LORD, and B herself by a pledge,
Job 5:18 he wounds, but he B up; he smites, but
12:18 bonds of kings, and B a waistcloth on their
26:8 He B up the waters in his thick clouds,
28:11 He B up the streams so that they do
30:18 seizes my garment; it B me about like the
36:13 for help when he B them.
Ps 147:3 heals the brokenhearted, and B up their wounds.
Prov 26:8 Like one who B the stone in the sling
Is 30:26 day when the LORD B up the hurt of
Mt 12:29 goods, unless he first B the strong man?
Mk 3:27 goods, unless he first B the strong man; then
Col 3:14 put on love, which B everything together in perfect

BINE-A (2)

1Chr 8:37 was the father of B; Raphah was his son,
9:43 was the father of B; and Rephaiah was his

BINNUI (7)

Ezra 8:33 son of Jeshua and No-adiah the son of B
10:30 Benaiah, Ma-aseiah, Mattaniah, Bezalel, B, and
10:38 Of the sons of B: Shimei,
Neh 3:24 After him B the son of Henadad repaired another
7:15 The sons of B, six hundred and forty-eight.
10:9 the son of Azaniah, B of the sons of
12:8 the Levites: Jeshua, B, Kadmi-el, Sherebiah, Judah,

BIRD (46)

Gen 1:21 kinds, and every winged B according to its kind.
1:30 earth, and to every B of the air, and
2:19 the field and every B of the air, and
7:14 its kind, and every B according to its kind,
7:14 to its kind, every B of every sort.
8:19 creeping thing, and every B, everything that moves
8:20 and of every clean B, and offered burnt offerings
9:2 earth, and upon every B of the air, upon
Lev 11:46 pertaining to beast and B and every living creature
14:6 shall take the living B with the cedarwood and
14:6 them and the living B in the blood of
14:6 the blood of the B that was killed over
14:7 shall let the living B go into the open
14:51 along with the living B, and dip them in
14:51 the blood of the B that was killed and
14:52 the blood of the B, and with the running
14:52 and with the living B, and with the cedarwood
14:53 shall let the living B go out of the
17:13 hunting any beast or B that may be eaten
20:25 and between the unclean B and the clean; you
20:25 by beast or by B or by anything with
Deut 4:17 likeness of any winged B that flies in the
22:6 to come upon a B's nest, in any tree
Job 28:7 "That path no B of prey knows, and the
41:5 him as with a B, or will you put
Ps 11:1 me, "Flee like a B to the mountains;
102:7 am like a lonely B on the housetop.
124:7 have escaped as a B from the snare of
Prov 1:17 the sight of any B;
6:5 the hunter, like a B from the hand of
7:23 its entrails; as a B rushes into a snare;
27:8 Like a B that strays from its nest, is
Eccl 10:20 the rich; for a B of the air will
12:4 the voice of a B, and all the daughters
Wis 5:11 or as, when a B flies through the air,
Sir 27:19 as you allow a B to escape from your
Is 46:11 my purpose,' calling a B of prey from the
Jer 12:9 me like a speckled B of prey?
Lam 3:52 been hunted like a B by those who were
Bar 6:71 garden, on which every B sits; or like a
Ezek 44:31 eat of anything, whether B or beast, that has
Dan 7:6 four wings of a B on its back; and
Hos 9:11 fly away like a B—no birth, no pregnancy,
Amos 3:5 Does a B fall in a snare on the
Jas 3:7 kind of beast and B, of reptile and sea
Rev 18:2 every foul and hateful B;

BIRDS (106)

Gen 1:20 living creatures, and let B fly above the earth
1:22 the seas, and let B multiply on the earth."
1:26 sea, and over the B of the air, and
1:28 sea and over the B of the air and
2:20 cattle, and to the B of the air, and
6:7 and creeping things and B of the air, for
6:20 Of the B according to their kinds, and of
7:3 seven pairs of the B of the air also,
7:8 not clean, and of B, and of everything that
7:21 moved upon the earth, B, cattle, beasts, all swarming
7:23 and creeping things and B of the air; they
8:17 you of all flesh— B and animals and every
9:10 is with you, the B, the cattle, and every
15:10 did not cut the B in two.
15:11 And when B of prey came down upon the
40:17 for Pharaoh, but the B were eating it out
40:19 a tree; and the B will eat the flesh
Lev 1:14 a burnt offering of B, then he shall bring
11:13 in abomination among the B, they shall not be
14:4 cleansed two living clean B and cedarwood and
14:5 kill one of the B in an earthen vessel
14:49 shall take two small B, with cedarwood and scarlet
14:50 kill one of the B in an earthen vessel
Deut 14:11 "You may eat all clean B
28:26 be food for all B of the air, and
1Sam 17:44 your flesh to the B of the air and
17:46 this day to the B of the air and
2Sam 21:10 did not allow the B of the air to
1Kgs 4:33 of beasts, and of B, and of reptiles, and
14:11 the open country the B of the air shall
16:4 in the field the B of the air shall
21:24 the open country the B of the air shall
Jud 11:7 the cattle and the B of the air will
Esth 16:24 most hateful for all time to beasts and B
Job 12:7 will teach you; the B of the air, and
28:21 and concealed from the B of the air.
35:11 us wiser than the B of the air?'
Ps 8:8 of the field, the B of the air, and
50:11 I know all the B of the air, and
78:27 them like dust, winged B like the sand of
79:2 thy servants to the B of the air for
104:12 By them the B of the air have their
104:17 In them the B build their nests; the stork
148:10 Beasts and all cattle, creeping things and flying B
Eccl 9:12 evil net, and like B which are caught in
Wis 17:18 a melodious sound of B in wide-spreading branches,
19:11 a new kind of B, when desire led them
Sir 17:4 and granted them dominion over beasts and B
22:18 throws a stone at B scares them away, and
27:9 B flock with their kind; so truth returns to
43:14 are opened, and the clouds fly forth like B
43:17 scatters the snow like B flying down, and its
Is 16:2 Like fluttering B, like scattered nestlings, so are the
18:6 be left to the B of prey of the
18:6 And the B of prey will summer upon them,
31:5 Like B hovering, so the LORD of hosts will
Jer 4:25 man, and all the B of the air had
5:27 a basket full of B, their houses are full
7:33 be food for the B of the air, and
9:10 not heard; both the B of the air and
12:4 the beasts and the B are swept away, because
12:9 Are the B of prey against her round about?
15:3 to tear, and the B of the air and
16:4 be food for the B of the air and
19:7 for food to the B of the air and
34:20 be food for the B of the air and
Bar 3:17 have sport with the B of the air, and

6:22 Bats, swallows, and B light on their bodies and
Ezek 13:20 the souls that you hunt go free like B
17:23 shade of its branches B of every sort will
29:5 earth and to the B of the air I
31:6 All the B of the air made their nests
31:13 will dwell all the B of the air, and
32:4 will cause all the B of the air to
38:20 the sea, and the B of the air, and
39:4 will give you to B of prey of every
39:17 GOD: Speak to the B of every sort and
Dan 2:38 the field, and the B of the air, making
3:81 Bless the Lord, all B of the air, sing
4:12 under it, and the B of the air dwelt
4:14 under it and the B from its branches.
4:21 in whose branches the B of the air dwelt--
4:33 his nails were like B claws.
Hos 2:18 of the field, the B of the air, and
4:3 the field, and the B of the air; and
7:13 bring them down like B of the air; I
11:11 shall come trembling like B from Egypt, and like
Zeph 1:3 will sweep away the B of the air and
2Mac 9:15 the beasts, for the B to pick, he would
15:33 it piecemeal to the B and hang up these
Mt 6:26 Look at the B of the air: they neither
8:20 "Foxes have holes, and B of the air have
13:4 the path, and the B came and devoured them.
13:32 tree, so that the B of the air come
Mk 4:4 the path, and the B came and devoured it.
4:32 branches, so that the B of the air can
Lk 8:5 under foot, and the B of the air devoured
9:58 "Foxes have holes, and B of the air have
12:24 how much more value are you than the B
13:19 a tree, and the B of the air made
Acts 10:12 animals and reptiles and B of the air.
11:6 prey and reptiles and B of the air.
Rom 1:23 resembling mortal man or B or animals or reptiles.
1Cor 15:39 for animals, another for B, and another for fish.
Rev 19:17 called to all the B that fly in midheaven,
19:21 mouth; and all the B were gorged with their

BIRSHA

Gen 14:2 Bera king of Sodom, B king of Gomorrah, Shinab

BIRTH (71)

Gen 5:7 Seth lived after the B of Enosh eight hundred
5:10 Enosh lived after the B of Kenan eight hundred
5:13 Kenan lived after the B of Mahalalel eight hundred
5:16 Mahalalel lived after the B of Jared eight hundred
5:19 Jared lived after the B of Enoch eight hundred
5:22 with God after the B of Methuselah three hundred
5:26 Methuselah lived after the B of Lamech seven
5:30 Lamech lived after the B of Noah five hundred
11:11 Shem lived after the B of Arpachshad five hundred
11:13 Arpachshad lived after the B of Shelah four hundred
11:15 Shelah lived after the B of Eber four hundred
11:17 Eber lived after the B of Peleg four hundred
11:19 Peleg lived after the B of Reu two hundred
11:21 Reu lived after the B of Serug two hundred
11:23 Serug lived after the B of Nahor two hundred
11:25 Nahor lived after the B of Terah a hundred
11:28 the land of his B, in Ur of the
24:7 the land of my B, and who spoke to
25:13 the order of their B: Nebaioth, the first-born of
31:13 land, and return to the land of your B
Ex 28:10 the other stone, in the order of their B
Deut 32:18 and you forgot the God who gave you B
Judg 13:5 Nazirite to God from B; and he shall begin
13:7 Nazirite to God from B to the day of
1Sam 4:19 of Phinehas, was with child, about to give B
4:19 she bowed and gave B; for her pains came
1Kgs 3:17 house; and I gave B to a child while
3:18 this woman also gave B; and we were alone;
2Kgs 19:3 have come to the B, and there is no
Job 3:1 his mouth and cursed the day of his B
3:11 I not die at B, come forth from the
3:16 as a hidden untimely B, as infants that never
38:29 and who has given B to the hoarfrost of
Ps 22:10 I cast from my B, and since my mother
58:3 they err from their B, speaking lies.
58:8 slime, like the untimely B that never sees the
71:6 have leaned from my B; thou art he who
Eccl 6:3 say that an untimely B is better off than
7:1 the day of death, than the day of B
Wis 8:3 She glorifies her noble B by living with God,
Sir 22:3 undisciplined son, and the B of a daughter is
23:14 and you will curse the day of your B
50:22 exalts our days from B, and deals with us
Is 14:19 like a loathed untimely B, clothed with the slain,
23:4 neither travailed nor given B, I have neither reared
37:3 have come to the B, and there is no
46:3 by me from your B, carried from the womb;
48:8 treacherously, and that from B you were called a
66:7 in labor she gave B; before her pain came
66:9 I bring to the B and not cause to
Jer 2:27 stone, 'You gave me B For they have turned
46:16 the land of our B, because of the sword
Ezek 16:3 Your origin and your B are of the land
16:4 And as for your B, on the day you
Dan 9:1 son of Ahasuerus, by B a Mede, who became
Hos 9:11 like a bird--no B, no pregnancy, no conception!
2Mac 5:22 at Jerusalem, Philip, by B a Phrygian and in
14:42 sinners and suffer outrages unworthy of his noble B
Mt 1:18 Now the B of Jesus Christ took place in
19:12 have been so from B, and there are eunuchs
Mk 7:25 the woman was a Greek, a Syrophoenician by B
Lk 1:14 will rejoice at his B;
1:57 delivered, and she gave B to a son.
2:7 And she gave B to her first-born son and
Jn 9:1 by, he saw a man blind from his B
Acts 3:2 a man lame from B was being carried, whom
14:8 was a cripple from B, who had never walked.
1Cor 1:26 many were of noble B;
Gal 2:15 who are Jews by B and not Gentile sinners,
Jas 1:14 it has conceived gives B to sin; and sin
Rev 12:2 in her pangs of B, in anguish for delivery.

BIRTH-PANGS (3)

Sir 7:27 do not forget the B of your mother.
Mt 24:8 all this is but the beginning of the B
Mk 13:8 famines; this is but the beginning of the B

BIRTHDAY (4)

Gen 40:20 day, which was Pharaoh's B, he made a feast
2Mac 6:7 celebration of the king's B, the Jews were taken,
Mt 14:6 when Herod's B came, the daughter of Herodi-as
Mk 6:21 when Herod on his B gave a banquet for

BIRTHRIGHT (10)

Gen 25:31 Jacob said, "First sell me your B
25:32 what use is a B to me?"
25:33 him, and sold his B to Jacob.
25:34 Thus Esau despised his B
27:36 He took away my B; and behold, now he
43:33 first-born according to his B and the youngest
1Chr 5:1 his father's couch, his B was given to the
5:1 genealogy according to the B;
5:2 from him, yet the B belonged to Joseph),
Heb 12:16 Esau, who sold his B for a single meal.

BIRTHSTOOL

Ex 1:15 see them upon the B, if it is a

BIRZAITH

1Chr 7:31 Heber and Malchi-el, who was the father of B

BISHLAM

Ezra 4:7 the days of Artaxerxes, B and Mithredath and Tabeel

BISHOP (3)

1Tim 3:1 to the office of B, he desires a noble
3:2 Now a B must be above reproach, the husband
Tit 1:6 For a B, as God's steward, must be blameless;

BISHOPS

Phil 1:1 at Philippi, with the B and deacons:

BIT (6)

Num 21:6 the people, and they B the people, so that
21:9 and if a serpent B any man, he would
2Kgs 19:28 your nose and my B in your mouth, and
Ps 32:9 must be curbed with B and bridle, else it
Is 37:29 your nose and my B in your mouth, and
Amos 5:19 wall, and a serpent B him.

BITE (5)

Eccl 10:8 and a serpent will B him who breaks through
Sir 21:2 approach sin, it will B you.
Jer 8:17 charmed, and they shall B you," says the LORD.
Amos 9:3 serpent, and it shall B them.
Gal 5:15 But if you B and devour one another take

BITES (5)

Gen 49:17 by the path, that B the horse's heels so
Prov 23:32 At the last it B like a serpent, and
Eccl 10:11 If the serpent B before it is charmed, there
Wis 16:5 being destroyed by the B of writhing serpents, thy
16:9 were killed by the B of locusts and flies,

BITHI-AH

1Chr 4:17 are the sons of B, the daughter of Pharaoh,

BITHYNIA (2)

Acts 16:7 attempted to go into B, but the Spirit of
1Pet 1:1 Galatia, Cappadocia, Asia, and B,

BITS (2)

Amos 6:11 smitten into fragments, and the little house into B
Jas 3:3 If we put B into the mouths of horses

BITTEN (3)

Num 21:8 every one who is B, when he sees it,
Wis 16:11 thy oracles they were B, and then were quickly
Sir 12:13 pity a snake charmer B by a serpent, or

BITTER (52)

Gen 26:35 and they made life B for Isaac and Rebekah.
27:34 an exceedingly great and B cry, and said to
Ex 1:13 and made their lives B with hard service, in
12:8 with unleavened bread and B herbs they shall eat
15:23 Marah because it was B; therefore it was named
Num 5:24 into her and cause B pain.
5:27 into her and cause B pain, and her body
9:11 with unleavened bread and B herbs.
Deut 29:18 root bearing poisonous and B fruit,
32:32 poison, their clusters are B;
Ruth 1:13 for it is exceedingly B to me for your
1Sam 30:6 all the people were B in soul, each for
2Sam 2:26 you not know that the end will be B
2Kgs 4:27 for she is in B distress; and the LORD
14:26 of Israel was very B, for there was none
Esth 4:1 with a loud and B cry;
14:8 that we are in B slavery, but they have
Job 3:20 and life to the B in soul,
13:26 For thou writest B things against me, and makest
23:2 also my complaint is B, his hand is heavy
27:2 has made my soul B;
Ps 64:3 like swords, who aim B words like arrows,
106:33 they made his spirit B, and he spoke words
Prov 5:4 the end she is B as wormwood, sharp as
27:7 who is hungry everything B is sweet.
31:6 wine to those in B distress;
Eccl 7:26 And I found more B than death the woman
Wis 19:13 they practiced a more B hatred of strangers.
Sir 7:11 a man who is B in soul, for there
29:25 this you will hear B words:
38:17 Let your weeping be B and your wailing fervent;
41:1 O death, how B is the reminder of you
Is 5:20 for darkness, who put B for sweet and sweet
5:20 who put bitter for sweet and sweet for B
22:4 me, let me weep B tears; do not labor
24:9 singing; strong drink is B to those who drink
Jer 2:19 it is evil and B for you to forsake
4:18 doom, and it is B; it has reached your
6:26 an only son, most B lamentation; for suddenly the
31:15 in Ramah, lamentation and B weeping.
Ezek 21:6 with breaking heart and B grief before their eyes.
27:31 bitterness of soul, with B mourning.
Hos 12:14 Ephraim has given B provocation; so his LORD will
Amos 8:10 of it like a B day.
Mic 2:4 you, and wail with B lamentation, and say, "We
Hab 1:6 rousing the Chaldeans, that B and hasty nation, who
Zeph 1:14 of the LORD is B, the mighty man cries
2Mac 6:7 Jews were taken, under B constraint, to partake of
Jas 3:14 But if you have B jealousy and selfish ambition
Rev 8:11 died of the water, because it was made B
10:9 eat; it will be B to your stomach, but
10:10 I had eaten it my stomach was made B

BITTERLY (19)

Judg 5:23 of the LORD, curse B its inhabitants, because they
21:2 and they lifted up their voices and wept B
Ruth 1:20 Almighty has dealt very B with me.
1Sam 1:10 distressed and prayed to the LORD, and wept B
2Sam 13:36 king also and all his servants wept very B
2Kgs 20:3 And Hezekiah wept B
Ezra 10:1 him out of Israel; for the people wept B
Sir 22:9 lacks intelligence; weep less B for the dead, for
25:17 among the neighbors, and he cannot help sighing B
Is 33:7 ones cry without; the envoys of peace weep B
38:3 And Hezekiah wept B
Jer 13:17 my eyes will weep B and run down with
22:10 bemoan him; but weep B for him who goes
Lam 1:2 She weeps B in the night, tears on her
1:4 have been dragged away, and she herself suffers B
Ezek 27:30 shore and wail aloud over you, and cry B
Zech 12:10 only child, and weep B over him, as one
Mt 26:75 And he went out and wept B
Lk 22:60 And he went out and wept B

BITTERNESS (27)

Num 5:18 have the water of B that brings the curse.
5:19 from this water of B that brings the curse.
5:23 into the water of B;
5:24 drink the water of B that brings the curse,
1Sam 15:32 Agag said, "Surely the B of death is past."
Job 7:11 will complain in the B of my soul.
9:18 me get my breath, but fills me with B
10:1 will speak in the B of my soul.
21:25 Another dies in B of soul, never having tasted
Prov 14:10 heart knows its own B, and no stranger shares
17:25 to his father and B to her who bore
Wis 8:16 with her has no B, and life with her
Sir 4:6 you; for if in B of soul he calls
21:12 taught, but there is a cleverness which increases B
31:29 drunk to excess is B of soul, with provocation
Is 38:15 fled because of the B of my soul.
38:17 that I had great B; but thou hast held
Lam 1:7 of her affliction and B all the precious things
3:5 and enveloped me with B and tribulation;
3:15 has filled me with B, he has sated me
3:19 my affliction and my B, the wormwood and the
Ezek 3:14 and I went in B in the heat of
27:31 weep over you in B of soul, with bitter
Acts 8:23 in the gall of B and in the bond
Rom 3:14 "Their mouth is full of curses and B
Eph 4:31 Let all B and wrath and anger and clamor
Heb 12:15 the grace of God; that no "root of B

BITUMEN (3)

Gen 11:3 brick for stone, and B for mortar.
14:10 Siddim was full of B pits; and as the
Ex 2:3 and daubed it with B and pitch; and she

BIZIOTHIAH

Josh 15:28 Heshmon, Beth-pelet, Hazar-shual, Beer-sheba, B,

BIZTHA

Esth 1:10 wine, he commanded Mehuman, B, Harbona, Bigtha

BLACK (16)

Gen 30:32 spotted sheep and every B lamb, and the spotted
30:33 among the goats and B among the lambs, if
30:35 every lamb that was B, and put them in
30:40 striped and all the B in the flock of
Lev 13:31 and there is no B hair in it, then
13:37 itch is checked, and B hair has grown in
1Kgs 18:45 while the heavens grew B with clouds and wind,
Job 30:30 My skin turns B and falls from me, and
Song 5:11 his locks are wavy, B as a raven.
Jer 4:28 the heavens above be B; for I have spoken,
Mic 3:6 the day shall be B over them;
Zech 6:2 red horses, the second B horses,
6:6 The chariot with the B horses goes toward the
Mt 5:36 for you cannot make one hair white or B
Rev 6:5 saw, and behold, a B horse, and its rider
6:12 and the sun became B as sackcloth, the full

BLACKENED (2)

Job 30:28 I go about B, but not by the sun;
Bar 6:21 their faces have been B by the smoke of

BLACKER

Lam 4:8 Now their visage is B than soot, they are

BLACKNESS (3)

Job 3:5 upon it; let the B of the day terrify
Is 50:3 clothe the heavens with B, and make sackcloth their
Joel 2:2 Like B there is spread upon the mountains a

BLADE (4)

Judg 3:22 went in after the B, and the fat closed
3:22 fat closed over the B, for he did not
Job 31:22 then let my shoulder B fall from my shoulder,

Mk 4:28 of itself, first the B, then the ear, then

BLAME (8)

Gen 43:9 let me bear the B for ever;
44:32 I shall bear the B in the sight of
Sir 11:29 evil, and to worthy actions he will attach B
41:7 Children will B an ungodly father, for they suffer
1Mac 11:5 had done, to throw B on him; but the
11:11 He threw B on Alexander because he coveted his
2Mac 13:4 this man was to B for all the trouble,
2Cor 8:20 that no one should B us about this liberal

BLAMED

Wis 13:6 are little to be B, for perhaps they go

BLAMELESS (60)

Gen 6:9 was a righteous man, B in his generation; Noah
17:1 am God Almighty; walk before me, and be B
44:10 slave, and the rest of you shall be B
Deut 18:13 You shall be B before the LORD your God.
Judg 15:3 time I shall be B in regard to the
1Sam 29:9 that you are as B in my sight as
2Sam 22:24 I was B before him, and I kept myself
22:26 thyself loyal; with the B man thou dost show
22:26 thou dost show thyself B;
2Chr 15:17 heart of Asa was B all his days.
16:9 those whose heart is B toward him.
25:2 yet not with a B heart.
Esth 16:13 and of Esth, the B partner of our kingdom,
Job 1:1 and that man was B and upright, one who
1:8 on the earth, a B and upright man, who
2:3 on the earth, a B and upright man, who
8:20 will not reject a B man, nor take the
9:20 me; though I am B, he would prove me
9:21 I am B; I regard not myself; I loathe
9:22 he destroys both the B and the wicked.
12:4 me, a just and B man, am a laughingstock.
22:3 gain to him if you make your ways B
Ps 18:23 I was B before him, and I kept myself
18:25 thyself loyal; with the B man thou dost show
18:25 thou dost show thyself B;
19:13 Then I shall be B, and innocent of great
37:18 the days of the B, and their heritage will
37:37 Mark the B man, and behold the upright, for
51:4 in thy sentence and B in thy judgment.
64:4 from ambush at the B, shooting at him suddenly
101:2 will give heed to the way that is B
101:6 the way that is B shall minister to me.
119:1 those whose way is B, who walk in the
119:80 May my heart be B in thy statutes, that
Prov 11:5 The righteousness of the B keeps his way straight,
11:20 LORD, but those of B ways are his delight.
28:10 own pit; but the B will have a goodly
29:10 hate one who is B, and the wicked seek
Wis 2:22 discern the prize for B souls;
4:9 for men, and a B life is ripe old
10:5 man and preserved him B before God, and kept
10:15 A holy people and B race wisdom delivered from
18:21 For a B man was quick to act as
Sir 31:8 man who is found B, and who does not
40:19 man's name, but a B wife is accounted better
Ezek 28:15 You were B in your ways from the day
Dan 6:22 because I was found B before him; and also
1Mac 4:42 He chose B priests devoted to the law,
Lk 1:6 all the commandments and ordinances of the Lord B
Eph 1:4 should be holy and B before him.
Phil 1:10 may be pure and B for the day of
2:15 that you may be B and innocent, children of
3:6 the church, as to righteousness under the law B
Col 1:22 present you holy and B and irreproachable before
1Thes 2:10 holy and righteous and B was our behavior to
5:23 be kept sound and B at the coming of
1Tim 3:10 if they prove themselves B let them serve as
Tit 1:5 if any man is B, the husband of one
1:6 God's steward, must be B; he must not be
Heb 7:26 a high priest, holy, B, unstained, separated from

BLAMELESSLY

Ps 15:2 He who walks B, and does what is right,

BLASPHEME (3)

Acts 26:11 tried to make them B; and in raging fury
1Tim 1:20 to Satan that they may learn not to B
Jas 2:7 it not they who B that honorable name which

BLASPHEMED (6)

Lev 24:11 the Israelite woman's son B the Name, and cursed.
Ezek 20:27 again your fathers B me, by dealing treacherously
Dan 14:9 shall die, because he B against Bel." And Daniel
2Mac 10:34 strength of the place, B terribly and hurled out
Rom 2:24 name of God is B among the Gentiles because
1Tim 1:13 though I formerly B and persecuted and insulted

BLASPHEMER (3)

Wis 1:6 will not free a B from the guilt of
Sir 3:16 father is like a B, and whoever angers his
2Mac 9:28 So the murderer and B, having endured the more

BLASPHEMERS (3)

2Mac 10:36 fires and burned the B alive.
15:24 thy arm may these B who come against thy
Acts 19:37 are neither sacrilegious nor B of our goddess.

BLASPHEMES (4)

Lev 24:16 He who B the name of the LORD shall
24:16 the native, when he B the Name, shall be
Mk 3:29 they utter; but whoever B against the Holy Spirit
Lk 12:10 forgiven; but he who B against the Holy Spirit

BLASPHEMIES (9)

Neh 9:18 and had committed great B,
9:26 them back to thee, and they committed great B
1Mac 2:6 He saw the B being committed in Judah and
7:38 the sword; remember their B, and let them live
2Mac 8:4 innocent babies and the B committed against his
10:35 anger because of the B, bravely stormed the wall
Mk 3:28 of men, and whatever B they utter;
Lk 5:21 to question, saying, "Who is this that speaks B
Rev 13:6 its mouth to utter B against God, blaspheming his

BLASPHEMING (5)

1Sam 3:13 because his sons were B God, and he did
2Mac 12:14 at them and even B and saying unholy things.
Mt 9:3 the scribes said to themselves, "This man is B
Jn 10:36 the world, 'You are B because I said, 'I
Rev 13:6 utter blasphemies against God, B his name and his

BLASPHEMOUS (6)

2Mac 10:4 be handed over to B and barbarous nations.
13:11 the hands of the B Gentiles.
Acts 6:11 have heard him speak B words against Moses and
Rev 13:1 its horns and a B name upon its heads.
13:5 mouth uttering haughty and B words, and it was
17:3 which was full of B names, and it had

BLASPHEMY (8)

1Mac 7:41 from the king spoke B, thy angel went forth
Mt 12:31 you, every sin and B will be forgiven men,
12:31 forgiven men, but the B against the Spirit will
26:65 tore his robes, and said, "He has uttered B
26:65 You have now heard his B
Mk 2:7 It is B
14:64 You have heard his B
Jn 10:33 stone you but for B; because you, being a

BLAST (11)

Ex 15:8 At the B of thy nostrils the waters piled
19:13 trumpet sounds a long B, they shall come up
19:16 a very loud trumpet B, so that all the
Lev 23:24 a memorial proclaimed with B of trumpets, a holy
Josh 6:5 they make a long B with the ram's horn,
2Sam 22:16 the LORD, at the B of the breath of
Job 4:9 perish, and by the B of his anger they
Ps 18:15 O LORD, at the B of the breath of
Is 25:4 the heat; for the B of the ruthless is
27:8 them with his fierce B in the day of
Zeph 1:16 a day of trumpet B and battle cry against

BLASTING

Deut 28:22 with drought, and with B, and with mildew; they

BLASTS

Rev 8:13 the earth, at the B of the other trumpets

BLASTUS

Acts 12:20 and having persuaded B, the king's chamberlain,

BLAZE (2)

Num 16:37 censers out of the B; then scatter the fire
2Mac 4:22 ushered in with a B of torches and with

BLAZED (5)
Num 11:10 anger of the LORD B hotly, and Moses was
Ps 118:12 me like bees, they B like a fire of
Wis 16:22 by the fire that B in the hail and
2Mac 1:22 out, a great fire B up, so that all
1:32 was done, a flame B up; but when the

BLAZES
Hos 7:7 in the morning it B like a flaming fire.

BLAZING (7)
Ps 21:9 make them as a B oven when you appear.
Sir 3:28 Water extinguishes a B fire: so almsgiving atones for
Ezek 20:47 every dry tree; the B flame shall not be
38:19 jealousy and in my B wrath I declare, On
Zech 12:6 of Judah like a B pot in the midst
Heb 12:18 may be touched, a B fire, and darkness, and
Rev 8:10 star fell from heaven, B like a torch, and

BLEACH
Mk 9:3 fuller on earth could B them.

BLEAT
Tob 2:13 when she returned to me it began to B

BLEATING
1Sam 15:14 "What then is this B of the sheep in

BLEEDING
Is 1:6 bruises and sores and B wounds; they are not

BLEMISH (73)
Ex 12:5 lamb shall be without B, a male a year
29:1 and two rams without B,
Lev 1:3 offer a male without B; he shall offer it
1:10 offer a male without B;
3:1 shall offer it without B before the LORD.
3:6 male or female, he shall offer it without B
4:3 a young bull without B to the LORD for
4:23 goat, a male without B,
4:28 goat, a female without B, for his sin which
4:32 bring a female without B,
5:15 LORD, a ram without B out of the flock,
5:18 priest a ram without B out of the flock,
6:6 LORD, a ram without B out of the flock,
9:2 burnt offering, both without B, and offer them before
9:3 a year old without B, for a burnt offering,
14:10 two male lambs without B, and one ewe lamb
14:10 a year old without B, and a cereal offering
21:17 generations who has a B may approach to offer
21:18 one who has a B shall draw near, a
21:21 priest who has a B shall come near to
21:21 since he has a B, he shall not come
21:23 because he has a B, that he may not
22:19 offer a male without B, of the bulls or
22:20 anything that has a B, for it will not
22:21 there shall be no B in it.
22:25 Since there is a B in them, because of
23:12 a year old without B as a burnt offering
23:18 a year old without B, and one young bull,
Num 6:14 a year old without B for a burnt offering,
6:14 a year old without B as a sin offering,
6:14 and one ram without B as a peace offering,
19:2 which there is no B, and upon which a
28:3 a year old without B, day by day, as
28:9 a year old without B, and two tenths of
28:11 a year old without B;
28:19 that they are without B;
28:31 See that they are without B
29:2 a year old without B;
29:8 be to you without B;
29:13 they shall be without B;
29:17 a year old without B,
29:20 a year old without B,
29:23 a year old without B,
29:26 a year old without B,
29:29 a year old without B,
29:32 a year old without B,
29:36 a year old without B,
Deut 15:21 if it has any B, if it is lame
15:21 or has any serious B whatever, you shall not
17:1 in which is a B, any defect whatever; for
32:5 children because of their B; they are a perverse
2Sam 14:25 head there was no B in him.
Job 11:15 up your face without B; you will be secure,
Wis 13:14 red and covering every B in it with paint;
Sir 11:31 devises evil, lest he give you a lasting B
Ezek 43:22 offer a he-goat without B for a sin offering;
43:23 offer a bull without B and a ram from
43:23 blemish and a ram from the flock without B
43:25 from the flock, without B, shall be provided.
45:18 a young bull without B, and cleanse the sanctuary.
45:23 and seven rams without B, on each of the
46:4 be six lambs without B and a ram without
46:4 and a ram without B;
46:6 a young bull without B, and six lambs and
46:6 which shall be without B;
46:13 a year old without B for a burnt offering
Dan 1:4 the nobility, youths without B, handsome and skillful
Eph 5:27 thing, that she might be holy and without B
Phil 2:15 children of God without B in the midst of
Heb 9:14 Spirit offered himself without B to God, purify your
1Pet 1:19 of a lamb without B or spot.
2Pet 3:14 him without spot or B, and at peace.
Jude 1:24 to present you without B before the presence of

BLEMISHED (2)
Sir 34:18 obtained, the offering is B; the gifts of the
Mal 1:14 the Lord what is B; for I am a

BLEMISHES (2)
2Pet 2:13 They are blots and B, reveling in their dissipation,
Jude 1:12 These are B on your love feasts, as they

BLENDED (3)
Ex 30:25 a sacred anointing oil B as by the perfumer;
30:35 and make an incense B as by the perfumer,
37:29 the pure fragrant incense, B as by the perfumer.

BLENDING
Sir 49:1 Josiah is like a B of incense prepared by

BLESS (179)
Gen 12:2 nation, and I will B you, and make your
12:3 I will B those who bless you, and him
12:3 will bless those who B you, and him who
12:3 of the earth shall B themselves.
17:16 I will B her, and moreover I will give
17:16 by her; I will B her, and she shall
17:20 you; behold, I will B him and make him
18:18 of the earth shall B themselves by him?
22:17 son, I will indeed B you, and I will
22:18 nations of the earth B themselves, because you have
26:3 with you, and will B you; for to you
26:4 of the earth shall B themselves:
26:24 with you and will B you and multiply your
27:4 eat; that I may B you before I die."
27:7 may eat it, and B you before the LORD
27:10 so that he may B you before he dies."
27:19 game, that you may B me."
27:25 my son's game and B you." So he brought
27:31 game, that you may B me."
27:34 said to his father, B me, even me also,
27:38 B me, even me also, O my father." And
28:3 God Almighty B you and make you fruitful and
28:14 families of the earth B themselves.
32:26 you go, unless you B me."
48:9 you, that I may B them."
48:16 me from all evil, B the lads; and in
49:25 God Almighty who will B you with blessings of
Ex 12:32 and be gone; and B me also!"
20:24 come to you and B you.
23:25 God, and I will B your bread and your
Num 6:23 sons, Thus you shall B the people of Israel:
6:24 to them, The LORD B you and keep you:
6:27 Israel, and I will B them."
22:6 that he whom you B is blessed, and he
23:11 have done nothing but B them."
23:20 received a command to B: he has blessed, and
23:25 them at all, nor B them at all."
24:1 pleased the LORD to B Israel, he did not
Deut 1:11 as you are, and B you, as he has
7:13 he will love you, B you, and multiply you;
7:13 you; he will also B the fruit of your
8:10 full, and you shall B the LORD your God
10:8 to him and to B in his name, to
14:29 LORD your God may B you in all the
15:4 (for the LORD will B you in the land
15:6 LORD your God will B you, as he promised
15:10 LORD your God will B you in all your
15:18 LORD your God will B you in all that
16:15 LORD your God will B you in all your

B

B

	21:5	to him and to B in the name of
	23:20	LORD your God may B you in all that
	24:13	in his cloak and B you; and it shall
	24:19	LORD your God may B you in all the
	26:15	habitation, from heaven, and B thy people Israel and
	27:12	upon Mount Gerizim to B the people: Simeon, Levi,
	28:8	undertake; and he will B you in the land
	28:12	its season and to B all the work of
	30:16	LORD your God will B you in the land
	33:11	B, O LORD, his substance, and accept the work
Josh	8:33	first, that they should B the people of Israel.
Judg	5:2	people offered themselves willingly, B the LORD!
	5:9	B the LORD.
Ruth	2:4	they answered, "The LORD B you."
1Sam	2:20	Then Eli would B Elkanah and his wife, and
	9:13	comes, since he must B the sacrifice; afterward
2Sam	6:20	And David returned to B his household.
	7:29	it please thee to B the house of thy
	21:3	expiation, that you may B the heritage of the
1Chr	4:10	"Oh that thou wouldst B me and enlarge my
	16:43	David went home to B his household.
	17:27	it please thee to B the house of thy
	29:20	to all the assembly, B the LORD your God."
Neh	9:5	said, "Stand up and B the LORD your God
Tob	4:19	B the Lord God on every occasion; ask him
	8:5	and all thy creatures B thee.
	8:15	and all thy creatures B thee; let all thy
	8:15	and thy chosen people B thee for ever.
Jud	15:10	May the Almighty Lord B you for ever!" And
Ps	5:12	For thou dost B the righteous, O LORD; thou
	16:7	I B the LORD who gives me counsel; in
	26:12	great congregation I will B the LORD.
	28:9	save thy people, and B thy heritage; be thou
	29:11	May the LORD B his people with peace!
	34:1	I will B the LORD at all times; his
	62:4	They B with their mouths, but inwardly they curse.
	63:4	So I will B thee as long as I
	66:8	[Selah] B our God, O peoples, let the sound
	67:1	gracious to us and B us and make his
	68:26	them maidens playing timbrels: B God in the great
	72:17	May men B themselves by him, all nations call
	96:2	Sing to the LORD, B his name; tell of
	100:4	Give thanks to him, B his name!
	103:1	B the LORD, O my soul; and all that
	103:1	that is within me, B his holy name!
	103:2	B the LORD, O my soul, and forget not
	103:20	B the LORD, O you his angels, you mighty
	103:21	B the LORD, all his hosts, his ministers that
	103:22	B the LORD, all his works, in all places
	103:22	B the LORD, O my soul!
	104:1	B the LORD, O my soul!
	104:35	B the LORD, O my soul!
	109:28	Let them curse, but do thou B
	115:12	of us; he will B us; he will bless
	115:12	bless us; he will B the house of Israel;
	115:12	of Israel; he will B the house of Aaron;
	115:13	of Aaron; he will B those who fear the
	115:18	But we will B the LORD from this time
	118:26	We B you from the house of the LORD.
	128:5	The LORD B you from Zion!
	129:8	We B you in the name of the LORD!"
	132:15	I will abundantly B her provisions; I will satisfy
	134:1	Come, B the LORD, all you servants of the
	134:2	the holy place, and B the LORD!
	134:3	May the LORD B you from Zion, he who
	135:19	O house of Israel, B the LORD!
	135:19	O house of Aaron, B the LORD!
	135:20	O house of Levi, B the LORD!
	135:20	that fear the LORD, B the LORD!
	145:1	God and King, and B thy name for ever
	145:2	Every day I will B thee, and praise thy
	145:10	all thy saints shall B thee!
	145:21	and let all flesh B his holy name for
Prov	30:11	fathers and do not B their mothers.
Sir	4:13	and the Lord will B the place she enters.
	32:13	And for these things B him who made you
	39:14	a hymn of praise; B the Lord for all
	39:35	heart and voice, and B the name of the
	45:15	serve as priest and B his people in his
	50:22	And now B the God of all, who in
	51:12	thee, and I will B the name of the
Is	65:16	in the land shall B himself by the God
Jer	4:2	uprightness, then nations shall B themselves in him,
	31:23	their fortunes: 'The LORD B you, O habitation of
Bar	6:66	can neither curse nor B kings;
Ezek	37:26	them; and I will B them and multiply them,
Dan	3:58	B the Lord, all works of the Lord, sing
	3:59	B the Lord, you heavens, sing praise to him
	3:60	B the Lord, you angels of the Lord, sing
	3:61	B the Lord, all waters above the heaven, sing
	3:62	B the Lord, all powers, sing praise to him
	3:63	B the Lord, sun and moon, sing praise to
	3:64	B the Lord, stars of heaven, sing praise to
	3:65	B the Lord, all rain and dew, sing praise
	3:66	B the Lord, all winds, sing praise to him
	3:67	B the Lord, fire and heat, sing praise to
	3:68	B the Lord, winter cold and summer heat, sing
	3:69	B the Lord, dews and snows, sing praise to
	3:70	B the Lord, nights and days, sing praise to
	3:71	B the Lord, light and darkness, sing praise to
	3:72	B the Lord, ice and cold, sing praise to
	3:73	B the Lord, frosts and snows, sing praise to
	3:74	B the Lord, lightnings and clouds, sing praise to
	3:75	Let the earth B the Lord; let it sing
	3:76	B the Lord, mountains and hills, sing praise to
	3:77	B the Lord, all things that grow on the
	3:78	B the Lord, you springs, sing praise to him
	3:79	B the Lord, seas and rivers, sing praise to
	3:80	B the Lord, you whales and all creatures that
	3:81	B the Lord, all birds of the air, sing
	3:82	B the Lord, all beasts and cattle, sing praise
	3:83	B the Lord, you sons of men, sing praise
	3:84	B the Lord, O Israel, sing praise to him
	3:85	B the Lord, you priests of the Lord, sing
	3:86	B the Lord, you servants of the Lord, sing
	3:87	B the Lord, spirits and souls of the righteous,
	3:88	B the Lord, you who are holy and humble
	3:89	B the Lord, Hananiah, Azariah, and Mishael, sing
	3:91	B him, all who worship the Lord, the God
Hag	2:19	day on I will B you."
Lk	6:28	those who hate you, B those who curse you,
Acts	3:26	to you first, to B you in turning every
Rom	12:14	B those who persecute you; bless and do not
	12:14	those who persecute you; B and do not curse
1Cor	4:12	When reviled, we B; when persecuted, we endure;
	10:16	of blessing which we B, is it not a
	14:16	Otherwise, if you B with the spirit, how can
Heb	6:14	saying, "Surely I will B you and multiply you."
Jas	3:9	With it we B the Lord and Father, and
1Pet	3:9	but on the contrary B, for to this you

BLESSED (354)

Gen	1:22	And God B them, saying, "Be fruitful and multiply
	1:28	And God B them, and God said to them,
	2:3	So God B the seventh day and hallowed it,
	5:2	created them, and he B them and named them
	9:1	And God B Noah and his sons, and said
	9:26	He also said, B by the LORD my God
	14:19	And he B him and said, "Blessed be Abram
	14:19	blessed him and said, B be Abram by God
	14:20	heaven and earth; and B be God Most High,
	24:1	and the LORD had B Abraham in all things.
	24:27	the LORD, and said, B be the LORD, the
	24:31	said, "Come in, O B of the LORD; why
	24:35	The LORD has greatly B my master, and he
	24:48	worshiped the LORD, and B the LORD, the God
	24:60	And they B Rebekah, and said to her, "Our
	25:11	death of Abraham God B Isaac his son.
	26:12	The LORD B him,
	26:29	You are now the B of the LORD."
	27:23	Esau's hands; so he B him.
	27:27	of his garments, and B him, and said, "See,
	27:27	smell of a field which the LORD has B
	27:29	who curses you, and B be every one who
	27:33	came, and I have B him?--yes, and he
	27:33	have blessed him?--yes, and he shall be B
	27:41	which his father had B him, and Esau said
	28:1	Isaac called Jacob and B him, and charged him,
	28:6	saw that Isaac had B Jacob and sent him
	28:6	and that as he B him he charged him,
	30:27	that the LORD has B me because of you;
	30:30	and the LORD has B you wherever I turned.
	31:55	and his daughters and B them; then he departed
	32:29	And there he B him.
	35:9	came from Paddan-aram, and B him.
	39:5	he had the LORD B the Egyptian's house for
	47:7	before Pharaoh, and Jacob B Pharaoh.
	47:10	And Jacob B Pharaoh, and went out from the
	48:3	land of Canaan and B me,
	48:15	And he B Joseph, and said, "The God before
	48:20	So he B them that day, saying, "By you
	49:28	to them as he B them, blessing each with

Ex 18:10 And Jethro said, B be the LORD, who has
20:11 day; therefore the LORD B the sabbath day and
39:43 And Moses B them.
Lev 9:22 toward the people and B them; and he came
9:23 they came out they B the people, and the
Num 22:6 whom you bless is B, and he whom you
22:12 shall not curse the people, for they are B
23:20 to bless: he has B, and I cannot revoke
24:9 B be every one who blesses you, and cursed
24:10 and behold, you have B them these three times.
Deut 2:7 LORD your God has B you in all the
7:14 You shall be B above all peoples; there shall
12:7 LORD your God has B you.
15:14 LORD your God has B you, you shall give
28:3 B shall you be in the city, and blessed
28:3 in the city, and B shall you be in
28:4 B shall be the fruit of your body, and
28:5 B shall be your basket and your kneading-trough.
28:6 B shall you be when you come in, and
28:6 you come in, and B shall you be when
33:1 the man of God B the children of Israel
33:13 of Joseph he said, B by the LORD be
33:20 of Gad he said, B be he who enlarges
33:24 of Asher he said, B above sons be Asher;
Josh 14:13 Then Joshua B him; and he gave Hebron to
17:14 hitherto the LORD has B me?"
22:6 So Joshua B them, and sent them away; and
22:7 to their homes and B them,
22:33 the people of Israel B God and spoke no
24:10 to Balaam; therefore he B you; so I delivered
Judg 5:24 "Most B of women be Jael, the wife of
5:24 of Heber the Kenite, of tent-dwelling women most B
13:24 grew, and the LORD B him.
17:2 And his mother said, B be my son by
Ruth 2:19 B be the man who took notice of you."
2:20 said to her daughter-in-law, B be he by the
3:10 said, "May you be B by the LORD, my
4:14 women said to Naomi, B be the LORD, who
1Sam 15:13 Saul said to him, B be you to the
23:21 said, "May you be B by the LORD; for
25:32 David said to Abigail, B be the LORD, the
25:33 B be your discretion, and blessed be you, who
25:33 be your discretion, and B be you, who have
25:39 was dead, he said, B be the LORD who
26:25 Saul said to David, B be you, my son
2Sam 2:5 them, "May you be B by the LORD, because
6:11 months; and the LORD B Obed-edom and all his
6:12 David, "The LORD has B the household of
6:18 the peace offerings, he B the people in the
7:29 of thy servant be B for ever."
14:22 and did obeisance, and B the king; and Joab
18:28 the earth, and said, B be the LORD your
19:39 king kissed Barzillai and B him, and he returned
22:47 "The LORD lives; and B be my rock, and
1Kgs 1:48 the king also said, B be the LORD, the
2:45 King Solomon shall be B, and the throne of
5:7 rejoiced greatly, and said, B be the LORD this
8:14 king faced about, and B all the assembly of
8:15 And he said, B be the LORD, the God
8:55 and he stood, and B all the assembly of
8:56 a loud voice, saying, B be the LORD who
8:66 people away; and they B the king, and went
10:9 B be the LORD your God, who has delighted
1Chr 13:14 and the LORD B the household of Obed-edom
16:2 the peace offerings, he B the people in the
16:36 B be the LORD, the God of Israel, from
17:27 thou, O LORD, hast B is blessed for ever."
17:27 LORD, hast blessed is B for ever."
26:5 the eighth; for God B him.
29:10 Therefore David B the LORD in the presence of
29:10 assembly; and David said: B art thou, O LORD,
29:20 And all the assembly B the LORD, the God
2Chr 2:12 Huram also said, B be the LORD God of
6:3 king faced about, and B all the assembly of
6:4 And he said, B be the LORD, the God
9:8 B be the LORD your God, who has delighted
20:26 Beracah, for there they B the LORD; therefore the
30:27 the Levites arose and B the people, and their
31:8 saw the heaps, they B the LORD and his
31:10 for the LORD has B his people, so that
Ezra 7:27 B be the LORD, the God of our fathers,
Neh 8:6 And Ezra B the LORD, the great God; and
9:5 B be thy glorious name which is exalted above
11:2 And the people B all the men who willingly
Tob 3:11 her window and said, B art thou, O Lord
3:11 Lord my God, and B is thy holy and
4:12 They were B in their children, and their posterity
7:7 And he B him and exclaimed, "Son of that
7:13 And he B them.
8:5 Tobias began to pray, B art thou, O God
8:5 of our fathers, and B by thy holy and
8:15 Then Raguel B God and said, "Blessed art thou,
8:15 blessed God and said, B art thou, O God,
8:16 B art thou, because thou hast made me glad.
8:17 B art thou, because thou hast had compassion on
9:6 And Gabael B Tobias and his wife.
10:11 And when he had B them he sent them
11:1 And he B Raguel and his wife Edna.
11:14 he wept and said, B art thou, O God,
11:14 thou, O God, and B is thy name for
11:14 name for ever, and B are all thy holy
11:17 Sarah his daughter-in-law, he B her, saying,
11:17 B is God who has brought you to us,
11:17 you to us, and B are your father and
13:1 of rejoicing, and said: B is God who lives
13:1 lives for ever, and B is his kingdom.
13:12 all who hate you; B for ever will be
13:14 How B are those who love you!
13:14 B are those who grieved over all your afflictions;
13:18 will give praise, saying, B is God, who has
Jud 13:17 said with one accord, B art thou, our God,
13:18 "O daughter, you are B by the Most High
13:18 women on earth; and B be the Lord God,
14:7 before her, and said, B are you in every
15:9 met her they all B her with one accord
15:12 to see her, and B her, and some of
Job 1:10 Thou hast B the work of his hands, and
1:21 LORD has taken away; B be the name of
29:11 heard, it called me B, and when the eye
31:20 his loins have not B me, and if he
42:12 And the LORD B the latter days of Job
Ps 1:1 B is the man who
2:12 B are all who take refuge in him.
18:46 The LORD lives; and B be my rock, and
21:6 dost make him most B for ever; thou dost
28:6 B be the LORD!
31:21 B be the LORD, for he has wondrously shown
32:1 B is he whose transgression is forgiven, whose sin
32:2 B is the man to whom the LORD imputes
33:12 B is the nation whose God is the LORD,
37:22 and gives; for those B by the LORD shall
40:4 B is the man who makes the LORD his
41:1 B is he who considers the poor!
41:2 alive; he is called B in the land; thou
41:13 B be the LORD, the God of Israel, from
45:2 lips; therefore God has B you for ever.
65:4 B is he whom thou dost choose and bring
66:20 B be God, because he has not rejected my
67:6 God, our God, has B us.
67:7 God has B us; let all the ends of
68:19 B be the Lord, who daily bears us up;
68:35 B be God!
72:17 bless themselves by him, all nations call him B
72:18 B be the LORD, the God of Israel, who
72:19 B be his glorious name for ever; may his
84:4 B are those who dwell in thy house, ever
84:5 [Selah] B are the men whose strength is in
84:12 O LORD of hosts, B is the man who
89:15 B are the people who know the festal shout,
89:52 B be the LORD for ever!
94:12 B is the man whom thou dost chasten, O
106:3 B are they who observe justice, who do
106:48 B be the LORD, the God of Israel, from
112:1 B is the man who fears the LORD, who
112:2 land; the generation of the upright will be B
113:2 B be the name of the LORD from this
115:15 May you be B by the LORD, who made
118:26 B be he who enters in the name of
119:1 B are those whose way is blameless, who walk
119:2 B are those who keep his testimonies, who seek
119:12 B be thou, O LORD; teach me thy statutes!
124:6 B be the LORD, who has not given us
128:1 B is every one who fears the LORD, who
128:4 shall the man be B who fears the LORD.
135:21 B be the LORD from Zion, he who dwells
144:1 B be the LORD, my rock, who trains my
Prov 5:18 Let your fountain be B, and rejoice in the
20:7 in his integrity-- B are his sons after
20:21 the beginning will in the end not be B
22:9 bountiful eye will be B, for he shares his
28:14 B is the man who fears the LORD always;
29:18 cast off restraint, but B is he who keeps

B

31:28 up and call her B; her husband also, and
Wis 3:13 For B is the barren woman who is undefiled,
3:14 B also is the eunuch whose hands have done
14:7 For B is the wood by which righteousness comes.
Sir 1:11 the day of his death he will be B
14:1 B is the man who does not blunder with
14:2 B is he whose heart does not condemn him,
14:20 B is the man who meditates on wisdom and
31:8 B is the rich man who is found blameless,
31:9 we will call him B, for he has done
33:12 some of them he B and exalted, and some
34:15 B is the soul of the man who fears
44:22 the nations would be B through his posterity; that
45:1 by God and man, Moses, whose memory is B
45:7 He B him with splendid vestments, and put a
46:11 from the Lord-- may their memory be B
48:11 B are those who saw you, and those who
50:28 B is he who concerns himself with these things,
Is 19:25 LORD of hosts has B, saying, "Blessed be Egypt
19:25 hosts has blessed, saying, B be Egypt my people,
30:18 a God of justice; B are all those who
51:2 called him, and I B him and made him
56:2 B is the man who does this, and the
61:9 they are a people whom the LORD has B
65:23 the offspring of the B of the LORD, and
Jer 17:7 B is the man who trusts in the LORD,
20:14 my mother bore me, let it not be B
Dan 2:19 Then Daniel B the God of heaven.
2:20 Daniel said: B be the name of God for
3:26 his mouth and said: B art thou, O Lord,
3:51 praised and glorified and B God in the furnace,
3:52 in the furnace, saying: B art thou, O Lord,
3:53 exalted for ever; And B is thy glorious, holy
3:54 highly exalted for ever; B art thou in the
3:55 B art thou, who sittest upon cherubim and lookest
3:56 B art thou upon the throne of thy kingdom
3:57 B art thou in the firmament of heaven and
3:96 Nebuchadnezzar said, B be the God of Shadrach,
4:34 to me, and I B the Most High, and
12:12 B is he who waits and comes to the
13:60 assembly shouted loudly and B God, who saves those
Zech 11:5 who sell them say, B be the LORD, I
Mal 3:12 nations will call you B, for you will be
3:15 we deem the arrogant B; evildoers not only prosper
1Mac 2:69 Then he B them, and was gathered to his
3:7 and his memory is B for ever.
4:30 strong, he prayed, saying, B art thou, O Savior
4:55 faces and worshiped and B Heaven, who had
2Mac 1:17 B in every way be our God, who has
10:38 hymns and thanksgivings they B the Lord who shows
12:41 So they all B the ways of the Lord,
15:29 and tumult, and they B the Sovereign Lord in
15:34 all, looking to heaven, B the Lord who had
15:34 had manifested himself, saying, B is he who has
Mt 5:3 and taught them, saying: B are the poor in
5:4 B are those who mourn, for they shall be
5:5 B are the meek, for they shall inherit the
5:6 B are those who hunger and thirst for righteousness,
5:7 B are the merciful, for they shall obtain mercy.
5:8 B are the pure in heart, for they shall
5:9 B are the peacemakers, for they shall be called
5:10 B are those who are persecuted for righteousness'
5:11 B are you when men revile you and persecute
11:6 And B is he who takes no offense at
13:16 to heal them.' But B are your eyes, for
14:19 up to heaven, and B, and broke and gave
16:17 Jesus answered him, B are you, Simon Bar-Jona!
21:9 B is he who comes in the name of
23:38 again, until you say, B is he who comes
24:46 B is that servant whom his master when he
25:34 right hand, 'Come, O B of my Father, inherit
26:26 Jesus took bread, and B, and broke it, and
Mk 6:41 up to heaven, and B, and broke the loaves,
8:7 small fish; and having B them, he commanded that
10:16 in his arms and B them, laying his hands
11:9 B is he who comes in the name of
11:10 B is the kingdom of our father David that
14:22 he took bread, and B, and broke it, and
14:61 "Are you the Christ, the Son of the B
Lk 1:42 with a loud cry, B are you among women,
1:42 you among women, and B is the fruit of
1:45 And B is she who believed that there would
1:48 generations will call me B;
1:68 Spirit, and prophesied, saying, B be the Lord God
2:28 in his arms and B God and said,
2:34 about him; and Simeon B them and said to
6:20 his disciples, and said: B are you poor, for
6:21 B are you that hunger now, for you shall
6:21 B are you that weep now, for you shall
6:22 B are you when men hate you, and when
7:23 And B is he who takes no offense at
9:16 up to heaven, and B and broke them, and
10:23 disciples he said privately, B are the eyes which
11:27 and said to him, B is the womb that
11:28 But he said, B rather are those who hear
12:37 B are those servants whom the master finds awake
12:38 and finds them so, B are those servants!
12:43 B is that servant whom his master when he
13:35 me until you say, B is he who comes
14:14 and you will be B, because they cannot repay
14:15 he said to him, B is he who shall
19:38 they had seen, saying, B is the King who
23:28 when they will say, B are the barren, and
24:30 took the bread and B, and broke it, and
24:50 up his hands he B them.
24:51 While he B them, he parted from them, and
Jn 12:13 B is he who comes in the name of
13:17 you know these things, B are you if you
20:29 B are those who have not seen and yet
Acts 3:25 of the earth be B
20:35 said, 'It is more B to give than to
Rom 1:25 the Creator, who is B for ever!
4:7 righteousness apart from works: B are those whose
4:8 whose sins are covered; B is the man against
9:5 is over all be B for ever.
2Cor 1:3 B be the God and Father of our Lord
11:31 Jesus, he who is B for ever, knows that
Gal 3:8 saying, "In you shall all the nations be B
3:9 men of faith are B with Abraham who had
Eph 1:3 B be the God and Father of our Lord
1:3 Jesus Christ, who has B us in Christ with
1Tim 1:11 glorious gospel of the B God with which I
6:15 proper time by the B and only Sovereign, the
Tit 2:13 this world, awaiting our B hope, the appearing of
Heb 7:1 of the kings and B him;
7:6 tithes from Abraham and B him who had the
7:7 that the inferior is B by the superior.
11:21 faith Jacob, when dying, B each of the sons
Jas 1:11 B is the man who endures trial, for when
1:24 acts, he shall be B in his doing.
1Pet 1:3 B be the God and Father of our Lord
3:14 do suffer for righteousness' sake, you will be B
4:14 of Christ, you are B, because the spirit of
Rev 1:3 B is he who reads aloud the words of
1:3 of the prophecy, and B are those who hear,
14:13 heaven saying, "Write this: B are the dead who
14:13 B indeed," says the Spirit, "that they may rest
16:15 B is he who is awake, keeping his garments
19:9 to me, "Write this: B are those who are
20:6 B and holy is he who shares in the
22:7 B is he who keeps the words of the
22:14 B are those who wash their robes, that they

BLESSES (10)

Gen 27:29 be every one who B you!"
Num 24:9 be every one who B you, and cursed be
Deut 14:24 the LORD your God B you, because the place
16:10 the LORD your God B you;
29:19 of this sworn covenant, B himself in his heart,
Ps 147:13 of your gates; he B your sons within you.
Prov 3:33 the wicked, but he B the abode of the
27:14 He who B his neighbor with a loud voice,
Is 65:16 So that he who B himself in the land
66:3 frankincense, like him who B an idol.

BLESSING (88)

Gen 12:2 name great, so that you will be a B
27:12 bring a curse upon myself and not a B
27:30 as Isaac had finished B Jacob, when Jacob had
27:35 with guile, and he has taken away your B
27:36 and behold, now he has taken away my B
27:36 you not reserved a B for me?"
27:38 "Have you but one B, my father?
27:41 Jacob because of the B with which his father
28:4 May he give the B of Abraham to you
39:5 for Joseph's sake; the B of the LORD was
49:28 as he blessed them, B each with the blessing
49:28 blessing each with the B suitable to him.
Ex 32:29 he may bestow a B upon you this day."
Lev 25:21 I will command my B upon you in the
Deut 11:26 you this day a B and a curse:
11:27 and a curse: the B, if you obey the

11:29 you shall set the B on Mount Gerizim and
12:15 desire, according to the B of the LORD your
16:17 able, according to the B of the LORD your
23:5 the curse into a B for you, because the
28:8 LORD will command the B upon you in your
30:1 come upon you, the B and the curse, which
30:19 you life and death, B and curse; therefore choose
33:1 This is the B with which Moses the man
33:23 and full of the B of the LORD, possess
Josh 8:34 of the law, the B and the curse, according
2Sam 7:29 spoken, and with thy B shall the house of
13:25 he would not go but gave him his B
Neh 9:5 is exalted above all B and praise."
13:2 yet our God turned the curse into a B
Tob 8:15 thou, O God, with every pure and holy B
Job 29:13 The B of him who was about to perish
Ps 3:8 to the LORD; thy B be upon thy people!
24:5 He will receive B from the LORD, and vindication
37:26 liberally and lending, and his children become a B
65:10 it with showers, and B its growth.
107:38 By his B they multiply greatly; and he does
109:17 He did not like B; may it be far
119:56 This B has fallen to me, that I have
129:8 do not say, "The B of the LORD be
133:3 LORD has commanded the B, life for evermore.
Prov 10:7 the righteous is a B, but the name of
10:22 The B of the LORD makes rich, and he
11:11 By the B of the upright a city is
11:26 back grain, but a B is on the head
24:25 delight, and a good B will be upon them.
Wis 15:19 escaped both the praise of God and his B
Sir 3:8 and deed, that a B from him may come
3:9 For a father's B strengthens the houses of the
7:32 poor, so that your B may be complete.
11:20 The B of the Lord is the reward of
11:20 quickly God causes his B to flourish.
26:3 wife is a great B; she will be granted
33:16 the grape-gatherers; by the B of the Lord I
34:17 to the eyes; he grants healing, life, and B
36:17 servants, according to the B of Aaron for thy
39:22 His B covers the dry land like a river,
40:27 like a garden of B, and covers a man
44:24 The B of all men and the covenant he
50:20 Israel, to pronounce the B of the Lord with
50:21 time, to receive the B from the Most High.
Is 19:24 Egypt and Assyria, a B in the midst of
44:3 your descendants, and my B on your offspring.
65:8 for there is a B in it,' so I
Ezek 34:26 about my hill a B; and I will send
34:26 in their season; they shall be showers of B
44:30 coarse meal, that a B may rest on your
Dan 3:24 hymns to God and B the Lord.
Joel 2:14 repent, and leave a B behind him, a cereal
Zech 8:13 I save you and you shall be a B
Mal 3:10 you and pour down for you an overflowing B
Lk 1:64 loosed, and he spoke, B God.
24:53 continually in the temple B God.
Rom 4:6 also David pronounces a B upon the man to
4:9 Is this B pronounced only upon the circumcised, or
15:29 the fulness of the B of Christ.
1Cor 10:16 The cup of B which we bless, is it
2Cor 1:11 our behalf for the B granted us in answer
9:8 provide you with every B in abundance, so that
Gal 3:14 in Christ Jesus the B of Abraham might come
Eph 1:3 Christ with every spiritual B in the heavenly places,
Heb 6:7 is cultivated, receives a B from God.
12:17 desired to inherit the B, he was rejected, for
Jas 3:10 the same mouth come B and cursing.
1Pet 3:9 have been called, that you may obtain a B
Rev 5:12 wisdom and might and honor and glory and B
5:13 to the Lamb be B and honor and glory
7:12 B and glory and wisdom and thanksgiving and honor

BLESSINGS (25)

Gen 48:20 you Israel will pronounce B, saying, 'God make you
49:25 will bless you with B of heaven above, blessings
49:25 blessings of heaven above, B of the deep that
49:25 deep that couches beneath, B of the breasts and
49:26 The B of your father are mighty beyond the
49:26 are mighty beyond the B of the eternal mountains,
Deut 28:2 And all these B shall come upon you and
1Chr 23:13 to him and pronounce B in his name for
Jud 13:20 he visit you with B, because you did not
Ps 21:3 meet him with goodly B; thou dost set a
72:15 for him continually, and B invoked for him all
144:15 people to whom such B fall!
Prov 10:6 B are on the head of the righteous, but
28:20 man will abound with B, but he who hastens
Wis 18:9 the same things, both B and dangers; and already
Sir 26:3 be granted among the B of the man who
40:17 like a garden of B, and almsgiving endures for
44:24 acknowledged him with his B, and gave him his
47:6 praised him for the B of the Lord, when
Mal 2:2 I will curse your B; indeed I have already
Acts 13:34 the holy and sure B of David.'
Rom 15:27 share in their spiritual B, they ought also to
15:27 to be of service to them in material B
1Cor 9:23 the gospel, that I may share in its B
Heb 11:20 faith Isaac invoked future B on Jacob and Esau.

BLEW (27)

Josh 6:9 before the priests who B the trumpets, and the
6:9 ark, while the trumpets B continually.
6:13 LORD, while the trumpets B continually.
Judg 7:19 the watch; and they B the trumpets and smashed
7:20 And the three companies B the trumpets and broke
7:22 When they B the three hundred trumpets, the LORD
1Sam 13:3 And Saul B the trumpet throughout all the land,
2Sam 2:28 So Joab B the trumpet; and all the men
18:16 Then Joab B the trumpet, and the troops came
20:1 a Benjaminite; and he B the trumpet, and said,
20:22 So he B the trumpet, and they dispersed from
1Kgs 1:39 Then they B the trumpet; and all the people
2Kgs 9:13 bare steps, and they B the trumpet, and proclaimed,
2Chr 13:14 LORD, and the priests B the trumpets.
Hag 1:9 brought it home, I B it away.
1Mac 4:13 the men with Judas B their trumpets
9:12 men with Judas also B their trumpets.
Mt 7:25 came, and the winds B and beat upon that
7:27 came, and the winds B and beat against that
Acts 27:13 when the south wind B gently, supposing that they
Rev 8:7 The first angel B his trumpet, and there followed
8:8 The second angel B his trumpet, and something like
8:10 The third angel B his trumpet, and a great
8:12 The fourth angel B his trumpet, and a third
9:1 And the fifth angel B his trumpet, and I
9:13 Then the sixth angel B his trumpet, and I
11:15 Then the seventh angel B his trumpet, and there

BLIGHT (4)

1Kgs 8:37 there is pestilence or B or mildew or locust
2Chr 6:28 there is pestilence or B or mildew or locust
Amos 4:9 "I smote you with B and mildew; I laid
Hag 2:17 of your toil with B and mildew and hail;

BLIGHTED (5)

Gen 41:6 seven ears, thin and B by the east wind.
41:23 ears, withered, thin, and B by the east wind,
41:27 the seven empty ears B by the east wind
2Kgs 19:26 grass on the housetops; B before it is grown?
Is 37:27 grass on the housetops, B before it is grown.

BLIND (81)

Ex 4:11 makes him dumb, or deaf, or seeing, or B
Lev 19:14 stumbling block before the B, but you shall fear
21:18 draw near, a man B or lame, or one
22:22 Animals B or disabled or mutilated or having a
Deut 15:21 it is lame or B, or has any serious
27:18 he who misleads a B man on the road.'
28:29 at noonday, as the B grope in darkness, and
1Sam 12:3 taken a bribe to B my eyes with it?
2Sam 5:6 in here, but the B and the lame will
5:8 the lame and the B, who are hated by
5:8 it is said, "The B and the lame shall
Job 29:15 was eyes to the B, and feet to the
Ps 146:8 free; the LORD opens the eyes of the B
Sir 20:28 Presents and gifts B the eyes of the wise;
Is 29:9 be in a stupor, B yourselves and be blind!
29:9 be in a stupor, blind yourselves and be B
29:18 the eyes of the B shall see.
35:5 the eyes of the B shall be opened, and
42:7 the eyes that are B, to bring out the
42:16 I will lead the B in a way that
42:18 deaf; and look, you B, that you may see!
42:19 Who is B but my servant, or deaf as
42:19 Who is B as my dedicated one, or blind
42:19 my dedicated one, or B as the servant of
43:8 the people who are B, yet have eyes, who
56:10 watchmen are B, they are all without knowledge;
59:10 the wall like the B, we grope like those
Jer 31:8 earth, among them the B and the lame, the
Lam 4:14 They wandered, B, through the streets, so defiled

Bar 6:37 restore sight to a B man; they cannot rescue
Zeph 1:17 shall walk like the B, because they have sinned
Mal 1:8 When you offer B animals in sacrifice, is that
Mt 9:27 on from there, two B men followed him, crying
9:28 entered the house, the B men came to him;
11:5 hear and see: the B receive their sight and
12:22 Then a B and dumb demoniac was brought to
15:14 them alone; they are B guides.
15:14 And if a B man leads a blind man,
15:14 blind man leads a B man, both will fall
15:30 lame, the maimed, the B, the dumb, and many
15:31 lame walking, and the B seeing; and they glorified
20:30 And behold, two B men sitting by the roadside,
21:14 And the B and the lame came to him
23:15 "Woe to you, B guides, who say, 'If any
23:16 by his oath.' You B fools!
23:18 by his oath.' You B men!
23:23 You B guides, straining out a gnat and swallowing
23:25 You B Pharisee!
Mk 8:22 brought to him a B man, and begged him
8:23 And he took the B man by the hand,
10:46 great multitude, Bartimaeus, a B beggar, the son of
10:49 And they called the B man, saying to him,
10:51 And the B man said to him, "Master, let
Lk 4:18 of sight to the B, to set at liberty
6:39 a parable: "Can a B man lead a blind
6:39 blind man lead a B man?
7:21 on many that were B he bestowed sight.
7:22 seen and heard: the B receive their sight, the
14:13 maimed, the lame, the B,
14:21 poor and maimed and B and lame.'
18:35 near to Jericho, a B man was sitting by
Jn 5:3 a multitude of invalids, B, lame, paralyzed.
9:1 he saw a man B from his birth.
9:2 man or his parents, that he was born B
9:13 the Pharisees the man who had formerly been B
9:17 again said to the B man, "What do you
9:18 that he had been B and had received his
9:19 this your son, who you say was born B
9:20 that he was born B;
9:24 man who had been B, and said to him,
9:25 that though I was B, now I see."
9:32 one opened the eyes of a man born B
9:39 see, and that those who see may become B
9:40 and they said to him, "Are we also B
9:41 them, "If you were B, you would have no
10:21 Can a demon open the eyes of the B
11:37 the eyes of the B man have kept this
Acts 13:11 and you shall be B and unable to see
Rom 2:19 a guide to the B, a light to those
2Pet 1:9 lacks these things is B and shortsighted and has
Rev 3:17 are wretched, pitiable, poor, B, and naked.

BLINDED (7)

Wis 2:21 astray, for their wickedness B them,
Ezek 6:9 departed from me, and B their eyes which turn
Zech 11:17 arm be wholly withered, his right eye utterly B
2Mac 10:30 so that, confused and B, they were thrown into
Jn 12:40 again said, "He has B their eyes and hardened
2Cor 4:4 of this world has B the minds of the
1Jn 2:11 because the darkness has B his eyes.

BLINDFOLDED

Lk 22:62 beat him; they also B him and asked him,

BLINDNESS (5)

Gen 19:11 And they struck with B the men who were
Deut 28:28 you with madness and B and confusion of mind;
2Kgs 6:18 said, "Strike this people, I pray thee, with B
6:18 he struck them with B in accordance with the
Zech 12:4 I strike every horse of the peoples with B

BLINDS (3)

Ex 23:8 bribe, for a bribe B the officials, and subverts
Deut 16:19 bribe, for a bribe B the eyes of the
Sir 43:4 with bright beams it B the eyes.

BLOCK (16)

Lev 19:14 or put a stumbling B before the blind, but
Sir 31:7 It is a stumbling B to those who are
Is 44:19 fall down before a B of wood?"
Ezek 3:20 I lay a stumbling B before him, he shall
7:19 it was the stumbling B of their iniquity.
14:3 and set the stumbling B of their iniquity before
14:4 and sets the stumbling B of his iniquity before
14:7 and putting the stumbling B of his iniquity before
39:11 the sea; it will B the travelers, for there
44:12 and became a stumbling B of iniquity to the
1Mac 2:36 stone at them or B up their hiding places,
Rom 14:13 to put a stumbling B or hindrance in the
1Cor 1:23 Christ crucified, a stumbling B to Jews and folly
8:9 somehow become a stumbling B to the weak.
Gal 5:11 that case the stumbling B of the cross has
Rev 2:14 to put a stumbling B before the sons of

BLOCKED (3)

Jud 16:4 his warriors; their multitude B up the valleys, their
Lam 3:9 my prayer; he has B my ways with hewn
1Mac 5:47 shut them out and B up the gates with

BLOCKS (2)

Jer 6:21 before this people stumbling B against which they
2Mac 4:41 picked up stones, some B of wood, and others

BLOOD (453)

Gen 4:10 voice of your brother's B is crying to me
4:11 to receive your brother's B from your hand.
9:4 eat flesh with its life, that is, its B
9:6 Whoever sheds the B of man, by man shall
9:6 by man shall his B be shed; for God
37:22 to them, "Shed no B; cast him into this
37:26 if we slay our brother and conceal his B
37:31 the robe in the B;
42:22 So now there comes a reckoning for his B
49:11 his vesture in the B of grapes;
Ex 4:9 the Nile will become B upon the dry ground."
4:25 are a bridegroom of B to me!"
4:26 that she said, "You are a bridegroom of B
7:17 shall be turned to B,
7:19 that they may become B; and there shall be
7:19 and there shall be B throughout all the land
7:20 water that was in the Nile turned to B
7:21 Nile; and there was B throughout all the land
12:7 take some of the B, and put it on
12:13 The B shall be a sign for you, upon
12:13 when I see the B, I will pass over
12:22 dip it in the B which is in the
12:22 two doorposts with the B which is in the
12:23 when he sees the B on the lintel and
23:18 shall not offer the B of my sacrifice with
24:6 took half of the B and put it in
24:6 and half of the B he threw against the
24:8 And Moses took the B and threw it upon
24:8 and said, "Behold the B of the covenant which
29:12 take part of the B of the bull and
29:12 the rest of the B you shall pour out
29:16 and shall take its B and throw it against
29:20 take part of its B and put it upon
29:20 the rest of the B against the altar round
29:21 take part of the B that is on the
30:10 a year; with the B of the sin offering
34:25 shall not offer the B of my sacrifice with
Lev 1:5 priests shall present the B, and throw the blood
1:5 blood, and throw the B round about against the
1:11 priests shall throw its B against the altar round
1:15 the altar; and its B shall be drained out
3:2 priests shall throw the B against the altar round
3:8 sons shall throw its B against the altar round
3:13 Aaron shall throw its B against the altar round
3:17 dwelling places, that you eat neither fat nor B
4:5 take some of the B of the bull and
4:6 his finger in the B and sprinkle part of
4:6 sprinkle part of the B seven times before the
4:7 put some of the B on the horns of
4:7 the rest of the B of the bull he
4:16 bring some of the B of the bull to
4:17 his finger in the B and sprinkle it seven
4:18 put some of the B on the horns of
4:18 the rest of the B he shall pour out
4:25 take some of the B of the sin offering
4:25 the rest of its B at the base of
4:30 take some of its B with his finger and
4:30 the rest of its B at the base of
4:34 take some of the B of the sin offering
4:34 the rest of its B at the base of
5:9 sprinkle some of the B of the sin offering
5:9 the rest of the B shall be drained out
6:27 when any of its B is sprinkled on a
6:30 eaten from which any B is brought into the
7:2 guilt offering, and its B shall be thrown on
7:14 priest who throws the B of the peace offerings.
7:26 you shall eat no B whatever, whether of fowl

7:27 Whoever eats any B, that person shall be cut
7:33 Aaron who offers the B of the peace offerings
8:15 it, and took the B, and with his finger
8:15 and poured out the B at the base of
8:19 it, and threw the B upon the altar round
8:23 took some of its B and put it on
8:24 put some of the B on the tips of
8:24 and Moses threw the B upon the altar round
8:30 oil and of the B which was on the
9:9 of Aaron presented the B to him, and he
9:9 his finger in the B and put it on
9:9 and poured out the B at the base of
9:12 delivered to him the B, and he threw it
9:18 delivered to him the B, which he threw upon
10:18 Behold, its B was not brought into the inner
12:4 thirty-three days in the B of her purifying; she
12:5 shall continue in the B of her purifying for
12:7 shall be clean from the flow of her B
14:6 living bird in the B of the bird that
14:14 take some of the B of the guilt offering,
14:17 right foot, upon the B of the guilt offering;
14:25 take some of the B of the guilt offering,
14:28 the place where the B of the guilt offering
14:51 dip them in the B of the bird that
14:52 the house with the B of the bird, and
15:19 has a discharge of B which is her regular
15:25 has a discharge of B for many days, not
16:14 take some of the B of the bull, and
16:14 he shall sprinkle the B with his finger seven
16:15 people, and bring its B within the veil, and
16:15 and do with its B as he did with
16:15 he did with the B of the bull, sprinkling
16:18 take some of the B of the bull and
16:18 bull and of the B of the goat, and
16:19 sprinkle some of the B upon it with his
16:27 the sin offering, whose B was brought in to
17:4 man; he has shed B; and that man shall
17:6 priest shall sprinkle the B on the altar of
17:10 among them eats any B, I will set my
17:10 that person who eats B, and will cut him
17:11 flesh is in the B; and I have given
17:11 for it is the B that makes atonement, by
17:12 among you shall eat B, neither shall any stranger
17:12 shall any stranger who sojourns among you eat B
17:13 shall pour out its B and cover it with
17:14 every creature is the B of it; therefore I
17:14 shall not eat the B of any creature, for
17:14 every creature is its B; whoever eats it shall
19:26 any flesh with the B in it.
20:9 or his mother, his B is upon him.
20:11 put to death, their B is upon them.
20:12 have committed incest, their B is upon them.
20:13 put to death, their B is upon them.
20:16 put to death, their B is upon them.
20:18 the fountain of her B; both of them shall
20:27 stoned with stones, their B shall be upon them."
Num 18:17 You shall sprinkle their B upon the altar, and
19:4 take some of her B with his finger, and
19:4 sprinkle some of her B toward the front of
19:5 her flesh, and her B, with her dung, shall
23:24 prey, and drinks the B of the slain."
35:19 The avenger of B shall himself put the murderer
35:21 murderer; the avenger of B shall put the murderer
35:24 and the avenger of B, in accordance with these
35:25 of the avenger of B, and the congregation shall
35:27 and the avenger of B finds him outside the
35:27 and the avenger of B slays the manslayer, he
35:27 the manslayer, he shall not be guilty of B
35:33 which you live; for B pollutes the land, and
35:33 the land, for the B that is shed in
35:33 it, except by the B of him who shed
Deut 12:16 shall not eat the B; you shall pour it
12:23 do not eat the B; for the blood is
12:23 the blood; for the B is the life, and
12:27 the flesh and the B, on the altar of
12:27 LORD your God; the B of your sacrifices shall
15:23 shall not eat its B; you shall pour it
19:6 lest the avenger of B in hot anger pursue
19:10 these three, lest innocent B be shed in your
19:12 to the avenger of B, so that he may
19:13 the guilt of innocent B from Israel, so that
21:7 did not shed this B, neither did our eyes
21:8 the guilt of innocent B in the midst of
21:8 let the guilt of B be forgiven them.'
21:9 the guilt of innocent B from your midst, when
22:8 bring the guilt of B upon your house, if

32:14 wheat--and of the B of the grape you
32:42 my arrows drunk with B, and my sword shall
32:42 devour flesh--with the B of the slain and
32:43 for he avenges the B of his servants, and
Josh 2:19 into the street, his B shall be upon his
2:19 in the house, his B shall be on our
20:3 for you a refuge from the avenger of B
20:5 if the avenger of B pursues him, they shall
20:9 of the avenger of B, till he stood before
Judg 9:24 might come and their B be laid upon Abimelech
1Sam 14:32 ground; and the people ate them with the B
14:33 sinning against the LORD, by eating with the B
14:34 sin against the LORD by eating with the B
19:5 you sin against innocent B by killing David without
25:31 conscience, for having shed B without cause or for
26:20 therefore, let not my B fall to the earth
2Sam 1:16 said to him, "Your B be upon your head;
1:22 "From the B of the slain, from the fat
3:27 he died, for the B of Asahel his brother.
3:28 the LORD for the B of Abner the son
4:11 not now require his B at your hand, and
14:11 that the avenger of B slay no more, and
16:7 begone, you man of B, you worthless fellow!
16:8 upon you all the B of the house of
16:8 on you; for you are a man of B
20:12 lay wallowing in his B in the highway.
23:17 Shall I drink the B of the men who
1Kgs 2:5 in time of peace B which had been shed
2:5 war, and putting innocent B upon the girdle about
2:9 gray head down with B to Sheol."
2:31 the guilt for the B which Joab shed without
2:33 So shall their B come back upon the head
2:37 you shall die; your B shall be upon your
18:28 and lances, until the B gushed out upon them.
21:19 dogs licked up the B of Naboth shall dogs
21:19 blood of Naboth shall dogs lick your own B
22:35 he died; and the B of the wound flowed
22:38 dogs licked up his B, and the harlots washed
2Kgs 3:22 saw the water opposite them as red as B
3:23 they said, "This is B; the kings have surely
9:7 avenge on Jezebel the B of my servants the
9:7 the prophets, and the B of all the servants
9:26 I saw yesterday the B of Naboth and the
9:26 of Naboth and the B of his sons--says
9:33 and some of her B spattered on the wall
16:13 offering, and threw the B of his peace offerings
16:15 upon it all the B of the burnt offering,
16:15 offering, and all the B of the sacrifice; but
21:16 shed very much innocent B, till he had filled
24:4 also for the innocent B that he had shed;
24:4 filled Jerusalem with innocent B, and the LORD
1Chr 22:8 'You have shed much B and have waged great
22:8 have shed so much B before me upon the
28:3 warrior and have shed B
2Chr 24:25 him because of the B of the son of
29:22 the priests received the B and threw it against
29:22 the rams and their B was thrown against the
29:22 the lambs and their B was thrown against the
29:24 sin offering with their B on the altar, to
30:16 the priests sprinkled the B which they received from
35:11 the priests sprinkled the B which they received from
Jud 6:4 be drunk with their B, and their fields will
9:3 to be stained with B, and thou didst strike
9:4 the pollution of their B, and called on thee
Esth 16:5 the shedding of innocent B, and have been involved
16:10 alien to the Persian B, and quite devoid of
Job 16:18 earth, cover not my B, and let my cry
39:30 young ones suck up B; and where the slain
Ps 9:12 For he who avenges B is mindful of them;
16:4 sorrows; their libations of B I will not pour
50:13 bulls, or drink the B of goats?
55:23 lowest pit; men of B and treachery shall not
58:10 his feet in the B of the wicked.
68:23 bathe your feet in B, that the tongues of
72:14 and precious is their B in his sight.
78:44 turned their rivers to B, so that they could
79:3 have poured out their B like water round about
79:10 avenging of the outpoured B of thy servants be
105:29 turned their waters into B, and caused their fish
106:38 they poured out innocent B, the blood of their
106:38 out innocent blood, the B of their sons and
106:38 of Canaan; and the land was polluted with B
139:19 and that men of B would depart from me,
Prov 1:11 lie in wait for B, let us wantonly ambush
1:16 to evil, and they make haste to shed B
1:18 wait for their own B, they set an ambush

6:17 hands that shed innocent B,
12:6 lie in wait for B, but the mouth of
28:17 is burdened with the B of another, let him
30:33 pressing the nose produces B, and pressing anger
Wis 7:2 ten months, compacted with B, from the seed of
11:6 up and defiled with B
12:5 and their sacrificial feasting on human flesh and B
14:25 a raging riot of B and murder, theft and
Sir 8:16 wilderness with him; because B is as nothing in
9:9 to her, and in B you be plunged into
11:30 and a sinner lies in wait to shed B
12:16 opportunity his thirst for B will be insatiable.
14:18 generations of flesh and B: one dies and another
17:26 So flesh and B devise evil.
28:11 hasty quarrel kindles fire, and urgent strife sheds B
33:30 as yourself, because you have bought him with B
34:21 deprives them of it is a man of B
34:22 an employee of his wages is to shed B
39:26 milk and honey, the B of the grape, and
50:15 a libation of the B of the grape; he
Is 1:11 not delight in the B of bulls, or of
1:15 will not listen; your hands are full of B
9:5 every garment rolled in B will be burned as
15:9 Dibon are full of B; yet I will bring
26:21 earth will disclose the B shed upon her, and
34:3 shall rise; the mountains shall flow with their B
34:6 it is sated with B, it is gorged with
34:6 with fat, with the B of lambs and goats,
34:7 shall be soaked with B, and their soil made
49:26 drunk with their own B as with wine.
59:3 hands are defiled with B and your fingers with
59:7 haste to shed innocent B; their thoughts are thoughts
66:3 him who offers swine's B; he who makes a
Jer 7:6 widow, or shed innocent B in this place, and
19:4 this place with the B of innocents,
22:3 widow, nor shed innocent B in this place.
22:17 gain, for shedding innocent B, and for practicing
26:15 you will bring innocent B upon yourselves and upon
46:10 be sated, and drink its fill of their B
51:35 "My B be upon the inhabitants of Chaldea," let
Lam 4:13 midst of her the B of the righteous.
4:14 streets, so defiled with B that none could touch
Ezek 3:18 his iniquity; but his B I will require at
3:20 be remembered; but his B I will require at
5:17 your children; pestilence and B shall pass through
9:9 land is full of B, and the city full
14:19 wrath upon it with B, to cut off from
16:6 you weltering in your B, I said to you
16:6 to you in your B, 'Live,
16:9 and washed off your B from you, and anointed
16:22 you were naked and bare, weltering in your B
16:36 and because of the B of your children that
16:38 break wedlock and shed B are judged, and bring
16:38 bring upon you the B of wrath and jealousy.
18:10 robber, a shedder of B,
18:13 shall surely die; his B shall be upon himself.
21:32 for the fire; your B shall be in the
22:3 A city that sheds B in the midst of
22:4 become guilty by the B which you have shed,
22:6 to his power, have been bent on shedding B
22:9 who slander to shed B, and men in you
22:12 take bribes to shed B; you take interest and
22:13 made, and at the B which has been in
22:27 tearing the prey, shedding B, destroying lives to get
23:37 have committed adultery, and B is upon their hands;
23:45 women that shed B; because they are adulteresses,
23:45 they are adulteresses, and B is upon their hands."
24:7 For the B she has shed is still in
24:8 the bare rock the B she has shed, that
28:23 pestilence into her, and B into her streets; and
32:6 with your flowing B; and the watercourses
33:4 takes him away, his B shall be upon his
33:5 not take warning; his B shall be upon himself.
33:6 his iniquity, but his B I will require at
33:8 his iniquity, but his B I will require at
33:25 eat flesh with the B, and lift up your
33:25 your idols, and shed B; shall you then possess
35:6 will prepare you for B, and blood shall pursue
35:6 you for blood, and B shall pursue you; because
35:6 you are guilty of B, therefore blood shall pursue
35:6 guilty of blood, therefore B shall pursue you.
36:18 upon them for the B which they had shed
39:17 Israel, and you shall eat flesh and drink B
39:18 mighty, and drink the B of the princes of
39:19 are filled, and drink B till you are drunk,
43:18 it and for throwing B against it,
43:20 take some of its B, and put it on
44:7 to me my food, the fat and the B
44:15 the fat and the B, says the Lord GOD;
45:19 take some of the B of the sin offering
Dan 13:46 am innocent of the B of this woman."
13:62 Thus innocent B was saved that day.
Hos 1:4 of Jehu for the B of Jezreel, and I
6:8 Gilead is a city of evildoers, tracked with B
Joel 2:30 and on the earth, B and fire and columns
2:31 and the moon to B, before the great and
3:19 they have shed innocent B in their land.
3:21 I will avenge their B, and I will not
Jon 1:14 not on us innocent B; for thou, O LORD,
Mic 3:10 who build Zion with B and Jerusalem with wrong.
7:2 lie in wait for B, and each hunts his
Hab 2:8 plunder you, for the B of men and violence
2:12 builds a town with B, and founds a city
2:17 terrify you, for the B of men and violence
Zeph 1:17 against the LORD; their B shall be poured out
Zech 9:7 will take away its B from its mouth, and
9:11 also, because of the B of my covenant with
9:15 they shall drink their B like wine, and be
1Mac 1:37 sanctuary they shed innocent B; they even defiled the
7:17 thy saints and their B they poured out round
9:38 And they remembered the B of John their brother,
9:42 had fully avenged the B of their brother, they
2Mac 1:8 kingdom and burned the gate and shed innocent B
8:3 to hearken to the B that cried out to
12:16 mile wide, appeared to be running over with B
14:45 rose, and though his B gushed forth and his
14:46 steep rock, with his B now completely drained from
Mt 16:17 For flesh and B has not revealed this to
23:29 them in shedding the B of the prophets.'
23:34 come all the righteous B shed on earth, from
23:34 on earth, from the B of innocent Abel to
23:34 innocent Abel to the B of Zechariah the son
26:28 for this is my B of the covenant, which
27:4 elders, saying, "I have sinned in betraying innocent B
27:6 treasury, since they are B money."
27:8 called the Field of B to this day.
27:24 of this righteous man's B; see to it yourselves."
27:25 the people answered, "His B be on us and
Mk 5:25 had a flow of B for twelve years,
14:24 them, "This is my B of the covenant, which
Lk 8:43 had a flow of B for twelve years and
8:44 immediately her flow of B ceased.
11:50 and persecute,' that the B of all the prophets,
11:51 this generation, from the B of Abel to the
11:51 of Abel to the B of Zechariah, who perished
13:1 of the Galileans whose B Pilate had mingled with
22:20 for you is the new covenant in my B
Jn 1:13 were born, not of B nor of the will
6:53 man and drink his B, you have no life
6:54 flesh and drinks my B has eternal life, and
6:55 food indeed, and my B is drink indeed.
6:56 flesh and drinks my B abides in me, and
19:34 once there came out B and water.
Acts 1:19 that is, Field of B
2:19 on the earth beneath, B, and fire, and vapor
2:20 and the moon into B, before the day of
5:28 to bring this man's B upon us."
15:20 unchastity and from what is strangled and from B
15:29 to idols and from B and from what is
18:6 said to them, "Your B be upon your heads!
20:26 am innocent of the B of all of you,
20:28 he obtained with the B of his own.
21:25 to idols and from B and from what is
22:20 And when the B of Stephen thy witness was
Rom 3:15 are swift to shed B,
3:25 an expiation by his B, to be received by
5:9 now justified by his B, much more shall we
1Cor 10:16 a participation in the B of Christ?
11:25 "This cup is the new covenant in my B
11:27 profaning the body and B of the Lord.
15:50 brethren: flesh and B cannot inherit the kingdom
Gal 1:16 confer with flesh and B,
Eph 1:7 have redemption through his B, the forgiveness of
2:13 brought near in the B of Christ.
6:12 contending against flesh and B, but against the
Col 1:20 making peace by the B of his cross.
Heb 2:14 share in flesh and B, he himself likewise partook
9:7 and not without taking B which he offers for
9:12 Place, taking not the B of goats and calves
9:12 calves but his own B, thus securing an eternal
9:13 defiled persons with the B of goats and bulls
9:14 much more shall the B of Christ, who through

9:18 even the first covenant was not ratified without B
9:19 people, he took the B of calves and goats,
9:20 saying, "This is the B of the covenant which
9:21 he sprinkled with the B both the tent and
9:22 everything is purified with B, and without the
9:22 without the shedding of B there is no forgiveness
9:25 Holy Place yearly with B not his own;
10:4 is impossible that the B of bulls and goats
10:19 the sanctuary by the B of Jesus,
10:29 God, and profaned the B of the covenant by
11:28 Passover and sprinkled the B, so that the Destroyer
12:4 yet resisted to the point of shedding your B
12:24 and to the sprinkled B that speaks more graciously
12:24 more graciously than the B of Abel.
13:11 of those animals whose B is brought into the
13:12 order to sanctify the people through his own B
13:20 the sheep, by the B of the eternal covenant,
1Pet 1:2 for sprinkling with his B: May grace and peace
1:19 but with the precious B of Christ, like that
1Jn 1:7 one another, and the B of Jesus his Son
5:6 came by water and B, Jesus Christ, not with
5:6 water only but with the water and the B
5:8 the water, and the B; and these three agree.
Rev 1:5 our sins by his B
5:9 slain and by thy B didst ransom men for
6:10 judge and avenge our B on those who dwell
6:12 full moon became like B,
7:14 them white in the B of the Lamb.
8:7 and fire, mixed with B, which fell on the
8:9 of the sea became B, a third of the
11:6 to turn them into B, and to smite the
12:11 conquered him by the B of the Lamb and
14:20 outside the city, and B flowed from the wine
16:3 it became like the B of a dead man,
16:4 and the fountains of water, and they became B
16:6 men have shed the B of saints and prophets,
16:6 thou hast given them B to drink.
17:6 woman, drunk with the B of the saints and
17:6 the saints and the B of the martyrs of
18:24 her was found the B of prophets and of
19:2 avenged on her the B of his servants."
19:13 a robe dipped in B, and the name by

BLOODGUILT (7)

Ex 22:3 there shall be no B for him;
22:4 him, there shall be B for him.
Lev 17:4 tabernacle of the LORD, B shall be imputed to
1Sam 25:26 restrained you from B, and from taking vengeance
25:33 me this day from B and from avenging myself
2Sam 21:1 LORD said, "There is B on Saul and on
Hos 12:14 LORD will leave his B upon him, and will

BLOODGUILTINESS

Ps 51:14 Deliver me from B, O God, thou God of

BLOODSHED (10)

Deut 19:10 so the guilt of B be upon you.
2Chr 19:10 in their cities, concerning B, law or commandment,
Sir 22:22 the furnace precede the fire; so insults precede B
27:15 the proud leads to B, and their abuse is
40:9 more, are death and B and strife and sword,
Is 5:7 justice, but behold, B; for righteousness, but behold,
33:15 ears from hearing of B and shuts his eyes
Jer 48:10 is he who keeps back his sword from B
Ezek 38:22 With pestilence and B I will enter into judgment
2Mac 14:18 their country, shrank from deciding the issue by B

BLOODSTAINS

Is 4:4 Zion and cleansed the B of Jerusalem from its

BLOODTHIRSTY (5)

Ps 5:6 lies; the LORD abhors B and deceitful men.
26:9 nor my life with B men,
59:2 and save me from B men.
Prov 29:10 B men hate one who is blameless, and the
2Mac 4:38 there he dispatched the B fellow.

BLOODY (6)

1Kgs 2:32 will bring back his B deeds upon his own
Ezek 7:23 land is full of B crimes and the city
22:2 will you judge the B city?
24:6 GOD: Woe to the B city, to the pot
24:9 GOD: Woe to the B city!
Nah 3:1 Woe to the B city, all full of lies

BLOOM (3)

Song 6:11 had budded, whether the pomegranates were in B
7:12 have opened and the pomegranates are in B
Nah 1:4 and Carmel wither, the B of Lebanon fades.

BLOSSOM (15)

Job 15:30 his shoots, and his B will be swept away
15:33 and cast off his B, like the olive tree.
Ps 72:16 Lebanon; and may men B forth from the cities
Song 2:13 the vines are in B; they give forth fragrance.
2:15 spoil the vineyards, for our vineyards are in B
Sir 51:15 From B to ripening grape my heart delighted in
Is 5:24 as rottenness, and their B go up like dust;
17:11 them, and make them B in the morning that
18:5 the harvest, when the B is over, and the
27:6 take root, Israel shall B and put forth shoots,
35:1 desert shall rejoice and B; like the crocus
35:2 the crocus it shall B abundantly, and rejoice with
Hos 14:5 to Israel; he shall B as the lily, he
14:7 a garden; they shall B as the vine, their
Hab 3:17 fig tree do not B, nor fruit be on

BLOSSOMED

Ezek 7:10 has come, injustice has B, pride has budded.

BLOSSOMS (8)

Gen 40:10 as it budded, its B shot forth, and the
Num 17:8 forth buds, and produced B, and it bore ripe
Eccl 12:5 way; the almond tree B, the grasshopper drags itself
Song 1:14 a cluster of henna B in the vineyards of
6:11 to look at the B of the valley, to
7:12 budded, whether the grape B have opened and the
Sir 24:17 to bud, and my B became glorious and abundant
39:14 frankincense, and put forth B like a lily.

BLOT (20)

Gen 6:7 LORD said, "I will B out man whom I
7:4 have made I will B out from the face
Ex 17:14 that I will utterly B out the remembrance of
23:23 the Jebusites, and I B them out,
32:32 sin–and if not, B me, I pray thee,
32:33 me, him will I B out of my book.
Deut 9:14 may destroy them and B out their name from
25:19 to possess, you shall B out the remembrance of
29:20 and the LORD would B out his name from
2Kgs 14:27 said that he would B out the name of
Ps 51:1 to thy abundant mercy B out my transgressions.
51:9 from my sins, and B out all my iniquities.
Sir 7:6 and thus put a B on your integrity.
20:23 lie is an ugly B on a man; it
46:20 earth in prophecy, to B out the wickedness of
47:22 perish; he will never B out the descendants of
Jer 18:23 not their iniquity, nor B out their sin from
Ezek 32:7 When I B you out, I will cover the
1Mac 12:53 war on them and B out the memory of
Rev 3:5 and I will not B his name out of

BLOTS (2)

Is 43:25 I am He who B out your transgressions for
2Pet 2:13 They are B and blemishes, reveling in their

BLOTTED (18)

Gen 7:23 He B out every living thing that was upon
7:23 the air; they were B out from the earth.
Deut 25:6 name may not be B out of Israel.
Judg 21:17 a tribe be not B out from Israel.
Neh 4:5 not their sin be B out from thy sight;
Tob 4:19 not let them be B out of your mind.
Ps 9:5 the wicked; thou hast B out their name for
69:28 Let them be B out of the book of
109:13 may his name be B out in the second
109:14 of his mother be B out!
Sir 23:26 disgrace will not be B out.
39:9 it will never be B out; his memory will
40:12 and injustice will be B out, but good faith
41:11 of sinners will be B out.
44:14 glory will not be B out.
44:19 flesh should not be B out by a flood.
2Mac 12:42 committed might be wholly B out.
Acts 3:19 your sins may be B out, that times of

BLOW (50)

Gen 8:1 God made a wind B over the earth, and
Ex 15:10 destroy them.' Thou didst B with thy wind, the
Num 10:4 But if they B only one, then the leaders,
10:5 When you B an alarm, the camps that are

10:6 And when you B an alarm the second time,
10:7 gathered together, you shall B, but you shall not
10:8 Aaron, the priests, shall B the trumpets.
10:10 your months, you shall B the trumpets over your
29:1 day for you to B the trumpets,
35:21 he who struck the B shall be put to
Judg 5:26 she struck Sisera a B, she crushed his head,
7:18 When I B the trumpet, I and all who
7:18 are with me, then B the trumpets also on
7:20 hands the trumpets to B; and they cried, "A
2Sam 20:10 without striking a second B; and he died.
1Kgs 1:34 king over Israel; then B the trumpet, and say,
1Chr 15:24 Eliezer, the priests, should B the trumpets before the
16:6 the priests were to B trumpets continually, before
Ps 78:26 the east wind to B in the heavens, and
81:3 B the trumpet at the new moon, at the
147:18 he makes his wind B, and the waters flow.
Song 4:16 B upon my garden, let its fragrance be wafted
Wis 12:9 destroy them at one B by dread wild beasts
Sir 22:20 secrets, or a treacherous B -- in these cases
27:25 head; and a treacherous B opens up wounds.
28:12 If you B on a spark, it will glow;
28:17 The B of a whip raises a welt, but
28:17 a welt, but a B of the tongue crushes
Is 30:26 people, and heals the wounds inflicted by his B
30:30 heard and the descending B of his arm to
Jer 4:5 in Jerusalem, and say, B the trumpet through the
6:1 B the trumpet in Tekoa, and raise a signal
6:29 The bellows B fiercely, the lead is consumed by
14:17 with a great wound, with a very grievous B
30:14 have dealt you the B of an enemy, the
51:27 standard on the earth, B the trumpet among the
Ezek 21:31 upon you; I will B upon you with the
22:20 into a furnace, to B the fire upon it
22:21 will gather you and B upon you with the
33:6 coming and does not B the trumpet, so that
Hos 5:8 B the horn in Gibe-ah, the trumpet in Ramah.
Joel 2:1 B the trumpet in Zion; sound the alarm on
2:15 B the trumpet in Zion; sanctify a fast; call
1Mac 1:30 dealt it a severe B, and destroyed many people
5:3 dealt them a heavy B and humbled them and
5:34 before him, and he dealt them a heavy B
2Mac 9:5 of Israel, struck him an incurable and unseen B
Rev 7:1 that no wind might B on earth or sea
8:6 trumpets made ready to B them.
8:13 trumpets which the three angels are about to B

BLOWING (7)

Josh 6:4 seven times, the priests B the trumpets.
6:8 the LORD went forward, B the trumpets, with the
6:13 the LORD passed on, B the trumpets continually; and
2Kgs 11:14 the land rejoicing and B trumpets.
2Chr 23:13 the land rejoicing and B trumpets, and the singers
Lk 12:55 see the south wind B, you say, 'There will
Jn 6:18 The sea rose because a strong wind was B

BLOWN (9)

Num 10:3 And when both are B, all the congregation shall
10:6 alarm is to be B whenever they are to
Josh 6:16 when the priests had B the trumpets, Joshua said
6:20 So the people shouted, and the trumpets were B
Job 20:26 treasures; a fire not B upon will devour him;
Is 18:3 When a trumpet is B, hear!
27:13 great trumpet will be B, and those who were
Ezek 7:14 "They have B the trumpet and made all ready;
Amos 3:6 Is a trumpet B in a city, and the

BLOWS (17)

Ps 39:10 am spent by the B of thy hand.
Prov 17:10 understanding than a hundred B into a fool.
20:30 B that wound cleanse away evil; strokes make clean
Eccl 1:6 The wind B to the south, and goes round
Sir 43:16 are shaken; at his will the south wind B
43:20 The cold north wind B, and ice freezes over
Is 14:6 in wrath with unceasing B, that ruled the nations
40:7 breath of the LORD B upon it; surely the
40:24 the earth, when he B upon them, and they
54:16 created the smith who B the fire of coals,
Bar 6:61 and the wind likewise B in every land.
Ezek 33:3 upon the land and B the trumpet and warns
2Mac 3:26 him continuously, inflicting many B on him.
6:30 to die under the B, he groaned aloud and
Mk 14:65 And the guards received him with B
Jn 3:8 born anew.' The wind B where it wills, and
Acts 16:23 they had inflicted many B upon them, they threw

BLUE (50)

Ex 25:4 gold, silver, and bronze, B and purple and scarlet
26:1 fine twined linen and B and purple and scarlet
26:4 shall make loops of B on the edge of
26:31 make a veil of B and purple and scarlet
26:36 of the tent, of B and purple and scarlet
27:16 twenty cubits long, of B and purple and scarlet
28:5 "They shall receive gold, B and purple and scarlet
28:6 ephod of gold, of B and purple and scarlet
28:8 and materials, of gold, B and purple and scarlet
28:15 make it; of gold, B and purple and scarlet
28:28 with a lace of B, that it may lie
28:31 make the robe of the ephod all of B
28:33 make pomegranates of B and purple and scarlet
28:37 by a lace of B; it shall be on
35:6 gold, silver, and bronze; B and purple and scarlet
35:23 with whom was found B or purple or scarlet
35:25 they had spun in B and purple and scarlet
35:35 by an embroiderer in B and purple and scarlet
36:8 fine twined linen and B and purple and scarlet
36:11 he made loops of B on the edge of
36:35 made the veil of B and purple and scarlet
36:37 of the tent, of B and purple and scarlet
38:18 embroidered with needlework in B and purple and
38:23 designer and embroiderer in B and purple and
39:1 And of the B and purple and scarlet stuff
39:2 the ephod of gold, B and purple and scarlet
39:3 to work into the B and purple and the
39:5 and workmanship, of gold, B and purple and scarlet
39:8 the ephod, of gold, B and purple and scarlet
39:21 with a lace of B, so that it should
39:22 ephod woven all of B;
39:24 they made pomegranates of B and purple and scarlet
39:29 twined linen and of B and purple and scarlet
39:31 it a lace of B, to fasten it on
Num 4:6 a cloth all of B, and shall put in
4:7 spread a cloth of B, and put upon it
4:9 take a cloth of B, and cover the lampstand
4:11 spread a cloth of B, and cover it with
4:12 in a cloth of B, and cover them with
15:38 corner a cord of B;
2Chr 2:7 in purple, crimson, and B fabrics, trained also in
2:14 wood, and in purple, B, and crimson fabrics and
3:14 made the veil of B and purple and crimson
Esth 1:6 white cotton curtains and B hangings caught up with
8:15 in royal robes of B and white, with a
Sir 6:30 ornament, and her bonds are a cord of B
45:10 garment, of gold and B and purple, the work
Ezek 27:7 serving as your ensign; B and purple from the
27:24 garments, in clothes of B and embroidered work, and
1Mac 4:23 silver, and cloth dyed B and sea purple, and

BLUNDER

Sir 14:1 man who does not B with his lips and

BLUNT

Eccl 10:10 If the iron is B, and one does not

BLUSH (4)

Ezra 9:6 I am ashamed and B to lift my face
Is 1:29 delighted; and you shall B for the gardens which
Jer 6:15 all ashamed; they did not know how to B
8:12 all ashamed; they did not know how to B

BLUSHED

Tob 2:14 the owners; and I B for her.

BO-ANERGES

Mk 3:17 James, whom he surnamed B, that is, sons of

BOAR

Ps 80:13 The B from the forest ravages it, and all

BOARD (5)

Jon 1:3 fare, and went on B, to go with them
Acts 20:14 we took him on B and came to Mitylene.
21:6 Then we went on B the ship, and they
27:6 Alexandria sailing for Italy, and put us on B
28:10 sailed, they put on B whatever we needed.

BOARDS (6)

Ex 27:8 make it hollow, with B; as it has been
38:7 it with them; he made it hollow, with B
1Kgs 6:15 on the inside with B of cedar; from the
6:15 of the house with B of cypress.
6:16 of the house with B of cedar from the

Song 8:9 will enclose her with B of cedar.

BOAST (52)

1Kgs 20:11 girds on his armor B himself as he that
Ps 20:7 Some B of chariots, and some of horses; but
20:7 of horses; but we B of the name of
34:2 My soul makes its B in the LORD; let
38:16 rejoice over me, who B against me when my
49:6 in their wealth and B of the abundance of
52:1 Why do you B, O mighty man, of mischief
75:4 [Selah] I say to the boastful, "Do not B
94:4 their arrogant words, they B, all the evildoers.
97:7 shame, who make their B in worthless idols; all
Prov 27:1 Do not B about tomorrow, for you do not
Wis 6:2 rule over multitudes, and B of many nations.
Sir 11:4 Do not B about wearing fine clothes, nor exalt
25:6 the aged, and their B is the fear of
30:2 by him, and will B of him among acquaintances.
48:4 has the right to B which you have?
Is 20:5 of Ethiopia their hope and of Egypt their B
Jer 49:4 Why do you B of your valleys, O faithless
Rom 2:17 upon the law and B of your relation to
2:23 You who B in the law, do you dishonor
4:2 he has something to B about, but not before
11:18 olive tree, do not B over the branches.
11:18 If you do B, remember it is not you
1Cor 1:29 no human being might B in the presence of
1:31 "Let him who boasts, B of the Lord."
3:21 So let no one B of men.
4:7 it, why do you B as if it were
2Cor 1:12 For our B is this, the testimony of our
9:2 readiness, of which I B about you to the
10:8 For even if I B a little too much
10:13 But we will not B beyond limit, but will
10:15 We do not B beyond limit, in other men's
10:17 "Let him who boasts, B of the Lord."
11:10 is in me, this B of mine shall not
11:16 that I too may B a little.
11:18 boastful confidence; since many B of worldly things,
11:18 things, I too will B
11:21 any one dares to B of--I am speaking
11:21 I also dare to B of that.
11:30 If I must B, I will boast of the
11:30 must boast, I will B of the things that
12:1 I must B; there is nothing to be gained
12:5 this man I will B, but on my own
12:5 behalf I will not B, except of my weaknesses.
12:6 if I wish to B, I shall not be
12:9 all the more gladly B of my weaknesses, that
Gal 6:4 then his reason to B will be in himself
Eph 2:9 not because of works, lest any man should B
2Thes 1:4 Therefore we ourselves B of you in the churches
Jas 1:8 Let the lowly brother B in his exaltation,
3:14 your hearts, do not B and be false to
4:16 As it is, you B in your arrogance.

BOASTED (7)

Jud 16:5 He B that he would burn up my territory,
Ps 44:8 In God we have B continually, and we will
Wis 5:8 what good has our B wealth brought us?
17:7 lay humbled, and their B wisdom was scornfully
Obad 1:12 you should not have B in the day of
Zeph 2:10 because they scoffed and B against the people of
2Cor 11:12 claim that in their B mission they work on

BOASTERS

Jude 1:16 own passions, loud-mouthed B, flattering people to

BOASTFUL (5)

Ps 5:5 The B may not stand before thy eyes; thou
75:4 I say to the B, "Do not boast," and
Rom 1:30 of God, insolent, haughty, B, inventors of evil,
1Cor 13:4 is not jealous or B;
2Cor 11:17 a fool, in this B confidence;

BOASTFULLY (2)

Jud 6:17 Holofernes had said so B against the house of
2Mac 15:32 arm, which had been B stretched out against the

BOASTFULNESS (2)

2Chr 25:19 and your heart has lifted you up in B
2Mac 15:6 Nicanor in his utter B and arrogance had determined

BOASTING (14)

Sir 10:26 one who goes about B, but lacks bread.
31:10 Let it be for him a ground for B
47:4 and struck down the B of Goliath?
Is 10:12 will punish the arrogant B of the king of
Rom 3:27 Then what becomes of our B
1Cor 5:6 Your B is not good.
9:15 any one deprive me of my ground for B
9:16 the gospel, that gives me no ground for B
2Cor 7:14 was true, so our B before Titus has proved
8:24 love and of our B about you to these
9:3 brethren so that our B about you may not
10:16 lands beyond you, without B of work already done
1Thes 2:19 joy or crown of B before our Lord Jesus
Jas 4:16 All such B is evil.

BOASTS (14)

Esth 16:4 carried away by the B of those who know
Ps 10:3 For the wicked B of the desires of his
12:3 tongue that makes great B,
Prov 20:14 buyer; but when he goes away, then he B
25:14 is a man who B of a gift he
Wis 2:16 the righteous happy, and B that God is his
Sir 48:18 Zion and made great B in his arrogance.
Is 16:6 his insolence-- his B are false.
Jer 48:30 says the LORD; his B are false, his deeds
Zeph 2:8 my people and made B against their territory.
1Cor 1:31 written, "Let him who B, boast of the Lord."
2Cor 10:17 "Let him who B, boast of the Lord."
Jas 3:5 a little member and B of great things.
2Pet 2:18 For, uttering loud B of folly, they entice with

BOAT (48)

Sir 33:2 it is like a B in a storm.
Mt 4:21 his brother, in the B with Zebedee their father,
4:22 Immediately they left the B and their father, and
8:23 he got into the B, his disciples followed him.
8:24 sea, so that the B was being swamped by
9:1 And getting into a B he crossed over and
13:2 he got into a B and sat there; and
14:13 from there in a B to a lonely place
14:22 disciples get into the B and go before him
14:24 there alone, but the B by this time was
14:29 got out of the B and walked on the
14:32 they got into the B, the wind ceased.
14:33 And those in the B worshipped him, saying, "Truly
15:39 he got into the B and went to the
Mk 1:19 who were in their B mending the nets.
1:20 father Zebedee in the B with the hired servants,
3:9 disciples to have a B ready for him because
4:1 he got into a B and sat in it
4:36 with them in the B, just as he was.
4:37 waves beat into the B, so that the boat
4:37 boat, so that the B was already filling.
5:2 come out of the B, there met him out
5:18 was getting into the B, the man who had
5:21 crossed again in the B to the other side,
6:32 went away in the B to a lonely place
6:45 disciples get into the B and go before him
6:47 when evening came, the B was out on the
6:51 he got into the B with them and the
6:54 got out of the B, immediately the people recognized
8:10 he got into the B with his disciples, and
8:13 and getting into the B again he departed to
8:14 had only one loaf with them in the B
Lk 5:3 sat down and taught the people from the B
5:7 partners in the other B to come and help
8:22 he got into a B with his disciples, and
8:37 he got into the B and returned.
Jn 6:17 sea, got into a B, and started across the
6:19 on the sea and drawing near to the B
6:21 take him into the B, and immediately the boat
6:21 boat, and immediately the B was at the land
6:22 had been only one B there, and that Jesus
6:22 had not entered the B with his disciples, but
21:3 and got into the B; but that night they
21:6 right side of the B, and you will find
21:8 disciples came in the B, dragging the net full
Acts 27:16 difficulty to secure the B;
27:30 and had lowered the B into the sea, under
27:32 the ropes of the B, and let it go.

BOATS (9)

2Mac 12:3 wives and children, on B which they had provided,
12:6 night, and burned the B, and massacred those who
Mk 4:36 And other B were with him.
Lk 5:2 And he saw two B by the lake; but
5:3 into one of the B, which was Simons, he
5:7 and filled both the B, so that they began

5:11 they had brought their B to land, they left
Jn 6:23 However, B from Tiberi-as came near the place
6:24 themselves got into the B and went to Caperna-um,

BOAZ (28)

Ruth 2:1 of the family of Elimelech, whose name was B
2:3 the field belonging to B, who was of the
2:4 And behold, B came from Bethlehem; and he said
2:5 Then B said to his servant who was in
2:8 Then B said to Ruth, "Now, listen, my daughter,
2:11 But B answered her, "All that you have done
2:14 And at mealtime B said to her, "Come here,
2:15 she rose to glean, B instructed his young men,
2:19 man's name with whom I worked today is B
2:23 to the maidens of B, gleaning until the end
3:2 Now is not B our kinsman, with whose maidens
3:7 And when B had eaten and drunk, and his
4:1 And B went up to the gate and sat
4:1 of kin, of whom B had spoken, came by.
4:1 So B said, "Turn aside, friend; sit down here";
4:5 Then B said, "The day you buy the field
4:8 of kin said to B, "Buy it for yourself,"
4:9 Then B said to the elders and all the
4:13 So B took Ruth and she became his wife;
4:21 of Salmon, Salmon of B, Boaz of Obed,
4:21 Salmon, Salmon of Boaz, B of Obed,
1Kgs 7:21 pillar on the north and called its name B
1Chr 2:11 of Salma, Salma of B,
2:12 Salma, Salma of Boaz, B of Obed, Obed of
2Chr 3:17 he called Jachin, and that on the north B
Mt 1:5 Salmon the father of B by Rahab, and Boaz
1:5 Boaz by Rahab, and B the father of Obed
Lk 3:32 Obed, the son of B, the son of Sala,

BOCHERU (2)

1Chr 8:38 names: Azrikam, B, Ishmael, She-ariah, Obadiah,
9:44 are their names: Azrikam, B, Ishmael, She-ariah,

BOCHIM (2)

Judg 2:1 of the LORD went up from Gilgal to B
2:5 name of that place B; and they sacrificed there

BODIES (65)

Gen 47:18 my lord but our B and our lands.
Ex 30:32 be poured upon the B of ordinary men, and
Lev 26:30 and cast your dead B upon the dead bodies
26:30 bodies upon the dead B of your idols; and
Num 14:29 to you: your dead B shall fall in this
14:32 for you, your dead B shall fall in this
14:33 last of your dead B lies in the wilderness.
1Sam 17:46 will give the dead B of the host of
31:12 of Saul and the B of his sons from
2Kgs 19:35 in the morning, behold, these were all dead B
1Chr 10:12 of Saul and the B of his sons, and
2Chr 20:24 behold, they were dead B lying on the ground;
Neh 9:37 power also over our B and over our cattle
Tob 1:18 When the B were sought by the king, they
Ps 73:4 have no pangs; their B are sound and sleek.
79:2 They have given the B of thy servants to
Sir 41:11 men is about their B, but the evil name
44:15 Their B were buried in peace, and their name
Is 26:19 dead shall live, their B shall rise.
37:36 in the morning, behold, these were all dead B
66:24 look on the dead B of the men that
Jer 7:33 And the dead B of this people will be
9:22 the LORD: 'The dead B of men shall fall
16:4 famine, and their dead B shall be food for
19:7 will give their dead B for food to the
31:40 valley of the dead B and the ashes, and
33:5 them with the dead B of men whom I
34:20 Their dead B shall be food for the birds
41:5 clothes torn, and their B gashed, bringing cereal
41:9 Ishmael cast all the B of the men whom
Lam 4:7 whiter than milk; their B were more ruddy than
Bar 2:17 been taken from their B, will not ascribe glory
6:22 birds light on their B and heads; and so
Ezek 1:11 the wing of another, while two covered their B
6:5 will lay the dead B of the people of
43:7 and by the dead B of their kings,
43:9 idolatry and the dead B of their kings far
Dan 3:95 any power over the B of those men; the
3:96 and yielded up their B rather than serve and
14:32 been given two human B and two sheep; but
Amos 8:3 Lord GOD; "the dead B shall be many; in
Nah 3:3 heaps of corpses, dead B without end--they stumble
3:3 dead bodies without end--they stumble over the B
1Mac 11:4 about, and the charred B of those whom Jonathan
2Mac 12:39 to take up the B of the fallen and
Mt 27:52 were opened, and many B of the saints who
Jn 19:31 order to prevent the B from remaining on the
Rom 1:24 the dishonoring of their B among themselves,
6:12 reign in your mortal B, to make you obey
8:10 in you, although your B are dead because of
8:11 life to your mortal B also through his Spirit
8:23 for adoption as sons, the redemption of our B
12:1 God, to present your B as a living sacrifice,
1Cor 6:15 not know that your B are members of Christ?
15:40 There are celestial B and there are terrestrial
15:40 and there are terrestrial B; but the glory of
2Cor 4:10 of Jesus may also be manifested in our B
7:5 came into Macedonia, our B had no rest but
Eph 5:28 husbands should love their wives as their own B
Heb 3:17 those who sinned, whose B fell in the wilderness?
10:22 evil conscience and our B washed with pure water.
13:11 For the B of those animals whose blood is
Jas 3:3 they may obey us, we guide their whole B
Rev 11:8 them, and their dead B will lie in the
11:9 gaze at their dead B and refuse to let

BODILY (8)

2Mac 3:17 For terror and B trembling had come over the
Lk 3:22 descended upon him in B form, as a dove,
2Cor 10:10 and strong, but his B presence is weak, and
Gal 4:13 was because of a B ailment that I preached
Eph 4:16 is working properly, makes B growth and upbuilds
Col 2:9 fulness of deity dwells B,
1Tim 4:8 in godliness; for while B training is of some
Heb 7:16 a legal requirement concerning B descent but by the

BODY (277)

Gen 25:25 forth red, all his B like a hairy mantle;
Ex 22:27 his mantle for his B; in what else shall
Lev 6:10 linen breeches upon his B, and he shall take
13:2 the skin of his B a swelling or an
13:2 the skin of his B, then he shall be
13:3 the skin of his B; and if the hair
13:3 the skin of his B, it is a leprous
13:4 the skin of his B, and appears no deeper
13:11 the skin of his B, and the priest shall
13:13 has covered all his B, he shall pronounce him
13:18 the skin of one's B a boil that has
13:24 "Or, when the B has a burn on its
13:38 the skin of the B, white spots,
13:39 the skin of the B are of a dull
13:43 the skin of the B,
14:9 clothes, and bathe his B in water, and he
15:2 a discharge from his B, his discharge is unclean.
15:3 a discharge: whether his B runs with his discharge,
15:3 his discharge, or his B is stopped from discharge,
15:7 And whoever touches the B of him who has
15:13 he shall bathe his B in running water, and
15:16 shall bathe his whole B in water, and be
15:19 regular discharge from her B, she shall be in
16:4 linen breeches on his B, be girded with the
16:4 He shall bathe his B in water, and then
16:24 he shall bathe his B in water in a
16:26 clothes and bathe his B in water, and afterward
16:28 clothes and bathe his B in water, and afterward
21:11 in to any dead B, nor defile himself, even
22:6 he has bathed his B in water.
Num 5:21 fall away and your B swell;
5:22 bowels and make your B swell and your thigh
5:27 bitter pain, and her B shall swell, and her
6:6 LORD he shall not go near a dead B
6:11 because he sinned by reason of the dead B
8:7 razor over all their B, and wash their clothes
9:6 through touching the dead B of a man, so
9:7 through touching the dead B of a man; why
9:10 through touching a dead B, or is afar off
19:7 clothes and bathe his B in water, and afterwards
19:8 water and bathe his B in water, and shall
19:11 who touches the dead B of any person shall
19:13 a dead person, the B of any man who
19:16 sword, or a dead B, or a bone of
25:8 man of Israel and the woman, through her B
Deut 7:13 the fruit of your B and the fruit of
21:23 on a tree, his B shall not remain all
28:4 the fruit of your B, and the fruit of
28:11 the fruit of your B, and in the fruit
28:18 the fruit of your B, and the fruit of
28:26 And your dead B shall be food for all
28:53 offspring of your own B, the flesh of your

30:9 the fruit of your B, and in the fruit
Josh 8:29 and they took his B down from the tree,
Judg 14:8 of bees in the B of the lion, and
1Sam 31:10 and they fastened his B to the wall of
31:12 night, and took the B of Saul and the
2Sam 7:12 come forth from your B, and I will establish
20:10 with it in the B, and shed his bowels
1Kgs 13:22 drink no water"; your B shall not come to
13:24 And his B was thrown in the road, and
13:24 beside it; the lion also stood beside the B
13:25 by, and saw the B thrown in the road,
13:25 the road, and the lion standing by the B
13:28 went and found his B thrown in the road,
13:28 the ass and the lion standing beside the B
13:28 had not eaten the B or torn the ass.
13:29 prophet took up the B of the man of
13:30 And he laid the B in his own grave;
2Kgs 6:30 sackcloth beneath upon his B --
1Chr 10:12 and took away the B of Saul and the
Tob 2:4 up and removed the B to a place of
2:7 went and dug a grave and buried the B
Jud 1:16 combined forces, a vast B of troops; and there
10:3 garments, and bathed her B with water, and anointed
13:8 all her might, and severed it from his B
13:9 Then she tumbled his B off the bed and
Esth 14:2 she utterly humbled her B, and every part that
Job 14:22 pain of his own B, and he mourns only
20:25 comes out of his B, the glittering point comes
21:24 ease and secure, his B full of fat and
Ps 16:9 my soul rejoices; my B also dwells secure.
31:9 my soul and my B also.
32:3 not my sin, my B wasted away through my
42:10 deadly wound in my B, my adversaries taunt me,
44:25 to the dust; our B cleaves to the ground.
109:18 it soak into his B like water, like oil
109:24 weak through fasting; my B has become gaunt.
132:11 the sons of your B I will set on
Prov 5:11 when your flesh and B are consumed,
16:24 sweetness to the soul and health to the B
18:8 go down into the inner parts of the B
26:22 go down into the inner parts of the B
Eccl 2:3 how to cheer my B with wine--my mind
11:10 away pain from your B; for youth and the
Song 5:14 His B is ivory work, encrusted with sapphires.
Wis 1:4 nor dwell in a B enslaved to sin.
2:3 it is extinguished, the B will turn to ashes,
8:20 or rather, being good, I entered an undefiled B
9:15 fail, for a perishable B weighs down the soul,
18:22 not by strength of B, and not by force
Sir 30:14 a rich man who is severely afflicted in B
30:15 gold, and a robust B than countless riches.
30:16 better than health of B, and there is no
34:25 after touching a dead B, and touches it again,
38:16 Lay out his B with the honor due him,
47:19 women, and through your B you were brought into
48:13 he was dead his B prophesied.
51:2 and hast delivered my B from destruction and from
Is 10:18 destroy, both soul and B, and it will be
14:19 Pit, like a dead B trodden under foot.
49:1 the womb, from the B of my mother he
Jer 26:23 and cast his dead B into the burial place
36:30 David, and his dead B shall be cast out
Bar 6:71 or like a dead B cast out in the
Ezek 1:23 and each creature had two wings covering its B
Dan 4:33 an ox, and his B was wet with the
5:21 an ox, and his B was wet with the
7:11 was slain, and its B destroyed and given over
10:6 His B was like beryl, his face like the
Mic 6:7 the fruit of my B for the sin of
Hab 3:16 I hear, and my B trembles, my lips quiver
Hag 2:13 contact with a dead B touches any of these,
1Mac 3:13 large company, including a B of faithful men who
7:12 scribes appeared in a B before Alcimus and
2Mac 4:9 a gymnasium and a B of youth for it,
6:30 terrible sufferings in my B under this beating, but
6:31 but to the great B of his nation.
7:7 rather than have your B punished limb by limb?"
7:37 my brothers, give up B and life for the
9:7 hard as to torture every limb of his B
9:9 so the ungodly man's B swarmed with worms, and
9:29 his courtiers, took his B home; then, fearing the
14:38 with all zeal risked B and life.
15:12 hands for the whole B of the Jews.
15:30 who was ever in B and soul the defender
Mt 5:29 than that your whole B be thrown into hell.
5:30 than that your whole B go into hell.
6:22 "The eye is the lamp of the B
6:22 is sound, your whole B will be full of
6:23 not sound, your whole B will be full of
6:25 drink, nor about your B, what you shall put
6:25 than food, and the B more than clothing?
10:28 those who kill the B but cannot kill the
10:28 destroy both soul and B in hell.
14:12 came and took the B and buried it; and
24:28 Wherever the B is, there the eagles will be
26:12 this ointment on my B she has done it
26:26 disciples and said, "Take, eat; this is my B
27:58 and asked for the B of Jesus.
27:59 And Joseph took the B, and wrapped it in
Mk 5:29 she felt in her B that she was healed
6:29 came and took his B, and laid it in
14:8 she has anointed my B beforehand for burying.
14:22 to them, and said, "Take; this is my B
14:51 linen cloth about his B; and they seized him,
15:42 and asked for the B of Jesus.
15:44 dead, he granted the B to Joseph.
Lk 11:34 the lamp of your B; when your eye is
11:34 is sound, your whole B is full of light;
11:34 is not sound, your B is full of darkness.
11:36 If then your whole B is full of light,
12:4 those who kill the B, and after that have
12:22 eat, nor about your B, what you shall put
12:23 than food, and the B more than clothing.
17:36 to them, "Where the B is, there the eagles
22:19 saying, "This is my B which is given for
23:51 and asked for the B of Jesus.
23:54 tomb, and how his B was laid;
24:3 they went in they did not find the B
24:23 did not find his B; and they came back
Jn 2:21 But he spoke of the temple of his B
7:23 made a man's whole B well?
19:38 might take away the B of Jesus, and Pilate
19:38 So he came and took away his B
19:40 They took the B of Jesus, and bound it
20:12 white, sitting where the B of Jesus had lain,
Acts 6:2 the twelve summoned the B of the disciples and
9:40 then turning to the B he said, "Tabitha, rise."
12:20 to him in a B, and having persuaded Blastus,
19:12 carried away from his B to the sick, and
Rom 4:19 he considered his own B, which was as good
6:6 so that the sinful B might be destroyed, and
7:4 the law through the B of Christ, so that
7:24 deliver me from this B of death?
8:13 the deeds of the B you will live.
12:4 For as in one B we have many members,
12:5 though many, are one B in Christ, and individually
1Cor 5:3 For though absent in B I am present in
6:13 The B is not meant for immorality, but for
6:13 for the Lord, and the Lord for the B
6:16 a prostitute becomes one B with her?
6:18 commits is outside the B; but the immoral man
6:18 but the immoral man sins against his own B
6:19 not know that your B is a temple of
6:20 So glorify God in your B
7:4 rule over her own B, but the husband does;
7:4 rule over his own B, but the wife does.
7:34 to be holy in B and spirit; but the
9:27 but I pommel my B and subdue it, lest
10:16 a participation in the B of Christ?
10:17 are many are one B, for we all partake
11:24 said, "This is my B which is for you.
11:27 guilty of profaning the B and blood of the
11:29 drinks without discerning the B eats and drinks
12:12 For just as the B is one and has
12:12 the members of the B, though many, are one
12:12 though many, are one B, so it is with
12:13 all baptized into one B --Jews or Greeks, slaves
12:14 For the B does not consist of one member
12:15 a hand, I do not belong to the B
12:15 make it any less a part of the B
12:16 an eye, I do not belong to the B
12:16 make it any less a part of the B
12:17 If the whole B were an eye, where would
12:17 If the whole B were an ear, where would
12:18 the organs in the B, each one of them,
12:19 organ, where would the B be?
12:20 it is, there are many parts, yet one B
12:22 the parts of the B which seem to be
12:23 those parts of the B which we think less
12:24 has so composed the B, giving the greater honor
12:25 no discord in the B, but that the members
12:27 Now you are the B of Christ and individually

13:3 if I deliver my B to be burned, but
15:35 With what kind of B do they come?"
15:37 sow is not the B which is to be,
15:38 God gives it a B as he has chosen,
15:38 and to each kind of seed its own B
15:44 is sown a physical B, it is raised a
15:44 a physical body, it is raised a spiritual B
15:44 there is a physical B, there is also a
15:44 a physical body, there is also a spiritual B
2Cor 4:10 always carrying in the B the death of Jesus,
5:6 at home in the B we are away from
5:8 be away from the B and at home with
5:10 according to what he has done in the B
7:1 from every defilement of B and spirit, and make
12:2 heaven--whether in the B or out of the
12:2 or out of the B I do not know,
12:3 Paradise--whether in the B or out of the
12:3 or out of the B I do not know,
Gal 6:17 I bear on my B the marks of Jesus.
Eph 1:23 church, which is his B, the fulness of him
2:3 following the desires of B and mind, and so
2:16 to God in one B through the cross, thereby
3:6 members of the same B, and partakers of the
4:4 There is one B and one Spirit, just as
4:12 for building up the B of Christ,
4:16 from whom the whole B, joined and knit together
5:23 of the church, his B, and is himself its
5:30 the church, because we are members of his B
Phil 1:20 be honored in my B, whether by life or
3:21 will change our lowly B to be like his
3:21 be like his glorious B, by the power which
Col 1:18 the head of the B, the church; he is
1:22 now reconciled in his B of flesh by his
1:24 the sake of his B, that is, the church,
2:5 I am absent in B, yet I am with
2:11 by putting off the B of flesh in the
2:19 from whom the whole B, nourished and knit together
2:23 and severity to the B, but they are of
3:15 which indeed you were called in the one B
1Thes 5:23 spirit and soul and B be kept sound and
Heb 9:10 ablutions, regulations for the B imposed until the
10:5 not desired, but a B hast thou prepared for
10:10 the offering of the B of Jesus Christ once
13:3 are ill-treated, since you also are in the B
Jas 2:16 things needed for the B, what does it profit?
2:26 For as the B apart from the spirit is
3:2 to bridle the whole B also.
3:6 members, staining the whole B, setting on fire the
1Pet 2:24 our sins in his B on the tree, that
3:21 of dirt from the B but as an appeal
2Pet 1:13 I am in this B, to arouse you by
1:14 putting off of my B will be soon, as
Jude 1:9 devil, disputed about the B of Moses, he did

BODYGUARD (9)
1Sam 22:14 and captain over your B, and honored in your
28:2 will make you my B for life."
2Sam 23:23 And David set him over his B
2Kgs 25:8 the captain of the B, a servant of the
1Chr 11:25 And David set him over his B
Jer 52:12 the captain of the B who served the king
1Mac 13:40 be enrolled in our B, let them be enrolled,
2Mac 3:24 the treasury with his B, then and there the
3:28 retinue and all his B but was now unable

BOG
Ps 40:2 out of the miry B, and set my feet

BOHAN (2)
Josh 15:6 to the stone of B the son of Reuben;
18:17 to the Stone of B the son of Reuben;

BOIL (22)
Ex 16:23 you will bake and B what you will boil,
16:23 boil what you will B, and all that is
23:19 "You shall not B a kid in its mother's
29:31 ram of ordination, and B its flesh in a
34:26 You shall not B a kid in its mother's
Lev 8:31 Aaron and his sons, B the flesh at the
13:18 of one's body a B that has healed,
13:19 the place of the B there comes a white
13:20 of leprosy, it has broken out in the B
13:23 the scar of the B; and the priest shall
Deut 14:21 "You shall not B a kid in its mother's
16:7 And you shall B it and eat it at
2Kgs 4:38 the great pot, and B pottage for the sons
20:7 lay it on the B, that he may recover."
Job 41:31 He makes the deep B like a pot; he
Is 38:21 apply it to the B, that he may recover."
64:2 fire causes water to B -- to make thy
Ezek 24:5 the logs under it; B its pieces, seethe also
24:10 logs, kindle the fire, B well the flesh, and
46:20 where the priests shall B the guilt offering and
46:24 at the temple shall B the sacrifices of the
Zech 14:21 take of them and B the flesh of the

BOILED (12)
Ex 12:9 of it raw or B with water, but roasted,
Lev 6:28 in which it is B shall be broken; but
6:28 but if it is B in a bronze vessel,
Num 6:19 ram, when it is B, and one unleavened cake
11:8 it in mortars, and B it in pots, and
1Sam 2:15 he will not accept B meat from you, but
1Kgs 19:21 and slew them, and B their flesh with the
2Kgs 6:29 son tomorrow.' So we B my son, and ate
2Chr 35:13 the ordinance; and they B the holy offerings in
Lam 4:10 of compassionate women have B their own children;
Dan 14:27 fat, and hair, and B them together and made
14:33 He had B pottage and had broken bread into

BOILING (4)
Gen 25:29 Once when Jacob was B pottage, Esau came in
1Sam 2:13 while the meat was B, with a three-pronged fork
Job 41:20 smoke, as from a B pot and burning rushes.
Jer 1:13 said, "I see a B pot, facing away from

BOILS (6)
Ex 9:9 of Egypt, and become B breaking out in sores
9:10 heaven, and it became B breaking out in sores
9:11 Moses because of the B, for the boils were
9:11 the boils, for the B were upon the magicians
Deut 28:27 smite you with the B of Egypt, and with
28:35 the legs with grievous B of which you cannot

BOLD (13)
Jud 14:13 slaves have been so B as to come down
Prov 21:29 man puts on a B face, but an upright
28:1 but the righteous are B as a lion.
Wis 11:17 multitude of bears, or B lions,
Sir 6:11 your equal, and be B with your servants;
Dan 8:23 a king of B countenance, one who understands
2Mac 3:24 who had been so B as to accompany him
Rom 10:20 Then Isaiah is so B as to say, "I
2Cor 3:12 hope, we are very B,
10:1 face with you, but B to you when I
Phil 1:14 and are much more B to speak the word
Philem 1:8 Accordingly, though I am B enough in Christ to
2Pet 2:10 B and wilful, they are not afraid to revile

BOLDLY (12)
Prov 10:10 trouble, but he who B reproves makes peace.
1Mac 4:18 and fight them, and afterward seize the plunder B
Acts 9:27 Damascus he had preached B in the name of
9:29 them at Jerusalem, preaching B in the name of
13:46 and Barnabas spoke out B, saying, "It was necessary
14:3 a long time, speaking B for the Lord, who
18:26 He began to speak B in the synagogue; but
19:8 for three months spoke B, arguing and pleading
Rom 15:15 written to you very B by way of reminder,
Eph 6:19 in opening my mouth B to proclaim the mystery
6:20 I may declare it B, as I ought to
Jude 1:12 love feasts, as they B carouse together, looking after

BOLDNESS (9)
Jud 16:10 Persians trembled at her B, the Medes were daunted
Sir 25:24 to water, and no B of speech in an
1Mac 4:32 with cowardice; melt the B of their strength; let
4:35 troops and observed the B which inspired those of
Acts 4:13 when they saw the B of Peter and John,
4:29 thy word with all B,
4:31 Spirit and spoke the word of God with B
2Cor 10:2 not have to show B with such confidence as
Eph 3:12 in whom we have B and confidence of access

BOLT (3)
2Sam 13:17 of my presence, and B the door after her."
Song 5:5 with liquid myrrh, upon the handles of the B
Sir 28:25 a door and a B for your mouth.

BOLTED
2Sam 13:18 put her out, and B the door after her.

BOLTS (7)

Neh	3:3	set its doors, its B, and its bars.
	3:6	set its doors, its B, and its bars.
	3:13	set its doors, its B, and its bars, and
	3:14	set its doors, its B, and its bars.
	3:15	set its doors, its B, and its bars; and
1Mac	12:38	Shephelah; he fortified it and installed gates with B
	13:33	walls and gates and B, and he stored food

BOND (9)

Deut	32:36	there is none remaining, B or free.
1Kgs	14:10	Jeroboam every male, both B and free in Israel,
	21:21	from Ahab every male, B or free, in Israel;
2Kgs	9:8	from Ahab every male, B or free, in Israel.
	14:26	there was none left, B or free, and there
Lk	13:16	be loosed from this B on the sabbath day?"
Acts	8:23	bitterness and in the B of iniquity."
Eph	4:3	the Spirit in the B of peace.
Col	2:14	trespasses, having canceled the B which stood

BONDAGE (28)

Ex	2:23	Israel groaned under their B, and cried out for
	2:23	and their cry under B came up to God.
	6:5	the Egyptians hold in B and I have remembered
	6:6	deliver you from their B, and I will redeem
	6:9	because of their broken spirit and their cruel B
	13:3	of the house of B, for by strength of
	13:14	us out of Egypt, from the house of B
	20:2	land of Egypt, out of the house of B
Deut	5:6	land of Egypt, out of the house of B
	6:12	land of Egypt, out of the house of B
	7:8	from the house of B, from the hand of
	8:14	of the house of B,
	13:5	of the house of B, to make you leave
	13:10	land of Egypt, out of the house of B
	26:6	and afflicted us, and laid upon us hard B
Josh	24:17	of the house of B, and who did those
Judg	6:8	of the house of B;
Ezra	9:8	and grant us a little reviving in our B
	9:9	forsaken us in our B, but has extended to
Neh	9:17	to return to their B in Egypt.
Wis	14:21	mankind, because men, in B to misfortune or to
Jer	34:13	of the house of B, saying,
Mic	6:4	from the house of B; and I sent before
Jn	8:33	have never been in B to any one.
Rom	8:21	set free from its B to decay and obtain
Gal	2:4	might bring us into B --
	4:8	God, you were in B to beings that by
Heb	2:15	through fear of death were subject to lifelong B

BONDED

Sir	22:14	A wooden beam firmly B into a building will

BONDMAID

Ex	23:12	the son of your B, and the alien, may

BONDMAN

Deut	15:17	he shall be your B for ever.

BONDMEN

Ezra	9:9	For we are B; yet our God has not

BONDS (19)

Judg	15:14	caught fire, and his B melted off his hands.
2Kgs	23:33	Neco put him in B at Riblah in the
Job	12:18	He looses the B of kings, and binds a
	39:5	Who has loosed the B of the swift ass,
Ps	2:3	"Let us burst their B asunder, and cast their
	69:33	does not despise his own that are in B
	107:14	gloom, and broke their B asunder.
	116:16	Thou hast loosed my B
Sir	6:25	carry her, and do not fret under her B
	6:30	golden ornament, and her B are a cord of
Is	28:22	not scoff, lest your B be made strong; for
	52:2	captive Jerusalem; loose the B from your neck, O
	58:6	choose: to loose the B of wickedness, to undo
Jer	2:20	yoke and burst your B; and you said, 'I
	5:5	had broken the yoke, they had burst the B
	30:8	I will burst their B, and strangers shall no
Nah	1:13	and will burst your B asunder."
Lk	8:29	but he broke the B and was driven by
Acts	22:5	and bring them in B to Jerusalem to be

BONDWOMAN

Deut	15:17	And to your B you shall do likewise.

BONE (17)

Gen	2:23	"This at last is B of my bones and
	29:14	"Surely you are my B and my flesh!" And
Ex	12:46	shall not break a B of it.
Num	9:12	morning, nor break a B of it; according to
	19:16	dead body, or a B of a man, or
	19:18	him who touched the B, or the slain, or
Judg	9:2	that I am your B and your flesh."
2Sam	5:1	"Behold, we are your B and flesh.
	19:12	kinsmen, you are my B and my flesh; why
	19:13	'Are you not my B and my flesh?
1Chr	11:1	"Behold, we are your B and flesh.
Job	2:5	now, and touch his B and his flesh, and
Prov	25:15	persuaded, and a soft tongue will break a B
Ezek	37:7	the bones came together, B to its bone.
	37:7	and the bones came together, bone to its B
	39:15	one sees a man's B, then he shall set
Jn	19:36	be fulfilled, "Not a B of him shall be

BONES (98)

Gen	2:23	is bone of my B and flesh of my
	50:25	shall carry up my B from here."
Ex	13:19	And Moses took the B of Joseph with him;
	13:19	you must carry my B with you from here."
Num	24:8	and shall break their B in pieces, and pierce
Josh	24:32	The B of Joseph which the people of Israel
1Sam	31:13	And they took their B and buried them under
2Sam	21:12	went and took the B of Saul and the
	21:12	of Saul and the B of his son Jonathan
	21:13	up from there the B of Saul and the
	21:13	of Saul and the B of his son Jonathan;
	21:13	and they gathered the B of those who were
	21:14	And they buried the B of Saul and his
1Kgs	13:2	upon you, and men's B shall be burned upon
	13:31	is buried; lay my B beside his bones.
	13:31	God is buried; lay my bones beside his B
2Kgs	13:21	the man touched the B of Elisha, he revived,
	23:14	their places with the B of men.
	23:16	sent and took the B out of the tombs,
	23:18	"Let him be; let no man move his B
	23:18	So they let his B alone, with the bones
	23:18	bones alone, with the B of the prophet who
	23:20	altars, and burned the B of men upon them.
1Chr	10:12	And they buried their B under the oak in
2Chr	34:5	He also burned the B of the priests on
Job	4:14	which made all my B shake.
	7:15	would choose strangling and death rather than my B
	10:11	knit me together with B and sinews.
	19:20	My B cleave to my skin and to my
	20:11	His B are full of youthful vigor, but it
	21:24	the marrow of his B moist.
	30:17	The night racks my B, and the pain that
	30:30	from me, and my B burn with heat.
	33:19	continual strife in his B;
	33:21	be seen; and his B which were not seen
	40:18	His B are tubes of bronze, his limbs like
Ps	6:2	heal me, for my B are troubled.
	22:14	water, and all my B are out of joint;
	22:17	can count all my B -- they stare and
	31:10	my misery, and my B waste away.
	34:20	He keeps all his B; not one of them
	35:10	All my B shall say, "O LORD, who is
	38:3	no health in my B because of my sin.
	51:8	and gladness; let the B which thou hast broken
	53:5	God will scatter the B of the ungodly; they
	102:3	like smoke, and my B burn like a furnace.
	102:5	my loud groaning my B cleave to my flesh.
	109:18	his body like water, like oil into his B
	141:7	land, so shall their B be strewn at the
Prov	3:8	healing to your flesh and refreshment to your B
	12:4	who brings shame is like rottenness in his B
	14:30	but passion makes the B rot.
	15:30	rejoices the heart, and good news refreshes the B
	17:22	medicine, but a downcast spirit dries up the B
Eccl	11:5	spirit comes to the B in the womb of
Sir	26:13	husband, and her skill puts fat on his B
	28:17	but a blow of the tongue crushes the B
	46:12	May their B revive from where they lie, and
	49:10	May the B of the twelve prophets revive from
	49:15	been born, and his B are cared for.
Is	38:13	he breaks all my B; from day to night
	58:11	things, and make your B strong; and you shall
	66:14	heart shall rejoice; your B shall flourish like the
Jer	8:1	says the LORD, the B of the kings of
	8:1	kings of Judah, the B of its princes, the
	8:1	of its princes, the B of the priests, the

8:1 of the priests, the B of the prophets, and
8:1 the prophets, and the B of the inhabitants of
20:9 shut up in my B, and I am weary
23:9 within me, all my B shake; I am like
50:17 Nebuchadrezzar king of Babylon has gnawed his B
Lam 1:13 sent fire; into my B he made it descend;
3:4 away, and broken my B;
4:8 has shriveled upon their B, it has become as
Bar 2:24 the prophets, that the B of our kings and
2:24 our kings and the B of our fathers would
Ezek 6:5 I will scatter your B round about your altars.
24:4 thigh and the shoulder; fill it with choice B
24:5 pieces, seethe also its B in it.
24:10 broth, and let the B be burned up.
32:27 shields are upon their B; for the terror of
37:1 midst of the valley; it was full of B
37:3 of man, can these B live?" And I answered,
37:4 me, "Prophesy to these B, and say to them,
37:4 to them, O dry B, hear the word of
37:5 Lord GOD to these B: Behold, I will cause
37:7 a rattling; and the B came together, bone to
37:11 "Son of man, these B are the whole house
37:11 Behold, they say, 'Our B are dried up, and
Dan 6:24 and broke all their B in pieces.
Amos 2:1 burned to lime the B of the king of
6:10 up to bring the B out of the house,
Mic 3:2 flesh from off their B;
3:3 them, and break their B in pieces, and chop
Hab 3:16 rottenness enters into my B, my steps totter beneath
1Mac 13:25 sent and took the B of Jonathan his brother,
Mt 23:26 full of dead men's B and all uncleanness.
Lk 24:39 has not flesh and B as you see that

BOOK (173)

Gen 5:1 This is the B of the generations of Adam.
Ex 17:14 a memorial in a B and recite it in
24:7 Then he took the B of the covenant, and
32:32 thee, out of thy B which thou hast written."
32:33 me, him will I blot out of my B
Num 5:23 these curses in a B, and wash them off
21:14 is said in the B of the Wars of
Deut 17:18 for himself in a B a copy of this
28:58 are written in this B, that you may fear
28:61 not recorded in the B of this law, the
29:20 curses written in this B would settle upon him,
29:21 covenant written in this B of the law.
29:27 curses written in this B;
30:10 are written in this B of the law, if
31:24 this law in a B, to the very end,
31:26 the LORD, "Take this B of the law, and
Josh 1:8 This B of the law shall not depart out
8:31 is written in the B of the law of
8:34 is written in the B of the law.
10:13 not written in the B of Jashar?
18:9 set down in a B a description of it
23:6 is written in the B of the law of
24:26 these words in the B of the law of
1Sam 10:25 wrote them in a B and laid it up
2Sam 1:18 is written in the B of Jashar.
1Kgs 11:41 not written in the B of the acts of
14:19 are written in the B of the Chronicles of
14:29 not written in the B of the Chronicles of
15:7 not written in the B of the Chronicles of
15:23 not written in the B of the Chronicles of
15:31 not written in the B of the Chronicles of
16:5 not written in the B of the Chronicles of
16:14 not written in the B of the Chronicles of
16:20 not written in the B of the Chronicles of
16:27 not written in the B of the Chronicles of
22:39 not written in the B of the Chronicles of
22:45 not written in the B of the Chronicles of
2Kgs 1:18 not written in the B of the Chronicles of
8:23 not written in the B of the Chronicles of
10:34 not written in the B of the Chronicles of
12:19 not written in the B of the Chronicles of
13:8 not written in the B of the Chronicles of
13:12 not written in the B of the Chronicles of
14:6 is written in the B of the law of
14:15 not written in the B of the Chronicles of
14:18 not written in the B of the Chronicles of
14:28 not written in the B of the Chronicles of
15:6 not written in the B of the Chronicles of
15:11 are written in the B of the Chronicles of
15:15 are written in the B of the Chronicles of
15:21 not written in the B of the Chronicles of
15:26 are written in the B of the Chronicles of
15:31 are written in the B of the Chronicles of
15:36 not written in the B of the Chronicles of
16:19 not written in the B of the Chronicles of
20:20 not written in the B of the Chronicles of
21:17 not written in the B of the Chronicles of
21:25 not written in the B of the Chronicles of
22:8 "I have found the B of the law in
22:8 And Hilkiah gave the B to Shaphan, and he
22:10 king, "Hilkiah the priest has given me a B
22:11 the words of the B of the law, he
22:13 the words of this B that has been found;
22:13 the words of this B, to do according to
22:16 the words of the B which the king of
23:2 the words of the B of the covenant which
23:3 were written in this B; and all the people
23:21 is written in this B of the covenant."
23:24 were written in the B that Hilkiah the priest
23:28 not written in the B of the Chronicles of
24:5 not written in the B of the Chronicles of
1Chr 9:1 are written in the B of the Kings of
2Chr 16:11 are written in the B of the Kings of
17:9 in Judah, having the B of the law of
20:34 are recorded in the B of the Kings of
24:27 the Commentary on the B of the Kings.
25:4 the law, in the B of Moses, where the
25:26 not written in the B of the Kings of
27:7 are written in the B of the Kings of
28:26 are written in the B of the Kings of
32:32 of Amoz, in the B of the Kings of
34:14 the priest found the B of the law of
34:15 "I have found the B of the law in
34:15 and Hilkiah gave the B to Shaphan.
34:16 Shaphan brought the B to the king, and further
34:18 king, "Hilkiah the priest has given me a B
34:21 the words of the B that has been found;
34:21 according to all that is written in this B
34:24 are written in the B which was read before
34:30 the words of the B of the covenant which
34:31 of the covenant that were written in this B
35:12 is written in the B of Moses.
35:27 are written in the B of the Kings of
36:8 are written in the B of the Kings of
Ezra 4:15 be made in the B of the records of
4:15 will find in the B of the records and
6:18 is written in the B of Moses.
Neh 7:5 And I found the B of the genealogy of
8:1 scribe to bring the B of the law of
8:3 were attentive to the B of the law.
8:5 And Ezra opened the B in the sight of
8:8 they read from the B, from the law of
8:18 he read from the B of the law of
9:3 and read from the B of the law of
12:23 were written in the B of the Chronicles until
13:1 they read from the B of Moses in the
Tob 1:1 The B of the acts of
12:20 Write in a B everything that has happened."
Esth 2:23 was recorded in the B of the Chronicles in
6:1 orders to bring the B of memorable deeds, the
10:2 not written in the B of the Chronicles of
Job 19:23 Oh that they were inscribed in a B
Ps 40:7 the roll of the B it is written of
56:8 Are they not in thy B
69:28 blotted out of the B of the living; let
139:16 unformed substance; in thy B were written, every
Sir 24:22 All this is the B of the covenant of
50:27 have written in this B, Jesus the son of
Is 29:11 the words of a B that is sealed.
29:12 when they give the B to one who cannot
29:18 the words of a B, and out of their
30:8 inscribe it in a B, that it may be
34:16 and read from the B of the LORD: Not
Jer 25:13 written in this B, which Jeremiah prophesied against
30:2 Israel: Write in a B all the words that
45:1 these words in a B at the dictation of
51:60 Jeremiah wrote in a B all the evil that
51:63 you finish reading this B, bind a stone to
Bar 1:1 the words of the B which Baruch the son
1:3 the words of this B in the hearing of
1:3 came to hear the B,
1:14 you shall read this B which we are sending
4:1 She is the B of the commandments of God,
Dan 10:21 is inscribed in the B of truth: there is
12:1 whose name shall be found written in the B
12:4 words, and seal the B, until the time of
Nah 1:1 The B of the vision of Nah of Elkosh.
Mal 3:16 heard them, and a B of remembrance was written

1Mac 1:57 Where the B of the covenant was found in
3:48 And they opened the B of the law to
2Mac 2:23 we shall attempt to condense into a single B
6:12 those who read this B not to be depressed
8:23 aloud from the holy B, and gave the watchword,
Mt 1:1 THE B of the genealogy of
Mk 12:26 not read in the B of Moses, in the
Lk 3:4 is written in the B of the words of
4:17 given to him the B of the prophet Isaiah.
4:17 He opened the B and found the place where
4:20 And he closed the B, and gave it back
20:42 himself says in the B of Psalms, 'The Lord
Jn 20:30 not written in this B;
Acts 1:1 In the first B, O Theophilus, I have
1:20 is written in the B of Psalms, 'Let his
7:42 is written in the B of the prophets: 'Did
Gal 3:10 things written in the B of the law, and
Phil 4:3 names are in the B of life.
Heb 9:19 and sprinkled both the B itself and all the
10:7 written of me in the roll of the B
Rev 1:11 you see in a B and send it to
3:5 name out of the B of life; I will
13:8 the world in the B of life of the
17:8 been written in the B of life from the
20:12 Also another B was opened, which is the book
20:12 opened, which is the B of life.
20:15 found written in the B of life, he was
21:27 written in the Lamb's B of life.
22:7 keeps the words of the prophecy of this B
22:9 with those who keep the words of this B
22:10 the prophecy of this B, for the time is
22:18 the prophecy of this B: if any one adds
22:18 plagues described in this B,
22:19 the words of the B of this prophecy, God
22:19 the holy city, which are described in this B

BOOKS (12)

Eccl 12:12 Of making many B there is no end, and
Dan 7:10 in judgment, and the B were opened.
9:2 Daniel, perceived in the B the number of years
1Mac 1:56 The B of the law which they found they
12:9 as encouragement the holy B which are in our
2Mac 2:13 library and collected the B about the kings and
2:14 also collected all the B that had been lost
Jn 21:25 could not contain the B that would be written.
Acts 19:19 magic arts brought their B together and burned
2Tim 4:13 at Troas, also the B, and above all the
Rev 20:12 before the throne, and B were opened.
20:12 was written in the B, by what they had

BOOR

Sir 21:23 A B peers into the house from the door,

BOOT

Is 9:5 For every B of the tramping warrior in battle

BOOTH (5)

Job 27:18 spider's web, like a B which a watchman makes.
Is 1:8 is left like a B in a vineyard, like
Lam 2:6 has broken down his B like that of a
Amos 9:11 will raise up the B of David that is
Jon 4:5 city, and made a B for himself there.

BOOTHS (27)

Gen 33:17 a house, and made B for his cattle; therefore
Lev 23:34 is the feast of B to the LORD.
23:42 You shall dwell in B for seven days; all
23:42 Israel shall dwell in B,
23:43 of Israel dwell in B when I brought them
Deut 16:13 keep the feast of B seven days, when you
16:16 feast of weeks, and at the feast of B
31:10 at the feast of B,
2Sam 11:11 and Judah dwell in B; and my lord Joab
1Kgs 20:12 the kings in the B, he said to his
20:16 himself drunk in the B, he and the thirty-two
Ezra 3:4 kept the feast of B, as it is written,
Neh 8:14 Israel should dwell in B during the feast of
8:15 leafy trees to make B, as it is written."
8:16 brought them and made B for themselves, each on
8:17 from the captivity made B and dwelt in the
8:17 and dwelt in the B; for from the days
Zech 14:16 of hosts, and to keep the feast of B
14:18 not go up to keep the feast of B
14:19 not go up to keep the feast of B
2Mac 1:9 keep the feast of B in the month of
1:18 celebrate the feast of B and the feast of
10:6 of the feast of B, remembering how not long
10:6 during the feast of B, they had been wandering
Mt 17:4 I will make three B here, one for you
Mk 9:5 let us make three B, one for you and
Lk 9:33 let us make three B, one for you and

BOOTY (24)

Num 31:9 and they took as B all their cattle, their
31:11 spoil and all the B, both of man and
31:12 the captives and the B and the spoil to
31:26 the count of the B that was taken, both
31:27 congregation; and divide the B into two parts,
31:32 Now the B remaining of the spoil that the
31:53 of war had taken B, every man for himself.)
Deut 2:35 for ourselves, with the B of the cities which
3:7 spoil of the cities we took as our B
20:14 you shall take as B for yourselves; and you
Josh 8:2 you shall take as B for yourselves; lay an
8:27 Israel took as their B, according to the word
11:14 Israel took for their B; but every man they
2Chr 14:13 The men of Judah carried away very much B
Jud 4:12 and their wives as B, and the cities they
9:4 captivity, and all their B to be divided among
15:7 a great amount of B, for there was a
16:5 children as prey, and take my virgins as B
Jer 49:32 Their camels shall become B, their herds of cattle
Bar 6:58 go off with this B, and they will not
Nah 3:1 full of lies and B –no end to the
Hab 2:7 Then you will be B for them.
1Mac 10:87 those with him returned to Jerusalem with much B
2Mac 8:20 one hundred and twenty thousand and took much B

BORASHAN

1Sam 30:30 Kenites, in Hormah, in B, in Athach,

BORDER (41)

Gen 14:6 as El-paran on the B of the wilderness;
49:13 for ships, and his B shall be at Sidon.
Ex 16:35 they came to the B of the land of
19:12 mountain or touch the B of it; whoever touches
Lev 19:9 field to its very B, neither shall you gather
23:22 field to its very B, nor shall you gather
Num 20:23 Mount Hor, on the B of the land of
21:15 and leans to the B of Moab."
Deut 3:14 as far as the B of the Geshurites and
19:8 your God enlarges your B, as he has sworn
Josh 4:19 Gilgal on the east B of Jericho.
13:23 And the B of the people of Reuben was
18:16 goes down to the B of the mountain that
18:19 end of the Jordan: this is the southern B
Judg 1:36 And the B of the Amorites ran from the
7:22 as far as the B of Abel-meholah, by Tabbath.
1Sam 6:12 as far as the B of Beth-shemesh.
13:18 company turned toward the B that looks down upon
1Kgs 4:21 Philistines and to the B of Egypt; they brought
2Kgs 14:25 He restored the B of Israel from the entrance
1Chr 4:10 me and enlarge my B, and that thy hand
2Chr 9:26 Philistines, and to the B of Egypt.
26:8 spread even to the B of Egypt, for he
Is 19:19 and a pillar to the LORD at its B
28:25 in its proper place, and spelt as the B
Ezek 11:10 judge you at the B of Israel; and you
11:11 judge you at the B of Israel;
29:10 as far as the B of Ethiopia.
47:16 (which lies on the B between Damascus and
47:16 which is on the B of Hauran.
47:17 is on the northern B of Damascus, with the
47:17 of Damascus, with the B of Hamath to the
48:1 Beginning at the northern B, from the sea by
48:1 is on the northern B of Damascus over against
48:21 portion to the east B, and westward from the
48:21 cubits to the west B, parallel to the tribal
Joel 3:6 the Greeks, removing them far from their own B
Amos 1:13 child in Gilead, that they might enlarge their B
Obad 1:7 driven you to the B; your confederates have
Mic 5:6 comes into our land and treads within our B
Mal 1:5 the LORD, beyond the B of Israel!"

BORDERING

1Mac 11:34 with all the region B them, were added to

BORDERS (25)

Ex 34:24 you, and enlarge your B; neither shall any man
Josh 17:18 it to its farthest B; for you shall drive
1Sam 27:1 any longer within the B of Israel, and I
1Chr 6:54 their settlements within their B: to the sons of

7:29 also along the B of the Manassites, Beth-shean
Jud 1:5 which is on the B of Ragae.
1:10 as far as the B of Ethiopia.
2:25 came to the southern B of Japheth, fronting toward
14:4 who live within the B of Israel shall pursue
15:5 great slaughter, even beyond Damascus and its B
Ps 147:14 makes peace in your B; he fills you with
Is 26:15 hast enlarged all the B of the land.
60:18 or destruction within your B; you shall call your
Ezek 27:4 perfect in beauty.' Your B are in the heart
Zech 9:2 Israel; Hamath also, which B thereon, Tyre and
1Mac 2:46 they found within the B of Israel.
3:32 river Euphrates to the B of Egypt.
5:60 were pursued to the B of Judea; as many
6:25 but also against all the lands on their B
11:59 of Tyre to the B of Egypt.
14:6 He extended the B of his nation, and gained
14:33 and Bethzur on the B of Judea, where formerly
14:34 which is on the B of Azotus, where the
15:30 have conquered outside the B of Judea;
2Mac 9:25 the princes along the B and the neighbors to

BORE (159)

Gen 4:1 and she conceived and B Cain, saying, "I have
4:2 And again, she B his brother Abel.
4:17 and she conceived and B Enoch; and he built
4:20 Adah B Jabal; he was the father of those
4:22 Zillah B Tubal-cain; he was the forger of all
4:25 wife again, and she B a son and called
6:4 of men, and they B children to them.
7:17 the waters increased, and B up the ark, and
16:1 Now Sarai, Abram's wife, B him no children.
16:15 And Hagar B Abram a son; and Abram called
16:15 his son, whom Hagar B, Ishmael.
16:16 years old when Hagar B Ishmael to Abram.
19:37 The first-born B a son, and called his name
19:38 The younger also B a son, and called his
20:17 slaves so that they B children.
21:2 And Sarah conceived, and B Abraham a son in
21:3 to him, whom Sarah B him, Isaac.
22:23 These eight Milcah B to Nahor, Abraham's brother.
22:24 whose name was Reumah, B Tebah, Gaham, Tahash,
24:24 of Milcah, whom she B to Nahor."
24:36 Sarah my master's wife B a son to my
24:47 Nahor's son, whom Milcah B to him.' So I
25:2 She B him Zimran, Jokshan, Medan, Midian, Ishbak,
25:12 the Egyptian, Sarah's maid, B to Abraham.
25:26 years old when she B them.
29:32 And Leah conceived and B a son, and she
29:33 She conceived again and B a son, and said,
29:34 Again she conceived and B a son, and said,
29:35 she conceived again and B a son, and said,
30:1 Rachel saw that she B Jacob no children, she
30:5 And Bilhah conceived and B Jacob a son.
30:7 Bilhah conceived again and B Jacob a second son.
30:10 Then Leah's maid Zilpah B Jacob a son.
30:12 Leah's maid Zilpah B Jacob a second son.
30:17 and she conceived and B Jacob a fifth son.
30:19 conceived again, and she B Jacob a sixth son.
30:21 Afterwards she B a daughter, and called her name
30:23 She conceived and B a son, and said, "God
31:8 then all the flock B spotted; and if he
31:8 then all the flock B striped.
31:39 bring to you; I B the loss of it
36:4 And Adah B to Esau, Eliphaz; Basemath bore Reuel;
36:4 to Esau, Eliphaz; Basemath B Reuel;
36:5 Reuel; and Oholibamah B Jeush, Jalam, and Korah.
36:12 Eliphaz, Esau's son; she B Amalek to Eliphaz.) These
36:14 Zibeon, Esau's wife: she B to Esau Jeush, Jalam,
38:3 and she conceived and B a son, and he
38:4 Again she conceived and B a son, and she
38:5 Yet again she B a son, and she called
38:5 in Chezib when she B him.
41:50 Potiphera priest of On, B to him.
44:27 know that my wife B me two sons;
46:15 of Leah, whom she B to Jacob in Paddan-aram,
46:18 and these she B to Jacob--sixteen persons).
46:20 the priest of On, B to him.
46:25 daughter, and these she B to Jacob--seven persons
Ex 2:2 The woman conceived and B a son; and when
2:22 She B a son, and he called his name
6:20 father's sister and she B him Aaron and Moses,
6:23 of Nahshon; and she B him Nadab, Abihu, Eleazar,
6:25 of Puti-el; and she B him Phinehas.
19:4 Egyptians, and how I B you on eagles' wings
21:6 and his master shall B his ear through with
Num 17:8 produced blossoms, and it B ripe almonds.
26:59 in Egypt; and she B to Amram Aaron and
Deut 1:31 the LORD your God B you, as a man
9:19 displeasure which the LORD B against you, so that
Josh 3:15 and when those who B the ark had come
3:17 ground, the priests who B the ark of the
4:10 For the priests who B the ark stood in
Judg 4:24 the people of Israel B harder and harder on
8:31 was in Shechem also B him a son, and
11:2 And Gilead's wife also B him sons; and when
13:24 And the woman B a son, and called his
Ruth 4:12 of Perez, whom Tamar B to Judah, because of
4:13 her conception, and she B a son.
1Sam 1:20 time Hannah conceived and B a son, and she
2:21 and she conceived and B three sons and two
14:1 the young man who B his armor, "Come, let
14:6 the young man who B his armor, "Come, let
2Sam 6:13 and when those who B the ark of the
11:27 became his wife, and B him a son.
12:15 child that Uriah's wife B to David, and it
12:24 with her; and she B a son, and he
21:8 of Aiah, whom she B to Saul, Armoni and
21:8 of Saul, whom she B to Adriel the son
1Kgs 2:26 to death, because you B the ark of the
11:20 the sister of Tahpenes B him Genubath his son,
14:28 the LORD, the guard B them and brought them
2Kgs 4:17 woman conceived, and she B a son about that
1Chr 1:32 Keturah, Abraham's concubine: she B Zimran,
2:3 three Bath-shua the Canaanitess B to him.
2:4 His daughter-in-law Tamar also B him Perez and
2:17 Abigail B Amasa, and the father of Amasa was
2:19 Caleb married Ephrath, who B him Hur.
2:21 years old; and she B him Segub;
2:24 his father, and she B him Ashhur, the father
2:29 was Abihail, and she B him Ahban and Molid.
2:35 his slave; and she B him Attai.
2:46 Ephah also, Caleb's concubine, B Haran, Moza, and
2:48 Maacah, Caleb's concubine, B Sheber and Tirhanah.
2:49 She also B Shaaph the father of Madmannah, Sheva
4:6 Helah and Naarah; Naarah B him Ahuzzam, Hepher,
4:9 Jabez, saying, "Because I B him in pain."
4:17 and she conceived and B Miriam, Shammai, and
4:18 And his Jewish wife B Jered the father of
7:14 whom his Aramean concubine B; she bore Machir
7:14 Aramean concubine bore; she B Machir the father of
7:16 the wife of Machir B a son, and she
7:18 And his sister Hammolecheth B Ishhod, Abi-ezer, and
7:23 and she conceived and B a son; and he
2Chr 11:19 of Jesse; and she B him sons, Jeush, Shemariah,
11:20 daughter of Absalom, who B him Abijah, Attai, Ziza,
12:11 the guard came and B them, and brought them
Ps 22:10 and since my mother B me thou hast been
68:11 host of those who B the tidings:
Prov 17:25 bitterness to her who B him.
23:25 glad, let her who B you rejoice.
Song 6:9 flawless to her that B her.
8:5 you, there she who B you was in travail.
Is 8:3 and she conceived and B a son.
22:6 And Elam B the quiver with chariots and horsemen,
51:2 and to Sarah who B you; for when he
53:12 the transgressors; yet he B the sin of many,
Jer 15:9 She who B seven has languished; she has swooned
15:10 my mother, that you B me, a man of
16:3 concerning the mothers who B them and the fathers
20:14 day when my mother B me, let it not
22:26 and the mother who B you into another country,
31:19 was confounded, because I B the disgrace of my
50:12 shamed, and she who B you shall be disgraced.
Ezek 23:4 became mine, and they B sons and daughters.
Hos 1:3 and she conceived and B him a son.
1:6 She conceived again and B a daughter.
1:8 pitied, she conceived and B a son.
Zech 13:3 father and mother who B him will say to
13:3 father and mother who B him shall pierce him
2Mac 3:36 And he B testimony to all men of the
7:6 in his song which B witness against the people
7:20 a single day, she B it with good courage
12:30 Jews who dwelt there B witness to the good
12:35 of the Thracian horsemen B down upon him and
Mt 8:17 took our infirmities and B our diseases."
13:26 plants came up and B grain, then the weeds
Mk 14:56 For many B false witness against him, and their
14:57 some stood up and B false witness against him,
Lk 11:27 is the womb that B you, and the breasts
23:28 the wombs that never B, and the breasts that
Jn 1:15 (John B witness to him, and cried, "This was

1:32 And John B witness, "I saw the Spirit descend
3:26 Jordan, to whom you B witness, here he is,
12:17 him from the dead B witness.
Acts 13:18 about forty years he B with them in the
14:3 for the Lord, who B witness to the word
15:8 who knows the heart B witness to them, giving
Heb 2:4 him, while God also B witness by signs and
1Pet 2:24 He himself B our sins in his body on
Rev 1:2 his servant John, who B witness to the word
16:2 upon the men who B the mark of the

BORED

2Kgs 12:9 took a chest, and B a hole in the

BORN (157)

Gen 4:18 To Enoch was B Irad; and Irad was the
4:26 also a son was B, and he called his
6:1 ground, and daughters were B to them,
10:1 and Japheth; sons were B to them after the
10:21 Eber, the elder brother of Japheth, children were B
10:25 To Eber were B two sons: the name of
14:14 forth his trained men, B in his house, three
15:3 offspring; and a slave B in my house will
17:12 throughout your generations, whether B in your
17:13 both he that is B in your house and
17:17 "Shall a child be B to a man who
17:23 and all the slaves B in his house or
17:27 of his house, those B in the house and
21:3 his son who was B to him, whom Sarah
21:5 his son Isaac was B to him.
24:15 behold, Rebekah, who was B to Bethuel the son
25:23 womb, and two peoples, B of you, shall be
35:26 of Jacob who were B to him in Paddan-aram.
36:5 of Esau who were B to him in the
36:18 these are the chiefs B of Oholibamah the daughter
46:20 land of Egypt were B Manasseh and Ephraim, whom
46:22 of Rachel, who were B to Jacob--fourteen persons
46:27 of Joseph, who were B to him in Egypt,
48:5 two sons, who were B to you in the
48:6 And the offspring B to you after them shall
50:23 son of Manasseh were B upon Joseph's knees.
Ex 1:21 "Every son that is B to the Hebrews you
Lev 18:9 of your mother, whether B at home or born
18:9 born at home or B abroad.
22:11 and those that are B in his house may
22:27 sheep or goat is B, it shall remain seven
25:45 you, who have been B in your land; and
Num 26:59 of Levi, who was B to Levi in Egypt;
26:60 And to Aaron were B Nadab, Abihu, Eleazar and
Deut 15:19 firstling males that are B of your herd and
23:8 third generation that are B to them may enter
Josh 5:5 the people that were B on the way in
Judg 13:8 to do with the boy that will be B
18:29 their ancestor, who was B to Israel; but the
Ruth 4:17 "A son has been B to Naomi." They named
2Sam 3:2 And sons were B to David at Hebron: his
3:5 These were B to David in Hebron.
5:13 sons and daughters were B to David.
5:14 of those who were B to him in Jerusalem:
12:14 the child that is B to you shall die."
14:27 There were B to Absalom three sons, and one
1Kgs 1:6 man; and he was B next after Absalom.
8:19 son who shall be B to you shall build
13:2 a son shall be B to the house of
2Kgs 20:18 own sons, who are B to you, shall be
1Chr 1:19 To Eber were B two sons: the name of
2:9 of Hezron, that were B to him: Jerahmeel, Ram,
3:1 of David that were B to him in Hebron:
3:4 wife Eglah; six were B to him in Hebron,
3:5 These were B to him in Jerusalem: Shimea, Shobab,
7:21 of Gath who were B in the land slew,
22:9 a son shall be B to you; he shall
26:6 son Shemaiah were sons B who were rulers in
2Chr 6:9 son who shall be B to you shall build
Jud 12:18 than in all the days since I was B
12:20 drunk in any one day since he was B
Esth 14:5 Ever since I was B I have heard in
Job 1:2 There were B to him seven sons and three
3:3 perish wherein I was B, and the night which
5:7 ground; but man is B to trouble as the
11:12 wild ass's colt is B a man.
14:1 "Man that is B of a woman is of
15:7 "Are you the first man that was B
15:14 Or he that is B of a woman, that
25:4 can he who is B of woman be clean?
38:21 know, for you were B then, and the number
Ps 87:4 "This one was B there," they say.
87:5 and that one were B in her"; for the
87:6 peoples, "This one was B there." [Selah]
Prov 17:17 and a brother is B for adversity.
Eccl 2:7 had slaves who were B in my house; I
3:2 a time to be B, and a time to
4:14 own kingdom had been B poor.
Wis 2:2 Because we were B by mere chance, and hereafter
4:6 For children B of unlawful unions are witnesses of
5:13 soon as we were B, ceased to be, and
7:3 And when I was B, I began to breathe
Sir 7:28 your parents you were B; and what can you
10:18 fierce anger for those B of women.
14:18 flesh and blood: one dies and another is B
23:14 you had never been B, and you will curse
41:9 When you are B, you are born to a
41:9 are born, you are B to a curse; and
44:10 they had not been B, and so have their
49:15 like Joseph has been B, and his bones are
Is 9:6 us a child is B, to us a son
39:7 own sons, who are B to you, shall be
49:20 The children B in the time of your bereavement
66:8 Shall a land be B in one day?
Jer 1:5 and before you were B I consecrated you; I
16:3 and daughters who are B in this place, and
20:14 Cursed be the day on which I was B
20:15 father, "A son is B to you," making him
22:26 where you were not B, and there you shall
Bar 3:26 The giants were B there, who were famous of
Ezek 16:4 the day you were B your navel string was
16:5 were abhorred, on the day that you were B
Hos 2:3 the day she was B, and make her like
1Mac 2:7 Why was I B to see this, the ruin
Mt 1:16 of whom Jesus was B, who is called Christ.
2:1 Now when Jesus was B in Bethlehem of Judea
2:2 he who has been B king of the Jews?
2:4 of them where the Christ was to be B
11:11 to you, among those B of women there has
26:24 for that man if he had not been B
Mk 14:21 for that man if he had not been B
Lk 1:35 the child to be B will be called holy,
2:11 for to you is B this day in the
7:28 tell you, among those B of women none is
Jn 1:13 of God; who were B, not of blood nor
3:3 you, unless one is B anew, he cannot see
3:4 can a man be B when he is old?
3:4 second time into his mother's womb and be B
3:5 you, unless one is B of water and the
3:6 That which is B of the flesh is flesh,
3:6 and that which is B of the Spirit is
3:7 you, 'You must be B anew.'
3:8 every one who is B of the Spirit."
8:41 him, "We were not B of fornication; we have
9:2 parents, that he was B blind?"
9:19 who you say was B blind?
9:20 and that he was B blind;
9:32 eyes of a man B blind.
9:34 answered him, "You were B in utter sin, and
16:21 that a child is B into the world.
18:37 For this I was B, and for this I
Acts 7:20 this time Moses was B, and was beautiful before
22:3 "I am a Jew, B at Tarsus in Cilicia,
22:28 said, "But I was B a citizen."
Rom 9:11 they were not yet B and had done nothing
1Cor 11:12 so man is now B of woman.
15:8 as to one untimely B, he appeared also to
Gal 1:15 apart before I was B, and had called me
4:4 sent forth his Son, B of woman, born under
4:4 Son, born of woman, B under the law,
4:23 of the slave was B according to the flesh,
4:29 time he who was B according to the flesh
4:29 persecuted him who was B according to the Spirit,
Phil 2:7 of a servant, being B in the likeness of
3:5 of Benjamin, a Hebrew B of Hebrews; as to
Heb 11:12 good as dead, were B descendants as many as
11:23 Moses, when he was B, was hid for three
1Pet 1:3 mercy we have been B anew to a living
1:23 You have been B anew, not of perishable seed
2Pet 2:12 animals, creatures of instinct, B to be caught and
1Jn 2:29 who does right is B of him.
3:9 No one B of God commits sin; for God's
3:9 sin because he is B of God.
4:7 he who loves is B of God and knows
5:4 For whatever is B of God overcomes the world;
5:18 know that any one B of God does not
5:18 but He who was B of God keeps him,

B

BORNE (41)
Gen 21:7 Yet I have B him a son in his
21:9 Egyptian, whom she had B to Abraham, playing with
22:20 "Behold, Milcah also has B children to your brother
29:34 me, because I have B him three sons"; therefore
30:20 me, because I have B him six sons"; so
30:25 When Rachel had B Joseph, Jacob said to Laban,
31:43 daughters, or to their children whom they have B
34:1 Leah, whom she had B to Jacob, went out
Deut 21:15 disliked, and they have B him children, both the
Ruth 4:15 than seven sons, has B him."
1Sam 2:5 The barren has B seven, but she who has
4:20 not, for you have B a son." But she
1Kgs 3:21 it was not the child that I had B
Job 21:32 When he is B to the grave, watch is
34:31 to God, 'I have B chastisement; I will not
Ps 69:7 sake that I have B reproach, that shame has
Sir 28:19 anger, who has not B its yoke, and has
Is 46:3 Israel, who have been B by me from your
49:21 your heart: 'Who has B me these?
51:18 the sons she has B; there is none to
53:4 Surely he has B our griefs and carried our
Jer 49:29 their camels shall be B away from them, and
Ezek 16:20 daughters, whom you had B to me, and these
23:37 sons whom they had B to me.
Dan 13:43 that these men have B false witness against me.
13:49 For these men have B false witness against her."
Hos 5:7 LORD; for they have B alien children.
Mt 1:25 not until she had B a son; and he
20:12 to us who have B the burden of the
Jn 1:34 have seen and have B witness that this is
5:32 John, and he has B witness to the truth.
5:36 sent me has himself B witness to me.
19:35 who saw it has B witness--his testimony is
1Cor 15:49 Just as we have B the image of the
1Tim 2:6 testimony to which was B at the proper time.
2Pet 1:17 and the voice was B to him by the
1:18 we heard this voice B from heaven, for we
1Jn 5:9 God that he has B witness to his Son.
5:10 testimony that God has B to his Son.
Rev 6:9 the witness they had B;
12:13 the woman who had B the male child.

BORROW (4)
Deut 15:6 but you shall not B; and you shall rule
28:12 lend to many nations, but you shall not B
2Kgs 4:3 he said, "Go outside, B vessels of all your
Mt 5:42 refuse him who would B from you.

BORROWED (5)
2Kgs 6:5 It was B
Neh 5:4 who said, "We have B money for the king's
Wis 15:16 one whose spirit is B formed them; for no
Sir 18:32 beggar by feasting with B money, when you have
Jer 15:10 lent, nor have I B, yet all of them

BORROWER (3)
Prov 22:7 the poor, and the B is the slave of
Sir 29:6 he does not, the B has robbed him of
Is 24:2 lender, so with the B; as with the creditor,

BORROWS (2)
Ex 22:14 "If a man B anything of his neighbor, and
Ps 37:21 The wicked B, and cannot pay back, but the

BOSOM (40)
Ex 4:6 said to him, "Put your hand into your B
4:6 his hand into his B; and when he took
4:7 God said, "Put your hand back into your B
4:7 hand back into his B; and when he took
Num 11:12 'Carry them in your B, as a nurse carries
Deut 13:6 the wife of your B, or your friend who
28:54 the wife of his B, and to the last
28:56 the husband of her B, to her son and
Ruth 4:16 laid him in her B, and became his nurse.
2Sam 12:3 and lie in his B, and it was like
12:8 master's wives into your B, and gave you the
1Kgs 1:2 her lie in your B, that my lord the
3:20 laid it in her B, and laid her dead
3:20 bosom, and laid her dead son in my B
17:19 took him from her B, and carried him up
Job 23:12 have treasured in my B the words of his
31:33 my iniquity in my B,
Ps 35:13 head bowed on my B,
41:9 Even my B friend in whom I trusted, who
74:11 dost thou keep thy right hand in thy B
79:12 Return sevenfold into the B of our neighbors the
89:50 I bear in my B the insults of the
129:7 binder of sheaves his B,
Prov 5:20 woman and embrace the B of an adventuress?
6:27 carry fire in his B and his clothes not
17:23 a bribe from the B to pervert the ways
21:14 a bribe in the B, strong wrath.
Eccl 7:9 anger lodges in the B of fools.
Sir 9:1 the wife of your B, and do not teach
Is 40:11 carry them in his B, and gently lead those
49:22 your sons in their B, and your daughters shall
65:6 will repay into their B
65:7 will measure into their B payment for their former
Lam 2:12 their life is poured out on their mothers' B
Ezek 23:8 and handled her virgin B and poured out their
23:21 the Egyptians handled your B and pressed your
Mic 7:5 who lies in your B;
Lk 16:22 and was carried by the angels to Abraham's B
16:23 and saw Abraham far-off and Lazarus in his B
Jn 1:18 who is in the B of the Father, he

BOSOMS
Ezek 23:3 pressed and their virgin B handled.

BOSOR (2)
1Mac 5:26 up in Bozrah and B, in Alema and Chaspho,
5:36 took Chaspho, Maked, and B, and the other cities

BOTH (306)
Gen 2:25 and his wife were B naked, and were not
3:7 Then the eyes of B were opened, and they
9:23 garment, laid it upon B their shoulders, and walked
13:6 land could not support B of them dwelling together;
17:13 not of your offspring, B he that is born
19:4 the men of Sodom, B young and old, all
19:11 door of the house, B small and great, so
19:36 Thus B the daughters of Lot were with child
21:31 called Beer-sheba; because there B of them swore
22:6 So they went B of them together.
22:8 So they went B of them together.
24:25 She added, "We have B straw and provender enough,
27:45 be bereft of you B in one day?"
34:30 I shall be destroyed, B I and my household."
40:5 And one night they B dreamed--the butler and
43:8 live and not die, B we and you and
44:16 are my lord's slaves, B we and he also
46:34 youth even until now, B we and our fathers,'
47:19 die before your eyes, B we and our land?
48:13 And Joseph took them B, Ephraim in his right
50:9 went up with him B chariots and horsemen; it
Ex 7:19 the land of Egypt, B in vessels of wood
9:25 the land of Egypt, B man and beast; and
12:12 the land of Egypt, B man and beast; and
12:31 from among my people, B you and the people
12:38 and very many cattle, B flocks and herds.
13:2 the people of Israel, B of man and of
13:15 the land of Egypt, B the first-born of man
22:9 it,' the case of B parties shall come before
22:11 shall be between them B to see whether he
26:24 shall it be with B of them; they shall
32:15 that were written on B sides; on the one
35:22 So they came, B men and women; all who
35:34 inspired him to teach, B him and Oholiab the
Lev 9:2 for a burnt offering, B without blemish, and offer
9:3 calf and a lamb, B a year old without
15:18 an emission of semen, B of them shall bathe
16:21 and Aaron shall lay B his hands upon the
20:10 wife of his neighbor, B the adulterer and the
20:11 uncovered his father's nakedness; B of them shall be
20:12 lies with his daughter-in-law, B of them shall be
20:13 as with a woman, B of them have committed
20:14 be burned with fire, B he and they, that
20:18 fountain of her blood; B of them shall be
21:22 bread of his God, B of the most holy
22:28 you shall not kill B her and her young
27:10 beast for beast, then B it and that for
27:33 he exchanges it, then B it and that for
Num 3:13 the first-born in Israel, B of man and of
5:3 you shall put out B male and female, putting
7:13 shekel of the sanctuary, B of them full of
7:19 shekel of the sanctuary, B of them full of
7:25 shekel of the sanctuary, B of them full of
7:31 shekel of the sanctuary, B of them full of
7:37 shekel of the sanctuary, B of them full of
7:43 shekel of the sanctuary, B of them full of
7:49 shekel of the sanctuary, B of them full of

7:55 shekel of the sanctuary, B of them full of
7:61 shekel of the sanctuary, B of them full of
7:67 shekel of the sanctuary, B of them full of
7:73 shekel of the sanctuary, B of them full of
7:79 shekel of the sanctuary, B of them full of
8:17 of Israel are mine, B of man and of
9:14 shall have one statute, B for the sojourner and
10:3 And when B are blown, all the congregation shall
12:5 and Miriam; and they B came forward.
20:4 we should die here, B we and our cattle?
25:8 inner room, and pierced B of them, the man
27:21 they shall come in, B he and all the
31:11 and all the booty, B of man and of
31:26 booty that was taken, B of man and of
31:47 one of every fifty, B of persons and of
Deut 19:17 him of wrongdoing, then B parties to the dispute
21:15 have borne him children, B the loved and the
22:22 wife of another man, B of them shall die,
22:24 you shall bring them B out to the gate
23:18 for any vow; for B of these are an
29:11 is in your camp, B he who hews your
32:25 shall be terror, destroying B young man and virgin,
Josh 6:21 all in the city, B men and women, young
8:25 who fell that day, B men and women, were
17:16 have chariots of iron, B those in Beth-shean and
Judg 6:5 like locusts for number; B they and their camels
19:8 So they ate, B of them.
Ruth 1:5 about ten years; and B Mahlon and Chilion died,
1Sam 2:26 Samuel continued to grow B in stature and in
2:34 the sign to you: B of them shall die
5:4 head of Dagon and B his hands were lying
5:6 afflicted them with tumors, B Ashdod and its
5:9 men of the city, B young and old, so
6:18 to the five lords, B fortified cities and unwalled
9:26 So Saul arose, and B he and Samuel went
12:14 the LORD, and if B you and the king
12:25 shall be swept away, B you and your king."
14:11 So B of them showed themselves to the garrison
15:3 spare them, but kill B man and woman, infant
17:36 Your servant has killed B lions and bears; and
20:11 So they B went out into the field.
20:42 as we have sworn B of us in the
22:19 put to the sword; B men and women, children
25:16 a wall to us B by night and by
25:43 Ahino-am of Jezreel; and B of them became his
30:2 who were in it, B small and great; they
2Sam 6:19 whole multitude of Israel, B men and women, to
9:13 he was lame in B his feet.
10:9 was set against him B in front and in
15:25 and let me see B it and his habitation;
16:23 counsel of Ahithophel esteemed, B by David and by
17:18 and told Absalom; so B of them went away
19:14 to the king, "Return, B you and all your
1Kgs 3:13 you have not asked, B riches and honor, so
6:5 walls of the house, B the nave and the
6:25 also measured ten cubits; B cherubim had the same
7:29 Upon the frames, B above and below the lions
14:10 from Jeroboam every male, B bond and free in
16:7 Baasha and his house, B because of all the
2Kgs 2:7 from them, as they B were standing by the
23:2 prophets, all the people, B small and great; and
25:26 Then all the people, B small and great, and
1Chr 7:24 Sheerah, who built B Lower and Upper Beth-horon,
12:3 was Ahiezer, then Joash, B sons of Shemaah of
16:3 distributed to all Israel, B men and women, to
19:10 was set against him B in front and in
24:5 officers of God among B the sons of Eleazar
29:12 B riches and honor come from thee, and thou
2Chr 24:14 house of the LORD, B for the service and
26:10 he had large herds, B in the Shephelah and
32:26 pride of his heart, B he and the inhabitants
34:30 Levites, all the people B great and small; and
Neh 8:2 law before the assembly, B men and women and
12:40 So B companies of those who gave thanks stood
Tob 3:16 The prayer of B was heard in the presence
5:15 your wages if you B return safe and sound."
5:16 for the journey, and good success to you B
5:16 So they B went out and departed, and the
6:5 And they B continued on their way until they
6:17 approach her, rise up, B of you, and cry
7:12 God will guide you B for the best."
8:9 Then they B went to sleep for the night.
8:13 in, and found them B asleep.
9:6 In the morning they B got up early and
11:9 And they B wept.
12:16 They were B alarmed; and they fell upon their
Jud 4:2 approach, and were alarmed B for Jerusalem and for
13:13 They all ran together, B small and great, for
Esth 1:5 in Susa the capital, B great and small, a
2:23 so, the men were B hanged on the gallows.
9:20 provinces of King Ahasuerus, B near and far,
11:6 great dragons came forward, B ready to fight, and
16:16 has directed the kingdom B for us an for
16:23 commemorative festivals, so that B now and
Job 9:22 I say, he destroys B the blameless and the
9:33 us, who might lay his hand upon us B
15:10 B the gray-haired and the aged are among us,
Ps 4:8 In peace I will B lie down and sleep;
49:2 inhabitants of the world, B low and high, rich
76:6 O God of Jacob, B rider and horse lay
104:25 things innumerable, living things B small and great.
106:6 B we and our fathers have sinned; we have
115:13 who fear the LORD, B small and great.
135:8 the first-born of Egypt, B of man and of
Prov 17:15 condemns the righteous are B alike an abomination
20:10 and diverse measures are B alike an abomination to
20:12 the seeing eye, the LORD has made them B
24:22 knows the ruin that will come from them B
27:3 weighty, but a fool's provocation is heavier than B
29:13 the LORD gives light to the eyes of B
Eccl 2:8 provinces; I got singers, B men and women, and
4:3 alive; but better than B is he who has
11:6 or that, or whether B alike will be good.
Wis 4:1 because it is known B by God and by
6:7 because he himself made B small and great, and
7:16 For B we and our words are in his
7:21 of roots; I learned B what is secret and
15:7 of the same clay B the vessels that serve
15:19 but they have escaped B the praise of God
18:9 alike the same things, B blessings and dangers; and
Sir 5:6 for B mercy and wrath are with him, and
10:7 and before men, and injustice is outrageous to B
18:16 B are to be found in a gracious man.
20:24 but the lot of B is ruin.
22:5 father and husband, and will be despised by B
28:12 be put out; and B come out of your
40:8 With all flesh, B man and beast, and upon
40:18 he who finds treasure is better off than B
40:19 but a blameless wife is accounted better than B
40:20 but the love of wisdom is better than B
40:21 melody, but a pleasant voice is better than B
40:22 but the green shoots of grain more than B
40:23 a wife with her husband is better than B
40:24 time of trouble, but almsgiving rescues better than B
40:25 sure, but good counsel is esteemed more than B
40:26 the fear of the Lord is better than B
Is 1:31 work a spark, and B of them shall burn
8:14 rock of stumbling to B houses of Israel, a
10:18 the LORD will destroy, B soul and body, and
20:4 and the Ethiopians exiles, B the young and the
Jer 4:9 LORD, courage shall fail B king and princes; the
6:11 of young men, also; B husband and wife shall
9:10 cattle is not heard; B the birds of the
10:8 They are B stupid and foolish; the instruction of
14:18 For B prophet and priest ply their trade through
16:6 B great and small shall die in this land;
21:6 inhabitants of this city, B man and beast; they
23:11 B prophet and priest are ungodly; even in my
32:14 Israel: Take these deeds, B this sealed deed of
44:17 her, as we did, B we and our fathers,
46:12 against warrior; they have B fallen together."
50:3 shall dwell in it; B man and beast shall
51:12 for the LORD has B planned and done what
Ezek 15:4 the fire has consumed B ends of it, and
16:53 will restore their fortunes, B the fortunes of Sodom
16:61 I take your sisters, B your elder and your
21:3 cut off from you B righteous and wicked.
21:4 cut off from you B righteous and wicked, therefore
21:19 of Babylon to come; B of them shall come
23:13 she was defiled; they B took the same way.
30:22 will break his arms, B the strong arm and
45:7 belong the land on B sides of the holy
47:12 on the banks, on B sides of the river,
48:21 "What remains on B sides of the holy portion
Dan 1:3 the people of Israel, B of the royal family
8:3 had two horns; and B horns were high, but
9:24 everlasting righteousness, to seal B vision and
13:10 B were overwhelmed with passion for her, but they
13:57 This is how you B have been dealing with
13:59 you in two, that he may destroy you B
Zech 5:4 house and consume it, B timber and stones."
6:13 shall be between them B

B

1Mac	1:16	he might reign over B kingdoms.
	4:34	Then B sides attacked, and there fell of the
	6:26	it; they have fortified B the sanctuary and Bethzur;
	6:45	parted before him on B sides.
	8:30	terms are in effect B parties shall determine to
	9:17	desperate, and many on B sides were wounded and
	11:34	confirmed as their possession B the territory of
	12:11	constantly on every occasion, B in our feasts and
2Mac	4:5	in view the welfare, B public and private, of
	5:15	had become a traitor B to the laws and
	8:19	came to their ancestors; B the time of Sennacherib,
	14:46	entrails, took them with B hands and hurled them
Mt	9:17	fresh wineskins, and so B are preserved."
	10:28	him who can destroy B soul and body in
	13:30	Let B grow together until the harvest; and at
	15:14	leads a blind man, B will fall into a
	22:10	all whom they found, B bad and good; so
Lk	1:6	And they were B righteous before God, walking in
	1:7	Elizabeth was barren, and B were advanced in years.
	5:7	they came and filled B the boats, so that
	6:39	Will they not B fall into a pit?
	7:42	When they could not pay, he forgave them B
	14:9	he who invited you B will come and say
	22:64	the people gathered together, B chief priests and
Jn	11:48	will come and destroy B our holy place and
	15:24	have seen and hated B me and my Father.
	20:4	They B ran, but the other disciple outran Peter
Acts	2:10	and visitors from Rome, B Jews and proselytes,
	2:29	patriarch David that he B died and was buried,
	2:36	God has made him B Lord and Christ, this
	4:27	whom thou didst anoint, B Herod and Pontius Pilate,
	5:14	to the Lord, multitudes B of men and women,
	7:35	judge?' God sent as B ruler and deliverer by
	8:12	Christ, they were baptized, B men and women.
	8:37	to stop, and they B went down into the
	10:39	all that he did B in the country of
	14:1	a great company believed, B of Jews and of
	14:5	attempt was made by B Gentiles and Jews, with
	15:3	they passed through B Phoenicia and Samaria,
	15:23	following letter: "The brethren, B the apostles and
	19:10	word of the Lord, B Jews and Greeks.
	19:17	all residents of Ephesus, B Jews and Greeks; and
	20:21	house to house, testifying B to Jews and to
	22:4	and delivering to prison B men and women,
	24:14	be a resurrection of B the just and the
	25:24	Jewish people petitioned me, B at Jerusalem and
	26:22	I stand here testifying B to small and great,
	26:23	he would proclaim light B to the people and
	28:23	convince them about Jesus B from the law of
Rom	1:12	by each other's faith, B yours and mine.
	1:14	I am under obligation B to Greeks and to
	1:14	Greeks and to barbarians, B to the wise and
	3:9	charged that all men, B Jews and Greeks, are
	14:9	he might be Lord B of the dead and
1Cor	1:2	our Lord Jesus Christ, B their Lord and ours:
	1:24	those who are called, B Jews and Greeks, Christ
	6:13	and God will destroy B one and the other.
Eph	2:14	who has made us B one, and has broken
	2:16	and might reconcile us B to God in one
	2:18	for through him we B have access in one
	6:9	that he who is B their Master and yours
Phil	1:7	with me of grace, B in my imprisonment and
	2:13	at work in you, B to will and to
1Thes	2:15	the Jews, who killed B the Lord Jesus and
1Tim	4:16	doing you will save B yourself and your hearers.
Philem	1:16	much more to you, B in the flesh and
Heb	9:19	and hyssop, and sprinkled B the book itself and
	9:21	sprinkled with the blood B the tent and all
2Pet	3:1	you, beloved, and in B of them I have
	3:18	him be the glory B now and to the
2Jn	1:9	in the doctrine has B the Father and the
Rev	11:18	who fear thy name, B small and great, and
	13:16	Also it causes all, B small and great, both
	13:16	both small and great, B rich and poor, both
	13:16	both rich and poor, B free and slave, to
	19:18	flesh of all men, B free and slave, both
	19:18	both free and slave, B small and great."

BOTHER

Lk	11:7	from within, 'Do not B me; the door is

BOTHERS

Lk	18:5	yet because this widow B me, I will vindicate

BOTTLE (3)

Jud	10:5	gave her maid a B of wine and a
Ps	33:7	sea as in a B; he put the deeps
	56:8	my tossings; put thou my tears in thy B

BOTTOM (7)

1Kgs	22:35	wound flowed into the B of the chariot.
Ezek	46:23	hearths made at the B of the rows round
Dan	6:24	before they reached the B of the den the
Amos	9:3	my sight at the B of the sea, there
Mt	27:51	two, from top to B; and the earth shook,
Mk	15:37	temple was torn in two, from top to B
Jn	19:23	woven from top to B;

BOTTOMLESS (6)

Rev	9:1	the shaft of the B pit;
	9:2	the shaft of the B pit, and from the
	9:11	the angel of the B pit; his name in
	11:7	that ascends from the B pit will make war
	17:8	to ascend from the B pit and go to
	20:1	the key of the B pit and a great

BOUGAEAN

Esth	12:6	son of Hammedatha, a B, was in great honor

BOUGH (3)

Gen	49:22	Joseph is a fruitful B, a fruitful bough by
	49:22	fruitful bough, a fruitful B by a spring; his
Is	17:6	top of the highest B, four or five on

BOUGHS (12)

Lev	23:40	of palm trees, and B of leafy trees, and
Deut	24:20	not go over the B again; it shall be
Wis	4:4	if they put forth B for a while, standing
Sir	14:26	will camp under her B
Is	10:33	hosts will lop the B with terrifying power; the
	27:11	When its B are dry, they are broken; women
Ezek	17:23	it may bring forth B and bear fruit, and
	19:11	aloft among the thick B; it was seen in
	31:5	of the forest; its B grew large and its
	31:6	their nests in its B; under its branches all
	31:8	fir trees equal its B; the plane trees were
	31:12	will fall, and its B will lie broken in

BOUGHT (51)

Gen	17:12	in your house, or B with your money from
	17:13	and he that is B with your money, shall
	17:23	in his house or B with his money, every
	17:27	the house and those B with money from a
	33:19	Hamor, Shechem's father, he B for a hundred pieces
	39:1	the guard, an Egyptian, B him from the Ishmaelites
	47:14	the grain which they B; and Joseph brought the
	47:20	So Joseph B all the land of Egypt for
	47:23	I have this day B you and your land
	49:30	of Canaan, which Abraham B with the field from
	50:13	of Mamre, which Abraham B with the field from
Ex	12:44	every slave that is B for money may eat
Lev	25:28	hand of him who B it until the year
	25:30	perpetuity to him who B it, throughout his
	25:50	reckon with him who B him from the year
	27:22	field which he has B, which is not a
	27:24	from whom it was B, to whom the land
Josh	24:32	of ground which Jacob B from the sons of
Ruth	4:9	day that I have B from the hand of
	4:10	of Mahlon, I have B to be my wife,
2Sam	12:3	but one little ewe lamb, which he had B
	24:24	So David B the threshing floor and the oxen
1Kgs	16:24	He B the hill of Samaria from Shemer for
Neh	5:8	we are able, have B back our Jewish brethren
Eccl	2:7	I B male and female slaves, and had slaves
Sir	33:30	yourself, because you have B him with blood.
Is	43:24	You have not B me sweet cane with money,
Jer	13:2	So I B a waistcloth according to the word
	13:4	waistcloth which you have B, which is upon your
	32:9	"And I B the field at Anathoth from Hanamel
	32:15	vineyards shall again be B in this land.'
	32:43	Fields shall be B in this land of which
	32:44	Fields shall be B for money, and deeds shall
Lam	5:4	we drink, the wood we get must be B
Bar	6:25	They are B at any cost, but there is
Hos	3:2	So I B her for fifteen shekels of silver
Mt	13:46	that he had and B it.
	21:12	all who sold and B in the temple, and
	27:7	they took counsel, and B with them the potter's
Mk	11:15	sold and those who B in the temple, and
	15:45	And he B a linen shroud, and taking him
	16:1	of James, and Salome, B spices, so that they
Lk	14:18	to him, 'I have B a field, and I

14:19 another said, 'I have B five yoke of oxen,
17:28 ate, they drank, they B, they sold, they planted,
Acts 1:18 (Now this man B a field with the reward
7:16 tomb that Abraham had B for a sum of
22:28 The tribune answered, "I B this citizenship for a
1Cor 6:20 your own; you were B with a price.
7:23 You were B with a price; do not become
2Pet 2:1 denying the Master who B them, bringing upon

BOUND (96)

Gen 22:9 wood in order, and B Isaac his son, and
38:28 the midwife took and B on his hand a
42:24 Simeon from them and B him before their eyes.
44:30 as his life is B up in the lad's
Ex 12:34 their kneading bowls being B up in their mantles
39:21 And they B the breastpiece by its rings to
Lev 8:13 them with girdles, and B caps on them, as
Num 30:4 by which she has B herself, and says nothing
30:4 by which she has B herself shall stand.
30:5 by which she has B herself, shall stand; and
30:6 by which she has B herself,
30:7 by which she has B herself shall stand.
30:8 lips, by which she B herself; and the LORD
30:9 by which she has B herself, shall stand against
30:10 her husband's house, or B herself by a pledge
30:11 pledge by which she B herself shall stand.
Josh 2:21 they departed; and she B the scarlet cord in
Judg 15:13 So they B him with two new ropes, and
16:6 how you might be B, that one could subdue
16:8 been dried, and she B him with them.
16:10 lies; please tell me how you might be B
16:12 took new ropes and B him with them, and
16:13 me lies; tell me how you might be B
16:21 down to Gaza, and B him with bronze fetters;
1Sam 25:29 my lord shall be B in the bundle of
2Sam 3:34 Your hands were not B, your feet were not
2Kgs 17:4 shut him up, and B him in prison.
25:7 eyes of Zedekiah, and B him in fetters, and
2Chr 33:11 Manasseh with hooks and B him with fetters of
36:6 king of Babylon, and B him in fetters to
Neh 6:18 many in Judah were B by oath to him,
Tob 8:3 Egypt, and the angel B him.
Jud 6:13 the hill and they B Achior and left him
Job 13:27 paths; thou settest a B to the soles of
28:3 out to the farthest B the ore in gloom
36:8 And if they are B in fetters and caught
Ps 104:9 Thou didst set a B which they should not
122:3 a city which is B firmly together,
Prov 22:15 Folly is B up in the heart of a
Wis 17:17 with one chain of darkness they all were B
Sir 28:19 and has not been B with its fetters;
Is 1:6 not pressed out, or B up, or softened with
61:1 to those who are B;
Jer 5:22 the sand as the B for the sea, a
39:7 eyes of Zedekiah, and B him in fetters to
40:1 when he took him B in chains along with
52:11 eyes of Zedekiah, and B him in fetters, and
Lam 1:14 "My transgressions were B into a yoke; by his
Ezek 3:25 and you shall be B with them, so that
27:24 carpets of colored stuff, B with cords and made
30:21 it has not been B up, to heal it
34:4 crippled you have not B up, the strayed you
Dan 3:21 Then these men were B in their mantles, their
3:23 Meshach, and Abednego, fell B into the burning fiery
3:92 not cast three men B into the fire?" They
4:15 roots in the earth, B with a band of
4:23 roots in the earth, B with a band of
Hos 13:12 iniquity of Ephraim is B up, his sin is
Nah 3:10 her great men were B in chains.
Mt 14:3 had seized John and B him and put him
16:19 on earth shall be B in heaven, and whatever
18:17 on earth shall be B in heaven, and whatever
23:15 the temple, he is B by his oath.'
23:17 the altar, he is B by his oath.'
27:2 to death; and they B him and led him
Mk 5:4 he had often been B with fetters and chains,
6:17 and seized John, and B him in prison for
15:1 a consultation; and they B Jesus and led him
Lk 8:29 kept under guard, and B with chains and fetters,
10:34 went to him and B up his wounds, pouring
13:16 of Abraham whom Satan B for eighteen years, be
Jn 11:44 his hands and feet B with bandages, and his
18:12 Jews seized Jesus and B him.
18:24 Annas then sent him B to Caiaphas the high
19:40 body of Jesus, and B it in linen cloths
Acts 9:2 he might bring them B to Jerusalem.
9:21 purpose, to bring them B before the chief priests."
12:6 sleeping between two soldiers, B with two chains,
20:22 am going to Jerusalem, B in the Spirit, not
21:11 took Paul's girdle and B his own feet and
21:33 ordered him to be B with two chains.
22:29 and that he had B him.
23:12 made a plot and B themselves by an oath
23:14 said, "We have strictly B ourselves by an oath
23:21 ambush for him, having B themselves by an oath
28:20 Israel that I am B with this chain."
Rom 7:2 a married woman is B by law to her
1Cor 7:15 a case the brother or sister is not B
7:27 Are you B to a wife?
7:39 A wife is B to her husband as long
Gal 5:3 circumcision that he is B to keep the whole
2Thes 1:3 We are B to give thanks to God always
2:13 But we are B to give thanks to God
Heb 5:3 of this he is B to offer sacrifice for
Rev 9:14 four angels who are B at the great river
20:2 Devil and Satan, and B him for a thousand

B

BOUNDARIES (5)

Num 34:12 your land with its B all round."
Prov 15:25 house of the proud, but maintains the widow's B
Is 10:13 I have removed the B of peoples, and have
Ezek 47:13 GOD: "These are the B by which you shall
Acts 17:26 allotted periods and the B of their habitation,

BOUNDARY (90)

Num 21:13 that extends from the B of the Amorites; for
21:13 the Arnon is the B of Moab, between Moab
21:24 for Jazer was the B of the Ammonites.
22:36 of Moab, on the B formed by the Arnon,
22:36 by the Arnon, at the extremity of the B
34:3 Edom, and your southern B shall be from the
34:4 the east; and your B shall turn south of
34:5 to Azmon; and the B shall turn from Azmon
34:6 "For the western B, you shall have the Great
34:6 and its coast; this shall be your western B
34:7 shall be your northern B: from the Great Sea
34:8 the end of the B shall be at Zeded;
34:9 at Zeded; then the B shall extend to Ziphron,
34:9 be at Hazar-enan; this shall be your northern B
34:10 mark out your eastern B from Hazar-enan to
34:11 to Shepham; and the B shall go down from
34:11 of Ain; and the B shall go down, and
34:12 the east; and the B shall go down to
Deut 2:18 to pass over the B of Moab at Ar;
3:16 the valley as a B, as far over as
3:16 the river Jabbok, the B of the Ammonites;
3:17 the Jordan as the B, from Chinnereth as far
Josh 12:2 the river Jabbok, the B of the Ammonites, that
12:5 all Bashan to the B of the Geshurites and
12:5 of Gilead to the B of Sihon king of
13:3 Egypt, northward to the B of Ekron, it is
13:4 to Aphek, to the B of the Amorites,
13:10 as far as the B of the Ammonites;
13:23 people of Reuben was the Jordan as a B
13:27 the Jordan as a B, to the lower end
15:1 reached southward to the B of Edom, to the
15:2 And their south B ran from the end of
15:4 This shall be your south B
15:5 And the east B is the Salt Sea, to
15:5 And the B on the north side runs from
15:6 the Jordan; and the B goes up to Beth-hoglah,
15:6 of Beth-arabah; and the B goes up to the
15:7 of Reuben; and the B goes up to Debir
15:7 the valley; and the B passes along to the
15:8 at En-rogel; then the B goes up by the
15:8 is, Jerusalem); and the B goes up to the
15:9 of Rephaim; then the B extends from the top
15:9 Mount Ephron; then the B bends round to Baalah
15:10 is, Kiriath-jearim); and the B circles west of Baalah
15:11 along by Timnah; the B goes out to the
15:11 of Ekron, then the B bends round to Shikkeron,
15:11 to Jabneel; then the B comes to an end
15:12 And the west B was the Great Sea with
15:12 This is the B round about the people of
15:21 extreme South, toward the B of Edom, were
16:5 was as follows: the B of their inheritance on
16:6 Upper Beth-horon, and the B goes thence to the
16:6 on the east the B turns round toward Taanath-shiloh,
16:8 From Tappuah the B goes westward to the brook
17:7 of Shechem; then the B goes along southward to
17:8 of Tappuah on the B of Manasseh belonged to
17:9 Then the B went down to the brook Kanah.

17:9 Then the B of Manasseh goes on the north
17:10 the sea forming its B; on the north Asher
18:12 the north side their B began at the Jordan;
18:12 the Jordan; then the B goes up to the
18:13 From there the B passes along southward in the
18:13 is Bethel), then the B goes down to Ataroth-addar,
18:14 Then the B goes in another direction, turning on
18:15 of Kiriath-jearim; and the B goes from there to
18:16 of Nephtoah; then the B goes down to the
18:19 the Arabah; then the B passes on to the
18:19 of Beth-hoglah; and the B ends at the northern
18:20 The Jordan forms its B on the eastern side.
18:20 according to its families, B by boundary round about.
18:20 its families, boundary by B round about.
19:11 as Sarid; then its B goes up westward, and
19:12 the sunrise to the B of Chisloth-tabor; thence it
19:14 on the north the B turns about to Hannathon,
19:22 En-gannim, En-haddah, Beth-pazzez; the B also
19:22 and Beth-shemesh, and its B ends at the Jordan--
19:29 the Great; then the B turns to Ramah, reaching
19:29 of Tyre; then the B turns to Hosah, and
19:33 And its B ran from Heleph, from the oak
19:34 Jordan; then the B turns westward to Aznoth-tabor,
22:25 made the Jordan a B between us and you,
Judg 11:18 the Arnon was the B of Moab.
Job 26:10 the waters at the B between light and darkness.
Ezek 45:7 western to the eastern B of the land.
47:15 "This shall be the B of the land: On
47:17 So the B shall run from the sea to
47:18 the east side, the B shall run from Hazar-enon
47:20 Sea shall be the B to a point opposite
48:28 to the south, the B shall run from Tamar
Mic 7:11 In that day the B shall be far extended.

BOUNDING (2)

Song 2:8 leaping upon the mountains, B over the hills.
Nah 3:2 wheel, galloping horse and B chariot!

BOUNDLESS

Sir 16:15 my soul in the B creation?

BOUNDS (16)

Ex 19:12 And you shall set B for the people round
19:23 charge us, saying, 'Set B about the mountain, and
23:31 I will set your B from the Red Sea
Num 35:26 time go beyond the B of his city of
35:27 finds him outside the B of his city of
Deut 32:8 men, he fixed the B of the peoples according
Judg 2:9 buried him within the B of his inheritance in
1Kgs 21:23 eat Jezebel within the B of Jezreel.'
Job 14:5 thou hast appointed his B that he cannot pass,
38:10 swaddling band, and prescribed B for it, and set
Ps 65:8 dwell at earth's farthest B are afraid at thy
74:17 hast fixed all the B of the earth; thou
148:6 ever; he fixed their B which cannot be passed.
Jer 5:28 They know no B in deeds of wickedness; they
Bar 3:25 great and has no B; it is high and
Hos 4:2 adultery; they break all B and murder follows

BOUNTIES

Gen 49:26 the eternal mountains, the B of the everlasting hills;

BOUNTIFUL (2)

Prov 22:9 He who has a B eye will be blessed,
2Mac 1:25 kind, who alone art B, who alone art just

BOUNTIFULLY (6)

Ps 13:6 because he has dealt B with me.
116:7 the LORD has dealt B with you.
119:17 Deal B with thy servant, that I may live
142:7 for thou wilt deal B with me.
2Cor 9:6 and he who sows B will also reap bountifully.
9:6 and he who sows bountifully will also reap B

BOUNTY (5)

1Kgs 10:13 given her by the B of King Solomon.
Esth 1:7 lavished according to the B of the king.
Ps 65:11 the year with thy B; the tracks of thy
116:12 LORD for all his B to me?
Wis 16:25 it served thy all-nourishing B, according to the desire

BOW (114)

Gen 9:13 generations: I set my B in the cloud, and
9:14 the earth and the B is seen in the
9:16 When the B is in the clouds, I will
21:20 the wilderness, and became an expert with the B
27:3 your quiver and your B, and go out to
27:29 serve you, and nations B down to you.
27:29 may your mother's sons B down to you.
37:10 brothers indeed come to B ourselves to the ground
41:43 they cried before him, B the knee!" Thus he
48:22 the Amorites with my sword and with my B
49:8 your father's sons shall B down before you.
49:24 him sorely; yet his B remained unmoved, his arms
Ex 11:8 down to me, and B down to me, saying,
20:5 earth; you shall not B down to them or
23:24 out, you shall not B down to their gods,
34:8 Moses made haste to B his head toward the
Lev 26:1 in your land, to B down to them; for
Deut 5:9 earth; you shall not B down to them or
Josh 23:7 or serve them, or B down yourselves to them,
23:16 serve other gods and B down to them.
24:12 was not by your sword or by your B
1Sam 18:4 his sword and his B and his girdle.
2Sam 1:22 of the mighty, the B of Jonathan turned not
22:35 arms can bend a B of bronze.
1Kgs 22:34 certain man drew his B at a venture, and
2Kgs 5:18 my arm, and I B myself in the house
5:18 of Rimmon, when I B myself in the house
6:22 taken captive with your sword and with your B
9:24 And Jehu drew his B with his full strength,
13:15 to him, "Take a B and arrows"; so he
13:15 so he took a B and arrows.
13:16 of Israel, "Draw the B; and he drew it.
17:35 fear other gods or B yourselves to them or
17:36 outstretched arm; you shall B yourselves to him, and
1Chr 5:18 sword, and drew the B, expert in war, forty-four
2Chr 17:17 thousand men armed with B and shield,
18:33 certain man drew his B at a venture, and
Jud 9:7 shield and spear, in B and sling, and know
Esth 3:2 But Mordecai did not B down or do obeisance.
3:5 that Mordecai did not B down or do obeisance
13:12 this, and refused to B down to this proud
13:14 and I will not B down to any one
Job 29:20 with me, and my B ever new in my
31:10 another, and let others B down upon her.
Ps 7:12 bent and strung his B;
11:2 the wicked bend the B, they have fitted their
18:34 arms can bend a B of bronze.
22:29 proud of the earth B down; before him shall
22:29 down; before him shall B all who go down
44:6 For not in my B do I trust, nor
45:11 he is your lord, B to him;
46:9 earth; he breaks the B, and shatters the spear,
60:4 fear thee, to rally to it from the B
72:9 May his foes B down before him, and his
78:9 Ephraimites, armed with the B, turned back on the
78:57 like their fathers; they twisted like a deceitful B
81:9 you; you shall not B down to a foreign
86:9 made shall come and B down before thee, O
95:6 let us worship and B down, let us kneel
97:7 worthless idols; all gods B down before him.
138:2 sing thy praise; I B down toward thy holy
144:5 B thy heavens, O LORD, and come down!
Prov 14:19 The evil B down before the good, the wicked
Wis 5:21 as from a well-drawn B of clouds,
Sir 4:7 beloved in the congregation; B your head low to
30:12 B down his neck in his youth, and beat
33:26 Yoke and thong will B the neck, and for
Is 2:8 filled with idols; they B down to the work
7:24 With B and arrows men will come there, for
21:15 sword, from the bent B, and from the press
22:3 fled together, without the B they were captured.
41:2 with his sword, like driven stubble with his B
45:14 over in chains and B down to you.
45:23 me every knee shall B, every tongue shall swear.'
46:2 They stoop, they B down together, they cannot save
49:23 the ground they shall B down to you, and
51:23 have said to you, B down, that we may
58:5 Is it to B down his head like a
60:14 who despised you shall B down at your feet;
65:12 all of you shall B down to the slaughter;
66:19 Lud, who draw the B, to Tubal and Javan,
Jer 6:23 They lay hold on B and spear, they are
9:3 their tongue like a B; falsehood and not truth
46:9 shield, men of Lud, skilled in handling the B
49:35 I will break the B of Elam, the mainstay
50:14 you that bend the B; shoot at her, spare
50:29 archers against Babylon, all those who bend the B
50:42 They lay hold of B and spear; they are
51:3 the archer bend his B, and let him not
Lam 2:4 He has bent his B like an enemy, with

3:12 desolate; he bent his B and set me as
Ezek 1:28 the appearance of the B that is in the
39:3 I will strike your B from your left hand,
Hos 1:5 I will break the B of Israel in the
1:7 not deliver them by B, nor by sword, nor
2:18 I will abolish the B, the sword, and war
7:17 are like a treacherous B, their princes shall fall
Amos 2:15 he who handles the B shall not stand, and
Mic 5:13 you, and you shall B down no more to
6:6 before the LORD, and B myself before God on
Hab 3:9 the sheath from thy B, and put the arrows
Zeph 1:5 idolatrous priests; those who B down on the roofs
1:5 the heavens; those who B down and swear to
2:11 and to him shall B down, each in its
Zech 9:10 Jerusalem; and the battle B shall be cut off,
9:13 bent Judah as my B; I have made Ephraim
10:4 of them the battle B, out of them every
Acts 27:30 out anchors from the B,
27:41 the vessel aground; the B stuck and remained
Rom 14:11 Lord, every knee shall B to me, and every
Eph 3:14 For this reason I B my knees before the
Phil 2:10 Jesus every knee should B, in heaven and on
Rev 3:9 make them come and B down before your feet,
6:2 its rider had a B; and a crown was

BOWED (72)

Gen 18:2 to meet them, and B himself to the earth,
19:1 to meet them, and B himself with his face
23:7 Abraham rose and B to the Hittites, the people
23:12 Then Abraham B down before the people of the
24:26 The man B his head and worshiped the LORD,
24:48 Then I B my head and worshiped the LORD,
24:52 heard their words, he B himself to the earth
33:6 and their children, and B down;
33:7 children drew near and B down; and last Joseph
33:7 drew near, and they B down.
37:7 gathered round it, and B down to my sheaf."
42:6 Joseph's brothers came, and B themselves before
43:26 had with them, and B down to him to
43:28 And they B their heads and made obeisance.
47:31 Then Israel B himself upon the head of his
48:12 his knees, and he B himself with his face
49:15 was pleasant; so he B his shoulder to bear,
Ex 4:31 their affliction, they B their heads and worshiped.
12:27 And the people B their heads and worshiped.
Num 22:31 his hand; and he B his head, and fell
25:2 the people ate, and B down to their gods.
Judg 2:12 round about them, and B down to them; and
2:17 after other gods and B down to them; they
16:30 Then he B with all his might; and the
1Sam 4:19 husband were dead, she B and gave birth; for
20:41 to the ground, and B three times; and they
24:8 looked behind him, David B with his face to
25:23 on her face, and B to the ground.
25:41 And she rose and B with her face to
28:14 was Samuel, and he B with his face to
2Sam 14:33 to the king, and B himself on his face
18:21 The Cushite B before Joab, and ran.
18:28 And he B before the king with his face
22:10 He B the heavens, and came down; thick darkness
1Kgs 1:16 Bathsheba B and did obeisance to the king, and
1:23 before the king, he B before the king, with
1:31 Then Bathsheba B with her face to the ground,
1:47 throne.' And the king B himself upon the bed.
2:19 to meet her, and B down to her; then
18:42 of Carmel; and he B himself down upon the
19:18 knees that have not B to Baal, and every
2Kgs 2:15 to meet him, and B to the ground before
1Chr 29:20 of their fathers, and B their heads, and worshiped
2Chr 7:3 upon the temple, they B down with their faces
20:18 Then Jehoshaphat B his head with his face to
29:29 were present with him B themselves and worshiped.
29:30 with gladness, and they B down and worshiped.
Neh 8:6 their hands; and they B their heads and worshiped
Jud 13:17 greatly astonished, and B down and worshipped God,
Esth 3:2 at the king's gate B down and did obeisance
16:11 father and was continually B sown to by all
Job 9:13 his anger; beneath him B the helpers of Rahab.
Ps 18:9 He B the heavens, and came down; thick darkness
35:13 I prayed with head B on my bosom,
35:14 who laments his mother, B down and in mourning.
38:6 foolishness, I am utterly B down and prostrate; all
44:25 For our soul is B down to the dust;
57:6 steps; my soul was B down.
107:12 Their hearts were B down with hard labor; they
145:14 up all who are B down.
146:8 up those who are B down; the LORD loves
Sir 19:23 There is a rascal B down in mourning, but
50:21 his name; and they B down in worship a
Is 5:15 Man is B down, and men are brought low,
21:3 in travail; I am B down so that I
51:14 He who is B down shall speedily be released;
Jer 2:20 every green tree you B down as a harlot.
Lam 2:10 maidens of Jerusalem have B their heads to the
3:20 of it and is B down within me.
Lk 24:5 they were frightened and B their faces to the
Jn 19:30 is finished"; and he B his head and gave
Rom 11:4 men who have not B the knee to Baal."

BOWELS (10)

Num 5:22 curse pass into your B and make your body
2Sam 20:10 body, and shed his B to the ground, without
2Chr 21:15 a disease of your B, until your bowels come
21:15 your bowels, until your B come out because of
21:18 smote him in his B with an incurable disease.
21:19 of two years, his B came out because of
Sir 10:9 even in life his B decay.
2Mac 9:5 a pain in his B for which there was
9:6 he had tortured the B of others with many
Acts 1:18 middle and all his B gushed out.

BOWING (6)

Gen 33:3 went on before them, B himself to the ground
37:9 and eleven stars were B down to me."
Judg 2:19 gods, serving them and B down to them; they
Ruth 2:10 fell on her face, B to the ground, and
2Kgs 4:37 fell at his feet, B to the ground; then
Heb 11:21 the sons of Joseph, B in worship over the

BOWL (19)

Judg 5:25 milk, she brought him curds in a lordly B
6:38 fleece to fill a B with water.
2Kgs 2:20 "Bring me a new B, and put salt in
Eccl 12:6 snapped, or the golden B is broken, or the
Song 7:2 navel is a rounded B that never lacks mixed
Is 51:17 to the dregs the B of staggering.
51:22 cup of staggering; the B of my wrath you
Dan 14:33 broken bread into a B, and was going into
Zech 4:2 of gold, with a B on the top of
4:3 the right of the B and the other on
9:15 be full like a B, drenched like the corners
Jn 19:29 A B full of vinegar stood there; so they
Rev 16:2 went and poured his B on the earth, and
16:3 second angel poured his B into the sea, and
16:4 third angel poured his B into the rivers and
16:8 fourth angel poured his B on the sun, and
16:10 fifth angel poured his B on the throne of
16:12 sixth angel poured his B on the great river
16:17 seventh angel poured his B into the air, and

BOWLS (29)

Ex 8:3 ovens and your kneading B;
12:34 was leavened, their kneading B being bound up in
25:29 and its flagons and B with which to pour
37:16 for incense, and its B and flagons with which
Num 4:7 dishes for incense, the B, and the flagons for
1Kgs 7:41 two pillars, the two B of the capitals that
7:41 to cover the two B of the capitals that
7:42 to cover the two B of the capitals that
2Kgs 12:13 basins of silver, snuffers, B, trumpets, or any vessels
25:15 the temple service, the firepans also, and the B
1Chr 28:17 cups; for the golden B and the weight of
28:17 each; for the silver B and the weight of
2Chr 4:12 the two pillars, the B, and the two capitals
4:12 to cover the two B of the capitals that
4:13 to cover the two B of the capitals that
Ezra 1:10 silver, twenty-nine censers, thirty B of gold, two
1:10 four hundred and ten B of silver, and a
8:27 talents of gold, twenty B of gold worth a
Jud 15:11 his beds and his B and all his furniture;
Jer 52:19 service; also the small B, and the firepans, and
52:19 for incense, and the B for libation.
Amos 6:6 who drink wine in B, and anoint themselves with
Zech 14:20 shall be as the B before the altar;
1Mac 1:22 for drink offerings, the B, the golden censers, the
Rev 5:8 harp, and with golden B full of incense, which
15:7 seven angels seven golden B full of the wrath
16:1 the earth the seven B of the wrath of
17:1 who had the seven B came and said to
21:9 who had the seven B full of the seven

BOWMEN (2)

1Chr 8:40 who were mighty warriors, B, having many sons and
12:2 They were B, and could shoot arrows and sling

BOWS (13)

1Sam 2:4 The B of the mighty are broken, but the
2Chr 14:8 carried shields and drew B; all these were mighty
26:14 helmets, coats of mail, B, and stones for slinging.
Neh 4:13 families, with their swords, their spears, and their B
4:16 held the spears, shields, B, and coats of mail;
Ps 21:12 you will aim at their faces with your B
37:14 sword and bend their B, to bring down the
37:15 own heart, and their B shall be broken.
Is 5:28 are sharp, all their B bent, their horses' hoofs
13:18 Their B will slaughter the young men; they will
46:1 Bel B down, Nebo stoops, their idols are on
Jer 51:56 warriors are taken, their B are broken in pieces;
Ezek 39:9 them, shields and bucklers, B and arrows, handpikes

BOWSHOT

Gen 21:16 the distance of a B; for she said, "Let

BOWSTRINGS (3)

Judg 16:7 me with seven fresh B which have not been
16:8 brought her seven fresh B which had not been
16:9 But he snapped the B, as a string of

BOX (6)

1Sam 6:8 and put in a B at its side the
6:11 the cart, and the B with the golden mice
6:15 the LORD and the B that was beside it,
Jn 12:6 he had the money B he used to take
13:29 Judas had the money B, Jesus was telling him,
1Cor 9:26 aimlessly, I do not B as one beating the

BOXES

Is 3:20 the sashes, the perfume B, and the amulets;

BOY (21)

Judg 13:5 his head, for the B shall be a Nazirite
13:7 nothing unclean, for the B shall be a Nazirite
13:8 to do with the B that will be born."
13:12 is to be the B's manner of life, and
13:24 name Samson; and the B grew, and the LORD
1Sam 2:11 And the B ministered to the LORD, in the
2:18 before the LORD, a B girded with a linen
2:21 And the B Samuel grew in the presence of
2:26 Now the B Samuel continued to grow both in
3:1 Now the B Samuel was ministering to the LORD
3:8 Eli perceived that the LORD was calling the B
2Chr 34:3 he was yet a B, he began to seek
Joel 3:3 and have given a B for a harlot, and
1Mac 6:17 him up as a B, and he named him
11:54 with him the young B Antiochus who began to
Mt 17:18 of him, and the B was cured instantly.
Mk 9:20 And they brought the B to him; and when
9:20 immediately it convulsed the B, and he fell on
9:26 came out, and the B was like a corpse;
Lk 2:43 they were returning, the B Jesus stayed behind in
9:42 spirit, and healed the B, and gave him back

BOYS (9)

Gen 25:27 When the B grew up, Esau was a skilful
2Kgs 2:23 the way, some small B came out of the
2:24 of the woods and tore forty-two of the B
Is 3:4 And I will make B their princes, and babes
Lam 5:13 at the mill; and B stagger under loads of
Zech 8:5 shall be full of B and girls playing in
1Mac 2:46 circumcised all the uncircumcised B that they found
2Mac 5:13 and old, destruction of B, women, and children, and
5:24 sell the women and B as slaves.

BOZEZ

1Sam 14:4 of the one was B, and the name of

BOZKATH (2)

Josh 15:39 Dilean, Mizpeh, Joktheel, Lachish, B, Eglon,
2Kgs 22:1 name was Jedidah the daughter of Adaiah of B

BOZRAH (10)

Gen 36:33 son of Zerah of B reigned in his stead.
1Chr 1:44 son of Zerah of B reigned in his stead.
Is 34:6 has a sacrifice in B, a great slaughter in
63:1 in crimsoned garments from B, he that is glorious
Jer 48:24 Beth-meon, and Kerioth, and B, and all the cities
49:13 says the LORD, that B shall become a horror,
49:22 spread his wings against B, and the heart of
Amos 1:12 Teman, and it shall devour the strongholds of B
1Mac 5:26 been shut up in B and Bosor, in Alema
5:28 the wilderness road to B; and he took the

BRACELET

Sir 21:21 ornament, and like a B on the right arm.

BRACELETS (8)

Gen 24:22 a half-shekel, and two B for her arms weighing
24:30 the ring, and the B on his sister's arms,
24:47 her nose, and the B on her arms.
Num 31:50 of gold, armlets and B, signet rings, earrings, and
Jud 10:4 on her anklets and B and rings, and her
Is 3:19 crescents; the pendants, the B, and the scarfs;
Ezek 16:11 with ornaments, and put B on your arms, and
23:42 wilderness; and they put B upon the hands of

BRACKISH

Jas 3:11 forth from the same opening fresh water and B

BRAGGART

Sir 20:6 right moment, but a B and fool goes beyond

BRAIDED

1Tim 2:9 seemly apparel, not with B hair or gold or

BRAIDING

1Pet 3:3 the outward adorning with B of hair, decoration of

BRAMBLE (4)

Judg 9:14 trees said to the B, 'Come you, and reign
9:15 over us.' And the B said to the trees,
9:15 come out of the B and devour the cedars
Lk 6:44 grapes picked from a B bush.

BRAMBLES

Song 2:2 As a lily among B, so is my love

BRAN

Bar 6:43 along the passageways, burning B for incense; and

BRANCH (25)

Ex 25:33 and flower, on one B, and three cups made
25:33 flower, on the other B --so for the six
37:19 and flower, on one B, and three cups made
37:19 flower, on the other B --so for the
Num 13:23 down from there a B with a single cluster
Job 15:32 his time, and his B will not be green.
Is 4:2 In that day the B of the LORD shall
9:14 head and tail, palm B and reed in one
11:1 of Jesse, and a B shall grow out of
19:15 head or tail, palm B or reed, may do.
Jer 23:5 for David a righteous B, and he shall reign
33:15 will cause a righteous B to spring forth for
Ezek 8:17 Lo, they put the B to their nose.
15:2 any wood, the vine B which is among the
Dan 11:7 "In those times a B from her roots shall
Zech 3:8 omen: behold, I will bring my servant the B
6:12 whose name is the B: for he shall grow
Mal 4:1 that it will leave them neither root nor B
1Mac 13:37 crown and the palm B which you sent, and
Mt 24:32 as soon as its B becomes tender and puts
Mk 13:28 as soon as its B becomes tender and puts
Jn 15:2 Every B of mine that bears no fruit, he
15:2 takes away, and every B that does bear fruit
15:4 As the B cannot bear fruit by itself, unless
15:6 cast forth as a B and withers; and the

BRANCHES (86)

Gen 40:10 vine there were three B; as soon as it
40:12 its interpretation: the three B are three days;
49:22 by a spring; his B run over the wall.
Ex 25:32 there shall be six B going out of its
25:32 of its sides, three B of the lampstand out
25:32 of it and three B of the lampstand out
25:33 so for the six B going out of the
25:35 pair of the six B going out from the
25:36 Their capitals and their B shall be of one
37:18 And there were six B going out of its
37:18 of its sides, three B of the lampstand out
37:18 of it and three B of the lampstand out
37:19 so for the six B going out of the
37:21 pair of the six B going out of it.
37:22 Their capitals and their B were of one piece
Lev 23:40 fruit of goodly trees, B of palm trees, and

2Sam	18:9	went under the thick B of a great oak,
Neh	8:15	the hills and bring B of olive, wild olive,
Jud	15:12	her; and she took B in her hands and
Job	14:9	bud and put forth B like a young plant.
	18:16	up beneath, and his B wither above.
	29:19	all night on my B,
Ps	80:10	mighty cedars with its B;
	80:11	it sent out its B to the sea, and
	104:12	air have their habitation; they sing among the B
	118:27	the festal procession with B, up to the horns
Song	7:8	the palm tree and lay hold of its B
Wis	4:5	The B will be broken off before they come
	17:18	of birds in wide-spreading B, or the rhythm of
Sir	1:18	of wisdom, and her B are long life.
	23:25	take root, and her B will not bear fruit.
	24:16	I spread out my B, and my branches are
	24:16	my branches, and my B are glorious and graceful.
	40:15	not put forth many B; they are unhealthy roots
Is	16:8	have struck down its B, which reached to Jazer
	17:6	or five on the B of a fruit tree,
	18:5	hooks, and the spreading B he will hew away.
	19:6	become foul, and the B of Egypt's Nile will
	27:10	grazes, there he lies down, and strips its B
Jer	5:10	end; strip away her B, for they are not
	6:9	a grape-gatherer pass your hand again over its B
	11:16	to it, and its B will be consumed.
	48:32	Your B passed over the sea, reached as far
Ezek	17:6	spreading vine, and its B turned toward him, and
	17:6	vine, and brought forth B and put forth foliage.
	17:7	and shot forth its B toward him that he
	17:8	it might bring forth B, and bear fruit, and
	17:9	and cut off its B, so that all its
	17:23	the shade of its B birds of every sort
	19:10	fruitful and full of B by reason of abundant
	19:11	in its height with the mass of its B
	19:14	stem, has consumed its B and fruit, so that
	31:3	in Lebanon, with fair B and forest shade, and
	31:5	grew large and its B long, from abundant water
	31:6	its boughs; under its B all the beasts of
	31:7	the length of its B; for its roots went
	31:8	nothing compared with its B; no tree in the
	31:9	the mass of its B, and all the trees
	31:12	all the valleys its B will fall, and its
	31:13	air, and upon its B will be all the
	36:8	shall shoot forth your B, and yield your fruit
Dan	4:12	air dwelt in its B, and all flesh was
	4:14	and cut off its B, strip off its leaves
	4:14	from under it and the birds from its B
	4:21	shade, and in whose B the birds of the
Joel	1:7	thrown it down; their B are made white.
Nah	2:2	them and ruined their B
Zech	4:12	"What are these two B of the olive trees,
1Mac	13:51	with praise and palm B, and with harps and
2Mac	10:7	ivy-wreathed wands and beautiful B and also fronds
	14:4	of the customary olive B from the temple.
Mt	13:32	the air come and make nests in its B
	21:8	road, and others cut B from the trees and
Mk	4:32	and puts forth large B, so that the birds
	11:8	and others spread leafy B which they had cut
Lk	13:19	birds of the air made nests in its B
Jn	12:13	So they took B of palm trees and went
	15:5	I am the vine, you are the B
	15:6	and withers; and the B are gathered, thrown into
Rom	11:16	if the root is holy, so are the B
	11:17	if some of the B were broken off, and
	11:18	the olive tree, do not boast over the B
	11:19	You will say, B were broken off so that
	11:21	not spare the natural B, neither will he spare
	11:24	more will these natural B be grafted back into
Rev	7:9	white robes, with palm B in their hands,

BRAND (2)

Amos	4:11	you were as a B plucked out of the
Zech	3:2	Is not this a B plucked from the fire?"

BRANDISH (2)

Ezek	32:10	of you, when I B my sword before them;
Zech	9:13	I will B your sons, O Zion, over your

BRANDISHED

Is	30:32	and lyres; battling with B arm he will fight

BRANDISHING (2)

2Mac	5:3	side and on that, B of shields, massing of
	11:8	clothed in white and B weapons of gold.

BRANDS (2)

Is	50:11	a fire, who set B alight.
	50:11	fire, and by the B which you have kindled!

BRASS (6)

Lev	26:19	and your earth like B;
Deut	28:23	your head shall be B, and the earth under
Is	48:4	sinew and your forehead B,
Dan	14:7	but clay inside and B outside, and it never
1Mac	6:35	of mail, and with B helmets on their heads;
	6:39	shields of gold and B, the hills were ablaze

BRAVE (11)

Tob	7:18	said to her, "Be B, my child; the Lord
	7:18	Be B, my daughter."
Sir	19:10	Be B
1Mac	5:56	forces, heard of their B deeds and of the
	5:61	thinking to do a B deed, they did not
	5:67	wished to do a B deed, fell in battle,
	8:2	wars and of the B deeds which they were
	9:22	his wars and the B deeds that he did,
	10:15	had fought, of the B deeds that they had
	16:23	his wars and the B deeds which he did,
2Mac	15:11	with the inspiration of B words, and he cheered

BRAVELY (4)

1Mac	9:10	come, let us die B for our brethren, and
2Mac	10:35	because of the blasphemies, B stormed the wall and
	14:43	He B ran up on the wall, and manfully
	15:17	campaign but to attack B, and to decide the

BRAVEST (2)

Judg	21:10	twelve thousand of their B men, and commanded
2Mac	13:15	picked force of the B young men, he attacked

BRAWLER

Prov	20:1	mocker, strong drink a B; and whoever is led

BRAY (2)

Job	6:5	Does the wild ass B when he has grass,
	30:7	Among the bushes they B; under the nettles they

BRAZEN

Ezek	16:30	the deeds of a B harlot;

BRAZIER (3)

Jer	36:22	fire burning in the B before him.
	36:23	the fire in the B, until the entire scroll
	36:23	consumed in the fire that was in the B

BREACH (18)

Gen	38:29	she said, "What a B you have made for
Ex	22:9	"For every B of trust, whether it is for
Lev	5:15	any one commits a B of faith and sins
	6:2	sins and commits a B of faith against the
Josh	22:22	in rebellion or in B of faith toward the
Judg	21:15	LORD had made a B in the tribes of
1Kgs	11:27	and closed up the B of the city of
2Kgs	25:4	Then a B was made in the city; the
Neh	6:1	that there was no B left in it (although
Job	16:14	He breaks me with B upon breach; he runs
	16:14	me with breach upon B; he runs upon me
	30:14	As through a wide B they come; amid the
Ps	106:23	one, stood in the B before him, to turn
Is	58:12	the repairer of the B, the restorer of streets
Jer	39:2	of the month, a B was made in the
	52:7	Then a B was made in the city; and
Ezek	22:30	and stand in the B before me for the
Mic	2:13	He who opens the B will go up before

BREACHED (3)

Ps	89:40	Thou hast B all his walls; thou hast laid
Ezek	26:10	as one enters a city which has been B
	30:16	agony; Thebes shall be B, and its walls broken

BREACHES (6)

Neh	4:7	forward and that the B were beginning to be
Ps	60:2	it open; repair its B, for it totters.
Is	22:9	you saw that the B of the city of
Ezek	13:5	gone up into the B, or built up a
Amos	4:3	go out through the B, every one straight before
	9:11	fallen and repair its B, and raise up its

BREAD (346)

Gen	3:19	face you shall eat B till you return to
	14:18	of Salem brought out B and wine; he was

B

	18:5	fetch a morsel of B, that you may refresh
	19:3	feast, and baked unleavened B, and they ate.
	21:14	the morning, and took B and a skin of
	25:34	Then Jacob gave Esau B and pottage of lentils,
	27:17	savory food and the B, which she had prepared,
	28:20	and will give me B to eat and clothing
	31:54	his kinsmen to eat B; and they ate bread
	31:54	bread; and they ate B and tarried all night
	41:54	in all the land of Egypt there was B
	41:55	cried to Pharaoh for B; and Pharaoh said to
	43:25	that they should eat B there.
	43:32	Egyptians might not eat B with the Hebrews, for
	45:23	she-asses loaded with grain, B, and provision for his
Ex	2:20	Call him, that he may eat B
	12:8	night, roasted; with unleavened B and bitter herbs
	12:15	you shall eat unleavened B; on the first day
	12:17	the feast of unleavened B, for on this very
	12:18	you shall eat unleavened B, and so until the
	12:20	in all your dwellings you shall eat unleavened B
	13:3	this place; no leavened B shall be eaten.
	13:6	you shall eat unleavened B, and on the seventh
	13:7	Unleavened B shall be eaten for seven days; no
	13:7	seven days; no leavened B shall be seen with
	16:3	the fleshpots and ate B to the full; for
	16:4	"Behold, I will rain B from heaven for you;
	16:8	and in the morning B to the full, because
	16:12	shall be filled with B; then you shall know
	16:15	them, "It is the B which the LORD has
	16:22	gathered twice as much B, two omers apiece; and
	16:29	day he gives you B for two days; remain
	16:32	they may see the B with which I fed
	18:12	of Israel to eat B with Moses' father-in-law before
	23:15	the feast of unleavened B; as I commanded you,
	23:15	you shall eat unleavened B for seven days at
	23:18	my sacrifice with leavened B, or let the fat
	23:25	I will bless your B and your water; and
	25:30	you shall set the B of the Presence on
	29:2	blemish, and unleavened B, unleavened cakes mixed
	29:23	and one loaf of B, and one cake of
	29:23	and one cake of B with oil, and one
	29:23	the basket of unleavened B that is before the
	29:32	the ram and the B that is in the
	29:34	ordination, or of the B, remain until the morning,
	34:18	he feast of unleavened B you shall keep.
	34:18	you shall eat unleavened B, as I commanded you,
	34:28	nights; he neither ate B nor drank water.
	35:13	its utensils, and the B of the Presence;
	39:36	its utensils, and the B of the Presence;
Lev	7:13	shall bring his offering with cakes of leavened B
	8:2	the basket of unleavened B;
	8:26	the basket of unleavened B which was before the
	8:26	and one cake of B with oil, and one
	8:31	eat it and the B that is in the
	8:32	the flesh and the B you shall burn with
	21:6	to the LORD, the B of their God; therefore
	21:8	for he offers the B of your God; he
	21:17	approach to offer the B of his God.
	21:21	near to offer the B of his God.
	21:22	He may eat the B of his God, both
	22:25	you offer as the B of your God any
	23:6	the feast of unleavened B to the LORD; seven
	23:6	the LORD; seven days you shall eat unleavened B
	23:14	you shall eat neither B nor grain parched or
	23:17	dwellings two loaves of B to be waved, made
	23:18	shall present with the B seven lambs a year
	23:20	wave them with the B of the first fruits
	24:7	may go with the B as a memorial portion
	26:5	you shall eat your B to the full, and
	26:26	break your staff of B, ten women shall bake
	26:26	women shall bake your B in one oven, and
	26:26	and shall deliver your B again by weight; and
Num	4:7	the table of the B of the Presence they
	4:7	drink offering; the continual B also shall be on
	6:15	a basket of unleavened B, cakes of fine flour
	6:17	the basket of unleavened B; the priest shall offer
	9:11	eat it with unleavened B and bitter herbs.
	14:9	land, for they are B for us; their protection
	28:17	seven days shall unleavened B be eaten.
Deut	8:3	does not live by B alone, but that man
	8:9	which you will eat B without scarcity, in which
	9:9	nights; I neither ate B nor drank water.
	9:18	nights; I neither ate B nor drank water, because
	16:3	shall eat no leavened B with it; seven days
	16:3	eat it with unleavened B, the bread of affliction–
	16:3	with unleavened bread, the B of affliction–for you
	16:8	you shall eat unleavened B; and on the seventh

	16:16	the feast of unleavened B, at the feast of
	23:4	not meet you with B and with water on
	29:6	you have not eaten B, and you have not
Josh	9:12	us."' Here is our B; it was still warm
Judg	7:13	a cake of barley B tumbled into the camp
	8:5	"Pray, give loaves of B to the people who
	8:6	that we should give B to your army?"
	8:15	that we should give B to your men who
	19:5	with a morsel of B, and after that you
	19:19	for our asses, with B and wine for me
Ruth	2:14	here, and eat some B, and dip your morsel
1Sam	2:5	hired themselves out for B, but those who were
	2:36	or a loaf of B, and shall say, 'Put
	2:36	places, that I may eat a morsel of B
	9:7	For the B in our sacks is gone, and
	10:3	carrying three loaves of B, and another carrying a
	10:4	you two loaves of B, which you shall accept
	16:20	an ass laden with B, and a skin of
	21:3	me five loaves of B, or whatever is here."
	21:4	"I have no common B at hand, but there
	21:4	but there is holy B; if only the young
	21:6	gave him the holy B; for there was no
	21:6	for there was no B there but the bread
	21:6	bread there but the B of the Presence, which
	21:6	be replaced by hot B on the day it
	22:13	you have given him B and a sword, and
	25:11	Shall I take my B and my water and
	28:22	set a morsel of B before you; and eat,
	28:24	it and baked unleavened B of it,
	30:11	and they gave him B and he ate, they
	30:12	he had not eaten B or drunk water for
2Sam	3:29	is slain by the sword, or who lacks B
	3:35	persuade David to eat B while it was yet
	3:35	also, if I taste B or anything else till
	6:19	each a cake of B, a portion of meat,
	9:10	master's son may have B to eat; but Mephibosheth
	13:5	come and give me B to eat, and prepare
	16:1	two hundred loaves of B, a hundred bunches of
	16:2	to ride on, the B and summer fruit for
1Kgs	7:48	golden table for the B of the Presence,
	13:8	I will not eat B or drink water in
	13:9	'You shall neither eat B, nor drink water, nor
	13:15	to him, "Come home with me and eat B
	13:16	neither will I eat B nor drink water with
	13:17	'You shall neither eat B nor drink water there,
	13:18	that he may eat B and drink water."' But
	13:19	with him, and ate B in his house, and
	13:22	back, and have eaten B and drunk water in
	13:22	to you, "Eat no B, and drink no water";
	13:23	after he had eaten B and drunk, he saddled
	17:6	the ravens brought him B and meat in the
	17:6	in the morning, and B and meat in the
	17:11	me a morsel of B in your hand."
	18:4	and fed them with B and water.)
	18:13	and fed them with B and water?
	21:7	Arise, and eat B, and let your heart be
	22:27	with scant fare of B and water, until I
2Kgs	4:42	the man of God B of the first fruits,
	6:22	Set B and water before them, that they may
	18:32	wine, a land of B and vineyards, a land
	23:9	but they ate unleavened B among their brethren.
1Chr	16:3	each a loaf of B, a portion of meat,
	23:29	the wafers of unleavened B, the baked offering, the
2Chr	4:19	the tables for the B of the Presence,
	8:13	the feast of unleavened B, the feast of weeks,
	18:26	with scant fare of B and water, until I
	30:13	the feast of unleavened B in the second month,
	30:21	the feast of unleavened B seven days with great
	35:17	the feast of unleavened B seven days.
Ezra	6:22	the feast of unleavened B seven days with joy;
	10:6	the night, neither eating B nor drinking water; for
Neh	9:15	Thou didst give them B from heaven for their
	13:2	children of Israel with B and water, but hired
Tob	1:17	I would give my B to the hungry and
	4:16	Give of your B to the hungry, and of
	4:17	Place your B on the grave of the righteous,
Jud	10:5	dried fruit and fine B; and she wrapped up
Job	3:24	sighing comes as my B, and my groanings are
	15:23	He wanders abroad for B, saying, 'Where is it?'
	22:7	and you have withheld B from the hungry.
	28:5	out of it comes B; but underneath it is
	33:20	that his life loathes B, and his appetite dainty
	42:11	him before, and ate B with him in his
Ps	14:4	people as they eat B, and do not call
	37:25	seen the righteous forsaken or his children begging B
	41:9	who ate of my B, has lifted his heel

BREAD

53:4 people as they eat B, and do not call
78:20 Can he also give B, or provide meat for
78:25 Man ate of the B of the angels; he
80:5 fed them with the B of tears, and given
102:4 grass, and withered; I forget to eat my B
102:9 I eat ashes like B, and mingle tears with
104:15 his face shine, and B to strengthen man's heart.
105:16 broke every staff of B,
105:40 quails, and gave them B from heaven in abundance.
127:2 to rest, eating the B of anxious toil; for
132:15 her provisions; I will satisfy her poor with B
Prov 4:18 For they eat the B of wickedness and drink
6:26 for a loaf of B, but an adulteress stalks
9:5 "Come, eat of my B and drink of the
9:17 water is sweet, and B eaten in secret is
12:9 one who plays the great man but lacks B
12:11 will have plenty of B, but he who follows
20:13 your eyes, and you will have plenty of B
20:17 B gained by deceit is sweet to a man,
22:9 for he shares his B with the poor.
23:6 Do not eat the B of a man who
25:21 is hungry, give him B to eat; and if
28:19 will have plenty of B, but he who follows
28:21 for a piece of B a man will do
31:27 does not eat the B of idleness.
Eccl 9:7 Go, eat your B with enjoyment, and drink your
9:11 to the strong, nor B to the wise, nor
10:19 B is made for laughter, and wine gladdens life,
11:1 Cast your B upon the waters, for you will
Wis 16:20 them from heaven with B ready to eat, providing
16:21 thy children; and the B, ministering to the desire
Sir 10:26 than one who goes about boasting, but lacks B
12:5 ungodly; hold back his B, and do not give
14:10 stingy man's eye begrudges B, and it is lacking
15:3 feed him with the B of understanding, and give
20:15 those who eat my B speak unkindly."
23:17 To a fornicator all B tastes sweet; he will
29:21 life are water and B and clothing and a
33:24 burdens for an ass; B and discipline and work
34:21 The B of the needy is the life of
45:20 first fruits, he prepared B of first fruits in
Is 3:1 the whole stay of B, and the whole stay
3:7 house there is neither B nor mantle; you shall
4:1 will eat our own B and wear our own
21:14 meet the fugitive with B, O inhabitants of the
28:28 Does one crush B grain?
30:20 Lord give you the B of adversity and the
33:16 fortresses of rocks; his B will be given him,
36:17 wine, a land of B and vineyards.
44:15 a fire and bakes B; also he makes a
44:19 fire, I also baked B on its coals, I
51:14 Pit, neither shall his B fail.
55:2 that which is not B, and your labor for
55:10 to the sower and B to the eater,
58:7 not to share your B with the hungry, and
Jer 16:7 No one shall break B for the mourner, to
37:21 and a loaf of B was given him daily
37:21 street, until all the B of the city was
38:9 for there is no B left in the city."
41:1 As they ate B together there at Mizpah,
42:14 or be hungry for B, and we will dwell
Lam 1:11 as they search for B; they trade their treasures
2:12 their mothers, "Where is B and wine?" as they
5:6 to Assyria, to get B enough.
5:9 We get our B at the peril of our
Ezek 4:9 single vessel, and make B of them.
4:13 of Israel eat their B unclean, among the nations
4:15 human dung, on which you may prepare your B
4:16 break the staff of B in Jerusalem; they shall
4:16 Jerusalem; they shall eat B by weight and with
4:17 that they may lack B and water, and look
5:16 famine upon you, and break your staff of B
12:18 of man, eat your B with quaking, and drink
12:19 They shall eat their B with fearfulness, and drink
13:19 and for pieces of B, putting to death persons
14:13 break its staff of B and send famine upon
16:19 Also my B which I gave you—I fed
18:7 no robbery, gives his B to the hungry and
18:16 robbery, but gives his B to the hungry and
24:17 lips, nor eat the B of mourners."
24:22 lips, nor eat the B of mourners.
44:3 in it to eat B before the LORD; he
45:21 for seven days unleavened B shall be eaten.
Dan 14:33 pottage and had broken B into a bowl, and
Hos 2:5 who give me my B and my water, my
9:4 Their B shall be like mourners' bread; all who
9:4 shall be like mourners' B; all who eat of
9:4 be defiled; for their B shall be for their
Amos 4:6 cities, and lack of B in all your places,
7:12 of Judah, and eat B there, and prophesy there;
8:11 not a famine of B, nor a thirst for
Hag 2:12 touches with his skirt B, or pottage, or wine,
1Mac 1:22 the table for the B of the Presence, the
4:51 They placed the B on the table and hung
2Mac 10:3 and set out the B of the Presence.
Mt 4:3 God, command these stones to become loaves of B
4:4 shall not live by B alone, but by every
6:11 this day our daily B;
7:9 son asks him for B, will give him a
12:4 God and ate the B of the Presence, which
15:26 to take the children's B and throw it to
15:33 are we to get B enough in the desert
16:5 other side, they had forgotten to bring any B
16:7 it among themselves, saying, "We brought no B
16:8 among yourselves the fact that you have no B
16:11 to perceive that I did not speak about B
16:12 of the leaven of B, but of the teaching
26:17 first day of Unleavened B the disciples came to
26:26 were eating, Jesus took B, and blessed, and broke
Mk 2:26 priest, and ate the B of the Presence, which
6:8 except a staff; no B, no bag, no money
6:37 hundred denarii worth of B, and give it to
7:26 to take the children's B and throw it to
8:4 feed these men with B here in the desert?"
8:14 had forgotten to bring B; and they had only
8:16 it with one another, saying, "We have no B
8:17 you discuss the fact that you have no B
14:1 before the Passover and the feast of Unleavened B
14:12 first day of Unleavened B, when they sacrificed the
14:20 one who is dipping B into the dish with
14:22 were eating, he took B, and blessed, and broke
Lk 4:3 Son of God, command this stone to become B
4:4 shall not live by B alone.'"
6:4 took and ate the B of the Presence, which
7:33 has come eating no B and drinking no wine;
9:3 staff, nor bag, nor B, nor money; and do
11:3 each day our daily B;
14:15 he who shall eat B in the kingdom of
15:17 father's hired servants have B enough and to spare,
22:1 the feast of Unleavened B drew near, which is
22:7 the day of Unleavened B, on which the passover
22:19 And he took B, and when he had given
24:30 them, he took the B and blessed, and broke
24:35 known to them in the breaking of the B
Jn 6:5 are we to buy B, so that these people
6:7 would not buy enough B for each of them
6:23 where they ate the B after the Lord had
6:31 written, 'He gave them B from heaven to eat.'"
6:32 who gave you the B from heaven; my Father
6:32 gives you the true B from heaven.
6:33 For the B of God is that which comes
6:34 "Lord, give us this B always."
6:35 them, "I am the B of life; he who
6:41 said, "I am the B which came down from
6:48 I am the B of life.
6:50 This is the B which comes down from heaven,
6:51 I am the living B which came down from
6:51 one eats of this B, he will live for
6:51 for ever; and the B which I shall give
6:58 This is the B which came down from heaven,
6:58 he who eats this B will live for ever."
13:18 'He who ate my B has lifted his heel
21:9 fire there, with fish lying on it, and B
21:13 came and took the B and gave it to
Acts 2:42 to the breaking of B and the prayers.
2:46 temple together and breaking B in their homes, they
12:3 This was during the days of Unleavened B
20:6 the days of Unleavened B, and in five days
20:7 gathered together to break B, Paul talked with
20:11 up and had broken B and eaten, he conversed
27:35 said this, he took B, and giving thanks to
1Cor 5:8 but with the unleavened B of sincerity and truth.
10:16 The B which we break, is it not a
10:17 Because there is one B, we who are many
10:17 body, for we all partake of the one B
11:23 he was betrayed took B,
11:26 as you eat this B and drink the cup,
11:27 Whoever, therefore, eats the B or drinks the cup
11:28 so eat of the B and drink of the
2Cor 9:10 to the sower and B for food will supply
2Thes 3:8 not eat any one's B without paying, but with
Heb 9:2 the table and the B of the Presence; it

BREADTH (73)

Gen	6:15	three hundred cubits, its B fifty cubits, and its
	13:17	the length and the B of the land, for
Ex	25:10	and a half its B, and a cubit and
	25:17	length, and a cubit and a half its B
	25:23	length, a cubit its B, and a cubit and
	26:2	twenty-eight cubits, and the B of each curtain four
	26:8	thirty cubits, and the B of each curtain four
	26:16	and a half the B of each frame.
	27:12	And for the B of the court on the
	27:13	The B of the court on the front to
	27:18	a hundred cubits, the B fifty, and the height
	28:16	a span its length and a span its B
	30:2	and a cubit its B; it shall be square,
	36:9	twenty-eight cubits, and the B of each curtain four
	36:15	thirty cubits, and the B of each curtain four
	36:21	and a half the B of each frame.
	37:1	and a half its B, and a cubit and
	37:6	length, and a cubit and a half its B
	37:10	length, a cubit its B, and a cubit and
	37:25	a cubit, and its B was a cubit; it
	38:1	and five cubits its B; it was square, and
	38:18	cubits high in its B, corresponding to the hangings
	39:9	and a span its B when doubled.
Deut	3:11	and four cubits its B, according to the common
1Kgs	7:2	hundred cubits, and its B fifty cubits, and its
	7:6	fifty cubits, and its B thirty cubits; there was
2Chr	3:3	sixty cubits, and the B twenty cubits.
	3:8	length, corresponding to the B of the house, was
	3:8	twenty cubits, and its B was twenty cubits; he
Ezra	6:3	sixty cubits and its B sixty cubits,
Jud	7:3	they spread out in B over Dothan as far
Sir	1:3	height of heaven, the B of the earth, the
Is	8:8	wings will fill the B of your land, O
Jer	8:19	from the length and B of the land: "Is
Ezek	40:11	Then he measured the B of the opening of
	40:11	ten cubits; and the B of the gateway, thirteen
	40:13	of the other, a B of five and twenty
	40:20	He measured its length and its B
	40:21	fifty cubits, and its B twenty-five cubits.
	40:25	fifty cubits, and its B twenty-five cubits.
	40:29	fifty cubits, and its B twenty-five cubits.
	40:33	fifty cubits, and its B twenty-five cubits.
	40:36	fifty cubits, and its B twenty-five cubits.
	40:48	either side; and the B of the gate was
	40:49	twenty cubits, and the B twelve cubits; and ten
	41:1	six cubits was the B of the jambs.
	41:2	And the B of the entrance was ten cubits;
	41:2	forty cubits, and its B, twenty cubits.
	41:3	two cubits; and the B of the entrance, six
	41:4	twenty cubits, and its B, twenty cubits, beyond the
	41:5	cubits thick; and the B of the side chambers,
	41:10	the court was a B of twenty cubits round
	41:11	the south; and the B of the part that
	41:14	cubits long; also the B of the east front
	42:2	hundred cubits, and the B fifty cubits.
	42:11	the same length and B, with the same exits
	43:14	two cubits, with a B of one cubit; and
	43:14	four cubits, with a B of one cubit;
	48:8	twenty-five thousand cubits in B, and in length equal
	48:9	thousand cubits in length, and twenty thousand in B
	48:10	ten thousand cubits in B on the western side,
	48:10	side, ten thousand in B on the eastern side,
	48:13	thousand cubits in length and ten thousand in B
	48:13	thousand cubits and the B twenty thousand.
	48:15	five thousand cubits in B and twenty-five thousand in
Dan	3:1	sixty cubits and its B six cubits.
Jon	3:3	an exceedingly great city, three days' journey in B
Hab	1:6	who march through the B of the earth, to
Zech	2:2	see what is its B and what is its
	5:2	twenty cubits, and its B ten cubits."
Eph	3:18	saints what is the B and length and height
Rev	21:16	the same as its B; and he measured the
	21:16	stadia; its length and B and height are equal.

BREAK (142)

Gen	19:9	and drew near to B the door.
	27:40	brother; but when you B loose you shall break
	27:40	break loose you shall B his yoke from your
Ex	12:46	and you shall not B a bone of it.
	13:13	redeem it you shall B its neck.
	19:21	the people, lest they B through to the LORD
	19:22	themselves, lest the LORD B out upon them."
	19:24	priests and the people B through to come up
	19:24	the LORD, lest he B out against them."
	23:24	utterly overthrow them and B their pillars in pieces.
	32:25	Aaron had let them B loose, to their shame
	34:13	down their altars, and B their pillars, and cut
	34:20	redeem it you shall B its neck.
Lev	2:6	with oil; you shall B it in pieces, and
	11:33	unclean, and you shall B it.
	14:45	And he shall B down the house, its stones
	26:15	all my commandments, but B my covenant,
	26:19	sins, and I will B the pride of your
	26:26	When I B your staff of bread, ten women
	26:44	destroy them utterly and B my covenant with them;
Num	9:12	until the morning, nor B a bone of it;
	24:8	his adversaries, and shall B their bones in pieces,
	24:17	forehead of Moab, and B down all the sons
	30:2	pledge, he shall not B his word; he shall
Deut	7:5	with them: you shall B down their altars, and
	21:4	nor sown, and shall B the heifer's neck there
	31:16	will forsake me and B my covenant which I
	31:20	and despise me and B my covenant.
Josh	22:20	the son of Zerah B faith in the matter
Judg	2:1	said, 'I will never B my covenant with you,
	2:2	this land; you shall B down their altars.' But
	8:9	in peace, I will B down this tower."
	19:25	the dawn began to B, they let her go.
1Sam	9:26	Then at the B of dawn Samuel called to
1Kgs	15:19	silver and gold; go, B your league with Baasha
2Kgs	3:26	seven hundred swordsmen to B through, opposite the
2Chr	16:3	silver and gold; go, B your league with Baasha
Ezra	9:14	as this, shall we B thy commandments again and
Neh	4:3	on it he will B down their stone wall!"
	4:21	the spears from the B of dawn till the
Jud	7:1	had joined him, to B camp and move against
	8:30	made us take an oath which we cannot B
	9:8	B their strength by thy might, and bring down
Job	19:2	you torment me, and B me in pieces with
	30:13	They B up my path, they promote my calamity;
Ps	2:9	You shall B them with a rod of iron,
	3:7	the cheek, thou dost B the teeth of the
	10:15	B thou the arm of the wicked and evildoer;
	28:5	his hands, he will B them down and build
	52:5	But God will B you down for ever; he
	58:6	O God, B the teeth in their mouths; tear
	74:13	thy might; thou didst B the heads of the
	98:4	LORD, all the earth; B forth into joyous song
Prov	18:1	estranged seeks pretexts to B out against all sound
	25:15	a soft tongue will B a bone.
Eccl	3:3	heal; a time to B down, and a time
Sir	22:18	reviles a friend will B off the friendship.
Is	5:5	be devoured; I will B down its wall, and
	14:7	rest and quiet; they B forth into singing.
	14:25	stand, that I will B the Assyrian in my
	30:13	to you like a B in a high wall,
	35:6	For waters shall B forth in the wilderness, and
	42:3	reed he will not B, and a dimly burning
	43:14	send to Babylon and B down all the bars,
	44:23	depths of the earth; B forth into singing, O
	45:2	the mountains, I will B in pieces the doors
	49:13	and exult, O earth; B forth, O mountains, into
	52:9	B forth together into singing, you waste places of
	54:1	who did not bear; B forth into singing and
	55:12	hills before you shall B forth into singing, and
	58:6	go free, and to B every yoke?
	58:8	Then shall your light B forth like the dawn,
Jer	1:10	pluck up and to B down, to destroy and
	1:14	the north evil shall B forth upon all the
	4:3	inhabitants of Jerusalem: B up your fallow ground,
	14:21	remember and do not B thy covenant with us.
	15:12	Can one B iron, iron from the north, and
	16:7	No one shall B bread for the mourner, to
	18:7	will pluck up and B down and destroy it,
	19:10	them.' "Then you shall B the flask in the
	19:11	hosts: So will I B this people and this
	28:4	LORD, for I will B the yoke of the
	28:11	Even so will I B the yoke of Nebuchadnezzar
	30:8	hosts, that I will B the yoke from off
	31:28	to pluck up and B down, to overthrow, destroy,
	33:20	LORD: If you can B my covenant with the
	43:13	He shall B the obelisks of Heliopolis which is
	48:12	empty his vessels, and B his jars in pieces.
	49:35	hosts: "Behold, I will B the bow of Elam,
	51:20	war: with you I B nations in pieces; with
	51:21	kingdoms; with you I B in pieces the horse
	51:21	rider; with you I B in pieces the chariot
	51:22	charioteer; with you I B in pieces man and
	51:22	woman; with you I B in pieces the old
	51:22	youth; with you I B in pieces the young
	51:23	maiden; with you I B in pieces the shepherd

51:23 flock; with you I B in pieces the farmer
51:23 team; with you I B in pieces governors and
Ezek 4:16 man, behold, I will B the staff of bread
5:16 famine upon you, and B your staff of bread.
13:11 and a stormy wind B out;
13:13 make a stormy wind B out in my wrath;
13:14 And I will B down the wall that you
14:13 hand against it, and B its staff of bread
16:38 you as women who B wedlock and shed blood
16:39 your vaulted chamber and B down your lofty places;
17:15 Can he B the covenant and yet escape?
17:22 it out; I will B off from the topmost
26:4 walls of Tyre, and B down her towers; and
26:9 his axes he will B down your towers.
26:12 your merchandise; they will B down your walls and
30:18 be dark, when I B there the dominion of
30:22 of Egypt, and will B his arms, both the
30:24 hand; but I will B the arms of Pharaoh,
34:27 the LORD, when I B the bars of their
Dan 2:40 which crushes, it shall B and crush all these.
2:44 It shall B in pieces all these kingdoms and
3:34 utterly, and do not B thy covenant,
4:27 be acceptable to you; B off your sins by
6:19 Then, at B of day, the king arose and
7:23 trample it down, and B it to pieces.
Hos 1:5 that day, I will B the bow of Israel
4:2 and committing adultery; they B all bounds and
10:2 The LORD will B down their altars, and destroy
10:12 fruit of steadfast love; B up your fallow ground,
Amos 1:5 I will B the bar of Damascus, and cut
5:6 and live, lest he B out like fire in
Jon 1:4 the ship threatened to B up.
Mic 2:13 before them; they will B through and pass the
3:3 from off them, and B their bones in pieces,
Nah 1:13 And now I will B his yoke from off
Mt 6:19 consume and where thieves B in and steal,
6:20 where thieves do not B in and steal.
12:20 streets; he will not B a bruised reed or
Mk 6:26 did not want to B his word to her.
Jn 19:33 dead, they did not B his legs.
Acts 20:7 were gathered together to B bread, Paul talked with
Rom 2:25 law; but if you B the law, your circumcision
2:27 code and circumcision but B the law.
1Cor 10:16 The bread which we B, is it not a
Gal 4:27 who does not bear; B forth and shout, you
Rev 5:2 open the scroll and B its seals?"

BREAKFAST (2)

Jn 21:12 Jesus said to them, "Come and have B
21:15 When they had finished B, Jesus said to Simon

BREAKING (22)

Gen 32:24 with him until the B of the day.
32:26 said, "Let me go, for the day is B
Ex 9:9 Egypt, and become boils B out in sores on
9:10 and it became boils B out in sores on
22:3 a thief is found B in, and is struck
Lev 13:42 spot, it is leprosy B out on his bald
Num 5:6 that men commit by B faith with the LORD,
10:2 the congregation, and for B camp.
1Sam 25:10 servants nowadays who are B away from their
Is 30:14 an instant; and its B is like that of
Jer 2:34 did not find them B in.
45:4 have built I am B down, and what I
Ezek 16:59 despised the oath in B the covenant,
21:6 of man; sigh with B heart and bitter grief
2Mac 10:28 Just as dawn was B, the two armies joined
Lk 5:6 as their nets were B,
24:35 to them in the B of the bread.
Jn 21:4 Just as day was B, Jesus stood on the
Acts 2:42 and fellowship, to the B of bread and the
2:46 the temple together and B bread in their homes,
21:13 you doing, weeping and B my heart?
Rom 2:23 you dishonor God by B the law?

BREAKS (23)

Ex 22:6 "When fire B out and catches in thorns so
Lev 13:12 And if the leprosy B out in the skin,
14:43 "If the disease B out again in the house,
Job 7:5 my skin hardens, then B out afresh.
8:14 His confidence B in sunder, and his trust is
16:14 He B me with breach upon breach; he runs
19:10 He B me down on every side, and I
Ps 29:5 voice of the LORD B the cedars, the LORD
29:5 the cedars, the LORD B the cedars of Lebanon.
46:9 of the earth; he B the bow, and shatters
Prov 15:4 but perverseness in it B the spirit.
17:14 quit before the quarrel B out.
Eccl 10:8 will bite him who B through a wall.
Sir 23:18 A man who B his marriage vows says to
35:18 of the insolent, and B the scepters of the
48:10 of God before it B out in fury, to
Is 38:13 like a lion he B all my bones; from
66:3 lamb, like him who B a dog's neck; he
Jer 19:11 this city, as one B a potter's vessel, so
23:29 like a hammer which B the rock in pieces?
Bar 6:55 When fire B out in a temple of wooden
Dan 2:40 as iron, because iron B to pieces and shatters
Hos 7:2 deal falsely, the thief B in, and the bandits

BREAST (25)

Ex 29:26 you shall take the B of the ram of
29:27 you shall consecrate the B of the wave offering,
Lev 7:30 the fat with the B, that the breast may
7:30 the breast, that the B may be waved as
7:31 the altar, but the B shall be for Aaron
7:34 For the B that is waved and the thigh
8:29 And Moses took the B, and waved it for
10:14 But the B that is waved and the thigh
10:15 is offered and the B that is waved they
Num 6:20 priest, together with the B that is waved and
18:18 be yours, as the B that is waved and
Job 24:9 fatherless child from the B, and take in pledge
Ps 22:14 is melted within my B;
131:2 quieted at its mother's B; like a child that
Song 8:1 brother to me, that nursed at my mother's B
Is 28:9 weaned from the milk, those taken from the B
60:16 you shall suck the B of kings; and you
Lam 4:3 the jackals give the B and suckle their young,
Dan 2:32 of fine gold, its B and arms of silver,
Hos 13:8 will tear open their B, and there I will
Lk 18:13 heaven, but beat his B, saying, 'God, be merciful
Jn 13:23 lying close to the B of Jesus;
13:25 thus, close to the B of Jesus, he said
21:20 lain close to his B at the supper and
Rev 1:13 golden girdle round his B;

BREASTPIECE (25)

Ex 25:7 for setting, for the ephod and for the B
28:4 they shall make: a B, an ephod, a robe,
28:15 you shall make a B of judgment, in skilled
28:22 shall make for the B twisted chains like cords,
28:23 shall make for the B two rings of gold,
28:23 two rings on the two edges of the B
28:24 the edges of the B;
28:26 two ends of the B, on its inside edge
28:28 they shall bind the B by its rings to
28:28 ephod, and that the B shall not come loose
28:29 of Israel in the B of judgment upon his
28:30 And in the B of judgment you shall put
29:5 the ephod, and the B, and gird him with
35:9 for setting, for the ephod and for the B
35:27 ephod and for the B,
39:8 He made the B, in skilled work, like the
39:9 It was square; the B was made double, a
39:15 they made on the B twisted chains like cords,
39:16 two edges of the B;
39:17 the two rings at the edges of the B
39:19 two ends of the B, on its inside edge
39:21 And they bound the B by its rings to
39:21 ephod, and that the B should not come loose
Lev 8:8 And he placed the B on him, and in
8:8 him, and in the B he put the Urim

BREASTPLATE (8)

1Kgs 22:34 scale armor and the B; therefore he said to
2Chr 18:33 scale armor and the B; therefore he said to
Wis 5:18 on righteousness as a B, and wear impartial justice
Sir 43:20 and the water puts it on like a B
Is 59:17 on righteousness as a B, and a helmet of
1Mac 3:3 he put on his B; he girded on his
Eph 6:14 having put on the B of righteousness,
1Thes 5:8 and put on the B of faith and love,

BREASTPLATES (3)

1Mac 6:2 rich, containing golden shields, B, and weapons left
Rev 9:9 had scales like iron B, and the noise of
9:17 vision: the riders wore B the color of fire

BREASTS (27)

Gen 49:25 beneath, blessings of the B and of the womb.
Lev 9:20 the fat upon the B, and he burned the

9:21 the altar, but the B and the right thigh
Job 3:12 Or why the B, that I should suck?
Ps 22:9 thou didst keep me safe upon my mother's B
Song 1:13 a bag of myrrh, that lies between my B
4:5 Your two B are like two fawns, twins of
7:3 Your two B are like two fawns, twins of
7:7 palm tree, and your B are like its clusters.
7:8 Oh, may your B be like clusters of the
8:8 have a little sister, and she has no B
8:10 a wall, and my B were like towers; then
Is 32:12 Beat upon your B for the pleasant fields, for
66:11 satisfied with her consoling B; that you may drink
Ezek 16:7 at full maidenhood; your B were formed, and your
23:3 their youth; there their B were pressed and their
23:21 handled your bosom and pressed your young B
23:34 hair, and tear your B; for I have spoken,
Hos 2:2 adultery from between her B;
9:14 Give them a miscarrying womb and dry B
Nah 2:7 lamenting, moaning like doves, and beating their B
2Mac 3:19 with sackcloth under their B, thronged the streets.
6:10 babies hung at their B, then hurled them down
Lk 11:27 bore you, and the B that you sucked!"
23:28 never bore, and the B that never gave suck!'
23:47 had taken place, returned home beating their B
Rev 15:6 bright linen, and their B girded with golden girdles.

BREATH (73)

Gen 1:30 everything that has the B of life, I have
2:7 into his nostrils the B of life; and man
6:17 in which is the B of life from under
7:15 which there was the B of life.
7:22 whose nostrils was the B of life died.
2Sam 22:16 the blast of the B of his nostrils.
1Kgs 17:17 that there was no B left in him.
Jud 7:28 see our wives and children draw their last B
Job 4:9 By the B of God they perish, and by
7:7 my life is a B; my eye will never
7:16 Let me alone, for my days are a B
9:18 let me get my B, but fills me with
12:10 living thing and the B of all mankind.
27:3 as long as my B is in me, and
32:8 in a man, the B of the Almighty, that
33:4 made me, and the B of the Almighty gives
34:14 gather to himself his B,
37:10 By the B of God ice is given, and
41:21 His B kindles coals, and a flame comes forth
Ps 18:15 the blast of the B of thy nostrils.
33:6 their host by the B of his mouth.
39:5 Surely every man stands as a mere B
39:11 to him; surely every man is a mere B
62:9 estate are but a B, men of high estate
62:9 go up; they are together lighter than a B
78:33 days vanish like a B, and their years in
94:11 thoughts of man, that they are but a B
104:29 thou takest away their B, they die and return
135:17 nor is there any B in their mouths.
144:4 Man is like a B, his days are like
146:4 When his B departs he returns to his earth;
Eccl 3:19 all have the same B, and man has no
Song 7:8 the scent of your B like apples,
Wis 2:2 never been; because the B in our nostrils is
7:25 For she is a B of the power of
11:18 as breathe out fiery B, or belch forth a
11:20 fall at a single B when pursued by justice
11:20 and scattered by the B of thy power.
15:15 with which to draw B, nor ears with which
Sir 33:20 still alive and have B in you, do not
38:28 handiwork in iron; the B of the fire melts
Is 2:22 in whose nostrils is B, for of what account
11:4 mouth, and with the B of his lips he
30:28 a devouring fire; his B is like an overflowing
30:33 wood in abundance; the B of the LORD, like
33:11 bring forth stubble; your B is a fire that
40:7 flower fades, when the B of the LORD blows
42:5 from it, who gives B to the people upon
57:13 carry them off, a B will take them away.
57:16 I have made the B of life.
Jer 4:31 of Zion gasping for B, stretching out her hands,
10:14 and there is no B in them.
51:17 and there is no B in them.
Lam 4:20 The B of our nostrils, the LORD's anointed, was
Bar 6:25 but there is no B in them.
Ezek 37:5 Behold, I will cause B to enter you, and
37:6 with skin, and put B in you, and you
37:8 but there was no B in them.
37:9 me, "Prophesy to the B, prophesy, son of man,
37:9 and say to the B, Thus says the Lord
37:9 the four winds, O B, and breathe upon these
37:10 commanded me, and the B came into them, and
Dan 5:23 whose hand is your B, and whose are all
10:17 in me, and no B is left in me."
Hab 2:19 and there is no B at all in it.
2Mac 3:31 one who was lying quite at his last B
7:9 was at his last B, he said, "You accursed
7:22 gave you life and B, nor I who set
7:23 mercy give life and B back to you again,
Acts 17:25 all men life and B and everything.
2Thes 2:8 slay him with the B of his mouth and
Rev 11:11 a half days a B of life from God
13:15 was allowed to give B to the image of

BREATHE (6)

Job 11:20 their hope is to B their last."
Ps 27:12 against me, and they B out violence.
Wis 7:3 born, I began to B the common air, and
11:18 rage, or such as B out fiery breath, or
Sir 31:19 He does not B heavily upon his bed.
Ezek 37:9 winds, O breath, and B upon these slain, that

BREATHED (14)

Gen 2:7 from the ground, and B into his nostrils the
25:8 Abraham B his last and died in a good
25:17 and thirty-seven years; he B his last and died,
35:29 And Isaac B his last; and he died and
49:33 into the bed, and B his last, and was
Josh 10:40 utterly destroyed all that B, as the LORD God
11:11 was none left that B, and he burned Hazor
11:14 them, and they did not leave any that B
1Kgs 15:29 Jeroboam not one that B, until he had destroyed
Wis 15:11 an active soul and B into him a living
Mk 15:36 a loud cry, and B his last.
15:38 saw that he thus B his last, he said,
Lk 23:45 having said this he B his last.
Jn 20:22 had said this, he B on them, and said

BREATHES (8)

Deut 20:16 save alive nothing that B,
Job 14:10 is laid low; man B his last, and where
Ps 150:6 Let everything that B praise the LORD!
Prov 6:19 a false witness who B out lies, and a
14:5 but a false witness B out lies.
Song 2:17 Until the day B and the shadows flee, turn,
4:6 Until the day B and the shadows flee, I
Sir 43:4 times as much; it B out fiery vapors, and

BREATHING (3)

2Mac 7:5 to the fire, still B, and to fry him
9:7 more filled with arrogance, B fire in his rage
Acts 9:1 But Saul, still B threats and murder against the

BRED (7)

Gen 30:38 And since they B when they came to drink,
30:39 to drink, the flocks B in front of the
Ex 16:20 the morning, and it B worms and became foul;
Deut 28:54 most tender and delicately B among you will grudge
28:56 most tender and delicately B woman among you,
Esth 8:10 in the king's service, B from the royal stud.
Jer 6:2 The comely and delicately B I will destroy, the

BREECHES (6)

Ex 28:42 make for them linen B to cover their naked
39:28 linen, and the linen B of fine twined linen,
Lev 6:10 and put his linen B upon his body, and
16:4 shall have the linen B on his body, be
Sir 45:8 of authority, the linen B, the long robe, and
Ezek 44:18 their heads, and linen B upon their loins; they

BREED (4)

Gen 8:17 earth—that they may B abundantly on the earth,
30:41 flock, that they might B among the rods,
Lev 19:19 not let your cattle B with a different kind;
2Tim 2:23 you know that they B quarrels.

BREEDER

2Kgs 3:4 Moab was a sheep B; and he had to

BREEDING

Gen 30:41 of the flock were B Jacob laid the rods

BREEDS

Job 21:10 Their bull B without fail; their cow calves, and

BRETHREN (398)

Lev 10:4 "Draw near, carry your B from before the sanctuary
10:6 the congregation; but your B, the whole house of
21:10 is chief among his B, upon whose head the
25:46 them, but over your B the people of Israel
Num 8:26 but minister to their B in the tent of
16:10 him, and all your B the sons of Levi
18:2 with you bring your B also, the tribe of
18:6 I have taken your B the Levites from among
20:3 had died when our B died before the LORD!
27:4 Give to us a possession among our father's B
27:7 inheritance among their father's B and cause the
32:6 of Reuben, "Shall your B go to the war
Deut 1:16 the cases between your B, and judge righteously
1:28 Our B have made our hearts melt, saying, "The
2:4 the territory of your B the sons of Esau,
2:8 on, away from our B the sons of Esau
3:18 over armed before your B the people of Israel.
3:20 gives rest to your B, as to you, and
15:7 man, one of your B, in any of your
17:15 One from among your B you shall set as
17:20 lifted up above his B, and that he may
18:2 no inheritance among their B; the LORD is their
18:15 among you, from your B --him you shall heed--
18:18 you from among their B; and I will put
24:7 stealing one of his B, the people of Israel,
24:14 is one of your B or one of the
Josh 1:14 over armed before your B and shall help them,
1:15 gives rest to your B as well as to
14:8 But my B who went up with me made
17:4 to give us an inheritance along with our B
17:4 an inheritance among the B of their father.
22:3 have not forsaken your B these many days, down
22:4 given rest to your B, as he promised them;
22:7 a possession beside their B in the land west
22:8 divide the spoil of your enemies with your B
Judg 18:8 they came to their B at Zorah and Eshtaol,
18:8 Zorah and Eshtaol, their B said to them, "What
18:14 Laish said to their B, "Do you know that
19:23 to them, "No, my B, do not act so
20:13 the voice of their B, the people of Israel.
20:23 to battle against our B the Benjaminites?" And the
20:28 to battle against our B the Benjaminites, or shall
Ruth 4:10 off from among his B and from the gate
2Sam 2:26 your people turn from the pursuit of their B
2:27 the pursuit of their B in the morning."
15:20 back, and take your B with you; and may
19:41 king, "Why have our B the men of Judah
2Kgs 23:9 but they ate unleavened bread among their B
1Chr 6:44 left hand were their B the sons of Merari:
6:48 of Levi; and their B the Levites were appointed
12:39 and drinking, for their B had made preparation for
13:2 send abroad to our B who remain in all
15:5 and twenty of his B;
15:6 and twenty of his B;
15:7 and thirty of his B;
15:8 two hundred of his B;
15:9 with eighty of his B;
15:10 chief, with a hundred and twelve of his B
15:12 yourselves, you and your B, so that you may
15:16 Levites to appoint their B as the singers who
15:17 Joel; and of his B Asaph the son of
15:17 sons of Merari, their B, Ethan the son of
15:18 and with them their B of the second order,
16:7 sung to the LORD by Asaph and his B
16:37 left Asaph and his B there before the ark
16:38 Obed-edom and his sixty-eight B; while Obed-edom,
16:39 the priest and his B the priests before the
23:32 sons of Aaron, their B, for the service of
24:31 lots, just as their B the sons of Aaron,
25:7 them along with their B, who were trained in
25:9 to him and his B and his sons, twelve;
25:10 his sons and his B, twelve;
25:11 his sons and his B, twelve;
25:12 his sons and his B, twelve;
25:13 his sons and his B, twelve;
25:14 his sons and his B, twelve;
25:15 his sons and his B, twelve;
25:16 his sons and his B, twelve;
25:17 his sons and his B, twelve;
25:18 his sons and his B, twelve;
25:19 his sons and his B, twelve;
25:20 his sons and his B, twelve;
25:21 his sons and his B, twelve;
25:22 his sons and his B, twelve;
25:23 his sons and his B, twelve;
25:24 his sons and his B, twelve;
25:25 his sons and his B, twelve;
25:26 his sons and his B, twelve;
25:27 his sons and his B, twelve;
25:28 his sons and his B, twelve;
25:29 his sons and his B, twelve;
25:30 his sons and his B, twelve;
25:31 his sons and his B, twelve.
26:7 Obed, and Elzabad, whose B were able men, Elihu
26:8 with their sons and B, able men qualified for
26:9 Meshelemiah had sons and B, able men, eighteen.
26:11 all the sons and B of Hosah were thirteen.
26:12 duties, just as their B did, ministering in the
26:25 His B: from Eliezer were his son Rehabiah, and
26:26 This Shelomoth and his B were in charge of
26:28 were in the care of Shelomoth and his B
26:30 Hashabiah and his B, one thousand seven hundred
26:32 appointed him and his B, two thousand seven
28:2 said: "Hear me, my B and my people.
2Chr 11:4 shall not go up or fight against your B
19:10 to you from your B who live in their
19:10 wrath may not come upon you and your B
29:15 gathered their B, and sanctified themselves, and
29:34 had sanctified themselves their B the Levites helped
30:7 your fathers and your B, who were faithless to
30:9 to the LORD, your B and your children will
31:15 the portions to their B, old and young alike,
35:5 fathers' houses of your B the lay people, and
35:6 and prepare for your B, to do according to
35:15 their service, for their B the Levites prepared for
Ezra 3:8 the rest of their B, the priests and the
7:18 to you and your B to do with the
8:17 to Iddo and his B the temple servants at
10:18 of Jeshua the son of Jozadak and his B
Neh 1:2 Hanani, one of my B, came with certain men
3:1 rose up with his B the priests and they
3:18 After him their B repaired: Bavvai the son of
4:2 the presence of his B and of the army
4:14 and fight for your B, your sons, your daughters,
4:23 neither I nor my B nor my servants nor
5:1 people and of their wives against their Jewish B
5:5 the flesh of our B, our children are as
5:8 bought back our Jewish B who have been sold
5:8 you even sell your B that they may be
5:10 Moreover I and my B and my servants are
5:14 neither I nor my B ate the food allowance
10:10 Henadad, Kadmi-el; and their B, Shebaniah, Hodiah,
10:29 understanding, join with their B, their nobles, and
11:12 of God, and their B who did the work
11:13 of Malchijah, and his B, heads of fathers' houses,
11:14 of Immer, and their B, mighty men of valor,
11:17 the second among his B; and Abda the son
11:19 Akkub, Talmon and their B, who kept watch at
12:7 priests and of their B in the days of
12:8 Mattaniah, who with his B was in charge of
12:9 Bakbukiah and Unno their B stood opposite them in
12:24 of Kadmi-el, with their B over against them, to
13:13 and their duty was to distribute to their B
Tob 1:3 of charity to my B and countrymen who went
1:10 to Nineveh, all my B and my relatives ate
1:16 I performed many acts of charity to my B
2:2 poor man of our B you may find who
4:12 of old, all took wives from among their B
4:13 my son, love your B, and in your heart
4:13 do not disdain your B and the sons and
5:13 not go astray in the error of our B
7:3 And Raguel asked them, "Where are you from, B
11:17 rejoicing among all his B in Nineveh.
14:4 Our B will be scattered over the earth from
14:7 righteousness will rejoice, showing mercy to our B
Jud 8:14 No, my B, do not provoke the Lord our
8:22 the slaughter of our B and the captivity of
8:24 "Now therefore, B, let us set an example to
8:24 an example to our B, for their lives depend
14:1 "Listen to me, my B, and take this head
Esth 10:3 the multitude of his B, for he sought the
Job 6:15 My B are treacherous as a torrent-bed, as freshets
19:13 "He has put my B far from me, and
Ps 22:22 thy name to my B; in the midst of
69:8 a stranger to my B, an alien to my
122:8 For my B and companions' sake I will say,
Sir 50:1 The leader of his B and the pride of
50:12 with a garland of B around him, he was
Is 66:5 at his word: "Your B who hate you and
66:20 shall bring all your B from all the nations
Ezek 11:15 "Son of man, your B, even your brethren, your

	11:15	your brethren, even your B, your fellow exiles, the
Mic	5:3	the rest of his B shall return to the
1Mac	2:40	all do as our B have done and refuse
	2:41	all die as our B died in their hiding
	5:13	fallen, and all our B who were in the
	5:16	should do for their B who were in distress
	5:17	go and rescue your B in Galilee; I and
	5:25	had happened to their B in Gilead:
	5:32	men of his forces, "Fight today for your B
	6:22	fail to do justice and to avenge our B
	9:9	come back with our B and fight them; we
	9:10	die bravely for our B, and leave no cause
	12:6	Jewish people to their B the Spartans, greeting.
	12:7	that you are our B, as the appended copy
	12:11	as it is right and proper to remember B
	12:21	Jews that they are B and are of the
	14:20	the Jewish people, our B, greeting.
	14:40	friends and allies and B, and that the Romans
2Mac	1:1	The Jewish B in Jerusalem and those
	1:1	Judea, To their Jewish B in Egypt, Greeting, and
	10:21	of having sold their B for money by setting
	11:7	risk their lives with him to aid their B
	12:6	the righteous Judge, attacked the murderers of his B
	12:25	him go, for the sake of saving their B
	15:14	man who loves the B and prays much for
	15:18	children, and also for B and relatives, lay upon
Mt	5:47	you salute only your B, what more are you
	12:46	his mother and his B stood outside, asking to
	12:47	"Who is my mother, and who are my B
	12:48	he said, "Here are my mother and my B
	13:55	And are not his B James and Joseph and
	23:8	you have one teacher, and you are all B
	25:40	least of these my B, you did it to
	28:10	go and tell my B to go to Galilee,
Mk	3:31	his mother and his B came; and standing outside
	3:32	"Your mother and your B are outside, asking for
	3:33	he replied, "Who are my mother and my B
	3:34	he said, "Here are my mother and my B
Lk	8:19	his mother and his B came to him, but
	8:21	"My mother and my B are those who hear
	22:32	and when you have turned again, strengthen your B
Jn	20:17	but go to my B and say to them,
	21:23	spread abroad among the B that this disciple was
Acts	1:15	stood up among the B (the company of persons
	1:16	and twenty), and said, B, the scripture had to
	2:29	gladness with thy presence.' B, I may say to
	2:37	rest of the apostles, B, what shall we do?"
	3:17	"And now, B, I know that you acted in
	3:22	a prophet from your B as he raised me
	6:3	Therefore, B, pick out from among you seven men
	7:2	And Stephen said: B and fathers, hear me.
	7:23	heart to visit his B, the sons of Israel.
	7:25	He supposed that his B understood that God was
	7:26	saying, 'Men, you are B, why do you wrong
	7:37	a prophet from your B as he raised me
	9:30	And when the B knew it, they brought him
	10:23	and some of the B from Joppa accompanied him.
	11:1	the apostles and the B who were in Judea
	11:12	These six B also accompanied me, and we entered
	11:29	send relief to the B who lived in Judea;
	12:17	said, "Tell this to James and to the B
	13:15	sent to them, saying, B, if you have any
	13:26	not worthy to untie.' B, sons of the family
	13:38	known to you therefore, B, that through this man
	14:2	the Gentiles and poisoned their minds against the B
	15:1	were teaching the B, "Unless you are circumcised
	15:3	and they gave great joy to all the B
	15:7	and said to them, B, you know that in
	15:13	finished speaking, James replied, B, listen to me.
	15:22	leading men among the B,
	15:23	the following letter: "The B, both the apostles and
	15:23	the elders, to the B who are of the
	15:32	prophets, exhorted the B with many words and
	15:33	in peace by the B to those who had
	15:35	return and visit the B in every city where
	15:39	being commended by the B to the grace of
	16:2	spoken of by the B at Lystra and Iconium.
	16:40	they had seen the B, they exhorted them and
	17:6	and some of the B before the city authorities,
	17:10	The B immediately sent Paul and Silas away by
	17:14	Then the B immediately sent Paul off on his
	18:18	took leave of the B and sailed for Syria,
	18:27	cross to Achaia, the B encouraged him, and wrote
	21:7	and we greeted the B and stayed with them
	21:17	come to Jerusalem, the B received us gladly.
	22:1	the Hebrew language, saying: B and fathers, hear
	22:5	received letters to the B, and I journeyed to
	23:1	at the council, said, B, I have lived before
	23:5	"I did not know, B, that he was the
	23:6	out in the council, B, I am a Pharisee,
	28:14	There we found B, and were invited to stay
	28:15	And the B there, when they heard of us,
	28:17	he said to them, B, though I had done
	28:21	and none of the B coming here has reported
Rom	1:13	want you to know, B, that I have often
	7:1	Do you not know, B --for I am speaking
	7:4	Likewise, my B, you have died to the law
	8:12	So then, B, we are debtors, not to the
	8:29	that he might be the first-born among many B
	9:3	the sake of my B, my kinsmen by race.
	10:1	B, my heart's desire and prayer to God for
	11:25	to understand this mystery, B: a hardening has come
	12:1	appeal to you therefore, B, by the mercies of
	15:14	satisfied about you, my B, that you yourselves are
	15:30	I appeal to you, B, by our Lord Jesus
	16:14	Patrobas, Hermas, and the B who are with them.
	16:17	I appeal to you, B, to take note of
1Cor	1:10	I appeal to you, B, by the name of
	1:11	people that there is quarreling among you, my B
	1:26	For consider your call, B; not many of you
	2:1	I came to you, B, I did not come
	3:1	But I, B, could not address you as spiritual
	4:6	Apollos for your benefit, B, that you may learn
	6:8	wrong and defraud, and that even your own B
	7:24	So, B, in whatever state each was called, there
	7:29	I mean, B, the appointed time has grown very
	8:12	sinning against your B and wounding their
	10:1	want you to know, B, that our fathers were
	11:33	So then, my B, when you come together to
	12:1	Now concerning spiritual gifts, B, I do not want
	14:6	Now, B, if I come to you speaking in
	14:20	B, do not be children in your thinking; be
	14:26	What then, B
	14:39	So, my B, earnestly desire to prophesy, and do
	15:1	I would remind you, B, in what terms I
	15:6	more than five hundred B at one time, most
	15:31	I protest, B, by my pride in you which
	15:50	I tell you this, B: flesh and blood cannot
	15:58	my beloved B, be steadfast, immovable, always
	16:11	me; for I am expecting him with the B
	16:12	you with the other B, but it was not
	16:15	Now, B, you know that the household of Stephanas
	16:20	All the B send greetings.
2Cor	1:8	you to be ignorant, B, of the affliction we
	8:1	want you to know, B, about the grace of
	8:23	and as for our B, they are messengers of
	9:3	I am sending the B so that our boasting
	9:5	necessary to urge the B to go on to
	11:9	were supplied by the B who came from Macedonia.
	11:26	sea, danger from false B;
	13:11	Finally, B, farewell.
Gal	1:2	and all the B who are with me,
	1:11	would have you know, B, that the gospel which
	2:4	But because of false B secretly brought in, who
	3:15	give a human example, B: no one annuls even
	4:12	B, I beseech you, become as I am, for
	4:28	Now we, B, like Isaac, are children of promise.
	4:31	So, B, we are not children of the slave
	5:11	But if I, B, still preach circumcision, why am
	5:13	were called to freedom, B; only do not use
	6:1	B, if a man is overtaken in any trespass,
	6:18	our Lord Jesus Christ be with your spirit, B
Eph	6:23	Peace be to the B, and love with faith,
Phil	1:12	want you to know, B, that what has happened
	1:14	and most of the B have been made confident
	3:1	Finally, my B, rejoice in the Lord.
	3:13	B, I do not consider that I have made
	3:17	B, join in imitating me, and mark those who
	4:1	Therefore, my B, whom I love and long for,
	4:8	Finally, B, whatever is true, whatever is honorable,
	4:21	The B who are with me greet you.
Col	1:2	the saints and faithful B in Christ at Colossae:
	4:15	my greetings to the B at La-odicea, and to
1Thes	1:4	For we know, B beloved by God, that he
	2:1	For you yourselves know, B, that our visit to
	2:9	our labor and toil, B; we worked night and
	2:14	For you, B, became imitators of the churches of
	2:17	were bereft of you, B, for a short time,
	3:7	for this reason, B, in all our distress
	4:1	Finally, B, we beseech and exhort you in the
	4:9	concerning love of the B you have no need
	4:10	do love all the B throughout Macedonia.

4:10 But we exhort you, B, to do so more
4:13 not have you ignorant, B, concerning those who are
5:1 times and the seasons, B, you have no need
5:4 are not in darkness, B, for that day to
5:12 But we beseech you, B, to respect those who
5:14 we exhort you, B, admonish the idlers, encourage
5:25 B, pray for us.
5:26 Greet all the B with a holy kiss.
5:27 that this letter be read to all the B
2Thes 1:3 God always for you, B, as is fitting, because
2:1 him, we beg you, B,
2:13 God always for you, B beloved by the Lord,
2:15 So then, B, stand firm and hold to the
3:1 Finally, B, pray for us, that the word of
3:6 Now we command you, B, in the name of
3:13 B, do not be weary in well-doing.
1Tim 4:6 these instructions before the B, you will be a
6:2 ground that they are B; rather they must serve
2Tim 4:21 Pudens and Linus and Claudia and all the B
Heb 2:11 ashamed to call them B,
2:12 thy name to my B, in the midst of
2:17 be made like his B in every respect, so
3:1 Therefore, holy B, who share in a heavenly call,
3:12 Take care, B, lest there be in any of
7:5 that is, from their B, though these also are
10:19 Therefore, B, since we have confidence to enter the
13:22 I appeal to you, B, bear with my word
Jas 1:2 it all joy, my B, when you meet various
1:15 Do not be deceived, my beloved B
1:18 Know this, my beloved B
2:1 My B, show no partiality as you hold the
2:5 Listen, my beloved B
2:14 does it profit, my B, if a man says
3:1 you become teachers, my B, for you know that
3:10 My B, this ought not to be so.
3:12 a fig tree, my B, yield olives, or a
4:11 Do not speak evil against one another, B
5:7 Be patient, therefore, B, until the coming of the
5:9 Do not grumble, B, against one another, that you
5:10 of suffering and patience, B, take the prophets who
5:12 But above all, my B, do not swear, either
5:19 My B, if any one among you wanders from
1Pet 1:22 sincere love of the B, love one another earnestly
3:8 sympathy, love of the B, a tender heart and
2Pet 1:10 Therefore, B, be the more zealous to confirm your
1Jn 3:13 Do not wonder, B, that the world hates you.
3:14 of death into life, because we love the B
3:16 ought to lay down our lives for the B
3Jn 1:3 when some of the B arrived and testified to
1:5 any service to the B, especially to strangers,
1:10 himself to welcome the B, and also stops those
Rev 6:11 fellow servants and their B should be complete, who
12:10 the accuser of our B has been thrown down,
19:10 with you and your B who hold the testimony
22:9 with you and your B the prophets, and with

BREVITY

2Mac 2:31 allowed to strive for B of expression and to

BRIBE (22)

Ex 18:21 and who hate a B; and place such men
23:8 you shall take no B, for a bribe blinds
23:8 no bribe, for a B blinds the officials, and
Deut 10:17 God, who is not partial and takes no B
16:19 shall not take a B, for a bribe blinds
16:19 a bribe, for a B blinds the eyes of
27:25 he who takes a B to slay an innocent
1Sam 12:3 have I taken a B to blind my eyes
Job 6:22 your wealth offer a B for me?
Ps 15:5 does not take a B against the innocent.
Prov 17:8 A B is like a magic stone in the
17:23 wicked man accepts a B from the bosom to
21:14 averts anger; and a B in the bosom, strong
Eccl 7:7 man foolish, and a B corrupts the mind.
Sir 35:12 not offer him a B, for he will not
Is 1:23 Every one loves a B and runs after gifts.
5:23 the guilty for a B, and deprive the innocent
33:15 lest they hold a B, who stops his ears
Amos 5:12 righteous, who take a B, and turn aside the
Mic 3:11 give judgment for a B, its priests teach for
7:3 judge ask for a B, and the great man
2Mac 4:45 beaten, promised a substantial B to Ptolemy son of

BRIBED

2Mac 10:20 who were money-hungry, were B by some of those

BRIBERY (2)

Job 15:34 is barren, and fire consumes the tents of B
Sir 40:12 All B and injustice will be blotted out, but

BRIBES (5)

1Sam 8:3 after gain; they took B and perverted justice.
2Chr 19:7 the LORD our God, or partiality, or taking B
Ps 26:10 devices, and whose right hands are full of B
Prov 15:27 but he who hates B will live.
Ezek 22:12 In you men take B to shed blood; you

BRIBING

Ezek 16:33 to all your lovers, B them to come to

BRICK (4)

Gen 11:3 And they had B for stone, and bitumen for
Ex 1:13 service, in mortar and B, and in all kinds
Ezek 4:1 of man, take a B and lay it before
Nah 3:14 take hold of the B mold!

BRICKKILNS

2Sam 12:31 them toil at the B; and thus he did

BRICKS (10)

Gen 11:3 "Come, let us make B, and burn them thoroughly."
Ex 5:7 people straw to make B, as heretofore; let them
5:8 But the number of B which they made heretofore
5:14 your task of making B today, as hitherto?"
5:16 say to us, 'Make B And behold, your servants
5:18 yet you shall deliver the same number of B
5:19 by no means lessen your daily number of B
Jud 5:11 set them to making B, and humbled them and
Is 9:10 arrogance of heart: "The B have fallen, but we
65:3 and burning incense upon B;

BRIDAL (3)

Tob 6:13 each died in the B chamber.
6:16 When you enter the B chamber, you shall take
1Mac 1:27 who sat in the B chamber was mourning.

BRIDE (27)

2Sam 17:3 to you as a B comes home to her
Song 4:8 me from Lebanon, my B; come with me from
4:9 heart, my sister, my B, you have ravished my
4:10 How sweet is your love, my sister, my B
4:11 lips distil nectar, my B; honey and milk are
4:12 is my sister, my B, a garden locked, a
5:1 garden, my sister, my B, I gather my myrrh
Wis 8:2 take her for my B, and I became enamored
Is 49:18 them on as a B does.
61:10 garland, and as a B adorns herself with her
62:5 bridegroom rejoices over the B, so shall your God
Jer 2:2 your love as a B, how you followed me
2:32 her ornaments, or a B her attire?
7:34 the voice of the B; for the land shall
16:9 of the bridegroom and the voice of the B
25:10 the voice of the B, the grinding of the
33:11 the voice of the B, the voices of those
Bar 2:23 the voice of the B, and the whole land
Joel 2:16 his room, and the B her chamber.
1Mac 9:37 and are conducting the B, a daughter of one
Jn 3:29 He who has the B is the bridegroom; the
2Cor 11:2 you as a pure B to her one husband.
Rev 18:23 voice of bridegroom and B shall be heard in
19:7 has come, and his B has made herself ready;
21:2 God, prepared as a B adorned for her husband;
21:9 will show you the B, the wife of the
22:17 The Spirit and the B say, "Come." And let

BRIDEGROOM (30)

Ex 4:25 "Surely you are a B of blood to me!"
4:26 said, "You are a B of blood," because of
Ps 19:5 comes forth like a B leaving his chamber, and
Is 61:10 of righteousness, as a B decks himself with a
62:5 you, and as the B rejoices over the bride,
Jer 7:34 the voice of the B and the voice of
16:9 the voice of the B and the voice of
25:10 the voice of the B and the voice of
33:11 the voice of the B and the voice of
Bar 2:23 the voice of the B and the voice of
Joel 1:8 with sackcloth for the B of her youth.
2:16 Let the B leave his room, and the bride
1Mac 1:27 Every B took up the lament; she who sat
9:39 much baggage; and the B came out with his
Mt 9:15 as long as the B is with them?
9:15 will come, when the B is taken away from

B

	25:1	took their lamps and went to meet the B
	25:5	As the B was delayed, they all slumbered and
	25:6	at midnight there was a cry, 'Behold, the B
	25:10	went to buy, the B came, and those who
Mk	2:19	guests fast while the B is with them?
	2:19	as they have the B with them, they cannot
	2:20	will come, when the B is taken away from
Lk	5:34	guests fast while the B is with them?
	5:35	will come, when the B is taken away from
Jn	2:9	the feast called the B
	3:29	the bride is the B; the friend of the
	3:29	the friend of the B, who stands and hears
	3:29	rejoices greatly at the B's voice; therefore this joy
Rev	18:23	and the voice of B and bride shall be

BRIDES (2)

Hos	4:13	the harlot, and your B commit adultery.
	4:14	the harlot, nor your B when they commit adultery;

BRIDLE (7)

Ps	32:9	curbed with bit and B, else it will not
	39:1	my tongue; I will B my mouth, so long
Prov	26:3	for the horse, a B for the ass, and
Is	30:28	of the peoples a B that leads astray.
Jas	1:25	religious, and does not B his tongue but deceives
	3:2	perfect man, able to B the whole body also.
Rev	14:20	high as a horse's B, for one thousand six

BRIDLES

2Mac	10:29	on horses with golden B, and they were leading

BRIEF (6)

Ezra	9:8	But now for a B moment favor has been
Wis	15:9	that his life is B, but he competes with
Is	54:7	For a B moment I forsook you, but with
2Mac	6:25	sake of living a B moment longer, they should
	7:36	brothers after enduring a B suffering have drunk of
	10:10	and will give a B summary of the principal

BRIEFLY (5)

2Mac	6:17	we must go on B with the story.
Acts	24:4	beg you in your kindness to hear us B
Eph	3:3	to me by revelation, as I have written B
Heb	13:22	of exhortation, for I have written to you B
1Pet	5:12	him, I have written B to you, exhorting and

BRIER (3)

Is	55:13	cypress; instead of the B shall come up the
Ezek	28:24	be no more a B to prick or a
Mic	7:4	them is like a B, the most upright of

BRIERS (11)

Judg	8:7	with the thorns of the wilderness and with B
	8:16	of the wilderness and B and with them taught
Is	5:6	pruned or hoed, and B and thorns shall grow
	7:23	of silver, will become B and thorns.
	7:24	the land will be B and thorns;
	7:25	there for fear of B and thorns; but they
	9:18	a fire, it consumes B and thorns; it kindles
	10:17	devour his thorns and B in one day.
	27:4	I had thorns and B to battle!
	32:13	up in thorns and B; yea, for all the
Ezek	2:6	of their words, though B and thorns are with

BRIGHT (19)

1Sam	14:27	hand to his mouth; and his eyes became B
	14:29	my eyes have become B, because I tasted a
Ezra	8:27	two vessels of fine B bronze as precious as
Job	25:5	the moon is not B and the stars are
	37:21	light when it is B in the skies, when
Ps	139:12	thee, the night is B as the day; for
Song	6:10	fair as the moon, B as the sun, terrible
Sir	43:4	fiery vapors, and with B beams it blinds the
Ezek	1:13	and the fire was B, and out of the
	32:8	All the B lights of heaven will I make
Mt	17:5	speaking, when lo, a B cloud overshadowed them,
Lk	11:36	it will be wholly B, as when a lamp
Acts	10:30	stood before me in B apparel,
Rev	6:4	out came another horse, B red; its rider was
	15:6	plagues, robed in pure B linen, and their breasts
	18:1	the earth was made B with his splendor.
	19:8	clothed with fine linen, B and pure"– for
	22:1	the water of life, B as crystal, flowing from
	22:16	offspring of David, the B morning star."

BRIGHTEN

Ezra	9:8	that our God may B our eyes and grant

BRIGHTER (6)

Job	11:17	your life will be B than the noonday; its
Prov	4:19	of dawn, which shines B and brighter until full
	4:19	which shines brighter and B until full day.
Sir	17:26	What is B than the sun?
	23:19	are ten thousand times B than the sun; they
Acts	26:13	a light from heaven, B than the sun, shining

BRIGHTNESS (18)

2Sam	22:13	Out of the B before him coals of fire
Ps	18:12	Out of the B before him there broke through
Sir	43:11	him who made it, exceedingly beautiful in its B
Is	59:9	behold, darkness, and for B, but we walk in
	60:3	and kings to the B of your rising.
	60:19	by day, nor for B shall the moon give
	62:1	vindication goes forth as B, and her salvation as
Ezek	1:4	a great cloud, with B round about it, and
	1:27	fire, and there was B round about him.
	1:28	the appearance of the B round about.
	8:2	like the appearance of B, like gleaming bronze.
	10:4	was full of the B of the glory of
Dan	2:31	mighty and of exceeding B, stood before you, and
	12:3	shall shine like the B of the firmament; and
Amos	5:20	and gloom with no B in it?
Hab	3:4	Selah His B was like the light, rays flashed
Acts	22:11	see because of the B of that light, I
2Cor	3:7	face because of its B, fading as this was,

BRILLIANT (2)

Wis	17:5	light, nor did the B flames of the stars
	17:20	world was illumined with B light, and was engaged

BRIM (10)

1Kgs	7:23	round, ten cubits from B to brim, and five
	7:23	cubits from brim to B, and five cubits high,
	7:24	its B were gourds, for thirty cubits, compassing
	7:26	a handbreadth; and its B was made like the
	7:26	was made like the B of a cup, like
2Chr	4:2	round, ten cubits from B to brim, and five
	4:2	cubits from brim to B, and five cubits high,
	4:5	a handbreadth; and its B was made like the
	4:5	was made like the B of a cup, like
Jn	2:7	And they filled them up to the B

BRIMSTONE (7)

Gen	19:24	on Sodom and Gomorrah B and fire from the
Deut	29:23	the whole land B and salt, and a
Job	18:15	is none of his; B is scattered upon his
Ps	11:6	coals of fire and B; a scorching wind shall
Is	30:33	like a stream of B, kindles it.
	34:9	and her soil into B; her land shall become
Ezek	38:22	with him, torrential rains and hailstones, fire and B

BRING (720)

Gen	1:20	said, "Let the waters B forth swarms of living
	1:24	"Let the earth B forth living creatures according
	3:16	in pain you shall B forth children, yet your
	3:18	and thistles it shall B forth to you; and
	5:29	cursed this one shall B us relief from our
	6:17	For behold, I will B a flood of waters
	6:19	all flesh, you shall B two of every sort
	8:17	B forth with you every living thing that is
	9:7	be fruitful and multiply, B forth abundantly on the
	9:14	When I B clouds over the earth and the
	15:9	He said to him, B me a heifer three
	15:14	years; but I will B judgment on the nation
	18:19	that the LORD may B to Abraham what he
	19:5	B them out to us, that we may know
	19:8	known man; let me B them out to you,
	19:12	have in the city, B them out of the
	27:4	as I love, and B it to me that
	27:5	hunt for game and B it,
	27:7	to your brother Esau, B me game, and prepare
	27:10	loves; and you shall B it to your father
	27:12	be mocking him, and B a curse upon myself
	27:25	Then he said, B it to me, that I
	28:15	you go, and will B you back to this
	31:39	beasts I did not B to you; I bore
	37:14	with the flock; and B me word again." So
	38:24	And Judah said, B her out, and let her
	41:32	and God will shortly B it to pass.
	42:16	you, and let him B your brother, while you
	42:20	of your households, and B your youngest brother to

42:34 B your youngest brother to me; then I shall
42:37 if I do not B him back to you;
42:37 hands, and I will B him back to you."
42:38 to make, you would B down my gray hairs
43:7 that he would say, B your brother down'?"
43:9 If I do not B him back to you
43:16 steward of his house, B the men into the
44:21 said to your servants, B him down to me,
44:29 befalls him, you will B down my gray hairs
44:31 and your servants will B down the gray hairs
44:32 'If I do not B him back to you,
45:13 Make haste and B my father down here."
45:19 for your wives, and B your father, and come.
46:4 and I will also B you up again; and
48:9 And he said, B them to me, I pray
48:21 with you, and will B you again to the
50:20 it for good, to B it about that many
50:24 will visit you, and B you up out of
Ex 3:8 the Egyptians, and to B them up out of
3:10 Pharaoh that you may B forth my people, the
3:11 go to Pharaoh, and B the sons of Israel
3:17 promise that I will B you up out of
6:6 LORD, and I will B you out from under
6:8 And I will B you into the land which
6:13 king of Egypt to B the people of Israel
6:26 whom the LORD said: B out the people of
7:4 hand upon Egypt and B forth my hosts, my
7:5 hand upon Egypt and B out the people of
8:18 their secret arts to B forth gnats, but they
10:4 behold, tomorrow I will B locusts into your country,
11:1 plague more I will B upon Pharaoh and upon
12:42 by the LORD, to B them out of the
15:17 Thou wilt B them in, and plant them on
16:5 they prepare what they B in, it will be
17:3 said, "Why did you B us up out of
18:19 people before God, and B their cases to God;
18:22 great matter they shall B to you, but any
21:6 then his master shall B him to God, and
21:6 God, and he shall B him to the door
22:13 by beasts, let him B it as evidence; he
23:4 going astray, you shall B it back to him.
23:19 your ground you shall B into the house of
23:20 the way and to B you to the place
26:33 from the clasps, and B the ark of the
27:20 of Israel that they B to you pure beaten
28:1 "Then B near to you Aaron your brother, and
28:29 the holy place, to B them to continual remembrance
28:43 holy place; lest they B guilt upon themselves and
29:3 in one basket and B them in the basket,
29:3 in the basket, and B the bull and the
29:4 You shall B Aaron and his sons to the
29:8 Then you shall B his sons, and put coats
29:10 "Then you shall B the bull before the tent
30:16 meeting; that it may B the people of Israel
32:2 and your daughters, and B them to me."
32:12 evil intent did he B them forth, to slay
33:12 thou sayest to me, B up this people'; but
34:26 your ground you shall B to the house of
35:5 generous heart, let him B the LORD's offering: gold,
35:29 heart moved them to B anything for the work
36:5 to Moses, "The people B much more than enough
Lev 1:2 the LORD, you shall B your offering of cattle
1:14 birds, then he shall B his offering of turtledoves
1:15 And the priest shall B it to the altar
2:2 frankincense on it, and B it to Aaron's sons
2:4 "When you B a cereal offering baked in the
2:8 And you shall B the cereal offering that is
2:8 the priest, he shall B it to the altar.
2:11 cereal offering which you B to the LORD shall
2:12 first fruits you may B them to the LORD,
4:4 He shall B the bull to the door of
4:5 of the bull and B it to the tent
4:14 a sin offering and B it before the tent
4:16 the anointed priest shall B some of the blood
4:23 to him, he shall B as his offering a
4:28 to him he shall B for his offering a
4:32 sin offering, he shall B a female without blemish,
5:6 committed, and he shall B his guilt offering to
5:7 lamb, then he shall B, as his guilt offering
5:8 He shall B them to the priest, who shall
5:11 pigeons, then he shall B, as his offering for
5:12 And he shall B it to the priest, and
5:15 the LORD, he shall B, as his guilt offering
5:18 He shall B to the priest a ram without
6:6 And he shall B to the priest his guilt
6:21 a griddle; you shall B it well mixed, in

7:13 for thanksgiving he shall B his offering with cakes
7:29 to the LORD shall B his offering to the
7:30 peace offerings he shall B with his own hands
7:30 the LORD; he shall B the fat with the
7:38 people of Israel to B their offerings to the
9:7 for the people; and B the offering of the
10:15 is waved they shall B with the offerings by
12:6 a daughter, she shall B to the priest at
14:23 eighth day he shall B them for his cleansing
15:29 two young pigeons, and B them to the priest,
16:12 small; and he shall B it within the veil
16:15 for the people, and B its blood within the
17:4 camp, and does not B it to the door
17:5 people of Israel may B their sacrifices which they
17:5 field, that they may B them to the LORD,
17:9 sacrifice, and does not B it to the door
19:21 free; but he shall B a guilt offering for
23:10 its harvest, you shall B the sheaf of the
23:17 You shall B from your dwellings two loaves of
24:2 people of Israel to B you pure oil from
24:14 LORD said to Moses, B out of the camp
25:21 so that it will B forth fruit for three
26:21 to me, I will B more plagues upon you,
26:25 And I will B a sword upon you, that
27:8 valuation, then he shall B the person before the
27:11 then the man shall B the animal before the
Num 3:6 LORD said to Moses, B the tribe of Levi
5:9 of Israel, which they B to the priest, shall
5:15 then the man shall B his wife to the
5:15 to the priest, and B the offering required of
5:16 "And the priest shall B her near, and set
5:25 before the LORD and B it to the altar;
6:10 eighth day he shall B two turtledoves or two
6:12 of his separation, and B a male lamb a
11:12 Did I B them forth, that thou shouldst say
11:16 officers over them; and B them to the tent
13:20 of good courage, and B some of the fruit
14:3 Why does the LORD B us into this land,
14:8 in us, he will B us into this land
14:13 it, for thou didst B up this people in
14:16 was not able to B this people into the
14:24 me fully, I will B into the land into
14:31 a prey, I will B in, and they shall
15:18 land to which I B you
16:9 congregation of Israel, to B you near to himself,
16:17 every one of you B before the LORD his
18:2 And with you B your brethren also, the tribe
18:13 their land, which they B to the LORD, shall
19:2 people of Israel to B you a red heifer
20:5 out of Egypt, to B us to this evil
20:8 water; so you shall B water out of the
20:10 you rebels; shall we B forth water for you
20:12 therefore you shall not B this assembly into the
20:25 Eleazar his son, and B them up to Mount
22:8 night, and I will B back word to you,
27:17 lead them out and B them in; that the
Deut 1:17 for you, you shall B to me, and I
1:22 land for us, and B us word again of
4:38 mightier than yourselves, to B you in, to give
6:23 there, that he might B us in and give
7:26 And you shall not B an abominable thing into
9:28 from which thou didst B us say, "Because the
9:28 was not able to B them into the land
9:29 heritage, whom thou didst B out by thy great
12:6 and thither you shall B your burnt offerings and
12:11 there, thither you shall B all that I command
14:24 are not able to B the tithe, when the
14:28 three years you shall B forth all the tithe
17:5 Israel, then you shall B forth to your gates
21:4 of that city shall B the heifer down to
21:12 wife, then you shall B her home to your
21:19 hold of him and B him out to the
22:2 know him, you shall B it home to your
22:8 that you may not B the guilt of blood
22:15 mother shall take and B out the tokens of
22:21 woman, then they shall B out the young woman
22:24 her, then you shall B them both out to
23:18 You shall not B the hire of a harlot,
24:4 and you shall not B guilt upon the land
24:11 make the loan shall B the pledge out to
26:10 And behold, now I B the first of the
28:36 "The LORD will B you, and your king whom
28:49 The LORD will B a nation against you from
28:59 then the LORD will B on you and your
28:60 And he will B upon you again all the
28:61 law, the LORD will B upon you, until you

B

28:68 And the LORD will B you back in ships
30:5 LORD your God will B you into the land
30:12 us to heaven, and B it to us, that
30:13 sea for us, and B it to us, that
31:23 courage; for you shall B the children of Israel
33:7 voice of Judah, and B him in to his
Josh 2:3 sent to Rahab, saying, B forth the men that
6:18 thing for destruction, and B trouble upon it.
6:22 the harlot's house, and B out from it the
7:25 said, "Why did you B trouble on us?
10:22 of the cave, and B those five kings out
18:6 in seven divisions and B the description here to
23:15 so the LORD will B upon you all the
Judg 6:13 'Did not the LORD B us up from Egypt?'
6:18 come to thee, and B out my present, and
6:30 town said to Joash, B out your son, that
11:5 of Gilead went to B Jephthah from the land
11:9 of Gilead, "If you B me home again to
19:3 kindly to her and B her back.
19:22 master of the house, B out the man who
19:24 his concubine; let me B them out now.
20:10 of ten thousand, to B provisions for the people,
Ruth 3:15 And he said, B the mantle you are wearing
1Sam 1:22 is weaned, I will B him, that he may
4:3 Let us B the ark of the covenant of
9:7 go, what can we B the man?
9:7 is no present to B to the man of
9:23 said to the cook, B the portion I gave
11:12 Saul reign over us?' B the men, that we
13:9 So Saul said, B the burnt offering here to
14:18 Saul said to Ahijah, B hither the ark of
14:34 them, 'Let every man B his ox or his
15:32 Then Samuel said, B here to me Agag the
16:17 can play well, and B him to me."
17:18 your brothers fare, and B some token from them."
19:15 to see David, saying, B him up to me
20:8 for why should you B me to your father?"
23:9 to Abiathar the priest, B the ephod here."
27:11 nor woman alive, to B tidings to Gath, thinking,
28:8 by a spirit, and B up for me whomever
28:9 for my life to B about my death?"
28:11 said, "Whom shall I B up for you?" He
28:11 He said, B up Samuel for me."
30:7 the son of Ahimelech, B me the ephod." So
2Sam 3:12 be with you to B over all Israel to
3:13 face, unless you first B Michal, Saul's daughter, when
3:18 Now then B it about; for the LORD has
6:2 him from Baale-judah, to B up from there the
9:10 for him, and shall B in the produce, that
12:23 Can I B him back again?
13:10 Amnon said to Tamar, B the food into the
14:10 says anything to you, B him to me, and
14:13 the king does not B his banished one home
14:21 I grant this; go, B back the young man
15:8 the LORD will indeed B me back to Jerusalem,
15:14 overtake us quickly, and B down evil upon us,
15:25 the LORD, he will B me back and let
17:3 only, and I will B all the people back
17:13 then all Israel will B ropes to that city,
17:14 that the LORD might B evil upon Absalom.
19:11 be the last to B the king back to
19:12 be the last to B back the king?'
19:15 the king and to B the king over the
19:18 crossed the ford to B over the king's household,
22:28 upon the haughty to B them down.
1Kgs 1:33 my own mule, and B him down to Gihon;
1:42 a worthy man and B good news."
2:9 him, and you shall B his gray head down
2:32 The LORD will B back his bloody deeds upon
2:44 so the LORD will B back your evil upon
3:24 And the king said, B me a sword." So
5:9 My servants shall B it down to the sea
8:1 Solomon in Jerusalem, to B up the ark of
8:34 thy people Israel, and B them again to the
8:51 heritage, which thou didst B out of Egypt, from
8:53 servant, when thou didst B our fathers out of
13:18 of the LORD, saying, B him back with you
14:10 therefore behold, I will B evil upon the house
17:10 to her and said, B me a little water
17:11 she was going to B it, he called to
17:11 to her and said, B me a morsel of
17:13 cake of it and B it to me, and
17:18 come to me to B my sin to remembrance,
20:33 he said, "Go and B him." Then Ben-hadad came
21:10 him, and let them B a charge against him,
21:21 Behold, I will B evil upon you; I will
21:29 me, I will not B the evil in his
21:29 son's days I will B the evil upon his
22:9 an officer and said, B quickly Micaiah the son
2Kgs 2:20 He said, B me a new bowl, and put
3:15 But now B me a minstrel." And when the
4:6 said to her son, B me another vessel." And
4:41 He said, "Then B meal." And he threw it
6:19 me, and I will B you to the man
10:22 charge of the wardrobe, B out the vestments for
11:15 set over the army, B her out between the
12:4 heart prompts him to B into the house of
19:3 is no strength to B them forth.
19:25 old what now I B to pass, that you
20:7 And Isaiah said, B a cake of figs.
22:16 LORD, Behold, I will B evil upon this place
22:20 evil which I will B upon this place.'" And
23:4 of the threshold, to B out of the temple
1Chr 13:3 Then let us B again the ark of our
13:5 entrance of Hamath, to B the ark of God
13:6 belongs to Judah, to B up from there the
13:12 said, "How can I B the ark of God
15:3 Israel at Jerusalem, to B up the ark of
15:12 so that you may B up the ark of
15:14 Levites sanctified themselves to B up the ark of
15:25 of thousands, went to B up the ark of
16:29 glory due his name; B an offering, and come
21:2 Beer-sheba to Dan, and B me a report, that
21:3 Why should he B guilt upon Israel?"
2Chr 2:16 need from Lebanon, and B it to you in
5:2 Israel, in Jerusalem, to B up the ark of
6:25 thy people Israel, and B them again to the
18:8 an officer and said, B quickly Micaiah the son
21:14 behold, the LORD will B a great plague on
23:14 army, saying to them, B her out between the
24:6 required the Levites to B in from Judah and
24:9 Judah and Jerusalem, to B in for the LORD
24:19 prophets among them to B them back to the
26:18 wrong, and it will B you no honor from
28:13 them, "You shall not B the captives in here,
28:13 for you propose to B upon us guilt against
28:27 for they did not B him into the tombs
29:31 LORD; come near, B sacrifices and thank offerings
31:10 "Since they began to B the contributions into the
34:24 LORD, Behold, I will B evil upon this place
34:28 evil which I will B upon this place and
Ezra 1:11 All these did Shesh-bazzar B up, when the exiles
3:7 and the Tyrians to B cedar trees from Lebanon
8:30 and the vessels, to B them to Jerusalem, to
Neh 1:9 gather them thence and B them to the place
8:1 Ezra the scribe to B the book of the
8:15 to the hills and B branches of olive, wild
9:7 didst choose Abram and B him forth out of
9:15 for their hunger and B forth water for them
9:23 heaven, and thou didst B them into the land
10:31 peoples of the land B in wares or any
10:34 the wood offering, to B it into the house
10:35 We obligate ourselves to B the first fruits of
10:36 the LORD; also to B to the house of
10:37 our flocks; and to B the first of our
10:37 our God; and to B to the Levites the
10:38 and the Levites shall B up the tithe of
10:39 sons of Levi shall B the contribution of grain,
11:1 people cast lots to B one out of ten
12:27 all their places, to B them to Jerusalem to
13:18 did not our God B all this evil on
13:18 Yet you B more wrath upon Israel by profaning
Tob 2:2 my son, "Go and B whatever poor man of
3:10 him, and I shall B his old age down
6:14 I may die and B the lives of my
8:17 mercy, O Lord; and B their lives to fulfilment
9:2 money for me; and B him to the wedding
10:12 "The Lord of heaven B you back safely, dear
14:5 mercy on them, and B them back into their
Jud 8:22 all this he will B upon our heads among
8:23 our slavery will not B us into favor, but
9:8 by thy might, and B down their power in
11:14 been doing this, to B back to them permission
11:22 our hands and to B destruction upon those who
12:1 he commanded them to B her in where his
14:5 you do all this, B Achior the Ammonite to
Esth 1:11 Ahasuerus as chamberlains, to B Queen Vashti before
5:5 Then said the king, B Haman quickly, that we
6:1 he gave orders to B the book of memorable
Job 10:17 toward me; thou dost B fresh hosts against me.
10:18 "Why didst thou B me forth from the womb?
12:6 God are secure, who B their god in their

14:3 such a one and B him into judgment with
14:4 Who can B a clean thing out of an
15:35 They conceive mischief and B forth evil and their
30:23 know that thou wilt B me to death, and
33:22 life to those who B death.
33:30 with a man, to B back his soul from
38:26 for the thunderbolt, to B rain on a land
39:1 when the mountain goats B forth?
39:2 the time when they B forth,
39:3 forth, when they crouch, B forth their offspring, and
39:12 he will return, and B your grain to your
40:12 that is proud, and B him low; and tread
40:19 him who made him B near his sword!
Ps 18:27 haughty eyes thou dost B down.
25:17 of my heart, and B me out of my
37:6 He will B forth your vindication as the light,
37:14 bend their bows, to B down the poor and
43:3 lead me, let them B me to thy holy
55:3 For they B trouble upon me, and in anger
59:11 by thy power, and B them down, O Lord,
60:9 Who will B me to the fortified city?
64:8 their tongue he will B them to ruin; all
65:4 thou dost choose and B near, to dwell in
66:11 Thou didst B us into the net; thou didst
68:22 Lord said, "I will B them back from Bashan,
68:22 from Bashan, I will B them back from the
71:20 the earth thou wilt B me up again.
72:10 of Sheba and Seba B gifts!
76:11 let all around him B gifts to him who
80:8 Thou didst B a vine out of Egypt; thou
92:14 They still B forth fruit in old age, they
94:23 He will B back on them their iniquity and
96:8 glory due his name; B an offering, and come
104:14 cultivate, that he may B forth food from the
108:10 Who will B me to the fortified city?
109:6 him; let an accuser B him to trial.
142:7 B me out of prison, that I may give
143:11 In thy righteousness B me out of trouble!
144:13 store; may our sheep B forth thousands and ten
Prov 16:15 like the clouds that B the spring rain.
18:6 A fool's lips B strife, and his mouth invites
19:24 and will not even B it back to his
25:8 seen do not hastily B into court; for what
25:10 he who hears you B shame upon you, and
26:15 wears him out to B it back to his
27:1 what a day may B forth.
29:23 A man's pride will B him low, but he
Eccl 3:22 his lot; who can B him to see what
11:9 these things God will B you into judgment.
12:14 For God will B every deed into judgment, with
Song 8:2 would lead you and B you into the house
8:11 each one was to B for its fruit a
Wis 1:12 of your life, nor B on destruction by the
16:14 another, but he cannot B back the departed spirit,
Sir 1:27 you fall, and thus B dishonor upon yourself.
4:17 tortuous paths, she will B fear and cowardice upon
4:20 evil; and do not B shame on yourself.
11:27 Do not B every man into your home, for
17:18 them, and he will B their recompense on their
33:22 all that you do; B no stain upon your
46:8 people on foot, to B them into their inheritance,
Is 1:13 B no more vain offerings; incense is an abomination
7:17 The LORD will B upon you and upon your
14:2 will take them and B them to their place,
15:9 blood; yet I will B upon Dibon even more,
21:2 she has caused I B to an end.
21:14 To the thirsty B water, meet the fugitive with
25:12 his walls he will B down, lay low, and
33:11 You conceive chaff, you B forth stubble; your breath
37:3 is no strength to B them forth.
37:26 old what now I B to pass, that you
38:12 to night thou dost B me to an end;
38:13 to night thou dost B me to an end.
41:21 case, says the LORD; B your proofs, says the
41:22 Let them B them, and tell us what is
42:1 upon him, he will B forth justice to the
42:3 quench; he will faithfully B forth justice.
42:7 that are blind, to B out the prisoners from
43:5 with you; I will B your offspring from the
43:6 south, Do not withhold; B my sons from afar
43:8 B forth the people who are blind, yet have
43:9 Let them B their witnesses to justify them, and
46:11 spoken, and I will B it to pass; I
46:13 far from deliverance: I B near my deliverance, it
49:5 be his servant, to B Jacob back to him,
49:22 peoples; and they shall B your sons in their
55:10 the earth, making it B forth and sprout, giving
56:7 these I will B to my holy mountain,
58:7 with the hungry, and B the homeless poor into
59:4 they conceive mischief and B forth iniquity.
60:6 They shall B gold and frankincense, and shall
60:9 of Tarshish first, to B your sons from far,
60:11 shut; that men may B to you the wealth
60:17 of bronze I will B gold, and instead of
60:17 of iron I will B silver; instead of wood,
61:1 has anointed me to B good tidings to the
65:9 I will B forth descendants from Jacob, and from
66:4 affliction for them, and B their fears upon them;
66:9 Shall I B to the birth and not cause
66:9 and not cause to B forth?
66:9 I, who cause to B forth, shut the womb?
66:20 And they shall B all your brethren from all
66:20 just as the Israelites B their cereal offering in
Jer 2:35 me.' Behold, I will B you to judgment for
3:14 family, and I will B you to Zion.
4:6 stay not, for I B evil from the north,
10:18 time, and I will B distress on them, that
10:24 thy anger, lest thou B me to nothing.
11:23 For I will B evil upon the men of
12:2 root; they grow and B forth fruit; thou art
12:9 all the wild beasts; B them to devour.
12:15 them, and I will B them again each to
14:22 the nations that can B rain?
16:15 them.' For I will B them back to their
17:18 me not be dismayed; B upon them the day
17:21 the sabbath day or B it in by the
17:24 says the LORD, and B in no burden by
21:4 walls; and I will B them together into the
23:3 them, and I will B them back to their
23:12 fall; for I will B evil upon them in
23:40 And I will B upon you everlasting reproach and
24:6 good, and I will B them back to this
25:9 servant, and I will B them against this land
25:13 I will B upon that land all the words
26:15 to death, you will B innocent blood upon yourselves
26:19 we are about to B great evil upon ourselves."
27:11 any nation which will B its neck under the
27:12 spoke in like manner: B your necks under the
27:22 Then I will B them back and restore them
28:3 two years I will B back to this place
28:4 I will also B back to this place Jeconiah
28:6 prophesied come true, and B back to this place
29:10 you my promise and B you back to this
29:14 LORD, and I will B you back to the
30:3 LORD, and I will B them back to the
31:8 Israel.' Behold, I will B them from the north
31:18 like an untrained calf; B me back that I
31:28 to overthrow, destroy, and B evil, so I will
31:32 by the hand to B them out of the
32:21 Thou didst B thy people Israel out of the
32:37 great indignation; I will B them back to this
32:42 people, so I will B upon them all the
33:6 Behold, I will B to it health and healing,
33:11 who sing, as they B thank offerings to the
34:22 the LORD, and will B them back to this
35:2 speak with them, and B them to the house
36:31 their iniquity; I will B upon them, and upon
42:17 evil which I will B upon them.
48:35 And I will B to an end in Moab,
48:44 For I will B these things upon Moab in
49:5 me?' Behold, I will B terror upon you, says
49:8 For I will B the calamity of Esau upon
49:16 the eagles, I will B you down from there,
49:32 hair, and I will B their calamity from every
49:36 might; and I will B upon Elam the four
49:37 their life; I will B evil upon them, my
51:27 a marshal against her, B up horses like bristling
51:40 I will B them down like lambs to the
Lam 1:21 B thou the day thou hast announced, and let
Bar 2:11 of Israel, who didst B thy people out of
2:19 our kings that we B before thee our prayer
2:34 I will B them again into the land which
4:29 calamities upon you will B you everlasting joy with
5:6 enemies; but God will B them back to you,
6:3 after that I will B you away from there
6:41 who cannot speak, they B him and pray Bel
Ezek 5:16 you, and when I B more and more famine
5:17 you; and I will B the sword upon you.
6:3 I, even I, will B a sword upon you,
7:24 of violence, I will B the worst of the
11:8 sword; and I will B the sword upon you,
11:9 And I will B you forth out of the

12:4 You shall B out your baggage by day in
12:13 snare; and I will B him to Babylon in
13:14 daubed with whitewash, and B it down to the
14:17 Or if I B a sword upon that land,
16:38 blood are judged, and B upon you the blood
16:40 They shall B up a host against you, and
17:8 waters, that it might B forth branches, and bear
17:20 snare, and I will B him to Babylon and
17:23 it, that it may B forth boughs and bear
17:24 that I the LORD B low the high tree,
20:6 them that I would B them out of the
20:15 that I would not B them into the land
20:34 I will B you out from the peoples and
20:35 out; and I will B you into the wilderness
20:38 against me; I will B them out of the
20:41 accept you, when I B you out from the
20:42 the LORD, when I B you into the land
23:22 disgust, and I will B them against you from
23:46 says the Lord GOD: B up a host against
26:3 O Tyre, and will B up many nations against
26:7 GOD: Behold, I will B upon Tyre from the
26:19 not inhabited, when I B up the deep over
26:21 I will B you to a dreadful end, and
28:7 therefore, behold, I will B strangers upon you, the
29:8 GOD: Behold, I will B a sword upon you,
29:14 fortunes of Egypt, and B them back to the
30:12 evil men; I will B desolation upon the land
32:12 "They shall B to nought the pride of Egypt,
33:2 to them, If I B the sword upon a
34:13 And I will B them out from the peoples,
34:13 the countries, and will B them into their own
34:16 lost, and I will B back the strayed, and
36:24 all the countries, and B you into your own
37:12 people; and I will B you home into the
37:21 from all sides, and B them to their own
38:4 jaws, and I will B you forth, and all
38:16 latter days I will B you against my land,
38:17 years that I would B you against them?
39:2 drive you forward, and B you up from the
46:20 in order not to B them out into the
Dan 1:3 his chief eunuch, to B some of the people
2:24 wise men of Babylon; B me in before the
2:44 all these kingdoms and B them to an end,
5:7 king cried aloud to B in the enchanters, the
9:15 our God, who didst B thy people out of
9:24 atone for iniquity, to B in everlasting righteousness,
11:17 kingdom, and he shall B terms of peace and
13:17 said to her maids, B me oil and ointments,
13:18 the side doors to B what they had been
13:56 and commanded them to B the other.
14:14 ordered his servants to B ashes and they sifted
Hos 2:14 will allure her, and B her into the wilderness,
7:13 my net; I will B them down like birds
9:12 Even if they B up children, I will bereave
9:16 Even though they B forth, I will slay their
Joel 3:2 all the nations and B them down to the
3:11 B down thy warriors, O LORD.
Amos 3:11 surround the land, and B down your defenses from
4:1 say to their husbands, B, that we may drink!'
4:4 and multiply transgression; B your sacrifices every
5:25 "Did you B to me sacrifices and offerings the
6:3 the evil day, and B near the seat of
6:10 take him up to B the bones out of
8:4 upon the needy, and B the poor of the
8:10 into lamentation; I will B sackcloth upon all loins,
9:2 from there I will B them down.
9:7 "Did I not B up Israel from the land
Obad 1:3 your heart, "Who will B me down to the
1:4 stars, thence I will B you down, says the
Jon 1:13 men rowed hard to B the ship back to
2:6 ever; yet thou didst B up my life from
Mic 1:15 I will again B a conqueror upon you, inhabitants
7:9 He will B me forth to the light; I
Zeph 1:17 I will B distress on men, so that they
3:10 my dispersed ones, shall B my offering.
Hag 1:8 to the hills and B wood and build the
Zech 3:8 omen: behold, I will B my servant the Branch.
4:7 plain; and he shall B forward the top stone
8:8 country; and I will B them to dwell in
10:6 I will B them back because I have compassion
10:10 I will B them home from the land of
10:10 Assyria; and I will B them to the land
Mal 1:13 You B what has been taken by violence or
1:13 sick, and this you B as your offering!
2:12 or answer, or to B an offering to the
3:10 B the full tithes into the storehouse, that there

1Mac 4:45 it down, lest it B reproach upon them, for
6:15 Antiochus his son and B him up to be
6:55 living had appointed to B up Antiochus his son
7:2 Antiochus and Lysias to B them to him.
9:58 So now let us B Bacchides back, and he
10:63 no one is to B charges against him about
2Mac 1:4 commandments, and may he B peace.
1:20 dip it out and B it.
6:21 privately urged him to B meat of his own
7:38 and my brothers to B to an end the
12:39 the fallen and to B them back to lie
Mt 2:8 you have found him B me word, that I
10:34 I have come to B peace on earth; I
10:34 have not come to B peace, but a sword.
14:18 And he said, B them here to me."
16:5 they had forgotten to B any bread.
17:17 B him here to me."
21:2 her; untie them and B them to me.
Mk 6:27 and gave orders to B his head.
6:55 neighborhood and began to B sick people on their
8:14 they had forgotten to B bread; and they had
9:19 B him to me."
11:2 sat; untie it and B it.
12:15 B me a coin, and let me look at
13:11 And when they B you to trial and deliver
15:4 how many charges they B against you."
Lk 1:19 to you, and to B you this good news.
2:10 afraid; for behold, I B you good news of
5:18 and they sought to B him in and lay
5:19 finding no way to B him in, because of
8:15 and good heart, and B forth fruit with patience.
9:41 B your son here."
12:11 And when they B you before the synagogues and
14:21 of the city, and B in the poor and
15:22 said to his servants, B quickly the best robe,
15:23 on his feet; and B the fatted calf and
19:27 to reign over them, B them here and slay
19:30 sat; untie it and B it here.
Jn 7:45 "Why did you not B him?"
8:6 have some charge to B against him.
10:16 this fold; I must B them also, and they
14:26 you all things, and B to your remembrance all
18:29 "What accusation do you B against this man?"
21:10 Jesus said to them, B some of the fish
Acts 5:28 and you intend to B this man's blood upon
9:2 or women, he might B them bound to Jerusalem.
9:21 for this purpose, to B them bound before the
10:5 men to Joppa, and B one Simon who is
11:13 'Send to Joppa and B Simon called Peter;
12:4 after the Passover to B him out to the
12:6 Herod was about to B him out, Peter was
13:32 And we B you the good news that what
13:47 Gentiles, that you may B salvation to the uttermost
14:15 nature with you, and B you good news, that
17:5 of Jason, seeking to B them out to the
17:20 For you B some strange things to our ears;
19:38 are proconsuls; let them B charges against one
22:5 who were there and B them in bonds to
23:10 from among them and B him into the barracks.
23:15 to the tribune to B him down to you,
23:18 and asked me to B this young man to
23:20 to ask you to B Paul down to the
23:24 Paul to ride, and B him safely to Felix
24:12 you what they now B up against me.
24:16 years I came to B to my nation alms
27:39 planned if possible to B the ship ashore.
28:19 had no charge to B against my nation.
Rom 1:5 grace and apostleship to B about the obedience of
7:13 which is good, then, B death to me?
8:33 Who shall B any charge against God's elect?
10:6 (that is, to B Christ down)
10:7 (that is, to B Christ up from the dead).
16:25 the eternal God, to B about the obedience of
1Cor 1:28 that are not, to B to nothing things that
4:5 Lord comes, who will B to light the things
14:6 benefit you unless I B you some revelation or
2Cor 4:14 also with Jesus and B us with you into
Gal 2:4 Jesus, that they might B us into bondage--
Eph 6:4 children to anger, but B them up in the
Phil 1:6 work in you will B it to completion at
1Thes 4:14 through Jesus, God will B with him those who
2Tim 4:11 Get Mark and B him with you; for he
4:13 When you come, B the cloak that I left
1Pet 3:18 unrighteous, that he might B us to God, being
2Pet 2:1 you, who will secretly B in destructive heresies, even
2Jn 1:10 you and does not B this doctrine, do not

3Jn 1:10 I come, I will B up what he is
Rev 21:24 of the earth shall B their glory into it,
21:26 night there; they shall B into it the glory

BRINGEST

Jer 18:22 their houses, when thou B the marauder suddenly

BRINGING (66)

Ex 6:27 king of Egypt about B out the people of
14:11 done to us, in B us out of Egypt?
19:24 down, and come up B Aaron with you; but
36:3 still kept B him freewill offerings every morning,
36:6 people were restrained from B;
Lev 4:3 priest who sins, thus B guilt on the people,
18:3 to which I am B you.
20:22 land where I am B you to dwell may
Num 5:15 cereal offering of remembrance, B iniquity to
14:36 murmur against him by B up an evil report
Deut 8:7 LORD your God is B you into a good
28:63 will take delight in B ruin upon you and
29:27 kindled against this land, B upon it all the
1Sam 28:15 you disturbed me by B me up?" Saul answered,
2Sam 3:22 Joab from a raid, B much spoil with them.
4:10 and thought he was B good news, I seized
19:10 you say nothing about B the king back?"
19:43 first to speak of B back our king?" But
1Kgs 8:32 condemning the guilty by B his conduct upon his
10:22 Tarshish used to come B gold, silver, ivory, apes,
2Kgs 4:42 man came from Baal-shalishah, B the man of God
10:6 the city, who were B them up.
21:12 Israel, Behold, I am B upon Jerusalem and Judah
1Chr 12:40 Zebulun and Naphtali, came B food on asses and
2Chr 6:23 requiting the guilty by B his conduct upon his
9:21 Tarshish used to come B gold, silver, ivory, apes,
34:14 While they were B out the money that had
Neh 13:15 on the sabbath, and B in heaps of grain
Ps 126:6 with shouts of joy, B his sheaves with him.
Is 8:7 behold, the Lord is B up against them the
Jer 4:31 anguish as of one B forth her first child,
5:15 Behold, I am B upon you a nation from
6:19 earth; behold, I am B evil upon this people,
11:11 LORD, Behold, I am B evil upon them which
17:26 and from the Negeb, B burnt offerings and sacrifices,
17:26 offerings and frankincense, and B thank offerings to
19:3 Israel, Behold, I am B such evil upon this
19:15 Israel, Behold, I am B upon this city and
35:17 Israel: Behold, I am B on Judah and all
41:5 their bodies gashed, B cereal offerings and incense
45:5 for, behold, I am B evil upon all flesh,
46:25 said: "Behold, I am B punishment upon Amon of
50:9 am stirring up and B against Babylon a company
50:18 Israel: Behold, I am B punishment on the king
51:64 evil that I am B upon her.'" Thus far
Ezek 20:9 known to them in B them out of the
Dan 9:12 who ruled us, by B upon us a great
1Mac 11:39 the Arab, who was B up Antiochus, the young
Mt 15:30 crowds came to him, B with them the lame,
25:20 five talents came forward, B five talents more,
Mk 2:3 And they came, B to him a paralytic carried
10:13 And they were B children to him, that he
Lk 5:18 And behold, men were B on a bed a
8:1 and villages, preaching and B the good news of
18:15 Now they were B even infants to him that
22:52 and led him away, B him into the high
Jn 19:4 them, "See, I am B him out to you,
19:39 him by night, came B a mixture of myrrh
Acts 5:16 the towns around Jerusalem, B the sick and those
12:25 had fulfilled their mission, B with them John whose
21:16 Caesarea went with us, B us to the house
25:7 Jerusalem stood about him, B against him many
Eph 2:16 through the cross, thereby B the hostility to an
Heb 2:10 all things exist, in B many sons to glory,
2Pet 2:1 Master who bought them, B upon themselves swift.
Rev 22:12 I am coming soon, B my recompense, to repay

BRINGS (91)

Ex 13:5 And when the LORD B you into the land
13:11 "And when the LORD B you into the land
23:23 goes before you, and B you in to the
Lev 1:2 any man of you B an offering to the
2:1 "When any one B a cereal offering as an
4:32 "If he B a lamb as his offering for
Num 5:18 water of bitterness that B the curse.
5:19 water of bitterness that B the curse.
5:22 may this water that B the curse pass into
5:24 water of bitterness that B the curse, and the
5:24 and the water that B the curse shall enter
5:27 husband, the water that B the curse shall enter
15:4 LORD, then he who B his offering shall offer
23:22 God B them out of Egypt; they have as
24:8 God B him out of Egypt; he has as
Deut 6:10 the LORD your God B you into the land
7:1 the LORD your God B you into the land
11:29 the LORD your God B you into the land
22:14 with shameful conduct, and B an evil name upon
Josh 7:25 The LORD B trouble on you today." And all
1Sam 2:6 The LORD kills and B to life; he brings
2:6 brings to life; he B down to Sheol and
2:7 and makes rich; he B low, he also exalts.
2Sam 18:26 king said, "He also B tidings."
Tob 13:2 down to Hades, and B up again, and there
Job 9:23 When disaster B sudden death, he mocks at the
12:22 out of darkness, and B deep darkness to light.
19:29 the sword, for wrath B the punishment of the
28:11 that is hid he B forth to light.
Ps 7:14 pregnant with mischief, and B forth lies.
33:10 The LORD B the counsel of the nations to
50:23 He who B thanksgiving as his sacrifice honors me;
135:7 for the rain and B forth the wind from
146:9 of the wicked he B to ruin.
Prov 10:5 who sleeps in harvest B shame.
10:14 babbling of a fool B ruin near.
10:31 mouth of the righteous B forth wisdom, but the
12:4 husband, but she who B shame is like rottenness
12:18 tongue of the wise B healing.
13:13 who despises the word B destruction on himself, but
13:17 but a faithful envoy B healing.
16:30 who compresses his lips B evil to pass.
18:16 room for him and B him before great men.
19:3 When a man's folly B his way to ruin,
19:4 Wealth B many new friends, but a poor man
19:26 who causes shame and B reproach.
21:22 of the mighty and B down the stronghold in
21:27 much more when he B it with evil intent.
25:23 The north wind B forth rain; and a backbiting
29:15 child left to himself B shame to his mother.
31:14 of the merchant, she B her food from afar.
Song 8:10 eyes as one who B peace.
Wis 6:19 of immortality, and immortality B one near to God;
Sir 4:21 is a shame which B sin, and there is
20:9 is a gift that B a double return.
20:25 disposition of a liar B disgrace, and his shame
22:4 one who acts shamefully B grief to her father.
30:24 shorten life, and anxiety B on old age too
37:30 to food; for overeating B sickness, and gluttony leads
42:14 is a woman who B shame and disgrace.
Is 30:5 cannot profit them, that B neither help nor profit,
31:2 he is wise and B disaster, he does not
40:23 to dwell in; who B princes to nought, and
40:26 He who B out their host by number, calling
43:17 the mighty waters, who B forth chariot and horse,
52:7 feet of him who B good tidings, who publishes
52:7 who publishes peace, who B good tidings of good,
61:11 For as the earth B forth its shoots, and
Jer 10:13 the rain, and he B forth the wind from
13:16 your God before he B darkness, before your feet
51:16 the rain, and he B forth the wind from
Ezek 21:23 solemn oaths; but he B their guilt to remembrance,
26:3 you, as the sea B up its waves.
Nah 1:15 feet of him who B good tidings, who proclaims
Hab 1:15 He B all of them up with a hook,
Hag 1:11 upon what the ground B forth, upon men and
2Mac 3:39 that place himself and B it aid, and he
Mt 12:20 smoldering wick, till he B justice to victory;
12:35 of his good treasure B forth good, and the
12:35 of his evil treasure B forth evil.
12:45 Then he goes and B with him seven other
13:52 like a householder who B out of his treasure
Lk 11:26 Then he goes and B seven other spirits more
Rom 4:15 For the law B wrath, but where there is
5:16 gift following many trespasses B justification.
2Cor 7:10 leads to salvation and B no regret, but worldly
Heb 1:6 And again, when he B the first-born into the
6:7 falls upon it, and B forth vegetation useful to
Jas 1:14 when it is full-grown B forth death.
5:19 truth and some one B him back,
5:20 him know that whoever B back a sinner from

BRINK (5)

Ex 2:3 placed it among the reeds at the river's B
7:15 him by the river's B, and take in your
Josh 3:8 you come to the B of the waters of

3:15 were dipped in the B of the water (the
Is 19:7 the Nile, on the B of the Nile, and

BRISTLING

Jer 51:27 bring up horses like B locusts.

B

BRITTLE

Dan 2:42 the kingdom shall be partly strong and partly B

BROAD (37)

Ex 3:8 to a good and B land, a land flowing
27:1 long and five cubits B; the altar shall be
Judg 18:10 The land is B; yea, God has given it
2Sam 22:20 me forth into a B place; he delivered me,
1Kgs 6:6 story was five cubits B, the middle one was
6:6 one was six cubits B, and the third was
6:6 third was seven cubits B; for around the outside
1Chr 4:40 the land was very B, quiet, and peaceful; for
Neh 3:8 as far as the B Wall.
12:38 the Ovens, to the B Wall,
Job 36:16 of distress into a B place where there was
37:10 is given, and the B waters are frozen fast.
Ps 18:19 me forth into a B place; he delivered me,
31:8 my feet in a B place.
119:96 perfection, but thy commandment is exceedingly B
Is 33:21 us a place of B rivers and streams, where
Jer 51:58 LORD of hosts: The B wall of Babylon shall
Ezek 40:7 long, and one reed B; and the space between
40:30 round about, twenty-five cubits long and five cubits B
40:42 cubit and a half B, and one cubit high,
40:47 and a hundred cubits B, foursquare; and the altar
41:12 side was seventy cubits B; and the wall of
41:22 long, and two cubits B; its corners, its base,
42:20 and five hundred cubits B, to make a separation
43:13 high, and one cubit B, with a rim of
43:16 shall be square, twelve cubits long by twelve B
43:17 cubits long by fourteen B, with a rim around
43:17 it half a cubit B, and its base one
45:1 and twenty thousand cubits B; it shall be holy
45:3 long and ten thousand B, in which shall be
45:5 and ten thousand cubits B, shall be for the
45:6 area five thousand cubits B, and twenty-five thousand
46:22 cubits long and thirty B; the four were of
Hos 4:16 a lamb in a B pasture?
Amos 8:9 darken the earth in B daylight.
Mt 23:5 they make their phylacteries B and their fringes
Rev 20:9 marched up over the B earth and surrounded the

BROADER (2)

Job 11:9 than the earth, and B than the sea.
Ezek 41:7 the side chambers became B as they rose from

BROILED

Lk 24:42 him a piece of B fish,

BROKE (95)

Ex 32:19 of his hands and B them at the foot
34:1 that were on the first tables, which you B
Deut 9:17 my two hands, and B them before your eyes.
10:2 first tables which you B, and you shall put
32:51 his people; because you B faith with me in
Josh 7:1 the people of Israel B faith in regard to
Judg 7:20 blew the trumpets and B the jars, holding in
8:17 And he B down the tower of Penuel, and
1Sam 5:9 old, so that tumors B out upon them.
2Sam 2:32 night, and the day B upon them at Hebron.
23:16 the three mighty men B through the camp of
1Kgs 19:11 rent the mountains, and B in pieces the rocks
2Kgs 11:18 and his images they B in pieces, and they
14:13 came to Jerusalem, and B down the wall of
18:4 the high places, and B the pillars, and cut
18:4 And he B in pieces the bronze serpent that
23:7 And he B down the houses of the male
23:8 to Beer-sheba; and he B down the high places
23:12 he pulled down and B in pieces, and cast
23:14 And he B in pieces the pillars, and cut
23:15 pulled down and he B in pieces its stones,
25:10 captain of the guard, B down the walls around
25:13 the LORD, the Chaldeans B in pieces, and carried
1Chr 11:18 the three mighty men B through the camp of
15:13 the LORD our God B forth upon us, because
2Chr 14:3 the high places, and B down the pillars and
23:17 and his images they B in pieces, and they
25:23 him to Jerusalem, and B down the wall of
26:6 against the Philistines, and B down the wall of
26:19 with the priests leprosy B out on his forehead,
31:1 cities of Judah and B in pieces the pillars
31:1 down the Asherim and B down the high places
34:4 And they B down the altars of the Baals
34:4 above them; and he B in pieces the Asherim
34:7 ruins round about, he B down the altars, and
36:19 house of God, and B down the wall of
Job 16:12 at ease, and he B me asunder; he seized
29:17 I B the fangs of the unrighteous, and made
Ps 18:12 brightness before him there B through his clouds
74:6 its carved wood they B down with hatchets and
76:3 There he B the flashing arrows, the shield, the
105:16 on the land, and B every staff of bread,
106:18 Fire also B out in their company; the flame
106:29 doings, and a plague B out among them.
107:14 darkness and gloom, and B their bonds asunder.
Prov 3:20 his knowledge the deeps B forth, and the clouds
Is 22:10 of Jerusalem, and you B down the houses to
Jer 2:20 "For long ago you B your yoke and burst
28:10 Jeremiah the prophet, and B them.
31:32 my covenant which they B, though I was their
39:8 of the people, and B down the walls of
52:14 captain of the guard, B down all the walls
52:17 the LORD, the Chaldeans B in pieces, and carried
Ezek 17:4 of the cedar; he B off the topmost of
17:16 covenant with him he B, in Babylon he shall
17:18 despised the oath and B the covenant, because he
17:19 my covenant which he B, I will requite upon
29:7 with the hand, you B, and tore all their
29:7 leaned upon you, you B, and made all their
Dan 2:34 iron and clay, and B them in pieces;
2:45 hand, and that it B in pieces the iron,
3:48 forty-nine cubits, and it B through and burned those
6:24 lions overpowered them and B all their bones in
7:7 teeth; it devoured and B in pieces, and stamped
7:19 and which devoured and B in pieces, and stamped
8:7 struck the ram and B his two horns; and
Zech 11:10 staff Grace, and I B it, annulling the covenant
11:14 Then I B my second staff Union, annulling the
1Mac 6:62 the place was, he B the oath he had
11:53 But he B his word about all that he
12:32 Then he B camp and went to Damascus, and
13:19 hundred talents, but Trypho B his word and did
15:27 receive them, and he B all the agreements he
2Mac 10:36 Others B open the gates and let in the
Mt 14:19 heaven, and blessed, and B and gave the loaves
15:36 having given thanks he B them and gave them
26:26 bread, and blessed, and B it, and gave it
Mk 5:4 and the fetters he B in pieces; and no
6:41 heaven, and blessed, and B the loaves, and gave
8:6 having given thanks he B them and gave them
8:19 When I B the five loaves for the five
14:3 very costly, and she B the flask and poured
14:22 bread, and blessed, and B it, and gave it
14:72 And he B down and wept.
Lk 6:48 flood arose, the stream B against that house, and
6:49 against which the stream B, and immediately it fell,
8:29 and fetters, but he B the bonds and was
9:16 heaven, and blessed and B them, and gave them
22:19 had given thanks he B it and gave it
24:30 bread and blessed, and B it, and gave it
Jn 5:17 because he not only B the sabbath but also
19:32 the soldiers came and B the legs of the
Acts 13:43 meeting of the synagogue B up, many Jews and
27:35 presence of all he B it and began to
1Cor 11:24 had given thanks, he B it, and said, "This

BROKEN (152)

Gen 17:14 his people; he has B my covenant."
Ex 6:9 Moses, because of their B spirit and their cruel
32:25 that the people had B loose (for Aaron had
Lev 6:28 is boiled shall be B; but if it is
11:35 stove, it shall be B in pieces; they are
13:20 of leprosy, it has B out in the boil.
13:25 is leprosy; it has B out in the burn,
13:39 is tetter that has B out in the skin;
15:12 discharge touches shall be B; and every vessel of
26:13 slaves; and I have B the bars of your
Num 15:31 the LORD, and has B his commandment, that person
Deut 21:6 heifer whose neck was B in the valley;
Judg 6:28 altar of Baal was B down, and the Asherah
1Sam 2:4 of the mighty are B, but the feeble gird
2:10 the LORD shall be B to pieces; against them
4:18 and his neck was B and he died, for
2Sam 5:20 said, "The LORD has B through my enemies before
6:8 because the LORD had B forth upon Uzzah; and
1Kgs 5:9 I will have them B up there, and you

2Kgs 18:21 now on Egypt, that B reed of a staff,
1Chr 13:11 because the LORD had B forth upon Uzzah; and
14:11 David said, "God has B through my enemies by
2Chr 14:13 alive; for they were B before the LORD and
15:6 They were B in pieces, nation against nation and
24:7 that wicked woman, had B into the house of
32:5 the wall that was B down, and raised towers
33:3 his father Hezekiah had B down, and erected altars
Ezra 10:2 addressed Ezra: "We have B faith with our God
Neh 1:3 wall of Jerusalem is B down, and its gates
2:13 of Jerusalem which were B down and its gates
Job 4:10 lion, the teeth of the young lions, are B
17:1 My spirit is B, my days are extinct, the
17:11 past, my plans are B off, the desires of
24:20 remembered; so wickedness is B like a tree.'
31:22 let my arm be B from its socket.
38:15 light is withheld, and their uplifted arm is B
Ps 31:12 have become like a B vessel.
34:20 all his bones; not one of them is B
37:15 their own heart, and their bows shall be B
37:17 the wicked shall be B; but the LORD upholds
44:19 that thou shouldst have B us in the place
51:8 bones which thou hast B rejoice.
51:17 to God is a B spirit; a broken and
51:17 a broken spirit; a B and contrite heart, O
60:1 thou hast rejected us, B our defenses; thou hast
69:20 Insults have B my heart, so that I am
80:12 Why then hast thou B down its walls, so
102:23 He has B my strength in mid-course; he has
119:126 LORD to act, for thy law has been B
124:7 fowlers; the snare is B, and we have escaped!
Prov 6:15 moment he will be B beyond healing.
15:13 but by sorrow of heart the spirit is B
18:14 endure sickness; but a B spirit who can bear?
24:31 its stone wall was B down.
25:28 is like a city B into and left without
29:1 neck will suddenly be B beyond healing.
Eccl 4:12 A threefold cord is not quickly B
12:6 the golden bowl is B, or the pitcher is
12:6 or the pitcher is B at the fountain, or
12:6 fountain, or the wheel B at the cistern,
Wis 4:5 The branches will be B off before they come
Sir 13:2 will strike against it, and will itself be B
21:14 fool is like a B jar; it will hold
43:15 and the hailstones are B in pieces.
Is 5:27 loose, not a sandal-thong B;
7:8 years Ephraim will be B to pieces so that
8:9 Be B, you peoples, and be dismayed; give ear,
8:15 shall fall and be B; they shall be snared
9:4 his oppressor, thou hast B as on the day
14:5 The LORD has B the staff of the wicked,
14:29 which smote you is B, for from the serpent's
24:5 violated the statutes, B the everlasting covenant.
24:10 city of chaos is B down, every house is
24:19 The earth is utterly B, the earth is rent
27:11 are dry, they are B; women come and make
28:13 fall backward, and be B, and snared, and taken.
33:8 Covenants are B, witnesses are despised, there is no
33:20 up, nor will any of its cords be B
36:6 relying on Egypt, that B reed of a staff,
Jer 2:13 out cisterns for themselves, B cisterns, that can hold
2:16 Memphis and Tahpanhes have B the crown of your
5:5 they all alike had B the yoke, they had
10:20 all my cords are B; my children have gone
11:10 house of Judah have B my covenant which I
22:28 man Coniah a despised, B pot, a vessel no
23:9 prophets: My heart is B within me, all my
28:2 of Israel: I have B the yoke of the
28:12 the prophet Hananiah had B the yoke-bars from off
28:13 the LORD: You have B wooden bars, but I
33:21 my servant may be B, so that he shall
48:1 put to shame and B down;
48:17 the mighty scepter is B, the glorious staff.'
48:20 shame, for it is B; wail and cry!
48:25 and his arm is B, says the LORD.
48:38 lamentation; for I have B Moab like a vessel
48:39 How it is B
50:23 of the whole earth is cut down and B
51:8 has fallen and been B; wail for her!
51:30 her dwellings are on fire, her bars are B
51:56 taken, their bows are B in pieces; for the
Lam 2:2 his wrath he has B down the strongholds of
2:6 He has B down his booth like that of
2:9 he has ruined and B her bars; her king
3:4 skin waste away, and B my bones;
Bar 6:17 useless when it is B, so are the gods
6:43 attractive as herself and her cord was not B
Ezek 6:4 incense altars shall be B; and I will cast
6:6 and ruined, your idols B and destroyed, your incense
6:9 captive, when I have B their wanton heart which
26:2 of the peoples is B, it has swung open
30:8 fire to Egypt, and all her helpers are B
30:16 breached, and its walls B down.
30:21 of man, I have B the arm of Pharaoh
30:22 the one that was B; and I will make
31:12 its boughs will lie B in all the watercourses
32:28 So you shall be B and lie among the
44:7 You have B my covenant, in addition to all
Dan 2:35 gold, all together were B in pieces, and became
3:44 power and dominion, and let their strength be B
8:8 the great horn was B, and instead of it
8:22 the horn that was B, in place of which
8:25 but, by no human hand, he shall be B
11:4 his kingdom shall be B and divided toward the
11:20 days he shall be B, neither in anger nor
11:22 away before him and B, and the prince of
14:33 boiled pottage and had B bread into a bowl,
Hos 8:1 LORD, because they have B my covenant, and
8:6 of Samaria shall be B to pieces.
Nah 1:6 and the rocks are B asunder by him.
2Mac 9:11 Then it was that, B in spirit, he began
Mt 14:20 baskets full of the B pieces left over.
15:37 baskets full of the B pieces left over.
21:44 this stone will be B to pieces; but when
24:43 let his house be B into.
Mk 6:43 twelve baskets full of B pieces and of the
8:8 they took up the B pieces left over, seven
8:19 many baskets full of B pieces did you take
8:20 many baskets full of B pieces did you take
Lk 9:17 over, twelve baskets of B pieces.
12:39 his house to be B into.
20:18 that stone will be B to pieces; but when
Jn 7:23 Moses may not be B, are you angry with
10:35 (and scripture cannot be B,
19:31 their legs might be B, and that they might
19:36 fulfilled, "Not a bone of him shall be B
Acts 20:11 gone up and had B bread and eaten, he
27:41 and the stern was B up by the surf.
Rom 11:17 of the branches were B off, and you, a
11:19 will say, "Branches were B off so that I
11:20 They were B off because of their unbelief, but
Eph 2:14 both one, and has B down the dividing wall
Rev 2:27 when earthen pots are B in pieces, even as

BROKENHEARTED (4)

Ps 34:18 is near to the B, and saves the crushed
109:16 and needy and the B to their death.
147:3 He heals the B, and binds up their wounds.
Is 61:1 to bind up the B, to proclaim liberty to

BRONZE (161)

Gen 4:22 of all instruments of B and iron.
Ex 25:3 them: gold, silver, and B,
26:11 make fifty clasps of B, and put the clasps
26:37 cast five bases of B for them.
27:2 with it, and you shall overlay it with B
27:3 firepans; all its utensils you shall make of B
27:4 grating, a network of B; and upon the net
27:4 you shall make four B rings at its four
27:6 and overlay them with B;
27:10 their bases twenty, of B, but the hooks of
27:11 their bases twenty, of B, but the hooks of
27:17 shall be of silver, and their bases of B
27:18 hangings of fine twined linen and bases of B
27:19 the pegs of the court, shall be of B
30:18 make a laver of B, with its base of
30:18 with its base of B, for washing.
31:4 in gold, silver, and B,
35:5 offering: gold, silver, and B;
35:16 with its grating of B, its poles, and all
35:24 offering of silver or B brought it as the
35:32 gold and silver and B,
36:18 made fifty clasps of B to couple the tent
36:38 of gold, but their five bases were of B
38:2 piece with it, and he overlaid it with B
38:3 the firepans: all its utensils he made of B
38:4 grating, a network of B, under its ledge, extending
38:5 four corners of the B grating as holders for
38:6 poles of acacia wood, and overlaid them with B
38:8 made the laver of B and its base of
38:8 and its base of B, from the mirrors of
38:10 their bases twenty, of B, but the hooks of

B

38:11 their bases twenty, of B, but the hooks of
38:17 the pillars were of B, but the hooks of
38:19 four bases were of B, their hooks of silver,
38:20 and for the court round about were of B
38:29 And the B that was contributed was seventy talents,
38:30 tent of meeting, the B altar and the bronze
38:30 bronze altar and the B grating for it and
39:39 of the tent; the B altar, and its grating
39:39 and its grating of B, its poles, and all
Lev 6:28 is boiled in a B vessel, that shall be
Num 16:39 the priest took the B censers, which those who
21:9 So Moses made a B serpent, and set it
21:9 would look at the B serpent and live.
31:22 gold, the silver, the B, the iron, the tin,
Deut 33:25 shall be iron and B; and as your days,
Josh 6:19 gold, and vessels of B and iron, are sacred
6:24 and the vessels of B and of iron, they
22:8 cattle, with silver, gold, B, and iron, and with
Judg 16:21 and bound him with B fetters; and he ground
1Sam 17:5 had a helmet of B on his head, and
17:5 of the coat was five thousand shekels of B
17:6 he had greaves of B upon his legs, and
17:6 and a javelin of B slung between his shoulders.
17:38 put a helmet of B on his head, and
2Sam 8:8 cities of Hadadezer, King David took very much B
8:10 of gold, and of B;
21:16 three hundred shekels of B, and who was girded
22:35 that my arms can bend a bow of B
1Kgs 4:13 cities with walls and B bars);
7:14 Tyre, a worker in B; and he was full
7:14 understanding, and skill, for making any work in B
7:15 He cast two pillars of B
7:16 two capitals of molten B, to set upon the
7:27 the ten stands of B; each stand was four
7:30 each stand had four B wheels and axles of
7:30 wheels and axles of B; and at the four
7:38 made ten lavers of B; each laver held forty
7:45 Hiram made for King Solomon, were of burnished B
7:47 the weight of the B was not found out.
8:64 peace offerings, because the B altar that was before
14:27 their stead shields of B, and committed them to
2Kgs 16:14 And the B altar which was before the LORD
16:15 the sacrifice; but the B altar shall be for
16:17 sea from off the B oxen that were under
18:4 broke in pieces the B serpent that Moses had
25:13 And the pillars of B that were in the
25:13 the stands and the B sea that were in
25:13 pieces, and carried the B to Babylon.
25:14 all the vessels of B used in the temple
25:16 of the LORD, the B of all these vessels
25:17 was a capital of B; the height of the
25:17 and pomegranates, all of B, were upon the capital
1Chr 15:19 Ethan, were to sound B cymbals;
18:8 David took very much B; with it Solomon made
18:8 it Solomon made the B sea and the pillars
18:8 sea and the pillars and the vessels of B
18:10 of silver, and of B;
22:3 clamps, as well as B in quantities beyond weighing,
22:14 talents of silver, and B and iron beyond weighing,
22:16 in working gold, silver, B, and iron.
29:2 of silver, and the B for the things of
29:2 for the things of B, the iron for the
29:7 eighteen thousand talents of B, and a hundred
2Chr 1:5 in Jerusalem.) Moreover the B altar that Bezalel the
1:6 up there to the B altar before the LORD,
2:7 work in gold, silver, B, and iron, and in
2:14 work in gold, silver, B, iron, stone, and wood,
4:1 made an altar of B, twenty cubits long, and
4:9 overlaid their doors with B;
4:16 Huram-abi made of burnished B for King Solomon
4:18 the weight of the B was not ascertained.
6:13 Solomon had made a B platform five cubits long,
7:7 peace offerings, because the B altar Solomon had
12:10 their stead shields of B, and committed them to
24:12 workers in iron and B to repair the house
33:11 him with fetters of B and brought him to
Ezra 8:27 vessels of fine bright B as precious as gold.
Job 6:12 the strength of stones, or is my flesh B
20:24 an iron weapon; a B arrow will strike him
40:18 bones are tubes of B, his limbs like bars
41:27 iron as straw, and B as rotten wood.
Ps 18:34 that my arms can bend a bow of B
68:31 Let B be brought from Egypt; let Ethiopia hasten
107:16 shatters the doors of B, and cuts in two
Sir 28:20 fetters are fetters of B;
Is 45:2 pieces the doors of B and cut asunder the
60:17 Instead of B I will bring gold, and instead
60:17 silver; instead of wood, B, instead of stones, iron.
Jer 1:18 an iron pillar, and B walls, against the whole
6:28 with slanders; they are B and iron, all of
15:12 one break iron, iron from the north, and B
15:20 a fortified wall of B; they will fight against
52:17 And the pillars of B that were in the
52:17 the stands and the B sea that were in
52:17 and carried all the B to Babylon.
52:18 all the vessels of B used in the temple
52:20 one sea, the twelve B bulls which were under
52:20 of the LORD, the B of all these things
52:22 was a capital of B; the height of the
52:22 and pomegranates, all of B, were upon the capital
Ezek 1:4 midst of the fire, as it were gleaming B
1:7 a calf's foot; and they sparkled like burnished B
1:27 as it were gleaming B, like the appearance of
8:2 like the appearance of brightness, like gleaming B
9:2 and stood beside the B altar.
22:18 of them, silver and B and tin and iron
22:20 men gather silver and B and iron and lead
27:13 men and vessels of B for your merchandise.
40:3 whose appearance was like B, with a line of
Dan 2:32 belly and thighs of B,
2:35 iron, the clay, the B, the silver, and the
2:39 a third kingdom of B, which shall rule over
2:45 pieces the iron, the B, the clay, the silver,
4:15 band of iron and B, amid the tender grass
4:23 band of iron and B, in the tender grass
5:4 of gold and silver, B, iron, wood, and stone.
5:23 silver and gold, of B, iron, wood, and stone,
7:19 iron and claws of B; and which devoured and
10:6 the gleam of burnished B, and the sound of
Mic 4:13 iron and your hoofs B; you shall beat in
Zech 6:1 mountains; and the mountains were mountains of B
1Mac 8:22 wrote in reply, on B tablets, and sent to
14:18 wrote to him on B tablets to renew with
14:27 made a record on B tablets and put it
14:48 inscribe this decree upon B tablets, to put them
Mk 7:4 washing of cups and pots and vessels of B
Rev 1:15 feet were like burnished B, refined as in a
2:18 of fire, and whose feet are like burnished B
9:20 gold and silver and B and stone and wood,
18:12 articles of costly wood, B, iron and marble,

BROOCHES

Ex 35:22 a willing heart brought B and earrings and signet

BROOD (10)

Num 32:14 your fathers' stead, a B of sinful men, to
Job 30:8 A senseless, a disreputable B, they have been
Wis 4:3 But the prolific B of the ungodly will be
Jer 17:11 partridge that gathers a B which she did not
Mt 3:7 said to them, "You B of vipers!
12:34 You B of vipers!
23:32 You serpents, you B of vipers, how are you
23:36 a hen gathers her B under her wings, and
Lk 3:7 baptized by him, "You B of vipers!
13:34 a hen gathers her B under her wings, and

BROOK (48)

Lev 23:40 and willows of the B; and you shall rejoice
Num 34:5 from Azmon to the B of Egypt, and its
Deut 2:13 and go over the B Zered.' So we went
2:13 we went over the B Zered.
2:14 until we crossed the B Zered was thirty-eight years,
9:21 of it into the B that descended out of
Josh 15:4 goes out by the B of Egypt, and comes
15:47 its villages; to the B of Egypt, and the
16:8 goes westward to the B Kanah, and ends at
17:9 went down to the B Kanah.
17:9 the south of the B, among the cities of
17:9 north side of the B and ends at the
19:11 touches Dabbesheth, then the B which is east of
1Sam 17:40 smooth stones from the B, and put them in
30:9 they came to the B Besor, where those stayed
30:10 exhausted to cross the B Besor.
30:21 been left at the B Besor; and they went
2Sam 15:23 the king crossed the B Kidron, and all the
17:20 have gone over the B of water." And when
1Kgs 2:37 forth, and cross the B Kidron, know for certain
8:65 of Hamath to the B of Egypt, before the
15:13 burned it at the B Kidron.
17:3 hide yourself by the B Cherith, that is east
17:4 shall drink from the B, and I have commanded
17:5 and dwelt by the B Cherith that is east

17:6 in the evening; and he drank from the B
17:7 after a while the B dried up, because there
18:40 them down to the B Kishon, and killed them
2Kgs 23:6 outside Jerusalem, to the B Kidron, and burned it
23:6 burned it at the B Kidron, and beat it
23:12 of them into the B Kidron.
24:7 of Egypt from the B of Egypt to the
2Chr 7:8 of Hamath to the B of Egypt.
15:16 burned it at the B Kidron.
29:16 it out to the B Kidron.
32:4 the springs and the B that flowed through the
Jud 2:8 their valleys, and every B and river shall be
2:24 hilltop cities along the B Abron, as far as
7:18 near Chusi beside the B Mochmur.
Job 40:22 the willows of the B surround him.
Ps 110:7 will drink from the B by the way; therefore
Is 15:7 carry away over the B of the Willows.
27:12 river Euphrates to the B of Egypt the LORD
Jer 15:18 me like a deceitful B, like waters that fail?
31:40 as far as the B Kidron, to the corner
Ezek 47:19 Meribath-kadesh, thence along the B of Egypt to the
48:28 Meribath-kadesh, thence along the B of Egypt to the
Amos 6:14 of Hamath to the B of the Arabah."

BROOKS (8)

Deut 8:7 land, a land of B of water, of fountains
10:7 Jotbathah, a land with B of water.
2Sam 23:30 Pirathon, Hiddai of the B of Gaash,
1Chr 11:32 Pirathon, Hurai of the B of Gaash, Abiel the
Ps 74:15 cleave open springs and B; thou didst dry up
Is 30:25 hill there will be B running with water, in
Jer 31:9 make them walk by B of water, in a
Joel 1:19 thee because the water B are dried up, and

BROOM (5)

1Kgs 19:4 sat down under a B tree; and he asked
19:5 and slept under a B tree; and behold, an
Job 30:4 and to warm themselves the roots of the B
Ps 120:4 glowing coals of the B tree!
Is 14:23 sweep it with the B of destruction, says the

BROTH (4)

Judg 6:19 a basket, and the B he put in a
6:20 rock, and pour the B over them." And he
Is 65:4 eat swine's flesh, and B of abominable things is
Ezek 24:10 and empty out the B, and let the bones

BROTHEL

Bar 6:11 some of it to the harlots in the B

BROTHER (444)

Gen 4:2 again, she bore his B Abel.
4:8 said to Abel his B, "Let us go out
4:8 rose up against his B Abel, and killed him.
4:9 LORD said to Cain, "Where is Abel your B
4:9 know; am I my B's keeper?"
4:10 The voice of your B's blood is crying to
4:11 mouth to receive your B's blood from your hand.
4:21 His B's name was Jubal; he was the father
9:5 man; of every man's B I will require the
10:21 of Eber, the elder B of Japheth, children were
10:25 was divided, and his B's name was Joktan.
12:5 wife, and Lot his B's son, and all their
14:12 the son of Abram's B, who dwelt in Sodom,
14:13 of Mamre the Amorite, B of Eshcol and of
20:5 said, 'He is my B In the integrity of
20:13 we come, say of me, He is my B
20:16 I have given your B a thousand pieces of
22:20 borne children to your B Nahor:
22:21 the first-born, Buz his B, Kemuel the father of
22:23 These eight Milcah bore to Nahor, Abraham's B
24:15 wife of Nahor, Abraham's B, came out with her
24:29 Rebekah had a B whose name was Laban; and
24:53 also gave to her B and to her mother
24:55 Her B and her mother said, "Let the maiden
25:26 Afterward his B came forth, and his hand had
27:6 father speak to your B Esau,
27:11 his mother, "Behold, my B Esau is a hairy
27:23 were hairy like his B Esau's hands; so he
27:30 his father, Esau his B came in from his
27:35 But he said, "Your B came with guile, and
27:40 you shall serve your B; but when you break
27:41 I will kill my B Jacob."
27:42 to him, "Behold, your B Esau comforts himself by
27:43 flee to Laban my B in Haran,
27:44 a while, until your B's fury turns away;
27:45 turns away; until your B's anger turns away, and
28:2 one of the daughters of Laban your mother's B
28:5 Bethuel the Aramean, the B of Rebekah, Jacob's and
29:10 of Laban his mother's B, and the sheep of
29:10 of Laban his mother's B, Jacob went up and
29:10 and watered the flock of Laban his mother's B
32:3 him to Esau his B in the land of
32:6 "We came to your B Esau, and he is
32:11 the hand of my B, from the hand of
32:13 a present for his B Esau,
32:17 foremost, "When Esau my B meets you, and asks
33:3 seven times, until he came near to his B
33:9 "I have enough, my B; keep what you have
35:1 you fled from your B Esau."
35:7 himself to him when he fled from his B
36:6 land away from his B Jacob.
37:26 if we slay our B and conceal his blood?
37:27 for he is our B, our own flesh." And
38:8 "Go in to your B's wife, and perform the
38:8 to her, and raise up offspring for your B
38:9 went in to his B's wife he spilled the
38:9 ground, lest he should give offspring to his B
38:29 his hand, behold, his B came out; and she
38:30 Afterward his B came out with the scarlet thread
42:4 not send Benjamin, Joseph's B, with his brothers, for
42:15 place unless your youngest B comes here.
42:16 let him bring your B, while you remain in
42:20 and bring your youngest B to me; so your
42:21 are guilty concerning our B, in that we saw
42:34 Bring your youngest B to me; then I shall
42:34 deliver to you your B, and you shall trade
42:38 with you, for his B is dead, and he
43:3 my face, unless your B is with you.'
43:4 you will send our B with us, we will
43:5 my face, unless your B is with you.'"
43:6 to tell the man that you had another B
43:7 Have you another B What we told him was
43:7 would say, 'Bring your B down'?"
43:13 Take also your B, and arise, go again to
43:14 send back your other B and Benjamin.
43:29 eyes, and saw his B Benjamin, his mother's son,
43:29 "Is this your youngest B, of whom you spoke
43:30 heart yearned for his B, and he sought a
44:19 a father, or a B
44:20 man, and a young B, the child of his
44:20 old age; and his B is dead, and he
44:23 servants, 'Unless your youngest B comes down with
44:26 If our youngest B goes with us, then we
44:26 face unless our youngest B is with us.'
45:4 said, "I am your B, Joseph, whom you sold
45:12 the eyes of my B Benjamin see, that it
45:14 he fell upon his B Benjamin's neck and wept;
48:19 great; nevertheless his younger B shall be greater
Ex 4:14 there not Aaron, your B, the Levite?
7:1 Pharaoh; and Aaron your B shall be your prophet.
7:2 you; and Aaron your B shall tell Pharaoh to
28:1 to you Aaron your B, and his sons with
28:2 garments for Aaron your B, for glory and for
28:4 garments for Aaron your B and his sons to
28:41 them upon Aaron your B, and upon his sons
32:27 slay every man his B, and every man his
32:29 son and of his B, that he may bestow
Lev 16:2 Moses, "Tell Aaron your B not to come at
18:14 nakedness of your father's B, that is, you shall
18:16 the nakedness of your B's wife; she is your
18:16 wife; she is your B's nakedness.
19:17 shall not hate your B in your heart, but
20:21 a man takes his B's wife, it is impurity;
20:21 he has uncovered his B's nakedness, they shall be
21:2 son, his daughter, his B,
25:25 "If your B becomes poor, and sells part of
25:25 and redeem what his B has sold.
25:35 "And if your B becomes poor, and cannot maintain
25:36 your God; that your B may live beside you.
25:39 "And if your B becomes poor beside you, and
25:47 becomes rich, and your B beside him becomes poor
Num 6:7 his mother, nor for B or sister, if they
20:8 you and Aaron your B, and tell the rock
20:14 Edom, "Thus says your B Israel: You know all
27:13 your people, as your B Aaron was gathered,
36:2 inheritance of Zelophehad our B to his daughters.
Deut 1:16 a man and his B or the alien that
13:6 "If your B, the son of your mother, or
15:2 of his neighbor, his B, because the LORD's release
15:3 yours is with your B your hand shall release.
15:7 hand against your poor B,

B

15:9 hostile to your poor B, and you give him
15:11 your hand to your B, to the needy and
15:12 "If your B, a Hebrew man, or a Hebrew
17:15 a foreigner over you, who is not your B
19:18 and has accused his B falsely,
19:19 to do to his B; so you shall purge
22:1 shall not see your B's ox or his sheep
22:1 them; you shall take them back to your B
22:2 with you until your B seeks it; then you
22:4 shall not see your B's ass or his ox
23:7 for he is your B; you shall not abhor
23:19 upon interest to your B, interest on money, interest
23:20 interest, but to your B you shall not lend
25:3 stripes than these, your B be degraded in your
25:5 a stranger; her husband's B shall go in to
25:5 duty of a husband's B to her.
25:6 the name of his B who is dead, that
25:7 wish to take his B's wife, then his brother's
25:7 brother's wife, then his B's wife shall go up
25:7 and say, 'My husband's B refuses to perpetuate his
25:7 refuses to perpetuate his B's name in Israel; he
25:7 duty of a husband's B to me.'
25:9 take her,' then his B's wife shall go up
25:9 not build up his B's house.'
28:54 grudge food to his B, to the wife of
32:50 people, as Aaron your B died in Mount Hor
Josh 15:17 son of Kenaz, the B of Caleb, took it;
Judg 1:3 said to Simeon his B, "Come up with me
1:13 of Kenaz, Caleb's younger B, took it; and he
1:17 went with Simeon his B, and they defeated the
3:9 them, Othni-el the son of Kenaz, Caleb's younger B
9:3 follow Abimelech, for they said, "He is our B
9:21 and dwelt there, for fear of Abimelech his B
9:24 laid upon Abimelech their B, who slew them, and
21:6 compassion for Benjamin their B, and said, "One
1Sam 14:3 son of Ahitub, Ichabod's B, son of Phinehas, son
17:28 Now Eliab his eldest B heard when he spoke
20:29 the city, and my B has commanded me to
26:6 Hittite, and to Joab's B Abishai the son of
2Sam 1:26 distressed for you, my B Jonathan; very pleasant
2:22 my face to your B Joab?"
3:27 he died, for the blood of Asahel his B
3:30 Joab and Abishai his B slew Abner, because he
3:30 he had killed their B Asahel in the battle
4:6 Rechab and Baanah his B slipped in.
4:9 Rechab and Baanah his B, the sons of Rimmon
10:10 charge of Abishai his B, and he arrayed them
13:3 son of Shimeah, David's B; and Jonadab was a
13:4 "I love Tamar, my B Absalom's sister."
13:7 saying, "Go to your B Amnon's house, and prepare
13:8 Tamar went to her B Amnon's house, where he
13:10 brought them into the chamber to Amnon her B
13:12 answered him, "No, my B, do not force me;
13:16 to him, "No, my B; for this wrong in
13:20 And her B Absalom said to her, "Has Amnon
13:20 her, "Has Amnon your B been with you?
13:20 sister; he is your B; do not take this
13:20 desolate woman, in her B Absalom's house.
13:26 not, pray let my B Amnon go with us."
13:32 son of Shimeah, David's B, said, "Let not my
14:7 man who struck his B, that we may kill
14:7 the life of his B whom he slew'; and
18:2 son of Zeruiah, Joab's B, and one third under
20:9 to Amasa, "Is it well with you, my B
20:10 Joab and Abishai his B pursued Sheba the son
21:21 son of Shimei, David's B, slew him.
23:18 Now Abishai, the B of Joab, the son of
23:24 Asahel the B of Joab was one of the
1Kgs 1:10 Benaiah or the mighty men or Solomon his B
2:7 met me when I fled from Absalom your B
2:21 given to Adonijah your B as his wife."
2:22 he is my elder B, and on his side
9:13 are these which you have given me, my B
13:30 and they mourned over him, saying, "Alas, my B
20:32 He is my B
20:33 and said, "Yes, your B Ben-hadad." Then he said,
2Kgs 1:17 Jehoram, his B, became king in his stead in
1Chr 1:19 the name of his B Joktan.
2:32 sons of Jada, Shammai's B: Jether and Jonathan;
2:42 sons of Caleb the B of Jerahmeel: Mareshah his
4:11 Chelub, the B of Shuhah, was the father of
6:39 of Israel; and his B Asaph, who stood on
7:16 the name of his B was Sheresh; and his
7:34 sons of Shemer his B: Rohgah, Jehubbah, and Aram.
7:35 sons of Helem his B: Zophah, Imna, Shelesh, and
8:39 sons of Eshek his B: Ulam his first-born, Jeush
11:20 Now Abishai, the B of Joab, was chief of
11:26 armies were Asahel the B of Joab, Elhanan the
11:38 of Ezbai, Joel the B of Nathan, Mibhar the
11:45 Shimri, and Joha his B, the Tizite,
19:11 charge of Abishai his B, and they were arrayed
19:15 fled before Abishai, Joab's B, and entered the city.
20:5 Jair slew Lahmi the B of Goliath the Gittite,
20:7 son of Shimea, David's B, slew him.
24:25 The B of Micah, Isshiah; of the sons of
24:31 house and his younger B alike, cast lots, just
26:22 Zetham and Joel his B, were in charge of
27:7 Asahel the B of Joab was fourth, for the
2Chr 31:12 Levite, with Shimei his B as second;
31:13 Conaniah and Shimei his B, by the appointment of
36:4 Egypt made Eliakim his B king over Judah and
36:4 Neco took Jehoahaz his B and carried him to
36:10 LORD, and made his B Zedekiah king over Judah
Neh 5:7 them, "You are exacting interest, each from his B
7:2 appointed, I gave my B Hanani and Hananiah the
Tob 1:14 trust with Gabael, the B of Gabrias.
1:21 the son of my B Anael, over all the
5:6 have stayed with our B Gabael."
5:10 said to him, "My B, to what tribe and
5:11 like to know, my B, your people and your
5:13 Tobit said to him, "You are welcome, my B
5:13 My B, you come of good stock.
6:6 said to the angel, B Azarias, of what use
6:10 to the young man, B, today we shall stay
6:13 said to the angel, B Azarias, I have heard
6:15 Now listen to me, B, for she will become
7:4 "Do you know our B Tobit?" And they said,
7:8 Tobias said to Raphael, B Azarias, speak of those
9:2 and said to him, B Azarias, take a servant
10:12 you back safely, dear B, and grant me to
11:2 "Are you not aware, B, of how you left
Jud 8:26 was keeping the sheep of Laban, his mother's B
Esth 15:9 I am your B
Job 1:13 wine in their eldest B's house;
1:18 wine in their eldest B's house;
30:29 I am a B of jackals, and a companion
Ps 35:14 my friend or my B; I went about as
50:20 and speak against your B; you slander your own
Prov 17:17 all times, and a B is born for adversity.
18:9 his work is a B to him who destroys.
18:19 A B helped is like a strong city, but
18:24 is a friend who sticks closer than a B
27:10 not go to your B's house in the day
27:10 is near than a B who is far away.
Eccl 4:8 one, either son or B, yet there is no
Song 8:1 you were like a B to me, that nursed
Wis 10:3 he perished because in rage he slew his B
10:10 man fled from his B's wrath, she guided him
Sir 7:12 a lie against your B, nor do the like
7:18 money, or a real B for the gold of
29:10 the sake of a B or a friend, and
29:27 an honored person; my B has come to stay
33:19 son or wife, to B or friend, do not
33:31 treat him as a B, for as your own
45:6 He exalted Aaron, the B of Moses, a holy
Is 3:6 takes hold of his B in the house of
9:19 fuel for the fire; no man spares his B
19:2 every man against his B and every man against
41:6 and says to his B, "Take courage!"
Jer 9:4 no trust in any B; for every brother is
9:4 any brother; for every B is a supplanter, and
22:18 him, saying, 'Ah my B or 'Ah sister!' They
23:35 every one to his B, 'What has the LORD
31:34 neighbor and each his B, saying, 'Know the LORD,'
34:9 that no one should enslave a Jew, his B
34:17 every one to his B and to his neighbor;
Ezek 18:18 practiced extortion, robbed his B, and did what is
33:30 another, each to his B, 'Come, and hear what
38:21 GOD; every man's sword will be against his B
44:25 son or daughter, for B or unmarried sister they
Hos 2:1 Say to your B, "My people," and to your
12:3 womb he took his B by the heel, and
Amos 1:11 because he pursued his B with the sword, and
Obad 1:10 violence done to your B Jacob, shame shall cover
1:12 the day of your B in the day of
Mic 7:2 and each hunts his B with a net.
Zech 7:9 mercy each to his B,
7:10 devise evil against his B in your heart."
Mal 1:2 "Is not Esau Jacob's B
1Mac 2:65 know that Simeon your B is wise in counsel;
5:17 said to Simon his B, "Choose your men and
5:17 I and Jonathan my B will go to Gilead."

5:24 Maccabeus and Jonathan his B crossed the Jordan
5:55 Gilead and Simon his B was in Galilee before
9:19 Simon took Judas their B and buried him in
9:29 the death of your B Judas there has been
9:31 leadership and took the place of Judas his B
9:33 Jonathan and Simon his B and all who were
9:35 And Jonathan sent his B as leader of the
9:37 Jonathan and Simon his B, "The sons of Jambri
9:38 blood of John their B, and went up and
9:42 the blood of their B, they returned to the
9:65 Jonathan left Simon his B in the city, while
10:18 "King Alexander to his B Jonathan, greeting.
10:74 Jerusalem, and Simon his B met him to help
11:30 Demetrius to Jonathan his B and to the nation
11:59 Simon his B he made governor from the Ladder
11:64 them, but left his B Simon in the country.
13:8 leader in place of Judas and Jonathan your B
13:14 place of Jonathan his B, and that he was
13:15 money that Jonathan your B owed the royal treasury,
13:25 bones of Jonathan his B, and buried him in
14:17 heard that Simon his B had become high priest
16:3 my place and my B's, and go out and
16:9 that time Judas the B of John was wounded,
2Mac 4:7 the kingdom, Jason the B of Onias obtained the
4:23 Jason sent Menelaus, the B of the previously
4:26 after supplanting his own B was supplanted by
4:29 Menelaus left his own B Lysimachus as deputy in
7:7 After the first B had died in this way,
7:8 tortures as the first B had done.
7:24 The youngest B being still alive, Antiochus not only
10:37 a cistern, and his B Chaereas, and Apollophanes.
11:22 "King Antiochus to his B Lysias, greeting.
14:17 Simon, the B of Judas, had encountered Nicanor, but
Mt 4:18 Peter and Andrew his B, casting a net into
4:21 Zebedee and John his B, in the boat with
5:22 is angry with his B shall be liable to
5:22 judgment; whoever insults his B shall be liable to
5:23 there remember that your B has something against
5:24 be reconciled to your B, and then come and
7:3 that is in your B's eye, but do not
7:4 you say to your B, 'Let me take the
7:5 speck out of your B's eye.
10:2 Peter, and Andrew his B; James the son of
10:2 Zebedee, and John his B;
10:21 B will deliver up brother to death, and the
10:21 Brother will deliver up B to death, and the
12:49 in heaven is my B, and sister, and mother."
14:3 sake of Herodi-as, his B Philip's wife;
17:1 James and John his B, and led them up
18:14 "If your B sins against you, go and tell
18:14 he listens to you, you have gained your B
18:20 how often shall my B sin against me, and
18:34 do not forgive your B from your heart."
22:24 having no children, his B must marry the widow,
22:24 up children for his B
22:25 having no children left his wife to his B
Mk 1:16 Simon and Andrew the B of Simon casting a
1:19 Zebedee and John his B, who were in their
3:17 Zebedee and John the B of James, whom he
3:35 of God is my B, and sister, and mother."
5:37 James and John the B of James.
6:3 son of Mary and B of James and Joses
6:17 sake of Herodi-as, his B Philip's wife; because he
6:18 you to have your B's wife."
12:19 that if a man's B dies and leaves a
12:19 the wife, and raise up children for his B
13:12 And B will deliver up brother to death, and
13:12 brother will deliver up B to death, and the
Lk 3:1 of Galilee, and his B Philip tetrarch of the
3:19 him for Herodi-as, his B's wife, and for all
6:14 Peter, and Andrew his B, and James and John,
6:41 that is in your B's eye, but do not
6:42 you say to your B, 'Brother, let me take
6:42 say to your brother, B, let me take out
6:42 that is in your B's eye.
12:13 him, "Teacher, bid my B divide the inheritance with
15:27 said to him, 'Your B has come, and your
15:32 glad, for this your B was dead, and is
17:3 to yourselves; if your B sins, rebuke him, and
20:28 that if a man's B dies, having a wife
20:28 the wife and raise up children for his B
Jn 1:40 and followed him, was Andrew, Simon Peter's B
1:41 He first found his B Simon, and said to
6:8 disciples, Andrew, Simon Peter's B, said to him,
11:2 with her hair, whose B Lazarus was ill.
11:19 and Mary to console them concerning their B
11:21 had been here, my B would not have died.
11:23 said to her, "Your B will rise again."
11:32 had been here, my B would not have died."
Acts 9:17 on him he said, B Saul, the Lord Jesus
12:2 He killed James the B of John with the
21:20 to him, "You see, B, how many thousands there
22:13 me said to me, B Saul, receive your sight.'
Rom 14:10 Why do you pass judgment on your B
14:10 Or you, why do you despise your B
14:13 block or hindrance in the way of a B
14:15 If your B is being injured by what you
14:21 anything that makes your B stumble.
16:23 city treasurer, and our B Quartus, greet you.
1Cor 1:1 Christ Jesus, and our B Sosthenes,
5:11 bears the name of B if he is guilty
6:1 a grievance against a B, does he dare go
6:6 of the brotherhood, but B goes to law against
6:6 goes to law against B, and that before unbelievers?
7:12 Lord, that if any B has a wife who
7:15 such a case the B or sister is not
8:11 man is destroyed, the B for whom Christ died.
8:13 a cause of my B's falling, I will never
8:13 lest I cause my B to fall.
16:12 As for our B Apollos, I strongly urged him
2Cor 1:1 by the will of God, and Timothy our B
2:13 did not find my B Titus there.
8:18 we are sending the B who is famous among
8:22 we are sending our B whom we have often
12:18 go, and sent the B with him.
Gal 1:19 of the other apostles except James the Lord's B
Eph 6:21 doing, Tychicus the beloved B and faithful minister in
Phil 2:25 to you Epaphroditus my B and fellow worker and
Col 1:1 God, and Timothy our B,
4:7 he is a beloved B and faithful minister and
4:9 the faithful and beloved B, who is one of
1Thes 3:2 we sent Timothy, our B and God's servant in
4:6 transgress, and wrong his B in this matter, because
2Thes 3:6 keep away from any B who is living in
3:15 as an enemy, but warn him as a B
Philem 1:1 Jesus, and Timothy our B, To Philemon our beloved
1:7 from your love, my B, because the hearts of
1:16 slave, as a beloved B, especially to me but
1:20 Yes, B, I want some benefit from you in
Heb 8:11 or every one his B, saying, 'Know the Lord,'
13:23 should understand that our B Timothy has been
Jas 1:8 Let the lowly B boast in his exaltation,
2:15 If a B or sister is ill-clad and in
4:11 speaks evil against a B or judges his brother,
4:11 brother or judges his B, speaks evil against the
1Pet 5:12 By Silvanus, a faithful B as I regard him,
2Pet 3:15 So also our beloved B Paul wrote to you
1Jn 2:9 light and hates his B is in the darkness
2:10 He who loves his B abides in the light,
2:11 he who hates his B is in the darkness
3:10 God, nor he who does not love his B
3:12 was of the evil one and murdered his B
3:12 were evil and his B's righteous.
3:15 one who hates his B is a murderer, and
3:17 goods and sees his B in need, yet closes
4:20 and hates his B, he is a liar; for
4:20 does not love his B whom he has seen,
4:21 God should love his B also.
5:16 any one sees his B committing what is not
Jude 1:1 of Jesus Christ and B of James, to those
Rev 1:9 I John, your B, who share with you in

BROTHER-IN-LAW

Gen 38:8 the duty of a B to her, and raise

BROTHERHOOD (7)

Amos 1:9 Edom, and did not remember the covenant of B
Zech 11:14 Union, annulling the B between Judah and Israel.
1Mac 12:10 send to renew our B and friendship with you,
12:17 letter from us concerning the renewal of our B
1Cor 6:5 between members of the B,
1Pet 2:17 Love the B
5:9 is required of your B throughout the world.

BROTHERLY (4)

Rom 12:10 love one another with B affection; outdo one another
Heb 13:1 Let B love continue.
2Pet 1:7 godliness with B affection, and brotherly affection
1:7 with brotherly affection, and B affection with love.

BROTHERS (193)

Gen 9:22 and told his two B outside.

BROTHERS

	9:25	slave of slaves shall he be to his B
	19:7	"I beg you, my B, do not act so
	27:29	Be lord over your B, and may your mother's
	27:37	lord, and all his B I have given to
	29:4	said to them, "My B, where do you come
	34:11	father and to her B, "Let me find favor
	34:25	Simeon and Levi, Dinah's B, took their swords and
	37:2	the flock with his B; he was a lad
	37:4	But when his B saw that their father loved
	37:4	more than all his B, they hated him, and
	37:5	told it to his B they only hated him
	37:8	His B said to him, "Are you indeed to
	37:9	told it to his B, and said, "Behold, I
	37:10	father and to his B, his father rebuked him,
	37:10	your mother and your B indeed come to bow
	37:11	And his B were jealous of him, but his
	37:12	Now his B went to pasture their father's flock
	37:13	Joseph, "Are not your B pasturing the flock at
	37:14	is well with your B, and with the flock;
	37:16	"I am seeking my B
	37:17	Joseph went after his B, and found them at
	37:23	Joseph came to his B, they stripped him of
	37:26	Judah said to his B, "What profit is it
	37:27	And his B heeded him.
	37:30	and returned to his B, and said, "The lad
	38:1	went down from his B, and turned in to
	38:11	he feared that he would die, like his B
	42:3	So ten of Joseph's B went down to buy
	42:4	Joseph's brother, with his B, for he feared that
	42:6	And Joseph's B came, and bowed themselves before
	42:7	Joseph saw his B, and knew them, but he
	42:8	Thus Joseph knew his B, but they did not
	42:13	your servants, are twelve B, the sons of one
	42:19	let one of your B remain confined in your
	42:28	he said to his B, "My money has been
	42:32	spies; we are twelve B, sons of our father;
	42:33	leave one of your B with me, and take
	44:14	When Judah and his B came to Joseph's house,
	44:33	and let the lad go back with his B
	45:1	him when Joseph made himself known to his B
	45:3	Joseph said to his B, "I am Joseph; is
	45:3	But his B could not answer him, for they
	45:4	Joseph said to his B, "Come near to me,
	45:15	he kissed all his B and wept upon them;
	45:15	and after that his B talked with him.
	45:16	Pharaoh's house, "Joseph's B have come," it pleased
	45:17	Joseph, "Say to your B, 'Do this: load your
	45:24	Then he sent his B away, and as they
	46:31	Joseph said to his B and to his father's
	46:31	say to him, 'My B and my father's household,
	47:1	"My father and my B, with their flocks and
	47:2	And from among his B he took five men
	47:3	Pharaoh said to his B, "What is your occupation?"
	47:5	"Your father and your B have come to you.
	47:6	your father and your B in the best of
	47:11	his father and his B, and gave them a
	47:12	provided his father, his B, and all his father's
	48:6	the name of their B in their inheritance.
	48:22	rather than to your B one mountain slope which
	49:5	Simeon and Levi are B; weapons of violence are
	49:8	Judah, your B shall praise you; your hand shall
	49:26	brow of him who was separate from his B
	50:8	of Joseph, his B, and his father's household;
	50:14	to Egypt with his B and all who had
	50:15	When Joseph's B saw that their father was dead,
	50:17	the transgression of your B and their sin, because
	50:18	His B also came and fell down before him,
	50:24	Joseph said to his B, "I am about to
Ex	1:5	died, and all his B, and all that generation.
Lev	25:48	redeemed; one of his B may redeem him,
Num	27:9	then you shall give his inheritance to his B
	27:10	if he has no B, then you shall give
	27:10	you shall give his inheritance to his father's B
	27:11	his father has no B, then you shall give
	36:11	Zelophehad, were married to sons of their father's B
Deut	10:9	or inheritance with his B; the LORD is his
	22:3	lost thing of your B, which he loses and
	25:5	"If B dwell together, and one of them dies
	33:9	not'; he disowned his B, and ignored his children.
	33:16	head of him that is prince among his B
	33:24	the favorite of his B, and let him dip
Josh	2:13	father and mother, my B and sisters, and all
	2:18	father and mother, your B, and all your father's
	6:23	father and mother and B and all who belonged
Judg	8:19	said, "They were my B, the sons of my
	9:5	Ophrah, and slew his B the sons of Jerubbaal,
	9:24	Shechem, who strengthened his hands to slay his B
	9:56	in killing his seventy B;
	11:3	Jephthah fled from his B, and dwelt in the
	16:31	Then his B and all his family came down
	21:22	their fathers or their B come to complain to
1Sam	16:13	the midst of his B; and the Spirit of
	17:17	son, "Take for your B an ephah of this
	17:17	the camp to your B;
	17:18	See how your B fare, and bring some token
	17:22	to the ranks, and went and greeted his B
	20:29	away, and see my B For this reason he
	22:1	Adullam; and when his B and all his father's
	30:23	not do so, my B, with what the LORD
2Sam	3:8	your father, to his B, and to his friends,
1Kgs	1:9	he invited all his B, the king's sons, and
	2:15	about and become my B, for it was his
1Chr	4:9	more honorable than his B; and his mother called
	4:27	six daughters; but his B had not many children,
	5:2	became strong among his B and a prince was
	7:22	many days, and his B came to comfort him.
	27:18	Elihu, one of David's B; for Issachar, Omri the
2Chr	11:22	chief prince among his B, for he intended to
	21:2	He had B, the sons of Jehoshaphat: Azariah, Jehiel,
	21:4	he slew all his B with the sword, and
	21:13	you have killed your B, of your father's house,
	22:8	the sons of Ahaziah's B, who attended Ahaziah, and
	35:9	and Nethanel his B, and Hashabiah and Je-iel
Jud	7:31	And Uzziah said to them, "Have courage, my B
Job	22:6	exacted pledges of your B for nothing, and stripped
	42:11	to him all his B and sisters and all
	42:15	their father gave them inheritance among their B
Ps	133:1	pleasant it is when B dwell in unity!
Prov	6:19	lies, and a man who sows discord among B
	17:2	will share the inheritance as one of the B
	19:7	All a poor man's B hate him; how much
Sir	10:20	Among B their leader is worthy of honor, and
	25:1	men; agreement between B, friendship between
	40:24	B and help are for a time of trouble,
Jer	12:6	For even your B and the house of your
	35:3	of Habazziniah, and his B, and all his sons,
	49:10	are destroyed, and his B, and his neighbors; and
1Mac	2:17	in this city, and supported by sons and B
	2:20	my sons and my B will live by the
	3:2	All his B and all who had joined his
	3:25	Then Judas and his B began to be feared,
	3:42	Now Judas and his B saw that misfortunes had
	4:36	said Judas and his B, "Behold, our enemies are
	4:59	Then Judas and his B and all the assembly
	5:10	to Judas and his B a letter which said,
	5:61	they did not listen to Judas and his B
	5:63	man Judas and his B were greatly honored in
	5:65	Then Judas and his B went forth and fought
	7:6	people: "Judas and his B have destroyed all your
	7:10	to Judas and his B with peaceable but treacherous
	7:27	to Judas and his B this peaceable message,
	8:20	called Maccabeus, and his B and the people of
	9:39	his friends and his B to meet them with
	9:66	down Odomera and his B and the sons of
	10:5	him and to his B and his nation."
	10:15	that Jonathan and his B had fought, of the
	13:3	things I and my B and the house of
	13:4	of this all my B have perished for the
	13:5	distress, for I am not better than my B
	13:27	his father and his B; he made it high
	13:28	another, for his father and mother and four B
	14:18	they had established with Judas and Jonathan his B
	14:26	For he and his B and the house of
	14:29	of Joarib, and his B, exposed themselves to danger
	16:2	them: "I and my B and the house of
	16:21	that his father and B had perished, and that
2Mac	2:19	Judas Maccabeus and his B, and the purification of
	7:1	happened also that seven B and their mother were
	7:4	the rest of the B and the mother looked
	7:5	spread widely, but the B and their mother
	7:29	fear this butcher, but prove worthy of your B
	7:29	I may get you back again with your B
	7:36	For our B after enduring a brief suffering have
	7:37	I, like my B, give up body and life
	7:38	through me and my B to bring to an
	8:22	He appointed his B also, Simon and Joseph and
	12:24	of them and the B of some and no
Mt	1:2	of Judah and his B,
	1:11	of Jechoniah and his B, at the time of
	4:18	Galilee, he saw two B, Simon who is called
	4:21	he saw two other B, James the son of
	19:29	has left houses or B or sisters or father

20:24 heard it, they were indignant at the two B
22:25 Now there were seven B among us; the first
Mk 10:29 has left house or B or sisters or mother
10:30 this time, houses and B and sisters and mothers
12:20 There were seven B; the first took a wife,
Lk 14:12 your friends or your B or your kinsmen or
14:26 wife and children and B and sisters, yes, and
16:28 for I have five B, so that he may
18:29 house or wife or B or parents or children,
20:29 Now there were seven B; the first took a
21:16 even by parents and B and kinsmen and friends,
Jn 2:12 his mother and his B and his disciples; and
7:3 So his B said to him, "Leave here and
7:5 For even his B did not believe in him.
7:10 But after his B had gone up to the
Acts 1:14 Mary the mother of Jesus, and with his B
7:13 himself known to his B, and Joseph's family became
28:11 Alexandria, with the Twin B as figurehead.
1Cor 9:5 other apostles and the B of the Lord and
1Tim 5:1 treat younger men like B,

BROUGHT (858)
Gen 1:12 The earth B forth vegetation, plants yielding seed
2:19 of the air, and B them to the man
2:22 into a woman and B her to the man.
4:3 course of time Cain B to the LORD an
4:4 the ground, and Abel B of the firstlings of
8:9 and took her and B her into the ark
14:16 Then he B back all the goods, and also
14:16 the goods, and also B back his kinsman Lot
14:18 Melchizedek king of Salem B out bread and wine;
15:5 And he B him outside and said, "Look toward
15:7 am the LORD who B you from Ur of
15:10 And he B him all these, cut them in
18:4 a little water be B, and wash your feet,
19:10 forth their hands and B Lot into the house
19:16 to him, and they B him forth and set
19:17 And when they had B them forth, they said,
20:9 you, that you have B on me and my
24:53 And the servant B forth jewelry of silver and
24:67 Then Isaac B her into the tent, and took
26:10 and you would have B guilt upon us."
27:14 and took them and B them to his mother;
27:25 So he B it to him, and he ate;
27:25 he ate; and he B him wine, and he
27:31 prepared savory food, and B it to his father.
27:33 that hunted game and B it to me, and
29:13 and kissed him, and B him to his house.
29:23 his daughter Leah and B her to Jacob; and
30:14 in the field, and B them to his mother
30:39 and so the flocks B forth striped, speckled, and
33:11 my gift that is B to you, because God
34:30 and Levi, "You have B trouble on me by
37:2 father's wives; and Joseph B an ill report of
37:32 robe with sleeves and B it to their father,
38:25 As she was being B out, she sent word
39:1 the Ishmaelites who had B him down there.
39:14 them, "See, he has B among us a Hebrew
39:17 servant, whom you have B among us, came in
41:14 called Joseph, and they B him hastily out of
41:47 plenteous years the earth B forth abundantly,
43:2 grain which they had B from Egypt, their father
43:17 Joseph bade him, and B the men to Joseph's
43:18 afraid because they were B to Joseph's house, and
43:18 time, that we are B in, so that he
43:21 weight; so we have B it again with us,
43:22 us, and we have B other money down in
43:23 Then he B Simeon out to them.
43:24 when the man had B the men into Joseph's
43:26 Joseph came home, they B into the house to
44:8 of our sacks, we B back to you from
46:7 all his offspring he B with him into Egypt.
46:32 cattle; and they have B their flocks, and their
47:7 Then Joseph B in Jacob his father, and set
47:14 they bought; and Joseph B the money into Pharaoh's
47:17 So they B their cattle to Joseph; and Joseph
48:10 So Joseph B them near him; and he kissed
48:13 Israel's right hand, and B them near him.
Ex 2:10 child grew, and she B him to Pharaoh's daughter,
3:12 you: when you have B forth the people out
6:7 your God, who has B you out from under
8:7 their secret arts, and B frogs upon the land
9:19 field and is not B home, and they shall
10:8 Moses and Aaron were B back to Pharaoh; and
10:13 Egypt, and the LORD B an east wind upon
10:13 the east wind had B the locusts.
12:17 this very day I B your hosts out of
12:39 dough which they had B out of Egypt, for
12:51 very day the LORD B the people of Israel
13:3 of hand the LORD B you out from this
13:9 hand the LORD has B you out of Egypt.
13:14 of hand the LORD B us out of Egypt,
13:16 strong hand the LORD B us out of Egypt."
15:19 the sea, the LORD B back the waters of
16:3 full; for you have B us out into this
16:6 was the LORD who B you out of the
16:32 the wilderness, when I B you out of the
18:1 how the LORD had B Israel out of Egypt.
18:26 times; hard cases they B to Moses, but any
19:4 on eagles' wings and B you to myself.
19:17 Then Moses B the people out of the camp
20:2 LORD your God, who B you out of the
29:46 LORD their God, who B them forth out of
32:1 Moses, the man who B us up out of
32:3 in their ears, and B them to Aaron.
32:4 gods, O Israel, who B you up out of
32:6 offered burnt offerings and B peace offerings; and
32:7 your people, whom you B up out of the
32:8 gods, O Israel, who B you up out of
32:11 people, whom thou hast B forth out of the
32:21 you that you have B a great sin upon
32:23 Moses, the man who B us up out of
33:1 people whom you have B up out of the
35:21 spirit moved him, and B the LORD's offering to
35:22 of a willing heart B brooches and earrings and
35:23 rams' skins or goatskins, B them.
35:24 of silver or bronze B it as the LORD's
35:24 use in the work, B it.
35:25 with their hands, and B what they had spun
35:27 And the leaders B onyx stones and stones to
35:29 Moses to be done, B it as their freewill
36:3 people of Israel had B for doing the work
39:33 And they B the tabernacle to Moses, the tent
Lev 6:30 which any blood is B into the tent of
8:6 And Moses B Aaron and his sons, and washed
8:13 And Moses B Aaron's sons, and clothed them with
8:14 Then he B the bull of the sin offering;
8:24 And Aaron's sons were B, and Moses put some
9:5 And they B what Moses commanded before the tent
10:18 its blood was not B into the inner part
11:45 am the LORD who B you up out of
13:2 then he shall be B to Aaron the priest
13:9 leprosy, he shall be B to the priest;
14:2 He shall be B to the priest;
16:27 offering, whose blood was B in to make atonement
19:36 LORD your God, who B you out of the
22:33 who sanctify you, who B you out of the
23:14 day, until you have B the offering of your
23:15 the day that you B the sheaf of the
23:43 in booths when I B them out of the
24:11 And they B him to Moses.
24:23 of Israel; and they B him who had cursed
25:38 LORD your God, who B you forth out of
25:42 my servants, whom I B forth out of the
25:55 my servants whom I B forth out of the
26:13 LORD your God, who B you forth out of
26:41 contrary to them and B them into the land
26:45 their forefathers, whom I B forth out of the
Num 6:13 completed: he shall be B to the door of
7:3 were numbered, offered and B their offerings before
11:31 the LORD, and it B quails from the sea,
12:14 that she may be B in again."
12:15 march till Miriam was B in again.
13:23 two of them; they B also some pomegranates and
13:26 Paran, at Kadesh; they B back word to them
13:32 So they B to the people of Israel an
14:37 land, the men who B up an evil report
15:25 error, and they have B their offering, an offering
15:33 found him gathering sticks B him to Moses and
15:36 And all the congregation B him outside the camp,
15:41 LORD your God, who B you out of the
16:10 and that he has B you near him, and
16:13 thing that you have B us up out of
16:14 Moreover you have not B us into a land
17:9 Then Moses B out all the rods from before
20:4 Why have you B the assembly of the LORD
20:16 sent an angel and B us forth out of
21:5 Moses, "Why have you B us up out of
22:41 Balak took Balaam and B him up to Bamoth-baal;
23:7 "From Aram Balak has B me, the king of
25:6 of Israel came and B a Midianite woman to
27:5 Moses B their case before the LORD.

BROUGHT

B

31:12 Then they B the captives and the booty and
31:50 And we have B the LORD's offering, what each
31:54 and of hundreds, and B it into the tent
32:17 Israel, until we have B them to their place;
Deut 1:25 of the land and B it down to us,
1:25 down to us, and B us word again, and
1:27 hated us he has B us forth out of
4:20 has taken you, and B you forth out of
4:37 descendants after them, and B you out of Egypt
5:6 LORD your God, who B you out of the
5:15 the LORD your God B you out thence with
6:12 forget the LORD, who B you out of the
6:21 Egypt; and the LORD B us out of Egypt
6:23 our eyes; and he B us out from there,
7:8 that the LORD has B you out with a
7:19 the LORD your God B you out; so will
8:14 LORD your God, who B you out of the
8:15 was no water, who B you water out of
9:4 that the LORD has B me in to possess
9:12 people whom you have B from Egypt have acted
9:26 greatness, whom thou hast B out of Egypt with
9:28 hated them, he has B them out to slay
13:5 LORD your God, who B you out of the
13:10 LORD your God, who B you out of the
16:1 the LORD your God B you out of Egypt
20:1 is with you, who B you up out of
22:19 woman, because he has B an evil name upon
26:8 oppression; and the LORD B us out of Egypt
26:9 and wonders; and he B us into this place
29:25 with them when he B them out of the
31:20 For when I have B them into the land
31:21 forming, before I have B them into the land
Josh 2:6 But she had B them up to the roof,
6:23 spies went in, and B out Rahab, and her
6:23 to her; and they B all her kindred, and
7:7 GOD, why hast thou B this people over the
7:14 therefore you shall be B near by your tribes;
7:16 in the morning, and B Israel near tribe by
7:17 was taken; and he B near the families of
7:17 was taken; and he B near the family of
7:18 was taken; and he B near his household man
7:23 of the tent and B them to Joshua and
7:24 he had; and they B them up to the
8:23 they took alive, and B him to Joshua.
10:23 they did so, and B those five kings out
10:24 And when they B those kings out to Joshua,
14:7 the land; and I B him word again as
22:32 people of Israel, and B back word to them.
24:5 it; and afterwards I B you out.
24:6 Then I B your fathers out of Egypt, and
24:8 Then I B you to the land of the
24:17 LORD our God who B us and our fathers
24:32 the people of Israel B up from Egypt were
Judg 1:7 And they B him to Jerusalem, and he died
2:1 And he said, "I B you up from Egypt,
2:1 up from Egypt, and B you into the land
2:12 their fathers, who had B them out of the
5:25 gave him milk, she B him curds in a
6:6 And Israel was B very low because of Midian;
6:8 up from Egypt, and B you out of the
6:19 in a pot, and B them to him under
7:5 So he B the people down to the water;
7:25 pursued Midian; and they B the heads of Oreb
11:35 you have B me very low, and you have
12:9 and thirty daughters he B in from outside for
14:11 people saw him, they B thirty companions to be
15:13 two new ropes, and B him up from the
16:8 lords of the Philistines B her seven fresh bowstrings
16:18 up to her, and B the money in their
16:21 out his eyes, and B him down to Gaza,
16:31 and took him and B him up and buried
18:3 said to him, "Who B you here?
19:21 So he B him into his house, and gave
20:3 how was this wickedness B to pass?"
21:12 with him; and they B them to the camp
Ruth 1:21 and the LORD has B me back empty.
1:21 and the Almighty has B calamity upon me?"
2:18 gleaned, and she also B out and gave her
1Sam 1:24 of wine; and she B him to the house
1:25 the bull, and they B the child to Eli.
2:14 all that the fork B up the priest would
4:4 sent to Shiloh, and B from there the ark
4:17 He who B the tidings answered and said, "Israel
5:2 ark of God and B it into the house
5:8 God of Israel be B around to Gath." So
5:8 So they B the ark of the God of
5:9 But after they had B it around, the hand
5:10 cried out, "They have B around to us the
7:1 of the LORD, and B it to the house
8:8 from the day I B them up out of
9:22 and his servant and B them into the hall
10:18 God of Israel, 'I B up Israel out of
10:20 Then Samuel B all the tribes of Israel near,
10:21 He B the tribe of Benjamin near by its
10:21 by lot; finally he B the family of the
10:27 they despised him, and B him no present.
12:6 Moses and Aaron and B your fathers up out
12:8 Moses and Aaron, who B forth your fathers out
14:34 one of the people B his ox with him
15:15 Saul said, "They have B them from the Amalekites;
15:20 sent me, I have B Agag the king of
16:12 And he sent, and B him in.
17:54 of the Philistine and B it to Jerusalem; but
17:57 Abner took him, and B him before Saul with
18:27 the Philistines; and David B their foreskins, which
19:7 And Jonathan B David to Saul, and he was
20:8 servant, for you have B your servant into a
21:8 For I have B neither my sword nor my
21:14 why then have you B him to me?
21:15 madmen, that you have B this fellow to play
23:5 with the Philistines, and B away their cattle, and
25:27 which your servant has B to my lord be
25:35 hand what she had B him; and he said
30:7 So Abiathar B the ephod to David.
30:11 the open country, and B him to David; and
30:19 had been taken; David B back all.
2Sam 1:10 arm, and I have B them here to my
2:3 And David B up his men who were with
2:8 son of Saul, and B him over to Mahanaim;
3:26 after Abner, and they B him back from the
4:8 Arabah all night, and B the head of Ish-bosheth
5:2 that led out and B in Israel; and the
6:3 a new cart, and B it out of the
6:12 So David went and B up the ark of
6:15 the house of Israel B up the ark of
6:17 And they B in the ark of the LORD,
7:6 since the day I B up the people of
7:18 house, that thou hast B me thus far?
8:2 servants to David and B tribute.
8:6 servants to David and B tribute.
8:7 servants of Hadadezer, and B them to Jerusalem.
8:10 And Joram B with him articles of silver, of
9:5 King David sent and B him from the house
10:16 And Hadadezer sent, and B out the Syrians who
11:27 over, David sent and B her to his house,
12:3 And he B it up, and it grew up
12:30 And he B forth the spoil of the city,
12:31 And he B forth the people who were in
13:10 she had made, and B them into the chamber
13:11 But when she B them near him to eat,
14:23 went to Geshur, and B Absalom to Jerusalem.
16:2 Ziba, "Why have you B these?" Ziba answered, "The
17:28 Gileadite from Rogelim, B beds, basins, and earthen
19:40 the people of Israel, B the king on his
19:41 stolen you away, and B the king and his
21:13 on Gilboa; and he B up from there the
22:20 He B me forth into a broad place; he
22:48 gave me vengeance and B down peoples under me,
22:49 peoples under me, who B me out from my
23:16 gate, and took and B it to David.
1Kgs 1:3 Abishag the Shunammite, and B her to the king.
1:27 Has this thing been B about by my lord
1:38 King David's mule, and B him to Gihon.
1:53 Solomon sent, and they B him down from the
2:19 and had a seat B for the king's mother;
2:30 Then Benaiah B the king word again, saying, "Thus
2:40 slaves; Shimei went and B his slaves from Gath.
3:1 took Pharaoh's daughter, and B her into the city
3:24 So a sword was B before the king.
4:21 border of Egypt; they B tribute and served Solomon
4:28 and swift steeds they B to the place where
7:13 King Solomon sent and B Hiram from Tyre.
7:51 And Solomon B in the things which David his
8:4 And they B up the ark of the LORD,
8:4 priests and the Levites B them up.
8:6 Then the priests B the ark of the covenant
8:16 the day that I B my people Israel out
8:21 our fathers, when he B them out of the
9:9 LORD their God who B their fathers out of
9:9 therefore the LORD has B all this evil upon
9:28 went to Ophir, and B from there gold, to
9:28 twenty talents; and they B it to King Solomon.

BROUGHT

10:11 fleet of Hiram, which B gold from Ophir, brought
10:11 brought gold from Ophir, B from Ophir a very
10:25 Every one of them B his present, articles of
12:15 a turn of affairs B about by the LORD
12:28 gods, O Israel, who B you up out of
13:20 the prophet who had B him back;
13:23 prophet whom he had B back.
13:26 the prophet who had B him back from the
13:29 upon the ass, and B it back to the
14:28 guard bore them and B them back to the
15:15 And he B into the house of the LORD
17:6 And the ravens B him bread and meat in
17:20 my God, hast thou B calamity even upon the
17:23 took the child, and B him down from the
18:40 seized them; and Elijah B them down to the
20:9 the messengers departed and B him word again.
20:39 a soldier turned and B a man to me,
21:13 and the base fellows B a charge against Naboth,
22:37 king died, and was B to Samaria; and they
2Kgs 2:20 So they B it to him.
4:5 as she poured they B the vessels to her.
4:20 had lifted him, and B him to his mother,
5:6 And he B the letter to the king of
5:20 in not accepting from his hand what he B
10:8 told him, "They have B the heads of the
10:22 So he B out the vestments for them.
10:26 of Baal and they B out the pillar that
11:4 year Jehoiada sent and B the captains of the
11:9 priest commanded, and each B his men who were
11:12 Then he B out the king's son, and put
11:19 the land; and they B the king down from
12:4 holy things which is B into the house of
12:9 the money that was B into the house of
12:13 the money that was B into the house of
12:16 sin offerings was not B into the house of
14:20 And they B him upon horses; and he was
17:7 their God, who had B them up out of
17:24 the king of Assyria B people from Babylon, Cuthah,
17:36 fear the LORD, who B you out of the
20:11 the LORD; and he B the shadow back ten
20:20 and the conduit and B water into the city,
22:4 money which has been B into the house of
22:20 And they B back word to the king.
23:6 And he B out the Asherah from the house
23:8 And he B all the priests out of the
23:30 chariot from Megiddo, and B him to Jerusalem, and
24:16 the king of Babylon B captive to Babylon all
25:6 captured the king, and B him up to the
25:20 guard took them, and B them to the king
1Chr 5:26 half-tribe of Manasseh, and B them to Halah, Habor,
9:28 them when they were B in and taken out.
10:12 of his sons, and B them to Jabesh.
11:2 that led out and B in Israel; and the
11:18 gate, and took and B it to David.
11:19 of their lives they B it." Therefore he would
14:17 lands, and the LORD B the fear of him
15:28 So all Israel B up the ark of the
16:1 And they B the ark of God, and set
17:16 house, that thou hast B me thus far?
18:2 servants to David and B tribute.
18:6 servants to David, and B tribute.
18:7 servants of Hadadezer, and B them to Jerusalem.
19:16 they sent messengers and B out the Syrians who
20:2 And he B forth the spoil of the city,
20:3 And he B forth the people who were in
22:4 the Sidonians and Tyrians B great quantities of cedar
22:19 of God may be B into a house built
2Chr 1:4 (But David had B up the ark of God
5:1 And Solomon B in the things which David his
5:5 And they B up the ark, the tent of
5:5 priests and the Levites B them up.
5:7 So the priests B the ark of the covenant
6:5 the day that I B my people out of
7:22 of their fathers who B them out of the
7:22 them; therefore he has B all this evil upon
8:11 Solomon B Pharaoh's daughter up from the city of
8:18 talents of gold and B it to King Solomon.
9:10 servants of Solomon, who B gold from Ophir, brought
9:10 brought gold from Ophir, B algum wood and precious
9:12 besides what she had B to the king.
9:14 the traders and merchants B; and all the kings
9:14 governors of the land B gold and silver to
9:24 Every one of them B his present, articles of
10:15 a turn of affairs B about by God that
12:11 and bore them, and B them back to the
15:11 spoil which they had B, seven hundred oxen and
15:18 And he B into the house of God the
17:5 hand; and all Judah B tribute to Jehoshaphat; and
17:11 of the Philistines B Jehoshaphat presents, and silver
17:11 and the Arabs also B him seven thousand seven
19:4 country of Ephraim, and B them back to the
22:9 Samaria, and he was B to Jehu and put
23:8 They each B his men, who were to go
23:11 Then he B out the king's son, and put
23:14 Then Jehoiada the priest B out the captains who
23:20 the land; and they B the king down from
24:10 the people rejoiced and B their tax and dropped
24:11 whenever the chest was B to the king's officers
24:14 they had finished, they B the rest of the
25:14 of the Edomites, he B the gods of the
25:23 Ahaziah, at Beth-shemesh, and B him to Jerusalem,
25:28 And they B him upon horses; and he was
28:5 of his people and B them to Damascus.
28:8 spoil from them and B the spoil to Samaria.
28:15 them on asses, they B them to their kinsfolk
28:19 For the LORD B Judah low because of Ahaz
29:4 He B in the priests and the Levites, and
29:16 cleanse it, and they B out all the uncleanness
29:21 And they B seven bulls, seven rams, seven lambs,
29:23 the sin offering were B to the king and
29:31 And the assembly B sacrifices and thank offerings;
29:31 of a willing heart B burnt offerings.
29:32 offerings which the assembly B was seventy bulls, a
30:15 they sanctified themselves, and B burnt offerings into
31:5 the field; and they B in abundantly the tithe
31:6 cities of Judah also B in the tithe of
31:12 And they faithfully B in the contributions, the tithes
32:23 And many B gifts to the LORD to Jerusalem
33:11 Therefore the LORD B upon them the commanders
33:11 fetters of bronze and B him to Babylon.
33:13 heard his supplication and B him again to Jerusalem
34:9 money that had been B into the house of
34:14 money that had been B into the house of
34:16 Shaphan B the book to the king, and further
34:28 And they B back word to the king.
35:24 his second chariot and B him to Jerusalem.
36:10 King Nebuchadnezzar sent and B him to Babylon,
36:17 Therefore he B up against them the king of
36:18 princes, all these he B to Babylon.
Ezra 1:7 Cyrus the king also B out the vessels of
1:8 Cyrus king of Persia B these out in charge
1:11 when the exiles were B up from Babylonia to
4:2 king of Assyria who B us here."
5:14 was in Jerusalem and B into the temple of
6:3 and burnt offerings are B; its height shall be
6:5 is in Jerusalem and B to Babylon, be restored
6:5 Babylon, be restored and B back to the temple
8:18 God upon us, they B us a man of
Neh 5:7 with myself, and I B charges against the nobles
8:2 And Ezra the priest B the law before the
8:16 people went out and B them and made booths
9:18 is your God who B you up out of
12:31 Then I B up the princes of Judah upon
13:9 the chambers; and I B back thither the vessels
13:12 Then all Judah B the tithe of the grain,
13:15 of burdens, which they B into Jerusalem on the
13:16 lived in the city, B in fish and all
13:19 no burden might be B in on the sabbath
Tob 7:1 her greeting, and she B them into the house.
9:5 the receipt, and Gabael B out the money bags
11:17 is God who has B you to us, and
12:2 of what I have B back.
12:5 that you two have B back."
12:12 daughter-in-law Sarah prayed, I B a reminder of
14:10 reared him, how he B him from light into
Jud 6:14 they untied him and B him into Bethulia and
10:17 her maid, and they B them to the tent
11:2 them; but they have B all this on themselves.
12:2 the things I have B with me."
12:5 the servants of Holofernes B her into the tent,
13:17 our God, who hast B into contempt this day
13:20 when our nation was B low, but have avenged
14:18 One Hebrew woman has B disgrace upon the house
16:3 of my pursuers, and B me to his camp,
Esth 1:17 Queen Vashti to be B before him, and she
2:7 He had B up Hadassah, that is Esther, the
2:20 as when she was B up by him.
6:8 let royal robes be B, which the king has
6:14 king's eunuchs arrived and B Haman in haste to
11:1 and Ptolemy his son B to Egypt the preceding
11:4 king of Babylon had B from Jerusalem with
13:4 honorably intend cannot be B about.

 BROUGHT

14:18 day that I was B here until now, except
Job 4:12 "Now a word was B to me stealthily, my
5:13 of the wily are B to a quick end.
14:21 know it; they are B low, and he perceives
15:7 Or were you B forth before the hills?
18:14 he trusted, and is B to the king of
31:13 my maidservant, when they B a complaint against
42:11 that the LORD had B upon him; and each
Ps 18:19 He B me forth into a broad place; he
30:3 O LORD, thou hast B up my soul from
37:33 condemned when he is B to trial.
40:14 be turned back and B to dishonor who desire
51:5 Behold, I was B forth in iniquity, and in
66:12 water; yet thou hast B us forth to a
68:31 Let bronze be B from Egypt; let Ethiopia hasten
69:6 who seek thee be B to dishonor through me,
70:2 be turned back and B to dishonor who desire
78:54 And he B them to his holy land, to
78:71 that had young he B him to be the
79:8 us, for we are B very low.
81:10 LORD your God, who B you up out of
90:2 Before the mountains were B forth, or ever thou
105:40 They asked, and he B quails, and gave them
106:42 them, and they were B into subjection under their
106:43 their purposes, and were B low through their iniquity.
107:14 from their distress; he B them out of darkness
107:30 had quiet, and he B them to their desired
107:39 they are diminished and B low through oppression,
116:6 simple; when I was B low, he saved me.
136:11 endures for ever; and B Israel out from among
142:6 cry; for I am B very low!
Prov 8:24 no depths I was B forth, when there were
8:25 the hills, I was B forth;
Eccl 12:4 daughters of song are B low;
Song 1:4 The king has B me into his chambers.
2:4 He B me to the banqueting house, and his
3:4 go until I had B him into my mother's
Wis 5:8 has our boasted wealth B us?
10:14 leave him, until she B him the scepter of
10:18 She B them over the Red Sea, and led
18:21 as their champion; he B forward the shield of
19:10 producing animals the earth B forth gnats, and
Sir 2:4 Accept whatever is B upon you, and in changes
6:12 but if you are B low he will turn
10:13 Therefore the Lord B upon them extraordinary
23:23 adultery through harlotry and B forth children by
23:24 She herself will be B before the assembly, and
33:12 he made holy and B near to himself; but
33:12 them he cursed and B low, and he turned
45:1 his descendants the Lord B forth a man of
47:19 your body you were B into subjection.
47:20 posterity, so that you B wrath upon your children
48:2 He B a famine upon them, and by his
48:3 and also three times B down fire.
48:6 the Most High; who B kings down to destruction,
48:12 ruler, and no one B him into subjection.
48:17 fortified his city, and B water into the midst
Is 1:2 have I reared and B up, but they have
2:9 humbled, and men are B low— forgive them
2:11 of man shall be B low, and the pride
2:17 of men shall be B low; and the LORD
3:9 For they have B evil upon themselves.
5:15 down, and men are B low, and the eyes
9:1 the former time he B into contempt the land
10:13 a bull I have B down those who sat
10:33 the lofty will be B low.
14:11 us!' Your pomp is B down to Sheol, the
14:15 High.' But you are B down to Sheol, to
16:14 of Moab will be B into contempt, in spite
17:4 of Jacob will be B low, and the fat
18:7 time gifts will be B to the LORD of
23:4 reared young men nor B up virgins."
26:5 For he has B low the inhabitants of the
26:18 have as it were B forth wind.
43:23 You have not B me your sheep for burnt
48:15 called him, I have B him, and he will
49:21 away, but who has B up these?
51:18 the sons she has B up.
57:6 drink offering, you have B a cereal offering.
59:16 then his own arm B him victory, and his
63:5 so my own arm B me victory, and my
63:11 Where is he who B up out of the
66:8 Shall a nation be B forth in one moment?
66:8 was in labor she B forth her sons.
Jer 2:6 is the LORD who B us up from the
2:7 man dwells?' And I B you into a plentiful
2:17 Have you not B this upon yourself by forsaking
4:18 and your doings have B this upon you.
7:22 the day that I B them out of the
8:1 of Jerusalem shall be B out of their tombs;
10:9 Beaten silver is B from Tarshish, and gold from
11:4 your fathers when I B them out of the
11:7 your fathers when I B them up out of
11:8 Therefore I B upon them all the words of
15:8 the seas; I have B against the mothers of
16:14 the LORD lives who B up the people of
16:15 the LORD lives who B up the people of
20:15 be the man who B the news to my
23:7 the LORD lives who B up the people of
23:8 the LORD lives who B up and led the
24:1 the smiths, and had B them to Babylon, the
26:23 Uriah from Egypt and B him to King Jehoiakim,
27:16 will now shortly be B back from Babylon,' for
32:42 Just as I have B all this great evil
34:11 had set free, and B them into subjection as
34:13 your fathers when I B them out of the
34:16 their desire, and you B them into subjection to
35:4 I B them to the house of the LORD
37:14 and seized Jeremiah and B him to the princes.
39:5 had taken him, they B him up to Nebuchadrezzar
40:3 place; the LORD has B it about, and has
41:16 and eunuchs, whom Johanan B back from Gibeon.
44:2 the evil that I B upon Jerusalem and upon
48:2 O Madmen, shall be B to silence; the sword
50:25 opened his armory, and B out the weapons of
51:10 The LORD has B forth our vindication; come, let
52:9 captured the king, and B him up to the
52:26 guard took them, and B them to the king
52:31 king of Judah and B him out of prison;
Lam 1:12 my sorrow which was B upon me, which the
2:2 of Judah; he has B down to the ground
2:6 feasts; the LORD has B to an end in
3:2 he has driven and B me into darkness without
4:5 streets; those who were B up in purple lie
Bar 1:9 of the land, and B them to Babylon.
1:19 day when the Lord B our fathers out of
1:20 the time when he B our fathers out of
2:5 They were B low and not raised up, because
2:9 and the Lord has B them upon us, for
2:24 our fathers would be B out of their graves;
3:29 and taken her, and B her down from the
4:8 the everlasting God, who B you up, and you
4:9 of Zion, God has B great sorrow upon me;
4:10 daughters, which the Everlasting B upon them.
4:14 daughters, which the Everlasting B upon them.
4:15 For he B against them a nation from afar,
4:18 For he who B these calamities upon you will
4:27 remembered by him who B this upon you.
4:29 For he who B these calamities upon you will
Ezek 8:3 earth and heaven, and B me in visions of
8:7 And he B me to the door of the
8:14 Then he B me to the entrance of the
8:16 And he B me into the inner court of
9:11 case at his side, B back word, saying, "I
11:1 lifted me up, and B me to the east
11:7 but you shall be B forth out of the
11:24 lifted me up and B me in the vision
12:7 I B out my baggage by day, as baggage
14:22 evil that I have B upon Jerusalem, for all
14:22 all that I have B upon it.
17:6 became a vine, and B forth branches and put
17:12 and her princes and B them to him to
19:3 And she B up one of her whelps; he
19:4 their pit; and they B him with hooks to
19:9 in a cage, and B him to the king
19:9 king of Babylon; they B him into custody, that
20:10 land of Egypt and B them into the wilderness.
20:14 whose sight I had B them out.
20:22 whose sight I had B them out.
20:28 For when I had B them into the land
22:4 made; and you have B your day near, the
23:27 lewdness and your harlotry B from the land of
23:30 and your harlotry have B this upon you, because
23:42 common sort drunkards were B from the wilderness;
27:15 own special markets, they B you in payment ivory
27:26 Your rowers have B you out into the high
28:18 your sanctuaries; so I B forth fire from the
30:11 the nations, shall be B in to destroy the
31:6 beasts of the field B forth their young; and
31:18 You shall be B down with the trees of
34:4 strayed you have not B back, the lost you
37:1 upon me, and he B me out by the

	38:8	waste; its people were B out from the nations
	39:8	and it will be B about, says the Lord
	39:27	afraid, when I have B them back from the
	40:2	was upon me, and B me in the visions
	40:3	When he B me there, behold, there was a
	40:4	you, for you were B here in order that
	40:17	Then he B me into the outer court; and
	40:28	Then he B me to the inner court by
	40:32	Then he B me to the inner court on
	40:35	Then he B me to the north gate, and
	40:44	Then he B me from without into the inner
	40:48	Then he B me to the vestibule of the
	41:1	Then he B me to the nave, and measured
	42:1	the north, and he B me to the chambers
	43:1	Afterward he B me to the gate, the gate
	43:5	lifted me up, and B me into the inner
	44:1	Then he B me back to the outer gate
	44:4	Then he B me by way of the north
	46:19	Then he B me through the entrance, which was
	46:21	Then he B me forth to the outer court,
	47:1	Then he B me back to the door of
	47:2	Then he B me out by way of the
Dan	1:2	of God; and he B them to the land
	1:18	that they should be B in, the chief of
	1:18	chief of the eunuchs B them in before.
	2:25	Then Arioch B in Daniel before the king in
	3:13	that Shadrach, Meshach, and Abednego be B
	3:13	Then they B these men before the king.
	3:28	all that thou hast B upon us and upon
	3:28	and justice thou hast B all this upon us
	3:31	all that thou hast B upon us, and all
	3:37	any nation, and are B low this day in
	4:6	of Babylon should be B before me, that they
	5:2	temple in Jerusalem be B, that the king and
	5:3	Then they B in the golden and silver vessels
	5:13	Then Daniel was B in before the king.
	5:13	the king my father B from Judah.
	5:15	the enchanters, have been B in before me to
	5:23	his house have been B in before you, and
	5:26	of your kingdom and B it to an end;
	6:16	commanded, and Daniel was B and cast into the
	6:17	And a stone was B and laid upon the
	6:18	fasting; no diversions were B to him, and sleep
	6:24	had accused Daniel were B and cast into the
	9:14	the calamity and has B it upon us; for
Hos	12:13	a prophet the LORD B Israel up from Egypt,
Amos	2:10	Also I B you up out of the land
	3:1	whole family which I B up out of the
Mic	5:3	is in travail has B forth; then the rest
	6:4	For I B you up from the land of
Nah	2:11	lions, where the lion B his prey, where his
Hag	1:9	little; and when you B it home, I blew
1Mac	1:6	officers, who had been B up with him from
	3:49	They also B the garments of the priesthood and
	4:49	new holy vessels, and B the lampstand, the altar
	6:17	Lysias had B him up as a boy, and
	7:6	And they B to the king this accusation against
	7:7	ruin which Judas has B upon us and upon
	7:25	to the king and B wicked charges against them.
	7:47	arrogantly stretched out, and B them and displayed
	9:26	friends of Judas, and B them to Bacchides, and
	10:82	Then Simon B forward his force and engaged the
	13:32	of Asia; and he B great calamity upon the
	13:43	made a siege engine, B it up to the
	14:29	be perserved; and they B great glory to their
	15:18	the Jews, and have B a gold shield weighing
2Mac	1:17	our God, who has B judgment upon those who
	2:5	a cave, and he B there the tent and
	3:18	was about to be B into contempt.
	4:43	Charges were B against Menelaus about this
	6:4	sacred precincts, and besides B in things for sacrifice
	6:10	two women were B in for having circumcised
	7:7	in this way, they B forward the second for
	7:15	Next they B forward the fifth and maltreated him.
	7:18	After him they B forward the sixth.
	7:27	have reared you and B you up to this
	8:34	thrice-accursed Nicanor, who had B the thousand
	9:8	in a balance, was B down to earth and
	11:18	that needed to be B before him, and he
	14:41	ordered that fire be B and the doors burned.
Mt	4:24	all Syria, and they B him all the sick,
	8:16	That evening they B to him many who were
	9:2	And behold, they B to him a paralytic, lying
	9:32	a dumb demoniac was B to him.
	11:23	You shall be B down to Hades.
	12:22	and dumb demoniac was B to him, and he
	13:8	on good soil and B forth grain, some a
	14:11	and his head was B on a platter and
	14:11	the girl, and she B it to her mother.
	14:35	all that region and B to him all that
	16:7	among themselves, saying, "We B no bread."
	17:16	And I B him to your disciples, and they
	18:23	the reckoning, one was B to him who owed
	19:13	Then children were B to him that he might
	21:7	had directed them; they B the ass and the
	21:16	and sucklings thou hast B perfect praise'?"
	22:19	And they B him a coin.
	27:3	condemned, he repented and B back the thirty
Mk	1:32	evening, at sundown, they B to him all who
	4:8	into good soil and B forth grain, growing up
	4:21	them, "Is a lamp B in to be put
	6:28	in the prison, and B his head on a
	7:31	And they B to him a man who was
	8:22	And some people B to him a blind man,
	9:17	answered him, "Teacher, I B my son to you,
	9:20	And they B the boy to him; and when
	11:7	And they B the colt to Jesus, and threw
	12:16	And they B one.
	15:22	And they B him to the place called Golgotha
Lk	2:22	law of Moses, they B him up to Jerusalem
	2:27	and when the parents B in the child Jesus,
	3:5	and hill shall be B low, and the crooked
	4:16	where he had been B up; and he went
	4:40	sick with various diseases B them to him; and
	5:11	And when they had B their boats to land,
	7:37	in the Pharisee's house, B an alabaster flask of
	10:15	You shall be B down to Hades.
	10:34	his own beast and B him to an inn,
	12:16	of a rich man B forth plentifully;
	16:1	steward, and charges were B to him that this
	18:40	commanded him to be B to him; and when
	19:35	And they B it to Jesus, and throwing their
	21:12	and you will be B before kings and governors
	23:1	of them arose, and B him before Pilate.
	23:14	said to them, "You B me this man as
Jn	1:42	He B him to Jesus.
	4:33	another, "Has any one B him food?"
	8:3	scribes and the Pharisees B a woman who had
	9:13	They B to the Pharisees the man who had
	10:4	When he has B out all his own, he
	18:16	kept the door, and B Peter in.
	19:13	heard these words, he B Jesus out and sat
Acts	4:34	houses sold them, and B the proceeds of what
	4:37	belonged to him, and B the money and laid
	5:2	of the proceeds, and B only a part and
	5:19	the prison doors and B them out and said,
	5:21	and sent to the prison to have them B
	5:26	the officers went and B them, but without violence,
	5:27	And when they had B them, they set them
	6:12	and seized him and B him before the council,
	7:20	And he was B up for three months in
	7:21	daughter adopted him and B him up as her
	7:45	Our fathers in turn B it in with Joshua
	9:8	by the hand and B him into Damascus.
	9:27	Barnabas took him, and B him to the apostles,
	9:30	brethren knew it, they B him down to Caesarea,
	11:26	had found him, he B him to Antioch.
	12:17	how the Lord had B him out of the
	13:23	man's posterity God has B to Israel a Savior,
	14:13	front of the city, B oxen and garlands to
	16:16	spirit of divination and B her owners much gain
	16:20	and when they had B them to the magistrates
	16:30	Paul and Silas, and B them out and said,
	16:34	Then he B them up into his house, and
	17:15	Those who conducted Paul B him as far as
	17:19	hold of him and B him to the Are-opagus,
	18:12	attack upon Paul and B him before the tribunal,
	19:19	who practiced magic arts B their books together and
	19:24	silver shrines of Artemis, B no little business to
	19:37	For you have B these men here who are
	20:38	And they B him to the ship.
	21:5	with wives and children, B us on our way
	21:28	place; moreover he also B Greeks into the temple,
	21:29	supposed that Paul had B him into the temple.
	21:34	ordered him to be B into the barracks.
	21:37	was about to be B into the barracks, he
	22:3	Tarsus in Cilicia, but B up in this city
	22:24	commanded him to be B into the barracks, and
	22:30	to meet, and he B Paul down and set
	23:18	he took him and B him to the tribune
	23:28	they accused him, I B him down to their
	23:31	instructions, took Paul and B him by night to

25:6 on the tribunal and ordered Paul to be B
25:17 the man to be B in.
25:18 accusers stood up, they B no charge in his
25:23 of Festus Paul was B in.
25:26 Therefore I have B him before you, and, especially
Rom 5:16 following one trespass B condemnation, but the free
6:13 men who have been B from death to life,
Gal 2:4 of false brethren secretly B in, who slipped in
Eph 2:13 were far-off have been B near in the blood
1Thes 3:6 from you, and has B us the good news
1Tim 5:10 as one who has B up children, shown hospitality,
6:7 with contentment; for we B nothing into the world,
2Tim 1:10 who abolished death and B life and immortality to
Heb 13:11 animals whose blood is B into the sanctuary by
13:20 God of peace who B again from the dead
Jas 1:17 his own will he B us forth by the
5:18 rain, and the earth B forth its fruit.
2Pet 2:5 other persons, when he B a flood upon the
Rev 12:4 her child when she B it forth;
12:5 brought it forth; she B forth a male child,

BROW (3)
Gen 49:26 Joseph, and on the B of him who was
Jer 3:3 you have a harlot's B, you refuse to be
Lk 4:29 led him to the B of the hill on

BRRETHREN
Lk 8:20 "Your mother and your B are standing outside,

BRUISE (3)
Gen 3:15 her seed; he shall B your head, and you
3:15 head, and you shall B his heel."
Is 53:10 of the LORD to B him; he has put

BRUISED (4)
Lev 22:24 which has its testicles B or crushed or torn
Is 42:3 in the street; a B reed he will not
53:5 our transgressions, he was B for our iniquities; upon
Mt 12:20 will not break a B reed or quench a

BRUISES (2)
Sir 23:10 torture will not lack B, so also the man
Is 1:6 soundness in it, but B and sores and bleeding

BRUISING
Mk 5:5 always crying out, and B himself with stones.

BRUSH
Dan 3:46 the furnace fires with naphtha, pitch, tow, and B

BRUSHWOOD (2)
Judg 9:48 down a bundle of B, and took it up
Is 64:2 as when fire kindles B and the fire causes

BRUTAL
Ezek 21:31 into the hands of B men, skilful to destroy.

BUCKET
Is 40:15 a drop from a B, and are accounted as

BUCKETS
Num 24:7 shall flow from his B, and his seed shall

BUCKLE (3)
1Mac 10:89 to him a golden B, such as it is
11:58 and dress in purple and wear a gold B
14:44 clothed in purple or put on a gold B

BUCKLER (5)
Ps 35:2 hold of shield and B, and rise for my
91:4 find refuge; his faithfulness is a shield and B
Jer 46:3 king of Judah: "Prepare B and shield, and advance
Ezek 23:24 on every side with B, shield, and helmet, and
38:4 all of them with B and shield, wielding swords;

BUCKLERS (3)
2Chr 14:8 from Judah, armed with B and spears, and two
Song 4:4 whereon hang a thousand B, all of them shields
Ezek 39:9 burn them, shields and B, bows and arrows,

BUD (4)
Ex 9:31 in the ear and the flax was in B
Job 14:9 of water it will B and put forth branches
Sir 24:17 I caused loveliness to B, and my blossoms became
39:13 you holy sons, and B like a rose growing

BUDDED (5)
Gen 40:10 as soon as it B, its blossoms shot forth,
Song 6:11 whether the vines had B, whether the pomegranates
7:12 the vines have B, whether the grape blossoms
Ezek 7:10 doom has come, injustice has blossomed, pride has B
Heb 9:4 and Aaron's rod that B, and the tables of

BUDS
Num 17:8 sprouted and put forth B, and produced blossoms,

BUFFETED
1Cor 4:11 we are ill-clad and B and homeless,

BUGLE
1Cor 14:8 And if the B gives an indistinct sound, who

BUILD (154)
Gen 11:4 said, "Come, let us B ourselves a city, and
Ex 20:25 stone, you shall not B it of hewn stones;
Num 23:1 Balaam said to Balak, B for me here seven
23:29 Balaam said to Balak, B for me here seven
32:16 and said, "We will B sheepfolds here for our
32:24 B cities for your little ones, and folds for
Deut 6:10 which you did not B,
20:20 down that you may B siegeworks against the city
22:8 "When you B a new house, you shall make
25:9 man who does not B up his brother's house.'
27:5 And there you shall B an altar to the
27:6 You shall B an altar to the LORD your
28:30 with her; you shall B a house, and you
Josh 22:26 said, 'Let us now B an altar, not for
Judg 6:26 is beside it; and B an altar to the
1Sam 2:35 mind; and I will B him a sure house,
2Sam 7:5 the LORD: Would you B me a house to
7:13 He shall B a house for my name, and
7:27 servant, saying, 'I will B you a house'; therefore
24:21 you, in order to B an altar to the
1Kgs 2:36 and said to him, B yourself a house in
5:3 my father could not B a house for the
5:5 so I purpose to B a house for the
5:5 in your place, shall B the house for my
5:18 and the stone to B the house.
6:1 month, he began to B the house of the
8:16 Israel in which to B a house, that my
8:17 David my father to B a house for the
8:18 in your heart to B a house for my
8:19 nevertheless you shall not B the house, but your
8:19 born to you shall B the house for my
9:1 that Solomon desired to B,
9:15 King Solomon levied to B the house of the
9:19 Solomon desired to B in Jerusalem, in Lebanon,
11:38 with you, and will B you a sure house,
1Chr 14:1 masons and carpenters to B a house for him.
17:4 LORD: You shall not B me a house to
17:10 that the LORD will B you a house.
17:12 He shall B a house for me, and I
17:25 servant that thou wilt B a house for him;
21:22 floor that I may B on it an altar
22:6 and charged him to B a house for the
22:7 in my heart to B a house to the
22:8 wars; you shall not B a house to my
22:10 He shall B a house for my name.
22:19 Arise and B the sanctuary of the LORD God,
28:2 in my heart to B a house of rest
28:3 me, 'You may not B a house for my
28:6 your son who shall B my house and my
28:10 has chosen you to B a house for the
29:19 and that he may B the palace for which
2Chr 2:1 Now Solomon purposed to B a temple for the
2:3 sent him cedar to B himself a house to
2:4 I am about to B a house for the
2:5 which I am to B will be great, for
2:6 who is able to B him a house, since
2:6 Who am I to B a house for him,
2:9 house I am to B will be great and
2:12 and understanding, who will B a temple for the
3:1 Then Solomon began to B the house of the
3:2 He began to B in the second month of
6:5 Israel in which to B a house, that my
6:7 David my father to B a house for the
6:8 in your heart to B a house for my
6:9 nevertheless you shall not B the house, but your
6:9 born to you shall B the house for my
8:6 Solomon desired to B in Jerusalem, in Lebanon,
14:7 to Judah, "Let us B these cities, and surround
36:23 has charged me to B him a house at

Ezra 1:2 has charged me to B him a house at
4:2 to them, "Let us B with you; for we
4:3 but we alone will B to the LORD, the
4:4 made them afraid to B,
5:3 you a decree to B this house and to
5:9 you a decree to B this house and to
Neh 2:17 Come, let us B the wall of Jerusalem, that
2:18 And they said, "Let us rise up and B
2:20 servants will arise and B; but you have no
Job 20:19 has seized a house which he did not B
Ps 28:5 break them down and B them up no more.
89:4 descendants for ever, and B your throne for all
102:16 For the LORD will B up Zion, he will
104:17 In them the birds B their nests; the stork
127:1 the house, those who B it labor in vain.
Prov 24:27 field; and after that B your house.
Eccl 3:3 and a time to B up;
Song 8:9 a wall, we will B upon her a battlement
Wis 9:8 hast given command to B a temple on thy
Sir 47:13 side, that he might B a house for his
49:7 destroy, and likewise to B and to plant.
Is 9:10 fallen, but we will B with dressed stones; the
45:13 his ways; he shall B my city and set
57:14 it shall be said, B up, build up, prepare
57:14 be said, "Build up, B up, prepare the way,
60:10 Foreigners shall B up your walls, and their kings
61:4 They shall B up the ancient ruins, they shall
62:10 way for the people; B up, build up the
62:10 the people; build up, B up the highway, clear
65:21 They shall B houses and inhabit them; they shall
65:22 They shall not B and another inhabit; they shall
66:1 house which you would B for me, and what
Jer 1:10 and to overthrow, to B and to plant."
18:9 kingdom that I will B and plant it,
22:14 who says, 'I will B myself a great house
24:6 I will B them up, and not tear them
29:5 from Jerusalem to Babylon: B houses and live in
29:28 exile will be long; B houses and live in
31:4 Again I will B you, and you shall be
31:28 watch over them to B and to plant, says
35:7 ever; you shall not B a house; you shall
35:9 daughters, and not to B houses to dwell in.
42:10 land, then I will B you up and not
Ezek 4:2 siegeworks against it, and B a siege wall against
11:3 is not near to B houses; this city is
13:10 because, when the people B a wall, these prophets
21:22 cast up mounds, to B siege towers.
22:30 among them who should B up the wall and
28:26 it, and they shall B houses and plant vineyards.
Dan 9:25 word to restore and B Jerusalem to the coming
Hos 2:6 thorns; and I will B a wall against her,
Mic 3:10 pervert all equity, who B Zion with blood and
Zeph 1:13 Though they B houses, they shall not inhabit them;
Hag 1:8 and bring wood and B the house, that I
Zech 5:11 land of Shinar, to B a house for it;
6:12 place, and he shall B the temple of the
6:13 is he who shall B the temple of the
6:15 come and help to B the temple of the
Mal 1:4 hosts says, "They may B, but I will tear
1Mac 1:47 and the priests, to B altars and sacred precincts
10:11 doing the work to B the walls and encircle
12:35 planned with them to B strongholds in Judea,
12:36 strongholds in Judea, to B the walls of Jerusalem
12:37 they gathered together to B up the city; part
15:39 and commanded him to B up Kedron and fortify
2Mac 14:33 altar, and I will B here a splendid temple
Mt 16:18 this rock I will B my church, and the
23:28 for you B the tombs of the prophets and
26:61 of God, and to B it in three days.'"
27:40 destroy the temple and B it in three days,
Mk 14:58 three days I will B another, not made with
15:28 destroy the temple and B it in three days,
Lk 11:47 for you B the tombs of the prophets whom
11:48 killed them, and you B their tombs.
12:18 down my barns, and B larger ones; and there
14:28 of you, desiring to B a tower, does not
14:30 'This man began to B, and was not able
Jn 2:20 taken forty-six years to B this temple, and will
Acts 7:49 What house will you B for me, says the
20:32 which is able to B you up and to
Rom 15:20 been named, lest I B on another man's foundation,
1Cor 10:23 but not all things B up.
Gal 2:18 But if I B up again those things which
1Thes 5:11 encourage one another and B one another up, just
Jude 1:20 But you, beloved, B yourselves up on your most

BUILDER (5)
2Mac 2:29 For as the master B of a new house
1Cor 3:10 like a skilled master B I laid a foundation,
Heb 3:3 than Moses as the B of a house has
3:4 some one, but the B of all things is
11:10 which has foundations, whose B and maker is God.

BUILDERS (16)
1Kgs 5:18 So Solomon's B and Hiram's builders and the men
5:18 Solomon's builders and Hiram's B and the men of
2Kgs 12:11 the carpenters and the B who worked upon the
22:6 carpenters, and to the B, and to the masons,
2Chr 34:11 the carpenters and the B to buy quarried stone,
Ezra 3:10 And when the B laid the foundation of the
Neh 4:5 they have provoked thee to anger before the B
4:18 And each of the B had his sword girded
Ps 118:22 The stone which the B rejected has become the
Is 49:17 Your B outstrip your destroyers, and those who laid
Ezek 27:4 of the seas; your B made perfect your beauty.
Mt 21:42 very stone which the B rejected has become the
Mk 12:10 very stone which the B rejected has become the
Lk 20:17 very stone which the B rejected has become the
Acts 4:11 was rejected by you B, but which has become
1Pet 2:7 very stone which the B rejected has become the

BUILDING (56)
Gen 11:8 and they left off B the city.
Josh 22:16 following the LORD, by B yourselves an altar this
22:19 us as rebels by B yourselves an altar other
22:23 us not today for B an altar to turn
22:29 following the LORD by B an altar for burnt
1Kgs 3:1 until he had finished B his own house and
6:12 house which you are B, if you will walk
6:38 was seven years in B it.
7:1 Solomon was B his own house thirteen years, and
9:1 When Solomon had finished B the house of the
15:21 of it, he stopped B Ramah, and he dwelt
15:22 which Baasha had been B; and with them King
1Chr 22:2 prepare dressed stones for B the house of God.
22:11 you may succeed in B the house of the
28:2 of our God; and I made preparations for B
29:16 we have provided for B thee a house for
2Chr 3:3 Solomon's measurements for B the house of God:
16:5 of it, he stopped B Ramah, and let his
16:6 which Baasha had been B, and with them he
20:36 He joined him in B ships to go to
27:3 LORD, and did much B on the wall of
Ezra 4:1 the returned exiles were B a temple to the
4:3 do with us in B a house to our
5:4 the men who are B this building?"
5:4 names of the men who are building this B
5:16 it has been in B, and it is not
6:14 They finished their B by command of the God
Neh 4:1 heard that we were B the wall, he was
4:3 "Yes, what they are B – if a fox
4:17 of Judah, who were B on the wall.
6:6 is why you are B the wall; and you
Tob 14:5 there with a glorious B for all generations for
Eccl 9:14 it and besieged it, B great siegeworks against it.
Sir 22:14 firmly bonded into a B will not be torn
40:19 Children and the B of a city establish a
Ezek 16:31 of a brazen harlot; B your vaulted chamber at
41:12 The B that was facing the temple yard on
41:12 the wall of the B was five cubits thick
41:13 the yard and the B with its walls, a
41:15 the length of the B facing the yard which
42:1 yard and opposite the B on the north.
42:2 The length of the B which was on the
42:5 from the lower and middle chambers in the B
42:10 yard and opposite the B, there were chambers
Mic 7:11 A day for the B of your walls!
1Mac 3:56 to those who were B houses, or were betrothed,
16:23 he did, and the B of the walls which
Lk 6:48 is like a man B a house, who dug
1Cor 3:9 God's fellow workers; you are God's field, God's B
3:10 and another man is B upon it.
14:12 strive to excel in B up the church.
2Cor 5:1 destroyed, we have a B from God, a house
10:8 the Lord gave for B you up and not
13:10 has given me for B up and not for
Eph 4:12 work of ministry, for B up the body of
1Pet 3:20 of Noah, during the B of the ark, in

BUILDINGS (5)
2Chr 34:11 and beams for the B which the kings of
Jud 3:3 Behold, our B, and all our land, and all

Mt 24:1 out to him the B of the temple.
Mk 13:1 what wonderful stones and what wonderful B
13:2 said to him, "Do you see these great B

BUILDS (12)

Job 27:18 The house which he B is like a spider's
Ps 127:1 Unless the LORD B the house, those who build
147:2 The LORD B up Jerusalem; he gathers the outcasts
Prov 14:1 Wisdom B her house, but folly with her own
Sir 21:8 A man who B his house with other people's
34:23 When one B and another tears down, what do
Jer 22:13 "Woe to him who B his house by unrighteousness,
Amos 9:6 Nile of Egypt; who B his upper chambers in
Hab 2:12 Woe to him who B a town with blood,
1Cor 3:10 take care how he B upon it.
3:12 Now if any one B on the foundation with
8:1 puffs up, but love B up.

BUILT (233)

Gen 4:17 bore Enoch; and he B a city, and called
8:20 Then Noah B an altar to the LORD, and
10:11 into Assyria, and B Nineveh, Rehoboth-Ir, Calah, and
11:5 the tower, which the sons of men had B
12:7 So he B there an altar to the LORD,
12:8 east; and there he B an altar to the
13:18 Hebron; and there he B an altar to the
22:9 had told him, Abraham B an altar there, and
26:25 So he B an altar there and called upon
33:17 journeyed to Succoth, and B himself a house, and
35:7 him, and there he B an altar, and called
Ex 1:10 heavy burdens; and they B for Pharaoh store-cities,
17:15 And Moses B an altar and called the name
24:4 in the morning, and B an altar at the
32:5 Aaron saw this, he B an altar before it;
Num 13:22 (Hebron was B seven years before Zoan in Egypt.)
21:27 Heshbon, let it be B, let the city of
23:14 top of Pisgah, and B seven altars, and offered
32:34 the sons of Gad B Dibon, Ataroth, Aroer,
32:37 the sons of Reuben B Heshbon, Elealeh, Kiriathaim,
32:38 gave other names to the cities which they B
Deut 8:12 are full, and have B goodly houses and live
13:16 it shall not be B again.
20:5 is there that has B a new house and
Josh 2:15 for her house was B into the city wall,
8:30 Then Joshua B an altar in Mount Ebal to
22:10 the half-tribe of Manasseh B there an altar by
22:11 half-tribe of Manasseh have B an altar at the
24:13 which you had not B, and you dwell therein;
Judg 1:26 of the Hittites and B a city, and called
6:24 Then Gideon B an altar there to the LORD,
6:28 was offered upon the altar which had been B
21:4 people rose early, and B there an altar, and
Ruth 4:11 and Leah, who together B up the house of
1Sam 7:17 And he B there an altar to the LORD.
14:35 And Saul B an altar to the LORD; it
14:35 first altar that he B to the LORD.
2Sam 5:9 And David B the city round about from the
5:11 carpenters and masons who B David a house.
7:7 "Why have you not B me a house of
24:25 And David B there an altar to the LORD,
1Kgs 3:2 house had yet been B for the name of
6:2 house which King Solomon B for the LORD was
6:5 He also B a structure against the wall of
6:7 When the house was B, it was with stone
6:7 heard in the temple, while it was being B
6:9 So he B the house, and finished it; and
6:10 He B the structure against the whole house, each
6:14 So Solomon B the house, and finished it.
6:16 He B twenty cubits of the rear of the
6:16 the rafters, and he B this within as an
6:36 He B the inner court with three courses of
7:2 He B the House of the Forest of Lebanon;
7:2 cubits, and it was B upon three rows of
8:13 I have B thee an exalted house, a place
8:20 promised, and I have B the house for the
8:27 how much less this house which I have B
8:43 house which I have B is called by thy
8:44 house which I have B for thy name,
8:48 house which I have B for thy name;
9:3 house which you have B, and put my name
9:10 in which Solomon had B the two houses, the
9:24 house which Solomon had B for her; then he
9:24 for her; then he B the Millo.
9:25 the altar which he B to the LORD, burning
9:26 King Solomon B a fleet of ships at Ezion-geber,
10:4 house that he had B,
11:7 Then Solomon B a high place for Chemosh the
11:27 Solomon B the Millo, and closed up the breach
11:38 sure house, as I B for David, and I
12:25 Then Jeroboam B Shechem in the hill country of
12:25 out from there and B Penuel.
14:23 For they also B for themselves high places, and
15:17 up against Judah, and B Ramah, that he might
15:22 with them King Asa B Geba of Benjamin and
15:23 the cities which he B, are they not written
16:24 the city which he B, Samaria, after the name
16:32 of Baal, which he B in Samaria.
16:34 days Hiel of Bethel B Jericho; he laid its
18:32 with the stones he B an altar in the
22:39 ivory house which he B, and all the cities
22:39 the cities that he B, are they not written
2Kgs 14:22 He B Elath and restored it to Judah, after
15:35 He B the upper gate of the house of
16:11 And Uriah the priest B the altar; in accordance
16:18 sabbath which had been B inside the palace, and
17:9 They B for themselves high places at all their
21:4 And he B altars in the house of the
21:5 And he B altars for all the host of
23:13 king of Israel had B for Ashtoreth the abomination
25:1 to it; and they B siegeworks against it round
1Chr 6:10 the house that Solomon B in Jerusalem).
6:32 meeting, until Solomon had B the house of the
7:24 daughter was Sheerah, who B both Lower and
8:12 Misham, and Shemed, who B Ono and Lod with
11:8 And he B the city round about from the
15:1 David B houses for himself in the city of
17:6 "Why have you not B me a house of
21:26 And David B there an altar to the LORD
22:5 that is to be B for the LORD must
22:19 brought into a house B for the name of
2Chr 6:2 I have B thee an exalted house, a place
6:10 promised, and I have B the house for the
6:18 how much less this house which I have B
6:33 house which I have B is called by thy
6:34 house which I have B for thy name,
6:38 house which I have B for thy name,
8:1 in which Solomon had B the house of the
8:4 He B Tadmor in the wilderness and all the
8:4 the store-cities which he B in Hamath.
8:5 He also B Upper Beth-horon and Lower Beth-horon,
8:11 house which he had B for her, for he
8:12 LORD which he had B before the vestibule,
9:3 house that he had B,
11:5 in Jerusalem, and he B cities for defense in
11:6 He B Bethlehem, Etam, Tekoa,
14:6 He B fortified cities in Judah, for the land
14:7 So they B and prospered.
16:1 up against Judah, and B Ramah, that he might
16:6 and with them he B Geba and Mizpah.
17:12 He B in Judah fortresses and store-cities,
20:8 in it, and have B thee in it a
20:36 to Tarshish, and they B the ships in Ezion-geber.
26:2 He B Eloth and restored it to Judah, after
26:6 of Ashdod; and he B cities in the territory
26:9 Moreover Uzziah B towers in Jerusalem at the
26:10 And he B towers in the wilderness, and hewed
27:3 He B the upper gate of the house of
27:4 Moreover he B cities in the hill country of
32:5 to work resolutely and B up all the wall
32:5 and outside it he B another wall; and he
33:4 And he B altars in the house of the
33:5 And he B altars for all the host of
33:14 Afterwards he B an outer wall for the city
33:15 altars that he had B on the mountain of
33:19 sites on which he B high places and set
35:3 David, king of Israel, B; you need no longer
Ezra 3:2 his kinsmen, and they B the altar of the
5:8 It is being B with huge stones, and timber
5:11 the house that was B many years ago, which
5:11 great king of Israel B and finished.
6:14 elders of the Jews B and prospered, through the
Neh 3:1 the priests and they B the Sheep Gate.
3:2 And next to him the men of Jericho B
3:2 next to them Zaccur the son of Imri B
3:3 the sons of Hassenaah B the Fish Gate; they
3:15 its bars; and he B the wall of the
4:6 So we B the wall; and all the wall
4:18 his sword girded at his side while he B
6:1 enemies that I had B the wall and that
7:1 the wall had been B and I had set
7:4 it were few and no houses had been B
12:29 for the singers had B for themselves villages around

Tob	13:16	For Jerusalem will be B with sapphires and
Jud	1:2	is the king who B walls about Ecbatana with
	1:3	at the gates he B towers a hundred cubits
Ps	78:69	He B his sanctuary like the high heavens, like
	122:3	Jerusalem, B as a city which is bound firmly
Prov	9:1	Wisdom has B her house, she has set up
	24:3	wisdom a house is B, and by understanding it
Eccl	2:4	made great works; I B houses and planted vineyards
Song	4:4	the tower of David, B for an arsenal, whereon
Wis	14:2	was the craftsman who B it;
Sir	48:17	rock with iron and B pools for water.
	49:12	in their days they B the house and raised
Is	5:2	with choice vines; he B a watchtower in the
	44:26	Judah, 'They shall be B, and I will raise
	44:28	Jerusalem, 'She shall be B and of the temple,
Jer	7:31	And they have B the high place of Topheth,
	12:16	then they shall be B up in the midst
	19:5	of innocents, and have B the high places of
	31:4	and you shall be B, O virgin Israel!
	32:31	the day it was B to this day, so
	32:35	They B the high places of Baal in the
	45:4	Behold, what I have B I am breaking down,
	52:4	siege to it and B siegeworks against it round
Ezek	13:5	into the breaches, or B up a wall for
	16:24	the Lord GOD), you B yourself a vaulted chamber,
	16:25	of every street you B your lofty place and
	17:17	up and siege walls B to cut off many
Dan	4:30	Babylon, which I have B by my mighty power
	9:25	weeks it shall be B again with squares and
Hos	8:14	forgotten his Maker, and B palaces; and Judah has
	10:1	the more altars he B; as his country improved
Amos	5:11	of wheat, you have B houses of hewn stone,
	7:7	standing beside a wall B with a plumb line,
Zech	1:16	my house shall be B in it, says the
	8:9	hosts was laid, that the temple might be B
	9:3	Tyre has B herself a rampart, and heaped up
1Mac	1:14	So they B a gymnasium in Jerusalem, according to
	1:54	They also B altars in the surrounding cities of
	4:47	the law directs, and B a new altar like
	4:53	new altar of burnt offering which they had B
	5:1	the altar had been B and the sanctuary dedicated
	6:20	fiftieth year; and he B siege towers and other
	6:31	days they fought and B engines of war; but
	8:15	pride, but they have B for themselves a senate
	9:50	returned to Jerusalem and B strong cities in Judea:
	10:12	strongholds that Bacchides had B fled;
	11:20	in Jerusalem, and he B many engines of war
	12:38	And Simon B Adida in the Shephelah; he fortified
	13:27	And Simon B a monument over the tomb of
	13:30	the tomb which he B in Modein; it remains
	13:33	But Simon B up the strongholds of Judea and
	13:38	strongholds that you have B be your possession.
	13:48	strengthened its fortifications and B in it a house
	14:36	in Jerusalem, who had B themselves a citadel from
	14:37	of the city, and B the walls of Jerusalem
	15:7	strongholds which you have B and now hold shall
	15:41	He B up Kedron and stationed there horsemen and
	16:9	until Cendebeus reached Kedron, which he had B
	16:15	Dok, which he had B; he gave them a
	16:23	the walls which he B, and his achievements,
2Mac	1:18	given when Nehemiah, who B the temple and the
	10:2	altars which had been B in the public square
Mt	7:24	a wise man who B his house upon the
	7:26	a foolish man who B his house upon the
	21:33	press in it, and B a tower, and let
Mk	12:1	the wine press, and B a tower, and let
Lk	4:29	which their city was B, that they might throw
	6:48	not shake it, because it had been well B
	6:49	like a man who B a house on the
	7:5	our nation, and he B us our synagogue."
	17:28	sold, they planted, they B,
Acts	7:47	it was Solomon who B a house for him.
	9:31	had peace and was B up; and walking in
1Cor	3:14	which any man has B on the foundation survives,
Eph	2:20	the household of God, B upon the foundation of
	2:22	whom you also are B into it for a
Col	2:7	in him, rooted and B up in him and
Heb	3:4	(For every house is B by some one, but
1Pet	2:5	living stones be yourselves B into a spiritual house,
Rev	21:18	The wall was B of jasper, while the city

BUKKI (5)

Num	34:22	of Dan a leader, B the son of Jogli.
1Chr	6:5	of Abishua, Abishua of B, Bukki of Uzzi,
	6:5	Abishua, Abishua of Bukki, B of Uzzi,
	6:51	son, Abishua his son, B his son, Uzzi his
Ezra	7:4	of Uzzi, son of B,

BUKKIAH (2)

1Chr	25:4	the sons of Heman: B, Mattaniah, Uzziel, Shebuel,
	25:13	twelve; the sixth to B, his sons and his

BUL

1Kgs	6:38	in the month of B, which is the eighth

BULGING

Is	30:13	in a high wall, B out, and about to

BULL (104)

Ex	29:1	Take one young B and two rams without blemish,
	29:3	basket, and bring the B and the two rams.
	29:10	you shall bring the B before the tent of
	29:10	the head of the B,
	29:11	you shall kill the B before the LORD, at
	29:12	the blood of the B and put it upon
	29:14	the flesh of the B, and its skin, and
	29:36	you shall offer a B as a sin offering
Lev	1:5	he shall kill the B before the LORD; and
	4:3	has committed a young B without blemish to the
	4:4	He shall bring the B to the door of
	4:4	the head of the B, and kill the bull
	4:4	bull, and kill the B before the LORD.
	4:5	the blood of the B and bring it to
	4:7	the blood of the B he shall pour out
	4:8	the fat of the B of the sin offering
	4:11	the skin of the B and all its flesh,
	4:12	its dung, the whole B he shall carry forth
	4:14	shall offer a young B for a sin offering
	4:15	the head of the B before the LORD, and
	4:15	the LORD, and the B shall be killed before
	4:16	the blood of the B to the tent of
	4:20	he do with the B; as he did with
	4:20	he did with the B of the sin offering,
	4:21	shall carry forth the B outside the camp, and
	4:21	he burned the first B; it is the sin
	8:2	anointing oil, and the B of the sin offering,
	8:14	Then he brought the B of the sin offering;
	8:14	the head of the B of the sin offering.
	8:17	But the B, and its skin, and its flesh,
	9:2	to Aaron, "Take a B calf for a sin
	16:3	place: with a young B for a sin offering
	16:6	Aaron shall offer the B as a sin offering
	16:11	"Aaron shall present the B as a sin offering
	16:11	he shall kill the B as a sin offering
	16:14	the blood of the B, and sprinkle it with
	16:15	the blood of the B, sprinkling it upon the
	16:18	the blood of the B and of the blood
	16:27	And the B for the sin offering and the
	22:23	A B or a lamb which has a part
	22:27	to Moses, "When a B or sheep or goat
	23:18	blemish, and one young B, and two rams; they
Num	7:15	of incense; one young B, one ram, one male
	7:21	of incense; one young B, one ram, one male
	7:27	of incense; one young B, one ram, one male
	7:33	of incense; one young B, one ram, one male
	7:39	of incense; one young B, one ram, one male
	7:45	of incense; one young B, one ram, one male
	7:51	of incense; one young B, one ram, one male
	7:57	of incense; one young B, one ram, one male
	7:63	of incense; one young B, one ram, one male
	7:69	of incense; one young B, one ram, one male
	7:75	of incense; one young B, one ram, one male
	7:81	of incense; one young B, one ram, one male
	8:8	them take a young B and its cereal offering
	8:8	shall take another young B for a sin offering.
	15:8	when you prepare a B for a burnt offering,
	15:9	shall offer with the B a cereal offering of
	15:11	be done for each B or ram, or for
	15:24	shall offer one young B for a burnt offering,
	23:2	on each altar a B and a ram.
	23:4	upon each altar a B and a ram."
	23:14	altars, and offered a B and a ram on
	23:30	said, and offered a B and a ram on
	28:12	with oil, for each B; and two tenths of
	28:14	of wine for a B, a third of a
	28:20	you offer for a B, and two tenths for
	28:28	an ephah for each B, two tenths for one
	29:2	the LORD: one young B, one ram, seven male
	29:3	an ephah for the B, two tenths for the
	29:8	pleasing odor: one young B, one ram, seven male
	29:9	an ephah for the B, two tenths for the
	29:36	to the LORD: one B, one ram, seven male

B

29:37 drink offerings for the B, for the ram, and
Deut 33:17 His firstling B has majesty, and his horns are
Judg 6:25 him, "Take your father's B, the second bull seven
6:25 father's bull, the second B seven years old, and
6:26 then take the second B, and offer it as
6:28 down, and the second B was offered upon the
1Sam 1:24 along with a three-year-old B, an ephah of flour,
1:25 Then they slew the B, and they brought the
1Kgs 18:23 let them choose one B for themselves, and cut
18:23 will prepare the other B and lay it on
18:25 "Choose for yourselves one B and prepare it first,
18:26 And they took the B which was given them,
18:33 order, and cut the B in pieces and laid
2Chr 13:9 himself with a young B or seven rams becomes
Job 21:10 Their B breeds without fail; their cow calves, and
Ps 50:9 I will accept no B from your house, nor
69:31 an ox or a B with horns and hoofs.
Sir 6:2 your soul be torn in pieces like a B
Is 10:13 their treasures; like a B I have brought down
Jer 46:15 Why did not your B stand?
Ezek 43:19 the Lord GOD, a B for a sin offering.
43:21 shall also take the B of the sin offering,
43:22 be cleansed, as it was cleansed with the B
43:23 you shall offer a B without blemish and a
43:25 sin offering; also a B and a ram from
45:18 shall take a young B without blemish, and cleanse
45:22 the land a young B for a sin offering.
45:24 an ephah for each B, an ephah for each
46:6 shall offer a young B without blemish, and six
46:7 an ephah with the B and an ephah with
46:11 offering with a young B shall be an ephah,

BULLS (59)

Gen 32:15 forty cows and ten B, twenty she-asses and ten
Lev 22:19 without blemish, of the B or the sheep or
Num 7:87 the burnt offering twelve B, twelve rams, twelve
7:88 of peace offerings twenty-four B, the rams sixty, the
8:12 the heads of the B; and you shall offer
23:1 for me here seven B and seven rams."
23:29 for me here seven B and seven rams."
28:11 the LORD: two young B, one ram, seven male
28:19 the LORD: two young B, one ram, and seven
28:27 the LORD; two young B, one ram, seven male
29:13 the LORD, thirteen young B, two rams, fourteen
29:14 each of the thirteen B, two tenths for each
29:17 second day twelve young B, two rams, fourteen male
29:18 drink offerings for the B, for the rams, and
29:20 the third day eleven B, two rams, fourteen male
29:21 drink offerings for the B, for the rams, and
29:23 the fourth day ten B, two rams, fourteen male
29:24 drink offerings for the B, for the rams, and
29:26 the fifth day nine B, two rams, fourteen male
29:27 drink offerings for the B, for the rams, and
29:29 the sixth day eight B, two rams, fourteen male
29:30 drink offerings for the B, for the rams, and
29:32 the seventh day seven B, two rams, fourteen male
29:33 drink offerings for the B, for the rams, and
1Kgs 18:23 Let two B be given to us; and let
1Chr 15:26 LORD, they sacrificed seven B and seven rams.
29:21 the LORD, a thousand B, a thousand rams, and
2Chr 29:21 And they brought seven B, seven rams, seven lambs,
29:22 So they killed the B, and the priests received
29:32 assembly brought was seventy B, a hundred rams,
29:33 offerings were six hundred B and three thousand
30:24 the assembly a thousand B and seven thousand sheep
30:24 the assembly a thousand B and ten thousand sheep.
35:7 thousand, and three thousand B; these were from the
35:8 six hundred lambs and kids and three hundred B
35:9 five thousand lambs and kids and five hundred B
35:12 And so they did with the B
Ezra 6:9 is needed-- young B, rams, or sheep for
6:17 of God one hundred B, two hundred rams, four
7:17 with all diligence buy B, rams, and lambs, with
8:35 God of Israel, twelve B for all Israel, ninety-six
Job 42:8 Now therefore take seven B and seven rams, and
Ps 22:12 Many B encompass me, strong bulls of Bashan
22:12 bulls encompass me, strong B of Bashan surround
50:13 eat the flesh of B, or drink the blood
51:19 whole burnt offerings; then B will be offered on
66:15 make an offering of B and goats.
68:30 reeds, the herd of B with the calves of
Sir 38:25 with their work, and whose talk is about B
Is 1:11 in the blood of B, or of lambs, or
34:7 with them, and young steers with the mighty B
Jer 50:27 Slay all her B, let them go down to
52:20 sea, the twelve bronze B which were under the
Ezek 39:18 and of goats, of B, all of them fatlings
45:23 the LORD seven young B and seven rams without
Dan 3:39 offerings of rams and B, and with tens of
Hos 12:11 in Gilgal they sacrifice B, their altars also shall
Heb 9:13 blood of goats and B and with the ashes
10:4 that the blood of B and goats should take

BULRUSHES

Ex 2:3 a basket made of B, and daubed it with

BULWARK (2)

Ps 8:2 thou hast founded a B because of thy foes,
1Tim 3:15 God, the pillar and B of the truth.

BULWARKS (3)

Is 26:1 city; he sets up salvation as walls and B
Jer 50:15 she has surrendered; her B have fallen, her walls
51:32 have been seized, the B are burned with fire,

BUNAH

1Chr 2:25 Hezron: Ram, his first-born, B, Oren, Ozem, and

BUNCH

Ex 12:22 Take a B of hyssop and dip it in

BUNCHES

2Sam 16:1 of bread, a hundred B of raisins, a hundred

BUNDLE (6)

Gen 42:35 sacks, behold, every man's B of money was in
Judg 9:48 and cut down a B of brushwood, and took
9:49 people cut down his B and following Abimelech put
1Sam 25:29 be bound in the B of the living in
Jer 10:17 Gather up your B from the ground, O you
Acts 28:3 Paul had gathered a B of sticks and put

BUNDLES (3)

Gen 42:35 their father saw their B of money, they were
Ruth 2:16 out some from the B for her, and leave
Mt 13:30 and bind them in B to be burned, but

BUNNI (3)

Neh 9:4 Bani, Kadmi-el, Shebaniah, B, Sherebiah, Bani, and
10:15 Pahath-moab, Elam, Zattu, Bani, B, Azgad, Bebai,
11:15 of Hashabiah, son of B;

BURDEN (47)

Ex 18:22 they will bear the B with you.
23:5 you lying under its B, you shall refrain from
Num 4:19 task and to his B,
11:11 thou dost lay the B of all this people
11:14 this people alone, the B is too heavy for
11:17 they shall bear the B of the people with
Deut 1:12 alone the weight and B of you and your
2Sam 15:33 you will be a B to me.
19:35 servant be an added B to my lord the
2Kgs 5:17 your servant two mules' B of earth; for henceforth
Neh 13:19 the gates, that no B might be brought in
Job 7:20 have I become a B to thee?
Ps 38:4 they weigh like a B too heavy for me.
55:22 Cast your B on the LORD, and he will
81:6 your shoulder of the B; your hands were freed
Wis 2:15 of him is a B to us, because his
Sir 21:16 narration is like a B on a journey, but
Is 1:14 they have become a B to me, I am
9:4 the yoke of his B, and the staff for
10:27 in that day his B will depart from your
14:25 from them, and his B from their shoulder."
22:25 and fall, and the B that was upon it
46:2 they cannot save the B, but themselves go into
Jer 17:21 do not bear a B on the sabbath day
17:22 do not carry a B out of your houses
17:24 and bring in no B by the gates of
17:27 not to bear a B and enter by the
23:33 you, 'What is the B of the LORD?' you
23:33 them, 'You are the B, and I will cast
23:34 people who says, 'The B of the LORD,' I
23:36 LORD spoken?' But 'the B of the LORD' you
23:36 no more, for the B is every man's own
23:38 if you say, 'The B of the LORD,' thus
23:38 said these words, "The B of the LORD," when
23:38 shall not say, 'The B of the LORD,"
Lam 3:14 of all peoples, the B of their songs all
3:63 rising; I am the B of their songs.
Mt 11:30 is easy, and my B is light."
20:12 who have borne the B of the day and

Acts 15:28 upon you no greater B than these necessary things:
2Cor 11:9 want, I did not B any one, for my
12:13 I myself did not B you?
12:14 will not be a B, for I seek not
12:16 I myself did not B you, I was crafty,
1Thes 2:9 that we might not B any of you, while
2Thes 3:8 that we might not B any of you.
Rev 2:24 upon you any other B;

BURDEN-BEARERS (3)

1Kgs 5:15 had seventy thousand B and eighty thousand hewers
2Chr 34:13 music, were over the B and directed all who
Neh 4:10 "The strength of the B is failing, and there

BURDENED (7)

Prov 28:17 If a man is B with the blood of
Sir 3:25 stubborn mind will be B by troubles, and the
Is 43:23 I have not B you with offerings, or wearied
43:24 But you have B me with your sins, you
2Cor 8:13 be eased and you B,
1Tim 5:16 the church not be B, so that it may
2Tim 3:6 and capture weak women, B with sins and swayed

BURDENING

2Cor 11:9 and will refrain from B you in any way.

BURDENS (20)

Ex 1:10 afflict them with heavy B; and they built for
2:11 and looked on their B; and he saw an
5:4 Get to your B
5:5 many and you make them rest from their B
6:6 out from under the B of the Egyptians, and
6:7 out from under the B of the Egyptians.
Num 4:24 in serving and bearing B:
4:47 the work of bearing B in the tent of
2Chr 2:2 thousand men to bear B and eighty thousand to
2:18 he assigned to bear B, eighty thousand to quarry
Neh 4:17 Those who carried B were laden in such a
5:15 before me laid heavy B upon the people, and
13:15 and all kinds of B, which they brought into
Wis 9:15 and this earthy tent B the thoughtful mind.
Sir 33:24 and a stick and B for an ass; bread
Is 46:1 carry are loaded as B on weary beasts.
Mt 23:4 They bind heavy B, hard to bear, and lay
Lk 11:46 you load men with B hard to bear, and
11:46 do not touch the B with one of your
Gal 6:2 Bear one another's B, and so fulfil the law

BURDENSOME (3)

2Sam 13:25 go, lest we be B to you." He pressed
Sir 8:15 fellow, lest he be B to you; for he
1Jn 5:3 And his commandments are not B

BURIAL (14)

Deut 34:6 the place of his B to this day.
2Chr 26:23 his fathers in the B field which belonged to
Eccl 6:3 and also has no B, I say that an
Sir 21:8 gathers stones for his B mound.
38:16 honor due him, and do not neglect his B
Is 14:20 joined with them in B, because you have destroyed
Jer 22:19 his majesty!' With the B of an ass he
26:23 dead body into the B place of the common
Ezek 39:11 Gog a place for B in Israel, the Valley
2Mac 13:7 lawbreaker died, without even B in the earth.
Mt 26:12 she has done it to prepare me for B
Jn 12:7 her keep it for the day of my B
19:40 spices, as is the B custom of the Jews.
Heb 11:22 of the Israelites and gave directions concerning his B

BURIED (117)

Gen 15:15 peace; you shall be B in a good old
23:19 After this, Abraham B Sarah his wife in the
25:9 and Ishmael his sons B him in the cave
25:10 There Abraham was B, with Sarah his wife.
35:8 died, and she was B under an oak below
35:19 died, and she was B on the way to
35:29 sons Esau and Jacob B him.
48:7 to Ephrath; and I B her there on the
49:31 There they B Abraham and Sarah his wife; there
49:31 his wife; there they B Isaac and Rebekah his
49:31 wife; and there I B Leah—
50:13 land of Canaan, and B him in the cave
50:14 After he had B his father, Joseph returned to
Num 11:34 Kibroth-hattaavah, because there they B the people
20:1 died there, and was B there.
Deut 10:6 and there he was B; and his son Eleazar
34:6 the LORD, and he B him in the valley
Josh 24:30 And they B him in his own inheritance at
24:32 up from Egypt were B at Shechem, in the
24:33 Aaron died; and they B him at Gibe-ah, the
Judg 2:9 And they B him within the bounds of his
8:32 old age, and was B in the tomb of
10:2 he died, and was B at Shamir.
10:5 Jair died, and was B in Kamon.
12:7 Gileadite died, and was B in his city in
12:10 Ibzan died, and was B at Bethlehem.
12:12 Zebulunite died, and was B at Aijalon in the
12:15 Pirathonite died, and was B at Pirathon in the
16:31 brought him up and B him between Zorah and
Ruth 1:17 I will die, and there will I be B
1Sam 25:1 for him, and they B him in his house
28:3 mourned for him and B him in Ramah, his
31:13 took their bones and B them under the tamarisk
2Sam 2:4 men of Jabesh-gilead who B Saul,"
2:5 Saul your lord, and B him!
2:32 took up Asahel, and B him in the tomb
3:32 They B Abner at Hebron; and the king lifted
4:12 head of Ish-bosheth, and B it in the tomb
17:23 he died, and was B in the tomb of
21:14 And they B the bones of Saul and his
1Kgs 2:10 his fathers, and was B in the city of
2:34 him; and he was B in his own house
11:43 his fathers, and was B in the city of
13:31 And after he had B him, he said to
13:31 man of God is B; lay my bones beside
14:18 And all Israel B him and mourned for him,
14:31 his fathers and was B with his fathers in
15:8 his fathers; and they B him in the city
15:24 his fathers, and was B with his fathers in
16:6 his fathers, and was B at Tirzah; and Elah
16:28 his fathers, and was B in Samaria; and Ahab
22:37 to Samaria; and they B the king in Samaria.
22:50 his fathers, and was B with his fathers in
2Kgs 8:24 his fathers, and was B with his fathers in
9:28 chariot to Jerusalem, and B him in his tomb
10:35 his fathers, and they B him in Samaria.
12:21 And they B him with his fathers in the
13:9 his fathers, and they B him in Samaria; and
13:13 throne; and Joash was B in Samaria with the
13:20 Elisha died, and they B him.
13:21 a man was being B, lo, a marauding band
14:16 his fathers, and was B in Samaria with the
14:20 horses; and he was B in Jerusalem with his
15:7 his fathers, and they B him with his fathers
15:38 his fathers, and was B with his fathers in
16:20 his fathers, and was B with his fathers in
21:18 his fathers, and was B in the garden of
21:26 And he was B in his tomb in the
23:30 him to Jerusalem, and B him in his own
1Chr 10:12 And they B their bones under the oak in
2Chr 9:31 his fathers, and was B in the city of
12:16 his fathers, and was B in the city of
14:1 his fathers, and they B him in the city
16:14 They B him in the tomb which he had
21:1 his fathers, and was B with his fathers in
21:20 They B him in the city of David, but
22:9 They B him, for they said, "He is the
24:16 And they B him in the city of David
24:25 he died; and they B him in the city
25:28 horses; and he was B with his fathers in
26:23 his fathers, and they B him with his fathers
27:9 his fathers, and they B him in the city
28:27 his fathers, and they B him in the city,
32:33 his fathers, and they B him in the ascent
33:20 his fathers, and they B him in his house;
35:24 he died, and was B in the tombs of
Tob 1:18 fleeing from Judea, I B them secretly.
2:7 dug a grave and B the body.
12:12 One; and when you B the dead, I was
14:12 when Anna died he B her with his father.
Jud 8:3 So they B him with his fathers in the
16:23 in Bethulia, and they B her in the cave
Eccl 8:10 I saw the wicked B; they used to go
Sir 44:15 Their bodies were B in peace, and their name
Jer 8:2 not be gathered or B; they shall be as
16:4 nor shall they be B; they shall be as
16:6 they shall not be B, and no one shall
20:6 there you shall be B, you and all your
22:19 ass he shall be B, dragged and cast forth
25:33 lamented, or gathered, or B; they shall be dung
Ezek 29:5 the open field, and not be gathered and B
39:11 his multitude will be B; it will be called

B

39:15 till the buriers have B it in the Valley
1Mac 2:70 forty-sixth year and was B in the tomb of
9:19 Judas their brother and B him in the tomb
13:23 Jonathan, and he was B there.
13:25 Jonathan his brother, and B him in Modein, the
Mt 14:12 took the body and B it; and they went
Lk 16:22 also died and was B;
Acts 2:29 both died and was B, and his tomb is
5:6 carried him out and B him.
5:9 of those that have B your husband are at
5:10 carried her out and B her beside her husband.
8:2 Devout men B Stephen, and made great lamentation
Rom 6:4 We were B therefore with him by baptism into
1Cor 15:4 scriptures, that he was B, that he was raised
Col 2:12 Christ; and you were B with him in baptism,

BURIERS
Ezek 39:15 by it, till the B have buried it in

BURIES (3)
Job 27:15 survive him the pestilence B, and their widows make
Prov 19:24 The sluggard B his hand in the dish, and
26:15 The sluggard B his hand in the dish; it

BURLAP
Sir 40:4 who is clothed in B;

BURN (147)
Gen 11:3 us make bricks, and B them thoroughly." And they
44:18 let not your anger B against your servant; for
Ex 12:10 anything that remains until the morning you shall B
21:25 hand, foot for foot, B for burn, wound for
21:25 for foot, burn for B, wound for wound, stripe
22:24 and my wrath will B, and I will kill
27:20 be set up to B continually.
29:13 is on them, and B them upon the altar.
29:14 its dung, you shall B with fire outside the
29:18 and its head, and B the whole ram upon
29:25 from their hands, and B them on the altar
29:34 morning, then you shall B the remainder with fire;
30:1 make an altar to B incense upon; of acacia
30:7 And Aaron shall B fragrant incense on it; every
30:7 the lamps he shall B it,
30:8 the evening, he shall B it, a perpetual incense
30:20 altar to minister, to B an offering by fire
32:10 that my wrath may B hot against them and
32:11 why does thy wrath B hot against thy people,
32:22 anger of my lord B hot; you know the
Lev 1:9 And the priest shall B the whole on the
1:13 offer the whole, and B it on the altar;
1:15 off its head, and B it on the altar;
1:17 And the priest shall B it on the altar,
2:2 and the priest shall B this as its memorial
2:9 its memorial portion and B this on the altar,
2:11 leaven; for you shall B no leaven nor any
2:16 And the priest shall B as its memorial portion
3:5 Then Aaron's sons shall B it on the altar
3:11 And the priest shall B it on the altar
3:16 And the priest shall B them on the altar
4:10 and the priest shall B them upon the altar
4:12 poured out, and shall B it on a fire
4:19 take from it and B upon the altar.
4:21 outside the camp, and B it as he burned
4:26 its fat he shall B on the altar, like
4:31 and the priest shall B it upon the altar
4:35 and the priest shall B it on the altar,
5:12 its memorial portion and B this on the altar,
6:12 out; the priest shall B wood on it every
6:12 upon it, and shall B on it the fat
6:15 the cereal offering, and B this as its memorial
7:5 kidneys; the priest shall B them on the altar
7:31 The priest shall B the fat on the altar,
8:32 the bread you shall B with fire.
13:24 the body has a B on its skin and
13:24 raw flesh of the B becomes a spot, reddish-white
13:25 broken out in the B, and the priest shall
13:28 a swelling from the B, and the priest shall
13:28 clean; for it is the scar of the B
13:52 And he shall B the garment, whether diseased in
13:55 is unclean; you shall B it in the fire,
13:57 is spreading; you shall B with fire that in
16:25 sin offering he shall B upon the altar.
17:6 tent of meeting, and B the fat for a
Num 5:26 its memorial portion, and B it upon the altar,
16:40 should draw near to B incense before the LORD,
18:17 the altar, and shall B their fat as an
Deut 7:5 down their Asherim, and B their graven images with
7:25 their gods you shall B with fire; you shall
12:3 pieces their pillars, and B their Asherim with fire;
12:31 gods; for they even B their sons and their
13:16 its open square, and B the city and all
Josh 11:6 hamstring their horses, and B their chariots with
11:13 on mounds did Israel B, except Hazor only; that
Judg 6:39 "Let not thy anger B against me, let me
9:52 of the tower to B it with fire.
12:1 We will B your house over you with fire."
14:15 riddle is, lest we B you and your father's
1Sam 2:16 to him, "Let them B the fat first, and
2:28 to my altar, to B incense, to wear an
1Kgs 12:33 to the altar to B incense.
13:1 by the altar to B incense.
13:2 the high places who B incense upon you, and
2Kgs 12:3 continued to sacrifice and B incense on the high
16:15 "Upon the great altar B the morning burnt offering,
23:5 Judah had ordained to B incense in the high
23:10 that no one might B his son or his
1Chr 23:13 sons for ever should B incense before the LORD,
2Chr 2:6 as a place to B incense before him?
4:20 of pure gold to B before the inner sanctuary,
13:11 that its lamps may B every evening; for we
26:16 of the LORD to B incense on the altar
26:18 for you, Uzziah, to B incense to the LORD,
26:18 who are consecrated to B incense.
26:19 in his hand to B incense, and when he
28:25 made high places to B incense to other gods,
29:11 be his ministers and B incense to him."
32:12 upon it you shall B your sacrifices"?
Neh 10:34 year by year, to B upon the altar of
Jud 6:4 We will B them up, and their mountains will
16:5 boasted that he would B up my territory, and
Job 30:30 me, and my bones B with heat.
31:12 Abaddon, and it would B to the root all
Ps 79:5 Will thy jealous wrath B like fire?
89:46 long will thy wrath B like fire?
102:3 smoke, and my bones B like a furnace.
Wis 13:12 serves life's needs, and B the castoff pieces of
Sir 28:23 its power; it will B among them and will
Is 1:31 both of them shall B together, with none to
10:17 flame; and it will B and devour his thorns
27:4 against them, I would B them up together.
57:5 of deceit, you who B with lust among the
Jer 4:4 forth like fire, and B with none to quench
7:9 commit adultery, swear falsely, B incense to Baal,
7:20 the ground; it will B and not be quenched."
7:31 son of Hinnom, to B their sons and their
11:12 gods to whom they B incense, but they cannot
11:13 to shame, altars to B incense to Baal.
15:14 is kindled which shall B for ever."
17:4 is kindled which shall B for ever."
18:15 have forgotten me, they B incense to false gods;
19:5 places of Baal to B their sons in the
21:10 Babylon, and he shall B it with fire.'
21:12 forth like fire, and B with none to quench
32:29 city on fire, and B it, with the houses
33:18 offer burnt offerings, to B cereal offerings, and to
34:2 Babylon, and he shall B it with fire.
34:5 you, so men shall B spices for you and
34:22 and take it, and B it with fire.
36:25 the king not to B the scroll, he would
37:8 shall take it and B it with fire.
37:10 would rise up and B this city with fire.'"
38:18 Chaldeans, and they shall B it with fire, and
43:12 Egypt; and he shall B them and carry them
43:13 of Egypt he shall B with fire.'"
44:3 that they went to B incense and serve other
44:5 from their wickedness and B no incense to other
44:17 that we have vowed, B incense to the queen
44:25 we have made, to B incense to the queen
Ezek 5:2 third part you shall B in the fire in
5:4 into the fire, and B them in the fire;
16:41 And they shall B your houses and execute judgments
23:47 and their daughters, and B up their houses.
24:11 and its copper may B, that its filthiness may
39:9 of the weapons and B them, shields and bucklers,
Hos 7:7 an oven their hearts B with intrigue; all night
Obad 1:18 Esau stubble; they shall B them and consume them,
Nah 2:13 hosts, and I will B your chariots in smoke,
Mal 4:1 day that comes shall B them up, says the
1Mac 7:35 return safely I will B up this house." And
Mt 3:12 the chaff he will B with unquenchable fire."
Lk 1:9 of the Lord and B incense.
3:17 the chaff he will B with unquenchable fire."

24:32 "Did not our hearts B within us while he
Rev 4:5 and before the throne B seven torches of fire,
17:16 devour her flesh and B her up with fire,

BURNED (184)

Gen 38:24 said, "Bring her out, and let her be B
Ex 32:19 the dancing, Moses' anger B hot, and he threw
Lev 4:12 the ashes are poured out it shall be B
4:21 burn it as he B the first bull; it
6:22 for ever; the whole of it shall be B
6:23 priest shall be wholly B; it shall not be
6:30 place; it shall be B with fire.
7:17 third day shall be B with fire.
7:19 eaten; it shall be B with fire.
8:16 their fat, and Moses B them on the altar.
8:17 and its dung, he B with fire outside the
8:20 cut into pieces, Moses B the head and the
8:21 washed with water, Moses B the whole ram on
8:28 from their hands, and B them on the altar
9:10 the sin offering he B upon the altar, as
9:11 and the skin he B with fire outside the
9:13 the head; and he B them upon the altar.
9:14 and the legs, and B them with the burnt
9:17 hand from it, and B it upon the altar,
9:20 the breasts, and he B the fat upon the
10:16 of the sin offering, and behold, it was B
13:52 leprosy; it shall be B in the fire.
16:27 their dung shall be B with fire.
19:6 third day shall be B with fire.
20:14 wickedness; they shall be B with fire, both he
21:9 father; she shall be B with fire.
Num 11:1 fire of the LORD B among them, and consumed
11:3 fire of the LORD B among them.
16:39 which those who were B had offered; and they
19:5 the heifer shall be B in his sight; her
19:5 her dung, shall be B;
31:10 all their encampments, they B with fire,
Deut 4:11 mountain, while the mountain B with fire to the
9:21 you had made, and B it with fire and
Josh 6:24 And they B the city with fire, and all
7:1 anger of the LORD B against the people of
7:15 devoted things shall be B with fire, he and
7:25 him with stones; they B them with fire, and
8:28 So Joshua B Ai, and made it for ever
11:9 hamstrung their horses, and B their chariots with
11:11 that breathed, and he B Hazor with fire.
11:13 did Israel burn, except Hazor only; that Joshua B
Judg 15:5 of the Philistines, and B up the shocks and
15:6 Philistines came up, and B her and her father
18:27 of the sword, and B the city with fire.
1Sam 2:15 before the fat was B, the priest's servant would
30:1 had overcome Ziklag, and B it with fire,
30:3 city, they found it B with fire, and their
30:14 of Caleb; and we B Ziklag with fire."
1Kgs 11:8 his foreign wives, who B incense and sacrificed to
13:2 men's bones shall be B upon you.'"
15:13 down her image and B it at the brook
16:18 the king's house, and B the king's house over
22:43 people still sacrificed and B incense on the high
2Kgs 10:26 house of Baal, and B it.
14:4 people still sacrificed and B incense on the high
15:4 people still sacrificed and B incense on the high
15:35 people still sacrificed and B incense on the high
16:3 He even B his son as an offering, according
16:4 And he sacrificed and B incense on the high
16:13 up on it, and B his burnt offering and
17:11 tree; and there they B incense on all the
17:17 And they B their sons and their daughters as
17:31 Tartak; and the Sepharvites B their children in the
18:4 people of Israel had B incense to it; it
21:6 And he B his son as an offering, and
22:17 forsaken me and have B incense to other gods,
23:4 host of heaven; he B them outside Jerusalem in
23:5 Jerusalem; those also who B incense to Baal, to
23:6 the brook Kidron, and B it at the brook
23:8 where the priests had B incense, from Geba to
23:11 the precincts; and he B the chariots of the
23:15 to dust; also he B the Asherah.
23:16 of the tombs, and B them upon the altar,
23:20 upon the altars, and B the bones of men
25:9 And he B the house of the LORD, and
25:9 every great house he B down.
1Chr 14:12 there, and David gave command, and they were B
2Chr 15:16 image, crushed it, and B it at the brook
28:3 the Baals; and he B incense in the valley
28:3 son of Hinnom, and B his sons as an
28:4 And he sacrificed and B incense on the high
29:7 lamps, and have not B incense or offered burnt
33:6 And he B his sons as an offering in
34:5 He also B the bones of the priests on
34:25 forsaken me and have B incense to other gods,
36:19 And they B the house of God, and broke
36:19 wall of Jerusalem, and B all its palaces with
Neh 2:17 how Jerusalem lies in ruins with its gates B
4:2 heaps of rubbish, and B ones at that?"
Tob 14:4 in it will be B down and will be
Jud 2:26 all the Midianites, and B their tents and plundered
2:27 the wheat harvest, and B all their fields and
Esth 1:12 enraged, and his anger B within him.
Job 1:16 fell from heaven and B up the sheep and
Ps 39:3 I mused, the fire B; then I spoke with
74:8 utterly subdue them"; they B all the meeting places
80:16 They have B it with fire, they have cut
106:18 their company; the flame B up the wicked.
Prov 6:27 in his bosom and his clothes not be B
Wis 16:19 midst of water it B more intensely than fire,
Sir 8:10 sinner, lest you be B in his flaming fire.
28:22 they will not be B in its flame.
45:14 sacrifices shall be wholly B twice every day
48:1 fire, and his word B like a torch.
Is 1:7 desolate, your cities are B with fire; in your
6:13 it, it will be B again, like a terebinth
9:5 in blood will be B as fuel for the
9:19 hosts the land is B, and the people are
33:12 will be as if B to lime, like thorns
33:12 cut down, that are B in the fire."
42:25 did not understand; it B him, but he did
43:2 you shall not be B, and the flame shall
44:19 "Half of it I B in the fire, I
64:11 praised thee, has been B by fire, and all
65:7 the LORD; because they B incense upon the
Jer 1:16 forsaking me; they have B incense to other gods,
19:13 roofs incense has been B to all the host
34:5 And as spices were B for your fathers, the
36:27 after the king had B the scroll with the
36:28 scroll, which Jehoiakim the king of Judah has B
36:29 the LORD, You have B this scroll, saying, "Why
36:32 king of Judah had B in the fire; and
38:17 city shall not be B with fire, and you
38:23 this city shall be B with fire."
39:8 The Chaldeans B the king's house and the house
44:19 women said, "When we B incense to the queen
44:21 the incense that you B in the cities of
44:23 It is because you B incense, and because you
49:2 its villages shall be B with fire; then Israel
51:32 seized, the bulwarks are B with fire, and the
51:58 high gates shall be B with fire.
52:13 And he B the house of the LORD, and
52:13 every great house he B down.
Lam 2:3 the enemy; he has B like a flaming fire
Bar 1:2 Chaldeans took Jerusalem and B it with fire.
Ezek 24:10 let the bones be B up.
Dan 3:48 it broke through and B those of the Chaldeans
7:11 given over to be B with fire.
Hos 2:13 the Baals when she B incense to them and
Joel 1:18 wilderness, and flame has B all the trees of
Amos 2:1 the punishment; because he B to lime the bones
Mic 1:7 her hires shall be B with fire, and all
1Mac 1:31 He plundered the city, B it with fire, and
1:55 cities of Judah, and B incense at the doors
1:56 tore to pieces and B with fire.
2:24 Mattathias saw it, be B with zeal and his
2:26 Thus he B with zeal for the law, as
3:5 pursued the lawless; he B those who troubled his
4:38 desolate, the altar profaned, and the gates B
4:50 Then they B incense on the altar and lighted
5:5 their complete destruction, and B with fire their
5:28 all its spoils and B it with fire.
5:35 it, plundered it, and B it with fire.
5:44 took the city and B the sacred precincts with
5:65 down its strongholds and B its towers round about.
5:68 of their gods he B with fire; he plundered
6:31 Jews sallied out and B these with fire, and
10:84 But Jonathan B Azotus and the surrounding towns
10:84 refuge in it he B with fire.
10:85 the sword, with those B alive, came to eight
11:4 the temple of Dagon B down, and Azotus and
11:4 those whom Jonathan had B in the war, for
11:61 he beseiged it and B its suburbs with fire
16:10 of Azotus, and John B it with fire, and
2Mac 1:8 and the kingdom and B the gate and shed
1:33 and his associates had B the materials of the

	6:11	Philip and were all B together, because their piety
	8:33	of their fathers, they B those who had set
	10:3	two years, and they B incense and lighted lamps
	10:36	they kindled fires and B the blasphemers alive.
	12:6	harbor by night, and B the boats, and massacred
	14:41	ordered that fire be brought and the doors B
Mt	13:30	in bundles to be B, but gather the wheat
	13:40	weeds are gathered and B with fire, so will
	22:7	destroyed those murderers and B their city.
Jn	15:6	branches are gathered, thrown into the fire and B
Acts	19:19	their books together and B them in the sight
1Cor	3:15	any man's work is B up, he will suffer
	13:3	my body to be B, but have not love,
Heb	6:8	to being cursed; its end is to be B
	13:11	sacrifice for sin are B outside the camp.
2Pet	3:10	upon it will be B up.
Rev	18:8	and she shall be B with fire; for mighty

BURNING (67)

Ex	3:2	lo, the bush was B, yet it was not
Lev	6:9	altar shall be kept B on it.
	6:12	altar shall be kept B on it, it shall
	6:13	Fire shall be kept B upon the altar continually;
	10:6	Israel, may bewail the B which the LORD has
	24:2	light may be kept B continually.
Num	19:6	the midst of the B of the heifer.
Deut	5:23	while the mountain was B with fire, you came
	9:15	and the mountain was B with fire; and the
	32:24	hunger, and devoured with B heat and poisonous
Josh	7:26	LORD turned from his B anger.
1Kgs	9:25	built to the LORD, B incense before the LORD.
2Chr	2:4	to him for the B of incense of sweet
	30:14	all the altars for B incense they took away
Jud	8:3	was overcome by the B heat, and took to
Job	41:20	a boiling pot and B rushes.
Ps	38:7	loins are filled with B, and there is no
	69:24	them, and let thy B anger overtake them.
	140:10	Let B coals fall upon them!
Sir	11:30	of fire come many B coals, and a sinner
	23:16	soul heated like a B fire will not be
	28:10	so will be the B, and in proportion to
	28:10	strife will be the B; in proportion to the
	43:3	who can withstand its B heat?
	43:4	a furnace works in B heat, but the sun
Is	4:4	spirit of judgment and by a spirit of B
	6:6	in his hand a B coal which he had
	10:16	under his glory a B will be kindled, like
	10:16	be kindled, like the B of fire.
	30:27	LORD comes from far, B with his anger, and
	30:33	For a B place has long been prepared; yea,
	34:9	her land shall become B pitch.
	35:7	in the desert; the B sand shall become a
	42:3	break, and a dimly B wick he will not
	62:1	her salvation as a B torch.
	65:3	sacrificing in gardens and B incense upon bricks;
Jer	11:17	me to anger by B incense to Baal."
	19:4	profaned this place by B incense in it to
	20:9	as it were a B fire shut up in
	36:22	there was a fire B in the brazier before
	44:8	works of your hands, B incense to other gods
	44:18	since we left off B incense to the queen
Lam	5:10	an oven with the B heat of famine.
Bar	6:43	sit along the passageways, B bran for incense; and
Ezek	1:13	something that looked like B coals of fire, like
	10:2	fill your hands with B coals from between the
Dan	3:6	be cast into a B fiery furnace."
	3:11	be cast into a B fiery furnace.
	3:15	be cast into a B fiery furnace; and who
	3:17	deliver us from the B fiery furnace; and he
	3:20	cast them into the B fiery furnace.
	3:21	were cast into the B fiery furnace.
	3:23	fell bound into the B fiery furnace.
	3:89	the midst of the B fiery furnace; from the
	3:94	the door of the B fiery furnace and said,
	7:9	flames, its wheels were B fire.
Hos	11:2	to the Baals, and B incense to idols.
Amos	4:11	plucked out of the B; yet you did not
Mal	4:1	behold, the day comes, B like an oven, when
1Mac	4:20	that the Jews were B the camp, for the
	12:29	it until morning, for they saw the fires B
Lk	12:35	girded and your lamps B,
Jn	5:34	He was a B and shining lamp, and you
Rom	12:20	doing you will heap B coals upon his head."
Rev	8:8	like a great mountain, B with fire, was thrown
	18:9	the smoke of her B;
	18:18	the smoke of her B, "What city was like

BURNINGS

Is	33:14	Who among us can dwell with everlasting B

BURNISHED (6)

1Kgs	7:45	King Solomon, were of B bronze.
2Chr	4:16	Huram-abi made of B bronze for King Solomon
Ezek	1:7	and they sparkled like B bronze.
Dan	10:6	like the gleam of B bronze, and the sound
Rev	1:15	his feet were like B bronze, refined as in
	2:18	whose feet are like B bronze.

BURNS (20)

Lev	16:28	And he who B them shall wash his clothes
Num	19:8	He who B the heifer shall wash his clothes
Deut	18:10	you any one who B his son or his
	32:22	my anger, and it B to the depths of
1Kgs	14:10	Jeroboam, as a man B up dung until it
Ps	46:9	shatters the spear, he B the chariots with fire!
	97:3	goes before him, and B up his adversaries round
Sir	23:16	cease until the fire B him up.
	43:4	heat, but the sun B the mountains three times
	43:21	consumes the mountains and B up the wilderness,
Is	9:18	For wickedness B like a fire, it consumes briers
	44:16	Half of it he B in the fire; over
	65:5	nostrils, a fire that B all the day.
Jer	48:35	the high place and B incense to his god.
Hos	8:5	My anger B against them.
Joel	2:3	devours before them, and behind them a flame B
Amos	6:10	man's kinsman, he who B him, shall take him
Hab	1:16	to his net and B incense to his seine;
Rev	19:20	lake of fire that B with sulphur.
	21:8	in the lake that B with fire and sulphur,

BURNT (326)

Gen	8:20	clean bird, and offered B offerings on the altar.
	22:2	him there as a B offering upon one of
	22:3	the wood for the B offering, and arose and
	22:6	the wood of the B offering, and laid it
	22:7	the lamb for a B offering?"
	22:8	the lamb for a B offering, my son." So
	22:13	it up as a B offering instead of his
Ex	3:3	this great sight, why the bush is not B
	10:25	us have sacrifices and B offerings, that we may
	18:12	Moses' father-in-law, offered a B offering and
	20:24	sacrifice on it your B offerings and your peace
	24:5	of Israel, who offered B offerings and sacrificed
	29:18	altar; it is a B offering to the LORD;
	29:25	in addition to the B offering, as a pleasing
	29:42	shall be a continual B offering throughout your
	30:9	unholy incense thereon, nor B offering, nor cereal
	30:28	and the altar of B offering with all its
	31:9	and the altar of B offering with all its
	32:6	the morrow, and offered B offerings and brought
	32:20	they had made, and B it with fire, and
	35:16	tabernacle; the altar of B offering, with its grating
	38:1	made the altar of B offering also of acacia
Lev	1:3	his offering is a B offering from the herd,
	1:4	the head of the B offering, and it shall
	1:6	he shall flay the B offering and cut it
	1:9	the altar, as a B offering, an offering by
	1:10	his gift for a B offering is from the
	1:13	altar; it is a B offering, an offering by
	1:14	the LORD is a B offering of birds, then
	1:17	fire; it is a B offering, an offering by
	3:5	the altar upon the B offering, which is upon
	4:7	of the altar of B offering which is at
	4:10	upon the altar of B offering.
	4:18	of the altar of B offering which is at
	4:24	where they kill the B offering before the LORD;
	4:25	of the altar of B offering, and pour out
	4:25	of the altar of B offering.
	4:29	in the place of B offering.
	4:30	of the altar of B offering, and pour out
	4:33	where they kill the B offering.
	4:34	of the altar of B offering, and pour out
	5:7	the other for a B offering.
	5:10	the second for a B offering according to the
	6:9	the law of the B offering.
	6:9	The B offering shall be on the hearth upon
	6:10	fire has consumed the B offering on the altar,
	6:12	he shall lay the B offering in order upon
	6:25	the place where the B offering is killed shall
	7:2	where they kill the B offering they shall kill
	7:8	who offers any man's B offering shall have for
	7:8	the skin of the B offering which he has
	7:37	the law of the B offering, of the cereal

8:18 the ram of the B offering; and Aaron and
8:21 the altar, as a B offering, a pleasing odor,
8:28 the altar with the B offering, as an ordination
9:2 a ram for a B offering, both without blemish,
9:3 without blemish, for a B offering,
9:7 sin offering and your B offering, and make
9:12 And he killed the B offering; and Aaron's sons
9:13 And they delivered the B offering to him, piece
9:14 burned them with the B offering on the altar.
9:16 And he presented the B offering, and offered it
9:17 the altar, besides the B offering of the morning.
9:22 sin offering and the B offering and the peace
9:24 LORD and consumed the B offering and the fat
10:19 sin offering and their B offering before the LORD;
12:6 year old for a B offering, and a young
12:8 pigeons, one for a B offering and the other
14:13 sin offering and the B offering, in the holy
14:19 he shall kill the B offering;
14:20 priest shall offer the B offering and the cereal
14:22 and the other a B offering.
14:31 the other for a B offering, along with a
15:15 the other for a B offering; and the priest
15:30 the other for a B offering; and the priest
16:3 a ram for a B offering.
16:5 one ram for a B offering.
16:24 forth, and offer his B offering and the burnt
16:24 burnt offering and the B offering of the people,
17:8 them, who offers a B offering or sacrifice,
22:18 the LORD as a B offering,
23:12 without blemish as a B offering to the LORD.
23:18 they shall be a B offering to the LORD,
23:37 LORD offerings by fire, B offerings and cereal
Num 6:11 the other for a B offering, and make atonement
6:14 without blemish for a B offering, and one ewe
6:16 sin offering and his B offering,
7:15 year old, for a B offering;
7:21 year old, for a B offering;
7:27 year old, for a B offering;
7:33 year old, for a B offering;
7:39 year old, for a B offering;
7:45 year old, for a B offering;
7:51 year old, for a B offering;
7:57 year old, for a B offering;
7:63 year old, for a B offering;
7:69 year old, for a B offering;
7:75 year old, for a B offering;
7:81 year old, for a B offering;
7:87 the cattle for the B offering twelve bulls, twelve
8:12 the other for a B offering to the LORD,
10:10 the trumpets over your B offerings and over the
15:3 by fire or a B offering or a sacrifice,
15:5 shall prepare with the B offering, or for the
15:8 a bull for a B offering, or for a
15:24 young bull for a B offering, a pleasing odor
19:17 some ashes of the B sin offering, and running
23:3 Balak, "Stand beside your B offering, and I will
23:6 were standing beside his B offering.
23:15 "Stand here beside your B offering, while I meet
23:17 was standing beside his B offering, and the princes
28:6 It is a continual B offering, which was ordained
28:10 offering: this is the B offering of every sabbath,
28:10 sabbath, besides the continual B offering and its
28:11 you shall offer a B offering to the LORD:
28:13 every lamb; for a B offering of pleasing odor,
28:14 lamb; this is the B offering of each month
28:15 offered besides the continual B offering and its drink
28:19 offering by fire, a B offering to the LORD:
28:23 offer these besides the B offering of the morning,
28:23 is for a continual B offering.
28:24 offered besides the continual B offering and its drink
28:27 work, but offer a B offering, a pleasing odor
28:31 Besides the continual B offering and its cereal
29:2 you shall offer a B offering, a pleasing odor
29:6 for you; besides the B offering of the new
29:6 offering, and the continual B offering and its cereal
29:8 you shall offer a B offering to the LORD,
29:11 atonement, and the continual B offering and its
29:13 you shall offer a B offering, an offering by
29:16 offering, besides the continual B offering, its cereal
29:19 offering, besides the continual B offering and its
29:22 offering, besides the continual B offering and its
29:25 offering, besides the continual B offering, its cereal
29:28 offering; besides the continual B offering and its
29:31 offering; besides the continual B offering, its cereal
29:34 offering; besides the continual B offering, its cereal
29:36 you shall offer a B offering, an offering by
29:38 offering; besides the continual B offering and its
29:39 freewill offerings, for your B offerings, and for your
Deut 12:6 you shall bring your B offerings and your sacrifices,
12:11 I command you: your B offerings and your sacrifices,
12:13 do not offer your B offerings at every place
12:14 you shall offer your B offerings, and there you
12:27 choose, and offer your B offerings, the flesh and
13:16 fire, as a whole B offering to the LORD
27:6 and you shall offer B offerings on it to
33:10 before thee, and whole B offering upon thy altar.
Josh 8:31 they offered on it B offerings to the LORD,
22:23 did so to offer B offerings or cereal offerings
22:26 an altar, not for B offering, nor for sacrifice,
22:27 his presence with our B offerings and sacrifices and
22:28 fathers made, not for B offerings, nor for sacrifice,
22:29 building an altar for B offering, cereal offering, or
Judg 6:26 offer it as a B offering with the wood
11:31 him up for a B offering."
13:16 you make ready a B offering, then offer it
13:23 not have accepted a B offering and a cereal
20:26 until evening, and offered B offerings and peace
21:4 an altar, and offered B offerings and peace offerings.
1Sam 6:14 the cows as a B offering to the LORD.
6:15 of Beth-shemesh offered B offerings and sacrificed
7:9 it as a whole B offering to the LORD;
7:10 was offering up the B offering, the Philistines drew
10:8 to you to offer B offerings and to sacrifice
13:9 Saul said, "Bring the B offering here to me,
13:9 And he offered the B offering.
13:10 had finished offering the B offering, behold, Samuel
13:12 myself, and offered the B offering."
15:22 as great delight in B offerings and sacrifices, as
31:12 came to Jabesh and B them there.
2Sam 6:17 it; and David offered B offerings and peace offerings
6:18 had finished offering the B offerings and the peace
24:22 the oxen for the B offering, and the threshing
24:24 I will not offer B offerings to the LORD
24:25 the LORD, and offered B offerings and peace
1Kgs 3:3 only, he sacrificed and B incense at the high
3:4 to offer a thousand B offerings upon that altar.
3:15 LORD, and offered up B offerings and peace
8:64 there he offered the B offering and the cereal
8:64 small to receive the B offering and the cereal
9:16 and captured Gezer and B it with fire, and
9:25 used to offer up B offerings and peace offerings
10:5 his cupbearers, and his B offerings which he offered
18:33 pour it on the B offering, and on the
18:38 fell, and consumed the B offering, and the wood,
2Kgs 3:27 offered him for a B offering upon the wall.
5:17 servant will not offer B offering or sacrifice to
10:24 to offer sacrifices and B offerings.
10:25 end of offering the B offering, Jehu said to
16:13 it, and burned his B offering and his cereal
16:15 altar burn the morning B offering, and the evening
16:15 offering, and the king's B offering, and his cereal
16:15 cereal offering, with the B offering of all the
16:15 the blood of the B offering, and all the
1Chr 6:49 upon the altar of B offering and upon the
16:1 it; and they offered B offerings and peace offerings
16:2 had finished offering the B offerings and the peace
16:40 at Gibeon, to offer B offerings to the LORD
16:40 upon the altar of B offering continually morning and
21:23 give the oxen for B offerings, and the threshing
21:24 is yours, nor offer B offerings which cost me
21:26 the LORD and presented B offerings and peace
21:26 upon the altar of B offering.
21:29 and the altar of B offering were at that
22:1 here the altar of B offering for Israel."
23:31 at evening, and whenever B offerings are offered to
29:21 the next day offered B offerings to the LORD,
2Chr 1:6 and offered a thousand B offerings upon it.
2:4 the showbread, and for B offerings morning and
4:6 was used for the B offering, and the sea
7:1 heaven and consumed the B offering and the
7:7 there he offered the B offering and the fat
7:7 could not hold the B offering and the cereal
8:12 Then Solomon offered up B offerings to the LORD
9:4 their clothing, and his B offerings which he offered
13:11 morning and every evening B offerings and incense
23:18 the LORD, to offer B offerings to the LORD,
24:14 service and for the B offerings, and dishes for
24:14 And they offered B offerings in the house of
29:7 burned incense or offered B offerings in the holy
29:18 LORD, the altar of B offering and all its
29:24 king commanded that the B offering and the sin
29:27 Hezekiah commanded that the B offering be offered

29:27 And when the B offering began, the song to
29:28 this continued until the B offering was finished.
29:31 a willing heart brought B offerings.
29:32 The number of the B offerings which the assembly
29:32 these were for a B offering to the LORD.
29:34 not flay all the B offerings, so until other
29:35 the great number of B offerings there was the
29:35 the libations for the B offerings.
30:15 sanctified themselves, and brought B offerings into
31:2 and the Levites, for B offerings and peace offerings,
31:3 possessions was for the B offerings: the burnt
31:3 the burnt offerings: the B offerings of morning and
31:3 and evening, and the B offerings for the sabbaths,
35:12 they set aside the B offerings that they might
35:14 busied in offering the B offerings and the fat
35:16 passover and to offer B offerings on the altar
Ezra 3:2 of Israel, to offer B offerings upon it, as
3:3 lands, and they offered B offerings upon it to
3:3 it to the LORD, B offerings morning and evening.
3:4 and offered the daily B offerings by number
3:5 after that the continual B offerings, the offerings at
3:6 they began to offer B offerings to the LORD.
6:3 sacrifices are offered and B offerings are brought; its
6:9 rams, or sheep for B offerings to the God
8:35 the returned exiles, offered B offerings to the God
8:35 all this was a B offering to the LORD.
Neh 10:33 cereal offering, the continual B offering, the
Jud 4:14 sackcloth, offered the continual B offerings and the
16:16 and all fat for B offerings to thee is
16:18 purified, they offered their B offerings, their freewill,
Job 1:5 the morning and offer B offerings according to the
42:8 up for yourselves a B offering; and my servant
Ps 20:3 regard with favor your B sacrifices!
40:6 B offering and sin offering thou hast not required.
50:8 for your sacrifices; your B offerings are continually
51:16 I to give a B offering, thou wouldst not
51:19 in right sacrifices, in B offerings and whole burnt
51:19 burnt offerings and whole B offerings; then bulls will
66:13 into thy house with B offerings; I will pay
66:15 will offer to thee B offerings of fatlings, with
Wis 3:6 and like a sacrificial B offering he accepted them.
Is 1:11 have had enough of B offerings of rams and
19:21 worship with sacrifice and B offering, and they will
40:16 beasts enough for a B offering.
43:23 me your sheep for B offerings, or honored me
56:7 house of prayer; their B offerings and their sacrifices
Jer 6:20 Your B offerings are not acceptable, nor your
7:21 of Israel: "Add your B offerings to your sacrifices,
7:22 or command them concerning B offerings and.
14:12 and though they offer B offering and cereal offering,
17:26 from the Negeb, bringing B offerings and sacrifices,
19:5 in the fire as B offerings to Baal, which
33:18 my presence to offer B offerings, to burn cereal
51:25 and make you a B mountain.
Bar 1:10 buy with the money B offerings and sin offerings
6:55 the gods will be B in two like beams.
Ezek 40:38 the gate, where the B offering was to be
40:39 side, on which the B offering and the sin
40:42 hewn stone for the B offering, a cubit and
40:42 laid with which the B offerings and the sacrifices
43:18 is erected for offering B offerings upon it and
43:21 and it shall be B in the appointed place
43:24 them up as a B offering to the LORD.
43:27 upon the altar your B offerings and your peace
44:11 they shall slay the B offering and the sacrifice
45:15 offering for cereal offerings, B offerings, and peace,
45:17 duty to furnish the B offerings, cereal offerings, and
45:17 sin offerings, cereal offerings, B offerings, and peace,
45:23 shall provide as a B offering to the LORD
45:25 provision for sin offerings, B offerings, and cereal,
46:2 priests shall offer his B offering and his peace
46:4 The B offering that the prince offers to the
46:12 freewill offering, either a B offering or peace
46:12 he shall offer his B offering or his peace
46:13 without blemish for a B offering to the LORD
46:14 ordinance for the continual B offering.
46:15 morning, for a continual B offering.
Dan 3:38 prophet, or leader, no B offering, or sacrifice, or
3:39 though it were with B offerings of rams and
8:11 host; and the continual B offering was taken away
8:12 with the continual B offering through transgression;
8:13 vision concerning the continual B offering, the
11:31 take away the continual B offering.
12:11 time that the continual B offering is taken away,
Hos 6:6 of God, rather than B offerings.
Amos 5:22 you offer me your B offerings and cereal offerings,
Mic 6:6 come before him with B offerings, with calves a
1Mac 1:45 the land, to forbid B offerings and sacrifices and
1:54 upon the altar of B offering.
1:59 upon the altar of B offering.
4:44 about the altar of B offering, which had been
4:53 the new altar of B offering which they had
4:56 eight days, and offered B offerings with gladness;
5:54 and joy, and offered B offerings, because not one
7:33 to show him the B offering that was being
2Mac 2:10 and consumed the whole B offerings.
Mk 12:33 more than all whole B offerings and sacrifices."
Heb 10:6 prepared for me; in B offerings and sin offerings
10:8 sacrifices and offerings and B offerings and sin
Rev 8:7 of the earth was B up, and a third
8:7 of the trees were B up, and all green
8:7 all green grass was B up.

BURNT-OUT

Deut 29:23 and salt, and a B waste, unsown, and growing

BURST (20)

Gen 7:11 of the great deep B forth, and the windows
Josh 9:13 and behold, they are B; and these garments and
Job 32:19 vent; like new wineskins, it is ready to B
38:8 with doors, when it B forth from the womb;
Ps 2:3 anointed, saying, "Let us B their bonds asunder, and
Sir 1:20 and then joy will B forth for him.
19:10 It will not make you B
Jer 2:20 broke your yoke and B your bonds; and you
5:5 the yoke, they had B the bonds.
23:19 whirling tempest; it will B upon the head of
30:8 neck, and I will B their bonds, and strangers
30:23 whirling tempest; it will B upon the head of
Ezek 32:2 in the seas; you B forth in your rivers,
Dan 14:27 dragon ate them, and B open.
Joel 2:8 in his path; they B through the weapons and
Nah 1:13 off you and will B your bonds asunder."
Mt 9:17 it is, the skins B, and the wine is
Mk 2:22 does, the wine will B the skins, and the
Lk 5:37 the new wine will B the skins and it
Acts 1:18 and falling headlong he B open in the middle

BURSTING (3)

2Sam 5:20 before me, like a B flood." Therefore the name
1Chr 14:11 my hand, like a B flood." Therefore the name
Prov 3:10 your vats will be B with wine.

BURY (46)

Gen 23:4 place, that I may B my dead out of
23:6 B your dead in the choicest of our sepulchres;
23:8 willing that I should B my dead out of
23:11 give it to you; B your dead."
23:13 me, that I may B my dead there."
23:15 B your dead."
47:29 Do not B me in Egypt,
47:30 out of Egypt and B me in their burying
49:29 gathered to my people; B me with my fathers
50:5 Canaan, there shall you B me.' Now therefore let
50:5 I pray you, and B my father; then I
50:6 answered, "Go up, and B your father, as he
50:7 Joseph went up to B his father; and with
50:14 up with him to B his father.
Deut 21:23 tree, but you shall B him the same day,
1Kgs 2:31 strike him down and B him; and thus take
11:15 army went up to B the slain, he slew
13:29 to mourn and to B him.
13:31 sons, "When I die, B me in the grave
14:13 mourn for him, and B him; for he only
2Kgs 9:10 Jezreel, and none shall B her." Then he opened
9:34 this cursed woman, and B her; for she is
9:35 when they went to B her, they found no
2Chr 24:25 but they did not B him in the tombs
Tob 1:17 of Nineveh, I would B him.
4:3 son, when I die, B me, and do not
4:4 When she dies B her beside me in the
6:14 no other son to B them."
8:12 is not, let us B him without any one
14:6 in truth, and will B their idols.
14:10 B me properly, and your mother with me.
Ps 79:3 there was none to B them.
Wis 18:12 not sufficient even to B them, since in one
Jer 7:32 Slaughter: for they will B in Topheth, because there
14:16 sword, with none to B them—them, their wives,
19:11 Men shall B in Topheth because there will be
19:11 because there will be no place else to B
Ezek 39:13 of the land will B them; and it will

39:14 the land continually and B those remaining upon the
Hos 9:6 gather them, Memphis shall B them.
1Mac 7:17 there was none to B them."
Mt 8:21 me first go and B my father."
8:22 leave the dead to B their own dead."
27:7 the potter's field, to B strangers in.
Lk 9:59 me first go and B my father."
9:60 "Leave the dead to B their own dead; but

BURYING (14)
Gen 23:4 among you for a B place, that I may
23:6 or hinder you from B your dead."
23:9 a possession for a B place."
23:20 a possession for a B place by the Hittites.
47:30 bury me in their B place." He answered, "I
49:30 to possess as a B place.
50:13 to possess as a B place.
Num 33:4 while the Egyptians were B all their first-born,
Tob 1:19 me, that I was B them; so I hid
2:8 and here he is B the dead again!"
2:9 night I returned from B him, and because I
Ezek 39:12 of Israel will be B them, in order to
2Mac 9:15 had not considered worth B but had planned to
Mk 14:8 could; she has anointed my body beforehand for B

BUSH (11)
Ex 3:2 the midst of a B; and he looked, and
3:2 looked, and lo, the B was burning, yet it
3:3 great sight, why the B is not burnt."
3:4 him out of the B, "Moses, Moses!" And he
Deut 33:16 the favor of him that dwelt in the B
Bar 6:71 and like a thorn B in a garden, on
Mk 12:26 the passage about the B, how God said to
Lk 6:44 thorns, nor are grapes picked from a bramble B
20:37 the passage about the B, where he calls the
Acts 7:30 Sinai, in a flame of fire in a B
7:35 the angel that appeared to him in the B

BUSHEL (3)
Mt 5:15 put it under a B, but on a stand,
Mk 4:21 be put under a B, or under a bed,
Lk 11:33 cellar or under a B, but on a stand,

BUSHELS
Dan 14:3 spent on it twelve B of fine flour and

BUSHES (4)
Gen 21:15 she cast the child under one of the B
Job 30:4 and the leaves of B, and to warm themselves
30:7 Among the B they bray; under the nettles they
1Mac 4:38 the courts they saw B sprung up as in

BUSIED
2Chr 35:14 sons of Aaron were B in offering the burnt

BUSINESS (21)
Deut 24:5 be charged with any B; he shall be free
Josh 2:14 do not tell this B of ours, then we
2:20 if you tell this B of ours, then we
Judg 18:3 What is your B here?"
1Sam 21:8 me, because the king's B required haste."
25:2 man in Maon, whose B was in Carmel.
Esth 3:9 charge of the king's B, that they may put
Ps 107:23 sea in ships, doing B on the great waters;
Eccl 1:13 it is an unhappy B that God has given
3:10 I have seen the B that God has given
4:8 This also is vanity and an unhappy B
5:3 dream comes with much B, and a fool's voice
8:16 and to see the B that is done on
Sir 38:24 he who has little B may become wise.
Dan 8:27 went about the king's B; but I was appalled
2Mac 4:23 king and to complete the records of essential B
15:5 to take up arms and finish the king's B
Mt 22:5 farm, another to his B,
Jn 2:14 and pigeons, and the money-changers at their B
Acts 19:24 Artemis, brought no little B to the craftsmen.
19:25 know that from this B we have our wealth.

BUSY (8)
1Kgs 20:40 as your servant was B here and there, he
Ps 141:4 to any evil, to B myself with wicked deeds
Eccl 1:13 of men to be B with.
3:10 of men to be B with
Wis 19:3 while they were still B at mourning, and were
Sir 8:8 of the sages, but B yourself with their maxims;
11:10 My son, do not B yourself with many matters;

Hag 1:9 in ruins, while you B yourselves each with his

BUSYBODIES (2)
2Thes 3:11 living in idleness, mere B, not doing any work.
1Tim 5:13 idlers but gossips and B, saying what they should

BUTCHER
2Mac 7:29 Do not fear this B, but prove worthy of

BUTLER (9)
Gen 40:1 time after this, the B of the king of
40:2 two officers, the chief B and the chief baker,
40:5 they both dreamed--the B and the baker of
40:9 So the chief B told his dream to Joseph,
40:13 his hand as formerly, when you were his B
40:20 head of the chief B and the head of
40:21 He restored the chief B to his butlership, and
40:23 Yet the chief B did not remember Joseph, but
41:9 Then the chief B said to Pharaoh, "I remember

BUTLERSHIP
Gen 40:21 chief butler to his B, and he placed the

BUTT
2Sam 2:23 the belly with the B of his spear, so

BUTTER
Ps 55:21 speech was smoother than B, yet war was in

BUTTOCKS
Is 20:4 naked and barefoot, with B uncovered, to the shame

BUY (65)
Gen 41:57 Egypt to Joseph to B grain, because the famine
42:2 Egypt; go down and B grain for us there,
42:3 brothers went down to B grain in Egypt.
42:5 of Israel came to B among the others who
42:7 land of Canaan, to B food."
42:10 my lord, but to B food have your servants
43:2 to them, "Go again, B us a little food."
43:4 will go down and B you food;
43:20 the first time to B food;
43:22 in our hand to B food.
44:25 father said, 'Go again, B us a little food,'
47:19 B us and our land for food, and we
47:22 priests he did not B; for the priests had
Ex 21:2 When you B a Hebrew slave, he shall serve
Lev 25:14 to your neighbor or B from your neighbor, you
25:15 the jubilee, you shall B from your neighbor, and
25:44 may have: you may B male and female slaves
25:45 You may also B from among the strangers who
27:27 animal, then he shall B it back at your
Deut 2:6 and you shall also B water of them for
28:68 but no man will B you."
Ruth 4:4 of it, and say, B it in the presence
4:5 said, "The day you B the field from the
4:8 kin said to Boaz, B it for yourself," he
2Sam 24:21 David said, "To B the threshing floor of you,
24:24 "No, but I will B it of you for
2Kgs 12:12 as well as to B timber and quarried stone
1Chr 21:24 "No, but I will B it for the full
2Chr 34:11 and the builders to B quarried stone, and timber
Ezra 7:17 shall with all diligence B bulls, rams, and lambs,
Neh 10:31 sell, we will not B from them on the
Prov 17:16 in his hand to B wisdom, when he has
23:23 B truth, and do not sell it; buy wisdom,
23:23 do not sell it; B wisdom, instruction, and
Is 55:1 has no money, come, B and eat!
55:1 Come, B wine and milk without money and without
Jer 13:1 to me, "Go and B a linen waistcloth, and
19:1 said the LORD, "Go, B a potter's earthen flask,
32:7 to you and say, B my field which is
32:8 and said to me, B my field which is
32:8 and redemption is yours; B it for yourself.' Then
32:25 hast said to me, B the field for money
Bar 1:10 send you money; so B with the money burnt
3:30 found her, and will B her for pure gold?
Amos 8:6 balances, that we may B the poor for silver
Zech 11:5 Those who B them slay them and go unpunished;
1Mac 12:36 its garrison could neither B nor sell.
13:49 country and back to B and sell.
2Mac 8:11 seacoast, inviting them to B Jewish slaves and
8:25 who had come to B them as slaves.
8:34 the thousand merchants to B the Jews,
Mt 14:15 into the villages and B food for themselves."
25:9 to the dealers and B for yourselves.'

25:10 while they went to B, the bridegroom came, and
Mk 6:36 villages round about and B themselves something to
6:37 "Shall we go and B two hundred denarii worth
Lk 9:13 are to go and B food for all these
22:36 sell his mantle and B one.
Jn 4:8 into the city to B food.
6:5 "How are we to B bread, so that these
6:7 hundred denarii would not B enough bread for each
13:29 Jesus was telling him, B what we need for
1Cor 7:30 rejoicing, and those who B as though they had
Rev 3:18 I counsel you to B from me gold refined
13:17 that no one can B or sell unless he

BUYER (5)
Tob 1:13 and I was his B of provisions.
Prov 20:14 says the B; but when he goes away, then
Sir 37:11 barter or with a B about selling, with a
Is 24:2 mistress; as with the B, so with the seller;
Ezek 7:12 Let not the B rejoice, nor the seller mourn,

BUYING (3)
Ruth 4:5 Naomi, you are also B Ruth the Moabitess, the
2Kgs 22:6 as well as for B timber and quarried stone
Sir 27:2 so sin is wedged in between selling and B

BUYS (5)
Lev 22:11 but if a priest B a slave as his
Prov 31:16 considers a field and B it; with the fruit
Sir 20:11 is a man who B much for a little,
Mt 13:44 that he has and B that field.
Rev 18:11 her, since no one B their cargo any more,

BUZ (3)
Gen 22:21 Nahor: Uz the first-born, B his brother, Kemuel the
1Chr 5:14 of Jahdo, son of B;
Jer 25:23 the sea; Dedan, Tema, B, and all who cut

BUZI
Ezek 1:3 priest, the son of B, in the land of

BUZITE (2)
Job 32:2 son of Barachel the B, of the family of
32:6 son of Barachel the B answered: "I am young

BUZZARD
Deut 14:13 vulture, the osprey, the B, the kite, after their

BYGONE
Job 8:8 I pray you, of B ages, and consider what

BYPATHS
Jer 18:15 and have gone into B, not the highway,

BYSTANDERS (6)
Mt 26:71 she said to the B, "This man was with
26:73 a little while the B came up and said
27:47 And some of the B hearing it said, "This
Mk 14:69 to say to the B, "This man is one
14:70 little while again the B said to Peter, "Certainly
15:34 And some of the B hearing it said, "Behold,

BYWAYS
Judg 5:6 Jael, caravans ceased and travelers kept to the B

BYWORD (17)
Deut 28:37 a proverb, and a B, among all the peoples
1Kgs 9:7 a proverb and a B among all peoples.
2Chr 7:20 a proverb and a B among all peoples.
Tob 3:4 thou madest us a B of reproach in all
Job 17:6 has made me a B of the peoples, and
30:9 song, I am a B to them.
Ps 44:14 hast made us a B among the nations, a
69:11 clothing, I became a B to them.
Wis 5:4 derision and made a B of reproach--we fools!
Sir 42:11 to your enemies, a B in the city and
Jer 24:9 be a reproach, a B, a taunt, and a
Ezek 14:8 a sign and a B and cut him off
16:56 your sister Sodom a B in your mouth in
23:10 and she became a B among women, when judgment
Dan 9:16 people have become a B among all who are
Joel 2:17 heritage a reproach, a B among the nations.
Zech 8:13 you have been a B of cursing among the

C

CA-INAN (2)
Lk 3:36 Shelah, the son of C, the son of Arphaxad,
3:37 Mahalale-el, the son of C,

CABBON
Josh 15:40 Lachish, Bozkath, Eglon, C, Lahmam, Chitlish,

CABUL (2)
Josh 19:27 in the north to C,
1Kgs 9:13 called the land of C to this day.

CAESAR (23)
Mt 22:17 to pay taxes to C, or not?"
22:21 them, "Render therefore to C the things that are
Mk 12:14 to pay taxes to C, or not?
12:17 to them, "Render to C the things that are
Lk 2:1 decree went out from C Augustus that all the
3:1 the reign of Tiberi-us C, Pontius Pilate being
20:22 to give tribute to C, or not?"
20:25 them, "Then render to C the things that are
23:2 to give tribute to C, and saying that he
Jn 19:12 man, you are not C's friend; every one who
19:12 who makes himself a king sets himself against C
19:15 chief priests answered, "We have no king but C
Acts 17:7 against the decrees of C, saying that there is
25:8 the temple, nor against C have I offended at
25:10 "I am standing before C's tribunal, where I ought
25:11 I appeal to C
25:12 "You have appealed to C; to Caesar you shall
25:12 appealed to Caesar; to C you shall go."
25:21 be held until I could send him to C
26:32 set free if he had not appealed to C
27:24 you must stand before C; and lo, God has
28:19 compelled to appeal to C --though I had no
Phil 4:22 you, especially those of C's household.

CAESAREA (17)
Mt 16:13 into the district of C Philippi, he asked his
Mk 8:27 to the villages of C Philippi; and on the
Acts 8:39 to all the towns till he came to C
9:30 brought him down to C, and sent him off
10:1 At C there was a man named Cornelius, a
10:24 And on the following day they entered C
11:11 in which we were, sent to me from C
12:19 down from Judea to C, and remained there.
18:22 he had landed at C, he went up and
21:8 departed and came to C; and we entered the
21:16 of the disciples from C went with us, bringing
23:23 two hundred spearmen to go as far as C
23:33 When they came to C and delivered the letter
25:1 three days he went up to Jerusalem from C
25:4 was being kept at C, and that he himself
25:6 he went down to C; and the next day
25:13 and Bernice arrived at C to welcome Festus.

CAESARS (6)
Mt 22:21 They said, C
22:21 the things that are C, and to God the
Mk 12:16 They said to him, C
12:17 the things that are C, and to God the
Lk 20:24 They said, C
20:25 the things that are C, and to God the

CAGE (2)
Sir 11:28 decoy partridge in a C, so is the mind
Ezek 19:9 put him in a C, and brought him to

CAIAPHAS (9)
Mt 26:3 priest, who was called C,
26:57 Jesus led him to C the high priest, where
Lk 3:2 high-priesthood of Annas and C, the word of God
Jn 11:49 But one of them, C, who was high priest
18:13 was the father-in-law of C, who was high priest
18:14 It was C who had given counsel to the
18:24 sent him bound to C the high priest.
18:28 from the house of C to the praetorium.
Acts 4:6 the high priest and C and John and Alexander,

CAIN (19)
Gen 4:1 she conceived and bore C, saying, "I have gotten
4:2 keeper of sheep, and C a tiller of the
4:3 the course of time C brought to the LORD
4:5 his offering, but for C and his offering he
4:5 So C was very angry, and his countenance fell.

4:6 The LORD said to C, "Why are you angry,
4:8 C said to Abel his brother, "Let us go
4:8 were in the field, C rose up against his
4:9 the LORD said to C, "Where is Abel your
4:13 C said to the LORD, "My punishment is greater
4:15 If any one slays C, vengeance shall be taken
4:15 put a mark on C, lest any who came
4:16 Then C went away from the presence of the
4:17 C knew his wife, and she conceived and bore
4:24 If C is avenged sevenfold, truly Lamech
4:25 instead of Abel, for C slew him."
Heb 11:4 more acceptable sacrifice than C, through which he
1 Jn 3:12 and not be like C who was of the
Jude 1:11 in the way of C, and abandon themselves for

CAKE (20)
Gen 40:16 dream: there were three C baskets on my head,
Ex 29:23 of bread, and one C of bread with oil,
Lev 7:14 he shall offer one C from each offering, as
8:26 he took one unleavened C, and one cake of
8:26 unleavened cake, and one C of bread with oil,
24:5 tenths of an ephah shall be in each C
Num 6:19 boiled, and one unleavened C out of the basket,
15:20 you shall present a C as an offering; as
Judg 7:13 dream; and lo, a C of barley bread tumbled
1Sam 30:12 a piece of a C of figs and two
2Sam 6:19 women, to each a C of bread, a portion
6:19 of meat, and a C of raisins.
1Kgs 17:13 make me a little C of it and bring
19:6 at his head a C baked on hot stones
2Kgs 20:7 Isaiah said, "Bring a C of figs.
1Chr 16:3 of meat, and a C of raisins.
Jud 10:5 parched grain and a C of dried fruit and
Is 38:21 "Let them take a C of figs, and apply
Ezek 4:12 it as a barley C, baking it in their
Hos 7:9 peoples; Ephraim is a C not turned.

CAKES (28)
Gen 18:6 measures of fine meal, knead it, and make C
Ex 12:39 And they baked unleavened C of the dough which
29:2 and unleavened bread, unleavened C mixed with oil,
Lev 2:4 it shall be unleavened C of fine flour mixed
7:12 thank offering unleavened C mixed with oil,
7:12 spread with oil, and C of fine flour well
7:13 bring his offering with C of leavened bread.
24:5 flour, and bake twelve C of it; two tenths
Num 6:15 basket of unleavened bread, C of fine flour mixed
11:8 in pots, and made C of it; and the
11:8 like the taste of C baked with oil.
Josh 5:11 of the land, unleavened C and parched grain.
Judg 6:19 a kid, and unleavened C from an ephah of
6:20 meat and the unleavened C, and put them on
6:21 meat and the unleavened C; and there sprang up
6:21 flesh and the unleavened C; and the angel of
1Sam 25:18 raisins, and two hundred C of figs, and laid
2Sam 13:6 make a couple of C in my sight, that
13:8 kneaded it, and made C in his sight, and
13:8 made cakes in his sight, and baked the C
13:10 And Tamar took the C she had made, and
1Kgs 14:3 you ten loaves, some C, and a jar of
1Chr 9:31 Korahite, was in charge of making the flat C
12:40 abundant provisions of meal, C of figs, clusters of
Jer 7:18 knead dough, to make C for the queen of
44:19 approval that we made C for her bearing her
Dan 14:27 them together and made C, which he fed to
Hos 3:1 other gods and love C of raisins."

CALAH (2)
Gen 10:11 and built Nineveh, Rehoboth-Ir, C, and
10:12 Resen between Nineveh and C; that is the great

CALAMITIES (16)
1Sam 10:19 you from all your C and your distresses; and
Esth 16:5 been involved in irremediable C, by the persuasion of
Sir 23:11 justified, for his house will be filled with C
40:9 and strife and sword, C, famine and affliction and
Bar 1:20 clung to us the C and the curse which
2:7 All those C with which the Lord threatened us
2:9 Lord has kept the C ready, and the Lord
3:4 their God, so that C have clung to us.
4:18 he who brought these C upon you will deliver
4:29 he who brought these C upon you will bring
2Mac 6:12 be depressed by such C, but to recognize that
6:16 he disciplines us with C, he does not forsake
10:10 summary of the principal C of the wars.
14:14 that the misfortunes and C of the Jews would

2Cor 6:4 endurance, in afflictions, hardships, C,
12:10 insults, hardships, persecutions, and C; for when I am

CALAMITY (49)
Deut 29:21 tribes of Israel for C, in accordance with all
32:35 the day of their C is at hand, and
Ruth 1:21 the Almighty has brought C upon me?"
2Sam 22:19 the day of my C; but the LORD was
1Kgs 17:20 God, hast thou brought C even upon the widow
Esth 8:6 endure to see the C that is coming to
Job 6:2 weighed, and all my C laid in the balances!
6:21 me; you see my C, and are afraid.
6:30 Cannot my taste discern C
9:23 he mocks at the C of the innocent.
18:12 strength is hunger-bitten, and C is ready for his
21:17 That their C comes upon them?
21:30 in the day of C, that he is rescued
30:13 path, they promote my C; no one restrains them.
31:3 Does not C befall the unrighteous, and disaster the
31:23 was in terror of C from God, and I
Ps 18:18 the day of my C; but the LORD was
35:26 shame and confusion altogether who rejoice at my C
Prov 1:26 will laugh at your C; I will mock when
1:27 a storm, and your C comes like a whirlwind,
6:15 sowing discord; therefore C will come upon him
17:5 who is glad at C will not go unpunished.
17:20 and one with a perverse tongue falls into C
22:8 sows injustice will reap C, and the rod of
24:16 rises again; but the wicked are overthrown by C
27:10 your brother's house in the day of your C
28:14 he who hardens his heart will fall into C
Sir 2:2 and do not be hasty in time of C
5:8 will not benefit you in the day of C
11:22 have enough, and what C could happen to me
12:17 If C befalls you, you will find him there
38:19 In C sorrow continues, and the life of the
Is 57:1 is taken away from C,
65:23 or bear children for C; for they shall be
Jer 18:17 not my face, in the day of their C
46:21 the day of their C has come upon them,
48:16 The C of Moab is near at hand and
49:8 I will bring the C of Esau upon him,
49:32 I will bring their C from every side of
Bar 6:48 For when war or C comes upon them, the
6:49 for they cannot save themselves from war or C
Ezek 35:5 the time of their C, at the time of
Dan 9:12 upon us a great C; for under the whole
9:13 of Moses, all this C has come upon us,
9:14 has kept ready the C and has brought it
Obad 1:13 the day of his C; you should not have
1:13 the day of his C; you should not have
1:13 looted his goods in the day of his C
1Mac 13:32 and he brought great C upon the land.

CALAMUS (2)
Song 4:14 nard, nard and saffron, C and cinnamon, with all
Ezek 27:19 wrought iron, cassia, and C were bartered for your

CALCOL (2)
1Kgs 4:31 the Ezrahite, and Heman, C, and Darda, the sons
1Chr 2:6 Zerah: Zimri, Ethan, Heman, C, and Dara, five in

CALDRON (5)
1Sam 2:14 pan, or kettle, or C, or pot; all that
Ezek 11:3 this city is the C, and we are the
11:7 this city is the C; but you shall be
11:11 shall not be your C, nor shall you be
Mic 3:3 meat in a kettle, like flesh in a C

CALDRONS (2)
2Chr 35:13 offerings in pots, in C, and in pans, and
2Mac 7:3 orders that pans and C be heated.

CALEB (40)
Num 13:6 the tribe of Judah, C the son of Jephunneh;
13:30 But C quieted the people before Moses, and said,
14:6 son of Nun and C the son of Jephunneh,
14:24 But my servant C, because he has a different
14:30 make you dwell, except C the son of Jephunneh
14:38 son of Nun and C the son of Jephunneh
26:65 man of them, except C the son of Jephunneh
32:12 followed me; none except C the son of Jephunneh
34:19 the tribe of Judah, C the son of Jephunneh.
Deut 1:36 to your fathers, except C the son of Jephunneh;
Josh 14:6 Joshua at Gilgal; and C the son of Jephunneh
14:13 he gave Hebron to C the son of Jephunneh

C

C

14:14 became the inheritance of C the son of Jephunneh
15:13 Joshua, he gave to C the son of Jephunneh
15:14 And C drove out from there the three sons
15:16 And C said, "Whoever smites Kiriath-sepher, and
15:17 Kenaz, the brother of C, took it; and he
15:18 from her ass, and C said to her, "What
15:19 And C gave her the upper springs and the
21:12 had been given to C the son of Jephunneh
Judg 1:12 And C said, "He who attacks Kiriath-sepher and
1:13 the son of Kenaz, C's younger brother, took it;
1:14 from her ass, and C said to her, "What
1:15 And C gave her the upper springs and the
1:20 Hebron was given to C, as Moses had said;
3:9 the son of Kenaz, C's younger brother.
1Sam 30:14 upon the Negeb of C; and we burned Ziklag
1Chr 2:18 C the son of Hezron had children by his
2:19 When Azubah died, C married Ephrath, who bore
2:24 the death of Hezron, C went in to Ephrathah,
2:42 The sons of C the brother of Jerahmeel: Mareshah
2:46 Ephah also, C's concubine, bore Haran, Moza, and
2:48 Maacah, C's concubine, bore Sheber and Tirhanah.
2:49 and the daughter of C was Achsah.
2:50 These were the descendants of C
4:15 The sons of C the son of Jephunneh: Iru,
6:56 villages they gave to C the son of Jephunneh.
Sir 46:7 loyal deed, he and C the son of Jephunneh:
46:9 And the Lord gave C strength, which remained with
1Mac 2:56 C, because he testified in the assembly, received an

CALEBITE

1Sam 25:3 man was churlish and ill-behaved; he was a C

CALF (34)

Gen 18:7 herd, and took a C, tender and good, and
18:8 and milk, and the C which he had prepared,
Ex 32:4 and made a molten C; and they said, "These
32:8 for themselves a molten C, and have worshiped it
32:19 camp and saw the C and the dancing, Moses'
32:20 And he took the C which they had made,
32:24 into the fire, and there came out this C
32:35 because they made the C which Aaron made.
Lev 9:2 Aaron, "Take a bull C for a sin offering,
9:3 sin offering, and a C and a lamb, both
9:8 altar, and killed the C of the sin offering,
Deut 9:16 made yourselves a molten C; you had turned aside
9:21 the sinful thing, the C which you had made,
1Sam 28:24 woman had a fatted C in the house, and
1Kgs 10:19 the throne was a C's head, and on each
Neh 9:18 for themselves a molten C and said, 'This is
Tob 1:5 to sacrifice to the C Baal, and so did
Job 21:10 their cow calves, and does not cast her C
Ps 29:6 to skip like a C, and Sirion like a
106:19 They made a C in Horeb and worshiped a
Is 11:6 the kid, and the C and the lion and
27:10 the wilderness; there the C grazes, there he lies
Jer 14:5 field forsakes her newborn C because there is no
31:18 chastened, like an untrained C; bring me back that
34:18 will make like the C which they cut in
34:19 the parts of the C;
Ezek 1:7 the sole of a C's foot; and they sparkled
Hos 8:5 I have spurned your C, O Samaria.
8:6 The C of Samaria shall be broken to pieces.
10:5 Samaria tremble for the C of Beth-aven.
Lk 15:23 and bring the fatted C and kill it, and
15:27 has killed the fatted C, because he has received
15:30 for him the fatted C
Acts 7:41 And they made a C in those days, and

CALL (221)

Gen 2:19 see what he would C them; and whatever the
4:26 time men began to C upon the name of
16:11 a son; you shall C his name Ishmael; because
17:15 wife, you shall not C her name Sarai, but
17:19 son, and you shall C his name Isaac.
24:57 They said, "We will C the maiden, and ask
30:13 For the women will C me happy"; so she
Ex 2:7 "Shall I go and C you a nurse from
2:20 C him, that he may eat bread."
Num 16:12 And Moses sent to C Dathan and Abiram the
22:5 land of Amaw to C him, saying, "Behold, a
22:20 men have come to C you, rise, go with
22:37 send to you to C you?
Deut 2:11 Rephaim, but the Moabites C them Emim.
2:20 there, but the Ammonites C them Zamzummim,
3:9 Mount Hermon (the Sidonians C Hermon Sirion,
3:9 Sirion, while the Amorites C it Senir),
4:7 to us, whenever we C upon him?
4:26 him to anger, I C heaven and earth to
25:8 of his city shall C him, and speak to
30:1 before you, and you C them to mind among
30:19 I C heaven and earth to witness against you
31:14 when you must die; C Joshua, and present yourselves
31:28 in their ears and C heaven and earth to
33:19 They shall C peoples to their mountain; there they
Judg 8:1 to us, not to C us when you went
12:1 Ammonites, and did not C us to go with
16:25 were merry, they said, C Samson, that he may
Ruth 1:20 to them, "Do not C me Naomi, call me
1:20 not call me Naomi, C me Mara, for the
1:21 Why C me Naomi, when the LORD has afflicted
1Sam 3:5 said, "I did not C; lie down again." So
3:6 said, "I did not C, my son; lie down
12:17 I will C upon the LORD, that he may
2Sam 15:2 for judgment, Absalom would C to him, and say,
17:5 Then Absalom said, C Hushai the Archite also, and
20:4 king said to Amasa, C the men of Judah
22:4 I C upon the LORD, who is worthy to
1Kgs 1:28 Then King David answered, C Bathsheba to me." So
1:32 King David said, C to me Zadok the priest,
8:52 to them whenever they C to thee.
18:24 And you C on the name of your god
18:24 god and I will C on the name of
18:25 you are many; and C on the name of
2Kgs 4:12 to Gehazi his servant, C this Shunammite." When he
4:15 He said, C her." And when he had called
4:36 summoned Gehazi and said, C this Shunammite." So
5:11 me, and stand, and C on the name of
10:19 Now therefore C to me all the prophets of
1Chr 16:8 thanks to the LORD, C on his name, make
2Chr 13:12 trumpets to sound the C to battle against you.
Tob 4:2 Why do I not C my son Tobias so
5:8 He said, C him to me, so that I
Jud 3:8 tongues and tribes should C upon him as god.
7:27 Now C them in and surrender the whole city
7:29 We C to witness against you heaven and earth
8:17 his deliverance, let us C upon him to help
16:2 psalm; exalt him, and C upon his name.
Job 5:1 and that without wisdom?' C now; is there any
13:22 Then C, and I will answer; or let me
14:15 Thou wouldest C, and I would answer thee; thou
19:7 am not answered; I C aloud, but there is
19:16 I C to my servant, but he gives me
27:10 Will he C upon God at all times?
35:9 people cry out; they C for help because of
Ps 4:1 Answer me when I C, O God of my
4:3 LORD hears when I C to him.
10:13 heart, "Thou wilt not C to account"?
14:4 bread, and do not C upon the LORD?
17:6 I C upon thee, for thou wilt answer me,
18:3 I C upon the LORD, who is worthy to
20:9 the king, O LORD; answer us when we C
28:1 thee, O LORD, I C; my rock, be not
31:17 O LORD, for I C on thee; let the
50:15 the Most High; and C upon me in the
53:4 bread, and do not C upon God?
55:16 But I C upon God; and the LORD will
56:9 be turned back in the day when I C
61:2 of the earth I C to thee, when my
63:4 up my hands and C on thy name.
72:17 by him, all nations C him blessed!
75:1 we give thanks; we C on thy name and
77:11 I will C to mind the deeds of the
79:6 kingdoms that do not C on thy name!
80:18 life, and we will C on thy name!
86:5 love to all who C on thee.
86:7 of my trouble I C on thee, for thou
88:1 LORD, my God, I C for help by day;
88:9 Every day I C upon thee, O LORD; I
102:2 answer me speedily in the day when I C
105:1 thanks to the LORD, C on his name, make
116:2 me, therefore I will C on him as long
116:13 cup of salvation and C on the name of
116:17 sacrifice of thanksgiving and C on the name of
141:1 I C upon thee, O LORD; make haste to
141:1 my voice, when I C to thee!
145:18 near to all who C upon him, to all
145:18 him, to all who C upon him in truth.
Prov 1:28 Then they will C upon me, but I will
7:4 and C insight your intimate friend;
8:1 Does not wisdom C, does not understanding raise her
8:4 you, O men, I C, and my cry is
9:3 out her maids to C from the highest places

31:28 children rise up and C her blessed; her husband
Wis 14:22 to ignorance, and they C such great evils peace.
18:8 our enemies thou didst C us to thyself and
Sir 11:26 C no one happy before his death; a man
31:9 And we will C him blessed, for he has
37:24 who see him will C him happy.
42:15 I will now C to mind the works of
Is 5:20 Woe to those who C evil good and good
7:14 a son, and shall C his name Immanu-el.
8:3 said to me, C his name Maher-shalal-hash-baz;
8:12 people, saying: "Do not C conspiracy all that this
8:12 all that this people C conspiracy, and do not
12:4 thanks to the LORD, C upon his name; make
22:20 that day I will C my servant Eliakim the
31:2 disaster, he does not C back his words, but
41:25 sun, and he shall C on my name; he
43:22 "Yet you did not C upon me, O Jacob;
44:5 the LORD's,' another will C himself by the name
45:3 God of Israel, who C you by your name.
45:4 Israel my chosen, I C you by your name,
48:2 For they C themselves after the holy city, and
48:13 the heavens; when I C to them, they stand
55:5 Behold, you shall C nations that you know not,
55:6 he may be found, C upon him while he
58:5 Will you C this a fast, and a day
58:9 Then you shall C, and the LORD will answer;
58:13 my holy day, and C the sabbath a delight
60:14 your feet; they shall C you the City of
60:18 your borders; you shall C your walls Salvation, and
65:1 nation that did not C on my name.
65:15 his servants he will C by a different name.
65:24 Before they C I will answer, while they are
Jer 3:19 I thought you would C me, My Father, and
7:27 You shall C to them, but they will not
9:17 of hosts: "Consider, and C for the mourning women
10:25 upon the peoples that C not on thy name;
11:14 not listen when they C to me in the
20:3 "The LORD does not C your name Pashhur, but
29:12 Then you will C upon me and come and
31:6 day when watchmen will C in the hill country
33:3 LORD is his name: C to me and I
46:17 sword of the oppressor.' C the name of Pharaoh,
Lam 3:8 on me; though I C and cry for help,
3:21 But this I C to mind, and therefore I
Bar 3:7 order that we should C upon thy name; and
6:40 they are gods, or C them gods?
6:44 they are gods, or C them gods?
6:64 they are gods nor C them gods, for they
Hos 1:4 LORD said to him, C his name Jezreel; for
1:6 LORD said to him, C her name Not pitied,
1:9 And the LORD said, C his name Not my
2:16 the LORD, you will C me, 'My husband,' and
2:16 no longer will you C me, 'My Baal.'
Joel 1:13 Sanctify a fast, C a solemn assembly.
2:15 Zion; sanctify a fast; C a solemn assembly;
2:32 pass that all who C upon the name of
Amos 5:16 alas!' They shall C the farmers to mourning and
Jon 1:6 Arise, C upon your god!
Zeph 3:9 all of them may C on the name of
Zech 13:9 They will C on my name, and I will
Mal 3:12 Then all nations will C you blessed, for you
1Mac 7:45 kept sounding the battle C on the trumpets.
2Mac 3:31 friends asked Onias to C upon the Most High
4:14 wrestling arena after the C to the discus,
6:2 temple in Jerusalem and C it the temple of
6:2 Olympian Zeus, and to C the one in Gerizim
13:10 ordered the people to C upon the Lord day
Mt 1:21 son, and you shall C his name Jesus, for
9:13 I came not to C the righteous, but sinners."
20:8 said to his steward, C the laborers and pay
22:3 sent his servants to C those who were invited
23:9 And C no man your father on earth, for
24:31 with a loud trumpet C, and they will gather
Mk 2:17 I came not to C the righteous, but sinners."
10:18 him, "Why do you C me good?
10:49 Jesus stopped and said, C him." And they called
15:12 the man whom you C the King of the
Lk 1:13 son, and you shall C his name John.
1:31 son, and you shall C his name Jesus.
1:48 henceforth all generations will C me blessed;
5:32 have not come to C the righteous, but sinners
6:46 "Why do you C me 'Lord, Lord,' and not
18:19 him, "Why do you C me good?
Jn 4:16 said to her, "Go, C your husband, and come
13:13 You C me Teacher and Lord; and you are
15:15 No longer do I C you servants, for the
Acts 9:14 to bind all who C upon thy name."
10:15 cleansed, you must not C common."
10:28 that I should not C any man common or
11:9 cleansed you must not C common.'
24:13 the Way, which they C a sect, I worship
Rom 2:17 But if you C yourself a Jew and rely
9:11 but because of his C,
9:25 my people I will C 'my people,' and her
9:25 not beloved I will C 'my beloved.'"
10:12 riches upon all who C upon him.
10:14 how are men to C upon him in whom
11:29 the gifts and the C of God are irrevocable.
1Cor 1:2 who in every place C on the name of
1:26 For consider your C, brethren; not many of you
7:18 the time of his C already circumcised?
7:18 the time of his C uncircumcised?
2Cor 1:23 But I C God to witness against me—it
Eph 4:4 that belongs to your C,
Phil 3:14 prize of the upward C of God in Christ
1Thes 4:16 command, with the archangel's C, and with the sound
2Thes 1:11 you worthy of his C, and may fulfil every
2Tim 2:22 along with those who C upon the Lord from
Heb 2:11 is not ashamed to C them brethren,
3:1 share in a heavenly C, consider Jesus, the apostle
Jas 5:11 Behold, we C those happy who were steadfast.
5:14 Let him C for the elders of the church,
2Pet 1:10 zealous to confirm your C and election, for if
Rev 2:2 have tested those who C themselves apostles but are
2:24 not learned what some C the deep things of
10:7 days of the trumpet C to be sounded by
13:10 Here is a C for the endurance and faith
14:12 Here is a C for the endurance of the

CALLED (660)

Gen 1:5 God C the light Day, and the darkness he
1:5 and the darkness he C Night.
1:8 And God C the firmament Heaven.
1:10 God C the dry land Earth, and the waters
1:10 were gathered together he C Seas.
2:19 and whatever the man C every living creature, that
2:23 flesh; she shall be C Woman, because she was
3:9 But the LORD God C to the man, and
3:20 The man C his wife's name Eve, because she
4:17 built a city, and C the name of the
4:25 bore a son and C his name Seth, for
4:26 was born, and he C his name Enosh.
5:29 of a son, and C his name Noah, saying,
11:9 Therefore its name was C Babel, because there the
12:8 to the LORD and C on the name of
12:18 So Pharaoh C Abram, and said, "What is this
13:4 first; and there Abram C on the name of
16:13 So she C the name of the LORD who
16:14 Therefore the well was C Beer-lahai-roi; it lies
16:15 a son; and Abram C the name of his
19:5 the house; and they C to Lot, "Where are
19:22 of the city was C Zoar.
19:37 bore a son, and C his name Moab; he
19:38 bore a son, and C his name Ben-ammi; he
20:8 in the morning, and C all his servants, and
20:9 Then Abimelech C Abraham, and said to him, "What
21:3 Abraham C the name of his son who was
21:17 the angel of God C to Hagar from heaven,
21:31 Therefore that place was C Beer-sheba; because
21:33 tree in Beer-sheba, and C there on the name
22:11 angel of the LORD C to him from heaven,
22:14 So Abraham C the name of that place The
22:15 angel of the LORD C to Abraham a second
24:58 And they C Rebekah, and said to her, "Will
25:25 hairy mantle; so they C his name Esau.
25:26 so his name was C Jacob.
25:30 (Therefore his name was C Edom.
26:9 So Abimelech C Isaac, and said, "Behold, she is
26:20 So he C the name of the well Esek,
26:21 that also; so he C its name Sitnah.
26:22 not quarrel; so he C its name Rehoboth, saying,
26:25 an altar there and C upon the name of
26:33 He C it Shibah; therefore the name of the
27:1 could not see, he C Esau his older son,
27:42 so she sent and C Jacob her younger son,
28:1 Then Isaac C Jacob and blessed him, and charged
28:19 He C the name of that place Bethel; but
29:32 a son, and she C his name Reuben; for
29:33 son also"; and she C his name Simeon.
29:34 therefore his name was C Levi.
29:35 the LORD"; therefore she C his name Judah; then
30:6 a son"; therefore she C his name Dan.

CALLED

C

30:8 have prevailed"; so she C his name Naphtali.
30:11 so she C his name Gad.
30:13 me happy"; so she C his name Asher.
30:18 my husband"; so she C his name Issachar.
30:20 six sons"; so she C his name Zebulun.
30:21 bore a daughter, and C her name Dinah.
30:24 my reproach"; and she C his name Joseph, saying,
31:4 So Jacob sent and C Rachel and Leah into
31:47 Laban C it Jegar-sahadutha: but Jacob called it
31:47 it Jegar-sahadutha: but Jacob C it Galeed.
31:54 on the mountain and C his kinsmen to eat
32:2 So he C the name of that place Mahanaim.
32:28 shall no more be C Jacob, but Israel, for
32:30 So Jacob C the name of the place Peniel,
33:17 of the place is C Succoth.
33:20 erected an altar and C it El-Elohe-Israel.
35:7 built an altar, and C the place El-bethel, because
35:8 name of it was C Allon-bacuth.
35:10 shall your name be C Jacob, but Israel shall
35:10 So his name was C Israel.
35:15 So Jacob C the name of the place where
35:18 (for she died), she C his name Ben-oni; but
35:18 Ben-oni; but his father C his name Benjamin.
38:3 a son, and he C his name Er.
38:4 a son, and she C his name Onan.
38:5 a son, and she C his name Shelah.
38:29 Therefore his name was C Perez.
38:30 and his name was C Zerah.
39:14 of the house, she C to the men of
41:8 and he sent and C for all the magicians
41:14 Then Pharaoh sent and C Joseph, and they brought
41:45 And Pharaoh C Joseph's name Zaphenath-paneah;
41:51 Joseph C the name of the first-born Manasseh, "For,"
41:52 of the second he C Ephraim, "For God has
47:29 Israel must die, he C his son Joseph and
48:6 yours; they shall be C by the name of
49:1 Then Jacob C his sons, and said, "Gather yourselves
Ex 1:17 the king of Egypt C the midwives, and said
2:8 the girl went and C the child's mother.
2:22 a son, and he C his name Gershom; for
3:4 aside to see, God C to him out of
8:8 Then Pharaoh C Moses and Aaron, and said,
8:25 Then Pharaoh C Moses and Aaron, and said, "Go,
9:27 Then Pharaoh sent, and C Moses and Aaron, and
10:16 Then Pharaoh C Moses and Aaron in haste, and
10:24 Then Pharaoh C Moses, and said, "Go, serve the
12:21 Then Moses C all the elders of Israel, and
16:31 the house of Israel C its name manna; it
17:7 And he C the name of the place Massah
17:15 built an altar and C the name of it,
19:3 God, and the LORD C to him out of
19:7 So Moses came and C the elders of the
19:20 mountain; and the LORD C Moses to the top
24:16 the seventh day he C to Moses out of
31:2 Moses, "See, I have C by name Bezalel the
33:7 the camp; and he C it the tent of
34:31 But Moses C to them; and Aaron and all
35:30 "See, the LORD has C by name Bezalel the
36:2 And Moses C Bezalel and Oholiab and every able
Lev 1:1 The LORD C Moses, and spoke to
9:1 the eighth day Moses C Aaron and his sons
10:4 And Moses C Mishael and Elzaphan, the sons of
Num 11:3 of that place was C Taberah, because the fire
11:34 of that place was C Kibroth-hattaavah, because
12:5 of the tent, and C Aaron and Miriam; and
13:16 And Moses C Hoshea the son of Nun Joshua.
13:24 That place was C the Valley of Eshcol, because
21:3 of the place was C Hormah.
24:10 said to Balaam, "I C you to curse my
32:41 took their villages, and C them Havvoth-jair.
32:42 and its villages, and C it Nobah, after his
Deut 3:13 of that Bashan is C the land of Rephaim.
3:14 and the Ma-acathites, and C the villages after his
25:10 his house shall be C in Israel, The house
28:10 see that you are C by the name of
Josh 4:4 Then Joshua C the twelve men from the people
5:9 of that place is C Gilgal to this day.
6:6 the son of Nun C the priests and said
7:26 of that place is C the Valley of Achor.
8:16 in the city were C together to pursue them,
22:34 Reubenites and the Gadites C the altar Witness;
Judg 1:17 of the city was C Hormah.
1:26 built a city, and C its name Luz; that
2:5 And they C the name of that place Bochim;
4:13 to Mount Tabor, Sisera C out all his chariots,
6:24 to the LORD, and C it, The LORD is
6:32 that day he was C Jerubbaal, that is to
6:34 and the Abiezrites were C out to follow him.
6:35 and they too were C out to follow him.
7:23 men of Israel were C out from Naphtali and
7:24 men of Ephraim were C out, and they seized
8:31 a son, and he C his name Abimelech.
9:54 Then he C hastily to the young man his
10:4 they had thirty cities, C Havvoth-jair to this day,
10:17 Then the Ammonites were C to arms, and they
12:1 men of Ephraim were C to arms, and they
12:2 Ammonites; and when I C you, you did not
13:24 bore a son, and C his name Samson; and
15:17 and that place was C Ramathlehi.
15:18 very thirsty, and he C on the LORD and
15:19 name of it was C En-hakkore; it is at
16:18 mind, she sent and C the lords of the
16:19 her knees; and she C a man, and had
16:25 So they C Samson out of the prison, and
16:28 Then Samson C to the LORD and said, "O
18:12 account that place is C Mahaneh-dan to this day;
18:22 near Micah's house were C out, and they overtook
1Sam 1:20 a son, and she C his name Samuel, for
3:4 Then the LORD C, "Samuel!
3:5 I am, for you C me." But he said,
3:6 And the LORD C again, "Samuel!" And Samuel
3:6 I am, for you C me." But he said,
3:8 And the LORD C Samuel again the third time.
3:8 I am, for you C me." Then Eli perceived
3:16 But Eli C Samuel and said, "Samuel, my son."
6:2 And the Philistines C for the priests and the
7:12 Mizpah and Jeshanah, and C its name Ebenezer; for
9:9 he who is now C a prophet was formerly
9:9 a prophet was formerly C a seer.)
9:26 break of dawn Samuel C to Saul upon the
10:17 Now Samuel C the people together to the LORD
12:18 So Samuel C upon the LORD, and the LORD
13:4 And the people were C out to join Saul
16:8 Then Jesse C Abinadab, and made him pass before
19:7 And Jonathan C David, and Jonathan showed him all
20:37 Jonathan had shot, Jonathan C after the lad and
20:38 And Jonathan C after the lad, "Hurry, make haste,
23:28 therefore that place was C the Rock of Escape.
24:8 of the cave, and C after Saul, "My lord
26:14 between them; and David C to the army, and
29:6 Then Achish C David and said to him, "As
2Sam 1:7 he saw me, and C to me.
1:15 Then David C one of the young men and
2:16 Therefore that place was C Helkath-hazzurim, which
2:26 Then Abner C to Joab, "Shall the sword devour
5:9 in the stronghold, and C it the city of
5:20 of that place is C Baal-perazim.
6:2 of God, which is C by the name of
6:8 and that place is C Perez-uzzah, to this day.
9:2 was Ziba, and they C him to David; and
9:9 Then the king C Ziba, Saul's servant, and said
12:24 a son, and he C his name Solomon.
12:25 the prophet; so he C his name Jedidiah, because
12:28 city, and it be C by my name."
13:17 He C the young man who served him and
18:18 name in remembrance"; he C the pillar after his
18:18 name, and it is C Absalom's monument to this
18:25 And the watchman C out and told the king.
18:26 running; and the watchman C to the gate and
20:16 Then a wise woman C from the city, "Hear!
20:21 hill country of Ephraim, C Sheba the son of
21:2 So the king C the Gibeonites.
22:7 "In my distress I C upon the LORD; to
22:7 called upon the LORD; to my God I C
1Kgs 7:21 on the south and C its name Jachin; and
7:21 on the north and C its name Boaz.
8:43 I have built is C by thy name.
9:13 So they are C the land of Cabul to
12:3 And they sent and C him; and Jeroboam and
12:20 returned, they sent and C him to the assembly
16:24 fortified the hill, and C the name of the
17:10 gathering sticks; and he C to her and said,
17:11 to bring it, he C to her and said,
18:3 And Ahab C Obadiah, who was over the household.
18:26 they prepared it, and C on the name of
20:7 the king of Israel C all the elders of
2Kgs 3:10 The LORD has C these three kings to give
3:13 the LORD who has C these three kings to
3:21 to the oldest, were C out, and were drawn
4:12 When he had C her, she stood before him.
4:15 And when he had C her, she stood in
4:22 Then she C to her husband, and said, "Send

CALLED

Book	Ref	Context
	4:36	So he C her.
	6:11	this thing; and he C his servants and said
	7:10	So they came and C to the gatekeepers of
	7:11	Then the gatekeepers C out, and it was told
	8:1	for the LORD has C for a famine, and
	9:1	Then Elisha the prophet C one of the sons
	14:7	Sela by storm, and C it Joktheel, which is
	18:4	to it; it was C Nehushtan.
	18:18	And when they C for the king, there came
	18:28	the Rabshakeh stood and C out in a loud
1Chr	4:9	brothers; and his mother C his name Jabez, saying,
	4:10	Jabez C on the God of Israel, saying, "Oh
	7:16	a son, and she C his name Peresh; and
	7:23	a son; and he C his name Beriah, because
	11:7	stronghold; therefore it was C the city of David.
	13:6	of God, which is C by the name of
	13:11	and that place is C Perez-uzza to this day.
	14:11	of that place is C Baal-perazim.
	21:26	and peace offerings, and C upon the LORD, and
	22:6	Then he C for Solomon his son, and charged
2Chr	3:17	on the south he C Jachin, and that on
	6:33	I have built is C by thy name.
	7:14	my people who are C by my name humble
	10:3	And they sent and C him; and Jeroboam and
	20:26	that place has been C the Valley of Beracah
Ezra	2:61	the Gileadite, and was C by their name).
Neh	5:12	And I C the priests, and took an oath
	7:63	the Gileadite and was C by their name).
Tob	4:3	So he C him and said, "My son, when
	7:13	Then he C his daughter Sarah, and taking her
	7:14	Next he C his wife Edna, and took a
	7:16	And Raguel C his wife Edna and said to
	9:1	Then Tobias C Raphael and said to him,
	12:1	Tobit then C his son Tobias and said to
	12:5	So he C the angel and said to him,
	12:6	Then the angel C the two of them privately
	14:3	grown very old he C his son and grandsons,
Jud	2:2	He C together all his officers and all his
	2:4	king of the Assyrians C Holofernes, the chief general
	2:14	of his master, and C together all the commanders,
	5:2	So he C together all the princes of Moab
	6:16	They C together all the elders of the city,
	6:21	all that night they C on the God of
	9:4	of their blood, and C on thee for help--
	10:2	she lay prostrate and C her maid and went
	13:11	Judith C out from afar to the watchmen at
	13:12	the city gate and C together the elders of
Esth	4:5	Then Esther C for Hathach, one of the king's
	4:11	inner court without being C, there is but one
	4:11	I have not been C to come in to
	9:26	Therefore they C these days Purim, after the term
	16:11	nation that he was C our father and was
Job	12:4	my friends; I, who C upon God and he
	29:11	the ear heard, it C me blessed, and when
	31:24	gold my trust, or C fine gold my confidence;
	42:14	And he C the name of the first Jemimah;
Ps	18:6	In my distress I C upon the LORD; to
	41:2	him alive; he is C blessed in the land;
	81:7	In distress you C, and I delivered you; I
	99:6	was among those who C on his name.
	116:4	Then I C on the name of the LORD:
	118:5	of my distress I C on the LORD; the
	138:3	On the day I C, thou didst answer me,
Prov	1:24	Because I have C and you refused to listen,
	3:18	hold her fast are C happy.
	16:21	wise of heart is C a man of discernment,
	24:8	do evil will be C a mischief-maker.
Song	3:1	found him not; I C him, but he gave
	5:6	found him not; I C him, but he gave
	6:9	maidens saw her and C her happy; the queens
Wis	7:7	was given me; I C upon God, and the
	11:4	When they thirsted they C upon thee, and water
	11:25	how would anything not C forth by thee have
Sir	2:10	Or who ever C upon him and was overlooked?
	5:14	Do not be C a slanderer, and do not
	36:12	Lord, upon the people C by thy name, upon
	46:5	He C upon the Most High, the Mighty One,
	46:16	He C upon the Lord, the Mighty One, when
	46:19	his eternal sleep, Samuel C men to witness before
	47:18	Lord God, who is C the God of Israel,
	48:20	But they C upon the Lord who is merciful,
Is	1:26	Afterward you shall be C the city of righteousness,
	4:1	only let us be C by your name; take
	4:3	in Jerusalem will be C holy, every one who
	6:3	And one C to another and said: "Holy, holy,
	6:4	voice of him who C, and the house was
	9:6	his name will be C "Wonderful Counselor, Mighty
	19:18	of these will be C the City of the
	22:12	Lord GOD of hosts C to weeping and mourning,
	30:7	empty, therefore I have C her "Rahab who sits
	31:4	band of shepherds is C forth against him is
	32:5	will no more be C noble, nor the knave
	35:8	and it shall be C the Holy Way; the
	36:13	the Rabshakeh stood and C out in a loud
	41:9	of the earth, and C from its farthest corners,
	42:6	the LORD, I have C you in righteousness, I
	43:1	redeemed you; I have C you by name, you
	43:7	every one who is C by my name, whom
	47:1	shall no more be C tender and delicate.
	47:5	shall no more be C the mistress of kingdoms.
	48:1	of Jacob, who are C by the name of
	48:8	from birth you were C a rebel.
	48:12	to me, O Jacob, and Israel, whom I C
	48:15	I, have spoken and C him, I have brought
	49:1	The LORD C me from the womb, from the
	50:2	When I C, was there no one to answer?
	51:2	was but one I C him, and I blessed
	54:5	the God of the whole earth he is C
	54:6	For the LORD has C you like a wife
	56:7	my house shall be C a house of prayer
	58:12	generations; you shall be C the repairer of the
	61:3	that they may be C oaks of righteousness, the
	61:6	but you shall be C the priests of the
	62:2	and you shall be C by a new name
	62:4	but you shall be C My delight is in
	62:12	And they shall be C The holy people, The
	62:12	and you shall be C Sought out, a city
	63:19	those who are not C by thy name.
	65:12	slaughter; because, when I C, you did not answer,
	66:4	them; because, when I C, no one answered, when
Jer	3:4	you not just now C to me, 'My father,
	3:17	time Jerusalem shall be C the throne of the
	6:30	Refuse silver they are C, for the LORD has
	7:10	this house, which is C by my name, and
	7:11	this house, which is C by my name, become
	7:13	listen, and when I C you, you did not
	7:14	the house which is C by my name, and
	7:30	the house which is C by my name, to
	7:32	will no more be C Topheth, or the valley
	11:16	The LORD once C you, 'A green olive tree,
	14:9	us, and we are C by thy name; leave
	15:16	heart; for I am C by thy name, O
	19:6	shall no more be C Topheth, or the valley
	23:6	which he will be C: 'The LORD is our
	25:29	the city which is C by my name, and
	30:17	LORD, because they have C you an outcast: 'It
	32:34	the house which is C by my name, to
	33:16	which it will be C: 'The LORD is our
	34:15	the house which is C by my name;
	35:17	not listened, I have C to them and they
	36:4	Then Jeremiah C Baruch the son of Neriah, and
Lam	1:19	"I C to my lovers but they deceived me;
	2:15	the city which was C the perfection of beauty,
	3:55	I am lost.' "I C on thy name, O
	3:57	come near when I C on thee; thou didst
Bar	2:15	and his descendants are C by thy name.
	2:26	the house which is C by thy name thou
	3:33	light, and it goes, C it, and it obeyed
	3:34	and were glad; he C them, and they said,
	5:4	will for ever be C by God, "Peace of
	6:30	why should they be C gods?
Ezek	9:3	the house; and he C to the man clothed
	10:13	the wheels, they were C in my hearing the
	20:29	So its name is C Bamah to this day.)
	39:11	buried; it will be C the Valley of Hamon-gog.
Dan	1:7	them names: Daniel he C Belteshazzar, Hananiah he
	1:7	Belteshazzar, Hananiah he C Shadrach, Mishael he
	1:7	called Shadrach, Mishael he C Meshach, and Azariah
	1:7	Meshach, and Azariah he C Abednego.
	5:12	Now let Daniel be C, and he will show
	8:16	the Ulai, and it C, "Gabriel, make this man
	9:18	the city which is C by thy name; for
	9:19	and thy people are C by thy name."
	14:3	Babylonians had an idol C Bel, and every day
	14:8	was angry, and he C his priests and said
Hos	11:1	out of Egypt I C my son.
	11:2	The more I C them, the more they went
Amos	9:12	the nations who are C by my name," says
Jon	2:2	the fish, saying, "I C to the LORD, out
Hag	1:11	And I have C for a drought upon the
Zech	7:13	"As I C, and they would not hear, so
	7:13	not hear, so they C, and I would not

8:3 and Jerusalem shall be C the faithful city, and
Mal 1:4 down, till they are C the wicked country, the
1Mac 2:3 John surnamed Gaddi, Simon C Thassi,
2:4 Simon called Thassi, Judas C Maccabeus,
2:5 Judas called Maccabeus, Eleazar C Avaran, and
2:5 called Avaran, and Jonathan C Apphus.
3:1 his son, who was C Maccabeus, took command in
5:16 a great assembly was C to determine what they
6:10 So he C all his friends and said to
6:14 Then he C for Philip, one of his friends,
6:43 And Eleazar, C Avaran, saw that one of the
7:37 this house to be C by thy name, and
8:20 "Judas, who is also C Maccabeus, and his brothers
10:20 you are to be C the king's friend" (and
11:7 far as the river C Eleutherus; then he returned
11:47 So the king C the Jews to his aid,
12:31 the Arabs who are C Zabadeans, and he crushed
12:37 he repaired the section C Chaphenatha.
16:2 And Simon C in his two older sons Judas
16:15 in the little stronghold C Dok, which he had
2Mac 1:36 Nehemiah and his associates C this "nephthar,"
1:36 most people it is C naphtha.
3:15 their priestly garments and C toward heaven upon
4:7 and Antiochus who was C Epiphanes succeeded to
7:25 at all, the king C the mother to him
8:1 Judas, who was also C Maccabeus, and his
8:15 and because he had C them by his holy
9:2 had entered the city C Persepolis, and attempted to
10:9 of Antiochus, who was C Epiphanes.
10:12 Ptolemy, who was C Macron, took the lead in
10:13 He heard himself C a traitor at every turn,
10:32 to a stronghold C Gazara, especially well garrisoned,
12:17 the Jews who are C Toubiani.
12:21 baggage to a place C Carnaim; for that place
12:28 But the Jews C upon the Sovereign who with
12:32 the feast C Pentecost, they hastened against Gorgias,
12:36 and were weary, Judas C upon the Lord to
13:23 Antioch; he was dismayed, C in the Jews, yielded
14:6 the Jews who are C Hasideans, whose leader is
14:16 battle at a village C Dessau.
14:34 toward heaven and C upon the constant Defender
14:37 his good will was C father of the Jews.
15:21 hands toward heaven and C upon the Lord who
15:22 And he C upon him in these words: "O
15:31 arrived there and had C his countrymen together and
15:36 – which is C Adar in the Syrian
Mt 1:16 was born, who is C Christ.
1:23 his name shall be C Emmanuel" (which means, God
1:25 a son; and he C his name Jesus.
2:15 of Egypt have I C my son."
2:23 dwelt in a city C Nazareth, that what was
2:23 fulfilled, "He shall be C a Nazarene."
4:18 brothers, Simon who is C Peter and Andrew his
4:21 their nets, and he C them.
5:9 for they shall be C sons of God.
5:19 men so, shall be C least in the kingdom
5:19 teaches them shall be C great in the kingdom
9:9 he saw a man C Matthew sitting at the
10:1 And he C to him his twelve disciples and
10:2 first, Simon, who is C Peter, and Andrew his
10:25 If they have C the master of the house
13:55 Is not his mother C Mary?
15:10 And he C the people to him and said
15:32 Then Jesus C his disciples to him and said,
20:25 But Jesus C them to him and said, "You
20:32 And Jesus stopped and C them, saying, "What do
21:13 'My house shall be C a house of prayer';
22:14 teeth.' For many are C, but few are chosen."
23:7 market places, and being C rabbi by men.
23:8 are not to be C rabbi, for you have
23:10 Neither be C masters, for you have one master,
25:14 going on a journey C his servants and entrusted
26:3 high priest, who was C Caiaphas,
26:14 the twelve, who was C Judas Iscariot, went to
26:36 them to a place C Gethsemane, and he said
27:8 that field has been C the Field of Blood
27:16 then a notorious prisoner, C Barabbas.
27:17 or Jesus who is C Christ?"
27:22 with Jesus who is C Christ?" They all said,
27:33 came to a place C Golgotha (which means the
Mk 1:20 And immediately he C them; and they left their
3:13 on the mountain, and C to him those whom
3:23 And he C them to him, and said to
3:31 sent to him and C him.
6:7 And he C to him the twelve, and began
7:14 And he C the people to him again, and
8:1 nothing to eat, he C his disciples to him,
8:34 And he C to him the multitude with his
9:35 he sat down and C the twelve; and he
10:42 And Jesus C them to him and said to
10:49 And they C the blind man, saying to him,
11:17 'My house shall be C a house of prayer
12:43 And he C his disciples to him, and said
14:32 a place which was C Gethsemane; and he said
15:7 there was a man C Barabbas.
15:16 the praetorium); and they C together the whole
15:22 him to the place C Golgotha (which means the
Lk 1:32 great, and will be C the Son of the
1:35 be born will be C holy, the Son of
1:36 with her who was C barren.
1:60 so; he shall be C John."
1:61 of your kindred is C by this name."
1:62 his father, inquiring what he would have him C
1:76 you, child, will be C the prophet of the
2:4 of David, which is C Bethlehem, because he was
2:21 was circumcised, he was C Jesus, the name given
2:23 the womb shall be C holy to the Lord")
6:13 it was day, he C his disciples, and chose
6:15 and Simon who was C the Zealot,
7:11 went to a city C Nain, and his disciples
8:2 and infirmities: Mary, C Magdalene, from whom
8:8 he said this, he C out, "He who has
8:54 by the hand he C, saying, "Child, arise."
9:1 And he C the twelve together and gave them
9:10 apart to a city C Beth-saida.
10:39 she had a sister C Mary, who sat at
13:12 Jesus saw her, he C her and said to
15:19 longer worthy to be C your son; treat me
15:21 longer worthy to be C your son.'
15:26 And he C one of the servants and asked
16:2 And he C him and said to him, 'What
16:24 And he C out, 'Father Abraham, have mercy upon
18:16 But Jesus C them to him, saying, "Let the
19:15 the money, to be C to him, that he
19:29 the mount that is C Olivet, he sent two
21:37 lodged on the mount C Olivet.
22:1 drew near, which is C the Passover.
22:3 Satan entered into Judas C Iscariot, who was of
22:25 authority over them are C benefactors.
22:45 crowd, and the man C Judas, one of the
23:13 Pilate then C together the chief priests and the
23:32 the place which is C The Skull, there they
Jn 1:42 You shall be C Cephas" (which means Peter).
1:48 answered him, "Before Philip C you, when you were
2:9 steward of the feast C the bridegroom
4:5 a city of Samaria, C Sychar, near the field
4:25 coming (he who is C Christ); when he comes,
5:2 a pool, in Hebrew C Beth-zatha, which has five
5:17 the sabbath but also C God his Father, making
9:11 He answered, "The man C Jesus made clay and
9:18 his sight, until they C the parents of the
9:24 the second time they C the man who had
10:35 If he C them gods to whom the word
11:16 Thomas, C the Twin, said to his fellow disciples,
11:28 this, she went and C her sister Mary, saying
11:54 wilderness, to a town C Ephraim; and there he
12:17 with him when he C Lazarus out of the
15:15 doing; but I have C you friends, for all
18:33 the praetorium again and C Jesus, and said to
19:13 seat at a place C The Pavement, and in
19:17 cross, to the place C the place of a
19:17 a skull, which is C in Hebrew Golgotha.
20:24 one of the twelve, C the Twin, was not
21:2 Simon Peter, Thomas C the Twin, Nathanael of Cana
Acts 1:12 Jerusalem from the mount C Olivet, which is near
1:19 that the field was C in their language Akeldama,
1:23 put forward two, Joseph C Barsabbas, who was
3:2 the temple which is C Beautiful to ask alms
3:11 them in the portico C Solomons, astounded.
4:18 So they C them and charged them not to
5:21 were with him and C together the council and
5:40 and when they had C in the apostles, they
6:9 Freedmen (as it was C, and of the Cyrenians,
7:14 And Joseph sent and C to him Jacob his
8:10 of God which is C Great."
9:11 go to the street C Straight, and inquire in
9:21 Jerusalem of those who C on this name?
10:5 one Simon who is C Peter;
10:7 him had departed, he C two of his servants
10:18 before the gate and C out to ask whether
10:18 whether Simon who was C Peter was lodging there.
10:23 So he C them in to be his guests.

10:24 expecting them and had C together his kinsmen and
10:32 for Simon who is C Peter; he is lodging
11:13 Joppa and bring Simon C Peter;
11:26 for the first time C Christians.
13:1 Barnabas, Simeon who was C Niger, Lucius of
13:2 to which I have C them."
13:9 Saul, who is also C Paul, filled with the
14:12 Barnabas they C Zeus, and Paul, because he was
14:12 the chief speaker, they C Hermes.
15:17 the Gentiles who are C by my name,
15:22 They sent Judas C Barsabbas, and Silas, leading men
15:36 take with them John C Mark.
16:10 concluding that God had C us to preach the
16:29 And he C for lights and rushed in, and
20:17 sent to Ephesus and C to him the elders
23:17 And Paul C one of the centurions and said,
23:18 said, "Paul the prisoner C me and asked me
23:23 Then he C two of the centurions and said,
24:2 and when he was C, Tertullus began to accuse
27:8 came to a place C Fair Havens, near which
27:14 soon a tempestuous wind, C the northeaster, struck
27:16 of a small island C Cauda, we managed with
28:1 that the island was C Malta.
28:17 After three days he C together the local leaders
Rom 1:1 servant of Jesus Christ, C to be an apostle,
1:6 including yourselves who are C to belong to Jesus
1:7 in Rome, who are C to be saints: Grace
7:3 Accordingly, she will be C an adulteress if she
8:28 love him, who are C according to his purpose.
8:30 he predestined he also C; and those whom he
8:30 and those whom he C he also justified; and
9:24 us whom he has C, not from the Jews
9:26 people,' they will be C 'sons of the living
1Cor 1:1 Paul, C by the will of
1:2 sanctified in Christ Jesus, C to be saints together
1:9 by whom you were C into the fellowship of
1:24 to those who are C, both Jews and Greeks,
7:15 For God has C us to peace.
7:17 in which God has C him.
7:20 remain in the state in which he was C
7:21 Were you a slave when C
7:22 For he who was C in the Lord as
7:22 who was free when C is a slave of
7:24 whatever state each was C, there let him remain
14:24 by all, he is C to account by all,
15:9 apostles, unfit to be C an apostle, because I
Gal 1:6 quickly deserting him who C you in the grace
1:15 was born, and had C me through his grace,
5:13 For you were C to freedom, brethren; only do
Eph 1:18 to which he has C you, what are the
2:11 Gentiles in the flesh, C the uncircumcision by what
2:11 uncircumcision by what is C the circumcision, which
4:1 which you have been C,
4:4 just as you were C to the one hope
Col 3:15 which indeed you were C in the one body.
4:11 and Jesus who is C Justus.
1Thes 4:7 For God has not C us for uncleanness, but
2Thes 2:14 To this he C you through our gospel, so
1Tim 6:12 to which you were C when you made the
6:20 of what is falsely C knowledge,
2Tim 1:9 who saved us and C us with a holy
Heb 3:13 long as it is C "today," that none of
5:4 himself, but he is C by God, just as
9:2 the Presence; it is C the Holy Place.
9:3 curtain stood a tent C the Holy of Holies,
9:15 that those who are C may receive the promised
11:8 obeyed when he was C to go out to
11:16 not ashamed to be C their God, for he
11:24 up, refused to be C the son of Pharaoh's
Jas 2:23 righteousness"; and he was C the friend of God.
1Pet 1:15 but as he who C you is holy, be
2:9 deeds of him who C you out of darkness
2:21 this you have been C, because Christ also suffered
3:9 this you have been C, that you may obtain
5:10 all grace, who has C you to his eternal
2Pet 1:3 knowledge of him who C us to his own
1 Jn 3:1 that we should be C children of God; and
Jude 1:1 to those who are C, beloved in God the
Rev 1:9 was on the island C Patmos on account of
7:2 living God, and he C with a loud voice
9:11 in Greek he is C Apollyon.
10:3 on the land, and C out with a loud
10:3 lion roaring; when he C out, the seven thunders
11:8 city which is allegorically C Sodom and Egypt, where
12:9 ancient serpent, who is C the Devil and Satan,
14:18 over fire, and he C with a loud voice
16:16 the place which is C in Hebrew Armageddon.
17:14 those with him are C and chosen and faithful."
18:2 And he C out with a mighty voice, "Fallen,
19:11 sat upon it is C Faithful and True, and
19:13 by which he is C is The Word of
19:17 a loud voice he C to all the birds

CALLING (33)

Josh 19:47 and settled in it, C Leshem, Dan, after the
1Sam 3:8 that the LORD was C the boy.
3:10 came and stood forth, C as at other times,
Esth 13:8 prayed to the Lord, C to remembrance all the
Prov 9:15 places of the town, C to those who pass
Is 1:13 and sabbath and the C of assemblies– I
21:11 One is C to me from Seir, "Watchman, what
40:26 their host by number, C them all by name;
41:4 performed and done this, C the generations from the
46:11 accomplish all my purpose,' C a bird of prey
Jer 1:15 For, lo, I am C all the tribes of
Hos 7:12 silly and without sense, C to Egypt, going to
Amos 7:4 the Lord GOD was C for a judgment by
2Mac 3:22 While they were C upon the Almighty Lord that
12:6 to his men and, C upon God the righteous
12:15 Judas and his men, C upon the great Sovereign
14:46 them at the crowd, C upon the Lord of
Mt 11:16 the market places and C to their playmates,
18:2 And C to him a child, he put him
27:47 said, "This man is C Elijah."
Mk 10:49 heart; rise, he is C you."
15:34 said, "Behold, he is C Elijah."
Lk 7:19 And John, C to him two of his disciples,
7:32 the market place and C to one another, 'We
19:13 C ten of his servants, he gave them ten
Jn 11:28 is here and is C for you."
Acts 9:41 Then C the saints and widows he presented her
22:16 wash away your sins, C on his name.'
Eph 4:1 life worthy of the C to which you have
2Tim 1:9 us with a holy C, not in virtue of
1Pet 3:6 as Sarah obeyed Abraham, C him lord.
Rev 6:16 rocks of the mountains, C to the mountains and
14:15 out of the temple, C with a loud voice

CALLISTHENES

2Mac 8:33 to the sacred gates, C and some others, who

CALLOUS

Eph 4:19 heart; they have become C and have given

CALLS (39)

Gen 46:33 they have.' When Pharaoh C you, and says, 'What
1Sam 3:9 down; and if he C you, you shall say,
26:14 "Who are you that C to the king?"
1Kgs 8:43 for which the foreigner C to thee; in order
2Chr 6:33 for which the foreigner C to thee; in order
Job 11:10 through, and imprisons, and C to judgment, who can
Ps 42:7 Deep C to deep at the thunder of thy
50:4 He C to the heavens above and to the
72:12 the needy when he C, the poor and him
91:15 When he C to me, I will answer him;
Wis 2:13 knowledge of God, and C himself a child of
2:16 ways as unclean; he C the last end of
14:1 voyage over raging waves C upon a piece of
Sir 4:6 bitterness of soul he C down a curse upon
Is 64:7 is no one that C upon thy name, that
Hos 7:8 and none of them C upon me.
Joel 2:32 the survivors shall be those whom the LORD C
Amos 5:8 day into night, who C for the waters of
9:6 upon the earth; who C for the waters of
2Mac 2:26 no light matter but C for sweat and loss
Mt 22:43 inspired by the Spirit, C him Lord, saying,
22:45 If David thus C him Lord, how is he
Mk 12:37 thy feet.' David himself C him Lord; so how
Lk 15:6 he comes home, he C together his friends and
15:9 has found it, she C together her friends and
20:37 the bush, where he C the Lord the God
20:44 thy feet.' David thus C him Lord; so how
Jn 10:3 his voice, and he C his own sheep by
Acts 2:21 shall be that whoever C on the name of
2:39 the Lord our God C to him."
Rom 4:17 to the dead and C into existence the things
10:13 For, "every one who C upon the name of
Gal 5:8 not from him who C you.
1Thes 2:12 worthy of God, who C you into his own
5:24 He who C you is faithful, and he will
1Pet 3:15 to any one who C you to account for
Rev 2:20 the woman Jezebel, who C herself a prophetess and

13:18 This C for wisdom: let him who has understanding
17:9 This C for a mind with wisdom: the seven

CALM (6)

Sir 39:28 out their strength and C the anger of their
48:10 it is written, to C the wrath of God
Ezek 16:42 you; I will be C, and will no more
Mt 8:26 and the sea; and there was a great C
Mk 4:39 the wind ceased, and there was a great C
Lk 8:24 waves; and they ceased, and there was a C

CALMED

Ps 131:2 But I have C and quieted my soul, like

CALNEH

Amos 6:2 Pass over to C, and see; and thence go

CALNO

Is 10:9 Is not C like Carchemish?

CALVES (19)

1Sam 6:7 cart, but take their C home, away from them.
6:10 and shut up their C at home.
14:32 sheep and oxen and C, and slew them on
1Kgs 12:28 counsel, and made two C of gold.
12:32 Bethel, sacrificing to the C that he had made.
2Kgs 10:29 to sin, the golden C that were in Bethel,
17:16 molten images of two C; and they made an
2Chr 11:15 satyrs, and for the C which he had made.
13:8 with you the golden C which Jeroboam made you
Job 21:10 without fail; their cow C, and does not cast
Ps 68:30 of bulls with the C of the peoples.
Jer 46:21 midst are like fatted C; yea, they have turned
Hos 13:2 Men kiss C
Amos 6:4 from the flock, and C from the midst of
Mic 6:6 with burnt offerings, with C a year old?
Mal 4:2 go forth leaping like C from the stall.
Mt 22:4 oxen and my fat C are killed, and everything
Heb 9:12 blood of goats and C but his own blood,
9:19 took the blood of C and goats, with water

CALVING

Job 39:1 Do you observe the C of the hinds?

CAME (1,750)

Gen 4:15 Cain, lest any who C upon him should kill
6:4 the sons of God C in to the daughters
7:6 the flood of waters C upon the earth.
7:10 waters of the flood C upon the earth.
8:4 the month, the ark C to rest upon the
8:11 ark; and the dove C back to him in
9:10 you, as many as C out of the ark.
10:14 Casluhim (whence C the Philistines), and C
11:5 And the LORD C down to see the city
11:31 Canaan; but when they C to Haran, they settled
13:18 moved his tent, and C and dwelt by the
14:5 who were with him C and subdued the Rephaim
14:7 they turned back and C to Enmishpat (that is,
14:13 one who had escaped C, and told Abram the
15:1 word of the LORD C to Abram in a
15:4 word of the LORD C to him, "This man
15:11 when birds of prey C down upon the carcasses,
19:1 The two angels C to Sodom in the evening;
19:5 are the men who C to you tonight?
19:9 they said, "This fellow C to sojourn, and he
19:23 the earth when Lot C to Zoar.
20:3 But God C to Abimelech in a dream by
22:9 When they C to the place of which God
24:5 son back to the land from which you C
24:15 of Nahor, Abraham's brother, C out with her water
24:16 filled her jar, and C up.
24:32 So the man C into the house; and Laban
24:42 from my oath.' "I C today to the spring,
24:45 my heart, behold, Rebekah C out with her water
25:25 The first C forth red, all his body like
25:26 Afterward his brother C forth, and his hand had
25:29 was boiling pottage, Esau C in from the field,
26:32 same day Isaac's servants C and told him about
27:27 So he C near and kissed him; and he
27:30 father, Esau his brother C in from his hunting.
27:33 it all before you C, and I have blessed
27:35 he said, "Your brother C with guile, and he
28:11 And he C to a certain place, and stayed
29:1 on his journey, and C to the land of
29:9 with them, Rachel C with her father's sheep;
30:16 When Jacob C from the field in the evening,
30:30 had little before I C, and it has increased
30:38 troughs, where the flocks C to drink.
30:38 they bred when they C to drink,
31:24 But God C to Laban the Aramean in a
32:6 to Jacob, saying, "We C to your brother Esau,
33:3 seven times, until he C near to his brother.
33:18 And Jacob C safely to the city of Shechem,
34:5 field, so Jacob held his peace until they C
34:7 The sons of Jacob C in from the field
34:20 and his son Shechem C to the gate of
34:25 took their swords and C upon the city unawares,
34:27 the sons of Jacob C upon the slain, and
35:6 And Jacob C to Luz (that is, Bethel), which
35:9 Jacob again, when he C from Paddan-aram, and
35:27 And Jacob C to his father Isaac at Mamre,
37:14 of Hebron, and he C to Shechem.
37:18 off, and before he C near to them they
37:23 So when Joseph C to his brothers, they stripped
38:27 time of her delivery C, there were twins in
38:28 scarlet thread, saying, "This C out first."
38:29 hand, behold, his brother C out; and she said,
38:30 Afterward his brother C out with the scarlet thread
39:14 to insult us; he C in to me to
39:16 her until his master C home,
39:17 have brought among us, C in to me to
40:6 When Joseph C to them in the morning and
41:2 Nile, and behold, there C up out of the
41:3 cows, gaunt and thin, C up out of the
41:13 to us, so it C to pass; I was
41:14 changed his clothes, he C in before Pharaoh.
41:18 cows, fat and sleek, C up out of the
41:19 and seven other cows C up after them, poor
41:27 and gaunt cows that C up after them are
41:50 the year of famine C, Joseph had two sons,
41:53 the land of Egypt C to an end;
41:57 Moreover, all the earth C to Egypt to Joseph
42:5 the sons of Israel C to buy among the
42:5 among the others who C, for the famine was
42:6 And Joseph's brothers C, and bowed themselves
42:29 When they C to Jacob their father in the
43:20 "Oh, my lord, we C down the first time
43:21 food; and when we C to the lodging place
43:26 When Joseph C home, they brought into the house
43:31 washed his face and C out; and controlling himself
44:14 Judah and his brothers C to Joseph's house, he
45:4 And they C near.
45:25 out of Egypt, and C to the land of
46:1 that he had, and C to Beer-sheba, and offered
46:6 land of Canaan, and C into Egypt, Jacob and
46:8 descendants of Israel, who C into Egypt, Jacob and
46:26 belonging to Jacob who C into Egypt, who were
46:27 house of Jacob, that C into Egypt, were seventy.
46:28 in Goshen; and they C into the land of
47:15 Canaan, all the Egyptians C to Joseph, and said,
47:18 year was ended, they C to him the following
48:5 of Egypt before I C to you in Egypt,
48:7 For when I C from Paddan, Rachel to my
50:10 When they C to the threshing floor of Atad,
50:18 His brothers also C and fell down before him,
Ex 1:1 sons of Israel who C to Egypt with Jacob,
2:5 the daughter of Pharaoh C down to bathe at
2:16 seven daughters; and they C and drew water, and
2:17 The shepherds C and drove them away; but Moses
2:18 When they C to their father Reuel, he said,
2:23 their cry under bondage C up to God.
3:1 of the wilderness, and C to Horeb, the mountain
5:15 the people of Israel C and cried to Pharaoh,
5:20 for them, as they C forth from Pharaoh;
5:23 For since I C to Pharaoh to speak in
8:6 Egypt; and the frogs C up and covered the
8:17 the earth, and there C gnats on man and
8:24 LORD did so; there C great swarms of flies
10:6 from the day they C on earth to this
10:14 And the locusts C up over all the land
13:3 day, in which you C out from Egypt, out
13:8 for me when I C out of Egypt.'
15:23 When they C to Marah, they could not drink
15:27 Then they C to Elim, where there were twelve
16:1 the people of Israel C to the wilderness of
16:13 In the evening quails C up and covered the
16:22 leaders of the congregation C and told Moses,
16:35 forty years, till they C to a habitable land;
16:35 the manna, till they C to the border of
17:8 Then C Amalek and fought with Israel at Rephidim.
18:5 And Jethro, Moses' father-in-law, C with his sons and
18:12 to God; and Aaron C with all the elders

	19:1	on that day they C into the wilderness of
	19:2	out from Rephidim and C into the wilderness of
	19:7	So Moses C and called the elders of the
	19:20	And the LORD C down upon Mount Sinai, to
	22:15	it was hired, it C for its hire.
	23:15	for in it you C out of Egypt.
	24:3	Moses C and told the people all the words
	32:19	as soon as he C near the camp and
	32:24	the fire, and there C out this calf."
	34:18	the month Abib you C out from Egypt.
	34:29	When Moses C down from Mount Sinai, with the
	34:29	his hand as he C down from the mountain,
	34:32	the people of Israel C near, and he gave
	34:34	veil off, until he C out; and when he
	34:34	out; and when he C out, and told the
	35:21	And they C, every one whose heart stirred him,
	35:22	So they C, both men and women; all who
	36:4	task on the sanctuary C, each from the task
Lev	9:22	blessed them; and he C down from offering the
	9:23	meeting; and when they C out they blessed the
	9:24	And fire C forth from before the LORD and
	10:2	And fire C forth from the presence of the
Num	3:38	any one else who C near was to be
	9:6	that day; and they C before Moses and Aaron
	11:25	Then the LORD C down in the cloud and
	12:4	the three of them C out.
	12:5	And the LORD C down in a pillar of
	12:5	Miriam; and they both C forward.
	13:22	into the Negeb, and C to Hebron; and Ahiman,
	13:23	in Egypt.) And they C to the Valley of
	13:26	And they C to Moses and Aaron and to
	13:27	they told him, "We C to the land to
	14:45	in that hill country C down, and defeated them
	16:27	and Dathan and Abiram C out and stood at
	16:35	And fire C forth from the LORD, and consumed
	16:43	And Moses and Aaron C to the front of
	20:1	Israel, the whole congregation, C into the wilderness
	20:11	rod twice; and water C forth abundantly, and the
	20:20	And Edom C out against them with many men,
	20:22	Israel, the whole congregation, C to Mount Hor.
	20:28	Then Moses and Eleazar C down from the mountain.
	21:7	And the people C to Moses, and said, "We
	21:23	to the wilderness, and C to Jahaz, and fought
	21:33	the king of Bashan C out against them, he
	22:7	their hand; and they C to Balaam, and gave
	22:9	And God C to Balaam and said, "Who are
	22:16	And they C to Balaam and said to him,
	22:20	And God C to Balaam at night and said
	22:39	with Balak, and they C to Kiriath-huzoth.
	23:17	And he C to him, and, lo, he was
	24:2	the Spirit of God C upon him,
	25:6	the people of Israel C and brought a Midianite
	26:4	people of Israel, who C forth out of the
	31:16	and so the plague C among the congregation of
	31:48	the captains of hundreds, C near to Moses,
	32:2	the sons of Reuben C and said to Moses
	32:11	of the men who C up out of Egypt,
	32:16	Then they C near to him, and said, "We
	33:9	out from Marah, and C to Elim; at Elim
	36:1	the sons of Joseph, C near and spoke before
Deut	1:19	commanded us; and we C to Kadesh-barnea.
	1:22	Then all of you C near me, and said,
	1:24	the hill country, and C to the Valley of
	1:31	you went until you C to this place.'
	1:44	in that hill country C out against you and
	2:23	Gaza, the Caphtorim, who C from Caphtor, destroyed
	2:32	his land.' Then Sihon C out against us, he
	3:1	the king of Bashan C out against us, he
	4:11	children so.' And you C near and stood at
	4:45	of Israel when they C out of Egypt,
	4:46	Israel defeated when they C out of Egypt.
	5:23	burning with fire, you C near to me, all
	9:7	from the day you C out of the land
	9:7	of Egypt, until you C to this place, you
	9:15	So I turned and C down from the mountain,
	10:5	Then I turned and C down from the mountain,
	11:5	the wilderness, until you C to this place;
	16:3	of affliction—for you C out of the land
	16:3	the day when you C out of the land
	16:6	at the time you C out of Egypt.
	22:14	woman, and when I C near her, I did
	22:27	his neighbor; because he C upon her in the
	23:4	the way, when you C forth out of Egypt,
	24:9	the way as you C forth out of Egypt.
	25:17	the way as you C out of Egypt,
	29:7	And when you C to this place, Sihon the
	29:7	the king of Bashan C out against us to
	29:16	Egypt, and how we C through the midst of
	32:44	Moses C and recited all the words of this
	33:2	He said, "The LORD C from Sinai, and dawned
	33:2	from Mount Paran, he C from the ten thousands
	33:21	was reserved; and he C to the heads of
Josh	2:1	And they went, and C into the house of
	2:4	she said, "True, men C to me, but I
	2:4	not know where they C from;
	2:8	they lay down, she C up to them on
	2:10	before you when you C out of Egypt, and
	2:23	Then the two men C down again from the
	2:23	and passed over and C to Joshua the son
	3:1	of Israel; and they C to the Jordan, and
	4:18	covenant of the LORD C up from the midst
	4:19	The people C up out of the Jordan on
	5:4	of the people who C out of Egypt, all
	5:5	all the people who C out had been circumcised,
	5:6	men of war that C forth out of Egypt,
	6:1	went out, and none C in.
	6:9	and the rear guard C after the ark, while
	6:11	it once; and they C into the camp, and
	6:13	and the rear guard C after the ark of
	8:22	And the others C forth from the city against
	10:9	So Joshua C upon them suddenly, having marched up
	10:24	Then they C near, and put their feet on
	10:33	Horam king of Gezer C up to help Lachish;
	11:4	And they C out, with all their troops, a
	11:5	joined their forces, and C and encamped together at
	11:7	So Joshua C suddenly upon them with all his
	11:21	And Joshua C at that time, and wiped out
	14:6	the people of Judah C to Joshua at Gilgal;
	15:18	When she C to him, she urged him to
	17:4	They C before Eleazar the priest and Joshua the
	18:9	seven divisions; then they C to Joshua in the
	18:11	according to its families C up, and the territory
	19:1	The second lot C out for Simeon, for the
	19:10	The third lot C up for the tribe of
	19:17	The fourth lot C out for Issachar, for the
	19:24	The fifth lot C out for the tribe of
	19:32	The sixth lot C out for the tribe of
	19:40	The seventh lot C out for the tribe of
	21:1	houses of the Levites C to Eleazar the priest
	21:4	The lot C out for the families of the
	21:45	Israel had failed; all C to pass.
	22:10	And when they C to the region about the
	22:15	And they C to the Reubenites, the Gadites, and
	22:17	and for which there C a plague upon the
	24:6	of Egypt, and you C to the sea; and
	24:11	over the Jordan and C to Jericho, and the
Judg	1:5	They C upon Adoni-bezek at Bezek, and fought
	1:14	When she C to him, she urged him to
	3:10	Spirit of the LORD C upon him, and he
	3:20	And Ehud C to him, as he was sitting
	3:22	belly; and the dirt C out.
	3:24	had gone, the servants C; and when they saw
	4:5	the people of Israel C up to her for
	4:18	And Jael C out to meet Sisera, and said
	5:15	the princes of Issachar C with Deborah, and Issachar
	5:19	"The kings C, they fought; then fought the kings
	5:23	its inhabitants, because they C not to the help
	6:5	the land as they C in.
	6:11	angel of the LORD C and sat under the
	6:33	people of the East C together, and crossing the
	7:13	When Gideon C, behold, a man was telling a
	7:13	camp of Midian, and C to the tent, and
	7:19	who were with him C to the outskirts of
	8:4	And Gideon C to the Jordan and passed over,
	8:15	And he C to the men of Succoth, and
	9:6	citizens of Shechem C together, and all Beth-millo,
	9:52	And Abimelech C to the tower, and fought against
	9:57	heads, and upon them C the curse of Jotham
	10:17	the people of Israel C together, and they encamped
	11:16	Ammonites, but when they C up from Egypt, Israel
	11:16	the Red Sea and C to Kadesh.
	11:29	Spirit of the LORD C upon Jephthah, and he
	11:34	Then Jephthah C to his home at Mizpah; and
	11:34	and behold, his daughter C out to meet him
	13:6	Then the woman C and told her husband, "A
	13:6	"A man of God C to me, and his
	13:9	the angel of God C again to the woman
	13:10	"Behold, the man who C to me the other
	13:11	after his wife, and C to the man and
	14:2	Then he C up, and told his father and
	14:5	to Timnah, and he C to the vineyards of
	14:6	Spirit of the LORD C mightily upon him, and

14:9 he went; and he C to his father and
14:14 "Out of the eater C something to eat.
14:14 Out of the strong C something sweet." And they
14:19 Spirit of the LORD C mightily upon him, and
15:6 And the Philistines C up, and burned her and
15:9 Then the Philistines C up and encamped in Judah,
15:14 When he C to Lehi, the Philistines came shouting
15:14 to Lehi, the Philistines C shouting to meet him;
15:14 Spirit of the LORD C mightily upon him, and
15:19 at Lehi, and there C water from it; and
16:5 lords of the Philistines C to her and said
16:18 lords of the Philistines C up to her, and
16:31 and all his family C down and took him
17:8 as he journeyed, he C to the hill country
18:2 And they C to the hill country of Ephraim,
18:7 five men departed, and C to Laish, and saw
18:8 And when they C to their brethren at Zorah
18:13 country of Ephraim, and C to the house of
18:15 turned aside thither, and C to the house of
18:27 to him, the Danites C to Laish, to a
19:3 And he C to her father's house; and when
19:3 father saw him, he C with joy to meet
19:22 out the man who C into your house, that
19:26 morning appeared, the woman C and fell down at
19:30 the people of Israel C up out of the
20:1 the people of Israel C out, from Dan to
20:4 answered and said, "I C to Gibe-ah that belongs
20:14 And the Benjaminites C together out of the cities
20:21 The Benjaminites C out of Gibe-ah, and felled to
20:24 the people of Israel C near against the Benjaminites
20:26 army, went up and C to Bethel and wept;
20:34 And there C against Gibe-ah ten thousand picked
20:42 them, and those who C out of the cities
21:2 And the people C to Bethel, and sat there
Ruth 1:19 went on until they C to Bethlehem.
1:19 And when they C to Bethlehem, the whole town
1:22 And they C to Bethlehem at the beginning of
2:4 And behold, Boaz C from Bethlehem; and he said
2:6 the Moabite maiden, who C back with Naomi from
2:7 the reapers.' So she C, and she has continued
2:11 your native land and C to a people that
3:7 Then she C softly, and uncovered his feet, and
3:14 known that the woman C to the threshing floor."
3:16 And when she C to her mother-in-law, she said,
4:1 whom Boaz had spoken, C by.
1Sam 2:14 all the Israelites who C there.
2:27 And there C a man of God to Eli,
3:10 And the LORD C and stood forth, calling as
4:1 the word of Samuel C to all Israel.
4:3 And when the troops C to the camp, the
4:5 covenant of the LORD C into the camp, all
4:12 the battle line, and C to Shiloh the same
4:13 And when the man C into the city and
4:14 the man hastened and C and told Eli.
4:19 birth; for her pains C upon her.
5:10 the ark of God C to Ekron, the people
6:14 The cart C into the field of Joshua of
7:1 the men of Kiriath-jearim C and took up the
8:4 Israel gathered together and C to Samuel at Ramah,
9:5 When they C to the land of Zuph, Saul
9:15 the day before Saul C, the LORD had revealed
9:25 And when they C down from the high place
10:9 and all these signs C to pass that day.
10:10 When they C to Gibe-ah, behold, a band of
10:10 the spirit of God C mightily upon him, and
10:13 had finished prophesying, he C to the high place.
11:4 When the messengers C to Gibe-ah of Saul, they
11:6 the spirit of God C mightily upon Saul when
11:7 the people, and they C out as one man.
11:9 When the messengers C and told the men of
11:11 three companies; and they C into the midst of
12:12 king of the Ammonites C against you, you said
13:5 seashore in multitude; they C up and encamped in
13:10 burnt offering, behold, Samuel C; and Saul went out
13:17 And raiders C out of the camp of the
14:25 And all the people C into the forest; and
15:2 the way, when they C up out of Egypt.
15:5 And Saul C to the city of Amalek, and
15:6 of Israel when they C up out of Egypt."
15:10 word of the LORD C to Samuel:
15:12 was told Samuel, "Saul C to Carmel, and behold,
15:13 And Samuel C to Saul, and Saul said to
15:32 And Agag C to him cheerfully.
16:4 the LORD commanded, and C to Bethlehem.
16:4 elders of the city C to meet him trembling,
16:6 When they C, he looked on Eliab and thought,
16:13 Spirit of the LORD C mightily upon David from
16:21 And David C to Saul, and entered his service.
17:4 And there C out from the camp of the
17:16 forty days the Philistine C forward and took his
17:20 commanded him; and he C to the encampment as
17:23 Gath, Goliath by name, C up out of the
17:34 father; and when there C a lion, or a
17:41 And the Philistine C on and drew near to
17:48 the Philistine arose and C and drew near to
17:53 the Israelites C back from chasing the Philistines,
18:6 the Philistine, the women C out of all the
18:13 he went out and C in before the people.
18:16 he went out and C in before them.
18:30 princes of the Philistines C out to battle, and
18:30 as often as they C out David had more
19:9 spirit from the LORD C upon Saul, as he
19:16 And when the messengers C in, behold, the image
19:18 and escaped, and he C to Samuel at Ramah,
19:20 the Spirit of God C upon the messengers of
19:22 went to Ramah, and C to the great well
19:23 the Spirit of God C upon him also, and
19:23 he prophesied, until he C to Naioth in Ramah.
20:1 Naioth in Ramah, and C and said before Jonathan,
20:24 when the new moon C, the king sat down
20:37 And when the lad C to the place of
20:38 up the arrows, and C to his master.
21:1 Then C David to Nob to Ahimelech the priest;
21:1 the priest; and Ahimelech C to meet David trembling,
22:11 and all of them C to the king.
23:6 David to Keilah, he C down with an ephod
23:27 them, when a messenger C to Saul, saying, "Make
24:3 And he C to the sheepfolds by the way,
25:9 When David's young men C, they said all this
25:12 men turned away, and C back and told him
25:20 on the ass, and C down under cover of
25:20 David and his men C down toward her; and
25:36 And Abigail C to Nabal; and, lo, he was
25:40 the servants of David C to Abigail at Carmel,
26:1 Then the Ziphites C to Saul at Gibe-ah, saying,
26:3 he saw that Saul C after him into the
26:5 Then David rose and C to the place where
26:15 one of the people C in to destroy the
27:9 and the garments, and C back to Achish.
28:4 The Philistines assembled, and C and encamped at
28:8 with him; and they C to the woman by
28:21 And the woman C to Saul, and when she
29:10 of your lord who C with you; and start
30:1 David and his men C to Ziklag on the
30:3 David and his men C to the city, they
30:9 with him, and they C to the brook Besor,
30:21 Then David C to the two hundred men, who
30:23 hand the band that C against us.
30:26 When David C to Ziklag, he sent part of
31:7 fled; and the Philistines C and dwelt in them.
31:8 morrow, when the Philistines C to strip the slain,
31:12 of Beth-shan; and they C to Jabesh and burnt
2Sam 1:2 day, behold, a man C from Saul's camp, with
1:2 And when he C to David, he fell to
2:4 the men of Judah C, and there they anointed
2:23 so that the spear C out at his back;
2:23 And all who C to the place where Asahel
2:24 was going down they C to the hill of
2:29 the whole forenoon they C to Mahanaim.
3:20 When Abner C with twenty men to David at
3:23 that was with him C, it was told Joab,
3:23 the son of Ner C to the king, and
3:24 Behold, Abner C to you; why is it that
3:25 the son of Ner C to deceive you, and
3:26 When Joab C out from David's presence, he sent
3:35 Then all the people C to persuade David to
4:4 about Saul and Jonathan C from Jezreel; and his
4:5 of the day they C to the house of
4:7 When they C into the house, as he lay
5:1 the tribes of Israel C to David at Hebron,
5:3 the elders of Israel C to the king at
5:13 from Jerusalem, after he C from Hebron; and more
5:20 And David C to Baal-perazim, and David defeated
5:22 And the Philistines C up yet again, and spread
6:6 And when they C to the threshing floor of
6:16 ark of the LORD C into the city of
6:20 the daughter of Saul C out to meet David,
7:4 word of the LORD C to Nathan,
8:5 the Syrians of Damascus C to help Hadadezer king
9:6 Jonathan, son of Saul, C to David, and fell
10:2 And David's servants C into the land of the
10:8 And the Ammonites C out and drew up in

10:14 against the Ammonites, and C to Jerusalem.
10:16 the Euphrates; and they C to Helam, with Shobach
10:17 crossed the Jordan, and C to Helam.
11:4 took her; and she C to him, and he
11:7 When Uriah C to him, David asked how Joab
11:17 men of the city C out and fought with
11:22 the messenger went, and C and told David all
11:23 advantage over us, and C out against us in
12:1 He C to him, and said to him, "There
12:4 Now there C a traveler to the rich man,
13:6 and when the king C to see him, Amnon
13:24 And Absalom C to the king, and said, "Behold,
13:30 on the way, tidings C to David, "Absalom has
13:36 behold, the king's sons C, and lifted up their
14:4 the woman of Tekoa C to the king, she
14:33 So he C to the king, and bowed himself
15:5 And whenever a man C near to do obeisance
15:6 all of Israel who C to the king for
15:13 And a messenger C to David, saying, "The hearts
15:20 You C only yesterday, and shall I today make
15:24 And Abiathar C up, and lo, Zadok came also,
15:24 up, and lo, Zadok C also, with all the
15:32 When David C to the summit, where God was
15:32 behold, Hushai the Archite C to meet him with
15:37 So Hushai, David's friend, C into the city, just
16:5 When King David C to Bahurim, there came out
16:5 came to Bahurim, there C out a man of
16:5 Gera; and as he C he cursed continually.
16:15 the men of Israel, C to Jerusalem, and Ahithophel
16:16 the Archite, David's friend, C to Absalom, Hushai said
17:6 And when Hushai C to Absalom, Absalom said to
17:18 went away quickly, and C to the house of
17:20 When Absalom's servants C to the woman at the
17:21 had gone, the men C up out of the
17:24 Then David C to Mahanaim.
17:27 When David C to Mahanaim, Shobi the son of
18:16 trumpet, and the troops C back from pursuing Israel;
18:25 And he C apace, and drew near.
18:31 And behold, the Cushite C; and the Cushite said,
19:5 Then Joab C into the house to the king,
19:8 and all the people C before the king.
19:15 So the king C back to the Jordan; and
19:15 the Jordan; and Judah C to Gilgal to meet
19:24 the son of Saul C down to meet the
19:24 until the day he C back in safety.
19:25 And when he C from Jerusalem to meet the
19:41 the men of Israel C to the king, and
20:3 And David C to his house at Jerusalem; and
20:8 is in Gibeon, Amasa C to meet them.
20:12 And any one who C by, seeing him, stopped;
20:15 who were with Joab C and besieged him in
20:17 And he C near her; and the woman said,
21:17 the son of Zeruiah C to his aid, and
22:7 voice, and my cry C to his ears.
22:10 bowed the heavens, and C down; thick darkness was
22:19 They C upon me in the day of my
22:45 Foreigners C cringing to me; as soon as they
22:46 Foreigners lost heart, and C trembling out of their
23:13 men went down, and C about harvest time to
24:6 Then they C to Gilead, and to Kadesh in
24:6 the Hittites; and they C to Dan, and from
24:7 around to Sidon, and C to the fortress of
24:8 all the land, they C to Jerusalem at the
24:11 word of the LORD C to the prophet Gad,
24:13 So Gad C to David and told him, and
24:18 And Gad C that day to David, and said
1Kgs 1:22 king, Nathan the prophet C in.
1:23 And when he C in before the king, he
1:28 So she C into the king's presence, and stood
1:32 So they C before the king.
1:42 of Abiathar the priest C; and Adonijah said, "Come
1:47 Moreover the king's servants C to congratulate our
1:53 And he C and did obeisance to King Solomon;
2:8 Mahanaim; but when he C down to meet me
2:13 the son of Haggith C to Bathsheba the mother
2:28 When the news C to Joab --for Joab
2:30 So Benaiah C to the tent of the LORD,
3:15 Then he C to Jerusalem, and stood before the
3:16 Then two harlots C to the king, and stood
4:27 and for all who C to King Solomon's table,
4:34 And men C from all peoples to hear the
6:1 the people of Israel C out of the land
6:11 word of the LORD C to Solomon,
7:14 He C to King Solomon, and did all his
8:3 the elders of Israel C, and the priests took
8:9 of Israel, when they C out of the land
8:10 And when the priests C out of the holy
9:12 But when Hiram C from Tyre to see the
10:1 of the LORD, she C to test him with
10:2 She C to Jerusalem with a very great retinue,
10:2 stones; and when she C to Solomon, she told
10:7 the reports until I C and my own eyes
10:10 precious stones; never again C such an abundance of
10:14 weight of gold that C to Solomon in one
10:15 gold, besides that which C from the traders and
11:18 out from Midian and C to Paran, and took
11:18 them from Paran and C to Egypt, to Pharaoh
12:3 the assembly of Israel C and said to Rehoboam,
12:12 and all the people C to Rehoboam the third
12:21 When Rehoboam C to Jerusalem, he assembled all
12:22 the word of God C to Shemaiah the man
13:1 a man of God C out of Judah by
13:9 water, nor return by the way that you C
13:10 the way that he C to Bethel.
13:11 And his sons C and told him all that
13:12 man of God who C from Judah had gone.
13:14 man of God who C from Judah?" And he
13:17 there, nor return by the way that you C
13:20 word of the LORD C to the prophet who
13:21 man of God who C from Judah, "Thus says
13:25 And they C and told it in the city
14:4 went to Shiloh, and C to the house of
14:5 When she C, she pretended to be another woman.
14:6 her feet, as she C in at the door,
14:17 arose, and departed, and C to Tirzah.
14:17 And as she C to the threshold of the
14:25 Shishak king of Egypt C up against Jerusalem;
16:1 word of the LORD C to Jehu the son
16:7 word of the LORD C by the prophet Jehu
16:10 household in Tirzah, Zimri C in and struck him
17:2 word of the LORD C to him,
17:8 word of the LORD C to him,
17:10 Zarephath; and when he C to the gate of
17:22 soul of the child C into him again, and
18:1 word of the LORD C to Elijah, in the
18:21 And Elijah C near to all the people, and
18:30 and all the people C near to him.
18:31 word of the LORD C, saying, "Israel shall be
18:36 oblation, Elijah the prophet C near and said, "O
19:3 for his life, and C to Beer-sheba, which belongs
19:4 into the wilderness, and C and sat down under
19:7 angel of the LORD C again a second time,
19:9 And there he C to a cave, and lodged
19:9 word of the LORD C to him, and he
19:13 And behold, there C a voice to him, and
20:5 messengers C again, and said, "Thus says Ben-hadad:
20:13 And behold, a prophet C near to Ahab king
20:22 Then the prophet C near to the king of
20:28 a man of God C near and said to
20:33 Then Ben-hadad C forth to him; and he caused
20:43 resentful and sullen, and C to Samaria.
21:5 But Jezebel his wife C to him, and said
21:13 the two base fellows C in and sat opposite
21:17 word of the LORD C to Elijah the Tishbite,
21:28 word of the LORD C to Elijah the Tishbite,
22:2 the king of Judah C down to the king
22:21 Then a spirit C forward and stood before the
22:24 the son of Chenaanah C near and struck Micaiah
2Kgs 1:6 said to him, "There C a man to meet
1:7 man was he who C to meet you and
1:10 Then fire C down from heaven, and consumed him
1:12 the fire of God C down from heaven and
1:13 fifty went up, and C and fell on his
1:14 Lo, fire C down from heaven, and consumed the
2:3 who were in Bethel C out to Elisha, and
2:4 So they C to Jericho.
2:15 And they C to meet him, and bowed to
2:18 And they C back to him, while he tarried
2:23 way, some small boys C out of the city
2:24 And two she-bears C out of the woods and
3:15 power of the LORD C upon him.
3:20 the sacrifice, behold, water C from the direction of
3:24 But when they C to the camp of Israel,
3:27 And there C great wrath upon Israel; and they
4:7 She C and told the man of God, and
4:11 One day he C there, and he turned into
4:25 she set out, and C to the man of
4:27 And when she C to the mountain to the
4:27 And Gehazi C to thrust her away.
4:32 When Elisha C into the house, he saw the
4:36 And when she C to him, he said, "Take
4:37 She C and fell at his feet, bowing to

4:38 And Elisha C again to Gilgal when there was
4:39 of wild gourds, and C and cut them up
4:42 A man C from Baal-shalishah, bringing the man of
5:9 So Naaman C with his horses and chariots, and
5:13 But his servants C near and said to him,
5:15 his company, and he C and stood before him;
5:24 And when he C to the hill, he took
6:4 And when they C to the Jordan, they cut
6:14 great army; and they C by night, and surrounded
6:18 And when the Syrians C down against him, Elisha
6:23 And the Syrians C no more on raids into
6:33 with them, the king C down to him and
7:5 Syrians; but when they C to the edge of
7:8 And when these lepers C to the edge of
7:8 hid them; then they C back, and entered another
7:10 So they C and called to the gatekeepers of
7:10 and told them, "We C to the camp of
7:17 said when the king C down to him.
8:7 Now Elisha C to Damascus.
8:9 When he C and stood before him, he said,
8:14 departed from Elisha, and C to his master, who
9:5 And when he C, behold, the commanders of the
9:11 When Jehu C out to the servants of his
9:17 of Jehu as he C, and said, "I see
9:19 a second horseman, who C to them, and said,
9:30 When Jehu C to Jezreel, Jezebel heard of it;
9:36 When they C back and told him, he said,
10:7 And when the letter C to them, they took
10:8 When the messenger C and told him, "They have
10:13 of Ahaziah, and we C down to visit the
10:17 And when he C to Samaria, he slew all
10:21 the worshipers of Baal C, so that there was
11:9 on the sabbath, and C to Jehoiada the priest.
12:10 and the high priest C up and they counted
14:13 Ahaziah, at Beth-shemesh, and C to Jerusalem, and
15:12 And so it C to pass.)
15:14 the son of Gadi C up from Tirzah and
15:14 up from Tirzah and C to Samaria, and he
15:19 the king of Assyria C against the land; and
15:29 king of Assyria C and captured Ijon, Abel-beth-ma
16:5 Remaliah, king of Israel, C up to wage war
16:6 Elath; and the Edomites C to Elath, where they
16:12 And when the king C from Damascus, the king
17:3 Against him C up Shalmaneser king of Assyria; and
17:5 all the land and C to Samaria, and for
17:28 carried away from Samaria C and dwelt in Bethel,
18:9 Shalmaneser king of Assyria C up against Samaria
18:13 Sennacherib king of Assyria C up against all the
18:17 they went up and C to Jerusalem.
18:17 When they arrived, they C and stood by the
18:18 for the king, there C out to them Eliakim
18:37 of Asaph, the recorder, C to Hezekiah with their
19:5 servants of King Hezekiah C to Isaiah,
19:28 you back on the way by which you C
19:33 the way that he C, by the same he
20:1 the son of Amoz C to him, and said
20:4 word of the LORD C to him:
20:14 Then Isaiah the prophet C to King Hezekiah, and
21:15 the day their fathers C out of Egypt, even
22:9 And Shaphan the secretary C to the king, and
23:17 man of God who C from Judah and predicted
23:18 of the prophet who C out of Samaria.
23:34 Jehoahaz away; and he C to Egypt, and died
24:1 Nebuchadnezzar king of Babylon C up, and
24:3 Surely this C upon Judah at the command of
24:10 Nebuchadnezzar king of Babylon C up to Jerusalem,
24:11 Nebuchadnezzar king of Babylon C to the city, while
24:20 of the LORD it C to the point in
25:1 Nebuchadnezzar king of Babylon C with all his army
25:8 the king of Babylon, C to Jerusalem.
25:23 appointed Gedaliah governor, they C with their men
25:25 of the royal family, C with ten men, and
1Chr 1:12 Naph-tuhim, Pathrusim, Casluhim (whence C the
2:53 the Mishra-ites; from these C the Zorathites and the
2:55 are the Kenites who C from Hammath, the father
4:41 These, registered by name, C in the days of
7:21 land slew, because they C down to raid their
7:22 days, and his brothers C to comfort him.
10:7 fled; and the Philistines C and dwelt in them.
10:8 morrow, when the Philistines C to strip the slain,
11:3 the elders of Israel C to the king at
12:1 are the men who C to David at Ziklag,
12:16 of Benjamin and Judah C to the stronghold to
12:18 Then the Spirit C upon Amasai, chief of the
12:19 to David when he C with the Philistines for
12:23 the armed troops, who C to David in Hebron,
12:38 arrayed in battle order, C to Hebron with full
12:40 and Zebulun and Naphtali, C bringing food on asses
13:9 And when they C to the threshing floor of
15:29 covenant of the LORD C to the city of
17:3 word of the LORD C to Nathan,
18:5 the Syrians of Damascus C to help Hadadezer king
19:2 And David's servants C to Hanun in the land
19:7 with his army, who C and encamped before Medeba.
19:7 from their cities and C to battle.
19:9 And the Ammonites C out and drew up in
19:15 Then Joab C to Jerusalem.
19:17 crossed the Jordan, and C to them, and drew
20:1 of the Ammonites, and C and besieged Rabbah.
21:4 throughout all Israel, and C back to Jerusalem.
21:11 So Gad C to David and said to him,
21:21 As David C to Ornan, Ornan looked and saw
22:8 word of the LORD C to me, saying, 'You
26:14 counselor, and his lot C out for the north.
26:15 Obed-edom's C out for the south, and to his
26:16 Shuppim and Hosah it C out for the west,
27:1 concerning the divisions that C and went, month
27:24 not finish; yet wrath C upon Israel for this,
29:30 of the circumstances that C upon him and upon
2Chr 1:13 So Solomon C from the high place at Gibeon,
5:4 the elders of Israel C, and the Levites took
5:10 of Israel, when they C out of Egypt.
5:11 Now when the priests C out of the holy
7:1 ended his prayer, fire C down from heaven and
9:1 fame of Solomon she C to Jerusalem to test
9:1 When she C to Solomon, she told him all
9:6 the reports until I C and my own eyes
9:13 weight of gold that C to Solomon in one
10:3 Jeroboam and all Israel C and said to Rehoboam,
10:12 and all the people C to Rehoboam the third
11:1 When Rehoboam C to Jerusalem, he assembled the
11:2 word of the LORD C to Shemaiah the man
11:14 and their holdings and C to Judah and Jerusalem,
11:16 LORD God of Israel C after them from all
12:2 Shishak king of Egypt C up against Jerusalem
12:3 were without number who C with him from Egypt--
12:4 cities of Judah and C as far as Jerusalem.
12:5 Then Shemaiah the prophet C to Rehoboam and to
12:7 word of the LORD C to Shemaiah: "They have
12:9 Shishak king of Egypt C up against Jerusalem; he
12:11 the LORD, the guard C and bore them, and
14:9 Zerah the Ethiopian C out against them with an
14:9 three hundred chariots, and C as far as Mareshah.
15:1 The Spirit of God C upon Azariah the son
15:5 or to him who C in, for great disturbances
16:7 time Hanani the seer C to Asa king of
18:20 Then a spirit C forward and stood before the
18:23 the son of Chenaanah C near and struck Micaiah
20:1 some of the Me-unites, C against Jehoshaphat for
20:2 Some men C and told Jehoshaphat, "A great
20:4 cities of Judah they C to seek the LORD.
20:10 Israel invade when they C from the land of
20:14 Spirit of the LORD C upon Jahaziel the son
20:24 When Judah C to the watchtower of the wilderness,
20:25 Jehoshaphat and his people C to take the spoil
20:28 They C to Jerusalem, with harps and lyres and
20:29 the fear of God C on all the kingdoms
21:12 And a letter C to him from Elijah the
21:17 the Ethiopians; and they C up against Judah, and
21:19 two years, his bowels C out because of the
22:1 band of men that C with the Arabs to
22:7 For when he C there he went out with
23:2 of Israel, and they C to Jerusalem.
24:17 the princes of Judah C and did obeisance to
24:18 And wrath C upon Judah and Jerusalem for this
24:23 army of the Syrians C up against Joash.
24:23 They C to Judah and Jerusalem, and destroyed all
25:7 a man of God C to him and said,
25:14 After Amaziah C from the slaughter of the Edomites,
28:9 meet the army that C to Samaria, and said
28:20 Tilgath-pilneser king of Assyria C against him, and
29:8 wrath of the LORD C on Judah and Jerusalem,
29:17 of the month they C to the vestibule of
29:36 people; for the thing C about suddenly.
30:11 Zebulun humbled themselves and C to Jerusalem.
30:13 And many people C together in Jerusalem to keep
30:25 the whole assembly that C out of Israel, and
30:25 and the sojourners who C out of the land
30:27 heard, and their prayer C to his holy habitation
31:8 Hezekiah and the princes C and saw the heaps,
32:1 Sennacherib king of Assyria C and invaded Judah
32:21 And when he C into the house of his

	32:25	wrath C upon him and Judah and Jerusalem.
	34:9	They C to Hilkiah the high priest and delivered
	36:6	Against him C up Nebuchadnezzar king of Babylon,
Ezra	2:1	of the province who C up out of the
	2:2	They C with Zerubbabel, Jeshua, Nehemiah,
	2:59	following were those who C up from Tel-melah,
	2:68	of families, when they C to the house of
	3:1	When the seventh month C, and the sons of
	3:10	priests in their vestments C forward with trumpets,
	4:12	that the Jews who C up from you to
	5:3	Shethar-bozenai and their associates C to them and
	5:16	Then this Shesh-bazzar C and laid the foundations of
	7:8	And he C to Jerusalem in the fifth month,
	7:9	the fifth month he C to Jerusalem, for the
	8:13	of Adonikam, those who C later, their names being
	8:32	We C to Jerusalem, and there we remained three
Neh	1:2	one of my brethren, C with certain men out
	2:9	Then I C to the governors of the province
	2:11	So I C to Jerusalem and was there three
	4:12	who lived by them C they said to us
	4:21	dawn till the stars C out.
	5:17	officials, besides those who C to us from the
	6:17	Tobiah, and Tobiah's letters C to them.
	7:5	genealogy of those who C up at the first,
	7:6	of the province who C up out of the
	7:7	They C with Zerubbabel, Jeshua, Nehemiah, Azariah,
	7:61	following were those who C up from Tel-melah,
	8:13	priests and the Levites, C together to Ezra the
	12:1	and the Levites who C up with Zerubbabel the
	12:39	Sheep Gate; and they C to a halt at
	13:7	of the king and C to Jerusalem, and I
Tob	1:18	to death any who C fleeing from Judea, I
	2:3	But he C back and said, "Father, one of
	3:17	the daughter of Raguel C down from her upper
	6:1	on their way they C at evening to the
	6:5	their way until they C near to Ecbatana.
	7:11	husbands, and when each C to her he died
	8:14	And she C out and told them that he
	9:6	got up early and C to the wedding feast.
	11:1	his way until they C near to Nineveh.
	11:17	When Tobit C near to Sarah his daughter-in-law, he
	11:18	and his nephew Nadab C,
Jud	1:14	of his cities, and C to Ecbatana, captured its
	2:25	who resisted him, and C to the southern borders
	3:5	The men C to Holofernes and told him all
	3:9	Then he C to the edge of Esdraelon, near
	6:5	on this race that C out of Egypt.
	6:11	the hill country and C to the springs below
	6:14	the men of Israel C down from their city
	7:8	commanders of the coastland C to him and said,
	8:11	They C to her, and she said to them,
	9:5	things thou didst intend C to pass,
	10:18	to tent, and they C and stood around her
	10:20	and all his servants C out and led her
	10:22	him of her he C forward to the front
	10:23	And when Judith C into the presence of Holofernes
	12:8	When she C up from the spring she prayed
	12:16	Then Judith C in and lay down, and Holofernes'
	13:1	evening C, his slaves quickly withdrew, and Bagoas
	13:7	She C close to his bed and took hold
	13:10	mountain to Bethulia and C to its gates.
	14:6	And when he C and saw the head of
	14:13	So they C to Holofernes' tent and said to
	15:2	Fear and trembling C over them, so that they
	15:5	the hill country also C, for they were told
	15:8	who lived at Jerusalem, C to witness the good
	16:4	The Assyrian C down from the mountains of the
	16:4	of the north; he C with myriads of his
Esth	2:12	Now when the turn C for each maiden to
	2:14	in the morning she C back to the second
	2:15	When the turn C for Esther the daughter of
	2:22	And this C to the knowledge of Mordecai, and
	4:3	and his decree C, there was great mourning
	4:4	maids and her eunuchs C and told her, the
	5:5	the king and Haman C to the dinner that
	6:6	So Haman C in, and the king said to
	8:1	And Mordecai C before the king, for Esther had
	8:17	command and his edict C, there was gladness and
	9:25	them; but when Esther C before the king, he
	10:11	And these two lots C to the hour and
	11:6	behold, two great dragons C forward, both ready to
	11:10	a tiny spring there C a great river, with
	11:11	with abundant water; light C, and the sun rose,
	15:8	his arms until she C to herself.
Job	1:6	the sons of God C to present themselves before
	1:6	LORD, and Satan also C among them.
	1:14	brother's house; and there C a messenger to Job,
	1:16	was yet speaking, there C another, and said, "The
	1:17	was yet speaking, there C another, and said, "The
	1:18	was yet speaking, there C another, and said, "Your
	1:19	behold, a great wind C across the wilderness, and
	1:21	he said, "Naked I C from my mother's womb,
	2:1	the sons of God C to present themselves before
	2:1	LORD, and Satan also C among them to present
	2:11	come upon him, they C each from his own
	4:14	falls on men, dread C upon me, and trembling,
	29:13	was about to perish C upon me, and I
	30:26	looked for good, evil C; and when I waited
	30:26	came; and when I waited for light, darkness C
	42:11	Then C to him all his brothers and sisters
Ps	18:9	bowed the heavens, and C down; thick darkness was
	18:10	cherub, and flew; he C swiftly upon the wings
	18:18	They C upon me in the day of my
	18:44	they obeyed me; foreigners C cringing to me.
	18:45	Foreigners lost heart, and C trembling out of their
	33:9	he spoke, and it C to be; he commanded,
	48:4	the kings assembled, they C on together.
	68:17	upon thousands, the Lord C from Sinai into the
	105:19	what he had said C to pass the word
	105:23	Then Israel C to Egypt; Jacob sojourned in the
	105:31	He spoke, and there C swarms of flies, and
	105:34	spoke, and the locusts C, and young locusts without
Eccl	5:15	As he C from his mother's womb he shall
	5:15	again, naked as he C, and shall take nothing
	5:16	evil: just as he C, so shall he go;
	9:14	and a great king C against it and besieged
Wis	6:22	is and how she C to be, and I
	7:7	the spirit of wisdom C to me.
	7:11	All good things C to me along with her,
	12:27	Therefore the utmost condemnation C upon them.
	16:5	rage of wild beasts C upon thy people and
	16:10	serpents, for thy mercy C to their help and
	17:18	Whether there C a whistling wind, or a melodious
	18:20	righteous, and a plague C upon the multitude in
	19:12	give them relief, quails C up from the sea.
	19:14	receive strangers when they C to them, but these
Sir	24:3	she will glory: "I C forth from the mouth
	27:27	not know where it C from.
	40:7	wonders that his fear C to nothing.
	40:10	the wicked, and on their account the flood C
	44:18	was left to the earth when the flood C
	47:25	of wickedness, till vengeance C upon them.
	48:18	In his days Sennacherib C up, and sent the
	48:25	hidden things before they C to pass.
	49:4	the kings of Judah C to an end;
	50:5	round him as he C out of the inner
	50:20	Then Simon C down, and lifted up his hands
Is	7:1	the king of Israel C up to Jerusalem to
	11:16	for Israel when they C up from the land
	14:28	that King Ahaz died C this oracle:
	20:1	the king of Assyria, C to Ashdod and fought
	36:1	Sennacherib king of Assyria C up against all the
	36:3	And there C out to him Eliakim the son
	36:22	of Asaph, the recorder, C to Hezekiah with their
	37:5	servants of King Hezekiah C to Isaiah,
	37:24	its choicest cypresses; I C to its remotest height,
	37:29	way by which you C
	37:34	the way that he C, by the same he
	38:1	the son of Amoz C to him, and said
	38:4	word of the LORD C to Isaiah:
	39:3	Then Isaiah the prophet C to King Hezekiah, and
	48:1	of Israel, and who C forth from the loins
	48:3	did them and they C to pass.
	48:5	of old, before they C to pass I announced
	48:16	from the time it C to be I have
	50:2	Why, when I C, was there no man?
	66:7	birth; before her pain C upon her she was
Jer	1:2	word of the LORD C in the days of
	1:3	It C also in the days of Jehoiakim the
	1:4	word of the LORD C to me saying,
	1:11	word of the LORD C to me, saying, "Jeremiah,
	1:13	word of the LORD C to me a second
	2:1	word of the LORD C to me, saying,
	2:3	it became guilty; evil C upon them, says the
	2:7	But when you C in you defiled my land,
	7:1	The word that C to Jeremiah from the LORD:
	7:25	day that your fathers C out of the land
	8:15	peace, but no good C, for a time of
	11:1	The word that C to Jeremiah from the LORD:
	13:3	word of the LORD C to me a second
	13:8	word of the LORD C to me:
	14:1	of the LORD which C to Jeremiah concerning the

14:19 peace, but no good C; for a time of
16:1 word of the LORD C to me:
17:16 thou knowest; that which C out of my lips
18:1 The word that C to Jeremiah from the LORD:
18:5 word of the LORD C to me:
19:14 Then Jeremiah C from Topheth, where the LORD
21:1 is the word which C to Jeremiah from the
24:4 word of the LORD C to me:
25:1 The word that C to Jeremiah concerning all the
26:1 of Judah, this word C from the LORD,
26:10 heard these things, they C up from the king's
27:1 of Judah, this word C to Jeremiah from the
28:12 word of the LORD C to Jeremiah:
29:30 word of the LORD C to Jeremiah:
30:1 The word that C to Jeremiah from the LORD:
32:1 The word that C to Jeremiah from the LORD
32:6 word of the LORD C to me:
32:8 Then Hanamel my cousin C to me in the
32:26 word of the LORD C to Jeremiah:
33:1 word of the LORD C to Jeremiah a second
33:19 word of the LORD C to Jeremiah:
33:23 word of the LORD C to Jeremiah:
34:1 The word which C to Jeremiah from the LORD,
34:8 The word which C to Jeremiah from the LORD,
34:12 word of the LORD C to Jeremiah from the
35:1 The word which C to Jeremiah from the LORD
35:11 Nebuchadrezzar king of Babylon C up against the
35:12 word of the LORD C to Jeremiah:
36:1 of Judah, this word C to Jeremiah from the
36:9 all the people who C from the cities of
36:14 in his hand and C to them.
36:27 word of the LORD C to Jeremiah:
37:6 word of the LORD C to Jeremiah the prophet:
37:7 'Behold, Pharaoh's army which C to help you is
38:27 Then all the princes C to Jeremiah and asked
39:1 and all his army C against Jerusalem and besieged
39:3 the king of Babylon C and sat in the
39:15 word of the LORD C to Jeremiah while he
40:1 The word that C to Jeremiah from the LORD
40:12 had been driven and C to the land of
40:13 in the open country C to Gedaliah at Mizpah
41:1 officers of the king, C with ten men to
41:6 the son of Nethaniah C out from Mizpah to
41:6 from Mizpah to meet them, weeping as he C
41:7 When they C into the city, Ishmael the son
41:12 They C upon him at the great pool which
41:14 Mizpah turned about and C back, and went to
42:1 least to the greatest, C near
42:7 word of the LORD C to Jeremiah.
43:7 And they C into the land of Egypt, for
43:8 word of the LORD C to Jeremiah in Tahpanhes:
44:1 The word that C to Jeremiah concerning all the
44:28 remnant of Judah, who C to the land of
46:1 of the LORD which C to Jeremiah the prophet
47:1 of the LORD that C to Jeremiah the prophet
49:9 If grape-gatherers C to you, would they not leave
49:9 If thieves C by night, would they not destroy
49:34 of the LORD that C to Jeremiah the prophet
52:3 of the LORD things C to such a pass
52:4 Nebuchadrezzar king of Babylon C with all his army
Lam 3:37 has commanded and it C to pass, unless the
Bar 1:3 all the people who C to hear the book,
4:9 saw the wrath that C upon you from God,
Ezek 1:3 word of the LORD C to Ezekiel the priest,
1:4 behold, a stormy wind C out of the north,
1:5 the midst of it C the likeness of four
1:25 And there C a voice from above the firmament
3:15 upon me; and I C to the exiles at
3:16 word of the LORD C to me:
6:1 word of the LORD C to me:
7:1 word of the LORD C to me:
9:2 And lo, six men C from the direction of
11:13 And it C to pass, while I was prophesying,
11:14 word of the LORD C to me:
12:1 word of the LORD C to me:
12:8 word of the LORD C to me:
12:17 word of the LORD C to me:
12:21 word of the LORD C to me:
12:26 word of the LORD C to me:
13:1 word of the LORD C to me:
14:1 Then C certain of the elders of Israel to
14:2 word of the LORD C to me:
14:12 word of the LORD C to me:
15:1 word of the LORD C to me:
16:1 word of the LORD C to me:
16:13 grew exceedingly beautiful, and C to regal estate.
17:1 word of the LORD C to me:
17:3 plumage of many colors, C to Lebanon and took
17:11 word of the LORD C to me:
17:12 the king of Babylon C to Jerusalem, and took
18:1 word of the LORD C to me again:
20:1 the elders of Israel C to inquire of the
20:2 word of the LORD C to me:
20:45 word of the LORD C to me:
21:1 word of the LORD C to me:
21:8 word of the LORD C to me:
21:18 word of the LORD C to me again:
22:1 word of the LORD C to me, saying,
22:17 word of the LORD C to me:
22:23 word of the LORD C to me:
23:1 word of the LORD C to me:
23:17 And the Babylonians C to her into the bed
23:39 the same day they C into my sanctuary to
23:40 whom a messenger was sent, and lo, they C
24:1 word of the LORD C to me:
24:15 word of the LORD C to me:
24:20 word of the LORD C to me:
25:1 word of the LORD C to me:
26:1 word of the LORD C to me:
27:1 word of the LORD C to me:
27:33 When your wares C from the seas, you satisfied
28:1 word of the LORD C to me:
28:11 word of the LORD C to me:
28:20 word of the LORD C to me:
29:1 word of the LORD C to me:
29:17 word of the LORD C to me:
30:1 word of the LORD C to me:
30:20 word of the LORD C to me:
31:1 word of the LORD C to me:
32:1 word of the LORD C to me:
32:17 word of the LORD C to me:
33:1 word of the LORD C to me:
33:21 had escaped from Jerusalem C to me and said,
33:22 evening before the fugitive C; and he had opened
33:22 the time the man C to me in the
33:23 word of the LORD C to me:
34:1 word of the LORD C to me:
35:1 word of the LORD C to me:
36:16 word of the LORD C to me:
36:20 But when they C to the nations, wherever they
36:20 the nations, wherever they C, they profaned my holy
36:21 be profaned among the nations to which they C
36:22 have profaned among the nations to which you C
37:7 rattling; and the bones C together, bone to its
37:10 me, and the breath C into them, and they
37:15 word of the LORD C to me:
38:1 word of the LORD C to me:
43:2 the God of Israel C from the east; and
43:3 had seen when he C to destroy the city,
Dan 1:1 Nebuchadnezzar king of Babylon C to Jerusalem
2:2 So they C in and stood before the king.
2:29 you lay in bed C thoughts of what would
3:8 time certain Chaldeans C forward and maliciously
3:49 angel of the Lord C down into the furnace
3:94 Then Nebuchadnezzar C near to the door of the
3:94 Shadrach, Meshach, and Abednego C out from the
4:7 Chaldeans, and the astrologers C in; and I told
4:8 At last Daniel C in before me--he who
4:13 watcher, a holy one, C down from heaven.
4:28 All this C upon King Nebuchadnezzar.
5:8 the king's wise men C in, but they could
5:10 king and his lords, C into the banqueting hall;
6:6 these presidents and satraps C by agreement to the
6:11 Then these men C by agreement and found Daniel
6:12 Then they C near and said before the king,
6:15 Then these men C by agreement to the king,
6:20 When he C near to the den where Daniel
7:3 And four great beasts C up out of the
7:8 horns, and behold, there C up among them another
7:10 of fire issued and C forth from before him;
7:13 clouds of heaven there C one like a son
7:13 of man, and he C to the Ancient of
7:20 the other horn which C up and before which
7:22 the Ancient of Days C, and judgment was given
7:22 High, and the time C when the saints received
8:3 and the higher one C up last.
8:5 considering, behold, a he-goat C from the west
8:6 He C to the ram with the two horns,
8:8 instead of it there C up four conspicuous horns
8:9 of one of them C forth a little horn,
8:17 So he C near where I stood; and when
8:17 stood; and when he C, I was frightened and

9:21 vision at the first, C to me in swift
9:22 He C and he said to me, "O Daniel,
10:13 of the chief princes, C to help me, so
10:14 kingdom of Persia and C to make you understand
13:5 Lord had said: "Iniquity C forth from Babylon, from
13:6 had suits at law C to them.
13:28 Joakim, the two elders C, full of their wicked
13:30 And she C, with her parents, her children, and
13:36 garden alone, this woman C in with two maids,
13:37 who had been hidden, C to her and lay
14:15 the night the priests C with their wives and
14:16 the king rose and C, and Daniel with him.
14:40 seventh day the king C to mourn for Daniel.
14:40 When he C to the den he looked in,
Hos 1:1 of the LORD that C to Hosea the son
2:15 the time when she C out of the land
9:10 But they C to Baal-peor, and consecrated themselves
Joel 1:1 of the LORD that C to Joel, the son
Obad 1:5 If thieves C to you, if plunderers by night—
1:5 If grape-gatherers C to you, would they not leave
Jon 1:1 word of the LORD C to Jonah the son
1:6 So the captain C and said to him, "What
2:7 LORD; and my prayer C to thee, into thy
3:1 word of the LORD C to Jonah the second
4:7 But when dawn C up the next day, God
4:10 make it grow, which C into being in a
Mic 1:1 of the LORD that C to Micah of Moresheth
7:15 the days when you C out of the land
Hab 3:3 God C from Teman, and the Holy One from
3:14 of his warriors, who C like a whirlwind to
Zeph 1:1 of the LORD which C to Zephaniah the son
Hag 1:1 word of the LORD C by Haggai the prophet
1:3 word of the LORD C by Haggai the prophet,
1:9 much, and, lo, it C to little; and when
1:14 the people; and they C and worked on the
2:1 word of the LORD C by Haggai the prophet,
2:5 made you when you C out of Egypt.
2:10 word of the LORD C by Haggai the prophet,
2:16 When one C to a heap of twenty measures,
2:16 but ten; when one C to the winevat to
2:20 word of the LORD C a second time to
Zech 1:1 word of the LORD C to Zechariah the son
1:7 word of the LORD C to Zechariah the son
2:3 who talked with me C forward, and another angel
2:3 forward, and another angel C forward to meet him,
4:1 who talked with me C again, and waked me,
4:8 word of the LORD C to me, saying,
5:5 who talked with me C forward and said to
6:1 and behold, four chariots C out from between two
6:7 When the steeds C out, they were impatient to
6:9 word of the LORD C to me:
7:1 word of the LORD C to Zechariah in the
7:4 the LORD of hosts C to me;
7:8 word of the LORD C to Zechariah, saying,
7:12 Therefore great wrath C from the LORD of hosts.
8:1 the LORD of hosts C to me, saying,
8:10 who went out or C in; for I set
8:18 the LORD of hosts C to me, saying,
1Mac 1:1 Philip, the Macedonian, who C from the land of
1:10 them C forth a sinful root, Antiochus Epiphanes,
1:11 those days lawless men C forth from Israel, and
1:20 up against Israel and C to Jerusalem with a
1:29 of tribute, and he C to Jerusalem with a
1:64 And very great wrath C upon Israel.
2:15 were enforcing the apostasy C to the city of
2:16 Many from Israel C to them; and Mattathias and
2:23 these words, a Jew C forward in the sight
4:29 They C into Idumea and encamped at Bethzur, and
5:14 with their garments rent, C from Galilee and made
5:33 Then he C up behind them in three companies,
5:46 So they C to Ephron.
5:53 the way till he C to the land of
5:59 Gorgias and his men C out of the city
6:3 So he C and tried to take the city
6:5 Then some one C to him in Persia and
6:29 And mercenary forces C to him from other kingdoms
6:31 They C through Idumea and encamped against
7:5 Then there C to him all the lawless and
7:10 they marched away and C with a large force
7:27 So Nicanor C to Jerusalem with a large force,
7:29 So he C to Judas, and they greeted one
7:33 Some of the priests C out of the sanctuary,
7:46 And men C out of all the villages of
8:1 friendship to those who C to them,
8:4 subdued the kings who C against them from the
9:36 of Jambri from Medeba C out and seized John
9:39 baggage; and the bridegroom C out with his friends
9:43 heard of this, he C with a large force
9:64 Then he C and encamped against Bethbasi; he
9:72 his own land, and C no more into their
10:7 Then Jonathan C to Jerusalem and read the letter
10:57 Cleopatra his daughter, and C to Ptolemais in the
10:67 the son of Demetrius C from Crete to the
10:85 with those burned alive, C to eight thousand men.
10:86 men of the city C out to meet him
11:15 heard of it and C against him in battle.
11:22 he set out and C to Ptolemais; and he
11:44 Antioch, and when they C to the king, the
11:60 When he C to Askalon, the people of the
12:40 he marched forth and C to Beth-shan.
12:41 fighting men, and he C to Beth-shan.
13:20 After this Trypho C to invade the country and
15:11 pursued him, and he C in his flight to
15:32 friend of the king C to Jerusalem, and when
15:40 So Cendebeus C to Jamnia and began to provoke
16:22 seized the men who C to destroy him and
2Mac 1:7 the critical distress which C upon us in those
1:14 to marry her, Antiochus C to the place together
2:5 And Jeremiah C and found a cave, and he
2:6 those who followed him C up to mark the
2:10 the Lord, and fire C down from heaven and
2:10 prayed, and the fire C down and consumed the
2:21 and the appearances which C from heaven to those
3:2 hatred of wickedness, it C about that the kings
3:27 ground and deep darkness C over him, his men
4:10 king assented and Jason C to office, he at
4:34 Andronicus C to Onias, and resorting to treachery
4:44 When the king C to Tyre, three men sent
5:18 as soon as he C forward, just as Heliodorus
5:26 sword all those who C out to see them,
6:7 the feast of Dionysus C, they were compelled to
7:22 not know how you C into being in my
8:12 Word C to Judas concerning Nicanor's invasion; and
8:19 the times when help C to their ancestors; both
8:20 by the help that C to them from heaven,
9:3 was in Ecbatana, news C to him of what
9:7 And so it C about that he fell out
9:24 or any unwelcome news C, the people throughout
9:28 had inflicted on others, C to the end of
10:21 of what had happened C to Maccabeus, he gathered
10:24 He C on, intending to take Judea by storm.
10:27 city; and when they C near to the enemy
10:36 Others who C up in the same way wheeled
11:2 all his cavalry and C against the Jews.
12:17 miles from there, they C to Charax, to the
12:22 appeared, terror and fear C over the enemy at
12:33 And he C out with three thousand infantry and
13:1 and forty-ninth year word C to Judas and his
13:7 such a fate it C about that Menelaus the
14:1 Three years later, word C to Judas and his
14:21 A chariot C forward from each army; seats of
14:28 When this message C to Nicanor, he was troubled
Mt 1:18 to Joseph, before they C together she was found
2:1 men from the East C to Jerusalem, saying,
2:9 before them, till it C to rest over the
3:1 In those days C John the Baptist, preaching in
3:13 Then Jesus C from Galilee to the Jordan to
4:3 And the tempter C and said to him, "If
4:11 him, and behold, angels C and ministered to him.
5:1 sat down his disciples C to him.
7:25 fell, and the floods C, and the winds blew
7:27 fell, and the floods C, and the winds blew
8:1 When he C down from the mountain, great crowds
8:2 and behold, a leper C to him and knelt
8:5 entered Caperna-um, a centurion C forward to him,
8:19 And a scribe C up and said to him,
8:28 And when he C to the other side, to
8:32 So they C out and went into the swine;
8:34 behold, all the city C out to meet Jesus;
9:1 he crossed over and C to his own city.
9:10 tax collectors and sinners C and sat down with
9:13 not sacrifice.' For I C not to call the
9:14 the disciples of John C to him, saying, "Why
9:18 them, behold, a ruler C in and knelt before
9:20 hemorrhage for twelve years C up behind him and
9:23 And when Jesus C to the ruler's house, and
9:28 house, the blind men C to him; and Jesus
11:18 not mourn.' For John C neither eating nor drinking,
11:19 the Son of man C eating and drinking, and
12:42 condemn it; for she C from the ends of
12:44 house from which I C. And when he comes
13:4 path, and the birds C and devoured them.

C

13:10 Then the disciples C and said to him, "Why
13:25 were sleeping, his enemy C and sowed weeds among
13:26 So when the plants C up and bore grain,
13:27 servants of the householder C and said to him,
13:36 And his disciples C to him, saying, "Explain to
14:6 when Herod's birthday C, the daughter of Herodi-as
14:12 And his disciples C and took the body and
14:15 was evening, the disciples C to him and said,
14:23 When evening C, he was there alone,
14:25 of the night he C to them, walking on
14:29 on the water and C to Jesus;
14:34 had crossed over, they C to land at Gennesaret.
15:1 Then Pharisees and scribes C to Jesus from
15:12 Then the disciples C and said to him, "Do
15:22 woman from that region C out and cried, "Have
15:23 And his disciples C and begged him, saying, "Send
15:25 But she C and knelt before him, saying, "Lord,
15:30 And great crowds C to him, bringing with them
16:1 the Pharisees and Sadducees C, and to test him
16:13 Now when Jesus C into the district of Caesarea
17:7 But Jesus C and touched them, saying, "Rise, and
17:14 And when they C to the crowd, a man
17:14 the crowd, a man C up to him and
17:18 him, and the demon C out of him, and
17:19 Then the disciples C to Jesus privately and said,
17:23 When they C to Caperna-um, the collectors of the
17:24 And when he C home, Jesus spoke to him
18:1 that time the disciples C to Jesus, saying, "Who
18:20 Then Peter C up and said to him, "Lord,
18:27 as he went out, C upon one of his
19:3 And Pharisees C up to him and tested him
19:16 And behold, one C up to him, saying, "Teacher,
20:8 too.' And when evening C, the owner of the
20:9 about the eleventh hour C, each of them received
20:10 Now when the first C, they thought they would
20:20 the sons of Zebedee C up to him, with
20:28 the Son of man C not to be served
21:1 near to Jerusalem and C to Bethphage, to the
21:14 blind and the lame C to him in the
21:23 elders of the people C up to him as
21:32 For John C to you in the way of
22:11 "But when the king C in to look at
22:23 The same day Sadducees C to him, who say
22:34 silenced the Sadducees, they C together.
24:1 away, when his disciples C to point out to
24:3 of Olives, the disciples C to him privately, saying,
24:39 know until the flood C and swept them all
25:10 to buy, the bridegroom C, and those who were
25:11 Afterward the other maidens C also, saying, 'Lord,
25:19 master of those servants C and settled accounts with
25:20 received the five talents C forward, bringing five
25:22 had the two talents C forward, saying, 'Master, you
25:24 received the one talent C forward, saying, 'Master, I
25:36 in prison and you C to me.'
26:7 the leper, a woman C up to him with
26:17 Unleavened Bread the disciples C to Jesus, saying,
26:40 And he C to the disciples and found them
26:43 And again he C and found them sleeping, for
26:45 Then he C to the disciples and said to
26:47 was still speaking, Judas C, one of the twelve,
26:49 And he C up to Jesus at once and
26:50 Then they C up and laid hands on Jesus
26:60 though many false witnesses C forward.
26:60 At last two C forward
26:69 And a maid C up to him, and said,
26:73 little while the bystanders C up and said to
27:1 When morning C, all the chief priests and the
27:32 they went out, they C upon a man of
27:33 And when they C to a place called Golgotha
27:57 it was evening, there C a rich man from
28:2 descended from heaven and C and rolled back the
28:9 And they C up and took hold of his
28:13 "Tell people, 'His disciples C by night and stole
28:18 And Jesus C and said to them, "All authority
Mk 1:9 In those days Jesus C from Nazareth of Galilee
1:10 And when he C up out of the water,
1:11 dove; and a voice C from heaven, "Thou art
1:14 John was arrested, Jesus C into Galilee, preaching
1:26 with a loud voice, C out of him.
1:31 And he C and took her by the hand
1:38 that is why I C out."
1:40 And a leper C to him beseeching him, and
1:45 the country; and people C to him from every
2:3 And they C, bringing to him a paralytic carried
2:17 who are sick; I C not to call the
2:18 were fasting; and people C and said to him,
3:8 all that he did, C to him.
3:13 he desired; and they C to him.
3:20 home; and the crowd C together again, so that
3:22 And the scribes who C down from Jerusalem said,
3:31 mother and his brethren C; and standing outside they
4:4 path, and the birds C and devoured it.
5:1 They C to the other side of the sea,
5:13 And the unclean spirits C out, and entered the
5:14 And people C to see what it was that
5:15 And they C to Jesus, and saw the demoniac
5:22 Then C one of the rulers of the synagogue,
5:27 reports about Jesus, and C up behind him in
5:33 been done to her, C in fear and trembling
5:35 was still speaking, there C from the ruler's house
5:38 When they C to the house of the ruler
6:1 away from there and C to his own country;
6:21 But an opportunity C when Herod on his birthday
6:22 For when Herodi-as' daughter C in and danced, she
6:25 And she C in immediately with haste to the
6:29 heard of it, they C and took his body,
6:35 grew late, his disciples C to him and said,
6:47 And when evening C, the boat was out on
6:48 of the night he C to them, walking on
6:53 had crossed over, they C to land at Gennesaret,
6:56 And wherever he C, in villages, cities, or country,
7:24 heard of him, and C and fell down at
8:11 The Pharisees C and began to argue with him,
8:22 And they C to Beth-saida.
9:7 them, and a voice C out of the cloud,
9:14 And when they C to the disciples, they saw
9:25 saw that a crowd C running together, he rebuked
9:26 convulsing him terribly, it C out, and the boy
9:33 And they C to Caperna-um; and when he was
10:2 And Pharisees C up and in order to test
10:35 the sons of Zebedee, C forward to him, and
10:45 Son of man also C not to be served
10:46 And they C to Jericho; and as he was
10:50 he sprang up and C to Jesus.
11:12 following day, when they C from Bethany, he was
11:13 When he C to it, he found nothing but
11:15 And they C to Jerusalem.
11:19 And when evening C they went out of the
11:26 And they C again to Jerusalem.
11:26 scribes and the elders C to him,
12:2 When the time C, he sent a servant to
12:14 And they C and said to him, "Teacher, we
12:18 And Sadducees C to him, who say that there
12:28 one of the scribes C up and heard them
12:42 And a poor widow C, and put in two
13:1 And as he C out of the temple, one
14:3 at table, a woman C with an alabaster flask
14:17 it was evening he C with the twelve.
14:37 And he C and found them sleeping, and he
14:40 And again he C and found them sleeping, for
14:41 And he C the third time, and said to
14:43 was still speaking, Judas C, one of the twelve,
14:45 And when he C, he went up to him
14:66 of the high priest C;
15:8 And the crowd C up and began to ask
15:40 many other women who C up with him to
Lk 1:22 And when he C out, he could not speak
1:28 And he C to her and said, "Hail, full
1:44 voice of your greeting C to my ears, the
1:57 Now the time C for Elizabeth to be delivered,
1:59 the eighth day they C to circumcise the child;
1:65 And fear C on all their neighbors.
2:6 were there, the time C for her to be
2:22 And when the time C for their purification according
2:27 by the Spirit he C into the temple; and
2:51 down with them and C to Nazareth, and was
3:2 the word of God C to John the son
3:7 to the multitudes that C out to be baptized
3:12 Tax collectors also C to be baptized, and said
3:22 dove, and a voice C from heaven, "Thou art
4:16 And he C to Nazareth, where he had been
4:25 six months, when there C a great famine over
4:35 in the midst, he C out of him, having
4:41 And demons also C out of many, crying, "You
4:42 people sought him and C to him, and would
5:7 And they C and filled both the boats, so
5:12 of the cities, there C a man full of
6:17 And he C down with them and stood on
6:17 Tyre and Sidon, who C to hear him and
6:19 touch him, for power C forth from him and
7:4 And when they C to Jesus, they besought him
7:14 And he C and touched the bier, and the

CAME

7:45 from the time I C in she has not
8:4 when a great crowd C together and people from
8:4 from town after town C to him, he said
8:19 mother and his brethren C to him, but they
8:23 a storm of wind C down on the lake,
8:33 Then the demons C out of the man and
8:35 had happened, and they C to Jesus, and found
8:41 And there C a man named Jairus, who was
8:44 be healed by anyone C up behind him, and
8:47 was not hidden, she C trembling, and falling down
8:49 from the ruler's house C and said, "Your daughter
8:51 And when he C to the house, he permitted
9:12 away; and the twelve C and said to him,
9:34 said this, a cloud C and overshadowed them; and
9:35 And a voice C out of the cloud, saying,
10:32 a Levite, when he C to the place and
10:33 Samaritan, as he journeyed, C to where he was;
11:24 house from which I C
11:31 condemn them; for she C from the ends of
12:49 "I C to cast fire upon the earth; and
13:6 his vineyard; and he C seeking fruit on it
13:31 very hour some Pharisees C, and said to him,
14:21 come.' So the servant C and reported this to
15:17 But when he C to himself he said, 'How
15:20 And he arose and C to his father.
15:25 field; and as he C and drew near to
15:28 His father C out and entreated him,
15:30 this son of yours C, who has devoured your
16:21 table; moreover the dogs C and licked his sores.
17:27 ark, and the flood C and destroyed them all.
18:40 him; and when he C near, he asked him,
19:5 And when Jesus C to the place, he looked
19:6 he made haste and C down, and received him
19:10 the Son of man C to seek and to
19:16 The first C before him, saying, 'Lord, your pound
19:18 cities.' And the second C, saying, 'Lord, your pound
19:20 five cities.' Then another C, saying, 'Lord, here is
20:1 scribes with the elders C up
20:10 When the time C, he sent a servant to
20:27 There C to him some Sadducees, those who say
21:38 morning all the people C to him in the
22:7 Then C the day of Unleavened Bread, on which
22:14 And when the hour C, he sat at table,
22:39 And he C out, and went, as was his
22:40 And when he C to the place he said
22:43 rose from prayer, he C to the disciples and
22:45 was still speaking, there C a crowd, and the
22:64 When day C, the assembly of the elders of
23:32 And when they C to the place which is
24:23 his body; and they C back saying that they
Jn 1:7 He C for testimony, to bear witness to the
1:8 not the light, but C to bear witness to
1:11 He C to his own home, and his own
1:17 Moses; grace and truth C through Jesus Christ.
1:31 but for this I C baptizing with water, that
1:39 They C and saw where he was staying; and
2:9 not know where it C from (though the servants
3:2 This man C to Jesus by night and said
3:23 water there; and people C and were baptized.
3:26 And they C to John, and said to him,
4:5 So he C to a city of Samaria, called
4:7 There C a woman of Samaria to draw water.
4:27 Just then his disciples C
4:40 So when the Samaritans C to him, they asked
4:45 So when he C to Galilee, the Galileans welcomed
4:46 So he C again to Cana in Galilee, where
6:16 When evening C, his disciples went down to the
6:23 However, boats from Tiberi-as C near the place
6:41 am the bread which C down from heaven."
6:51 the living bread which C down from heaven; if
6:58 is the bread which C down from heaven, not
8:2 in the morning he C again to the temple;
8:2 temple; all the people C to him, and he
8:42 for I proceeded and C forth from God; I
8:42 forth from God; I C not of my own
9:7 went and washed and C back seeing.
9:39 said, "For judgment I C into this world, that
10:8 All who C before me are thieves and robbers;
10:10 kill and destroy; I C that they may have
10:35 the word of God C (and scripture cannot be
10:41 And many C to him; and they said, "John
11:17 Now when Jesus C, he found that Lazarus had
11:32 Then Mary, when she C where Jesus was and
11:33 and the Jews who C with her also weeping,
11:38 Jesus, deeply moved again, C to the tomb; it
11:44 The dead man C out, his hands and feet
12:1 the Passover, Jesus C to Bethany, where Lazarus
12:9 he was there, they C, not only on account
12:21 So these C to Philip, who was from Beth-saida
12:28 Then a voice C from heaven, "I have glorified
13:6 He C to Simon Peter; and Peter said to
16:27 have believed that I C from the Father.
16:28 I C from the Father and have come into
16:30 we believe that you C from God."
17:8 in truth that I C from thee; and they
18:4 was to befall him, C forward and said to
19:3 a purple robe; they C up to him, saying,
19:5 So Jesus C out, wearing the crown of thorns
19:32 So the soldiers C and broke the legs of
19:33 him; but when they C to Jesus and saw
19:34 and at once there C out blood and water.
19:38 So he C and took away his body.
19:39 to him by night, C bringing a mixture of
20:1 the week Mary Magdalene C to the tomb early,
20:3 Peter then C out with the other disciple, and
20:6 Then Simon Peter C, following him, and went into
20:19 of the Jews, Jesus C and stood among them
20:24 the Twin, was not with them when Jesus C
20:26 were shut, but Jesus C and stood among them,
21:8 But the other disciples C in the boat, dragging
21:13 Jesus C and took the bread and gave it
Acts 2:2 And suddenly a sound C from heaven like the
2:6 this sound the multitude C together, and they were
2:43 And fear C upon every soul; and many wonders
3:24 Samuel and those who C afterwards, also
4:1 temple and the Sadducees C upon them,
4:4 number of the men C to about five thousand.
5:5 And great fear C upon all who heard of
5:7 three hours his wife C in, not knowing what
5:10 When the young men C in they found her
5:11 And great fear C upon the whole church, and
5:15 pallets, that as Peter C by at least his
5:21 Now the high priest C and those who were
5:22 But when the officers C, they did not find
5:25 And some one C and told them, "The men
5:36 him were dispersed and C to nothing.
6:12 the scribes, and they C upon him and seized
7:11 Now there C a famine throughout all Egypt and
7:23 forty years old, it C into his heart to
7:31 voice of the Lord C,
8:7 For unclean spirits C out of many who were
8:15 Peter and John, who C down and prayed for
8:36 along the road they C to some water, and
8:38 And when they C up out of the water,
8:39 the towns till he C to Caesarea.
9:17 road by which you C, has sent me that
9:32 among them all, he C down also to the
10:13 And there C a voice to him, "Rise, Peter;
10:15 And the voice C to him again a second
10:29 was sent for, I C without objection.
10:45 the circumcised who C with Peter were amazed,
11:5 four corners; and it C down to me.
11:22 News of this C to the ears of the
11:23 When he C and saw the grace of God,
11:27 in these days prophets C down from Jerusalem to
12:10 the second guard, they C to the iron gate
12:11 And Peter C to himself, and said, "Now I
12:13 a maid named Rhoda C to answer.
12:18 Now when day C, there was no small stir
12:20 and Sidon; and they C to him in a
13:6 far as Paphos, they C upon a certain magician,
13:13 sail from Paphos, and C to Perga in Pamphylia.
13:14 on from Perga and C to Antioch of Pisidia.
13:31 appeared to those who C up with him from
14:19 But Jews C there from Antioch and Iconium; and
14:24 passed through Pisidia, and C to Pamphylia.
15:1 But some men C down from Judea and were
15:4 When they C to Jerusalem, they were welcomed by
16:1 And he C also to Derbe and to Lystra.
16:18 And it C out that very hour.
16:39 Roman citizens; so they C and apologized to them.
17:1 Amphipolis and Apollonia, they C to Thessalonica,
17:13 at Beroea also, they C there too, stirring up
18:19 And they C to Ephesus, and he left them
18:24 a native of Alexandria, C to Ephesus.
19:1 the upper country and C to Ephesus.
19:6 them, the Holy Spirit C on them; and they
19:12 and the evil spirits C out of them.
19:18 who were now believers C, confessing and divulging
19:19 them and found it C to fifty thousand pieces
20:2 them much encouragement, he C to Greece.
20:6 in five days we C to them at Troas,

20:14 him on board and C to Mitylene.
20:15 sailing from there we C the following day opposite
20:15 day after that we C to Miletus.
20:18 And when they C to him, he said to
21:1 and set sail, we C by a straight course
21:8 morrow we departed and C to Caesarea; and we
21:10 a prophet named Agabus C down from Judea.
21:31 to kill him, word C to the tribune of
21:33 Then the tribune C up and arrested him, and
21:35 And when he C to the steps, he was
22:11 were with me, and C into Damascus.
22:13 Jews who lived there, C to me, and standing
22:27 So the tribune C and said to him, "Tell
23:27 by them, when I C upon them with the
23:33 When they C to Caesarea and delivered the letter
24:1 the high priest Ananias C down with some elders
24:16 after some years I C to bring to my
24:23 After some days Felix C with his wife Drusilla,
25:17 When therefore they C together here, I made no
25:23 morrow Agrippa and Bernice C with great pomp, and
27:5 Cilicia and Pamphylia, we C to Myra in Lycia.
27:8 it with difficulty, we C to a place called
27:21 without food, Paul then C forward among them and
28:3 fire, when a viper C out because of the
28:9 who had diseases also C and were cured.
28:13 the second day we C to Puteoli.
28:14 And so we C to Rome.
28:15 they heard of us, C as far as the
28:16 And when we C into Rome, Paul was allowed
28:23 day for him, they C to him at his
28:29 and welcomed all who C to him,
Rom 5:12 Therefore as sin C into the world through one
5:20 Law C in, to increase the trespass; but where
7:9 but when the commandment C, sin revived and I
1Cor 2:1 When I C to you, brethren, I did not
15:21 as by a man C death, by a man
2Cor 2:3 so that when I C I might not suffer
2:12 When I C to Troas to preach the gospel
3:7 in letters on stone, C with such splendor that
3:11 if what faded away C with splendor, what is
7:5 For even when we C into Macedonia, our bodies
11:9 by the brethren who C from Macedonia.
Gal 1:12 taught it, but it C through a revelation of
2:11 But when Cephas C to Antioch I opposed him
2:12 For before certain men C from James, he ate
2:12 Gentiles; but when they C he drew back and
3:17 mean: the law, which C four hundred and thirty
3:23 Now before faith C, we were confined under the
3:24 our custodian until Christ C, that we might be
Eph 2:17 And he C and preached peace to you who
1Thes 1:5 you; for our gospel C to you not only
1Tim 1:15 acceptance, that Christ Jesus C into the world to
Heb 4:2 For good news C to us just as to
7:28 of the oath, which C later than the law,
10:5 Consequently, when Christ C into the world, he said,
2Pet 1:21 because no prophecy ever C by the impulse of
1 Jn 5:6 This is he who C by water and blood,
Jude 1:14 saying, "Behold, the Lord C with his holy myriads,
Rev 2:8 last, who died and C to life.
6:4 And out C another horse, bright red; its rider
8:3 And another angel C and stood at the altar
9:3 Then from the smoke C locusts on the earth,
11:18 raged, but thy wrath C, and the time for
12:16 But the earth C to the help of the
14:15 And another angel C out of the temple, calling
14:17 And another angel C out of the temple in
14:18 Then another angel C out from the altar, the
15:6 out of the temple C the seven angels with
16:2 foul and evil sores C upon the men who
16:17 and a loud voice C out of the temple,
17:1 had the seven bowls C and said to me,
19:5 And from the throne C a voice crying, "Praise
20:4 They C to life, and reigned with Christ a
20:9 beloved city; but fire C down from heaven and
21:9 Then C one of the seven angels who had

CAMEL (14)

Gen 24:64 she alighted from the C,
31:34 put them in the C's saddle, and sat upon
Lev 11:4 not eat these: The C, because it chews the
Deut 14:7 not eat these: the C, the hare, and the
1Sam 15:3 suckling, ox and sheep, C and ass.'"
2Kgs 8:9 goods of Damascus, forty C loads.
Sir 24:15 Like cassia and C's thorn I gave forth the
Jer 2:23 done–a restive young C interlacing her tracks,
Mt 3:4 wore a garment of C's hair, and a leather
19:24 is easier for a C to go through the
23:23 guides, straining out a gnat and swallowing a C
Mk 1:6 John was clothed with C's hair, and had a
10:25 is easier for a C to go through the
Lk 18:25 is easier for a C to go through the

CAMELS (50)

Gen 12:16 had sheep, oxen, he-asses, menservants,
24:10 ten of his master's C and departed, taking all
24:11 And he made the C kneel down outside the
24:14 I will water your C –let her be the
24:19 will draw for your C also, until they have
24:20 to draw, and she drew for all his C
24:22 When the C had done drinking, the man took
24:30 was standing by the C at the spring.
24:31 prepared the house and a place for the C
24:32 and Laban ungirded the C, and gave him straw
24:32 and provender for the C, and water to wash
24:35 gold, menservants and maidservants, C and asses.
24:44 will draw for your C also," let her be
24:46 I will give your C drink also.' So I
24:46 and she gave the C drink also.
24:61 and rode upon the C and followed the man;
24:63 and behold, there were C coming.
30:43 maidservants and menservants, and C and asses.
31:17 and his wives on C;
32:7 flocks and herds and C, into two companies,
32:15 twenty rams, thirty milch C and their colts, forty
37:25 from Gilead, with their C bearing gum, balm, and
Ex 9:3 horses, the asses, the C, the herds, and the
Judg 6:5 both they and their C could not be counted;
7:12 for multitude; and their C were without number, as
8:21 crescents that were on the necks of their C
8:26 collars that were about the necks of their C
1Sam 27:9 oxen, the asses, the C, and the garments, and
30:17 young men, who mounted C and fled.
1Kgs 10:2 very great retinue, with C bearing spices, and very
1Chr 5:21 fifty thousand of their C, two hundred and fifty
12:40 on asses and on C and on mules and
27:30 Over the C was Obil the Ishmaelite; and over
2Chr 9:1 very great retinue and C bearing spices and very
14:15 cattle, and carried away sheep in abundance and C
Ezra 2:67 hundred and forty-five, their C were four hundred
Neh 7:69 and forty-five, their C four hundred and thirty-five,
Tob 9:2 a servant and two C with you and go
Jud 2:17 a vast number of C and asses and mules
Job 1:3 thousand sheep, three thousand C, five hundred yoke
1:17 a raid upon the C and took them, and
42:12 thousand sheep, six thousand C, a thousand yoke of
Is 21:7 on asses, riders on C, let him listen diligently,
30:6 on the humps of C, to a people that
60:6 A multitude of C shall cover you, the young
60:6 cover you, the young C of Midian and Ephah;
Jer 49:29 all their goods; their C shall be borne away
49:32 Their C shall become booty, their herds of cattle
Ezek 25:5 Rabbah a pasture for C and the cities of
Zech 14:15 horses, the mules, the C, the asses, and whatever

CAMEST

Is 64:3 looked not for, thou C down, the mountains quaked

CAMP (200)

Gen 32:21 and he himself lodged that night in the C
Ex 16:13 up and covered the C; and in the morning
16:13 in the morning dew lay round about the C
19:16 who were in the C trembled.
19:17 people out of the C to meet God; and
29:14 with fire outside the C; it is a sin
32:17 "There is a noise of war in the C
32:19 he came near the C and saw the calf
32:26 the gate of the C, and said, "Who is
32:27 to gate throughout the C, and slay every man
33:7 pitch it outside the C, far-off from the camp;
33:7 camp, far-off from the C; and he called it
33:7 the tent of meeting, which was outside the C
33:11 turned again into the C, his servant Joshua the
36:6 was proclaimed throughout the C, "Let neither man
Lev 4:12 carry forth outside the C to a clean place,
4:21 the bull outside the C, and burn it as
6:11 the ashes outside the C to a clean place.
8:17 with fire outside the C, as the LORD commanded
9:11 the skin he burned with fire outside the C
10:4 brethren from before the sanctuary out of the C
10:5 coats out of the C, as Moses had said.
13:46 shall dwell alone in a habitation outside the C
14:3 go out of the C, and the priest shall

14:8 shall come into the C, but shall dwell outside
16:26 water, and afterward he may come into the C
16:27 carried forth outside the C; their skin and their
16:28 water, and afterward he may come into the C
17:3 a goat in the C, or kills it outside
17:3 kills it outside the C,
24:10 Israel quarreled in the C,
24:14 "Bring out of the C him who cursed; and
24:23 cursed out of the C, and stoned him with
Num 1:52 man by his own C and every man by
2:3 the standard of the C of Judah by their
2:9 whole number of the C of Judah, by their
2:10 the standard of the C of Reuben by their
2:16 whole number of the C of Reuben, by their
2:17 set out, with the C of the Levites in
2:18 the standard of the C of Ephraim by their
2:24 whole number of the C of Ephraim, by their
2:25 the standard of the C of Dan by their
2:31 whole number of the C of Dan is a
4:5 When the C is to set out, Aaron and
4:15 the sanctuary, as the C sets out, after that
5:2 put out of the C every leper, and every
5:3 putting them outside the C, that they may not
5:3 may not defile their C, in the midst of
5:4 drove them outside the C; as the LORD said
9:18 cloud rested over the tabernacle, they remained in C
9:20 LORD they remained in C; then according to the
9:22 of Israel remained in C and did not set
10:2 for summoning the congregation, and for breaking C
10:14 The standard of the C of the men of
10:18 the standard of the C of Reuben set out
10:22 the standard of the C of the men of
10:25 the standard of the C of the men of
10:34 by day, whenever they set out from the C
11:1 them, and consumed some outlying parts of the C
11:9 dew fell upon the C in the night, the
11:26 men remained in the C, one named Eldad, and
11:26 the tent, and so they prophesied in the C
11:27 Moses, "Eldad and Medad are prophesying in the C
11:30 and the elders of Israel returned to the C
11:31 them fall beside the C, about a day's journey
11:31 side, round about the C, and about two cubits
11:32 spread them out for themselves all around the C
12:14 shut up outside the C seven days, and after
12:15 shut up outside the C seven days; and the
14:44 the LORD, nor Moses, departed out of the C
15:35 shall stone him with stones outside the C
15:36 brought him outside the C, and stoned him to
19:3 be taken outside the C and slaughtered before him;
19:7 shall come into the C; and the priest shall
19:9 deposit them outside the C in a clean place;
31:12 of Israel, at the C on the plains of
31:13 congregation, went forth to meet them outside the C
31:19 Encamp outside the C seven days; whoever of you
31:24 clean; and afterward you shall come into the C
Deut 2:14 had perished from the C, as the LORD had
2:15 destroy them from the C, until they had perished.
23:9 enemies and are in C, then you shall keep
23:10 shall go outside the C, he shall not come
23:10 not come within the C;
23:11 sun is down, he may come within the C
23:12 a place outside the C and you shall go
23:14 the midst of your C, to save you and
23:14 before you, therefore your C must be holy, that
29:11 who is in your C, both he who hews
Josh 1:11 "Pass through the C, and command the people,
3:2 officers went through the C
5:8 their places in the C till they were healed.
6:11 they came into the C, and spent the night
6:11 the camp, and spent the night in the C
6:14 around the city once, and returned into the C
6:18 things and make the C of Israel a thing
6:23 set them outside the C of Israel.
9:6 to Joshua in the C at Gilgal, and said
10:6 to Joshua at the C in Gilgal, saying, "Do
10:15 with him, to the C at Gilgal.
10:21 to Joshua in the C at Makkedah; not a
10:43 with him, to the C at Gilgal.
18:9 to Joshua in the C at Shiloh,
Judg 7:1 of Harod; and the C of Midian was north
7:8 hundred men; and the C of Midian was below
7:9 go down against the C; for I have given
7:10 go down to the C with Purah your servant;
7:11 shall be strengthened to go down against the C
7:11 of the armed men that were in the C
7:13 bread tumbled into the C of Midian, and came
7:15 he returned to the C of Israel, and said,
7:17 the outskirts of the C, do as I do.
7:18 side of all the C, and shout, 'For the
7:19 the outskirts of the C at the beginning of
7:21 place round about the C, and all the army
21:8 had come to the C from Jabesh-gilead, to the
21:12 brought them to the C at Shiloh, which is
1Sam 4:3 troops came to the C, the elders of Israel
4:5 LORD came into the C, all Israel gave a
4:6 great shouting in the C of the Hebrews mean?"
4:6 had come to the C,
4:7 they said, "A god has come into the C
11:11 the midst of the C in the morning watch,
13:17 came out of the C of the Philistines in
14:15 a panic in the C, in the field, and
14:19 the tumult in the C of the Philistines increased
14:21 with them into the C, even they also turned
17:4 came out from the C of the Philistines a
17:17 them quickly to the C to your brothers;
17:53 chasing the Philistines, and they plundered their C
26:6 with me into the C to Saul?" And Abishai
2Sam 1:2 man came from Saul's C, with his clothes rent
1:3 have escaped from the C of Israel."
23:16 men broke through the C of the Philistines, and
1Kgs 16:16 army, king over Israel that day in the C
2Kgs 3:24 they came to the C of Israel, the Israelites
6:8 such and such a place shall be my C
7:4 go over to the C of the Syrians; if
7:5 to go to the C of the Syrians; but
7:5 the edge of the C of the Syrians, behold,
7:7 their asses, leaving the C as it was, and
7:8 the edge of the C, they went into a
7:10 "We came to the C of the Syrians, and
7:12 gone out of the C to hide themselves in
7:16 out, and plundered the C of the Syrians.
19:35 eighty-five thousand in the C of the Assyrians; and
1Chr 9:18 the gatekeepers of the C of the Levites.
9:19 in charge of the C of the LORD, keepers
11:18 men broke through the C of the Philistines, and
2Chr 22:1 the Arabs to the C had slain all the
31:2 the gates of the C of the LORD and
32:21 and officers in the C of the king of
Jud 6:11 him out of the C into the plain, and
7:1 joined him, to break C and move against Bethulia,
7:2 their warriors moved their C that day; their force
7:12 Remain in your C, and keep all the men
7:13 the nearby mountains and C there to keep watch
10:18 excitement in the whole C, for her arrival was
12:7 she remained in the C for three days, and
12:7 Bethulia, and bathed at the spring in the C
13:10 they passed through the C and circled around the
14:3 and go into the C and rouse the officers
14:19 and shouts arose in the midst of the C
15:5 had happened in the C of the enemy; and
15:6 fell upon the Assyrian C and plundered it, and
15:11 the people plundered the C for thirty days.
16:3 brought me to his C, in the midst of
Ps 69:25 May their C be a desolation, let no one
78:28 the midst of their C, all around their habitations.
106:16 When men in the C were jealous of Moses
Wis 19:7 seen overshadowing the C, and dry land emerging
Sir 14:26 her shelter, and will C under her boughs
48:21 The Lord smote the C of the Assyrians, and
Is 37:36 eighty-five thousand in the C of the Assyrians; and
Amos 4:10 the stench of your C go up into your
1Mac 3:41 and went to the C to get the sons
4:2 to fall upon the C of the Jews and
4:4 while the division was still absent from the C
4:5 When Gorgias entered the C of Judas by night,
4:7 And they saw the C of the Gentiles, strong
4:13 went forth from their C to battle.
4:20 Jews were burning the C, for the smoke that
4:23 returned to plunder the C, and they seized much
4:30 and didst give the C of the Philistines into
5:38 to spy out the C, and they reported to
6:32 at Beth-zechariah, opposite the C of the king.
9:6 slipped away from the C, until no more than
9:11 marched out from the C and took its stand
11:73 as Kadesh, to their C, and there they encamped.
12:26 sent spies to their C, and they returned and
12:27 for battle, and he stationed outposts around the C
12:28 kindled fires in their C and withdrew.
12:32 Then he broke C and went to Damascus, and
2Mac 13:14 commonwealth, he pitched his C near Modein.
13:15 as many as two thousand men in the C
13:16 end they filled the C with terror and confusion

15:22 eighty-five thousand in the C of Sennacherib.
Heb 13:11 a sacrifice for sin are burned outside the C
13:13 to him outside the C and bear the abuse
Rev 20:9 earth and surrounded the C of the saints and

CAMPAIGN (3)
1Sam 29:6 with me in the C; for I have found
Jud 2:16 as a great army is marshaled for a C
2Mac 15:17 to carry on a C but to attack bravely,

CAMPED (9)
Gen 33:18 from Paddan-aram; and he C before the city.
Ex 17:1 of the LORD, and C at Rephidim; but there
Judg 11:18 land of Moab, and C on the other side
Tob 6:1 the Tigris river and C there.
Jud 2:21 plain of Bectileth, and C opposite Bectileth near the
3:10 of Judea; here he C between Geba and Scythopolis,
15:3 Those who had C in the hills around Bethulia
1Mac 9:33 wilderness of Tekoa and C by the water of
16:4 marched against Cendebeus and C for the night in

CAMPING
2Sam 11:11 of my lord are C in the open field;

CAMPS (9)
Num 2:17 the midst of the C; as they encamp, so
2:32 houses; all in the C who were numbered by
10:5 blow an alarm, the C that are on the
10:6 the second time, the C that are on the
10:25 guard of all the C, set out by their
13:19 they dwell in are C or strongholds,
Ezek 4:2 mound against it; set C also against it, and
Zech 14:15 asses, and whatever beasts may be in those C
1Mac 5:41 he shows fear and C on the other side

CANA (4)
Jn 2:1 was a marriage at C in Galilee, and the
2:11 signs, Jesus did at C in Galilee, and manifested
4:46 he came again to C in Galilee, where he
21:2 the Twin, Nathanael of C in Galilee, the sons

CANAAN (92)
Gen 9:18 Ham was the father of C
9:22 Ham, the father of C, saw the nakedness of
9:25 he said, "Cursed be C; a slave of slaves
9:26 be Shem; and let C be his slave.
9:27 of Shem; and let C be his slave."
10:6 The sons of Ham: Cush, Egypt, Put, and C
10:15 C became the father of Sidon his first-born, and
11:31 into the land of C; but when they came
12:5 set forth to go to the land of C
12:5 to the land of C,
13:12 in the land of C, while Lot dwelt among
16:3 in the land of C, Sarai, Abram's wife, took
17:8 all the land of C, for an everlasting possession;
23:2 in the land of C; and Abraham went in
23:19 Mamre (that is, Hebron) in the land of C
31:18 to the land of C to his father Isaac.
33:18 in the land of C, on his way from
35:6 in the land of C, he and all the
36:5 were born to him in the land of C
36:6 in the land of C; and he went into
37:1 of his father's sojournings, in the land of C
42:5 for the famine was in the land of C
42:7 "From the land of C, to buy food."
42:13 in the land of C; and behold, the youngest
42:29 in the land of C, they told him all
42:32 in the land of C
44:8 from the land of C; how then should we
45:17 to the land of C;
45:25 to the land of C to their father Jacob.
46:6 in the land of C, and came into Egypt,
46:12 in the land of C; and the sons of
46:31 in the land of C, have come to me;
47:1 from the land of C; they are now in
47:4 in the land of C; and now, we pray
47:13 and the land of C languished by reason of
47:14 in the land of C, for the grain which
47:15 in the land of C, all the Egyptians came
48:3 in the land of C and blessed me,
48:7 in the land of C on the way, when
49:30 in the land of C, which Abraham bought with
50:5 in the land of C, there shall you bury
50:13 to the land of C, and buried him in
Ex 6:4 them the land of C, the land in which
15:15 all the inhabitants of C have melted away.
16:35 came to the border of the land of C
Lev 14:34 into the land of C, which I give you
18:3 in the land of C, to which I am
25:38 you the land of C, and to be your
Num 13:2 out the land of C, which I give to
13:17 out the land of C, and said to them,
26:19 Er and Onan died in the land of C
32:30 have possessions among you in the land of C
32:32 into the land of C, and the possession of
33:40 in the land of C, heard of the coming
33:51 into the land of C,
34:2 enter the land of C (this is the land
34:2 inheritance, the land of C in its full extent),
34:29 the people of Israel in the land of C
35:10 into the land of C,
35:14 in the land of C, to be cities of
Deut 32:49 view the land of C, which I give to
Josh 5:12 of the land of C that year.
14:1 in the land of C, which Eleazar the priest,
21:2 in the land of C, "The LORD commanded through
22:9 in the land of C, to go to the
22:10 in the land of C, the Reubenites and the
22:11 of the land of C, in the region about
22:32 to the land of C, to the people of
24:3 all the land of C, and made his offspring
Judg 3:1 of any war in C;
4:2 of Jabin king of C, who reigned in Hazor;
4:23 Jabin the king of C before the people of
4:24 Jabin the king of C, until they destroyed Jabin
4:24 of Canaan, until they destroyed Jabin king of C
5:19 fought the kings of C, at Taanach, by the
21:12 at Shiloh, which is in the land of C
1Chr 1:8 The sons of Ham: Cush, Egypt, Put, and C
1:13 C was the father of Sidon his first-born, and
16:18 give the land of C, as your portion for
Jud 5:9 were living and go to the land of C
5:10 a famine spread over C they went down to
Ps 105:11 give the land of C as your portion for
106:38 to the idols of C; and the land was
135:11 all the kingdoms of C,
Is 19:18 speak the language of C and swear allegiance to
23:11 command concerning C to destroy its strongholds.
Bar 3:22 been heard of in C, nor seen in Teman;
Dan 13:56 him, "You offspring of C and not of Judah,
Zeph 2:5 is against you, O C, land of the Philistines;
1Mac 9:37 the great nobles of C, from Nadabath with a
Acts 7:11 throughout all Egypt and C, and great affliction, and
13:19 in the land of C, he gave them their

CANAANITE (11)
Gen 28:1 marry one of the C women.
28:6 marry one of the C women,"
28:8 Esau saw that the C women did not please
38:2 daughter of a certain C whose name was Shua;
Ex 6:15 the son of a C woman; these are the
23:28 shall drive out Hivite, C, and Hittite from before
Num 21:1 When the C, the king of Arad, who dwelt
33:40 And the C, the king of Arad, who dwelt
Josh 13:3 it is reckoned as C; there are five rulers
Neh 9:8 the land of the C, the Hittite, the Amorite,
Mt 15:22 And behold, a C woman from that region came

CANAANITES (63)
Gen 10:18 the families of the C spread abroad.
10:19 the territory of the C extended from Sidon, in
12:6 At that time the C were in the land.
13:7 At that time the C and the Perizzites dwelt
15:21 Rephaim, the Amorites, the C, the Girgashites and
24:3 the daughters of the C, among whom I dwell,
24:37 the daughters of the C, in whose land I
34:30 of the land, the C and the Perizzites; my
36:2 his wives from the C: Adah the daughter of
50:11 of the land, the C, saw the mourning on
Ex 3:8 the place of the C, the Hittites, the Amorites,
3:17 the land of the C, the Hittites, the Amorites,
13:5 the land of the C, the Hittites, the Amorites,
13:11 the land of the C, as he swore to
23:23 the Perizzites, and the C, the Hivites, and the
33:2 will drive out the C, the Amorites, the Hittites,
34:11 you the Amorites, the C, the Hittites, the Perizzites,
Num 13:29 hill country; and the C dwell by the sea,
14:25 the Amalekites and the C dwell in the valleys,
14:43 the Amalekites and the C are before you, and
14:45 the Amalekites and the C who dwelt in that
21:3 and gave over the C; and they utterly destroyed
Deut 1:7 the land of the C, and Lebanon, as far

7:1 Girgashites, the Amorites, the C, the Perizzites, the
11:30 the land of the C who live in the
20:17 and the Amorites, the C and the Perizzites, the
Josh 3:10 from before you the C, the Hittites, the Hivites,
5:1 the kings of the C that were by the
7:9 For the C and all the inhabitants of the
9:1 Hittites, the Amorites, the C, the Perizzites, the
11:3 the west, to the C in the east and
12:8 Hittites, the Amorites, the C, the Perizzites, the
13:4 the land of the C, and Mearah which belongs
16:10 not drive out the C that dwelt in Gezer:
16:10 in Gezer: so the C have dwelt in the
17:12 those cities; but the C persisted in dwelling in
17:13 strong, they put the C to forced labor, and
17:16 us; yet all the C who dwell in the
17:18 shall drive out the C, though they have chariots
24:11 Amorites, the Perizzites, the C, the Hittites, the
Judg 1:1 for us against the C, to fight against them?"
1:3 may fight against the C; and I likewise will
1:4 the LORD gave the C and the Perizzites into
1:5 him, and defeated the C and the Perizzites.
1:9 to fight against the C who dwelt in the
1:10 Judah went against the C who dwelt in Hebron
1:17 and they defeated the C who inhabited Zephath, and
1:27 its villages; but the C persisted in dwelling in
1:28 strong, they put the C to forced labor, but
1:29 not drive out the C who dwelt in Gezer;
1:29 in Gezer; but the C dwelt in Gezer among
1:30 of Nahalol; but the C dwelt among them, and
1:32 Asherites dwelt among the C, the inhabitants of the
1:33 but dwelt among the C, the inhabitants of the
3:3 Philistines, and all the C, and the Sidonians, and
3:5 Israel dwelt among the C, the Hittites, the Amorites,
2Sam 24:7 of the Hivites and C; and they went out
1Kgs 9:16 and had slain the C who dwelt in the
Ezra 9:1 their abominations, from the C, the Hittites, the
Neh 9:24 of the land, the C, and didst give them
Jud 5:3 them, "Tell me, you C, what people is this
5:16 out before them the C and the Perizzites and
Ezek 16:3 the land of the C; your father was an

CANAANITESS

1Chr 2:3 these three Bath-shua the C bore to him.

CANAANITISH

Gen 46:10 the son of a C woman.

CANAL (2)

Sir 24:28 went forth like a C from a river and
24:29 plot"; and lo, my C became a river, and

CANALS (3)

Ex 7:19 over their rivers, their C, and their ponds, and
8:5 the rivers, over the C, and over the pools,
Is 19:6 and dry; and its C will become foul, and

CANANAEAN (2)

Mt 10:4 and Thaddaeus; Simon the C, and Judas Iscariot,
Mk 3:18 Thaddaeus, and Simon the C,

CANCEL (2)

1Mac 10:33 and let all officials C also the taxes on
13:39 to this day, and C the crown tax which

CANCELED (4)

1Mac 10:42 temple, this too is C, because it belongs to
11:36 these grants shall be C from this time forth
15:8 future debts shall be C for you from henceforth
Col 2:14 all our trespasses, having C the bond which stood

CANDACE

Acts 8:27 a minister of the C, queen of the Ethiopians,

CANE (3)

Ex 30:23 fifty, and of aromatic C two hundred and fifty,
Is 43:24 not bought me sweet C with money, or satisfied
Jer 6:20 from Sheba, or sweet C from a distant land?

CANNEH

Ezek 27:23 Haran, C, Eden, Asshur, and Chilmad traded with

CANNOT (273)

Gen 16:10 descendants that they C be numbered for multitude."
19:19 my life; but I C flee to the hills,
24:50 from the LORD; we C speak to you bad
29:8 But they said, "We C until all the flocks
31:35 be angry that I C rise before you, for
32:12 of the sea, which C be numbered for multitude.'"
34:14 said to them, "We C do this thing, to
44:22 my lord, 'The lad C leave his father, for
44:26 food,' we said, 'We C go down.
44:26 go down; for we C see the man's face
Ex 19:23 the LORD, "The people C come up to Mount
33:20 he said, "you C see my face; for man
Lev 5:7 "But if he C afford a lamb, then he
5:11 "But if he C afford two turtledoves or two
12:8 And if she C afford a lamb, then she
14:21 he is poor and C afford so much, then
14:32 a leprous disease, who C afford the offerings for
22:23 a votive offering it C be accepted.
25:35 brother becomes poor, and C maintain himself with
Num 23:20 has blessed, and I C revoke it.
31:23 of impurity; and whatever C stand the fire, you
Deut 28:27 itch, of which you C be healed.
28:35 boils of which you C be healed, from the
Josh 7:12 the people of Israel C stand before their enemies;
7:13 you, O Israel; you C stand before your enemies,
24:19 to the people, "You C serve the LORD; for
Judg 11:35 the LORD, and I C take back my vow."
14:13 garments; but if you C tell me what it
21:18 Yet we C give them wives of our daughters."
Ruth 4:6 of kin said, "I C redeem it for myself,
4:6 redemption yourself, for I C redeem it."
1Sam 12:21 after vain things which C profit or save, for
17:39 said to Saul, "I C go with these; for
17:55 lives, O king, I C tell."
25:17 so ill-natured that one C speak to him."
2Sam 5:6 you off"--thinking, "David C come in here."
14:14 on the ground, which C be gathered up again;
14:19 lord the king, one C turn to the right
23:6 thrown away; for they C be taken with the
1Kgs 3:8 a great people, that C be numbered or counted
8:27 and the highest heaven C contain thee; how much
18:12 tell Ahab and he C find you, he will
20:9 but this thing I C do.'" And the messengers
2Chr 2:6 heaven, even highest heaven, C contain him?
6:18 and the highest heaven C contain thee; how much
13:12 your fathers; for you C succeed."
24:20 LORD, so that you C prosper?
Ezra 10:13 of heavy rain; we C stand in the open.
Neh 6:3 great work and I C come down.
Tob 6:12 the law of Moses, C give her to another
Jud 6:3 They C resist the might of our cavalry.
6:4 They C withstand us, but will utterly perish.
8:14 You C plumb the depths of the human heart,
8:30 an oath which we C break.
11:10 is true: our nation C be punished, nor can
12:2 But Judith said, "I C eat it, lest it
Esth 8:8 with the king's ring C be revoked."
13:4 which we honorably intend C be brought about.
Job 6:30 C my taste discern calamity?
9:15 I am innocent, I C answer him; I must
10:15 I am righteous, I C lift up my head,
14:5 his bounds that he C pass,
19:8 way, so that I C pass, and he has
22:11 darkened, so that you C see, and a flood
23:8 and backward, but I C perceive him;
23:9 seek him, but I C behold him; I turn
23:9 right hand, but I C see him.
28:15 not with me.' It C be gotten for gold,
28:15 for gold, and silver C be weighed as its
28:16 It C be valued in the gold of Ophir,
28:17 Gold and glass C equal it, nor can it
28:19 The topaz of Ethiopia C compare with it, nor
33:21 wasted away that it C be seen; and his
37:5 great things which we C comprehend.
37:19 say to him; we C draw up our case
37:21 "And now men C look on the light when
37:23 The Almighty--we C find him; he is great
39:24 swallows the ground; he C stand still at the
41:17 clasp each other and C be separated.
41:28 The arrow C make him flee; for him slingstones
Ps 22:29 dust, and he who C keep himself alive.
33:17 its great might it C save.
36:2 eyes that his iniquity C be found out and
37:21 The wicked borrows, and C pay back, but the
40:12 overtaken me, till I C see; they are more
49:12 Man C abide in his pomp, he is like
49:20 Man C abide in his pomp, he is like
69:23 darkened, so that they C see; and make their
77:4 so troubled that I C speak.
88:8 in so that I C escape;

92:6 The dull man C know, the stupid cannot understand
92:6 cannot know, the stupid C understand this:
125:1 like Mount Zion, which C be moved, but abides
139:6 it is high, I C attain it.
148:6 fixed their bounds which C be passed.
Prov 4:17 For they C sleep unless they have done wrong;
8:11 that you may desire C compare with her.
30:21 trembles; under four it C bear up:
Eccl 1:8 of weariness; a man C utter it; the eye
1:15 What is crooked C be made straight, and what
1:15 and what is lacking C be numbered.
3:11 yet so that he C find out what God
8:17 of God, that man C find out the work
8:17 claims to know, he C find it out.
Song 8:7 Many waters C quench love, neither can floods
Wis 13:16 he knows that it C help itself, for it
13:18 journey, a thing that C take a step;
16:14 kills another, but he C bring back the departed
Sir 1:19 Unrighteous anger C be justified, for a man's anger
14:16 because in Hades one C look for luxury.
17:25 For all things C be in men, since a
21:12 who is not clever C be taught, but there
25:17 the neighbors, and he C help sighing bitterly.
38:32 Without them a city C be established, and men
38:33 sentence of judgment; they C expound discipline or
40:29 of another, his existence C be considered as life.
43:27 we speak much we C reach the end, and
43:30 grow weary, for you C praise him enough.
Is 1:13 of assemblies-- I C endure iniquity and solemn
21:3 down so that I C hear, I am dismayed
21:3 dismayed so that I C see.
29:11 he says, "I C, for it is sealed."
29:12 book to one who C read, saying, "Read this,"
29:12 he says, "I C read."
30:5 through a people that C profit them, that brings
30:6 to a people that C profit them.
33:19 obscure speech which you C comprehend,
33:19 a tongue which you C understand.
33:23 tackle hangs loose; it C hold the mast firm
38:18 For Sheol C thank thee, death cannot praise thee;
38:18 cannot thank thee, death C praise thee; those who
38:18 down to the pit C hope for thy faithfulness.
41:7 nails so that it C be moved.
43:17 they lie down, they C rise, they are extinguished,
44:18 eyes, so that they C see, and their minds,
44:18 minds, so that they C understand.
44:20 him astray, and he C deliver himself or say,
45:20 to a god that C save.
46:2 bow down together, they C save the burden, but
46:7 it stands there; it C move from its place.
47:11 you, for which you C atone; disaster shall fall
47:14 fire consumes them; they C deliver themselves from
50:2 hand shortened, that it C redeem?
56:10 all dumb dogs, they C bark; dreaming, lying down,
57:20 tossing sea; for it C rest, and its waters
59:1 not shortened, that it C save, or his ear
59:1 ear dull, that it C hear;
59:14 public squares, and uprightness C enter.
Jer 4:19 is beating wildly; I C keep silent; for I
5:22 perpetual barrier which it C pass; though the waves
5:22 the waves toss, they C prevail, though they roar,
5:22 though they roar, they C pass over it.
6:10 ears are closed, they C listen; behold, the word
8:17 you serpents, adders which C be charmed, and they
10:4 nails so that it C move.
10:5 cucumber field, and they C speak; they have to
10:5 be carried, for they C walk.
10:5 of them, for they C do evil, neither is
10:10 quakes, and the nations C endure his indignation.
11:11 upon them which they C escape; though they cry
11:12 burn incense, but they C save them in the
14:9 a mighty man who C save?
20:9 am weary with holding it in, and I C
23:24 places so that I C see him?
24:3 so bad that they C be eaten."
24:8 are so bad they C be eaten, so will
29:17 are so bad they C be eaten.
33:22 the host of heaven C be numbered and the
33:22 sands of the sea C be measured, so I
46:6 The swift C flee away, nor the warrior escape;
49:23 like the sea which C be quiet.
Lam 1:14 of those whom I C withstand.
3:7 about so that I C escape; he has put
Bar 6:8 they are false and C speak.
6:12 gold and wood, which C save themselves from rust
6:15 an axe; but it C save itself from war
6:27 of them upright, it C move itself; and if
6:27 is tipped over, it C straighten itself; but gifts
6:34 They C set up a king or depose one.
6:36 They C save a man from death or rescue
6:37 They C restore sight to a blind man; they
6:37 a blind man; they C rescue a man who
6:38 They C take pity on a widow or do
6:41 a dumb man, who C speak, they bring him
6:42 Yet they themselves C perceive this and abandon
6:49 not gods, for they C save themselves from war
6:53 For they C set up a king over a
6:54 They C judge their own cause or deliver one
6:67 nor bless kings; they C show signs in the
Ezek 3:6 language, whose words you C understand.
3:25 them, so that you C go out among the
4:8 you, so that you C turn from one side
7:19 of the LORD; they C satisfy their hunger or
Dan 3:33 And now we C open our mouths; shame and
6:8 document, so that it C be changed, according to
6:8 and the Persians, which C be revoked."
6:12 Medes and Persians, which C be revoked."
14:24 said to Daniel, "You C deny that this is
Hos 2:6 her, so that she C find her paths.
Mic 2:3 evil, from which you C remove your necks; and
1Mac 10:72 tell you that you C stand before us, for
2Mac 7:14 death, he said, "One C but choose to die
Mt 5:14 set on a hill C be hid.
5:36 your head, for you C make one hair white
6:24 You C serve God and mammon.
7:18 A sound tree C bear evil fruit, nor can
10:28 kill the body but C kill the soul; rather
16:3 the sky, but you C interpret the signs of
26:42 "My Father, if this C pass unless I drink
26:53 you think that I C appeal to my Father,
27:42 "He saved others; he C save himself.
Mk 2:19 bridegroom with them, they C fast.
3:24 against itself, that kingdom C stand.
3:26 and is divided, he C stand, but is coming
7:17 a man from outside C defile him,
9:29 to them, "This kind C be driven out by
15:30 "He saved others; he C save himself.
Lk 11:7 me in bed; I C get up and give
13:33 day following; for it C be that a prophet
14:14 be blessed, because they C repay you.
14:20 wife, and therefore I C come.'
14:26 his own life, he C be my disciple.
14:27 and come after me, C be my disciple.
14:33 all that he has C be my disciple.
16:13 You C serve God and mammon."
20:36 in marriage, for they C die any more, because
Jn 3:3 is born anew, he C see the kingdom of
3:5 and the Spirit, he C enter the kingdom of
7:7 The world C hate you, but it hates me
7:34 where I am you C come."
7:36 'Where I am you C come'?"
8:21 I am going, you C come."
8:22 I am going, you C come'?"
8:43 It is because you C bear to hear my
10:35 God came (and scripture C be broken),
13:33 I am going you C come.'
13:36 I am going you C follow me now; but
13:37 to him, "Lord, why C I follow you now?
14:17 truth, whom the world C receive, because it neither
15:4 As the branch C bear fruit by itself, unless
16:12 to you, but you C bear them now.
Acts 4:16 of Jerusalem, and we C deny it.
4:20 must judge; for we C but speak of what
15:1 custom of Moses, you C be saved."
19:36 then that these things C be contradicted, you ought
27:31 in the ship, you C be saved."
Rom 7:18 is right, but I C do it.
8:7 God's law, indeed it C;
8:8 are in the flesh C please God.
11:10 darkened so that they C see, and bend their
1Cor 7:9 But if they C exercise self-control, they should marry.
10:21 You C drink the cup of the Lord and
10:21 You C partake of the table of the Lord
12:21 The eye C say to the hand, "I have
15:50 brethren: flesh and blood C inherit the kingdom of
2Cor 12:4 he heard things that C be told, which man
13:8 For we C do anything against the truth, but
Phil 1:22 I shall choose I C tell.
Col 3:11 Here there C be Greek and Jew, circumcised and
1Tim 5:25 they are not, they C remain hidden.
6:7 the world, and we C take anything out of
2Tim 2:13 faithful-- for he C deny himself.

Tit 2:8 and sound speech that C be censured, so that
Heb 9:5 Of these things we C now speak in detail.
9:9 sacrifices are offered which C perfect the conscience
12:27 in order that what C be shaken may remain.
12:28 receiving a kingdom that C be shaken, and thus
Jas 1:12 by God"; for God C be tempted with evil
4:2 And you covet and C obtain; so you fight
1 Jn 3:9 in him, and he C sin because he is
4:20 whom he has seen, C love God whom he
Rev 2:2 endurance, and how you C bear evil men but
9:20 stone and wood, which C either see or hear

CANOPY (10)

2Sam 22:12 darkness around him his C, thick clouds, a gathering
1Kgs 7:6 with pillars, and a C before them.
Jud 10:21 his bed, under a C which was woven with
13:9 and pulled down the C from the posts; after
13:15 and here is the C beneath which he lay
16:19 given her; and the C which she took for
Ps 18:11 covering around him, his C thick clouds dark with
Is 4:5 there will be a C and a pavilion.
Jer 43:10 will spread his royal C over them.
Ezek 41:25 and there was a C of wood in front

CANST (4)

Job 42:2 "I know that thou C do all things, and
Wis 11:23 to all, for thou C do all things, and
14:4 waves, showing that thou C save from every danger,
Hab 1:13 to behold evil and C not look on wrong,

CAPABLE

Wis 8:15 I shall show myself C, and courageous in war.

CAPARISONED

2Mac 3:25 to them a magnificently C horse, with a rider

CAPERNA-UM (16)

Mt 4:13 went and dwelt in C by the sea, in
8:5 As he entered C, a centurion came forward to
11:23 And you, C, will you be exalted to heaven?
17:23 When they came to C, the collectors of the
Mk 1:21 And they went into C; and immediately on the
2:1 when he returned to C after some days, it
9:33 And they came to C; and when he was
Lk 4:23 heard you did at C, do here also in
4:31 he went down to C, a city of Galilee.
7:1 in the hearing of the people he entered C
10:15 And you, C, will you be exalted to heaven?
Jn 2:12 he went down to C, with his mother and
4:46 And at C there was an official whose son
6:17 a boat, and started across the sea to C
6:24 boats and went to C, seeking Jesus.
6:59 said in the synagogue, as he taught at C

CAPHAR-SALAMA

1Mac 7:31 went out to meet Judas in battle near C

CAPHTOR (3)

Deut 2:23 Caphtorim, who came from C, destroyed them and
Jer 47:4 the Philistines, the remnant of the coastland of C
Amos 9:7 and the Philistines from C and the Syrians from

CAPHTORIM (3)

Gen 10:14 Naph-tuhim, Pathrusim, Casluhim (whence came the
Deut 2:23 far as Gaza, the C, who came from Caphtor,
1Chr 1:12 Naph-tuhim, Pathrusim, Casluhim (whence came the

CAPITAL (34)

Ex 25:33 like almonds, each with C and flower, on one
25:33 like almonds, each with C and flower, on the
25:35 and flowers, and a C of one piece with
37:19 like almonds, each with C and flower, on one
37:19 like almonds, each with C and flower, on the
37:21 and flowers, and a C of one piece with
1Kgs 7:16 height of the one C was five cubits, and
7:16 height of the other C was five cubits.
7:17 net for the one C, and a net for
7:17 one capital, and a net for the other C
7:18 network, to cover the C that was upon the
7:18 and he did the same with the other C
7:20 rows round about; and so with the other C
2Kgs 25:17 upon it was a C of bronze; the height
25:17 the height of the C was three cubits; a
25:17 bronze, were upon the C round about.
2Chr 3:15 cubits high, with a C of five cubits on
Ezra 6:2 And in Ecbatana, the C which is in the
Neh 1:1 was in Susa the C,
Esth 1:2 throne in Susa the C,
1:5 present in Susa the C, both great and small,
2:3 harem in Susa the C, under custody of Hegai
2:5 Jew in Susa the C whose name was Mordecai,
2:8 gathered in Susa the C in custody of Hegai,
3:15 and the decree was issued in Susa the C
8:14 and the decree was issued in Susa the C
9:6 In Susa the C itself the Jews slew and
9:11 slain in Susa the C was reported to the
9:12 Esther, "In Susa the C the Jews have slain
Jer 52:22 Upon it was a C of bronze; the height
52:22 height of the one C was five cubits; a
52:22 bronze, were upon the C round about.
Dan 8:2 was in Susa the C, which is in the
1Mac 3:37 departed from Antioch his C in the one hundred

CAPITALS (22)

Ex 25:31 work; its cups, its C, and its flowers shall
25:34 like almonds, with their C and flowers,
25:36 Their C and their branches shall be of one
36:38 He overlaid their C, and their fillets were of
37:17 work; its cups, its C, and its flowers were
37:20 like almonds, with their C and flowers,
37:22 Their C and their branches were of one piece
38:17 the overlaying of their C was also of silver,
38:19 the overlaying of their C and their fillets of
38:28 pillars, and overlaid their C and made fillets for
1Kgs 7:16 He also made two C of molten bronze, to
7:17 chain work for the C upon the tops of
7:19 Now the C that were upon the tops of
7:20 The C were upon the two pillars and also
7:41 two bowls of the C that were on the
7:41 two bowls of the C that were on the
7:42 two bowls of the C that were upon the
2Chr 4:12 bowls, and the two C on the top of
4:12 two bowls of the C that were on the
4:13 two bowls of the C that were upon the
Amos 9:1 he said: "Smite the C until the thresholds shake,
Zeph 2:14 shall lodge in her C; the owl shall hoot

CAPPADOCIA (2)

Acts 2:9 of Mesopotamia, Judea and C, Pontus and Asia,
1Pet 1:1 dispersion in Pontus, Galatia, C, Asia, and Bithynia,

CAPS (4)

Ex 28:40 coats and girdles and C; you shall make them
29:9 with girdles and bind C on them; and the
39:28 fine linen, and the C of fine linen, and
Lev 8:13 with girdles, and bound C on them, as the

CAPTAIN (57)

Gen 37:36 officer of Pharaoh, the C of the guard.
39:1 officer of Pharaoh, the C of the guard, an
40:3 the house of the C of the guard, in
40:4 The C of the guard charged Joseph with them,
41:10 the house of the C of the guard,
41:12 a servant of the C of the guard; and
Num 14:4 "Let us choose a C, and go back to
1Sam 22:2 him; and he became C over them.
22:14 the king's son-in-law, and C over your bodyguard, and
2Kgs 1:9 sent to him a C of fifty men with
1:10 But Elijah answered the C of fifty, "If I
1:11 sent to him another C of fifty men with
1:13 the king sent the C of a third fifty
1:13 And the third C of fifty went up, and
7:2 Then the C on whose hand the king leaned
7:17 king had appointed the C on whose hand he
7:19 the C had answered the man of God, "If
15:25 son of Remaliah, his C, conspired against him with
18:24 you repulse a single C among the least of
25:8 of Babylon—Nebuzaradan, the C of the bodyguard, a
25:10 who were with the C of the guard, broke
25:11 the multitude, Nebuzaradan the C of the guard
25:12 But the C of the guard left some of
25:15 was of gold the C of the guard took
25:18 And the C of the guard took Seraiah the
25:20 And Nebuzaradan the C of the guard took them,
Jud 14:2 city, and set a C over them, as if
Is 3:3 and the elder, the C of fifty and the
36:9 you repulse a single C among the least of
Jer 39:9 Then Nebuzaradan, the C of the guard, carried into
39:10 Nebuzaradan, the C of the guard, left in the
39:11 Jeremiah through Nebuzaradan, the C of the guard,
39:13 So Nebuzaradan the C of the guard, Nebushazban

40:1 LORD after Nebuzaradan the C of the guard had
40:2 The C of the guard took Jeremiah and said
40:5 So the C of the guard gave him an
41:10 Mizpah, whom Nebuzaradan, the C of the guard, had
43:6 person whom Nebuzaradan the C of the guard had
52:12 of Babylon--Nebuzaradan the C of the bodyguard
52:14 who were with the C of the guard, broke
52:15 And Nebuzaradan the C of the guard carried away
52:16 But Nebuzaradan the C of the guard left some
52:19 was of gold the C of the guard took
52:24 And the C of the guard took Seraiah the
52:26 And Nebuzaradan the C of the guard took them,
52:30 of Nebuchadrezzar, Nebuzaradan the C of the guard
Dan 2:14 discretion to Arioch, the C of the king's guard,
2:15 to Arioch, the king's C, "Why is the decree
Jon 1:6 So the C came and said to him, "What
2Mac 3:4 who had been made C of the temple, had
4:28 When Sostratus the C of the citadel kept requesting
5:24 Antiochus sent Apollonius, the C of the Mysians, with
Jn 18:12 of soldiers and their C and the officers of
Acts 4:1 the priests and the C of the temple and
5:24 Now when the C of the temple and the
5:26 Then the C with the officers went and brought
27:11 more attention to the C and to the owner

CAPTAINS (29)

Num 31:48 of the army, the C of thousands and the
31:48 of thousands and the C of hundreds, came near
2Sam 4:2 two men who were C of raiding bands; the
1Kgs 9:22 his commanders, his C, his chariot commanders and
22:31 commanded the thirty-two C of his chariots, "Fight
22:32 And when the C of the chariots saw Jehoshaphat,
22:33 And when the C of the chariots saw that
2Kgs 1:14 consumed the two former C of fifty men with
11:4 sent and brought the C of the Carites and
11:9 The C did according to all that Jehoiada the
11:10 priest delivered to the C the spears and shields
11:14 the custom, and the C and the trumpeters beside
11:15 the priest commanded the C who were set over
11:19 And he took the C, the Carites, the guards,
25:23 Now when all the C of the forces in
25:26 and great, and the C of the forces arose,
2Chr 18:30 Syria had commanded the C of his chariots, "Fight
18:31 And when the C of the chariots saw Jehoshaphat,
18:32 him, for when the C of the chariots saw
23:9 priest delivered to the C the spears and the
23:13 the entrance, and the C and the trumpeters beside
23:14 priest brought out the C who were set over
23:20 And he took the C, the nobles, the governors
Jud 14:12 the generals and the C and to all their
Job 39:25 the thunder of the C, and the shouting.
Jer 40:7 When all the C of the forces in the
1Mac 16:19 sent letters to the C asking them to come
2Mac 12:19 Sosipater, who were C under Maccabeus, marched
Rev 19:18 kings, the flesh of C, the flesh of mighty

CAPTIVATED

Jud 16:9 his eyes, her beauty C his mind, and the

CAPTIVE (63)

Gen 14:14 kinsman had been taken C, he led forth his
Ex 12:29 the first-born of the C who was in the
Num 21:1 fought against Israel, and took some of them C
24:22 How long shall Asshur take you away C
31:9 people of Israel took C the women of Midian
Deut 21:10 and you take them C,
21:13 shall put off her C's garb, and shall remain
1Sam 30:2 with fire, and taken C the women and all
30:3 and their wives and sons and daughters taken C
30:5 also had been taken C, Ahino-am of Jezreel, and
1Kgs 8:46 they are carried away C to the land of
8:47 they have been carried C, and repent, and make
8:48 enemies, who carried them C, and pray to thee
8:50 those who carried them C, that they may have
2Kgs 6:22 whom you have taken C with your sword and
15:29 he carried the people C to Assyria.
16:9 it, carrying its people C to Kir, and he
24:16 king of Babylon brought C to Babylon all the
1Chr 3:17 sons of Jeconiah, the C: Shealtiel his son,
2Chr 6:36 they are carried away C to a land far
6:37 they have been carried C, and repent, and make
6:38 which they were carried C, and pray toward their
28:5 defeated him and took C a great number of
28:8 men of Israel took C two hundred thousand of
Ezra 2:1 of Babylon had carried C to Babylonia; they returned
Tob 1:10 I was carried away C to Nineveh, all my
Jud 2:9 will lead them away C to the ends of
5:18 and were led away C to a foreign country;
Ps 106:46 be pitied by all those who held them C
Prov 11:6 the treacherous are taken C by their lust.
Song 7:5 a king is held C in the tresses.
Sir 31:7 fool will be taken C by it.
48:15 they were carried away C from their land and
Is 14:2 slaves; they will take C those who were their
52:2 the dust, arise, O C Jerusalem; loose the bonds
52:2 from your neck, O C daughter of Zion.
Jer 13:17 tears, because the LORD's flock has been taken C
20:4 he shall carry them C to Babylon, and shall
22:12 they have carried him C, there shall he die,
41:10 Then Ishmael took C all the rest of the
41:10 of Nethaniah took them C and set out to
41:14 Ishmael had carried away C from Mizpah turned
41:16 Nethaniah had carried away C from Mizpah after he
43:12 and carry them away C; and he shall clean
48:46 sons have been taken C, and your daughters into
50:33 all who took them C have held them fast,
52:15 the guard carried away C some of the poorest
52:27 So Judah was carried C out of its land.
52:28 Nebuchadrezzar carried away C: in the seventh year,
52:29 he carried away C from Jerusalem eight hundred
52:30 the guard carried away C of the Jews seven
Ezek 6:9 where they are carried C, when I have broken
32:9 when I carry you C among the nations, into
1Mac 1:32 And they took C the women and children, and
8:10 and the Romans took C their wives and children;
10:33 Jews taken as a C from the land of
15:40 and take the people C and kill them.
2Mac 1:19 fathers were being led C to Persia, the pious
Lk 21:24 sword, and be led C among all nations; and
Rom 7:6 that which held us C, so that we serve
7:23 mind and making me C to the law of
2Cor 10:5 and take every thought C to obey Christ,
Rev 13:10 is to be taken C, to captivity he goes;

CAPTIVES (35)

Gen 31:26 away my daughters like C of the sword?
Num 21:29 fugitives, and his daughters C, to an Amorite king,
31:12 Then they brought the C and the booty and
31:19 purify yourselves and your C on the third day
Deut 21:11 and see among the C a beautiful woman, and
32:42 the slain and the C, from the long-haired heads
Judg 5:12 Barak, lead away your C, O son of Abino-am.
2Kgs 24:14 of valor, ten thousand C, and all the craftsmen
2Chr 28:11 and send back the C from your kinsfolk whom
28:13 shall not bring the C in here, for you
28:14 armed men left the C and the spoil before
28:15 rose and took the C, and with the spoil
28:17 invaded and defeated Judah, and carried away C
Neh 4:4 be plundered in a land where they are C
Tob 7:3 of Naphtali, who are C in Nineveh."
13:10 within you who are C, and love those within
Esth 2:6 Jerusalem among the C carried away with Jeconiah
11:4 was one of the C whom Nebuchadnezzar king of
Ps 68:18 the high mount, leading C in thy train, and
Wis 17:2 they themselves lay as C of darkness and prisoners
Is 20:4 lead away the Egyptians C and the Ethiopians exiles,
49:24 the mighty, or the C of a tyrant be
49:25 the LORD: "Even the C of the mighty shall
61:1 proclaim liberty to the C, and the opening of
Jer 40:1 along with all the C of Jerusalem and Judah
Lam 1:5 children have gone away, C before the foe.
Bar 6:1 taken to Babylon as C by the king of
6:2 taken to Babylon as C by Nebuchadnezzar, king of
Hab 1:9 They gather C like sand.
Zech 9:11 I will set your C free from the waterless
1Mac 9:70 peace with him and obtain release of the C
9:72 restored to him the C whom he had formerly
14:7 gathered a host of C; he ruled over Gazara
Lk 4:18 proclaim release to the C and recovering of sight
Eph 4:8 led a host of C, and he gave gifts

CAPTIVITY (45)

Deut 28:41 not be yours; for they shall go into C
Judg 18:30 the day of the C of the land.
2Kgs 24:15 land, he took into C from Jerusalem to Babylon.
2Chr 6:37 the land of their C, saying, 'We have sinned,
6:38 the land of their C, to which they were
29:9 our wives are in C for this.
Ezra 2:1 up out of the C of those exiles whom
3:8 all who had come to Jerusalem from the C
8:35 who had come from C, the returned exiles, offered
9:7 to the sword, to C, to plundering, and to

Neh 7:6 up out of the C of those exiles whom
8:17 had returned from the C made booths and dwelt
Tob 1:2 Assyrians, was taken into C from Thisbe, which is
3:4 us over to plunder, C, and death; thou madest
3:15 of my father in the land of my C
13:6 the land of my C, and I show his
14:5 the places of their C, and will rebuild Jerusalem
Jud 4:3 recently returned from the C, and all the people
8:22 our brethren and the C of the land and
9:4 and their daughters to C, and all their booty
Ps 78:61 delivered his power to C, his glory to the
Is 46:2 cannot save the burden, but themselves go into C
Jer 1:3 of Judah, until the C of Jerusalem in the
15:2 those who are for C, to captivity.'"
15:2 are for captivity, to C
20:6 house, shall go into C; to Babylon you shall
22:22 lovers shall go into C; then you will be
30:10 and your offspring from the land of their C
30:16 them, shall go into C; those who despoil you
43:11 to the pestilence, to C those who are doomed
43:11 who are doomed to C, and to the sword
46:27 and your offspring from the land of their C
48:46 have been taken captive, and your daughters into C
52:31 thirty-seventh year of the C of Jehoiachin king of
Lam 1:18 maidens and my young men have gone into C
Bar 4:10 I have seen the C of my sons and
Ezek 12:11 go into exile, into C
30:17 the sword; and the women shall go into C
30:18 a cloud, and her daughters shall go into C
39:23 of Israel went into C for their iniquity, because
Dan 11:33 sword and flame, by C and plunder, for some
Amos 9:4 though they go into C before their enemies, there
Nah 3:10 away, she went into C; her little ones were
1Mac 2:9 honor; her glorious vessels have been carried into C
Rev 13:10 be taken captive, to C he goes; if any

CAPTORS (5)

1Kgs 8:47 the land of their C, saying, 'We have sinned,
2Chr 30:9 find compassion with their C, and return to this
Ps 137:3 For there our C required of us songs, and
Is 14:2 those who were their C, and rule over those
Mic 2:4 Among our C he divides our fields."

CAPTURE (14)

1Sam 23:26 and his men to C them,
Jud 10:13 he can go and C all the hill country
Prov 6:25 do not let her C you with her eyelashes;
Jer 50:46 the sound of the C of Babylon the earth
Bar 4:14 Zion come; remember the C of my sons and
4:24 have now seen your C, so they soon will
1Mac 5:11 preparing to come and C the stronghold to which
5:30 engines of war to C the stronghold, and attacking
9:58 back, and he will C them all in one
2Mac 8:36 the Romans by the C of the people of
14:41 troops were about to C the tower and were
Mt 26:55 swords and clubs to C me?
Mk 14:48 swords and clubs to C me?
2Tim 3:6 way into households and C weak women, burdened

CAPTURED (43)

Gen 34:29 in the houses, they C and made their prey.
Deut 2:34 And we C all his cities at that time
2:35 with the booty of the cities which we C
1Sam 4:11 ark of God was C; and the two sons
4:17 dead, and the ark of God has been C
4:19 ark of God was C, and that her father-in-law
4:21 of God had been C and because of her
4:22 Israel, for the ark of God has been C
5:1 When the Philistines C the ark of God, they
30:20 David also C all the flocks and herds; and
1Kgs 9:16 had gone up and C Gezer and burnt it
20:21 Israel went out, and C the horses and chariots,
2Kgs 14:13 Jehoash king of Israel C Amaziah king of Judah,
15:29 came and C Ijon, Abel-beth-maacah, Jan-oah,
17:6 the king of Assyria C Samaria, and he carried
25:6 Then they C the king, and brought him up
2Chr 22:9 Ahaziah, and he was C while hiding in Samaria,
25:12 The men of Judah C another ten thousand alive,
25:23 Joash king of Israel C Amaziah king of Judah,
Neh 9:25 And they C fortified cities and a rich land,
Tob 14:15 destruction of Nineveh, which Nebuchadnezzar and
Jud 1:14 and came to Ecbatana, C its towers, plundered its
1:15 He C Arphaxad in the mountains of Ragae and
5:18 and their cities were C by their enemies.
7:28 for us to be C by them; for we
8:21 For if we are C all Judea will be
8:21 all Judea will be C and our sanctuary will
10:13 one of his men, C or slain."
Is 22:3 have fled together, without the bow they were C
22:3 who were found were C, though they had fled
Jer 34:3 but shall surely be C and delivered into his
52:9 Then they C the king, and brought him up
Ezek 21:23 their guilt to remembrance, that they may be C
1Mac 1:19 And they C the fortified cities in the land
5:13 killed; the enemy have C their wives and children
11:56 And Trypho C the elephants and gained control of
13:43 city, and battered and C one tower.
2Mac 8:6 He C strategic positions and put to flight not
8:10 talents, by selling the C Jews into slavery.
8:25 They C the money of those who had come
10:22 turned traitor, and immediately C the two towers.
2Tim 2:26 the devil, after being C by him to do
Rev 19:20 And the beast was C, and with it the

CAPTURING

Josh 19:47 against Leshem, and after C it and putting it

CARAVAN (2)

Gen 37:25 up they saw a C of Ishmaelites coming from
Judg 8:11 went up by the C route east of Nobah

CARAVANS (4)

Judg 5:6 the days of Jael, C ceased and travelers kept
Job 6:18 The C turn aside from their course; they go
6:19 The C of Tema look, the travelers of Sheba
Is 21:13 you will lodge, O C of Dedanites.

CARBUNCLE (3)

Ex 28:17 of sardius, topaz, and C shall be the first
39:10 of sardius, topaz, and C was the first row;
Ezek 28:13 beryl, and onyx, sapphire, C, and emerald; and

CARBUNCLES

Is 54:12 agate, your gates of C, and all your wall

CARCASS (18)

Lev 5:2 unclean thing, whether the C of an unclean beast
5:2 unclean beast or a C of unclean cattle or
5:2 unclean cattle or a C of unclean swarming things,
11:24 unclean; whoever touches their C shall be unclean
11:25 any part of their C shall wash his clothes
11:27 you; whoever touches their C shall be unclean until
11:28 he who carries their C shall wash his clothes
11:35 any part of their C falls shall be unclean;
11:36 but whatever touches their C shall be unclean.
11:37 any part of their C falls upon any seed
11:38 any part of their C falls on it, it
11:39 he who touches its C shall be unclean until
11:40 who eats of its C shall wash his clothes
11:40 also who carries the C shall wash his clothes
Judg 14:8 aside to see the C of the lion, and
14:9 the honey from the C of the lion.
Ps 89:10 crush Rahab like a C, thou didst scatter thy
Ezek 32:5 the mountains, and fill the valleys with your C

CARCASSES (5)

Gen 15:11 came down upon the C, Abram drove them away.
Lev 11:8 not eat, and their C you shall not touch;
11:11 not eat, and their C you shall have in
Deut 14:8 not eat, and their C you shall not touch.
Jer 16:18 my land with the C of their detestable idols,

CARCHEMISH (3)

2Chr 35:20 up to fight at C on the Euphrates and
Is 10:9 Is not Calno like C
Jer 46:2 the river Euphrates at C and which Nebuchadrezzar

CARE (63)

Gen 33:13 giving suck are a C to me; and if
39:22 prison committed to Joseph's C all the prisoners who
39:23 that was in Joseph's C, because the LORD was
Num 7:9 were charged with the C of the holy things
Josh 22:5 Take good C to observe the commandment and the
Judg 2:22 whether they will take C to walk in the
19:20 to you; I will C for all your wants;
1Sam 9:5 my father cease to C about the asses and
10:2 father has ceased to C about the asses and
25:29 the living in the C of the LORD your
2Sam 18:3 flee, they will not C about us.
18:3 die, they will not C about us.
20:3 he had left to C for the house, and
1Chr 15:13 because we did not C for it in the

23:28 the LORD, having the C of the courts and
26:28 gifts were in the C of Shelomoth and his
29:8 the LORD, in the C of Jehiel the Gershonite.
2Chr 13:11 of pure gold, and C for the golden lampstand
Ezra 4:22 And take C not to be slack in this
Tob 2:10 Ahikar, however, took C of me until he went
Jud 2:13 And you--take C not to transgress any of
12:11 who is in your C to join us and
Esth 16:8 future we will take C to render our kingdom
Job 10:12 steadfast love; and thy C has preserved my spirit.
21:21 For what do they C for their houses after
Ps 8:4 man that thou dost C for him?
Eccl 12:9 and studying and arranging proverbs with great C
Wis 5:15 the Most High takes C of them.
6:15 soon be free from C,
7:4 I was nursed with C in swaddling cloths.
12:13 god besides thee, whose C is for all men,
12:20 punish with such great C and indulgence the enemies
13:13 takes and carves with C in his leisure, and
Sir 13:5 will drain your resources and he will not C
13:8 Take C not to be led astray, and not
18:18 you fall ill, take C of your health.
32:1 of them; take good C of them and then
38:15 he fall into the C of a physician.
Jer 2:10 Kedar and examine with C; see if there has
23:2 concerning the shepherds who C for my people: "You
23:4 over them who will C for them, and they
30:14 have forgotten you; they C nothing for you; for
Lam 2:20 eat their offspring, the children of their tender C
Bar 6:5 So take C not to become at all like
Zech 11:16 shepherd who does not C for the perishing, or
1Mac 3:33 was also to take C of Antiochus his son
11:37 Now therefore take C to make a copy of
2Mac 7:27 life, and have taken C of you.
Mt 22:16 of God truthfully, and C for no man; for
Mk 4:38 "Teacher, do you not C if we perish?"
12:14 you are true, and C for no man; for
Lk 10:34 an inn, and took C of him.
10:35 the innkeeper, saying, 'Take C of him; and whatever
10:40 "Lord, do you not C that my sister has
Acts 5:35 "Men of Israel, take C what you do with
20:28 made you overseers, to C for the church of
1Cor 3:10 Let each man take C how he builds upon
8:9 Only take C lest this liberty of yours somehow
12:25 may have the same C for one another.
2Cor 8:16 puts the same earnest C for you into the
1Thes 2:7 like a nurse taking C of her children.
1Tim 3:5 household, how can he C for God's church?
Heb 3:12 Take C, brethren, lest there be in any of

CARED (5)

Deut 32:10 he encircled him, he C for him, he kept
Esth 4:8 lowliness, when you were C for by me, because
Sir 49:15 and his bones are C for.
Jn 12:6 said, not that he C for the poor but
Acts 27:3 his friends and be C for.

CAREFREE

Ezek 23:42 The sound of a C multitude was with her;

CAREFUL (47)

Deut 5:1 learn them and be C to do them.
5:32 possess.' You shall be C to do therefore as
6:3 O Israel, and be C to do them; that
6:25 us, if we are C to do all this
7:11 You shall therefore be C to do the commandment,
8:1 day you shall be C to do, that you
11:22 if you will be C to do all this
11:32 it, you shall be C to do all the
12:1 which you shall be C to do in the
12:28 Be C to heed all these words which I
12:32 you, you shall be C to do; you shall
15:5 LORD your God, being C to do all this
16:12 and you shall be C to observe these statutes.
17:10 and you shall be C to do according to
19:9 provided you are C to keep all this
23:23 You shall be C to perform what has passed
24:8 leprosy, to be very C to do according to
24:8 so you shall be C to do.
26:16 you shall therefore be C to do them with
28:1 LORD your God, being C to do all his
28:13 you this day, being C to do them,
28:15 your God or be C to do all his
28:58 "If you are not C to do all the
29:9 Therefore be C to do the words of this
31:12 your God, and be C to do all the
32:46 that they may be C to do all the
Josh 1:7 and very courageous, being C to do according to
1:8 that you may be C to do according to
22:3 day, but have been C to keep the charge
2Kgs 10:31 But Jehu was not C to walk in the
17:37 you shall always be C to do.
21:8 only they will be C to do according to
1Chr 22:13 prosper if you are C to observe the statutes
2Chr 33:8 only they will be C to do all that
Sir 37:31 but he who is C to avoid it prolongs
38:26 furrows, and he is C about fodder for the
38:27 image, and he is C to finish his work.
38:28 handiwork, and he is C to complete its decoration.
38:30 glazing, and he is C to clean the furnace.
Ezek 18:9 my statutes, and is C to observe my ordinances
18:19 right, and has been C to observe all my
20:19 my statutes, and be C to observe my ordinances,
20:21 statutes, and were not C to observe my ordinances,
36:27 my statutes and be C to observe my ordinances.
37:24 my ordinances and be C to observe my statutes.
Lk 11:35 Therefore be C lest the light in you be
Tit 3:8 in God may be C to apply themselves to

CAREFULLY (6)

Gen 43:7 "The man questioned us C about ourselves and our
Job 13:17 Listen C to my words, and let my declaration
21:2 Then Job answered: "Listen C to my words, and
Prov 23:1 with a ruler, observe C what is before you;
2Mac 8:31 they stored them all C in strategic places, and
Eph 5:15 Look C then how you walk, not as unwise

CARELESS (2)

Prov 14:16 but a fool throws off restraint and is C
Mt 12:36 render account for every C word they utter;

CARES (14)

Deut 11:12 the LORD your God C for; the eyes of
Ps 94:19 When the C of my heart are many, thy
142:4 to me, no man C for me.
Wis 8:9 counsel and encouragement in C and grief.
Jer 22:28 a vessel no one C for?
30:17 for whom no one C
48:38 for which no one C, says the LORD.
Zech 10:3 the LORD of hosts C for his flock, the
Mt 13:22 the word, but the C of the world and
Mk 4:19 the word, but the C of the world, and
Lk 8:14 are choked by the C and riches and pleasures
21:34 dissipation and drunkenness and C of this life, and
Jn 10:13 is a hireling and C nothing for the sheep.
1Pet 5:7 on him, for he C about you.

CAREST

Heb 2:6 of man, that thou C for him?

CARGO (5)

Acts 21:3 for there the ship was to unload its C
27:10 not only of the C and the ship, but
27:18 day to throw the C overboard;
Rev 18:11 no one buys their C any more,
18:12 their cargo any more, C of gold, silver, jewels

CARIA

1Mac 15:23 to Sicyon, and to C, and to Samos, and

CARING

2Mac 11:23 kingdom be undisturbed in C for their own affairs.

CARITES (2)

2Kgs 11:4 the captains of the C and of the guards,
11:19 took the captains, the C, the guards, and all

CARKAS

Esth 1:10 and Abagtha, Zethar and C, the seven eunuchs who

CARMEL (29)

Josh 12:22 king of Jokne-am in C, one;
15:55 Maon, C, Ziph, Juttah,
19:26 the west it touches C and Shihor-libnath,
1Sam 15:12 Samuel, "Saul came to C, and behold, he set
25:2 a man in Maon, whose business was in C
25:2 He was shearing his sheep in C
25:5 men, "Go up to C, and go to Nabal,
25:7 missed nothing, all the time they were in C
25:40 came to Abigail at C, they said to her,
27:3 Jezreel, and Abigail of C, Nabal's widow.
30:5 Jezreel, and Abigail the widow of Nabal of C

2Sam 2:2 Jezreel, and Abigail the widow of Nabal of C
3:3 widow of Nabal of C; and the third, Absalom
23:35 of Gilo, Hezro of C, Paarai the Arbite,
1Kgs 18:19 to me at Mount C, and the four hundred
18:20 and gathered the prophets together at Mount C
18:42 to the top of C; and he bowed himself
2Kgs 2:25 went on to Mount C, and thence he returned
4:25 came to the man of God at Mount C
1Chr 11:37 the Pelonite, Hezro of C, Naarai the son of
Jud 1:8 among the nations of C and Gilead, and Upper
Song 7:5 head crowns you like C, and your flowing locks
Is 33:9 desert; and Bashan and C shake off their leaves.
35:2 it, the majesty of C and Sharon.
Jer 46:18 the mountains, and like C by the sea, shall
50:19 he shall feed on C and in Bashan, and
Amos 1:2 and the top of C withers."
9:3 on the top of C, from there I will
Nah 1:4 the rivers; Bashan and C wither, the bloom of

CARMELITESS
1Chr 3:1 Daniel, by Abigail the C,

CARMI (8)
Gen 46:9 the sons of Reuben: Hanoch, Pallu, Hezron, and C
Ex 6:14 Hanoch, Pallu, Hezron, and C; these are the families
Num 26:6 of the Hezronites; of C, the family of the
Josh 7:1 Achan the son of C, son of Zabdi, son
7:18 Achan the son of C, son of Zabdi, son
1Chr 2:7 The sons of C: Achar, the troubler of Israel,
4:1 of Judah: Perez, Hezron, C, Hur, and Shobal.
5:3 the first-born of Israel: Hanoch, Pallu, Hezron, and C

CARMITES
Num 26:6 the Hezronites; of Carmi, the family of the C

CARNAIM (5)
1Mac 5:26 and Bosor, in Alema and Chaspho, Maked and C
5:43 arms and fled into the sacred precincts at C
5:44 Thus C was conquered; they could stand before Judas
2Mac 12:21 to a place called C; for that place was
12:26 Then Judas marched against C and the temple of

CARNAL
Rom 7:14 spiritual; but I am C, sold under sin.

CARNALLY (3)
Lev 18:20 you shall not lie C with your neighbor's wife,
19:20 "If a man lies C with a woman who
Num 5:13 man lies with her C, and it is hidden

CARNELIAN (3)
Ezek 28:13 stone was your covering, C, topaz, and jasper,
Rev 4:3 appeared like jasper and C, and round the throne
21:20 fifth onyx, the sixth C, the seventh chrysolite, the

CAROUSE
Jude 1:12 feasts, as they boldly C together, looking after

CAROUSING (3)
Gal 5:21 party spirit, envy, drunkenness, C, and the like.
1Pet 4:3 passions, drunkenness, revels, C, and lawless idol
2Pet 2:13 reveling in their dissipation, C with you.

CARPENTER (3)
Is 44:13 The C stretches a line, he marks it out
Mt 13:55 Is not this the C's son?
Mk 6:3 Is not this the C, the son of Mary

CARPENTERS (9)
2Sam 5:11 and cedar trees, also C and masons who built
2Kgs 12:11 it out to the C and the builders who
22:6 that is, to the C, and to the builders,
1Chr 14:1 trees, also masons and C to build a house
22:15 of workmen: stonecutters, masons, C, and all kinds of
2Chr 24:12 they hired masons and C to restore the house
34:11 gave it to the C and the builders to
Ezra 3:7 the masons and the C, and food, drink, and
Bar 6:45 They are made by C and goldsmiths; they can

CARPETS (2)
Judg 5:10 who sit on rich C and you who walk
Ezek 27:24 embroidered work, and in C of colored stuff, bound

CARPUS
2Tim 4:13 that I left with C at Troas, also the

CARRIED (164)
Gen 31:26 have cheated me, and C away my daughters like
46:5 the sons of Israel C Jacob their father, their
50:13 them; for his sons C him to the land
Ex 25:28 the table shall be C with these.
27:7 two sides of the altar, when it is C
Lev 10:5 they drew near, and C them in their coats
16:27 holy place, shall be C forth outside the camp;
Num 7:9 which had to be C on the shoulder.
10:17 sons of Merari, who C the tabernacle, set out.
13:23 of grapes, and they C it on a pole
Deut 31:9 sons of Levi, who C the ark of the
31:25 commanded the Levites who C the ark of the
Josh 3:3 LORD your God being C by the Levitical priests,
4:8 told Joshua; and they C them over with them
8:33 the Levitical priests who C the ark of the
Judg 3:18 away the people that C the tribute.
16:3 on his shoulders and C them to the top
21:23 the dancers whom they C off; then they went
1Sam 5:1 ark of God, they C it from Ebenezer to
30:2 killed no one, but C them off, and went
2Sam 5:21 David and his men C them away.
6:3 And they C the ark of God upon a
8:7 of gold which were C by the servants of
15:29 So Zadok and Abiathar C the ark of God
20:12 the people stopped, he C Amasa out of the
1Kgs 5:16 of the people who C on the work.
8:46 so that they are C away captive to the
8:47 which they have been C captive, and repent, and
8:48 of their enemies, who C them captive, and pray
8:50 sight of those who C them captive, that they
9:23 of the people who C on the work.
15:22 was exempt, and they C away the stones of
17:19 from her bosom, and C him up into the
2Kgs 5:2 of their raids had C off a little maid
5:23 his servants; and they C them before Gehazi.
7:8 and drank, and they C off silver and gold
7:8 entered another tent, and C off things from it,
9:28 His servants C him in a chariot to Jerusalem,
15:29 of Naphtali; and he C the people captive to
17:6 captured Samaria, and he C the Israelites away to
17:11 did whom the LORD C away before them.
17:26 nations which you have C away and placed in
17:27 the priests whom you C away thence; and let
17:28 priests whom they had C away from Samaria came
17:33 whom they had been C away.
18:11 The king of Assyria C the Israelites away to
20:17 this day, shall be C to Babylon; nothing shall
23:4 of the Kidron, and C their ashes to Bethel.
23:30 And his servants C him dead in a chariot
24:13 of his reign, and C off all the treasures
24:14 He C away all Jerusalem, and all the princes,
24:15 And he C away Jehoiachin to Babylon; the king's
25:11 captain of the guard C into exile.
25:13 broke in pieces, and C the bronze to Babylon.
1Chr 5:6 Tilgath-pilneser king of Assyria C away into exile; he
5:18 had valiant men, who C shield and sword, and
5:21 They C off their livestock: fifty thousand of their
5:26 of Assyria, and he C them away, namely, the
8:6 Geba, and they were C into exile to Manahath):
13:7 And they C the ark of God upon a
15:15 And the Levites C the ark of God upon
18:7 of gold which were C by the servants of
18:11 gold which he had C off from all the
2Chr 6:36 so that they are C away captive to a
6:37 which they have been C captive, and repent, and
6:38 to which they were C captive, and pray toward
14:8 men from Benjamin, that C shields and drew bows;
14:13 The men of Judah C away very much booty.
14:15 who had cattle, and C away sheep in abundance
16:6 all Judah, and they C away the stones of
21:17 and invaded it, and C away all the possessions
28:17 and defeated Judah, and C away captives.
29:16 Levites took it and C it out to the
33:14 the Fish Gate, and C it round Ophel, and
35:13 and in pans, and C them quickly to all
35:24 of the chariot and C him in his second
36:4 Jehoahaz his brother and C him to Egypt.
36:7 Nebuchadnezzar also C part of the vessels of the
Ezra 1:7 LORD which Nebuchadnezzar had C away from
2:1 king of Babylon had C captive to Babylonia; they
5:12 destroyed this house and C away the people to
Neh 4:17 Those who C burdens were laden in such a
7:6 king of Babylon had C into exile; they returned
Tob 1:10 Now when I was C away captive to Nineveh,
Jud 10:22 tent, with silver lamps C before him.

Esth 2:6 Benjaminite, who had been C away from Jerusalem
2:6 Jerusalem among the captives C away with Jeconiah
2:6 king of Babylon had C away.
16:4 from among men, but, C away by the boasts
Job 10:19 I had not been, C from the womb to
20:28 his house will be C away, dragged off in
24:18 say, "They are swiftly C away upon the face
Wis 5:14 man is like chaff C by the wind, and
Sir 48:15 sins, till they were C away captive from their
Is 8:4 of Samaria will be C away before the king
23:7 of old, whose feet C her to settle afar?
39:6 this day, shall be C to Babylon; nothing shall
46:3 me from your birth, C from the womb;
49:22 your daughters shall be C on their shoulders.
53:4 borne our griefs and C our sorrows; yet we
60:4 your daughters shall be C in the arms.
63:9 lifted them up and C them all the days
66:12 suck, you shall be C upon her hip, and
Jer 10:5 they have to be C, for they cannot walk.
22:12 place where they have C him captive, there shall
27:22 Jerusalem: They shall be C to Babylon and remain
28:3 from this place and C to Babylon.
39:9 captain of the guard, C into exile to Babylon
41:14 people whom Ishmael had C away captive from
41:16 son of Nethaniah had C away captive from Mizpah
52:15 captain of the guard C away captive some of
52:17 broke in pieces, and C all the bronze to
52:27 So Judah was C captive out of its land.
52:28 the people whom Nebuchadrezzar C away captive:
52:29 year of Nebuchadrezzar he C away captive from
52:30 captain of the guard C away captive of the
Lam 2:17 what he purposed, has C out his threat; as
Bar 1:8 Lord, which had been C away from the temple,
1:9 of Babylon had C away from Jerusalem Jeconiah
2:14 of those who have C us into exile;
4:26 away like a flock C off by the enemy.
5:6 them back to you, C in glory, as on
6:4 and wood, which are C on men's shoulders and
6:26 no feet, they are C on men's shoulders, revealing
Ezek 6:9 nations where they are C captive, when I have
17:4 its young twigs and C it to a land
23:14 But she C her harlotry further; she saw men
23:18 When she C on her harlotry so openly and
30:4 and her wealth is C away, and her foundations
Dan 2:35 floors; and the wind C them away, so that
Hos 10:6 thing itself shall be C to Assyria, as tribute
12:1 Assyria, and oil is C to Egypt.
Joel 3:5 my gold, and have C my rich treasures into
Amos 1:6 the punishment; because they C into exile a whole
4:10 with the sword; I C away your horses; and
Obad 1:11 the day that strangers C off his wealth, and
Nah 2:7 is stripped, she is C off, her maidens lamenting,
3:10 Yet she was C away, she went into captivity;
1Mac 2:9 glorious vessels have been C into captivity.
4:30 of the man who C his armor.
2Mac 3:28 on a stretcher and C him away, this man
4:19 Those who C the money, however, thought best not
5:21 So Antiochus C off eighteen hundred talents from
7:27 I C you nine months in my womb, and
8:31 in strategic places, and C the rest of the
9:8 down to earth and C in a litter, making
Mk 2:3 to him a paralytic C by four men.
Lk 7:12 had died was being C out, the only son
16:22 man died and was C by the angels to
24:51 from them, and was C up into heaven.
Jn 20:15 "Sir, if you have C him away, tell me
Acts 3:2 from birth was being C, whom they laid daily
5:6 wrapped him up and C him out and buried
5:10 her dead, and they C her out and buried
5:15 so that they even C out the sick into
7:16 fathers, and they were C back to Shechem and
19:12 handkerchiefs or aprons were C away from his body
21:35 steps, he was actually C by the soldiers because
Gal 2:13 that even Barnabas was C away by their insincerity.
Eph 4:14 to and fro and C about with every wind
2Pet 3:17 beware lest you be C away with the error
Jude 1:12 waterless clouds, C along by winds; fruitless
Rev 17:3 And he C me away in the Spirit into
21:10 in the Spirit he C me away to a

CARRIERS

2Mac 4:20 the decision of its C it was applied to

CARRIES (14)

Lev 11:25 the evening, and whoever C any part of their
11:28 evening, and he who C their carcass shall wash
11:40 evening; he also who C the carcass shall wash
15:10 evening; and he who C such a thing shall
Num 11:12 bosom, as a nurse C the sucking child, to
Jud 12:4 me before the Lord C out by my hand
Job 21:18 chaff that the storm C away?
27:20 the night a whirlwind C him off.
Ps 37:7 over the man who C out evil devices!
Wis 14:1 than the ship which C him.
Sir 31:2 and a severe illness C off sleep.
Is 40:24 wither, and the tempest C them off like stubble.
Hag 2:12 this question, 'If one C holy flesh in the
Rev 17:7 and ten horns that C her.

CARRION (2)

Lev 11:18 hen, the pelican, the C vulture,
Deut 14:17 and the pelican, the C vulture and the cormorant,

CARRY (118)

Gen 37:25 on their way to C it down to Egypt.
42:19 the rest go and C grain for the famine
43:11 in your bags, and C down to the man
43:12 the money with you; C back with you the
44:1 much as they can C, and put each man's
45:27 Joseph had sent to C him, the spirit of
46:5 Pharaoh had sent to C him.
47:30 lie with my fathers; C me out of Egypt
50:25 you, and you shall C up my bones from
Ex 12:46 eaten; you shall not C forth any of the
13:19 you; then you must C my bones with you
25:14 of the ark, to C the ark by them.
25:27 for the poles to C the table.
30:4 poles with which to C it.
33:15 with me, do not C us up from here.
37:5 of the ark, to C the ark.
37:14 for the poles to C the table.
37:15 of acacia wood to C the table, and overlaid
37:27 poles with which to C it.
38:7 of the altar, to C it with them; he
Lev 4:12 whole bull he shall C forth outside the camp
4:21 And he shall C forth the bull outside the
6:11 on other garments, and C forth the ashes outside
10:4 to them, "Draw near, C your brethren from before
14:45 house; and he shall C them forth out of
Num 1:50 it; they are to C the tabernacle and all
4:15 Kohath shall come to C these, but they must
4:15 meeting which the sons of Kohath are to C
4:25 bearing burdens: they shall C the curtains of the
4:27 that they are to C, and in all that
4:27 to their charge all that they are to C
4:31 they are charged to C, as the whole of
4:32 name the objects which they are required to C
11:12 shouldst say to me, C them in your bosom,
11:14 am not able to C all this people alone,
16:46 incense on it, and C it quickly to the
Deut 10:8 tribe of Levi to C the ark of the
28:38 You shall C much seed into the field, and
Josh 4:3 priests' feet stood, and C them over with you,
1Sam 17:17 these ten loaves, and C them quickly to the
20:40 to him, "Go and C them to the city."
28:18 LORD, and did not C out his fierce wrath
31:9 of the Philistines, to C the good news to
2Sam 13:13 me, where could I C my shame?
15:25 king said to Zadok, C the ark of God
18:19 "Let me run, and C tidings to the king
18:20 "You are not to C tidings today; you may
18:20 tidings today; you may C tidings another day, but
18:20 but today you shall C no tidings, because the
1Kgs 18:12 of the LORD will C you whither I know
22:34 chariot, "Turn about, and C me out of the
2Kgs 4:19 said to his servant, C him to his mother."
1Chr 10:9 of the Philistines, to C the good news to
15:2 but the Levites may C the ark of God,
15:2 LORD chose them to C the ark of the
15:13 Because you did not C it the first time,
23:26 no longer need to C the tabernacle or any
2Chr 18:33 chariot, "Turn about, and C me out of the
20:25 themselves until they could C no more.
29:5 of your fathers, and C out the filth from
35:3 you need no longer C it upon your shoulders.
Jud 2:13 but be sure to C them out just as
10:5 her vessels and gave them to her to C
13:5 thy inheritance, and to C out my undertaking for
Job 15:12 Why does your heart C you away, and why
24:10 without clothing; hungry, they C the sheaves;
31:36 Surely I would C it on my shoulder; I
Ps 28:9 thou their shepherd, and C them for ever.

	49:17	he dies he will C nothing away; his glory
Prov	6:27	Can a man C fire in his bosom and
Eccl	5:15	toil, which he may C away in his hand.
	10:20	of the air will C your voice, or some
Sir	6:25	shoulder under her and C her, and do not
Is	5:29	seize their prey, they C it off, and none
	15:7	have laid up they C away over the Brook
	30:1	says the LORD, "who C out a plan, but
	30:6	the flying serpent, they C their riches on the
	40:11	his arms, he will C them in his bosom,
	41:16	and the wind shall C them away, and the
	45:20	have no knowledge who C about their wooden idols,
	46:1	cattle; these things you C are loaded as burdens
	46:4	gray hairs I will C you.
	46:4	will bear; I will C and will save.
	46:7	upon their shoulders, they C it, they set it
	57:13	The wind will C them off, a breath will
Jer	17:22	And do not C a burden out of your
	20:4	of Babylon; he shall C them captive to Babylon,
	20:5	and seize them, and C them to Babylon.
	43:12	shall burn them and C them away captive; and
Bar	6:62	the whole world, they C out his command.
Ezek	12:6	upon your shoulder, and C it out in the
	29:19	Babylon; and he shall C off its wealth and
	32:9	many peoples, when I C you captive among the
	38:12	to seize spoil and C off plunder; to assail
	38:13	assembled your hosts to C off plunder, to carry
	38:13	carry off plunder, to C away silver and gold,
Dan	11:8	He shall also C off to Egypt their gods
	11:10	through, and again shall C the war as far
Hos	5:14	go away, I will C off, and none shall
2Mac	3:8	but in fact to C out the king's purpose.
	4:19	citizens from Jerusalem, to C three hundred silver
	4:23	previously mentioned Simon, to C the money to the
	9:10	one was able to C the man who a
	15:17	they determined not to C on a campaign but
	15:23	a good angel to C terror and trembling before
	15:30	head and arm and C them to Jerusalem.
Mt	3:11	am not worthy to C; he will baptize you
	27:32	man they compelled to C his cross.
Mk	11:16	allow any one to C anything through the temple.
	15:21	Alexander and Rufus, to C his cross.
Lk	10:4	C no purse, no bag, no sandals; and salute
	23:25	him the cross, to C it behind Jesus.
Jn	5:9	lawful for you to C your pallet."
	21:18	will gird you and C you where you do
Acts	5:9	door, and they will C you out."
	9:15	instrument of mine to C my name before the
1Cor	16:3	accredit by letter to C your gift to Jerusalem.
Rev	17:17	into their hearts to C out his purpose by

CARRYING (24)

Num	4:10	put it upon the C frame.
	4:12	put them on the C frame.
	4:49	task of serving or C; thus they were numbered
	10:21	the Kohathites set out, C the holy things, and
1Sam	10:3	meet you there, one C three kids, another carrying
	10:3	carrying three kids, another C three loaves of bread,
	10:3	of bread, and another C a skin of wine.
2Kgs	10:30	have done well in C out what is right
	16:9	Damascus, and took it, C its people captive to
1Chr	15:26	the Levites who were C the ark of the
	15:27	the Levites who were C the ark, and the
2Chr	28:15	and anointed them; and C all the feeble among
Jud	2:1	of the Assyrians about C out his revenge on
Esth	15:4	while the other followed C her train.
Wis	18:16	doomed, a stern warrior C the sharp sword of
Ezek	12:7	forth in the dark, C my outfit upon my
1Mac	5:30	could not be counted, C ladders and engines of
2Mac	15:5	did not succeed in C out his abominable design.
Mk	14:13	city, and a man C a jar of water
Lk	22:10	the city, a man C a jar of water
Acts	27:43	Paul, kept them from C out their purpose.
2Cor	4:10	but not destroyed; always C in the body the
	8:19	work which we are C on, for the glory
	10:3	world we are not C on a worldly war,

CARSHENA

Esth	1:14	to him being C, Shethar, Admatha, Tarshish, Meres,

CART (16)

1Sam	6:7	and prepare a new C and two milch cows
	6:7	the cows to the C, but take their calves
	6:8	place it on the C, and put in a
	6:10	yoked them to the C, and shut up their
	6:11	the LORD on the C, and the box with
	6:14	The C came into the field of Joshua of
	6:14	the wood of the C and offered the cows
2Sam	6:3	God upon a new C, and brought it out
	6:3	were driving the new C
1Chr	13:7	God upon a new C, from the house of
	13:7	Abinadab, and Uzzah and Ahio were driving the C
Sir	33:5	fool is like a C wheel, and his thoughts
Is	5:18	draw sin as with C ropes,
	28:27	sledge, nor is a C wheel rolled over cummin;
	28:28	when he drives his C wheel over it with
Amos	2:13	your place, as a C full of sheaves presses

CARTS

Jud	15:11	and hitched up her C and piled the things

CARVE

Is	22:16	on the height, and C a habitation for yourself

CARVED (15)

1Kgs	6:18	within the house was C in the form of
	6:29	He C all the walls of the house round
	6:29	house round about with C figures of cherubim and
	6:35	On them he C cherubim and palm trees and
	6:35	evenly applied upon the C work.
	7:36	on its panels, he C cherubim, lions, and palm
2Chr	3:7	its doors; and he C cherubim on the walls.
Ps	74:6	And then all its C wood they broke down
Ezek	41:17	and the nave were C likenesses
	41:19	They were C on the whole temple round about;
	41:20	and palm trees were C on the wall.
	41:25	of the nave were C cherubim and palm trees,
	41:25	trees, such as were C on the walls; and
1Mac	13:29	the suits of armor C ships, so that they
2Cor	3:7	the dispensation of death, C in letters on stone,

CARVES

Wis	13:13	knots, he takes and C with care in his

CARVING (2)

Ex	31:5	for setting, and in C wood, for work in
	35:33	for setting, and in C wood, for work in

CARVINGS (2)

1Kgs	6:32	doors of olivewood with C of cherubim, palm trees,
	7:31	its opening there were C; and its panels were

CASE (51)

Ex	22:9	'This is it,' the C of both parties shall
Num	8:19	people of Israel in C the people of Israel
	27:5	Moses brought their C before the LORD.
Deut	1:17	is Gods; and the C that is too hard
	17:8	"If any C arises requiring decision between one kind
	17:8	assault and another, any C within your towns which
	22:26	by death, for this C is like that of
Josh	20:4	city, and explain his C to the elders of
2Chr	19:10	whole heart: whenever a C comes to you from
Job	13:3	desire to argue my C with God.
	13:8	will you plead the C for God?
	13:18	I have prepared my C; I know that I
	23:4	I would lay my C before him and fill
	35:14	see him, that the C is before him, and
	37:19	cannot draw up our C because of darkness.
Prov	18:17	He who states his C first seems right, until
	25:9	Argue your C with your neighbor himself, and do
Sir	4:9	and do not be fainthearted in judging a C
	11:9	nor sit with sinners when they judge a C
	35:13	show partiality in the C of a poor man;
	35:19	till he judges the C of his people and
Is	41:21	Set forth your C, says the LORD; bring your
	43:26	together; set forth your C, that you may be
	45:21	Declare and present your C; let them take counsel
Jer	12:1	I would plead my C before thee.
Bar	6:64	either to decide a C or to do good
Ezek	9:2	linen, with a writing C at his side.
	9:3	who had the writing C at his side.
	9:11	linen, with the writing C at his side, brought
Mic	6:1	says: Arise, plead your C before the mountains, and
2Mac	2:8	were shown in the C of Moses, and as
	2:29	my judgment is the C with us.
	3:13	money must in any C be confiscated for the
	4:44	the senate presented the C before him.
	6:14	For in the C of the other nations the
Mt	13:23	and yields, in one C a hundredfold, in another
	19:10	"If such is the C of a man with
Acts	5:38	So in the present C I tell you, keep
	23:15	going to determine his C more exactly.

24:1 before the governor their C against Paul;
24:21 the tribune comes down, I will decide your C
25:14 days, Festus laid Paul's C before the king, saying,
25:18 no charge in his C of such evils as
28:18 no reason for the death penalty in my C
1Cor 7:15 so; in such a C the brother or sister
2Cor 3:10 Indeed, in this C, what once had splendor has
4:4 In their C the god of this world has
9:3 prove vain in this C, so that you may
Gal 5:11 In that C the stumbling block of the cross
Heb 6:9 thus, yet in your C, beloved, we feel sure
1Pet 2:12 Gentiles, so that in C they speak against you

CASES (9)
Ex 18:19 God, and bring their C to God;
18:26 at all times; hard C they brought to Moses,
Num 5:29 is the law in C of jealousy, when a
Deut 1:16 that time, 'Hear the C between your brethren, and
2Chr 19:8 judgment for the LORD and to decide disputed C
Sir 22:20 blow– in these C any friend will flee.
1Cor 6:2 by you, are you incompetent to try trivial C
6:4 then you have such C, why do you lay
Tit 3:14 so as to help C of urgent need, and

CASIPHIA (2)
Ezra 8:17 man at the place C, telling them what to
8:17 servants at the place C, namely, to send us

CASLUHIM (2)
Gen 10:14 Lehabim, Naph-tuhim, Pathrusim, C (whence came
1Chr 1:12 Anamim, Lehabim, Naph-tuhim, Pathrusim, C

CASPIN
2Mac 12:13 Its name was C

CASSIA (4)
Ex 30:24 and fifty, and of C five hundred, according to
Ps 45:8 are all fragrant with myrrh and aloes and C
Sir 24:15 Like C and camel's thorn I gave forth the
Ezek 27:19 wares; wrought iron, C, and calamus were bartered

CAST (300)
Gen 21:10 she said to Abraham, C out this slave woman
21:15 skin was gone, she C the child under one
37:22 them, "Shed no blood; C him into this pit
37:24 they took him and C him into a pit.
39:7 time his master's wife C her eyes upon Joseph,
Ex 1:21 the Hebrews you shall C into the Nile, but
4:3 And he said, C it on the ground." So
4:3 So he C it on the ground, and it
7:9 'Take your rod and C it down before Pharaoh,
7:10 the LORD commanded; Aaron C down his rod before
7:12 For every man C down his rod, and they
15:4 and his host he C into the sea; and
22:31 the field; you shall C it to the dogs.
23:26 None shall C her young or be barren in
25:12 And you shall C four rings of gold for
26:37 gold, and you shall C five bases of bronze
34:24 For I will C out nations before you, and
36:36 of gold, and he C for them four bases
37:3 And he C for it four rings of gold
37:13 He C for it four rings of gold, and
38:5 He C four rings on the four corners of
Lev 1:16 with the feathers, and C it beside the altar
16:8 meeting; and Aaron shall C lots upon the two
26:30 your incense altars, and C your dead bodies upon
Num 19:6 and scarlet stuff, and C them into the midst
35:23 and without seeing him C it upon him, so
Deut 9:17 the two tables, and C them out of my
29:28 and great wrath, and C them into another land,
Josh 8:29 from the tree, and C it at the entrance
18:6 me; and I will C lots for you here
18:8 me; and I will C lots for you here
18:10 at Shiloh, and Joshua C lots for them in
Judg 6:13 now the LORD has C us off, and given
8:25 garment, and every man C in it the earrings
1Sam 12:22 the LORD will not C away his people, for
14:42 Then Saul said, C the lot between me and
18:11 his hand; and Saul C the spear, for he
20:33 But Saul C his spear at him to smite
2Sam 11:21 Did not a woman C an upper millstone upon
20:15 Abel of Beth-maacah; they C up a mound against
1Kgs 7:15 He C two pillars of bronze.
7:24 were in two rows, C with it when it
7:24 two rows, cast with it when it was C
7:30 The supports were C, with wreaths at the side
7:33 rims, their spokes, and their hubs, were all C
7:37 all of them were C alike, of the same
7:46 the Jordan the king C them, in the clay
9:7 my name I will C out of my sight;
14:9 to anger, and have C me behind your back;
19:19 passed by him and C his mantle upon him.
21:26 done, whom the LORD C out before the people
2Kgs 2:16 caught him up and C him upon some mountain
9:25 "Take him up, and C him on the plot
9:26 take him up and C him on the plot
10:25 guard and the officers C them out and went
13:21 and the man was C into the grave of
13:23 them; nor has he C them from his presence
17:20 spoilers, until he had C them out of his
19:18 their lands, and have C their gods into the
19:32 with a shield or C up a siege mound
21:14 And I will C off the remnant of my
23:6 it to dust and C the dust of it
23:12 broke in pieces, and C the dust of them
23:27 Israel, and I will C off this city which
24:20 and Judah that he C them out from his
1Chr 24:31 his younger brother alike, C lots, just as their
25:8 And they C lots for their duties, small and
26:13 the LORD; and they C lots by fathers' houses,
26:14 They C lots also for his son Zechariah, a
28:9 forsake him, he will C you off for ever.
2Chr 4:3 were in two rows, C with it when it
4:3 two rows, cast with it when it was C
4:17 the Jordan the king C them, in the clay
7:20 my name, I will C out of my sight,
11:14 Jeroboam and his sons C them out from serving
25:8 for war, God will C you down before the
25:8 to help or to C down."
32:17 he wrote letters to C contempt on the LORD
Neh 9:11 land; and thou didst C their pursuers into the
9:26 rebelled against thee and C thy law behind their
10:34 We have likewise C lots, the priests, the Levites,
11:1 rest of the people C lots to bring one
Jud 9:8 name rests, and to C down the horn of
Esth 3:7 of King Ahasuerus, they C Pur, that is the
3:7 after day; and they C it month after month
9:24 destroy them, and had C Pur, that is the
Job 6:27 You would even C lots over the fatherless, and
15:33 like the vine, and C off his blossom, like
18:8 For he is C into a net by his
19:3 ten times you have C reproach upon me; are
19:12 on together; they have C up siegeworks against me,
21:10 calves, and does not C her calf.
29:24 countenance they did not C down.
30:11 humbled me, they have C off restraint in my
30:12 drive me forth, they C up against me their
30:19 God has C me into the mire, and I
41:23 flesh cleave together, firmly C upon him and
Ps 2:3 their bonds asunder, and C their cords from us."
5:10 of their many transgressions C them out, for they
17:11 set their eyes to C me to the ground.
18:42 before the wind; I C them out like the
22:10 Upon thee was I C from my birth, and
22:18 for my raiment they C lots.
27:9 C me not off, forsake me not, O God
37:24 he shall not be C headlong, for the LORD
42:5 Why are you C down, O my soul, and
42:6 My soul is C down within me, therefore I
42:11 Why are you C down, O my soul, and
43:2 refuge; why hast thou C me off?
43:5 Why are you C down, O my soul, and
44:9 [Selah] Yet thou hast C us off and abased
44:23 Do not C us off for ever!
50:17 hate discipline, and you C my words behind you.
51:11 C me not away from thy presence, and take
55:22 C your burden on the LORD, and he will
55:23 thou, O God, wilt C them down into the
56:7 their crime; in wrath C down the peoples, O
60:8 washbasin; upon Edom I C my shoe; over Philistia
71:9 Do not C me off in the time of
74:1 God, why dost thou C us off for ever?
88:14 LORD, why dost thou C me off?
89:38 But now thou hast C off and rejected, thou
89:44 from his hand, and C his throne to the
108:9 washbasin; upon Edom I C my shoe; over Philistia
140:10 Let them be C into pits, no more to
Prov 16:33 The lot is C into the lap, but the
21:12 wicked; the wicked are C down to ruin.
29:18 no prophecy the people C off restraint, but blessed
Eccl 3:5 dance; a time to C away stones, and a
3:6 and a time to C away;

11:1 C your bread upon the waters, for you will
Wis 10:19 drowned their enemies, and C them up from the
11:14 long before had been C out and exposed, at
Sir 1:27 reveal your secrets and C you down in the
6:21 not be slow to C her off.
7:26 pleases you, do not C her out; but do
10:14 The Lord has C down the thrones of rulers,
37:8 himself– lest he C the lot against you
Is 2:20 that day men will C forth their idols of
14:19 tomb; but you are C out, away from your
19:8 and lament, all who C hook in the Nile;
22:19 and you will be C down from your station.
25:7 the covering that is C over all peoples, the
25:12 down, lay low, and C to the ground, even
28:2 overflowing waters, he will C down to the earth
31:7 day every one shall C away his idols of
34:3 Their slain shall be C out, and the stench
34:17 He has C the lot for them, his hand
37:19 their lands, and have C their gods into the
37:33 with a shield, or C up a siege mound
38:8 will make the shadow C by the declining sun
38:17 destruction, for thou hast C all my sins behind
41:9 chosen you and not C you off";
54:6 youth when she is C off, says your God.
66:5 who hate you and C you out for my
Jer 6:6 "Hew down her trees; C up a siege mound
7:15 And I will C you out of my sight,
7:15 my sight, as I C out all your kinsmen,
7:29 off your hair and C it away; raise a
9:19 land, because they have C down our dwellings.'"
14:16 they prophesy shall be C out in the streets
22:7 your choicest cedars, and C them into the fire.
22:19 be buried, dragged and C forth beyond the gates
22:28 his children hurled and C into a land which
23:33 burden, and I will C you off, says the
23:39 lift you up and C you away from my
26:23 with the sword and C his dead body into
31:37 explored, then I will C off all the descendants
36:30 dead body shall be C out to the heat
38:6 they took Jeremiah and C him into the cistern
41:7 him slew them, and C them into a cistern.
41:9 cistern into which Ishmael C all the bodies of
51:63 stone to it, and C it into the midst
52:3 and Judah that he C them out from his
Lam 2:1 He has C down from heaven to earth the
2:10 in silence; they have C dust on their heads
3:31 the Lord will not C off for ever,
3:53 into the pit and C stones on me;
Bar 2:25 behold, they have been C out to the heat
6:24 when they were being C, they had no feeling.
6:71 like a dead body C out in the darkness.
Ezek 4:2 wall against it, and C up a mound against
5:4 shall take some, and C them into the fire,
6:4 broken; and I will C down your slain before
7:19 They C their silver into the streets, and their
16:5 you; but you were C out on the open
17:17 war, when mounds are C up and siege walls
18:31 C away from you all the transgressions which you
19:12 plucked up in fury, C down to the ground;
20:7 I said to them, C away the detestable things
20:8 did not every man C away the detestable things
21:22 against the gates, to C up mounds, to build
23:35 have forgotten me and C me behind your back,
26:12 and soil they will C into the midst of
27:30 They C dust on their heads and wallow in
28:16 you sinned; so I C you as a profane
28:17 I C you to the ground; I exposed you
29:5 And I will C you forth into the wilderness,
31:11 I have C it out.
31:16 its fall, when I C it down to Sheol
32:4 And I will C you on the ground, on
Dan 3:6 worship shall immediately be C into a burning fiery
3:11 and worship shall be C into a burning fiery
3:15 you shall immediately be C into a burning fiery
3:20 and Abednego, and to C them into the burning
3:21 garments, and they were C into the burning fiery
3:92 counselors, "Did we not C three men bound into
6:7 O king, shall be C into the den of
6:12 O king, shall be C into the den of
6:16 Daniel was brought and C into the den of
6:24 Daniel were brought and C into the den of
8:7 before him, but he C him down to the
8:10 of the stars it C down to the ground,
8:12 transgression; and truth was C down to the ground,
11:12 exalted, and he shall C down tens of thousands,
Hos 9:17 My God will C them off, because they have
Joel 3:3 my land, and have C lots for my people,
Amos 1:11 with the sword, and C off all pity, and
4:3 and you shall be C forth into Harmon," says
5:7 justice to wormwood, and C down righteousness to
8:3 place they shall be C out in silence."
Obad 1:11 entered his gates and C lots for Jerusalem, you
Jon 1:7 another, "Come, let us C lots, that we may
1:7 So they C lots, and the lot fell upon
2:3 For thou didst C me into the deep, into
2:4 I said, 'I am C out from thy presence;
Mic 2:5 will have none to C the line by lot
4:7 and those who were C off, a strong nation;
7:19 Thou wilt C all our sins into the depths
Nah 3:10 honored men lots were C, and all her great
Zeph 3:15 against you, he has C out your enemies.
Zech 1:21 to terrify them, to C down the horns of
11:13 LORD said to me, C it into the treasury"
11:13 shekels of silver and C them into the treasury
1Mac 11:55 troops that Demetrius had C off gathered around
13:48 He C out of it all uncleanness, and settled
2Mac 5:8 fellow citizens, he was C ashore in Egypt;
5:10 He who had C out many to lie unburied
Mt 7:22 in your name, and C out demons in your
8:16 with demons; and he C out the spirits with
8:31 begged him, "If you C us out, send us
9:33 the demon had been C out, the dumb man
10:1 over unclean spirits, to C them out, and to
10:8 the dead, cleanse lepers, C out demons.
12:27 And if I C out demons by Be-elzebul, by
12:27 whom do your sons C them out?
12:28 of God that I C out demons, then the
17:19 "Why could we not C it out?"
17:26 to the sea and C a hook, and take
21:21 'Be taken up and C into the sea,' it
21:39 they took him and C him out of the
22:13 hand and foot, and C him into the outer
25:30 And C the worthless servant into the outer darkness;
Mk 1:34 with various diseases, and C out many demons; and
3:15 and have authority to C out demons:
3:23 parables, "How can Satan C out Satan?
6:13 And they C out many demons, and anointed with
7:25 she begged him to C the demon out of
9:18 asked your disciples to C it out, and they
9:22 And it has often C him into the fire
9:28 "Why could we not C it out?"
11:23 'Be taken up and C into the sea,' and
12:8 and killed him, and C him out of the
16:9 from whom he had C out seven demons.
16:17 my name they will C out demons; they will
Lk 6:22 and revile you, and C out your name as
9:40 begged your disciples to C it out, but they
11:18 you say that I C out demons by Be-elzebul.
11:19 And if I C out demons by Be-elzebul, by
11:19 whom do your sons C them out?
11:20 of God that I C out demons, then the
12:5 killed, has power to C into hell; yes, I
12:49 "I came to C fire upon the earth; and
13:32 that fox, 'Behold, I C out demons and perform
17:2 neck and he were C into the sea, than
19:43 when your enemies will C up a bank about
20:12 one they wounded and C out.
20:15 be ours.' And they C him out of the
23:33 And they C lots to divide his garments.
Jn 6:37 me I will not C out.
9:34 And they C him out.
9:35 heard that they had C him out, and having
12:31 of this world be C out;
15:6 in me, he is C forth as a branch
19:24 not tear it, but C lots for it to
19:24 for my clothing they C lots."
21:6 He said to them, C the net on the
21:6 So they C it, and now they were not
Acts 1:26 And they C lots for them, and the lot
7:58 Then they C him out of the city and
16:37 and do they now C us out secretly?
26:10 put to death I C my vote against them.
27:19 the third day they C out with their own
27:40 So they C off the anchors and left them
Rom 13:12 Let us then C off the works of darkness
Gal 4:30 C out the slave and her son; for the
1Pet 5:7 C all your anxieties on him, for he cares
2Pet 2:4 when they sinned, but C them into hell and
Rev 4:10 ever and ever; they C their crowns before the
12:4 stars of heaven, and C them to the earth.

CASTANETS
2Sam 6:5 harps and tambourines and C and cymbals.

CASTING (15)
Ex 38:27 of silver were for C the bases of the
Lev 18:24 the nations I am C out before you defiled
20:23 nation which I am C out before you; for
Ezra 10:1 made confession, weeping and C himself down
Jud 6:12 from coming up by C stones at them.
Jer 38:9 Jeremiah the prophet by C him into the cistern;
Mt 4:18 and Andrew his brother, C a net into the
27:35 garments among them by C lots;
Mk 1:16 the brother of Simon C a net in the
1:39 in their synagogues and C out demons.
9:38 we saw a man C out demons in your
15:24 his garments among them, C lots for them, to
Lk 9:49 we saw a man C out demons in your
11:14 Now he was C out a demon that was
Jude 1:13 waves of the sea, C up the foam of

CASTLE (2)
Neh 7:2 the governor of the C charge over Jerusalem, for
Prov 18:19 but quarreling is like the bars of a C

CASTOFF (2)
Wis 13:12 needs, and burn the C pieces of his work
13:13 But a C piece from among them, useful for

CASTS (16)
Job 16:11 to the ungodly, and C me into the hands
20:15 them up again; God C them out of his
Ps 147:6 up the downtrodden, he C the wicked to the
147:17 He C forth his ice like morsels; who can
Prov 19:15 Slothfulness C into a deep sleep, and an idle
Sir 21:15 he dislikes it and C it behind his back.
Is 26:5 low to the ground, C it to the dust.
40:19 a workman C it, and a goldsmith overlays it
40:19 it with gold, and C for it silver chains.
44:10 fashions a god or C an image, that is
Mt 9:34 the Pharisees said, "He C out demons by the
12:24 demons, that this man C out demons."
12:26 stand; and if Satan C out Satan, he is
Mk 3:22 prince of demons he C out the demons."
Lk 11:15 of them said, "He C out demons by Be-elzebul,
1 Jn 4:18 love, but perfect love C out fear.

CATAPULT
Wis 5:22 hurled as from a C; the water of the

CATAPULTS
1Mac 6:51 fire and stones, machines to shoot arrows, and C

CATARACTS
Ps 42:7 the thunder of thy C; all thy waves and

CATASTROPHE
Jud 8:19 they suffered a great C before our enemies.

CATCH (13)
Tob 6:3 angel said to him, C the fish." So the
Prov 12:27 slothful man will not C his prey, but the
Song 2:15 C us the foxes, the little foxes, that spoil
Sir 27:19 go, and will not C him again.
Jer 5:26 set a trap; they C men.
16:16 LORD, and they shall C them; and afterwards I
Ezek 19:3 and he learned to C prey; he devoured men.
19:6 and he learned to C prey; he devoured men.
Dan 13:58 what tree did you C them being intimate with
Lk 5:4 deep and let down your nets for a C
5:9 with him, at the C of fish which they
11:54 wait for him, to C at something he might
20:26 of the people to C him by what he

CATCHES (3)
Ex 22:6 fire breaks out and C in thorns so that
Sir 34:2 As one who C at a shadow and pursues
1Cor 3:19 it is written, "He C the wise in their

CATCHING (2)
Deut 32:11 spreading out its wings, C them, bearing them on
Lk 5:10 henceforth you will be C men."

CATERPILLAR (4)
1Kgs 8:37 mildew or locust or C; if their enemy besieges
2Chr 6:28 mildew or locust or C; if their enemies besiege
Ps 78:46 their crops to the C, and the fruit of
Is 33:4 is gathered as the C gathers; as locusts leap,

CATS
Bar 6:22 on their bodies and heads; and so do C

CATTLE (150)
Gen 1:24 according to their kinds: C and creeping things and
1:25 their kinds and the C according to their kinds,
1:26 air, and over the C, and over all the
2:20 gave names to all C, and to the birds
3:14 are you above all C, and above all wild
4:20 of those who dwell in tents and have C
7:14 kind, and all the C according to their kinds,
7:21 the earth, birds, C, beasts, all swarming creatures
8:1 beasts and all the C that were with him
9:10 you, the birds, the C, and every beast of
13:2 was very rich in C, in silver, and in
13:7 the herdsmen of Abram's C and the herdsmen of
13:7 of Abram's cattle and the herdsmen of Lot's C
30:29 you, and how your C have fared with me.
31:9 has taken away the C of your father, and
31:18 drove away all his C, all his livestock which
31:18 he had gained, the C in his possession which
33:14 the pace of the C which are before me
33:17 made booths for his C; therefore the name of
34:5 sons were with his C in the field, so
34:23 Will not their C, their property and all their
36:6 of his household, his C, all his beasts, and
36:7 could not support them because of their C
46:6 They also took their C and their goods, which
46:32 have been keepers of C; and they have brought
46:34 have been keepers of C from our youth even
47:6 among them, put them in charge of my C
47:16 Joseph answered, "Give your C, and I will give
47:16 in exchange for your C, if your money is
47:17 So they brought their C to Joseph; and Joseph
47:17 exchange for all their C that year.
47:18 and the herds of C are my lords; there
Ex 9:3 severe plague upon your C which are in the
9:4 a distinction between the C of Israel and the
9:4 of Israel and the C of Egypt, so that
9:6 this thing; all the C of the Egyptians died,
9:6 died, but of the C of the people of
9:7 not one of the C of the Israelites was
9:19 therefore send, get your C and all that you
9:20 his slaves and his C flee into the houses;
9:21 his slaves and his C in the field.
10:26 Our C also must go with us; not a
11:5 the mill; and all the first-born of the C
12:29 the dungeon, and all the first-born of the C
12:38 them, and very many C, both flocks and herds.
13:12 the firstlings of your C that are males shall
13:15 the first-born of man and the first-born of C
17:3 our children and our C with thirst?"
20:10 your maidservant, or your C, or the sojourner who
34:19 mine, all your male C, the firstlings of cow
Lev 1:2 bring your offering of C from the herd or
5:2 a carcass of unclean C or a carcass of
19:19 shall not let your C breed with a different
25:7 with you; for your C also and for the
26:22 children, and destroy your C, and make you few
Num 3:41 of Israel, and the C of the Levites instead
3:41 the firstlings among the C of the people of
3:45 of Israel, and the C of the Levites instead
3:45 Levites instead of their C; and the Levites shall
7:87 twenty shekels; all the C for the burnt offering
7:88 offering; and all the C for the sacrifice of
20:4 we should die here, both we and our C
20:8 shall give drink to the congregation and their C
20:11 abundantly, and the congregation drank, and their C
20:19 water, I and my C, then I will pay
31:9 as booty all their C, their flocks, and all
31:30 flocks, of all the C, and give them to
31:33 thousand sheep, seventy-two thousand C,
31:38 The C were thirty-six thousand, of which the LORD's
31:44 hundred sheep, thirty-six thousand C,
32:1 very great multitude of C; and they saw the
32:1 and behold, the place was a place for C
32:4 is a land for C; and your servants have
32:4 a land for cattle; and your servants have C
32:26 flocks, and all our C, shall remain there in
35:3 shall be for their C and for their livestock
Deut 2:35 none remaining; only the C we took as spoil
3:7 But all the C and the spoil of the
3:19 little ones, and your C (I know that you
3:19 that you have many C shall remain in the

5:14 or any of your C, or the sojourner who
7:13 the increase of your C and the young of
7:14 or female barren among you, or among your C
11:15 your fields for your C, and you shall eat
13:15 in it and its C, with the edge of
20:14 the little ones, the C, and everything else in
28:4 the increase of your C, and the young of
28:11 the fruit of your C, and in the fruit
28:18 the increase of your C, and the young of
28:51 the offspring of your C and the fruit of
28:51 the increase of your C or the young of
30:9 the fruit of your C, and in the fruit
Josh 1:14 little ones, and your C shall remain in the
8:2 its spoil and its C you shall take as
8:27 Only the C and the spoil of that city
11:14 these cities and the C, the people of Israel
14:4 pasture lands for their C and their substance.
21:2 in, along with their pasture lands for our C
22:8 and with very many C, with silver, gold, bronze,
Judg 6:5 come up with their C and their tents, coming
18:21 little ones and the C and the goods in
1Sam 8:16 the best of your C and your asses, and
23:5 and brought away their C, and made a great
30:20 the people drove those C before him, and said,
1Kgs 4:23 oxen, and twenty pasture-fed C, a hundred sheep,
2Kgs 3:17 shall drink, you, your C, and your beasts.'
1Chr 5:9 the Euphrates, because their C had multiplied in the
7:21 slew, because they came down to raid their C
28:1 all the property and C of the king and
2Chr 14:15 of those who had C, and carried away sheep
20:25 from them, they found C in great numbers, goods,
31:6 in the tithe of C and sheep, and the
32:28 for all kinds of C, and sheepfolds.
Neh 9:37 bodies and over our C at their pleasure, and
10:36 sons and of our C, as it is written
Tob 10:10 his property in slaves, C, and money.
Jud 4:10 their children and their C and every resident alien
5:9 with much gold and silver and very many C
8:7 and women slaves, and C, and fields; and she
11:7 the field and the C and the birds of
11:12 planned to kill their C and have determined to
Job 18:3 Why are we counted as C
Ps 50:10 forest is mine, the C on a thousand hills.
78:48 He gave over their C to the hail, and
104:14 to grow for the C, and plants for man
107:38 does not let their C decrease.
144:14 our fields; may our C be heavy with young,
148:10 Beasts and all C, creeping things and flying birds!
Sir 7:22 Do you have C
Is 7:25 become a place where C are let loose and
30:23 In that day your C will graze in large
46:1 are on beasts and C; these things you carry
63:14 Like C that go down into the valley, the
Jer 9:10 and the lowing of C is not heard; both
49:32 booty, their herds of C a spoil.
Ezek 38:12 nations, who have gotten C and goods, who dwell
38:13 gold, to take away C and goods, to seize
Dan 3:82 Lord, all beasts and C, sing praise to him
Joel 1:17 The herds of C are perplexed because there is
Jon 4:11 right hand from their left, and also much C
Hag 1:11 forth, upon men and C, and upon all their
Zech 2:4 multitude of men and C in it.
1Mac 1:32 captive the women and children, and seized the C
2:30 their wives, and their C, because evils pressed heavily
2:38 wives and children and C, to the number of
10:33 all officials cancel also the taxes on their C
12:23 to you that your C and your property belong
2Mac 12:11 promising to give him C and to help his
Jn 4:12 from it himself, and his sons, and his C
Rev 18:13 fine flour and wheat, C and sheep, horses and

CAUDA

Acts 27:16 a small island called C, we managed with difficulty

CAUGHT (52)

Gen 22:13 him was a ram, C in a thicket by
39:12 in the house, she C him by his garment,
Ex 4:4 out his hand and C it, and it became
Judg 1:6 they pursued him, and C him, and cut off
8:14 And he C a young man of Succoth, and
15:4 So Samson went and C three hundred foxes, and
15:14 as flax that has C fire, and his bonds
1Sam 17:35 arose against me, I C him by his beard,
2Sam 2:16 And each C his opponent by the head, and
18:9 oak, and his head C fast in the oak,
1Kgs 1:50 arose, and went, and C hold of the horns
2:28 of the LORD and C hold of the horns
2Kgs 2:16 of the LORD has C him up and cast
4:27 man of God, she C hold of his feet.
Tob 11:6 And she C sight of him coming, and said
Jud 6:12 city saw them, they C up their weapons and
Esth 1:6 curtains and blue hangings C up with cords of
Job 36:8 bound in fetters and C in the cords of
Ps 9:15 which they hid has their own foot been C
10:2 poor; let them be C in the schemes which
Prov 3:26 confidence and will keep your foot from being C
5:22 him, and he is C in the toils of
6:2 utterance of your lips, C in the words of
6:31 And if he is C, he will pay sevenfold;
7:22 as a stag is C fast
Eccl 9:12 like birds which are C in a snare, so
Wis 4:11 He was C up lest evil change his understanding
Sir 9:4 singer, lest you be C in her intrigues.
23:7 the one who observes it will never be C
27:26 a snare will be C in it.
27:29 the godly will be C in a snare, and
Is 13:15 through, and whoever is C will fall by the
24:18 the pit shall be C in the snare.
Jer 2:26 thief is shamed when C, so the house of
48:44 the pit shall be C in the snare.
50:24 you were found and C, because you strove against
Dan 3:48 the Chaldeans whom it C about the furnace.
1Mac 6:24 us as they have C, and they have seized
2Mac 12:35 was a strong man, C hold of Gorgias, and
13:21 he was sought for, C, and put in prison.
Mt 14:31 out his hand and C him, saying to him,
Jn 8:3 woman who had been C in adultery, and placing
8:4 this woman has been C in the act of
21:3 but that night they C nothing.
21:10 some of the fish that you have just C
Acts 8:38 Spirit of the Lord C up Philip; and the
27:15 when the ship was C and could not face
2Cor 12:2 fourteen years ago was C up to the third
12:3 that this man was C up into Paradise—whether
1Thes 4:17 are left, shall be C up together with them
2Pet 2:12 instinct, born to be C and killed, reviling in
Rev 12:5 but her child was C up to God and

CAULKERS

Ezek 27:27 and your pilots, your C, your dealers in merchandise,

CAULKING

Ezek 27:9 men were in you, C your seams; all the

CAUSE (145)

Ex 8:5 over the pools, and C frogs to come upon
9:18 this time I will C very heavy hail to
20:24 every place where I C my name to be
23:8 officials, and subverts the C of those who are
24:14 you; whoever has a C, let him go to
Lev 14:41 city; and he shall C the inside of the
22:16 the LORD, and so C them to bear iniquity
26:16 waste the eyes and C life to pine away.
Num 5:24 enter into her and C bitter pain.
5:27 enter into her and C bitter pain, and her
8:13 And you shall C the Levites to attend Aaron
16:5 is holy, and will C him to come near
16:5 will choose he will C to come near to
27:7 their father's brethren and C the inheritance of their
27:8 son, then you shall C his inheritance to pass
27:19 your hand upon him; C him to stand before
Deut 1:38 him, for he shall C Israel to inherit it.
16:19 wise and subverts the C of the righteous.
17:16 horses for himself, or C the people to return
25:2 beaten, the judge shall C him to lie down
28:7 "The LORD will C your enemies who rise against
28:25 "The LORD will C you to be defeated before
Josh 1:6 courage; for you shall C this people to inherit
Judg 6:31 Or will you defend his C
11:35 you have become the C of great trouble to
1Sam 19:5 sin against innocent blood by killing David without C
24:15 it, and plead my C, and deliver me from
25:31 lord shall have no C of grief, or pangs
25:31 having shed blood without C or for my lord
2Sam 15:4 with a suit or C might come to me,
20:6 himself fortified cities, and C us trouble.
23:5 For will he not C to prosper all my
1Kgs 1:33 of your lord, and C Solomon my son to
2:31 guilt for the blood which Joab shed without C
8:45 prayer and their supplication, and maintain their C
8:49 supplication, and maintain their C
8:59 may he maintain the C of his servant, and

C

	8:59	his servant, and the C of his people Israel,
	17:18	to remembrance, and to C the death of my
2Kgs	19:7	land; and I will C him to fall by
	21:8	and I will not C the feet of Israel
2Chr	6:35	prayer and their supplication, and maintain their C
	6:39	supplications, and maintain their C and forgive thy
Neh	4:8	against Jerusalem and to C confusion in it.
Tob	11:8	rub them, and will C the white films to
Jud	9:14	And C thy whole nation and every tribe to
Job	2:3	moved me against him, to destroy him without C
	5:8	would I commit my C;
	9:17	multiplies my wounds without C;
	29:16	I searched out the C of him whom I
	31:13	I have rejected the C of my manservant or
Ps	7:4	plundered my enemy without C,
	9:4	hast maintained my just C; thou hast sat on
	17:1	Hear a just C, O LORD; attend to my
	22:8	heads; "He committed his C to the LORD; let
	35:7	For without C they hid their net for me;
	35:7	net for me; without C they dug a pit
	35:19	those wink the eye who hate me without C
	35:23	my right, for my C, my God and my
	38:19	are my foes without C are mighty, and many
	43:1	God, and defend my C against an ungodly people;
	45:4	forth victoriously for the C of truth and to
	45:17	I will C your name to be celebrated in
	56:5	seek to injure my C; all their thoughts are
	69:4	who hate me without C; mighty are those who
	72:4	May he defend the C of the poor of
	74:22	O God, plead thy C; remember how the impious
	104:14	Thou dost C the grass to grow for the
	109:3	with words of hate, and attack me without C
	119:154	Plead my C and redeem me; give me life
	119:161	Princes persecute me without C, but my heart stands
	140:12	the LORD maintains the C of the afflicted, and
Prov	22:23	LORD will plead their C and despoil of life
	23:11	he will plead their C against you.
	23:29	Who has wounds without C
	24:28	against your neighbor without C, and do not deceive
Wis	14:27	is the beginning and C and end of every
Sir	18:14	your good deeds, nor C grief by your words
	29:4	as a windfall, and C trouble to those who
	36:2	look upon us, and C the fear of thee
	36:20	A perverse mind will C grief, but a man
	44:22	like the stars, and C them to inherit from
	47:22	up his mercy, nor C any of his works
Is	1:23	fatherless, and the widow's C does not come to
	30:30	And the LORD will C his majestic voice to
	34:8	of recompense for the C of Zion.
	45:8	forth, and let it C righteousness to spring up
	51:22	God who pleads the C of his people: "Behold,
	61:11	the Lord GOD will C righteousness and praise to
	66:9	the birth and not C to bring forth?
	66:9	LORD; shall I, who C to bring forth, shut
Jer	5:28	not with justice the C of the fatherless, to
	11:20	them, for to thee have I committed my C
	19:7	and Jerusalem, and will C their people to fall
	20:12	them, for to thee have I committed my C
	22:16	He judged the C of the poor and needy;
	30:13	none to uphold your C, no medicine for your
	32:35	do this abomination, to C Judah to sin.
	33:15	that time I will C a righteous Branch to
	49:2	LORD, when I will C the battle cry to
	50:34	will surely plead their C, that he may give
	51:36	I will plead your C and take vengeance for
Lam	3:32	ever, but, though he C grief, he will have
	3:36	a man in his C, the Lord does not
	3:51	and sees; my eyes C me grief at the
	3:52	were my enemies without C;
	3:58	hast taken up my C, O Lord, thou hast
	3:59	done to me, O LORD; judge thou my C
Bar	6:54	cannot judge their own C or deliver one who
Ezek	14:15	If I C wild beasts to pass through the
	14:23	have not done without C all that I have
	29:21	that day I will C a horn to spring
	32:4	fling you, and will C all the birds of
	32:12	I will C your multitude to fall by the
	32:14	their waters clear, and C their rivers to run
	36:11	fruitful; and I will C you to be inhabited
	36:15	peoples and no longer C your nation to stumble,
	36:27	spirit within you, and C you to walk in
	36:33	your iniquities, I will C the cities to be
	37:5	bones: Behold, I will C breath to enter you,
	37:6	upon you, and will C flesh to come upon
Dan	8:24	great, and he shall C fearful destruction, and shall
	9:17	own sake, O Lord, C thy face to shine
	9:27	the week he shall C sacrifice and offering to
Mic	7:9	until he pleads my C and executes judgment for
Zech	8:12	dew; and I will C the remnant of this
	11:6	Lo, I will C men to fall each into
1Mac	3:42	to the people to C their final destruction.
	9:10	brethren, and leave no C to question our honor."
2Mac	4:1	had been the real C of the misfortune.
	4:47	Menelaus, the C of all the evil, he acquitted
Mt	19:3	it lawful to divorce one's wife for any C
Lk	17:2	than that he should C one of these little
Jn	15:25	hated me without a C
Acts	19:40	today, there being no C that we can give
Rom	14:15	let what you eat C the ruin of one
1Cor	8:13	if food is a C of my brother's falling,
	8:13	eat meat, lest I C my brother to fall.
2Cor	2:2	For if I C you pain, who is there
	2:4	many tears, not to C you pain but to
	5:12	again but giving you C to be proud of
Phil	1:26	you may have ample C to glory in Christ
Heb	12:15	spring up and C trouble, and by it the
1 Jn	2:10	it there is no C for stumbling.
Rev	13:15	even speak, and to C those who would not

CAUSED (45)

Gen	2:5	LORD God had not C it to rain upon
	2:21	So the LORD God C a deep sleep to
	20:13	And when God C me to wander from my
	39:3	and that the LORD C all that he did
Num	27:22	he took Joshua and C him to stand before
	31:16	Behold, these C the people of Israel, by the
Deut	28:51	flock, until they have C you to perish.
Josh	6:11	So he C the ark of the LORD to
1Kgs	1:38	Pelethites, went down and C Solomon to ride on
	1:44	Pelethites; and they have C him to ride on
	20:33	to him; and he C him to come up
Ezra	6:12	the God who has C his name to dwell
Job	29:13	upon me, and I C the widow's heart to
	31:16	poor desired, or have C the eyes of the
	31:39	yield without payment, and C the death of its
	34:28	ways, so that they C the cry of the
	38:12	your days began, and C the dawn to know
Ps	78:16	of the rock, and C waters to flow down
	78:26	He C the east wind to blow in the
	88:8	[Selah] Thou hast C my companions to shun me;
	88:18	Thou hast C lover and friend to shun me;
	105:29	waters into blood, and C their fish to die.
	106:46	He C them to be pitied by all those
	111:4	He has C his wonderful works to be remembered;
Sir	3:23	and wrong opinion has C their thoughts to slip.
	24:17	Like a vine I C loveliness to bud, and
	25:22	a wounded heart are C by an evil wife.
	25:22	and weak knees are C by the wife who
	35:15	against him who has C them to fall?
	45:3	By his words he C signs to cease; the
	47:23	Rehoboam, whose policy C the people to revolt.
	47:23	son of Nebat, who C Israel to sin and
Is	21:2	the sighing she has C I bring to an
	63:12	his holy Spirit, who C his glorious arm to
Lam	1:14	upon my neck; he C my strength to fail;
	2:8	hand from destroying; he C rampart and wall to
Ezek	32:30	the terror which they C by their might; they
	36:21	the house of Israel C to be profaned among
Mal	2:8	the way; you have C many to stumble by
1Mac	1:9	many years; and they C many evils on the
	3:29	disaster which he had C in the land by
	15:31	destruction that you have C and the tribute money
2Mac	3:24	and of all authority C so great a manifestation
2Cor	2:5	if any one has C pain, he has caused
	2:5	caused pain, he has C it not to me,

CAUSELESS

Prov	26:2	a curse that is C does not alight.

CAUSES (27)

Ex	22:5	"When a man C a field or vineyard to
Lev	24:19	When a man C a disfigurement in his neighbor,
Job	37:13	or for love, he C it to happen.
	37:15	command upon them, and C the lightning of his
Prov	10:4	A slack hand C poverty, but the hand of
	10:10	who winks the eye C trouble, but he who
	19:26	is a son who C shame and brings reproach.
	29:22	man given to anger C much transgression.
Wis	12:16	thy sovereignty over all C thee to spare all.
	17:13	prefers ignorance of what C the torment.
Sir	11:20	godly, and quickly God C his blessing to flourish.
Is	61:11	and as a garden C what is sown in

	64:2	brushwood and the fire C water to boil--
Ezek	44:18	themselves with anything that C sweat.
Mt	5:29	If your right eye C you to sin, pluck
	5:30	if your right hand C you to sin, cut
	13:41	of his kingdom all C of sin and all
	18:6	receives me; but whoever C one of these little
	18:8	hand or your foot C you to sin, cut
	18:9	And if your eye C you to sin, pluck
Mk	9:42	"Whoever C one of these little ones who believe
	9:43	And if your hand C you to sin, cut
	9:44	And if your foot C you to sin, cut
	9:45	And if your eye C you to sin, pluck
Jas	4:1	What C wars, and what causes fightings among you?
	4:1	causes wars, and what C fightings among you?
Rev	13:16	Also it C all, both small and great, both

CAUSING (3)

1Sam	5:9	was against the city, C a very great panic,
Esth	1:17	known to all women, C them to look with
1Mac	15:35	you demand, they were C great damage among the

CAUTIONED

Mk	8:15	And he C them, saying, "Take heed, beware of

CAUTIOUS (2)

Prov	14:16	A wise man is C and turns away from
Sir	18:26	A wise man is C in everything, and in

CAVALRY (36)

Jud	1:13	Arphaxad, and all his C and all his chariots.
	2:5	twenty thousand foot soldiers and twelve thousand C
	2:22	whole army, his infantry, C, and chariots, and went
	6:3	They cannot resist the might of our C
	7:2	infantry and twelve thousand C, together with the
	7:6	led out all his C in full view of
	7:20	chariots, and C, surrounded them for thirty-four
	16:4	up the valleys, their C covered the hills.
1Mac	1:17	chariots and elephants and C and with a large
	3:39	infantry and seven thousand C to go into the
	4:1	and a thousand picked C, and this division moved
	4:7	strong and fortified, with C round about it; and
	4:28	infantrymen and five thousand C to subdue them.
	4:31	them be ashamed of their troops and their C
	8:6	twenty elephants and with C and chariots and a
	9:4	twenty thousand foot soldiers and two thousand C
	9:11	The C was divided into two companies, and the
	10:73	able to withstand my C and such an army
	10:77	he mustered three thousand C and a large army,
	10:77	a large troop of C and put confidence in
	10:79	secretly left a thousand C behind them.
	10:82	in battle (for the C was exhausted); they were
	10:83	and fled, and the C was dispersed in the
	12:49	Trypho sent troops and C into Galilee and the
	13:22	Trypho got all his C ready to go, but
	15:13	twenty thousand warriors and eight thousand C
	15:38	country, and gave him troops of infantry and C
	16:7	the infantry, for the C of the enemy were
2Mac	10:24	mercenaries and collected the C from Asia in no
	11:2	men and all his C and came against the
	11:4	and his thousands of C, and his eighty elephants.
	12:20	thousand infantry and two thousand five hundred C
	12:33	out with three thousand infantry and four hundred C
	13:2	thousand three hundred C, twenty-two elephants,
	15:20	strategically stationed and the C deployed on the
Rev	9:16	of the troops of C was twice ten thousand

CAVE (35)

Gen	19:30	he dwelt in a C with his two daughters.
	23:9	may give me the C of Mach-pelah, which he
	23:11	I give you the C that is in it;
	23:17	the field with the C which was in it
	23:19	his wife in the C of the field of
	23:20	The field and the C that is in it
	25:9	buried him in the C of Mach-pelah, in the
	49:29	my fathers in the C that is in the
	49:30	the Hittite, in the C that is in the
	49:32	the field and the C that is in it
	50:13	buried him in the C of the field at
Josh	10:16	hid themselves in the C at Makkedah.
	10:17	found, hidden in the C at Makkedah."
	10:18	the mouth of the C, and set men by
	10:22	the mouth of the C, and bring those five
	10:22	those five kings out to me from the C
	10:23	to him from the C, the king of Jerusalem,
	10:27	threw them into the C where they had hidden
	10:27	the mouth of the C, which remain to this
1Sam	22:1	and escaped to the C of Adullam; and when
	24:3	where there was a C; and Saul went in
	24:3	were sitting in the innermost parts of the C
	24:7	up and left the C, and went upon his
	24:8	went out of the C, and called after Saul,
	24:10	my hand in the C; and some bade me
2Sam	23:13	to David at the C of Adullam, when a
1Kgs	18:4	by fifties in a C, and fed them with
	18:13	by fifties in a C, and fed them with
	19:9	he came to a C, and lodged there; and
	19:13	out and stood at the entrance of the C
1Chr	11:15	to David at the C of Adullam, when the
Jud	16:23	buried her in the C of her husband Manasseh,
Nah	2:11	the lions' den, the C of the young lions,
2Mac	2:5	came and found a C, and he brought there
Jn	11:38	tomb; it was a C, and a stone lay

CAVERNS

Is	2:21	bats, to enter the C of the rocks and

CAVES (9)

Judg	6:2	the mountains, and the C and the strongholds.
1Sam	13:6	people hid themselves in C and in holes and
Is	2:19	men shall enter the C of the rocks and
Ezek	33:27	in strongholds and in C shall die by pestilence.
Nah	2:12	lionesses; he filled his C with prey and his
2Mac	6:11	had assembled in the C near by, to observe
	10:6	in the mountains and C like wild animals.
Heb	11:38	and in dens and C of the earth.
Rev	6:15	free, hid in the C and among the rocks

CEASE (49)

Gen	8:22	summer and winter, day and night, shall not C
Ex	9:29	LORD; the thunder will C, and there will be
Num	17:5	I will make to C from me the murmurings
Deut	15:11	the poor will never C out of the land;
	32:26	the remembrance of them C from among men,"
Josh	22:25	might make our children C to worship the LORD.
Judg	20:28	against our brethren the Benjaminites, or shall we C
1Sam	7:8	to Samuel, "Do not C to cry to the
	9:5	back, lest my father C to care about the
2Chr	16:5	he stopped building Ramah, and let his work C
	35:21	C opposing God, who is with me, lest he
Ezra	4:21	men be made to C, and that this city
	4:23	Jerusalem and by force and power made them C
Esth	9:28	commemoration of these days C among their
Job	3:17	There the wicked C from troubling, and there the
	14:7	sprout again, and that its shoots will not C
Ps	46:9	He makes wars C to the end of the
Prov	19:27	C, my son, to hear instruction only to stray
	22:10	will go out, and quarreling and abuse will C
Eccl	12:3	bent, and the grinders C because they are few,
Sir	16:25	and they do not C from their labors.
	23:16	of kin will never C until the fire burns
	23:17	sweet; he will never C until he dies.
	24:9	eternity I shall not C to exist.
	28:6	of your life, and C from enmity, remember
	38:23	rest, let his remembrance C, and be comforted for
	45:3	he caused signs to C; the Lord glorified him
Is	1:16	from before my eyes; C to do evil,
	17:1	Behold, Damascus will C to be a city, and
	29:20	nought and the scoffer C, and all who watch
Jer	7:34	I will make to C from the cities of
	14:17	and let them not C, for the virgin daughter
	16:9	I will make to C from this place, before
	17:8	for it does not C to bear fruit."
	31:36	the descendants of Israel C from being a nation
	48:33	have made the wine C from the wine presses;
Bar	2:23	I will make to C from the cities of
Ezek	45:9	execute justice and righteousness; C your evictions of
Dan	3:46	them in did not C feeding the furnace fires
	9:27	sacrifice and offering to C; and upon the wing
Hos	8:10	And they shall C for a little while from
Amos	7:5	said, "O Lord GOD, C, I beseech thee!
2Mac	6:1	of their fathers and C to live by the
	15:7	But Maccabeus did not C to trust with all
Acts	5:42	home they did not C teaching and preaching Jesus
	20:31	years I did not C night or day to
1Cor	13:8	for tongues, they will C; as for knowledge, it
Eph	1:16	saints, I do not C to give thanks for
Rev	4:8	and night they never C to sing, "Holy, holy,

CEASED (45)

Gen	18:11	in age; it had C to be with Sarah
	29:35	name Judah; then she C bearing.
	30:9	saw that she had C bearing children, she took

C

41:49 the sea, until he C to measure it, for
Ex 9:33 thunder and the hail C, and the rain no
9:34 and the thunder had C, he sinned yet again,
Josh 5:12 And the manna C on the morrow, when they
Judg 5:6 days of Jael, caravans C and travelers kept to
5:7 The peasantry C in Israel, they ceased until you
5:7 ceased in Israel, they C until you arose, Deborah,
1Sam 2:5 who were hungry have C to hunger.
10:2 now your father has C to care about the
Ezra 4:24 Jerusalem stopped; and it C until the second year
Jud 10:1 When Judith had C crying out to the God
Job 32:1 So these three men C to answer Job, because
Ps 36:3 and deceit; he has C to act wisely and
77:8 Has his steadfast love for ever C
Wis 5:13 as we were born, C to be, and we
Sir 17:23 not exist, thanksgiving has C; he who is alive
Is 14:4 "How the oppressor has C, the insolent fury ceased!
14:4 "How the oppressor has ceased, the insolent fury C
16:4 more, and destruction has C, and he who tramples
24:8 of the jubilant has C, the mirth of the
33:1 When you have C to destroy, you will be
Jer 51:30 warriors of Babylon have C fighting, they remain in
Lam 5:15 of our hearts has C; our dancing has been
Jon 1:15 sea; and the sea C from its raging.
1Mac 3:45 flute and the harp C to play.
9:27 the time that prophets C to appear among them.
9:73 Thus the sword C from Israel.
2Mac 9:5 As soon as he C speaking he was seized
Mt 14:32 when they got into the boat, the wind C
Mk 4:39 And the wind C, and there was a great
5:29 And immediately the hemorrhage C; and she felt in
6:51 into the boat with them and the wind C
Lk 5:4 And when he had C speaking, he said to
7:45 in she has not C to kiss my feet.
8:24 raging waves; and they C, and there was a
8:44 his garment; and immediately her flow of blood C
11:1 place, and when he C, one of his disciples
Acts 20:1 After the uproar C, Paul sent for the disciples
21:14 not be persuaded, we C and said, "The will
Col 1:9 it, we have not C to pray for you,
Heb 10:2 would they not have C to be offered?
1Pet 4:1 in the flesh has C from sin,

CEASES (8)

Prov 26:20 out; and where there is no whisperer, quarreling C
Wis 7:10 her rather than light, because her radiance never C
Sir 14:19 Every product decays and C to exist, and the
Is 33:8 The highways lie waste, the wayfaring man C
Lam 3:22 of the LORD never C, his mercies never come
Hos 7:5 heated oven, whose baker C to stir the fire,
Acts 6:13 said, "This man never C to speak words against
Heb 4:10 enters God's rest also C from his labors as

CEASING (5)

1Sam 12:23 against the LORD by C to pray for you;
Ps 35:15 not slandered me without C;
Lam 3:49 eyes will flow without C, without respite,
2Mac 13:12 for three days without C, Judas exhorted them and
Rom 1:9 his Son, that without C I mention you always

CEDAR (53)

Num 24:6 LORD has planted, like C trees beside the waters.
2Sam 5:11 messengers to David, and C trees, also carpenters
7:2 in a house of C, but the ark of
7:7 me a house of C
1Kgs 4:33 of trees, from the C that is in Lebanon
5:8 in the matter of C and cypress timber.
5:10 all the timber of C and cypress that he
6:9 of the house of beams and planks of C
6:10 was joined to the house with timbers of C
6:15 inside with boards of C; from the floor of
6:16 house with boards of C from the floor to
6:18 The C within the house was carved in the
6:18 open flowers; all was C, no stone was seen.
6:20 He also made an altar of C
6:36 and one course of C beams.
7:2 upon three rows of C pillars, with cedar beams
7:2 of cedar pillars, with C beams upon the pillars.
7:3 it was covered with C above the chambers that
7:7 it was finished with C from floor to rafters.
7:11 stones, hewn according to measurement, and C
7:12 and a course of C beams; so had the
9:11 had supplied Solomon with C and cypress timber and
10:27 stone, and he made C as plentiful as the
2Kgs 14:9 Lebanon sent to a C on Lebanon, saying, 'Give
1Chr 14:1 messengers to David, and C trees, also masons and
17:1 In a house of C, but the ark of
17:6 me a house of C
22:4 beyond weighing, and C timbers without number;
22:4 brought great quantities of C to David.
2Chr 1:15 stone, and he made C as plentiful as the
2:3 father and sent him C to build himself a
2:8 Send me also C, cypress, and algum timber from
9:27 Jerusalem as stone, and C as plentiful as the
25:18 Lebanon sent to a C on Lebanon, saying, 'Give
Ezra 3:7 the Tyrians to bring C trees from Lebanon to
Job 40:17 tail stiff like a C; the sinews of his
Ps 37:35 and towering like a C of Lebanon.
92:12 and grow like a C in Lebanon.
Song 1:17 of our house are C, our rafters are pine.
8:9 door, we will enclose her with boards of C
Sir 24:13 grew tall like a C in Lebanon, and like
50:12 was like a young C on Lebanon; and they
Is 41:19 in the wilderness the C, the acacia, the myrtle,
44:14 forest; he plants a C and the rain nourishes
Jer 22:14 it, paneling it with C, and painting it with
22:15 you are a king because you compete in C
Ezek 17:3 the top of the C;
17:22 lofty top of the C, and will set it
17:23 and become a noble C; and under it will
27:5 Senir; they took a C from Lebanon to make
31:3 liken you to a C in Lebanon, with fair
Zeph 2:14 the threshold; for her C work will be laid
Zech 11:2 O cypress, for the C has fallen, for the

CEDARS (19)

Judg 9:15 bramble and devour the C of Lebanon.'
1Kgs 5:6 Now therefore command that C of Lebanon be cut
2Kgs 19:23 I felled its tallest C, its choicest cypresses; I
Ps 29:5 the LORD breaks the C, the LORD breaks the
29:5 the LORD breaks the C of Lebanon.
80:10 its shade, the mighty C with its branches;
104:16 are watered abundantly, the C of Lebanon which he
148:9 Mountains and all hills, fruit trees and all C
Song 5:15 His appearance is like Lebanon, choice as the C
Is 2:13 high; against all the C of Lebanon, lofty and
9:10 but we will put C in their place."
14:8 rejoice at you, the C of Lebanon, saying, 'Since
37:24 I felled its tallest C, its choicest cypresses; I
44:14 He cuts down C; or he chooses a holm
Jer 22:7 cut down your choicest C, and cast them into
22:23 Lebanon, nested among the C, how you will groan
Ezek 31:8 The C in the garden of God could not
Amos 2:9 the height of the C, and who was as
Zech 11:1 O Lebanon, that the fire may devour your C

CEDARWOOD (6)

Lev 14:4 living clean birds and C and scarlet stuff and
14:6 living bird with the C and the scarlet stuff
14:49 two small birds, with C and scarlet stuff and
14:51 and shall take the C and the hyssop and
14:52 bird, and with the C and hyssop and scarlet
Num 19:6 the priest shall take C and hyssop and scarlet

CEILING (3)

1Kgs 6:9 and he made the C of the house of
6:15 the rafters of the C, he covered them on
2Mac 1:16 secret door in the C, they threw stones and

CELEBRATE (10)

Neh 12:27 them to Jerusalem to C the dedication with gladness,
Tob 6:12 from Rages we will C the marriage.
Wis 14:23 in their initiations, or C secret mysteries, or hold
Ezek 45:21 the month, you shall C the feast of the
1Mac 13:52 every year they should C this day with rejoicing.
2Mac 1:18 of Chislev we shall C the purification of the
1:18 that you also may C the feast of booths
2:16 we are about to C the purification, we write
15:36 go unobserved, but to C the thirteenth day of
1Cor 5:8 Let us, therefore, C the festival, not with the

CELEBRATED (8)

Ezra 6:16 of the returned exiles, C the dedication of this
Tob 11:19 and Tobias' marriage was C for seven days with
Ps 45:17 your name to be C in all generations; therefore
1Mac 4:56 So they C the dedication of the altar for
7:48 people rejoiced greatly and C that day as a
7:49 this day should be C each year on the
10:58 in marriage, and C her wedding at Ptolemais
2Mac 10:6 And they C it for eight days with rejoicing,

CELEBRATING (2)
1Mac 9:37 sons of Jambri are C a great wedding, and
2Mac 8:33 While they were C the victory in the city

CELEBRATION (3)
2Chr 23:13 with their musical instruments leading in the C
Sir 36:14 Fill Zion with the C of thy wondrous deeds,
2Mac 6:7 On the monthly C of the king's birthday, the

CELEBRATIONS
Wis 19:16 receiving them with festal C, afflicted with terrible

CELESTIAL (2)
1Cor 15:40 There are C bodies and there are terrestrial bodies;
15:40 the glory of the C is one, and the

CELL
Acts 12:7 light shone in the C; and he struck Peter

CELLAR
Lk 11:33 puts it in a C or under a bushel,

CELLARS
1Chr 27:27 vineyards for the wine C was Zabdi the Shiphmite.

CELLS
Jer 37:16 come to the dungeon C, and remained there many

CEMETERY (2)
2Mac 9:4 will make Jerusalem a C of Jews."
9:14 and to make a C, he was now declaring

CENCHRE-AE (2)
Acts 18:18 At C he cut his hair, for he had
Rom 16:1 of the church at C,

CENDEBEUS (6)
1Mac 15:38 Then the king made C commander-in-chief of the
15:40 So C came to Jamnia and began to provoke
16:1 Simon his father what C had done.
16:4 and they marched against C and camped for the
16:8 sounded the trumpets, and C and his army were
16:9 John pursued them until C reached Kedron, which he

CENSER (12)
Lev 10:1 Aaron, each took his C, and put fire in
16:12 he shall take a C full of coals of
Num 16:17 of you take his C, and put incense upon
16:17 before the LORD his C, two hundred and fifty
16:17 fifty censers; you also, and Aaron, each his C
16:18 every man took his C, and they put fire
16:46 to Aaron, "Take your C, and put fire therein
2Chr 26:19 Now he had a C in his hand to
Sir 50:9 and incense in the C, like a vessel of
Ezek 8:11 Each had his C in his hand, and the
Rev 8:3 altar with a golden C; and he was given
8:5 the angel took the C and filled it with

CENSERS (7)
Num 16:6 Do this: take C, Korah and all his company;
16:17 two hundred and fifty C; you also, and Aaron,
16:37 to take up the C out of the blaze;
16:38 they are holy, the C of these men who
16:39 priest took the bronze C, which those who were
Ezra 1:9 basins of silver, twenty-nine C,
1Mac 1:22 the bowls, the golden C, the curtain, the crowns,

CENSURE
Job 20:3 I hear C which insults me, and out of

CENSURED
Tit 2:8 speech that cannot be C, so that an opponent

CENSUS (13)
Ex 30:12 "When you take the C of the people of
30:13 is numbered in the C shall give this: half
30:14 is numbered in the C, from twenty years old
38:26 was numbered in the C, from twenty years old
Num 1:2 Egypt, saying, "Take a C of all the congregation
1:49 shall not take a C of them among the
4:2 and Aaron, "Take a C of the sons of
4:22 to Moses, "Take a C of the sons of
26:2 the priest, "Take a C of all the congregation
26:4 Jericho, saying, "Take a C of the people, from
2Chr 2:17 Then Solomon took a C of all the aliens
2:17 of Israel, after the C of them which David
Acts 5:37 the days of the C and drew away some

CENTER (3)
Judg 9:37 coming down from the C of the land, and
Ezek 5:5 set her in the C of the nations, with
38:12 who dwell at the C of the earth.

CENTURION (20)
Mt 8:5 he entered Caperna-um, a C came forward to him,
8:8 But the C answered him, "Lord, I am not
8:13 And to the C Jesus said, "Go; be it
27:54 When the C and those who were with him,
Mk 15:38 And when the C, who stood facing him, saw
15:43 dead; and summoning the C, he asked him whether
15:44 he learned from the C that he was dead,
Lk 7:2 Now a C had a slave who was dear
7:6 from the house, the C sent friends to him,
23:46 Now when the C saw what had taken place,
Acts 10:1 man named Cornelius, a C of what was known
10:22 they said, "Cornelius, a C, an upright and God-fearing
22:25 Paul said to the C who was standing by,
22:26 When the C heard that, he went to the
24:22 gave orders to the C that he should be
27:1 other prisoners to a C of the Augustan Cohort,
27:6 There the C found a ship of Alexandria sailing
27:11 But the C paid more attention to the captain
27:31 Paul said to the C and the soldiers, "Unless
27:43 and escape; but the C, wishing to save Paul,

CENTURIONS (3)
Acts 21:32 once took soldiers and C, and ran down to
23:17 called one of the C and said, "Take this
23:23 called two of the C and said, "At the

CEPHAS (9)
Jn 1:42 You shall be called C
1Cor 1:12 or "I belong to C
3:22 Paul or Apollos or C or the world or
9:5 apostles and the brothers of the Lord and C
15:5 that he appeared to C, then to the twelve.
Gal 1:18 to Jerusalem to visit C, and remained with him
2:9 to me, James and C and John, who were
2:11 But when C came to Antioch I opposed him
2:14 gospel, I said to C before them all, "If

CEREAL (143)
Ex 29:41 offer with it a C offering and its libation,
30:9 nor burnt offering, nor C offering; and you shall
Lev 2:1 any one brings a C offering as an offering
2:3 is left of the C offering shall be for
2:4 "When you bring a C offering baked in the
2:5 your offering is a C offering baked on a
2:6 it; it is a C offering.
2:7 your offering is a C offering cooked in a
2:8 you shall bring the C offering that is made
2:9 shall take from the C offering its memorial portion
2:10 is left of the C offering shall be for
2:11 "No C offering which you bring to the LORD
2:13 shall season all your C offerings with salt; you
2:13 be lacking from your C offering; with all your
2:14 "If you offer a C offering of first fruits
2:14 shall offer for the C offering of your first
2:15 it; it is a C offering.
5:13 priest, as in the C offering."
6:14 the law of the C offering.
6:15 fine flour of the C offering with its oil
6:15 which is on the C offering, and burn this
6:20 flour as a regular C offering, half of it
6:21 baked pieces like a C offering, and offer it
6:23 Every C offering of a priest shall be wholly
7:9 And every C offering baked in the oven and
7:10 And every C offering, mixed with oil or dry,
7:37 burnt offering, of the C offering, of the sin
9:4 the LORD, and a C offering mixed with oil;
9:17 And he presented the C offering, and filled his
10:12 were left, "Take the C offering that remains of
14:10 without blemish, and a C offering of three tenths
14:20 burnt offering and the C offering on the altar.
14:21 with oil for a C offering, and a log
14:31 offering, along with a C offering; and the priest
23:13 And the C offering with it shall be two
23:16 you shall present a C offering of new grain
23:18 the LORD, with their C offering and their drink
23:37 fire, burnt offerings and C offerings, sacrifices and
Num 4:16 fragrant incense, the continual C offering, and the
5:15 for it is a C offering of jealousy, a

5:15 offering of jealousy, a C offering of remembrance,
5:18 in her hands the C offering of remembrance, which
5:18 remembrance, which is the C offering of jealousy.
5:25 priest shall take the C offering of jealousy out
5:25 and shall wave the C offering before the LORD
5:26 a handful of the C offering, as its memorial
6:15 with oil, and their C offering and their drink
6:17 shall offer also its C offering and its drink
7:13 with oil for a C offering;
7:19 with oil for a C offering;
7:25 with oil for a C offering;
7:31 with oil for a C offering;
7:37 with oil for a C offering;
7:43 with oil for a C offering;
7:49 with oil for a C offering;
7:55 with oil for a C offering;
7:61 with oil for a C offering;
7:67 with oil for a C offering;
7:73 with oil for a C offering;
7:79 with oil for a C offering;
7:87 year old, with their C offering; and twelve male
8:8 young bull and its C offering of fine flour
15:4 to the LORD a C offering of a tenth
15:6 shall prepare for a C offering two tenths of
15:9 with the bull a C offering of three tenths
15:24 the LORD, with its C offering and its drink
18:9 offering of theirs, every C offering of theirs and
28:5 fine flour for a C offering, mixed with a
28:8 the evening; like the C offering of the morning,
28:9 fine flour for a C offering, mixed with oil,
28:12 fine flour for a C offering, mixed with oil,
28:12 fine flour for a C offering, mixed with oil,
28:13 with oil as a C offering for every lamb;
28:20 without blemish; also their C offering of fine flour
28:26 when you offer a C offering of new grain
28:28 year old; also their C offering of fine flour
28:31 burnt offering and its C offering, you shall offer
29:3 without blemish; also their C offering of fine flour
29:6 new moon, and its C offering, and the continual
29:6 burnt offering and its C offering, and their drink
29:9 without blemish; and their C offering of fine flour
29:11 burnt offering and its C offering, and their drink
29:14 without blemish; and their C offering of fine flour
29:16 continual burnt offering, its C offering and its drink
29:18 without blemish, with the C offering and the drink
29:19 burnt offering and its C offering, and their drink
29:21 without blemish, with the C offering and the drink
29:22 burnt offering and its C offering and its drink
29:24 without blemish, with the C offering and the drink
29:25 continual burnt offering, its C offering and its drink
29:27 without blemish, with the C offering and the drink
29:28 burnt offering and its C offering and its drink
29:30 without blemish, with the C offering and the drink
29:31 continual burnt offering, its C offering, and its drink
29:33 without blemish, with the C offering and the drink
29:34 continual burnt offering, its C offering, and its drink
29:37 without blemish, and the C offering and the drink
29:38 burnt offering and its C offering and its drink
29:39 offerings, and for your C offerings, and for your
Josh 22:23 offer burnt offerings or C offerings or peace
22:29 altar for burnt offering, C offering, or sacrifice, other
Judg 13:19 the kid with the C offering, and offered it
13:23 burnt offering and a C offering at our hands,
1Kgs 8:64 burnt offering and the C offering and the fat
8:64 burnt offering and the C offering and the fat
2Kgs 16:13 burnt offering and his C offering, and poured his
16:15 offering, and the evening C offering, and the king's
16:15 burnt offering, and his C offering, with the burnt
16:15 the land, and their C offering, and their drink
1Chr 21:23 the wheat for a C offering.
23:29 the flour for the C offering, the wafers of
2Chr 7:7 burnt offering and the C offering and the fat.
Ezra 7:17 and lambs, with their C offerings and their drink
Neh 10:33 showbread, the continual C offering, the continual
13:5 had previously put the C offering, the frankincense,
13:9 of God, with the C offering and the frankincense.
Is 57:6 you have brought a C offering.
66:3 he who presents a C offering, like him who
66:20 the Israelites bring their C offering in a clean
Jer 14:12 offer burnt offering and C offering, I will not
17:26 offerings and sacrifices, C offerings and frankincense,
33:18 burnt offerings, to burn C offerings, and to make
41:5 their bodies gashed, bringing C offerings and incense
Bar 1:10 incense, and prepare a C offering, and offer them
Ezek 42:13 most holy offerings--the C offering, the sin offering,
44:29 They shall eat the C offering, the sin offering,
45:15 is the offering for C offerings, burnt offerings, and
45:17 furnish the burnt offerings, C offerings, and drink
45:17 provide the sin offerings, C offerings, burnt offerings,
45:24 shall provide as a C offering an ephah for
45:25 offerings, burnt offerings, and C offerings, and for the
46:5 without blemish; and the C offering with the ram
46:5 an ephah, and the C offering with the lambs
46:7 without blemish; as a C offering he shall provide
46:11 the appointed seasons the C offering with a young
46:14 he shall provide a C offering with it morning
46:14 the flour, as a C offering to the LORD;
46:20 they shall bake the C offering, in order not
Joel 1:9 The C offering and the drink offering are cut
1:12 Because C offering and drink offering are withheld
2:14 blessing behind him, a C offering and a drink
Amos 5:22 your burnt offerings and C offerings, I will not
2Mac 1:8 we offered sacrifice and C offering, and we lighted

CERTAIN (62)

Gen 28:11 he came to a C place, and stayed there
38:1 turned in to a C Adullamite, whose name was
38:2 the daughter of a C Canaanite whose name was
Num 9:6 And there were C men who were unclean through
Deut 13:13 to dwell there, that C base fellows have gone
13:14 it be true and C that such an abominable
17:4 it is true and C that such an abominable
Josh 2:2 king of Jericho, "Behold, C men of Israel have
Judg 9:53 And a C woman threw an upper millstone upon
13:2 And there was a C man of Zorah, of
19:1 king in Israel, a C Levite was sojourning in
Ruth 1:1 the land, and a C man of Bethlehem in
1Sam 1:1 There was a C man of Ramathaim-zophim of
21:7 Now a C man of the servants of Saul
2Sam 12:1 two men in a C city, the one rich
18:10 And a C man saw it, and told Joab,
1Kgs 2:37 brook Kidron, know for C that you shall die;
2:42 you, saying, 'Know for C that on the day
11:17 to Egypt, together with C Edomites of his father's
20:35 And a C man of the sons of the
22:34 But a C man drew his bow at a
1Chr 16:4 Moreover he appointed C of the Levites as ministers
25:1 apart for the service C of the sons of
2Chr 13:7 against his lord; and C worthless scoundrels gathered
18:33 But a C man drew his bow at a
19:8 Jerusalem Jehoshaphat appointed C Levites and
:12 C chiefs also of the men of Ephraim, Azariah
Neh 1:2 my brethren, came with C men out of Judah;
11:4 And in Jerusalem lived C of the sons of
11:36 And C divisions of the Levites in Judah were
12:35 Shemaiah, and Jeremiah, and C of the priests' sons
Esth 3:8 Ahasuerus, "There is a C people scattered abroad
13:4 there is scattered a C hostile people, who have
Jer 26:15 Only know for C that if you put me
26:17 And C of the elders of the land arose
26:22 Jehoiakim sent to Egypt C men, Elnathan the son
Ezek 14:1 Then came C of the elders of Israel to
20:1 day of the month, C of the elders of
Dan 2:45 The dream is C, and its interpretation sure."
3:8 Therefore at that time C Chaldeans came forward
3:12 There are C Jews whom you have appointed over
3:20 And he ordered C mighty men of his army
1Mac 11:21 But C lawless men who hated their nation went
11:25 Although C lawless men of his nation kept making
15:3 Whereas C pestilent men have gained control of the
2Mac 4:40 the leadership of a C Auranus, a man advanced
12:13 He also attacked a C city which was strongly
12:35 But a C Dositheus, one of Bacenor's men, who
14:3 Now a C Alcimus, who had formerly been high
14:37 A C Razis, one of the elders of Jerusalem,
Mt 26:18 the city to a C one, and say to
Lk 7:41 "A C creditor had two debtors; one owed five
11:1 was praying in a C place, and when he
18:2 He said, "In a C city there was a
Jn 11:1 Now a C man was ill, Lazarus of Bethany,
Acts 13:6 they came upon a C magician, a Jewish false
25:19 supposed; but they had C points of dispute with
Gal 2:12 For before C men came from James, he ate
1Tim 1:3 that you may charge C persons not to teach
1:6 C persons by swerving from these have wandered
1:19 conscience, C persons have made shipwreck of
Heb 4:7 again he sets a C day, "Today," saying through

CERTAINLY (21)

Lev 10:18 You C ought to have eaten it in the
Num 24:11 I said, 'I will C honor you,' but the
1Sam 25:28 for the LORD will C make my lord a

2Sam 5:19 up; for I will C give the Philistines into
2Kgs 8:10 to him, 'You shall C recover'; but the LORD
8:10 me that he shall C die."
8:14 me that you would C recover."
Sir 12:2 if not by him, C by the Most High.
31:12 not say, "There is C much upon it!"
Jer 36:29 king of Babylon will C come and destroy this
Bar 6:46 that make them will C not live very long
2Mac 3:38 at all, for there C is about the place
7:31 against the Hebrews, will C not escape the hands
Mt 26:73 and said to Peter, C you are also one
Mk 14:70 bystanders said to Peter, C you are one of
Lk 22:57 still another insisted, saying, C this man also was
23:46 praised God, and said, C this man was innocent!"
Acts 21:22 They will C hear that you have come.
Rom 6:5 like his, we shall C be united with him
Gal 2:17 C not!
3:21 C not; for if a law had been given

CERTAINTY (5)

Josh 9:24 your servants for a C that the LORD your
1Sam 26:4 and learned of a C that Saul had come.
Jer 42:19 Egypt.' Know for a C that I have warned
42:22 therefore know for a C that you shall die
Dan 2:8 answered, "I know with C that you are trying

CERTIFICATE (3)

Mt 5:31 him give her a C of divorce.'
19:7 one to give a C of divorce, and to
Mk 10:4 man to write a C of divorce, and to

CHABRIS (3)

Jud 6:15 tribe of Simeon, and C the son of Gothoniel,
8:10 she possessed, to summon C and Charmis, the elders
10:6 elders of the city, C and Charmis

CHAEREAS (2)

2Mac 10:32 especially well garrisoned, where C was commander.
10:37 cistern, and his brother C, and Apollophanes.

CHAFES

Sir 26:7 an ox yoke which C; taking hold of her

CHAFF (16)

Job 13:25 thou frighten a driven leaf and pursue dry C
21:18 the wind, and like C that the storm carries
Ps 1:4 so, but are like C which the wind drives
35:5 Let them be like C before the wind, with
83:13 like whirling dust, like C before the wind.
Wis 5:14 ungodly man is like C carried by the wind,
Is 17:13 far away, chased like C on the mountains before
29:5 and the multitude of the ruthless like passing C
33:11 You conceive C, you bring forth stubble; your breath
41:15 make the hills like C;
Jer 13:24 will scatter you like C driven by the wind
Dan 2:35 and became like the C of the summer threshing
Hos 13:3 early away, like the C that swirls from the
Zeph 2:2 away like the drifting C, before there comes upon
Mt 3:12 the granary, but the C he will burn with
Lk 3:17 his granary, but the C he will burn with

CHAIN (10)

Gen 41:42 and put a gold C about his neck;
1Kgs 7:17 work with wreaths of C work for the capitals
Wis 17:17 fate; for with one C of darkness they all
Ezek 16:11 your arms, and a C on your neck.
Dan 5:7 purple, and have a C of gold about his
5:16 purple, and have a C of gold about your
5:29 clothed with purple, a C of gold was put
Mk 5:3 more, even with a C;
Acts 28:20 of Israel that I am bound with this C
Rev 20:1 key of the bottomless pit and a great C

CHAINS (27)

Ex 28:14 gold filigree, and two C of pure gold, twisted
28:14 shall attach the corded C to the settings.
28:22 for the breastpiece twisted C like cords, of pure
39:15 on the breastpiece twisted C like cords, of pure
1Kgs 6:21 gold, and he drew C of gold across, in
2Chr 3:5 and made palms and C on it.
3:16 He made C like a necklace and put them
3:16 a hundred pomegranates, and put them on the C
Job 38:31 "Can you bind the C of the Pleiades, or
Ps 149:8 bind their kings with C and their nobles with
Is 40:19 it with gold, and casts for it silver C
45:14 shall come over in C and bow down to
Jer 40:1 took him bound in C along with all the
40:4 you today from the C on your hands.
Lam 3:7 he has put heavy C on me;
Nah 3:10 and all her great men were bound in C
Mk 5:4 bound with fetters and C, but the chains he
5:4 and chains, but the C he wrenched apart, and
Lk 8:29 guard, and bound with C and fetters, but he
Acts 12:6 soldiers, bound with two C, and sentries before the
12:7 And the C fell off his hands.
21:33 and ordered him to be bound with two C
26:29 become such as I am—except for these C
Eph 6:20 am an ambassador in C; that I may declare
2Tim 1:16 not ashamed of my C,
Heb 11:36 and scourging, and even C and imprisonment.
Jude 1:6 by him in eternal C in the nether gloom

CHAIR

2Kgs 4:10 bed, a table, a C, and a lamp, so

CHALDEA (10)

Jud 5:7 the gods of their fathers who were in C
Is 48:20 from Babylon, flee from C, declare this with a
Jer 50:10 C shall be plundered; all who plunder her shall
51:1 against the inhabitants of C;
51:24 all the inhabitants of C before your very eyes
51:35 "My blood be upon the inhabitants of C
Ezek 11:24 Spirit of God into C, to the exiles.
16:29 the trading land of C; and even with this
23:15 a picture of Babylonians whose native land was C
23:16 upon them, and sent messengers to them in C

CHALDEAN (6)

2Kgs 25:24 afraid because of the C officials; dwell in the
Ezra 5:12 king of Babylon, the C, who destroyed this house
Jer 37:11 when the C army had withdrawn from Jerusalem
41:3 at Mizpah, and the C soldiers who happened to
Dan 2:10 a thing of any magician or enchanter or C
5:30 very night Belshazzar the C king was slain.

CHALDEANS (82)

Gen 11:28 land of his birth, in Ur of the C
11:31 from Ur of the C to go into the
15:7 from Ur of the C, to give you this
2Kgs 24:2 him bands of the C, and bands of the
25:4 king's garden, though the C were around the city.
25:5 the army of the C pursued the king, and
25:10 the army of the C, who were with the
25:13 of the LORD, the C broke in pieces, and
25:25 the Jews and the C who were with him
25:26 to Egypt; for they were afraid of the C
2Chr 36:17 the king of the C, who slew their young
Neh 9:7 of Ur of the C and give him the
Jud 1:6 Many nations joined the forces of the C
5:6 This people is descended from the C
Job 1:17 another, and said, "The C formed three companies,
Is 13:19 and pride of the C, will be like Sodom
23:13 Behold the land of the C
43:14 the shouting of the C will be turned to
47:1 ground without a throne, O daughter of the C
47:5 O daughter of the C; for you shall no
48:14 Babylon, and his arm shall be against the C
Jer 21:4 Babylon and against the C who are besieging you
21:9 and surrenders to the C who are besieging you
22:25 of Babylon and into the hand of the C
24:5 from this place to the land of the C
25:12 the land of the C, for their iniquity, says
32:4 the hand of the C, but shall surely be
32:5 you fight against the C, you shall not succeed'?"
32:24 the hands of the C who are fighting against
32:25 city is given into the hands of the C
32:28 the hands of the C and into the hand
32:29 The C who are fighting against this city shall
32:43 it is given into the hands of the C
33:5 before the sword: The C are coming in to
35:11 the army of the C and the army of
37:5 and when the C who were besieging Jerusalem
37:8 And the C shall come back and fight against
37:9 deceive yourselves, saying, "The C will surely stay
37:10 the whole army of C who are fighting against
37:13 the prophet, saying, "You are deserting to the C
37:14 is false; I am not deserting to the C
38:2 goes out to the C shall live; he shall
38:18 the hand of the C, and they shall burn
38:19 have deserted to the C, lest I be handed
38:23 led out to the C, and you yourself shall
39:5 the army of the C pursued them, and overtook

39:8 The C burned the king's house and the house
40:9 saying, "Do not be afraid to serve the C
40:10 for you before the C who will come to
41:18 Egypt because of the C; for they were afraid
43:3 the hand of the C, that they may kill
50:1 the land of the C, by Jeremiah the prophet:
50:8 the land of the C, and be as he-goats
50:25 work to do in the land of the C
50:35 "A sword upon the C, says the LORD, and
50:45 the land of the C: Surely the little ones
51:4 the land of the C, and wounded in her
51:5 the land of the C is full of guilt
51:54 of great destruction from the land of the C
52:7 king's garden, while the C were round about the
52:8 the army of the C pursued the king, and
52:14 the army of the C, who were with the
52:17 of the LORD, the C broke in pieces, and
Bar 1:2 the time when the C took Jerusalem and burned
6:40 Besides, even the C themselves dishonor them;
Ezek 1:3 the land of the C by the river Chebar;
12:13 the land of the C, yet he shall not
23:14 the images of the C portrayed in vermilion,
23:23 Babylonians and all the C, Pekod and Shoa and
Dan 1:4 teach them the letters and language of the C
2:2 the sorcerers, and the C be summoned, to tell
2:4 Then the C said to the king, "O king,
2:5 The king answered the C, "The word from me
2:10 The C answered the king, "There is not a
3:8 at that time certain C came forward and maliciously
3:48 burned those of the C whom it caught about
4:7 magicians, the enchanters, the C, and the astrologers
5:7 in the enchanters, the C, and the astrologers.
5:11 of the magicians, enchanters, C, and astrologers,
9:1 the realm of the C --
Hab 1:6 I am rousing the C, that bitter and hasty
Acts 7:4 the land of the C, and lived in Haran.

CHALKSTONES

Is 27:9 of the altars like C crushed to pieces, no

CHALPHI

1Mac 11:70 Judas the son of C, commanders of the forces

CHAMBER (59)

Gen 43:30 And he entered his C and wept there.
Judg 3:20 he was sitting alone in his cool roof C
3:23 doors of the roof C upon him, and locked
3:24 doors of the roof C were locked, they thought,
3:24 relieving himself in the closet of the cool C
3:25 doors of the roof C, they took the key
15:1 will go in to my wife in the C
16:9 had men lying in wait in an inner C
16:12 men lying in wait were in an inner C
2Sam 13:10 the food into the C, that I may eat
13:10 brought them into the C to Amnon her brother.
18:33 went up to the C over the gate, and
1Kgs 1:15 the king into his C (now the king was
17:19 up into the upper C, where he lodged, and
17:23 down from the upper C into the house, and
20:30 and entered an inner C in the city.
22:25 go into an inner C to hide yourself."
2Kgs 1:2 lattice in his upper C in Samaria, and lay
4:10 make a small roof C with walls, and put
4:11 he turned into the C and rested there.
9:2 his fellows, and lead him to an inner C
23:11 LORD, by the C of Nathan-melech the chamberlain,
23:12 roof of the upper C of Ahaz, which the
2Chr 18:24 go into an inner C to hide yourself."
Ezra 10:6 and went to the C of Jehohanan the son
Neh 3:30 the son of Berechiah repaired opposite his C
3:31 and to the upper C of the corner.
3:32 And between the upper C of the corner and
13:5 for Tobiah a large C where they had previously
13:7 preparing for him a C in the courts of
13:8 the household furniture of Tobiah out of the C
Tob 6:13 husbands and that each died in the bridal C
6:16 you enter the bridal C, you shall take live
Job 37:9 From its C comes the whirlwind, and cold from
Ps 19:5 a bridegroom leaving his C, and like a strong
45:13 is decked in her C with gold-woven robes;
Song 3:4 house, and into the C of her that conceived
8:2 mother, and into the C of her that conceived
Wis 17:4 not even the inner C that held them protected
Jer 35:4 the LORD into the C of the sons of
35:4 which was near the C of the princes, above
35:4 the princes, above the C of Ma-aseiah the son
36:10 the LORD, in the C of Gemariah the son
36:12 house, into the secretary's C; and all the princes
36:20 the scroll in the C of Elishama the secretary;
36:21 took it from the C of Elishama the secretary;
Ezek 16:24 built yourself a vaulted C, and made yourself a
16:31 harlot; building your vaulted C at the head of
16:39 throw down your vaulted C and break down your
40:38 There was a C with its door in the
40:45 said to me, This C which faces south is
40:46 the temple, and the C which faces north is
Dan 6:10 windows in his upper C open toward Jerusalem; and
Joel 2:16 bridegroom leave his room, and the bride her C
1Mac 1:27 sat in the bridal C was mourning.
8:15 for themselves a senate C, and every day three
8:19 they entered the senate C and spoke as follows:
12:3 and entered the senate C and said, "Jonathan the
Acts 20:8 lights in the upper C where we were gathered.

CHAMBERLAIN (2)

2Kgs 23:11 chamber of Nathan-melech the C, which was in the
Acts 12:20 persuaded Blastus, the king's C, they asked for peace,

CHAMBERLAINS

Esth 1:10 served King Ahasuerus as C,

CHAMBERS (55)

Deut 32:25 bereave, and in the C shall be terror, destroying
1Kgs 6:5 and he made side C all around.
7:3 with cedar above the C that were upon the
1Chr 9:26 in charge of the C and the treasures of
9:33 Levites, dwelling in the C of the temple free
23:28 the courts and the C, the cleansing of all
28:11 rooms, and its inner C, and of the room
28:12 LORD, all the surrounding C, the treasuries of the
2Chr 3:9 he overlaid the upper C with gold.
31:11 commanded them to prepare C in the house of
Ezra 8:29 at Jerusalem, within the C of the house of
Neh 10:37 the priests, to the C of the house of
10:38 our God, to the C, to the storehouse.
10:39 and oil to the C, where are the vessels
12:44 were appointed over the C for the stores, the
13:4 was appointed over the C of the house of
13:9 and they cleansed the C; and I brought back
Job 9:9 the Pleiades and the C of the south;
Ps 104:3 the beams of thy C on the waters, who
105:30 frogs, even in the C of their kings.
Prov 7:27 going down to the C of death.
Song 1:4 The king has brought me into his C
Is 26:20 my people, enter your C, and shut your doors
Jer 35:2 into one of the C; then offer them wine
Ezek 40:17 and behold, there were C and a pavement, round
40:17 about the court; thirty C fronted on the pavement.
40:44 behold, there were two C in the inner court,
41:5 breadth of the side C, four cubits, round about
41:6 And the side C were in three stories, one
41:6 supports for the side C, so that they should
41:7 And the side C became broader as they rose
41:8 foundations of the side C measured a full reed
41:9 wall of the side C was five cubits; and
41:10 the temple and the C of the court was
41:11 doors of the side C opened on the part
42:1 brought me to the C which were opposite the
42:4 And before the C was a passage inward, ten
42:5 Now the upper C were narrower, for the galleries
42:5 the lower and middle C in the building.
42:6 court; hence the upper C were set back from
42:7 outside parallel to the C, toward the outer court,
42:7 outer court, opposite the C, fifty cubits long.
42:8 For the C on the outer court were fifty
42:9 Below these C was an entrance on the east
42:10 the building, there were C
42:11 were similar to the C on the north, of
42:12 And below the south C was an entrance on
42:13 to me, "The north C and the south chambers
42:13 chambers and the south C opposite the yard are
42:13 yard are the holy C, where the priests who
44:19 them in the holy C; and they shall put
46:19 row of the holy C for the priests; and
Amos 9:6 who builds his upper C in the heavens, and
1Mac 4:38 They saw also the C of the priests in
4:57 the gates and the C for the priests, and

CHAMELEON

Lev 11:30 crocodile, the lizard, the sand lizard, and the C

CHAMPION (4)

1Sam 17:4 of the Philistines a C named Goliath, of Gath,
17:23 with them, behold, the C, the Philistine of Gath,
17:51 Philistines saw that their C was dead, they fled.
Wis 18:21 to act as their C; he brought forward the

CHANCE (10)

Deut 22:6 "If you C to come upon a bird's nest,
1Sam 6:9 that struck us, it happened to us by C
2Sam 1:6 told him said, "By C I happened to be
Eccl 9:11 skill; but time and C happen to them all.
Wis 2:2 were born by mere C, and hereafter we shall
12:10 thou gavest them a C to repent, though thou
Sir 27:12 people watch for a C to leave, but among
Lk 10:31 Now by C a priest was going down that
Acts 27:12 from there, on the C that somehow they could
Heb 12:17 for he found no C to repent, though he

CHANCED (2)

2Sam 18:9 And Absalom C to meet the servants of David.
Acts 17:17 day with those who C to be there.

CHANCES

Deut 23:10 by reason of what C to him by night,

CHANGE (31)

Gen 35:2 and purify yourselves, and C your garments;
2Sam 14:20 In order to C the course of affairs your
Ps 15:4 hurt and does not C;
46:2 the earth should C, though the mountains shake
110:4 sworn and will not C his mind, "You are
Wis 4:11 caught up lest evil C his understanding or guile
12:10 and that their way of thinking would never C
19:2 them forth, they would C their minds and pursue
Sir 12:18 and whisper much, and C his expression.
18:25 morning to evening conditions C, and all things move
33:19 to another, lest you C your mind and must
Jer 13:23 Can the Ethiopian C his skin or the leopard
Dan 2:9 and corrupt words before me till the times C
5:10 not your thoughts alarm you or your color C
7:25 and shall think to C the times and the
Hos 4:7 against me; I will C their glory into shame.
Zeph 3:9 that time I will C the speech of the
3:19 outcast, and I will C their shame into praise
Mal 3:6 the LORD do not C; therefore you, O sons
1Mac 1:49 forget the law and C all the ordinances.
2Mac 3:16 his face and the C in his color disclosed
4:46 induced the king to C his mind.
6:9 did not choose to C over to Greek customs.
11:24 consent to our father's C to Greek customs but
Acts 6:14 this place, and will C the customs which Moses
Gal 4:20 you now and to C my tone, for I
Phil 3:21 Jesus Christ, who will C our lowly body to
Heb 7:12 when there is a C in the priesthood, there
7:12 there is necessarily a C in the law as
7:21 sworn and will not C his mind, 'Thou art
Jas 1:16 there is no variation or shadow due to C

CHANGED (41)

Gen 31:7 has cheated me and C my wages ten times,
31:41 flock, and you have C my wages ten times.
41:14 had shaved himself and C his clothes, he came
Ex 14:5 and his servants was C toward the people, and
Lev 13:16 turns again and is C to white, then he
13:55 diseased spot has not C color, though the disease
Num 32:38 (their names to be C, and Sibmah; and they
1Sam 21:13 So he C his behavior before them, and feigned
2Sam 12:20 and anointed himself, and C his clothes; and he
2Kgs 23:34 Josiah his father, and C his name to Jehoiakim.
24:17 in his stead, and C his name to Zedekiah.
2Chr 36:4 Judah and Jerusalem, and C his name to Jehoiakim;
Jud 10:7 altered and her clothing C, they greatly admired her
Esth 9:1 but which had been C to a day when
15:8 Then God C the spirit of the king to
Job 38:14 It is C like clay under the seal, and
Ps 77:10 the right hand of the Most High has C
Eccl 8:1 shine, and the hardness of his countenance is C
Wis 16:21 who took it, was C to suit every one's
16:25 at that time also, C into all forms, it
19:18 For the elements C places with one another, as
Sir 6:28 and she will be C into joy for you.
Jer 2:11 Has a nation C its gods, even though they
2:11 But my people have C their glory for that
48:11 remains in him, and his scent is not C
Lam 4:1 has grown dim, how the pure gold is C
Dan 3:19 of his face was C against Shadrach, Meshach, and
4:16 let his mind be C from a mans, and
5:6 Then the king's color C, and his thoughts alarmed
5:9 alarmed, and his color C; and his lords were
6:8 that it cannot be C, according to the law
6:15 or ordinance which the king establishes can be C
6:17 that nothing might be C concerning Daniel.
7:28 me, and my color C; but I kept the
10:8 radiant appearance was fearfully C, and I retained
2Mac 6:29 with good will now C to ill will, because
Acts 28:6 come to him, they C their minds and said
1Cor 15:51 we shall all be C,
15:52 will be raised imperishable, and we shall be C
2Cor 3:18 the Lord, are being C into his likeness from
Heb 1:12 wilt roll them up, and they will be C

CHANGES (9)

Wis 7:18 the solstices and the C of the seasons,
Sir 2:4 upon you, and in C that humble you be
6:9 is a friend who C into an enemy, and
13:24 A man's heart C his countenance, either for good
25:16 wickedness of a wife C her appearance, and darkens
27:11 wise, but the fool C like the moon.
37:17 As a clue to C of heart
Dan 2:21 He C times and seasons; he removes kings and
Mic 2:4 are utterly ruined; he C the portion of my

CHANGEST (2)

Job 14:20 and he passes; thou C his countenance, and sendest
Ps 102:26 Thou C them like raiment, and they pass away;

CHANGING (2)

Esth 16:9 for all men, by C our methods and always
Jer 2:36 lightly you gad about, C your way!

CHANNEL (2)

Job 38:25 "Who has cleft a C for the torrents of
Sir 24:28 and like a water C into a garden.

CHANNELS (5)

2Sam 22:16 Then the C of the sea were seen, the
Job 28:10 He cuts out C in the rocks, and his
Ps 18:15 Then the C of the sea were seen, and
Is 8:7 rise over all its C and go over all
11:15 smite it into seven C that men may cross

CHANT (2)

Ezek 32:16 of the nations shall C it; over Egypt, and
32:16 her multitude, shall they C it, says the Lord

CHANTED (2)

Ps 8:1 above the heavens is C
Ezek 32:16 lamentation which shall be C; the daughters of the

CHAOS (5)

Job 10:22 land of gloom and C, where light is as
Is 24:10 The city of C is broken down, every house
34:11 and the plummet of C over its nobles.
45:18 not create it a C, he formed it to
45:19 Jacob, 'Seek me in C I the LORD speak

CHAPHENATHA

1Mac 12:37 had fallen, and he repaired the section called C

CHARACTER (4)

2Mac 5:22 a Phrygian and in C more barbarous than the
Rom 5:4 and endurance produces C, and character produces
5:4 endurance produces character, and C produces hope,
Heb 6:17 the promise the unchangeable C of his purpose, he

CHARACTERS

Is 8:1 in common C, 'Belonging to Maher-shalal-hash-baz.'"

CHARAX

2Mac 12:17 there, they came to C, to the Jews who

CHARCOAL (3)

Prov 26:21 As C to hot embers and wood to fire,
Jn 18:18 officers had made a C fire, because it was
21:9 land, they saw a C fire there, with fish

CHARGE (164)

Gen 18:19 him, that he may C his children and his
24:2 his house, who had C of all that he
26:5 voice and kept my C, my commandments, my
30:35 and put them in C of his sons;
39:4 and put him in C of all that he

39:6 he had in Joseph's C; and having him he
47:6 them, put them in C of my cattle."
Ex 6:13 and gave them a C to the people of
19:23 for thou thyself didst C us, saying, 'Set bounds
23:7 far from a false C, and do not slay
Lev 18:30 So keep my C never to practice any of
22:9 shall therefore keep my C, lest they bear sin
Num 1:53 the Levites shall keep C of the tabernacle of
3:8 tabernacle; they shall have C of all the furnishings
3:25 And the C of the sons of Gershon in
3:31 And their C was to be the ark, the
3:32 of those who had C of the sanctuary.
3:36 And the appointed C of the sons of Merari
3:38 and his sons, having C of the rites within
4:16 the priest shall have C of the oil for
4:27 shall assign to their C all that they are
8:26 meeting, to keep the C, and they shall do
9:19 of Israel kept the C of the LORD, and
9:23 out; they kept the C of the LORD, at
31:30 the Levites who have C of the tabernacle of
31:47 the Levites who had C of the tabernacle of
Deut 3:28 But C Joshua, and encourage and strengthen him; for
11:1 God, and keep his C, his statutes, his ordinances,
17:18 which is in the C of the Levitical priests;
19:15 three witnesses, shall a C be sustained.
Josh 22:3 careful to keep the C of the LORD your
Ruth 2:5 servant who was in C of the reapers, "Whose
2:6 servant who was in C of the reapers answered,
1Sam 7:1 son, Eleazar, to have C of the ark of
13:21 his sickle; and the C was a pim for
14:27 not heard his father C the people with the
17:22 left the things in C of the keeper of
2Sam 3:8 David; and yet you C me today with a
10:10 he put in the C of Abishai his brother,
20:24 and Adoram was in C of the forced labor;
1Kgs 2:3 man, and keep the C of the LORD your
4:6 friend; Ahishar was in C of the palace; and
4:6 of Abda was in C of the forced labor.
4:28 where it was required, each according to his C
5:14 home; Adoniram was in C of the levy.
5:16 the work, who had C of the people who
9:23 and fifty, who had C of the people who
11:28 industrious he gave him C over all the forced
21:10 let them bring a C against him, saying, 'You
21:13 base fellows brought a C against Naboth, in the
2Kgs 6:1 we dwell under your C is too small for
7:17 he leaned to have C of the gate; and
10:22 him who was in C of the wardrobe, "Bring
1Chr 6:31 whom David put in C of the service of
9:19 the Korahites, were in C of the work of
9:19 fathers had been in C of the camp of
9:23 their sons were in C of the gates of
9:26 were Levites, were in C of the chambers and
9:27 watching, and they had C of opening it every
9:28 Some of them had C of the utensils of
9:31 the Korahite, was in C of making the flat
9:32 of the Kohathites had C of the showbread, to
19:11 he put in the C of Abishai his brother,
22:12 when he gives you C over Israel you may
23:4 David said, "shall have C of the work in
23:32 Thus they shall keep C of the tent of
26:20 the Levites, Ahijah had C of the treasuries of
26:22 his brother, were in C of the treasuries of
26:24 was chief officer in C of the treasuries.
26:26 his brethren were in C of all the treasuries
27:2 of Zabdiel was in C of the first division
27:4 the Ahohite was in C of the division of
27:6 his son was in C of his division.
2Chr 13:11 for we keep the C of the LORD our
23:6 people shall keep the C of the LORD.
23:18 organized to be in C of the house of
24:12 to those who had C of the work of
31:12 The chief officer in C of them was Conaniah
Ezra 1:8 brought these out in C of Mithredath the treasurer,
Neh 7:2 governor of the castle C over Jerusalem, for he
10:32 ourselves the obligation to C ourselves yearly with
12:8 his brethren was in C of the songs of
Tob 1:22 the signet, and in C of administration of the
Jud 8:10 maid, who was in C of all she possessed,
12:11 the eunuch who had C of his personal affairs,
14:13 to the steward in C of all his personal
Esth 2:3 eunuch who is in C of the women; let
2:8 of Hegai who had C of the women.
2:14 eunuch who was in C of the concubines; she
2:15 king's eunuch, who had C of the women, advised.
3:9 of those who have C of the king's business,
4:8 it to her and C her to go to
13:6 Haman, who is in C of affairs and is
Job 1:22 did not sin or C God with wrong.
34:13 Who gave him C over the earth and who
Ps 50:21 you, and lay the C before you.
91:11 will give his angels C of you to guard
Jer 23:32 not send them or C them; so they do
27:4 Give them this C for their masters: 'Thus says
29:26 the priest, to have C in the house of
47:7 quiet, when the LORD has given it a C
Ezek 40:45 the priests who have C of the temple,
40:46 the priests who have C of the altar; these
44:8 you have not kept C of my holy things;
44:8 foreigners to keep my C in my sanctuary.
44:14 appoint them to keep C of the temple, to
44:15 Zadok, who kept the C of my sanctuary when
44:16 minister to me, and they shall keep my C
48:11 Zadok, who kept my C, who did not go
Dan 12:1 great prince who has C of your people.
Joel 2:7 Like warriors they C, like soldiers they scale the
Zech 3:7 ways and keep my C, then you shall rule
3:7 my house and have C of my courts, and
Mal 3:14 of our keeping his C or of walking as
1Mac 3:32 of royal lineage, in C of the king's affairs
3:55 of the people, in C of thousands and hundreds
4:8 fear their numbers or be afraid when they C
5:19 them this command, "Take C of this people, but
7:20 He placed Alcimus in C of the country and
9:25 and put them in C of the country.
14:42 that he should take C of the sanctuary and
14:42 that he should take C of the sanctuary,
2Mac 3:7 Heliodorus, who was in C of his affairs, and
6:21 Those who were in C of that unlawful sacrifice
10:11 one Lysias to have C of the government and
11:1 kinsman, who was in C of the government, being
13:2 his guardian, who had C of the government.
13:23 had been left in C of the government, had
Mt 4:6 will give his angels C of you,' and 'On
27:14 even to a single C; so that the governor
27:37 head they put the C against him, which read,
Mk 13:34 puts his servants in C, each with his work,
15:26 the inscription of the C against him read, "The
Lk 4:10 will give his angels C of you, to guard
Jn 8:6 they might have some C to bring against him.
10:18 take it again; this C I have received from
Acts 8:27 of the Ethiopians, in C of all her treasure,
13:28 Though they could C him with nothing deserving
15:5 circumcise them, and to C them to keep the
16:18 to the spirit, "I C you in the name
16:24 Having received this C, he put them into the
23:28 desiring to know the C on which they accused
24:8 also joined in the C, affirming that all this
25:16 his defense concerning the C laid against him.
25:18 up, they brought no C in his case of
28:19 though I had no C to bring against my
Rom 3:8 as some people slanderously C us with saying.
8:33 Who shall bring any C against God's elect?
1Cor 7:10 the married I give C, not I but the
9:18 the gospel free of C, not making full use
2Cor 13:1 Any C must be sustained by the evidence of
1Tim 1:3 Ephesus that you may C certain persons not to
1:5 the aim of our C is love that issues
1:18 This C I commit to you, Timothy, my son,
5:19 Never admit any C against an elder except on
5:21 the elect angels I C you to keep these
6:14 the good confession, I C you to keep the
6:17 rich in this world, C them not to be
2Tim 2:14 them of this, and C them before the Lord
4:1 I C you in the presence of God and
Tit 1:5 not open to the C of being profligate or
Philem 1:18 or owes you anything, C that to my account.
1Pet 5:2 God that is your C, not by constraint but
5:3 over those in your C but being examples to

CHARGED (49)
Gen 28:1 and blessed him, and C him, "You shall not
28:6 he blessed him he C him, "You shall not
40:4 captain of the guard C Joseph with them, and
49:29 Then he C them, and said to them, "I
Ex 4:28 signs which he had C him to do.
Lev 8:35 what the LORD has C, lest you die; for
Num 4:31 is what they are C to carry, as the
7:9 none, because they were C with the care of
Deut 1:16 And I C your judges at that time, 'Hear
24:5 the army or be C with any business; he
27:11 And Moses C the people the same day, saying,

Josh 18:8 their way; and Joshua C those who went to
Ruth 2:9 Have I not C the young men not to
1Sam 14:28 said, "Your father strictly C the people with an
21:2 priest, "The king has C me with a matter,
21:2 with which I have C you.' I have made
1Kgs 2:1 die drew near, he C Solomon his son, saying,
2:43 commandment with which I C you?"
14:6 For I am C with heavy tidings for you.
1Chr 22:6 Solomon his son, and C him to build a
2Chr 19:9 And he C them: "Thus you shall do in
36:23 earth, and he has C me to build him
Ezra 1:2 earth, and he has C me to build him
Esth 2:10 kindred, for Mordecai had C her not to make
2:20 people, as Mordecai had C her; for Esther obeyed
Jer 32:13 I C Baruch in their presence, saying,
2Mac 12:37 with hymns; then he C against Gorgias' men when
Mt 9:30 And Jesus sternly C them, "See that no one
16:20 Then he strictly C the disciples to tell no
Mk 1:43 And he sternly C him, and sent him away
5:43 And he strictly C them that no one should
6:8 He C them to take nothing for their journey
7:35 And he C them to tell no one; but
7:35 but the more he C them, the more zealously
8:30 And he C them to tell no one about
9:9 down the mountain, he C them to tell no
Lk 5:14 And he C him to tell no one; but
8:56 were amazed; but he C them to tell no
9:21 But he C and commanded them to tell this
Acts 1:4 staying with them he C them not to depart
4:18 they called them and C them not to speak
5:28 them, saying, "We strictly C you not to teach
5:40 they beat them and C them not to speak
19:40 in danger of being C with rioting today, there
23:29 of their law, but C with nothing deserving death
Rom 3:9 for I have already C that all men, both
1Thes 2:11 and encouraged you and C you
4:11 your hands, as we C you;
2Tim 4:16 May it not be C against them!

CHARGERS

Nah 2:3 mustered in array; the C prance.

CHARGES (16)

Deut 22:14 then spurns her, and C her with shameful conduct,
22:17 he has made shameful C against her, saying, "I
Neh 5:7 myself, and I brought C against the nobles and
Job 4:18 and his angels he C with error;
1Mac 7:25 king and brought wicked C against them.
10:63 one is to bring C against him about any
2Mac 4:43 C were brought against Menelaus about this
4:47 he acquitted of the C against him, while he
Mk 15:4 See how many C they bring against you."
Lk 16:1 had a steward, and C were brought to him
23:14 of any of your C against him;
Acts 19:38 proconsuls; let them bring C against one another.
25:7 against him many serious C which they could not
25:9 be tried on these C before me?"
25:11 is nothing in their C against me, no one
25:27 not to indicate the C against him."

CHARGING (8)

Gen 49:33 When Jacob finished C his sons, he drew up
Prov 28:15 roaring lion or a C bear is a wicked
Dan 8:4 I saw the ram C westward and northward and
Nah 3:3 Horsemen C, flashing sword and glittering spear,
2Mac 5:2 appeared golden-clad horsemen C through the air, in
Mt 10:5 twelve Jesus sent out, C them, "Go nowhere among
Acts 16:23 threw them into prison, C the jailer to keep
23:22 dismissed the young man, C him, "Tell no one

CHARIOT (63)

Gen 41:43 ride in his second C; and they cried before
46:29 Joseph made ready his C and went up to
Ex 14:6 he made ready his C and took his army
14:25 the Egyptians, clogging their C wheels so that they
Judg 4:15 Sisera alighted from his C and fled away on
5:28 lattice: 'Why is his C so long in coming?
2Sam 8:4 David hamstrung all the C horses, but left enough
15:1 Absalom got himself a C and horses, and fifty
1Kgs 7:33 were made like a C wheel; their axles, their
9:22 his captains, his C commanders and his horsemen.
10:26 he stationed in the C cities and with the
10:29 A C could be imported from Egypt for six
12:18 haste to mount his C, to flee to Jerusalem.
18:44 to Ahab, 'Prepare your C and go down, lest
20:25 horse for horse, and C for chariot; then we
20:25 horse, and chariot for C; then we will fight
20:33 he caused him to come up into the C
22:34 the driver of his C, "Turn about, and carry
22:35 propped up in his C facing the Syrians, until
22:35 the wound flowed into the bottom of the C
22:38 And they washed the C by the pool of
2Kgs 2:11 and talked, behold, a C of fire and horses
5:21 he alighted from the C to meet him, and
5:26 man turned from his C to meet you?
8:21 and he and his C commanders smote the Edomites
9:16 Then Jehu mounted his C, and went to Jezreel,
9:21 And they made ready his C
9:21 out, each in his C, and went to meet
9:24 pierced his heart, and he sank in his C
9:27 shot him in the C at the ascent of
9:28 carried him in a C to Jerusalem, and buried
10:15 Jehu took him up with him into the C
10:16 So he had him ride in his C
23:30 him dead in a C from Megiddo, and brought
1Chr 18:4 David hamstrung all the C horses, but left enough
28:18 plan for the golden C of the cherubim that
2Chr 1:14 he stationed in the C cities and with the
1:17 They imported a C from Egypt for six hundred
9:25 he stationed in the C cities and with the
10:18 haste to mount his C, to flee to Jerusalem.
18:33 the driver of his C, "Turn about, and carry
18:34 himself up in his C facing the Syrians until
21:9 surrounded him and his C commanders.
35:24 him out of the C and carried him in
35:24 him in his second C and brought him to
Ps 65:11 the tracks of thy C drip with fatness.
104:3 makest the clouds thy C, who ridest on the
Song 6:12 set me in a C beside my prince.
Sir 48:9 of fire, in a C with horses of fire;
49:8 showed him above the C of the cherubim.
Is 43:17 waters, who brings forth C and horse, army and
Jer 51:21 break in pieces the C and the charioteer;
Nah 3:2 and rumble of wheel, galloping horse and bounding C
Hab 3:8 thy horses, upon thy C of victory?
Zech 6:2 The first C had red horses, the second black
6:3 horses, and the fourth C dappled gray horses.
6:6 The C with the black horses goes toward the
9:10 will cut off the C from Ephraim and the
2Mac 9:7 fell out of his C as it was rushing
14:21 A C came forward from each army; seats of
Acts 8:28 returning; seated in his C, he was reading the
8:29 said to Philip, "Go up and join this C
8:37 And he commanded the C to stop, and they

CHARIOTEER (2)

Jer 51:21 the chariot and the C;
2Mac 9:4 so he ordered his C to drive without stopping

CHARIOTRY

Ps 68:17 With mighty C, twice ten thousand, thousands upon

CHARIOTS (115)

Gen 50:9 up with him both C and horsemen; it was
Ex 14:7 took six hundred picked C and all the other
14:7 and all the other C of Egypt with officers
14:9 all Pharaoh's horses and C and his horsemen and
14:17 all his host, his C, and his horsemen.
14:18 glory over Pharaoh, his C, and his horsemen."
14:23 all Pharaoh's horses, his C, and his horsemen.
14:26 Egyptians, upon their C, and upon their horsemen."
14:28 returned and covered the C and the horsemen and
15:4 "Pharaoh's C and his host he cast into the
15:19 of Pharaoh with his C and his horsemen went
Deut 11:4 horses and to their C; how he made the
20:1 and see horses and C and an army larger
Josh 11:4 upon the seashore, with very many horses and C
11:6 horses, and burn their C with fire."
11:9 horses, and burned their C with fire.
17:16 in the plain have C of iron, both those
17:18 Canaanites, though they have C of iron, and though
24:6 pursued your fathers with C and horsemen to the
Judg 1:19 plain, because they had C of iron.
4:3 he had nine hundred C of iron, and oppressed
4:7 river Kishon with his C and his troops; and
4:13 called out all his C, nine hundred chariots of
4:13 his chariots, nine hundred C of iron, and all
4:15 Sisera and all his C and all his army
4:16 And Barak pursued the C and the army to
5:28 the hoofbeats of his C
1Sam 8:11 appoint them to his C and to be his
8:11 to run before his C;

8:12 implements of war and the equipment of his C
13:5 Israel, thirty thousand C, and six thousand horsemen,
2Sam 1:6 spear; and lo, the C and the horsemen were
8:4 chariot horses, but left enough for a hundred C
10:18 of seven hundred C, and forty thousand horsemen,
1Kgs 1:5 he prepared for himself C and horsemen, and fifty
4:26 of horses for his C, and twelve thousand horsemen.
9:19 the cities for his C, and the cities for
10:26 And Solomon gathered together C and horsemen; he
10:26 fourteen hundred C and twelve thousand horsemen,
16:9 commander of half his C, conspired against him.
20:1 him, and horses and C; and he went up
20:21 captured the horses and C, and killed the Syrians
22:31 thirty-two captains of his C, "Fight with neither
22:32 the captains of the C saw Jehoshaphat, they said,
22:33 the captains of the C saw that it was
2Kgs 2:12 the C of Israel and its horsemen!" And he
5:9 with his horses and C, and halted at the
6:14 sent there horses and C and a great army;
6:15 army with horses and C was round about the
6:17 full of horses and C of fire round about
7:6 hear the sound of C, and of horses, the
8:21 Zair with all his C, and rose by night,
10:2 there are with you C and horses, fortified cities
13:7 fifty horsemen and ten C and ten thousand footmen;
13:14 The C of Israel and its horsemen!"
18:24 rely on Egypt for C and for horsemen?
19:23 said, 'With my many C I have gone up
23:11 and he burned the C of the sun with
1Chr 18:4 from him a thousand C, seven thousand horsemen,
18:4 chariot horses, but left enough for a hundred C
19:6 of silver to hire C and horsemen from Mesopotamia,
19:7 They hired thirty-two thousand C and the king of
19:18 men of seven thousand C, and forty thousand foot
2Chr 1:14 Solomon gathered together C and horsemen; he had
1:14 fourteen hundred C and twelve thousand horsemen,
8:6 the cities for his C, and the cities for
8:9 the commanders of his C, and his horsemen.
9:25 stalls for horses and C, and twelve thousand
12:3 Jerusalem with twelve hundred C and sixty thousand
14:9 men and three hundred C, and came as far
16:8 army with exceedingly many C and horsemen?
18:30 the captains of his C, "Fight with neither small
18:31 the captains of the C saw Jehoshaphat, they said,
18:32 the captains of the C saw that it was
21:9 commanders and all his C, and he rose by
Jud 1:13 Arphaxad, and all his cavalry and all his C
2:19 the west with their C and horsemen and picked
2:22 his infantry, cavalry, and C, and went up into
7:20 Assyrian army, their infantry, C, and cavalry,
Ps 20:7 Some boast of C, and some of horses; but
46:9 spear, he burns the C with fire!
Song 1:9 you, my love, to a mare of Pharaoh's C
Is 2:7 horses, and there is no end to their C
22:6 bore the quiver with C and horsemen, and Kir
22:7 valleys were full of C, and the horsemen took
22:18 shall be your splendid C, you shame of your
31:1 horses, who trust in C because they are many
36:9 rely on Egypt for C and for horsemen?
37:24 said, With my many C I have gone up
66:15 in fire, and his C like the stormwind, to
66:20 upon horses, and in C, and in litters, and
Jer 4:13 up like clouds, his C like the whirlwind; his
17:25 of David, riding in C and on horses, they
22:4 of David, riding in C and on horses, they,
46:9 Advance, O horses, and rage, O C
47:3 the rushing of his C, at the rumbling of
50:37 horses and upon her C, and upon all the
Ezek 23:24 from the north with C and wagons and a
26:7 kings, with horses and C, and with horsemen and
26:10 horsemen and wagons and C, when he enters your
Dan 11:40 like a whirlwind, with C and horsemen, and with
Hos 10:13 have trusted in your C and in the multitude
Joel 2:5 with the rumbling of C, they leap on the
Mic 1:13 the steeds to the C, inhabitants of Lachish; you
5:10 and will destroy your C;
Nah 2:3 The C flash like flame when mustered in array;
2:4 The C rage in the streets, they rush to
2:13 I will burn your C in smoke, and the
Hag 2:22 nations, and overthrow the C and their riders; and
Zech 6:1 saw, and behold, four C came out from between
1Mac 1:17 a strong force, with C and elephants and cavalry
8:6 and with cavalry and C and a very large
2Mac 13:2 elephants, and three hundred C armed with scythes.
Rev 9:9 the noise of many C with horses rushing into
18:13 and sheep, horses and C, and slaves, that is,

CHARITIES

Tob 2:14 me, "Where are your C and your righteous deeds?

CHARITY (8)

Tob 1:3 performed many acts of C to my brethren and
1:16 performed many acts of C to my brethren.
4:10 For C delivers from death and keeps you from
4:11 all who practice it C is an excellent offering
4:16 all your surplus to C, and do not let
12:9 who perform deeds of C and of righteousness will
Sir 31:11 and the assembly will relate his acts of C
Acts 9:36 was full of good works and acts of C

CHARM (6)

Prov 31:30 C is deceitful, and beauty is vain, but a
Wis 14:20 multitude, attracted by the C of his work, now
Sir 7:19 good wife, for her C is worth more than
26:13 A wife's C delights her husband, and her skill
26:15 A modest wife adds C to charm, and no
26:15 wife adds charm to C, and no balance can

CHARMED (2)

Eccl 10:11 bites before it is C, there is no advantage
Jer 8:17 adders which cannot be C, and they shall bite

CHARMER (3)

Deut 18:11 a sorcerer, or a C, or a medium, or
Eccl 10:11 is charmed, there is no advantage in a C
Sir 12:13 will pity a snake C bitten by a serpent,

CHARMERS

Ps 58:5 hear the voice of C or of the cunning

CHARMIS (3)

Jud 6:15 son of Gothoniel, and C the son of Melchiel.
8:10 to summon Chabris and C, the elders of her
10:6 the city, Chabris and C

CHARMS (3)

Is 3:3 and the skilful magician and the expert in C
Nah 3:4 graceful and of deadly C, who betrays nations with
3:4 nations with her harlotries, and peoples with her C

CHARRED (3)

Ezek 15:4 middle of it is C, is it useful for
15:5 it and it is C, can it ever be
1Mac 11:4 lying about, and the C bodies of those whom

CHASE (5)

Lev 26:7 And you shall C your enemies, and they shall
26:8 Five of you shall C a hundred, and a
26:8 hundred of you shall C ten thousand; and your
Deut 32:30 How should one C a thousand, and two put
Job 18:11 on every side, and C him at his heels.

CHASED (10)

Deut 1:44 out against you and C you as bees do
Josh 7:5 men of them, and C them before the gate
10:10 slaughter at Gibeon, and C them by the way
11:8 who smote them and C them as far as
Judg 9:40 And Abimelech C him, and he fled before him;
Neh 13:28 the Horonite; therefore I C him from me.
Job 20:8 found; he will be C away like a vision
Wis 2:4 like mist that is C by the rays of
Is 17:13 will flee far away, C like chaff on the
Lam 4:19 in the heavens; they C us on the mountains,

CHASES

Prov 19:26 to his father and C away his mother is

CHASING

1Sam 17:53 Israelites came back from C the Philistines, and they

CHASM

Lk 16:26 and you a great C has been fixed, in

CHASPHO (2)

1Mac 5:26 Bosor, in Alema and C, Maked and Carnaim" –
5:36 marched on and took C, Maked, and Bosor, and

CHASTE (4)

Sir 26:15 the value of a C soul.
Tit 2:5 to be sensible, C, domestic, kind, and submissive
1Pet 3:2 see your reverent and C behavior.
Rev 14:4 women, for they are C; it is these who

CHASTEN (9)

2Sam 7:14 commits iniquity, I will C him with the rod
Ps 6:1 in thy anger, nor C me in thy wrath.
38:1 in thy anger, nor C me in thy wrath!
39:11 When thou dost C man with rebukes for sin,
94:12 man whom thou dost C, O LORD, and whom
Jer 2:19 Your wickedness will C you, and your apostasy will
30:11 I will C you in just measure, and I
46:28 I will C you in just measure, and I
Rev 3:19 love, I reprove and C; so be zealous and

CHASTENED (6)

Job 33:19 "Man is also C with pain upon his bed,
Ps 73:14 have been stricken, and C every morning.
118:18 The LORD has C me sorely, but he has
Jer 31:18 Ephraim bemoaning, 'Thou hast C me, and I was
31:18 me, and I was C, like an untrained calf;
1Cor 11:32 the Lord, we are C so that we may

CHASTENING (3)

Job 5:17 therefore despise not the C of the Almighty.
Wis 12:22 So while C us thou scourgest our enemies ten
Is 26:16 a prayer when thy C was upon them.

CHASTENS

Ps 94:10 He who C the nations, does he not chastise?

CHASTISE (13)

Lev 26:18 me, then I will C you again sevenfold for
26:28 you in fury, and C you myself sevenfold for
Deut 21:18 mother, and, though they C him, will not give
1Kgs 12:11 whips, but I will C you with scorpions.'"
12:14 whips, but I will C you with scorpions."
2Chr 10:11 whips, but I will C you with scorpions.'"
10:14 whips, but I will C you with scorpions."
Ps 94:10 He who chastens the nations, does he not C
Hos 5:2 Shittim; but I will C all of them.
7:13 the air; I will C them for their wicked
10:10 the wayward people to C them; and nations shall
Lk 23:16 him; I will therefore C him and release him."
23:21 death; I will therefore C him and release him."

CHASTISED (5)

1Kgs 12:11 My father C you with whips, but I will
12:14 your yoke; my father C you with whips, but
2Chr 10:11 My father C you with whips, but I will
10:14 to it; my father C you with whips, but
Hos 10:10 them when they are C for their double iniquity.

CHASTISEMENT (6)

Job 34:31 God, 'I have borne C; I will not offend
Ps 149:7 on the nations and C on the peoples,
Prov 16:22 but folly is the C of fools.
Is 53:5 upon him was the C that made us whole,
Lam 4:6 For the C of the daughter of my people
Hab 1:12 and thou, O Rock, hast established them for C

CHASTISEMENTS (2)

Ezek 5:15 fury, and with furious C --I, the LORD, have
25:17 execute great vengeance upon them with wrathful C

CHASTISES

Heb 12:6 whom he loves, and C every son whom he

CHASTISING

Sir 22:6 the wrong time, but C and discipline are wisdom

CHASTITY

Sir 7:24 Be concerned for their C, and do not show

CHATTER (2)

1Tim 6:20 Avoid the godless C and contradictions of what is
2Tim 2:16 Avoid such godless C, for it will lead people

CHATTERER

Sir 8:3 not argue with a C, nor heap wood on

CHEAPER

Wis 15:10 ashes, his hope is C than dirt, and his

CHEAT (2)

Gen 31:27 you flee secretly, and C me, and did not
Mal 1:14 Cursed be the C who has a male in

CHEATED (2)

Gen 31:7 yet your father has C me and changed my
31:26 done, that you have C me, and carried away

CHEBAR (8)

Ezek 1:1 exiles by the river C, the heavens were opened,
1:3 Chaldeans by the river C; and the hand of
3:15 exiles at Tel-abib, who dwelt by the river C
3:23 seen by the river C; and I fell on
10:15 living creatures that I saw by the river C
10:20 Israel by the river C; and I knew that
10:22 whose appearance I had seen by the river C
43:3 seen by the river C; and I fell upon

CHECKED (3)

Lev 13:5 eyes the disease is C and the disease has
13:37 eyes the itch is C, and black hair has
2Mac 14:17 but had been temporarily C because of the sudden

CHECKER (3)

Ex 28:4 robe, a coat of C work, a turban, and
28:39 weave the coat in C work of fine linen,
1Kgs 7:17 made two nets of C work with wreaths of

CHECKING

Col 2:23 of no value in C the indulgence of the

CHED-OR-LAOMER (5)

Gen 14:1 Arioch king of Ellasar, C king of Elam, and
14:4 years they had served C, but in the thirteenth
14:5 In the fourteenth year C and the kings who
14:9 Valley of Siddim with C king of Elam, Tidal
14:17 from the defeat of C and the kings who

CHEEK (9)

1Kgs 22:24 struck Micaiah on the C, and said, "How did
2Chr 18:23 struck Micaiah on the C, and said, "Which way
Job 16:10 insolently upon the C, they mass themselves together
Ps 3:7 my enemies on the C, thou dost break the
Sir 35:15 widow run down her C as she cries out
Lam 3:30 let him give his C to the smiter, and
Mic 5:1 they strike upon the C the ruler of Israel.
Mt 5:39 you on the right C, turn to him the
Lk 6:29 strikes you on the C, offer the other also;

CHEEKS (7)

Deut 18:3 shoulder and the two C and the stomach.
Song 1:10 Your C are comely with ornaments, your neck with
4:3 Your C are like halves of a pomegranate behind
5:13 His C are like beds of spices, yielding fragrance.
6:7 Your C are like halves of a pomegranate behind
Is 50:6 the smiters, and my C to those who pulled
Lam 1:2 night, tears on her C; among all her lovers

CHEER (9)

Tob 11:11 saying, "Be of good C, father."
13:10 May he C those within you who are captives,
Esth 16:22 this with all good C as a notable day
Job 9:27 and be of good C
Ps 94:19 are many, thy consolations C my soul.
Eccl 2:3 my mind how to C my body with wine--
11:9 and let your heart C you in the days
2Mac 11:26 and be of good C and go on happily
Jn 16:33 but be of good C, I have overcome the

CHEERED (2)

2Mac 15:11 brave words, and he C them all by relating
Phil 2:19 that I may be C by news of you.

CHEERFUL (11)

1Kgs 21:7 let your heart be C; I will give you
Prov 15:13 glad heart makes a C countenance, but by sorrow
15:15 are evil, but a C heart has a continual
17:22 A C heart is a good medicine, but a
Sir 13:25 happy heart is a C face, but to devise
26:4 glad, and at all times his face is C
30:25 A man of C and good heart will give
35:9 every gift show a C face, and dedicate your
Zech 8:19 joy and gladness, and C feasts; therefore love truth
2Cor 9:7 for God loves a C giver.
Jas 5:13 Is any C

CHEERFULLY (2)

1Sam 15:32 And Agag came to him C
Acts 24:9 over this nation, I C make my defense.

CHEERFULNESS

Rom 12:8 zeal; he who does acts of mercy, with C

CHEERS
Judg 9:13 leave my wine which C gods and men, and

CHEESE (2)
2Sam 17:29 curds and sheep and C from the herd, for
Job 10:10 me out like milk and curdle me like C

CHEESES
1Sam 17:18 also take these ten C to the commander of

CHELAL
Ezra 10:30 sons of Pahath-moab: Adna, C, Benaiah, Ma-aseiah,

CHELLEANS
Jud 2:23 the desert, south of the country of the C

CHELOUS
Jud 1:9 Jerusalem and Bethany and C and Kadesh and the

CHELUB (2)
1Chr 4:11 C, the brother of Shuhah, was the father of
27:26 Ezri the son of C;

CHELUBAI
1Chr 2:9 that were born to him: Jerahmeel, Ram, and C

CHELUHI
Ezra 10:35 Amram, Uel, Benaiah, Bedeiah, C,

CHEMOSH (8)
Num 21:29 You are undone, O people of C
Judg 11:24 you not possess what C your god gives you
1Kgs 11:7 a high place for C the abomination of Moab,
11:33 goddess of the Sidonians, C the god of Moab,
2Kgs 23:13 the Sidonians, and for C the abomination of Moab,
Jer 48:7 shall be taken; and C shall go forth into
48:13 shall be ashamed of C, as the house of
48:46 The people of C is undone; for your sons

CHENAANAH (5)
1Kgs 22:11 Zedekiah the son of C made for himself horns
22:24 Zedekiah the son of C came near and struck
1Chr 7:10 Jeush, Benjamin, Ehud, C, Zethan, Tarshish, and Ahi
2Chr 18:10 Zedekiah the son of C made for himself horns
18:23 Zedekiah the son of C came near and struck

CHENANI
Neh 9:4 Bunni, Sherebiah, Bani, and C; and they cried with

CHENANIAH (3)
1Chr 15:22 C, leader of the Levites in music, should direct
15:27 and the singers, and C the leader of the
26:29 Of the Izharites, C and his sons were appointed

CHEPHAR-AMMONI
Josh 18:24 Avvim, Parah, Ophrah, C, Ophni, Geba--twelve cities

CHEPHIRAH (4)
Josh 9:17 cities were Gibeon, C, Be-eroth, and Kiriath-jearim.
18:26 Gibeon, Ramah, Be-eroth, Mizpeh, C, Mozah,
Ezra 2:25 The sons of Kiriatharim, C, and Be-eroth, seven
Neh 7:29 The men of Kiriath-jearim, C, and Be-eroth, seven

CHERAN (2)
Gen 36:26 the sons of Dishon: Hemdan, Eshban, Ithran, and C
1Chr 1:41 The sons of Dishon: Hamran, Eshban, Ithran, and C

CHERETHITES (10)
1Sam 30:14 the Negeb of the C and upon that which
2Sam 8:18 Jehoiada was over the C and the Pelethites; and
15:18 him; and all the C, and all the Pelethites,
20:7 Abishai, Joab and the C and the Pelethites, and
20:23 in command of the C and the Pelethites;
1Kgs 1:38 of Jehoiada, and the C and the Pelethites, went
1:44 of Jehoiada, and the C and the Pelethites; and
1Chr 18:17 Jehoiada was over the C and the Pelethites; and
Ezek 25:16 will cut off the C, and destroy the rest
Zeph 2:5 inhabitants of the seacoast, you nation of the C

CHERISH (4)
Job 36:13 "The godless in heart C anger; they do not
Ps 55:3 and in anger they C enmity against me.
Hos 4:10 forsaken the LORD to C harlotry.
2Mac 7:14 of men and to C the hope that God

CHERISHED (2)
Ps 66:18 If I had C iniquity in my heart, the
Ezek 35:5 Because you C perpetual enmity, and gave over the

CHERISHES
Eph 5:29 flesh, but nourishes and C it, as Christ does

CHERITH (2)
1Kgs 17:3 yourself by the brook C, that is east of
17:5 dwelt by the brook C that is east of

CHERUB (25)
Ex 25:19 Make one C on the one end, and one
25:19 one end, and one C on the other end;
37:8 he made them, one C on the one end,
37:8 one end, and one C on the other end;
2Sam 22:11 He rode on a C, and flew; he was
1Kgs 6:24 one wing of the C, and five cubits the
6:24 other wing of the C; it was ten cubits
6:25 The other C also measured ten cubits; both cherubim
6:26 The height of one C was ten cubits, and
6:26 cubits, and so was that of the other C
6:27 wing of the other C touched the other wall;
2Chr 3:11 wing of the other C;
3:12 cherub; and of this C, one wing, of five
3:12 was joined to the wing of the first C
Ezra 2:59 up from Tel-melah, Tel-harsha, C, Addan, and Immer,
Neh 7:61 up from Tel-melah, Tel-harsha, C, Addon, and Immer,
Ps 18:10 He rode on a C, and flew; he came
Ezek 10:7 And a C stretched forth his hand from between
10:9 cherubim, one beside each C; and the appearance of
10:14 the face of the C, and the second face
28:14 With an anointed guardian C I placed you; you
28:16 God, and the guardian C drove you out from
41:18 a palm tree between C and cherub.
41:18 palm trees, a palm tree between cherub and C
41:18 Every C had two faces:

CHERUBIM (71)
Gen 3:24 Eden he placed the C, and a flaming sword
Ex 25:18 you shall make two C of gold; of hammered
25:19 shall you make the C on its two ends.
25:20 The C shall spread out their wings above,
25:20 the faces of the C be.
25:22 from between the two C that are upon the
26:1 and scarlet stuff; with C skilfully worked shall you
26:31 it be made, with C;
36:8 and scarlet stuff, with C skilfully worked.
36:35 fine twined linen; with C skilfully worked he made
37:7 And he made two C of hammered gold; on
37:8 seat he made the C on its two ends.
37:9 The C spread out their wings above, overshadowing
37:9 the mercy seat were the faces of the C
Num 7:89 from between the two C; and it spoke to
1Sam 4:4 is enthroned on the C; and the two sons
2Sam 6:2 LORD of hosts who sits enthroned on the C
1Kgs 6:23 sanctuary he made two C of olivewood, each ten
6:25 measured ten cubits; both C had the same measure
6:27 He put the C in the innermost part of
6:27 the wings of the C were spread out so
6:28 And he overlaid the C with gold.
6:29 with carved figures of C and palm trees and
6:32 olivewood with carvings of C, palm trees, and open
6:32 spread gold upon the C and upon the palm
6:35 On them he carved C and palm trees and
7:29 set in the frames were lions, oxen, and C
7:36 its panels, he carved C, lions, and palm trees,
8:6 most holy place, underneath the wings of the C
8:7 For the C spread out their wings over the
8:7 ark, so that the C made a covering above
2Kgs 19:15 art enthroned above the C, thou art the God,
1Chr 13:6 of the LORD who sits enthroned above the C
28:18 golden chariot of the C that spread their wings
2Chr 3:7 doors; and he carved C on the walls.
3:10 place he made two C of wood and overlaid
3:11 The wings of the C together extended twenty cubits:
3:13 The wings of these C extended twenty cubits; the
3:13 extended twenty cubits; the C stood on their feet,
3:14 fine linen, and worked C on it.
5:7 most holy place, underneath the wings of the C
5:8 For the C spread out their wings over the
5:8 ark, so that the C made a covering above
Ps 80:1 art enthroned upon the C, shine forth
99:1 sits enthroned upon the C; let the earth quake!
Sir 49:8 God showed him above the chariot of the C
Is 37:16 art enthroned above the C, thou art the God,

Ezek 9:3 gone up from the C on which it rested
10:1 the heads of the C there appeared above them
10:2 whirling wheels underneath the C; fill your hands
10:2 coals from between the C, and scatter them over
10:3 Now the C were standing on the south side
10:4 went up from the C to the threshold of
10:5 the wings of the C was heard as far
10:6 between the whirling wheels, from between the C
10:7 hand from between the C to the fire that
10:7 that was between the C, and took some of
10:8 The C appeared to have the form of a
10:9 four wheels beside the C, one beside each cherub;
10:15 And the C mounted up.
10:16 And when the C went, the wheels went beside
10:16 them; and when the C lifted up their wings
10:18 threshold of the house, and stood over the C
10:19 And the C lifted up their wings and mounted
10:20 river Chebar; and I knew that they were C
11:22 Then the C lifted up their wings, with the
41:18 were carved likenesses of C and palm trees, a
41:20 to above the door C and palm trees were
41:25 the nave were carved C and palm trees, such
Dan 3:55 thou, who sittest upon C and lookest upon the
Heb 9:5 above it were the C of glory overshadowing the

CHESALON

Josh 15:10 Mount Jearim (that is, C, and goes down to

CHESED

Gen 22:22 the father of Aram, C, Hazo, Pildash, Jidlaph, and

CHESIL

Josh 15:30 Baalah, Iim, Ezem, Eltolad, C, Hormah,

CHEST (6)

2Kgs 12:9 the priest took a C, and bored a hole
12:10 much money in the C, the king's secretary and
2Chr 24:8 and they made a C, and set it outside
24:10 dropped it into the C until they had finished.
24:11 And whenever the C was brought to the king's
24:11 come and empty the C and take it and

CHESULLOTH

Josh 19:18 Its territory included Jezreel, C, Shunem,

CHEW (7)

Lev 11:4 Nevertheless among those that C the cud or part
11:7 cloven-footed but does not C the cud, is unclean
11:26 cloven-footed or does not C the cud is unclean
Deut 14:7 Yet of those that C the cud or have
14:7 rock badger, because they C the cud but do
14:8 hoof but does not C the cud, is unclean
Sir 31:16 you, and do not C greedily, lest you be

CHEWS (5)

Lev 11:3 and is cloven-footed and C the cud, among the
11:4 The camel, because it C the cud but does
11:5 rock badger, because it C the cud but does
11:6 the hare, because it C the cud but does
Deut 14:6 cloven in two, and C the cud, among the

CHEZIB

Gen 38:5 She was in C when she bore him.

CHIDE

Ps 103:9 He will not always C, nor will he keep

CHIDON

1Chr 13:9 the threshing floor of C, Uzzah put out his

CHIEF (178)

Gen 40:2 his two officers, the C butler and the chief
40:2 chief butler and the C baker,
40:9 So the C butler told his dream to Joseph,
40:16 When the C baker saw that the interpretation was
40:20 the head of the C butler and the head
40:20 the head of the C baker among his servants.
40:21 He restored the C butler to his butlership, and
40:22 but he hanged the C baker, as Joseph had
40:23 Yet the C butler did not remember Joseph, but
41:9 Then the C butler said to Pharaoh, "I remember
41:10 put me and the C baker in custody in
Ex 24:11 his hand on the C men of the people
Lev 21:10 "The priest who is C among his brethren, upon
Num 3:32 priest was to be C over the leaders of
1Sam 21:7 Doeg the Edomite, the C of Saul's herdsmen.
2Sam 23:8 a Tah-chemonite; he was C of the three; he
23:13 three of the thirty C men went down, and
23:18 son of Zeruiah, was C of the thirty.
1Kgs 5:16 three thousand three hundred C officers who were
9:23 These were the C officers who were over Solomon's
2Kgs 24:15 his officials, and the C men of the land,
25:18 guard took Seraiah the C priest, and Zephaniah the
1Chr 5:7 was reckoned: the C, Je-iel, and Zechariah,
5:12 as Salecah: Joel the C, Shapham the second, Janai,
5:15 son of Guni, was C in their fathers' houses;
7:3 five, all of them C men;
7:40 houses, approved, mighty warriors, C of the princes.
8:28 according to their generations, C men.
9:11 son of Ahitub, the C officer of the house
9:17 kinsmen (Shallum being the C,
9:26 these; for the four C gatekeepers, who were Levites,
11:6 Jebusites first shall be C and commander." And Joab
11:6 of Zeruiah went up first, so he became C
11:11 Jashobe-am, a Hachmonite, was C of the three; he
11:15 Three of the thirty C men went down to
11:20 brother of Joab, was C of the thirty.
12:3 The C was Ahiezer, then Joash, both sons of
12:9 mountains: Ezer the C, Obadiah second, Eliab third,
12:18 Spirit came upon Amasai, C of the thirty, and
15:5 of Kohath, Uriel the C, with a hundred and
15:6 of Merari, Asaiah the C, with two hundred and
15:7 of Gershom, Joel the C, with a hundred and
15:8 of Eli-zaphan, Shemaiah the C, with two hundred of
15:9 of Hebron, Eliel the C, with eighty of his
15:10 of Uzziel, Amminadab the C, with a hundred and
16:5 Asaph was the C, and second to him were
18:17 David's sons were the C officials in the service
23:8 of Ladan: Jehiel the C, and Zetham, and Joel,
23:11 Jahath was the C, and Zizah the second; but
23:16 The sons of Gershom: Shebuel the C
23:17 of Eliezer: Rehabiah the C; Eliezer had no other
23:18 The sons of Izhar: Shelomith the C
23:19 Hebron: Jeriah the C, Amariah the second, Jahaziel
23:20 of Uzziel: Micah the C and Isshiah the second.
24:4 Since more C men were found among the sons
24:21 Rehabiah: of the sons of Rehabiah, Isshiah the C
24:23 Hebron: Jeriah the C, Amariah the second, Jahaziel
26:10 had sons: Shimri the C (for though he was
26:10 his father made him C,
26:12 corresponding to their C men, had duties, just
26:24 son of Moses, was C officer in charge of
26:31 the Hebronites, Jerijah was C of the Hebronites of
27:3 of Perez, and was C of all the commanders
27:5 Jehoiada the priest, as C; in his division were
27:16 son of Zichri was C officer; for the Simeonites,
2Chr 8:10 And these were the C officers of King Solomon,
11:22 son of Maacah as C prince among his brothers,
19:11 And behold, Amariah the C priest is over you
24:6 king summoned Jehoiada the C, and said to him,
24:11 the officer of the C priest would come and
26:20 And Azariah the C priest, and all the priests,
31:10 Azariah the C priest, who was of the house
31:12 The C officer in charge of them was Conaniah
31:13 king and Azariah the C officer of the house
35:8 Zechariah, and Jehiel, the C officers of the house
Ezra 7:5 son of Aaron the C priest--
8:29 weigh them before the C priests and the Levites
9:2 of the officials and C men has been foremost."
Neh 12:46 old there was a C of the singers, and
Jud 2:4 Assyrians called Holofernes, the C general of his
Job 29:25 way, and sat as C, and I dwelt like
Prov 6:7 Without having any C, officer or ruler,
Song 4:14 and aloes, with all C spices--
Jer 20:1 of Immer, who was C officer in the house
31:7 raise shouts for the C of the nations; proclaim,
39:13 Rabmag, and all the C officers of the king
41:1 family, one of the C officers of the king,
52:24 guard took Seraiah the C priest, and Zephaniah the
Ezek 17:13 (The C men of the land he had taken
38:2 land of Magog, the C prince of Meshech and
38:3 against you, O Gog, C prince of Meshech and
39:1 against you, O Gog, C prince of Meshech and
Dan 1:3 king commanded Ashpenaz, his C eunuch, to bring
1:7 And the C of the eunuchs gave them names:
1:8 therefore he asked the C of the eunuchs to
1:9 the sight of the C of the eunuchs;
1:10 the eunuchs; and the C of the eunuchs said
1:11 the steward whom the C of the eunuchs had
1:18 be brought in, the C of the eunuchs brought
2:48 province of Babylon, and C prefect over all the

4:9 dream, saying, "O Belteshazzar, C of the magicians,
5:11 your father, made him C of the magicians,
10:13 Michael, one of the C princes, came to help
1Mac 1:29 cities of Judah a C collector of tribute, and
9:11 as did all the C warriors.
10:65 enrolled him among his C friends, and made him
11:27 as one of his C friends.
2Mac 4:50 wickedness, having become the C plotter against his
8:9 one of the king's C friends, and sent him,
10:11 government and to be C governor of Coelesyria and
Mt 2:4 and assembling all the C priests and scribes of
16:21 from the elders and C priests and scribes, and
20:18 be delivered to the C priests and scribes, and
21:15 But when the C priests and the scribes saw
21:23 entered the temple, the C priests and the elders
21:45 When the C priests and the Pharisees heard his
26:3 Then the C priests and the elders of the
26:14 Iscariot, went to the C priests
26:47 and clubs, from the C priests and the elders
26:59 Now the C priests and the whole council sought
27:1 morning came, all the C priests and the elders
27:3 of silver to the C priests and the elders,
27:6 But the C priests, taking the pieces of silver,
27:12 was accused by the C priests and elders, he
27:20 Now the C priests and the elders persuaded the
27:41 So also the C priests, with the scribes and
27:62 day of Preparation, the C priests and the Pharisees
28:11 city and told the C priests all that had
Mk 8:31 the elders and the C priests and the scribes,
10:33 be delivered to the C priests and the scribes,
11:18 And the C priests and the scribes heard it
11:26 in the temple, the C priests and the scribes
14:1 And the C priests and the scribes were seeking
14:10 twelve, went to the C priests in order to
14:43 and clubs, from the C priests and the scribes
14:53 priest; and all the C priests and the elders
14:55 Now the C priests and the whole council sought
15:1 it was morning the C priests, with the elders
15:3 And the C priests accused him of many things.
15:10 of envy that the C priests had delivered him
15:11 But the C priests stirred up the crowd to
15:30 So also the C priests mocked him to one
Lk 9:22 by the elders and C priests and scribes, and
19:2 Zacchaeus; he was a C tax collector, and rich.
19:47 The C priests and the scribes and the principal
20:1 preaching the gospel, the C priests and the scribes
20:19 The scribes and the C priests tried to lay
22:2 And the C priests and the scribes were seeking
22:4 and conferred with the C priests and officers how
22:50 Jesus said to the C priests and officers of
22:64 people gathered together, both C priests and scribes;
23:4 Pilate said to the C priests and the multitudes,
23:10 The C priests and the scribes stood by, vehemently
23:13 then called together the C priests and the rulers
24:20 people, and how our C priests and rulers delivered
Jn 7:32 about him, and the C priests and Pharisees sent
7:45 went back to the C priests and Pharisees, who
11:47 So the C priests and the Pharisees gathered the
11:57 Now the C priests and the Pharisees had given
12:10 So the C priests planned to put Lazarus also
18:3 some officers from the C priests and the Pharisees,
18:35 own nation and the C priests have handed you
19:6 When the C priests and the officers saw him,
19:15 The C priests answered, "We have no king but
19:21 The C priests of the Jews then said to
Acts 4:23 and reported what the C priests and the elders
5:24 the temple and the C priests heard these words,
9:14 has authority from the C priests to bind all
9:21 them bound before the C priests."
14:12 because he was the C speaker, they called Hermes.
22:30 him, and commanded the C priests and all the
23:14 they went to the C priests and elders, and
25:2 And the C priests and the principal men of
25:15 was at Jerusalem, the C priests and the elders
26:10 by authority from the C priests, but when they
26:12 and commission of the C priests.
28:7 lands belonging to the C man of the island,
1Pet 5:4 And when the C Shepherd is manifested you will

CHIEFLY

2Mac 8:35 Antioch, having succeeded C in the destruction

CHIEFS (41)

Gen 36:15 These are the C of the sons of Esau.
36:15 first-born of Esau: the C Teman, Omar, Zepho, Kenaz,
36:16 Amalek; these are the C of Eliphaz in the
36:17 Reuel, Esau's son: the C Nahath, Zerah, Shammah,
36:17 Mizzah; these are the C of Reuel in the
36:18 Oholibamah, Esau's wife: the C Jeush, Jalam, and
36:18 Korah; these are the C born of Oholibamah the
36:19 Esau (that is, Edom), and these are their C
36:21 Dishan; these are the C of the Horites, the
36:29 These are the C of the Horites: the chiefs
36:29 of the Horites: the C Lotan, Shobal, Zibeon, Anah,
36:30 Dishan; these are the C of the Horites, according
36:40 the names of the C of Esau, according to
36:40 by their names: the C Timna, Alvah, Jetheth,
36:43 Iram; these are the C of Edom (that is,
Ex 15:15 Now are the C of Edom dismayed; the leaders
Num 25:4 Moses, "Take all the C of the people, and
Josh 10:24 and said to the C of the men of
22:14 and with him ten C, one from each of
22:30 the priest and the C of the congregation, the
22:32 the priest, and the C, returned from the Reubenites
Judg 20:2 And the C of all the people, of all
1Chr 1:51 The C of Edom were: chiefs Timna, Aliah, Jetheth,
1:51 chiefs of Edom were: C Timna, Aliah, Jetheth,
1:54 Iram; these are the C of Edom.
11:10 Now these are the C of David's mighty men,
12:20 Elihu, and Zillethai, C of thousands in Manasseh.
12:32 to do, two hundred C, and all their kinsmen
15:16 David also commanded the C of the Levites to
25:1 David and the C of the service also set
2Chr 28:12 Certain C also of the men of Ephraim, Azariah
35:9 Je-iel and Jozabad, the C of the Levites, gave
Neh 10:14 The C of the people: Parosh, Pahath-moab, Elam,
11:3 These are the C of the province who lived
11:16 and Jozabad, of the C of the Levites, who
12:7 These were the C of the priests and of
12:24 And the C of the Levites: Hashabiah, Sherebiah, and
Esth 1:3 and servants, the army C of Persia and Media
Job 12:24 away understanding from the C of the people of
Ps 110:6 corpses; he will shatter C over the wide earth.
Ezek 32:21 The mighty C shall speak of them, with their

CHIEFTAIN

1Chr 5:6 exile; he was a C of the Reubenites.

CHIEFTAINS

Jud 7:8 Then all the C of the people of Esau

CHILD (207)

Gen 4:25 appointed for me another C instead of Abel, for
11:30 Now Sarai was barren; she had no C
16:11 "Behold, you are with C, and shall bear a
17:17 to himself, "Shall a C be born to a
17:17 Sarah, who is ninety years old, bear a C
18:13 I indeed bear a C, now that I am
19:36 of Lot were with C by their father.
21:8 And the C grew, and was weaned; and Abraham
21:14 shoulder, along with the C, and sent her away.
21:15 gone, she cast the C under one of the
21:16 me not look upon the death of the C
21:16 over against him, the C lifted up his voice
38:24 moreover she is with C by harlotry." And Judah
38:25 man to whom these belong, I am with C
44:20 a young brother, the C of his old age;
Ex 2:2 he was a goodly C, she hid him three
2:3 and she put the C in it and placed
2:6 it she saw the C; and lo, the babe
2:7 women to nurse the C for you?"
2:8 went and called the C's mother.
2:9 to her, "Take this C away, and nurse him
2:9 the woman took the C and nursed him.
2:10 And the C grew, and she brought him to
21:22 hurt a woman with C, so that there is
Lev 12:2 and bears a male C, then she shall be
12:5 she bears a female C, then she shall be
12:7 her who bears a C, either male or female.
22:13 divorced, and has no C, and returns to her
Num 11:12 nurse carries the sucking C, to the land which
Deut 32:25 and virgin, the sucking C with the man of
Judg 11:34 she was his only C; beside her he had
Ruth 4:16 Then Naomi took the C and laid him in
1Sam 1:22 "As soon as the C is weaned, I will
1:24 at Shiloh; and the C was young.
1:25 and they brought the C to Eli.
1:27 For this C I prayed; and the LORD has
4:19 of Phinehas, was with C, about to give birth.
4:21 And she named the C Ichabod, saying, "The glory
2Sam 6:23 of Saul had no C to the day of
11:5 she sent and told David, "I am with C

C

	12:14	scorned the LORD, the C that is born to
	12:15	the LORD struck the C that Uriah's wife bore
	12:16	besought God for the C; and David fasted, and
	12:18	the seventh day the C died.
	12:18	tell him that the C was dead; for they
	12:18	said, "Behold, while the C was yet alive, we
	12:18	say to him the C is dead?
	12:19	David perceived that the C was dead; and David
	12:19	his servants, "Is the C dead?" They said, "He
	12:21	and wept for the C while it was alive;
	12:21	alive; but when the C died, you arose and
	12:22	He said, "While the C was still alive, I
	12:22	to me, that the C may live?'
1Kgs	3:7	am but a little C; I do not know
	3:17	gave birth to a C while she was in
	3:21	morning to nurse my C, behold, it was dead;
	3:21	it was not the C that I had borne."
	3:22	said, "No, the living C is mine, and the
	3:22	mine, and the dead C is yours." The first
	3:22	said, "No, the dead C is yours, and the
	3:22	yours, and the living C is mine." Thus they
	3:25	said, "Divide the living C in two, and give
	3:26	give her the living C, and by no means
	3:27	said, "Give the living C to the first woman,
	11:17	his father's servants, Hadad being yet a little C
	14:3	will tell you what shall happen to the C
	14:12	enter the city, the C shall die.
	14:17	of the house, the C died.
	17:21	stretched himself upon the C three times, and cried
	17:21	my God, let this C's soul come into him
	17:22	the soul of the C came into him again,
	17:23	And Elijah took the C, and brought him down
2Kgs	4:18	When the C had grown, he went out one
	4:20	to his mother, the C sat on her lap
	4:26	Is it well with the C
	4:29	lay my staff upon the face of the C
	4:30	the mother of the C said, "As the LORD
	4:31	the face of the C, but there was no
	4:31	and told him, "The C has not awaked."
	4:32	house, he saw the C lying dead on his
	4:34	and lay upon the C, putting his mouth upon
	4:34	the flesh of the C became warm.
	4:35	himself upon him; the C sneezed seven times, and
	4:35	seven times, and the C opened his eyes.
	5:14	flesh of a little C, and he was clean.
	8:12	little ones, and rip up their women with C
	15:16	all the women in it who were with C
Tob	3:10	"I am the only C of my father; if
	3:15	am my father's only C, and he has no
	3:15	and he has no C to be his heir,
	5:17	have you sent our C away?
	5:18	consider it as rubbish as compared to our C
	7:10	for it is your right to take my C
	7:18	her, "Be brave, my C; the Lord of heaven
	10:5	I not distressed, my C, that I let you
	10:7	stop deceiving me; my C has perished." And she
	11:9	have seen you, my C; now I am ready
Job	24:9	who snatch the fatherless C from the breast, and
Ps	131:2	my soul, like a C quieted at its mother's
	131:2	mother's breast; like a C that is quieted is
Prov	20:11	Even a C makes himself known by his acts,
	22:6	Train up a C in the way he should
	22:15	the heart of a C, but the rod of
	23:13	withhold discipline from a C; if you beat him
	29:15	give wisdom, but a C left to himself brings
Eccl	10:16	your king is a C, and your princes feast
	11:5	of a woman with C, so you do not
Wis	2:13	and calls himself a C of the Lord.
	7:1	descendant of the first-formed C of earth; and in
	8:19	As a C I was by nature well endowed,
	10:5	in the face of his compassion for his C
	14:15	an image of his C, who had been suddenly
	18:5	holy ones, and one C had been exposed and
Sir	19:11	pangs like a woman in labor with a C
	30:9	Pamper a C, and he will frighten you; play
Is	7:16	For before the C knows how to refuse the
	8:4	for before the C knows how to cry
	9:6	For to us a C is born, to us
	10:19	so few that a C can write them down.
	11:6	together, and a little C shall lead them.
	11:8	The sucking C shall play over the hole of
	11:8	asp, and the weaned C shall put his hand
	26:17	Like a woman with C, who writhes and cries
	26:18	LORD; we were with C, we writhed, we have
	49:15	woman forget her sucking C, that she should have
	65:20	his days, for the C shall die a hundred
Jer	4:31	bringing forth her first C, the cry of the
	30:6	now, and see, can a man bear a C
	31:8	lame, the woman with C and her who is
	31:20	Is he my darling C
	44:7	and woman, infant and C, from the midst of
Bar	4:15	old man, and had no pity for a C
Dan	11:6	and her attendants, her C, and he who got
Hos	11:1	When Israel was a C, I loved him, and
Amos	1:13	ripped up women with C in Gilead, that they
Zech	12:10	mourns for an only C, and weep bitterly over
2Mac	7:28	I beseech you, my C, to look at the
Mt	1:18	found to be with C of the Holy Spirit;
	2:8	search diligently for the C, and when you have
	2:9	the place where the C was.
	2:11	house they saw the C with Mary his mother,
	2:13	said, "Rise, take the C and his mother, and
	2:13	to search for the C, to destroy him."
	2:14	rose and took the C and his mother by
	2:20	saying, "Rise, take the C and his mother, and
	2:20	those who sought the C's life are dead."
	2:21	rose and took the C and his mother, and
	10:21	and the father his C, and children will rise
	18:2	calling to him a C, he put him in
	18:4	humbles himself like this C, he is the greatest
	18:5	"Whoever receives one such C in my name receives
	23:14	twice as much a C of hell as yourselves.
	24:19	those who are with C and for those who
Mk	5:39	The C is not dead but sleeping."
	5:40	outside, and took the C's father and mother and
	5:40	went in where the C was.
	7:29	home, and found the C lying in bed, and
	9:24	the father of the C cried out and said,
	9:36	And he took a C, and put him in
	9:37	"Whoever receives one such C in my name receives
	10:15	of God like a C shall not enter it."
	12:19	wife, but leaves no C, the man must take
	13:12	and the father his C, and children will rise
	13:17	those who are with C and for those who
Lk	1:7	But they had no C, because Elizabeth was barren,
	1:35	overshadow you; therefore the C to be born will
	1:59	came to circumcise the C; and they would have
	1:66	"What then will this C be?" For the hand
	1:76	And you, C, will be called the prophet of
	1:80	And the C grew and became strong in spirit,
	2:5	enrolled with Mary, his betrothed, who was with C
	2:17	told them concerning this C;
	2:27	parents brought in the C Jesus, to do for
	2:34	his mother, "Behold, this C is set for the
	2:40	And the C grew and became strong, filled with
	8:51	James, and the father and mother of the C
	8:54	hand he called, saying, C, arise."
	9:38	he is my only C;
	9:47	hearts, he took a C and put him by
	9:48	them, "Whoever receives this C in my name receives
	18:17	of God like a C shall not enter it."
	21:23	those who are with C and for those who
Jn	4:49	come down before my C dies."
	16:21	is delivered of the C, she no longer remembers
	16:21	for joy that a C is born into the
Acts	7:5	his posterity after him, though he had no C
1Cor	4:17	my beloved and faithful C in the Lord, to
	13:11	When I was a C, I spoke like a
	13:11	I spoke like a C, I thought like a
	13:11	I thought like a C, I reasoned like a
	13:11	I reasoned like a C; when I became a
Gal	4:1	as he is a C, is no better than
1Thes	5:3	upon a woman with C, and there will be
1Tim	1:2	To Timothy, my true C in the faith: Grace,
2Tim	1:2	To Timothy, my beloved C: Grace, mercy, and peace
Tit	1:3	To Titus, my true C in a common faith:
Philem	1:10	to you for my C, Onesimus, whose father I
Heb	5:13	the word of righteousness, for he is a C
	11:23	they saw that the C was beautiful; and they
1Jn	5:1	the Christ is a C of God, and every
	5:1	every one who loves the parent loves the C
Rev	12:2	stars; she was with C and she cried out
	12:4	about to bear a C, that he might devour
	12:4	he might devour her C when she brought it
	12:5	brought forth a male C, one who is to
	12:5	of iron, but her C was caught up to
	12:13	pursued the woman who had borne the male C

CHILDBEARING

Gen	3:16	multiply your pain in C; in pain you shall

C

CHILDBIRTH (2)

Bar 6:29 be touched by women in menstruation or at C
Hos 13:13 The pangs of C come for him, but he

CHILDHOOD (5)

Prov 29:21 pampers his servant from C, will in the end
2Mac 6:23 excellent life even from C, and moreover according to
15:12 had been trained from C in all that belongs
Mk 9:21 And he said, "From C
2Tim 3:15 it and how from C you have been acquainted

CHILDISH

1Cor 13:11 man, I gave up C ways.

CHILDLESS (11)

Gen 15:2 me, for I continue C, and the heir of
Lev 20:20 they shall bear their sin, they shall die C
20:21 uncovered his brother's nakedness, they shall be C
1Sam 15:33 sword has made women C, so shall your mother
15:33 shall your mother be C among women." And Samuel
1Chr 2:30 of Nadab: Seled and Appa-im; and Seled died C
2:32 brother: Jether and Jonathan; and Jether died C
Job 24:21 feed on the barren C woman, and do no
Sir 16:3 thousand, and to die C is better than to
Jer 18:21 let their wives become C and widowed.
22:30 this man down as C, a man who shall

CHILDLESSNESS

Wis 4:1 Better than this is C with virtue, for in

CHILDREN (550)

Gen 3:16 you shall bring forth C, yet your desire shall
6:4 men, and they bore C to them.
10:21 father of all the C of Eber, the elder
10:21 elder brother of Japheth, C were born.
16:1 Now Sarai, Abram's wife, bore him no C
16:2 prevented me from bearing C; go in to my
16:2 that I shall obtain C by her." And Abram
18:19 he may charge his C and his household after
20:17 wife and female slaves so that they bore C
21:7 have said to Abraham that Sarah would suckle C
22:20 Milcah also has borne C to your brother Nahor:
25:4 All these were the C of Keturah.
25:22 The C struggled together within her; and she said,
30:1 she bore Jacob no C, she envied her sister;
30:1 to Jacob, "Give me C, or I shall die!"
30:3 even I may have C through her."
30:9 she had ceased bearing C, she took her maid
30:26 my wives and my C for whom I have
31:16 us and to our C; now then, whatever God
31:43 are my daughters, the C are my children, the
31:43 the children are my C, the flocks are my
31:43 daughters, or to their C whom they have borne?
32:11 and slay us all, the mothers with the C
32:22 maids, and his eleven C, and crossed the ford
33:1 So he divided the C among Leah and Rachel
33:2 the maids with their C in front, then Leah
33:2 then Leah with her C, and Rachel and Joseph
33:5 saw the women and C, he said, "Who are
33:5 Jacob said, "The C whom God has graciously given
33:6 near, they and their C, and bowed down;
33:7 Leah likewise and her C drew near and bowed
33:13 lord knows that the C are frail, and that
33:14 the pace of the C, until I come to
36:25 These are the C of Anah: Dishon and Oholibamah
37:3 any other of his C, because he was the
42:36 bereaved me of my C: Joseph is no more,
43:14 am bereaved of my C, I am bereaved."
44:20 left of his mother's C; and his father loves
45:10 me, you and your C and your children's children,
45:10 your children and your C's children, and your flocks,
45:10 children and your children's C, and your flocks, your
48:11 let me see your C also."
50:8 father's household; only their C, their flocks, and
50:23 And Joseph saw Ephraim's C of the third generation;
50:23 the third generation; the C also of Machir the
Ex 1:16 but let the male C live.
1:17 and let the male C live?"
2:6 and said, "This is one of the Hebrews' C
10:20 did not let the C of Israel go.
10:24 serve the LORD; your C also may go with
12:26 And when your C say to you, 'What do
12:37 hundred thousand men on foot, besides women and C
17:3 kill us and our C and our cattle with
17:7 the faultfinding of the C of Israel, and because
19:6 shall speak to the C of Israel."
20:5 the fathers upon the C to the third and
21:4 the wife and her C shall be her master's
21:5 my wife, and my C; I will not go
22:24 become widows and your C fatherless.
34:7 the fathers upon the C and the children's children,
34:7 the children and the C's children, to the third
34:7 children and the children's C, to the third and
Lev 6:18 Every male among the C of Aaron may eat
18:21 give any of your C to devote them by
20:2 gives any of his C to Molech shall be
20:3 given one of his C to Molech, defiling my
20:4 gives one of his C to Molech, and do
20:17 the sight of the C of their people; he
21:15 may not profane his C among his people; for
25:41 you, he and his C with him, and go
25:54 jubilee, he and his C with him.
26:22 rob you of your C, and destroy your cattle,
Num 3:4 the wilderness of Sinai; and they had no C
5:28 then she shall be free and shall conceive C
14:18 iniquity of fathers upon C, upon the third and
14:33 And your C shall be shepherds in the wilderness
Deut 1:36 him and to his C I will give the
1:39 a prey, and your C, who this day have
2:34 city, men, women, and C; we left none remaining;
3:6 Heshbon, destroying every city, men, women, and C
4:9 them known to your C and your children's children—
4:9 your children and your C's children—
4:9 children and your children's C –
4:10 they may teach their C so.'
4:25 "When you beget C and children's children, and have
4:25 you beget children and C's children, and have grown
4:25 beget children and children's C, and have grown old
4:40 you, and with your C after you, and that
4:44 Moses set before the C of Israel;
4:45 Moses spoke to the C of Israel when they
4:46 whom Moses and the C of Israel defeated when
5:9 the fathers upon the C to the third and
5:29 them and with their C for ever!
6:7 them diligently to your C, and shall talk of
11:2 not speaking to your C who have not known
11:19 teach them to your C, talking of them when
11:21 the days of your C may be multiplied in
12:25 you and with your C after you, when you
12:28 you and with your C after you for ever,
17:20 kingdom, he and his C, in Israel.
21:15 they have borne him C, both the loved and
23:8 The C of the third generation that are born
24:16 to death for the C, nor shall the children
24:16 children, nor shall the C be put to death
28:54 the last of the C who remain to him;
28:55 the flesh of his C whom he is eating,
28:57 her feet and her C whom she bears, because
29:22 generation to come, your C who rise up after
29:29 us and to our C for ever, that we
30:2 God, you and your C, and obey his voice
31:13 law, and that their C, who have not known
31:23 you shall bring the C of Israel into the
32:5 are no longer his C because of their blemish;
32:20 are a perverse generation, C in whom is no
32:46 command them to your C, that they may be
33:1 of God blessed the C of Israel before his
33:9 not'; he disowned his brothers, and ignored his C
Josh 4:6 among you, when your C ask in time to
4:21 of Israel, "When your C ask their fathers in
4:22 you shall let your C know, 'Israel passed over
5:7 So it was their C, whom he raised up
14:9 for you and your C for ever, because you
22:24 time to come your C might say to our
22:24 might say to our C, 'What have you to
22:25 the LORD.' So your C might make our children
22:25 children might make our C cease to worship the
22:27 peace offerings; lest your C say to our children
22:27 children say to our C in time to come,
24:4 but Jacob and his C went down to Egypt.
Judg 10:8 crushed and oppressed the C of Israel that year.
13:2 and his wife was barren and had no C
13:3 barren and have no C; but you shall conceive
Ruth 4:12 Judah, because of the C that the LORD will
1Sam 1:2 And Peninnah had C, but Hannah had no children.
1:2 And Peninnah had children, but Hannah had no C
2:5 she who has many C is forlorn.
2:20 "The LORD give you C by this woman for
22:19 both men and women, C and sucklings, oxen, asses
30:22 away his wife and C, and depart."
2Sam 12:3 him and with his C; it used to eat

1Kgs 6:13 will dwell among the C of Israel, and will
8:39 hearts of all the C of men);
9:6 me, you or your C, and do not keep
20:3 your fairest wives and C also are mine.'"
20:5 your wives and your C;
20:7 my wives and my C, and for my silver
2Kgs 4:1 to take my two C to be his slaves."
14:6 put to death the C of the murderers; according
14:6 to death for the C, or the children be
14:6 the children, or the C be put to death
17:31 the Sepharvites burned their C in the fire to
17:34 the LORD commanded the C of Jacob, whom he
17:41 graven images; their C likewise, and their children's
17:41 likewise, and their C's children--as their fathers
17:41 likewise, and their children's C--as their fathers did,
19:3 rebuke, and of disgrace; C have come to the
1Chr 2:18 son of Hezron had C by his wife Azubah,
4:27 brothers had not many C, nor did all their
6:3 The C of Amram: Aaron, Moses, and Miriam.
14:4 the names of the C whom he had in
24:2 father, and had no C, so Eleazar and Ithamar
28:8 an inheritance to your C after you for ever.
6:30 the hearts of the C of men);
7:3 When all the C of Israel saw the fire
20:13 with their little ones, their wives, and their C
21:14 on your people, your C, your wives, and all
25:4 did not put their C to death, according to
25:4 to death for the C, or the children be
25:4 the children, or the C be put to death
30:9 your brethren and your C will find compassion with
31:18 with all their little C, their wives, their sons,
Ezra 8:21 way for ourselves, our C, and all our goods.
9:12 an inheritance to your C for ever.'
10:1 of men, women, and C, gathered to him out
10:3 these wives and their C, according to the counsel
10:44 women, and they put them away with their C
Neh 2:10 the welfare of the C of Israel.
5:5 of our brethren, our C are as their children;
5:5 children are as their C; yet we are forcing
7:73 month had come, the C of Israel were in
12:43 joy; the women and C also rejoiced.
13:2 did not meet the C of Israel with bread
13:24 and half of their C spoke the language of
Tob 4:12 were blessed in their C, and their posterity will
6:17 that you will have C by her." When Tobias
8:17 because thou hast had compassion on two only C
10:11 will prosper you, my C, before I die."
10:12 me to see your C by my daughter Sarah,
14:11 now, my C, consider what almsgiving accomplishes
Jud 4:10 their wives and their C and their cattle and
4:11 of Israel, and their C, living at Jerusalem, prostrated
7:14 and their wives and C will waste away with
7:23 Their C lost heart, and the
7:24 the women, and the C, gathered about Uzziah and
7:28 see our wives and C draw their last breath.
7:33 The women and C he sent home.
9:13 Zion, and against the house possessed by thy C
16:5 ground and seize my C as prey, and take
16:12 were wounded like the C of fugitives, they perished
Esth 3:13 and old, women and C, in one day, the
8:11 attack them, with their C and women, and to
13:6 with their wives and C, be utterly destroyed by
Job 8:4 If your C have sinned against him, he has
17:5 the eyes of his C will fail.
19:18 Even young C despise me; when I rise they
20:10 His C will seek the favor of the poor,
21:8 Their C are established in their presence, and their
21:11 a flock, and their C dance.
24:5 prey in the wilderness as food for their C
27:14 the Almighty: If his C are multiplied, it is
29:5 with me, when my C were about me;
38:32 or can you guide the Bear with its C
Ps 11:4 his eyelids test, the C of men.
14:2 from heaven upon the C of men, to see
17:14 for them; may their C have more than enough;
21:10 the earth, and their C from among the sons
25:13 in prosperity, and his C shall possess the land.
36:7 The C of men take refuge in the shadow
37:25 righteous forsaken or his C begging bread.
37:26 and lending, and his C become a blessing.
37:28 for ever, but the C of the wicked shall
69:36 and possess it; the C of his servants shall
73:15 have been untrue to the generation of thy C
78:4 hide them from their C, but tell to the
78:5 to teach to their C;
78:6 might know them, the C yet unborn, and arise
78:6 tell them to their C,
83:8 strong arm of the C of Lot.
89:30 If his C forsake my law and do not
90:3 sayest, "Turn back, O C of men!"
90:16 thy servants, and thy glorious power to their C
102:28 The C of thy servants shall dwell secure; their
103:13 a father pities his C, so the LORD pities
103:17 and his righteousness to C's children,
103:17 his righteousness to children's C,
109:9 May his C be fatherless, and his wife a
109:10 May his C wander about and beg; may they
109:12 to him, nor any to pity his fatherless C
113:9 a home, making her the joyous mother of C
115:14 the LORD give you increase, you and your C
128:3 within your house; your C will be like olive
128:6 May you see your C's children!
128:6 May you see your children's C
148:12 Young men and maidens together, old men and C
Prov 13:22 an inheritance to his C's children, but the sinner's
13:22 inheritance to his children's C, but the sinner's wealth
14:26 strong confidence, and his C will have a refuge.
31:28 Her C rise up and call her blessed; her
Eccl 6:3 man begets a hundred C, and lives many years,
Wis 3:12 are foolish, and their C evil;
3:16 But C of adulterers will not come to maturity,
4:6 For C born of unlawful unions are witnesses of
12:5 merciless slaughter of C, and their sacrificial feasting
12:25 Therefore, as to thoughtless C, thou didst send thy
13:17 and his marriage and C, he is not ashamed
14:23 For whether they kill C in their initiations, or
16:21 sweetness toward thy C; and the bread, ministering
18:5 a multitude of their C; and thou didst destroy
18:9 in secret the holy C of good men offered
18:10 piteous lament for their C was spread abroad.
18:12 instant their most valued C had been destroyed.
19:6 thy commands, that thy C might be kept unharmed.
Sir 3:1 me your father, O C; and act accordingly, that
3:2 the father above the C, and he confirmed the
3:5 gladdened by his own C, and when he prays
3:9 the houses of the C, but a mother's curse
3:11 is a disgrace for C not to respect their
7:23 Do you have C
11:26 death; a man will be known through his C
14:26 he will place his C under her shelter, and
16:1 a multitude of useless C, nor rejoice in ungodly
16:3 die childless is better than to have ungodly C
23:7 Listen, my C, to instruction concerning speech; the
23:23 harlotry and brought forth C by another man.
23:24 the assembly, and punishment will fall on her C
23:25 Her C will not take root, and her branches
25:7 man rejoicing in his C; a man who lives
33:21 is better that your C should ask from you
40:15 The C of the ungodly will not put forth
40:19 C and the building of a city establish a
41:5 The C of sinners are abominable children, and they
41:5 of sinners are abominable C, and they frequent the
41:6 The inheritance of the C of sinners will perish,
41:7 C will blame an ungodly father, for they suffer
41:14 My C, observe instruction and be at peace; hidden
42:5 of much discipline of C, and of whipping a
44:10 and so have their C after them.
44:12 their inheritance to their C's children.
44:12 and their inheritance to their children's C
44:13 by the covenants; their C also, for their sake.
46:9 hill country, and his C obtained it for an
47:20 brought wrath upon your C and they were grieved
Is 3:12 My people-- C are their oppressors, and women
8:18 Behold, I and the C whom the LORD has
13:18 of the womb; their eyes will not pity C
17:3 the glory of the C of Israel, says the
17:9 deserted because of the C of Israel, and there
29:23 when he sees his C, the work of my
30:1 "Woe to the rebellious C
37:3 rebuke, and of disgrace; C have come to the
38:19 makes known to the C thy faithfulness.
45:11 question me about my C, or command me concerning
47:8 know the loss of C:
47:9 day; the loss of C and widowhood shall come
49:20 The C born in the time of your bereavement
49:25 contend with you, and I will save your C
54:1 For the C of the desolate one will be
54:1 be more than the C of her that is
57:4 Are you not C of transgression, the offspring of
57:5 tree; who slay your C in the valleys, under
59:21 the mouth of your C, or out of the
59:21 the mouth of your C's children, says the LORD,

59:21 mouth of your children's C, says the LORD, from
65:23 in vain, or bear C for calamity; for they
65:23 the LORD, and their C with them.
Jer 2:9 LORD, and with your C's children I will contend.
2:9 and with your children's C I will contend.
2:30 have I smitten your C, they took no correction;
3:14 Return, O faithless C, says the LORD; for I
4:22 not; they are stupid C, they have no understanding.
5:7 Your C have forsaken me, and have sworn by
6:11 it out upon the C in the street, and
7:18 The C gather wood, the fathers kindle fire, and
9:21 palaces, cutting off the C from the streets and
10:20 cords are broken; my C have gone from me,
17:2 their altars, while their C remember their altars and
18:21 Therefore deliver up their C to famine; give them
22:28 are he and his C hurled and cast into
30:20 Their C shall be as they were of old,
31:15 is weeping for her C; she refuses to be
31:15 be comforted for her C, because they are not."
31:17 the LORD, and your C shall come back to
31:29 sour grapes, and the C's teeth are set on
32:18 of fathers to their C after them, O great
32:39 the good of their C after them.
40:7 him men, women, and C, those of the poorest
41:16 soldiers, women, C, and eunuchs, whom Johanan
43:6 men, the women, the C, the princesses, and every
47:3 not back to their C, so feeble are their
49:10 His C are destroyed, and his brothers, and his
49:11 Leave your fatherless C, I will keep them alive;
Lam 1:5 of her transgressions; her C have gone away, captives
1:16 revive my courage; my C are desolate, for the
2:19 the lives of your C, who faint for hunger
2:20 eat their offspring, the C of their tender care?
4:4 mouth for thirst; the C beg for food, but
4:10 have boiled their own C; they became their food
Bar 4:12 the sins of my C, because they turned away
4:19 Go, my C, go; for I have been left
4:21 "Take courage, my C, cry to God, and he
4:25 My C, endure with patience the wrath that has
4:27 "Take courage, my C, and cry to God, for
4:32 the cities which your C served as slaves; wretched
5:5 east, and see your C gathered from west and
6:33 of their gods to clothe their wives and C
Ezek 5:17 rob you of your C; pestilence and blood shall
9:6 men and maidens, little C and women, but touch
16:21 that you slaughtered my C and delivered them up
16:36 the blood of your C that you gave to
16:45 her husband and her C; and you are the
16:45 your sisters, who loathed their husbands and their C
18:2 sour grapes, and the C's teeth are set on
20:18 I said to their C in the wilderness, Do
20:21 But the C rebelled against me; they did not
23:39 they had slaughtered their C in sacrifice to their
36:12 and you shall no longer bereave them of C
36:13 bereave your nation of C
36:14 bereave your nation of C, says the Lord GOD;
37:16 'For Judah, and the C of Israel associated with
37:25 Jacob; they and their C and their children's children
37:25 their children and their C's children shall dwell there
37:25 children and their children's C shall dwell there for
47:22 you and have begotten C among you.
Dan 6:24 of lions–they, their C, and their wives; and
13:30 with her parents, her C, and all her kindred.
14:10 seventy priests of Bel, besides their wives and C
14:15 with their wives and C, as they were accustomed
14:20 see the footsteps of men and women and C
14:21 and their wives and C; and they showed him
Hos 1:2 of harlotry and have C of harlotry, for the
2:4 Upon her C also I will have no pity,
2:4 pity, because they are C of harlotry.
3:4 For the C of Israel shall dwell many days
3:5 Afterward the C of Israel shall return and seek
4:6 of your God, I also will forget your C
5:7 with the LORD; for they have borne alien C
9:12 if they bring up C, I will bereave them
9:16 they bring forth, I will slay their beloved C
10:14 battle; mothers were dashed in pieces with their C
Joel 1:3 Tell your C of it, and let your children
1:3 it, and let your C tell their children, and
1:3 your children tell their C, and their children another
1:3 their children, and their C another generation.
2:16 the elders; gather the C, even nursing infants.
Mic 1:16 your hair, for the C of your delight; make
2:9 houses; from their young C you take away my
Zech 10:7 Their C shall see it and rejoice, their hearts
10:9 me, and with their C they shall live and
Mal 4:6 of fathers to their C and the hearts of
4:6 and the hearts of C to their fathers, lest
1Mac 1:32 captive the women and C, and seized the cattle.
1:38 her offspring, and her C forsook her.
1:60 women who had their C circumcised,
2:38 with their wives and C and cattle, to the
2:50 Now, my C, show zeal for the law, and
2:64 My C, be courageous and grow strong in the
3:20 our wives and our C, and to despoil us;
3:45 not one of her C went in or out.
5:13 captured their wives and C and goods, and have
5:23 with their wives and C, and all they possessed,
5:45 with their wives and C and goods, a very
8:10 captive their wives and C; they plundered them,
13:6 and your wives and C, for all the nations
13:45 with their wives and C, went up on the
2Mac 5:13 of boys, women, and C, and slaughter of virgins
6:10 were brought in for having circumcised their C
7:34 your hand against the C of heaven.
8:28 distributed the rest among themselves and their C
9:15 throw out with their C to the beasts, for
9:20 If you and your C are well and your
12:3 with their wives and C, on boats which they
12:21 the women and the C and also the baggage
14:25 to marry and have C; so he married, settled
15:18 concern for wives and C, and also for brethren
Mt 2:16 killed all the male C in Bethlehem and in
2:18 Rachel weeping for her C; she refused to be
3:9 stones to raise up C to Abraham.
7:11 good gifts to your C, how much more will
10:21 father his child, and C will rise against parents
11:16 It is like C sitting in the market places
14:21 were about five thousand men, besides women and C
15:26 fair to take the C's bread and throw it
15:38 ate were four thousand men, besides women and C
18:3 turn and become like C, you will never enter
18:24 with his wife and C and all that he
19:13 Then C were brought to him that he might
19:14 Jesus said, "Let the C come to me, and
19:29 father or mother or C or lands, for my
21:15 he did, and the C crying out in the
22:24 man dies, having no C, his brother must marry
22:24 widow, and raise up C for his brother.'
22:25 died, and having no C left his wife to
23:36 I have gathered your C together as a hen
27:25 "His blood be on us and on our C
Mk 7:26 to her, "Let the C first be fed, for
7:26 right to take the C's bread and throw it
7:27 the table eat the C's crumbs."
10:13 And they were bringing C to him, that he
10:14 to them, "Let the C come to me, do
10:24 said to them again, C, how hard it is
10:29 mother or father or C or lands, for my
10:30 and mothers and C and lands, with persecutions,
12:19 wife, and raise up C for his brother.
12:20 he died left no C;
12:21 and died, leaving no C; and the third likewise;
12:22 the third likewise; and the seven left no C
13:12 father his child, and C will rise against parents
Lk 1:17 the fathers to the C, and the disobedient to
3:8 stones to raise up C to Abraham.
7:32 They are like C sitting in the market place
7:35 sinners!' Yet wisdom is justified by all her C
11:7 now shut, and my C are with me in
11:13 good gifts to your C, how much more will
13:34 I have gathered your C together as a hen
14:26 mother and wife and C and brothers and sisters,
18:16 him, saying, "Let the C come to me, and
18:29 brothers or parents or C, for the sake of
19:44 ground, you and your C within you, and they
20:28 a wife but no C, the man must take
20:28 wife and raise up C for his brother.
20:29 wife, and died without C;
20:31 all seven left no C and died.
23:27 me, but weep for yourselves and for your C
Jn 1:12 gave power to become C of God;
8:39 "If you were Abraham's C, you would do what
11:52 gather into one the C of God who are
13:33 Little C, yet a little while I am with
21:5 Jesus said to them, C, have you any fish?"
Acts 2:39 you and to your C and to all that
13:33 fulfilled to us their C by raising Jesus; as
21:5 all, with wives and C, brought us on our
21:21 not to circumcise their C or observe the customs.
Rom 2:20 foolish, a teacher of C, having in the law
8:16 spirit that we are C of God,

	8:17	of God, and if C, then heirs, heirs of
	8:21	glorious liberty of the C of God.
	9:7	and not all are C of Abraham because they
	9:8	it is not the C of the flesh who
	9:8	flesh who are the C of God, but the
	9:8	of God, but the C of the promise are
	9:10	when Rebecca had conceived C by one man, our
	9:29	had not left us C, we would have fared
1Cor	4:14	ashamed, but to admonish you as my beloved C
	7:14	Otherwise, your C would be unclean, but as it
	14:20	Brethren, do not be C in your thinking; be
2Cor	6:13	I speak as to C --widen your hearts also.
	12:14	yours but you; for C ought not to lay
	12:14	up for their parents, but parents for their C
Gal	4:3	us; when we were C, we were slaves to
	4:19	My little C, with whom I am again in
	4:24	from Mount Sinai, bearing C for slavery; she is
	4:25	Jerusalem, for she is in slavery with her C
	4:27	in travail; for the C of the desolate one
	4:27	many more than the C of her that is
	4:28	brethren, like Isaac, are C of promise.
	4:31	brethren, we are not C of the slave but
Eph	2:3	we were by nature C of wrath, like the
	4:14	may no longer be C, tossed to and fro
	5:1	Therefore be imitators of God, as beloved C
	5:8	the Lord; walk as C of light
	6:1	C, obey your parents in the Lord, for this
	6:4	do not provoke your C to anger, but bring
Phil	2:15	be blameless and innocent, C of God without blemish
Col	3:20	C, obey your parents in everything, for this pleases
	3:21	do not provoke your C, lest they become discouraged.
1Thes	2:7	you, like a nurse taking care of her C
	2:11	a father with his C, we exhorted each one
1Tim	2:15	be saved through bearing C, if she continues in
	3:4	household well, keeping his C submissive and
	3:12	let them manage their C and their households well;
	5:4	If a widow has C or grandchildren, let them
	5:10	who has brought up C, shown hospitality, washed the
	5:14	younger widows marry, bear C, rule their households,
Tit	1:5	one wife, and his C are believers and not
	2:4	love their husbands and C,
Heb	2:13	am I, and the C God has given me."
	2:14	Since therefore the C share in flesh and blood,
	12:8	then you are illegitimate C and not sons.
1Pet	1:14	As obedient C, do not be conformed to the
	3:6	you are now her C if you do right
2Pet	2:14	Accursed C
1Jn	2:1	My little C, I am writing this to you
	2:12	writing to you, little C, because your sins are
	2:13	I write to you, C, because you know the
	2:18	C, it is the last hour; and as you
	2:28	And now, little C, abide in him, so that
	3:1	we should be called C of God; and so
	3:2	Beloved, we are God's C now; it does not
	3:7	Little C, let no one deceive you.
	3:10	seen who are the C of God, and who
	3:10	and who are the C of the devil: whoever
	3:18	Little C, let us not love in word or
	4:4	Little C, you are of God, and have overcome
	5:2	that we love the C of God, when we
	5:21	Little C, keep yourselves from idols.
2Jn	1:1	elect lady and her C, whom I love in
	1:4	find some of your C following the truth, just
	1:13	The C of your elect sister greet you.
3Jn	1:4	to hear that my C follow the truth.
Rev	2:23	I will strike her C dead.

CHILE-AB

2Sam	3:3	Jezreel; and his second, C, of Abigail the widow

CHILION (3)

Ruth	1:2	sons were Mahlon and C; they were Ephrathites
	1:5	and both Mahlon and C died, so that the
	4:9	all that belonged to C and to Mahlon.

CHILMAD

Ezek	27:23	Canneh, Eden, Asshur, and C traded with you.

CHIMHAM (4)

2Sam	19:37	here is your servant C; let him go over
	19:38	And the king answered, C shall go over with
	19:40	on to Gilgal, and C went on with him;
Jer	41:17	and stayed at Geruth C near Bethlehem, intending to

CHINNERETH (4)

Num	34:11	of the sea of C on the east;
Deut	3:17	as the boundary, from C as far as the
Josh	13:27	of the Sea of C, eastward beyond the Jordan.
	19:35	Ziddim, Zer, Hammath, Rakkath, C,

CHINNEROTH (3)

Josh	11:2	the Arabah south of C, and in the lowland,
	12:3	to the Sea of C eastward, and in the
1Kgs	15:20	Dan, Abel-beth-maacah, and all C, with all the land

CHIOS

Acts	20:15	the following day opposite C; the next day we

CHIP

Hos	10:7	shall perish, like a C on the face of

CHIRP

Is	8:19	and the wizards who C and mutter," should not

CHIRPED

Is	10:14	moved a wing, or opened the mouth, or C

CHISLEV (8)

Neh	1:1	in the month of C, in the twentieth year,
Zech	7:1	fourth day of the ninth month, which is C
1Mac	1:54	the fifteenth day of C, in the one hundred
	4:52	is the month of C, in the one hundred
	4:59	with the twenty-fifth day of the month of C
2Mac	1:9	in the month of C, in the one hundred
	1:18	the twenty-fifth day of C we shall celebrate the
	10:5	twenty-fifth day of the same month, which was C

CHISLON

Num	34:21	the tribe of Benjamin, Elidad the son of C

CHISLOTH-TABOR

Josh	19:12	to the boundary of C; thence it goes to

CHITLISH

Josh	15:40	Bozkath, Eglon, Cabbon, Lahmam, C,

CHLOE

1Cor	1:11	reported to me by C's people that there is

CHOBA (3)

Jud	4:4	and Jericho and to C and Aesora and the
	15:4	Betomasthaim and Bebai and C and Kola, and to
	15:5	enemy, and cut them down as far as C

CHOICE (24)

Gen	24:10	taking all sorts of C gifts from his master;
	43:11	take some of the C fruits of the land
	49:11	ass's colt to the C vine, he washes his
2Kgs	3:19	fortified city, and every C city, and shall fell
Neh	5:18	one ox and six C sheep; fowls likewise were
Esth	9:19	on which they send C portions to one another.
	9:22	gladness, days for sending C portions to one another
Prov	8:10	and knowledge rather than C gold;
	8:19	and my yield than C silver.
	10:20	of the righteous is C silver; the mind of
Song	5:15	appearance is like Lebanon, C as the cedars.
	7:13	our doors are all C fruits, new as well
Sir	15:15	act faithfully is a matter of your own C
	24:15	of spices, and like C myrrh I spread a
Is	5:2	and planted it with C vines; he built a
Jer	2:21	I planted you a C vine, wholly of pure
	25:34	you shall fall like C rams.
Ezek	24:4	shoulder; fill it with C bones.
	24:6	of it piece after piece, without making any C
	27:24	traded with you in C garments, in clothes of
	31:16	trees of Eden, the C and best of Lebanon,
	48:14	shall not alienate this C portion of the land,
1Mac	10:32	men of his own C to guard it.
Acts	15:7	early days God made C among you, that by

CHOICEST (14)

Gen	23:6	your dead in the C of our sepulchres; none
Deut	33:13	his land, with the C gifts of heaven above,
	33:14	couches beneath, with the C fruits of the sun,
1Sam	2:29	yourselves upon the C parts of every offering
2Kgs	19:23	its tallest cedars, its C cypresses; I entered its
Song	4:13	of pomegranates with all C fruits, henna with nard,
	4:16	garden, and eat its C fruits.
Is	22:7	Your C valleys were full of chariots, and the
	37:24	its tallest cedars, its C cypresses; I came to
Jer	22:7	shall cut down your C cedars, and cast them
	48:15	come up, and the C of his young men

Ezek 20:40 your contributions and the C of your gifts, with
23:7 harlotries upon them, the C men of Assyria all
24:5 Take the C one of the flock, pile the

CHOIRMASTER

Hab 3:19 To the C: with stringed instruments.

CHOKE (2)

Mt 13:22 the delight in riches C the word, and it
Mk 4:19 things, enter in and C the word, and it

CHOKED (4)

Mt 13:7 thorns grew up and C them.
Mk 4:7 thorns grew up and C it, and it yielded
Lk 8:7 grew with it and C it.
8:14 their way they are C by the cares and

CHOKING

Sir 51:4 that I endured, from C fire on every side

CHOOSE (79)

Ex 17:9 Moses said to Joshua, C for us men, and
18:21 Moreover C able men from all the people, such
Num 14:4 one another, "Let us C a captain, and go
16:5 him whom he will C he will cause to
17:5 the man whom I C shall sprout; thus I
Deut 1:13 C wise, understanding, and experienced men
12:5 LORD your God will C out of all your
12:11 LORD your God will C, to make his name
12:14 which the LORD will C in one of your
12:18 LORD your God will C, you and your son
12:21 LORD your God will C to put his name
12:26 which the LORD will C,
14:23 place which he will C, to make his name
15:20 year at the place which the LORD will C
16:2 which the LORD will C, to make his name
16:6 LORD your God will C, to make his name
16:7 LORD your God will C; and in the morning
16:11 LORD your God will C, to make his name
16:15 which the LORD will C; because the LORD your
16:16 place which he will C: at the feast of
17:8 LORD your God will C,
17:10 which the LORD will C; and you shall be
17:15 you him whom the LORD your God will C
18:6 which the LORD will C,
23:16 place which he shall C within one of your
26:2 LORD your God will C, to make his name
30:19 blessing and curse; therefore C life, that you and
31:11 place which he will C, you shall read this
Josh 9:27 this day, in the place which he should C
24:15 to serve the LORD, C this day whom you
1Sam 17:8 C a man for yourselves, and let him come
2Sam 17:1 to Absalom, "Let me C twelve thousand men, and
24:12 things I offer you; C one of them, that
1Kgs 18:23 us; and let them C one bull for themselves,
18:25 the prophets of Baal, C for yourselves one bull
1Chr 21:10 things I offer you; C one of them, that
Neh 9:7 the God who didst C Abram and bring him
Jud 8:15 if he does not C to help us within
Job 7:15 so that I would C strangling and death rather
15:5 your mouth, and you C the tongue of the
34:4 Let us C what is right; let us determine
34:33 For you must C, and not I; therefore declare
Ps 16:4 Those who C another god multiply their sorrows;
25:12 he instruct in the way that he should C
65:4 he whom thou dost C and bring near, to
78:67 Joseph, he did not C the tribe of Ephraim;
Prov 1:29 knowledge and did not C the fear of the
3:31 violence and do not C any of his ways;
Wis 12:18 thou hast power to act whenever thou dost C
Sir 6:18 from your youth up C instruction, and until you
Is 7:15 refuse the evil and C the good.
7:16 refuse the evil and C the good, the land
14:1 Jacob and will again C Israel, and will set
56:4 keep my sabbaths, who C the things that please
58:5 the fast that I C, a day for a
58:6 the fast that I C: to loose the bonds
66:4 abominations; I also will C affliction for them, and
Jer 33:26 servant and will not C one of his descendants
49:19 and I will appoint over her whomever I C
50:44 and I will appoint over her whomever I C
Bar 3:27 God did not C them, nor give them the
Dan 13:23 I C not to do it and to fall
Zech 1:17 comfort Zion and again C Jerusalem.'"
2:12 land, and will again C Jerusalem."
1Mac 5:17 to Simon his brother, C your men and go
7:37 and said, "Thou didst C this house to be
12:45 to their homes and C for yourself a few
2Mac 1:25 every evil, who didst C the fathers and consecrate
5:19 the Lord did not C the nation for the
6:9 those who did not C to change over to
7:14 said, "One cannot but C to die at the
11:25 Accordingly, since we C that this nation also be
Mt 20:14 you, and go; I C to give to this
20:15 to do what I C with what belongs to
Jn 6:70 them, "Did I not C you, the twelve, and
15:16 You did not C me, but I chose you
Acts 15:22 the whole church, to C men from among them
15:25 to one accord, to C men and send them
Phil 1:22 Yet which I shall C I cannot tell.

CHOOSES (9)

Num 16:7 man whom the LORD C shall be the holy
Deut 14:24 the LORD your God C, to set his name
14:25 the LORD your God C,
Sir 15:17 death, and whichever he C will be given to
Is 40:20 He who is impoverished C for an offering wood
41:24 abomination is he who C you.
44:14 down cedars; or he C a holm tree or
Mt 11:27 to whom the Son C to reveal him.
Lk 10:22 to whom the Son C to reveal him."

CHOOSING (2)

Job 9:14 can I answer him, C my words with him?
Heb 11:25 Pharaoh's daughter, C rather to share ill-treatment

CHOP

Mic 3:3 bones in pieces, and C them up like meat

CHORAZIN (2)

Mt 11:21 "Woe to you, C
Lk 10:13 "Woe to you, C

CHOSE (63)

Gen 6:2 took to wife such of them as they C
13:11 So Lot C for himself all the Jordan valley,
Ex 18:25 Moses C able men out of all Israel, and
Deut 4:37 loved your fathers and C their descendants after
7:7 love upon you and C you, for you were
10:15 upon your fathers and C their descendants after
33:21 He C the best of the land for himself,
Josh 8:3 to Ai; and Joshua C thirty thousand mighty men
1Sam 2:28 And I C him out of all the tribes
13:2 Saul C three thousand men of Israel; two thousand
17:40 in his hand, and C five smooth stones from
2Sam 6:21 before the LORD, who C me above your father,
10:9 in the rear, he C some of the picked
1Kgs 8:16 out of Egypt, I C no city in all
8:16 be there; but I C David to be over
11:34 my servant whom I C, who kept my commandments
1Chr 15:2 God, for the LORD C them to carry the
19:10 in the rear, he C some of the picked
28:4 LORD God of Israel C me from all my
28:4 for ever; for he C Judah as leader, and
6:5 land of Egypt, I C no city in all
6:5 be there, and I C no man as prince
Jud 10:17 They C from their number a hundred men to
11:1 hurt any one who C to serve Nebuchadnezzar, the
Job 29:25 I C their way, and sat as chief, and
Ps 47:4 He C our heritage for us, the pride of
78:68 of Ephraim; but he C the tribe of Judah,
78:70 He C David his servant, and took him from
Wis 7:10 and beauty, and I C to have her rather
Sir 45:4 faithfulness and meekness; he C him out of all
45:16 He C him out of all the living to
Is 65:12 in my eyes, and C what I did not
66:4 in my eyes, and C that in which I
Jer 33:24 LORD has rejected the two families which he C
Ezek 20:5 the day when I C Israel, I swore to
1Mac 1:63 They C to die rather than to be defiled
3:38 Lysias C Ptolemy the son of Dorymenes, and Nicanor
4:42 He C blameless priests devoted to the law,
7:8 So the king C Bacchides, one of the king's
8:17 So Judas C Eupolemus the son of John, son
9:25 And Bacchides C the ungodly and put them in
10:74 He C ten thousand men and set out from
11:23 the siege; and he C some of the elders
12:1 favorable for him, he C men and sent them
13:34 Simon also C men and sent them to Demetrius
16:4 So John C out of the country twenty thousand
2Mac 3:7 The king C Heliodorus, who was in charge of
14:12 And he immediately C Nicanor, who had been in

Mk 13:20 the elect, whom he C, he shortened the days.
Lk 6:13 called his disciples, and C from them twelve, whom
14:7 he marked how they C the places of honor,
Jn 15:16 choose me, but I C you and appointed you
15:19 the world, but I C you out of the
Acts 6:5 whole multitude, and they C Stephen, a man full
13:17 of this people Israel C our fathers and made
15:39 to Cyprus, but Paul C Silas and departed, being
1Cor 1:27 noble birth; but God C what is foolish in
1:27 shame the wise, God C what is weak in
1:28 shame the strong, God C what is low and
12:18 the body, each one of them, as he C
Eph 1:4 places, even as he C us in him before
Col 1:27 To them God C to make known how great
2Thes 2:13 the Lord, because God C you from the beginning

CHOSEN (118)

Gen 18:19 No, for I have C him, that he may
Num 1:16 These were the ones C from the congregation, the
11:28 Moses, one of his C men, said, "My lord
16:2 leaders of the congregation, C from the assembly,
26:9 the Dathan and Abiram, C from the congregation,
Deut 7:6 LORD your God has C you to be a
14:2 and the LORD has C you to be a
18:5 LORD your God has C him out of all
21:5 LORD your God has C them to minister to
Josh 24:22 yourselves that you have C the LORD, to serve
Judg 5:8 When new gods were C, then war was in
10:14 gods whom you have C; let them deliver you
1Sam 8:18 king, whom you have C for yourselves; but the
10:24 "Do you see him whom the LORD has C
12:13 king whom you have C, for whom you have
16:8 "Neither has the LORD C this one."
16:9 "Neither has the LORD C this one."
16:10 "The LORD has not C these."
20:30 know that you have C the son of Jesse
24:2 Saul took three thousand C men out of all
26:2 Ziph, with three thousand C men of Israel, to
2Sam 6:1 again gathered all the C men of Israel, thirty
16:18 men of Israel have C, his I will be,
1Kgs 3:8 people whom thou hast C, a great people, that
8:44 city which thou hast C and the house which
8:48 city which thou hast C, and the house which
11:13 for the sake of Jerusalem which I have C
11:32 city which I have C out of all the
11:36 city where I have C to put my name.
12:21 hundred and eighty thousand C warriors, to fight
14:21 which the LORD had C out of all the
2Kgs 21:7 Jerusalem, which I have C out of all the
23:27 city which I have C, Jerusalem, and the house
1Chr 9:22 All these, who were C as gatekeepers at the
16:13 sons of Jacob, his C ones!
16:41 the rest of those C and expressly named to
24:6 one father's house being C for Eleazar and one
24:6 for Eleazar and one C for Ithamar.
28:5 many sons) he has C Solomon my son to
28:6 courts, for I have C him to be my
28:10 for the LORD has C you to build a
29:1 whom alone God has C, is young and inexperienced,
6:6 Israel; but I have C Jerusalem that my name
6:6 there and I have C David to be over
6:34 city which thou hast C and the house which
6:38 city which thou hast C, and the house which
7:12 your prayer, and have C this place for myself
7:16 For now I have C and consecrated this house
11:1 hundred and eighty thousand C warriors, to fight
12:13 which the LORD had C out of all the
29:11 for the LORD has C you to stand in
33:7 Jerusalem, which I have C out of all the
Neh 1:9 place which I have C, to make my name
Tob 1:4 place which had been C from among all the
8:15 thy angels and thy C people bless thee for
Esth 2:9 food, and with seven C maids from the king's
16:21 a joy to his C people instead of a
Job 36:21 for this you have C rather than affliction.
Ps 16:5 The LORD is my C portion and my cup;
33:12 people whom he has C as his heritage!
89:3 a covenant with my C one, I have sworn
89:19 I have exalted one C from the people.
105:6 sons of Jacob, his C ones!
105:26 Moses his servant, and Aaron whom he had C
105:43 people with joy, his C ones with singing.
106:5 the prosperity of thy C ones, that I may
106:23 had not Moses, his C one, stood in the
119:30 I have C the way of faithfulness, I set
119:173 me, for I have C thy precepts.
132:13 For the LORD has C Zion; he has desired
135:4 For the LORD has C Jacob for himself, Israel
Prov 16:16 understanding is to be C rather than silver.
22:1 name is to be C rather than great riches,
Wis 9:7 Thou hast C me to be king of thy
Sir 47:22 the descendants of his C one, nor destroy the
49:6 set fire to the C city of the sanctuary,
Is 1:29 shall blush for the gardens which you have C
41:8 Jacob, whom I have C, the offspring of Abraham,
41:9 my servant, I have C you and not cast
42:1 whom I uphold, my C, in whom my soul
43:10 servant whom I have C, that you may know
43:20 give drink to my C people,
44:1 O Jacob my servant, Israel whom I have C
44:2 O Jacob my servant, Jeshurun whom I have C
45:4 Jacob, and Israel my C, I call you by
49:7 of Israel, who has C you."
65:9 of my mountains; my C shall inherit it, and
65:15 your name to my C for a curse, and
65:22 people be, and my C shall long enjoy the
66:3 These have C their own ways, and their soul
Hag 2:23 ring; for I have C you, says the LORD
Zech 3:2 The LORD who has C Jerusalem rebuke you!
1Mac 2:19 obey him, and have C to do his commandments,
9:30 So now we have C you today to take
12:16 We therefore have C Numenius the son of Antiochus
2Mac 4:19 vile Jason sent envoys, C as being Antiochian citizens
Mt 12:18 servant whom I have C, my beloved with whom
22:14 teeth.' For many are called, but few are C
Lk 9:35 is my Son, my C; listen to him!"
10:42 Mary has C the good portion, which shall not
23:34 Christ of God, his C One!"
Jn 13:18 know whom I have C; it is that the
Acts 1:2 Holy Spirit to the apostles whom he had C
1:24 these two thou hast C
9:15 for he is a C instrument of mine to
10:41 to us who were C by God as witnesses,
Rom 11:5 there is a remnant, C by grace.
1Cor 15:38 body as he has C, and to each kind
Col 3:12 on then, as God's C ones, holy and beloved,
1Thes 1:4 God, that he has C you;
Heb 5:1 For every high priest C from among men is
Jas 2:5 Has not God C those who are poor in
1Pet 1:2 Asia, and Bithynia, C and destined by God
2:4 but in God's sight C and precious;
2:6 a stone, a cornerstone C and precious, and he
2:9 But you are a C race, a royal priesthood,
5:13 Babylon, who is likewise C, sends you greetings; and
Rev 17:14 him are called and C and faithful."

CHRIST (528)

Mt 1:1 the genealogy of Jesus C, the son of David,
1:16 of whom Jesus was born, who is called C
1:17 to Babylon to the C fourteen generations.
1:18 the birth of Jesus C took place in this
2:4 of them where the C was to be born.
11:2 the deeds of the C, he sent word by
16:16 replied, "You are the C, the Son of the
16:20 to tell no one that he was the C
22:42 question, saying, "What do you think of the C
23:10 called masters, for you have one master, the C
24:5 saying, 'I am the C and they will lead
24:23 'Lo, here is the C or 'There he is!'
26:63 if you are the C, the Son of God."
26:68 some slapped him, saying, "Prophesy to us, you C
27:17 for you, Barabbas or Jesus who is called C
27:22 shall I do with Jesus who is called C
Mk 1:1 the gospel of Jesus C, the Son of God.
8:29 Peter answered him, "You are the C
9:41 bear the name of C, will by no means
12:35 scribes say that the C is the son of
13:21 'Look, here is the C or 'Look, there he
14:61 him, "Are you the C, the Son of the
15:31 Let the C, the King of Israel, come down
Lk 2:11 a Savior, who is C the Lord.
2:26 see death before he had seen the Lord's C
3:15 perhaps he were the C,
4:41 speak, because they knew that he was the C
9:20 And Peter answered, "The C of God."
20:41 they say that the C is David's son?
22:65 "If you are the C, tell us." But he
23:2 that he himself is C a king."
23:34 if he is the C of God, his Chosen
23:38 railed at him, saying, "Are you not the C
24:26 not necessary that the C should suffer these things
24:46 is written, that the C should suffer and on

C

Jn	1:17	Moses; grace and truth came through Jesus C
	1:20	not deny, but confessed, "I am not the C
	1:25	you are neither the C, nor Elijah, nor the
	1:41	(which means C
	3:28	I am not the C, but I have been
	4:25	(he who is called C; when he comes, he
	4:29	Can this be the C
	7:26	the authorities really know that this is the C
	7:27	from; and when the C appears, no one will
	7:31	they said, "When the C appears, will he do
	7:41	Others said, "This is the C
	7:41	some said, "Is the C to come from Galilee?
	7:42	scripture said that the C is descended from David,
	9:22	confess him to be C, he was to be
	10:24	If you are the C, tell us plainly."
	11:27	that you are the C, the Son of God,
	12:34	the law that the C remains for ever.
	17:3	true God, and Jesus C whom thou hast sent.
	20:31	that Jesus is the C, the Son of God,
Acts	2:31	the resurrection of the C, that he was not
	2:36	him both Lord and C, this Jesus whom you
	2:38	the name of Jesus C for the forgiveness of
	3:6	the name of Jesus C of Nazareth, walk."
	3:18	the prophets, that his C should suffer, he thus
	3:20	he may send the C appointed for you, Jesus,
	4:10	the name of Jesus C of Nazareth, whom you
	5:42	not cease teaching and preaching Jesus as the C
	8:5	city of Samaria, and proclaimed to them the C
	8:12	the name of Jesus C, they were baptized, both
	9:22	in Damascus by proving that Jesus was the C
	9:34	to him, "Aeneas, Jesus C heals you; rise and
	10:36	of peace by Jesus C (he is Lord of
	10:48	to be baptized in the name of Jesus C
	11:17	in the Lord Jesus C, who was I that
	15:26	lives for the sake of our Lord Jesus C
	16:18	the name of Jesus C to come out of
	17:3	was necessary for the C to suffer and to
	17:3	Jesus, whom I proclaim to you, is the C
	18:5	the Jews that the C was Jesus.
	18:28	the scriptures that the C was Jesus.
	20:21	God and of faith in our Lord Jesus C
	24:23	speak upon faith in C Jesus.
	26:23	to pass: that the C must suffer, and that,
	28:30	about the Lord Jesus C quite openly and unhindered.
Rom	1:1	a servant of Jesus C, called to be an
	1:4	from the dead, Jesus C our Lord,
	1:6	to belong to Jesus C;
	1:7	from God our Father and the Lord Jesus C
	1:8	my God through Jesus C for all of you,
	2:16	secrets of men by C Jesus.
	3:22	through faith in Jesus C for all who believe.
	3:24	redemption which is in C Jesus,
	5:1	have peace with God through our Lord Jesus C
	5:6	at the right time C died for the ungodly.
	5:8	we were yet sinners C died for us.
	5:11	through our Lord Jesus C, through whom we have
	5:15	that one man Jesus C abounded for many.
	5:17	reign in life through the one man Jesus C
	5:21	eternal life through Jesus C our Lord.
	6:3	have been baptized into C Jesus were baptized into
	6:4	death, so that as C was raised from the
	6:8	we have died with C, we believe that we
	6:9	For we know that C being raised from the
	6:11	alive to God in C Jesus.
	6:23	is eternal life in C Jesus our Lord.
	7:4	through the body of C, so that you may
	7:25	to God through Jesus C our Lord!
	8:1	those who are in C Jesus.
	8:2	Spirit of life in C Jesus has set me
	8:9	have the Spirit of C does not belong to
	8:10	But if C is in you, although your bodies
	8:11	you, he who raised C Jesus from the dead
	8:17	and fellow heirs with C, provided we suffer with
	8:34	Is it C Jesus, who died, yes, who was
	8:35	Who shall separate us from the love of C
	8:39	love of God in C Jesus our Lord.
	9:1	speaking the truth in C, I am not lying;
	9:3	and cut off from C for the sake of
	9:5	their race, according to the flesh, is the C
	10:4	For C is the end of the law, that
	10:6	(that is, to bring C down)
	10:7	(that is, to bring C up from the dead).
	10:17	what is heard comes by the preaching of C
	12:5	are one body in C, and individually members one
	13:14	on the Lord Jesus C, and make no provision
	14:9	For to this end C died and lived again,
	14:15	of one for whom C died.
	14:18	he who thus serves C is acceptable to God
	15:3	For C did not please himself; but, as it
	15:5	another, in accord with C Jesus,
	15:6	the God and Father of our Lord Jesus C
	15:7	one another, therefore, as C has welcomed you, for
	15:8	I tell you that C became a servant to
	15:16	be a minister of C Jesus to the Gentiles
	15:17	In C Jesus, then, I have reason to be
	15:18	of anything except what C has wrought through me
	15:19	preached the gospel of C,
	15:20	the gospel, not where C has already been named,
	15:29	come in the fulness of the blessing of C
	15:30	by our Lord Jesus C and by the love
	16:3	my fellow workers in C Jesus,
	16:5	who was the first convert in Asia for C
	16:7	and they were in C before me.
	16:9	our fellow worker in C, and my beloved Stachys.
	16:10	Greet Apelles, who is approved in C
	16:16	All the churches of C greet you.
	16:18	not serve our Lord C, but their own appetites,
	16:20	of our Lord Jesus C be with you.
	16:24	the preaching of Jesus C, according to the revelation
	16:26	wise God be glory for evermore through Jesus C
1Cor	1:1	be an apostle of C Jesus, and our brother
	1:2	to those sanctified in C Jesus, called to be
	1:2	of our Lord Jesus C, both their Lord and
	1:3	from God our Father and the Lord Jesus C
	1:4	was given you in C Jesus,
	1:6	as the testimony to C was confirmed among you--
	1:7	of our Lord Jesus C;
	1:8	guiltless in the day of our Lord Jesus C
	1:9	of his Son, Jesus C our Lord.
	1:10	of our Lord Jesus C, that all of you
	1:12	or "I belong to C
	1:13	Is C divided?
	1:17	any one else.) For C did not send me
	1:17	lest the cross of C be emptied of its
	1:23	wisdom, but we preach C crucified, a stumbling block
	1:24	both Jews and Greeks, C the power of God
	1:30	of your life in C Jesus, whom God made
	2:2	among you except Jesus C and him crucified.
	2:16	But we have the mind of C
	3:1	as men of the flesh, as babes in C
	3:11	than that which is laid, which is Jesus C
	3:23	you are Christs; and C is Gods.
	4:1	us, as servants of C and stewards of the
	4:10	We are fools for C's sake, but you are
	4:10	for Christ's sake, but you are wise in C
	4:15	have countless guides in C, you do not have
	4:15	became your father in C Jesus through the gospel.
	4:17	of my ways in C, as I teach them
	5:7	For C, our paschal lamb, has been sacrificed.
	6:11	of the Lord Jesus C and in the Spirit
	6:15	not know that your bodies are members of C
	6:15	take the members of C and make them members
	7:22	was free when called is a slave of C
	8:6	and one Lord, Jesus C, through whom are all
	8:11	the brother for whom C died.
	8:12	conscience when it is weak, you sin against C
	9:12	obstacle in the way of the gospel of C
	9:21	under the law of C --that I might win
	10:4	Rock which followed them, and the Rock was C
	10:16	it not a participation in the blood of C
	10:16	it not a participation in the body of C
	11:1	Be imitators of me, as I am of C
	11:3	of every man is C, the head of a
	11:3	and the head of C is God.
	12:12	many, are one body, so it is with C
	12:27	are the body of C and individually members of
	15:3	I also received, that C died for our sins
	15:12	Now if C is preached as raised from the
	15:13	of the dead, then C has not been raised;
	15:14	not been raised; if C has not been raised,
	15:15	God that he raised C, whom he did not
	15:16	are not raised, then C has not been raised.
	15:17	If C has not been raised, your faith is
	15:18	have fallen asleep in C have perished.
	15:19	we have hoped in C, we are of all
	15:20	But in fact C has been raised from the
	15:22	die, so also in C shall all be made
	15:23	in his own order: C the first fruits, then
	15:23	then at his coming those who belong to C
	15:31	which I have in C Jesus our Lord, I
	15:57	gives us the victory through our Lord Jesus C
	16:24	with you all in C Jesus.

2Cor 1:1 Paul, an apostle of C Jesus by the will
1:2 from God our Father and the Lord Jesus C
1:3 of our Lord Jesus C, the Father of mercies
1:5 share abundantly in C's sufferings, so through Christ
1:5 Christ's sufferings, so through C we share abundantly
1:19 Son of God, Jesus C, whom we preached among
1:21 us with you in C, and has commissioned us;
2:10 in the presence of C,
2:12 preach the gospel of C, a door was opened
2:14 to God, who in C always leads us in
2:15 are the aroma of C to God among those
2:17 in the sight of God we speak in C
3:3 are a letter from C delivered by us, written
3:4 that we have through C toward God.
3:14 unlifted, because only through C is it taken away.
4:4 of the glory of C, who is the likeness
4:5 not ourselves, but Jesus C as Lord, with ourselves
4:6 the glory of God in the face of C
5:10 the judgment seat of C, so that each one
5:14 For the love of C controls us, because we
5:16 though we once regarded C from a human point
5:17 any one is in C, he is a new
5:18 from God, who through C reconciled us to himself
5:19 reconciliation; that is, in C God was reconciling the
5:20 we are ambassadors for C, God making his appeal
5:20 you on behalf of C, be reconciled to God.
6:15 What accord has C with Belial?
8:9 of our Lord Jesus C, that though he was
8:23 are messengers of the churches, the glory of C
9:13 acknowledging the gospel of C, and by the generosity
10:1 meekness and gentleness of C --I who am humble
10:5 thought captive to obey C,
10:14 the way to you with the gospel of C
11:2 I betrothed you to C to present you as
11:3 astray from a sincere and pure devotion to C
11:10 As the truth of C is in me, this
11:13 workmen, disguising themselves as apostles of C
11:23 Are they servants of C
12:2 know a man in C who fourteen years ago
12:9 that the power of C may rest upon me.
12:10 For the sake of C, then, I am content
12:19 have been speaking in C, and all for your
13:3 you desire proof that C is speaking in me.
13:5 not realize that Jesus C is in you?--unless
13:14 of the Lord Jesus C and the love of
Gal 1:1 man, but through Jesus C and God the Father,
1:3 and our Lord Jesus C,
1:6 in the grace of C and turning to a
1:7 you and want to pervert the gospel of C
1:10 men, I should not be a servant of C
1:12 but it came through a revelation of Jesus C
1:22 to the churches of C in Judea;
2:4 which we have in C Jesus, that they might
2:16 through faith in Jesus C, even we have believed
2:16 we have believed in C Jesus, in order to
2:16 justified by faith in C, and not by works
2:17 to be justified in C, we ourselves were found
2:17 to be sinners, is C then an agent of
2:20 have been crucified with C; it is no longer
2:20 I who live, but C who lives in me;
2:21 through the law, then C died to no purpose.
3:1 before whose eyes Jesus C was publicly portrayed as
3:13 C redeemed us from the curse of the law,
3:14 tree"-- that in C Jesus the blessing of
3:16 which is C
3:22 to faith in Jesus C might be given to
3:24 was our custodian until C came, that we might
3:26 a custodian; for in C Jesus you are all
3:27 as were baptized into C have put on Christ.
3:27 as were baptized into Christ have put on C
3:28 are all one in C Jesus.
4:14 angel of God, as C Jesus.
4:19 again in travail until C be formed in you!
5:1 For freedom C has set us free; stand fast
5:2 if you receive circumcision, C will be of no
5:4 You are severed from C, you who would be
5:6 For in C Jesus neither circumcision nor
5:24 those who belong to C Jesus have crucified the
6:2 another's burdens, and so fulfil the law of C
6:12 may not be persecuted for the cross of C
6:14 of our Lord Jesus C, by which the world
6:18 of our Lord Jesus C be with your spirit,
Eph 1:1 Paul, an apostle of C Jesus by the will
1:1 are also faithful in C Jesus:
1:2 from God our Father and the Lord Jesus C
1:3 of our Lord Jesus C, who has blessed us
1:3 has blessed us in C with every spiritual blessing
1:5 his sons through Jesus C, according to the purpose
1:9 he set forth in C
1:12 who first hoped in C have been destined and
1:17 of our Lord Jesus C, the Father of glory,
1:20 which he accomplished in C when he raised him
2:5 us alive together with C (by grace you have
2:6 the heavenly places in C Jesus,
2:7 kindness toward us in C Jesus.
2:10 his workmanship, created in C Jesus for good works,
2:12 separated from C, alienated from the commonwealth
2:13 But now in C Jesus you who once were
2:13 have been brought near in the blood of C
2:20 the apostles and prophets, C Jesus himself being the
3:1 Paul, a prisoner for C Jesus on behalf of
3:4 into the mystery of C,
3:6 of the promise in C Jesus through the gospel.
3:8 the unsearchable riches of C,
3:11 he has realized in C Jesus our Lord,
3:17 inner man, and that C may dwell in your
3:19 know the love of C which surpasses knowledge, that
3:21 the church and in C Jesus to all generations,
4:7 to the measure of C's gift.
4:12 up the body of C,
4:13 of the fulness of C;
4:15 is the head, into C,
4:20 did not so learn C –
4:32 another, as God in C forgave you.
5:2 walk in love, as C loved us and gave
5:5 in the kingdom of C and of God.
5:14 from the dead, and C shall give you light."
5:20 of our Lord Jesus C to God the Father.
5:21 subject to one another out of reverence for C
5:23 of the wife as C is the head of
5:24 church is subject to C, so let wives also
5:25 love your wives, as C loved the church and
5:29 and cherishes it, as C does the church,
5:32 that it refers to C and the church;
6:5 of heart, as to C;
6:6 but as servants of C, doing the will of
6:23 from God the Father and the Lord Jesus C
6:24 love our Lord Jesus C with love undying.
Phil 1:1 and Timothy, servants of C Jesus, To all the
1:1 all the saints in C Jesus who are at
1:2 from God our Father and the Lord Jesus C
1:6 it to completion at the day of Jesus C
1:8 with the affection of C Jesus.
1:10 for the day of C,
1:11 which come through Jesus C, to the glory and
1:13 my imprisonment is for C;
1:15 Some indeed preach C from envy and rivalry, but
1:17 gospel; the former proclaim C out of partisanship,
1:18 pretense or in truth, C is proclaimed; and in
1:19 the Spirit of Jesus C this will turn out
1:20 courage now as always C will be honored in
1:21 me to live is C, and to die is
1:23 depart and be with C, for that is far
1:26 cause to glory in C Jesus, because of my
1:27 of the gospel of C, so that whether I
1:29 for the sake of C you should not only
2:1 is any encouragement in C, any incentive of love,
2:5 which is yours in C Jesus,
2:11 tongue confess that Jesus C is Lord, to the
2:16 in the day of C I may be proud
2:21 after their own interests, not those of Jesus C
2:30 for the work of C, risking his life to
3:3 spirit, and glory in C Jesus, and put no
3:7 I counted as loss for the sake of C
3:8 surpassing worth of knowing C Jesus my Lord.
3:8 that I may gain C
3:9 is through faith in C, the righteousness from God
3:12 it my own, because C Jesus has made me
3:14 call of God in C Jesus.
3:18 tears, live as enemies of the cross of C
3:20 Savior, the Lord Jesus C,
4:7 and your minds in C Jesus.
4:19 riches in glory in C Jesus.
4:21 Greet every saint in C Jesus.
4:23 of the Lord Jesus C be with your spirit.
Col 1:1 Paul, an apostle of C Jesus by the will
1:2 and faithful brethren in C at Colossae: Grace to
1:3 of our Lord Jesus C, when we pray for
1:4 of your faith in C Jesus and of the
1:7 a faithful minister of C on our behalf
1:24 what is lacking in C's afflictions for the sake
1:27 this mystery, which is C in you, the hope

1:28 that we may present every man mature in C
2:2 of God's mystery, of C,
2:5 order and the firmness of your faith in C
2:6 As therefore you received C Jesus the Lord, so
2:8 spirits of the universe, and not according to C
2:11 in the circumcision of C;
2:17 is to come; but the substance belongs to C
2:20 If with C you died to the elemental spirits
3:1 have been raised with C, seek the things that
3:1 that are above, where C is, seated at the
3:3 life is hid with C in God.
3:4 When C who is our life appears, then you
3:11 slave, free man, but C is all, and in
3:15 let the peace of C rule in your hearts,
3:16 Let the word of C dwell in you richly,
3:24 as your reward; you are serving the Lord C
4:3 declare the mystery of C, on account of which
4:12 yourselves, a servant of C Jesus, greets you, always
1Thes 1:1 and the Lord Jesus C: Grace to you and
1:3 and steadfastness of hope in our Lord Jesus C
2:6 we might have made demands as apostles of C
2:14 churches of God in C Jesus which are in
3:2 in the gospel of C, to establish you in
4:16 And the dead in C will rise first;
5:9 through our Lord Jesus C,
5:18 will of God in C Jesus for you.
5:23 blameless at the coming of our Lord Jesus C
5:28 of our Lord Jesus C be with you.
2Thes 1:1 and the Lord Jesus C:
1:2 from God the Father and the Lord Jesus C
1:12 grace of our God and the Lord Jesus C
2:1 of our Lord Jesus C and our assembling to
2:14 may obtain the glory of our Lord Jesus C
2:16 may our Lord Jesus C himself, and God our
3:5 love of God and to the steadfastness of C
3:6 of our Lord Jesus C, that you keep away
3:12 in the Lord Jesus C to do their work
3:18 of our Lord Jesus C be with you all.
1Tim 1:1 Paul, an apostle of C Jesus by command of
1:1 our Savior and of C Jesus our hope,
1:2 God the Father and C Jesus our Lord.
1:12 me strength for this, C Jesus our Lord, because
1:14 love that are in C Jesus.
1:15 of full acceptance, that C Jesus came into the
1:16 as the foremost, Jesus C might display his perfect
2:5 and men, the man C Jesus,
3:13 faith which is in C Jesus.
4:6 a good minister of C Jesus, nourished on the
5:11 they grow wanton against C they desire to marry,
5:21 of God and of C Jesus and of the
6:3 of our Lord Jesus C and the teaching which
6:13 all things, and of C Jesus who in his
6:14 of our Lord Jesus C;
2Tim 1:1 Paul, an apostle of C Jesus by the will
1:1 life which is in C Jesus,
1:2 God the Father and C Jesus our Lord.
1:9 he gave us in C Jesus ages ago,
1:10 of our Savior C Jesus, who abolished death
1:13 love which are in C Jesus;
2:1 grace that is in C Jesus,
2:3 a good soldier of C Jesus.
2:8 Remember Jesus C, risen from the dead, descended
2:10 may obtain salvation in C Jesus with its eternal
3:12 a godly life in C Jesus will be persecuted,
3:15 salvation through faith in C Jesus.
4:1 of God and of C Jesus who is to
Tit 1:1 an apostle of Jesus C, to further the faith
1:3 God the Father and C Jesus our Savior.
2:13 God and Savior Jesus C,
3:6 us richly through Jesus C our Savior,
Philem 1:1 Paul, a prisoner for C Jesus, and Timothy our
1:3 from God our Father and the Lord Jesus C
1:6 of all the good that is ours in C
1:8 am bold enough in C to command you to
1:9 a prisoner also for C Jesus--
1:20 Refresh my heart in C
1:23 my fellow prisoner in C Jesus, sends greetings to
1:25 of the Lord Jesus C be with your spirit.
Heb 3:6 be spoken later, but C was faithful over God's
3:14 For we share in C, if only we hold
5:5 So also C did not exalt himself to be
6:1 the elementary doctrine of C and go on to
8:6 But as it is, C has obtained a ministry
9:11 But when C appeared as a high priest of
9:14 shall the blood of C, who through the eternal
9:24 For C has entered, not into a sanctuary made
9:28 that comes judgment, so C, having been offered once
10:5 Consequently, when C came into the world, he said,
10:10 the body of Jesus C once for all.
10:12 But when C had offered for all time a
11:26 abuse suffered for the C greater wealth than the
13:8 Jesus C is the same yesterday and today and
13:21 his sight, through Jesus C; to whom be glory
Jas 1:1 of the LORD Jesus C, to the twelve tribes
2:1 of our Lord Jesus C, the Lord of glory.
1Pet 1:1 an apostle of Jesus C, to the Exiles of
1:2 for obedience to Jesus C and for sprinkling with
1:3 the God and Father of our Lord Jesus C
1:3 the resurrection of Jesus C from the dead,
1:7 glory and honor at the revelation of Jesus C
1:11 by the Spirit of C within them when predicting
1:11 predicting the sufferings of C and the subsequent
1:13 coming to you at the revelation of Jesus C
1:19 the precious blood of C, like that of a
2:5 sacrifices acceptable to God through Jesus C
2:21 have been called, because C also suffered for you,
3:15 in your hearts reverence C as Lord.
3:16 your good behavior in C may be put to
3:18 For C also died for sins once for all,
3:21 the resurrection of Jesus C,
4:1 Since therefore C suffered in the flesh, arm
4:11 in everything God may be glorified through Jesus C
4:13 far as you share C's sufferings, that you may
4:14 for the name of C, you are blessed, because
5:1 of the sufferings of C as well as a
5:10 his eternal glory in C, will himself restore, establish,
5:14 Peace to all of you that are in C
2Pet 1:1 and apostle of Jesus C, To those who have
1:1 God and Savior Jesus C:
1:8 unfruitful in the knowledge of our Lord Jesus C
1:11 eternal kingdom of our Lord and Savior Jesus C
1:14 as our Lord Jesus C showed me.
1:16 of our Lord Jesus C, but we were eyewitnesses
2:20 Lord and Savior Jesus C, they are again entangled
3:18 and knowledge of our Lord and Savior Jesus C
1Jn 1:3 with the Father and with his Son Jesus C
2:1 with the Father, Jesus C the righteous;
2:22 but he who denies that Jesus is the C
3:23 of his Son Jesus C and love one another,
4:2 which confesses that Jesus C has come in the
5:1 that Jesus is the C is a child of
5:6 water and blood, Jesus C, not with the water
5:20 him who is true, in his Son Jesus C
2Jn 1:3 Father and from Jesus C the Father's Son, in
1:7 the coming of Jesus C in the flesh; such
1:9 in the doctrine of C does not have God;
Jude 1:1 a servant of Jesus C and brother of James,
1:1 and kept for Jesus C:
1:4 and deny our only Master and Lord, Jesus C
1:17 of our Lord Jesus C;
1:21 of our Lord Jesus C unto eternal life.
1:25 our Savior through Jesus C our Lord, be glory,
Rev 1:1 THE revelation of Jesus C, which God gave him
1:2 the testimony of Jesus C, even to all that
1:5 throne, and from Jesus C the faithful witness, the
11:15 Lord and of his C, and he shall reign
12:10 the authority of his C have come, for the
20:4 life, and reigned with C a thousand years.
20:6 of God and of C, and they shall reign

CHRISTIAN (2)

Acts 26:28 short time you think to make me a C
1Pet 4:16 one suffers as a C, let him not be

CHRISTIANS

Acts 11:26 the disciples were for the first time called C

CHRISTS (6)

Mt 24:24 For false C and false prophets will arise and
Mk 13:22 False C and false prophets will arise and show
1Cor 3:23 yours; and you are C; and Christ is Gods.
2Cor 10:7 confident that he is C, let him remind himself
10:7 that as he is C, so are we.
Gal 3:29 And if you are C, then you are Abraham's

CHRONIC (2)

Lev 13:11 swelling, it is a C leprosy in the skin
Sir 30:17 and eternal rest than C sickness.

CHRONICLES (46)

1Kgs 14:19 the Book of the C of the Kings of
14:29 the Book of the C of the Kings of

15:7 the Book of the C of the Kings of
15:23 the Book of the C of the Kings of
15:31 the Book of the C of the Kings of
16:5 the Book of the C of the Kings of
16:14 the Book of the C of the Kings of
16:20 the Book of the C of the Kings of
16:27 the Book of the C of the Kings of
22:39 the Book of the C of the Kings of
22:45 the Book of the C of the Kings of
2Kgs 1:18 the Book of the C of the Kings of
8:23 the Book of the C of the Kings of
10:34 the Book of the C of the Kings of
12:19 the Book of the C of the Kings of
13:8 the Book of the C of the Kings of
13:12 the Book of the C of the Kings of
14:15 the Book of the C of the Kings of
14:18 the Book of the C of the Kings of
14:28 the Book of the C of the Kings of
15:6 the Book of the C of the Kings of
15:11 the Book of the C of the Kings of
15:15 the Book of the C of the Kings of
15:21 the Book of the C of the Kings of
15:26 the Book of the C of the Kings of
15:31 the Book of the C of the Kings of
15:36 the Book of the C of the Kings of
16:19 the Book of the C of the Kings of
20:20 the Book of the C of the Kings of
21:17 the Book of the C of the Kings of
21:25 the Book of the C of the Kings of
23:28 the Book of the C of the Kings of
24:5 the Book of the C of the Kings of
1Chr 27:24 not entered in the C of King David.
29:29 are written in the C of Samuel the seer,
29:29 seer, and in the C of Nathan the prophet,
29:29 prophet, and in the C of Gad the seer,
12:15 not written in the C of Shemaiah the prophet
20:34 are written in the C of Jehu the son
33:18 they are in the C of the Kings of
33:19 are written in the C of the Seers.
Neh 12:23 the Book of the C until the days of
Esth 2:23 the Book of the C in the presence of
6:1 of memorable deeds, the C, and they were read
10:2 the Book of the C of the kings of
1Mac 16:24 are written in the C of his high-priesthood, from

CHRYSOLITE (4)

Ezek 1:16 the gleaming of a C; and the four had
10:9 the appearance of the wheels was like sparkling C
28:13 topaz, and jasper, C, beryl, and onyx, sapphire,
Rev 21:20 sixth carnelian, the seventh C, the eighth beryl, the

CHRYSOPRASE

Rev 21:20 ninth topaz, the tenth C, the eleventh jacinth, the

CHURCH (74)

Mt 16:18 I will build my C, and the powers of
18:16 tell it to the C; and if he refuses
18:16 listen even to the C, let him be to
Acts 5:11 came upon the whole C, and upon all who
8:1 persecution arose against the C in Jerusalem; and
8:3 Saul was ravaging the C, and entering house after
9:31 So the C throughout all Judea and Galilee and
11:22 the ears of the C in Jerusalem, and they
11:26 they met with the C, and taught a large
12:1 violent hands upon some who belonged to the C
12:5 for him was made to God by the C
13:1 Now in the C at Antioch there were prophets
14:23 for them in every C, with prayer and fasting
14:27 arrived, they gathered the C together and declared
15:3 their way by the C, they passed through both
15:4 were welcomed by the C and the apostles and
15:22 elders, with the whole C, to choose men from
18:22 up and greeted the C, and then went down
20:17 and called to him the elders of the C
20:28 to care for the C of the LORD which
Rom 16:1 a deaconess of the C at Cenchre-ae,
16:5 thanks; greet also the C in their house.
16:23 and to the whole C, greets you.
1Cor 1:2 brother Sosthenes, To the C of God which is
4:17 Christ, as I teach them everywhere in every C
5:12 not those inside the C whom you are to
6:4 before those who are least esteemed by the C
10:32 Greeks or to the C of God,
11:18 you assemble as a C, I hear that there
11:22 do you despise the C of God and humiliate
12:28 has appointed in the C first apostles, second prophets,
14:4 edifies himself, but he who prophesies edifies the C
14:5 interprets, so that the C may be edified.
14:12 Spirit, strive to excel in building up the C
14:19 you all; nevertheless, in C I would rather speak
14:23 If, therefore, the whole C assembles and all speak
14:28 them keep silence in C and speak to himself
14:35 is shameful for a woman to speak in C
15:9 because I persecuted the C of God.
16:19 Prisca, together with the C in their house, send
2Cor 1:1 To the C of God which is at Corinth,
Gal 1:13 how I persecuted the C of God violently and
Eph 1:22 all things for the C,
3:10 things; that through the C the manifold wisdom of
3:21 be glory in the C and in Christ Jesus
5:23 the head of the C, his body, and is
5:24 As the C is subject to Christ, so let
5:25 as Christ loved the C and gave himself up
5:27 he might present the C to himself in splendor,
5:29 as Christ does the C,
5:32 to Christ and the C;
Phil 3:6 a persecutor of the C, as to righteousness under
4:15 I left Macedonia, no C entered into partnership with
Col 1:18 of the body, the C; he is the beginning,
1:24 body, that is, the C,
4:15 to Nympha and the C in her house.
4:16 read also in the C of the La-odiceans; and
1Thes 1:1 and Timothy, to the C of the Thessalonians in
2Thes 1:1 and Timothy, to the C of the Thessalonians in
1Tim 3:5 own household, how can he care for God's C
3:15 God, which is the C of the living God,
5:16 assist them; let the C not be burdened, so
Philem 1:2 fellow soldier, and the C in your house:
Jas 5:14 the elders of the C, and let them pray
3Jn 1:6 who have testified to your love before the C
1:9 written something to the C; but Diotrephes, who
1:10 welcome them and puts them out of the C
Rev 2:1 the angel of the C in Ephesus write: 'The
2:8 the angel of the C in Smyrna write: 'The
2:12 the angel of the C in Pergamum write: 'The
2:18 the angel of the C in Thyatira write: 'The
3:1 the angel of the C in Sardis write: 'The
3:7 the angel of the C in Philadelphia write: 'The
3:14 the angel of the C in La-odicea write: 'The

CHURCHES (35)

Acts 15:40 went through Syria and Cilicia, strengthening the C
16:5 So the C were strengthened in the faith, and
Rom 16:4 but also all the C of the Gentiles give
16:16 All the C of Christ greet you.
1Cor 7:17 This is my rule in all the C
11:16 practice, nor do the C of God.
14:33 As in all the C of the saints,
14:34 saints, the women should keep silence in the C
16:1 as I directed the C of Galatia, so you
16:19 The C of Asia send greetings.
2Cor 8:1 been shown in the C of Macedonia,
8:18 famous among all the C for his preaching of
8:19 been appointed by the C to travel with us
8:23 are messengers of the C, the glory of Christ.
8:24 give proof, before the C, of your love and
11:8 I robbed other C by accepting support from them
11:28 upon me of my anxiety for all the C
12:13 the rest of the C, except that I myself
Gal 1:2 with me, To the C of Galatia:
1:22 by sight to the C of Christ in Judea;
1Thes 2:14 became imitators of the C of God in Christ
2Thes 1:4 of you in the C of God for your
Rev 1:4 John to the seven C that are in Asia:
1:11 it to the seven C, to Ephesus and to
1:20 angels of the seven C and the seven lampstands
1:20 churches and the seven lampstands are the seven C
2:7 him hear what the Spirit says to the C
2:11 him hear what the Spirit says to the C
2:17 him hear what the Spirit says to the C
2:23 And all the C shall know that I am
2:29 Spirit says to the C
3:6 Spirit says to the C
3:13 Spirit says to the C
3:22 him hear what the Spirit says to the C
22:16 angel to you with this testimony for the C

CHURLISH

1Sam 25:3 but the man was C and ill-behaved; he was

CHUSI

Jud 7:18 Acraba, which is near C beside the brook Mochmur.

CHUZA
Lk 8:3 Joanna, the wife of C, Herod's steward, and Susanna,

CILICIA (14)
Jud 1:7 those who lived in C and Damascus and Lebanon
1:12 the whole territory of C and Damascus and Syria,
2:21 mountain which is to the north of Upper C
2:25 seized the territory of C, and killed every one
1Mac 11:14 the king was in C at that time, because
2Mac 4:36 from the region of C, the Jews in the
Acts 6:9 and of those from C and Asia, arose and
15:23 Antioch and Syria and C, greeting.
15:40 through Syria and C, strengthening the churches.
21:39 Jew, from Tarsus in C, a citizen of no
22:3 born at Tarsus in C, but brought up in
23:34 that he was from C
27:5 sea which is off C and Pamphylia, we came
Gal 1:21 I went into the regions of Syria and C

CINNAMON (4)
Ex 30:23 shekels, and of sweet-smelling C half as much, that
Prov 7:17 have perfumed my bed with myrrh, aloes, and C
Song 4:14 and saffron, calamus and C, with all trees of
Rev 18:13 bronze, iron and marble, C, spice, incense, myrrh,

CIRCLE (4)
Job 26:10 He has described a C upon the face of
Prov 8:27 when he drew a C on the face of
Wis 13:2 swift air, or the C of the stars, or
Is 40:22 who sits above the C of the earth, and

CIRCLED (2)
Jud 13:10 through the camp and C around the valley and
1Mac 13:20 destroy it, and he C around by the way

CIRCLES
Josh 15:10 Kiriath-jearim); and the boundary C west of Baalah

CIRCUIT (6)
1Sam 7:16 he went on a C year by year to
1Chr 11:8 the Millo in complete C; and Joab repaired the
Neh 12:28 gathered together from the C round Jerusalem and
from
Ps 19:6 the heavens, and its C to the end of
Sir 24:5 I have made the C of the vault of
Acts 28:13 there we made a C and arrived at Rhegium;

CIRCUITOUS
2Kgs 3:9 they had made a C march of seven days,

CIRCUITS
Eccl 1:6 wind, and on its C the wind returns.

CIRCUMCISE (8)
Deut 10:16 C therefore the foreskin of your heart, and be
30:6 LORD your God will C your heart and the
Josh 5:2 "Make flint knives and C the people of Israel
Jer 4:4 C yourselves to the LORD, remove the foreskin of
Lk 1:59 day they came to C the child; and they
Jn 7:22 the fathers), and you C a man upon the
Acts 15:5 "It is necessary to C them, and to charge
21:21 telling them not to C their children or observe

CIRCUMCISED (55)
Gen 17:10 after you: Every male among you shall be C
17:11 You shall be C in the flesh of your
17:12 among you shall be C; every male throughout your
17:13 that is bought with your money, shall be C
17:14 male who is not C in the flesh of
17:23 Abraham's house, and he C the flesh of their
17:24 old when he was C in the flesh of
17:25 old when he was C in the flesh of
17:26 his son Ishmael were C;
17:27 from a foreigner, were C with him.
21:4 And Abraham C his son Isaac when he was
34:15 we are and every male of you be C
34:17 to us and be C, then we will take
34:22 male among us be C as they are circumcised.
34:22 male among us be circumcised as they are C
34:24 and every male was C, all who went out
Ex 12:44 it after you have C him.
12:48 all his males be C, then he may come
Lev 12:3 day the flesh of his foreskin shall be C
Josh 5:3 made flint knives, and C the people of Israel
5:4 the reason why Joshua C them: all the males
5:5 came out had been C, yet all the people
5:5 had come out of Egypt had not been C
5:7 stead, that Joshua C; for they were uncircumcised,
5:7 they had not been C on the way.
Jud 14:10 in God, and was C, and joined the house
Jer 9:25 all those who are C but yet uncircumcised--
1Mac 1:60 who had their children C,
1:61 families and those who C them; and they hung
2:46 the altars; they forcibly C all the uncircumcised boys
2Mac 6:10 brought in for having C their children.
Lk 2:21 days, when he was C, he was called Jesus,
Acts 7:8 father of Isaac, and C him on the eighth
10:45 believers from among the C who came with Peter
15:1 brethren, "Unless you are C according to the custom
16:3 he took him and C him because of the
Rom 3:30 he will justify the C on the ground of
4:9 pronounced only upon the C, or also upon the
4:10 Was it before or after he had been C
4:10 It was not after, but before he was C
4:11 who believe without being C and who thus have
4:12 the father of the C who are not merely
4:12 who are not merely C but also follow the
4:12 which our father Abraham had before he was C
15:8 a servant to the C to show God's truthfulness,
1Cor 7:18 one at the time of his call already C
Gal 2:3 not compelled to be C, though he was a
2:7 the gospel to the C
2:8 the mission to the C worked through me also
2:9 and they to the C;
6:12 compel you to be C, and only in order
6:13 desire to have you C that they may glory
Phil 3:5 flesh, I have more: C on the eighth day,
Col 2:11 him also you were C with a circumcision made
3:11 be Greek and Jew, C and uncircumcised, barbarian,

CIRCUMCISING
Josh 5:8 When the C of all the nation was done,

CIRCUMCISION (30)
Ex 4:26 because of the C
1Mac 1:15 removed the marks of C, and abandoned the holy
Jn 7:22 Moses gave you C (not that it is from
7:23 sabbath a man receives C, so that the law
Acts 7:8 place.' And he gave him the covenant of C
11:2 up to Jerusalem, the C party criticized him,
Rom 2:25 C indeed is of value if you obey the
2:25 break the law, your C becomes uncircumcision.
2:26 law, will not his uncircumcision be regarded as C
2:27 the written code and C but break the law.
2:28 outwardly, nor is true C something external and
2:29 one inwardly, and real C is a matter of
3:1 Or what is the value of C
4:11 He received C as a sign or seal of
1Cor 7:18 him not seek to remove the marks of C
7:18 Let him not seek C
7:19 For neither C counts for anything nor uncircumcision,
Gal 2:12 separated himself, fearing the C party.
5:2 that if you receive C, Christ will be of
5:3 every man who receives C that he is bound
5:6 in Christ Jesus neither C nor uncircumcision is of
5:11 I, brethren, still preach C, why am I still
6:13 even those who receive C do not themselves keep
6:15 For neither C counts for anything, nor
Eph 2:11 what is called the C, which is made in
Phil 3:3 we are the true C, who worship God in
Col 2:11 were circumcised with a C made without hands, by
2:11 of flesh in the C of Christ;
4:11 only men of the C among my fellow workers
Tit 1:9 and deceivers, especially the C party;

CIRCUMFERENCE (6)
1Kgs 7:15 twelve cubits measured its C; it was hollow, and
7:23 and a line of thirty cubits measured its C
4:2 and a line of thirty cubits measured its C
Sir 50:3 quarried out, a reservoir like the sea in C
Jer 52:21 was eighteen cubits, its C was twelve cubits, and
Ezek 48:35 The C of the city shall be eighteen thousand

CIRCUMSTANCES (5)
1Chr 29:30 might and of the C that came upon him
Sir 20:10 men who have raised their heads from humble C
29:8 a man in humble C, and do not make
Phil 4:12 in any and all C I have learned the
1Thes 5:18 give thanks in all C; for this is the

CISTERN (20)
Lev 11:36 a spring or a C holding water shall be

2Sam 3:26 him back from the C of Sirah; but David
2Kgs 18:31 water of his own C;
Prov 5:15 water from your own C, flowing water from your
Eccl 12:6 wheel broken at the C,
Sir 50:3 In his days a C for water was quarried
Is 30:14 or to dip up water out of the C
36:16 water of his own C;
Jer 38:6 cast him into the C of Malchiah, the king's
38:6 no water in the C, but only mire, and
38:7 put Jeremiah into the C --the king was sitting
38:9 casting him into the C; and he will die
38:10 prophet out of the C before he dies."
38:11 to Jeremiah in the C by ropes.
38:13 with ropes and lifted him out of the C
41:7 him slew them, and cast them into a C
41:9 Now the C into which Ishmael cast all the
41:9 slain was the large C which King Asa had
2Mac 1:19 hollow of a dry C, where they took such
10:37 was hidden in a C, and his brother Chaereas,

CISTERNS (9)

Deut 6:11 did not fill, and C hewn out, which you
1Sam 13:6 in tombs and in C,
26:10 and hewed out many C, for he had large
Neh 9:25 of all good things, C hewn out, vineyards, olive
Jud 7:21 Bethulia were empty; their C were going dry, and
8:31 rain to fill our C and we will no
Jer 2:13 waters, and hewed out C for themselves, broken
2:13 cisterns for themselves, broken C, that can hold no
14:3 they come to the C, they find no water,

CITADEL (33)

1Kgs 16:18 he went into the C of the king's house,
2Kgs 15:25 in Samaria, in the C of the king's house;
1Mac 1:33 wall and strong towers, and it became their C
3:45 of aliens held the C; it was a lodging
4:2 Men from the C were his guides.
4:41 against those in the C until he had cleansed
6:18 the men in the C kept hemming Israel in
6:20 together and besieged the C in the one hundred
6:24 our people besieged the C and became hostile to
6:26 have encamped against the C in Jerusalem to take
6:32 away from the C and encamped at Beth-zechariah,
9:52 and Gazara, and the C, and in them he
9:53 under guard in the C at Jerusalem.
10:6 the hostages in the C should be released to
10:7 the people and of the men in the C
10:9 the men in the C released the hostages to
10:32 my control of the C in Jerusalem and give
11:20 Judea to attack the C in Jerusalem, and he
11:21 reported to him that Jonathan was besieging the C
11:41 the troops of the C from Jerusalem, and the
12:36 high barrier between the C and the city to
13:21 the men in the C kept sending envoys to
13:49 The men in the C at Jerusalem were prevented
13:50 there and cleansed the C from its pollutions.
13:52 temple hill alongside the C, and he and his
14:7 and Bethzur and the C, and he removed its
14:36 had built themselves a C from which they used
15:28 and Gazara and the C in Jerusalem; they are
2Mac 4:12 gymnasium right under the C, and he induced the
4:28 the captain of the C kept requesting payment, for
5:5 was being taken, Menelaus took refuge in the C
15:31 he sent for those who were in the C
15:35 Nicanor's head from the C, a clear and conspicuous

CITADELS (2)

Ps 48:3 Within her C God has shown himself a sure
48:13 ramparts, go through her C; that you may tell

CITIES (465)

Gen 13:12 Lot dwelt among the C of the valley and
19:25 and he overthrew those C, and all the valley,
19:25 the inhabitants of the C, and what grew on
19:29 when God destroyed the C of the valley, God
19:29 when he overthrew the C in which Lot dwelt.
35:5 God fell upon the C that were round about
41:35 for food in the C, and let them keep
41:48 up food in the C; he stored up in
Lev 25:32 Nevertheless the C of the Levites, the houses in
25:32 the houses in the C of their possession, the
25:33 the houses in the C of the Levites are
25:34 land belonging to their C may not be sold;
26:25 you gather within your C I will send pestilence
26:31 I will lay your C waste, and will make
26:33 a desolation, and your C shall be a waste.
Num 13:19 bad, and whether the C that they dwell in
13:28 are strong, and the C are fortified and very
21:2 my hand, then I will utterly destroy their C
21:3 destroyed them and their C; so the name of
21:25 Israel took all these C, and Israel settled in
21:25 settled in all the C of the Amorites, in
24:19 and the survivors of C be destroyed!"
31:10 All their C in the places where they dwelt,
32:16 for our flocks, and C for our little ones,
32:17 live in the fortified C because of the inhabitants
32:24 Build C for your little ones, and folds for
32:26 remain there in the C of Gilead;
32:33 the land and its C with their territories, the
32:33 with their territories, the C of the land throughout
32:36 Beth-nimrah and Beth-haran, fortified C, and folds
32:38 other names to the C which they built.
35:2 inheritance of their possession, C to dwell in; and
35:2 to the Levites pasture lands round about the C
35:3 The C shall be theirs to dwell in, and
35:4 pasture lands of the C, which you shall give
35:5 belong to them as pasture land for their C
35:6 The C which you give to the Levites shall
35:6 shall be the six C of refuge, where you
35:6 in addition to them you shall give forty-two C
35:7 All the C which you give to the Levites
35:8 And as for the C which you shall give
35:8 shall give of its C to the Levites."
35:11 then you shall select C to be cities of
35:11 select cities to be C of refuge for you,
35:12 The C shall be for you a refuge from
35:13 And the C which you give shall be your
35:13 shall be your six C of refuge.
35:14 You shall give three C beyond the Jordan, and
35:14 the Jordan, and three C in the land of
35:14 of Canaan, to be C of refuge.
35:15 These six C shall be for refuge for the
Deut 1:22 go up and the C into which we shall
1:28 taller than we; the C are great and fortified
2:34 we captured all his C at that time and
2:35 the booty of the C which we captured.
2:37 river Jabbok and the C of the hill country,
3:4 we took all his C at that time--there
3:4 take from them--sixty C, the whole region of
3:5 All these were C fortified with high walls, gates,
3:7 the spoil of the C we took as our
3:10 it Senir), all the C of the tableland and
3:10 as Salecah and Edre-i, C of the kingdom of
3:12 of Gilead with its C;
3:19 shall remain in the C which I have given
4:41 Moses set apart three C in the east beyond
4:42 to one of these C he might save his
6:10 with great and goodly C, which you did not
9:1 mightier than yourselves, C great and fortified up
13:12 in one of your C, which the LORD your
19:1 and dwell in their C and in their houses,
19:2 shall set apart three C for you in the
19:5 to one of these C and save his life;
19:7 I command you, You shall set apart three C
19:9 shall add three other C to these three,
19:11 into one of these C,
20:15 do to all the C which are very far
20:15 you, which are not C of the nations here.
20:16 But in the C of these peoples that the
21:2 the distance to the C which are around him
Josh 9:17 out and reached their C on the third day.
9:17 Now their C were Gibeon, Chephirah, Be-eroth
10:2 one of the royal C, and because it was
10:19 let them enter their C; for the LORD your
10:20 entered into the fortified C,
11:12 And all the C of those kings, and all
11:13 But none of the C that stood on mounds
11:14 the spoil of these C and the cattle, the
11:21 of Israel; Joshua utterly destroyed them with their C
13:10 Dibon; and all the C of Sihon king of
13:17 Heshbon, and all its C that are in the
13:21 that is, all the C of the tableland, and
13:23 their families with their C and villages.
13:25 Jazer, and all the C of Gilead, and half
13:28 their families, with their C and villages.
13:30 are in Bashan, sixty C,
13:31 Ashtaroth, and Edre-i, the C of the kingdom of
14:4 the land, but only C to dwell in, with
14:12 there, with great fortified C: it may be that
15:9 from there to the C of Mount Ephron; then
15:21 The C belonging to the tribe of the people
15:32 Rimmon: in all, twenty-nine C, with their villages.

C

15:36 Gederothaim: fourteen C with their villages.
15:41 and Makkedah: sixteen C with their villages.
15:44 Achzib, and Mareshah: nine C with their villages.
15:51 Holon, and Giloh: eleven C with their villages.
15:54 Hebron), and Zior: nine C with their villages.
15:57 Gibe-ah, and Timnah: ten C with their villages.
15:59 Beth-anoth, and Eltekon: six C with their villages.
15:60 Kiriath-jearim), and Rabbah: two C with their.
15:62 Salt, and Engedi: six C with their villages.
17:9 The C here, to the south of the brook,
17:9 the brook, among the C of Manasseh, belong to
17:12 take possession of those C; but the Canaanites
18:21 Now the C of the tribe of Benjamin according
18:24 Chephar-ammoni, Ophni, Geba--twelve C with their
18:28 Gibe-ah and Kiriath-jearim--fourteen C with their
19:6 and Sharuhen-- thirteen C with their villages;
19:7 Ether, and Ashan--four C with their villages;
19:8 villages round about these C as far as Baalath-beer,
19:15 Idalah, and Bethlehem--twelve C with their villages.
19:16 to its families--these C with their villages.
19:22 at the Jordan--sixteen C with their villages.
19:23 to its families--the C with their villages.
19:30 Aphek and Rehob--twenty-two C with their villages.
19:31 to its families--these C with their villages.
19:35 The fortified C are Ziddim, Zer, Hammath, Rakkath
19:38 and Beth-shemesh-- nineteen C with their villages.
19:39 to its families--the C with their villages.
19:48 to their families--these C with their villages.
20:2 of Israel, 'Appoint the C of refuge, of which
20:4 to one of these C and shall stand at
20:9 These were the C designated for all the people
21:2 that we be given C to dwell in, along
21:3 the Levites the following C and pasture lands out
21:4 tribes of Judah, Simeon, and Benjamin, thirteen C
21:5 of Dan and the half-tribe of Manasseh, ten C
21:6 the half-tribe of Manasseh in Bashan, thirteen C
21:7 of Gad, and the tribe of Zebulun, twelve C
21:8 These C and their pasture lands the people of
21:9 they gave the following C mentioned by name,
21:16 its pasture lands--nine C out of these two
21:18 lands, and Almon with its pasture lands--four C
21:19 The C of the descendants of Aaron, the priests,
21:19 were in all thirteen C with their pasture lands.
21:20 of the Levites, the C allotted to them were
21:22 its pasture lands--four C;
21:24 its pasture lands--four C;
21:25 and Gath-rimmon with its pasture lands--two C
21:26 The C of the families of the rest of
21:27 its pasture lands--two C;
21:29 its pasture lands--four C;
21:31 its pasture lands--four C;
21:32 lands, and Kartan with its pasture lands--three C
21:33 The C of the several families of the Gershonites
21:33 were in all thirteen C with their pasture lands.
21:35 its pasture lands--four C;
21:37 its pasture lands--four C;
21:39 its pasture lands--four C in all.
21:40 As for the C of the several Merarite families,
21:40 those allotted to them were in all twelve C
21:41 The C of the Levites in the midst of
21:41 were in all forty-eight C with their pasture lands.
21:42 These C had each its pasture lands round about
21:42 about it; so it was with all these C
24:13 had not labored, and C which you had not
Judg 10:4 and they had thirty C, called Havvoth-jair to this
11:26 and in all the C that are on the
11:33 neighborhood of Minnith, twenty C, and as far as
20:14 together out of the C to Gibe-ah, to go
20:15 mustered out of their C on that day twenty-six
20:42 came out of the C destroyed them in the
1Sam 6:18 number of all the C of the Philistines belonging
6:18 five lords, both fortified C and unwalled villages.
7:14 The C which the Philistines had taken from Israel
18:6 out of all the C of Israel, singing and
30:29 in Racal, in the C of the Jerahmeelites, in
30:29 the Jerahmeelites, in the C of the Kenites,
31:7 dead, they forsook their C and fled; and the
2Sam 2:1 into any of the C of Judah?" And the
8:8 and from Berothai, C of Hadadezer, King David
10:12 people, and for the C of our God; and
12:31 did to all the C of the Ammonites.
20:6 he get himself fortified C, and cause us trouble.
24:7 and to all the C of the Hivites and
1Kgs 4:13 in Bashan, sixty great C with walls and bronze
8:37 in any of their C; whatever plague, whatever sickness
9:11 gave to Hiram twenty C in the land of
9:12 Tyre to see the C which Solomon had given
9:13 said, "What kind of C are these which you
9:19 Solomon had, and the C for his chariots, and
9:19 his chariots, and the C for his horsemen, and
10:26 stationed in the chariot C and with the king
12:17 who dwelt in the C of Judah.
13:32 which are in the C of Samaria, shall surely
15:20 his armies against the C of Israel, and conquered
15:23 he did, and the C which he built, are
20:34 said to him, "The C which my father took
22:39 built, and all the C that he built, are
2Kgs 3:25 And they overthrew the C, and on every good
10:2 chariots and horses, fortified C also, and weapons,
13:25 son of Hazael the C which he had taken
13:25 him and recovered the C of Israel.
17:6 Gozan, and in the C of the Medes.
17:24 placed them in the C of Samaria instead of
17:24 took possession of Samaria, and dwelt in its C
17:26 and placed in the C of Samaria do not
17:29 every nation in the C in which they dwelt;
18:11 Gozan, and in the C of the Medes,
18:13 against all the fortified C of Judah and took
19:25 you should turn fortified C into heaps of ruins,
23:5 high places at the C of Judah and round
23:8 priests out of the C of Judah, and defiled
23:19 that were in the C of Samaria, which kings
1Chr 2:22 Jair, who had twenty-three C in the land of
4:31 These were their C until David reigned.
4:32 Tochen, and Ashan, five C,
4:33 were round about these C as far as Baal.
6:57 Aaron they gave the C of refuge: Hebron, Libnah
6:60 All their C throughout their families were thirteen.
6:61 of the half-tribe, the half of Manasseh, ten C
6:62 families were allotted thirteen C out of the tribes
6:63 families were allotted twelve C out of the tribes
6:64 gave the Levites the C with their pasture lands.
6:65 Simeon, and Benjamin these C which are mentioned
6:66 sons of Kohath had C of their territory out
6:67 They were given the C of refuge: Shechem with
9:2 their possessions in their C were Israel, the priests,
10:7 dead, they forsook their C and fled; and the
13:2 and Levites in the C that have pasture lands,
18:8 Tibhath and from Cun, C of Hadadezer, David took
19:7 were mustered from their C and came to battle.
19:13 people, and for the C of our God; and
20:3 did to all the C of the Ammonites.
27:25 the country, in the C, in the villages and
1:14 stationed in the chariot C and with the king
6:28 in any of their C; whatever plague, whatever sickness
8:2 house, Solomon rebuilt the C which Huram had
8:5 and Lower Beth-horon, fortified C with walls, gates,
8:6 had, and all the C for his chariots, and
8:6 his chariots, and the C for his horsemen, and
9:25 stationed in the chariot C and with the king
10:17 who dwelt in the C of Judah.
11:5 Jerusalem, and he built C for defense in Judah.
11:10 Aijalon, and Hebron, fortified C which are in Judah
11:12 spears in all the C, and made them very
11:23 in all the fortified C; and he gave them
12:4 he took the fortified C of Judah and came
13:19 pursued Jeroboam, and took C from him, Bethel with
14:5 out of all the C of Judah the high
14:6 He built fortified C in Judah, for the land
14:7 "Let us build these C, and surround them with
14:14 they smote all the C round about Gerar, for
14:14 They plundered all the C, for there was much
15:8 Benjamin and from the C which he had taken
16:4 his armies against the C of Israel, and they
17:2 in all the fortified C of Judah, and set
17:2 Judah, and in the C of Ephraim which Asa
17:7 to teach in the C of Judah;
17:9 about through all the C of Judah and taught
17:13 great stores in the C of Judah.
17:19 placed in the fortified C throughout all Judah.
19:5 in all the fortified C of Judah, city by
19:10 who live in their C, concerning bloodshed, law or
20:4 LORD; from all the C of Judah they came
21:3 possessions, together with fortified C in Judah; but
23:2 Levites from all the C of Judah, and the
24:5 "Go out to the C of Judah, and gather
25:13 battle, fell upon the C of Judah, from Samaria
26:6 Ashdod; and he built C in the territory of
27:4 Moreover he built C in the hill country of
28:18 made raids on the C in the Shephelah and
31:1 went out to the C of Judah and broke
31:1 Israel returned to their C, every man to his

31:6 who lived in the C of Judah also brought
31:15 assisting him in the C of the priests, to
31:19 land belonging to their C, there were men in
31:19 men in the several C who were designated by
32:1 encamped against the fortified C, thinking to win
32:29 He likewise provided C for himself, and flocks and
33:14 in all the fortified C in Judah.
34:6 And in the C of Manasseh, Ephraim, and Simeon,
Ezra 4:10 and settled in the C of Samaria and in
10:14 let all in our C who have taken foreign
Neh 9:25 And they captured fortified C and a rich land,
Jud 1:14 took possession of his C, and came to Ecbatana,
2:24 destroyed all the hilltop C along the brook Abron,
2:27 herds and sacked their C and ravaged their lands
3:4 Our C also and their inhabitants are your slaves;
3:6 garrisons in the hilltop C and took picked men
4:12 as booty, and the C they had inherited to
5:3 What C do they inhabit?
5:18 the ground, and their C were captured by their
6:7 in one of the C beside the passes,
Esth 9:2 Jews gathered in their C throughout all the provinces
Job 15:28 has lived in desolate C, in houses which no
Ps 9:6 in everlasting ruins; their C thou hast rooted out;
69:35 Zion and rebuild the C of Judah; and his
72:16 blossom forth from the C like the grass of
Wis 10:6 escaped the fire that descended on the Five C
Sir 28:14 nation, and destroyed strong C, and overturned the
46:2 hands and stretched out his sword against the C
Is 1:7 country lies desolate, your C are burned with fire;
6:11 And he said: "Until C lie waste without inhabitant,
14:17 desert and overthrew its C, who did not let
14:21 and fill the face of the world with C
17:2 Her C will be deserted for ever; they will
17:9 that day their strong C will be like the
19:18 there will be five C in the land of
25:3 peoples will glorify thee; C of ruthless nations will
36:1 against all the fortified C of Judah and took
37:26 you should make fortified C crash into heaps of
40:9 not; say to the C of Judah, "Behold your
42:11 the desert and its C lift up their voice,
44:26 inhabited,' and of the C of Judah, 'They shall
54:3 possess the nations and will people the desolate C
61:4 shall repair the ruined C, the devastations of many
64:10 Thy holy C have become a wilderness, Zion has
Jer 1:15 and against all the C of Judah.
2:15 land a waste; his C are in ruins, without
2:28 as many as your C are your gods, O
4:5 go into the fortified C
4:7 land a waste; your C will be ruins without
4:16 they shout against the C of Judah.
4:26 desert, and all its C were laid in ruins
4:29 among rocks; all the C are forsaken, and no
5:6 is watching against their C, every one who goes
5:17 fig trees; your fortified C in which you trust
7:17 are doing in the C of Judah and in
7:34 to cease from the C of Judah and from
8:14 go into the fortified C and perish there; for
9:11 I will make the C of Judah a desolation,
10:22 country to make the C of Judah a desolation,
11:6 these words in the C of Judah, and in
11:12 Then the C of Judah and the inhabitants of
11:13 as many as your C, O Judah; and as
13:19 The C of the Negeb are shut up, with
17:26 shall come from the C of Judah and the
20:16 man be like the C which the LORD overthrew
25:18 it: Jerusalem and the C of Judah, its kings
26:2 speak to all the C of Judah which come
31:21 Return, O virgin Israel, return to these your C
31:23 Judah and in its C, when I restore their
31:24 Judah and all its C shall dwell there together,
32:44 Jerusalem, and in the C of Judah, in the
32:44 of Judah, in the C of the hill country,
32:44 hill country, in the C of the Shephelah, and
32:44 Shephelah, and in the C of the Negeb; for
33:10 or beast,' in the C of Judah and the
33:12 in all of its C, there shall again be
33:13 In the C of the hill country, in the
33:13 hill country, in the C of the Shephelah, and
33:13 Shephelah, and in the C of the Negeb, in
33:13 Jerusalem, and in the C of Judah, flocks shall
34:1 and all of its C:
34:7 and against all the C of Judah that were
34:7 were the only fortified C of Judah that remained.
34:22 I will make the C of Judah a desolation
36:6 men of Judah who come out of their C
36:9 who came from the C of Judah to Jerusalem
40:5 appointed governor of the C of Judah, and dwell
40:10 and dwell in your C that you have taken."
44:2 and upon all the C of Judah.
44:6 and kindled in the C of Judah and in
44:17 our princes, in the C of Judah and in
44:21 you burned in the C of Judah and in
46:8 earth, I will destroy C and their inhabitants.
48:9 would fly away; her C shall become a desolation,
48:15 of Moab and his C has come up, and
48:24 Bozrah, and all the C of the land of
48:28 "Leave the C, and dwell in the rock, O
48:41 wings against Moab; the C shall be taken and
49:1 dispossessed Gad, and his people settled in its C
49:13 curse; and all her C shall be perpetual wastes."
49:18 Gomorrah and their neighbor C were overthrown
50:32 a fire in his C, and it will devour
50:40 Gomorrah and their neighbor C, says the LORD, so
51:43 Her C have become a horror, a land of
Lam 1:1 a princess among the C has become a vassal.
Bar 2:23 to cease from the C of Judah and from
4:32 Wretched will be the C which your children served
Ezek 6:6 Wherever you dwell your C shall be waste and
12:20 And the inhabited C shall be laid waste, and
19:7 and laid waste their C; and the land was
25:5 for camels and the C of the Ammonites a
25:9 of Moab from the C on its frontier, the
26:19 laid waste, like the C that are not inhabited,
29:12 desolated countries; and her C shall be a desolation
29:12 desolation forty years among C that are laid waste.
30:7 desolated countries and her C shall be in the
30:7 in the midst of C that are laid waste.
35:4 I will lay your C waste, and you shall
35:9 desolation, and your C shall not be inhabited.
36:4 wastes and the deserted C, which have become a
36:10 all of it; the C shall be inhabited and
36:33 I will cause the C to be inhabited, and
36:35 and desolate and ruined C are now inhabited and
36:38 so shall the waste C be filled with flocks
39:9 who dwell in the C of Israel will go
45:5 as their possession for C to live in.
Hos 8:14 Judah has multiplied fortified C; but I will send
8:14 a fire upon his C, and it shall devour
11:6 shall rage against their C, consume the bars of
Amos 4:6 teeth in all your C, and lack of bread
4:8 so two or three C wandered to one city
9:14 shall rebuild the ruined C and inhabit them; they
Obad 1:20 Sepharad shall possess the C of the Negeb.
Mic 5:11 will cut off the C of your land and
5:14 your Asherim from among you and destroy your C
Hab 2:8 to the earth, to C and all who dwell
2:17 to the earth, to C and all who dwell
Zeph 1:16 cry against the fortified C and against the lofty
3:6 walks in them; their C have been made desolate,
Zech 1:12 on Jerusalem and the C of Judah, against which
1:17 LORD of hosts: My C shall again overflow with
7:7 in prosperity, with her C round about her, and
8:20 the inhabitants of many C;
9:1 the LORD belong the C of Aram, even as
1Mac 1:19 they captured the fortified C in the land of
1:29 king sent to the C of Judah a chief
1:44 to Jerusalem and the C of Judah; he directed
1:51 people and commanded the C of Judah to offer
1:54 altars in the surrounding C of Judah,
1:58 against those found month after month in the C
3:8 He went through the C of Judah; he destroyed
5:26 —all these C were strong and large—
5:27 up in the other C of Gilead; the enemy
5:36 Bosor, and the other C of Gilead.
5:68 fire; he plundered the C and returned to the
9:50 Jerusalem and built strong C in Judea: the fortress
10:71 I have with me the power of the C
11:2 the people of the C opened their gates to
11:3 when Ptolemy entered the C he stationed forces as
11:8 control of the coastal C as far as Seleucia
11:60 river and among the C, and all the army
14:10 He supplied the C with food, and furnished them
14:17 the country and the C in it
14:33 He fortified the C of Judea, and Bethzur on
14:34 and provided in those C whatever was necessary for
15:4 who have devastated many C in my kingdom,
15:19 against them and their C and their country, or
15:28 in Jerusalem; they are C of my kingdom.
15:30 then, hand over the C which you have seized
15:31 tribute money of the C, five hundred talents more.
16:14 Simon was visiting the C of the country and
16:18 over to him the C and the country.

2Mac 3:8 of inspection of the C of Coelesyria and Phoenicia,
4:30 Mallus revolted because their C had been given as
4:32 he had sold to Tyre and the neighboring C
6:8 to the neighboring Greek C, that they should adopt
8:11 immediately sent to the C on the seacoast, inviting
Mt 9:35 went about all the C and villages, teaching in
11:1 from there to teach and preach in their C
11:20 began to upbraid the C where most of his
Mk 6:56 he came, in villages, C, or country, they laid
Lk 4:43 God to the other C also; for I was
5:12 in one of the C, there came a man
8:1 he went on through C and villages, preaching and
19:17 have authority over ten C
19:19 to be over five C
Acts 14:6 to Lystra and Derbe, C of Lycaonia, and to
16:4 their way through the C, they delivered to them
26:11 against them, I persecuted them even to foreign C
2Pet 2:6 if by turning the C of Sodom and Gomorrah
Jude 1:7 the surrounding C, which likewise acted immorally
Rev 16:19 three parts, and the C of the nations fell,

CITIZEN (7)
Acts 21:39 Tarsus in Cilicia, a C of no mean city;
22:25 who is a Roman C, and uncondemned?"
22:26 For this man is a Roman C
22:27 to him, "Tell me, are you a Roman C
22:28 Paul said, "But I was born a C
22:29 Paul was a Roman C and that he had
23:27 him, having learned that he was a Roman C

CITIZENS (23)
Judg 9:2 ears of all the C of Shechem, 'Which is
9:6 And all the C of Shechem came together, and
9:18 maidservant, king over the C of Shechem, because
9:20 Abimelech, and devour the C of Shechem, and
9:20 come out from the C of Shechem, and from
2Mac 4:5 not accusing his fellow C but having in view
4:9 men of Jerusalem as C of Antioch.
4:19 chosen as being Antiochian C from Jerusalem, to
4:50 having become the chief plotter against his fellow C
5:6 slaughtering his fellow C, not realizing that success
5:8 country and his fellow C, he was cast ashore
5:23 it over his fellow C worse than the others
5:23 malice toward the Jewish C,
9:15 of them, equal to C of Athens;
9:19 "To his worthy Jewish C, Antiochus their king and
14:8 because I have regard also for my fellow C
14:37 who loved his fellow C and was very well
15:30 defender of his fellow C, the man who maintained
Lk 15:15 to one of the C of that country, who
19:14 I come.' But his C hated him and sent
Acts 16:37 men who are Roman C, and have thrown us
16:38 that they were Roman C;
Eph 2:19 but you are fellow C with the saints and

CITIZENSHIP
Acts 22:28 answered, "I bought this C for a large sum."

CITY (982)
Gen 4:17 and he built a C, and called the name
4:17 the name of the C after the name of
10:12 between Nineveh and Calah; that is the great C
11:4 us build ourselves a C, and a tower with
11:5 down to see the C and the tower, which
11:8 the earth, and they left off building the C
18:24 fifty righteous within the C; wilt thou then destroy
18:26 fifty righteous in the C, I will spare the
18:28 thou destroy the whole C for lack of five?"
19:4 the men of the C, the men of Sodom,
19:12 you have in the C, bring them out of
19:14 for the LORD is about to destroy the C
19:15 you be consumed in the punishment of the C
19:16 brought him forth and set him outside the C
19:20 Behold, yonder C is near enough to flee to,
19:21 will not overthrow the C of which you have
19:22 the name of the C was called Zoar.
23:10 the gate of his C,
23:18 who went in at the gate of his C
24:10 to Mesopotamia, to the C of Nahor.
24:11 kneel down outside the C by the well of
24:13 the men of the C are coming out to
26:33 the name of the C is Beer-sheba to this
28:19 the name of the C was Luz at the
33:18 came safely to the C of Shechem, which is
33:18 from Paddan-aram; and he camped before the C
34:20 the gate of their C and spoke to the
34:20 the men of their C, saying,
34:24 the gate of his C hearkened to Hamor and
34:24 who went out of the gate of his C
34:25 and came upon the C unawares, and killed all
34:27 slain, and plundered the C, because their sister had
34:28 whatever was in the C and in the field;
36:32 the name of his C being Dinhabah.
36:35 the name of his C being Avith.
36:39 the name of his C being Pau; his wife's
41:48 stored up in every C the food from the
44:4 short distance from the C, Joseph said to his
44:13 loaded his ass, and they returned to the C
Ex 9:29 gone out of the C, I will stretch out
9:33 went out of the C from Pharaoh, and stretched
Lev 14:40 unclean place outside the C;
14:41 unclean place outside the C;
14:45 forth out of the C to an unclean place.
14:53 go out of the C into the open field;
25:29 house in a walled C, he may redeem it
25:30 is in the walled C shall be made sure
25:33 was sold in a C of their possession shall
Num 20:16 are in Kadesh, a C on the edge of
21:26 For Heshbon was the C of Sihon the king
21:27 be built, let the C of Sihon be established.
21:28 Heshbon, flame from the C of Sihon.
22:36 meet him at the C of Moab, on the
35:4 the wall of the C outward a thousand cubits
35:5 shall measure, outside the C, for the east side
35:5 two thousand cubits, the C being in the middle;
35:25 restore him to his C of refuge, to which
35:26 the bounds of his C of refuge to which
35:27 the bounds of his C of refuge, and the
35:28 must remain in his C of refuge until the
35:32 has fled to his C of refuge, that he
Deut 2:34 utterly destroyed every C, men, women, and children;
2:36 Arnon, and from the C that is in the
2:36 there was not a C too high for us;
3:4 there was not a C which we did not
3:6 destroying every C, men, women, and children.
13:13 the inhabitants of the C, saying, 'Let us go
13:15 the inhabitants of that C to the sword, destroying
13:16 square, and burn the C and all its spoil
19:12 the elders of his C shall send and fetch
20:10 draw near to a C to fight against it,
20:14 everything else in the C, all its spoil, you
20:19 "When you besiege a C for a long time,
20:20 build siegeworks against the C that makes war with
21:3 the elders of the C which is nearest to
21:4 the elders of that C shall bring the heifer
21:6 the elders of that C nearest to the slain
21:19 the elders of his C at the gate of
21:20 the elders of his C, 'This our son is
21:21 the men of the C shall stone him to
22:15 the elders of the C in the gate;
22:17 spread the garment before the elders of the C
22:18 the elders of that C shall take the man
22:21 the men of her C shall stone her to
22:23 meets her in the C and lies with her,
22:24 the gate of that C, and you shall stone
22:24 she was in the C, and the man because
25:8 the elders of his C shall call him, and
28:3 you be in the C, and blessed shall you
28:16 you be in the C, and cursed shall you
34:3 valley of Jericho the C of palm trees, as
Josh 2:15 was built into the C wall, so that she
3:16 far-off, at Adam, the C that is beside Zarethan,
6:3 shall march around the C, all the men of
6:3 war going around the C once.
6:4 shall march around the C seven times, the priests
6:5 the wall of the C will fall down flat,
6:7 forward; march around the C, and let the armed
6:11 LORD to compass the C, going about it once;
6:14 they marched around the C once, and returned into
6:15 and marched around the C in the same manner
6:15 they marched around the C seven times.
6:16 "Shout; for the LORD has given you the C
6:17 And the C and all that is within it
6:20 went up into the C, every man straight before
6:20 man straight before him, and they took the C
6:21 destroyed all in the C, both men and women,
6:24 And they burned the C with fire, and all
6:26 up and rebuilds this C, Jericho.
8:1 and his people, his C, and his land;
8:2 an ambush against the C, behind it."
8:4 in ambush against the C, behind it; do not
8:4 very far from the C, but hold yourselves all

8:5 people who are with me, will approach the C
8:6 them away from the C; for they will say,
8:7 ambush, and seize the C; for the LORD your
8:8 you have taken the C, you shall set the
8:8 you shall set the C on fire, doing as
8:11 drew near before the C, and encamped on the
8:12 Bethel and Ai, to the west of the C
8:13 was north of the C and its rear guard
8:13 city and its rear guard west of the C
8:14 the men of the C, made haste and went
8:14 there was an ambush against him behind the C
8:16 who were in the C were called together to
8:16 pursued Joshua they were drawn away from the C
8:17 Israel; they left the C open, and pursued Israel.
8:18 javelin that was in his hand toward the C
8:19 ran and entered the C and took it; and
8:19 haste to set the C on fire.
8:20 the smoke of the C went up to heaven;
8:21 ambush had taken the C, and that the smoke
8:21 the smoke of the C went up, then they
8:22 came forth from the C against them; so they
8:27 the spoil of that C Israel took as their
8:29 the gate of the C, and raised over it
10:2 Gibeon was a great C, like one of the
11:19 There was not a C that made peace with
13:9 the Arnon, and the C that is in the
13:16 the Arnon, and the C that is in the
15:62 Middin, Secacah, Nibshan, the C of Salt, and Engedi:
18:14 (that is, Kiriath-jearim), a C belonging to the tribe
19:29 reaching to the fortified C of Tyre; then the
19:50 they gave him the C which he asked, Timnath-serah
19:50 and he rebuilt the C, and settled in it.
20:4 the gate of the C, and explain his case
20:4 the elders of that C; then they shall take
20:4 take him into the C, and give him a
20:6 shall remain in that C until he has stood
21:12 the fields of the C and its villages had
21:13 they gave Hebron, the C of refuge for the
21:21 were given Shechem, the C of refuge for the
21:27 its pasture lands, the C of refuge for the
21:32 its pasture lands, the C of refuge for the
21:38 its pasture lands, the C of refuge for the
Judg 1:8 sword, and set the C on fire.
1:16 of Judah from the C of palms into the
1:17 the name of the C was called Hormah.
1:23 the name of the C was formerly Luz.)
1:24 coming out of the C, and they said to
1:24 the way into the C, and we will deal
1:25 the way into the C; and they smote the
1:25 and they smote the C with the edge of
1:26 Hittites and built a C, and called its name
3:13 took possession of the C of palms.
8:16 the elders of the C and he took thorns
8:17 of Penuel, and slew the men of the C
8:27 put it in his C, in Ophrah; and all
9:30 the ruler of the C heard the words of
9:31 are stirring up the C against you.
9:33 and rush upon the C; and when he and
9:35 the gate of the C; and Abimelech and the
9:43 coming out of the C, and he rose against
9:44 the gate of the C, while the two companies
9:45 Abimelech fought against the C all that day; he
9:45 day; he took the C, and killed the people
9:45 and he razed the C and sowed it with
9:51 strong tower within the C, and all the people
9:51 the people of the C fled to it, all
12:7 was buried in his C in Gilead.
14:18 the men of the C said to him on
16:2 him all night at the gate of the C
16:3 the gate of the C and the two posts,
18:27 sword, and burned the C with fire.
18:28 And they rebuilt the C, and dwelt in it.
18:29 And they named the C Dan, after the name
18:29 the name of the C was Laish at the
19:11 turn aside to this C of the Jebusites, and
19:12 turn aside into the C of foreigners, who do
19:15 open square of the C; for no man took
19:17 open square of the C; and the old man
19:22 the men of the C, base fellows, beset the
20:11 Israel gathered against the C, united as one man.
20:31 drawn away from the C; and as at other
20:32 them away from the C to the highways."
20:37 and smote all the C with the edge of
20:38 up out of the C
20:40 rise out of the C in a column of
20:40 the whole of the C went up in smoke

Ruth 2:18 and went into the C; she showed her mother-in-law
3:15 it upon her; then she went into the C
4:2 the elders of the C, and said, "Sit down
1Sam 1:3 by year from his C to worship and to
4:13 man came into the C and told the news,
4:13 the news, all the C cried out.
5:9 LORD was against the C, causing a very great
5:9 the men of the C, both young and old,
5:11 there was a deathly panic throughout the whole C
5:12 the cry of the C went up to heaven.
8:22 men of Israel, "Go every man to his C
9:6 of God in this C, and he is a
9:10 they went to the C where the man of
9:11 the hill to the C, they met young maidens
9:12 just now to the C, because the people have
9:13 as you enter the C, you will find him,
9:14 So they went up to the C
9:14 they were entering the C, they saw Samuel coming
9:25 high place into the C, a bed was spread
9:27 the outskirts of the C, Samuel said to Saul,
10:5 you come to the C, you will meet a
15:5 Saul came to the C of Amalek, and lay
16:4 The elders of the C came to meet him
20:6 run to Bethlehem his C; for there is a
20:29 a sacrifice in the C, and my brother has
20:40 to him, "Go and carry them to the C
20:42 rose and departed; and Jonathan went into the C
22:19 And Nob, the C of the priests, he put
23:10 Keilah, to destroy the C on my account.
27:5 dwell in the royal C with you?"
28:3 him and buried him in Ramah, his own C
30:3 men came to the C, they found it burned
2Sam 5:7 Zion, that is, the C of David.
5:9 and called it the C of David.
5:9 And David built the C round about from the
6:10 the LORD into the C of David; but David
6:12 of Obed-edom to the C of David with rejoicing;
6:16 LORD came into the C of David, Michal the
10:3 you to search the C, and to spy it
10:14 they likewise fled before Abishai, and entered the C
11:16 Joab was besieging the C, he assigned Uriah to
11:17 the men of the C came out and fought
11:20 go so near the C to fight?
11:25 your attack upon the C, and overthrow it.' And
12:1 men in a certain C, the one rich and
12:26 Rabbah of the Ammonites, and took the royal C
12:27 I have taken the C of waters.
12:28 and encamp against the C, and take it; lest
12:28 lest I take the C, and it be called
12:30 the spoil of the C, a very great amount.
15:2 and say, "From what C are you?" And when
15:12 David's counselor, from his C Giloh.
15:14 us, and smite the C with the edge of
15:24 the people had all passed out of the C
15:25 "Carry the ark of God back into the C
15:27 go back to the C in peace, you and
15:34 you return to the C, and say to Absalom,
15:37 friend, came into the C, just as Absalom was
17:13 he withdraws into a C, then all Israel will
17:13 bring ropes to that C, and we shall drag
17:17 for they must not be seen entering the C
17:23 ass, and went off home to his own C
18:3 better that you send us help from the C
19:3 people stole into the C that day as people
19:37 die in my own C, near the grave of
20:15 a mound against the C, and it stood against
20:16 woman called from the C, "Hear!
20:19 seek to destroy a C which is a mother
20:21 him alone, and I will withdraw from the C
20:22 they dispersed from the C, every man to his
24:5 Aroer, and from the C that is in the
1Kgs 1:41 this uproar in the C mean?"
1:45 rejoicing, so that the C is in an uproar.
2:10 was buried in the C of David.
3:1 brought her into the C of David, until he
8:1 LORD out of the C of David, which is
8:16 Egypt, I chose no C in all the tribes
8:44 the LORD toward the C which thou hast chosen
8:48 to their fathers, the C which thou hast chosen,
9:16 who dwelt in the C, and had given it
9:24 went up from the C of David to her
11:27 the breach of the C of David his father.
11:32 sake of Jerusalem, the C which I have chosen
11:36 me in Jerusalem, the C where I have chosen
11:43 was buried in the C of David his father;
13:25 told it in the C where the old prophet

	13:29	it back to the C, to mourn and to
	14:11	who dies in the C the dogs shall eat;
	14:12	your feet enter the C, the child shall die.
	14:21	years in Jerusalem, the C which the LORD had
	14:31	his fathers in the C of David.
	15:8	buried him in the C of David.
	15:24	his fathers in the C of David his father;
	16:4	who dies in the C the dogs shall eat;
	16:18	Zimri saw that the C was taken, he went
	16:24	the name of the C which he built, Samaria,
	17:10	the gate of the C, behold, a widow was
	20:2	sent messengers into the C to Ahab king of
	20:12	And they took their positions against the C
	20:19	went out of the C, the servants of the
	20:30	rest fled into the C of Aphek; and the
	20:30	fled, and entered an inner chamber in the C
	21:8	the nobles who dwelt with Naboth in his C
	21:11	the men of his C, the elders and the
	21:11	who dwelt in his C, did as Jezebel had
	21:13	took him outside the C, and stoned him to
	21:24	who dies in the C the dogs shall eat;
	22:26	the governor of the C and to Joash the
	22:36	"Every man to his C, and every man to
	22:50	his fathers in the C of David his father;
2Kgs	2:19	the men of the C said to Elisha, "Behold,
	2:19	the situation of this C is pleasant, as my
	2:23	came out of the C and jeered at him,
	3:19	shall conquer every fortified C, and every choice city,
	3:19	city, and every choice C, and shall fell every
	6:14	and they came by night, and surrounded the C
	6:15	with horses and chariots was round about the C
	6:19	this is not the C; follow me, and I
	7:4	'Let us enter the C the famine is in
	7:4	famine is in the C, and we shall die
	7:10	the gatekeepers of the C, and told them, "We
	7:12	come out of the C, we shall take them
	7:12	shall take them alive and get into the C
	8:24	his fathers in the C of David; and Ahaziah
	9:15	slip out of the C to go and tell
	9:28	his fathers in the C of David.
	10:1	the rulers of the C, to the elders, and
	10:5	who was over the C, together with the elders
	10:6	great men of the C, who were bringing them
	11:20	land rejoiced; and the C was quiet after Athaliah
	12:21	his fathers in the C of David, and Amaziah
	14:20	his fathers in the C of David.
	15:7	his fathers in the C of David, and Jotham
	15:38	his fathers in the C of David his father;
	16:20	his fathers in the C of David; and Hezekiah
	17:9	from watchtower to fortified C;
	18:8	Gaza and its territory, from watchtower to fortified C
	18:30	deliver us, and this C will not be given
	19:13	the king of the C of Sepharvaim, the king
	19:32	not come into this C or shoot an arrow
	19:33	not come into this C, says the LORD.
	19:34	I will defend this C to save it, for
	20:6	deliver you and this C out of the hand
	20:6	I will defend this C for my own sake
	20:20	brought water into the C, are they not written
	23:8	the governor of the C, which were on one's
	23:8	on one's left at the gate of the C
	23:17	the men of the C told him, "It is
	23:27	will cast off this C which I have chosen,
	24:10	to Jerusalem, and the C was besieged.
	24:11	Babylon came to the C, while his servants were
	25:2	So the C was besieged till the eleventh year
	25:3	so severe in the C that there was no
	25:4	was made in the C; the king with all
	25:4	garden, though the Chaldeans were around the C
	25:11	were left in the C and the deserters who
	25:19	threshold; and from the C he took an officer
	25:19	were found in the C; and the secretary of
	25:19	of the land who were found in the C
1Chr	1:43	the name of whose C was Dinhabah.
	1:46	the name of his C was Avith.
	1:50	the name of his C was Pai, and his
	6:56	the fields of the C and its villages they
	11:5	Zion, that is, the C of David.
	11:7	it was called the C of David.
	11:8	And he built the C round about from the
	11:8	circuit; and Joab repaired the rest of the C
	13:13	ark home into the C of David, but took
	15:1	for himself in the C of David; and he
	15:29	LORD came to the C of David, Michal the
	19:9	the entrance of the C, and the kings who
	19:15	fled before Abishai, Joab's brother, and entered the C
	20:2	the spoil of the C, a very great amount.
	5:2	LORD out of the C of David, which is
	6:5	Egypt, I chose no C in all the tribes
	6:34	to thee toward this C which thou hast chosen
	6:38	to their fathers, the C which thou hast chosen,
	8:11	daughter up from the C of David to the
	9:31	was buried in the C of David his father;
	12:13	years in Jerusalem, the C which the LORD had
	12:16	was buried in the C of David; and Abijah
	14:1	buried him in the C of David; and Asa
	15:6	nation against nation and C against city, for God
	15:6	nation and city against C, for God troubled them
	16:14	for himself in the C of David.
	18:25	the governor of the C and to Joash the
	19:5	fortified cities of Judah, C by city,
	19:5	of Judah, city by C,
	21:1	his fathers in the C of David; and Jehoram
	21:20	buried him in the C of David, but not
	23:21	land rejoiced; and the C was quiet, after Athaliah
	24:16	buried him in the C of David among the
	24:25	buried him in the C of David, but they
	25:28	his fathers in the C of David.
	27:9	buried him in the C of David; and Ahaz
	28:15	kinsfolk at Jericho, the C of palm trees.
	28:25	In every C of Judah he made high places
	28:27	buried him in the C, in Jerusalem, for they
	29:20	the officials of the C, and went up to
	30:10	the couriers went from C to city through the
	30:10	went from city to C through the country of
	32:3	that were outside the C; and they helped him.
	32:5	the Millo in the C of David.
	32:6	the gate of the C and spoke encouragingly to
	32:18	them, in order that they might take the C
	32:30	west side of the C of David.
	33:14	outer wall for the C of David west of
	33:15	Jerusalem, and he threw them outside of the C
	34:8	the governor of the C, and Joah the son
Ezra	4:12	that rebellious and wicked C; they are finishing the
	4:13	king that, if this C is rebuilt and the
	4:15	and learn that this C is a rebellious city,
	4:15	city is a rebellious C, hurtful to kings and
	4:15	That was why this C was laid waste.
	4:16	king that, if this C is rebuilt and its
	4:19	been found that this C from of old has
	4:21	cease, and that this C be not rebuilt, until
	10:14	and judges of every C, till the fierce wrath
Neh	2:3	be sad, when the C, the place of my
	2:5	to Judah, to the C of my fathers' sepulchres,
	2:8	the wall of the C, and for the house
	3:15	go down from the C of David.
	7:4	The C was wide and large, but the people
	11:1	in Jerusalem the holy C, while nine tenths remained
	11:9	the son of Hassenuah was second over the C
	11:18	Levites in the holy C were two hundred and
	12:37	the stairs of the C of David, at the
	13:16	who lived in the C, brought in fish and
	13:18	all this evil on us and on this C
Tob	13:9	O Jerusalem, the holy C, he will afflict you
Jud	1:1	Assyrians in the great C of Nineveh, in the
	6:12	the men of the C saw them, they caught
	6:12	ran out of the C to the top of
	6:14	came down from their C and found him; and
	6:14	the magistrates of their C,
	6:16	the elders of the C, and all their young
	7:7	the approaches to the C, and visited the springs
	7:13	destroy them, and they will give up their C
	7:13	that not a man gets out of the C
	7:23	the streets of the C and in the passages
	7:24	the rulers of the C and cried out with
	7:27	and surrender the whole C to the army of
	7:33	up on the walls and towers of their C
	7:33	And they were greatly depressed in the C
	8:3	to his bed and died in Bethulia his C
	8:9	oath to surrender the C to the Assyrians after
	8:10	summon Chabris and Charmis, the elders of her C
	8:11	promising to surrender the C to our enemies unless
	8:18	family or people or C of ours which worshiped
	8:33	Stand at the C gate tonight, and I will
	8:33	promised to surrender the C to our enemies, the
	10:6	went out to the C gate of Bethulia, and
	10:6	the elders of the C, Chabris and Charmis
	10:9	the gate of the C to be opened for
	10:10	the men of the C watched her until she
	13:12	the men of her C heard her voice, they
	13:12	hurried down to the C gate and called together
	13:12	gate and called together the elders of the C

14:2 go out of the C, and set a captain
14:9 shout and made a joyful noise in their C
Esth 3:15 to drink; but the C of Susa was perplexed.
4:1 the midst of the C, wailing with a loud
4:6 open square of the C in front of the
6:9 open square of the C, proclaiming before him: 'Thus
6:11 open square of the C, proclaiming, "Thus shall it
8:11 who were in every C to gather and defend
8:15 and purple, while the C of Susa shouted and
8:17 and in every C, wherever the king's command
9:28 every family, province, and C, and that these days
11:3 Jew, dwelling in the C of Susa, a great
16:24 "Every C and country, without exception, which does
Job 24:12 From out of the C the dying groan, and
29:7 the gate of the C, when I prepared my
39:7 the tumult of the C; he hears not the
Ps 31:21 when I was beset as in a besieged C
46:4 streams make glad the C of God, the holy
48:1 be praised in the C of our God!
48:2 the far north, the C of the great King.
48:8 we seen in the C of the LORD of
48:8 of hosts, in the C of our God, which
55:9 for I see violence and strife in the C
59:6 back, howling like dogs and prowling about the C
59:14 back, howling like dogs and prowling about the C
60:9 Who will bring me to the fortified C
87:1 holy mount stands the C he founded;
87:3 spoken of you, O C of God.
101:8 the evildoers from the C of the LORD.
107:4 no way to a C to dwell in;
107:7 till they reached a C to dwell in.
107:36 and they establish a C to live in;
108:10 Who will bring me to the fortified C
122:3 Jerusalem, built as a C which is bound firmly
127:1 LORD watches over the C, the watchman stays
Prov 1:21 the entrance of the C gates she speaks:
10:15 wealth is his strong C; the poverty of the
11:10 with the righteous, the C rejoices; and when the
11:11 of the upright a C is exalted, but it
16:32 rules his spirit than he who takes a C
18:11 wealth is his strong C, and like a high
18:19 is like a strong C, but quarreling is like
21:22 wise man scales the C of the mighty and
25:28 self-control is like a C broken into and left
29:8 Scoffers set a C aflame, but wise men turn
Eccl 7:19 more than ten rulers that are in a C
8:10 were praised in the C where they had done
9:14 There was a little C with few men in
9:15 man, and he by his wisdom delivered the C
10:15 he does not know the way to the C
Song 3:2 and go about the C, in the streets and
3:3 found me, as they went about in the C
5:7 went about in the C; they beat me, they
Wis 9:8 an altar in the C of thy habitation, a
Sir 9:7 the streets of a C, nor wander about in
9:13 going about on the C battlements.
9:18 is feared in his C, and the man who
10:2 the ruler of the C, so are all its
10:3 his people, but a C will grow through the
16:4 man of understanding a C will be filled with
23:21 the streets of the C, and where he least
24:11 In the beloved C likewise he gave me a
26:5 The slander of a C, the gathering of a
31:24 The C will complain of the one who is
36:13 Have pity on the C of thy sanctuary, Jerusalem,
36:26 robber that skips from C to city?
36:26 a nimble robber that skips from city to C
38:32 Without them a C cannot be established, and men
40:19 the building of a C establish a man's name,
42:11 a byword in the C and notorious among the
48:17 Hezekiah fortified his C, and brought water into the
49:6 fire to the chosen C of the sanctuary, and
50:4 ruin, and fortified the C to withstand a seige.
Is 1:8 lodge in a cucumber field, like a besieged C
1:21 How the faithful C has become a harlot, she
1:26 shall be called the C of righteousness, the faithful
1:26 be called the city of righteousness, the faithful C
14:31 O gate; cry, O C; melt in fear, O
17:1 cease to be a C, and will become a
19:2 man against his neighbor, C against C, kingdom
19:18 will be called the C of the Sun.
22:2 full of shoutings, tumultuous C, exultant town?
22:9 the breaches of the C of David were many,
23:7 Is this your exultant C whose origin is from
23:16 harp, go about the C, O forgotten harlot!
24:10 The C of chaos is broken down, every house
24:12 is left in the C, the gates are battered
25:2 thou hast made the C a heap, the fortified
25:2 a heap, the fortified C a ruin; the palace
25:2 of aliens is a C no more, it will
26:1 "We have a strong C; he sets up salvation
26:5 low the inhabitants of the height, the lofty C
27:10 For the fortified C is solitary, a habitation deserted
29:1 Ho Ariel, Ariel, the C where David encamped!
32:13 for all the joyous houses in the joyful C
32:14 be forsaken, the populous C deserted; the hill and
32:19 go down, and the C will be utterly laid
33:20 Look upon Zion, the C of our appointed feasts!
36:15 surely deliver us; this C will not be given
37:13 the king of the C of Sepharvaim, the king
37:33 not come into this C, or shoot an arrow
37:34 not come into this C, says the LORD.
37:35 I will defend this C to save it, for
38:6 deliver you and this C out of the hand
38:6 of the king of Assyria, and defend this C
45:13 he shall build my C and set my exiles
48:2 themselves after the holy C, and stay themselves on
52:1 O Jerusalem, the holy C; for there shall no
60:14 shall call you the C of the LORD, the
62:12 called Sought out, a C not forsaken.
66:6 "Hark, an uproar from the C
Jer 1:18 this day a fortified C, an iron pillar, and
3:14 you, one from a C and two from a
4:29 horseman and archer every C takes to flight; they
6:6 This is the C which must be punished; there
8:16 that fills it, the C and those who dwell
14:18 if I enter the C, behold, the diseases of
17:24 the gates of this C on the sabbath day,
17:25 the gates of this C kings who sit on
17:25 of Jerusalem; and this C shall be inhabited for
19:8 I will make this C a horror, a thing
19:11 this people and this C, as one breaks a
19:12 its inhabitants, making this C like Topheth.
19:15 am bringing upon this C and upon all its
20:5 the wealth of the C, all its gains, all
21:4 bring them together into the midst of this C
21:6 the inhabitants of this C, both man and beast;
21:7 the people in this C who survive the pestilence,
21:9 who stays in this C shall die by the
21:10 my face against this C for evil and not
22:6 I will make you a desert, an uninhabited C
22:8 will pass by this C, and every man will
22:8 has the LORD dealt thus with this great C
23:39 presence, you and the C which I gave to
25:29 work evil at the C which is called by
26:6 I will make this C a curse for all
26:9 like Shiloh, and this C shall be desolate, without
26:11 has prophesied against this C, as you have heard
26:12 this house and this C all the words you
26:15 yourselves and upon this C and its inhabitants, for
26:20 He prophesied against this C and against this land
27:17 Why should this C become a desolation?
27:19 are left in this C,
29:7 the welfare of the C where I have sent
29:16 who dwell in this C, your kinsmen who did
30:18 on his dwellings; the C shall be rebuilt upon
31:38 the LORD, when the C shall be rebuilt for
32:3 I am giving this C into the hand of
32:24 come up to the C to take it, and
32:24 famine and pestilence the C is given into the
32:25 get witnesses"--though the C is given into the
32:28 I am giving this C into the hands of
32:29 are fighting against this C shall come and set
32:29 come and set this C on fire, and burn
32:31 This C has aroused my anger and wrath, from
32:36 of Israel, concerning this C of which you say,
33:4 the houses of this C and the houses of
33:5 my face from this C because of all their
33:9 And this C shall be to me a name
34:2 I am giving this C into the hand of
34:22 them back to this C; and they will fight
37:8 and fight against this C; they shall take it
37:10 up and burn this C with fire.'"
37:21 the bread of the C was gone.
38:2 who stays in this C shall die by the
38:3 says the LORD, This C shall surely be given
38:4 are left in this C, and the hands of
38:9 for there is no bread left in the C
38:17 be spared, and this C shall not be burned
38:18 of Babylon, then this C shall be given into
38:23 of Babylon; and this C shall be burned with
39:2 the month, a breach was made in the C

	39:4	going out of the C at night by way
	39:9	were left in the C, those who had deserted
	39:16	my words against this C for evil and not
	41:7	they came into the C, Ishmael the son of
	47:2	that fills it, the C and those who dwell
	48:8	shall come upon every C, and no city shall
	48:8	every city, and no C shall escape; the valley
	49:25	How the famous C is forsaken, the joyful city!
	49:25	How the famous city is forsaken, the joyful C
	51:31	of Babylon that his C is taken on every
	52:5	So the C was besieged till the eleventh year
	52:6	so severe in the C, that there was no
	52:7	was made in the C; and all the men
	52:7	went out from the C by night by the
	52:7	garden, while the Chaldeans were round about the C
	52:15	were left in the C and the deserters who
	52:25	threshold; and from the C he took an officer
	52:25	were found in the C; and the secretary of
	52:25	who were found in the midst of the C
Lam	1:1	How lonely sits the C that was full of
	1:19	elders perished in the C, while they sought food
	2:11	and babes faint in the streets of the C
	2:12	the streets of the C, as their life is
	2:15	Jerusalem; "Is this the C which was called the
	3:51	the fate of all the maidens of my C
	5:14	men have quit the C gate, the young men
Bar	4:32	wretched will be the C which received your sons.
Ezek	4:1	portray upon it a C, even Jerusalem;
	4:3	between you and the C; and set your face
	4:7	arm bared; and you shall prophesy against the C
	5:2	the midst of the C, when the days of
	5:2	sword round about the C; and a third part
	7:15	that is in the C famine and pestilence devour.
	7:23	bloody crimes and the C is full of violence,
	9:1	you executioners of the C, each with his destroying
	9:4	him, "Go through the C, through Jerusalem, and put
	9:5	hearing, "Pass through the C after him, and smite;
	9:7	So they went forth, and smote in the C
	9:9	of blood, and the C full of injustice; for
	10:2	between the cherubim, and scatter them over the C
	11:2	wicked counsel in this C;
	11:3	to build houses; this C is the caldron, and
	11:6	your slain in this C, and have filled its
	11:7	the flesh, and this C is the caldron; but
	11:11	This C shall not be your caldron, nor shall
	11:23	the midst of the C, and stood upon the
	11:23	which is on the east side of the C
	17:4	set it in a C of merchants.
	21:19	the way to a C;
	22:2	will you judge, will you judge the bloody C
	22:3	the Lord GOD: A C that sheds blood in
	24:6	Woe to the bloody C, to the pot whose
	24:9	says the Lord GOD: Woe to the bloody C
	26:10	as one enters a C which has been breached.
	26:17	from the seas, O C renowned, that was mighty
	26:19	I make you a C laid waste, like the
	33:21	me and said, "The C has fallen."
	39:16	(A C Hamonah is there also.) Thus shall they
	40:1	fourteenth year after the C was conquered, on that
	40:2	a structure like a C opposite me.
	43:3	came to destroy the C, and like the vision
	45:6	the possession of the C an area five thousand
	45:7	the property of the C, alongside the holy district
	45:7	the property of the C, on the west and
	48:15	ordinary use for the C, for dwellings and for
	48:15	it shall be the C;
	48:17	And the C shall have open land: on the
	48:18	shall be food for the workers of the C
	48:19	the workers of the C, from all the tribes
	48:20	holy portion together with the property of the C
	48:21	the property of the C shall belong to the
	48:22	the property of the C, shall be in the
	48:30	the exits of the C: On the north side,
	48:31	the gates of the C being named after the
	48:35	circumference of the C shall be eighteen thousand
	48:35	the name of the C henceforth shall be, The
Dan	3:28	upon Jerusalem, the holy C of our fathers, for
	9:16	turn away from thy C Jerusalem, thy holy hill;
	9:18	our desolations, and the C which is called by
	9:19	my God, because thy C and thy people are
	9:24	people and your holy C, to finish the transgression,
	9:26	come shall destroy the C and the sanctuary.
	11:15	and throw up siegeworks, and take a well-fortified C
Hos	6:8	Gilead is a C of evildoers, tracked with blood.
Joel	2:9	They leap upon the C, they run upon the
Amos	3:6	trumpet blown in a C, and the people are
	3:6	Does evil befall a C, unless the LORD has
	4:7	send rain upon one C, and send no rain
	4:7	no rain upon another C; one field would be
	4:8	cities wandered to one C to drink water, and
	5:3	the Lord GOD: "The C that went forth a
	6:8	will deliver up the C and all that is
	7:17	a harlot in the C, and your sons and
Jon	1:2	to Nineveh, that great C, and cry against it;
	3:2	to Nineveh, that great C, and proclaim to it
	3:3	was an exceedingly great C, three days' journey in
	3:4	to go into the C, going a day's journey.
	4:5	went out of the C and sat to the
	4:5	the east of the C, and made a booth
	4:5	he should see what would become of the C
	4:11	pity Nineveh, that great C, in which there are
Mic	4:10	go forth from the C and dwell in the
	6:9	LORD cries to the C --and it is sound
	6:9	name: "Hear, O tribe and assembly of the C
Nah	3:1	Woe to the bloody C, all full of lies
Hab	2:12	blood, and founds a C on iniquity!
Zeph	2:15	This is the exultant C that dwelt secure, that
	3:1	her that is rebellious and defiled, the oppressing C
Zech	8:3	be called the faithful C, and the mountain of
	8:5	the streets of the C shall be full of
	8:21	the inhabitants of one C shall go to another,
	14:2	to battle, and the C shall be taken and
	14:2	ravished; half of the C shall go into exile,
	14:2	people shall not be cut off from the C
1Mac	1:30	suddenly fell upon the C, dealt it a severe
	1:31	He plundered the C, burned it with fire, and
	1:33	Then they fortified the C of David with a
	1:51	Judah to offer sacrifice, C by city.
	1:51	cities of Judah to offer sacrifice, city by C
	2:7	ruin of the holy C, and to dwell there
	2:15	apostasy came to the C of Modein to make
	2:17	and great in this C, and supported by sons
	2:27	cried out in the C with a loud voice,
	2:28	and left all that they had in the C
	2:31	troops in Jerusalem the C of David, that men
	5:28	and he took the C, and killed every male
	5:31	the cry of the C went up to Heaven
	5:44	But he took the C and burned the sacred
	5:46	large and very strong C on the road, and
	5:47	the men of the C shut them out and
	5:50	he fought against the C all that day and
	5:50	the night, and the C was delivered into his
	5:51	of the sword, and razed and plundered the C
	5:51	he passed through the C over the slain.
	5:59	came out of the C to meet them in
	6:1	in Persia was a C famed for its wealth
	6:3	tried to take the C and plunder it, but
	6:3	the men of the C
	6:7	high walls as before, and also Bethzur, his C
	6:49	and they evacuated the C, because they had no
	6:63	in control of the C, but he fought against
	6:63	him, and took the C by force.
	7:1	few men to a C by the sea, and
	7:24	prevented those in the C from going out into
	7:32	rest fled into the C of David.
	9:52	He also fortified the C of Bethzur, and Gazara,
	9:65	his brother in the C, while he went out
	9:67	sallied out from the C and set fire to
	10:10	Jerusalem and began to rebuild and restore the C
	10:63	the middle of the C and proclaim that no
	10:75	the men of the C closed its gates, for
	10:76	the men of the C became afraid and opened
	10:86	the men of the C came out to meet
	11:3	he stationed forces as a garrison in each C
	11:45	the men of the C assembled within the city,
	11:45	city assembled within the C, to the number of
	11:46	the men of the C seized the main streets
	11:46	main streets of the C and began to fight.
	11:47	spread out through the C; and they killed on
	11:48	set fire to the C and seized much spoil
	11:49	the men of the C saw that the Jews
	11:49	gained control of the C as they pleased, their
	11:50	the Jews stop fighting against us and our C
	11:60	the people of the C met him and paid
	11:66	took possession of the C, and set a garrison
	12:36	the citadel and the C to separate it from
	12:36	separate it from the C, in order to isolate
	12:37	to build up the C; part of the wall
	13:25	him in Modein, the C of his fathers.
	13:43	it up to the C, and battered and captured
	13:44	leaped out into the C, and a great tumult
	13:44	city, and a great tumult arose in the C

13:45 The men in the C, with their wives and
13:47 expelled them from the C and cleansed the houses
14:20 "The rulers and the C of the Spartans to
14:36 the men in the C of David in Jerusalem,
14:37 country and of the C, and built the walls
15:14 He surrounded the C, and the ships joined battle
15:14 sea; he pressed the C hard from land and
2Mac 1:12 drove out those who fought against the holy C
2:22 world and freed the C and restored the laws
3:1 While the holy C was inhabited in unbroken peace
3:4 the administration of the C market;
3:9 high priest of the C, he told about the
3:14 There was no little distress throughout the whole C
4:2 the benefactor of the C, the protector of his
4:22 by Jason and the C, and ushered in with
4:36 the Jews in the C appealed to him with
4:38 him about the whole C to that very place
4:39 been committed in the C by Lysimachus with the
4:48 had spoken for the C and the villages and
5:2 that over all the C, for almost forty days,
5:5 men and suddenly made an assault upon the C
5:5 and at last the C was being taken, Menelaus
5:8 the Arabs, fleeing from C to city, pursued by
5:8 fleeing from city to C, pursued by all men,
5:11 Egypt and took the C by storm.
5:17 who dwelt in the C, and that therefore he
5:26 then rushed into the C with his armed men
6:10 publicly paraded about the C, with their babies hung
8:3 have mercy on the C which was being destroyed
8:17 torture of the derided C, and besides, the overthrow
8:33 the victory in the C of their fathers, they
9:2 had entered the C called Persepolis, and attempted
9:2 attempted to rob the temples and control the C
9:14 stating that the holy C, which he was hastening
10:1 the temple and the C;
10:27 considerable distance from the C; and when they
10:36 rest of the force, and they occupied the C
11:2 intended to make the C a home for Greeks,
12:4 this was done by public vote of the C
12:7 Then, because the C's gates were closed, he
12:13 also attacked a certain C which was strongly
12:16 They took the C by the will of God,
12:27 against Ephron, a fortified C where Lysias dwelt with
12:28 and they got the C into their hands, and
12:38 and went to the C of Adullam.
13:13 could enter Judea and get possession of the C
13:14 for the laws, temple, C, country, and commonwealth,
15:14 people and the holy C, Jeremiah, the prophet of
15:17 all courage, because the C and the sanctuary and
15:19 to remain in the C were in no little
15:37 from that time the C has been in the
Mt 2:23 and dwelt in a C called Nazareth, that what
4:5 him to the holy C, and set him on
5:14 A C set on a hill cannot be hid.
5:35 for it is the C of the great King.
8:33 and going into the C they told everything, and
8:34 And behold, all the C came out to meet
9:1 he crossed over and came to his own C
12:25 laid waste, and no C or house divided against
21:10 Jerusalem, all the C was stirred, saying, "Who
21:17 went out of the C to Bethany and lodged
21:18 was returning to the C, he was hungry.
22:7 and destroyed those murderers and burned their C
26:18 said, "Go into the C to a certain one,
27:53 went into the holy C and appeared to many.
28:11 guard went into the C and told the chief
Mk 1:33 And the whole C was gathered together about the
5:14 told it in the C and in the country.
11:19 when evening came they went out of the C
14:13 them, "Go into the C, and a man carrying
14:16 and went to the C, and found it as
Lk 1:26 from God to a C of Galilee named Nazareth,
1:39 hill country, to a C of Judah,
2:3 went to be enrolled, each to his own C
2:4 from Galilee, from the C of Nazareth, to Judea,
2:4 to Judea, to the C of David, which is
2:11 this day in the C of David a Savior,
2:39 Galilee, to their own C, Nazareth.
4:29 him out of the C, and led him to
4:29 hill on which their C was built, that they
4:31 down to Caperna-um, a C of Galilee.
7:11 he went to a C called Nain, and his
7:12 the gate of the C, behold, a man who
7:12 large crowd from the C was with her.
7:37 a woman of the C, who was a sinner,
8:27 a man from the C who had demons; for
8:34 told it in the C and in the country.
8:39 proclaiming throughout the whole C how much Jesus
9:10 withdrew apart to a C called Beth-saida.
14:21 and lanes of the C, and bring in the
18:2 said, "In a certain C there was a judge
18:3 a widow in that C who kept coming to
19:41 near and saw the C he wept over it,
21:21 who are inside the C depart, and let not
22:10 you have entered the C, a man carrying a
23:18 insurrection started in the C, and for murder.
24:49 but stay in the C, until you are clothed
Jn 1:44 was from Beth-saida, the C of Andrew and Peter.
4:5 he came to a C of Samaria, called Sychar,
4:8 gone away into the C to buy food.
4:28 went away into the C, and said to the
4:30 went out of the C and were coming to
4:39 Many Samaritans from that C believed in him
19:20 crucified was near the C; and it was written
Acts 4:27 for truly in this C there were gathered together
7:58 him out of the C and stoned him; and
8:5 went down to a C of Samaria, and proclaimed
8:8 So there was much joy in that C
8:9 practiced magic in the C and amazed the nation
9:6 rise and enter the C, and you will be
10:9 and coming near the C, Peter went up on
11:5 "I was in the C of Joppa praying; and
12:10 came to the iron gate leading into the C
13:44 sabbath almost the whole C gathered together to
13:50 leading men of the C, and stirred up persecution
14:4 the people of the C were divided; some sided
14:13 in front of the C, brought oxen and garlands
14:19 him out of the C, supposing that he was
14:20 up and entered the C; and on the next
14:21 the gospel to that C and had made many
15:21 has had in every C those who preach him,
15:35 the brethren in every C where we proclaimed the
16:12 which is the leading C of the district of
16:12 We remained in this C some days;
16:14 named Lydia, from the C of Thyatira, a seller
16:20 men are Jews and they are disturbing our C
16:39 them out and asked them to leave the C
17:5 a crowd, set the C in an uproar, and
17:6 the brethren before the C authorities, crying, "These
17:8 the people and the C authorities were disturbed
17:16 he saw that the C was full of idols.
18:10 you; for I have many people in this C
19:29 So the C was filled with the confusion; and
19:35 not know that the C of the Ephesians is
20:23 to me in every C that imprisonment and afflictions
21:5 we were outside the C; and kneeling down on
21:29 with him in the C, and they supposed that
21:30 Then all the C was aroused, and the people
21:39 citizen of no mean C; I beg you, let
22:3 brought up in this C at the feet of
24:11 temple or in the synagogues, or in the C
25:23 military tribunes and the prominent men of the C
27:8 near which was the C of Lasea.
Rom 16:23 Erastus, the C treasurer, and our brother Quartus,
2Cor 11:26 Gentiles, danger in the C, danger in the wilderness,
11:32 King Aretas guarded the C of Damascus in order
Heb 11:10 looked forward to the C which has foundations,
11:16 God, for he has prepared for them a C
12:22 Zion and to the C of the living God,
13:14 we have no lasting C, but we seek the
13:14 but we seek the C which is to come.
Rev 3:12 the name of the C of my God, the
11:2 trample over the holy C for forty-two months.
11:8 street of the great C which is allegorically called
11:13 a tenth of the C fell; seven thousand people
14:20 was trodden outside the C, and blood flowed from
16:19 The great C was split into three parts, and
17:18 saw is the great C which has dominion over
18:10 thou great C, thou mighty city, Babylon!
18:10 great city, thou mighty C, Babylon!
18:16 alas, for the great C that was clothed in
18:18 of her burning, "What C was like the great
18:18 her burning, "What city was like the great C
18:19 alas, for the great C where all who had
18:21 shall Babylon the great C be thrown down with
20:9 saints and the beloved C; but fire came down
21:2 I saw the holy C, new Jerusalem, coming down
21:10 showed me the holy C Jerusalem coming down out
21:14 the wall of the C had twelve foundations, and
21:15 gold to measure the C and its gates and
21:16 The C lies foursquare, its length the same as
21:16 and he measured the C with his rod, twelve

21:18 of jasper, while the C was pure gold, clear
21:19 the wall of the C were adorned with every
21:21 the street of the C was pure gold, transparent
21:22 no temple in the C, for its temple is
21:23 And the C has no need of sun or
22:2 the street of the C; also, on either side
22:14 they may enter the C by the gates.
22:19 and in the holy C, which are described in

CIVILIAN
2Tim 2:4 service gets entangled in C pursuits, since his aim

CLAD (5)
2Sam 13:18 daughters of the king C of old.
1Kgs 11:29 Now Ahijah had C himself with a new garment;
Rev 3:5 who conquers shall be C thus in white garments,
4:4 were twenty-four elders, C in white garments, with
19:13 He is C in a robe dipped in blood,

CLAIM (7)
Job 3:5 gloom and deep darkness C it.
1Mac 15:3 I intend to lay C to the kingdom so
Jn 8:53 Who do you C to be?"
1Cor 9:12 others share this rightful C upon you, do not
2Cor 3:5 competent of ourselves to C anything as coming
11:12 order to undermine the C of those who would
11:12 who would like to C that in their boasted

CLAIMING
Rom 1:22 C to be wise, they became fools,

CLAIMS (2)
2Sam 15:3 to him, "See, your C are good and right;
Eccl 8:17 though a wise man C to know, he cannot

CLAMOR (6)
Ps 74:23 Do not forget the C of thy foes, the
Is 38:14 or a crane I C, I moan like a
Jer 25:31 The C will resound to the ends of the
Lam 2:7 of her palaces; a C was raised in the
Acts 23:9 Then a great C arose; and some of the
Eph 4:31 wrath and anger and C and slander be put

CLAMPS
1Chr 22:3 the gates and for C, as well as bronze

CLAN (5)
Judg 6:15 Behold, my C is the weakest in Manasseh, and
9:1 and to the whole C of his mother's family,
12:9 in marriage outside his C, and thirty daughters he
Is 60:22 one shall become a C, and the smallest one
Zech 9:7 shall be like a C in Judah, and Ekron

CLANGING
1Cor 13:1 noisy gong or a C cymbal.

CLANKING
1Mac 6:41 the multitude and the C of their arms, trembled,

CLANS (8)
Gen 36:30 Horites, according to their C in the land of
Num 1:16 the heads of the C of Israel.
Josh 22:14 a family among the C of Israel.
Judg 5:15 Among the C of Reuben there were great searchings
5:16 Among the C of Reuben there were great searchings
Mic 5:2 to be among the C of Judah, from you
Zech 12:5 Then the C of Judah shall say to themselves,
12:6 I will make the C of Judah like a

CLAP (10)
Ps 47:1 [Selah] C your hands, all peoples!
98:8 Let the floods C their hands; let the hills
Sir 12:18 shake his head, and C his hands, and whisper
40:13 crash like a loud C of thunder in a
Is 55:12 of the field shall C their hands.
Lam 2:15 pass along the way C their hands at you;
Ezek 6:11 says the Lord GOD: C your hands, and stamp
21:14 therefore, son of man; C your hands and let
21:17 I also will C my hands, and I will
Nah 3:19 the news of you C their hands over you.

CLAPPED (2)
2Kgs 11:12 anointed him; and they C their hands, and said,
Ezek 25:6 GOD: Because you have C your hands and stamped

CLAPS (2)
Job 27:23 It C its hands at him, and hisses at
34:37 to his sin; he C his hands among us,

CLASHING
Ps 150:5 praise him with loud C cymbals!

CLASP
Job 41:17 one to another; they C each other and cannot

CLASPS (8)
Ex 26:6 you shall make fifty C of gold, and couple
26:6 the other with the C, that the tabernacle may
26:11 you shall make fifty C of bronze, and put
26:11 bronze, and put the C into the loops, and
26:33 the veil from the C, and bring the ark
36:13 And he made fifty C of gold, and coupled
36:13 to the other with C; so the tabernacle was
36:18 And he made fifty C of bronze to couple

CLASS
2Cor 10:12 that we venture to C or compare ourselves with

CLAUDIA
2Tim 4:21 Pudens and Linus and C and all the brethren.

CLAUDIUS (3)
Acts 11:28 and this took place in the days of C
18:2 his wife Priscilla, because C had commanded all the
23:26 letter to this effect: C Lysias to his Excellency

CLAWS (2)
Dan 4:33 eagles' feathers, and his nails were like birds' C
7:19 teeth of iron and C of bronze; and which

CLAY (39)
1Kgs 7:46 cast them, in the C ground between Succoth and
4:17 cast them, in the C ground between Succoth and
Job 4:19 dwell in houses of C, whose foundation is in
10:9 hast made me of C; and wilt thou turn
13:12 proverbs of ashes, your defenses are defenses of C
27:16 pile up clothing like C;
33:6 I too was formed from a piece of C
38:14 It is changed like C under the seal, and
Wis 7:9 will be accounted as C before her.
15:7 out of the same C both the vessels that
15:7 these the worker in C decides.
15:8 god from the same C -- this man who
15:10 of less worth than C,
Sir 13:2 How can the C pot associate with the iron
33:13 As C in the hand of the potter--
38:30 He moulds the C with his arm and makes
Is 29:16 be regarded as the C; that the thing made
41:25 rulers as on mortar, as the potter treads C
45:9 Does the C say to him who fashions it,
64:8 Father; we are the C, and thou art our
Jer 18:4 he was making of C was spoiled in the
18:6 Behold, like the C in the potter's hand, so
Dan 2:33 its feet partly of iron and partly of C
2:34 feet of iron and C, and broke them in
2:35 then the iron, the C, the bronze, the silver,
2:41 toes partly of potter's C and partly of iron,
2:41 as you saw iron mixed with the miry C
2:42 partly iron and partly C, so the kingdom shall
2:43 iron mixed with miry C, so they will mix
2:43 together, just as iron does not mix with C
2:45 iron, the bronze, the C, the silver, and the
14:7 for this is but C inside and brass outside,
Nah 3:14 forts; go into the C, tread the mortar, take
Jn 9:6 the ground and made C of the spittle and
9:6 man's eyes with the C,
9:11 man called Jesus made C and anointed my eyes
9:14 when Jesus made the C and opened his eyes.
9:15 to them, "He put C on my eyes, and
Rom 9:21 no right over the C, to make out of

CLEAN (127)
Gen 7:2 seven pairs of all C animals, the male and
7:2 animals that are not C, the male and his
7:8 Of C animals, and of animals that are not
7:8 animals that are not C, and of birds, and
8:20 and took of every C animal and of every
8:20 animal and of every C bird, and offered burnt
Lev 4:12 the camp to a C place, where the ashes
6:11 the camp to a C place.
7:19 All who are C may eat flesh,

10:10 the unclean and the C;
10:14 shall eat in any C place, you and your
11:32 unclean until the evening; then it shall be C
11:36 holding water shall be C; but whatever touches their
11:37 be sown, it is C;
11:47 the unclean and the C and between the living
12:7 then she shall be C from the flow of
12:8 make atonement for her, and she shall be C
13:6 priest shall pronounce him C; it is only an
13:6 and he shall wash his clothes, and be C
13:13 he shall pronounce him C of the disease; it
13:13 it has all turned white, and he is C
13:17 pronounce the diseased person C; he is clean.
13:17 shall pronounce the diseased person clean; he is C
13:23 the boil; and the priest shall pronounce him C
13:28 priest shall pronounce him C; for it is the
13:34 priest shall pronounce him C; and he shall wash
13:34 and he shall wash his clothes, and be C
13:37 is healed, he is C; and the priest shall
13:37 is clean; and the priest shall pronounce him C
13:39 has broken out in the skin; he is C
13:40 his head, he is bald but he is C
13:41 has baldness of the forehead but he is C
13:58 then be washed a second time, and be C
13:59 decide whether it is C or unclean.
14:4 be cleansed two living C birds and cedarwood and
14:7 he shall pronounce him C, and shall let the
14:8 and he shall be C; and after that he
14:9 his body in water, and he shall be C
14:20 make atonement for him, and he shall be C
14:48 shall pronounce the house C, for the disease is
14:53 atonement for the house, and it shall be C
14:57 when it is unclean and when it is C
15:8 on one who is C, then he shall wash
15:13 his body in running water, and shall be C
15:28 seven days, and after that she shall be C
16:30 sins you shall be C before the LORD.
17:15 unclean until the evening; then he shall be C
20:25 a distinction between the C beast and the unclean,
20:25 unclean bird and the C; you shall not make
22:4 eat of the holy things until he is C
22:7 down he shall be C; and afterward he may
Num 5:28 defiled herself and is C, then she shall be
9:13 the man who is C and is not on
18:11 every one who is C in your house may
18:13 every one who is C in your house may
19:9 a man who is C shall gather up the
19:9 the camp in a C place; and they shall
19:12 day, and so be C; but if he does
19:12 on the seventh day, he will not become C
19:18 a vessel; then a C person shall take hyssop,
19:19 the grave; and the C person shall sprinkle upon
19:19 in water, and at evening he shall be C
31:23 pass through the fire, and it shall be C
31:24 and you shall be C; and afterward you shall
Deut 12:15 the unclean and the C may eat of it,
12:22 the unclean and the C alike may eat of
14:11 "You may eat all C birds.
14:20 All C winged things you may eat.
15:22 the unclean and the C alike may eat it,
23:10 man who is not C by reason of what
1Sam 20:26 him; he is not C, surely he is not
20:26 he is not clean, surely he is not C
2Kgs 5:10 flesh shall be restored, and you shall be C
5:12 Could I not wash in them, and be C
5:13 when he says to you, 'Wash, and be C
5:14 flesh of a little child, and he was C
30:17 one who was not C, to make it holy
Ezra 6:20 had purified themselves together; all of them were C
Jud 12:9 So she returned C and stayed in the tent
Job 11:4 pure, and I am C in God's eyes.'
14:4 Who can bring a C thing out of an
15:14 What is man, that he can be C
15:15 the heavens are not C in his sight;
17:9 and he that has C hands grows stronger and
25:4 can he who is born of woman be C
25:5 the stars are not C in his sight;
33:9 You say, 'I am C, without transgression; I am
Ps 19:9 of the LORD is C, enduring for ever; the
24:4 He who has C hands and a pure heart,
51:7 and I shall be C; wash me, and I
51:10 Create in me a C heart, O God, and
73:13 I kept my heart C and washed my hands
Prov 20:9 have made my heart C; I am pure from
20:30 away evil; strokes make C the innermost parts.
Eccl 9:2 the evil, to the C and the unclean, to
Wis 15:7 the vessels that serve C uses and those for
Sir 34:4 From an unclean thing what will be made C
38:30 he is careful to C the furnace.
Is 1:16 Wash yourselves; make yourselves C; remove the evil
66:20 cereal offering in a C vessel to the house
Jer 13:27 long will it be before you are made C
43:12 captive; and he shall C the land of Egypt,
Ezek 22:26 the unclean and the C, and they have disregarded
36:25 I will sprinkle C water upon you, and you
36:25 and you shall be C from all your uncleannesses,
37:11 is lost; we are C cut off.'
44:23 how to distinguish between the unclean and the C
44:26 himself seven days, and then he shall be C
Zech 3:5 "Let them put a C turban on his head."
3:5 So they put a C turban on his head
Mt 8:2 "Lord, if you will, you can make me C
8:3 hand and touched him, saying, "I will; be C
23:25 the plate, that the outside also may be C
27:59 wrapped it in a C linen shroud,
Mk 1:40 him, "If you will, you can make me C
1:41 him, and said to him, "I will; be C
1:42 the leprosy left him, and he was made C
7:18 he declared all foods C
Lk 5:12 "Lord, if you will, you can make me C
5:13 hand, and touched him, saying, "I will; be C
11:41 and behold, everything is C for you.
Jn 13:10 feet, but he is C all over; and you
13:10 over; and you are C, but not every one
13:11 was why he said, "You are not all C
15:3 You are already made C by the word which
Rom 14:20 Everything is indeed C, but it is wrong for
Heb 10:22 with our hearts sprinkled C from an evil conscience

CLEANING

2Sam 4:6 the house had been C wheat, but she grew

CLEANNESS (7)

2Sam 22:21 righteousness; according to the C of my hands he
22:25 righteousness, according to my C in his sight.
30:19 though not according to the sanctuary's rules of C
Job 22:30 be delivered through the C of your hands."
Ps 18:20 righteousness; according to the C of my hands he
18:24 righteousness, according to the C of my hands in
Amos 4:6 "I gave you C of teeth in all your

CLEANS

Jer 43:12 Egypt, as a shepherd C his cloak of vermin;

CLEANSE (40)

Lev 14:52 Thus he shall C the house with the blood
16:19 finger seven times, and C it and hallow it
16:30 made for you, to C you; from all your
Num 8:6 people of Israel, and C them.
8:7 do to them, to C them: sprinkle the water
8:7 wash their clothes and C themselves.
8:21 atonement for them to C them.
19:12 seven days; he shall C himself with the water
19:12 if he does not C himself on the third
19:13 died, and does not C himself, defiles the tabernacle
19:19 seventh day he shall C him, and he shall
19:20 unclean and does not C himself, that person shall
29:15 of the LORD, to C the house of the
29:16 of the LORD to C it, and they brought
Job 9:30 myself with snow, and C my hands with lye,
Ps 51:2 from my iniquity, and C me from my sin!
Prov 20:30 Blows that wound C away evil; strokes make clean
Sir 38:10 your hands aright, and C your heart from all
Jer 4:11 not to winnow or C,
33:8 I will C them from all the guilt of
Ezek 16:4 washed with water to C you, nor rubbed with
36:25 your idols I will C you.
36:33 the day that I C you from all your
37:23 have sinned, and will C them; and they shall
39:12 them, in order to C the land.
39:14 land, so as to C it; at the end
39:16 also.) Thus shall they C the land.
43:20 about; thus you shall C the altar and make
45:18 bull without blemish, and C the sanctuary.
Dan 11:35 to refine and to C them and to make
Zech 13:1 inhabitants of Jerusalem to C them from sin and
1Mac 4:36 us go up to C the sanctuary and dedicate
Mt 10:8 sick, raise the dead, C lepers, cast out demons.
23:24 for you C the outside of the cup and
23:25 first C the inside of the cup and of
Lk 11:39 him, "Now you Pharisees C the outside of the
1Cor 5:7 C out the old leaven that you may be

	91:14	Because he C to me in love, I will
	119:25	My soul C to the dust; revive me according
	141:7	a rock which one C and shatters on the
Lam	4:4	tongue of the nursling C to the roof of

CLEAVING (2)

Deut	11:22	all his ways, and C to him,
	30:20	obeying his voice, and C to him; for that

CLEFT (8)

Ex	33:22	put you in a C of the rock, and
Judg	15:8	and stayed in the C of the rock of
	15:11	went down to the C of the rock of
Job	38:25	"Who has C a channel for the torrents of
Ps	78:15	He C rocks in the wilderness, and gave them
Is	48:21	from the rock; he C the rock and the
Jer	13:4	it there in a C of the rock."
Mic	1:4	the valleys will be C, like wax before the

CLEFTS (7)

Song	2:14	my dove, in the C of the rock, in
Is	2:21	the rocks and the C of the cliffs, from
	7:19	ravines, and in the C of the rocks, and
	57:5	the valleys, under the C of the rocks?
Jer	16:16	and out of the C of the rocks.
	49:16	who live in the C of the rock, who
Obad	1:3	who live in the C of the rock, whose

CLEMENT

Phil	4:3	the gospel together with C and the rest of

CLEOPAS

Lk	24:18	one of them, named C, answered him, "Are you

CLEOPATRA (3)

Esth	11:1	reign of Ptolemy and C, Dositheus, who said that
1Mac	10:57	from Egypt, he and C his daughter, and came
	10:58	and Ptolemy gave him C his daughter in marriage,

CLERK

Acts	19:35	And when the town C had quieted the crowd,

CLEVER (5)

Sir	1:5	Her C devices--who knows them?
	6:32	and if you apply yourself you will become C
	21:12	He who is not C cannot be taught, but
	21:20	he laughs, but a C man smiles quietly.
1Cor	1:19	the cleverness of the C I will thwart."

CLEVERLY (2)

2Mac	14:31	that he had been C outwitted by the man,
2Pet	1:16	we did not follow C devised myths when we

CLEVERNESS (6)

Sir	19:20	There is a C which is abominable, but there
	19:22	There is a C which is scrupulous but unjust,
	21:12	but there is a C which increases bitterness.
	32:4	do not display your C out of season.
	34:10	things, but he that has traveled acquires much C
1Cor	1:19	the wise, and the C of the clever I

CLIFF

Song	2:14	the covert of the C, let me see your

CLIFFS (2)

Is	2:21	the clefts of the C, from before the terror
Ezek	38:20	thrown down, and the C shall fall, and every

CLIMB (4)

Song	7:8	I say I will C the palm tree and
Jer	4:29	they enter thickets; they C among rocks; all the
Joel	2:9	upon the walls; they C up into the houses,
Amos	9:2	take them; though they C up to heaven, from

CLIMBED (2)

1Sam	14:13	Then Jonathan C up on his hands and feet,
Lk	19:4	ran on ahead and C up into a sycamore

CLIMBS (3)

Is	24:18	pit; and he who C out of the pit
Jer	48:44	pit, and he who C out of the pit
Jn	10:1	by the door but C in by another way,

CLING (2)

Job	24:8	of the mountains, and C to the rock for
Jer	13:11	whole house of Judah C to me, says the

CLINGS (6)

Ps	63:8	My soul C to thee; thy right hand upholds
Sir	10:13	and the man who C to it pours out
	13:15	species, and a man C to one like himself.
Jer	13:11	For as the waistcloth C to the loins of
Lk	10:11	of your town that C to our feet, we
Heb	12:1	weight, and sin which C so closely, and let

CLOAK (9)

Deut	22:12	four corners of your C with which you cover
	24:13	may sleep in his C and bless you; and
Jer	43:12	a shepherd cleans his C of vermin; and he
2Mac	12:35	Gorgias, and grasping his C was dragging him off
Mt	5:40	let him have your C as well;
Mk	15:17	him in a purple C, and plaiting a crown
	15:20	him of the purple C, and put his own
1Thes	2:5	you know, or a C for greed, as God
2Tim	4:13	you come, bring the C that I left with

CLOAKS

Is	3:22	robes, the mantles, the C, and the handbags;

CLODS (3)

Job	21:33	The C of the valley are sweet to him;
	38:38	a mass and the C cleave fast together?
Joel	1:16	shrivels under the C, the storehouses are desolate;

CLOGGING

Ex	14:25	host of the Egyptians, C their chariot wheels so

CLOPAS

Jn	19:25	Mary the wife of C, and Mary Magdalene.

CLOSE (46)

Gen	31:23	seven days and followed C after him into the
	46:4	and Joseph's hand shall C your eyes."
Ex	25:27	C to the frame the rings shall lie, as
	37:14	C to the frame were the rings, as holders
Lev	3:9	entire, taking it away C by the backbone, and
Judg	19:9	day draws to its C; lodge here and let
	20:34	know that disaster was C upon them.
	20:41	saw that disaster was C upon them.
Ruth	2:8	this one, but keep C to my maidens.
	2:21	me, 'You shall keep C by my servants, till
	2:23	So she kept C to the maidens of Boaz,
2Sam	1:6	and the horsemen were C upon him.
Neh	6:10	temple, and let us C the doors of the
Jud	13:7	She came C to his bed and took hold
Esth	16:7	from investigation of matters C at hand.
Job	19:14	My kinsfolk and my C friends have failed me;
Ps	17:10	They C their hearts to pity; with their mouths
	69:15	up, or the pit C its mouth over me.
	88:15	Afflicted and C to death from my youth up,
	88:17	all day long; they C in upon me together.
Prov	16:28	and a whisperer separates C friends.
Sir	11:25	luxury, and at the C of a man's life
	16:22	acquire knowledge, and pay C attention to my words.
	51:26	is to be found C by.
Is	13:22	palaces; its time is C at hand and its
Lam	3:56	my plea, 'Do not C thine ear to my
Dan	8:7	I saw him come C to the ram, and
Hab	3:5	pestilence, and plague followed C behind.
1Mac	9:16	they turned and followed C behind Judas and his
	12:50	and kept marching in C formation, ready for battle.
2Mac	4:42	robber himself they killed C by the treasury.
	7:27	But, leaning C to him, she spoke in their
	12:31	feast of weeks was C at hand.
	15:20	the enemy was already C at hand with their
Mt	13:39	the harvest is the C of the age, and
	13:40	it be at the C of the age.
	13:49	will be at the C of the age.
	24:3	coming and of the C of the age?"
	28:20	you always, to the C of the age."
Jn	13:23	Jesus loved, was lying C to the breast of
	13:25	So lying thus, C to the breast of Jesus,
	19:42	as the tomb was C at hand, they laid
	21:20	loved, who had lain C to his breast at
Acts	10:24	together his kinsmen and C friends.
	27:13	and sailed along Crete, C inshore.
Rom	7:21	do right, evil lies C at hand.

CLOSED (31)

Gen	2:21	of his ribs and C up its place with
	8:2	of the heavens were C, the rain from the
	20:18	For the LORD had C all the wombs of
Num	16:33	Sheol; and the earth C over them, and they

Josh 2:5 gate was to be C, at dark, the men
Judg 3:22 blade, and the fat C over the blade, for
3:23 into the vestibule, and C the doors of the
1Sam 1:5 because the LORD had C her womb.
1:6 because the LORD had C her womb.
1Kgs 11:27 built the Millo, and C up the breach of
32:30 This same Hezekiah C the upper outlet of the
Neh 4:7 were beginning to be C, they were very angry;
Jud 5:1 for war and had C the passes in the
13:1 quickly withdrew, and Bagoas C the tent from
Job 17:4 Since thou hast C their minds to understanding,
19:6 in the wrong, and C his net about me.
Sir 30:18 a mouth that is C are like offerings of
Is 29:10 deep sleep, and has C your eyes, the prophets,
32:3 see will not be C, and the ears of
45:1 gates may not be C:
Jer 6:10 Behold, their ears are C, they cannot listen; behold,
Lam 3:54 stones on me; water C over my head; 'I
Jon 2:5 holy temple?' The waters C in over me, the
2:6 the land whose bars C upon me for ever;
1Mac 10:75 men of the city C its gates, for Apollonius
12:48 the men of Ptolemais C the gates and seized
2Mac 1:15 the sacred precinct, they C the temple as soon
12:7 the city's gates were C, he withdrew, intending to
Mt 13:15 their eyes they have C, lest they should perceive
Lk 4:20 And he C the book, and gave it back
Acts 28:27 their eyes they have C; lest they should perceive

CLOSELY (6)

1Kgs 3:21 I looked at it C in the morning, behold,
Job 41:15 of shields, shut up C as with a seal.
Lk 1:3 having followed all things C for some time past,
Acts 11:6 Looking at it C I observed animals and beasts
23:20 to inquire somewhat more C about him.
Heb 12:1 sin which clings so C, and let us run

CLOSER (2)

Prov 18:24 a friend who sticks C than a brother.
Heb 2:1 we must pay the C attention to what we

CLOSES (3)

Prov 17:28 considered wise; when he C his lips, he is
21:13 He who C his ear to the cry of
1Jn 3:17 brother in need, yet C his heart against him,

CLOSET

Judg 3:24 relieving himself in the C of the cool chamber."

CLOSING (2)

1Sam 23:26 and his men were C in upon David and
Ps 77:4 hold my eyelids from C; I am so troubled

CLOTH (17)

Lev 19:19 you a garment of C made of two kinds
Num 4:6 spread over that a C all of blue, and
4:7 they shall spread a C of blue, and put
4:8 spread over them a C of scarlet, and cover
4:9 they shall take a C of blue, and cover
4:11 they shall spread a C of blue, and cover
4:12 put them in a C of blue, and cover
4:13 and spread a purple C over it;
1Sam 21:9 here wrapped in a C behind the ephod; if
Ezek 16:10 you also with embroidered C and shod you with
16:13 and silk, and embroidered C; you ate fine flour
1Mac 4:23 gold and silver, and C dyed blue and sea
Mt 9:16 a piece of unshrunk C on an old garment,
Mk 2:21 a piece of unshrunk C on an old garment;
14:51 nothing but a linen C about his body; and
14:52 he left the linen C and ran away naked.
Jn 11:44 with bandages, and his face wrapped with a C

CLOTHE (23)

Esth 4:4 she sent garments to C Mordecai, so that he
Job 10:11 Thou didst C me with skin and flesh, and
39:19 Do you C his neck with strength?
40:10 with majesty and dignity; C yourself with glory and
Ps 65:13 with joy, the meadows C themselves with flocks, the
132:16 Her priests I will C with salvation, and her
132:18 His enemies I will C with shame, but upon
Prov 23:21 poverty, and drowsiness will C a man with rags.
Is 22:21 Hilkiah, and I will C him with your robe,
50:3 I C the heavens with blackness, and make sackcloth
Bar 6:33 of their gods to C their wives and children.
Ezek 26:16 garments; they will C themselves with trembling;
31:15 be stopped; I will C Lebanon in gloom for
34:3 eat the fat, you C yourselves with the wool,
Hag 1:6 have your fill; you C yourselves, but no one
Zech 3:4 you, and I will C you with rich apparel."
1Mac 10:62 Jonathan's garments and to C him in purple, and
Mt 6:30 he not much more C you, O men of
25:38 thee, or naked and C thee?
25:43 and you did not C me, sick and in
Lk 12:28 much more will he C you, O men of
1Pet 5:5 C yourselves, all of you, with humility toward one
Rev 3:18 and white garments to C you and to keep

CLOTHED (70)

Gen 3:21 garments of skins, and C them.
Lev 8:7 with the girdle, and C him with the robe,
8:13 brought Aaron's sons, and C them with coats, and
1Sam 17:38 Then Saul C David with his armor; he put
17:38 on his head, and C him with a coat
2Sam 1:24 weep over Saul, who C you daintily in scarlet,
1Chr 15:27 David was C with a robe of fine linen,
21:16 David and the elders, C in sackcloth, fell upon
6:41 O LORD God, be C with salvation, and let
28:15 with the spoil they C all that were naked
28:15 naked among them; they C them, gave them sandals,
Esth 4:2 enter the king's gate C with sackcloth.
15:6 on his royal throne, C in the full array
Job 7:5 My flesh is C with worms and dirt; my
8:22 hate you will be C with shame, and the
29:14 on righteousness, and it C me; my justice was
37:22 golden splendor; God is C with terrible majesty.
Ps 35:26 Let them be C with shame and dishonor who
104:1 Thou art C with honor and majesty,
109:18 He C himself with cursing as his coat, may
109:29 May my accusers be C with dishonor; may they
132:9 Let thy priests be C with righteousness, and let
Prov 31:21 all her household are C in scarlet.
Sir 40:4 the one who is C in burlap;
45:8 He C him with superb perfection, and strengthened
50:11 his glorious robe and C himself with superb
Is 14:19 a loathed untimely birth, C with the slain, those
37:2 and the senior priests, C with sackcloth, to the
61:10 God; for he has C me with the garments
Ezek 9:2 them was a man C in linen, with a
9:3 called to the man C in linen, who had
9:11 And lo, the man C in linen, with the
10:2 said to the man C in linen, "Go in
10:6 he commanded the man C in linen, "Take fire
10:7 hands of the man C in linen, who took
16:10 I C you also with embroidered cloth and shod
23:6 lovers the Assyrians, warriors C in purple, governors
23:12 governors and commanders, warriors C in full armor,
38:4 horsemen, all of them C in full armor, a
Dan 5:7 its interpretation, shall be C with purple, and have
5:16 interpretation, you shall be C with purple, and have
5:29 commanded, and Daniel was C with purple, a chain
10:5 and behold, a man C in linen, whose loins
12:6 said to the man C in linen, who was
12:7 The man C in linen, who was above the
Nah 2:3 red, his soldiers are C in scarlet.
Zech 3:3 standing before the angel, C with filthy garments.
3:5 on his head and C him with garments; and
1Mac 1:28 house of Jacob was C with shame.
10:64 proclamation, and saw him C in purple, they all
14:43 that he should be C in purple and wear
14:44 permission, or to be C in purple or put
2Mac 11:8 appeared at their head, C in white and brandishing
Mt 11:8 To see a man C in soft raiment?
25:36 was naked and you C me, I was sick
Mk 1:6 Now John was C with camel's hair, and had
5:15 the demoniac sitting there, C and in his right
15:17 And they C him in a purple cloak, and
Lk 7:25 A man C in soft clothing?
8:35 the feet of Jesus, C and in his right
16:19 rich man, who was C in purple and fine
24:49 city, until you are C with power from on
2Cor 5:4 we would be further C, so that what is
Rev 1:13 a son of man, C with a long robe
7:9 and before the Lamb, C in white robes, with
7:13 saying, "Who are these, C in white robes, and
11:3 hundred and sixty days, C in sackcloth."
12:1 in heaven, a woman C with the sun, with
18:16 great city that was C in fine linen, in
19:8 granted her to be C with fine linen, bright

CLOTHES (94)

Gen 37:29 pit, he rent his C
41:14 himself and changed his C, he came in before
44:13 Then they rent their C, and every man loaded

Lev 10:6 do not rend your C, lest you die, and
11:25 carcass shall wash his C and be unclean until
11:28 carcass shall wash his C and be unclean until
11:40 carcass shall wash his C and be unclean until
11:40 carcass shall wash his C and be unclean until
13:6 he shall wash his C, and be clean.
13:34 he shall wash his C, and be clean.
13:45 disease shall wear torn C and let the hair
14:8 cleansed shall wash his C, and shave off all
14:9 he shall wash his C, and bathe his body
14:47 house shall wash his C; and he who eats
14:47 who eats in the house shall wash his C
15:5 bed shall wash his C, and bathe himself in
15:6 sat shall wash his C, and bathe himself in
15:7 discharge shall wash his C, and bathe himself in
15:8 he shall wash his C, and bathe himself in
15:10 thing shall wash his C, and bathe himself in
15:11 water shall wash his C, and bathe himself in
15:13 cleansing, and wash his C; and he shall bathe
15:21 bed shall wash his C, and bathe himself in
15:22 sits shall wash his C, and bathe himself in
15:27 and shall wash his C, and bathe himself in
16:26 Azazel shall wash his C and bathe his body
16:28 them shall wash his C and bathe his body
17:15 sojourner, shall wash his C, and bathe himself in
21:10 loose, nor rend his C;
Num 8:7 body, and wash their C and cleanse themselves.
8:21 sin, and washed their C; and Aaron offered them
14:6 the land, rent their C,
19:7 priest shall wash his C and bathe his body
19:8 heifer shall wash his C in water and bathe
19:10 heifer shall wash his C, and be unclean until
19:19 he shall wash his C and bathe himself in
19:21 impurity shall wash his C; and he who touches
31:24 You must wash your C on the seventh day,
Deut 29:5 in the wilderness; your C have not worn-out upon
Josh 7:6 Then Joshua rent his C, and fell to the
9:5 their feet, and worn-out C; and all their provisions
Judg 3:16 girded it on his right thigh under his C
11:35 her, he rent his C, and said, "Alas, my
Ruth 3:3 put on your best C and go down to
1Sam 4:12 same day, with his C rent and with earth
19:13 at its head, and covered it with the C
19:24 too stripped off his C, and he too prophesied
2Sam 1:2 Saul's camp, with his C rent and earth upon
1:11 took hold of his C, and rent them; and
3:31 with him, "Rend your C, and gird on sackcloth,
12:20 himself, and changed his C; and he went into
19:24 beard, nor washed his C, from the day the
1Kgs 1:1 they covered him with C, he could not get
21:27 words, he rent his C, and put sackcloth upon
2Kgs 2:12 hold of his own C and rent them in
5:7 letter, he rent his C and said, "Am I
5:8 Israel had rent his C, he sent to the
5:8 the king, saying, "Why have you rent your C
6:30 woman he rent his C –now he was passing
11:14 And Athaliah rent her C, and cried, "Treason!
18:37 to Hezekiah with their C rent, and told him
19:1 it, he rent his C, and covered himself with
22:11 the book of the law, he rent his C
22:19 you have rent your C and wept before me,
23:13 And Athaliah rent her C, and cried, "Treason!
34:19 the words of the law he rent his C
34:27 and have rent your C and wept before me,
Neh 4:23 us took off our C; each kept his weapon
9:21 they lacked nothing; their C did not wear out
Esth 4:1 done, Mordecai rent his C and put on sackcloth
Job 9:31 pit, and my own C will abhor me.
Prov 6:27 his bosom and his C not be burned?
Sir 11:4 boast about wearing fine C, nor exalt yourself in
Is 4:1 and wear our own C, only let us be
36:22 to Hezekiah with their C rent, and told him
37:1 it, he rent his C, and covered himself with
Jer 38:11 old rags and worn-out C, which he let down
38:12 "Put the rags and C between your armpits and
41:5 beards shaved and their C torn, and their bodies
Bar 6:31 priests sit with their C rent, their heads and
Ezek 16:39 strip you of your C and take your fair
23:26 strip you of your C and take away your
27:24 in choice garments, in C of blue and embroidered
1Mac 2:14 his sons rent their C, put on sackcloth, and
3:47 sprinkled ashes on their heads, and rent their C
4:39 Then they rent their C, and mourned with great
13:45 the wall with their C rent, and they cried
Mt 6:30 But if God so C the grass of the
27:31 and put his own C on him, and led
Mk 15:20 and put his own C on him.
Lk 8:27 he had worn no C, and he lived not
12:28 But if God so C the grass which is
24:12 he saw the linen C by themselves; and he
Jn 21:7 he put on his C, for he was stripped

CLOTHING (45)

Gen 28:20 bread to eat and C to wear,
Ex 3:22 and of gold, and C, and you shall put
12:35 and of gold, and C;
21:10 diminish her food, her C, or her marital rights.
22:9 ass, for sheep, for C, or for any kind
Deut 8:4 Your C did not wear out upon you, and
10:18 and loves the sojourner, giving him food and C
Josh 22:8 iron, and with much C; divide the spoil of
1Kgs 10:5 of his servants, their C, his cupbearers, and his
2Kgs 7:8 silver and gold and C, and went and hid
9:4 his servants, and their C, his cupbearers, and their
9:4 his cupbearers, and their C, and his burnt offerings
20:25 in great numbers, goods, C, and precious things,
Tob 1:17 the hungry and my C to the naked; and
4:16 hungry, and of your C to the naked.
Jud 10:7 was altered and her C changed, they greatly admired
Job 22:6 for nothing, and stripped the naked of their C
24:7 all night naked, without C, and have no covering
24:10 go about naked, without C; hungry, they carry the
27:16 dust, and pile up C like clay;
31:19 perish for lack of C, or a poor man
Ps 69:11 I made sackcloth my C, I became a byword
Prov 27:26 lambs will provide your C, and the goats the
31:22 makes herself coverings; her C is fine linen and
31:25 and dignity are her C, and she laughs at
Sir 29:21 water and bread and C and a house to
39:26 the blood of the grape, and oil and C
Is 23:18 abundant food and fine C for those who dwell
59:6 will not serve as C; men will not cover
59:17 garments of vengeance for C, and wrapped himself
Jer 10:9 of the goldsmith; their C is violet and purple;
Bar 6:33 take some of the C of their gods to
1Mac 11:24 silver and gold and C and numerous other gifts.
2Mac 3:33 dressed in the same C, and they stood and
Mt 6:25 more than food, and the body more than C
6:28 And why are you anxious about C
7:15 to you in sheep's C but inwardly are ravenous
Lk 7:25 A man clothed in soft C
12:23 more than food, and the body more than C
Jn 19:24 them, and for my C they cast lots."
1Tim 6:8 we have food and C, with these we shall
Jas 2:2 rings and in fine C comes into your assembly,
2:2 poor man in shabby C also comes in,
2:3 who wears the fine C and say, "Have a
1Pet 3:3 and wearing of fine C,

CLOTHS (7)

Wis 7:4 I was nursed with care in swaddling C
Lk 2:7 wrapped him in swaddling C, and laid him in
2:12 babe wrapped in swaddling C and lying in a
Jn 19:40 bound it in linen C with the spices, as
20:5 he saw the linen C lying there, but he
20:6 he saw the linen C lying,
20:7 lying with the linen C but rolled up in

CLOUD (101)

Gen 9:13 my bow in the C, and it shall be
Ex 13:21 in a pillar of C to lead them along
13:22 night; the pillar of C by day and the
14:19 and the pillar of C moved from before them
14:20 And there was the C and the darkness; and
14:24 of fire and of C looked down upon the
16:10 the glory of the LORD appeared in the C
19:9 you in a thick C, that the people may
19:16 lightnings, and a thick C upon the mountain, and
24:15 the mountain, and the C covered the mountain.
24:16 Mount Sinai, and the C covered it six days;
24:16 to Moses out of the midst of the C
24:18 And Moses entered the C, and went up on
33:9 tent, the pillar of C would descend and stand
33:10 saw the pillar of C standing at the door
34:5 LORD descended in the C and stood with him
Lev 16:2 will appear in the C upon the mercy seat.
16:13 the LORD, that the C of the incense may
Num 9:15 was set up, the C covered the tabernacle, the
9:16 it was continually; the C covered it by day,
9:17 And whenever the C was taken up from over
9:17 the place where the C settled down, there the
9:18 as long as the C rested over the tabernacle,

C

9:19 Even when the C continued over the tabernacle
9:20 Sometimes the C was a few days over the
9:21 And sometimes the C remained from evening until
9:21 morning; and when the C was taken up in
9:21 a night, when the C was taken up they
9:22 time, that the C continued over the tabernacle,
10:11 of the month, the C was taken up from
10:12 of Sinai; and the C settled down in the
10:34 And the C of the LORD was over them
11:25 came down in the C and spoke to him,
12:5 in a pillar of C, and stood at the
12:10 departed; and when the C removed from over the
14:14 to face, and thy C stands over them and
14:14 in a pillar of C by day and in
16:42 meeting; and behold, the C covered it, and the
Deut 1:33 go, and in the C by day.
4:11 heaven, wrapped in darkness, C, and gloom.
5:22 of the fire, the C, and the thick darkness,
31:15 in a pillar of C; and the pillar of
31:15 and the pillar of C stood by the door
Judg 20:38 they made a great C of smoke rise up
1Kgs 8:10 the holy place, a C filled the house of
8:11 minister because of the C; for the glory of
18:44 said, "Behold, a little C like a man's hand
5:13 was filled with a C,
5:14 minister because of the C; for the glory of
Neh 9:12 By a pillar of C thou didst lead them
9:19 wilderness; the pillar of C which led them in
Job 7:9 As the C fades and vanishes, so he who
26:8 thick clouds, and the C is not rent under
26:9 of the moon, and spreads over it his C
30:15 and my prosperity has passed away like a C
37:11 He loads the thick C with moisture; the clouds
37:15 the lightning of his C to shine?
Ps 78:14 led them with a C, and all the night
99:7 in the pillar of C; they kept his testimonies,
105:39 He spread a C for a covering, and fire
Wis 2:4 the traces of a C, and be scattered like
19:7 The C was seen overshadowing the camp, and dry
Sir 24:4 and my throne was in a pillar of C
Is 4:5 over her assemblies a C by day, and smoke
18:4 in sunshine, like a C of dew in the
19:1 riding on a swift C and comes to Egypt;
25:5 the shade of a C, so the song of
44:22 your transgressions like a C, and your sins like
60:8 that fly like a C, and like doves to
Lam 2:1 has set the daughter of Zion under a C
3:44 wrapped thyself with a C so that no prayer
Ezek 1:4 north, and a great C, with brightness round about
1:28 that is in the C on the day of
8:11 the smoke of the C of incense went up.
10:3 went in; and a C filled the inner court.
10:4 was filled with the C, and the court was
30:18 be covered by a C, and her daughters shall
32:7 the sun with a C, and the moon shall
38:9 will be like a C covering the land you
38:16 people Israel, like a C covering the land.
Hos 6:4 is like a morning C, like the dew that
2Mac 2:8 the Lord and the C will appear, as they
Mt 17:5 when lo, a bright C overshadowed them, and a
17:5 a voice from the C said, "This is my
Mk 9:7 And a C overshadowed them, and a voice came
9:7 came out of the C, "This is my beloved
Lk 9:34 he said this, a C came and overshadowed them;
9:34 and they were afraid as they entered the C
9:35 came out of the C, saying, "This is my
12:54 "When you see a C rising in the west,
21:27 man coming in a C with power and great
Acts 1:9 lifted up, and a C took him out of
1Cor 10:1 were all under the C, and all passed through
10:2 into Moses in the C and in the sea,
Heb 12:1 by so great a C of witnesses, let us
Rev 10:1 heaven, wrapped in a C, with a rainbow over
11:12 foes they went up to heaven in a C
14:14 and lo, a white C, and seated on the
14:14 and seated on the C one like a son
14:15 who sat upon the C, "Put in your sickle,
14:16 who sat upon the C swung his sickle on

CLOUDBURST

Is 30:30 devouring fire, with a C and tempest and hailstones.

CLOUDED

2Mac 1:22 sun, which had been C over, shone out, a

CLOUDLESS

2Sam 23:4 shining forth upon a C morning, like rain that

CLOUDS (70)

Gen 9:14 When I bring C over the earth and the
9:14 is seen in the C,
9:16 bow is in the C, I will look upon
Judg 5:4 heavens dropped, yea, the C dropped water.
2Sam 22:12 him his canopy, thick C, a gathering of water.
1Kgs 18:45 heavens grew black with C and wind, and there
Job 3:5 Let C dwell upon it; let the blackness of
20:6 head reach to the C,
22:14 Thick C enwrap him, so that he does not
26:8 waters in his thick C, and the cloud is
35:5 see; and behold the C, which are higher than
36:29 the spreading of the C, the thunderings of his
37:11 cloud with moisture; the C scatter his lightning.
37:16 the balancings of the C, the wondrous works of
38:9 womb; when I made C its garment, and thick
38:34 your voice to the C, that a flood of
38:36 put wisdom in the C, or given understanding to
38:37 Who can number the C by wisdom?
Ps 18:11 him, his canopy thick C dark with water.
18:12 there broke through his C hailstones and coals of
36:5 extends to the heavens, thy faithfulness to the C
57:10 great to the heavens, thy faithfulness to the C
68:4 who rides upon the C; his name is the
77:17 The C poured out water; the skies gave forth
97:2 C and thick darkness are round about him;
104:3 waters, who makest the C thy chariot, who ridest
108:4 above the heavens, thy faithfulness reaches to the C
135:7 is who makes the C rise at the end
147:8 covers the heavens with C, he prepares rain for
Prov 3:20 broke forth, and the C drop down the dew.
16:15 favor is like the C that bring the spring
25:14 Like C and wind without rain is a man
Eccl 11:3 If the C are full of rain, they empty
11:4 he who regards the C will not reap.
12:2 are darkened and the C return after the rain;
Wis 5:21 a well-drawn bow of C,
Sir 13:22 they extol to the C what he says.
35:16 accepted, and his prayer will reach to the C
35:17 the humble pierces the C, and he will not
35:20 he afflicts them as C of rain in the
43:14 are opened, and the C fly forth like birds.
43:15 majesty he amasses the C, and the hailstones are
50:6 morning star among the C, like the moon when
50:7 rainbow gleaming in glorious C;
50:10 fruit, and like a cypress towering in the C
Is 5:6 will also command the C that they rain no
5:30 distress; and the light is darkened by its C
14:14 the heights of the C, I will make myself
Jer 4:13 he comes up like C, his chariots like the
Bar 3:29 taken her, and brought her down from the C
6:62 When God commands the C to go over the
Ezek 30:3 be a day of C, a time of doom
31:3 and of great height, its top among the C
31:10 its top among the C, and its heart was
31:14 their tops among the C, and that no trees
34:12 on a day of C and thick darkness.
Dan 3:74 the Lord, lightnings and C, sing praise to him
7:13 and behold, with the C of heaven there came
Joel 2:2 gloom, a day of C and thick darkness!
Nah 1:3 and storm, and the C are the dust of
3:17 grasshoppers, your scribes like C of locusts settling
Zeph 1:15 gloom, a day of C and thick darkness,
Zech 10:1 who makes the storm C, who gives men showers
Mt 24:30 man coming on the C of heaven with power
26:64 and coming on the C of heaven."
Mk 13:26 of man coming in C with great power and
14:62 and coming with the C of heaven."
1Thes 4:17 with them in the C to meet the Lord
Jude 1:12 themselves; waterless C, carried along by winds;
Rev 1:7 is coming with the C, and every eye will

CLOVEN (2)

Deut 14:6 and has the hoof C in two, and chews
14:7 or have the hoof C you shall not eat

CLOVEN-FOOTED (3)

Lev 11:3 the hoof and is C and chews the cud,
11:7 the hoof and is C but does not chew
11:26 hoof but is not C or does not chew

CLUB (2)

Prov 25:18 is like a war C, or a sword, or

Dan 14:26 I will slay the dragon without sword or C

CLUBS (6)

Job 41:29 C are counted as stubble; he laughs at the
Mt 26:47 crowd with swords and C, from the chief priests
26:55 robber, with swords and C to capture me?
Mk 14:43 crowd with swords and C, from the chief priests
14:48 robber, with swords and C to capture me?
Lk 22:50 out as against a robber, with swords and C

CLUE

Sir 37:17 As a C to changes of heart

CLUNG (6)

Ruth 1:14 her mother-in-law, but Ruth C to her.
1Kgs 11:2 after their gods"; Solomon C to these in love.
2Kgs 3:3 Nevertheless he C to the sin of Jeroboam the
Bar 1:20 this day there have C to us the calamities
3:4 so that calamities have C to us.
Acts 3:11 While he C to Peter and John, all the

CLUSTER (5)

Num 13:23 branch with a single C of grapes, and they
13:24 Eshcol, because of the C which the men of
Song 1:14 is to me a C of henna blossoms in
Is 65:8 is found in the C, and they say, 'Do
Mic 7:1 gleaned: there is no C to eat, no first-ripe

CLUSTERS (8)

Gen 40:10 shot forth, and the C ripened into grapes.
Deut 32:32 grapes of poison, their C are bitter;
1Sam 25:18 grain, and a hundred C of raisins, and two
30:12 of figs and two C of raisins.
1Chr 12:40 meal, cakes of figs, C of raisins, and wine
Song 7:7 palm tree, and your breasts are like its C
7:8 your breasts be like C of the vine, and
Rev 14:18 sickle, and gather the C of the vine of

CNIDUS (2)

1Mac 15:23 Aradus and Gortyna and C and Cyprus and Cyrene.
Acts 27:7 arrived with difficulty off C, and as the wind

COAL (3)

2Sam 14:7 they would quench my C which is left, and
Is 6:6 his hand a burning C which he had taken
47:14 No C for warming oneself is this, no fire

COALS (21)

Lev 16:12 a censer full of C of fire from the
2Sam 22:9 from his mouth; glowing C flamed forth from him.
22:13 the brightness before him C of fire flamed forth.
Job 41:21 His breath kindles C, and a flame comes forth
Ps 11:6 wicked he will rain C of fire and brimstone;
18:8 from his mouth; glowing C flamed forth from him.
18:12 his clouds hailstones and C of fire.
18:13 his voice, hailstones and C of fire.
120:4 sharp arrows, with glowing C of the broom tree!
140:10 Let burning C fall upon them!
Prov 6:28 one walk upon hot C and his feet not
25:22 for you will heap C of fire on his
Sir 8:10 Do not kindle the C of a sinner, lest
11:30 fire come many burning C, and a sinner lies
Is 44:12 works it over the C; he shapes it with
44:19 baked bread on its C, I roasted flesh and
54:16 blows the fire of C, and produces a weapon
Ezek 1:13 that looked like burning C of fire, like torches
10:2 hands with burning C from between the cherubim,
24:11 it empty upon the C, that it may become
Rom 12:20 you will heap burning C upon his head."

COARSE (4)

Num 15:20 the first of your C meal you shall present
15:21 the first of your C meal you shall give
Neh 10:37 the first of our C meal, and our contributions,
Ezek 44:30 the first of your C meal, that a blessing

COAST (6)

Num 34:6 Great Sea and its C; this shall be your
Josh 9:1 lowland all along the C of the Great Sea
Judg 5:17 sat still at the C of the sea, settling
Is 23:2 O inhabitants of the C, O merchants of Sidon;
23:6 over to Tarshish, wail, O inhabitants of the C
Acts 27:2 the ports along the C of Asia, we put

COAST-LINE (2)

Josh 15:12 west boundary was the Great Sea with its C
15:47 of Egypt, and the Great Sea with its C

COASTAL (2)

1Mac 11:8 gained control of the C cities as far as
15:38 Cendebeus commander-in-chief of the C country, and

COASTING

Acts 27:8 C along it with difficulty, we came to a

COASTLAND (6)

Gen 10:5 From these the C peoples spread.
Jud 5:2 the governors of the C,
7:8 the commanders of the C came to him and
Is 20:6 the inhabitants of this C will say in that
Jer 25:22 the kings of the C across the sea;
47:4 the remnant of the C of Caphtor.

COASTLANDS (21)

Esth 10:1 land and on the C of the sea.
Ps 97:1 rejoice; let the many C be glad!
Is 11:11 Hamath, and from the C of the sea.
24:15 the LORD; in the C of the sea, to
41:1 me in silence, O C; let the peoples renew
41:5 The C have seen and are afraid, the ends
42:4 the earth; and the C wait for his law.
42:10 that fills it, the C and their inhabitants.
42:12 the LORD, and declare his praise in the C
49:1 Listen to me, O C, and hearken, you peoples
51:5 rule the peoples; the C wait for me, and
59:18 his enemies; to the C he will render requital.
60:9 For the C shall wait for me, the ships
66:19 and Javan, to the C afar off, that have
Jer 31:10 declare it in the C afar off; say, 'He
Ezek 26:15 Tyre: Will not the C shake at the sound
27:3 the peoples on many C, thus says the Lord
27:15 traded with you; many C were your own special
27:35 the inhabitants of the C are appalled at you;
39:6 dwell securely in the C; and they shall know
Dan 11:18 his face to the C, and shall take many

COASTS (4)

Jud 1:12 as far as the C of the two seas.
Jer 2:10 For cross to the C of Cyprus and see,
Ezek 27:6 of pines from the C of Cyprus, inlaid with
27:7 and purple from the C of Elishah was your

COAT (15)

Ex 28:4 ephod, a robe, a C of checker work, a
28:39 you shall weave the C in checker work of
29:5 put on Aaron the C and the robe of
Lev 8:7 put on him the C, and girded him with
16:4 on the holy linen C, and shall have the
1Sam 17:5 was armed with a C of mail, and the
17:5 the weight of the C was five thousand shekels
17:38 clothed him with a C of mail.
2Sam 15:32 meet him with his C rent and earth upon
Job 41:13 can penetrate his double C of mail?
Ps 109:18 with cursing as his C, may it soak into
Wis 13:14 animal, giving it a C of red paint and
Jer 51:3 stand up in his C of mail.
Mt 5:40 you and take your C, let him have your
Lk 6:29 who takes away your C do not withhold even

COATS (10)

Ex 28:40 sons you shall make C and girdles and caps;
29:8 his sons, and put C on them,
39:27 They also made the C, woven of fine linen,
Lev 8:13 and clothed them with C, and girded them with
10:5 carried them in their C out of the camp,
26:14 army shields, spears, helmets, C of mail, bows, and
Neh 4:16 spears, shields, bows, and C of mail; and the
Jer 46:4 spears, put on your C of mail!
1Mac 6:35 thousand men armed with C of mail, and with
Lk 3:11 "He who has two C, let him share with

COCK (12)

Prov 30:31 before any; the strutting C, the he-goat, and a
Mt 26:34 very night, before the C crows, you will deny
26:74 And immediately the C crowed.
26:75 of Jesus, "Before the C crows, you will deny
Mk 14:30 very night, before the C crows twice, you will
14:72 And immediately the C crowed a second time.
14:72 to him, "Before the C crows twice, you will
Lk 22:34 tell you, Peter, the C will not crow this
22:58 was still speaking, the C crowed.
22:59 to him, "Before the C crows today, you will

Jn 13:38 say to you, the C will not crow, till
18:27 and at once the C crowed.

COCKCROW
Mk 13:35 at midnight, or at C, or in the morning–

CODE (4)
Rom 2:27 who have the written C and circumcision but break
7:6 under the old written C but in the new
2Cor 3:6 not in a written C but in the Spirit;
3:6 Spirit; for the written C kills, but the Spirit

COELESYRIA (6)
1Mac 10:69 Apollonius the governor of C, and he assembled a
2Mac 3:5 time was governor of C and Phoenicia.
3:8 of the cities of C and Phoenicia, but in
4:4 Menestheus and governor of C and Phoenicia, was
8:8 Ptolemy, the governor of C and Phoenicia, for aid
10:11 be chief governor of C and Phoenicia.

COFFERS
1Mac 3:28 And he opened his C and gave a year's

COFFIN
Gen 50:26 was put in a C in Egypt.

COHORT (3)
Acts 10:1 known as the Italian C,
21:31 the tribune of the C that all Jerusalem was
27:1 centurion of the Augustan C, named Julius.

COIN (5)
Mt 22:19 And they brought him a C
Mk 12:15 Bring me a C, and let me look at
Lk 15:8 if she loses one C, does not light a
15:9 I have found the C which I had lost.'
20:24 craftiness, and said to them, "Show me a C

COINAGE
1Mac 15:6 to mint your own C as money for your

COINS (4)
Mk 12:42 put in two copper C, which make a penny.
Lk 15:8 woman, having ten silver C, if she loses one
21:2 saw a poor widow put in two copper C
Jn 2:15 he poured out the C of the money-changers and

COLD (22)
Gen 8:22 remains, seedtime and harvest, C and heat, summer
31:40 consumed me, and the C by night, and my
Job 24:7 without clothing, and have no covering in the C
37:9 the whirlwind, and C from the scattering winds.
Ps 147:17 ice like morsels; who can stand before his C
Prov 25:13 Like the C of snow in the time of
25:20 a garment on a C day, and like vinegar
25:25 Like C water to a thirsty soul, so is
Sir 43:20 The C north wind blows, and ice freezes over
Jer 18:14 waters run dry, the C flowing streams?
Dan 3:68 Bless the Lord, winter C and summer heat, sing
3:72 the Lord, ice and C, sing praise to him
Nah 3:17 in a day of C —when the sun rises,
Zech 14:6 there shall be neither C nor frost.
Mt 10:42 even a cup of C water because he is
24:12 is multiplied, most men's love will grow C
Jn 18:18 fire, because it was C, and they were standing
Acts 28:2 because it had begun to rain and was C
2Cor 11:27 often without food, in C and exposure.
Rev 3:15 works: you are neither C nor hot.
3:15 Would that you were C or hot!
3:16 are lukewarm, and neither C nor hot, I will

COLHOZEH (2)
Neh 3:15 Shallum the son of C, ruler of the district
11:5 of Baruch, son of C, son of Hazaiah, son

COLIC
Sir 31:20 and of nausea and C are with the glutton.

COLLAPSE (2)
Ps 20:8 They will C and fall; but we shall rise
Is 30:13 out, and about to C, whose crash comes suddenly,

COLLAPSED
Esth 15:7 pale and faint, and C upon the head of

COLLAR (6)
Job 30:18 me about like the C of my tunic.
Ps 105:18 was put in a C of iron;
133:2 running down on the C of his robes!
Sir 6:24 into her fetters, and your neck into her C
6:29 strong protection, and her C a glorious robe.
Jer 29:26 prophesies, to put him in the stocks and C

COLLARS
Judg 8:26 Midian, and besides the C that were about the

COLLECT (5)
Neh 10:37 is the Levites who C the tithes in all
Nah 2:1 road; gird your loins; C all your strength.
1Mac 3:31 go to Persia and C the revenues from those
10:30 I will not C them from the land of
Lk 3:13 he said to them, C no more than is

COLLECTED (16)
Judg 11:3 Tob; and worthless fellows C round Jephthah, and
2Kgs 22:4 of the threshold have C from the people;
24:11 day after day, and C money in abundance.
34:9 of the threshold, had C from Manasseh and Ephraim
Jud 2:17 He C a vast number of camels and asses
Eccl 12:11 firmly fixed are the C sayings which are given
Is 22:9 were many, and you C the waters of the
Bar 1:6 the Lord; and they C money, each giving what
Zech 14:14 round about shall be C, gold, silver, and garments
1Mac 13:39 other tax has been C in Jerusalem shall be
13:39 in Jerusalem shall be C no longer.
2Mac 2:13 founded a library and C the books about the
2:14 same way Judas also C all the books that
8:27 And when they had C the arms of the
10:24 force of mercenaries and C the cavalry from Asia
Lk 19:23 coming I should have C it with interest?'

COLLECTING (3)
1Mac 1:35 arms and food, and C the spoils of Jerusalem
10:30 levies, and instead of C the third of the
2Mac 8:31 C the arms of the enemy, they stored them

COLLECTION (3)
Is 57:13 cry out, let your C of idols deliver you!
2Mac 4:28 requesting payment, for the C of the revenue was
12:43 also took up a C, man by man, to

COLLECTOR (8)
1Mac 1:29 of Judah a chief C of tribute, and he
Mt 10:3 and Matthew the tax C; James the son of
18:16 to you as a Gentile and a tax C
Lk 5:27 and saw a tax C, named Levi, sitting at
18:10 one a Pharisee and the other a tax C
18:11 unjust, adulterers, or even like this tax C
18:13 get.' But the tax C, standing far-off, would not
19:2 was a chief tax C, and rich.

COLLECTORS (16)
Mt 5:46 not even the tax C do the same?
9:10 house, behold, many tax C and sinners came and
9:11 teacher eat with tax C and sinners?"
11:19 a friend of tax C and sinners!' Yet wisdom
17:23 came to Caperna-um, the C of the half-shekel tax
21:31 to you, the tax C and the harlots go
21:32 him, but the tax C and the harlots believed
Mk 2:15 his house, many tax C and sinners were sitting
2:16 with sinners and tax C, said to his disciples,
2:16 he eat with tax C and sinners?"
Lk 3:12 Tax C also came to be baptized, and said
5:29 large company of tax C and others sitting at
5:30 and drink with tax C and sinners?"
7:29 people and the tax C justified God, having been
7:34 a friend of tax C and sinners!'
15:1 Now the tax C and sinners were all drawing

COLLECTS
Hab 2:5 himself all nations, and C as his own all

COLONNADE (2)
Sir 22:15 the stucco decoration on the wall of a C
2Mac 4:46 king aside into a C as if for refreshment,

COLONY (2)
Wis 12:7 might receive a worthy C of the servants of
Acts 16:12 of the district of Macedonia, and a Roman C

COLOR (7)
Lev 13:55 spot has not changed C, though the disease has
Dan 5:6 Then the king's C changed, and his thoughts alarmed
5:9 greatly alarmed, and his C changed; and his lords
5:10 alarm you or your C change.
7:28 alarmed me, and my C changed; but I kept
2Mac 3:16 the change in his C disclosed the anguish of
Rev 9:17 riders wore breastplates the C of fire and of

COLORED (3)
1Chr 29:2 stones for setting, antimony, C stones, all sorts of
Prov 7:16 couch with coverings, C spreads of Egyptian linen;
Ezek 27:24 and in carpets of C stuff, bound with cords

COLORING
Wis 13:14 of red paint and C its surface red and

COLORS (2)
Wis 15:4 figure stained with varied C,
Ezek 17:3 in plumage of many C, came to Lebanon and

COLOSSAE
Col 1:2 brethren in Christ at C: Grace to you and

COLT (15)
Gen 49:11 vine and his ass's C to the choice vine,
Job 11:12 when a wild ass's C is born a man.
Zech 9:9 an ass, on a C the foal of an
Mt 21:2 ass tied, and a C with her; untie them
21:5 ass, and on a C, the foal of an
21:7 the ass and the C, and put their garments
Mk 11:2 you will find a C tied, on which no
11:4 away, and found a C tied at the door
11:5 to them, "What are you doing, untying the C
11:7 And they brought the C to Jesus, and threw
Lk 19:30 you will find a C tied, on which no
19:33 they were untying the C, its owners said to
19:33 said to them, "Why are you untying the C
19:35 their garments on the C they set Jesus upon
Jn 12:15 your king is coming, sitting on an ass's C

COLTS
Gen 32:15 milch camels and their C, forty cows and ten

COLUMN (3)
Judg 20:40 the city in a C of smoke, the Benjaminites
Song 3:6 the wilderness, like a C of smoke, perfumed with
Is 9:18 roll upward in a C of smoke.

COLUMNS (5)
Song 5:15 His legs are alabaster C, set upon bases of
Jer 36:23 read three or four C, the king would cut
Joel 2:30 blood and fire and C of smoke.
1Mac 13:29 erecting about them great C, and upon the columns
13:29 columns, and upon the C he put suits of

COMBAT
32:6 And he set C commanders over the people, and

COMBED (2)
Jud 10:3 with precious ointment, and C her hair and put
Is 19:9 The workers in C flax will be in despair,

COMBINED
Jud 1:16 he and all his C forces, a vast body

COME (1,692)
Gen 6:18 you; and you shall C into the ark, you,
6:20 of every sort shall C in to you, to
11:3 said to one another, C, let us make bricks,
11:4 Then they said, C, let us build ourselves a
11:7 C, let us go down, and there confuse their
12:5 When they had C to the land of Canaan,
15:14 afterward they shall C out with great possessions.
15:16 And they shall C back here in the fourth
16:8 Sarai, where have you C from and where are
17:6 you, and kings shall C forth from you.
17:16 kings of peoples shall C from her."
18:5 on—since you have C to your servant." So
18:21 the outcry which has C to me; and if
19:8 men, for they have C under the shelter of
19:31 man on earth to C in to us after
19:32 C, let us make our father drink wine, and
20:13 place to which we C, say of me, He
22:5 yonder and worship, and C again to you."
24:31 He said, C in, O blessed of the LORD;
24:41 my oath, when you C to my kindred; and
24:62 Now Isaac had C from Beer-lahai-roi, and was
26:27 them, "Why have you C to me, seeing that
27:21 Isaac said to Jacob, C near, that I may
27:26 Isaac said to him, C near and kiss me,
28:21 wear, so that I C again to my father's
29:4 brothers, where do you C from?" They said, "We
30:16 and said, "You must C in to me; for
30:33 me later, when you C to look into my
31:44 C now, let us make a covenant, you and
32:11 fear him, lest he C and slay us all,
33:14 the children, until I C to my lord in
35:11 company of nations shall C from you, and kings
37:10 and your brothers indeed C to bow ourselves to
37:13 C, I will send you to them." And he
37:20 C now, let us kill him and throw him
37:27 C, let us sell him to the Ishmaelites, and
38:16 road side, and said, C, let me come in
38:16 said, "Come, let me C in to you," for
38:16 me, that you may C in to me?"
41:29 There will C seven years of great plenty throughout
41:54 of famine began to C, as Joseph had said.
42:7 "Where do you C from?" he said.
42:9 are spies, you have C to see the weakness
42:10 lord, but to buy food have your servants C
42:12 land that you have C to see."
42:21 therefore is this distress C upon us."
42:36 Benjamin; all this has C upon me."
44:30 Now therefore, when I C to your servant my
44:34 the evil that would C upon my father."
45:4 said to his brothers, C near to me, I
45:9 lord of all Egypt; C down to me, do
45:11 years of famine to C; lest you and your
45:11 all that you have, C to poverty.'
45:16 heard in Pharaoh's house, "Joseph's brothers have C
45:18 and your households, and C to me, and I
45:19 for your wives, and bring your father, and C
46:31 land of Canaan, have C to me;
47:1 that they possess, have C from the land of
47:4 to Pharaoh, "We have C to sojourn in the
47:5 and your brothers have C to you.
48:2 "Your son Joseph has C to you"; then Israel
49:1 you what shall befall you in days to C
49:6 O my soul, C not into their council; O
Ex 1:9 C, let us deal shrewdly with them, lest they
2:18 it that you have C so soon today?"
3:5 he said, "Do not C near; put off your
3:8 sufferings, and I have C down to deliver them
3:9 people of Israel has C to me, and I
3:10 C, I will send you to Pharaoh that you
3:13 to God, "If I C to the people of
8:3 with frogs which shall C up into your house,
8:4 bowls; the frogs shall C up on you and
8:5 and cause frogs to C upon the land of
9:19 for the hail shall C down upon every man
10:12 locusts, that they may C upon the land of
11:8 these your servants shall C down to me, and
12:25 And when you C to the land which the
12:48 circumcised, then he may C near and keep it;
13:14 when in time to C your son asks you,
14:26 that the water may C back upon the Egyptians,
16:9 the people of Israel, C near before the LORD,
17:6 rock, and water shall C out of it, that
18:8 the hardship that had C upon them in the
18:15 father-in-law, "Because the people C to me to
18:16 have a dispute, they C to me and I
19:11 day the LORD will C down upon Mount Sinai
19:13 long blast, they shall C up to the mountain."
19:22 let the priests who C near to the LORD
19:23 LORD, "The people cannot C up to Mount Sinai;
19:24 him, "Go down, and C up bringing Aaron with
19:24 people break through to C up to the LORD,
20:20 fear; for God has C to prove you, and
20:24 be remembered I will C to you and bless
22:8 of the house shall C near to God, to
22:9 of both parties shall C before God; he whom
23:27 against whom you shall C, and I will make
24:1 he said to Moses, C up to the LORD,
24:2 Moses alone shall C near to the LORD; but
24:2 the others shall not C near, and the people
24:2 the people shall not C up with him."
24:12 LORD said to Moses, C up to me on
24:14 for us, until we C to you again; and,
28:28 the breastpiece shall not C loose from the ephod.
28:43 meeting, or when they C near the altar to
30:20 meeting, or when they C near the altar to

32:1 that Moses delayed to C down from the mountain,
32:26 C to me." And all the sons of Levi
34:2 in the morning, and C up in the morning
34:3 No man shall C up with you, and let
34:30 they were afraid to C near him.
35:10 able man among you C and make all that
36:2 stirred him up to C to do the work;
39:21 the breastpiece should not C loose from the ephod;
Lev 5:1 he has seen or C to know the matter,
10:6 die, and lest wrath C upon all the congregation;
11:34 upon which water may C, shall be unclean; and
12:4 any hallowed thing, nor C into the sanctuary, until
13:16 white, then he shall C to the priest,
14:8 after that he shall C into the camp, but
14:34 and Aaron, "When you C into the land of
14:35 owns the house shall C and tell the priest,
14:39 And the priest shall C again on the seventh
15:14 two young pigeons, and C before the LORD to
16:2 your brother not to C at all times into
16:3 But thus shall Aaron C into the holy place:
16:23 "Then Aaron shall C into the tent of meeting,
16:24 on his garments, and C forth, and offer his
16:26 and afterward he may C into the camp.
16:28 and afterward he may C into the camp.
19:19 seed; nor shall there C upon you a garment
19:23 "When you C into the land and plant all
21:21 has a blemish shall C near to offer the
21:21 blemish, he shall not C near to offer the
21:23 but he shall not C near the veil or
23:10 of Israel, When you C into the land which
25:2 of Israel, When you C into the land which
25:25 next of kin shall C and redeem what his
Num 1:1 year after they had C out of the land
4:15 sons of Kohath shall C to carry these, but
4:19 not die when they C near to the most
6:5 separation no razor shall C upon his head; until
8:19 people of Israel should C near the sanctuary."
9:1 year after they had C out of the land
10:29 give it to you'; C with us, and we
11:17 And I will C down and talk with you
11:20 saying, 'Why did we C forth out of Egypt?'"
11:23 whether my word will C true for you or
12:4 to Aaron and Miriam, C out, you three, to
13:33 sons of Anak, who C from the Nephilim); and
14:30 me, not one shall C into the land where
14:35 this wilderness they shall C to a full end,
15:2 of Israel, When you C into the land you
15:18 of Israel, When you C into the land to
16:5 will cause him to C near to him; him
16:5 he will cause to C near to him.
16:12 said, "We will not C up.
16:14 We will not C up."
18:3 tent; but shall not C near to the vessels
18:4 no one else shall C near you.
18:22 of Israel shall not C near the tent of
19:2 blemish, and upon which a yoke has never C
19:7 and afterwards he shall C into the camp; and
20:5 have you made us C up out of Egypt,
20:18 pass through, lest I C out with the sword
21:27 the ballad singers say, C to Heshbon, let it
22:5 "Behold, a people has C out of Egypt; they
22:6 C now, curse this people for me, since they
22:11 'Behold, a people has C out of Egypt, and
22:11 of the earth; now C, curse them for me;
22:14 said, "Balaam refuses to C with us."
22:17 me I will do; C, curse this people for
22:20 "If the men have C to call you, rise,
22:32 Behold, I have C forth to withstand you, because
22:36 heard that Balaam had C, he went out to
22:37 Why did you not C to me?
22:38 Balak, "Lo, I have C to you!
23:3 perhaps the LORD will C to meet me; and
23:7 from the eastern mountains: C, curse Jacob for me,
23:7 Jacob for me, and C, denounce Israel!'
23:13 Balak said to him, C with me to another
23:27 Balak said to Balaam, C now, I will take
24:14 going to my people; C, I will let you
24:17 nigh: a star shall C forth out of Jacob,
24:20 the end he shall C to destruction."
24:24 But ships shall C from Kittim and shall afflict
24:24 and he also shall C to destruction."
27:17 out before them and C in before them, who
27:21 his word they shall C in, both he and
31:14 of hundreds, who had C from service in the
31:24 and afterward you shall C into the camp."
32:19 because our inheritance has C to us on this
33:38 people of Israel had C out of the land
Deut 1:20 to you, 'You have C to the hill country
1:22 into which we shall C
4:30 and all these things C upon you in the
6:20 you in time to C, 'What is the meaning
10:1 like the first, and C up to me on
11:10 from which you have C, where you sowed your
12:9 have not as yet C to the rest and
14:29 within your towns, shall C and eat and be
17:14 "When you C to the land which the LORD
18:6 lives--and he may C when he desires--to
18:9 "When you C into the land which the LORD
18:22 the word does not C to pass or come
18:22 come to pass or C true, that is a
20:2 battle, the priest shall C forward and speak to
21:2 and your judges shall C forth, and they shall
21:5 sons of Levi shall C forward, for the LORD
22:6 "If you chance to C upon a bird's nest,
23:10 camp, he shall not C within the camp;
23:11 is down, he may C within the camp.
25:1 between men, and they C into court, and the
26:1 "When you C into the land which the LORD
26:3 God that I have C into the land which
28:2 all these blessings shall C upon you and overtake
28:6 you be when you C in, and blessed shall
28:7 before you; they shall C out against you one
28:15 all these curses shall C upon you and overtake
28:19 you be when you C in, and cursed shall
28:24 from heaven it shall C down upon you until
28:43 higher; and you shall C down lower and lower.
28:45 All these curses shall C upon you and pursue
28:52 in which you trusted, C down throughout all your
29:22 And the generation to C, your children who rise
30:1 when all these things C upon you, the blessing
31:2 to go out and C in.
31:17 evils and troubles will C upon them, so that
31:17 'Have not these evils C upon us because our
31:21 evils and troubles have C upon them, this song
31:29 in the days to C evil will befall you,
32:17 new gods that had C in of late, whom
33:16 Let these C upon the head of Joseph, and
33:29 Your enemies shall C fawning to you; and you
Josh 2:2 men of Israel have C here tonight to search
2:3 the men that have C to you, who entered
2:3 house; for they have C to search out all
2:18 Behold, when we C into the land, you shall
3:4 thousand cubits; do not C near it."
3:8 the covenant, 'When you C to the brink of
3:9 the people of Israel, C hither, and hear the
3:15 bore the ark had C to the Jordan, and
4:6 ask in time to C, 'What do those stones
4:16 of the testimony to C up out of the
4:17 therefore commanded the priests, C up out of the
4:21 fathers in time to C, 'What do these stones
5:4 wilderness after they had C out of Egypt.
5:5 wilderness after they had C out of Egypt had
5:14 the army of the LORD I have now C
7:14 the LORD takes shall C near by families; and
7:14 the LORD takes shall C near by households; and
7:14 the LORD takes shall C near man by man.
8:5 And when they C out against us, as before,
8:6 them; and they will C out after us, till
9:6 of Israel, "We have C from a far country;
9:8 And where do you C from?"
9:9 country your servants have C, because of the name
9:11 "We are your servants; C now, make a covenant
9:12 we set forth to C to you, but now,
10:4 king of Eglon, saying, C up to me, and
10:6 hand from your servants; C up to us quickly,
10:24 had gone with him, C near, put your feet
11:20 hearts that they should C against Israel in battle,
18:4 their inheritances, and then C to me.
18:8 of the land, and C again to me; and
22:24 that in time to C your children might say
22:27 children in time to C, "You have no portion
22:28 descendants in time to C, we should say, 'Behold
23:14 concerning you; all have C to pass for you,
24:7 and made the sea C upon them and cover
Judg 1:3 to Simeon his brother, C up with me into
1:34 not allow them to C down to the plain;
4:22 and said to him, C, and I will show
6:3 of the East would C up and attack them;
6:5 For they would C up with their cattle and
6:18 pray thee, until I C to thee, and bring
7:17 do likewise; when I C to the outskirts of
7:24 of Ephraim, saying, C down against the Midianites

8:9 of Penuel, "When I C again in peace, I
9:10 to the fig tree, C you, and reign over
9:12 said to the vine, C you, and reign over
9:14 said to the bramble, C you, and reign over
9:15 king over you, then C and take refuge in
9:15 if not, let fire C out of the bramble
9:20 if not, let fire C out from Abimelech, and
9:20 Beth-millo; and let fire C out from the citizens
9:24 sons of Jerubbaal might C and their blood be
9:29 'Increase your army, and C out.'"
9:31 and his kinsmen have C to Shechem, and they
9:33 that are with him C out against you, you
11:6 they said to Jephthah, C and be our leader,
11:7 Why have you C to me now when you
11:12 me, that you have C to me to fight
12:3 why then have you C up to me this
13:5 No razor shall C upon his head, for the
13:8 whom thou didst send C again to us, and
13:12 "Now when your words C true, what is to
13:17 that, when your words C true, we may honor
15:10 said, "Why have you C up against us?" They
15:10 They said, "We have C up to bind Samson,
15:12 to him, "We have C down to bind you,
16:2 were told, "Samson has C here," and they
16:17 "A razor has never C upon my head; for
16:18 of the Philistines, saying, C up this once, for
17:9 Micah said to him, "From where do you C
18:10 you go, you will C to an unsuspecting people.
18:19 upon your mouth, and C with us, and be
18:23 ails you that you C with such a company?"
19:11 said to his master, C now, let us turn
19:13 said to his servant, C and let us draw
19:17 and whence do you C
19:18 the hill country of Ephraim, from which I C
19:23 that this man has C into my house, do
20:10 people, that when they C they may requite Gibe-ah
21:3 Israel, why has this C to pass in Israel,
21:5 of Israel did not C up in the assembly
21:5 him who did not C up to the LORD
21:8 Israel that did not C up to the LORD
21:8 behold, no one had C to the camp from
21:21 the daughters of Shiloh C out to dance in
21:21 in the dances, then C out of the vineyards
21:22 fathers or their brothers C to complain to us,
Ruth 2:3 and she happened to C to the part of
2:12 whose wings you have C to take refuge!"
2:14 Boaz said to her, C here, and eat some
4:3 kin, "Naomi, who has C back from the country
4:4 redeem it, and I C after you." And he
1Sam 2:3 proudly, let not arrogance C from your mouth; for
2:13 the priest's servant would C, while the meat was
2:15 the priest's servant would C and say to the
2:36 in your house shall C to implore him for
4:3 Shiloh, that he may C among us and save
4:6 of the LORD had C to the camp,
4:7 said, "A god has C into the camp." And
4:16 am he who has C from the battle; I
6:7 which there has never C a yoke, and yoke
6:21 C down and take it up to you."
7:17 Then he would C back to Ramah, for his
9:5 who was with him, C, let us go back,
9:9 of God, he said, C, let us go to
9:10 his servant, "Well said; C, let us go." So
9:12 Make haste; he has C just now to the
9:16 because their cry has C to me."
10:3 from there further and C to the oak of
10:5 After that you shall C to Gibe-ath-elohim, where
10:5 and there, as you C to the city, you
10:6 of the LORD will C mightily upon you, and
10:8 shall wait, until I C to you and show
10:11 one another, "What has C over the son of
10:22 LORD, "Did the man C hither?" and the LORD
11:7 saying, "Whoever does not C out after Saul and
11:9 the messengers who had C, "Thus shall you say
11:14 said to the people, C, let us go to
13:8 but Samuel did not C to Gilgal, and the
13:11 that you did not C within the days appointed,
13:12 'Now the Philistines will C down upon me at
14:1 who bore his armor, C, let us go over
14:6 who bore his armor, C, let us go over
14:9 us, 'Wait until we C to you,' then we
14:10 But if they say, C up to us,' then
14:12 his armor-bearer, and said, C up to us, and
14:12 said to his armor-bearer, C up after me; for
14:38 And Saul said, C hither, all you leaders of
16:2 and say, 'I have C to sacrifice to the
16:4 and said, "Do you C peaceably?"
16:5 said, "Peaceably; I have C to sacrifice to the
16:5 LORD; consecrate yourselves, and C with me to the
17:8 Israel, "Why have you C out to draw up
17:8 yourselves, and let him C down to me.
17:25 this man who has C up?
17:25 Surely he has C up to defy Israel; and
17:28 said, "Why have you C down?
17:28 heart; for you have C down to see the
17:43 a dog, that you C to me with sticks?"
17:44 Philistine said to David, C to me, and I
17:45 to the Philistine, "You C to me with a
17:45 a javelin; but I C to you in the
20:9 father that evil should C upon you, would I
20:11 Jonathan said to David, C, let us go out
20:21 then you are to C, for, as the LORD
20:27 the son of Jesse C to the meal, either
20:29 reason he has not C to the king's table."
21:15 Shall this fellow C into my house?"
23:7 Saul that David had C to Keilah.
23:10 that Saul seeks to C to Keilah, to destroy
23:11 Will Saul C down, as thy servant has heard?
23:11 LORD said, "He will C down."
23:15 afraid because Saul had C out to seek his
23:20 Now C down, O king, according to all your
23:20 your heart's desire to C down; and our part
23:23 where he hides, and C back to me with
23:27 saying, "Make haste and C; for the Philistines have
24:14 the king of Israel C out?
25:8 your eyes; for we C on a feast day.
25:11 it to men who C from I do not
25:19 before me; behold, I C after you." But she
25:34 had made haste and C to meet me, truly
26:4 and learned of a certainty that Saul had C
26:10 or his day shall C to die; or he
26:20 king of Israel has C out to seek my
26:22 of the young men C over and fetch it.
28:10 lives, no punishment shall C upon you for this
31:4 it, lest these uncircumcised C and thrust me through,
2Sam 1:3 him, "Where do you C from?" And he said
1:13 him, "Where do you C from?" And he answered,
3:13 Saul's daughter, when you C to see my face."
5:6 David, "You will not C in here, but the
5:6 off"–thinking, "David cannot C in here."
5:8 the lame shall not C into the house."
5:18 Now the Philistines had C and spread out in
5:23 to their rear, and C upon them opposite the
6:9 ark of the LORD C to me?"
7:12 after you, who shall C forth from your body,
7:19 a great while to C, and hast shown me
10:11 you, then I will C and help you.
11:10 Uriah, "Have you not C from a journey?
12:4 the wayfarer who had C to him, but he
12:4 the man who had C to him."
13:5 'Let my sister Tamar C and give me bread
13:6 let my sister Tamar C and make a couple
13:11 and said to her, C, lie with me, my
13:35 the king's sons have C; as your servant said,
13:35 said, so it has C about."
14:15 Now I have C to say this to my
14:24 he is not to C into my presence." So
14:24 house, and did not C into the king's presence.
14:29 but Joab would not C to him.
14:29 sent a second time, but Joab would not C
14:32 sent word to you, C here, that I may
14:32 ask, "Why have I C from Geshur?
15:2 had a suit to C before the king for
15:4 suit or cause might C to me, and I
17:2 I will C upon him while he is weary
17:12 So we shall C upon him in some place
18:22 said again to Joab, C what may, let me
18:23 C what may," he said, "I will run." So
19:7 the evil that has C upon you from your
19:11 of all Israel has C to the king?
19:16 Bahurim, made haste to C down with the men
19:20 therefore, behold, I have C this day, the first
19:20 house of Joseph to C down to meet my
19:30 lord the king has C safely home."
19:31 Barzillai the Gileadite had C down from Rogelim;
19:33 king said to Barzillai, C over with me, and
20:16 Tell Joab, C here, that I may speak to
21:10 of the air to C upon them by day,
24:13 three years of famine C to you in your
24:21 my lord the king C to his servant?" David
1Kgs 1:12 Now therefore C, let me give you counsel, that
1:14 king, I also will C in after you and

1:21 Otherwise it will C to pass, when my lord
1:35 Solomon!' You shall then C up after him, and
1:35 him, and he shall C and sit upon my
1:42 came; and Adonijah said, C in, for you are
2:13 said, "Do you C peaceably?" He said, "Peaceably."
2:30 him, "The king commands, C forth.'" But he said,
2:33 So shall their blood C back upon the head
3:7 to go out or C in.
10:12 such almug wood has C or been seen, to
10:22 of Tarshish used to C bringing gold, silver, ivory,
12:1 for all Israel had C to Shechem to make
12:5 for three days, then C again to me." So
12:12 as the king said, C to me again the
13:7 the man of God, C home with me, and
13:15 he said to him, C home with me and
13:22 commanded you, but have C back, and have eaten
13:22 your body shall not C to the tomb of
13:32 of Samaria, shall surely C to pass."
14:6 the door, he said, C in, wife of Jeroboam;
14:13 only of Jeroboam shall C to the grave, because
15:17 to go out or C in to Asa king
17:18 You have C to me to bring my sin
17:21 let this child's soul C into him again."
18:12 and so, when I C and tell Ahab and
18:30 to all the people, C near to me"; and
20:18 said, "If they have C out for peace, take
20:18 or if they have C out for war, take
20:22 and said to him, C, strengthen yourself, and consider
20:22 king of Syria will C up against you."
20:33 he caused him to C up into the chariot.
22:15 And when he had C to the king, the
22:27 and water, until I C in peace.'"'"
2Kgs 1:4 LORD, 'You shall not C down from the bed
1:6 Therefore you shall not C down from the bed
1:9 God, the king says, C down.'"
1:10 of God, let fire C down from heaven and
1:11 is the king's order, C down quickly!'"
1:12 of God, let fire C down from heaven and
1:16 therefore you shall not C down from the bed
2:21 death nor miscarriage shall C from it."
3:21 that the kings had C up to fight against
4:1 but the creditor has C to take my two
4:22 man of God, and C back again."
5:8 Let him C now to me, that he may
5:11 that he would surely C out to me, and
5:22 'There have just now C to me from the
7:4 So now C, let us go over to the
7:6 kings of Egypt to C upon us."
7:9 overtake us; now therefore C, let us go and
7:12 country, thinking, 'When they C out of the city,
8:1 famine, and it will C upon the land for
8:7 man of God has C here,"
9:11 did this mad fellow C to you?" And he
9:16 king of Judah had C down to visit Joram.
10:6 your master's sons, and C to me at Jezreel
10:16 And he said, C with me, and see my
10:21 was not a man left who did not C
11:4 guards, and had them C to him in the
11:5 of you, those who C off duty on the
11:7 divisions of you, which C on duty in force
11:9 those who were to C on duty on the
14:8 king of Israel, saying, C, let us look one
16:7 C up, and rescue me from the hand of
18:23 C now, make a wager with my master the
18:25 LORD that I have C up against this place
18:31 peace with me and C out to me; then
18:32 own cistern; until I C and take you away
19:3 of disgrace; children have C to the birth, and
19:28 and your arrogance has C into my ears, I
19:32 Assyria, He shall not C into this city or
19:32 an arrow there, or C before it with a
19:33 and he shall not C into this city, says
20:14 And whence did they C to you?" And Hezekiah
20:14 Hezekiah said, "They have C from a far country,
23:9 high places did not C up to the altar
24:7 of Egypt did not C again out of his
1Chr 9:25 villages were obliged to C in every seven days,
10:4 it, lest these uncircumcised C and make sport of
11:5 David, "You will not C in here." Nevertheless David
12:17 them, "If you have C to me in friendship
12:31 were expressly named to C and make David king.
13:2 lands, that they may C together to us.
14:9 Now the Philistines had C and made a raid
14:14 them; go around and C upon them opposite the
16:29 bring an offering, and C before him!
17:17 a great while to C, and hast shown me
19:3 Have not his servants C to you to search
19:9 the kings who had C were by themselves in
24:19 in their service to C into the house of
29:12 Both riches and honor C from thee, and thou
29:14 For all things C from thee, and of thy
1:10 to go out and C in before this people,
7:3 Israel saw the fire C down and the glory
8:11 of the LORD has C are holy."
9:21 of Tarshish used to C bringing gold, silver, ivory,
10:1 for all Israel had C to Shechem to make
10:5 He said to them, C to me again in
10:12 as the king said, C to me again the
13:13 an ambush around to C on them from behind;
14:11 thy name we have C against this multitude.
16:1 to go out or C in to Asa king
18:14 And when he had C to the king, the
19:10 and wrath may not C upon you and your
20:16 them; behold, they will C up by the ascent
20:22 Mount Seir, who had C against Judah, so that
21:15 bowels, until your bowels C out because of the
22:7 downfall of Ahaziah should C about through his going
23:4 priests and Levites who C off duty on the
23:8 those who were to C on duty on the
24:11 the chief priest would C and empty the chest
24:24 of the Syrians had C with few men, the
25:10 the army that had C to him from Ephraim,
25:17 king of Israel, saying, C, let us look one
29:31 yourselves to the LORD; C near, bring sacrifices and
30:1 Manasseh, that they should C to the house of
30:5 that the people should C and keep the passover
30:8 to the LORD, and C to his sanctuary, which
32:2 saw that Sennacherib had C and intended to fight
32:4 the kings of Assyria C and find much water?"
32:26 the LORD did not C upon them in the
Ezra 3:8 and all who had C to Jerusalem from the
8:35 time those who had C from captivity, the returned
9:13 after all that has C upon us for our
10:8 any one did not C within three days, by
10:14 have taken foreign wives C at appointed times, and
10:17 first month they had C to the end of
Neh 2:7 pass through until I C to Judah;
2:10 that some one had C to seek the welfare
2:17 C, let us build the wall of Jerusalem, that
4:8 all plotted together to C and fight against Jerusalem
4:11 or see till we C into the midst of
4:12 they live they will C up against us."
6:2 sent to me, saying, C and let us meet
6:3 work and I cannot C down.
6:3 I leave it and C down to you?"
6:7 So now C, and let us take counsel together."
7:73 the seventh month had C, the children of Israel
9:13 Thou didst C down upon Mount Sinai, and speak
9:32 to thee that has C upon us, upon our
9:33 in all that has C upon us, for thou
13:21 on they did not C on the sabbath.
13:22 should purify themselves and C and guard the gates,
Tob 5:13 My brother, you C of good stock.
5:21 successful, and he will C back safe and sound."
12:18 For I did not C as a favor on
13:11 Many nations will C from afar to the name
Jud 3:4 inhabitants are your slaves; C and deal with them
5:4 the west, refused to C out and meet me?"
5:5 No falsehood shall C from your servant's mouth.
5:8 the God they had C to know; hence they
5:19 their God, and have C back from the places
9:5 that are now, and those that are to C
11:3 from them and have C over to us--since
11:3 us--since you have C to safety.
11:18 And I will C and tell you, and then
11:19 of Judea, till you C to Jerusalem; and I
12:13 beautiful maidservant will please C to my lord and
13:3 wait for her to C out, as she did
14:3 Then fear will C over them, and they will
14:13 so bold as to C down against us to
Esth 1:12 Queen Vashti refused to C at the king's command
1:17 and she did not C
1:19 that Vashti is to C no more before King
4:11 not been called to C in to the king
4:14 whether you have not C to the kingdom for
5:4 the king and Haman C this day to a
5:8 the king and Haman C tomorrow to the dinner
5:12 Esther let no one C with the king to
6:5 king said, "Let him C in."
9:25 against the Jews should C upon his own head,
10:4 said, "These things have C from God.
15:10 C near."

Job 1:7 The LORD said to Satan, "Whence have you C
2:2 the LORD said to Satan, "Whence have you C
2:11 this evil that had C upon him, they came
2:11 an appointment together to C to condole with him
3:6 year, let it not C into the number of
3:11 not die at birth, C forth from the womb
4:5 But now it has C to you, and you
5:6 For affliction does not C from the dust, nor
5:26 You shall C to your grave in ripe old
6:20 were confident; they C thither and are confounded.
7:6 a weaver's shuttle, and C to their end without
7:9 to Sheol does not C up;
9:32 him, that we should C to trial together.
13:13 will speak, and let C on me what may.
13:16 godless man shall not C before him.
14:14 service I would wait, till my release should C
14:21 His sons C to honor, and he does not
15:21 prosperity the destroyer will C upon him.
16:22 a few years have C I shall go the
17:10 But you, C on again, all of you, and
19:12 His troops C on together; they have cast up
20:22 force of misery will C upon him.
20:25 of his gall; terrors C upon him.
22:21 peace; thereby good will C to you.
23:3 him, that I might C even to his seat!
23:10 tried me, I shall C forth as gold.
26:4 and whose spirit has C forth from you?
30:14 a wide breach they C; amid the crash they
30:27 still; days of affliction C to meet me.
34:28 of the poor to C to him, and he
38:11 'Thus far shall you C, and no farther, and
38:29 womb did the ice C forth, and who has
41:16 that no air can C between them.
Ps 7:9 evil of the wicked C to an end, but
14:7 deliverance for Israel would C out of Zion!
17:2 From thee let my vindication C
24:7 King of glory may C in.
24:9 King of glory may C in.
34:11 C, O sons, listen to me, I will teach
35:8 Let ruin C upon them unawares!
36:11 the foot of arrogance C upon me, nor the
38:2 and thy hand has C down on me.
40:7 I said, "Lo, I C; in the roll of
42:2 When shall I C and behold the face of
44:17 All this has C upon us, though we have
44:26 Rise up, C to our help!
46:8 [Selah] C, behold the works of the LORD, how
53:6 deliverance for Israel would C from Zion!
55:5 Fear and trembling C upon me, and horror
55:15 Let death C upon them; let them go down
59:4 Rouse thyself, C to my help, and see!
59:6 [Selah] Each evening they C back, howling like dogs
59:14 [Selah] Each evening they C back, howling like dogs
65:2 thee shall all flesh C
66:5 [Selah] C and see what God has done: he
66:13 I will C into thy house with burnt offerings;
66:16 [Selah] C and hear, all you who fear God,
69:1 For the waters have C up to my neck.
69:2 no foothold; I have C into deep waters, and
71:16 Lord GOD I will C, I will praise thy
71:18 proclaim thy might to all the generations to C
78:16 He made streams C out of the rock, and
79:1 God, the heathen have C into thy inheritance; they
79:8 forefathers; let thy compassion C speedily to meet us,
79:11 groans of the prisoners C before thee; according to
80:2 up thy might, and C to save us!
83:4 They say, C, let us wipe them out as
86:9 thou hast made shall C and bow down before
88:2 Let my prayer C before thee, incline thy ear
90:9 thy wrath, our years C to an end like
91:7 but it will not C near you.
91:10 befall you, no scourge C near your tent.
95:1 O C, let us sing to the LORD; let
95:2 Let us C into his presence with thanksgiving; let
95:6 O C, let us worship and bow down, let
96:8 bring an offering, and C into his courts!
100:2 C into his presence with singing!
101:2 Oh when wilt thou C to me?
102:1 LORD; let my cry C to thee!
102:13 time to favor her; the appointed time has C
102:18 for a generation to C, so that a people
109:7 is tried, let him C forth guilty; let his
109:17 to curse; let curses C on him!
110:3 dew your youth will C to you.
119:41 Let thy steadfast love C to me, O LORD,
119:77 Let thy mercy C to me, that I may
119:143 Trouble and anguish have C upon me, but thy
119:169 Let my cry C before thee, O LORD; give
119:170 Let my supplication C before thee; deliver me
121:1 From whence does my help C
126:6 seed for sowing, shall C home with shouts of
134:1 C, bless the LORD, all you servants of the
144:5 heavens, O LORD, and C down!
Prov 1:11 If they say, C with us, let us lie
1:27 when distress and anguish C upon you.
2:6 wisdom; from his mouth C knowledge and
2:10 path; for wisdom will C into your heart, and
2:19 who go to her C back nor do they
3:28 your neighbor, "Go, and C again, tomorrow I will
6:3 yourself, for you have C into your neighbor's power:
6:11 rest, and poverty will C upon you like a
6:15 discord; therefore calamity will C upon him suddenly;
7:15 so now I have C out to meet you,
7:18 C, let us take our fill of love till
7:20 full moon he will C home."
8:6 from my lips will C what is right;
9:5 without sense she says, C, eat of my bread
10:8 a prating fool will C to ruin.
10:24 the wicked dreads will C upon him, but the
13:18 Poverty and disgrace C to him who ignores
14:4 grain; but abundant crops C by the strength of
20:13 not sleep, lest you C to poverty; open your
22:16 the rich, will only C to want.
23:21 and the glutton will C to poverty, and drowsiness
24:22 the ruin that will C from them both?
24:34 rest, and poverty will C upon you like a
25:7 better to be told, C up here," than to
26:27 and a stone will C back upon him who
28:22 know that want will C upon him.
30:4 ascended to heaven and C down?
31:25 clothing, and she laughs at the time to C
Eccl 1:11 happen among those who C after.
2:1 I said to myself, C now, I will make
2:16 in the days to C all will have been
2:18 the man who will C after me;
4:4 all skill in work C from a man's envy
4:16 Yet those who C later will not rejoice in
6:10 Whatever has C to be has already been named,
7:18 who fears God shall C forth from them all.
12:1 before the evil days C, and the years draw
Song 2:10 my fair one, and C away;
2:12 time of singing has C, and the voice of
2:13 my fair one, and C away.
4:2 shorn ewes that have C up from the washing,
4:8 C with me from Lebanon, my bride; come with
4:8 from Lebanon, my bride; C with me from Lebanon.
4:16 O north wind, and C, O south wind!
4:16 Let my beloved C to his garden, and eat
5:1 I C to my garden, my sister, my bride,
6:6 of ewes, that have C up from the washing,
7:11 C, my beloved, let us go forth into the
Wis 1:9 of his words will C to the Lord, to
2:6 C, therefore, let us enjoy the good things that
3:16 of adulterers will not C to maturity, and the
4:5 broken off before they C to maturity, and their
4:20 They will C with dread when their sins are
6:5 of God, he will C upon you terribly and
7:14 for the gifts that C from instruction.
8:8 infers the things to C; she understands turns of
8:13 remembrance to those who C after me.
12:12 Or who will C before thee to plead as
14:5 on a raft they C safely to land.
16:4 oppressors inexorable want should C, while to these
17:12 of the helps that C from reason;
19:13 The punishments did not C upon the sinners without
19:15 of some sort will C upon the former for
Sir 1:27 because you did not C in the fear of
2:1 My son, if you C forward to serve the
3:8 blessing from him may C upon you.
4:18 Then she will C straight back to him and
5:13 Glory and dishonor C from speaking, and a man's
6:19 C to her like one who plows and sows,
6:26 C to her with all your soul, and keep
11:14 death, poverty and wealth, C from the Lord.
11:30 a spark of fire C many burning coals, and
12:3 No good will C to the man who persists
15:2 She will C to meet him like a mother,
24:18 C to me, you who desire me, and eat
28:12 put out; and both C out of your mouth.
29:26 will hear bitter words: C here, stranger, prepare the
29:27 person; my brother has C to stay with me;
31:6 Many have C to ruin because of gold, and

39:31 and when their times C they will not transgress
40:1 from the day they C forth from their mother's
Is 1:12 "When you C to appear before me, who requires
1:18 C now, let us reason together, says the LORD:
1:23 widow's cause does not C to them.
2:2 It shall C to pass in the latter days
2:3 and many peoples shall C, and say: "Come, let
2:3 shall come, and say: C, let us go up
2:5 O house of Jacob, C, let us walk in
5:19 near, and let it C, that we may know
7:7 and it shall not C to pass.
7:17 days as have not C since the day that
7:19 And they will all C and settle in the
7:24 and arrows men will C there, for all the
7:25 hoe, you will not C there for fear of
8:10 together, but it will C to nought; speak a
10:3 the storm which will C from afar?
10:25 while my indignation will C to an end, and
10:28 from Rimmon, he has C to Aiath; he has
11:1 There shall C forth a shoot from the stump
13:5 They C from a distant land, from the end
13:6 near; as destruction from the Almighty it will C
14:9 meet you when you C, it rouses the shades
14:29 the serpent's root will C forth an adder, and
19:23 and the Assyrian will C into Egypt, and the
21:9 And, behold, here C riders, horsemen in pairs!" And
21:12 you will inquire, inquire; C back again."
21:16 glory of Kedar will C to an end;
22:15 Lord GOD of hosts, C, go to this steward,
26:20 C, my people, enter your chambers, and shut your
27:6 In days to C Jacob shall take root, Israel
27:11 they are broken; women C and make a fire
27:13 land of Egypt will C and worship the LORD
28:15 through it will not C to us; for we
29:4 dust your words shall C; your voice shall come
29:4 come; your voice shall C from the ground like
29:20 For the ruthless shall C to nought and the
29:24 err in spirit will C to understanding, and those
30:6 and anguish, from where C the lioness and the
30:8 for the time to C as a witness for
31:4 LORD of hosts will C down to fight upon
32:10 vintage will fail, the fruit harvest will not C
35:4 Behold, your God will C with vengeance, with the
35:4 He will C and save you."
35:9 shall any ravenous beast C up on it; they
35:10 LORD shall return, and C to Zion with singing;
36:8 C now, make a wager with my master the
36:10 LORD that I have C up against this land
36:16 peace with me and C out to me; then
36:17 own cistern; until I C and take you away
37:3 of disgrace; children have C to the birth, and
37:29 and your arrogance has C to my ears, I
37:33 Assyria: He shall not C into this city, or
37:33 an arrow there, or C before it with a
37:34 and he shall not C into this city, says
39:3 And whence did they C to you?" Hezekiah said,
39:3 Hezekiah said, "They have C to me from a
41:5 the earth tremble; they have drawn near and C
41:22 outcome; or declare to us the things to C
41:23 us what is to C hereafter, that we may
41:25 north, and he has C, from the rising of
42:9 the former things have C to pass, and new
42:23 will attend and listen for the time to C
44:7 has announced from of old the things to C
45:14 men of stature, shall C over to you and
45:14 follow you; they shall C over in chains and
45:20 "Assemble yourselves and C, draw near together, you
45:24 strength; to him shall C and be ashamed, all
47:1 C down and sit in the dust, O virgin
47:9 These two things shall C to you in a
47:9 children and widowhood shall C upon you in full
47:11 But evil shall C upon you, for which you
47:11 expiate; and ruin shall C on you suddenly, of
49:9 saying to the prisoners, C forth,' to those who
49:12 Lo, these shall C from afar, and lo, these
49:18 they all gather, they C to you.
49:21 I was left alone; whence then have these C
50:8 Let him C near to me.
51:11 LORD shall return, and C to Zion with singing;
52:1 there shall no more C into you the uncircumcised
54:14 for it shall not C near you.
55:1 every one who thirsts, C to the waters; and
55:1 who has no money, C, buy and eat!
55:1 C, buy wine and milk without money and without
55:3 Incline your ear, and C to me; hear, that
55:10 rain and the snow C down from heaven, and
55:13 of the thorn shall C up the cypress; instead
55:13 of the brier shall C up the myrtle; and
56:1 soon my salvation will C, and my deliverance be
56:9 beasts of the field, C to devour-- all
56:12 C," they say, "let us get wine, let us fill
59:19 sun; for he will C like a rushing stream,
59:20 "And he will C to Zion as Redeemer, to
60:1 for your light has C, and the glory of
60:3 And nations shall C to your light, and kings
60:4 all gather together, they C to you; your sons
60:4 you; your sons shall C from far, and your
60:5 of the nations shall C to you.
60:6 Midian and Ephah; all those from Sheba shall C
60:7 to you; they shall C up with acceptance on
60:13 glory of Lebanon shall C to you, the cypress,
60:14 who oppressed you shall C bending low to you;
63:4 my heart, and my year of redemption has C
64:1 rend the heavens and C down, that the mountains
65:5 to yourself, do not C near me, for I
65:17 not be remembered or C into mind.
66:15 behold, the LORD will C in fire, and his
66:17 abomination and mice, shall C to an end together,
66:18 tongues; and they shall C and shall see my
66:23 sabbath, all flesh shall C to worship before me,
Jer 1:15 LORD; and they shall C and every one shall
2:31 are free, we will C no more to thee?
2:37 it too you will C away with your hands
3:3 spring rain has not C; yet you have a
3:16 It shall not C to mind, or be remembered,
3:18 and together they shall C from the land of
3:22 "Behold, we C to thee; for thou art the
4:16 to Jerusalem, "Besiegers C from a distant land;
5:12 nothing; no evil will C upon us, nor shall
6:3 with their flocks shall C against her; they shall
6:20 purpose does frankincense C to me from Sheba,
6:26 suddenly the destroyer will C upon us.
7:10 not known, and then C and stand before me
7:31 command, nor did it C into my mind.
8:16 They C and devour the land and all that
9:17 the mourning women to C; send for the skilful
9:17 the skilful women to C;
9:21 For death has C up into our windows, it
12:12 the desert destroyers have C; for the sword of
12:16 And it shall C to pass, if they will
13:18 your beautiful crown has C down from your head."
13:20 and see those who C from the north.
13:22 'Why have these things C upon me?' it is
14:3 servants for water; they C to the cisterns, they
14:15 and famine shall not C on this land: By
16:19 thee shall the nations C from the ends of
17:6 the desert, and shall not see any good C
17:15 Let it C
17:26 And people shall C from the cities of Judah
18:18 Then they said, C, let us make plots against
18:18 C, let us smite him with the tongue, and
19:5 decree, nor did it C into my mind;
20:18 Why did I C forth from the womb to
21:13 who say, 'Who shall C down against us, or
22:23 will groan when pangs C upon you, pain as
23:17 say, 'No evil shall C upon you.'"
25:3 of the LORD has C to me, and I
25:34 slaughter and dispersion have C, and you shall fall
26:2 cities of Judah which C to worship in the
27:3 the envoys who have C to Jerusalem to Zedekiah
28:6 which you have prophesied C true, and bring back
29:12 call upon me and C and pray to me,
30:8 "And it shall C to pass in that day,
30:19 Out of them shall C songs of thanksgiving, and
30:21 themselves, their ruler shall C forth from their midst;
31:9 With weeping they shall C, and with consolations I
31:12 They shall C and sing aloud on the height
31:16 LORD, and they shall C back from the land
31:17 and your children shall C back to their own
31:28 And it shall C to pass that as I
32:7 Shallum your uncle will C to you and say,
32:23 made all this evil C upon them.
32:24 the siege mounds have C up to the city
32:24 thou didst speak has C to pass, and behold,
32:29 against this city shall C and set this city
33:20 and night will not C at their appointed time,
35:11 the land, we said, C, and let us go
36:6 men of Judah who C out of their cities.
36:7 that their supplication will C before the LORD, and
36:14 read in the hearing of the people, and C
36:29 of Babylon will certainly C and destroy this land,
37:5 army of Pharaoh had C out of Egypt; and

37:8 And the Chaldeans shall C back and fight against
37:16 When Jeremiah had C to the dungeon cells, and
37:19 of Babylon will not C against you and against
37:20 let my humble plea C before you, and do
38:25 spoken with you and C to you and say
40:3 voice, this thing has C upon you.
40:4 good to you to C with me to Babylon,
40:4 with me to Babylon, C, and I will look
40:4 wrong to you to C with me to Babylon,
40:4 to come with me to Babylon, do not C
40:10 the Chaldeans who will C to us; but as
41:6 he said to them, C in to Gedaliah the
42:2 prophet, "Let our supplication C before you, and pray
43:11 He shall C and smite the land of Egypt,
44:8 Egypt where you have C to live, that you
44:12 set their faces to C to the land of
44:14 of Judah who have C to live in the
44:21 Did it not C into his mind?
46:18 and like Carmel by the sea, shall one C
46:20 from the north has C upon her.
46:21 of their calamity has C upon them, the time
46:22 march in force, and C against her with axes,
47:5 Baldness has C upon Gaza, Ashkelon has perished.
48:2 planned evil against her: C, let us cut her
48:8 The destroyer shall C upon every city, and no
48:15 and his cities has C up, and the choicest
48:18 broken, the glorious staff.' C down from your glory,
48:18 destroyer of Moab has C up against you; he
48:21 "Judgment has C upon the tableland, upon Holon,
49:4 treasures, saying, 'Who will C against me?'
49:14 "Gather yourselves together and C against her, and
49:36 which those driven out of Elam shall not C
50:3 north a nation has C up against her, which
50:4 people of Judah shall C together, weeping as they
50:4 together, weeping as they C; and they shall seek
50:5 turned toward it, saying, C, let us join ourselves
50:26 C against her from every quarter; open her
50:27 for their day has C, the time of their
50:31 for your day has C, the time when I
51:2 her land, when they C against her from every
51:10 brought forth our vindication; C, let us declare in
51:13 treasures, your end has C, the thread of your
51:33 while and the time of her harvest will C
51:42 The sea has C up on Babylon; she is
51:48 for the destroyers shall C against them out of
51:50 afar, and let Jerusalem C into your mind:
51:51 face, for aliens have C into the holy places
51:53 height, yet destroyers would C from me upon her,
51:56 for a destroyer has C upon her, upon Babylon;
51:60 the evil that should C upon Babylon, all these
51:61 to Seraiah: "When you C to Babylon, see that
Lam 1:4 Zion mourn, for none C to the appointed feasts;
1:22 "Let all their evil-doing C before thee; and deal
3:22 ceases, his mercies never C to an end;
3:38 of the Most High that good and evil C
3:47 panic and pitfall have C upon us, devastation and
3:57 for help!' Thou didst C near when I called
4:18 our days were numbered; for our end had C
Bar 2:7 Lord threatened us have C upon us.
2:30 their exile they will C to themselves,
4:14 the neighbors of Zion C; remember the capture of
4:22 you, and joy has C to me from the
4:22 mercy which soon will C to you from your
4:24 by God, which will C to you with great
4:25 the wrath that has C upon you from God.
4:35 For fire will C upon her from the Everlasting
5:9 mercy and righteousness that C from him.
6:3 Therefore when you have C to Babylon you will
6:47 reproach for those who C after.
Ezek 4:14 nor has foul flesh C into my mouth."
5:4 there a fire will C forth into all the
7:2 The end has C upon the four corners of
7:6 An end has C, the end has come; it
7:6 come, the end has C; it has awakened against
7:7 Your doom has C to you, O inhabitant of
7:7 land; the time has C, the day is near,
7:10 Your doom has C, injustice has blossomed, pride has
7:12 The time has C, the day draws near.
11:5 know the things that C into your mind.
11:18 Israel.' And when they C there, they will remove
14:22 and daughters, when they C forth to you, and
16:33 lovers, bribing them to C to you from every
20:3 Is it to inquire of me that you C
21:14 and let the sword C down twice, yea thrice,
21:19 king of Babylon to C; both of them shall
21:19 both of them shall C forth from the same
21:20 for the sword to C to Rabbah of the
21:24 appear--because you have C to remembrance, you
21:25 Israel, whose day has C, the time of your
21:29 wicked, whose day has C, the time of their
22:3 that her time may C, and that makes idols
22:4 near, the appointed time of your years has C
23:24 And they shall C against you from the north
23:40 sent for men to C from far, to whom
24:14 have spoken; it shall C to pass, I will
24:26 day a fugitive will C to you to report
27:29 down from their ships C all that handle the
27:36 at you; you have C to a dreadful end
28:19 at you; you have C to a dreadful end
30:4 A sword shall C upon Egypt, and anguish shall
30:6 her proud might shall C down; from Migdol to
30:9 Ethiopians; and anguish shall C upon them on the
30:18 her proud might shall C to an end; she
32:11 king of Babylon shall C upon you.
32:21 of Sheol: 'They have C down, they lie still,
33:28 her proud might shall C to an end; and
33:30 each to his brother, C, and hear what the
33:31 the LORD.' And they C to you as people
33:31 to you as people C, and they sit before
33:33 When this comes--and C it will!--then they
35:7 from it all who C and go.
36:8 for they will soon C home.
37:6 will cause flesh to C upon you, and cover
37:8 them, and flesh had C upon them, and skin
37:9 says the Lord GOD: C from the four winds,
38:10 that day thoughts will C into your mind, and
38:13 to you, 'Have you C to seize spoil?
38:15 will bestir yourself and C from your place out
38:16 mighty army; you will C up against my people
38:18 day, when Gog shall C against the land of
39:17 the field, 'Assemble and C, gather from all sides
40:46 sons of Levi may C near to the LORD
44:13 They shall not C near to me, to serve
44:13 me as priest, nor C near any of my
44:15 astray from me, shall C near to me to
46:9 people of the land C before the LORD at
Dan 3:2 of the provinces to C to the dedication of
3:94 God, C forth, and C here!" Then Shadrach,
3:95 smell of fire had C upon them.
4:24 Most High, which has C upon my lord the
8:7 I saw him C close to the ram, and
9:13 all this calamity has C upon us, yet we
9:22 Daniel, I have now C out to give you
9:23 forth, and I have C to tell it to
9:26 prince who is to C shall destroy the city
9:26 Its end shall C with a flood, and to
9:27 of abominations shall C one who makes desolate,
10:12 heard, and I have C because of your words.
10:14 For the vision is for days yet to C
10:16 the vision pains have C upon me, and I
10:20 know why I have C to you?
10:20 with him, lo, the prince of Greece will C
11:6 of the south shall C to the king of
11:7 his place; he shall C against the army and
11:9 Then the latter shall C into the realm of
11:10 great forces, which shall C on and overflow and
11:11 moved with anger, shall C out and fight with
11:13 some years he shall C on with a great
11:15 of the north shall C and throw up siegeworks,
11:17 set his face to C with the strength of
11:21 been given; he shall C in without warning and
11:24 Without warning he shall C into the richest parts
11:29 he shall return and C into the south; but
11:30 ships of Kittim shall C against him, and he
11:40 ships; and he shall C into countries and shall
11:41 He shall C into the glorious land.
11:45 mountain; yet he shall C to his end, with
13:4 the Jews used to C to him because he
13:42 all things before they C to be,
13:50 elders said to him, C, sit among us and
13:52 your sins have now C home, which you have
Hos 3:5 king; and they shall C in fear to the
4:14 people without understanding shall C to ruin.
6:1 they seek me, saying, C, let us return to
6:3 the dawn; he will C to us as the
9:4 only; it shall not C to the house of
9:7 days of punishment have C, the days of recompense
9:7 days of recompense have C; Israel shall know it.
10:10 I will C against the wayward people to chastise
10:12 LORD, that he may C and rain salvation upon
11:9 and I will not C to destroy.
11:10 and his sons shall C trembling from the west;

	11:11	the west; they shall C trembling like birds from
	12:11	Gilead they shall surely C to nought; if in
	13:13	The pangs of childbirth C for him, but he
	13:15	of the LORD, shall C, rising from the wilderness;
Joel	1:6	For a nation has C up against my land,
	2:28	"And it shall C to pass afterward, that I
	2:32	And it shall C to pass that all who
	3:9	draw near, let them C up.
	3:11	Hasten and C, all you nations round about, gather
	3:12	nations bestir themselves, and C up to the valley
	3:18	and a fountain shall C forth from the house
Amos	3:15	the great houses shall C to an end," says
	4:4	C to Bethel, and transgress; to Gilgal, and multiply
	5:5	exile, and Bethel shall C to nought."
	6:1	the nations, to whom the house of Israel C
	8:2	me, "The end has C upon my people Israel;
Jon	1:2	for their wickedness has C up before me."
	1:7	said to one another, C, let us cast lots,
	1:7	account this evil has C upon us." So they
	1:8	account this evil has C upon us?
	1:8	And whence do you C
	1:12	this great tempest has C upon you."
	4:6	plant, and made it C up over Jonah, that
Mic	1:3	his place, and will C down and tread upon
	1:9	incurable; and it has C to Judah, it has
	1:11	of Zaanan do not C forth; the wailing of
	1:12	good, because evil has C down from the LORD
	1:15	glory of Israel shall C to Adullam.
	3:11	No evil shall C upon us."
	4:1	It shall C to pass in the latter days
	4:2	and many nations shall C, and say: "Come, let
	4:2	shall come, and say: C, let us go up
	4:8	to you shall it C, the former dominion shall
	4:8	the former dominion shall C, the kingdom of the
	5:2	Judah, from you shall C forth for me one
	6:6	"With what shall I C before the LORD, and
	6:6	Shall I C before him with burnt offerings, with
	7:4	of their punishment, has C; now their confusion is
	7:12	that day they will C to you, from Assyria
	7:17	the earth; they shall C trembling out of their
Nah	1:11	Did one not C out from you, who plotted
	1:15	again shall the wicked C against you, he is
	2:1	The shatterer has C up against you.
	3:19	upon whom has not C your unceasing evil?
Hab	1:8	Yea, their horsemen C from afar; they fly like
	1:9	They all C for violence; terror of them goes
	2:3	it; it will surely C, it will not delay.
	2:16	LORD's right hand will C around to you, and
	2:16	you, and shame will C upon your glory!
	3:16	day of trouble to C upon people who invade
Zeph	2:1	C together and hold assembly, O shameless nation,
Hag	1:2	time has not yet C to rebuild the house
	2:7	of all nations shall C in, and I will
	2:15	now, consider what will C to pass from this
Zech	1:21	head; and these have C to terrify them, to
	2:10	Zion; for lo, I C and I will dwell
	6:15	who are far-off shall C and help to build
	6:15	And this shall C to pass, if you will
	8:20	hosts: Peoples shall yet C, even the inhabitants of
	8:22	and strong nations shall C to seek the LORD
	10:4	Out of them shall C the cornerstone, out of
	12:3	of the earth will C together against it.
	12:9	all the nations that C against Jerusalem.
	14:5	LORD your God will C, and all the holy
	14:16	the nations that have C against Jerusalem shall go
	14:18	then upon them shall C the plague with which
	14:21	all who sacrifice may C and take of them
Mal	3:1	you seek will suddenly C to his temple; the
	4:6	their fathers, lest I C and smite the land
1Mac	1:11	them many evils have C upon us."
	2:18	be the first to C and do what the
	2:27	and supports the covenant C out with me!"
	2:33	C out and do what the king commands, and
	2:34	said, "We will not C out, nor will we
	3:20	They C against us in great pride and lawlessness
	4:46	hill until there should C a prophet to tell
	5:11	They are preparing to C and capture the stronghold
	5:12	Now then C and rescue us from their hands,
	5:39	the stream, ready to C and fight against you."
	6:11	said to myself, 'To what distress I have C
	6:13	that these evils have C upon me; and behold,
	6:58	Now then let us C to terms with these
	7:11	saw that they had C with a large force.
	7:14	line of Aaron has C with the army, and
	7:28	and you; I shall C with a few men
	7:30	Judas that Nicanor had C to him with treacherous
	8:9	The Greeks planned to C and destroy them,
	9:9	now, and let us C back with our brethren
	9:10	If our time has C, let us die bravely
	9:60	He started to C with a large force, and
	9:69	had counseled him to C into the country, and
	10:16	C now, we will make him our friend and
	10:59	wrote to Jonathan to C to meet him.
	10:71	confidence in your forces, C down to the plain
	11:9	Demetrius the king, saying, C, let us make a
	11:63	officers of Demetrius had C to Kadesh in Galilee
	12:42	saw that he had C with a large army,
	12:45	stay with you, and C with me to Ptolemais.
	13:21	Trypho urging him to C to them by way
	14:22	of the Jews, have C to us to renew
	15:17	of the Jews have C to us as our
	15:31	Otherwise we will C and conquer you."
	16:19	captains asking them to C to him so that
2Mac	1:15	treasures and Antiochus had C with a few men
	2:14	the war which had C upon us, and they
	3:9	stated why he had C, and he inquired whether
	3:17	and bodily trembling had C over the man, which
	3:39	and destroys those who C to do it injury."
	4:34	suspicion persuaded Onias to C out from the place
	6:9	the misery that had C upon them.
	8:25	of those who had C to buy them as
	9:11	his arrogance and to C to his senses under
	9:18	of God had justly C upon him, he gave
	12:7	he withdrew, intending to C again and root out
	14:7	and have now C here,
	15:8	times when help had C to them from heaven,
	15:24	these blasphemers who C against thy holy people
Mt	2:2	the East, and have C to worship him."
	2:6	for from you shall C a ruler who will
	2:8	that I too may C and worship him."
	3:7	warned you to flee from the wrath to C
	3:14	you, and do you C to me?"
	5:17	not that I have C to abolish the law
	5:17	the prophets; I have C not to abolish them
	5:24	your brother, and then C and offer your gift.
	6:10	Thy kingdom C
	7:15	of false prophets, who C to you in sheep's
	8:7	to him, "I will C and heal him."
	8:8	worthy to have you C under my roof; but
	8:9	goes, and to another, C and he comes, and
	8:11	tell you, many will C from east and west
	8:29	Have you C here to torment us before the
	9:15	The days will C, when the bridegroom is taken
	9:18	has just died; but C and lay your hand
	10:13	worthy, let your peace C upon it; but if
	10:34	think that I have C to bring peace on
	10:34	earth; I have not C to bring peace, but
	10:35	For I have C to set a man against
	11:3	he who is to C, or shall we look
	11:14	accept it, he is Elijah who is to C
	11:28	C to me, all who labor and are heavy
	12:28	kingdom of God has C upon you.
	12:32	in this age or in the age to C
	13:32	birds of the air C and make nests in
	13:49	The angels will C out and separate the evil
	14:28	is you, bid me C to you on the
	14:29	He said, C
	15:19	out of the heart C evil thoughts, murder, adultery,
	16:24	"If any man would C after me, let him
	16:27	of man is to C with his angels in
	17:10	do the scribes say that first Elijah must C
	17:11	He replied, "Elijah does C, and he is to
	17:12	that Elijah has already C, and they did not
	18:7	is necessary that temptations C, but woe to the
	19:14	said, "Let the children C to me, and do
	19:21	treasure in heaven; and C, follow me."
	21:19	"May no fruit ever C from you again!" And
	21:38	'This is the heir; C, let us kill him
	22:3	to the marriage feast; but they would not C
	22:4	and everything is ready; C to the marriage feast.'
	23:34	that upon you may C all the righteous blood
	23:35	you, all this will C upon this generation.
	24:5	For many will C in my name, saying, 'I
	24:14	to all nations; and then the end will C
	24:50	of that servant will C on a day when
	25:6	C out to meet him.'
	25:34	at his right hand, C, O blessed of my
	26:55	the crowds, "Have you C out as against a
	27:40	the Son of God, C down from the cross."
	27:42	of Israel; let him C down now from the
	27:49	see whether Elijah will C to save him."
	28:6	C, see the place where he lay.

Mk 1:24 Have you C to destroy us?
1:25 saying, "Be silent, and C out of him!"
2:20 The days will C, when the bridegroom is taken
3:3 had the withered hand, C here."
4:22 anything secret, except to C to light.
4:29 puts in the sickle, because the harvest has C
4:35 day, when evening had C, he said to them,
5:2 And when he had C out of the boat,
5:8 had said to him, C out of the man,
5:23 C and lay your hands on her, so that
6:31 he said to them, C away by yourselves to
7:1 the scribes, who had C from Jerusalem,
7:4 elders; and when they C from the market place,
7:15 but the things which C out of a man
7:20 the heart of man, C evil thoughts, fornication, theft,
7:22 All these evil things C from within, and they
8:3 some of them have C a long way."
8:34 "If any man would C after me, let him
9:1 kingdom of God has C with power."
9:11 do the scribes say that first Elijah must C
9:12 to them, "Elijah does C first to restore all
9:13 you that Elijah has C, and they did to
9:25 spirit, I command you, C out of him, and
10:14 them, "Let the children C to me, do not
10:21 treasure in heaven; and C, follow me."
10:30 in the age to C eternal life.
11:23 what he says will C to pass, it will
12:7 'This is the heir; C, let us kill him,
12:9 He will C and destroy the tenants, and give
13:6 Many will C in my name, saying, 'I am
13:33 you do not know when the time will C
13:35 of the house will C, in the evening, or
13:36 morning– lest he C suddenly and find you
14:41 enough; the hour has C; the Son of man
14:48 to them, "Have you C out as against a
15:29 days, save yourself, and C down from the cross!"
15:31 the King of Israel, C down now from the
15:32 the sixth hour had C, there was darkness over
15:35 see whether Elijah will C to take him down."
15:41 And when evening had C, since it was the
16:8 trembling and astonishment had C upon them; and
Lk 1:20 day that these things C to pass, because you
1:35 "The Holy Spirit will C upon you, and the
1:43 of my Lord should C to me?
2:10 great joy which will C to all the people;
3:7 warned you to flee from the wrath to C
4:34 Have you C to destroy us?
4:35 saying, "Be silent, and C out of him!" And
4:36 unclean spirits, and they C out."
5:7 the other boat to C and help them.
5:17 sitting by, who had C from every village of
5:32 sick; I have not C to call the righteous,
5:35 The days will C, when the bridegroom is taken
6:8 had the withered hand, C and stand here." And
7:3 Jews, asking him to C and heal his slave.
7:6 worthy to have you C under my roof;
7:7 did not presume to C to you.
7:8 goes; and to another, C and he comes; and
7:19 he who is to C, or shall we look
7:20 when the men had C to him, they said,
7:20 he who is to C, or shall we look
7:33 John the Baptist has C eating no bread and
7:34 Son of man has C eating and drinking; and
8:17 not be known and C to light.
8:29 the unclean spirit to C out of the man.
8:41 he besought him to C to his house,
9:23 "If any man would C after me, let him
9:37 day, when they had C down from the mountain,
9:54 us to bid fire C down from heaven and
10:1 and place where he himself was about to C
10:9 kingdom of God has C near to you.'
10:11 kingdom of God has C near.'
10:35 repay you when I C back.'
11:2 Thy kingdom C
11:20 kingdom of God has C upon you.
12:36 for their master to C home from the marriage
12:37 table, and he will C and serve them.
12:46 of that servant will C on a day when
12:51 think that I have C to give peace on
13:7 three years I have C seeking fruit on this
13:14 ought to be done; C on those days and
13:25 not know where you C from.'
13:27 not know where you C from; depart from me,
13:29 And men will C from east and west, and
14:9 invited you both will C and say to you,
14:17 who had been invited, C; for all is now
14:20 and therefore I cannot C
14:23 and compel people to C in, that my house
14:27 his own cross and C after me, cannot be
15:27 him, 'Your brother has C, and your father has
16:28 them, lest they also C into this place of
17:1 sin are sure to C; but woe to him
17:1 come; but woe to him by whom they C
17:7 him when he has C in from the field,
17:7 in from the field, C at once and sit
17:31 in the house, not C down to take them
18:16 saying, "Let the children C to me, and do
18:22 treasure in heaven; and C, follow me."
18:30 in the age to C eternal life."
19:5 "Zacchaeus, make haste and C down; for I must
19:9 him, "Today salvation has C to this house, since
19:13 with these till I C
19:43 For the days shall C upon you, when your
20:16 He will C and destroy those tenants, and give
21:6 see, the days will C when there shall not
21:8 astray; for many will C in my name, saying,
21:20 that its desolation has C near.
21:30 as soon as they C out in leaf, you
21:34 life, and that day C upon you suddenly like
21:35 snare; for it will C upon all who dwell
22:50 and elders, who had C out against him, "Have
22:50 against him, "Have you C out as against a
23:41 remember me when you C into your kingdom."
23:54 The women who had C with him from Galilee
Jn 1:39 He said to them, C and see." They came
1:46 him, "Can anything good C out of Nazareth?" Philip
1:46 Philip said to him, C and see."
2:4 My hour has not yet C
3:2 you are a teacher C from God; for no
3:19 that the light has C into the world, and
3:20 light, and does not C to the light, lest
4:15 may not thirst, nor C here to draw."
4:16 call your husband, and C here."
4:29 said to the people, C, see a man who
4:47 heard that Jesus had C from Judea to Galilee,
4:47 and begged him to C down and heal his
4:49 said to him, "Sir, C down before my child
4:54 did when he had C from Judea to Galilee.
5:23 life; he does not C into judgment, but has
5:28 hear his voice and C forth, those who have
5:39 yet you refuse to C to me that you
5:42 I have C in my Father's name, and you
6:14 prophet who is to C into the world!"
6:15 they were about to C and take him by
6:17 Jesus had not yet C to them.
6:25 "Rabbi, when did you C here?"
6:37 Father gives me will C to me; and him
6:38 For I have C down from heaven, not to
6:42 now say, 'I have C down from heaven'?"
6:44 No one can C to me unless the Father
6:65 that no one can C to me unless it
6:69 have believed, and have C to know, that you
7:6 time has not yet C, but your time is
7:8 feast, for my time has not yet fully C
7:28 you know where I C from?
7:28 But I have not C of my own accord;
7:29 know him, for I C from him, and he
7:30 on him, because his hour had not yet C
7:34 not find me; where I am you cannot C
7:36 find me,' and, 'Where I am you cannot C
7:37 one thirst, let him C to me and drink.
7:41 "Is the Christ to C from Galilee?
8:14 know whence I have C and whither I am
8:14 not know whence I C or whither I am
8:20 arrested him, because his hour had not yet C
8:21 your sin; where I am going, you cannot C
8:22 he says, 'Where I am going, you cannot C
11:19 of the Jews had C to Martha and Mary
11:30 Jesus had not yet C to the village, but
11:34 said to him, "Lord, C and see."
11:43 a loud voice, "Lazarus, C out."
11:45 Jews therefore, who had C with Mary and had
11:48 and the Romans will C and destroy both our
11:56 That he will not C to the feast?"
12:12 great crowd who had C to the feast heard
12:23 them, "The hour has C for the Son of
12:27 this purpose I have C to this hour.
12:30 answered, "This voice has C for your sake, not
12:46 I have C as light into the world, that
12:47 for I did not C to judge the world
13:1 that his hour had C to depart out of
13:3 and that he had C from God and was

C

13:33 am going you cannot C
14:3 for you, I will C again and will take
14:18 you desolate; I will C to you.
14:23 him, and we will C to him and make
14:28 away, and I will C to you.' If you
15:22 If I had not C and spoken to them,
16:7 the Counselor will not C to you; but if
16:13 declare to you the things that are to C
16:21 because her hour has C; but when she is
16:28 the Father and have C into the world; again,
16:32 coming, indeed it has C, when you will be
17:1 "Father, the hour has C; glorify thy Son that
18:20 temple, where all Jews C together; I have said
18:37 for this I have C into the world, to
19:39 who had at first C to him by night,
21:12 Jesus said to them, C and have breakfast." Now
21:22 he remain until I C, what is that to
21:23 he remain until I C, what is that to
Acts 1:6 So when they had C together, they asked him,
1:8 the Holy Spirit has C upon you; and you
1:11 you into heaven, will C in the same way
2:1 day of Pentecost had C, they were all together
3:19 times of refreshing may C from the presence of
5:24 wondering what this would C to.
7:7 after that they shall C out and worship me
7:34 groaning, and I have C down to deliver them.
7:34 And now C, I will send you to Egypt.'
8:24 you have said may C upon me."
8:27 all her treasure, had C to Jerusalem to worship
8:31 he invited Philip to C up and sit with
9:12 a man named Ananias C in and lay his
9:21 And he has C here for this purpose, to
9:26 And when he had C to Jerusalem he attempted
9:38 him entreating him, "Please C to us without delay."
9:39 And when he had C, they took him to
10:22 send for you to C to his house, and
10:33 once, and you have been kind enough to C
13:40 Beware, therefore, lest there C upon you what is
14:11 Lycaonian, "The gods have C down to us in
15:25 good to us, having C to one accord, to
15:35 Paul said to Barnabas, C, let us return and
16:7 when they had C opposite Mysia, they attempted
16:9 beseeching him and saying, C over to Macedonia and
16:13 the women who had C together.
16:15 faithful to the Lord, C to my house and
16:18 of Jesus Christ to C out of her." And
16:36 you go; now therefore C out and go in
16:37 let them C themselves and take us out."
17:6 world upside down have C here also,
17:15 Silas and Timothy to C to him as soon
18:2 native of Pontus, lately C from Italy with his
19:4 one who was to C after him, that is,
19:27 trade of ours may C into disrepute but also
19:32 know why they had C together.
20:29 departure fierce wolves will C in among you, not
21:3 When we had C in sight of Cyprus, leaving
21:17 When we had C to Jerusalem, the brethren received
21:22 They will certainly hear that you have C
25:1 Now when Festus had C into his province, after
25:7 And when he had C, the Jews who had
26:22 and Moses said would C to pass:
27:27 the fourteenth night had C, as we were drifting
27:29 from the stern, and prayed for day to C
28:6 and saw no misfortune C to him, they changed
Rom 1:13 have often intended to C to you (but thus
3:8 evil that good may C --as some people slanderously
4:13 the world, did not C through the law but
5:14 a type of the one who was to C
8:38 present, nor things to C, nor powers,
11:11 their trespass salvation has C to the Gentiles, so
11:25 brethren: a hardening has C upon part of Israel,
11:25 number of the Gentiles C in,
11:26 written, "The Deliverer will C from Zion, he will
15:12 root of Jesse shall C, he who rises to
15:23 for many years to C to you,
15:27 if the Gentiles have C to share in their
15:29 know that when I C to you I shall
15:29 to you I shall C in the fulness of
15:32 God's will I may C to you with joy
1Cor 2:1 brethren, I did not C proclaiming to you the
4:19 But I will C to you soon, if the
4:21 Shall I C to you with a rod, or
7:5 to prayer; but then C together again, lest Satan
10:11 upon whom the end of the ages has C
11:17 you, because when you C together it is not
11:33 my brethren, when you C together to eat, wait
11:34 at home--lest you C together to be condemned.
11:34 other things I will give directions when I C
14:6 Now, brethren, if I C to you speaking in
14:26 When you C together, each one has a hymn,
15:21 by a man has C also the resurrection of
15:34 C to your right mind, and sin no more.
15:35 With what kind of body do they C
15:36 you sow does not C to life unless it
15:54 on immortality, then shall C to pass the saying
16:2 that contributions need not be made when I C
16:12 all his will to C now.
16:12 He will C when he has opportunity.
16:22 Our Lord, C
2Cor 1:15 this, I wanted to C to you first, so
1:16 to Macedonia, and to C back to you from
3:10 once had splendor has C to have no splendor
5:17 old has passed away, behold, the new has C
6:17 Therefore C out from them, and be separate from
9:4 lest if some Macedonians C with me and find
10:14 were the first to C all the way to
12:14 I am ready to C to you.
12:20 that perhaps I may C and find you not
12:21 fear that when I C again my God may
13:2 visit, that if I C again I will not
13:10 order that when I C I may not have
Gal 3:14 blessing of Abraham might C upon the Gentiles, that
3:19 till the offspring should C to whom the promise
3:25 now that faith has C, we are no longer
4:4 the time had fully C, God sent forth his
4:9 now that you have C to know God, or
Eph 1:21 that which is to C;
4:29 Let no evil talk C out of your mouths,
Phil 1:11 fruits of righteousness which C through Jesus Christ,
1:27 so that whether I C and see you or
2:24 shortly I myself shall C also.
Col 1:6 the gospel which has C to you, as indeed
2:10 bodily, and you have C to fulness of life
2:17 of what is to C; but the substance belongs
1Thes 1:10 Jesus who delivers us from the wrath to C
2:16 But God's wrath has C upon them at last!
2:18 because we wanted to C to you--I, Paul,
3:4 just as it has C to pass, and as
3:6 now that Timothy has C to us from you,
5:2 of the Lord will C like a thief in
5:3 then sudden destruction will C upon them as travail
2Thes 2:2 effect that the day of the Lord has C
2:3 that day will not C, unless the rebellion comes
1Tim 2:4 be saved and to C to the knowledge of
3:14 I hope to C to you soon, but I
4:8 present life and also for the life to C
4:13 Till I C, attend to the public reading of
2Tim 2:25 they will repent and C to know the truth,
3:1 last days there will C times of stress.
4:6 being sacrificed; the time of my departure has C
4:9 Do your best to C to me soon.
4:13 When you C, bring the cloak that I left
4:21 Do your best to C before winter.
Tit 3:12 do your best to C to me at Nicopolis,
Heb 2:5 subjected the world to C, of which we are
6:5 of the age to C,
8:8 says: "The days will C, says the Lord, when
9:11 good things that have C, then through the greater
10:1 the good things to C instead of the true
10:7 said, 'Lo, I have C to do thy will,
10:9 added, "Lo, I have C to do thy will."
10:37 the coming one shall C and shall not tarry;
12:18 For you have not C to what may be
12:22 But you have C to Mount Zion and to
13:14 but we seek the city which is to C
13:24 Those who C from Italy send you greetings.
Jas 3:10 From the same mouth C blessing and cursing.
4:13 C now, you who say, "Today or tomorrow we
5:1 C now, you rich, weep and howl for the
1Pet 2:4 C to him, to that living stone, rejected by
4:17 For the time has C for judgment to begin
2Pet 3:3 this, that scoffers will C in the last days
3:10 of the Lord will C like a thief, and
1Jn 2:18 now many antichrists have C; therefore we know
4:2 that Jesus Christ has C in the flesh is
5:20 Son of God has C and has given us
2Jn 1:12 but I hope to C to see you and
3Jn 1:10 So if I C, I will bring up what
Rev 1:4 and who is to C, and from the seven
1:8 and who is to C, the Almighty.
2:5 If not, I will C to you and remove
2:16 If not, I will C to you soon and

2:25 only hold fast what you have, until I C
3:3 not awake, I will C like a thief, and
3:3 what hour I will C upon you.
3:9 I will make them C and bow down before
3:20 the door, I will C in to him and
4:1 like a trumpet, said, C up hither, and I
4:8 Almighty, who was and is and is to C
6:1 creatures say, as with a voice of thunder, C
6:3 seal, I heard the second living creature say, C
6:5 seal, I heard the third living creature say, C
6:7 the voice of the fourth living creature say, C
6:17 of their wrath has C, and who can stand
7:13 clothed in white robes, and whence have they C
7:14 are they who have C out of the great
9:12 has passed; behold, two woes are still to C
11:12 heaven saying to them, C up hither!" And in
11:14 passed; behold, the third woe is soon to C
12:10 of his Christ have C, for the accuser of
12:12 for the devil has C down to you in
13:13 signs, even making fire C down from heaven to
14:7 of his judgment has C; and worship him who
14:15 hour to reap has C, for the harvest of
15:4 All nations shall C and worship thee, for thy
17:1 and said to me, C, I will show you
17:8 it was and is not and is to C
17:10 other has not yet C, and when he comes
18:4 voice from heaven saying, C out of her, my
18:8 so shall her plagues C in a single day,
18:10 In one hour has thy judgment C
19:7 of the Lamb has C, and his Bride has
19:17 that fly in midheaven, C, gather for the great
20:5 the dead did not C to life until the
20:8 his prison and will C out to deceive the
21:9 spoke to me, saying, C, I will show you
22:17 The Spirit and the Bride say, C
22:17 And let him who hears say, C
22:17 him who is thirsty C, let him who desires
22:20 C, Lord Jesus!

COMELINESS

Is 53:2 had no form or C that we should look

COMELY (7)

Gen 49:21 let loose, that bears C fawns.
1Sam 17:42 a youth, ruddy and C in appearance.
Song 1:5 am very dark, but C, O daughters of Jerusalem,
1:10 Your cheeks are C with ornaments, your neck with
2:14 your voice is sweet, and your face is C
6:4 as Tirzah, my love, C as Jerusalem, terrible as
Jer 6:2 The C and delicately bred I will destroy, the

COMES (313)

Gen 24:43 the young woman who C out to draw, to
24:50 Bethuel answered, "The thing C from the LORD; we
32:8 companies, thinking, "If Esau C to the one company
37:19 to one another, "Here C this dreamer.
42:15 unless your youngest brother C here.
42:22 So now there C a reckoning for his blood."
44:23 'Unless your youngest brother C down with you, you
49:10 his feet, until he C to whom it belongs;
Ex 1:18 delivered before the midwife C to them."
21:3 If he C in single, he shall go out
21:3 out single; if he C in married, then his
28:35 LORD, and when he C out, lest he die.
29:30 seven days, when he C into the tent of
Lev 5:3 from him, when he C to know it he
5:4 from him, when he C to know it he
13:19 of the boil there C a white swelling or
14:48 "But if the priest C and makes an examination,
15:17 on which the semen C shall be washed with
16:17 holy place until he C out and has made
25:22 year, when its produce C in, you shall eat
Num 1:51 if any one else C near, he shall be
3:10 if any one else C near, he shall be
5:14 the spirit of jealousy C upon him, and he
5:14 the spirit of jealousy C upon him, and he
5:30 the spirit of jealousy C upon a man and
11:20 whole month, until it C out at your nostrils
12:12 half consumed when he C out of his mother's
17:13 Every one who C near, who comes near to
17:13 who comes near, who C near to the tabernacle
18:7 any one else who C near shall be put
19:14 tent: every one who C into the tent, and
30:8 day that her husband C to hear of it,
36:4 the people of Israel C, then their inheritance will
Deut 13:2 which he tells you C to pass, and if
14:22 of your seed, which C forth from the field
18:6 "And if a Levite C from any of your
23:11 camp; but when evening C on, he shall bathe
28:57 daughter, her afterbirth that C out from between her
29:22 and the foreigner who C from a far land,
31:11 booths, when all Israel C to appear before the
32:32 For their vine C from the vine of Sodom,
32:35 hand, and their doom C swiftly.
Josh 15:4 Brook of Egypt, and C to its end at
15:11 Jabneel; then the boundary C to an end at
Judg 4:20 and if any man C and asks you, 'Is
11:31 my hand, then whoever C forth from the doors
13:14 eat of anything that C from the vine, neither
1Sam 9:6 all that he says C true.
9:13 not eat till he C, since he must bless
16:11 sit down till he C here."
24:13 'Out of the wicked C forth wickedness'; but my
2Sam 13:5 and when your father C to see you, say
15:28 the wilderness, until word C from you to inform
17:3 you as a bride C home to her husband.
18:27 a good man, and C with good tidings."
1Kgs 8:31 take an oath, and C and swears his oath
8:41 of thy people Israel, C from a far country
8:42 outstretched arm), when he C and prays toward this
2Kgs 4:10 so that whenever he C to us, he can
4:16 season, when the time C round, you shall embrace
6:32 Look, when the messenger C, shut the door, and
10:2 soon as this letter C to you, seeing your
11:8 out and when he C in."
1Chr 16:33 the LORD, for he C to judge the earth.
29:16 for thy holy name C from thy hand and
6:22 take an oath, and C and swears his oath
6:32 of thy people Israel, C from a far country
6:32 outstretched arm, when he C and prays toward this
13:9 Whoever C to consecrate himself with a young bull
19:10 heart: whenever a case C to you from your
20:9 name, saying, 'If evil C upon us, the sword,
23:7 the king when he C in, and when he
Jud 7:32 by, and no help C for us, I will
14:2 as soon as morning C and the sun rises,
Esth 16:9 and always judging what C before our eyes with
Job 3:21 for death, but it C not, and dig for
3:24 For my sighing C as my bread, and my
3:25 thing that I fear C upon me, and what
3:26 I quiet; I have no rest; but trouble C
5:21 tongue, and shall not fear destruction when it C
5:26 a shock of grain C up to the threshing
14:2 He C forth like a flower, and withers; he
20:25 is drawn forth and C out of his body,
20:25 body, the glittering point C out of his gall;
21:17 That their calamity C upon them?
27:9 his cry, when trouble C upon him?
28:5 earth, out of it C bread; but underneath it
28:20 "Whence then C wisdom?
33:26 he accepts him, he C into his presence with
37:2 and the rumbling that C from his mouth.
37:9 From its chamber C the whirlwind, and cold from
37:22 Out of the north C golden splendor; God is
41:20 Out of his nostrils C forth smoke, as from
41:21 coals, and a flame C forth from his mouth.
Ps 19:5 for the sun, which C forth like a bridegroom
22:25 From thee C my praise in the great congregation;
30:5 the night, but joy C with the morning.
41:6 And when one C to see me, he utters
50:3 Our God C, he does not keep silence, before
62:1 in silence; from him C my salvation.
75:6 not from the wilderness C lifting up;
78:39 wind that passes and C not again.
88:13 the morning my prayer C before thee.
96:13 the LORD, for he C, for he comes to
96:13 he comes, for he C to judge the earth.
98:9 the LORD, for he C to judge the earth.
112:10 of the wicked man C to nought.
121:2 My help C from the LORD, who made heaven
Prov 1:27 storm, and your calamity C like a whirlwind, when
3:25 the wicked, when it C;
10:28 expectation of the wicked C to nought.
11:2 When pride C, then comes disgrace; but with the
11:2 When pride comes, then C disgrace; but with the
11:7 expectation of the godless C to nought.
11:27 seeks favor, but evil C to him who searches
12:12 tower of the wicked C to ruin, but the
12:14 of a man's hand C back to him.
13:3 opens wide his lips C to ruin.
18:3 wickedness C, contempt C also; and with dishonor
18:3 also; and with dishonor C disgrace.

18:17 right, until the other C and examines him.
21:5 one who is hasty C only to want.
Eccl 1:4 goes, and a generation C, but the earth remains
2:12 the man do who C after the king?
2:14 perceived that one fate C to all of them.
5:3 For a dream C with much business, and a
6:4 For it C into vanity and goes into darkness,
9:2 vanity, since one fate C to all, to the
9:3 sun, that one fate C to all; also the
11:5 know how the spirit C to the bones in
11:8 All that C is vanity.
Song 2:8 Behold, he C, leaping upon the mountains, bounding
Wis 2:1 remedy when a man C to his end, and
5:12 the air, thus divided, C together at once, so
9:6 without the wisdom that C from thee he will
13:5 of created things C a corresponding perception of
14:7 For blessed is the wood by which righteousness C
Sir 1:1 All wisdom C from the Lord and
3:11 For a man's glory C from honoring his father,
5:14 your tongue; for shame C to the thief, and
19:9 and when the time C he will hate you.
21:5 God, and his judgment C speedily.
26:19 of a third anger C over me: a warrior
38:2 created him; for healing C from the Most High,
42:13 women; for from garments C the moth, and from
42:13 and from a woman C woman's wickedness.
43:7 From the moon C the sign for feast days,
Is 5:26 of the earth; and lo, swiftly, speedily it C
13:9 day of the LORD C, cruel, with wrath and
14:8 laid low, no hewer C up against us.'
14:31 For smoke C out of the north, and there
16:12 high place, when he C to his sanctuary to
19:1 a swift cloud and C to Egypt; and the
21:1 Negeb sweep on, it C from the desert, from
21:12 The watchman says: "Morning C, and also the night.
23:5 When the report C to Egypt, they will be
28:29 This also C from the LORD of hosts; he
30:5 reach Hanes, every one C to shame through a
30:13 to collapse, whose crash C suddenly, in an instant;
30:27 name of the LORD C from far, burning with
34:1 world, and all that C from it.
40:10 Behold, the Lord GOD C with might, and his
42:5 the earth and what C from it, who gives
62:11 Zion, "Behold, your salvation C; behold, his reward is
63:1 Who is this that C from Edom, in crimsoned
Jer 4:12 too full for this C for me.
4:13 Behold, he C up like clouds, his chariots like
5:31 but what will you do when the end C
10:22 Behold, it C –a great commotion out of the
17:8 not fear when heat C, for its leaves remain
27:7 of his own land C; then many nations and
28:9 word of that prophet C to pass, then it
50:41 "Behold, a people C from the north; a mighty
51:46 land, when a report C in one year and
Bar 6:48 when war or calamity C upon them, the priests
Ezek 7:5 Behold, it C
7:6 Behold, it C
7:10 Behold, it C
7:25 When anguish C, they will seek peace, but there
7:26 Disaster C upon disaster, rumor follows rumor; they
12:22 long, and every vision C to nought?
14:4 his face, and yet C to the prophet, I
14:7 his face, and yet C to a prophet to
21:7 When it C, every heart will melt and all
21:7 Behold, it C and it will be fulfilled," says
21:22 Into his right hand C the lot for Jerusalem,
21:27 of it until he C whose right it is;
24:24 When this C, then you will know that I
30:9 the day of Egypt's doom; for, lo, it C
33:4 warning, and the sword C and takes him away,
33:6 warned, and the sword C, and takes any one
33:30 the word is that C forth from the LORD.'
33:33 When this C –and come it will!–then they
Dan 11:16 But he who C against him shall do according
12:7 of the holy people C to an end all
12:12 he who waits and C to the thousand three
Hos 14:8 evergreen cypress, from me C your fruit.
Joel 1:14 near, and as destruction from the Almighty it C
2:31 the great and terrible day of the LORD C
Amos 5:9 strong, so that destruction C upon the fortress.
Mic 5:5 peace, when the Assyrian C into our land and
5:6 the Assyrian when he C into our land and
Zeph 2:2 drifting chaff, before there C upon you the fierce
2:2 the LORD, before there C upon you the day
Zech 9:9 Lo, your king C to you; triumphant and victorious
Mal 4:1 "For behold, the day C, burning like an oven,
4:1 stubble; the day that C shall burn them up,
4:5 the great and terrible day of the LORD C
1Mac 2:41 against every man who C to attack us on
3:19 battle depends, but strength C from Heaven.
8:24 If war C first to Rome or to any
8:27 same way, if war C first to the nation
12:15 have the help which C from Heaven for our
16:3 may the help which C from Heaven be with
2Mac 7:28 Thus also mankind C into being.
Mt 5:37 anything more than this C from evil.
8:9 another, 'Come,' and he C, and to my slave,
10:23 towns of Israel, before the Son of man C
12:44 came.' And when he C he finds it empty,
13:19 it, the evil one C and snatches away what
15:11 a man, but what C out of the mouth,
15:18 But what C out of the mouth proceeds from
17:26 the first fish that C up, and when you
18:7 woe to the man by whom the temptation C
21:9 Blessed is he who C in the name of
21:40 owner of the vineyard C, what will he do
23:38 'Blessed is he who C in the name of
24:27 For as the lightning C from the east and
24:46 his master when he C will find so doing.
25:31 the Son of man C in his glory, and
28:14 asleep.' And if this C to the governor's ears,
Mk 1:7 preached, saying, "After me C he who is mightier
4:15 they hear, Satan immediately C and takes away the
7:19 And he said, "What C out of a man
8:38 be ashamed, when he C in the glory of
11:9 Blessed is he who C in the name of
Lk 6:47 Every one who C to me and hears my
7:8 another, 'Come,' and he C; and to my slave,
8:12 heard; then the devil C and takes away the
9:26 be ashamed when he C in his glory and
11:25 came.' And when he C he finds it swept
12:36 at once when he C and knocks.
12:37 finds awake when he C; truly, I say to
12:38 If he C in the second watch, or in
12:43 his master when he C will find so doing.
13:35 'Blessed is he who C in the name of
14:10 that when your host C he may say to
14:26 them, "If any one C to me and does
14:31 to meet him who C against him with twenty
15:6 And when he C home, he calls together his
18:8 the Son of man C, will he find faith
19:38 is the King who C in the name of
22:18 of the vine until the kingdom of God C
Jn 1:15 I said, 'He who C after me ranks before
1:27 know, even he who C after me, the thong
1:30 I said, 'After me C a man who ranks
3:8 not know whence it C or whither it goes;
3:21 does what is true C to the light, that
3:31 He who C from above is above all; he
3:31 he speaks; he who C from heaven is above
4:25 called Christ); when he C, he will show us
4:35 yet four months, then C the harvest?
5:42 receive me; if another C in his own name,
5:43 seek the glory that C from the only God?
6:33 God is that which C down from heaven, and
6:35 of life; he who C to me shall not
6:37 me; and him who C to me I will
6:45 learned from the Father C to me.
6:50 is the bread which C down from heaven, that
7:27 know where this man C from; and when the
7:27 will know where he C from."
7:42 descended from David, and C from Bethlehem, the
9:4 it is day; night C, when no one can
9:29 not know where he C from."
9:30 not know where he C from, and yet he
10:10 The thief C only to steal and kill and
12:13 Blessed is he who C in the name of
14:6 the life; no one C to the Father, but
15:26 But when the Counselor C, whom I shall send
16:4 that when their hour C you may remember that
16:8 And when he C, he will convince the world
16:13 the Spirit of truth C, he will guide you
Acts 2:20 day of the Lord C, the great and manifest
23:15 kill him before he C near."
24:21 "When Lysias the tribune C down, I will decide
26:22 had the help that C from God, and so
Rom 3:20 since through the law C knowledge of sin.
10:3 of the righteousness that C from God, and seeking
10:17 So faith C from what is heard, and what
10:17 and what is heard C by the preaching of
1Cor 4:5 time, before the Lord C, who will bring to
11:26 cup, you proclaim the Lord's death until he C

13:10 but when the perfect C, the imperfect will pass
15:24 Then C the end, when he delivers the kingdom
16:10 When Timothy C, see that you put him at
2Cor 3:18 to another; for this C from the Lord who
11:4 For if some one C and preaches another Jesus
Eph 5:6 the wrath of God C upon the sons of
Col 4:10 received instructions–if he C to you, receive him),
1Thes 5:3 upon them as travail C upon a woman with
2Thes 1:10 his might, when he C on that day to
2:3 come, unless the rebellion C first, and the man
Heb 9:27 once, and after that C judgment,
11:7 of the righteousness which C by faith.
13:23 see you if he C soon.
Jas 2:2 and in fine clothing C into your assembly, and
2:2 in shabby clothing also C in,
3:15 is not such as C down from above, but
1Pet 4:12 the fiery ordeal which C upon you to prove
2Jn 1:10 If any one C to you and does not
Rev 3:12 the new Jerusalem which C down from my God
17:10 come, and when he C he must remain only

COMFORT (52)

Gen 37:35 daughters rose up to C him; but he refused
1Chr 7:22 his brothers came to C him.
Esth 15:16 his servants sought to C her.
Job 2:11 condole with him and C him.
7:13 say, 'My bed will C me, my couch will
10:20 may find a little C
21:34 How then will you C me with empty nothings?
Ps 23:4 and thy staff, they C me.
71:21 increase my honor, and C me again.
119:50 This is my C in my affliction that thy
119:52 of old, I take C, O LORD.
119:76 love be ready to C me according to thy
119:82 ask, "When wilt thou C me?"
Eccl 4:1 had no one to C them!
4:1 was no one to C them.
Sir 30:23 Delight your soul and C your heart, and remove
Is 12:1 away, and thou didst C me.
22:4 do not labor to C me for the destruction
40:1 C, comfort my people, says your God.
40:1 Comfort, C my people, says your God.
51:3 For the LORD will C Zion; he will comfort
51:3 comfort Zion; he will C all her waste places,
51:19 and sword; who will C you?
57:18 and requite him with C, creating for his mourners
61:2 of our God; to C all who mourn;
66:13 comforts, so I will C you; you shall be
Jer 16:7 for the mourner, to C him for the dead;
31:13 into joy, I will C them, and give them
Lam 1:2 she has none to C her; all her friends
1:17 there is none to C her; the LORD has
1:21 there is none to C me.
2:13 you, that I may C you, O virgin daughter
Bar 4:30 who named you will C you.
Ezek 32:31 sees them, he will C himself for all his
Zech 1:17 the LORD will again C Zion and again choose
Acts 9:31 Lord and in the C of the Holy Spirit
2Cor 1:3 and God of all C,
1:4 may be able to C those who are in
1:4 any affliction, with the C with which we ourselves
1:5 we share abundantly in C too.
1:6 it is for your C and salvation; and if
1:6 it is for your C, which you experience when
1:7 our sufferings, you will also share in our C
2:7 turn to forgive and C him, or he may
7:4 great pride in you; I am filled with C
7:7 but also by the C with which he was
7:13 And besides our own C we rejoiced still more
Col 4:11 they have been a C to me.
1Thes 4:18 Therefore C one another with these words.
2Thes 2:16 and gave us eternal C and good hope through
2:17 good hope through grace, C your hearts and establish
Philem 1:7 derived much joy and C from your love, my

COMFORTED (31)

Gen 24:67 So Isaac was C after his mother's death.
37:35 he refused to be C, and said, "No, I
38:12 and when Judah was C, he went up to
50:21 he reassured them and C them.
Ruth 2:13 lord, for you have C me and spoken kindly
2Sam 12:24 Then David C his wife, Bathsheba, and went in
13:39 Absalom; for he was C about Amnon, seeing he
Tob 7:17 But the mother C her daughter in her tears,
Esth 15:8 And he C her with soothing words, and said
Job 42:11 showed him sympathy and C him for all the
Ps 77:2 out without wearying; my soul refuses to be C
86:17 hast helped me and C me.
Sir 38:17 avoid criticism; then be C for your sorrow.
38:23 remembrance cease, and be C for him when his
48:24 the last things, and C those who mourned in
49:10 they lie, for they C the people of Jacob
Is 49:13 For the LORD has C his people, and will
52:9 for the LORD has C his people, he has
54:11 one, storm-tossed, and not C, behold, I will set
66:13 you; you shall be C in Jerusalem.
Jer 31:15 she refuses to be C for her children, because
Ezek 31:16 drink water, will be C in the nether world.
Mt 5:4 are those who mourn, for they shall be C
Lk 16:25 but now he is C here, and you are
Acts 20:12 lad away alive, and were not a little C
2Cor 1:4 which we ourselves are C by God.
1:6 and if we are C, it is for your
7:6 who comforts the downcast, C us by the coming
7:7 with which he was C in you, as he
7:13 Therefore we are C
1Thes 3:7 affliction we have been C about you through your

COMFORTER (2)

Lam 1:9 therefore her fall is terrible, she has no C
1:16 with tears; for a C is far from me,

COMFORTERS (5)

2Sam 10:3 because David has sent C to you, that he
1Chr 19:3 because David has sent C to you, that he
Job 16:2 many such things; miserable C are you all.
Ps 69:20 was none; and for C, but I found none.
Nah 3:7 whence shall I seek C for her?

COMFORTING

Zech 1:13 LORD answered gracious and C words to the angel

COMFORTS (6)

Gen 27:42 "Behold, your brother Esau C himself by planning to
Job 29:25 troops, like one who C mourners.
Is 51:12 I am he that C you; who are you
66:13 one whom his mother C, so I will comfort
2Cor 1:4 of all comfort, who C us in all our
7:6 But God, who C the downcast, comforted us by

COMING (260)

Gen 24:13 of the city are C out to draw water.
24:63 eyes and looked, and behold, there were camels C
29:6 Rachel his daughter is C with the sheep!"
32:6 Esau, and he is C to meet you, and
33:1 and behold, Esau was C, and four hundred men
37:25 a caravan of Ishmaelites C from Gilead, with their
41:35 good years that are C, and lay up grain
43:25 the present for Joseph's C at noon, for they
Ex 4:14 and behold, he is C out to meet you,
9:32 they are late in C up.)
14:20 and stood behind them, C between the host of
14:20 night passed without one C near the other all
18:6 your father-in-law Jethro is C to you with your
19:9 Moses, "Lo, I am C to you in a
Num 21:1 heard that Israel was C by the way of
22:16 nothing hinder you from C to me;
33:40 Canaan, heard of the C of the people of
Deut 17:9 God will choose, and C to the Levitical priests,
Josh 3:13 flowing, and the waters C down from above shall
3:16 of harvest), the waters C down from above stood
14:11 was then, for war, and for going and C
Judg 1:24 spies saw a man C out of the city,
5:28 lattice: 'Why is his chariot so long in C
6:5 cattle and their tents, C like locusts for number;
9:36 Zebul, "Look, men are C down from the mountain
9:37 said, "Look, men are C down from the center
9:37 and one company is C from the direction of
9:43 and saw the men C out of the city,
11:13 Jephthah, "Because Israel on C from Egypt took
19:16 an old man was C from his work in
Ruth 4:11 the woman, who is C into your house, like
1Sam 2:31 Behold, the days are C, when I will cut
9:11 they met young maidens C out to draw water,
9:14 city, they saw Samuel C out toward them on
10:5 a band of prophets C down from the high
10:8 and behold, I am C to you to offer
11:5 Now Saul was C from the field behind the
14:11 said, "Look, Hebrews are C out of the holes
18:6 As they were C home, when David returned from
22:9 the son of Jesse C to Nob, to Ahimelech
28:13 "I see a god C up out of the

28:14 "An old man is C up; and he is
29:6 the day of your C to me to this
2Sam 3:25 going out and your C in, and to know
13:34 behold, many people were C from the Horonaim
14:28 in Jerusalem, without C into the king's presence.
24:20 king and his servants C on toward him; and
1Kgs 14:5 wife of Jeroboam is C to inquire of you
20:17 to him, "Men are C out from Samaria."
2Kgs 4:25 of God saw her C, he said to Gehazi
9:18 but he is not C back."
9:20 but he is not C back.
10:15 the son of Rechab C to meet him; and
19:27 your going out and C in, and your raging
20:17 Behold, the days are C, when all that is
1Chr 12:22 to day men kept C to David to help
20:2 "A great multitude is C against you from Edom,
20:11 they reward us by C to drive us out
20:12 great multitude that is C against us.
28:12 against those who were C from the war,
35:21 I am not C against you this day, but
Ezra 3:8 second year of their C to the house of
Neh 6:10 temple; for they are C to kill you, at
6:10 at night they are C to kill you."
Tob 11:6 caught sight of him C, and said to his
11:6 "Behold, your son is C, and so is the
Jud 2:7 water, for I am C against them in my
6:12 slingers kept them from C up by casting stones
10:12 and where are you C from, and where are
Esth 8:6 the calamity that is C to my people?
Ps 22:30 the Lord to the C generation,
37:13 wicked, for he sees that his day is C
78:4 but tell to the C generation the glorious deeds
121:8 going out and your C in from this time
Song 3:6 What is that C up from the wilderness, like
8:5 Who is that C up from the wilderness, leaning
Wis 5:11 no sign of its C is found there;
Sir 38:21 forget, there is no C back; you do the
Is 26:21 behold, the LORD is C forth out of his
37:28 your going out and C in, and your raging
39:6 Behold, the days are C, when all that is
66:18 thoughts, and I am C to gather all nations
Jer 4:16 that he is C; announce to Jerusalem, "Besiegers
6:22 "Behold, a people is C from the north country,
7:32 behold, the days are C, says the LORD, when
8:7 the time of their C; but my people know
9:25 "Behold, the days are C, says the LORD, when
16:14 behold, the days are C, says the LORD, when
19:6 therefore, behold, days are C, says the LORD, when
23:5 "Behold, the days are C, says the LORD, when
23:7 behold, the days are C, says the LORD, when
30:3 For behold, days are C, says the LORD, when
31:27 "Behold, the days are C, says the LORD, when
31:31 "Behold, the days are C, says the LORD, when
31:38 "Behold, the days are C, says the LORD, when
33:5 sword: The Chaldeans are C in to fight and
33:14 "Behold, the days are C, says the LORD, when
46:13 the prophet about the C of Nebuchadrezzar king of
47:4 the day that is C to destroy all the
48:12 behold, the days are C, says the LORD, when
49:2 behold, the days are C, says the LORD, when
49:19 Behold, like a lion C up from the jungle
50:44 "Behold, like a lion C up from the jungle
51:47 behold, the days are C when I will punish
51:52 behold, the days are C, says the LORD, when
Bar 4:36 the joy that is C to you from God!
4:37 Behold, your sons are C, whom you sent away;
4:37 sent away; they are C, gathered from east and
Ezek 33:3 he sees the sword C upon the land and
33:6 watchman sees the sword C and does not blow
38:9 You will advance, C on like a storm, you
39:8 Behold, it is C and it will be brought
43:2 the sound of his C was like the sound
47:2 and the water was C out on the south
Dan 4:23 watcher, a holy one, C down from heaven and
9:25 build Jerusalem to the C of an anointed one,
Joel 2:1 of the LORD is C, it is near,
Amos 4:2 behold, the days are C upon you, when they
8:11 "Behold, the days are C
9:13 "Behold, the days are C
Mic 1:3 behold, the LORD is C forth out of his
Zech 1:21 said, "What are these C to do?" He answered,
5:9 and behold, two women C forward!
14:1 of the LORD is C, when the spoil taken
Mal 3:1 delight, behold, he is C, says the LORD of
3:2 the day of his C, and who can stand
1Mac 3:17 they saw the army C to meet them, they
4:12 up and saw them C against them,
4:19 speech, a detachment appeared, C out of the hills.
4:60 keep the Gentiles from C and trampling them down
14:21 glory and honor, and we rejoiced at their C
16:5 infantry and horsemen was C to meet them; and
2Mac 8:6 C without warning, he would set fire to towns
8:16 Gentiles who were wickedly C against them, but to
8:18 down those who are C against us and even
12:38 the seventh day was C on, they purified themselves
13:1 that Antiochus Eupator was C with a great army
13:9 with barbarous arrogance was C to show the Jews
14:15 Jews heard of Nicanor's C and the gathering of
15:20 looking forward to the C decision, and the enemy
Mt 3:7 the Pharisees and Sadducees C for baptism, he said
3:11 but he who is C after me is mightier
8:28 two demoniacs met him, C out of the tombs,
13:54 away from there, and C to his own country
16:28 the Son of man C in his kingdom."
17:9 And as they were C down the mountain, Jesus
21:5 Behold, your king is C to you, humble, and
24:3 the sign of your C and of the close
24:27 so will be the C of the Son of
24:30 the Son of man C on the clouds of
24:37 so will be the C of the Son of
24:39 so will be the C of the Son of
24:42 not know on what day your Lord is C
24:43 night the thief was C, he would have watched
24:44 Son of man is C at an hour you
25:27 bankers, and at my C I should have received
26:2 days the Passover is C, and the Son of
26:64 hand of Power, and C on the clouds of
27:53 asleep were raised, and C out of the tombs
Mk 3:26 cannot stand, but is C to an end.
6:31 For many were C and going, and they had
9:9 And as they were C down the mountain, he
11:10 the kingdom of our father David that is C
13:26 the Son of man C in clouds with great
14:62 hand of Power, and C with the clouds of
15:21 of Cyrene, who was C in from the country,
Lk 2:38 And C up at that very hour she gave
3:16 mightier than I is C, the thong of whose
9:42 While he was C, the demon tore him and
12:39 hour the thief was C, he would have been
12:40 Son of man is C at an unexpected hour."
12:45 master is delayed in C and begins to beat
12:54 once, 'A shower is C; and so it happens.
17:20 kingdom of God was C, he answered them, "The
17:20 of God is not C with signs to be
17:22 disciples, "The days are C when you will desire
18:3 that city who kept C to him and saying,
18:5 she will wear me out by her continual C
19:23 bank, and at my C I should have collected
21:26 foreboding of what is C on the world; for
21:27 the Son of man C in a cloud with
23:25 of Cyrene, who was C in from the country,
23:28 behold, the days are C when they will say,
23:35 soldiers also mocked him, C up and offering him
Jn 1:9 enlightens every man was C into the world.
1:29 day he saw Jesus C toward him, and said,
1:47 Jesus saw Nathanael C to him, and said of
4:21 me, the hour is C when neither on this
4:23 But the hour is C, and now is, when
4:25 know that Messiah is C (he who is called
4:30 the city and were C to him.
5:24 you, the hour is C, and now is, when
5:27 for the hour is C when all who are
6:5 that a multitude was C to him, Jesus said
10:12 not, sees the wolf C and leaves the sheep
11:20 heard that Jesus was C, she went and met
11:27 God, he who is C into the world."
12:12 heard that Jesus was C to Jerusalem.
12:15 behold, your king is C, sitting on an ass's
14:30 you, for the ruler of this world is C
16:2 indeed, the hour is C when whoever kills you
16:25 figures; the hour is C when I shall no
16:32 The hour is C, indeed it has come, when
17:11 world, and I am C to thee.
17:13 But now I am C to thee; and these
Acts 7:52 announced beforehand the C of the Righteous One,
10:3 an angel of God C in and saying to
10:9 on their journey and C near the city, Peter
10:21 looking for; what is the reason for your C
11:20 and Cyrene, who on C to Antioch spoke to
13:24 Before his C John had preached a baptism of
13:25 after me one is C, the sandals of whose
21:11 And C to us he took Paul's girdle and

28:21 none of the brethren C here has reported or
Rom 1:10 at last succeed in C to you.
15:22 often been hindered from C to you.
1Cor 4:18 though I were not C to you.
15:23 fruits, then at his C those who belong to
16:17 I rejoice at the C of Stephanas and Fortunatus
2Cor 1:23 that I refrained from C to Corinth.
3:5 to claim anything as C from us; our competence
7:6 comforted us by the C of Titus,
7:7 not only by his C but also by the
13:1 third time I am C to you.
Eph 2:7 Jesus, that in the C ages he might show
Phil 1:26 Jesus, because of my C to you again.
Col 3:6 account of these the wrath of God is C
1Thes 2:19 of boasting before our Lord Jesus at his C
3:13 and Father, at the C of our Lord Jesus
4:15 are left until the C of the Lord, shall
5:23 and blameless at the C of our Lord Jesus
2Thes 2:1 Now concerning the C of our Lord Jesus Christ
2:8 and destroy him by his appearing and his C
2:9 The C of the lawless one by the activity
2Tim 4:3 For the time is C when people will not
Heb 10:37 little while, and the C one shall come and
Jas 1:16 gift is from above, C down from the Father
5:1 the miseries that are C upon you.
5:7 therefore, brethren, until the C of the Lord.
5:8 your hearts, for the C of the Lord is
1Pet 1:13 the grace that is C to you at the
2Pet 1:16 you the power and C of our Lord Jesus
3:4 and saying, "Where is the promise of his C
3:12 for and hastening the C of the day of
1Jn 2:18 heard that antichrist is C, so now many antichrists
2:28 not shrink from him in shame at his C
4:3 heard that it was C, and now it is
2Jn 1:7 will not acknowledge the C of Jesus Christ in
Rev 1:7 Behold, he is C with the clouds, and every
3:10 of trial which is C on the whole world,
3:11 I am C soon; hold fast what you have,
10:1 saw another mighty angel C down from heaven
16:15 ("Lo, I am C like a thief!
18:1 I saw another angel C down from heaven, having
20:1 I saw an angel C down from heaven, holding
21:2 holy city, new Jerusalem, C down out of heaven
21:10 the holy city Jerusalem C down out of heaven
22:7 And behold, I am C soon." Blessed is he
22:12 "Behold, I am C soon, bringing my recompense, to
22:20 says, "Surely I am C soon." Amen.

COMMAND (245)

Gen 27:8 my word as I C you.
41:40 order themselves as you C; only as regards the
45:19 fat of the land.' C them also, 'Do this:
45:21 wagons, according to the C of Pharaoh, and gave
50:16 "Your father gave this C before he died,
Ex 7:2 speak all that I C you; and Aaron your
8:9 Pharaoh, "Be pleased to C me when I am
8:27 God as he will C us."
27:20 "And you shall C the people of Israel that
34:11 "Observe what I C you this day.
36:6 So Moses gave C, and word was proclaimed
Lev 6:9 LORD said to Moses, C Aaron and his sons,
13:54 then the priest shall C that they wash the
14:4 leper, the priest shall C them to take for
14:5 and the priest shall C them to kill one
14:36 Then the priest shall C that they empty the
14:40 then the priest shall C that they take out
24:2 LORD said to Moses, C the people of Israel
25:21 our crop?' I will C my blessing upon you
Num 4:27 shall be at the C of Aaron and his
5:2 LORD said to Moses, C the people of Israel
9:8 what the LORD will C concerning you."
9:18 At the C of the LORD the people of
9:18 out, and at the C of the LORD they
9:20 and according to the C of the LORD they
9:20 then according to the C of the LORD they
9:23 At the C of the LORD they encamped, and
9:23 encamped, and at the C of the LORD they
9:23 the LORD, at the C of the LORD by
10:13 first time at the C of the LORD by
13:3 Paran, according to the C of the LORD, all
14:41 are you transgressing the C of the LORD, for
20:24 you rebelled against my C at the waters of
22:18 not go beyond the C of the LORD my
23:20 Behold, I received a C to bless: he has
28:2 LORD said to Moses, C the people of Israel,
31:49 who are under our C, and there is not
32:28 So Moses gave C concerning them to Eleazar the
33:2 stage by stage, by C of the LORD; and
33:38 Mount Hor at the C of the LORD, and
34:2 LORD said to Moses, C the people of Israel,
35:2 the Jordan at Jericho, C the people of Israel,
Deut 1:26 but rebelled against the C of the LORD your
1:43 you rebelled against the C of the LORD, and
2:4 And C the people, You are about to pass
4:2 the word which I C you, nor take from
4:2 your God which I C you.
4:40 his commandments, which I C you this day, that
6:2 his commandments, which I C you, all the days
6:6 these words which I C you this day shall
7:11 the ordinances, which I C you this day.
8:1 the commandment which I C you this day you
8:11 his statutes, which I C you this day:
10:13 the LORD, which I C you this day for
11:8 the commandment which I C you this day, that
11:13 my commandments which I C you this day, to
11:22 this commandment which I C you to do, loving
11:27 your God, which I C you this day,
11:28 the way which I C you this day, to
12:11 bring all that I C you: your burnt offerings
12:28 these words which I C you, that it may
12:32 "Everything that I C you, you shall be careful
13:18 his commandments which I C you this day, and
15:5 this commandment which I C you this day.
15:11 the land; therefore I C you, You shall open
15:15 redeemed you; therefore I C you this today.
18:18 them all that I C him.
19:7 Therefore I C you, You shall set apart three
19:9 this commandment, which I C you this day, by
24:18 from there; therefore I C you to do this.
24:22 of Egypt; therefore I C you to do this.
27:1 the commandment which I C you this day.
27:4 stones, concerning which I C you this day, on
27:10 his statutes, which I C you this day."
28:1 his commandments which I C you this day, the
28:8 The LORD will C the blessing upon you in
28:13 your God, which I C you this day, being
28:14 the words which I C you this day, to
28:15 his statutes which I C you this day, then
30:2 in all that I C you this day, with
30:8 his commandments which I C you this day.
30:11 this commandment which I C you this day is
30:16 your God which I C you this day, by
32:46 day, that you may C them to your children,
Josh 1:11 through the camp, and C the people, 'Prepare your
1:18 your words, whatever you C him, shall be put
3:8 And you shall C the priests who bear the
4:3 tribe a man, and C them, 'Take twelve stones
4:16 LORD said to Joshua, C the priests who bear
19:50 By C of the LORD they gave him the
21:3 So by C of the LORD the people of
22:9 had possessed themselves by C of the LORD through
Judg 2:2 their altars.' But you have not obeyed my C
1Sam 16:16 Let our lord now C your servants, who are
2Sam 13:32 dead, for by the C of Absalom this has
18:2 one third under the C of Joab, one third
18:2 one third under the C of Abishai the son
18:2 one third under the C of Ittai the Gittite.
20:23 Now Joab was in C of all the army
20:23 of Jehoiada was in C of the Cherethites and
1Kgs 4:4 of Jehoiada was in C of the army; Zadok
5:6 my name.' Now therefore C that cedars of Lebanon
5:17 At the king's C, they quarried out great, costly
11:38 to all that I C you, and will walk
20:35 his fellow at the C of the LORD, "Strike
2Kgs 18:36 word, for the king's C was, "Do not answer
23:35 money according to the C of Pharaoh.
24:3 upon Judah at the C of the LORD, to
25:19 who had been in C of the men of
1Chr 10:13 did not keep the C of the LORD, and
12:32 hundred chiefs, and all their kinsmen under their C
14:12 there, and David gave C, and they were burned.
21:6 numbering, for the king's C was abhorrent to Joab.
21:17 not I who gave C to number the people?
27:6 the thirty and in C of the thirty; Ammizabad
28:21 all the people will be wholly at your C
7:13 is no rain, or C the locust to devour
24:21 against him, and by C of the king they
26:13 Under their C was an army of three hundred
31:5 As soon as the C was spread abroad, the
35:10 Levites in their divisions according to the king's C
35:15 place according to the C of David, and Asaph,
35:16 LORD, according to the C of King Josiah.

C

Ezra 6:14 finished their building by C of the God of
9:11 commandments, which thou didst C by thy servants
Neh 1:7 ordinances which thou didst C thy servant Moses.
1:8 word which thou didst C thy servant Moses, saying,
9:14 thy holy sabbath and C them commandments and
11:23 For there was a C from the king concerning
12:45 gatekeepers, according to the C of David and his
Tob 3:6 according to thy pleasure; C my spirit to be
3:6 C that I now be released from my distress
3:13 C that I be released from the earth and
3:15 to take my life, C that respect be shown
Jud 2:3 had not obeyed his C should be destroyed.
12:6 "Let my lord now C that your servant be
Esth 1:12 come at the king's C conveyed by the eunuchs.
1:15 has not performed the C of King Ahasuerus conveyed
3:3 to Mordecai, "Why do you transgress the king's C
4:3 province, wherever the king's C and his decree came,
8:14 urged by the king's C; and the decree was
8:17 city, wherever the king's C and his edict came,
9:1 same, when the king's C and edict were about
9:32 The C of Queen Esther fixed these practices of
Job 37:15 how God lays his C upon them, and causes
39:27 Is it at your C that the eagle mounts
Ps 68:11 The Lord gives the C; great is the host
147:15 He sends forth his C to the earth; his
148:8 hail, snow and frost, stormy wind fulfilling his C
Prov 8:29 might not transgress his C, when he marked out
Eccl 8:2 Keep the king's C, and because of your sacred
8:5 He who obeys a C will meet no harm,
Wis 9:8 Thou hast given C to build a temple on
14:16 law, and at the C of monarchs graven images
16:6 of deliverance to remind them of thy law's C
18:16 sword of thy authentic C, and stood and filled
Sir 39:18 At his C whatever pleases him is done, and
43:5 it; and at his C it hastens on its
43:10 At the C of the Holy One they stand
43:13 By his C he sends the driving snow and
Is 5:6 up; I will also C the clouds that they
10:6 of my wrath I C him, to take spoil
23:11 the LORD has given C concerning Canaan to destroy
36:21 word, for the king's C was, "Do not answer
45:11 about my children, or C me concerning the work
Jer 1:7 go, and whatever I C you you shall speak.
1:17 them everything that I C you.
7:22 to your fathers or C them concerning burnt offerings
7:23 But this C I gave them, 'Obey my voice,
7:23 the way that I C you, that it may
7:31 which I did not C, nor did it come
11:4 do all that I C you.
14:14 them, nor did I C them or speak to
19:5 which I did not C or decree, nor did
26:2 the words that I C you to speak to
29:23 which I did not C them.
32:23 of all thou didst C them to do.
32:35 though I did not C them, nor did it
34:22 Behold, I will C, says the LORD, and will
35:14 The C which Jonadab the son of Rechab gave
35:14 this day, for they have obeyed their father's C
35:16 Rechab have kept the C which their father gave
35:18 you have obeyed the C of Jonadab your father,
39:11 gave C concerning Jeremiah through Nebuzaradan,
52:25 who had been in C of the men of
Bar 2:28 day when thou didst C him to write thy
5:8 every fragrant tree have shaded Israel at God's C
6:62 over the whole world, they carry out his C
Ezek 9:11 done as thou didst C me."
Dan 3:96 at nought the king's C, and yielded up their
Amos 9:3 sea, there I will C the serpent, and it
9:4 enemies, there I will C the sword, and it
9:9 "For lo, I will C, and shake the house
Zech 9:10 off, and he shall C peace to the nations;
Mal 2:1 now, O priests, this C is for you.
2:4 I have sent this C to you, that my
1Mac 1:43 the Gentiles accepted the C of the king.
1:50 does not obey the C of the king shall
2:23 the altar in Modein, according to the king's C
2:31 had rejected the king's C had gone down to
2:55 because he fulfilled the C, became a judge in
2:66 his youth; he shall C the army for you
3:1 was called Maccabeus, took C in his place.
3:14 Judas and his companions, who scorn the king's C
5:19 he gave them this C, "Take charge of this
5:42 and gave them this C, "Permit no man to
12:23 We therefore C that our envoys report to you
2Mac 7:30 not obey the king's C, but I obey the
7:30 but I obey the C of the law that
8:9 and sent him, in C of no fewer than
8:22 and Jonathan, each to C a division, putting fifteen
9:8 thinking that he could C the waves of the
10:13 Unable to C the respect due his office, he
12:20 divisions, set men in C of the divisions, and
14:12 who had been in C of the elephants, appointed
14:16 At the C of the leader, they set out
15:5 on earth, and I C you to take up
Mt 4:3 the Son of God, C these stones to become
19:7 "Why then did Moses C one to give a
20:21 She said to him, C that these two sons
Mk 9:25 and deaf spirit, I C you, come out of
10:3 them, "What did Moses C you?"
Lk 4:3 the Son of God, C this stone to become
8:31 begged him not to C them to depart into
15:29 I never disobeyed your C; yet you never gave
Jn 15:14 you do what I C you.
15:17 This I C you, to love one another.
Acts 17:15 Athens; and receiving a C for Silas and Timothy
25:23 Then by C of Festus Paul was brought in.
Rom 16:25 nations, according to the C of the eternal God,
1Cor 7:6 say this by way of concession, not of C
7:25 unmarried, I have no C of the Lord, but
14:37 to you is a C of the Lord.
2Cor 8:8 this not as a C, but to prove by
1Thes 4:12 so that you may C the respect of outsiders,
4:16 with a cry of C, with the archangel's call,
2Thes 3:4 doing and will do the things which we C
3:6 Now we C you, brethren, in the name of
3:10 we gave you this C: If any one will
3:12 Now such persons we C and exhort in the
1Tim 1:1 of Christ Jesus by C of God our Savior
4:11 C and teach these things.
5:7 C this, so that they may be without reproach.
Tit 1:3 have been entrusted by C of God our Savior;
Philem 1:8 enough in Christ to C you to do what

COMMANDED (418)

Gen 2:16 And the LORD God C the man, saying, "You
3:11 tree of which I C you not to eat?"
3:17 tree of which I C you, 'You shall not
6:22 did all that God C him.
7:5 that the LORD had C him.
7:9 Noah, as God had C Noah.
7:16 in as God had C him; and the LORD
21:4 old, as God had C him.
44:1 Then he C the steward of his house, "Fill
47:11 in the land of Rameses, as Pharaoh had C
50:2 And Joseph C his servants the physicians to embalm
50:12 him as he had C them;
Ex 1:16 the king of Egypt C them, but let the
1:21 Then Pharaoh C all his people, "Every son that
5:6 The same day Pharaoh C the taskmasters of the
7:6 did as the LORD C them.
7:10 did as the LORD C; Aaron cast down his
7:20 did as the LORD C; in the sight of
12:28 as the LORD had C Moses and Aaron, so
12:50 Israel; as the LORD C Moses and Aaron, so
16:16 what the LORD has C: 'Gather of it, every
16:23 what the LORD has C: 'Tomorrow is a day
16:32 what the LORD has C: 'Let an omer of
16:34 As the LORD C Moses, so Aaron placed it
19:7 which the LORD had C him.
23:15 unleavened bread; as I C you, you shall eat
29:35 all that I have C you; through seven days
31:6 all that I have C you:
31:11 all that I have C you they shall do."
32:8 the way which I C them; they have made
34:4 as the LORD had C him, and took in
34:18 unleavened bread, as I C you, at the time
34:34 Israel what he was C,
35:1 which the LORD has C you to do.
35:4 "This is the thing which the LORD has C
35:10 that the LORD has C: the tabernacle,
35:29 which the LORD had C by Moses to be
36:1 in accordance with all that the LORD has C
36:5 which the LORD has C us to do."
38:22 all that the LORD C Moses;
39:1 as the LORD had C Moses.
39:5 as the LORD had C Moses.
39:7 as the LORD had C Moses.
39:21 as the LORD had C Moses.
39:26 as the LORD had C Moses.
39:29 as the LORD had C Moses.
39:31 as the LORD had C Moses.
39:32 that the LORD had C Moses; so had they

39:42 that the LORD had C Moses, so the people
39:43 as the LORD had C, so had they done
Lev 4:2 which the LORD has C not to be done,
4:13 which the LORD has C not to be done
4:22 LORD his God has C not to be done,
4:27 which the LORD has C not to be done,
5:17 which the LORD has C not to be done,
7:36 the LORD; the LORD C this to be given
7:38 offerings, which the LORD C Moses on Mount Sinai,
7:38 the day that he C the people of Israel
8:4 did as the LORD C him; and the congregation
8:5 which the LORD has C to be done."
8:9 crown, as the LORD C Moses.
8:13 them, as the LORD C Moses.
8:17 camp, as the LORD C Moses.
8:21 LORD, as the LORD C Moses.
8:29 ordination, as the LORD C Moses.
8:31 ordination offerings, as I C, saying, 'Aaron and his
8:34 today, the LORD has C to be done to
8:35 charged, lest you die; for so I am C
8:36 things which the LORD C by Moses.
9:5 they brought what Moses C before the tent of
9:6 thing which the LORD C you to do; and
9:7 make atonement for them; as the LORD has C
9:10 altar, as the LORD C Moses.
9:21 a wave offering before the LORD; as Moses C
10:1 as he had not C them.
10:13 fire to the LORD; for so I am C
10:15 a due for ever; as the LORD has C
10:18 have eaten it in the sanctuary, as I C
16:34 did as the LORD C him.
17:2 This is the thing which the LORD has C
24:23 did as the LORD C Moses.
27:34 commandments which the LORD C Moses for the
Num 1:19 head, as the LORD C Moses.
1:54 all that the LORD C Moses.
2:33 Israel, as the LORD C Moses.
2:34 all that the LORD C Moses, so they encamped
3:16 the word of the LORD, as he was C
3:42 Israel, as the LORD C him.
3:51 LORD, as the LORD C Moses.
4:49 him, as the LORD C Moses.
8:3 lampstand, as the LORD C Moses.
8:20 all that the LORD C Moses concerning the Levites,
8:22 as the LORD had C Moses concerning the Levites,
9:5 all that the LORD C Moses, so the people
15:23 that the LORD has C you by Moses, from
15:36 stones, as the LORD C Moses.
17:11 Moses; as the LORD C him, so he did.
19:2 which the LORD has C: Tell the people of
20:9 the LORD, as he C him.
20:27 did as the LORD C; and they went up
26:4 as the LORD C Moses.
27:11 ordinance, as the LORD C Moses.'"
27:22 did as the LORD C him; he took Joshua
29:40 as the LORD had C Moses.
30:1 of Israel, "This is what the LORD has C
30:16 statutes which the LORD C Moses, as between a
31:7 Midian, as the LORD C Moses, and slew every
31:21 which the LORD has C Moses:
31:31 did as the LORD C Moses.
31:41 priest, as the LORD C Moses.
31:47 LORD; as the LORD C Moses.
34:13 Moses C the people of Israel, saying, "This is
34:13 which the LORD has C to give to the
34:29 men whom the LORD C to divide the inheritance
36:2 they said, "The LORD C my lord to give
36:2 and my lord was C by the LORD to
36:5 And Moses C the people of Israel according to
36:10 did as the LORD C Moses;
36:13 ordinances which the LORD C by Moses to the
Deut 1:18 hear it.' And I C you at that time
1:19 the LORD our God C us; and we came
1:41 the LORD our God C us.' And every man
3:18 "And I C you at that time, saying, 'The
3:21 given you.' And I C Joshua at that time,
4:5 the LORD my God C me, that you should
4:13 his covenant, which he C you to perform, that
4:14 And the LORD C me at that time to
5:12 the LORD your God C you.
5:15 the LORD your God C you to keep the
5:16 the LORD your God C you; that your days
5:32 LORD your God has C you; you shall not
5:33 LORD your God has C you, that you may
6:1 the LORD your God C me to teach you,
6:17 statutes, which he has C you.
6:20 LORD our God has C you?'
6:24 And the LORD C us to do all these
6:25 God, as he has C us.'
9:12 the way which I C them; they have made
9:16 which the LORD had C you.
10:5 are, as the LORD C me.
12:21 you, as I have C you; and you may
13:5 the LORD your God C you to walk.
18:20 which I have not C him to speak, or
20:17 LORD your God has C;
24:8 direct you; as I C them, so you shall
26:13 commandment which thou hast C me; I have not
26:14 all that thou hast C me.
27:1 the elders of Israel C the people, saying, "Keep
28:45 his statutes which he C you.
29:1 covenant which the LORD C Moses to make with
31:5 commandment which I have C you.
31:10 And Moses C them, "At the end of every
31:25 the very end, Moses C the Levites who carried
31:29 way which I have C you; and in the
33:4 from thee, when Moses C us a law, as
34:9 as the LORD had C Moses.
Josh 1:7 which Moses my servant C you; turn not from
1:9 Have I not C you?
1:10 Then Joshua C the officers of the people,
1:13 servant of the LORD C you, saying, 'The LORD
1:16 "All that you have C us we will do,
3:3 through the camp and C the people, "When you
4:8 Israel did as Joshua C, and took up twelve
4:10 finished that the LORD C Joshua to tell the
4:10 all that Moses had C Joshua.
4:17 Joshua therefore C the priests, "Come up out of
6:8 And as Joshua had C the people, the seven
6:10 But Joshua C the people, "You shall not shout
7:11 my covenant which I C them; they have taken
8:4 And he C them, "Behold, you shall lie in
8:8 bidden; see, I have C you."
8:27 the LORD which he C Joshua.
8:29 of the sun Joshua C, and they took his
8:31 of the LORD had C the people of Israel,
8:33 of the LORD had C at the first, that
8:35 of all that Moses C which Joshua did not
9:24 LORD your God had C his servant Moses to
10:27 of the sun, Joshua C, and they took them
10:40 that breathed, as the LORD God of Israel C
11:12 as Moses the servant of the LORD had C
11:15 As the LORD had C Moses his servant, so
11:15 his servant, so Moses C Joshua, and so Joshua
11:15 that the LORD had C Moses.
11:20 exterminated, as the LORD C Moses.
13:6 inheritance, as I have C you.
14:2 as the LORD had C Moses for the nine
14:5 did as the LORD C Moses; they allotted the
17:4 and said, "The LORD C Moses to give us
21:2 of Canaan, "The LORD C through Moses that we
21:8 as the LORD had C through Moses.
22:2 servant of the LORD C you, and have obeyed
22:2 all that I have C you;
22:5 servant of the LORD C you, to love the
23:16 your God, which he C you, and go and
Judg 2:20 my covenant which I C their fathers, and have
3:4 the LORD, which he C their fathers by Moses.
3:19 And he C, "Silence." And all his attendants went
13:14 thing; all that I C her let her observe."
21:10 their bravest men, and C them, "Go and smite
21:20 And they C the Benjaminites, saying, "Go and lie
1Sam 2:29 my offerings which I C, and honor your sons
13:13 your God, which he C you; for now the
13:14 kept what the LORD C you."
16:4 did what the LORD C, and came to Bethlehem.
17:20 went, as Jesse had C him; and he came
18:22 And Saul C his servants, "Speak to David in
20:29 and my brother has C me to be there.
2Sam 4:12 And David C his young men, and they killed
5:25 did as the LORD C him, and smote the
7:7 of Israel, whom I C to shepherd my people
13:28 Absalom C his servants, "Mark when Amnon's heart
13:28 not; have I not C you?
13:29 of Absalom did to Amnon as Absalom had C
18:12 our hearing the king C you and Abishai and
21:14 father; and they did all that the king C
24:19 went up at Gad's word, as the LORD C
1Kgs 2:46 Then the king C Benaiah the son of Jehoiada;
8:58 his ordinances, which he C our fathers.
9:4 all that I have C you, and keeping my
11:10 him twice, and had C him concerning this thing,

 COMMANDED

11:10 but he did not keep what the LORD C
11:11 statutes which I have C you, I will surely
13:9 for so was it C me by the word
13:21 the LORD your God C you,
15:5 from anything that he C him all the days
17:4 brook, and I have C the ravens to feed
17:9 Behold, I have C a widow there to feed
22:31 king of Syria had C the thirty-two captains of
2Kgs 5:13 if the prophet had C you to do some
11:5 And he C them, "This is the thing that
11:9 that Jehoiada the priest C, and each brought his
11:15 Then Jehoiada the priest C the captains who were
14:6 Moses, where the LORD C, "The fathers shall not
16:15 And King Ahaz C Uriah the priest, saying, "Upon
16:16 the priest did all this, as King Ahaz C
17:13 the law which I C your fathers, and which
17:15 whom the LORD had C them that they should
17:27 the king of Assyria C, "Send there one of
17:34 which the LORD C the children of Jacob,
17:35 covenant with them, and C them, "You shall not
18:6 commandments which the LORD C Moses.
18:12 servant of the LORD C; they neither listened nor
21:8 all that I have C them, and according to
21:8 that my servant Moses C them."
22:12 And the king C Hilkiah the priest, and Ahikam
23:4 And the king C Hilkiah, the high priest, and
23:21 And the king C all the people, "Keep the
1Chr 6:49 all that Moses the servant of God had C
14:16 David did as God C him, and they smote
15:15 poles, as Moses had C according to the word
15:16 David also C the chiefs of the Levites to
16:15 the word that he C, for a thousand generations,
16:40 the LORD which he C Israel.
17:6 of Israel, whom I C to shepherd my people,
21:18 angel of the LORD C Gad to say to
21:27 Then the LORD C the angel; and he put
22:2 David C to gather together the aliens who were
22:13 ordinances which the LORD C Moses for Israel.
22:17 David also C all the leaders of Israel to
24:19 God of Israel had C him.
7:17 all that I have C you and keeping my
8:14 for so David the man of God had C
8:15 what the king had C the priests and Levites
14:4 down the Asherim, and C Judah to seek the
18:30 king of Syria had C the captains of his
23:8 did according to all that Jehoiada the priest C
24:8 So the king C, and they made a chest,
25:4 Moses, where the LORD C, "The fathers shall not
29:15 as the king had C, by the words of
29:21 And he C the priests the sons of Aaron
29:24 For the king C that the burnt offering and
29:27 Then Hezekiah C that the burnt offering be offered
29:30 king and the princes C the Levites to sing
30:6 as the king had C, saying, "O people of
30:12 king and the princes C by the word of
31:4 And he C the people who lived in Jerusalem
31:11 Then Hezekiah C them to prepare chambers in the
32:12 and his altars and C Judah and Jerusalem, "Before
33:8 all that I have C them, all the law,
33:16 of thanksgiving; and he C Judah to serve the
34:20 And the king C Hilkiah, Ahikam the son of
35:21 war; and God has C me to make haste.
Ezra 4:3 king of Persia has C us."
7:23 Whatever is C by the God of heaven, let
Neh 8:14 that the LORD had C by Moses that the
13:19 before the sabbath, I C that the doors should
13:22 And I C the Levites that they should purify
Tob 1:8 my father's mother had C me, for I was
5:1 everything that you have C me;
6:15 with which your father C you to take a
Jud 5:9 Then their God C them to leave the place
12:1 Then he C them to bring her in where
12:7 So Holofernes C his guards not to hinder her.
Esth 1:10 merry with wine, he C Mehuman, Biztha, Harbona,
1:17 will say, 'King Ahasuerus C Queen Vashti to be
3:2 the king had so C concerning him.
3:12 to all that Haman C, was written to the
8:9 to all that Mordecai C concerning the Jews to
9:14 So the king C this to be done; a
Job 38:12 "Have you C the morning since your days began,
Ps 33:9 came to be; he C, and it stood forth.
78:5 in Israel, which he C our fathers to teach
78:23 Yet he C the skies above, and opened the
105:8 the word that he C, for a thousand generations,
106:34 peoples, as the LORD C them,
107:25 For he C, and raised the stormy wind, which
111:9 his people; he has C his covenant for ever.
119:4 Thou hast C thy precepts to be kept diligently.
133:3 there the LORD has C the blessing, life for
148:5 For he C and they were created.
Sir 7:31 his portion, as is C you: the first fruits,
15:20 He has not C any one to be ungodly,
24:22 the law which Moses C us as an inheritance
48:22 which Isaiah the prophet C, who was great and
Is 13:3 I myself have C my consecrated ones, have
34:16 of the LORD has C, and his Spirit has
45:12 the heavens, and I C all their host.
48:5 and my molten image C them.'
Jer 11:4 this covenant which I C your fathers when I
11:8 this covenant, which I C them to do, but
13:5 Euphrates, as the LORD C me.
13:6 the waistcloth which I C you to hide there."
17:22 day holy, as I C your fathers.
26:8 that the LORD had C him to speak to
35:6 of Rechab, our father, C us, 'You shall not
35:8 in all that he C us, to drink no
35:10 that Jonadab our father C us.
35:18 done all that he C you,
36:26 And the king C Jerahmeel the king's son and
38:10 the king C Ebed-melech, the Ethiopian, "Take three
50:21 all that I have C you.
51:59 which Jeremiah the prophet C Seraiah the son of
Lam 1:17 her; the LORD has C against Jacob that his
3:37 Who has C and it came to pass, unless
Bar 2:9 works which he has C us to do.
6:1 message which God had C him.
Ezek 10:6 And when he C the man clothed in linen,
12:7 And I did as I was C
24:18 the next morning I did as I was C
37:7 prophesied as I was C; and as I prophesied,
37:10 I prophesied as he C me, and the breath
Dan 1:3 Then the king C Ashpenaz, his chief eunuch, to
1:18 when the king had C that they should be
2:2 Then the king C that the magicians, the enchanters,
2:12 and very furious, and C that all the wise
2:46 homage to Daniel, and C that an offering and
3:4 proclaimed aloud, "You are C, O peoples, nations,
3:13 Nebuchadnezzar in furious rage C that Shadrach,
3:30 them, as thou hast C us that it might
4:26 And as it was C to leave the stump
5:2 he tasted the wine, C that the vessels of
5:29 Belshazzar C, and Daniel was clothed with purple,
6:16 Then the king C, and Daniel was brought and
6:23 was exceedingly glad, and C that Daniel be taken
6:24 And the king C, and those men who had
13:18 what they had been C; and they did not
13:56 put him aside, and C them to bring the
Amos 2:12 Nazirites drink wine, and C the prophets, saying, 'You
Zech 1:6 my statutes, which I C my servants the prophets,
Mal 4:4 and ordinances that I C him at Horeb for
1Mac 1:51 all the people and C the cities of Judah
3:39 Judah and destroy it, as the king had C
3:42 what the king had C to do to the
4:27 as the king had C him.
7:9 high priest; and he C him to take vengeance
7:26 detested Israel, and he C him to destroy the
10:6 his ally; and he C that the hostages in
10:37 as the king has C in the land of
10:81 stood fast, as Jonathan C, and the enemy's horses
11:2 Alexander the king had C them to meet him,
12:17 We have C them to go also to you
12:27 the sun set, Jonathan C his men to be
12:43 gave him gifts and C his friends and his
15:39 He C him to encamp against Judea, and commanded
15:39 encamp against Judea, and C him to build up
2Mac 5:12 And he C his soldiers to cut down relentlessly
5:24 of twenty-two thousand, and C him to slay all
6:21 meal which had been C by the king,
7:4 heated immediately, and he C that the tongue of
14:31 the customary sacrifices, and C them to hand the
15:3 in heaven who had C the keeping of the
Mt 1:24 angel of the Lord C him; he took his
8:4 the gift that Moses C, for a proof to
14:9 and his guests he C it to be given;
15:4 For God C, 'Honor your father and your mother,'
17:9 down the mountain, Jesus C them, "Tell no one
28:20 all that I have C you; and lo, I
Mk 1:44 your cleansing what Moses C, for a proof to
6:39 Then he C them all to sit down by
8:6 And he C the crowd to sit down on
8:7 having blessed them, he C that these also should
Lk 5:14 your cleansing, as Moses C, for a proof to

	8:29	For he had C the unclean spirit to come
	9:21	But he charged and C them to tell this
	14:22	said, 'Sir, what you C has been done, and
	17:9	thank the servant because he did what was C
	17:10	done all that is C you, say, 'We are
	18:40	And Jesus stopped, and C him to be brought
	19:15	the kingly power, he C these servants, to whom
Jn	8:5	in the law Moses C us to stone such.
	14:31	as the Father has C me, so that the
Acts	4:15	But when they had C them to go aside
	8:37	And he C the chariot to stop, and they
	10:33	that you have been C by the Lord."
	10:42	And he C us to preach to the people,
	10:48	And he C them to be baptized in the
	13:47	so the Lord has C us, saying, 'I have
	18:2	Priscilla, because Claudius had C all the Jews to
	22:24	the air, the tribune C him to be brought
	22:30	he unbound him, and C the chief priests and
	23:2	the high priest Ananias C those who stood by
	23:10	in pieces by them, C the soldiers to go
	23:35	And he C him to be guarded in Herod's
	25:21	of the emperor, I C him to be held
1Cor	9:14	same way, the Lord C that those who proclaim
Heb	9:20	the covenant which God C you."
1Jn	3:23	just as he has C us.
2Jn	1:4	as we have been C by the Father.

COMMANDER (57)

Gen	21:22	Abimelech and Phicol the C of his army said
	21:32	Abimelech and Phicol the C of his army rose
	26:26	adviser and Phicol the C of his army.
Deut	33:21	himself, for there a C's portion was reserved; and
Josh	5:14	said, "No; but as C of the army of
	5:15	And the C of the LORD's army said to
Judg	4:2	reigned in Hazor; the C of his army was
1Sam	12:9	the hand of Sisera, C of the army of
	14:50	the name of the C of his army was
	17:18	ten cheeses to the C of their thousand.
	17:55	said to Abner, the C of the army, "Abner,
	18:13	and made him a C of a thousand; and
	26:5	son of Ner, the C of his army; Saul
2Sam	2:8	the son of Ner, C of Saul's army, had
	10:16	Helam, with Shobach the C of the army of
	10:18	and wounded Shobach the C of their army, so
	19:13	if you are not C of my army henceforth
	23:19	thirty, and became their C; but he did not
1Kgs	1:19	priest, and Joab the C of the army; but
	1:25	king's sons, Joab the C of the army, and
	2:32	the son of Ner, C of the army of
	2:32	the son of Jether, C of the army of
	11:15	Edom, and Joab the C of the army went
	11:21	and that Joab the C of the army was
	16:9	But his servant Zimri, C of half his chariots,
	16:16	Israel made Omri, the C of the army, king
2Kgs	4:13	king or to the C of the army?" She
	5:1	Naaman, C of the army of the king of
	9:5	said, "I have an errand to you, O C
	9:5	And he said, "To you, O C
	25:19	the secretary of the C of the army who
1Chr	11:6	smite the Jebusites first shall be chief and C
	11:21	thirty, and became their C; but he did not
	19:16	Euphrates, with Shophach the C of the army of
	19:18	killed also Shophach the C of their army.
	27:5	The third C, for the third month, was Benaiah,
	27:8	The fifth C, for the fifth month, was Shamhuth,
	27:34	Joab was C of the king's army.
	17:14	of thousands: Adnah the C, with three hundred
	17:15	to him Jehohanan the C, with two hundred and
	28:7	son and Azrikam the C of the palace and
Ezra	4:8	Rehum the C and Shimshai the scribe wrote a
	4:9	then wrote Rehum the C, Shimshai the scribe, and
	4:17	answer: "To Rehum the C and Shimshai the scribe
Jud	6:1	died down, Holofernes, the C of the Assyrian army,
	10:13	presence of Holofernes the C of your army, to
	13:15	head of Holofernes, the C of the Assyrian army,
Is	55:4	peoples, a leader and C for the peoples.
Jer	52:25	the secretary of the C of the army who
Dan	11:18	of them; but a C shall put an end
1Mac	3:13	Now when Seron, the C of the Syrian army,
	13:42	great high priest and C and leader of the
	13:53	so he made him C of all the forces,
	14:47	high priest, to be C and ethnarch of the
2Mac	4:29	Sostratus left Crates, the C of the Cyprian troops.
	8:32	They killed the C of Timothy's forces, a most
	10:32	especially well garrisoned, where Chaereas was C

COMMANDER-IN-CHIEF (2)

Is	20:1	the year that the C, who was sent by
1Mac	15:38	the king made Cendebeus C of the coastal country,

COMMANDERS (83)

Num	31:14	of the army, the C of thousands and the
	31:14	of thousands and the C of hundreds, who had
	31:52	the LORD, from the C of thousands and the
	31:52	of thousands and the C of hundreds, was sixteen
	31:54	the gold from the C of thousands and of
Deut	1:15	as heads over you, C of thousands, commanders of
	1:15	you, C of thousands, C of hundreds, C of fifties
	1:15	of fifties, C of tens, and officers,
	20:9	to the people, then C shall be appointed at
Judg	5:9	goes out to the C of Israel who offered
	5:14	Machir marched down the C, and from Zebulun
1Sam	8:12	appoint for himself C of thousands and commanders
	8:12	commanders of thousands and C of fifties, and some
	22:7	he make you all C of thousands and commanders
	22:7	commanders of thousands and C of hundreds,
	29:3	rear with Achish, the C of the Philistines said,
	29:3	Achish said to the C of the Philistines, "Is
	29:4	But the C of the Philistines were angry with
	29:4	with him; and the C of the Philistines said
	29:9	of God; nevertheless the C of the Philistines have
2Sam	18:1	and set over them C of thousands and commanders
	18:1	commanders of thousands and C of hundreds.
	18:5	orders to all the C about Absalom.
	19:6	it clear today that C and servants are nothing
	24:2	to Joab and the C of the army, who
	24:4	against Joab and the C of the army.
	24:4	So Joab and the C of the army went
1Kgs	2:5	dealt with the two C of the armies of
	9:22	were his officials, his C, his captains, his chariot
	9:22	his captains, his chariot C and his horsemen.
	15:20	Asa, and sent the C of his armies against
	20:24	his post, and put C in their places;
2Kgs	8:21	he and his chariot C smote the Edomites who
	9:5	he came, behold, the C of the army were
1Chr	12:21	of valor, and were C in the army.
	12:28	in valor, and twenty-two C from his own father's
	12:34	Of Naphtali a thousand C with whom were
	13:1	David consulted with the C of thousands and of
	15:25	of Israel, and the C of thousands, went to
	21:2	to Joab and the C of the army, "Go,
	26:26	the hundreds, and the C of the army, had
	27:1	of fathers' houses, the C of thousands and hundreds,
	27:3	chief of all the C of the army for
	28:1	C of thousands, the C of hundreds, the stewards
	29:6	of the tribes, the C of thousands and of
	1:2	all Israel, to the C of thousands and of
	8:9	and his officers, the C of his chariots, and
	11:11	fortresses strong, and put C in them, and stores
	16:4	Asa, and sent the C of his armies against
	17:14	houses: Of Judah, the C of thousands: Adnah the
	21:9	passed over with his C and all his chariots,
	21:9	Edomites who had surrounded him and his chariot C
	23:1	a compact with the C of hundreds, Azariah the
	25:5	by fathers' houses under C of thousands and of
	26:11	the direction of Hananiah, one of the king's C
	32:6	And he set combat C over the people, and
	32:21	the mighty warriors and C and officers in the
	33:11	brought upon them the C of the army of
	33:14	height; he also put C of the army in
Jud	2:14	called together all the C, generals, and officers of
	5:2	of Moab and the C of Ammon and all
	7:8	the Moabites and the C of the coastland came
	14:12	sent word to their C, and they went to
Is	10:8	says: "Are not my C all kings?
Jer	42:1	Then all the C of the forces, and Johanan
	42:8	Kareah and all the C of the forces who
	43:4	Kareah and all the C of the forces and
	43:5	Kareah and all the C of the forces took
	51:23	with you I break in pieces governors and C
	51:57	men, her governors, her C, and her warriors; they
Ezek	23:6	in purple, governors and C, all of them desirable
	23:12	the Assyrians, governors and C, warriors clothed in
	23:23	young men, governors and C all of them, officers
1Mac	5:56	Zechariah, and Azariah, the C of the forces, heard
	6:28	all his friends, the C of his forces and
	6:57	the king, to the C of the forces, and
	6:60	the king and the C, and he sent to
	6:61	the king and the C gave them their oath.
	11:70	the son of Chalphi, C of the forces of
	12:24	Jonathan heard that the C of Demetrius had
	14:2	sent one of his C to take him alive.

C

COMMANDING (3)

Deut 12:14 all that I am C you.
2Mac 14:27 with the covenant and C him to send Maccabeus
Mt 15:35 And C the crowd to sit down on the

COMMANDMENT (100)

Ex 17:1 stages, according to the C of the LORD, and
24:12 the law and the C, which I have written
25:22 will give you in C for the people of
34:32 he gave them in C all that the LORD
38:21 were counted at the C of Moses, for the
Num 3:39 Aaron numbered at the C of the LORD, by
4:37 numbered according to the C of the LORD by
4:41 numbered according to the C of the LORD.
4:45 numbered according to the C of the LORD by
4:49 According to the C of the LORD through Moses
15:23 that the LORD gave C, and onward throughout your
15:31 and has broken his C, that person shall be
Deut 1:3 had given him in C to them,
5:31 tell you all the C and the statutes and
6:1 "Now this is the C, the statutes and the
6:25 to do all this C before the LORD our
7:11 careful to do the C, and the statutes, and
8:1 "All the C which I command you this day
9:23 you rebelled against the C of the LORD your
11:8 therefore keep all the C which I command you
11:22 to do all this C which I command you
15:5 to do all this C which I command you
17:20 turn aside from the C, either to the right
19:9 to keep all this C, which I command you
26:13 according to all thy C which thou hast commanded
27:1 saying, "Keep all the C which I command you
30:11 "For this C which I command you this day
31:5 according to all the C which I have commanded
Josh 1:18 Whoever rebels against your C and disobeys your
15:13 According to the C of the LORD to Joshua,
17:4 So according to the C of the LORD he
22:5 care to observe the C and the law which
1Sam 12:14 not rebel against the C of the LORD, and
12:15 but rebel against the C of the LORD, then
13:13 have not kept the C of the LORD your
15:13 I have performed the C of the LORD."
15:24 I have transgressed the C of the LORD and
1Kgs 2:43 the LORD and the C with which I charged
13:21 have not kept the C which the LORD your
2Kgs 17:34 the law or the C which the LORD commanded
17:37 the law and the C which he wrote for
8:13 offering according to the C of Moses for the
14:4 fathers, and to keep the law and the C
19:10 bloodshed, law or C, statutes or ordinances, then
29:25 lyres, according to the C of David and of
29:25 the prophet; for the C was from the LORD
Ezra 10:3 who tremble at the C of our God; and
Neh 12:24 thanks, according to the C of David the man
13:5 which were given by C to the Levites, singers,
Job 23:12 not departed from the C of his lips; I
Ps 19:8 rejoicing the heart; the C of the LORD is
119:96 all perfection, but thy C is exceedingly broad.
119:98 Thy C makes me wiser than my enemies, for
Prov 6:20 son, keep your father's C, and forsake not your
6:23 For the C is a lamp and the teaching
13:13 he who respects the C will be rewarded.
19:16 He who keeps the C keeps his life; he
Sir 17:12 And he gave C to each of them concerning
24:8 things gave me a C, and the one who
29:9 poor man for the C's sake, and because of
35:5 things are to be done because of the C
Is 29:13 of me is a C of men learned by
Nah 1:14 The LORD has given C about you: "No more
1Mac 2:53 his distress kept the C, and became lord of
Mt 15:3 do you transgress the C of God for the
22:36 which is the great C in the law?"
22:38 This is the great and first C
Mk 7:8 men.' You leave the C of God, and hold
7:9 way of rejecting the C of God, in order
10:5 your hardness of heart he wrote you this C
12:28 well, asked him, "Which C is the first of
12:31 There is no other C greater than these."
Lk 23:55 On the sabbath they rested according to the C
Jn 12:49 has himself given me C what to say and
12:50 I know that his C is eternal life.
13:34 cannot come.' A new C I give to you,
15:12 "This is my C, that you love one another
Acts 1:2 after he had given C through the Holy Spirit
Rom 7:8 finding opportunity in the C, wrought in me all
7:9 law, but when the C came, sin revived and
7:10 I died; the very C which promised life proved
7:11 finding opportunity in the C, deceived me and by
7:12 is holy, and the C is holy and just
7:13 sin, and through the C might become sinful beyond
13:9 and any other C, are summed up in this
Eph 6:2 (this is the first C with a promise),
1Tim 6:14 you to keep the C unstained and free from
Heb 7:5 priestly office have a C in the law to
7:18 one hand, a former C is set aside because
9:19 For when every C of the law had been
2Pet 2:21 back from the holy C delivered to them.
3:2 holy prophets and the C of the Lord and
1Jn 2:7 writing you no new C, but an old commandment
2:7 commandment, but an old C which you had from
2:7 the beginning; the old C is the word which
2:8 writing you a new C, which is true in
3:23 And this is his C, that we should believe
4:21 And this C we have from him, that he
2Jn 1:5 writing you a new C, but the one we
1:6 commandments; this is the C, as you have heard

COMMANDMENTS (170)

Gen 26:5 kept my charge, my C, my statutes, and my
Ex 15:26 give heed to his C and keep all his
16:28 refuse to keep my C and my laws?
20:6 of those who love me and keep my C
34:28 tables the words of the covenant, the ten C
Lev 22:31 you shall keep my C and do them: I
26:3 statutes and observe my C and do them,
26:14 not do all these C,
26:15 not do all my C, but break my covenant,
27:34 These are the C which the LORD commanded Moses
Num 15:22 not observe all these C which the LORD has
15:39 and remember all the C of the LORD, to
15:40 and do all my C, and be holy to
36:13 These are the C and the ordinances which the
Deut 4:2 you may keep the C of the LORD your
4:13 that is, the ten C; and he wrote them
4:40 his statutes and his C, which I command you
5:10 of those who love me and keep my C
5:29 to keep all my C, that it might go
6:2 his statutes and his C, which I command you,
6:17 shall diligently keep the C of the LORD your
7:9 him and keep his C, to a thousand generations,
8:2 you would keep his C, or not.
8:6 you shall keep the C of the LORD your
8:11 by not keeping his C and his ordinances and
10:4 first writing, the ten C which the LORD had
10:13 and to keep the C and statutes of the
11:1 his ordinances, and his C always.
11:13 you will obey my C which I command you
11:27 if you obey the C of the LORD your
11:28 do not obey the C of the LORD your
13:4 him, and keep his C and obey his voice,
13:18 God, keeping all his C which I command you
26:13 transgressed any of thy C, neither have I forgotten
26:17 his statutes and his C and his ordinances, and
26:18 to keep all his C,
27:10 your God, keeping his C and his statutes, which
28:1 to do all his C which I command you
28:9 if you keep the C of the LORD your
28:13 if you obey the C of the LORD your
28:15 to do all his C and his statutes which
28:45 God, to keep his C and his statutes which
30:8 and keep all his C which I command you
30:10 God, to keep his C and his statutes which
30:16 If you obey the C of the LORD your
30:16 and by keeping his C and his statutes and
Josh 22:5 and to keep his C, and to cleave to
Judg 2:17 who had obeyed the C of the LORD, and
3:4 Israel would obey the C of the LORD, which
1Sam 15:11 from following me, and has not performed my C
1Kgs 2:3 keeping his statutes, his C, his ordinances, and his
3:14 my statutes and my C, as your father David
6:12 and keep all my C and walk in them,
8:58 and to keep his C, his statutes, and his
8:61 statutes and keeping his C, as at this day."
9:6 do not keep my C and my statutes which
11:34 chose, who kept my C and my statutes;
11:38 my statutes and my C, as David my servant
14:8 David, who kept my C, and followed me with
18:18 you have forsaken the C of the LORD and
2Kgs 17:13 ways and keep my C and my statutes, in
17:16 they forsook all the C of the LORD their
17:19 did not keep the C of the LORD their
18:6 him, but kept the C which the LORD commanded

	23:3	and to keep his C and his testimonies and
1Chr	28:7	resolute in keeping my C and my ordinances, as
	28:8	seek out all the C of the LORD your
	29:19	he may keep thy C, thy testimonies, and thy
2Chr	7:19	my statutes and my C which I have set
	17:4	and walked in his C, and not according to
	24:20	do you transgress the C of the LORD, so
	31:21	the law and the C, seeking his God, he
	34:31	and to keep his C and his testimonies and
Ezra	7:11	in matters of the C of the LORD and
	9:10	we have forsaken thy C,
	9:14	shall we break thy C again and intermarry with
Neh	1:5	him and keep his C;
	1:7	have not kept the C, the statutes, and the
	1:9	me and keep my C and do them, though
	9:13	laws, good statutes and C,
	9:14	sabbath and command them C and statutes and a
	9:16	did not obey thy C;
	9:29	did not obey thy C, but sinned against thy
	9:34	law or heeded thy C and thy warnings which
	10:29	and do all the C of the LORD our
Tob	3:4	For they disobeyed thy C, and thou gavest us
	3:5	my fathers, because we did not keep thy C
	4:5	and refuse to sin or to transgress his C
	14:9	the law and the C, and be merciful and
Ps	78:7	God, but keep his C;
	89:31	do not keep my C,
	103:18	keep his covenant and remember to do his C
	112:1	fears the LORD, who greatly delights in his C
	119:6	shame, having my eyes fixed on all thy C
	119:10	seek thee; let me not wander from thy C
	119:19	earth; hide not thy C from me!
	119:21	who wander from thy C;
	119:32	the way of thy C when thou enlargest my
	119:35	the path of thy C, for I delight in
	119:47	my delight in thy C, which I love.
	119:48	I revere thy C, which I love, and I
	119:60	hasten and do not delay to keep thy C
	119:66	judgment and knowledge, for I believe in thy C
	119:73	give me understanding that I may learn thy C
	119:86	All thy C are sure; they persecute me with
	119:115	I may keep the C of my God.
	119:127	Therefore I love thy C above gold, above fine
	119:131	mouth I pant, because I long for thy C
	119:143	upon me, but thy C are my delight.
	119:151	LORD, and all thy C are true.
	119:166	thy salvation, O LORD, and I do thy C
	119:172	word, for all thy C are right.
	119:176	thy servant, for I do not forget thy C
Prov	2:1	and treasure up my C with you,
	3:1	your heart keep my C;
	4:5	my words; keep my C, and live;
	7:1	and treasure up my C with you;
	7:2	with you; keep my C and live, keep my
	10:8	of heart will heed C, but a prating fool
Eccl	12:13	God, and keep his C; for this is the
Wis	9:9	sight and what is right according to thy C
Sir	1:23	desire wisdom, keep the C, and the Lord will
	6:37	Lord, and meditate at all times on his C
	10:19	Those who transgress the C
	15:15	you can keep the C, and to act faithfully
	23:27	than to heed the C of the Lord.
	28:6	destruction and death, and be true to the C
	28:7	Remember the C, and do not be angry with
	29:1	that strengthens him with his hand keeps the C
	29:11	treasure according to the C of the Most High,
	32:23	act, for this is the keeping of the C
	32:24	gives heed to the C, and he who trusts
	35:1	he who heeds the C sacrifices a peace offering.
	37:12	a keeper of the C, whose soul is in
	45:5	and gave him the C face to face, the
	45:17	In his C he gave him authority and statutes
Is	48:18	O that you had hearkened to my C
Bar	3:9	Hear the C of life, O Israel; give ear,
	4:1	the book of the C of God, and the
	4:13	the ways of God's C, nor tread the paths
Dan	3:29	have not obeyed thy C;
	9:4	him and keep his C,
	9:5	turning aside from thy C and ordinances;
1Mac	2:19	chosen to do his C, departing each one from
	10:14	the law and the C, for it served as
2Mac	1:4	his law and his C, and may he bring
	2:2	not to forget the C of the Lord, nor
Mt	5:19	the least of these C and teaches men so,
	19:17	If you would enter life, keep the C
	22:40	On these two C depend all the law and
Mk	10:19	You know the C: 'Do not kill, Do not
Lk	1:6	walking in all the C and ordinances of the
	18:20	You know the C: 'Do not commit adultery, Do
Jn	14:15	"If you love me, you will keep my C
	14:21	He who has my C and keeps them, he
	15:10	If you keep my C, you will abide in
	15:10	have kept my Father's C and abide in his
Rom	13:9	The C, "You shall not commit adultery, You shall
1Cor	7:19	uncircumcision, but keeping the C of God.
Eph	2:15	flesh the law of C and ordinances, that he
1 Jn	2:3	that we know him, if we keep his C
	2:4	but disobeys his C is a liar, and the
	3:22	because we keep his C and do what pleases
	3:24	All who keep his C abide in him, and
	5:2	God, when we love God and obey his C
	5:3	the love of God, that we keep his C
	5:3	And his C are not burdensome.
2 Jn	1:6	that we follow his C; this is the commandment,
Rev	12:17	those who keep the C of God and bear
	14:12	those who keep the C of God and the

COMMANDS (37)

Ex	18:23	this, and God so C you, then you will
Num	32:25	Moses, "Your servants will do as my lord C
	36:6	is what the LORD C concerning the daughters of
Deut	26:16	the LORD your God C you to do these
	33:21	Israel he executed the C and just decrees of
Judg	4:6	the God of Israel, C you, 'Go, gather your
2Sam	9:11	my lord the king C his servant, so will
1Kgs	2:30	to him, "The king C, 'Come forth.'" But he
Tob	4:19	my son, remember my C, and do not let
Jud	2:13	any of your sovereign's C, but be sure to
Job	9:7	its pillars tremble; who C the sun, and it
	36:10	ears to instruction, and C that they return from
	36:32	with the lightning, and C it to strike the
	37:12	accomplish all that he C them on the face
Ps	42:8	By day the LORD C his steadfast love; and
	119:158	with disgust, because they do not keep thy C
Wis	19:6	anew, complying with thy C, that thy children might
Sir	39:16	good, and whatever he C will be done in
	39:31	will rejoice in his C, and be made ready
	45:3	He gave him C for his people, and showed
Bar	6:62	When God C the clouds to go over the
Amos	6:11	For behold, the LORD C, and the great house
Zeph	2:3	land, who do his C; seek righteousness, seek humility;
1Mac	2:18	do what the king C, as all the Gentiles
	2:33	do what the king C, and you will live."
	2:34	do what the king C and so profane the
	2:68	Gentiles in full, and heed what the law C
	6:23	by what he said and to follow his C
	9:55	a word or give C concerning his house.
2Mac	3:7	and sent him with C to effect the removal
	3:13	because of the king's C which he had, said
Mk	1:27	With authority he C even the unclean spirits, and
	13:34	with his work, and C the doorkeeper to be
Lk	4:36	authority and power he C the unclean spirits, and
	8:25	is this, that he C even wind and water,
Acts	17:30	overlooked, but now he C all men everywhere to
Tit	1:13	Jewish myths or to C of men who reject

COMMEMORATION

Esth	9:28	Jews, nor should the C of these days cease

COMMEMORATIVE

Esth	16:22	notable day among your C festivals,

COMMEND (11)

Eccl	8:15	And I C enjoyment, for man has no good
Acts	20:32	And now I C you to God and to
Rom	16:1	I C to you our sister Phoebe, a deaconess
1Cor	8:8	Food will not C us to God.
	11:2	I C you because you remember me in everything
	11:17	instructions I do not C you, because when you
	11:22	Shall I C you in this?
2Cor	3:1	Are we beginning to C ourselves again?
	4:2	the truth we would C ourselves to every man's
	6:4	servants of God we C ourselves in every way:
	10:12	some of those who C themselves.

COMMENDATION

1Cor	4:5	man will receive his C from God.

COMMENDED (8)

Prov	12:8	A man is C according to his good sense,
Wis	7:14	obtain friendship with God, C for the gifts that
1Mac	12:43	him with honor and C him to all his

C

2Mac 9:25 have often entrusted and C to most of you
Lk 16:8 write eighty.' The master C the dishonest steward for
Acts 14:26 where they had been C to the grace of
15:39 Silas and departed, being C by the brethren to
2Cor 12:11 ought to have been C by you.

COMMENDING

2Cor 5:12 We are not C ourselves to you again but

COMMENDS (2)

2Cor 10:18 not the man who C himself that is accepted,
10:18 is accepted, but the man whom the Lord C

COMMENTARY

2Chr 24:27 are written in the C on the Book of

COMMISSION (4)

Num 27:19 congregation, and you shall C him in their sight.
Deut 31:14 meeting, that I may C him." And Moses and
Acts 26:12 with the authority and C of the chief priests.
1Cor 9:17 my own will, I am entrusted with a C

COMMISSIONED (5)

Num 27:23 hands upon him, and C him as the LORD
Deut 31:23 And the LORD C Joshua the son of Nun
2Mac 1:20 God, Nehemiah, having been C by the king of
2Cor 1:21 in Christ, and has C us;
2:17 men of sincerity, as C by God, in the

COMMISSIONS

Ezra 8:36 also delivered the king's C to the king's satraps

COMMIT (45)

Ex 20:14 "You shall not C adultery.
Num 5:6 the sins that men C by breaking faith with
Deut 5:18 "'Neither shall you C adultery.
19:20 and shall never again C any such evil among
2Kgs 17:21 LORD and made them C great sin.
Tob 12:10 life; but those who C sin are the enemies
Job 5:8 to God would I C my cause;
Ps 31:5 Into thy hand I C my spirit; thou hast
37:5 C your way to the LORD; trust in him,
Prov 16:3 C your work to the LORD, and your plans
Wis 14:28 live unrighteously, or readily C perjury;
Sir 7:8 Do not C a sin twice; even for one
Is 22:21 on him, and will C your authority to his
Jer 7:9 Will you steal, murder, C adultery, swear falsely, burn
9:5 to speak lies; they C iniquity and are too
23:14 a horrible thing: they C adultery and walk in
44:7 Israel: Why do you C this great evil against
Ezek 8:13 will see still greater abominations which they C
8:17 house of Judah to C the abominations which they
8:17 the abominations which they C here, that they should
22:9 upon the mountains; men C lewdness in your midst.
23:24 helmet, and I will C the judgment to them,
23:43 Do not men now C adultery when they practice
23:44 and to Oholibah to C lewdness.
23:48 take warning and not C lewdness as you have
33:26 to the sword, you C abominations and each of
Hos 4:13 harlot, and your brides C adultery.
4:14 your brides when they C adultery; for the men
6:9 to Shechem, yea, they C villainy.
Mt 5:27 said, 'You shall not C adultery.'
19:18 kill, You shall not C adultery, You shall not
Mk 10:19 not kill, Do not C adultery, Do not steal,
Lk 12:48 him to whom men C much they will demand
18:20 the commandments: 'Do not C adultery, Do not kill,
23:45 into thy hands I C my spirit!" And having
Rom 2:22 that one must not C adultery, do you commit
2:22 commit adultery, do you C adultery?
13:9 commandments, "You shall not C adultery, You shall
2Cor 11:7 Did I C a sin in abasing myself so
1Tim 1:18 This charge I C to you, Timothy, my son,
Heb 6:6 come, if they then C apostasy, since they crucify
Jas 2:9 you show partiality, you C sin, and are convicted
2:11 who said, "Do not C adultery," said also, "Do
2:11 If you do not C adultery but do kill,
Rev 2:22 sickbed, and those who C adultery with her I

COMMITS (33)

Lev 4:13 whole congregation of Israel C a sin unwittingly and
5:15 Moses, "If any one C a breach of faith
6:2 any one sins and C a breach of faith
20:10 "If a man C adultery with the wife of
Num 5:6 a man or woman C any of the sins
15:28 for the person who C an error, when he
2Sam 7:14 When he C iniquity, I will chasten him with
Ps 10:14 thy hands; the hapless C himself to thee; thou
Prov 6:32 He who C adultery has no sense; he who
Sir 23:16 consumed; a man who C fornication with his near
Ezek 3:20 from his righteousness and C iniquity, and I lay
18:7 the debtor his pledge, C no robbery, gives his
18:12 the poor and needy, C robbery, does not restore
18:12 eyes to the idols, C abomination,
18:16 one, exacts no pledge, C no robbery, but gives
18:24 from his righteousness and C iniquity and does the
18:26 from his righteousness and C iniquity, he shall die
22:11 One C abomination with his neighbor's wife; another
33:13 in his righteousness and C iniquity, none of his
33:18 from his righteousness, and C iniquity, he shall die
Hos 1:2 harlotry, for the land C great harlotry by forsaking
Mt 5:32 marries a divorced woman C adultery.
19:9 unchastity, and marries another, C adultery; and he
19:9 marries a divorced woman, C adultery."
Mk 10:11 wife and marries another, C adultery against her;
10:12 and marries another, she C adultery."
Lk 16:18 wife and marries another C adultery, and he who
16:18 divorced from her husband C adultery.
Jn 8:34 you, every one who C sin is a slave
1Cor 6:18 sin which a man C is outside the body;
1 Jn 3:4 Every one who C sin is guilty of lawlessness;
3:8 He who C sin is of the devil; for
3:9 one born of God C sin; for God's nature

COMMITTED (115)

Gen 39:22 keeper of the prison C to Joseph's care all
Lev 4:3 sin which he has C a young bull without
4:14 sin which they have C becomes known, the assembly
4:23 sin which he has C is made known to
4:28 sin which he has C is made known to
4:28 without blemish, for his sin which he has C
4:35 sin which he has C, and he shall be
5:5 the sin he has C,
5:6 sin which he has C, a female from the
5:7 sin which he has C, two turtledoves or two
5:10 sin which he has C, and he shall be
5:11 sin which he has C, a tenth of an
5:13 sin which he has C in any one of
5:18 the error which he C unwittingly, and he shall
6:4 the deposit which was C to him, or the
19:22 sin which he has C; and the sin which
19:22 sin which he has C shall be forgiven him.
20:12 to death; they have C incest, their blood is
20:13 both of them have C an abomination; they shall
26:40 their treachery which they C against me, and also
Num 5:7 sin which he has C; and he shall make
Deut 9:18 sin which you had C, in doing what was
19:15 offense that he has C; only on the evidence
21:22 if a man has C a crime punishable by
Josh 22:16 treachery which you have C against the God of
22:31 because you have not C this treachery against the
Judg 9:56 of Abimelech, which he C against his father in
20:6 Israel; for they have C abomination and wantonness
20:10 crime which they have C in Israel."
1Kgs 8:50 transgressions which they have C against thee; and
14:22 their sins which they C, more than all that
14:27 shields of bronze, and C them to the hands
16:19 his sins which he C, doing evil in the
16:19 his sin which he C, making Israel to sin.
2Kgs 21:11 king of Judah has C these abominations, and has
21:17 the sin that he C, are they not written
2Chr 12:10 shields of bronze, and C them to the hands
34:16 king, "All that was C to your servants they
Neh 9:18 of Egypt,' and had C great blasphemies,
9:26 to thee, and they C great blasphemies.
Tob 3:3 those which my fathers C before thee.
Jud 11:17 me when they have C their sins.
13:16 destruction, and yet he C no act of sin
Ps 22:8 wag their heads; "He C his cause to the
106:6 have sinned; we have C iniquity, we have done
Sir 23:23 High; second, she has C an offense against her
23:23 and third, she has C adultery through harlotry and
27:1 Many have C sin for a trifle, and whoever
Jer 2:13 for my people have C two evils: they have
5:7 to the full, they C adultery and trooped to
6:15 they ashamed when they C abomination?
8:12 they ashamed when they C abomination?
11:20 to thee have I C my cause.
16:10 sin that we have C against the LORD our
20:12 to thee have I C my cause.
29:23 because they have C folly in Israel, they have
29:23 in Israel, they have C adultery with their neighbors'

37:21 gave orders, and they C Jeremiah to the court
40:7 the land, and had C to him men, women,
41:10 of the guard, had C to Gedaliah the son
44:3 the wickedness which they C, provoking me to anger,
44:9 your wives, which they C in the land of
44:22 the abominations which you C; therefore your land
Bar 6:2 sins which you have C before God, you will
Ezek 6:9 evils which they have C, for all their abominations.
9:4 the abominations that are C in it."
16:43 "Have you not C lewdness in addition to all
16:51 Samaria has not C half your sins; you have
16:51 your sins; you have C more abominations than they,
16:51 righteous by all the abominations which you have C
17:20 the treason he has C against me.
18:21 sins which he has C and keeps all my
18:22 transgressions which he has C shall be remembered
18:24 the sin he has C, he shall die.
18:26 iniquity which he has C he shall die.
18:27 the wickedness he has C and does what is
18:28 transgressions which he had C, he shall surely live,
18:31 transgressions which you have C against me, and get
20:43 yourselves for all the evils that you have C
22:29 have practiced extortion and C robbery; they have
23:37 For they have C adultery, and blood is upon
23:37 their idols they have C adultery; and they have
33:13 iniquity that he has C he shall die.
33:16 sins that he has C shall be remembered against
33:29 because of all their abominations which they have C
43:8 abominations which they have C, so I have consumed
44:13 because of the abominations which they have C
Dan 9:7 treachery which they have C against thee.
13:52 home, which you have C in the past,
Mal 2:11 and abomination has been C in Israel and in
1Mac 1:24 He C deeds of murder, and spoke with great
2:6 the blasphemies being C in Judah and Jerusalem,
13:39 any errors and offenses C to this day, and
16:17 So he C an act of great treachery and
2Mac 4:3 that even murders were C by one of Simon's
4:38 place where he had C the outrage against Onias,
4:39 of sacrilege had been C in the city by
8:4 babies and the blasphemies C against his name, and
8:17 which the Gentiles had C against the holy place,
12:42 sin which had been C might be wholly blotted
13:8 just; because he had C many sins against the
Mt 5:28 woman lustfully has already C adultery with her in
Mk 15:7 in prison, who had C murder in the insurrection,
Acts 8:3 men and women and C them to prison.
14:23 prayer and fasting they C them to the Lord
25:11 a wrongdoer, and have C anything for which I
Rom 6:17 to which you were C,
Jas 5:15 and if he has C sins, he will be
1Pet 2:22 He C no sin; no guile was found on
2Pet 2:4 them into hell and C them to pits of
Jude 1:15 ungodliness which they have C in such an ungodly
Rev 17:2 of the earth have C fornication, and with the
18:3 of the earth have C fornication with her, and
18:9 of the earth, who C fornication and were wanton
20:4 on them were those to whom judgment was C

COMMITTING (8)

Jer 3:9 she polluted the land, C adultery with stone and
Ezek 8:6 house of Israel are C here, to drive me
8:9 abominations that they are C here."
33:15 the statutes of life, C no iniquity; he shall
Hos 4:2 lying, killing, stealing, and C adultery; they break all
2Mac 13:14 So, C the decision to the Creator of the
Rom 1:27 for one another, men C shameless acts with men
1 Jn 5:16 one sees his brother C what is not a

COMMON (40)

Lev 4:27 any one of the C people sins unwittingly in
10:10 the holy and the C, and between the unclean
25:34 But the fields of C land belonging to their
Num 16:29 these men die the C death of all men,
Deut 3:11 breadth, according to the C cubit.
1Sam 21:4 David, "I have no C bread at hand, but
21:5 when it is a C journey; how much more
1Kgs 10:27 king made silver as C in Jerusalem as stone,
2Kgs 23:6 the graves of the C people.
2Chr 1:15 silver and gold as C in Jerusalem as stone,
9:27 king made silver as C in Jerusalem as stone,
11:14 the Levites left their C lands and their holdings
31:19 in the fields of C land belonging to their
Wis 7:3 began to breathe the C air, and fell upon
7:6 into life, and a C departure.
18:11 the master, and the C man suffered the same
Is 8:1 write upon it in C characters, 'Belonging to
Jer 23:28 What has straw in C with wheat?
26:23 burial place of the C people.
Ezek 22:26 the holy and the C, neither have they taught
23:42 with men of the C sort drunkards were brought
42:20 make a separation between the holy and the C
44:23 the holy and the C, and show them how
2Mac 8:29 done this, they made C supplication and besought the
11:15 having regard for the C good, agreed to all
14:25 down, and shared the C life.
Acts 2:44 had all things in C;
4:13 that they were uneducated, C men, they wondered;
4:32 was his own, but they had everything in C
5:18 put them in the C prison.
10:14 eaten anything that is C or unclean."
10:15 "What God has cleansed, you must not call C
10:28 not call any man C or unclean.
11:8 'No, Lord; for nothing C or unclean has ever
11:9 you must not call C
1Cor 10:13 you that is not C to man.
12:7 the Spirit for the C good.
2Cor 6:15 has a believer in C with an unbeliever?
Tit 1:3 true child in a C faith: Grace and peace
Jude 1:3 to you of our C salvation, I found it

COMMONWEALTH (3)

2Mac 13:14 temple, city, country, and C, he pitched his camp
Eph 2:12 Christ, alienated from the C of Israel, and strangers
Phil 3:20 But our C is in heaven, and from it

COMMOTION (3)

Sir 11:32 will upset you with C, and will estrange you
Jer 10:22 it comes!–a great C out of the north
Acts 19:40 cause that we can give to justify this C

COMMUNE (2)

Ps 4:4 angry, but sin not; C with your own hearts
77:6 I C with my heart in the night; I

COMMUNICATE (2)

Ezek 44:19 other garments, lest they C holiness to the people
46:20 outer court and so C holiness to the people."

COMMUNICATED

Tob 7:9 So he C the proposal to Raguel.

COMMUNICATION

2Mac 11:17 have delivered your signed C and have asked about

COMMUNITY (2)

1Mac 1:25 mourned deeply in every C,
2Mac 12:7 root out the whole C of Joppa.

COMPACT

2Chr 23:1 and entered into a C with the commanders of

COMPACTED

Wis 7:2 period of ten months, C with blood, from the

COMPANIES (32)

Gen 32:7 and camels, into two C,
32:10 this Jordan; and now I have become two C
Num 1:52 their tents by their C, every man by his
2:3 of Judah by their C, the leader of the
2:9 of Judah, by their C, is a hundred and
2:10 of Reuben by their C, the leader of the
2:16 of Reuben, by their C, is a hundred and
2:18 of Ephraim by their C, the leader of the
2:24 of Ephraim, by their C, is a hundred and
2:25 of Dan by their C, the leader of the
2:32 were numbered by their C were six hundred and
10:14 out first by their C; and over their host
10:18 set out by their C; and over their host
10:22 set out by their C; and over their host
10:25 set out by their C; and over their host
Judg 7:16 hundred men into three C, and put trumpets into
7:20 And the three C blew the trumpets and broke
9:34 night, and laid wait against Shechem in four C
9:43 divided them into three C, and laid wait in
9:44 city, while the two C rushed upon all who
1Sam 11:11 the people in three C; and they came into
13:17 the Philistines in three C; one company turned
Neh 12:31 and appointed two great C which gave thanks and
12:40 So both C of those who gave thanks stood
Jud 14:11 they went out in C to the passes in
Job 1:17 "The Chaldeans formed three C, and made a raid

C

Mt 13:24 of heaven may be C to a man who
18:22 of heaven may be C to a king who
22:2 of heaven may be C to a king who
25:1 of heaven shall be C to ten maidens who

COMPARING

Rom 8:18 time are not worth C with the glory that

COMPARISON (4)

Judg 8:2 I done now in C with you?
8:3 able to do in C with you?" Then their
Wis 7:8 wealth as nothing in C with her.
2Cor 4:17 of glory beyond all C,

COMPASS (2)

Josh 6:11 of the LORD to C the city, going about
Is 44:13 marks it with a C; he shapes it into

COMPASSING (2)

1Kgs 7:24 gourds, for thirty cubits, C the sea round about;
2Chr 4:3 gourds, for thirty cubits, C the sea round about;

COMPASSION (60)

Deut 13:17 you mercy, and have C on you, and multiply
30:3 your fortunes, and have C upon you, and he
32:36 his people and have C on his servants, when
Judg 21:6 people of Israel had C for Benjamin their brother,
21:15 And the people had C on Benjamin because the
1Sam 23:21 for you have had C on me.
1Kgs 8:50 thee; and grant them C in the sight of
8:50 that they may have C on them
2Kgs 13:23 to them and had C on them, and he
2Chr 30:9 your children will find C with their captors, and
36:15 messengers, because he had C on his people and
36:17 sanctuary, and had no C on young man or
Tob 8:17 because thou hast had C on two only children.
Ps 77:9 Has he in anger shut up his C
79:8 our forefathers; let thy C come speedily to meet
135:14 his people, and have C on his servants.
145:9 to all, and his C is over all that
Wis 10:5 the face of his C for his child.
Sir 18:12 The C of man is for his neighbor, but
18:12 his neighbor, but the C of the Lord is
18:13 He has C on those who accept his discipline
Is 9:17 men, and has no C on their fatherless and
14:1 The LORD will have C on Jacob and will
27:11 them will not have C on them, he that
49:13 people, and will have C on his afflicted.
49:15 she should have no C on the son of
54:7 you, but with great C I will gather you.
54:8 love I will have C on you, says the
54:10 the LORD, who has C on you.
63:15 thy heart and thy C are withheld from me.
Jer 12:15 I will again have C on them, and I
13:14 or spare or have C, that I should not
21:7 spare them, or have C
30:18 of Jacob, and have C on his dwellings; the
Lam 3:32 grief, he will have C according to the abundance
Bar 2:27 in all thy great C,
Ezek 16:5 to you out of C for you; but you
Dan 1:9 gave Daniel favor and C in the sight of
Hos 11:4 them with cords of C, with the bands of
11:8 recoils within me, my C grows warm and tender.
13:14 C is hid from my eyes.
Mic 7:19 He will again have C upon us, he will
Zech 1:16 returned to Jerusalem with C; my house shall be
10:6 back because I have C on them, and they
12:10 Jerusalem a spirit of C and supplication, so that,
1Mac 3:44 and to pray and ask for mercy and C
2Mac 7:6 and in truth has C on us, as Moses
7:6 ïAnd he will have C on his servants.'"
Mt 9:36 the crowds, he had C for them, because they
14:14 throng; and he had C on them, and healed
15:32 and said, "I have C on the crowd, because
Mk 6:34 throng, and he had C on them, because they
8:2 to them, "I have C on the crowd, because
Lk 7:13 saw her, he had C on her and said
10:33 saw him, he had C,
15:20 saw him and had C, and ran and embraced
Rom 9:15 and I will have C on whom I have
9:15 I will have compassion on whom I have C
Col 3:12 holy and beloved, C, kindness, lowliness, meekness,
Heb 10:34 For you had C on the prisoners, and you

COMPASSIONATE (5)

Ex 22:27 to me, I will hear, for I am C
Ps 78:38 Yet he, being C, forgave their iniquity, and did
Sir 2:11 For the Lord is C and merciful; he forgives
Lam 4:10 The hands of C women have boiled their own
Jas 5:11 how the Lord is C and merciful.

COMPEL (4)

2Mac 6:1 an Athenian senator to C the Jews to forsake
Lk 14:23 highways and hedges, and C people to come in,
Gal 2:14 Jew, how can you C the Gentiles to live
6:12 the flesh that would C you to be circumcised,

COMPELLED (12)

Ex 3:19 let you go unless C by a mighty hand.
Jud 8:30 very thirsty, and they C us to do for
Esth 1:8 law, no one was C; for the king had
Wis 19:3 they had begged and C to depart.
Lam 5:13 Young men are C to grind at the mill;
2Mac 6:7 Dionysus came, they were C to walk in the
7:1 arrested and were being C by the king, under
15:2 the Jews who were C to follow him said,
Mt 27:32 name; this man they C to carry his cross.
Mk 15:21 And they C a passer-by, Simon of Cyrene, who
Acts 28:19 Jews objected, I was C to appeal to Caesar--
Gal 2:3 with me, was not C to be circumcised, though

COMPELS

Prov 7:21 her smooth talk she C him.

COMPENSATION

Prov 6:35 He will accept no C, nor be appeased though

COMPETE (3)

Jer 12:5 you, how will you C with horses?
22:15 a king because you C in cedar?
1Cor 9:24 race all the runners C, but only one receives

COMPETENCE

2Cor 3:5 coming from us; our C is from God,

COMPETENT (3)

Dan 1:4 knowledge, understanding learning, and C to serve in
2Cor 3:5 Not that we are C of ourselves to claim
3:6 who has made us C to be ministers of

COMPETES (2)

Wis 15:9 is brief, but he C with workers in gold
2Tim 2:5 not crowned unless he C according to the rules.

COMPILE

Lk 1:1 many have undertaken to C a narrative of the

COMPILER

2Mac 2:28 exact details to the C, while devoting our effort

COMPLACENCE

Prov 1:32 turning away, and the C of fools destroys them;

COMPLACENT (3)

Is 32:9 hear my voice; you C daughters, give ear to
32:10 you will shudder, you C women; for the vintage
32:11 at ease, shudder, you C ones; strip, and make

COMPLAIN (8)

Judg 21:22 their brothers come to C to us, we will
Jud 5:22 the tent began to C; Holofernes' officers and all
Job 7:11 my spirit; I will C in the bitterness of
Sir 31:24 The city will C of the one who is
Jer 2:29 "Why do you C against me?
12:1 O LORD, when I C to thee; yet I
Lam 3:39 should a living man C, a man, about the
Phil 4:11 Not that I C of want; for I have

COMPLAINED (2)

Gen 21:25 When Abraham C to Abimelech about a well of
Num 11:1 And the people C in the hearing of the

COMPLAINING

Prov 23:29 Who has C

COMPLAINT (15)

Job 7:13 couch will ease my C
9:27 'I will forget my C, I will put off
10:1 free utterance to my C; I will speak in
21:4 for me, is my C against man?
23:2 answered: "Today also my C is bitter, his hand
31:13 when they brought a C against me;

Ps 55:17 noon I utter my C and moan, and he
64:1 O God, in my C; preserve my life from
142:2 I pour out my C before him, I tell
Dan 6:4 find a ground for C against Daniel with regard
6:4 find no ground for C or any fault, because
6:5 find any ground for C against this Daniel unless
Hab 2:1 me, and what I will answer concerning my C
Acts 19:38 with him have a C against any one, the
Col 3:13 if one has a C against another, forgiving each

COMPLAINTS

1Mac 11:25 his nation kept making C against him,

COMPLETE (28)

Gen 15:16 the iniquity of the Amorites is not yet C
29:27 C the week of this one, and we will
Ex 5:13 taskmasters were urgent, saying, C your work, your
1Chr 11:8 from the Millo in C circuit; and Joab repaired
2Chr 12:12 not to make a C destruction; moreover, conditions
Job 23:14 For he will C what he appoints for me;
36:11 and serve him, they C their days in prosperity,
Wis 15:3 to know thee is C righteousness, and to know
Sir 7:32 the poor, so that your blessing may be C
26:2 husband, and he will C his years in peace.
38:28 he is careful to C its decoration.
Zech 4:9 his hands shall also C it.
1Mac 5:5 against them, vowed their C destruction, and burned
13:10 warriors and hastened to C the walls of Jerusalem,
2Mac 4:23 the king and to C the records of essential
15:1 to attack them with C safety on the day
Lk 14:28 he has enough to C it?
2Cor 8:6 beginning, he should also C among you this gracious
8:10 for you now to C what a year ago
10:6 punish every disobedience, when your obedience is C
Phil 2:2 any affection and sympathy, C my joy by being
2:30 risking his life to C your service to me.
Col 1:24 in my flesh I C what is lacking in
2Tim 3:17 of God may be C, equipped for every good
Jas 1:4 may be perfect and C, lacking in nothing.
1 Jn 1:4 are writing this that our joy may be C
2 Jn 1:12 to face, so that our joy may be C
Rev 6:11 their brethren should be C, who were to be

COMPLETED (22)

Gen 29:21 go in to her, for my time is C
29:28 Jacob did so, and C her week; then Laban
Lev 8:33 of your ordination are C, for it will take
12:4 sanctuary, until the days of her purifying are C
12:6 of her purifying are C, whether for a son
Num 6:5 until the time is C for which he separates
6:13 his separation has been C: he shall be brought
2Chr 8:16 So the house of the LORD was C
Tob 14:5 one until the times of the age are C
Esth 1:5 when these days were C, the king gave for
Sir 50:19 was ended; so they C his service.
Jer 25:12 after seventy years are C, I will punish the
29:10 When seventy years are C for Babylon, I will
Ezek 4:6 And when you have C these, you shall lie
4:8 other, till you have C the days of your
5:2 of the siege are C; and a third part
43:27 And when they have C these days, then from
1Mac 3:49 the Nazirites who had C their days;
2Mac 9:4 without stopping until he C the journey.
Acts 21:27 seven days were almost C, the Jews from Asia,
Rom 15:28 When therefore I have C this, and have delivered
Jas 2:22 works, and faith was C by works,

COMPLETELY (7)

Ex 11:1 lets you go, he will drive you away C
Jud 14:13 to give battle, in order to be destroyed C
Esth 13:7 our government C secure and untroubled hereafter."
Prov 28:5 but those who seek the LORD understand it C
1Mac 8:18 of the Greeks was C enslaving Israel.
2Mac 4:16 and wished to imitate C became their enemies and
14:46 with his blood now C drained from him, he

COMPLETENESS

Wis 12:17 when men doubt the C of thy power, and

COMPLETING (2)

Sir 37:11 for a year about C his work, with a
2Cor 8:11 be matched by your C it out of what

COMPLETION (2)

2Mac 2:9 for the dedication and C of the temple.
Phil 1:6 will bring it to C at the day of

COMPLIMENTARY

Prov 25:27 so be sparing of C words.

COMPLYING

Wis 19:6 nature was fashioned anew, C with thy commands,

COMPOSED (2)

Sir 44:5 of instruction; those who C musical tunes, and set
1Cor 12:24 But God has so C the body, giving the

COMPOSITION (2)

Ex 30:32 other like it in C; it is holy, and
30:37 make according to its C, you shall not make

COMPOUND

Sir 38:8 away pain; the pharmacist makes of them a C

COMPOUNDS

Ex 30:33 Whoever C any like it or whoever puts any

COMPREHEND (4)

Jud 8:14 out his mind or C his thought?
Job 37:5 voice; he does great things which we cannot C
Is 33:19 speech which you cannot C, stammering in a tongue
Eph 3:18 may have power to C with all the saints

COMPREHENDED

Job 38:18 Have you C the expanse of the earth?

COMPREHENDS

1Cor 2:11 So also no one C the thoughts of God

COMPREHENSION

Sir 1:17 down knowledge and discerning C, and he exalted

COMPRESSES

Prov 16:30 perverse things, he who C his lips brings evil

COMPULSION (3)

Dan 14:30 him hard, and under C he handed Daniel over
2Cor 9:7 not reluctantly or under C, for God loves a
Philem 1:14 might not be by C but of your own

COMPUTE (2)

Lev 27:18 then the priest shall C the money-value for it
27:23 then the priest shall C the valuation for it

COMRADE (2)

Judg 7:13 a dream to his C; and he said, "Behold,
7:14 And his C answered, "This is no other than

COMRADES

Heb 1:9 thee with the oil of gladness beyond thy C

CONANIAH (3)

2Chr 31:12 charge of them was C the Levite, with Shimei
31:13 Benaiah were overseers assisting C and Shimei his
35:9 C also, and Shemaiah and Nethanel his brothers, and

CONCEAL (9)

Gen 37:26 slay our brother and C his blood?
Deut 13:8 him, nor shall you C him;
Tob 12:11 "I will not C anything from you.
Job 14:13 Sheol, that thou wouldest C me until thy wrath
27:11 what is with the Almighty I will not C
Ps 27:5 of trouble; he will C me under the cover
Prov 25:2 glory of God to C things, but the glory
Jer 49:10 is not able to C himself.
50:2 a banner and proclaim, C it not, and say:

CONCEALED (7)

Job 28:21 of all living, and C from the birds of
31:33 wayfarer); if I have C my transgressions from men,
Ps 40:10 salvation; I have not C thy steadfast love and
Sir 11:4 and his works are C from men.
16:19 can see, so most of his works are C
Jer 16:17 nor is their iniquity C from my eyes.
Lk 9:45 saying, and it was C from them, that they

CONCEALS (5)

Prov 10:6 mouth of the wicked C violence.
10:11 mouth of the wicked C violence.
10:18 He who C hatred has lying lips, and he
12:23 A prudent man C his knowledge, but fools proclaim
28:13 He who C his transgressions will not prosper, but

CONCEIT (6)

Job	37:24	regard any who are wise in their own C
2Cor	12:20	anger, selfishness, slander, gossip, C, and disorder.
Phil	2:3	nothing from selfishness or C, but in humility count
1Tim	3:6	be puffed up with C and fall into the
	6:4	is puffed up with C, he knows nothing; he
2Tim	3:4	reckless, swollen with C, lovers of pleasure rather

CONCEITED

Rom	12:16	haughty, but associate with the lowly; never be C

CONCEITS

Rom	11:25	wise in your own C, I want you to

CONCEIVE (14)

Num	5:28	be free and shall C children.
	11:12	Did I C all this people?
Judg	13:3	children; but you shall C and bear a son.
	13:5	for lo, you shall C and bear a son.
	13:7	me, 'Behold, you shall C and bear a son;
Job	15:35	They C mischief and bring forth evil and their
Ps	35:20	in the land they C words of deceit.
	51:5	sin did my mother C me.
Is	7:14	a young woman shall C and bear a son,
	33:11	You C chaff, you bring forth stubble; your breath
	59:4	they speak lies, they C mischief and bring forth
Mt	1:23	"Behold, a virgin shall C and bear a son,
Lk	1:31	And behold, you will C in your womb and
Heb	11:11	herself received power to C, even when she was

CONCEIVED (43)

Gen	4:1	his wife, and she C and bore Cain, saying,
	4:17	his wife, and she C and bore Enoch; and
	16:4	to Hagar, and she C; and when she saw
	16:4	saw that she had C, she looked with contempt
	16:5	saw that she had C, she looked on me
	21:2	And Sarah C, and bore Abraham a son in
	25:21	LORD granted his prayer, and Rebekah his wife C
	29:32	And Leah C and bore a son, and she
	29:33	She C again and bore a son, and said,
	29:34	Again she C and bore a son, and said,
	29:35	And she C again and bore a son, and
	30:5	And Bilhah C and bore Jacob a son.
	30:7	Rachel's maid Bilhah C again and bore Jacob a
	30:17	to Leah, and she C and bore Jacob a
	30:19	And Leah C again, and she bore Jacob a
	30:23	She C and bore a son, and said, "God
	38:3	to her, and she C and bore a son,
	38:4	Again she C and bore a son, and she
	38:18	to her, and she C by him.
Ex	2:2	The woman C and bore a son; and when
1Sam	1:20	in due time Hannah C and bore a son,
	2:21	visited Hannah, and she C and bore three sons
2Sam	11:5	And the woman C; and she sent and told
2Kgs	4:17	But the woman C, and she bore a son
1Chr	4:17	Mered married; and she C and bore Miriam,
	7:23	his wife, and she C and bore a son;
Job	3:3	said, 'A man-child is C
Ps	64:6	thought out a cunningly C plot." For the inward
Song	3:4	chamber of her that C me.
	8:2	chamber of her that C me.
Is	8:3	the prophetess, and she C and bore a son.
Hos	1:3	of Diblaim, and she C and bore him a
	1:6	She C again and bore a daughter.
	1:8	weaned Not pitied, she C and bore a son.
	2:5	the harlot; she that C them has acted shamefully.
2Mac	9:4	Transported with rage, he C the idea of turning
Mt	1:20	for that which is C in her is of
Lk	1:24	days his wife Elizabeth C, and for five months
	1:36	old age has also C a son; and this
	2:21	angel before he was C in the womb.
Rom	9:10	also when Rebecca had C children by one man,
1Cor	2:9	the heart of man C, what God has prepared
Jas	1:14	desire when it has C gives birth to sin;

CONCEIVES (2)

Lev	12:2	Israel, If a woman C, and bears a male
Ps	7:14	Behold, the wicked man C evil, and is pregnant

CONCEIVING

Is	59:13	speaking oppression and revolt, C and uttering from

CONCEPTION (2)

Ruth	4:13	the LORD gave her C, and she bore a
Hos	9:11	like a bird--no birth, no pregnancy, no C

CONCERN (7)

Gen	39:6	him he had no C for anything but the
	39:8	my master has no C about anything in the
Wis	6:17	desire for instruction, and C for instruction is love
Sir	11:9	matter which does not C you, nor sit with
Ezek	36:21	land.' But I had C for my holy name,
2Mac	15:18	Their C for wives and children, and also for
Phil	4:10	you have revived your C for me; you were

CONCERNED (11)

Wis	15:9	But he is not C that he is destined
Sir	7:24	Be C for their chastity, and do not show
	8:13	you give surety, be C as one who must
	38:29	he is always deeply C over his work, and
	39:1	ancients, and will be C with prophecies;
Bar	3:31	to her, or is C about the path to
2Mac	2:29	new house must be C with the whole construction,
	14:8	because I am genuinely C for the interests of
1Cor	9:9	Is it for oxen that God is C
Phil	4:10	me; you were indeed C for me, but you
Heb	2:16	angels that he is C but with the descendants

CONCERNING (230)

Gen	12:20	Pharaoh gave men orders C him; and they set
	24:9	and swore to him C this matter.
	42:21	truth we are guilty C our brother, in that
	47:26	made it a statute C the land of Egypt,
Ex	8:12	cried to the LORD C the frogs, as he
	25:9	that I show you C the pattern of the
Num	8:20	the LORD commanded Moses C the Levites, the
	8:22	LORD had commanded Moses C the Levites, so they
	9:8	the LORD will command C you."
	30:12	out of her lips C her vows, or concerning
	30:12	concerning her vows, or C her pledge of herself,
	32:28	So Moses gave command C them to Eleazar the
	36:6	what the LORD commands C the daughters of
Deut	26:17	have declared this day C the LORD that he
	26:18	has declared this day C you that you are
	27:4	set up these stones, C which I command you
Josh	14:6	of God in Kadesh-barnea C you and me.
	23:14	LORD your God promised C you; all have come
	23:15	LORD your God promised C you have been fulfilled
Judg	21:5	taken a great oath C him who did not
Ruth	4:7	former times in Israel C redeeming and exchanging:
1Sam	3:12	that I have spoken C his house, from beginning
	12:7	you before the LORD C all the saving deeds
	25:30	that he has spoken C you, and has appointed
2Sam	3:8	today with a fault C a woman.
	7:25	which thou hast spoken C thy servant and concerning
	7:25	concerning thy servant and C his house, and do
	10:2	servants to console him C his father.
	14:8	I will give orders C you."
1Kgs	2:4	word which he spoke C me, saying, 'If your
	2:27	which he had spoken C the house of Eli
	6:12	LORD came to Solomon, C this house which you
	10:1	the fame of Solomon C the name of the
	11:2	women, from the nations C which the LORD had
	11:10	and had commanded him C this thing, that he
	14:5	to inquire of you C her son; for he
	22:8	he never prophesies good C me, but evil." And
	22:18	would not prophesy good C me, but evil?"
	22:23	LORD has spoken evil C you."
2Kgs	10:10	which the LORD spoke C the house of Ahab;
	17:15	were round about them, C whom the LORD had
	19:9	when the king heard C Tirhakah king of Ethiopia,
	19:21	the LORD has spoken C him: "She despises you,
	19:32	thus says the LORD C the king of Assyria,
	22:13	and for all Judah, C the words of this
	22:13	all that is written C us."
1Chr	11:10	word of the LORD C Israel.
	17:23	which thou hast spoken C thy servant and concerning
	17:23	concerning thy servant and C his house be
	19:2	messengers to console him C his father.
	19:5	When David was told C the men, he sent
	22:11	as he has spoken C you.
	27:1	king in all matters C the divisions that came
	28:19	hand of the LORD C it, all the work
2Chr	8:15	the priests and Levites C any matter and concerning
	8:15	concerning any matter and C the treasuries.
	9:29	of Iddo the seer C Jeroboam the son of
	18:7	he never prophesies good C me, but always evil."
	18:17	would not prophesy good C me, but evil?"
	18:22	LORD has spoken evil C you."
	19:10	live in their cities, C bloodshed, law or
	23:3	as the LORD spoke C the sons of David.
	34:21	Israel and in Judah, C the words of the

Ezra 5:5 be returned by letter C it.
6:3 king issued a decree: C the house of God
Neh 1:2 and I asked them C the Jews that survived,
1:2 had escaped exile, and C Jerusalem.
6:7 up prophets to proclaim C you in Jerusalem, 'There
11:23 command from the king C them, and a settled
11:24 hand in all matters C the people.
13:14 me, O my God, C this, and wipe not
Esth 3:2 king had so commanded C him.
4:8 speak to the king C us and deliver us
8:9 all that Mordecai commanded C the Jews to the
10:5 dream that I had C these matters, and none
12:2 he informed the king C them.
Job 27:11 I will teach you C the hand of God;
36:33 Its crashing declares C him, who is jealous with
41:12 will not keep silence C his limbs, or his
Ps 71:10 For my enemies speak C me, those who watch
Sir 17:12 to each of them C his neighbor.
23:7 my children, to instruction C speech; the one who
Is 1:1 Amoz, which he saw C Judah and Jerusalem in
2:1 son of Amoz saw C Judah and Jerusalem.
5:1 beloved a love song C his vineyard: My beloved
13:1 The oracle C Babylon which Isaiah the son of
14:26 purpose that is purposed C the whole earth; and
15:1 An oracle C Moab.
16:13 which the LORD spoke C Moab in the past.
17:1 An oracle C Damascus.
19:1 An oracle C Egypt.
21:1 The oracle C the wilderness of the sea.
21:11 The oracle C Dumah.
21:13 The oracle C Arabia.
22:1 The oracle C the valley of vision.
23:1 The oracle C Tyre.
23:11 LORD has given command C Canaan to destroy its
29:22 LORD, who redeemed Abraham, C the house of
32:6 ungodliness, to utter error C the LORD, to leave
37:9 Now the king heard C Tirhakah king of Ethiopia,
37:21 have prayed to me C Sennacherib king of Assyria,
37:22 the LORD has spoken C him: 'She despises you,
37:33 thus says the LORD C the king of Assyria:
45:11 children, or command me C the work of my
Jer 7:22 fathers or command them C burnt offerings and
11:21 thus says the LORD C the men of Anathoth,
12:14 Thus says the LORD C all my evil neighbors
14:1 which came to Jeremiah C the drought:
14:10 Thus says the LORD C this people: "They have
14:15 thus says the LORD C the prophets who prophesy
16:3 thus says the LORD C the sons and daughters
16:3 in this place, and C the mothers who bore
18:7 any time I declare C a nation or a
18:8 and if that nation, C which I have spoken,
18:9 any time I declare C a nation or a
22:6 thus says the LORD C the house of the
22:11 thus says the LORD C Shallum the son of
22:18 thus says the LORD C Jehoiakim the son of
23:2 the God of Israel, C the shepherds who care
23:9 C the prophets: My heart is broken within me,
23:15 the LORD of hosts C the prophets: "Behold, I
25:1 that came to Jeremiah C all the people of
27:13 the LORD has spoken C any nation which will
27:19 the LORD of hosts C the pillars, the sea,
27:21 the God of Israel, C the vessels which are
29:16 Thus says the LORD C the king who sits
29:16 throne of David, and C all the people who
29:21 the God of Israel, C Ahab the son of
29:31 'Thus says the LORD C Shemaiah of Nehelam:
30:4 which the LORD spoke C Israel and Judah:
32:36 the God of Israel, C this city of which
33:4 the God of Israel, C the houses of this
34:4 Thus says the LORD C you: 'You shall not
36:29 And C Jehoiakim king of Judah you shall say,
36:30 thus says the LORD C Jehoiakim king of Judah,
39:11 Babylon gave command C Jeremiah through
44:1 that came to Jeremiah C all the Jews that
46:1 to Jeremiah the prophet C the nations.
46:2 C the army of Pharaoh Neco, king of Egypt,
47:1 to Jeremiah the prophet C the Philistines, before
48:1 C Moab.
49:1 C the Ammonites.
49:7 C Edom.
49:23 C Damascus.
49:28 C Kedar and the kingdoms of Hazor which
49:34 to Jeremiah the prophet C Elam, in the beginning
50:1 which the LORD spoke C Babylon, concerning the
50:1 LORD spoke concerning Babylon, C the land of the
51:11 Medes, because his purpose C Babylon is to destroy
51:12 done what he spoke C the inhabitants of Babylon.
51:60 words that are written C Babylon.
51:62 LORD, thou hast said C this place that thou
Ezek 12:19 says the Lord GOD C the inhabitants of Jerusalem
13:16 of Israel who prophesied C Jerusalem and saw
18:2 by repeating this proverb C the land of Israel,
21:28 says the Lord GOD C the Ammonites, and concerning
21:28 the Ammonites, and C their reproach; say, A
26:2 man, because Tyre said C Jerusalem, 'Aha, the gate
36:6 Therefore prophesy C the land of Israel, and say
44:5 I shall tell you C all the ordinances of
44:12 therefore I have sworn C them, says the Lord
Dan 1:20 of wisdom and understanding C which the king
2:18 the God of heaven C this mystery, so that
5:29 and proclamation was made C him, that he should
6:12 said before the king, C the interdict, "O king!
6:17 nothing might be changed C Daniel.
7:16 asked him the truth C all this.
7:19 to know the truth C the fourth beast, which
7:20 with its feet; and C the ten horns that
8:13 long is the vision C the continual burnt offering,
9:24 of years are decreed C your people and your
13:5 C them the Lord had said: "Iniquity came forth
Amos 1:1 Tekoa, which he saw C Israel in the days
7:3 The LORD repented C this; "It shall not be,"
7:6 The LORD repented C this; "This also shall not
Obad 1:1 says the Lord GOD C Edom: We have heard
Mic 1:1 Judah, which he saw C Samaria and Jerusalem.
3:5 Thus says the LORD C the prophets who lead
Nah 1:1 An oracle C Nineveh.
Hab 2:1 what I will answer C my complaint.
Zech 12:1 word of the LORD C Israel: Thus says the
1Mac 8:15 senators constantly deliberate C the people, to
8:31 "And C the wrongs which King Demetrius is doing
9:55 word or give commands C his house.
11:31 letter which we wrote C you to Lasthenes our
12:17 this letter from us C the renewal of our
12:21 been found in writing C the Spartans and the
12:22 this, please write us C your welfare;
2Mac 8:12 Word came to Judas C Nicanor's invasion; and when
11:20 And C these matters and their details, I have
Mt 11:7 speak to the crowds C John: "What did you
Mk 4:10 the twelve asked him C the parables.
Lk 1:4 may know the truth C the things of which
2:17 had been told them C this child;
3:15 questioned in their hearts C John, whether perhaps
4:14 Galilee, and a report C him went out through
5:15 the report went abroad C him; and great multitudes
7:17 And this report C him spread through the whole
7:24 speak to the crowds C John: "What did you
24:19 they said to him, C Jesus of Nazareth, who
24:27 the scriptures the things C himself.
Jn 11:19 Mary to console them C their brother.
16:8 will convince the world C sin and righteousness and
16:9 and righteousness and judgment: C sin, because they
16:10 not believe in me; C righteousness, because I go
16:11 see me no more; C judgment, because the ruler
Acts 1:16 the mouth of David, C Judas who was guide
2:25 For David says C him, 'I saw the Lord
4:9 are being examined today C a good deed done
18:25 taught accurately the things C Jesus, though he knew
19:23 arose no little stir C the Way.
25:16 to make his defense C the charge laid against
Rom 1:3 holy scriptures, the gospel C his Son, who was
4:20 distrust made him waver C the promise of God,
7:2 discharged from the law C the husband.
9:27 And Isaiah cries out C Israel: "Though the number
1Cor 7:1 Now C the matters about which you wrote.
7:25 Now C the unmarried, I have no command of
8:1 Now C food offered to idols: we know that
12:1 Now C spiritual gifts, brethren, I do not want
16:1 Now C the contribution for the saints: as I
Col 4:10 the cousin of Barnabas C whom you have received
1Thes 1:9 For they themselves report C us what a welcome
4:9 But C love of the brethren you have no
4:13 have you ignorant, brethren, C those who are asleep,
2Thes 2:1 Now C the coming of our Lord Jesus Christ
Heb 7:16 to a legal requirement C bodily descent but by
11:7 being warned by God C events as yet unseen,
11:22 Israelites and gave directions C his burial.
1 Jn 1:1 touched with our hands, C the word of life—

CONCERNS (4)

Num 18:7 priesthood for all that C the altar and that
Job 35:8 Your wickedness C a man like yourself, and your
Sir 50:28 Blessed is he who C himself with these things,

Ezek 12:10 Lord GOD: This oracle C the prince in Jerusalem

CONCERT

Sir 32:5 of gold is a C of music at a

CONCESSION

1Cor 7:6 this by way of C, not of command.

CONCESSIONS

2Mac 4:11 aside the existing royal C to the Jews, secured

CONCILIATE

1Cor 4:13 slandered, we try to C; we have become, and

CONCISELY

Sir 32:8 Speak C, say much in few words; be as

CONCLUDED (2)

1Mac 6:9 gripped him, and he C that he was dying.
2Mac 14:30 had been his custom, C that this austerity did

CONCLUDING

Acts 16:10 go on into Macedonia, C that God had called

CONCUBINE (23)

Gen 22:24 Moreover, his C, whose name was Reumah, bore
35:22 with Bilhah his father's C; and Israel heard of
36:12 (Timna was a C of Eliphaz, Esau's son; she
Judg 8:31 And his C who was in Shechem also bore
19:1 took to himself a C from Bethlehem in Judah.
19:2 And his C became angry with him, and she
19:9 the man and his C and his servant rose
19:10 saddled asses, and his C was with him.
19:24 virgin daughter and his C; let me bring them
19:25 the man seized his C, and put her out
19:27 behold, there was his C lying at the door
19:29 laying hold of his C he divided her, limb
20:4 Benjamin, I and my C, to spend the night.
20:5 and they ravished my C, and she is dead.
20:6 And I took my C and cut her in
2Sam 3:7 Now Saul had a C, whose name was Rizpah,
3:7 "Why have you gone in to my father's C
21:11 daughter of Aiah, the C of Saul, had done,
1Chr 1:32 sons of Keturah, Abraham's C: she bore Zimran,
2:46 Ephah also, Caleb's C, bore Haran, Moza, and Gazez;
2:48 Maacah, Caleb's C, bore Sheber and Tirhanah.
7:14 Asriel, whom his Aramean C bore; she bore Machir
2Mac 4:30 given as a present to Antiochis, the king's C

CONCUBINES (18)

Gen 25:6 the sons of his C Abraham gave gifts, and
2Sam 5:13 And David took more C and wives from Jerusalem,
15:16 the king left ten C to keep the house.
16:21 in to your father's C, whom he has left
16:22 in to his father's C in the sight of
19:5 your wives and your C,
20:3 king took the ten C whom he had left
1Kgs 11:3 princesses, and three hundred C; and his wives
1Chr 3:9 the sons of the C; and Tamar was their
2Chr 11:21 all his wives and C (he took eighteen wives
11:21 eighteen wives and sixty C, and had twenty-eight
Esth 2:14 in charge of the C; she did not go
Eccl 2:8 and women, and many C, man's delight.
Song 6:8 sixty queens and eighty C, and maidens without
6:9 happy; the queens and C also, and they praised
Dan 5:2 his wives, and his C might drink from them.
5:3 his wives, and his C drank from them.
5:23 your wives, and your C have drunk wine from

CONDEMN (30)

Ex 22:9 he whom God shall C shall pay double to
Job 9:20 my own mouth would C me; though I am
10:2 to God, Do not C me; let me know
34:17 Will you C him who is righteous and mighty,
34:29 afflicted-- When he is quiet, who can C
40:8 Will you C me that you may be justified?
Ps 94:21 of the righteous, and C the innocent to death.
109:31 him from those who C him to death.
141:6 to those who shall C them, then they shall
Wis 2:20 Let us C him to a shameful death, for,
4:16 who had died will C the ungodly who are
4:16 is quickly perfected will C the prolonged old age
12:15 to thy power to C him who does not
Sir 14:2 whose heart does not C him, and who has
Mt 12:41 with this generation and C it; for they repented
12:42 with this generation and C it; for she came
20:18 scribes, and they will C him to death,
Mk 10:33 scribes, and they will C him to death, and
Lk 6:37 will not be judged; C not, and you will
11:31 of this generation and C them; for she came
11:32 with this generation and C it; for they repented
19:22 to him, 'I will C you out of your
Jn 3:17 the world, not to C the world, but that
8:11 said, "Neither do I C you; go, and do
Rom 2:1 judgment upon him you C yourself, because you, the
2:27 keep the law will C you who have the
8:34 It is God who justifies; who is to C
2Cor 7:3 not say this to C you, for I said
1 Jn 3:20 him whenever our hearts C us; for God is
3:21 our hearts do not C us, we have confidence

CONDEMNATION (17)

Prov 19:29 C is ready for scoffers, and flogging for the
Wis 11:10 the ungodly as a stern king does in C
12:27 Therefore the utmost C came upon them.
Sir 5:14 the thief, and severe C to the double-tongued.
Mk 12:40 They will receive the greater C
Lk 20:47 They will receive the greater C
23:39 since you are under the same sentence of C
Rom 3:8 Their C is just.
5:16 following one trespass brought C, but the free gift
5:18 man's trespass led to C for all men, so
8:1 is therefore now no C for those who are
2Cor 3:9 dispensation of C, the dispensation of righteousness
1Tim 3:6 and fall into the C of the devil;
5:12 and so they incur C for having violated their
Jas 5:12 be no, that you may not fall under C
2Pet 2:3 from of old their C has not been idle,
Jude 1:4 designated for this C, ungodly persons who pervert

CONDEMNED (29)

Job 9:29 I shall be C; why then do I labor
Ps 34:21 and those who hate the righteous will be C
34:22 those who take refuge in him will be C
37:33 or let him be C when he is brought
Wis 17:11 is a cowardly thing, C by its own testimony;
Sir 19:5 in wickedness will be C,
Dan 13:41 and judges; and they C her to death.
13:48 Have you C a daughter of Israel without examination
1Mac 1:57 decree of the king C him to death.
Mt 12:7 you would not have C the guiltless.
12:37 justified, and by your words you will be C
27:3 saw that he was C, he repented and brought
Mk 14:64 And they all C him as deserving death.
16:16 but he who does not believe will be C
Lk 6:37 you will not be C; forgive, and you will
24:20 him up to be C to death, and crucified
Jn 3:18 in him is not C; he who does not
3:18 does not believe is C already, because he has
8:10 Has no one C you?"
Rom 3:7 am I still being C as a sinner?
8:3 and for sin, he C sin in the flesh,
14:23 who has doubts is C, if he eats, because
1Cor 11:32 we may not be C along with the world.
11:34 at home--lest you come together to be C
Gal 2:11 opposed him to his face, because he stood C
2Thes 2:12 that all may be C who did not believe
Heb 11:7 household; by this he C the world and became
Jas 5:6 You have C, you have killed the righteous man;
2Pet 2:6 Gomorrah to ashes he C them to extinction and

CONDEMNING (4)

Deut 25:1 acquitting the innocent and C the guilty,
1Kgs 8:32 and judge thy servants, C the guilty by bringing
Dan 13:53 pronouncing unjust judgments, C the innocent and
Acts 13:27 sabbath, fulfilled these by C him.

CONDEMNS (3)

Job 15:6 Your own mouth C you, and not I; your
Prov 12:2 LORD, but a man of evil devices he C
17:15 wicked and he who C the righteous are both

CONDENSATION

2Mac 2:28 effort to arriving at the outlines of the C

CONDENSE

2Mac 2:23 we shall attempt to C into a single book.

CONDITION (9)

Gen 34:15 Only on this C will we consent to you:
34:22 Only on this C will the men agree to
Ex 2:25 the people of Israel, and God knew their C

C

Gal 5:10 I have C in the Lord that you will
Eph 3:12 we have boldness and C of access through our
Phil 3:3 Jesus, and put no C in the flesh.
3:4 myself have reason for C in the flesh also.
3:4 he has reason for C in the flesh, I
2Thes 3:4 And we have C in the Lord about you,
1Tim 3:13 themselves and also great C in the faith which
Heb 3:6 we hold fast our C and pride in our
3:14 we hold our first C firm to the end,
4:16 Let us then with C draw near to the
10:19 brethren, since we have C to enter the sanctuary
10:35 not throw away your C, which has a great
1Pet 1:21 Through him you have C in God, who raised
1 Jn 2:28 appears we may have C and not shrink from
3:21 condemn us, we have C before God;
4:17 that we may have C for the day of
5:14 And this is the C which we have in

CONFIDENT (10)

Jud 2:5 take with you men C in their strength, to
Job 6:20 disappointed because they were C; they come thither
40:23 not frightened; he is C though Jordan rushes against
Ps 27:3 war arise against me, yet I will be C
Sir 5:5 Do not be so C of atonement that you
49:10 and delivered them with C hope.
2Cor 9:4 to say nothing of you--for being so C
10:7 If any one is C that he is Christs,
Phil 1:14 brethren have been made C in the Lord because
Philem 1:21 C of your obedience, I write to you, knowing

CONFIDENTLY (3)

Sir 41:16 and not everything is C esteemed by every one.
Acts 2:29 may say to you C of the patriarch David
Heb 13:6 Hence we can C say, "The Lord is my

CONFINED (6)

Gen 39:20 the king's prisoners were C, and he was there
40:3 the guard, in the prison where Joseph was C
40:5 of Egypt, who were C in the prison--each
42:19 of your brothers remain C in your prison, and
Sir 23:19 His fear is C to the eyes of men,
Gal 3:23 faith came, we were C under the law, kept

CONFIRM (19)

Lev 26:9 multiply you, and will C my covenant with you.
Deut 8:18 wealth; that he may C his covenant which he
9:5 and that he may C the word which the
27:26 he who does not C the words of this
Ruth 4:7 redeeming and exchanging: to C a transaction, the
2Sam 7:25 now, O LORD God, C for ever the word
1Kgs 1:14 in after you and C your words."
2Kgs 15:19 might help him to C his hold of the
1Chr 17:14 you, but I will C him in my house
Ps 119:38 C to thy servant thy promise, which is for
Sir 29:3 C your word and keep faith with him, and
Jer 44:25 libations to her.' Then C your vows and perform
Dan 11:1 I stood up to C and strengthen him.
1Mac 11:57 to Jonathan, saying, "I C you in the high-priesthood
12:1 them to Rome to C and renew the friendship
14:24 a thousand minas, to C the alliance with the
15:5 kingdom, now therefore I C to you all the
Rom 15:8 truthfulness, in order to C the promises given to
2Pet 1:10 the more zealous to C your call and election,

CONFIRMATION (2)

Phil 1:7 in the defense and C of the gospel.
Heb 6:16 all their disputes an oath is final for C

CONFIRMED (16)

1Kgs 8:26 let thy word be C, which thou hast spoken
1Chr 16:17 to Isaac, which he C as a statute to
2Chr 6:17 let thy word be C, which thou hast spoken
Ps 105:10 to Isaac, which he C to Jacob as a
119:106 sworn an oath and C it, to observe thy
Sir 3:2 the children, and he C the right of the
Bar 2:1 "So the Lord C his word, which he spoke
2:24 Babylon; and thou hast C thy words, which thou
Dan 9:12 He has C his words, which he spoke against
1Mac 11:27 He C him in the high-priesthood and in as
11:34 We have C as their possession both the territory
14:38 things King Demetrius C him in the high-priesthood,
2Mac 12:25 many words he had C his solemn promise to
Mt 18:15 every word may be C by the evidence of
Mk 16:20 worked with them and C the message by the
1Cor 1:6 testimony to Christ was C among you—

CONFIRMING

Esth 9:29 gave full written authority, C this second letter about

CONFIRMS (2)

Sir 42:25 One C the good things of the other, and
Is 44:26 their knowledge foolish; who C the word of his

CONFISCATED (2)

Tob 1:20 all my property was C and nothing was left
2Mac 3:13 in any case be C for the king's treasury.

CONFISCATION

Ezra 7:26 for banishment or for C of his goods or

CONFLICT (2)

Dan 10:1 word was true, and it was a great C
Phil 1:30 engaged in the same C which you saw and

CONFLICTING

Rom 2:15 bears witness and their C thoughts accuse or perhaps

CONFORM

Ps 119:85 men who do not C to thy law.

CONFORMED (3)

Rom 8:29 also predestined to be C to the image of
12:2 Do not be C to this world but be
1Pet 1:14 children, do not be C to the passions of

CONFOUND (3)

Ps 14:6 You would C the plans of the poor, but
Is 19:3 out, and I will C their plans; and they
Zech 10:5 them, and they shall C the riders on horses.

CONFOUNDED (23)

2Kgs 19:26 strength, are dismayed and C, and have become like
Job 6:20 they were confident; they come thither and are C
Ps 35:4 be turned back and C who devise evil against
Wis 10:5 agreement had been C, recognized the righteous
Is 20:5 shall be dismayed and C because of Ethiopia their
24:23 the moon will be C, and the sun ashamed;
33:9 languishes; Lebanon is C and withers away; Sharon
37:27 strength, are dismayed and C, and have become like
41:11 put to shame and C; those who strive against
45:16 put to shame and C, the makers of idols
45:17 put to shame or C to all eternity.
50:7 I have not been C; therefore I have set
54:4 be ashamed; be not C, for you will not
Jer 14:3 they are ashamed and C and cover their heads.
22:22 will be ashamed and C because of all your
31:19 ashamed, and I was C, because I bore the
49:23 "Hamath and Arpad are C, for they have heard
Ezek 16:63 may remember and be C, and never open your
36:32 Be ashamed and C for your ways, O house
Joel 1:10 Be C, O tillers of the soil, wail, O
Zech 9:5 in anguish; Ekron also, because its hopes are C
1Mac 3:6 all the evildoers were C; and deliverance prospered
Acts 9:22 more in strength, and C the Jews who lived

CONFRONT (3)

Deut 31:21 them, this song shall C them as a witness
Ps 17:13 C them, overthrow them!
Wis 12:14 any king or monarch C thee about those whom

CONFRONTED (2)

2Sam 22:6 the snares of death C me.
Ps 18:5 the snares of death C me.

CONFRONTING

Sir 34:3 likeness of a face C a face.

CONFUSE (3)

Gen 11:7 go down, and there C their language, that they
Ps 55:9 their plans, O Lord, C their tongues; for I
Is 3:12 leaders mislead you, and C the course of your

CONFUSED (4)

Gen 11:9 because there the LORD C the language of all
Is 28:7 strong drink, they are C with wine, they stagger
Jer 14:9 be like a man C, like a mighty man
2Mac 10:30 the enemy, so that, C and blinded, they were

CONFUSES

Sir 40:5 his sleep at night C his mind.

C

CONFUSION (30)

Ex 23:27 and will throw into C all the people against
Deut 7:23 throw them into great C, until they are destroyed.
28:20 send upon you curses, C, and frustration, in all
28:28 madness and blindness and C of mind;
1Sam 7:10 and threw them into C; and they were routed
14:20 against his fellow, and there was very great C
Neh 4:8 Jerusalem and to cause C in it.
Tob 4:13 is ruin and great C; and in shiftlessness there
Esth 11:5 Behold, noise and C, thunders and earthquake,
Ps 35:26 put to shame and C altogether who rejoice at
40:14 put to shame and C altogether who seek to
44:7 and hast put to C those who hate us.
70:2 put to shame and C who seek my life!
Wis 14:26 faithlessness, tumult, perjury, C over what is good,
Is 19:14 her a spirit of C; and they have made
22:5 tumult and trampling and C in the valley of
34:11 stretch the line of C over it, and the
45:16 of idols go in C together.
Jer 7:19 Is it not themselves, to their own C
Bar 1:15 Lord our God, but C of face, as at
2:6 Lord our God, but C of face to us
Dan 9:7 righteousness, but to us C of face, as at
9:8 us, O Lord, belongs C of face, to our
Mic 7:4 has come; now their C is at hand.
2Mac 4:41 threw them in wild C at Lysimachus and his
13:16 camp with terror and C and withdrew in triumph.
Acts 19:29 was filled with the C; and they rushed together
19:32 the assembly was in C, and most of them
21:31 of the cohort that all Jerusalem was in C
1Cor 14:33 not a God of C but of peace.

CONFUTE (2)

Is 54:17 prosper, and you shall C every tongue that rises
Tit 1:8 doctrine and also to C those who contradict it.

CONFUTED (2)

Job 32:12 there was none that C Job, or that answered
Acts 18:28 believed, for he powerfully C the Jews in public,

CONGEALED

Ex 15:8 a heap; the deeps C in the heart of

CONGENIAL

Sir 27:16 will never find a C friend.

CONGRATULATE (3)

2Sam 8:10 greet him, and to C him because he had
1Kgs 1:47 king's servants came to C our lord King David,
1Chr 18:10 greet him, and to C him because he had

CONGREGATION (155)

Ex 12:3 Tell all the C of Israel that on the
12:6 whole assembly of the C of Israel shall kill
12:19 cut off from the C of Israel, whether he
12:47 All the C of Israel shall keep it.
16:1 Elim, and all the C of the people of
16:2 And the whole C of the people of Israel
16:9 "Say to the whole C of the people of
16:10 spoke to the whole C of the people of
16:22 the leaders of the C came and told Moses,
17:1 an ephah.) All the C of the people of
34:31 the leaders of the C returned to him, and
35:1 Moses assembled all the C of the people of
35:4 said to all the C of the people of
35:20 Then all the C of the people of Israel
38:25 from those of the C who were numbered was
Lev 4:13 "If the whole C of Israel commits a sin
4:15 the elders of the C shall lay their hands
8:3 and assemble all the C at the door of
8:4 commanded him; and the C was assembled at the
8:5 Moses said to the C, "This is the thing
9:5 meeting; and all the C drew near and stood
10:6 come upon all the C; but your brethren, the
10:17 the iniquity of the C, to make atonement for
16:5 shall take from the C of the people of
19:2 "Say to all the C of the people of
24:14 and let all the C stone him.
24:16 to death; all the C shall stone him; the
Num 1:2 census of all the C of the people of
1:16 ones chosen from the C, the leaders of their
1:18 they assembled the whole C together, who registered
1:53 no wrath upon the C of the people of
3:7 and for the whole C before the tent of
4:34 the leaders of the C numbered the sons of
8:9 and assemble the whole C of the people of
8:20 Aaron and all the C of the people of
10:2 them for summoning the C, and for breaking camp.
10:3 are blown, all the C shall gather themselves to
13:26 and to all the C of the people of
13:26 and to all the C, and showed them the
14:1 Then all the C raised a loud cry; and
14:2 and Aaron; the whole C said to them, "Would
14:5 the assembly of the C of the people of
14:7 said to all the C of the people of
14:10 But all the C said to stone them with
14:27 long shall this wicked C murmur against me?
14:35 to all this wicked C that are gathered together
14:36 and made all the C to murmur against him
15:24 the knowledge of the C, all the congregation shall
15:24 the congregation, all the C shall offer one young
15:25 atonement for all the C of the people of
15:26 And all the C of the people of Israel
15:33 to Moses and Aaron, and to all the C
15:35 to death; all the C shall stone him with
15:36 And all the C brought him outside the camp,
16:2 fifty leaders of the C, chosen from the assembly,
16:3 For all the C are holy, every one of
16:9 separated you from the C of Israel, to bring
16:9 to stand before the C to minister to them;
16:19 Korah assembled all the C against them at the
16:19 glory of the LORD appeared to all the C
16:21 yourselves from among this C, that I may consume
16:22 and wilt thou be angry with all the C
16:24 Moses, "Say to the C, Get away from about
16:26 he said to the C, "Depart, I pray you,
16:41 the morrow all the C of the people of
16:42 And when the C had assembled against Moses and
16:45 the midst of this C, that I may consume
16:46 it quickly to the C, and make atonement for
19:9 be kept for the C of the people of
20:1 of Israel, the whole C, came into the wilderness
20:2 no water for the C; and they assembled themselves
20:8 rod, and assemble the C, you and Aaron your
20:8 give drink to the C and their cattle."
20:11 forth abundantly, and the C drank, and their cattle.
20:22 of Israel, the whole C, came to Mount Hor.
20:27 Mount Hor in the sight of all the C
20:29 And when all the C saw that Aaron was
25:6 sight of the whole C of the people of
25:7 rose and left the C, and took a spear
26:2 census of all the C of the people of
26:9 Abiram, chosen from the C, who contended against
27:2 leaders and all the C, at the door of
27:14 the strife of the C, to sanctify me at
27:16 a man over the C,
27:17 them in; that the C of the LORD may
27:19 priest and all the C, and you shall commission
27:20 authority, that all the C of the people of
27:21 the people of Israel with him, the whole C
27:22 priest and the whole C,
31:12 priest, and to the C of the people of
31:13 the leaders of the C, went forth to meet
31:16 plague came among the C of the LORD.
31:26 fathers' houses of the C;
31:27 who went out to battle and all the C
31:43 war-- now the C's half was three hundred
32:2 the leaders of the C,
32:4 LORD smote before the C of Israel, is a
35:12 he stands before the C for judgment.
35:24 his harm; then the C shall judge between the
35:25 ordinances; and the C shall rescue the manslayer
35:25 of blood, and the C shall restore him to
Josh 9:15 the leaders of the C swore to them.
9:18 the leaders of the C had sworn to them
9:18 Then all the C murmured against the leaders.
9:19 said to all the C, "We have sworn to
9:21 water for all the C, as the leaders had
9:27 of water for the C and for the altar
18:1 Then the whole C of the people of Israel
20:6 has stood before the C for judgment, until the
20:9 avenger of blood, till he stood before the C
22:16 "Thus says the whole C of the LORD, 'What
22:17 a plague upon the C of the LORD,
22:18 angry with the whole C of Israel tomorrow.
22:20 fell upon all the C of Israel?
22:30 the chiefs of the C, the heads of the
Judg 20:1 of Gilead, and the C assembled as one man
21:10 So the C sent thither twelve thousand of their
21:13 Then the whole C sent word to the Benjaminites
21:16 the elders of the C said, "What shall we
1Kgs 8:5 Solomon and all the C of Israel, who had

2Chr 5:6 Solomon and all the C of Israel, who had
7:8 him, a very great C, from the entrance of
24:6 the LORD, on the C of Israel for the
Ezra 10:8 himself banned from the C of the exiles.
Ps 1:5 nor sinners in the C of the righteous;
22:22 the midst of the C I will praise thee:
22:25 praise in the great C; my vows I will
26:12 ground; in the great C I will bless the
35:18 thee in the great C; in the mighty throng
40:9 deliverance in the great C; lo, I have not
40:10 steadfast love and thy faithfulness from the great C
68:26 God in the great C, the LORD, O you
74:2 Remember thy C, which thou hast gotten of old,
107:32 extol him in the C of the people, and
111:1 in the company of the upright, in the C
Prov 5:14 the point of utter ruin in the assembled C
Sir 1:27 the midst of the C, because you did not
4:7 yourself beloved in the C; bow your head low
33:18 you leaders of the C, hearken.
39:10 his wisdom, and the C will proclaim his praise;
41:18 of iniquity, before a C or the people; of
44:16 their wisdom, and the C proclaims their praise.
46:7 Jephunneh: they withstood the C, restrained the
46:14 Lord he judged the C, and the Lord watched
50:13 hands, before the whole C of Israel.
50:20 hands over the whole C of the sons of
Jer 6:18 nations, and know, O C, what will happen to
30:20 of old, and their C shall be established before
Lam 1:10 those whom thou didst forbid to enter thy C
Joel 2:16 Sanctify the C; assemble the elders; gather the
1Mac 3:44 And the C assembled to be ready for battle,
Acts 7:38 who was in the C in the wilderness with
15:30 and having gathered the C together, they delivered
19:9 the Way before the C, he withdrew from them,
Heb 2:12 the midst of the C I will praise thee."

CONGREGATIONS

Sir 24:22 an inheritance for the C of Jacob.

CONIAH (3)

Jer 22:24 says the LORD, though C the son of Jehoiakim,
22:28 Is this man C a despised, broken pot, a
37:1 Judah, reigned instead of C the son of Jehoiakim.

CONJUGAL

1Cor 7:3 to his wife her C rights, and likewise the

CONNECTED (2)

Neh 13:4 God, and who was C with Tobiah,
2Mac 3:3 revenues all the expenses C with the service of

CONNECTING

Ex 36:17 edge of the other C curtain.

CONNECTION (6)

Num 18:1 shall bear iniquity in C with the sanctuary; and
18:1 shall bear iniquity in C with your priesthood.
Deut 19:15 for any wrong in C with any offense that
Dan 6:5 we find it in C with the law of
1Mac 13:15 the royal treasury, in C with the offices he
Heb 7:14 from Judah, and in C with that tribe Moses

CONNIVANCE

2Mac 4:39 by Lysimachus with the C of Menelaus, and when

CONQUER (9)

2Kgs 3:19 hand, and you shall C every fortified city, and
16:5 Ahaz but could not C him.
Is 7:1 but they could not C it.
7:6 it, and let us C it for ourselves, and
1Mac 15:31 we will come and C you."
Rev 6:2 him, and he went out conquering and to C
11:7 war upon them and C them and kill them,
13:7 the saints and to C them.
17:14 and the Lamb will C them, for he is

CONQUERED (16)

1Kgs 15:20 cities of Israel, and C Ijon, Dan, Abel-beth-maacah,
2Kgs 3:25 the slingers surrounded and C it.
2Chr 16:4 of Israel, and they C Ijon, Dan, Abel-maim, and
Wis 16:10 thy sons were not C even by the teeth
18:22 He C the wrath not by strength of body,
Ezek 40:1 after the city was C, on that very day,
1Mac 1:2 He fought many battles, C strongholds, and put to
5:44 Thus Carnaim was C; they could stand before Judas
8:5 up against them, they crushed in battle and C
8:10 children; they plundered them, C the land, tore down
15:30 places which you have C outside the borders of
Heb 11:33 through faith C kingdoms, enforced justice, received
Rev 3:21 throne, as I myself C and sat down with
5:5 Root of David, has C, so that he can
12:11 And they have C him by the blood of
15:2 and those who had C the beast and its

CONQUERING (3)

Is 18:2 a nation mighty and C, whose land the rivers
18:7 a nation mighty and C, whose land the rivers
Rev 6:2 and he went out C and to conquer.

CONQUEROR

Mic 1:15 will again bring a C upon you, inhabitants of

CONQUERORS (2)

Jer 8:10 and their fields to C, because from the least
Rom 8:37 we are more than C through him who loved

CONQUERS (8)

Rev 2:7 To him who C I will grant to eat
2:11 He who C shall not be hurt by the
2:17 To him who C I will give some of
2:26 He who C and who keeps my works until
3:5 He who C shall be clad thus in white
3:12 He who C, I will make him a pillar
3:21 He who C, I will grant him to sit
21:7 He who C shall have this heritage, and I

CONSCIENCE (28)

1Sam 25:31 grief, or pangs of C, for having shed blood
Wis 17:11 testimony; distressed by C, it has always exaggerated
Acts 23:1 God in all good C up to this day."
24:15 to have a clear C toward God and toward
Rom 2:15 their hearts, while their C also bears witness and
9:1 am not lying; my C bears me witness in
13:5 God's wrath but also for the sake of C
1Cor 8:7 an idol; and their C, being weak, is defiled.
8:10 be encouraged, if his C is weak, to eat
8:12 brethren and wounding their C when it is weak,
10:25 without raising any question on the ground of C
10:27 without raising any question on the ground of C
10:28 informed you, and for C sake--
10:29 I mean his C, not yours--do not
2Cor 1:12 the testimony of our C that we have behaved
4:2 ourselves to every man's C in the sight of
5:11 I hope it is known also to your C
1Tim 1:5 heart and a good C and sincere faith.
1:19 the good warfare, holding faith and a good C
1:19 By rejecting C, certain persons have made shipwreck
3:9 the mystery of the faith with a clear C
2Tim 1:3 serve with a clear C, as did my fathers,
Heb 9:9 which cannot perfect the C of the worshiper,
9:14 to God, purify your C from dead works to
10:22 clean from an evil C and our bodies washed
13:18 we have a clear C, desiring to act honorably
1Pet 3:16 reverence; and keep your C clear, so that, when
3:21 God for a clear C, through the resurrection of

CONSCIENCES (2)

1Tim 4:2 pretensions of liars whose C are seared,
Tit 1:14 their very minds and C are corrupted.

CONSCIOUSNESS

Heb 10:2 no longer have any C of sin.

CONSECRATE (30)

Ex 13:2 LORD said to Moses, C to me all the
19:10 to the people and C them today and tomorrow,
19:22 near to the LORD C themselves, lest the LORD
19:23 about the mountain, and C it.'"
28:3 make Aaron's garments to C him for my priesthood.
28:41 and ordain them and C them, that they may
29:1 do to them to C them, that they may
29:27 And you shall C the breast of the wave
29:33 made, to ordain and C them, but an outsider
29:36 shall anoint it, to C it.
29:37 for the altar, and C it, and the altar
29:44 my glory; I will C the tent of meeting
29:44 his sons I will C, to serve me as
30:29 its base; you shall C them, that they may
30:30 and his sons, and C them, that they may
Lev 8:11 and its base, to C them.
8:12 and anointed him, to C him.
11:44 the LORD your God; C yourselves therefore, and be

Phil 3:13 Brethren, I do not C that I have made
Philem 1:17 So if you C me your partner, receive him
Heb 3:1 in a heavenly call, C Jesus, the apostle and
10:24 faithful; and let us C how to stir up
12:3 C him who endured from sinners such hostility
13:7 the word of God; C the outcome of their

CONSIDERABLE (4)

1Mac 12:10 estranged from you, for C time has passed since
13:11 and with him a C army; he drove out
2Mac 10:27 arms and advanced a C distance from the city;
Acts 19:26 and turned away a C company of people, saying

CONSIDERATELY

1Pet 3:7 Likewise you husbands, live C with your wives,

CONSIDERATION (3)

Esth 16:9 what comes before our eyes with more equitable C
2Mac 12:24 of some and no C would be shown them.
1Cor 10:28 then out of C for the man who informed

CONSIDERED (27)

1Kgs 10:21 silver, it was not C as anything in the
2Chr 9:20 gold; silver was not C as anything in the
Job 1:8 to Satan, "Have you C my servant Job, that
2:3 to Satan, "Have you C my servant Job, that
Prov 17:28 who keeps silent is C wise; when he closes
24:32 Then I saw and C it; I looked and
Eccl 2:11 Then I C all that my hands had done
Wis 2:16 We are C by him as something base, and
8:17 When I C these things inwardly, and thought upon
15:12 But he C our existence an idle game, and
Sir 40:29 his existence cannot be C as life.
50:4 He C how to save his people from ruin,
Is 53:8 for his generation, who C that he was cut
Ezek 18:28 Because he C and turned away from all the
Dan 7:8 I C the horns, and behold, there came up
1Mac 10:38 Judea that they are C to be under one
2Mac 9:15 whom he had not C worth burying but had
11:36 soon as you have C them, send some one
14:20 terms had been fully C, and the leader had
Mt 1:20 But as he C this, behold, an angel of
Lk 1:29 at the saying, and C in her mind what
Rom 4:19 in faith when he C his own body, which
4:19 old, or when he C the barrenness of Sarah's
1Tim 5:17 who rule well be C worthy of double honor,
Heb 11:11 the age, since she C him faithful who had
11:19 He C that God was able to raise men
11:26 He C abuse suffered for the Christ greater wealth

CONSIDERING (3)

Wis 1:16 and deeds summoned death; C him a friend, they
Dan 8:5 As I was C, behold, a he-goat came from
2Mac 2:24 For C the flood of numbers involved and the

CONSIDERS (6)

Ps 41:1 Blessed is he who C the poor!
90:11 Who C the power of thy anger, and thy
Prov 21:29 but an upright man C his ways.
31:16 She C a field and buys it; with the
Sir 42:18 hearts of men, and C their crafty devices.
Is 44:19 No one C, nor is there knowledge or discernment

CONSIGNED (4)

Esth 16:15 the Jews, who were C to annihilation by this
Is 38:10 must depart; I am C to the gates of
Rom 11:32 For God has C all men to disobedience, that
Gal 3:22 But the scripture C all things to sin, that

CONSIST (4)

Jud 5:3 and in what does their power or strength C
Lk 12:15 man's life does not C in the abundance of
1Cor 4:20 of God does not C in talk but in
12:14 the body does not C of one member but

CONSISTENT

Sir 5:10 in your understanding, and let your speech be C

CONSOLATION (9)

Job 6:10 This would be my C; I would even exult
21:2 to my words, and let this be your C
Wis 3:18 no hope and no C in the day of
Jer 16:7 him the cup of C to drink for his
Ezek 16:54 have done, becoming a C to them.
Zech 10:2 the dreamers tell false dreams, and give empty C
Lk 2:25 devout, looking for the C of Israel, and the
6:24 that are rich, for you have received your C
1Cor 14:3 for their upbuilding and encouragement and C

CONSOLATIONS (3)

Job 15:11 Are the C of God too small for you,
Ps 94:19 heart are many, thy C cheer my soul.
Jer 31:9 shall come, and with C I will lead them

CONSOLE (5)

2Sam 10:2 by his servants to C him concerning his father.
1Chr 19:2 David sent messengers to C him concerning his
19:2 of the Ammonites, to C him.
Ezek 14:23 They will C you, when you see their ways
Jn 11:19 Martha and Mary to C them concerning their

CONSOLED (4)

Jud 6:20 Then they C Achior, and praised him greatly.
Sir 35:17 he will not be C until it reaches the
Ezek 14:22 doings, you will be C for the evil that
Mt 2:18 she refused to be C, because they were no

CONSOLING (2)

Is 66:11 be satisfied with her C breasts; that you may
Jn 11:31 her in the house, C her, saw Mary rise

CONSORT

Ps 26:4 men, nor do I C with dissemblers;

CONSORTS

Sir 19:2 and the man who C with harlots is very

CONSPICUOUS (7)

Dan 8:5 the goat had a C horn between his eyes.
8:8 there came up four C horns toward the four
1Mac 11:37 put up in a C place on the holy
14:48 them up in a C place in the precincts
2Mac 15:35 citadel, a clear and C sign to every one
1Tim 5:24 of some men are C, pointing to judgment, but
5:25 also good deeds are C; and even when they

CONSPIRACY (11)

2Sam 15:12 And the C grew strong, and the people with
1Kgs 16:20 of Zimri, and the C which he made, are
2Kgs 12:20 arose and made a C, and slew Joash in
14:19 And they made a C against him in Jerusalem,
15:15 of Shallum, and the C which he made, behold,
15:30 of Elah made a C against Pekah the son
2Chr 25:27 LORD they made a C against him in Jerusalem,
Is 8:12 saying: "Do not call C all that this people
8:12 that this people call C, and do not fear
2Mac 5:7 only disgrace from his C, and fled again into
Acts 23:13 There were more than forty who made this C

CONSPIRATOR

2Mac 14:26 he had appointed that C against the kingdom, Judas,

CONSPIRATORS

2Sam 15:31 "Ahithophel is among the C with Absalom." And

CONSPIRE (2)

Ps 2:1 Why do the nations C, and the peoples plot
83:5 Yea, they C with one accord; against thee they

CONSPIRED (20)

Gen 37:18 near to them they C against him to kill
1Sam 22:8 all of you have C against me?
22:13 him, "Why have you C against me, you and
1Kgs 15:27 the house of Issachar, C against him; and Baasha
16:9 of half his chariots, C against him.
16:16 it said, "Zimri has C, and he has killed
2Kgs 9:14 the son of Nimshi C against Joram.
10:9 It was I who C against my master, and
15:10 the son of Jabesh C against him, and struck
15:25 of Remaliah, his captain, C against him with fifty
21:23 the servants of Amon C against him, and killed
21:24 all those who had C against King Amon, and
2Chr 24:21 But they C against him, and by command of
24:25 severely wounded, his servants C against him
24:26 Those who C against him were Zabad the son
33:24 And his servants C against him and killed him
33:25 all those who had C against King Amon; and
Sir 45:18 Outsiders C against him, and envied him in the
Dan 14:28 were very indignant and C against the king, saying,
Amos 7:10 Israel, saying, "Amos has C against you in the

CONSTANT (2)
2Mac 14:34 and called upon the C Defender of our nation,
Rom 12:12 patient in tribulation, be C in prayer.

CONSTANTLY (9)
Esth 13:5 and it alone, stands C in opposition to all
Sir 37:12 But stay C with a godly man whom you
1Mac 8:15 and twenty senators C deliberate concerning the
12:11 We therefore remember you C on every occasion,
Acts 10:2 the people, and prayed C to God.
1Thes 1:2 always for you all, C mentioning you in our
2:13 we also thank God C for this, that when
5:17 Rejoice always, pray C,
2Tim 1:3 when I remember you C in my prayers.

CONSTELLATION
Wis 7:29 sun, and excels every C of the stars.

CONSTELLATIONS (3)
2Kgs 23:5 the moon, and the C, and all the host
Wis 7:19 the year and the C of the stars,
Is 13:10 the heavens and their C will not give their

CONSTERNATION (2)
Ps 116:11 I said in my C, "Men are all a
2Mac 14:17 because of the sudden C created by the enemy.

CONSTITUTION
Sir 30:14 well and strong in C than a rich man

CONSTRAINED (2)
Lk 12:50 and how I am C until it is accomplished!
24:29 going further, but they C him, saying, "Stay with

CONSTRAINING
2Mac 11:14 would persuade the king, C him to be their

CONSTRAINS
Job 32:18 the spirit within me C me.

CONSTRAINT (2)
2Mac 6:7 were taken, under bitter C, to partake of the
1Pet 5:2 your charge, not by C but willingly, not for

CONSTRUCTED
Heb 11:7 unseen, took heed and C an ark for the

CONSTRUCTION (8)
Ex 36:1 any work in the C of the sanctuary shall
38:24 work, in all the C of the sanctuary, the
1Kgs 7:28 This was the C of the stands: they had
Neh 4:16 my servants worked on C, and half held the
Ezek 1:16 the wheels and their C: their appearance was like
1:16 the same likeness, their C being as it were
2Mac 2:29 concerned with the whole C, while the one who
4:20 was applied to the C of triremes.

CONSUL (2)
1Mac 15:16 following was written: "Lucius, C of the Romans, to
15:22 The C wrote the same thing to Demetrius the

CONSULT (15)
Deut 17:9 those days, you shall C them, and they shall
Ezra 2:63 be a priest to C Urim and Thummim.
Ps 71:10 watch for my life C together,
83:3 against thy people; they C together against thy
Sir 8:17 Do not C with a fool, for he will
9:14 know your neighbors, and C with the wise.
37:10 Do not C the one who looks at you
37:11 Do not C with a woman about her rival
Is 8:19 they say to you, C the mediums and the
8:19 should not a people C their God?
8:19 Should they C the dead on behalf of the
19:3 plans; and they will C the idols and the
31:1 One of Israel or C the LORD!
40:14 Whom did he C for his enlightenment, and who
Bar 6:48 upon them, the priests C together as to where

CONSULTATION
Mk 15:1 whole council held a C; and they bound Jesus

CONSULTED (4)
2Sam 16:23 was as if one C the oracle of God;
1Chr 10:13 the LORD, and also C a medium, seeking guidance,
13:1 David C with the commanders of thousands and of
1Mac 9:59 And they went and C with him.

CONSULTING (2)
1Mac 3:48 which the Gentiles were C the images of their
2Mac 13:13 After C privately with the elders, he determined to

CONSULTS
Ezek 21:21 shakes the arrows, he C the teraphim, he looks

CONSUME (40)
Gen 41:30 Egypt; the famine will C the land,
Ex 32:10 them and I may C them; but of you
32:12 the mountains, and to C them from the face
33:3 among you, lest I C you in the way,
33:5 among you, I would C you.
Num 16:21 congregation, that I may C them in a moment."
16:45 congregation, that I may C them in a moment."
25:11 that I did not C the people of Israel
Deut 5:25 this great fire will C us; if we hear
28:38 for the locust shall C it.
Josh 24:20 do you harm, and C you, after having done
1Kgs 14:10 Israel, and will utterly C the house of Jeroboam,
2Kgs 1:10 down from heaven and C you and your fifty."
1:12 down from heaven and C you and your fifty."
Ezra 9:14 us till thou wouldst C us, so that there
Jud 11:13 They have decided to C the first fruits of
Ps 21:9 wrath; and fire will C them.
39:11 for sin, thou dost C like a moth what
59:13 lies which they utter, C them in wrath, consume
59:13 consume them in wrath, C them till they are
Eccl 10:12 lips of a fool C him.
Wis 16:18 that it might not C the creatures sent against
19:21 the contrary, failed to C the flesh of perishable
Sir 27:29 snare, and pain will C them before their death.
45:19 wonders against them to C them in flaming fire.
Is 26:11 fire for thy adversaries C them.
33:11 a fire that will C you.
43:2 the flame shall not C you.
Jer 14:12 them; but I will C them by the sword,
Bar 6:63 sent from above to C mountains and woods does
Ezek 15:7 the fire shall yet C them; and you will
22:15 countries, and I will C your filthiness out of
Dan 14:13 go in regularly and C the provisions.
Hos 11:6 rage against their cities, C the bars of their
Obad 1:18 shall burn them and C them, and there shall
Zech 5:4 in his house and C it, both timber and
Mt 6:19 where moth and rust C and where thieves break
Lk 9:54 down from heaven and C them?"
Jn 2:17 for thy house will C me."
Heb 10:27 of fire which will C the adversaries.

CONSUMED (81)
Gen 19:15 here, lest you be C in the punishment of
19:17 valley; flee to the hills, lest you be C
31:40 by day the heat C me, and the cold
Ex 3:2 the bush was burning, yet it was not C
22:6 or the field is C, he that kindled the
Lev 6:10 which the fire has C the burnt offering on
9:24 before the LORD and C the burnt offering and
Num 11:1 burned among them, and C some outlying parts of
11:33 teeth, before it was C, the anger of the
12:12 the flesh is half C when he comes out
16:35 from the LORD, and C the two hundred and
32:13 evil in the sight of the LORD was C
Deut 28:21 you until he has C you off the land
Judg 6:21 from the rock and C the flesh and the
1Sam 15:18 them until they are C
2Sam 21:5 king, "The man who C us and planned to
22:38 and did not turn back until they were C
22:39 I C them; I thrust them through, so that
23:7 and they are utterly C with fire."
1Kgs 18:38 the LORD fell, and C the burnt offering, and
2Kgs 1:10 down from heaven, and C him and his fifty.
1:12 down from heaven and C him and his fifty.
1:14 down from heaven, and C the two former captains
2Chr 7:1 down from heaven and C the burnt offering and
Esth 11:11 lowly were exalted and C those held in honor.
Job 1:16 and the servants, and C them; and I alone
4:9 by the blast of his anger they are C
18:13 disease his skin is C, the first-born of death
20:26 what is left in his tent will be C
22:20 left the fire has C
Ps 18:37 and did not turn back till they were C
69:9 for thy house has C me, and the insults
71:13 put to shame and C; with scorn and disgrace
90:7 For we are C by thy anger; by thy
104:35 Let sinners be C from the earth, and let
119:20 My soul is C with longing for thy ordinances

Prov 5:11 flesh and body are C,
Wis 5:13 to show, but were C in our wickedness."
14:15 For a father, C with grief at an untimely
16:16 relentless storms, and utterly C by fire.
Sir 23:16 quenched until it is C; a man who commits
36:9 him who survives be C in the fiery wrath,
Is 1:28 and those who forsake the LORD shall be C
Jer 5:3 no anguish; thou hast C them, but they refused
6:29 fiercely, the lead is C by the fire; in
9:16 them, until I have C them."
10:25 have devoured him and C him, and have laid
11:16 fire to it, and its branches will be C
14:15 By sword and famine those prophets shall be C
27:8 LORD, until I have C it by his hand.
36:23 the entire scroll was C in the fire that
44:12 they shall all be C; in the land of
44:12 famine they shall be C; from the least to
44:18 everything and have been C by the sword and
44:27 of Egypt shall be C by the sword and
49:37 them, until I have C them;
Lam 4:11 fire in Zion, which C its foundations.
Bar 6:72 will finally themselves be C, and be a reproach
Ezek 5:12 of pestilence and be C with famine in the
15:4 when the fire has C both ends of it,
15:5 when the fire has C it and it is
19:12 was withered; the fire C it.
19:14 from its stem, has C its branches and fruit,
22:31 upon them; I have C them with the fire
24:11 filthiness may be melted in it, its rust C
28:18 midst of you; it C you, and I turned
34:29 shall no more be C with hunger in the
43:8 committed, so I have C them in my anger.
Dan 7:26 taken away, to be C and destroyed to the
Nah 1:10 entangled thorns they are C, like dry stubble.
Zeph 1:18 the earth shall be C; for a full, yea,
3:8 my jealous wrath all the earth shall be C
Mal 3:6 therefore you, O sons of Jacob, are not C
1Mac 6:53 from the Gentiles had C the last of the
2Mac 1:23 the sacrifice was being C, the priests offered prayer
1:31 of the sacrifice were C, Nehemiah ordered that the
2:10 fire came down and C the whole burnt offerings.
2:11 Moses said, "They were C because the sin offering
Rom 1:27 with women and were C with passion for one
Gal 5:15 that you are not C by one another.
Rev 20:9 down from heaven and C them,

CONSUMES (11)

Ex 15:7 forth thy fury, it C them like stubble.
Job 15:34 is barren, and fire C the tents of bribery.
18:13 the first-born of death C his limbs.
31:12 be a fire which C unto Abaddon, and it
Ps 83:14 As fire C the forest, as the flame sets
119:139 My zeal C me, because my foes forget thy
Sir 43:21 He C the mountains and burns up the wilderness,
Is 9:18 like a fire, it C briers and thorns; it
47:14 like stubble, the fire C them; they cannot deliver
Mt 6:20 neither moth nor rust C and where thieves do
Rev 11:5 from their mouth and C their foes; if any

CONSUMING (2)

Lam 2:3 flaming fire in Jacob, C all around.
Heb 12:29 our God is a C fire.

CONSUMMATION

Sir 39:28 in the time of C they will pour out

CONSUMPTION (2)

Lev 26:16 over you sudden terror, C, and fever that waste
Deut 28:22 will smite you with C, and with fever, inflammation,

CONTACT (3)

Lev 22:4 that is unclean through C with the dead or
Num 5:2 that is unclean through C with the dead;
Hag 2:13 who is unclean by C with a dead body

CONTAIN (5)

1Kgs 8:27 the highest heaven cannot C thee; how much less
18:32 as great as would C two measures of seed.
2Chr 2:6 even highest heaven, cannot C him?
6:18 the highest heaven cannot C thee; how much less
Jn 21:25 world itself could not C the books that would

CONTAINED (2)

1Mac 12:8 received the letter, which C a clear declaration of
Heb 9:4 sides with gold, which C a golden urn holding

CONTAINING (3)

Jer 32:11 sealed deed of purchase, C the terms and conditions,
Ezek 45:11 same measure, the bath C one tenth of a
1Mac 6:2 temple was very rich, C golden shields, breastplates,

CONTAINS (3)

Ezek 12:19 stripped of all it C, on account of the
23:32 in derision, for it C much;
45:14 cor, like the homer, C ten baths);

CONTEMPT (34)

Gen 16:4 conceived, she looked with C on her mistress.
16:5 she had conceived, she looked on me with C
1Sam 2:17 men treated the offering of the LORD with C
2Chr 32:17 wrote letters to cast C on the LORD the
Jud 13:17 who hast brought into C this day the enemies
Esth 1:17 them to look with C upon their husbands, since
1:18 and there will be C and wrath in plenty.
Job 12:5 at ease there is C for misfortune; it is
12:21 He pours C on princes, and looses the belt
31:34 the multitude, and the C of families terrified me,
Ps 31:18 speak insolently against the righteous in pride and C
107:40 and sorrow, he pours C upon princes and makes
119:22 me their scorn and C, for I have kept
123:3 for we have had more than enough of C
123:4 are at ease, the C of the proud.
Prov 18:3 When wickedness comes, C comes also; and with
Wis 4:18 see, and will have C for him, but the
14:30 they swore unrighteously through C for holiness.
Is 9:1 time he brought into C the land of Zebulun
16:14 will be brought into C, in spite of all
Ezek 22:7 mother are treated with C in you; the sojourner
28:24 all their neighbors who have treated them with C
28:26 all their neighbors who have treated them with C
36:5 wholehearted joy and utter C, that they might
Dan 12:2 everlasting life, and some to shame and everlasting C
Mic 7:6 treats the father with C, the daughter rises up
Nah 3:6 and treat you with C, and make you a
Hab 2:16 will be sated with C instead of glory.
1Mac 1:39 her sabbaths into a reproach, her honor into C
2Mac 3:18 holy place was about to be brought into C
7:24 was being treated with C, and he was suspicious
Mk 9:12 should suffer many things and be treated with C
Lk 23:11 soldiers treated him with C and mocked him; then,
Heb 6:6 their own account and hold him up to C

CONTEMPTIBLE (2)

2Sam 6:22 make myself yet more C than this, and I
Dan 11:21 place shall arise a C person to whom royal

CONTEMPTUOUSLY

Sir 26:19 men who are treated C; a man who turns

CONTEND (30)

Deut 2:5 good heed; do not C with them; for I
2:9 not harass Moab or C with them in battle,
2:19 not harass them or C with them, for I
2:24 to take possession, and C with him in battle.
33:7 With thy hands C for him, and be a
Judg 6:31 against him, "Will you C for Baal?
6:31 a god, let him C for himself, because his
6:32 to say, "Let Baal C against him," because he
Job 9:3 If one wished to C with him, one could
10:2 know why thou dost C against me.
13:19 is there that will C with me?
23:6 Would he C with me in the greatness of
33:13 Why do you C against him, saying, 'He will
40:2 Job: "Shall a faultfinder C with the Almighty?
Ps 35:1 C, O LORD, with those who contend with me;
35:1 LORD, with those who C with me; fight against
Prov 3:30 Do not C with a man for no reason,
Sir 8:1 Do not C with a powerful man, lest you
Is 3:13 taken his place to C, he stands to judge
27:8 by exile thou didst C with them; he removed
41:12 shall seek those who C with you, but you
49:25 rescued, for I will C with those who contend
49:25 contend with those who C with you, and I
50:8 Who will C with me?
57:16 For I will not C for ever, nor will
Jer 2:9 "Therefore I still C with you, says the LORD,
2:9 LORD, and with your children's children I will C
Hos 4:4 Yet let no one C, and let none accuse,
Mic 6:2 people, and he will C with Israel.
Jude 1:3 appealing to you to C for the faith which

CONTENDED (7)

Gen 26:20 well Esek, because they C with him.
Num 20:3 And the people C with Moses, and said, "Would
20:13 the people of Israel C with the LORD, and
26:9 from the congregation, who C against Moses and Aaron
26:9 of Korah, when they C against the LORD,
Neh 13:25 And I C with them and cursed them and
Acts 23:9 party stood up and C, "We find nothing wrong

CONTENDERS

Prov 18:18 an end to disputes and decides between powerful C

CONTENDING (2)

Eph 6:12 For we are not C against flesh and blood,
Jude 1:9 the archangel Michael, C with the devil, disputed

CONTENDS (2)

Judg 6:31 Whoever C for him shall be put to death
Dan 10:21 there is none who C by my side against

CONTENT (15)

Ex 2:21 And Moses was C to dwell with the man,
Lev 10:20 And when Moses heard that, he was C
Josh 7:7 that we had been C to dwell beyond the
Judg 17:11 And the Levite was C to dwell with the
2Kgs 14:10 Be C with your glory, and stay at home;
Sir 29:23 Be C with little or much.
Ezek 16:47 Yet you were not C to walk in their
2Mac 5:15 Not C with this, Antiochus dared to enter the
9:18 This was its C:
Lk 3:14 false accusation, and be C with your wages."
2Cor 12:10 Christ, then, I am C with weaknesses, insults,
Phil 4:11 learned, in whatever state I am, to be C
1Tim 6:8 food and clothing, with these we shall be C
Heb 13:5 of money, and be C with what you have;
3 Jn 1:10 And not C with that, he refuses himself to

CONTENTION (5)

Prov 15:18 but he who is slow to anger quiets C
Jer 15:10 man of strife and C to the whole land!
Hos 4:4 with you is my C, O priest.
Hab 1:3 before me; strife and C arise.
Acts 15:38 there arose a sharp C, so that they separated

CONTENTIOUS (5)

Prov 21:9 house shared with a C woman.
21:19 land than with a C and fretful woman.
25:24 house shared with a C woman.
27:15 rainy day and a C woman are alike;
1Cor 11:16 is disposed to be C, we recognize no other

CONTENTMENT

1Tim 6:6 gain in godliness with C;

CONTENTS (3)

Bar 6:59 house that protects its C, than these false gods;
1Mac 11:29 all these things; its C were as follows:
15:2 all the nation; its C were as follows: "King

CONTEST (3)

Job 9:19 If it is a C of strength, behold him!
Wis 4:2 triumph, victor in the C for prizes that are
10:12 him; in his arduous C she gave him the

CONTINGENTS

Jud 6:1 of all the foreign C:

CONTINUAL (40)

Ex 28:29 to bring them to C remembrance before the LORD.
29:42 It shall be a C burnt offering throughout your
Num 4:7 the drink offering; the C bread also shall be
4:16 the fragrant incense, the C cereal offering, and the
28:3 by day, as a C offering.
28:6 It is a C burnt offering, which was ordained
28:10 every sabbath, besides the C burnt offering and its
28:15 be offered besides the C burnt offering and its
28:23 which is for a C burnt offering.
28:24 be offered besides the C burnt offering and its
28:31 Besides the C burnt offering and its cereal offering,
29:6 cereal offering, and the C burnt offering and its
29:11 of atonement, and the C burnt offering and its
29:16 sin offering, besides the C burnt offering, its cereal
29:19 sin offering, besides the C burnt offering and its
29:22 sin offering, besides the C burnt offering and its
29:25 sin offering, besides the C burnt offering, its cereal
29:28 sin offering; besides the C burnt offering and its
29:31 sin offering; besides the C burnt offering, its cereal
29:34 sin offering; besides the C burnt offering, its cereal
29:38 sin offering; besides the C burnt offering and its
2Chr 2:4 him, and for the C offering of the showbread,
12:15 were C wars between Rehoboam and Jeroboam.
Ezra 3:5 and after that the C burnt offerings, the offerings
Neh 10:33 the showbread, the C cereal offering, the continual
10:33 continual cereal offering, the C burnt offering, the
Jud 4:14 with sackcloth, offered the C burnt offerings and the
Job 33:19 his bed, and with C strife in his bones;
Prov 15:15 cheerful heart has a C feast.
19:13 wife's quarreling is a C dripping of rain.
27:15 A C dripping on a rainy day and a
Ezek 38:8 which had been a C waste; its people were
46:14 the ordinance for the C burnt offering.
46:15 by morning, for a C burnt offering.
Dan 8:11 the host; and the C burnt offering was taken
8:12 it together with the C burnt offering through
8:13 the vision concerning the C burnt offering, the
11:31 shall take away the C burnt offering.
12:11 the time that the C burnt offering is taken
Lk 18:5 me out by her C coming.'"

CONTINUALLY (84)

Gen 6:5 the thoughts of his heart was only evil C
8:3 restrained, and the waters receded from the earth C
Ex 9:24 hail, and fire flashing C in the midst of
27:20 a lamp may be set up to burn C
28:30 of Israel upon his heart before the LORD C
29:38 two lambs a year old day by day C
Lev 6:13 burning upon the altar C; it shall not go
24:2 lamp, that a light may be kept burning C
24:3 morning before the LORD C; it shall be a
24:4 the lampstand of pure gold before the LORD C
24:8 order before the LORD C on behalf of the
Num 9:16 So it was C; the cloud covered it by
Deut 28:29 only oppressed and robbed C, and there shall be
28:33 only oppressed and crushed C;
Josh 6:9 came after the ark, while the trumpets blew C
6:13 on, blowing the trumpets C; and the armed men
6:13 ark of the LORD, while the trumpets blew C
1Sam 18:29 So Saul was David's enemy C
2Sam 16:5 of Gera; and as he came he cursed C
1Kgs 10:8 these your servants, who C stand before you and
14:30 there was war between Rehoboam and Jeroboam C
2Kgs 4:9 of God, who is C passing our way.
13:3 and he gave them C into the hand of
1Chr 16:6 were to blow trumpets C, before the ark of
16:11 the LORD and his strength, seek his presence C
16:37 the LORD to minister C before the ark as
16:40 altar of burnt offering C morning and evening,
23:31 number required of them, C before the LORD.
2Chr 9:7 these your servants, who C stand before you and
24:14 house of the LORD C all the days of
Esth 13:4 of every nation and C disregard the ordinances of
16:11 our father and was C bowed sown to by
Job 1:5 Thus Job did C
Ps 34:1 times; his praise shall C be in my mouth.
40:16 love thy salvation say C, "Great is the LORD!"
42:3 men say to me C, "Where is your God?"
42:10 they say to me C, "Where is your God?"
44:8 God we have boasted C, and we will give
50:8 your burnt offerings are C before me.
69:23 they cannot see; and make their loins tremble C
71:6 My praise is C of thee.
71:14 But I will hope C, and will praise thee
72:15 be made for him C, and blessings invoked for
73:23 Nevertheless I am C with thee; thou dost hold
74:23 the uproar of thy adversaries which goes up C
105:4 the LORD and his strength, seek his presence C
109:15 be before the LORD C; and may his memory
119:44 will keep thy law C, for ever and ever;
119:109 life in my hand C, but I do not
119:117 be safe and have regard for thy statutes C
140:2 things in their heart, and stir up wars C
141:5 for my prayer is C against their wicked deeds.
Prov 6:14 perverted heart devises evil, C sowing discord;
Wis 10:7 wickedness still remains: a C smoking wasteland,
Sir 17:15 and his eyes are C upon their ways.
20:18 wrong time, which is C on the lips of
20:23 a man; it is C on the lips of
23:10 a servant who is C examined under torture will
37:18 is the tongue that C rules them.
45:14 sacrifices shall be wholly burned twice every day C
51:11 will praise thy name C, and will sing praise

Is 21:8 I stand, O Lord, C by day, and at
28:24 Does he who plows for sowing plow C
28:24 does he C open and harrow his ground?
49:16 hands; your walls are C before me.
51:13 the earth, and fear C all the day because
52:5 says the LORD, and C all the day my
58:11 LORD will guide you C, and satisfy your desire
60:11 gates shall be open C; day and night they
65:3 me to my face C, sacrificing in gardens and
Jer 23:17 They say C to those who despise the word
Lam 3:20 My soul C thinks of it and is bowed
Ezek 1:4 and fire flashing forth C, and in the midst
39:14 pass through the land C and bury those remaining
Dan 6:16 God, whom you serve C, deliver you!"
6:20 God, whom you serve C, been able to deliver
Hos 12:6 and justice, and wait C for your God."
1Mac 1:36 against the sanctuary, an evil adversary of Israel C
6:9 days, because deep grief C gripped him, and he
15:25 king besieged Dor anew, C throwing his forces
Lk 24:53 great joy, and were C in the temple blessing
Heb 9:6 made, the priests go C into the outer tent,
10:1 same sacrifices which are C offered year after year,
13:15 him then let us C offer up a sacrifice

CONTINUE (40)

Gen 15:2 give me, for I C childless, and the heir
Lev 12:4 Then she shall C for thirty-three days in the
12:5 menstruation; and she shall C in the blood of
15:25 the discharge she shall C in uncleanness; as in
Deut 17:20 so that he may C long in his kingdom,
Josh 9:27 of the LORD, to C to this day, in
23:13 your God will not C to drive out these
1Sam 13:14 your kingdom shall not C; the LORD has sought
2Sam 7:29 servant, that it may C for ever before thee;
1Chr 17:27 servant, that it may C for ever before thee;
Jud 16:15 fear thee thou wilt C to show mercy.
Ps 36:10 O C thy steadfast love to those who know
49:9 suffice, that he should C to live on for
72:17 for ever, his fame C as long as the
101:7 who utters lies shall C in my presence.
Prov 23:17 heart envy sinners, but C in the fear of
28:2 understanding and knowledge its stability will long C
Wis 16:5 thy wrath did not C to the end;
18:20 the desert, but the wrath did not long C
Sir 44:14 Their posterity will C for ever, and their glory
Is 1:5 be smitten, that you C to rebel?
Zech 14:8 western sea; it shall C in summer as in
1Mac 10:27 And now C still to keep faith with us,
11:22 wrote Jonathan not to C the siege, but to
11:23 he gave orders to C the siege; and he
2Mac 8:26 reason they did not C their pursuit.
Jn 8:31 in him, "If you C in my word, you
8:35 The slave does not C in the house for
Acts 13:43 and urged them to C in the grace of
14:22 disciples, exhorting them to C in the faith, and
Rom 6:1 Are we to C in sin that grace may
9:11 purpose of election might C, not because of works
11:22 to you, provided you C in his kindness; otherwise
2Cor 11:12 I do I will C to do, in order
Phil 1:25 I shall remain and C with you all, for
Col 1:23 him, provided that you C in the faith, stable
4:2 C steadfastly in prayer, being watchful in it with
2Tim 3:14 But as for you, C in what you have
Heb 8:9 for they did not C in my covenant, and
13:1 Let brotherly love C

CONTINUED (35)

Gen 7:17 The flood C forty days upon the earth; and
8:5 And the waters C to abate until the tenth
40:4 on them; and they C for some time in
Num 9:19 Even when the cloud C over the tabernacle many
9:21 out, or if it C for a day and
9:22 time, that the cloud C over the tabernacle, abiding
21:16 And from there they C to Beer; that is
Deut 31:1 So Moses C to speak these words to all
Ruth 2:7 came, and she has C from early morning until
1Sam 1:12 As she C praying before the LORD, Eli observed
2:26 Now the boy Samuel C to grow both in
1Kgs 22:1 years Syria and Israel C without war.
2Kgs 12:3 taken away; the people C to sacrifice and burn
2Chr 29:28 trumpeters sounded; all this C until the burnt
Neh 1:4 for days; and I C fasting and praying before
Tob 6:5 And they both C on their way until they
11:1 So he C on his way until they came
14:2 gave alms, and he C to fear the Lord
Jud 16:20 So the people C feasting in Jerusalem before the
Job 36:1 And Elihu C, and said:
Jer 31:3 love; therefore I have C my faithfulness to you.
Dan 1:21 And Daniel C until the first year of King
Hos 10:9 you have sinned, O Israel; there they have C
1Mac 10:26 with us and have C your friendship with us,
2Mac 5:27 wild animals do; they C to live on what
8:1 enlisted those who had C in the Jewish faith,
Lk 6:12 and all night he C in prayer to God.
22:28 are those who have C with me in my
Jn 8:7 And as they C to ask him, he stood
Acts 8:13 after being baptized he C with Philip.
12:16 But Peter C knocking; and when they opened, they
19:10 This C for two years, so that all the
27:33 day that you have C in suspense and without
2Pet 3:4 asleep, all things have C as they were from
1 Jn 2:19 us, they would have C with us; but they

CONTINUES (9)

Josh 19:27 and Neiel; then it C in the north to
1Chr 28:7 for ever if he C resolute in keeping my
Job 14:2 like a shadow, and C not.
Sir 38:19 In calamity sorrow C, and the life of the
Jn 8:35 for ever; the son C for ever.
1Tim 2:15 bearing children, if she C in faith and love
5:5 hope on God and C in supplications and prayers
Heb 7:3 Son of God he C a priest for ever.
7:24 priesthood permanently, because he C for ever.

CONTINUING (2)

Josh 18:5 into seven portions, Judah C in his territory on
Heb 7:23 prevented by death from C in office;

CONTINUOUS

Zech 14:7 And there shall be C day (it is known

CONTINUOUSLY

2Mac 3:26 him and scourged him C, inflicting many blows on

CONTRACT

Tob 7:14 and wrote out the C; and they set their

CONTRACTS (2)

1Mac 13:42 in their documents and C, "In the first year
14:43 all, and that all C in the country should

CONTRADICT (2)

Lk 21:15 your adversaries will be able to withstand or C
Tit 1:8 to confute those who C it.

CONTRADICTED (2)

Acts 13:45 filled with jealousy, and C what was spoken by
19:36 these things cannot be C, you ought to be

CONTRADICTIONS

1Tim 6:20 the godless chatter and C of what is falsely

CONTRARY (25)

Lev 26:21 "Then if you walk C to me, and will
26:23 to me, but walk C to me,
26:24 I also will walk C to you, and I
26:27 to me, but walk C to me,
26:28 then I will walk C to you in fury,
26:40 and also in walking C to me,
26:41 so that I walked C to them and brought
Esth 13:4 people, who have laws C to those of every
Wis 15:7 uses and those for C uses, making all in
19:21 Flames, on the C, failed to consume the flesh
Sir 41:2 to one who is C, and has lost his
1Mac 14:45 Whoever acts C to these decisions or nullifies any
2Mac 4:11 and introduced new customs C to the law.
Acts 18:13 men to worship God C to the law."
23:3 the law, and yet C to the law you
Rom 3:31 On the C, we uphold the law.
10:21 to a disobedient and C people."
11:24 olive tree, and grafted, C to nature, into a
1Cor 12:22 On the C, the parts of the body which
15:10 On the C, I worked harder than any of
Gal 1:8 to you a gospel C to that which we
1:9 to you a gospel C to that which you
2:7 me; but on the C, when they saw that
1Tim 1:10 and whatever else is C to sound doctrine,
1Pet 3:9 reviling; but on the C bless, for to this

CONTRIBUTE

Rom 12:13 C to the needs of the saints, practice hospitality.

C

CONTRIBUTED (5)
Ex 38:29 the bronze that was C was seventy talents, and
2Chr 35:7 Then Josiah C to the lay people, as passover
35:8 And his princes C willingly to the people, to
Mk 12:44 For they all C out of their abundance; but
Lk 21:4 them; for they all C out of their abundance,

CONTRIBUTES
Rom 12:8 his exhortation; he who C, in liberality; he who

CONTRIBUTING
Mk 12:43 all those who are C to the treasury.

CONTRIBUTION (6)
2Chr 31:3 The C of the king from his own possessions
31:14 God, to apportion the C reserved for the LORD
Neh 10:39 Levi shall bring the C of grain, wine, and
Rom 15:26 pleased to make some C for the poor among
1Cor 16:1 Now concerning the C for the saints: as I
2Cor 9:13 the generosity of your C for them and for

CONTRIBUTIONS (7)
2Chr 31:10 began to bring the C into the house of
31:12 faithfully brought in the C, the tithes and the
Neh 10:37 coarse meal, and our C, the fruit of every
12:44 for the stores, the C, the first fruits, and
13:5 and gatekeepers, and the C for the priests.
Ezek 20:40 I will require your C and the choicest of
1Cor 16:2 may prosper, so that C need not be made

CONTRITE (5)
Ps 51:17 spirit; a broken and C heart, O God, thou
Is 57:15 who is of a C and humble spirit, to
57:15 humble, and to revive the heart of the C
66:2 that is humble and C in spirit, and trembles
Dan 3:39 Yet with a C heart and a humble spirit

CONTRIVED (2)
2Mac 7:31 But you, who have C all sorts of evil
Acts 5:4 it that you have C this deed in your

CONTROL (24)
Gen 45:1 Then Joseph could not C himself before all those
1Mac 6:56 was trying to seize C of the government.
6:63 He found Philip in C of the city, but
7:22 They gained C of the land of Judah and
8:3 of Spain to get C of the silver and
8:4 how they had gained C of the whole region
8:16 over them and to C all their land; they
10:32 I release also my C of the citadel in
10:52 crushed Demetrius and gained C of our country;
11:8 So King Ptolemy gained C of the coastal cities
11:49 the Jews had gained C of the city as
11:56 the elephants and gained C of Antioch.
14:6 nation, and gained full C of the country.
15:3 pestilent men have gained C of the kingdom of
15:9 When we gain C of our kingdom, we will
15:28 him, saying, "You hold C of Joppa and Gazara
16:13 he determined to get C of the country, and
2Mac 3:6 to fall under the C of the king.
5:7 He did not gain C of the government, however;
9:2 rob the temples and C the city.
10:15 the Idumeans, who had C of important strongholds,
1Cor 7:37 having his desire under C, and has determined this
Tit 2:6 the younger men to C themselves.
Heb 2:8 subjection to him, he left nothing outside his C

CONTROLLING
Gen 43:31 and came out; and C himself he said, "Let

CONTROLS (2)
Sir 21:11 Whoever keeps the law C his thoughts, and wisdom
2Cor 5:14 the love of Christ C us, because we are

CONTROVERSIES (3)
Acts 26:3 with all customs and C of the Jews; therefore
2Tim 2:23 do with stupid, senseless C; you know that they
Tit 3:9 avoid stupid C, genealogies, dissensions, and quarrels

CONTROVERSY (5)
Ezek 44:24 In a C they shall act as judges, and
Hos 4:1 the LORD has a C with the inhabitants of
Mic 6:2 Hear, you mountains, the C of the LORD, and
6:2 the LORD has a C with his people, and
1Tim 6:4 a morbid craving for C and for disputes about

CONVENE
1Mac 14:44 he says, or to C an assembly in the

CONVENED
1Mac 12:35 When Jonathan returned he C the elders of the

CONVENIENCE
Sir 6:8 such at his own C, but will not stand

CONVENIENT
1Mac 4:46 the stones in a C place on the temple

CONVERGED
1Mac 15:12 knew that troubles had C upon him, and his

CONVERSATION (6)
Esth 12:2 He overheard their C their conversation and inquired
12:2 overheard their conversation their C and inquired
Sir 9:15 Let your C be with men of understanding, and
19:7 Never repeat a C, and you will lose nothing
Jer 38:27 with him, for the C had not been overheard.
Lk 24:17 them, "What is this C which you are holding

CONVERSE
Ps 55:14 used to hold sweet C together; within God's house

CONVERSED (2)
Acts 20:11 bread and eaten, he C with them a long
24:25 for him often and C with him.

CONVERSION
Acts 15:3 and Samaria, reporting the C of the Gentiles, and

CONVERT (2)
Rom 16:5 who was the first C in Asia for Christ.
1Tim 3:6 not be a recent C, or he may be

CONVERTING
Sir 49:2 was led aright in C the people, and took

CONVERTS (2)
Acts 13:43 many Jews and devout C to Judaism followed Paul
1Cor 16:15 Stephanas were the first C in Achaia, and they

CONVEY
Ezra 7:15 hand, and also to C the silver and gold

CONVEYED (2)
Esth 1:12 at the king's command C by the eunuchs.
1:15 command of King Ahasuerus C by the eunuchs?"

CONVICT (3)
Wis 1:9 to the Lord, to C him of his lawless
4:20 their lawless deeds will C them to their face.
Jude 1:15 on all, and to C all the ungodly of

CONVICTED (3)
Dan 13:61 own mouths Daniel had C them of bearing false
1Cor 14:24 outsider enters, he is C by all, he is
Jas 2:9 commit sin, and are C by the law as

CONVICTION (2)
1Thes 1:5 and in the Holy Spirit and with full C
Heb 11:1 things hoped for, the C of things not seen.

CONVICTS (3)
2Sam 14:13 this decision the king C himself, inasmuch as the
Wis 1:3 power is tested, it C the foolish;
Jn 8:46 Which of you C me of sin?

CONVINCE (5)
Wis 16:8 this also thou didst C our enemies that it
Jn 16:8 he comes, he will C the world concerning sin
Acts 28:23 God and trying to C them about Jesus both
2Tim 4:2 and out of season, C, rebuke, and exhort, be
Jude 1:22 And C some, who doubt;

CONVINCED (10)
Sir 39:32 beginning I have been C, and have thought this
2Mac 13:26 the best possible defense, C them, appeased them,
Lk 16:31 neither will they be C if some one should
20:6 us; for they are C that John was a
Acts 26:9 "I myself was C that I ought to do
28:24 And some were C by what he said, while
Rom 4:21 glory to God, fully C that God was able
14:5 every one be fully C in his own mind.

2Cor 5:14 us, because we are C that one has died
Phil 1:25 C of this, I know that I shall remain

CONVINCINGLY

Heb 6:17 desired to show more C to the heirs of

CONVOCATION (15)

Lev 23:3 solemn rest, a holy C; you shall do no
23:7 shall have a holy C; you shall do no
23:8 day is a holy C; you shall do no
23:21 shall hold a holy C; you shall do no
23:24 proclaimed with blast of trumpets, a holy C
23:27 a time of holy C, and you shall afflict
23:35 shall be a holy C; you shall do no
23:36 shall hold a holy C and present an offering
23:37 as times of holy C, for presenting to the
Num 28:18 shall be a holy C: you shall do no
28:25 shall have a holy C; you shall do no
28:26 shall have a holy C; you shall do no
29:1 shall have a holy C; you shall do no
29:7 shall have a holy C, and afflict yourselves; you
29:12 shall have a holy C; you shall do no

CONVOCATIONS (2)

Lev 23:2 shall proclaim as holy C, my appointed feasts, are
23:4 the LORD, the holy C, which you shall proclaim

CONVULSED (3)

Ezek 27:35 their kings are horribly afraid, their faces are C
Mk 9:20 saw him, immediately it C the boy, and he
Lk 9:42 demon tore him and C him.

CONVULSES

Lk 9:39 suddenly cries out; it C him till he foams,

CONVULSING (2)

Mk 1:26 And the unclean spirit, C him and crying with
9:26 after crying out and C him terribly, it came

COOK (2)

1Sam 9:23 Samuel said to the C, "Bring the portion I
9:24 So the C took up the leg and the

COOKED

Lev 2:7 is a cereal offering C in a pan, it

COOKS

1Sam 8:13 to be perfumers and C and bakers.

COOL (5)

Gen 3:8 the garden in the C of the day, and
Judg 3:20 sitting alone in his C roof chamber.
3:24 the closet of the C chamber."
Prov 17:27 he who has a C spirit is a man
Lk 16:24 finger in water and C my tongue; for I

COPIED

Prov 25:1 which the men of Hezekiah king of Judah C

COPIES (2)

1Mac 14:49 sanctuary, and to deposit C of them in the
Heb 9:23 was necessary for the C of the heavenly things

COPING

1Kgs 7:9 the foundation to the C, and from the court

COPPER (9)

Deut 8:9 and out of whose hills you can dig C
Job 28:2 of the earth, and C is smelted from the
Wis 15:9 and imitates workers in C; and he counts it
Sir 12:10 like the rusting of C, so is his wickedness.
Ezek 24:11 become hot, and its C may burn, that its
Mt 10:9 gold, nor silver, nor C in your belts,
Mk 12:42 and put in two C coins, which make a
Lk 12:59 out till you have paid the very last C
21:2 widow put in two C coins.

COPPERSMITH

2Tim 4:14 Alexander the C did me great harm; the Lord

COPY (29)

Deut 17:18 in a book a C of this law, from
Josh 8:32 upon the stones a C of the law of
22:28 should say, 'Behold the C of the altar of
Ezra 4:11 now this is a C of the letter that
4:23 Then, when the C of King Artaxerxes' letter was
5:6 The C of the letter which Tattenai the governor
7:11 This is a C of the letter which King
Esth 3:14 A C of the document was to be issued
4:8 also gave him a C of the written decree
8:13 A C of what was written was to be
13:1 This is a C of the letter: "The Great
16:1 The following is a C of this letter: "The
16:19 'Therefore post a C of this letter publicly in
Wis 9:8 of thy habitation, a C of the holy tent
Jer 32:11 conditions, and the open C;
Bar 6:1 A C of a letter which Jeremiah sent to
1Mac 8:22 and this is a C of the letter which
11:31 This C of the letter which we wrote concerning
11:37 care to make a C of this, and let
12:5 This is a C of the letter which Jonathan
12:7 brethren, as the appended C shows.
12:19 This is a C of the letter which they
14:20 This is a C of the letter which the
14:23 and to put a C of their words in
14:23 they have sent a C of this to Simon
14:27 This is a C of what they wrote: "On
15:24 They also sent a C of these things to
Heb 8:5 They serve a C and shadow of the heavenly
9:24 made with hands, a C of the true one,

COR (2)

Ezek 45:14 a bath from each C (the cor, like the
45:14 from each cor (the C, like the homer, contains

CORAL (3)

Job 28:18 shall be made of C or of crystal; the
Lam 4:7 were more ruddy than C, the beauty of their
Ezek 27:16 embroidered work, fine linen, C, and agate.

CORBAN

Mk 7:11 gained from me is C (that is, given to

CORD (11)

Gen 38:18 "Your signet and your C, and your staff that
38:25 the signet and the C and the staff."
Num 15:38 of each corner a C of blue;
Josh 2:18 shall bind this scarlet C in the window through
2:21 she bound the scarlet C in the window.
Job 30:11 God has loosed my C and humbled me, they
41:1 fishhook, or press down his tongue with a C
Eccl 4:12 A threefold C is not quickly broken.
12:6 streets; before the silver C is snapped, or the
Sir 6:30 her bonds are a C of blue.
Bar 6:43 as herself and her C was not broken.

CORDED

Ex 28:14 you shall attach the C chains to the settings.

CORDS (34)

Ex 28:14 pure gold, twisted like C; and you shall attach
28:22 breastpiece twisted chains like C, of pure gold;
28:24 shall put the two C of gold in the
28:25 ends of the two C you shall attach to
35:18 the court, and their C;
39:15 breastpiece twisted chains like C, of pure gold;
39:17 they put the two C of gold in the
39:18 ends of the two C they had attached to
39:40 of the court, its C, and its pegs; and
Num 3:26 the altar, and its C; all the service pertaining
3:37 round about, with their bases and pegs and C
4:26 the altar, and their C, and all the equipment
4:32 their bases, pegs, and C, with all their equipment
2Sam 22:6 perdition assailed me; the C of Sheol entangled me,
Esth 1:6 hangings caught up with C of fine linen and
Job 36:8 and caught in the C of affliction,
38:31 Pleiades, or loose the C of Orion?
Ps 2:3 asunder, and cast their C from us."
18:4 The C of death encompassed me, the torrents of
18:5 perdition assailed me; the C of Sheol entangled me,
119:61 Though the C of the wicked ensnare me, I
129:4 he has cut the C of the wicked.
140:5 for me, and with C they have spread a
Is 5:18 who draw iniquity with C of falsehood, who draw
33:20 will any of its C be broken.
54:2 back, lengthen your C and strengthen your stakes.
Jer 10:20 destroyed, and all my C are broken; my children
Bar 6:43 And the women, with C about them, sit along
Ezek 3:25 son of man, behold, C will be placed upon
4:8 behold, I will put C upon you, so that
27:24 colored stuff, bound with C and made secure; in
Hos 11:4 I led them with C of compassion, with the

2Mac 7:1 torture with whips and C, to partake of unlawful
Jn 2:15 making a whip of C, he drove them all,

CORIANDER (2)

Ex 16:31 manna; it was like C seed, white, and the
Num 11:7 the manna was like C seed, and its appearance

CORINTH (6)

Acts 18:1 After this he left Athens and went to C
19:1 While Apollos was at C, Paul passed through the
1Cor 1:2 God which is at C, to those sanctified in
2Cor 1:1 God which is at C, with all the saints
1:23 spare you that I refrained from coming to C
2Tim 4:20 Erastus remained at C; Trophimus I left ill at

CORINTHIANS (2)

Acts 18:8 and many of the C hearing Paul believed and
2Cor 6:11 is open to you, C; our heart is wide.

CORMORANT (2)

Lev 11:17 kind, the owl, the C, the ibis,
Deut 14:17 carrion vulture and the C,

CORNELIUS (8)

Acts 10:1 was a man named C, a centurion of what
10:3 of God coming in and saying to him, C
10:17 that were sent by C, having made inquiry for
10:22 And they said, C, a centurion, an upright and
10:24 C was expecting them and had called together his
10:25 When Peter entered, C met him and fell down
10:30 And C said, "Four days ago, about this hour,
10:31 in bright apparel, saying, C, your prayer has been

CORNER (30)

Num 15:38 the tassel of each C a cord of blue;
1Kgs 7:39 sea on the southeast C of the house.
2Kgs 14:13 Ephraim Gate to the C Gate.
2Chr 4:10 sea at the southeast C of the house.
25:23 Ephraim Gate to the C Gate.
26:9 in Jerusalem at the C Gate and at the
28:24 himself altars in every C of Jerusalem.
Neh 3:25 of Azariah to the Angle and to the C
3:31 Gate, and to the upper chamber of the C
3:32 upper chamber of the C and the Sheep Gate
9:22 allot to them every C; so they took possession
Ps 118:22 builders rejected has become the head of the C
144:12 full-grown, our daughters like C pillars cut for the
Prov 7:8 the street near her C, taking the road to
7:12 market, and at every C she lies in wait.
21:9 to live in a C of the housetop than
25:24 to live in a C of the housetop than
Jer 31:38 of Hananel to the C Gate.
31:40 brook Kidron, to the C of the Horse Gate
51:26 from you for a C and no stone for
Ezek 46:21 court; and in each C of the court there
Dan 13:38 We were in a C of the garden, and
Amos 3:12 be rescued, with the C of a couch and
Zech 14:10 former gate, to the C Gate, and from the
Mt 21:42 the head of the C; this was the Lord's
Mk 12:10 the head of the C;
Lk 20:17 builders rejected has become the head of the C
Acts 4:11 but which has become the head of the C
26:26 notice, for this was not done in a C
1Pet 2:7 builders rejected has become the head of the C

CORNERS (36)

Ex 25:26 rings to the four C at its four legs.
26:23 make two frames for C of the tabernacle in
26:24 both of them; they shall form the two C
27:2 it on its four C; its horns shall be
27:4 shall make four bronze rings at its four C
36:28 made two frames for C of the tabernacle in
36:29 made two of them thus, for the two C
37:3 gold for its four C, two rings on its
37:13 rings to the four C at its four legs.
38:2 it on its four C; its horns were of
38:5 rings on the four C of the bronze grating
Num 15:38 make tassels on the C of their garments throughout
Deut 22:12 tassels on the four C of your cloak with
1Kgs 7:30 and at the four C were supports for a
7:34 supports at the four C of each stand; the
2Chr 26:15 the towers and the C, to shoot arrows and
Tob 11:13 scaled off from the C of his eyes.
Job 1:19 and struck the four C of the house, and
37:3 his lightning to the C of the earth.
Is 11:12 Judah from the four C of the earth.
41:9 called from its farthest C, saying to you, "You
Jer 9:26 desert that cut the C of their hair; for
25:23 all who cut the C of their hair;
49:32 those who cut the C of their hair, and
Ezek 7:2 come upon the four C of the land.
41:22 two cubits broad; its C, its base, and its
43:20 and on the four C of the ledge, and
45:19 the temple, the four C of the ledge of
46:21 me to the four C of the court; and
46:22 in the four C of the court were
Zech 9:15 bowl, drenched like the C of the altar.
Mt 6:5 and at the street C, that they may be
Acts 10:11 let down by four C upon the earth.
11:5 from heaven by four C; and it came down
Rev 7:1 standing at the four C of the earth, holding
20:8 are at the four C of the earth, that

CORNERSTONE (5)

Job 38:6 or who laid its C,
Is 28:16 tested stone, a precious C, of a sure foundation:
Zech 10:4 them shall come the C, out of them the
Eph 2:20 Jesus himself being the C,
1Pet 2:6 Zion a stone, a C chosen and precious, and

CORNERSTONES

Is 19:13 those who are the C of her tribes have

CORONATION

2Mac 4:21 to Egypt for the C of Philometor as king,

CORPSE (3)

2Kgs 9:37 of Jezebel; and the C of Jezebel shall be
Sir 48:5 You who raised a C from death and from
Mk 9:26 boy was like a C; so that most of

CORPSES (7)

Ps 110:6 nations, filling them with C; he will shatter chiefs
Wis 4:18 they will become dishonored C, and an outrage
18:12 form of death, had C too many to count.
Is 5:25 mountains quaked; and their C were as refuse in
34:3 the stench of their C shall rise; the mountains
Nah 3:3 of slain, heaps of C, dead bodies without end–
1Mac 11:4 suburbs destroyed, and the C lying about, and the

CORRECT (3)

Wis 12:2 Therefore thou dost C little by little those who
Is 1:17 seek justice, C oppression; defend the fatherless,
Jer 10:24 C me, O LORD, but in just measure; not

CORRECTING

2Tim 2:25 an apt teacher, forbearing, C his opponents with

CORRECTION (6)

Job 37:13 Whether for C, or for his land, or for
Jer 2:30 children, they took no C; your own sword devoured
5:3 hast consumed them, but they refused to take C
Zeph 3:2 She listens to no voice, she accepts no C
3:7 me, she will accept C; she will not lose
2Tim 3:16 teaching, for reproof, for C, and for training in

CORRECTOR (2)

Wis 7:15 of wisdom and the C of the wise.
Rom 2:20 are in darkness, a C of the foolish, a

CORRECTS

Prov 9:7 He who C a scoffer gets himself abuse, and

CORRESPOND

2Cor 11:15 Their end will C to their deeds.

CORRESPONDED

1Chr 26:16 Watch C to watch.

CORRESPONDING (9)

Ex 38:18 high in its breadth, C to the hangings of
1Chr 23:6 organized them in divisions C to the sons of
26:12 divisions of the gatekeepers, C to their chief men,
2Chr 3:8 holy place; its length, C to the breadth of
Neh 12:24 man of God, watch C to watch.
Wis 13:5 created things comes a C perception of their Creator.
Ezek 40:18 side of the gates, C to the length of
41:7 from story to story, C to the enlargement of
45:7 and on the east, C in length to one

CORRESPONDS (2)

Gal 4:25 Sinai in Arabia; she C to the present Jerusalem,

1Pet 3:21 Baptism, which C to this, now saves you, not

CORROSION

Bar 6:12 wood, which cannot save themselves from rust and C

CORRUPT (16)

Gen 6:11 Now the earth was C in God's sight, and
6:12 and behold, it was C; for all flesh had
2Chr 27:2 the people still followed C practices.
Job 15:16 who is abominable and C, a man who drinks
Ps 14:1 They are C, they do abominable deeds, there is
14:3 they are all alike C; there is none that
53:1 They are C, doing abominable iniquity; there is none
Jer 17:9 all things, and desperately C; who can understand it?
Ezek 16:47 time you were more C than they in all
20:44 nor according to your C doings, O house of
23:11 yet she was more C than she in her
Dan 2:9 to speak lying and C words before me till
Zeph 3:7 they were eager to make all their deeds C
Eph 4:22 of life and is C through deceitful lusts,
2Tim 3:8 the truth, men of C mind and counterfeit faith;
Tit 1:14 pure, but to the C and unbelieving nothing is

CORRUPTED (8)

Gen 6:12 for all flesh had C their way upon the
Ex 32:7 land of Egypt, have C themselves;
Ezek 28:17 of your beauty; you C your wisdom for the
Hos 9:9 They have deeply C themselves as in the days
Mal 2:8 your instruction; you have C the covenant of Levi,
2Cor 7:2 no one, we have C no one, we have
Tit 1:14 is pure; their very minds and consciences are C
Rev 19:2 the great harlot who C the earth with her

CORRUPTION (14)

2Kgs 23:13 of the mount of C, which Solomon the king
Wis 14:12 of them was the C of life,
14:25 murder, theft and deceit, C, faithlessness, tumult,
Hos 7:2 would heal Israel, the C of Ephraim is revealed,
2Mac 4:7 obtained the high-priesthood by C,
Acts 2:27 to Hades, nor let thy Holy One see C
2:31 abandoned to Hades, nor did his flesh see C
13:34 more to return to C, he spoke in this
13:35 thy Holy One see C
13:36 his fathers, and saw C;
13:37 but he whom God raised up saw no C
Gal 6:8 from the flesh reap C; but he who sows
2Pet 1:4 may escape from the C that is in the
2:19 themselves are slaves of C; for whatever overcomes

CORRUPTLY (8)

Deut 4:16 beware lest you act C by making a graven
4:25 land, if you act C by making a graven
9:12 from Egypt have acted C; they have turned aside
31:29 you will surely act C, and turn aside from
32:5 They have dealt C with him, they are no
Neh 1:7 We have acted very C against thee, and have
Is 1:4 with iniquity, offspring of evildoers, sons who deal C
Jer 6:28 are bronze and iron, all of them act C

CORRUPTS

Eccl 7:7 foolish, and a bribe C the mind.

CORS (8)

1Kgs 4:22 one day was thirty C of fine flour, and
4:22 fine flour, and sixty C of meal,
5:11 gave Hiram twenty thousand C of wheat as food
5:11 household, and twenty thousand C of beaten oil.
2Chr 2:10 cut timber, twenty thousand C of crushed wheat,
2:10 crushed wheat, twenty thousand C of barley, twenty
27:5 silver, and ten thousand C of wheat and ten
Ezra 7:22 of silver, a hundred C of wheat, a hundred

COS (2)

1Mac 15:23 to Phaselis, and to C, and to Side, and
Acts 21:1 a straight course to C, and the next day

COSAM

Lk 3:28 Addi, the son of C, the son of Elmadam,

COST (21)

Ex 32:29 each one at the C of his son and
Num 16:38 have sinned at the C of their lives; so
Deut 15:18 for at half the C of a hired servant
Josh 6:26 At the C of his first-born shall he lay
6:26 foundation, and at the C of his youngest son
2Sam 24:24 LORD my God which C me nothing." So David
1Kgs 2:23 this word does not C Adonijah his life!
16:34 its foundation at the C of Abiram his first-born,
16:34 its gates at the C of his youngest son
1Chr 21:24 offer burnt offerings which C me nothing."
Ezra 6:4 of timber; let the C be paid from the
6:8 house of God; the C is to be paid
Prov 7:23 know that it will C him his life.
Jer 42:20 gone astray at the C of your lives.
Bar 6:25 are bought at any C, but there is no
1Mac 10:44 "Let the C of rebuilding and restoring the structures
10:45 And let the C of rebuilding the walls of
10:45 round about, and the C of rebuilding the walls
2Mac 5:6 that success at the C of one's kindred is
Lk 14:28 down and count the C, whether he has enough
2Cor 11:7 preached God's gospel without C to you?

COSTLY (17)

Gen 24:53 and to her mother C ornaments.
1Kgs 5:17 they quarried out great, C stones in order to
7:9 these were made of C stones, hewn according to
7:10 The foundation was of C stones, huge stones, stones
7:11 above were C stones, hewn according to
2Chr 32:27 for all kinds of C vessels;
Ezra 1:6 with beasts, and with C wares, besides all that
Esth 14:2 mourning, and instead of C perfumes she covered her
Ps 49:8 of his life is C, and can never suffice,
Prov 20:15 gold, and abundance of C stones; but the lips
Wis 2:7 take our fill of C wine and perfumes, and
Dan 11:38 with precious stones and C gifts.
1Mac 1:23 the gold, and the C vessels; he took also
Mk 14:3 of pure nard, very C, and she broke the
Jn 12:3 took a pound of C ointment of pure nard
1Tim 2:9 gold or pearls or C attire
Rev 18:12 ivory, all articles of C wood, bronze, iron and

COTTON (2)

Esth 1:6 There were white C curtains and blue hangings
Is 19:9 be in despair, and the weavers of white C

COUCH (13)

Gen 49:4 you defiled it--you went up to my C
2Sam 11:2 David arose from his C and was walking upon
11:13 to lie on his C with the servants of
1Chr 5:1 he polluted his father's C, his birthright was given
Esth 7:8 was falling on the C where Esther was; and
Job 7:13 will comfort me, my C will ease my complaint,'
17:13 if I spread my C in darkness,
Ps 6:6 tears; I drench my C with my weeping.
Prov 7:16 I have decked my C with coverings, colored spreads
Song 1:12 king was on his C, my nard gave forth
1:16 Our C is green;
Ezek 23:41 sat upon a stately C, with a table spread
Amos 3:12 the corner of a C and part of a

COUCHED (3)

Gen 49:9 He stooped down, he C as a lion, and
Num 24:9 He C, he lay down like a lion, and
Ezek 19:2 She C in the midst of young lions, rearing

COUCHES (6)

Gen 49:25 of the deep that C beneath, blessings of the
Deut 33:13 of the deep that C beneath,
33:20 Gad C like a lion, he tears the arm,
Esth 1:6 marble pillars, and also C of gold and silver
Ps 149:5 glory; let them sing for joy on their C
Amos 6:4 stretch themselves upon their C, and eat lambs from

COUCHING

Gen 4:7 do well, sin is C at the door; its

COUNCIL (40)

Gen 49:6 come not into their C; O my spirit, be
2Kgs 9:5 the army were in C; and he said, "I
25:19 men of the king's C who were found in
Jud 6:1 the men outside the C died down, Holofernes, the
6:17 taken place at the C of Holofernes, and all
11:9 Achior said in your C, we have heard his
Job 15:8 you listened in the C of God?
Ps 82:1 place in the divine C; in the midst of
89:7 God feared in the C of the holy ones,
Sir 38:33 sought out for the C of the people, nor
Jer 23:18 has stood in the C of the LORD to
23:22 had stood in my C, then they would have
52:25 men of the king's C, who were found in
Ezek 13:9 not be in the C of my people, nor
2Mac 14:5 a meeting of the C and was asked about

C

Mt 5:22 be liable to the C, and whoever says, 'You
26:59 priests and the whole C sought false testimony
Mk 14:55 and the whole C sought testimony against Jesus
15:1 scribes, and the whole C held a consultation; and
15:42 respected member of the C, who was also himself
Lk 22:64 him away to their C, and they said,
23:49 a member of the C, a good and righteous
Jn 11:47 the Pharisees gathered the C, and said, "What are
Acts 4:15 aside out of the C, they conferred with one
5:21 and called together the C and all the senate
5:27 had brought them, they set them before the C
5:34 a Pharisee in the C named Gamali-el, a teacher
5:41 the presence of the C, rejoicing that they were
6:12 brought him before the C,
6:15 who sat in the C saw that his face
22:5 priest and the whole C of elders bear me
22:30 priests and all the C to meet, and he
23:1 looking intently at the C, said, "Brethren, I have
23:6 cried out in the C, "Brethren, I am a
23:15 therefore, along with the C, give notice now to
23:20 Paul down to the C tomorrow, as though they
23:28 accused him, I brought him down to their C
24:19 I stood before the C,
25:12 conferred with his C, answered, "You have appealed
1Tim 4:14 prophetic utterance when the C of elders laid their

COUNCILS (2)

Mt 10:17 deliver you up to C, and flog you in
Mk 13:9 deliver you up to C; and you will be

COUNSEL (118)

Ex 18:19 I will give you C, and God be with
Num 31:16 of Israel, by the C of Balaam, to act
Deut 32:28 a nation void of C, and there is no
Judg 19:30 day; consider it, take C, and speak."
20:7 give your advice and C here."
2Sam 15:31 pray thee, turn the C of Ahithophel into foolishness."
15:34 defeat for me the C of Ahithophel.
16:20 to Ahithophel, "Give your C; what shall we do?"
16:23 in those days the C which Ahithophel gave was
16:23 so was all the C of Ahithophel esteemed, both
17:7 Absalom, "This time the C which Ahithophel has
17:11 But my C is that all Israel be gathered
17:14 of Israel said, "The C of Hushai the Archite
17:14 is better than the C of Ahithophel." For the
17:14 to defeat the good C of Ahithophel, so that
17:15 and so did Ahithophel C Absalom and the elders
17:23 Ahithophel saw that his C was not followed, he
20:18 'Let them but ask C at Abel'; and so
1Kgs 1:12 let me give you C, that you may save
12:6 Then King Rehoboam took C with the old men,
12:8 But he forsook the C which the old men
12:8 gave him, and took C with the young men
12:13 harshly, and forsaking the C which the old men
12:14 them according to the C of the young men,
12:28 So the king took C, and made two calves
2Kgs 6:8 against Israel, he took C with his servants, saying,
1Chr 12:19 of the Philistines took C and sent him away,
2Chr 10:6 Then King Rehoboam took C with the old men,
10:8 But he forsook the C which the old men
10:8 gave him, and took C with the young men
10:13 harshly, and forsaking the C of the old men,
10:14 them according to the C of the young men,
20:21 when he had taken C with the people, he
22:5 He even followed their C, and went with Jehoram
25:16 done this and have not listened to my C
25:17 king of Judah took C and sent to Joash
30:2 in Jerusalem had taken C to keep the passover
Ezra 10:3 children, according to the C of my lord and
Neh 5:7 I took C with myself, and I brought charges
6:7 and let us take C together."
Tob 4:18 wise man, and do not despise any useful C
Esth 5:14 This C pleased Haman, and he had the gallows
Job 12:13 and might; he has C and understanding.
21:16 The C of the wicked is far from me.
22:18 things— but the C of the wicked is
29:21 me, and waited, and kept silence for my C
38:2 is this that darkens C by words without knowledge?
42:3 is this that hides C without knowledge?' Therefore I
Ps 1:1 walks not in the C of the wicked, nor
2:2 and the rulers take C together, against the LORD
16:7 LORD who gives me C; in the night also
32:8 should go; I will C you with my eye
33:10 The LORD brings the C of the nations to
33:11 The C of the LORD stands for ever, the
73:24 guide me with thy C, and afterward thou wilt
106:13 his works; they did not wait for his C
107:11 God, and spurned the C of the Most High.
Prov 1:25 have ignored all my C and would have none
1:30 have none of my C, and despised all my
8:14 I have C and sound wisdom, I have insight,
15:22 Without C plans go wrong, but with many advisers
20:18 Plans are established by C; by wise guidance wage
21:30 wisdom, no understanding, no C, can avail against
Wis 8:9 would give me good C and encouragement in cares
9:13 man can learn the C of God?
9:17 Who has learned thy C, unless thou hast given
Sir 6:2 yourself through your soul's C, lest your soul be
6:23 and accept my judgment; do not reject my C
19:19 wisdom, nor is there prudence where sinners take C
21:13 a flood, and his C like a flowing spring.
22:14 fixed on a reasonable C will not be afraid
23:1 abandon me to their C, and let me not
24:27 the sea, and her C deeper than the great
25:4 men, and for the aged to possess good C
25:5 aged, and understanding and C in honorable men!
37:7 Every counselor praises C, but some give counsel in
37:7 counsel, but some give C in their own interest.
37:10 you suspiciously; hide your C from those who are
37:11 no attention to these in any matter of C
37:13 And establish the C of your own heart, for
37:16 of every work, and C precedes every undertaking.
39:7 He will direct his C and knowledge aright, and
40:25 stand sure, but good C is esteemed more than
43:23 By his C he stilled the great deep and
44:3 for their power, giving C by their understanding, and
Is 8:10 Take C together, but it will come to nought;
11:2 understanding, the spirit of C and might, the spirit
16:3 "Give C, grant justice; make your shade like night
19:11 foolish; the wise counselors of Pharaoh give stupid C
28:29 he is wonderful in C, and excellent in wisdom.
29:15 from the LORD their C, whose deeds are in
30:2 without asking for my C, to take refuge in
44:26 servant, and performs the C of his messengers; who
45:21 case; let them take C together!
46:10 yet done, saying, 'My C shall stand, and I
46:11 the man of my C from a far country.
Jer 18:18 from the priest, nor C from the wise, nor
32:19 of hosts, great in C and mighty in deed;
38:15 if I give you C, you will not listen
49:7 Has C perished from the prudent?
Ezek 7:26 from the priest, and C from the elders.
11:2 and who give wicked C in this city;
Dan 4:27 O king, let my C be acceptable to you;
1Mac 2:65 brother is wise in C; always listen to him;
Mt 12:14 went out and took C against him, how to
22:15 Pharisees went and took C how to entangle him
26:4 called Caiaphas, and took C together in order to
27:1 of the people took C against Jesus to put
27:7 So they took C, and bought with them the
28:12 the elders and taken C, they gave a sum
Mk 3:6 out, and immediately held C with the Herodi-ans
Lk 14:31 down first and take C whether he is able
Jn 11:53 day on they took C how to put him
18:14 Caiaphas who had given C to the Jews that
Acts 13:36 he had served the C of God in his
20:27 to you the whole C of God.
Eph 1:11 things according to the C of his will,
Rev 3:18 Therefore I C you to buy from me gold

COUNSELED (5)

2Sam 17:15 of Israel; and thus and so have I C
17:21 and so has Ahithophel C against you."
Job 26:3 How you have C him who has no wisdom,
Nah 1:11 against the LORD, and C villainy?
1Mac 9:69 lawless men who had C him to come into

COUNSELOR (19)

2Sam 15:12 Ahithophel the Gilonite, David's C, from his city
1Chr 26:14 son Zechariah, a shrewd C, and his lot came
27:32 David's uncle, was a C, being a man of
27:33 Ahithophel was the king's C, and Hushai the Archite
2Chr 22:3 his mother was his C in doing wickedly.
25:16 to him, "Have we made you a royal C
Sir 37:7 Every C praises counsel, but some give counsel in
37:8 Be wary of a C, and learn first what
42:21 and he needs no one to be his C
Is 3:3 man of rank, the C and the skilful magician
9:6 called "Wonderful C, Mighty God, Everlasting Father,
40:13 LORD, or as his C has instructed him?
41:28 these there is no C who, when I ask,
Mic 4:9 Has your C perished, that pangs have seized you

Jn 14:16 will give you another C, to be with you
14:26 But the C, the Holy Spirit, whom the Father
15:26 cause.' But when the C comes, whom I shall
16:7 not go away, the C will not come to
Rom 11:34 of the Lord, or who has been his C

COUNSELORS (20)

2Chr 22:4 father they were his C, to his undoing.
Ezra 4:5 to build, and hired C against them to frustrate
7:14 king and his seven C to make inquiries about
7:15 the king and his C have freely offered to
7:28 the king and his C, and before all the
8:25 the king and his C and his lords and
Esth 13:3 "When I asked my C how this might be
Job 3:14 rest, with kings and C of the earth who
12:17 He leads C away stripped, and judges he makes
Ps 119:24 Thy testimonies are my delight, they are my C
Prov 11:14 in an abundance of C there is safety.
24:6 and in abundance of C there is victory.
Is 1:26 the first, and your C as at the beginning.
19:11 utterly foolish; the wise C of Pharaoh give stupid
Dan 3:2 and the governors, the C, the treasurers, the justices,
3:3 and the governors, the C, the treasurers, the justices,
3:92 He said to his C, "Did we not cast
3:95 governors, and the king's C gathered together and
4:36 My C and my lords sought me, and I
6:7 and the satraps, the C and the governors are

COUNSELS (7)

Ps 5:10 fall by their own C; because of their many
81:12 to their stubborn hearts, to follow their own C
Prov 12:5 righteous are just; the C of the wicked are
Wis 1:9 be made into the C of an ungodly man,
Is 47:13 wearied with your many C; let them stand forth
Jer 7:24 walked in their own C and the stubbornness of
Mic 6:16 have walked in their C; that I may make

COUNT (34)

Gen 13:16 that if one can C the dust of the
Ex 12:4 you shall make your C for the lamb.
Lev 15:13 discharge, then he shall C for himself seven days
15:28 her discharge, she shall C for herself seven days,
19:23 food, then you shall C their fruit as forbidden;
23:15 "And you shall C from the morrow after the
25:8 "And you shall C seven weeks of years, seven
Num 23:10 Who can C the dust of Jacob, or number
31:26 to Moses, "Take the C of the booty that
Deut 16:9 "You shall C seven weeks; begin to count the
seven weeks; begin to C the seven weeks from
1Chr 9:28 they were required to C them when they were
Job 13:24 hide thy face, and C me as thy enemy?
19:15 forgotten me; my maidservants C me as a stranger;
Ps 22:17 feet-- I can C all my bones--
56:8 Thou hast kept C of my tossings; put thou
119:119 the earth thou dost C as dross; therefore I
139:18 If I would C them, they are more than
139:22 with perfect hatred; I C them my enemies.
Wis 18:12 form of death, had corpses too many to C
Sir 1:2 of eternity--who can C them?
7:16 Do not C yourself among the crowd of sinners;
Ezek 44:26 is defiled, he shall C for himself seven days,
Lk 14:28 first sit down and C the cost, whether he
Acts 19:27 great goddess Artemis may C for nothing, and that
2Cor 10:2 such confidence as I C on showing against some
Phil 2:3 but in humility C others better than yourselves.
2:6 of God, did not C equality with God a
3:8 Indeed I C everything as loss because of the
3:8 of all things, and C them as refuse, in
Jas 1:2 C it all joy, my brethren, when you meet
2Pet 2:13 They C it pleasure to revel in the daytime.
3:9 his promise as some C slowness, but is forbearing
3:15 And C the forbearance of our Lord as salvation.

COUNTED (32)

Gen 13:16 of the earth, your descendants also can be C
30:33 with me, shall be C stolen."
Ex 38:21 testimony, as they were C at the commandment of
Num 31:49 Moses, "Your servants have C the men of war
Judg 6:5 camels could not be C; so that they wasted
1Kgs 1:21 son Solomon will be C offenders."
3:8 cannot be numbered or C for multitude.
8:5 they could not be C or numbered.
2Kgs 12:10 came up and they C and tied up in
2Chr 5:6 they could not be C or numbered.
Ezra 1:8 the treasurer, who C them out to Shesh-bazzar
8:34 The whole was C and weighed, and the weight
Neh 13:13 Mattaniah, for they were C faithful; and their duty
Jud 2:20 the earth--a multitude that could not be C
5:10 so great that they could not be C
Job 18:3 Why are we C as cattle?
34:6 my right I am C a liar; my wound
41:29 Clubs are C as stubble; he laughs at the
Ps 109:7 let his prayer be C as sin!
141:2 Let my prayer be C as incense before thee,
Prov 27:14 the morning, will be C as cursing.
Wis 18:1 see their forms, and C them happy for not
Is 22:10 lower pool, and you C the houses of Jerusalem,
33:18 "Where is he who C, where is he who
33:18 Where is he who C the towers?"
Bar 3:11 dead, that you are C among those in Hades?
1Mac 5:30 that could not be C, carrying ladders and engines
Acts 5:41 rejoicing that they were C worthy to suffer dishonor
19:19 of all; and they C the value of them
Rom 5:13 but sin is not C where there is no
Phil 3:7 gain I had, I C as loss for the
Heb 3:3 Yet Jesus has been C worthy of as much

COUNTENANCE (26)

Gen 4:5 very angry, and his C fell.
4:6 and why has your C fallen?
Num 6:26 LORD lift up his C upon you, and give
Deut 28:50 a nation of stern C, who shall not regard
Judg 13:6 to me, and his C was like the countenance
13:6 countenance was like the C of the angel of
1Sam 1:18 and ate, and her C was no longer sad.
Jud 16:7 Merari undid him with the beauty of her C
Esth 15:14 my lord, and your C is full of grace."
Job 9:27 put off my sad C, and be of good
14:20 passes; thou changest his C, and sendest him away.
29:24 the light of my C they did not cast
Ps 4:6 the light of thy C upon us, O LORD!"
10:4 the pride of his C the wicked does not
44:3 the light of thy C; for thou didst delight
80:16 may they perish at the rebuke of thy C
89:15 the light of thy C,
90:8 our secret sins in the light of thy C
Prov 15:13 heart makes a cheerful C, but by sorrow of
Eccl 7:3 for by sadness of C the heart is made
8:1 the hardness of his C is changed.
Sir 13:24 man's heart changes his C, either for good or
36:22 woman's beauty gladdens the C, and surpasses every
Dan 8:23 a king of bold C, one who understands riddles,
Mk 10:22 At that saying his C fell, and he went
Lk 9:29 the appearance of his C was altered, and his

COUNTERATTACKS

2Mac 5:3 drawn up, attacks and C made on this side

COUNTERFEIT (2)

Wis 15:9 glory that he molds C gods.
2Tim 3:8 of corrupt mind and C faith;

COUNTING (4)

Lev 23:16 weeks shall they be, C fifty days to the
Tob 9:4 but my father is C the days, and if
10:1 his father Tobit was C each day, and when
2Cor 5:19 world to himself, not C their trespasses against them,

COUNTLESS (4)

Sir 30:15 a robust body than C riches.
Nah 3:4 And all for the C harlotries of the harlot,
1Cor 4:15 For though you have C guides in Christ, you
2Cor 11:23 far more imprisonments, with C beatings, and often

COUNTRIES (44)

2Kgs 18:35 the gods of the C have delivered their countries
18:35 countries have delivered their C out of my hand,
1Chr 29:30 Israel, and upon all the kingdoms of the C
2Chr 12:8 and the service of the kingdoms of the C
20:29 the kingdoms of the C when they heard that
Sir 47:17 for your interpretations, the C marveled at you.
Is 8:9 ear, all you far C; gird yourselves and be
36:20 the gods of these C have delivered their countries
36:20 countries have delivered their C out of my hand,
Jer 16:15 out of all the C where he had driven
23:3 out of all the C where I have driven
23:8 out of all the C where he had driven
28:8 and pestilence against many C and great kingdoms.
32:37 them from all the C to which I drove
Ezek 5:5 of the nations, with C round about her.
5:6 statutes more than the C round about her, by
6:8 are scattered through the C,

C

11:16 scattered them among the C, yet I have been
11:16 a while in the C where they have gone.'
11:17 you out of the C where you have been
12:15 among the nations and scatter them through the C
20:23 disperse them through the C,
20:32 the tribes of the C, and worship wood and
20:34 you out of the C where you are scattered,
20:41 you out of the C where you have been
22:4 the nations, and a mocking to all the C
22:15 disperse you through the C, and I will consume
25:7 perish out of the C; I will destroy you.
29:12 the midst of desolated C; and her cities shall
29:12 among the nations, and disperse them among the C
30:7 the midst of desolated C and her cities shall
30:26 the nations and disperse them throughout the C
32:9 the nations, into the C which you have not
34:13 gather them from the C, and will bring them
35:10 nations and these two C shall be mine, and
36:19 were dispersed through the C; in accordance with
36:24 you from all the C, and bring you into
Dan 11:40 he shall come into C and shall overflow and
11:42 his hand against the C, and the land of
Zech 10:9 nations, yet in far C they shall remember me,
1Mac 1:4 army and ruled over C, nations, and princes, and
15:15 to the kings and C, in which the following
15:19 to the kings and C that they should not
15:23 and to all the C, and to Sampsames, and

COUNTRY (316)
Gen 10:30 Sephar to the hill C of the east.
12:1 Abram, "Go from your C and your kindred and
14:7 and subdued all the C of the Amalekites, and
24:4 will go to my C and to my kindred,
25:6 from his son Isaac, eastward to the east C
29:26 so done in our C, to give the younger
30:25 I may go to my own home and C
31:21 face toward the hill C of Gilead.
31:23 him into the hill C of Gilead.
31:25 tent in the hill C, and Laban with his
31:25 encamped in the hill C of Gilead.
32:3 land of Seir, the C of Edom,
32:9 me, 'Return to your C and to your kindred,
36:8 dwelt in the hill C of Seir; Esau is
36:9 Edomites in the hill C of Seir.
36:35 defeated Midian in the C of Moab, reigned in
Ex 8:2 will plague all your C with frogs;
10:4 bring locusts into your C,
10:14 settled on the whole C of Egypt, such a
10:19 left in all the C of Egypt.
18:27 and he went his way to his own C
Lev 25:24 And in all the C you possess, you shall
25:31 the fields of the C; they may be redeemed,
Num 13:17 up into the hill C,
13:29 dwell in the hill C; and the Canaanites dwell
14:40 heights of the hill C, saying, "See, we are
14:44 heights of the hill C, although neither the ark
14:45 dwelt in that hill C came down, and defeated
32:33 territories, the cities of the land throughout the C
Deut 1:7 go to the hill C of the Amorites, and
1:7 Arabah, in the hill C and in the lowland,
1:19 way to the hill C of the Amorites, as
1:20 come to the hill C of the Amorites, which
1:24 up into the hill C, and came to the
1:41 it easy to go up into the hill C
1:43 were presumptuous and went up into the hill C
1:44 lived in that hill C came out against you
2:3 about this mountain C long enough; turn northward.
2:37 cities of the hill C, and wherever the LORD
3:12 and half the hill C of Gilead with its
3:25 Jordan, that goodly hill C, and Lebanon.'
21:1 lying in the open C, and it is not
22:25 if in the open C a man meets a
22:27 her in the open C, and though the betrothed
Josh 9:1 Jordan in the hill C and in the lowland
9:6 come from a far C; so now make a
9:9 "From a very far C your servants have come,
9:11 the inhabitants of our C said to us, 'Take
10:6 dwell in the hill C are gathered against us."
10:40 whole land, the hill C and the Negeb and
10:41 Gaza, and all the C of Goshen, as far
11:2 in the northern hill C, and in the Arabah
11:3 Jebusites in the hill C, and the Hivites under
11:16 that land, the hill C and all the Negeb
11:16 Arabah and the hill C of Israel and its
11:21 Anakim from the hill C, from Hebron, from Debir,
11:21 from all the hill C of Judah, and from
11:21 from all the hill C of Israel; Joshua utterly
12:8 allotments, in the hill C, in the lowland, in
13:6 of the hill C from Lebanon to Misrephoth-maim,
14:12 give me this hill C of which the LORD
15:48 And in the hill C, Shamir, Jattir, Socoh,
16:1 Jericho into the hill C to Bethel;
17:15 Rephaim, since the hill C of Ephraim is too
17:16 Joseph said, "The hill C is not enough for
17:18 only, but the hill C shall be yours, for
18:12 up through the hill C westward; and it ends
19:50 Timnath-serah in the hill C of Ephraim; and he
20:7 Galilee in the hill C of Naphtali, and Shechem
20:7 Shechem in the hill C of Ephraim, and Kiriath-arba
20:7 Hebron) in the hill C of Judah.
21:11 Hebron, in the hill C of Judah, along with
21:21 lands in the hill C of Ephraim, Gezer with
24:4 gave Esau the hill C of Seir to possess,
24:30 is in the hill C of Ephraim, north of
24:33 him in the hill C of Ephraim.
Judg 1:9 dwelt in the hill C, in the Negeb, and
1:19 possession of the hill C, but he could not
1:34 back into the hill C, for they did not
2:9 Timnath-heres, in the hill C of Ephraim, north of
3:27 trumpet in the hill C of Ephraim; and the
3:27 him from the hill C, having him at their
4:5 Bethel in the hill C of Ephraim; and the
7:24 throughout all the hill C of Ephraim, saying, "Come
10:1 Shamir in the hill C of Ephraim.
11:19 your land to our C
11:21 the land of the Amorites, who inhabited that C
12:15 Ephraim, in the hill C of the Amalekites.
16:24 the ravager of our C, who has slain many
17:1 man of the hill C of Ephraim, whose name
17:8 came to the hill C of Ephraim to the
18:2 came to the hill C of Ephraim, to the
18:13 there to the hill C of Ephraim, and came
18:14 to spy out the C of Laish said to
19:1 parts of the hill C of Ephraim, who took
19:16 was from the hill C of Ephraim, and he
19:18 parts of the hill C of Ephraim, from which
20:6 her throughout all the C of the inheritance of
20:31 and in the open C, about thirty men of
Ruth 1:1 to sojourn in the C of Moab, he and
1:2 They went into the C of Moab and remained
1:6 to return from the C of Moab, for she
1:6 had heard in the C of Moab that the
1:22 who returned from the C of Moab.
2:6 with Naomi from the C of Moab.
4:3 come back from the C of Moab, is selling
1Sam 1:1 Ramathaim-zophim of the hill C of Ephraim, whose
6:1 LORD was in the C of the Philistines seven
9:4 passed through the hill C of Ephraim and passed
13:2 Michmash and the hill C of Bethel, and a
14:22 themselves in the hill C of Ephraim heard that
23:14 wilderness, in the hill C of the Wilderness of
27:5 in one of the C towns, that I may
27:7 David dwelt in the C of the Philistines was
27:11 he dwelt in the C of the Philistines.
30:11 Egyptian in the open C, and brought him to
2Sam 10:8 and Maacah, were by themselves in the open C
15:23 And all the C wept aloud as all the
18:8 face of all the C; and the forest devoured
20:21 man of the hill C of Ephraim, called Sheba
1Kgs 4:8 Ben-hur, in the hill C of Ephraim;
4:19 land of Gilead, the C of Sihon king of
5:15 stone in the hill C,
8:41 comes from a far C for thy name's sake
11:21 depart, that I may go to my own C
11:22 are now seeking to go to your own C
11:29 two of them were alone in the open C
12:25 Shechem in the hill C of Ephraim, and dwelt
14:11 dies in the open C the birds of the
20:27 flocks of goats, but the Syrians filled the C
21:24 dies in the open C the birds of the
22:36 to his city, and every man to his C
2Kgs 3:20 of Edom, till the C was filled with water.
5:22 me from the hill C of Ephraim two young
7:12 themselves in the open C, thinking, 'When they come
20:14 come from a far C, from Babylon."
25:23 forces in the open C and their men heard
1Chr 1:46 defeated Midian in the C of Moab, reigned in
6:67 lands in the hill C of Ephraim, Gezer with
8:8 had sons in the C of Moab after he
19:9 had come were by themselves in the open C
20:1 army, and ravaged the C of the Ammonites, and
27:25 the treasuries in the C, in the cities, in

2Chr	2:2	quarry in the hill C, and three thousand six
	2:18	quarry in the hill C, and three thousand six
	6:32	comes from a far C for the sake of
	13:4	is in the hill C of Ephraim, and said,
	15:8	taken in the hill C of Ephraim, and he
	19:4	Beer-sheba to the hill C of Ephraim, and brought
	21:11	places in the hill C of Judah, and led
	27:4	cities in the hill C of Judah, and forts
	30:10	to city through the C of Ephraim and Manasseh,
Tob	1:4	was in my own C, in the land of
Jud	1:6	people of the hill C and all those who
	2:6	attack the whole west C, because they disobeyed my
	2:22	up into the hill C
	2:23	desert, south of the C of the Chelleans.
	3:7	and all in the C round about welcomed him
	5:3	people is this that lives in the hill C
	5:15	Jordan they took possession of all the hill C
	5:18	captive to a foreign C; the temple of their
	5:19	settled in the hill C, because it was uninhabited.
	6:7	back into the hill C and put you in
	6:11	up into the hill C and came to the
	7:1	up into the hill C and make war on
	7:18	encamped in the hill C opposite Dothan; and they
	10:13	capture all the hill C without losing one of
	11:2	live in the hill C had not slighted me,
	15:2	path across the plain and through the hill C
	15:5	and all the hill C also came, for they
	15:7	towns in the hill C and in the plain
	16:21	was honored in her time throughout the whole C
Esth	8:17	the peoples of the C declared themselves Jews, for
	16:24	"Every city and C, without exception, which does not
Ps	105:31	came swarms of flies, and gnats throughout their C
	105:33	fig trees, and shattered the trees of their C
Prov	25:25	soul, so is good news from a far C
Sir	46:9	up to the hill C, and his children obtained
Is	1:7	Your C lies desolate, your cities are burned with
	39:3	me from a far C, from Babylon."
	46:11	the man of my counsel from a far C
Jer	6:22	coming from the north C, a great nation is
	10:22	out of the north C to make the cities
	16:15	out of the north C and out of all
	17:3	high hills, on the mountains in the open C
	17:26	Shephelah, from the hill C, and from the Negeb,
	22:26	bore you into another C, where you were not
	23:8	out of the north C and out of all
	31:6	call in the hill C of Ephraim: 'Arise, and
	31:8	them from the north C, and gather them from
	31:17	your children shall come back to their own C
	32:44	cities of the hill C, in the cities of
	33:13	cities of the hill C, in the cities of
	40:7	forces in the open C and their men heard
	40:13	forces in the open C came to Gedaliah at
	46:10	sacrifice in the north C by the river Euphrates.
	50:9	nations, from the north C; and they shall array
	51:9	each to his own C; for her judgment has
Bar	3:10	old in a foreign C, that you are defiled
	6:53	a king over a C or give rain to
Ezek	20:42	land of Israel, the C which I swore to
	25:9	the glory of the C, Beth-jeshimoth, Baal-meon, and
	34:13	and in all the inhabited places of the C
	48:15	for the city, for dwellings and for open C
Hos	10:1	he built; as his C improved he improved his
Jon	1:8	What is your C
	4:2	I said when I was yet in my C
Mic	1:6	heap in the open C, a place for planting
	4:10	dwell in the open C; you shall go to
Zech	6:6	goes toward the north C, the white ones go
	6:6	go toward the west C, and the dappled ones
	6:6	and the dappled ones go toward the south C
	6:8	go toward the north C have set my Spirit
	6:8	set my Spirit at rest in the north C
	8:7	people from the east C and from the west
	8:7	and from the west C;
Mal	1:3	laid waste his hill C and left his heritage
	1:4	are called the wicked C, the people with whom
1Mac	3:29	the revenues from the C were small because of
	7:20	in charge of the C and left with him
	7:24	in the city from going out into the C
	8:8	their best provinces, the C of India and Media
	9:24	famine occurred, and the C deserted with them to
	9:25	ungodly and put them in charge of the C
	9:61	the men of the C who were leaders in
	9:65	went out into the C; and he went with
	9:69	to come into the C, and he killed many
	10:38	to Judea from the C of Samaria, let them
	10:52	gained control of our C;
	10:70	you assume authority against us in the hill C
	11:62	he passed through the C as far as Damascus.
	11:64	them, but left his brother Simon in the C
	12:25	gave them no opportunity to invade his own C
	12:33	and marched through the C as far as Askalon
	13:20	came to invade the C and destroy it, and
	13:34	grant relief to the C, for all that Trypho
	13:49	going out to the C and back to buy
	14:6	his nation, and gained full control of the C
	14:17	was ruling over the C and the cities in
	14:28	the elders of the C, the following was proclaimed
	14:29	often occurred in the C, Simon the son of
	14:31	decided to invade their C and lay hands on
	14:36	put out of the C, as were also the
	14:37	the safety of the C and of the city,
	14:42	tasks and over the C and the weapons and
	14:43	all contracts in the C should be written in
	14:44	an assembly in the C without his permission, or
	15:4	a landing in the C so that I may
	15:4	who have destroyed our C and those who have
	15:6	as money for your C,
	15:19	their cities and their C, or make alliance with
	15:21	to you from their C, hand them over to
	15:38	commander-in-chief of the coastal C, and gave him
	16:4	chose out of the C twenty thousand warriors and
	16:13	get control of the C, and made treacherous plans
	16:14	the cities of the C and attending to their
	16:18	turn over to him the cities and the C
2Mac	4:1	money against his own C, slandered Onias, saying
	5:7	fled again into the C of the Ammonites.
	5:8	the executioner of his C and his fellow citizens,
	5:9	many from their own C into exile died in
	5:15	traitor both to the laws and to his C
	8:21	their laws and their C; then he divided his
	8:35	runaway slave across the C till he reached Antioch,
	9:23	expeditions into the upper C, appointed his successor,
	13:3	the sake of his C's welfare, but because he
	13:10	the law and their C and the holy temple,
	13:14	laws, temple, city, C, and commonwealth, he pitched
	14:2	taken possession of the C, having made away with
	14:9	take thought for our C and our hard-pressed nation
	14:18	in battle for their C, shrank from deciding the
	15:19	being anxious over the encounter in the open C
Mt	2:12	departed to their own C by another way.
	8:28	other side, to the C of the Gadarenes, two
	13:54	coming to his own C he taught them in
	13:57	except in his own C and in his own
	21:33	it out to tenants, and went into another C
Mk	1:5	to him all the C of Judea, and all
	1:45	was out in the C; and people came to
	5:1	the sea, to the C of the Gerasenes.
	5:10	eagerly not to send them out of the C
	5:14	told it in the city and in the C
	6:1	came to his own C; and his disciples followed
	6:4	except in his own C, and among his own
	6:36	to go into the C and villages round about
	6:56	in villages, cities, or C, they laid the sick
	12:1	it out to tenants, and went into another C
	15:21	coming in from the C, the father of Alexander
	16:12	of them, as they were walking into the C
Lk	1:39	haste into the hill C, to a city of
	1:65	through all the hill C of Judea;
	4:14	him went out through all the surrounding C
	4:23	at Caperna-um, do here also in your own C
	4:24	you, no prophet is acceptable in his own C
	7:17	the whole of Judea and all the surrounding C
	8:26	they arrived at the C of the Gerasenes, which
	8:34	told it in the city and in the C
	8:37	people of the surrounding C of the Gerasenes asked
	9:12	into the villages and C round about, to lodge
	15:13	journey into a far C, and there he squandered
	15:14	famine arose in that C, and he began to
	15:15	the citizens of that C, who sent him into
	19:12	went into a far C to receive a kingly
	20:9	and went into another C for a long while.
	21:21	are out in the C enter it;
	23:25	coming in from the C, and laid on him
Jn	4:44	a prophet has no honor in his own C
	11:54	from there to the C near the wilderness, to
	11:55	went up from the C to Jerusalem before the
Acts	10:39	did both in the C of the Jews and
	12:20	for peace, because their C depended on the king's
	12:20	depended on the king's C for food.
	14:6	and to the surrounding C;
	19:1	passed through the upper C and came to Ephesus.
	26:20	and throughout all the C of Judea, and also

Heb 11:16 they desire a better C, that is, a heavenly

COUNTRYMEN (10)

Judg 14:16 a riddle to my C, and you have not
14:17 Then she told the riddle to her C
Tob 1:3 to my brethren and C who went with me
2Mac 4:2 protector of his fellow C, and a zealot for
4:10 at once shifted his C over to the Greek
5:6 of victory over enemies and not over fellow C
12:5 cruelty visited on his C, he gave orders to
15:30 good will toward his C, ordered them to cut
15:31 and had called his C together and stationed the
1Thes 2:14 things from your own C as they did from

COUNTRYSIDE

Ezek 27:28 of your pilots the C shakes,

COUNTS (9)

Job 19:11 wrath against me, and C me as his adversary.
33:10 occasions against me, he C me as his enemy;
41:27 He C iron as straw, and bronze as rotten
Ps 49:18 while he lives, he C himself happy, and though
Wis 14:30 overtake them on two C: because they thought
15:9 in copper; and he C it his glory that
Jer 33:13 of the one who C them, says the LORD.
1Cor 7:19 For neither circumcision C for anything nor
Gal 6:15 circumcision C for anything, nor uncircumcision, but

COUPLE (9)

Ex 26:6 clasps of gold, and C the curtains one to
26:9 And you shall C five curtains by themselves, and
26:11 into the loops, and C the tent together that
36:18 clasps of bronze to C the tent together that
Judg 19:3 his servant and a C of asses.
19:10 had with him a C of saddled asses, and
2Sam 13:6 come and make a C of cakes in my
16:1 met him, with a C of asses saddled, bearing
1Kgs 17:12 I am gathering a C of sticks, that I

COUPLED (6)

Ex 26:3 Five curtains shall be C to one another; and
26:3 five curtains shall be C to one another.
36:10 And he C five curtains to one another, and
36:10 other five curtains he C to one another.
36:13 clasps of gold, and C the curtains one to
36:16 He C five curtains by themselves, and six curtains

COURAGE (65)

Num 13:20 Be of good C, and bring some of the
Deut 31:6 strong and of good C, do not fear or
31:7 strong and of good C; for you shall go
31:23 strong and of good C; for you shall bring
Josh 1:6 strong and of good C; for you shall cause
1:9 strong and of good C; be not frightened, neither
1:18 Only be strong and of good C
2:11 and there was no C left in any man,
10:25 strong and of good C; for thus the LORD
Judg 20:22 men of Israel, took C, and again formed the
1Sam 4:9 Take C, and acquit yourselves like men, O Philistines,
2Sam 4:1 died at Hebron, his C failed, and all Israel
7:27 thy servant has found C to pray this prayer
10:12 Be of good C, and let us play the
1Chr 17:25 thy servant has found C to pray before thee.
19:13 Be of good C, and let us play the
22:13 Be strong, and of good C
28:20 strong and of good C, and do it.
2Chr 15:7 But you, take C
15:8 of Oded, he took C, and put away the
23:1 seventh year Jehoiada took C, and entered into a
25:11 But Amaziah took C, and led out his people,
32:7 to them, saying, "Be strong and of good C
Ezra 7:28 I took C, for the hand of the LORD
Jud 7:19 their God, for their C failed, because all their
7:31 said to them, "Have C, my brothers!
11:1 said to her, "Take C, woman, and do not
11:4 Have C; you will live, tonight and from now
Esth 14:12 affliction, and give me C, O King of the
15:9 Take C;
Ps 27:14 let your heart take C; yea, wait for the
31:24 let your heart take C, all you who wait
107:26 to the depths; their C melted away in their
Wis 8:7 and prudence, justice and C; nothing in life is
Is 41:6 his neighbor, and says to his brother, "Take C
Jer 4:9 day, says the LORD, C shall fail both king
Lam 1:16 one to revive my C; my children are desolate,
Bar 4:5 Take C, my people, O memorial of Israel!
4:21 "Take C, my children, cry to God, and he
4:27 "Take C, my children, and cry to God, for
4:30 Take C, O Jerusalem, for he who named you
6:59 king who shows his C, or a household utensil
Ezek 22:14 Can your C endure, or can your hands be
Dan 10:19 be with you; be strong and of good C
11:25 his power and his C against the king of
Hag 2:4 Yet now take C, O Zerubbabel, says the LORD;
2:4 says the LORD; take C, O Joshua, son of
2:4 the high priest; take C, all you people of
1Mac 11:49 as they pleased, their C failed and they cried
2Mac 6:20 go who have the C to refuse things that
6:31 and a memorial of C, not only to the
7:20 bore it with good C because of her hope
7:21 reasoning with a man's C, and said to them,
8:21 filled them with good C and made them ready
14:18 his men and their C in battle for their
15:10 he had aroused their C, he gave his orders,
15:17 fighting hand-to-hand with all C, because the city and
Mk 15:42 kingdom of God, took C and went to Pilate,
Acts 23:11 him and said, "Take C, for as you have
28:15 On seeing them Paul thanked God and took C
2Cor 5:6 are always of good C; we know that while
5:8 We are of good C, and we would rather
Phil 1:20 but that with full C now as always Christ
1Thes 2:2 you know, we had C in our God to
Heb 12:5 the Lord, nor lose C when you are punished

COURAGEOUS (7)

Josh 1:7 be strong and very C, being careful to do
2Sam 13:28 Be C and be valiant."
2Chr 17:6 His heart was C in the ways of the
Wis 8:15 show myself capable, and C in war.
Sir 28:15 Slander has driven away C women, and deprived
1Mac 2:64 My children, be C and grow strong in the
1Cor 16:13 in your faith, be C, be strong.

COURAGEOUSLY (3)

2Chr 19:11 Deal C, and may the LORD be with the
1Mac 6:45 He C ran into the midst of the phalanx
2Mac 7:10 out his tongue and C stretched forth his hands,

COURIERS (6)

2Chr 30:6 So C went throughout all Israel and Judah with
30:10 So the C went from city to city through
Esth 3:13 Letters were sent by C to all the king's
3:15 The C went in haste by order of the
8:10 were sent by mounted C riding on swift horses
8:14 So the C, mounted on their swift horses that

COURSE (25)

Gen 4:3 In the C of time Cain brought to the
38:12 In C of time the wife of Judah, Shua's
Ex 2:23 In the C of those many days the king
2Sam 14:20 order to change the C of affairs your servant
1Kgs 6:36 hewn stone and one C of cedar beams.
7:12 round about, and a C of cedar beams; so
2Chr 21:19 In C of time, at the end of two
Ezra 6:4 great stones and one C of timber; let the
Job 1:5 feast had run their C, Job would send and
6:18 turn aside from their C; they go up into
Ps 19:5 strong man runs its C with joy.
Wis 6:22 I will trace her C from the beginning of
14:3 Father, that steers its C, because thou hast given
18:14 night in its swift C was now half gone,
Sir 19:17 the law of the Most High take its C
43:5 and at his command it hastens on its C
Is 3:12 you, and confuse the C of your paths.
Jer 2:33 well you direct your C to seek lovers!
8:6 turns to his own C, like a horse plunging
23:10 Their C is evil, and their might is not
Lk 13:32 tomorrow, and the third day I finish my C
Acts 13:25 John was finishing his C, he said, 'What do
20:24 I may accomplish my C and the ministry which
21:1 came by a straight C to Cos, and the
Eph 2:2 once walked, following the C of this world, following

COURSES (5)

Judg 5:20 the stars, from their C they fought against Sisera.
1Kgs 6:36 inner court with three C of hewn stone and
7:12 great court had three C of hewn stone round
Ezra 6:4 sixty cubits, with three C of great stones and
6:18 the Levites in their C, for the service of

COURT (131)

Ex 27:9 "You shall make the C of the tabernacle.

27:9 the south side the C shall have hangings of
27:12 the breadth of the C on the west side
27:13 The breadth of the C on the front to
27:16 the gate of the C there shall be a
27:17 the pillars around the C shall be filleted with
27:18 The length of the C shall be a hundred
27:19 the pegs of the C, shall be of bronze.
35:17 the hangings of the C, its pillars and its
35:17 the gate of the C;
35:18 the pegs of the C, and their cords;
38:9 And he made the C; for the south side
38:9 the hangings of the C were of fine twined
38:15 the gate of the C were hangings of fifteen
38:16 hangings round about the C were of fine twined
38:17 the pillars of the C were filleted with silver.
38:18 the gate of the C was embroidered with needlework
38:18 its breadth, corresponding to the hangings of the C
38:20 tabernacle and for the C round about were of
38:31 bases round about the C, and the bases of
38:31 the gate of the C, all the pegs of
38:31 tabernacle, and all the pegs round about the C
39:40 the hangings of the C, its pillars, and its
39:40 the gate of the C, its cords, and its
Lev 6:16 holy place; in the C of the tent of
6:26 be eaten, in the C of the tent of
Num 3:26 the hangings of the C, the screen for the
3:26 the door of the C which is around the
3:37 the pillars of the C round about, with their
4:26 the hangings of the C, and the screen for
4:26 the gate of the C which is around the
4:32 the pillars of the C round about with their
Deut 25:1 and they come into C, and the judges decide
1Kgs 6:36 He built the inner C with three courses of
7:8 dwell, in the other C back of the hall,
7:9 coping, and from the C of the house of
7:9 the house of the LORD to the great C
7:12 The great C had three courses of hewn stone
7:12 so had the inner C of the house of
8:64 the middle of the C that was before the
2Kgs 20:4 out of the middle C, the word of the
2Chr 4:9 He made the C of the priests, and the
4:9 priests, and the great C, and doors for the
4:9 and doors for the C, and overlaid their doors
6:13 set it in the C; and he stood upon
7:7 the middle of the C that was before the
20:5 LORD, before the new C,
24:21 with stones in the C of the house of
29:16 the LORD into the C of the house of
Neh 3:25 the king at the C of the guard.
Esth 1:5 seven days, in the C of the garden of
2:11 in front of the C of the harem, to
4:11 king inside the inner C without being called, there
5:1 stood in the inner C of the king's palace,
5:2 Esther standing in the C, she found favor in
6:4 And the king said, "Who is in the C
6:4 just entered the outer C of the king's palace
6:5 told him, "Haman is there, standing in the C
11:3 man, serving in the C of the king.
12:5 to serve in the C and rewarded him for
Prov 25:8 not hastily bring into C; for what will you
Sir 50:11 altar, he made the C of the sanctuary glorious.
Jer 19:14 he stood in the C of the LORD's house,
26:2 LORD: Stand in the C of the LORD's house,
32:2 shut up in the C of the guard which
32:8 to me in the C of the guard, in
32:12 were sitting in the C of the guard.
33:1 shut up in the C of the guard:
36:10 was in the upper C, at the entry of
36:20 they went into the C to the king, having
37:21 committed Jeremiah to the C of the guard; and
37:21 Jeremiah remained in the C of the guard.
38:6 which was in the C of the guard, letting
38:13 Jeremiah remained in the C of the guard.
38:28 Jeremiah remained in the C of the guard until
39:14 took Jeremiah from the C of the guard.
39:15 shut up in the C of the guard:
Ezek 8:3 gateway of the inner C that faces north, where
8:7 the door of the C; and when I looked,
8:16 me into the inner C of the house of
10:3 went in; and a cloud filled the inner C
10:4 the cloud, and the C was full of the
10:5 far as the outer C, like the voice of
40:14 about the vestibule of the gateway was the C
40:17 me into the outer C; and behold, there were
40:17 round about the C; thirty chambers fronted on
40:19 front of the inner C, a hundred cubits.
40:20 faced toward the north, belonging to the outer C
40:23 gate to the inner C; and he measured from
40:27 south of the inner C; and he measured from
40:28 me to the inner C by the south gate,
40:31 vestibule faced the outer C, and palm trees were
40:32 me to the inner C on the east side,
40:34 vestibule faced the outer C, and it had palm
40:37 vestibule faced the outer C, and it had palm
40:44 without into the inner C, and behold, there were
40:44 chambers in the inner C, one at the side
40:47 And he measured the C, a hundred cubits long,
41:10 the chambers of the C was a breadth of
42:1 out into the inner C, toward the north, and
42:3 belonged to the inner C, and facing the pavement
42:3 belonged to the outer C, was gallery against gallery
42:6 pillars of the outer C; hence the upper chambers
42:7 toward the outer C, opposite the chambers, fifty
42:8 chambers on the outer C were fifty cubits long,
42:9 them from the outer C,
42:14 it into the outer C without laying there the
43:5 me into the inner C; and behold, the glory
44:17 gates of the inner C, they shall wear linen
44:17 gates of the inner C, and within.
44:19 out into the outer C to the people, they
44:21 shall drink wine, when he enters the inner C
44:27 place, into the inner C, to minister in the
45:19 the posts of the gate of the inner C
46:1 gate of the inner C that faces east shall
46:20 out into the outer C and so communicate holiness
46:21 forth to the outer C, and led me to
46:21 four corners of the C; and in each corner
46:21 each corner of the C there was a court--
46:21 court there was a C –
46:22 four corners of the C were small courts, forty
Dan 2:49 of Babylon; but Daniel remained at the king's C
7:10 stood before him; the C sat in judgment, and
7:26 But the C shall sit in judgment, and his
1Mac 9:54 wall of the inner C of the sanctuary.
Mt 5:25 going with him to C, lest your accuser hand
Jn 18:15 priest, he entered the C of the high priest
Acts 13:1 a member of the C of Herod the tetrarch,
1Cor 4:3 be judged by you or by any human C
Jas 2:6 is it not they who drag you into C
Rev 11:2 do not measure the C outside the temple; leave

COURTESIES (2)

Sir 6:5 multiplies friends, and a gracious tongue multiplies C
20:12 his words, but the C of fools are wasted.

COURTESY

Tit 3:2 and to show perfect C toward all men.

COURTIERS (2)

2Mac 9:29 Philip, one of his C, took his body home;
Mk 6:21 a banquet for his C and officers and the

COURTS (28)

2Kgs 21:5 heaven in the two C of the house of
23:12 made in the two C of the house of
1Chr 23:28 the care of the C and the chambers, the
28:6 my house and my C, for I have chosen
28:12 in mind for the C of the house of
2Chr 23:5 shall be in the C of the house of
33:5 heaven in the two C of the house of
Neh 8:16 roof, and in their C and in the courts
8:16 courts and in the C of the house of
13:7 a chamber in the C of the house of
Ps 65:4 choose and bring near, to dwell in thy C
84:2 yea, faints for the C of the LORD; my
84:10 a day in thy C is better than a
92:13 they flourish in the C of our God.
96:8 name; bring an offering, and come into his C
100:4 with thanksgiving, and his C with praise!
116:19 his people, in the C of the house of
135:2 the LORD, in the C of the house of
Is 1:12 who requires of you this trampling of my C
62:9 drink it in the C of my sanctuary."
Ezek 9:7 house, and fill the C with the slain.
46:22 the court were small C, forty cubits long and
46:23 each of the four C was a row of
Zech 3:7 have charge of my C, and I will give
1Mac 4:38 In the C they saw bushes sprung up as
4:48 the interior of the temple, and consecrated the C
Lk 7:25 appareled and live in luxury are in kings' C
Acts 19:38 against any one, the C are open, and there

COURTYARD (10)
2Sam 17:18 a well in his C; and they went down
Tob 2:9 the wall of the C, and my face was
Esth 12:1 his rest in the C with Gabatha and Tharra,
12:1 of the king who kept watch in the C
2Mac 14:41 the door of the C, they ordered that fire
Mt 26:58 as far as the C of the high priest,
26:69 Now Peter was sitting outside in the C
Mk 14:54 distance, right into the C of the high priest;
14:66 was below in the C, one of the maids
Lk 22:53 the middle of the C and sat down together,

COURTYARDS
Ex 8:13 of the houses and C and out of the

COUSIN (6)
Lev 25:49 his uncle, or his C may redeem him, or
Tob 7:2 young man resembles my C Tobit!"
Jer 32:8 yours.' Then Hanamel my C came to me in
32:9 Anathoth from Hanamel my C, and weighed out the
32:12 presence of Hanamel my C, in the presence of
Col 4:10 you, and Mark the C of Barnabas (concerning whom

COVENANT (344)
Gen 6:18 I will establish my C with you; and you
9:9 "Behold, I establish my C with you and your
9:11 I establish my C with you, that never again
9:12 the sign of the C which I make between
9:13 a sign of the C between me and the
9:15 I will remember my C which is between me
9:16 and remember the everlasting C between God and
9:17 the sign of the C which I have established
15:18 the LORD made a C with Abram, saying, "To
17:2 I will make my C between me and you,
17:4 to him, "Behold, my C is with you, and
17:7 I will establish my C between me and you
17:7 generations for an everlasting C, to be God to
17:9 you shall keep my C, you and your descendants
17:10 This is my C, which you shall keep, between
17:11 a sign of the C between me and you.
17:13 So shall my C be in your flesh an
17:13 my covenant be in your flesh an everlasting C
17:14 off from his people; he has broken my C
17:19 I will establish my C with him as an
17:19 him as an everlasting C for his descendants after
17:21 I will establish my C with Isaac, whom Sarah
21:27 to Abimelech, and the two men made a C
21:32 So they made a C at Beer-sheba.
26:28 let us make a C with you,
31:44 let us make a C, you and I; and
Ex 2:24 God remembered his C with Abraham, with Isaac,
6:4 I also established my C with them, to give
6:5 hold in bondage and I have remembered my C
19:5 voice and keep my C, you shall be my
23:32 You shall make no C with them or with
24:7 the book of the C, and read it in
24:8 the blood of the C which the LORD has
31:16 throughout their generations, as a perpetual C
34:10 And he said, "Behold, I make a C
34:12 lest you make a C with the inhabitants of
34:15 lest you make a C with the inhabitants of
34:27 I have made a C with you and with
34:28 the words of the C, the ten commandments.
Lev 2:13 the salt of the C with your God be
24:8 of Israel as a C for ever.
26:9 and will confirm my C with you.
26:15 commandments, but break my C,
26:25 execute vengeance for the C; and if you gather
26:42 I will remember my C with Jacob, and I
26:42 I will remember my C with Isaac and my
26:42 with Isaac and my C with Abraham, and I
26:44 utterly and break my C with them; for I
26:45 their sake remember the C with their forefathers,
Num 10:33 the ark of the C of the LORD went
14:44 the ark of the C of the LORD, nor
18:19 due; it is a C of salt for ever
25:12 give to him my C of peace;
25:13 descendants after him, the C of a perpetual
Deut 4:13 declared to you his C, which he commanded you
4:23 lest you forget the C of the LORD your
4:31 you or forget the C with your fathers which
5:2 our God made a C with us in Horeb.
5:3 the LORD make this C, but with us, who
7:2 you shall make no C with them, and show
7:9 faithful God who keeps C and steadfast love with
7:12 keep with you the C and the steadfast love
8:18 he may confirm his C which he swore to
9:9 the tables of the C which the LORD made
9:11 two tables of stone, the tables of the C
9:15 two tables of the C were in my two
10:8 the ark of the C of the LORD, to
17:2 God, in transgressing his C,
29:1 the words of the C which the LORD commanded
29:1 of Moab, besides the C which he had made
29:9 the words of this C, that you may prosper
29:12 enter into the sworn C of the LORD your
29:14 I make this sworn C,
29:19 words of this sworn C, blesses himself in his
29:21 the curses of the C written in this book
29:25 because they forsook the C of the LORD, the
31:9 the ark of the C of the LORD, and
31:16 me and break my C which I have made
31:20 serve them, and despise me and break my C
31:25 the ark of the C of the LORD,
31:26 the ark of the C of the LORD your
33:9 For they observed thy word, and kept thy C
Josh 3:3 the ark of the C of the LORD your
3:6 the ark of the C, and pass on before
3:6 the ark of the C, and went before the
3:8 the ark of the C, 'When you come to
3:11 the ark of the C of the Lord of
3:14 the ark of the C before the people,
3:17 the ark of the C of the LORD stood
4:7 the ark of the C of the LORD; when
4:9 the ark of the C had stood; and they
4:18 the ark of the C of the LORD came
6:6 the ark of the C, and let seven priests
6:8 the ark of the C of the LORD following
7:11 they have transgressed my C which I commanded
7:15 he has transgressed the C of the LORD, and
8:33 the ark of the C of the LORD, half
9:6 so now make a C with us."
9:7 can we make a C with you?"
9:11 come now, make a C with us."'
9:15 them, and made a C with them, to let
9:16 they had made a C with them, they heard
23:16 if you transgress the C of the LORD your
24:25 So Joshua made a C with the people that
Judg 2:1 will never break my C with you,
2:2 you shall make no C with the inhabitants of
2:20 people have transgressed my C which I commanded
20:27 the ark of the C of God was there
1Sam 4:3 the ark of the C of the LORD here
4:4 the ark of the C of the LORD of
4:4 the ark of the C of God.
4:5 the ark of the C of the LORD came
18:3 Then Jonathan made a C with David, because he
20:8 servant into a sacred C with you.
23:18 of them made a C before the LORD; David
2Sam 3:12 Make your C with me, and behold, my hand
3:13 I will make a C with you; but one
3:21 they may make a C with you, and that
5:3 King David made a C with them at Hebron
15:24 the ark of the C of God; and they
23:5 with me an everlasting C, ordered in all things
1Kgs 3:15 the ark of the C of the LORD, and
6:19 the ark of the C of the LORD.
8:1 the ark of the C of the LORD out
8:6 the ark of the C of the LORD to
8:9 the LORD made a C with the people of
8:21 in which is the C of the LORD which
8:23 earth beneath, keeping C and showing steadfast love
11:11 have not kept my C and my statutes which
19:10 Israel have forsaken thy C, thrown down thy altars,
19:14 Israel have forsaken thy C, thrown down thy altars,
20:34 So he made a C with him and let
2Kgs 11:4 and he made a C with them and put
11:17 And Jehoiada made a C between the LORD and
13:23 them, because of his C with Abraham, Isaac, and
17:15 his statutes, and his C that he made with
17:35 The LORD made a C with them, and commanded
17:38 shall not forget the C that I have made
18:12 God but transgressed his C, even all that Moses
23:2 the book of the C which had been found
23:3 pillar and made a C before the LORD, to
23:3 the words of this C that were written in
23:3 book; and all the people joined in the C
23:21 it is written in this book of the C
1Chr 11:3 and David made a C with them at Hebron
15:25 the ark of the C of the LORD from
15:26 the ark of the C of the LORD, they
15:28 the ark of the C of the LORD with

15:29 the ark of the C of the LORD came
16:6 the ark of the C of God.
16:15 is mindful of his C for ever, of the
16:16 a thousand generations, the C which he made with
16:17 Jacob, as an everlasting C to Israel,
16:37 the ark of the C of the LORD to
17:1 the ark of the C of the LORD is
22:19 the ark of the C of the LORD and
28:2 the ark of the C of the LORD, and
28:18 the ark of the C of the LORD.
2Chr 5:2 the ark of the C of the LORD out
5:7 the ark of the C of the LORD to
5:10 the LORD made a C with the people of
6:11 in which is the C of the LORD which
6:14 or on earth, keeping C and showing steadfast love
13:5 his sons by a C of salt?
15:12 they entered into a C to seek the LORD,
21:7 David, because of the C which he had made
23:3 the assembly made a C with the king in
23:16 And Jehoiada made a C between himself and all
29:10 heart to make a C with the LORD, the
34:30 the book of the C which had been found
34:31 place and made a C before the LORD, to
34:31 the words of the C that were written in
34:32 did according to the C of God, the God
Ezra 10:3 let us make a C with our God to
Neh 1:5 terrible God who keeps C and steadfast love with
9:8 make with him the C to give to his
9:32 terrible God, who keepest C and steadfast love, let
9:38 we make a firm C and write it, and
13:29 the priesthood and the C of the priesthood and
Jud 9:13 cruel things against thy C, and against thy
Job 31:1 "I have made a C with my eyes; how
41:4 Will he make a C with you to take
Ps 25:10 those who keep his C and his testimonies.
25:14 him, and he makes known to them his C
44:17 not forgotten thee, or been false to thy C
50:5 ones, who made a C with me by sacrifice!"
50:16 statutes, or take my C on your lips?
55:20 his hand against his friends, he violated his C
74:20 Have regard for thy C; for the dark places
78:10 did not keep God's C, but refused to walk
78:37 toward him; they were not true to his C
83:5 thee they make a C --
89:3 "I have made a C with my chosen one,
89:28 for ever, and my C will stand firm for
89:34 will not violate my C, or alter the word
89:39 Thou hast renounced the C with thy servant; thou
103:18 those who keep his C and remember to do
105:8 is mindful of his C for ever, of the
105:9 a thousand generations, the C which he made with
105:10 Israel as an everlasting C,
106:45 for their sake his C, and relented according to
111:5 fear him; he is ever mindful of his C
111:9 he has commanded his C for ever.
132:12 your sons keep my C and my testimonies which
Prov 2:17 youth and forgets the C of her God;
Wis 1:16 and they made a C with him, because they
Sir 11:18 Stand by your C and attend to it, and
16:20 For the C is far-off."
17:10 with them an eternal C, and showed them his
24:22 the book of the C of the Most High
28:7 your neighbor; remember the C of the Most High,
39:8 will glory in the law of the Lord's C
41:19 ashamed before the truth of God and his C
42:2 Most High and his C, and of rendering judgment
44:21 and was taken into C with him; he established
44:21 him; he established the C in his flesh, and
44:24 all men and the C he made to rest
45:5 to teach Jacob the C, and Israel his judgments.
45:7 He made an everlasting C with him, and gave
45:15 it was an everlasting C for him and for
45:24 Therefore a C of peace was established with him,
45:25 A C was also established with David, the son
47:11 he gave him the C of kings and a
Is 24:5 laws, violated the statutes, broken the everlasting C
28:15 "We have made a C with death, and with
28:18 Then your C with death will be annulled, and
42:6 given you as a C to the people, a
49:8 given you as a C to the people, to
54:10 from you, and my C of peace shall not
55:3 with you an everlasting C, my steadfast, sure love
56:4 and hold fast my C,
56:6 and holds fast my C --
59:21 me, this is my C with them, says the
61:8 will make an everlasting C with them.
Jer 3:16 "The ark of the C of the LORD." It
11:2 the words of this C, and speak to the
11:3 the words of this C
11:6 the words of this C and do them.
11:8 the words of this C, which I commanded them
11:10 Judah have broken my C which I made with
14:21 do not break thy C with us.
22:9 "Because they forsook the C of the LORD their
31:31 will make a new C with the house of
31:32 Judah, not like the C which I made with
31:32 land of Egypt, my C which they broke, though
31:33 But this is the C which I will make
32:40 with them an everlasting C, that I will not
33:20 you can break my C with the day and
33:20 the day and my C with the night, so
33:21 time, then also my C with David my servant
33:21 his throne, and my C with the Levitical priests
33:25 have not established my C with day and night
34:8 Zedekiah had made a C with all the people
34:10 had entered into the C that every one would
34:13 Israel: I made a C with your fathers when
34:15 and you made a C before me in the
34:18 men who transgressed my C and did not keep
34:18 the terms of the C which they made before
50:5 LORD in an everlasting C which will never be
Bar 2:35 will make an everlasting C with them to be
Ezek 16:8 and entered into a C with you, says the
16:59 oath in breaking the C,
16:60 I will remember my C with you in the
16:60 and I will establish with you an everlasting C
16:61 on account of the C with you.
16:62 I will establish my C with you, and you
17:13 royal and made a C with him, putting him
17:14 that by keeping his C it might stand.)
17:15 Can he break the C and yet escape?
17:16 he despised, and whose C with him he broke,
17:18 oath and broke the C, because he gave his
17:19 he despised, and my C which he broke, I
34:25 make with them a C of peace and banish
37:26 I will make a C of peace with them;
37:26 shall be an everlasting C with them; and I
44:7 You have broken my C, in addition to all
Dan 3:34 do not break thy C,
9:4 terrible God, who keepest C and steadfast love with
9:27 shall make a strong C with many for one
11:22 the prince of the C also.
11:28 his heart shall be set against the holy C
11:30 be enraged and take action against the holy C
11:30 give heed to those who forsake the holy C
11:32 those who violate the C; but the people who
Hos 2:18 make for you a C on that day with
6:7 Adam they transgressed the C; there they dealt
8:1 they have broken my C, and transgressed my law.
Amos 1:9 did not remember the C of brotherhood.
Zech 9:11 the blood of my C with you, I will
11:10 broke it, annulling the C which I had made
Mal 2:4 to you, that my C with Levi may hold,
2:5 My C with him was a covenant of life
2:5 with him was a C of life and peace,
2:8 you have corrupted the C of Levi, says the
2:10 one another, profaning the C of our fathers?
2:14 was witness to the C between you and the
2:14 she is your companion and your wife by C
3:1 the messenger of the C in whom you delight,
1Mac 1:11 go and make a C with the Gentiles round
1:15 the marks of circumcision, and abandoned the holy C
1:57 the book of the C was found in the
1:63 to profane the holy C; and they did die.
2:20 will live by the C of our fathers.
2:27 law and supports the C come out with me!"
2:50 your lives for the C of our fathers.
2:54 zealous, received the C of everlasting priesthood.
4:10 us and remember his C with our fathers and
11:9 let us make a C with each other, and
2Mac 1:2 may he remember his C with Abraham and Isaac
7:36 everflowing life under God's C; but you, by the
14:20 were of one mind, they agreed to the C
14:26 another, he took the C that had been made
14:27 was displeased with the C and commanding him to
Mt 26:28 my blood of the C, which is poured out
Mk 14:24 my blood of the C, which is poured out
Lk 1:72 to remember his holy C,
22:20 you is the new C in my blood.
Acts 3:25 prophets and of the C which God gave to
7:8 he gave him the C of circumcision.
Rom 11:27 this will be my C with them when I

1Cor 11:25 cup is the new C in my blood.
2Cor 3:6 ministers of a new C, not in a written
3:14 they read the old C, that same veil remains
Gal 3:17 does not annul a C previously ratified by God,
Heb 7:22 This makes Jesus the surety of a better C
8:6 the old as the C he mediates is better,
8:7 For if that first C had been faultless, there
8:8 will establish a new C with the house of
8:9 Judah; not like the C that I made with
8:9 not continue in my C, and so I paid
8:10 This is the C that I will make with
8:13 speaking of a new C he treats the first
9:1 Now even the first C had regulations for worship
9:4 the ark of the C covered on all sides
9:4 the tables of the C;
9:15 mediator of a new C, so that those who
9:15 them from the transgressions under the first C
9:18 Hence even the first C was not ratified without
9:20 the blood of the C which God commanded you."
10:16 saying, "This is the C that I will make
10:29 the blood of the C by which he was
12:24 mediator of a new C, and to the sprinkled
13:20 blood of the eternal C,
Rev 11:19 the ark of his C was seen within his

COVENANTED (2)

2Chr 7:18 royal throne, as I C with David your father,
Esth 14:8 slavery, but they have C with their idols

COVENANTS (10)

Wis 12:21 thou gavest oaths and C full of good promises!
18:22 to the oaths and C given to our fathers.
Sir 44:13 descendants stand by the C; their children also, for
44:19 Everlasting C were made with him that all flesh
Is 33:8 C are broken, witnesses are despised, there is no
Hos 10:4 empty oaths they make C; so judgment springs up
2Mac 8:15 the sake of the C made with their fathers,
Rom 9:4 sonship, the glory, the C, the giving of the
Gal 4:24 this is an allegory: these women are two C
Eph 2:12 and strangers to the C of promise, having no

COVER (78)

Gen 6:14 in the ark, and C it inside and out
Ex 10:5 country, and they shall C the face of the
15:5 The floods C them; they went down into the
21:33 pit and does not C it, and an ox
26:13 and that side, to C it.
28:42 them linen breeches to C their naked flesh; from
33:22 rock, and I will C you with my hand
Lev 13:45 loose, and he shall C his upper lip and
16:13 of the incense may C the mercy seat which
17:13 out its blood and C it with dust.
Num 4:5 of the screen, and C the ark of the
4:8 cloth of scarlet, and C the same with a
4:9 cloth of blue, and C the lampstand for the
4:11 cloth of blue, and C it with a covering
4:12 cloth of blue, and C them with a covering
19:15 vessel, which has no C fastened upon it, is
22:5 out of Egypt; they C the face of the
Deut 22:12 cloak with which you C yourself.
23:13 and turn back and C up your excrement.
Josh 24:7 come upon them and C them; and your eyes
1Sam 25:20 and came down under C of the mountain, behold,
1Kgs 7:18 the one network, to C the capital that was
7:41 the two networks to C the two bowls of
7:42 for each network, to C the two bowls of
2Chr 4:12 the two networks to C the two bowls of
4:13 for each network, to C the two bowls of
Neh 4:5 Do not C their guilt, and let not their
Jud 2:7 my anger, and will C the whole face of
2:19 King Nebuchadnezzar and to C the whole face of
Job 14:17 bag, and thou wouldest C over my iniquity.
16:18 "O earth, C not my blood, and let my
21:26 dust, and the worms C them.
38:34 flood of waters may C you?
40:22 shade the lotus trees C him; the willows of
Ps 5:12 O LORD; thou dost C him with favor as
27:5 conceal me under the C of his tent, he
91:4 deadly pestilence; he will C you with his pinions,
104:6 Thou didst C it with the deep as with
104:9 they might not again C the earth.
139:11 say, "Let only darkness C me, and the light
Wis 5:16 right hand he will C them, and with his
Sir 29:21 and a house to C one's nakedness.
37:3 were you formed to C the land with deceit?
Is 11:9 LORD as the waters C the sea.
26:21 and will no more C her slain.
58:7 see the naked, to C him, and not to
59:6 clothing; men will not C themselves with what they
60:2 For behold, darkness shall C the earth, and thick
60:6 multitude of camels shall C you, the young camels
Jer 3:25 and let our dishonor C us; for we have
14:3 ashamed and confounded and C their heads.
14:4 farmers are ashamed, they C their heads.
46:8 will rise, I will C the earth, I will
Bar 6:68 they can flee to C and help themselves.
Ezek 12:6 the dark; you shall C your face, that you
12:12 through it; he shall C his face, that he
16:18 your embroidered garments to C them, and set my
24:7 upon the ground to C it with dust.
24:17 your feet; do not C your lips, nor eat
24:22 done; you shall not C your lips, nor eat
26:10 that their dust will C you; your walls will
26:19 and the great waters C you,
32:7 you out, I will C the heavens, and make
32:7 stars dark; I will C the sun with a
37:6 come upon you, and C you with skin, and
Hos 2:9 flax, which were to C her nakedness.
10:8 say to the mountains, C us, and to the
Obad 1:10 brother Jacob, shame shall C you, and you shall
Mic 3:7 shame; they shall all C their lips, for there
7:10 see, and shame will C her who said to
Hab 2:14 LORD, as the waters C the sea.
Zech 5:7 And behold, the leaden C was lifted, and there
Mal 2:13 You C the LORD's altar with tears, with weeping
1Mac 9:38 up and hid under C of the mountain.
Mk 14:65 on him, and to C his face, and to
Lk 23:29 and to the hills, C us.'
1Cor 11:7 man ought not to C his head, since he
Jas 5:20 from death and will C a multitude of sins.

COVERED (86)

Gen 7:19 the whole heaven were C;
9:23 and walked backward and C the nakedness of their
24:65 took her veil and C herself.
38:15 harlot, for she had C her face.
Ex 8:6 frogs came up and C the land of Egypt.
10:15 For they C the face of the whole land,
14:28 The waters returned and C the chariots and the
15:10 thy wind, the sea C them; they sank as
16:13 quails came up and C the camp; and in
24:15 mountain, and the cloud C the mountain.
24:16 Sinai, and the cloud C it six days; and
Lev 13:13 if the leprosy has C all his body, he
Num 7:3 before the LORD, six C wagons and twelve oxen,
9:15 set up, the cloud C the tabernacle, the tent
9:16 was continually; the cloud C it by day, and
16:42 and behold, the cloud C it, and the glory
Judg 4:18 the tent, and she C him with a rug.
4:19 him a drink and C him.
1Sam 19:13 at its head, and C it with the clothes.
2Sam 15:30 and with his head C; and all the people
15:30 who were with him C their heads, and they
19:4 The king C his face, and the king cried
19:5 said, "You have today C with shame the faces
1Kgs 1:1 years, and although they C him with clothes, he
6:15 of the ceiling, he C them on the inside
6:15 with wood; and he C the floor of the
6:32 He C the two doors of olivewood with carvings
7:3 And it was C with cedar above the chambers
2Kgs 3:25 stone, until it was C; they stopped every spring
16:18 And the C way for the sabbath which had
19:1 rent his clothes, and C himself with sackcloth, and
19:2 and the senior priests, C with sackcloth, to the
1Chr 28:18 spread their wings and C the ark of the
2Chr 3:5 lined with cypress, and C it with fine gold,
Neh 3:15 he rebuilt it and C it and set its
Jud 7:18 in the plain, and C the whole face of
16:4 the valleys, their cavalry C the hills.
Esth 6:12 to his house, mourning and with his head C
7:8 of the king, they C Haman's face.
14:2 of costly perfumes she C her head with ashes
14:2 loved to adorn she C with her tangled hair.
15:6 of his majesty, all C with gold and precious
Job 15:27 shield; because he has C his face with his
Ps 32:1 he whose transgression is forgiven, whose sin is C
44:15 me, and shame has C my face,
44:19 place of jackals, and C us with deep darkness.
68:13 wings of a dove C with silver, its pinions
69:7 reproach, that shame has C my face.
71:13 disgrace may they be C who seek my hurt.
80:10 The mountains were C with its shade, the mighty

89:45 his youth; thou hast C him with shame.
106:11 And the waters C their adversaries; not one of
106:17 swallowed up Dathan, and C the company of Abiram.
140:7 strong deliverer, thou hast C my head in the
Prov 24:31 thorns; the ground was C with nettles, and its
26:26 though his hatred be C with guile, his wickedness
Eccl 6:4 darkness its name is C;
Sir 16:28 of living beings he C its surface, and to
24:3 the Most High, and C the earth like a
47:15 Your soul C the earth, and you filled it
48:12 was Elijah who was C by the whirlwind, and
Is 6:2 wings: with two he C his face, and with
6:2 and with two he C his feet, and with
29:10 eyes, the prophets, and C your heads, the seers.
37:1 rent his clothes, and C himself with sackcloth, and
61:10 of salvation, he has C me with the robe
Jer 51:42 on Babylon; she is C with its tumultuous waves.
51:51 heard reproach; dishonor has C our face, for aliens
Ezek 1:11 of another, while two C their bodies.
16:8 skirt over you, and C your nakedness: yea, I
16:10 in fine linen and C you with silk.
24:8 she has shed, that it may not be C
30:18 end; she shall be C by a cloud, and
37:8 them, and skin had C them; but there was
41:16 (now the windows were C,
Jon 3:6 removed his robe, and C himself with sackcloth, and
3:8 man and beast be C with sackcloth, and let
Hab 3:3 His glory C the heavens, and the earth was
1Mac 6:37 wooden towers, strong and C; they were fastened
2Mac 6:5 The altar was C with abominable offerings which
Mt 10:26 them; for nothing is C that will not be
13:44 a man found and C up; then in his
Lk 12:2 Nothing is C up that will not be revealed,
Rom 4:7 and whose sins are C;
1Cor 11:4 prophesies with his head C dishonors his head,
Heb 9:4 ark of the covenant C on all sides with

COVEREST

Ps 104:2 honor and majesty, who C thyself with light as

COVERING (42)

Gen 7:20 prevailed above the mountains, C them fifteen cubits
8:13 and Noah removed the C of the ark, and
Ex 22:27 that is his only C, it is his mantle
26:14 for the tent a C of tanned rams' skins
35:11 its tent and its C, its hooks and its
36:19 for the tent a C of tanned rams' skins
39:34 and its bases; the C of tanned rams' skins
Lev 3:3 shall offer the fat C the entrails and all
3:14 the LORD, the fat C the entrails, and all
Num 3:25 the tent with its C, the screen for the
4:6 put on it a C of goatskin, and spread
4:8 the same with a C of goatskin, and shall
4:10 its utensils in a C of goatskin and put
4:11 cover it with a C of goatskin, and shall
4:12 cover them with a C of goatskin, and put
4:14 spread upon it a C of goatskin, and shall
4:15 his sons have finished C the sanctuary and all
4:25 of meeting with its C, and the covering of
4:25 its covering, and the C of goatskin that is
16:38 hammered plates as a C for the altar, for
16:39 hammered out as a C for the altar,
2Sam 17:19 took and spread a C over the well's mouth,
1Kgs 8:7 the cherubim made a C above the ark and
2Chr 5:8 the cherubim made a C above the ark and
Job 24:7 clothing, and have no C in the cold.
26:6 is naked before God, and Abaddon has no C
31:19 a poor man without C;
Ps 18:11 He made darkness his C around him, his canopy
105:39 a cloud for a C, and fire to give
Prov 26:23 Like the glaze C an earthen vessel are smooth
Wis 13:14 its surface red and C every blemish in it
Is 14:11 the bed beneath you, and worms are your C
22:8 has taken away the C of Judah.
25:7 on this mountain the C that is cast over
28:20 on it, and the C too narrow to wrap
50:3 heavens with blackness, and make sackcloth their C
Ezek 1:23 creature had two wings C its body.
28:13 precious stone was your C, carnelian, topaz, and
38:9 be like a cloud C the land you and
38:16 Israel, like a cloud C the land.
Mal 2:16 God of Israel, and C one's garment with violence,
1Cor 11:15 her hair is given to her for a C

COVERINGS (2)

Prov 7:16 decked my couch with C, colored spreads of
31:22 She makes herself C; her clothing is fine linen

COVERLET

2Kgs 8:15 morrow he took the C and dipped it in

COVERS (25)

Ex 29:13 all the fat that C the entrails, and the
29:22 and the fat that C the entrails, and the
Lev 3:9 and the fat that C the entrails, and all
4:8 it, the fat that C the entrails and all
7:3 tail, the fat that C the entrails,
9:19 tail, and that which C the entrails, and the
13:12 so that the leprosy C all the skin of
Num 22:11 of Egypt, and it C the face of the
Job 9:24 of the wicked; he C the faces of its
22:11 a flood of water C you.
23:17 darkness, and thick darkness C my face.
26:9 He C the face of the moon, and spreads
36:30 lightning about him, and C the roots of the
36:32 He C his hands with the lightning, and commands
Ps 73:6 is their necklace; violence C them as a garment.
84:6 the early rain also C it with pools.
147:8 He C the heavens with clouds, he prepares rain
Prov 10:12 up strife, but love C all offenses.
Sir 39:22 His blessing C the dry land like a river,
40:27 garden of blessing, and C a man better than
Ezek 7:18 with sackcloth, and horror C them; shame is upon
18:7 to the hungry and C the naked with a
18:16 to the hungry and C the naked with a
Lk 8:16 after lighting a lamp C it with a vessel,
1Pet 4:8 one another, since love C a multitude of sins.

COVERT (7)

Job 38:40 their dens, or lie in wait in their C
40:21 he lies, in the C of the reeds and
Ps 10:9 a lion in his C; he lurks that he
31:20 In the C of thy presence thou hidest them
Song 2:14 the rock, in the C of the cliff, let
Is 32:2 from the wind, a C from the tempest, like
Jer 25:38 he has left his C, for their land has

COVET (9)

Ex 20:17 "You shall not C your neighbor's house; you shall
20:17 house; you shall not C your neighbor's wife, or
Deut 5:21 "'Neither shall you C your neighbor's wife; and you
7:25 fire; you shall not C the silver or the
Mic 2:2 They C fields, and seize them; and houses, and
Rom 7:7 what it is to C if the law had
7:7 the law had not said, "You shall not C
13:9 kill, You shall not steal, You shall not C
Jas 4:2 And you C and cannot obtain; so you fight

COVETED (3)

Josh 7:21 fifty shekels, then I C them, and took them;
1Mac 11:11 on Alexander because he C his kingdom.
Acts 20:33 I C no one's silver or gold or apparel.

COVETING

Mk 7:21 fornication, theft, murder, adultery, C, wickedness,

COVETOUS (2)

Wis 10:11 When his oppressors were C, she stood by him
Eph 5:5 or one who is C (that is, an idolater),

COVETOUSNESS (6)

Is 57:17 the iniquity of his C I was angry, I
Lk 12:15 and beware of all C; for a man's life
Rom 1:29 manner of wickedness, evil, C, malice.
7:8 the commandment, wrought in me all kinds of C
Eph 5:3 and all impurity or C must not even be
Col 3:5 passion, evil desire, and C, which is idolatry.

COVETS (2)

Ps 34:12 who desires life, and C many days, that he
Prov 21:26 day long the wicked C, but the righteous gives

COW (7)

Ex 34:19 cattle, the firstlings of C and sheep.
Lev 22:28 the mother is a C or a ewe, you
Num 18:17 the firstling of a C, or the firstling of
Job 21:10 breeds without fail; their C calves, and does not
Is 7:21 keep alive a young C and two sheep;
11:7 The C and the bear shall feed; their young
Ezek 4:15 will let you have C's dung instead of human

C

C

COWARD (2)
Sir 34:14 timid, nor play the C, for he is his
37:11 rival or with a C about war, with a

COWARDICE (2)
Sir 4:17 will bring fear and C upon him, and will
1Mac 4:32 Fill them with C; melt the boldness of their

COWARDLY (3)
Wis 17:11 For wickedness is a C thing, condemned by its
2Mac 8:13 army, those who were C and distrustful of God's
Rev 21:8 But as for the C, the faithless, the polluted,

COWER (2)
Sir 32:18 proud man will not C in fear.
Lam 3:16 gravel, and made me C in ashes;

COWS (18)
Gen 32:15 and their colts, forty C and ten bulls, twenty
41:2 of the Nile seven C sleek and fat, and
41:3 And behold, seven other C, gaunt and thin, came
41:3 stood by the other C on the bank of
41:4 the gaunt and thin C ate up the seven
41:4 cows ate up the seven sleek and fat C
41:18 the Nile; and seven C, fat and sleek, came
41:19 grass; and seven other C came up after them,
41:20 the thin and gaunt C ate up the first
41:20 the first seven fat C,
41:26 The seven good C are seven years, and the
41:27 seven lean and gaunt C that came up after
1Sam 6:7 cart and two milch C upon which there has
6:7 yoke, and yoke the C to the cart, but
6:10 and took two milch C and yoked them to
6:12 And the C went straight in the direction of
6:14 cart and offered the C as a burnt offering
Amos 4:1 "Hear this word, you C of Bashan, who are

COZBI (2)
Num 25:15 who was slain was C the daughter of Zur,
25:18 in the matter of C, the daughter of the

COZEBA
1Chr 4:22 and the men of C, and Joash, and Saraph,

CRACK
Nah 3:2 The C of whip, and rumble of wheel, galloping

CRACKLING (2)
Eccl 7:6 For as the C of thorns under a pot,
Joel 2:5 the mountains, like the C of a flame of

CRAFT (5)
Ex 31:5 and in carving wood, for work in every C
35:33 in carving wood, for work in every skilled C
Esth 16:13 life, and with intricate C and deceit asked for
Is 2:16 ships of Tarshish, and against all the beautiful C
Rev 18:22 a craftsman of any C shall be found in

CRAFTILY (2)
Ps 105:25 his people, to deal C with his servants.
Acts 7:19 He dealt C with our race and forced our

CRAFTINESS (4)
Job 5:13 wise in their own C; and the schemes of
Lk 20:23 But he perceived their C, and said to them,
1Cor 3:19 is written, "He catches the wise in their C
Eph 4:14 of men, by their C in deceitful wiles.

CRAFTS
Wis 7:16 hand, as are all understanding and skill in C

CRAFTSMAN (14)
Ex 35:35 work done by a C or by a designer
38:23 tribe of Dan, a C and designer and embroiderer
Deut 27:15 the hands of a C, and sets it up
Wis 13:1 did they recognize the C while paying heed to
14:2 and wisdom was the C who built it;
14:18 the ambition of the C impelled even those who
Sir 38:27 So too is every C and master workman who
45:11 the work of a C; with precious stones engraved
Is 40:20 seeks out a skilful C to set up an
41:7 The C encourages the goldsmith, and he who
Jer 10:3 with an axe by the hands of a C
10:9 the work of the C and of the hands
Bar 6:8 are smoothed by the C, and they themselves are
Rev 18:22 no more; and a C of any craft shall

CRAFTSMANSHIP (2)
Ex 31:3 with knowledge and all C,
35:31 knowledge, and with all C,

CRAFTSMEN (16)
2Kgs 24:14 captives, and all the C and the smiths; none
24:16 seven thousand, and the C and the smiths, one
1Chr 4:14 of Ge-harashim, so-called because they were C
22:15 and all kinds of C without number, skilled in
29:5 to be done by C, gold for the things
2Chr 2:14 assigned him, with your C, the craftsmen of my
2:14 with your craftsmen, the C of my lord, David
Neh 11:35 Zeboim, Neballat, Lod, and Ono, the valley of C
Sir 9:17 the skill of the C; so a people's leader
Is 44:11 to shame, and the C are but men; let
Jer 24:1 princes of Judah, the C, and the smiths, and
29:2 Judah and Jerusalem, the C, and the smiths had
Bar 6:45 nothing but what the C wish them to be.
Hos 13:2 their silver, all of them the work of C
Acts 19:24 of Artemis, brought no little business to the C
19:38 therefore Demetrius and the C with him have a

CRAFTY (7)
2Sam 13:3 Jonadab was a very C man.
Job 5:12 the devices of the C, so that their hands
15:5 mouth, and you choose the tongue of the C
Ps 83:3 They lay C plans against thy people; they consult
Sir 11:27 home, for many are the wiles of the C
42:18 men, and considers their C devices.
2Cor 12:16 burden you, I was C, you say, and got

CRAG (4)
1Sam 14:4 there was a rocky C on the one side
14:4 side and a rocky C on the other side;
14:5 The one C rose on the north in front
Job 39:28 his home in the fastness of the rocky C

CRAGS (2)
Jer 18:14 of Lebanon leave the C of Sirion?
51:25 you down from the C, and make you a

CRAMPING
Job 36:16 where there was no C, and what was set

CRANE (2)
Is 38:14 a swallow or a C I clamor, I moan
Jer 8:7 the turtledove, swallow, and C keep the time of

CRASH (7)
Job 30:14 they come; amid the C they roll on.
Ps 77:18 The C of thy thunder was in the whirlwind;
Wis 17:19 water, or the harsh C of rocks hurled down,
Sir 40:13 like a torrent, and C like a loud clap
Is 30:13 about to collapse, whose C comes suddenly, in an
37:26 should make fortified cities C into heaps of ruins,
Zeph 1:10 Second Quarter, a loud C from the hills.

CRASHING (2)
Job 36:33 Its C declares concerning him, who is jealous with
41:25 are afraid; at the C they are beside themselves.

CRATES
2Mac 4:29 high-priesthood, while Sostratus left C, the

CRAVE
Deut 12:20 eat flesh,' because you C flesh, you may eat

CRAVED (2)
Ps 78:18 in their heart by demanding the food they C
78:29 well filled, for he gave them what they C

CRAVES (2)
Deut 14:26 drink, whatever your appetite C; and you shall eat
Prov 13:4 soul of the sluggard C, and gets nothing, while

CRAVING (8)
Num 11:4 them had a strong C; and the people of
11:34 there they buried the people who had the C
Ps 78:30 they had sated their C, while the food was
106:14 they had a wanton C in the wilderness, and
Prov 10:3 but he thwarts the C of the wicked.
Is 32:6 LORD, to leave the C of the hungry unsatisfied,
1Tim 6:4 he has a morbid C for controversy and for
6:10 it is through this C that some have wandered

CRAWLING (3)
Deut 32:24 them, with venom of C things of the dust.
Mic 7:17 a serpent, like the C things of the earth;
Hab 1:14 of the sea, like C things that have no

CRAWLS
Lev 11:44 any swarming thing that C upon the earth.

CRAZED
Jer 25:16 and stagger and be C because of the sword

CREATE (12)
Ps 51:10 C in me a clean heart, O God, and
Sir 36:15 those whom thou didst C in the beginning, and
Is 4:5 Then the LORD will C over the whole site
45:7 I form light and C darkness, I make weal
45:7 I make weal and C woe, I am the
45:18 it; he did not C it a chaos, he
65:17 "For behold, I C new heavens and a new
65:18 in that which I C; for behold, I create
65:18 create; for behold, I C Jerusalem a rejoicing, and
Rom 16:17 note of those who C dissensions and difficulties, in
Eph 2:15 ordinances, that he might C in himself one new
Rev 4:11 power, for thou didst C all things, and by

CREATED (81)
Gen 1:1 IN the beginning God C the heavens and the
1:21 So God C the great sea monsters and every
1:27 So God C man in his own image, in
1:27 image of God he C him; male and female
1:27 male and female he C them.
2:4 the heavens and the earth when they were C
5:1 When God C man, he made him in the
5:2 Male and female he C them, and he blessed
5:2 them and named them Man when they were C
6:7 man whom I have C from the face of
Deut 4:32 the day that God C man upon the earth,
32:6 he your father, who C you, who made you
Jud 13:18 the Lord God, who C the heavens and the
Ps 89:12 the south, thou hast C them; Tabor and Hermon
89:47 what vanity thou hast C all the sons of
104:30 thy Spirit, they are C; and thou renewest the
148:5 For he commanded and they were C
Prov 8:22 The LORD C me at the beginning of his
Wis 1:14 For he C all things that they might exist,
2:23 blameless souls; for God C man for incorruption, and
10:1 he alone had been C; she delivered him from
11:17 thy all-powerful hand, which C the world out of
11:18 bold lions, or newly C unknown beasts full of
13:3 the author of beauty C them.
13:5 greatness and beauty of C things comes a
14:11 part of what God C, they became an abomination,
Sir 1:4 Wisdom was C before all things, and prudent
1:7 The Lord himself C wisdom; he saw her and
1:12 of wisdom she is C with the faithful in
7:15 farm work, which were C by the Most High.
10:18 Pride was not C for men, nor fierce anger
15:14 It was he who C man in the beginning,
17:1 The Lord C man out of earth, and turned
18:1 who lives for ever C the whole universe;
23:20 Before the universe was C, it was known to
24:8 and the one who C me assigned a place
24:9 in the beginning, he C me, and for eternity
31:13 What has been C more greedy than the eye?
31:27 It has been C to make men glad.
33:10 ground, and Adam was C of the dust.
38:1 him, for the Lord C him;
38:4 The Lord C medicines from the earth, and a
38:12 place, for the Lord C him; let him not
39:21 for everything has been C for its use.
39:25 beginning good things were C for good people, just
39:28 winds that have been C for vengeance, and in
39:29 all these have been C for vengeance;
40:1 Much labor was C for every man, and a
40:10 All these were C for the wicked, and on
49:14 like Enoch has been C on earth, for he
Is 40:26 high and see: who C these?
41:20 One of Israel has C it.
42:5 God, the LORD, who C the heavens and stretched
43:1 the LORD, he who C you, O Jacob, he
43:7 my name, whom I C for my glory, whom
45:8 I the LORD have C it.
45:12 made the earth, and C man upon it; it
45:18 says the LORD, who C the heavens (he is
48:7 They are C now, not long ago; before today
54:16 Behold, I have C the smith who blows the
54:16 I have also C the ravager to destroy;
Jer 31:22 For the LORD has C a new thing on
Ezek 21:30 place where you were C, in the land of
28:13 day that you were C they were prepared.
28:15 the day you were C, till iniquity was found
Dan 14:5 the living God, who C heaven and earth and
Mal 2:10 Has not one God C us?
2Mac 14:17 of the sudden consternation C by the enemy.
Mk 13:19 the creation which God C until now, and never
1Cor 11:9 Neither was man C for woman, but woman for
Eph 2:10 we are his workmanship, C in Christ Jesus for
3:9 ages in God who C all things;
4:24 on the new nature, C after the likeness of
Col 1:16 him all things were C, in heaven and on
1:16 authorities--all things were C through him and for
1Tim 4:3 from foods which God C to be received with
4:4 For everything C by God is good, and nothing
Heb 1:2 through whom also he C the world.
11:3 that the world was C by the word of
Rev 4:11 and by thy will they existed and were C
10:6 ever and ever, who C heaven and what is

CREATES (2)
Num 16:30 But if the LORD C something new, and the
Amos 4:13 forms the mountains, and C the wind, and declares

CREATING
Is 57:18 requite him with comfort, C for his mourners the

CREATION (28)
Gen 2:3 all his work which he had done in C
Jud 9:12 King of all thy C, hear my prayer!
Wis 2:6 make use of the C to the full as
5:17 and will arm all C to repel his enemies;
5:20 for a sword, and C will join with him
6:22 from the beginning of C, and make knowledge of
16:24 For C, serving thee who hast made it, exerts
19:6 For the whole C in its nature was fashioned
Sir 16:15 for what is my soul in the boundless C
16:24 the beginning by his C, and when he made
49:16 and Adam above every living being in the C
Hab 2:18 trusts in his own C when he makes dumb
Mk 10:6 from the beginning of C, 'God made them male
13:19 the beginning of the C which God created until
16:15 world and preach the gospel to the whole C
Rom 1:20 Ever since the C of the world his invisible
8:19 For the C waits with eager longing for the
8:20 of God; for the C was subjected to futility,
8:21 in hope; because the C itself will be set
8:22 know that the whole C has been groaning in
8:23 and not only the C, but we ourselves, who
8:39 anything else in all C, will be able to
2Cor 5:17 he is a new C; the old has passed
Gal 6:15 counts for anything, nor uncircumcision, but a new C
Col 1:15 the first-born of all C;
Heb 9:11 is, not of this C
2Pet 3:4 continued as they were from the beginning of C
Rev 3:14 faithful and true witness, the beginning of God's C

CREATOR (13)
Jud 9:12 of heaven and earth, C of the waters, King
Eccl 12:1 Remember also your C in the days of your
Wis 13:5 things comes a corresponding perception of their C
Sir 4:6 curse upon you, his C will hear his prayer.
24:8 Then the C of all things gave me a
Is 40:28 the everlasting God, the C of the ends of
43:15 your Holy One, the C of Israel, your King."
2Mac 1:24 "O Lord, Lord God, C of all things, who
7:23 Therefore the C of the world, who shaped the
13:14 the decision to the C of the world and
Rom 1:25 creature rather than the C, who is blessed for
Col 3:10 renewed in knowledge after the image of its C
1Pet 4:19 right and entrust their souls to a faithful C

CREATURE (35)
Gen 1:21 monsters and every living C that moves, with which
2:19 man called every living C, that was its name.
3:1 than any other wild C that the LORD God
8:21 again destroy every living C as I have done.
9:10 and with every living C that is with you,
9:12 you and every living C that is with you,
9:15 you and every living C of all flesh; and
9:16 God and every living C of all flesh that
Lev 11:46 bird and every living C that moves through the
11:46 the waters and every C that swarms upon the
11:47 and between the living C that may be eaten

	11:47	eaten and the living C that may not be
	17:14	the life of every C is the blood of
	17:14	the blood of any C, for the life of
	17:14	the life of every C is its blood; whoever
Job	41:33	not his like, a C without fear.
Eccl	10:20	voice, or some winged C tell the matter.
Sir	13:14	Every C loves its like, and every person his
Ezek	1:11	spread out above; each C had two wings, each
	1:23	toward another; and each C had two wings covering
	47:9	river goes every living C which swarms will live,
Acts	28:4	the natives saw the C hanging from his hand,
	28:5	however, shook off the C into the fire and
Rom	1:25	worshiped and served the C rather than the Creator,
Col	1:23	been preached to every C under heaven, and of
Heb	4:13	And before him no C is hidden, but all
Jas	3:7	of reptile and sea C, can be tamed and
Rev	4:7	behind: the first living C like a lion, the
	4:7	lion, the second living C like an ox, the
	4:7	ox, the third living C with the face of
	4:7	and the fourth living C like a flying eagle.
	5:13	And I heard every C in heaven and on
	6:3	heard the second living C say, "Come!"
	6:5	heard the third living C say, "Come!" And I
	6:7	of the fourth living C say, "Come!"

CREATURES (56)

Gen	1:20	forth swarms of living C, and let birds fly
	1:24	earth bring forth living C according to their kinds:
	7:21	cattle, beasts, all swarming C that swarm upon the
Lev	11:10	scales, of the swarming C in the waters and
	11:10	and of the living C that are in the
Tob	8:5	heavens and all thy C bless thee.
	8:15	saints and all thy C bless thee; let all
Jud	16:14	Let all thy C serve thee, for thou didst
Ps	74:14	as food for the C of the wilderness.
	104:24	them all; the earth is full of thy C
Wis	9:2	have dominion over the C thou hast made,
	11:15	a multitude of irrational C to punish them,
	12:27	became incensed at those C which they had thought
	16:1	punished through such C, and were tormented by
	16:3	because of the odious C sent to them, while
	16:18	might not consume the C sent against the ungodly,
	19:19	transformed into water C, and creatures that swim
	19:19	into water creatures, and C that swim moved over
	19:21	the flesh of perishable C that walked among them,
Sir	11:3	is small among flying C, but her product is
	43:25	living things, and huge C of the sea.
Is	13:21	be full of howling C; there ostriches will dwell,
Bar	3:32	filled it with four-footed C;
Ezek	1:5	of it came the likeness of four living C
	1:13	midst of the living C there was something that
	1:13	fro among the living C; and the fire was
	1:14	And the living C darted to and fro, like
	1:15	looked at the living C, I saw a wheel
	1:15	earth beside the living C, one for each of
	1:19	And when the living C went, the wheels went
	1:19	and when the living C rose from the earth,
	1:20	spirit of the living C was in the wheels.
	1:21	spirit of the living C was in the wheels.
	1:22	heads of the living C there was the likeness
	3:13	wings of the living C as they touched one
	10:15	These were the living C that I saw by
	10:17	spirit of the living C was in them.
	10:20	These were the living C that I saw underneath
Dan	3:80	you whales and all C that move in the
Jas	1:17	be a kind of first fruits of his C
	4:4	Unfaithful C
2Pet	2:12	these, like irrational animals, C of instinct, born to
Rev	4:6	throne, are four living C, full of eyes in
	4:8	And the four living C, each of them with
	4:9	And whenever the living C give glory and honor
	5:6	and the four living C and among the elders,
	5:8	scroll, the four living C and the twenty-four elders
	5:11	throne and the living C and the elders the
	5:14	And the four living C said, "Amen!" and the
	6:1	of the four living C say, as with a
	6:6	of the four living C saying, "A quart of
	7:11	and the four living C, and they fell on
	8:9	third of the living C in the sea died,
	14:3	before the four living C and before the elders.
	15:7	of the four living C gave the seven angels
	19:4	and the four living C fell down and worshiped

CREDIT (5)

Lk	6:32	who love you, what C is that to you?
	6:33	good to you, what C is that to you?
	6:34	hope to receive, what C is that to you?
Phil	4:17	I seek the fruit which increases to your C
1Pet	2:20	For what C is it, if when you do

CREDITED (2)

Lev	7:18	neither shall it be C to him; it shall
Sir	3:14	sins it will be C to you;

CREDITOR (6)

Ex	22:25	to him as a C, and you shall not
Deut	15:2	of the release: every C shall release what he
2Kgs	4:1	the LORD, but the C has come to take
Ps	109:11	May the C seize all that he has; may
Is	24:2	borrower; as with the C, so with the debtor.
Lk	7:41	"A certain C had two debtors; one owed five

CREDITORS

Is	50:1	Or which of my C is it to whom

CREEP (2)

Ps	104:20	beasts of the forest C forth.
Ezek	38:20	all creeping things that C on the ground, and

CREEPING (14)

Gen	1:24	their kinds: cattle and C things and beasts of
	1:26	earth, and over every C thing that creeps upon
	6:7	man and beast and C things and birds of
	6:20	their kinds, of every C thing of the ground
	7:14	their kinds, and every C thing that creeps on
	7:23	man and animals and C things and birds of
	8:17	and animals and every C thing that creeps on
	8:19	And every beast, every C thing, and every bird,
Lev	22:5	and whoever touches a C thing by which he
Ps	148:10	Beasts and all cattle, C things and flying birds!
Sir	10:11	dead he will inherit C things, and wild beasts,
Ezek	8:10	were all kinds of C things, and loathsome beasts,
	38:20	the field, and all C things that creep on
Hos	2:18	the air, and the C things of the ground;

CREEPS (8)

Gen	1:25	kinds, and everything that C upon the ground
	1:26	every creeping thing that C upon the earth."
	1:30	and to everything that C on the earth, everything
	7:8	and of everything that C on the ground,
	7:14	every creeping thing that C on the earth according
	8:17	every creeping thing that C on the earth--that
	9:2	air, upon everything that C on the ground and
Deut	4:18	likeness of anything that C on the ground, the

CRESCENS

2Tim	4:10	and gone to Thessalonica; C has gone to Galatia,

CRESCENTS (3)

Judg	8:21	and he took the C that were on the
	8:26	of gold; besides the C and the pendants and
Is	3:18	the headbands, and the C;

CRETANS (2)

Acts	2:11	both Jews and proselytes, C and Arabians, we hear
Tit	1:11	of their own, said, C are always liars, evil

CRETE (6)

1Mac	10:67	of Demetrius came from C to the land of
Acts	27:7	under the lee of C off Salmone.
	27:12	Phoenix, a harbor of C, looking northeast and
	27:13	anchor and sailed along C, close inshore.
	27:21	have set sail from C and incurred this injury
Tit	1:4	I left you in C, that you might amend

CREW

Ezek	27:34	merchandise and all your C have sunk with you.

CRIB (2)

Job	39:9	Will he spend the night at your C
Is	1:3	the ass its master's C; but Israel does not

CRICKET

Lev	11:22	to its kind, the C according to its kind,

CRIED (161)

Gen	27:34	of his father, he C out with an exceedingly
	39:14	with me, and I C out with a loud
	39:15	up my voice and C, he left his garment
	39:18	up my voice and C, he left his garment
	41:43	second chariot; and they C before him, "Bow the
	41:55	was famished, the people C to Pharaoh for bread;

	45:1	by him; and he C, "Make every one go
Ex	2:23	under their bondage, and C out for help, and
	5:15	of Israel came and C to Pharaoh, "Why do
	8:12	from Pharaoh; and Moses C to the LORD concerning
	14:10	the people of Israel C out to the LORD;
	15:25	And he C to the LORD; and the LORD
	17:4	So Moses C to the LORD, "What shall I
Num	11:2	Then the people C to Moses; and Moses prayed
	12:13	And Moses C to the LORD, "Heal her, O
	20:16	fathers; and when we C to the LORD, he
Deut	22:27	the betrothed young woman C for help there was
	26:7	Then we C to the LORD the God of
Josh	24:7	And when they C to the LORD, he put
Judg	3:9	the people of Israel C to the LORD, the
	3:15	the people of Israel C to the LORD, the
	4:3	the people of Israel C to the LORD for
	6:6	the people of Israel C for help to the
	6:7	the people of Israel C to the LORD on
	7:20	to blow; and they C, "A sword for the
	7:21	the army ran; they C out and fled.
	9:7	of Mount Gerizim, and C aloud and said to
	10:10	the people of Israel C to the LORD, saying,
	10:12	oppressed you; and you C to me, and I
1Sam	4:13	news, all the city C out.
	5:10	the people of Ekron C out, "They have brought
	7:9	the LORD; and Samuel C to the LORD for
	12:8	them, then your fathers C to the LORD and
	12:10	And they C to the LORD, and said, 'We
	15:11	was angry; and he C to the LORD all
	28:12	woman saw Samuel, she C out with a loud
2Sam	18:28	Then Ahima-az C out to the king, "All is
	19:4	face, and the king C with a loud voice,
	22:42	none to save; they C to the LORD, but
1Kgs	13:2	And the man C against the altar by the
	13:4	of God, which he C against the altar at
	13:21	him back; and he C to the man of
	13:32	the saying which he C by the word of
	17:20	And he C to the LORD, "O LORD my
	17:21	child three times, and C to the LORD, "O
	18:28	And they C aloud, and cut themselves after their
	20:39	the king passed, he C to the king and
	22:32	against him; and Jehoshaphat C out.
2Kgs	2:12	saw it and he C, "My father, my father!
	4:1	sons of the prophets C to Elisha, "Your servant
	4:40	of the pottage, they C out, "O man of
	6:5	the water; and he C out, "Alas, my master!
	6:26	the wall, a woman C out to him, saying,
	11:14	rent her clothes, and C, "Treason!
	20:11	And Isaiah the prophet C to the LORD; and
1Chr	5:20	their hands, for they C to God in the
2Chr	13:14	behind them; and they C to the LORD, and
	14:11	And Asa C to the LORD his God, "O
	18:31	against him; and Jehoshaphat C out, and the LORD
	23:13	rent her clothes, and C, "Treason!
	32:20	because of this and C to heaven.
Neh	9:4	and Chenani; and they C with a loud voice
	9:27	of their suffering they C to thee and thou
	9:28	when they turned and C to thee thou didst
Jud	4:9	every man of Israel C out to God with
	4:12	altar with sackcloth and C out in unison, praying
	4:15	upon their turbans, they C out to the Lord
	5:12	Then they C out to their God, and he
	6:18	and worshiped God, and C out to him, and
	7:19	The people of Israel C out to the Lord
	7:24	of the city and C out with a loud
	7:30	the assembly, and they C out to the Lord
	9:1	God in Jerusalem, Judith C out to the Lord
	14:16	And he C out with a loud voice and
Esth	10:9	this is Israel, who C out to God and
	11:10	Then they C to God; and from their cry,
	13:18	And all Israel C out mightily, for their death
Job	29:12	delivered the poor who C, and the fatherless who
	31:38	"If my land has C out against me, and
Ps	18:6	to my God I C for help.
	18:41	They C for help, but there was none to
	18:41	none to save, they C to the LORD, but
	22:5	To thee they C, and were saved; in thee
	22:24	has heard, when he C to him.
	30:2	LORD my God, I C to thee for help,
	30:8	thee, O LORD, I C; and to the LORD
	31:22	my supplications, when I C to thee for help.
	34:6	This poor man C, and the LORD heard him,
	66:17	I C aloud to him, and he was extolled
	99:6	They C to the LORD, and he answered them.
	107:6	Then they C to the LORD in their trouble,
	107:13	Then they C to the LORD in their trouble,
	107:19	Then they C to the LORD in their trouble,
	107:28	Then they C to the LORD in their trouble,
Is	21:8	Then he who saw C: "Upon a watchtower I
Lam	4:15	men C at them; "Away!
Ezek	9:1	Then he C in my ears with a loud
	9:8	upon my face, and C, "Ah Lord GOD!
	11:13	upon my face, and C with a loud voice,
Dan	4:14	He C aloud and said thus, 'Hew down the
	5:7	The king C aloud to bring in the enchanters,
	6:20	where Daniel was, he C out in a tone
	13:24	Then Susanna C out with a loud voice, and
	13:42	Then Susanna C out with a loud voice, and
	13:46	named Daniel; and he C with a loud voice,
Jon	1:5	were afraid, and each C to his god; and
	1:14	Therefore they C to the LORD, "We beseech thee,
	2:2	belly of Sheol I C, and thou didst hear
	3:4	And he C, "Yet forty days, and Nineveh shall
Zech	1:4	whom the former prophets C out, 'Thus says the
	6:8	Then he C to me, "Behold, those who go
1Mac	2:27	Then Mattathias C out in the city with a
	3:50	their days; and they C aloud to Heaven, saying,
	4:40	on the trumpets, and C out to Heaven.
	5:33	sounded their trumpets and C aloud in prayer.
	11:49	courage failed and they C out to the king
	13:45	clothes rent, and they C out with a loud
	13:50	Then they C to Simon to make peace with
2Mac	8:3	to the blood that C out to him,
Mt	8:29	And behold, they C out, "What have you to
	14:26	And they C out for fear.
	14:30	beginning to sink he C out, "Lord, save me."
	15:22	region came out and C, "Have mercy on me,
	20:30	Jesus was passing by, C out, "Have mercy on
	20:31	be silent; but they C out the more, "Lord,
	27:46	the ninth hour Jesus C with a loud voice,
	27:50	And Jesus C again with a loud voice and
Mk	1:24	unclean spirit; and he C out, "What have you
	3:11	down before him and C out, "You are the
	6:49	was a ghost, and C out;
	9:24	father of the child C out and said, "I
	10:48	be silent; but he C out all the more,
	11:9	and those who followed C out, "Hosanna!
	15:13	And they C out again, "Crucify him."
	15:33	the ninth hour Jesus C with a loud voice,
Lk	4:33	unclean demon; and he C out with a loud
	8:28	he saw Jesus, he C out and fell down
	9:38	man from the crowd C, "Teacher, I beg you
	18:38	And he C, "Jesus, Son of David, have mercy
	18:39	be silent; but he C out all the more,
	23:17	But they all C out together, "Away with this
Jn	1:15	witness to him, and C, "This was he of
	11:43	had said this, he C with a loud voice,
	12:44	And Jesus C out and said, "He who believes
	18:40	They C out again, "Not this man, but Barabbas!"
	19:6	officers saw him, they C out, "Crucify him, crucify
	19:12	him, but the Jews C out, "If you release
	19:15	They C out, "Away with him, away with him,
Acts	7:57	But they C out with a loud voice and
	7:60	he knelt down and C with a loud voice,
	16:28	But Paul C with a loud voice, "Do not
	19:28	they were enraged, and C out, "Great is Artemis
	19:32	Now some C one thing, some another; for the
	19:34	all with one voice C out, "Great is Artemis
	22:23	And as they C out and waved their garments
	23:6	the other Pharisees, he C out in the council,
	24:20	one thing which I C out while standing among
Rev	6:10	they had borne; they C out with a loud
	12:2	with child and she C out in her pangs
	18:18	sea, stood far-off and C out as they saw
	19:3	Once more they C, "Hallelujah!

CRIES (19)

Ex	22:27	And if he C to me, I will hear,
Jud	14:19	dismayed, and their loud C and shouts arose in
Job	24:12	soul of the wounded C for help; yet God
Prov	1:20	Wisdom's Warning Wisdom C aloud in the street; in
	1:21	of the walls she C out; at the entrance
	8:3	of the portals she C aloud:
Sir	35:15	her cheek as she C out against him who
Is	15:5	My heart C out for Moab; his fugitives flee
	26:17	child, who writhes and C out in her pangs,
	40:3	A voice C: "In the wilderness prepare the way
	42:13	up his fury; he C out, he shouts aloud,
	46:7	If one C to it, it does not answer
Mic	6:9	voice of the LORD C to the city--and
Zeph	1:14	bitter, the mighty man C aloud there.
Lk	9:39	him, and he suddenly C out; it convulses him

C

23:22 urgent, demanding with loud C that he should be
Rom 9:27 And Isaiah C out concerning Israel: "Though the
Heb 5:7 and supplications, with loud C and tears, to him
Jas 5:4 cry out; and the C of the harvesters have

CRIME (14)
Deut 19:15 a man for any C or for any wrong
21:22 man has committed a C punishable by death and
Judg 9:56 Thus God requited the C of Abimelech, which he
20:10 for all the wanton C which they have committed
Job 31:11 would be a heinous C; that would be an
Ps 56:7 recompense them for their C; in wrath cast down
2Mac 4:36 and the Greeks shared their hatred of the C
4:49 their hatred of the C, provided magnificently for their
Lk 23:4 multitudes, "I find no C in this man."
23:21 found in him no C deserving death; I will
Jn 18:38 them, "I find no C in him.
19:4 that I find no C in him."
19:6 for I find no C in him."
Acts 18:14 of wrongdoing or vicious C, I should have reason

CRIMES (3)
Ps 64:6 Who can search out our C
Ezek 7:23 is full of bloody C and the city is
2Mac 13:6 man guilty of sacrilege or notorious for other C

CRIMINAL
2Tim 2:9 I am suffering and wearing fetters like a C

CRIMINALS (3)
Lk 23:31 others also, who were C, were led away to
23:32 crucified him, and the C, one on the right
23:38 One of the C who were hanged railed at

CRIMSON (4)
2Chr 2:7 iron, and in purple, C, and blue fabrics, trained
2:14 in purple, blue, and C fabrics and fine linen,
3:14 blue and purple and C fabrics and fine linen,
Is 1:18 they are red like C, they shall become like

CRIMSONED
Is 63:1 comes from Edom, in C garments from Bozrah, he

CRINGE (2)
Ps 66:3 power that thy enemies C before thee.
81:15 hate the LORD would C toward him, and their

CRINGING (3)
2Sam 22:45 Foreigners came C to me; as soon as they
Ps 18:44 obeyed me; foreigners came C to me.
Sir 12:11 himself and goes about C, watch yourself, and be

CRIPPLE (2)
Acts 4:9 deed done to a C, by what means this
14:8 feet; he was a C from birth, who had

CRIPPLED (4)
2Sam 4:4 a son who was C in his feet.
9:3 of Jonathan; he is C in his feet."
Ezek 34:4 have not healed, the C you have not bound
34:16 will bind up the C, and I will strengthen

CRIPPLES
Ps 35:15 gathered together against me; C whom I knew not

CRISIS (2)
Sir 22:14 reasonable counsel will not be afraid in a C
Bar 3:5 fathers, but in this C remember thy power and

CRISPUS (2)
Acts 18:8 C, the ruler of the synagogue, believed in the
1Cor 1:14 none of you except C and Gaius;

CRITICAL
2Mac 1:7 to you, in the C distress which came upon

CRITICISM
Sir 38:17 or two, to avoid C; then be comforted for

CRITICIZED
Acts 11:2 Jerusalem, the circumcision party C him,

CROAK
Zeph 2:14 the window, the raven C on the threshold; for

CROCODILE
Lev 11:30 the gecko, the land C, the lizard, the sand

CROCUS
Is 35:1 and blossom; like the C

CROOKED (19)
Deut 32:5 are a perverse and C generation.
2Sam 22:27 pure, and with the C thou dost show thyself
Ps 18:26 pure; and with the C thou dost show thyself
125:5 turn aside upon their C ways the LORD will
Prov 2:15 men whose paths are C, and who are devious
4:25 Put away from you C speech, and put devious
6:12 man, goes about with C speech,
8:8 is nothing twisted or C in them.
17:20 A man of C mind does not prosper, and
21:8 of the guilty is C, but the conduct of
Eccl 1:15 What is C cannot be made straight, and what
7:13 who can make straight what he has made C
Wis 13:13 for nothing, a stick C and full of knots,
Is 59:8 have made their roads C, no one who goes
Lam 3:9 with hewn stones, he has made my paths C
Lk 3:5 brought low, and the C shall be made straight,
Acts 2:40 "Save yourselves from this C generation."
13:10 you not stop making C the straight paths of
Phil 2:15 the midst of a C and perverse generation, among

CROOKEDNESS
Prov 11:3 guides them, but the C of the treacherous destroys

CROP (5)
Lev 1:16 shall take away its C with the feathers, and
25:20 or gather in our C
Deut 22:9 to the sanctuary, the C which you have sown
Sir 7:3 injustice, and you will not reap a sevenfold C
1Cor 9:10 thresh in hope of a share in the C

CROPS (11)
Lev 25:15 number of years for C he shall sell to
25:16 the number of the C that he is selling
Neh 10:31 we will forego the C of the seventh year
Ps 78:46 He gave their C to the caterpillar, and the
Prov 14:4 no grain; but abundant C come by the strength
Wis 16:19 fire, to destroy the C of the unrighteous land.
16:22 might know that the C of their enemies were
16:26 not the production of C that feeds man, but
1Mac 11:34 each year, from the C of the land and
Lk 12:17 nowhere to store my C
2Tim 2:6 ought to have the first share of the C

CROSS (45)
Num 34:4 ascent of Akrabbim, and C to Zin, and its
35:10 of Israel, When you C the Jordan into the
Deut 4:21 that I should not C the Jordan, and that
Judg 12:1 Jephthah, "Why did you C over to fight against
1Sam 14:8 Jonathan, "Behold, we will C over to the men,
30:10 were too exhausted to C the brook Besor.
2Sam 19:18 he was about to C the Jordan,
1Kgs 2:37 you go forth, and C the brook Kidron, know
Sir 8:16 man, and do not C the wilderness with him;
Is 11:15 channels that men may C dryshod.
Jer 2:10 For C to the coasts of Cyprus and see,
41:10 and set out to C over to the Ammonites.
Amos 5:5 enter into Gilgal or C over to Beer-sheba; for
1Mac 5:41 the river, we will C over to him and
9:48 the enemy did not C the Jordan to attack
16:6 soldiers were afraid to C the stream, so he
Mt 10:38 does not take his C and follow me is
16:24 and take up his C and follow me.
27:32 name; this man they compelled to carry his C
27:40 the Son of God, come down from the C
27:42 down now from the C, and we will believe
Mk 8:34 and take up his C and follow me.
15:21 father of Alexander and Rufus, to carry his C
15:29 days, save yourself, and come down from the C
15:31 down now from the C, that we may see
Lk 9:23 and take up his C daily and follow me.
14:27 not bear his own C and come after me,
16:26 able, and none may C from there to us.'
23:25 laid on him the C, to carry it behind
Jn 19:17 out, bearing his own C, to the place called
19:19 put it on the C; it read, "Jesus of
19:25 But standing by the C of Jesus were his
19:31 from remaining on the C on the sabbath (for
Acts 18:27 when he wished to C to Achaia, the brethren
1Cor 1:17 eloquent wisdom, lest the C of Christ be emptied

1:18 the word of the C is folly to those
Gal 5:11 stumbling block of the C has been removed.
6:12 be persecuted for the C of Christ.
6:14 glory except in the C of our Lord Jesus
Eph 2:16 one body through the C, thereby bringing the
Phil 2:8 became obedient unto death, even death on a C
3:18 as enemies of the C of Christ.
Col 1:20 heaven, making peace by the blood of his C
2:14 this he set aside, nailing it to the C
Heb 12:2 before him endured the C, despising the shame, and

CROSSED (36)

Gen 31:21 had, and arose and C the Euphrates, and set
32:10 only my staff I C this Jordan; and now
32:22 his eleven children, and C the ford of the
Deut 2:14 leaving Kadesh-barnea until we C the brook Zered
Josh 5:1 Israel until they had C over, their heart melted,
Judg 10:9 And the Ammonites C the Jordan to fight also
11:32 So Jephthah C over to the Ammonites to fight
12:1 to arms, and they C to Zaphon and said
12:3 in my hand, and C over against the Ammonites,
1Sam 13:7 and in cisterns, or C the fords of the
2Sam 2:29 the Arabah; they C the Jordan, and marching
10:17 all Israel together, and C the Jordan, and came
15:23 by, and the king C the brook Kidron, and
17:22 with him, and they C the Jordan; by daybreak
17:22 left who had not C the Jordan.
17:24 And Absalom C the Jordan with all the men
19:18 the king, and they C the ford to bring
24:5 They C the Jordan, and began from Aroer, and
2Kgs 2:9 When they had C, Elijah said to Elisha, "Ask
1Chr 12:15 are the men who C the Jordan in the
19:17 all Israel together, and C the Jordan, and came
Is 10:29 his baggage; they have C over the pass, at
1Mac 3:37 He C the Euphrates river and went through the
5:6 Then he C over to attack the Ammonites, where
5:24 and Jonathan his brother C the Jordan and went
5:43 Then he C over against them first, and the
5:52 And they C the Jordan into the large plain
9:34 with all his army C the Jordan.
12:30 them, for they had C the Eleutherus river.
16:6 the stream, so he C over first; and when
16:6 men saw him, they C over after him.
Mt 9:1 into a boat he C over and came to
14:34 And when they had C over, they came to
Mk 5:21 And when Jesus had C again in the boat
6:53 And when they had C over, they came to
Heb 11:29 By faith the people C the Red Sea as

CROSSES

1Mac 5:40 his forces, "If he C over to us first,

CROSSING (4)

Gen 48:14 the head of Manasseh, C his hands, for Manasseh
Judg 6:33 East came together, and C the Jordan they
Jud 5:15 inhabitants of Heshbon; and C over the Jordan they
Acts 21:2 having found a ship C to Phoenicia, we went

CROUCH (3)

Job 38:40 young lions, when they C in their dens, or
39:3 bring forth, when they C, bring forth their offspring,
Is 10:4 Nothing remains but to C among the prisoners or

CROUCHING

Gen 49:14 is a strong ass, C between the sheepfolds;

CROW (2)

Lk 22:34 the cock will not C this day, until you
Jn 13:38 the cock will not C, till you have denied

CROWD (82)

Jud 2:20 them went a mixed C like a swarm of
Sir 7:16 count yourself among the C of sinners; remember
16:26 They do not C one another aside, and they
31:14 see, and do not C your neighbor at the
2Mac 14:43 hit exactly, and the C was now rushing in
14:43 wall, and manfully threw himself down into the C
14:45 he ran through the C; and standing upon a
14:46 hurled them at the C, calling upon the Lord
Mt 9:23 flute players, and the C making a tumult,
9:25 But when the C had been put outside, he
13:2 there; and the whole C stood on the beach.
15:32 have compassion on the C, because they have been
15:33 in the desert to feed so great a C
15:35 And commanding the C to sit down on the
17:14 they came to the C, a man came up
20:29 of Jericho, a great C followed him.
20:31 The C rebuked them, telling them to be silent;
21:8 Most of the C spread their garments on the
22:33 And when the C heard it, they were astonished
26:47 with him a great C with swords and clubs,
27:15 to release for the C any one prisoner whom
27:24 his hands before the C, saying, "I am innocent
Mk 2:4 him because of the C, they removed the roof
2:13 sea; and all the C gathered about him, and
3:9 him because of the C, lest they should crush
3:20 went home; and the C came together again, so
3:32 And a C was sitting about him; and they
4:1 And a very large C gathered about him, so
4:1 sea; and the whole C was beside the sea
4:36 And leaving the C, they took him with them
5:21 other side, a great C gathered about him; and
5:24 And a great C followed him and thronged about
5:27 behind him in the C and touched his garment.
5:30 turned about in the C, and said, "Who touched
5:31 him, "You see the C pressing around you, and
6:45 other side, to Beth-saida, while he dismissed the C
8:1 when again a great C had gathered, and they
8:2 have compassion on the C, because they have been
8:6 And he commanded the C to sit down on
8:6 the people; and they set them before the C
9:14 they saw a great C about them, and scribes
9:15 And immediately all the C, when they saw him,
9:17 And one of the C answered him, "Teacher, I
9:25 Jesus saw that a C came running together, he
14:43 and with him a C with swords and clubs,
15:8 And the C came up and began to ask
15:11 priests stirred up the C to have him release
15:15 wishing to satisfy the C, released for them Barabbas;
Lk 5:19 in, because of the C, they went up on
6:17 place, with a great C of his disciples and
6:19 And all the C sought to touch him, for
7:11 disciples and a great C went with him.
7:12 widow; and a large C from the city was
8:4 And when a great C came together and people
8:19 but they could not reach him for the C
8:40 when Jesus returned, the C welcomed him, for they
9:12 to him, "Send the C away, to go into
9:16 them to the disciples to set before the C
9:37 the mountain, a great C met him.
9:38 a man from the C cried, "Teacher, I beg
11:27 a woman in the C raised her voice and
19:3 on account of the C, because he was small
22:45 speaking, there came a C, and the man called
Jn 5:12 as there was a C in the place.
7:32 The Pharisees heard the C thus muttering about him,
7:49 But this C, who do not know the law,
12:9 When the great C of the Jews learned that
12:12 next day a great C who had come to
12:17 The C that had been with him when he
12:18 The reason why the C went to meet him
12:29 The C standing by heard it and said that
12:34 The C answered him, "We have heard from the
Acts 16:22 The C joined in attacking them; and the magistrates
17:5 rabble, they gathered a C, set the city in
19:30 go in among the C, but the disciples would
19:33 Some of the C prompted Alexander, whom the Jews
19:35 clerk had quieted the C, he said, "Men of
21:27 stirred up all the C, and laid hands on
21:34 Some in the C shouted one thing, some another;
21:35 the violence of the C;
24:11 or stirring up a C, either in the temple
24:17 the temple, without any C or tumult.

CROWDS (34)

2Mac 3:18 of their houses in C to make a general
4:40 And since the C were becoming aroused and filled
Mt 4:25 And great C followed him from Galilee and the
5:1 Seeing the C, he went up on the mountain,
7:28 finished these sayings, the C were astonished at his
8:1 from the mountain, great C followed him;
8:18 when Jesus saw great C around him, he gave
9:8 When the C saw it, they were afraid, and
9:33 man spoke; and the C marveled, saying, "Never was
9:36 When he saw the C, he had compassion for
11:7 to speak to the C concerning John: "What did
13:2 And great C gathered about him, so that he
13:34 Jesus said to the C in parables; indeed he
13:36 Then he left the C and went into the
14:13 But when the C heard it, they followed him
14:15 now over; send the C away to go into
14:19 Then he ordered the C to sit down on

14:19 disciples, and the disciples gave them to the C
14:22 to the other side, while he dismissed the C
14:23 he had dismissed the C, he went up on
15:30 And great C came to him, bringing with them
15:36 disciples, and the disciples gave them to the C
15:39 And sending away the C, he got into the
19:2 the Jordan; and large C followed him, and he
21:9 And the C that went before him and that
21:11 And the C said, "This is the prophet Jesus
23:1 said Jesus to the C and to his disciples,
26:55 Jesus said to the C, "Have you come out
Mk 10:1 beyond the Jordan, and C gathered to him again;
Lk 7:24 to speak to the C concerning John: "What did
9:11 When the C learned it, they followed him; and
11:29 When the C were increasing, he began to say,
Acts 14:11 And when the C saw what Paul had done,
17:13 came there too, stirring up and inciting the C

CROWED (4)

Mt 26:74 And immediately the cock C
Mk 14:72 And immediately the cock C a second time.
Lk 22:58 immediately, while he was still speaking, the cock C
Jn 18:27 again denied it; and at once the cock C

CROWN (85)

Ex 29:6 and put the holy C upon the turban.
39:30 plate of the holy C of pure gold, and
Lev 8:9 golden plate, the holy C, as the LORD commanded
Deut 28:35 your foot to the C of your head.
33:16 Joseph, and upon the C of the head of
33:20 the arm, and the C of the head.
2Sam 1:10 and I took the C which was on his
12:30 And he took the C of their king from
14:25 his foot to the C of his head there
1Kgs 7:31 opening was within a C which projected upward one
2Kgs 11:12 son, and put the C upon him, and gave
1Chr 20:2 And David took the C of their king from
2Chr 23:11 son, and put the C upon him, and gave
Esth 1:11 king with her royal C, in order to show
2:17 he set the royal C on her head and
6:8 whose head a royal C is set;
8:15 with a great golden C and a mantle of
Job 2:7 his foot to the C of his head.
19:9 glory, and taken the C from my head.
31:36 on me as a C;
Ps 8:5 than God, and dost C him with glory and
21:3 thou dost set a C of fine gold upon
68:21 his enemies, the hairy C of him who walks
89:19 "I have set the C upon one who is
89:39 thou hast defiled his C in the dust.
132:18 but upon himself his C will shed its luster."
Prov 4:10 garland; she will bestow on you a beautiful C
12:4 good wife is the C of her husband, but
14:24 The C of the wise is their wisdom, but
16:31 hoary head is a C of glory; it is
17:6 Grandchildren are the C of the aged, and the
27:24 ever; and does a C endure to all generations?
Song 3:11 King Solomon, with the C with which his mother
Wis 2:8 Let us C ourselves with rosebuds before they wither.
5:16 will receive a glorious C and a beautiful diadem
Sir 1:9 and gladness and a C of rejoicing.
1:16 the Lord is the C of wisdom, making peace
6:31 her on like a C of gladness.
11:5 who was never thought of has worn a C
15:6 find gladness and a C of rejoicing, and will
25:6 Rich experience is the C of the aged, and
40:4 wears purple and a C to the one who
45:12 Israel; with a gold C upon his turban, inscribed
Is 28:1 Woe to the proud C of the drunkards of
28:3 The proud C of the drunkards of Ephraim will
28:5 hosts will be a C of glory, and a
62:3 You shall be a C of beauty in the
Jer 2:16 Tahpanhes have broken the C of your head.
13:18 seat, for your beautiful C has come down from
48:45 forehead of Moab, the C of the sons of
Lam 5:16 The C has fallen from our head; woe to
Ezek 16:12 ears, and a beautiful C upon your head.
21:26 and take off the C; things shall not remain
Dan 14:36 took him by the C of his head, and
Zech 6:11 gold, and make a C, and set it upon
6:14 them both."' And the C shall be in the
9:16 the jewels of a C they shall shine on
1Mac 6:15 He gave him the C and his robe and
8:14 has put on a C or worn purple as
10:20 robe and a golden C "and you are to
10:29 and salt tax and C levies,
11:13 and put on the C of Asia.
11:13 upon his head, the C of Egypt and that
11:35 salt pits and the C taxes due to us
11:54 who began to reign and put on the C
12:39 and put on the C, and to raise his
13:32 place, putting on the C of Asia; and he
13:37 have received the gold C and the palm branch
13:39 day, and cancel the C tax which you owe;
14:5 To C all his honors he took Joppa for
2Mac 14:4 presenting to him a C of gold and a
Mt 27:29 him, and plaiting a C of thorns they put
Mk 15:17 cloak, and plaiting a C of thorns they put
Jn 19:2 the soldiers plaited a C of thorns, and put
19:5 came out, wearing the C of thorns and the
Phil 4:1 for, my joy and C, stand firm thus in
1Thes 2:19 hope or joy or C of boasting before our
2Tim 4:8 up for me the C of righteousness, which the
Jas 1:11 he will receive the C of life which God
1Pet 5:4 will obtain the unfading C of glory.
Rev 2:10 will give you the C of life.
3:11 have, so that no one may seize your C
6:2 a bow; and a C was given to him,
12:1 on her head a C of twelve stars;
14:14 man, with a golden C on his head, and

CROWNED (7)

Jud 15:13 with her; and they C themselves with olive wreaths,
Prov 14:18 but the prudent are C with knowledge.
Song 3:11 with which his mother C him on the day
Wis 4:2 all time it marches C in triumph, victor in
2Tim 2:5 An athlete is not C unless he competes according
Heb 2:7 the angels, thou hast C him with glory and
2:9 lower than the angels, C with glory and honor

CROWNEST

Ps 65:11 Thou C the year with thy bounty; the tracks

CROWNS (12)

Ps 103:4 from the Pit, who C you with steadfast love
Song 7:5 Your head C you like Carmel, and your flowing
Is 23:8 Tyre, the bestower of C, whose merchants were
Bar 6:9 take gold and make C for the heads of
Ezek 23:42 the women, and beautiful C upon their heads.
1Mac 1:9 They all put on C after his death, and
1:22 censers, the curtain, the C, and the gold decoration
4:57 the temple with golden C and small shields; they
11:13 Thus he put two C upon his head, the
Rev 4:4 white garments, with golden C upon their heads.
4:10 ever; they cast their C before the throne, singing,
9:7 were what looked like C of gold; their faces

CROWS (6)

Bar 6:54 power; they are like C between heaven and earth.
Mt 26:34 night, before the cock C, you will deny me
26:75 Jesus, "Before the cock C, you will deny me
Mk 14:30 night, before the cock C twice, you will deny
14:72 him, "Before the cock C twice, you will deny
Lk 22:59 him, "Before the cock C today, you will deny

CRUCIAL

Sir 4:23 from speaking at the C time, and do not

CRUCIBLE (2)

Prov 17:3 The C is for silver, and the furnace is
27:21 The C is for silver, and the furnace is

CRUCIFIED (39)

Mt 20:19 mocked and scourged and C, and he will be
26:2 of man will be delivered up to be C
27:22 They all said, "Let him be C
27:23 they shouted all the more, "Let him be C
27:26 and having scourged Jesus, delivered him to be C
27:35 And when they had C him, they divided his
27:38 Then two robbers were C with him, one on
27:44 the robbers who were C with him also reviled
28:5 I know that you seek Jesus who was C
Mk 15:15 having scourged Jesus, he delivered him to be C
15:24 And they C him, and divided his garments among
15:25 third hour, when they C him.
15:27 And with him they C two robbers, one on
15:31 Those who were C with him also reviled him.
16:6 amazed; you seek Jesus of Nazareth, who was C
Lk 23:22 demanding with loud cries that he should be C
23:32 The Skull, there they C him, and the criminals,
24:7 sinful men, and be C, and on the third
24:20 condemned to death, and C him.

Jn 19:16 he handed him over to them to be C
19:18 There they C him, and with him two others,
19:20 place where Jesus was C was near the city;
19:23 When the soldiers had C Jesus they took his
19:32 other who had been C with him;
19:41 place where he was C there was a garden,
Acts 2:23 foreknowledge of God, you C and killed by the
2:36 both Lord and Christ, this Jesus whom you C
4:10 of Nazareth, whom you C, whom God raised from
Rom 6:6 our old self was C with him so that
1Cor 1:13 Was Paul C for you?
1:23 but we preach Christ C, a stumbling block to
2:2 nothing among you except Jesus Christ and him C
2:8 they would not have C the Lord of glory.
2Cor 13:4 For he was C in weakness, but lives by
Gal 2:20 I have been C with Christ; it is no
3:1 whose eyes Jesus Christ was publicly portrayed as C
5:24 to Christ Jesus have C the flesh with its
6:14 the world has been C to me, and I
Rev 11:8 called Sodom and Egypt, where their Lord was C

CRUCIFY (14)

Mt 23:33 you will kill and C, and some you will
27:31 led him away to C him.
Mk 15:13 they cried out again, C him."
15:14 shouted all the more, C him."
15:20 led him out to C him.
Lk 23:20 but they shouted out, C, crucify him!"
23:20 they shouted out, "Crucify, C him!"
Jn 19:6 him, they cried out, C him, crucify him!" Pilate
19:6 cried out, "Crucify him, C him!" Pilate said to
19:6 "Take him yourselves and C him, for I find
19:10 you, and power to C you?"
19:15 him, away with him, C him!" Pilate said to
19:15 to them, "Shall I C your King?" The chief
Heb 6:6 commit apostasy, since they C the Son of God

CRUEL (20)

Gen 49:7 is fierce; and their wrath, for it is C
Ex 6:9 broken spirit and their C bondage.
Deut 32:33 of serpents, and the C venom of asps.
Jud 9:13 for they have planned C things against thy covenant,
Job 30:21 Thou hast turned C to me; with the might
Ps 71:4 of the unjust and C man.
144:11 Rescue me from the C sword, and deliver me
Prov 11:17 benefits himself, but a C man hurts himself.
12:10 beast, but the mercy of the wicked is C
17:11 only rebellion, and a C messenger will be sent
27:4 Wrath is C, anger is overwhelming; but who can
28:16 lacks understanding is a C oppressor; but he who
Song 8:6 as death, jealousy is C as the grave.
Sir 13:12 C is he who does not keep words to
Is 13:9 of the LORD comes, C, with wrath and fierce
Jer 6:23 and spear, they are C and have no mercy,
50:42 and spear; they are C, and have no mercy.
Lam 4:3 my people has become C, like the ostriches in
2Mac 4:25 hot temper of a C tyrant and the rage
7:27 as follows, deriding the C tyrant: "My son, have

CRUELLY (2)

Judg 4:3 the people of Israel C for twenty years.
Job 39:16 She deals C with her young, as if they

CRUELTIES

2Chr 16:10 And Asa inflicted C upon some of the people

CRUELTY

2Mac 12:5 Judas heard of the C visited on his countrymen,

CRUMBLES

Job 14:18 the mountain falls and C away, and the rock

CRUMBS (2)

Mt 15:27 the dogs eat the C that fall from their
Mk 7:27 the dogs under the table eat the children's C

CRUSE (3)

1Kgs 17:12 little oil in a C; and now, I am
17:14 be spent, and the C of oil shall not
17:16 spent, neither did the C of oil fail, according

CRUSH (33)

Num 24:17 of Israel; it shall C the forehead of Moab,
Deut 33:11 work of his hands; C the loins of his
2Sam 22:30 by thee I can C a troop, and by
Jud 9:10 prince with his servant; C their arrogance by the
Esth 9:24 is the lot, to C and destroy them;
Job 6:9 would please God to C me, that he would
39:15 that a foot may C them, and that the
Ps 18:29 by thee I can C a troop; and by
72:4 to the needy, and C the oppressor!
74:14 Thou didst C the heads of Leviathan, thou didst
89:10 Thou didst C Rahab like a carcass, thou didst
89:23 I will C his foes before him and strike
94:5 They C thy people, O LORD, and afflict thy
Prov 22:22 he is poor, or C the afflicted at the
27:22 C a fool in a mortar with a pestle
Sir 36:10 C the heads of the rulers of the enemy,
Is 28:28 Does one C bread grain?
28:28 horses, he does not C it.
41:15 thresh the mountains and C them, and you shall
Lam 1:15 assembly against me to C my young men; the
3:34 To C under foot all the prisoners of the
Dan 2:40 it shall break and C all these.
Amos 4:1 oppress the poor, who C the needy, who say
Hab 3:13 Thou didst C the head of the wicked, laying
Zech 11:6 king; and they shall C the earth, and I
1Mac 3:22 He himself will C them before us; as for
4:10 with our fathers and C this army before us
4:30 of Israel, who didst C the attack of the
7:42 So also C this army before us today; let
Mt 21:44 any one, it will C him."
Mk 3:9 crowd, lest they should C him;
Lk 20:18 any one it will C him."
Rom 16:20 of peace will soon C Satan under your feet.

CRUSHED (50)

Lev 2:14 of your first fruits C new grain from fresh
2:16 portion part of the C grain and of the
21:20 disease or scabs or C testicles;
22:24 its testicles bruised or C or torn or cut,
Deut 9:21 it with fire and C it, grinding it very
23:1 "He whose testicles are C or whose male member
28:33 be only oppressed and C continually;
Judg 5:26 Sisera a blow, she C his head, she shattered
9:53 upon Abimelech's head, and C his skull.
10:8 Ammonites, and they C and oppressed the children
2Sam 22:43 of the earth, I C them and stamped them
2Chr 2:10 twenty thousand cors of C wheat, twenty thousand
15:16 cut down her image, C it, and burned it
Job 4:19 the dust, who are C before the moth.
5:4 from safety, they are C in the gate, and
20:19 For he has C and abandoned the poor, he
22:9 empty, and the arms of the fatherless were C
34:25 overturns them in the night, and they are C
Ps 10:10 The hapless is C, sinks down, and falls by
34:18 brokenhearted, and saves the C in spirit.
38:8 am utterly spent and C; I groan because of
143:3 pursued me; he has C my life to the
Prov 27:22 a pestle along with C grain, yet his folly
Sir 47:7 adversaries the Philistines; he C their power even to
Is 19:10 the land will be C, and all who work
27:9 the altars like chalkstones C to pieces, no Asherim
59:5 from one which is C a viper is hatched.
Jer 51:34 devoured me, he has C me; he has made
Ezek 36:3 made you desolate, and C you from all sides,
Hos 5:11 Ephraim is oppressed, C in judgment, because he
1Mac 3:23 army, and they were C before him.
4:14 The Gentiles were C and fled into the plain,
4:36 "Behold, our enemies are C; let us go up
5:7 them and they were C before him; he struck
5:21 and the Gentiles were C before him.
7:43 army of Nicanor was C, and he himself was
8:4 the earth, until they C them and inflicted great
8:5 up against them, they C in battle and conquered.
8:6 He was C by them;
9:7 was imminent, he was C in spirit, for he
9:15 with him, and they C the right wing, and
9:16 the right wing was C, they turned and followed
9:68 Bacchides, and he was C by them.
10:52 – for I C Demetrius and gained control
10:53 and his army were C by us, and we
12:31 called Zabadeans, and he C them and plundered
13:51 great enemy had been C and removed from Israel.
14:13 and the kings were C in those days.
2Cor 1:8 were so utterly, unbearably C that we despaired of
4:8 every way, but not C; perplexed, but not driven

CRUSHES (5)

Jud 16:3 is the Lord who C wars; for he has
Job 9:17 For he C me with a tempest, and multiplies
Sir 28:17 blow of the tongue C the bones.

C

35:18 with them, till he C the loins of the
Dan 2:40 and like iron which C, it shall break and

CRUSHEST

Jud 9:7 art the Lord who C wars; the Lord is

CRUSHING (2)

2Kgs 23:15 in pieces its stones, C them to dust; also
Is 3:15 do you mean by C my people, by grinding

CRY (204)

Gen 27:34 exceedingly great and bitter C, and said to his
Ex 2:23 for help, and their C under bondage came up
3:7 and have heard their C because of their taskmasters;
3:9 And now, behold, the C of the people of
5:8 are idle; therefore they C, 'Let us go and
11:6 shall be a great C throughout all the land
12:30 there was a great C in Egypt, for there
14:15 Moses, "Why do you C to me?
22:23 afflict them, and they C out to me, I
22:23 will surely hear their C;
32:18 the sound of the C of defeat, but the
Lev 13:45 his upper lip and C, 'Unclean, unclean.'
Num 14:1 congregation raised a loud C; and the people wept
16:34 them fled at their C; for they said, "Lest
Deut 15:9 him nothing, and he C to the LORD against
22:24 because she did not C for help though she
24:15 upon it); lest he C against you to the
Judg 10:14 Go and C to the gods whom you have
1Sam 5:12 with tumors, and the C of the city went
7:8 "Do not cease to C to the LORD our
8:18 that day you will C out because of your
9:16 my people, because their C has come to me."
17:20 forth to the battle line, shouting the war C
2Sam 19:28 have I, then, to C to the king?"
22:7 my voice, and my C came to his ears.
1Kgs 8:28 God, hearkening to the C and to the prayer
18:27 Elijah mocked them, saying, C aloud, for he is
22:36 And about sunset a C went through the army,
2Chr 6:19 God, hearkening to the C and to the prayer
20:9 in this house, and C to thee in our
Neh 9:9 Egypt and hear their C at the Red Sea,
Tob 6:17 both of you, and C out to the merciful
13:18 all her lanes will C 'Hallelujah!' and will give
Esth 4:1 a loud and bitter C;
11:10 God; and from their C, as though from a
Job 3:7 barren; let no joyful C be heard in it.
16:18 blood, and let my C find no resting place.
19:7 Behold, I C out, 'Violence!' but I am not
27:9 Will God hear his C, when trouble comes upon
30:20 I C to thee and thou dost not answer
30:24 and in his disaster C for help?
30:28 in the assembly, and C for help.
34:28 that they caused the C of the poor to
34:28 and he heard the C of the afflicted--
35:9 multitude of oppressions people C out; they call for
35:12 the air?' There they C out, but he does
35:13 not hear an empty C, nor does the Almighty
36:13 anger; they do not C for help when he
36:19 Will your C avail to keep you from distress,
38:41 when its young ones C to God, and wander
Ps 3:4 I C aloud to the LORD, and he answers
5:2 the sound of my C, my King and my
9:12 does not forget the C of the afflicted.
17:1 a just cause, O LORD; attend to my C
18:6 my voice, and my C to him reached his
22:2 O my God, I C by day, but thou
27:7 O LORD, when I C aloud, be gracious to
28:2 my supplication, as I C to thee for help,
29:9 in his temple all C, "Glory!"
34:15 toward the righteous, and his ears toward their C
34:17 When the righteous C for help, the LORD hears,
39:12 give ear to my C; hold not thy peace
40:1 LORD; he inclined to me and heard my C
57:2 I C to God Most High, to God who
61:1 Hear my C, O God, listen to my prayer;
77:1 I C aloud to God, aloud to God, that
86:3 to thee do I C all the day.
86:6 prayer; hearken to my C of supplication.
88:1 help by day; I C out in the night
88:2 come before thee, incline thy ear to my C
88:13 But I, O LORD, C to thee; in the
89:26 He shall C to me, 'Thou art my Father,
102:1 O LORD; let my C come to thee!
106:44 he regarded their distress, when he heard their C
119:145 my whole heart I C; answer me, O LORD!
119:146 I C to thee; save me, that I may
119:147 rise before dawn and C for help; I hope
119:169 Let my C come before thee, O LORD; give
120:1 In my distress I C to the LORD, that
130:1 of the depths I C to thee, O LORD!
142:1 I C with my voice to the LORD, with
142:5 I C to thee, O LORD; I say, Thou
142:6 Give heed to my C; for I am brought
144:14 may there be no C of distress in our
145:19 he also hears their C, and saves them.
147:9 their food, and to the young ravens which C
Prov 2:3 understanding; yes, if you C out for insight and
8:4 I call, and my C is to the sons
21:13 his ear to the C of the poor will
21:13 the poor will himself C out and not be
30:15 they C
Wis 7:3 first sound was a C, like that of all.
18:10 But the discordant C of their enemies echoed back,
Sir 30:7 and his feelings will be troubled at every C
Is 5:7 bloodshed; for righteousness, but behold, a C
8:4 child knows how to C 'My father' or 'My
10:30 C aloud, O daughter of Gallim!
13:2 hill raise a signal, C aloud to them; wave
13:22 Hyenas will C in its towers, and jackals in
14:31 Wail, O gate; C, O city; melt in fear,
15:4 Heshbon and Ele-aleh C out, their voice is heard
15:4 armed men of Moab C aloud; his soul trembles.
15:5 Horonaim they raise a C of destruction;
15:8 For a C has gone round the land of
19:20 of Egypt; when they C to the LORD because
30:19 the sound of your C; when he hears it,
33:7 Behold, the valiant ones C without; the envoys of
34:14 hyenas, the satyr shall C to his fellow; yea,
38:13 to an end; I C for help until morning;
40:2 tenderly to Jerusalem, and C to her that her
40:6 A voice says, C
40:6 And I said, "What shall I C
42:2 He will not C or lift up his voice,
42:14 myself; now I will C out like a woman
54:1 forth into singing and C aloud, you who have
57:13 When you C out, let your collection of idols
58:1 C aloud, spare not, lift up your voice like
58:9 will answer; you shall C, and he will say,
65:14 heart, but you shall C out for pain of
65:19 of weeping and the C of distress.
Jer 4:5 through the land; C aloud and say, 'Assemble,
4:31 For I heard a C as of a woman
4:31 her first child, the C of the daughter of
7:16 people, or lift up C or prayer for them,
8:19 Hark, the C of the daughter of my people
11:11 cannot escape; though they C to me, I will
11:12 Jerusalem will go and C to the gods to
11:14 or lift up a C or prayer on their
12:6 they are in full C after you; believe them
14:2 the ground, and the C of Jerusalem goes up.
14:12 will not hear their C, and though they offer
18:22 May a C be heard from their houses, when
20:8 whenever I speak, I C out, I shout, "Violence
20:16 let him hear a C in the morning and
22:20 up to Lebanon, and C out, and lift up
22:20 your voice in Bashan; C from Abarim, for all
25:34 "Wail, you shepherds, and C, and roll in ashes,
25:36 Hark, the C of the shepherds, and the wail
30:5 We have heard a C of panic, of terror,
30:15 Why do you C out over your hurt?
46:12 is full of your C; for warrior has stumbled
47:2 Men shall C out, and every inhabitant of the
48:3 a C from Horonaim, 'Desolation and great
48:4 Moab is destroyed; a C is heard as far
48:5 they have heard the C of destruction.
48:20 to shame, for it is broken; wail and C
48:31 wail for Moab; I C out for all Moab;
48:34 "Heshbon and Ele-aleh C out; as far as Jahaz
49:2 will cause the battle C to be heard against
49:3 C, O daughters of Rabbah!
49:21 the sound of their C shall be heard at
49:29 them, and men shall C to them: 'Terror on
50:46 shall tremble, and her C shall be heard among
51:54 a C from Babylon!
Lam 2:12 They C to their mothers, "Where is bread and
2:16 gnash their teeth, they C: "We have destroyed her!
2:18 C aloud to the Lord!
2:19 Arise, C out in the night, at the beginning
3:8 though I call and C for help, he shuts
3:56 thine ear to my C for help!'
Bar 3:1 and the wearied spirit C out to thee.

4:20 my supplication; I will C to the Everlasting all
4:21 "Take courage, my children, C to God, and he
4:27 courage, my children, and C to God, for you
Ezek 8:18 pity; and though they C in my ears with
21:12 C and wail, son of man, for it is
21:22 the mouth with a C, to lift up the
27:28 the sound of the C of your pilots the
27:30 aloud over you, and C bitterly.
Dan 13:44 The Lord heard her C
Hos 7:15 They do not C to me from the heart,
8:2 To me they C, My God, we Israel know
Joel 1:13 LORD your God; and C to the LORD.
1:18 Unto thee, O LORD, I C
1:19 Even the wild beasts C to thee because the
Amos 3:4 Does a young lion C out from his den,
Jon 1:2 that great city, and C against it; for their
3:8 sackcloth, and let them C mightily to God; yea,
Mic 3:4 Then they will C to the LORD, but he
3:5 my people astray, who C "Peace" when they have
4:9 Now why do you C aloud?
Nah 2:8 they C; but none turns back.
Hab 1:2 how long shall I C for help, and thou
1:2 Or C to thee "Violence!" and thou wilt not
2:11 For the stone will C out from the wall,
Zeph 1:10 says the LORD, "a C will be heard from
1:16 trumpet blast and battle C against the fortified cities
Zech 1:14 me said to me, C out, Thus says the
1:17 C again, Thus says the LORD of hosts: My
1Mac 4:10 And now let us C to Heaven, to see
5:31 begun and that the C of the city went
9:46 C out now to Heaven that you may be
2Mac 12:37 he raised the battle C, with hymns; then he
Mt 12:19 will not wrangle or C aloud, nor will any
25:6 midnight there was a C, 'Behold, the bridegroom!
Mk 10:47 Nazareth, he began to C out and say, "Jesus,
15:36 Jesus uttered a loud C, and breathed his last.
Lk 1:42 exclaimed with a loud C, "Blessed are you among
18:7 vindicate his elect, who C to him day and
19:40 the very stones would C out."
Rom 8:15 When we C, "Abba!
1Thes 4:16 from heaven with a C of command, with the
Jas 5:4 kept back by fraud, C out; and the cries
Rev 16:7 I heard the altar C, "Yea, Lord God the

CRYING (34)

Gen 4:10 your brother's blood is C to me from the
Ex 2:6 saw the child; and lo, the babe was C
2Sam 13:19 head, and went away, C aloud as she went.
2Kgs 13:14 and wept before him, C, "My father, my father!
Jud 10:1 When Judith had ceased C out to the God
Ps 69:3 am weary with my C; my throat is parched.
Mt 3:3 "The voice of one C in the wilderness: Prepare
9:27 blind men followed him, C aloud, "Have mercy on
15:23 away, for she is C after us."
21:15 did, and the children C out in the temple,
Mk 1:3 the voice of one C in the wilderness: Prepare
1:26 spirit, convulsing him and C with a loud voice,
5:5 mountains he was always C out, and bruising himself
5:7 and worshiped him; and C out with a loud
9:26 And after C out and convulsing him terribly, it
Lk 3:4 "The voice of one C in the wilderness: Prepare
4:41 came out of many, C, "You are the Son
23:45 Then Jesus, C with a loud voice, said, "Father,
Jn 1:23 the voice of one C in the wilderness, 'Make
12:13 out to meet him, C, "Hosanna!
Acts 8:7 many who were possessed, C with a loud voice;
14:14 out among the multitude, C,
16:17 followed Paul and us, C, "These men are servants
17:6 before the city authorities, C, "These men who have
21:28 laid hands on him, C out, "Men of Israel,
21:36 of the people followed, C, "Away with him!"
Gal 4:6 Son into our hearts, C, "Abba!
Rev 7:10 in their hands, and C out with a loud
8:13 I heard an eagle C with a loud voice,
18:19 they wept and mourned, C out, "Alas, alas, for
19:1 great multitude in heaven, C, "Hallelujah!
19:5 throne came a voice C, "Praise our God, all
19:6 sound of mighty thunderpeals, C, "Hallelujah!
21:4 there be mourning nor C nor pain any more,

CRYSTAL (5)

Job 28:18 of coral or of C; the price of wisdom
Ezek 1:22 a firmament, shining like C, spread out above their
Rev 4:6 as it were a sea of glass, like C
21:11 most rare jewel, like a jasper, clear as C
22:1 of life, bright as C, flowing from the throne

CRYSTALLINE

Wis 19:21 did they melt the C, easily melted kind of

CUB

1Mac 3:4 deeds, like a lion's C roaring for prey.

CUBIT (41)

Gen 6:16 finish it to a C above; and set the
Ex 25:10 be its length, a C and a half its
25:10 its breadth, and a C and a half its
25:17 its length, and a C and a half its
25:23 be its length, a C its breadth, and a
25:23 its breadth, and a C and a half its
26:13 And the C on the one side, and the
26:13 one side, and the C on the other side,
26:16 a frame, and a C and a half the
30:2 A C shall be its length, and a cubit
30:2 its length, and a C its breadth; it shall
36:21 a frame, and a C and a half the
37:1 was its length, a C and a half its
37:1 its breadth, and a C and a half its
37:6 its length, and a C and a half its
37:10 was its length, a C its breadth, and a
37:10 its breadth, and a C and a half its
37:25 its length was a C, and its breadth was
37:25 its breadth was a C; it was square, and
Deut 3:11 four cubits its breadth, according to the common C
Judg 3:16 with two edges, a C in length; and he
1Kgs 7:31 which projected upward one C; its opening was
7:31 pedestal is made, a C and a half deep.
7:32 a wheel was a C and a half.
7:35 round band half a C high; and on the
Ezek 40:5 cubits, each being a C and a handbreadth in
40:12 the side rooms, one C on either side; and
40:42 the burnt offering, a C and a half long,
40:42 half long, and a C and a half broad,
40:42 half broad, and one C high, on which the
43:13 altar by cubits (the C being a cubit and
43:13 (the cubit being a C and a handbreadth): its
43:13 base shall be one C high, and one cubit
43:13 cubit high, and one C broad, with a rim
43:14 a breadth of one C; and from the smaller
43:14 a breadth of one C;
43:15 upward, four horns, one C high.
43:17 around it half a C broad, and its base
43:17 and its base one C round about.
Mt 6:27 anxious can add one C to his span of
Lk 12:25 anxious can add a C to his span of

CUBITS (255)

Gen 6:15 the ark three hundred C, its breadth fifty cubits,
6:15 cubits, its breadth fifty C, and its height thirty
6:15 its breadth fifty cubits, and its height thirty C
7:20 mountains, covering them fifteen C deep.
Ex 25:10 of acacia wood; two C and a half shall
25:17 of pure gold; two C and a half shall
25:23 of acacia wood; two C shall be its length,
26:2 curtain shall be twenty-eight C, and the breadth of
26:2 of each curtain four C; all the curtains shall
26:8 curtain shall be thirty C, and the breadth of
26:8 of each curtain four C; the eleven curtains shall
26:16 Ten C shall be the length of a frame,
27:1 of acacia wood, five C long and five cubits
27:1 cubits long and five C broad; the altar shall
27:1 be square, and its height shall be three C
27:9 twined linen a hundred C long for one side;
27:11 be hangings a hundred C long, their pillars twenty
27:12 be hangings for fifty C, with ten pillars and
27:13 the front to the east shall be fifty C
27:14 gate shall be fifteen C, with three pillars and
27:15 hangings shall be fifteen C, with three pillars and
27:16 be a screen twenty C long, of blue and
27:18 shall be a hundred C, the breadth fifty, and
27:18 and the height five C, with hangings of fine
30:2 be square, and two C shall be its height;
36:9 each curtain was twenty-eight C, and the breadth of
36:9 of each curtain four C; all the curtains had
36:15 each curtain was thirty C, and the breadth of
36:15 of each curtain four C; the eleven curtains had
36:21 Ten C was the length of a frame, and
37:1 of acacia wood; two C and a half was
37:6 of pure gold; two C and a half was
37:10 of acacia wood; two C was its length, a
37:25 was square, and two C was its height; its
38:1 of acacia wood; five C was its length, and
38:1 its length, and five C its breadth; it was

 CUBITS

38:1 was square, and three C was its height.
38:9 twined linen, a hundred C;
38:11 north side a hundred C, their pillars twenty, their
38:12 were hangings of fifty C, their pillars ten, and
38:13 And for the front to the east, fifty C
38:14 the gate were fifteen C, with three pillars and
38:15 were hangings of fifteen C, with three pillars and
38:18 linen; it was twenty C long and five cubits
38:18 cubits long and five C high in its breadth,
Num 11:31 camp, and about two C above the face of
35:4 city outward a thousand C all round.
35:5 east side two thousand C, and for the south
35:5 south side two thousand C, and for the west
35:5 west side two thousand C, and for the north
35:5 north side two thousand C, the city being in
Deut 3:11 Nine C was its length, and four cubits its
3:11 its length, and four C its breadth, according to
Josh 3:4 of about two thousand C; do not come near
1Sam 17:4 whose height was six C and a span.
1Kgs 6:2 the LORD was sixty C long, twenty cubits wide,
6:2 sixty cubits long, twenty C wide, and thirty cubits
6:2 cubits wide, and thirty C high.
6:3 the house was twenty C long, equal to the
6:3 the house, and ten C deep in front of
6:6 lowest story was five C broad, the middle one
6:6 middle one was six C broad, and the third
6:6 the third was seven C broad; for around the
6:10 house, each story five C high, and it was
6:16 He built twenty C of the rear of the
6:17 inner sanctuary, was forty C long.
6:20 inner sanctuary was twenty C long, twenty cubits
6:20 twenty cubits long, twenty C wide, and twenty cubits
6:20 cubits wide, and twenty C high; and he overlaid
6:23 of olivewood, each ten C high.
6:24 Five C was the length of one wing of
6:24 the cherub, and five C the length of the
6:24 cherub; it was ten C from the tip of
6:25 cherub also measured ten C; both cherubim had the
6:26 one cherub was ten C, and so was that
7:2 length was a hundred C, and its breadth fifty
7:2 and its breadth fifty C, and its height thirty
7:2 and its height thirty C, and it was built
7:6 its length was fifty C, and its breadth thirty
7:6 and its breadth thirty C; there was a porch
7:10 stones, huge stones, stones of eight and ten C
7:15 Eighteen C was the height of one pillar, and
7:15 a line of twelve C measured its circumference; it
7:16 one capital was five C, and the height of
7:16 the height of the other capital was five C
7:19 pillars in the vestibule were of lily-work, four C
7:23 it was round, ten C from brim to brim,
7:23 to brim, and five C high, and a line
7:23 a line of thirty C measured its circumference.
7:24 were gourds, for thirty C, compassing the sea round
7:27 each stand was four C long, four cubits wide,
7:27 four cubits long, four C wide, and three cubits
7:27 cubits wide, and three C high.
7:38 each laver measured four C, and there was a
2Kgs 14:13 Jerusalem for four hundred C, from the Ephraim
25:17 one pillar was eighteen C, and upon it was
25:17 capital was three C; a network and pomegranates,
1Chr 11:23 of great stature, five C tall.
2Chr 3:3 God: the length, in C of the old standard,
3:3 old standard, was sixty C, and the breadth twenty
3:3 standard, was sixty cubits, and the breadth twenty C
3:4 the house was twenty C long, equal to the
3:4 and its height was a hundred and twenty C
3:8 the house, was twenty C, and its breadth was
3:8 its breadth was twenty C; he overlaid it with
3:11 cherubim together extended twenty C: one wing of
3:11 the one, of five C, touched the wall of
3:11 other wing, of five C, touched the wing of
3:12 one wing, of five C, touched the wall of
3:12 wing, also of five C, was joined to the
3:13 cherubim extended twenty C; the cherubim stood on
3:15 made two pillars thirty-five C high, with a capital
3:15 a capital of five C on the top of
4:1 altar of bronze, twenty C long, and twenty cubits
4:1 cubits long, and twenty C wide, and ten cubits
4:1 cubits wide, and ten C high.
4:2 it was round, ten C from brim to brim,
4:2 to brim, and five C high, and a line
4:2 a line of thirty C measured its circumference.
4:3 of gourds, for thirty C, compassing the sea round
6:13 a bronze platform five C long, five cubits wide,
6:13 five cubits long, five C wide, and three cubits
6:13 cubits wide, and three C high, and had set
25:23 Jerusalem for four hundred C, from the Ephraim
Ezra 6:3 height shall be sixty C and its breadth sixty
6:3 and its breadth sixty C,
Neh 3:13 and repaired a thousand C of the wall, as
Jud 1:2 with hewn stones three C thick and six cubits
1:2 cubits thick and six C long; he made the
1:2 made the walls seventy C high and fifty cubits
1:2 cubits high and fifty C wide;
1:3 built towers a hundred C high and sixty cubits
1:3 cubits high and sixty C wide at the foundations;
1:4 gates, which were seventy C high and forty cubits
1:4 cubits high and forty C wide, so that his
Esth 5:14 "Let a gallows fifty C high be made, and
7:9 in Haman's house, fifty C high."
Jer 52:21 pillar was eighteen C, its circumference was twelve
52:21 its circumference was twelve C, and its thickness
52:22 one capital was five C; a network and pomegranates,
Ezek 40:5 hand was six long C, each being a cubit
40:7 the side rooms, five C; and the threshold of
40:8 of the gateway, eight C;
40:9 and its jambs, two C; and the vestibule of
40:11 of the gateway, ten C; and the breadth of
40:11 cubits; and the breadth of the gateway, thirteen C
40:12 side rooms were six C on either side.
40:13 of five and twenty C, from door to door.
40:14 also the vestibule, twenty C; and round about the
40:15 the inner vestibule of the gate was fifty C
40:19 outer front of the inner court, a hundred C
40:21 its length was fifty C, and its breadth twenty-five
40:21 length was fifty cubits, and its breadth twenty-five C
40:23 he measured from gate to gate, a hundred C
40:25 its length was fifty C, and its breadth twenty-five
40:25 length was fifty cubits, and its breadth twenty-five C
40:27 gate to gate toward the south, a hundred C
40:29 its length was fifty C, and its breadth twenty-five
40:29 length was fifty cubits, and its breadth twenty-five C
40:30 vestibules round about, twenty-five C long and five
40:30 cubits long and five C broad.
40:33 its length was fifty C, and its breadth twenty-five
40:33 length was fifty cubits, and its breadth twenty-five C
40:36 its length was fifty C, and its breadth twenty-five
40:36 length was fifty cubits, and its breadth twenty-five C
40:47 the court, a hundred C long, and a hundred
40:47 long, and a hundred C broad, foursquare; and the
40:48 of the vestibule, five C on either side; and
40:48 the gate was fourteen C; and the sidewalls of
40:48 the gate were three C on either side.
40:49 the vestibule was twenty C, and the breadth twelve
40:49 and the breadth twelve C; and ten steps led
41:1 on each side six C was the breadth of
41:2 the entrance was ten C; and the sidewalls of
41:2 the entrance were five C on either side; and
41:2 of the nave forty C, and its breadth, twenty
41:2 the nave forty cubits, and its breadth, twenty C
41:3 of the entrance, two C; and the breadth of
41:3 of the entrance, six C; and the sidewalls of
41:3 cubits; and the sidewalls of the entrance, seven C
41:4 of the room, twenty C, and its breadth, twenty
41:4 and its breadth, twenty C, beyond the nave.
41:5 of the temple, six C thick; and the breadth
41:5 the side chambers, four C, round about the temple.
41:8 chambers measured a full reed of six long C
41:9 side chambers was five C; and the part of
41:9 the platform which was left free was five C
41:10 a breadth of twenty C round about the temple
41:11 left free was five C round about.
41:12 west side was seventy C broad; and the wall
41:12 the building was five C thick round about, and
41:12 cubits thick round about, and its length ninety C
41:13 the temple, a hundred C long; and the yard
41:13 its walls, a hundred C long;
41:14 of the temple and the yard, a hundred C
41:15 and its walls on either side, a hundred C
41:22 altar of wood, three C high, two cubits long,
41:22 three cubits high, two C long, and two cubits
41:22 cubits long, and two C broad; its corners, its
42:2 side was a hundred C, and the breadth fifty
42:2 was a hundred cubits, and the breadth fifty C
42:3 Adjoining the twenty C which belonged to the inner
42:4 a passage inward, ten C wide and a hundred
42:4 wide and a hundred C long, and their doors
42:7 opposite the chambers, fifty C long.
42:8 outer court were fifty C long, while those opposite
42:8 temple were a hundred C long.
42:16 measuring reed, five hundred C by the measuring

42:17 north side, five hundred C by the measuring reed.
42:18 south side, five hundred C by the measuring reed.
42:19 and measured, five hundred C by the measuring reed.
42:20 around it, five hundred C long and five hundred
42:20 long and five hundred C broad, to make a
43:13 of the altar by C (the cubit being a
43:14 the lower ledge, two C, with a breadth of
43:14 the larger ledge, four C, with a breadth of
43:15 the altar hearth, four C; and from the altar
43:16 shall be square, twelve C long by twelve broad.
43:17 shall be square, fourteen C long by fourteen broad,
45:1 holy district, twenty-five thousand C long and twenty
45:1 long and twenty thousand C broad; it shall be
45:2 hundred by five hundred C shall be for the
45:2 the sanctuary, with fifty C for an open space
45:3 a section twenty-five thousand C long and ten
45:5 Another section, twenty-five thousand C long and ten
45:5 long and ten thousand C broad, shall be for
45:6 an area five thousand C broad, and twenty-five
45:6 broad, and twenty-five thousand C long; it shall
46:22 were small courts, forty C long and thirty broad;
47:3 man measured a thousand C, and then led me
48:8 set apart, twenty-five thousand C in breadth, and in
48:9 shall be twenty-five thousand C in length, and twenty
48:10 measuring twenty-five thousand C on the northern
48:10 northern side, ten thousand C in breadth on the
48:13 an allotment twenty-five thousand C in length and
48:13 shall be twenty-five thousand C and the breadth
48:15 "The remainder, five thousand C in breadth and
48:16 four thousand five hundred C, the south side four
48:17 two hundred and fifty C, on the south two
48:18 shall be ten thousand C to the east, and
48:20 shall be twenty-five thousand C square, that is, the
48:21 from the twenty-five thousand C of the holy portion
48:21 from the twenty-five thousand C to the west border,
48:30 four thousand five hundred C by measure,
48:32 four thousand five hundred C, three gates, the gate
48:33 four thousand five hundred C by measure, three
48:34 four thousand five hundred C, three gates, the gate
48:35 of the city shall be eighteen thousand C
Dan 3:1 whose height was sixty C and its breadth six
3:1 height was sixty cubits and its breadth six C
3:47 above the furnace forty-nine C,
Zech 5:2 its length is twenty C, and its breadth ten
5:2 length is twenty cubits, and its breadth ten C
2Mac 13:5 in that place, fifty C high, full of ashes,
Rev 21:17 a hundred and forty-four C by a man's measure,

CUBS (4)
2Sam 17:8 bear robbed of her C in the field.
Prov 17:12 she-bear robbed of her C, rather than a fool
Hos 13:8 bear robbed of her C, I will tear open
Nah 2:11 his prey, where his C were, with none to

CUCUMBER (3)
Is 1:8 a lodge in a C field, like a besieged
Jer 10:5 like scarecrows in a C field, and they cannot
Bar 6:70 a scarecrow in a C bed, that guards nothing,

CUCUMBERS
Num 11:5 Egypt for nothing, the C, the melons, the leeks,

CUD (11)
Lev 11:3 cloven-footed and chews the C, among the animals,
11:4 those that chew the C or part the hoof,
11:4 because it chews the C but does not part
11:5 because it chews the C but does not part
11:6 because it chews the C but does not part
11:7 does not chew the C, is unclean to you.
11:26 does not chew the C is unclean to you;
Deut 14:6 two, and chews the C, among the animals, you
14:7 those that chew the C or have the hoof
14:7 because they chew the C but do not part
14:8 does not chew the C, is unclean for you.

CULT (8)
Deut 23:17 "There shall be no C prostitute of the daughters
23:17 shall there be a C prostitute of the sons
1Kgs 14:24 there were also male C prostitutes in the land.
15:12 put away the male C prostitutes out of the
22:46 remnant of the male C prostitutes who remained in
2Kgs 23:7 houses of the male C prostitutes which were in
Wis 12:5 midst of a heathen C,
Hos 4:14 harlots, and sacrifice with C prostitutes, and a people

CULTIVATE
Ps 104:14 plants for man to C, that he may bring

CULTIVATED (4)
Eccl 5:9 to a land with C fields.
Sir 21:23 the door, but a C man remains outside.
Rom 11:24 to nature, into a C olive tree, how much
Heb 6:7 whose sake it is C, receives a blessing from

CULTIVATES
Sir 20:27 Whoever C the soil will heap up his harvest,

CULTIVATION (2)
Sir 27:6 The fruit discloses the C of a tree; so
27:6 a thought discloses the C of a man's mind.

CUMI
Mk 5:41 said to her, "Talitha C; which means, "Little girl,

CUMMIN (4)
Is 28:25 not scatter dill, sow C, and put in wheat
28:27 cart wheel rolled over C; but dill is beaten
28:27 with a stick, and C with a rod.
Mt 23:22 mint and dill and C, and have neglected the

CUN
1Chr 18:8 from Tibhath and from C, cities of Hadadezer, David

CUNNING (9)
Josh 9:4 their part acted with C, and went and made
1Sam 23:22 it is told me that he is very C
2Kgs 10:19 Jehu did it with C in order to destroy
Ps 58:5 charmers or of the C enchanter.
119:118 thy statutes; yea, their C is in vain.
Dan 8:25 By his C he shall make deceit prosper under
2Cor 4:2 we refuse to practice C or to tamper with
11:3 deceived Eve by his C, your thoughts will be
Eph 4:14 of doctrine, by the C of men, by their

CUNNINGLY
Ps 64:6 have thought out a C conceived plot." For the

CUP (67)
Gen 40:11 Pharaoh's C was in my hand; and I took
40:11 pressed them into Pharaoh's C, and placed the cup
40:11 cup, and placed the C in Pharaoh's hand."
40:13 you shall place Pharaoh's C in his hand as
40:21 and he placed the C in Pharaoh's hand;
44:2 sack, and put my C, the silver cup, in
44:2 my cup, the silver C, in the mouth of
44:4 Why have you stolen my silver C
44:12 the youngest; and the C was found in Benjamin's
44:16 in whose hand the C has been found."
44:17 in whose hand the C was found shall be
2Sam 12:3 and drink from his C, and lie in his
1Kgs 7:26 the brim of a C, like the flower of
2Chr 4:5 the brim of a C, like the flower of
Ps 11:6 scorching wind shall be the portion of their C
16:5 chosen portion and my C; thou holdest my lot.
23:5 head with oil, my C overflows.
75:8 LORD there is a C, with foaming wine, well
116:13 will lift up the C of salvation and call
Prov 23:31 it sparkles in the C and goes down smoothly.
Sir 50:15 his hand to the C and poured a libation
Is 51:17 of the LORD the C of his wrath, who
51:22 from your hand the C of staggering; the bowl
Jer 16:7 one give him the C of consolation to drink
25:15 from my hand this C of the wine of
25:17 So I took the C from the LORD's hand,
25:28 refuse to accept the C from your hand to
49:12 deserve to drink the C must drink it, will
51:7 Babylon was a golden C in the LORD's hand,
Lam 4:21 to you also the C shall pass; you shall
Ezek 23:31 I will give her C into your hand.
23:32 shall drink your sister's C which is deep and
23:33 A C of horror and desolation, is the cup
23:33 and desolation, is the C of your sister Samaria;
Hab 2:15 neighbors drink of the C of his wrath, and
2:16 The C in the LORD's right hand will come
Zech 12:2 to make Jerusalem a C of reeling to all
Mt 10:42 little ones even a C of cold water because
20:22 able to drink the C that I am to
20:23 "You will drink my C, but to sit at
23:24 the outside of the C and of the plate,
23:25 the inside of the C and of the plate,
26:27 And he took a C, and when he had

26:39 be possible, let this C pass from me; nevertheless,
Mk 9:41 whoever gives you a C of water to drink
10:38 able to drink the C that I drink, or
10:39 said to them, "The C that I drink you
14:23 And he took a C, and when he had
14:36 to thee; remove this C from me; yet not
Lk 11:39 the outside of the C and of the dish,
22:17 And he took a C, and when he had
22:20 And likewise the C after supper, saying, "This cup
22:20 after supper, saying, "This C which is poured out
22:42 art willing, remove this C from me; nevertheless not
Jn 18:11 I not drink the C which the Father has
1Cor 10:16 The C of blessing which we bless, is it
10:21 You cannot drink the C of the Lord and
10:21 the Lord and the C of demons.
11:25 same way also the C, after supper, saying, "This
11:25 after supper, saying, "This C is the new covenant
11:26 bread and drink the C, you proclaim the Lord's
11:27 bread or drinks the C of the Lord in
11:28 eat of the bread and drink of the C
Rev 14:10 poured unmixed into the C of his anger, and
16:19 make her drain the C of the fury of
17:4 her hand a golden C full of abominations and
18:6 for her in the C she mixed.

CUPBEARER (2)
Neh 1:11 Now I was C to the king.
Tob 1:22 Now Ahikar was C, keeper of the signet, and

CUPBEARERS (2)
1Kgs 10:5 servants, their clothing, his C, and his burnt offerings
2Chr 9:4 and their clothing, his C, and their clothing, and

CUPIDITY
2Mac 4:50 Menelaus, because of the C of those in power,

CUPS (16)
Ex 25:31 of hammered work; its C, its capitals, and its
25:33 side of it; three C made like almonds, each
25:33 one branch, and three C made like almonds, each
25:34 the lampstand itself four C made like almonds, with
37:17 of hammered work; its C, its capitals, and its
37:19 side of it; three C made like almonds, each
37:19 one branch, and three C made like almonds, each
37:20 lampstand itself were four C made like almonds,
1Kgs 7:50 tongs, of gold; the C, snuffers, basins, dishes for
1Chr 28:17 the basins, and the C; for the golden bowls
Is 22:24 small vessel, from the C to all the flagons.
65:11 for Fortune and fill C of mixed wine for
Jer 35:5 full of wine, and C; and I said to
1Mac 1:22 of the Presence, the C for drink offerings, the
11:58 to drink from gold C and dress in purple
Mk 7:4 observe, the washing of C and pots and vessels

CURBED
Ps 32:9 understanding, which must be C with bit and bridle,

CURDLE
Job 10:10 out like milk and C me like cheese?

CURDS (9)
Gen 18:8 Then he took C, and milk, and the calf
Deut 32:14 C from the herd, and milk from the flock,
Judg 5:25 milk, she brought him C in a lordly bowl.
2Sam 17:29 and lentils, honey and C and sheep and cheese
Job 20:17 the rivers, the streams flowing with honey and C
Prov 30:33 For pressing milk produces C, pressing the nose
Is 7:15 He shall eat C and honey when he knows
7:22 give, he will eat C; for every one that
7:22 the land will eat C and honey.

CURE (6)
2Kgs 5:3 He would C him of his leprosy."
5:6 servant, that you may C him of his leprosy."
5:7 word to me to C a man of his
5:11 over the place, and C the leper.
Hos 5:13 is not able to C you or heal your
Lk 9:1 all demons and to C diseases,

CURED (9)
Tob 6:8 films in his eyes, and he will be C
12:3 to you safely, he C my wife, he obtained
Wis 16:12 neither herb nor poultice C them, but it was
Mt 17:18 and the boy was C instantly.
Lk 6:18 those who were troubled with unclean spirits were C
7:21 In that hour he C many of diseases and
9:11 kingdom of God, and C those who had need
Jn 5:9 the man who was C, "It is the sabbath,
Acts 28:9 island who had diseases also came and were C

CURES
Lk 13:32 out demons and perform C today and tomorrow, and

CURRENT (2)
Gen 23:16 according to the weights C among the merchants.
Sir 4:26 try to stop the C of a river.

CURSE (108)
Gen 8:21 "I will never again C the ground because of
12:3 curses you I will C; and by you all
27:12 him, and bring a C upon myself and not
27:13 "Upon me be your C, my son; only obey
Ex 22:28 not revile God, nor C a ruler of your
Lev 19:14 You shall not C the deaf or put a
Num 5:18 have the water of bitterness that brings the C
5:19 from this water of bitterness that brings the C
5:21 the oath of the C, and say to the
5:22 water that brings the C pass into your bowels
5:24 bitterness that brings the C, and the water that
5:24 water that brings the C shall enter into her
5:27 water that brings the C shall enter into her
22:6 Come now, C this people for me, since they
22:6 and he whom you C is cursed."
22:11 the earth; now come, C them for me; perhaps
22:12 them; you shall not C the people, for they
22:17 I will do; come, C this people for me.'"
23:7 the eastern mountains: 'Come, C Jacob for me, and
23:8 Israel!' How can I C whom God has not
23:11 I took you to C my enemies, and behold,
23:13 see them all; then C them for me from
23:25 said to Balaam, "Neither C them at all, nor
23:27 God that you may C them for me from
24:10 "I called you to C my enemies, and behold,
Deut 11:26 a blessing and a C:
11:28 this day, and the C, if you do not
11:29 Mount Gerizim and the C on Mount Ebal.
23:4 Pethor of Mesopotamia, to C you.
23:5 your God turned the C into a blessing for
27:13 Mount Ebal for the C: Reuben, Gad, Asher, Zebulun,
30:1 the blessing and the C, which I have set
30:19 and death, blessing and C; therefore choose life, that
Josh 8:34 the blessing and the C, according to all that
24:9 son of Beor to C you,
Judg 5:23 C Meroz, says the angel of the LORD, curse
5:23 angel of the LORD, C bitterly its inhabitants, because
9:57 upon them came the C of Jotham the son
17:2 which you uttered a C, and also spoke it
2Sam 16:9 should this dead dog C my lord the king?
16:10 has said to him, C David,' who then shall
16:11 alone, and let him C; for the LORD has
1Kgs 2:8 me with a grievous C on the day when
2Kgs 22:19 a desolation and a C, and you have rent
Neh 10:29 and enter into a C and an oath to
13:2 Balaam against them to C them– yet our
13:2 our God turned the C into a blessing.
Job 1:11 has, and he will C thee to thy face."
2:5 flesh, and he will C thee to thy face."
2:9 C God, and die."
3:8 Let those C it who curse the day, who
3:8 those curse it who C the day, who are
31:30 his life with a C;
Ps 62:4 They bless with their mouths, but inwardly they C
102:8 who deride me use my name for a C
109:17 He loved to C; let curses come on him!
109:28 Let them C, but do thou bless!
Prov 3:33 The LORD's C is on the house of the
11:26 The people C him who holds back grain, but
26:2 in its flying, a C that is causeless does
28:27 who hides his eyes will get many a C
29:24 life; he hears the C, but discloses nothing.
30:10 his master, lest he C you, and you be
30:11 There are those who C their fathers and do
Eccl 10:20 your thought, do not C the king, nor in
10:20 nor in your bedchamber C the rich; for a
Sir 3:9 children, but a mother's C uproots their foundations.
4:5 a man occasion to C you;
4:6 he calls down a C upon you, his Creator
23:14 born, and you will C the day of your
23:26 her memory for a C, and her disgrace will
28:13 C the whisperer and deceiver, for he has destroyed
41:9 are born to a C; and when you die,
41:9 when you die, a C is your lot.

41:10 the ungodly go from C to destruction.
Is 8:21 be enraged and will C their king and their
24:6 Therefore a C devours the earth, and its inhabitants
65:15 my chosen for a C, and the Lord GOD
Jer 15:10 yet all of them C me.
23:10 adulterers; because of the C the land mourns, and
24:9 a taunt, and a C in all the places
25:18 a hissing and a C, as at this day;
26:6 make this city a C for all the nations
29:18 earth, to be a C, a terror, a hissing,
29:22 Because of them this C shall be used by
42:18 execration, a horror, a C, and a taunt.
44:8 off and become a C and a taunt among
44:12 execration, a horror, a C, and a taunt.
44:22 a waste and a C, without inhabitant, as it
49:13 a waste, and a C; and all her cities
Lam 3:65 dullness of heart; thy C will be on them.
Bar 1:20 the calamities and the C which the Lord declared
6:66 For they can neither C nor bless kings;
Dan 9:11 And the C and oath which are written in
Zech 5:3 me, "This is the C that goes out over
14:11 shall be no more C; Jerusalem shall dwell in
Mal 2:2 I will send the C upon you and I
2:2 you and I will C your blessings; indeed I
3:9 are cursed with a C, for you are robbing
4:6 I come and smite the land with a C
Mt 26:74 began to invoke a C on himself and to
Mk 14:71 began to invoke a C on himself and to
Lk 6:28 you, bless those who C you, pray for those
Rom 12:14 bless and do not C them.
Gal 3:10 law are under a C; for it is written,
3:13 redeemed us from the C of the law, having
3:13 law, having become a C for us—for it
Jas 3:9 and with it we C men, who are made

CURSED (78)

Gen 3:14 you have done this, C are you above all
3:17 not eat of it,' C is the ground because
4:11 And now you are C from the ground, which
5:29 which the LORD has C this one shall bring
9:25 to him, he said, C be Canaan; a slave
27:29 C be every one who curses you, and blessed
49:7 C be their anger, for it is fierce; and
Lev 20:9 to death; he has C his father or his
24:11 Israelite woman's son blasphemed the Name, and C
24:14 the camp him who C; and let all who
24:23 brought him who had C out of the camp,
Num 22:6 is blessed, and he whom you curse is C
23:8 How can I curse whom God has not C
24:9 who blesses you, and C be every one who
Deut 27:15 with a loud voice: C be the man who
27:16 answer and say, 'Amen.' C be he who dishonors
27:17 people shall say, 'Amen.' C be he who removes
27:18 people shall say, 'Amen.' C be he who misleads
27:19 people shall say, 'Amen.' C be he who perverts
27:20 people shall say, 'Amen.' C be he who lies
27:21 people shall say, 'Amen.' C be he who lies
27:22 people shall say, 'Amen.' C be he who lies
27:23 people shall say, 'Amen.' C be he who lies
27:24 people shall say, 'Amen.' C be he who slays
27:25 people shall say, 'Amen.' C be he who takes
27:26 people shall say, 'Amen.' C be he who does
28:16 C shall you be in the city, and cursed
28:16 in the city, and C shall you be in
28:17 C shall be your basket and your kneading-trough.
28:18 C shall be the fruit of your body, and
28:19 C shall you be when you come in, and
28:19 you come in, and C shall you be when
Josh 6:26 at that time, saying, C before the LORD be
9:23 Now therefore you are C, and some of you
Judg 21:18 of Israel had sworn, C be he who gives
1Sam 14:24 on the people, saying, C be the man who
14:28 with an oath, saying, C be the man who
17:43 And the Philistine C David by his gods.
26:19 men, may they be C before the LORD, for
2Sam 16:5 as he came he C continually.
16:7 Shimei said as he C, "Begone, begone, you man
16:13 hillside opposite him and C as he went, and
19:21 for this, because he C the LORD's anointed?"
1Kgs 2:8 Benjaminite from Bahurim, who C me with a
21:10 him, saying, 'You have C God and the king.'
21:13 the people, saying, "Naboth C God and the king."
2Kgs 2:24 he saw them, he C them in the name
9:34 "See now to this C woman, and bury her;
Neh 13:25 contended with them and C them and beat some
Tob 13:12 C are all who hate you; blessed for ever
Job 1:5 sons have sinned, and C God in their hearts."
3:1 opened his mouth and C the day of his
5:3 root, but suddenly I C his dwelling.
24:18 waters; their portion is C in the land; no
Ps 37:22 the land, but those C by him shall be
Prov 24:24 will be C by peoples, abhorred by nations;
Eccl 7:22 times you have yourself C others.
Sir 3:16 angers his mother is C by the Lord.
33:12 some of them he C and brought low, and
Jer 11:3 the God of Israel: C be the man who
17:5 Thus says the LORD: C is the man who
20:14 C be the day on which I was born!
20:15 C be the man who brought the news to
48:10 C is he who does the work of the
48:10 LORD with slackness; and C is he who keeps
Bar 3:8 to be reproached and C and punished for all
Mal 1:14 C be the cheat who has a male in
2:2 indeed I have already C them, because you do
3:9 You are C with a curse, for you are
Mt 25:41 'Depart from me, you C, into the eternal fire
Mk 11:21 fig tree which you C has withered."
1Cor 12:3 the Spirit of God ever says "Jesus be C
Gal 3:10 for it is written, C be every one who
3:13 for it is written, C be every one who
Heb 6:8 and near to being C; its end is to
Rev 16:9 fierce heat, and they C the name of God
16:11 tongues in anguish and C the God of heaven
16:21 from heaven, till men C God for the plague

CURSES (23)

Gen 12:3 you, and him who C you I will curse;
27:29 be every one who C you, and blessed be
Ex 21:17 "Whoever C his father or his mother shall be
Lev 20:9 For every one who C his father or his
24:15 people of Israel, Whoever C his God shall bear
Num 5:23 priest shall write these C in a book, and
24:9 be every one who C you."
Deut 28:15 day, then all these C shall come upon you
28:20 will send upon you C, confusion, and frustration, in
28:45 All these C shall come upon you and pursue
29:20 that man, and the C written in this book
29:21 accordance with all the C of the covenant written
29:27 upon it all the C written in this book;
30:7 will put all these C upon your foes and
2Chr 34:24 its inhabitants, all the C that are written in
Ps 10:3 man greedy for gain C and renounces the LORD.
109:17 loved to curse; let C come on him!
Prov 20:20 If one C his father or his mother, his
Sir 21:27 When an ungodly man C his adversary, he curses
21:27 curses his adversary, he C his own soul.
29:6 will repay him with C and reproaches, and instead
34:24 one prays and another C, to whose voice will
Rom 3:14 mouth is full of C and bitterness."

CURSING (9)

2Sam 16:10 If he is C because the LORD has said
16:12 with good for this C of me today."
Ps 10:7 mouth is filled with C and deceit and oppression;
59:12 For the C and lies which they utter,
109:18 He clothed himself with C as his coat, may
Prov 27:14 early in the morning, will be counted as C
Eccl 7:21 you hear your servant C you;
Zech 8:13 been a byword of C among the nations, O
Jas 3:10 From the same mouth come blessing and C

CURTAIN (31)

Ex 26:2 The length of each C shall be twenty-eight cubits,
26:2 the breadth of each C four cubits; all the
26:4 edge of the outmost C in the first set;
26:4 edge of the outmost C in the second set.
26:5 make on the one C, and fifty loops you
26:5 the edge of the C that is in the
26:8 The length of each C shall be thirty cubits,
26:8 the breadth of each C four cubits; the eleven
26:9 themselves, and the sixth C you shall double over
26:10 the edge of the C that is outmost in
26:10 the edge of the C which is outmost in
26:12 the tent, the half C that remains, shall hang
36:9 The length of each C was twenty-eight cubits, and
36:9 the breadth of each C four cubits; all the
36:11 edge of the outmost C of the first set;
36:11 edge of the outmost C of the second set;
36:12 loops on the one C, and he made fifty
36:12 the edge of the C that was in the
36:15 The length of each C was thirty cubits, and
36:15 the breadth of each C four cubits; the eleven

36:17 edge of the outmost C of the one set,
36:17 loops on the edge of the other connecting C
Wis 17:3 unobserved behind a dark C of forgetfulness, they
Is 40:22 the heavens like a C, and spreads them like
1Mac 1:22 the golden censers, the C, the crowns, and the
Mt 27:51 And behold, the C of the temple was torn
Mk 15:37 And the C of the temple was torn in
Lk 23:44 light failed; and the C of the temple was
Heb 6:19 inner shrine behind the C,
9:3 Behind the second C stood a tent called the
10:20 for us through the C, that is, through his

CURTAINS (31)

Ex 26:1 the tabernacle with ten C of fine twined linen
26:2 four cubits; all the C shall have one measure.
26:3 Five C shall be coupled to one another; and
26:3 and the other five C shall be coupled to
26:6 gold, and couple the C one to the other
26:7 "You shall also make C of goats' hair for
26:7 over the tabernacle; eleven C shall you make.
26:8 four cubits; the eleven C shall have the same
26:9 you shall couple five C by themselves, and six
26:9 by themselves, and six C by themselves, and the
26:12 that remains of the C of the tent, the
26:13 the length of the C of the tent shall
36:8 the tabernacle with ten C; they were made of
36:9 four cubits; all the C had the same measure.
36:10 And he coupled five C to one another, and
36:10 and the other five C he coupled to one
36:13 gold, and coupled the C one to the other
36:14 He also made C of goats' hair for a
36:14 a tent over the tabernacle; he made eleven C
36:15 four cubits; the eleven C had the same measure.
36:16 He coupled five C by themselves, and six curtains
36:16 by themselves, and six C by themselves.
Num 4:25 they shall carry the C of the tabernacle, and
Esth 1:6 There were white cotton C and blue hangings caught
Song 1:5 of Kedar, like the C of Solomon.
Is 54:2 tent, and let the C of your habitations be
Jer 4:20 tents are destroyed, my C in a moment.
10:20 my tent again, and to set up my C
49:29 shall be taken, their C and all their goods;
Hab 3:7 Cushan in affliction; the C of the land of
1Mac 4:51 bread on the table and hung up the C

CUSH (8)

Gen 2:13 one which flows around the whole land of C
10:6 The sons of Ham: C, Egypt, Put, and Canaan.
10:7 The sons of C: Seba, Havilah, Sabtah, Raamah, and
10:8 C became the father of Nimrod; he was the
1Chr 1:8 The sons of Ham: C, Egypt, Put, and Canaan.
1:9 The sons of C: Seba, Havilah, Sabta, Raama, and
1:10 C was the father of Nimrod; he began to
Ezek 38:5 shield, wielding swords; Persia, C, and Put are with

CUSHAN

Hab 3:7 saw the tents of C in affliction; the curtains

CUSHAN-RISHATHAIM (4)

Judg 3:8 into the hand of C king of Mesopotamia; and
3:8 people of Israel served C eight years.
3:10 and the LORD gave C king of Mesopotamia into
3:10 into his hand; and his hand prevailed over C

CUSHI (2)

Jer 36:14 of Shelemiah, son of C, to say to Baruch,
Zeph 1:1 Zephaniah the son of C, son of Gedaliah, son

CUSHION

Mk 4:38 stern, asleep on the C; and they woke him

CUSHITE (10)

Num 12:1 Moses because of the C woman whom he had
12:1 he had married a C woman;
2Sam 18:21 Joab said to the C, "Go, tell the king
18:21 The C bowed before Joab, and ran.
18:22 what may, let me also run after the C
18:23 the way of the plain, and outran the C
18:31 And behold, the C came; and the Cushite said,
18:31 Cushite came; and the C said, "Good tidings for
18:32 king said to the C, "Is it well with
18:32 And the C answered, "May the enemies of my

CUSTODIAN (2)

Gal 3:24 the law was our C until Christ came, that
3:25 no longer under a C;

CUSTODY (15)

Gen 40:3 he put them in C in the house of
40:4 them; and they continued for some time in C
40:7 were with him in C in his master's house,
41:10 the chief baker in C in the house of
Lev 24:12 they put him in C, till the will of
Num 15:34 They put him in C, because it had not
Jud 10:12 and took her into C, and asked her, "To
Esth 2:3 Susa the capital, under C of Hegai the king's
2:8 Susa the capital in C of Hegai, Esther also
2:8 palace and put in C of Hegai who had
2:14 the second harem in C of Sha-ashgaz the king's
Ezek 19:9 they brought him into C, that his voice should
Acts 4:3 and put them in C until the morrow, for
24:22 should be kept in C but should have some
25:21 to be kept in C for the decision of

CUSTOM (26)

Judg 11:39 And it became a C in Israel
Ruth 4:7 Now this was the C in former times in
1Sam 2:13 The C of the priests with the people was
27:11 Such was his C all the while he dwelt
1Kgs 18:28 cut themselves after their C with swords and lances,
2Kgs 11:14 pillar, according to the C, and the captains and
Ezra 4:13 will not pay tribute, C, or toll, and the
4:20 River, to whom tribute, C, and toll were paid.
7:24 lawful to impose tribute, C, or toll upon any
Wis 14:16 Then the ungodly C, grown strong with time, was
1Mac 1:14 Jerusalem, according to Gentile C,
10:89 as it is the C to give to the
2Mac 12:38 themselves according to the C, and they kept the
13:4 method which is the C in that place.
14:30 than had been his C, concluded that this austerity
Mk 10:1 and again, as his C was, he taught them.
Lk 1:9 duty, according to the C of the priesthood, it
2:27 him according to the C of the law,
2:42 went up according to C;
4:16 the synagogue, as his C was, on the sabbath
22:39 went, as was his C, to the Mount of
Jn 18:39 But you have a C that I should release
19:40 as is the burial C of the Jews.
Acts 15:1 circumcised according to the C of Moses, you cannot
17:2 in, as was his C, and for three weeks
25:16 it was not the C of the Romans to

CUSTOMARY (2)

2Mac 14:4 these some of the C olive branches from the
14:31 priests were offering the C sacrifices, and

CUSTOMS (19)

Lev 18:30 any of these abominable C which were practiced
20:23 not walk in the C of the nation which
2Kgs 17:8 and walked in the C of the nations whom
17:8 Israel, and in the C which the kings of
17:19 but walked in the C which Israel had introduced.
Wis 14:23 frenzied revels with strange C,
Jer 10:3 at them, for the C of the peoples are
1Mac 1:42 people, and that each should give up his C
1:44 directed them to follow C strange to the land,
2Mac 4:11 living and introduced new C contrary to the law.
6:9 did not choose to change over to Greek C
11:24 father's change to Greek C but prefer their own
11:24 ask that their own C be allowed them.
11:25 live according to the C of their ancestors.
Acts 6:14 and will change the C which Moses delivered to
16:21 They advocate C which it is not lawful for
21:21 not to circumcise their children or observe the C
26:3 especially familiar with all C and controversies of the
28:17 the people or the C of our fathers, yet

CUT (307)

Gen 9:11 shall all flesh be C off by the waters
15:10 brought him all these, C them in two, and
15:10 but he did not C the birds in two.
17:14 his foreskin shall be C off from his people;
22:3 son Isaac; and he C the wood for the
Ex 4:25 took a flint and C off her son's foreskin,
9:15 you would have been C off from the earth;
12:15 that person shall be C off from Israel.
12:19 that person shall be C off from the congregation
29:17 Then you shall C the ram into pieces, and
30:33 an outsider shall be C off from his people.'"
30:38 as perfume shall be C off from his people."
31:14 that soul shall be C off from among his
34:1 LORD said to Moses, C two tables of stone
34:4 So Moses C two tables of stone like the

34:13 break their pillars, and C down their Asherim
39:3 was hammered out and C into threads to work
Lev 1:6 the burnt offering and C it into pieces;
1:12 And he shall C it into pieces, with its
7:20 that person shall be C off from his people.
7:21 that person shall be C off from his people."
7:25 the LORD shall be C off from his people.
7:27 that person shall be C off from his people."
8:20 when the ram was C into pieces, Moses burned
17:4 that man shall be C off from among his
17:9 that man shall be C off from his people.
17:10 eats blood, and will C him off from among
17:14 eats it shall be C off.
18:29 do them shall be C off from among their
19:8 that person shall be C off from his people.
20:3 that man, and will C him off from among
20:5 his family, and will C them off from among
20:6 that person, and will C him off from among
20:17 and they shall be C off in the sight
20:18 of them shall be C off from among their
22:3 that person shall be C off from my presence:
22:24 crushed or torn or C, you shall not offer
23:29 same day shall be C off from his people.
26:30 your high places, and C down your incense altars,
Num 9:13 that person shall be C off from his people,
13:23 Valley of Eshcol, and C down from there a
13:24 the men of Israel C down from there.
15:30 that person shall be C off from among his
15:31 person shall be utterly C off; his iniquity shall
19:13 that person shall be C off from Israel; because
19:20 that person shall be C off from the midst
Deut 14:1 God; you shall not C yourselves or make any
19:5 with his neighbor to C wood, and his hand
19:5 swings the axe to C down a tree, and
20:19 but you shall not C them down.
20:20 you may destroy and C down that you may
23:1 whose male member is C off shall not enter
25:12 parts, then you shall C off her hand; your
25:18 faint and weary, and C off at your rear
Josh 3:16 Salt Sea, were wholly C off; and the people
4:7 of the Jordan were C off before the ark
4:7 of the Jordan were C off.
7:9 will surround us, and C off our name from
23:4 that I have already C off, from the Jordan
Judg 1:6 and caught him, and C off his thumbs and
1:7 and their great toes C off used to pick
6:25 your father has, and C down the Asherah that
6:26 Asherah which you shall C down."
6:28 Asherah beside it was C down, and the second
6:30 altar of Baal and C down the Asherah beside
9:48 in his hand, and C down a bundle of
9:49 one of the people C down his bundle and
20:6 took my concubine and C her in pieces, and
20:45 men of them were C down in the highways,
21:6 said, "One tribe is C off from Israel this
Ruth 4:10 dead may not be C off from among his
1Sam 2:9 the wicked shall be C off in darkness; for
2:31 coming, when I will C off your strength and
2:33 whom I shall not C off from my altar
5:4 his hands were lying C off upon the threshold;
11:7 yoke of oxen, and C them in pieces and
11:11 the morning watch, and C down the Ammonites until
17:46 strike you down, and C off your head; and
17:51 and killed him, and C off his head with
20:15 die; and do not C off your loyalty from
20:16 name of Jonathan be C off from the house
24:4 David arose and stealthily C off the skirt of
24:5 him, because he had C off Saul's skirt.
24:11 the fact that I C off the skirt of
24:21 that you will not C off my descendants after
28:9 done, how he has C off the mediums and
31:9 And they C off his head, and stripped off
2Sam 4:12 they killed them, and C off their hands and
7:9 you went, and have C off all your enemies
10:4 beard of each, and C off their garments in
14:26 And when he C the hair of his head
14:26 year he used to C it; when it was
14:26 heavy on him, he C it), he weighed the
20:22 And they C off the head of Sheba the
1Kgs 5:6 cedars of Lebanon be C for me; and my
5:6 who knows how to C timber like the Sidonians."
9:7 them, then I will C off Israel from the
11:16 months, until he had C off every male in
13:34 Jeroboam, so as to C it off and to
14:10 of Jeroboam, and will C off from Jeroboam every
14:14 over Israel, who shall C off the house of

15:13 for Asherah; and Asa C down her image and
18:4 greatly; and when Jezebel C off the prophets of
18:23 bull for themselves, and C it in pieces and
18:28 they cried aloud, and C themselves after their custom
18:33 wood in order, and C the bull in pieces
21:21 you away, and will C off from Ahab every
2Kgs 4:39 gourds, and came and C them up into the
6:4 to the Jordan, they C down trees.
6:6 him the place, he C off a stick, and
9:8 perish; and I will C off from Ahab every
10:32 the LORD began to C off parts of Israel.
16:17 And King Ahaz C off the frames of the
18:4 broke the pillars, and C down the Asherah.
23:14 pieces the pillars, and C down the Asherim, and
24:13 the king's house, and C in pieces all the
1Chr 17:8 you went, and have C off all your enemies
19:4 and shaved them, and C off their garments in
2Chr 2:8 servants know how to C timber in Lebanon.
2:10 servants, the hewers who C timber, twenty thousand
2:16 servants; and we will C whatever timber you need
15:16 Asa C down her image, crushed it, and burned
28:24 house of God and C in pieces the vessels
32:21 sent an angel, who C off all the mighty
Tob 6:4 angel said to him, C open the fish and
Jud 3:8 all their shrines and C down their sacred groves;
14:4 shall pursue them and C them down as they
14:15 dead, with his head C off and missing.
15:5 upon the enemy, and C them down as far
Job 4:7 where were the upright C off?
6:9 loose his hand and C me off!
8:12 in flower and not C down, they wither before
14:7 tree, if it be C down, that it will
21:21 of their months is C off?
22:20 'Surely our adversaries are C off, and what they
24:24 the mallow; they are C off like the heads
33:17 from his deed, and C off pride from man;
36:20 night, when peoples are C off in their place.
Ps 12:3 May the LORD C off all flattering lips, the
34:16 is against evildoers, to C off the remembrance of
37:9 the wicked shall be C off; but those who
37:22 by him shall be C off.
37:28 the wicked shall be C off.
37:38 the wicked shall be C off.
75:10 the wicked he will C off, but the horns
80:16 with fire, they have C it down; may they
88:5 more, for they are C off from thy hand.
89:45 Thou hast C short the days of his youth;
109:13 May his posterity be C off; may his name
109:15 may his memory be C off from the earth!
118:10 of the LORD I C them off!
118:11 of the LORD I C them off!
118:12 of the LORD I C them off!
129:4 is righteous; he has C the cords of the
143:12 in thy steadfast love C off my enemies, and
144:12 daughters like corner pillars C for the structure of
Prov 2:22 the wicked will be C off from the land,
10:31 perverse tongue will be C off.
23:18 hope will not be C off.
24:14 hope will not be C off.
Wis 18:23 back the wrath, and C off its way to
Sir 38:27 by day; those who C the signets of seals,
Is 9:10 the sycamores have been C down, but we will
9:14 So the LORD C off from Israel head and
10:7 to destroy, and to C off nations not a
10:34 He will C down the thickets of the forest
11:13 harass Judah shall be C off; Ephraim shall not
14:12 How you are C down to the ground, you
14:22 of hosts, "and will C off from Babylon name
18:5 ripening grape, he will C off the shoots with
22:25 and it will be C down and fall, and
22:25 upon it will be C off, for the LORD
29:20 do evil shall be C off,
33:12 to lime, like thorns C down, that are burned
45:2 doors of bronze and C asunder the bars of
48:9 that I may not C you off.
48:19 name would never be C off or destroyed from
51:9 not thou that didst C Rahab in pieces, that
53:8 considered that he was C off out of the
55:13 which shall not be C off."
56:5 which shall not be C off.
Jer 7:28 has perished; it is C off from their lips.
7:29 C off your hair and cast it away; raise
9:26 in the desert that C the corners of their
10:3 from the forest is C down, and worked with
11:19 its fruit, let us C him off from the
16:6 lament for them or C himself or make himself

22:7 weapons; and they shall C down your choicest cedars,
25:23 Buz, and all who C the corners of their
34:18 the calf which they C in two and passed
36:23 columns, the king would C them off with a
36:29 this land, and will C off from it man
44:7 evil against yourselves, to C off from you man
44:8 that you may be C off and become a
44:11 you for evil, to C off all Judah.
46:23 They shall C down her forest, says the LORD,
47:4 all the Philistines, to C off from Tyre and
48:2 her: 'Come, let us C her off from being
48:25 horn of Moab is C off, and his arm
48:37 shaved and every beard C off; upon all the
49:32 every wind those who C the corners of their
50:16 C off from Babylon the sower, and the one
50:23 the whole earth is C down and broken!
51:6 Be not C off in her punishment, for this
51:13 has come, the thread of your life is C
51:62 place that thou wilt C it off, so that
Lam 2:3 He has C down in fierce anger all the
Ezek 5:11 abominations, therefore I will C you down; my eye
6:6 destroyed, your incense altars C down, and your
14:8 and a byword and C him off from the
14:13 famine upon it, and C off from it man
14:17 the land; and I C off from it man
14:19 it with blood, to C off from it man
14:21 beasts, and pestilence, to C off from it man
16:4 navel string was not C, nor were you washed
16:40 shall stone you and C you to pieces with
17:9 up its roots and C off its branches, so
17:17 siege walls built to C off many lives.
21:3 its sheath, and will C off from you both
21:4 Because I will C off from you both righteous
21:16 C sharply to right and left where your edge
23:25 They shall C off your nose and your ears,
25:7 nations; and I will C you off from the
25:13 hand against Edom, and C off from it man
25:16 Philistines, and I will C off the Cherethites, and
29:8 upon you, and will C off from you man
30:15 stronghold of Egypt, and C off the multitude of
31:12 of the nations, will C it down and leave
35:7 desolation; and I will C off from it all
37:11 lost; we are clean C off.'
39:10 of the field or C down any out of
Dan 2:34 looked, a stone was C out by no human
2:45 that a stone was C from a mountain by
4:14 down the tree and C off its branches, strip
9:26 anointed one shall be C off, and shall have
13:55 God and will immediately C you in two."
Hos 10:15 Israel shall be utterly C off.
Joel 1:5 wine, for it is C off from your mouth.
1:9 the drink offering are C off from the house
1:15 Is not the food C off before our eyes,
Amos 1:5 bar of Damascus, and C off the inhabitants from
1:8 I will C off the inhabitants from Ashdod, and
2:3 the trumpet; I will C off the ruler from
3:14 the altar shall be C off and fall to
Obad 1:9 Mount Esau will be C off by slaughter.
1:10 and you shall be C off for ever.
1:14 of the ways to C off his fugitives; you
Mic 1:16 Make yourselves bald and C off your hair, for
5:9 your enemies shall be C off.
5:10 the LORD, I will C off your horses from
5:11 chariots; and I will C off the cities of
5:12 strongholds; and I will C off sorceries from your
5:13 soothsayers; and I will C off your images and
Nah 1:12 many, they will be C off and pass away.
1:14 your gods I will C off the graven image
1:15 you, he is utterly C off.
2:13 young lions; I will C off your prey from
3:15 you, the sword will C you off.
Hab 3:17 food, the flock be C off from the fold
Zeph 1:3 the wicked; I will C off mankind from the
1:4 Jerusalem; and I will C off from this place
1:11 weigh out silver are C off.
3:6 "I have C off nations; their battlements are in
Zech 5:3 who steals shall be C off henceforth according to
5:3 swears falsely shall be C off henceforth according to
9:10 I will C off the chariot from Ephraim and
9:10 battle bow shall be C off, and he shall
13:2 of hosts, I will C off the names of
13:8 two thirds shall be C off and perish, and
14:2 people shall not be C off from the city.
Mal 2:12 May the LORD C off from the tents of
1Mac 6:6 the armies they had C down;
7:47 the plunder, and they C off Nicanor's head and
11:17 And Zabdiel the Arab C off the head of
2Mac 1:13 seemed irresistible, they were C to pieces in the
1:16 and dismembered them and C off their heads and
5:12 commanded his soldiers to C down relentlessly every
7:4 of their spokesman be C out and that they
7:4 they scalp him and C off his hands and
10:30 thrown into disorder and C to pieces.
10:35 and with savage fury C down every one they
12:35 down upon him and C off his arm; so
15:30 countrymen, ordered them to C off Nicanor's head
15:33 the Almighty; and he C out the tongue of
Mt 3:10 bear good fruit is C down and thrown into
5:30 causes you to sin, C it off and throw
7:19 bear good fruit is C down and thrown into
18:8 causes you to sin, C it off and throw
21:8 the road, and others C branches from the trees
26:51 the high priest, and C off his ear.
Mk 9:43 causes you to sin, C it off; it is
9:44 causes you to sin, C it off; it is
11:8 branches which they had C from the fields.
14:47 the high priest and C off his ear.
Lk 3:9 bear good fruit is C down and thrown into
13:7 C it down; why should it use up the
13:9 if not, you can C it down.'"
22:48 the high priest and C off his right ear.
Jn 18:10 high priest's slave and C off his right ear.
18:26 whose ear Peter had C off, asked, "Did I
Acts 2:37 heard this they were C to the heart, and
18:18 At Cenchre-ae he C his hair, for he had
27:32 Then the soldiers C away the ropes of the
Rom 9:3 myself were accursed and C off from Christ for
11:22 you too will be C off.
11:24 if you have been C from what is by
1Cor 11:6 herself, then she should C off her hair; but

CUTH

2Kgs 17:30 Succoth-benoth, the men of C made Nergal, the men

CUTHAH

2Kgs 17:24 brought people from Babylon, C, Avva, Hamath, and

CUTS (11)

Deut 12:29 the LORD your God C off before you the
19:1 the LORD your God C off the nations whose
1Sam 20:15 When the LORD C off every one of the
Job 27:8 the godless when God C him off, when God
28:10 He C out channels in the rocks, and his
Ps 76:12 to be feared, who C off the spirit of
107:16 doors of bronze, and C in two the bars
Prov 26:6 hand of a fool C off his own feet
Is 38:12 up my life; he C me off from the
44:14 He C down cedars; or he chooses a holm
Jer 22:14 spacious upper rooms,' and C out windows for it,

CUTTER

Joel 2:25 the destroyer, and the C, my great army, which

CUTTING (8)

Ex 31:5 silver, and bronze, in C stones for setting, and
35:33 silver and bronze, in C stones for setting, and
Judg 20:43 C down the Benjaminites, they pursued them and
Ps 101:8 wicked in the land, C off all the evildoers
Jer 9:21 has entered our palaces, C off the children from
Joel 1:4 What the C locust left, the swarming locust has
Hab 2:10 to your house by C off many peoples; you
2Mac 2:32 lengthen the preface while C short the history itself.

CUTTINGS (2)

Lev 19:28 shall not make any C in your flesh on
21:5 beards, nor make any C in their flesh.

CYAMON

Jud 7:3 length from Bethulia to C, which faces Esdraelon.

CYCLE

Jas 3:6 setting on fire the C of nature, and set

CYCLES

Wis 7:19 of the seasons, the C of the year and

CYMBAL

1Cor 13:1 I am a noisy gong or a clanging C

CYMBALS (19)

2Sam 6:5 and harps and tambourines and castanets and C
1Chr 13:8 harps and tambourines and C and trumpets.

15:16 harps and lyres and C, to raise sounds of
15:19 were to sound bronze C;
15:28 the horn, trumpets, and C, and made loud music
16:5 was to sound the C,
16:42 Jeduthun had trumpets and C for the music and
25:1 should prophesy with lyres, with harps, and with C
25:6 of the LORD with C, harps, and lyres for
2Chr 5:12 in fine linen, with C, harps, and lyres, stood
5:13 with trumpets and C and other musical instruments,
29:25 of the LORD with C, harps, and lyres, according
Ezra 3:10 sons of Asaph, with C, to praise the LORD,
Neh 12:27 and with singing, with C, harps, and lyres.
Jud 16:2 God with tambourines, sing to my Lord with C
Ps 150:5 Praise him with sounding C; praise him with loud
150:5 sounding cymbals; praise him with loud clashing C
1Mac 4:54 dedicated with songs and harps and lutes and C
13:51 and with harps and C and stringed instruments, and

CYPRESS (14)

1Kgs 5:8 matter of cedar and C timber.
5:10 timber of cedar and C that he desired,
6:15 the floor of the house with boards of C
6:34 and two doors of C wood; the two leaves
9:11 Solomon with cedar and C timber and gold, as
2Chr 2:8 Send me also cedar, C, and algum timber from
3:5 nave he lined with C, and covered it with
Sir 24:13 Lebanon, and like a C on the heights of
50:10 fruit, and like a C towering in the clouds.
Is 41:19 in the desert the C, the plane and the
55:13 shall come up the C; instead of the brier
60:13 come to you, the C, the plane, and the
Hos 14:8 am like an evergreen C, from me comes your
Zech 11:2 Wail, O C, for the cedar has fallen, for

CYPRESSES (3)

2Kgs 19:23 tallest cedars, its choicest C; I entered its farthest
Is 14:8 The C rejoice at you, the cedars of Lebanon,
37:24 tallest cedars, its choicest C; I came to its

CYPRIAN

2Mac 4:29 the commander of the C troops.

CYPRUS (15)

Is 23:1 From the land of C it is revealed to
23:12 arise, pass over to C, even there you will
Jer 2:10 to the coasts of C and see, or send
Ezek 27:6 from the coasts of C, inlaid with ivory.
1Mac 15:23 Gortyna and Cnidus and C and Cyrene.
2Mac 10:13 because he had abandoned C, which Philometor had
12:2 Nicanor the governor of C, would not let them
Acts 4:36 Levite, a native of C,
11:19 far as Phoenicia and C and Antioch, speaking the
11:20 of them, men of C and Cyrene, who on
13:4 to Seleucia; and from there they sailed to C
15:38 and sailed away to C,
21:3 come in sight of C, leaving it on the
21:16 house of Mnason of C, an early disciple, with
27:4 under the lee of C, because the winds were

CYRENE (8)

1Mac 15:23 Aradus and Gortyna and Cnidus and Cyprus and C
2Mac 2:23 forth by Jason of C in five volumes, we
Mt 27:32 upon a man of C, Simon by name; this
Mk 15:21 a passer-by, Simon of C, who was coming in
Lk 23:25 seized one Simon of C, who was coming in
Acts 2:10 of Libya belonging to C, and visitors from Rome,
11:20 men of Cyprus and C, who on coming to
13:1 called Niger, Lucius of C, Mana-en a member of

CYRENIANS

Acts 6:9 called), and of the C, and of the Alexandrians,

CYRUS (24)

2Chr 36:22 the first year of C king of Persia, that
36:22 up the spirit of C king of Persia so
36:23 in writing: "Thus says C king of Persia, 'The
Ezra 1:1 the first year of C King of Persia, that
1:1 up the spirit of C king of Persia so
1:2 in writing: "Thus says C king of Persia: The
1:7 C the king also brought out the vessels of
1:8 C king of Persia brought these out in charge
3:7 which they had from C king of Persia.
4:3 of Israel, as King C the king of Persia
4:5 all the days of C king of Persia, even
5:13 the first year of C king of Babylon, Cyrus
5:13 Cyrus king of Babylon, C the king made a
5:14 temple of Babylon, these C the king took out
5:17 decree was issued by C the king for the
6:3 the first year of C the king, Cyrus the
6:3 of Cyrus the king, C the king issued a
6:14 and by decree of C and Darius and Artaxerxes
Is 44:28 rivers'; who says of C, 'He is my shepherd,
45:1 to his anointed, to C, whose right hand I
Dan 1:21 Daniel continued until the first year of King C
6:28 and the reign of C the Persian.
10:1 the third year of C king of Persia a
14:1 laid with his fathers, C the Persian received his

D

DABBESHETH

Josh 19:11 to Mareal, and touches D, then the brook which

DABERATH (3)

Josh 19:12 thence it goes to D, then up to Japhia;
21:28 with its pasture lands, D with its pasture lands,
1Chr 6:72 with its pasture lands, D with its pasture lands,

DAGGER

Bar 6:15 It has a D in its right hand, and

DAGON (15)

Judg 16:23 a great sacrifice to D their god, and to
1Sam 5:2 into the house of D and set it up
5:2 house of Dagon and set it up beside D
5:3 the next day, behold, D had fallen face downward
5:3 So they took D and put him back in
5:4 next morning, behold, D had fallen face downward
5:4 and the head of D and both his hands
5:4 only the trunk of D was left to him.
5:5 why the priests of D and all who enter
5:5 enter the house of D do not tread on
5:5 on the threshold of D in Ashdod to this
5:7 upon us and upon D our god."
1Chr 10:10 and fastened his head in the temple of D
1Mac 10:84 and the temple of D, and those who had
11:4 him the temple of D burned down, and Azotus

DAILY (31)

Ex 5:13 "Complete your work, your D task, as when there
5:19 no means lessen your D number of bricks."
16:5 will be twice as much as they gather D
Num 28:24 way you shall offer D, for seven days, the
Ezra 3:4 written, and offered the D burnt offerings by number
Neh 12:47 of Nehemiah gave the D portions for the singers
Jud 12:15 from Bagoas for her D use, so that she
Ps 68:19 be the Lord, who D bears us up; God
109:19 belt with which he D girds himself!
Prov 8:30 workman; and I was D his delight, rejoicing before
8:34 listens to me, watching D at my gates, waiting
Is 58:2 Yet they seek me D, and delight to know
Jer 37:21 bread was given him D from the bakers' street,
Ezek 43:25 days you shall provide D a goat for a
45:23 days; and a he-goat D for a sin offering.
46:13 offering to the LORD D; morning by morning he
Dan 1:5 king assigned them a D portion of the rich
1Mac 6:57 to the men, "We D grow weaker, our food
Mt 6:11 us this day our D bread;
Lk 9:23 take up his cross D and follow me.
11:3 us each day our D bread;
19:47 And he was teaching D in the temple.
Acts 3:2 carried, whom they laid D at that gate of
6:1 were neglected in the D distribution.
16:5 in the faith, and they increased in numbers D
17:11 eagerness, examining the scriptures D to see if these
19:9 with him, and argued D in the hall of
2Cor 11:28 things, there is the D pressure upon me of
Heb 7:27 priests, to offer sacrifices D, first for his own
10:11 And every priest stands D at his service, offering
Jas 2:15 and in lack of D food,

DAINTIES (5)

Gen 49:20 shall be rich, and he shall yield royal D
Ps 141:4 iniquity; and let me not eat of their D
Sir 31:3 when he rests he fills himself with his D
Lam 4:5 Those who feasted on D perish in the streets;
Rev 18:14 thee, and all thy D and thy splendor are

DAINTILY (2)

2Sam 1:24 Saul, who clothed you D in scarlet, who put

Esth 15:3 maids with her, leaning D on one,

DAINTY
Job 33:20 bread, and his appetite D food.

DALLIED
2Mac 6:4 by the Gentiles, who D with harlots and had

DALMANUTHA
Mk 8:10 his disciples, and went to the district of D

DALMATIA
2Tim 4:10 Crescens has gone to Galatia, Titus to D

DALPHON
Esth 9:7 also slew Par-shan-datha and D and Aspatha

DAM
Ex 22:30 shall be with its D; on the eighth day

DAMAGE (6)
Ezra 4:22 this matter; why should D grow to the hurt
Wis 11:19 not only could their D exterminate men, but the
1Mac 7:22 Judah and did great D in Israel.
14:36 sanctuary and do great D to its purity.
15:29 you have done great D in the land, and
15:35 they were causing great D among the people and

DAMARIS
Acts 17:34 and a woman named D and others with them.

DAMASCUS (67)
Gen 14:15 them and pursued them to Hobah, north of D
15:2 the heir of my house is Eliezer of D
2Sam 8:5 when the Syrians of D came to help Hadadezer
8:6 garrisons in Aram of D; and the Syrians became
1Kgs 11:24 and they went to D, and dwelt there, and
11:24 and dwelt there, and made him king in D
15:18 Syria, who dwelt in D, saying,
19:15 to the wilderness of D; and when you arrive,
20:34 bazaars for yourself in D, as my father did
2Kgs 5:12 Pharpar, the rivers of D, better than all the
8:7 Now Elisha came to D
8:9 kinds of goods of D, forty camel loads.
14:28 he recovered for Israel D and Hamath, which had
16:9 Assyria marched up against D, and took it, carrying
16:10 King Ahaz went to D to meet Tiglath-pileser king
16:10 Assyria, he saw the altar that was at D
16:11 Ahaz had sent from D, so Uriah the priest
16:11 priest made it, before King Ahaz arrived from D
16:12 the king came from D, the king viewed the
1Chr 18:5 when the Syrians of D came to help Hadadezer
18:6 garrisons in Syria of D; and the Syrians became
2Chr 16:2 Syria, who dwelt in D, saying,
24:23 sent all their spoil to the king of D
28:5 number of his people and brought them to D
28:23 to the gods of D which had defeated him,
Jud 1:7 lived in Cilicia and D and Lebanon and Antilebanon
1:12 territory of Cilicia and D and Syria, that he
2:27 into the plain of D during the wheat harvest,
15:5 great slaughter, even beyond D and its borders.
Song 7:4 nose is like a tower of Lebanon, overlooking D
Is 7:8 head of Syria is D, and the head of
7:8 and the head of D is Rezin.
8:4 mother,' the wealth of D and the spoil of
10:9 Is not Samaria like D
17:1 An oracle concerning D
17:1 Behold, D will cease to be a city, and
17:3 and the kingdom from D; and the remnant of
Jer 49:23 Concerning D
49:24 D has become feeble, she turned to flee, and
49:27 in the wall of D, and it shall devour
Ezek 27:18 D trafficked with you for your abundant goods,
47:16 on the border between D and Hamath), as far
47:17 the northern border of D, with the border of
47:18 Hazar-enon between Hauran and D; along the
48:1 the northern border of D over against Hamath), and
Amos 1:3 "For three transgressions of D, and for four, I
1:5 break the bar of D, and cut off the
5:27 therefore I will take you into exile beyond D
Zech 9:1 the land of Hadrach and will rest upon D
1Mac 11:62 he passed through the country as far as D
12:32 camp and went to D, and marched through all
Acts 9:2 to the synagogues at D, so that if he
9:3 he journeyed he approached D, and suddenly a light
9:8 him by the hand and brought him into D
9:10 was a disciple at D named Ananias.
9:19 several days he was with the disciples at D
9:22 Jews who lived in D by proving that Jesus
9:27 him, and how at D he had preached boldly
22:5 and I journeyed to D to take those also
22:6 and drew near to D, about noon a great
22:10 'Rise, and go into D, and there you will
22:11 those who were with me, and came into D
26:12 "Thus I journeyed to D with the authority and
26:20 first to those at D, then at Jerusalem and
2Cor 11:32 At D, the governor under King Aretas guarded the
11:32 guarded the city of D in order to seize
Gal 1:17 away into Arabia; and again I returned to D

DAN (62)
Gen 14:14 them, and went in pursuit as far as D
30:6 me a son"; therefore she called his name D
35:25 of Bilhah, Rachel's maid: D and Naphtali.
46:23 The sons of D: Hushim.
49:16 D shall judge his people as one of the
49:17 D shall be a serpent in the way, a
Ex 1:3 Zebulun, and Benjamin, D and Naphtali, Gad and
31:6 of the tribe of D; and I have given
35:34 the son of Ahisamach of the tribe of D
38:23 of the tribe of D, a craftsman and designer
Lev 24:11 the daughter of Dibri, of the tribe of D
Num 1:12 son of Gideoni; from D, Ahiezer the son of
1:38 Of the people of D, their generations, by their
1:39 of the tribe of D was sixty-two thousand seven
2:25 of the camp of D by their companies, the
2:25 of the people of D being Ahiezer the son
2:31 of the camp of D is a hundred and
7:66 of the men of D:
10:25 of the men of D, acting as the rear
13:12 from the tribe of D, Ammiel the son of
26:42 are the sons of D according to their families:
26:42 are the families of D according to their families.
34:22 of the sons of D a leader, Bukki the
Deut 27:13 Reuben, Gad, Asher, Zebulun, D, and Naphtali.
33:22 And of D he said, "Dan is a lion's
33:22 of Dan he said, D is a lion's whelp,
34:1 Gilead as far as D,
Josh 19:40 for the tribe of D, according to its families.
19:47 in it, calling Leshem, D, after the name of
19:47 after the name of D their ancestor.
19:48 of the tribe of D, according to their families--
21:5 from the tribe of D and the half-tribe of
21:23 of the tribe of D, Elteke with its pasture
Judg 5:17 beyond the Jordan; and D, why did he abide
18:11 of the tribe of D, armed with weapons of
18:29 they named the city D, after the name of
18:29 after the name of D their ancestor, who was
20:1 Israel came out, from D to Beer-sheba, including the
1Sam 3:20 And all Israel from D to Beer-sheba knew that
2Sam 3:10 and over Judah, from D to Beer-sheba."
17:11 gathered to you, from D to Beer-sheba, as the
24:2 tribes of Israel, from D to Beer-sheba, and number
24:6 and they came to D, and from Dan they
24:6 to Dan, and from D they went around to
24:15 of the people from D to Beer-sheba seventy thousand
1Kgs 4:25 dwelt in safety, from D even to Beer-sheba, every
12:29 in Bethel, and the other he put in D
12:30 Bethel and to the other as far as D
15:20 Israel, and conquered Ijon, D, Abel-beth-maacah, and
2Kgs 10:29 golden calves that were in Bethel, and in D
1Chr 2:2 Levi, Judah, Issachar, Zebulun, D, Joseph, Benjamin,
21:2 Israel, from Beer-sheba to D, and bring me a
27:22 son of Abner; for D, Azarel the son of
2Chr 2:14 of the daughters of D, and his father was
16:4 and they conquered Ijon, D, Abel-maim, and all the
30:5 Israel, from Beer-sheba to D, that the people should
Jer 4:15 a voice declares from D and proclaims evil from
8:16 horses is heard from D; at the sound of
Ezek 48:1 side to the west, D, one portion.
48:2 Adjoining the territory of D, from the east side
48:32 the gate of Benjamin, and the gate of D
Amos 8:14 thy god lives, O D and, 'As the way

DANCE (13)
Judg 21:21 Shiloh come out to D in the dances, then
Jud 15:12 of them performed a D for her; and she
15:13 the people in the D, leading all the women,
Job 21:11 little ones like a flock, and their children D
Ps 150:4 him with timbrel and D; praise him with strings
Eccl 3:4 and a time to D;
Song 6:13 Shulammite, as upon a D before two armies?

14:24 the king said to D, "You cannot deny that
14:25 D said, "I will worship the Lord my God,
14:27 Then D took pitch, fat, and hair, and boiled
14:27 And D said, "See what you have been worshiping!"
14:29 king, they said, "Hand D over to us, or
14:30 under compulsion he handed D over to them.
14:31 They threw D into the lions' den, and he
14:32 to them now, so that they might devour D
14:34 have to Babylon, to D, in the lions' den."
14:37 Then Habakkuk shouted, D, Daniel!
14:37 Then Habakkuk shouted, "Daniel, D
14:38 And D said, "Thou hast remembered me, O God,
14:39 So D arose and ate.
14:40 seventh day the king came to mourn for D
14:40 the den he looked in, and there sat D
14:41 O Lord God of D, and there is no
14:42 And he pulled D out, and threw into the
1Mac 2:60 D because of his innocence was delivered from the
Mt 24:15 of by the prophet D, standing in the holy

DANITES (15)
Josh 19:47 the territory of the D was lost to them,
19:47 lost to them, the D went up and fought
Judg 1:34 The Amorites pressed the D back into the hill
13:2 the tribe of the D, whose name was Manoah;
18:1 the tribe of the D was seeking for itself
18:2 So the D sent five able men from the
18:16 hundred men of the D, armed with their weapons
18:22 house were called out, and they overtook the D
18:23 they shouted to the D, who turned round and
18:25 And the D said to him, "Do not let
18:26 Then the D went their way; and when Micah
18:27 belonged to him, the D came to Laish, to
18:30 And the D set up the graven image for
18:30 the tribe of the D until the day of
1Chr 12:35 Of the D twenty-eight thousand six hundred men

DANNAH
Josh 15:49 Shamir, Jattir, Socoh, D, Kiriath-sannah (that is,

DAPHNE
2Mac 4:33 place of sanctuary at D near Antioch.

DAPPLED (2)
Zech 6:3 and the fourth chariot D gray horses.
6:6 west country, and the D ones go toward the

DARA
1Chr 2:6 Ethan, Heman, Calcol, and D, five in all.

DARDA
1Kgs 4:31 and Heman, Calcol, and D, the sons of Mahol;

DARE (6)
Jer 30:21 me, for who would D of himself to approach
Mt 22:46 day did any one D to ask him any
Acts 7:32 trembled and did not D to look.
Rom 5:7 good man one will D even to die.
1Cor 6:1 a brother, does he D go to law before
2Cor 11:21 a fool--I also D to boast of that.

DARED (6)
2Mac 4:2 He D to designate as a plotter against the
5:15 content with this, Antiochus D to enter the most
Mk 12:34 after that no one D to ask him any
Lk 20:40 For they no longer D to ask him any
Jn 21:12 none of the disciples D ask him, "Who are
Acts 5:13 None of the rest D join them, but the

DARES (3)
Gen 49:9 as a lioness; who D rouse him up?
Job 41:10 so fierce that he D to stir him up.
2Cor 11:21 But whatever any one D to boast of--I

DARICS (6)
1Chr 29:7 talents and ten thousand D of gold, ten thousand
Ezra 2:69 the work sixty-one thousand D of gold, five thousand
8:27 gold worth a thousand D, and two vessels of
Neh 7:70 the treasury a thousand D of gold, fifty basins,
7:71 the work twenty thousand D of gold and two
7:72 gave was twenty thousand D of gold, two thousand

DARING (3)
Jud 16:10 her boldness, the Medes were daunted at her D
2Mac 8:18 "For they trust to arms and acts of D
13:18 a taste of the D of the Jews, tried

DARIUS (27)
Ezra 4:5 until the reign of D king of Persia.
4:24 of the reign of D king of Persia.
5:5 a report should reach D and then answer be
5:6 the River sent to D the king;
5:7 written as follows: "To D the king, all peace.
6:1 Then D the king made a decree, and search
6:12 I D make a decree; let it be done
6:13 the word sent by D the king, Tattenai, the
6:13 with all diligence what D the king had ordered.
6:14 decree of Cyrus and D and Artaxerxes king of
6:15 of the reign of D the king.
Neh 12:22 until the reign of D the Persian.
Dan 5:31 And D the Mede received the kingdom, being about
6:1 It pleased D to set over the kingdom a
6:6 to him, "O King D, live for ever!
6:9 Therefore King D signed the document and interdict.
6:25 Then King D wrote to all the peoples, nations,
6:28 during the reign of D and the reign of
9:1 the first year of D the son of Ahasuerus,
11:1 the first year of D the Mede, I stood
Hag 1:1 the second year of D the king, in the
2:1 the second year of D the king, in the
2:10 the second year of D, the word of the
Zech 1:1 the second year of D, the word of the
1:7 the second year of D, the word of the
7:1 fourth year of King D, the word of the
1Mac 1:1 of Kittim, had defeated D, king of the Persians

DARK (35)
Gen 15:17 down and it was D, behold, a smoking fire
Num 12:8 clearly, and not in D speech; and he beholds
Josh 2:5 to be closed, at D, the men went out;
Neh 13:19 it began to be D at the gates of
Job 3:9 of its dawn be D; let it hope for
6:16 pass away, which are D with ice, and where
12:25 They grope in the D without light; and he
18:6 The light is D in his tent, and his
24:14 murderer rises in the D, that he may kill
24:16 In the D they dig through houses; by day
Ps 11:2 to shoot in the D at the upright in
18:11 his canopy thick clouds D with water.
35:6 Let their way be D and slippery, with the
74:20 thy covenant; for the D places of the land
78:2 parable; I will utter D sayings from of old,
88:6 Pit, in the regions D and deep.
105:28 and made the land D; they rebelled against his
139:12 the darkness is not D to thee, the night
Song 1:5 I am very D, but comely, O daughters of
Wis 17:3 were unobserved behind a D curtain of forgetfulness,
Is 13:10 the sun will be D at its rising and
29:15 deeds are in the D, and who say, "Who
Ezek 8:12 are doing in the D, every man in his
12:6 it out in the D; you shall cover your
12:7 went forth in the D, carrying my outfit upon
12:12 his shoulder in the D, and shall go forth;
30:18 the day shall be D, when I break there
32:7 and make their stars D; I will cover the
32:8 heaven will I make D over you, and put
Mt 10:27 tell you in the D, utter in the light;
Lk 11:36 light, having no part D, it will be wholly
12:3 have said in the D shall be heard in
Jn 6:17 It was now D, and Jesus had not yet
20:1 while it was still D, and saw that the
2Pet 1:19 lamp shining in a D place, until the day

DARKEN
Amos 8:9 down at noon, and D the earth in broad

DARKENED (14)
Ex 10:15 that the land was D, and they ate all
Job 22:11 you; your light is D, so that you cannot
Ps 69:23 Let their eyes be D, so that they cannot
Eccl 12:2 and the stars are D and the clouds return
Is 5:30 and the light is D by its clouds.
Joel 2:10 and the moon are D, and the stars withdraw
3:15 and the moon are D, and the stars withdraw
Mt 24:29 the sun will be D, and the moon will
Mk 13:24 the sun will be D, and the moon will
Rom 1:21 in their thinking and their senseless minds were D
11:10 let their eyes be D so that they cannot
Eph 4:18 their minds; they are D in their understanding,
Rev 8:12 of their light was D; a third of the
9:2 and the air were D with the smoke from

DARKENS (3)

Job	38:2	"Who is this that D counsel by words without
Sir	25:16	changes her appearance, and D her face like that
Amos	5:8	into the morning, and D the day into night,

DARKNESS (186)

Gen	1:2	form and void, and D was upon the face
	1:4	good; and God separated the light from the D
	1:5	light Day, and the D he called Night.
	1:18	night, and to separate the light from the D
	15:12	a dread and great D fell upon him.
Ex	10:21	that there may be D over the land of
	10:21	land of Egypt, a D to be felt."
	10:22	and there was thick D in all the land
	14:20	the cloud and the D; and the night passed
	20:21	near to the thick D where God was.
Deut	4:11	of heaven, wrapped in D, cloud, and gloom.
	5:22	cloud, and the thick D, with a loud voice;
	5:23	the midst of the D, while the mountain was
	28:29	the blind grope in D, and you shall not
Josh	24:7	the LORD, he put D between you and the
1Sam	2:9	be cut off in D; for not by might
2Sam	22:10	and came down; thick D was under his feet.
	22:12	He made D around him his canopy, thick clouds,
	22:29	lamp, O LORD, and my God lightens my D
1Kgs	8:12	has said that he would dwell in thick D
2Chr	6:1	has said that he would dwell in thick D
Tob	4:10	you from entering the D;
	14:10	him from light into D, and with what he
	14:10	repayment as he himself went down into the D
Esth	11:8	behold, a day of D and gloom, tribulation and
Job	3:4	'A man-child is conceived.' Let that day be D
	3:5	Let gloom and deep D claim it.
	3:6	That night--let thick D seize it!
	5:14	They meet with D in the daytime, and grope
	10:21	of gloom and deep D,
	10:22	of gloom and chaos, where light is as D
	11:17	than the noonday; its D will be like the
	12:22	the deeps out of D, and brings deep darkness
	12:22	darkness, and brings deep D to light.
	15:22	will return out of D, and he is destined
	15:23	that a day of D is ready at his
	15:30	will not escape from D; the flame will dry
	16:16	my eyelids is deep D;
	17:12	'is near to the D
	17:13	spread my couch in D,
	18:18	thrust from light into D, and driven out of
	19:8	and he has set D upon my paths.
	20:26	Utter D is laid up for his treasures; a
	22:13	Can he judge through the deep D
	23:17	am hemmed in by D, and thick darkness covers
	23:17	by darkness, and thick D covers my face.
	24:17	For deep D is morning to all of them;
	24:17	they are friends with the terrors of deep D
	26:10	the waters at the boundary between light and D
	28:3	put an end to D, and search out to
	28:3	farthest bound the ore in gloom and deep D
	29:3	light I walked through D;
	30:26	I waited for light, D came.
	34:22	no gloom or deep D where evildoers may hide
	37:19	we cannot draw up our case because of D
	38:9	its garment, and thick D its swaddling band,
	38:17	or have you seen the gates of deep D
	38:19	is the place of D,
Ps	18:9	and came down; thick D was under his feet.
	18:11	He made D his covering around him, his canopy
	18:28	my lamp; the LORD my God lightens my D
	44:19	place of jackals, and covered us with deep D
	82:5	they walk about in D; all the foundations of
	88:12	wonders known in the D, or thy saving help
	88:18	friend to shun me; my companions are in D
	91:6	pestilence that stalks in D, nor the destruction that
	97:2	Clouds and thick D are round about him;
	104:20	Thou makest D, and it is night, when all
	105:28	He sent D, and made the land dark; they
	107:10	Some sat in D and in gloom, prisoners in
	107:14	brought them out of D and gloom, and broke
	112:4	Light rises in the D for the upright; the
	139:11	I say, "Let only D cover me, and the
	139:12	even the D is not dark to thee, the
	139:12	as the day; for D is as light with
	143:3	made me sit in D like those long dead.
Prov	2:13	in the ways of D,
	4:20	wicked is like deep D; they do not know
	7:9	the evening, at the time of night and D
	20:20	his lamp will be put out in utter D
Eccl	2:13	saw that wisdom excels folly as light excels D
	2:14	the fool walks in D; and yet I perceived
	5:17	all his days in D and grief, in much
	6:4	vanity and goes into D, and in darkness its
	6:4	into darkness, and in D its name is covered;
	11:8	that the days of D will be many.
Wis	17:2	lay as captives of D and prisoners of long
	17:17	with one chain of D they all were bound.
	17:21	an image of the D that was destined to
	17:21	but still heavier than D were they to themselves.
	18:4	light and imprisoned in D, those who had kept
	19:17	when, surrounded by yawning D, each tried to find
Sir	23:18	D surrounds me, and the walls hide me, and
	45:5	him into the thick D, and gave him the
Is	5:20	good evil, who put D for light and light
	5:20	light and light for D, who put bitter for
	5:30	to the land, behold, D and distress; and the
	8:22	but behold, distress and D, the gloom of anguish;
	8:22	anguish; and they will be thrust into thick D
	9:2	people who walked in D have seen a great
	9:2	a land of deep D, on them has light
	29:18	of their gloom and D the eyes of the
	42:7	dungeon, from the prison those who sit in D
	42:16	I will turn the D before them into light,
	45:3	you the treasures of D and the hoards in
	45:7	form light and create D, I make weal and
	45:19	in a land of D; I did not say
	47:5	silence, and go into D, O daughter of the
	49:9	those who are in D, 'Appear.' They shall feed
	50:10	servant, who walks in D and has no light,
	58:10	light rise in the D and your gloom be
	59:9	for light, and behold, D, and for brightness, but
	60:2	For behold, D shall cover the earth, and thick
	60:2	the earth, and thick D the peoples; but the
Jer	2:6	of drought and deep D, in a land that
	2:31	wilderness to Israel, or a land of thick D
	13:16	God before he brings D, before your feet stumble
	13:16	turns it into gloom and makes it deep D
	23:12	slippery paths in the D, into which they shall
Lam	3:2	and brought me into D without any light;
	3:6	made me dwell in D like the dead of
Bar	6:71	like a dead body cast out in the D
Ezek	32:8	over you, and put D upon your land, says
	34:12	scattered on a day of clouds and thick D
Dan	2:22	what is in the D, and the light dwells
	3:71	the Lord, light and D, sing praise to him
Joel	2:2	near, a day of D and gloom, a day
	2:2	and gloom, a day of clouds and thick D
	2:31	shall be turned to D, and the moon to
Amos	4:13	who makes the morning D, and treads on the
	5:8	Orion, and turns deep D into the morning, and
	5:18	It is D, and not light;
	5:20	day of the LORD D, and not light, and
Mic	3:6	you, without vision, and D to you, without divination.
	7:8	when I sit in D, the LORD will be
Nah	1:8	his adversaries, and will pursue his enemies into D
Zeph	1:15	devastation, a day of D and gloom, a day
	1:15	of clouds and thick D,
2Mac	3:27	the ground and deep D came over him, his
Mt	4:16	people who sat in D have seen a great
	6:23	sound, your whole body will be full of D
	6:23	light in you is D, how great is the
	6:23	in you is darkness, how great is the D
	8:12	thrown into the outer D; there men will weep
	22:13	him into the outer D; there men will weep
	25:30	servant into the outer D; there men will weep
	27:45	sixth hour there was D over all the land
Mk	15:32	had come, there was D over the whole land
Lk	1:79	those who sit in D and in the shadow
	11:34	is not sound, your body is full of D
	11:35	be careful lest the light in you be D
	22:51	this is your hour, and the power of D
	23:43	hour, and there was D over the whole land
Jn	1:5	light shines in the D, and the darkness has
	1:5	the darkness, and the D has not overcome it.
	3:19	world, and men loved D rather than light, because
	8:12	will not walk in D, but will have the
	12:35	the light, lest the D overtake you; he who
	12:35	who walks in the D does not know where
	12:46	whoever believes in me may not remain in D
Acts	2:20	shall be turned into D and the moon into
	13:11	Immediately mist and D fell upon him and he
	26:18	they may turn from D to light and from
Rom	2:19	those who are in D,
	13:12	off the works of D and put on the
1Cor	4:5	things now hidden in D and will disclose the

2Cor 4:6 God who said, "Let light shine out of D
6:14 Or what fellowship has light with D
Eph 5:8 for once you were D, but now you are
5:11 the unfruitful works of D, but instead expose them.
6:12 rulers of this present D, against the spiritual hosts
Col 1:13 from the dominion of D and transferred us to
1Thes 5:4 you are not in D, brethren, for that day
5:5 we are not of the night or of D
Heb 12:18 a blazing fire, and D, and gloom, and a
1Pet 2:9 called you out of D into his marvelous light.
2Pet 2:17 the nether gloom of D has been reserved.
1 Jn 1:5 in him is no D at all.
1:6 while we walk in D, we lie and do
2:8 in you, because the D is passing away and
2:9 brother is in the D still.
2:11 brother is in the D and walks in the
2:11 and walks in the D, and does not know
2:11 is going, because the D has blinded his eyes.
Jude 1:13 the nether gloom of D has been reserved for
Rev 16:10 its kingdom was in D; men gnawed their tongues

DARKON (2)
Ezra 2:56 Jaalah, the sons of D, the sons of Giddel,
Neh 7:58 Jaala, the sons of D, the sons of Giddel,

DARLING (2)
Song 6:9 is only one, the D of her mother, flawless
Jer 31:20 Is he my D child?

DART (2)
Job 41:26 nor the spear, the D, or the javelin.
Nah 2:4 gleam like torches, they D like lightning.

DARTED
Ezek 1:14 And the living creatures D to and fro, like

DARTS (2)
2Sam 18:14 And he took three D in his hand, and
Eph 6:16 quench all the flaming D of the evil one.

DASH (9)
Deut 7:5 down their altars, and D in pieces their pillars,
12:3 down their altars, and D in pieces their pillars,
2Kgs 8:12 with the sword, and D in pieces their little
Jud 16:5 with the sword, and D my infants to the
Ps 2:9 rod of iron, and D them in pieces like
91:12 you up, lest you D your foot against a
Wis 4:19 ever; because he will D them speechless to the
Jer 13:14 And I will D them one against another, fathers
Lk 19:44 on every side, and D you to the ground,

DASHED (7)
2Chr 25:12 and they were all D to pieces.
Job 16:12 by the neck and D me to pieces; he
Is 13:16 Their infants will be D in pieces before their
Dan 13:39 opened the doors and D out.
Hos 10:14 of battle; mothers were D in pieces with their
13:16 little ones shall be D in pieces, and their
Nah 3:10 her little ones were D in pieces at the

DASHES (2)
Ps 137:9 your little ones and D them against the rock!
Mk 9:18 it seizes him, it D him down; and he

DATE
Gal 4:2 and trustees until the D set by the father.

DATHAN (11)
Num 16:1 son of Levi, and D and Abiram the sons
16:12 Moses sent to call D and Abiram the sons
16:24 the dwelling of Korah, D, and Abiram."
16:25 rose and went to D and Abiram; and the
16:27 the dwelling of Korah, D, and Abiram; and Dathan
16:27 Dathan, and Abiram; and D and Abiram came out
26:9 sons of Eliab: Nemuel, D, and Abiram.
26:9 These are the D and Abiram, chosen from the
Deut 11:6 what he did to D and Abiram the sons
Ps 106:17 opened and swallowed up D, and covered the
Sir 45:18 him in the wilderness, D and Abiram and their

DATHEMA (2)
1Mac 5:9 to the stronghold of D,
5:29 went all the way to the stronghold of D

DAUB (2)
Ezek 13:10 a wall, these prophets D it with whitewash;
13:11 say to those who D it with whitewash that

DAUBED (6)
Ex 2:3 made of bulrushes, and D it with bitumen and
Ezek 13:12 daubing with which you D it?'
13:14 wall that you have D with whitewash, and bring
13:15 upon those who have D it with whitewash; and
13:15 more, nor those who D it,
22:28 And her prophets have D for them with whitewash,

DAUBING
Ezek 13:12 you, 'Where is the D with which you daubed

DAUGHTER (333)
Gen 11:29 Nahor's wife, Milcah, the D of Haran the father
20:12 indeed my sister, the D of my father but
20:12 father but not the D of my mother; and
24:23 said, "Tell me whose D you are.
24:24 him, "I am the D of Bethuel the son
24:47 I asked her, 'Whose D are you?' She said,
24:47 you?' She said, The D of Bethuel, Nahor's son,
24:48 way to take the D of my master's kinsman
25:20 to wife Rebekah, the D of Bethuel the Aramean
26:34 to wife Judith the D of Be-eri the Hittite,
26:34 Hittite, and Basemath the D of Elon the Hittite;
28:9 he had, Mahalath the D of Ishmael Abraham's son,
29:6 and see, Rachel his D is coming with the
29:10 Jacob saw Rachel the D of Laban his mother's
29:18 years for your younger D Rachel."
29:23 evening he took his D Leah and brought her
29:24 maid Zilpah to his D Leah to be her
29:28 Laban gave him his D Rachel to wife.
29:29 maid Bilhah to his D Rachel to be her
30:21 Afterwards she bore a D, and called her name
34:1 Now Dinah the D of Leah, whom she had
34:3 drawn to Dinah the D of Jacob; he loved
34:5 he had defiled his D Dinah; but his sons
34:7 by lying with Jacob's D, for such a thing
34:8 Shechem longs for your D; I pray you, give
34:17 we will take our D, and we will be
34:19 the thing, because he had delight in Jacob's D
36:2 the Canaanites: Adah the D of Elon the Hittite,
36:2 the Hittite, Oholibamah the D of Anah the son
36:3 and Basemath, Ishmael's D, the sister of Nebaioth.
36:14 sons of Oholibamah the D of Anah the son
36:18 born of Oholibamah the D of Anah, Esau's wife.
36:25 Dishon and Oholibamah the D of Anah.
36:39 name was Mehetabel, the D of Matred, daughter of
36:39 the daughter of Matred, D of Mezahab.
38:2 There Judah saw the D of a certain Canaanite
38:12 wife of Judah, Shua's D, died; and when Judah
41:45 in marriage Asenath, the D of Potiphera priest of
41:50 sons, whom Asenath, the D of Potiphera priest of
46:15 Paddan-aram, together with his D Dinah; altogether
46:18 gave to Leah his D; and these she bore
46:20 Ephraim, whom Asenath, the D of Potiphera the
46:25 gave to Rachel his D, and these she bore
Ex 1:15 if it is a D, she shall live."
1:21 you shall let every D live."
2:1 took to wife a D of Levi.
2:5 Now the D of Pharaoh came down to bathe
2:7 sister said to Pharaoh's D, "Shall I go and
2:8 And Pharaoh's D said to her, "Go." So the
2:9 And Pharaoh's D said to her, "Take this child
2:10 brought him to Pharaoh's D, and he became her
2:21 he gave Moses his D Zipporah.
6:23 to wife Elisheba, the D of Amminadab and the
20:10 your son, or your D, your manservant, or your
21:7 a man sells his D as a slave, she
21:9 he shall deal with her as with a D
21:31 a man's son or D, he shall be dealt
Lev 12:6 son or for a D, she shall bring to
18:9 of your sister, the D of your father or
18:9 your father or the D of your mother, whether
18:10 nakedness of your son's D or of your daughter's
18:10 daughter or of your D's daughter, for their nakedness
18:10 or of your daughter's D, for their nakedness is
18:11 of your father's wife's D, begotten by your father,
18:17 woman and of her D, and you shall not
18:17 not take her son's D or her daughter's daughter
18:17 son's daughter or her D's daughter to uncover her
18:17 or her daughter's D to uncover her nakedness;
19:29 "Do not profane your D by making her a
20:17 takes his sister, a D of his father or
20:17 his father or a D of his mother, and
21:2 father, his son, his D, his brother,

21:9 And the D of any priest, if she profanes
22:12 If a priest's D is married to an outsider
22:13 But if a priest's D is a widow or
24:11 name was Shelomith, the D of Dibri, of the
Num 25:15 slain was Cozbi the D of Zur, who was
25:18 matter of Cozbi, the D of the prince of
26:46 the name of the D of Asher was Serah.
26:59 wife was Jochebed the D of Levi, who was
27:8 shall cause his inheritance to pass to his D
27:9 if he has no D, then you shall give
30:16 a father and his D, while in her youth,
36:8 And every D who possesses an inheritance in any
Deut 5:14 your son, or your D, or your manservant, or
12:18 your son and your D, your manservant and your
13:6 your son, or your D, or the wife of
16:11 your son and your D, your manservant and your
16:14 your son and your D, your manservant and your
18:10 his son or his D as an offering, any
22:16 elders, 'I gave my D to this man to
22:17 not find in your D the tokens of virginity."
22:17 the tokens of my D's virginity.' And they shall
27:22 his sister, whether the D of his father or
27:22 his father or the D of his mother.' And
28:56 son and to her D,
Josh 15:16 I give Achsah my D as wife."
15:17 gave him Achsah his D as wife.
Judg 1:12 give him Achsah my D as wife."
1:13 gave him Achsah his D as wife.
11:34 Mizpah; and behold, his D came out to meet
11:34 child; beside her he had neither son nor D
11:35 he rent his clothes, and said, "Alas, my D
11:40 year to lament the D of Jephthah the Gileadite
19:24 here are my virgin D and his concubine; let
21:1 us shall give his D in marriage to Benjamin."
Ruth 2:2 And she said to her, "Go, my D
2:8 Ruth, "Now, listen, my D, do not go to
2:22 "It is well, my D, that you go out
3:1 said to her, "My D, should I not seek
3:10 by the LORD, my D; you have made this
3:11 And now, my D, do not fear, I will
3:16 mother-in-law, she said, "How did you fare, my D
3:18 She replied, "Wait, my D, until you learn how
1Sam 14:50 wife was Ahino-am the D of Ahima-az.
17:25 will give him his D, and make his father's
18:17 "Here is my elder D Merab; I will give
18:19 time when Merab, Saul's D, should have been given
18:20 Now Saul's D Michal loved David; and they told
18:27 Saul gave him his D Michal for a wife.
25:44 had given Michal his D, David's wife, to Palti
2Sam 3:3 son of Maacah the D of Talmai king of
3:7 name was Rizpah, the D of Aiah; and Ish-bosheth
3:13 first bring Michal, Saul's D, when you come to
6:16 of David, Michal the D of Saul looked out
6:20 But Michal the D of Saul came out to
6:23 And Michal the D of Saul had no child
11:3 not this Bathsheba, the D of Eliam, the wife
12:3 it was like a D to him.
14:27 three sons, and one D whose name was Tamar;
17:25 had married Abigal the D of Nahash, sister of
21:8 sons of Rizpah the D of Aiah, whom she
21:8 sons of Merab the D of Saul, whom she
21:10 Then Rizpah the D of Aiah took sackcloth, and
21:11 told what Rizpah the D of Aiah, the concubine
1Kgs 3:1 Egypt; he took Pharaoh's D, and brought her into
4:11 (he had Taphath the D of Solomon as his
4:15 had taken Basemath the D of Solomon as his
7:8 this hall for Pharaoh's D whom he had taken
9:16 as dowry to his D, Solomon's wife;
9:24 But Pharaoh's D went up from the city of
11:1 foreign women: the D of Pharaoh, and Moabite,
15:2 name was Maacah the D of Abishalom.
15:10 name was Maacah the D of Abishalom.
16:31 for wife Jezebel the D of Ethbaal king of
22:42 name was Azubah the D of Shilhi.
2Kgs 8:18 had done, for the D of Ahab was his
9:34 and bury her; for she is a king's D
11:2 But Jehosheba, the D of King Joram, sister of
14:9 Lebanon, saying, 'Give your D to my son for
15:33 name was Jerusha the D of Zadok.
18:2 name was Abi the D of Zechariah.
19:21 scorns you--the virgin D of Zion; she wags
19:21 head behind you--the D of Jerusalem.
21:19 name was Meshullemeth the D of Haruz of Jotbah.
22:1 name was Jedidah the D of Adaiah of Bozkath.
23:10 his son or his D as an offering to
23:31 name was Hamutal the D of Jeremiah of Libnah.
23:36 name was Zebidah the D of Pedaiah of Rumah.
24:8 name was Nehushta the D of Elnathan of Jerusalem.
24:18 name was Hamutal the D of Jeremiah of Libnah.
1Chr 1:50 name Mehetabel the D of Matred, the daughter
1:50 daughter of Matred, the D of Mezahab.
2:21 went in to the D of Machir the father
2:35 So Sheshan gave his D in marriage to Jarha
2:49 of Gibe-a; and the D of Caleb was Achsah.
3:2 mother was Maacah, the D of Talmai, king of
3:5 four by Bath-shua, the D of Ammiel;
4:17 sons of Bithi-ah, the D of Pharaoh, whom Mered
7:24 His D was Sheerah, who built both Lower and
15:29 of David, Michal the D of Saul looked out
2Chr 8:11 Solomon brought Pharaoh's D up from the city of
11:18 as wife Mahalath the D of Jerimoth the son
11:18 and of Abihail the D of Eliab the son
11:20 he took Maacah the D of Absalom, who bore
11:21 Rehoboam loved Maacah the D of Absalom above all
13:2 name was Micaiah the D of Uriel of Gibe-ah.
20:31 name was Azubah the D of Shilhi.
21:6 had done; for the D of Ahab was his
22:11 But Jeho-shabe-ath, the D of the king, took Joash
22:11 Jeho-shabe-ath, the D of King Jehoram and wife
25:18 Lebanon, saying, 'Give your D to my son for
27:1 name was Jerushah the D of Zadok.
29:1 name was Abijah the D of Zechariah.
Neh 6:18 Jehohanan had taken the D of Meshullam the son
Tob 3:7 that Sarah, the D of Raguel, was reproached
3:9 see a son or D of yours!"
3:17 to give Sarah the D of Raguel in marriage
3:17 house and Sarah the D of Raguel came down
6:10 he has an only D named Sarah.
7:8 wife Edna and his D Sarah wept.
7:11 I have given my D to seven husbands, and
7:13 Then he called his D Sarah, and taking her
7:17 the mother comforted her D in her tears, and
7:18 Be brave, my D
10:12 said also to his D, "Honor your father-in-law and
10:12 your children by my D Sarah, that I may
10:12 I am entrusting my D to you; do nothing
11:17 Sarah his daughter-in-law, he blessed her, saying,
Jud 8:1 things: she was the D of Merari the son
10:12 replied, "I am a D of the Hebrews, but
13:18 said to her, "O D, you are blessed by
16:7 him; but Judith the D of Merari undid him
Esth 2:7 that is Esther, the D of his uncle, for
2:7 mother died, Mordecai adopted her as his own D
2:15 came for Esther the D of Abihail the uncle
2:15 her as his own D, to go in to
9:29 Then Queen Esther, the D of Abihail, and Mordecai
Ps 9:14 the gates of the D of Zion I may
45:10 Hear, O D, consider, and incline your ear; forget
137:8 O D of Babylon, you devastator!
Sir 7:25 Give a D in marriage; you will have finished
22:3 the birth of a D is a loss.
22:4 A sensible D obtains her husband, but one who
22:5 An impudent D disgraces father and husband, and
26:10 watch over a headstrong D, lest, when she finds
36:21 any man, but one D is better than another.
42:9 A D keeps her father secretly wakeful, and worry
42:11 watch over a headstrong D, lest she make you
Is 1:8 And the D of Zion is left like a
10:30 Cry aloud, O D of Gallim!
10:32 the mount of the D of Zion, the hill
15:2 The D of Dibon has gone up to the
16:1 the mount of the D of Zion.
22:4 the destruction of the D of my people."
23:10 like the Nile, O D of Tarshish; there is
23:12 exult, O oppressed virgin D of Sidon; arise, pass
37:22 you-- the virgin D of Zion; she wags
37:22 behind you-- the D of Jerusalem.
47:1 the dust, O virgin D of Babylon; sit on
47:1 without a throne, O D of the Chaldeans!
47:5 go into darkness, O D of the Chaldeans; for
52:2 your neck, O captive D of Zion.
62:11 earth: Say to the D of Zion, "Behold, your
Jer 4:11 the desert toward the D of my people, not
4:31 the cry of the D of Zion gasping for
6:2 I will destroy, the D of Zion.
6:23 battle, against you, O D of Zion!"
6:26 O D of my people, gird on sackcloth, and
8:19 the cry of the D of my people from
8:21 the wound of the D of my people is
8:22 the health of the D of my people not
9:1 the slain of the D of my people!
14:17 cease, for the virgin D of my people is

31:22 How long will you waver, O faithless D
46:11 take balm, O virgin D of Egypt!
46:24 The D of Egypt shall be put to shame,
49:4 your valleys, O faithless D, who trusted in her
50:42 battle against you, O D of Babylon!
51:33 God of Israel: The D of Babylon is like
52:1 name was Hamutal the D of Jeremiah of Libnah.
Lam 1:6 From the D of Zion has departed all her
1:15 wine press the virgin D of Judah.
2:1 anger has set the D of Zion under a
2:2 the strongholds of the D of Judah; he has
2:4 the tent of the D of Zion; he has
2:5 has multiplied in the D of Judah mourning and
2:8 the wall of the D of Zion; he marked
2:10 The elders of the D of Zion sit on
2:11 the destruction of the D of my people, because
2:13 what compare you, O D of Jerusalem?
2:13 comfort you, O virgin D of Zion?
2:15 their heads at the D of Jerusalem; "Is this
2:18 O D of Zion!
3:48 the destruction of the D of my people.
4:3 their young, but the D of my people has
4:6 the chastisement of the D of my people has
4:10 the destruction of the D of my people.
4:21 and be glad, O D of Edom, dweller in
4:22 of your iniquity, O D of Zion, is accomplished,
4:22 but your iniquity, O D of Edom, he will
Bar 2:3 his son and another the flesh of his D
Ezek 14:20 deliver neither son nor D; they would deliver but
16:44 you, 'Like mother, like D
16:45 daughter.' You are the D of your mother, who
22:11 another in you defiles his sister, his father's D
44:25 mother, for son or D, for brother or unmarried
Dan 11:6 an alliance, and the D of the king of
11:17 shall give him the D of women to destroy
13:2 wife named Susanna, the D of Hilkiah, a very
13:3 and had taught their D according to the law
13:29 "Send for Susanna, the D of Hilkiah, who is
13:48 Have you condemned a D of Israel without
13:57 through fear; but a D of Judah would not
13:63 praised God for their D Susanna, and so did
Hos 1:3 and took Gomer the D of Diblaim, and she
1:6 She conceived again and bore a D
Mic 1:13 of sin to the D of Zion, for in
4:8 flock, hill of the D of Zion, to you
4:8 the kingdom of the D of Jerusalem.
4:10 Writhe and groan, O D of Zion, like a
4:13 Arise and thresh, O D of Zion, for I
7:6 father with contempt, the D rises up against her
Zeph 3:10 Ethiopia my suppliants, the D of my dispersed ones,
3:14 Sing aloud, O D of Zion; shout, O Israel!
3:14 all your heart, O D of Jerusalem!
Zech 2:7 who dwell with the D of Babylon.
2:10 Sing and rejoice, O D of Zion; for lo,
9:9 Rejoice greatly, O D of Zion!
9:9 Shout aloud, O D of Jerusalem!
Mal 2:11 and has married the D of a foreign god.
1Mac 9:37 conducting the bride, a D of one of the
10:54 give me now your D as my wife, and
10:57 he and Cleopatra his D, and came to Ptolemais
10:58 gave him Cleopatra his D in marriage, and
11:9 you in marriage my D who was Alexander's wife,
11:10 I gave him my D, for he has tried
11:12 So he took his D away from him and
Mt 9:18 before him, saying, "My D has just died; but
9:22 he said, "Take heart, D; your faith has made
10:35 his father, and a D against her mother, and
10:37 who loves son or D more than me is
14:6 Herod's birthday came, the D of Herodi-as danced
15:22 Son of David; my D is severely possessed by
15:28 And her D was healed instantly.
21:5 prophet, saying, "Tell the D of Zion, Behold, your
Mk 5:23 him, saying, "My little D is at the point
5:34 he said to her, D, your faith has made
5:35 some who said, "Your D is dead.
6:22 For when Herodi-as' D came in and danced, she
7:24 a woman, whose little D was possessed by an
7:25 him to cast the demon out of her D
7:28 go your way; the demon has left your D
Lk 2:36 a prophetess, Anna, the D of Phanu-el, of the
8:42 he had an only D, about twelve years of
8:48 he said to her, D, your faith has made
8:49 came and said, "Your D is dead; do not
12:53 father, mother against D and D against her
13:16 not this woman, a D of Abraham whom Satan
Jn 12:15 is written, "Fear not, D of Zion; behold, your
Acts 7:21 he was exposed, Pharaoh's D adopted him and
Heb 11:24 the son of Pharaoh's D,

DAUGHTER-IN-LAW (21)

Gen 11:31 grandson, and Sarai his D, his son Abram's wife,
38:11 said to Tamar his D, "Remain a widow in
38:16 he did not know that she was his D
38:24 was told, "Tamar your D has played the harlot;
Lev 18:15 the nakedness of your D; she is your son's
20:12 man lies with his D, both of them shall
Ruth 1:22 Ruth the Moabitess her D with her, who returned
2:20 Naomi said to her D, "Blessed be he by
2:22 said to Ruth, her D, "It is well, my
4:15 old age; for your D who loves you, who
1Sam 4:19 Now his D, the wife of Phinehas, was with
1Chr 2:4 His D Tamar also bore him Perez and Zerah.
Tob 11:16 out to meet his D at the gate of
11:17 near to Sarah his D, he blessed her, saying,
12:12 when you and your D Sarah prayed, I brought
12:14 heal you and your D Sarah.
Ezek 22:11 another lewdly defiles his D; another in you defiles
Mic 7:6 against her mother, the D against her mother-in-law;
Mt 10:35 her mother, and a D against her mother-in-law;
Lk 12:53 mother, mother-in-law against her D and D against

DAUGHTERS (245)

Gen 5:4 hundred years; and he had other sons and D
5:7 and seven years, and had other sons and D
5:10 and fifteen years, and had other sons and D
5:13 and forty years, and had other sons and D
5:16 and thirty years, and had other sons and D
5:19 eight hundred years, and had other sons and D
5:22 three hundred years, and had other sons and D
5:26 and eighty-two years, and had other sons and D
5:30 and ninety-five years, and had other sons and D
6:1 of the ground, and D were born to them,
6:2 God saw that the D of men were fair;
6:4 came in to the D of men, and they
11:11 five hundred years, and had other sons and D
11:13 and three years, and had other sons and D
11:15 and three years, and had other sons and D
11:17 and thirty years, and had other sons and D
11:19 and nine years, and had other sons and D
11:21 and seven years, and had other sons and D
11:23 two hundred years, and had other sons and D
11:25 and nineteen years, and had other sons and D
19:8 Behold, I have two D who have not known
19:12 Sons-in-law, sons, D, or any one you have in
19:14 were to marry his D, "Up, get out of
19:15 wife and your two D who are here, lest
19:16 wife and his two D by the hand, the
19:30 hills with his two D, for he was afraid
19:30 he dwelt in a cave with his two D
19:36 Thus both the D of Lot were with child
24:3 my son from the D of the Canaanites, among
24:13 of water, and the D of the men of
24:37 my son from the D of the Canaanites, in
28:2 there one of the D of Laban your mother's
29:16 Now Laban had two D; the name of the
31:26 and carried away my D like captives of the
31:28 my sons and my D farewell?
31:31 you would take your D from me by force.
31:41 years for your two D, and six years for
31:43 said to Jacob, "The D are my daughters, the
31:43 "The daughters are my D, the children are my
31:43 day to these my D, or to their children
31:50 If you ill-treat my D, or if you take
31:50 take wives besides my D, although no man is
31:55 his grandchildren and his D and blessed them; then
34:9 with us; give your D to us, and take
34:9 us, and take our D for yourselves.
34:16 we will give our D to you, and we
34:16 we will take your D to ourselves, and we
34:21 let us take their D in marriage, and let
34:21 in marriage, and let us give them our D
36:6 wives, his sons, his D, and all the members
37:35 sons and all his D rose up to comfort
46:7 sons with him, his D, and his sons' daughters;
46:7 daughters, and his sons' D; all his offspring he
46:15 his sons and his D numbered thirty-three).
Ex 2:16 of Midian had seven D; and they came and
2:20 He said to his D, "And where is he?
3:22 sons and on your D; thus you shall despoil
6:25 wife one of the D of Puti-el; and she
10:9 with our sons and D and with our flocks
21:4 bears him sons or D, the wife and her

32:2 your sons, and your D, and bring them to
34:16 you take of their D for your sons, and
34:16 your sons, and their D play the harlot after
Lev 10:14 your sons and your D with you; for they
26:29 and you shall eat the flesh of your D
Num 18:11 to your sons and D with you, as a
18:19 to your sons and D with you, as a
21:29 sons fugitives, and his D captives, to an Amorite
25:1 the harlot with the D of Moab.
26:33 had no sons, but D: and the names of
26:33 the names of the D of Zelophehad were Mahlah,
27:1 Then drew near the D of Zelophehad the son
27:1 The names of his D were: Mahlah, Noah, Hoglah,
27:7 said to Moses, "The D of Zelophehad are right;
36:2 the inheritance of Zelophehad our brother to his D
36:6 LORD commands concerning the D of Zelophehad,
36:10 The D of Zelophehad did as the LORD commanded
36:11 and Noah, the D of Zelophehad, were married
Deut 7:3 with them, giving your D to their sons or
7:3 sons or taking their D for your sons.
12:12 your sons and your D, your menservants and your
12:31 their sons and their D in the fire to
23:17 cult prostitute of the D of Israel, neither shall
28:32 Your sons and your D shall be given to
28:41 shall beget sons and D, but they shall not
28:53 of your sons and D, whom the LORD your
32:19 of the provocation of his sons and his D
Josh 7:24 and his sons and D, and his oxen and
17:3 no sons, but only D; and these are the
17:3 the names of his D: Mahlah, Noah, Hoglah, Milcah,
17:6 the Jordan; because the D of Manasseh received an
Judg 3:6 and they took their D to themselves for wives,
3:6 wives, and their own D they gave to their
11:40 in Israel that the D of Israel went year
12:9 thirty sons; and thirty D he gave in marriage
12:9 his clan, and thirty D he brought in from
14:1 saw one of the D of the Philistines.
14:2 saw one of the D of the Philistines at
14:3 a woman among the D of your kinsmen, or
21:7 them any of our D for wives?"
21:18 Yet we cannot give them wives of our D
21:21 and watch; if the D of Shiloh come out
21:21 his wife from the D of Shiloh, and go
Ruth 1:11 said, "Turn back, my D, why will you go
1:12 Turn back, my D, go your way, for I
1:13 No, my D, for it is exceedingly bitter to
1Sam 1:4 all her sons and D;
2:21 she conceived and bore three sons and two D
8:13 He will take your D to be perfumers and
14:49 names of his two D were these: the name
30:3 wives and sons and D taken captive.
30:6 bitter in soul, each for his sons and D
30:19 or great, sons or D, spoil or anything that
2Sam 1:20 of Ashkelon; lest the D of the Philistines rejoice,
1:20 Philistines rejoice, lest the D of the uncircumcised
1:24 "Ye D of Israel, weep over Saul, who clothed
5:13 and more sons and D were born to David.
13:18 thus were the virgin D of the king clad
19:5 your sons and your D, and the lives of
2Kgs 17:17 their sons and their D as offerings, and used
1Chr 2:34 had no sons, only D; but Sheshan had an
4:27 sixteen sons and six D; but his brothers had
7:15 the second was Zelophehad; and Zelophehad had D
14:3 in Jerusalem, and David begot more sons and D
23:22 no sons, but only D; their kinsmen, the sons
25:5 God had given Heman fourteen sons and three D
2Chr 2:14 a woman of the D of Dan, and his
11:21 twenty-eight sons and sixty D;
13:21 wives, and had twenty-two sons and sixteen D
24:3 him two wives, and he had sons and D
28:8 kinsfolk, women, sons, and D; they also took much
29:9 our sons and our D and our wives are
31:18 their sons, and their D, the whole multitude; for
Ezra 2:61 a wife from the D of Barzillai the Gileadite,
9:2 taken some of their D to be wives for
9:12 Therefore give not your D to their sons, neither
9:12 sons, neither take their D for your sons, and
Neh 3:12 the district of Jerusalem, repaired, he and his D
4:14 brethren, your sons, your D, your wives, and your
5:2 our sons and our D, we are many; let
5:5 our sons and our D to be slaves, and
5:5 and some of our D have already been enslaved;
7:63 a wife of the D of Barzillai the Gileadite
10:28 wives, their sons, their D, all who have knowledge
10:30 will not give our D to the peoples of
10:30 land or take their D for our sons;
13:25 shall not give your D to their sons, or
13:25 sons, or take their D for your sons or
Tob 4:13 and the sons and D of your people by
Jud 9:4 a prey and their D to captivity, and all
12:13 like one of the D of the Assyrians who
Job 1:2 were born to him seven sons and three D
1:13 when his sons and D were eating and drinking
1:18 said, "Your sons and D were eating and drinking
42:13 He had also seven sons and three D
42:15 so fair as Job's D; and their father gave
Ps 45:9 instruments make you glad; D of kings are among
48:11 Let the D of Judah rejoice because of thy
97:8 is glad, and the D of Judah rejoice, because
106:37 their sons and their D to the demons;
106:38 of their sons and D, whom they sacrificed to
144:12 like plants full-grown, our D like corner pillars cut
Prov 30:15 The leech has two D; "Give, give," they cry.
Eccl 12:4 bird, and all the D of song are brought
Song 1:5 dark, but comely, O D of Jerusalem, like the
2:7 I adjure you, O D of Jerusalem, by the
3:5 I adjure you, O D of Jerusalem, by the
3:10 wrought within by the D of Jerusalem.
3:11 Go forth, O D of Zion, and behold King
5:8 I adjure you, O D of Jerusalem, if you
5:16 is my friend, O D of Jerusalem.
8:4 I adjure you, O D of Jerusalem, that you
Wis 9:7 and to be judge over thy sons and D
Sir 7:24 Do you have D
Is 3:16 LORD said: Because the D of Zion are haughty
3:17 the heads of the D of Zion, and the
4:4 the filth of the D of Zion and cleansed
16:2 nestlings, so are the D of Moab at the
32:9 my voice; you complacent D, give ear to my
43:6 from afar and my D from the end of
49:22 their bosom, and your D shall be carried on
56:5 better than sons and D; I will give them
60:4 from far, and your D shall be carried in
Jer 3:24 flocks and their herds, their sons and their D
5:17 your sons and your D; they shall eat up
7:31 their sons and their D in the fire; which
9:20 mouth; teach to your D a lament, and each
11:22 their sons and their D shall die by famine;
14:16 them--them, their wives, their sons, and their D
16:2 you have sons or D in this place.
16:3 concerning the sons and D who are born in
19:9 their sons and their D, and every one shall
29:6 and have sons and D; take wives for your
29:6 sons, and give your D in marriage, that they
29:6 may bear sons and D; multiply there, and do
32:35 up their sons and D to Molech, though I
35:8 our sons, or our D,
41:10 in Mizpah, the king's D and all the people
48:46 taken captive, and your D into captivity.
49:3 Cry, O D of Rabbah!
Bar 4:10 of my sons and D, which the Everlasting brought
4:14 of my sons and D, which the Everlasting brought
4:16 sons, and bereaved the lonely woman of her D
Ezek 13:17 your face against the D of your people, who
14:16 deliver neither sons nor D; they alone would be
14:18 deliver neither sons nor D, but they alone would
14:22 lead out sons and D, when they come forth
16:20 your sons and your D, whom you had borne
16:27 of your enemies, the D of the Philistines, who
16:46 who lived with her D to the north of
16:46 the south of you, is Sodom with her D
16:48 sister Sodom and her D have not done as
16:48 as you and your D have done.
16:49 Sodom: she and her D had pride, surfeit of
16:53 of Sodom and her D, and the fortunes of
16:53 of Samaria and her D, and I will restore
16:55 sisters, Sodom and her D shall return to their
16:55 and Samaria and her D shall return to their
16:55 and you and your D shall return to your
16:57 of reproach for the D of Edom and all
16:57 neighbors, and for the D of the Philistines, those
16:61 them to you as D, but not on account
23:2 were two women, the D of one mother;
23:4 They became mine, and they bore sons and D
23:10 her sons and her D; and her they slew
23:25 your sons and your D, and your survivors shall
23:47 their sons and their D, and burn up their
24:21 your sons and your D whom you left behind
24:25 also their sons and D,
26:6 the nations; and her D on the mainland shall
26:8 with the sword your D on the mainland; he
30:18 a cloud, and her D shall go into captivity.

	32:16	shall be chanted; the D of the nations shall
	32:18	down, her and the D of majestic nations, to
Dan	13:57	been dealing with the D of Israel, and they
Hos	4:13	Therefore your D play the harlot, and your brides
	4:14	will not punish your D when they play the
Joel	2:28	your sons and your D shall prophesy, your old
	3:8	your sons and your D into the hand of
Amos	7:17	your sons and your D shall fall by the
Lk	1:5	a wife of the D of Aaron, and her
	23:27	turning to them said, D of Jerusalem, do not
Acts	2:17	your sons and your D shall prophesy, and your
	21:9	he had four unmarried D, who prophesied.
2Cor	6:18	be my sons and D, says the Lord Almighty."

D

DAUGHTERS-IN-LAW (3)

Ruth	1:6	she started with her D to return from the
	1:7	was, with her two D, and they went on
	1:8	said to her two D, "Go, return each of

DAUNTED (2)

Jud	16:10	boldness, the Medes were D at her daring.
Is	31:4	by their shouting or D at their noise, so

DAVID (1,077)

Ruth	4:17	was the father of Jesse, the father of D
	4:22	of Obed, Obed of Jesse, and Jesse of D
1Sam	16:13	LORD came mightily upon D from that day forward.
	16:19	and said, "Send me D your son, who is
	16:20	and sent them by D his son to Saul.
	16:21	And D came to Saul, and entered his service.
	16:22	to Jesse, saying, "Let D remain in my service,
	16:23	God was upon Saul, D took the lyre and
	17:12	Now D was the son of an Ephrathite of
	17:14	D was the youngest; the three eldest followed Saul,
	17:15	eldest followed Saul, but D went back and forth
	17:17	And Jesse said to D his son, "Take for
	17:20	And D rose early in the morning, and left
	17:22	And D left the things in charge of the
	17:23	And D heard him.
	17:26	And D said to the men who stood by
	17:28	anger was kindled against D, and he said, "Why
	17:29	And D said, "What have I done now?
	17:31	When the words which D spoke were heard, they
	17:32	And D said to Saul, "Let no man's heart
	17:33	And Saul said to D, "You are not able
	17:34	But D said to Saul, "Your servant used to
	17:37	And D said, "The LORD who delivered me from
	17:37	And Saul said to D, "Go, and the LORD
	17:38	Then Saul clothed D with his armor; he put
	17:39	And D girded his sword over his armor, and
	17:39	Then D said to Saul, "I cannot go with
	17:39	And D put them off.
	17:41	and drew near to D, with his shield-bearer in
	17:42	Philistine looked, and saw D, he disdained him; for
	17:43	the Philistine said to D, "Am I a dog,
	17:43	And the Philistine cursed D by his gods.
	17:44	The Philistine said to D, "Come to me, and
	17:45	Then D said to the Philistine, "You come to
	17:48	drew near to meet D, David ran quickly toward
	17:48	near to meet David, D ran quickly toward the
	17:49	And D put his hand in his bag and
	17:50	So D prevailed over the Philistine with a sling
	17:50	there was no sword in the hand of D
	17:51	Then D ran and stood over the Philistine, and
	17:54	And D took the head of the Philistine and
	17:55	When Saul saw D go forth against the Philistine,
	17:57	And as D returned from the slaughter of the
	17:58	And D answered, "I am the son of your
	18:1	to the soul of D, and Jonathan loved him
	18:3	made a covenant with D, because he loved him
	18:4	and gave it to D, and his armor, and
	18:5	And D went out and was successful wherever Saul
	18:6	were coming home, when D returned from slaying
	18:7	slain his thousands, and D his ten thousands."
	18:8	"They have ascribed to D ten thousands, and to
	18:9	And Saul eyed D from that day on.
	18:10	within his house, while D was playing the lyre,
	18:11	thought, "I will pin D to the wall." But
	18:11	But D evaded him twice.
	18:12	Saul was afraid of D, because the LORD was
	18:14	And D had success in all his undertakings; for
	18:16	Israel and Judah loved D; for he went out
	18:17	Then Saul said to D, "Here is my elder
	18:18	And D said to Saul, "Who am I, and
	18:19	have been given to D, she was given to
	18:20	Saul's daughter Michal loved D; and they told Saul,
	18:21	Therefore Saul said to D a second time, "You
	18:22	his servants, "Speak to D in private and say,
	18:23	servants spoke those words in the ears of D
	18:23	And D said, "Does it seem to you a
	18:24	"Thus and so did D speak."
	18:25	shall you say to D, 'The king desires no
	18:25	Saul thought to make D fall by the hand
	18:26	when his servants told D these words, it pleased
	18:26	these words, it pleased D well to be the
	18:27	the time had expired, D arose and went, along
	18:27	of the Philistines; and D brought their foreskins,
	18:28	the LORD was with D, and that all Israel
	18:29	loved him, Saul was still more afraid of D
	18:29	So Saul was D's enemy continually.
	18:30	as they came out D had more success than
	19:1	to all his servants, that they should kill D
	19:1	But Jonathan, Saul's son, delighted much in D
	19:2	And Jonathan told D, "Saul my father seeks to
	19:4	Jonathan spoke well of D to Saul his father,
	19:4	sin against his servant D; because he has not
	19:5	innocent blood by killing D without cause?"
	19:7	And Jonathan called D, and Jonathan showed him all
	19:7	And Jonathan brought D to Saul, and he was
	19:8	was war again; and D went out and fought
	19:9	in his hand; and D was playing the lyre.
	19:10	Saul sought to pin D to the wall with
	19:10	And D fled, and escaped.
	19:11	Saul sent messengers to D's house to watch him,
	19:11	But Michal, D's wife, told him, "If you do
	19:12	So Michal let D down through the window; and
	19:14	sent messengers to take D, she said, "He is
	19:15	the messengers to see D, saying, "Bring him up
	19:18	Now D fled and escaped, and he came to
	19:19	was told Saul, "Behold, D is at Naioth in
	19:20	sent messengers to take D; and when they saw
	19:22	Secu; and he asked, "Where are Samuel and D
	20:1	Then D fled from Naioth in Ramah, and came
	20:3	But D replied, "Your father knows well that I
	20:4	Then said Jonathan to D, "Whatever you say, I
	20:5	D said to Jonathan, "Behold, tomorrow is the new
	20:6	at all, then say, D earnestly asked leave of
	20:10	Then said D to Jonathan, "Who will tell me
	20:11	And Jonathan said to D, "Come, let us go
	20:12	And Jonathan said to D, "The LORD, the God
	20:12	he is well-disposed toward D, shall I not then
	20:15	of the enemies of D from the face of
	20:16	Jonathan be cut off from the house of D
	20:16	LORD take vengeance on D's enemies."
	20:17	And Jonathan made D swear again by his love
	20:24	So D hid himself in the field; and when
	20:25	by Saul's side, but D's place was empty.
	20:27	after the new moon, D's place was empty.
	20:28	Jonathan answered Saul, D earnestly asked leave of
	20:33	was determined to put D to death.
	20:34	he was grieved for D, because his father had
	20:35	to the appointment with D, and with him a
	20:39	nothing; only Jonathan and D knew the matter.
	20:41	the lad had gone, D rose from beside the
	20:41	with one another, until D recovered himself.
	20:42	Then Jonathan said to D, "Go in peace, forasmuch
	21:1	Then came D to Nob to Ahimelech the priest;
	21:1	Ahimelech came to meet D trembling, and said to
	21:2	And D said to Ahimelech the priest, "The king
	21:4	And the priest answered D, "I have no common
	21:5	And D answered the priest, "Of a truth women
	21:8	And D said to Ahimelech, "And have you not
	21:9	And D said, "There is none like that; give
	21:10	And D rose and fled that day from Saul,
	21:11	him, "Is not this D the king of the
	21:11	slain his thousands, and D his ten thousands'?"
	21:12	And D took these words to heart, and was
	22:1	D departed from there and escaped to the cave
	22:3	And D went from there to Mizpeh of Moab;
	22:4	all the time that D was in the stronghold.
	22:5	prophet Gad said to D, "Do not remain in
	22:5	So D departed, and went into the forest of
	22:6	Now Saul heard that D was discovered, and the
	22:14	is so faithful as D, who is the king's
	22:17	hand also is with D, and they knew that
	22:20	of Ahitub, named Abiathar, escaped and fled after D
	22:21	And Abiathar told D that Saul had killed the
	22:22	And D said to Abiathar, "I knew on that
	23:1	Now they told D, "Behold, the Philistines are fighting
	23:2	Therefore D inquired of the LORD, "Shall I go
	23:2	the LORD said to D, "Go and attack the
	23:3	But D's men said to him, "Behold, we are

23:4 Then D inquired of the LORD again.
23:5 And D and his men went to Keilah, and
23:5 So D delivered the inhabitants of Keilah.
23:6 of Ahimelech fled to D to Keilah, he came
23:7 was told Saul that D had come to Keilah.
23:8 to Keilah, to besiege D and his men.
23:9 D knew that Saul was plotting evil against him;
23:10 Then said D, "O LORD, the God of Israel,
23:12 Then said D, "Will the men of Keilah surrender
23:13 Then D and his men, who were about six
23:13 Saul was told that D had escaped from Keilah,
23:14 And D remained in the strongholds in the wilderness,
23:15 And D was afraid because Saul had come out
23:15 D was in the Wilderness of Ziph at Horesh.
23:16 rose, and went to D at Horesh, and strengthened
23:18 covenant before the LORD; D remained at Horesh,
23:19 Gibe-ah, saying, "Does not D hide among us in
23:24 Now D and his men were in the wilderness
23:25 And D was told; therefore he went down to
23:25 that, he pursued after D in the wilderness of
23:26 of the mountain, and D and his men on
23:26 of the mountain; and D was making haste to
23:26 were closing in upon D and his men to
23:28 returned from pursuing after D, and went against the
23:29 And D went up from there, and dwelt in
24:1 he was told, "Behold, D is in the wilderness
24:2 and went to seek D and his men in
24:3 Now D and his men were sitting in the
24:4 And the men of D said to him, "Here
24:4 Then D arose and stealthily cut off the skirt
24:5 And afterward D's heart smote him, because he had
24:7 So D persuaded his men with these words, and
24:8 Afterward D also arose, and went out of the
24:8 Saul looked behind him, D bowed with his face
24:9 And D said to Saul, "Why do you listen
24:9 men who say, 'Behold, D seeks your hurt?
24:16 When D had finished speaking these words to Saul,
24:16 Saul said, "Is this your voice, my son D
24:17 He said to D, "You are more righteous than
24:22 And D swore this to Saul.
24:22 Saul went home; but D and his men went
25:1 Then D rose and went down to the wilderness
25:4 D heard in the wilderness that Nabal was shearing
25:5 So D sent ten young men; and David said
25:5 ten young men; and D said to the young
25:8 hand to your servants and to your son D
25:9 When D's young men came, they said all this
25:9 in the name of D; and then they waited.
25:10 And Nabal answered D's servants, "Who is David?
25:10 And Nabal answered David's servants, "Who is D
25:12 So D's young men turned away, and came back
25:13 And D said to his men, "Every man gird
25:13 girded on his sword; D also girded on his
25:13 men went up after D, while two hundred remained
25:14 Abigail, Nabal's wife, "Behold, D sent messengers
25:20 of the mountain, behold, D and his men came
25:21 Now D had said, "Surely in vain have I
25:22 God do so to D and more also, if
25:23 When Abigail saw D, she made haste, and alighted
25:23 ass, and fell before D on her face, and
25:32 And D said to Abigail, "Blessed be the LORD,
25:35 Then D received from her hand what she had
25:39 When D heard that Nabal was dead, he said,
25:39 Then D sent and wooed Abigail, to make her
25:40 when the servants of D came to Abigail at
25:40 they said to her, D has sent us to
25:42 after the messengers of D, and became his wife.
25:43 D also took Ahino-am of Jezreel; and both of
25:44 given Michal his daughter, D's wife, to Palti the
26:1 Gibe-ah, saying, "Is not D hiding himself on the
26:2 of Israel, to seek D in the wilderness of
26:3 But D remained in the wilderness; and when he
26:4 him into the wilderness, D sent out spies, and
26:5 Then D rose and came to the place where
26:5 Saul had encamped; and D saw the place where
26:6 Then D said to Ahimelech the Hittite, and to
26:7 So D and Abishai went to the army by
26:8 Then said Abishai to D, "God has given your
26:9 But D said to Abishai, "Do not destroy him;
26:10 And D said, "As the LORD lives, the LORD
26:12 So D took the spear and the jar of
26:13 Then D went over to the other side, and
26:14 space between them; and D called to the army,
26:15 And D said to Abner, "Are you not a
26:17 Saul recognized D's voice, and said, "Is this your
26:17 and said, "Is this your voice, my son D
26:17 And D said, "It is my voice, my lord,
26:21 wrong; return, my son D, for I will no
26:22 And D made answer, "Here is the spear, O
26:25 Then Saul said to D, "Blessed be you, my
26:25 said to David, "Blessed be you, my son D
26:25 So D went his way, and Saul returned to
27:1 And D said in his heart, "I shall now
27:2 So D arose and went over, he and the
27:3 And D dwelt with Achish at Gath, he and
27:3 with his household, and D with his two wives,
27:4 was told Saul that D had fled to Gath,
27:5 Then D said to Achish, "If I have found
27:7 of the days that D dwelt in the country
27:8 Now D and his men went up, and made
27:9 And D smote the land, and left neither man
27:10 D would say, "Against the Negeb of Judah," or
27:11 And D saved neither man nor woman alive, to
27:11 us, and say, 'So D has done.'" Such was
27:12 And Achish trusted D, thinking, "He has made
28:1 And Achish said to D, "Understand that you and
28:2 D said to Achish, "Very well, you shall know
28:2 And Achish said to D, "Very well, I will
28:17 your hand, and given it to your neighbor, D
29:2 and by thousands, and D and his men were
29:3 Philistines, "Is not this D, the servant of Saul,
29:5 Is not this D, of whom they sing to
29:5 slain his thousands, and D his ten thousands'?"
29:6 Then Achish called D and said to him, "As
29:8 And D said to Achish, "But what have I
29:9 Achish made answer to D, "I know that you
29:11 So D set out with his men early in
30:1 Now when D and his men came to Ziklag
30:3 And when D and his men came to the
30:4 Then D and the people who were with him
30:5 D's two wives also had been taken captive, Ahino-am
30:6 And D was greatly distressed; for the people spoke
30:6 But D strengthened himself in the LORD his God.
30:7 And D said to Abiathar the priest, the son
30:7 So Abiathar brought the ephod to D
30:8 And D inquired of the LORD, "Shall I pursue
30:9 So D set out, and the six hundred men
30:10 But D went on with the pursuit, he and
30:11 and brought him to D; and they gave him
30:13 And D said to him, "To whom do you
30:15 And D said to him, "Will you take me
30:17 And D smote them from twilight until the evening
30:18 D recovered all that the Amalekites had taken; and
30:18 Amalekites had taken; and D rescued his two wives.
30:19 that had been taken; D brought back all.
30:20 D also captured all the flocks and herds; and
30:20 and said, "This is D's spoil."
30:21 Then D came to the two hundred men, who
30:21 too exhausted to follow D, and who had been
30:21 went out to meet D and to meet the
30:21 with him; and when D drew near to the
30:22 who had gone with D said, "Because they did
30:23 But D said, "You shall not do so, my
30:26 When D came to Ziklag, he sent part of
30:31 all the places where D and his men had
2Sam 1:1 death of Saul, when D had returned from the
1:1 slaughter of the Amalekites, D remained two days in
1:2 when he came to D, he fell to the
1:3 D said to him, "Where do you come from?"
1:4 And D said to him, "How did it go?
1:5 Then D said to the young man who told
1:11 Then D took hold of his clothes, and rent
1:13 And D said to the young man who told
1:14 D said to him, "How is it you were
1:15 Then D called one of the young men and
1:16 And D said to him, "Your blood be upon
1:17 And D lamented with this lamentation over Saul and
2:1 After this D inquired of the LORD, "Shall I
2:1 D said, "To which shall I go up?" And
2:2 So D went up there, and his two wives
2:3 And D brought up his men who were with
2:4 and there they anointed D king over the house
2:4 When they told D, "It was the men of
2:5 D sent messengers to the men of Jabesh-gilead, and
2:10 But the house of Judah followed D
2:11 And the time that D was king in Hebron
2:13 and the servants of D, went out and met
2:15 of Saul, and twelve of the servants of D
2:17 of Israel were beaten before the servants of D
2:30 there were missing of D's servants nineteen men
2:31 But the servants of D had slain of Benjamin
3:1 and the house of D; and David grew stronger

D

3:1 house of David; and D grew stronger and stronger,
3:2 sons were born to D at Hebron: his first-born
3:5 sixth, Ithre-am, of Eglah, D's wife.
3:5 These were born to D in Hebron.
3:6 and the house of D, Abner was making himself
3:8 into the hand of D; and yet you charge
3:9 do not accomplish for D what the LORD has
3:10 up the throne of D over Israel and over
3:12 Abner sent messengers to D at Hebron, saying, "To
3:14 Then D sent messengers to Ish-bosheth Saul's son,
3:17 you have been seeking D as king over you.
3:18 the LORD has promised D, saying, 'By the hand
3:18 hand of my servant D I will save my
3:19 Abner went to tell D at Hebron all that
3:20 with twenty men to D at Hebron, David made
3:20 to David at Hebron, D made a feast for
3:21 And Abner said to D, "I will arise and
3:21 So D sent Abner away; and he went in
3:22 then the servants of D arrived with Joab from
3:22 Abner was not with D at Hebron, for he
3:26 Joab came out from D's presence, he sent
3:26 cistern of Sirah; but D did not know about
3:28 Afterward, when D heard of it, he said, "I
3:31 Then D said to Joab and to all the
3:31 And King D followed the bier.
3:35 people came to persuade D to eat bread while
3:35 was yet day; but D swore, saying, "God do
4:8 head of Ish-bosheth to D at Hebron.
4:9 But D answered Rechab and Baanah his brother, the
4:12 And D commanded his young men, and they killed
5:1 of Israel came to D at Hebron, and said,
5:3 at Hebron; and King D made a covenant with
5:3 LORD, and they anointed D king over Israel.
5:4 D was thirty years old when he began to
5:6 land, who said to D, "You will not come
5:6 ward you off"–thinking, D cannot come in here."
5:7 Nevertheless D took the stronghold of Zion, that is,
5:7 stronghold of Zion, that is, the city of D
5:8 And D said on that day, "Whoever would smite
5:8 who are hated by D's soul." Therefore it is
5:9 And D dwelt in the stronghold, and called it
5:9 the stronghold, and called it the city of D
5:9 And D built the city round about from the
5:10 And D became greater and greater, for the LORD,
5:11 Tyre sent messengers to D, and cedar trees, also
5:11 and masons who built D a house.
5:12 And D perceived that the LORD had established him
5:13 And D took more concubines and wives from
5:13 and more sons and daughters were born to D
5:17 the Philistines heard that D had been anointed king
5:17 up in search of D; but David heard of
5:17 search of David; but D heard of it and
5:19 And D inquired of the LORD, "Shall I go
5:19 the LORD said to D, "Go up; for I
5:20 And D came to Baal-perazim, and David defeated
5:20 came to Baal-perazim, and D defeated them there;
5:21 their idols there, and D and his men carried
5:23 And when D inquired of the LORD, he said,
5:25 And D did as the LORD commanded him, and
6:1 D again gathered all the chosen men of Israel,
6:2 And D arose and went with all the people
6:5 And D and all the house of Israel were
6:8 And D was angry because the LORD had broken
6:9 And D was afraid of the LORD that day;
6:10 So D was not willing to take the ark
6:10 into the city of D; but David took it
6:10 city of David; but D took it aside to
6:12 it was told King D, "The LORD has blessed
6:12 So D went and brought up the ark of
6:12 to the city of D with rejoicing;
6:14 And D danced before the LORD with all his
6:14 all his might; and D was girded with a
6:15 So D and all the house of Israel brought
6:16 into the city of D, Michal the daughter of
6:16 window, and saw King D leaping and dancing before
6:17 inside the tent which D had pitched for it;
6:17 pitched for it; and D offered burnt offerings and
6:18 And when D had finished offering the burnt offerings
6:20 And D returned to bless his household.
6:20 came out to meet D, and said, "How the
6:21 And D said to Michal, "It was before the
7:5 and tell my servant D, 'Thus says the LORD:
7:8 say to my servant D, 'Thus says the LORD
7:17 accordance with all this vision, Nathan spoke to D
7:18 Then King D went in and sat before the
7:20 And what more can D say to thee?
7:26 house of thy servant D will be established before
8:1 After this D defeated the Philistines and subdued
8:1 and subdued them, and D took Metheg-ammah out
8:2 Moabites became servants to D and brought tribute.
8:3 D also defeated Hadadezer the son of Rehob, king
8:4 And D took from him a thousand and seven
8:4 thousand foot soldiers; and D hamstrung all the
8:5 Hadadezer king of Zobah, D slew twenty-two
8:6 Then D put garrisons in Aram of Damascus; and
8:6 Syrians became servants to D and brought tribute.
8:6 LORD gave victory to D wherever he went.
8:7 And D took the shields of gold which were
8:8 cities of Hadadezer, King D took very much bronze.
8:9 of Hamath heard that D had defeated the whole
8:10 son Joram to King D, to greet him, and
8:11 bronze; these also King D dedicated to the LORD,
8:13 And D won a name for himself.
8:14 all the Edomites became D's servants.
8:14 LORD gave victory to D wherever he went.
8:15 So D reigned over all Israel; and David administered
8:15 over all Israel; and D administered justice and equity
8:18 and the Pelethites; and D's sons were priests.
9:1 And D said, "Is there still any one left
9:2 they called him to D; and the king said
9:5 Then King D sent and brought him from the
9:6 of Saul, came to D, and fell on his
9:6 D said, "Mephibosheth!" And he answered, "Behold,
9:7 And D said to him, "Do not fear; for
9:11 So Mephibosheth ate at D's table, like one of
10:2 And D said, "I will deal loyally with Hanun
10:2 So D sent by his servants to console him
10:2 And D's servants came into the land of the
10:3 "Do you think, because D has sent comforters to
10:3 Has not D sent his servants to you to
10:4 So Hanun took D's servants, and shaved off half
10:5 When it was told D, he sent to meet
10:6 had become odious to D, the Ammonites sent and
10:7 And when D heard of it, he sent Joab
10:17 when it was told D, he gathered all Israel
10:17 Syrians arrayed themselves against D, and fought
10:18 fled before Israel; and D slew of the Syrians
11:1 go forth to battle, D sent Joab, and his
11:1 But D remained at Jerusalem.
11:2 late one afternoon, when D arose from his couch
11:3 And D sent and inquired about the woman.
11:4 So D sent messengers, and took her; and she
11:5 she sent and told D, "I am with child."
11:6 So D sent word to Joab, "Send me Uriah
11:6 And Joab sent Uriah to D
11:7 Uriah came to him, D asked how Joab was
11:8 Then D said to Uriah, "Go down to your
11:10 When they told D, "Uriah did not go down
11:10 D said to Uriah, "Have you not come from
11:11 Uriah said to D, "The ark and Israel and
11:12 Then D said to Uriah, "Remain here today also,
11:13 And D invited him, and he ate in his
11:14 In the morning D wrote a letter to Joab,
11:17 of the servants of D among the people fell.
11:18 Joab sent and told D all the news about
11:22 and came and told D all that Joab had
11:23 The messenger said to D, "The men gained an
11:25 D said to the messenger, "Thus shall you say
11:27 the mourning was over, D sent and brought her
11:27 But the thing that D had done displeased the
12:1 And the LORD sent Nathan to D
12:5 Then D's anger was greatly kindled against the man;
12:7 Nathan said to D, "You are the man.
12:13 D said to Nathan, "I have sinned against the
12:13 And Nathan said to D, "The LORD also has
12:15 Uriah's wife bore to D, and it became sick.
12:16 D therefore besought God for the child; and David
12:16 for the child; and D fasted, and went in
12:18 And the servants of D feared to tell him
12:19 But when D saw that his servants were whispering
12:19 servants were whispering together, D perceived that
12:19 child was dead; and D said to his servants,
12:20 Then D arose from the earth, and washed, and
12:24 Then D comforted his wife, Bathsheba, and went in
12:27 Joab sent messengers to D, and said, "I have
12:29 So D gathered all the people together and went
12:30 it was placed on D's head.
12:31 Then D and all the people returned to Jerusalem.
13:1 Now Absalom, D's son, had a beautiful sister, whose
13:1 after a time Amnon, D's son, loved her.
13:3 the son of Shimeah, D's brother; and Jonadab was
13:7 Then D sent home to Tamar, saying, "Go to

13:21 When King D heard of all these things, he
13:30 way, tidings came to D, "Absalom has slain all
13:32 the son of Shimeah, D's brother, said, "Let not
13:37 And D mourned for his son day after day.
15:12 Ahithophel the Gilonite, D's counselor, from his city
15:13 a messenger came to D, saying, "The hearts of
15:14 Then D said to all his servants who were
15:22 And D said to Ittai, "Go then, pass on."
15:30 But D went up the ascent of the Mount
15:31 And it was told D, "Ahithophel is among the
15:31 And D said, "O LORD, I pray thee, turn
15:32 When D came to the summit, where God was
15:33 D said to him, "If you go on with
15:37 So Hushai, D's friend, came into the city, just
16:1 When D had passed a little beyond the summit,
16:5 When King D came to Bahurim, there came out
16:6 he threw stones at D, and at all the
16:6 the servants of King D; and all the people
16:10 said to him, 'Curse D who then shall say,
16:11 And D said to Abishai and to all his
16:13 So D and his men went on the road,
16:16 Hushai the Archite, D's friend, came to Absalom,
16:23 Ahithophel esteemed, both by D and by Absalom.
17:1 set out and pursue D tonight.
17:16 send quickly and tell D, 'Do not lodge tonight
17:17 go and tell King D; for they must not
17:21 of the well, and went and told King D
17:21 They said to D, "Arise, and go quickly over
17:22 Then D arose, and all the people who were
17:24 Then D came to Mahanaim.
17:27 When D came to Mahanaim, Shobi the son of
17:29 from the herd, for D and the people with
18:1 Then D mustered the men who were with him,
18:2 And D sent forth the army, one third under
18:7 by the servants of D, and the slaughter there
18:9 And Absalom chanced to meet the servants of D
18:24 Now D was sitting between the two gates; and
19:11 And King D sent this message to Zadok and
19:16 Judah to meet King D;
19:22 But D said, "What have I to do with
19:41 the Jordan, and all D's men with him?"
19:43 the king, and in D also we have more
20:1 have no portion in D, and we have no
20:2 of Israel withdrew from D, and followed Sheba the
20:3 And D came to his house at Jerusalem; and
20:6 And D said to Abishai, "Now Sheba the son
20:11 and whoever is for D, let him follow Joab."
20:21 his hand against King D; give up him alone,
20:26 the Jairite was also D's priest.
21:1 in the days of D for three years, year
21:1 year after year; and D sought the face of
21:3 And D said to the Gibeonites, "What shall I
21:7 was between them, between D and Jonathan the son
21:11 When D was told what Rizpah the daughter of
21:12 of Saul, had done, D went and took the
21:15 again with Israel, and D went down together with
21:15 against the Philistines; and D grew weary.
21:16 girded with a new sword, thought to kill D
21:17 Then D's men adjured him, "You shall no more
21:21 the son of Shimei, D's brother, slew him.
21:22 by the hand of D and by the hand
22:1 And D spoke to the LORD the words of
22:51 to his anointed, to D, and his descendants for
23:1 the last words of D: The oracle of David,
23:1 David: The oracle of D, the son of Jesse,
23:8 men whom D had: Josheb-basshebeth a
23:9 He was with D when they defied the Philistines
23:13 about harvest time to D at the cave of
23:14 D was then in the stronghold; and the garrison
23:15 And D said longingly, "O that some one would
23:16 the gate, and took and brought it to D
23:23 And D set him over his bodyguard.
24:1 Israel, and he incited D against them, saying, "Go,
24:10 But D's heart smote him after he had numbered
24:10 And D said to the LORD, "I have sinned
24:11 And when D arose in the morning, the word
24:11 to the prophet Gad, D's seer, saying,
24:12 "Go and say to D, 'Thus says the LORD,
24:13 So Gad came to D and told him, and
24:14 Then D said to Gad, "I am in great
24:17 Then D spoke to the LORD when he saw
24:18 came that day to D, and said to him,
24:19 So D went up at Gad's word, as the
24:21 D said, "To buy the threshing floor of you,
24:22 Then Araunah said to D, "Let my lord the
24:24 So D bought the threshing floor and the oxen
24:25 And D built there an altar to the LORD,
1Kgs 1:1 Now King D was old and advanced
1:8 Shimei, and Rei, and D's mighty men were not
1:11 has become king and D our lord does not
1:13 at once to King D, and say to him,
1:28 Then King D answered, "Call Bathsheba to me." So
1:31 "May my lord King D live for ever!"
1:32 King D said, "Call to me Zadok the priest,
1:37 greater than the throne of my lord King D
1:38 to ride on King D's mule, and brought him
1:43 for our lord King D has made Solomon king;
1:47 congratulate our lord King D, saying, 'Your God make
2:1 When D's time to die drew near, he charged
2:10 Then D slept with his fathers, and was buried
2:10 fathers, and was buried in the city of D
2:11 And the time that D reigned over Israel was
2:12 upon the throne of D his father; and his
2:24 on the throne of D my father, and who
2:26 the Lord GOD before D my father, and because
2:32 knowledge of my father D, he attacked and slew
2:33 for ever; but to D, and to his descendants,
2:44 that you did to D my father; so the
2:45 and the throne of D shall be established before
3:1 into the city of D, until he had finished
3:3 in the statutes of D his father; only, he
3:6 love to thy servant D my father, because he
3:7 king in place of D my father, although I
3:14 commandments, as your father D walked, then I will
5:1 place of his father; for Hiram always loved D
5:3 Hiram, "You know that D my father could not
5:5 the LORD said to D my father, 'Your son,
5:7 who has given to D a wise son to
6:12 which I spoke to D your father.
7:51 in the things which D his father had dedicated,
8:1 of the city of D, which is Zion.
8:15 with his mouth to D my father, saying,
8:16 there; but I chose D to be over my
8:17 in the heart of D my father to build
8:18 the LORD said to D my father, 'Whereas it
8:20 in the place of D my father, and sit
8:24 kept with thy servant D my father what thou
8:25 keep with thy servant D my father what thou
8:26 spoken to thy servant D my father.
8:66 LORD had shown to D his servant and to
9:4 walk before me, as D your father walked, with
9:5 ever, as I promised D your father, saying, 'There
9:24 from the city of D to her own house
11:4 was the heart of D his father.
11:6 follow the LORD, as D his father had done.
11:12 for the sake of D your father I will
11:13 for the sake of D my servant and for
11:15 For when D was in Edom, and Joab the
11:21 heard in Egypt that D slept with his fathers
11:24 after the slaughter by D; and they went to
11:27 of the city of D his father.
11:32 sake of my servant D and for the sake
11:33 and my ordinances, as D his father did.
11:34 for the sake of D my servant whom I
11:36 give one tribe, that D my servant may always
11:38 and my commandments, as D my servant did, I
11:38 as I built for D, and I will give
11:39 afflict the descendants of D, but not for ever.'"
11:43 in the city of D his father; and Rehoboam
12:16 answered the king, "What portion have we in D
12:16 Look now to your own house, D
12:19 against the house of D to this day.
12:20 followed the house of D, but the tribe of
12:26 to the house of D;
13:2 to the house of D, Josiah by name; and
14:8 from the house of D and gave it to
14:8 like my servant D, who kept my commandments,
14:31 buried with his fathers in the city of D
15:3 as the heart of D his father.
15:4 Nevertheless for D's sake the LORD his God gave
15:5 and establishing Jerusalem; because D did what was
15:8 and they buried him in the city of D
15:11 of the LORD, as D his father had done.
15:24 in the city of D his father; and Jehoshaphat
22:50 in the city of D his father; and Jehoram
2Kgs 8:19 for the sake of D his servant, since he
8:24 in the city of D; and Ahaziah his son
9:28 tomb with his fathers in the city of D
12:21 in the city of D, and Amaziah his son
14:3 LORD, yet not like D his father; he did
14:20 Jerusalem with his fathers in the city of D
15:7 in the city of D, and Jotham his son

15:38 in the city of D his father; and Ahaz
16:2 God, as his father D had done,
16:20 in the city of D; and Hezekiah his son
17:21 from the house of D they made Jeroboam the
18:3 according to all that D his father had done.
19:34 sake and for the sake of my servant D
20:5 LORD, the God of D your father: I have
20:6 and for my servant D's sake."
21:7 the LORD said to D and to Solomon his
22:2 all the way of D his father, and he
1Chr 2:15 fifth, Ozem the sixth, D the seventh;
3:1 are the sons of D that were born to
3:9 All these were D's sons, besides the sons of
4:31 were their cities until D reigned.
6:31 are the men whom D put in charge of
7:2 in the days of D being twenty-two thousand six
9:22 D and Samuel the seer established them in their
10:14 the kingdom over to D the son of Jesse.
11:1 Israel gathered together to D at Hebron, and said,
11:3 king at Hebron; and D made a covenant with
11:3 LORD, and they anointed D king over Israel,
11:4 And D and all Israel went to Jerusalem, that
11:5 of Jebus said to D, "You will not come
11:5 Nevertheless D took the stronghold of Zion, that is,
11:5 stronghold of Zion, that is, the city of D
11:6 D said, "Whoever shall smite the Jebusites first shall
11:7 And D dwelt in the stronghold; therefore it was
11:7 stronghold; therefore it was called the city of D
11:9 And D became greater and greater, for the LORD
11:10 are the chiefs of D's mighty men, who gave
11:11 is an account of D's mighty men: Jashobe-am, a
11:13 He was with D at Pas-dammim when the Philistines
11:15 to the rock to D at the cave of
11:16 D was then in the stronghold; and the garrison
11:17 And D said longingly, "O that some one would
11:18 the gate, and took and brought it to D
11:18 But D would not drink of it; he poured
11:25 And D set him over his bodyguard.
12:1 men who came to D at Ziklag, while he
12:8 there went over to D at the stronghold in
12:16 Benjamin and Judah came to the stronghold to D
12:17 D went out to meet them and said to
12:18 "We are yours, O D; and with you, O
12:18 Then D received them, and made them officers of
12:19 of Manasseh deserted to D when he came with
12:21 They helped D against the band of raiders; for
12:22 men kept coming to D to help him, until
12:23 troops, who came to D in Hebron, to turn
12:31 to come and make D king.
12:33 of war, to help D with singleness of purpose.
12:38 full intent to make D king over all Israel;
12:38 single mind to make D king.
12:39 they were there with D for three days, eating
13:1 D consulted with the commanders of thousands and
13:2 And D said to all the assembly of Israel,
13:5 So D assembled all Israel from the Shihor of
13:6 And D and all Israel went up to Baalah,
13:8 And D and all Israel were making merry before
13:11 And D was angry because the LORD had broken
13:12 And D was afraid of God that day; and
13:13 So D did not take the ark home into
13:13 into the city of D, but took it aside
14:1 Tyre sent messengers to D, and cedar trees, also
14:2 And D perceived that the LORD had established him
14:3 And D took more wives in Jerusalem, and David
14:3 wives in Jerusalem, and D begot more sons and
14:8 the Philistines heard that D had been anointed king
14:8 up in search of D; and David heard of
14:8 search of David; and D heard of it and
14:10 And D inquired of God, "Shall I go up
14:11 up to Baal-perazim, and D defeated them there; and
14:11 defeated them there; and D said, "God has broken
14:12 their gods there, and D gave command, and they
14:14 And when D again inquired of God, God said
14:16 And D did as God commanded him, and they
14:17 And the fame of D went out into all
15:1 D built houses for himself in the city of
15:1 in the city of D; and he prepared a
15:2 Then D said, "No one but the Levites may
15:3 And D assembled all Israel at Jerusalem, to bring
15:4 And D gathered together the sons of Aaron and
15:11 Then D summoned the priests Zadok and Abiathar,
15:16 D also commanded the chiefs of the Levites to
15:25 So D and the elders of Israel, and the
15:27 D was clothed with a robe of fine linen,
15:27 of the singers; and D wore a linen ephod.

15:29 to the city of D, Michal the daughter of
15:29 window, and saw King D dancing and making merry;
16:1 inside the tent which D had pitched for it;
16:2 And when D had finished offering the burnt offerings
16:7 Then on that day D first appointed that thanksgiving
16:37 So D left Asaph and his brethren there before
16:43 to his house, and D went home to bless
17:1 Now when D dwelt in his house, David said
17:1 dwelt in his house, D said to Nathan the
17:2 And Nathan said to D, "Do all that is
17:4 and tell my servant D, 'Thus says the LORD:
17:7 say to my servant D, 'Thus says the LORD
17:15 accordance with all this vision, Nathan spoke to D
17:16 Then King D went in and sat before the
17:18 And what more can D say to thee for
17:24 house of thy servant D will be established before
18:1 After this D defeated the Philistines and subdued
18:2 Moabites became servants to D and brought tribute.
18:3 D also defeated Hadadezer king of Zobah, toward
18:4 And D took from him a thousand chariots, seven
18:4 thousand foot soldiers; and D hamstrung all the
18:5 king of Zobah, D slew twenty-two thousand men
18:6 Then D put garrisons in Syria of Damascus; and
18:6 Syrians became servants to D, and brought tribute.
18:6 LORD gave victory to D wherever he went.
18:7 And D took the shields of gold which were
18:8 Cun, cities of Hadadezer, D took very much bronze;
18:9 of Hamath heard that D had defeated the whole
18:10 son Hadoram to King D, to greet him, and
18:11 bronze; these also King D dedicated to the LORD,
18:13 all the Edomites became D's servants.
18:13 LORD gave victory to D wherever he went.
18:14 So D reigned over all Israel; and he administered
18:17 and the Pelethites; and D's sons were the chief
19:2 And D said, "I will deal loyally with Hanun
19:2 So D sent messengers to console him concerning his
19:2 And D's servants came to Hanun in the land
19:3 "Do you think, because D has sent comforters to
19:4 So Hanun took D's servants, and shaved them, and
19:5 When D was told concerning the men, he sent
19:6 themselves odious to D, Hanun and the Ammonites
19:8 When D heard of it, he sent Joab and
19:17 when it was told D, he gathered all Israel
19:17 And when D set the battle in array against
19:18 fled before Israel; and D slew of the Syrians
19:19 they made peace with D, and became subject to
20:1 But D remained at Jerusalem.
20:2 And D took the crown of their king from
20:2 it was placed on D's head.
20:3 and axes; and thus D did to all the
20:3 Then D and all the people returned to Jerusalem.
20:7 the son of Shimea, D's brother, slew him.
20:8 by the hand of D and by the hand
21:1 against Israel, and incited D to number Israel.
21:2 So D said to Joab and the commanders of
21:5 sum of the numbering of the people to D
21:8 And D said to God, "I have sinned greatly
21:9 LORD spoke to Gad, D's seer, saying,
21:10 "Go and say to D, 'Thus says the LORD,
21:11 So Gad came to D and said to him,
21:13 Then D said to Gad, "I am in great
21:16 And D lifted his eyes and saw the angel
21:16 Then D and the elders, clothed in sackcloth, fell
21:17 And D said to God, "Was it not I
21:18 Gad to say to D that David should go
21:18 say to David that D should go up and
21:19 So D went up at Gad's word, which he
21:21 As D came to Ornan, Ornan looked and saw
21:21 Ornan looked and saw D and went forth from
21:21 and did obeisance to D with his face to
21:22 And D said to Ornan, "Give me the site
21:23 Then Ornan said to D, "Take it; and let
21:24 But King D said to Ornan, "No, but I
21:25 So D paid Ornan six hundred shekels of gold
21:26 And D built there an altar to the LORD
21:28 At that time, when D saw that the LORD
21:30 place at Gibeon; but D could not go before
22:1 Then D said, "Here shall be the house of
22:2 D commanded to gather together the aliens who
22:3 D also provided great stores of iron for nails
22:4 and Tyrians brought great quantities of cedar to D
22:5 For D said, "Solomon my son is young and
22:5 So D provided materials in great quantity before his
22:7 D said to Solomon, "My son, I had it
22:17 D also commanded all the leaders of Israel to
23:1 When D was old and full of days, he

23:2 D assembled all the leaders of Israel and the
23:4 D said, "shall have charge of the work in
23:6 And D organized them in divisions corresponding to
23:25 For D said, "The LORD, the God of Israel,
23:27 the last words of D these were the number
24:3 the sons of Ithamar, D organized them according to
24:31 the presence of King D, Zadok, Ahimelech, and the
25:1 D and the chiefs of the service also set
26:26 the dedicated gifts which D the king, and the
26:31 the fortieth year of D's reign search was made
26:32 Jazer in Gilead.) King D appointed him and his
27:18 Judah, Elihu, one of D's brothers; for Issachar, Omri
27:23 D did not number those below twenty years of
27:24 was not entered in the chronicles of King D
27:31 were stewards of King D's property.
27:32 Jonathan, D's uncle, was a counselor, being a man
28:1 D assembled at Jerusalem all the officials of Israel,
28:2 Then King D rose to his feet and said:
28:11 Then D gave Solomon his son the plan of
28:20 Then D said to Solomon his son, "Be strong
29:1 And D the king said to all the assembly,
29:9 freely to the LORD; D the king also rejoiced
29:10 Therefore D blessed the LORD in the presence of
29:10 all the assembly; and D said: "Blessed art thou,
29:20 Then D said to all the assembly, "Bless the
29:22 Solomon the son of D king the second time,
29:23 as king instead of D his father; and he
29:24 the sons of King D, pledged their allegiance to
29:26 Thus D the son of Jesse reigned over all
29:29 the acts of King D, from first to last,
2Chr 1:1 Solomon the son of D established himself in his
1:4 (But D had brought up the ark of God
1:4 to the place that D had prepared for it,
1:8 and steadfast love to D my father, and hast
1:9 let thy promise to D my father be now
2:3 "As you dealt with D my father and sent
2:7 Judah and Jerusalem, whom D my father provided.
2:12 who has given King D a wise son, endued
2:14 craftsmen of my lord, D your father.
2:17 census of them which D his father had taken;
3:1 LORD had appeared to D his father, at the
3:1 at the place that D had appointed, on the
5:1 in the things which D his father had dedicated,
5:2 of the city of D, which is Zion.
6:4 with his mouth to D my father, saying,
6:6 and I have chosen D to be over my
6:7 in the heart of D my father to build
6:8 the LORD said to D my father, 'Whereas it
6:10 in the place of D my father, and sit
6:15 kept with thy servant D my father what thou
6:16 keep with thy servant D my father what thou
6:17 confirmed, which thou hast spoken to thy servant D
6:42 thy steadfast love for D thy servant."
7:6 the LORD which King D had made for giving
7:6 endures for ever--whenever D offered praises by
7:10 LORD had shown to D and to Solomon and
7:17 walk before me, as D your father walked, doing
7:18 as I covenanted with D your father, saying, 'There
8:11 from the city of D to the house which
8:11 in the house of D king of Israel, for
8:14 to the ordinance of D his father, he appointed
8:14 several gates; for so D the man of God
9:31 in the city of D his father; and Rehoboam
10:16 answered the king, "What portion have we in D
10:16 Look now to your own house, D
10:19 against the house of D to this day.
11:17 in the way of D and Solomon.
11:18 Jerimoth the son of D, and of Abihail the
12:16 in the city of D; and Abijah his son
13:5 Israel for ever to D and his sons by
13:6 Solomon the son of D, rose up and rebelled
13:8 of the sons of D, because you are a
14:1 in the city of D; and Asa his son
16:14 hewn out for himself in the city of D
21:1 in the city of D; and Jehoram his son
21:7 destroy the house of D, because of the covenant
21:7 he had made with D, and since he had
21:12 LORD, the God of D your father, 'Because you
21:20 in the city of D, but not in the
23:3 as the LORD spoke concerning the sons of D
23:18 and the Levites whom D had organized to be
23:18 and with singing, according to the order of D
24:16 in the city of D among the kings, because
24:25 in the city of D, but they did not
25:28 buried with his fathers in the city of D
27:9 in the city of D; and Ahaz his son
28:1 LORD, like his father D,
29:2 according to all that D his father had done.
29:25 to the commandment of D and of Gad the
29:26 with the instruments of D, and the priests with
29:27 by the instruments of D king of Israel.
29:30 with the words of D and of Asaph the
30:26 Solomon the son of D king of Israel there
32:5 he strengthened the Millo in the city of D
32:30 to the west side of the city of D
32:33 of the sons of D; and all Judah and
33:7 which God said to D and to Solomon his
33:14 for the city of D west of Gihon, in
34:2 in the ways of D his father; and he
34:3 seek the God of D his father; and in
35:3 Solomon the son of D, king of Israel, built;
35:4 following the directions of D king of Israel and
35:15 to the command of D, and Asaph, and Heman,
Ezra 3:10 to the directions of D king of Israel;
8:2 Of the sons of D, Hattush,
8:20 the temple servants, whom D and his officials had
Neh 3:15 stairs that go down from the City of D
3:16 opposite the sepulchres of D, to the artificial pool,
12:24 to the commandment of D the man of God,
12:36 the musical instruments of D the man of God;
12:37 of the city of D, at the ascent of
12:37 above the house of D, to the Water Gate
12:45 to the command of D and his son Solomon.
12:46 in the days of D and Asaph of old
Ps 18:50 to his anointed, to D and his descendants for
72:20 The prayers of D, the son of Jesse, are
78:70 He chose D his servant, and took him from
89:3 I have sworn to D my servant:
89:20 I have found D, my servant; with my holy
89:35 by my holiness; I will not lie to D
89:49 which by thy faithfulness thou didst swear to D
122:5 were set, the thrones of the house of D
132:1 Remember, O LORD, in D's favor, all the hardships
132:10 For thy servant D's sake do not turn away
132:11 The LORD swore to D a sure oath from
132:17 horn to sprout for D; I have prepared a
144:10 to kings, who rescuest D thy servant.
Prov 1:1 of Solomon, son of D, king of Israel:
Eccl 1:1 Preacher, the son of D, king in Jerusalem.
Song 4:4 like the tower of D, built for an arsenal,
Sir 45:25 was also established with D, the son of Jesse,
47:1 rose up to prophesy in the days of D
47:2 the peace offering, so D was selected from the
47:22 to Jacob, and to D a root of his
48:15 number, but with rulers from the house of D
48:22 to the ways of D his father, which Isaiah
49:4 Except D and Hezekiah and Josiah they all sinned
Is 7:2 When the house of D was told, "Syria is
7:13 And he said, "Hear then, O house of D
9:7 upon the throne of D, and over his kingdom,
16:5 in the tent of D one who judges and
22:9 of the city of D were many, and you
22:22 of the house of D; he shall open, and
29:1 Ariel, the city where D encamped!
37:35 sake and for the sake of my servant D
38:5 LORD, the God of D your father: I have
55:3 an everlasting covenant, my steadfast, sure love for D
Jer 13:13 kings who sit on D's throne, the priests, the
17:25 on the throne of D, riding in chariots and
21:12 the word of the LORD, O house of D
22:2 on the throne of D, you, and your servants,
22:4 on the throne of D, riding in chariots and
22:30 on the throne of D, and ruling again in
23:5 will raise up for D a righteous Branch, and
29:16 on the throne of D, and concerning all the
30:9 LORD their God and D their king, whom I
33:15 to spring forth for D; and he shall execute
33:17 thus says the LORD: D shall never lack a
33:21 also my covenant with D my servant may be
33:22 multiply the descendants of D my servant, and the
33:26 descendants of Jacob and D my servant and will
36:30 upon the throne of D, and his dead body
Ezek 34:23 one shepherd, my servant D, and he shall feed
34:24 God, and my servant D shall be prince among
37:24 "My servant D shall be king over them; and
37:25 there for ever; and D my servant shall be
Hos 3:5 LORD their God, and D their king; and they
Amos 6:5 harp, and like D invent for themselves instruments
9:11 up the booth of D that is fallen and
Zech 12:7 of the house of D and the glory of
12:8 day shall be like D, and the house of
12:8 and the house of D shall be like God,

D

12:10 on the house of D and the inhabitants of
12:12 of the house of D by itself, and their
13:1 for the house of D and the inhabitants of
1Mac 1:33 fortified the city of D with a great strong
2:31 Jerusalem the city of D, that men who had
2:57 D, because he was merciful, inherited the throne of
4:30 hand of thy servant D, and didst give the
7:32 and the rest fled into the city of D
14:36 in the city of D in Jerusalem, who had
2Mac 2:13 and the writings of D, and letters of kings
Mt 1:1 Christ, the son of D, the son of Abraham.
1:6 Jesse the father of D the king.
1:6 And D was the father of Solomon by the
1:17 from Abraham to D were fourteen generations, and
1:17 fourteen generations, and from D to the deportation
1:20 saying, "Joseph, son of D, do not fear to
9:27 crying aloud, "Have mercy on us, Son of D
12:3 you not read what D did, when he was
12:23 and said, "Can this be the Son of D
15:22 O Lord, Son of D; my daughter is severely
20:30 cried out, "Have mercy on us, Son of D
20:31 more, "Lord, have mercy on us, Son of D
21:9 followed him shouted, "Hosanna to the Son of D
21:15 in the temple, "Hosanna to the Son of D
22:42 They said to him, "The son of D
22:43 is it then that D, inspired by the Spirit,
22:45 If D thus calls him Lord, how is he
Mk 2:25 you never read what D did, when he was
10:47 say, "Jesus, Son of D, have mercy on me!"
10:48 the more, "Son of D, have mercy on me!"
11:10 kingdom of our father D that is coming!
12:35 say that the Christ is the son of D
12:36 D himself, inspired by the Holy Spirit, declared, 'The
12:37 enemies under thy feet.' D himself calls him Lord;
Lk 1:27 of the house of D; and the virgin's name
1:32 throne of his father D,
1:69 house of his servant D,
2:4 to the city of D, which is called Bethlehem,
2:4 house and lineage of D,
2:11 in the city of D a Savior, who is
3:31 Nathan, the son of D,
6:3 you not read what D did when he was
18:38 cried, "Jesus, Son of D, have mercy on me!"
18:39 the more, "Son of D, have mercy on me!"
20:41 that the Christ is D's son?
20:42 For D himself says in the Book of Psalms,
20:44 stool for thy feet.' D thus calls him Lord;
Jn 7:42 Christ is descended from D, and comes from
7:42 Bethlehem, the village where D was?"
Acts 1:16 by the mouth of D, concerning Judas who was
2:25 For D says concerning him, 'I saw the Lord
2:29 confidently of the patriarch D that he both died
2:34 For D did not ascend into the heavens; but
4:25 mouth of our father D, thy servant, didst say
7:45 until the days of D,
13:22 him, he raised up D to be their king;
13:22 'I have found in D the son of Jesse
13:34 and sure blessings of D
13:36 One see corruption.' For D, after he had served
15:16 rebuild the dwelling of D, which has fallen; I
Rom 1:3 who was descended from D according to the flesh
4:6 So also D pronounces a blessing upon the man
11:9 And D says, "Let their table become a snare
2Tim 2:8 the dead, descended from D, as preached in my
Heb 4:7 saying through D so long afterward, in the words
11:32 Barak, Samson, Jephthah, of D and Samuel and the
Rev 3:7 has the key of D, who opens and no
5:5 Judah, the Root of D, has conquered, so that
22:16 and the offspring of D, the bright morning star."

DAVIDS (2)
2Kgs 11:10 that had been King D, which were in the
2Chr 23:9 that had been King D, which were in the

DAWN (29)
Josh 6:15 rose early at the D of day, and marched
Judg 19:25 And as the D began to break, they let
1Sam 9:26 at the break of D Samuel called to Saul
Neh 4:21 from the break of D till the stars came
Jud 14:11 soon as it was D they hung the head
Job 3:9 the stars of its D be dark; let it
7:4 and I am full of tossing till the D
38:12 began, and caused the D to know its place,
41:18 his eyes are like the eyelids of the D
Ps 57:8 I will awake the D
108:2 I will awake the D
119:147 I rise before D and cry for help; I
Prov 4:19 like the light of D, which shines brighter and
Eccl 11:10 for youth and the D of life are vanity.
Song 6:10 looks forth like the D, fair as the moon,
Sir 24:30 shine forth like the D, and I will make
Is 8:20 this word which they speak there is no D
14:12 fallen from heaven, O Day Star, son of D
58:8 break forth like the D, and your healing shall
Hos 6:3 is sure as the D; he will come to
Jon 4:7 But when D came up the next day, God
Zeph 3:5 forth his justice, each D he does not fail;
1Mac 5:30 At D they looked up, and behold, a large
2Mac 10:28 Just as D was breaking, the two armies joined
10:35 But at D of the fifth day, twenty young
Mt 28:1 the sabbath, toward the D of the first day
Lk 1:78 when the day shall D upon us from on
24:1 the week, at early D, they went to the
Acts 27:33 day was about to D, Paul urged them all

DAWNED (3)
Gen 19:15 When morning D, the angels urged Lot, saying,
Deut 33:2 came from Sinai, and D from Seir upon us;
Mt 4:16 the region and shadow of death light has D

DAWNING (2)
Wis 16:28 to thee at the D of the light;
2Mac 13:17 just as day was D, because the Lord's help

DAWNS (4)
2Sam 23:4 fear of God, he D on them like the
Ps 97:11 Light D for the righteous, and joy for the
Mic 2:1 When the morning D, they perform it, because it
2Pet 1:19 place, until the day D and the morning star

DAY (1,806)
Gen 1:5 God called the light D, and the darkness he
1:5 there was evening and there was morning, one D
1:8 was evening and there was morning, a second D
1:13 was evening and there was morning, a third D
1:14 heavens to separate the D from the night; and
1:16 light to rule the D, and the lesser light
1:18 to rule over the D and over the night,
1:19 was evening and there was morning, a fourth D
1:23 was evening and there was morning, a fifth D
1:31 was evening and there was morning, a sixth D
2:2 And on the seventh D God finished his work
2:2 rested on the seventh D from all his work
2:3 God blessed the seventh D and hallowed it, because
2:4 In the D that the LORD God made the
2:17 eat, for in the D that you eat of
3:8 the cool of the D, and the man and
4:14 hast driven me this D away from the ground;
7:11 month, on the seventeenth D of the month, on
7:11 the month, on that D all the fountains of
7:13 On the very same D Noah and his sons,
8:4 month, on the seventeenth D of the month, the
8:5 month, on the first D of the month, the
8:13 first month, the first D of the month, the
8:14 month, on the twenty-seventh D of the month, the
8:22 heat, summer and winter, D and night, shall not
15:18 On that D the LORD made a covenant with
17:23 their foreskins that very D, as God had said
17:26 That very D Abraham and his son Ishmael were
18:1 of his tent in the heat of the D
19:34 And on the next D, the first-born said to
19:37 is the father of the Moabites to this D
19:38 is the father of the Ammonites to this D
21:8 great feast on the D that Isaac was weaned.
22:4 On the third D Abraham lifted up his eyes
22:14 is said to this D, "On the mount of
26:32 That same D Isaac's servants came and told him
26:33 name of the city is Beer-sheba to this D
27:2 do not know the D of my death.
27:45 I be bereft of you both in one D
29:7 it is still high D, it is not time
30:35 But that D Laban removed the he-goats that were
31:22 Laban on the third D that Jacob had fled,
31:39 it, whether stolen by D or stolen by night.
31:40 Thus I was; by D the heat consumed me,
31:43 can I do this D to these my daughters,
32:24 wrestled with him until the breaking of the D
32:26 me go, for the D is breaking." But Jacob
32:32 Therefore to this D the Israelites do not eat
33:13 are overdriven for one D, all the flocks will
33:16 So Esau returned that D on his way to
34:25 On the third D, when they were sore, two

35:3 answered me in the D of my distress and
35:20 of Rachel's tomb, which is there to this D
39:10 she spoke to Joseph D after day, he would
39:10 to Joseph day after D, he would not listen
39:11 But one D, when he went into the house
40:20 On the third D, which was Pharaoh's birthday, he
42:13 the youngest is this D with our father, and
42:18 On the third D Joseph said to them, "Do
42:32 the youngest is this D with our father in
47:23 "Behold, I have this D bought you and your
47:26 it stands to this D, that Pharaoh should have
48:15 life long to this D,
48:20 he blessed them that D, saying, "By you Israel
Ex 2:11 One D, when Moses had grown up, he went
2:13 went out the next D, behold, two Hebrews were
5:6 The same D Pharaoh commanded the taskmasters
6:28 On the D when the LORD spoke to Moses
8:22 But on that D I will set apart the
9:18 in Egypt from the D it was founded until
10:6 have seen, from the D they came on earth
10:6 the day they came on earth to this D
10:13 the land all that D and all that night;
10:28 again; for in the D you see my face
12:3 that on the tenth D of this month they
12:6 it until the fourteenth D of this month, when
12:14 "This D shall be for you a memorial day,
12:14 for you a memorial D, and you shall keep
12:15 bread; on the first D you shall put away
12:15 leavened, from the first D until the seventh day,
12:15 day until the seventh D, that person shall be
12:16 On the first D you shall hold a holy
12:16 and on the seventh D a holy assembly; no
12:17 for on this very D I brought your hosts
12:17 shall observe this D, throughout your generations, as
12:18 month, on the fourteenth D of the month at
12:18 so until the twenty-first D of the month at
12:41 years, on that very D, all the hosts of
12:51 And on that very D the LORD brought the
13:3 the people, "Remember this D, in which you came
13:4 This D you are to go forth, in the
13:6 and on the seventh D there shall be a
13:8 your son on that D, 'It is because of
13:21 went before them by D in a pillar of
13:21 they might travel by D and by night;
13:22 pillar of cloud by D and the pillar of
14:30 LORD saved Israel that D from the hand of
16:1 Sinai, on the fifteenth D of the second month
16:4 out and gather a D's portion every day, that
16:4 a day's portion every D, that I may prove
16:5 On the sixth D, when they prepare what they
16:22 On the sixth D they gathered twice as much
16:23 commanded: 'Tomorrow is a D of solemn rest, a
16:26 but on the seventh D, which is a sabbath,
16:27 On the seventh D some of the people went
16:29 therefore on the sixth D he gives you bread
16:29 go out of his place on the seventh D
16:30 So the people rested on the seventh D
19:1 of Egypt, on that D they came into the
19:11 ready by the third D; for on the third
19:11 for on the third D the LORD will come
19:15 ready by the third D; do not go near
19:16 morning of the third D there were thunders and
20:8 "Remember the sabbath D, to keep it holy.
20:10 work; but the seventh D is a sabbath to
20:11 rested the seventh D; therefore the LORD blessed
20:11 LORD blessed the sabbath D and hallowed it.
21:21 the slave survives a D or two, he is
22:30 dam; on the eighth D you shall give it
23:12 but on the seventh D you shall rest; that
24:16 and on the seventh D he called to Moses
29:36 ordain them, and every D you shall offer a
29:38 lambs a year old D by day continually.
29:38 year old day by D continually.
31:15 done, but the seventh D is a sabbath of
31:15 work on the sabbath D shall be put to
31:17 and on the seventh D he rested, and was
32:28 of the people that D about three thousand men.
32:29 he may bestow a blessing upon you this D
32:34 Nevertheless, in the D when I visit, I will
34:11 "Observe what I command you this D
34:21 but on the seventh D you shall rest; in
35:2 but on the seventh D you shall have a
35:3 fire in all your habitations on the sabbath D
Lev 6:5 it belongs, on the D of his guilt offering.
6:20 the LORD on the D when he is anointed:
7:15 be eaten on the D of his offering; he
7:16 be eaten on the D that he offers his
7:17 sacrifice on the third D shall be burned with
7:18 eaten on the third D, he who offers it
7:35 to them on the D they were presented to
7:36 of Israel, on the D that they were anointed;
7:38 Mount Sinai, on the D that he commanded the
8:35 meeting you shall remain D and night for seven
9:1 On the eighth D Moses called Aaron and his
12:3 And on the eighth D the flesh of his
13:5 him on the seventh D, and if in his
13:6 again on the seventh D, and if the diseased
13:27 examine him the seventh D; if it is spreading
13:32 and on the seventh D the priest shall examine
13:34 and on the seventh D the priest shall examine
13:51 he shall examine the disease on the seventh D
14:2 the leper for the D of his cleansing.
14:9 And on the seventh D he shall shave all
14:10 "And on the eighth D he shall take two
14:23 And on the eighth D he shall bring them
14:39 again on the seventh D, and look; and if
15:14 And on the eighth D he shall take two
15:29 And on the eighth D she shall take two
16:29 month, on the tenth D of the month, you
16:30 you; for on this D shall atonement be made
19:6 be eaten the same D you offer it, or
19:6 over until the third D shall be burned with
19:7 all on the third D, it is an abomination;
22:27 and from the eighth D on it shall be
22:28 kill both her and her young in one D
22:30 eaten on the same D, you shall leave none
23:3 but on the seventh D is a sabbath of
23:5 month, on the fourteenth D of the month in
23:6 And on the fifteenth D of the same month
23:7 On the first D you shall have a holy
23:8 days; on the seventh D is a holy convocation;
23:12 And on the D when you wave the sheaf,
23:14 fresh until this same D, until you have brought
23:15 the sabbath, from the D that you brought the
23:21 proclamation on the same D; you shall hold a
23:24 month, on the first D of the month, you
23:24 you shall observe a D of solemn rest, a
23:27 Moses, "On the tenth D of this seventh month
23:27 seventh month is the D of atonement; it shall
23:28 work on this same D; for it is a
23:28 for it is a D of atonement, to make
23:29 afflicted on this same D shall be cut off
23:30 work on this same D, that person I will
23:32 yourselves; on the ninth D of the month beginning
23:34 Israel, On the fifteenth D of this seventh month
23:35 On the first D shall be a holy convocation;
23:36 LORD; on the eighth D you shall hold a
23:37 each on its proper D;
23:39 "On the fifteenth D of the seventh month, when
23:39 days; on the first D shall be a solemn
23:39 and on the eighth D shall be a solemn
23:40 take on the first D the fruit of goodly
24:8 Every sabbath D Aaron shall set it in order
25:9 trumpet on the tenth D of the seventh month;
25:9 seventh month; on the D of atonement you shall
27:23 the valuation on that D as a holy thing
Num 1:1 meeting, on the first D of the second month,
1:18 and on the first D of the second month,
3:13 are mine; on the D that I slew all
6:9 his head on the D of his cleansing; on
6:9 cleansing; on the seventh D he shall shave it.
6:10 On the eighth D he shall bring two turtledoves
6:11 his head that same D,
7:1 On the D when Moses had finished setting up
7:10 the altar on the D it was anointed; and
7:11 offerings, one leader each D, for the dedication of
7:12 his offering the first D was Nahshon the son
7:18 On the second D Nethanel the son of Zuar,
7:24 On the third D Eliab the son of Helon,
7:30 On the fourth D Elizur the son of Shedeur,
7:36 On the fifth D Shelumi-el the son of Zurishaddai,
7:42 On the sixth D Eliasaph the son of Deuel,
7:48 On the seventh D Elishama the son of Ammihud,
7:54 On the eighth D Gamaliel the son of Pedahzur,
7:60 On the ninth D Abidan the son of Gideoni,
7:66 On the tenth D Ahiezer the son of Ammishaddai,
7:72 On the eleventh D Pagiel the son of Ochran,
7:78 On the twelfth D Ahira the son of Enan,
7:84 the altar, on the D when it was anointed,
8:17 of beast; on the D that I slew all
9:3 On the fourteenth D of this month, in the
9:5 month, on the fourteenth D of the month, in

9:6 the passover on that D; and they came before
9:6 and Aaron on that D;
9:11 month on the fourteenth D in the evening they
9:15 On the D that the tabernacle was set up,
9:16 cloud covered it by D, and the appearance of
9:21 it continued for a D and a night, when
10:10 On the D of your gladness also, and at
10:11 month, on the twentieth D of the month, the
10:34 was over them by D, whenever they set out
11:19 shall not eat one D, or two days, or
11:31 the camp, about a D's journey on this side
11:31 this side and a D's journey on the other
11:32 people rose all that D, and all night, and
11:32 and all the next D, and gathered the quails;
14:14 pillar of cloud by D and in a pillar
14:34 forty days, for every D a year, you shall
15:23 by Moses, from the D that the LORD gave
15:32 found a man gathering sticks on the sabbath D
19:12 water on the third D and on the seventh
19:12 and on the seventh D, and so be clean;
19:12 himself on the third D and on the seventh
19:12 and on the seventh D, he will not become
19:19 unclean on the third D and on the seventh
19:19 and on the seventh D; thus on the seventh
19:19 thus on the seventh D he shall cleanse him,
22:30 have ridden all your life long to this D
25:18 was slain on the D of the plague on
28:3 year old without blemish, D by day, as a
28:3 without blemish, day by D, as a continual offering.
28:9 "On the sabbath D two male lambs a year
28:16 "On the fourteenth D of the first month is
28:17 And on the fifteenth D of this month is
28:18 On the first D there shall be a holy
28:25 And on the seventh D you shall have a
28:26 "On the D of the first fruits, when you
29:1 "On the first D of the seventh month you
29:1 It is a D for you to blow the
29:7 "On the tenth D of this seventh month you
29:12 "On the fifteenth D of the seventh month you
29:17 "On the second D twelve young bulls, two rams,
29:20 "On the third D eleven bulls, two rams, fourteen
29:23 "On the fourth D ten bulls, two rams, fourteen
29:26 "On the fifth D nine bulls, two rams, fourteen
29:29 "On the sixth D eight bulls, two rams, fourteen
29:32 "On the seventh D seven bulls, two rams, fourteen
29:35 "On the eighth D you shall have a solemn
30:5 to her on the D that he hears of
30:7 to her on the D that he hears; then
30:8 But if, on the D that her husband comes
30:12 and void on the D that he hears them,
30:14 nothing to her from D to day, then he
30:14 her from day to D, then he establishes all
30:14 to her on the D that he heard of
31:19 captives on the third D and on the seventh
31:19 on the third day and on the seventh D
31:24 clothes on the seventh D, and you shall be
32:10 was kindled on that D, and he swore, saying,
33:3 month, on the fifteenth D of the first month;
33:3 first month; on the D after the passover the
33:38 Egypt, on the first D of the fifth month.
Deut 1:3 year, on the first D of the eleventh month,
1:10 behold, you are this D as the stars of
1:33 you should go, and in the cloud by D
1:39 your children, who this D have no knowledge of
2:18 said to me, 'This D you are to pass
2:22 and settled in their stead even to this D
2:25 This D I will begin to put the dread
2:30 give him into your hand, as at this D
3:14 it is to this D
4:4 the LORD your God are all alive this D
4:8 this law which I set before you this D
4:10 how on the D that you stood before
4:15 no form on the D that the LORD spoke
4:20 people of his own possession, as at this D
4:26 witness against you this D, that you will soon
4:32 before you, since the D that God created man
4:38 inheritance, as at this D;
4:39 day; know therefore this D, and lay it to
4:40 I command you this D, that it may go
5:1 in your hearing this D, and you shall learn
5:3 who are all of us here alive this D
5:12 "'Observe the sabbath D, to keep it holy, as
5:14 work; but the seventh D is a sabbath to
5:15 your God commanded you to keep the sabbath D
5:24 fire; we have this D seen God speak with
6:6 I command you this D shall be upon your
6:24 he might preserve us alive, as at this D
7:11 and the ordinances, which I command you this D
8:1 I command you this D you shall be careful
8:11 I command you this D:
8:18 he swore to your fathers, as at this D
8:19 solemnly warn you this D that you shall surely
9:1 over the Jordan this D, to go in to
9:3 Anak?' Know therefore this D that he who goes
9:7 the wilderness; from the D you came out of
9:10 the fire on the D of the assembly.
9:24 the LORD from the D that I knew you.
10:4 the fire on the D of the assembly; and
10:8 and to bless in his name, to this D
10:13 I command you this D for your good?
10:15 them, you above all peoples, as at this D
11:2 And consider this D (since I am not speaking
11:4 destroyed them to this D;
11:8 I command you this D, that you may be
11:13 I command you this D, to love the LORD
11:26 set before you this D a blessing and a
11:27 I command you this D,
11:28 I command you this D, to go after other
11:32 the ordinances which I set before you this D
12:8 are doing here this D, every man doing whatever
13:18 I command you this D, and doing what is
15:5 all this commandment which I command you this D
16:3 you may remember the D when you came out
16:4 evening of the first D remain all night until
16:8 and on the seventh D there shall be a
18:16 at Horeb on the D of the assembly, when
19:9 I command you this D, by loving the LORD
20:3 you draw near this D to battle against your
21:16 disliked, then on the D when he assigns his
21:23 bury him the same D, for a hanged man
24:15 his hire on the D he earns it, before
26:3 him, 'I declare this D to the LORD your
26:16 milk and honey.' "This D the LORD your God
26:17 You have declared this D concerning the LORD that
26:18 LORD has declared this D concerning you that you
27:1 all the commandment which I command you this D
27:2 And on the D you pass over the Jordan
27:4 I command you this D, on Mount Ebal, and
27:9 hear, O Israel: this D you have become the
27:10 and his statutes, which I command you this D
27:11 the people the same D, saying,
28:1 I command you this D, the LORD your God
28:13 I command you this D, being careful to do
28:14 I command you this D, to the right hand
28:15 I command you this D, then all these curses
28:32 for them all the D; and it shall not
28:66 before you; night and D you shall be in
29:4 wonders; but to this D the LORD has not
29:10 "You stand this D all of you before the
29:12 makes with you this D;
29:13 may establish you this D as his people, and
29:15 here with us this D as well as with
29:15 here with us this D before the LORD our
29:18 heart turns away this D from the LORD our
29:28 land, as at this D
30:2 I command you this D, with all your heart
30:8 all his commandments which I command you this D
30:11 I command you this D is not too hard
30:15 set before you this D life and good, death
30:16 I command you this D, by loving the LORD
30:18 declare to you this D, that you shall perish;
30:19 witness against you this D, that I have set
31:2 twenty years old this D; I am no longer
31:17 against them in that D, and I will forsake
31:17 will say in that D, 'Have not these evils
31:18 my face in that D on account of all
31:22 this song the same D, and taught it to
32:35 shall slip; for the D of their calamity is
32:46 enjoin upon you this D, that you may command
32:48 to Moses that very D,
33:12 encompasses him all the D long, and makes his
34:6 knows the place of his burial to this D
Josh 1:8 shall meditate on it D and night, that you
3:7 said to Joshua, "This D I will begin to
4:9 had stood; and they are there to this D
4:14 On that D the LORD exalted Joshua in the
4:19 Jordan on the tenth D of the first month,
5:9 said to Joshua, "This D I have rolled away
5:9 of that place is called Gilgal to this D
5:10 passover on the fourteenth D of the month at
5:11 passover, on that very D, they ate of the
6:4 and on the seventh D you shall march around

6:10 your mouth, until the D I bid you shout;
6:14 And the second D they marched around the city
6:15 On the seventh D they rose early at the
6:15 at the dawn of D, and marched around the
6:15 was only on that D that they marched around
6:25 in Israel to this D, because she hid the
7:26 that remains to this D; then the LORD turned
7:26 Therefore to this D the name of that place
8:25 all who fell that D, both men and women,
8:28 heap of ruins, as it is to this D
8:29 heap of stones, which stands there to this D
9:12 the journey, on the D we set forth to
9:17 out and reached their cities on the third D
9:27 Joshua made them that D hewers of wood and
9:27 to continue to this D, in the place which
10:12 the LORD in the D when the LORD gave
10:13 hasten to go down for about a whole D
10:14 There has been no D like it before or
10:27 of the cave, which remain to this very D
10:28 took Makkedah on that D, and smote it and
10:32 it on the second D, and smote it with
10:35 took it on that D, and smote it with
10:35 he utterly destroyed that D, as he had done
13:13 dwell in the midst of Israel to this D
14:9 Moses swore on that D, saying, 'Surely the land
14:10 lo, I am this D eighty-five years old.
14:11 as strong to this D as I was in
14:11 I was in the D that Moses sent me;
14:12 LORD spoke on that D; for you heard on
14:12 you heard on that D how the Anakim were
14:14 the Kenizzite to this D, because he wholly followed
15:63 the people of Judah at Jerusalem to this D
16:10 of Ephraim to this D but have become slaves
22:3 days, down to this D, but have been careful
22:16 in turning away this D from following the LORD,
22:16 yourselves an altar this D in rebellion against the
22:18 must turn away this D from following the LORD?
22:29 and turn away this D from following the LORD
23:8 your God as you have done to this D
23:9 has been able to withstand you to this D
24:15 the LORD, choose this D whom you will serve,
24:25 with the people that D, and made statutes and
Judg 1:21 the people of Benjamin in Jerusalem to this D
1:26 name Luz; that is its name to this D
3:30 Moab was subdued that D under the hand of
4:14 For this is the D in which the LORD
4:23 So on that D God subdued Jabin the king
5:1 of Abino-am on that D:
6:24 To this D it still stands at Ophrah, which
6:27 to do it by D, he did it by
6:32 Therefore on that D he was called Jerubbaal, that
9:18 my father's house this D, and have slain his
9:19 with his house this D, then rejoice in Abimelech,
9:42 On the following D the men went out into
9:45 the city all that D; he took the city,
10:4 called Havvoth-jair to this D, which are in the
10:15 thee; only deliver us, we pray thee, this D
11:27 the Judge, decide this D between the people of
12:3 up to me this D, to fight against me?"
13:7 from birth to the D of his death.'"
13:10 to me the other D has appeared to me."
14:15 On the fourth D they said to Samson's wife,
14:17 and on the seventh D he told her, because
14:18 him on the seventh D before the sun went
15:19 called En-hakkore; it is at Lehi to this D
16:16 hard with her words D after day, and urged
16:16 her words day after D, and urged him, his
18:12 called Mahaneh-dan to this D; behold, it is west
18:30 the Danites until the D of the captivity of
19:5 And on the fourth D they arose early in
19:8 And on the fifth D he arose early in
19:8 and tarry until the D declines." So they ate,
19:9 him, "Behold, now the D has waned toward evening;
19:9 Behold, the D draws to its close; lodge here
19:11 were near Jebus, the D was far spent, and
19:30 been seen from the D that the people of
19:30 of Egypt until this D; consider it, take counsel,
20:15 their cities on that D twenty-six thousand men that
20:21 the ground on that D twenty-two thousand men of
20:22 where they had formed it on the first D
20:24 came near against the Benjaminites the second D
20:25 of Gibe-ah the second D, and felled to the
20:26 LORD, and fasted that D until evening, and offered
20:30 Benjaminites on the third D, and set themselves in
20:35 men of Benjamin that D; all these were men
20:46 all who fell that D of Benjamin were twenty-five
21:6 "One tribe is cut off from Israel this D
Ruth 4:5 Then Boaz said, "The D you buy the field
4:9 "You are witnesses this D that I have bought
4:10 of his native place; you are witnesses this D
4:14 not left you this D without next of kin;
1Sam 1:4 On the D when Elkanah sacrificed, he would give
2:34 both of them shall die on the same D
3:12 On that D I will fulfil against Eli all
4:12 to Shiloh the same D, with his clothes rent
5:3 rose early the next D, behold, Dagon had fallen
5:5 the threshold of Dagon in Ashdod to this D
6:15 sacrificed sacrifices on that D to the LORD.
6:16 it, they returned that D to Ekron.
6:18 a witness to this D in the field of
7:2 From the D that the ark was lodged at
7:6 and fasted on that D, and said there, "We
7:10 a mighty voice that D against the Philistines and
8:8 to me, from the D I brought them up
8:8 Egypt even to this D, forsaking me and serving
8:18 And in that D you will cry out because
8:18 the LORD will not answer you in that D
9:15 Now the D before Saul came, the LORD had
9:24 So Saul ate with Samuel that D
10:9 and all these signs came to pass that D
10:19 But you have this D rejected your God, who
11:11 the heat of the D; and those who survived
11:13 put to death this D, for today the LORD
12:2 walked before you from my youth until this D
12:5 anointed is witness this D, that you have not
12:18 thunder and rain that D; and all the people
13:22 So on the D of the battle there was
14:1 One D Jonathan the son of Saul said to
14:23 LORD delivered Israel that D; and the battle passed
14:24 Israel were distressed that D; for Saul laid an
14:28 'Cursed be the man who eats food this D
14:31 the Philistines that D from Michmash to Aijalon.
14:37 But he did not answer him that D
14:41 why hast thou not answered thy servant this D
14:45 ground; for he has wrought with God this D
15:28 Israel from you this D, and has given it
15:35 Saul again until the D of his death, but
16:13 upon David from that D forward.
17:10 ranks of Israel this D; give me a man,
17:46 This D the LORD will deliver you into my
17:46 of the Philistines this D to the birds of
18:2 Saul took him that D, and would not let
18:9 eyed David from that D on.
18:10 lyre, as he did D by day.
18:10 playing the lyre, as he did day by D
19:24 lay naked all that D and all that night.
20:5 field till the third D at evening.
20:12 tomorrow, or the third D, behold, if he is
20:19 And on the third D you will be greatly
20:26 not say anything that D; for he thought, "Something
20:27 But on the second D, the morrow after the
20:34 no food the second D of the month, for
21:6 hot bread on the D it is taken away.
21:7 Saul was there that D, detained before the LORD;
21:10 rose and fled that D from Saul, and went
22:8 me, to lie in wait, as at this D
22:13 me, to lie in wait, as at this D
22:18 he killed on that D eighty-five persons who wore
22:22 "I knew on that D, when Doeg the Edomite
23:14 Saul sought him every D, but God did not
24:4 him, "Here is the D of which the LORD
24:10 Lo, this D your eyes have seen how the
24:18 you have declared this D how you have dealt
24:19 for what you have done to me this D
25:8 your eyes; for we come on a feast D
25:16 by night and by D, all the while we
25:32 who sent you this D to meet me!
25:33 have kept me this D from bloodguilt and from
26:8 into your hand this D; now therefore let me
26:10 smite him; or his D shall come to die;
26:19 driven me out this D that I should have
26:21 in your eyes this D; behold, I have played
26:24 life was precious this D in my sight, so
27:1 shall now perish one D by the hand of
27:6 So that D Achish gave him Ziklag; therefore Ziklag
27:6 belonged to the kings of Judah to this D
28:18 LORD has done this thing to you this D
28:20 had eaten nothing all D and all night.
29:3 have found no fault in him to this D
29:6 in you from the D of your coming to
29:6 day of your coming to me to this D
29:8 your servant from the D I entered your service

30:1 Ziklag on the third D, the Amalekites had made
30:17 evening of the next D; and not a man
30:25 And from that D forward he made it a
30:25 statute and an ordinance for Israel to this D
31:6 men, on the same D together.
2Sam 1:2 and on the third D, behold, a man came
2:17 was very fierce that D; and Abner and the
2:32 all night, and the D broke upon them at
3:8 This D I keep showing loyalty to the house
3:35 while it was yet D; but David swore, saying,
3:37 all Israel understood that D that it had not
3:38 man has fallen this D in Israel?
3:39 And I am this D weak, though anointed king;
4:3 Gittaim, and have been sojourners there to this D
4:5 the heat of the D they came to the
4:8 lord the king this D on Saul and on
5:8 David said on that D, "Whoever would smite the
6:8 and that place is called Perez-uzzah, to this D
6:9 of the LORD that D; and he said, "How
6:23 no child to the D of her death.
7:6 a house since the D I brought up the
7:6 from Egypt to this D, but I have been
11:12 remained in Jerusalem that D, and the next.
12:18 On the seventh D the child died.
13:32 been determined from the D he forced his sister
13:37 mourned for his son D after day.
13:37 And David mourned for his son day after D
18:7 was great on that D, twenty thousand men.
18:8 devoured more people that D than the sword.
18:18 and it is called Absalom's monument to this D
18:20 may carry tidings another D, but today you shall
18:31 has delivered you this D from the power of
19:2 So the victory that D was turned into mourning
19:2 the people heard that D, "The king is grieving
19:3 into the city that D as people steal in
19:5 servants, who have this D saved your life, and
19:19 did wrong on the D my lord the king
19:20 I have come this D, the first of all
19:22 that you should this D be as an adversary
19:22 one be put to death in Israel this D
19:22 that I am this D king over Israel?"
19:24 his clothes, from the D the king departed until
19:24 king departed until the D he came back in
19:35 I am this D eighty years old; can I
20:3 shut up until the D of their death, living
21:10 come upon them by D, or the beasts of
21:12 hanged them, on the D the Philistines killed Saul
22:1 this song on the D when the LORD delivered
22:19 upon me in the D of my calamity; but
23:10 a great victory that D; and the men returned
23:20 a pit on a D when snow had fallen.
24:18 And Gad came that D to David, and said
1Kgs 1:25 has gone down this D, and has sacrificed oxen,
1:30 my stead'; even so will I do this D
1:48 on my throne this D, my own eyes seeing
2:8 grievous curse on the D when I went to
2:24 promised, Adonijah shall be put to death this D
2:37 For on the D you go forth, and cross
2:42 certain that on the D you go forth and
3:6 a son to sit on his throne this D
3:18 Then on the third D after I was delivered,
4:22 Solomon's provision for one D was thirty cors of
5:7 be the LORD this D, who has given to
8:8 from outside; and they are there to this D
8:16 father, saying, 'Since the D that I brought my
8:24 and with thy hand hast fulfilled it this D
8:28 prays before thee this D;
8:29 be open night and D toward this house, the
8:59 the LORD our God D and night, and may
8:59 people Israel, as each D requires;
8:61 statutes and keeping his commandments, as at this D
8:64 The same D the king consecrated the middle of
8:66 On the eighth D he sent the people away;
9:13 are called the land of Cabul to this D
9:21 of slaves, and so they are to this D
10:12 wood has come or been seen, to this D
12:12 to Rehoboam the third D, as the king said,
12:12 king said, "Come to me again the third D
12:19 rebellion against the house of David to this D
12:32 feast on the fifteenth D of the eighth month
12:33 Bethel on the fifteenth D in the eighth month,
13:3 a sign the same D, saying, "This is the
13:11 God had done that D in Bethel; the words
16:16 king over Israel that D in the camp.
17:14 not fail, until the D that the LORD sends
18:36 it be known this D that thou art God
19:4 he himself went a D's journey into the wilderness,
20:13 into your hand this D; and you shall know
20:29 Then on the seventh D the battle was joined;
20:29 Syrians a hundred thousand foot soldiers in one D
22:25 shall see on that D when you go into
22:35 battle grew hot that D, and the king was
2Kgs 2:22 been wholesome to this D, according to the word
4:8 One D Elisha went on to Shunem, where a
4:11 One D he came there, and he turned into
4:18 he went out one D to his father among
6:29 And on the next D I said to her,
7:9 This D is a day of good news; if
7:9 This day is a D of good news; if
8:6 the fields from the D that she left the
8:22 revolted from the rule of Judah to this D
10:27 Baal, and made it a latrine to this D
14:7 it Joktheel, which is its name to this D
15:5 a leper to the D of his death, and
16:6 came to Elath, where they dwell to this D
17:23 from their own land to Assyria until this D
17:34 To this D they do according to the former
17:41 their fathers did, so they do to this D
19:3 "Thus says Hezekiah, This D is a day of
19:3 This day is a D of distress, of rebuke,
20:5 you; on the third D you shall go up
20:8 the house of the LORD on the third D
20:17 stored up till this D, shall be carried to
21:15 to anger, since the D their fathers came out
21:15 fathers came out of Egypt, even to this D
25:1 month, on the tenth D of the month, Nebuchadnezzar
25:3 On the ninth D of the fourth month the
25:8 month, on the seventh D of the month--which
25:27 twenty-seventh D of the month, Evil-merodach
25:29 And every D of his life he dined regularly
25:30 by the king, every D a portion, as long
1Chr 4:41 exterminated them to this D, and settled in their
4:43 escaped, and they have dwelt there to this D
5:26 Habor, Hara, and the river Gozan, to this D
9:33 they were on duty D and night.
11:22 a pit on a D when snow had fallen.
12:22 For from D to day men kept coming to
12:22 For from day to D men kept coming to
13:11 and that place is called Perez-uzza to this D
13:12 afraid of God that D; and he said, "How
16:7 on that D David first appointed that thanksgiving
16:23 of his salvation from D to day.
16:23 Tell of his salvation from day to D
16:37 the ark as each D required,
17:5 a house since the D I led up Israel
17:5 up Israel to this D, but I have gone
26:17 there were six each D, on the north four
26:17 the north four each D, on the south four
26:17 the south four each D, as well as two
29:21 and on the next D offered burnt offerings to
29:22 the LORD on that D with great gladness.
2Chr 5:9 from outside; and they are there to this D
6:5 father, saying, 'Since the D that I brought my
6:15 and with thy hand hast fulfilled it this D
6:20 eyes may be open D and night toward this
7:9 And on the eighth D they held a solemn
7:10 On the twenty-third D of the seventh month he
8:8 forced levy and so they are to this D
8:13 the duty of each D required, offering according to
8:14 the duty of each D required, and the gatekeepers
8:16 of Solomon from the D the foundation of the
10:12 to Rehoboam the third D, as the king said,
10:12 king said, "Come to me again the third D
10:19 rebellion against the house of David to this D
15:11 the LORD on that D, from the spoil which
18:24 shall see on that D when you go into
18:34 battle grew hot that D, and the king of
20:26 On the fourth D they assembled in the Valley
20:26 been called the Valley of Beracah to this D
21:10 revolted from the rule of Judah to this D
21:15 because of the disease, D by day.'''
21:15 come out because of the disease, day by D
24:11 Thus they did D after day, and collected money
24:11 they did day after D, and collected money in
26:21 a leper to the D of his death, and
28:6 in Judah in one D, all of them men
29:17 sanctify on the first D of the first month,
29:17 and on the eighth D of the month they
29:17 and on the sixteenth D of the first month
30:15 lamb on the fourteenth D of the second month.
30:21 priests praised the LORD D by day, singing with
30:21 the LORD day by D, singing with all their

31:16 the duty of each D required, for their service
35:1 lamb on the fourteenth D of the first month.
35:16 LORD was prepared that D, to keep the passover
35:21 coming against you this D, but against the house
35:25 spoken of Josiah in their laments to this D
Ezra 3:4 the ordinance, as each D required,
3:6 From the first D of the seventh month they
6:9 be given to them D by day without fail,
6:9 to them day by D without fail,
6:15 finished on the third D of the month of
6:19 On the fourteenth D of the first month the
7:9 for on the first D of the first month
7:9 and on the first D of the fifth month
8:31 Ahava on the twelfth D of the first month,
8:33 On the fourth D, within the house of our
9:7 our fathers to this D we have been in
9:7 plundering, and to utter shame, as at this D
9:15 a remnant that has escaped, as at this D
10:9 month, on the twentieth D of the month.
10:13 a work for one D or for two; for
10:16 On the first D of the tenth month they
10:17 and by the first D of the first month
Neh 1:6 now pray before thee D and night for the
4:2 Will they finish up in a D
4:9 a protection against them D and night.
4:16 From that D on, half of my servants worked
4:22 for us by night and may labor by D
5:11 to them this very D their fields, their vineyards,
5:18 was prepared for one D was one ox and
6:15 finished on the twenty-fifth D of the month Elul,
8:2 understanding, on the first D of the seventh month.
8:9 all the people, "This D is holy to the
8:10 is prepared; for this D is holy to our
8:11 "Be quiet, for this D is holy; do not
8:13 On the second D the heads of fathers' houses
8:17 of Nun to that D the people of Israel
8:18 And D by day, from the first day to
8:18 And day by D, from the first day to
8:18 day, from the first D to the last day,
8:18 day to the last D, he read from the
8:18 and on the eighth D there was a solemn
9:1 Now on the twenty-fourth D of this month the
9:3 a fourth of the D; for another fourth of
9:10 thee a name, as it is to this D
9:12 lead them in the D, and by a pillar
9:19 depart from them by D, nor the pillar of
9:32 time of the kings of Assyria until this D
9:36 we are slaves this D; in the land that
10:31 grain on the sabbath D to sell, we will
10:31 or on a holy D; and we will forego
11:23 the singers, as every D required.
12:43 offered great sacrifices that D and rejoiced, for God
12:44 On that D men were appointed over the chambers
13:1 On that D they read from the book of
13:15 Jerusalem on the sabbath D; and I warned them
13:15 warned them on the D when they sold food.
13:17 thing which you are doing, profaning the sabbath D
13:19 burden might be brought in on the sabbath D
13:22 to keep the sabbath D holy.
Tob 3:7 On the same D, at Ecbatana in Media, it
4:1 On that D Tobit remembered the money which he
4:9 for yourself against the D of necessity.
4:14 over till the next D the wages of any
5:14 you--a drachma a D, and expenses for yourself
10:1 Tobit was counting each D, and when the days
10:7 she went out every D to the road by
Jud 1:15 spears; and he utterly destroyed him, to this D
2:1 year, on the twenty-second D of the first month,
2:10 for me till the D of their punishment.
6:5 these words on the D of your iniquity, you
6:5 face again from this D until I take revenge
6:19 people, and look this D upon the faces of
7:1 The next D Holofernes ordered his whole army, and
7:2 moved their camp that D; their force of men
7:6 On the second D Holofernes led out all his
7:21 fill for a single D, because it was measured
7:29 him not do this D the things which we
8:6 her widowhood, except the D before the sabbath and
8:6 the sabbath itself, the D before the new moon
8:6 new moon and the D of the new moon,
8:12 to the test this D, and are setting yourselves
11:15 this, on that very D they will be handed
11:17 the God of heaven D and night; therefore, my
12:10 On the fourth D Holofernes held a banquet for
12:14 to me until the D of my death!"
12:16 her, ever since the D he first saw her.
12:20 drunk in any one D since he was born.
13:3 as she did every D; for she said she
13:7 "Give me strength this D, O Lord God of
13:11 our enemies, even as he has done this D
13:17 brought into contempt this D the enemies of thy
14:8 had done, from the D she left until the
14:10 the house of Israel, remaining so to this D
16:17 on them in the D of judgment; fire and
Esth 1:10 On the seventh D, when the heart of the
1:18 not come.' This very D the ladies of Persia
2:11 And every D Mordecai walked in front of the
3:4 they spoke to him D after day and he
3:4 to him day after D and he would not
3:7 the lot, before Haman D after day; and they
3:7 before Haman day after D; and they cast it
3:12 summoned on the thirteenth D of the first month,
3:13 and children, in one D, the thirteenth day of
3:13 one day, the thirteenth D of the twelfth month,
3:14 all the peoples to be ready for that D
4:16 eat nor drink for three days, night or D
5:1 On the third D Esther put on her royal
5:4 and Haman come this D to a dinner that
5:9 Haman went out that D joyful and glad of
7:2 And on the second D, as they were drinking
8:1 On that D King Ahasuerus gave to Queen Esther
8:9 Sivan, on the twenty-third D; and an edict was
8:12 their goods, upon one D throughout all the provinces
8:12 Ahasuerus, on the thirteenth D of the twelfth month,
8:13 be ready on that D to avenge themselves upon
9:1 Adar, on the thirteenth D of the same, when
9:1 executed, on the very D when the enemies of
9:1 been changed to a D when the Jews should
9:11 That very D the number of those slain in
9:13 do according to this D's edict.
9:15 also on the fourteenth D of the month of
9:17 was on the thirteenth D of the month of
9:17 and on the fourteenth D they rested and made
9:17 and made that a D of feasting and gladness.
9:18 gathered on the thirteenth D and on the fourteenth,
9:18 rested on the fifteenth D, making that a day
9:18 day, making that a D of feasting and gladness.
9:19 towns, hold the fourteenth D of the month of
9:19 of Adar as a D for gladness and feasting
9:19 and holiday-making, and a D on which they send
9:21 should keep the fourteenth D of the month Adar
9:21 and also the fifteenth D of the same, year
10:11 hour and moment and D of decision before God
11:2 Great, on the first D of Nisan, Mordecai the
11:8 And behold, a D of darkness and gloom, tribulation
11:12 mind and sought all D to understand it in
13:6 mercy, on the fourteenth D of the twelfth month,
13:7 hostile may in one D go down in violence
14:18 no joy since the D that I was brought
15:1 On the third D, when she ended her prayer,
16:20 that on the thirteenth D of the twelfth month,
16:20 Adar, on that very D they may defend themselves
16:21 things, has made this D to be a joy
16:21 people instead of a D of destruction for them.
16:22 as a notable D among your commemorative festivals,
Job 1:4 of each on his D; and they would send
1:6 Now there was a D when the sons of
1:13 Now there was a D when his sons and
2:1 Again there was a D when the sons of
3:1 mouth and cursed the D of his birth.
3:3 Job said: "Let the D perish wherein I was
3:4 is conceived.' Let that D be darkness!
3:5 the blackness of the D terrify it.
3:8 it who curse the D, who are skilled to
14:6 that he may enjoy, like a hireling, his D
15:23 He knows that a D of darkness is ready
17:12 They make night into D; 'The light,' they say,
18:20 are appalled at his D, and horror seizes them
20:28 dragged off in the D of God's wrath.
21:30 is spared in the D of calamity, that he
21:30 is rescued in the D of wrath?
24:16 dig through houses; by D they shut themselves up;
30:25 weep for him whose D was hard?
38:23 of trouble, for the D of battle and war?
Ps 1:2 his law he meditates D and night.
7:11 judge, and a God who has indignation every D
13:2 and have sorrow in my heart all the D
18:18 upon me in the D of my calamity; but
19:2 D to day pours forth speech, and night to
19:2 Day to D pours forth speech, and night to
20:1 answer you in the D of trouble!
22:2 God, I cry by D, but thou dost not

D

25:5 I wait all the D long.
27:5 his shelter in the D of trouble; he will
32:3 through my groaning all D long.
32:4 For D and night thy hand was heavy upon
35:28 thy praise all the D long.
37:13 he sees that his D is coming.
38:6 and prostrate; all the D I go about mourning.
38:12 meditate treachery all the D long.
41:1 delivers him in the D of trouble;
42:3 have been my food D and night, while men
42:8 By D the LORD commands his steadfast love; and
44:15 All D long my disgrace is before me, and
44:22 are slain all the D long, and accounted as
50:15 upon me in the D of trouble; I will
52:1 All the D
55:10 D and night they go around it on its
56:1 trample upon me; all D long foemen oppress me;
56:2 trample upon me all D long, for many fight
56:5 All D long they seek to injure my cause;
56:9 turned back in the D when I call.
59:16 a refuge in the D of my distress.
61:8 I pay my vows D after day.
61:8 name, as I pay my vows day after D
71:8 thy praise, and with thy glory all the D
71:15 of salvation all the D, for their number is
71:24 righteous help all the D long, for they have
72:15 continually, and blessings invoked for him all the D
73:14 For all the D long I have been stricken,
74:16 Thine is the D, thine also the night; thou
74:22 how the impious scoff at thee all the D
77:2 In the D of my trouble I seek the
78:9 turned back on the D of battle.
78:42 his power, or the D when he redeemed them
81:3 moon, at the full moon, on our feast D
84:10 For a D in thy courts is better than
86:3 for to thee do I cry all the D
86:7 In the D of my trouble I call on
88:1 call for help by D; I cry out in
88:9 Every D I call upon thee, O LORD; I
88:17 like a flood all D long; they close in
89:16 thy name all the D, and extol thy righteousness.
91:5 arrow that flies by D,
95:8 Meribah, as on the D at Massah in the
96:2 of his salvation from D to day.
96:2 name; tell of his salvation from day to D
102:2 from me in the D of my distress!
102:2 me speedily in the D when I call!
102:8 All the D my enemies taunt me, those who
110:3 themselves freely on the D you lead your host
110:5 shatter kings on the D of his wrath.
118:24 This is the D which the LORD has made;
119:91 appointment they stand this D; for all things are
119:97 It is my meditation all the D
119:164 Seven times a D I praise thee for thy
121:6 not smite you by D, nor the moon by
136:8 to rule over the D, for his steadfast love
137:7 against the Edomites the D of Jerusalem, how they
138:3 On the D I called, thou didst answer me,
139:12 is bright as the D; for darkness is as
140:7 my head in the D of battle.
145:2 Every D I will bless thee, and praise thy
146:4 earth; on that very D his plans perish.
Prov 4:19 dawn, which shines brighter and brighter until full D
11:4 not profit in the D of wrath, but righteousness
16:4 the wicked for the D of trouble.
21:26 All D long the wicked covets, but the righteous
21:31 made ready for the D of battle, but the
23:17 in the fear of the LORD all the D
24:10 you faint in the D of adversity, your strength
25:20 garment on a cold D, and like vinegar on
27:1 not know what a D may bring forth.
27:10 brother's house in the D of your calamity.
27:15 dripping on a rainy D and a contentious woman
Eccl 7:1 precious ointment; and the D of death, than the
7:1 of death, than the D of birth.
7:14 In the D of prosperity be joyful, and in
7:14 joyful, and in the D of adversity consider; God
8:8 or authority over the D of death; there is
8:16 on earth, how neither D nor night one's eyes
12:3 the rain; in the D when the keepers of
Song 2:17 Until the D breathes and the shadows flee, turn,
3:11 crowned him on the D of his wedding, on
3:11 his wedding, on the D of the gladness of
4:6 Until the D breathes and the shadows flee, I
8:8 our sister, on the D when she is spoken
Wis 3:18 no consolation in the D of decision.
5:14 remembrance of a guest who stays but a D
10:17 shelter to them by D, and a starry flame
Sir 1:11 the end; on the D of his death he
3:15 to you; in the D of your affliction it
5:7 nor postpone it from D to day; for suddenly
5:7 it from day to D; for suddenly the wrath
5:8 benefit you in the D of calamity.
6:8 by you in your D of trouble.
6:10 by you in your D of trouble.
11:4 exalt yourself in the D that you are honored;
11:23 In the D of prosperity, adversity is forgotten, and
11:23 forgotten, and in the D of adversity, prosperity is
11:24 a man on the D of death according to
14:14 yourself of a happy D; let not your share
18:9 few years in the D of eternity.
18:23 his wrath on the D of death, and of
23:14 you will curse the D of your birth.
33:7 Why is any D better than another, when all
36:8 Hasten the D, and remember the appointed time, and
38:17 his merit, for one D, or two, to avoid
38:27 as well as by D; those who cut the
40:1 of Adam, from the D they come forth from
40:1 mother's womb till the D they return to the
40:2 anxious thought is the D of death,
45:14 wholly burned twice every D continually.
46:4 And did not one D become as long as
47:7 Philistines; he crushed their power even to this D
50:8 Lebanon on a summer D;
Is 2:11 the LORD alone will be exalted in that D
2:12 of hosts has a D against all that is
2:17 the LORD alone will be exalted in that D
2:20 In that D men will cast forth their idols
3:7 your rule"; in that D he will speak out,
3:18 In that D the Lord will take away the
4:1 one man in that D, saying, "We will eat
4:2 In that D the branch of the LORD shall
4:5 assemblies a cloud by D, and smoke and the
4:6 for a shade by D from the heat, and
5:30 over it on that D, like the roaring of
7:17 not come since the D that Ephraim departed from
7:18 In that D the LORD will whistle for the
7:20 In that D the Lord will shave with a
7:21 In that D a man will keep alive a
7:23 In that D every place where there used to
9:4 broken as on the D of Midian.
9:14 and reed in one D —
10:3 you do on the D of punishment, in the
10:17 and devour his thorns and briers in one D
10:20 In that D the remnant of Israel and the
10:27 And in that D his burden will depart from
10:32 This very D he will halt at Nob, he
11:10 In that D the root of Jesse shall stand
11:11 In that D the Lord will extend his hand
12:1 will say in that D: "I will give thanks
12:4 will say in that D: "Give thanks to the
13:6 Wail, for the D of the LORD is near;
13:9 Behold, the D of the LORD comes, cruel, with
13:13 of hosts in the D of his fierce anger.
14:12 fallen from heaven, O D Star, son of Dawn!
17:4 And in that D the glory of Jacob will
17:7 In that D men will regard their Maker, and
17:9 In that D their strong cities will be like
17:11 them grow on the D that you plant them,
17:11 flee away in a D of grief and incurable
19:16 In that D the Egyptians will be like women,
19:18 In that D there will be five cities in
19:19 In that D there will be an altar to
19:21 the LORD in that D and worship with sacrifice
19:23 In that D there will be a highway from
19:24 In that D Israel will be the third with
20:6 will say in that D, 'Behold, this is what
21:8 O Lord, continually by D, and at my post
22:5 of hosts has a D of tumult and trampling
22:8 In that D you looked to the weapons of
22:12 In that D the Lord GOD of hosts called
22:20 In that D I will call my servant Eliakim
22:25 In that D, says the LORD of hosts, the
23:15 In that D Tyre will be forgotten for seventy
24:21 On that D the LORD will punish the host
25:9 be said on that D, "Lo, this is our
26:1 In that D this song will be sung in
27:1 In that D the LORD with his hard and
27:2 In that D: "A pleasant vineyard, sing of it!
27:3 guard it night and D;
27:8 fierce blast in the D of the east wind.
27:12 In that D from the river Euphrates to the

27:13 And in that D a great trumpet will be
28:5 In that D the LORD of hosts will be
28:19 will pass through, by D and by night; and
29:18 In that D the deaf shall hear the words
30:23 In that D your cattle will graze in large
30:25 with water, in the D of the great slaughter,
30:26 seven days, in the D when the LORD binds
31:7 For in that D every one shall cast away
34:8 the LORD has a D of vengeance, a year
34:10 Night and D it shall not be quenched; its
37:3 "Thus says Hezekiah, 'This D is a day of
37:3 'This day is a D of distress, of rebuke,
38:12 from the loom; from D to night thou dost
38:13 all my bones; from D to night thou dost
38:19 as I do this D; the father makes known
39:6 stored up till this D, shall be carried to
47:9 a moment, in one D; the loss of children
49:8 answered you, in a D of salvation I have
51:13 fear continually all the D because of the fury
52:5 and continually all the D my name is despised.
52:6 name; therefore in that D they shall know that
56:12 will be like this D, great beyond measure."
58:3 it?' Behold, in the D of your fast you
58:4 Fasting like yours this D will not make your
58:5 that I choose, a D for a man to
58:5 a fast, and a D acceptable to the LORD?
58:13 pleasure on my holy D, and call the sabbath
58:13 delight and the holy D of the LORD honorable;
60:11 shall be open continually; D and night they shall
60:19 more your light by D, nor for brightness shall
61:2 LORD's favor, and the D of vengeance of our
62:6 set watchmen; all the D and all the night
63:4 For the D of vengeance was in my heart,
65:2 my hands all the D to a rebellious people,
65:5 my nostrils, a fire that burns all the D
66:8 Shall a land be born in one D
Jer 1:10 have set you this D over nations and over
1:18 I make you this D a fortified city, an
3:25 youth even to this D; and we have not
4:9 "In that D, says the LORD, courage shall fail
6:4 to us, for the D declines, for the shadows
7:22 For in the D that I brought them out
7:25 From the D that your fathers came out of
7:25 of Egypt to this D, I have persistently sent
7:25 the prophets to them, D after day;
7:25 to them, day after D;
9:1 that I might weep D and night for the
11:5 flowing with milk and honey, as at this D
11:7 persistently, even to this D, saying, Obey my voice.
12:3 them apart for the D of slaughter.
14:17 with tears night and D, and let them not
15:9 while it was yet D; she has been shamed
16:13 shall serve other gods D and night, for I
16:19 my refuge in the D of trouble, to thee
17:16 have I desired the D of disaster, thou knowest;
17:17 my refuge in the D of evil.
17:18 bring upon them the D of evil; destroy them
17:21 burden on the sabbath D or bring it in
17:22 but keep the sabbath D holy, as I commanded
17:24 city on the sabbath D, but keep the sabbath
17:24 but keep the sabbath D holy and do no
17:27 to keep the sabbath D holy, and not to
17:27 Jerusalem on the sabbath D, then I will kindle
18:17 my face, in the D of their calamity."
20:7 a laughingstock all the D; every one mocks me.
20:8 reproach and derision all D long.
20:14 Cursed be the D on which I was born!
20:14 The D when my mother bore me, let it
25:3 of Judah, to this D, the word of the
25:18 curse, as at this D;
25:33 the LORD on that D shall extend from one
27:22 remain there until the D when I give attention
30:7 that D is so great there is none like
30:8 to pass in that D, says the LORD of
31:6 there shall be a D when watchmen will call
31:35 sun for light by D and the fixed order
32:20 Egypt, and to this D in Israel and among
32:20 hast made thee a name, as at this D
32:31 and wrath, from the D it was built to
32:31 was built to this D, so that I will
33:20 my covenant with the D and my covenant with
33:20 the night, so that D and night will not
33:25 established my covenant with D and night and the
35:14 drink none to this D, for they have obeyed
36:2 the nations, from the D I spoke to you,
36:6 and on a fast D in the hearing of
36:30 to the heat by D and the frost by
38:28 the guard until the D that Jerusalem was taken.
39:2 month, on the ninth D of the month, a
39:16 they shall be accomplished before you on that D
39:17 deliver you on that D, says the LORD, and
41:4 On the D after the murder of Gedaliah, before
42:19 have warned you this D
42:21 And I have this D declared it to you,
44:2 Behold, this D they are a desolation, and no
44:6 a waste and a desolation, as at this D
44:10 themselves even to this D, nor have they feared,
44:22 a curse, without inhabitant, as it is this D
44:23 this evil has befallen you, as at this D
46:10 That D is the day of the Lord GOD
46:10 That day is the D of the Lord GOD
46:10 GOD of hosts, a D of vengeance, to avenge
46:21 not stand; for the D of their calamity has
47:4 hands, because of the D that is coming to
48:41 shall be in that D like the heart of
49:22 shall be in that D like the heart of
49:26 be destroyed in that D, says the LORD of
50:27 to them, for their D has come, the time
50:30 be destroyed on that D, says the LORD.
50:31 of hosts; for your D has come, the time
51:2 every side on the D of trouble.
52:4 month, on the tenth D of the month, Nebuchadrezzar
52:6 On the ninth D of the fourth month the
52:11 in prison till the D of his death.
52:12 month, on the tenth D of the month--which
52:31 on the twenty-fifth D of the month, Evil-merodach
52:33 And every D of his life he dined regularly
52:34 the king until the D of his death as
Lam 1:12 LORD inflicted on the D of his fierce anger.
1:13 stunned, faint all the D long.
1:21 Bring thou the D thou hast announced, and let
2:1 his footstool in the D of his anger.
2:7 LORD as on the D of an appointed feast.
2:16 Ah, this is the D we longed for; now
2:18 down like a torrent D and night!
2:21 the sword; in the D of thy anger thou
2:22 invite as to the D of an appointed feast
2:22 side; and on the D of the anger of
3:3 and again the whole D long.
3:14 of their songs all D long.
3:62 against me all the D long.
Bar 1:2 year, on the seventh D of the month, at
1:8 time, on the tenth D of Sivan, Baruch took
1:13 God, and to this D the anger of the
1:15 face, as at this D, to us, to the
1:19 From the D when the Lord brought our fathers
1:20 So to this D there have clung to us
2:6 to us and our fathers, as at this D
2:11 name, as at this D,
2:25 to the heat of D and the frost of
2:28 servant Moses on the D when thou didst command
3:20 seen the light of D, and have dwelt upon
Ezek 1:1 month, on the fifth D of the in month,
1:2 On the fifth D of the month (it was
1:28 the cloud on the D of rain, so was
2:3 fathers have transgressed against me to this very D
4:6 I assign you, a D for each year.
4:10 weight, twenty shekels a D; once a day you
4:10 a day; once a D you shall eat it.
4:11 a hin; once a D you shall drink.
7:7 time has come, the D is near, a day
7:7 day is near, a D of tumult, and not
7:10 "Behold, the D
7:12 time has come, the D draws near.
7:19 deliver them in the D of the wrath of
8:1 month, on the fifth D of the month, as
12:3 go into exile by D in their sight; you
12:4 out your baggage by D in their sight, as
12:7 out my baggage by D, as baggage for exile,
13:5 in battle in the D of the LORD.
16:4 your birth, on the D you were born your
16:5 were abhorred, on the D that you were born.
16:56 your mouth in the D of your pride,
20:1 month, on the tenth D of the month, certain
20:5 Lord GOD: On the D when I chose Israel,
20:6 On that D I swore to them that I
20:29 called Bamah to this D
20:31 defile yourselves with all your idols to this D
21:25 prince of Israel, whose D has come, the time
21:29 the unhallowed wicked, whose D has come, the time
22:4 you have brought your D near, the appointed time
22:24 rained upon in the D of indignation.

D

23:38 sanctuary on the same D and profaned my sabbaths.
23:39 idols, on the same D they came into my
24:1 month, on the tenth D of the month, the
24:2 the name of this D, this very day.
24:2 down the name of this day, this very D
24:2 Babylon has laid siege to Jerusalem this very D
24:25 of man, on the D when I take from
24:26 and daughters, on that D a fugitive will come
24:27 On that D your mouth will be opened to
26:1 year, on the first D of the month, the
26:18 isles tremble on the D of your fall; yea,
27:27 the seas on the D of your ruin.
28:13 On the D that you were created they were
28:15 your ways from the D you were created, till
29:1 month, on the twelfth D of the month, the
29:17 month, on the first D of the month, the
29:21 "On that D I will cause a horn to
30:2 "Wail, 'Alas for the D
30:3 the day!' For the D is near, the day
30:3 day is near, the D of the LORD is
30:3 it will be a D of clouds, a time
30:9 "On that D swift messengers shall go forth from
30:9 upon them on the D of Egypt's doom; for,
30:18 At Tehaphnehes the D shall be dark, when I
30:20 month, on the seventh D of the month, the
31:1 month, on the first D of the month, the
32:1 month, on the first D of the month, the
32:10 own life, on the D of your downfall.
32:17 month, on the fifteenth D of the month, the
33:21 month, on the fifth D of the month, a
34:12 been scattered on a D of clouds and thick
36:33 Lord GOD: On the D that I cleanse you
38:10 Lord GOD: On that D thoughts will come into
38:14 Lord GOD: On that D when my people Israel
38:18 But on that D, when Gog shall come against
38:19 I declare, On that D there shall be a
39:8 That is the D of which I have spoken.
39:11 "On that D I will give to Gog a
39:13 their honor on the D that I show my
39:22 their God, from that D forward.
40:1 year, on the tenth D of the month, in
40:1 conquered, on that very D, the hand of the
43:18 the altar: On the D when it is erected
43:22 And on the second D you shall offer a
43:27 then from the eighth D onward the priests shall
44:27 And on the D that he goes into the
45:18 month, on the first D of the month, you
45:20 same on the seventh D of the month for
45:21 month, on the fourteenth D of the month, you
45:22 On that D the prince shall provide for himself
45:25 month, on the fifteenth D of the month and
46:1 but on the sabbath D it shall be opened
46:1 opened and on the D of the new moon
46:4 LORD on the sabbath D shall be six lambs
46:6 On the D of the new moon he shall
46:12 peace offerings as he does on the sabbath D
Dan 3:37 are brought low this D in all the world
3:40 in thy sight this D, and may we wholly
6:10 knees three times a D and prayed and gave
6:13 signed, but makes his petition three times a D
6:19 Then, at break of D, the king arose and
9:7 face, as at this D, to the men of
9:15 name, as at this D, we have sinned, we
10:4 On the twenty-fourth D of the first month, as
10:12 for from the first D that you set your
13:8 to see her every D, going in and walking
13:12 And they watched eagerly, D after day, to see
13:12 watched eagerly, day after D, to see her.
13:15 watching for an opportune D, she went in as
13:28 The next D, when the people gathered at the
13:62 Thus innocent blood was saved that D
13:64 And from that D onward Daniel had a great
14:3 called Bel, and every D they spent on it
14:4 it and went every D to worship it.
14:6 see how much he eats and drinks every D
14:32 the den, and every D they had been given
14:40 On the seventh D the king came to mourn
Hos 1:5 And on that D, I will break the bow
1:11 great shall be the D of Jezreel.
2:3 her as in the D she was born, and
2:16 "And in that D, says the LORD, you will
2:18 a covenant on that D with the beasts of
2:21 "And in that D, says the LORD, I will
4:5 You shall stumble by D, the prophet also shall
5:9 a desolation in the D of punishment; among the
6:2 us; on the third D he will raise us
7:6 On the D of our king the princes became
9:5 you do on the D of appointed festival, and
9:5 festival, and on the D of the feast of
10:14 destroyed Beth-arbel on the D of battle; mothers
12:1 the east wind all D long; they multiply falsehood
Joel 1:14 Alas for the D
1:14 For the D of the LORD is near, and
2:1 land tremble, for the D of the LORD is
2:2 it is near, a D of darkness and gloom,
2:2 darkness and gloom, a D of clouds and thick
2:11 For the D of the LORD is great and
2:31 the great and terrible D of the LORD comes.
3:14 For the D of the LORD is near in
3:18 "And in that D the mountains shall drip sweet
Amos 1:14 with shouting in the D of battle, with a
1:14 a tempest in the D of the whirlwind;
2:16 the mighty shall flee away naked in that D
3:14 hosts, "that on the D I punish Israel for
5:8 morning, and darkens the D into night, who calls
5:18 you who desire the D of the LORD!
5:18 would you have the D of the LORD?
5:20 Is not the D of the LORD darkness, and
6:3 far away the evil D, and bring near the
8:3 of the temple shall become wailings in that D
8:9 "And on that D
8:10 and the end of it like a bitter D
8:13 "In that D the fair virgins and the young
9:11 meet us.' "In that D I will raise up
Obad 1:8 I not on that D, says the LORD, destroy
1:11 On the D that you stood aloof, on the
1:11 stood aloof, on the D that strangers carried off
1:12 have gloated over the D of your brother in
1:12 your brother in the D of his misfortune; you
1:12 of Judah in the D of their ruin; you
1:12 have boasted in the D of distress.
1:13 my people in the D of his calamity; you
1:13 his disaster in the D of his calamity; you
1:13 his goods in the D of his calamity.
1:14 his survivors in the D of distress.
1:15 For the D of the LORD is near upon
Jon 3:4 the city, going a D's journey.
4:7 came up the next D, God appointed a worm
Mic 2:4 In that D they shall take up a taunt
3:6 the prophets, and the D shall be black over
4:6 In that D, says the LORD, I will assemble
5:10 And in that D, says the LORD, I will
7:4 The D of their watchmen, of their punishment, has
7:11 A D for the building of your walls!
7:11 In that D the boundary shall be far extended.
7:12 In that D they will come to you, from
Nah 1:7 a stronghold in the D of trouble; he knows
3:17 the fences in a D of cold--when the
Hab 3:16 quietly wait for the D of trouble to come
Zeph 1:7 For the D of the LORD is at hand;
1:8 And on the D of the LORD's sacrifice--"I
1:9 On that D I will punish every one who
1:10 "On that D
1:14 The great D of the LORD is near, near
1:14 the sound of the D of the LORD is
1:15 A D of wrath is that day, a day
1:15 of wrath is that D, a day of distress
1:15 is that day, a D of distress and anguish,
1:15 distress and anguish, a D of ruin and devastation,
1:15 ruin and devastation, a D of darkness and gloom,
1:15 darkness and gloom, a D of clouds and thick
1:16 and thick darkness, a D of trumpet blast and
1:18 deliver them on the D of the wrath of
2:2 comes upon you the D of the wrath of
2:3 be hidden on the D of the wrath of
3:8 the LORD, "for the D when I arise as
3:11 "On that D you shall not be put to
3:16 On that D it shall be said to Jerusalem:
3:18 singing as on a D of festival.
Hag 1:1 month, on the first D of the month, the
1:15 God, on the twenty-fourth D of the month, in
2:1 month, on the twenty-first D of the month, the
2:10 On the twenty-fourth D of the ninth month, in
2:15 to pass from this D onward.
2:18 from this D onward, from the twenty-fourth D
2:18 Since the D that the foundation of the LORD's
2:19 From this D on I will bless you."
2:20 Haggai on the twenty-fourth D of the month,
2:23 On that D, says the LORD of hosts, I
Zech 1:7 On the twenty-fourth D of the eleventh month which
2:11 the LORD in that D, and shall be my
3:9 the guilt of this land in a single D

	3:10	In that D, says the LORD of hosts, every
	4:10	whoever has despised the D of small things shall
	6:10	and go the same D to the house of
	7:1	Zechariah in the fourth D of the ninth month,
	8:9	the prophets, since the D that the foundation of
	9:16	On that D the LORD their God will save
	11:11	was annulled on that D, and the traffickers in
	12:3	On that D I will make Jerusalem a heavy
	12:4	On that D, says the LORD, I will strike
	12:6	their God.' "On that D I will make the
	12:8	On that D the LORD will put a shield
	12:8	among them on that D shall be like David,
	12:9	And on that D I will seek to destroy
	12:11	On that D the mourning in Jerusalem will be
	13:1	"On that D there shall be a fountain opened
	13:2	"And on that D, says the LORD of hosts,
	13:4	On that D every prophet will be ashamed of
	14:1	Behold, a D of the LORD is coming, when
	14:3	he fights on a D of battle.
	14:4	On that D his feet shall stand on the
	14:6	On that D there shall be neither cold nor
	14:7	there shall be continuous D (it is known to
	14:7	to the LORD), not D and not night, for
	14:8	On that D living waters shall flow out from
	14:9	the earth; on that D the LORD will be
	14:13	And on that D a great panic from the
	14:20	And on that D there shall be inscribed on
	14:21	house of the LORD of hosts on that D
Mal	3:2	who can endure the D of his coming, and
	3:17	special possession on the D when I act, and
	4:1	"For behold, the D comes, burning like an oven,
	4:1	will be stubble; the D that comes shall burn
	4:3	your feet, on the D when I act, says
	4:5	the great and terrible D of the LORD comes.
1Mac	1:54	Now on the fifteenth D of Chislev, in the
	1:59	And on the twenty-fifth D of the month they
	2:32	prepared for battle against them on the sabbath D
	2:34	the king commands and so profane the sabbath D
	2:41	made this decision that D: "Let us fight against
	2:41	us on the sabbath D; let us not all
	3:47	They fasted that D, put on sackcloth and sprinkled
	4:25	Thus Israel had a great deliverance that D
	4:52	morning on the twenty-fifth D of the ninth month,
	4:54	and on the very D that the Gentiles had
	4:59	beginning with the twenty-fifth D of the month of
	5:27	take and destroy all these men in one D
	5:34	many as eight thousand of them fell that D
	5:50	the city all that D and all the night,
	5:60	thousand of the people of Israel fell that D
	5:67	On that D some priests, who wished to do
	7:16	killed them in one D, in accordance with the
	7:43	battle on the thirteenth D of the month of
	7:45	Jews pursued them a D's journey, from Adasa as
	7:48	greatly and celebrated that D as a day of
	7:48	that day as a D of great gladness.
	7:49	they decreed that this D should be celebrated each
	7:49	year on the thirteenth D of Adar.
	8:10	down their strongholds, and enslaved them to this D
	8:15	senate chamber, and every D three hundred and
	9:34	out on the sabbath D, and he with all
	9:43	force on the sabbath D to the banks of
	9:49	about one thousand of Bacchides' men fell that D
	10:30	release them from this D and henceforth.
	10:30	and Galilee, from this D and for all time.
	10:50	the sun set, and Demetrius fell on that D
	10:55	said, "Happy was the D on which you returned
	11:47	they killed on that D as many as a
	11:48	much spoil on that D, and they saved the
	11:74	as three thousand of the foreigners fell that D
	13:30	he built in Modein; it remains to this D
	13:39	offenses committed to this D, and cancel the crown
	13:51	On the twenty-third D of the second month, in
	13:52	they should celebrate this D with rejoicing.
	14:27	wrote: "On the eighteenth D of Elul, in the
	16:2	our youth until this D, and things have prospered
2Mac	1:18	Since on the twenty-fifth D of Chislev we shall
	3:14	So he set a D and went in to
	5:25	until the holy sabbath D; then, finding the Jews
	6:11	to observe the seventh D secretly, were betrayed to
	6:11	view of their regard for that most holy D
	7:20	perish within a single D, she bore it with
	8:26	For it was the D before the sabbath, and
	8:27	preserved them for that D and allotted it to
	10:5	that on the same D on which the sanctuary
	10:5	is, on the twenty-fifth D of the same month,
	10:35	dawn of the fifth D, twenty young men in
	11:30	home by the thirtieth D of Xanthicus will have
	12:38	As the seventh D was coming on, they purified
	12:39	On the next D, as by that time it
	13:10	call upon the Lord D and night, now if
	13:17	This happened, just as D was dawning, because the
	14:4	During that D he kept quiet.
	14:21	the leaders set a D on which to meet
	15:1	complete safety on the D of rest.
	15:2	show respect for the D which he who sees
	15:3	who had commanded the keeping of the sabbath D
	15:4	heaven, who ordered us to observe the seventh D
	15:36	never to let this D go unobserved, but to
	15:36	to celebrate the thirteenth D of the twelfth month
	15:36	language – the D before Mordecai's day.
	15:36	Syrian language – the day before Mordecai's D
Mt	6:11	Give us this D our daily bread;
	6:34	Let the D's own trouble be sufficient for the D
	7:22	On that D many will say to me, 'Lord,
	10:15	more tolerable on the D of judgment for the
	11:22	more tolerable on the D of judgment for Tyre
	11:23	in Sodom, it would have remained until this D
	11:24	more tolerable on the D of judgment for the
	12:36	tell you, on the D of judgment men will
	13:1	That same D Jesus went out of the house
	14:15	lonely place, and the D is now over; send
	16:21	and on the third D be raised.
	17:22	and he will be raised on the third D
	20:2	for a denarius a D, he sent them into
	20:6	stand here idle all D
	20:12	the burden of the D and the scorching heat.'
	20:19	and he will be raised on the third D
	22:23	The same D Sadducees came to him, who say
	22:46	word, nor from that D did any one dare
	24:36	"But of that D and hour no one knows,
	24:38	in marriage, until the D when Noah entered the
	24:42	not know on what D your Lord is coming.
	24:50	will come on a D when he does not
	25:13	you know neither the D nor the hour.
	26:17	Now on the first D of Unleavened Bread the
	26:29	the vine until that D when I drink it
	26:55	D after day I sat in the temple teaching,
	26:55	Day after D I sat in the temple teaching,
	27:8	been called the Field of Blood to this D
	27:62	Next D, that is, after the day of Preparation,
	27:62	that is, after the D of Preparation, the chief
	27:64	secure until the third D, lest his disciples go
	28:1	dawn of the first D of the week, Mary
	28:15	has been spread among the Jews to this D
Mk	1:35	a great while before D, he rose and went
	2:20	them, and then they will fast in that D
	4:27	and rise night and D, and the seed should
	4:35	On that D, when evening had come, he said
	5:5	Night and D among the tombs and on the
	11:12	On the following D, when they came from Bethany,
	13:32	"But of that D or that hour no one
	14:12	And on the first D of Unleavened Bread, when
	14:25	the vine until that D when I drink it
	14:49	D after day I was with you in the
	14:49	Day after D I was with you in the
	15:41	since it was the D of Preparation, that is,
	15:41	Preparation, that is, the D before the sabbath,
	16:2	early on the first D of the week they
	16:9	early on the first D of the week, he
Lk	1:20	to speak until the D that these things come
	1:59	And on the eighth D they came to circumcise
	1:78	our God, when the D shall dawn upon us
	1:80	the wilderness till the D of his manifestation to
	2:11	you is born this D in the city of
	2:37	worshiping with fasting and prayer night and D
	2:44	company they went a D's journey, and they sought
	4:16	synagogue, as his custom was, on the sabbath D
	4:42	And when it was D he departed and went
	6:13	And when it was D, he called his disciples,
	6:23	Rejoice in that D, and leap for joy, for
	8:22	One D he got into a boat with his
	9:12	Now the D began to wear away; and the
	9:22	and on the third D be raised."
	9:37	On the next D, when they had come down
	10:12	more tolerable on that D for Sodom than for
	10:35	And the next D he took out two denarii
	11:3	Give us each D our daily bread;
	12:46	will come on a D when he does not
	13:14	and be healed, and not on the sabbath D
	13:16	be loosed from this bond on the sabbath D
	13:32	tomorrow, and the third D I finish my course.
	13:33	and tomorrow and the D following; for it cannot

	14:5	not immediately pull him out on a sabbath D
	16:19	and fine linen and who feasted sumptuously every D
	17:4	seven times in the D, and turns to you
	17:24	will the Son of man be in his D
	17:27	in marriage, until the D when Noah entered the
	17:29	built, but on the D when Lot went out
	17:30	it be on the D when the Son of
	17:31	On that D, let him who is on the
	18:7	who cry to him D and night?
	18:33	and on the third D he will rise."
	20:1	One D, as he was teaching the people in
	21:34	this life, and that D come upon you suddenly
	21:37	And every D he was teaching in the temple,
	22:7	Then came the D of Unleavened Bread, on which
	22:34	will not crow this D, until you three times
	22:51	I was with you D after day in the
	22:51	with you day after D in the temple, you
	22:64	When D came, the assembly of the elders of
	23:12	each other that very D, for before this they
	23:53	It was the D of Preparation, and the sabbath
	24:1	But on the first D of the week, at
	24:7	and on the third D rise."
	24:13	That very D two of them were going to
	24:21	is now the third D since this happened.
	24:29	toward evening and the D is now far spent."
	24:46	and on the third D rise from the dead,
Jn	1:29	The next D he saw Jesus coming toward him,
	1:35	The next D again John was standing with two
	1:39	stayed with him that D, for it was about
	1:43	The next D Jesus decided to go to Galilee.
	2:1	On the third D there was a marriage at
	5:8	Now that D was the sabbath.
	6:22	On the next D the people who remained on
	6:39	me, but raise it up at the last D
	6:40	I will raise him up at the last D
	6:44	I will raise him up at the last D
	6:54	I will raise him up at the last D
	7:37	On the last D of the feast, the great
	7:37	the feast, the great D, Jesus stood up and
	8:56	was to see my D; he saw it and
	9:4	me, while it is D; night comes, when no
	9:14	it was a sabbath D when Jesus made the
	11:9	answered, "Are there not twelve hours in the D
	11:9	one walks in the D, he does not stumble,
	11:24	rise again in the resurrection at the last D
	11:53	So from that D on they took counsel how
	12:7	keep it for the D of my burial.
	12:12	The next D a great crowd who had come
	12:48	spoken will be his judge on the last D
	14:20	In that D you will know that I am
	16:23	In that D you will ask nothing of me.
	16:26	In that D you will ask in my name;
	19:14	Now it was the D of Preparation of the
	19:31	Since it was the D of Preparation, in order
	19:31	sabbath was a high D, the Jews asked Pilate
	19:42	because of the Jewish D of Preparation, as the
	20:1	Now on the first D of the week Mary
	20:19	the evening of that D, the first day of
	20:19	that day, the first D of the week, the
	21:4	Just as D was breaking, Jesus stood on the
Acts	1:2	and teach, until the D when he was taken
	1:12	near Jerusalem, a sabbath D's journey away;
	1:22	of John until the D when he was taken
	2:1	When the D of Pentecost had come, they were
	2:15	third hour of the D;
	2:20	into blood, before the D of the Lord comes,
	2:20	of the Lord comes, the great and manifest D
	2:29	and his tomb is with us to this D
	2:41	there were added that D about three thousand souls.
	2:46	And D by day, attending the temple together and
	2:46	And day by D, attending the temple together and
	2:47	added to their number D by day those who
	2:47	their number day by D those who were being
	5:42	And every D in the temple and at home
	7:8	him on the eighth D; and Isaac became the
	7:26	And on the following D he appeared to them
	8:1	And on that D a great persecution arose against
	9:24	were watching the gates D and night, to kill
	10:3	ninth hour of the D he saw clearly in
	10:9	The next D, as they were on their journey
	10:23	The next D he rose and went off with
	10:24	And on the following D they entered Caesarea.
	10:40	him on the third D and made him manifest;
	12:18	Now when D came, there was no small stir
	12:21	On an appointed D Herod put on his royal
	13:14	And on the sabbath D they went into the
	14:20	and on the next D he went on with
	16:11	Samothrace, and the following D to Ne-apolis,
	16:13	and on the sabbath D we went outside the
	16:35	But when it was D, the magistrates sent the
	17:17	the market place every D with those who chanced
	17:31	he has fixed a D on which he will
	20:7	On the first D of the week, when we
	20:15	we came the following D opposite Chios; the next
	20:15	opposite Chios; the next D we touched at Samos;
	20:15	at Samos; and the D after that we came
	20:16	if possible, on the D of Pentecost.
	20:18	time from the first D that I set foot
	20:26	testify to you this D that I am innocent
	20:31	not cease night or D to admonish every one
	21:1	Cos, and the next D to Rhodes, and from
	21:7	the brethren and stayed with them for one D
	21:18	On the following D Paul went in with us
	21:26	men, and the next D he purified himself with
	22:3	zealous for God as you all are this D
	23:1	God in all good conscience up to this D
	23:12	When it was D, the Jews made a plot
	24:20	dead I am on trial before you this D
	25:6	Caesarea; and the next D he took his seat
	25:17	but on the next D took my seat on
	26:7	to attain, as they earnestly worship night and D
	26:22	To this D I have had the help that
	26:29	who hear me this D might become such as
	27:3	The next D we put in at Sidon; and
	27:18	storm-tossed, they began next D to throw the cargo
	27:19	overboard; and the third D they cast out with
	27:20	appeared for many a D, and no small tempest
	27:29	stern, and prayed for D to come.
	27:33	As D was about to dawn, Paul urged them
	27:33	"Today is the fourteenth D that you have continued
	27:39	Now when it was D, they did not recognize
	28:13	Rhegium; and after one D a south wind sprang
	28:13	and on the second D we came to Puteoli.
	28:23	they had appointed a D for him, they came
Rom	2:5	for yourself on the D of wrath when God's
	2:16	excuse them on that D when, according to my
	8:36	being killed all the D long; we are regarded
	10:21	Israel he says, "All D long I have held
	11:8	that should not hear, down to this very D
	13:12	is far gone, the D is at hand.
	13:13	becomingly as in the D, not in reveling and
	14:5	One man esteems one D as better than another,
	14:6	He who observes the D, observes it in honor
1Cor	1:8	end, guiltless in the D of our Lord Jesus
	3:13	become manifest; for the D will disclose it, because
	5:5	be saved in the D of the Lord Jesus.
	10:8	did, and twenty-three thousand fell in a single D
	15:4	raised on the third D in accordance with the
	15:31	in Christ Jesus our Lord, I die every D
	16:2	On the first D of every week, each of
2Cor	1:14	of you, on the D of the Lord Jesus.
	3:14	hardened; for to this D, when they read the
	3:15	Yes, to this D whenever Moses is read a
	4:16	away, our inner nature is being renewed every D
	6:2	helped you on the D of salvation." Behold, now
	6:2	behold, now is the D of salvation.
	11:25	a night and a D I have been adrift
Eph	4:30	were sealed for the D of redemption.
	6:13	withstand in the evil D, and having done all,
Phil	1:5	gospel from the first D until now.
	1:6	to completion at the D of Jesus Christ.
	1:10	and blameless for the D of Christ,
	2:16	so that in the D of Christ I may
	3:5	circumcised on the eighth D, of the people of
Col	1:6	yourselves, from the D you heard and understood
	1:9	And so, from the D we heard of it,
1Thes	2:9	we worked night and D, that we might not
	3:10	praying earnestly night and D that we may see
	5:2	know well that the D of the Lord will
	5:4	darkness, brethren, for that D to surprise you like
	5:5	and sons of the D; we are not of
	5:8	we belong to the D, let us be sober,
2Thes	1:10	he comes on that D to be glorified in
	2:2	the effect that the D of the Lord has
	2:3	any way; for that D will not come, unless
	3:8	we worked night and D, that we might not
1Tim	5:5	and prayers night and D;
2Tim	1:4	I long night and D to see you, that
	1:12	to guard until that D what has been entrusted
	1:18	the Lord on that D –and you well know
	4:8	to me on that D, and not only to
Heb	3:8	the rebellion, on the D of testing in the

3:13 exhort one another every D, as long as it
4:4 spoken of the seventh D in this way, "And
4:4 rested on the seventh D from all his works."
4:7 he sets a certain D, "Today," saying through David
4:8 rest, God would not speak later of another D
8:9 their fathers on the D when I took them
10:25 as you see the D drawing near.
Jas 5:5 your hearts in a D of slaughter.
1Pet 2:12 glorify God on the D of visitation.
2Pet 1:19 dark place, until the D dawns and the morning
2:8 in his righteous soul D after day with their
2:8 righteous soul day after D with their lawless deeds),
2:9 under punishment until the D of judgment,
3:7 being kept until the D of judgment and destruction
3:8 with the Lord one D is as a thousand
3:8 thousand years, and a thousand years as one D
3:10 But the D of the Lord will come like
3:12 the coming of the D of God, because of
3:18 now and to the D of eternity.
1 Jn 4:17 have confidence for the D of judgment, because as
Jude 1:6 judgment of the great D;
Rev 1:10 Spirit on the Lord's D, and I heard behind
4:8 round and within, and D and night they never
6:17 Lamb; for the great D of their wrath has
7:15 God, and serve him D and night within his
8:12 a third of the D was kept from shining,
9:15 for the hour, the D, the month, and the
12:10 down, who accuses them D and night before our
14:11 they have no rest, D or night, these worshipers
16:14 battle on the great D of God the Almighty.
18:8 come in a single D, pestilence and mourning and
20:10 they will be tormented D and night for ever
21:25 never be shut by D--and there shall be

DAYBREAK (4)

2Sam 17:22 crossed the Jordan; by D not one was left
1Mac 4:6 At D Judas appeared in the plain with three
Acts 5:21 entered the temple at D and taught.
20:11 a long while, until D, and so departed.

DAYLIGHT (2)

Sir 33:7 another, when all the D in the year is
Amos 8:9 at noon, and darken the earth in broad D

DAYS (951)

Gen 1:14 for seasons and for D and years,
3:14 shall eat all the D of your life.
3:17 of it all the D of your life;
5:4 The D of Adam after he became the father
5:5 Thus all the D that Adam lived were nine
5:8 Thus all the D of Seth were nine hundred
5:11 Thus all the D of Enosh were nine hundred
5:14 Thus all the D of Kenan were nine hundred
5:17 Thus all the D of Mahalalel were eight hundred
5:20 Thus all the D of Jared were nine hundred
5:23 Thus all the D of Enoch were three hundred
5:27 Thus all the D of Methuselah were nine hundred
5:31 Thus all the D of Lamech were seven hundred
6:3 is flesh, but his D shall be a hundred
6:4 the earth in those D, and also afterward, when
7:4 For in seven D I will send rain upon
7:4 upon the earth forty D and forty nights; and
7:10 And after seven D the waters of the flood
7:12 upon the earth forty D and forty nights.
7:17 The flood continued forty D upon the earth; and
7:24 prevailed upon the earth a hundred and fifty D
8:3 a hundred and fifty D the waters had abated;
8:6 the end of forty D Noah opened the window
8:10 He waited another seven D, and again he sent
8:12 he waited another seven D, and sent forth the
9:29 All the D of Noah were nine hundred and
10:25 Peleg, for in his D the earth was divided,
11:32 The D of Terah were two hundred and five
14:1 In the D of Amraphel king of Shinar, Arioch
17:12 He that is eight D old among you shall
21:4 when he was eight D old, as God had
21:34 And Abraham sojourned many D in the land of
24:55 while, at least ten D; after that she may
25:7 These are the D of the years of Abraham's
25:24 When her D to be delivered were fulfilled, behold,
26:1 that was in the D of Abraham.
26:15 had dug in the D of Abraham his father.)
26:18 been dug in the D of Abraham his father;
27:41 said to himself, "The D of mourning for my
29:20 him but a few D because of the love
30:14 In the D of wheat harvest Reuben went and
30:36 a distance of three D journey between himself and
31:23 pursued him for seven D and followed close after
35:28 Now the D of Isaac were a hundred and
35:29 old and full of D; and his sons Esau
37:34 his loins, and mourned for his son many D
40:12 three branches are three D;
40:13 three days; within three D Pharaoh will lift up
40:18 three baskets are three D;
40:19 three days; within three D Pharaoh will lift up
42:17 put them all together in prison for three D
47:8 "How many are the D of the years of
47:9 said to Pharaoh, "The D of the years of
47:9 evil have been the D of the years of
47:9 not attained to the D of the years of
47:9 my fathers in the D of their sojourning."
47:28 seventeen years; so the D of Jacob, the years
49:1 shall befall you in D to come.
50:3 physicians embalmed Israel; forty D were required
50:3 And the Egyptians wept for him seventy D
50:4 And when the D of weeping for him were
50:10 he made a mourning for his father seven D
Ex 2:23 course of those many D the king of Egypt
3:18 us go a three D journey into the wilderness,
5:3 we pray, a three D journey into the wilderness,
7:25 Seven D passed after the LORD had struck the
8:27 We must go three D journey into the wilderness
10:22 land of Egypt three D;
10:23 his place for three D; but all the people
12:15 Seven D you shall eat unleavened bread; on the
12:16 be done on those D; but what every one
12:19 For seven D no leaven shall be found in
13:6 Seven D you shall eat unleavened bread, and on
13:7 be eaten for seven D; no leavened bread shall
15:22 Shur; they went three D in the wilderness and
16:26 Six D you shall gather it; but on the
16:29 you bread for two D; remain every man of
20:9 Six D you shall labor, and do all your
20:11 gates; for in six D the LORD made heaven
20:12 your mother, that your D may be long in
22:30 with your sheep: seven D it shall be with
23:12 "Six D you shall do your work, but on
23:15 unleavened bread for seven D at the appointed time
23:26 land; I will fulfil the number of your D
24:16 cloud covered it six D; and on the seventh
24:18 on the mountain forty D and forty nights.
29:30 shall wear them seven D, when he comes into
29:35 commanded you; through seven D shall you ordain
29:37 Seven D you shall make atonement for the altar,
31:15 Six D shall work be done, but the seventh
31:17 Israel that in six D the LORD made heaven
34:18 Seven D you shall eat unleavened bread, as I
34:21 "Six D you shall work, but on the seventh
34:28 with the LORD forty D and forty nights; he
35:2 Six D shall work be done, but on the
Lev 8:33 of meeting for seven D, until the days of
8:33 seven days, until the D of your ordination are
8:33 it will take seven D to ordain you.
8:35 and night for seven D, performing what the LORD
12:2 shall be unclean seven D; as at the time
12:4 shall continue for thirty-three D in the blood of
12:4 the sanctuary, until the D of her purifying are
12:5 in the blood of her purifying for sixty-six D
12:6 "And when the D of her purifying are completed,
13:4 diseased person for seven D;
13:5 shut him up seven D more;
13:21 shut him up seven D;
13:26 shut him up seven D,
13:31 itching disease for seven D,
13:33 itching disease for seven D more;
13:50 the disease for seven D;
13:54 shut it up seven D more;
14:8 camp, but shall dwell outside his tent seven D
14:38 the house, and shut up the house seven D
15:13 count for himself seven D for his cleansing, and
15:19 her impurity for seven D, and whoever touches her
15:24 shall be unclean seven D; and every bed on
15:25 of blood for many D, not at the time
15:25 her impurity, all the D of the discharge she
15:25 uncleanness; as in the D of her impurity, she
15:26 she lies, all the D of her discharge, shall
15:28 count for herself seven D, and after that she
22:27 it shall remain seven D with its mother; and
23:3 Six D shall work be done; but on the
23:6 to the LORD; seven D you shall eat unleavened
23:8 to the LORD seven D; on the seventh day
23:16 they be, counting fifty D to the morrow after

D

23:34 month and for seven D is the feast of
23:36 Seven D you shall present offerings by fire to
23:39 of the LORD seven D; on the first day
23:40 shall rejoice before the LORD your God seven D
23:41 to the LORD seven D in the year; it
23:42 in booths for seven D; all that are native
Num 6:4 All the D of his separation he shall eat
6:5 "All the D of his vow of separation no
6:6 "All the D that he separates himself to the
6:8 All the D of his separation he is holy
6:12 the LORD for the D of his separation, and
9:19 over the tabernacle many D, the people of Israel
9:20 cloud was a few D over the tabernacle, and
9:22 Whether it was two D, or a month, or
10:33 of the LORD three D journey; and the ark
10:33 went before them three D journey, to seek out
11:19 one day, or two D, or five days, or
11:19 two days, or five D, or ten days, or
11:19 five days, or ten D, or twenty days,
11:19 ten days, or twenty D,
12:14 her face, should she not be shamed seven D
12:14 outside the camp seven D, and after that she
12:15 outside the camp seven D; and the people did
13:25 the end of forty D they returned from spying
14:34 the number of the D in which you spied
14:34 out the land, forty D, for every day a
19:11 shall be unclean seven D;
19:14 is in the tent, shall be unclean seven D
19:16 man, or a grave, shall be unclean seven D
20:29 the house of Israel wept for Aaron thirty D
24:14 will do to your people in the latter D
28:17 is a feast; seven D shall unleavened bread be
28:24 offer daily, for seven D, the food of an
29:12 to the LORD seven D;
31:19 outside the camp seven D; whoever of you has
33:8 they went a three D journey in the wilderness
Deut 1:2 It is eleven D journey from Horeb by the
1:46 remained at Kadesh many D, the days that you
1:46 Kadesh many days, the D that you remained there.
2:1 me; and for many D we went about Mount
4:9 your heart all the D of your life; make
4:10 fear me all the D that they live upon
4:30 you in the latter D, you will return to
4:32 ask now of the D that are past, which
4:40 you may prolong your D in the land which
5:13 Six D you shall labor, and do all your
5:16 commanded you; that your D may be prolonged, and
6:2 command you, all the D of your life; and
6:2 life; and that your D may be prolonged.
9:9 on the mountain forty D and forty nights; I
9:11 the end of forty D and forty nights the
9:18 LORD as before, forty D and forty nights; I
9:25 LORD for these forty D and forty nights, because
10:10 the first time, forty D and forty nights, and
11:21 your gates, that your D and the days of
11:21 your days and the D of your children may
12:1 to possess, all the D that you live upon
16:3 bread with it; seven D you shall eat it
16:3 flight--that all the D of your life you
16:4 your territory for seven D; nor shall any of
16:8 For six D you shall eat unleavened bread; and
16:13 feast of booths seven D, when you make your
16:15 For seven D you shall keep the feast to
17:9 in office in those D, you shall consult them,
17:19 in it all the D of his life, that
19:17 in office in those D;
22:19 he may not put her away all his D
22:29 he may not put her away all his D
23:6 their prosperity all your D for ever.
25:15 shall have; that your D may be prolonged in
30:20 you and length of D, that you may dwell
31:14 to Moses, "Behold, the D approach when you must
31:29 you; and in the D to come evil will
32:7 Remember the D of old, consider the years of
33:25 bronze; and as your D, so shall your strength
34:8 plains of Moab thirty D; then the days of
34:8 thirty days; then the D of weeping and mourning
Josh 1:5 before you all the D of your life; as
1:11 provisions; for within three D you are to pass
2:16 hide yourselves there three D, until the pursuers have
2:22 remained there three D, until the pursuers returned;
3:2 the end of three D the officers went through
4:14 of Moses, all the D of his life.
6:3 Thus shall you do for six D
6:14 So they did for six D
9:16 the end of three D after they had made
22:3 your brethren these many D, down to this day,
24:31 the LORD all the D of Joshua, and all
24:31 Joshua, and all the D of the elders who
Judg 2:7 the LORD all the D of Joshua, and all
2:7 Joshua, and all the D of the elders who
2:18 their enemies all the D of the judge; for
5:6 "In the D of Shamgar, son of Anath, in
5:6 of Anath, in the D of Jael, caravans ceased
8:28 forty years in the D of Gideon.
11:40 Jephthah the Gileadite four D in the year.
14:12 is, within the seven D of the feast, and
14:14 could not in three D tell what the riddle
14:17 before him the seven D that their feast lasted;
15:20 judged Israel in the D of the Philistines twenty
17:6 In those D there was no king in Israel;
18:1 In those D there was no king in Israel.
18:1 And in those D the tribe of the Danites
19:1 In those D, when there was no king in
19:4 remained with him three D; so they ate and
20:27 was there in those D,
20:28 before it in those D, saying, "Shall we yet
21:25 In those D there was no king in Israel;
Ruth 1:1 In the D when the judges ruled
1Sam 1:11 the LORD all the D of his life, and
2:31 Behold, the D are coming, when I will cut
3:1 was rare in those D; there was no frequent
7:13 the Philistines all the D of Samuel.
7:15 judged Israel all the D of his life.
9:20 that were lost three D ago, do not set
10:8 Seven D you shall wait, until I come to
11:3 him, "Give us seven D respite that we may
13:8 He waited seven D, the time appointed by Samuel;
13:11 not come within the D appointed, and that the
14:52 the Philistines all the D of Saul; and when
17:12 In the D of Saul the man was already
17:16 For forty D the Philistine came forward and took
25:38 And about ten D later the LORD smote Nabal;
27:7 the number of the D that David dwelt in
28:1 In those D the Philistines gathered their forces for
29:3 with me now for D and years, and since
30:12 drunk water for three D and three nights.
30:13 I fell sick three D ago.
31:13 the tamarisk tree in Jabesh, and fasted seven D
2Sam 1:1 Amalekites, David remained two D in Ziklag;
7:12 When your D are fulfilled and you lie down
14:2 has been mourning many D for the dead;
16:23 Now in those D the counsel which Ahithophel gave
20:4 to me within three D, and be here yourself."
21:1 a famine in the D of David for three
21:9 death in the first D of harvest, at the
24:8 at the end of nine months and twenty D
24:13 shall there be three D pestilence in your land?
1Kgs 2:38 So Shimei dwelt in Jerusalem many D
3:13 other king shall compare with you, all your D
3:14 father David walked, then I will lengthen your D
4:21 served Solomon all the D of his life.
4:25 fig tree, all the D of Solomon.
8:40 fear thee all the D that they live in
8:65 of Egypt, before the LORD our God, seven D
10:21 as anything in the D of Solomon.
11:12 do it in your D, but I will tear
11:25 of Israel all the D of Solomon, doing mischief
11:34 him ruler all the D of his life, for
12:5 them, "Depart for three D, then come again to
15:5 commanded him all the D of his life, except
15:6 and Jeroboam all the D of his life.
15:14 was wholly true to the LORD all his D
15:16 Asa and Baasha king of Israel all their D
15:32 Asa and Baasha king of Israel all their D
16:15 Judah, Zimri reigned seven D in Tirzah.
16:34 In his D Hiel of Bethel built Jericho; he
17:15 and he, and her household ate for many D
18:1 After many D the word of the LORD came
19:8 of that food forty D and forty nights to
20:29 And they encamped opposite one another seven D
21:29 the evil in his D; but in his son's
21:29 but in his son's D I will bring the
22:46 who remained in the D of his father Asa,
2Kgs 2:17 men; and for three D they sought him but
3:9 circuitous march of seven D, there was no water
8:20 In his D Edom revolted from the rule of
10:32 In those D the LORD began to cut off
12:2 the LORD all his D, because Jehoiada the priest
13:22 oppressed Israel all the D of Jehoahaz.
15:18 not depart all his D from all the sins
15:29 In the D of Pekah king of Israel Tiglath-pileser

15:37 In those D the LORD began to send Rezin
18:4 made, for until those D the people of Israel
19:25 I planned from D of old what now I
20:1 In those D Hezekiah became sick and was at
20:17 the LORD: Behold, the D are coming, when all
20:19 there will be peace and security in my D
23:22 been kept since the D of the judges who
23:22 or during all the D of the kings of
23:29 In his D Pharaoh Neco king of Egypt went
24:1 In his D Nebuchadnezzar king of Babylon came up,
1Chr 1:19 Peleg (for in his D the earth was divided),
4:41 name, came in the D of Hezekiah, king of
5:10 And in the D of Saul they made war
5:17 by genealogies in the D of Jotham king of
5:17 Judah, and in the D of Jeroboam king of
7:2 their number in the D of David being twenty-two
7:22 their father mourned many D, and his brothers came
9:25 come in every seven D, from time to time,
10:12 under the oak in Jabesh, and fasted seven D
12:39 with David for three D, eating and drinking, for
13:3 neglected it in the D of Saul."
17:11 When your D are fulfilled to go to be
21:12 you; or else three D of the sword of
22:9 give peace and quiet to Israel in his D
23:1 old and full of D, he made Solomon his
23:31 new moons, and feast D, according to the number
29:15 our fathers were; our D on the earth are
29:28 old age, full of D, riches, and honor; and
2Chr 6:31 thy ways all the D that they live in
7:8 the feast for seven D, and all Israel with
7:9 of the altar seven D and the feast seven
7:9 the altar seven days and the feast seven D
9:20 as anything in the D of Solomon.
10:5 to them, "Come to me again in three D
13:20 his power in the D of Abijah; and the
14:1 In his D the land had rest for ten
15:17 the heart of Asa was blameless all his D
20:25 They were three D in taking the spoil, it
21:8 In his D Edom revolted from the rule of
24:2 the LORD all the D of Jehoiada the priest.
24:14 LORD continually all the D of Jehoiada.
24:15 old and full of D, and died; he was
26:5 seek God in the D of Zechariah, who instructed
29:17 LORD; then for eight D they sanctified the house
30:21 of unleavened bread seven D with great gladness;
30:22 the festival for seven D, sacrificing peace offerings
30:23 feast for another seven D; so they kept it
30:23 it for another seven D with gladness.
32:24 In those D Hezekiah became sick and was at
32:26 upon them in the D of Hezekiah.
34:33 All his D they did not turn away from
35:17 time, and the feast of unleavened bread seven D
35:18 in Israel since the D of Samuel the prophet;
36:9 three months and ten D in Jerusalem.
36:21 All the D that it lay desolate it kept
Ezra 4:2 him ever since the D of Esarhaddon king of
4:5 their purpose, all the D of Cyrus king of
4:7 And in the D of Artaxerxes, Bishlam and Mithredath
6:22 of unleavened bread seven D with joy; for the
8:15 runs to Ahava, and there we encamped three D
8:32 came to Jerusalem, and there we remained three D
9:7 From the D of our fathers to this day
10:8 not come within three D, by order of the
10:9 Jerusalem within the three D; it was the ninth
Neh 1:4 wept, and mourned for D; and I continued fasting
2:11 I came to Jerusalem and was there three D
5:18 me, and every ten D skins of wine in
6:15 twenty-fifth day of the month Elul, in fifty-two D
6:17 Moreover in those D the nobles of Judah sent
8:17 booths; for from the D of Jeshua the son
8:18 kept the feast seven D; and on the eighth
12:7 their brethren in the D of Jeshua.
12:12 And in the D of Joiakim were priests, heads
12:22 the Levites, in the D of Eliashib, Joiada, Johanan,
12:23 the Chronicles until the D of Johanan the son
12:26 These were in the D of Joiakim the son
12:26 Jozadak, and in the D of Nehemiah the governor
12:46 For in the D of David and Asaph of
12:47 all Israel in the D of Zerubbabel and in
12:47 Zerubbabel and in the D of Nehemiah gave the
13:15 In those D I saw in Judah men treading
13:23 In those D also I saw the Jews who
Tob 1:2 Naphtali, who in the D of Shalmaneser, king of
1:3 and righteousness all the D of my life, and
1:16 In the D of Shalmaneser I performed many acts
1:21 But not fifty D passed before two of Sennacherib's
4:3 Honor her all the D of your life; do
4:5 our God all your D, my son, and refuse
4:5 Live uprightly all the D of your life, and
8:19 a wedding feast for them which lasted fourteen D
8:20 And before the D of the feast were over,
8:20 leave until the fourteen D of the wedding feast
9:4 father is counting the D, and if I delay
10:1 day, and when the D for the journey had
10:7 Tobias, until the fourteen D of the wedding feast
11:19 was celebrated for seven D with great festivity.
12:19 All these D I merely appeared to you and
Jud 1:1 of Nineveh, in the D of Arphaxad, who ruled
1:5 it was in those D that King Nebuchadnezzar made
1:16 rested and feasted for one hundred and twenty D
2:21 They marched for three D from Nineveh to the
4:13 the people fasted many D throughout Judea and in
6:15 city, who in those D were Uzziah the son
7:20 surrounded them for thirty-four D, until all the
7:31 out for five more D; by that time the
7:32 But if these D pass by, and no help
8:6 She fasted all the D of her widowhood, except
8:6 and the feasts and D of rejoicing of the
8:9 the Assyrians after five D,
8:11 Lord turns and helps us within so many D
8:15 us within these five D, he has power to
8:18 nor in these present D, has there been any
8:18 as was done in D gone by--
8:33 maid; and within the D after which you have
10:2 and on her feast D;
12:7 the camp for three D, and went out each
12:18 than in all the D since I was born."
14:8 tell me what you have done during these D
15:11 all the people plundered the camp for thirty D
16:22 a widow all the D of her life after
16:24 the house of Israel mourned for her seven D
16:25 of Israel in the D of Judith, or for
Esth 1:1 In the D of Ahasuerus, the Ahasuerus
1:2 provinces, in those D when King Ahasuerus sat
1:4 his majesty for many D, a hundred and eighty
1:4 majesty for many days, a hundred and eighty D
1:5 And when these D were completed, the king gave
1:5 banquet lasting for seven D, in the court of
2:21 And in those D, as Mordecai was sitting at
4:8 "Remembering the D of your lowliness, when you
4:11 to come in to the king these thirty D
4:16 nor drink for three D, night or day.
9:22 by year, as the D on which the Jews
9:22 they should make them D of feasting and gladness,
9:22 feasting and gladness, D for sending choice portions
9:26 Therefore they called these D Purim, after the term
9:27 would keep these two D according to what was
9:28 every year, that these D should be remembered and
9:28 city, and that these D of Purim should never
9:28 commemoration of these D cease among their
9:31 and truth, that these D of Purim should be
10:13 they will observe these D in the month of
14:16 my head on the D when I appear in
14:16 wear it on the D when I am at
Job 1:5 And when the D of the feast had run
2:13 on the ground seven D and seven nights, and
3:6 not rejoice among the D of the year, let
7:1 and are not his D like the days of
7:1 his days like the D of a hireling?
7:6 My D are swifter than a weaver's shuttle, and
7:16 me alone, for my D are a breath.
8:7 was small, your latter D will be very great.
8:9 know nothing, for our D on earth are a
9:25 "My D are swifter than a runner; they flee
10:5 Are thy D as the days of man, or
10:5 thy days as the D of man, or thy
10:20 Are not the D of my life few?
12:12 with the aged, and understanding in length of D
14:1 woman is of few D, and full of trouble.
14:5 Since his D are determined, and the number of
14:14 All the D of my service I would wait,
15:20 in pain all his D, through all the years
17:1 spirit is broken, my D are extinct, the grave
17:11 My D are past, my plans are broken off,
21:13 They spend their D in prosperity, and in peace
24:1 do those who know him never see his D
27:6 does not reproach me for any of my D
29:2 old, as in the D when God watched over
29:4 was in my autumn D, when the friendship of
29:18 I shall multiply my D as the sand,
30:16 poured out within me; D of affliction have taken
30:27 and is never still; D of affliction come to

D

D

32:7 I said, 'Let D speak, and many years teach
33:25 him return to the D of his youthful vigor';
36:11 him, they complete their D in prosperity, and their
38:12 the morning since your D began, and caused the
38:21 the number of your D is great!
42:12 LORD blessed the latter D of Job more than
42:17 Job died, an old man, and full of D
Ps 21:4 to him, length of D for ever and ever.
23:6 follow me all the D of my life; and
27:4 the LORD all the D of my life, to
34:12 life, and covets many D, that he may enjoy
37:18 The LORD knows the D of the blameless, and
37:19 evil times, in the D of famine they have
39:4 the measure of my D; let me know how
39:5 thou hast made my D a few handbreadths, and
44:1 didst perform in their D, in the days of
44:1 their days, in the D of old:
55:23 and treachery shall not live out half their D
72:7 In his D may righteousness flourish, and peace
77:5 I consider the D of old, I remember the
78:33 So he made their D vanish like a breath,
89:29 his throne as the D of the heavens.
89:45 hast cut short the D of his youth; thou
90:9 For all our D pass away under thy wrath,
90:12 us to number our D that we may get
90:14 we may rejoice and be glad all our D
90:15 us glad as many D as thou hast afflicted
94:13 give him respite from D of trouble, until a
102:3 For my D pass away like smoke, and my
102:11 My D are like an evening shadow; I wither
102:23 my strength in mid-course; he has shortened my D
102:24 the midst of my D, thou whose years endure
103:15 As for man, his D are like grass; he
109:8 May his D be few; may another seize his
128:5 of Jerusalem all the D of your life!
139:16 one of them, the D that were formed for
143:5 I remember the D of old, I meditate on
144:4 like a breath, his D are like a passing
Prov 3:2 commandments; for length of D and years of life
9:11 For by me your D will be multiplied, and
15:15 All the D of the afflicted are evil, but
28:16 he who hates unjust gain will prolong his D
31:12 not harm, all the D of her life.
Eccl 2:3 heaven during the few D of their life.
2:16 seeing that in the D to come all will
2:23 For all his D are full of pain, and
5:17 and spent all his D in darkness and grief,
5:18 the sun the few D of his life which
5:20 not much remember the D of his life because
6:3 years, so that the D of his years are
6:12 he lives the few D of his vain life,
7:10 "Why were the former D better than these?" For
8:13 will he prolong his D like a shadow, because
8:15 his toil through the D of life which God
9:9 you love, all the D of your vain life
11:1 waters, for you will find it after many D
11:8 him remember that the D of darkness will be
11:9 cheer you in the D of your youth; walk
12:1 your Creator in the D of your youth, before
12:1 youth, before the evil D come, and the years
Sir 1:2 of rain, and the D of eternity—who can
17:2 gave to men few D, a limited time, but
18:8 number of a man's D is great if he
18:24 of hunger; in the D of wealth think of
18:26 in everything, and in D of sin he guards
22:10 the dead lasts seven D, but for a fool
23:15 words will never become disciplined all his D
26:1 the number of his D will be doubled.
30:22 the rejoicing of a man is length of D
33:9 hallowed, and some of them he made ordinary D
33:23 when you end the D of your life, in
37:25 man is numbered by D, but the days of
37:25 by days, but the D of Israel are without
41:3 death; remember your former D and the end of
41:13 The D of a good life are numbered, but
43:7 the sign for feast D, a light that wanes
45:15 his descendants all the D of heaven, to minister
46:7 And in the D of Moses he did a
47:1 to prophesy in the D of David.
47:13 him; Solomon reigned in D of peace, and God
48:12 spirit; in all his D he did not tremble
48:18 In his D Sennacherib came up, and sent the
48:23 In his D the sun went backward, and he
49:3 the Lord; in the D of wicked men he
49:12 of Jozadak; in their D they built the house
50:3 In his D a cistern for water was quarried
50:8 like roses in the D of the first fruits,
50:22 things; who exalts our D from birth, and deals
50:23 may be in our D in Israel, as in
50:23 Israel, as in the D of old.
50:24 And let him deliver us in our D
51:10 forsake me in the D of affliction, at the
Is 1:1 and Jerusalem in the D of Uzziah, Jotham, Ahaz,
2:2 pass in the latter D that the mountain of
7:1 In the D of Ahaz the son of Jotham,
7:17 your father's house such D as have not come
13:22 at hand and its D will not be prolonged.
23:7 whose origin is from D of old, whose feet
23:15 seventy years, like the D of one king.
24:22 prison, and after many D they will be punished.
27:6 In D to come Jacob shall take root, Israel
30:26 the light of seven D, in the day when
37:26 I planned from D of old what now I
38:1 In those D Hezekiah became sick and was at
38:10 the noontide of my D I must depart; I
38:20 stringed instruments all the D of our life, at
39:6 of hosts: Behold, the D are coming, when all
39:8 "There will be peace and security in my D
51:9 LORD; awake, as in D of old, the generations
53:10 he shall prolong his D; the will of the
54:9 this is like the D of Noah to me:
60:20 everlasting light, and your D of mourning shall be
63:9 carried them all the D of old.
63:11 Then he remembered the D of old, of Moses
65:20 lives but a few D, or an old man
65:20 not fill out his D, for the child shall
65:22 eat; for like the D of a tree shall
65:22 a tree shall the D of my people be,
Jer 1:2 LORD came in the D of Josiah the son
1:3 came also in the D of Jehoiakim the son
2:32 people have forgotten me D without number.
3:6 to me in the D of King Josiah: "Have
3:16 the land, in those D, says the LORD, they
3:18 In those D the house of Judah shall join
5:18 "But even in those D, says the LORD, I
7:32 Therefore, behold, the D are coming, says the LORD,
9:25 "Behold, the D are coming, says the LORD, when
13:6 And after many D the LORD said to me,
16:9 eyes and in your D, the voice of mirth
16:14 favor.' "Therefore, behold, the D are coming, says the
17:11 the midst of his D they will leave him,
19:6 my mind; therefore, behold, D are coming, says the
20:18 sorrow, and spend my D in shame?
22:30 not succeed in his D; for none of his
23:5 "Behold, the D are coming, says the LORD, when
23:6 In his D Judah will be saved, and Israel
23:7 righteousness.' "Therefore, behold, the D are coming,
23:20 In the latter D you will understand it clearly.
25:34 the flock, for the D of your slaughter and
26:18 Moresheth prophesied in the D of Hezekiah king of
30:3 For behold, D are coming, says the LORD, when
30:24 In the latter D you will understand this.
31:27 "Behold, the D are coming, says the LORD, when
31:29 In those D they shall no longer say: 'The
31:31 "Behold, the D are coming, says the LORD, when
31:33 of Israel after those D, says the LORD: I
31:38 "Behold, the D are coming, says the LORD, when
33:14 "Behold, the D are coming, says the LORD, when
33:15 In those D and at that time I will
33:16 In those D Judah will be saved and Jerusalem
35:1 the LORD in the D of Jehoiakim the son
35:7 in tents all your D, that you may live
35:7 you may live many D in the land where
35:8 no wine all our D, ourselves, our wives, our
36:2 to you, from the D of Josiah until today.
37:16 and remained there many D,
42:7 the end of ten D the word of the
46:26 inhabited as in the D of old, says the
48:12 behold, the D are coming, says the LORD,
48:47 Moab in the latter D, says the LORD." Thus
49:2 Therefore, behold, the D are coming, says the LORD,
49:39 "But in the latter D I will restore the
50:4 "In those D and in that time, says the
50:20 In those D and in that time, says the
51:47 "Therefore, behold, the D are coming when I will
51:52 house.' "Therefore, behold, the D are coming, says
Lam 1:7 Jerusalem remembers in the D of her affliction and
1:7 that were hers from D of old.
4:18 end drew near; our D were numbered; for our
5:21 Renew our D as of old!
Bar 1:11 his son, that their D on earth may be
1:11 may be like the D of heaven.

DAYS

1:12 shall serve them many D and find favor in
1:14 the Lord on the D of the feasts and
3:14 there is length of D, and life, where there
4:20 I will cry to the Everlasting all my D
4:35 the Everlasting for many D, and for a long
Ezek 3:15 And I sat there overwhelmed among them seven D
3:16 the end of seven D, the word of the
4:4 the number of the D that you lie upon
4:5 you a number of D, three hundred and ninety
4:5 three hundred and ninety D, equal to the number
4:6 house of Judah; forty D I assign you, a
4:8 you have completed the D of your siege.
4:9 During the number of D that you lie upon
4:9 three hundred and ninety D, you shall eat it.
5:2 the city, when the D of the siege are
12:22 of Israel, saying, 'The D grow long, and every
12:23 say to them, The D are at hand, and
12:25 delayed, but in your D, O rebellious house, I
12:27 sees is for many D hence, and he prophesies
16:22 did not remember the D of your youth, when
16:43 have not remembered the D of your youth, but
16:60 with you in the D of your youth, and
22:14 be strong, in the D that I shall deal
23:8 had practiced since her D in Egypt; for in
23:19 her harlotry, remembering the D of her youth, when
38:8 After many D you will be mustered; in the
38:16 In the latter D I will bring you against
38:17 I spoke in former D by my servants the
38:17 Israel, who in those D prophesied for years that
43:25 For seven D you shall provide daily a goat
43:26 Seven D shall they make atonement for the altar
43:27 they have completed these D, then from the eighth
44:26 count for himself seven D, and then he shall
45:21 passover, and for seven D unleavened bread shall be
45:23 And on the seven D of the festival he
45:23 each of the seven D; and a he-goat daily
45:25 and for the seven D of the feast, he
46:1 on the six working D; but on the sabbath
Dan 1:12 your servants for ten D; let us be given
1:14 in this matter, and tested them for ten D
1:15 the end of ten D it was seen that
2:28 King Nebuchadnezzar what will be in the latter D
2:44 And in the D of those kings the God
3:70 the Lord, nights and D, sing praise to him
4:34 the end of the D I, Nebuchadnezzar, lifted my
5:11 In the D of your father light and understanding
5:26 God has numbered the D of your kingdom and
6:7 or man for thirty D, except to you, O
6:12 or man within thirty D except to you, O
7:9 that was ancient of D took his seat; his
7:13 to the Ancient of D and was presented before
7:22 until the Ancient of D came, and judgment was
8:26 it pertains to many D hence."
8:27 lay sick for some D; then I rose and
10:2 In those D I, Daniel, was mourning for three
10:13 Persia withstood me twenty-one D; but Michael, one
10:14 is to befall your people in the latter D
10:14 the vision is for D yet to come."
11:20 but within a few D he shall be broken,
11:33 and flame, by captivity and plunder, for some D
12:11 shall be a thousand two hundred and ninety D
12:12 to the thousand three hundred and thirty-five D
12:13 your allotted place at the end of the D
13:52 old relic of wicked D, your sins have now
14:31 lions' den, and he was there for six D
Hos 1:1 of Be-eri, in the D of Uzziah, Jotham, Ahaz,
1:1 Judah, and in the D of Jeroboam the son
2:13 her for the feast D of the Baals when
2:15 answer as in the D of her youth, as
3:3 as mine for many D; you shall not play
3:4 Israel shall dwell many D without king or prince,
3:5 LORD and to his goodness in the latter D
6:2 After two D he will revive us; on the
9:7 The D of punishment have come, the days of
9:7 punishment have come, the D of recompense have
9:9 themselves as in the D of Gibe-ah: he will
10:9 From the D of Gibe-ah, you have sinned, O
12:9 tents, as in the D of the appointed feast.
Joel 1:2 thing happened in your D, or in the days
1:2 days, or in the D of your fathers?
2:29 and maidservants in those D, I will pour out
3:1 "For behold, in those D and at that time,
Amos 1:1 concerning Israel in the D of Uzziah king of
1:1 Judah and in the D of Jeroboam the son
4:2 holiness that, behold, the D are coming upon you,
4:4 your tithes every three D;
8:11 "Behold, the D are coming," says the Lord GOD,
9:11 as in the D of old;
9:13 "Behold, the D are coming," says the LORD, "when
Jon 1:17 of the fish three D and three nights.
3:3 exceedingly great city, three D journey in breadth.
3:4 he cried, "Yet forty D, and Nineveh shall be
Mic 1:1 of Moresheth in the D of Jotham, Ahaz, and
4:1 pass in the latter D that the mountain of
5:2 whose origin is from of old, from ancient D
7:14 Gilead as in the D of old.
7:15 As in the D when you came out of
7:20 our fathers from the D of old.
Hab 1:5 a work in your D that you would not
Zeph 1:1 of Hezekiah, in the D of Josiah the son
Zech 8:6 this people in these D, should it also be
8:9 you who in these D have been hearing these
8:10 For before those D there was no wage for
8:11 as in the former D, says the LORD of
8:15 I purposed in these D to do good to
8:23 of hosts: In those D ten men from the
14:5 the earthquake in the D of Uzziah king of
Mal 3:4 LORD as in the D of old and as
3:7 From the D of your fathers you have turned
1Mac 1:11 In those D lawless men came forth from Israel,
2:1 In those D Mattathias the son of John, son
2:49 Now the D drew near for Mattathias to die,
3:29 the laws that had existed from the earliest D
3:49 who had completed their D;
4:56 the altar for eight D, and offered burnt offerings
4:59 at that season the D of dedication of the
4:59 and joy for eight D, beginning with the twenty-fifth
5:24 Jordan and went three D journey into the
6:9 lay there for many D, because deep grief continually
6:31 Bethzur, and for many D they fought and built
6:51 Then he encamped before the sanctuary for many D
6:52 war to match theirs, and fought for many D
7:50 land of Judah had rest for a few D
9:20 him; they mourned many D and said,
9:24 In those D a very great famine occurred, and
9:64 against it for many D and made machines of
10:34 new moons and appointed D, and the three days
10:34 days, and the three D before a feast and
10:34 let them all be D of immunity and release
10:47 them, and they remained his allies all his D
11:18 King Ptolemy died three D later, and his troops
11:20 In those D Jonathan assembled the men of Judea
11:40 had for him; and he stayed there many D
11:65 against it for many D and hemmed it in.
12:11 and on other appropriate D, at the sacrifices which
13:26 great lamentation, and mourned for him many D
13:43 In those D Simon encamped against Gazara and
14:4 had rest all the D of Simon.
14:4 as was the honor shown him, all his D
14:13 them, and the kings were crushed in those D
14:36 And in his D things prospered in his hands,
2Mac 2:12 Likewise Solomon also kept the eight D
2:16 Will you therefore please keep the D
5:2 forty D, there appeared golden-clad horsemen
5:14 the total of three D eighty thousand were destroyed,
10:6 celebrated it for eight D with rejoicing, in the
10:8 Jews should observe these D every year.
10:33 glad, and they besieged the fort for four D
12:15 overthrew Jericho in the D of Joshua, rushed
13:12 lying prostrate for three D without ceasing, Judas
15:2 all things has honored and hallowed above other D
Mt 2:1 of Judea in the D of Herod the king,
3:1 In those D came John the Baptist, preaching in
4:2 And he fasted forty D and forty nights, and
9:15 The D will come, when the bridegroom is taken
11:12 From the D of John the Baptist until now
12:40 as Jonah was three D and three nights in
12:40 of man be three D and three nights in
15:32 with me now three D, and have nothing to
17:1 And after six D Jesus took with him Peter
23:29 had lived in the D of our fathers, we
24:19 and for those who give suck in those D
24:22 And if those D had not been shortened, no
24:22 of the elect those D will be shortened.
24:29 the tribulation of those D the sun will be
24:37 As were the D of Noah, so will be
24:38 For as in those D before the flood they
26:2 know that after two D the Passover is coming,
26:61 of God, and to build it in three D
27:40 build it in three D, save yourself!
27:63 still alive, 'After three D I will rise again.'
Mk 1:9 In those D Jesus came from Nazareth of Galilee

1:13 in the wilderness forty D, tempted by Satan; and
2:1 to Caperna-um after some D, it was reported that
2:20 The D will come, when the bridegroom is taken
8:1 In those D, when again a great crowd had
8:2 with me now three D, and have nothing to
8:31 killed, and after three D rise again.
9:2 And after six D Jesus took with him Peter
9:31 is killed, after three D he will rise."
10:34 him; and after three D he will rise."
13:17 and for those who give suck in those D
13:19 For in those D there will be such tribulation
13:20 had not shortened the D, no human being would
13:20 the elect, whom he chose, he shortened the D
13:24 "But in those D, after that tribulation, the sun
14:1 It was now two D before the Passover and
14:58 hands, and in three D I will build another,
15:28 build it in three D,
Lk 1:5 In the D of Herod, king of Judea, there
1:24 After these D his wife Elizabeth conceived, and for
1:25 to me in the D when he looked on
1:39 In those D Mary arose and went with haste
1:75 before him all the D of our life.
2:1 In those D a decree went out from Caesar
2:21 the end of eight D, when he was circumcised,
2:46 After three D they found him in the temple,
4:2 the Spirit for forty D in the wilderness, tempted
4:2 ate nothing in those D; and when they were
4:25 in Israel in the D of Elijah, when the
5:17 On one of those D, as he was teaching,
5:35 The D will come, when the bridegroom is taken
5:35 them, and then they will fast in those D
6:12 In these D he went out to the mountain
9:28 Now about eight D after these sayings he took
9:36 no one in those D anything of what they
9:51 When the D drew near for him to be
13:14 people, "There are six D on which work ought
13:14 done; come on those D and be healed, and
15:13 Not many D later, the younger son gathered all
17:22 to the disciples, "The D are coming when you
17:22 see one of the D of the Son of
17:26 it was in the D of Noah, so will
17:26 it be in the D of the Son of
17:28 it was in the D of Lot--they ate,
19:43 For the D shall come upon you, when your
21:6 which you see, the D will come when there
21:22 it; for these are D of vengeance, to fulfil
21:23 and for those who give suck in those D
23:28 For behold, the D are coming when they will
24:18 the things that have happened there in these D
Jn 2:12 disciples; and there they stayed for a few D
2:19 temple, and in three D I will raise it
2:20 and will you raise it up in three D
4:40 stay with them; and he stayed there two D
4:43 After the two D he departed to Galilee.
11:6 ill, he stayed two D longer in the place
11:17 Lazarus had already been in the tomb four D
11:39 an odor, for he has been dead four D
12:1 Six D before the Passover, Jesus came to Bethany,
20:26 Eight D later, his disciples were again in the
Acts 1:3 to them during forty D, and speaking of the
1:5 water, but before many D you shall be baptized
1:15 In those D Peter stood up among the brethren
2:17 'And in the last D it shall be, God
2:18 my maidservants in those D I will pour out
3:24 those who came afterwards, also proclaimed these D
5:36 For before these D Theudas arose, giving himself out
5:37 Galilean arose in the D of the census and
6:1 Now in these D when the disciples were increasing
7:41 a calf in those D, and offered a sacrifice
7:45 it was until the D of David,
9:9 And for three D he was without sight, and
9:19 For several D he was with the disciples at
9:23 When many D had passed, the Jews plotted to
9:37 In those D she fell sick and died; and
9:43 in Joppa for many D with one Simon, a
10:30 And Cornelius said, "Four D ago, about this hour,
10:48 Then they asked him to remain for some D
11:27 Now in these D prophets came down from Jerusalem
11:28 took place in the D of Claudius.
12:3 This was during the D of Unleavened Bread.
13:31 dead; and for many D he appeared to those
13:41 a deed in your D, a deed you will
15:7 that in the early D God made choice among
15:35 And after some D Paul said to Barnabas, "Come,
16:12 in this city some D;
16:18 And this she did for many D
18:18 this Paul stayed many D longer, and then took
20:6 from Philippi after the D of Unleavened Bread, and
20:6 Bread, and in five D we came to them
20:6 them at Troas, where we stayed for seven D
21:4 out the disciples, we stayed there for seven D
21:5 And when our D there were ended, we departed
21:10 were staying for some D, a prophet named Agabus
21:15 After these D we made ready and went up
21:26 give notice when the D of purification would be
21:27 When the seven D were almost completed, the Jews
24:1 And after five D the high priest Ananias came
24:10 not more than twelve D since I went up
24:23 After some D Felix came with his wife Drusilla,
25:1 his province, after three D he went up to
25:6 than eight or ten D, he went down to
25:13 Now when some D had passed, Agrippa the king
25:14 they stayed there many D, Festus laid Paul's case
27:7 for a number of D, and arrived with difficulty
28:7 received us and entertained us hospitably for three D
28:12 in at Syracuse, we stayed there for three D
28:14 were invited to stay with them for seven D
28:17 After three D he called together the local leaders
Rom 14:5 another man esteems all D alike.
15:4 was written in former D was written for our
Gal 1:18 to visit Cephas, and remained with him fifteen D
4:10 You observe D, and months, and seasons, and years!
Eph 5:16 the time, because the D are evil.
2Tim 3:1 that in the last D there will come times
Tit 3:3 and pleasures, passing our D in malice and envy,
Heb 1:2 but in these last D he has spoken to
5:7 In the D of his flesh, Jesus offered up
7:3 has neither beginning of D nor end of life,
8:8 when he says: "The D will come, says the
8:10 of Israel after those D, says the Lord: I
10:16 with them after those D, says the Lord: I
10:32 But recall the former D when, after you were
11:30 down after they had been encircled for seven D
Jas 5:3 You have laid up treasure for the last D
1Pet 3:10 life and see good D, let him keep his
3:20 patience waited in the D of Noah, during the
2Pet 3:3 come in the last D with scoffing, following their
Rev 2:10 tested, and for ten D you will have tribulation.
2:13 faith even in the D of Antipas my witness,
9:6 And in those D men will seek death and
10:7 but that in the D of the trumpet call
11:3 two hundred and sixty D, clothed in sackcloth."
11:6 may fall during the D of their prophesying, and
11:9 For three D and a half men from the
11:11 three and a half D a breath of life
12:6 nourished for one thousand two hundred and sixty D

DAYTIME (4)

Tob 10:7 ate nothing in the D, and throughout the nights
Job 5:14 with darkness in the D, and grope at noonday
Ps 78:14 In the D he led them with a cloud,
2Pet 2:13 They count it pleasure to revel in the D

DAZED

Nah 3:11 drunken, you will be D; you will seek a

DAZZLING (2)

Lk 9:29 and his raiment became D white.
24:4 stood by them in D apparel;

DEACONESS

Rom 16:1 our sister Phoebe, a D of the church at

DEACONS (5)

Phil 1:1 with the bishops and D:
1Tim 3:8 D likewise must be serious, not double-tongued, not
3:10 they prove themselves blameless let them serve as D
3:12 Let D be the husband of one wife, and
3:13 who serve well as D gain a good standing

DEAD (354)

Gen 20:3 "Behold, you are a D man, because of the
23:3 up from before his D, and said to the
23:4 I may bury my D out of my sight."
23:6 Bury your D in the choicest of our sepulchres;
23:6 his sepulchre, or hinder you from burying your D
23:8 I should bury my D out of my sight,
23:11 people I give it to you; bury your D
23:13 I may bury my D there."
23:15 Bury your D
42:38 for his brother is D, and he only is
44:20 and his brother is D, and he alone is

	50:15	that their father was D, they said, "It may
Ex	4:19	the men who were seeking your life are D
	9:7	one of the cattle of the Israelites was D
	12:30	was not a house where one was not D
	12:33	said, "We are all D men."
	14:30	Israel saw the Egyptians D upon the seashore.
	21:34	its owner, and the D beast shall be his.
	21:35	of it; and the D beast also they shall
	21:36	for ox, and the D beast shall be his.
Lev	11:31	them when they are D shall be unclean until
	11:32	falls when they are D shall be unclean, whether
	19:28	on account of the D or tattoo any marks
	21:1	defile himself for the D among his people,
	21:11	go in to any D body, nor defile himself,
	22:4	through contact with the D or a man who
	26:30	altars, and cast your D bodies upon the dead
	26:30	dead bodies upon the D bodies of your idols;
Num	5:2	through contact with the D;
	6:6	not go near a D body.
	6:11	by reason of the D body.
	9:6	unclean through touching the D body of a man,
	9:7	unclean through touching the D body of a man;
	9:10	unclean through touching a D body, or is afar
	12:12	not be as one D, of whom the flesh
	14:29	do to you: your D bodies shall fall in
	14:32	as for you, your D bodies shall fall in
	14:33	the last of your D bodies lies in the
	16:48	he stood between the D and the living; and
	19:11	"He who touches the D body of any person
	19:13	Whoever touches a D person, the body of any
	19:16	a sword, or a D body, or a bone
	19:18	the slain, or the D, or the grave;
	20:29	saw that Aaron was D, all the house of
Deut	2:16	had perished and were D from among the people,
	14:1	make any baldness on your foreheads for the D
	25:5	the wife of the D shall not be married
	25:6	his brother who is D, that his name may
	26:14	of it to the D; I have obeyed the
	28:26	And your D body shall be food for all
Josh	1:2	"Moses my servant is D; now therefore arise, go
Judg	3:25	there lay their lord D on the floor.
	4:22	and there lay Sisera D, with the tent peg
	5:27	he fell; where he sank, there he fell D
	9:55	saw that Abimelech was D, they departed every man
	16:30	So the D whom he slew at his death
	20:5	and they ravished my concubine, and she is D
Ruth	1:8	have dealt with the D and with me.
	2:20	kindness has not forsaken the living or the D
	4:5	the widow of the D, in order to restore
	4:5	the name of the D to his inheritance."
	4:10	the name of the D in his inheritance, that
	4:10	the name of the D may not be cut
1Sam	4:17	Hophni and Phinehas, are D, and the ark of
	4:19	and her husband were D, she bowed and gave
	17:46	I will give the D bodies of the host
	17:51	that their champion was D, they fled.
	24:14	After a D dog!
	25:39	heard that Nabal was D, he said, "Blessed be
	31:5	saw that Saul was D, he also fell upon
	31:7	and his sons were D, they forsook their cities
2Sam	1:4	have fallen and are D; and Saul and his
	1:4	and Saul and his son Jonathan are also D
	1:5	know that Saul and his son Jonathan are D
	2:7	Saul your lord is D, and the house of
	4:10	me, 'Behold, Saul is D and thought he was
	9:8	should look upon a D dog such as I?"
	11:21	Uriah the Hittite is D also.'"
	11:24	the king's servants are D; and your servant Uriah
	11:24	Uriah the Hittite is D also."
	11:26	Uriah her husband was D, she made lamentation for
	12:18	that the child was D; for they said, "Behold,
	12:18	can we say to him the child is D
	12:19	that the child was D; and David said to
	12:19	David said to his servants, "Is the child D
	12:19	They said, "He is D
	12:23	But now he is D; why should I fast?
	13:32	for Amnon alone is D, for by the command
	13:33	the king's sons are D; for Amnon alone is
	13:33	king's sons are dead; for Amnon alone is D
	13:39	he was comforted about Amnon, seeing he was D
	14:2	many days for the D;
	14:5	"Alas, I am a widow; my husband is D
	16:9	king, "Why should this D dog curse my lord
	18:20	carry no tidings, because the king's son is D
	19:6	all of us were D today, then you would
	19:10	anointed over us, is D in battle.
1Kgs	3:20	bosom, and laid her D son in my bosom.
	3:21	child, behold, it was D; but when I looked
	3:22	is mine, and the D child is yours." The
	3:22	first said, "No, the D child is yours, and
	3:23	and your son is D; and the other says,
	3:23	but your son is D, and my son is
	11:21	of the army was D, Hadad said to Pharaoh,
	21:14	Jezebel, saying, "Naboth has been stoned; he is D
	21:15	been stoned and was D, Jezebel said to Ahab,
	21:15	for money; for Naboth is not alive, but D
	21:16	heard that Naboth was D, Ahab arose to go
2Kgs	4:1	servant my husband is D; and you know that
	4:32	saw the child lying D on his bed.
	8:5	Elisha had restored the D to life, behold, the
	11:1	that her son was D, she arose and destroyed
	19:35	behold, these were all D bodies.
	23:30	his servants carried him D in a chariot from
1Chr	10:5	saw that Saul was D, he also fell upon
	10:7	and his sons were D, they forsook their cities
2Chr	20:24	and behold, they were D bodies lying on the
	22:10	that her son was D, she arose and destroyed
Tob	1:17	one of my people D and thrown out behind
	2:8	he is burying the D again!"
	3:9	If they are D, go with them!
	3:15	Already seven husbands of mine are D
	12:12	when you buried the D, I was likewise present
	12:13	and lay out the D, your good deed was
Jud	2:8	be filled with their D, and overflow;
	6:4	and their fields will be full of their D
	14:15	down on the platform D, with his head cut
Job	1:19	people, and they are D; and I alone have
Ps	31:12	like one who is D; I have become like
	88:5	one forsaken among the D, like the slain that
	88:10	Dost thou work wonders for the D
	106:28	sacrifices offered to the D;
	115:17	The D do not praise the LORD, nor do
	143:3	made me sit in darkness like those long D
Prov	9:18	not know that the D are there, that her
	21:16	understanding will rest in the assembly of the D
Eccl	4:2	And I thought the D who are already dead
	4:2	dead who are already D more fortunate than the
	9:3	live, and after that they go to the D
	9:4	is better than a D lion.
	9:5	will die, but the D know nothing, and they
	10:1	D flies make the perfumer's ointment give off an
Wis	4:18	an outrage among the D for ever;
	13:10	their hopes set on D things, are the men
	13:18	a thing that is D; for aid he entreats
	14:15	what was once a D human being, and handed
	15:5	lifeless form of a D image.
	15:17	with lawless hands is D, for he is better
	18:18	there, hurled down half D, made known why they
	18:23	For when the D had already fallen on one
	19:3	the graves of their D, they reached another foolish
Sir	7:33	the living, and withhold not kindness from the D
	10:11	when a man is D he will inherit creeping
	17:23	From the D, as from one who does not
	22:9	Weep for the D, for he lacks the light;
	22:9	less bitterly for the D, for he has attained
	22:10	Mourning for the D lasts seven days, but for
	30:4	yet he is not D, for he has left
	34:25	washes after touching a D body, and touches it
	38:16	tears fall for the D, and as one who
	38:21	back; you do the D no good, and you
	38:23	When the D is at rest, let his remembrance
	48:13	and when he was D his body prophesied.
Is	8:19	Should they consult the D on behalf of the
	14:19	the Pit, like a D body trodden under foot.
	22:2	with the sword or D in battle.
	26:14	They are D, they will not live; they are
	26:19	Thy D shall live, their bodies shall rise.
	37:36	behold, these were all D bodies.
	59:10	vigor we are like D men.
	66:24	and look on the D bodies of the men
Jer	7:33	And the D bodies of this people will be
	9:22	says the LORD: 'The D bodies of men shall
	16:4	by famine, and their D bodies shall be food
	16:7	comfort him for the D; nor shall any one
	19:7	I will give their D bodies for food to
	22:10	for him who is D, nor bemoan him; but
	26:23	sword and cast his D body into the burial
	31:40	whole valley of the D bodies and the ashes,
	33:5	fill them with the D bodies of men whom
	34:20	Their D bodies shall be food for the birds
	36:30	of David, and his D body shall be cast
Lam	3:6	in darkness like the D of long ago.

Bar 2:17 and see; for the D who are in Hades,
3:4 the prayer of the D of Israel and of
3:10 are defiled with the D,
6:27 are placed before them just as before the D
6:71 sits; or like a D body cast out in
Ezek 6:5 I will lay the D bodies of the people
24:17 but not aloud; make no mourning for the D
43:7 harlotry, and by the D bodies of their kings,
43:9 their idolatry and the D bodies of their kings
44:25 going near to a D person; however, for father
Amos 8:3 the Lord GOD; "the D bodies shall be many;
Nah 3:3 slain, heaps of corpses, D bodies without end--they
Hag 2:13 by contact with a D body touches any of
1Mac 6:17 that the king was D, he set up Antiochus
9:57 saw that Alcimus was D, he returned to the
2Mac 5:5 arose that Antiochus was D, Jason took no less
12:40 every one of the D they found sacred tokens
12:44 been superfluous and foolish to pray for the D
12:45 made atonement for the D, that they might be
15:28 they recognized Nicanor, lying D, in full armor.
Mt 2:20 for those who sought the child's life are D
8:22 me, and leave the D to bury their own
8:22 and leave the dead to bury their own D
9:24 the girl is not D but sleeping." And they
10:8 the sick, raise the D, cleanse lepers, cast out
11:5 deaf hear, and the D are raised up, and
14:2 been raised from the D; that is why these
17:9 the Son of man is raised from the D
22:31 the resurrection of the D, have you not read
22:32 not God of the D, but of the living."
23:26 they are full of D men's bones and all
27:64 has risen from the D and the last fraud
28:4 trembled and became like D men.
28:7 has risen from the D, and behold, he is
Mk 5:35 ruler's house some who said, "Your daughter is D
5:39 The child is not D but sleeping."
6:14 been raised from the D; that is why these
9:9 Son of man should have risen from the D
9:10 the rising from the D meant.
9:26 so that most of them said, "He is D
12:25 they rise from the D, they neither marry nor
12:26 And as for the D being raised, have you
12:27 not God of the D, but of the living;
15:43 if he were already D; and summoning the centurion,
15:43 centurion, he asked him whether he was already D
15:44 centurion that he was D, he granted the body
Lk 7:15 And the D man sat up, and began to
7:22 the deaf hear, the D are raised up, the
8:49 said, "Your daughter is D; do not trouble the
8:52 for she is not D but sleeping."
8:53 they laughed at him, knowing that she was D
9:7 been raised from the D,
9:60 to him, "Leave the D to bury their own
9:60 to bury their own D; but as for you,
10:30 and beat him, and departed, leaving him half D
15:24 this my son was D, and is alive again;
15:32 this your brother was D, and is alive; he
16:30 to them from the D, they will repent.'
16:31 convinced if some one should rise from the D
20:35 the resurrection from the D neither marry nor are
20:37 But that the D are raised, even Moses showed,
20:38 not God of the D, but of the living;
24:5 "Why do you seek the living among the D
24:46 day rise from the D,
Jn 2:22 was raised from the D, his disciples remembered
5:20 the Father raises the D and gives them life,
5:24 now is, when the D will hear the voice
11:14 them plainly, "Lazarus is D;
11:39 the sister of the D man, said to him,
11:39 for he has been D four days."
11:44 The D man came out, his hands and feet
12:1 Lazarus was, whom Jesus had raised from the D
12:9 see Lazarus, whom he had raised from the D
12:17 raised him from the D bore witness.
19:33 that he was already D, they did not break
20:9 the scripture, that he must rise from the D
21:14 the disciples after he was raised from the D
Acts 3:15 Author of life, whom God raised from the D
4:2 and proclaiming in Jesus the resurrection from the D
4:10 God raised from the D, by him this man
5:10 in they found her D, and they carried her
10:41 drank with him after he rose from the D
10:42 to be judge of the living and the D
13:30 raised him from the D;
13:34 raised him from the D, no more to return
14:19 out of the city, supposing that he was D
17:3 to rise from the D, and saying, "This Jesus,
17:31 to all men by raising him from the D
17:32 the resurrection of the D, some mocked; but others
20:9 from the third story and was taken up D
23:6 the resurrection of the D I am on trial."
24:20 the resurrection of the D I am on trial
25:19 one Jesus, who was D, but whom Paul asserted
26:8 by any of you that God raises the D
26:23 to rise from the D, he would proclaim light
28:6 or suddenly fall down D; but when they had
Rom 1:4 his resurrection from the D, Jesus Christ our Lord,
4:17 gives life to the D and calls into existence
4:19 was as good as D because he was about
4:24 that raised from the D Jesus our Lord,
6:4 was raised from the D by the glory of
6:9 being raised from the D will never die again;
6:11 also must consider yourselves D to sin and alive
7:4 been raised from the D in order that we
7:6 discharged from the law, D to that which held
7:8 Apart from the law sin lies D
8:10 although your bodies are D because of sin, your
8:11 raised Jesus from the D dwells in you, he
8:11 Christ Jesus from the D will give life to
8:34 was raised from the D, who is at the
10:7 (that is, to bring Christ up from the D
10:9 raised him from the D, you will be saved.
11:15 will their acceptance mean but life from the D
14:9 Lord both of the D and of the living.
1Cor 15:12 as raised from the D, how can some of
15:12 say that there is no resurrection of the D
15:13 no resurrection of the D, then Christ has not
15:15 is true that the D are not raised.
15:16 For if the D are not raised, then Christ
15:20 been raised from the D, the first fruits of
15:21 man has come also the resurrection of the D
15:29 mean by being baptized on behalf of the D
15:29 If the D are not raised at all, why
15:32 If the D are not raised, "Let us eat
15:35 ask, "How are the D raised?
15:42 So is it with the resurrection of the D
15:52 will sound, and the D will be raised imperishable,
2Cor 1:9 God who raises the D;
Gal 1:1 raised him from the D --
Eph 1:20 raised him from the D and made him sit
2:1 alive, when you were D through the trespasses and
2:5 even when we were D through our trespasses, made
5:14 and arise from the D, and Christ shall give
Phil 3:11 possible I may attain the resurrection from the D
Col 1:18 the first-born from the D, that in everything he
2:12 working of God, who raised him from the D
2:13 And you, who were D in trespasses and the
1Thes 1:10 he raised from the D, Jesus who delivers us
4:16 And the D in Christ will rise first;
1Tim 5:6 who is self-indulgent is D even while she lives.
2Tim 2:8 Christ, risen from the D, descended from David, as
4:1 the living and the D, and by his appearing
Heb 6:1 foundation of repentance from D works and of faith
6:2 the resurrection of the D, and eternal judgment.
9:14 purify your conscience from D works to serve the
11:12 him as good as D, were born descendants as
11:19 men even from the D; hence, figuratively speaking,
11:35 Women received their D by resurrection.
13:20 brought again from the D our Lord Jesus, the
Jas 2:17 by itself, if it has no works, is D
2:26 from the spirit is D, so faith apart from
2:26 is dead, so faith apart from works is D
1Pet 1:3 Jesus Christ from the D,
1:21 raised him from the D and gave him glory,
4:5 is ready to judge the living and the D
4:6 preached even to the D, that though judged in
Jude 1:12 in late autumn, twice D, uprooted;
Rev 1:5 the first-born of the D, and the ruler of
1:17 him, I fell at his feet as though D
2:23 her doings; and I will strike her children D
3:1 the name of being alive, and you are D
11:8 kill them, and their D bodies will lie in
11:9 nations gaze at their D bodies and refuse to
11:18 the time for the D to be judged, for
14:13 this: Blessed are the D who die in the
16:3 the blood of a D man, and every living
20:5 The rest of the D did not come to
20:12 And I saw the D, great and small, standing
20:12 And the D were judged by what was written
20:13 sea gave up the D in it, Death and
20:13 Hades gave up the D in them, and all

DEADLY (12)
Ps 7:13 he has prepared his D weapons, making his arrows
17:9 who despoil me, my D enemies who surround me.
41:8 They say, "A D thing has fastened upon him;
42:10 As with a D wound in my body, my
91:3 fowler and from the D pestilence;
Jer 9:8 Their tongue is a D arrow; it speaks deceitfully;
16:4 They shall die of D diseases.
Ezek 5:16 loose against you my D arrows of famine, arrows
Nah 3:4 harlot, graceful and of D charms, who betrays
Mk 16:18 if they drink any D thing, it will not
2Cor 1:10 delivered us from so D a peril, and he
Jas 3:8 restless evil, full of D poison.

DEAF (16)
Ex 4:11 makes him dumb, or D, or seeing, or blind?
Lev 19:14 shall not curse the D or put a stumbling
Ps 28:1 my rock, be not D to me, lest, if
38:13 I am like a D man, I do not
58:4 a serpent, like the D adder that stops its
Is 29:18 In that day the D shall hear the words
35:5 the ears of the D unstopped;
42:18 Hear, you D; and look, you blind, that you
42:19 but my servant, or D as my messenger whom
43:8 have eyes, who are D, yet have ears!
Mic 7:16 their ears shall be D;
Mt 11:5 are cleansed and the D hear, and the dead
Mk 7:31 a man who was D and had an impediment
7:36 he even makes the D hear and the dumb
9:25 it, "You dumb and D spirit, I command you,
Lk 7:22 are cleansed, and the D hear, the dead are

DEAL (71)
Gen 19:9 Now we will D worse with you than with
21:23 that you will not D falsely with me or
21:23 with you, you will D with me and with
24:49 then, if you will D loyally and truly with
47:29 thigh, and promise to D loyally and truly with
Ex 1:9 Come, let us D shrewdly with them, lest they
5:15 Pharaoh, "Why do you D thus with your servants?
8:29 only let not Pharaoh D falsely again by not
21:9 his son, he shall D with her as with
Lev 19:11 shall not steal, nor D falsely, nor lie to
Num 4:19 among the Levites; but D thus with them, that
11:15 If thou wilt D thus with me, kill me
Deut 7:5 But thus shall you D with them: you shall
Josh 2:12 you, you also will D kindly with my father's
2:14 ours, then we will D kindly and faithfully with
24:27 against you, lest you D falsely with your God."
Judg 1:24 city, and we will D kindly with you."
Ruth 1:8 May the LORD D kindly with you, as you
1Sam 20:8 Therefore D kindly with your servant, for you have
2Sam 10:2 David said, "I will D loyally with Hanun the
18:5 and Abishai and Ittai, D gently for my sake
1Kgs 2:7 But D loyally with the sons of Barzillai the
2Kgs 22:7 their hand, for they D honestly."
1Chr 19:2 David said, "I will D loyally with Hanun the
2Chr 2:3 to dwell in, so D with me.
19:11 D courageously, and may the LORD be with the
Tob 3:6 And now D with me according to thy pleasure;
Jud 3:4 your slaves; come and D with them in any
Job 42:8 his prayer not to D with you according to
Ps 58:2 devise wrongs; your hands D out violence on earth.
103:10 He does not D with us according to our
105:25 hate his people, to D craftily with his servants.
109:21 O GOD my Lord, D on my behalf for
119:17 D bountifully with thy servant, that I may live
119:124 D with thy servant according to thy steadfast love,
142:7 me; for thou wilt D bountifully with me.
Sir 42:7 Whatever you D out, let it be by number
Is 1:4 of evildoers, sons who D corruptly!
24:16 D treacherously, the treacherous D very
48:8 knew that you would D very treacherously, and that
63:8 sons who will not D falsely; and he became
Jer 18:23 be overthrown before thee; D with them in the
21:2 perhaps the LORD will D with us according to
23:5 reign as king and D wisely, and shall execute
39:12 him no harm, but D with him as he
Lam 1:22 come before thee; and D with them as thou
Ezek 8:18 Therefore I will D in wrath; my eye will
16:59 Lord GOD: I will D with you as you
20:44 the LORD, when I D with you for my
22:14 days that I shall D with you?
23:25 you, that they may D with you in fury.
23:29 disgust; and they shall D with you in hatred,
31:11 nations; he shall surely D with it as its
35:11 Lord GOD, I will D with you according to
35:15 desolate, so I will D with you; you shall
Dan 1:13 to what you see D with your servants."
3:42 us to shame, but D with us in thy
11:7 north, and he shall D with them and shall
11:39 He shall D with the strongest fortresses by the
Hos 7:2 of Samaria; for they D falsely, the thief breaks
Amos 8:5 the shekel great, and D deceitfully with false
Zeph 3:19 that time I will D with all your oppressors.
Zech 1:6 of hosts purposed to D with us for our
8:11 now I will not D with the remnant of
1Mac 9:29 and Bacchides, and to D with those of our
2Mac 6:14 but he does not D in this way with
1Cor 7:31 goods, and those who D with the world as
Heb 5:2 He can D gently with the ignorant and wayward,
9:10 of the worshiper, but D only with food and
9:28 second time, not to D with sin but to

DEALERS (3)
Ezek 27:21 Kedar were your favored D in lambs, rams, and
27:27 pilots, your caulkers, your D in merchandise, and all
Mt 25:9 go rather to the D and buy for yourselves.'

DEALING (9)
Prov 1:3 receive instruction in wise D, righteousness, justice,
Sir 41:18 the people; of unjust D, before your partner or
42:5 little; of profit from D with merchants, and of
Is 33:1 made an end of D treacherously, you will be
Ezek 20:27 fathers blasphemed me, by D treacherously with me.
Dan 13:57 you both have been D with the daughters of
Lk 16:8 are more shrewd in D with their own generation
2Cor 13:3 is not weak in D with you, but is
13:4 in him, but in D with you we shall

DEALINGS (6)
Judg 18:7 Sidonians and had no D with any one.
18:28 and they had no D with any one.
1Sam 2:23 hear of your evil D from all the people.
2Mac 14:30 more austere in his D with him and was
Jn 4:9 For Jews have no D with Samaritans.
1Cor 7:31 though they had no D with it.

DEALS (10)
Job 15:11 or the word that D gently with you?
39:16 She D cruelly with her young, as if they
Ps 55:12 not an adversary who D insolently with me--
112:5 with the man who D generously and lends, who
Prov 14:35 A servant who D wisely has the king's favor,
17:2 A slave who D wisely will rule over a
Sir 50:22 days from birth, and D with us according to
Is 26:10 land of uprightness he D perversely and does not
Jer 6:13 to priest, every one D falsely.
8:10 to priest every one D falsely.

DEALT (57)
Gen 12:16 for her sake he D well with Abram; and
16:6 Then Sarai D harshly with her, and she fled
21:23 but as I have D loyally with you, you
33:11 you, because God has D graciously with me, and
Ex 1:19 So God D well with the midwives; and the
18:11 the Egyptians, when they D arrogantly with them."
21:8 people, since he has D faithlessly with her.
21:31 daughter, he shall be D with according to this
Num 11:11 LORD, "Why hast thou D ill with thy servant?
20:15 time; and the Egyptians D harshly with us and
Deut 32:5 They have D corruptly with him, they are no
Josh 2:12 that as I have D kindly with you, you
Judg 9:16 and if you have D well with Jerubbaal and
9:23 men of Shechem D treacherously with Abimelech;
18:4 and thus has Micah D with me: he has
Ruth 1:8 you, as you have D with the dead and
1:20 for the Almighty has D very bitterly with me.
1Sam 14:33 he said, "You have D treacherously; roll a great
24:18 day how you have D well with me, in
25:31 when the LORD has D well with my lord,
2Sam 10:2 Nahash, as his father D loyally with me." So
18:13 hand, if I had D treacherously against his life
1Kgs 2:5 to me, how he D with the two commanders
2Kgs 12:15 the workmen, for they D honestly.
21:6 soothsaying and augury, and D with mediums and
1Chr 19:2 Nahash, for his father D loyally with me." So
2Chr 2:3 of Tyre: "As you D with David my father
11:23 And he D wisely, and distributed some of his
28:19 Israel, for he had D wantonly in Judah and
33:6 augury and sorcery, and D with mediums and with
Neh 9:33 us, for thou hast D faithfully and we have

D

Ps 13:6 LORD, because he has D bountifully with me.
116:7 for the LORD has D bountifully with you.
119:65 Thou hast D well with thy servant, O LORD,
147:20 He has not D thus with any other nation;
Is 33:1 with whom none has D treacherously!
33:1 treacherously, you will be D with treacherously.
Jer 12:6 father, even they have D treacherously with you; they
22:8 "Why has the LORD D thus with this great
30:14 you; for I have D you the blow of
Lam 1:2 all her friends have D treacherously with her, they
1:22 them as thou hast D with me because of
2:20 With whom hast thou D thus?
Bar 2:27 "Yet thou hast D with us, O Lord our
Ezek 39:23 their iniquity, because they D so treacherously with
39:24 I D with them according to their uncleanness and
Dan 5:20 hardened so that he D proudly, he was deposed
Hos 5:7 They have D faithlessly with the LORD; for they
6:7 the covenant; there they D faithlessly with me.
Joel 2:26 your God, who has D wondrously with you.
Zech 1:6 deeds, so has he D with us."
1Mac 1:30 fell upon the city, D it a severe blow,
5:3 He D them a heavy blow and humbled them
5:34 before him, and he D them a heavy blow.
13:31 Trypho D treacherously with the young king
Acts 1:1 O Theophilus, I have D with all that Jesus
7:19 He D craftily with our race and forced our

DEAR (6)

Tob 10:12 bring you back safely, D brother, and grant me
Ps 39:11 a moth what is D to him; surely every
102:14 servants hold her stones D, and have pity on
Jer 31:20 youth.' Is Ephraim my D son?
Lk 7:2 a slave who was D to him, who was
1Thes 2:8 you had become very D to us.

DEATH (483)

Gen 21:16 not look upon the D of the child." And
24:67 So Isaac was comforted after his mother's D
25:11 After the D of Abraham God blessed Isaac his
26:11 man or his wife shall be put to D
26:18 stopped them after the D of Abraham; and he
27:2 I do not know the day of my D
Ex 10:17 only to remove this D from me."
19:12 shall be put to D;
21:12 so that he dies shall be put to D
21:15 father or his mother shall be put to D
21:16 in possession of him, shall be put to D
21:17 father or his mother shall be put to D
21:28 or a woman to D, the ox shall be
21:29 and its owner also shall be put to D
22:19 lies with a beast shall be put to D
31:14 shall be put to D; whoever does any work
31:15 on the sabbath day shall be put to D
35:2 shall be put to D;
Lev 16:1 to Moses, after the D of the two sons
19:20 not be put to D, because she was not
20:2 shall be put to D; the people of the
20:4 not put him to D,
20:9 shall be put to D; he has cursed his
20:10 adulterer and the adulteress shall be put to D
20:11 shall be put to D, their blood is upon
20:12 shall be put to D; they have committed incest,
20:13 shall be put to D, their blood is upon
20:15 shall be put to D; and you shall kill
20:16 shall be put to D, their blood is upon
20:27 shall be put to D; they shall be stoned
24:16 shall be put to D; all the congregation shall
24:16 he blasphemes the Name, shall be put to D
24:17 who kills a man shall be put to D
24:21 who kills a man shall be put to D
27:29 shall be ransomed; he shall be put to D
Num 1:51 else comes near, he shall be put to D
3:10 else comes near, he shall be put to D
3:38 who came near was to be put to D
15:35 shall be put to D; all the congregation shall
15:36 and stoned him to D with stones, as the
16:29 men die the common D of all men, or
18:7 else who comes near shall be put to D
23:10 Let me die the D of the righteous, and
35:16 a murderer; the murderer shall be put to D
35:17 a murderer; the murderer shall be put to D
35:18 a murderer; the murderer shall be put to D
35:19 put the murderer to D; when he meets him,
35:19 he meets him, he shall put him to D
35:21 shall be put to D; he is a murderer;
35:21 put the murderer to D, when he meets him.
35:25 in it until the D of the high priest
35:28 of refuge until the D of the high priest;
35:28 priest; but after the D of the high priest
35:30 shall be put to D on the evidence of
35:30 shall be put to D on the testimony of
35:31 who is guilty of D; but he shall be
35:31 of death; but he shall be put to D
35:32 the land before the D of the high priest.
Deut 13:5 shall be put to D, because he has taught
13:9 to put him to D, and afterwards the hand
13:10 shall stone him to D with stones, because he
17:5 man or woman to D with stones.
17:6 shall be put to D; a person shall not
17:6 not be put to D on the evidence of
17:7 to put him to D, and afterward the hand
21:21 shall stone him to D with stones; so you
21:22 a crime punishable by D and he is put
21:22 he is put to D, and you hang him
22:21 shall stone her to D with stones, because she
22:24 shall stone them to D with stones, the young
22:26 no offense punishable by D, for this case is
24:16 not be put to D for the children, nor
24:16 children be put to D for the fathers; every
24:16 shall be put to D for his own sin.
30:15 day life and good, D and evil.
30:19 before you life and D, blessing and curse; therefore
31:27 against the LORD; how much more after my D
31:29 know that after my D you will surely act
33:1 God blessed the children of Israel before his D
Josh 1:1 After the D of Moses the servant
1:18 whatever you command him, shall be put to D
2:13 belong to them, and deliver our lives from D
10:26 and put them to D, and he hung them
11:17 kings, and smote them, and put them to D
20:6 for judgment, until the D of him who is
Judg 1:1 After the D of Joshua the people
5:18 their lives to the D; Naphtali too, on the
6:31 shall be put to D by morning.
13:7 God from birth to the day of his D
16:16 and urged him, his soul was vexed to D
16:30 he slew at his D were more than those
20:13 may put them to D, and put away evil
21:5 to Mizpah, saying, "He shall be put to D
Ruth 1:17 more also if even D parts me from you."
2:11 your mother-in-law since the D of your husband has
1Sam 4:20 the time of her D the women attending her
11:12 the men, that we may put them to D
11:13 shall be put to D this day, for today
15:32 "Surely the bitterness of D is past."
15:35 the day of his D, but Samuel grieved over
19:6 LORD lives, he shall not be put to D
20:3 there is but a step between me and D
20:32 his father, "Why should he be put to D
20:33 his father was determined to put David to D
22:22 I have occasioned the D of all the persons
28:9 snare for my life to bring about my D
2Sam 1:1 After the D of Saul, when David
1:23 In life and in D they were not divided;
6:23 had no child to the day of her D
8:2 to be put to D, and one full line
15:21 shall be, whether for D or for life, there
19:21 Shimei be put to D for this, because he
19:22 one be put to D in Israel this day?
19:28 but men doomed to D before my lord the
20:3 the day of their D, living as if in
21:1 his house, because he put the Gibeonites to D
21:4 put any man to D in Israel." And he
21:9 They were put to D in the first days
22:5 "For the waves of D encompassed me, the torrents
22:6 me, the snares of D confronted me.
1Kgs 2:8 not put you to D with the sword.'
2:24 shall be put to D this day."
2:26 to Anathoth, to your estate; for you deserve D
2:26 time put you to D, because you bore the
11:40 in Egypt until the D of Solomon.
12:18 Israel stoned him to D with stones.
17:18 and to cause the D of my son!"
21:10 Then take him out, and stone him to D
21:13 and stoned him to D with stones.
2Kgs 1:1 After the D of Ahab, Moab rebelled
2:21 wholesome; henceforth neither D nor miscarriage
4:40 of God, there is D in the pot!" And
14:6 did not put to D the children of the
14:6 not be put to D for the children, or
14:6 children be put to D for the fathers; but
14:17 fifteen years after the D of Jehoash son of

	15:5	the day of his D, and he dwelt in
	20:1	became sick and was at the point of D
	25:21	and put them to D at Riblah in the
1Chr	2:24	After the D of Hezron, Caleb went in to
	22:5	provided materials in great quantity before his D
2Chr	10:18	Israel stoned him to D with stones.
	15:13	should be put to D, whether young or old,
	22:4	done; for after the D of his father they
	22:9	he was brought to Jehu and put to D
	24:15	a hundred and thirty years old at his D
	24:17	Now after the D of Jehoiada the princes of
	25:4	put their children to D, according to what is
	25:4	not be put to D for the children, or
	25:4	children be put to D for the fathers; but
	25:16	Why should you be put to D
	25:25	fifteen years after the D of Joash the son
	26:21	the day of his D, and being a leper
	32:24	at the point of D, and he prayed to
	32:33	inhabitants of Jerusalem did him honor at his D
Ezra	7:26	upon him, whether for D or for banishment or
Tob	1:18	the king put to D any who came fleeing
	1:18	For in his anger he put many to D
	1:19	to be put to D, I left home in
	2:8	will be put to D for doing this; he
	3:4	to plunder, captivity, and D; thou madest us a
	4:2	he said to himself; "I have asked for D
	4:10	For charity delivers from D and keeps you from
	6:12	incurring the penalty of D, because you rather than
	12:9	For almsgiving delivers from D, and it will purge
	14:15	Before his D he rejoiced over Nineveh.
Jud	2:27	lands and put to D all their young men
	5:22	Moab insisted that he must be put to D
	7:28	shall not witness the D of our babes before
	11:11	and his purpose frustrated, D will fall upon them,
	12:14	joy to me until the day of my D
	14:5	sent him to us as if to his D
	16:25	Judith, or for a long time after her D
Esth	4:8	the king concerning us and deliver us from D
	4:11	to be put to D, except the one to
	13:18	out mightily, for their D was before their eyes.
Job	3:21	soul, who long for D, but it comes not,
	5:20	will redeem you from D, and in war from
	7:15	would choose strangling and D rather than my bones.
	9:23	When disaster brings sudden D, he mocks at the
	18:13	consumed, the first-born of D consumes his limbs.
	28:22	Abaddon and D say, 'We have heard a rumor
	30:23	wilt bring me to D, and to the house
	31:39	payment, and caused the D of its owners;
	33:22	Pit, and his life to those who bring D
	38:17	Have the gates of D been revealed to you,
Ps	6:5	For in D there is no remembrance of thee;
	9:13	from the gates of D,
	13:3	sleep the sleep of D;
	18:4	The cords of D encompassed me, the torrents of
	18:5	me, the snares of D confronted me.
	22:15	thou dost lay me in the dust of D
	23:4	of the shadow of D, I fear no evil;
	30:9	is there in my D, if I go down
	33:19	deliver their soul from D, and keep them alive
	49:14	are appointed for Sheol; D shall be their shepherd;
	55:4	me, the terrors of D have fallen upon me.
	55:15	Let D come upon them; let them go down
	56:13	delivered my soul from D, yea, my feet from
	68:20	and to GOD, the Lord, belongs escape from D
	78:50	not spare them from D, but gave their lives
	88:15	Afflicted and close to D from my youth up,
	89:48	What man can live and never see D
	94:21	of the righteous, and condemn the innocent to D
	107:18	and they drew near to the gates of D
	109:16	poor and needy and the brokenhearted to their D
	109:31	save him from those who condemn him to D
	116:3	The snares of D encompassed me; the pangs of
	116:8	delivered my soul from D, my eyes from tears,
	116:15	the LORD is the D of his saints.
	118:18	but he has not given me over to D
Prov	2:18	house sinks down to D, and her paths to
	5:5	feet go down to D; her steps follow the
	7:27	to Sheol, going down to the chambers of D
	8:36	me injures himself; all who hate me love D
	10:2	do not profit, but righteousness delivers from D
	11:4	the day of wrath, but righteousness delivers from D
	12:28	life, but the way of error leads to D
	13:14	life, that one may avoid the snares of D
	14:12	man, but its end is the way to D
	14:27	life, that one may avoid the snares of D
	16:14	is a messenger of D, and a wise man
	16:25	man, but its end is the way to D
	18:21	D and life are in the power of the
	21:6	is a fleeting vapor and a snare of D
	24:11	being taken away to D; hold back those who
	26:18	throws firebrands, arrows, and D,
	28:17	be a fugitive until D; let no one help
Eccl	7:1	and the day of D, than the day of
	7:26	found more bitter than D the woman whose heart
	8:8	over the day of D; there is no discharge
Song	8:6	love is strong as D, jealousy is cruel as
Wis	1:12	Do not invite D by the error of your
	1:13	God did not make D, and he does not
	1:13	not delight in the D of the living.
	1:16	and deeds summoned D; considering him a friend,
	2:5	no return from our D, because it is sealed
	2:20	him to a shameful D, for, according to what
	2:24	through the devil's envy D entered the world, and
	12:20	and those deserving of D, granting them time and
	16:13	power over life and D; thou dost lead men
	18:12	the one form of D, had corpses too many
	18:16	filled all things with D, and touched heaven while
	18:20	The experience of D touched also the righteous, and
	19:5	journey, but they themselves might meet a strange D
Sir	1:11	the day of his D he will be blessed.
	4:28	Strive even to D for the truth and the
	8:7	rejoice over any one's D; remember that we all
	9:13	will not be worried by the fear of D
	11:14	and bad, life and D, poverty and wealth, come
	11:24	on the day of D according to his conduct.
	11:26	one happy before his D; a man will be
	14:12	Remember that D will not delay, and the decree
	15:17	man are life and D, and whichever he chooses
	18:21	do not wait until D to be released from
	18:23	on the day of D, and of the moment
	22:9	the life of the fool is worse than D
	23:12	which is comparable to D; may it never be
	26:5	and false accusation--all these are worse than D
	27:29	snare, and pain will consume them before their D
	28:6	enmity, remember destruction and D, and be true to
	28:21	fetters of bronze; its D is an evil death,
	28:21	death is an evil D, and Hades is preferable
	30:17	D is better than a miserable life, and eternal
	33:14	life the opposite of D; so the sinner is
	33:23	in the hour of D, distribute your inheritance.
	34:12	been in danger of D, but have escaped because
	37:2	a grief to the D when a companion and
	37:18	and evil, life and D; and it is the
	38:18	For sorrow results in D, and sorrow of heart
	40:2	is the day of D,
	40:5	unrest, and fear of D, and fury and strife.
	40:9	seven times more, are D and bloodshed and strife
	41:1	O D, how bitter is the reminder of you
	41:2	O D, how welcome is your sentence to one
	41:3	fear the sentence of D; remember your former days
	46:20	to the king his D, and lifted up his
	48:5	raised a corpse from D and from Hades, by
	48:14	did wonders, so in D his deeds were marvelous.
	51:6	soul drew near to D, and my life was
	51:9	from the earth, and prayed for deliverance from D
Is	25:8	He will swallow up D for ever, and the
	28:15	made a covenant with D, and with Sheol we
	28:18	Then your covenant with D will be annulled, and
	38:1	became sick and was at the point of D
	38:18	Sheol cannot thank thee, D cannot praise thee; those
	53:9	rich man in his D, although he had done
	53:12	out his soul to D, and was numbered with
Jer	8:3	D shall be preferred to life by all the
	9:21	For D has come up into our windows, it
	18:21	May their men meet D by pestilence, their youths
	21:8	the way of life and the way of D
	26:11	deserves the sentence of D, because he has
	26:15	you put me to D, you will bring innocent
	26:16	deserve the sentence of D, for he has spoken
	26:19	of Judah and all Judah put him to D
	26:21	to put him to D; but when Uriah heard
	26:24	over to the people to be put to D
	38:4	man be put to D, for he is weakening
	38:15	you not be sure to put me to D
	38:16	not put you to D or deliver you into
	38:25	not put you to D
	52:11	him in prison till the day of his D
	52:27	and put them to D at Riblah in the
	52:34	the day of his D as long as he
Lam	1:20	sword bereaves; in the house it is like D
Bar	6:18	he were sentenced to D, so the priests make
	6:36	save a man from D or rescue the weak

Ezek 13:19 of bread, putting to D persons who should not
18:23 any pleasure in the D of the wicked, says
18:32 no pleasure in the D of any one, says
28:8 you shall die the D of the slain in
28:10 You shall die the D of the uncircumcised by
31:14 all given over to D, to the nether world
33:11 no pleasure in the D of the wicked, but
Dan 3:89 from the hand of D, and delivered us from
13:22 this thing, it is D for me; and if
13:28 their wicked plot to have Susanna put to D
13:41 people and judges; and they condemned her to D
13:45 to be put to D, God aroused the holy
13:53 'Do not put to D an innocent and righteous
13:62 the law of Moses, they put them to D
14:22 king put them to D, and gave Bel over
Hos 13:14 Shall I redeem them from D
13:14 O D, where are your plagues?
Hab 2:5 wide as Sheol; like D he has never enough.
1Mac 1:2 strongholds, and put to D the kings of the
1:9 on crowns after his D, and so did their
1:57 the decree of the king condemned him to D
1:60 decree, they put to D the women who had
6:24 they have put to D as many of us
9:23 After the D of Judas, the lawless emerged in
9:29 to Jonathan, "Since the D of your brother Judas
2Mac 4:47 while he sentenced to D those unfortunate men, who
6:19 But he, welcoming D with honor rather than life
6:22 might be saved from D, and be treated kindly
6:28 to die a good D willingly and nobly for
6:30 have been saved from D, I am enduring terrible
6:31 died, leaving in his D an example of nobility
7:14 when he was near D, he said, "One cannot
7:29 Accept D, so that in God's mercy I may
13:4 to put him to D by the method which
13:8 holy, he met his D in ashes.
13:14 fight nobly to the D for the laws, temple,
14:46 This was the manner of his D
Mt 2:15 remained there until the D of Herod.
4:16 region and shadow of D light has dawned."
10:21 deliver up brother to D, and the father his
10:21 have them put to D;
14:5 to put him to D, he feared the people,
16:18 and the powers of D shall not prevail against
16:28 who will not taste D before they see the
20:18 will condemn him to D,
21:41 wretches to a miserable D, and let out the
24:9 and put you to D; and you will be
26:38 very sorrowful, even to D; remain here, and watch
26:59 might put him to D,
26:66 They answered, "He deserves D
27:1 to put him to D;
Mk 5:23 "My little daughter is at the point of D
9:1 who will not taste D before they see that
10:33 will condemn him to D, and deliver him to
13:12 deliver up brother to D, and the father his
13:12 have them put to D;
14:34 very sorrowful, even to D; remain here, and watch."
14:55 to put him to D; but they found none.
14:64 And they all condemned him as deserving D
Lk 1:79 in the shadow of D, to guide our feet
2:26 he should not see D before he had seen
7:2 who was sick and at the point of D
9:27 who will not taste D before they see the
21:16 they will put to D;
22:2 to put him to D; for they feared the
22:33 to go with you to prison and to D
23:15 Behold, nothing deserving D has been done by him;
23:21 him no crime deserving D; I will therefore chastise
23:31 to be put to D with him.
24:20 to be condemned to D, and crucified him.
Jn 4:47 son, for he was at the point of D
5:23 but has passed from D to life.
8:51 one keeps my word, he will never see D
8:52 he will never taste D
11:4 illness is not unto D; it is for the
11:13 had spoken of his D, but they thought that
11:53 they took counsel how to put him to D
12:10 put Lazarus also to D,
12:33 to show by what D he was to die.
18:31 lawful for us to put any man to D
18:32 to show by what D he was to die.
21:19 to show by what D he was to glorify
Acts 2:24 loosed the pangs of D, because it was not
8:1 And Saul was consenting to his D
10:39 They put him to D by hanging him on
12:19 and ordered that they should be put to D
13:28 him with nothing deserving D, yet they asked Pilate
22:4 this Way to the D, binding and delivering to
23:29 charged with nothing deserving D or imprisonment.
25:11 not seek to escape D; but if there is
25:25 had done nothing deserving D; and as he himself
26:10 they were put to D I cast my vote
26:31 doing nothing to deserve D or imprisonment."
28:18 no reason for the D penalty in my case.
Rom 4:25 who was put to D for our trespasses and
5:10 to God by the D of his Son, much
5:12 through one man and D through sin, and so
5:12 through sin, and so D spread to all men
5:14 Yet D reigned from Adam to Moses, even over
5:17 of one man's trespass, D reigned through that one
5:21 as sin reigned in D, grace also might reign
6:3 baptized into Christ Jesus were baptized into his D
6:4 him by baptism into D, so that as Christ
6:5 with him in a D like his, we shall
6:9 will never die again; D no longer has dominion
6:10 The D he died he died to sin, once
6:13 have been brought from D to life, and your
6:16 sin, which leads to D, or of obedience, which
6:21 The end of those things is D
6:23 wages of sin is D, but the free gift
7:5 work in our members to bear fruit for D
7:10 life proved to be D to me.
7:13 is good, then, bring D to me?
7:13 It was sin, working D in me through what
7:24 Who will deliver me from this body of D
8:2 me free from the law of sin and D
8:6 on the flesh is D, but to set the
8:13 Spirit you put to D the deeds of the
8:38 am sure that neither D, nor life, nor angels,
1Cor 3:22 world or life or D or the present or
4:9 like men sentenced to D; because we have become
11:26 you proclaim the Lord's D until he comes.
15:21 by a man came D, by a man has
15:26 The last enemy to be destroyed is D
15:54 saying that is written: D is swallowed up in
15:55 "O D, where is thy victory?
15:55 O D, where is thy sting?"
15:56 The sting of D is sin, and the power
2Cor 1:9 received the sentence of D; but that was to
2:16 one a fragrance from D to death, to the
2:16 fragrance from death to D, to the other a
3:7 if the dispensation of D, carved in letters on
4:10 in the body the D of Jesus, so that
4:11 being given up to D for Jesus' sake, so
4:12 So D is at work in us, but life
7:10 and brings no regret, but worldly grief produces D
11:23 with countless beatings, and often near D
Phil 1:20 in my body, whether by life or by D
2:8 and became obedient unto D, even death on a
2:8 obedient unto death, even D on a cross.
2:27 Indeed he was ill, near to D
3:10 like him in his D,
Col 1:22 of flesh by his D, in order to present
3:5 Put to D therefore what is earthly in you:
2Tim 1:10 Christ Jesus, who abolished D and brought life and
Heb 2:9 of the suffering of D, so that by the
2:9 God he might taste D for every one.
2:14 same nature, that through D he might destroy him
2:14 has the power of D, that is, the devil,
2:15 who through fear of D were subject to lifelong
5:7 to save him from D, and he was heard
7:23 they were prevented by D from continuing in office;
9:15 inheritance, since a D has occurred which redeems
9:16 will is involved, the D of the one who
9:17 takes effect only at D, since it is not
11:5 he should not see D; and he was not
Jas 1:14 and sin when it is full-grown brings forth D
5:20 save his soul from D and will cover a
1Pet 3:18 God, being put to D in the flesh but
1 Jn 3:14 have passed out of D into life, because we
3:14 He who does not love abides in D
Rev 1:18 have the keys of D and Hades.
2:10 Be faithful unto D, and I will give you
2:11 hurt by the second D
3:2 on the point of D, for I have not
6:8 its rider's name was D, and Hades followed him;
9:6 days men will seek D and will not find
9:6 long to die, and D will fly from them.
12:11 for they loved not their lives even unto D
20:6 Over such the second D has no power, but
20:13 the dead in it, D and Hades gave up
20:14 Then D and Hades were thrown into the lake

20:14 This is the second D, the lake of fire;
21:4 from their eyes, and D shall be no more,
21:8 with fire and sulphur, which is the second D

DEATHLY (2)
1Sam 5:11 For there was a D panic throughout the whole
Esth 14:1 the queen, seized with D anxiety, fled to the

DEATHTRAP
Tob 14:10 alms and escaped the D which Nadab had set

DEBARRED
Jer 36:5 Baruch, saying, "I am D from going to the

DEBATE (2)
Acts 15:2 no small dissension and D with them, Paul and
15:7 there had been much D, Peter rose and said

DEBATER
1Cor 1:20 Where is the D of this age?

DEBAUCHERY (4)
Wis 14:26 souls, sex perversion, disorder in marriage, adultery, and D
2Mac 6:4 temple was filled with D and reveling by the
Rom 13:13 and drunkenness, not in D and licentiousness, not in
Eph 5:18 wine, for that is D; but be filled with

DEBIR (14)
Josh 10:3 of Lachish, and to D king of Eglon, saying,
10:38 Israel, turned back to D and assaulted it,
10:39 so he did to D and to its king.
11:21 country, from Hebron, from D, from Anab, and from
12:13 one; the king of D, one; the king of
13:26 to the territory of D,
15:7 boundary goes up to D from the Valley of
15:15 against the inhabitants of D; now the name of
15:15 now the name of D formerly was Kiriath-sepher.
15:49 Dannah, Kiriath-sannah (that is, D,
21:15 with its pasture lands, D with its pasture lands,
Judg 1:11 From there they went against the inhabitants of D
1:11 The name of D was formerly Kiriath-sepher.
1Chr 6:58 with its pasture lands, D with its pasture lands,

DEBORAH (11)
Gen 35:8 And D, Rebekah's nurse, died, and she was buried
Judg 4:4 Now D, a prophetess, the wife of Lappidoth, was
4:5 under the palm of D between Ramah and Bethel
4:9 Then D arose, and went with Barak to Kedesh.
4:10 at his heels; and D went up with him.
4:14 And D said to Barak, "Up!
5:1 Then sang D and Barak the son of Abino-am
5:7 ceased until you arose, D, arose as a mother
5:12 "Awake, awake, D
5:15 of Issachar came with D, and Issachar faithful to
Tob 1:8 was my duty, as D my father's mother had

DEBT (9)
1Sam 22:2 one who was in D, and every one who
Neh 10:31 the seventh year and the exaction of every D
1Mac 10:43 king or has any D, let him be released
15:8 Every D you owe to the royal treasury and
Mt 18:26 that servant released him and forgave him the D
18:29 him in prison till he should pay the D
18:31 forgave you all that D because you besought me;
18:33 the jailers, till he should pay all his D
Rom 15:27 indeed they are in D to them, for if

DEBTOR (2)
Is 24:2 borrower; as with the creditor, so with the D
Ezek 18:7 but restores to the D his pledge, commits no

DEBTORS (5)
Hab 2:7 Will not your D suddenly arise, and those awake
Mt 6:12 also have forgiven our D;
Lk 7:41 certain creditor had two D; one owed five hundred
16:5 So, summoning his master's D one by one, he
Rom 8:12 then, brethren, we are D, not to the flesh,

DEBTS (4)
2Kgs 4:7 oil and pay your D, and you and your
Prov 22:26 those who give pledges, who become surety for D
1Mac 15:8 and any such future D shall be canceled for
Mt 6:12 And forgive us our D, As we also have

DECAPOLIS (3)
Mt 4:25 from Galilee and the D and Jerusalem and Judea
Mk 5:20 to proclaim in the D how much Jesus had
7:30 Sea of Galilee, through the region of the D

DECAY (4)
Sir 10:9 for even in life his bowels D
19:3 D and worms will inherit him, and the reckless
2Mac 9:9 stench the whole army felt revulsion at his D
Rom 8:21 from its bondage to D and obtain the glorious

DECAYS
Sir 14:19 Every product D and ceases to exist, and the

D

DECEASED
2Mac 4:37 good conduct of the D;

DECEIT (39)
Jud 9:3 was ashamed of the D they had practiced, to
9:10 By the D of my lips strike down the
Esth 16:13 with intricate craft and D asked for destruction of
Job 15:35 and bring forth evil and their heart prepares D
27:4 speak falsehood, and my tongue will not utter D
31:5 foot has hastened to D;
Ps 10:7 filled with cursing and D and oppression; under his
17:1 ear to my prayer from lips free of D
32:2 iniquity, and in whose spirit there is no D
34:13 tongue from evil, and your lips from speaking D
35:20 quiet in the land they conceive words of D
36:3 mouth are mischief and D; he has ceased to
50:19 free rein for evil, and your tongue frames D
101:7 No man who practices D shall dwell in my
Prov 12:17 gives honest evidence, but a false witness utters D
12:20 D is in the heart of those who devise
20:17 Bread gained by D is sweet to a man,
26:24 his lips and harbors D in his heart;
Wis 1:5 spirit will flee from D, and will rise and
14:25 theft and D, corruption, faithlessness, tumult, perjury,
14:30 idols, and because in D they swore unrighteously
Sir 1:27 the Lord, and your heart was full of D
19:23 in mourning, but inwardly he is full of D
37:3 were you formed to cover the land with D
Is 53:9 and there was no D in his mouth.
57:4 transgression, the offspring of D,
Jer 8:5 They hold fast to D, they refuse to return.
9:6 oppression upon oppression, and D upon deceit, they
9:6 oppression, and deceit upon D, they refuse to know
14:14 worthless divination, and the D of their own minds.
23:26 and who prophesy the D of their own heart,
Dan 8:25 cunning he shall make D prosper under his hand,
14:18 you there is no D, none at all."
Hos 11:12 house of Israel with D; but Judah is still
1Mac 8:28 shall keep these obligations and do so without D
Mk 7:21 adultery, coveting, wickedness, D, licentiousness, ,
Acts 13:10 righteousness, full of all D and villainy, will you
Rom 1:29 of envy, murder, strife, D, malignity, they are gossips,
Col 2:8 by philosophy and empty D, according to human

DECEITFUL (20)
Jud 9:13 Make my D words to be their wound and
Ps 5:6 LORD abhors bloodthirsty and D men.
43:1 an ungodly people; from D and unjust men deliver
52:4 words that devour, O D tongue.
78:57 they twisted like a D bow.
109:2 For wicked and D mouths are opened against me,
120:2 lying lips, from a D tongue."
120:3 done to you, you D tongue?
Prov 31:30 Charm is D, and beauty is vain, but a
Wis 1:4 will not enter a D soul, nor dwell in
Jer 15:18 to me like a D brook, like waters that
17:9 The heart is D above all things, and desperately
Mic 1:14 Achzib shall be a D thing to the kings
6:11 with a bag of D weights?
6:12 and their tongue is D in their mouth.
Zeph 3:13 in their mouth a D tongue.
2Cor 11:13 men are false apostles, D workmen, disguising
Eph 4:14 by their craftiness in D wiles.
4:22 and is corrupt through D lusts,
1Tim 4:1 by giving heed to D spirits and doctrines of

DECEITFULLY (8)
Gen 34:13 and his father Hamor D, because he had defiled
Job 13:7 for God, and speak D for him?
Ps 24:4 to what is false, and does not swear D
Jer 9:8 deadly arrow; it speaks D; with his mouth each
Dan 11:23 him he shall act D; and he shall become

Amos 8:5 shekel great, and deal D with false balances,
1Mac 1:30 D he spoke peaceable words to them, and they
13:17 that they were speaking D to him, but he

DECEITFULNESS

Heb 3:13 be hardened by the D of sin.

DECEIVE (28)

Josh 9:22 them, "Why did you D us, saying, 'We are
2Sam 3:25 of Ner came to D you, and to know
2Kgs 4:28 not say, Do not D me?"
18:29 'Do not let Hezekiah D you, for he will
19:10 on whom you rely D you by promising that
2Chr 32:15 do not let Hezekiah D you or mislead you
Jud 12:16 for an opportunity to D her, ever since the
16:8 a linen gown to D him.
Job 13:9 Or can you D him, as one deceives a
Prov 24:28 cause, and do not D with your lips.
Wis 4:11 his understanding or guile D his soul.
Sir 13:6 needs you he will D you, he will smile
Is 36:14 'Do not let Hezekiah D you, for he will
37:10 on whom you rely D you by promising that
Jer 29:8 who are among you D you, and do not
37:9 the LORD, Do not D yourselves, saying, "The
Zech 13:4 mantle in order to D,
2Mac 7:18 he said, "Do not D yourself in vain.
Rom 3:13 an open grave, they use their tongues to D
16:18 and flattering words they D the hearts of the
1Cor 3:18 Let no one D himself.
Eph 5:6 Let no one D you with empty words, for
2Thes 2:3 Let no one D you in any way; for
1 Jn 1:8 have no sin, we D ourselves, and the truth
2:26 about those who would D you;
3:7 children, let no one D you.
Rev 20:3 him, that he should D the nations no more,
20:8 will come out to D the nations which are

DECEIVED (33)

Gen 29:25 Why then have you D me?"
Deut 11:16 lest your heart be D, and you turn aside
1Sam 19:17 Michal, "Why have you D me thus, and let
28:12 Saul, "Why have you D me?
2Sam 19:26 O king, my servant D me; for your servant
Job 12:16 strength and wisdom; the D and the deceiver are
Wis 12:24 enemies despised; they were D like foolish babes.
Sir 34:7 For dreams have D many, and those who put
Jer 4:10 surely thou hast utterly D this people and Jerusalem,
20:7 O LORD, thou hast D me, and I was
20:7 me, and I was D; thou art stronger than
20:10 "Perhaps he will be D, then we can overcome
38:22 'Your trusted friends have D you and prevailed
49:16 horror you inspire has D you, and the pride
Lam 1:19 my lovers but they D me; my priests and
Ezek 14:9 if the prophet be D and speak a word,
14:9 I, the LORD, have D that prophet, and I
Dan 13:56 of Judah, beauty has D you and lust has
14:7 said, "Do not be D, O king; for this
Obad 1:3 of your heart has D you, you who live
1:7 All your allies have D you, they have driven
Rom 7:11 opportunity in the commandment, D me and by it
1Cor 6:9 Do not be D; neither the immoral, nor idolaters,
15:33 Do not be D: "Bad company ruins good morals."
2Cor 11:3 that as the serpent D Eve by his cunning,
Gal 6:7 Do not be D; God is not mocked, for
1Tim 2:14 and Adam was not D, but the woman was
2:14 but the woman was D and became a transgressor.
2Tim 3:13 go on from bad to worse, deceivers and D
Jas 1:15 Do not be D, my beloved brethren.
Rev 18:23 and all nations were D by thy sorcery.
19:20 signs by which he D those who had received
20:10 the devil who had D them was thrown into

DECEIVER (4)

Job 12:16 the deceived and the D are his.
Sir 28:13 Curse the whisperer and D, for he has destroyed
2 Jn 1:7 a one is the D and the antichrist.
Rev 12:9 Devil and Satan, the D of the whole world--

DECEIVERS (3)

2Tim 3:13 from bad to worse, D and deceived.
Tit 1:9 talkers and D, especially the circumcision party;
2 Jn 1:7 For many D have gone out into the world,

DECEIVES (6)

Job 13:9 deceive him, as one D a man?
Prov 26:19 is the man who D his neighbor and says,
Jer 9:5 Every one D his neighbor, and no one speaks
Gal 6:3 he is nothing, he D himself.
Jas 1:25 bridle his tongue but D his heart, this man's
Rev 13:14 of the beast, it D those who dwell on

DECEIVING (5)

Lev 6:2 against the LORD by D his neighbor in a
Tob 10:7 "Be still and stop D me; my child has
Job 15:31 not trust in emptiness, D himself; for emptiness will
Prov 14:8 his way, but the folly of fools is D
Jas 1:21 and not hearers only, D yourselves.

DECENTLY

1Cor 14:40 things should be done D and in order.

DECEPTION (2)

2Mac 1:13 of Nanea by a D employed by the priests
2Thes 2:10 and with all wicked D for those who are

DECEPTIONS

Sir 34:8 Without such D the law will be fulfilled, and

DECEPTIVE (5)

Prov 11:18 A wicked man earns D wages, but one who
23:3 delicacies, for they are D food.
Jer 7:4 not trust in these D words: 'This is the
7:8 "Behold, you trust in D words to no avail.
Lam 2:14 for you false and D visions; they have not

DECIDE (22)

Gen 31:37 kinsmen, that they may D between us two.
Ex 18:16 to me and I D between a man and
18:22 small matter they shall D themselves; so it will
Lev 13:59 anything of skin, to D whether it is clean
Deut 25:1 court, and the judges D between them, acquitting the
Judg 11:27 the LORD, the Judge, D this day between the
2Sam 24:13 Now consider, and D what answer I shall return
1Chr 21:12 territory of Israel.' Now D what answer I shall
2Chr 19:8 the LORD and to D disputed cases.
Job 22:28 You will D on a matter, and it will
Is 2:4 the nations, and shall D for many peoples; and
11:3 his eyes see, or D by what his ears
11:4 judge the poor, and D with equity for the
Bar 6:64 not able either to D a case or to
Mic 4:3 many peoples, and shall D for strong nations afar
Hag 2:11 Ask the priests to D this question,
2Mac 13:13 to march out and D the matter by the
15:17 attack bravely, and to D the matter, by fighting
Mk 15:24 lots for them, to D what each should take.
Acts 24:21 comes down, I will D your case."
Rom 14:13 one another, but rather D never to put a
1Cor 6:5 you wise enough to D between members of the

DECIDED (23)

Ex 18:26 any small matter they D themselves.
2Sam 19:29 I have D: you and Ziba shall divide the
1Kgs 20:40 be; you yourself have D it."
2Chr 24:4 After this Joash D to restore the house of
Jud 2:3 region; and it was D that every one who
11:13 They have D to consume the first fruits of
1Mac 6:19 So Judas D to destroy them, and assembled all
8:26 ships, as Rome has D; and they shall keep
8:28 ships, as Rome has D; and they shall keep
9:69 Then he D to depart to his own land.
14:31 And when their enemies D to invade their country
14:41 Jews and their priests D that Simon should be
15:19 We therefore have D to write to the kings
2Mac 3:23 it, Heliodorus went on with what had been D
11:36 the matters which he D are to be referred
Lk 16:4 I have D what to do, so that people
Jn 1:43 The next day Jesus D to go to Galilee.
Acts 3:13 Pilate, when he had D to release him.
20:16 For Paul had D to sail past Ephesus, so
25:25 to the emperor, I D to send him.
27:1 And when it was D that we should sail
1Cor 2:2 For I D to know nothing among you except
Tit 3:12 Nicopolis, for I have D to spend the winter

DECIDES (5)

2Sam 15:15 ready to do whatever my lord the king D
Prov 18:18 end to disputes and D between powerful contenders.
Wis 15:7 of each of these the worker in clay D
Sir 33:13 who made them, to give them as he D
2Mac 15:21 but as the Lord D, that he gains the

DECIDING

2Mac 14:18 their country, shrank from D the issue by bloodshed.

DECISION (22)

Deut 17:8 any case arises requiring D between one kind of
17:9 them, and they shall declare to you the D
17:11 and according to the D which they pronounce to
2Sam 14:13 For in giving this D the king convicts himself,
Esth 10:11 moment and day of D before God and among
Prov 16:33 the lap, but the D is wholly from the
Wis 3:18 hope and no consolation in the day of D
19:3 reached another foolish D, and pursued as fugitives
Sir 8:14 a judge, for the D will favor him because
32:17 and will find a D according to his liking.
33:8 By the Lord's D they were distinguished, and he
Dan 4:17 of the watchers, the D by the word of
Joel 3:14 Multitudes, multitudes, in the valley of D
3:14 the LORD is near in the valley of D
Zeph 3:8 For my D is to gather nations, to assemble
1Mac 2:41 So they made this D that day: "Let us
2Mac 4:20 Hercules, but by the D of its carriers it
11:25 free from disturbance, our D is that their temple
13:14 So, committing the D to the Creator of the
15:20 forward to the coming D, and the enemy was
Mk 14:64 What is your D
Acts 25:21 in custody for the D of the emperor, I

DECISIONS (7)

Ex 18:16 them know the statutes of God and his D
18:20 the statutes and the D, and make them know
Prov 16:10 Inspired D are on the lips of a king;
1Mac 14:44 nullify any of these D or to oppose what
14:45 acts contrary to these D or nullifies any of
14:46 the right to act in accord with these D
Acts 16:4 them for observance the D which had been reached

DECK (6)

Job 40:10 D yourself with majesty and dignity; clothe yourself
Ps 65:13 with flocks, the valleys D themselves with grain, they
Jer 4:30 in scarlet, that you D yourself with ornaments of
10:4 Men D it with silver and gold; they fasten
Bar 6:11 They D their gods out with garments like men--
Ezek 27:6 oars; they made your D of pines from the

DECKED (7)

Ps 45:13 The princess is D in her chamber with gold-woven
Prov 7:16 I have D my couch with coverings, colored spreads
Ezek 16:11 And I D you with ornaments, and put bracelets
16:13 Thus you were D with gold and silver; and
16:16 made for yourself gaily D shrines, and on them
23:40 painted your eyes, and D yourself with ornaments;
Hos 2:13 incense to them and D herself with her ring

DECKS (2)

Gen 6:16 side; make it with lower, second, and third D
Is 61:10 righteousness, as a bridegroom D himself with a

DECLARATION (2)

Job 13:17 words, and let my D be in your ears.
1Mac 12:8 which contained a clear D of alliance and friendship.

DECLARE (84)

Deut 5:5 at that time, to D to you the word
17:9 them, and they shall D to you the decision.
17:10 according to what they D to you from that
17:11 the verdict which they D to you, either to
26:3 say to him, 'I D this day to the
27:14 And the Levites shall D to all the men
30:18 and serve them, I D to you this day,
1Kgs 8:24 father what thou didst D to him; yea, thou
8:53 heritage, as thou didst D through Moses, thy servant,
1Chr 16:24 D his glory among the nations, his marvelous works
17:10 Moreover I D to you that the LORD will
2Chr 6:15 father what thou didst D to him; yea, thou
Job 12:8 of the sea will D to you.
15:17 have seen I will D
32:6 timid and afraid to D my opinion to you.
32:10 me; let me also D my opinion.'
32:17 answer; I also will D my opinion.
33:3 My words D the uprightness of my heart, and
33:23 of the thousand, to D to man what is
34:33 and not I; therefore D what you know.
38:3 you, and you shall D to me.
38:18 D, if you know all this.
40:7 question you, and you D to me.
42:4 question you, and you D to me.'
Ps 50:6 The heavens D his righteousness, for God himself is
92:2 O Most High; to D thy steadfast love in
96:3 D his glory among the nations, his marvelous works
102:21 die; that men may D in Zion the name
119:13 With my lips I D all the ordinances of
145:4 to another, and shall D thy mighty acts.
145:6 acts, and I will D thy greatness.
Sir 16:23 instruction by weight, and D knowledge accurately.
39:10 Nations will D his wisdom, and the congregation will
42:15 the Lord, and will D what I have seen.
44:9 name, so that men D their praise.
44:16 Peoples will D their wisdom, and the congregation
Is 41:22 know their outcome; or D to us the things
42:9 new things I now D; before they spring forth
42:12 to the LORD, and D his praise in the
43:9 Who among them can D this, and show us
43:21 myself that they might D my praise.
44:7 proclaim it, let him D and set it forth
45:19 speak the truth, I D what is right.
45:21 D and present your case; let them take counsel
48:6 and will you not D it?
48:20 Babylon, flee from Chaldea, D this with a shout
50:9 helps me; who will D me guilty?
58:1 voice like a trumpet; D to my people their
66:19 glory; and they shall D my glory among the
Jer 4:5 D in Judah, and proclaim in Jerusalem, and say,
5:20 D this in the house of Jacob, proclaim it
9:12 spoken, that he may D it?
18:7 at any time I D concerning a nation or
18:9 at any time I D concerning a nation or
31:10 LORD, O nations, and D it in the coastlands
42:20 LORD our God says D to us and we
46:14 the land of Egypt: D in Egypt, and proclaim
50:2 by Jeremiah the prophet: D among the nations and
50:28 land of Babylon, to D in Zion the vengeance
51:10 vindication; come, let us D in Zion the work
Bar 2:20 us, as thou didst D by thy servants the
Ezek 22:2 Then D to her all her abominable deeds.
23:36 Then D to them their abominable deeds.
38:19 my blazing wrath I D, On that day there
40:4 show it to you; D all that you see
Dan 4:18 And you, O Belteshazzar, D the interpretation,
Hos 5:9 tribes of Israel I D what is sure.
Mic 3:5 something to eat, but D war against him who
3:8 justice and might, to D to Jacob his transgression
Zech 9:12 of hope; today I D that I will restore
Mt 7:23 And then will I D to them, 'I never
Lk 8:39 to your home, and D how much God has
Jn 8:26 is true, and I D to the world what
16:13 speak, and he will D to you the things
16:14 what is mine and D it to you.
16:15 what is mine and D it to you.
Acts 11:14 called Peter; he will D to you a message
1Cor 14:25 will worship God and D that God is really
Eph 6:20 chains; that I may D it boldly, as I
Col 4:3 for the word, to D the mystery of Christ,
1Thes 2:2 in our God to D to you the gospel
4:15 For this we D to you by the word
Tit 2:15 D these things; exhort and reprove with all authority.
1Pet 2:9 people, that you may D the wonderful deeds of

DECLARED (48)

Ex 9:16 my name may be D throughout all the earth.
Lev 14:36 in the house be D unclean; and afterward the
23:44 Thus Moses D to the people of Israel the
24:12 the LORD should be D to them.
Deut 4:13 And he D to you his covenant, which he
26:17 You have D this day concerning the LORD that
26:18 and the LORD has D this day concerning you
1Sam 24:18 And you have D this day how you have
Neh 8:12 the words that were D to them.
Tob 8:20 feast were over, Raguel D by oath to Tobias
Esth 8:17 peoples of the country D themselves Jews, for the
Job 26:3 no wisdom, and plentifully D sound knowledge!
28:27 he saw it and D it; he established it,
32:3 answer, although they had D Job to be in
Ps 32:3 When I D not my sin, my body wasted
88:11 Is thy steadfast love D in the grave, or
Sir 18:2 Lord alone will be D righteous.
26:20 tradesman will not be D innocent of sin.
Is 41:26 Who D it from the beginning, that we might
41:26 There was none who D it, none who proclaimed,
41:27 I first have D it to Zion, and I
43:12 I D and saved and proclaimed, when there was
44:8 from of old and D it?
45:21 Who D it of old?

48:3 "The former things I D of old, they went
48:5 your forehead brass, I D them to you from
48:14 Who among them has D these things?
Jer 42:21 I have this day D it to you, but
44:25 and your wives have D with your mouths, and
Bar 1:20 curse which the Lord D through Moses his servant
2Mac 2:7 he rebuked them and D: "The place shall be
6:23 holy God-given law, he D himself quickly, telling
7:6 on us, as Moses D in his song which
14:32 And when they D on oath that they did
15:4 And when they D, "It is the living Lord
Mt 11:25 At that time Jesus D, "I thank thee, Father,
26:33 Peter D to him, "Though they all fall away
Mk 7:18 (Thus he D all foods clean.)
12:36 by the Holy Spirit, D, 'The Lord said to
Lk 8:47 falling down before him D in the presence of
Acts 9:27 to the apostles, and D to them how on
10:46 Then Peter D,
14:27 the church together and D all that God had
15:4 the elders, and they D all that God had
26:20 the heavenly vision, but D first to those at
Heb 2:2 For if the message D by angels was valid
2:3 It was D at first by the Lord, and
9:19 the law had been D by Moses to all

DECLARES (14)

1Sam 2:30 the God of Israel D: 'I promised that your
2:30 but now the LORD D: 'Far be it from
2Sam 7:11 Moreover the LORD D to you that the LORD
Job 21:31 Who D his way to his face, and who
36:9 of affliction, then he D to them their work
36:33 Its crashing D concerning him, who is jealous with
Ps 19:2 and night to night D knowledge.
147:19 He D his word to Jacob, his statutes and
Sir 42:19 He D what has been and what is to
Jer 4:15 For a voice D from Dan and proclaims evil
Amos 4:13 creates the wind, and D to man what is
2Mac 10:26 an adversary to their adversaries, as the law D
Acts 2:17 it shall be, God D, that I will pour
13:41 never believe, if one D it to you.'"

DECLARING (6)

Tob 12:6 exalt his name, worthily D the works of God.
Is 46:10 is none like me, D the end from the
2Mac 9:14 cemetery, he was now D to be free;
Acts 20:20 did not shrink from D to you anything that
20:27 did not shrink from D to you the whole
1Pet 5:12 to you, exhorting and D that this is the

DECLINED (3)

2Kgs 20:11 which the sun had D on the dial of
Is 38:8 dial the ten steps by which it had D
Acts 18:20 a longer period, he D;

DECLINES (2)

Judg 19:8 "Strengthen your heart, and tarry until the day D
Jer 6:4 us, for the day D, for the shadows of

DECLINING

Is 38:8 shadow cast by the D sun on the dial

DECORATED

1Mac 4:57 They D the front of the temple with golden

DECORATION (5)

Sir 22:15 is like the stucco D on the wall of
38:28 handiwork, and he is careful to complete its D
1Mac 1:22 crowns, and the gold D on the front of
2Mac 2:29 undertakes its painting and D has to consider only
1Pet 3:3 with braiding of hair, D of gold, and wearing

DECOY

Sir 11:28 Like a D partridge in a cage, so is

DECREASE (3)

Ps 107:38 greatly; and he does not let their cattle D
Jer 29:6 sons and daughters; multiply there, and do not D
Jn 3:30 He must increase, but I must D

DECREE (52)

Ezra 4:19 And I made a D, and search has been
4:21 Therefore make a D that these men be made
4:21 not rebuilt, until a D is made by me.
5:3 "Who gave you a D to build this house
5:9 'Who gave you a D to build this house
5:13 the king made a D that this house of
5:17 to see whether a D was issued by Cyrus
6:1 the king made a D, and search was made
6:3 the king issued a D: Concerning the house of
6:8 Moreover I make a D regarding what you shall
6:11 Also I make a D that if any one
6:12 I Darius make a D; let it be done
6:14 of Israel and by D of Cyrus and Darius
7:13 now I make a D that any one of
7:21 the king, make a D to all the treasurers
Tob 1:6 is ordained for all Israel by an everlasting D
Esth 1:20 So when the D made by the king is
3:14 be issued as a D in every province by
3:15 the king, and the D was issued in Susa
4:3 king's command and his D came, there was great
4:8 copy of the written D issued in Susa for
8:13 be issued as a D in every province, and
8:14 king's command; and the D was issued in Susa
9:14 to be done; a D was issued in Susa,
Job 28:26 when he made a D for the rain, and
Ps 2:7 will tell of the D of the LORD: He
58:1 Do you indeed D what is right, you gods?
81:5 He made it a D in Joseph, when he
Prov 8:15 kings reign, and rulers D what is just;
Wis 11:7 in rebuke for the D to slay the infants,
Sir 14:12 not delay, and the D of Hades has not
14:17 a garment, for the D from of old is,
41:3 life; this is the D from the Lord for
Is 10:1 Woe to those who D iniquitous decrees, and the
28:22 I have heard a D of destruction from the
Jer 3:8 her away with a D of divorce; yet her
19:5 did not command or D, nor did it come
Dan 2:13 So the D went forth that the wise men
2:15 captain, "Why is the D of the king so
3:10 king, have made a D, that every man who
3:97 Therefore I make a D: Any people, nation, or
4:6 Therefore I made a D that all the wise
4:17 sentence is by the D of the watchers, the
4:24 king: It is a D of the Most High,
6:26 I make a D, that in all my royal
Jon 3:7 through Nineveh, "By the D of the king and
1Mac 1:57 to the law, the D of the king condemned
1:60 According to the D, they put to death the
14:48 orders to inscribe this D upon bronze tablets, to
2Mac 6:8 suggestion of Ptolemy a D was issued to the
Lk 2:1 In those days a D went out from Caesar
Rom 1:32 Though they know God's D that those who do

DECREED (20)

Lev 6:18 eat of it, as D for ever throughout your
6:22 to the LORD as D for ever; the whole
2Chr 30:5 So they D to make a proclamation throughout all
Esth 2:1 and what had been D against her.
3:9 king, let it be D that they be destroyed,
13:6 "Therefore we have D that those indicated to you
Job 20:29 from God, the heritage D for him by God."
Ps 122:4 the LORD, as was D for Israel, to give
Prov 31:5 forget what has been D, and pervert the rights
Is 10:22 Destruction is D, overflowing with righteousness.
10:23 a full end, as D, in the midst of
Dan 9:24 weeks of years are D concerning your people and
9:26 the end there shall be war; desolations are D
9:27 makes desolate, until the D end is poured out
1Mac 7:49 And they D that this day should be celebrated
8:7 took him alive and D that he and those
13:52 And Simon D that every year they should celebrate
2Mac 10:8 They D by public ordinance and vote that the
15:36 And they all D by public vote never to
1Cor 2:7 of God, which God D before the ages for

DECREES (5)

Deut 33:21 the commands and just D of the LORD."
Ps 93:5 Thy D are very sure; holiness befits thy house,
Is 10:1 those who decree iniquitous D, and the writers who
1Mac 14:22 recorded in our public D, as follows, 'Numenius the
Acts 17:7 all acting against the D of Caesar, saying that

DEDAN (10)

Gen 10:7 The sons of Raamah: Sheba and D
25:3 Jokshan was the father of Sheba and D
25:3 sons of D were Asshurim, Letushim, and Le-ummim.
1Chr 1:9 The sons of Raamah: Sheba and D
1:32 The sons of Jokshan: Sheba and D
Jer 25:23 coastland across the sea; D, Tema, Buz, and all
49:8 back, dwell in the depths, O inhabitants of D
Ezek 25:13 from Teman even to D they shall fall by
27:20 D traded with you in saddlecloths for riding.

38:13 Sheba and D and the merchants of Tarshish and

DEDANITES

Is 21:13 in Arabia you will lodge, O caravans of D

DEDICATE (7)

Lev 22:2 of Israel, which they D to me, so that
22:3 the people of Israel D to the LORD, while
27:26 LORD, no man may D; whether ox or sheep,
Deut 20:5 battle and another man D it.
2Chr 2:4 LORD my God and D it to him for
Sir 35:9 a cheerful face, and D your tithe with gladness.
1Mac 4:36 cleanse the sanctuary and D it."

DEDICATED (25)

Deut 20:5 house and has not D it?
2Sam 8:11 these also King David D to the LORD, together
8:11 and gold which he D from all the nations
1Kgs 7:51 David his father had D, the silver, the gold,
8:63 the people of Israel D the house of the
2Kgs 12:18 kings of Judah, had D, and his own votive
23:11 kings of Judah had D to the sun, at
1Chr 18:11 these also King David D to the LORD, together
26:20 the treasuries of the D gifts.
26:26 the treasuries of the D gifts which David the
26:26 hundreds, and the commanders of the army, had D
26:27 won in battles they D gifts for the maintenance
26:28 son of Zeruiah had D --all dedicated gifts were
26:28 Zeruiah had dedicated--all D gifts were in the
28:12 and the treasuries for D gifts;
2Chr 5:1 David his father had D, and stored the silver,
7:5 and all the people D the house of God.
24:7 also used all the D things of the house
31:6 and sheep, and the D things which had been
31:12 the tithes and the D things.
Jud 16:19 Judith also D to God all the vessels of
Is 23:18 her hire will be D to the LORD; it
42:19 is blind as my D one, or blind as
1Mac 4:54 profaned it, it was D with songs and harps
5:1 built and the sanctuary D as it was before,

DEDICATES (7)

Lev 27:14 "When a man D his house to be holy
27:15 And if he who D it wishes to redeem
27:16 "If a man D to the LORD part of
27:17 If he D his field from the year of
27:18 valuation; but if he D his field after the
27:19 And if he who D the field wishes to
27:22 If he D to the LORD a field which

DEDICATING

Ex 35:22 gold objects, every man D an offering of gold

DEDICATION (16)

Num 7:10 offered offerings for the D of the altar on
7:11 each day, for the D of the altar."
7:84 This was the D offering for the altar, on
7:88 This was the D offering for the altar, after
2Chr 7:9 they had kept the D of the altar seven
Ezra 6:16 returned exiles, celebrated the D of this house of
6:17 They offered at the D of this house of
Neh 12:27 And at the D of the wall of Jerusalem
12:27 Jerusalem to celebrate the D with gladness, with
Dan 3:2 to come to the D of the image which
3:3 were assembled for the D of the image that
1Mac 4:56 So they celebrated the D of the altar for
4:59 season the days of D of the altar should
2Mac 2:9 offered sacrifice for the D and completion of the
2:19 great temple, and the D of the altar,
Jn 10:22 the feast of the D at Jerusalem;

DEDUCTION

Lev 27:18 of jubilee, and a D shall be made from

DEED (39)

Gen 44:15 said to them, "What D is this that you
2Sam 12:14 Nevertheless, because by this D you have utterly scorned
Tob 12:13 the dead, your good D was not hidden from
Esth 1:17 For this D of the queen will be made
Job 33:17 man aside from his D, and cut off pride
Prov 19:17 LORD, and he will repay him for his D
Eccl 8:11 sentence against an evil D is not executed speedily,
12:14 God will bring every D into judgment, with every
Wis 3:14 have done no lawless D, and who has not
Sir 3:8 father by word and D, that a blessing from
15:19 and he knows every D of man.
46:7 he did a loyal D, he and Caleb the
Is 28:21 Gibeon; to do his D-- strange is his
28:21 to do his deed-- strange is his D
Jer 32:10 I signed the D, sealed it, got witnesses, and
32:11 I took the sealed D of purchase, containing the
32:12 and I gave the D of purchase to Baruch
32:12 witnesses who signed the D of purchase, and in
32:14 deeds, both this sealed D of purchase and this
32:14 purchase and this open D, and put them in
32:16 I had given the D of purchase to Baruch
32:19 counsel and mighty in D; whose eyes are open
Joel 3:4 I will requite your D upon your own head
3:7 I will requite your D upon your own head.
1Mac 5:61 to do a brave D, they did not listen
5:67 to do a brave D, fell in battle, for
2Mac 12:3 did so ungodly a D as this: they invited
Mt 19:16 saying, "Teacher, what good D must I do, to
Lk 23:50 to their purpose and D, and he was looking
24:19 a prophet mighty in D and word before God
Jn 7:21 them, "I did one D, and you all marvel
Acts 4:9 today concerning a good D done to a cripple,
5:4 you have contrived this D in your heart?
13:41 for I do a D in your days, a
13:41 in your days, a D you will never believe,
Rom 15:18 Gentiles, by word and D,
Col 3:17 do, in word or D, do everything in the
Tit 1:15 they are detestable, disobedient, unfit for any good D
1 Jn 3:18 or speech but in D and in truth.

DEEDS (175)

Ex 15:11 holiness, terrible in glorious D, doing wonders?
Deut 11:3 his signs and his D which he did in
34:12 the great and terrible D which Moses wrought in
Judg 6:13 are all his wonderful D which our fathers recounted
9:16 to him as his D deserved--
1Sam 8:8 According to all the D which they have done
12:7 concerning all the saving D of the LORD which
19:4 you, and because his D have been of good
2Sam 23:20 a doer of great D; he smote two ariels
1Kgs 2:32 bring back his bloody D upon his own head,
2Kgs 14:18 the rest of the D of Amaziah, are they
15:11 the rest of the D of Zechariah, behold, they
15:15 the rest of the D of Shallum, and the
15:21 the rest of the D of Menahem, and all
15:26 the rest of the D of Pekahiah, and all
20:20 The rest of the D of Hezekiah, and all
24:5 the rest of the D of Jehoiakim, and all
1Chr 11:22 a doer of great D; he smote two ariels
16:8 name, make known his D among the peoples!
2Chr 25:26 the rest of the D of Amaziah, from first
32:32 Hezekiah, and his good D, behold, they are written
35:26 Josiah, and his good D according to what is
Ezra 9:13 us for our evil D and for our great
Neh 6:19 spoke of his good D in my presence, and
13:14 not out my good D that I have done
Tob 2:14 me, "Where are your charities and your righteous D
3:2 O Lord; all thy D and all thy ways
4:6 is true, your ways will prosper through your D
12:9 Those who perform D of charity and of righteousness
13:9 afflict you for the D of your sons, but
Esth 6:1 the book of memorable D, the chronicles, and they
Ps 9:1 heart; I will tell of all thy wonderful D
9:11 Tell among the peoples his D
11:7 righteous, he loves righteous D; the upright shall
14:1 corrupt, they do abominable D, there is none that
26:7 song of thanksgiving, and telling all thy wondrous D
28:4 the evil of their D; requite them according to
33:15 hearts of them all, and observes all their D
40:5 my God, thy wondrous D and thy thoughts toward
44:1 have told us, what D thou didst perform in
45:4 right; let your right hand teach you dread D
65:5 By dread D thou dost answer us with deliverance,
66:3 Say to God, "How terrible are thy D
66:5 is terrible in his D among men.
71:15 righteous acts, of thy D of salvation all the
71:16 With the mighty D of the Lord GOD I
71:17 taught me, and I still proclaim thy wondrous D
75:1 call on thy name and recount thy wondrous D
77:11 call to mind the D of the LORD; yea,
77:12 all thy work, and muse on thy mighty D
78:4 coming generation the glorious D of the LORD, and
105:1 name, make known his D among the peoples!
107:22 and tell of his D in songs of joy!
107:24 waters; they saw the D of the LORD, his
118:17 live, and recount the D of the LORD.

D

	141:4	busy myself with wicked D in company with men
	141:5	for my prayer is continually against their wicked D
	145:12	of men thy mighty D, and the glorious splendor
	145:13	all his words, and gracious in all his D
	150:2	him for his mighty D; praise him according to
Prov	14:14	a good man with the fruit of his D
Eccl	4:3	not seen the evil D that are done under
	8:14	happens according to the D of the wicked, and
	8:14	happens according to the D of the righteous.
	9:1	the wise and their D are in the hand
Wis	1:9	him of his lawless D;
	1:16	by their words and D summoned death; considering
	4:20	up, and their lawless D will convict them to
Sir	4:29	your speech, or sluggish and remiss in your D
	7:35	man, because for such D you will be loved.
	11:25	a man's life his D will be revealed.
	12:1	and you will be thanked for your good D
	16:12	reproof; he judges a man according to his D
	16:14	every one will receive in accordance with his D
	18:3	works; and who can search out his mighty D
	18:14	reproach with your good D, nor cause grief by
	20:15	gratitude for my good D; those who eat my
	27:22	his eye plans evil D, and no one can
	32:16	and like a light they will kindle righteous D
	35:19	man according to his D, and the works of
	36:8	appointed time, and let people recount thy mighty D
	36:14	celebration of thy wondrous D, and thy temple with
	44:11	of mercy, whose righteous D have not been forgotten;
	48:4	glorious you were, O Elijah, in your wondrous D
	48:14	so in death his D were marvelous.
Is	3:8	their speech and their D are against the LORD,
	3:10	for they shall eat the fruit of their D
	5:12	do not regard the D of the LORD, or
	12:4	make known his D among the nations, proclaim
	29:15	LORD their counsel, whose D are in the dark,
	59:6	works of iniquity, and D of violence are in
	59:18	According to their D, so will he repay, wrath
	64:6	and all our righteous D are like a polluted
Jer	5:28	know no bounds in D of wickedness; they judge
	11:15	in my house, when she has done vile D
	11:18	knew; then thou didst show me their evil D
	21:2	to all his wonderful D, and will make him
	25:14	them according to their D and the work of
	32:14	of Israel: Take these D, both this sealed deed
	32:44	bought for money, and D shall be signed and
	48:30	boasts are false, his D are false.
	50:29	her according to her D, do to her according
Bar	2:19	because of any righteous D of our fathers or
	2:33	stubbornness and their wicked D; for they will
Ezek	3:20	sin, and his righteous D which he has done
	9:10	I will requite their D upon their heads."
	11:21	I will requite their D upon their own heads,
	16:30	all these things, the D of a brazen harlot;
	16:43	I will requite your D upon your head, says
	18:24	None of the righteous D which he has done
	22:2	Then declare to her all her abominable D
	23:36	Then declare to them their abominable D
	33:13	none of his righteous D shall be remembered; but
	36:19	their conduct and their D I judged them.
	36:31	evil ways, and your D that were not good;
	36:31	for your iniquities and your abominable D
Hos	4:9	for their ways, and requite them for their D
	5:4	Their D do not permit them to return to
	7:2	revealed, and the wicked D of Samaria; for they
	7:3	Now their D encompass them, they are before my
	7:13	air; I will chastise them for their wicked D
	9:15	the wickedness of their D I will drive them
	12:2	his ways, and requite him according to his D
Amos	8:7	"Surely I will never forget any of their D
Obad	1:15	done to you, your D shall return on your
Mic	3:4	they have made their D evil.
Zeph	3:7	to make all their D corrupt."
	3:11	shame because of the D by which you have
Zech	1:4	and from your evil D But they did not
	1:6	for our ways and D, so has he dealt
1Mac	1:24	He committed D of murder, and spoke with great
	2:51	"Remember the D of the fathers, which they did
	3:4	a lion in his D, like a lion's cub
	3:7	Jacob glad by his D, and his memory is
	5:56	heard of their brave D and of the heroic
	8:2	and of the brave D which they were doing
	9:22	wars and the brave D that he did, and
	10:15	fought, of the brave D that they had done,
	16:23	wars and the brave D which he did, and
2Mac	3:36	all men of the D of the supreme God,
Mt	11:2	in prison about the D of the Christ, he
	11:19	and sinners!' Yet wisdom is justified by her D
	23:5	They do all their D to be seen by
Lk	11:48	and consent to the D of your fathers; for
	23:40	due reward of our D; but this man has
Jn	3:19	than light, because their D were evil.
	3:20	the light, lest his D should be exposed.
	3:21	clearly seen that his D have been wrought in
Acts	7:22	and he was mighty in his words and D
	26:20	to God and perform D worthy of their repentance.
Rom	8:13	put to death the D of the body you
2Cor	11:15	Their end will correspond to their D
Col	1:21	in mind, doing evil D,
1Tim	2:10	attire but by good D, as befits women who
	5:10	attested for her good D, as one who has
	5:25	So also good D are conspicuous; and even when
	6:18	be rich in good D, liberal and generous,
2Tim	4:14	harm; the Lord will requite him for his D
Tit	1:15	deny him by their D; they are detestable, disobedient,
	2:7	a model of good D, and in your teaching
	2:14	of his own who are zealous for good D
	3:5	us, not because of D done by us in
	3:8	apply themselves to good D; these are excellent and
	3:14	apply themselves to good D, so as to help
1Pet	1:17	impartially according to his D, conduct yourselves
	2:9	may declare the wonderful D of him who called
	2:12	may see your good D and glorify God on
2Pet	2:8	day with their lawless D,
1 Jn	3:12	Because his own D were evil and his brother's
Jude	1:15	ungodly of all their D of ungodliness which they
Rev	14:13	their labors, for their D follow them!"
	15:3	and wonderful are thy D, O Lord God the
	16:11	and sores, and did not repent of their D
	18:6	her double for her D; mix a double draught
	19:8	linen is the righteous D of the saints.

DEEM

Mal	3:15	Henceforth we D the arrogant blessed; evildoers not

DEEMED (5)

Prov	17:28	his lips, he is D intelligent.
Wis	17:6	and in terror they D the things which they
Sir	23:14	their presence, and be D a fool on account
Is	32:15	the fruitful field is D a forest.
2Mac	9:21	illness, and I have D it necessary to take

DEEMING

Wis	12:15	rulest all things righteously, D it alien to thy

DEEMS

2Thes	1:6	since indeed God D it just to repay

DEEP (97)

Gen	1:2	the face of the D; and the Spirit of
	2:21	LORD God caused a D sleep to fall upon
	7:11	fountains of the great D burst forth, and the
	7:20	above the mountains, covering them fifteen cubits D
	8:2	the fountains of the D and the windows of
	15:12	was going down, a D sleep fell on Abram;
	49:25	blessings of the D that couches beneath, blessings
Deut	33:13	above, and of the D that couches beneath,
1Sam	26:12	all asleep, because a D sleep from the LORD
2Sam	1:21	or rain upon you, nor upsurging of the D
1Kgs	6:3	house, and ten cubits D in front of the
	7:31	pedestal is made, a cubit and a half D
Job	3:5	Let gloom and D darkness claim it.
	4:13	of the night, when D sleep falls on men,
	10:21	land of gloom and D darkness,
	11:7	you find out the D things of God?
	12:22	of darkness, and brings D darkness to light.
	16:16	on my eyelids is D darkness;
	22:13	he judge through the D darkness?
	24:17	For D darkness is morning to all of them;
	24:17	with the terrors of D darkness.
	28:3	ore in gloom and D darkness.
	28:14	The D says, 'It is not in me,' and
	33:15	of the night, when D sleep falls upon men,
	34:22	is no gloom or D darkness where evildoers may
	38:16	sea, or walked in the recesses of the D
	38:17	seen the gates of D darkness?
	38:30	the face of the D is frozen.
	41:31	He makes the D boil like a pot; he
	41:32	one would think the D to be hoary.
Ps	36:1	speaks to the wicked D in his heart; there
	36:6	are like the great D; man and beast thou
	42:7	D calls to deep at the thunder of thy
	42:7	Deep calls to D at the thunder of thy

	44:19	and covered us with D darkness.
	64:6	inward mind and heart of a man are D
	69:2	I sink in D mire, where there is no
	69:2	I have come into D waters, and the flood
	69:14	enemies and from the D waters.
	69:15	over me, or the D swallow me up, or
	77:16	were afraid, yea, the D trembled.
	78:15	and gave them drink abundantly as from the D
	80:9	for it; it took D root and filled the
	88:6	of the Pit, in the regions dark and D
	92:5	Thy thoughts are very D
	104:6	cover it with the D as with a garment;
	106:9	led them through the D as through a desert.
	107:24	of the LORD, his wondrous works in the D
Prov	4:20	the wicked is like D darkness; they do not
	8:27	the face of the D,
	8:28	the fountains of the D,
	18:4	a man's mouth are D waters; the fountain of
	19:15	Slothfulness casts into a D sleep, and an idle
	20:5	man's mind is like D water, but a man
	22:14	loose woman is a D pit; he with whom
	23:27	a harlot is a D pit; an adventures is
Eccl	7:24	is, is far-off, and D, very deep; who can
	7:24	far-off, and deep, very D; who can find it
Wis	4:3	seedlings will strike a D root or take a
	10:18	and led them through D waters;
	16:11	they should fall into D forgetfulness and become
Sir	22:7	rouses a sleeper from D slumber.
	43:23	he stilled the great D and planted islands in
Is	7:11	God; let it be D as Sheol or high
	9:2	in a land of D darkness, on them has
	29:4	Then D from the earth you shall speak, from
	29:10	you a spirit of D sleep, and has closed
	29:15	to those who hide D from the LORD their
	30:33	ready, its pyre made D and wide, with fire
	44:27	who says to the D, 'Be dry, I will
	51:10	waters of the great D; that didst make the
Jer	2:6	land of drought and D darkness, in a land
	13:16	gloom and makes it D darkness.
Ezek	23:32	sister's cup which is D and large; you shall
	26:19	I bring up the D over you, and the
	31:4	waters nourished it, the D made it grow tall,
	31:15	I will make the D mourn for it, and
	40:6	the gate, one reed D;
	47:5	had risen; it was D enough to swim in,
Dan	2:22	understanding; he reveals D and mysterious things;
	8:18	I fell into a D sleep with my face
	10:9	my face in a D sleep with my face
Hos	5:2	And they have made D the pit of Shittim;
Amos	5:8	and Orion, and turns D darkness into the morning,
	7:4	it devoured the great D and was eating up
Jon	2:3	cast me into the D, into the heart of
	2:5	in over me, the D was round about me;
Hab	3:10	waters swept on; the D gave forth its voice,
1Mac	6:9	for many days, because D grief continually gripped
	6:13	I am perishing of D grief in a strange
2Mac	3:27	to the ground and D darkness came over him,
Lk	5:4	"Put out into the D and let down your
	6:48	a house, who dug D, and laid the foundation
Jn	4:11	and the well is D; where do you get
Acts	20:9	He sank into a D sleep as Paul talked
Rom	8:26	us with sighs too D for words.
Rev	2:24	what some call the D things of Satan, to

DEEPER (14)

Lev	13:3	disease appears to be D than the skin of
	13:4	body, and appears no D than the skin, and
	13:20	and if it appears D than the skin and
	13:21	and it is not D than the skin, but
	13:25	white and it appears D than the skin, then
	13:26	and it is no D than the skin, but
	13:30	and if it appears D than the skin, and
	13:31	and it appears no D than the skin and
	13:32	appears to be no D than the skin,
	13:34	appears to be no D than the skin, then
	14:37	it appears to be D than the surface,
Job	11:8	D than Sheol—what can you know?
Prov	17:10	A rebuke goes D into a man of understanding
Sir	24:27	sea, and her counsel D than the great abyss.

DEEPLY (20)

1Sam	1:10	She was D distressed and prayed to the LORD,
2Sam	18:33	And the king was D moved, and went up
Tob	3:10	these things she was D grieved, even to the
	6:17	with her and yearned D for her.
Esth	4:4	her, the queen was D distressed; she sent garments
Song	5:1	friends, and drink: drink D, O lovers!
Sir	38:29	feet; he is always D concerned over his work,
Is	31:6	from whom you have D revolted, O people of
	49:7	Holy One, to one D despised, abhorred by the
	66:11	that you may drink D with delight from the
Dan	13:22	Susanna sighed D, and said, "I am hemmed in
Hos	9:9	They have D corrupted themselves as in the days
1Mac	1:25	Israel mourned D in every community,
	2:39	friends learned of it, they mourned for them D
	2:54	because he was D zealous, received the covenant
	12:52	were in great fear; and all Israel mourned D
	14:16	died, and they were D grieved.
Mk	8:12	And he sighed D in his spirit, and said,
Jn	11:33	also weeping, he was D moved in spirit and
	11:38	Then Jesus, D moved again, came to the tomb;

DEEPS (7)

Ex	15:8	in a heap; the D congealed in the heart
Job	12:22	He uncovers the D out of darkness, and brings
Ps	33:7	bottle; he put the D in storehouses.
	135:6	and on earth, in the seas and all D
	148:7	sea monsters and all D,
Prov	3:20	by his knowledge the D broke forth, and the
Dan	3:55	and lookest upon the D, and to be praised

DEFAMED

1Tim	6:1	of God and the teaching may not be D

DEFEAT (12)

Gen	14:17	his return from the D of Ched-or-laomer and the
Ex	32:18	of the cry of D, but the sound of
Num	22:6	shall be able to D them and drive them
Deut	7:2	to you, and you D them; then you must
2Sam	15:34	servant,' then you will D for me the counsel
	17:14	LORD had ordained to D the good counsel of
Jud	5:20	will go up and D them.
Jer	37:10	even if you should D the whole army of
1Mac	5:40	for he will surely D us.
	5:41	over to him and D him."
2Mac	11:13	he pondered over the D which had befallen him,
1Cor	6:7	with one another is D for you.

DEFEATED (77)

Gen	36:35	son of Bedad, who D Midian in the country
Num	14:45	country came down, and D them and pursued them,
Deut	1:4	them, after he had D Sihon the king of
	1:42	you; lest you be D before your enemies.'
	2:33	to us; and we D him and his sons
	4:46	the children of Israel D when they came out
	28:7	against you to be D before you; they shall
	28:25	cause you to be D before your enemies; you
	29:7	to battle, but we D them;
Josh	10:40	So Joshua D the whole land, the hill country
	10:41	And Joshua D them from Kadesh-barnea to Gaza,
	12:1	the people of Israel D, and took possession of
	12:6	the people of Israel D them; and Moses the
	12:7	the people of Israel D on the west side
	13:12	Rephaim); these Moses had D and driven out.
	13:21	in Heshbon, whom Moses D with the leaders of
Judg	1:4	their hand; and they D ten thousand of them
	1:5	fought against him, and D the Canaanites and the
	1:10	Kiriath-arba); and they D Sheshai and Ahiman and
	1:17	his brother, and they D the Canaanites who inhabited
	3:13	Amalekites, and went and D Israel; and they took
	11:21	of Israel, and they D them; so Israel took
	20:35	And the LORD D Benjamin before Israel; and the
	20:36	So the Benjaminites saw that they were D
1Sam	4:2	battle spread, Israel was D by the Philistines, who
	4:10	fought, and Israel was D, and they fled, every
	13:3	Jonathan D the garrison of the Philistines which was
	13:4	said that Saul had D the garrison of the
	15:7	And Saul D the Amalekites, from Havilah as far
2Sam	5:20	to Baal-perazim, and David D them there; and he
	8:1	After this David D the Philistines and subdued them,
	8:2	And he D Moab, and measured them with a
	8:3	David also D Hadadezer the son of Rehob, king
	8:9	heard that David had D the whole army of
	8:10	fought against Hadadezer and D him; for Hadadezer
	10:15	that they had been D by Israel, they gathered
	10:19	that they had been D by Israel, they made
	18:7	men of Israel were D there by the servants
1Kgs	8:33	thy people Israel are D before the enemy because
2Kgs	10:32	Hazael D them throughout the territory of Israel:
	13:25	Three times Joash D him and recovered the cities
	14:12	And Judah was D by Israel, and every man
1Chr	1:46	son of Bedad, who D Midian in the country

	14:11	to Baal-perazim, and David D them there; and David
	18:1	After this David D the Philistines and subdued them,
	18:2	And he D Moab, and the Moabites became servants
	18:3	David also D Hadadezer king of Zobah, toward
	18:9	heard that David had D the whole army of
	18:10	fought against Hadadezer and D him; for Hadadezer
	19:16	that they had been D by Israel, they sent
	19:19	that they had been D by Israel, they made
2Chr	6:24	thy people Israel are D before the enemy because
	13:15	of Judah shouted, God D Jeroboam and all Israel
	14:12	So the LORD D the Ethiopians before Asa and
	25:22	And Judah was D by Israel, and every man
	28:5	king of Syria, who D him and took captive
	28:5	king of Israel, who D him with great slaughter.
	28:17	had again invaded and D Judah, and carried away
	28:23	of Damascus which had D him, and said, "Because
Jud	1:13	against King Arphaxad, and D him in battle, and
	5:18	them, they were utterly D in many battles and
	7:9	lord hear a word, lest his army be D
	11:11	lord may not be D and his purpose frustrated,
Jer	46:2	Nebuchadrezzar king of Babylon D in the fourth year
1Mac	1:1	land of Kittim, had D Darius, king of the
	3:11	meet him, and he D and killed him.
	5:43	All the Gentiles were D before him, and they
	8:2	Gauls, how they had D them and forced them
	8:6	They also D Antiochus the Great, king of Asia,
	10:49	Alexander pursued him and D them.
	14:3	And he went and D the army of Demetrius,
2Mac	9:2	and his men were D, with the result that
	10:24	Timothy, who had been D by the Jews before,
	12:11	The D nomads besought Judas to grant them pledges
	13:19	Jews, was turned back, attacked again, and was D
	13:22	and his men, was D
Rev	12:8	fought, but they were D and there was no

DEFECT (3)

Lev	21:20	a man with a D in his sight or
Num	19:2	a red heifer without D, in which there is
Deut	17:1	is a blemish, any D whatever; for that is

DEFECTIVE

Tit	1:4	might amend what was D, and appoint elders in

DEFEND (21)

Judg	6:31	Or will you D his cause?
2Kgs	19:34	For I will D this city to save it,
	20:6	Assyria, and I will D this city for my
Jud	5:21	for their Lord will D them, and their God
	6:2	because their God will D them?
Esth	8:11	city to gather and D their lives, to destroy,
	9:16	provinces also gathered to D their lives, and got
	16:20	very day they may D themselves against those who
Job	13:15	hope; yet I will D my ways to his
Ps	5:11	joy; and do thou D them, that those who
	43:1	me, O God, and D my cause against an
	45:4	of truth and to D the right; let your
	72:4	May he D the cause of the poor of
Is	1:17	seek justice, correct oppression; D the fatherless,
	1:23	They do not D the fatherless, and the widow's
	19:20	a savior, and will D and deliver them.
	37:35	For I will D this city to save it,
	38:6	king of Assyria, and D this city.
Jer	5:28	and they do not D the rights of the
Hos	13:10	all your princes, to D you --those of
1Mac	8:32	against you, we will D their rights and fight

DEFENDED (3)

2Sam	23:12	of the plot, and D it, and slew the
1Chr	11:14	of the plot, and D it, and slew the
Acts	7:24	them being wronged, he D the oppressed man and

DEFENDER (3)

2Mac	8:36	the Jews had a D, and that therefore the
	14:34	called upon the constant D of our nation, in
	15:30	body and soul the D of his fellow citizens,

DEFENDERS

2Mac	10:36	wheeled around against the D and set fire to

DEFENDING (3)

Wis	10:20	with one accord thy D hand,
2Mac	6:11	piety kept them from D themselves, in view of
2Cor	12:19	that we have been D ourselves before you?

DEFENDS

Wis	16:17	effect, for the universe D the righteous.

DEFENSE (23)

2Chr	11:5	he built cities for D in Judah.
Ps	48:3	her citadels God has shown himself a sure D
Wis	6:10	who have been taught them will find a D
Sir	34:16	against stumbling and a D against falling.
Is	33:16	heights; his place of D will be the fortresses
Jer	33:4	down to make a D against the siege mounds
	41:9	Asa had made for D against Baasha king of
1Mac	14:10	with the means of D, till his renown spread
2Mac	12:27	and made a vigorous D; and great stores of
	13:26	made the best possible D, convinced them, appeased
Acts	19:33	wishing to make a D to the people.
	22:1	and fathers, hear the D which I now make
	24:9	judge over this nation, I cheerfully make my D
	25:8	Paul said in his D, "Neither against the law
	25:16	opportunity to make his D concerning the charge laid
	26:1	hand and made his D:
	26:2	am to make my D today against all the
	26:24	he thus made his D, Festus said with a
1Cor	9:3	This is my D to those who would examine
Phil	1:7	imprisonment and in the D and confirmation of the
	1:16	put here for the D of the gospel;
2Tim	4:16	At my first D no one took my part;
1Pet	3:15	prepared to make a D to any one who

DEFENSELESS

Ps	141:8	in thee I seek refuge; leave me not D

DEFENSES (4)

Job	13:12	proverbs of ashes, your D are defenses of clay.
	13:12	ashes, your defenses are D of clay.
Ps	60:1	rejected us, broken our D; thou hast been angry;
Amos	3:11	and bring down your D from you, and your

DEFER (2)

Lev	19:15	to the poor or D to the great, but
Is	48:9	my name's sake I D my anger, for the

DEFERENCE (3)

Eccl	10:4	leave your place, for D will make amends for
Wis	6:7	any one, nor show D to greatness; because he
Sir	4:22	your own harm, or D, to your downfall.

DEFERRED

Prov	13:12	Hope D makes the heart sick, but a desire

DEFIANCE

Job	15:25	against God, and bids D to the Almighty,

DEFIANTLY

Ex	14:8	the people of Israel as they went forth D

DEFIED (5)

1Sam	17:36	them, seeing he has D the armies of the
	17:45	of the armies of Israel, whom you have D
2Sam	23:9	with David when they D the Philistines who were
2Chr	13:7	gathered about him and D Rehoboam the son of
Jer	50:29	for she has proudly D the LORD, the Holy

DEFILE (47)

Lev	11:43	and you shall not D yourselves with them, lest
	11:44	You shall not D yourselves with any swarming thing
	18:20	your neighbor's wife, and D yourself with her.
	18:23	with any beast and D yourself with it, neither
	18:24	"Do not D yourselves by any of these things,
	18:28	you out, when you D it, as it vomited
	18:30	you, and never to D yourselves by them: I
	21:1	none of them shall D himself for the dead
	21:3	for her he may D himself).
	21:4	He shall not D himself as a husband among
	21:11	any dead body, nor D himself, even for his
Num	5:3	that they may not D their camp, in the
	35:34	You shall not D the land in which you
Deut	21:23	God; you shall not D your land which the
Jud	9:2	of a virgin to D her, and uncovered her
	9:8	for they intend to D thy sanctuary, and to
	13:16	sin with me, to D and shame me."
Is	23:9	has purposed it, to D the pride of all
	30:22	Then you will D your silver-covered graven images
Jer	7:30	by my name, to D it.
	32:34	by my name, to D it.
Ezek	9:7	he said to them, D the house, and fill
	14:11	astray from me, nor D themselves any more with
	18:6	of Israel, does not D his neighbor's wife or
	18:15	of Israel, does not D his neighbor's wife,
	20:7	you, and do not D yourselves with the idols

20:18 their ordinances, nor D yourselves with their idols.
20:30 Lord GOD: Will you D yourselves after the manner
20:31 sons by fire, you D yourselves with all your
22:3 that makes idols to D herself!
28:7 of your wisdom and D your splendor.
37:23 They shall not D themselves any more with their
43:7 Israel shall no more D my holy name, neither
44:25 They shall not D themselves by going near to
44:25 unmarried sister they may D themselves.
Dan 1:8 that he would not D himself with the king's
1:8 allow him not to D himself.
1Mac 1:46 sabbaths and feasts, to D the sanctuary and the
14:36 to sally forth and D the environs of the
2Mac 6:25 of me, while I D and disgrace my old
Mt 15:20 These are what D a man; but to eat
15:20 unwashed hands does not D a man."
Mk 7:15 going into him can D him; but the things
7:15 a man are what D him."
7:17 man from outside cannot D him,
7:22 from within, and they D a man."
Jude 1:8 men in their dreamings D the flesh, reject authority,

DEFILED (70)

Gen 34:5 heard that he had D his daughter Dinah; but
34:13 deceitfully, because he had D their sister Dinah.
34:27 their sister had been D;
49:4 father's bed; then you D it—you went up
Lev 18:24 casting out before you D themselves;
18:25 and the land became D, so that I punished
18:27 that the land became D;
19:31 them out, to be D by them: I am
21:7 woman who has been D; neither shall they marry
21:14 woman who has been D, or a harlot, these
Num 5:13 undetected though she has D herself, and there is
5:14 his wife who has D herself; or if the
5:14 though she has not D herself;
5:20 and if you have D yourself, and some man
5:27 then, if she has D herself and has acted
5:28 the woman has not D herself and is clean,
6:12 time shall be void, because his separation was D
19:20 assembly, since he has D the sanctuary of the
Deut 24:4 after she has been D; for that is an
2Sam 1:21 of the mighty was D, the shield of Saul,
2Kgs 23:8 cities of Judah, and D the high places where
23:10 And he D Topheth, which is in the valley
23:13 And the king D the high places that were
23:16 upon the altar, and D it, according to the
Neh 13:29 God, because they have D the priesthood and the
Tob 2:9 and because I was D I slept by the
Ps 79:1 thy inheritance; they have D thy holy temple; they
89:39 thy servant; thou hast D his crown in the
Wis 7:25 Almighty; therefore nothing D gains entrance into
11:6 river, stirred up and D with blood
Sir 13:1 touches pitch will be D, and whoever associates with
42:10 virgin, lest she be D or become pregnant in
47:20 upon your honor, and D your posterity, so that
Is 59:3 For your hands are D with blood and your
Jer 2:7 you came in you D my land, and made
2:23 say, 'I am not D, I have not gone
19:13 other gods—shall be D like the place of
Lam 4:14 through the streets, so D with blood that none
Bar 3:10 country, that you are D with the dead,
Ezek 4:14 behold, I have never D myself; from my youth
5:11 surely, because you have D my sanctuary with all
20:26 have life; and I D them through their very
22:4 you have shed, and D by the idols which
23:7 of them; and she D herself with all the
23:13 saw that she was D; they both took the
23:17 of love, and they D her with their lust;
23:38 to me: they have D my sanctuary on the
36:17 their own land, they D it by their ways
36:18 with which they had D it.
43:8 They have D my holy name by their abominations
44:26 After he is D, he shall count for himself
Hos 5:3 Ephraim, you have played the harlot, Israel is D
6:10 horrible thing; Ephraim's harlotry is there, Israel is D
9:4 of it shall be D; for their bread shall
Zeph 3:1 that is rebellious and D, the oppressing city!
1Mac 1:37 innocent blood; they even D the sanctuary.
1:63 rather than to be D by food or to
4:43 sanctuary and removed the D stones to an unclean
4:45 for the Gentiles had D it.
7:34 and derided them and D them and spoke arrogantly,
2Mac 7:34 unholy wretch, you most D of all men, do
14:3 priest but had wilfully D himself in the times
Mk 7:2 disciples ate with hands D, that is, unwashed.
7:5 tradition of the elders, but eat with hands D
Jn 18:28 they might not be D, but might eat the
Acts 21:28 temple, and he has D this holy place."
1Cor 8:7 an idol; and their conscience, being weak, is D
Heb 9:13 if the sprinkling of D persons with the blood
12:15 it the many become D;
Rev 14:4 these who have not D themselves with women, for

DEFILEMENT (2)

2Mac 5:27 so that they might not share in the D
2Cor 7:1 cleanse ourselves from every D of body and spirit,

DEFILEMENTS

2Pet 2:20 they have escaped the D of the world through

DEFILES (12)

Num 5:29 authority, goes astray and D herself,
6:9 beside him, and he D his consecrated head, then
19:13 does not cleanse himself, D the tabernacle of the
Sir 21:28 A whisperer D his own soul and is hated
Ezek 18:11 eats upon the mountains, D his neighbor's wife,
22:11 wife; another lewdly D his daughter-in-law; another
22:11 daughter-in-law; another in you D his sister, his
33:26 and each of you D his neighbor's wife; shall
Mt 15:11 goes into the mouth D a man, but what
15:11 of the mouth, this D a man."
15:18 the heart, and this D a man.
Mk 7:19 a man is what D a man.

DEFILING (4)

Lev 15:31 in their uncleanness by D my tabernacle that is
20:3 his children to Molech, D my sanctuary and
22:8 he shall not eat, D himself by it: I
2Pet 2:10 in the lust of D passion and despise authority.

DEFINITE (2)

Acts 2:23 up according to the D plan and foreknowledge of
25:26 But I have nothing D to write to my

DEFRAUD (2)

Mk 10:19 false witness, Do not D, Honor your father and
1Cor 6:8 you yourselves wrong and D, and that even your

DEFRAUDED (5)

1Sam 12:3 Or whom have I D
12:4 said, "You have not D us or oppressed us
Sir 29:7 been afraid of being D needlessly.
Lk 19:8 and if I have D any one of anything,
1Cor 6:7 Why not rather be D

DEFRAYED

2Mac 3:3 the king of Asia, D from his own revenues

DEFY (4)

1Sam 17:10 the Philistine said, "I D the ranks of Israel
17:25 has come up to D Israel; and the man
17:26 Philistine, that he should D the armies of the
Ps 139:20 me, men who maliciously D thee, who lift themselves

DEFYING

Is 3:8 are against the LORD, D his glorious presence.

DEGENERATE

Jer 2:21 then have you turned D and become a wild

DEGRADED

Deut 25:3 these, your brother be D in your sight.

DEGRADING

1Cor 11:14 wear long hair is D to him,

DEGREE (3)

2Mac 4:3 progressed to such a D that even murders were
Lk 1:52 exalted those of low D;
2Cor 3:18 his likeness from one D of glory to another;

DEIGN

2Mac 14:9 details of this matter, D to take thought for

DEITY (3)

Acts 17:29 to think that the D is like gold, or
Rom 1:20 his eternal power and D, has been clearly perceived
Col 2:9 the whole fulness of D dwells bodily,

DEJECTED

Sir 25:22 A D mind, a gloomy face, and a wounded

D

DEJECTEDLY
1Kgs 21:27 fasted and lay in sackcloth, and went about D

DEJECTION
Jas 4:9 be turned to mourning and your joy to D

DELAIAH (7)
1Chr 3:24 Eliashib, Pelaiah, Akkub, Johanan, D, and Anani,
24:18 the twenty-third to D, the twenty-fourth to Ma-aziah.
Ezra 2:60 Israel: the sons of D, the sons of Tobiah,
Neh 6:10 Shemaiah the son of D, son of Mehetabel, who
7:62 Israel: the sons of D, the sons of Tobiah,
Jer 36:12 Elishama the secretary, D the son of Shemaiah,
36:25 Even when Elnathan and D and Gemariah urged the

DELAY (25)
Gen 24:56 to them, "Do not D me, since the LORD
34:19 young man did not D to do the thing,
Ex 22:29 "You shall not D to offer from the fulness
Ezra 6:8 in full and without D from the royal revenue,
Tob 5:8 he said to him, "Go, and do not D
9:4 days, and if I D long he will be
10:4 has perished; his long D proves it." Then she
Jud 2:13 you; and do not D about it."
Ps 119:60 hasten and do not D to keep thy commandments.
Eccl 5:4 to God, do not D paying it; for he
8:3 his presence, do not D when the matter is
Sir 4:3 an angry mind, nor D your gift to a
5:7 Do not D to turn to the Lord, nor
7:16 crowd of sinners; remember that wrath does not D
14:12 that death will not D, and the decree of
29:5 for repayment he will D, and will pay in
35:18 the Lord will not D, neither will he be
Dan 9:19 give heed and act; D not, for thy own
Hab 2:3 it; it will surely come, it will not D
2Mac 14:27 send Maccabeus to Antioch as a prisoner without D
Lk 1:21 they wondered at his D in the temple.
18:7 Will he D long over them?
Acts 9:38 him entreating him, "Please come to us without D
25:17 here, I made no D, but on the next
Rev 10:6 should be no more D,

DELAYED (10)
Gen 43:10 if we had not D, we would now have
Ex 32:1 people saw that Moses D to come down from
Judg 3:26 Ehud escaped while they D, and passed beyond the
2Sam 20:5 summon Judah; but he D beyond the set time
Ezek 12:25 will no longer be D, but in your days,
12:28 my words will be D any longer, but the
Mt 24:48 himself, 'My master is D
25:5 As the bridegroom was D, they all slumbered and
Lk 12:45 himself, 'My master is D in coming,' and begins
1Tim 3:15 that, if I am D, you may know how

DELECTABLE
Song 7:6 are, O loved one, D maiden!

DELETE
1Mac 8:30 determine to add or D anything, they shall do

DELETION
1Mac 8:30 and any addition or D that they may make

DELIBERATE (2)
Sir 5:11 to hear, and be D in answering.
1Mac 8:15 twenty senators constantly D concerning the people,

DELIBERATED
1Mac 4:44 They D what to do about the altar of

DELIBERATELY (3)
Sir 30:21 over to sorrow, and do not afflict yourself D
Heb 10:26 For if we sin D after receiving the knowledge
2Pet 3:5 They D ignore this fact, that by the word

DELIBERATION
Sir 32:19 Do nothing without D; and when you have acted,

DELIBERATIONS
Sir 44:4 the people in their D and in understanding of

DELICACIES (5)
Prov 23:3 Do not desire his D, for they are deceptive
23:6 do not desire his D;
Wis 16:3 suffering want a short time, might partake of D
Jer 51:34 his belly with my D, he has rinsed me
Dan 10:3 I ate no D, no meat or wine entered

DELICACY
Wis 16:2 quails to eat, a D to satisfy the desire

DELICATE (2)
Deut 28:56 because she is so D and tender, will grudge
Is 47:1 you shall no more be called tender and D

DELICATELY (3)
Deut 28:54 the most tender and D bred among you will
28:56 The most tender and D bred woman among you,
Jer 6:2 The comely and D bred I will destroy, the

DELICIOUS (3)
Prov 18:8 a whisperer are like D morsels; they go down
26:22 a whisperer are like D morsels; they go down
2Mac 15:39 water is sweet and D and enhances one's enjoyment,

DELIGHT (84)
Gen 3:6 that it was a D to the eyes, and
34:19 thing, because he had D in Jacob's daughter.
Deut 21:14 if you have no D in her, you shall
28:63 as the LORD took D in doing you good
28:63 the LORD will take D in bringing ruin upon
30:9 LORD will again take D in prospering you, as
30:9 you, as he took D in your fathers,
1Sam 15:22 the LORD as great D in burnt offerings and
18:22 'Behold, the king has D in you, and all
2Sam 24:3 my lord the king D in this thing?"
Neh 1:11 of thy servants who D to fear thy name;
Esth 6:6 "Whom would the king D to honor more than
Job 22:26 silver; then you will D yourself in the Almighty,
27:10 Will he take D in the Almighty?
34:9 that he should take D in God.'
Ps 1:2 of scoffers; but his D is in the law
16:3 are the noble, in whom is all my D
37:4 Take D in the LORD, and he will give
37:11 possess the land, and D themselves in abundant
40:8 written of me; I D to do thy will,
44:3 countenance; for thou didst D in them.
51:16 For thou hast no D in sacrifice; were I
51:19 Jerusalem, then wilt thou D in right sacrifices, in
68:30 scatter the peoples who D in war.
119:14 of thy testimonies I D as much as in
119:16 I will D in thy statutes; I will not
119:24 Thy testimonies are my D, they are my counselors.
119:35 thy commandments, for I D in it.
119:47 for I find my D in thy commandments, which
119:70 like fat, but I D in thy law.
119:77 I may live; for thy law is my D
119:92 had not been my D, I should have perished
119:143 come upon me, but thy commandments are my D
119:174 salvation, O LORD, and thy law is my D
147:10 His D is not in the strength of the
Prov 1:22 How long will scoffers D in their scoffing and
2:14 in doing evil and D in the perverseness of
5:19 at all times with D, be infatuated always with
7:18 till morning; let us D ourselves with love.
8:30 I was daily his D, rejoicing before him always,
11:1 the LORD, but a just weight is his D
11:20 LORD, but those of blameless ways are his D
12:22 LORD, but those who act faithfully are his D
15:8 but the prayer of the upright is his D
16:13 Righteous lips are the D of a king, and
24:25 the wicked will have D, and a good blessing
29:17 rest; he will give D to your heart.
Eccl 2:8 men and women, and many concubines, man's D
Song 2:3 With great D I sat in his shadow, and
Wis 1:13 and he does not D in the death of
3:14 a place of great D in the temple of
6:21 Therefore if you D in thrones and scepters, O
8:18 friendship with her, pure D, and in the labors
13:3 If through D in the beauty of these things
Sir 9:12 Do not D in what pleases the ungodly; remember
21:16 on a journey, but D will be found in
30:23 D your soul and comfort your heart, and remove
45:12 of an expert, the D of the eyes, richly
Is 1:11 beasts; I do not D in the blood of
11:3 And his D shall be in the fear of
13:17 silver and do not D in gold.
44:9 and the things they D in do not profit;
55:2 what is good, and D yourselves in fatness.
58:2 seek me daily, and D to know my ways,
58:2 me righteous judgments, they D to draw near to
58:13 call the sabbath a D and the holy day

	58:14	then you shall take D in the LORD, and
	62:4	shall be called My D is in her, and
	65:12	what I did not D in."
	66:4	and chose that in which I did not D
	66:11	may drink deeply with D from the abundance of
Jer	9:24	in these things I D, says the LORD."
	15:16	a joy and the D of my heart; for
Ezek	24:16	about to take the D of your eyes away
	24:21	of your power, the D of your eyes, and
	24:25	joy and glory, the D of their eyes and
Hos	8:13	the LORD has no D in them.
Amos	5:21	and I take no D in your solemn assemblies.
Mic	1:16	the children of your D; make yourselves as bald
Mal	3:1	covenant in whom you D, behold, he is coming,
	3:12	be a land of D, says the LORD of
Mt	13:22	the world and the D in riches choke the
Mk	4:19	the world, and the D in riches, and the
Rom	7:22	For I D in the law of God, in

DELIGHTED (9)

1Sam	19:1	But Jonathan, Saul's son, D much in David.
2Sam	22:20	delivered me, because he D in me.
1Kgs	10:9	your God, who has D in you and set
2Chr	9:8	your God, who has D in you and set
Neh	9:25	and became fat, and D themselves in thy great
Esth	2:14	again, unless the king D in her and she
Ps	18:19	delivered me, because he D in me.
Sir	51:15	ripening grape my heart D in her; my foot
Is	1:29	oaks in which you D; and you shall blush

DELIGHTING

Prov	8:31	his inhabited world and D in the sons of

DELIGHTS (23)

Num	14:8	If the LORD D in us, he will bring
Esth	6:6	man whom the king D to honor?" And Haman
	6:7	man whom the king D to honor,
	6:9	man whom the king D to honor, and let
	6:9	man whom the king D to honor.'"
	6:11	man whom the king D to honor."
Job	20:20	he will not save anything in which he D
Ps	5:4	not a God who D in wickedness; evil may
	22:8	rescue him, for he D in him!"
	35:27	is the LORD, who D in the welfare of
	36:8	givest them drink from the river of thy D
	37:23	in whose way he D;
	112:1	the LORD, who greatly D in his commandments!
Prov	3:12	as a father the son in whom he D
Sir	1:10	fear of the Lord D the heart, and gives
	1:24	and instruction, and he D in fidelity and meekness.
	26:13	A wife's charm D her husband, and her skill
Is	42:1	in whom my soul D; I have put my
	62:4	Married; for the LORD D in you, and your
	66:3	ways, and their soul D in their abominations;
Mic	7:18	for ever because he D in steadfast love.
Mal	2:17	the LORD, and he D in them." Or by
2Mac	15:39	style of the story D the ears of those

DELILAH (7)

Judg	16:4	in the valley of Sorek, whose name was D
	16:6	And D said to Samson, "Please tell me wherein
	16:10	And D said to Samson, "Behold, you have mocked
	16:12	So D took new ropes and bound him with
	16:13	And D said to Samson, "Until now you have
	16:14	So while he slept, D took the seven locks
	16:18	When D saw that he had told her all

DELIVER (195)

Gen	32:11	D me, I pray thee, from the hand of
	42:34	men, and I will D to you your brother,
Ex	3:8	have come down to D them out of the
	5:18	you, yet you shall D the same number of
	6:6	Egyptians, and I will D you from their bondage,
	23:31	Euphrates; for I will D the inhabitants of the
Lev	26:26	one oven, and shall D your bread again by
Deut	32:39	is none that can D out of my hand.
Josh	2:13	belong to them, and D our lives from death."
Judg	6:14	might of yours and D Israel from the hand
	6:15	Lord, how can I D Israel?
	6:36	God, "If thou wilt D Israel by my hand,
	6:37	know that thou wilt D Israel by my hand,
	7:7	that lapped I will D you, and give the
	10:1	Abimelech there arose to D Israel Tola the son
	10:11	Israel, "Did I not D you from the Egyptians
	10:13	gods; therefore I will D you no more.
	10:14	have chosen; let them D you in the time
	10:15	good to thee; only D us, we pray thee,
	12:2	you, you did not D me from their hand.
	12:3	that you would not D me, I took my
	13:5	he shall begin to D Israel from the hand
1Sam	4:8	Who can D us from the power of these
	7:3	only, and he will D you out of the
	12:10	the Ashtaroth; but now D us out of the
	17:37	of the bear, will D me from the hand
	17:46	day the LORD will D you into my hand,
	24:15	plead my cause, and D me from your hand."
	26:24	LORD, and may he D me out of all
	30:15	not kill me, or D me into the hands
2Sam	14:16	king will hear, and D his servant from the
	22:28	Thou dost D a humble people, but thy eyes
	22:44	"Thou didst D me from strife with the peoples;
	22:49	my adversaries, thou didst D me from men of
1Kgs	20:5	sent to you, saying, D to me your silver
2Kgs	3:4	and he had to D annually to the king
	17:39	God, and he will D you out of the
	18:29	not be able to D you out of my
	18:30	The LORD will surely D us, and this city
	18:32	saying, The LORD will D us.
	18:35	that the LORD should D Jerusalem out of my
	20:6	I will D you and this city out of
1Chr	16:35	Say also: D us, O God of our salvation,
2Chr	25:15	people, which did not D their own people from
	32:11	LORD our God will D us from the hand
	32:13	at all able to D their lands out of
	32:14	destroyed was able to D his people from my
	32:14	should be able to D you from my hand?
	32:15	has been able to D his people from my
	32:15	less will your God D you out of my
	32:17	of Hezekiah will not D his people from my
Ezra	7:19	your God, you shall D before the God of
Neh	9:28	many times thou didst D them according to thy
Jud	6:3	their God will not D them--we the king's
	8:33	enemies, the Lord will D Israel by my hand.
Esth	4:8	king concerning us and D us from death."
Job	5:4	is no one to D them.
	5:19	He will D you from six troubles; in seven
	6:23	Or, D me from the adversary's hand?
	10:7	there is none to D out of thy hand?
	33:24	to him, and says, D him from going down
Ps	3:7	D me, O my God!
	6:4	LORD, save my life; D me for the sake
	7:1	all my pursuers, and D me,
	17:13	D my life from the wicked by thy sword,
	18:27	For thou dost D a humble people; but the
	18:43	Thou didst D me from strife with the peoples;
	18:48	my adversaries; thou didst D me from men of
	22:4	trusted, and thou didst D them.
	22:8	the LORD; let him D him, let him rescue
	22:20	D my soul from the sword, my life from
	25:20	guard my life, and D me; let me not
	31:1	shame; in thy righteousness D me!
	31:15	are in thy hand; D me from the hand
	33:19	love, that he may D their soul from death,
	39:8	D me from all my transgressions.
	40:13	pleased, O LORD, to D me!
	43:1	deceitful and unjust men D me!
	44:26	D us for the sake of thy steadfast love!
	50:15	of trouble; I will D you, and you shall
	50:22	lest I rend, and there be none to D
	51:14	D me from bloodguiltiness, O God, thou God of
	55:18	He will D my soul in safety from the
	59:1	D me from my enemies, O my God, protect
	59:2	rise up against me, D me from those who
	70:1	pleased, O God, to D me!
	71:2	In thy righteousness D me and rescue me; incline
	71:11	there is none to D him."
	74:19	Do not D the soul of thy dove to
	79:9	glory of thy name; D us, and forgive our
	82:4	weak and the needy; D them from the hand
	89:48	Who can D his soul from the power of
	91:3	For he will D you from the snare of
	91:14	in love, I will D him; I will protect
	109:21	steadfast love is good, D me!
	119:153	on my affliction and D me, for I do
	119:170	supplication come before thee; D me according to
	120:2	he may answer me: D me, O LORD, from
	140:1	D me, O LORD, from evil men; preserve me
	142:6	D me from my persecutors; for they are too
	143:9	D me, O LORD, from my enemies!
	144:7	high, rescue me and D me from the many
	144:11	the cruel sword, and D me from the hand
Prov	19:19	penalty; for if you D him, you will only

D

Eccl 8:8 war, nor will wickedness D those who are given
Wis 2:18 help him, and will D him from the hand
19:9 O Lord, who didst D them.
Sir 4:9 D him who is wronged from the hand of
33:1 in trial he will D him again and again.
50:24 And let him D us in our days!
51:3 my helper and didst D me, in the greatness
51:8 old, that thou dost D those who wait for
Is 19:20 and will defend and D them.
31:5 he will protect and D it, he will spare
36:14 not be able to D you.
36:15 "The LORD will surely D us; this city will
36:18 saying, "The LORD will D us." Has any of
36:20 that the LORD should D Jerusalem out of my
38:6 I will D you and this city out of
43:13 is none who can D from my hand; I
44:17 to it and says, D me, for thou art
44:20 astray, and he cannot D himself or say, "Is
47:14 consumes them; they cannot D themselves from the
50:2 Or have I no power to D
57:13 your collection of idols D you!
Jer 1:8 am with you to D you, says the LORD."
1:19 says the LORD, to D you."
15:20 to save you and D you, says the LORD.
15:21 I will D you out of the hand of
18:21 Therefore D up their children to famine; give them
21:12 in the morning, and D from the hand of
22:3 justice and righteousness, and D from the hand of
29:21 name: Behold, I will D them into the hand
38:16 you to death or D you into the hand
39:17 But I will D you on that day, says
42:11 save you and to D you from his hand.
43:3 you against us, to D us into the hand
46:26 I will D them into the hand of those
Lam 5:8 there is none to D us from their hand.
Bar 2:14 for thy own sake D us, and grant us
4:18 calamities upon you will D you from the hand
4:21 God, and he will D you from the power
6:54 their own cause or D one who is wronged,
Ezek 7:19 are not able to D them in the day
13:21 will tear off, and D my people out of
13:23 practice divination; I will D my people out of
14:14 in it, they would D but their own lives
14:16 Lord GOD, they would D neither sons nor daughters;
14:18 Lord GOD, they would D neither sons nor daughters,
14:20 Lord GOD, they would D neither son nor daughter;
14:20 nor daughter; they would D but their own lives
21:31 wrath; and I will D you into the hands
23:28 GOD: Behold, I will D you into the hands
33:12 the righteous shall not D him when he transgresses;
34:27 of their yoke, and D them from the hand
36:29 And I will D you from all your uncleannesses;
Dan 3:15 the god that will D you out of my
3:17 serve is able to D us from the burning
3:17 furnace; and he will D us out of your
3:43 D us in accordance with thy marvelous works, and
3:97 who is able to D in this way."
6:14 set his mind to D Daniel; and he labored
6:16 whom you serve continually, D you!"
6:20 continually, been able to D you from the lions?"
Hos 1:7 Judah, and I will D them by the LORD
1:7 God; I will not D them by bow, nor
Amos 1:6 a whole people to D them up to Edom.
6:8 strongholds; and I will D up the city and
Mic 5:6 sword; and they shall D us from the Assyrian
5:8 tears in pieces, and there is none to D
Zeph 1:18 shall be able to D them on the day
Zech 11:6 earth, and I will D none from their hand."
1Mac 12:17 and greet you and D to you this letter
Mt 6:13 not into temptation, But D us from evil.
10:17 men; for they will D you up to councils,
10:19 When they D you up, do not be anxious
10:21 Brother will D up brother to death, and the
20:19 him to death, and D him to the Gentiles
24:9 "Then they will D you up to tribulation, and
26:15 give me if I D him to you?" And
27:43 in God; let God D him now, if he
Mk 10:33 him to death, and D him to the Gentiles;
13:9 yourselves; for they will D you up to councils;
13:11 you to trial and D you up, do not
13:12 And brother will D up brother to death, and
Lk 20:20 said, so as to D him up to the
Acts 7:34 have come down to D them.
21:11 owns this girdle and D him into the hands
Rom 7:24 Who will D me from this body of death?
1Cor 5:5 Jesus, you are to D this man to Satan
13:3 have, and if I D my body to be
2Cor 1:10 peril, and he will D us; on him we
1:10 hope that he will D us again.
Gal 1:4 for our sins to D us from the present
Heb 2:15 is, the devil, and D all those who through

DELIVERANCE (38)

Judg 15:18 hast granted this great D by the hand of
1Sam 11:9 time the sun is hot, you shall have D
11:13 the LORD has wrought D in Israel."
2Chr 12:7 will grant them some D, and my wrath shall
Jud 8:17 we wait for his D, let us call upon
Esth 4:14 as this, relief and D will rise for the
Ps 3:8 D belongs to the LORD; thy blessing be upon
9:14 daughter of Zion I may rejoice in thy D
14:7 O that D for Israel would come out of
22:31 generation, and proclaim his D to a people yet
32:7 me from trouble; thou dost encompass me with D
35:3 Say to my soul, "I am your D
35:9 shall rejoice in the LORD, exulting in his D
40:9 the glad news of D in the great congregation;
51:14 and my tongue will sing aloud of thy D
53:6 O that D for Israel would come from Zion!
62:7 On God rests my D and my honor; my
65:5 dost answer us with D, O God of our
72:4 of the people, give D to the needy, and
Wis 16:6 received a token of D to remind them of
18:7 The D of the righteous and the destruction of
Sir 51:9 earth, and prayed for D from death.
Is 26:18 We have wrought no D in the earth, and
46:12 who are far from D:
46:13 I bring near my D, it is not far-off,
51:1 me, you who pursue D, you who seek the
51:5 My D draws near speedily, my salvation has gone
51:6 for ever, and my D will never be ended.
51:8 like wool; but my D will be for ever,
56:1 will come, and my D be revealed.
Jon 2:9 D belongs to the LORD!"
Mic 7:9 forth to the light; I shall behold his D
1Mac 3:6 evildoers were confounded; and D prospered by his
4:25 Israel had a great D that day.
4:56 offered a sacrifice of D and praise.
5:62 those men through whom D was given to Israel.
Acts 7:25 God was giving them D by his hand, but
Phil 1:19 turn out for my D,

DELIVERED (191)

Gen 9:2 of the sea; into your hand they are D
14:20 Most High, who has D your enemies into your
25:24 her days to be D were fulfilled, behold, there
32:16 These he D into the hand of his servants,
37:21 Reuben heard it, he D him out of their
Ex 1:18 are vigorous and are D before the midwife comes
2:19 They said, "An Egyptian D us out of the
5:23 and thou hast not D thy people at all."
18:4 was my help, and D me from the sword
18:8 how the LORD had D them.
18:9 in that he had D them out of the
18:10 the LORD, who has D you out of the
18:11 all gods, because he D the people from under
Lev 9:12 offering; and Aaron's sons D to him the blood,
9:13 And they D the burnt offering to him, piece
9:18 people; and Aaron's sons D to him the blood,
26:25 and you shall be D into the hand of
Josh 9:26 did to them, and D them out of the
24:10 blessed you; so I D you out of his
Judg 3:9 people of Israel, who D them, Othni-el the son
3:31 oxgoad; and he too D Israel.
6:9 of bondage; and I D you from the hand
7:2 'My own hand has D me.'
8:22 also; for you have D us out of the
10:12 to me, and I D you out of their
1Sam 10:18 of Egypt, and I D you from the hand
12:11 Jephthah, and Samuel, and D you out of the
14:23 So the LORD D Israel that day; and the
14:48 smote the Amalekites, and D Israel out of the
17:35 and smote him and D it out of his
17:37 said, "The LORD who D me from the paw
23:5 So David D the inhabitants of Keilah.
2Sam 12:7 over Israel, and I D you out of the
18:19 that the LORD has D him from the power
18:28 your God, who has D up the men who
18:31 For the LORD has D you this day from
19:9 Israel, saying, "The king D us from the hand
22:1 day when the LORD D him from the hand
22:18 He D me from my strong enemy, from those

22:20 a broad place; he D me, because he delighted
1Kgs 3:18 day after I was D, this woman also gave
17:23 into the house, and D him to his mother;
2Kgs 11:10 And the priest D to the captains the spears
12:15 into whose hand they D the money to pay
18:33 of the nations ever D his land out of
18:34 Have they D Samaria out of my hand?
18:35 of the countries have D their countries out of
19:11 And shall you be D
19:12 gods of the nations D them, the nations which
22:7 the money which is D into their hand, for
22:9 the house, and have D it into the hand
1Chr 22:18 For he has D the inhabitants of the land
2Chr 23:9 And Jehoiada the priest D to the captains the
24:24 few men, the LORD D into their hand a
32:17 lands who have not D their people from my
34:9 the high priest and D the money that had
34:10 They D it to the workmen who had the
34:17 the LORD and have D it into the hand
Ezra 5:14 Babylon, and they were D to one whose name
8:31 upon us, and he D us from the hand
8:36 They also D the king's commissions to the king's
Jud 16:3 wars; for he has D me out of the
Esth 10:9 people; the Lord has D us from all these
Job 8:4 against him, he has D them into the power
22:30 man; you will be D through the cleanness of
29:12 it approved; because I D the poor who cried,
39:3 their offspring, and are D of their young?
Ps 18:17 He D me from my strong enemy, and from
18:19 a broad place; he D me, because he delighted
18:48 peoples under me; who D me from my enemies;
31:8 adversities, and hast not D me into the hand
33:16 a warrior is not D by his great strength.
34:4 he answered me, and D me from all my
54:7 For thou hast D me from every trouble, and
56:13 For thou hast D my soul from death, yea,
60:5 thy beloved may be D, give victory by thy
69:14 mire; let me be D from my enemies and
78:61 dwelt among men, and D his power to captivity,
81:7 you called, and I D you; I answered you
86:13 toward me; thou hast D my soul from the
106:10 of the foe, and D them from the power
106:43 Many times he D them, but they were rebellious
107:6 their trouble, and he D them from their distress;
107:13 their trouble, and he D them from their distress;
107:19 their trouble, and he D them from their distress;
107:20 and healed them, and D them from destruction.
107:28 their trouble, and he D them from their distress;
108:6 thy beloved may be D, give help by thy
116:8 For thou hast D my soul from death, my
Prov 11:8 The righteous is D from trouble, and the wicked
11:9 his neighbor, but by knowledge the righteous are D
11:21 unpunished, but those who are righteous will be D
28:18 in integrity will be D, but he who is
28:26 but he who walks in wisdom will be D
Eccl 9:15 he by his wisdom D the city.
Wis 10:1 had been created; she D him from his transgression,
10:13 not desert him, but D him from sin.
10:15 and blameless race wisdom D from a nation of
16:11 and then were quickly D, lest they should fall
Sir 48:20 them from heaven, and D them by the hand
49:10 people of Jacob and D them with confident hope.
51:2 and helper and hast D my body from destruction
Is 20:6 for help to be D from the king of
36:18 gods of the nations D his land out of
36:19 Have they D Samaria out of my hand?
36:20 of these countries have D their countries out of
37:11 And shall you be D
37:12 gods of the nations D them, the nations which
43:28 of the sanctuary, I D Jacob to utter destruction
64:7 from us, and hast D us into the hand
66:7 upon her she was D of a son.
Jer 7:10 and say, 'We are D –only to go on
20:13 For he has D the life of the needy
34:3 surely be captured and D into his hand; you
37:17 said, "You shall be D into the hand of
46:24 shame, she shall be D into the hand of
Lam 2:7 his sanctuary; he has D into the hand of
Ezek 14:16 they alone would be D, but the land would
14:18 sons nor daughters, but they alone would be D
16:21 slaughtered my children and D them up as an
16:27 your allotted portion, and D you to the greed
21:12 of Israel; they are D over to the sword
23:9 Therefore I D her into the hands of her
Dan 3:89 hand of death, and D us from the midst
3:89 the fire he has D us.
3:96 sent his angel and D his servants, who trusted
11:41 but these shall be D out of his hand:
12:1 your people shall be D, every one whose name
Joel 2:32 the LORD shall be D; for in Mount Zion
Amos 1:9 the punishment; because they D up a whole people
Obad 1:14 you should not have D up his survivors in
1Mac 2:60 of his innocence was D from the mouth of
5:50 and the city was D into his hands.
7:35 and his army are D into my hands this
9:46 that you may be D from the hands of
12:15 aid; and we were D from our enemies and
16:2 so that we have D Israel many times.
2Mac 11:15 the Jews which Maccabeus D to Lysias in writing.
11:17 sent by you, have D your signed communication and
12:45 that they might be D from their sin.
Mt 11:27 All things have been D to me by my
17:21 man is to be D into the hands of
18:33 in anger his lord D him to the jailers,
20:18 of man will be D to the chief priests
25:20 more, saying, 'Master, you D to me five talents;
25:22 forward, saying, 'Master, you D to me two talents;
26:2 of man will be D up to be crucified."
27:2 led him away and D him to Pilate the
27:18 envy that they had D him up.
27:26 and having scourged Jesus, D him to be crucified.
Mk 9:31 of man will be D into the hands of
10:33 of man will be D to the chief priests
15:1 led him away and D him to Pilate.
15:10 the chief priests had D him up.
15:15 having scourged Jesus, he D him to be crucified.
Lk 1:2 just as they were D to us by those
1:57 for Elizabeth to be D, and she gave birth
1:74 us that we, being D from the hand of
2:6 there, the time came for her to be D
4:6 for it has been D to me, and I
9:44 man is to be D into the hands of
10:22 All things have been D to me by my
18:32 For he will be D to the Gentiles, and
21:16 You will be D up even by parents and
23:24 for; but Jesus he D up to their will.
24:7 of man must be D into the hands of
24:20 chief priests and rulers D him up to be
Jn 16:21 but when she is D of the child, she
19:11 above; therefore he who D me to you has
Acts 2:23 know-- this Jesus, D up according to the
3:13 servant Jesus, whom you D up and denied in
6:14 the customs which Moses D to us."
7:53 received the law as D by angels and did
12:4 him in prison, and D him to four squads
15:30 the congregation together, they D the letter.
16:4 through the cities, they D to them for observance
23:33 came to Caesarea and D the letter to the
27:1 sail for Italy, they D Paul and some other
28:17 fathers, yet I was D prisoner from Jerusalem into
Rom 15:28 completed this, and have D to them what has
15:31 that I may be D from the unbelievers in
1Cor 11:2 even as I have D them to you.
11:23 Lord what I also D to you, that the
15:3 For I D to you as of first importance
2Cor 1:10 raises the dead; he D us from so deadly
3:3 a letter from Christ D by us, written not
Col 1:13 He has D us from the dominion of darkness
2Thes 3:2 that we may be D from wicked and evil
1Tim 1:20 Alexander, whom I have D to Satan that they
2Pet 2:21 from the holy commandment D to them.
Jude 1:3 was once for all D to the saints.

DELIVERER (11)

Judg 3:9 LORD raised up a D for the people of
3:15 up for them a D, Ehud, the son of
18:28 And there was no D because it was far
2Sam 22:2 my fortress, and my D,
Ps 18:2 my fortress, and my D, my God, my rock,
40:17 my help and my D; do not tarry, O
70:5 my help and my D; O LORD, do not
140:7 my Lord, my strong D, thou hast covered my
144:2 my stronghold and my D, my shield and he
Acts 7:35 as both ruler and D by the hand of
Rom 11:26 it is written, "The D will come from Zion,

DELIVEREST (3)

Ps 35:10 like thee, thou who D the weak from him
106:4 help me when thou D them;
Wis 16:8 it is thou who D from every evil.

D

DELIVERING (4)

Prov	2:12	understanding will guard you; D you from the way
Lk	21:12	you and persecute you, D you up to the
Acts	22:4	the death, binding and D to prison both men
	26:17	will appear to you, D you from the people

DELIVERS (24)

Ex	22:7	"If a man D to his neighbor money or
	22:10	"If a man D to his neighbor an ass
Tob	4:10	For charity D from death and keeps you from
	12:9	For almsgiving D from death, and it will purge
	14:11	children, consider what almsgiving accomplishes
Job	22:30	He D the innocent man; you will be delivered
	36:15	He D the afflicted by their affliction, and opens
Ps	34:7	who fear him, and D them.
	34:17	the LORD hears, and D them out of all
	34:19	righteous; but the LORD D him out of them
	37:40	LORD helps them and D them; he delivers them
	37:40	and delivers them; he D them from the wicked,
	41:1	The LORD D him in the day of trouble;
	72:12	For he D the needy when he calls, the
	97:10	of his saints; he D them from the hand
	138:7	and thy right hand D me.
Prov	10:2	not profit, but righteousness D from death.
	11:4	of wrath, but righteousness D from death.
	11:6	righteousness of the upright D them, but the
	12:6	mouth of the upright D men.
	31:24	and sells them; she D girdles to the merchant.
Dan	6:27	He D and rescues, he works signs and wonders
1Cor	15:24	the end, when he D the kingdom to God
1Thes	1:10	the dead, Jesus who D us from the wrath

DELIVERY (2)

Gen	38:27	the time of her D came, there were twins
Rev	12:2	in her pangs of birth, in anguish for D

DELOS

1Mac	15:23	the Spartans, and to D, and to Myndos, and

DELUDE

Col	2:4	that no one may D you with beguiling speech.

DELUDED (2)

Is	19:13	princes of Memphis are D; those who are the
	44:20	feeds on ashes; a D mind has led him

DELUGE (2)

Ezek	13:11	There will be a D of rain, great hailstones
	13:13	there shall be a D of rain in my

DELUGED

2Pet	3:6	that then existed was D with water and perished.

DELUSION (6)

Ps	62:9	high estate are a D; in the balances they
Is	41:29	they are all a D; their works are nothing;
Jer	3:23	the hills are a D, the orgies on the
	10:15	worthless, a work of D; at the time of
	51:18	worthless, a work of D; at the time of
2Thes	2:11	upon them a strong D, to make them believe

DELUSIONS (2)

Wis	17:7	The D of their magic art lay humbled, and
Ezek	13:8	"Because you have uttered D and seen lies,

DELUSIVE (3)

Ezek	13:7	you not seen a D vision, and uttered a
	13:9	the prophets who see D visions and who give
	13:23	shall no more see D visions nor practice divination;

DELVED

Num	21:18	nobles of the people D, with the scepter and

DEMAND (6)

Neh	5:18	this I did not D the food allowance of
Dan	2:10	can meet the king's D; for no great and
1Mac	15:35	and Gazara, which you D, they were causing great
Lk	12:48	commit much they will D the more.
	23:23	gave sentence that their D should be granted.
1Cor	1:22	For Jews D signs and Greeks seek wisdom,

DEMANDED (3)

1Kgs	20:9	'All that you first D of your servant I
2Mac	7:10	When it was D, he quickly put out his
Lk	22:31	"Simon, Simon, behold, Satan D to have you, that

DEMANDING (3)

Ps	44:12	people for a trifle, D no high price for
	78:18	in their heart by D the food they craved.
Lk	23:22	But they were urgent, D with loud cries that

DEMANDS (3)

Sir	31:31	afflict him by making D of him.
Col	2:14	us with its legal D; this he set aside,
1Thes	2:6	we might have made D as apostles of Christ.

DEMAS (3)

Col	4:14	the beloved physician and D greet you.
2Tim	4:10	For D, in love with this present world, has
Philem	1:24	so do Mark, Aristarchus, D, and Luke, my fellow

DEMETRIUS (53)

1Mac	7:1	hundred and fifty-first year D the son of Seleucus
	7:4	army killed them, and D took his seat upon
	8:31	the wrongs which King D is doing to them
	9:1	When D heard that Nicanor and his army had
	10:2	When D the king heard of it, he assembled
	10:3	And D sent Jonathan a letter in peaceable words
	10:6	So D gave him authority to recruit troops, to
	10:15	all the promises which D had sent to Jonathan,
	10:22	When D heard of these things he was grieved
	10:25	the following words: "King D to the nation of
	10:46	the great wrongs which D had done in Israel
	10:48	assembled large forces and encamped opposite D
	10:49	and the army of D fled, and Alexander pursued
	10:50	the sun set, and D fell on that day.
	10:52	for I crushed D and gained control of
	10:67	hundred and sixty-fifth year D the son of Demetrius
	10:67	Demetrius the son of D came from Crete to
	10:69	And D appointed Apollonius the governor of
	11:9	He sent envoys to D the king, saying, "Come,
	11:12	daughter away from him and gave her to D
	11:19	So D became king in the one hundred and
	11:30	were as follows: "King D to Jonathan his brother
	11:32	'King D to Lasthenes his father, greeting.
	11:38	Now when D the king saw that the land
	11:39	saw that all the troops were murmuring against D
	11:40	reported to Imalkue what D had done and told
	11:40	which the troops of D had for him; and
	11:41	Now Jonathan sent to D the king the request
	11:42	And D sent this message to Jonathan, "Not only
	11:52	So D the king sat on the throne of
	11:55	All the troops that D had cast off gathered
	11:55	and they fought against D, and he fled and
	11:63	that the officers of D had come to Kadesh
	12:24	that the commanders of D had returned, with a
	12:34	to the men whom D had sent.
	13:34	and sent them to D the king with a
	13:35	D the king sent him a favorable reply to
	13:36	letter as follows, "King D to Simon, the high
	14:1	and seventy-second year D the king assembled his
	14:2	and Media heard that D had invaded his territory,
	14:3	defeated the army of D, and seized him and
	14:38	of these things King D confirmed him in the
	15:1	Antiochus, the son of D the king, sent a
	15:22	the same thing to D the king and to
2Mac	1:7	In the reign of D, in the one hundred
	14:1	and his men that D, the son of Seleucus,
	14:4	and went to King D in about the one
	14:5	he was invited by D to a meeting of
	14:11	to Judas, quickly inflamed D still more.
	14:26	covenant that had been made and went to D
Acts	19:24	For a man named D, a silversmith, who made
	19:38	If therefore D and the craftsmen with him have
3 Jn	1:12	D has testimony from every one, and from the

DEMOLISH

Num	33:52	their molten images, and D all their high places;

DEMOLISHED (6)

2Kgs	10:27	And they D the pillar of Baal, and demolished
	10:27	pillar of Baal, and D the house of Baal,
Jud	3:8	And he D all their shrines and cut down
Lam	2:17	long ago, he has D without pity; he has
1Mac	9:62	it that had been D, and they fortified it.
Rom	11:3	thy prophets, they have D thy altars, and I

DEMON (28)

Tob	3:8	husbands, and the evil D Asmodeus had slain each
	3:17	bind Asmodeus the evil D, because Tobias was
	6:7	and liver, if a D or evil spirit gives
	6:14	me did, for a D is in love with

6:15 not worry about the D, for this very night
6:17 Then the D will smell it and flee away,
8:3 And when the D smelled the odor he fled
Mt 9:33 And when the D had been cast out, the
11:18 say, 'He has a D;
15:22 David; my daughter is severely possessed by a D
17:18 rebuked him, and the D came out of him,
Mk 7:25 him to cast the D out of her daughter.
7:28 go your way; the D has left your daughter."
7:29 in bed, and the D gone.
Lk 4:33 spirit of an unclean D; and he cried out
4:35 And when the D had thrown him down in
7:33 say, 'He has a D
8:29 was driven by the D into the desert.)
9:42 he was coming, the D tore him and convulsed
11:14 was casting out a D that was dumb; when
11:14 was dumb; when the D had gone out, the
Jn 7:20 The people answered, "You have a D
8:48 that you are a Samaritan and have a D
8:49 "I have not a D; but I honor my
8:52 him, "Now we know that you have a D
10:20 said, "He has a D, and he is mad;
10:21 not the sayings of one who has a D
10:21 Can a D open the eyes of the blind?"

DEMONIAC (4)

Mt 9:32 away, behold, a dumb D was brought to him.
12:22 a blind and dumb D was brought to him,
Mk 5:15 Jesus, and saw the D sitting there, clothed and
5:16 had happened to the D and to the swine.

DEMONIACS (3)

Mt 4:24 diseases and pains, D, epileptics, and paralytics, and
8:28 of the Gadarenes, two D met him, coming out
8:33 told everything, and what had happened to the D

DEMONIC

Rev 16:14 frogs; for they are D spirits, performing signs, who

DEMONS (51)

Deut 32:17 They sacrificed to D which were no gods, to
Ps 106:37 their daughters to the D;
Bar 4:7 you, by sacrificing to D and not to God.
4:35 a long time she will be inhabited by D
Mt 7:22 name, and cast out D in your name, and
8:16 who were possessed with D; and he cast out
8:31 And the D begged him, "If you cast us
9:34 said, "He casts out D by the prince of
9:34 "He casts out demons by the prince of D
10:8 sick, raise the dead, cleanse lepers, cast out D
12:24 Be-elzebul, the prince of D, that this man casts
12:24 prince of demons, that this man casts out D
12:27 if I cast out D by Be-elzebul, by whom
12:28 that I cast out D, then the kingdom of
Mk 1:32 him all who were sick or possessed with D
1:34 and cast out many D; and he would not
1:34 would not permit the D to speak, because they
1:39 preaching in their synagogues and casting out D
3:15 authority to cast out D:
3:22 by the prince of D he casts out the
3:22 the prince of demons he casts out the D
5:18 had been possessed with D begged him that he
6:13 they cast out many D, and anointed with oil
9:38 a man casting out D in your name, and
16:9 Magdalene, from whom he had cast out seven D
16:17 they will cast out D; they will speak in
Lk 4:41 And D also came out of many, crying, "You
8:2 Magdalene, from whom seven D had gone out,
8:27 the city who had D; for a long time
8:30 said, "Legion"; for many D had entered him.
8:33 Then the D came out of the man and
8:35 man from whom the D had gone, sitting at
8:36 had been possessed with D was healed.
8:38 man from whom the D had gone begged that
9:1 and authority over all D and to cure diseases,
9:49 a man casting out D in your name, and
10:17 saying, "Lord, even the D are subject to us
11:15 said, "He casts out D by Be-elzebul, the prince
11:15 Be-elzebul, the prince of D;
11:18 that I cast out D by Be-elzebul.
11:19 if I cast out D by Be-elzebul, by whom
11:20 that I cast out D, then the kingdom of
13:32 'Behold, I cast out D and perform cures today
1Cor 10:20 sacrifice they offer to D and not to God.
10:20 do not want you to be partners with D
10:21 cup of the Lord and the cup of D
10:21 table of the Lord and the table of D
1Tim 4:1 spirits and doctrines of D,
Jas 2:19 Even the D believe--and shudder.
Rev 9:20 nor give up worshiping D and idols of gold
18:2 a dwelling place of D, a haunt of every

DEMONSTRATION

1Cor 2:4 of wisdom, but in D of the Spirit and

DEMOPHON

2Mac 12:2 well as Hieronymus and D, and in addition to

DEN (24)

Is 11:8 child shall put his hand on the adder's D
Jer 7:11 my name, become a D of robbers in your
Dan 6:7 be cast into the D of lions.
6:12 be cast into the D of lions?" The king
6:16 and cast into the D of lions.
6:17 the mouth of the D, and the king sealed
6:19 in haste to the D of lions.
6:20 came near to the D where Daniel was, he
6:23 that Daniel be taken up out of the D
6:23 up out of the D, and no kind of
6:24 and cast into the D of lions--they, their
6:24 the bottom of the D the lions overpowered them
14:31 Daniel into the lions' D, and he was there
14:32 seven lions in the D, and every day they
14:34 have to Babylon, to Daniel, in the lions' D
14:35 seen Babylon, and I know nothing about the D
14:36 Babylon, right over the D, with the rushing sound
14:40 he came to the D he looked in, and
14:42 and threw into the D the men who had
Amos 3:4 cry out from his D, if he has taken
Nah 2:11 Where is the lions' D, the cave of the
Mt 21:13 you make it a D of robbers."
Mk 11:17 have made it a D of robbers."
Lk 19:46 have made it a D of robbers."

DENARII (7)

Mt 18:27 owed him a hundred D; and seizing him by
Mk 6:37 and buy two hundred D worth of bread, and
14:5 more than three hundred D, and given to the
Lk 7:41 one owed five hundred D, and the other fifty.
10:35 he took out two D and gave them to
Jn 6:7 answered him, "Two hundred D would not buy
12:5 sold for three hundred D and given to the

DENARIUS (6)

Mt 20:2 the laborers for a D a day, he sent
20:9 eleventh hour came, each of them received a D
20:10 more; but each of them also received a D
20:13 did you not agree with me for a D
Rev 6:6 of wheat for a D, and three quarts of
6:6 of barley for a D; but do not harm

DENIED (16)

Gen 18:15 But Sarah D, saying, "I did not laugh"; for
Job 6:10 for I have not D the words of the
Mt 26:70 But he D it before them all, saying, "I
26:72 And again he D it with an oath, "I
Mk 14:68 But he D it, saying, "I neither know nor
14:70 But again he D it.
Lk 8:45 When all D it, Peter said, "Master, the multitudes
12:9 before men will be D before the angels of
22:55 But he D it, saying, "Woman, I do not
Jn 13:38 crow, till you have D me three times.
18:25 He D it and said, "I am not."
18:27 Peter again D it; and at once the cock
Acts 3:13 you delivered up and D in the presence of
3:14 But you D the Holy and Righteous One, and
8:33 his humiliation justice was D him.
Rev 3:8 word and have not D my name.

DENIES (5)

Mt 10:33 in heaven; but whoever D me before men, I
Lk 12:9 God; but he who D me before men will
1 Jn 2:22 liar but he who D that Jesus is the
2:22 the antichrist, he who D the Father and the
2:23 No one who D the Son has the Father.

DENOUNCE (4)

Num 23:7 for me, and come, D Israel!'
23:8 How can I D whom the LORD has not
Jer 20:10 D him!
20:10 Let us D him!" say all my familiar friends,

DENOUNCED (3)

Num 23:8 can I denounce whom the LORD has not D
2Mac 14:37 elders of Jerusalem, was D to Nicanor as a
1Cor 10:30 thankfulness, why am I D because of that for

DENS (8)

Judg 6:2 made for themselves the D which are in the
Job 37:8 go into their lairs, and remain in their D
38:40 they crouch in their D, or lie in wait
Ps 104:22 get them away and lie down in their D
Song 4:8 and Hermon, from the D of lions, from the
Is 32:14 the watchtower will become D for ever, a joy
Nah 2:12 with prey and his D with torn flesh.
Heb 11:38 and mountains, and in D and caves of the

DENSE

Ex 10:14 of Egypt, such a D swarm of locusts as

DENSEST (2)

2Kgs 19:23 its farthest retreat, its D forest.
Is 37:24 its remotest height, its D forest.

DENY (25)

Jud 8:28 no one who can D your words.
Job 8:18 place, then it will D him, saying, 'I have
Prov 30:7 I ask of thee; D them not to me
30:9 I be full, and D thee, and say, "Who
Dan 14:24 to Daniel, "You cannot D that this is a
Mt 10:33 men, I also will D before my Father who
16:24 after me, let him D himself and take up
26:34 cock crows, you will D me three times."
26:35 you, I will not D you." And so said
26:75 cock crows, you will D me three times." And
Mk 8:34 after me, let him D himself and take up
14:30 crows twice, you will D me three times."
14:31 you, I will not D you." And they all
14:72 crows twice, you will D me three times." And
Lk 9:23 after me, let him D himself and take up
22:34 until you three times D that you know me."
22:59 crows today, you will D me three times."
Jn 1:20 confessed, he did not D, but confessed, "I am
Acts 4:16 Jerusalem, and we cannot D it.
2Tim 2:12 with him; if we D him, he also will
2:12 him, he also will D us;
2:13 for he cannot D himself.
Tit 1:15 know God, but they D him by their deeds;
Jude 1:4 God into licentiousness and D our only Master and
Rev 2:13 and you did not D my faith even in

DENYING (3)

Is 59:13 our iniquities: transgressing, and D the LORD, and
2Tim 3:5 form of religion but D the power of it.
2Pet 2:1 in destructive heresies, even D the Master who

DEPART (96)

Gen 49:10 The scepter shall not D from Judah, nor the
Ex 8:11 The frogs shall D from you and your houses
8:29 swarms of flies may D from Pharaoh, from his
13:22 by night did not D from before the people.
18:27 Moses let his father-in-law D, and he went his
33:1 LORD said to Moses, D, go up hence, you
33:11 young man, did not D from the tent.
Num 10:30 not go; I will D to my own land
16:26 said to the congregation, D, I pray you, from
Deut 4:9 seen, and lest they D from your heart all
Josh 1:8 the law shall not D out of your mouth,
Judg 6:18 Do not D from here, I pray thee, until
19:8 in the morning to D; and the girl's father
19:9 servant rose up to D, his father-in-law, the girl's
1Sam 10:2 When you D from me today you will meet
15:6 to the Kenites, "Go, D, go down from among
22:5 remain in the stronghold; D, and go into the
29:10 in the morning, and D as soon as you
30:22 may lead away his wife and children, and D
2Sam 11:12 today also, and tomorrow I will let you D
12:10 the sword shall never D from your house, because
1Kgs 11:21 to Pharaoh, "Let me D, that I may go
12:5 He said to them, D for three days, then
17:3 LORD came to him, D from here and turn
2Kgs 3:3 sin; he did not D from it.
8:1 to life, "Arise, and D with your household, and
13:2 sin; he did not D from them.
13:6 Nevertheless they did not D from the sins of
13:11 LORD; he did not D from all the sins
14:24 LORD; he did not D from all the sins
15:9 He did not D from the sins of Jeroboam
15:18 LORD; he did not D all his days from
15:28 LORD; he did not D from the sins of
17:22 did; they did not D from them,
18:6 LORD; he did not D from following him, but
2Chr 35:15 did not need to D from their service, for
Neh 9:19 the way did not D from them by day,
Tob 3:6 up, that I may D and become dust.
14:3 and am about to D this life.
Jud 13:19 Your hope will never D from the hearts of
Job 21:14 They say to God, D from us!
22:17 They said to God, D from us,' and 'What
28:28 is wisdom; and to D from evil is understanding.'"
Ps 9:17 Selah] The wicked shall D to Sheol, all the
34:14 D from evil, and do good; seek peace, and
37:27 D from evil, and do good; so shall you
39:13 know gladness, before I D and be no more!"
55:11 and fraud do not D from its market place.
119:115 D from me, you evildoers, that I may keep
139:19 men of blood would D from me,
Prov 5:7 me, and do not D from the words of
17:13 good, evil will not D from his house.
22:6 old he will not D from it.
27:22 his folly will not D from him.
Song 4:8 D from the peak of Amana, from the peak
Wis 1:5 and will rise and D from foolish thoughts, and
19:2 permitted thy people to D and hastily sent them
19:3 those whom they had begged and compelled to D
Sir 2:3 him and do not D, that you may be
10:12 man's pride is to D from the Lord; his
Is 10:27 day his burden will D from your shoulder, and
11:13 jealousy of Ephraim shall D, and those who harass
14:25 and his yoke shall D from them, and his
38:10 my days I must D; I am consigned to
52:11 D, depart, go out thence, touch no unclean thing;
52:11 Depart, D, go out thence, touch no unclean thing;
54:10 For the mountains may D and the hills be
54:10 steadfast love shall not D from you, and my
59:21 your mouth, shall not D out of your mouth,
Ezek 16:42 and my jealousy shall D from you; I will
Hos 9:12 to them when I D from them!
Zech 10:11 laid low, and the scepter of Egypt shall D
1Mac 6:57 quickly gave orders to D, and said to the
9:69 Then he decided to D to his own land.
2Mac 2:3 the law should not D from their hearts.
Mt 7:23 'I never knew you; D from me, you evildoers.'
9:24 a tumult, he said, D; for the girl is
10:11 in it, and stay with him until you D
25:41 at his left hand, D from me, you cursed,
Mk 5:17 to beg Jesus to D from their neighborhood.
Lk 2:29 lettest thou thy servant D in peace, according to
2:37 She did not D from the temple, worshiping with
5:8 at Jesus' knees, saying, D from me, for I
8:31 to command them to D into the abyss.
8:37 Gerasenes asked him to D from them; for they
9:4 house you enter, stay there, and from there D
13:27 where you come from; D from me, all you
21:21 are inside the city D, and let not those
Jn 13:1 hour had come to D out of this world
Acts 1:4 charged them not to D from Jerusalem, but to
7:3 and said to him, D from your land and
20:7 with them, intending to D on the morrow; and
22:21 he said to me, D; for I will send
Phil 1:23 My desire is to D and be with Christ,
1Tim 4:1 later times some will D from the faith by
2Tim 2:19 name of the Lord D from iniquity."

DEPARTED (119)

Gen 12:4 years old when he D from Haran.
14:12 who dwelt in Sodom, and his goods, and D
21:14 And she D, and wandered in the wilderness of
24:10 his master's camels and D, taking all sorts of
26:17 So Isaac D from there, and encamped in the
26:31 their way, and they D from him in peace.
31:55 blessed them; then he D and returned home.
42:26 they loaded their asses with their grain, and D
45:24 away, and as they D, he said to them,
Ex 16:1 month after they had D from the land of
35:20 the people of Israel D from the presence of
Num 12:9 against them, and he D;
14:44 the LORD, nor Moses, D out of the camp.
22:7 the elders of Midian D with the fees for
Josh 2:21 them away, and they D; and she bound the
2:22 They D, and went into the hills, and remained
Judg 9:55 Abimelech was dead, they D every man to his
11:38 two months; and she D, she and her companions,
17:8 And the man D from the town of Bethlehem

18:7 Then the five men D, and came to Laish,
18:21 So they turned and D, putting the little ones
19:10 he rose up and D, and arrived opposite Jebus
21:24 the people of Israel D from there at that
1Sam 4:21 saying, "The glory has D from Israel!" because the
4:22 said, "The glory has D from Israel, for the
6:6 not they let the people go, and they D
15:6 So the Kenites D from among the Amalekites.
16:14 Spirit of the LORD D from Saul, and an
16:23 and the evil spirit D from him.
18:12 with him but had D from Saul.
20:42 And he rose and D; and Jonathan went into
22:1 David D from there and escaped to the cave
22:5 So David D, and went into the forest of
23:13 six hundred, arose and D from Keilah, and they
2Sam 6:19 Then all the people D, each to his house.
19:24 the day the king D until the day he
22:22 and have not wickedly D from my God.
1Kgs 12:16 So Israel D to their tents.
14:17 Jeroboam's wife arose, and D, and came to Tirzah.
19:19 So he D from there, and found Elisha the
20:9 And the messengers D and brought him word again.
20:36 soon as he had D from him, a lion
20:38 So the prophet D, and waited for the king
2Kgs 5:24 and he sent the men away, and they D
8:14 Then he D from Elisha, and came to his
10:15 And when he D from there, he met Jehonadab
19:36 Sennacherib king of Assyria D, and went home, and
1Chr 16:43 Then all the people D each to his house,
19:5 their hips, and sent them away; and they D
21:4 So Joab D and went throughout all Israel, and
2Chr 10:16 So all Israel D to their tents.
21:20 in Jerusalem; and he D with no one's regret.
24:25 When they had D from him, leaving him severely
Ezra 8:31 Then we D from the river Ahava on the
Tob 5:16 both went out and D, and the young man's
Jud 5:18 But when they D from the way which he
Job 23:12 I have not D from the commandment of his
Ps 18:21 and have not wickedly D from my God.
44:18 nor have our steps D from thy way,
105:38 was glad when they D, for dread of them
Wis 10:3 when an unrighteous man D from her in his
16:14 cannot bring back the D spirit, nor set free
Sir 38:23 be comforted for him when his spirit is D
Is 7:17 the day that Ephraim D from Judah-- the
37:37 Sennacherib king of Assyria D, and went home and
Jer 29:2 and the smiths had D from Jerusalem.
Lam 1:6 daughter of Zion has D all her majesty.
Ezek 6:9 wanton heart which has D from me, and blinded
Dan 3:29 have sinfully and lawlessly D from thee, and have
4:31 spoken: The kingdom has D from you,
13:7 When the people D at noon, Susanna would go
14:14 and sealed it with the king's signet, and D
Hos 10:5 its glory which has D from it.
1Mac 1:24 Taking them all, he D to his own land.
3:37 of his troops and D from Antioch his capital
3:40 so they D with their entire force, and when
4:35 to die nobly, he D to Antioch and enlisted
5:29 He D from there at night, and they went
6:4 and in great grief D from there to return
6:63 Then he D with haste and returned to Antioch.
7:19 Then Bacchides D from Jerusalem and encamped in
9:36 that he had, and D with it.
9:72 then he turned and D to his own land,
10:13 left his place and D to his own land.
10:86 Then Jonathan D from there and encamped against
11:61 From there he D to Gaza, but the men
13:12 Then Trypho D from Ptolemais with a large army
13:24 Trypho turned back and D to his own land.
2Mac 12:12 receiving his pledges they D to their tents.
12:18 he had by then D from the region without
Mt 2:12 return to Herod, they D to their own country
2:13 Now when they had D, behold, an angel of
2:14 mother by night, and D to Egypt,
16:4 So he left them and D
27:5 in the temple, he D; and he went and
27:60 stone to the door of the tomb, and D
28:8 So they D quickly from the tomb with fear
Mk 8:13 the boat again he D to the other side.
Lk 1:38 And the angel D from her.
4:13 ended every temptation, he D from him until an
4:42 it was day he D and went into a
9:6 And they D and went through the villages, preaching
10:30 and beat him, and D, leaving him half dead.
Jn 4:3 he left Judea and D again to Galilee.
4:43 the two days he D to Galilee.
12:36 had said this, he D and hid himself from
Acts 7:4 show you.' Then he D from the land of
9:17 So Ananias D and entered the house.
10:7 spoke to him had D, he called two of
12:17 Then he D and went to another place.
15:39 Paul chose Silas and D, being commended by the
16:40 had seen the brethren, they exhorted them and D
17:15 come to him as soon as possible, they D
18:23 some time there he D and went from place
20:1 leave of them and D for Macedonia.
20:11 them a long while, until daybreak, and so D
21:5 there were ended, we D and went on our
21:8 On the morrow we D and came to Caesarea;
28:25 disagreed among themselves, they D, after Paul had

DEPARTING (2)
Gen 35:18 as her soul was D (for she died), she
1Mac 2:19 to do his commandments, D each one from the

DEPARTS (6)
Lev 13:58 from which the disease D when you have washed
Deut 24:1 his house, and she D out of his house,
Ps 146:4 When his breath D he returns to his earth;
Is 59:15 lacking, and he who D from evil makes himself
Jer 31:36 "If this fixed order D from before me, says
1Mac 6:10 said to them, "Sleep D from my eyes and

DEPARTURE (6)
Wis 3:2 have died, and their D was thought to be
7:6 mankind one entrance into life, and a common D
Lk 9:31 and spoke of his D, which he was to
Acts 20:29 know that after my D fierce wolves will come
2Tim 4:6 the time of my D has come.
2Pet 1:15 it that after my D you may be able

DEPEND (4)
Jud 8:24 brethren, for their lives D upon us, and the
Job 39:11 Will you D on him because his strength is
Sir 5:8 Do not D on dishonest wealth, for it will
Mt 22:40 On these two commandments D all the law and

DEPENDABLE
Sir 33:3 the law is as D as an inquiry by

DEPENDED
Acts 12:20 peace, because their country D on the king's country

DEPENDENT
1Thes 4:12 of outsiders, and be D on nobody.

DEPENDENTS (2)
Gen 47:12 with food, according to the number of their D
Wis 14:15 handed on to his D secret rites and initiations.

DEPENDS (8)
Jud 9:11 "For thy power D not upon numbers, nor thy
Sir 31:20 Healthy sleep D on moderate eating; he rises early,
38:24 wisdom of the scribe D on the opportunity of
1Mac 3:19 that victory in battle D, but strength comes from
Rom 4:16 That is why it D on faith, in order
9:16 So it D not upon man's will or exertion,
12:18 so far as it D upon you, live peaceably
Phil 3:9 righteousness from God that D on faith;

DEPICTED
Wis 18:24 the whole world was D, and the glories of

DEPLOYED
2Mac 15:20 stationed and the cavalry D on the flanks,

DEPORTATION (4)
Mt 1:11 the time of the D to Babylon.
1:12 And after the D to Babylon: Jechoniah was the
1:17 from David to the D to Babylon fourteen generations,
1:17 generations, and from the D to Babylon to the

DEPORTED (3)
Ezra 4:10 great and noble Osnappar D and settled in the
2Mac 2:1 those who were being D to take some of
2:2 those who were being D not to forget the

DEPOSE (2)
Bar 6:34 up a king or D one.
1Mac 8:13 whom they wish they D; and they have been

DEPOSED (4)
2Kgs 23:5 And he D the idolatrous priests whom the kings
2Chr 36:3 the king of Egypt D him in Jerusalem and
Dan 5:20 dealt proudly, he was D from his kingly throne,
Acts 19:27 she may even be D from her magnificence, she

DEPOSIT (5)
Lev 6:2 in a matter of D or security, or through
6:4 by oppression, or the D which was committed to
Num 17:4 Then you shall D them in the tent of
19:9 of the heifer, and D them outside the camp
1Mac 14:49 the sanctuary, and to D copies of them in

DEPOSITED (2)
Num 17:7 And Moses D the rods before the LORD in
2Mac 3:15 for those who had D them.

DEPOSITS (2)
2Mac 3:10 that there were some D belonging to widows and
3:15 given the law about D, that he should keep

DEPRAVED (3)
Ps 53:3 they are all alike D; there is none that
2Mac 14:27 false accusations of that D man, wrote to Nicanor,
1Tim 6:5 among men who are D in mind and bereft

DEPRESSED (2)
Jud 7:33 And they were greatly D in the city.
2Mac 6:12 book not to be D by such calamities, but

DEPRIVE (9)
Esth 16:12 arrogance, he undertook to D us of our kingdom
Prov 18:5 wicked man, or to D a righteous man of
Sir 4:1 My son, D not the poor of his living,
7:19 Do not D yourself of a wise and good
14:14 Do not D yourself of a happy day; let
34:22 to murder him; to D an employee of his
Is 5:23 for a bribe, and D the innocent of his
32:6 hungry unsatisfied, and to D the thirsty of drink.
1Cor 9:15 than have any one D me of my ground

DEPRIVED (5)
Wis 18:4 enemies deserved to be D of light and imprisoned
Sir 28:15 away courageous women, and D them of the fruit
Dan 3:44 them be disgraced and D of all power and
2Mac 3:29 the divine intervention and D of any hope of
13:10 the point of being D of the law and

DEPRIVES (2)
Job 12:20 He D of speech those who are trusted, and
Sir 34:21 of the poor; whoever D them of it is

DEPRIVING (2)
Eccl 4:8 am I toiling and D myself of pleasure?" This
Sir 14:4 Whoever accumulates by D himself, accumulates for others; and

DEPTH (8)
Prov 25:3 and the earth for D, so the mind of
Wis 10:19 them up from the D of the sea.
Mt 13:5 since they had no D of soil,
18:6 be drowned in the D of the sea.
Mk 4:5 since it had no D of soil;
Rom 8:39 powers, nor height, nor D, nor anything else in
11:33 O the D of the riches and wisdom and
Eph 3:18 length and height and D,

DEPTHS (28)
Ex 15:5 went down into the D like a stone.
Deut 32:22 it burns to the D of Sheol, devours the
Neh 9:11 their pursuers into the D, as a stone into
Jud 8:14 You cannot plumb the D of the human heart,
Ps 63:9 go down into the D of the earth;
68:22 them back from the D of the sea,
71:20 me again; from the D of the earth thou
86:13 my soul from the D of Sheol.
88:6 put me in the D of the Pit, in
95:4 his hand are the D of the earth; the
107:26 went down to the D; their courage melted away
130:1 Out of the D I cry to thee, O
139:15 intricately wrought in the D of the earth.
Prov 8:24 When there were no D I was brought forth,
9:18 guests are in the D of Sheol.
Sir 24:5 have walked in the D of the abyss.
51:5 not kindle, from the D of the belly of
Is 14:15 to Sheol, to the D of the Pit.
44:23 done it; shout, O D of the earth; break
51:10 that didst make the D of the sea a
63:13 an everlasting name, who led them through the D
Jer 49:8 back, dwell in the D, O inhabitants of Dedan!
49:30 away, dwell in the D, O inhabitants of Hazor!
Lam 3:55 O LORD, from the D of the pit;
Ezek 27:34 the seas, in the D of the waters; your
Mic 7:19 our sins into the D of the sea.
Zech 10:11 smitten, and all the D of the Nile dried
1Cor 2:10 searches everything, even the D of God.

DEPUTED
2Sam 15:3 there is no man D by the king to

DEPUTIES
Jer 51:28 with their governors and D, and every land under

DEPUTY (3)
1Kgs 22:47 king in Edom; a D was king.
2Mac 4:29 own brother Lysimachus as D in the high-priesthood,
4:31 man of high rank, to act as his D

DERBE (4)
Acts 14:6 fled to Lystra and D, cities of Lycaonia, and
14:20 next day he went on with Barnabas to D
16:1 he came also to D and to Lystra.
20:4 Secundus; and Gaius of D, and Timothy; and the

DERIDE (3)
Ps 102:8 taunt me, those who D me use my name
119:51 Godless men utterly D me, but I do not
Sir 13:7 and finally he will D you.

DERIDED (6)
Neh 2:19 heard of it, they D us and despised us
Ps 79:4 our neighbors, mocked and D by those round about
1Mac 7:34 he mocked them and D them and defiled them
2Mac 8:17 the torture of the D city, and besides, the
Mt 27:39 those who passed by D him, wagging their heads
Mk 15:28 those who passed by D him, wagging their heads,

DERIDES (2)
1Sam 2:1 My mouth D my enemies, because I rejoice in
Bar 6:43 is lain with, she D the woman next to

DERIDING
2Mac 7:27 native tongue as follows, D the cruel tyrant: "My

DERISION (12)
Ps 2:4 the heavens laughs; the LORD has them in D
44:13 of our neighbors, the D and scorn of those
59:8 them; thou dost hold all the nations in D
Wis 5:4 we once held in D and made a byword
Jer 20:8 me a reproach and D all day long.
48:26 vomit, and he too shall be held in D
48:27 Was not Israel a D to you?
48:39 Moab has become a D and a horror to
Ezek 23:32 at and held in D, for it contains much;
36:4 become a prey and D to the rest of
Hos 7:17 This shall be their D in the land of
Hab 2:6 against him, in scoffing D of him, and say,

DERIVED
Philem 1:7 For I have D much joy and comfort from

DESCEND (9)
Ex 33:9 pillar of cloud would D and stand at the
Job 17:16 Shall we D together into the dust?"
Ps 49:14 to the grave they D, and their form shall
Lam 1:13 bones he made it D; he spread a net
Ezek 26:20 down with those who D into the Pit, to
Jn 1:32 "I saw the Spirit D as a dove from
1:33 you see the Spirit D and remain, this is
Rom 10:7 down) or "Who will D into the abyss?" (that
1Thes 4:16 the Lord himself will D from heaven with a

DESCENDANT (4)
1Chr 27:3 He was a D of Perez, and was chief
Job 18:19 has no offspring or D among his people, and
Wis 7:1 like all men, a D of the first-formed child
Rom 11:1 am an Israelite, a D of Abraham, a member

DESCENDANTS (157)
Gen 9:9 with you and your D after you,
11:10 These are the D of Shem.
11:27 Now these are the D of Terah.

12:7 and said, "To your D I will give this
13:15 you and to your D for ever.
13:16 I will make your D as the dust of
13:16 of the earth, your D also can be counted.
15:5 him, "So shall your D be."
15:13 a surety that your D will be sojourners in
15:18 Abram, saying, "To your D I give this land,
16:10 so greatly multiply your D that they cannot be
17:7 and you and your D after you throughout their
17:7 you and to your D after you.
17:8 you, and to your D after you, the land
17:9 covenant, you and your D after you throughout their
17:10 and you and your D after you: Every male
17:19 everlasting covenant for his D after him.
21:12 through Isaac shall your D be named.
22:17 I will multiply your D as the stars of
22:17 And your D shall possess the gate of their
22:18 enemies, and by your D shall all the nations
24:7 to me, 'To your D I will give this
24:60 thousands; and may your D possess the gate of
25:12 These are the D of Ishmael, Abraham's son, whom
25:19 These are the D of Isaac, Abraham's son: Abraham
26:3 you and to your D I will give all
26:4 I will multiply your D as the stars of
26:4 will give to your D all these lands; and
26:4 lands; and by your D all the nations of
26:24 you and multiply your D for my servant Abraham's
28:4 you and to your D with you, that you
28:13 you and to your D;
28:14 your descendants; and your D shall be like the
28:14 by you and your D shall all the families
32:12 good, and make your D as the sand of
35:12 the land to your D after you."
36:1 These are the D of Esau (that is, Edom).
36:9 These are the D of Esau the father of
46:8 the names of the D of Israel, who came
48:4 this land to your D after you for an
48:19 than he, and his D shall become a multitude
Ex 1:6 But the D of Israel were fruitful and increased
28:43 him and for his D after him.
30:21 him and to his D throughout their generations."
32:13 'I will multiply your D as the stars of
32:13 will give to your D, and they shall inherit
33:1 Jacob, saying, 'To your D I will give it.'
Lev 21:17 Aaron, None of your D throughout their generations
21:21 no man of the D of Aaron the priest
22:3 one of all your D throughout your generations
Num 9:10 you or of your D is unclean through touching
13:22 Sheshai, and Talmai, the D of Anak, were there.
13:28 besides, we saw the D of Anak there.
14:24 he went, and his D shall possess it.
16:40 is not of the D of Aaron, should draw
25:13 him, and to his D after him, the covenant
Deut 1:8 them and to their D after them.'
4:37 fathers and chose their D after them, and brought
10:15 fathers and chose their D after them, you above
11:9 them and to their D, a land flowing with
23:2 generation none of his D shall enter the assembly
28:46 wonder, and upon your D for ever.
30:19 that you and your D may live,
31:21 the mouths of their D; for I know the
34:4 give it to your D I have let you
Josh 15:14 Ahiman and Talmai, the D of Anak.
16:1 The allotment of the D of Joseph went from
17:2 these were the male D of Manasseh the son
21:4 those Levites who were D of Aaron the priest
21:10 which went to the D of Aaron, one of
21:13 And to the D of Aaron the priest they
21:19 The cities of the D of Aaron, the priests,
22:28 us or to our D in time to come,
24:32 an inheritance of the D of Joseph.
Judg 1:16 And the D of the Kenite, Moses' father-in-law, went
4:11 from the Kenites, the D of Hobab the father-in-law
Ruth 4:18 Now these are the D of Perez: Perez was
1Sam 20:42 you, and between my D and your descendants, for
20:42 my descendants and your D, for ever.'" And he
24:21 not cut off my D after me, and that
2Sam 21:16 Ishbi-benob, one of the D of the giants, whose
21:18 was one of the D of the giants.
22:51 to David, and his D for ever."
1Kgs 2:33 the head of his D for ever; but to
2:33 David, and to his D, and to his house,
9:21 of Israel– their D who were left after
11:39 for this afflict the D of David, but not
2Kgs 5:27 you, and to your D for ever." So he
17:20 LORD rejected all the D of Israel, and afflicted
1Chr 1:33 All these were the D of Keturah.
2:23 All these were D of Machir, the father of
2:33 These were the D of Jerahmeel.
2:50 These were the D of Caleb.
3:10 The D of Solomon: Rehoboam, Abijah his son, Asa
3:16 The D of Jehoiakim: Jeconiah his son, Zedekiah his
20:4 was one of the D of the giants; and
2Chr 8:8 of Israel, from their D who were left after
20:7 for ever to the D of Abraham thy friend?
Neh 9:8 to give to his D the land of the
9:23 Thou didst multiply their D as the stars of
9:24 So the D went in and possessed the land,
11:3 temple servants, and the D of Solomon's servants.
Tob 1:1 of Gabael, of the D of Asiel and the
4:12 wife from among the D of your fathers and
Jud 8:32 will go down through all generations of our D
Esth 9:27 upon themselves and their D and all who joined
9:28 commemoration of these days cease among their D
9:31 themselves and for their D, with regard to their
Job 5:25 know also that your D shall be many, and
Ps 18:50 to David and his D for ever.
89:4 'I will establish your D for ever, and build
106:27 and would disperse their D among the nations,
112:2 His D will be mighty in the land; the
Sir 1:13 foundation, and among their D she will be trusted.
4:16 obtain her; and his D will remain in possession
44:12 will remain with their D, and their inheritance to
44:13 Their D stand by the covenants; their children also,
45:1 From his D the Lord brought forth a man
45:13 his sons and his D perpetually.
45:15 him and for his D all the days of
45:21 Lord, which he gave to him and his D
45:24 that he and his D should have the dignity
45:25 so the heritage of Aaron is for his D
47:22 never blot out the D of his chosen one,
Is 14:20 "May the D of evildoers nevermore be named!
44:3 my Spirit upon your D, and my blessing on
48:19 the sand, and your D like its grains; their
54:3 the left, and your D will possess the nations
61:9 Their D shall be known among the nations, and
65:9 I will bring forth D from Jacob, and from
66:22 LORD; so shall your D and your name remain.
Jer 23:8 up and led the D of the house of
29:32 of Nehelam and his D; he shall not have
31:36 LORD, then shall the D of Israel cease from
31:37 cast off all the D of Israel for all
33:22 I will multiply the D of David my servant,
33:26 I will reject the D of Jacob and David
33:26 choose one of his D to rule over the
Bar 2:15 for Israel and his D are called by thy
Dan 3:36 promise to make their D as many as the
1Mac 5:2 determined to destroy the D of Jacob who lived
2Mac 1:20 of Persia, sent the D of the priests who
7:17 his mighty power will torture you and your D
Jn 8:33 answered him, "We are D of Abraham, and have
8:37 know that you are D of Abraham; yet you
Acts 2:30 set one of his D upon his throne,
Rom 4:13 to Abraham and his D, that they should inherit
4:16 guaranteed to all his D – not only to
4:18 told, "So shall your D be."
9:7 because they are his D; but "Through Isaac shall
9:7 "Through Isaac shall your D be named."
9:8 the children of the promise are reckoned as D
2Cor 11:22 Are they D of Abraham?
Heb 2:16 concerned but with the D of Abraham.
7:5 And those D of Levi who receive the priestly
11:12 as dead, were born D as many as the
11:18 "Through Isaac shall your D be named."

DESCENDED (21)

Ex 19:18 smoke, because the LORD D upon it in fire;
34:5 And the LORD D in the cloud and stood
Deut 9:21 into the brook that D out of the mountain.
2Sam 21:20 and he also was D from the giants.
21:22 These four were D from the giants in Gath;
1Chr 20:6 and he also was D from the giants.
20:8 These were D from the giants in Gath; and
Jud 5:6 This people is D from the Chaldeans.
Wis 10:6 escaped the fire that D on the Five Cities.
10:13 She D with him into the dungeon,
Mt 28:2 angel of the Lord D from heaven and came
Lk 3:22 and the Holy Spirit D upon him in bodily
Jn 3:13 heaven but he who D from heaven, the Son
7:42 that the Christ is D from David, and comes
Rom 1:3 his Son, who was D from David according to
9:6 not all who are D from Israel belong to

Eph 4:9 that he had also D into the lower parts
4:10 He who D is he who also ascended far
2Tim 2:8 risen from the dead, D from David, as preached
Heb 7:5 though these also are D from Abraham.
7:14 that our Lord was D from Judah, and in

DESCENDING (7)

Gen 28:12 God were ascending and D on it!
Is 30:30 be heard and the D blow of his arm
Mt 3:16 the Spirit of God D like a dove, and
Mk 1:10 opened and the Spirit D upon him like a
Jn 1:51 of God ascending and D upon the Son of
Acts 10:11 heaven opened, and something D, like a great sheet,
11:5 saw a vision, something D, like a great sheet,

DESCENDS (2)

Ps 7:16 head, and on his own pate his violence D
Is 34:5 the heavens; behold, it D for judgment upon Edom,

DESCENT (11)

Josh 7:5 far as Shebarim, and slew them at the D
8:14 out early to the D toward the Arabah to
Ezra 2:59 fathers' houses or their D, whether they belonged to
Neh 7:61 fathers' houses nor their D, whether they belonged to
13:3 they separated from Israel all those of foreign D
Sir 43:17 flying down, and its D is like locusts alighting.
46:6 nation, and at the D of Beth-horon he destroyed
Jer 48:5 weeping; for at the D of Horonaim they have
1Mac 3:24 pursued them down the D of Beth-horon to the
Lk 19:37 drawing near, at the D of the Mount of
Heb 7:16 legal requirement concerning bodily D but by the

DESCRIBE (5)

Josh 18:6 And you shall D the land in seven divisions
Wis 17:1 judgments and hard to D; therefore unintructed souls
Sir 43:31 seen him and can D him?
Ezek 43:10 you, son of man, D to the house of
Acts 8:33 Who can D his generation?

DESCRIBED (6)

Jud 7:29 do this day the things which we have D
14:8 Then Judith D to him in the presence of
Job 26:10 He has D a circle upon the face of
Acts 12:17 to be silent, he D to them how the
Rev 22:18 to him the plagues D in this book,
22:19 holy city, which are D in this book.

DESCRIPTION (5)

Josh 18:4 the land, writing a D of it with a
18:6 divisions and bring the D here to me; and
18:8 went to write the D of the land, saying,
18:8 down and write a D of the land, and
18:9 in a book a D of it by towns

DESECRATED (2)

Jud 4:12 to be profaned and D to the malicious joy
Ps 74:7 to the ground they D the dwelling place of

DESECRATION

Jud 8:21 will exact of us the penalty for its D

DESERT (56)

Num 21:20 top of Pisgah which looks down upon the D
23:28 to the top of Peor, that overlooks the D
Deut 32:10 found him in a D land, and in the
1Chr 5:9 the entrance of the D this side of the
12:19 our heads he will D to his master Saul.")
Jud 2:23 who lived along the D, south of the country
Job 24:5 wild asses in the D they go forth to
38:26 man is, on the D in which there is
Ps 78:17 him, rebelling against the Most High in the D
78:40 in the wilderness and grieved him in the D
105:41 it flowed through the D like a river.
106:9 led them through the deep as through a D
106:14 the test in the D;
107:4 Some wandered in D wastes, finding no way to
107:33 turns rivers into a D, springs of water into
107:35 He turns a D into pools of water, a
Prov 21:19 to live in a D land than with a
Wis 10:13 sold, wisdom did not D him, but delivered him
18:20 the multitude in the D, but the wrath did
Is 14:17 the world like a D and overthrew its cities,
16:1 by way of the D, to the mount of
16:8 and strayed to the D; its shoots spread abroad
21:1 it comes from the D, from a terrible land.
31:9 terror, and his officers D the standard in panic,"
33:9 Sharon is like a D; and Bashan and Carmel
35:1 shall be glad, the D shall rejoice and blossom;
35:6 and streams in the D;
40:3 make straight in the D a highway for our
41:19 will set in the D the cypress, the plane
42:11 Let the D and its cities lift up their
43:19 way in the wilderness and rivers in the D
43:20 wilderness, rivers in the D, to give drink to
50:2 make the rivers a D; their fish stink for
51:3 wilderness like Eden, her D like the garden of
63:13 a horse in the D, they did not stumble.
Jer 4:11 bare heights in the D toward the daughter of
4:26 fruitful land was a D, and all its cities
5:6 a wolf from the D shall destroy them.
9:2 I had in the D a wayfarers' lodging place,
9:26 who dwell in the D that cut the corners
12:12 bare heights in the D destroyers have come; for
13:24 like chaff driven by the wind from the D
17:6 a shrub in the D, and shall not see
22:6 will make you a D, an uninhabited city.
25:24 that dwell in the D;
48:6 Be like a wild ass in the D
50:12 last of the nations, a wilderness dry and D
51:43 of drought and a D, a land in which
Zeph 2:13 Nineveh a desolation, a dry waste like the D
Mal 1:3 and left his heritage to jackals of the D
1Mac 1:39 became desolate as a D; her feasts were turned
2:21 it from us to D the law and the
Mt 15:33 bread enough in the D to feed so great
Mk 8:4 feed these men with bread here in the D
Lk 8:29 the demon into the D
Acts 8:26 This is a D road.

DESERTED (25)

1Sam 29:3 years, and since he D to me I have
2Kgs 25:11 the deserters who had D to the king of
1Chr 12:19 the men of Manasseh D to David when he
12:20 these men of Manasseh D to him: Adnah, Jozabad,
2Chr 15:9 for great numbers had D to him from Israel
Tob 1:4 of Naphtali my forefather D the house of Jerusalem.
Prov 19:4 a poor man is D by his friend.
Sir 9:7 wander about in its D sections.
Is 7:16 two kings you are in dread will be D
17:2 Her cities will be D for ever; they will
17:9 will be like the D places of the Hivites
17:9 the Amorites, which they D because of the children
27:10 is solitary, a habitation D and forsaken, like the
32:14 forsaken, the populous city D; the hill and the
Jer 38:19 the Jews who have D to the Chaldeans, lest
39:9 city, those who had D to him, and the
52:15 the deserters who had D to the king of
Ezek 36:4 desolate wastes and the D cities, which have become
Zeph 2:4 For Gaza shall be D, and Ashkelon shall become
1Mac 7:19 the men who had D to him, and some
7:24 the men who had D, and he prevented those
9:24 occurred, and the country D with them to the
15:12 and his troops had D him.
2Tim 4:10 this present world, has D me and gone to
4:16 took my part; all D me.

DESERTERS (2)

2Kgs 25:11 the city and the D who had deserted to
Jer 52:15 the city and the D who had deserted to

DESERTING (4)

Is 57:8 up your symbol; for, D me, you have uncovered
Jer 37:13 prophet, saying, "You are D to the Chaldeans."
37:14 false; I am not D to the Chaldeans." But
Gal 1:6 you are so quickly D him who called you

DESERTS (6)

Ps 94:2 of the earth; render to the proud their D
Wis 5:7 we journeyed through trackless D, but the way of
Is 48:21 led them through the D; he made water flow
Jer 2:6 in a land of D and pits, in a
Zech 11:17 my worthless shepherd, who D the flock!
Heb 11:38 worthy-- wandering over D and mountains, and in

DESERVE (12)

Deut 19:6 the man did not D to die, since he
1Sam 26:16 the LORD lives, you D to die, because you
1Kgs 2:26 your estate; for you D death.
Wis 12:15 him who does not D to be punished.
Sir 8:5 remember that we all D punishment.
Jer 26:16 "This man does not D the sentence of death,
49:12 those who did not D to drink the cup

2Mac 15:21 victory for those who D it.
Acts 25:11 anything for which I D to die, I do
26:31 is doing nothing to D death or imprisonment."
Rom 1:32 who do such things D to die, they not
Rev 2:23 give to each of you as your works D

DESERVED (10)

Judg 9:16 him as his deeds D --
Ezra 9:13 less than our iniquities D and hast given us
Esth 16:18 has speedily inflicted on him the punishment he D
Wis 12:26 rebukes will experience the D judgment of God.
16:9 for them, because they D to be punished by
18:4 For their enemies D to be deprived of light
19:4 For the fate they D drew them on to
2Mac 4:38 Lord thus repaid him with the punishment he D
Lk 12:48 know, and did what D a beating, shall receive
Heb 10:29 you think will be D by the man who

DESERVEDLY

Wis 16:1 Therefore those men were D punished through such

DESERVES (11)

Deut 25:2 if the guilty man D to be beaten, the
2Sam 12:5 who has done this D to die;
Tob 12:4 old man said, "He D it."
Job 11:6 God exacts of you less than your guilt D
Wis 3:10 punished as their reasoning D, who disregarded the
Jer 26:11 the people, "This man D the sentence of death,
Ezek 31:11 shall surely deal with it as its wickedness D
Mt 10:10 staff; for the laborer D his food.
26:66 They answered, "He D death."
Lk 10:7 provide, for the laborer D his wages; do not
1Tim 5:18 and, "The laborer D his wages."

DESERVING (7)

Wis 12:20 thy servants and those D of death, granting them
Mk 14:64 all condemned him as D death.
Lk 23:15 Behold, nothing D death has been done by him;
23:21 in him no crime D death; I will therefore
Acts 13:28 charge him with nothing D death, yet they asked
23:29 but charged with nothing D death or imprisonment.
25:25 he had done nothing D death; and as he

DESIGN (4)

Ex 39:3 and into the fine twined linen, in skilled D
2Chr 2:14 engraving and execute any D that may be assigned
Esth 8:3 to avert the evil D of Haman the Agagite
2Mac 15:5 did not succeed in carrying out his abominable D

DESIGNATE

2Mac 4:2 He dared to D as a plotter against the

DESIGNATED (7)

Ex 21:8 her master, who has D her for himself, then
Josh 20:9 These were the cities D for all the people
2Chr 31:19 several cities who were D by name to distribute
Ezra 10:16 houses, each of them D by name.
Rom 1:4 to the flesh and D Son of God in
Heb 5:10 who obey him, being D by God a high
Jude 1:4 who long ago were D for this condemnation, ungodly

DESIGNATES

Ex 21:9 If he D her for his son, he shall

DESIGNED (2)

Jud 9:5 that followed; thou hast D the things that are
2Mac 6:12 that these punishments were D not to destroy but

DESIGNER (3)

Ex 35:35 craftsman or by a D or by an embroiderer
35:35 weaver--by any sort of workman or skilled D
38:23 Dan, a craftsman and D and embroiderer in blue

DESIGNS (6)

Ex 31:4 craftsmanship, to devise artistic D, to work in gold,
35:32 craftsmanship, to devise artistic D, to work in gold
Job 10:3 hands and favor the D of the wicked?
Wis 9:14 is worthless, and our D are likely to fail,
1Mac 11:8 he kept devising evil D against Alexander.
2Cor 2:11 us; for we are not ignorant of his D

DESIRABLE (7)

1Sam 9:20 is all that is D in Israel?
Song 5:16 speech is most sweet, and he is altogether D
Wis 8:5 If riches are a D possession in life, what
Sir 1:15 whole house with D goods, and their storehouses
Ezek 23:6 commanders, all of them D young men, horsemen
23:12 horses, all of them D young men.
23:23 the Assyrians with them, D young men, governors

DESIRE (128)

Gen 3:16 forth children, yet your D shall be for your
4:7 at the door; its D is for you, but
Ex 10:11 serve the LORD, for that is what you D
15:9 divide the spoil, my D shall have its fill
34:24 neither shall any man D your land, when you
Deut 5:21 and you shall not D your neighbor's house, his
12:15 as much as you D, according to the blessing
12:20 you may eat as much flesh as you D
12:21 eat within your towns as much as you D
14:26 money for whatever you D, oxen, or sheep, or
21:11 woman, and you have D for her and would
1Sam 23:20 to all your heart's D to come down; and
2Sam 19:38 and all that you D of me I will
23:5 cause to prosper all my help and my D
1Kgs 1:16 king, and the king said, "What do you D
5:8 to do all you D in the matter of
2Chr 15:15 him with their whole D, and he was found
Jud 12:16 was moved with great D to possess her; for
Esth 13:2 extent, to re-establish the peace which all men D
13:15 annihilate us, and they D to destroy the inheritance
Job 6:8 God would grant my D;
13:3 the Almighty, and I D to argue my case
21:14 We do not D the knowledge of thy ways.
33:32 me; speak, for I D to justify you.
Ps 10:17 thou wilt hear the D of the meek; thou
20:4 grant you your heart's D, and fulfil all your
21:2 given him his heart's D, and hast not withheld
35:25 say to themselves, "Aha, we have our heart's D
35:27 Let those who D my vindication shout for joy
40:6 offering thou dost not D; but thou hast given
40:14 brought to dishonor who D my hurt!
45:11 and the king will D your beauty.
70:2 brought to dishonor who D my hurt!
73:25 upon earth that I D besides thee.
112:8 until he sees his D on his adversaries.
112:10 and melts away; the D of the wicked man
145:16 hand, thou satisfiest the D of every living thing.
145:19 He fulfils the D of all who fear him,
Prov 3:15 jewels, and nothing you D can compare with her.
6:25 Do not D her beauty in your heart, and
8:11 all that you may D cannot compare with her.
10:24 upon him, but the D of the righteous will
11:23 The D of the righteous ends only in good;
13:2 eats good, but the D of the treacherous is
13:12 heart sick, but a D fulfilled is a tree
13:19 A D fulfilled is sweet to the soul; but
21:25 The D of the sluggard kills him for his
23:3 Do not D his delicacies, for they are deceptive
23:6 is stingy; do not D his delicacies;
24:1 of evil men, nor D to be with them;
31:4 or for rulers to D strong drink;
Eccl 6:9 than the wandering of D; this also is vanity
12:5 drags itself along and D fails; because man goes
Song 7:10 my beloveds, and his D is for me.
Wis 4:12 is good, and roving D perverts the innocent mind.
6:11 Therefore set your D on my words; long for
6:13 known to those who D her.
6:17 is the most sincere D for instruction, and concern
6:20 to God; so the D for wisdom leads to
14:2 For it was D for gain that planned that
15:5 fools, so that they D the lifeless form of
15:6 who either make or D or worship them.
15:19 appearance that one would D them, but they have
16:2 delicacy to satisfy the D of appetite;
16:21 bread, ministering to the D of the one who
16:25 bounty, according to the D of those who had
19:11 kind of birds, when D led them to ask
Sir 1:23 If you D wisdom, keep the commandments, and the
3:27 and an attentive ear is the wise man's D
6:37 your mind, and your D for wisdom will be
16:1 Do not D a multitude of useless children, nor
18:30 take pleasure in base D, it will make you
20:3 Like a eunuch's D to violate a maiden is
23:5 me haughty eyes, and remove from me evil D
24:18 to me, you who D me, and eat your
25:20 beauty, and do not D a woman for her
36:22 countenance, and surpasses every human D
Is 26:8 memorial name is the D of our soul.
53:2 beauty that we should D him.
58:10 hungry and satisfy the D of the afflicted, then
58:11 continually, and satisfy your D with good things, and

Jer 34:16 free according to their D, and you brought them
42:22 the place where you D to go to live."
44:14 Judah, to which they D to return to dwell
50:19 in Bashan, and his D shall be satisfied on
Ezek 24:21 your eyes, and the D of your soul; and
24:25 eyes and their heart's D, and also their sons
Dan 13:8 and they began to D her.
13:11 to disclose their lustful D to possess her.
Hos 6:6 For I D steadfast love and not sacrifice, the
Amos 5:18 Woe to you who D the day of the
Mic 7:3 man utters the evil D of his soul; thus
Mal 2:15 And what does he D
2Mac 11:23 to the gods, we D that the subjects of
11:28 If you are well, it is as we D
Mt 9:13 what this means, 'I D mercy, and not sacrifice.'
12:7 what this means, 'I D mercy, and not sacrifice,'
15:28 Be it done for you as you D
Mk 4:19 in riches, and the D for other things, enter
Lk 17:22 coming when you will D to see one of
Jn 17:24 Father, I D that they also, whom thou hast
Acts 28:22 But we D to hear from you what your
Rom 10:1 Brethren, my heart's D and prayer to God for
1Cor 7:37 necessity but having his D under control, and has
10:6 for us, not to D evil as they did.
12:31 But earnestly D the higher gifts.
14:1 your aim, and earnestly D the spiritual gifts,
14:35 there is anything they D to know, let them
14:39 So, my brethren, earnestly D to prophesy, and do
2Cor 8:10 to do but to D,
13:3 them-- since you D proof that Christ is
Gal 4:21 Tell me, you who D to be under law,
6:13 the law, but they D to have you circumcised
Phil 1:23 My D is to depart and be with Christ,
Col 3:5 impurity, passion, evil D, and covetousness,
1Thes 2:17 eagerly and with great D to see you face
1Tim 2:8 I D then that in every place the men
5:11 wanton against Christ they D to marry,
6:9 But those who D to be rich fall into
2Tim 3:12 Indeed all who D to live a godly life
Tit 3:8 I D you to insist on these things, so
Heb 6:11 And we D each one of you to show
11:16 as it is, they D a better country, that
Jas 1:13 he is lured and enticed by his own D
1:14 Then D when it has conceived gives birth to
4:2 You D and do not have; so you kill.
Jude 1:5 Now I D to remind you, though you were
Rev 11:6 earth with every plague, as often as they D

DESIRED (38)

Gen 3:6 tree was to be D to make one wise,
Deut 18:16 just as you D of the LORD your
1Kgs 5:10 and cypress that he D,
9:1 and all that Solomon D to build,
9:11 as much as he D, King Solomon gave to
9:19 and whatever Solomon D to build in Jerusalem,
10:13 Sheba all that she D, whatever she asked besides
2Chr 8:6 horsemen, and whatever Solomon D to build in,
9:12 Sheba all that she D, whatever she asked besides
Jud 16:22 Many D to marry her, but she remained a
Esth 1:8 of his palace to do as every man D
2:13 was given whatever she D to take with her
Job 31:16 anything that the poor D, or have caused the
Ps 19:10 More to be D are they than gold, even
68:16 the mount which God D for his abode, yea,
107:30 brought them to their D haven.
132:13 chosen Zion; he has D it for his habitation:
132:14 dwell, for I have D it.
Prov 19:22 What is D in a man is loyalty, and
Eccl 2:10 And whatever my eyes D I did not keep
Wis 8:2 my youth, and I D to take her for
16:3 those men, when they D food, might lose the
Sir 14:14 not your share of D good pass by you.
42:22 How greatly to be D are all his works,
Jer 17:16 evil, nor have I D the day of disaster,
Dan 7:19 and ever.' "Then I D to know the truth
1Mac 4:6 not have armor and swords such as they D
2Mac 15:38 is what I myself D; if it is poorly
Mk 3:13 him those whom he D; and they came to
Lk 10:24 many prophets and kings D to see what you
16:21 full of sores, who D to be fed with
22:15 them, "I have earnestly D to eat this passover
23:8 for he had long D to see him, because
Acts 10:10 he became hungry and D something to eat; but
Heb 6:17 So when God D to show more convincingly to
10:5 offerings thou hast not D, but a body hast
10:8 above, "Thou hast neither D nor taken pleasure in
12:17 that afterward, when he D to inherit the blessing,

DESIRES (31)

Deut 18:6 may come when he D --to the place which
1Sam 18:25 to David, 'The king D no marriage present except
2Sam 3:21 you may reign over all that your heart D
1Kgs 11:37 all that your soul D, and you shall be
Esth 5:5 Haman quickly, that we may do as Esther D
Job 17:11 are broken off, the D of my heart.
23:13 What he D, that he does.
Ps 10:3 wicked boasts of the D of his heart, and
34:12 man is there who D life, and covets many
37:4 will give you the D of your heart.
140:8 not, O LORD, the D of the wicked; do
Prov 21:10 soul of the wicked D evil; his neighbor finds
Eccl 6:2 of all that he D, yet God does not
Sir 5:2 walking according to the D of your heart.
18:29 not follow your base D, but restrain your appetites.
40:22 The eye D grace and beauty, but the green
Mic 7:1 to eat, no first-ripe fig which my soul D
Mt 27:43 him now, if he D him; for he said,
Lk 5:39 after drinking old wine D new; for he says,
Jn 8:44 and your will is to do your father's D
Rom 13:14 no provision for the flesh, to gratify its D
1Cor 7:15 if the unbelieving partner D to separate, let it
Gal 5:16 do not gratify the D of the flesh.
5:17 For the D of the flesh are against the
5:17 the Spirit, and the D of the Spirit are
5:24 have crucified the flesh with its passions and D
Eph 2:3 our flesh, following the D of body and mind,
1Tim 2:4 God our Savior, who D all men to be
3:1 office of bishop, he D a noble task.
6:9 many senseless and hurtful D that plunge men into
Rev 22:17 come, let him who D take the water of

DESIREST

Ps 51:6 Behold, thou D truth in the inward being; therefore

DESIRING (12)

Wis 13:6 while seeking God and D to find him.
Lk 8:20 brrethren are standing outside, D to see you."
10:29 But he, D to justify himself, said to Jesus,
14:28 For which of you, D to build a tower,
23:19 addressed them once more, D to release Jesus;
Acts 22:30 But on the morrow, D to know the real
23:28 And D to know the charge on which they
24:26 by Porcius Festus; and D to do the Jews
Rom 9:22 What if God, D to show his wrath and
2Cor 8:11 that your readiness in D it may be matched
1Tim 1:7 away into vain discussion, D to be teachers of
Heb 13:18 have a clear conscience, D to act honorably in

DESIROUS

1Thes 2:8 So, being affectionately D of you, we were ready

DESIST (3)

Job 14:6 away from him, and D, that he may enjoy,
Prov 23:4 toil to acquire wealth; be wise enough to D
Sir 35:17 Lord; he will not D until the Most High

DESOLATE (87)

Gen 47:19 die, and that the land may not be D
Ex 23:29 lest the land become D and the wild beasts
Lev 26:22 in number, so that your ways shall become D
26:31 will make your sanctuaries D, and I will not
26:34 long as it lies D, while you are in
26:35 long as it lies D it shall have rest,
26:43 sabbaths while it lies D without them; and they
2Sam 13:20 So Tamar dwelt, a D woman, in her brother
2Chr 36:21 days that it lay D it kept sabbath, to
Tob 14:4 from the good land, and Jerusalem will be D
Job 15:28 and has lived in D cities, in houses which
16:7 out; he has made D all my company.
30:3 gnaw the dry and D ground;
38:27 satisfy the waste and D land, and to make
Ps 40:2 me up from the D pit, out of the
68:6 God gives the D a home to dwell in;
Prov 31:8 for the rights of all who are left D
Sir 16:4 tribe of lawless men it will be made D
49:6 and made her streets D, according to the word
Is 1:7 Your country lies D, your cities are burned with
1:7 your land; it is D, as overthrown by aliens.
5:9 many houses shall be D, large and beautiful houses,
6:11 the land is utterly D,
24:1 earth and make it D, and he will twist
49:8 land, to apportion the D heritages;

49:19 your waste and your D places and your devastated
54:1 the children of the D one will be more
54:3 and will people the D cities.
62:4 no more be termed D; but you shall be
Jer 2:12 be shocked, be utterly D, says the LORD,
4:30 And you, O D one, what do you mean
12:10 my pleasant portion a D wilderness.
12:11 made it a desolation; D, it mourns to me.
12:11 whole land is made D, but no man lays
26:9 this city shall be D, without inhabitant'?" And all
33:10 of Jerusalem that are D, without man or inhabitant
48:34 For the waters of Nimrim also have become D
49:2 it shall become a D mound, and its villages
51:62 and it shall be D for ever.'
Lam 1:4 all her gates are D, her priests groan; her
1:16 courage; my children are D, for the enemy has
3:11 he has made me D;
5:18 Mount Zion which lies D; jackals prowl over it.
Bar 4:12 many; I was left D because of the sins
4:19 my children, go; for I have been left D
Ezek 6:4 Your altars shall become D, and your incense altars
6:14 and make the land D and waste, throughout all
14:15 and it be made D, so that no man
14:16 would be delivered, but the land would be D
15:8 will make the land D, because they have acted
25:3 when it was made D, and over the house
25:13 I will make it D; from Teman even to
32:15 the land of Egypt D and when the land
33:28 Israel shall be so D that none will pass
35:12 saying, 'They are laid D, they are given us
35:14 of the whole earth I will make you D
35:15 Israel, because it was D, so I will deal
35:15 you; you shall be D, Mount Seir, and all
36:3 because they made you D, and crushed you from
36:4 and the valleys, the D wastes and the deserted
36:34 the land that was D shall be tilled, instead
36:35 'This land that was D has become like the
36:35 and the waste and D and ruined cities are
36:36 replanted that which was D; I, the LORD, have
Dan 8:13 the transgression that makes D, and the giving over
9:17 face to shine upon thy sanctuary, which is D
9:27 come one who makes D, until the decreed end
11:31 they shall set up the abomination that makes D
12:11 the abomination that makes D is set up, there
Joel 1:16 clods, the storehouses are D; the granaries are
2:3 but after them a D wilderness, and nothing escapes
2:20 into a parched and D land, his front into
3:19 desolation and Edom a D wilderness, for the violence
Amos 7:9 Isaac shall be made D, and the sanctuaries of
Mic 6:13 smite you, making you D because of your sins.
7:13 the earth will be D because of its inhabitants,
Nah 2:10 D! D and ruin
Zeph 3:6 cities have been made D, without a man, without
Zech 7:14 land they left was D, so that no one
7:14 and fro, and the pleasant land was made D
1Mac 1:39 Her sanctuary became D as a desert; her feasts
4:38 they saw the sanctuary D, the altar profaned, and
Mt 23:37 Behold, your house is forsaken and D
Jn 14:18 will not leave you D; I will come to
Acts 1:20 'Let his habitation become D, and let there be
Gal 4:27 the children of the D one are many more
Rev 17:16 they will make her D and naked, and devour

DESOLATED (3)

Ezek 29:12 in the midst of D countries; and her cities
30:7 And she shall be D in the midst of
30:7 in the midst of D countries and her cities

DESOLATING (3)

1Mac 1:54 year, they erected a D sacrilege upon the altar
Mt 24:15 when you see the D sacrilege spoken of by
Mk 13:14 when you see the D sacrilege set up where

DESOLATION (57)

Lev 26:33 land shall be a D, and your cities shall
2Kgs 22:19 they should become a D and a curse, and
2Chr 30:7 he made them a D, as you see.
Jud 8:22 the land and the D of our inheritance--all
Ps 69:25 their camp be a D, let no one dwell
Is 13:9 make the earth a D and to destroy its
15:6 of Nimrim are a D; the grass is withered,
17:9 the children of Israel, and there will be D
24:12 D is left in the city, the gates are
59:7 are thoughts of iniquity, D and destruction are in
64:10 Zion has become a wilderness, Jerusalem a D
Jer 4:27 land shall be a D; yet I will not
6:8 I make you a D, an uninhabited land."
9:11 cities of Judah a D, without inhabitant."
10:22 cities of Judah a D, a lair of jackals.
12:11 have made it a D; desolate, it mourns to
22:5 the LORD, that this house shall become a D
25:18 to make them a D and a waste, a
27:17 Why should this city become a D
32:43 saying, It is a D, without man or beast;
34:22 cities of Judah a D without inhabitant."
44:2 day they are a D, and no one dwells
44:6 a waste and a D, as at this day.
44:22 land has become a D and a waste and
48:3 a cry from Horonaim, D and great destruction!'
48:9 cities shall become a D, with no inhabitant in
50:3 make her land a D, and none shall dwell
50:13 shall be an utter D; every one who passes
51:29 land of Babylon a D, without inhabitant.
Bar 2:4 a reproach and a D among all the surrounding
2:23 land will be a D without inhabitants."
4:33 so she will be grieved at her own D
Ezek 5:14 will make you a D and an object of
7:23 shall enter and profane it, and make a D
12:20 land shall become a D; and you shall know
23:33 cup of horror and D, is the cup of
29:9 Egypt shall be a D and a waste.
29:10 an utter waste and D, from Migdol to Syene,
29:12 land of Egypt a D in the midst of
29:12 cities shall be a D forty years among cities
30:12 men; I will bring D upon the land and
30:14 will make Pathros a D, and will set fire
33:28 make the land a D and a waste; and
33:29 made the land a D and a waste because
35:3 will make you a D and a waste.
35:4 you shall become a D; and you shall know
35:7 a waste and a D; and I will cut
35:9 make you a perpetual D, and your cities shall
36:34 instead of being the D that it was in
Hos 5:9 Ephraim shall become a D in the day of
Joel 3:19 "Egypt shall become a D and Edom a desolate
Mic 6:16 may make you a D, and your inhabitants a
Nah 2:10 D and ruin!
Zeph 2:4 Ashkelon shall become a D; Ashdod's people shall be
2:13 will make Nineveh a D, a dry waste like
2:15 What a D she has become, a lair for
Lk 21:20 then know that its D has come near.

DESOLATIONS (4)

Ps 46:8 how he has wrought D in the earth.
Dan 9:2 the end of the D of Jerusalem, namely, seventy
9:18 eyes and behold our D, and the city which
9:26 there shall be war; D are decreed.

DESOLATOR

Dan 9:27 the decreed end is poured out on the D

DESPAIR (9)

1Sam 27:1 Philistines; then Saul will D of seeking me any
Job 24:22 rise up when they D of life.
Ps 69:20 broken my heart, so that I am in D
Eccl 2:20 my heart up to D over all the toil
Sir 22:19 a friend, do not D, for a renewal of
Is 19:9 flax will be in D, and the weavers of
Ezek 7:27 prince is wrapped in D, and the hands of
2Mac 9:22 I do not D of my condition, for I
2Cor 4:8 but not driven to D;

DESPAIRED

2Cor 1:8 unbearably crushed that we D of life itself.

DESPAIRING (2)

Esth 14:19 the voice of the D, and save us from
Job 6:26 the speech of a D man is wind?

DESPERATE

1Mac 9:17 The battle became D, and many on both sides

DESPERATELY

Jer 17:9 above all things, and D corrupt; who can understand

DESPISE (44)

Num 14:11 long will this people D me?
Deut 31:20 and serve them, and D me and break my
1Sam 2:30 honor, and those who D me shall be lightly
2Sam 19:43 Why then did you D us?
Tob 4:18 man, and do not D any useful counsel.
Jud 10:19 his neighbor, "Who can D these people, who have

Job 5:17 whom God reproves; therefore D not the chastening
10:3 thee to oppress, to D the work of thy
19:18 Even young children D me; when I rise they
36:5 mighty, and does not D any; he is mighty
42:6 sees thee; therefore I D myself, and repent in
Ps 51:17 and contrite heart, O God, thou wilt not D
69:33 needy, and does not D his own that are
73:20 awakes, on awaking you D their phantoms.
102:17 destitute, and will not D their supplication.
Prov 1:7 beginning of knowledge; fools D wisdom and
3:11 My son, do not D the LORD's discipline or
6:30 Do not men D a thief if he steals
23:9 fool, for he will D the wisdom of your
23:22 you, and do not D your mother when she
Song 8:1 you, and none would D me.
Sir 3:13 your strength do not D him.
10:22 is not right to D an intelligent poor man,
31:31 wine, and do not D him in his merrymaking;
38:4 sensible man will not D them.
Is 30:12 of Israel, "Because you D this word, and trust
Jer 4:30 Your lovers D you; they seek your life.
23:17 continually to those who D the word of the
Lam 1:8 all who honored her D her, for they have
Ezek 16:57 those round about who D you.
21:13 it do if you D the rod?" says the
Amos 5:21 "I hate, I D your feasts, and I take
Mal 1:6 you, O priests, who D my name.
Mt 6:24 to the one and D the other.
18:10 that you do not D one of these little
Lk 16:13 to the one and D the other.
Rom 14:3 not him who eats D him who abstains, and
14:10 you, why do you D your brother?
1Cor 11:22 Or do you D the church of God and
16:11 So let no one D him.
Gal 4:14 did not scorn or D me, but received me
1Thes 5:20 the Spirit, do not D prophesying,
1Tim 4:12 Let no one D your youth, but set the
2Pet 2:10 of defiling passion and D authority.

DESPISED (54)

Gen 25:34 Thus Esau D his birthright.
Num 14:23 none of those who D me shall see it.
14:31 they shall know the land which you have D
15:31 Because he has D the word of the LORD,
16:30 that these men have D the LORD."
Judg 9:38 him?' Are not these the men whom you D
1Sam 10:27 And they D him, and brought him no present.
15:9 them; all that was D and worthless they utterly
2Sam 6:16 the LORD; and she D him in her heart.
12:9 Why have you D the word of the LORD,
12:10 house, because you have D me, and have taken
2Kgs 17:15 They D his statutes, and his covenant that he
1Chr 15:29 making merry; and she D him in her heart.
Neh 2:19 they derided us and D us and said, "What
4:4 God, for we are D; turn back their taunt
Jud 14:5 recognize the man who D the house of Israel
Ps 15:4 eyes a reprobate is D, but who honors those
22:6 scorned by men, and D by the people.
22:24 For he has not D or abhorred the affliction
106:24 Then they D the pleasant land, having no faith
119:141 I am small and D, yet I do not
Prov 1:30 of my counsel, and D all my reproof,
5:12 discipline, and my heart D reproof!
12:8 good sense, but one of perverse mind is D
Eccl 9:16 poor man's wisdom is D, and his words are
Wis 12:24 which even their enemies D; they were deceived like
Sir 22:5 husband, and will be D by both.
Is 1:4 the LORD, they have D the Holy One of
5:24 of hosts, and have D the word of the
33:8 are broken, witnesses are D, there is no regard
49:7 One, to one deeply D, abhorred by the nations,
52:5 and continually all the day my name is D
53:3 He was D and rejected by men; a man
53:3 their faces he was D, and we esteemed him
60:14 you; and all who D you shall bow down
Jer 22:28 this man Coniah a D, broken pot, a vessel
33:24 Thus they have D my people so that they
49:15 small among the nations, D among men.
Lam 1:11 "Look, O LORD, and behold, for I am D
Ezek 16:59 have done, who have D the oath in breaking
17:16 king, whose oath he D, and whose covenant with
17:18 Because he D the oath and broke the covenant,
17:19 my oath which he D, and my covenant which
21:10 You have D the rod, my son, with everything
22:8 You have D my holy things, and profaned my
Obad 1:2 small among the nations, you shall be utterly D
Zech 4:10 For whoever has D the day of small things
Mal 1:6 say, 'How have we D thy name?'
1:7 By thinking that the LORD's table may be D
1:12 polluted, and the food for it may be D
2:9 so I make you D and abased before all
2Mac 1:27 who are rejected and D, and let the Gentiles
Lk 18:9 they were righteous and D others:
1Cor 1:28 what is low and D in the world, even

DESPISES (12)

2Kgs 19:21 spoken concerning him: "She D you, she scorns you—
Prov 13:13 He who D the word brings destruction on himself,
14:2 devious in his ways D him.
14:21 He who D his neighbor is a sinner, but
15:5 A fool D his father's instruction, but he who
15:20 but a foolish man D his mother.
15:32 He who ignores instruction D himself, but he who
19:16 his life; he who D the word will die.
Wis 3:11 the Lord; for whoever D wisdom and instruction is
Sir 19:1 become rich; he who D small things will fail
Is 33:15 and speaks uprightly, who D the gain of oppressions,
37:22 spoken concerning him: 'She D you, she scorns you—

DESPISING (3)

2Chr 36:16 the messengers of God, D his words, and scoffing
2Mac 4:14 D the sanctuary and neglecting the sacrifices, they
Heb 12:2 him endured the cross, D the shame, and is

DESPITE

Ps 78:32 this they still sinned; D his wonders they did

DESPOIL (11)

Ex 3:22 daughters; thus you shall D the Egyptians."
1Sam 14:36 Philistines by night and D them until the morning
Ps 17:9 from the wicked who D me, my deadly enemies
89:41 All that pass by D him; he has become
Prov 22:23 plead their cause and D of life those who
22:23 of life those who D them.
Is 17:14 portion of those who D us, and the lot
Jer 30:16 into captivity; those who D you shall become a
Ezek 29:19 off its wealth and D it and plunder it;
39:10 the weapons; they will D those who despoiled them,
1Mac 3:20 our children, and to D us;

DESPOILED (7)

Ex 12:36 Thus they D the Egyptians.
Ps 12:5 "Because the poor are D, because the needy groan,
Is 24:3 laid waste and utterly D; for the LORD has
Ezek 39:10 will despoil those who D them, and plunder those
Zech 11:3 wail of the shepherds, for their glory is D
1Mac 5:3 and humbled them and D them.
5:22 Gentiles fell, and he D them.

DESPOILING

Jer 25:36 For the LORD is D their pasture,

DESPOILS

Ps 35:10 needy from him who D him?"

DESSAU

2Mac 14:16 engaged them in battle at a village called D

DESTINE

Is 65:12 for Destiny; I will D you to the sword,

DESTINED (13)

Tob 6:17 afraid, for she was D for you from eternity.
Job 15:22 darkness, and he is D for the sword.
15:28 should inhabit, which were D to become heaps of
Wis 15:9 concerned that he is D to die or that
17:21 the darkness that was D to receive them; but
Is 23:13 They D Tyre for wild beasts.
Hos 9:13 I have seen, are D for a prey; Ephraim
Eph 1:5 He D us in love to be his sons
1:12 in Christ have been D and appointed to live
1Thes 5:9 For God has not D us for wrath, but
1Pet 1:2 and Bithynia, chosen and D by God the Father
1:20 He was D before the foundation of the world
2:8 word, as they were D to do.

DESTINY

Is 65:11 of mixed wine for D;

DESTITUTE (4)

Ps 82:3 maintain the right of the afflicted and the D
102:17 the prayer of the D, and will not despise

Sir 37:20 hated; he will be D of all food,
Heb 11:37 of sheep and goats, D, afflicted, ill-treated—

DESTROY (276)

Gen 6:13 them; behold, I will D them with the earth.
6:17 upon the earth, to D all flesh in which
8:21 will I ever again D every living creature as
9:11 be a flood to D the earth."
9:15 become a flood to D all flesh.
18:23 said, "Wilt thou indeed D the righteous with the
18:24 city; wilt thou then D the place and not
18:28 Wilt thou D the whole city for lack of
18:28 said, "I will not D it if I find
18:31 twenty I will not D it."
18:32 ten I will not D it."
19:13 we are about to D this place, because the
19:13 has sent us to D it."
19:14 LORD is about to D the city." But he
Ex 12:13 fall upon you to D you, when I smite
15:9 sword, my hand shall D them.'
Lev 23:30 that person I will D from among his people.
26:22 of your children, and D your cattle, and make
26:30 And I will D your high places, and cut
26:44 them so as to D them utterly and break
Num 21:2 then I will utterly D their cities."
32:15 wilderness; and you will D all this people."
33:52 from before you, and D all their figured stones,
33:52 their figured stones, and D all their molten images,
Deut 1:27 of the Amorites, to D us.
2:15 was against them, to D them from the camp,
4:31 not fail you or D you or forget the
6:15 against you, and he D you from off the
7:2 then you must utterly D them; you shall make
7:4 you, and he would D you quickly.
7:16 And you shall D all the peoples that the
9:3 your God; he will D them and subdue them
9:8 he was ready to D you.
9:14 alone, that I may D them and blot out
9:19 he was ready to D you.
9:20 he was ready to D him; and I prayed
9:25 had said he would D you.
9:26 LORD, 'O Lord GOD, D not thy people and
10:10 LORD was unwilling to D you.
12:2 You shall surely D all the places where the
12:3 of their gods, and D their name out of
20:17 but you shall utterly D them, the Hittites and
20:19 it, you shall not D its trees by wielding
20:20 for food you may D and cut down that
31:3 before you; he will D these nations before you,
33:27 thrust out the enemy before you, and said, D
Josh 7:7 of the Amorites, to D us?
7:12 no more, unless you D the devoted things from
9:24 the land, and to D all the inhabitants of
22:33 war against them, to D the land where the
Judg 6:4 encamp against them and D the produce of the
21:11 has lain with a male you shall utterly D
1Sam 15:3 smite Amalek, and utterly D all that they have;
15:6 the Amalekites, lest I D you with them; for
15:9 and would not utterly D them; all that was
15:18 and said, 'Go, utterly D the sinners, the Amalekites,
23:10 come to Keilah, to D the city on my
24:21 that you will not D my name out of
26:9 to Abishai, "Do not D him; for who can
26:15 people came in to D the king your lord.
2Sam 1:14 forth your hand to D the LORD's anointed?"
4:11 at your hand, and D you from the earth?"
14:7 and so they would D the heir also.
14:16 the man who would D me and my son
20:19 Israel; you seek to D a city which is
20:20 be it, that I should swallow up or D
21:5 us and planned to D us, so that we
24:16 hand toward Jerusalem to D it, the LORD repented
1Kgs 9:21 Israel were unable to D utterly—these Solomon
13:34 it off and to D it from the face
2Kgs 8:19 the LORD would not D Judah, for the sake
10:19 cunning in order to D the worshipers of Baal.
13:23 Jacob, and would not D them; nor has he
18:25 against this place to D it?
18:25 against this land, and D it.'"
24:2 them against Judah to D it, according to the
1Chr 21:15 angel to Jerusalem to D it; but when he
21:15 he was about to D it, the LORD saw,
2Chr 12:7 themselves; I will not D them, but I will
20:10 avoided and did not D —
20:23 they all helped to D one another.
20:37 Ahaziah, the LORD will D what you have made."
21:7 the LORD would not D the house of David,
22:7 LORD had anointed to D the house of Ahab.
25:16 God has determined to D you, because you have
35:21 with me, lest he D you."
Ezra 6:12 alter this, or to D this house of God
Jud 3:8 given to him to D all the gods of
6:3 his forces and will D them from the face
6:3 the king's servants will D them as one man.
7:13 So thirst will D them, and they will give
8:15 pleases, or even to D us in the presence
15:4 upon their enemies to D them.
Esth 3:6 Mordecai, Haman sought to D all the Jews, the
3:13 the king's provinces, to D, to slay, and to
8:5 which he wrote to D the Jews who are
8:11 defend their lives, to D, to slay, and to
9:24 against the Jews to D them, and had cast
9:24 lot, to crush and D them;
10:8 those that gathered to D the name of the
13:15 and they desire to D the inheritance that has
13:17 O Lord; do not D the mouth of those
14:9 has ordained and to D thy inheritance, to stop
Job 2:3 me against him, to D him without cause."
10:8 dost turn about and D me.
Ps 21:10 You will D their offspring from the earth, and
55:9 D their plans, O Lord, confuse their tongues; for
63:9 those who seek to D my life shall go
69:4 are those who would D me, those who attack
78:38 iniquity, and did not D them; he restrained his
88:16 me; thy dread assaults D me.
101:5 Him who slanders his neighbor secretly I will D
101:8 by morning I will D all the wicked in
106:23 he said he would D them— had not
106:34 They did not D the peoples, as the LORD
119:95 lie in wait to D me; but I consider
143:12 off my enemies, and D all my adversaries, for
145:20 love him; but all the wicked he will D
Prov 11:9 the godless man would D his neighbor, but by
31:3 ways to those who D kings.
Eccl 5:6 at your voice, and D the work of your
7:16 overwise; why should you D yourself?
Wis 12:6 thou didst will to D by the hands of
12:8 of thy army, to D them little by little,
12:9 in battle, or to D them at one blow
16:19 intensely than fire, to D the crops of the
18:5 children; and thou didst D them all together by
Sir 6:3 devour your leaves and D your fruit, and will
6:4 An evil soul will D him who has it,
21:2 are lion's teeth, and D the souls of men.
22:25 my tongue may not D me!
36:7 pour out thy wrath; D the adversary and wipe
47:22 his chosen one, nor D the posterity of him
49:7 up and afflict and D, and likewise to build
Is 10:7 in his mind to D, and to cut off
10:18 land the LORD will D, both soul and body,
11:9 shall not hurt or D in all my holy
11:15 the LORD will utterly D the tongue of the
13:5 of his indignation, to D the whole earth.
13:9 a desolation and to D its sinners from it.
23:11 command concerning Canaan to D its strongholds.
25:7 And he will D on this mountain the covering
33:1 you have ceased to D, you will be destroyed;
36:10 against this land to D it?
36:10 against this land, and D it.'"
51:13 of the oppressor, when he sets himself to D
54:16 created the ravager to D;
65:8 they say, 'Do not D it, for there is
65:8 servants' sake, and not D them all.
65:25 shall not hurt or D in all my holy
Jer 1:10 to break down, to D and to overthrow, to
5:6 from the desert shall D them.
5:10 through her vine-rows and D, but make not a
5:17 you trust they shall D with the sword."
6:2 delicately bred I will D, the daughter of Zion.
6:5 attack by night, and D her palaces!"
11:19 schemes, saying, "Let us D the tree with its
12:17 pluck it up and D it, says the LORD."
13:14 that I should not D them.'"
15:3 the beasts of the earth to devour and D
17:18 the day of evil; D them with double destruction!
18:7 and break down and D it,
23:1 to the shepherds who D and scatter the sheep
25:9 about; I will utterly D them, and make them
31:28 break down, to overthrow, D, and bring evil, so
36:29 will certainly come and D this land, and will
46:8 the earth, I will D cities and their inhabitants.
47:4 that is coming to D all the Philistines, to

49:9 night, would they not D only enough for themselves?
49:28 D the people of the east!
49:38 throne in Elam, and D their king and princes,
50:21 Slay, and utterly D after them, says the LORD,
50:26 heaps of grain, and D her utterly; let nothing
51:3 her young men; utterly D all her host.
51:11 concerning Babylon is to D it, for that is
51:20 pieces; with you I D kingdoms;
Lam 3:66 them in anger and D them from under thy
Bar 6:14 scepter, though unable to D any one who offends
Ezek 5:16 I will loose to D you, and when I
6:3 you, and I will D your high places.
9:8 wilt thou D all that remains of Israel in
13:13 hailstones in wrath to D it.
14:9 against him, and will D him from the midst
20:17 and I did not D them or make a
21:31 into the hands of brutal men, skilful to D
22:30 that I should not D it; but I found
25:7 the countries; I will D you.
25:15 malice of heart to D in never-ending enmity;
25:16 off the Cherethites, and D the rest of the
26:4 They shall D the walls of Tyre, and break
26:12 down your walls and D your pleasant houses; your
30:11 be brought in to D the land; and they
30:13 Lord GOD: I will D the idols, and put
32:13 I will D all its beasts from beside many
43:3 when he came to D the city, and like
Dan 2:24 king had appointed to D the wise men of
2:24 to him, "Do not D the wise men of
4:23 down the tree and D it, but leave the
8:24 what he does, and D mighty men and the
8:25 Without warning he shall D many; and he shall
9:26 is to come shall D the city and the
11:17 daughter of women to D the kingdom; but it
11:44 to exterminate and utterly D many.
13:59 two, that he may D you both."
Hos 4:5 night; and I will D your mother.
10:2 down their altars, and D their pillars.
11:9 I will not again D Ephraim; for I am
11:9 your midst, and I will not come to D
13:9 I will D you, O Israel; who can help
Amos 9:8 kingdom, and I will D it from the surface
9:8 I will not utterly D the house of Jacob,"
Obad 1:8 day, says the LORD, D the wise men out
Mic 5:10 among you and will D your chariots;
5:14 from among you and D your cities.
Zeph 2:5 Philistines; and I will D you till no inhabitant
2:13 against the north, and D Assyria; and he will
Hag 2:22 I am about to D the strength of the
Zech 12:9 I will seek to D all the nations that
Mal 3:11 that it will not D the fruits of your
1Mac 2:40 ordinances, they will quickly D us from the earth."
3:20 pride and lawlessness to D us and our wives
3:35 to wipe out and D the strength of Israel
3:39 land of Judah and D it, as the king
3:52 assembled against us to D us; thou knowest what
3:58 assembled against us to D us and our sanctuary.
5:2 and they determined to D the descendants of Jacob
5:2 began to kill and D among the people.
5:9 territory, and planned to D them.
5:10 together against us to D us.
5:27 tomorrow and take and D all these men in
6:12 and I sent to D the inhabitants of Judah
6:19 So Judas decided to D them, and assembled all
7:26 he commanded him to D the people.
8:9 planned to come and D them,
12:49 the Great Plain to D all Jonathan's soldiers.
12:53 about them tried to D them, for they said,
13:1 land of Judah and D it,
13:6 out of hatred to D us."
13:20 invade the country and D it, and he circled
16:22 men who came to D him and killed them,
16:22 they were seeking to D him.
2Mac 6:12 were designed not to D but to discipline our
15:2 him said, "Do not D so savagely and barbarously,
Mt 2:13 for the child, to D him."
10:28 fear him who can D both soul and body
12:14 against him, how to D him.
26:61 'I am able to D the temple of God,
27:20 ask for Barabbas and D Jesus.
27:40 saying, "You who would D the temple and build
Mk 1:24 Have you come to D us?
3:6 against him, how to D him.
9:22 into the water, to D him; but if you
11:18 sought a way to D him; for they feared
12:9 He will come and D the tenants, and give
14:58 him say, 'I will D this temple that is
15:28 You who would D the temple and build it
Lk 4:34 Have you come to D us?
6:9 save life or to D it?"
19:47 the people sought to D him;
20:16 He will come and D those tenants, and give
Jn 2:19 Jesus answered them, D this temple, and in three
10:10 steal and kill and D; I came that they
11:48 Romans will come and D both our holy place
Acts 6:14 Jesus of Nazareth will D this place, and will
Rom 14:20 the sake of food, D the work of God.
1Cor 1:19 is written, "I will D the wisdom of the
3:17 God's temple, God will D him.
6:13 food"—and God will D both one and the
2Cor 10:4 have divine power to D strongholds.
10:5 We D arguments and every proud obstacle to the
Gal 1:13 violently and tried to D it;
1:23 now preaching the faith he once tried to D
2Thes 2:8 of his mouth and D him by his appearing
Heb 2:14 through death he might D him who has the
Jas 4:12 he who is able to save and to D
1 Jn 3:8 God appeared was to D the works of the

DESTROYED (211)

Gen 13:10 was before the LORD D Sodom and Gomorrah.
19:29 was that, when God D the cities of the
34:30 me, I shall be D, both I and my
Ex 8:9 that the frogs be D from you and your
22:20 save to the LORD only, shall be utterly D
Lev 27:29 is to be utterly D from among men, shall
Num 4:18 of the Kohathites be D from among the Levites;
21:3 Canaanites; and they utterly D them and their cities;
24:19 be exercised, and the survivors of cities be D
Deut 2:12 Esau dispossessed them, and D them from before
2:21 Anakim; but the LORD D them before them; and
2:22 in Seir, when he D the Horites before them,
2:23 who came from Caphtor, D them and settled in
2:34 that time and utterly D every city, men, women,
3:6 And we utterly D them, as we did to
4:3 the LORD your God D from among you all
4:26 live long upon it, but will be utterly D
7:20 are left and hide themselves from you are D
7:23 throw them into great confusion, until they are D
7:24 you, until you have D them.
11:4 how the LORD has D them to this day;
12:30 after they have been D before you, and that
28:20 do, until you are D and perish quickly, on
28:24 shall come down upon you until you are D
28:45 you, till you are D, because you did not
28:48 neck, until he has D you.
28:51 ground, until you are D; who also shall not
28:61 LORD will bring upon you, until you are D
31:4 their land, when he D them.
Josh 2:10 Jordan, to Sihon and Og, whom you utterly D
6:21 Then they utterly D all in the city, both
8:26 until he had utterly D all the inhabitants of
10:1 Ai, and had utterly D it, doing to Ai
10:28 the sword; he utterly D every person in it,
10:35 in it he utterly D that day, as he
10:37 to Eglon, and utterly D it with every person
10:39 the sword, and utterly D every person in it;
10:40 none remaining, but utterly D all that breathed, as
11:14 sword, until they had D them, and they did
11:20 they should be utterly D, and should receive no
11:21 of Israel; Joshua utterly D them with their cities.
23:15 things, until he have D you from off this
24:8 their land, and I D them before you.
Judg 1:17 inhabited Zephath, and utterly D it.
4:24 of Canaan, until they D Jabin king of Canaan.
20:35 the men of Israel D twenty-five thousand one
20:42 out of the cities D them in the midst
21:16 since the women are D out of Benjamin?"
1Sam 15:8 Amalekites alive, and utterly D all the people with
15:9 all that was despised and worthless they utterly D
15:15 your God; and the rest we have utterly D
15:20 and I have utterly D the Amalekites.
2Sam 14:11 slay no more, and my son be not D
22:38 pursued my enemies and D them, and did not
22:41 hated me, and I D them.
1Kgs 15:29 breathed, until he had D it, according to the
16:7 and also because he D it.
16:12 Thus Zimri D all the house of Baasha, according
22:11 you shall push the Syrians until they are D
2Kgs 11:1 dead, she arose and D all the royal family.
13:7 king of Syria had D them and made them
19:12 nations which my fathers D, Gozan, Haran, Rezeph,

	19:18	men's hands, wood and stone; therefore they were D
	21:3	Hezekiah his father had D; and he erected altars
	21:9	done whom the LORD D before the people of
1Chr	4:41	king of Judah, and D their tents and the
	4:43	of Ishi; and they D the remnant of the
	5:25	land, whom God had D before them.
2Chr	8:8	of Israel had not D –these Solomon made a
	18:10	you shall push the Syrians until they are D
	19:3	in you, for you D the Asherahs out of
	22:10	dead, she arose and D all the royal family
	24:23	Judah and Jerusalem, and D all the princes of
	31:1	Manasseh, until they had D them all.
	32:14	which my fathers utterly D was able to deliver
	33:9	nations whom the LORD D before the people of
	36:19	palaces with fire, and D all its precious vessels.
Ezra	5:12	Babylon, the Chaldean, who D this house and carried
Neh	1:3	and its gates are D by fire."
	2:3	its gates have been D by fire?"
	2:13	gates which had been D by fire.
Jud	1:15	spears; and he utterly D him, to this day.
	2:3	who had not obeyed his command should be D
	2:24	passed through Mesopotamia and D all the hilltop
	2:27	all their fields and D their flocks and herds
	4:1	he had plundered and D all their temples;
	4:12	had inherited to be D, and the sanctuary to
	5:15	and by their might D all the inhabitants of
	11:15	will be handed over to you to be D
	13:14	of Israel, but has D our enemies by my
	14:13	in order to be D completely."
Esth	3:9	decreed that they be D, and I will pay
	7:4	my people, to be D, to be slain, and
	9:6	the Jews slew and D five hundred men,
	13:6	and children, be utterly D by the sword of
	16:24	act accordingly, shall be D in wrath with spear
Job	4:20	and evening they are D; they perish for ever
	8:18	If he is D from his place, then it
	19:26	skin has been thus D, then from my flesh
Ps	9:5	the nations, thou hast D the wicked; thou hast
	11:3	if the foundations are D, what can the righteous
	18:40	to me, and those who hated me I D
	37:38	transgressors shall be altogether D; the posterity of
	73:19	How they are D in a moment, swept away
	74:3	ruins; the enemy has D everything in the sanctuary!
	78:45	them, and frogs, which D them.
	78:47	He D their vines with hail, and their sycamores
	83:10	river Kishon, who were D at Endor, who became
Prov	14:11	the wicked will be D, but the tent of
Wis	16:5	and they were being D by the bites of
	16:22	their enemies were being D by the fire that
	16:27	For what was not D by fire was melted
	18:12	one instant their most valued children had been D
	18:13	when their first-born were D, they acknowledged thy
Sir	10:13	them extraordinary afflictions, and D them utterly.
	10:16	the nations, and has D them to the foundations
	10:17	some of them and D them, and has extinguished
	16:9	to destruction, for those D in their sins;
	27:18	enemy, so you have D the friendship of your
	28:13	deceiver, for he has D many who were at
	28:14	nation to nation, and D strong cities, and overturned
	30:23	you, for sorrow has D many, and there is
	31:25	wine, for wine has D many.
	45:19	his anger they were D; he wrought wonders against
	46:6	descent of Beth-horon he D those who resisted, so
Is	1:28	and sinners shall be D together, and those who
	10:27	his yoke will be D from your neck." He
	14:20	burial, because you have D your land, you have
	33:1	yourself have not been D; you treacherous one, with
	33:1	destroy, you will be D; and when you have
	37:12	nations which my fathers D, Gozan, Haran, Rezeph,
	37:19	men's hands, wood and stone; therefore they were D
	48:19	be cut off or D from before me."
Jer	4:20	Suddenly my tents are D, my curtains in a
	10:20	My tent is D, and all my cords are
	12:10	Many shepherds have D my vineyard, they have
	15:6	hand against you and D you;--I am weary
	15:7	bereaved them, I have D my people; they did
	22:20	cry from Abarim, for all your lovers are D
	24:10	they shall be utterly D from the land which
	48:4	great destruction!' Moab is D; a cry is heard
	48:8	the plain shall be D, as the LORD has
	48:18	against you; he has D your strongholds.
	48:42	pangs; Moab shall be D and be no longer
	48:45	of Sihon; it has D the forehead of Moab,
	49:10	His children are D, and his brothers, and his
	49:26	her soldiers shall be D in that day, says
	50:30	her soldiers shall be D on that day, says
	50:36	sword upon her warriors, that they may be D
Lam	2:2	The Lord has D without mercy all the habitations
	2:5	an enemy, he has D Israel; he has destroyed
	2:5	destroyed Israel; he has D all its palaces, laid
	2:16	they cry: "We have D her!
	2:22	those whom I dandled and reared my enemy D
Ezek	6:6	your idols broken and D, your incense altars cut
	27:32	you: 'Who was ever D like Tyre in the
Dan	2:12	that all the wise men of Babylon be D
	2:44	which shall never be D, nor shall its sovereignty
	6:26	kingdom shall never be D, and his dominion shall
	7:11	slain, and its body D and given over to
	7:14	and his kingdom one that shall not be D
	7:26	to be consumed and D to the end.
	14:22	over to Daniel, who D it and its temple.
	14:28	a Jew; he has D Bel, and slain the
Hos	4:6	My people are D for lack of knowledge; because
	10:8	of Aven, the sin of Israel, shall be D
	10:14	your fortresses shall be D, as Shalman destroyed
	10:14	be destroyed, as Shalman D Beth-arbel on the day
Joel	1:10	because the grain is D, the wine fails, the
Amos	2:9	"Yet I D the Amorite before them, whose height
	2:9	as the oaks; I D his fruit above, and
Obad	1:5	how you have been D –would they not steal
Zech	11:8	In one month I D the three shepherds.
	11:9	what is to be D, let it be destroyed;
	11:9	destroyed, let it be D; and let those that
1Mac	1:30	a severe blow, and D many people of Israel.
	3:8	cities of Judah; he D the ungodly out of
	5:13	and goods, and have D about a thousand men
	5:51	He D every male by the edge of the
	7:6	and his brothers have D all your friends, and
	8:11	ever opposed them, they D and enslaved;
	9:73	the people, and he D the ungodly out of
	11:4	Azotus and its suburbs D, and the corpses lying
	15:4	against those who have D our country and those
2Mac	4:11	the Romans; and he D the lawful ways of
	5:14	days eighty thousand were D, forty thousand
	8:3	city which was being D and about to be
	8:20	to them from heaven, D one hundred and twenty
	10:2	the foreigners, and also D the sacred precincts.
	10:23	everything he undertook, he D more than twenty
	12:19	Maccabeus, marched out and D those whom Timothy
	12:23	to the sword, and D as many as thirty
Mt	9:17	and the skins are D; but new wine is
	22:7	sent his troops and D those murderers and burned
Lk	5:37	will be spilled, and the skins will be D
	17:27	the flood came and D them all.
	17:29	rained from heaven and D them all–
Acts	3:23	that prophet shall be D from the people.'
	13:19	And when he had D seven nations in the
Rom	6:6	sinful body might be D, and we might no
1Cor	8:11	this weak man is D, the brother for whom
	10:9	them did and were D by serpents;
	10:10	them did and were D by the Destroyer.
	15:26	last enemy to be D is death.
2Cor	4:9	struck down, but not D;
	5:1	we live in is D, we have a building
Heb	10:39	shrink back and are D, but of those who
2Pet	2:12	are ignorant, will be D in the same destruction
Jude	1:5	land of Egypt, afterward D those who did not
	1:10	by instinct as irrational animals do, they are D
Rev	8:9	died, and a third of the ships were D

DESTROYER (18)

Ex	12:23	will not allow the D to enter your houses
Job	15:21	ears; in prosperity the D will come upon him.
Wis	18:25	To these the D yielded, these he feared; for
Is	16:4	you; be a refuge to them from the D
	21:2	plunderer plunders, and the D destroys.
	33:1	Woe to you, D, who yourself have not been
Jer	4:7	from his thicket, a D of nations has set
	6:26	lamentation; for suddenly the D will come upon us.
	15:8	of young men a D at noonday; I have
	48:8	The D shall come upon every city, and no
	48:15	The D of Moab and his cities has come
	48:18	For the D of Moab has come up against
	48:32	and your vintage the D has fallen.
	51:1	the spirit of a D against Babylon, against the
	51:56	is raised; for a D has come upon her,
Joel	2:25	eaten, the hopper, the D, and the cutter, my
1Cor	10:10	of them did and were destroyed by the D
Heb	11:28	blood, so that the D of the first-born might

DESTROYERS (7)

Is	49:17	Your builders outstrip your D, and those who laid

Jer	12:12	heights in the desert D have come; for the
	15:3	them four kinds of D, says the LORD: the
	22:7	I will prepare D against you, each with his
	51:48	over Babylon; for the D shall come against them
	51:53	her strong height, yet D would come from me
Rev	11:18	and for destroying the D of the earth."

DESTROYEST (2)

Job	14:19	the earth; so thou D the hope of man.
Ps	5:6	Thou D those who speak lies; the LORD abhors

DESTROYING (25)

Deut	3:6	the king of Heshbon, D every city, men, women,
	7:10	who hate him, by D them; he will not
	13:15	city to the sword, D it utterly, all who
	28:63	ruin upon you and D you; and you shall
	32:25	chambers shall be terror, D both young man and
Josh	11:11	were in it, utterly D them; there was none
	11:12	of the sword, utterly D them, as Moses the
2Kgs	19:11	done to all lands, D them utterly.
1Chr	21:12	angel of the LORD D throughout all the territory
	21:15	he said to the D angel, "It is enough;
2Chr	20:23	inhabitants of Mount Seir, D them utterly, and when
Esth	9:5	the sword, slaughtering, and D them, and did as
Ps	78:49	distress, a company of D angels.
	106:23	away his wrath from D them.
Is	28:2	storm of hail, a D tempest, like a storm
	37:11	done to all lands, D them utterly.
Jer	47:4	For the LORD is D the Philistines, the remnant
	51:25	am against you, O D mountain, says the LORD,
Lam	2:8	not his hand from D; he caused rampart and
Ezek	9:1	city, each with his D weapon in his hand."
	22:27	the prey, shedding blood, D lives to get dishonest
Joel	1:4	hopping locust left, the D locust has eaten.
1Cor	15:24	God the Father after D every rule and every
2Cor	10:8	up and not for D you, I shall not
Rev	11:18	and great, and for D the destroyers of the

DESTROYS (19)

Gen	32:8	the one company and D it, then the company
Ex	21:26	male or female, and D it, he shall let
Job	9:22	therefore I say, he D both the blameless and
	12:23	nations great, and he D them: he enlarges nations,
Prov	1:32	the complacence of fools D them;
	6:32	he who does it D himself.
	11:3	crookedness of the treacherous D them.
	18:9	his work is a brother to him who D
	28:24	is the companion of a man who D
Eccl	9:18	war, but one sinner D much good.
Wis	1:11	and a lying mouth D the soul.
Sir	27:16	Whoever betrays secrets D confidence, and he will
	27:18	For as a man D his enemy, so you
Is	21:2	to me; the plunderer plunders, and the destroyer D
Jer	51:25	says the LORD, which D the whole earth; I
Mic	2:10	because of uncleanness that D with a grievous
2Mac	3:39	and he strikes and D those who come to
Lk	12:33	fail, where no thief approaches and no moth D
1Cor	3:17	If any one D God's temple, God will destroy

DESTRUCTION (120)

Num	24:20	but in the end he shall come to D
	24:24	and Eber; and he also shall come to D
Josh	6:17	to the LORD for D; only Rahab the harlot
	6:18	the things devoted to D, lest when you have
	6:18	Israel a thing for D, and bring trouble upon
	7:12	enemies, because they have become a thing for D
1Sam	15:21	the things devoted to D, to sacrifice to the
2Sam	24:16	angel who was working D among the people, "It
1Kgs	20:42	I had devoted to D, therefore your life shall
2Chr	12:12	to make a complete D; moreover, conditions were
	26:16	he was strong he grew proud, to his D
Tob	14:15	heard of the D of Nineveh, which Nebuchadnezzar
Jud	7:26	the ground before them with thirst and utter D
	11:22	hands and to bring D upon those who have
	13:5	my undertaking for the D of the enemies who
	13:16	tricked him to his D, and yet he committed
Esth	4:7	king's treasuries for the D of the Jews.
	4:8	in Susa for their D, that he might show
	4:8	to the king, spoke against us for our D
	8:6	endure to see the D of my kindred?"
	16:13	and deceit asked for D of Mordecai, our savior
	16:21	of a day of D for them.
	16:23	against us it may be a reminder of D
Job	5:21	and shall not fear D when it comes.
	5:22	At D and famine you shall laugh, and shall
	21:20	own eyes see their D, and let them drink
	30:12	they cast up against me their ways of D
Ps	5:9	mouth; their heart is D, their throat is an
	37:34	will look on the D of the wicked.
	52:2	All the day you are plotting D
	57:1	till the storms of D pass by.
	91:6	in darkness, nor the D that wastes at noonday.
	92:7	they are doomed to D for ever,
	107:20	word, and healed them, and delivered them from D
Prov	10:29	way is upright, but D to evildoers.
	13:13	despises the word brings D on himself, but he
	16:18	Pride goes before D, and a haughty spirit before
	17:19	strife; he who makes his door high seeks D
	18:12	Before D a man's heart is haughty, but humility
	19:18	d o not set your heart on his D
Wis	1:12	life, nor bring on D by the works of
	3:3	us to be their D; but they are at
	5:7	paths of lawlessness and D, and we journeyed
	12:12	accuse thee for the D of nations which thou
	18:7	the righteous and the D of their enemies were
Sir	9:9	her, and in blood you be plunged into D
	16:9	a nation devoted to D, for those destroyed in
	28:6	cease from enmity, remember D and death, and be
	31:6	of gold, and their D has met them face
	36:9	and may those who harm thy people meet D
	39:30	punishes the ungodly with D;
	41:10	dust; so the ungodly go from curse to D
	48:6	brought kings down to D, and famous men from
	51:2	delivered my body from D and from the snare
	51:12	didst save me from D and rescue me from
Is	10:22	D is decreed, overflowing with righteousness.
	10:25	and my anger will be directed to their D
	13:6	LORD is near; as D from the Almighty it
	14:23	with the broom of D, says the LORD of
	15:5	raise a cry of D;
	16:4	is no more, and D has ceased, and he
	22:4	comfort me for the D of the daughter of
	26:14	hast visited them with D and wiped out all
	28:22	heard a decree of D from the Lord GOD
	30:28	with the sieve of D, and to place on
	38:17	from the pit of D, for thou hast cast
	43:28	delivered Jacob to utter D and Israel to reviling.
	51:19	you?– devastation and D, famine and sword; who
	59:7	of iniquity, desolation and D are in their highways.
	60:18	your land, devastation or D within your borders; you
Jer	4:6	I bring evil from the north, and great D
	6:1	evil looms out of the north, and great D
	6:7	wickedness; violence and D are heard within her;
	17:18	the day of evil; destroy them with double D
	20:8	speak, I cry out, I shout, "Violence and D
	48:3	Horonaim, 'Desolation and great D
	48:5	of Horonaim they have heard the cry of D
	50:22	of battle is in the land, and great D
	51:54	The noise of great D from the land of
Lam	2:11	grief because of the D of the daughter of
	3:47	upon us, devastation and D;
	3:48	tears because of the D of the daughter of
	4:10	their food in the D of the daughter of
Bar	4:6	It was not for D that you were sold
	4:25	will soon see their D and will tread upon
Ezek	5:16	of famine, arrows for D, which I will loose
Dan	8:24	he shall cause fearful D, and shall succeed in
	14:42	who had attempted his D, and they were devoured
Hos	7:14	D to them, for they have rebelled against me!
	8:4	and gold they made idols for their own D
	13:14	O Sheol, where is your D
Joel	1:14	is near, and as D from the Almighty it
Amos	5:9	his name, who makes D flash forth against the
	5:9	the strong, so that D comes upon the fortress.
Mic	2:10	of uncleanness that destroys with a grievous D
Hab	1:3	D and violence are before me; strife and contention
	2:17	will overwhelm you; the D of the beasts will
1Mac	3:42	do to the people to cause their final D
	3:43	"Let us repair the D of our people, and
	4:32	of their strength; let them tremble in their D
	5:5	them, vowed their complete D, and burned with fire
	15:31	silver, and for the D that you have caused
2Mac	5:13	of young and old, D of boys, women, and
	8:4	remember also the lawless D of the innocent babies
	8:35	succeeded chiefly in the D of his own army!
	12:27	After the rout and D of these, he marched
	13:6	they all push to D any man guilty of
Mt	7:13	easy, that leads to D, and those who enter
Rom	9:22	of wrath made for D,
1Cor	5:5	to Satan for the D of the flesh, that
Phil	1:28	to them of their D, but of your salvation,
	3:19	Their end is D, their god is the belly,

1Thes 5:3 then sudden D will come upon them as travail
2Thes 1:9 the punishment of eternal D and exclusion from the
1Tim 6:9 hurtful desires that plunge men into ruin and D
2Pet 2:1 bought them, bringing upon themselves swift D
2:3 been idle, and their D has not been asleep.
2:12 destroyed in the same D with them,
3:7 day of judgment and D of ungodly men.
3:16 twist to their own D, as they do the

DESTRUCTIVE (2)
Wis 1:14 and there is no D poison in them; and
2Pet 2:1 will secretly bring in D heresies, even denying the

DETACHMENT
1Mac 4:19 finishing this speech, a D appeared, coming out of

DETAIL (2)
Esth 11:12 sought all day to understand it in every D
Heb 9:5 Of these things we cannot now speak in D

DETAILED
1Mac 4:41 Then Judas D men to fight against those in

DETAILS (5)
2Kgs 16:10 altar, and its pattern, exact in all its D
2Mac 2:28 the responsibility for exact D to the compiler, while
2:30 to take trouble with D,
11:20 these matters and their D, I have ordered these
14:9 O king, with the D of this matter, deign

DETAIN (3)
Judg 13:15 LORD, "Pray, let us D you, and prepare a
13:16 to Manoah, "If you D me, I will not
Acts 24:4 But, to D you no further, I beg you

DETAINED (2)
1Sam 21:7 was there that day, D before the LORD; his
Tob 10:2 said, "Is it possible that he has been D

DETAINING
1Mac 13:15 held, that we are D him.

DETECTS
Sir 36:19 so an intelligent mind D false words.

DETERMINE (5)
Ex 21:22 him; and he shall pay as the judges D
Job 34:4 is right; let us D among ourselves what is
1Mac 5:16 assembly was called to D what they should do
8:30 effect both parties shall D to add or delete
Acts 23:15 you were going to D his case more exactly.

DETERMINED (39)
Gen 6:13 to Noah, "I have D to make an end
Ruth 1:18 saw that she was D to go with her,
1Sam 20:7 know that evil is D by him.
20:9 knew that it was D by my father that
20:33 that his father was D to put David to
25:17 do; for evil is D against our master and
2Sam 13:32 Absalom this has been D from the day he
2Kgs 19:25 not heard that I D it long ago?
2Chr 25:16 know that God has D to destroy you, because
Jud 11:12 their cattle and have D to use all that
12:4 hand what he has D to do."
Esth 7:7 saw that evil was D against him by the
11:12 dream what God had D to do, and after
13:2 with kindness, I have D to settle the lives
Job 14:5 Since his days are D, and the number of
38:5 Who D its measurements--surely you know!
Wis 8:9 Therefore I D to take her to live with
Sir 16:24 he made them, he D their divisions.
44:24 him his inheritance; he D his portions, and
Is 37:26 not heard that I D it long ago?
Lam 2:8 The LORD D to lay in ruins the wall
Dan 11:36 accomplished; for what is D shall be done.
Hos 5:11 judgment, because he was D to go after vanity.
1Mac 1:16 kingdom was established, he D to become king of
3:31 perplexed in mind, and D to go to Persia
4:59 the assembly of Israel D that every year at
5:2 very angry, and they D to destroy the descendants
11:33 to us, we have D to do good, because
16:13 was lifted up; he D to get control of
2Mac 8:10 Nicanor D to make up for the king the
13:13 with the elders, he D to march out and
15:6 boastfulness and arrogance had D to erect a public
15:17 of the young, they D not to carry on

Lk 22:22 as it has been D; but woe to that
Acts 11:29 And the disciples D, every one according to his
17:26 of the earth, having D allotted periods and the
20:3 sail for Syria, he D to return through Macedonia.
1Cor 7:37 under control, and has D this in his heart,
10:29 should my liberty be D by another man's scruples?

DETERMINES
Ps 147:4 He D the number of the stars, he gives

DETEST (2)
Deut 7:26 it; you shall utterly D and abhor it; for
Sir 7:26 do not trust yourself to one whom you D

DETESTABLE (13)
Deut 29:17 you have seen their D things, their idols of
Wis 12:4 didst hate for their D practices, their works of
Jer 16:18 the carcasses of their D idols, and have filled
Ezek 5:11 sanctuary with all your D things and with all
7:20 abominable images and their D things of it; therefore
11:18 from it all its D things and all its
11:21 heart goes after their D things and their
20:7 them, Cast away the D things your eyes feast
20:8 man cast away the D things their eyes feasted
20:30 go astray after their D things?
37:23 their idols and their D things, or with any
Hos 9:10 to Baal, and became D like the thing they
Tit 1:15 their deeds; they are D, disobedient, unfit for any

DETESTED (3)
Sir 20:4 wise, while another is D for being too talkative.
Zech 11:8 them, and they also D me.
1Mac 7:26 princes, who hated and D Israel, and he commanded

DEUEL (4)
Num 1:14 Eliasaph the son of D;
7:42 Eliasaph the son of D, the leader of the
7:47 was the offering of Eliasaph the son of D
10:20 men of Gad was Eliasaph the son of D

DEVASTATE
Lev 26:32 And I will D the land, so that your

DEVASTATED (4)
Is 49:19 desolate places and your D land-- surely now
Jer 25:37 the peaceful folds are D, because of the fierce
1Mac 15:4 and those who have D many cities in my
15:29 You have D their territory, you have done great

DEVASTATION (5)
1Chr 21:12 or three months of D by your foes, while
Is 51:19 condole with you?-- D and destruction, famine and
60:18 heard in your land, D or destruction within your
Lam 3:47 have come upon us, D and destruction;
Zeph 1:15 day of ruin and D, a day of darkness

DEVASTATIONS (2)
Is 61:4 raise up the former D; they shall repair the
61:4 the ruined cities, the D of many generations.

DEVASTATOR
Ps 137:8 O daughter of Babylon, you D

DEVICES (14)
Job 5:12 He frustrates the D of the crafty, so that
Ps 26:10 whose hands are evil D, and whose right hands
37:7 way, over the man who carries out evil D
Prov 1:31 their way and be sated with their own D
12:2 a man of evil D he condemns.
Eccl 7:29 man upright, but they have sought out many D
Sir 1:5 Her clever D --who knows them?
35:19 men according to their D; till he judges the
42:18 the hearts of men, and considers their crafty D
Is 32:7 evil; he devises wicked D to ruin the poor
65:2 good, following their own D;
Jer 6:19 the fruit of their D, because they have not
Lam 3:60 their vengeance, all their D against me.
3:61 O LORD, all their D against me.

DEVIL (35)
Wis 2:24 eternity, but through the D's envy death entered the
Mt 4:1 into the wilderness to be tempted by the D
4:5 Then the D took him to the holy city,
4:8 Again, the D took him to a very high
4:11 Then the D left him, and behold, angels came
13:39 sowed them is the D; the harvest is the

25:41 fire prepared for the D and his angels;
Lk 4:2 forty days in the wilderness, tempted by the D
4:3 The D said to him, "If you are the
4:5 And the D took him up, and showed him
4:13 And when the D had ended every temptation, he
8:12 have heard; then the D comes and takes away
Jn 6:70 the twelve, and one of you is a D
8:44 of your father the D, and your will is
13:2 during supper, when the D had already put it
Acts 10:38 were oppressed by the D, for God was with
13:10 "You son of the D, you enemy of all
Eph 4:27 your anger, and give no opportunity to the D
6:11 able to stand against the wiles of the D
1Tim 3:6 the condemnation of the D;
3:7 fall into reproach and the snare of the D
2Tim 2:26 the snare of the D, after being captured by
Heb 2:14 death, that is, the D,
Jas 4:7 Resist the D and he will flee from you.
1Pet 5:8 Your adversary the D prowls around like a roaring
1 Jn 3:8 sin is of the D; for the devil has
3:8 the devil; for the D has sinned from the
3:8 appeared was to destroy the works of the D
3:10 the children of the D: whoever does not do
Jude 1:9 Michael, contending with the D, disputed about the
Rev 2:10 Behold, the D is about to throw some of
12:9 who is called the D and Satan, the deceiver
12:12 and sea, for the D has come down to
20:2 serpent, who is the D and Satan, and bound
20:10 consumed them, and the D who had deceived them

DEVILISH

Jas 3:15 comes down from above, but is earthly, unspiritual, D

DEVIOUS (3)

Prov 2:15 crooked, and who are D in their ways.
4:25 crooked speech, and put D talk far from you.
14:2 but he who is D in his ways despises

DEVISE (19)

Ex 31:4 and all craftsmanship, to D artistic designs, to work
35:32 with all craftsmanship, to D artistic designs, to work
Ps 21:11 against you, if they D mischief, they will not
35:4 back and confounded who D evil against me!
58:2 in your hearts you D wrongs; your hands deal
Prov 12:20 heart of those who D evil, but those who
14:22 they not err that D evil?
14:22 Those who D good meet loyalty and faithfulness.
24:2 them; for their minds D violence, and their lips
Sir 7:12 Do not D a lie against your brother, nor
13:25 cheerful face, but to D proverbs requires painful
17:26 So flesh and blood D evil.
Ezek 11:2 are the men who D iniquity and who give
38:10 mind, and you will D an evil scheme
Dan 11:24 He shall D plans against strongholds, but only for
Hos 7:16 their arms, yet they D evil against me.
Mic 2:1 Woe to those who D wickedness and work evil
Zech 7:10 let none of you D evil against his brother
8:17 for peace, do not D evil in your hearts

DEVISED (14)

1Kgs 12:33 month which he had D of his own heart;
Esth 8:3 plot which he had D against the Jews.
8:5 to revoke the letters D by Haman the Agagite,
9:25 plot which he had D against the Jews should
Ps 10:2 be caught in the schemes which they have D
Wis 3:14 and who has not D wicked things against the
Is 7:5 son of Remaliah, has D evil against you, saying,
Jer 11:19 was against me they D schemes, saying, "Let us
Dan 11:25 for plots shall be D against him.
Mic 6:5 Balak king of Moab D, and what Balaam the
Hab 2:10 You have D shame to your house by cutting
1Mac 13:29 for the pyramids he D an elaborate setting, erecting
2Mac 7:23 beginning of man and D the origin of all
2Pet 1:16 did not follow cleverly D myths when we made

DEVISES (6)

2Sam 14:14 life of him who D means not to keep
Prov 6:14 with perverted heart D evil, continually sowing
6:18 blood, a heart that D wicked plans, feet that
Sir 11:31 a scoundrel, for he D evil, lest he give
Is 32:7 knave are evil; he D wicked devices to ruin
32:8 he who is noble D noble things, and by

DEVISING (5)

Prov 24:9 The D of folly is sin, and the scoffer
30:32 if you have been D evil, put your hand

Jer 18:11 evil against you and D a plan against you.
Mic 2:3 this family I am D evil, from which you
1Mac 11:8 sea, and he kept D evil designs against Alexander.

DEVOID (3)

Esth 16:10 Persian blood, and quite D of our kindliness), having
Sir 16:21 This is what one D of understanding thinks; a
Jude 1:19 up divisions, worldly people, D of the Spirit.

DEVOTE (5)

Lev 18:21 of your children to D them by fire to
Mic 4:13 many peoples, and shall D their gain to the
Acts 6:4 But we will D ourselves to prayer and to
1Cor 7:5 season, that you may D yourselves to prayer; but
1Tim 4:15 Practice these duties, D yourself to them, so that

DEVOTED (31)

Lev 27:21 field that has been D; the priest shall be
27:28 "But no D thing that a man devotes to
27:28 sold or redeemed; every D thing is most holy
27:29 No one D, who is to be utterly destroyed
Num 18:14 Every D thing in Israel shall be yours.
Deut 13:17 None of the D things shall cleave to your
Josh 6:17 within it shall be D to the LORD for
6:18 yourselves from the things D to destruction, lest
6:18 lest when you have D them you take any
6:18 take any of the D things and make the
7:1 in regard to the D things; for Achan the
7:1 took some of the D things; and the anger
7:11 taken some of the D things; they have stolen,
7:12 unless you destroy the D things from among you.
7:13 of Israel, "There are D things in the midst
7:13 you take away the D things from among you."
7:15 is taken with the D things shall be burned
22:20 the matter of the D things, and wrath fell
1Sam 15:21 best of the things D to destruction, to sacrifice
1Kgs 20:42 man whom I had D to destruction, therefore your
1Chr 2:7 the matter of the D thing;
Sir 16:9 pity for a nation D to destruction, for those
31:7 to those who are D to it, and every
Ezek 44:29 guilt offering; and every D thing in Israel shall
1Mac 4:42 He chose blameless priests D to the law,
Mt 6:24 or he will be D to the one and
Lk 16:13 or he will be D to the one and
Acts 1:14 these with one accord D themselves to prayer,
2:42 And they D themselves to the apostles' teaching and
1Cor 16:15 Achaia, and they have D themselves to the service
1Tim 5:10 relieved the afflicted, and D herself to doing good

DEVOTES (3)

Lev 27:28 thing that a man D to the LORD, of
Sir 7:20 a hired laborer who D himself to you.
39:1 other hand he who D himself to the study

DEVOTING (2)

Wis 14:30 wickedly of God in D themselves to idols, and
2Mac 2:28 to the compiler, while D our effort to arriving

DEVOTION (6)

1Chr 29:3 and because of my D to the house of
Jud 8:8 of her, for she feared God with great D
Jer 2:2 LORD, I remember the D of your youth, your
1Cor 7:35 to secure your undivided D to the Lord.
2Cor 11:3 a sincere and pure D to Christ.
Col 2:23 in promoting rigor of D and self-abasement and

DEVOUR (71)

Deut 32:42 and my sword shall D flesh--with the blood
Judg 9:15 of the bramble and D the cedars of Lebanon.'
9:20 out from Abimelech, and D the citizens of Shechem,
9:20 and from Beth-millo, and D Abimelech."
2Sam 2:26 Joab, "Shall the sword D for ever?
2Chr 7:13 command the locust to D the land, or send
Job 20:26 not blown upon will D him; what is left
Ps 52:4 love all words that D, O deceitful tongue.
57:4 of lions that greedily D the sons of men;
Prov 30:14 teeth are knives, to D the poor from off
Sir 6:3 You will D your leaves and destroy your fruit,
51:3 of teeth about to D me, from the hand
Is 1:7 your very presence aliens D your land; it is
9:12 Philistines on the west D Israel with open mouth.
9:20 still hungry, and they D on the left, but
10:17 it will burn and D his thorns and briers
31:8 not of man, shall D him; and he shall
56:9 the field, come to D -- all you beasts
Jer 5:14 and the fire shall D them.

8:16 They come and D the land and all that
12:9 assemble all the wild beasts; bring them to D
15:3 of the earth to D and destroy.
17:27 gates, and it shall D the palaces of Jerusalem
21:14 forest, and it shall D all that is round
30:16 Therefore all who D you shall be devoured, and
46:10 The sword shall D and be sated, and drink
46:14 for the sword shall D round about you.'
49:27 and it shall D the strongholds of Ben-hadad."
50:32 cities, and it will D all that is round
Bar 6:20 worms from the earth D them and their robes.
Ezek 7:15 that is in the city famine and pestilence D
20:47 you, and it shall D every green tree in
34:28 beasts of the land D them; they shall dwell
35:12 are given us to D
36:13 say to you, 'You D men, and you bereave
36:14 you shall no longer D men and no longer
Dan 7:5 it was told, 'Arise, D much flesh.'
7:23 kingdoms, and it shall D the whole earth, and
14:21 accustomed to enter and D what was on the
14:32 so that they might D Daniel.
Hos 2:12 of the field shall D them.
5:7 the new moon shall D them with their fields.
7:8 an oven, and they D their rulers.
7:10 Aliens D his strength, and he knows it not;
8:7 to yield, aliens would D it.
8:14 cities, and it shall D his strongholds.
11:6 of their gates, and D them in their fortresses.
13:8 and there I will D them like a lion,
Amos 1:4 Hazael, and it shall D the strongholds of Ben-hadad.
1:7 Gaza, and it shall D her strongholds.
1:10 Tyre, and it shall D her strongholds."
1:12 Teman, and it shall D the strongholds of Bozrah."
1:14 Rabbah, and it shall D her strongholds, with shouting
2:2 Moab, and it shall D the strongholds of Kerioth,
2:5 Judah, and it shall D the strongholds of Jerusalem."
5:6 of Joseph, and it D, with none to quench
Nah 2:13 and the sword shall D your young lions; I
3:15 There will the fire D you, the sword will
3:15 It will D you like the locust.
Hab 1:8 afar; they fly like an eagle swift to D
3:14 rejoicing as if to D the poor in secret.
Zech 9:15 them, and they shall D and tread down the
11:1 that the fire may D your cedars!
11:9 those that are left D the flesh of one
12:6 sheaves; and they shall D to the right and
Mk 12:40 honor at feasts, who D widows' houses and for
Lk 20:47 honor at feasts, who D widows' houses and for
Gal 5:15 if you bite and D one another take heed
1Pet 5:8 like a roaring lion, seeking some one to D
Rev 12:4 child, that he might D her child when she
17:16 desolate and naked, and D her flesh and burn

DEVOURED (46)

Gen 37:20 a wild beast has D him, and we shall
37:33 a wild beast has D him; Joseph is without
Lev 10:2 of the LORD and D them, and they died
Num 21:28 It D Ar of Moab, the lords of the
26:10 died, when the fire D two hundred and fifty
Deut 31:17 and they will be D; and many evils and
32:24 wasted with hunger, and D with burning heat and
2Sam 18:8 country; and the forest D more people that day
Jud 5:24 and they will be D by your vast army."
10:12 to be handed over to you to be D
Ps 78:45 swarms of flies, which D them, and frogs, which
78:63 Fire D their young men, and their maidens had
79:7 For they have D Jacob, and laid waste his
105:35 locusts without number; which D all the vegetation
in
Is 1:20 rebel, you shall be D by the sword; for
3:14 is you who have D the vineyard, the spoil
5:5 and it shall be D; I will break down
Jer 2:30 correction; your own sword D your prophets like a
3:24 the shameful thing has D all for which our
10:25 name; for they have D Jacob; they have devoured
10:25 devoured Jacob; they have D him and consumed him,
30:16 devour you shall be D, and all your foes,
50:7 who found them have D them, and their enemies
50:17 the king of Assyria D him, and now at
51:34 king of Babylon has D me, he has crushed
Ezek 16:20 and these you sacrificed to them to be D
19:3 to catch prey; he D men.
19:6 to catch prey; he D men.
22:25 the prey; they have D human lives; they have
23:25 your survivors shall be D by fire.
33:27 the beasts to be D; and those who are
39:4 sort and to the wild beasts to be D
Dan 7:7 great iron teeth; it D and broke in pieces,
7:19 of bronze; and which D and broke in pieces,
14:42 destruction, and they were D immediately before his
Joel 1:18 For fire has D the pastures of the wilderness,
1:19 up, and fire has D the pastures of the
Amos 4:9 olive trees the locust D; yet you did not
7:4 by fire, and it D the great deep and
Nah 3:13 your foes; fire has D your bars.
Zech 9:4 and she shall be D by fire.
2Mac 2:10 down from heaven and D the sacrifices, so also
Mt 13:4 the birds came and D them.
Mk 4:4 the birds came and D it.
Lk 8:5 birds of the air D it.
15:30 yours came, who has D your living with harlots,

DEVOURER

Mal 3:11 I will rebuke the D for you, so that

DEVOURING (12)

Gen 49:27 wolf, in the morning D the prey, and at
Ex 24:17 LORD was like a D fire on the top
Deut 4:24 your God is a D fire, a jealous God.
9:3 before you as a D fire is the LORD
2Sam 22:9 from his nostrils, and D fire from his mouth;
Ps 18:8 from his nostrils, and D fire from his mouth;
50:3 before him is a D fire, round about him
Is 29:6 the flame of a D fire.
30:27 tongue is like a D fire;
30:30 and a flame of D fire, with a cloudburst
33:14 can dwell with the D fire?
Joel 2:5 a flame of fire D the stubble, like a

DEVOURS (12)

Num 13:32 is a land that D its inhabitants; and all
23:24 lie down till it D the prey, and drinks
Deut 32:22 the depths of Sheol, D the earth and its
2Sam 11:25 you, for the sword D now one and now
Prov 19:28 mouth of the wicked D iniquity.
21:20 but a foolish man D it.
Is 5:24 the tongue of fire D the stubble, and as
9:20 are not satisfied; each D his neighbor's flesh,
24:6 Therefore a curse D the earth, and its inhabitants
Jer 12:12 sword of the LORD D from one end of
Joel 2:3 Fire D before them, and behind them a flame
Zech 11:16 nourish the sound, but D the flesh of the

DEVOUT (12)

Jud 8:31 since you are a D woman, and the Lord
Is 57:1 lays it to heart; D men are taken away,
Lk 2:25 man was righteous and D, looking for the consolation
Acts 2:5 dwelling in Jerusalem Jews, D men from every
8:2 D men buried Stephen, and made great lamentation
10:2 the Italian Cohort, a D man who feared God
10:7 his servants and a D soldier from among those
13:43 up, many Jews and D converts to Judaism followed
13:50 the Jews incited the D women of high standing
17:4 great many of the D Greeks and not a
17:17 the Jews and the D persons, and in the
22:12 "And one Ananias, a D man according to the

DEW (39)

Gen 27:28 give you of the D of heaven, and of
27:39 and away from the D of heaven on high.
Ex 16:13 and in the morning D lay round about the
16:14 And when the D had gone up, there was
Num 11:9 When the D fell upon the camp in the
Deut 32:2 speech distil as the D, as the gentle rain
33:28 grain and wine; yea, his heavens drop down D
Judg 6:37 floor; if there is D on the fleece alone,
6:38 fleece, he wrung enough D from the fleece to
6:39 and on all the ground let there be D
6:40 only, and on all the ground there was D
2Sam 1:21 let there be no D or rain upon you,
17:12 upon him as the D falls on the ground;
1Kgs 17:1 there shall be neither D nor rain these years,
Job 29:19 the waters, with the D all night on my
38:28 father, or who has begotten the drops of D
Ps 110:3 of the morning like D your youth will come
133:3 It is like the D of Hermon, which falls
Prov 3:20 broke forth, and the clouds drop down the D
19:12 his favor is like D upon the grass.
Song 5:2 head is wet with D, my locks with the
Wis 11:22 a drop of morning D that falls upon the
Sir 18:15 Does not the D assuage the scorching heat?
43:22 all things; when the D appears, it refreshes from

Is 18:4 like a cloud of D in the heat of
26:19 For thy D is a dew of light, and
26:19 thy dew is a D of light, and on
Dan 3:65 Lord, all rain and D, sing praise to him
4:15 be wet with the D of heaven; let his
4:23 be wet with the D of heaven; and let
4:25 be wet with the D of heaven, and seven
4:33 was wet with the D of heaven till his
5:21 was wet with the D of heaven, until he
Hos 6:4 morning cloud, like the D that goes early away.
13:3 mist or like the D that goes early away,
14:5 will be as the D to Israel; he shall
Mic 5:7 of many peoples like D from the LORD, like
Hag 1:10 you have withheld the D, and the earth has
Zech 8:12 heavens shall give their D; and I will cause

DEWS
Dan 3:69 Bless the Lord, D and snows, sing praise to

DIADEM (6)
Wis 5:16 crown and a beautiful D from the hand of
18:24 thy majesty on the D upon his head.
Sir 47:6 Lord, when the glorious D was bestowed upon him.
Is 28:5 of glory, and a D of beauty, to the
62:3 LORD, and a royal D in the hand of
Bar 5:2 on your head the D of the glory of

DIADEMS (3)
Rev 12:3 ten horns, and seven D upon his heads.
13:1 seven heads, with ten D upon its horns and
19:12 his head are many D; and he has a

DIAGNOSIS
Sir 38:14 grant them success in D and in healing, for

DIAL (3)
2Kgs 20:11 had declined on the D of Ahaz.
Is 38:8 declining sun on the D of Ahaz turn back
38:8 turned back on the D the ten steps by

DIAMOND (3)
Ex 28:18 a sapphire, and a D;
39:11 a sapphire, and a D;
Jer 17:1 with a point of D it is engraved on

DIBLAIM
Hos 1:3 Gomer the daughter of D, and she conceived and

DIBON (11)
Num 21:30 Heshbon, as far as D, and we laid waste
32:3 congregation, "Ataroth, D, Jazer, Nimrah, Heshbon,
32:34 sons of Gad built D, Ataroth, Aroer,
Josh 13:9 Medeba as far as D;
13:17 tableland; D, and Bamoth-baal, and Beth-baal-meon,
Neh 11:25 its villages, and in D and its villages, and
Is 15:2 The daughter of D has gone up to the
15:9 For the waters of D are full of blood;
15:9 I will bring upon D even more, a lion
Jer 48:18 sit on the parched ground, O inhabitant of D
48:22 Mephaath, and D, and Nebo, and Beth-diblathaim,

DIBON-GAD (2)
Num 33:45 they set out from Iyim, and encamped at D
33:46 out from D, and encamped at Almon-diblathaim.

DIBRI
Lev 24:11 Shelomith, the daughter of D, of the tribe of

DICTATED
Jer 36:18 Baruch answered them, "He D all these words to

DICTATION (6)
Jer 36:4 a scroll at the D of Jeremiah all the
36:6 the scroll which you have written at my D
36:17 Was it at his D
36:27 Baruch wrote at Jeremiah's D, the word of the
36:32 on it at the D of Jeremiah all the
45:1 a book at the D of Jeremiah, in the

DIDST (240)
Gen 32:9 Isaac, O LORD who D say to me, 'Return
32:12 But thou D say, 'I will do you good,
Ex 5:22 Why D thou ever send me?
15:10 shall destroy them.' Thou D blow with thy wind,
15:12 Thou D stretch out thy right hand, the earth
19:23 Sinai; for thou thyself D charge us, saying, 'Set
32:13 servants, to whom thou D swear by thine own
32:13 thine own self, and D say to them, 'I
Num 11:12 the land which thou D swear to give their
14:13 of it, for thou D bring up this people
22:34 not know that thou D stand in the road
Deut 9:28 land from which thou D bring us say, "Because
9:29 thy heritage, whom thou D bring out by thy
26:15 given us, as thou D swear to our fathers,
33:8 godly one, whom thou D test at Massah, with
33:8 Massah, with whom thou D strive at the waters
Judg 5:4 "LORD, when thou D go forth from Seir, when
5:4 from Seir, when thou D march from the region
13:8 of God whom thou D send come again to
2Sam 7:24 And thou D establish for thyself thy people Israel
7:24 and thou, O LORD, D become their God.
22:37 Thou D give a wide place for my steps
22:40 For thou D gird me with strength for the
22:40 for the battle; thou D make my assailants sink
22:41 Thou D make my enemies turn their backs to
22:44 "Thou D deliver me from strife with the peoples;
22:44 with the peoples; thou D keep me as the
22:49 from my enemies; thou D exalt me above my
22:49 above my adversaries, thou D deliver me from men
1Kgs 8:24 my father what thou D declare to him; yea,
8:24 to him; yea, thou D speak with thy mouth,
8:51 thy heritage, which thou D bring out of Egypt,
8:53 For thou D separate them from among all the
8:53 thy heritage, as thou D declare through Moses, thy
8:53 thy servant, when thou D bring our fathers out
1Chr 17:21 thy people whom thou D redeem from Egypt?
17:22 And thou D make thy people Israel to be
17:22 and thou, O LORD, D become their God.
2Chr 6:15 my father what thou D declare to him; yea,
6:15 to him; yea, thou D speak with thy mouth,
20:7 D thou not, O our God, drive out the
Ezra 9:11 thy commandments, which thou D command by thy
Neh 1:7 the ordinances which thou D command thy servant
1:8 the word which thou D command thy servant Moses,
9:7 LORD, the God who D choose Abram and bring
9:8 name Abraham; and thou D find his heart faithful
9:8 faithful before thee, and D make with him the
9:9 "And thou D see the affliction of our fathers
9:10 the Red Sea, and D perform signs and wonders
9:10 our fathers; and thou D get thee a name,
9:11 And thou D divide the sea before them, so
9:11 dry land; and thou D cast their pursuers into
9:12 pillar of cloud thou D lead them in the
9:13 Thou D come down upon Mount Sinai, and speak
9:14 and commandments, and thou D make known to
9:15 Thou D give them bread from heaven for their
9:15 their thirst, and thou D tell them to go
9:17 the wonders which thou D perform among them; but
9:17 in steadfast love, and D not forsake them.
9:19 in thy great mercies D not forsake them in
9:20 to instruct them, and D not withhold thy manna
9:21 Forty years D thou sustain them in the wilderness,
9:22 And thou D give them kingdoms and peoples, and
9:22 kingdoms and peoples, and D allot to them every
9:23 Thou D multiply their descendants as the stars of
9:23 of heaven, and thou D bring them into the
9:24 the land, and thou D subdue before them the
9:24 land, the Canaanites, and D give them into their
9:27 Therefore thou D give them into the hand of
9:27 to thee and thou D hear them from heaven;
9:27 thy great mercies thou D give them saviors who
9:28 before thee, and thou D abandon them to the
9:28 cried to thee thou D hear from heaven, and
9:28 and many times thou D deliver them according to
9:29 And thou D warn them in order to turn
9:30 Many years thou D bear with them, and didst
9:30 bear with them, and D warn them by thy
9:30 Therefore thou D give them into the hand of
9:31 thy great mercies thou D not make an end
9:34 thy warnings which thou D give them.
9:35 rich land which thou D set before them; and
Tob 8:6 Thou D say, 'It is not good that the
Jud 9:3 with blood, and thou D strike down slaves along
9:5 Yea, the things thou D intend came to pass,
9:6 and the things thou D will presented themselves and
16:14 serve thee, for thou D speak, and they were
16:14 Thou D send forth thy Spirit, and it formed
Esth 13:16 thy portion, which thou D redeem for thyself out
14:5 that thou, O Lord, D take Israel out of
14:5 inheritance, and that thou D do for them all
14:5 them all that thou D promise.
Job 10:10 D thou not pour me out like milk and

10:11 Thou D clothe me with skin and flesh, and
10:13 Yet these things thou D hide in thy heart;
10:18 "Why D thou bring me forth from the womb?
Ps 18:36 Thou D give a wide place for my steps
18:39 For thou D gird me with strength for the
18:39 for the battle; thou D make my assailants sink
18:40 Thou D make my enemies turn their backs to
18:43 Thou D deliver me from strife with the peoples;
18:43 with the peoples; thou D make me the head
18:48 my enemies; yea, thou D exalt me above my
18:48 above my adversaries; thou D deliver me from men
22:4 they trusted, and thou D deliver them.
22:9 from the womb; thou D keep me safe upon
30:7 a strong mountain; thou D hide thy face, I
31:22 But thou D hear my supplications, when I cried
32:5 the LORD"; then thou D forgive the guilt of
44:1 us, what deeds thou D perform in their days,
44:2 with thy own hand D drive out the nations,
44:2 nations, but them thou D plant; thou didst afflict
44:2 thou didst plant; thou D afflict the peoples, but
44:2 peoples, but them thou D set free;
44:3 thy countenance; for thou D delight in them.
48:7 the east wind thou D shatter the ships of
66:11 Thou D bring us into the net; thou didst
66:11 into the net; thou D lay affliction on our
66:12 on our loins; thou D let men ride over
68:7 O God, when thou D go forth before thy
68:7 thy people, when thou D march through the
68:9 abundance, O God, thou D shed abroad; thou didst
68:9 didst shed abroad; thou D restore thy heritage as
68:10 goodness, O God, thou D provide for the needy.
68:18 Thou D ascend the high mount, leading captives in
74:13 Thou D divide the sea by thy might; thou
74:13 by thy might; thou D break the heads of
74:14 Thou D crush the heads of Leviathan, thou didst
74:14 heads of Leviathan, thou D give him as food
74:15 Thou D cleave open springs and brooks; thou didst
74:15 springs and brooks; thou D dry up ever-flowing
76:8 From the heavens thou D utter judgment; the earth
77:15 Thou D with thy arm redeem thy people, the
77:20 Thou D lead thy people like a flock by
80:8 Thou D bring a vine out of Egypt; thou
80:8 out of Egypt; thou D drive out the nations
80:9 Thou D clear the ground for it; it took
83:9 to them as thou D to Midian, as to
85:1 to thy land; thou D restore the fortunes of
85:2 Thou D forgive the iniquity of thy people; thou
85:2 of thy people; thou D pardon all their sin.
85:3 [Selah] Thou D withdraw all thy wrath; thou didst
85:3 all thy wrath; thou D turn from thy hot
89:10 Thou D crush Rahab like a carcass, thou didst
89:10 like a carcass, thou D scatter thy enemies with
89:19 Of old thou D speak in a vision to
89:49 by thy faithfulness thou D swear to David?
99:8 LORD our God, thou D answer them; thou wast
102:25 Of old thou D lay the foundation of the
104:5 Thou D set the earth on its foundations, so
104:6 Thou D cover it with the deep as with
104:8 the place which thou D appoint for them.
104:9 Thou D set a bound which they should not
104:26 and Leviathan which thou D form to sport in
119:26 of my ways, thou D answer me; teach me
138:3 day I called, thou D answer me, my strength
138:3 strength of soul thou D increase.
139:13 For thou D form my inward parts, thou didst
139:13 my inward parts, thou D knit me together in
Wis 9:8 holy tent which thou D prepare from the beginning.
9:9 was present when thou D make the world, and
11:8 that time how thou D punish their enemies.
11:10 For thou D test them as a father does
11:10 in warning, but thou D examine the ungodly as
11:15 and worthless animals, thou D send upon them a
12:4 thy holy land thou D hate for their detestable
12:6 murder helpless lives, thou D will to destroy by
12:8 But even these thou D spare, since they were
12:8 were but men, and D send wasps as forerunners
12:11 any one that thou D leave them unpunished for
12:12 of nations which thou D make?
12:20 For if thou D punish with such great care
12:23 life lived unrighteously thou D torment through their
12:25 to thoughtless children, thou D send thy judgment to
16:2 of this punishment thou D show kindness to thy
16:2 thy people, and thou D prepare quails to eat,
16:8 by this also thou D convince our enemies that
16:20 of these things thou D give thy people food
16:20 without their toil thou D supply them from heaven
16:26 thy sons, whom thou D love, O Lord, might
18:3 Therefore thou D provide a flaming pillar of fire
18:5 exposed and rescued, thou D in punishment take
18:5 their children; and thou D destroy them all together
18:8 means by which thou D punish our enemies thou
18:8 punish our enemies thou D call us to thyself
19:9 thee, O Lord, who D deliver them.
Sir 36:15 to those whom thou D create in the beginning,
51:3 wast my helper and D deliver me, in the
51:12 was heard, for thou D save me from destruction
Is 12:1 turned away, and thou D comfort me.
27:8 measure, by exile thou D contend with them; he
51:9 it not thou that D cut Rahab in pieces,
51:9 Rahab in pieces, that D pierce the dragon?
51:10 it not thou that D dry up the sea,
51:10 the great deep; that D make the depths of
63:14 So thou D lead thy people, to make for
64:3 When thou D terrible things which we looked not
Jer 11:18 I knew; then thou D show me their evil
32:21 Thou D bring thy people Israel out of the
32:22 this land, which thou D swear to their fathers
32:23 nothing of all thou D command them to do.
32:24 What thou D speak has come to pass, and
Lam 1:10 sanctuary, those whom thou D forbid to enter thy
2:22 Thou D invite as to the day of an
3:56 of the pit; thou D hear my plea, 'Do
3:57 cry for help!' Thou D come near when I
3:57 called on thee; thou D say, 'Do not fear!'
Bar 2:11 God of Israel, who D bring thy people out
2:20 upon us, as thou D declare by thy servants
2:24 thy words, which thou D speak by thy servants
2:28 great compassion, as thou D speak by thy servant
2:28 the day when thou D command him to write
Ezek 9:11 have done as thou D command me."
Dan 3:36 one, to whom thou D promise to make their
9:15 Lord our God, who D bring thy people out
Jon 2:2 I cried, and thou D hear my voice.
2:3 For thou D cast me into the deep, into
2:6 for ever; yet thou D bring up my life
Hab 3:8 the sea, when thou D ride upon thy horses,
3:9 Thou D strip the sheath from thy bow, and
3:9 Selah Thou D cleave the earth with rivers.
3:12 Thou D bestride the earth in fury, thou didst
3:12 earth in fury, thou D trample the nations in
3:13 Thou D crush the head of the wicked, laying
3:14 Selah Thou D pierce with thy shafts the head
3:15 Thou D trample the sea with thy horses, the
1Mac 4:30 Savior of Israel, who D crush the attack of
4:30 thy servant David, and D give the camp of
7:37 wept and said, "Thou D choose this house to
2Mac 1:25 from every evil, who D choose the fathers and
15:22 words: "O Lord, thou D send thy angel in
Jn 11:42 may believe that thou D send me."
17:8 have believed that thou D send me.
17:18 As thou D send me into the world, so
Acts 4:24 said, "Sovereign Lord, who D make the heaven and
4:25 father David, thy servant, D say by the Holy
4:27 servant Jesus, whom thou D anoint, both Herod and
Heb 1:10 And, "Thou, Lord, D found the earth in the
2:7 Thou D make him for a little while lower
Rev 4:11 and power, for thou D create all things, and
5:9 and by thy blood D ransom men for God

DIE (341)

Gen 2:17 day that you eat of it you shall D
3:3 garden, neither shall you touch it, lest you D
3:4 serpent said to the woman, "You will not D
6:17 heaven; everything that is on the earth shall D
19:19 hills, lest the disaster overtake me, and I D
20:7 that you shall surely D, you, and all that
25:32 "I am about to D; of what use is
26:9 I thought, 'Lest I D because of her.'"
27:4 eat; that I may bless you before I D
27:7 the LORD before I D
30:1 to Jacob, "Give me children, or I shall D
33:13 overdriven for one day, all the flocks will D
38:11 feared that he would D, like his brothers.
42:2 us there, that we may live, and not D
42:20 words will be verified, and you shall not D
43:8 may live and not D, both we and you
44:9 be found, let him D, and we also will
44:22 father, his father would D
44:31 with us, he will D; and your servants will
45:28 I will go and see him before I D
46:30 Joseph, "Now let me D, since I have seen
47:15 food; why should we D before your eyes?

	47:19	Why should we D before your eyes, both we
	47:19	may live, and not D, and that the land
	47:29	near that Israel must D, he called his son
	48:21	I am about to D, but God will be
	50:5	'I am about to D: in my tomb which
	50:24	"I am about to D; but God will visit
Ex	7:18	in the Nile shall D, and the Nile shall
	9:4	so that nothing shall D of all that belongs
	9:19	and is not brought home, and they shall D
	10:28	the day you see my face you shall D
	11:5	land of Egypt shall D, from the first-born of
	14:11	taken us away to D in the wilderness?
	14:12	the Egyptians than to D in the wilderness."
	20:19	let not God speak to us, lest we D
	21:14	take him from my altar, that he may D
	21:18	the man does not D but keeps his bed,
	28:35	LORD, and when he comes out, lest he D
	28:43	place; lest they bring guilt upon themselves and D
	30:20	LORD, they shall wash with water, lest they D
	30:21	their feet, lest they D: it shall be a
Lev	8:35	has charged, lest you D; for so I am
	10:6	your clothes, lest you D, and lest wrath come
	10:7	of meeting, lest you D; for the anointing oil
	10:9	of meeting, lest you D; it shall be a
	15:31	their uncleanness, lest they D in their uncleanness by
	16:2	the ark, lest he D; for I will appear
	16:13	the testimony, lest he D;
	20:20	their sin, they shall D childless.
	22:9	sin for it and D thereby when they profane
Num	4:15	must not touch the holy things, lest they D
	4:19	may live and not D when they come near
	4:20	holy things even for a moment, lest they D
	6:7	or sister, if they D, shall he make himself
	14:35	to a full end, and there they shall D
	16:29	If these men D the common death of all
	17:10	end of their murmurings against me, lest they D
	17:13	near to the tabernacle of the LORD, shall D
	18:3	or to the altar, lest they, and you, D
	18:22	tent of meeting, lest they bear sin and D
	18:32	things of the people of Israel, lest you D
	20:4	wilderness, that we should D here, both we and
	20:26	his people, and shall D there."
	21:5	out of Egypt to D in the wilderness?
	23:10	Let me D the death of the righteous, and
	26:11	Notwithstanding, the sons of Korah did not D
	26:65	of them, "They shall D in the wilderness." There
	35:12	the manslayer may not D until he stands before
	35:17	which a man may D, and he died, he
	35:18	which a man may D, and he died, he
	35:23	which a man may D, and without seeing him
Deut	4:22	For I must D in this land, I must
	5:25	Now therefore why should we D
	5:25	the LORD our God any more, we shall D
	17:6	he that is to D shall be put to
	17:12	judge, that man shall D; so you shall purge
	18:16	any more, lest I D
	18:20	that same prophet shall D
	19:6	did not deserve to D, since he was not
	19:12	the avenger of blood, so that he may D
	20:5	his house, lest he D in the battle and
	20:6	his house, lest he D in the battle and
	20:7	his house, lest he D in the battle and
	22:22	both of them shall D, the man who lay
	22:25	only the man who lay with her shall D
	24:7	then that thief shall D; so you shall purge
	31:14	approach when you must D; call Joshua, and present
	32:50	for a possession; and D on the mountain which
	33:6	Reuben live, and not D, nor let his men
Josh	20:9	that he might not D by the hand of
Judg	6:23	to you; do not fear, you shall not D
	6:30	son, that he may D, for he has pulled
	13:22	wife, "We shall surely D, for we have seen
	15:18	and shall I now D of thirst, and fall
	16:30	Samson said, "Let me D with the Philistines." Then
Ruth	1:17	my God; where you D I will die, and
	1:17	you die I will D, and there will I
1Sam	2:33	of your house shall D by the sword of
	2:34	both of them shall D on the same day.
	5:12	men who did not D were stricken with tumors,
	12:19	that we may not D; for we have added
	14:39	be in Jonathan my son, he shall surely D
	14:43	in my hand; here I am, I will D
	14:44	also; you shall surely D, Jonathan."
	14:45	to Saul, "Shall Jonathan D, who has wrought this
	14:45	the people ransomed Jonathan, that he did not D
	20:2	You shall not D
	20:14	that I may not D;
	20:31	fetch him to me, for he shall surely D
	22:16	said, "You shall surely D, Ahimelech, you and all
	26:10	day shall come to D; or he shall go
	26:16	lives, you deserve to D, because you have not
2Sam	3:33	Abner, saying, "Should Abner D as a fool dies?
	11:15	him, that he may be struck down, and D
	12:5	done this deserves to D;
	12:13	has put away your sin; you shall not D
	12:14	the child that is born to you shall D
	14:14	We must all D, we are like water spilt
	18:3	If half of us D, they will not care
	19:23	the king said to Shimei, "You shall not D
	19:37	return, that I may D in my own city,
1Kgs	1:52	if wickedness is found in him, he shall D
	2:1	When David's time to D drew near, he charged
	2:30	said, "No, I will D here." Then Benaiah brought
	2:37	certain that you shall D; your blood shall be
	2:42	and go to any place whatever, you shall D
	13:31	his sons, "When I D, bury me in the
	14:12	your feet enter the city, the child shall D
	17:12	my son, that we may eat it, and D
	19:4	asked that he might D, saying, "It is enough;
2Kgs	1:4	which you have gone, but you shall surely D
	1:6	to which you have gone, but shall surely D
	1:16	which you have gone, but you shall surely D
	7:3	another, "Why do we sit here till we D
	7:4	city, and we shall D there; and if we
	7:4	we sit here, we D also.
	7:4	and if they kill us we shall but D
	8:10	LORD has shown me that he shall certainly D
	13:14	which he was to D, Joash king of Israel
	14:6	but every man shall D for his own sin."
	18:32	and honey, that you may live, and not D
	20:1	order; for you shall D, you shall not recover.'"
2Chr	25:4	but every man shall D for his own sin."
	32:11	give you over to D by famine and by
Tob	3:6	better for me to D than to live, because
	4:2	explain to him about the money before I D
	4:3	"My son, when I D, bury me, and do
	6:14	go in I will D as those before me
	6:14	fear that I may D and bring the lives
	8:10	grave, with the thought, "Perhaps he too will D
	8:21	would be his "when my wife and I D
	10:11	heaven will prosper you, my children, before I D
	11:9	you, my child; now I am ready to D
Jud	6:8	and you will not D until you perish along
Esth	15:10	courage; you shall not D, for our law applies
Job	2:9	Curse God, and D
	3:11	"Why did I not D at birth, come forth
	4:21	them, do they not D, and that without wisdom?'
	12:2	people, and wisdom will D with you.
	13:19	For then I would be silent and D
	14:8	earth, and its stump D in the ground,
	14:14	If a man D, shall he live again?
	27:5	are right; till I D I will not put
	29:18	I thought, 'I shall D in my nest, and
	34:20	In a moment they D; at midnight the people
	36:12	by the sword, and D without knowledge.
	36:14	They D in youth, and their life ends in
Ps	41:5	malice: "When will he D, and his name perish?"
	49:10	that even the wise D, the fool and the
	79:11	to thy great power preserve those doomed to D
	82:7	you; nevertheless, you shall D like men, and fall
	102:20	who were doomed to D;
	104:29	away their breath, they D and return to their
	105:29	waters into blood, and caused their fish to D
	118:17	I shall not D, but I shall live, and
Prov	10:21	feed many, but fools D for lack of sense.
	11:19	will live, but he who pursues evil will D
	15:10	forsakes the way; he who hates reproof will D
	19:16	his life; he who despises the word will D
	23:13	beat him with a rod, he will not D
	30:7	to me before I D:
Eccl	3:2	and a time to D; a time to plant,
	7:17	fool; why should you D before your time?
	9:5	know that they will D, but the dead know
Wis	3:18	If they D young, they will have no hope
	4:7	righteous man, though he D early, will be at
	15:9	he is destined to D or that his life
Sir	8:7	any one's death; remember that we all must D
	10:10	king of today will D tomorrow.
	14:13	a friend before you D, and reach out and
	14:17	decree from of old is, "You must surely D
	16:3	a thousand, and to D childless is better than
	19:10	Let it D with you.

	25:23	its beginning, and because of her we all D
	30:4	The father may D, and yet he is not
	40:28	it is better to D than to beg.
	41:9	curse; and when you D, a curse is your
Is	22:13	"Let us eat and drink, for tomorrow we D
	22:14	iniquity will not be forgiven you till you D
	22:18	land; there you shall D, and there shall be
	38:1	order; for you shall D, you shall not recover."
	50:2	lack of water, and D of thirst.
	51:6	dwell in it will D like gnats; but my
	51:14	released; he shall not D and go down to
	65:20	for the child shall D a hundred years old,
	66:24	their worm shall not D, their fire shall not
Jer	11:21	LORD, or you will D by our hand"--
	11:22	the young men shall D by the sword; their
	11:22	and their daughters shall D by famine;
	16:4	this land: They shall D of deadly diseases.
	16:6	great and small shall D in this land; they
	20:6	and there you shall D, and there you shall
	21:6	and beast; they shall D of a great pestilence.
	21:9	in this city shall D by the sword, by
	22:12	captive, there shall he D, and he shall never
	22:26	you were not born, and there you shall D
	26:8	people laid hold of him, saying, "You shall D
	27:13	you and your people D by the sword, by
	28:16	very year you shall D, because you have uttered
	31:30	But every one shall D for his own sin;
	34:4	you: 'You shall not D by the sword.
	34:5	You shall D in peace.
	37:20	the secretary, lest I D there."
	38:2	in this city shall D by the sword, by
	38:9	cistern; and he will D there of hunger, for
	38:24	know of these words and you shall not D
	38:26	house of Jonathan to D there."'
	42:16	after you to Egypt; and there you shall D
	42:17	to live there shall D by the sword, by
	42:22	certainty that you shall D by the sword, by
	44:12	the greatest, they shall D by the sword and
Bar	4:1	will live, and those who forsake her will D
Ezek	3:18	wicked, 'You shall surely D and you give him
	3:18	that wicked man shall D in his iniquity; but
	3:19	wicked way, he shall D in his iniquity; but
	3:20	before him, he shall D; because you have not
	3:20	warned him, he shall D for his sin, and
	5:12	part of you shall D of pestilence and be
	6:12	that is far-off shall D of pestilence; and he
	6:12	and is preserved shall D of famine.
	12:13	it; and he shall D there.
	13:19	persons who should not D and keeping alive persons
	17:16	with him he broke, in Babylon he shall D
	18:4	son is mine: the soul that sins shall D
	18:13	things; he shall surely D; his blood shall be
	18:17	statutes; he shall not D for his father's iniquity;
	18:18	people, behold, he shall D for his iniquity.
	18:20	The soul that sins shall D
	18:21	right, he shall surely live; he shall not D
	18:24	and the sin he has committed, he shall D
	18:26	commits iniquity, he shall D for it; for the
	18:26	the iniquity which he has committed he shall D
	18:28	committed, he shall surely live, he shall not D
	18:31	Why will you D, O house of Israel?
	28:8	Pit, and you shall D the death of the
	28:10	You shall D the death of the uncircumcised by
	33:8	man, you shall surely D, and you do not
	33:8	that wicked man shall D in his iniquity, but
	33:9	his way; he shall D in his iniquity, but
	33:11	for why will you D, O house of Israel?
	33:13	the iniquity that he has committed he shall D
	33:14	wicked, 'You shall surely D yet if he turns
	33:15	iniquity; he shall surely live, he shall not D
	33:18	commits iniquity, he shall D for it.
	33:27	and in caves shall D by pestilence.
Dan	13:43	And now I am to D
	14:8	me who is eating these provisions, you shall D
	14:9	eating them, Daniel shall D, because he blasphemed
	14:12	it all, we will D; or else Daniel will,
Amos	2:2	Kerioth, and Moab shall D amid uproar, amid
	6:9	ten men remain in one house, they shall D
	7:11	has said, 'Jeroboam shall D by the sword, and
	7:17	line; you yourself shall D in an unclean land,
	9:10	of my people shall D by the sword, who
Jon	4:3	better for me to D than to live."
	4:8	asked that he might D, and said, "It is
	4:8	better for me to D than to live."
	4:9	do well to be angry, angry enough to D
Hab	1:12	We shall not D
Zech	11:9	What is to D, let it die; what is
	11:9	to die, let it D; what is to be
1Mac	1:50	not obey the command of the king shall D
	1:63	They chose to D rather than to be defiled
	1:63	to profane the holy covenant; and they did D
	2:37	said, "Let us all D in our innocence; heaven
	2:41	let us not all D as our brethren died
	2:49	near for Mattathias to D, and he said to
	3:59	better for us to D in battle than to
	4:35	to live or to D nobly, he departed to
	9:10	has come, let us D bravely for our brethren,
2Mac	6:26	whether I live or D I shall not escape
	6:28	example of how to D a good death willingly
	6:30	he was about to D under the blows, he
	7:2	we are ready to D rather than transgress the
	7:5	encouraged one another to D nobly, saying,
	7:14	cannot but choose to D at the hands of
	7:18	he was about to D, he said, "Do not
	8:21	made them ready to D for their laws and
	14:42	own sword, preferring to D nobly rather than to
Mt	15:4	mother, let him surely D
	26:35	"Even if I must D with you, I will
Mk	7:10	mother, let him surely D;
	9:46	their worm does not D, and the fire is
	14:31	vehemently, "If I must D with you, I will
Lk	20:36	marriage, for they cannot D any more, because they
Jn	6:50	a man may eat of it and not D
	8:21	will seek me and D in your sin; where
	8:24	you that you would D in your sins, for
	8:24	sins, for you will D in your sins unless
	11:16	go, that we may D with him."
	11:25	in me, though he D, yet shall he live,
	11:26	whoever lives and believes in me shall never D
	11:50	that one man should D for the people, and
	11:51	prophesied that Jesus should D for the nation,
	12:33	to show by what death he was to D
	18:14	that one man should D for the people.
	18:32	to show by what death he was to D
	19:7	law he ought to D, because he has made
	21:23	disciple was not to D; yet Jesus did not
	21:23	he was not to D, but, "If it is
Acts	21:13	imprisoned but even to D at Jerusalem for the
	25:11	which I deserve to D, I do not seek
Rom	1:32	such things deserve to D, they not only do
	5:7	Why, one will hardly D for a righteous man--
	5:7	a good man one will dare even to D
	6:9	the dead will never D again; death no longer
	8:13	the flesh you will D, but if by the
	14:8	Lord, and if we D, we die to the
	14:8	if we die, we D to the Lord; so
	14:8	live or whether we D, we are the Lords.
1Cor	9:15	For I would rather D than have any one
	15:22	as in Adam all D, so also in Christ
	15:31	Jesus our Lord, I D every day!
	15:32	"Let us eat and drink, for tomorrow we D
2Cor	7:3	in our hearts, to D together and to live
Phil	1:21	is Christ, and to D is gain.
Heb	9:27	appointed for men to D once, and after that
1Pet	2:24	tree, that we might D to sin and live
Rev	9:6	they will long to D, and death will fly
	14:13	are the dead who D in the Lord henceforth."

DIED (273)

Gen	5:5	were nine hundred and thirty years; and he D
	5:8	were nine hundred and twelve years; and he D
	5:11	were nine hundred and five years; and he D
	5:14	were nine hundred and ten years; and he D
	5:17	were eight hundred and ninety-five years; and he D
	5:20	were nine hundred and sixty-two years; and he D
	5:27	were nine hundred and sixty-nine years; and he D
	5:31	were seven hundred and seventy-seven years; and he
D		
	7:21	And all flesh D that moved upon the earth,
	7:22	in whose nostrils was the breath of life D
	9:29	were nine hundred and fifty years; and he D
	11:28	Haran D before his father Terah in the land
	11:32	five years; and Terah D in Haran.
	23:2	And Sarah D at Kiriath-arba (that is, Hebron) in
	25:8	breathed his last and D in a good old
	25:17	breathed his last and D, and was gathered to
	35:8	And Deborah, Rebekah's nurse, D, and she was
	35:18	was departing (for she D, she called his name
	35:19	So Rachel D, and she was buried on the
	35:29	his last; and he D and was gathered to
	36:33	Bela D, and Jobab the son of Zerah of
	36:34	Jobab D, and Husham of the land of the

36:35 Husham D, and Hadad the son of Bedad, who
36:36 Hadad D, and Samlah of Masrekah reigned in his
36:37 Samlah D, and Shaul of Rehoboth on the Euphrates
36:38 Shaul D, and Baal-hanan the son of Achbor reigned
36:39 the son of Achbor D, and Hadar reigned in
38:12 of Judah, Shua's daughter, D; and when Judah was
46:12 (but Er and Onan D in the land of
48:7 Rachel to my sorrow D in the land of
50:16 this command before he D,
50:26 So Joseph D, being a hundred and ten years
Ex 1:5 Then Joseph D, and all his brothers, and all
2:23 of those many days the king of Egypt D
7:21 fish in the Nile D; and the Nile became
8:13 of Moses; the frogs D out of the houses
9:6 cattle of the Egyptians D, but of the cattle
9:6 cattle of the people of Israel not one D
16:3 "Would that we had D by the hand of
Lev 10:2 devoured them, and they D before the LORD.
16:1 before the LORD and D;
Num 3:4 But Nadab and Abihu D before the LORD when
14:2 "Would that we had D in the land of
14:2 would that we had D in this wilderness!
14:37 report of the land, D by plague before the
16:49 Now those who D by the plague were fourteen
16:49 hundred, besides those who D in the affair of
19:13 any man who has D, and does not cleanse
20:1 in Kadesh; and Miriam D there, and was buried
20:3 "Would that we had D when our brethren died
20:3 died when our brethren D before the LORD!
20:28 his son; and Aaron D there on the top
21:6 the people, so that many people of Israel D
25:9 those that D by the plague were twenty-four
26:10 Korah, when that company D, when the fire devoured
26:19 and Er and Onan D in the land of
26:61 But Nadab and Abihu D when they offered unholy
27:3 meeting, saying, "Our father D in the wilderness; he
27:3 company of Korah, but D for his own sin;
33:38 of the LORD, and D there, in the fortieth
33:39 years old when he D on Mount Hor.
35:16 iron, so that he D, he is a murderer;
35:17 may die, and he D, he is a murderer;
35:18 may die, and he D, he is a murderer;
35:20 wait, so that he D,
35:21 hand, so that he D, then he who struck
35:23 him, so that he D, though he was not
Deut 10:6 There Aaron D, and there he was buried; and
32:50 as Aaron your brother D in Mount Hor and
34:5 servant of the LORD D there in the land
34:7 years old when he D; his eye was not
Josh 5:4 men of war, had D on the way in
10:11 as Azekah, and they D; there were more who
10:11 there were more who D because of the hailstones
24:29 servant of the LORD, D, being a hundred and
24:33 the son of Aaron D; and they buried him
Judg 1:7 to Jerusalem, and he D there.
2:8 servant of the LORD, D at the age of
2:19 But whenever the judge D, they turned back and
2:21 Joshua left when he D,
3:11 Then Othni-el the son of Kenaz D
4:1 in the sight of the LORD, after Ehud D
4:21 So he D
8:32 the son of Joash D in a good old
8:33 As soon as Gideon D, the people of Israel
9:49 Tower of Shechem also D, about a thousand men
9:54 his young man thrust him through, and he D
10:2 Then he D, and was buried at Shamir.
10:5 And Jair D, and was buried in Kamon.
12:7 Then Jephthah the Gileadite D, and was buried in
12:10 Then Ibzan D, and was buried at Bethlehem.
12:12 Then Elon the Zebulunite D, and was buried at
12:15 of Hillel the Pirathonite D, and was buried at
Ruth 1:3 the husband of Naomi, D, and she was left
1:5 both Mahlon and Chilion D, so that the woman
1Sam 4:18 was broken and he D, for he was an
25:1 Now Samuel D; and all Israel assembled and
25:37 things, and his heart D within him, and he
25:38 days later the LORD smote Nabal; and he D
28:3 Now Samuel had D, and all Israel had mourned
31:5 upon his sword, and D with him.
31:6 Thus Saul D, and his three sons, and his
2Sam 1:15 And he smote him so that he D
2:23 he fell there, and D where he was.
2:23 Asahel had fallen and D, stood still.
3:27 belly, so that he D, for the blood of
4:1 heard that Abner had D at Hebron, his courage
6:7 the ark; and he D there beside the ark
10:1 king of the Ammonites D, and Hanun his son
10:18 army, so that he D there.
11:21 wall, so that he D at Thebez?
12:18 On the seventh day the child D
12:21 but when the child D, you arose and ate
17:23 hanged himself; and he D, and was buried in
18:33 Would I had D instead of you, O Absalom,
20:10 ground, without striking a second blow; and he D
24:15 appointed time; and there D of the people from
1Kgs 2:25 Jehoiada; and he struck him down, and he D
2:46 went out and struck him down, and he D
3:19 And this woman's son D in the night, because
14:17 to the threshold of the house, the child D
16:18 him with fire, and D,
16:22 of Ginath; so Tibni D, and Omri became king.
22:35 until at evening he D; and the blood of
22:37 So the king D, and was brought to Samaria;
2Kgs 1:17 So he D according to the word of the
3:5 But when Ahab D, the king of Moab rebelled
4:20 on her lap till noon, and then he D
7:17 gate, so that he D, as the man of
7:20 trod upon him in the gate and he D
8:15 and spread it over his face, till he D
9:27 fled to Megiddo, and D there.
12:21 servants, who struck him down, so that he D
13:20 So Elisha D, and they buried him.
13:24 Hazael king of Syria D, Ben-hadad his son became
23:34 came to Egypt, and D there.
1Chr 1:44 When Bela D, Jobab the son of Zerah of
1:45 When Jobab D, Husham of the land of the
1:46 When Husham D, Hadad the son of Bedad, who
1:47 When Hadad D, Samlah of Masrekah reigned in his
1:48 Samlah D, Shaul of Rehoboth on the Euphrates
1:49 When Shaul D, Baal-hanan, the son of Achbor,
1:50 When Baal-hanan D, Hadad reigned in his stead; and
1:51 And Hadad D
2:19 When Azubah D, Caleb married Ephrath, who bore
2:30 and Appa-im; and Seled D childless.
2:32 and Jonathan; and Jether D childless.
10:5 dead, he also fell upon his sword, and D
10:6 Thus Saul D; he and his three sons and
10:6 and all his house D together.
10:13 So Saul D for his unfaithfulness; he was unfaithful
13:10 the ark; and he D there before God.
19:1 king of the Ammonites D, and his son reigned
23:22 Eleazar D having no sons, but only daughters; their
24:2 But Nadab and Abihu D before their father, and
29:28 Then he D in a good old age, full
2Chr 13:20 Abijah; and the LORD smote him, and he D
18:34 the Syrians until evening; then at sunset he D
21:19 the disease, and he D in great agony.
24:15 full of days, and D; he was a hundred
24:25 So he D; and they buried him in the
35:24 And he D, and was buried in the tombs
Tob 1:15 when Shalmaneser D, Sennacherib his son reigned
6:13 husbands and that each D in the bridal chamber.
7:11 came to her he D in the night.
10:2 possible that Gabael has D and there is no
14:11 he said this he D in his bed.
14:12 And when Anna D he buried her with his
14:14 He D in Ecbatana of Media at the age
14:15 But before he D he heard of the destruction
Jud 6:1 men outside the council D down, Holofernes, the
8:2 tribe and family, had D during the barley harvest.
8:3 to his bed and D in Bethulia his city.
16:22 after Manasseh her husband D and was gathered to
16:23 She D in Bethulia, and they buried her in
16:24 Before she D she distributed her property to all
Esth 2:7 father and her mother D, Mordecai adopted her as
Job 10:18 Would that I had D before any eye had
42:17 And Job D, an old man, and full of
Wis 3:2 they seemed to have D, and their departure was
4:16 righteous man who had D will condemn the ungodly
Sir 30:5 rejoiced, and when he D he was not grieved;
37:31 Many have D of gluttony, but he who is
Is 6:1 year that King Uzziah D I saw the Lord
14:28 year that King Ahaz D came this oracle:
Jer 28:17 year, in the seventh month, the prophet Hananiah D
Bar 6:32 a funeral feast for a man who has D
Ezek 4:14 have never eaten what D of itself or was
11:13 was prophesying, that Pelatiah the son of Benaiah D
24:18 in the morning, and at evening my wife D
44:31 or beast, that has D of itself or is
Hos 13:1 Israel; but he incurred guilt through Baal and D
1Mac 1:7 And after Alexander had reigned twelve years, he D
2:38 the sabbath, and they D, with their wives and

2:41 die as our brethren D in their hiding places."
2:70 He D in the one hundred and forty-sixth year
6:16 Thus Antiochus the king D there in the one
6:46 fell to the ground upon him and he D
9:56 And Alcimus D at that time in great agony.
11:18 But King Ptolemy D three days later, and his
14:16 Sparta, that Jonathan had D, and they were deeply
2Mac 4:7 Seleucus D and Antiochus who was called Epiphanes
5:9 own country into exile D in exile, having embarked
6:31 in this way he D, leaving in his death
7:7 the first brother had D in this way, they
7:9 life, because we have D for his laws."
7:13 When he too had D, they maltreated and tortured
7:40 So he D in his integrity, putting his whole
7:41 of all, the mother D, after her sons.
13:7 that Menelaus the lawbreaker D, without even burial
in
Mt 2:19 But when Herod D, behold, an angel of the
9:18 "My daughter has just D; but come and lay
22:25 the first married, and D, and having no children
22:27 After them all, the woman D
Mk 12:20 wife, and when he D left no children;
12:21 second took her, and D, leaving no children; and
12:22 Last of all the woman also D
Lk 7:12 a man who had D was being carried out,
16:22 The poor man D and was carried by the
16:22 The rich man also D and was buried;
20:29 took a wife, and D without children;
20:31 and likewise all seven left no children and D
20:32 Afterward the woman also D
Jn 6:49 ate the manna in the wilderness, and they D
6:58 the fathers ate and D; he who eats this
8:52 Abraham D, as did the prophets; and you say,
8:53 Are you greater than our father Abraham, who D
8:53 And the prophets D
11:21 had been here, my brother would not have D
11:32 had been here, my brother would not have D
Acts 2:29 David that he both D and was buried, and
5:5 Ananias heard these words, he fell down and D
5:10 Immediately she fell down at his feet and D
7:4 And after his father D, God removed him from
7:15 And he D, himself and our fathers,
9:37 she fell sick and D; and when they had
12:23 glory; and he was eaten by worms and D
Rom 5:6 the right time Christ D for the ungodly.
5:8 were yet sinners Christ D for us.
5:15 For if many D through one man's trespass, much
6:2 How can we who D to sin still live
6:7 For he who has D is freed from sin.
6:8 But if we have D with Christ, we believe
6:10 The death he D he died to sin, once
6:10 death he died he D to sin, once for
7:4 my brethren, you have D to the law through
7:9 sin revived and I D;
8:34 it Christ Jesus, who D, yes, who was raised
14:9 to this end Christ D and lived again, that
14:15 cause the ruin of one for whom Christ D
1Cor 8:11 man is destroyed, the brother for whom Christ D
11:30 you are weak and ill, and some have D
15:3 also received, that Christ D for our sins in
2Cor 5:14 convinced that one has D for all; therefore all
5:14 one has died for all; therefore all have D
5:15 And he D for all, that those who live
5:15 who for their sake D and was raised.
Gal 2:19 I through the law D to the law, that
2:21 the law, then Christ D to no purpose.
Phil 2:30 men, for he nearly D for the work of
Col 2:20 If with Christ you D to the elemental spirits
3:3 For you have D, and your life is hid
1Thes 4:14 we believe that Jesus D and rose again, even
5:10 Lord Jesus Christ, who D for us so that
2Tim 2:11 sure: If we have D with him, we shall
Heb 11:4 accepting his gifts; he D, but through his faith
11:13 These all D in faith, not having received what
1Pet 3:18 For Christ also D for sins once for all,
Rev 1:18 the living one; I D, and behold I am
2:8 and the last, who D and came to life.
8:9 creatures in the sea D, and a third of
8:11 wormwood, and many men D of the water, because
16:3 and every living thing D that was in the

DIES (55)

Gen 27:10 so that he may bless you before he D
Ex 21:12 man so that he D shall be put to
21:20 rod and the slave D under his hand, he
21:35 anothers, so that it D, then they shall sell
22:3 struck so that he D, there shall be no
22:10 to keep, and it D or is hurt or
22:14 it is hurt or D, the owner not being
Lev 7:24 of an animal that D of itself, and the
11:39 which you may eat D, he who touches its
17:15 person that eats what D of itself or what
22:8 That which D of itself or is torn by
Num 6:9 "And if any man D very suddenly beside him,
19:14 law when a man D in a tent: every
27:8 Israel, 'If a man D, and has no son,
Deut 14:21 not eat anything that D of itself; you may
19:5 neighbor so that he D —he may flee to
19:11 mortally so that he D, and the man flees
24:3 if the latter husband D, who took her to
25:5 and one of them D and has no son,
2Sam 3:33 Abner, saying, "Should Abner die as a fool D
1Kgs 14:11 belonging to Jeroboam who D in the city the
14:11 and any one who D in the open country
16:4 belonging to Baasha who D in the city the
16:4 one of his who D in the field the
21:24 belonging to Ahab who D in the city the
21:24 one of his who D in the open country
Tob 4:4 When she D bury her beside me in the
Job 14:10 But man D, and is laid low; man breathes
21:23 One D in full prosperity, being wholly at ease
21:25 Another D in bitterness of soul, never having tasted
Ps 49:17 For when he D he will carry nothing away;
Prov 5:23 He D for lack of discipline, and because of
11:7 When the wicked D, his hope perishes, and the
Eccl 2:16 How the wise man D just like the fool!
3:19 the same; as one D, so dies the other.
3:19 as one dies, so D the other.
Sir 11:17 pass until he leaves them to others and D
14:18 flesh and blood: one D and another is born.
23:17 tastes sweet; he will never cease until he D
Is 51:12 afraid of man who D, of the son of
59:5 who eats their eggs D, and from one which
Jer 38:10 the prophet out of the cistern before he D
Ezek 7:15 is in the field D by the sword; and
Mt 22:24 said, 'If a man D, having no children, his
Mk 12:19 if a man's brother D and leaves a wife,
Lk 20:28 if a man's brother D, having a wife but
Jn 4:49 to him, "Sir, come down before my child D
12:24 into the earth and D, it remains alone; but
12:24 alone; but if it D, it bears much fruit.
Rom 7:2 but if her husband D she is discharged from
7:3 But if her husband D she is free from
14:7 and none of us D to himself.
1Cor 7:39 If the husband D, she is free to be
15:36 sow does not come to life unless it D
Heb 10:28 the law of Moses D without mercy at the

DIFFER

Rom 12:6 Having gifts that D according to the grace given

DIFFERENCE (4)

Ezek 22:26 have they taught the D between the unclean and
44:23 teach my people the D between the holy and
1Mac 3:18 Heaven there is no D between saving by many
Gal 2:6 they were makes no D to me; God shows

DIFFERENT (22)

Lev 19:19 cattle breed with a D kind; you shall not
Num 14:24 because he has a D spirit and has followed
1Kgs 18:21 go limping with two D opinions?
Esth 1:7 golden goblets, goblets of D kinds, and the royal
3:8 kingdom; their laws are D from those of every
Wis 7:5 king has had a D beginning of existence;
Sir 33:8 and he appointed the D seasons and feasts;
33:11 them and appointed their D ways;
Is 65:15 will call by a D name.
Ezek 16:34 So you were D from other women in your
16:34 hire was given to you; therefore you were D
Dan 7:3 out of the sea, D from one another.
7:7 It was D from all the beasts that were
7:19 fourth beast, which was D from all the rest,
7:23 earth, which shall be D from all the kingdoms,
7:24 them; he shall be D from the former ones,
1Cor 4:7 For who sees anything D in you?
14:10 There are doubtless many D languages in the world,
2Cor 11:4 if you receive a D spirit from the one
11:4 if you accept a D gospel from the one
Gal 1:6 and turning to a D gospel–
1Tim 1:3 not to teach any D doctrine,

DIFFERS
1Cor 15:41 the stars; for star D from star in glory.

DIFFICULT (5)
Deut 17:8 towns which is too D for you, then you
Sir 3:20 not what is too D for you, nor investigate
Dan 2:11 the king asks is D, and none can show
4:9 that no mystery is D for you, here is
2Mac 12:21 hard to besiege and D of access because of

DIFFICULTIES (3)
Wis 17:11 by conscience, it has always exaggerated the D
1Mac 13:3 the wars and the D which we have seen.
Rom 16:17 who create dissensions and D, in opposition to the

DIFFICULTY (5)
Wis 6:14 her will have no D, for he will find
2Mac 2:24 numbers involved and the D there is for those
Acts 27:7 days, and arrived with D off Cnidus, and as
27:8 Coasting along it with D, we came to a
27:16 Cauda, we managed with D to secure the boat;

DIG (10)
Deut 8:9 whose hills you can D copper.
23:13 down outside, you shall D a hole with it,
Job 3:21 it comes not, and D for it more than
24:16 In the dark they D through houses; by day
Ezek 8:8 me, "Son of man, D in the wall"; and
12:5 D through the wall in their sight, and go
12:12 go forth; he shall D through the wall and
Amos 9:2 "Though they D into Sheol, from there shall my
Lk 13:8 year also, till I D about it and put
16:3 not strong enough to D, and I am ashamed

DIGGED (2)
Is 5:2 He D it and cleared it of stones, and
51:1 and to the quarry from which you were D

DIGGING
Ps 7:15 He makes a pit, D it out, and falls

DIGNIFIED
1Tim 3:2 one wife, temperate, sensible, D, hospitable, an apt

DIGNITY (7)
Esth 6:3 said, "What honor or D has been bestowed on
Job 40:10 yourself with majesty and D; clothe yourself with
Prov 31:25 Strength and D are her clothing, and she laughs
Sir 45:24 descendants should have the D of the priesthood for
Hab 1:7 they; their justice and D proceed from themselves.
2Mac 6:23 his years and the D of his old age
15:13 his gray hair and D, and of marvelous majesty

DIGS (4)
Ex 21:33 or when a man D a pit and does
Prov 26:27 He who D a pit will fall into it,
Eccl 10:8 He who D a pit will fall into it;
Sir 27:26 He who D a pit will fall into it,

DIKLAH (2)
Gen 10:27 Hazarmaveth, Jerah, Hadoram, Uzal, D,
1Chr 1:21 Hazarmaveth, Jerah, Hadoram, Uzal, D,

DILEAN
Josh 15:38 Zenan, Hadashah, Migdal-gad, D, Mizpeh, Joktheel,

DILIGENCE (5)
Ezra 6:12 a decree; let it be done with all D
6:13 associates did with all D what Darius the king
7:17 you shall with all D buy bulls, rams, and
7:21 it done with all D,
Sir 11:16 is rich through his D and self-denial, and this

DILIGENT (7)
Prov 10:4 the hand of the D makes rich.
12:24 The hand of the D will rule, while the
12:27 his prey, but the D man will get precious
13:4 the soul of the D is richly supplied.
13:24 who loves him is D to discipline him.
21:5 The plans of the D lead surely to abundance,
Sir 38:27 of seals, each is D in making a great

DILIGENTLY (21)
Ex 15:26 saying, "If you will D hearken to the voice
Lev 10:16 Now Moses D inquired about the goat of the
Deut 4:9 and keep your soul D, lest you forget the
6:7 you shall teach them D to your children, and
6:17 You shall D keep the commandments of the LORD
13:14 make search and ask D; and behold, if it
17:4 then you shall inquire D, and if it is
19:18 the judges shall inquire D, and if the witness
Ezra 5:8 this work goes on D and prospers in their
Ps 119:4 Thou hast commanded thy precepts to be kept D
Prov 1:28 they will seek me D but will not find
8:17 those who seek me D find me.
11:27 He who D seeks good seeks favor, but evil
Is 21:7 camels, let him listen D, very diligently."
21:7 riders on camels, let him listen diligently, very D
55:2 Hearken D to me, and eat what is good,
Jer 12:16 pass, if they will D learn the ways of
Mic 7:3 evil, to do it D; the prince and the
Zech 6:15 pass, if you will D obey the voice of
Mt 2:8 saying, "Go and search D for the child, and
Lk 15:8 the house and seek D until she finds it?

DILL (4)
Is 28:25 does he not scatter D, sow cummin, and put
28:27 D is not threshed with a threshing sledge, nor
28:27 rolled over cummin; but D is beaten out with
Mt 23:22 you tithe mint and D and cummin, and have

DIM (16)
Gen 27:1 and his eyes were D so that he could
48:10 eyes of Israel were D with age, so that
Lev 13:6 the diseased spot is D and the disease has
13:21 the skin, but is D, then the priest shall
13:26 the skin, but is D, the priest shall shut
13:28 the skin, but is D, it is a swelling
13:56 and the disease is D after it is washed,
Deut 34:7 his eye was not D, nor his natural force
1Sam 3:2 had begun to grow D, so that he could
1Kgs 14:4 for his eyes were D because of his age.
Job 17:7 My eye has grown D from grief, and all
Ps 69:3 My eyes grow D with waiting for my God.
88:9 escape; my eye grows D through sorrow.
Sir 18:17 gift of a grudging man makes the eyes D
Lam 4:1 the gold has grown D, how the pure gold
5:17 our eyes have grown D,

DIMENSIONS (2)
Ezek 43:13 "These are the D of the altar by cubits
48:16 these shall be its D: the north side four

DIMINISH (4)
Ex 21:10 himself, he shall not D her food, her clothing,
Lev 25:16 are few you shall D the price, for it
Sir 18:5 is not possible to D or increase them, nor
Is 19:6 of Egypt's Nile will D and dry up, reeds

DIMINISHED (3)
Ps 107:39 When they are D and brought low through
Bar 2:34 will increase them, and they will not be D
Ezek 16:27 hand against you, and D your allotted portion, and

DIMINISHES
Sir 31:4 toils as his livelihood D, and when he rests

DIMLY (2)
Is 42:3 not break, and a D burning wick he will
1Cor 13:12 see in a mirror D, but then face to

DIMMED
Eccl 12:3 through the windows are D,

DIMNAH
Josh 21:35 with its pasture lands, D with its pasture lands,

DIMONAH
Josh 15:22 Kabzeel, Eder, Jagur, Kinah, D, Adadah,

DINAH (8)
Gen 30:21 she bore a daughter, and called her name D
34:1 Now D the daughter of Leah, whom she had
34:3 soul was drawn to D the daughter of Jacob;
34:5 had defiled his daughter D; but his sons were
34:13 deceitfully, because he had defiled their sister D
34:25 Jacob, Simeon and Levi, D's brothers, took their
34:26 the sword, and took D out of Shechem's house,
46:15 together with his daughter D; altogether his sons and

DINE (4)
Gen 43:16 the men are to D with me at noon."

Sir 9:9 Never D with another man's wife, nor revel with
Lk 11:37 Pharisee asked him to D with him; so he
14:1 when he went to D at the house of

DINED (2)

2Kgs 25:29 of his life he D regularly at the king's
Jer 52:33 of his life he D regularly at the king's

DINHABAH (2)

Gen 36:32 in Edom, the name of his city being D
1Chr 1:43 of Beor, the name of whose city was D

DINNER (14)

Tob 2:1 seven weeks, a good D was prepared for me
12:13 rise and leave your D in order to go
Esth 5:4 this day to a D that I have prepared
5:5 Haman came to the D that Esther had prepared.
5:8 come tomorrow to the D which I will prepare
5:14 then go merrily with the king to the D
Prov 15:17 Better is a D of herbs where love is
Sir 9:16 righteous men be your D companions, and let your
Dan 14:34 to Habakkuk, "Take the D which you have to
14:37 Take the D which God has sent you."
Mt 22:4 have made ready my D, my oxen and my
Lk 11:38 see that he did not first wash before D
14:12 "When you give a D or a banquet, do
1Cor 10:27 unbelievers invites you to D and you are disposed

DIONYSIUS

Acts 17:34 and believed, among them D the Are-opagite and a

DIONYSUS (3)

2Mac 6:7 when the feast of D came, they were compelled
6:7 procession in honor of D, wearing wreaths of ivy.
14:33 I will build here a splendid temple to D

DIOSCORINTHIUS

2Mac 11:21 hundred and forty-eighth year, D twenty-fourth."

DIOTREPHES

3 Jn 1:9 to the church; but D, who likes to put

DIP (13)

Ex 12:22 bunch of hyssop and D it in the blood
Lev 4:6 and the priest shall D his finger in the
4:17 and the priest shall D his finger in the
14:6 and the hyssop, and D them and the living
14:16 own left hand, and D his right finger in
14:51 the living bird, and D them in the blood
Num 19:18 shall take hyssop, and D it in the water,
Deut 33:24 brothers, and let him D his foot in oil.
Ruth 2:14 eat some bread, and D your morsel in the
Is 30:14 the hearth, or to D up water out of
Jer 13:1 loins, and do not D it in water."
2Mac 1:20 he ordered them to D it out and bring
Lk 16:24 and send Lazarus to D the end of his

DIPHATH

1Chr 1:6 sons of Gomer: Ashkenaz, D, and Togarmah.

DIPPED (10)

Gen 37:31 killed a goat, and D the robe in the
Lev 9:9 to him, and he D his finger in the
Josh 3:15 bearing the ark were D in the brink of
1Sam 14:27 in his hand, and D it in the honeycomb,
2Kgs 5:14 he went down and D himself seven times in
8:15 took the coverlet and D it in water and
Mt 26:23 answered, "He who has D his hand in the
Jn 13:26 morsel when I have D it." So when he
13:26 So when he had D the morsel, he gave
Rev 19:13 clad in a robe D in blood, and the

DIPPING

Mk 14:20 twelve, one who is D bread into the dish

DIRECT (23)

Deut 17:10 to all that they D you;
24:8 the Levitical priests shall D you; as I commanded
1Sam 7:3 from among you, and D your heart to the
1Kgs 5:9 to the place you D, and I will have
1Chr 15:22 Levites in music, should D the music, for he
29:18 of thy people, and D their hearts toward thee.
Jud 11:7 had sent you to D every living soul, not
12:8 God of Israel to D her way for the
Ps 74:3 D thy steps to the perpetual ruins; the enemy
119:128 Therefore I D my steps by all thy precepts;
Prov 23:19 and be wise, and D your mind in the
Sir 25:25 not go as you D, separate her from yourself.
37:15 High that he may D your way in truth.
38:10 up your faults and D your hands aright, and
39:7 He will D his counsel and knowledge aright, and
Jer 2:33 "How well you D your course to seek lovers!
10:23 man who walks to D his steps.
Ezek 23:25 And I will D my indignation against you, that
26:9 He will D the shock of his battering-rams against
2Mac 3:14 and went in to D the inspection of these
Acts 16:11 Troas, we made a D voyage to Samothrace, and
1Thes 3:11 and our Lord Jesus, D our way to you;
2Thes 3:5 May the Lord D your hearts to the love

DIRECTED (24)

Num 27:23 him as the LORD D through Moses.
2Chr 32:30 waters of Gihon and D them down to the
34:13 over the burden-bearers and D all who did work
Esth 16:16 living God, who has D the kingdom both for
Job 32:14 man.' He has not D his words against me,
Wis 6:9 monarchs, my words are D, that you may learn
Sir 49:9 good to those who D their ways aright.
51:20 I D my soul to her, and through purification
Is 10:25 my anger will be D to their destruction.
40:13 Who has D the Spirit of the LORD, or
Ezek 21:16 to right and left where your edge is D
1Mac 1:44 cities of Judah; he D them to follow customs
10:11 He D those who were doing the work to
Mt 21:6 did as Jesus had D them;
26:19 did as Jesus had D them, and they prepared
27:10 field, as the Lord D me."
28:15 did as they were D; and this story has
28:16 to which Jesus had D them.
Lk 8:55 at once; and he D that something should be
Acts 3:4 And Peter D his gaze at him, with John,
7:44 who spoke to Moses D him to make it,
10:22 whole Jewish nation, was D by a holy angel
1Cor 16:1 the saints: as I D the churches of Galatia,
Tit 1:4 every town as I D you,

DIRECTION (38)

Gen 10:19 from Sidon, in the D of Gerar, as far
10:19 Gaza, and in the D of Sodom, Gomorrah, Admah,
10:30 from Mesha in the D of Sephar to the
13:10 of Egypt, in the D of Zoar; this was
25:18 opposite Egypt in the D of Assyria; he settled
Ex 38:21 the Levites under the D of Ithamar the son
Num 7:8 their service, under the D of Ithamar the son
Deut 1:40 the wilderness in the D of the Red Sea.'
2:1 the wilderness in the D of the Red Sea,
2:8 and went in the D of the wilderness of
33:3 in thy steps, receiving D from thee,
Josh 8:15 and fled in the D of the wilderness.
9:14 and did not ask D from the LORD.
12:3 eastward, and in the D of Beth-jeshimoth, to the
18:13 along southward in the D of Luz, to the
18:14 boundary goes in another D, turning on the western
18:17 bends in a northerly D going on to En-shemesh,
19:12 goes in the other D eastward toward the sunrise
Judg 9:37 is coming from the D of the Diviners' Oak."
20:42 of Israel in the D of the wilderness; but
1Sam 6:12 went straight in the D of Beth-shemesh along one
1Kgs 18:6 Ahab went in one D by himself, and Obadiah
18:6 Obadiah went in another D by himself.
2Kgs 3:20 water came from the D of Edom, till the
9:27 he fled in the D of Beth-haggan.
25:4 they went in the D of the Arabah.
1Chr 25:2 of Asaph, under the D of Asaph, who prophesied
25:2 who prophesied under the D of the king.
25:3 Mattithiah, six, under the D of their father Jeduthun,
25:6 were all under the D of their father in
2Chr 23:18 the LORD under the D of the Levitical priests
26:11 the officer, under the D of Hananiah, one of
Is 47:15 each in his own D; there is no one
Jer 5:31 priests rule at their D; my people love to
52:7 they went in the D of the Arabah.
Ezek 8:5 eyes now in the D of the north." So
9:2 men came from the D of the upper gate,
10:11 went, but in whatever D the front wheel faced

DIRECTIONS (7)

2Chr 35:4 your divisions, following the D of David king of
35:4 of Israel and the D of Solomon his son.
Ezra 3:10 LORD, according to the D of David king of
Ezek 1:17 any of their four D without turning as they
10:11 any of their four D without turning as they

1Cor 11:34 things I will give D when I come.
Heb 11:22 the Israelites and gave D concerning his burial.

DIRECTLY
Prov 4:26 Let your eyes look D forward, and your gaze

DIRECTS (5)
Prov 16:9 way, but the LORD D his steps.
Sir 6:17 Whoever fears the Lord D his friendship aright, for
1Mac 4:47 stones, as the law D, and built a new
4:53 sacrifice, as the law D, on the new altar
Jas 3:4 small rudder wherever the will of the pilot D

D

DIRGE (2)
Jer 9:20 a lament, and each to her neighbor a D
1Mac 9:41 the voice of their musicians into a funeral D

DIRT (6)
Judg 3:22 his belly; and the D came out.
Job 7:5 clothed with worms and D; my skin hardens, then
Wis 15:10 hope is cheaper than D, and his life is
Is 57:20 rest, and its waters toss up mire and D
Zech 9:3 and gold like the D of the streets.
1Pet 3:21 as a removal of D from the body but

DISABLED (2)
Lev 22:22 Animals blind or D or mutilated or having a
2Mac 8:24 enemy, and wounded and D most of Nicanor's army,

DISAGREED
Acts 28:25 So, as they D among themselves, they departed, after

DISAGREEMENT
2Mac 3:4 the temple, had a D with the high priest

DISAPPEAR (3)
Job 6:17 time of heat they D; when it is hot,
Sir 39:9 his memory will not D, and his name will
Is 17:3 The fortress will D from Ephraim, and the kingdom

DISAPPOINT
Rom 5:5 and hope does not D us, because God's love

DISAPPOINTED (3)
Job 6:20 They are D because they were confident; they come
41:9 of a man is D; he is laid low
Ps 22:5 saved; in thee they trusted, and were not D

DISAPPROVAL (2)
Num 30:5 if her father expresses D to her on the
30:8 of it, he expresses D, then he shall make

DISARMED
Col 2:15 He D the principalities and powers and made a

DISASTER (23)
Gen 19:19 the hills, lest the D overtake me, and I
Judg 20:34 did not know that D was close upon them.
20:41 for they saw that D was close upon them.
Job 9:23 When D brings sudden death, he mocks at the
30:24 hand, and in his D cry for help?
31:3 befall the unrighteous, and D the workers of
Prov 24:22 either of them; for D from them will rise
Wis 18:21 an end to the D, showing that he was
Is 31:2 is wise and brings D, he does not call
47:11 which you cannot atone; D shall fall upon you,
Jer 4:20 D follows hard on disaster, the whole land is
4:20 Disaster follows hard on D, the whole land is
17:16 desired the day of D, thou knowest; that which
Ezek 7:5 says the Lord GOD: D after disaster!
7:5 "Thus says the Lord GOD: Disaster after D
7:26 D comes upon disaster, rumor follows rumor; they
7:26 Disaster comes upon D, rumor follows rumor; they
Obad 1:13 have gloated over his D in the day of
Zeph 3:18 "I will remove D from you, so that you
Zech 1:15 was angry but a little they furthered the D
1Mac 3:29 of the dissension and D which he had caused
8:4 them and inflicted great D upon them; the rest
2Mac 4:16 For this reason heavy D overtook them, and those

DISASTERS (2)
Jer 19:8 horrified and will hiss because of all its D
49:17 horrified and will hiss because of all its D

DISBELIEVED (4)
Wis 18:13 For though they had D everything because of their
Lk 24:41 And while they still D for joy, and wondered,
Acts 19:9 some were stubborn and D, speaking evil of the
28:24 were convinced by what he said, while others D

DISCARDED
2Chr 29:19 utensils which King Ahaz D in his reign when

DISCERN (15)
Deut 32:29 understand this, they would D their latter end!
2Sam 14:17 angel of God to D good and evil.
19:35 years old; can I D what is pleasant and
1Kgs 3:9 people, that I may D between good and evil;
3:11 for yourself understanding to D what is right,
Job 4:16 but I could not D its appearance.
6:30 Cannot my taste D calamity?
38:20 and that you may D the paths to its
Ps 19:12 But who can D his errors?
Prov 14:8 prudent man is to D his way, but the
Wis 2:22 wages of holiness, nor D the prize for blameless
9:13 Or who can D what the Lord wills?
Is 44:18 not, nor do they D; for he has shut
Bar 3:14 at the same time D where there is length
Dan 13:42 eternal God, who dost D what is secret, who

DISCERNED (2)
Wis 6:12 and she is easily D by those who love
1Cor 2:14 understand them because they are spiritually D

DISCERNEST
Ps 139:2 I rise up; thou D my thoughts from afar.

DISCERNING (6)
1Kgs 3:12 you a wise and D mind, so that none
Sir 1:17 rained down knowledge and D comprehension, and
Is 29:14 the discernment of their D men shall be hid."
Hos 14:9 these things; whoever is D, let him know them;
1Cor 11:29 eats and drinks without D the body eats and
Heb 4:12 joints and marrow, and D the thoughts and intentions

DISCERNMENT (6)
Job 12:20 and takes away the D of the elders.
Prov 16:21 called a man of D, and pleasant speech increases
Is 27:11 is a people without D; therefore he who made
29:14 shall perish, and the D of their discerning men
44:19 is there knowledge or D to say, "Half of
Phil 1:9 with knowledge and all D,

DISCHARGE (30)
Lev 15:2 any man has a D from his body, his
15:2 from his body, his D is unclean.
15:3 his uncleanness for a D: whether his body runs
15:3 body runs with his D, or his body is
15:3 body is stopped from D, it is uncleanness in
15:4 he who has the D lies shall be unclean;
15:6 he who has the D has sat shall wash
15:7 him who has the D shall wash his clothes,
15:8 he who has the D spits on one who
15:9 he who has the D rides shall be unclean.
15:11 he that has the D touches without having rinsed
15:12 he who has the D touches shall be broken;
15:13 he who has a D is cleansed of his
15:13 is cleansed of his D, then he shall count
15:15 atonement for him before the LORD for his D
15:19 a woman has a D of blood which is
15:19 which is her regular D from her body, she
15:25 a woman has a D of blood for many
15:25 if she has a D beyond the time of
15:25 the days of the D she shall continue in
15:26 the days of her D, shall be to her
15:28 is cleansed of her D, she shall count for
15:30 for her before the LORD for her unclean D
15:32 him who has a D and for him who
15:33 female, who has a D, and for the man
22:4 leper or suffers a D may eat of the
22:22 mutilated or having a D or an itch or
Num 5:2 every one having a D, and every one that
2Sam 3:29 one who has a D, or who is leprous,
Eccl 8:8 death; there is no D from war, nor will

DISCHARGED (3)
2Chr 25:10 Then Amaziah D the army that had come to
Rom 7:2 husband dies she is D from the law concerning
7:6 But now we are D from the law, dead

DISCIPLE (29)
Mt 10:24 "A D is not above his teacher, nor a

10:25 is enough for the D to be like his
10:42 because he is a D, truly, I say to
27:57 who also was a D of Jesus.
Lk 6:40 A D is not above his teacher, but every
14:26 even his own life, he cannot be my D
14:27 cross and come after me, cannot be my D
14:33 renounce all that he has cannot be my D
Jn 9:28 saying, "You are his D, but we are disciples
18:15 Simon Peter followed Jesus, and so did another D
18:15 As this D was known to the high priest,
18:16 So the other D, who was known to the
19:26 his mother, and the D whom he loved standing
19:27 he said to the D, "Behold, your mother!" And
19:27 from that hour the D took her to his
19:38 Arimathea, who was a D of Jesus, but secretly,
20:2 Peter and the other D, the one whom Jesus
20:3 out with the other D, and they went toward
20:4 ran, but the other D outran Peter and reached
20:8 Then the other D, who reached the tomb first,
21:7 That D whom Jesus loved said to Peter, "It
21:20 saw following them the D whom Jesus loved, who
21:23 the brethren that this D was not to die;
21:24 This is the D who is bearing witness to
Acts 9:10 Now there was a D at Damascus named Ananias.
9:26 they did not believe that he was a D
9:36 was at Joppa a D named Tabitha, which means
16:1 A D was there, named Timothy, the son of
21:16 of Cyprus, an early D, with whom we should

DISCIPLES (240)

Is 8:16 up the testimony, seal the teaching among my D
Mt 5:1 he sat down his D came to him.
8:21 Another of the D said to him, "Lord, let
8:23 into the boat, his D followed him.
9:10 came and sat down with Jesus and his D
9:11 they said to his D, "Why does your teacher
9:14 Then the D of John came to him, saying,
9:14 Pharisees fast, but your D do not fast?"
9:19 And Jesus rose and followed him, with his D
9:37 he said to his D, "The harvest is plentiful,
10:1 to him his twelve D and gave them authority
11:1 finished instructing his twelve D, he went on from
11:2 sent word by his D
12:1 on the sabbath; his D were hungry, and they
12:2 to him, "Look, your D are doing what is
12:48 his hand toward his D, he said, "Here are
13:10 Then the D came and said to him, "Why
13:36 And his D came to him, saying, "Explain to
14:12 And his D came and took the body and
14:15 it was evening, the D came to him and
14:19 the loaves to the D, and the disciples gave
14:19 the disciples, and the D gave them to the
14:22 Then he made the D get into the boat
14:26 But when the D saw him walking on the
15:2 said, "Why do your D transgress the tradition of
15:12 Then the D came and said to him, "Do
15:23 And his D came and begged him, saying, "Send
15:32 Then Jesus called his D to him and said,
15:33 And the D said to him, "Where are we
15:36 gave them to the D, and the disciples gave
15:36 the disciples, and the D gave them to the
16:5 When the D reached the other side, they had
16:13 Philippi, he asked his D, "Who do men say
16:20 he strictly charged the D to tell no one
16:21 began to show his D that he must go
16:24 Then Jesus told his D, "If any man would
17:6 When the D heard this, they fell on their
17:10 And the D asked him, "Then why do the
17:13 Then the D understood that he was speaking to
17:16 brought him to your D, and they could not
17:19 Then the D came to Jesus privately and said,
18:1 At that time the D came to Jesus, saying,
19:10 The D said to him, "If such is the
19:13 The D rebuked the people;
19:23 Jesus said to his D, "Truly, I say to
19:25 When the D heard this they were greatly astonished,
20:17 he took the twelve D aside, and on the
21:1 then Jesus sent two D,
21:6 The D went and did as Jesus had directed
21:20 When the D saw it they marveled, saying, "How
22:16 And they sent their D to him, along with
23:1 crowds and to his D,
24:1 going away, when his D came to point out
24:3 Mount of Olives, the D came to him privately,
26:1 he said to his D,
26:8 But when the D saw it, they were indignant,
26:17 of Unleavened Bread the D came to Jesus, saying,
26:18 keep the passover at your house with my D
26:19 And the D did as Jesus had directed them,
26:20 table with the twelve D;
26:26 gave it to the D and said, "Take, eat;
26:35 And so said all the D
26:36 he said to his D, "Sit here, while I
26:40 he came to the D and found them sleeping;
26:45 he came to the D and said to them,
26:56 Then all the D forsook him and fled.
27:64 third day, lest his D go and steal him
28:7 quickly and tell his D that he has risen
28:8 and great joy, and ran to tell his D
28:13 said, "Tell people, 'His D came by night and
28:16 Now the eleven D went to Galilee, to the
28:19 Go therefore and make D of all nations, baptizing
Mk 2:15 with Jesus and his D; for there were many
2:16 collectors, said to his D, "Why does he eat
2:18 Now John's D and the Pharisees were fasting; and
2:18 him, "Why do John's D and the disciples of
2:18 John's disciples and the D of the Pharisees fast,
2:18 Pharisees fast, but your D do not fast?"
2:23 made their way his D began to pluck heads
3:7 Jesus withdrew with his D to the sea, and
3:9 And he told his D to have a boat
4:34 privately to his own D he explained everything.
5:31 And his D said to him, "You see the
6:1 own country; and his D followed him.
6:29 When his D heard of it, they came and
6:35 it grew late, his D came to him and
6:41 gave them to the D to set before the
6:45 Immediately he made his D get into the boat
7:2 that some of his D ate with hands defiled,
7:5 him, "Why do your D not live according to
7:16 left the people, his D asked him about the
8:1 eat, he called his D to him, and said
8:4 And his D answered him, "How can one feed
8:6 gave them to his D to set before the
8:10 the boat with his D, and went to the
8:27 went on with his D, to the villages of
8:27 way he asked his D, "Who do men say
8:33 turning and seeing his D, he rebuked Peter, and
8:34 the multitude with his D, and said to them,
9:14 they came to the D, they saw a great
9:18 and I asked your D to cast it out,
9:28 entered the house, his D asked him privately, "Why
9:31 he was teaching his D, saying to them, "The
10:10 in the house the D asked him again about
10:13 touch them; and the D rebuked them.
10:23 and said to his D, "How hard it will
10:24 And the D were amazed at his words.
10:46 leaving Jericho with his D and a great multitude,
11:1 sent two of his D,
11:14 And his D heard it.
12:43 And he called his D to him, and said
13:1 temple, one of his D said to him, "Look,
14:12 the passover lamb, his D said to him, "Where
14:13 sent two of his D, and said to them,
14:14 the passover with my D
14:16 And the D set out and went to the
14:32 he said to his D, "Sit here, while I
16:7 But go, tell his D and Peter that he
Lk 5:30 scribes murmured against his D, saying, "Why do you
5:33 said to him, "The D of John fast often
5:33 and so do the D of the Pharisees, but
6:1 through the grainfields, his D plucked and ate some
6:13 day, he called his D, and chose from them
6:17 great crowd of his D and a great multitude
6:20 his eyes on his D, and said: "Blessed are
7:11 called Nain, and his D and a great crowd
7:18 The D of John told him of all these
7:19 him two of his D, sent them to the
8:9 And when his D asked him what this parable
8:22 a boat with his D, and he said to
9:14 he said to his D, "Make them sit down
9:16 gave them to the D to set before the
9:18 was praying alone the D were with him; and
9:40 And I begged your D to cast it out,
9:43 he said to his D,
9:54 And when his D James and John saw it,
10:23 Then turning to the D he said privately, "Blessed
11:1 ceased, one of his D said to him, "Lord,
11:1 teach us to pray, as John taught his D
12:1 to say to his D first, "Beware of the
12:22 he said to his D, "Therefore I tell you,
16:1 also said to the D, "There was a rich

17:1 he said to his D, "Temptations to sin are
17:22 he said to the D, "The days are coming
18:15 them; and when the D saw it, they rebuked
19:29 sent two of the D,
19:37 whole multitude of the D began to rejoice and
19:39 the multitude said to him, "Teacher, rebuke your D
20:45 he said to his D,
22:11 the passover with my D
22:39 of Olives; and the D followed him.
22:43 he came to the D and found them sleeping
Jn 1:35 with two of his D;
1:37 The two D heard him say this, and they
2:2 also was invited to the marriage, with his D
2:11 his glory; and his D believed in him.
2:12 his brothers and his D; and there they stayed
2:17 His D remembered that it was written, "Zeal for
2:22 from the dead, his D remembered that he had
3:22 this Jesus and his D went into the land
3:25 discussion arose between John's D and a Jew over
4:1 making and baptizing more D than John
4:2 baptize, but only his D,
4:8 For his D had gone away into the city
4:27 Just then his D came.
4:31 Meanwhile the D besought him, saying, "Rabbi, eat."
4:33 So the D said to one another, "Has any
6:3 the mountain, and there sat down with his D
6:8 One of his D, Andrew, Simon Peter's brother, said
6:12 fill, he told his D, "Gather up the fragments
6:16 When evening came, his D went down to the
6:22 the boat with his D, but that his disciples
6:22 disciples, but that his D had gone away alone.
6:24 not there, nor his D, they themselves got into
6:60 Many of his D, when they heard it, said,
6:61 in himself that his D murmured at it, said
6:66 this many of his D drew back and no
7:3 to Judea, that your D may see the works
8:31 you are truly my D,
9:2 And his D asked him, "Rabbi, who sinned, this
9:27 Do you too want to become his D
9:28 disciple, but we are D of Moses.
11:7 he said to the D, "Let us go into
11:8 The D said to him, "Rabbi, the Jews were
11:12 The D said to him, "Lord, if he has
11:16 said to his fellow D, "Let us also go,
11:54 called Ephraim; and there he stayed with the D
12:4 Iscariot, one of his D (he who was to
12:16 His D did not understand this at first; but
13:5 began to wash the D feet, and to wipe
13:22 The D looked at one another, uncertain of whom
13:23 One of his D, whom Jesus loved, was lying
13:35 that you are my D, if you have love
15:8 much fruit, and so prove to be my D
16:17 Some of his D said to one another, "What
16:29 His D said, "Ah, now you are speaking plainly,
18:1 went forth with his D across the Kidron valley,
18:1 which he and his D entered.
18:2 place; for Jesus often met there with his D
18:17 "Are not you also one of this man's D
18:19 questioned Jesus about his D and his teaching.
18:25 him, "Are not you also one of his D
20:10 Then the D went back to their homes.
20:18 and said to the D, "I have seen the
20:19 being shut where the D were, for fear of
20:20 Then the D were glad when they saw the
20:25 So the other D told him, "We have seen
20:26 Eight days later, his D were again in the
20:30 the presence of the D, which are not written
21:1 himself again to the D by the Sea of
21:2 two others of his D were together.
21:4 the beach; yet the D did not know that
21:8 But the other D came in the boat, dragging
21:12 Now none of the D dared ask him, "Who
21:14 was revealed to the D after he was raised
Acts 6:1 these days when the D were increasing in number,
6:2 the body of the D and said, "It is
6:7 the number of the D multiplied greatly in Jerusalem,
9:1 and murder against the D of the Lord, went
9:19 he was with the D at Damascus.
9:25 kill him; but his D took him by night
9:26 attempted to join the D; and they were all
9:38 was near Joppa, the D, hearing that Peter was
11:26 and in Antioch the D were for the first
11:29 And the D determined, every one according to his
13:52 And the D were filled with joy and with
14:20 But when the D gathered about him, he rose
14:21 and had made many D, they returned to Lystra
14:22 the souls of the D, exhorting them to continue
14:28 And they remained no little time with the D
15:10 the neck of the D which neither our fathers
18:23 of Galatia and Phrygia, strengthening all the D
18:27 and wrote to the D to receive him.
19:1 There he found some D
19:9 from them, taking the D with him, and argued
19:30 the crowd, but the D would not let him;
20:1 Paul sent for the D and having exhorted them
20:30 to draw away the D after them.
21:4 having sought out the D, we stayed there for
21:16 And some of the D from Caesarea went with

DISCIPLINE (36)

Lev 26:23 "And if by this D you are not turned
Deut 4:36 voice, that he might D you; and on earth
11:2 seen it), consider the D of the LORD your
Ps 50:17 For you hate D, and you cast my words
Prov 3:11 not despise the LORD's D or be weary of
5:12 say, "How I hated D, and my heart despised
5:23 dies for lack of D, and because of his
6:23 and the reproofs of D are the way of
12:1 Whoever loves D loves knowledge, but he who hates
13:24 him is diligent to D him.
15:10 There is severe D for him who forsakes the
19:18 D your son while there is hope; d o
22:15 but the rod of D drives it far from
23:13 Do not withhold D from a child; if you
29:17 D your son, and he will give you rest;
Sir 4:17 torment him by her D until she trusts him,
7:23 D them, and make them obedient from their youth.
18:13 those who accept his D and who are eager
22:6 time, but chastising and D are wisdom at all
23:2 my thoughts, and the D of wisdom over my
30:13 D your son and take pains with him, that
32:14 Lord will accept his D, and those who rise
33:24 an ass; bread and D and work for a
38:33 judgment; they cannot expound D or judgment, and
42:5 merchants, and of much D of children, and of
Jer 7:28 and did not accept D; truth has perished; it
Bar 4:13 tread the paths of D in his righteousness.
2Mac 6:12 to destroy but to D our people.
7:33 while, to rebuke and D us, he will again
Eph 6:4 them up in the D and instruction of the
Heb 12:5 not regard lightly the D of the Lord, nor
12:7 It is for D that you have to endure.
12:7 son is there whom his father does not D
12:8 you are left without D, in which all have
12:9 had earthly fathers to D us and we respected
12:11 For the moment all D seems painful rather than

DISCIPLINED (9)

Tob 4:14 you do, and be D in all your conduct.
Prov 29:19 a servant is not D, for though he understands,
Wis 1:5 For a holy and D spirit will flee from
3:5 Having been D a little, they will receive great
11:9 though they were being D in mercy, they learned
Sir 23:15 words will never become D all his days.
26:14 so precious as a D soul.
2Mac 10:4 sin, they might be D by him with forbearance
Heb 12:10 For they D us for a short time at

DISCIPLINES (6)

Deut 8:5 that, as a man D his son, the LORD
8:5 the LORD your God D you.
Sir 30:2 He who D his son will profit by him,
2Mac 6:16 Though he D us with calamities, he does not
Heb 12:6 For the Lord D him whom he loves, and
12:10 their pleasure, but he D us for our good,

DISCLOSE (11)

1Sam 20:12 not then send and D it to you?
20:13 if I do not D it to you, and
22:17 fled, and did not D it to me." But
Prov 25:9 himself, and do not D another's secret;
Sir 6:9 an enemy, and will D a quarrel to your
19:8 for you, do not D it;
Is 26:21 and the earth will D the blood shed upon
Dan 13:11 they were ashamed to D their lustful desire to
2Mac 2:8 then the Lord will D these things, and the
1Cor 3:13 for the Day will D it, because it will
4:5 in darkness and will D the purposes of the

DISCLOSED (5)

1Mac 7:31 his plan had been D, he went out to
2Mac 3:16 change in his color D the anguish of his

Acts 23:30 And when it was D to me that there
Rom 16:25 ages but is now D and through the prophetic
1Cor 14:25 of his heart are D; and so, falling on

DISCLOSES (5)

1Sam 22:8 No one D to me when my son makes
22:8 sorry for me or D to me that my
Prov 29:24 hears the curse, but D nothing.
Sir 27:6 The fruit D the cultivation of a tree; so
27:6 expression of a thought D the cultivation of a

DISCLOSING

1Sam 20:2 great or small without D it to me; and

DISCLOSURE (2)

Sir 22:20 as for reviling, arrogance, D of secrets, or a
2Mac 3:9 he told about the D that had been made

DISCOMFITED (2)

Ex 14:24 of the Egyptians, and D the host of the
Job 32:15 "They are D, they answer no more; they have

DISCOMFORT

Jon 4:6 over his head, to save him from his D

DISCONTENTED

1Sam 22:2 every one who was D, gathered to him; and

DISCORD (3)

Prov 6:14 devises evil, continually sowing D;
6:19 a man who sows D among brothers.
1Cor 12:25 there may be no D in the body, but

DISCORDANT

Wis 18:10 But the D cry of their enemies echoed back,

DISCOURAGE

Num 32:7 Why will you D the heart of the people

DISCOURAGED (6)

Num 32:9 saw the land, they D the heart of the
2Sam 17:2 he is weary and D, and throw him into
Ezra 4:4 people of the land D the people of Judah,
Is 42:4 not fail or be D till he has established
1Mac 4:27 he was perplexed and D, for things had not
Col 3:21 do not provoke your children, lest they become D

DISCOURSE (12)

Num 23:7 Balaam took up his D, and said, "From Aram
23:18 Balaam took up his D, and said, "Rise, Balak,
24:3 he took up his D, and said, "The oracle
24:15 he took up his D, and said, "The oracle
24:20 and took up his D, and said, "Amalek was
24:21 and took up his D, and said, "Enduring is
24:23 he took up his D, and said, "Alas, who
Job 27:1 again took up his D, and said:
29:1 again took up his D, and said:
Sir 8:8 Do not slight the D of the sages, but
8:9 Do not disregard the D of the aged, for
39:2 he will preserve the D of notable men and

DISCOVER

Ps 44:21 god, would not God D this?

DISCOVERED (3)

1Sam 22:6 heard that David was D, and the men who
2Kgs 12:5 the house wherever any need of repairs is D
Neh 13:7 Jerusalem, and I then D the evil that Eliashib

DISCREDITED

Tit 2:5 that the word of God may not be D

DISCREET (3)

Gen 41:33 Pharaoh select a man D and wise, and set
41:39 there is none so D and wise as you
Sir 21:24 a door, and a D man is grieved by

DISCREETLY

Prov 26:16 own eyes than seven men who can answer D

DISCRETION (14)

1Sam 25:33 Blessed be your D, and blessed be you, who
1Chr 22:12 the LORD grant you D and understanding, that when
2Chr 2:12 wise son, endued with D and understanding, who will
Ezra 8:18 us a man of D, of the sons of
Prov 1:4 the simple, knowledge and D to the youth—
2:11 pleasant to your soul; D will watch over you;
3:21 keep sound wisdom and D; let them not escape
5:2 that you may keep D, and your lips may
8:12 dwell in prudence, and I find knowledge and D
11:22 a swine's snout is a beautiful woman without D
14:17 but a man of D is patient.
Sir 33:29 toward anybody, and do nothing without D
Dan 2:14 replied with prudence and D to Arioch, the captain
1Mac 8:30 do so at their D, and any addition or

DISCUS

2Mac 4:14 the call to the D,

DISCUSS (3)

2Mac 2:30 the ground and to D matters from every side
Mt 16:8 faith, why do you D among yourselves the fact
Mk 8:17 them, "Why do you D the fact that you

DISCUSSED (5)

Mt 16:7 And they D it among themselves, saying, "We
Mk 8:16 And they D it with one another, saying, "We
9:34 the way they had D with one another who
Lk 6:11 filled with fury and D with one another what
20:5 And they D it with one another, saying, "If

DISCUSSING (3)

Mk 9:16 them, "What are you D with them?"
9:33 them, "What were you D on the way?"
Lk 24:15 they were talking and D together, Jesus himself drew

DISCUSSION (3)

Sir 9:15 and let all your D be about the law
Jn 3:25 Now a D arose between John's disciples and a
1Tim 1:6 wandered away into vain D,

DISDAIN (4)

Tob 4:13 your heart do not D your brethren and the
Jud 8:20 that he will not D us or any of
Sir 8:6 Do not D a man when he is old,
2Mac 7:11 of his laws I D them, and from him

DISDAINED (3)

1Sam 17:42 and saw David, he D him; for he was
Esth 3:6 But he D to lay hands on Mordecai alone.
Job 30:1 fathers I would have D to set with the

DISDAINING

2Mac 4:15 call to the discus, D the honors prized by

DISEASE (63)

Lev 13:2 turns into a leprous D on the skin of
13:3 turned white and the D appears to be deeper
13:3 it is a leprous D; when the priest has
13:5 in his eyes the D is checked and the
13:5 is checked and the D has not spread in
13:6 is dim and the D has not spread in
13:13 him clean of the D; it has all turned
13:17 him, and if the D has turned white, then
13:20 unclean; it is the D of leprosy, it has
13:25 shall pronounce him unclean; it is a leprous D
13:27 shall pronounce him unclean; it is a leprous D
13:29 or woman has a D on the head or
13:30 priest shall examine the D; and if it appears
13:31 priest examines the itching D, and it appears no
13:31 person with the itching D for seven days,
13:32 priest shall examine the D; and if the itch
13:33 person with the itching D for seven days more;
13:44 pronounce him unclean; his D is on his head.
13:45 leper who has the D shall wear torn clothes
13:46 as he has the D; he is unclean; he
13:47 there is a leprous D in a garment, whether
13:49 of skin, if the D shows greenish or reddish
13:49 it is a leprous D and shall be shown
13:50 priest shall examine the D, and shut up that
13:50 that which has the D for seven days;
13:51 he shall examine the D on the seventh day.
13:51 If the D has spread in the garment, in
13:51 of the skin, the D is a malignant leprosy;
13:53 priest examines, and the D has not spread in
13:54 in which is the D, and he shall shut
13:55 changed color, though the D has not spread, it
13:56 priest examines, and the D is dim after it
13:57 burn with fire that in which is the D
13:58 skin from which the D departs when you have
13:59 law for a leprous D in a garment of
14:3 Then, if the leprous D is healed in the

14:32 whom is a leprous D, who cannot afford the
14:34 I put a leprous D in a house in
14:35 be some sort of D in my house.'
14:36 goes to examine the D, lest all that is
14:37 he shall examine the D; and if the disease
14:37 disease; and if the D is in the walls
14:39 look; and if the D has spread in the
14:40 in which is the D and throw them into
14:43 "If the D breaks out again in the house,
14:44 look; and if the D has spread in the
14:48 an examination, and the D has not spread in
14:48 house clean, for the D is healed.
14:54 law for any leprous D: for an itch,
21:20 sight or an itching D or scabs or crushed
2Chr 16:12 his feet, and his D became severe; yet even
16:12 yet even in his D he did not seek
21:15 severe sickness with a D of your bowels, until
21:15 out because of the D, day by day.'"
21:18 smote him in his bowels with an incurable D
21:19 out because of the D, and he died in
Job 18:13 By D his skin is consumed, the first-born of
Ps 106:15 but sent a wasting D among them.
Mt 4:23 kingdom and healing every D and every infirmity
9:35 kingdom, and healing every D and every infirmity.
10:1 and to heal every D and every infirmity.
Mk 5:29 her body that she was healed of her D
5:34 go in peace, and be healed of your D

DISEASED (15)
Lev 13:3 priest shall examine the D spot on the skin
13:3 the hair in the D spot has turned white
13:4 shall shut up the D person for seven days;
13:6 day, and if the D spot is dim and
13:12 the skin of the D person from head to
13:17 priest shall pronounce the D person clean; he is
13:22 the priest shall pronounce him unclean; it is D
13:42 bald forehead a reddish-white D spot, it is leprosy
13:43 him, and if the D swelling is reddish-white on
13:52 burn the garment, whether D in warp or woof,
13:55 priest shall examine the D thing after it has
13:55 And if the D spot has not changed color,
1Kgs 15:23 old age he was D in his feet.
2Chr 16:12 his reign Asa was D in his feet, and
Jn 6:2 signs which he did on those who were D

DISEASES (16)
Ex 15:26 put none of the D upon you which I
Deut 7:15 none of the evil D of Egypt, which you
28:60 you again all the D of Egypt, which you
Ps 103:3 who heals all your D,
Jer 14:18 the city, behold, the D of famine!
16:4 in this land: They shall die of deadly D
Mt 4:24 those afflicted with various D and pains, demoniacs,
8:17 Isaiah, "He took our infirmities and bore our D
Mk 1:34 were sick with various D, and cast out many
3:10 that all who had D pressed upon him to
Lk 4:40 were sick with various D brought them to him;
6:17 be healed of their D;
7:21 he cured many of D and plagues and evil
9:1 demons and to cure D,
Acts 19:12 to the sick, and D left them and the
28:9 the island who had D also came and were

DISFIGURE
Mt 6:16 the hypocrites, for they D their faces that their

DISFIGURED (2)
Lev 24:20 tooth; as he has D a man, he shall
24:20 he has disfigured a man, he shall be D

DISFIGUREMENT
Lev 24:19 a man causes a D in his neighbor, as

DISGRACE (40)
Gen 34:14 that would be a D to us.
1Sam 11:2 eyes, and thus put D upon all Israel."
2Kgs 19:3 of rebuke, and of D; children have come to
Neh 2:17 of Jerusalem, that we may no longer suffer D
Tob 3:10 it will be a D to him, and I
Jud 9:2 polluted her womb to D her; for thou hast
12:12 it will be a D if we let such
14:18 Hebrew woman has brought D upon the house of
Job 10:15 I am filled with D and look upon my
Ps 44:15 All day long my D is before me, and
71:13 consumed; with scorn and D may they be covered
83:17 and dismayed for ever; let them perish in D
Prov 3:35 The wise will inherit honor, but fools get D
6:33 he get, and his D will not be wiped
11:2 pride comes, then comes D; but with the humble
13:18 Poverty and D come to him who ignores instruction,
18:3 contempt comes also; and with dishonor comes D
Sir 3:11 and it is a D for children not to
6:9 enemy, and will disclose a quarrel to your D
7:7 public, and do not D yourself among the people.
20:25 of a liar brings D, and his shame is
21:24 and a discreet man is grieved by the D
22:1 filthy stone, and every one hisses at his D
22:3 It is a D to be the father of
23:26 a curse, and her D will not be blotted
25:21 and impudence and great D when a wife supports
42:14 it is a woman who brings shame and D
Is 30:5 brings neither help nor profit, but shame and D
37:3 of rebuke, and of D; children have come to
Jer 31:19 because I bore the D of my youth.'
Lam 5:1 what has befallen us; behold, and see our D
Ezek 16:52 Bear your D, you also, for you have made
16:52 also, and bear your D, for you have made
16:54 you may bear your D and be ashamed of
36:15 no longer bear the D of the peoples and
36:30 never again suffer the D of famine among the
Dan 3:33 our mouths; shame and D have befallen thy servants
Mic 2:6 preach of such things; D will not overtake us."
2Mac 5:7 the end got only D from his conspiracy, and
6:25 while I defile and D my old age.

DISGRACED (8)
1Sam 20:34 because his father had D him.
Ps 71:24 put to shame and D who sought to do
Sir 8:4 with an ill-bred person, lest your ancestors be D
11:6 rulers have been greatly D, and illustrious men have
Jer 15:9 was yet day; she has been shamed and D
50:12 shamed, and she who bore you shall be D
Dan 3:44 shame; let them be D and deprived of all
Mic 3:7 the seers shall be D, and the diviners put

DISGRACEFUL (3)
2Mac 11:12 Lysias himself escaped by D flight.
1Cor 11:6 but if it is D for a woman to
2Cor 4:2 We have renounced D, underhanded ways; we refuse

DISGRACEFULLY
Prov 13:5 falsehood, but a wicked man acts shamefully and D

DISGRACES
Sir 22:5 An impudent daughter D father and husband, and

DISGUISE (4)
1Kgs 14:2 his wife, "Arise, and D yourself, that it be
22:30 to Jehoshaphat, "I will D myself and go into
2Chr 18:29 to Jehoshaphat, "I will D myself and go into
2Cor 11:15 if his servants also D themselves as servants of

DISGUISED (4)
1Sam 28:8 So Saul D himself and put on other garments,
1Kgs 22:30 the king of Israel D himself and went into
2Chr 18:29 the king of Israel D himself; and they went
35:22 away from him, but D himself in order to

DISGUISES (2)
Job 24:15 see me'; and he D his face.
2Cor 11:14 wonder, for even Satan D himself as an angel

DISGUISING (2)
1Kgs 20:38 king by the way, D himself with a bandage
2Cor 11:13 deceitful workmen, D themselves as apostles of

DISGUST (5)
Ps 119:158 at the faithless with D, because they do not
Ezek 23:17 polluted by them, she turned from them in D
23:18 nakedness, I turned in D from her, as I
23:22 whom you turned in D, and I will bring
23:28 whom you turned in D;

DISH (20)
Num 7:14 cereal offering; one golden D of ten shekels, full
7:20 cereal offering; one golden D of ten shekels, full
7:26 cereal offering; one golden D of ten shekels, full
7:32 cereal offering; one golden D of ten shekels, full
7:38 cereal offering; one golden D of ten shekels, full
7:44 cereal offering; one golden D of ten shekels, full
7:50 cereal offering; one golden D of ten shekels, full
7:56 cereal offering; one golden D of ten shekels, full

	7:62	cereal offering; one golden D of ten shekels, full
	7:68	cereal offering; one golden D of ten shekels, full
	7:74	cereal offering; one golden D of ten shekels, full
	7:80	cereal offering; one golden D of ten shekels, full
2Kgs	21:13	as one wipes a D, wiping it and turning
Prov	19:24	his hand in the D, and will not even
	26:15	his hand in the D; it wears him out
Sir	31:14	and do not crowd your neighbor at the D
Bar	6:17	For just as one's D is useless when it
Mt	26:23	his hand in the D with me, will betray
Mk	14:20	dipping bread into the D with me.
Lk	11:39	cup and of the D, but inside you are

DISHAN (5)

Gen	36:21	Anah, Dishon, Ezer, and D; these are the chiefs
	36:28	are the sons of D: Uz and Aran.
	36:30	Anah, Dishon, Ezer, and D; these are the chiefs
1Chr	1:38	Lotan, Shobal, Zibeon, Anah, Dishon, Ezer, and D
	1:42	The sons of D: Uz and Aran.

DISHEARTENED (2)

Ezek	13:22	Because you have D the righteous falsely, although I
	13:22	although I have not D him, and you have

DISHES (14)

Ex	25:29	make its plates and D for incense, and its
	37:16	table, its plates and D for incense, and its
Num	4:7	it the plates, the D for incense, the bowls,
	7:84	silver basins, twelve golden D,
	7:86	sanctuary, the twelve golden D, full of incense,
	7:86	the gold of the D being a hundred and
1Kgs	7:50	the cups, snuffers, basins, D for incense, and firepans,
2Kgs	25:14	the snuffers, and the D for incense and all
2Chr	4:22	gold; the snuffers, basins, D for incense, and firepans,
	24:14	the burnt offerings, and D for incense, and vessels
Jud	12:1	in where his silver D were kept, and ordered
	15:11	and all his silver D and his beds and
Jer	52:18	the basins, and the D for incense, and all
	52:19	the lampstands, and the D for incense, and the

DISHON (7)

Gen	36:21	Lotan, Shobal, Zibeon, Anah, D, Ezer, and Dishan;
	36:25	the children of Anah: D and Oholibamah the
	36:26	are the sons of D: Hemdan, Eshban, Ithran, and
	36:30	Lotan, Shobal, Zibeon, Anah, D, Ezer, and Dishan;
1Chr	1:38	Lotan, Shobal, Zibeon, Anah, D, Ezer, and Dishan.
	1:41	The sons of Anah: D
	1:41	The sons of D: Hamran, Eshban, Ithran, and Cheran.

DISHONEST (7)

Sir	5:8	Do not depend on D wealth, for it will
Jer	22:17	heart only for your D gain, for shedding innocent
Ezek	22:13	hands together at the D gain which you have
	22:27	destroying lives to get D gain.
Lk	16:8	The master commended the D steward for his
	16:10	and he who is D in a very little
	16:10	a very little is D also in much.

DISHONESTLY

Deut	25:16	things, all who act D, are an abomination to

DISHONOR (29)

Ezra	4:14	to witness the king's D, therefore we send and
Jud	8:23	the Lord our God will turn it to D
Ps	35:4	put to shame and D who seek after my
	35:26	clothed with shame and D who magnify themselves
	40:14	back and brought to D who desire my hurt!
	69:6	thee be brought to D through me, O God
	69:19	my shame and my D; my foes are all
	70:2	back and brought to D who desire my hurt!
	109:29	accusers be clothed with D; may they be wrapped
Prov	6:33	Wounds and D will he get, and his disgrace
	18:3	comes also; and with D comes disgrace.
Sir	1:27	fall, and thus bring D upon yourself.
	3:10	father, for your father's D is no glory to
	5:13	Glory and D come from speaking, and a man's
	29:6	and instead of glory will repay him with D
Is	23:9	of all glory, to D all the honored of
	61:7	double portion, instead of D you shall rejoice in
Jer	3:25	shame, and let our D cover us; for we
	14:21	name's sake; do not D thy glorious throne; remember
	20:11	Their eternal D will never be forgotten.
	51:51	we have heard reproach; D has covered our face,
Lam	2:2	to the ground in D the kingdom and its
Bar	6:40	even the Chaldeans themselves D them;
1Mac	1:40	Her D now grew as great as her glory;
Jn	8:49	my Father, and you D me.
Acts	5:41	counted worthy to suffer D for the name.
Rom	2:23	the law, do you D God by breaking the
1Cor	15:43	It is sown in D, it is raised in
2Cor	6:8	left; in honor and D, in ill repute and

DISHONORABLE

Rom	1:26	gave them up to D passions.

DISHONORED (3)

Wis	4:18	this they will become D corpses, and an outrage
Sir	10:30	And a man D in wealth, how much more
Jas	2:6	But you have D the poor man.

DISHONORING (2)

Sir	3:10	not glorify yourself by D your father, for your
Rom	1:24	to impurity, to the D of their bodies among

DISHONORS (4)

Deut	27:16	"'Cursed be he who D his father or his
Sir	10:28	honor the man that D his own life?
1Cor	11:4	with his head covered D his head,
	11:5	with her head unveiled D her head—it is

DISINHERIT

Num	14:12	with the pestilence and D them, and I will

DISLIKED (6)

Deut	21:15	loved and the other D, and they have borne
	21:15	the loved and the D, and if the first-born
	21:15	is hers that is D,
	21:16	the son of the D, who is the first-born,
	21:17	the son of the D, by giving him a
Prov	14:20	The poor is D even by his neighbor, but

DISLIKES (2)

Deut	24:3	and the latter husband D her and writes her
Sir	21:15	reveler hears it, he D it and casts it

DISLOYAL

2Mac	14:26	him that Nicanor was D to the government, for

DISMAL (2)

Wis	17:4	out around them, and D phantoms with gloomy faces
Mt	6:16	fast, do not look D, like the hypocrites, for

DISMAY (7)

Prov	21:15	to the righteous, but D to evildoers.
Jer	1:17	by them, lest I D you before them.
	8:21	wounded, I mourn, and D has taken hold on
Ezek	4:16	they shall drink water by measure and in D
	4:17	at one another in D, and waste away under
	12:19	and drink water in D, because their land will
Nah	2:6	the palace is in D;

DISMAYED (55)

Gen	42:35	father saw their bundles of money, they were D
	45:3	him, for they were D at his presence.
Ex	15:15	the chiefs of Edom D; the leaders of Moab,
Deut	1:21	not fear or be D
	31:8	or forsake you; do not fear or be D
Josh	1:9	not frightened, neither be D; for the LORD your
	8:1	not fear or be D; take all the fighting
	10:25	not be afraid or D; be strong and of
Judg	20:41	men of Benjamin were D, for they saw that
1Sam	17:11	the Philistine, they were D and greatly afraid.
2Sam	4:1	Hebron, his courage failed, and all Israel was D
2Kgs	19:26	shorn of strength, are D and confounded, and have
1Chr	22:13	Fear not; be not D
	28:20	Fear not, be not D; for the LORD God,
2Chr	20:15	not, and be not D at this great multitude;
	20:17	not, and be not D; tomorrow go out against
	32:7	not be afraid or D before the king of
Jud	14:19	tunics and were greatly D, and their loud cries
Job	4:5	are impatient; it touches you, and you are D
	21:6	of it I am D, and shuddering seizes my
	39:22	fear, and is not D; he does not turn
Ps	30:7	mountain; thou didst hide thy face, I was D
	83:17	put to shame and D for ever; let them
	104:29	thy face, they are D; when thou takest away
Eccl	8:2	sacred oath be not D;
Is	8:9	you peoples, and be D; give ear, all you
	8:9	gird yourselves and be D; gird yourselves and be
	8:9	and be dismayed; gird yourselves and be D
	13:8	man's heart will melt, and they will be D
	20:5	Then they shall be D and confounded because of

21:3 cannot hear, I am D so that I cannot
37:27 shorn of strength, are D and confounded, and have
41:10 with you, be not D, for I am your
41:23 that we may be D and terrified.
51:7 men, and be not D at their revilings.
Jer 1:17 Do not be D by them, lest I dismay
8:9 shame, they shall be D and taken; lo, they
10:2 the nations, nor be D at the signs of
10:2 because the nations are D at them,
14:4 the ground which is D, since there is no
17:18 shame; let them be D, but let me not
17:18 let me not be D; bring upon them the
23:4 no more, nor be D, neither shall any be
30:10 the LORD, nor be D, O Israel; for lo,
46:5 They are D and have turned backward.
46:27 my servant, nor be D, O Israel; for lo,
50:2 taken, Bel is put to shame, Merodach is D
50:2 shame, her idols are D
Ezek 2:6 their words, nor be D at their looks, for
3:9 them not, nor be D at their looks, for
26:18 in the sea are D at your passing.'
Dan 4:19 name was Belteshazzar, was D for a moment, and
Joel 1:17 for them; even the flocks of sheep are D
Obad 1:9 mighty men shall be D, O Teman, so that
2Mac 13:23 in Antioch; he was D, called in the Jews,

DISMEMBERED

2Mac 1:16 and his men, and D them and cut off

DISMISS (3)

2Chr 23:8 the priest did not D the divisions.
1Mac 12:45 D them now to their homes and choose for
2Mac 7:9 "You accursed wretch, you D us from this present

DISMISSED (10)

Judg 2:6 When Joshua D the people, the people of Israel
Jud 7:33 Then he D the people to their various posts,
Dan 13:36 the garden doors, and D the maids.
1Mac 11:38 opposition to him, he D all his troops, each
2Mac 14:23 of the way, but D the flocks of people
Mt 14:22 other side, while he D the crowds.
14:23 And after he had D the crowds, he went
Mk 6:45 to Beth-saida, while he D the crowd.
Acts 19:41 had said this, he D the assembly.
23:22 So the tribune D the young man, charging him,

DISOBEDIENCE (9)

Rom 5:19 as by one man's D many were made sinners,
11:30 mercy because of their D,
11:32 consigned all men to D, that he may have
2Cor 10:6 ready to punish every D, when your obedience is
Eph 2:2 is now at work in the sons of D
5:6 wrath of God comes upon the sons of D
Heb 2:2 and every transgression or D received a just
4:6 to enter because of D,
4:11 no one fall by the same sort of D

DISOBEDIENT (16)

Neh 9:26 "Nevertheless they were D and rebelled against thee
and
Sir 16:6 kindled, and in a D nation wrath was kindled.
47:21 was divided and a D kingdom arose out of
Bar 1:19 today, we have been D to the Lord our
Lk 1:17 the children, and the D to the wisdom of
Acts 26:19 Agrippa, I was not D to the heavenly vision,
Rom 1:30 boastful, inventors of evil, D to parents,
10:21 my hands to a D and contrary people."
11:30 as you were once D to God but now
11:31 they have now been D in order that by
1Tim 1:9 for the lawless and D, for the ungodly and
2Tim 3:2 money, proud, arrogant, abusive, D to their parents,
Tit 1:15 deeds; they are detestable, D, unfit for any good
3:3 ourselves were once foolish, D, led astray, slaves to
Heb 3:18 enter his rest, but to those who were D
11:31 with those who were D, because she had given

DISOBEY (6)

Prov 24:21 king, and do not D either of them;
Sir 1:25 Do not D the fear of the Lord; do
2:15 the Lord will not D his words, and those
16:26 and they will never D his word.
30:12 he become stubborn and D you, and you have
1Pet 2:8 they stumble because they D the word, as they

DISOBEYED (7)

1Kgs 13:21 LORD, 'Because you have D the word of the
13:26 man of God, who D the word of the
Tob 3:4 For they D thy commandments, and thou gavest us
Jud 2:6 west country, because they D my orders.
Sir 23:23 of all, she has D the law of the
Bar 1:18 the Lord, and have D him, and have not
Lk 15:29 you, and I never D your command; yet you

DISOBEYING

Jer 42:13 remain in this land,' D the voice of the

DISOBEYS (2)

Josh 1:18 against your commandment and D your words,
1 Jn 2:4 but D his commandments is a liar, and the

DISORDER (5)

Wis 14:26 of souls, sex perversion, D in marriage, adultery, and
2Mac 9:1 Antiochus had retreated in D from the region of
10:30 they were thrown into D and cut to pieces.
2Cor 12:20 selfishness, slander, gossip, conceit and D
Jas 3:16 exist, there will be D and every vile practice.

DISORDERS

Wis 17:8 off the fears and D of a sick soul

DISOWNED (3)

Deut 33:9 regard them not'; he D his brothers, and ignored
Lam 2:7 has scorned his altar, D his sanctuary; he has
1Tim 5:8 own family, he has D the faith and is

DISPATCH (2)

Ezek 23:47 shall stone them and D them with their swords;
Rom 9:28 his sentence upon the earth with rigor and D

DISPATCHED (2)

2Kgs 6:32 Now the king had D a man from his
2Mac 4:38 Onias, and there he D the bloodthirsty fellow.

DISPENSATION (4)

2Cor 3:7 Now if the D of death, carved in letters
3:8 was, will not the D of the Spirit be
3:9 D of condemnation, the D of righteousness must far

DISPENSES

Prov 15:2 tongue of the wise D knowledge, but the mouths

DISPERSE (8)

1Sam 14:34 And Saul said, D yourselves among the people, and
Ps 106:27 the wilderness, and would D their descendants
Ezek 12:15 the LORD, when I D them among the nations
20:23 among the nations and D them through the countries,
22:15 among the nations and D you through the countries,
29:12 among the nations, and D them among the countries.
30:23 among the nations, and D them throughout the lands.
30:26 among the nations and D them throughout the

DISPERSED (10)

2Sam 20:22 the trumpet, and they D from the city, every
Neh 1:9 do them, though your D be under the farthest
Tob 3:4 all the nations among which we have been D
Esth 3:8 people scattered abroad and D among the peoples in
Wis 5:14 a storm; it is D like smoke before the
Is 11:12 Israel, and gather the D of Judah from the
Ezek 36:19 nations, and they were D through the countries; in
Zeph 3:10 the daughter of my D ones, shall bring my
1Mac 10:83 and the cavalry was D in the plain.
Acts 5:36 who followed him were D and came to nothing.

DISPERSION (4)

Jer 25:34 of your slaughter and D have come, and you
Jn 7:35 to go to the D among the Greeks and
Jas 1:1 twelve tribes in the D: Greeting.
1Pet 1:1 the Exiles of the D in Pontus, Galatia, Cappadocia,

DISPLAY (4)

Sir 7:5 before the Lord, nor D your wisdom before the
10:25 Do not make a D of your wisdom when
32:4 out talk; do not D your cleverness out of
1Tim 1:16 foremost, Jesus Christ might D his perfect patience

DISPLAYED

1Mac 7:47 and brought them and D them just outside
Jerusalem.

DISPLEASE (2)

1Sam 29:7 that you may not D the lords of the
1Thes 2:15 drove us out, and D God and oppose all

DISPLEASED (14)
Gen 21:12 to Abraham, "Be not D because of the lad
48:17 head of Ephraim, it D him; and he took
Num 11:10 of the LORD blazed hotly, and Moses was D
1Sam 8:6 But the thing D Samuel when they said, "Give
18:8 angry, and this saying D him; he said, "They
2Sam 11:27 that David had done D the LORD.
1Kgs 1:6 never at any time D him by asking, "Why
1Chr 21:7 But God was D with this thing, and he
Neh 2:10 Ammonite, heard this, it D them greatly that some
Prov 24:18 see it, and be D, and turn away his
Is 59:15 saw it, and it D him that there was
Jon 4:1 But it D Jonah exceedingly, and he was angry.
2Mac 4:35 nations, were grieved and D at the unjust murder
14:27 stating that he was D with the covenant and

DISPLEASING (2)
Gen 21:11 the thing was very D to Abraham on account
38:10 what he did was D in the sight of

DISPLEASURE (2)
Num 14:34 you shall know my D
Deut 9:19 the anger and hot D which the LORD bore

DISPOSAL
Acts 5:4 it was sold, was it not at your D

DISPOSED (3)
2Mac 5:25 pretended to be peaceably D and waited until the
1Cor 10:27 dinner and you are D to go, eat whatever
11:16 If any one is D to be contentious, we

DISPOSITION (3)
Jud 8:29 understanding, for your heart's D is right.
Sir 20:25 The D of a liar brings disgrace, and his
2Mac 14:5 was asked about the D and intentions of the

DISPOSSESS (10)
Deut 7:17 I; how can I D them?'
9:1 to go in to D nations greater and mightier
11:23 you, and you will D nations greater and mightier
12:2 nations whom you shall D served their gods, upon
12:29 you go in to D, and you dispossess them
12:29 to dispossess, and you D them and dwell in
18:14 you are about to D, give heed to soothsayers
19:1 gives you, and you D them and dwell in
31:3 so that you shall D them; and Joshua will
Jer 49:2 fire; then Israel shall D those who dispossessed him,

DISPOSSESSED (13)
Num 21:32 took its villages, and D the Amorites that were
24:18 Edom shall be D, Seir also, his enemies, shall
24:18 his enemies, shall be D, while Israel does valiantly.
32:39 and took it, and D the Amorites who were
Deut 2:12 the sons of Esau D them, and destroyed them
2:21 before them; and they D them, and settled in
2:22 before them, and they D them, and settled in
Judg 11:23 the God of Israel, D the Amorites from before
11:24 LORD our God has D before us, we will
Jer 49:1 Why then has Milcom D Gad, and his people
49:2 shall dispossess those who D him, says the LORD.
Ezek 46:18 my people shall be D of his property."
Acts 7:45 with Joshua when they D the nations which God

DISPUTE (8)
Ex 18:16 when they have a D, they come to me
Deut 19:17 both parties to the D shall appear before the
21:5 by their word every D and every assault shall
25:1 "If there is a D between men, and they
Eccl 6:10 is not able to D with one stronger than
Lk 22:24 A D also arose among them, which of them
Acts 25:19 had certain points of D with him about their
Heb 7:7 It is beyond D that the inferior is blessed

DISPUTED (5)
2Chr 19:8 LORD and to decide D cases.
Jn 6:52 The Jews then D among themselves, saying, "How
Acts 6:9 and Asia, arose and D with Stephen.
9:29 And he spoke and D against the Hellenists; but
Jude 1:9 contending with the devil, D about the body of

DISPUTES (4)
Prov 18:18 puts an end to D and decides between powerful
Rom 14:1 him, but not for D over opinions.
1Tim 6:4 for controversy and for D about words, which
Heb 6:16 and in all their D an oath is final

DISPUTING (3)
Mk 12:28 up and heard them D with one another, and
Acts 24:11 did not find me D with any one or
2Tim 2:14 the Lord to avoid D about words, which does

DISQUALIFIED
1Cor 9:27 after preaching to others I myself should be D

DISQUALIFY
Col 2:18 Let no one D you, insisting on self-abasement and

DISQUIETED (3)
Ps 42:5 and why are you D within me?
42:11 and why are you D within me?
43:5 and why are you D within me?

DISREGARD (5)
Jud 11:10 and master, do not D what he said, but
Esth 13:4 every nation and continually D the ordinances of the
Sir 8:9 Do not D the discourse of the aged, for
31:22 son, and do not D me, and in the
Tit 2:15 Let no one D you.

DISREGARDED (4)
Jud 1:11 in the whole region D the orders of Nebuchadnezzar
Wis 3:10 their reasoning deserves, who D the righteous man
Is 40:27 and my right is D by my God"?
Ezek 22:26 clean, and they have D my sabbaths, so that

DISREGARDING
2Mac 5:17 that therefore he was D the holy place.

DISREGARDS (4)
Sir 14:8 averts his face and D people.
23:11 him, and if he D it, he sins doubly;
1Thes 4:8 Therefore whoever D this, D not man but God,

DISREPUTABLE
Job 30:8 A senseless, a D brood, they have been whipped

DISREPUTE (2)
Acts 19:27 ours may come into D but also that the
1Cor 4:10 You are held in honor, but we in D

DISRESPECTFUL
1Tim 6:2 masters must not be D on the ground that

DISSEMBLERS
Ps 26:4 do I consort with D;

DISSEMBLES
Prov 26:24 He who hates, D with his lips and harbors

DISSENSION (6)
1Mac 3:29 small because of the D and disaster which he
Acts 15:2 Barnabas had no small D and debate with them,
23:7 had said this, a D arose between the Pharisees
23:10 And when the D became violent, the tribune, afraid
Gal 5:20 strife, jealousy, anger, selfishness, D, party spirit,
1Tim 6:4 words, which produce envy, D, slander, base

DISSENSIONS (3)
Rom 16:17 of those who create D and difficulties, in opposition
1Cor 1:10 that there be no D among you, but that
Tit 3:9 avoid stupid controversies, genealogies, D, and

DISSIPATION (2)
Lk 21:34 be weighed down with D and drunkenness and cares
2Pet 2:13 blemishes, reveling in their D, carousing with you.

DISSOLVE
Wis 2:3 and the spirit will D like empty air.

DISSOLVED (3)
2Pet 3:10 the elements will be D with fire, and the
3:11 are thus to be D, what sort of persons
3:12 will be kindled and D, and the elements will

DISSOLVES
Ps 58:8 like the snail which D into slime, like the

DISSUADE
1Mac 9:9 But they tried to D him, saying, "We are

DISTAFF
Prov 31:19 her hands to the D, and her hands hold

DISTANCE (23)

Gen 21:16 way off, about the D of a bowshot; for
30:36 and he set a D of three days' journey
35:16 they were still some D from Ephrath, Rachel
44:4 gone but a short D from the city, Joseph
48:7 there was still some D to go to Ephrath;
Ex 2:4 sister stood at a D, to know what would
Deut 21:2 they shall measure the D to the cities which
Josh 3:4 you and it, a D of about two thousand
2Kgs 2:7 and stood at some D from them, as they
5:19 from him a short D,
Wis 14:17 they lived at a D, they imagined their appearance
Sir 13:10 not remain at a D, lest you be forgotten.
Ezek 40:19 Then he measured the D from the inner front
2Mac 8:25 pursuing them for some D, they were obliged to
10:27 and advanced a considerable D from the city; and
Mt 8:30 was feeding at some D from them.
26:58 followed him at a D, as far as the
Mk 11:13 And seeing in the D a fig tree in
14:54 followed him at a D, right into the courtyard
Lk 15:20 was yet at a D, his father saw him
17:12 who stood at a D
22:52 Peter followed at a D;
23:48 Galilee stood at a D and saw these things.

DISTANT (6)

Is 13:5 They come from a D land, from the end
Jer 4:16 "Besiegers come from a D land; they shout against
6:20 sweet cane from a D land?
1Mac 8:4 the place was far D from them.
2Mac 12:9 the light was seen in Jerusalem, thirty miles D
Mt 14:24 time was many furlongs D from the land, beaten

DISTIL (2)

Deut 32:2 the rain, my speech D as the dew, as
Song 4:11 Your lips D nectar, my bride; honey and milk

DISTILLING

Song 5:13 His lips are lilies, D liquid myrrh.

DISTILS

Job 36:27 drops of water, he D his mist in rain

DISTINCT (3)

Ex 33:16 so that we are D, I and thy people,
Wis 7:22 mobile, clear, unpolluted, D, invulnerable, loving
1Cor 14:7 harp, do not give D notes, how will any

DISTINCTION (11)

Ex 9:4 LORD will make a D between the cattle of
11:7 the LORD makes a D between the Egyptians and
Lev 11:47 earth, to make a D between the unclean and
20:25 shall therefore make a D between the clean beast
Sir 45:12 a D to be prized, the work of an
Ezek 22:26 they have made no D between the holy and
2Mac 6:23 he had reached with D and his excellent life
Acts 11:12 told me to go with them, making no D
15:9 and he made no D between us and them,
Rom 3:22 For there is no D;
10:12 For there is no D between Jew and Greek;

DISTINCTIONS

Jas 2:4 have you not made D among yourselves, and become

DISTINCTLY

Is 32:4 tongue of the stammerers will speak readily and D

DISTINGUISH (6)

Lev 10:10 You are to D between the holy and the
Ezra 3:13 the people could not D the sound of the
Ezek 44:23 show them how to D between the unclean and
Mal 3:18 once more you shall D between the righteous and
1Cor 12:10 another the ability to D between spirits, to another
Heb 5:14 trained by practice to D good from evil.

DISTINGUISHED (7)

Esth 13:3 sound judgment, and is D for his unchanging good
Song 5:10 all radiant and ruddy, D among ten thousand.
Sir 33:8 Lord's decision they were D, and he appointed the
33:11 his knowledge the Lord D them and appointed their
Dan 6:3 Then this Daniel became D above all the other
1Mac 3:32 He left Lysias, a D man of royal lineage,
2Mac 15:13 likewise a man appeared, D by his gray hair

DISTORT

Sir 19:22 there are people who D kindness to gain a

DISTRACTED (2)

Sir 41:2 strength, very old and D over everything; to one
Lk 10:40 But Martha was D with much serving; and she

DISTRACTIONS

Sir 41:1 to a man without D, who is prosperous in

DISTRAUGHT

Ps 55:2 I am D

DISTRESS (88)

Gen 35:3 the day of my D and has been with
42:21 that we saw the D of his soul, when
42:21 listen; therefore is this D come upon us."
Deut 28:53 siege and in the D with which your enemies
28:53 which your enemies shall D you.
28:55 siege and in the D with which your enemy
28:55 which your enemy shall D you in all your
28:57 siege and in the D with which your enemy
28:57 which your enemy shall D you in your towns.
Judg 10:14 them deliver you in the time of your D
1Sam 2:32 Then in D you will look with envious eye
22:2 one who was in D, and every one who
28:15 "I am in great D; for the Philistines are
2Sam 22:7 "In my D I called upon the LORD; to
24:14 "I am in great D; let us fall into
2Kgs 4:27 she is in bitter D; and the LORD has
19:3 is a day of D, of rebuke, and of
1Chr 21:13 "I am in great D; let me fall into
2Chr 15:4 but when in their D they turned to the
15:6 for God troubled them with every sort of D
28:22 the time of his D he became yet more
33:12 when he was in D he entreated the favor
Neh 9:37 at their pleasure, and we are in great D
Tob 3:6 be released from my D to go to the
Esth 11:8 and gloom, tribulation and D, affliction and great
14:2 on the garments of D and mourning, and instead
Job 15:24 ready at his hand; D and anguish terrify him;
36:16 allured you out of D into a broad place
36:19 to keep you from D, or all the force
Ps 4:1 hast given me room when I was in D
18:6 In my D I called upon the LORD; to
31:9 for I am in D; my eye is wasted
32:6 at a time of D, in the rush of
39:2 to no avail; my D grew worse,
59:16 and a refuge in the day of my D
69:17 for I am in D, make haste to answer
78:49 anger, wrath, indignation, and D, a company of
81:7 In D you called, and I delivered you; I
102:2 face from me in the day of my D
106:44 Nevertheless he regarded their D, when he heard
107:6 delivered them from their D;
107:13 delivered them from their D;
107:19 delivered them from their D;
107:28 delivered them from their D;
116:3 on me; I suffered D and anguish.
118:5 Out of my D I called on the LORD;
120:1 In my D I cry to the LORD, that
144:14 be no cry of D in our streets!
Prov 1:27 like a whirlwind, when D and anguish come upon
31:6 to those in bitter D;
Sir 31:20 The D of sleeplessness and of nausea and colic
Is 5:30 land, behold, darkness and D; and the light is
8:22 the earth, but behold, D and darkness, the gloom
25:4 the needy in his D, a shelter from the
26:16 O LORD, in D they sought thee, they poured
29:2 Yet I will D Ariel, and there shall be
29:7 and her stronghold and D her, shall be like
37:3 is a day of D, of rebuke, and of
65:19 the sound of weeping and the cry of D
Jer 10:18 and I will bring D on them, that they
15:11 time of trouble and in the time of D
19:9 siege and in the D, with which their enemies
30:7 is a time of D for Jacob; yet he
Lam 1:3 all overtaken her in the midst of her D
1:20 for I am in D, my soul is in
Bar 6:37 they cannot rescue a man who is in D
Dan 13:10 each other of their D,
Hos 5:15 face, and in their D they seek me, saying,
Obad 1:12 should not have boasted in the day of D
1:14 delivered up his survivors in the day of D
Jon 2:2 LORD, out of my D, and he answered me;
Zeph 1:15 day, a day of D and anguish, a day
1:17 I will bring D on men, so that they
1Mac 2:53 the time of his D kept the commandment, and
5:16 brethren who were in D and were being attacked

6:11 to myself, 'To what D I have come!
9:27 Thus there was great D in Israel, such as
13:5 in any time of D, for I am not
2Mac 1:7 you, in the critical D which came upon us
3:14 There was no little D throughout the whole city.
15:19 were in no little D, being anxious over the
Mt 8:6 servant is lying paralyzed at home, in terrible D
Lk 21:23 For great D shall be upon the earth and
21:25 and upon the earth D of nations in perplexity
Rom 2:9 will be tribulation and D for every human being
8:35 Shall tribulation, or D, or persecution, or famine, or
1Cor 7:26 view of the present D it is well for
1Thes 3:7 brethren, in all our D and affliction we have

DISTRESSED (23)

Gen 32:7 was greatly afraid and D; and he divided the
45:5 now do not be D, or angry with yourselves,
Judg 10:9 house of Ephraim; so that Israel was sorely D
1Sam 1:10 She was deeply D and prayed to the LORD,
14:24 men of Israel were D that day; for Saul
30:6 And David was greatly D; for the people spoke
2Sam 1:26 I am D for you, my brother Jonathan; very
Tob 9:4 if I delay long he will be greatly D
10:3 And he was greatly D
10:5 said, "Am I not D, my child, that I
13:10 within you who are D, to all generations for
Esth 4:4 the queen was deeply D; she sent garments to
Wis 11:11 present, they were equally D,
17:11 by its own testimony; D by conscience, it has
Is 8:21 through the land, greatly D and hungry; and when
Bar 2:18 person that is greatly D, that goes about bent
Dan 6:14 these words, was much D, and set his mind
1Mac 9:68 They D him greatly, for his plan and his
Mt 17:22 And they were greatly D
18:30 place, they were greatly D, and they went and
Mk 14:33 began to be greatly D and troubled.
Phil 2:26 all, and has been D because you heard that
2Pet 2:7 righteous Lot, greatly D by the licentiousness

DISTRESSES (2)

1Sam 10:19 your calamities and your D; and you have said,
Ps 25:17 my heart, and bring me out of my D

DISTRIBUTE (7)

2Chr 31:15 of the priests, to D the portions to their
31:19 designated by name to D portions to every male
35:12 offerings that they might D them according to the
Neh 13:13 their duty was to D to their brethren.
Sir 33:23 the hour of death, D your inheritance.
1Mac 3:36 all their territory, and D their land.
Lk 18:22 that you have and D to the poor, and

DISTRIBUTED (16)

Josh 13:32 the inheritances which Moses D in the plains of
14:1 the people of Israel D to them.
19:51 the people of Israel D by lot at Shiloh
2Sam 6:19 LORD of hosts, and D among all the people,
1Chr 16:3 of the LORD, and D to all Israel, both
2Chr 11:23 he dealt wisely, and D some of his sons
Jud 16:24 Before she died she D her property to all
Job 38:24 where the light is D, or where the east
Ps 112:9 He has D freely, he has given to the
Sir 44:24 determined his portions, and D them among twelve
1Mac 6:35 And they D the beasts among the phalanxes; with
2Mac 8:28 widows and orphans, and D the rest among
Jn 6:11 had given thanks, he D them to those who
Acts 2:3 tongues as of fire, D and resting on each
2:45 possessions and goods and D them to all, as
Heb 2:4 of the Holy Spirit D according to his own

DISTRIBUTES

Job 21:17 That God D pains in his anger?

DISTRIBUTING

Josh 19:49 When they had finished D the several territories of

DISTRIBUTION (2)

Acts 4:35 the apostles' feet; and D was made to each
6:1 because their widows were neglected in the daily D

DISTRICT (23)

Neh 3:9 ruler of half the D of Jerusalem, repaired.
3:12 ruler of half the D of Jerusalem, repaired, he
3:14 Rechab, ruler of the D of Beth-haccherem, repaired
3:15 Colhozeh, ruler of the D of Mizpah, repaired the
3:16 ruler of half the D of Bethzur, repaired to
3:17 ruler of half the D of Keilah, repaired for
3:17 half the district of Keilah, repaired for his D
3:18 ruler of half the D of Keilah;
Jud 4:4 they sent to every D of Samaria, and to
5:5 this people that dwells in the nearby mountain D
Ezek 45:1 land as a holy D, twenty-five thousand cubits long
45:3 And in the holy D you shall measure off
45:6 apart as the holy D you shall assign for
45:7 sides of the holy D and the property of
45:7 city, alongside the holy D and the property of
Mt 2:22 he withdrew to the D of Galilee.
9:26 the report of this went through all that D
9:31 away and spread his fame through all that D
15:21 and withdrew to the D of Tyre and Sidon.
16:13 Jesus came into the D of Caesarea Philippi, he
Mk 8:10 and went to the D of Dalmanutha.
Acts 13:50 and Barnabas, and drove them out of their D
16:12 leading city of the D of Macedonia, and a

DISTRICTS (10)

1Kgs 20:14 By the servants of the governors of the D
20:15 the governors of the D, and they were two
20:17 the governors of the D went out first.
20:19 the governors of the D, and the army which
2Chr 11:23 sons through all the D of Judah and Benjamin,
1Mac 10:30 or from the three D added to it from
10:38 "As for the three D that have been added
11:28 Judea and the three D of Samaria from tribute,
11:34 Judea and the three D of Aphairema and Lydda
11:57 you over the four D and make you one

DISTRUST (2)

Wis 1:2 those who do not D him.
Rom 4:20 No D made him waver concerning the promise of

DISTRUSTFUL

2Mac 8:13 who were cowardly and D of God's justice ran

DISTURB (3)

Song 6:5 from me, for they D me– Your hair
Sir 28:9 a sinful man will D friends and inject enmity
Nah 2:11 prey, where his cubs were, with none to D

DISTURBANCE (3)

Jud 6:1 When the D made by the men outside the
2Mac 3:30 full of fear and D, was filled with joy
11:25 also be free from D, our decision is that

DISTURBANCES

2Chr 15:5 came in, for great D afflicted all the inhabitants

DISTURBED (5)

1Sam 28:15 Saul, "Why have you D me by bringing me
2Sam 7:10 own place, and be D no more; and violent
1Chr 17:9 own place, and be D no more; and violent
Wis 18:19 for the dreams which D them forewarned them of
Acts 17:8 the city authorities were D when they heard this.

DISTURBING (2)

Wis 17:9 For even if nothing D frightened them, yet, scared
Acts 16:20 Jews and they are D our city.

DISUSE

Esth 9:28 should never fall into D among the Jews, nor

DIVERSE (4)

Prov 20:10 D weights and diverse measures are both alike an
20:10 Diverse weights and D measures are both alike an
20:23 D weights are an abomination to the LORD, and
Heb 13:9 be led away by D and strange teachings; for

DIVERSIONS

Dan 6:18 the night fasting; no D were brought to him,

DIVIDE (40)

Gen 49:7 I will D them in Jacob and scatter them
Ex 14:16 over the sea and D it, that the people
15:9 will overtake, I will D the spoil, my desire
21:35 the live ox and D the price of it;
21:35 it; and the dead beast also they shall D
Lev 1:17 wings, but shall not D it asunder.
Num 31:27 of the congregation; and D the booty into two
34:17 the men who shall D the land to you
34:18 of every tribe, to D the land for inheritance.
34:29 the LORD commanded to D the inheritance for the
Deut 19:3 prepare the roads, and D into three parts the

Josh 13:7 Now therefore D this land for an inheritance to
18:5 They shall D it into seven portions, Judah continuing
22:8 and with much clothing; D the spoil of your
2Sam 19:29 you and Ziba shall D the land."
1Kgs 3:25 And the king said, D the living child in
3:26 neither mine nor yours; D it."
Neh 9:11 And thou didst D the sea before them, so
Job 27:17 and the innocent will D the silver.
41:6 Will they D him up among the merchants?
Ps 22:18 gloat over me; they D my garments among them,
60:6 "With exultation I will D up Shechem and portion
68:12 The women at home D the spoil,
74:13 Thou didst D the sea by thy might; thou
108:7 "With exultation I will D up Shechem, and portion
Prov 16:19 the poor than to D the spoil with the
Is 9:3 men rejoice when they D the spoil.
18:2 mighty and conquering, whose land the rivers D
18:7 whose land the rivers D, to Mount Zion, the
47:13 save you, those who D the heavens, who gaze
53:12 Therefore I will D him a portion with the
53:12 great, and he shall D the spoil with the
Ezek 5:1 balances for weighing, and D the hair.
47:13 by which you shall D the land for inheritance
47:14 And you shall D it equally; I swore to
47:21 "So you shall D this land among you according
Dan 11:39 over many and shall D the land for a
Lk 12:13 "Teacher, bid my brother D the inheritance with
22:17 said, "Take this, and D it among yourselves;
23:33 they cast lots to D his garments.

DIVIDED (56)

Gen 2:10 garden, and there it D and became four rivers.
10:25 days the earth was D, and his brother's name
14:15 And he D his forces against them by night,
25:23 of you, shall be D; the one shall be
32:7 and distressed; and he D the people that were
33:1 So he D the children among Leah and Rachel
Ex 14:21 the sea dry land, and the waters were D
Num 26:53 the land shall be D for inheritance according to
26:55 the land shall be D by lot; according to
26:56 Their inheritance shall be D according to lot
Judg 7:16 And he D the three hundred men into three
9:43 took his men and D them into three companies,
19:29 of his concubine he D her, limb by limb,
2Sam 1:23 death they were not D; they were swifter than
1Kgs 16:21 people of Israel were D into two parts; half
18:6 So they D the land between them to pass
1Chr 1:19 days the earth was D, and the name of
Jud 9:4 their booty to be D among thy beloved sons,
Ps 78:13 He D the sea and let them pass through
136:13 ever; to him who D the Red Sea in
Wis 5:12 target, the air, thus D, comes together at once,
Sir 1:25 approach him with a D mind.
14:15 by toil to be D by lot?
47:21 that the sovereignty was D and a disobedient
Is 33:23 in abundance will be D; even the lame will
63:12 hand of Moses, who D the waters before them
Ezek 37:22 nations, and no longer D into two kingdoms.
Dan 2:41 it shall be a D kingdom; but some of
5:28 PERES, your kingdom is D and given to the
11:4 shall be broken and D toward the four winds
Joel 3:2 the nations, and have D up my land,
Zech 14:1 from you will be D in the midst of
1Mac 1:6 him from youth, and D his kingdom among them
9:11 The cavalry was D into two companies, and the
16:7 Then he D the army and placed the horsemen
2Mac 8:21 their country; then he D his army into four
8:30 high strongholds, and they D very much plunder,
Mt 12:25 to them, "Every kingdom D against itself is laid
12:25 no city or house D against itself will stand;
12:26 out Satan, he is D against himself; how then
27:35 had crucified him, they D his garments among them
Mk 3:24 If a kingdom is D against itself, that kingdom
3:25 if a house is D against itself, that house
3:26 against himself and is D, he cannot stand, but
6:41 the people; and he D the two fish among
15:24 they crucified him, and D his garments among them,
Lk 11:17 to them, "Every kingdom D against itself is laid
11:17 laid waste, and a D household falls.
11:18 if Satan also is D against himself, how will
12:52 there will be five D, three against two and
12:53 three; they will be D, father against son and
15:12 to me.' And he D his living between them.
Acts 14:4 of the city were D; some sided with the
23:7 the Sadducees; and the assembly was D
1Cor 1:13 Is Christ D
7:34 to please his wife, and his interests are D

DIVIDER

Lk 12:14 me a judge or D over you?"

DIVIDES (2)

Mic 2:4 Among our captors he D our fields."
Lk 11:22 which he trusted, and D his spoil.

DIVIDING (6)

Gen 49:27 prey, and at even D the spoil."
Josh 19:51 So they finished D the land.
Judg 5:30 they not finding and D the spoil?–A maiden
Sir 42:3 traveling companions, and of D the inheritance of
Ezek 42:12 opposite them was a D wall.
Eph 2:14 has broken down the D wall of hostility,

DIVINATION (14)

Gen 30:27 I have learned by D that the LORD has
Num 22:7 with the fees for D in their hand; and
23:23 enchantment against Jacob, no D against Israel; now
Deut 18:10 any one who practices D, a soothsayer, or an
1Sam 15:23 as the sin of D, and stubbornness is as
2Kgs 17:17 as offerings, and used D and sorcery, and sold
Jer 14:14 a lying vision, worthless D, and the deceit of
Ezek 12:24 false vision or flattering D within the house of
13:7 and uttered a lying D, whenever you have said,
13:23 delusive visions nor practice D; I will deliver my
21:21 two ways, to use D; he shakes the arrows,
21:23 seem like a false D; they have sworn solemn
Mic 3:6 you, without vision, and darkness to you, without D
Acts 16:16 had a spirit of D and brought her owners

DIVINATIONS (2)

Sir 34:5 D and omens and dreams are folly, and like
Ezek 13:9 and who give lying D; they shall not be

DIVINE (17)

Gen 44:15 that such a man as I can indeed D
1Sam 28:8 And he said, D for me by a spirit,
Ps 45:6 Your D throne endures for ever and ever.
82:1 his place in the D council; in the midst
Wis 18:9 accord agreed to the D law, that the saints
Ezek 21:29 false visions, while they D lies for you–to
Mic 3:11 for hire, its prophets D for money; yet they
2Mac 3:29 speechless because of the D intervention and
4:17 show irreverence to the D laws – a
Rom 3:25 righteousness, because in his D forbearance he had
2Cor 10:4 not worldly but have D power to destroy strongholds.
11:2 I feel a D jealousy for you, for I
Col 1:25 minister according to the D office which was given
1Tim 1:4 speculations rather than the D training that is in
Heb 11:2 men of old received D approval.
2Pet 1:3 His D power has granted to us all things
1:4 become partakers of the D nature.

DIVINED

Ezek 13:6 have spoken falsehood and D a lie; they say,

DIVINER

Is 3:2 and the prophet, the D and the elder,

DIVINERS (10)

Deut 18:14 to soothsayers and to D; but as for you,
Judg 9:37 the direction of the D Oak."
1Sam 6:2 the priests and the D and said, "What shall
Is 2:6 they are full of D from the east and
44:25 and makes fools of D; who turns wise men
Jer 27:9 to your prophets, your D, your dreamers, your
29:8 your prophets and your D who are among you
50:36 A sword upon the D, that they may become
Mic 3:7 be disgraced, and the D put to shame; they
Zech 10:2 utter nonsense, and the D see lies; the dreamers

DIVINES

Gen 44:5 my lord drinks, and by this that he D

DIVINING

Ezek 22:28 seeing false visions and D lies for them, saying,

DIVINITIES

Acts 17:18 a preacher of foreign D –because he preached Jesus

DIVISION (31)

Ex 8:23 I will put a D between my people and
1Chr 27:1 throughout the year, each D numbering twenty-four

27:2 charge of the first D in the first month;
27:2 first month; in his D were twenty-four thousand.
27:4 in charge of the D of the second month;
27:4 second month; in his D were twenty-four thousand.
27:5 as chief; in his D were twenty-four thousand.
27:6 Ammizabad his son was in charge of his D
27:7 after him; in his D were twenty-four thousand.
27:8 the Izrahite; in his D were twenty-four thousand.
27:9 the Tekoite; in his D were twenty-four thousand.
27:10 of Ephraim; in his D were twenty-four thousand.
27:11 the Zerahites; in his D were twenty-four thousand.
27:12 a Benjaminite; in his D were twenty-four thousand.
27:13 the Zerahites; in his D were twenty-four thousand.
27:14 of Ephraim; in his D were twenty-four thousand.
27:15 of Othni-el; in his D were twenty-four thousand.
2Chr 31:2 and of the Levites, D by division, each according
31:2 the Levites, division by D, each according to his
1Mac 4:1 picked cavalry, and this D moved out by night
4:4 in Emmaus while the D was still absent from
2Mac 8:22 each to command a D, putting fifteen hundred men
8:23 then, leading the first D himself, he joined battle
12:22 But when Judas' first D appeared, terror and fear
Lk 1:5 named Zechariah, of the D of Abijah; and he
1:8 before God when his D was on duty,
12:51 tell you, but rather D;
Jn 7:43 So there was a D among the people over
9:16 There was a D among them.
10:19 There was again a D among the Jews because
Heb 4:12 sword, piercing to the D of soul and spirit,

DIVISIONS (32)

Josh 18:6 the land in seven D and bring the description
18:9 by towns in seven D; then they came to
2Kgs 11:7 palace; and the two D of you, which come
1Chr 12:23 the numbers of the D of the armed troops,
23:6 David organized them in D corresponding to the sons
24:1 The D of the sons of Aaron were these.
26:1 As for the D of the gatekeepers: of the
26:12 These D of the gatekeepers, corresponding to their
26:19 These were the D of the gatekeepers among the
27:1 all matters concerning the D that came and went,
28:1 the officers of the D that served the king,
28:13 dedicated gifts; for the D of the priests and
28:21 And behold the D of the priests and the
2Chr 5:11 without regard to their D;
8:14 father, he appointed the D of the priests for
8:14 the gatekeepers in their D for the several gates;
23:8 for Jehoiada the priest did not dismiss the D
26:11 fit for war, in D according to the numbers
31:2 And Hezekiah appointed the D of the priests and
31:15 and young alike, by D,
31:16 their service according to their offices, by their D
31:17 upwards was according to their offices, by their D
35:4 fathers' houses by your D, following the directions of
35:10 the Levites in their D according to the king's
Ezra 6:18 the priests in their D and the Levites in
Neh 11:36 And certain D of the Levites in Judah were
Jud 2:15 the picked troops by D as his lord had
Sir 16:24 and when he made them, he determined their D
2Mac 12:20 arranged his army in D, set men in command
12:20 in command of the D, and hastened after Timothy,
1Cor 11:18 hear that there are D among you; and I
Jude 1:19 these who set up D, worldly people, devoid of

DIVORCE (14)

Deut 24:1 her a bill of D and puts it in
24:3 her a bill of D and puts it in
Is 50:1 your mother's bill of D, with which I put
Jer 3:8 with a decree of D; yet her false sister
Mal 2:16 "For I hate D, says the LORD the God
Mt 5:31 her a certificate of D
19:3 "Is it lawful to D one's wife for any
19:7 give a certificate of D, and to put her
19:8 Moses allowed you to D your wives, but from
Mk 10:2 for a man to D his wife?"
10:4 write a certificate of D, and to put her
1Cor 7:11 the husband should not D his wife.
7:12 him, he should not D her.
7:13 her, she should not D him.

DIVORCED (8)

Lev 21:7 they marry a woman D from her husband; for
21:14 A widow, or one D, or a woman who
22:13 is a widow or D, and has no child,
Num 30:9 widow or of a D woman, anything by which
Ezek 44:22 a widow, or a D woman, but only a
Mt 5:32 and whoever marries a D woman commits adultery.
19:9 he who marries a D woman, commits adultery."
Lk 16:18 who marries a woman D from her husband commits

DIVORCES (7)

Jer 3:1 "If a man D his wife and she goes
Mt 5:31 was also said, 'Whoever D his wife, let him
5:32 that every one who D his wife, except on
19:9 say to you: whoever D his wife, except for
Mk 10:11 said to them, "Whoever D his wife and marries
10:12 her; and if she D her husband and marries
Lk 16:18 "Every one who D his wife and marries another

DIVULGE

Sir 8:18 know what he will D

DIVULGING

Acts 19:18 believers came, confessing and D their practices.

DIZAHAB

Deut 1:1 between Paran and Tophel, Laban, Hazeroth, and D

DO-DAVAHU

2Chr 20:37 Eliezer the son of D of Mareshah prophesied against

DOCTRINE (13)

Job 11:4 For you say, 'My D is pure, and I
Rom 16:17 in opposition to the D which you have been
Eph 4:14 with every wind of D, by the cunning of
1Tim 1:3 to teach any different D,
1:10 is contrary to sound D,
4:6 and of the good D which you have followed.
Tit 1:8 give instruction in sound D and also to confute
2:1 But as for you, teach what befits sound D
2:10 they may adorn the D of God our Savior.
Heb 6:1 us leave the elementary D of Christ and go
2 Jn 1:9 not abide in the D of Christ does not
1:9 who abides in the D has both the Father
1:10 does not bring this D, do not receive him

DOCTRINES (4)

Mt 15:9 worship me, teaching as D the precepts of men.'"
Mk 7:7 worship me, teaching as D the precepts of men.'
Col 2:22 they are used), according to human precepts and D
1Tim 4:1 to deceitful spirits and D of demons,

DOCUMENT (4)

Esth 3:14 A copy of the D was to be issued
Dan 6:8 interdict and sign the D, so that it cannot
6:9 King Darius signed the D and interdict.
6:10 Daniel knew that the D had been signed, he

DOCUMENTS (2)

Ezra 6:1 the archives where the D were stored.
1Mac 13:42 to write in their D and contracts, "In the

DODAI

1Chr 27:4 D the Ahohite was in charge of the division

DODANIM

Gen 10:4 The sons of Javan: Elishah, Tarshish, Kittim, and D

DODO (5)

Judg 10:1 of Puah, son of D, a man of Issachar;
2Sam 23:9 Eleazar the son of D, son of Ahohi.
23:24 Elhanan the son of D of Bethlehem,
1Chr 11:12 Eleazar the son of D, the Ahohite.
11:26 Elhanan the son of D of Bethlehem,

DOE

Prov 5:19 of your youth, a lovely hind, a graceful D

DOEG (5)

1Sam 21:7 LORD; his name was D the Edomite, the chief
22:9 Then answered D the Edomite, who stood by the
22:18 the king said to D, "You turn and fall
22:18 And D the Edomite turned and fell upon the
22:22 on that day, when D the Edomite was there,

DOER (6)

Gen 39:22 there, he was the D of it;
2Sam 23:20 man of Kabzeel, a D of great deeds; he
1Chr 11:22 man of Kabzeel, a D of great deeds; he
Jas 1:22 word and not a D, he is like a
1:24 that forgets but a D that acts, he shall
4:11 you are not a D of the law but

D

DOERS (3)
1Mac 9:23 of Israel; all the D of injustice appeared.
Rom 2:13 before God, but the D of the law who
Jas 1:21 But be D of the word, and not hearers

DOEST (5)
Job 9:12 say to him, 'What D thou?
Ps 86:10 thou art great and D wondrous things, thou alone
119:68 Thou art good and D good; teach me thy
Jer 14:22 on thee, for thou D all these things.
Dan 4:35 say to him, "What D thou?"

D

DOG (19)
Ex 11:7 or beast, not a D shall growl; that you
Deut 23:18 the wages of a D, into the house of
Judg 7:5 his tongue, as a D laps, you shall set
1Sam 17:43 David, "Am I a D, that you come to
24:14 After a dead D
2Sam 3:8 said, "Am I a D's head of Judah?
9:8 look upon a dead D such as I?"
16:9 "Why should this dead D curse my lord the
2Kgs 8:13 who is but a D, that he should do
Tob 5:16 and the young man's D was with them.
11:4 their way, and the D went along behind them.
Jud 11:19 shepherd, and not a D will so much as
Ps 22:20 sword, my life from the power of the D
Prov 26:11 Like a D that returns to his vomit is
26:17 who takes a passing D by the ears.
Eccl 9:4 hope, for a living D is better than a
Sir 13:17 peace is there between a hyena and a D
Is 66:3 him who breaks a D's neck; he who presents
2Pet 2:22 the true proverb, The D turns back to his

DOGGED
Lam 4:18 Men D our steps so that we could not

DOGS (26)
Ex 22:31 the field; you shall cast it to the D
1Kgs 14:11 in the city the D shall eat; and any
16:4 in the city the D shall eat; and any
21:19 "In the place where D licked up the blood
21:19 blood of Naboth shall D lick your own blood."'"
21:23 LORD also said, 'The D shall eat Jezebel within
21:24 in the city the D shall eat; and any
22:38 of Samaria, and the D licked up his blood,
2Kgs 9:10 And the D shall eat Jezebel in the territory
9:36 territory of Jezreel the D shall eat the flesh
Job 30:1 to set with the D of my flock.
Ps 22:16 Yea, D are round about me; a company of
59:6 come back, howling like D and prowling about the
59:14 come back, howling like D and prowling about the
68:23 the tongues of your D may have their portion
Is 56:10 they are all dumb D, they cannot bark; dreaming,
56:11 The D have a mighty appetite; they never have
Jer 15:3 sword to slay, the D to tear, and the
Mt 7:6 "Do not give D what is holy; and do
15:26 the children's bread and throw it to the D
15:27 Lord, yet even the D eat the crumbs that
Mk 7:26 the children's bread and throw it to the D
7:27 Lord; yet even the D under the table eat
Lk 16:21 man's table; moreover the D came and licked his
Phil 3:2 Look out for the D, look out for the
Rev 22:15 Outside are the D and sorcerers and fornicators and

DOINGS (31)
Deut 28:20 the evil of your D, because you have forsaken
Ps 106:2 can utter the mighty D of the LORD, or
106:29 to anger with their D, and a plague broke
106:39 their acts, and played the harlot in their D
145:17 all his ways, and kind in all his D
Is 1:16 the evil of your D from before my eyes;
19:14 stagger in all her D as a drunken man
57:12 your righteousness and your D, but they will not
65:7 into their bosom payment for their former D
Jer 4:4 quench it, because of the evil of your D
4:18 Your ways and your D have brought this upon
7:3 your ways and your D, and I will let
7:5 your ways and your D, if you truly execute
17:10 his ways, according to the fruit of his D
18:11 your ways and your D
21:14 the fruit of your D, says the LORD; I
23:22 evil way, and from the evil of their D
25:5 evil way and wrong D, and dwell upon the
26:13 your ways and your D, and obey the voice
32:19 the fruit of his D;
35:15 way, and amend your D, and do not go
Ezek 14:22 their ways and their D, you will be consoled
14:23 their ways and their D; and you shall know
20:43 ways and all the D with which you have
20:44 according to your corrupt D, O house of Israel,
21:24 that in all your D your sins appear—because
24:14 your ways and your D I will judge you,
36:17 their ways and their D; their conduct before me
Mic 2:7 Are these his D
7:13 of its inhabitants, for the fruit of their D
Rev 2:22 they repent of her D;

DOK
1Mac 16:15 the little stronghold called D, which he had built;

DOMESTIC
Tit 2:5 to be sensible, chaste, D, kind, and submissive to

DOMINEERING
1Pet 5:3 but eagerly, not as D over those in your

DOMINION (60)
Gen 1:26 and let them have D over the fish of
1:28 subdue it; and have D over the fish of
37:8 you indeed to have D over us?" So they
Num 24:19 By Jacob shall D be exercised, and the survivors
Judg 14:4 time the Philistines had D over Israel.
1Kgs 4:24 For he had D over all the region west
9:19 Lebanon, and in all the land of his D
2Chr 8:6 Lebanon, and in all the land of his D
Neh 9:28 so that they had D over them; yet when
Esth 14:12 King of the gods and Master of all D
Job 25:2 Bildad the Shuhite answered: D and fear are with
Ps 8:6 Thou hast given him D over the works of
19:13 let them not have D over me!
22:28 For D belongs to the LORD, and he rules
72:8 May he have D from sea to sea, and
103:22 all his works, in all places of his D
114:2 language, Judah became his sanctuary, Israel his D
119:133 let no iniquity get D over me.
145:13 everlasting kingdom, and thy D endures throughout
Wis 1:14 in them; and the D of Hades is not
6:3 For your D was given you from the Lord,
9:2 formed man, to have D over the creatures thou
Sir 16:25 eternal order, and their D for all generations; they
17:4 beings, and granted them D over beasts and birds.
24:11 a resting place, and in Jerusalem was my D
Jer 34:1 the earth under his D and all the peoples
51:28 governors and deputies, and every land under their D
Ezek 30:18 I break there the D of Egypt, and her
Dan 3:44 of all power and D, and let their strength
4:3 everlasting kingdom, and his D is from generation to
4:22 to heaven, and your D to the ends of
4:34 for ever; for his D is an everlasting dominion,
4:34 dominion is an everlasting D, and his kingdom
6:26 in all my royal D men tremble and fear
6:26 be destroyed, and his D shall be to the
7:6 had four heads; and D was given to it.
7:12 of the beasts, their D was taken away, but
7:14 to him was given D and glory and kingdom,
7:14 should serve him; his D is an everlasting dominion,
7:14 dominion is an everlasting D, which shall not pass
7:26 in judgment, and his D shall be taken away,
7:27 the kingdom and the D and the greatness of
11:3 shall rule with great D and do according to
11:4 nor according to the D with which he ruled;
11:5 than he and his D shall be a great
11:5 he and his dominion shall be a great D
14:5 and earth and has D over all flesh."
Mic 4:8 it come, the former D shall come, the kingdom
Zech 9:10 to the nations; his D shall be from sea
1Mac 8:24 allies in all their D,
Rom 6:9 death no longer has D over him.
6:14 sin will have no D over you, since you
Eph 1:21 authority and power and D, and above every name
Col 1:13 delivered us from the D of darkness and transferred
1Tim 6:16 To him be honor and eternal D
1Pet 4:11 him belong glory and D for ever and ever.
5:11 To him be the D for ever and ever.
Jude 1:25 Lord, be glory, majesty, D, and authority, before all
Rev 1:6 him be glory and D for ever and ever.
17:18 great city which has D over the kings of

DOMINIONS (2)
Dan 7:27 everlasting kingdom, and all D shall serve and obey
Col 1:16 invisible, whether thrones or D or principalities or

DONNED
1Mac 14:9 things; and the youths D the glories and garments

DOOM (10)
Deut 32:35 at hand, and their D comes swiftly.
Ps 92:11 ears have heard the D of my evil assailants.
Sir 38:22 "Remember my D, for yours is like it: yesterday
Jer 4:18 This is your D, and it is bitter; it
11:15 Can vows and sacrificial flesh avert your D
Lam 1:9 no thought of her D; therefore her fall is
Ezek 7:7 Your D has come to you, O inhabitant of
7:10 Your D has come, injustice has blossomed, pride has
30:3 clouds, a time of D for the nations.
30:9 the day of Egypt's D; for, lo, it comes!

DOOMED (17)
2Sam 19:28 house were but men D to death before my
2Kgs 18:27 the wall, who are D with you to eat
Ps 79:11 great power preserve those D to die!
92:7 evildoers flourish, they are D to destruction for ever,
102:20 free those who were D to die;
Wis 18:15 the land that was D, a stern warrior
Is 34:2 their host, he has D them, has given them
34:5 judgment upon Edom, upon the people I have D
36:12 the wall, who are D with you to eat
Jer 8:14 LORD our God has D us to perish, and
43:11 pestilence those who are D to the pestilence, to
43:11 captivity those who are D to captivity, and to
43:11 sword those who are D to the sword.
Zech 11:4 shepherd of the flock D to slaughter.
11:7 shepherd of the flock D to be slain for
1Cor 2:6 this age, who are D to pass away.
Rev 11:5 them, thus he is D to be killed.

DOOR (165)
Gen 4:7 is couching at the D; its desire is for
6:16 above; and set the D of the ark in
18:1 he sat at the D of his tent in
18:2 ran from the tent D to meet them, and
18:10 listening at the tent D behind him.
19:6 went out of the D to the men, shut
19:6 the men, shut the D after him,
19:9 man Lot, and drew near to break the D
19:10 into the house to them, and shut the D
19:11 who were at the D of the house, both
19:11 so that they wearied themselves groping for the D
43:19 with him at the D of the house,
Ex 12:22 go out of the D of his house until
12:23 will pass over the D, and will not allow
21:6 bring him to the D or the doorpost; and
26:36 a screen for the D of the tent, of
29:4 his sons to the D of the tent of
29:11 the LORD, at the D of the tent of
29:32 the basket, at the D of the tent of
29:42 your generations at the D of the tent of
33:8 stood at his tent D, and looked after Moses,
33:9 and stand at the D of the tent, and
33:10 cloud standing at the D of the tent, all
33:10 up and worship, every man at his tent D
35:15 the screen for the D, at the door of
35:15 the door, at the D of the tabernacle;
36:37 a screen for the D of the tent, of
38:8 who ministered at the D of the tent of
38:30 the bases for the D of the tent of
39:38 the screen for the D of the tent;
Lev 1:3 offer it at the D of the tent of
1:5 that is at the D of the tent of
3:2 kill it at the D of the tent of
4:4 the bull to the D of the tent of
4:7 which is at the D of the tent of
4:18 which is at the D of the tent of
8:3 the congregation at the D of the tent of
8:4 was assembled at the D of the tent of
8:31 the flesh at the D of the tent of
8:33 go out from the D of the tent of
8:35 At the D of the tent of meeting you
10:7 go out from the D of the tent of
12:6 the priest at the D of the tent of
14:11 the LORD, at the D of the tent of
14:23 the priest, to the D of the tent of
14:38 the house to the D of the house, and
15:14 the LORD to the D of the tent of
15:29 the priest, to the D of the tent of
16:7 the LORD at the D of the tent of
17:4 bring it to the D of the tent of
17:5 the priest at the D of the tent of
17:6 the LORD at the D of the tent of
17:9 bring it to the D of the tent of
19:21 the LORD, to the D of the tent of
Num 3:25 the screen for the D of the tent of
3:26 the screen for the D of the court which
4:25 the screen for the D of the tent of
6:10 the priest to the D of the tent of
6:13 be brought to the D of the tent of
6:18 consecrated head at the D of the tent of
11:10 every man at the D of his tent; and
12:5 and stood at the D of the tent, and
16:27 and stood at the D of their tents, together
20:6 the assembly to the D of the tent of
25:6 were weeping at the D of the tent of
27:2 the congregation, at the D of the tent of
Deut 15:17 his ear into the D, and he shall be
22:21 young woman to the D of her father's house,
31:15 cloud stood by the D of the tent.
Josh 19:51 the LORD, at the D of the tent of
Judg 4:20 her, "Stand at the D of the tent, and
9:52 drew near to the D of the tower to
19:22 about, beating on the D; and they said to
19:26 fell down at the D of the man's house
19:27 concubine lying at the D of the house, with
2Sam 11:9 Uriah slept at the D of the king's house
13:17 presence, and bolt the D after her."
13:18 out, and bolted the D after her.
1Kgs 6:34 leaves of the one D were folding, and the
6:34 leaves of the other D were folding.
14:6 came in at the D, he said, "Come in,
14:27 guard, who kept the D of the king's house.
2Kgs 4:4 in, and shut the D upon yourself and your
4:5 him and shut the D upon herself and her
4:21 God, and shut the D upon him, and went
4:33 in and shut the D upon the two of
5:9 and halted at the D of Elisha's house.
6:32 messenger comes, shut the D, and hold the door
6:32 door, and hold the D fast against him.
9:3 Israel.' Then open the D and flee; do not
9:10 Then he opened the D, and fled.
2Chr 12:10 guard, who kept the D of the king's house.
Neh 3:20 the Angle to the D of the house of
3:21 another section from the D of the house of
Tob 8:4 When the D was shut and the two were
8:13 the maid opened the D and went in, and
11:10 Tobit started toward the D, and stumbled.
Jud 14:14 and knocked at the D of the tent, for
Job 31:9 wait at my neighbor's D;
Ps 141:3 keep watch over the D of my lips!
Prov 5:8 not go near the D of her house;
9:14 She sits at the D of her house, she
17:19 he who makes his D high seeks destruction.
26:14 As a D turns on its hinges, so does
Song 8:9 if she is a D, we will enclose her
Wis 19:17 were those at the D of the righteous man–
19:17 tried to find the way through his own D
Sir 21:23 the house from the D, but a cultivated man
21:24 to listen at a D, and a discreet man
28:25 words, and make a D and a bolt for
Is 57:8 Behind the D and the doorpost you have set
Bar 6:59 gods; better even the D of a house that
Ezek 8:7 brought me to the D of the court; and
8:8 dug in the wall, lo, there was a D
8:16 and behold, at the D of the temple of
10:19 they stood at the D of the east gate
11:1 And behold, at the D of the gateway there
40:13 and twenty cubits, from D to door.
40:13 of five and twenty cubits, from door to D
40:38 a chamber with its D in the vestibule of
41:11 was left free, one D toward the north, and
41:11 the north, and another D toward the south; and
41:17 the space above the D, even to the inner
41:20 floor to above the D cherubim and palm trees
41:23 and the holy place had each a double D
41:24 two leaves apiece, two swinging leaves for each D
47:1 me back to the D of the temple; and
Dan 3:94 came near to the D of the burning fiery
13:26 in at the side D to see what had
14:11 wine, and shut the D and seal it with
14:14 went out, shut the D and sealed it with
Hos 2:15 Valley of Achor a D of hope.
2Mac 1:16 Opening the secret D in the ceiling, they threw
14:41 and were forcing the D of the courtyard, they
Mt 6:6 room and shut the D and pray to your
25:10 marriage feast; and the D was shut.
27:60 great stone to the D of the tomb, and

D

Mk 1:33 the whole city was gathered together about the D
2:2 not even about the D; and he was preaching
11:4 colt tied at the D out in the open
15:45 a stone against the D of the tomb.
16:3 for us from the D of the tomb?"
Lk 11:7 not bother me; the D is now shut, and
13:24 enter by the narrow D; for many, I tell
13:25 up and shut the D, you will begin to
13:25 to knock at the D, saying, 'Lord, open to
Jn 10:1 the sheepfold by the D but climbs in by
10:2 who enters by the D is the shepherd of
10:7 you, I am the D of the sheep.
10:9 I am the D; if any one enters by
18:16 with Jesus, while Peter stood outside at the D
18:16 maid who kept the D, and brought Peter in.
18:17 maid who kept the D said to Peter, "Are
Acts 5:9 husband are at the D, and they will carry
12:6 and sentries before the D were guarding the prison;
12:13 he knocked at the D of the gateway, a
14:27 he had opened a D of faith to the
18:7 his house was next D to the synagogue.
1Cor 16:9 Pentecost, for a wide D for effective work has
2Cor 2:12 gospel of Christ, a D was opened for me
Col 4:3 open to us a D for the word, to
Rev 3:8 before you an open D, which no one is
3:20 I stand at the D and knock; if any
3:20 voice and opens the D, I will come in
4:1 I looked, and lo, in heaven an open D

DOORKEEPER (3)

2Sam 4:6 And behold, the D of the house had been
Ps 84:10 would rather be a D in the house of
Mk 13:34 work, and commands the D to be on the

DOORKEEPERS

Ezra 7:24 Levites, the singers, the D, the temple servants, or

DOORPOST (3)

Ex 21:6 the door or the D; and his master shall
1Sam 1:9 the seat beside the D of the temple of
Is 57:8 the door and the D you have set up

DOORPOSTS (12)

Ex 12:7 it on the two D and the lintel of
12:22 lintel and the two D with the blood which
12:23 and on the two D, the LORD will pass
Deut 6:9 write them on the D of your house and
11:20 write them upon the D of your house and
1Kgs 6:31 the lintel and the D formed a pentagon.
6:33 entrance to the nave D of olivewood, in the
2Kgs 18:16 LORD, and from the D which Hezekiah king of
Ezek 41:21 The D of the nave were squared; and in
43:8 my threshold and their D beside my doorposts, with
43:8 their doorposts beside my D, with only a wall
45:19 put it on the D of the temple, the

DOORS (83)

Josh 2:19 goes out of the D of your house into
Judg 3:23 vestibule, and closed the D of the roof chamber
3:24 they saw that the D of the roof chamber
3:25 did not open the D of the roof chamber,
11:31 comes forth from the D of my house to
16:3 took hold of the D of the gate of
19:27 when he opened the D of the house and
1Sam 3:15 then he opened the D of the house of
21:13 made marks on the D of the gate, and
1Kgs 6:31 inner sanctuary he made D of olivewood; the lintel
6:32 He covered the two D of olivewood with carvings
6:34 a square, and two D of cypress wood; the
7:50 of gold, for the D of the innermost part
7:50 place, and for the D of the nave of
2Kgs 18:16 the gold from the D of the temple of
1Chr 22:3 for nails for the D of the gates and
2Chr 3:7 its walls, and its D; and he carved cherubim
4:9 the great court, and D for the court, and
4:9 court, and overlaid their D with bronze;
4:22 temple, for the inner D to the most holy
4:22 place and for the D of the nave of
28:24 he shut up the D of the house of
29:3 month, he opened the D of the house of
29:7 They also shut the D of the vestibule and
Neh 3:1 it and set its D; they consecrated it as
3:3 beams and set its D, its bolts, and its
3:6 beams and set its D, its bolts, and its
3:13 it and set its D, its bolts, and its
3:14 it and set its D, its bolts, and its
3:15 it and set its D, its bolts, and its
6:1 not set up the D in the gates),
6:10 let us close the D of the temple; for
7:1 had set up the D, and the gatekeepers, the
7:3 standing guard let them shut and bar the D
13:19 I commanded that the D should be shut and
Esth 15:6 gone through all the D, she stood before the
Job 3:10 did not shut the D of my mother's womb,
31:32 I have opened my D to the wayfarer);
31:34 not go out of D --
38:8 in the sea with D, when it burst forth
38:10 and set bars and D,
41:14 Who can open the D of his face?
Ps 24:7 and be lifted up, O ancient D
24:9 and be lifted up, O ancient D
78:23 above, and opened the D of heaven;
107:16 For he shatters the D of bronze, and cuts
Prov 8:34 watching daily at my gates, waiting beside my D
Eccl 12:4 are dimmed, and the D on the street are
Song 7:13 fragrance, and over our D are all choice fruits,
Sir 14:23 also listen at her D;
Is 26:20 chambers, and shut your D behind you; hide
45:1 of kings, to open D before him that gates
45:2 break in pieces the D of bronze and cut
Bar 6:18 their temples secure with D and locks and bars,
Ezek 33:30 walls and at the D of the houses, say
41:11 And the D of the side chambers opened on
41:24 The D had two leaves apiece, two swinging leaves
41:25 And on the D of the nave were carved
42:4 cubits long, and their D were on the north.
42:11 with the same exits and arrangements and D
Dan 13:17 and shut the garden D so that I may
13:18 said, shut the garden D, and went out by
13:18 out by the side D to bring what they
13:20 said: "Look, the garden D are shut, no one
13:25 one of them ran and opened the garden D
13:36 maids, shut the garden D, and dismissed the maids.
13:39 and he opened the D and dashed out.
14:18 As soon as the D were opened, the king
14:21 showed him the secret D through which they were
Mic 7:5 a friend; guard the D of your mouth from
Zech 11:1 Open your D, O Lebanon, that the fire may
Mal 1:10 who would shut the D, that you might not
1Mac 1:55 burned incense at the D of the houses and
4:57 chambers for the priests, and furnished them with D
2Mac 14:41 be brought and the D burned.
14:43 the crowd was now rushing in through the D
Jn 20:19 of the week, the D being shut where the
20:26 The D were shut, but Jesus came and stood
Acts 5:19 Lord opened the prison D and brought them out
5:23 sentries standing at the D, but when we opened
16:26 and immediately all the D were opened and every
16:27 saw that the prison D were open, he drew
Jas 5:9 judged; behold, the Judge is standing at the D

DOORSTEP

Sir 6:36 him early; let your foot wear out his D

DOORWAY

2Kgs 4:15 he had called her, she stood in the D

DOORWAYS

1Kgs 7:5 All the D and windows had square frames, and

DOPHKAH (2)

Num 33:12 from the wilderness of Sin, and encamped at D
33:13 they set out from D, and encamped at Alush.

DOR (7)

Josh 12:23 one; the king of D in Naphath-dor, one; the
17:11 and the inhabitants of D and its villages, and
Judg 1:27 or the inhabitants of D and its villages, or
1Chr 7:29 Megiddo and its towns, D and its towns.
1Mac 15:11 in his flight to D, which is by the
15:13 So Antiochus encamped against D, and with him
15:25 Antiochus the king besieged D anew, continually

DORCAS (2)

Acts 9:36 at Joppa a disciple named Tabitha, which means D
9:39 and other garments which D made while she was

DORYMENES (2)

1Mac 3:38 Ptolemy the son of D, and Nicanor and Gorgias,
2Mac 4:45 to Ptolemy son of D to win over the

DOSITHEUS (4)
Esth 11:1 of Ptolemy and Cleopatra, D, who said that he
2Mac 12:19 D and Sosipater, who were captains under
12:24 into the hands of D and Sosipater and their
12:35 But a certain D, one of Bacenor's men, who

DOST (135)
Num 11:11 thy sight, that thou D lay the burden of
14:15 Now if thou D kill this people as one
2Sam 22:26 "With the loyal thou D show thyself loyal; with
22:26 the blameless man thou D show thyself blameless;
22:27 with the pure thou D show thyself pure, and
22:27 with the crooked thou D show thyself perverse.
22:28 Thou D deliver a humble people, but thy eyes
1Kgs 8:35 their sin, when thou D afflict them,
8:36 people Israel, when thou D teach them the good
8:46 angry with them, and D give them to an
2Chr 6:26 their sin, when thou D afflict them,
6:27 people Israel, when thou D teach them the good
6:36 angry with them, and D give them to an
20:6 D thou not rule over all the kingdoms of
Tob 3:2 and truth, and thou D render true and righteous
Job 7:14 my complaint,' then thou D scare me with dreams
7:17 is man, that thou D make so much of
7:17 him, and that thou D set thy mind upon
7:18 thy mind upon him, D visit him every morning,
7:21 Why D thou not pardon my transgression and take
10:2 me know why thou D contend against me.
10:4 D thou see as man sees?
10:6 man's years, that thou D seek out my iniquity
10:8 me; and now thou D turn about and destroy
10:14 If I sin, thou D mark me, and dost
10:14 dost mark me, and D not acquit me of
10:16 lift myself up, thou D hunt me like a
10:17 wonders against me; thou D renew thy witnesses
10:17 vexation toward me; thou D bring fresh hosts against
13:24 Why D thou hide thy face, and count me
14:3 And D thou open thy eyes upon such a
30:20 to thee and thou D not answer me; I
30:20 I stand, and thou D not heed me.
30:21 of thy hand thou D persecute me.
Ps 3:7 For thou D smite all my enemies on the
3:7 on the cheek, thou D break the teeth of
5:3 in the morning thou D hear my voice; in
5:12 For thou D bless the righteous, O LORD; thou
5:12 righteous, O LORD; thou D cover him with favor
8:4 of man that thou D care for him?
8:5 less than God, and D crown him with glory
10:1 [Selah] Why D thou stand afar off, O LORD?
10:1 Why D thou hide thyself in times of trouble?
10:14 Thou D see; yea, thou dost note trouble and
10:14 dost see; yea, thou D note trouble and vexation,
16:10 For thou D not give me up to Sheol,
16:11 Thou D show me the path of life; in
18:25 With the loyal thou D show thyself loyal; with
18:25 the blameless man thou D show thyself blameless;
18:26 with the pure thou D show thyself pure; and
18:26 with the crooked thou D show thyself perverse.
18:27 For thou D deliver a humble people; but the
18:27 the haughty eyes thou D bring down.
18:28 Yea, thou D light my lamp; the LORD my
21:3 [Selah] For thou D meet him with goodly blessings;
21:3 with goodly blessings; thou D set a crown of
21:5 splendor and majesty thou D bestow upon him.
21:6 Yea, thou D make him most blessed for ever;
21:6 blessed for ever; thou D make him glad with
22:2 by day, but thou D not answer; and by
22:15 to my jaws; thou D lay me in the
32:7 me from trouble; thou D encompass me with
39:11 When thou D chasten man with rebukes for sin,
39:11 rebukes for sin, thou D consume like a moth
40:6 Sacrifice and offering thou D not desire; but thou
41:2 in the land; thou D not give him up
44:24 Why D thou hide thy face?
44:24 Why D thou forget our affliction and oppression?
59:8 But thou, O LORD, D laugh at them; thou
59:8 laugh at them; thou D hold all the nations
60:10 Thou D not go forth, O God, with our
62:12 For thou D requite a man according to his
65:3 prevail over us, thou D forgive them.
65:4 is he whom thou D choose and bring near,
65:5 By dread deeds thou D answer us with deliverance,
65:7 girded with might; who D still the roaring of
67:4 for joy, for thou D judge the peoples with
73:18 Truly thou D set them in slippery places; thou
73:18 in slippery places; thou D make them fall to
73:23 continually with thee; thou D hold my right hand.
73:24 Thou D guide me with thy counsel, and afterward
73:27 thee shall perish; thou D put an end to
74:1 O God, why D thou cast us off for
74:11 Why D thou hold back thy hand, why dost
74:11 back thy hand, why D thou keep thy right
77:4 [Selah] Thou D hold my eyelids from closing; I
80:6 Thou D make us the scorn of our neighbors;
86:7 on thee, for thou D answer me.
88:5 like those whom thou D remember no more, for
88:7 upon me, and thou D overwhelm me with all
88:10 D thou work wonders for the dead?
88:14 O LORD, why D thou cast me off?
88:14 Why D thou hide thy face from me?
89:9 Thou D rule the raging of the sea; when
90:5 Thou D sweep men away; they are like a
94:12 the man whom thou D chasten, O LORD, and
94:12 LORD, and whom thou D teach out of thy
102:26 will perish, but thou D endure; they will all
104:14 Thou D cause the grass to grow for the
108:11 Thou D not go forth, O God, with our
119:21 Thou D rebuke the insolent, accursed ones, who
119:118 Thou D spurn all who go astray from thy
119:119 of the earth thou D count as dross; therefore
119:171 forth praise that thou D teach me thy statutes.
138:7 midst of trouble, thou D preserve my life; thou
138:7 preserve my life; thou D stretch out thy hand
139:5 Thou D beset me behind and before, and layest
144:3 is man that thou D regard him, or the
144:3 of man that thou D think of him?
Wis 11:23 all things, and thou D overlook men's sins, that
12:2 Therefore thou D correct little by little those who
12:2 those who trespass, and D remind and warn them
12:17 For thou D show thy strength when men doubt
12:17 of thy power, and D rebuke any insolence among
12:18 art sovereign in strength D judge with mildness, and
12:18 with great forbearance thou D govern us; for thou
12:18 to act whenever thou D choose.
16:13 life and death; thou D lead men down to
Sir 51:8 of old, that thou D deliver those who wait
51:8 wait for thee and D save them from the
Is 25:5 Thou D subdue the noise of the aliens; as
26:3 Thou D keep him in perfect peace, whose mind
26:7 righteous is level; thou D make smooth the path
38:12 day to night thou D bring me to an
38:13 day to night thou D bring me to an
63:17 O LORD, why D thou make us err from
Jer 32:18 love to thousands, but D requite the guilt of
Lam 5:19 But thou, O LORD, D reign for ever; thy
5:20 Why D thou forget us for ever, why dost
5:20 us for ever, why D thou so long forsake
Dan 13:42 "O eternal God, who D discern what is secret,
Hab 1:3 Why D thou make me see wrongs and look
1:13 look on wrong, why D thou look on faithless
1Mac 3:53 withstand them, if thou D not help us?"
2Mac 1:25 almighty and eternal, who D rescue Israel from

DOT (2)
Mt 5:18 an iota, not a D, will pass from the
Lk 16:17 away, than for one D of the law to

DOTED (6)
Ezek 23:5 was mine; and she D on her lovers the
23:7 the idols of every one on whom she D
23:9 the hands of the Assyrians, upon whom she D
23:12 She D upon the Assyrians, governors and
23:16 she saw them she D upon them, and sent
23:20 land of Egypt and D upon her paramours there,

DOTHAN (8)
Gen 37:17 I heard them say, 'Let us go to D
37:17 went after his brothers, and found them at D
2Kgs 6:13 It was told him, "Behold, he is in D
Jud 3:9 edge of Esdraelon, near D, fronting the great ridge
4:6 opposite the plain near D,
7:3 out in breadth over D as far as Balbaim
7:18 the hill country opposite D; and they sent some
8:3 in the field between D and Balamon.

DOTING
Ezek 23:11 than she in her D and in her harlotry,

DOUBLE (26)
Gen 43:12 Take D the money with you; carry back with
43:15 present, and they took D the money with them,
Ex 22:2 an ass or a sheep, he shall pay D

D

D

22:7 if the thief is found, he shall pay D
22:9 shall condemn shall pay D to his neighbor.
26:9 sixth curtain you shall D over at the front
28:16 shall be square and D, a span its length
39:9 the breastpiece was made D, a span its length
Deut 21:17 by giving him a D portion of all that
2Kgs 2:9 let me inherit a D share of your spirit."
Job 41:13 Who can penetrate his D coat of mail?
Ps 12:2 flattering lips and a D heart they speak.
Sir 20:9 gift that brings a D return.
50:2 foundations for the high D walls, the high retaining
Is 40:2 from the LORD's hand D for all her sins.
61:7 you shall have a D portion, instead of dishonor
61:7 you shall possess a D portion; yours shall be
Jer 17:18 evil; destroy them with D destruction!
Ezek 41:23 place had each a D door.
Hos 10:10 are chastised for their D iniquity.
Zech 9:12 I declare that I will restore to you D
2Cor 1:15 you might have a D pleasure;
1Tim 5:17 be considered worthy of D honor, especially those
Jas 4:8 hearts, you men of D mind.
Rev 18:6 rendered, and repay her D for her deeds; mix
18:6 her deeds; mix a D draught for her in

DOUBLE-MINDED (2)
Ps 119:113 I hate D men, but I love thy law.
Jas 1:7 not suppose that a D man, unstable in all

DOUBLE-TONGUED (4)
Sir 5:9 follow every path: the D sinner does that.
5:14 to the thief, and severe condemnation to the D
6:1 reproach: so fares the D sinner.
1Tim 3:8 must be serious, not D, not addicted to much

DOUBLED (2)
Ex 39:9 its length and a span its breadth when D
Sir 26:1 wife; the number of his days will be D

DOUBLING
Gen 41:32 And the D of Pharaoh's dream means that the

DOUBLY (2)
Sir 23:11 disregards it, he sins D; if he has sworn
Jer 16:18 And I will D recompense their iniquity and their

DOUBT (9)
Gen 37:33 him; Joseph is without D torn to pieces."
Deut 28:66 life shall hang in D before you; night and
Job 12:2 Then Job answered: "No D you are the people,
Wis 12:17 thy strength when men D the completeness of thy
Mt 14:31 "O man of little faith, why did you D
21:21 have faith and never D, you will not only
Mk 11:23 sea,' and does not D in his heart, but
Acts 28:4 to one another, "No D this man is a
Jude 1:22 And convince some, who D;

DOUBTED
Mt 28:17 they saw him they worshipped him; but some D

DOUBTING
Jas 1:6 in faith, with no D, for he who doubts

DOUBTLESS (2)
Lk 4:23 he said to them, D you will quote to
1Cor 14:10 There are D many different languages in the world,

DOUBTS (2)
Rom 14:23 But he who has D is condemned, if he
Jas 1:6 doubting, for he who D is like a wave

DOUGH (6)
Ex 12:34 the people took their D before it was leavened,
12:39 unleavened cakes of the D which they had brought
2Sam 13:8 And she took D, and kneaded it, and made
Jer 7:18 and the women knead D, to make cakes for
Hos 7:5 the kneading of the D until it is leavened.
Rom 11:16 If the D offered as first fruits is holy,

DOVE (19)
Gen 8:8 he sent forth a D from him, to see
8:9 the ground; but the D found no place to
8:10 he sent forth the D out of the ark;
8:11 the ark; and the D came back to him
8:12 and sent forth the D; and she did not
2Kgs 6:25 of a kab of D's dung for five shekels
Ps 55:6 say, "O that I had wings like a D
68:13 the wings of a D covered with silver, its
74:19 the soul of thy D to the wild beasts;
Song 2:14 O my D, in the clefts of the rock,
5:2 sister, my love, my D, my perfect one; for
6:9 My D, my perfect one, is only one, the
Is 38:14 a crane I clamor, I moan like a D
Jer 48:28 Be like the D that nests in the sides
Hos 7:12 Ephraim is like a D, silly and without sense,
Mt 3:16 God descending like a D, and alighting on him;
Mk 1:10 upon him like a D;
Lk 3:22 bodily form, as a D, and a voice came
Jn 1:32 Spirit descend as a D from heaven, and it

DOVES (9)
Song 1:15 love; behold, you are beautiful; your eyes are D
4:1 Your eyes are D behind your veil.
5:12 His eyes are like D beside springs of water,
Is 59:11 moan and moan like D; we look for justice,
60:8 a cloud, and like D to their windows?
Ezek 7:16 on the mountains, like D of the valleys, all
Hos 11:11 from Egypt, and like D from the land of
Nah 2:7 lamenting, moaning like D, and beating their breasts.
Mt 10:16 so be wise as serpents and innocent as D

DOWNCAST (4)
Gen 40:7 "Why are your faces D today?"
Jud 6:9 they will not be taken, do not look D
Prov 17:22 good medicine, but a D spirit dries up the
2Cor 7:6 God, who comforts the D, comforted us by the

DOWNFALL (11)
2Chr 22:7 by God that the D of Ahaziah should come
Esth 14:11 them mock at our D; but turn their plan
Ps 92:11 eyes have seen the D of my enemies, my
Prov 29:16 increases; but the righteous will look upon their D
Sir 4:22 to your own harm, or deference, to your D
5:13 from speaking, and a man's tongue is his D
13:13 for you are walking about with your own D
20:17 the tongue; so the D of the wicked will
25:7 lives to see the D of his foes;
Lam 1:7 the foe gloated over her, mocking at her D
Ezek 32:10 his own life, on the day of your D

DOWNHEARTED
1Mac 6:10 eyes and I am D with worry.

DOWNTRODDEN (2)
Ps 74:21 Let not the D be put to shame; let
147:6 LORD lifts up the D, he casts the wicked

DOWNWARD (7)
Deut 28:13 upward only, and not D; if you obey the
Josh 18:16 of the Jebusites, and D to En-rogel;
1Sam 5:3 Dagon had fallen face D on the ground before
5:4 Dagon had fallen face D on the ground before
2Kgs 19:30 shall again take root D, and bear fruit upward;
Is 37:31 shall again take root D, and bear fruit upward;
Ezek 1:27 enclosed round about; and D from what had the

DOWRY (3)
Gen 30:20 me with a good D; now my husband will
1Kgs 9:16 had given it as D to his daughter, Solomon's
2Mac 1:14 to secure most of its treasures as a D

DRACHMA
Tob 5:14 to pay you—a D a day, and expenses

DRACHMAS (3)
2Mac 4:19 carry three hundred silver D for the sacrifice to
10:20 on receiving seventy thousand D let some of them
12:43 amount of two thousand D of silver, and sent

DRAG (3)
2Sam 17:13 city, and we shall D it into the valley,
Lk 12:58 the way, lest he D you to the judge,
Jas 2:6 it not they who D you into court?

DRAGGED (11)
Job 20:28 will be carried away, D off in the day
Jer 22:19 he shall be buried, D and cast forth beyond
49:20 the flock shall be D away; surely their fold
50:45 their flock shall be D away; surely their fold
Lam 1:4 her maidens have been D away, and she herself
Mt 10:18 and you will be D before governors and kings
Acts 8:3 house after house, he D off men and women
14:19 they stoned Paul and D him out of the

16:19 Paul and Silas and D them into the market
17:6 not find them, they D Jason and some of
21:30 they seized Paul and D him out of the

DRAGGING (4)

Ps 7:2 lion they rend me, D me away, with none
2Mac 12:35 grasping his cloak was D him off by main
Jn 21:8 came in the boat, D the net full of
Acts 19:29 together into the theater, D with them Gaius and

DRAGNET

Ezek 32:3 and I will haul you up in my D

DRAGON (23)

Sir 25:15 a lion and a D than dwell with an
Is 27:1 he will slay the D that is in the
51:9 cut Rahab in pieces, that didst pierce the D
Ezek 29:3 of Egypt, the great D that lies in the
32:2 you are like a D in the seas; you
Dan 14:23 was also a great D, which the Babylonians revered.
14:26 I will slay the D without sword or club."
14:27 and made cakes, which he fed to the D
14:27 The D ate them, and burst open.
14:28 Bel, and slain the D, and slaughtered the priests."
Rev 12:3 behold, a great red D, with seven heads and
12:4 And the D stood before the woman who was
12:7 angels fighting against the D; and the dragon and
12:7 the dragon; and the D and his angels fought,
12:9 And the great D was thrown down, that ancient
12:13 And when the D saw that he had been
12:16 the river which the D had poured from his
12:17 Then the D was angry with the woman, and
13:2 And to it the D gave his power and
13:4 Men worshiped the D, for he had given his
13:11 like a lamb and it spoke like a D
16:13 the mouth of the D and from the mouth
20:2 And he seized the D, that ancient serpent, who

DRAGONS (3)

Esth 10:7 The two D are Haman and myself.
11:6 And behold, two great D came forward, both ready
Ps 74:13 the heads of the D on the waters.

DRAGS (2)

Eccl 12:5 tree blossoms, the grasshopper D itself along and
Hab 1:15 with a hook, he D them out with his

DRAIN (4)

Ps 75:8 of the earth shall D it down to the
Sir 13:5 with you; he will D your resources and he
Ezek 23:34 shall drink it and D it out, and pluck
Rev 16:19 Babylon, to make her D the cup of the

DRAINED (4)

Lev 1:15 its blood shall be D out on the side
5:9 the blood shall be D out at the base
Sir 13:7 foods, until he has D you two or three
2Mac 14:46 his blood now completely D from him, he tore

DRANK (49)

Gen 9:21 a vineyard; and he D of the wine, and
24:46 drink also.' So I D, and she gave the
24:54 with him ate and D, and they spent the
25:34 and he ate and D, and rose and went
26:30 made them a feast, and they ate and D
27:25 ate; and he brought him wine, and he D
43:34 So they D and were merry with him.
Ex 24:11 of Israel; they beheld God, and ate and D
34:28 neither ate bread nor D water.
Num 20:11 abundantly, and the congregation D, and their cattle.
Deut 9:9 neither ate bread nor D water.
9:18 neither ate bread nor D water, because of all
32:14 of the grape you D wine.
32:38 of their sacrifices, and D the wine of their
Judg 9:27 god, and ate and D and reviled Abimelech.
15:19 it; and when he D, his spirit returned, and
19:4 so they ate and D, and lodged there.
19:6 sat and ate and D together; and the girl's
19:21 and they washed their feet, and ate and D
2Sam 11:13 in his presence and D, so that he made
1Kgs 4:20 sea; they ate and D and were happy.
13:19 in his house, and D water.
17:6 the evening; and he D from the brook.
19:6 And he ate and D, and lay down again.
19:8 arose, and ate and D, and went in the
2Kgs 7:8 tent, and ate and D, and they carried off
9:34 in and ate and D; and he said, "See
19:24 I dug wells and D foreign waters, and I
1Chr 29:22 and they ate and D before the LORD on
Jud 12:19 took and ate and D before him what her
12:20 pleased with her, and D a great quantity of
Is 37:25 I dug wells and D waters, and I dried
Jer 51:7 earth drunken; the nations D of her wine, therefore
Dan 1:5 king ate, and of the wine which he D
1:8 the wine which he D; therefore he asked the
5:1 of his lords, and D wine in front of
5:3 wives, and his concubines D from them.
5:4 They D wine, and praised the gods of gold
14:7 it never ate or D anything."
14:15 do, and ate and D everything.
Mk 14:23 them, and they all D of it.
Lk 13:26 say, 'We ate and D in your presence, and
17:27 They ate, they D, they married, they were given
17:28 Lot—they ate, they D, they bought, they sold,
Jn 4:12 us the well, and D from it himself, and
Acts 9:9 he was without sight, and neither ate nor D
10:41 witnesses, who ate and D with him after he
1Cor 10:4 supernatural food and all D the same supernatural
10:4 For they D from the supernatural Rock which

DRAUGHT (2)

Ps 75:8 he will pour a D from it, and all
Rev 18:6 deeds; mix a double D for her in the

DRAW (84)

Gen 24:11 women go out to D water.
24:13 are coming out to D water.
24:19 she said, "I will D for your camels also,
24:20 to the well to D, and she drew for
24:43 who comes out to D, to whom I shall
24:44 "Drink, and I will D for your camels also,"
Ex 15:9 I will D my sword, my hand shall destroy
Lev 9:7 Moses said to Aaron, D near to the altar,
10:4 and said to them, D near, carry your brethren
21:18 has a blemish shall D near, a man blind
Num 16:40 descendants of Aaron, should D near to burn incense
Deut 2:37 Ammon you did not D near, that is, to
13:10 because he sought to D you away from the
20:2 And when you D near to the battle, the
20:3 'Hear, O Israel, you D near this day to
20:10 "When you D near to a city to fight
Josh 8:26 For Joshua did not D back his hand, with
Judg 3:22 for he did not D the sword out of
4:7 And I will D out Sisera, the general of
8:20 the youth did not D his sword; for he
9:54 and said to him, D your sword and kill
19:13 "Come and let us D near to one of
20:23 LORD, "Shall we again D near to battle against
20:32 "Let us flee, and D them away from the
1Sam 9:11 maidens coming out to D water, and said to
14:36 priest said, "Let us D near hither to God."
17:8 you come out to D up for battle?
31:4 said to his armor-bearer, D your sword, and thrust
2Sam 11:15 hardest fighting, and then D back from him, that
1Kgs 13:4 that he could not D it back to himself.
2Kgs 13:16 the king of Israel, D the bow"; and he
1Chr 10:4 said to his armor-bearer, D your sword, and thrust
Jud 7:28 our wives and children D their last breath.
8:27 Lord scourges those who D near to him, in
Job 37:19 to him; we cannot D up our case because
41:1 "Can you D out Leviathan with a fishhook, or
Ps 35:3 D the spear and javelin against my pursuers!
37:14 The wicked D the sword and bend their bows,
69:18 D near to me, redeem me, set me free
119:150 They D near who persecute me with evil purpose;
Prov 20:5 man of understanding will D it out.
Eccl 5:1 house of God; to D near to listen is
12:1 come, and the years D nigh, when you will
Song 1:4 D me after you, let us make haste.
Wis 15:15 nostrils with which to D breath, nor ears with
Sir 51:23 D near to me, you who are untaught, and
Is 5:18 Woe to those who D iniquity with cords of
5:18 cords of falsehood, who D sin as with cart
5:19 Holy One of Israel D near, and let it
12:3 With joy you will D water from the wells
29:13 said: "Because this people D near with their mouth
34:1 D near, O nations, to hear, and hearken, O
41:1 speak; let us together D near for judgment.
45:20 "Assemble yourselves and come, D near together,
48:16 D near to me, hear this: from the beginning
57:3 But you, D near hither, sons of the sorceress,
58:2 judgments, they delight to D near to God.

D

66:19 Put, and Lud, who D the bow, to Tubal
Jer 30:21 I will make him D near, and he shall
Ezek 9:1 a loud voice, saying, D near, you executioners of
21:3 against you, and will D forth my sword out
28:7 nations; and they shall D their swords against the
29:4 scales; and I will D you up out of
30:11 land; and they shall D their swords against Egypt,
43:19 family of Zadok, who D near to me to
Joel 3:9 the men of war D near, let them come
Nah 3:14 D water for the siege, strengthen your forts; go
Zeph 3:2 LORD, she does not D near to her God.
Hag 2:16 to the winevat to D fifty measures, there were
Mal 3:5 "Then I will D near to you for judgment;
Jn 2:8 said to them, "Now D some out, and take
4:7 woman of Samaria to D water.
4:11 you have nothing to D with, and the well
4:15 I may not thirst, nor come here to D
12:32 from the earth, will D all men to myself."
Acts 20:30 speaking perverse things, to D away the disciples
Heb 4:16 us then with confidence D near to the throne
7:19 introduced, through which we D near to God.
7:25 to save those who D near to God through
10:1 make perfect those who D near.
10:22 of God, let us D near with a true
11:6 For whoever would D near to God must believe
Jas 4:8 D near to God and he will draw near
4:8 God and he will D near to you.

DRAWERS (3)
Josh 9:21 hewers of wood and D of water for all
9:23 hewers of wood and D of water for the
9:27 hewers of wood and D of water for the

DRAWING (5)
Lk 15:1 and sinners were all D near to hear him.
19:37 As he was now D near, at the descent
21:28 because your redemption is D near."
Jn 6:19 on the sea and D near to the boat.
Heb 10:25 you see the Day D near.

DRAWN (31)
Gen 34:3 And his soul was D to Dinah the daughter
Num 22:23 the road, with a D sword in his hand;
22:31 the way, with his D sword in his hand;
31:30 you shall take one D out of every fifty,
Deut 4:19 of heaven, you be D away and worship them
13:13 among you and have D away the inhabitants of
30:17 not hear, but are D away to worship other
Josh 5:13 before him with his D sword in his hand;
8:6 us, till we have D them away from the
8:16 pursued Joshua they were D away from the city.
Judg 20:31 the people, and were D away from the city;
Ruth 2:9 vessels and drink what the young men have D
2Kgs 3:21 called out, and were D up at the frontier.
1Chr 21:16 in his hand a D sword stretched out over
Job 20:25 It is D forth and comes out of his
Ps 30:1 LORD, for thou hast D me up, and hast
55:21 oil, yet they were D swords.
Sir 22:19 Even if you have D your sword against a
Is 21:15 the swords, from the D sword, from the bent
41:5 earth tremble; they have D near and come.
Ezek 21:5 I the LORD have D my sword out of
21:28 sword, a sword is D for the slaughter, it
Joel 2:5 like a powerful army D up for battle.
Mic 5:6 of Nimrod with the D sword; and they shall
1Mac 4:21 the army of Judas D up in the plain
12:26 the enemy were being D up in formation to
2Mac 5:2 armed with lances and D swords--
5:3 troops of horsemen D up, attacks and counterattacks
15:20 hand with their army D up for battle, the
Jn 2:9 the servants who had D the water knew), the
Acts 11:10 times, and all was D up again into heaven.

DRAWS (10)
Deut 25:11 wife of the one D near to rescue her
29:11 wood and he who D your water,
Judg 19:9 Behold, the day D to its close; lodge here
Job 33:22 His soul D near the Pit, and his life
36:27 For he D up the drops of water, he
Ps 10:9 the poor when he D him into his net.
88:3 troubles, and my life D near to Sheol.
Is 51:5 My deliverance D near speedily, my salvation has
Ezek 7:12 has come, the day D near.
Jn 6:44 Father who sent me D him; and I will

DREAD (41)
Gen 9:2 of you and the D of you shall be
15:12 Abram; and lo, a D and great darkness fell
Ex 1:11 the Egyptians were in D of the people of
15:16 Terror and D fall upon them; because of the
Num 22:3 Moab was in great D of the people, because
Deut 1:29 'Do not be in D or afraid of them.
2:25 begin to put the D and fear of you
7:21 shall not be in D of them; for the
11:25 of you and the D of you upon all
20:3 tremble, or be in D of them;
28:66 you shall be in D, and have no assurance
28:67 morning!' because of the D which your heart shall
31:6 fear or be in D of them: for it
1Sam 11:7 Then the D of the LORD fell upon the
Job 3:25 me, and what I D befalls me.
4:14 sleep falls on men, D came upon me, and
9:34 me, and let not D of him terrify me.
13:11 terrify you, and the D of him fall upon
13:21 me, and let not D of thee terrify me.
23:15 consider, I am in D of him.
Ps 31:11 neighbors, an object of D to my acquaintances; those
45:4 right hand teach you D deeds!
64:1 preserve my life from D of the enemy,
65:5 By D deeds thou dost answer us with deliverance,
88:16 swept over me; thy D assaults destroy me.
105:38 when they departed, for D of them had fallen
119:39 the reproach which I D; for thy ordinances are
Prov 1:33 be at ease, without D of evil."
20:2 The D wrath of a king is like the
Wis 4:20 They will come with D when their sins are
8:15 be subject to me; D monarchs will be afraid
10:16 the Lord, and withstood D kings with wonders and
12:9 at one blow by D wild beasts or thy
Is 7:16 kings you are in D will be deserted.
8:12 not fear what they fear, nor be in D
8:13 be your fear, and let him be your D
57:11 Whom did you D and fear, so that you
Jer 20:11 with me as a D warrior; therefore my persecutors
Mic 7:17 they shall turn in D to the LORD our
Hab 1:7 D and terrible are they; their justice and dignity
1Mac 7:18 Then the fear and D of them fell upon

DREADED
Deut 32:17 in of late, whom your fathers had never D

DREADFUL (7)
Wis 5:2 will be shaken with D fear, and they will
17:6 to them except a D, self-kindled fire, and in
18:17 at once apparitions in D dreams greatly troubled
Ezek 26:21 bring you to a D end, and you shall
27:36 have come to a D end and shall be
28:19 have come to a D end and shall be
Dan 7:7 fourth beast, terrible and D and exceedingly strong;

DREADS
Prov 10:24 What the wicked D will come upon him, but

DREAM (78)
Gen 20:3 to Abimelech in a D by night, and said
20:6 to him in the D, "Yes, I know that
31:10 and saw in a D that the he-goats which
31:11 to me in the D, 'Jacob,' and I said,
31:24 the Aramean in a D by night, and said
37:5 Now Joseph had a D, and when he told
37:6 to them, "Hear this D which I have dreamed:
37:9 Then he dreamed another D, and told it to
37:9 I have dreamed another D; and behold, the sun,
37:10 him, "What is this D that you have dreamed?
40:5 prison--each his own D, and each dream with
40:5 own dream, and each D with its own meaning.
40:9 chief butler told his D to Joseph, and said
40:9 to him, "In my D there was a vine
40:16 "I also had a D: there were three cake
41:7 And Pharaoh awoke, and behold, it was a D
41:8 Pharaoh told them his D, but there was none
41:11 I, each having a D with its own meaning.
41:12 an interpretation to each man according to his D
41:15 "I have had a D, and there is no
41:15 when you hear a D you can interpret it."
41:17 Joseph, "Behold, in my D I was standing on
41:22 also saw in my D seven ears growing on
41:25 said to Pharaoh, "The D of Pharaoh is one;
41:26 are seven years; the D is one.
41:32 the doubling of Pharaoh's D means that the thing
Num 12:6 a vision, I speak with him in a D

Judg 7:13 man was telling a D to his comrade; and
7:13 "Behold, I dreamed a D; and lo, a cake
7:15 the telling of the D and its interpretation, he
1Kgs 3:5 to Solomon in a D by night; and God
3:15 And Solomon awoke, and behold, it was a D
Esth 10:5 For I remember the D that I had concerning
11:2 Kish, of the tribe of Benjamin, had a D
11:4 And this was his D:
11:12 Mordecai saw in his D what God had determined
Job 20:8 fly away like a D, and not be found;
33:15 In a D, in a vision of the night,
Ps 73:20 They are like a D when one awakes, on
90:5 they are like a D, like grass which is
126:1 fortunes of Zion, we were like those who D
Eccl 5:3 For a D comes with much business, and a
Is 29:7 shall be like a D, a vision of the
Jer 23:28 prophet who has a D tell the dream, but
23:28 a dream tell the D, but let him who
29:8 the dreams which they D,
Dan 2:3 them, "I had a D, and my spirit is
2:3 and my spirit is troubled to know the D
2:4 Tell your servants the D, and we will show
2:5 known to me the D and its interpretation, you
2:6 if you show the D and its interpretation, you
2:6 Therefore show me the D and its interpretation."
2:7 tell his servants the D, and we will show
2:9 do not make the D known to me, there
2:9 Therefore tell me the D, and I shall know
2:26 known to me the D that I have seen
2:28 Your D and the visions of your head as
2:36 "This was the D; now we will tell the
2:45 The D is certain, and its interpretation sure."
4:5 I had a D which made me afraid; as
4:6 make known to me the interpretation of the D
4:7 I told them the D, but they could not
4:8 I told him the D, saying,
4:9 you, here is the D which I saw; tell
4:18 lowliest of men.' This D I, King Nebuchadnezzar, saw.
4:19 "Belteshazzar, let not the D or the interpretation
4:19 "My lord, may the D be for those who
7:1 Babylon, Daniel had a D and visions of his
7:1 he wrote down the D, and told the sum
Joel 2:28 your old men shall D dreams, and your young
2Mac 15:11 all by relating a D, a sort of vision,
Mt 1:20 to him in a D, saying, "Joseph, son of
2:12 being warned in a D not to return to
2:13 to Joseph in a D and said, "Rise, take
2:19 Lord appeared in a D to Joseph in Egypt,
2:22 being warned in a D he withdrew to the
27:19 have suffered much over him today in a D
Acts 2:17 your old men shall D dreams;

DREAMED (13)

Gen 28:12 And he D that there was a ladder set
37:6 dream which I have D:
37:9 Then he D another dream, and told it to
37:9 said, "Behold, I have D another dream; and behold,
37:10 him, "What is this dream that you have D
40:5 one night they both D—the butler and the
41:1 two whole years, Pharaoh D that he was standing
41:5 he fell asleep and D a second time; and
41:11 of the guard, we D on the same night,
42:9 dreams which he had D of them; and he
Judg 7:13 he said, "Behold, I D a dream; and lo,
Jer 23:25 name, saying, 'I have D, I have dreamed!'
23:25 have dreamed, I have D

DREAMER (4)

Gen 37:19 They said to one another, "Here comes this D
Deut 13:1 among you, or a D of dreams, and gives
13:3 prophet or to that D of dreams; for the
13:5 that prophet or that D of dreams shall be

DREAMERS (2)

Jer 27:9 prophets, your diviners, your D, your soothsayers, or
Zech 10:2 diviners see lies; the D tell false dreams, and

DREAMING

Is 56:10 dogs, they cannot bark; D, lying down, loving to

DREAMINGS

Jude 1:8 these men in their D defile the flesh, reject

DREAMS (31)

Gen 37:8 yet more for his D and for his words.
37:20 we shall see what will become of his D
40:8 him, "We have had D, and there is no
41:12 him, he interpreted our D to us, giving an
42:9 And Joseph remembered the D which he had
Deut 13:1 or a dreamer of D, and gives you a
13:3 to that dreamer of D; for the LORD your
13:5 or that dreamer of D shall be put to
1Sam 28:6 answer him, either by D, or by Urim, or
28:15 by prophets or by D; therefore I have summoned
Job 7:14 dost scare me with D and terrify me with
Eccl 5:7 For when D increase, empty words grow many: but
Wis 18:17 once apparitions in dreadful D greatly troubled them,
18:19 were dying; for the D which disturbed them
Sir 34:1 and false hopes, and D give wings to fools.
34:2 wind, so is he who gives heed to D
34:3 The vision of D is this against that, the
34:5 Divinations and omens and D are folly, and like
34:7 For D have deceived many, and those who put
Is 29:8 when a hungry man D he is eating and
29:8 when a thirsty man D he is drinking and
Jer 23:27 my name by their D which they tell one
23:32 those who prophesy lying D, says the LORD, and
29:8 not listen to the D which they dream,
Dan 1:17 and Daniel had understanding in all visions and D
2:1 of Nebuchadnezzar, Nebuchadnezzar had D; and his
2:2 Chaldeans be summoned, to tell the king his D
5:12 understanding to interpret D, explain riddles, and
Joel 2:28 old men shall dream D, and your young men
Zech 10:2 the dreamers tell false D, and give empty
Acts 2:17 old men shall dream D;

DREGS (2)

Ps 75:8 the earth shall drain it down to the D
Is 51:17 have drunk to the D the bowl of staggering.

DRENCH (4)

Ps 6:6 bed with tears; I D my couch with my
Sir 24:29 water my orchard and D my garden plot"; and
Is 16:9 vine of Sibmah; I D you with my tears,
Ezek 32:6 I will D the land even to the mountains

DRENCHED

Zech 9:15 full like a bowl, D like the corners of

DRENCHES

Sir 39:22 like a river, and D it like a flood.

DRESS (4)

Deut 28:39 shall plant vineyards and D them, but you shall
Jer 4:30 you mean that you D in scarlet, that you
1Mac 11:58 from gold cups and D in purple and wear
Acts 12:8 angel said to him, D yourself and put on

DRESSED (10)

1Sam 25:18 and five sheep ready D, and five measures of
2Sam 19:24 king; he had neither D his feet, nor trimmed
1Kgs 5:17 of the house with D stones.
1Chr 22:2 set stonecutters to prepare D stones for building the
Prov 7:10 a woman meets him, D as a harlot, wily
Is 9:10 we will build with D stones; the sycamores have
Bar 6:12 When they have been D in purple robes,
2Mac 3:26 gloriously beautiful and splendidly D, who stood on
3:33 appeared again to Heliodorus D in the same clothing,
Mk 16:5 on the right side, D in a white robe;

DRESSER

Amos 7:14 a herdsman, and a D of sycamore trees,

DRESSES

Ex 30:7 every morning when he D the lamps he shall

DREW (105)

Gen 18:23 Then Abraham D near, and said, "Wilt thou indeed
19:9 the man Lot, and D near to break the
24:20 to draw, and she D for all his camels.
24:45 and she went down to the spring, and D
33:6 Then the maids D near, they and their children,
33:7 likewise and her children D near and bowed down;
33:7 last Joseph and Rachel D near, and they bowed
37:28 passed by; and they D Joseph up and lifted
38:29 But as he D back his hand, behold, his
47:29 And when the time D near that Israel must
49:33 charging his sons, he D up his feet into
Ex 2:10 she said, "Because I D him out of the
2:16 and they came and D water, and filled the
2:19 the shepherds, and even D water for us and
14:10 When Pharaoh D near, the people of Israel lifted

20:21 afar off, while Moses D near to the thick
Lev 9:5 and all the congregation D near and stood before
9:8 So Aaron D near to the altar, and killed
10:5 So they D near, and carried them in their
16:1 of Aaron, when they D near before the LORD
Num 27:1 Then D near the daughters of Zelophehad the son
Josh 8:11 him went up, and D near before the city,
Judg 8:10 twenty thousand men who D the sword.
9:52 fought against it, and D near to the door
20:2 men on foot that D the sword.
20:15 twenty-six thousand men that D the sword, besides
20:17 hundred thousand men that D sword; all these were
20:20 the men of Israel D up the battle line
20:25 these were men who D the sword.
20:35 these were men who D the sword.
20:46 twenty-five thousand men that D the sword, all of
Ruth 4:7 a transaction, the one D off his sandal and
4:8 he D off his sandal.
1Sam 4:2 The Philistines D up in line against Israel, and
7:6 gathered at Mizpah, and D water and poured it
7:10 burnt offering, the Philistines D near to attack
17:2 valley of Elah, and D up in line of
17:21 Israel and the Philistines D up for battle, army
17:40 his hand, and he D near to the Philistine.
17:41 Philistine came on and D near to David, with
17:48 arose and came and D near to meet David,
17:51 took his sword and D it out of its
30:21 him; and when David D near to the people
2Sam 10:8 Ammonites came out and D up in battle array
10:13 who were with him D near to battle against
18:25 he came apace, and D near.
22:17 he took me, he D me out of many
23:16 of the Philistines, and D water out of the
24:9 thousand valiant men who D the sword, and the
1Kgs 2:1 David's time to die D near, he charged Solomon
6:21 pure gold, and he D chains of gold across,
22:34 But a certain man D his bow at a
2Kgs 2:5 who were at Jericho D near to Elisha, and
9:24 And Jehu D his bow with his full strength,
13:16 the bow"; and he D it.
16:12 Then the king D near to the altar, and
1Chr 5:18 shield and sword, and D the bow, expert in
11:18 of the Philistines, and D water out of the
19:9 Ammonites came out and D up in battle array
19:14 who were with him D near before the Syrians
19:17 came to them, and D up his forces against
21:5 hundred thousand men who D the sword, and in
21:5 and seventy thousand who D the sword.
2Chr 13:3 picked men; and Jeroboam D up his line of
14:8 that carried shields and D bows; all these were
14:10 meet him, and they D up their lines of
18:31 God D them away from him,
18:33 But a certain man D his bow at a
Ps 18:16 he took me, he D me out of many
40:2 He D me up from the desolate pit, out
107:18 of food, and they D near to the gates
Prov 8:27 was there, when he D a circle on the
Wis 19:4 the fate they deserved D them on to this
Sir 51:6 My soul D near to death, and my life
Jer 38:13 Then they D Jeremiah up with ropes and lifted
Lam 4:18 our streets; our end D near; our days were
1Mac 2:49 Now the days D near for Mattathias to die,
5:40 Judas and his army D near to the stream
2Mac 10:25 As he D near, Maccabeus and his men sprinkled
14:44 But as they quickly D back, a space opened
Mt 13:48 it was full, men D it ashore and sat
21:1 And when they D near to Jerusalem and came
21:34 the season of fruit D near, he sent his
26:51 out his hand and D his sword, and struck
Mk 11:1 And when they D near to Jerusalem, to Bethphage
14:47 those who stood by D his sword, and struck
Lk 7:12 As he D near to the gate of the
9:51 When the days D near for him to be
15:25 as he came and D near to the house,
18:35 As he D near to Jericho, a blind man
19:29 When he D near to Bethphage and Bethany, at
19:41 And when he D near and saw the city
22:1 feast of Unleavened Bread D near, which is called
22:45 He D near to Jesus to kiss him;
24:15 discussing together, Jesus himself D near and went
24:28 So they D near to the village to which
Jn 6:66 many of his disciples D back and no longer
18:6 they D back and fell to the ground.
18:10 Peter, having a sword, D it and struck the
Acts 5:37 of the census and D away some of the
7:17 time of the promise D near, which God had
7:31 sight; and as he D near to look, the
16:27 doors were open, he D his sword and was
22:6 made my journey and D near to Damascus, about
Gal 2:12 when they came he D back and separated himself,

DRIED (27)

Gen 8:7 until the waters were D up from the earth.
8:13 month, the waters were D from off the earth;
Num 6:3 juice of grapes or eat grapes, fresh or D
11:6 now our strength is D up, and there is
Josh 2:10 heard how the LORD D up the water of
4:23 the LORD your God D up the waters of
4:23 Red Sea, which he D up for us until
5:1 that the LORD had D up the waters of
Judg 16:7 which have not been D, then I shall become
16:8 which had not been D, and she bound him
1Kgs 13:4 stretched out against him, D up, so that he
17:7 a while the brook D up, because there was
2Kgs 19:24 foreign waters, and I D up with the sole
Jud 5:13 Then God D up the Red Sea before them,
10:5 and a cake of D fruit and fine bread;
Ps 22:15 breast; my strength is D up like a potsherd,
32:4 me; my strength was D up as by the
Is 19:5 the Nile will be D up, and the river
37:25 drank waters, and I D up with the sole
Jer 23:10 of the wilderness are D up.
50:38 that they may be D up!
Ezek 19:12 ground; the east wind D it up; its fruit
37:11 say, 'Our bones are D up, and our hope
Hos 9:16 stricken, their root is D up, they shall bear
Joel 1:19 the water brooks are D up, and fire has
Zech 10:11 depths of the Nile D up.
Rev 16:12 and its water was D up, to prepare the

DRIES (3)

Job 14:11 river wastes away and D up,
Prov 17:22 but a downcast spirit D up the bones.
Nah 1:4 makes it dry, he D up all the rivers;

DRIFT

Heb 2:1 have heard, lest we D away from it.

DRIFTING (2)

Zeph 2:2 driven away like the D chaff, before there comes
Acts 27:27 come, as we were D across the sea of

DRINK (355)

Gen 19:32 us make our father D wine, and we will
19:33 they made their father D wine that night; and
19:34 let us make him D wine tonight also; then
19:35 they made their father D wine that night also;
21:19 skin with water, and gave the lad a D
24:14 jar that I may D and who shall say,
24:14 and who shall say, D, and I will water
24:17 a little water to D from your jar."
24:18 She said, D, my lord"; and she quickly let
24:18 jar upon her hand, and gave him a D
24:19 finished giving him a D, she said, "I will
24:43 me a little water from your jar to D
24:44 will say to me, D, and I will draw
24:45 her, 'Pray let me D
24:46 her shoulder, and said, D, and I will give
24:46 will give your camels D also.' So I drank,
24:46 she gave the camels D also.
30:38 the watering troughs, where the flocks came to D
30:38 when they came to D,
35:14 he poured out a D offering on it, and
Ex 7:18 Egyptians will loathe to D water from the Nile."'
7:21 the Egyptians could not D water from the Nile;
7:24 Nile for water to D, for they could not
7:24 for they could not D the water of the
15:23 Marah, they could not D the water of Marah
15:24 murmured against Moses, saying, "What shall we D
17:1 there was no water for the people to D
17:2 with Moses, and said, "Give us water to D
17:6 come out of it, that the people may D
32:6 down to eat and D, and rose up to
32:20 the people of Israel D it.
Lev 10:9 spoke to Aaron, saying, D no wine nor strong
10:9 no wine nor strong D, you nor your sons
11:34 be unclean; and all D which may be drunk
23:13 pleasing odor; and the D offering with it shall
23:18 cereal offering and their D offerings, an offering by
23:37 cereal offerings, sacrifices and D offerings, each on
Num 4:7 the flagons for the D offering; the continual bread
5:24 shall make the woman D the water of bitterness

5:26 shall make the woman D the water.
5:27 he has made her D the water, then, if
6:3 from wine and strong D; he shall drink no
6:3 strong drink; he shall D no vinegar made from
6:3 from wine or strong D, and shall not drink
6:3 drink, and shall not D any juice of grapes
6:15 cereal offering and their D offerings.
6:17 cereal offering and its D offering.
6:20 that the Nazirite may D wine.
15:5 and wine for the D offering, a fourth of
15:7 oil; and for the D offering you shall offer
15:10 shall offer for the D offering half a hin
15:24 cereal offering and its D offering, according to the
20:5 or pomegranates; and there is no water to D
20:8 so you shall give D to the congregation and
20:17 vineyard, neither will we D water from a well;
20:19 highway; and if we D of your water, I
21:22 vineyard; we will not D the water of a
28:7 Its D offering shall be a fourth of a
28:7 shall pour out a D offering of strong drink
28:7 drink offering of strong D to the LORD.
28:8 morning, and like its D offering, you shall offer
28:9 with oil, and its D offering:
28:10 burnt offering and its D offering.
28:14 Their D offerings shall be half a hin of
28:15 burnt offering and its D offering.
28:24 burnt offering and its D offering.
28:31 offer them and their D offering.
29:6 cereal offering, and their D offering, according to the
29:11 cereal offering, and their D offerings.
29:16 cereal offering and its D offering.
29:18 cereal offering and the D offerings for the bulls,
29:19 cereal offering, and their D offerings.
29:21 cereal offering and the D offerings for the bulls,
29:22 cereal offering and its D offering.
29:24 cereal offering and the D offerings for the bulls,
29:25 cereal offering and its D offering.
29:27 cereal offering and the D offerings for the bulls,
29:28 cereal offering and its D offering.
29:30 cereal offering and the D offerings for the bulls,
29:31 cereal offering, and its D offerings.
29:33 cereal offering and the D offerings for the bulls,
29:34 cereal offering, and its D offering.
29:37 cereal offering and the D offerings for the bull,
29:38 cereal offering and its D offering.
29:39 offerings, and for your D offerings, and for your
33:14 there was no water for the people to D
Deut 2:6 water of them for money, that you may D
2:28 money, that I may D; only let me pass
14:26 or wine or strong D, whatever your appetite craves;
28:39 but you shall neither D of the wine nor
29:6 drunk wine or strong D; that you may know
32:38 the wine of their D offering?
Judg 4:19 a little water to D; for I am thirsty."
4:19 and gave him a D and covered him.
7:5 himself; likewise every one that kneels down to D
7:6 people knelt down to D water.
13:4 Therefore beware, and D no wine or strong drink,
13:4 no wine or strong D, and eat nothing unclean,
13:7 a son; so then D no wine or strong
13:7 no wine or strong D, and eat nothing unclean,
13:14 vine, neither let her D wine or strong drink,
13:14 drink wine or strong D, or eat any unclean
Ruth 2:9 to the vessels and D what the young men
1Sam 1:15 neither wine nor strong D, but I have been
30:11 gave him water to D,
2Sam 11:11 to eat and to D, and to lie with
12:3 of his morsel, and D from his cup, and
16:2 for those who faint in the wilderness to D
23:15 give me water to D from the well of
23:16 But he would not D of it; he poured
23:17 Shall I D the blood of the men who
23:17 Therefore he would not D it.
1Kgs 13:8 not eat bread or D water in this place;
13:9 neither eat bread, nor D water, nor return by
13:16 I eat bread nor D water with you in
13:17 neither eat bread nor D water there, nor return
13:18 may eat bread and D water.'" But he lied
13:22 "Eat no bread, and D no water"; your body
17:4 You shall D from the brook, and I have
17:10 little water in a vessel, that I may D
18:41 "Go up, eat and D; for there is a
18:42 So Ahab went up to eat and to D
2Kgs 3:17 so that you shall D, you, your cattle, and
6:22 they may eat and D and go to their
16:13 offering, and poured his D offering, and threw the
16:15 cereal offering, and their D offering; and throw upon
18:27 own dung and to D their own urine?"
18:31 one of you will D the water of his
1Chr 11:17 give me water to D from the well of
11:18 But David would not D of it; he poured
11:19 Shall I D the lifeblood of these men?
11:19 Therefore he would not D it.
29:21 thousand lambs, with their D offerings, and sacrifices
2Chr 28:15 them with food and D, and anointed them; and
Ezra 3:7 the carpenters, and food, D, and oil to the
7:17 cereal offerings and their D offerings, and you shall
Neh 8:10 eat the fat and D sweet wine and send
8:12 way to eat and D and to send portions
Tob 4:15 Do not D wine to excess or let drunkenness
7:9 said to Tobias, "Eat, D, and be merry;
12:19 did not eat or D, but you were seeing
Jud 7:21 have enough water to D their fill for a
7:21 because it was measured out to them to D
12:11 us and eat and D with us.
12:13 in his presence, and D wine and be merry
12:17 D now, and be merry with us!"
12:18 Judith said, "I will D now, my lord, because
Esth 3:15 Haman sat down to D; but the city of
4:16 and neither eat nor D for three days, night
Job 1:4 sisters to eat and D with them.
21:20 destruction, and let them D of the wrath of
22:7 to the weary to D, and you have withheld
Ps 36:8 and thou givest them D from the river of
50:13 flesh of bulls, or D the blood of goats?
60:3 given us wine to D that made us reel.
69:21 for my thirst they gave me vinegar to D
78:15 wilderness, and gave them D abundantly as from the
78:44 that they could not D of their streams.
80:5 given them tears to D in full measure.
102:9 mingle tears with my D,
104:11 the hills, they give D to every beast of
110:7 He will D from the brook by the way;
Prov 4:18 bread of wickedness and D the wine of violence.
5:15 D water from your own cistern, flowing water from
9:5 of my bread and D of the wine I
20:1 is a mocker, strong D a brawler; and whoever
23:7 "Eat and D
23:35 I will seek another D
25:21 give him water to D;
31:4 not for kings to D wine, or for rulers
31:4 rulers to desire strong D;
31:5 strong drink; lest they D and forget what has
31:6 Give strong D to him who is perishing, and
31:7 bitter distress; let them D and forget their poverty,
Eccl 2:24 he should eat and D, and find enjoyment in
3:13 one should eat and D and take pleasure in
5:18 is to eat and D and find enjoyment in
8:15 but to eat and D, and enjoy himself, for
9:7 bread with enjoyment, and D your wine with a
Song 5:1 with my honey, I D my wine with my
5:1 Eat, O friends, and D: drink deeply, O lovers!
5:1 O friends, and drink: D deeply, O lovers!
8:2 you spiced wine to D, the juice of my
Sir 9:10 has aged you will D it with pleasure.
15:3 and give him the water of wisdom to D
24:20 more, and those who D me will thirst for
29:25 the host and provide D without being thanked, and
31:27 to men, if you D it in moderation.
Is 5:11 may run after strong D, who tarry late into
5:22 men in mixing strong D,
21:5 table, they spread the rugs, they eat, they D
22:13 "Let us eat and D, for tomorrow we die."
24:9 No more do they D wine with singing; strong
24:9 wine with singing; strong D is bitter to those
24:9 bitter to those who D it.
28:7 and stagger with strong D; the priest and the
28:7 prophet reel with strong D, they are confused with
28:7 they stagger with strong D; they err in vision,
29:9 not with wine; stagger, but not with strong D
32:6 hungry unsatisfied, and to deprive the thirsty of D
36:12 their own dung and D their own urine?"
36:16 one of you will D the water of his
43:20 the desert, to give D to my chosen people,
51:22 my wrath you shall D no more;
56:12 fill ourselves with strong D; and tomorrow will be
57:6 have poured out a D offering, you have brought
62:8 and foreigners shall not D your wine for which
62:9 who gather it shall D it in the courts
65:13 behold, my servants shall D, but you shall be
66:11 breasts; that you may D deeply with delight from
Jer 2:18 going to Egypt, to D the waters of the

D

2:18 going to Assyria, to D the waters of the
7:18 and they pour out D offerings to other gods,
8:14 us poisoned water to D, because we have sinned
9:15 wormwood, and give them poisonous water to D
16:7 cup of consolation to D for his father or
16:8 feasting to sit with them, to eat and D
19:13 host of heaven, and D offerings have been poured
22:15 your father eat and D and do justice and
23:15 them poisoned water to D; for from the prophets
25:15 whom I send you D it.
25:16 They shall D and stagger and be crazed because
25:17 the Lord sent me D it:
25:26 And after them the king of Babylon shall D
25:27 the God of Israel: D, be drunk and vomit,
25:28 from your hand to D, then you shall say
25:28 'Thus says the LORD of hosts: You must D
32:29 offered to Baal and D offerings have been poured
35:2 of the chambers; then offer them wine to D
35:5 I said to them, D wine."
35:6 they answered, "We will D no wine, for Jonadab
35:6 us, 'You shall not D wine, neither you nor
35:8 he commanded us, to D no wine all our
35:14 to his sons, to D no wine, has been
35:14 been kept; and they D none to this day,
46:10 and be sated, and D its fill of their
49:12 did not deserve to D the cup must drink
49:12 drink the cup must D it, will you go
49:12 You shall not go unpunished, but you must D
Lam 5:4 for the water we D, the wood we get
Ezek 4:11 And water you shall D by measure, the sixth
4:11 of a hin; once a day you shall D
4:16 fearfulness; and they shall D water by measure and
12:18 bread with quaking, and D water with trembling and
12:19 bread with fearfulness, and D water in dismay,
20:28 they poured out their D offerings.
23:32 Lord GOD: "You shall D your sister's cup which
23:34 sister Samaria; you shall D it and drain it
25:4 fruit, and they shall D your milk.
31:14 that no trees that D water may reach up
31:16 of Lebanon, all that D water, will be comforted
34:18 your pasture; and to D of clear water, that
34:19 with your feet, and D what you have fouled
39:17 shall eat flesh and D blood.
39:18 of the mighty, and D the blood of the
39:19 you are filled, and D blood till you are
44:21 No priest shall D wine, when he enters the
45:17 offerings, cereal offerings, and D offerings, at the
Dan 1:10 your food and your D, should see that you
1:12 be given vegetables to eat and water to D
1:16 wine they were to D, and gave them vegetables.
5:2 and his concubines might D from them.
Hos 2:5 my oil and my D
Joel 1:9 cereal offering and the D offering are cut off
1:12 Because cereal offering and D offering are withheld
2:14 cereal offering and a D offering for the LORD,
Amos 2:8 of their God they D the wine of those
2:12 you made the Nazirites D wine, and commanded the
4:1 'Bring, that we may D
4:8 to one city to D water, and were not
5:11 but you shall not D their wine.
6:6 instruments of music; who D wine in bowls, and
9:14 shall plant vineyards and D their wine, and they
Obad 1:16 nations round about shall D; they shall drink, and
1:16 shall drink; they shall D, and stagger, and shall
Jon 3:7 them not feed, or D water,
Mic 2:11 will preach to you of wine and strong D
6:15 tread grapes, but not D wine.
Hab 2:15 who makes his neighbors D of the cup of
2:16 D, yourself, and stagger!
Zeph 1:13 vineyards, they shall not D wine from them."
Hag 1:6 never have enough; you D, but you never have
Zech 7:6 eat and when you D, do you not eat
7:6 eat for yourselves and D for yourselves?
9:15 slingers; and they shall D their blood like wine,
1Mac 1:22 Presence, the cups for D offerings, the bowls, the
1:45 offerings and sacrifices and D offerings in the
11:58 him the right to D from gold cups and
2Mac 15:39 it is harmful to D wine alone, or, again,
15:39 alone, or, again, to D water alone, while wine
Mt 6:25 or what you shall D, nor about your body,
6:31 or 'What shall we D or 'What shall we
20:22 Are you able to D the cup that I
20:22 to drink the cup that I am to D
20:23 to them, "You will D my cup, but to
25:35 and you gave me D, I was a stranger
25:37 and feed thee, or thirsty and give thee D
25:42 you gave me no D,
26:27 it to them, saying, D of it, all of
26:29 you I shall not D again of this fruit
26:29 that day when I D it new with you
26:42 cannot pass unless I D it, thy will be
27:34 offered him wine to D, mingled with gall; but
27:34 it, he would not D it.
27:48 a reed, and gave it to him to D
Mk 9:41 cup of water to D because you bear the
10:38 Are you able to D the cup that I
10:38 the cup that I D, or to be baptized
10:39 "The cup that I D you will drink; and
10:39 I drink you will D; and with the baptism
14:25 you, I shall not D again of the fruit
14:25 that day when I D it new in the
15:35 it to him to D, saying, "Wait, let us
16:18 serpents, and if they D any deadly thing, it
Lk 1:15 Lord, and he shall D no wine nor strong
1:15 no wine nor strong D, and he will be
5:30 do you eat and D with tax collectors and
5:33 disciples of the Pharisees, but yours eat and D
12:19 take your ease, eat, D, be merry.'
12:29 what you are to D, nor be of anxious
12:45 and to eat and D and get drunk,
17:8 till I eat and D; and afterward you shall
17:8 and drink; and afterward you shall eat and D
22:18 on I shall not D of the fruit of
22:30 you may eat and D at my table in
Jn 4:7 Jesus said to her, "Give me a D
4:9 a Jew, ask a D of me, a woman
4:10 you, 'Give me a D you would have asked
6:53 Son of man and D his blood, you have
6:55 and my blood is D indeed.
7:37 one thirst, let him come to me and D
18:11 sheath; shall I not D the cup which the
Acts 23:12 neither to eat nor D till they had killed
23:21 neither to eat nor D till they have killed
Rom 12:20 is thirsty, give him D; for by so doing
14:17 is not food and D but righteousness and peace
14:21 to eat meat or D wine or do anything
1Cor 9:4 not have the right to our food and D
10:4 food and all drank the same supernatural D
10:7 down to eat and D and rose up to
10:21 You cannot D the cup of the Lord and
10:31 whether you eat or D, or whatever you do,
11:22 houses to eat and D in?
11:25 as often as you D it, in remembrance of
11:26 eat this bread and D the cup, you proclaim
11:28 of the bread and D of the cup.
12:13 all were made to D of one Spirit.
15:32 "Let us eat and D, for tomorrow we die."
Col 2:16 questions of food and D or with regard to
1Tim 5:23 No longer D only water, but use a little
Tit 2:3 slanderers or slaves to D; they are to teach
Heb 9:10 only with food and D and various ablutions,
Rev 14:8 who made all nations D the wine of her
14:10 hand, he also shall D the wine of God's
16:6 prophets, and thou hast given them blood to D

DRINKERS

Joel 1:5 and wail, all you D of wine, because of

DRINKING (28)

Gen 24:19 for your camels also, until they have done D
24:22 the camels had done D, the man took a
Ruth 3:3 the man until he has finished eating and D
1Sam 30:16 the land, eating and D and dancing, because of
1Kgs 1:25 they are eating and D before him, and saying,
10:21 All King Solomon's D vessels were of gold, and
16:9 he was at Tirzah, D himself drunk in the
20:12 message as he was D with the kings in
20:16 noon, while Ben-hadad was D himself drunk in the
1Chr 12:39 three days, eating and D, for their brethren had
2Chr 9:20 All King Solomon's D vessels were of gold, and
Ezra 10:6 neither eating bread nor D water; for he was
Esth 1:8 And D was according to the law, no one
5:6 And as they were D wine, the king said
7:2 day, as they were D wine, the king again
7:8 place where they were D wine, as Haman was
Job 1:13 daughters were eating and D wine in their eldest
1:18 daughters were eating and D wine in their eldest
Is 5:22 who are heroes at D wine, and valiant men
22:13 sheep, eating flesh and D wine.
29:8 man dreams he is D and awakes faint, with
Mt 11:18 came neither eating nor D, and they say, 'He
11:19 man came eating and D, and they say, 'Behold,

	24:38	they were eating and D, marrying and giving in
Lk	5:39	And no one after D old wine desires new;
	7:33	eating no bread and D no wine; and you
	7:34	has come eating and D; and you say, 'Behold,
	10:7	same house, eating and D what they provide, for

DRINKS (20)

Gen	44:5	this that my lord D, and by this that
Num	23:24	devours the prey, and D the blood of the
Deut	11:11	hills and valleys, which D water by the rain
2Sam	19:35	servant taste what he eats or what he D
Esth	1:7	D were served in golden goblets, goblets of different
Job	6:4	in me; my spirit D their poison; the terrors
	15:16	corrupt, a man who D iniquity like water!
	34:7	is like Job, who D up scoffing like water,
Prov	26:6	his own feet and D violence.
Sir	26:12	opens his mouth and D from any water near
Is	44:12	his strength fails, he D no water and is
Dan	14:6	much he eats and D every day?"
Mt	24:49	servants, and eats and D with the drunken,
Jn	4:13	her, "Every one who D of this water will
	4:14	thirst again, but whoever D of the water that
	6:54	eats my flesh and D my blood has eternal
	6:56	eats my flesh and D my blood abides in
1Cor	11:27	eats the bread or D the cup of the
	11:29	one who eats and D without discerning the body
	11:29	the body eats and D judgment upon himself.

DRIP (5)

Ps	65:11	tracks of thy chariot D with fatness.
	65:12	pastures of the wilderness D, the hills gird
Prov	5:3	of a loose woman D honey, and her speech
Joel	3:18	day the mountains shall D sweet wine, and the
Amos	9:13	seed; the mountains shall D sweet wine, and all

DRIPPED

Song	5:5	beloved, and my hands D with myrrh, my fingers

DRIPPING (2)

Prov	19:13	quarreling is a continual D of rain.
	27:15	A continual D on a rainy day and a

DRIPPINGS (2)

Ps	19:10	also than honey and D of the honeycomb.
Prov	24:13	is good, and the D of the honeycomb are

DRIVE (62)

Ex	6:1	strong hand he will D them out of his
	11:1	you go, he will D you away completely.
	23:28	before you, which shall D out Hivite, Canaanite, and
	23:29	I will not D them out from before you
	23:30	by little I will D them out from before
	23:31	hand, and you shall D them out before you.
	33:2	you, and I will D out the Canaanites, the
	34:11	Behold, I will D out before you the Amorites,
Num	22:6	to defeat them and D them from the land;
	22:11	fight against them and D them out.'"
	33:52	Canaan, then you shall D out all the inhabitants
	33:55	if you do not D out the inhabitants of
Deut	4:27	where the LORD will D you.
	9:3	you; so you shall D them out, and make
	11:23	then the LORD will D out all these nations
Josh	3:10	he will without fail D out from before you
	13:6	I will myself D them out from before the
	13:13	of Israel did not D out the Geshurites or
	14:12	me, and I shall D them out as the
	15:63	of Judah could not D out; so the Jebusites
	16:10	However they did not D out the Canaanites that
	17:13	and did not utterly D them out.
	17:18	borders; for you shall D out the Canaanites, though
	23:5	back before you, and D them out of your
	23:13	will not continue to D out these nations before
Judg	1:19	but he could not D out the inhabitants of
	1:21	of Benjamin did not D out the Jebusites who
	1:27	Manasseh did not D out the inhabitants of
	1:28	but did not utterly D them out.
	1:29	And Ephraim did not D out the Canaanites who
	1:30	Zebulun did not D out the inhabitants of Kitron,
	1:31	Asher did not D out the inhabitants of Acco,
	1:32	for they did not D them out.
	1:33	did not D out the inhabitants of Beth-shemesh,
	2:3	say, I will not D them out before you;
	2:21	I will not henceforth D out before them any
	11:7	not hate me, and D me out of my
2Chr	20:7	not, O our God, D out the inhabitants of
	20:11	us by coming to D us out of thy
Job	24:3	They D away the ass of the fatherless; they
	30:12	the rabble rise, they D me forth, they cast
Ps	36:11	hand of the wicked D me away.
	44:2	thy own hand didst D out the nations, but
	68:2	is driven away, so D them away; as wax
	80:8	of Egypt; thou didst D out the nations and
Prov	22:10	D out a scoffer, and strife will go out,
Wis	17:8	those who promised to D off the fears and
Sir	8:19	every one, lest you D away your good luck.
	38:20	your heart to sorrow; D it away, remembering the
Jer	24:9	places where I shall D them.
	27:10	land, and I will D you out, and you
	27:15	result that I will D you out and you
Ezek	4:13	nations whither I will D them."
	8:6	are committing here, to D me far from my
	39:2	turn you about and D you forward, and bring
Hos	9:15	their deeds I will D them out of my
Joel	2:20	far from you, and D him into a parched
Mic	2:9	of my people you D out from their pleasant
2Mac	9:4	ordered his charioteer to D without stopping until he
Mk	11:15	temple and began to D out those who sold
Lk	19:45	temple and began to D out those who sold,
1Cor	5:13	D out the wicked person from among you."

DRIVEN (64)

Gen	4:14	Behold, thou hast D me this day away from
Ex	10:11	And they were D out from Pharaoh's presence.
	22:10	is hurt or is D away, without any one
Lev	26:36	the sound of a D leaf shall put them
Num	32:21	LORD, until he has D out his enemies from
Deut	28:34	that you shall be D mad by the sight
	30:1	LORD your God has D you,
Josh	13:12	Moses had defeated and D out.
	23:9	For the LORD has D out before you great
1Sam	26:19	LORD, for they have D me out this day
2Chr	13:9	Have you not D out the priests of the
Job	6:13	and any resource is D from me.
	13:25	Wilt thou frighten a D leaf and pursue dry
	18:18	light into darkness, and D out of the world.
	30:5	They are D out from among men; they shout
Ps	31:22	my alarm, "I am D far from thy sight."
	68:2	As smoke is D away, so drive them away;
	109:10	beg; may they be D out of the ruins
Eccl	3:15	seeks what has been D away.
Wis	5:14	like a light hoarfrost D away by a storm;
	17:15	sleep, and now were D by monstrous specters, and
Sir	27:2	As a stake is D firmly into a fissure
	28:15	Slander has D away courageous women, and
	29:18	the sea; it has D men of power into
Is	19:7	will dry up, be D away, and be no
	27:13	and those who were D out to the land
	41:2	with his sword, like D stubble with his bow.
Jer	8:3	places where I have D them, says the LORD
	13:24	scatter you like chaff D by the wind from
	16:15	countries where he had D them.' For I will
	23:2	my flock, and have D them away, and you
	23:3	countries where I have D them, and I will
	23:8	countries where he had D them.' Then they shall
	23:12	which they shall be D and fall; for I
	29:14	places where I have D you, says the LORD,
	29:18	nations where I have D them,
	40:12	which they had been D and came to the
	43:5	which they had been D –
	46:28	to which I have D you, but of you
	49:5	and you shall be D out, every man straight
	49:36	nation to which those D out of Elam shall
	50:17	is a hunted sheep D away by lions.
Lam	3:2	his wrath; he has D and brought me into
	5:5	necks we are hard D; we are weary, we
Dan	4:25	that you shall be D from among men, and
	4:32	and you shall be D from among men, and
	4:33	He was D from among men, and ate grass
	5:21	from him; he was D from among men, and
	9:7	to which thou hast D them, because of the
Obad	1:7	deceived you, they have D you to the border;
Mic	4:6	those who have been D away, and those whom
Zeph	2:2	nation, before you are D away like the drifting
	2:4	Ashdod's people shall be D out at noon, and
1Mac	7:6	your friends, and have D us out of our
2Mac	4:26	by another man, was D as a fugitive into
	5:9	and he who had D many from their own
Mk	9:29	"This kind cannot be D out by anything but
Lk	8:29	the bonds and was D by the demon into
Acts	27:15	wind, we gave way to it and were D
	27:17	Syrtis, they lowered the gear, and so were D
2Cor	4:8	crushed; perplexed, but not D to despair;

D

Jas 1:6 the sea that is D and tossed by the
3:4 so great and are D by strong winds, they
2Pet 2:17 waterless springs and mists D by a storm; for

DRIVER (4)

1Kgs 22:34 he said to the D of his chariot, "Turn
2Chr 18:33 he said to the D of his chariot, "Turn
Job 39:7 city; he hears not the shouts of the D
1Mac 6:37 who fought from there, and also its Indian D

DRIVES (7)

2Kgs 9:20 of Nimshi; for he D furiously."
Ps 1:4 chaff which the wind D away.
Prov 20:26 winnows the wicked, and D the wheel over them.
22:15 the rod of discipline D it far from him.
Sir 38:25 of a goad, who D oxen and is occupied
Is 28:28 for ever; when he D his cart wheel over
59:19 rushing stream, which the wind of the LORD D

DRIVING (13)

Deut 4:38 by his great power, D out before you nations
9:4 that the LORD is D them out before you.
9:5 LORD your God is D them out from before
18:12 LORD your God is D them out before you.
Judg 2:23 left those nations, not D them out at once,
2Sam 6:3 sons of Abinadab, were D the new cart
7:23 and terrible things, by D out before his people
2Kgs 9:20 And the D is like the driving of Jehu
9:20 driving is like the D of Jehu the son
1Chr 13:7 Uzzah and Ahio were D the cart.
17:21 and terrible things, in D out nations before thy
Ps 35:5 angel of the LORD D them on!
Sir 43:13 command he sends the D snow and speeds the

DROMEDARIES

Is 66:20 upon mules, and upon D, to my holy mountain

DROOPING (2)

Sir 25:22 D hands and weak knees are caused by the
Heb 12:12 Therefore lift your D hands and strengthen your

DROP (12)

Deut 28:40 for your olives shall D off.
32:2 May my teaching D as the rain, my speech
33:28 wine; yea, his heavens D down dew.
Judg 2:19 them; they did not D any of their practices
Neh 6:9 thinking, "Their hands will D from the work, and
Job 29:17 unrighteous, and made him D his prey from his
36:28 skies pour down, and D upon man abundantly.
Prov 3:20 forth, and the clouds D down the dew.
Wis 11:22 scales, and like a D of morning dew that
Sir 18:9 Like a D of water from the sea and
Is 40:15 nations are like a D from a bucket, and
Ezek 39:3 will make your arrows D out of your right

DROPPED (5)

Judg 5:4 trembled, and the heavens D, yea, the clouds dropped
5:4 dropped, yea, the clouds D water.
2Chr 24:10 brought their tax and D it into the chest
Job 29:22 again, and my word D upon them.
Rev 16:21 heavy as a hundred-weight, D on men from heaven,

DROPPING

1Sam 14:26 behold, the honey was D, but no man put

DROPPINGS

Tob 2:10 wall and their fresh D fell into my open

DROPS (4)

Job 36:27 he draws up the D of water, he distils
38:28 who has begotten the D of dew?
Song 5:2 my locks with the D of the night."
Sir 1:2 of the sea, the D of rain, and the

DROPSY

Lk 14:2 there was a man before him who had D

DROSS (7)

Ps 119:119 thou dost count as D; therefore I love thy
Prov 25:4 Take away the D from the silver, and the
Is 1:22 Your silver has become D, your wine mixed with
1:25 will smelt away your D as with lye and
Ezek 22:18 of Israel has become D to me; all of
22:18 iron and lead in the furnace, have become D
22:19 you have all become D, therefore, behold, I will

DROUGHT (10)

Deut 28:22 fiery heat, and with D, and with blasting, and
Job 24:19 D and heat snatch away the snow waters; so
Sir 35:20 as clouds of rain in the time of D
Jer 2:6 in a land of D and deep darkness, in
14:1 to Jeremiah concerning the D:
17:8 in the year of D, for it does not
50:38 A D upon her waters, that they may be
51:43 horror, a land of D and a desert, a
Hos 13:5 in the land of D;
Hag 1:11 have called for a D upon the land and

DROVE (47)

Gen 3:24 He D out the man; and at the east
15:11 upon the carcasses, Abram D them away.
31:18 on camels; and he D away all his cattle,
32:16 of his servants, every D by itself, and said
32:16 put a space between D and drove."
32:16 me, and put a space between drove and D
Ex 2:17 The shepherds came and D them away; but Moses
10:19 lifted the locusts and D them into the Red
14:21 sea; and the LORD D the sea back by
14:25 wheels so that they D heavily; and the Egyptians
Num 5:4 Israel did so, and D them outside the camp;
Josh 15:14 And Caleb D out from there the three sons
24:12 hornet before you, which D them out before you,
24:18 passed; and the LORD D out before us all
Judg 1:20 had said; and he D out from it the
4:21 softly to him and D the peg into his
6:9 who oppressed you, and D them out before you,
9:41 at Arumah; and Zebul D out Gaal and his
1Sam 30:20 herds; and the people D those cattle before him,
2Sam 11:23 the field; but we D them back to the
1Kgs 14:24 nations which the LORD D out before the people
2Kgs 16:3 nations whom the LORD D out before the people
16:6 Elath for Edom, and D the men of Judah
17:8 nations whom the LORD D out before the people
17:21 And Jeroboam D Israel from following the LORD
and
21:2 nations whom the LORD D out before the people
2Chr 28:3 nations whom the LORD D out before the people
33:2 nations whom the LORD D out before the people
Jud 5:8 to know; hence they D them out from the
5:12 and so the Egyptians D them out of their
5:14 Sinai and Kadesh-barnea, and D out all the people
5:16 And they D out before them the Canaanites and
Ps 78:55 He D out nations before them; he apportioned them
Jer 32:37 countries to which I D them in my anger
Lam 3:13 He D into my heart the arrows of his
Ezek 28:16 and the guardian cherub D you out from the
Dan 3:49 and his companions, and D the fiery flame out
1Mac 1:53 in the land; they D Israel into hiding in
7:46 out-flanked the enemy and D them back to their
13:11 a considerable army; he D out its occupants and
2Mac 1:12 For he D out those who fought against the
Mt 21:12 temple of God and D out all who sold
Mk 1:12 The Spirit immediately D him out into the
Jn 2:15 whip of cords, he D them all, with the
Acts 13:50 Paul and Barnabas, and D them out of their
18:16 And he D them from the tribunal.
1Thes 2:15 and the prophets, and D us out, and displease

DROVES (2)

Gen 30:40 he put his own D apart, and did not
32:19 all who followed the D, "You shall say the

DROWN

Song 8:7 love, neither can floods D it.

DROWNED (6)

Wis 10:19 deep waters; but she D their enemies, and cast
2Mac 12:4 out to sea and D them, not less than
Mt 18:6 neck and to be D in the depth of
Mk 5:13 the sea, and were D in the sea.
Lk 8:33 the steep bank into the lake and were D
Heb 11:29 when they attempted to do the same, were D

DROWSINESS

Prov 23:21 come to poverty, and D will clothe a man

DROWSY (2)

2Sam 4:6 wheat, but she grew D and slept; so Rechab
Sir 22:8 tells it to a D man; and at the

DRUNK (50)

Gen 9:21 the wine, and became D, and lay uncovered in

Lev 11:34 drink which may be D from every such vessel
Deut 29:6 and you have not D wine or strong drink;
32:42 will make my arrows D with blood, and my
Ruth 3:7 Boaz had eaten and D, and his heart was
1Sam 1:9 they had eaten and D in Shiloh, Hannah rose.
1:15 sorely troubled; I have D neither wine nor strong
25:36 for he was very D; so she told him
30:12 not eaten bread or D water for three days
2Sam 11:13 that he made him D; and in the evening
1Kgs 13:22 have eaten bread and D water in the place
13:23 had eaten bread and D, he saddled the ass
16:9 at Tirzah, drinking himself D in the house of
20:16 Ben-hadad was drinking himself D in the booths, he
2Kgs 6:23 they had eaten and D, he sent them away,
Jud 6:4 their mountains will be D with their blood, and
12:20 than he had ever D in any one day
Esth 14:17 the king's feast or D the wine of the
Sir 31:28 Wine D in season and temperately is rejoicing of
31:29 Wine D to excess is bitterness of soul, with
Is 29:9 Be D, but not with wine; stagger, but not
34:5 For my sword has D its fill in the
49:26 and they shall be D with their own blood
51:17 Jerusalem, you who have D at the hand of
51:17 his wrath, who have D to the dregs the
51:21 are afflicted, who are D, but not with wine:
63:6 anger, I made them D in my wrath, and
Jer 25:27 of Israel: Drink, be D and vomit, fall and
48:26 "Make him D, because he magnified himself against
51:39 feast and make them D, till they swoon away
51:57 I will make D her princes and her wise
Lam 4:21 pass; you shall become D and strip yourself bare.
Ezek 39:19 blood till you are D, at the sacrificial feast
Dan 5:23 and your concubines have D wine from them; and
Joel 3:3 for wine, and have D it.
Obad 1:16 For as you have D upon my holy mountain,
Hab 2:15 wrath, and makes them D, to gaze on their
1Mac 16:16 and his sons were D, Ptolemy and his men
2Mac 7:36 a brief suffering have D of everflowing life under
Lk 12:45 and drink and get D,
Jn 2:10 and when men have D freely, then the poor
Acts 2:15 these men are not D, as you suppose, since
1Cor 11:21 meal, and one is hungry and another is D
Eph 5:18 And do not get D with wine, for that
1Thes 5:7 and those who get D are drunk at night.
5:7 who get drunk are D at night.
Heb 6:7 For land which has D the rain that often
Rev 17:2 fornication the dwellers on earth have become D
17:6 I saw the woman, D with the blood of
18:3 for all nations have D the wine of her

DRUNKARD (10)

Deut 21:20 a glutton and a D
Prov 23:21 of meat; for the D and the glutton will
26:9 the hand of a D is a proverb in
26:10 is he who hires a passing fool or D
Sir 19:1 workman who is a D will not become rich;
Mt 11:19 a glutton and a D, a friend of tax
Lk 7:34 a glutton and a D, a friend of tax
1Cor 5:11 is an idolater, reviler, D, or robber--not even
1Tim 3:3 an apt teacher, no D, not violent but gentle,
Tit 1:6 or quick-tempered or a D or violent or greedy

DRUNKARDS (7)

Ps 69:12 the gate, and the D make songs about me.
Is 28:1 proud crown of the D of Ephraim, and to
28:3 proud crown of the D of Ephraim will be
Ezek 23:42 of the common sort D were brought from the
Hos 4:18 A band of D, they give themselves to harlotry;
Joel 1:5 Awake, you D, and weep; and wail, all you
1Cor 6:10 nor the greedy, nor D, nor revilers, nor robbers

DRUNKEN (12)

1Sam 1:13 her to be a D woman.
1:14 said to her, "How long will you be D
Jud 13:15 he lay in his D stupor.
Job 12:25 them stagger like a D man.
Ps 107:27 reeled and staggered like D men, and were at
Sir 26:8 when a wife is D; she will not hide
Is 19:14 her doings as a D man staggers in his
24:20 earth staggers like a D man, it sways like
Jer 23:9 I am like a D man, like a man
51:7 making all the earth D; the nations drank of
Nah 3:11 You also will be D, you will be dazed;
Mt 24:49 and drinks with the D,

DRUNKENNESS (9)

Tob 4:15 to excess or let D go with you on
Eccl 10:17 the proper time, for strength, and not for D
Sir 31:30 D increases the anger of a fool to his
Jer 13:13 I will fill with D all the inhabitants of
Ezek 23:33 will be filled with D and sorrow.
Lk 21:34 down with dissipation and D and cares of this
Rom 13:13 not in reveling and D, not in debauchery and
Gal 5:21 dissension, party spirit, envy, D, carousing, and the
1Pet 4:3 living in licentiousness, passions, D, revels, carousing,

DRUSILLA

Acts 24:23 came with his wife D, who was a Jewess;

DRY (84)

Gen 1:9 place, and let the D land appear." And it
1:10 God called the D land Earth, and the waters
7:22 man; everything on the D land in whose nostrils
8:13 and behold, the face of the ground was D
8:14 twenty-seventh day of the month, the earth was D
Ex 4:9 pour it upon the D ground; and the water
4:9 become blood upon the D ground."
14:16 Israel may go on D ground through the sea.
14:21 and made the sea D land, and the waters
14:22 of the sea on D ground, the waters being
14:29 of Israel walked on D ground through the sea,
15:19 of Israel walked on D ground in the midst
Lev 7:10 mixed with oil or D, shall be for all
Deut 29:19 away of moist and D alike.
Josh 3:17 were passing over on D ground, the priests who
3:17 the LORD stood on D ground in the midst
4:18 were lifted up on D ground, the waters of
4:22 over this Jordan on D ground.'
9:5 all their provisions were D and moldy.
9:12 now, behold, it is D and moldy;
Judg 6:37 alone, and it is D on all the ground,
6:39 pray, let it be D only on the fleece,
6:40 night; for it was D on the fleece only,
2Kgs 2:8 could go over on D ground.
3:16 'I will make this D stream-bed full of pools.'
Neh 9:11 of the sea on D land; and thou didst
Jud 7:21 their cisterns were going D, and they did not
Job 12:15 withholds the waters, they D up; if he sends
13:25 driven leaf and pursue D chaff?
15:30 darkness; the flame will D up his shoots, and
18:16 His roots D up beneath, and his branches wither
30:3 hunger they gnaw the D and desolate ground;
Ps 63:1 thee, as in a D and weary land where
66:6 turned the sea into D land; men passed through
74:15 and brooks; thou didst D up ever-flowing streams.
95:5 his hands formed the D land.
106:9 Sea, and it became D; and he led them
Prov 17:1 Better is a D morsel with quiet than a
Wis 4:19 will be left utterly D and barren, and they
19:7 overshadowing the camp, and D land emerging
Sir 39:22 His blessing covers the D land like a river,
40:13 of the unjust will D up like a torrent,
Is 5:24 the stubble, and as D grass sinks down in
19:5 will be parched and D;
19:6 Nile will diminish and D up, reeds and rushes
19:7 by the Nile will D up, be driven away,
25:5 like heat in a D place.
27:11 When its boughs are D, they are broken; women
32:2 of water in a D place, like the shade
35:1 The wilderness and the D land shall be glad,
41:18 of water, and the D land springs of water.
42:15 mountains and hills, and D up all their herbage;
42:15 rivers into islands, and D up the pools.
44:3 and streams on the D ground; I will pour
44:27 to the deep, 'Be D, I will dry up
44:27 'Be dry, I will D up your rivers';
50:2 by my rebuke I D up the sea, I
51:10 not thou that didst D up the sea, the
53:2 a root out of D ground; he had no
56:3 "Behold, I am a D tree."
Jer 18:14 mountain waters run D, the cold flowing streams?
50:12 the nations, a wilderness D and desert.
51:36 I will D up her sea and make her
51:36 and make her fountain D;
Lam 4:8 it has become as D as wood.
Ezek 17:24 high the low tree, D up the green tree,
17:24 tree, and make the D tree flourish.
19:13 the wilderness, in a D and thirsty land.
20:47 in you and every D tree; the blazing flame
30:12 And I will D up the Nile, and will
37:2 upon the valley; and lo, they were very D

D

	37:4	say to them, O D bones, hear the word
Hos	5:12	to Ephraim, and like D rot to the house
	9:14	a miscarrying womb and D breasts.
	13:15	and his fountain shall D up, his spring shall
Jon	1:9	the sea and the D land."
	2:10	out Jonah upon the D land.
Nah	1:4	sea and makes it D, he dries up all
	1:10	they are consumed, like D stubble.
Zeph	2:13	Nineveh a desolation, a D waste like the desert.
Hag	2:6	the sea and the D land;
2Mac	1:19	the hollow of a D cistern, where they took
Lk	23:30	is green, what will happen when it is D
Heb	11:29	Sea as if on D land; but the Egyptians,

DRYSHOD

Is	11:15	it into seven channels that men may cross D

DUE (54)

Ex	23:6	not pervert the justice D to your poor in
	29:28	sons as a perpetual D from the people of
Lev	7:34	sons, as a perpetual D from the people of
	7:36	it is a perpetual D throughout their generations."
	10:13	because it is your D and your sons' due,
	10:13	due and your sons' D, from the offerings by
	10:14	are given as your D and your sons' due,
	10:14	due and your sons' D, from the sacrifices of
	10:15	with you, as a D for ever; as the
	24:9	offerings by fire to the LORD, a perpetual D
	25:52	the years of service D from him he shall
Num	18:8	portion, and to your sons as a perpetual D
	18:11	you, as a perpetual D; every one who is
	18:19	you, as a perpetual D; it is a covenant
	18:29	shall present every offering D to the LORD, from
	28:2	to me in its D season.'
Deut	12:26	holy things which are D from you, and your
	18:3	shall be the priests' D from the people, from
	24:17	not pervert the justice D to the sojourner or
	27:19	who perverts the justice D to the sojourner, the
Judg	6:26	with stones laid in D order; then take the
1Sam	1:20	remembered her; and in D time Hannah conceived
1Chr	6:32	performed their service in D order.
	16:29	the LORD the glory D his name; bring an
2Chr	31:4	to give the portion D to the priests and
Ps	7:17	the LORD the thanks D to his righteousness, and
	28:4	hands; render them their D reward.
	65:1	Praise is D to thee, O God, in Zion;
	96:8	the LORD the glory D his name; bring an
	104:27	them their food in D season.
	145:15	them their food in D season.
Prov	3:27	to whom it is D, when it is in
Wis	14:22	live in great strife D to ignorance, and they
Sir	38:1	physician with the honor D him, according to your
	38:16	body with the honor D him, and do not
Jer	10:7	For this is thy D; for among all the
1Mac	10:36	given them that is D to all the forces
	11:35	the other payments henceforth D to us of the
	11:35	tithes, and the taxes D to us, and the
	11:35	and the crown taxes D to us –
2Mac	8:10	the king the tribute D to the Romans, two
	10:13	to command the respect D his office, he took
Lk	23:40	we are receiving the D reward of our deeds;
Rom	1:27	their own persons the D penalty for their error.
	4:4	not reckoned as a gift but as his D
	13:7	to whom taxes are D, revenue to whom revenue
	13:7	to whom revenue is D, respect to whom respect
	13:7	to whom respect is D, honor to whom honor
	13:7	respect is due, honor to whom honor is D
Gal	6:9	in well-doing, for in D season we shall reap,
Eph	4:18	that is in them, D to their hardness of
Jas	1:16	no variation or shadow D to change.
1Pet	5:6	of God, that in D time he may exalt
Rev	16:6	It is their D

DUES (2)

Deut	18:1	by fire to the LORD, and his rightful D
Rom	13:7	all of them their D, taxes to whom taxes

DUG (28)

Gen	21:30	for me that I D this well."
	26:15	his father's servants had D in the days of
	26:18	And Isaac D again the wells of water which
	26:18	water which had been D in the days of
	26:19	But when Isaac's servants D in the valley and
	26:21	Then they D another well, and they quarreled over
	26:22	moved from there and D another well, and over
	26:25	And there Isaac's servants D a well.
	26:32	well which they had D, and said to him,
Ex	7:24	And all the Egyptians D round about the Nile
Num	21:18	well which the princes D, which the nobles of
2Kgs	19:24	I D wells and drank foreign waters, and I
Tob	2:7	set I went and D a grave and buried
	8:9	arose and went and D a grave,
Ps	35:7	me; without cause they D a pit for my
	57:6	They D a pit in my way, but they
	94:13	until a pit is D for the wicked.
	119:85	Godless men have D pitfalls for me, men who
Is	37:25	I D wells and drank waters, and I dried
Jer	13:7	to the Euphrates, and D, and I took the
	18:20	Yet they have D a pit for my life.
	18:22	For they have D a pit to take me,
Ezek	8:8	wall"; and when I D in the wall, lo,
	12:7	in the evening I D through the wall with
Mt	21:33	hedge around it, and D a wine press in
	25:18	one talent went and D in the ground and
Mk	12:1	hedge around it, and D a pit for the
Lk	6:48	building a house, who D deep, and laid the

DULL (6)

Lev	13:39	body are of a D white, it is tetter
Ps	92:6	The D man cannot know, the stupid cannot
Is	59:1	save, or his ear D, that it cannot hear;
Mt	13:15	people's heart has grown D, and their ears are
Acts	28:27	people's heart has grown D, and their ears are
Heb	5:11	since you have become D of hearing.

DULLEST

Ps	94:8	Understand, O D of the people!

DULLNESS

Lam	3:65	Thou wilt give them D of heart; thy curse

DUMAH (4)

Gen	25:14	Kedar, Adbeel, Mibsam, Mishma, D, Massa,
Josh	15:52	Arab, D, Eshan,
1Chr	1:30	Kedar, Adbeel, Mibsam, Mishma, D, Massa, Hadad,
Is	21:11	The oracle concerning D

DUMB (32)

Ex	4:11	Who makes him D, or deaf, or seeing, or
Ps	31:18	the lying lips be D, which speak insolently against
	38:13	not hear, like a D man who does not
	39:2	I was D and silent, I held my peace
	39:9	I am D, I do not open my mouth;
Prov	31:8	your mouth for the D, for the rights of
Wis	10:21	the mouth of the D, and made the tongues
Is	35:6	the tongue of the D sing for joy.
	53:7	before its shearers is D, so he opened not
	56:10	knowledge; they are all D dogs, they cannot bark;
Bar	6:41	when they see a D man, who cannot speak,
Ezek	3:26	that you shall be D and unable to reprove
	24:27	and you shall speak and be no longer D
	33:22	mouth was opened, and I was no longer D
Dan	10:15	turned my face toward the ground and was D
Hab	2:18	creation when he makes D idols!
	2:19	thing, Awake; to a D stone, Arise!
Mt	9:32	going away, behold, a D demoniac was brought to
	9:33	been cast out, the D man spoke; and the
	12:22	Then a blind and D demoniac was brought to
	12:22	him, so that the D man spoke and saw.
	15:30	maimed, the blind, the D, and many others, and
	15:31	when they saw the D speaking, the maimed whole,
Mk	7:36	deaf hear and the D speak."
	9:17	for he has a D spirit;
	9:25	saying to it, "You D and deaf spirit, I
Lk	1:22	and he made signs to them and remained D
	11:14	a demon that was D; when the demon had
	11:14	had gone out, the D man spoke, and the
Acts	8:32	before its shearer is D, so he opens not
1Cor	12:2	were led astray to D idols, however you may
2Pet	2:16	his own transgression; a D ass spoke with human

DUMBFOUNDED

Ps	31:17	shame, let them go D to Sheol.

DUNG (28)

Ex	29:14	its skin, and its D, you shall burn with
Lev	4:11	its entrails, and its D,
	8:17	its flesh, and its D, he burned with fire
	16:27	their flesh and their D shall be burned with
Num	19:5	her blood, with her D, shall be burned;
1Kgs	14:10	a man burns up D until it is all
2Kgs	6:25	a kab of dove's D for five shekels of

9:37 Jezebel shall be as D upon the face of
18:27 to eat their own D and to drink their
Neh 2:13 Well and to the D Gate, and I inspected
3:13 as far as the D Gate.
3:14 of Beth-haccherem, repaired the D Gate; he rebuilt
12:31 the wall to the D Gate;
Esth 14:2 head with ashes and D, and she utterly humbled
Job 20:7 ever like his own D; those who have seen
Ps 83:10 at Endor, who became D for the ground.
Is 36:12 to eat their own D and drink their own
Jer 8:2 they shall be as D on the surface of
9:22 men shall fall like D upon the open field,
16:4 they shall be as D on the surface of
25:33 buried; they shall be D on the surface of
Ezek 4:12 cake, baking it in their sight on human D
4:15 let you have cow's D instead of human dung,
4:15 dung instead of human D, on which you may
Zeph 1:17 poured out like dust, and their flesh like D
Mal 2:3 your offspring, and spread D upon your faces, the
2:3 upon your faces, the D of your offerings, and
1Mac 2:62 splendor will turn into D and worms.

DUNG-PIT

Is 25:10 place, as straw is trodden down in a D

DUNGEON (6)

Gen 40:15 nothing that they should put me into the D
41:14 hastily out of the D; and when he had
Ex 12:29 who was in the D, and all the first-born
Wis 10:13 with him into the D,
Is 42:7 the prisoners from the D, from the prison those
Jer 37:16 had come to the D cells, and remained there

DUNGHILL (2)

Ezra 6:11 it, and his house shall be made a D
Lk 14:35 land nor for the D; men throw it away.

DUNGHILLS

Sir 22:2 to the filth of D; any one that picks

DURA

Dan 3:1 on the plain of D, in the province of

DURING (27)

Gen 41:34 the land of Egypt D the seven plenteous years.
41:47 D the seven plenteous years the earth brought forth
Lev 15:20 upon which she lies D her impurity shall be
Num 27:14 the wilderness of Zin D the strife of the
Judg 16:30 whom he had slain D his life.
2Kgs 23:22 who judged Israel, or D all the days of
Neh 8:14 should dwell in booths D the feast of the
Jud 2:27 the plain of Damascus D the wheat harvest, and
8:2 and family, had died D the barley harvest.
14:8 what you have done D these days." Then Judith
Eccl 2:3 to do under heaven D the few days of
Ezek 4:9 D the number of days that you lie upon
36:38 the flock at Jerusalem D her appointed feasts, so
Dan 6:28 So this Daniel prospered D the reign of Darius
2Mac 10:6 how not long before, D the feast of booths,
14:4 D that day he kept quiet.
Mt 26:5 But they said, "Not D the feast, lest there
Mk 14:2 for they said, "Not D the feast, lest there
Jn 13:2 And D supper, when the devil had already put
Acts 1:3 proofs, appearing to them D forty days, and speaking
1:21 who have accompanied us D all the time that
12:3 This was D the days of Unleavened Bread.
13:17 made the people great D their stay in the
Rom 7:1 on a person only D his life?
Philem 1:13 me on your behalf D my imprisonment for the
1Pet 3:20 the days of Noah, D the building of the
Rev 11:6 no rain may fall D the days of their

DUST (125)

Gen 2:7 God formed man of D from the ground, and
3:14 you shall go, and D you shall eat all
3:19 were taken; you are D, and to dust you
3:19 are dust, and to D you shall return."
13:16 your descendants as the D of the earth; so
13:16 one can count the D of the earth, your
18:27 I who am but D and ashes.
28:14 shall be like the D of the earth, and
Ex 8:16 rod and strike the D of the earth, that
8:17 rod, and struck the D of the earth, and
8:17 and beast; all the D of the earth became
9:9 it shall become fine D over all the land
Lev 17:13 pour out its blood and cover it with D
Num 5:17 take some of the D that is on the
23:10 Who can count the D of Jacob, or number
Deut 9:21 was as fine as D; and I threw the
9:21 and I threw the D of it into the
28:24 your land powder and D; from heaven it shall
32:24 them, with venom of crawling things of the D
Josh 7:6 Israel; and they put D upon their heads.
1Sam 2:8 the poor from the D; he lifts the needy
2Sam 16:13 went, and threw stones at him and flung D
22:43 them fine as the D of the earth, I
1Kgs 16:2 you out of the D and made you leader
18:38 the stones, and the D, and licked up the
20:10 more also, if the D of Samaria shall suffice
2Kgs 13:7 made them like the D at threshing.
23:6 and beat it to D and cast the dust
23:6 dust and cast the D of it upon the
23:12 pieces, and cast the D of them into the
23:15 stones, crushing them to D; also he burned the
2Chr 1:9 as many as the D of the earth.
34:4 images, and he made D of them and strewed
Tob 3:6 taken up, that I may depart and become D
Jud 2:20 of locusts, like the D of the earth--a
Job 2:12 their robes and sprinkled D upon their heads toward
4:19 foundation is in the D, who are crushed before
5:6 not come from the D, nor does trouble sprout
10:9 thou turn me to D again?
16:15 skin, and have laid my strength in the D
17:16 Shall we descend together into the D
20:11 it will lie down with him in the D
21:26 down alike in the D, and the worms cover
22:24 lay gold in the D, and gold of Ophir
27:16 heap up silver like D, and pile up clothing
28:6 sapphires, and it has D of gold.
30:19 I have become like D and ashes.
34:15 would perish together, and man would return to D
38:38 the heavens, when the D runs into a mass
40:13 them all in the D together; bind their faces
42:6 myself, and repent in D and ashes."
Ps 7:5 the ground, and lay my soul in the D
18:42 beat them fine as D before the wind; I
22:15 lay me in the D of death.
22:29 go down to the D, and he who cannot
30:9 Will the D praise thee?
44:25 bowed down to the D; our body cleaves to
72:9 down before him, and his enemies lick the D
78:27 flesh upon them like D, winged birds like the
83:13 make them like whirling D, like chaff before the
89:39 servant; thou hast defiled his crown in the D
90:3 man back to the D, and sayest, "Turn back,
102:14 her stones dear, and have pity on her D
103:14 knows our frame; he remembers that we are D
104:29 their breath, they die and return to their D
113:7 the poor from the D, and lifts the needy
119:25 soul cleaves to the D; revive me according to
Prov 8:26 the first of the D of the world.
Eccl 3:20 all are from the D, and all turn to
3:20 and all turn to D again.
12:7 the cistern, and the D returns to the earth
Sir 10:9 can he who is D and ashes be proud?
17:27 but all men are D and ashes.
33:10 the ground, and Adam was created of the D
40:3 who is humbled in D and ashes,
41:10 Whatever is from the D returns to dust; so
41:10 the dust returns to D; so the ungodly go
44:22 multiply him like the D of the earth, and
Is 2:10 and hide in the D from before the terror
5:24 blossom go up like D; for they have rejected
17:13 the wind and whirling D before the storm.
25:12 and cast to the ground, even to the D
26:5 low to the ground, casts it to the D
26:19 O dwellers in the D, awake and sing for
29:4 from low in the D your words shall come;
29:4 and your speech shall whisper out of the D
29:5 shall be like small D, and the multitude of
40:12 a span, enclosed the D of the earth in
40:15 are accounted as the D on the scales; behold,
40:15 behold, he takes up the isles like fine D
41:2 he makes them like D with his sword, like
47:1 and sit in the D, O virgin daughter of
49:23 you, and lick the D of your feet.
52:2 yourself from the D, arise, O captive Jerusalem;
65:25 like the ox; and D shall be the serpent's
Lam 2:10 silence; they have cast D on their heads and
2:21 In the D of the streets lie the young
3:29 his mouth in the D -- there may yet
Bar 6:13 wiped because of the D from the temple, which

D

6:17 are full of the D raised by the feet
Ezek 24:7 it upon the ground to cover it with D
26:10 so many that their D will cover you; your
27:30 They cast D on their heads and wallow in
Dan 12:2 who sleep in the D of the earth shall
Amos 2:7 the poor into the D of the earth, and
Mic 1:10 at all; in Beth-le-aphrah roll yourselves in the D
7:17 they shall lick the D like a serpent, like
Nah 1:3 the clouds are the D of his feet.
Zeph 1:17 be poured out like D, and their flesh like
Zech 9:3 heaped up silver like D, and gold like the
1Mac 2:63 has returned to the D, and his plans will
11:71 his garments and put D on his head, and
2Mac 10:25 and his men sprinkled D upon their heads and
14:15 the Gentiles, they sprinkled D upon their heads and
Mt 10:14 words, shake off the D from your feet as
Mk 6:11 leave, shake off the D that is on your
Lk 9:5 town shake off the D from your feet as
10:11 and say, 'Even the D of your town that
Acts 13:51 they shook off the D from their feet against
22:23 their garments and threw D into the air,
1Cor 15:47 earth, a man of D; the second man is
15:48 was the man of D, so are those who
15:48 who are of the D; and as is the
15:49 of the man of D, we shall also bear
Rev 18:19 And they threw D on their heads, as they

DUTIES (19)

Num 3:7 They shall perform D for him and for the
3:8 and attend to the D for the people of
3:28 hundred, attending to the D of the sanctuary.
8:26 you do to the Levites in assigning their D
18:3 and attend to all D of the tent; but
18:5 shall attend to the D of the sanctuary and
18:5 the sanctuary and the D of the altar, that
1Sam 10:25 people the rights and D of the kingship; and
1Chr 24:3 according to the appointed D in their service.
25:1 work and of their D was:
25:8 cast lots for their D, small and great, teacher
26:12 their chief men, had D, just as their brethren
26:29 were appointed to outside D for Israel, as officers
Neh 13:30 and I established the D of the priests and
Sir 32:2 you have fulfilled your D, take your place, that
Ezek 18:11 does none of these D, but eats upon the
1Tim 4:15 Practice these D, devote yourself to them, so that
6:2 Teach and urge these D
Heb 9:6 tent, performing their ritual D;

DUTY (27)

Gen 38:8 wife, and perform the D of a brother-in-law to
Deut 25:5 wife, and perform the D of a husband's brother
25:7 will not perform the D of a husband's brother
2Kgs 11:5 those who come off D on the sabbath and
11:7 you, which come on D in force on the
11:9 were to go off D on the sabbath, with
11:9 were to come on D on the sabbath, and
1Chr 9:27 upon them lay the D of watching, and they
9:33 for they were on D day and night.
23:28 upward—"but their D shall be to assist
24:19 had as their appointed D in their service to
2Chr 5:13 and it was the D of the trumpeters and
8:13 the vestibule, as the D of each day required,
8:14 the priests as the D of each day required,
23:4 Levites who come off D on the sabbath, one
23:8 were to go off D on the sabbath, with
23:8 were to come on D on the sabbath; for
31:16 the LORD as the D of each day required,
Neh 13:13 counted faithful; and their D was to distribute to
Tob 1:8 whom it was my D, as Deborah my father's
Eccl 12:13 this is the whole D of man.
Ezek 45:17 shall be the prince's D to furnish the burnt
2Mac 2:30 It is the D of the original historian to
Lk 1:8 his division was on D,
17:10 servants; we have only done what was our D
Acts 6:3 of wisdom, whom we may appoint to this D
1Tim 5:4 first learn their religious D to their own family

DWARF

Lev 21:20 a hunchback, or a D, or a man with

DWELL (297)

Gen 4:20 father of those who D in tents and have
9:27 Japheth, and let him D in the tents of
13:6 that they could not D together,
16:12 him; and he shall D over against all his
19:30 he was afraid to D in Zoar; so he
20:15 land is before you; D where it pleases you."
24:3 Canaanites, among whom I D,
24:37 in whose land I D;
26:2 go down to Egypt; D in the land of
34:10 You shall D with us; and the land shall
34:10 be open to you; D and trade in it,
34:16 ourselves, and we will D with you and become
34:21 with us; let them D in the land and
34:22 the men agree to D with us, to become
34:23 them, and they will D with us."
35:1 up to Bethel, and D there; and make there
36:7 great for them to D together; the land of
45:10 not tarry; you shall D in the land of
46:34 order that you may D in the land of
47:4 you, let your servants D in the land of
47:6 the land; let them D in the land of
49:13 Zebulun shall D at the shore of the sea;
Ex 2:21 Moses was content to D with the man, and
8:22 Goshen, where my people D, so that no swarms
23:33 They shall not D in your land, lest they
25:8 sanctuary, that I may D in their midst.
29:45 And I will D among the people of Israel,
29:46 Egypt that I might D among them; I am
Lev 13:46 is unclean; he shall D alone in a habitation
14:8 the camp, but shall D outside his tent seven
20:22 am bringing you to D may not vomit you
23:42 You shall D in booths for seven days; all
23:42 native in Israel shall D in booths,
23:43 the people of Israel D in booths when I
25:18 them; so you will D in the land securely.
25:19 eat your fill, and D in it securely.
26:5 to the full, and D in your land securely.
Num 5:3 their camp, in the midst of which I D
13:18 whether the people who D in it are strong
13:19 the land that they D in is good or
13:19 the cities that they D in are camps or
13:28 Yet the people who D in the land are
13:29 The Amalekites D in the land of the Negeb;
13:29 Jebusites, and the Amorites D in the hill country;
13:29 country; and the Canaanites D by the sea, and
14:25 Amalekites and the Canaanites D in the valleys, turn
14:30 I would make you D, except Caleb the son
33:55 shall trouble you in the land where you D
35:2 their possession, cities to D in; and you shall
35:3 shall be theirs to D in, and their pasture
35:32 he may return to D in the land before
35:34 midst of which I D; for I the LORD
35:34 for I the LORD D in the midst of
Deut 12:11 to make his name D there, thither you shall
12:29 you dispossess them and D in their land,
13:12 God gives you to D there,
14:23 to make his name D there, you shall eat
16:2 to make his name D there.
16:6 to make his name D in it, there you
16:11 to make his name D there.
17:14 you possess it and D in it, and then
19:1 you dispossess them and D in their cities and
23:16 to you; he shall D with you, in your
25:5 "If brothers D together, and one of them dies
26:2 make his name to D there.
28:30 and you shall not D in it; you shall
30:20 days, that you may D in the land which
Josh 7:7 had been content to D beyond the Jordan!
9:22 from you,' when you D among us?
10:6 of the Amorites that D in the hill country
13:13 but Geshur and Maacath D in the midst of
14:4 but only cities to D in, with their pasture
15:63 out; so the Jebusites D with the people of
17:16 all the Canaanites who D in the plain have
21:2 be given cities to D in, along with their
24:13 not built, and you D therein; you eat the
24:15 in whose land you D; but as for me
Judg 6:10 in whose land you D But you have not
17:11 Levite was content to D with the man; and
18:1 itself an inheritance to D in; for until then
1Sam 12:8 Egypt, and made them D in this place.
27:5 towns, that I may D there; for why should
27:5 why should your servant D in the royal city
2Sam 7:2 prophet, "See now, I D in a house of
7:5 me a house to D in?
7:10 them, that they may D in their own place,
11:11 and Israel and Judah D in booths; and my
14:24 king said, "Let him D apart in his own
1Kgs 2:36 house in Jerusalem, and D there, and do not
3:17 this woman and I D in the same house;
6:13 And I will D among the children of Israel,

	7:8	where he was to D, in the other court
	8:12	said that he would D in thick darkness.
	8:13	place for thee to D in for ever."
	8:27	"But will God indeed D on the earth?
	17:9	belongs to Sidon, and D there.
2Kgs	4:13	She answered, "I D among my own people."
	6:1	the place where we D under your charge is
	6:2	place for us to D there." And he answered,
	16:6	to Elath, where they D to this day.
	17:27	let him go and D there, and teach them
	25:24	of the Chaldean officials; D in the land, and
1Chr	9:2	Now the first to D again in their possessions
	17:1	the prophet, "Behold, I D in a house of
	17:4	me a house to D in.
	17:9	them, that they may D in their own place,
2Chr	2:3	himself a house to D in, so deal with
	6:1	said that he would D in thick darkness.
	6:2	place for thee to D in for ever."
	6:18	"But will God D indeed with man on the
Ezra	6:12	caused his name to D there overthrow any king
Neh	1:9	to make my name D there.'
	8:14	people of Israel should D in booths during the
Job	3:5	Let clouds D upon it; let the blackness of
	4:19	much more those who D in houses of clay,
	11:14	and let not wickedness D in your tents.
	30:6	the torrents they must D, in holes of the
Ps	4:8	O LORD, makest me D in safety.
	15:1	Who shall D on thy holy hill?
	23:6	life; and I shall D in the house of
	24:1	world and those who D therein;
	27:4	after; that I may D in the house of
	37:3	good; so you will D in the land, and
	37:29	possess the land, and D upon it for ever.
	61:4	Let me D in thy tent for ever!
	65:4	and bring near, to D in thy courts!
	65:8	so that those who D at earth's farthest bounds
	68:6	desolate a home to D in; he leads out
	68:6	prosperity; but the rebellious D in a parched land.
	68:16	where the LORD will D for ever?
	68:18	the LORD God may D there.
	68:30	Rebuke the beasts that D among the reeds, the
	69:25	desolation, let no one D in their tents.
	69:35	and his servants shall D there and possess it;
	69:36	love his name shall D in it.
	84:4	Blessed are those who D in thy house, ever
	84:10	of my God than D in the tents of
	85:9	him, that glory may D in our land.
	98:7	world and those who D in it!
	101:6	land, that they may D with me; he who
	101:7	who practices deceit shall D in my house; no
	102:28	of thy servants shall D secure; their posterity shall
	107:4	to a city to D in;
	107:7	reached a city to D in.
	107:36	he lets the hungry D, and they establish a
	120:5	in Meshech, that I D among the tents of
	132:14	ever; here I will D, for I have desired
	133:1	it is when brothers D in unity!
	139:9	of the morning and D in the uttermost parts
	140:13	name; the upright shall D in thy presence.
Prov	1:33	listens to me will D secure and will be
	8:12	I, wisdom, D in prudence, and I find knowledge
	10:30	the wicked will not D in the land.
Song	8:13	O you who D in the gardens, my companions
Wis	1:4	a deceitful soul, nor D in a body enslaved
Sir	4:15	heed to her will D secure.
	14:27	the heat, and will D in the midst of
	25:15	I would rather D with a lion and a
	25:15	and a dragon than D with an evil wife.
	50:26	the foolish people that D in Shechem.
Is	5:8	you are made to D alone in the midst
	6:5	unclean lips, and I D in the midst of
	10:24	"O my people, who D in Zion, be not
	11:6	The wolf shall D with the lamb, and the
	13:21	creatures; there ostriches will D, and there satyrs
	18:3	the world, you who D on the earth, when
	23:18	clothing for those who D before the LORD.
	30:19	people in Zion who D at Jerusalem; you shall
	32:16	Then justice will D in the wilderness, and
	33:14	"Who among us can D with the devouring fire?
	33:14	Who among us can D with everlasting burnings?"
	33:16	upon evil, he will D on the heights; his
	33:24	sick"; the people who D there will be forgiven
	34:11	and the raven shall D in it.
	34:17	to generation they shall D in it.
	40:22	like a tent to D in;
	44:13	of a man, to D in a house.
	49:20	room for me to D in.'
	51:6	garment, and they who D in it will die
	57:15	name is Holy: "I D in the high and
	58:12	restorer of streets to D in.
	65:9	and my servants shall D there.
Jer	7:3	I will let you D in this place.
	7:7	I will let you D in this place, in
	7:12	I made my name D at first, and see
	8:16	city and those who D in it.
	9:26	Moab, and all who D in the desert that
	10:17	ground, O you who D under siege!
	12:4	wickedness of those who D in it the beasts
	17:6	He shall D in the parched places of the
	20:6	Pashhur, and all who D in your house, shall
	23:6	saved, and Israel will D securely.
	23:8	them.' Then they shall D in their own land."
	24:8	land, and those who D in the land of
	25:5	and wrong doings, and D upon the land which
	25:24	the mixed tribes that D in the desert;
	27:11	to till it and D there, says the LORD."'"
	29:16	all the people who D in this city, your
	31:24	all its cities shall D there together, and the
	32:37	I will make them D in safety.
	33:16	saved and Jerusalem will D securely.
	35:9	to build houses to D in.
	35:15	and then you shall D in the land which
	40:5	cities of Judah, and D with him among the
	40:9	D in the land, and serve the king of
	40:10	for me, I will D at Mizpah, to stand
	40:10	in your vessels, and D in your cities that
	42:14	bread, and we will D there,'
	44:13	will punish those who D in the land of
	44:14	desire to return to D there; for they shall
	44:26	you of Judah who D in the land of
	47:2	city and those who D in it.
	48:28	"Leave the cities, and D in the rock, O
	49:8	Flee, turn back, D in the depths, O inhabitants
	49:18	LORD, no man shall D there, no man shall
	49:30	Flee, wander far away, D in the depths, O
	49:33	waste; no man shall D there, no man shall
	50:3	desolation, and none shall D in it; both man
	50:39	"Therefore wild beasts shall D with hyenas in
	50:39	Babylon, and ostriches shall D in her; she shall
	50:40	so no man shall D there, and no son
	51:13	O you who D by many waters, rich in
	51:62	so that nothing shall D in it, neither man
Lam	3:6	he has made me D in darkness like the
Ezek	6:6	Wherever you D your cities shall be waste and
	12:2	"Son of man, you D in the midst of
	12:19	of all those who D in it.
	17:23	and under it will D all kinds of beasts;
	26:20	will make you to D in the nether world,
	28:25	nations, then they shall D in their own land
	28:26	And they shall D securely in it, and they
	28:26	They shall D securely, when I execute judgments
	31:13	Upon its ruin will D all the birds of
	32:15	I smite all who D in it, then they
	34:25	so that they may D securely in the wilderness
	34:28	devour them; they shall D securely, and none shall
	36:28	You shall D in the land which I gave
	37:25	They shall D in the land where your fathers
	37:25	their children's children shall D there for ever; and
	38:8	the nations and now D securely, all of them.
	38:11	the quiet people who D securely, all of them
	38:12	cattle and goods, who D at the center of
	39:6	and on those who D securely in the coastlands;
	39:9	"Then those who D in the cities of Israel
	39:26	against me, when they D securely in their land
	43:7	feet, where I will D in the midst of
	43:9	me, and I will D in their midst for
Dan	2:38	has given, wherever they D, the sons of men,
	4:1	nations, and languages, that D in all the earth:
	6:25	nations, and languages that D in all the earth:
Hos	3:3	to her, "You must D as mine for many
	3:4	children of Israel shall D many days without king
	4:3	mourns, and all who D in it languish, and
	12:9	will again make you D in tents, as in
	14:7	They shall return and D beneath my shadow, they
Joel	3:17	LORD your God, who D in Zion, my holy
Amos	3:12	people of Israel who D in Samaria be rescued,
	5:11	but you shall not D in them; you have
	9:5	melts, and all who D in it mourn, and
Mic	4:10	from the city and D in the open country;
	5:4	And they shall D secure, for now he shall
	7:14	of thy inheritance, who D alone in a forest
Nah	1:5	world and all that D therein.

D

Hab 2:8 cities and all who D therein.
2:17 cities and all who D therein.
Hag 1:4 for you yourselves to D in your paneled houses,
Zech 2:7 to Zion, you who D with the daughter of
2:10 come and I will D in the midst of
2:11 people; and I will D in the midst of
8:3 to Zion, and will D in the midst of
8:8 will bring them to D in the midst of
9:6 a mongrel people shall D in Ashdod; and I
14:11 more curse; Jerusalem shall D in security.
1Mac 2:7 holy city, and to D there when it was
2:29 to the wilderness to D there,
Mt 12:45 and they enter and D there; and the last
Lk 11:26 and they enter and D there; and the last
21:35 come upon all who D upon the face of
Acts 2:14 Judea and all who D in Jerusalem, let this
2:26 moreover my flesh will D in hope.
7:48 Most High does not D in houses made with
Eph 3:17 and that Christ may D in your hearts through
Col 1:19 God was pleased to D,
3:16 the word of Christ D in you richly, teach
Jas 4:5 he has made to D in us"?
Rev 2:13 "'I know where you D, where Satan's throne is;
3:10 to try those who D upon the earth.
6:10 blood on those who D upon the earth?"
8:13 woe to those who D on the earth, at
11:10 tomb, and those who D on the earth will
11:10 torment to those who D on the earth.
12:12 heaven and you that D therein!
13:6 that is, those who D in heaven.
13:8 nation, and all who D on earth will worship
13:14 it deceives those who D on earth, bidding them
14:6 proclaim to those who D on earth, to every
21:3 He will D with them, and they shall be

DWELLER

Lam 4:21 O daughter of Edom, D in the land of

DWELLERS (3)

Is 26:19 O D in the dust, awake and sing for
Rev 17:2 of whose fornication the D on earth have become
17:8 to perdition; and the D on earth whose names

DWELLING (76)

Gen 13:6 support both of them D together; for their
24:62 from Beer-lahai-roi, and was D in the Negeb.
25:27 was a quiet man, D in tents.
27:39 the earth shall your D be, and away from
36:40 their families and their D places, by their names:
36:43 Edom), according to their D places in the land
Lev 3:17 generations, in all your D places, that you eat
25:29 a man sells a D house in a walled
Num 16:24 away from about the D of Korah, Dathan, and
16:27 away from about the D of Korah, Dathan, and
22:5 earth, and they are D opposite me.
23:9 him; lo, a people D alone, and not reckoning
24:21 said, "Enduring is your D place, and your nest
Deut 33:12 long, and makes his D between his shoulders."
33:27 eternal God is your D place, and underneath are
Josh 17:12 the Canaanites persisted in D in that land.
Judg 1:27 the Canaanites persisted in D in that land.
1:35 the Amorites persisted in D in Har-heres, in Aijalon,
2Sam 7:6 been moving about in a tent for my D
1Kgs 8:30 thou in heaven thy D place; and when thou
8:39 thou in heaven thy D place, and forgive, and
8:43 thou in heaven thy D place, and do according
8:49 thou in heaven thy D place their prayer and
2Kgs 17:25 the beginning of their D there, they did not
1Chr 6:54 These are their D places according to their
9:33 houses of the Levites, D in the chambers of
17:5 to tent and from D to dwelling.
17:5 from tent to tent and from dwelling to D
2Chr 6:21 thou from heaven thy D place; and when thou
6:30 thou from heaven thy D place, and forgive, and
6:33 thou from heaven thy D place, and do according
6:39 thou from heaven thy D place their prayer and
36:15 people and on his D place;
Ezra 7:15 God of Israel, whose D is in Jerusalem,
Tob 1:4 the temple of the D of the Most High
Esth 11:3 He was a Jew, D in the city of
Job 5:3 fool taking root, but suddenly I cursed his D
38:19 the way to the D of light, and where
39:6 salt land for his D place?
Ps 43:3 me to thy holy hill and to thy D
49:11 homes for ever, their D places to all generations,
68:10 thy flock found a D in it; in thy
74:7 ground they desecrated the D place of thy name.
76:2 established in Salem, his D place in Zion.
78:60 He forsook his D at Shiloh, the tent where
84:1 How lovely is thy D place, O LORD of
87:2 more than all the D places of Jacob.
90:1 thou hast been our D place in all generations.
120:6 have I had my D among those who hate
132:5 for the LORD, a D place for the Mighty
132:7 us go to his D place; let us worship
Prov 21:20 in a wise man's D, but a foolish man
24:15 wicked man against the D of the righteous; do
Sir 24:8 he said, 'Make your D in Jacob, and in
Is 18:4 quietly look from my D like clear heat in
38:12 My D is plucked up and removed from me
Bar 3:13 God, you would be D in peace for ever.
Ezek 37:27 My D place shall be with them; and I
38:11 securely, all of them D without walls, and having
38:14 my people Israel are D securely, you will bestir
Dan 2:11 except the gods, whose D is not with flesh."
4:25 among men, and your D shall be with the
4:32 among men, and your D shall be with the
5:21 a beast, and his D was with the wild
Obad 1:3 of the rock, whose D is high, who say
Zech 2:13 for he has roused himself from his holy D
1Mac 1:38 fled; she became a D of strangers; she became
2Mac 3:39 he who has his D in heaven watches over
Acts 2:5 Now there were D in Jerusalem Jews, devout men
15:16 I will rebuild the D of David, which has
2Cor 5:2 put on our heavenly D,
Eph 2:22 into it for a D place of God in
Jude 1:6 but left their proper D have been kept by
Rev 13:6 his name and his D, that is, those who
18:2 It has become a D place of demons, a
21:3 throne saying, "Behold, the D of God is with

DWELLINGS (16)

Ex 12:20 leavened; in all your D you shall eat unleavened
Lev 7:26 fowl or of animal, in any of your D
23:3 a sabbath to the LORD in all your D
23:14 for ever throughout your generations in all your D
23:17 shall bring from your D two loaves of bread
23:21 ever in all your D throughout your generations.
23:31 for ever throughout your generations in all your D
Num 35:29 to you throughout your generations in all your D
Job 18:21 Surely such are the D of the ungodly, such
Is 11:10 nations seek, and his D shall be glorious.
32:18 peaceful habitation, in secure D, and in quiet resting
Jer 9:19 the land, because they have cast down our D
30:18 have compassion on his D; the city shall be
51:30 have become women; her D are on fire, her
Ezek 25:4 you and make their D in your midst; they
48:15 for the city, for D and for open country.

DWELLS (46)

Deut 33:12 of the LORD, he D in safety by him;
2Sam 7:2 the ark of God D in a tent."
1Chr 23:25 his people; and he D in Jerusalem for ever.
Tob 5:16 this man; God who D in heaven will prosper
Jud 5:5 about this people that D in the nearby mountain
Job 17:2 me, and my eye D on their provocation.
18:15 In his tent D that which is none of
39:28 On the rock he D and makes his home
Ps 9:11 to the LORD, who D in Zion!
16:9 rejoices; my body also D secure.
26:8 thy house, and the place where thy glory D
91:1 He who D in the shelter of the Most
135:21 from Zion, he who D in Jerusalem!
Prov 3:29 against your neighbor who D trustingly beside you.
Sir 1:8 She D with all flesh according to his gift,
Is 8:18 LORD of hosts, who D on Mount Zion.
33:5 is exalted, for he D on high; he will
Jer 2:6 through, where no man D
4:29 forsaken, and no man D in them.
44:2 desolation, and no one D in them,
49:31 nation at ease, that D securely, says the LORD,
49:31 gates or bars, that D alone.
51:43 in which no one D, and through which no
Lam 1:3 and hard servitude; she D now among the nations,
Ezek 17:16 place where the king D who made him king,
27:3 say to Tyre, who D at the entrance to
Dan 2:22 darkness, and the light D with him.
Joel 3:21 guilty, for the LORD D in Zion."
Amos 8:8 every one mourn who D in it, and all
Mt 23:20 and by him who D in it;
Jn 14:10 but the Father who D in me does his
14:17 know him, for he D with you, and will

Rom 7:17 it, but sin which D within me.
7:18 know that nothing good D within me, that is,
7:20 it, but sin which D within me.
7:23 law of sin which D in my members.
8:9 the Spirit of God D in you.
8:11 Jesus from the dead D in you, he who
8:11 through his Spirit which D in you.
1Cor 3:16 and that God's Spirit D in you?
Col 2:9 whole fulness of deity D bodily,
1Tim 6:16 alone has immortality and D in unapproachable light,
2Tim 1:5 now, I am sure, D in you.
1:14 the Holy Spirit who D within us.
2Pet 3:13 heavens and a new earth in which righteousness D
Rev 2:13 one, who was killed among you, where Satan D

DWELT (179)

Gen 4:16 of the LORD, and D in the land of
13:7 Canaanites and the Perizzites D in the land.
13:12 Abram D in the land of Canaan, while Lot
13:12 of Canaan, while Lot D among the cities of
13:18 tent, and came and D by the oaks of
14:7 also the Amorites who D in Hazazon-tamar.
14:12 of Abram's brother, who D in Sodom, and his
16:3 So, after Abram had D ten years in the
19:29 when he overthrew the cities in which Lot D
19:30 out of Zoar, and D in the hills with
19:30 in Zoar; so he D in a cave with
20:1 of the Negeb, and D between Kadesh and Shur;
22:19 to Beer-sheba; and Abraham D at Beer-sheba.
25:11 And Isaac D at Beer-lahai-roi.
25:18 to his kindred.) They D from Havilah to Shur,
26:6 So Isaac D in Gerar.
26:17 valley of Gerar and D there.
35:22 While Israel D in that land Reuben went and
36:8 So Esau D in the hill country of Seir;
37:1 Jacob D in the land of his father's sojournings,
38:11 So Tamar went and D in her father's house.
47:27 Thus Israel D in the land of Egypt, in
50:22 So Joseph D in Egypt, he and his father's
Ex 6:4 land in which they D as sojourners.
10:23 the people of Israel had light where they D
12:40 the people of Israel D in Egypt was four
Lev 18:3 of Egypt, where you D, and you shall not
26:35 your sabbaths when you D upon it.
Num 14:45 and the Canaanites who D in that hill country
20:15 to Egypt, and we D in Egypt a long
21:1 king of Arad, who D in the Negeb, heard
21:31 Thus Israel D in the land of the Amorites.
21:34 of the Amorites, who D at Heshbon."
25:1 While Israel D in Shittim the people began to
31:10 the places where they D, and all their encampments,
33:40 king of Arad, who D in the Negeb in
Deut 3:2 of the Amorites, who D at Heshbon.'
29:16 "You know how we D in the land of
33:16 favor of him that D in the bush.
33:28 So Israel D in safety, the fountain of Jacob
Josh 2:15 wall, so that she D in the wall.
6:25 saved alive; and she D in Israel to this
9:10 king of Bashan, who D in Ashtaroth.
9:16 neighbors, and that they D among them.
12:2 of the Amorites who D at Heshbon, and ruled
12:4 of the Rephaim, who D at Ashtaroth and at
13:21 princes of Sihon, who D in the land.
16:10 out the Canaanites that D in Gezer: so the
16:10 so the Canaanites have D in the midst of
Judg 1:9 against the Canaanites who D in the hill country,
1:10 against the Canaanites who D in Hebron (now the
1:21 out the Jebusites who D in Jerusalem; so the
1:21 so the Jebusites have D with the people of
1:29 out the Canaanites who D in Gezer; but the
1:29 Gezer; but the Canaanites D in Gezer among them.
1:30 Nahalol; but the Canaanites D among them, and
1:32 Rehob; but the Asherites D among the Canaanites,
1:33 inhabitants of Beth-anath, but D among the
3:3 and the Hivites who D on Mount Lebanon, from
3:5 the people of Israel D among the Canaanites, the
4:2 army was Sisera, who D in Harosheth-ha-goiim.
8:29 of Joash went and D in his own house.
9:21 went to Beer and D there, for fear of
9:41 And Abimelech D at Arumah; and Zebul drove out
11:3 from his brothers, and D in the land of
11:26 While Israel D in Heshbon and its villages, and
18:7 were there, how they D in security, after the
18:28 rebuilt the city, and D in it.
21:23 rebuilt the towns, and D in them.
1Sam 12:11 every side; and you D in safety.
19:18 and Samuel went and D at Naioth.
23:29 up from there, and D in the strongholds of
27:3 And David D with Achish at Gath, he and
27:7 the days that David D in the country of
27:11 all the while he D in the country of
31:7 the Philistines came and D in them.
2Sam 2:3 his household; and they D in the towns of
5:9 And David D in the stronghold, and called it
7:1 Now when the king D in his house, and
7:6 I have not D in a house since the
9:12 all who D in Ziba's house became Mephibosheth's
9:13 So Mephibosheth D in Jerusalem; for he ate always
13:20 So Tamar D, a desolate woman, in her brother
14:24 So Absalom D apart in his own house, and
14:28 So Absalom D two full years in Jerusalem, without
15:8 a vow while I D at Geshur in Aram,
1Kgs 2:38 So Shimei D in Jerusalem many days.
4:25 And Judah and Israel D in safety, from Dan
9:16 slain the Canaanites who D in the city, and
11:24 went to Damascus, and D there, and made him
12:17 people of Israel who D in the cities of
12:25 country of Ephraim, and D there; and he went
13:11 Now there D an old prophet in Bethel.
13:25 it in the city where the old prophet D
15:18 king of Syria, who D in Damascus, saying,
15:21 building Ramah, and he D in Tirzah.
17:5 LORD; he went and D by the brook Cherith
21:8 and the nobles who D with Naboth in his
21:11 and the nobles who D in his city, did
2Kgs 13:5 the people of Israel D in their homes as
15:5 his death, and he D in a separate house.
17:24 possession of Samaria, and D in its cities.
17:28 from Samaria came and D in Bethel, and taught
17:29 cities in which they D;
19:36 and went home, and D at Nineveh.
22:14 the wardrobe (now she D in Jerusalem in the
1Chr 2:55 of the scribes that D at Jabez: the Tirathites,
4:23 Netaim and Gederah; they D there with the king
4:28 They D in Beer-sheba, Moladah, Hazar-shual,
4:43 escaped, and they have D there to this day.
5:8 son of Joel, who D in Aroer, as far
5:9 He also D to the east as far as
5:10 their hand; and they D in their tents throughout
5:11 The sons of Gad D over against them in
5:16 fathers' houses; and they D in Gilead, in Bashan
5:22 And they D in their place until the exile.
5:23 the half-tribe of Manasseh D in the land; they
7:29 In these D the sons of Joseph the son
8:28 These D in Jerusalem.
8:29 the father of Gibeon D in Gibeon, and the
8:32 these also D opposite their kinsmen in Jerusalem,
9:3 Benjamin, Ephraim, and Manasseh D in Jerusalem:
9:16 son of Elkanah, who D in the villages of
9:35 In Gibeon D the father of Gibeon, Je-iel, and
9:38 Shimeam; and these also D opposite their kinsmen in
10:7 the Philistines came and D in them.
11:7 And David D in the stronghold; therefore it was
17:1 Now when David D in his house, David said
17:5 For I have not D in a house since
2Chr 10:17 people of Israel who D in the cities of
11:5 Rehoboam D in Jerusalem, and he built cities for
16:2 king of Syria, who D in Damascus, saying,
19:4 Jehoshaphat D at Jerusalem; and he went out again
20:8 And they have D in it, and have built
26:7 against the Arabs that D in Gurbaal, and against
26:21 and being a leper D in a separate house,
30:25 and the sojourners who D in Judah, rejoiced.
34:22 the wardrobe (now she D in Jerusalem in the
Neh 8:17 captivity made booths and D in the booths; for
Job 21:28 in which the wicked D
22:8 and the favored man D in it.
29:25 as chief, and I D like a king among
Ps 74:2 Remember Mount Zion, where thou hast D
78:60 the tent where he D among men,
94:17 soul would soon have D in the land of
Wis 12:3 Those who D of old in thy holy land
Sir 24:4 I D in high places, and my throne was
Is 9:2 great light; those who D in a land of
13:20 never be inhabited or D in for all generations;
37:37 and went home and D at Nineveh.
Jer 39:14 So he D among the people.
40:6 Ahikam, at Mizpah, and D with him among the
44:1 all the Jews that D in the land of
44:15 all the people who D in Pathros in the
Bar 1:4 and great, all who D in Babylon by the
3:20 of day, and have D upon the earth; but

Ezek 3:15 exiles at Tel-abib, who D by the river Chebar.
20:9 nations among whom they D, in whose sight I
31:6 and under its shadow D all great nations.
31:17 sword; yea, those who D under its shadow among
36:17 the house of Israel D in their own land,
37:25 land where your fathers D that I gave to
Dan 4:12 birds of the air D in its branches, and
4:21 birds of the air D –
Zeph 2:15 the exultant city that D secure, that said to
1Mac 9:73 And Jonathan D in Michmash.
10:10 And Jonathan D in Jerusalem and began to rebuild
13:52 he and his men D there.
13:53 the forces, and he D in Gazara.
14:34 the borders of Azotus, where the enemy formerly D
2Mac 5:17 sins of those who D in the city, and
6:2 did the people who D in that place.
12:27 fortified city where Lysias D with multitudes of
12:30 when the Jews who D there bore witness to
Mt 2:23 And he went and D in a city called
4:13 Nazareth he went and D in Caperna-um by the
Lk 13:4 all the others who D in Jerusalem?
Jn 1:14 Word became flesh and D among us, full of
2Tim 1:5 faith, a faith that D first in your grandmother

DWINDLE

Prov 13:11 Wealth hastily gotten will D, but he who gathers

DYED (5)

Judg 5:30 every man; spoil of D stuffs for Sisera, spoil
5:30 for Sisera, spoil of D stuffs embroidered, two pieces
5:30 embroidered, two pieces of D work embroidered for
Job 38:14 seal, and it is D like a garment.
1Mac 4:23 and silver, and cloth D blue and sea purple,

DYING (11)

2Chr 16:13 slept with his fathers, D in the forty-first year
24:22 And when he was D, he said, "May the
Job 24:12 of the city the D groan, and the soul
Wis 18:18 known why they were D;
Is 5:13 their honored men are D of hunger, and their
1Mac 1:5 he fell sick and perceived that he was D
6:9 gripped him, and he concluded that he was D
Lk 8:42 about twelve years of age, and she was D
Jn 11:37 the blind man have kept this man from D
2Cor 6:9 and yet well-known; as D, and behold we live;
Heb 11:21 By faith Jacob, when D, blessed each of the

DYSENTERY

Acts 28:8 sick with fever and D; and Paul visited him

E

EACH (421)

Gen 1:11 which is their seed, E according to its kind,
1:12 which is their seed, E according to its kind.
10:5 Japheth in their lands, E with his own language,
13:11 thus they separated from E other.
15:10 in two, and laid E half over against the
40:5 confined in the prison-- E his own dream, and
40:5 his own dream, and E dream with its own
41:11 night, he and I, E having a dream with
41:12 giving an interpretation to E man according to his
44:1 can carry, and put E man's money in the
45:22 To E and all of them he gave festal
49:28 he blessed them, blessing E with the blessing
Ex 1:1 to Egypt with Jacob, E with his household:
3:22 not go empty, but E woman shall ask of
12:4 persons; according to what E can eat you shall
16:16 of the persons whom E of you has in
16:18 little had no lack; E gathered according to what
16:21 morning they gathered it, E as much as he
18:7 him; and they asked E other of their welfare,
25:33 cups made like almonds, E with capital and flower,
25:33 cups made like almonds, E with capital and flower,
25:35 piece with it under E pair of the six
26:2 The length of E curtain shall be twenty-eight cubits,
26:2 and the breadth of E curtain four cubits; all
26:8 The length of E curtain shall be thirty cubits,
26:8 and the breadth of E curtain four cubits; the
26:16 half the breadth of E frame.
26:17 be two tenons in E frame, for fitting together;
28:21 shall be like signets, E engraved with its name,
30:12 people of Israel, then E shall give a ransom
30:13 E who is numbered in the census shall give
30:34 with pure frankincense (of E shall there be an
32:29 service of the LORD, E one at the cost
36:4 on the sanctuary came, E from the task that
36:9 The length of E curtain was twenty-eight cubits, and
36:9 and the breadth of E curtain four cubits; all
36:15 The length of E curtain was thirty cubits, and
36:15 and the breadth of E curtain four cubits; the
36:21 half the breadth of E frame.
36:22 E frame had two tenons, for fitting together; he
37:19 cups made like almonds, E with capital and flower,
37:19 cups made like almonds, E with capital and flower,
37:21 piece with it under E pair of the six
39:14 they were like signets, E engraved with its name,
Lev 7:14 offer one cake from E offering, as an offering
10:1 the sons of Aaron, E took his censer, and
23:37 sacrifices and drink offerings, E on its proper day;
24:5 ephah shall be in E cake.
24:7 put pure frankincense with E row, that it may
25:10 jubilee for you, when E of you shall return
25:10 to his property and E of you shall return
25:13 this year of jubilee E of you shall return
Num 1:4 you a man from E tribe, each man being
1:4 man from each tribe, E man being the head
1:44 of Israel, twelve men, E representing his fathers'
2:2 of Israel shall encamp E by his own standard,
2:17 shall they set out, E in position, standard by
4:19 in and appoint them E to his task and
4:49 Moses they were appointed, E to his task of
7:3 the leaders, and for E one an ox; they
7:5 to the Levites, to E man according to his
7:11 their offerings, one leader E day, for the dedication
7:85 basins, twelve golden dishes, E silver plate weighing
7:85 and thirty shekels and E basin seventy, all the
13:2 people of Israel; from E tribe of their fathers
15:5 for the sacrifice, for E lamb.
15:11 shall be done for E bull or ram, or
15:11 or ram, or for E of the male lambs
15:38 upon the tassel of E corner a cord of
16:17 you also, and Aaron, E his censer."
17:2 them rods, one for E fathers' house, from all
17:2 Write E man's name upon his rod,
17:3 for the head of E fathers' house.
17:6 him rods, one for E leader, according to their
17:9 and they looked, and E man took his rod.
23:2 and Balaam offered on E altar a bull and
23:4 I have offered upon E altar a bull and
23:14 and a ram on E altar.
23:30 and a ram on E altar.
28:7 of a hin for E lamb; in the holy
28:12 mixed with oil, for E bull; and two tenths
28:14 the burnt offering of E month throughout the months
28:21 shall you offer for E of the seven lambs;
28:28 of an ephah for E bull, two tenths for
28:29 ram, a tenth for E of the seven lambs;
29:4 and one tenth for E of the seven lambs;
29:10 ram, a tenth for E of the seven lambs:
29:14 of an ephah for E of the thirteen bulls,
29:14 bulls, two tenths for E of the two rams,
29:15 and a tenth for E of the fourteen lambs;
31:4 send a thousand from E of the tribes of
31:5 Israel, a thousand from E tribe, twelve thousand
31:6 war, a thousand from E tribe, together with Phinehas
31:50 the LORD's offering, what E man found, articles of
32:18 of Israel have inherited E his inheritance.
35:8 you shall take few; E, in proportion to the
36:9 tribe to another; for E of the tribes of
Deut 1:23 you, one man for E tribe;
Josh 3:12 tribes of Israel, from E tribe a man.
4:2 from the people, from E tribe a man,
4:4 appointed, a man from E tribe;
4:5 Jordan, and take up E of you a stone
18:4 Provide three men from E tribe, and I will
18:10 people of Israel, to E his portion.
21:42 These cities had E its pasture lands round about
22:14 ten chiefs, one from E of the tribal families
Judg 2:6 people of Israel went E to his inheritance to
15:4 put a torch between E pair of tails.
16:5 him; and we will E give you eleven hundred
21:21 the vineyards and seize E man his wife from
21:22 did not take for E man of them his
Ruth 1:8 two daughters-in-law, "Go, return E of you to her
1:9 may find a home, E of you in the
1Sam 2:19 take it to him E year, when she went
10:25 all the people away, E one to his home.
30:6 were bitter in soul, E for his sons and
30:22 have recovered, except that E man may lead away

2Sam 2:16 And E caught his opponent by the head, and
6:19 men and women, to E a cake of bread,
6:19 all the people departed, E to his house.
10:4 half the beard of E, and cut off their
13:29 king's sons arose, and E mounted his mule and
21:20 had six fingers on E hand, and six toes
21:20 and six toes on E foot, twenty-four in number;
1Kgs 1:49 trembled, and rose, and E went his own way.
4:7 king and his household; E man had to make
4:27 to King Solomon's table, E one in his month;
4:28 where it was required, E according to his charge.
6:10 against the whole house, E story five cubits high,
6:23 two cherubim of olivewood, E ten cubits high.
6:27 their other wings touched E other in the middle
7:3 forty-five pillars, fifteen in E row.
7:27 ten stands of bronze; E stand was four cubits
7:30 Moreover E stand had four bronze wheels and axles
7:30 were cast, with wreaths at the side of E
7:34 the four corners of E stand; the supports were
7:36 to the space of E, with wreaths round about.
7:38 ten lavers of bronze; E laver held forty baths,
7:38 laver held forty baths, E laver measured four cubits,
7:38 was a laver for E of the ten stands.
7:42 rows of pomegranates for E network, to cover the
8:38 all thy people Israel, E knowing the affliction of
8:39 act, and render to E whose heart thou knowest,
8:59 his people Israel, as E day requires;
10:16 of gold went into E shield.
10:17 of gold went into E shield; and the king
10:19 calf's head, and on E side of the seat
10:20 stood there, one on E end of a step
20:20 And E killed his man; the Syrians fled and
20:24 this: remove the kings, E from his post, and
22:17 have no master; let E return to his home
2Kgs 6:2 to the Jordan and E of us get there
9:21 of Judah set out, E in his chariot, and
11:8 shall surround the king, E with his weapons in
11:9 the priest commanded, and E brought his men who
12:4 the money for which E man is assessed--the
12:5 let the priests take, E from his acquaintance; and
1Chr 16:3 men and women, to E a loaf of bread,
16:37 before the ark as E day required,
16:43 all the people departed E to his house, and
20:6 had six fingers on E hand, and six toes
20:6 and six toes on E foot, twenty-four in number;
24:31 also, the head of E father's house and his
26:17 east there were six E day, on the north
26:17 on the north four E day, on the south
26:17 on the south four E day, as well as
27:1 throughout the year, E division numbering
28:14 all golden vessels for E service, the weight of
28:14 of silver vessels for E service,
28:15 weight of gold for E lampstand and its lamps,
28:15 to the use of E lampstand in the service,
28:16 weight of gold for E table for the showbread,
28:17 and the weight of E; for the silver bowls
28:17 and the weight of E;
2Chr 3:15 capital of five cubits on the top of E
4:13 rows of pomegranates for E network, to cover the
6:29 all thy people Israel, E knowing his own affliction,
6:30 forgive, and render to E whose heart thou knowest,
8:13 as the duty of E day required, offering according
8:14 as the duty of E day required, and the
9:15 beaten gold went into E shield.
9:16 of gold went into E shield; and the king
9:18 the throne, and on E side of the seat
9:19 stood there, one on E end of a step
10:16 E of you to your tents, O Israel!
18:16 have no master; let E return to his home
23:7 shall surround the king, E with his weapons in
23:8 They E brought his men, who were to go
31:2 Levites, division by division, E according to his
31:16 as the duty of E day required, for their
35:5 let there be for E a part of a
35:15 the gatekeepers were at E gate; they did not
35:21 we to do with E other, king of Judah?
Ezra 1:4 in Jerusalem; and let E survivor, in whatever place
2:1 to Jerusalem and Judah, E to his own town.
3:4 to the ordinance, as E day required,
6:5 which is in Jerusalem, E to its place; you
10:16 to their fathers' houses, E of them designated by
Neh 3:28 Gate the priests repaired, E one opposite his own
4:15 returned to the wall, E to his work.
4:17 such a way that E with one hand labored
4:18 And E of the builders had his sword girded
4:23 took off our clothes; E kept his weapon in
5:7 "You are exacting interest, E from his brother." And
7:3 the inhabitants of Jerusalem, E to his station and
7:3 to his station and E opposite his own house."
7:6 to Jerusalem and Judah, E to his town.
8:16 made booths for themselves, E on his roof, and
13:10 the work, had fled E to his field.
13:24 but the language of E people.
13:30 the priests and Levites, E in his work;
Tob 1:7 and spend the proceeds E year at Jerusalem;
3:8 demon Asmodeus had slain E of them before he
5:9 entered and they greeted E other.
6:13 seven husbands and that E died in the bridal
7:11 seven husbands, and when E came to her he
10:1 father Tobit was counting E day, and when the
Jud 7:5 Then E man took up his weapons, and when
12:7 days, and went out E night to the valley
Esth 2:12 the turn came for E maiden to go in
Job 1:4 in the house of E on his day; and
2:11 upon him, they came E from his own place,
41:17 to another; they clasp E other and cannot be
42:11 brought upon him; and E of them gave him
Ps 59:6 [Selah] E evening they come back, howling like dogs
59:14 [Selah] E evening they come back, howling like dogs
85:10 and peace will kiss E other.
Song 3:8 and expert in war, E with his sword at
8:11 the vineyard to keepers; E one was to bring
Wis 15:7 earth and laboriously molds E vessel for our service,
15:7 be the use of E of these the worker
19:17 surrounded by yawning darkness, E tried to find the
19:18 of the rhythm, while E note remains the same.
Sir 17:12 he gave commandment to E of them concerning his
38:27 the signets of seals, E is diligent in making
38:31 upon their hands, and E is skilful in his
Is 6:2 him stood the seraphim; E had six wings: with
9:20 but are not satisfied; E devours his neighbor's flesh,
14:18 nations lie in glory, E in his own tomb;
32:2 E will be like a hiding place from the
34:15 the kites be gathered, E one with her mate.
47:15 youth; they wander about E in his own direction;
56:11 to their own way, E to his own gain,
Jer 5:8 were well-fed lusty stallions, E neighing for his
6:3 her, they shall pasture, E in his place.
9:8 deceitfully; with his mouth E speaks peaceably to his
9:20 daughters a lament, and E to her neighbor a
12:15 will bring them again E to his heritage and
12:15 to his heritage and E to his land.
22:7 prepare destroyers against you, E with his weapons;
31:30 for his own sin; E man who eats sour
31:34 And no longer shall E man teach his neighbor
31:34 teach his neighbor and E his brother, saying, 'Know
34:14 end of six years E of you must set
34:15 eyes by proclaiming liberty, E to his neighbor, and
34:16 profaned my name when E of you took back
51:9 and let us go E to his own country;
Bar 1:6 and they collected money, E giving what he could;
1:21 to us, but we E followed the intent of
2:8 Lord by turning away, E of us, from the
Ezek 1:6 form of men, but E had four faces, and
1:6 had four faces, and E of them had four
1:10 likeness of their faces, E had the face of
1:11 were spread out above; E creature had two wings,
1:11 creature had two wings, E of which touched the
1:12 And E went straight forward; wherever the spirit
1:15 living creatures, one for E of the four of
1:23 one toward another; and E creature had two wings
4:6 you, a day for E year.
8:11 E had his censer in his hand, and the
9:1 executioners of the city, E with his destroying
10:9 the cherubim, one beside E cherub; and the
10:21 E had four faces, and each four wings, and
10:21 had four faces, and E four wings, and underneath
33:20 Israel, I will judge E of you according to
33:26 you commit abominations and E of you defiles his
33:30 say to one another, E to his brother, 'Come,
40:5 was six long cubits, E being a cubit and
41:1 measured the jambs; on E side six cubits was
41:6 over another, thirty in E story.
41:23 the holy place had E a double door.
41:24 two swinging leaves for E door.
45:13 of an ephah from E homer of wheat, and
45:13 of an ephah from E homer of barley,
45:14 of a bath from E cor (the cor, like
45:23 rams without blemish, on E of the seven days;
45:24 offering an ephah for E bull, an ephah for
45:24 bull, an ephah for E ram, and a hin
45:24 hin of oil to E ephah.

46:5 hin of oil to E ephah.
46:7 hin of oil to E ephah.
46:9 which he entered, but E shall go out straight
46:21 the court; and in E corner of the court
46:23 On the inside, around E of the four courts
Dan 13:10 they did not tell E other of their distress,
13:13 They said to E other, "Let us go home,
13:14 out, they parted from E other.
13:14 met again; and when E pressed the other for
13:51 "Separate them far from E other, and I will
13:52 they were separated from E other, he summoned one
13:54 being intimate with E other?" He answered, "Under
13:58 being intimate with E other?" He answered, "Under
Joel 2:7 They march E on his way, they do not
2:8 not jostle one another, E marches in his path;
Jon 1:5 mariners were afraid, and E cried to his god;
Mic 4:5 all the peoples walk E in the name of
7:2 wait for blood, and E hunts his brother with
Zeph 2:11 him shall bow down, E in its place, all
3:5 shows forth his justice, E dawn he does not
Hag 1:9 while you busy yourselves E with his own house.
Zech 4:2 with seven lips on E of the lamps which
7:9 show kindness and mercy E to his brother,
8:4 the streets of Jerusalem, E with staff in hand
11:6 cause men to fall E into the hand of
11:6 of his shepherd, and E into the hand of
12:12 The land shall mourn, E family by itself; the
12:14 families that are left, E by itself, and their
14:13 on them, so that E will lay hold on
1Mac 1:8 officers began to rule, E in his own place.
1:42 one people, and that E should give up his
2:19 commandments, departing E one from the religion
2:40 And E said to his neighbor: "If we all
3:56 or were fainthearted, that E should return to his
5:49 to the army that E should encamp where he
6:35 among the phalanxes; with E elephant they stationed
6:35 horsemen were assigned to E beast.
6:37 they were fastened upon E beast by special harness,
6:37 special harness, and upon E were four armed men
6:54 they had been scattered, E to his own place.
7:49 day should be celebrated E year on the thirteenth
8:16 They trust one man E year to rule over
10:13 Bacchides had built fled; E left his place and
10:71 us match strength with E other there, for I
11:3 as a garrison in E city.
11:9 make a covenant with E other, and I will
11:34 formerly received from them E year, from the crops
11:38 dismissed all his troops, E man to his own
14:12 E man sat under his vine and his fig
2Mac 3:26 dressed, who stood on E side of him and
7:21 She encouraged E of them in the language of
7:22 order the elements within E of you.
8:22 and Joseph and Jonathan, E to command a division,
8:22 a division, putting fifteen hundred men under E
9:26 your present good will, E of you, toward me
13:2 E of them had a Greek force of one
14:21 chariot came forward from E army; seats of honor
15:11 He armed E of them not so much with
Mt 20:9 the eleventh hour came, E of them received a
20:10 would receive more; but E of them also received
25:15 to another one, to E according to his ability.
Mk 13:34 his servants in charge, E with his work, and
15:24 them, to decide what E should take.
Lk 2:3 went to be enrolled, E to his own city.
6:44 bear good fruit; for E tree is known by
9:14 "Make them sit down in companies, about fifty E
11:3 Give us E day our daily bread;
13:15 Does not E of you on the sabbath untie
23:12 Pilate became friends with E other that very day,
23:12 been at enmity with E other.
24:14 Jerusalem, and talking with E other about all these
24:17 you are holding with E other as you walk?"
24:32 They said to E other, "Did not our hearts
Jn 2:6 Jewish rites of purification, E holding twenty or
6:7 buy enough bread for E of them to get
7:53 They went E to his own house.
19:23 four parts, one for E soldier; also his tunic.
Acts 2:3 distributed and resting on E one of them.
2:6 they were bewildered, because E one heard them
2:8 it that we hear, E of us in his
4:35 distribution was made to E as any had need.
7:26 why do you wrong E other?'
15:38 they separated from E other; Barnabas took Mark
17:27 is not far from E one of us,
Rom 1:12 be mutually encouraged by E other's faith, both
12:3 think with sober judgment, E according to the
14:12 So E of us shall give account of himself
15:2 to please ourselves; let E of us please his
1Cor 1:12 I mean is that E one of you says,
3:5 whom you believed, as the Lord assigned to E
3:8 waters are equal, and E shall receive his wages
3:10 Let E man take care how he builds upon
3:13 wood, hay, straw-- E man's work will become
3:13 what sort of work E one has done.
7:2 the temptation to immorality, E man should have his
7:2 his own wife and E woman her own husband.
7:7 But E has his own special gift from God,
7:24 brethren, in whatever state E was called, there let
11:21 For in eating, E one goes ahead with his
12:7 To E is given the manifestation of the Spirit
12:11 Spirit, who apportions to E one individually as he
12:18 organs in the body, E one of them, as
14:26 When you come together, E one has a hymn,
14:27 at most three, and E in turn; and let
14:28 one to interpret, let E of them keep silence
15:23 But E in his own order: Christ the first
15:38 has chosen, and to E kind of seed its
16:2 day of every week, E of you is to
2Cor 5:10 of Christ, so that E one may receive good
9:7 E one must do as he has made up
Gal 5:17 these are opposed to E other, to prevent you
6:4 But let E one test his own work, and
6:5 For E man will have to bear his own
Eph 4:7 grace was given to E of us according to
4:16 it is supplied, when E part is working properly,
5:33 the church; however, let E one of you love
Phil 2:4 Let E of you look not only to his
Col 3:13 against another, forgiving E other; as the Lord
1Thes 2:11 his children, we exhorted E one of you and
4:4 abstain from unchastity; that E one of you know
Heb 6:11 And we desire E one of you to show
11:21 Jacob, when dying, blessed E of the sons of
Jas 1:13 tempts no one; but E person is tempted when
1Pet 1:17 Father him who judges E one impartially according
4:10 As E has received a gift, employ it for
Rev 2:23 I will give to E of you as your
4:6 round the throne, on E side of the throne,
4:8 the four living creatures, E of them with six
5:8 down before the Lamb, E holding a harp, and
6:11 Then they were E given a white robe and
21:21 gates were twelve pearls, E of the gates made
22:2 fruit, yielding its fruit E month; and the leaves

EAGER (12)

Ps 17:12 are like a lion E to tear, as a
Sir 18:13 discipline and who are E for his judgments.
Zeph 3:7 the more they were E to make all their
2Mac 15:9 they had won, he made them the more E
Rom 1:15 foolish: so I am E to preach the gospel
8:19 the creation waits with E longing for the revealing
1Cor 14:12 yourselves; since you are E for manifestations of the
Gal 2:10 very thing I was E to do.
Eph 4:3 one another in love, E to maintain the unity
Phil 1:20 as it is my E expectation and hope that
2:28 I am the more E to send him, therefore,
Jude 1:3 Beloved, being very E to write to you of

EAGERLY (9)

Prov 7:15 you, to seek you E, and I have found
Dan 13:12 And they watched E, day after day, to see
1Mac 1:13 some of the people E went to the king.
2Mac 11:7 Then they E rushed off together.
Mk 5:10 And he begged him E not to send them
1Thes 2:17 we endeavored the more E and with great desire
2Tim 1:17 he searched for me E and found me--
Heb 9:28 save those who are E waiting for him.
1Pet 5:2 for shameful gain but E,

EAGERNESS (2)

Acts 17:11 the word with all E, examining the scriptures daily
2Cor 7:11 produced in you, what E to clear yourselves, what

EAGLE (20)

Lev 11:13 are an abomination: the E, the vulture, the osprey,
Deut 14:12 shall not eat: the E, the vulture, the osprey,
28:49 as swift as the E flies, a nation whose
32:11 Like an E that stirs up its nest, that
Job 9:26 of reed, like an E swooping on the prey.
39:27 your command that the E mounts up and makes
Prov 23:5 wings, flying like an E toward heaven.
30:19 the way of an E in the sky, the
Jer 48:40 fly swiftly like an E, and spread his wings

49:22 fly swiftly like an E, and spread his wings
Ezek 1:10 the face of an E at the back.
10:14 lion, and the fourth the face of an E
17:3 Lord GOD: A great E with great wings and
17:7 there was another great E with great wings and
Obad 1:4 soar aloft like the E, though your nest is
Mic 1:16 as bald as the E, for they shall go
Hab 1:8 they fly like an E swift to devour.
Rev 4:7 and the fourth living creature like a flying E
8:13 and I heard an E crying with a loud
12:14 wings of the great E that she might fly

EAGLES (10)

Ex 19:4 I bore you on E wings and brought you
2Sam 1:23 they were swifter than E, they were stronger than
Ps 103:5 so that your youth is renewed like the E
Is 40:31 up with wings like E, they shall run and
Jer 4:13 horses are swifter than E – woe to us,
49:16 as high as the E, I will bring you
Dan 4:33 grew as long as E feathers, and his nails
7:4 a lion and had E wings.
Mt 24:28 body is, there the E will be gathered together.
Lk 17:36 body is, there the E will be gathered together."

EAR (121)

Ex 9:31 barley was in the E and the flax was
21:6 master shall bore his E through with an awl;
29:20 tip of the right E of Aaron and upon
Lev 8:23 tip of Aaron's right E and on the thumb
14:14 tip of the right E of him who is
14:17 tip of the right E of him who is
14:25 tip of the right E of him who is
14:28 tip of the right E of him who is
Deut 1:45 your voice or give E to you.
15:17 thrust it through his E into the door, and
32:1 "Give E, O heavens, and I will speak; and
Judg 5:3 "Hear, O kings; give E, O princes; to the
1Kgs 8:52 thy people Israel, giving E to them whenever they
2Kgs 19:16 Incline thy E, O LORD, and hear; open thy
Neh 1:6 his commandments; let thy E be attentive, and thy
1:11 O Lord, let thy E be attentive to the
9:30 through thy prophets; yet they would not give E
Job 4:12 to me stealthily, my E received the whisper of
12:11 Does not the E try words as the palate
13:1 seen all this, my E has heard and understood
29:11 When the E heard, it called me blessed, and
34:2 wise men, and give E to me, you who
34:3 who know; for the E tests words as the
36:15 affliction, and opens their E by adversity.
42:5 the hearing of the E, but now my eye
Ps 5:1 Give E to my words, O LORD; give heed
10:17 thou wilt incline thy E
17:1 Give E to my prayer from lips free of
17:6 O God; incline thy E to me, hear my
31:2 Incline thy E to me, rescue me speedily!
39:12 O LORD, and give E to my cry; hold
40:6 desire; but thou hast given me an open E
45:10 consider, and incline your E; forget your people and
49:1 Give E, all inhabitants of the world,
49:4 I will incline my E to a proverb; I
54:2 prayer, O God; give E to the words of
55:1 Give E to my prayer, O God; and hide
55:19 God will give E, and humble them, he who
58:4 adder that stops its E,
71:2 rescue me; incline thy E to me, and save
78:1 Give E, O my people, to my teaching; incline
80:1 Give E, O Shepherd of Israel, thou who leadest
84:8 hear my prayer; give E, O God of Jacob!
86:1 Incline thy E, O LORD, and answer me, for
86:6 Give E, O LORD, to my prayer; hearken to
88:2 before thee, incline thy E to my cry!
94:9 He who planted the E, does he not hear?
102:2 Incline thy E to me; answer me speedily in
116:2 Because he inclined his E to me, therefore I
140:6 art my God; give E to the voice of
141:1 Give E to my voice, when I call to
143:1 prayer, O LORD; give E to my supplications!
Prov 2:2 with you, making your E attentive to wisdom and
4:21 my words; incline your E to my sayings.
5:1 my wisdom, incline your E to my understanding;
5:13 teachers or incline my E to my instructors.
15:31 He whose E heeds wholesome admonition will abide
18:15 acquires knowledge, and the E of the wise seeks
20:12 The hearing E and the seeing eye, the LORD
21:13 He who closes his E to the cry of
22:17 Incline your E, and hear the words of the
23:12 to instruction and your E to words of knowledge.
25:12 gold is a wise reprover to a listening E
28:9 one turns away his E from hearing the law,
Eccl 1:8 with seeing, nor the E filled with hearing.
Wis 1:10 deeds; because a jealous E hears all things, and
6:2 Give E, you that rule over multitudes, and boast
Sir 3:27 parable, and an attentive E is the wise man's
4:8 Incline your E to the poor, and answer him
6:33 if you incline your E you will become wise.
16:5 has seen, and my E has heard things more
38:28 furnace; he inclines his E to the sound of
51:16 I inclined my E a little and received her,
Is 1:2 O heavens, and give E, O earth; for the
1:10 Give E to the teaching of our God, you
8:9 and be dismayed; give E, all you far countries;
28:23 Give E, and hear my voice; hearken, and hear
32:9 you complacent daughters, give E to my speech.
37:17 Incline thy E, O LORD, and hear; open thy
42:23 among you will give E to this, will attend
48:8 from of old your E has not been opened.
50:4 wakens, he wakens my E to hear as those
50:5 GOD has opened my E, and I was not
51:4 my people, and give E to me, my nation;
55:3 Incline your E, and come to me; hear, that
59:1 cannot save, or his E dull, that it cannot
64:4 or perceived by the E, no eye has seen
Jer 7:24 obey or incline their E, but walked in their
7:26 me, or incline their E, but stiffened their neck.
9:20 LORD, and let your E receive the word of
11:8 obey or incline their E, but every one walked
13:15 Hear and give E; be not proud, for the
17:23 listen or incline their E, but stiffened their neck,
35:15 did not incline your E or listen to me.
44:5 listen or incline their E, to turn from their
Lam 3:56 'Do not close thine E to my cry for
Bar 2:16 Incline thy E, O Lord, and hear;
3:9 life, O Israel; give E, and learn wisdom!
Dan 9:18 my God, incline thy E and hear; open thy
Joel 1:2 you aged men, give E, all inhabitants of the
Amos 3:12 a piece of an E, so shall the people
Mt 26:51 of the high priest, and cut off his E
Mk 4:28 the blade, then the E, then the full grain
4:28 the ear, then the full grain in the E
14:47 of the high priest and cut off his E
Lk 22:48 the high priest and cut off his right E
22:49 And he touched his E and healed him.
Jn 18:10 high priest's slave and cut off his right E
18:26 of the man whose E Peter had cut off,
Acts 2:14 to you, and give E to my words.
1Cor 2:9 eye has seen, nor E heard, nor the heart
12:16 And if the E should say, "Because I am
12:17 whole body were an E, where would be the
Rev 2:7 He who has an E, let him hear what
2:11 He who has an E, let him hear what
2:17 He who has an E, let him hear what
2:29 He who has an E, let him hear what
3:6 He who has an E, let him hear what
3:13 He who has an E, let him hear what
3:22 He who has an E, let him hear what
13:9 any one has an E, let him hear:

EARLIER

2Chr 17:3 he walked in the E ways of his father;

EARLIEST

1Mac 3:29 had existed from the E days.

EARLY (87)

Gen 19:2 you may rise up E and go on your
19:27 And Abraham went E in the morning to the
20:8 So Abimelech rose E in the morning, and called
21:14 So Abraham rose E in the morning, and took
22:3 So Abraham rose E in the morning, saddled his
26:31 the morning they rose E and took oath with
28:18 So Jacob rose E in the morning, and he
31:55 E in the morning Laban arose, and kissed his
Ex 8:20 to Moses, "Rise up E in the morning and
9:13 to Moses, "Rise up E in the morning and
24:4 And he rose E in the morning, and built
32:6 And they rose up E on the morrow, and
34:4 first; and he rose E in the morning and
Num 14:40 And they rose E in the morning, and went
Deut 11:14 in its season, the E rain and the later
Josh 3:1 E in the morning Joshua rose and set out
6:12 Then Joshua rose E in the morning, and the
6:15 seventh day they rose E at the dawn of

7:16 So Joshua rose E in the morning, and brought
8:10 And Joshua arose E in the morning and mustered
8:14 haste and went out E to the descent toward
Judg 6:28 of the town rose E in the morning, behold,
6:38 When he rose E next morning and squeezed the
7:1 were with him rose E and encamped beside the
9:33 sun is up, rise E and rush upon the
19:5 fourth day they arose E in the morning, and
19:8 fifth day he arose E in the morning to
19:9 tomorrow you shall arise E in the morning for
21:4 morrow the people rose E, and built there an
Ruth 2:7 she has continued from E morning until now, without
1Sam 1:19 They rose E in the morning and worshiped before
5:3 people of Ashdod rose E the next day, behold,
5:4 But when they rose E on the next morning,
15:12 And Samuel rose E to meet Saul in the
17:20 And David rose E in the morning, and left
29:10 battle.' Now then rise E in the morning with
29:10 with you; and start E in the morning, and
29:11 out with his men E in the morning, to
2Sam 15:2 Absalom used to rise E and stand beside the
2Kgs 3:22 And when they rose E in the morning, and
6:15 man of God rose E in the morning and
19:35 and when men arose E in the morning, behold,
2Chr 20:20 And they rose E in the morning and went
29:20 Hezekiah the king rose E and gathered the officials
Neh 8:3 the Water Gate from E morning until midday, in
Tob 9:6 they both got up E and came to the
Job 1:5 and he would rise E in the morning and
Ps 46:5 not be moved; God will help her right E
84:6 place of springs; the E rain also covers it
127:2 that you rise up E and go late to
Prov 27:14 a loud voice, rising E in the morning, will
Song 7:12 let us go out E to the vineyards, and
Wis 4:7 man, though he die E, will be at rest.
6:14 He who rises E to seek her will have
Sir 4:12 those who seek her E will be filled with
6:36 intelligent man, visit him E; let your foot wear
31:20 moderate eating; he rises E, and feels fit.
32:14 and those who rise E to seek him will
39:5 his heart to rise E to seek the Lord
47:10 the sanctuary resounded from E morning.
Is 5:11 to those who rise E in the morning, that
37:36 and when men arose E in the morning, behold,
Ezek 27:17 merchandise wheat, olives and E figs, honey, oil, and
Dan 14:16 E in the morning the king rose and came,
Hos 6:4 the dew that goes E away.
13:3 the dew that goes E away, like the chaff
Joel 2:23 he has given the E rain for your vindication,
2:23 you abundant rain, the E and the latter rain,
1Mac 3:58 Be ready E in the morning to fight with
4:52 E in the morning on the twenty-fifth day of
6:33 E in the morning the king rose and took
10:80 at his men from E morning till late afternoon.
11:67 E in the morning they marched to the plain
16:5 E in the morning they arose and marched into
Mt 20:1 householder who went out E in the morning to
Mk 16:2 And very E on the first day of the
16:9 Now when he rose E on the first day
Lk 21:38 And E in the morning all the people came
24:1 of the week, at E dawn, they went to
24:22 were at the tomb E in the morning
Jn 8:2 E in the morning he came again to the
18:28 It was E
20:1 came to the tomb E, while it was still
Acts 15:7 know that in the E days God made choice
15:21 For from E generations Moses has had in every
21:16 Mnason of Cyprus, an E disciple, with whom we
Jas 5:7 until it receives the E and the late rain.

EARN

2Thes 3:12 in quietness and to E their own living.

EARNED

Tob 2:11 Then my wife Anna E money at women's work.

EARNEST (5)

Acts 12:5 kept in prison; but E prayer for him was
2Cor 8:16 who puts the same E care for you into
8:17 but being himself very E he is going to
8:22 often tested and found E in many matters, but
8:22 who is now more E than ever because of

EARNESTLY (16)

1Sam 20:6 all, then say, 'David E asked leave of me
20:28 Jonathan answered Saul, "David E asked leave of
Jud 4:12 out in unison, praying E to the God of
Ps 78:34 sought for him; they repented and sought God E
Is 26:9 my spirit within me E seeks thee.
Lk 7:4 Jesus, they besought him E, saying, "He is worthy
22:15 to them, "I have E desired to eat this
Acts 26:7 to attain, as they E worship night and day.
1Cor 12:31 But E desire the higher gifts.
14:1 love your aim, and E desire the spiritual gifts,
14:39 So, my brethren, E desire to prophesy, and do
2Cor 8:4 free will, begging us E for the favor of
Col 4:12 you, always remembering you E in his prayers, that
1Thes 3:10 before our God, praying E night and day that
Heb 13:19 urge you the more E to do this in
1Pet 1:22 brethren, love one another E from the heart.

EARNESTNESS (4)

2Cor 7:11 For see what E this godly grief has produced
8:7 in knowledge, in all E, and in your love
8:8 to prove by the E of others that your
Heb 6:11 to show the same E in realizing the full

EARNS (4)

Deut 24:15 on the day he E it, before the sun
Prov 11:18 A wicked man E deceptive wages, but one who
Hag 1:6 warm; and he who E wages earns wages to
1:6 he who earns wages E wages to put them

EARRINGS (8)

Ex 35:22 heart brought brooches and E and signet rings and
Num 31:50 and bracelets, signet rings, E, and beads, to make
Judg 8:24 man of you the E of his spoil." (For
8:24 (For they had golden E, because they were
8:25 cast in it the E of his spoil.
8:26 weight of the golden E that he requested was
Jud 10:4 and rings, and her E and all her ornaments,
Ezek 16:12 on your nose, and E in your ears, and

EARS (121)

Gen 35:4 that were in their E; and Jacob hid them
41:5 time; and behold, seven E of grain, plump and
41:6 after them sprouted seven E, thin and blighted by
41:7 And the thin E swallowed up the seven plump
41:7 ears swallowed up the seven plump and full E
41:22 in my dream seven E growing on one stalk,
41:23 and good; and seven E, withered, thin, and blighted
41:24 them, and the thin E swallowed up the seven
41:24 the thin ears swallowed up the seven good E
41:26 and the seven good E are seven years; the
41:27 and the seven empty E blighted by the east
44:18 word in my lord's E, and let not your
50:4 pray you, in the E of Pharaoh, saying,
Ex 17:14 recite it in the E of Joshua, that I
29:20 tips of the right E of his sons, and
32:2 which are in the E of your wives, your
32:3 which were in their E, and brought them to
Lev 2:14 new grain from fresh E, parched with fire.
8:24 tips of their right E and on the thumbs
Deut 23:25 you may pluck the E with your hand, but
29:4 eyes to see, or E to hear.
31:28 these words in their E and call heaven and
31:30 were finished, in the E of all the assembly
Judg 7:3 therefore proclaim in the E of the people, saying,
9:2 family, "Say in the E of all the citizens
9:3 his behalf in the E of all the men
17:2 spoke it in my E, behold, the silver is
Ruth 2:2 and glean among the E of grain after him
1Sam 3:11 at which the two E of every one that
8:21 repeated them in the E of the LORD.
11:4 the matter in the E of the people; and
15:14 the sheep in my E, and the lowing of
18:23 those words in the E of David.
25:24 handmaid speak in your E, and hear the words
2Sam 7:22 to all that we have heard with our E
22:7 my voice, and my cry came to his E
2Kgs 4:42 of barley, and fresh E of grain in his
19:28 has come into my E, I will put my
21:12 such evil that the E of every one who
1Chr 17:20 to all that we have heard with our E
2Chr 6:40 be open and thy E attentive to a prayer
7:15 be open and my E attentive to the prayer
Neh 8:3 could understand; and the E of all the people
Job 13:17 words, and let my declaration be in your E
15:21 sounds are in his E; in prosperity the destroyer
28:22 of it with our E
33:16 then he opens the E of men, and terrifies
36:10 He opens their E to instruction, and commands that

Ps 18:6 voice, and my cry to him reached his E
34:15 the righteous, and his E toward their cry.
44:1 have heard with our E, O God, our fathers
78:1 my teaching; incline your E to the words of
92:11 of my enemies, my E have heard the doom
115:6 They have E, but do not hear; noses, but
130:2 Let thy E be attentive to the voice of
135:17 see not, they have E, but they hear not,
Prov 26:17 one who takes a passing dog by the E
Wis 15:15 to draw breath, nor E with which to hear,
Sir 17:5 eyes; he gave them E and a mind for
17:11 glorious majesty, and their E heard the glory of
21:5 his lips to the E of God, and his
27:14 and their quarrels make a man stop his E
Is 6:10 people fat, and their E heavy, and shut their
6:10 and hear with their E, and understand with their
11:3 decide by what his E hear;
17:5 his arm harvests the E, and as when one
17:5 when one gleans the E of grain in the
22:14 revealed himself in my E: "Surely this iniquity will
30:21 And your E shall hear a word behind you,
32:3 be closed, and the E of those who hear
33:15 bribe, who stops his E from hearing of bloodshed
35:5 be opened, and the E of the deaf unstopped;
37:29 has come to my E, I will put my
42:20 not observe them; his E are open, but he
43:8 yet have eyes, who are deaf, yet have E
49:20 yet say in your E: 'The place is too
Jer 5:21 see not, who have E, but hear not.
6:10 Behold, their E are closed, they cannot listen; behold,
19:3 this place that the E of every one who
25:4 listened nor inclined your E to hear, although the
26:11 city, as you have heard with your own E
26:15 you to speak all these words in your E
34:14 me or incline their E to me.
Bar 2:31 heart that obeys and E that hear;
Ezek 3:10 receive in your heart, and hear with your E
8:18 they cry in my E with a loud voice,
9:1 he cried in my E with a loud voice,
12:2 see not, who have E to hear, but hear
16:12 and earrings in your E, and a beautiful crown
23:25 your nose and your E, and your survivors shall
40:4 and hear with your E, and set your mind
44:5 and hear with your E all that I shall
Mic 7:16 on their mouths; their E shall be deaf;
Zech 7:11 shoulder, and stopped their E that they might not
2Mac 15:39 the story delights the E of those who read
Mt 11:15 He who has E to hear, let him hear.
13:9 He who has E, let him hear."
13:15 grown dull, and their E are heavy of hearing,
13:15 and hear with their E, and understand with their
13:16 they see, and your E, for they hear.
13:43 He who has E, let him hear.
28:14 comes to the governor's E, we will satisfy him
Mk 4:9 said, "He who has E to hear, let him
4:23 If any man has E to hear, let him
7:32 his fingers into his E, and he spat and
7:34 And his E were opened, his tongue was released,
8:18 not see, and having E do you not hear?
Lk 1:44 greeting came to my E, the babe in my
8:8 out, "He who has E to hear, let him
9:44 words sink into your E; for the Son of
14:35 He who has E to hear, let him hear."
Acts 7:51 uncircumcised in heart and E, you always resist the
7:57 voice and stopped their E and rushed together upon
11:22 this came to the E of the church in
17:20 strange things to our E; we wish to know
28:27 grown dull, and their E are heavy of hearing,
28:27 and hear with their E, and understand with their
Rom 11:8 should not see and E that should not hear,
2Tim 4:3 teaching, but having itching E they will accumulate
Jas 5:4 harvesters have reached the E of the Lord of
1Pet 3:12 the righteous, and his E are open to their

EARTH (985)

Gen 1:1 the beginning God created the heavens and the E
1:2 The E was without form and void, and darkness
1:10 called the dry land E, and the waters that
1:11 God said, "Let the E put forth vegetation, plants
1:11 seed, each according to its kind, upon the E
1:12 The E brought forth vegetation, plants yielding seed
1:15 of the heavens to give light upon the E
1:17 give light upon the E,
1:20 birds fly above the E across the firmament of
1:22 the seas, and let birds multiply on the E
1:24 God said, "Let the E bring forth living creatures
1:24 and beasts of the E according to their kinds."
1:25 the beasts of the E according to their kinds
1:26 and over all the E, and over every creeping
1:26 over every creeping thing that creeps upon the E
1:28 multiply, and fill the E and subdue it; and
1:28 over every living thing that moves upon the E
1:29 face of all the E, and every tree with
1:30 every beast of the E, and to every bird
1:30 that creeps on the E, everything that has the
2:1 the heavens and the E were finished, and all
2:4 the heavens and the E when they were created.
2:4 LORD God made the E and the heavens,
2:5 was yet in the E and no herb of
2:5 to rain upon the E, and there was no
2:6 went up from the E and watered the whole
4:12 be a fugitive and a wanderer on the E
4:14 a wanderer on the E, and whoever finds me
6:4 Nephilim were on the E in those days, and
6:5 was great in the E, and that every imagination
6:6 made man on the E, and it grieved him
6:11 Now the E was corrupt in God's sight, and
6:11 God's sight, and the E was filled with violence.
6:12 And God saw the E, and behold, it was
6:12 all flesh had corrupted their way upon the E
6:13 all flesh; for the E is filled with violence
6:13 them; behold, I will destroy them with the E
6:17 of waters upon the E, to destroy all flesh
6:17 that is on the E shall die.
7:3 kind alive upon the face of all the E
7:4 send rain upon the E forty days and forty
7:6 when the flood of waters came upon the E
7:10 the waters of the flood came upon the E
7:12 rain fell upon the E forty days and forty
7:14 that creeps on the E according to its kind,
7:17 forty days upon the E; and the waters increased,
7:17 the ark, and it rose high above the E
7:18 increased greatly upon the E; and the ark floated
7:19 so mightily upon the E that all the high
7:21 that moved upon the E, birds, cattle, beasts, all
7:21 that swarm upon the E, and every man;
7:23 the air; they were blotted out from the E
7:24 waters prevailed upon the E a hundred and fifty
8:1 wind blow over the E, and the waters subsided;
8:3 waters receded from the E continually.
8:7 until the waters were dried up from the E
8:9 were still on the face of the whole E
8:11 knew that the waters had subsided from the E
8:13 dried from off the E; and Noah removed the
8:14 of the month, the E was dry.
8:17 that creeps on the E –that they may breed
8:17 breed abundantly on the E, and be fruitful and
8:17 earth, and be fruitful and multiply upon the E
8:19 that moves upon the E, went forth by families
8:22 While the E remains, seedtime and harvest, cold and
9:1 them, "Be fruitful and multiply, and fill the E
9:2 every beast of the E, and upon every bird
9:7 forth abundantly on the E and multiply in it."
9:10 every beast of the E with you, as many
9:11 shall there be a flood to destroy the E
9:13 sign of the covenant between me and the E
9:14 bring clouds over the E and the bow is
9:16 creature of all flesh that is upon the E
9:17 me and all flesh that is upon the E
9:19 from these the whole E was peopled.
10:8 was the first on E to be a mighty
10:25 in his days the E was divided, and his
10:32 spread abroad on the E after the flood.
11:1 Now the whole E had one language and few
11:4 scattered abroad upon the face of the whole E
11:8 face of all the E, and they left off
11:9 language of all the E; and from there the
11:9 them abroad over the face of all the E
12:3 the families of the E shall bless themselves.
13:16 the dust of the E; so that if one
13:16 the dust of the E, your descendants also can
14:19 maker of heaven and E;
14:22 maker of heaven and E,
18:2 bowed himself to the E,
18:18 the nations of the E shall bless themselves by
18:25 Judge of all the E do right?"
19:1 his face to the E,
19:23 had risen on the E when Lot came to
19:31 not a man on E to come in to
19:31 to us after the manner of all the E
22:18 the nations of the E bless themselves, because you
24:3 heaven and of the E, that you will not

E

24:52 bowed himself to the E before the LORD.
26:4 the nations of the E shall bless themselves:
26:15 stopped and filled with E all the wells which
27:28 the fatness of the E, and plenty of grain
27:39 the fatness of the E shall your dwelling be,
28:12 set up on the E, and the top of
28:14 the dust of the E, and you shall spread
28:14 the families of the E bless themselves.
41:47 seven plenteous years the E brought forth
41:57 Moreover, all the E came to Egypt to Joseph
41:57 because the famine was severe over all the E
45:7 you a remnant on E, and to keep alive
48:12 he bowed himself with his face to the E
48:16 into a multitude in the midst of the E
Ex 8:16 the dust of the E, that it may become
8:17 the dust of the E, and there came gnats
8:17 the dust of the E became gnats throughout all
8:22 am the LORD in the midst of the E
9:14 there is none like me in all the E
9:15 cut off from the E;
9:16 my name may be declared throughout all the E
9:23 and hail, and fire ran down to the E
9:29 may know that the E is the LORDs.
9:33 and the rain no longer poured upon the E
10:6 day they came on E to this day.'" Then
15:12 thy right hand, the E swallowed them.
19:5 peoples; for all the E is mine,
20:4 that is in the E beneath, or that is
20:4 the water under the E;
20:11 LORD made heaven and E, the sea, and all
20:24 An altar of E you shall make for me
31:17 LORD made heaven and E, and on the seventh
32:12 to consume them from the face of the E
33:16 people that are upon the face of the E
34:8 his head toward the E, and worshiped.
34:10 wrought in all the E or in any nation;
Lev 11:2 among all the beasts that are on the E
11:21 their feet, with which to leap on the E
11:29 that swarm upon the E: the weasel, the mouse,
11:41 that swarms upon the E is an abomination; it
11:42 that swarm upon the E, you shall not eat;
11:44 with any swarming thing that crawls upon the E
11:46 that swarms upon the E,
26:19 like iron and your E like brass;
Num 11:31 about two cubits above the face of the E
12:3 men that were on the face of the E
14:21 and as all the E shall be filled with
16:32 split asunder; and the E opened its mouth and
16:33 into Sheol; and the E closed over them, and
16:34 they said, "Lest the E swallow us up!"
22:5 the face of the E, and they are dwelling
22:11 the face of the E; now come, curse them
26:10 the LORD, and the E opened its mouth and
Deut 3:24 in heaven or on E who can do such
4:10 they live upon the E, and that they may
4:17 that is on the E, the likeness of any
4:18 fish that is in the water under the E
4:26 I call heaven and E to witness against you
4:32 created man upon the E, and ask from one
4:36 discipline you; and on E he let you see
4:39 above and on the E beneath; there is no
5:8 that is on the E beneath, or that is
5:8 the water under the E;
6:15 destroy you from off the face of the E
7:6 peoples that are on the face of the E
10:14 heaven of heavens, the E with all that is
11:6 of Reuben; how the E opened its mouth and
11:21 as long as the heavens are above the E
12:1 all the days that you live upon the E
12:16 it out upon the E like water.
12:24 it out upon the E like water.
13:7 one end of the E to the other,
14:2 peoples that are on the face of the E
28:1 you high above all the nations of the E
28:10 the peoples of the E shall see that you
28:23 be brass, and the E under you shall be
28:25 a horror to all the kingdoms of the E
28:26 the beasts of the E; and there shall be
28:49 the end of the E, as swift as the
28:64 one end of the E to the other; and
30:19 I call heaven and E to witness against you
31:28 and call heaven and E to witness against them.
32:1 speak; and let the E hear the words of
32:13 high places of the E, and he ate the
32:22 of Sheol, devours the E and its increase, and
33:16 best gifts of the E and its fulness, and
33:17 the ends of the E; such are the ten
Josh 2:11 heaven above and on E beneath.
3:11 Lord of all the E is to pass over
3:13 Lord of all the E, shall rest in the
4:24 the peoples of the E may know that the
5:14 his face to the E, and worshiped, and said
7:6 and fell to the E upon his face before
7:9 our name from the E; and what wilt thou
7:21 are hidden in the E inside my tent, with
23:14 way of all the E, and you know in
Judg 5:4 region of Edom, the E trembled, and the heavens
18:7 that is in the E, and possessing wealth, and
18:10 no lack of anything that is in the E
1Sam 2:8 the pillars of the E are the LORDS, and
2:10 the ends of the E; he will give strength
4:5 shout, so that the E resounded.
4:12 clothes rent and with E upon his head.
14:15 the raiders trembled; the E quaked; and it became
17:46 wild beasts of the E; that all the earth
17:46 earth; that all the E may know that there
20:15 the face of the E,
20:31 Jesse lives upon the E, neither you nor your
24:8 his face to the E, and did obeisance.
26:8 pin him to the E with one stroke of
26:20 blood fall to the E away from the presence
28:13 see a god coming up out of the E
28:23 he arose from the E, and sat upon the
2Sam 1:2 his clothes rent and E upon his head.
4:11 at your hand, and destroy you from the E
7:9 the name of the great ones of the E
7:23 What other nation on E is like thy people
12:20 David arose from the E, and washed, and anointed
13:31 and lay on the E; and all his servants
14:7 name nor remnant upon the face of the E
14:20 to know all things that are on the E
15:32 his coat rent and E upon his head.
18:9 hanging between heaven and E, while the mule that
18:28 his face to the E, and said, "Blessed be
22:8 "Then the E reeled and rocked; the foundations of
22:43 the dust of the E, I crushed them and
23:4 rain that makes grass to sprout from the E
1Kgs 1:40 joy, so that the E was split by their
1:52 shall fall to the E; but if wickedness is
2:2 about to go the way of all the E
4:34 the kings of the E, who had heard of
8:23 heaven above or on E beneath, keeping covenant and
8:27 "But will God indeed dwell on the E
8:43 the peoples of the E may know thy name
8:53 the peoples of the E, to be thy heritage,
8:60 the peoples of the E may know that the
10:23 the kings of the E in riches and in
10:24 And the whole E sought the presence of Solomon
13:34 to destroy it from the face of the E
17:14 day that the LORD sends rain upon the E
18:1 Ahab; and I will send rain upon the E
18:42 himself down upon the E, and put his face
2Kgs 5:15 God in all the E but in Israel; so
5:17 two mules' burden of E; for henceforth your servant
10:10 shall fall to the E nothing of the word
19:15 the kingdoms of the E; thou hast made heaven
19:15 of the earth; thou hast made heaven and E
19:19 the kingdoms of the E may know that thou,
1Chr 1:10 began to be a mighty one in the E
1:19 in his days the E was divided), and the
16:14 our God; his judgments are in all the E
16:23 Sing to the Lord, all the E
16:30 before him, all the E; yea, the world stands
16:31 glad, and let the E rejoice, and let them
16:33 the LORD, for he comes to judge the E
17:8 the name of the great ones of the E
17:21 What other nation on E is like thy people
21:16 the LORD standing between E and heaven, and in
22:8 shed so much blood before me upon the E
29:11 heavens and in the E is thine; thine is
29:15 our days on the E are like a shadow,
2Chr 1:9 people as many as the dust of the E
2:12 who made heaven and E, who has given King
6:14 in heaven or on E, keeping covenant and showing
6:18 will God dwell indeed with man on the E
6:33 the peoples of the E may know thy name
7:3 their faces to the E on the pavement, and
9:22 the kings of the E in riches and in
9:23 the kings of the E sought the presence of
16:9 fro throughout the whole E, to show his might
32:19 the peoples of the E, which are the work
36:23 the kingdoms of the E, and he has charged

Ezra 1:2 the kingdoms of the E, and he has charged
5:11 God of heaven and E, and we are rebuilding
Neh 9:1 in sackcloth, and with E upon their heads.
9:6 all their host, the E and all that is
Tob 3:13 be released from the E and that I hear
7:18 Lord of heaven and E grant you joy in
14:4 be scattered over the E from the good land,
Jud 2:5 lord of the whole E: When you leave my
2:7 Tell them to prepare E and water, for I
2:7 whole face of the E with the feet of
2:9 away captive to the ends of the whole E
2:19 whole face of the E to the west with
2:20 the dust of the E --a multitude that could
6:3 the face of the E, and their God will
6:4 says King Nebuchadnezzar, the lord of the whole E
7:29 against you heaven and E and our God, the
9:12 Lord of heaven and E, Creator of the waters,
11:1 to serve Nebuchadnezzar, the king of all the E
11:7 king of the whole E lives, and as his
11:21 one end of the E to the other, either
13:18 above all women on E; and blessed be the
13:18 the heavens and the E, who has guided you
Esth 11:5 thunders and earthquake, tumult upon the E
11:8 and distress, affliction and great tumult upon the E
13:10 hast made heaven and E and every wonderful thing
Job 1:7 and fro on the E, and from walking up
1:8 like him on the E, a blameless and upright
2:2 and fro on the E, and from walking up
2:3 like him on the E, a blameless and upright
3:14 and counselors of the E who rebuilt ruins for
5:10 gives rain upon the E and sends waters upon
5:22 and shall not fear the beasts of the E
5:25 and your offspring as the grass of the E
7:1 a hard service upon E, and are not his
7:21 shall lie in the E; thou wilt seek me,
8:9 for our days on E are a shadow.
8:19 and out of the E others will spring.
9:6 anger; who shakes the E out of its place,
9:24 The E is given into the hand of the
11:9 is longer than the E, and broader than the
12:8 the plants of the E, and they will teach
12:24 the people of the E, and makes them wander
14:8 grow old in the E, and its stump die
14:19 the soil of the E; so thou destroyest the
15:29 strike root in the E;
16:18 "O E, cover not my blood, and let my
18:4 your anger, shall the E be forsaken for you,
18:17 memory perishes from the E, and he has no
19:25 will stand upon the E;
20:4 man was placed upon E,
20:27 his iniquity, and the E will rise up against
24:4 the poor of the E all hide themselves.
26:7 void, and hangs the E upon nothing.
28:2 taken out of the E, and copper is smelted
28:5 As for the E, out of it comes bread;
28:24 the ends of the E, and sees everything under
30:6 in holes of the E and of the rocks.
34:13 him charge over the E and who laid on
35:11 the beasts of the E, and makes us wiser
37:3 and his lightning to the corners of the E
37:6 says, 'Fall on the E; and to the shower
37:17 are hot when the E is still because of
38:4 you when I laid the foundation of the E
38:13 the skirts of the E, and the wicked be
38:18 Have you comprehended the expanse of the E
38:24 where the east wind is scattered upon the E
38:33 Can you establish their rule on the E
39:14 her eggs to the E, and lets them be
41:33 Upon E there is not his like, a creature
Ps 2:2 The kings of the E set themselves, and the
2:8 the ends of the E your possession.
2:10 be wise; be warned, O rulers of the E
8:1 how majestic is thy name in all the E
8:9 how majestic is thy name in all the E
10:18 who is of the E may strike terror no
18:7 Then the E reeled and rocked; the foundations also
19:4 out through all the E, and their words to
21:10 their offspring from the E, and their children from
22:27 the ends of the E shall remember and turn
22:29 the proud of the E bow down; before him
24:1 The E is the LORD's and the fulness thereof,
33:5 righteousness and justice; the E is full of the
33:8 Let all the E fear the LORD, let all
33:14 the inhabitants of the E,
34:16 cut off the remembrance of them from the E
45:16 you will make them princes in all the E
46:2 not fear though the E should change, though the
46:6 utters his voice, the E melts.
46:8 LORD, how he has wrought desolations in the E
46:9 the end of the E; he breaks the bow,
46:10 among the nations, I am exalted in the E
47:2 is terrible, a great king over all the E
47:7 king of all the E; sing praises with a
47:9 the shields of the E belong to God; he
48:2 joy of all the E, Mount Zion, in the
48:10 thy praise reaches to the ends of the E
50:1 speaks and summons the E from the rising of
50:4 above and to the E, that he may judge
57:5 Let thy glory be over all the E
57:11 Let thy glory be over all the E
58:2 devise wrongs; your hands deal out violence on E
58:11 surely there is a God who judges on E
59:13 rules over Jacob to the ends of the E
61:2 the end of the E I call to thee,
63:9 the depths of the E;
65:5 the ends of the E, and of the farthest
65:8 those who dwell at E's farthest bounds are afraid
65:9 Thou visitest the E and waterest it, thou greatly
66:1 to God, all the E;
66:4 All the E worships thee; they sing praises to
67:2 may be known upon E, thy saving power among
67:4 peoples with equity and guide the nations upon E
67:6 The E has yielded its increase; God, our God,
67:7 the ends of the E fear him!
68:8 the wilderness, [Selah] the E quaked, the heavens
68:32 O kingdoms of the E; sing praises to the
69:34 Let heaven and E praise him, the seas and
71:20 the depths of the E thou wilt bring me
72:6 the mown grass, like showers that water the E
72:8 from the River to the ends of the E
72:19 for ever; may his glory fill the whole E
73:9 the heavens, and their tongue struts through the E
73:25 there is nothing upon E that I desire besides
74:12 old, working salvation in the midst of the E
74:17 the bounds of the E; thou hast made summer
75:3 When the E totters, and all its inhabitants, it
75:8 the wicked of the E shall drain it down
76:8 didst utter judgment; the E feared and was still,
76:9 judgment to save all the oppressed of the E
76:12 who is terrible to the kings of the E
77:18 up the world; the E trembled and shook.
78:69 high heavens, like the E, which he has founded
79:2 of thy saints to the beasts of the E
82:5 the foundations of the E are shaken.
82:8 O God, judge the E; for to thee belong
83:18 LORD, art the Most High over all the E
89:11 heavens are thine, the E also is thine; the
89:27 first-born, the highest of the kings of the E
90:2 thou hadst formed the E and the world, from
94:2 O judge of the E; render to the proud
95:4 the depths of the E; the heights of the
96:1 new song; sing to the LORD, all the E
96:9 in holy array; tremble before him, all the E
96:11 glad, and let the E rejoice; let the sea
96:13 he comes, for he comes to judge the E
97:1 LORD reigns; let the E rejoice; let the many
97:4 lighten the world; the E sees and trembles.
97:5 the LORD, before the Lord of all the E
97:9 high over all the E; thou art exalted far
98:3 the ends of the E have seen the victory
98:4 the LORD, all the E; break forth into joyous
98:9 the LORD, for he comes to judge the E
99:1 the cherubim; let the E quake!
102:15 the kings of the E thy glory.
102:19 LORD looked at the E,
102:25 the foundation of the E, and the heavens are
103:11 are high above the E, so great is his
104:5 Thou didst set the E on its foundations, so
104:9 so that they might not again cover the E
104:13 waterest the mountains; the E is satisfied with the
104:14 forth food from the E,
104:24 made them all; the E is full of thy
104:32 who looks on the E and it trembles, who
104:35 be consumed from the E, and let the wicked
105:7 our God; his judgments are in all the E
106:17 of the LORD, the E opened and swallowed up
108:5 Let thy glory be over all the E
109:15 may his memory be cut off from the E
110:6 corpses; he will shatter chiefs over the wide E
113:6 looks far down upon the heavens and the E
114:7 Tremble, O E, at the presence of the LORD,
115:15 blessed by the LORD, who made heaven and E

54:5 God of the whole E he is called.
54:9 more go over the E, so I have sworn
55:9 are higher than the E, so are my ways
55:10 thither but water the E, making it bring forth
58:14 the heights of the E; I will feed you
60:2 darkness shall cover the E, and thick darkness the
61:11 For as the E brings forth its shoots, and
62:7 Jerusalem and makes it a praise in the E
62:11 the end of the E: Say to the daughter
63:6 and I poured out their lifeblood on the E
65:17 heavens and a new E; and the former things
66:1 my throne and the E is my footstool; what
66:22 heavens and the new E which I will make
Jer 4:23 I looked on the E, and lo, it was
4:28 For this the E shall mourn, and the heavens
6:19 Hear, O E; behold, I am bringing evil upon
6:22 is stirring from the farthest parts of the E
7:33 the beasts of the E; and none will frighten
9:24 and righteousness in the E; for in these things
10:10 At his wrath the E quakes, and the nations
10:11 the heavens and the E shall perish from the
10:11 shall perish from the E and from under the
10:12 he who made the E by his power, who
10:13 the mist rise from the ends of the E
15:3 the beasts of the E to devour and destroy.
15:4 the kingdoms of the E because of what Manasseh
16:4 the air and for the beasts of the E
16:19 the ends of the E and say: "Our fathers
17:13 be written in the E, for they have forsaken
19:7 the air and to the beasts of the E
23:24 Do I not fill heaven and E
24:9 the kingdoms of the E, to be a reproach,
25:26 world which are on the face of the E
25:29 the inhabitants of the E, says the LORD of
25:30 tread grapes, against all the inhabitants of the E
25:31 the ends of the E, for the LORD has
25:32 is stirring from the farthest parts of the E
25:33 one end of the E to the other.
26:6 a curse for all the nations of the E
27:5 arm have made the E, with the men and
27:5 that are on the E, and I give it
28:16 will remove you from the face of the E
29:18 the kingdoms of the E, to be a curse,
31:8 farthest parts of the E, among them the blind
31:22 new thing on the E: a woman protects a
31:37 the foundations of the E below can be explored,
32:17 the heavens and the E by thy great power
33:2 LORD who made the E, the LORD who formed
33:9 the nations of the E who shall hear of
33:25 ordinances of heaven and E,
34:1 the kingdoms of the E under his dominion and
34:17 a horror to all the kingdoms of the E
34:20 of the air and the beasts of the E
44:8 a taunt among all the nations of the E
46:8 I will cover the E, I will destroy cities
46:12 your shame, and the E is full of your
49:21 of their fall the E shall tremble; the sound
50:23 hammer of the whole E is cut down and
50:34 give rest to the E, but unrest to the
50:41 are stirring from the farthest parts of the E
50:46 capture of Babylon the E shall tremble, and her
51:7 hand, making all the E drunken; the nations drank
51:15 he who made the E by his power, who
51:16 the mist rise from the ends of the E
51:25 which destroys the whole E; I will stretch out
51:27 a standard on the E, blow the trumpet among
51:41 praise of the whole E seized!
51:48 the heavens and the E, and all that is
51:49 Babylon have fallen the slain of all the E
Lam 2:1 down from heaven to E the splendor of Israel;
2:15 perfection of beauty, the joy of all the E
3:34 the prisoners of the E,
4:12 The kings of the E did not believe, or
Bar 1:11 that their days on E may be like the
2:15 exile; that all the E may know that thou
3:16 over the beasts on E;
3:20 have dwelt upon the E; but they have not
3:23 for understanding on the E, the merchants of Merran
3:32 He who prepared the E for all time filled
3:37 Afterward she appeared upon E and lived among
6:20 when worms from the E devour them and their
6:54 power; they are like crows between heaven and E
Ezek 1:15 a wheel upon the E beside the living creatures,
1:19 creatures rose from the E, the wheels rose.
1:21 those rose from the E, the wheels rose along
7:21 the wicked of the E for a spoil; and
8:3 lifted me up between E and heaven, and brought
10:16 mount up from the E, the wheels did not
10:19 mounted up from the E in my sight as
27:33 and merchandise you enriched the kings of the E
28:18 to ashes upon the E in the sight of
29:5 the beasts of the E and to the birds
31:12 the peoples of the E will go from its
32:4 beasts of the whole E with you.
34:6 the face of the E, with none to search
34:27 their fruit, and the E shall yield its increase,
35:14 rejoicing of the whole E I will make you
38:12 goods, who dwell at the center of the E
38:20 the face of the E, shall quake at my
39:18 the princes of the E –of rams, of lambs,
43:2 many waters; and the E shone with his glory.
Dan 2:10 not a man on E who can meet the
2:35 became a great mountain and filled the whole E
2:39 of bronze, which shall rule over all the E
3:75 Let the E bless the Lord; let it sing
3:77 that grow on the E, sing praise to him
4:1 dwell in all the E: Peace be multiplied to
4:10 the midst of the E; and its height was
4:11 was visible to the end of the whole E
4:15 its roots in the E, bound with a band
4:15 the grass of the E;
4:20 end of the whole E;
4:22 and your dominion to the ends of the E
4:23 its roots in the E, bound with a band
4:35 the inhabitants of the E are accounted as nothing;
4:35 the inhabitants of the E; and none can stay
6:25 dwell in all the E: "Peace be multiplied to
6:27 in heaven and on E, he who has saved
7:17 four kings who shall arise out of the E
7:23 a fourth kingdom on E, which shall be different
7:23 shall devour the whole E, and trample it down,
8:5 face of the whole E, without touching the ground;
12:2 the dust of the E shall awake, some to
14:5 who created heaven and E and has dominion over
Hos 2:21 they shall answer the E;
2:22 the earth; and the E shall answer the grain,
6:3 showers, as the spring rains that water the E
Joel 2:10 The E quakes before them, the heavens tremble.
2:30 heavens and on the E, blood and fire and
3:16 the heavens and the E shake.
Amos 2:7 the dust of the E, and turn aside the
3:2 the families of the E; therefore I will punish
3:5 a snare on the E, when there is no
4:13 the heights of the E –the LORD, the God
5:7 to wormwood, and cast down righteousness to the E
5:8 the surface of the E, the LORD is his
8:9 noon, and darken the E in broad daylight.
9:5 he who touches the E and it melts, and
9:6 his vault upon the E; who calls for the
9:6 the surface of the E – the LORD is
9:9 sieve, but no pebble shall fall upon the E
Mic 1:2 of you; hearken, O E, and all that is
1:3 and tread upon the high places of the E
4:13 their wealth to the Lord of the whole E
5:4 shall be great to the ends of the E
6:2 enduring foundations of the E; for the LORD has
7:2 has perished from the E, and there is none
7:13 But the E will be desolate because of its
7:17 crawling things of the E; they shall come trembling
Nah 1:5 the hills melt; the E is laid waste before
2:13 your prey from the E, and the voice of
Hab 1:6 the breadth of the E, to seize habitations not
1:10 for they heap up E and take it.
2:8 and violence to the E, to cities and all
2:14 For the E will be filled with the knowledge
2:17 and violence to the E, to cities and all
2:20 temple; let all the E keep silence before him.
3:3 the heavens, and the E was full of his
3:6 stood and measured the E; he looked and shook
3:9 Thou didst cleave the E with rivers.
3:12 Thou didst bestride the E in fury, thou didst
Zeph 1:2 sweep away everything from the face of the E
1:3 cut off mankind from the face of the E
1:18 jealous wrath, all the E shall be consumed; for
1:18 will make of all the inhabitants of the E
2:11 the gods of the E, and to him shall
3:8 jealous wrath all the E shall be consumed.
3:19 shame into praise and renown in all the E
Hag 1:10 the dew, and the E has withheld its produce.
2:6 the heavens and the E and the sea and
2:21 the heavens and the E,
Zech 1:10 sent to patrol the E

E

1:11 'We have patrolled the E, and behold, all the
1:11 and behold, all the E remains at rest.'
4:10 of the LORD, which range through the whole E
4:14 who stand by the Lord of the whole E
5:9 up the ephah between E and heaven.
6:5 presenting themselves before the LORD of all the E
6:7 were impatient to get off and patrol the E
6:7 And he said, "Go, patrol the E
6:7 So they patrolled the E
9:10 from the River to the ends of the E
11:6 they shall crush the E, and I will deliver
12:1 heavens and founded the E and formed the spirit
12:3 the nations of the E will come together against
14:9 king over all the E; on that day the
14:17 the families of the E do not go up
1Mac 1:2 and put to death the kings of the E
1:3 the ends of the E, and plundered many nations.
1:3 When the E became quiet before him, he was
1:9 years; and they caused many evils on the E
2:37 our innocence; heaven and E testify for us that
2:40 ordinances, they will quickly destroy us from the E
3:9 the ends of the E; he gathered in those
8:4 the ends of the E, until they crushed them
9:13 The E was shaken by the noise of the
14:10 his renown spread to the ends of the E
15:9 your glory will become manifest in all the E
2Mac 7:28 the heaven and the E and see everything that
9:8 was brought down to E and carried in a
13:7 the lawbreaker died, without even burial in the E
15:5 a sovereign also, on E, and I command you
Mt 5:5 are the meek, for they shall inherit the E
5:13 the salt of the E; but if salt has
5:18 you, till heaven and E pass away, not an
5:35 God, or by the E, for it is his
6:10 will be done, On E as it is in
6:19 for yourselves treasures on E, where moth and rust
9:6 man has authority on E to forgive sins"--he
10:34 to bring peace on E; I have not come
11:25 Lord of heaven and E, that thou hast hidden
12:40 and three nights in the heart of the E
12:42 the ends of the E to hear the wisdom
16:19 whatever you bind on E shall be bound in
16:19 whatever you loose on E shall be loosed in
17:24 do kings of the E take toll or tribute?
18:17 whatever you bind on E shall be bound in
18:17 whatever you loose on E shall be loosed in
18:18 of you agree on E about anything they ask,
23:9 man your father on E, for you have one
23:34 righteous blood shed on E, from the blood of
24:30 the tribes of the E will mourn, and they
24:35 Heaven and E will pass away, but my words
27:51 to bottom; and the E shook, and the rocks
28:18 in heaven and on E has been given to
Mk 2:10 man has authority on E to forgive sins"--he
4:28 The E produces of itself, first the blade, then
4:31 all the seeds on E;
9:3 as no fuller on E could bleach them.
13:27 the ends of the E to the ends of
13:31 Heaven and E will pass away, but my words
Lk 2:14 the highest, and on E peace among men with
5:24 man has authority on E to forgive sins"--he
10:21 Lord of heaven and E, that thou hast hidden
11:31 the ends of the E to hear the wisdom
12:49 cast fire upon the E; and would that it
12:51 that I have come to give peace on E
12:56 interpret the appearance of E and sky; but why
16:17 easier for heaven and E to pass away, than
18:8 of man comes, will he find faith on E
21:23 shall be upon the E and wrath upon this
21:25 stars, and upon the E distress of nations in
21:33 Heaven and E will pass away, but my words
21:35 who dwell upon the face of the whole E
Jn 3:31 who is of the E belongs to the earth,
3:31 earth belongs to the E, and of the earth
3:31 earth, and of the E he speaks; he who
12:24 wheat falls into the E and dies, it remains
12:32 lifted up from the E, will draw all men
17:4 I glorified thee on E, having accomplished the work
Acts 1:8 and Samaria and to the end of the E
2:19 and signs on the E beneath, blood, and fire,
3:25 the families of the E be blessed.'
4:24 the heaven and the E and the sea and
4:26 The kings of the E set themselves in array,
7:49 is my throne, and E my footstool.
8:33 For his life is taken up from the E
10:11 sheet, let down by four corners upon the E
13:47 bring salvation to the uttermost parts of the E
14:15 the heaven and the E and the sea and
17:24 Lord of heaven and E, does not live in
17:26 the face of the E, having determined allotted periods
22:22 said, "Away with such a fellow from the E
Rom 9:17 my name may be proclaimed in all the E
9:28 his sentence upon the E with rigor and dispatch."
10:18 out to all the E, and their words to
1Cor 8:5 in heaven or on E --as indeed there are
10:26 For "the E is the Lords, and everything in
15:47 man was from the E, a man of dust;
Eph 1:10 in him, things in heaven and things on E
3:15 in heaven and on E is named,
4:9 also descended into the lower parts of the E
6:3 and that you may live long on the E
Phil 2:10 in heaven and on E and under the earth,
2:10 earth and under the E,
Col 1:16 in heaven and on E, visible and invisible, whether
1:20 all things, whether on E or in heaven, making
3:2 are above, not on things that are on E
Heb 1:10 Lord, didst found the E in the beginning, and
8:4 if he were on E, he would not be
11:13 that they were strangers and exiles on the E
11:38 mountains, and in dens and caves of the E
12:25 who warned them on E, much less shall we
12:26 voice then shook the E; but now he has
12:26 shake not only the E but also the heaven."
Jas 5:5 have lived on the E in luxury and in
5:7 precious fruit of the E, being patient over it
5:12 by heaven or by E or with any other
5:17 six months it did not rain on the E
5:18 gave rain, and the E brought forth its fruit.
2Pet 3:5 long ago, and an E formed out of water
3:7 word the heavens and E that now exist have
3:10 with fire, and the E and the works that
3:13 heavens and a new E in which righteousness dwells.
Rev 1:5 the dead, and the ruler of kings on E
1:7 all tribes of the E will wail on account
3:10 world, to try those who dwell upon the E
5:3 in heaven or on E or under the earth
5:3 earth or under the E was able to open
5:6 out into all the E;
5:10 to our God, and they shall reign on E
5:13 in heaven and on E and under the earth
5:13 earth and under the E and in the sea,
6:4 take peace from the E, so that men should
6:8 a fourth of the E, to kill with sword
6:8 with pestilence and by wild beasts of the E
6:10 our blood on those who dwell upon the E
6:13 sky fell to the E as the fig tree
6:15 the kings of the E and the great men
7:1 four corners of the E, holding back the four
7:1 four winds of the E, that no wind might
7:1 wind might blow on E or sea or against
7:2 given power to harm E and sea,
7:3 "Do not harm the E or the sea or
8:5 threw it on the E; and there were peals
8:7 which fell on the E; and a third of
8:7 a third of the E was burnt up, and
8:13 who dwell on the E, at the blasts of
9:1 fallen from heaven to E, and he was given
9:3 came locusts on the E, and they were given
9:3 of scorpions of the E;
9:4 the grass of the E or any green growth
10:6 is in it, the E and what is in
11:4 lampstands which stand before the Lord of the E
11:6 and to smite the E with every plague, as
11:10 who dwell on the E will rejoice over them
11:10 a torment to those who dwell on the E
11:18 great, and for destroying the destroyers of the E
12:4 stars of heaven, and cast them to the E
12:9 thrown down to the E, and his angels were
12:12 woe to you, O E and sea, for the
12:13 thrown down to the E, he pursued the woman
12:16 But the E came to the help of the
12:16 the woman, and the E opened its mouth and
13:3 healed, and the whole E followed the beast with
13:8 all who dwell on E will worship it, every
13:11 rose out of the E; it had two horns
13:12 presence, and makes the E and its inhabitants
13:13 down from heaven to E in the sight of
13:14 those who dwell on E, bidding them make an
14:3 thousand who had been redeemed from the E
14:6 those who dwell on E, to every nation and
14:7 who made heaven and E, the sea and the
14:15 the harvest of the E is fully ripe."

14:16 his sickle on the E, and the earth was
14:16 the earth, and the E was reaped.
14:18 the vine of the E, for its grapes are
14:19 his sickle on the E and gathered the vintage
14:19 the vintage of the E, and threw it into
16:1 pour out on the E the seven bowls of
16:2 his bowl on the E, and foul and evil
16:18 men were on the E, so great was that
17:2 the kings of the E have committed fornication, and
17:2 fornication the dwellers on E have become drunk."
17:5 of harlots and of E's abominations."
17:8 and the dwellers on E whose names have not
17:18 which has dominion over the kings of the E
18:1 great authority; and the E was made bright with
18:3 the kings of the E have committed fornication with
18:3 the merchants of the E have grown rich with
18:9 the kings of the E, who committed fornication and
18:11 the merchants of the E weep and mourn for
18:23 great men of the E, and all nations were
18:24 and of all who have been slain on E
19:2 harlot who corrupted the E with her fornication, and
19:19 the kings of the E with their armies gathered
20:8 four corners of the E, that is, Gog and
20:9 up over the broad E and surrounded the camp
20:11 it; from his presence E and sky fled away,
21:1 heaven and a new E; for the first heaven
21:1 heaven and the first E had passed away, and
21:24 the kings of the E shall bring their glory

EARTHEN (13)

Lev 6:28 And the E vessel in which it is boiled
11:33 them falls into any E vessel, all that is
14:5 the birds in an E vessel over running water.
14:50 the birds in an E vessel over running water,
15:12 And the E vessel which he who has the
Num 5:17 holy water in an E vessel, and take some
2Sam 17:28 brought beds, basins, and E vessels, wheat, barley,
Prov 26:23 the glaze covering an E vessel are smooth lips
Is 45:9 with his Maker, an E vessel with the potter!
Jer 19:1 "Go, buy a potter's E flask, and take some
Lam 4:2 they are reckoned as E pots, the work of
2Cor 4:7 have this treasure in E vessels, to show that
Rev 2:27 of iron, as when E pots are broken in

EARTHENWARE (2)

Jer 32:14 put them in an E vessel, that they may
2Tim 2:20 also of wood and E, and some for noble

EARTHLY (10)

Jn 3:12 I have told you E things and you do
2Cor 1:12 godly sincerity, not by E wisdom but by the
5:1 know that if the E tent we live in
Eph 6:5 those who are your E masters, with fear and
Phil 3:19 with minds set on E things.
Col 3:5 death therefore what is E in you: fornication,
3:22 those who are your E masters, not with eye-service,
Heb 9:1 for worship and an E sanctuary.
12:9 this, we have had E fathers to discipline us
Jas 3:15 from above, but is E, unspiritual, devilish.

EARTHQUAKE (20)

1Kgs 19:11 after the wind an E, but the LORD was
19:11 was not in the E;
19:12 earthquake; and after the E a fire, but the
Esth 11:5 confusion, thunders and E, tumult upon the earth!
Sir 22:14 torn loose by an E; so the mind firmly
Is 29:6 with thunder and with E and great noise, with
Ezek 3:12 sound of a great E;
3:13 wheels beside them, that sounded like a great E
Amos 1:1 Joash, king of Israel, two years before the E
Zech 14:5 you fled from the E in the days of
Mt 27:54 over Jesus, saw the E and what took place,
28:2 there was a great E; for an angel of
Acts 16:26 there was a great E, so that the foundations
Rev 6:12 there was a great E; and the sun became
8:5 of thunder, voices, flashes of lightning, and an E
11:13 there was a great E, and a tenth of
11:13 were killed in the E, and the rest were
11:19 peals of thunder, an E, and heavy hail.
16:18 thunder, and a great E such as had never
16:18 were on the earth, so great was that E

EARTHQUAKES (3)

Mt 24:7 will be famines and E in various places:
Mk 13:8 kingdom; there will be E in various places, there
Lk 21:11 there will be great E, and in various places

EARTHWORKS

2Mac 12:13 was strongly fortified with E and walls, and inhabited

EARTHY (2)

Wis 9:15 the soul, and this E tent burdens the thoughtful
15:13 when he makes from E matter fragile vessels and

EASE (22)

Deut 28:65 you shall find no E, and there shall be
Job 3:18 the prisoners are at E together; they hear not
3:26 I am not at E, nor am I quiet;
7:13 me, my couch will E my complaint,'
12:5 one who is at E there is contempt for
16:12 I was at E, and he broke me asunder;
21:23 prosperity, being wholly at E and secure,
Ps 73:12 the wicked; always at E, they increase in riches.
123:4 those who are at E, the contempt of the
Prov 1:33 and will be at E, without dread of evil."
Is 32:9 women who are at E, hear my voice; you
32:11 women who are at E, shudder, you complacent ones;
Jer 30:10 and have quiet and E, and none shall make
46:27 and have quiet and E, and none shall make
48:11 "Moab has been at E from his youth and
49:31 against a nation at E, that dwells securely, says
Ezek 16:49 of food, and prosperous E, but did not aid
Dan 4:4 I, Nebuchadnezzar, was at E in my house and
Amos 6:1 those who are at E in Zion, and to
Zech 1:15 nations that are at E; for while I was
Lk 12:19 many years; take your E, eat, drink, be merry.'
1Cor 16:10 you put him at E among you, for he

EASED

2Cor 8:13 that others should be E and you burdened,

EASES

Hos 11:4 them as one, who E the yoke on their

EASIER (9)

Ex 18:22 so it will be E for you, and they
Sir 22:13 piece of iron are E to bear than a
Mt 9:5 For which is E, to say, 'Your sins are
19:24 tell you, it is E for a camel to
Mk 2:9 Which is E, to say to the paralytic, 'Your
10:25 It is E for a camel to go through
Lk 5:23 Which is E, to say, 'Your sins are forgiven
16:17 But it is E for heaven and earth to
18:25 For it is E for a camel to go

EASILY (3)

Gen 26:10 of the people might E have lain with your
Wis 6:12 unfading, and she is E discerned by those who
19:21 they melt the crystalline, E melted kind of heavenly

EAST (190)

Gen 2:8 in Eden, in the E; and there he put
2:14 is Tigris, which flows E of Assyria.
3:24 man; and at the E of the garden of
4:16 the land of Nod, E of Eden.
10:30 of Sephar to the hill country of the E
11:2 men migrated from the E, they found a plain
12:8 the mountain on the E of Bethel, and pitched
12:8 and Ai on the E; and there he built
13:11 valley, and Lot journeyed E; thus they separated
23:17 which was to the E of Mamre, the field
23:19 the field of Mach-pelah E of Mamre (that is,
25:6 Isaac, eastward to the E country.
25:9 of Zohar the Hittite, E of Mamre,
28:14 west and to the E and to the north
29:1 to the land of the people of the E
41:6 and blighted by the E wind.
41:23 and blighted by the E wind, sprouted after them,
41:27 ears blighted by the E wind are also seven
49:30 at Mach-pelah, to the E of Mamre, in the
50:13 at Mach-pelah, to the E of Mamre, which Abraham
Ex 10:13 the LORD brought an E wind upon the land
10:13 it was morning the E wind had brought the
14:21 back by a strong E wind all night, and
27:13 the front to the E shall be fifty cubits.
38:13 the front to the E, fifty cubits.
Lev 1:16 the altar on the E side, in the place
Num 2:3 to encamp on the E side toward the sunrise
3:38 the tabernacle on the E, before the tent of
10:5 that are on the E side shall set out.
32:19 on this side of the Jordan to the E
33:7 to Pi-hahiroth, which is E of Baal-zephon; and they
34:3 Salt Sea on the E;

34:11 to Riblah on the E side of Ain; and
34:11 of Chinnereth on the E;
35:5 the city, for the E side two thousand cubits,
Deut 3:17 Sea, under the slopes of Pisgah on the E
4:41 three cities in the E beyond the Jordan,
4:47 who lived to the E beyond the Jordan;
4:49 the Arabah on the E side of the Jordan
Josh 4:19 in Gilgal on the E border of Jericho.
7:2 which is near Beth-aven, E of Bethel, and said
11:3 the Canaanites in the E and the west, the
13:3 the Shihor, which is E of Egypt, northward to
13:25 to Aroer, which is E of Rabbah,
13:32 Moab, beyond the Jordan E of Jericho.
15:5 And the E boundary is the Salt Sea, to
16:1 the Jordan by Jericho, E of the waters of
16:5 their inheritance on the E was Ataroth-addar as far
16:6 Mich-methath; then on the E the boundary turns
16:6 beyond it on the E to Jan-oah,
17:7 to Mich-methath, which is E of Shechem; then the
17:10 reached, and on the E Issachar.
19:11 the brook which is E of Jokne-am;
19:13 passes along on the E toward the sunrise to
19:34 and Judah on the E at the Jordan.
20:8 And beyond the Jordan E of Jericho, they appointed
Judg 6:3 the people of the E would come up and
6:33 the people of the E came together, and crossing
7:12 the people of the E lay along the valley
8:10 the people of the E; for there had fallen
8:11 by the caravan route E of Nobah and Jogbehah,
11:18 and arrived on the E side of the land
20:43 Nohah as far as opposite Gibe-ah on the E
21:19 of Bethel, on the E of the highway that
1Sam 13:5 in Michmash, to the E of Beth-aven.
15:7 as Shur, which is E of Egypt.
26:1 which is on the E of Jeshimon?"
26:3 the road on the E of Jeshimon.
1Kgs 4:30 the people of the E, and all the wisdom
7:25 south, and three facing E; the sea was set
11:7 Ammonites, on the mountain E of Jerusalem.
17:3 brook Cherith, that is E of the Jordan.
17:5 brook Cherith that is E of the Jordan.
2Kgs 23:13 high places that were E of Jerusalem, to the
1Chr 4:39 of Gedor, to the E side of the valley,
5:9 also dwelt to the E as far as the
5:10 throughout all the region E of Gilead.
6:78 at Jericho, on the E side of the Jordan,
9:18 king's gate on the E side.
9:24 on the four sides, E, west, north, and south;
12:15 the valleys, to the E and to the west.
26:14 The lot for the E fell to Shelemiah.
26:17 On the E there were six each day, on
2Chr 4:4 south, and three facing E; the sea was set
5:12 harps, and lyres, stood E of the altar with
20:16 end of the valley, E of the wilderness of
29:4 the square on the E,
31:14 Levite, keeper of the E gate, was over the
Neh 3:26 Water Gate on the E and the projecting tower.
3:29 the keeper of the E Gate, repaired.
12:37 of David, to the Water Gate on the E
Jud 7:18 the south and the E, toward Acraba, which is
Job 1:3 the greatest of all the people of the E
15:2 fill himself with the E wind?
18:20 his day, and horror seizes them of the E
27:21 The E wind lifts him up and he is
38:24 distributed, or where the E wind is scattered
Ps 48:7 By the E wind thou didst shatter the ships
75:6 For not from the E or from the west
78:26 He caused the E wind to blow in the
103:12 as far as the E is from the west,
107:3 the lands, from the E and from the west,
Is 2:6 of diviners from the E and of soothsayers like
9:12 The Syrians on the E and the Philistines on
11:14 together they shall plunder the people of the E
24:15 Therefore in the E give glory to the LORD;
27:8 the day of the E wind.
41:2 up one from the E whom victory meets at
43:5 your offspring from the E, and from the west
46:11 of prey from the E, the man of my
Jer 18:17 Like the E wind I will scatter them before
31:40 Horse Gate toward the E, shall be sacred to
49:28 Destroy the people of the E
Bar 4:36 Look toward the E, O Jerusalem, and see the
4:37 are coming, gathered from E and west, at the
5:5 and look toward the E, and see your children
5:5 gathered from west and E, at the word of
Ezek 8:16 their faces toward the E, worshiping the sun
8:16 toward the east, worshiping the sun toward the E
10:19 the door of the E gate of the house
11:1 brought me to the E gate of the house
11:1 of the house of the LORD, which faces E
11:23 which is on the E side of the city.
17:10 utterly wither when the E wind strikes it--wither
19:12 to the ground; the E wind dried it up;
25:4 the people of the E for a possession, and
25:10 the people of the E as a possession, that
27:26 The E wind has wrecked you in the heart
39:11 Valley of the Travelers E of the sea; it
40:6 into the gateway facing E, going up its steps,
40:10 either side of the E gate; the three were
40:22 which faced toward the E; and seven steps led
40:23 north, as on the E, was a gate to
40:32 inner court on the E side, and he measured
41:14 the breadth of the E front of the temple
42:9 an entrance on the E side, as one enters
42:12 an entrance on the E side, where one enters
42:15 the gate which faced E, and measured the temple
42:16 He measured the E side with the measuring reed,
43:1 brought me to the gate, the gate facing E
43:2 Israel came from the E; and the sound of
43:4 by the gate facing E,
43:17 The steps of the altar shall face E
44:1 the sanctuary, which faces E; and it was shut.
45:7 west and on the E, corresponding in length to
46:1 inner court that faces E shall be shut on
46:12 LORD, the gate facing E shall be opened for
47:1 the temple toward the E (for the temple faced
47:1 (for the temple faced E; and the water was
47:2 that faces toward the E; and the water was
47:18 "On the E side, the boundary shall run from
47:18 This shall be the E side.
48:1 and extending from the E side to the west,
48:2 of Dan, from the E side to the west,
48:3 of Asher, from the E side to the west,
48:4 of Naphtali, from the E side to the west,
48:5 of Manasseh, from the E side to the west,
48:6 of Ephraim, from the E side to the west,
48:7 of Reuben, from the E side to the west,
48:8 of Judah, from the E side to the west,
48:8 tribal portions, from the E side to the west,
48:16 thousand five hundred, the E side four thousand five
48:17 and fifty, on the E two hundred and fifty,
48:18 thousand cubits to the E, and ten thousand to
48:21 holy portion to the E border, and westward from
48:23 the tribes: from the E side to the west,
48:24 of Benjamin, from the E side to the west,
48:25 of Simeon, from the E side to the west,
48:26 of Issachar, from the E side to the west,
48:27 of Zebulun, from the E side to the west,
48:32 On the E side, which is to be four
Dan 8:9 the south, toward the E, and toward the glorious
11:44 But tidings from the E and the north shall
Hos 12:1 wind, and pursues the E wind all day long;
13:15 the reed plant, the E wind, the wind of
Amos 8:12 and from north to E; they shall run to
Jon 4:5 and sat to the E of the city, and
4:8 God appointed a sultry E wind, and the sun
Zech 8:7 my people from the E country and from the
14:4 before Jerusalem on the E; and the Mount of
14:4 split in two from E to west by a
1Mac 12:37 the valley to the E had fallen, and he
Mt 2:1 wise men from the E came to Jerusalem, saying,
2:2 his star in the E, and have come to
2:9 had seen in the E went before them, till
8:11 many will come from E and west and sit
24:27 lightning comes from the E and shines as far
Lk 13:29 men will come from E and west, and from
Rev 16:12 prepare the way for the kings from the E
21:13 were inscribed; on the E three gates, on the

EASTERN (9)

Num 23:7 of Moab from the E mountains: 'Come, curse Jacob
34:10 shall mark out your E boundary from Hazar-enan to
Josh 18:20 its boundary on the E side.
Ezek 45:7 the western to the E boundary of the land.
47:8 water flows toward the E region and goes down
47:18 of Israel; to the E sea and as far
48:10 in breadth on the E side, and twenty-five thousand
Joel 2:20 his front into the E sea, and his rear
Zech 14:8 of them to the E sea and half of

EASTWARD (17)

Gen 13:14 northward and southward and E and westward;

	25:6	from his son Isaac, E to the east country.
Num	34:15	the Jordan at Jericho E, toward the sunrise."
Deut	3:27	northward and southward and E, and behold it with
Josh	11:8	Sidon and Misrephoth-maim, and E as far as the
	12:1	with all the Arabah E:
	12:3	the Sea of Chinneroth E, and in the direction
	13:8	them, beyond the Jordan E, as Moses the servant
	13:27	the Sea of Chinnereth, E beyond the Jordan.
	18:7	inheritance beyond the Jordan E, which Moses the
	19:12	in the other direction E toward the sunrise to
	19:27	Shihor-libnath, then it turns E, it goes to Beth-dagon,
1Kgs	17:3	from here and turn E, and hide yourself by
2Kgs	10:33	Israel: from the Jordan E, all the land of
	13:17	said, "Open the window E; and he opened it.
1Chr	7:28	and its towns, and E Naaran, and westward Gezer
Ezek	47:3	Going on E with a line in his hand,

EASY (13)

Deut	1:41	war, and thought it E to go up into
2Kgs	20:10	answered, "It is an E thing for the shadow
Jud	4:7	invaded, and it was E to stop any who
	7:10	for it is not E to reach the tops
Prov	14:6	vain, but knowledge is E for a man of
Wis	13:11	saw down a tree E to handle and skilfully
Sir	11:19	toil; for it is E in the sight of
	11:24	For it is E in the sight of the
1Mac	3:18	Judas replied, "It is E for many to be
2Mac	2:25	read, to make it E for those who are
	2:27	as it is not E for one who prepares
Mt	7:13	and the way is E, that leads to destruction,
	11:30	For my yoke is E, and my burden is

EAT (543)

Gen	2:16	saying, "You may freely E of every tree of
	2:17	evil you shall not E, for in the day
	2:17	the day that you E of it you shall
	3:1	say, 'You shall not E of any tree of
	3:2	the serpent, "We may E of the fruit of
	3:3	said, 'You shall not E of the fruit of
	3:5	knows that when you E of it your eyes
	3:11	tree of which I commanded you not to E
	3:14	and dust you shall E all the days of
	3:17	you, 'You shall not E of it,' cursed is
	3:17	in toil you shall E of it all the
	3:18	you; and you shall E the plants of the
	3:19	your face you shall E bread till you return
	3:22	tree of life, and E, and live for ever"–
	9:4	Only you shall not E flesh with its life,
	24:33	set before him to E; but he said, "I
	24:33	said, "I will not E until I have told
	25:30	to Jacob, "Let me E some of that red
	27:4	me that I may E; that I may bless
	27:7	food, that I may E it, and bless you
	27:10	to your father to E, so that he may
	27:19	now sit up and E of my game, that
	27:25	me, that I may E of my son's game
	27:31	my father arise, and E of his son's game,
	28:20	give me bread to E and clothing to wear,
	31:54	called his kinsmen to E bread; and they ate
	32:32	the Israelites do not E the sinew of the
	37:25	they sat down to E; and looking up they
	40:19	and the birds will E the flesh from you."
	43:25	heard that they should E bread there.
	43:32	the Egyptians might not E bread with the Hebrews,
	45:18	Egypt, and you shall E the fat of the
Ex	2:20	him, that he may E bread."
	10:5	land; and they shall E what is left to
	10:5	hail, and they shall E every tree of yours
	10:12	land of Egypt, and E every plant in the
	12:4	to what each can E you shall make your
	12:7	houses in which they E them.
	12:8	They shall E the flesh that night, roasted; with
	12:8	bitter herbs they shall E it.
	12:9	Do not E any of it raw or boiled
	12:11	this manner you shall E it: your loins girded,
	12:11	hand; and you shall E it in haste.
	12:15	Seven days you shall E unleavened bread; on the
	12:16	what every one must E, that only may be
	12:18	at evening, you shall E unleavened bread, and so
	12:20	You shall E nothing leavened; in all your dwellings
	12:20	your dwellings you shall E unleavened bread."
	12:43	passover: no foreigner shall E of it;
	12:44	bought for money may E of it after you
	12:45	or hired servant may E of it.
	12:48	no uncircumcised person shall E of it.
	13:6	Seven days you shall E unleavened bread, and on
	16:8	the evening flesh to E and in the morning
	16:12	'At twilight you shall E flesh, and in the
	16:15	bread which the LORD has given you to E
	16:16	much as he can E; you shall take an
	16:18	lack; each gathered according to what he could E
	16:21	much as he could E; but when the sun
	16:25	Moses said, E it today, for today is a
	18:12	elders of Israel to E bread with Moses' father-in-law
	22:31	therefore you shall not E any flesh that is
	23:11	of your people may E; and what they leave
	23:11	and what they leave the wild beasts may E
	23:15	commanded you, you shall E unleavened bread for
	29:32	and his sons shall E the flesh of the
	29:33	They shall E those things with which atonement was
	29:33	an outsider shall not E of them, because they
	32:6	people sat down to E and drink, and rose
	34:15	one invites you, you E of his sacrifice,
	34:18	Seven days you shall E unleavened bread, as I
Lev	3:17	dwelling places, that you E neither fat nor blood."
	6:16	and his sons shall E; it shall be eaten
	6:16	of meeting they shall E it.
	6:18	children of Aaron may E of it, as decreed
	6:26	it for sin shall E it; in a holy
	6:29	among the priests may E of it; it is
	7:6	among the priests may E of it; it shall
	7:19	who are clean may E flesh,
	7:23	of Israel, You shall E no fat, of ox,
	7:24	no account shall you E it.
	7:26	Moreover you shall E no blood whatever, whether of
	8:31	of meeting, and there E it and the bread
	8:31	and his sons shall E it';
	10:12	to the LORD, and E it unleavened beside the
	10:13	most holy; you shall E it in a holy
	10:14	is offered you shall E in any clean place,
	11:2	things which you may E among all the beasts
	11:3	chews the cud, among the animals, you may E
	11:4	hoof, you shall not E these: The camel, because
	11:8	flesh you shall not E, and their carcasses you
	11:9	"These you may E, of all that are in
	11:9	the seas or in the rivers, you may E
	11:11	flesh you shall not E, and their carcasses you
	11:21	all fours you may E those which have legs
	11:22	Of them you may E: the locust according to
	11:39	of which you may E dies, he who touches
	11:42	earth, you shall not E; for they are an
	17:12	person among you shall E blood, neither shall any
	17:12	who sojourns among you E blood.
	17:14	Israel, You shall not E the blood of any
	19:25	fifth year you may E of their fruit, that
	19:26	"You shall not E any flesh with the blood
	21:22	He may E the bread of his God, both
	22:4	suffers a discharge may E of the holy things
	22:6	evening and shall not E of the holy things
	22:7	and afterward he may E of the holy things,
	22:8	beasts he shall not E, defiling himself by it:
	22:10	"An outsider shall not E of a holy thing.
	22:10	hired servant shall not E of a holy thing;
	22:11	money, the slave may E of it; and those
	22:11	in his house may E of his food.
	22:12	outsider she shall not E of the offering of
	22:13	her youth, she may E of her father's food;
	22:13	yet no outsider shall E of it.
	23:6	seven days you shall E unleavened bread.
	23:14	And you shall E neither bread nor grain parched
	24:9	sons, and they shall E it in a holy
	25:12	to you; you shall E what it yields out
	25:19	fruit, and you will E your fill, and dwell
	25:20	say, 'What shall we E in the seventh year,
	25:22	comes in, you shall E the old.
	26:5	sowing; and you shall E your bread to the
	26:10	And you shall E old store long kept, and
	26:16	for your enemies shall E it;
	26:26	weight; and you shall E, and not be satisfied.
	26:29	You shall E the flesh of your sons, and
	26:29	sons, and you shall E the flesh of your
	26:38	of your enemies shall E you up.
Num	6:3	juice of grapes or E grapes, fresh or dried.
	6:4	his separation he shall E nothing that is produced
	9:11	keep it; they shall E it with unleavened bread
	11:4	and said, "O that we had meat to E
	11:13	meat, that we may E
	11:18	tomorrow, and you shall E meat; for you have
	11:18	LORD, saying, "Who will give us meat to E
	11:18	LORD will give you meat, and you shall E
	11:19	You shall not E one day, or two days,
	11:21	meat, that they may E a whole month!'

15:19 you and when you E of the food of
18:10 holy place shall you E of it; every male
18:10 it; every male may E of it; it is
18:11 in your house may E of it.
18:13 in your house may E of it.
18:31 press; and you may E it in any place,
24:8 wild ox, he shall E up the nations his
Deut 2:6 money, that you may E; and you shall also
2:28 money, that I may E, and give me water
4:28 see, nor hear, nor E, nor smell.
6:11 plant, and when you E and are full,
8:9 in which you will E bread without scarcity, in
8:10 And you shall E and be full, and you
11:15 cattle, and you shall E and be full.
12:7 and there you shall E before the LORD your
12:15 you may slaughter and E flesh within any of
12:15 and the clean may E of it, as of
12:16 Only you shall not E the blood; you shall
12:17 You may not E within your towns the tithe
12:18 present; but you shall E them before the LORD
12:20 you say, 'I will E flesh,' because you crave
12:20 crave flesh, you may E as much flesh as
12:21 you; and you may E within your towns as
12:22 eaten, so you may E of it; the unclean
12:22 the clean alike may E of it.
12:23 that you do not E the blood; for the
12:23 and you shall not E the life with the
12:24 You shall not E it; you shall pour it
12:25 You shall not E it; that all may go
12:27 LORD your God, but the flesh you may E
14:3 "You shall not E any abominable thing.
14:4 the animals you may E: the ox, the sheep,
14:6 chews the cud, among the animals, you may E
14:7 cloven you shall not E these: the camel, the
14:8 flesh you shall not E, and their carcasses you
14:9 the waters you may E these: whatever has fins
14:9 these: whatever has fins and scales you may E
14:10 scales you shall not E; it is unclean for
14:11 "You may E all clean birds.
14:12 which you shall not E: the eagle, the vulture,
14:20 All clean winged things you may E
14:21 "You shall not E anything that dies of itself;
14:21 towns, that he may E it, or you may
14:23 dwell there, you shall E the tithe of your
14:26 craves; and you shall E there before the LORD
14:29 towns, shall come and E and be filled; that
15:20 You shall E it, you and your household, before
15:22 You shall E it within your towns; the unclean
15:22 the clean alike may E it, as though it
15:23 Only you shall not E its blood; you shall
16:3 You shall E no leavened bread with it; seven
16:3 seven days you shall E it with unleavened bread,
16:7 shall boil it and E it at the place
16:8 six days you shall E unleavened bread; and on
18:1 with Israel; they shall E the offerings by fire
18:8 have equal portions to E, besides what he receives
20:19 them; for you may E of them, but you
23:24 neighbor's vineyard, you may E your fill of grapes,
26:12 widow, that they may E within your towns and
27:7 peace offerings, and shall E there; and you shall
28:31 and you shall not E of it; your ass
28:33 have not known shall E up the fruit of
28:39 for the worm shall E them.
28:51 the young, and shall E the offspring of your
28:53 And you shall E the offspring of your own
28:57 bears, because she will E them secretly, for want
Josh 24:13 you dwell therein; you E the fruit of vineyards
Judg 13:4 or strong drink, and E nothing unclean,
13:7 or strong drink, and E nothing unclean, for the
13:14 She may not E of anything that comes from
13:14 or strong drink, or E any unclean thing; all
13:16 me, I will not E of your food; but
14:14 them, "Out of the eater came something to E
Ruth 2:14 her, "Come here, and E some bread, and dip
1Sam 1:7 Therefore Hannah wept and would not E
1:8 And why do you not E
2:36 places, that I may E a morsel of bread."'
9:13 the high place to E; for the people will
9:13 the people will not E till he comes, since
9:13 the sacrifice; afterward those E who are invited.
9:19 for today you shall E with me, and in
9:24 E; because it was kept for you until the
9:24 appointed, that you might E with the guests." So
14:34 slay them here, and E; and do not sin
20:24 king sat down to E food.
28:22 bread before you; and E, that you may have
28:23 He refused, and said, "I will not E
2Sam 3:35 to persuade David to E bread while it was
9:7 father; and you shall E at my table always."
9:10 may have bread to E; but Mephibosheth your
9:10 master's son shall always E at my table." Now
11:11 to my house, to E and to drink, and
12:3 children; it used to E of his morsel, and
12:17 not, nor did he E food with them.
13:5 give me bread to E, and prepare the food
13:5 may see it, and E it from her hand."'
13:6 sight, that I may E from her hand."
13:9 it out before him, but he refused to E
13:10 chamber, that I may E from your hand." And
13:11 them near him to E, he took hold of
16:2 the young men to E, and the wine for
17:29 people with him to E; for they said, "The
19:28 servant among those who E at your table.
1Kgs 2:7 be among those who E at your table; for
13:8 And I will not E bread or drink water
13:9 saying, 'You shall neither E bread, nor drink water,
13:15 home with me and E bread."
13:16 you; neither will I E bread nor drink water
13:17 LORD, 'You shall neither E bread nor drink water
13:18 house that he may E bread and drink water."'
13:22 he said to you, E no bread, and drink
14:11 city the dogs shall E; and any one who
14:11 of the air shall E; for the LORD has
16:4 city the dogs shall E; and any one of
16:4 the field the birds of the air shall E
17:12 son, that we may E it, and die."
18:19 prophets of Asherah, who E at Jezebel's table."
18:41 to Ahab, "Go up, E and drink; for there
18:42 Ahab went up to E and to drink.
19:5 touched him, and said to him, "Arise and E
19:7 and said, "Arise and E, else the journey will
21:4 his face, and would E no food.
21:5 so vexed that you E no food?"
21:7 Arise, and E bread, and let your heart be
21:23 said, 'The dogs shall E Jezebel within the bounds
21:24 city the dogs shall E; and any one of
21:24 open country the birds of the air shall E
2Kgs 4:8 who urged him to E some food.
4:8 turn in there to E food.
4:40 And they poured out for the men to E
4:40 And they could not E it.
4:41 "Pour out for the men, that they may E
4:42 said, "Give to the men, that they may E
4:43 men, that they may E, for thus says the
4:43 the LORD, 'They shall E and have some left."'
6:22 them, that they may E and drink and go
6:28 son, that we may E him today, and we
6:28 today, and we will E my son tomorrow.'
6:29 son, that we may E him'; but she has
7:2 but you shall not E of it."
7:19 but you shall not E of it."
9:10 And the dogs shall E Jezebel in the territory
9:36 Jezreel the dogs shall E the flesh of Jezebel;
18:27 doomed with you to E their own dung and
18:31 one of you will E of his own vine,
19:29 this year you shall E what grows of itself,
19:29 and plant vineyards, and E their fruit.
Ezra 4:14 Now because we E the salt of the palace
9:12 may be strong, and E the good of the
Neh 5:2 grain, that we may E and keep alive."
8:10 them, "Go your way, E the fat and drink
8:12 went their way to E and drink and to
Tob 2:1 prepared for me and I sat down to E
2:13 is not right to E what is stolen."
7:9 Raguel said to Tobias, E, drink, and be merry;
7:11 Tobias said, "I will E nothing here until you
7:15 Then they began to E
12:19 you and did not E or drink, but you
Jud 11:12 God by his laws has forbidden them to E
12:2 Judith said, "I cannot E it, lest it be
12:11 to join us and E and drink with us.
Esth 4:16 my behalf, and neither E nor drink for three
Job 1:4 their three sisters to E and drink with them.
5:5 His harvest the hungry E, and he takes it
27:14 sword; and his offspring have not enough to E
31:8 me sow, and another E; and let what grows
Ps 14:4 all the evildoers who E up my people as
14:4 my people as they E bread, and do not
22:26 The afflicted shall E and be satisfied; those who
50:13 Do I E the flesh of bulls, or drink
53:4 evil no understanding, who E up my people as
53:4 my people as they E bread, and do not

78:24 upon them manna to E, and gave them the
102:4 withered; I forget to E my bread.
102:9 For I E ashes like bread, and mingle tears
128:2 You shall E the fruit of the labor of
141:4 and let me not E of their dainties!
Prov 1:31 reproof, therefore they shall E the fruit of their
4:18 For they E the bread of wickedness and drink
9:5 sense she says, "Come, E of my bread and
18:21 who love it will E its fruits.
23:1 you sit down to E with a ruler, observe
23:6 Do not E the bread of a man who
23:7 E and drink!" he says to you; but his
24:13 My son, E honey, for it is good, and
25:16 you have found honey, E only enough for you,
25:21 give him bread to E; and if he is
25:27 is not good to E much honey, so be
27:18 a fig tree will E its fruit, and he
31:27 household, and does not E the bread of idleness.
Eccl 2:24 than that he should E and drink, and find
2:25 from him who can E or who can have
3:13 that every one should E and drink and take
5:11 increase, they increase who E them; and what gain
5:18 be fitting is to E and drink and find
8:15 the sun but to E and drink, and enjoy
9:7 Go, E your bread with enjoyment, and drink your
Song 4:16 to his garden, and E its choicest fruits.
5:1 with my spice, I E my honeycomb with my
5:1 E, O friends, and drink: drink deeply, O lovers!
Wis 4:5 not ripe enough to E, and good for nothing.
13:12 prepare his food, and E his fill.
16:2 didst prepare quails to E, a delicacy to satisfy
16:20 with bread ready to E, providing every pleasure and
Sir 6:19 and soon you will E of her produce.
20:15 good deeds; those who E my bread speak unkindly."
24:18 who desire me, and E your fill of my
24:20 Those who E me will hunger for more, and
29:26 anything at hand, let me have it to E
30:19 For it can neither E nor smell.
31:16 E like a human being what is set before
45:21 in abundance; for they E the sacrifices to the
Is 1:19 and obedient, you shall E the good of the
3:10 them, for they shall E the fruit of their
4:1 day, saying, "We will E our own bread and
7:15 He shall E curds and honey when he knows
7:22 they give, he will E curds; for every one
7:22 in the land will E curds and honey.
11:7 and the lion shall E straw like the ox.
21:5 spread the rugs, they E, they drink.
22:13 "Let us E and drink, for tomorrow we die."
30:24 till the ground will E salted provender, which has
36:12 doomed with you to E their own dung and
36:16 one of you will E of his own vine,
37:30 for you: this year E what grows of itself,
37:30 and plant vineyards, and E their fruit.
49:26 will make your oppressors E their own flesh, and
50:9 garment; the moth will E them up.
51:8 For the moth will E them up like a
51:8 and the worm will E them like wool; but
55:1 he who has no money, come, buy and E
55:2 diligently to me, and E what is good, and
61:6 our God; you shall E the wealth of the
62:9 who garner it shall E it and praise the
65:4 in secret places; who E swine's flesh, and broth
65:13 "Behold, my servants shall E, but you shall be
65:21 shall plant vineyards and E their fruit.
65:22 not plant and another E; for like the days
65:25 together, the lion shall E straw like the ox;
Jer 5:17 They shall E up your harvest and your food;
5:17 your food; they shall E up your sons and
5:17 your daughters; they shall E up your flocks and
5:17 your herds; they shall E up your vines and
7:21 to your sacrifices, and E the flesh.
16:8 sit with them, to E and drink.
19:9 I will make them E the flesh of their
19:9 and every one shall E the flesh of his
22:15 Did not your father E and drink and do
29:5 them; plant gardens and E their produce.
29:28 and plant gardens and E their produce.'"'
Lam 2:20 Should women E their offspring, the children of their
Bar 2:3 Moses, that we should E, one the flesh of
Ezek 2:8 open your mouth, and E what I give you."
3:1 me, "Son of man, E what is offered to
3:1 is offered to you; E this scroll, and go,
3:2 mouth, and he gave me the scroll to E
3:3 me, "Son of man, E this scroll that I
4:9 ninety days, you shall E it.
4:10 the food which you E shall be by weight,
4:10 a day you shall E it.
4:12 And you shall E it as a barley cake,
4:13 the people of Israel E their bread unclean, among
4:16 in Jerusalem; they shall E bread by weight and
5:10 Therefore fathers shall E their sons in the midst
5:10 you, and sons shall E their fathers; and I
12:18 me: "Son of man, E your bread with quaking,
12:19 of Israel: They shall E their bread with fearfulness,
18:6 if he does not E upon the mountains or
18:15 likewise, who does not E upon the mountains or
22:9 men in you who E upon the mountains; men
24:17 cover your lips, nor E the bread of mourners."
24:22 cover your lips, nor E the bread of mourners.
25:4 your midst; they shall E your fruit, and they
33:25 the Lord GOD: You E flesh with the blood,
34:3 You E the fat, you clothe yourselves with the
34:19 And must my sheep E what you have trodden
39:17 Israel, and you shall E flesh and drink blood.
39:18 You shall E the flesh of the mighty, and
39:19 And you shall E fat till you are filled,
42:13 approach the LORD shall E the most holy offerings;
44:3 sit in it to E bread before the LORD;
44:29 They shall E the cereal offering, the sin offering,
44:31 The priests shall not E of anything, whether bird
Dan 1:12 be given vegetables to E and water to drink.
1:13 of the youths who E the king's rich food
4:25 shall be made to E grass like an ox,
4:32 shall be made to E grass like an ox;
11:26 Even those who E his rich food shall be
Hos 4:10 They shall E, but not be satisfied; they shall
8:13 they sacrifice flesh and E it; but the LORD
9:3 Egypt, and they shall E unclean food in Assyria.
9:4 mourners' bread; all who E of it shall be
Joel 2:26 "You shall E in plenty and be satisfied, and
Amos 6:4 upon their couches, and E lambs from the flock,
7:12 land of Judah, and E bread there, and prophesy
9:14 shall make gardens and E their fruit.
Mic 3:3 off their bones; who E the flesh of my
3:5 they have something to E, but declare war against
6:14 You shall E, but not be satisfied, and there
7:1 is no cluster to E, no first-ripe fig which
Hag 1:6 and harvested little; you E, but you never have
Zech 7:6 And when you E and when you drink, do
7:6 drink, do you not E for yourselves and drink
1Mac 1:62 their hearts not to E unclean food.
2Mac 6:18 open his mouth to E swine's flesh.
7:7 asked him, "Will you E rather than have your
Mt 6:25 life, what you shall E or what you shall
6:31 saying, 'What shall we E or 'What shall we
9:11 "Why does your teacher E with tax collectors and
12:1 began to pluck heads of grain and to E
12:4 lawful for him to E nor for those who
14:16 not go away; you give them something to E
15:2 they do not wash their hands when they E
15:20 a man; but to E with unwashed hands does
15:27 yet even the dogs E the crumbs that fall
15:32 and have nothing to E; and I am unwilling
26:17 prepare for you to E the passover?"
26:26 disciples and said, "Take, E; this is my body."
Mk 2:16 disciples, "Why does he E with tax collectors and
2:26 but the priests to E, and also gave it
3:20 together again, so that they could not even E
5:43 and told them to give her something to E
6:31 going, and they had no leisure even to E
6:36 round about and buy themselves something to E
6:37 he answered them, "You give them something to E
6:37 of bread, and give it to them to E
7:3 the Jews, do not E unless they wash their
7:4 place, they do not E unless they purify themselves;
7:5 of the elders, but E with hands defiled?"
7:27 dogs under the table E the children's crumbs."
8:1 they had nothing to E, he called his disciples
8:2 and have nothing to E;
11:14 "May no one ever E fruit from you again."
14:12 prepare for you to E the passover?"
14:14 where I am to E the passover with my
Lk 5:30 saying, "Why do you E and drink with tax
5:33 the Pharisees, but yours E and drink."
6:4 but the priests to E, and also gave it
7:36 Pharisees asked him to E with him, and he
8:55 directed that something should be given her to E
9:13 said to them, "You give them something to E
10:8 and they receive you, E what is set before
12:19 years; take your ease, E, drink, be merry.'
12:22 life, what you shall E, nor about your body,

	12:29	what you are to E and what you are
	12:45	the maidservants, and to E and drink and get
	14:15	is he who shall E bread in the kingdom
	15:23	it, and let us E and make merry;
	17:8	serve me, till I E and drink; and afterward
	17:8	and afterward you shall E and drink?
	22:8	us, that we may E it."
	22:11	where I am to E the passover with my
	22:15	have earnestly desired to E this passover with you
	22:16	you I shall not E it until it is
	22:30	kingdom, that you may E and drink at my
	24:41	said to them, "Have you anything here to E
Jn	4:31	the disciples besought him, saying, "Rabbi, E
	4:32	"I have food to E of which you do
	6:5	to buy bread, so that these people may E
	6:31	written, 'He gave them bread from heaven to E
	6:50	that a man may E of it and not
	6:52	can this man give us his flesh to E
	6:53	to you, unless you E the flesh of the
	18:28	be defiled, but might E the passover.
Acts	10:10	and desired something to E; but while they were
	10:13	a voice to him, "Rise, Peter; kill and E
	11:3	to uncircumcised men and E with them?"
	11:7	'Rise, Peter; kill and E
	23:12	an oath neither to E nor drink till they
	23:21	an oath neither to E nor drink till they
	27:35	of all he broke it and began to E
Rom	14:2	One believes he may E anything, while the weak
	14:15	injured by what you E, you are no longer
	14:15	not let what you E cause the ruin of
	14:21	is right not to E meat or drink wine
1Cor	5:11	robber--not even to E with such a one.
	8:7	hitherto accustomed to idols, E food as really offered
	8:8	if we do not E, and no better off
	8:10	conscience is weak, to E food offered to idols?
	8:13	falling, I will never E meat, lest I cause
	10:7	people sat down to E and drink and rose
	10:18	are not those who E the sacrifices partners in
	10:25	E whatever is sold in the meat market without
	10:27	are disposed to go, E whatever is set before
	10:29	not yours--do not E it.) For why should
	10:31	So, whether you E or drink, or whatever you
	11:20	it is not the Lord's supper that you E
	11:22	not have houses to E and drink in?
	11:26	as often as you E this bread and drink
	11:28	examine himself, and so E of the bread and
	11:33	you come together to E, wait for one another--
	11:34	is hungry, let him E at home--lest you
	15:32	not raised, "Let us E and drink, for tomorrow
2Thes	3:8	you, we did not E any one's bread without
	3:10	any one will not work, let him not E
2Tim	2:17	and their talk will E its way like gangrene.
Heb	13:10	who serve the tent have no right to E
Jas	5:3	against you and will E your flesh like fire.
Rev	2:7	I will grant to E of the tree of
	2:14	Israel, that they might E food sacrificed to idols
	2:20	practice immorality and to E food sacrificed to idols.
	3:20	in to him and E with him, and he
	10:9	me, "Take it and E; it will be bitter
	19:18	supper of God, to E the flesh of kings,

EATEN (89)

Gen	3:11	Have you E of the tree of which I
	3:17	your wife, and have E of the tree of
	6:21	of food that is E, and store it up;
	14:24	the young men have E, and the share of
	31:38	and I have not E the rams of your
	41:21	but when they had E them no one would
	41:21	known that they had E them, for they were
	43:2	And when they had E the grain which they
Ex	12:46	house shall it be E; you shall not carry
	13:3	from this place; no leavened bread shall be E
	13:7	Unleavened bread shall be E for seven days; no
	21:28	flesh shall not be E; but the owner of
	29:34	it shall not be E, because it is holy.
Lev	6:16	eat; it shall be E unleavened in a holy
	6:23	shall be wholly burned; it shall not be E
	6:26	place it shall be E, in the court of
	6:30	sin offering shall be E from which any blood
	7:6	it; it shall be E in a holy place;
	7:15	for thanksgiving shall be E on the day of
	7:16	offering, it shall be E on the day that
	7:16	of it shall be E,
	7:18	his peace offering is E on the third day,
	7:19	thing shall not be E; it shall be burned
	10:17	"Why have you not E the sin offering in
	10:18	certainly ought to have E it in the sanctuary,
	10:19	If I had E the sin offering today, would
	11:13	they shall not be E, they are an abomination:
	11:34	it which may be E, upon which water may
	11:41	earth is an abomination; it shall not be E
	11:47	creature that may be E and the living creature
	11:47	and the living creature that may not be E
	17:13	bird that may be E shall pour out its
	19:6	It shall be E the same day you offer
	19:7	If it is E at all on the third
	19:23	be forbidden to you, it must not be E
	22:30	It shall be E on the same day, you
Num	28:17	a feast; seven days shall unleavened bread be E
Deut	8:12	lest, when you have E and are full, and
	12:22	or the hart is E, so you may eat
	14:19	are unclean for you; they shall not be E
	26:14	them; I have not E of the tithe while
	29:6	feet; you have not E bread, and you have
	31:20	fathers, and they have E and are full and
Ruth	3:7	And when Boaz had E and drunk, and his
1Sam	1:9	After they had E and drunk in Shiloh, Hannah
	14:30	if the people had E freely today of the
	28:20	him, for he had E nothing all day and
	30:12	And when he had E, his spirit revived; for
	30:12	for he had not E bread or drunk water
2Sam	19:42	Have we E at all at the king's expense?
1Kgs	13:22	come back, and have E bread and drunk water
	13:23	And after he had E bread and drunk, he
	13:28	The lion had not E the body or torn
2Kgs	6:23	and when they had E and drunk, he sent
2Chr	31:10	the LORD we have E and had enough and
Ezra	6:21	for themselves; it was E by the people of
Esth	14:17	thy servant has not E at Haman's table, and
Job	6:6	which is tasteless be E without salt, or is
	20:21	left after he had E; therefore his prosperity will
	31:17	to fail, or have E my morsel alone, and
	31:17	the fatherless has not E of it
	31:39	together; if I have E its yield without payment,
Prov	9:17	is sweet, and bread E in secret is pleasant."
	23:8	morsels which you have E, and waste your pleasant
	30:17	of the valley and E by the vultures.
Is	44:19	roasted flesh and have E; and shall I make
Jer	24:2	figs, so bad that they could not be E
	24:3	very bad, so bad that they cannot be E
	24:8	bad they cannot be E, so will I treat
	29:17	figs which are so bad they cannot be E
	31:29	say: 'The fathers have E sour grapes, and the
Ezek	4:14	now I have never E what died of itself
	18:2	Israel, 'The fathers have E sour grapes, and the
	45:21	and for seven days unleavened bread shall be E
Dan	14:12	find that Bel has E it all, we will
Hos	10:13	reaped injustice, you have E the fruit of lies.
Joel	1:4	the cutting locust left, the swarming locust has E
	1:4	the hopping locust has E, and what the hopping
	1:4	the hopping locust left, the destroying locust has E
	2:25	the swarming locust has E, the hopper, the destroyer,
1Mac	3:17	faint, for we have E nothing today."
2Mac	2:11	consumed because the sin offering had not been E
Jn	6:12	And when they had E their fill, he told
	6:13	five barley loaves, left by those who had E
Acts	10:14	for I have never E anything that is common
	12:23	glory; and he was E by worms and died.
	20:11	had broken bread and E, he conversed with them
	27:38	And when they had E enough, they lightened the
Rev	10:10	but when I had E it my stomach was

EATER (3)

Judg	14:14	them, "Out of the E came something to eat.
Is	55:10	and bread to the E,
Nah	3:12	shaken they fall into the mouth of the E

EATERS

Prov	23:20	winebibbers, or among gluttonous E of meat;

EATING (44)

Gen	40:17	but the birds were E it out of the
Lev	22:16	iniquity and guilt, by E their holy things: for
	25:22	year, you will be E old produce; until the
Deut	28:55	children whom he is E, because he has nothing
Judg	14:9	hands, and went on, E as he went; and
Ruth	3:3	until he has finished E and drinking.
1Sam	14:33	against the LORD, by E with the blood." And
	14:34	against the LORD by E with the blood."' So
	30:16	over all the land, E and drinking and dancing,
1Kgs	1:25	and behold, they are E and drinking before him,
2Kgs	4:40	But while they were E of the pottage, they

1Chr 12:39 David for three days, E and drinking, for their
Ezra 10:6 spent the night, neither E bread nor drinking water;
Tob 1:11 I kept myself from E it,
8:1 When they had finished E, they escorted Tobias in
Job 1:13 sons and daughters were E and drinking wine in
1:18 sons and daughters were E and drinking wine in
Ps 127:2 go late to rest, E the bread of anxious
Sir 31:17 the first to stop E, for the sake of
31:20 sleep depends on moderate E; he rises early, and
Is 22:13 oxen and killing sheep, E flesh and drinking wine.
29:8 man dreams he is E and awakes with his
66:17 one in the midst, E swine's flesh and the
Dan 14:8 tell me who is E these provisions, you shall
14:9 prove that Bel is E them, Daniel shall die,
Amos 7:2 When they had finished E the grass of the
7:4 great deep and was E up the land.
2Mac 6:21 pretend that he was E the flesh of the
7:42 enough, then, about the E of sacrifices and the
Mt 11:18 For John came neither E nor drinking, and they
11:19 Son of man came E and drinking, and they
24:38 the flood they were E and drinking, marrying and
26:21 and as they were E, he said, "Truly, I
26:26 Now as they were E, Jesus took bread, and
Mk 2:16 saw that he was E with sinners and tax
14:18 they were at table E, Jesus said, "Truly, I
14:18 me, one who is E with me."
14:22 And as they were E, he took bread, and
Lk 7:33 the Baptist has come E no bread and drinking
7:34 of man has come E and drinking; and you
10:7 in the same house, E and drinking what they
1Cor 8:4 Hence, as to the E of food offered to
9:7 plants a vineyard without E any of its fruit?
11:21 For in E, each one goes ahead with his

EATS (48)

Ex 12:15 for if any one E what is leavened, from
12:19 for if any one E what is leavened, that
Lev 7:18 abomination, and he who E of it shall bear
7:20 but the person who E of the flesh of
7:21 unclean abomination, and then E of the flesh of
7:25 For every person who E of the fat of
7:27 Whoever E any blood, that person shall be cut
11:40 evening, and he who E of its carcass shall
14:47 clothes; and he who E in the house shall
17:10 that sojourn among them E any blood, I will
17:10 against that person who E blood, and will cut
17:14 is its blood; whoever E it shall be cut
17:15 And every person that E what dies of itself
19:8 and every one who E it shall bear his
22:14 And if a man E of a holy thing
1Sam 14:24 be the man who E food until it is
14:28 be the man who E food this day.'" And
2Sam 19:35 servant taste what he E or what he drinks?
Job 40:15 I made you; he E grass like an ox.
Ps 106:20 of an ox that E grass.
Prov 13:2 mouth a good man E good, but the desire
30:20 of an adulteress: she E, and wipes her mouth,
Eccl 4:5 folds his hands, and E his own flesh.
5:12 a laborer, whether he E little or much; but
Sir 30:25 heart will give heed to the food he E
Is 28:4 man sees it, he E it up as soon
44:16 over the half he E flesh, he roasts meat
59:5 spider's web; he who E their eggs dies, and
Jer 31:30 sin; each man who E sour grapes, his teeth
Ezek 18:11 of these duties, but E upon the mountains, defiles
Dan 14:6 see how much he E and drinks every day?"
Mt 24:49 his fellow servants, and E and drinks with the
Lk 15:2 man receives sinners and E with them."
Jn 6:51 heaven; if any one E of this bread, he
6:54 in you; he who E my flesh and drinks
6:56 He who E my flesh and drinks my blood
6:57 Father, so he who E me will live because
6:58 and died; he who E this bread will live
Rom 14:2 while the weak man E only vegetables.
14:3 Let not him who E despise him who abstains,
14:3 judgment on him who E; for God has welcomed
14:6 He also who E, eats in honor of the
14:6 He also who eats, E in honor of the
14:20 fall by what he E;
14:23 is condemned, if he E, because he does not
1Cor 11:27 Whoever, therefore, E the bread or drinks the cup
11:29 For any one who E and drinks without discerning
11:29 without discerning the body E and drinks judgment

EBAL (8)

Gen 36:23 of Shobal: Alvan, Manahath, E, Shepho, and Onam.
Deut 11:29 on Mount Gerizim and the curse on Mount E
27:4 this day, on Mount E, and you shall plaster
27:13 shall stand upon Mount E for the curse: Reuben,
Josh 8:30 an altar in Mount E to the LORD, the
8:33 in front of Mount E, as Moses the servant
1Chr 1:22 Hadoram, Uzal, Diklah, E, Abima-el, Sheba,
1:40 of Shobal: Alian, Manahath, E, Shephi, and Onam.

EBED (6)

Judg 9:26 Gaal the son of E moved into Shechem with
9:28 Gaal the son of E said, "Who is Abimelech,
9:30 Gaal the son of E, his anger was kindled.
9:31 Gaal the son of E and his kinsmen have
9:35 Gaal the son of E went out and stood
Ezra 8:6 the sons of Adin, E the son of Jonathan,

EBED-MELECH (6)

Jer 38:7 When E the Ethiopian, a eunuch, who was in
38:8 the Benjamin Gate-- E went from the king's
38:10 Then the king commanded E, the Ethiopian, "Take
38:11 So E took the men with him and went
38:12 Then E the Ethiopian said to Jeremiah, "Put the
39:16 "Go, and say to E the Ethiopian, 'Thus says

EBENEZER (3)

1Sam 4:1 Philistines; they encamped at E, and
5:1 they carried it from E to Ashdod;
7:12 and called its name E; for he said, "Hitherto

EBER (16)

Gen 10:21 all the children of E, the elder brother of
10:24 of Shelah; and Shelah became the father of E
10:25 To E were born two sons: the name of
11:14 became the father of E;
11:15 after the birth of E four hundred and three
11:16 When E had lived thirty-four years, he became the
11:17 father of Peleg; and E lived after the birth
Num 24:24 shall afflict Asshur and E; and he also shall
1Chr 1:18 of Shelah; and Shelah was the father of E
1:19 To E were born two sons: the name of
1:25 Shem, Arpachshad, Shelah; E, Peleg, Reu;
5:13 Jorai, Jacan, Zia, and E, seven.
8:12 The sons of Elpaal: E, Misham, and Shemed, who
8:22 Ishpan, E, Eliel,
Neh 12:20 Sallai, Kallai; of Amok, E;
Lk 3:35 Peleg, the son of E, the son of Shelah,

EBEZ

Josh 19:20 Shion, Anaharath, Rabbith, Kishion, E,

EBIASAPH (3)

1Chr 6:23 son, Elkanah his son, E his son, Assir his
6:37 of Assir, son of E, son of Korah,
9:19 of Kore, son of E, son of Korah, and

EBONY

Ezek 27:15 they brought you in payment ivory tusks and E

EBRON

Josh 19:28 the north to Cabul, E, Rehob, Hammon, Kanah, as

ECBATANA (11)

Ezra 6:2 And in E, the capital which is in the
Tob 3:7 the same day, at E in Media, it also
6:5 on their way until they came near to E
6:9 When they approached E,
7:1 When they reached E and arrived at the house
14:12 and his sons to E, to Raguel his father-in-law.
14:14 He died in E of Media at the age
Jud 1:1 over the Medes in E --
1:2 who built walls about E with hewn stones three
1:14 cities, and came to E, captured its towers, plundered
2Mac 9:3 While he was in E, news came to him

ECHO

Wis 17:19 roaring beasts, or an E thrown back from a

ECHOED

Wis 18:10 cry of their enemies E back, and their piteous

EDEN (19)

Gen 2:8 planted a garden in E, in the east; and
2:10 river flowed out of E to water the garden,
2:15 in the garden of E to till it and
3:23 from the garden of E, to till the ground
3:24 of the garden of E he placed the cherubim,

4:16 dwelt in the land of Nod, east of E
2Kgs 19:12 and the people of E who were in Tel-assar?
2Chr 29:12 son of Zimmah, and E the son of Joah;
31:15 E, Miniamin, Jeshua, Shemaiah, Amariah, and
Is 37:12 and the people of E who were in Tel-assar?
51:3 make her wilderness like E, her desert like the
Ezek 27:23 Haran, Canneh, E, Asshur, and Chilmad traded with
28:13 You were in E, the garden of God; every
31:9 all the trees of E envied it, that were
31:16 all the trees of E, the choice and best
31:18 glory and in greatness among the trees of E
31:18 with the trees of E to the nether world;
36:35 like the garden of E; and the waste and
Joel 2:3 like the garden of E before them, but after

E

EDER (5)

Gen 35:21 and pitched his tent beyond the tower of E
Josh 15:21 of Edom, were Kabzeel, E, Jagur,
1Chr 8:15 Zebadiah, Arad, E,
23:23 sons of Mushi: Mahli, E, and Jeremoth, three.
24:30 sons of Mushi: Mahli, E, and Jerimoth.

EDGE (65)

Ex 13:20 at Etham, on the E of the wilderness.
17:13 his people with the E of the sword.
26:4 of blue on the E of the outmost curtain
26:4 make loops on the E of the outmost curtain
26:5 shall make on the E of the curtain that
26:10 fifty loops on the E of the curtain that
26:10 fifty loops on the E of the curtain which
28:26 breastpiece, on its inside E next to the ephod.
36:11 of blue on the E of the outmost curtain
36:11 made them on the E of the outmost curtain
36:12 fifty loops on the E of the curtain that
36:17 fifty loops on the E of the outmost curtain
36:17 fifty loops on the E of the other connecting
39:19 breastpiece, on its inside E next to the ephod.
Num 20:16 a city on the E of your territory.
21:24 slew him with the E of the sword, and
33:6 which is on the E of the wilderness.
33:37 Mount Hor, on the E of the land of
Deut 2:36 which is on the E of the valley of
3:12 which is on the E of the valley of
4:48 which is on the E of the valley of
13:15 its cattle, with the E of the sword.
Josh 6:21 and asses, with the E of the sword.
8:24 had fallen by the E of the sword, all
8:24 smote it with the E of the sword.
10:28 its king with the E of the sword; he
10:30 smote it with the E of the sword, and
10:32 smote it with the E of the sword, and
10:35 smote it with the E of the sword; and
10:37 smote it with the E of the sword, and
10:39 smote them with the E of the sword, and
11:12 smote them with the E of the sword, utterly
11:14 they smote with the E of the sword, until
12:2 which is on the E of the valley of
13:9 which is on the E of the valley of
13:16 which is on the E of the valley of
Judg 1:8 smote it with the E of the sword, and
1:25 the city with the E of the sword, but
4:15 before Barak at the E of the sword; and
4:16 Sisera fell by the E of the sword; not
18:27 smote them with the E of the sword, and
20:37 the city with the E of the sword.
20:48 smote them with the E of the sword, men
21:10 of Jabesh-gilead with the E of the sword; also
1Sam 15:8 the people with the E of the sword.
2Sam 15:14 the city with the E of the sword."
2Kgs 7:5 they came to the E of the camp of
7:8 lepers came to the E of the camp, they
Jud 2:27 young men with the E of the sword.
3:9 he came to the E of Esdraelon, near Dothan,
Job 1:15 the servants with the E of the sword; and
1:17 the servants with the E of the sword; and
Ps 89:43 hast turned back the E of his sword, and
Eccl 10:10 does not whet the E, he must put forth
Sir 28:18 have fallen by the E of the sword, but
Jer 21:7 smite them with the E of the sword; he
31:29 teeth are set on E
31:30 sour grapes, his teeth shall be set on E
Ezek 18:2 grapes, and the children's teeth are set on E
21:16 and left where your E is directed.
43:13 with a rim of one span around its E
1Mac 5:28 every male by the E of the sword; then
5:51 every male by the E of the sword, and
Lk 21:24 will fall by the E of the sword, and
Heb 11:34 raging fire, escaped the E of the sword, won

EDGES (9)

Ex 28:7 attached to its two E, that it may be
28:23 rings on the two E of the breastpiece.
28:24 two rings at the E of the breastpiece;
39:4 ephod shoulder-pieces, joined to it at its two E
39:16 rings on the two E of the breastpiece;
39:17 two rings at the E of the breastpiece.
Lev 19:27 temples or mar the E of your beard.
21:5 nor shave off the E of their beards, nor
Judg 3:16 a sword with two E, a cubit in length;

EDICT (9)

Ezra 6:11 any one alters this E, a beam shall be
Esth 2:8 king's order and his E were proclaimed, and when
3:12 first month, and an E, according to all that
8:8 king's ring; for an E written in the name
8:9 twenty-third day; and an E was written according to
8:17 king's command and his E came, there was gladness
9:1 the king's command and E were about to be
9:13 tomorrow also to do according to this day's E
Heb 11:23 and they were not afraid of the king's E

EDIFICATION

1Cor 14:26 Let all things be done for E

EDIFIED (2)

1Cor 14:5 one interprets, so that the church may be E
14:17 well enough, but the other man is not E

EDIFIES (2)

1Cor 14:4 speaks in a tongue E himself, but he who
14:4 but he who prophesies E the church.

EDIFY

Rom 15:2 for his good, to E him.

EDIFYING

Eph 4:29 as is good for E, as fits the occasion,

EDNA (7)

Tob 7:2 said to his wife E, "How much the young
7:8 And his wife E and his daughter Sarah wept.
7:14 he called his wife E, and took a scroll
7:16 Raguel called his wife E and said to her,
8:12 said to his wife E, "Send one of the
10:12 And E said to Tobias, "The Lord of heaven
11:1 And he blessed Raguel and his wife E

EDOM (98)

Gen 25:30 (Therefore his name was called E
32:3 Seir, the country of E,
36:1 These are the descendants of Esau (that is, E
36:8 in the hill country of Seir; Esau is E
36:16 in the land of E; they are the sons
36:17 in the land of E; they are the sons
36:19 of Esau (that is, E, and these are their
36:21 the sons of Seir in the land of E
36:31 in the land of E, before any king reigned
36:32 of Beor reigned in E, the name of his
36:43 are the chiefs of E (that is, Esau, the
36:43 Esau, the father of E, according to their dwelling
Ex 15:15 are the chiefs of E dismayed; the leaders of
Num 20:14 to the king of E, "Thus says your brother
20:18 But E said to him, "You shall not pass
20:20 And E came out against them with many men,
20:21 Thus E refused to give Israel passage through his
20:23 of the land of E,
21:4 around the land of E; and the people became
24:18 E shall be dispossessed, Seir also, his enemies, shall
33:37 Hor, on the edge of the land of E
34:3 along the side of E, and your southern boundary
Josh 15:1 to the boundary of E, to the wilderness of
15:21 toward the boundary of E, were Kabzeel, Eder,
Judg 5:4 from the region of E, the earth trembled, and
11:17 to the king of E, saying, 'Let us pass,
11:17 but the king of E would not listen.
11:18 around the land of E and the land of
1Sam 14:47 against the Ammonites, against E, against the kings
2Sam 8:12 nations he subdued, from E, Moab, the Ammonites,
8:14 he put garrisons in E; throughout all Edom he
8:14 in Edom; throughout all E he put garrisons, and
1Kgs 9:26 of the Red Sea, in the land of E
11:14 Edomite; he was of the royal house in E

11:15 when David was in E, and Joab the commander
11:15 slew every male in E
11:16 off every male in E;
22:47 was no king in E; a deputy was king.
2Kgs 3:8 answered, "By the way of the wilderness of E
3:9 the king of Judah and the king of E
3:12 and the king of E went down to him.
3:20 from the direction of E, till the country was
3:26 opposite the king of E; but they could not.
8:20 In his days E revolted from the rule of
8:22 So E revolted from the rule of Judah to
14:10 You have indeed smitten E, and your heart has
16:6 time the king of E recovered Elath for Edom,
16:6 Edom recovered Elath for E, and drove the men
1Chr 1:43 in the land of E before any king reigned
1:51 The chiefs of E were: chiefs Timna, Aliah, Jetheth,
1:54 Magdiel, and Iram; these are the chiefs of E
18:11 all the nations, from E, Moab, the Ammonites, the
18:13 he put garrisons in E; and all the Edomites
2Chr 8:17 shore of the sea, in the land of E
20:2 coming against you from E, from beyond the sea;
21:8 In his days E revolted from the rule of
21:10 So E revolted from the rule of Judah to
25:19 'See, I have smitten E and your heart has
25:20 enemies, because they had sought the gods of E
Ps 60:8 is my washbasin; upon E I cast my shoe;
60:9 Who will lead me to E
83:6 the tents of E and the Ishmaelites, Moab
108:9 is my washbasin; upon E I cast my shoe;
108:10 Who will lead me to E
Is 11:14 forth their hand against E and Moab, and the
34:5 descends for judgment upon E, upon the people I
34:6 Bozrah, a great slaughter in the land of E
34:9 And the streams of E shall be turned into
63:1 this that comes from E, in crimsoned garments from
Jer 9:26 uncircumcised-- Egypt, Judah, E, the sons of Ammon,
25:21 the remnant of Ashdod); E, Moab, and the sons
27:3 to the king of E, the king of Moab,
40:11 the Ammonites and in E and in other lands
49:7 Concerning E
49:17 E shall become a horror; every one who passes
49:20 LORD has made against E and the purposes which
49:22 of the warriors of E shall be in that
Lam 4:21 glad, O daughter of E, dweller in the land
4:22 iniquity, O daughter of E, he will punish, he
Ezek 16:57 for the daughters of E and all her neighbors,
25:12 the Lord GOD: Because E acted revengefully against
25:13 out my hand against E, and cut off from
25:14 lay my vengeance upon E by the hand of
25:14 they shall do in E according to my anger
27:16 E trafficked with you because of your abundant
32:29 E is there, her kings and all her princes,
35:15 Mount Seir, and all E, all of it.
36:5 nations, and against all E, who gave my land
Dan 11:41 out of his hand: E and Moab and the
Joel 3:19 become a desolation and E a desolate wilderness, for
Amos 1:6 a whole people to deliver them up to E
1:9 a whole people to E, and did not remember
1:11 "For three transgressions of E, and for four, I
2:1 to lime the bones of the king of E
9:12 possess the remnant of E and all the nations
Obad 1:1 the Lord GOD concerning E: We have heard tidings
1:8 wise men out of E, and understanding out of
Mal 1:4 If E says, "We are shattered but we will

EDOMITE (7)

Deut 23:7 shall not abhor an E, for he is your
1Sam 21:7 name was Doeg the E, the chief of Saul's
22:9 Then answered Doeg the E, who stood by the
22:18 And Doeg the E turned and fell upon the
22:22 day, when Doeg the E was there, that he
1Kgs 11:1 Pharaoh, and Moabite, Ammonite, E, Sidonian, and
11:14 against Solomon, Hadad the E; he was of the

EDOMITES (13)

Gen 36:9 the father of the E in the hill country
2Sam 8:13 he slew eighteen thousand E in the Valley of
8:14 garrisons, and all the E became David's servants.
1Kgs 11:17 Egypt, together with certain E of his father's,
2Kgs 8:21 chariot commanders smote the E who had
14:7 He killed ten thousand E in the Valley of
16:6 from Elath; and the E came to Elath, where
1Chr 18:12 Zeruiah, slew eighteen thousand E in the Valley of
18:13 Edom; and all the E became David's servants.
2Chr 21:9 night and smote the E who had surrounded him
25:14 the slaughter of the E, he brought the gods
28:17 For the E had again invaded and defeated Judah,
Ps 137:7 O LORD, against the E the day of Jerusalem,

EDRE-I (8)

Num 21:33 he and all his people, to battle at E
Deut 1:4 of Bashan, who lived in Ashtaroth and in E
3:1 he and all his people, to battle at E
3:10 far as Salecah and E, cities of the kingdom
Josh 12:4 at Ashtaroth and at E
13:12 in Ashtaroth and in E (he alone was left
13:31 Gilead, and Ashtaroth, and E, the cities of the
19:37 Adamah, Ramah, Hazor, Kedesh, E, En-hazor,

EDUCATE

Sir 10:1 A wise magistrate will E his people, and the

EDUCATED (3)

Sir 34:9 An E man knows many things, and one with
Dan 1:5 They were to be E for three years, and
Acts 22:3 the feet of Gamali-el, E according to the strict

EDUCATION (3)

Sir 4:24 known through speech, and E through the words of
21:19 To a senseless man E is fetters on his
21:21 To a sensible man E is like a golden

EFFECT (16)

2Chr 34:22 Second Quarter) and spoke to her to that E
Wis 14:5 should not be without E; therefore men trust their
16:17 fire had still greater E, for the universe defends
Is 32:17 And the E of righteousness will be peace, and
1Mac 8:30 these terms are in E both parties shall determine
12:2 letters to the same E to the Spartans and
2Mac 1:24 prayer was to this E: "O Lord, Lord God,
3:7 him with commands to E the removal of the
11:16 Lysias was to this E: "Lysias to the people
Lk 18:1 a parable, to the E that they ought always
Acts 7:6 God spoke to this E, that his posterity would
23:25 a letter to this E:
Rom 5:16 is not like the E of that one man's
2Thes 2:2 from us, to the E that the day of
Heb 9:17 For a will takes E only at death, since
Jas 1:4 steadfastness have its full E, that you may be

EFFECTIVE (3)

Wis 8:6 And if understanding is E, who more than she
2Mac 15:17 so noble and so E in arousing valor and
1Cor 16:9 a wide door for E work has opened to

EFFECTS (2)

Wis 8:5 richer than wisdom who E all things?
Jas 5:16 a righteous man has great power in its E

EFFORT (3)

2Mac 2:28 compiler, while devoting our E to arriving at the
Lk 12:58 the magistrate, make an E to settle with him
2Pet 1:5 very reason make every E to supplement your faith

EGG

Lk 11:12 he asks for an E, will give him a

EGGS (6)

Deut 22:6 with young ones or E and the mother sitting
22:6 young or upon the E, you shall not take
Job 39:14 For she leaves her E to the earth, and
Is 10:14 and as men gather E that have been forsaken
59:5 They hatch adders' E, they weave the spider's web;
59:5 he who eats their E dies, and from one

EGLAH (2)

2Sam 3:5 the sixth, Ithre-am, of E, David's wife.
1Chr 3:3 Ithream, by his wife E;

EGLAIM

Is 15:8 the wailing reaches to E, the wailing reaches to

EGLATH-SHELISHIYAH (2)

Is 15:5 for Moab; his fugitives flee to Zoar, to E
Jer 48:34 utter their voice, from Zoar to Horonaim and E

EGLON (13)

Josh 10:3 to Debir king of E, saying,
10:5 and the king of E, gathered their forces, and
10:23 the king of Lachish, and the king of E
10:34 Israel from Lachish to E; and they laid siege
10:36 with all Israel from E to Hebron; and they

10:37 he had done to E, and utterly destroyed it
12:12 one; the king of E, one; the king of
15:39 Mizpeh, Joktheel, Lachish, Bozkath, E,
Judg 3:12 and the LORD strengthened E the king of Moab
3:14 people of Israel served E the king of Moab
3:15 tribute by him to E the king of Moab.
3:17 presented the tribute to E king of Moab.
3:17 Now E was a very fat man.

EGYPT (653)

Gen 10:6 sons of Ham: Cush, E, Put, and Canaan.
10:13 E became the father of Ludim, Anamim, Lehabim,
12:10 Abram went down to E to sojourn there, for
12:11 was about to enter E, he said to Sarai
12:14 When Abram entered E the Egyptians saw that the
13:1 Abram went up from E, he and his wife,
13:10 like the land of E, in the direction of
15:18 from the river of E to the great river,
21:21 a wife for him from the land of E
25:18 Shur, which is opposite E in the direction of
26:2 not go down to E; dwell in the land
37:25 on their way to carry it down to E
37:28 shekels of silver; and they took Joseph to E
37:36 had sold him in E to Potiphar, an officer
39:1 was taken down to E, and Potiphar, an officer
40:1 of the king of E and his baker offended
40:1 his baker offended their lord the king of E
40:5 of the king of E, who were confined in
41:8 all the magicians of E and all its wise
41:19 had never seen in all the land of E
41:29 all the land of E,
41:30 in the land of E; the famine will consume
41:33 wise, and set him over the land of E
41:34 of the land of E during the seven plenteous
41:36 befall the land of E, so that the land
41:41 have set you over all the land of E
41:43 he set him over all the land of E
41:44 hand or foot in all the land of E
41:45 So Joseph went out over the land of E
41:46 he entered the service of Pharaoh king of E
41:46 Pharaoh, and went through all the land of E
41:48 in the land of E, and stored up food
41:53 in the land of E came to an end;
41:54 all the land of E there was bread.
41:55 all the land of E was famished, the people
41:56 the famine was severe in the land of E
41:57 the earth came to E to Joseph to buy
42:1 there was grain in E, he said to his
42:2 there is grain in E; go down and buy
42:3 Joseph's brothers went down to buy grain in E
43:2 they had brought from E, their father said to
43:15 and went down to E, and stood before Joseph.
45:4 am your brother, Joseph, whom you sold into E
45:8 house and ruler over all the land of E
45:9 me lord of all E; come down to me,
45:13 all my splendor in E, and of all that
45:18 of the land of E, and you shall eat
45:19 from the land of E for your little ones
45:20 all the land of E is yours.'"
45:23 the good things of E, and ten she-asses loaded
45:25 went up out of E, and came to the
45:26 he is ruler over all the land of E
46:3 to go down to E; for I will there
46:4 down with you to E, and I will also
46:6 Canaan, and came into E, Jacob and all his
46:7 all his offspring he brought with him into E
46:8 Israel, who came into E, Jacob and his sons.
46:20 in the land of E were born Manasseh and
46:26 Jacob who came into E, who were his own
46:27 born to him in E, were two; all the
46:27 Jacob, that came into E, were seventy.
47:6 The land of E is before you; settle your
47:11 in the land of E, in the best of
47:13 that the land of E and the land of
47:14 in the land of E and in the land
47:15 in the land of E and in the land
47:20 all the land of E for Pharaoh; for all
47:21 from one end of E to the other.
47:26 concerning the land of E, and it stands to
47:27 in the land of E, in the land of
47:28 in the land of E seventeen years; so the
47:29 not bury me in E,
47:30 carry me out of E and bury me in
48:5 in the land of E before I came to
48:5 came to you in E, are mine; Ephraim and
50:7 of the land of E,
50:14 father, Joseph returned to E with his brothers and
50:22 So Joseph dwelt in E, he and his father's
50:26 and he was put in a coffin in E
Ex 1:1 Israel who came to E with Jacob, each with
1:4 were seventy persons; Joseph was already in E
1:7 a new king over E, who did not know
1:14 Then the king of E said to the Hebrew
1:16 as the king of E commanded them, but let
1:17 So the king of E called the midwives, and
2:23 days the king of E died.
3:7 people who are in E, and have heard their
3:10 my people, the sons of Israel, out of E
3:11 and bring the sons of Israel out of E
3:12 the people out of E, you shall serve God
3:16 done to you in E;
3:17 of the affliction of E, to the land of
3:18 to the king of E and say to him,
3:19 that the king of E will not let you
3:20 my hand and smite E with all the wonders
4:18 to my kinsmen in E and see whether they
4:19 Midian, "Go back to E; for all the men
4:20 to the land of E; and in his hand
4:21 you go back to E, see that you do
5:4 But the king of E said to them, "Moses
5:12 all the land of E, to gather stubble for
6:11 tell Pharaoh king of E to let the people
6:13 to Pharaoh king of E to bring the people
6:13 people of Israel out of the land of E
6:26 from the land of E by their hosts."
6:27 to Pharaoh king of E about bringing out the
6:27 people of Israel from E, this Moses and this
6:28 in the land of E,
6:29 tell Pharaoh king of E all that I say
7:3 in the land of E,
7:4 lay my hand upon E and bring forth my
7:4 of the land of E by great acts of
7:5 forth my hand upon E and bring out the
7:11 also, the magicians of E, did the same by
7:19 over the waters of E, over their rivers, their
7:19 all the land of E, both in vessels of
7:21 there was blood throughout all the land of E
7:22 But the magicians of E did the same by
8:5 cause frogs to come upon the land of E
8:6 over the waters of E; and the frogs came
8:6 frogs came up and covered the land of E
8:7 arts, and brought frogs upon the land of E
8:16 may become gnats throughout all the land of E
8:17 earth became gnats throughout all the land of E
8:24 all the land of E the land was ruined
9:4 and the cattle of E, so that nothing shall
9:9 all the land of E, and become boils breaking
9:9 man and beast throughout all the land of E
9:18 never has been in E from the day it
9:22 all the land of E, upon man and beast
9:22 plant of the field, throughout the land of E
9:23 upon the land of E;
9:24 all the land of E since it became a
9:25 all the land of E, both man and beast;
10:7 not yet understand that E is ruined?"
10:12 over the land of E for the locusts, that
10:12 upon the land of E, and eat every plant
10:13 over the land of E, and the LORD brought
10:14 all the land of E, and settled on the
10:14 the whole country of E, such a dense swarm
10:15 of the field, through all the land of E
10:19 locust was left in all the country of E
10:21 over the land of E, a darkness to be
10:22 all the land of E three days;
11:1 upon Pharaoh and upon E; afterwards he will let
11:3 in the land of E, in the sight of
11:4 in the midst of E;
11:5 in the land of E shall die, from the
11:6 all the land of E, such as there has
11:9 wonders may be multiplied in the land of E
12:1 in the land of E,
12:12 through the land of E that night, and I
12:12 in the land of E, both man and beast;
12:12 all the gods of E I will execute judgments:
12:13 destroy you, when I smite the land of E
12:17 of the land of E: therefore you shall observe
12:27 people of Israel in E, when he slew the
12:29 in the land of E, from the first-born of
12:30 a great cry in E, for there was not
12:39 had brought out of E, for it was not
12:39 were thrust out of E and could not tarry,
12:40 of Israel dwelt in E was four hundred and

12:41 the LORD went out from the land of E
12:42 of the land of E; so this same night
12:51 of the land of E by their hosts.
13:3 you came out from E, out of the house
13:8 I came out of E
13:9 hand the LORD has brought you out of E
13:14 brought us out of E, from the house of
13:15 in the land of E, both the first-born of
13:16 strong hand the LORD brought us out of E
13:17 repent when they see war, and return to E
13:18 of the land of E equipped for battle.
14:5 When the king of E was told that the
14:7 the other chariots of E with officers over all
14:8 of Pharaoh king of E and he pursued the
14:11 are no graves in E that you have taken
14:11 done to us, in bringing us out of E
14:12 said to you in E, 'Let us alone and
14:20 between the host of E and the host of
16:1 after they had departed from the land of E
16:3 in the land of E, when we sat by
16:6 of the land of E,
16:32 I brought you out of the land of E
17:3 us up out of E, to kill us and
18:1 how the LORD had brought Israel out of E
19:1 of the land of E, on that day they
20:2 of the land of E, out of the house
22:21 for you were strangers in the land of E
23:9 for you were strangers in the land of E
23:15 Abib, for in it you came out of E
29:46 of the land of E that I might dwell
32:1 of the land of E, we do not know
32:4 brought you up out of the land of E
32:7 of the land of E, have corrupted themselves;
32:8 brought you up out of the land of E
32:11 of the land of E with great power and
32:23 of the land of E, we do not know
33:1 of the land of E, to the land of
34:18 in the month Abib you came out from E
Lev 11:45 of the land of E, to be your God;
18:3 in the land of E, where you dwelt, and
19:34 in the land of E: I am the LORD
19:36 who brought you out of the land of E
22:33 of the land of E to be your God:
23:43 of the land of E: I am the LORD
25:38 of the land of E to give you the
25:42 of the land of E; they shall not be
25:55 of the land of E: I am the LORD
26:13 of the land of E, that you should not
26:45 of the land of E in the sight of
Num 1:1 of the land of E, saying,
3:13 in the land of E, I consecrated for my
8:17 in the land of E I consecrated them for
9:1 of the land of E, saying,
11:5 fish we ate in E for nothing, the cucumbers,
11:18 For it was well with us in E
11:20 saying, 'Why did we come forth out of E
13:22 years before Zoan in E
14:2 that we had died in the land of E
14:3 be better for us to go back to E
14:4 us choose a captain, and go back to E
14:19 forgiven this people, from E even until now."
14:22 which I wrought in E and in the wilderness,
15:41 of the land of E, to be your God:
20:5 come up out of E, to bring us to
20:15 fathers went down to E, and we dwelt in
20:15 and we dwelt in E a long time; and
20:16 us forth out of E; and here we are
21:5 us up out of E to die in the
22:5 has come out of E; they cover the face
22:11 has come out of E, and it covers the
23:22 brings them out of E; they have as it
24:8 brings him out of E; he has as it
26:4 of the land of E, were:
26:59 born to Levi in E; and she bore to
32:11 came up out of E, from twenty years old
33:1 of the land of E by their hosts under
33:38 of the land of E, on the first day
34:5 to the Brook of E, and its termination shall
Deut 1:27 of the land of E, to give us into
1:30 did for you in E before your eyes,
4:20 iron furnace, out of E, to be a people
4:34 did for you in E before your eyes?
4:37 brought you out of E with his own presence,
4:45 they came out of E,
4:46 of Israel defeated when they came out of E
5:6 of the land of E, out of the house
5:15 in the land of E, and the LORD your
6:12 of the land of E, out of the house
6:21 were Pharaoh's slaves in E; and the LORD brought
6:21 brought us out of E with a mighty hand;
6:22 great and grievous, against E and against Pharaoh
7:8 bondage, from the hand of Pharaoh king of E
7:15 the evil diseases of E, which you knew, will
7:18 Pharaoh and to all E,
8:14 of the land of E, out of the house
9:7 of the land of E, until you came to
9:12 you have brought from E have acted corruptly; they
9:26 hast brought out of E with a mighty hand.
10:19 for you were sojourners in the land of E
10:22 fathers went down to E seventy persons; and now
11:3 which he did in E to Pharaoh the king
11:3 Pharaoh the king of E and to all his
11:4 to the army of E, to their horses and
11:10 like the land of E, from which you have
13:5 of the land of E and redeemed you out
13:10 of the land of E, out of the house
15:15 in the land of E, and the LORD your
16:1 brought you out of E by night.
16:3 of the land of E in hurried flight--that
16:3 when you came out of the land of E
16:6 sun, at the time you came out of E
16:12 were a slave in E; and you shall be
17:16 people to return to E in order to multiply
20:1 brought you up out of the land of E
23:4 came forth out of E, and because they hired
24:9 the way as you came forth out of E
24:18 were a slave in E and the LORD your
24:22 in the land of E; therefore I command you
25:17 you came out of E,
26:5 he went down into E and sojourned there, few
26:8 brought us out of E with a mighty hand
28:27 with the boils of E, and with the ulcers
28:60 all the diseases of E, which you were afraid
28:68 back in ships to E, a journey which I
29:2 in the land of E, to Pharaoh and to
29:16 in the land of E, and how we came
29:25 of the land of E,
34:11 in the land of E, to Pharaoh and to
Josh 2:10 you came out of E, and what you did
5:4 who came out of E, all the men of
5:4 the wilderness after they had come out of E
5:5 had come out of E had not been circumcised.
5:6 came forth out of E, perished, because they did
5:9 away the reproach of E from you." And so
9:9 that he did in E,
13:3 which is east of E, northward to the boundary
15:4 by the Brook of E, and comes to its
15:47 to the Brook of E, and the Great Sea
24:4 but Jacob and his children went down to E
24:5 Aaron, and I plagued E with what I did
24:6 your fathers out of E, and you came to
24:7 what I did to E; and you lived in
24:14 the River, and in E, and serve the LORD.
24:17 from the land of E, out of the house
24:32 Israel brought up from E were buried at Shechem,
Judg 2:1 brought you up from E, and brought you into
2:12 of the land of E; they went after other
6:8 led you up from E, and brought you out
6:13 bring us up from E But now the LORD
11:13 Israel on coming from E took away my land,
11:16 they came up from E, Israel went through the
19:30 of the land of E until this day; consider
1Sam 2:27 when they were in E subject to the house
8:8 them up out of E even to this day,
10:18 up Israel out of E, and I delivered you
12:6 your fathers up out of the land of E
12:8 When Jacob went into E and the Egyptians
12:8 your fathers out of E, and made them dwell
15:2 the way, when they came up out of E
15:6 of Israel when they came up out of E
15:7 as far as Shur, which is east of E
27:8 as far as Shur, to the land of E
30:13 a young man of E, servant to an Amalekite;
2Sam 7:6 people of Israel from E to this day, but
1Kgs 3:1 with Pharaoh king of E; he took Pharaoh's daughter,
4:21 to the border of E; they brought tribute and
4:30 of the east, and all the wisdom of E
6:1 of the land of E, in the fourth year
8:9 when they came out of the land of E
8:16 people Israel out of E, I chose no city
8:21 he brought them out of the land of E
8:51 didst bring out of E, from the midst of

E

EGYPT

8:53 our fathers out of E, O Lord GOD."
8:65 to the Brook of E, before the LORD our
9:9 of the land of E, and laid hold on
9:16 Gezer (Pharaoh king of E had gone up and
10:28 of horses was from E and Kue, and the
10:29 could be imported from E for six hundred shekels
11:17 but Hadad fled to E, together with certain Edomites
11:18 Paran and came to E, to Pharaoh king of
11:18 to Pharaoh king of E, who gave him a
11:21 when Hadad heard in E that David slept with
11:40 arose, and fled into E, to Shishak king of
11:40 to Shishak king of E, and was in Egypt
11:40 Egypt, and was in E until the death of
12:2 he was still in E, whither he had fled
12:2 King Solomon), then Jeroboam returned from E
12:28 brought you up out of the land of E
14:25 Shishak king of E came up against Jerusalem;
2Kgs 7:6 and the kings of E to come upon us."
17:4 to So, king of E, and offered no tribute
17:7 of the land of E from under the hand
17:7 of Pharaoh king of E, and had feared other
17:36 of the land of E with great power and
18:21 are relying now on E, that broken reed of
18:21 is Pharaoh king of E to all who rely
18:24 when you rely on E for chariots and for
19:24 all the streams of E
21:15 fathers came out of E, even to this day."
23:29 Pharaoh Neco king of E went up to the
23:34 and he came to E, and died there.
24:7 And the king of E did not come again
24:7 to the king of E from the Brook of
24:7 from the Brook of E to the river Euphrates.
25:26 arose, and went to E; for they were afraid
1Chr 1:8 sons of Ham: Cush, E, Put, and Canaan.
1:11 E was the father of Ludim, Anamim, Lehabim,
13:5 from the Shihor of E to the entrance of
17:21 before thy people whom thou didst redeem from E
2Chr 1:16 of horses was from E and Kue, and the
1:17 imported a chariot from E for six hundred shekels
5:10 people of Israel, when they came out of E
6:5 of the land of E, I chose no city
7:8 the entrance of Hamath to the Brook of E
7:22 of the land of E, and laid hold on
9:26 of the Philistines, and to the border of E
9:28 imported for Solomon from E and from all lands.
10:2 (for he was in E, whither he had fled
10:2 King Solomon), then Jeroboam returned from E
12:2 LORD, Shishak king of E came up against Jerusalem
12:3 with him from E --Libyans, Sukki-im, and Ethiopians.
12:9 So Shishak king of E came up against Jerusalem;
20:10 from the land of E, and whom they avoided
26:8 to the border of E, for he became very
35:20 temple, Neco king of E went up to fight
36:3 Then the king of E deposed him in Jerusalem
36:4 And the king of E made Eliakim his brother
36:4 took Jehoahaz his brother and carried him to E
Neh 9:9 of our fathers in E and hear their cry
9:17 a leader to return to their bondage in E
9:18 you up out of E and had committed great
Tob 8:3 the remotest parts of E, and the angel bound
Jud 1:9 and the river of E, and Tahpanhes and Raamses
1:10 all who lived in E as far as the
1:12 and every one in E, as far as the
5:10 they went down to E and lived there as
5:11 So the king of E became hostile to them;
5:12 the whole land of E with incurable plagues; and
6:5 revenge on this race that came out of E
Esth 11:1 his son brought to E the preceding Letter of
13:16 redeem for thyself out of the land of E
Ps 68:31 bronze be brought from E; let Ethiopia hasten to
78:12 in the land of E, in the fields of
78:43 wrought his signs in E, and his miracles in
78:51 all the first-born in E, the first issue of
80:8 a vine out of E; thou didst drive out
81:5 when he went out over the land of E
81:10 brought you up out of the land of E
105:23 Then Israel came to E; Jacob sojourned in the
105:38 E was glad when they departed, for dread of
106:7 when they were in E, did not consider thy
106:21 done great things in E,
114:1 Israel went forth from E, the house of Jacob
135:8 smote the first-born of E, both of man and
135:9 in thy midst, O E, sent signs and wonders
136:10 smote the first-born of E, for his steadfast love
Is 7:18 of the streams of E, and for the bee
10:26 he will lift it as he did in E
11:11 from Assyria, from E, from Pathros, from Ethiopia,
11:15 of the sea of E; and will wave his
11:16 when they came up from the land of E
19:1 An oracle concerning E
19:1 cloud and comes to E; and the idols of
19:1 and the idols of E will tremble at his
19:6 and the branches of E's Nile will diminish and
19:12 what the LORD of hosts has purposed against E
19:13 her tribes have led E astray.
19:14 and they have made E stagger in all her
19:15 will be nothing for E which head or tail,
19:18 in the land of E which speak the language
19:19 of the land of E, and a pillar to
19:20 in the land of E; when they cry to
19:22 the LORD will smite E, smiting and healing, and
19:23 be a highway from E to Assyria, and the
19:23 Assyrian will come into E, and the Egyptian into
19:24 be the third with E and Assyria, a blessing
19:25 saying, "Blessed be E my people, and Assyria
20:3 and a portent against E and Ethiopia,
20:4 barefoot, with buttocks uncovered, to the shame of E
20:5 their hope and of E their boast.
23:5 the report comes to E, they will be in
27:12 to the Brook of E the LORD will thresh
27:13 to the land of E will come and worship
30:2 to go down to E, without asking for my
30:2 and to seek shelter in the shadow of E
30:3 in the shadow of E to your humiliation.
30:7 For E's help is worthless and empty, therefore I
31:1 who go down to E for help and rely
36:6 you are relying on E, that broken reed of
36:6 is Pharaoh king of E to all who rely
36:9 when you rely on E for chariots and for
37:25 sole of my foot all the streams of E
43:3 I give E as your ransom, Ethiopia and Seba
45:14 LORD: "The wealth of E and the merchandise of
52:4 at the first into E to sojourn there, and
Jer 2:6 from the land of E, who led us in
2:18 gain by going to E, to drink the waters
2:36 put to shame by E as you were put
7:22 of the land of E, I did not speak
7:25 of the land of E to this day, I
9:26 but yet uncircumcised-- E, Judah, Edom, the sons
11:4 of the land of E, from the iron furnace,
11:7 of the land of E, warning them persistently, even
16:14 of the land of E
23:7 of the land of E
24:8 and those who dwell in the land of E
25:19 day; Pharaoh king of E, his servants, his princes,
26:21 he was afraid and fled and escaped to E
26:22 King Jehoiakim sent to E certain men, Elnathan the
26:23 they fetched Uriah from E and brought him to
31:32 of the land of E, my covenant which they
32:20 in the land of E, and to this day
32:21 of the land of E with signs and wonders,
34:13 of the land of E, out of the house
37:5 had come out of E; and when the Chaldeans
37:7 about to return to E, to its own land.
41:17 intending to go to E
42:14 to the land of E, where we shall not
42:15 your faces to enter E and go to live
42:16 in the land of E; and the famine of
42:16 hard after you to E; and there you shall
42:17 faces to go to E to live there shall
42:18 poured out on you when you go to E
42:19 'Do not go to E Know for a certainty
43:2 'Do not go to E to live there';
43:7 into the land of E, for they did not
43:11 smite the land of E, giving to the pestilence
43:12 of the gods of E; and he shall burn
43:12 clean the land of E, as a shepherd cleans
43:13 in the land of E; and the temples of
43:13 of the gods of E he shall burn with
44:1 in the land of E, at Migdol, at Tahpanhes,
44:8 in the land of E where you have come
44:12 to the land of E to live, and they
44:12 in the land of E they shall fall; by
44:13 in the land of E, as I have punished
44:14 in the land of E shall escape or survive
44:15 in the land of E, answered Jeremiah:
44:24 in the land of E,
44:26 in the land of E: Behold, I have sworn
44:26 all the land of E, saying, 'As the Lord
44:27 in the land of E shall be consumed by
44:28 from the land of E to the land of
44:28 to the land of E to live, shall know

Is 19:23 into Egypt, and the E into Assyria, and the
Acts 7:24 oppressed man and avenged him by striking the E
7:28 as you killed the E yesterday?'
21:38 Are you not the E, then, who recently stirred

EGYPTIANS (104)

Gen 12:12 behold; and when the E see you, they will
12:14 Abram entered Egypt the E saw that the woman
41:55 said to all the E, "Go to Joseph; what
41:56 and sold to the E, for the famine was
43:32 by themselves, and the E who ate with him
43:32 by themselves, because the E might not eat bread
43:32 Hebrews, for that is an abomination to the E
45:2 aloud, so that the E heard it, and the
46:34 for every shepherd is an abomination to the E
47:15 of Canaan, all the E came to Joseph, and
47:20 Pharaoh; for all the E sold their fields, because
50:3 And the E wept for him seventy days.
50:11 said, "This is a grievous mourning to the E
Ex 1:11 And the E were in dread of the people
3:8 the hand of the E, and to bring them
3:9 oppression with which the E oppress them.
3:21 the sight of the E; and when you go,
3:22 on your daughters; thus you shall despoil the E
6:5 of Israel whom the E hold in bondage and
6:6 the burdens of the E, and I will deliver
6:7 you out from under the burdens of the E
7:5 And the E shall know that I am the
7:18 become foul, and the E will loathe to drink
7:21 foul, so that the E could not drink water
7:24 And all the E dug round about the Nile
8:21 the houses of the E shall be filled with
8:26 the LORD our God offerings abominable to the E
8:26 offerings abominable to the E before their eyes, will
9:6 the cattle of the E died, but of the
9:11 were upon the magicians and upon all the E
10:2 made sport of the E and what signs I
10:6 and of all the E; as neither your fathers
11:3 the people favor in the sight of the E
11:7 a distinction between the E and Israel.
12:23 through to slay the E; and when he sees
12:27 when he slew the E but spared our houses.'"
12:30 servants, and all the E; and there was a
12:33 And the E were urgent with the people, to
12:35 had asked of the E jewelry of silver and
12:36 the sight of the E, so that they let
12:36 Thus they despoiled the E
14:4 his host; and the E shall know that I
14:9 The E pursued them, all Pharaoh's horses and
14:10 eyes, and behold, the E were marching after them;
14:12 'Let us alone and let us serve the E
14:12 us to serve the E than to die in
14:13 you today; for the E whom you see today,
14:17 the hearts of the E so that they shall
14:18 And the E shall know that I am the
14:23 The E pursued, and went in after them into
14:24 the host of the E, and discomfited the host
14:24 the host of the E,
14:25 drove heavily; and the E said, "Let us flee
14:25 for the LORD fights for them against the E
14:26 come back upon the E, upon their chariots, and
14:27 morning appeared; and the E fled into it, and
14:27 the LORD routed the E in the midst of
14:30 the hand of the E; and Israel saw the
14:30 and Israel saw the E dead upon the seashore.
14:31 LORD did against the E, and the people feared
15:26 I put upon the E; for I am the
18:8 Pharaoh and to the E for Israel's sake, all
18:9 delivered them out of the hand of the E
18:10 the hand of the E and out of the
18:11 the hand of the E, when they dealt arrogantly
19:4 I did to the E, and how I bore
32:12 Why should the E say, 'With evil intent did
Num 14:13 the LORD, "Then the E will hear of it,
20:15 long time; and the E dealt harshly with us
33:3 sight of all the E,
33:4 the Egyptians, while the E were burying all their
Deut 26:6 And the E treated us harshly, and afflicted us,
Josh 24:6 the sea; and the E pursued your fathers with
24:7 between you and the E, and made the sea
Judg 6:9 the hand of the E, and from the hand
10:11 deliver you from the E and from the Amorites,
1Sam 4:8 gods who smote the E with every sort of
6:6 your hearts as the E and Pharaoh hardened their
10:18 the hand of the E and from the hand
12:8 into Egypt and the E oppressed them, then your
Ezra 9:1 Ammonites, the Moabites, the E, and the Amorites.
Jud 5:12 plagues; and so the E drove them out of
Is 10:24 against you as the E did.
19:1 the heart of the E will melt within them.
19:2 I will stir up E against Egyptians, and they
19:2 stir up Egyptians against E, and they will fight,
19:3 the spirit of the E within them will be
19:4 will give over the E into the hand of
19:16 In that day the E will be like women,
19:17 a terror to the E; every one to whom
19:21 himself known to the E; and the Egyptians will
19:21 the Egyptians; and the E will know the LORD
19:23 into Assyria, and the E will worship with the
20:4 Assyria lead away the E captives and the Ethiopians
31:3 The E are men, and not God; and their
Ezek 16:26 the harlot with the E, your lustful neighbors,
23:21 your youth, when the E handled your bosom and
23:27 your eyes to the E or remember them any
29:12 I will scatter the E among the nations, and
29:13 I will gather the E from the peoples among
30:23 I will scatter the E among the nations, and
30:26 I will scatter the E among the nations and
Acts 7:22 the wisdom of the E, and he was mighty
Heb 11:29 dry land; but the E, when they attempted to

EHI

Gen 46:21 Ashbel, Gera, Naaman, E, Rosh, Muppim, Huppim,

EHUD (11)

Judg 3:15 for them a deliverer, E, the son of Gera,
3:16 And E made for himself a sword with two
3:18 And when E had finished presenting the tribute, he
3:20 And E came to him, as he was sitting
3:20 And E said, "I have a message from God
3:21 And E reached with his left hand, took the
3:23 Then E went out into the vestibule, and closed
3:26 E escaped while they delayed, and passed beyond
4:1 of the LORD, after E died.
1Chr 7:10 of Bilhan: Jeush, Benjamin, E, Chenaanah, Zethan,
8:6 are the sons of E (they were heads of

EIGHT (66)

Gen 5:4 father of Seth were E hundred years; and he
5:7 the birth of Enosh E hundred and seven years,
5:10 the birth of Kenan E hundred and fifteen years,
5:13 the birth of Mahalalel E hundred and forty years,
5:16 the birth of Jared E hundred and thirty years,
5:17 days of Mahalalel were E hundred and ninety-five
5:19 the birth of Enoch E hundred years, and had
17:12 He that is E days old among you shall
21:4 Isaac when he was E days old, as God
22:23 These E Milcah bore to Nahor, Abraham's brother.
Ex 26:25 And there shall be E frames, with their bases
36:30 There were E frames with their bases of silver:
Num 2:24 is a hundred and E thousand one hundred.
3:28 and upward, there were E thousand six hundred,
4:48 numbered of them were E thousand five hundred
7:8 and four wagons and E oxen he gave to
29:29 "On the sixth day E bulls, two rams, fourteen
Judg 3:8 of Israel served Cushan-rishathaim E years.
12:14 and he judged Israel E years.
1Sam 17:12 named Jesse, who had E sons.
2Sam 23:8 wielded his spear against E hundred whom he slew
24:9 in Israel there were E hundred thousand valiant men
1Kgs 7:10 huge stones, stones of E and ten cubits.
2Kgs 8:17 king, and he reigned E years in Jerusalem.
22:1 Josiah was E years old when he began to
1Chr 12:24 spear were six thousand E hundred armed troops.
12:30 Ephraimites twenty thousand E hundred, mighty
24:4 sons of Eleazar, and E of the sons of
2Chr 13:3 battle against him with E hundred thousand picked
21:5 king, and he reigned E years in Jerusalem.
21:20 reign, and he reigned E years in Jerusalem; and
29:17 the LORD; then for E days they sanctified the
34:1 Josiah was E years old when he began to
36:9 Jehoiachin was E years old when he began to
Ezra 2:6 and Joab, two thousand E hundred and twelve.
Neh 7:11 and Joab, two thousand E hundred and eighteen.
7:13 The sons of Zattu, E hundred and forty-five.
11:12 work of the house, E hundred and twenty-two; and
Tob 14:2 his sight, and after E years he regained it.
Eccl 11:2 seven, or even to E, for you know not
Jer 41:15 escaped from Johanan with E men, and went to
52:29 captive from Jerusalem E hundred and thirty-two
Ezek 40:8 vestibule of the gateway, E cubits;
40:31 and its stairway had E steps.

40:34 and its stairway had E steps.
40:37 and its stairway had E steps.
40:41 side of the gate, E tables, on which the
Mic 5:5 him seven shepherds and E princes of men;
1Mac 3:24 Beth-horon to the plain; E hundred of them fell,
4:56 of the altar for E days, and offered burnt
4:59 gladness and joy for E days, beginning with the
5:20 go to Galilee, and E thousand to Judas for
5:34 As many as E thousand of them fell that
9:6 until no more than E hundred of them were
10:85 burned alive, came to E thousand men.
15:13 twenty thousand warriors and E thousand cavalry.
2Mac 2:12 Solomon also kept the E days.
8:20 place in Babylonia, when E thousand in all went
8:20 Macedonians were hard-pressed, the E thousand, by
10:6 they celebrated it for E days with rejoicing, in
Lk 2:21 at the end of E days, when he was
9:28 Now about E days after these sayings he took
Jn 20:26 E days later, his disciples were again in the
Acts 9:33 had been bedridden for E years and was paralyzed.
25:6 them not more than E or ten days, he
1Pet 3:20 a few, that is, E persons, were saved through

EIGHTEEN (23)
Gen 14:14 house, three hundred and E of them, and went
Judg 3:14 the king of Moab E years.
10:8 For E years they oppressed all the people of
20:25 felled to the ground E thousand men of the
20:44 E thousand men of Benjamin fell, all of them
2Sam 8:13 he returned, he slew E thousand Edomites in the
1Kgs 7:15 E cubits was the height of one pillar, and
2Kgs 24:8 Jehoiachin was E years old when he became king,
25:17 the one pillar was E cubits, and upon it
1Chr 12:31 the half-tribe of Manasseh E thousand, who were
18:12 son of Zeruiah, slew E thousand Edomites in the
26:9 Meshelemiah had sons and brethren, able men, E
29:7 thousand talents of silver, E thousand talents of
2Chr 11:21 and concubines (he took E wives and sixty
Ezra 8:9 him two hundred and E men.
8:18 his sons and kinsmen, E;
Neh 7:11 Jeshua and Joab, two thousand eight hundred and E
Jer 52:21 the one pillar was E cubits, its circumference was
Ezek 48:35 the city shall be E thousand cubits.
2Mac 5:21 So Antiochus carried off E hundred talents from the
Lk 13:4 Or those E upon whom the tower in Siloam
13:11 spirit of infirmity for E years; she was bent
13:16 whom Satan bound for E years, be loosed from

EIGHTEENTH (13)
1Kgs 15:1 Now in the E year of King Jeroboam the
2Kgs 3:1 In the E year of Jehoshaphat king of Judah,
22:3 In the E year of King Josiah, the king
23:23 Judah; but in the E year of King Josiah
1Chr 24:15 seventeenth to Hezir, the E to Happizzez,
25:25 brethren, twelve; to the E, to Hanani, his sons
2Chr 13:1 In the E year of King Jeroboam Abijah began
34:8 Now in the E year of his reign, when
35:19 In the E year of the reign of Josiah
Jud 2:1 In the E year, on the twenty-second day of
Jer 32:1 Judah, which was the E year of Nebuchadrezzar.
52:29 twenty-three Jews; in the E year of Nebuchadrezzar
1Mac 14:27 they wrote: "On the E day of Elul, in

EIGHTH (36)
Ex 22:30 its dam; on the E day you shall give
Lev 9:1 On the E day Moses called Aaron and his
12:3 And on the E day the flesh of his
14:10 "And on the E day he shall take two
14:23 And on the E day he shall bring them
15:14 And on the E day he shall take two
15:29 And on the E day she shall take two
22:27 mother; and from the E day on it shall
23:36 the LORD; on the E day you shall hold
23:39 rest, and on the E day shall be a
25:22 you sow in the E year, you will be
Num 6:10 On the E day he shall bring two turtledoves
7:54 On the E day Gamaliel the son of Pedahzur,
29:35 "On the E day you shall have a solemn
1Kgs 6:38 Bul, which is the E month, the house was
8:66 On the E day he sent the people away;
12:32 fifteenth day of the E month like the feast
12:33 fifteenth day in the E month, in the month
2Kgs 24:12 him prisoner in the E year of his reign,
1Chr 12:12 sixth, Eliel seventh, Johanan E, Elzabad ninth,
24:10 seventh to Hakkoz, the E to Abijah,
25:15 his brethren, twelve; the E to Jeshaiah, his sons
26:5 the seventh, Pe-ullethai the E; for God blessed him.
27:11 E, for the eighth month, was Sibbecai the
27:11 Eighth, for the E month, was Sibbecai the
2Chr 7:9 And on the E day they held a solemn
29:17 month, and on the E day of the month
34:3 For in the E year of his reign, while
Neh 8:18 days; and on the E day there was a
Ezek 43:27 days, then from the E day onward the priests
Zech 1:1 In the E month, in the second
Lk 1:59 And on the E day they came to circumcise
Acts 7:8 circumcised him on the E day; and Isaac became
Phil 3:5 more: circumcised on the E day, of the people
Rev 17:11 not, it is an E but it belongs to
21:20 the seventh chrysolite, the E beryl, the ninth topaz,

EIGHTIETH
1Kgs 6:1 the four hundred and E year after the people

EIGHTY (27)
Gen 35:28 were a hundred and E years.
Ex 7:7 Now Moses was E years old, and Aaron eighty-three
Num 4:48 of them were eight thousand five hundred and E
Judg 3:30 land had rest for E years.
2Sam 19:32 a very aged man, E years old; and he
19:35 I am this day E years old; can I
1Kgs 5:15 thousand burden-bearers and E thousand hewers
12:21 Benjamin, a hundred and E thousand chosen
2Kgs 6:25 head was sold for E shekels of silver, and
10:24 Now Jehu had stationed E men outside, and said,
1Chr 15:9 Eliel the chief, with E of his brethren;
2Chr 2:2 to bear burdens and E thousand to quarry in
2:18 assigned to bear burdens, E thousand to quarry in
11:1 Benjamin, a hundred and E thousand chosen
14:8 two hundred and E thousand men from Benjamin,
17:15 with two hundred and E thousand,
17:18 with a hundred and E thousand armed for war.
26:17 in after him, with E priests of the LORD
Ezra 8:8 Michael, and with him E men.
Esth 1:4 days, a hundred and E days.
Song 6:8 are sixty queens and E concubines, and maidens
Jer 41:5 one knew of it, E men arrived from Shechem
2Mac 4:8 another source of revenue, E talents.
5:14 total of three days E thousand were destroyed, forty
11:2 had happened, gathered about E thousand men and
11:4 of cavalry, and his E elephants.
Lk 16:7 your bill, and write E

EIGHTY-EIGHT (2)
1Chr 25:7 all who were skilful, was two hundred and E
Neh 7:26 men of Bethlehem and Netophah, a hundred and E

EIGHTY-EIGHTH
2Mac 1:9 the one hundred and E year.

EIGHTY-FIVE (7)
Josh 14:10 I am this day E years old.
1Sam 22:18 killed on that day E persons who wore the
2Kgs 19:35 slew a hundred and E thousand in the camp
Is 37:36 slew a hundred and E thousand in the camp
1Mac 7:41 down one hundred and E thousand of the Assyrians.
2Mac 8:19 when one hundred and E thousand perished,
15:22 fully a hundred and E thousand in the camp

EIGHTY-FOUR (2)
Neh 11:18 in the holy city were two hundred and E
Lk 2:37 virginity, and as a widow till she was E

EIGHTY-SEVEN (2)
Gen 5:25 lived a hundred and E years, he became the
1Chr 7:5 Issachar were in all E thousand mighty warriors,

EIGHTY-SIX (2)
Gen 16:16 Abram was E years old when Hagar bore Ishmael
Num 2:9 is a hundred and E thousand four hundred.

EIGHTY-THREE
Ex 7:7 years old, and Aaron E years old, when they

EIGHTY-TWO (2)
Gen 5:26 Lamech seven hundred and E years, and had other
5:28 lived a hundred and E years, he became the

EITHER (72)
Gen 31:24 a word to Jacob, E good or bad."
Ex 4:10 I am not eloquent, E heretofore or since thou
11:7 the people of Israel, E man or beast, not

E

Lev 12:7 who bears a child, E male or female.
13:59 of wool or linen, E in warp or woof,
16:29 shall do no work, E the native or the
18:26 none of these abominations, E the native or the
27:12 shall value it as E good or bad; as
27:14 shall value it as E good or bad; as
Num 6:2 people of Israel, When E a man or a
22:24 with a wall on E side.
22:26 no way to turn E to the right or
24:13 the LORD, to do E good or bad of
Deut 17:11 they declare to you, E to the right hand
17:20 aside from the commandment, E to the right hand
1Sam 20:2 my father does nothing E great or small without
20:27 come to the meal, E yesterday or today?"
28:6 did not answer him, E by dreams, or by
28:15 answers me no more, E by prophets or by
1Kgs 18:27 he is a god; E he is musing, or
1Chr 12:2 and sling stones with E the right or the
21:12 'Take which you will: E three years of famine;
Jud 11:21 earth to the other, E for beauty of face
13:4 out, and no one, E small or great, was
Prov 24:21 and do not disobey E of them;
Eccl 4:8 who has no one, E son or brother, yet
Wis 13:2 but they supposed that E fire or wind or
14:24 they no longer keep E their lives or their
14:24 marriages pure, but they E treacherously kill one
14:28 For their worshippers E rave in exultation, or
15:6 hope are those who E make or desire or
Sir 13:24 heart changes his countenance, E for good or for
20:29 advantage is there in E of them?
41:14 advantage is there in E of them?
Is 17:8 own fingers have made, E the Asherim or the
Bar 6:35 not able to give E wealth or money; if
6:64 they are not able E to decide a case
Ezek 40:10 three side rooms on E side of the east
40:10 and the jambs on E side were of the
40:12 rooms, one cubit on E side; and the side
40:12 were six cubits on E side.
40:21 side rooms, three on E side, and its jambs
40:26 its jambs, one on E side.
40:34 its jambs, one on E side; and its stairway
40:37 its jambs, one on E side; and its stairway
40:39 were two tables on E side, on which the
40:48 vestibule, five cubits on E side; and the breadth
40:48 were three cubits on E side.
40:49 beside the jambs on E side.
41:2 were five cubits on E side; and he measured
41:15 and its walls on E side, a hundred cubits.
41:26 and palm trees on E side, on the sidewalls
46:12 provides a freewill offering, E a burnt offering or
1Mac 4:35 how ready they were E to live or to
6:38 horsemen were stationed on E side, on the two
Mt 5:34 not swear at all, E by heaven, for it
6:24 serve two masters; for E he will hate the
12:32 will not be forgiven, E in this age or
12:33 E make the tree good, and its fruit good;
Lk 16:13 serve two masters; for E he will hate the
Jn 19:18 two others, one on E side, and Jesus between
Acts 24:11 stirring up a crowd, E in the temple or
Rom 6:16 one whom you obey, E of sin, which leads
9:11 and had done nothing E good or bad, in
1Thes 2:5 For we never used E words of flattery, as
2Thes 2:2 in mind or excited, E by spirit or by
2:15 were taught by us, E by word of mouth
1Tim 1:7 the law, without understanding E what they are
Jas 5:12 brethren, do not swear, E by heaven or by
1Jn 3:6 one who sins has E seen him or known
Rev 9:20 and wood, which cannot E see or hear or
22:2 the city; also, on E side of the river,

EKER

1Chr 2:27 the first-born of Jerahmeel: Maaz, Jamin, and E

EKRON (25)

Josh 13:3 to the boundary of E, it is reckoned as
13:3 Ashdod, Ashkelon, Gath, and E, and those of the
15:11 the hill north of E, then the boundary bends
15:45 E, with its towns and its villages;
15:46 and its villages; from E to the sea, all
19:43 Aijalon, Ithlah, Elon, Timnah, E,
Judg 1:18 with its territory, and E with its territory.
1Sam 5:10 So they sent the ark of God to E
5:10 of God came to E, the people of Ekron
5:10 Ekron, the people of E cried out, "They have
6:16 Philistines saw it, they returned that day to E
6:17 for Gath, one for E;
7:14 restored to Israel, from E to Gath; and Israel
17:52 and the gates of E, so that the wounded
17:52 way from Sha-araim as far as Gath and E
2Kgs 1:2 Baal-zebub, the god of E, whether I shall recover
1:3 Baal-zebub, the god of E
1:6 sending to inquire of Baal-zebub, the god of E
1:16 Baal-zebub, the god of E --is it because there
Jer 25:20 the Philistines (Ashkelon, Gaza, E, and the remnant
Amos 1:8 turn my hand against E; and the remnant of
Zeph 2:4 out at noon, and E shall be uprooted.
Zech 9:5 shall writhe in anguish; E also, because its hopes
9:7 clan in Judah, and E shall be like the
1Mac 10:89 He also gave him E and all its environs

EL-BERITH

Judg 9:46 they entered the stronghold of the house of E

EL-BETHEL

Gen 35:7 and called the place E, because there God had

EL-ELOHE-ISRAEL

Gen 33:20 There he erected an altar and called it E

EL-PARAN

Gen 14:6 Seir as far as E on the border of

ELA

1Kgs 4:18 Shimei the son of E, in Benjamin;

ELABORATE

1Mac 13:29 pyramids he devised an E setting, erecting about

ELAH (16)

Gen 36:41 Timna, Alvah, Jetheth, Oholibamah, E, Pinon,
1Sam 17:2 in the valley of E, and drew up in
17:19 in the valley of E, fighting with the Philistines.
21:9 in the valley of E, behold, it is here
1Kgs 16:6 buried at Tirzah; and E his son reigned in
16:8 Asa king of Judah, E the son of Baasha
16:13 and the sins of E his son which they
16:14 of the acts of E, and all that he
2Kgs 15:30 Hoshea the son of E made a conspiracy against
17:1 Hoshea the son of E began to reign in
18:1 of Hoshea son of E, king of Israel, Hezekiah
18:9 of Hoshea son of E, king of Israel, Shalmaneser
1Chr 1:52 Timna, Aliah, Jetheth, Oholibamah, E, Pinon,
4:15 son of Jephunneh: Iru, E, and Naam; and the
4:15 and the sons of E: Kenaz.
9:8 the son of Jeroham, E the son of Uzzi,

ELAM (28)

Gen 10:22 The sons of Shem: E, Asshur, Arpachshad, Lud, and
14:1 Ellasar, Ched-or-laomer king of E, and Tidal king of
14:9 with Ched-or-laomer king of E, Tidal king of Goiim,
1Chr 1:17 The sons of Shem: E, Asshur, Arpachshad, Lud, Aram,
8:24 Abdon, Zichri, Hanan, Hananiah, E, Anthothijah,
26:3 third, Jathni-el the fourth, E the fifth, Jehohanan the
Ezra 2:7 The sons of E, one thousand two hundred and
2:31 sons of the other E, one thousand two hundred
8:7 Of the sons of E, Jeshaiah the son of
10:2 of the sons of E, addressed Ezra: "We have
10:26 Of the sons of E: Mattaniah, Zechariah, Jehiel, Abdi,
Neh 7:12 The sons of E, a thousand two hundred and
7:34 sons of the other E, a thousand two hundred
10:14 the people: Parosh, Pahath-moab, E, Zattu, Bani,
12:42 Eleazar, Uzzi, Jehohanan, Malchijah, E, and Ezer.
Is 11:11 from Ethiopia, from E, from Shinar, from Hamath,
21:2 Go up, O E, lay siege, O Media; all
22:6 And E bore the quiver with chariots and horsemen,
Jer 25:25 all the kings of E, and all the kings
49:34 Jeremiah the prophet concerning E, in the beginning
49:35 break the bow of E, the mainstay of their
49:36 I will bring upon E the four winds from
49:36 those driven out of E shall not come.
49:37 I will terrify E before their enemies, and before
49:38 set my throne in E, and destroy their king
49:39 restore the fortunes of E, says the LORD."
Ezek 32:24 E is there, and all her multitude about her
Dan 8:2 in the province of E; and I saw in

ELAMITES (2)

Ezra 4:9 Susa, that is, the E,
Acts 2:9 Parthians and Medes and E and residents of

ELAPSED

Acts 24:26 when two years had E, Felix was succeeded by

ELASA

1Mac 9:5 Judas was encamped in E, and with him were

ELASAH (2)

Ezra 10:22 of Pashhur: Eli-o-enai, Ma-aseiah, Ishmael,
Jer 29:3 by the hand of E the son of Shaphan

ELATED (7)

Esth 13:2 the whole world, not E with presumption of authority
2Mac 5:17 Antiochus was E in spirit, and did not perceive
5:21 walk on the sea, because his mind was E
7:34 men, do not be E in vain and puffed
11:4 of God, but was E with his ten thousands
2Cor 12:7 me from being too E by the abundance of
12:7 harass me, to keep me from being too E

ELATH (5)

Deut 2:8 the Arabah road from E and Ezion-geber.
2Kgs 14:22 He built E and restored it to Judah, after
16:6 king of Edom recovered E for Edom, and drove
16:6 men of Judah from E; and the Edomites came
16:6 the Edomites came to E, where they dwell to

ELDAAH (2)

Gen 25:4 of Midian were Ephah, Epher, Hanoch, Abida, and E
1Chr 1:33 sons of Midian: Ephah, Epher, Hanoch, Abida, and E

ELDAD (2)

Num 11:26 the camp, one named E, and the other named
11:27 ran and told Moses, E and Medad are prophesying

ELDER (16)

Gen 10:21 children of Eber, the E brother of Japheth, children
25:23 than the other, the E shall serve the younger."
1Sam 18:17 David, "Here is my E daughter Merab; I will
1Kgs 2:22 for he is my E brother, and on his
Is 3:2 the diviner and the E,
3:5 be insolent to the E, and the base fellow
9:15 one day-- the E and honored man is
Ezek 16:46 And your E sister is Samaria, who lived with
16:61 your sisters, both your E and your younger, and
23:4 the name of the E and Oholibah the name
Lk 15:25 "Now his E son was in the field; and
Rom 9:12 she was told, "The E will serve the younger."
1Tim 5:19 any charge against an E except on the evidence
1Pet 5:1 you, as a fellow E and a witness of
2Jn 1:1 The E to the elect lady
3Jn 1:1 The E to the beloved Gaius,

ELDERS (219)

Gen 50:7 servants of Pharaoh, the E of his household, and
50:7 household, and all the E of the land of
Ex 3:16 Go and gather the E of Israel together, and
3:18 and you and the E of Israel shall go
4:29 gathered together all the E of the people of
12:21 Moses called all the E of Israel, and said
17:5 you some of the E of Israel; and take
17:6 the sight of the E of Israel.
18:12 came with all the E of Israel to eat
19:7 came and called the E of the people, and
24:1 and seventy of the E of Israel, and worship
24:9 and seventy of the E of Israel went up,
24:14 he said to the E, "Tarry here for us,
Lev 4:15 of meeting; and the E of the congregation shall
9:1 his sons and the E of Israel;
Num 11:16 seventy men of the E of Israel, whom you
11:16 know to be the E of the people and
11:24 seventy men of the E of the people, and
11:25 it upon the seventy E; and when the spirit
11:30 And Moses and the E of Israel returned to
16:25 and Abiram; and the E of Israel followed him.
22:4 Moab said to the E of Midian, "This horde
22:7 So the E of Moab and the elders of
22:7 of Moab and the E of Midian departed with
Deut 5:23 your tribes, and your E;
19:12 these cities, then the E of his city shall
21:2 killed him, then your E and your judges shall
21:3 is slain; and the E of the city which
21:4 And the E of that city shall bring the
21:6 And all the E of that city nearest to
21:19 him out to the E of his city at
21:20 shall say to the E of his city, 'This
22:15 her virginity to the E of the city in
22:16 shall say to the E, 'I gave my daughter
22:17 the garment before the E of the city.
22:18 Then the E of that city shall take the
25:7 the gate to the E, and say, 'My husband's
25:8 to me.' Then the E of his city shall
25:9 the presence of the E, and pull his sandal
27:1 Now Moses and the E of Israel commanded the
29:10 of your tribes, your E, and your officers, all
31:9 and to all the E of Israel.
31:28 to me all the E of your tribes, and
32:7 will show you; your E, and they will tell
Josh 7:6 evening, he and the E of Israel; and they
8:10 went up, with the E of Israel, before the
8:33 as homeborn, with their E and officers and their
9:11 And our E and all the inhabitants of our
20:4 his case to the E of that city; then
23:2 summoned all Israel, their E and heads, their judges
24:1 Shechem, and summoned the E, the heads, the
24:31 the days of the E who outlived Joshua and
Judg 2:7 the days of the E who outlived Joshua, who
8:14 him the officials and E of Succoth, seventy-seven
8:16 And he took the E of the city and
11:5 war against Israel, the E of Gilead went to
11:7 Jephthah said to the E of Gilead, "Did you
11:8 And the E of Gilead said to Jephthah, "That
11:9 Jephthah said to the E of Gilead, "If you
11:10 And the E of Gilead said to Jephthah, "The
11:11 Jephthah went with the E of Gilead, and the
21:16 Then the E of the congregation said, "What shall
Ruth 4:2 ten men of the E of the city, and
4:4 the presence of the E of my people.
4:9 Boaz said to the E and all the people,
4:11 the gate, and the E, said, "We are witnesses.
1Sam 4:3 to the camp, the E of Israel said, "Why
8:4 Then all the E of Israel gathered together and
11:3 The E of Jabesh said to him, "Give us
15:30 me now before the E of my people and
16:4 The E of the city came to meet him
30:26 to his friends, the E of Judah, saying, "Here
2Sam 3:17 Abner conferred with the E of Israel, saying, "For
5:3 So all the E of Israel came to the
12:17 And the E of his house stood beside him,
17:4 Absalom and all the E of Israel.
17:15 counsel Absalom and the E of Israel; and thus
19:11 priests, "Say to the E of Judah, 'Why should
1Kgs 8:1 Then Solomon assembled the E of Israel and all
8:3 And all the E of Israel came, and the
20:7 Israel called all the E of the land, and
20:8 And all the E and all the people said
21:8 the letters to the E and the nobles who
21:11 of his city, the E and the nobles who
2Kgs 6:32 his house, and the E were sitting with him.
6:32 Elisha said to the E, "Do you see how
10:1 the city, to the E, and to the guardians
10:5 city, together with the E and the guardians, sent
23:1 sent, and all the E of Judah and Jerusalem
1Chr 11:3 So all the E of Israel came to the
15:25 So David and the E of Israel, and the
21:16 Then David and the E, clothed in sackcloth, fell
2Chr 5:2 Then Solomon assembled the E of Israel and all
5:4 And all the E of Israel came, and the
34:29 gathered together all the E of Judah and Jerusalem.
Ezra 5:5 God was upon the E of the Jews, and
5:9 Then we asked those E and spoke to them
6:7 the Jews and the E of the Jews rebuild
6:8 shall do for these E of the Jews for
6:14 And the E of the Jews built and prospered,
10:8 the officials and the E all his property should
10:14 and with them the E and judges of every
Jud 6:16 called together all the E of the city, and
6:21 a banquet for the E; and all that night
7:24 said before all the E,
8:10 Chabris and Charmis, the E of her city.
10:6 standing there with the E of the city, Chabris
13:12 and called together the E of the city.
Job 12:20 trusted, and takes away the discernment of the E
Ps 105:22 and to teach his E wisdom.
107:32 and praise him in the assembly of the E
Prov 31:23 he sits among the E of the land.
Wis 8:10 the presence of the E, though I am young.
Sir 6:34 Stand in the assembly of the E
7:14 the assembly of the E, nor repeat yourself in
Is 3:14 into judgment with the E and princes of his
24:23 Jerusalem and before his E he will manifest his
Jer 19:1 take some of the E of the people and
26:17 And certain of the E of the land arose
29:1 from Jerusalem to the E of the exiles, and
Lam 1:19 me; my priests and E perished in the city,
2:10 The E of the daughter of Zion sit on

	4:16	shown to the priests, no favor to the E
	5:12	their hands; no respect is shown to the E
Bar	1:4	the hearing of the E, and in the hearing
Ezek	7:26	perishes from the priest, and counsel from the E
	8:1	my house, with the E of Judah sitting before
	8:11	seventy men of the E of the house of
	8:12	you seen what the E of the house of
	9:6	they began with the E who were before the
	14:1	came certain of the E of Israel to me;
	20:1	month, certain of the E of Israel came to
	20:3	man, speak to the E of Israel, and say
	27:9	The E of Gebal and her skilled men were
Dan	13:5	In that year two E from the people were
	13:5	forth from Babylon, from E who were judges, who
	13:8	The two E used to see her every day,
	13:16	there except the two E, who had hid themselves
	13:18	did not see the E, because they were hidden.
	13:19	gone out, the two E rose and ran to
	13:24	voice, and the two E shouted against her.
	13:27	And when the E told their tale, the servants
	13:28	husband Joakim, the two E came, full of their
	13:34	Then the two E stood up in the midst
	13:36	The E said, "As we were walking in the
	13:41	them, because they were E of the people and
	13:50	And the E said to him, "Come, sit among
	13:61	rose against the two E, for out of their
Joel	1:13	Gather the E and all the inhabitants of the
	2:16	congregation; assemble the E; gather the children,
1Mac	1:26	every community, rulers and E groaned, maidens and
	7:33	and some of the E of the people, to
	11:23	chose some of the E of Israel and some
	12:35	returned he convened the E of the people and
	13:36	kings, and to the E and nation of the
	14:20	priest and to the E and the priests and
	14:28	the nation and the E of the country, the
2Mac	13:13	consulting privately with the E, he determined to
	14:37	Razis, one of the E of Jerusalem, was denounced
Mt	15:2	do your disciples transgress the tradition of the E
	16:21	many things from the E and chief priests and
	21:23	chief priests and the E of the people came
	26:3	chief priests and the E of the people gathered
	26:47	chief priests and the E of the people.
	26:57	the scribes and the E had gathered.
	27:1	chief priests and the E of the people took
	27:3	chief priests and the E,
	27:12	the chief priests and E, he made no answer.
	27:20	chief priests and the E persuaded the people to
	27:41	with the scribes and E, mocked him, saying,
	28:12	had assembled with the E and taken counsel, they
Mk	7:3	the tradition of the E;
	7:5	the tradition of the E, but eat with hands
	8:31	be rejected by the E and the chief priests
	11:26	the scribes and the E came to him,
	14:43	the chief priests and the scribes and the E
	14:53	chief priests and the E and the scribes were
	15:1	chief priests, with the E and scribes, and the
Lk	7:3	he sent to him E of the Jews, asking
	9:22	be rejected by the E and chief priests and
	20:1	the scribes with the E came up
	22:50	of the temple and E, who had come out
	22:64	the assembly of the E of the people gathered
Acts	4:5	morrow their rulers and E and scribes were
	4:8	of the people and E,
	4:23	chief priests and the E had said to them.
	6:12	the people and the E and the scribes, and
	11:30	sending it to the E by the hand of
	14:23	when they had appointed E for them in every
	15:2	the apostles and the E about this question.
	15:4	the apostles and the E, and they declared all
	15:6	The apostles and the E were gathered together to
	15:22	the apostles and the E, with the whole church,
	15:23	the apostles and the E, to the brethren who
	16:4	by the apostles and E who were at Jerusalem.
	20:17	called to him the E of the church.
	21:18	James; and all the E were present.
	22:5	the whole council of E bear me witness.
	23:14	the chief priests and E, and said, "We have
	24:1	came down with some E and a spokesman, one
	25:15	chief priests and the E of the Jews gave
1Tim	4:14	when the council of E laid their hands upon
	5:17	Let the E who rule well be considered worthy
Tit	1:4	was defective, and appoint E in every town as
Jas	5:14	him call for the E of the church, and
1Pet	5:1	So I exhort the E among you, as a
	5:5	you that are younger be subject to the E
Rev	4:4	the thrones were twenty-four E, clad in white
	4:10	and ever, the twenty-four E fall down before him
	5:5	Then one of the E said to me, "Weep
	5:6	creatures and among the E, I saw a Lamb
	5:8	creatures and the twenty-four E fell down before the
	5:11	living creatures and the E the voice of many
	5:14	and the E fell down and worshiped.
	7:11	throne and round the E and the four living
	7:13	Then one of the E addressed me, saying, "Who
	11:16	And the twenty-four E who sit on their thrones
	14:3	before the four living creatures and before the E
	19:4	And the twenty-four E and the four living creatures

ELDEST (8)

Gen	44:12	searched, beginning with the E and ending with the
1Sam	17:13	The three E sons of Jesse had followed Saul
	17:14	the youngest; the three E followed Saul,
	17:28	Now Eliab his E brother heard when he spoke
2Kgs	3:27	Then he took his E son who was to
Job	1:13	drinking wine in their E brother's house;
	1:18	drinking wine in their E brother's house;
Jn	8:9	one, beginning with the E, and Jesus was left

ELE-AD

1Chr	7:21	son, and Ezer and E, whom the men of

ELE-ADAH

1Chr	7:20	son, Tahath his son, E his son, Tahath his

ELE-ALEH (3)

Is	15:4	Heshbon and E cry out, their voice is heard
	16:9	tears, O Heshbon and E; for upon your fruit
Jer	48:34	"Heshbon and E cry out; as far as Jahaz

ELE-ASAH (4)

1Chr	2:39	was the father of Helez, and Helez of E
	2:40	E was the father of Sismai, and Sismai of
	8:37	Raphah was his son, E his son, Azel his
	9:43	Rephaiah was his son, E his son, Azel his

ELEALEH (2)

Num	32:3	Dibon, Jazer, Nimrah, Heshbon, E, Sebam, Nebo
	32:37	of Reuben built Heshbon, E, Kiriathaim,

ELEAZAR (83)

Ex	6:23	bore him Nadab, Abihu, E, and Ithamar.
	6:25	E, Aaron's son, took to wife one of the
	28:1	sons, Nadab and Abihu, E and Ithamar.
Lev	10:6	to Aaron and to E and Ithamar, his sons,
	10:12	to Aaron and to E and Ithamar, his sons
	10:16	he was angry with E and Ithamar, the sons
Num	3:2	the first-born, and Abihu, E, and Ithamar;
	3:4	So E and Ithamar served as priests in the
	3:32	And E the son of Aaron the priest was
	4:16	"And E the son of Aaron the priest shall
	16:37	said to Moses, "Tell E the son of Aaron
	16:39	So E the priest took the bronze censers, which
	16:40	the LORD said to E through Moses.
	19:3	shall give her to E the priest, and she
	19:4	slaughtered before him; and E the priest shall take
	20:25	Take Aaron and E his son, and bring them
	20:26	and put them upon E his son; and Aaron
	20:28	and put them upon E his son; and Aaron
	20:28	Then Moses and E came down from the mountain.
	25:7	Phinehas the son of E, son of Aaron the
	25:11	"Phinehas the son of E, son of Aaron the
	26:1	to Moses and to E the son of Aaron,
	26:3	And Moses and E the priest spoke with them
	26:60	were born Nadab, Abihu, E and Ithamar.
	26:63	numbered by Moses and E the priest, who numbered
	27:2	before Moses, and before E the priest, and before
	27:19	him to stand before E the priest and all
	27:21	he shall stand before E the priest, who shall
	27:22	him to stand before E the priest and the
	31:6	Phinehas the son of E the priest, with the
	31:12	to Moses, and to E the priest, and to
	31:13	Moses, and E the priest, and all the leaders
	31:21	And E the priest said to the men of
	31:26	of beast, you and E the priest and the
	31:29	and give it to E the priest as an
	31:31	And Moses and E the priest did as the
	31:41	for the LORD, to E the priest, as the
	31:51	And Moses and E the priest received from them
	31:54	himself.) And Moses and E the priest received the
	32:2	to Moses and to E the priest and to
	32:28	command concerning them to E the priest, and to
	34:17	to you for inheritance: E the priest and Joshua

Deut 10:6 buried; and his son E ministered as priest in
Josh 14:1 land of Canaan, which E the priest, and Joshua
17:4 They came before E the priest and Joshua the
19:51 are the inheritances which E the priest and Joshua
21:1 the Levites came to E the priest and to
22:13 Phinehas the son of E the priest,
22:31 Phinehas the son of E the priest said to
22:32 Phinehas the son of E the priest, and the
24:33 And E the son of Aaron died; and they
Judg 20:28 Phinehas the son of E, son of Aaron, ministered
1Sam 7:1 they consecrated his son, E, to have charge of
2Sam 23:9 three mighty men was E the son of Dodo,
1Chr 6:3 of Aaron: Nadab, Abihu, E, and Ithamar.
6:4 E was the father of Phinehas, Phinehas of Abishua,
6:50 the sons of Aaron: E his son, Phinehas his
9:20 Phinehas the son of E was the ruler over
11:12 three mighty men was E the son of Dodo,
23:21 The sons of Mahli: E and Kish.
23:22 E died having no sons, but only daughters; their
24:1 of Aaron: Nadab, Abihu, E, and Ithamar.
24:2 had no children, so E and Ithamar became the
24:3 of the sons of E, and Ahimelech of the
24:4 among the sons of E than among the sons
24:4 of the sons of E, and eight of the
24:5 both the sons of E and the sons of
24:6 house being chosen for E and one chosen for
24:28 Of Mahli: E, who had no sons.
Ezra 7:5 of Phinehas, son of E, son of Aaron the
8:33 and with him was E the son of Phinehas,
10:25 Malchijah, Mijamin, E, Hashabiah, and Benaiah.
Neh 12:42 trumpets; and Ma-aseiah, Shemaiah, E, Uzzi,
Sir 45:23 Phinehas the son of E is the third in
50:27 of Sirach, son of E, of Jerusalem, who out
1Mac 2:5 Judas called Maccabeus, E called Avaran, and
6:43 And E, called Avaran, saw that one of the
8:17 Jason the son of E, and sent them to
2Mac 6:18 E, one of the scribes in high position, a
6:24 young should suppose that E in his ninetieth year
8:23 Besides, he appointed E to read aloud from the
Mt 1:15 Eliud the father of E, and Eleazar the father
1:15 father of Eleazar, and E the father of Matthan,

ELECT (17)

Wis 3:9 mercy are upon his E, and he watches over
4:15 mercy are with his E, and he watches over
Sir 46:1 great savior of God's E, to take vengeance on
Mt 24:22 the sake of the E those days will be
24:24 as to lead astray, if possible, even the E
24:31 they will gather his E from the four winds,
Mk 13:20 the sake of the E, whom he chose, he
13:22 and wonders, to lead astray, if possible, the E
13:27 angels, and gather his E from the four winds,
Lk 18:7 not God vindicate his E, who cry to him
Rom 8:33 Who shall bring any charge against God's E
11:7 The E obtained it, but the rest were hardened,
1Tim 5:21 Jesus and of the E angels I charge you
2Tim 2:10 the sake of the E, that they also may
Tit 1:1 the faith of God's E and their knowledge of
2Jn 1:1 The elder to the E lady and her children,
1:13 The children of your E sister greet you.

ELECTION (3)

Rom 9:11 that God's purpose of E might continue, not because
11:28 sake; but as regards E they are beloved for
2Pet 1:10 confirm your call and E, for if you do

ELEMENTAL (4)

Gal 4:3 were slaves to the E spirits of the universe.
4:9 the weak and beggarly E spirits, whose slaves you
Col 2:8 tradition, according to the E spirits of the universe,
2:20 you died to the E spirits of the universe,

ELEMENTARY

Heb 6:1 let us leave the E doctrine of Christ and

ELEMENTS (5)

Wis 7:17 the activity of the E;
19:18 For the E changed places with one another, as
2Mac 7:22 set in order the E within each of you.
2Pet 3:10 loud noise, and the E will be dissolved with
3:12 and dissolved, and the E will melt with fire!

ELEPHANT (3)

1Mac 6:35 the phalanxes; with each E they stationed a
6:46 He got under the E, stabbed it from beneath,
2Mac 13:15 He stabbed the leading E and its rider.

ELEPHANTS (12)

1Mac 1:17 force, with chariots and E and cavalry and with
3:34 his troops and the E, and gave him orders
6:30 thousand horsemen, and thirty-two E accustomed to
6:34 They showed the E the juice of grapes and
6:37 And upon the E were wooden towers, strong and
8:6 a hundred and twenty E and with cavalry and
11:56 And Trypho captured the E and gained control of
2Mac 11:4 and his thousands of cavalry, and his eighty E
13:2 three hundred cavalry, twenty-two E, and three
14:12 in command of the E, appointed him governor of
15:20 up for battle, the E strategically stationed and the
15:21 the savagery of the E, stretched out his hands

ELEUTHERUS (2)

1Mac 11:7 as the river called E; then he returned to
12:30 they had crossed the E river.

ELEVATION

Ps 48:2 holy mountain, beautiful in E, is the joy of

ELEVEN (24)

Gen 32:22 two maids, and his E children, and crossed the
37:9 sun, the moon, and E stars were bowing down
Ex 26:7 tent over the tabernacle; E curtains shall you make.
26:8 curtain four cubits; the E curtains shall have the
36:14 the tabernacle; he made E curtains.
36:15 curtain four cubits; the E curtains had the same
Num 29:20 "On the third day E bulls, two rams, fourteen
Deut 1:2 It is E days' journey from Horeb by the
Josh 15:51 Goshen, Holon, and Giloh: E cities with their villages.
Judg 16:5 will each give you E hundred pieces of silver."
17:2 to his mother, "The E hundred pieces of silver
17:3 And he restored the E hundred pieces of silver
2Kgs 23:36 reign, and he reigned E years in Jerusalem.
24:18 king, and he reigned E years in Jerusalem.
2Chr 36:5 reign, and he reigned E years in Jerusalem.
36:11 reign, and he reigned E years in Jerusalem.
Jer 52:1 king; and he reigned E years in Jerusalem.
2Mac 11:11 the enemy, and slew E thousand of them and
Mt 28:16 Now the E disciples went to Galilee, to the
Mk 16:14 he appeared to the E themselves as they sat
Lk 24:9 all this to the E and to all the
24:33 and they found the E gathered together and those
Acts 1:26 was enrolled with the E apostles.
2:14 Peter, standing with the E, lifted up his voice

ELEVENTH (21)

Num 7:72 On the E day Pagiel the son of Ochran,
Deut 1:3 first day of the E month, Moses spoke to
1Kgs 6:38 And in the E year, in the month of
2Kgs 9:29 In the E year of Joram the son of
25:2 was besieged till the E year of King Zedekiah.
1Chr 12:13 Johanan eighth, Elzabad ninth, Jeremiah tenth,
24:12 tenth to Shecaniah, the E to Eliashib, the twelfth
25:18 his brethren, twelve; the E to Azarel, his sons
27:14 E, for the eleventh month, was Benaiah of Pirathon,
27:14 Eleventh, for the E month, was Benaiah of Pirathon,
Jer 1:3 the end of the E year of Zedekiah, the
39:2 besieged it; in the E year of Zedekiah, in
52:5 was besieged till the E year of King Zedekiah.
Ezek 26:1 In the E year, on the first day of
30:20 In the E year, in the first month, on
31:1 In the E year, in the third month, on
Zech 1:7 twenty-fourth day of the E month which is the
1Mac 16:14 seventy-seventh year, in the E month, which is the
Mt 20:6 And about the E hour he went out and
20:9 those hired about the E hour came, each of
Rev 21:20 the tenth chrysoprase, the E jacinth, the twelfth

ELHANAN (4)

2Sam 21:19 Philistines at Gob; and E the son of Jaareoregim,
23:24 one of the thirty; E the son of Dodo
1Chr 11:26 the brother of Joab, E the son of Dodo
20:5 with the Philistines; and E the son of Jair

ELI (37)

1Sam 1:3 the two sons of E, Hophni and Phinehas, were
1:9 Now E the priest was sitting on the seat
1:12 praying before the LORD, E observed her mouth.
1:13 was not heard; therefore E took her to be
1:14 And E said to her, "How long will you
1:17 Then E answered, "Go in peace, and the God
1:25 the bull, and they brought the child to E
2:11 in the presence of E the priest.
2:12 Now the sons of E were worthless men; they

2:20 Then E would bless Elkanah and his wife, and
2:22 Now E was very old, and he heard all
2:27 man of God to E, and said to him,
3:1 boy Samuel was ministering to the LORD under E
3:2 At that time E, whose eyesight had begun to
3:5 and ran to E, and said, "Here I am,
3:6 arose and went to E, and said, "Here I
3:8 arose and went to E, and said, "Here I
3:8 Then E perceived that the LORD was calling the
3:9 Therefore E said to Samuel, "Go, lie down; and
3:12 I will fulfil against E all that I have
3:14 to the house of E that the iniquity of
3:14 that the iniquity of E's house shall not be
3:15 Samuel was afraid to tell the vision to E
3:16 But E called Samuel and said, "Samuel, my son."
3:17 And E said, "What was it that he told
4:4 the two sons of E, Hophni and Phinehas, were
4:11 the two sons of E, Hophni and Phinehas, were
4:13 When he arrived, E was sitting upon his seat
4:14 When E heard the sound of the outcry, he
4:14 Then the man hastened and came and told E
4:15 Now E was ninety-eight years old and his eyes
4:16 the man said to E, "I am he who
4:18 the ark of God, E fell over backward from
14:3 of Phinehas, son of E, the priest of the
1Kgs 2:27 concerning the house of E in Shiloh.
Mt 27:46 with a loud voice, E, Eli, lama sabach-thani?" that
27:46 a loud voice, "Eli, E, lama sabach-thani?" that is,

ELI-E-HO-ENAI (2)
1Chr 26:3 fifth, Jehohanan the sixth, E the seventh.
Ezra 8:4 the sons of Pahath-moab, E the son of Zerahiah,

ELI-ENAI
1Chr 8:20 Jakim, Zichri, Zabdi, E, Zillethai, Eliel,

ELI-O-ENAI (7)
1Chr 3:23 The sons of Neariah: E, Hizkiah, and Azrikam, three.
3:24 The sons of E: Hodaviah, Eliashib, Pelaiah, Akkub,
4:36 Seraiah, son of Asiel, E, Ja-akobah, Jeshohaiah,
7:8 Becher: Zemirah, Joash, Eliezer, E, Omri, Jeremoth,
Ezra 10:22 the sons of Pashhur: E, Ma-aseiah, Ishmael,
10:27 the sons of Zattu: E, Eliashib, Mattaniah, Jeremoth,
Neh 12:41 Ma-aseiah, Miniamin, Micaiah, E, Zechariah,

ELI-ZAPHAN (4)
Num 3:30 of the tabernacle, with E the son of Uzziel
34:25 of Zebulun a leader, E the son of Parnach.
1Chr 15:8 of the sons of E, Shemaiah the chief, with
2Chr 29:13 of the sons of E, Shimri and Jeuel; and

ELIAB (22)
Num 1:9 of Zuar; from Zebulun, E the son of Helon;
2:7 people of Zebulun being E the son of Helon,
7:24 On the third day E the son of Helon,
7:29 was the offering of E the son of Helon.
10:16 men of Zebulun was E the son of Helon.
16:1 Abiram the sons of E, and On the son
16:12 Abiram the sons of E; and they said, "We
26:8 And the sons of Pallu: E
26:9 The sons of E: Nemuel, Dathan, and Abiram.
Deut 11:6 Abiram the sons of E, son of Reuben; how
1Sam 16:6 came, he looked on E and thought, "Surely the
17:13 to the battle were E the first-born, and next
17:28 Now E his eldest brother heard when he spoke
17:28 to the men; and E's anger was kindled against
1Chr 2:13 was the father of E his first-born, Abinadab the
6:27 son, Nahath his son, E his son, Jeroham his
12:9 the chief, Obadiah second, E third,
15:18 Ja-aziel, Shemiramoth, Jehiel, Unni, E, Benaiah,
15:20 Azi-el, Shemiramoth, Jehiel, Unni, E, Ma-aseiah, and
16:5 Je-iel, Shemiramoth, Jehiel, Mattithiah, E, Benaiah,
2Chr 11:18 Abihail the daughter of E the son of Jesse;
Jud 8:1 of Hilkiah, son of E, son of Nathanael, son

ELIADA (4)
2Sam 5:16 Elishu-a, Nepheg, Japhia, Elishama, E, and
1Kgs 11:23 Rezon the son of E, who had fled from
1Chr 3:8 Nogah, Nepheg, Japhia, Elishama, E, and Eliphelet,
2Chr 17:17 Of Benjamin: E, a mighty man of valor, with

ELIAHBA (2)
2Sam 23:32 Arbathite, Azmaveth of Bahurim, E of Sha-albon, the
1Chr 11:33 Arbathite, Azmaveth of Baharum, E of Sha-albon,

ELIAKIM (15)
2Kgs 18:18 came out to them E the son of Hilkiah,
18:26 Then E the son of Hilkiah, and Shebnah, and
18:37 Then E the son of Hilkiah, who was over
19:2 And he sent E, who was over the household,
23:34 And Pharaoh Neco made E the son of Josiah
2Chr 36:4 king of Egypt made E his brother king over
Neh 12:41 me; and the priests E, Ma-aseiah, Miniamin,
Is 22:20 will call my servant E the son of Hilkiah,
36:3 came out to him E the son of Hilkiah,
36:11 Then E, Shebna, and Joah said to the Rabshakeh,
36:22 Then E the son of Hilkiah, who was over
37:2 And he sent E, who was over the household,
Mt 1:13 Abiud the father of E, and Eliakim the father
1:13 father of Eliakim, and E the father of Azor,
Lk 3:30 Jonam, the son of E,

ELIAM (2)
2Sam 11:3 Bathsheba, the daughter of E, the wife of Uriah
23:34 of Ahasbai of Maacah, E the son of Ahithophel

ELIASAPH (6)
Num 1:14 of Ochran; from Gad, E the son of Deuel;
2:14 people of Gad being E the son of Reuel,
3:24 on the west, with E, the son of Lael
7:42 On the sixth day E the son of Deuel,
7:47 was the offering of E the son of Deuel.
10:20 men of Gad was E the son of Deuel.

ELIASHIB (17)
1Chr 3:24 Eli-o-enai: Hodaviah, E, Pelaiah, Akkub, Johanan, D
24:12 Shecaniah, the eleventh to E, the twelfth to Jakim,
Ezra 10:6 Jehohanan the son of E, where he spent the
10:24 Of the singers: E
10:27 sons of Zattu: Eli-o-enai, E, Mattaniah, Jeremoth,
10:36 Bedeiah, Cheluhi, Vaniah, Meremoth, E,
Neh 3:1 Then E the high priest rose up with his
3:20 of the house of E the high priest.
3:21 of the house of E to the end of
3:21 Eliashib to the end of the house of E
12:10 Joiakim the father of E, Eliashib the father of
12:10 the father of Eliashib, E the father of Joiada,
12:22 in the days of E, Joiada, Johanan, and Jaddu-a,
12:23 until the days of Johanan the son of E
13:4 Now before this, E the priest, who was appointed
13:7 discovered the evil that E had done for Tobiah,
13:28 Jehoiada, the son of E the high priest, was

ELIATHAH (2)
1Chr 25:4 and Jerimoth, Hananiah, Hanani, E, Giddalti, and
25:27 to the twentieth, to E, his sons and his

ELIDAD
Num 34:21 the tribe of Benjamin, E the son of Chislon.

ELIEL (10)
1Chr 5:24 fathers' houses: Epher, Ishi, E, Azriel, Jeremiah,
6:34 of Jeroham, son of E, son of Toah,
8:20 Zichri, Zabdi, Eli-enai, Zillethai, E,
8:22 Ishpan, Eber, E,
11:46 his brother, the Tizite, E the Mahavite, and Jeribai,
11:47 and Ithmah the Moabite, E, and Obed, and Jaasiel
12:11 Jeremiah fifth, Attai sixth, E seventh,
15:9 the sons of Hebron, E the chief, with eighty
15:11 Uriel, Asaiah, Joel, Shemaiah, E, and Amminadab,
2Chr 31:13 Nahath, Asahel, Jerimoth, Jozabad, E, Ismachiah,

ELIEZER (15)
Gen 15:2 of my house is E of Damascus?"
Ex 18:4 name of the other, E (for he said, "The
1Chr 7:8 of Becher: Zemirah, Joash, E, Eli-o-enai, Omri,
15:24 Amasai, Zechariah, Benaiah, and E, the priests,
23:15 The sons of Moses: Gershom and E
23:17 The sons of E: Rehabiah the chief; Eliezer had
23:17 Eliezer: Rehabiah the chief; E had no other sons,
26:25 His brethren: from E were his son Rehabiah, and
27:16 Israel, for the Reubenites E the son of Zichri
2Chr 20:37 Then E the son of Do-davahu of Mareshah
Ezra 8:16 Then I sent for E, Ariel, Shemaiah, Elnathan, Jarib,
10:18 women were found Ma-aseiah, E, Jarib, and
10:23 Kelaiah (that is, Kelita), Pethahiah, Judah, and E
10:31 the sons of Harim: E, Isshijah, Malchijah, Shemaiah,
Lk 3:29 Joshua, the son of E, the son of Jorim,

ELIGIBLE
Tob 6:11 you are her only E kinsman.

ELIHOREPH

1Kgs	4:3	Zadok was the priest; E and Ahijah the sons

ELIHU (11)

1Sam	1:1	of Jeroham, son of E, son of Tohu, son
1Chr	12:20	Jedia-el, Michael, Jozabad, E, and Zillethai, chiefs
	26:7	brethren were able men, E and Semachiah.
	27:18	Aaron, Zadok; for Judah, E, one of David's brothers;
Job	32:2	Then E the son of Barachel the Buzite, of
	32:4	Now E had waited to speak to Job because
	32:5	And when E saw that there was no answer
	32:6	And E the son of Barachel the Buzite answered:
	34:1	Then E said:
	35:1	And E said:
	36:1	And E continued, and said:

ELIJAH (106)

1Kgs	17:1	Now E the Tishbite, of Tishbe in Gilead, said
	17:13	And E said to her, "Fear not; go and
	17:15	went and did as E said; and she, and
	17:16	word of the LORD which he spoke by E
	17:18	And she said to E, "What have you against
	17:22	to the voice of E; and the soul of
	17:23	And E took the child, and brought him down
	17:23	to his mother; and E said, "See, your son
	17:24	the woman said to E, "Now I know that
	18:1	the LORD came to E, in the third year,
	18:2	So E went to show himself to Ahab.
	18:7	on the way, behold, E met him; and Obadiah
	18:7	face, and said, "Is it you, my lord E
	18:8	tell your lord, 'Behold, E is here.'"
	18:11	tell your lord, "Behold, E is here."'
	18:14	tell your lord, "Behold, E is here"'; and he
	18:15	And E said, "As the LORD of hosts lives,
	18:16	and told him; and Ahab went to meet E
	18:17	When Ahab saw E, Ahab said to him, "Is
	18:21	And E came near to all the people, and
	18:22	Then E said to the people, "I, even I
	18:25	Then E said to the prophets of Baal, "Choose
	18:27	And at noon E mocked them, saying, "Cry aloud,
	18:30	Then E said to all the people, "Come near
	18:31	had been thrown down; E took twelve stones,
	18:36	offering of the oblation, E the prophet came near
	18:40	And E said to them, "Seize the prophets of
	18:40	they seized them; and E brought them down to
	18:41	And E said to Ahab, "Go up, eat and
	18:42	And E went up to the top of Carmel;
	18:46	the LORD was on E; and he girded up
	19:1	told Jezebel all that E had done, and how
	19:2	sent a messenger to E, saying, "So may the
	19:9	said to him, "What are you doing here, E
	19:13	And when E heard it, he wrapped his face
	19:13	him, and said, "What are you doing here, E
	19:19	E passed by him and cast his mantle upon
	19:20	oxen, and ran after E, and said, "Let me
	19:21	arose and went after E, and ministered to him.
	21:17	the LORD came to E the Tishbite, saying,
	21:20	Ahab said to E, "Have you found me, O
	21:28	the LORD came to E the Tishbite, saying,
2Kgs	1:3	the LORD said to E the Tishbite, "Arise, go
	1:4	So E went.
	1:8	he said, "It is E the Tishbite."
	1:9	He went up to E, who was sitting on
	1:10	But E answered the captain of fifty, "If I
	1:12	But E answered them, "If I am a man
	1:13	on his knees before E, and entreated him, "O
	1:15	the LORD said to E, "Go down with him;
	1:17	of the LORD which E had spoken.
	2:1	was about to take E up to heaven by
	2:1	heaven by a whirlwind, E and Elisha were on
	2:2	And E said to Elisha, "Tarry here, I pray
	2:4	E said to him, "Elisha, tarry here, I pray
	2:6	Then E said to him, "Tarry here, I pray
	2:8	Then E took his mantle, and rolled it up,
	2:9	When they had crossed, E said to Elisha, "Ask
	2:11	And E went up by a whirlwind into heaven.
	2:13	up the mantle of E that had fallen from
	2:14	took the mantle of E that had fallen from
	2:14	saying, "Where is the LORD, the God of E
	2:15	said, "The spirit of E rests on Elisha." And
	3:11	here, who poured water on the hands of E
	9:36	spoke by his servant E the Tishbite, 'In the
	10:10	has done what he said by his servant E
	10:17	word of the LORD which he spoke to E
1Chr	8:27	Shamsherai, Shehariah, Athaliah, Ja-areshiah, E,
2Chr	21:12	came to him from E the prophet, saying, "Thus
Ezra	10:21	sons of Harim: Ma-aseiah, E, Shemaiah, Jehiel,
	10:26	Zechariah, Jehiel, Abdi, Jeremoth, and E
Jud	8:1	of Ahitub, son of E, son of Hilkiah, son
Sir	48:1	Then the prophet E arose like a fire, and
	48:4	glorious you were, O E, in your wondrous deeds!
	48:12	It was E who was covered by the whirlwind,
Mal	4:5	I will send you E the prophet before the
1Mac	2:58	E because of great zeal for the law was
Mt	11:14	accept it, he is E who is to come.
	16:14	the Baptist, others say E, and others Jeremiah or
	17:3	to them Moses and E, talking with him.
	17:4	you and one for Moses and one for E
	17:10	scribes say that first E must come?"
	17:11	He replied, E does come, and he is to
	17:12	I tell you that E has already come, and
	27:47	bystanders hearing it said, "This man is calling E
	27:49	let us see whether E will come to save
Mk	6:15	But others said, "It is E
	8:28	Baptist; and others say, E; and others one of
	9:4	there appeared to them E with Moses; and they
	9:5	you and one for Moses and one for E
	9:11	scribes say that first E must come?"
	9:12	he said to them, E does come first to
	9:13	I tell you that E has come, and they
	15:34	bystanders hearing it said, "Behold, he is calling E
	15:35	let us see whether E will come to take
Lk	1:17	spirit and power of E, to turn the hearts
	4:25	in the days of E, when the heaven was
	4:26	all the land; and E was sent to none
	9:8	dead, by some that E had appeared, and by
	9:19	Baptist; but others say, E; and others, that one
	9:30	with him, Moses and E,
	9:33	Moses and one for E --not knowing what he
Jn	1:21	Are you E
	1:25	neither the Christ, nor E, nor the prophet?"
Rom	11:2	the scripture says of E, how he pleads with
Jas	5:17	E was a man of like nature with ourselves

ELIKA

2Sam	23:25	Bethlehem, Shammah of Harod, E of Harod,

ELIM (6)

Ex	15:27	Then they came to E, where there were twelve
	16:1	They set out from E, and all the congregation
	16:1	Sin, which is between E and Sinai, on the
Num	33:9	Marah, and came to E; at Elim there were
	33:9	came to Elim; at E there were twelve springs
	33:10	they set out from E, and encamped by the

ELIMELECH (6)

Ruth	1:2	of the man was E and the name of
	1:3	But E, the husband of Naomi, died, and she
	2:1	of the family of E, whose name was Boaz.
	2:3	to Boaz, who was of the family of E
	4:3	parcel of land which belonged to our kinsman E
	4:9	all that belonged to E and all that belonged

ELIPHAL

1Chr	11:35	of Sachar the Hararite, E the son of Ur,

ELIPHAZ (15)

Gen	36:4	Adah bore to Esau, E; Basemath bore Reuel;
	36:10	names of Esau's sons: E the son of Adah
	36:11	The sons of E were Teman, Omar, Zepho, Gatam,
	36:12	was a concubine of E, Esau's son; she bore
	36:12	she bore Amalek to E These are the sons
	36:15	The sons of E the first-born of Esau: the
	36:16	are the chiefs of E in the land of
1Chr	1:35	The sons of Esau: E, Reuel, Jeush, Jalam, and
	1:36	The sons of E: Teman, Omar, Zephi, Gatam, Kenaz,
Job	2:11	from his own place, E the Temanite, Bildad the
	4:1	Then E the Temanite answered:
	15:1	Then E the Temanite answered:
	22:1	Then E the Temanite answered:
	42:7	the LORD said to E the Temanite: "My wrath
	42:9	So E the Temanite and Bildad the Shuhite and

ELIPHELEHU (2)

1Chr	15:18	Eliab, Benaiah, Ma-aseiah, Mattithiah, E, and
	15:21	but Mattithiah, E, Mikneiah, Obed-edom, Je-iel, and

ELIPHELET (8)

2Sam	5:16	Elishu-a, Nepheg, Japhia, Elishama, Eliada, and E
	23:34	of Sharar the Hararite, E the son of Ahasbai
1Chr	3:6	Ammiel; then Ibhar, Elishama, E,
	3:8	Japhia, Elishama, Eliada, and E, nine.

8:39 Jeush the second, and E the third.
14:7 Nogah, Nepheg, Japhia, Elishama, Beeliada, and E
Ezra 8:13 later, their names being E, Jeuel, and Shemaiah, and
10:33 Hashum: Mattenai, Mattattah, Zabad, E, Jeremai,

ELISHA (63)

1Kgs 19:16 king over Israel; and E the son of Shaphat
19:17 sword of Jehu shall E slay.
19:19 from there, and found E the son of Shaphat,
2Kgs 2:1 a whirlwind, Elijah and E were on their way
2:2 And Elijah said to E, "Tarry here, I pray
2:2 But E said, "As the LORD lives, and as
2:3 Bethel came out to E, and said to him,
2:4 Elijah said to him, E, tarry here, I pray
2:5 Jericho drew near to E, and said to him,
2:9 crossed, Elijah said to E, "Ask what I shall
2:9 And E said, "I pray you, let me inherit
2:12 And E saw it and he cried, "My father,
2:14 to the other; and E went over.
2:15 they said, "The spirit of Elijah rests on E
2:19 the city said to E, "Behold, the situation of
2:22 to the word which E spoke.
3:11 of Israel's servants answered, E the son of Shaphat
3:13 And E said to the king of Israel, "What
3:14 And E said, "As the LORD of hosts lives,
4:1 the prophets cried to E, "Your servant my husband
4:2 And E said to her, "What shall I do
4:8 One day E went on to Shunem, where a
4:17 the following spring, as E had said to her.
4:32 When E came into the house, he saw the
4:38 And E came again to Gilgal when there was
4:42 And E said, "Give to the men, that they
5:8 But when E the man of God heard that
5:9 at the door of E's house.
5:10 And E sent a messenger to him, saying, "Go
5:20 Gehazi, the servant of E the man of God,
5:25 before his master, and E said to him, "Where
6:1 the prophets said to E, "See, the place where
6:12 lord, O king; but E, the prophet who is
6:17 Then E prayed, and said, "O LORD, I pray
6:17 of horses and chariots of fire round about E
6:18 came down against him, E prayed to the LORD,
6:18 with blindness in accordance with the prayer of E
6:19 And E said to them, "This is not the
6:20 as they entered Samaria, E said, "O LORD, open
6:21 them he said to E, "My father, shall I
6:31 if the head of E the son of Shaphat
6:32 E was sitting in his house, and the elders
6:32 before the messenger arrived E said to the elders,
7:1 But E said, "Hear the word of the LORD:
8:1 Now E had said to the woman whose son
8:4 the great things that E has done."
8:5 telling the king how E had restored the dead
8:5 is her son whom E restored to life."
8:7 Now E came to Damascus.
8:10 And E said to him, "Go, say to him,
8:13 E answered, "The LORD has shown me that you
8:14 Then he departed from E, and came to his
8:14 to him, "What did E say to you?" And
9:1 Then E the prophet called one of the sons
13:14 Now when E had fallen sick with the illness
13:15 And E said to him, "Take a bow and
13:16 And E laid his hands upon the king's hands.
13:17 Then E said, "Shoot"; and he shot.
13:20 So E died, and they buried him.
13:21 into the grave of E; and as soon as
13:21 touched the bones of E, he revived, and stood
Sir 48:12 by the whirlwind, and E was filled with his
Lk 4:27 time of the prophet E; and none of them

ELISHAH (3)

Gen 10:4 The sons of Javan: E, Tarshish, Kittim, and Dodanim.
1Chr 1:7 The sons of Javan: E, Tarshish, Kittim, and Rodanim.
Ezek 27:7 from the coasts of E was your awning.

ELISHAMA (17)

Num 1:10 of Joseph, from Ephraim, E the son of Ammihud,
2:18 people of Ephraim being E the son of Ammihud,
7:48 On the seventh day E the son of Ammihud,
7:53 was the offering of E the son of Ammihud.
10:22 over their host was E the son of Ammihud.
2Sam 5:16 Ibhar, Elishu-a, Nepheg, Japhia, E, Eliada, and
2Kgs 25:25 of Nethaniah, son of E, of the royal family,
1Chr 2:41 was the father of Jekamiah, and Jekamiah of E
3:6 of Ammiel; then Ibhar, E, Eliphelet,
3:8 Nogah, Nepheg, Japhia, E, Eliada, and Eliphelet,
7:26 son, Ammihud his son, E his son,
14:7 Nogah, Nepheg, Japhia, E, Beeliada, and Eliphelet.
2Chr 17:8 these Levites, the priests E and Jehoram.
Jer 36:12 princes were sitting there: E the secretary, Delaiah
36:20 in the chamber of E the secretary; and they
36:21 from the chamber of E the secretary; and Jehudi
41:1 of Nethaniah, son of E, of the royal family,

ELISHAPHAT

2Chr 23:1 son of Adaiah, and E the son of Zichri.

ELISHEBA

Ex 6:23 Aaron took to wife E, the daughter of Amminadab

ELISHU-A (2)

2Sam 5:15 Shobab, Nathan, Solomon, Ibhar, E, Nepheg, Japhia,
1Chr 14:5 Shobab, Nathan, Solomon, Ibhar, E, Elpelet,

ELIUD (2)

Mt 1:14 Achim the father of E,
1:15 father of Eliud, and E the father of Eleazar,

ELIXIR

Sir 6:16 faithful friend is an E of life; and those

ELIZABETH (9)

Lk 1:5 the daughters of Aaron, and her name was E
1:7 had no child, because E was barren, and both
1:13 heard, and your wife E will bear you a
1:24 these days his wife E conceived, and for five
1:36 And behold, your kinswoman E in her old age
1:40 she entered the house of Zechariah and greeted E
1:41 And when E heard the greeting of Mary, the
1:41 in her womb; and E was filled with the
1:57 the time came for E to be delivered, and

ELIZUR (5)

Num 1:5 From Reuben, E the son of Shedeur;
2:10 people of Reuben being E the son of Shedeur,
7:30 On the fourth day E the son of Shedeur,
7:35 was the offering of E the son of Shedeur.
10:18 over their host was E the son of Shedeur.

ELKANAH (20)

Ex 6:24 sons of Korah: Assir, E, and Abiasaph; these are
1Sam 1:1 Ephraim, whose name was E the son of Jeroham,
1:4 On the day when E sacrificed, he would give
1:8 And E, her husband, said to her, "Hannah, why
1:19 And E knew Hannah his wife, and the LORD
1:21 And the man E and all his house went
1:23 E her husband said to her, "Do what seems
2:11 Then E went home to Ramah.
2:20 Then Eli would bless E and his wife, and
1Chr 6:23 son, Assir his son, E his son, Ebiasaph his
6:25 The sons of E: Amasai and Ahimoth,
6:26 Elkanah: Amasai and Ahimoth, E his son, Zophai his
6:27 son, Jeroham his son, E his son.
6:34 of Samuel, son of E, son of Jeroham, son
6:35 of Zuph, son of E, son of Mahath, son
6:36 of Amasai, son of E, son of Joel, son
9:16 of Asa, son of E, who dwelt in the
12:6 Haruphite; E, Isshiah, Azarel, Jo-ezer,
15:23 Berechiah and E were to be gatekeepers for the
2Chr 28:7 of the palace and E the next in authority

ELKIAH

Jud 8:1 of Oziel, son of E, son of Ananias, son

ELKOSH

Nah 1:1 The book of the vision of Nah of E

ELLASAR (2)

Gen 14:1 Shinar, Arioch king of E, Ched-or-laomer king of
14:9 and Arioch king of E, four kings against five.

ELMADAM

Lk 3:28 Cosam, the son of E, the son of Er,

ELNA-AM

1Chr 11:46 Joshaviah, the sons of E, and Ithmah the Moabite,

ELNATHAN (7)

2Kgs 24:8 Nehushta the daughter of E of Jerusalem.
Ezra 8:16 for Eliezer, Ariel, Shemaiah, E, Jarib, Elnathan,
8:16 Ariel, Shemaiah, Elnathan, Jarib, E, Nathan,
8:16 and for Joiarib and E, who were men of

Jer 26:22 to Egypt certain men, E the son of Achbor
36:12 the son of Shemaiah, E the son of Achbor,
36:25 Even when E and Delaiah and Gemariah urged the

ELO-I (2)
Mk 15:33 with a loud voice, E, E lama sabach-thani?"

ELON (7)
Gen 26:34 Basemath the daughter of E the Hittite;
36:2 Adah the daughter of E the Hittite, Oholibamah the
46:14 sons of Zebulun: Sered, E, and Jahleel
Num 26:26 of the Seredites; of E, the family of the
Josh 19:43 Sha-alabbin, Aijalon, Ithlah, E, Timnah, Ekron,
Judg 12:11 After him E the Zebulunite judged Israel; and he
12:12 Then E the Zebulunite died, and was buried at

ELONBETH-HANAN
1Kgs 4:9 Makaz, Sha-albim, Beth-shemesh, and E;

ELONITES
Num 26:26 the family of the E; of Jahleel, the family

ELOQUENT (4)
Ex 4:10 Lord, I am not E, either heretofore or since
Esth 14:13 Put E speech in my mouth before the lion,
Acts 18:24 He was an E man, well versed in the
1Cor 1:17 gospel, and not with E wisdom, lest the cross

ELOTH (3)
1Kgs 9:26 Ezion-geber, which is near E on the shore of
2Chr 8:17 went to Ezion-geber and E on the shore of
26:2 He built E and restored it to Judah, after

ELPAAL (3)
1Chr 8:11 He also had sons by Hushim: Abitub and E
8:12 The sons of E: Eber, Misham, and Shemed, who
8:18 Ishmerai, Izliah, and Jobab were the sons of E

ELPELET
1Chr 14:5 Nathan, Solomon, Ibhar, Elishu-a, E,

ELSE (40)
Gen 19:12 "Have you any one E here?
42:16 truth in you; or E, by the life of
Ex 8:21 E, if you will not let my people go,
22:27 his body; in what E shall he sleep?
Num 1:51 And if any one E comes near, he shall
3:10 but if any one E comes near, he shall
3:38 Israel; and any one E who came near was
6:21 Nazirite, apart from what E he can afford; in
18:4 tent; and no one E shall come near you.
18:7 gift, and any one E who comes near shall
Deut 20:14 the cattle, and everything E in the city, all
Judg 21:22 give them to them, E you would now be
2Sam 3:35 taste bread or anything E till the sun goes
15:14 let us flee; or E there will be no
1Kgs 3:18 there was no one E with us in the
19:7 said, "Arise and eat, E the journey will be
20:39 for his life, or E you shall pay a
21:6 vineyard for money; or E, if it please you,
1Chr 21:12 enemies overtakes you; or E three days of the
Ezra 7:20 And whatever E is required for the house of
Neh 2:2 This is nothing E but sadness of the heart."
Job 32:22 know how to flatter, E would my Maker soon
Ps 32:9 with bit and bridle, E it will not keep
Jer 9:7 test them, for what E can I do, because
19:11 will be no place E to bury.
Dan 14:12 we will die; or E Daniel will, who is
14:29 over to us, or E we will kill you
Joel 2:27 LORD, am your God and there is none E
Zeph 2:15 to herself, "I am and there is none E
1Mac 15:31 borders of Judea; or E give me for them
Lk 22:56 little later some one E saw him and said,
Jn 14:11 Father in me; or E believe me for the
15:24 works which no one E did, they would not
Acts 4:12 salvation in no one E, for there is no
8:34 say this, about himself or about some one E
24:19 Or E let these men themselves say what wrongdoing
Rom 8:39 nor depth, nor anything E in all creation, will
1Cor 1:16 I baptized any one E
7:11 her remain single or E be reconciled to her
1Tim 1:10 liars, perjurers, and whatever E is contrary to sound

ELSEWHERE (3)
2Chr 26:6 territory of Ashdod and E among the Philistines.
Ps 84:10 in thy courts is better than a thousand E

Jer 7:32 bury in Topheth, because there is no room E

ELTEKE
Josh 21:23 the tribe of Dan, E with its pasture lands,

ELTEKEH
Josh 19:44 Elon, Timnah, Ekron, E, Gibbethon, Baalath,

ELTEKON
Josh 15:59 Gedor, Maarath, Beth-anoth, and E: six cities with

ELTOLAD (2)
Josh 15:30 Baalah, Iim, Ezem, E, Chesil, Hormah,
19:4 Hazar-shual, Balah, Ezem, E, Bethul, Hormah,

ELUDED (2)
1Sam 19:10 the spear; but he E Saul, so that he
1Mac 9:47 strike Bacchides, but he E him and went to

ELUL (2)
Neh 6:15 day of the month E, in fifty-two days.
1Mac 14:27 the eighteenth day of E, in the one hundred

ELUZAI
1Chr 12:5 Johanan, Jozabad of Gederah, E, Jerimoth, Bealiah,

ELYMAEANS
Jud 1:6 and in the plain where Arioch ruled the E

ELYMAIS (2)
Tob 2:10 took care of me until he went to E
1Mac 6:1 when he heard that E in Persia was a

ELYMAS
Acts 13:8 But E the magician (for that is the meaning

ELZABAD (2)
1Chr 12:12 Eliel seventh, Johanan eighth, E ninth,
26:7 Othni, Repha-el, Obed, and E, whose brethren were

ELZAPHAN (2)
Ex 6:22 sons of Uzziel: Mishael, E, and Sithri.
Lev 10:4 Moses called Mishael and E, the sons of Uzziel

EMANATION
Wis 7:25 God, and a pure E of the glory of

EMBALM
Gen 50:2 servants the physicians to E his father.

EMBALMED (2)
Gen 50:2 So the physicians E Israel;
50:26 years old; and they E him, and he was

EMBALMING
Gen 50:3 for it, for so many are required for E

EMBARK
2Mac 12:3 lived among them to E, with their wives and

EMBARKED (2)
1Mac 15:37 Now Trypho E on a ship and escaped to
2Mac 5:9 died in exile, having E to go to the

EMBARKING
Acts 27:2 And E in a ship of Adramyttium, which was

EMBASSY (2)
Lk 14:32 off, he sends an E and asks terms of
19:14 him and sent an E after him, saying, 'We

EMBERS
Prov 26:21 As charcoal to hot E and wood to fire,

EMBITTERED (2)
Ps 73:21 When my soul was E, when I was pricked
1Mac 3:7 He E many kings, but he made Jacob glad

EMBODIMENT
Rom 2:20 in the law the E of knowledge and truth—

EMBRACE (6)
Gen 16:5 my maid to your E, and when she saw
2Kgs 4:16 comes round, you shall E a son." And she
Jud 12:12 if we do not E her she will laugh
Prov 4:9 honor you if you E her.

5:20 a loose woman and E the bosom of an
Eccl 3:5 together; a time to E, and a time to

EMBRACED (10)
Gen 29:13 to meet him, and E him and kissed him,
33:4 to meet him, and E him, and fell on
48:10 he kissed them and E them.
Tob 11:9 to meet them, and E her son, and said
11:14 saw his son and E him, and he wept
Esth 15:12 her neck; and he E her, and said, "Speak
Song 2:6 that his right hand E me!
8:3 that his right hand E me!
Lk 15:20 compassion, and ran and E him and kissed him.
Acts 20:37 they all wept and E Paul and kissed him,

EMBRACES
Sir 30:20 like a eunuch who E a maiden and groans.

EMBRACING (3)
Eccl 3:5 time to refrain from E;
Dan 13:39 We saw them E, but we could not hold
Acts 20:10 bent over him, and E him said, "Do not

EMBROIDERED (15)
Ex 26:36 and fine twined linen, E with needlework.
27:16 and fine twined linen, E with needlework; it shall
28:39 shall make a girdle E with needlework.
36:37 and fine twined linen, E with needlework;
38:18 of the court was E with needlework in blue
39:29 purple and scarlet stuff, E with needlework; as the
Judg 5:30 spoil of dyed stuffs E, two pieces of dyed
5:30 pieces of dyed work E for my neck as
Ezek 16:10 clothed you also with E cloth and shod you
16:13 linen, and silk, and E cloth; you ate fine
16:18 and you took your E garments to cover them,
26:16 and strip off their E garments; they will clothe
27:7 Of fine E linen from Egypt was your sail,
27:16 your wares emeralds, purple, E work, fine linen,
27:24 clothes of blue and E work, and in carpets

EMBROIDERER (3)
Ex 35:35 designer or by an E in blue and purple
38:23 craftsman and designer and E in blue and purple
Sir 45:10 the work of an E; with the oracle of

EMEK-KEZIZ
Josh 18:21 families were Jericho, Beth-hoglah, E,

EMERALD (6)
Ex 28:18 the second row an E, a sapphire, and a
39:11 the second row, an E, a sapphire, and a
Sir 32:6 A seal of E in a rich setting of
Ezek 28:13 onyx, sapphire, carbuncle, and E; and wrought in
Rev 4:3 throne was a rainbow that looked like an E
21:19 third agate, the fourth E,

EMERALDS (3)
Tob 13:16 built with sapphires and E, her walls with precious
Jud 10:21 purple and gold and E and precious stones.
Ezek 27:16 exchanged for your wares E, purple, embroidered

EMERGED (2)
1Mac 9:23 of Judas, the lawless E in all parts of
11:69 the men in ambush E from their places and

EMERGING
Wis 19:7 camp, and dry land E where water had stood

EMIM (3)
Gen 14:5 Zuzim in Ham, the E in Shaveh-kiriathaim,
Deut 2:10 for a possession.' (The E formerly lived there, a
2:11 known as Rephaim, but the Moabites call them E

EMINENCE (2)
Ps 62:4 only plan to thrust him down from his E
Sir 38:33 nor do they attain E in the public assembly.

EMINENT (3)
Sir 10:21 The rich, and the E, and the poor--
Lk 14:8 honor, lest a more E man than you be
Rom 16:13 Greet Rufus, E in the Lord, also his mother

EMINENTLY
2Mac 13:8 And this was E just; because he had committed

EMISSION (4)
Lev 15:16 a man has an E of semen, he shall
15:18 woman and has an E of semen, both of
15:32 him who has an E of semen, becoming unclean
22:4 who has had an E of semen,

EMMANUEL
Mt 1:23 a son, and his name shall be called E

EMMAUS (5)
1Mac 3:40 arrived they encamped near E in the plain.
3:57 marched out and encamped to the south of E
4:3 the king's force in E
9:50 fortress in Jericho, and E, and Beth-horon, and
Lk 24:13 to a village named E, about seven miles from

EMPEROR (4)
Acts 25:21 the decision of the E, I commanded him to
25:25 himself appealed to the E, I decided to send
1Pet 2:13 it be to the E as supreme,
2:17 Honor the E

EMPLOY
1Pet 4:10 has received a gift, E it for one another,

EMPLOYED (2)
2Mac 1:13 Nanea by a deception E by the priests of
1Cor 9:13 that those who are E in the temple service

EMPLOYEE
Sir 34:22 him; to deprive an E of his wages is

EMPTIED (10)
Gen 24:20 So she quickly E her jar into the trough
42:35 As they E their sacks, behold, every man's bundle
2Sam 13:9 took the pan and E it out before him,
2Kgs 22:9 king, "Your servants have E out the money that
2Chr 34:17 They have E out the money that was found
Neh 5:13 So may he be shaken out and E
Is 19:3 within them will be E out, and I will
Jer 48:11 he has not been E from vessel to vessel,
1Cor 1:17 cross of Christ be E of its power.
Phil 2:7 to be grasped, but E himself, taking the form

EMPTINESS (4)
Job 7:3 am allotted months of E, and nights of misery
15:31 him not trust in E, deceiving himself; for emptiness
15:31 emptiness, deceiving himself; for E will be his
Is 40:17 accounted by him as less than nothing and E

EMPTY (44)
Gen 37:24 The pit was E, there was no water in
41:27 years, and the seven E ears blighted by the
Ex 3:21 you shall not go E,
34:20 And none shall appear before me E
Lev 14:36 shall command that they E the house before the
Judg 7:16 all of them and E jars, with torches inside
Ruth 1:21 full, and the LORD has brought me back E
1Sam 6:3 do not send it E, but by all means
20:18 will be missed, because your seat will be E
20:25 sat by Saul's side, but David's place was E
20:27 morrow after the new moon, David's place was E
2Sam 1:22 back, and the sword of Saul returned not E
2Kgs 4:3 of all your neighbors, E vessels and not too
2Chr 24:11 priest would come and E the chest and take
Jud 7:20 inhabitant of Bethulia were E;
Job 21:34 you comfort me with E nothings?
22:9 have sent widows away E, and the arms of
35:13 does not hear an E cry, nor does the
35:16 opens his mouth in E talk, he multiplies words
Ps 41:6 see me, he utters E words, while his heart
Eccl 5:7 For when dreams increase, E words grow many: but
11:3 full of rain, they E themselves on the earth;
Wis 2:3 spirit will dissolve like E air.
Sir 29:9 of his need do not send him away E
Is 29:21 gate, and with an E plea turn aside him
30:7 help is worthless and E, therefore I have called
41:29 their molten images are E wind.
55:11 not return to me E, but it shall accomplish
59:4 honestly; they rely on E pleas, they speak lies,
Jer 14:3 return with their vessels E; they are ashamed and
48:12 will tilt him, and E his vessels, and break
51:2 her, and they shall E her land, when they
51:34 has made me an E vessel, he has swallowed
Ezek 24:10 well the flesh, and E out the broth, and
24:11 Then set it E upon the coals, that it

Hos 10:4 utter mere words; with E oaths they make
Zech 10:2 false dreams, and give E consolation.
2Mac 14:44 the middle of the E space.
Mt 6:7 do not heap up E phrases as the Gentiles
12:44 comes he finds it E, swept, and put in
Lk 1:53 rich he has sent E away.
Eph 5:6 one deceive you with E words, for it is
Col 2:8 you by philosophy and E deceit, according to human
Tit 1:9 are many insubordinate men, E talkers and

EMPTY-HANDED (11)
Gen 31:42 surely now you would have sent me away E
Ex 23:15 None shall appear before me E
Deut 15:13 not let him go E;
16:16 appear before the LORD E;
Ruth 3:17 must not go back E to your mother-in-law.'"
Jud 1:11 sent back his messengers E and shamefaced.
Sir 35:4 appear before the Lord E,
Jer 50:9 like a skilled warrior who does not return E
Mk 12:3 him and beat him, and sent him away E
Lk 20:10 the tenants beat him, and sent him away E
20:11 beat and treated shamefully, and sent him away E

EMPTYING
Hab 1:17 then to keep on E his net, and mercilessly

EN
Judg 7:3 twenty-two thousand returned, and E thousand

EN-EGLAIM
Ezek 47:10 sea; from Engedi to E it will be a

EN-GANNIM (3)
Josh 15:34 Eshtaol, Zorah, Ashnah, Zanoah, E, Tappuah, Enam,
19:21 Kishion, Ebez, Remeth, E, En-haddah, Beth-pazzez;
21:29 with its pasture lands, E with its pasture lands--

EN-GEDI
Sir 24:14 a palm tree in E, and like rose plants

EN-HADDAH
Josh 19:21 Kishion, Ebez, Remeth, En-gannim, E, Beth-pazzez;

EN-HAKKORE
Judg 15:19 of it was called E; it is at Lehi

EN-HAZOR
Josh 19:37 Ramah, Hazor, Kedesh, Edre-i, E,

EN-RIMMON (2)
Josh 19:7 cities with their villages; E, Ether, and Ashan--four
Neh 11:29 and its villages, in E, in Zorah, in Jarmuth,

EN-ROGEL (4)
Josh 15:7 En-shemesh, and ends at E;
18:16 Jebusites, and downward to E;
2Sam 17:17 Ahima-az were waiting at E; a maidservant used to
1Kgs 1:9 Stone, which is beside E, and he invited all

EN-SHEMESH (2)
Josh 15:7 to the waters of E, and ends at En-rogel;
18:17 direction going on to E, and thence goes to

EN-TAPPUAH
Josh 17:7 goes along southward to the inhabitants of E

ENABLED
Sir 42:17 The Lord has not E his holy ones to

ENABLES
Phil 3:21 by the power which E him even to subject

ENACTED
Heb 8:6 better, since it is E on better promises.

ENAIM (2)
Gen 38:14 at the entrance to E, which is on the
38:21 harlot who was at E by the wayside?" And

ENAM
Josh 15:34 Ashnah, Zanoah, En-gannim, Tappuah, E,

ENAMORED
Wis 8:2 bride, and I became E of her beauty.

ENAN (5)
Num 1:15 of Deuel; from Naphtali, Ahira the son of E
2:29 Ahira the son of E,
7:78 Ahira the son of E, the leader of the
7:83 was the offering of Ahira the son of E
10:27 men of Naphtali was Ahira the son of E

ENCAM
Ex 14:2 to turn back and E in front of Pi-ha-hiroth,

ENCAMP (26)
Ex 14:2 of Baal-zephon; you shall E over against it, by
Num 1:50 tend it, and shall E around the tabernacle.
1:53 but the Levites shall E around the tabernacle of
2:2 people of Israel shall E each by his own
2:2 fathers' houses; they shall E facing the tent of
2:3 Those to E on the east side toward the
2:5 Those to E next to him shall be the
2:12 And those to E next to him shall be
2:17 the camps; as they E, so shall they set
2:27 And those to E next to him shall be
3:23 the Gershonites were to E behind the tabernacle on
3:29 of Kohath were to E on the south side
3:35 Abihail; they were to E on the north side
3:38 And those to E before the tabernacle on the
10:31 how we are to E in the wilderness, and
31:19 E outside the camp seven days; whoever of you
Judg 6:4 attack them; they would E against them and destroy
2Sam 12:28 the people together, and E against the city, and
Job 19:12 siegeworks against me, and E round about my tent.
Ps 27:3 Though a host E against me, my heart shall
Is 29:3 And I will E against you round about, and
Jer 50:29 E round about her; let no one escape.
Zech 9:8 Then I will E at my house as a
1Mac 5:42 "Permit no man to E, but make them all
5:49 army that each should E where he was.
15:39 He commanded him to E against Judea, and

ENCAMPED (133)
Gen 26:17 departed from there, and E in the valley of
31:25 Laban with his kinsmen E in the hill country
Ex 13:20 on from Succoth, and E at Etham, on the
14:9 army, and overtook them E at the sea, by
15:27 palm trees; and they E there by the water.
18:5 wilderness where he was E at the mountain of
19:2 wilderness of Sinai, they E in the wilderness; and
19:2 wilderness; and there Israel E before the mountain.
Num 2:34 commanded Moses, so they E by their standards, and
9:17 cloud settled down, there the people of Israel E
9:18 of the LORD they E; as long as the
9:23 of the LORD they E, and at the command
12:16 out from Hazeroth, and E in the wilderness of
21:10 Israel set out, and E in Oboth.
21:11 out from Oboth, and E at Iye-abarim, in the
21:12 they set out, and E in the Valley of
21:13 they set out, and E on the other side
22:1 Israel set out, and E in the plains of
33:5 out from Rameses, and E at Succoth.
33:6 out from Succoth, and E at Etham, which is
33:7 of Baal-zephon; and they E before Migdol.
33:8 wilderness of Etham, and E at Marah.
33:9 palm trees, and they E there.
33:10 out from Elim, and E by the Red Sea.
33:11 the Red Sea, and E in the wilderness of
33:12 wilderness of Sin, and E at Dophkah.
33:13 out from Dophkah, and E at Alush.
33:14 out from Alush, and E at Rephidim, where there
33:15 out from Rephidim, and E in the wilderness of
33:16 wilderness of Sinai, and E at Kibroth-hattaavah.
33:17 out from Kibroth-hattaavah, and E at Hazeroth.
33:18 out from Hazeroth, and E at Rithmah.
33:19 out from Rithmah, and E at Rimmon-perez.
33:20 out from Rimmon-perez, and E at Libnah.
33:21 out from Libnah, and E at Rissah.
33:22 out from Rissah, and E at Kehelathah.
33:23 out from Kehelathah, and E at Mount Shepher.
33:24 from Mount Shepher, and E at Haradah.
33:25 out from Haradah, and E at Makheloth.
33:26 out from Makheloth, and E at Tahath.
33:27 out from Tahath, and E at Terah.
33:28 out from Terah, and E at Mithkah.
33:29 out from Mithkah, and E at Hashmonah.
33:30 out from Hashmonah, and E at Moseroth.
33:31 out from Moseroth, and E at Bene-jaakan.
33:32 out from Bene-jaakan, and E at Hor-haggidgad.
33:33 out from Hor-haggidgad, and E at Jotbathah.

33:34 out from Jotbathah, and E at Abronah.
33:35 out from Abronah, and E at Ezion-geber.
33:36 out from Ezion-geber, and E in the wilderness of
33:37 out from Kadesh, and E at Mount Hor, on
33:41 from Mount Hor, and E at Zalmonah.
33:42 out from Zalmonah, and E at Punon.
33:43 out from Punon, and E at Oboth.
33:44 out from Oboth, and E at Iye-abarim, in the
33:45 out from Iyim, and E at Dibon-gad.
33:46 out from Dibon-gad, and E at Almon-diblathaim.
33:47 out from Almon-diblathaim, and E in the mountains
33:48 mountains of Abarim, and E in the plains of
33:49 Jordan at Jericho; they E by the Jordan from
Josh 4:19 first month, and they E in Gilgal on the
5:10 people of Israel were E in Gilgal they kept
8:11 before the city, and E on the north side
10:5 all their armies and E against Gibeon, and made
11:5 forces, and came and E together at the waters
Judg 6:33 crossing the Jordan they E in the Valley of
7:1 him rose early and E beside the spring of
9:50 went to Thebez, and E against Thebez, and took
10:17 to arms, and they E in Gilead; and the
10:17 came together, and they E at Mizpah.
11:20 his people together, and E at Jahaz, and fought
15:9 Philistines came up and E in Judah, and made
18:12 and went up and E at Kiriath-jearim in Judah.
20:19 in the morning, and E against Gibe-ah.
1Sam 4:1 against the Philistines; they E at Ebenezer, and the
4:1 Ebenezer, and the Philistines E at Aphek.
13:5 they came up and E in Michmash, to the
13:16 Benjamin; but the Philistines E in Michmash.
17:1 belongs to Judah, and E between Socoh and Azekah,
17:2 Israel were gathered, and E in the valley of
26:3 And Saul E on the hill of Hachilah, which
26:5 place where Saul had E; and David saw the
26:5 while the army was E around him.
28:4 assembled, and came and E at Shunem; and Saul
28:4 all Israel, and they E at Gilboa.
29:1 and the Israelites were E by the fountain which
2Sam 17:26 And Israel and Absalom E in the land of
23:13 band of Philistines was E in the valley of
1Kgs 16:15 Now the troops were E against Gibbethon, which
16:16 the troops who were E heard it said, "Zimri
20:27 the people of Israel E before them like two
20:29 And they E opposite one another seven days.
1Chr 11:15 army of Philistines was E in the valley of
19:7 army, who came and E before Medeba.
2Chr 32:1 and invaded Judah and E against the fortified cities,
Ezra 8:15 Ahava, and there we E three days.
Neh 11:30 So they E from Beer-sheba to the valley of
Jud 7:3 They E in the valley near Bethulia, beside the
7:17 thousand Assyrians, and they E in the valley and
7:18 Ammon went up and E in the hill country
7:18 of the Assyrian army E in the plain, and
Is 29:1 Ho Ariel, Ariel, the city where David E
1Mac 2:32 and overtook them; they E opposite them and
3:40 when they arrived they E near Emmaus in the
3:42 that the forces were E in their territory.
3:57 army marched out and E to the south of
4:29 came into Idumea and E at Bethzur, and Judas
5:5 their towers; and he E against them, vowed their
5:37 gathered another army and E opposite Raphon, on
5:39 them, and they are E across the stream, ready
5:50 men of the forces E, and he fought against
6:26 behold, today they have E against the citadel in
6:31 came through Idumea and E against Bethzur, and for
6:32 from the citadel and E at Beth-zechariah, opposite
6:48 them, and the king E in Judea and at
6:51 Then he E before the sanctuary for many days.
7:19 departed from Jerusalem and E in Beth-zaith.
7:39 out from Jerusalem and E in Beth-horon, and the
7:40 And Judas E in Adasa with three thousand men.
9:2 leads to Gilgal and E against Mesaloth in Arbela,
9:3 and fifty-second year they E against Jerusalem;
9:5 Now Judas was E in Elasa, and with him
9:64 Then he came and E against Bethbasi; he fought
10:48 assembled large forces and E opposite Demetrius.
10:69 a large force and E against Jamnia.
10:75 He E before Joppa, but the men of the
10:86 departed from there and E against Askalon, and the
11:65 Simon E before Bethzur and fought against it for
11:67 Jonathan and his army E by the waters of
11:73 as Kadesh, to their camp, and there they E
13:13 And Simon E in Adida, facing the plain.
13:43 In those days Simon E against Gazara and
15:13 So Antiochus E against Dor, and with him were

ENCAMPING

Num 24:2 eyes, and saw Israel E tribe by tribe.

ENCAMPMENT (4)

Josh 8:13 the forces, the main E which was north of
1Sam 17:20 he came to the E as the host was
26:5 was lying within the E, while the army was
26:7 Saul sleeping within the E, with his spear stuck

ENCAMPMENTS (4)

Gen 25:16 villages and by their E, twelve princes according to
Num 24:5 tents, O Jacob, your E, O Israel!
31:10 dwelt, and all their E, they burned with fire,
Ezek 25:4 they shall set their E among you and make

ENCAMPS (2)

Ps 34:7 angel of the LORD E around those who fear
Sir 14:24 her doors; he who E near her house will

ENCHANTER (2)

Ps 58:5 the voice of charmers or of the cunning E
Dan 2:10 of any magician or E or Chaldean.

ENCHANTERS (7)

Dan 1:20 all the magicians and E that were in all
2:2 that the magicians, the E, the sorcerers, and the
2:27 king, "No wise men, E, magicians, or astrologers can
4:7 Then the magicians, the E, the Chaldeans, and the
5:7 to bring in the E, the Chaldeans, and the
5:11 chief of the magicians, E, Chaldeans, and astrologers,
5:15 the wise men, the E, have been brought in

ENCHANTMENT

Num 23:23 For there is no E against Jacob, no divination

ENCHANTMENTS (2)

Is 47:9 many sorceries and the great power of your E
47:12 Stand fast in your E and your many sorceries,

ENCIRCLE (2)

Ps 22:16 a company of evildoers E me; they have pierced
1Mac 10:11 build the walls and E Mount Zion with squared

ENCIRCLED (5)

Deut 32:10 of the wilderness; he E him, he cared for
Song 7:2 a heap of wheat, E with lilies.
Sir 45:9 And he E him with pomegranates, with very many
1Mac 12:13 and many wars have E us; the kings round
Heb 11:30 after they had been E for seven days.

ENCIRCLES

Sir 43:12 It E the heaven with its glorious arc; the

ENCLOSE (2)

Ex 28:11 of Israel; you shall E them in settings of
Song 8:9 a door, we will E her with boards of

ENCLOSED (6)

Ex 39:6 onyx stones were prepared, E in settings of gold
39:13 a jasper; they were E in settings of gold
Is 40:12 heavens with a span, E the dust of the
Ezek 1:27 the appearance of fire E round about; and downward
2Mac 1:34 investigated the matter, and E the place and made
Lk 5:6 had done this, they E a great shoal of

ENCLOSURE

Sir 50:2 walls, the high retaining walls for the temple E

ENCOMPASS (3)

Ps 22:12 Many bulls E me, strong bulls of Bashan surround
32:7 from trouble; thou dost E me with deliverance.
Hos 7:3 Now their deeds E them, they are before my

ENCOMPASSED (5)

2Sam 22:5 the waves of death E me, the torrents of
Ps 18:4 The cords of death E me, the torrents of
40:12 For evils have E me without number; my iniquities
116:3 The snares of death E me; the pangs of
Hos 11:12 Ephraim has E me with lies, and the house

ENCOMPASSES (2)

Deut 33:12 safety by him; he E him all the day
Ezek 21:14 the great slaughter, which E them,

ENCOUNTER (3)

1Mac 9:11 the camp and took its stand for the E

2Mac 15:19 being anxious over the E in the open country.
Lk 14:31 what king, going to E another king in war,

ENCOUNTERED (3)

1Mac 5:25 They E the Nabateans, who met them peaceably and
2Mac 10:17 slew those whom they E, killing no fewer than
14:17 brother of Judas, had E Nicanor, but had been

ENCOUNTERS

2Mac 8:30 In E with the forces of Timothy and Bacchides

ENCOURAGE (8)

Deut 1:38 you, he shall enter; E him, for he shall
3:28 But charge Joshua, and E and strengthen him; for
2Sam 11:25 and overthrow it.' And E him."
2Mac 11:32 also sent Menelaus to E you.
Eph 6:22 and that he may E your hearts.
Col 4:8 and that he may E your hearts,
1Thes 5:11 Therefore E one another and build one another up,
5:14 brethren, admonish the idlers, E the fainthearted, help the

ENCOURAGED (14)

2Chr 35:2 to their offices and E them in the service
Ezek 13:22 him, and you have E the wicked, that he
1Mac 12:50 his men, and they E one another and kept
13:3 the people together he E them, saying to them,
2Mac 7:5 brothers and their mother E one another to die
7:21 She E each of them in the language of
15:17 E by the words of Judas, so noble and
Acts 18:27 to Achaia, the brethren E him, and wrote to
27:36 Then they all were E and ate some food
Rom 1:12 we may be mutually E by each other's faith,
1Cor 8:10 might he not be E, if his conscience is
14:31 learn and all be E;
Col 2:2 their hearts may be E as they are knit
1Thes 2:11 one of you and E you and charged you

ENCOURAGEMENT (10)

Wis 8:9 me good counsel and E in cares and grief.
1Mac 10:24 write them words of E and promise them honor
12:9 since we have as E the holy books which
Acts 4:36 (which means, Son of E, a Levite, a native
20:2 had given them much E, he came to Greece.
Rom 15:4 steadfastness and by the E of the scriptures we
15:5 God of steadfastness and E grant you to live
1Cor 14:3 for their upbuilding and E and consolation.
Phil 2:1 if there is any E in Christ, any incentive
Heb 6:18 refuge might have strong E to seize the hope

ENCOURAGES (2)

Sir 17:19 a return, and he E those whose endurance is
Is 41:7 The craftsman E the goldsmith, and he who smooths

ENCOURAGING (3)

1Mac 5:53 rallying the laggards and E the people all the
2Mac 15:9 E them from the law and the prophets, and
Heb 10:25 habit of some, but E one another, and all

ENCOURAGINGLY (2)

2Chr 30:22 And Hezekiah spoke E to all the Levites who
32:6 the city and spoke E to them, saying,

ENCRUSTED

Song 5:14 body is ivory work, E with sapphires.

END (340)

Gen 6:13 determined to make an E of all flesh; for
8:3 At the E of a hundred and fifty days
8:6 At the E of forty days Noah opened the
23:9 it is at the E of his field.
41:53 Egypt came to an E;
47:21 of them from one E of Egypt to the
Ex 12:41 And at the E of four hundred and thirty
23:16 of ingathering at the E of the year, when
25:19 cherub on the one E, and one cherub on
25:19 cherub on the other E; of one piece with
26:28 shall pass through from E to end.
26:28 the frames, shall pass through from end to E
31:18 he had made an E of speaking with him
34:22 and the feast of ingathering at the year's E
36:33 to pass through from E to end halfway up
36:33 through from end to E halfway up the frames.
37:8 cherub on the one E, and one cherub on
37:8 cherub on the other E; of one piece with
Lev 16:20 he has made an E of atoning for the
17:5 This is to the E that the people of
Num 13:25 At the E of forty days they returned from
14:35 come to a full E, and there they shall
17:10 you may make an E of their murmurings against
23:10 righteous, and let my E be like his!"
24:20 nations, but in the E he shall come to
34:3 shall be from the E of the Salt Sea
34:4 to Zin, and its E shall be south of
34:8 of Hamath, and the E of the boundary shall
34:9 to Ziphron, and its E shall be at Hazar-enan;
34:12 the Jordan, and its E shall be at the
Deut 4:32 and ask from one E of heaven to the
7:22 may not make an E of them at once,
8:16 test you, to do you good in the E
9:11 And at the E of forty days and forty
11:12 the year to the E of the year.
13:7 you, from the one E of the earth to
14:28 "At the E of every three years you shall
15:1 "At the E of every seven years you shall
20:9 officers have made an E of speaking to the
28:49 from afar, from the E of the earth, as
28:64 all peoples, from one E of the earth to
31:10 commanded them, "At the E of every seven years,
31:24 book, to the very E,
32:20 will see what their E will be, for they
32:29 understand this, they would discern their latter E
Josh 3:2 At the E of three days the officers went
9:16 At the E of three days after they had
13:27 boundary, to the lower E of the Sea of
15:2 boundary ran from the E of the Salt Sea,
15:4 and comes to its E at the sea.
15:8 west, at the northern E of the valley of
15:11 boundary comes to an E at the sea.
18:16 is at the north E of the valley of
18:19 Sea, at the south E of the Jordan: this
Judg 11:39 And at the E of two months, she returned
Ruth 2:23 Boaz, gleaning until the E of the barley and
3:7 lie down at the E of the heap of
1Sam 3:12 spoken concerning his house, from beginning to E
2Sam 2:26 not know that the E will be bitter?
14:26 head (for at the E of every year he
15:7 And at the E of four years Absalom said
24:8 to Jerusalem at the E of nine months and
1Kgs 2:39 it happened at the E of three years that
9:10 At the E of twenty years, in which Solomon
10:20 there, one on each E of a step on
2Kgs 8:3 And at the E of the seven years, when
10:21 was filled from one E to the other.
10:25 he had made an E of offering the burnt
13:17 you have made an E of them."
13:19 you had made an E of it, but now
18:10 it and at the E of three years he
21:16 filled Jerusalem from one E to another, besides the
2Chr 8:1 At the E of twenty years, in which Solomon
9:19 there, one on each E of a step on
20:16 find them at the E of the valley, east
20:23 they had made an E of the inhabitants of
21:19 of time, at the E of two years, his
24:23 At the E of the year the army of
Ezra 9:11 have filled it from E to end with their
9:11 it from end to E with their uncleanness.
10:17 had come to the E of all the men
Neh 3:21 of Eliashib to the E of the house of
9:31 didst not make an E of them or forsake
Jud 11:21 a woman from one E of the earth to
13:6 the post at the E of the bed, above
Esth 14:13 there may be an E of him and those
Job 5:13 of the wily are brought to a quick E
6:11 And what is my E, that I should be
7:6 and come to their E without hope.
16:3 Shall windy words have an E
22:5 There is no E to your iniquities.
28:3 Men put an E to darkness, and search out
32:22 Maker soon put an E to me.
34:36 were tried to the E, because he answers like
Ps 7:9 wicked come to an E, but establish thou the
19:4 their words to the E of the world.
19:6 rising is from the E of the heavens, and
19:6 its circuit to the E of them; and there
39:4 let me know my E, and what is the
46:9 wars cease to the E of the earth; he
49:13 have foolish confidence, the E of those who are
54:5 thy faithfulness put an E to them.
61:2 my prayer; from the E of the earth I
73:17 the sanctuary of God; then I perceived their E
73:27 thou dost put an E to those who are

E

77:8 his promises at an E for all time?
90:9 years come to an E like a sigh.
102:27 art the same, and thy years have no E
105:45 peoples' toil, to the E that they should keep
107:27 like drunken men, and were at their wits' E
119:33 statutes; and I will keep it to the E
119:87 have almost made an E of me on earth;
119:112 to perform thy statutes for ever, to the E
135:7 clouds rise at the E of the earth, who
Prov 5:4 oil; but in the E she is bitter as
5:11 alien; and at the E of your life you
14:12 a man, but its E is the way to
14:13 is sad, and the E of joy is grief.
16:25 a man, but its E is the way to
18:18 The lot puts an E to disputes and decides
20:21 beginning will in the E not be blessed.
25:8 you do in the E, when your neighbor puts
25:10 upon you, and your ill repute have no E
29:21 childhood, will in the E find him his heir.
Eccl 3:11 God has done from the beginning to the E
4:8 yet there is no E to all his toil,
4:16 place; there was no E of all the people;
7:2 for this is the E of all men, and
7:8 Better is the E of a thing than its
10:13 is foolishness, and the E of his talk is
12:12 books there is no E, and much study is
12:13 The E of the matter; all has been heard.
Wis 2:1 man comes to his E, and no one has
2:16 he calls the last E of the righteous happy,
2:17 will happen at the E of his life;
3:19 For the E of an unrighteous generation is grievous.
4:17 they will see the E of the wise man,
5:4 madness and that his E was without honor.
7:18 elements; the beginning and E and middle of times,
8:1 reaches mightily from one E of the earth to
11:14 and exposed, at the E of the events they
14:14 and therefore their speedy E has been planned.
14:27 beginning and cause and E of every evil.
16:5 not continue to the E;
18:21 anger and put an E to the disaster, showing
19:1 were assailed to the E by pitiless anger, for
19:4 them on to this E, and made them forget
Sir 1:11 go well at the E; on the day of
2:3 be honored at the E of your life.
3:24 be afflicted at the E, and whoever loves danger
7:36 you do, remember the E of your life, and
9:11 not know what his E will be.
14:7 it unintentionally, and betrays his baseness in the E
18:11 and recognizes that their E will be evil; therefore
21:9 gathered together, and their E is a flame of
21:10 stones, but at its E is the pit of
22:8 man; and at the E he will say, "What
27:14 one's hair stand on E, and their quarrels make
28:6 Remember the E of your life, and cease from
30:10 him, and in the E you will gnash your
31:22 me, and in the E you will appreciate my
33:23 the time when you E the days of your
38:20 it away, remembering the E of life.
41:3 former days and the E of life; this is
43:27 we cannot reach the E, and the sum of
48:25 to occur to the E of time, and the
49:4 Judah came to an E;
Is 2:7 and there is no E to their treasures; their
2:7 and there is no E to their chariots.
7:3 your son, at the E of the conduit of
9:7 there will be no E, upon the throne of
10:23 will make a full E, as decreed, in the
10:25 will come to an E, and my anger will
13:5 distant land, from the E of the heavens, the
13:11 I will put an E to the pride of
21:2 sighing she has caused I bring to an E
21:16 will come to an E;
23:15 At the E of seventy years, it will happen
23:17 At the E of seventy years, the LORD will
26:14 not arise; to that E thou hast visited them
33:1 you have made an E of dealing treacherously, you
38:12 bring me to an E;
38:13 to night thou dost bring me to an E
42:10 his praise from the E of the earth!
43:6 my daughters from the E of the earth,
46:10 like me, declaring the E from the beginning and
47:7 lay these things to heart or remember their E
48:20 it forth to the E of the earth; say,
49:6 may reach to the E of the earth."
62:11 has proclaimed to the E of the earth: Say
66:17 shall come to an E together, says the LORD.
Jer 1:3 Judah, and until the E of the eleventh year
3:5 be indignant to the E Behold, you have spoken,
4:27 desolation; yet I will not make a full E
5:10 make not a full E; strip away her branches,
5:18 not make a full E of you.
5:31 you do when the E comes?
12:4 men said, "He will not see our latter E
12:12 LORD devours from one E of the land to
17:11 him, and at his E he will be a
25:33 shall extend from one E of the earth to
30:11 will make a full E of all the nations
30:11 of you I will not make a full E
34:14 bondage, saying, 'At the E of six years each
42:7 At the E of ten days the word of
44:27 until there is an E of them.
46:28 will make a full E of all the nations
46:28 of you I will not make a full E
48:35 will bring to an E in Moab, says the
51:13 rich in treasures, your E has come, the thread
Lam 2:6 has brought to an E in Zion appointed feast
3:22 never come to an E;
4:18 in our streets; our E drew near; our days
4:18 were numbered; for our E had come.
Bar 3:17 and there is no E to their getting;
Ezek 3:16 And at the E of seven days, the word
7:2 Lord GOD to the land of Israel: An E
7:2 The E has come upon the four corners of
7:3 Now the E is upon you, and I will
7:6 An E has come, the end has come; it
7:6 end has come, the E has come; it has
7:24 I will put an E to their proud might,
11:13 thou make a full E of the remnant of
12:23 I will put an E to this proverb, and
20:13 to make a full E of them.
20:17 or make a full E of them in the
23:27 I will put an E to your lewdness and
23:48 will I put an E to lewdness in the
26:21 you to a dreadful E, and you shall be
27:36 come to a dreadful E and shall be no
28:19 come to a dreadful E and shall be no
29:13 Lord GOD: At the E of forty years I
30:10 I will put an E to the wealth of
30:13 idols, and put an E to the images, in
30:18 shall come to an E; she shall be covered
33:28 shall come to an E; and the mountains of
39:14 cleanse it; at the E of seven months they
40:7 gate at the inner E, one reed.
40:9 vestibule of the gate was at the inner E
40:15 the entrance to the E of the inner vestibule
44:6 let there be an E to all your abominations,
46:19 at the extreme western E of them.
47:1 from below the south E of the threshold of
Dan 1:5 years, and at the E of that time they
1:15 At the E of ten days it was seen
1:18 At the E of the time, when the king
2:44 bring them to an E, and it shall stand
4:11 was visible to the E of the whole earth.
4:17 holy ones, to the E that the living may
4:20 was visible to the E of the whole earth;
4:29 At the E of twelve months he was walking
4:34 At the E of the days I, Nebuchadnezzar, lifted
5:26 brought it to an E;
6:26 destroyed, and his dominion shall be to the E
7:26 away, to be consumed and destroyed to the E
7:28 them.'"Here is the E of the matter.
8:17 the vision is for the time of the E
8:19 be at the latter E of the indignation; for
8:19 it pertains to the appointed time of the E
8:23 And at the latter E of their rule, when
9:2 must pass before the E of the desolations of
9:24 transgression, to put an E to sin, and to
9:26 Its E shall come with a flood, and to
9:26 flood, and to the E there shall be war;
9:27 desolate, until the decreed E is poured out on
11:18 commander shall put an E to his insolence; indeed
11:27 no avail; for the E is yet to be
11:35 the time of the E, for it is yet
11:40 the time of the E the king of the
11:45 shall come to his E, with none to help
12:4 seal the book, until the time of the E
12:6 it be till the E of these wonders?"
12:7 people comes to an E all these things would
12:9 up and sealed until the time of the E
12:13 your way till the E; and you shall rest,
12:13 allotted place at the E of the days."
Hos 1:4 I will put an E to the kingdom of

2:11 I will put an E to all her mirth,
Amos 3:15 and the great houses shall come to an E
8:2 said to me, "The E has come upon my
8:4 the land to an E,
8:10 only son, and the E of it like a
Nah 1:8 will make a full E of his adversaries, and
1:9 will make a full E; he will not take
2:9 There is no E of treasure, or wealth of
3:1 lies and booty--no E to the plunder!
3:3 corpses, dead bodies without E --they stumble over
Hab 2:3 it hastens to the E --it will not lie.
Zeph 1:18 a full, yea, sudden E he will make of
Zech 9:6 I will make an E of the pride of
2Mac 5:7 however; and in the E got only disgrace from
5:8 Finally he met a miserable E
7:38 to bring to an E the wrath of the
9:28 others, came to the E of his life by
10:9 Such then was the E of Antiochus, who was
13:16 In the E they filled the camp with terror
15:37 I too will here E my story.
15:39 And here will be the E
Mt 10:22 who endures to the E will be saved.
24:6 take place, but the E is not yet.
24:13 who endures to the E will be saved.
24:14 nations; and then the E will come.
24:31 four winds, from one E of heaven to the
26:58 he sat with the guards to see the E
Mk 3:26 he cannot stand, but is coming to an E
13:7 take place, but the E is not yet.
13:13 who endures to the E will be saved.
Lk 1:33 and of his kingdom there will be no E
2:21 And at the E of eight days, when he
16:24 Lazarus to dip the E of his finger in
21:9 take place, but the E will not be at
Jn 13:1 in the world, he loved them to the E
Acts 1:8 Samaria and to the E of the earth."
Rom 6:21 The E of those things is death.
6:22 is sanctification and its E, eternal life.
10:4 For Christ is the E of the law, that
14:9 For to this E Christ died and lived again,
1Cor 1:8 sustain you to the E, guiltless in the day
10:11 instruction, upon whom the E of the ages has
15:24 Then comes the E, when he delivers the kingdom
2Cor 3:13 might not see the E of the fading splendor.
11:15 Their E will correspond to their deeds.
Eph 2:16 the cross, thereby bringing the hostility to an E
6:18 To that E keep alert with all perseverance, making
Phil 3:19 Their E is destruction, their god is the belly,
2Thes 1:11 To this E we always pray for you, that
1Tim 4:10 For to this E we toil and strive, because
Heb 1:12 art the same, and thy years will never E
3:14 confidence firm to the E,
6:8 to being cursed; its E is to be burned.
6:11 of hope until the E,
7:3 beginning of days nor E of life, but resembling
9:26 for all at the E of the age to
11:22 faith Joseph, at the E of his life, made
1Pet 1:20 made manifest at the E of the times for
4:7 The E of all things is at hand; therefore
4:17 what will be the E of those who do
Rev 2:26 my works until the E, I will give him
21:6 Alpha and the Omega, the beginning and the E
22:13 first and the last, the beginning and the E

ENDANGER

Dan 1:10 So you would E my head with the king."

ENDANGERED

Eccl 10:9 who splits logs is E by them.

ENDEAVOR (2)

2Mac 11:19 the government, I will E for the future to
Gal 2:17 But if, in our E to be justified in

ENDEAVORED (2)

2Mac 10:15 banished from Jerusalem, and E to keep up the
1Thes 2:17 not in heart, we E the more eagerly and

ENDED (28)

Gen 47:18 when that year was E, they came to him
Deut 34:8 days of weeping and mourning for Moses were E
Josh 19:33 as Lakkum; and it E at the Jordan;
2Chr 7:1 When Solomon had E his prayer, fire came down
Tob 8:20 the wedding feast were E,
14:1 Here Tobit E his words of praise.
Jud 10:1 of Israel, and had E all these words,
Esth 15:1 third day, when she E her prayer, she took
Job 31:40 The words of Job are E
Ps 72:20 prayers of David, the son of Jesse, are E
Sir 50:19 of the Lord was E; so they completed his
Is 40:2 that her warfare is E, that her iniquity is
51:6 for ever, and my deliverance will never be E
60:20 light, and your days of mourning shall be E
Jer 8:20 past, the summer is E, and we are not
2Mac 10:13 he took poison and E his life.
15:24 With these words he E his prayer.
Lk 1:23 time of service was E, he went to his
2:43 when the feast was E, as they were returning,
4:2 and when they were E, he was hungry.
4:13 when the devil had E every temptation, he departed
7:1 After he had E all his sayings in the
Acts 21:5 our days there were E, we departed and went
Rev 15:1 for with them the wrath of God is E
15:8 the seven plagues of the seven angels were E
20:3 nations no more, till the thousand years were E
20:5 come to life until the thousand years were E
20:7 the thousand years are E, Satan will be loosed

ENDING (3)

Gen 44:12 with the eldest and E with the youngest; and
Josh 16:7 Naarah, and touches Jericho, E at the Jordan.
Gal 3:3 Spirit, are you now E with the flesh?

ENDLESS

1Tim 1:4 themselves with myths and E genealogies which

ENDOR (3)

Josh 17:11 and the inhabitants of E and its villages, and
1Sam 28:7 to him, "Behold, there is a medium at E
Ps 83:10 who were destroyed at E, who became dung for

ENDOWED (5)

Gen 30:20 Leah said, "God has E me with a good
Ex 28:3 ability, whom I have E with an able mind,
Wis 8:19 was by nature well E, and a good soul
Sir 17:3 He E them with strength like his own, and
Dan 1:4 skillful in all wisdom, E with knowledge,

ENDOWING

Prov 8:21 the paths of justice, E with wealth those who

ENDOWMENT

Jas 1:16 Every good E and every perfect gift is from

ENDS (64)

Ex 25:18 them, on the two E of the mercy seat.
25:19 shall you make the cherubim on its two E
28:25 the breastpiece; the two E of the two cords
28:26 them at the two E of the breastpiece, on
37:7 gold; on the two E of the mercy seat
37:8 seat he made the cherubim on its two E
39:18 Two E of the two cords they had attached
39:19 them at the two E of the breastpiece, on
Deut 33:17 of them, to the E of the earth; such
Josh 15:7 waters of En-shemesh, and E at En-rogel;
16:3 to Gezer, and it E at the sea.
16:8 the brook Kanah, and E at the sea.
17:9 of the brook and E at the sea;
18:12 country westward; and it E at the wilderness of
18:14 opposite Beth-horon, and it E at Kiriath-baal (that is,
18:19 Beth-hoglah; and the boundary E at the northern bay
19:14 to Hannathon, and it E at the valley of
19:22 Beth-shemesh, and its boundary E at the Jordan--
19:29 to Hosah, and it E at the sea; Mahalab,
1Sam 2:10 LORD will judge the E of the earth; he
1Kgs 8:8 so long that the E of the poles were
2Chr 5:9 so long that the E of the poles were
Jud 2:9 away captive to the E of the whole earth.
Job 28:24 he looks to the E of the earth, and
36:14 youth, and their life E in shame.
Ps 2:8 your heritage, and the E of the earth your
22:27 All the E of the earth shall remember and
48:10 praise reaches to the E of the earth.
59:13 over Jacob to the E of the earth.
65:5 hope of all the E of the earth, and
67:7 us; let all the E of the earth fear
72:8 the River to the E of the earth!
98:3 All the E of the earth have seen the
Prov 10:28 hope of the righteous E in gladness, but the
11:23 desire of the righteous E only in good; the
17:24 fool are on the E of the earth.
30:4 has established all the E of the earth?

Wis 6:1 O judges of the E of the earth.
Sir 44:22 the River to the E of the earth.
Is 5:26 for it from the E of the earth; and
24:16 From the E of the earth we hear songs
40:28 the Creator of the E of the earth.
41:5 and are afraid, the E of the earth tremble;
41:9 I took from the E of the earth, and
45:22 be saved, all the E of the earth!
52:10 nations; and all the E of the earth shall
Jer 10:13 mist rise from the E of the earth.
16:19 nations come from the E of the earth and
25:31 will resound to the E of the earth, for
51:16 mist rise from the E of the earth.
Ezek 15:4 fire has consumed both E of it, and the
Dan 4:22 your dominion to the E of the earth.
Mic 5:4 be great to the E of the earth.
Zech 9:10 the River to the E of the earth.
1Mac 1:3 He advanced to the E of the earth, and
3:9 was renowned to the E of the earth; he
8:4 against them from the E of the earth, until
14:10 renown spread to the E of the earth.
Mt 12:42 she came from the E of the earth to
Mk 13:27 four winds, from the E of the earth to
13:27 the earth to the E of heaven.
Lk 11:31 she came from the E of the earth to
Rom 10:18 their words to the E of the world."
1Cor 13:8 Love never E; as for prophecies, they will pass

ENDUED (2)

2Chr 2:12 David a wise son, E with discretion and
2:13 sent a skilled man, E with understanding, Huram-abi,

ENDURANCE (14)

Sir 2:14 Woe to you who have lost your E
17:19 he encourages those whose E is failing.
Lk 21:19 By your E you will gain your lives.
Rom 5:3 knowing that suffering produces E,
5:4 suffering produces endurance, and E produces
2Cor 6:4 every way: through great E, in afflictions, hardships, ,
Col 1:11 glorious might, for all E and patience with joy,
Heb 10:36 you have need of E, so that you may
Rev 1:9 kingdom and the patient E, was on the island
2:2 toil and your patient E, and how you cannot
2:19 and service and patient E, and that your latter
3:10 my word of patient E, I will keep you
13:10 a call for the E and faith of the
14:12 a call for the E of the saints, those

ENDURE (43)

Ex 18:23 will be able to E, and all this people
Esth 8:6 For how can I E to see the calamity
8:6 Or how can I E to see the destruction
Job 8:15 lays hold of it, but it does not E
15:29 his wealth will not E, nor will he strike
20:21 he had eaten; therefore his prosperity will not E
Ps 61:6 king; may his years E to all generations!
72:17 May his name E for ever, his fame continue
89:36 His line shall E for ever, his throne as
89:37 ever; it shall stand firm while the skies E
101:5 haughty looks and arrogant heart I will not E
102:24 thou whose years E throughout all generations!"
102:26 perish, but thou dost E; they will all wear
104:31 glory of the LORD E for ever, may the
119:84 How long must thy servant E
Prov 12:19 Truthful lips E for ever, but a lying tongue
18:14 A man's spirit will E sickness; but a broken
21:28 the word of a man who hears will E
27:24 and does a crown E to all generations?
Sir 1:20 A patient man will E until the right moment,
45:26 that their glory may E throughout their generations.
Is 1:13 assemblies— I cannot E iniquity and solemn
Jer 10:10 and the nations cannot E his indignation.
Bar 4:25 My children, E with patience the wrath that has
Ezek 22:14 Can your courage E, or can your hands be
Dan 11:6 his offspring shall not E; but she shall be
13:57 of Judah would not E your wickedness.
Joel 2:11 very terrible; who can E it?
Nah 1:6 Who can E the heat of his anger?
Mal 3:2 But who can E the day of his coming,
2Mac 2:27 many we will gladly E the uncomfortable toil,
9:12 when he could not E his own stench, he
Mk 4:17 root in themselves, but E for a while; then,
1Cor 4:12 bless; when persecuted, we E;
9:12 this right, but we E anything rather than put
10:13 may be able to E it.
2Cor 1:6 experience when you patiently E the same sufferings
2Tim 2:10 Therefore I E everything for the sake of the
2:12 with him; if we E, we shall also reign
4:3 when people will not E sound teaching, but having
4:5 you, always be steady, E suffering, do the work
Heb 12:7 It is for discipline that you have to E
12:20 For they could not E the order that was

ENDURED (14)

Ps 132:1 all the hardships he E;
Wis 11:25 How would anything have E if thou hadst not
17:17 he was seized, and E the inescapable fate; for
Sir 51:3 many afflictions that I E,
1Mac 10:15 done, and of the troubles that they had E
2Mac 9:28 murderer and blasphemer, having E the more intense
Rom 9:22 known his power, has E with much patience the
2Tim 3:11 Lystra, what persecutions I E; yet from them all
Heb 6:15 thus Abraham, having patiently E, obtained the
10:32 you were enlightened, you E a hard struggle with
11:27 the king; for he E as seeing him who
12:2 was set before him E the cross, despising the
12:3 Consider him who E from sinners such hostility
13:13 outside the camp and bear the abuse he E

ENDURES (75)

1Chr 16:34 for his steadfast love E for ever!
16:41 for his steadfast love E for ever.
2Chr 5:13 for his steadfast love E for ever," the house,
7:3 for his steadfast love E for ever."
7:6 for his steadfast love E for ever—whenever David
20:21 for his steadfast love E for ever."
Ezra 3:11 for his steadfast love E for ever toward Israel."
Jud 11:7 and as his power E, who had sent you
Ps 45:6 Your divine throne E for ever and ever.
72:5 live while the sun E, and as long as
100:5 good; his steadfast love E for ever, and his
102:12 for ever; thy name E to all generations.
106:1 for his steadfast love E for ever!
107:1 for his steadfast love E for ever!
111:3 work, and his righteousness E for ever.
111:10 His praise E for ever!
112:3 house; and his righteousness E for ever.
112:9 the poor; his righteousness E for ever; his horn
117:2 faithfulness of the LORD E for ever.
118:1 good; his steadfast love E for ever!
118:2 say, "His steadfast love E for ever."
118:3 say, "His steadfast love E for ever."
118:4 say, "His steadfast love E for ever."
118:29 for his steadfast love E for ever!
119:90 Thy faithfulness E to all generations; thou hast
119:160 of thy righteous ordinances E for ever.
135:13 Thy name, O LORD, E for ever, thy renown,
136:1 for his steadfast love E for ever.
136:2 for his steadfast love E for ever.
136:3 for his steadfast love E for ever;
136:4 for his steadfast love E for ever;
136:5 for his steadfast love E for ever;
136:6 for his steadfast love E for ever;
136:7 for his steadfast love E for ever;
136:8 for his steadfast love E for ever;
136:9 for his steadfast love E for ever;
136:10 for his steadfast love E for ever;
136:11 for his steadfast love E for ever;
136:12 for his steadfast love E for ever;
136:13 for his steadfast love E for ever;
136:14 for his steadfast love E for ever;
136:15 for his steadfast love E for ever;
136:16 for his steadfast love E for ever;
136:17 for his steadfast love E for ever;
136:18 for his steadfast love E for ever;
136:19 for his steadfast love E for ever;
136:20 for his steadfast love E for ever;
136:21 for his steadfast love E for ever;
136:22 for his steadfast love E for ever.
136:23 for his steadfast love E for ever;
136:24 for his steadfast love E for ever;
136:25 for his steadfast love E for ever.
136:26 for his steadfast love E for ever.
138:8 steadfast love, O LORD, E for ever.
145:13 kingdom, and thy dominion E throughout all
Eccl 3:14 that whatever God does E for ever; nothing can
Sir 11:15 gift of the Lord E for those who are
40:17 of blessings, and almsgiving E for ever.
41:13 but a good name E for ever.
Jer 33:11 for his steadfast love E for ever!' For I
Lam 5:19 for ever; thy throne E to all generations.
Bar 4:1 and the law that E for ever.

Dan 3:90 good, for his mercy E for ever.
3:91 him, for his mercy E for ever."
4:34 dominion, and his kingdom E from generation to
1Mac 4:24 good, for his mercy E for ever.
Mt 10:22 But he who E to the end will be
13:21 root in himself, but E for a while, and
24:13 But he who E to the end will be
Mk 13:13 But he who E to the end will be
Jn 6:27 for the food which E to eternal life, which
1Cor 13:7 things, hopes all things, E all things.
2Cor 9:9 the poor; his righteousness E for ever."
Jas 1:11 is the man who E trial, for when he
1Pet 2:19 mindful of God, he E pain while suffering unjustly.

ENDURING (11)

Num 24:21 his discourse, and said, E is your dwelling place,
Ps 19:9 the LORD is clean, E for ever; the ordinances
Prov 8:18 honor are with me, E wealth and prosperity.
Eccl 2:16 fool there is no E remembrance, seeing that in
Jer 5:15 It is an E nation, it is an ancient
Dan 6:26 is the living God, E for ever; his kingdom
Mic 6:2 the LORD, and you E foundations of the earth;
2Mac 6:30 from death, I am E terrible sufferings in my
7:36 For our brothers after E a brief suffering have
2Thes 1:4 persecutions and in the afflictions which you are E
Rev 2:3 I know you are E patiently and bearing up

ENEMIES (305)

Gen 14:20 who has delivered your E into your hand!" And
22:17 the gate of their E,
49:8 the neck of your E; your father's sons shall
Ex 1:9 us, they join our E and fight against us
23:22 an enemy to your E and an adversary to
23:27 will make all your E turn their backs to
32:25 their shame among their E,
Lev 26:7 you shall chase your E, and they shall fall
26:8 ten thousand; and your E shall fall before you
26:16 in vain, for your E shall eat it;
26:17 be smitten before your E; those who hate you
26:32 land, so that your E who settle in it
26:34 you are in your E land; then the land
26:36 the lands of their E; the sound of a
26:37 shall have no power to stand before your E
26:38 the land of your E shall eat you up.
26:39 pine away in your E lands because of their
26:41 the land of their E; if then their uncircumcised
26:44 the land of their E, I will not spurn
Num 10:9 God, and you shall be saved from your E
10:35 LORD, and let thy E be scattered; and let
14:42 struck down before your E, for the LORD is
23:11 you to curse my E, and behold, you have
24:10 you to curse my E, and behold, you have
24:18 dispossessed, Seir also, his E, shall be dispossessed,
32:21 has driven out his E from before him
Deut 1:42 be defeated before your E
6:19 thrusting out all your E from before you, as
12:10 rest from all your E round about, so that
20:1 to war against your E, and see horses and
20:3 to battle against your E: let not your heart
20:4 for you against your E, to give you the
20:14 the spoil of your E, which the LORD your
21:10 to war against your E, and the LORD your
23:9 go forth against your E and are in camp,
23:14 to give up your E before you, therefore your
25:19 rest from all your E round about, in the
28:7 LORD will cause your E who rise against you
28:25 be defeated before your E; you shall go out
28:31 be given to your E, and there shall be
28:48 you shall serve your E whom the LORD will
28:53 distress with which your E shall distress you.
28:68 for sale to your E as male and female
30:7 upon your foes and E who persecuted you.
32:31 our Rock, even our E themselves being judges.
33:29 Your E shall come fawning to you; and you
Josh 7:8 when Israel has turned their backs before their E
7:12 cannot stand before their E; they turn their backs
7:12 their backs before their E, because they have
7:13 cannot stand before your E, until you take away
10:13 stayed, until the nation took vengeance on their E
10:19 there yourselves, pursue your E, fall upon their rear,
10:25 do to all your E against whom you fight."
21:44 one of all their E had withstood them, for
21:44 had given all their E into their hands.
22:8 the spoil of your E with your brethren."
23:1 Israel from all their E round about, and Joshua
Judg 2:14 the power of their E round about, so that
2:14 so that they could no longer withstand their E
2:18 the hand of their E all the days of
3:28 LORD has given your E the Moabites into your
5:31 "So perish all thine E, O LORD!
8:34 hand of all their E on every side;
11:36 avenged you on your E, on the Ammonites."
1Sam 2:1 My mouth derides my E, because I rejoice in
4:3 and save us from the power of our E
10:1 the hand of their E round about.
12:10 the hand of our E, and we will serve
12:11 the hand of your E on every side; and
14:24 is evening and I am avenged on my E
14:30 the spoil of their E which they found; for
14:47 fought against all his E on every side, against
18:25 that he may be avenged of the king's E
20:15 every one of the E of David from the
20:16 And may the LORD take vengeance on David's E
25:26 now then let your E and those who seek
25:29 the lives of your E he shall sling out
29:8 and fight against the E of my lord the
30:26 the spoil of the E of the LORD";
2Sam 3:18 Philistines, and from the hand of all their E
5:20 has broken through my E before me, like a
7:1 rest from all his E round about,
7:9 cut off all your E from before you; and
7:11 I will give you rest from all your E
18:19 has delivered him from the power of his E
18:32 Cushite answered, "May the E of my lord the
19:9 the hand of our E, and saved us from
22:1 hand of all his E, and from the hand
22:4 be praised, and I am saved from my E
22:38 slip; I pursued my E and destroyed them, and
22:41 Thou didst make my E turn their backs to
22:49 me out from my E; thou didst exalt me
1Kgs 3:11 the life of your E, but have asked for
5:3 warfare with which his E surrounded him, until the
8:48 the land of their E, who carried them captive,
2Kgs 17:39 you out of the hand of all your E
21:14 the hand of their E, and they shall become
21:14 spoil to all their E,
1Chr 14:11 has broken through my E by my hand, like
17:8 cut off all your E from before you; and
17:10 people Israel; and I will subdue all your E
21:12 the sword of your E overtakes you; or else
22:9 peace from all his E round about; for his
2Chr 6:28 or caterpillar; if their E besiege them in any
6:34 to battle against their E, by whatever way thou
20:27 the LORD had made them rejoice over their E
20:29 had fought against the E of Israel.
25:20 the hand of their E, because they had sought
32:22 hand of all his E; and he gave them
Neh 4:11 And our E said, "They will not know or
4:15 When our E heard that it was known to
5:9 to prevent the taunts of the nations our E
6:1 the rest of our E that I had built
6:16 And when all our E heard of it, all
9:27 the hand of their E, who made them suffer;
9:27 who saved them from the hand of their E
9:28 the hand of their E, so that they had
Tob 12:10 commit sin are the E of their own lives.
Jud 5:18 ground, and their cities were captured by their E
7:19 failed, because all their E had surrounded them and
8:11 the city to our E unless the Lord turns
8:15 to destroy us in the presence of our E
8:19 so they suffered a great catastrophe before our E
8:33 the city to our E, the Lord will deliver
8:35 go before you, to take revenge upon our E
13:5 the destruction of the E who have risen up
13:11 his strength against our E, even as he has
13:14 but has destroyed our E by my hand this
13:17 contempt this day the E of thy people."
13:18 strike the head of the leader of our E
15:4 rush out upon their E to destroy them.
Esth 8:13 on that day to avenge themselves upon their E
9:1 very day when the E of the Jews hoped
9:5 Jews smote all their E with the sword, slaughtering,
9:16 got relief from their E, and slew seventy-five
9:22 got relief from their E, and as the month
13:6 the sword of their E, without pity or mercy,
14:6 the hands of our E,
Ps 3:7 dost smite all my E on the cheek, thou
5:8 righteousness because of my E; make thy way
6:10 All my E shall be ashamed and sorely troubled;
7:6 the fury of my E; awake, O my God;
9:3 When my E turned back, they stumbled and perished
17:9 despoil me, my deadly E who surround me.

18:3 be praised, and I am saved from my E
18:37 I pursued my E and overtook them; and did
18:40 Thou didst make my E turn their backs to
18:48 delivered me from my E; yea, thou didst exalt
21:8 find out all your E; your right hand will
23:5 the presence of my E; thou anointest my head
25:2 shame; let not my E exult over me.
27:6 lifted up above my E round about me; and
27:11 me on a level path because of my E
31:15 the hand of my E and persecutors!
37:20 the wicked perish; the E of the LORD are
41:2 give him up to the will of his E
41:5 My E say of me in malice: "When will
44:10 the foe; and our E have gotten spoil.
45:5 heart of the king's E; the peoples fall under
54:5 He will requite my E with evil; in thy
54:7 my eye has looked in triumph on my E
56:2 foemen oppress me; my E trample upon me all
56:9 Then my E will be turned back in the
59:1 Deliver me from my E, O my God, protect
59:10 will let me look in triumph on my E
66:3 thy power that thy E cringe before thee.
68:1 God arise, let his E be scattered; let those
68:21 the heads of his E, the hairy crown of
69:14 be delivered from my E and from the deep
69:18 redeem me, set me free because of my E
71:10 For my E speak concerning me, those who watch
72:9 before him, and his E lick the dust!
78:53 were not afraid; but the sea overwhelmed their E
80:6 our neighbors; and our E laugh among themselves.
81:14 would soon subdue their E, and turn my hand
83:2 For lo, thy E are in tumult; those who
89:10 thou didst scatter thy E with thy mighty arm.
89:42 hast made all his E rejoice.
89:51 peoples, with which thy E taunt, O LORD, with
92:9 For, lo, thy E, O LORD, for, lo, thy
92:9 LORD, for, lo, thy E shall perish; all evildoers
92:11 the downfall of my E, my ears have heard
102:8 All the day my E taunt me, those who
106:42 Their E oppressed them, and they were brought into
110:1 till I make your E your footstool."
119:98 me wiser than my E, for it is ever
127:5 he speaks with his E in the gate.
132:18 His E I will clothe with shame, but upon
138:7 the wrath of my E, and thy right hand
139:22 them with perfect hatred; I count them my E
143:9 Deliver me, O LORD, from my E
143:12 love cut off my E, and destroy all my
Prov 16:7 he makes even his E to be at peace
Wis 5:17 creation to repel his E;
10:12 protected him from his E, and kept him safe
10:19 but she drowned their E, and cast them up
11:3 They withstood their E and fought off their foes.
11:5 things by which their E were punished, they
11:8 at that time how thou didst punish their E
12:20 care and indulgence the E of thy servants and
12:22 us thou scourgest our E ten thousand times more,
12:24 animals which even their E despised; they were
15:14 infant, are all the E who oppressed thy people.
15:18 The E of thy people worship even the most
16:4 merely shown how their E were being tormented.
16:8 thou didst convince our E that it is thou
16:22 the crops of their E were being destroyed by
18:1 Their E heard their voices but did not see
18:4 For their E deserved to be deprived of light
18:7 the destruction of their E were expected by thy
18:8 thou didst punish our E thou didst call us
18:10 discordant cry of their E echoed back, and their
Sir 6:4 it, and make him the laughingstock of his E
6:13 yourself far from your E, and be on guard
12:9 A man's E are grieved when he prospers, and
18:30 it will make you the laughingstock of your E
25:13 And any vengeance, but not the vengeance of E
30:3 son will make his E envious, and will glory
30:6 an avenger against his E, and one to repay
42:11 a laughingstock to your E, a byword in the
45:2 made him great in the fears of his E
46:1 take vengeance on the E that rose against them,
46:5 the Mighty One, when E pressed him on every
46:16 Mighty One, when his E pressed him on every
47:7 he wiped out his E on every side, and
49:9 For God remembered his E with storm, and did
51:8 dost save them from the hand of their E
Is 1:24 my wrath on my E, and avenge myself on
9:11 raises adversaries against them, and stirs up their E
59:18 adversaries, requital to his E; to the coastlands he
62:8 be food for your E, and foreigners shall not
66:6 voice of the LORD, rendering recompense to his E
66:14 his servants, and his indignation is against his E
Jer 12:7 of my soul into the hands of her E
15:9 the sword before their E, says the LORD."
15:14 make you serve your E in a land which
17:4 make you serve your E in a land which
19:7 the sword before their E, and by the hand
19:9 distress, with which their E and those who seek
20:4 the sword of their E while you look on.
20:5 the hand of their E, who shall plunder them,
21:7 the hand of their E, into the hand of
34:20 the hand of their E and into the hand
34:21 the hand of their E and into the hand
44:30 the hand of his E and into the hand
46:22 gliding away; for her E march in force, and
49:37 terrify Elam before their E, and before those who
50:7 devoured them, and their E have said, 'We are
Lam 1:2 treacherously with her, they have become her E
1:5 become the head, her E prosper, because the LORD
1:21 All my E have heard of my trouble; they
2:16 All your E rail against you; they hiss, they
3:46 "All our E rail against us;
3:52 those who were my E without cause;
Bar 3:10 the land of your E, that you are growing
4:6 handed over to your E because you angered God.
4:18 will deliver you from the hand of your E
5:6 led away by their E; but God will bring
6:56 offer no resistance to a king or any E
Ezek 16:27 the greed of your E, the daughters of the
39:27 gathered them from their E lands, and through them
Dan 3:32 the hands of lawless E, most hateful rebels, and
4:19 who hate you and its interpretation for your E
Amos 9:4 into captivity before their E, there I will command
Mic 4:10 will redeem you from the hand of your E
5:9 adversaries, and all your E shall be cut off.
7:6 her mother-in-law; a man's E are the men of
Nah 1:2 on his adversaries and keeps wrath for his E
1:8 and will pursue his E into darkness.
Zeph 3:15 judgments against you, he has cast out your E
1Mac 4:18 stand now against our E and fight them, and
4:36 his brothers, "Behold, our E are crushed; let us
5:16 were in distress and were being attacked by E
9:8 "Let us rise and go up against our E
9:29 to go against our E and Bacchides, and to
9:46 may be delivered from the hands of our E
10:26 not sided with our E, we have heard of
12:15 were delivered from our E and our enemies were
12:15 our enemies and our E were humbled.
14:26 fought and repulsed Israel's E and established its
14:29 danger and resisted the E of their nation, in
14:31 And when their E decided to invade their country
15:33 one time had been unjustly taken by our E
2Mac 4:16 imitate completely became their E and punished
5:6 trophies of victory over E and not over fellow
10:21 money by setting their E free to fight against
10:26 an enemy to their E and an adversary to
12:28 the might of his E, and they got the
Mt 5:44 to you, Love your E and pray for those
22:44 till I put thy E under thy feet?
Mk 12:36 till I put thy E under thy feet.'
Lk 1:71 be saved from our E, and from the hand
1:74 the hand of our E, might serve him without
6:27 that hear, Love your E, do good to those
6:35 But love your E, and do good, and lend,
19:27 But as for these E of mine, who did
19:43 upon you, when your E will cast up a
20:43 till I make thy E a stool for thy
Acts 2:35 till I make thy E a stool for thy
Rom 5:10 if while we were E we were reconciled to
11:28 the gospel they are E of God, for your
1Cor 15:25 has put all his E under his feet.
Phil 3:18 with tears, live as E of the cross of
Heb 1:13 till I make thy E a stool for thy
10:13 to wait until his E should be made a

ENEMY (161)

Gen 14:11 So the E took all the goods of Sodom
Ex 15:6 power, thy right hand, O LORD, shatters the E
15:9 The E said, 'I will pursue, I will overtake,
23:4 "If you meet your E's ox or his ass
23:22 I will be an E to your enemies and
Lev 26:25 shall be delivered into the hand of the E
Num 35:23 he was not his E, and did not seek
Deut 28:55 distress with which your E shall distress you in
28:57 distress with which your E shall distress you in

32:27 feared provocation by the E, lest their adversaries
32:42 long-haired heads of the E
33:27 he thrust out the E before you, and said,
Judg 16:23 has given Samson our E into our hand."
16:24 god has given our E into our hand, the
1Sam 18:29 So Saul was David's E continually.
19:17 thus, and let my E go, so that he
24:4 I will give your E into your hand, and
24:19 a man finds his E, will he let him
26:8 "God has given your E into your hand this
28:16 LORD has turned from you and become your E
2Sam 4:8 son of Saul, your E, who sought your life;
22:18 me from my strong E, from those who hated
1Kgs 8:33 are defeated before the E because they have sinned
8:37 or caterpillar; if their E besieges them in any
8:44 to battle against their E, by whatever way thou
8:46 give them to an E, so that they are
8:46 the land of the E, far-off or near;
21:20 to Elijah, "Have you found me, O my E
2Chr 6:24 are defeated before the E because they have sinned
6:36 give them to an E, so that they are
25:8 you down before the E; for God has power
26:13 mighty power, to help the king against the E
Ezra 8:22 protect us against the E on our way; since
8:31 the hand of the E and from ambushes by
Jud 15:5 they fell upon the E, and cut them down
15:5 the camp of the E; and those in Gilead
16:11 people shouted and the E trembled; they lifted up
16:11 their voices, and the E were turned back.
Esth 3:10 son of Hammedatha, the E of the Jews.
7:6 And Esther said, "A foe and E
8:1 house of Haman, the E of the Jews.
9:10 son of Hammedatha, the E of the Jews; but
9:24 son of Hammedatha, the E of all the Jews,
Job 13:24 hide thy face, and count me as thy E
27:7 "Let my E be as the wicked, and let
33:10 counts me as his E;
Ps 7:4 evil or plundered my E without cause,
7:5 without cause, let the E pursue me and overtake
8:2 foes, to still the E and the avenger.
9:6 The E have vanished in everlasting ruins; their cities
13:2 How long shall my E be exalted over me?
13:4 of death; lest my E say, "I have prevailed
18:17 me from my strong E, and from those who
31:8 the hand of the E; thou hast set my
41:11 me, in that my E has not triumphed over
42:9 I mourning because of the oppression of the E
43:2 I mourning because of the oppression of the E
44:16 the sight of the E and the avenger.
55:3 the noise of the E, because of the oppression
55:12 It is not an E who taunts me--
61:3 art my refuge, a strong tower against the E
64:1 from dread of the E,
74:3 the perpetual ruins; the E has destroyed everything
74:10 Is the E to revile thy name for ever?
74:18 O LORD, how the E scoffs, and an impious
89:22 The E shall not outwit him, the wicked shall
106:10 and delivered them from the power of the E
143:3 For the E has pursued me; he has crushed
Prov 24:17 not rejoice when your E falls, and let not
25:21 If your E is hungry, give him bread to
27:6 a friend; profuse are the kisses of an E
Sir 5:15 do not become an E instead of a friend.
6:9 who changes into an E, and will disclose a
12:8 prosperity, nor will an E be hidden in adversity.
12:10 Never trust your E, for like the rusting of
12:16 An E will speak sweetly with his lips, but
12:16 into a pit; an E will weep with his
20:22 to a friend, and needlessly make him an E
23:3 my adversaries, and my E will not rejoice over
25:14 wrath worse than an E's wrath.
27:18 a man destroys his E, so you have destroyed
29:6 needlessly made him his E; he will repay him
29:13 it will fight on your behalf against your E
36:7 wrath; destroy the adversary and wipe out the E
36:10 the rulers of the E, who say, "There is
Is 63:10 turned to be their E, and himself fought against
Jer 6:25 the road; for the E has a sword, terror
15:11 on behalf of the E in the time of
18:17 east wind I will scatter them before the E
30:14 the blow of an E, the punishment of a
31:16 shall come back from the land of the E
44:30 Babylon, who was his E and sought his life."
Lam 1:9 my affliction, for the E has triumphed!"
1:10 The E has stretched out his hands over all
1:16 are desolate, for the E has prevailed."
2:3 the face of the E; he has burned like
2:4 his bow like an E, with his right hand
2:5 has become like an E, he has destroyed Israel;
2:7 the hand of the E the walls of her
2:17 he has made the E rejoice over you, and
2:22 dandled and reared my E destroyed.
4:12 world, that foe or E could enter the gates
Bar 4:21 you from the power and hand of the E
4:25 Your E has overtaken you, but you will soon
4:26 away like a flock carried off by the E
Ezek 36:2 Lord GOD: Because the E said of you, 'Aha!'
Hos 8:3 spurned the good; the E shall pursue him.
Mic 2:8 my people as an E; you strip the robe
7:8 over me, O my E; when I fall, I
7:10 Then my E will see, and shame will cover
Nah 3:11 dazed; you will seek a refuge from the E
1Mac 2:7 given over to the E, the sanctuary given over
2:35 Then the E hastened to attack them.
5:13 have been killed; the E have captured their wives
5:27 cities of Gilead; the E are getting ready to
6:38 army, to harass the E while being themselves
7:29 But the E were ready to seize Judas.
7:46 and they out-flanked the E and drove them back
8:23 and may sword and E be far from them.
8:26 And to the E who makes war they shall
8:28 And to the E allies shall be given no
9:6 huge number of the E forces, they were greatly
9:24 and the country deserted with them to the E
9:48 other side, and the E did not cross the
10:81 Jonathan commanded, and the E's horses grew tired.
11:72 the battle against the E and routed them, and
12:26 to him that the E were being drawn up
12:28 When the E heard that Jonathan and his men
13:51 songs, because a great E had been crushed and
14:33 the arms of the E had been stored, and
14:34 of Azotus, where the E formerly dwelt.
16:7 the cavalry of the E were very numerous.
2Mac 3:38 "If you have any E or plotter against your
8:6 put to flight not a few of the E
8:16 be frightened by the E and not to fear
8:24 nine thousand of the E, and wounded and disabled
8:27 the arms of the E and stripped them of
8:31 the arms of the E, they stored them all
10:26 and to be an E to their enemies and
10:27 came near to the E they halted.
10:29 there appeared to the E from heaven five
10:30 and thunderbolts upon the E, so that, confused and
11:11 like lions against the E, and slew eleven thousand
12:22 fear came over the E at the manifestation to
13:21 secret information to the E; he was sought for,
14:17 of the sudden consternation created by the E
14:22 the part of the E; they held the proper
15:20 coming decision, and the E was already close at
15:26 his men met the E in battle with invocation
Mt 5:43 neighbor and hate your E
13:25 men were sleeping, his E came and sowed weeds
13:28 said to them, 'An E has done this.' The
13:39 evil one, and the E who sowed them is
Lk 10:19 the power of the E; and nothing shall hurt
Acts 13:10 of the devil, you E of all righteousness, full
Rom 12:20 No, "if your E is hungry, feed him; if
1Cor 15:26 The last E to be destroyed is death.
Gal 4:16 I then become your E by telling you the
2Thes 3:15 on him as an E, but warn him as
1Tim 5:14 households, and give the E no occasion to revile
Jas 4:4 world makes himself an E of God.

ENERGY

Col 1:29 striving with all the E which he mightily inspires

ENFORCE

Dan 6:7 establish an ordinance and E an interdict, that

ENFORCED

Heb 11:33 faith conquered kingdoms, E justice, received

ENFORCING

1Mac 2:15 king's officers who were E the apostasy came to

ENGAGE

1Mac 5:19 people, but do not E in battle with the

ENGAGED (10)

2Chr 24:13 So those who were E in the work labored,
Wis 17:20 brilliant light, and was E in unhindered work,
1Mac 1:18 He E Ptolemy king of Egypt in battle, and

4:14 blew their trumpets and E in battle.
5:7 He E in many battles with them and they
10:78 Azotus, and the armies E in battle.
10:82 forward his force and E the phalanx in battle
2Mac 14:16 from there immediately and E them in battle at
Lk 22:5 they were glad, and E to give him money.
Phil 1:30 suffer for his sake, E in the same conflict

ENGEDI (6)

Josh 15:62 City of Salt, and E: six cities with their
1Sam 23:29 from there, and dwelt in the strongholds of E
24:1 told, "Behold, David is in the wilderness of E
2Chr 20:2 (that is, E
Song 1:14 cluster of henna blossoms in the vineyards of E
Ezek 47:10 beside the sea; from E to En-eglaim it will

ENGINE (2)

1Mac 13:43 He made a siege E, brought it up to
13:44 men in the siege E leaped out into the

ENGINES (10)

2Chr 26:15 In Jerusalem he made E, invented by skilful men,
1Mac 5:30 counted, carrying ladders and E of war to capture
6:20 siege towers and other E of war.
6:31 they fought and built E of war; but the
6:51 set up siege towers, E of war to throw
6:52 The Jews also made E of war to match
11:20 and he built many E of war to use
15:25 against it and making E of war; and he
2Mac 12:15 battering-rams or E of war overthrew Jericho
12:27 great stores of war E and missiles were there.

ENGRAVE (4)

Ex 28:9 two onyx stones, and E on them the names
28:11 signets, so shall you E the two stones with
28:36 of pure gold, and E on it, like the
Zech 3:9 seven facets, I will E its inscription, says the

ENGRAVED (7)

Ex 28:21 be like signets, each E with its name, for
39:6 of gold filigree and E like the engravings of
39:14 were like signets, each E with its name, for
Wis 18:24 of the fathers were E on the four rows
Sir 45:11 craftsman; with precious stones E like signets, in a
45:11 for a reminder, in E letters, according to the
Jer 17:1 of diamond it is E on the tablet of

ENGRAVES

Ex 28:11 As a jeweler E signets, so shall you engrave

ENGRAVING (4)

Ex 28:36 on it, like the E of a signet, 'Holy
39:30 an inscription, like the E of a signet, "Holy
2Chr 2:7 fabrics, trained also in E, to be with the
2:14 do all sorts of E and execute any design

ENGRAVINGS (2)

Ex 39:6 and engraved like the E of a signet, according
Ezek 28:13 wrought in gold were your settings and your E

ENHANCE

2Mac 5:16 kings had made to E the glory and honor

ENHANCES

2Mac 15:39 sweet and delicious and E one's enjoyment, so also

ENJOIN (2)

Deut 32:46 the words which I E upon you this day,
1Tim 4:3 who forbid marriage and E abstinence from foods

ENJOINED (3)

Esth 9:31 Jew and Queen Esther E upon the Jews, and
Zeph 3:7 all that I have E upon her.' But all
Zech 3:6 angel of the LORD E Joshua,

ENJOINING

Esth 9:21 both near and far, E them that they should

ENJOY (30)

Lev 26:34 "Then the land shall E its sabbaths as long
26:34 land shall rest, and E its sabbaths.
26:43 left by them, and E its sabbaths while it
Deut 20:6 battle and another man E its fruit.
20:14 yourselves; and you shall E the spoil of your
Neh 9:36 to our fathers to E its fruit and its
Job 14:6 desist, that he may E, like a hireling, his
Ps 34:12 days, that he may E good?
37:3 in the land, and E security.
Prov 14:9 wicked, but the upright E his favor.
Eccl 2:1 a test of pleasure; E yourself." But behold, this
3:12 to be happy and E themselves as long as
3:22 that a man should E his work, for that
5:19 possessions and power to E them, and to accept
6:2 give him power to E them, but a stranger
6:3 but he does not E life's good things, and
6:6 years twice told, yet E no good–do not
8:15 eat and drink, and E himself, for this will
9:9 E life with the wife whom you love, all
Wis 2:6 "Come, therefore, let us E the good things that
Sir 11:17 and now I shall E my goods!" he does
14:5 He will not E his own riches.
41:1 has the vigor to E his food!
Is 65:22 my chosen shall long E the work of their
Jer 2:7 a plentiful land to E its fruits and its
31:5 shall plant, and shall E the fruit.
2Mac 11:31 for the Jews to E their own food and
Acts 24:2 "Since through you we E much peace, and since
1Tim 6:17 God who richly furnishes us with everything to E
Heb 11:25 of God than to E the fleeting pleasures of

ENJOYED (5)

Deut 20:6 vineyard and has not E its fruit?
2Chr 36:21 until the land had E its sabbaths.
Esth 16:11 our guest, so far E the good will that
Eccl 2:21 leave all to be E by a man who
Rom 15:24 you, once I have E your company for a

ENJOYING

Jud 12:12 a woman go without E her company, for if

ENJOYMENT (9)

Job 20:18 profit of his trading he will get no E
Eccl 2:24 and drink, and find E in his toil.
2:25 him who can eat or who can have E
5:18 and drink and find E in all the toil
5:19 his lot and find E in his toil–this
8:15 And I commend E, for man has no good
9:7 eat your bread with E, and drink your wine
Wis 2:9 us leave signs of E, because this is our
2Mac 15:39 delicious and enhances one's E, so also the style

ENJOYS (2)

Eccl 6:2 them, but a stranger E them; this is vanity;
Sir 37:28 and not every person E everything.

ENLARGE (6)

Gen 9:27 God E Japheth, and let him dwell in the
Ex 34:24 nations before you, and E your borders; neither shall
1Chr 4:10 wouldst bless me and E my border, and that
Is 54:2 E the place of your tent, and let the
Jer 4:30 of gold, that you E your eyes with paint?
Amos 1:13 Gilead, that they might E their border.

ENLARGED (3)

Is 5:14 Therefore Sheol has E its appetite and opened its
26:15 art glorified; thou hast E all the borders of
2Cor 10:15 you may be greatly E,

ENLARGEMENT

Ezek 41:7 story, corresponding to the E of the offset from

ENLARGES (4)

Deut 12:20 the LORD your God E your territory, as he
19:8 the LORD your God E your border, as he
33:20 "Blessed be he who E Gad!
Job 12:23 he destroys them: he E nations, and leads them

ENLARGEST

Ps 119:32 thy commandments when thou E my understanding!

ENLIGHTEN

Sir 45:17 the testimonies, and to E Israel with his law.

ENLIGHTENED (4)

Rom 10:2 a zeal for God, but it is not E
Eph 1:18 eyes of your hearts E, that you may know
Heb 6:4 who have once been E, who have tasted the
10:32 when, after you were E, you endured a hard

ENLIGHTENING

Ps 19:8 the LORD is pure, E the eyes;

ENLIGHTENMENT
Is 40:14 he consult for his E, and who taught him

ENLIGHTENS
Jn 1:9 The true light that E every man was coming

ENLISTED (3)
1Mac 4:35 departed to Antioch and E mercenaries, to invade
2Mac 8:1 summoned their kinsmen and E those who had
2Tim 2:4 satisfy the one who E him.

ENMISHPAT
Gen 14:7 back and came to E (that is, Kadesh), and

ENMITY (18)
Gen 3:15 I will put E between you and the woman,
Num 35:21 he died, or in E struck him down with
35:22 stabbed him suddenly without E, or hurled anything
Deut 4:42 unintentionally, without being at E with him in time
19:4 without having been at E with him in time
19:6 he was not at E with his neighbor in
Josh 20:5 unwittingly, having had no E against him in times
Ps 55:3 in anger they cherish E against me.
Sir 28:6 life, and cease from E, remember destruction and
28:9 disturb friends and inject E among those who are
37:2 death when a companion and friend turns to E
Ezek 25:15 to destroy in never-ending E;
35:5 Because you cherished perpetual E, and gave over
1Mac 11:12 from Alexander, and their E became manifest.
2Mac 14:39 wishing to exhibit the E which he had for
Lk 23:12 they had been at E with each other.
Gal 5:20 impurity, licentiousness, idolatry, sorcery, E, strife,
Jas 4:4 with the world is E with God?

ENOCH (15)
Gen 4:17 she conceived and bore E; and he built a
4:17 the city after the name of his son, E
4:18 To E was born Irad; and Irad was the
5:18 and sixty-two years he became the father of E
5:19 after the birth of E eight hundred years, and
5:21 When E had lived sixty-five years, he became the
5:22 E walked with God after the birth of Methuselah
5:23 all the days of E were three hundred and
5:24 E walked with God; and he was not, for
1Chr 1:3 Kenan, Mahalalel, Jared, E, Thuselah, Lamech,
Sir 44:17 E pleased the Lord, and was taken up; he
49:14 No one like E has been created on earth,
Lk 3:37 Methuselah, the son of E, the son of Jared,
Heb 11:5 By faith E was taken up so that he
Jude 1:14 of these also that E in the seventh generation

ENOS
Lk 3:38 Ca-inan, the son of E, the son of Seth,

ENOSH (8)
Gen 4:26 son was born, and he called his name E
5:6 and five years, he became the father of E
5:7 after the birth of E eight hundred and seven
5:9 When E had lived ninety years, he became the
5:10 E lived after the birth of Kenan eight hundred
5:11 all the days of E were nine hundred and
1Chr 1:1 Adam, Seth, E;
1:1 Seth, Enosh; Adam, Seth, E;

ENOUGH (72)
Gen 19:20 yonder city is near E to flee to, and
24:25 both straw and provender E, and room to lodge
33:9 Esau said, "I have E, my brother; keep what
33:11 dealt graciously with me, and because I have E
34:21 the land is large E for them; let us
45:28 Israel said, "It is E; Joseph my son is
Ex 9:28 for there has been E of this thunder and
36:5 bring much more than E for doing the work
Deut 1:6 'You have stayed long E at this mountain;
2:3 this mountain country long E; turn northward.
Josh 17:16 hill country is not E for us; yet all
22:17 Have we not had E of the sin at
Judg 6:38 the fleece, he wrung E dew from the fleece
2Sam 8:4 chariot horses, but left E for a hundred chariots.
24:16 the people, "It is E; now stay your hand."
1Kgs 12:28 people, "You have gone up to Jerusalem long E
19:4 die, saying, "It is E; now, O LORD, take
1Chr 18:4 chariot horses, but left E for a hundred chariots.
21:15 destroying angel, "It is E; now stay your hand."
2Chr 31:10 have eaten and had E and have plenty left;
Tob 5:19 by the Lord is E for us."

Jud 4:7 was narrow, only wide E for two men at
7:21 they did not have E water to drink their
Job 27:14 his offspring have not E to eat.
Ps 17:14 children have more than E; may they leave
123:3 have had more than E of contempt.
Prov 13:25 The righteous has E to satisfy his appetite, but
23:4 acquire wealth; be wise E to desist.
25:16 found honey, eat only E for you, lest you
27:27 field; there will be E goats' milk for your
30:15 satisfied; four never say, E:
30:16 for water, and the fire which never says, E
Wis 4:5 be useless, not ripe E to eat, and good
14:22 Afterward it was not E for them to err
18:25 feared; for merely to test the wrath was E
Sir 5:1 heart on your wealth, nor say, "I have E
11:22 not say, "I have E, and what calamity could
39:11 to rest, it is E for him.
42:25 and who can have E of beholding his glory?
43:30 not grow weary, for you cannot praise him E
Is 1:11 LORD; I have had E of burnt offerings of
40:16 nor are its beasts E for a burnt offering.
56:11 dogs have a mighty appetite; they never have E
Jer 49:9 they not destroy only E for themselves?
Lam 5:6 to Egypt, and to Assyria, to get bread E
Ezek 34:18 Is it not E for you to feed on
45:9 says the Lord GOD: E, O princes of Israel!
47:5 risen; it was deep E to swim in, a
Obad 1:5 they not steal only E for themselves?
Jon 4:9 to be angry, angry E to die."
Nah 2:12 The lion tore E for his whelps and strangled
Hab 2:5 wide as Sheol; like death he has never E
Hag 1:6 but you never have E; you drink, but you
1Mac 2:33 they said to them, E of this!
2Mac 7:42 Let this be E, then, about the eating of
Mt 10:25 his master; it is E for the disciple to
15:33 we to get bread E in the desert to
25:9 there will not be E for us and for
Mk 14:41 It is E; the hour has come; the Son
Lk 14:28 cost, whether he has E to complete it?
15:17 hired servants have bread E and to spare, but
16:3 I am not strong E to dig, and I
22:38 And he said to them, "It is E
Jn 6:7 denarii would not buy E bread for each of
Acts 10:33 you have been kind E to come.
27:38 when they had eaten E, they lightened the ship,
1Cor 6:5 man among you wise E to decide between members
14:17 may give thanks well E, but the other man
2Cor 2:6 by the majority is E;
9:8 you may always have E of everything and may
11:4 one you accepted, you submit to it readily E
Philem 1:8 though I am bold E in Christ to command

ENRAGED (15)
2Sam 17:8 and that they are E, like a bear robbed
Neh 4:1 was angry and greatly E, and he ridiculed the
Esth 1:12 this the king was E, and his anger burned
Is 8:21 hungry, they will be E and will curse their
34:2 For the LORD is E against all the nations,
Jer 37:15 And the princes were E at Jeremiah, and they
Ezek 16:43 your youth, but have E me with all these
Dan 8:7 ram, and he was E against him and struck
11:30 turn back and be E and take action against
14:21 Then the king was E, and he seized the
1Mac 6:28 The king was E when he heard this.
9:69 So he was greatly E at the lawless men
Acts 5:33 heard this they were E and wanted to kill
7:54 these things they were E, and they ground their
19:28 heard this they were E, and cried out, "Great

ENRICH (2)
1Sam 17:25 him, the king will E with great riches, and
Sir 11:19 of the Lord to E a poor man quickly

ENRICHED (6)
Jud 15:6 Assyrian camp and plundered it, and were greatly E
Prov 11:25 liberal man will be E, and one who waters
28:25 he who trusts in the LORD will be E
Ezek 27:33 wealth and merchandise you E the kings of the
1Cor 1:5 every way you were E in him with all
2Cor 9:11 You will be E in every way for great

ENRICHEST
Ps 65:9 waterest it, thou greatly E it; the river of

ENROL (2)
2Mac 4:9 for it, and to E the men of Jerusalem

1Tim 5:11 But refuse to E younger widows; for when they

ENROLLED (25)

1Chr 5:1 that he is not E in the genealogy according
5:17 All of these were E by genealogies in the
7:5 eighty-seven thousand mighty warriors, E by
7:40 Their number E by genealogies, for service in war,
9:1 So all Israel was E by genealogies; and these
9:22 They were E by genealogies in their villages.
2Chr 31:16 by divisions, except those E by genealogy, males
31:18 The priests were E with all their little children,
31:19 to every one among the Levites who was E
Ezra 2:62 their registration among those E in the genealogies,
Neh 7:5 the people to be E by genealogy.
7:64 their registration among those E in the genealogies,
Ps 69:28 let them not be E among the righteous.
Ezek 13:9 my people, nor be E in the register of
1Mac 8:20 that we may be E as your allies and
10:36 "Let Jews be E in the king's forces to
10:65 king honored him and E him among his chief
13:40 are qualified to be E in our bodyguard, let
13:40 bodyguard, let them be E, and let there be
Lk 2:1 Caesar Augustus that all the world should be E
2:3 all went to be E, each to his own
2:5 of David, to be E with Mary, his betrothed,
Acts 1:26 Matthias; and he was E with the eleven apostles.
1Tim 5:9 Let a widow be E if she is not
Heb 12:23 the first-born who are E in heaven, and to

ENROLLMENT (4)

1Chr 7:7 warriors; and their E by genealogies was twenty-two
7:9 of Becher; and their E by genealogies, according to
2Chr 31:17 The E of the priests was according to their
Lk 2:2 This was the first E, when Quirinius was governor

ENSIGN (4)

Is 11:10 shall stand as an E to the peoples; him
11:12 He will raise an E for the nations, and
62:10 stones, lift up an E over the peoples.
Ezek 27:7 sail, serving as your E; blue and purple from

ENSIGNS

Num 2:2 own standard, with the E of their fathers' houses;

ENSLAVE (2)

Jer 34:9 that no one should E a Jew, his brother.
Acts 7:6 to others, who would E them and ill-treat them

ENSLAVED (9)

Neh 5:5 daughters have already been E; but it is not
Wis 1:4 dwell in a body E to sin.
Jer 34:10 they would not be E again; they obeyed and
Ezek 34:27 hand of those who E them.
1Mac 8:10 down their strongholds, and E them to this day.
8:11 them, they destroyed and E;
Rom 6:6 might no longer be E to sin.
1Cor 6:12 I will not be E by anything.
2Pet 2:19 whatever overcomes a man, to that he is E

ENSLAVING

1Mac 8:18 the Greeks was completely E Israel.

ENSNARE (5)

Jud 10:19 will be able to E the whole world!"
Job 34:30 that he should not E the people.
Ps 35:8 net which they hid E them; let them fall
119:61 cords of the wicked E me, I do not
Prov 5:22 iniquities of the wicked E him, and he is

ENSNARED (5)

Deut 7:25 yourselves, lest you be E by it; for it
12:30 that you be not E to follow them, after
Prov 12:13 An evil man is E by the transgression of
29:6 An evil man is E in his transgression, but
Sir 25:20 Do not be E by a woman's beauty, and

ENTANGLE (2)

Prov 22:25 learn his ways and E yourself in a snare.
Mt 22:15 took counsel how to E him in his talk.

ENTANGLED (6)

Ex 14:3 of Israel, 'They are E in the land; the
2Sam 22:6 the cords of Sheol E me, the snares of
Ps 18:5 the cords of Sheol E me, the snares of
Nah 1:10 Like E thorns they are consumed, like dry stubble.
2Tim 2:4 soldier on service gets E in civilian pursuits, since
2Pet 2:20 Christ, they are again E in them and overpowered,

ENTER (185)

Gen 12:11 he was about to E Egypt, he said to
Ex 12:23 allow the destroyer to E your houses to slay
Num 4:3 old, all who can E the service, to do
4:23 them, all who can E for service, to do
4:30 every one that can E the service, to do
4:35 every one that could E the service, for work
4:39 every one that could E the service for work
4:43 every one that could E the service, for work
4:47 every one that could E to do the work
5:24 brings the curse shall E into her and cause
5:27 brings the curse shall E into her and cause
20:24 for he shall not E the land which I
34:2 to them, When you E the land of Canaan
Deut 1:38 before you, he shall E; encourage him, for he
4:21 that I should not E the good land which
23:1 cut off shall not E the assembly of the
23:2 "No bastard shall E the assembly of the LORD;
23:2 of his descendants shall E the assembly of the
23:3 Ammonite or Moabite shall E the assembly of the
23:3 belonging to them shall E the assembly of the
23:8 born to them may E the assembly of the
27:3 you pass over to E the land which the
29:12 water, that you may E into the sworn covenant
30:18 over the Jordan to E and possess.
Josh 10:19 do not let them E their cities; for the
Judg 11:18 but they did not E the territory of Moab,
18:9 slow to go, and E in and possess the
1Sam 5:5 Dagon and all who E the house of Dagon
7:13 and did not again E the territory of Israel.
9:13 As soon as you E the city, you will
1Kgs 11:2 Israel, "You shall not E into marriage with them,
14:12 When your feet E the city, the child shall
2Kgs 7:4 we say, 'Let us E the city,' the famine
2Chr 7:2 the priests could not E the house of the
23:6 Let no one E the house of the LORD
23:6 ministering Levites; they may E, for they are holy,
23:19 that no one should E who was in any
Neh 9:23 told their fathers to E and possess.
10:29 brethren, their nobles, and E into a curse and
13:1 or Moabite should ever E the assembly of God;
Tob 6:16 When you E the bridal chamber, you shall take
12:15 of the saints and E into the presence of
Jud 4:7 any who tried to E, for the approach was
Esth 4:2 for no one might E the king's gate clothed
Ps 5:7 thy steadfast love will E thy house, I will
37:15 uprightly; their sword shall E their own heart, and
45:15 led along as they E the palace of the
95:11 that they should not E my rest.
100:4 E his gates with thanksgiving, and his courts with
118:19 righteousness, that I may E through them and give
118:20 LORD; the righteous shall E through it.
132:3 Jacob, "I will not E my house or get
143:2 E not into judgment with thy servant; for no
Prov 4:15 Do not E the path of the wicked, and
23:10 an ancient landmark or E the fields of the
Wis 1:4 because wisdom will not E a deceitful soul, nor
8:16 When I E my house, I shall find rest
Is 2:10 E into the rock, and hide in the dust
2:19 And men shall E the caves of the rocks
2:21 to the bats, to E the caverns of the
13:2 hand for them to E the gates of the
24:10 house is shut up so that none can E
26:2 which keeps faith may E in.
26:20 Come, my people, E your chambers, and shut your
59:14 in the public squares, and uprightness cannot E
Jer 4:29 takes to flight; they E thickets; they climb among
7:2 men of Judah who E these gates to worship
14:18 And if I E the city, behold, the diseases
16:5 the LORD: Do not E the house of mourning,
17:19 the kings of Judah E and by which they
17:20 inhabitants of Jerusalem, who E by these gates.
17:25 it, then there shall E by the gates of
17:27 bear a burden and E by the gates of
21:13 us, or who shall E our habitations?'
22:2 and your people who E these gates.
22:4 word, then there shall E the gates of this
32:35 them, nor did it E into my mind, that
42:15 set your faces to E Egypt and go to
Lam 1:10 thou didst forbid to E thy congregation.
4:12 foe or enemy could E the gates of Jerusalem.
Bar 6:17 dust raised by the feet of those who E
Ezek 7:22 precious place; robbers shall E and profane it,
13:9 Israel, nor shall they E the land of Israel;

17:20 him to Babylon and E into judgment with him
20:35 and there I will E into judgment with you
20:36 Egypt, so I will E into judgment with you,
20:38 but they shall not E the land of Israel.
37:5 will cause breath to E you, and you shall
38:22 and bloodshed I will E into judgment with him;
42:14 When the priests E the holy place, they shall
44:2 and no one shall E by it; for the
44:3 the LORD; he shall E by way of the
44:9 people of Israel, shall E my sanctuary.
44:16 Lord GOD; they shall E my sanctuary, and they
44:17 When they E the gates of the inner court,
46:2 The prince shall E by the vestibule of the
Dan 11:7 against the army and E the fortress of the
14:21 they were accustomed to E and devour what was
Hos 4:15 E not into Gilgal, nor go up to Beth-aven,
Joel 2:9 into the houses, they E through the windows like
3:2 Jehoshaphat, and I will E into judgment with them
Amos 5:5 Bethel, and do not E into Gilgal or cross
Zech 5:4 hosts, and it shall E the house of the
1Mac 5:42 but make them all E the battle."
15:14 one to leave or E it.
2Mac 2:24 those who wish to E upon the narratives of
5:15 this, Antiochus dared to E the most holy temple
13:13 the king's army could E Judea and get possession
Mt 5:20 Pharisees, you will never E the kingdom of heaven.
7:13 E by the narrow gate; for the gate is
7:13 destruction, and those who E by it are many.
7:21 me, 'Lord, Lord,' shall E the kingdom of heaven,
10:5 among the Gentiles, and E no town of the
10:11 town or village you E, find out who is
10:12 As you E the house, salute it.
12:29 Or how can one E a strong man's house
12:45 than himself, and they E and dwell there; and
18:3 children, you will never E the kingdom of heaven.
18:8 better for you to E life maimed or lame
18:9 better for you to E life with one eye
19:17 If you would E life, keep the commandments."
19:23 a rich man to E the kingdom of heaven.
19:24 a rich man to E the kingdom of God."
23:13 men; for you neither E yourselves, nor allow those
23:13 allow those who would E to go in.
25:21 set you over much; E into the joy of
25:23 set you over much; E into the joy of
26:41 that you may not E into temptation; the spirit
Mk 1:45 could no longer openly E a town, but was
3:27 But no one can E a strong man's house
4:19 desire for other things, E in and choke the
5:12 the swine, let us E them."
6:10 to them, "Where you E a house, stay there
8:26 saying, "Do not even E the village."
9:25 of him, and never E him again."
9:43 better for you to E life maimed than with
9:44 better for you to E life lame than with
9:45 better for you to E the kingdom of God
10:15 a child shall not E it."
10:23 trust in riches to E the kingdom of God!"
10:24 trust in riches to E the kingdom of God!
10:25 a rich man to E the kingdom of God."
11:2 and immediately as you E it you will find
13:15 not go down, nor E his house, to take
14:38 that you may not E into temptation; the spirit
Lk 1:9 him by lot to E the temple of the
8:16 stand, that those who E may see the light.
8:32 him to let them E these.
8:51 permitted no one to E with him, except Peter
9:4 And whatever house you E, stay there, and from
10:5 Whatever house you E, first say, 'Peace be to
10:8 Whenever you E a town and they receive you,
10:10 you.' But whenever you E a town and they
11:26 than himself, and they E and dwell there; and
11:33 stand, that those who E may see the light.
11:52 knowledge; you did not E yourselves, and you
13:24 to them, "Strive to E by the narrow door;
13:24 you, will seek to E and will not be
18:17 a child shall not E it."
18:24 who have riches to E the kingdom of God!
18:25 a rich man to E the kingdom of God."
21:21 out in the country E it;
22:40 that you may not E into temptation."
22:44 that you may not E into temptation."
24:26 suffer these things and E into his glory?"
Jn 3:4 Can he E a second time into his mother's
3:5 the Spirit, he cannot E the kingdom of God.
10:1 he who does not E the sheepfold by the
18:28 They themselves did not E the praetorium, so that
Acts 9:6 persecuting; but rise and E the city, and you
14:22 many tribulations we must E the kingdom of God.
1Cor 14:23 and outsiders or unbelievers E, will they not say
Heb 3:11 wrath, 'They shall never E my rest.'"
3:18 that they should never E his rest, but to
3:19 they were unable to E because of unbelief.
4:3 we who have believed E that rest, as he
4:3 wrath, 'They shall never E my rest,'" although his
4:5 said, "They shall never E my rest."
4:6 remains for some to E it, and those who
4:6 good news failed to E because of disobedience,
4:11 us therefore strive to E that rest, that no
10:19 we have confidence to E the sanctuary by the
Rev 15:8 and no one could E the temple until the
21:27 But nothing unclean shall E it, nor any one
22:14 and that they may E the city by the

ENTERED (139)

Gen 7:13 his sons with them E the ark,
7:16 And they that E, male and female of all
12:14 When Abram E Egypt the Egyptians saw that the
19:3 aside to him and E his house; and he
31:33 of Leah's tent, and E Rachels.
41:46 years old when he E the service of Pharaoh
43:30 And he E his chamber and wept there.
Ex 24:18 And Moses E the cloud, and went up on
33:9 When Moses E the tent, the pillar of cloud
Josh 2:3 come to you, who E your house; for they
8:19 hand, they ran and E the city and took
10:20 remained of them had E into the fortified cities,
Judg 9:46 heard of it, they E the stronghold of the
18:17 land went up, and E and took the graven
19:29 And when he E his house, he took a
1Sam 14:26 And when the people E the forest, behold, the
16:21 came to Saul, and E his service.
29:8 from the day I E your service until now,
2Sam 10:14 fled before Abishai, and E the city.
1Kgs 20:30 Ben-hadad also fled, and E an inner chamber in
2Kgs 6:20 As soon as they E Samaria, Elisha said, "O
7:8 they came back, and E another tent, and carried
9:31 And as Jehu E the gate, she said, "Is
10:21 And they E the house of Baal, and the
12:9 right side as one E the house of the
19:23 its choicest cypresses; I E its farthest retreat, its
1Chr 19:15 Abishai, Joab's brother, and E the city.
27:24 the number was not E in the chronicles of
2Chr 15:12 And they E into a covenant to seek the
23:1 Jehoiada took courage, and E into a compact with
26:16 LORD his God, and E the temple of the
31:16 and upwards, all who E the house of the
Neh 2:15 I turned back and E by the Valley Gate,
Tob 3:17 moment Tobit returned and E his house and Sarah
5:9 invited him in; he E and they greeted each
Esth 6:4 Now Haman had just E the outer court of
Job 38:16 "Have you E into the springs of the sea,
38:22 "Have you E the storehouses of the snow, or
Wis 2:24 the devil's envy death E the world, and those
3:13 undefiled, who has not E into a sinful union;
8:20 rather, being good, I E an undefiled body.
10:16 She E the soul of a servant of the
14:14 vanity of men they E the world, and therefore
Sir 51:15 in her; my foot E upon the straight path;
Jer 9:21 our windows, it has E our palaces, cutting off
32:23 and honey; and they E and took possession of
34:10 the people who had E into the covenant that
52:12 the king of Babylon, E Jerusalem.
Bar 3:15 And who has E her storehouses?
Ezek 2:2 to me, the Spirit E into me and set
3:24 But the Spirit E into me, and set me
16:8 troth to you and E into a covenant with
20:36 As I E into judgment with your fathers in
43:4 glory of the LORD E the temple by the
44:2 God of Israel, has E by it; therefore it
46:9 gate by which he E, but each shall go
Dan 10:3 no meat or wine E my mouth, nor did
Obad 1:11 his wealth, and foreigners E his gates and cast
1:13 You should not have E the gate of my
1Mac 1:21 He arrogantly E the sanctuary and took the golden
4:5 When Gorgias E the camp of Judas by night,
6:62 But when the king E Mount Zion and saw
8:19 long journey; and they E the senate chamber and
10:83 fled to Azotus and E Beth-dagon, the temple of
11:3 But when Ptolemy E the cities he stationed forces
11:13 Then Ptolemy E Antioch and put on the crown
12:3 went to Rome and E the senate chamber and
12:48 But when Jonathan E Ptolemais, the men of

12:48 and all who had E with him they killed
13:47 idols were, and then E it with hymns and
13:51 seventy-first year, the Jews E it with praise and
2Mac 1:15 as soon as he E it.
3:28 man who had just E the aforesaid treasury with
8:1 and his companions secretly E the villages and
9:2 For he had E the city called Persepolis, and
Mt 8:5 As he E Caperna-um, a centurion came forward to
8:14 And when Jesus E Peter's house, he saw his
9:28 When he E the house, the blind men came
12:4 with him: how he E the house of God
12:9 on from there, and E their synagogue.
19:1 away from Galilee and E the region of Judea
21:10 And when he E Jerusalem, all the city was
21:12 And Jesus E the temple of God and drove
21:23 And when he E the temple, the chief priests
24:38 the day when Noah E the ark,
Mk 1:21 on the sabbath he E the synagogue and taught.
1:29 left the synagogue, and E the house of Simon
2:26 with him: how he E the house of God,
3:1 Again he E the synagogue, and a man was
5:13 spirits came out, and E the swine; and the
5:39 And when he had E, he said to them,
7:16 And when he had E the house, and left
7:23 And he E a house, and would not have
9:28 And when he had E the house, his disciples
11:11 And he E Jerusalem, and went into the temple;
11:15 And he E the temple and began to drive
Lk 1:40 of Judah, and she E the house of Zechariah
4:38 left the synagogue, and E Simon's house.
6:4 with him: how he E the house of God,
6:6 another sabbath, when he E the synagogue and
7:1 of the people he E Caperna-um.
7:44 I E your house, you gave me no water
8:30 for many demons had E him.
8:33 of the man and E the swine, and the
9:34 were afraid as they E the cloud.
9:52 him, who went and E a village of the
10:38 on their way, he E a village; and a
17:12 And as he E a village, he was met
17:27 the day when Noah E the ark, and the
19:1 He E Jericho and was passing through.
19:45 And he E the temple and began to drive
22:3 Then Satan E into Judas called Iscariot, who was
22:10 "Behold, when you have E the city, a man
Jn 4:38 labored, and you have E into their labor."
6:22 that Jesus had not E the boat with his
13:27 after the morsel, Satan E into him.
18:1 was a garden, which he and his disciples E
18:15 the high priest, he E the court of the
18:33 Pilate E the praetorium again and called Jesus, and
19:9 the more afraid; he E the praetorium again and
Acts 1:13 and when they had E, they went up to
3:2 alms of those who E the temple.
3:8 stood and walked and E the temple with them,
5:21 they heard this, they E the temple at daybreak
9:17 So Ananias departed and E the house.
10:24 the following day they E Caesarea.
10:25 When Peter E, Cornelius met him and fell down
11:8 or unclean has ever E my mouth.'
11:12 accompanied me, and we E the man's house.
14:1 Now at Iconium they E together into the Jewish
14:20 he rose up and E the city; and on
19:8 And he E the synagogue and for three months
21:8 to Caesarea; and we E the house of Philip
23:16 so he went and E the barracks and told
25:23 great pomp, and they E the audience hall with
Phil 4:15 left Macedonia, no church E into partnership with
Heb 9:12 of this creation) he E once for all into
9:24 For Christ has E, not into a sanctuary made
Rev 11:11 of life from God E them, and they stood

ENTERING (21)

Deut 4:5 land which you are E to take possession of
7:1 land which you are E to take possession of
11:10 land which you are E to take possession of
11:29 land which you are E to take possession of
23:20 land which you are E to take possession of
28:21 land which you are E to take possession of
28:63 land which you are E to take possession of
30:16 land which you are E to take possession of
1Sam 9:14 As they were E the city, they saw Samuel
23:7 shut himself in by E a town that has
2Sam 15:37 just as Absalom was E Jerusalem.
17:17 must not be seen E the city.
Ezra 9:11 land which you are E, to take possession of
Tob 4:10 and keeps you from E the darkness;
Jer 25:31 the nations; he is E into judgment with all
1Mac 7:2 As he was E the royal palace of his
Mk 16:5 And E the tomb, they saw a young man
Lk 11:52 yourselves, and you hindered those who were E
19:30 village opposite, where on E you will find a
Acts 8:3 ravaging the church, and E house after house, he
Heb 4:1 while the promise of E his rest remains, let

ENTERS (29)

Lev 14:46 Moreover he who E the house while it is
16:17 of meeting when he E to make atonement in
2Chr 23:7 his hand; and whoever E the house shall be
Job 22:4 he reproves you, and E into judgment with you?
Ps 118:26 Blessed be he who E in the name of
Sir 4:13 and the Lord will bless the place she E
Is 3:14 The LORD E into judgment with the elders and
57:2 away from calamity, he E into peace; they rest
59:4 No one E suit justly, no one goes to
Ezek 26:10 and chariots, when he E your gates as one
26:10 your gates as one E a city which has
42:9 east side, as one E them from the outer
42:12 east side, where one E the passage, and opposite
44:21 drink wine, when he E the inner court.
46:8 When the prince E, he shall go in by
46:9 appointed feasts, he who E by the north gate
46:9 gate; and he who E by the south gate
47:8 Arabah; and when it E the stagnant waters of
Hab 3:16 at the sound; rottenness E into my bones, my
Mk 7:18 defile him, since it E, not his heart but
14:14 him, and wherever he E, say to the householder,
Lk 16:16 preached, and every one E it violently.
22:10 the house which he E,
Jn 10:2 robber; but he who E by the door is
10:9 door; if any one E by me, he will
1Cor 14:24 an unbeliever or outsider E, he is convicted by
Heb 4:10 of God; for whoever E God's rest also ceases
6:19 soul, a hope that E into the inner shrine
9:25 as the high priest E the Holy Place yearly

ENTERTAINED (2)

Acts 28:7 who received us and E us hospitably for three
Heb 13:2 for thereby some have E angels unawares.

ENTERTAINMENT

Sir 32:4 Where there is E, do not pour out talk;

ENTHRONED (17)

1Sam 4:4 of hosts, who is E on the cherubim; and
2Sam 6:2 of hosts who sits E on the cherubim.
2Kgs 19:15 of Israel, who art E above the cherubim, thou
1Chr 13:6 the LORD who sits E above the cherubim.
Ps 9:7 But the LORD sits E for ever, he has
22:3 Yet thou art holy, E on the praises of
29:10 The LORD sits E over the flood; the LORD
29:10 flood; the LORD sits E as king for ever.
33:14 from where he sits E he looks forth on
55:19 them, he who is E from of old; because
61:7 May he be E for ever before God; bid
80:1 Thou who art E upon the cherubim, shine forth
99:1 He sits E upon the cherubim; let the earth
102:12 thou, O LORD, art E for ever; thy name
123:1 O thou who art E in the heavens!
Is 37:16 of Israel, who art E above the cherubim, thou
Bar 3:3 For thou art E for ever, and we are

ENTICE (13)

Judg 14:15 said to Samson's wife, E your husband to tell
16:5 and said to her, E him, and see wherein
1Kgs 22:20 LORD said, 'Who will E Ahab, that he may
22:21 LORD, saying, 'I will E him.'
22:22 said, 'You are to E him, and you shall
2Chr 18:19 LORD said, 'Who will E Ahab the king of
18:20 LORD, saying, 'I will E him.' And the LORD
18:21 said, 'You are to E him, and you shall
Jud 10:4 herself very beautiful, to E the eyes of all
Job 36:18 Beware lest wrath E you into scoffing; and let
Prov 1:10 My son, if sinners E you, do not consent.
2Pet 2:14 They E unsteady souls.
2:18 boasts of folly, they E with licentious passions of

ENTICED (3)

Job 31:9 my heart has been E to a woman, and
31:27 heart has been secretly E, and my mouth has
Jas 1:13 he is lured and E by his own desire.

ENTICES (2)
Deut 13:6 as your own soul, E you secretly, saying, 'Let
Prov 16:29 A man of violence E his neighbor and leads

ENTIRE (8)
Lev 3:9 fat, the fat tail E, taking it away close
Deut 2:14 thirty-eight years, until the E generation, that is, the
1Kgs 7:1 and he finished his E house.
2Kgs 6:24 of Syria mustered his E army, and went up,
Tob 1:21 kingdom and over the E administration.
Jer 36:23 the brazier, until the E scroll was consumed in
1Mac 3:40 they departed with their E force, and when they
Tit 2:10 pilfer, but to show E and true fidelity, so

ENTIRELY
1Cor 9:10 Does he not speak E for our sake?

ENTITLED (3)
Tob 3:17 demon, because Tobias was E to possess her.
6:11 marriage, because you are E to her and to
6:12 any other man are E to the inheritance."

ENTRAILS (22)
Ex 29:13 fat that covers the E, and the appendage of
29:17 pieces, and wash its E and its legs, and
29:22 fat that covers the E, and the appendage of
Lev 1:9 the altar; but its E and its legs he
1:13 the altar; but the E and the legs he
3:3 the fat covering the E and all the fat
3:3 that is on the E,
3:9 fat that covers the E, and all the fat
3:9 that is on the E,
3:14 the fat covering the E, and all the fat
3:14 that is on the E,
4:8 fat that covers the E and all the fat
4:8 that is on the E,
4:11 head, its legs, its E, and its dung,
7:3 fat that covers the E,
8:16 that was on the E, and the appendage of
8:21 And when the E and the legs were washed
8:25 that was on the E, and the appendage of
9:14 And he washed the E and the legs, and
9:19 that which covers the E, and the kidneys, and
Prov 7:23 an arrow pierces its E; as a bird rushes
2Mac 14:46 he tore out his E, took them with both

ENTRANCE (77)
Gen 38:14 and sat at the E to Enaim, which is
Num 4:26 the screen for the E of the gate of
10:3 to you at the E of the tent of
13:21 to Rehob, near the E of Hamath.
16:18 they stood at the E of the tent of
16:19 against them at the E of the tent of
16:50 to Moses at the E of the tent of
34:8 it out to the E of Hamath, and the
Josh 8:29 cast it at the E of the gate of
13:5 Mount Hermon to the E of Hamath,
20:4 shall stand at the E of the gate of
Judg 3:3 as far as the E of Hamath.
9:35 and stood in the E of the gate of
9:40 wounded, up to the E of the gate.
9:44 and stood at the E of the gate of
18:16 war, stood by the E of the gate;
18:17 priest stood by the E of the gate with
1Sam 2:22 who served at the E to the tent of
2Sam 10:8 battle array at the E of the gate; and
11:23 them back to the E of the gate.
1Kgs 6:8 The E for the lowest story was on the
6:31 For the E to the inner sanctuary he made
6:33 he made for the E to the nave doorposts
8:65 great assembly, from the E of Hamath to the
18:46 before Ahab to the E of Jezreel.
19:13 and stood at the E of the cave.
22:10 threshing floor at the E of the gate of
2Kgs 7:3 were lepers at the E to the gate; and
10:8 two heaps at the E of the gate until
11:16 went through the horses' E to the king's house,
14:25 of Israel from the E of Hamath as far
16:18 palace, and the outer E for the king he
23:8 that were at the E of the gate of
23:11 the sun, at the E to the house of
1Chr 4:39 They journeyed to the E of Gedor, to the
5:9 as far as the E of the desert this
9:19 the camp of the LORD, keepers of the E
9:21 was gatekeeper at the E of the tent of
13:5 of Egypt to the E of Hamath, to bring
19:9 battle array at the E of the city, and
2Chr 7:8 great congregation, from the E of Hamath to the
18:9 threshing floor at the E of the gate of
23:13 his pillar at the E, and the captains and
23:15 she went into the E of the horse gate
33:14 valley, and for the E into the Fish Gate,
Esth 4:2 went up to the E of the king's gate,
5:1 the palace opposite the E to the palace;
Ps 74:5 At the upper E they hacked the wooden trellis
Prov 1:21 cries out; at the E of the city gates
8:3 the town, at the E of the portals she
Wis 7:6 for all mankind one E into life, and a
7:25 therefore nothing defiled gains E into her.
Jer 1:15 his throne at the E of the gates of
38:14 him at the third E of the temple of
43:9 which is at the E to Pharaoh's palace in
Ezek 8:3 to Jerusalem, to the E of the gateway of
8:5 altar gate, in the E, was this image of
8:14 brought me to the E of the north gate
27:3 who dwells at the E to the sea, merchant
40:15 the gate at the E to the end of
40:40 the vestibule at the E of the north gate
41:2 the breadth of the E was ten cubits; and
41:2 the sidewalls of the E were five cubits on
41:3 the jambs of the E, two cubits; and the
41:3 the breadth of the E, six cubits; and the
41:3 the sidewalls of the E, seven cubits.
42:9 these chambers was an E on the east side,
42:12 south chambers was an E on the east side,
46:3 shall worship at the E of that gate before
46:19 brought me through the E, which was at the
47:15 of Hethlon to the E of Hamath, and on
47:20 a point opposite the E of Hamath.
48:1 of Hethlon to the E of Hamath, as far
Dan 14:13 had made a hidden E, through which they used
Amos 6:14 oppress you from the E of Hamath to the
2Mac 2:5 altar of incense, and he sealed up the E
2Pet 1:11 provided for you an E into the eternal kingdom

ENTRANCES
Ezek 43:11 its exits and its E, and its whole form;

ENTRAP
Mk 12:13 of the Herodi-ans, to E him in his talk.

ENTREAT (20)
Gen 23:8 sight, hear me, and E for me Ephron the
Ex 8:8 and Aaron, and said, E the LORD to take
8:9 when I am to E, for you and for
9:28 E the LORD; for there has been enough of
10:17 only this once, and E the LORD your God
Ruth 1:16 But Ruth said, E me not to leave you
1Kgs 13:6 the man of God, E now the favor of
Esth 4:8 supplication to him and E him for her people.
Job 11:19 you afraid; many will E your favor.
Ps 119:58 I E thy favor with all my heart; be
Jer 26:19 fear the LORD and E the favor of the
Zech 7:2 and their men, to E the favor of the
8:21 go at once to E the favor of the
8:22 in Jerusalem, and to E the favor of the
Mal 1:9 And now E the favor of God, that he
2Cor 6:1 with him, then, we E you not to accept
10:1 I, Paul, myself E you, by the meekness and
Phil 4:2 I E Eu-odia and I entreat Syntyche to agree
4:2 entreat Eu-odia and I E Syntyche to agree in
Heb 12:19 words made the hearers E that no further messages

ENTREATED (10)
Ex 10:18 out from Pharaoh, and E the LORD.
Judg 13:8 Then Manoah E the LORD, and said, "O, LORD,
1Sam 13:12 and I have not E the favor of the
1Kgs 13:6 the man of God E the LORD; and the
2Kgs 1:13 knees before Elijah, and E him, "O man of
2Chr 33:12 was in distress he E the favor of the
Jer 15:11 if I have not E thee for their good,
Bar 2:8 Yet we have not E the favor of the
Dan 9:13 yet we have not E the favor of the
Lk 15:28 father came out and E him,

ENTREATIES
Prov 18:23 The poor use E, but the rich answer roughly.

ENTREATING
Acts 9:38 two men to him E him, "Please come to

ENTREATS
Wis 13:18 dead; for aid he E a thing that is

ENTREATY (7)
Ex 8:28 Make E for me."
1Chr 5:20 and he granted their E because they trusted in
2Chr 33:13 and God received his E and heard his supplication
33:19 how God received his E, and all his sin
Ezra 8:23 God for this, and he listened to our E
1Mac 11:49 the king with this E,
2Mac 3:20 up their hands to heaven, they all made E

ENTRUST (5)
Sir 50:24 May he E to us his mercy!
2Mac 7:24 for his friend and E him with public affairs.
Lk 16:11 unrighteous mammon, who will E to you the true
2Tim 2:2 me before many witnesses E to faithful men who
1Pet 4:19 will do right and E their souls to a

ENTRUSTED (18)
Num 12:7 servant Moses; he is E with all my house.
Esth 16:5 friends who have been E with the administration of
Jer 39:14 They E him to Gedaliah the son of Ahikam,
2Mac 3:22 keep what had been E safe and secure for
3:22 for those who had E it,
9:25 whom I have often E and commended to most
10:13 Cyprus, which Philometor had E to him, and had
Mt 25:14 called his servants and E to them his property;
Rom 3:2 with, the Jews are E with the oracles of
1Cor 9:17 own will, I am E with a commission.
Gal 2:7 that I had been E with the gospel to
2:7 as Peter had been E with the gospel to
1Thes 2:4 by God to be E with the gospel, so
1Tim 1:11 the blessed God with which I have been E
6:20 guard what has been E to you.
2Tim 1:12 Day what has been E to me.
1:14 truth that has been E to you by the
Tit 1:3 which I have been E by command of God

ENTRUSTING (2)
Tob 10:12 See, I am E my daughter to you; do
2Cor 5:19 trespasses against them, and E to us the message

ENTRY (3)
Jer 19:2 of Hinnom at the E of the Potsherd Gate,
26:10 their seat in the E of the New Gate
36:10 upper court, at the E of the New Gate

ENVELOPED (2)
Wis 18:14 For while gentle silence E all things, and night
Lam 3:5 he has besieged and E me with bitterness and

ENVIABLE
2Mac 7:24 make him rich and E if he would turn

ENVIED (4)
Gen 26:14 so that the Philistines E him.
30:1 Jacob no children, she E her sister; and she
Sir 45:18 conspired against him, and E him in the wilderness,
Ezek 31:9 the trees of Eden E it, that were in

ENVIOUS (8)
1Sam 2:32 you will look with E eye on all the
Ps 37:1 the wicked, be not E of wrongdoers!
73:3 For I was E of the arrogant, when I
Prov 24:1 Be not E of evil men, nor desire to
24:19 evildoers, and be not E of the wicked;
Sir 14:3 is property to an E man?
26:6 when a wife is E of a rival, and
30:3 will make his enemies E, and will glory in

ENVIRONS (3)
1Mac 10:31 let Jerusalem and her E, her tithes and her
10:89 Ekron and all its E as his possession.
14:36 forth and defile the E of the sanctuary and

ENVOY (2)
Prov 13:17 trouble, but a faithful E brings healing.
1Mac 12:8 Onias welcomed the E with honor, and received the

ENVOYS (19)
2Kgs 20:12 king of Babylon, sent E with letters and a
2Chr 32:31 the matter of the E of the princes of
35:21 But he sent E to him, saying, "What have
Is 30:4 at Zoan and his E reach Hanes,
33:7 ones cry without; the E of peace weep bitterly.
39:1 king of Babylon, sent E with letters and a
57:9 perfumes; you sent your E far-off, and sent down
Jer 27:3 the hand of the E who have come to
1Mac 11:9 He sent E to Demetrius the king, saying, "Come,
12:4 to provide for the E safe conduct to the
12:23 therefore command that our E report to you
13:14 him, so he sent E to him and said,
13:21 the citadel kept sending E to Trypho urging him
14:21 The E who were sent to our people have
14:22 the son of Jason, E of the Jews, have
14:40 Romans had received the E of Simon with honor.
15:17 The E of the Jews have come to us
2Mac 4:19 the vile Jason sent E, chosen as being Antiochian
11:34 Memmius and Titus Manius, E of the Romans, to

ENVY (22)
Ps 68:16 Why look you with E, O many-peaked mountain, at
Prov 3:31 Do not E a man of violence and do
23:17 Let not your heart E sinners, but continue in
Eccl 4:4 come from a man's E of his neighbor.
9:6 their hate and their E have already perished, and
Wis 2:24 but through the devil's E death entered the world,
6:23 the company of sickly E, for envy does not
6:23 of sickly envy, for E does not associate with
Sir 9:11 Do not E the honors of a sinner, for
40:5 there is anger and E and trouble and unrest,
Ezek 35:11 to the anger and E which you showed because
1Mac 8:16 and there is no E or jealousy among them.
Mt 27:18 it was out of E that they had delivered
Mk 7:21 wickedness, deceit, licentiousness, E, slander, pride,
15:10 it was out of E that the chief priests
Rom 1:29 Full of E, murder, strife, deceit, malignity, they are
Gal 5:21 selfishness, dissension, party spirit, E, drunkenness,
5:26 of one another, no E of one another.
Phil 1:15 indeed preach Christ from E and rivalry, but others
1Tim 6:4 about words, which produce E, dissension, slander,
Tit 3:3 days in malice and E, hated by men and
1Pet 2:1 guile and insincerity and E and all slander.

ENWRAP
Job 22:14 Thick clouds E him, so that he does not

EPAENETUS
Rom 16:5 Greet my beloved E, who was the first convert

EPAPHRAS (3)
Col 1:7 you learned it from E our beloved fellow servant.
4:12 E, who is one of yourselves, a servant of
Philem 1:23 E, my fellow prisoner in Christ Jesus, sends greetings

EPAPHRODITUS (2)
Phil 2:25 to send to you E my brother and fellow
4:18 filled, having received from E the gifts you sent,

EPHAH (55)
Gen 25:4 sons of Midian were E, Epher, Hanoch, Abida, and
Ex 16:36 tenth part of an E
Lev 5:11 a tenth of an E of fine flour for
6:20 a tenth of an E of fine flour as
14:10 three tenths of an E of fine flour mixed
14:21 a tenth of an E of fine flour mixed
19:36 just weights, a just E, and a just hin:
23:13 two tenths of an E of fine flour mixed
23:17 two tenths of an E; they shall be of
24:5 two tenths of an E shall be in each
Num 5:15 a tenth of an E of barley meal; he
15:4 a tenth of an E of fine flour, mixed
15:6 two tenths of an E of fine flour mixed
15:9 three tenths of an E of fine flour, mixed
28:5 a tenth of an E of fine flour for
28:9 two tenths of an E of fine flour for
28:12 three tenths of an E of fine flour for
28:20 three tenths of an E shall you offer for
28:28 three tenths of an E for each bull, two
29:3 three tenths of an E for the bull, two
29:9 three tenths of an E for the bull, two
29:14 three tenths of an E for each of the
Judg 6:19 unleavened cakes from an E of flour; the meat
Ruth 2:17 it was about an E of barley.
1Sam 1:24 a three-year-old bull, an E of flour, and a
17:17 for your brothers an E of this parched grain,
1Chr 1:33 The sons of Midian: E, Epher, Hanoch, Abida, and
2:46 E also, Caleb's concubine, bore Haran, Moza, and
2:47 Regem, Jotham, Geshan, Pelet, E, and Shaaph.
Is 5:10 a homer of seed shall yield but an E
60:6 camels of Midian and E; all those from Sheba

Ezek 45:10 just balances, a just E, and a just bath.
45:11 The E and the bath shall be of the
45:11 a homer, and the E one tenth of a
45:13 one sixth of an E from each homer of
45:13 one sixth of an E from each homer of
45:24 a cereal offering an E for each bull, an
45:24 for each bull, an E for each ram, and
45:24 ram, and a hin of oil to each E
46:5 ram shall be an E, and the cereal offering
46:5 together with a hin of oil to each E
46:7 he shall provide an E with the bull and
46:7 the bull and an E with the ram, and
46:7 together with a hin of oil to each E
46:11 bull shall be an E, and with a ram
46:11 with a ram an E, and with the lambs
46:11 together with a hin of oil to an E
46:14 one sixth of an E, and one third of
Amos 8:5 we may make the E small and the shekel
Zech 5:6 said, "This is the E that goes forth." And
5:7 and there was a woman sitting in the E
5:8 her back into the E, and thrust down the
5:9 they lifted up the E between earth and heaven.
5:10 talked with me, "Where are they taking the E
5:11 they will set the E down there on its

EPHAI

Jer 40:8 Tanhumeth, the sons of E the Netophathite, Jezaniah

EPHER (4)

Gen 25:4 of Midian were Ephah, E, Hanoch, Abida, and
1Chr 1:33 sons of Midian: Ephah, E, Hanoch, Abida, and
4:17 of Ezrah: Jether, Mered, E, and Jalon.
5:24 of their fathers' houses: E, Ishi, Eliel, Azriel,

EPHES-DAMMIM

1Sam 17:1 and encamped between Socoh and Azekah, in E

EPHESIAN

Acts 21:29 previously seen Trophimus the E with him in the

EPHESIANS (3)

Acts 19:28 and cried out, "Great is Artemis of the E
19:34 voice cried out, "Great is Artemis of the E
19:35 the city of the E is temple keeper of

EPHESUS (16)

Acts 18:19 And they came to E, and he left them
18:21 and he set sail from E
18:24 named Apollos, a native of Alexandria, came to E
19:1 passed through the upper country and came to E
19:17 to all residents of E, both Jews and Greeks;
19:26 that not only at E but almost throughout all
19:35 he said, "Men of E, what man is there
20:16 decided to sail past E, so that he might
20:17 Miletus he sent to E and called to him
1Cor 15:32 if, humanly speaking, I fought with beasts at E
16:8 I will stay in E until Pentecost,
1Tim 1:3 to Macedonia, remain at E that you may charge
2Tim 1:18 well know all the service he rendered at E
4:12 Tychicus I have sent to E
Rev 1:11 the seven churches, to E and to Smyrna and
2:1 of the church in E write: 'The words of

EPHLAL (2)

1Chr 2:37 was the father of E, and Ephlal of Obed.
2:37 father of Ephlal, and E of Obed.

EPHOD (52)

Ex 25:7 for setting, for the E and for the breastpiece.
28:4 make: a breastpiece, an E, a robe, a coat
28:6 they shall make the E of gold, of blue
28:12 the shoulder-pieces of the E, as stones of
28:15 the work of the E you shall make it;
28:25 it in front to the shoulder-pieces of the E
28:26 breastpiece, on its inside edge next to the E
28:27 two shoulder-pieces of the E, at its joining above
28:27 joining above the skilfully woven band of the E
28:28 the rings of the E with a lace of
28:28 woven band of the E, and that the breastpiece
28:28 the breastpiece shall not come loose from the E
28:31 the robe of the E all of blue.
29:5 the robe of the E, and the ephod, and
29:5 the ephod, and the E, and the breastpiece, and
29:5 woven band of the E;
35:9 for setting, for the E and for the breastpiece.
35:27 be set, for the E and for the breastpiece,
39:2 And he made the E of gold, blue and
39:4 They made for the E shoulder-pieces, joined to it
39:7 the shoulder-pieces of the E, to be stones of
39:8 the work of the E, of gold, blue and
39:18 it in front to the shoulder-pieces of the E
39:19 breastpiece, on its inside edge next to the E
39:20 two shoulder-pieces of the E, at its joining above
39:20 joining above the skilfully woven band of the E
39:21 the rings of the E with a lace of
39:21 woven band of the E, and that the breastpiece
39:21 come loose from the E; as the LORD had
39:22 the robe of the E woven all of blue;
Lev 8:7 robe, and put the E upon him, and girded
8:7 woven band of the E, binding it to him
Num 34:23 of Manasseh a leader, Hanniel the son of E
Judg 8:27 And Gideon made an E of it and put
17:5 and he made an E and teraphim, and installed
18:14 houses there are an E, teraphim, a graven image,
18:17 the graven image, the E, the teraphim, and the
18:18 the graven image, the E, the teraphim, and the
18:20 glad; he took the E, and the teraphim, and
1Sam 2:18 the LORD, a boy girded with a linen E
2:28 incense, to wear an E before me; and I
14:3 priest of the LORD in Shiloh, wearing an E
21:9 a cloth behind the E; if you will take
22:18 that day eighty-five persons who wore the linen E
23:6 came down with an E in his hand.
23:9 the priest, "Bring the E here."
30:7 priest, the son of Ahimelech, "Bring me the E
30:7 So Abiathar brought the E to David.
2Sam 6:14 might; and David was girded with a linen E
1Chr 15:27 of the singers; and David wore a linen E
Sir 45:8 the linen breeches, the long robe, and the E
Hos 3:4 sacrifice or pillar, without E or teraphim.

EPHPHATHA

Mk 7:33 to heaven, he sighed, and said to him, E

EPHRAIM (176)

Gen 41:52 the second he called E, "For God has made
46:20 were born Manasseh and E, whom Asenath, the
48:1 took with him his two sons, Manasseh and E
48:5 in Egypt, are mine; E and Manasseh shall be
48:13 Joseph took them both, E in his right hand
48:14 upon the head of E, who was the younger,
48:17 upon the head of E, it displeased him; and
48:17 to remove it from E's head to Manasseh's head.
48:20 'God make you as E and as Manasseh'"; and
48:20 and thus he put E before Manasseh.
50:23 And Joseph saw E's children of the third generation;
Num 1:10 sons of Joseph, from E, Elishama the son of
1:32 of the people of E, their generations, by their
1:33 of the tribe of E was forty thousand five
2:18 of the camp of E by their companies, the
2:18 of the people of E being Elishama the son
2:24 of the camp of E, by their companies, is
7:48 of the men of E:
10:22 of the men of E set out by their
13:8 from the tribe of E, Hoshea the son of
26:28 Joseph according to their families: Manasseh and E
26:35 are the sons of E according to their families:
26:37 of the sons of E according to their number,
34:24 of the sons of E a leader, Kemuel the
Deut 33:17 the ten thousands of E, and such are the
34:2 Naphtali, the land of E and Manasseh, all the
Josh 14:4 two tribes, Manasseh and E; and no portion was
16:4 of Joseph, Manasseh and E, received their
16:10 in the midst of E to this day but
17:8 boundary of Manasseh belonged to the sons of E
17:9 brook, among the cities of Manasseh, belong to E
17:10 to the south being E's and that to the
17:15 the hill country of E is too narrow for
17:17 house of Joseph, to E and Manasseh, "You are
19:50 the hill country of E; and he rebuilt the
20:7 the hill country of E, and Kiriath-arba (that is,
21:5 of the tribe of E, from the tribe of
21:20 to them were out of the tribe of E
21:21 the hill country of E, Gezer with its pasture
24:30 the hill country of E, north of the mountain
24:33 been given him in the hill country of E
Judg 1:29 And E did not drive out the Canaanites who
2:9 the hill country of E, north of the mountain
3:27 the hill country of E; and the people of
4:5 the hill country of E; and the people of
5:14 From E they set out thither into the valley,
7:24 the hill country of E, saying, "Come down against

7:24 all the men of E were called out, and
8:1 And the men of E said to him, "What
8:2 of the grapes of E better than the vintage
10:1 lived at Shamir in the hill country of E
10:9 against the house of E; so that Israel was
12:1 The men of E were called to arms, and
12:4 Gilead and fought with E; and the men of
12:4 men of Gilead smote E, because they said, "You
12:4 "You are fugitives of E, you Gileadites, in the
12:4 in the midst of E and Manasseh."
12:5 of the fugitives of E said, "Let me go
12:15 in the land of E, in the hill country
17:1 the hill country of E, whose name was Micah.
17:8 the hill country of E to the house of
18:2 the hill country of E, to the house of
18:13 the hill country of E, and came to the
19:1 the hill country of E, who took to himself
19:16 the hill country of E, and he was sojourning
19:18 the hill country of E, from which I come.
1Sam 1:1 the hill country of E, whose name was Elkanah
9:4 the hill country of E and passed through the
14:22 the hill country of E heard that the Philistines
2Sam 2:9 Ashurites and Jezreel and E and Benjamin and all
13:23 Baal-hazor, which is near E, and Absalom invited all
18:6 the battle was fought in the forest of E
20:21 the hill country of E, called Sheba the son
1Kgs 4:8 the hill country of E;
12:25 the hill country of E, and dwelt there; and
2Kgs 5:22 the hill country of E two young men of
14:13 hundred cubits, from the E Gate to the Corner
1Chr 6:66 of their territory out of the tribe of E
6:67 the hill country of E, Gezer with its pasture
7:20 The sons of E: Shuthelah, and Bered his son,
7:22 And E their father mourned many days, and his
7:23 And E went in to his wife, and she
9:3 people of Judah, Benjamin, E, and Manasseh dwelt
27:10 of the sons of E; in his division were
27:14 of the sons of E; in his division were
2Chr 13:4 the hill country of E, and said, "Hear me,
15:8 the hill country of E, and he repaired the
15:9 Benjamin, and those from E, Manasseh, and Simeon
17:2 in the cities of E which Asa his father
19:4 the hill country of E, and brought them back
25:10 come to him from E, to go home again.
25:23 hundred cubits, from the E Gate to the Corner
28:7 a mighty man of E, slew Ma-aseiah the king's
28:12 of the men of E, Azariah the son of
30:1 wrote letters also to E and Manasseh, that they
30:10 through the country of E and Manasseh, and as
30:18 many of them from E, Manasseh, Issachar, and
31:1 and Benjamin, and in E and Manasseh, until they
34:6 the cities of Manasseh, E, and Simeon, and as
34:9 collected from Manasseh and E and from all the
Neh 8:16 and in the square at the Gate of E
12:39 above the Gate of E, and by the Old
Jud 6:2 and you hirelings of E, to prophesy among us
Ps 60:7 mine; Manasseh is mine; E is my helmet; Judah
78:67 choose the tribe of E;
80:2 cherubim, shine forth before E and Benjamin and
108:8 mine; Manasseh is mine; E is my helmet; Judah
Sir 47:21 divided and a disobedient kingdom arose out of E
47:23 to sin and gave E a sinful way.
Is 7:2 David was told, "Syria is in league with E
7:5 Because Syria, with E and the son of Remaliah,
7:8 (Within sixty-five years E will be broken to pieces
7:9 And the head of E is Samaria, and the
7:17 since the day that E departed from Judah—
9:9 the people will know, E and the inhabitants of
9:21 his neighbor's flesh, Manasseh E, and E
11:13 The jealousy of E shall depart, and those who
11:13 shall be cut off; E shall not be jealous
11:13 jealous of Judah, and Judah shall not harass E
17:3 fortress will disappear from E, and the kingdom
28:1 of the drunkards of E, and to the fading
28:3 of the drunkards of E will be trodden under
Jer 4:15 declares from Dan and proclaims evil from Mount E
7:15 out all your kinsmen, all the offspring of E
31:6 the hill country of E: 'Arise, and let us
31:9 father to Israel, and E is my first-born.
31:18 I have heard E bemoaning, 'Thou hast chastened me,
31:20 of my youth.' Is E my dear son?
50:19 on the hills of E and in Gilead.
Ezek 37:16 Joseph (the stick of E and all the house
37:19 in the hand of E and the tribes of
48:5 side to the west, E, one portion.
48:6 Adjoining the territory of E, from the east side
Hos 4:17 E is joined to idols, let him alone.
5:3 I know E, and Israel is not hid from
5:3 me; for now, O E, you have played the
5:5 testifies to his face; E shall stumble in his
5:9 E shall become a desolation in the day of
5:11 E is oppressed, crushed in judgment, because he was
5:12 like a moth to E, and like dry rot
5:13 When E saw his sickness, and Judah his wound,
5:13 Judah his wound, then E went to Assyria, and
5:14 like a lion to E, and like a young
6:4 What shall I do with you, O E
6:10 seen a horrible thing; E's harlotry is there, Israel
7:2 Israel, the corruption of E is revealed, and the
7:9 E mixes himself with the peoples; Ephraim is a
7:9 himself with the peoples; E is a cake not
7:12 E is like a dove, silly and without sense,
8:9 wild ass wandering alone; E has hired lovers.
8:11 Because E has multiplied altars for sinning, they
9:3 of the LORD; but E shall return to Egypt,
9:8 is the watchman of E, the people of my
9:11 E's glory shall fly away like a bird—no
9:13 E's sons, as I have seen, are destined for
9:13 destined for a prey; E must lead forth his
9:16 E is stricken, their root is dried up, they
10:6 E shall be put to shame, and Israel shall
10:11 E was a trained heifer that loved to thresh,
10:11 but I will put E to the yoke, Judah
11:3 was I who taught E to walk, I took
11:8 How can I give you up, O E
11:9 will not again destroy E; for I am God
11:12 E has encompassed me with lies, and the house
12:1 E herds the wind, and pursues the east wind
12:8 E has said, "Ah, but I am rich, I
12:14 E has given bitter provocation; so his LORD will
13:1 When E spoke, men trembled; he was exalted in
13:12 The iniquity of E is bound up, his sin
14:8 O E, what have I to do with idols?
Obad 1:19 possess the land of E and the land of
Zech 9:10 off the chariot from E and the war horse
9:13 bow; I have made E its arrow.
10:7 Then E shall become like a mighty warrior, and
Jn 11:54 to a town called E; and there he stayed

EPHRAIMITE (3)

Judg 12:5 of Gilead said to him, "Are you an E
1Sam 1:1 Elihu, son of Tohu, son of Zuph, an E
1Kgs 11:26 son of Nebat, an E of Zeredah, a servant

EPHRAIMITES (9)

Josh 16:5 The territory of the E by their families was
16:8 the tribe of the E by their families,
16:9 set apart for the E within the inheritance of
Judg 12:5 took the fords of the Jordan against the E
12:6 fell at that time forty-two thousand of the E
1Chr 12:30 Of the E twenty thousand eight hundred, mighty men
27:20 of Azriel; for the E, Hoshea the son of
2Chr 25:7 LORD is not with Israel, with all these E
Ps 78:9 The E, armed with the bow, turned back on

EPHRATH (5)

Gen 35:16 still some distance from E, Rachel travailed, and she
35:19 on the way to E (that is, Bethlehem),
48:7 distance to go to E; and I buried her
48:7 on the way to E (that is, Bethlehem)."
1Chr 2:19 Azubah died, Caleb married E, who bore him Hur.

EPHRATHAH (6)

Ruth 4:11 May you prosper in E and be renowned in
1Chr 2:24 Caleb went in to E, the wife of Hezron
2:50 Hur the first-born of E: Shobal the father of
4:4 Hur, the first-born of E, the father of Bethlehem.
Ps 132:6 heard of it in E, we found it in
Mic 5:2 But you, O Bethlehem E, who are little to

EPHRATHITE

1Sam 17:12 the son of an E of Bethlehem in Judah,

EPHRATHITES

Ruth 1:2 and Chilion; they were E from Bethlehem in Judah.

EPHRON (17)

Gen 23:8 and entreat for me E the son of Zohar,
23:10 Now E was sitting among the Hittites; and Ephron
23:10 the Hittites; and E the Hittite answered Abraham
23:13 And he said to E in the hearing of
23:14 E answered Abraham,

23:16 Abraham agreed with E; and Abraham weighed out
23:16 Abraham weighed out for E the silver which he
23:17 So the field of E in Mach-pelah, which was
25:9 in the field of E the son of Zohar
49:29 in the field of E the Hittite,
49:30 with the field from E the Hittite to possess
50:13 with the field from E the Hittite, to possess
Josh 15:9 the cities of Mount E; then the boundary bends
18:15 goes from there to E, to the spring of
2Chr 13:19 with its villages and E with its villages.
1Mac 5:46 So they came to E
2Mac 12:27 he marched also against E, a fortified city where

EPICUREAN
Acts 17:18 Some also of the E and Stoic philosophers met

EPILEPTIC
Mt 17:15 for he is an E and he suffers terribly;

EPILEPTICS
Mt 4:24 diseases and pains, demoniacs, E, and paralytics, and

EPIPHANES (6)
1Mac 1:10 a sinful root, Antiochus E, son of Antiochus the
10:1 and sixtieth year Alexander E, the son of Antiochus,
2Mac 2:20 the wars against Antiochus E and his son Eupator,
4:7 Antiochus who was called E succeeded to the
10:9 was the end of Antiochus, who was called E
10:13 to him, and had gone over to Antiochus E

EPISODE
2Mac 3:40 the outcome of the E of Heliodorus and the

EQUAL (23)
Ex 30:34 shall there be an E part),
Deut 18:8 They shall have E portions to eat, besides what
1Kgs 6:3 was twenty cubits long, E to the width of
2Chr 3:4 was twenty cubits long, E to the width of
Job 28:17 Gold and glass cannot E it, nor can it
Ps 55:13 it is you, my E, my companion, my familiar
Sir 6:11 will make himself your E, and be bold with
13:11 treat him as an E, nor trust his abundance
32:9 not act as their E; and when another is
45:2 He made him E in glory to the holy
Is 46:5 me and make me E, and compare me, that
Ezek 4:5 hundred and ninety days, E to the number of
31:8 nor the fir trees E its boughs; the plane
48:8 breadth, and in length E to one of the
2Mac 8:30 to the aged, shares E to their own.
9:12 think that he is E to God."
9:15 make, all of them, E to citizens of Athens;
Mt 20:12 you have made them E to us who have
Lk 20:36 more, because they are E to angels and are
Jn 5:17 his Father, making himself E with God.
1Cor 3:8 he who waters are E, and each shall receive
2Pet 1:1 obtained a faith of E standing with ours in
Rev 21:16 stadia; its length and breadth and height are E

EQUALITY (3)
2Cor 8:14 as a matter of E your abundance at the
8:14 may supply your want, that there may be E
Phil 2:6 God, did not count E with God a thing

EQUALLY (3)
Wis 11:11 or present, they were E distressed,
14:9 For E hateful to God are the ungodly man
Ezek 47:14 you shall divide it E; I swore to give

EQUALS
Sir 7:28 back to them that E their gift to you?

EQUIP (3)
1Mac 10:6 to recruit troops, to E them with arms, and
Eph 4:12 pastors and teachers, to E the saints for the
Heb 13:21 of the eternal covenant, E you with everything good

EQUIPMENT (7)
Num 4:26 cords, and all the E for their service; and
4:32 cords, with all their E and all their accessories;
1Sam 8:12 of war and the E of his chariots.
2Kgs 7:15 littered with garments and E which the Syrians had
2Chr 4:16 forks, and all the E for these Huram-abi made
1Mac 15:26 him, and silver and gold and much military E
Eph 6:15 your feet with the E of the gospel of

EQUIPPED (8)
Ex 13:18 the land of Egypt E for battle.
1Chr 12:33 fifty thousand seasoned troops, E for battle with all
12:35 thousand six hundred men E for battle.
1Mac 6:43 of the beasts was E with royal armor.
10:21 he recruited troops and E them with arms in
15:3 mercenary troops and have E warships,
2Mac 10:18 very strong towers well E to withstand a siege,
2Tim 3:17 God may be complete, E for every good work.

EQUITABLE
Esth 16:9 our eyes with more E consideration.

EQUITY (14)
2Sam 8:15 David administered justice and E to all his people.
1Chr 18:14 he administered justice and E to all his people.
Ps 9:8 with righteousness, he judges the peoples with E
45:6 is a scepter of E;
67:4 judge the peoples with E and guide the nations
75:2 time which I appoint I will judge with E
96:10 be moved; he will judge the peoples with E
98:9 the world with righteousness, and the peoples with E
99:4 justice, thou hast established E; thou hast executed
Prov 1:3 dealing, righteousness, justice, and E;
2:9 righteousness and justice and E, every good path;
29:14 judges the poor with E his throne will be
Is 11:4 poor, and decide with E for the meek of
Mic 3:9 justice and pervert all E,

EQUIVALENT
Ex 22:17 he shall pay money E to the marriage present

ER (11)
Gen 38:3 bore a son, and he called his name E
38:6 took a wife for E his first-born, and her
38:7 But E, Judah's first-born, was wicked in the sight
46:12 The sons of Judah: E, Onan, Shelah, Perez, and
46:12 Perez, and Zerah (but E and Onan died in
Num 26:19 sons of Judah were E and Onan; and Er
26:19 Er and Onan; and E and Onan died in
1Chr 2:3 The sons of Judah: E, Onan, and Shelah; these
2:3 Now E, Judah's first-born, was wicked in the sight
4:21 the son of Judah: E the father of Lecah,
Lk 3:28 Elmadam, the son of E,

ERAN
Num 26:36 sons of Shuthelah: of E, the family of the

ERANITES
Num 26:36 of Shuthelah: of Eran, the family of the E

ERASTUS (3)
Acts 19:22 his helpers, Timothy and E, he himself stayed in
Rom 16:23 E, the city treasurer, and our brother Quartus, greet
2Tim 4:20 E remained at Corinth; Trophimus I left ill at

ERECH (2)
Gen 10:10 his kingdom was Babel, E, and Accad, all of
Ezra 4:9 Persians, the men of E, the Babylonians, the men

ERECT (7)
Ex 26:30 And you shall E the tabernacle according to the
Lev 26:1 yourselves no idols and E no graven image or
26:13 bars of your yoke and made you walk E
Ezra 2:68 house of God, to E it on its site;
1Mac 12:36 still higher, and to E a high barrier between
2Mac 15:6 arrogance had determined to E a public monument
Heb 8:5 Moses was about to E the tent, he was

ERECTED (10)
Gen 33:20 There he E an altar and called it El-Elohe-Israel.
1Kgs 16:32 He E an altar for Baal in the house
2Kgs 21:3 had destroyed; and he E altars for Baal, and
23:15 Bethel, the high place E by Jeroboam the son
2Chr 33:3 had broken down, and E altars to the Baals,
Is 23:13 They E their siegetowers, they razed her palaces,
Ezek 43:18 day when it is E for offering burnt offerings
1Mac 1:54 and forty-fifth year, they E a desolating sacrilege
6:7 abomination which he had E upon the altar in
13:28 He also E seven pyramids, opposite one another, for

ERECTING
1Mac 13:29 devised an elaborate setting, E about them great

ERI (2)
Gen 46:16 Ziphion, Haggi, Shuni, Ezbon, E, Arodi, and Areli.

Num 26:16 of the Oznites; of E, the family of the

ERITES
Num 26:16 the family of the E;

ERR (10)
Num 15:22 "But if you E, and do not observe all
Ps 58:3 from the womb, they E from their birth, speaking
95:10 are a people who E in heart, and they
Prov 14:22 Do they not E that devise evil?
Wis 14:22 enough for them to E about the knowledge of
Sir 28:26 Beware lest you E with your tongue, lest you
Is 28:7 with strong drink; they E in vision, they stumble
29:24 And those who E in spirit will come to
35:8 and fools shall not E therein.
63:17 dost thou make us E from thy ways and

E

ERRAND (2)
Gen 24:33 will not eat until I have told my E
2Kgs 9:5 said, "I have an E to you, O commander."

ERRED (3)
1Sam 26:21 the fool, and have E exceedingly."
Job 6:24 be silent; make me understand how I have E
19:4 true that I have E, my error remains with

ERROR (23)
Lev 5:18 for him for the E which he committed unwittingly,
Num 15:25 because it was an E, and they have brought
15:25 their sin offering before the LORD, for their E
15:26 because the whole population was involved in the E
15:28 person who commits an E, when he sins unwittingly,
Tob 5:13 go astray in the E of our brethren.
Jud 5:20 there is any unwitting E in this people and
Job 4:18 angels he charges with E;
19:4 I have erred, my E remains with myself.
Prov 12:28 but the way of E leads to death.
Eccl 10:5 as it were an E proceeding from the ruler:
Wis 1:12 invite death by the E of your life, nor
12:24 on the paths of E, accepting as gods those
Is 32:6 ungodliness, to utter E concerning the LORD, to
Ezek 45:20 who has sinned through E or ignorance; so you
Dan 6:4 was faithful, and no E or fault was found
Rom 1:27 their own persons the due penalty for their E
1Thes 2:3 does not spring from E or uncleanness, nor is
Jas 5:20 a sinner from the E of his way will
2Pet 2:18 have barely escaped from those who live in E
3:17 carried away with the E of lawless men and
1Jn 4:6 the spirit of truth and the spirit of E
Jude 1:11 of gain to Balaam's E, and perish in Korah's

ERRORS (6)
Ps 19:12 But who can discern his E
Sir 23:2 spare me in my E, and that it may
23:12 For all these E will be far from the
30:11 in his youth, and do not ignore his E
1Mac 13:39 We pardon any E and offenses committed to this
Heb 9:7 himself and for the E of the people.

ERUPTION (5)
Lev 13:2 a swelling or an E or a spot, and
13:6 it is only an E; and he shall wash
13:7 But if the E spreads in the skin, after
13:8 examination, and if the E has spread in the
14:56 a swelling or an E or a spot,

ESARHADDON (5)
2Kgs 19:37 And E his son reigned in his stead.
Ezra 4:2 since the days of E king of Assyria who
Tob 1:21 Then E, his son, reigned in his place; and
1:22 of the accounts, for E had appointed him second
Is 37:38 And E his son reigned in his stead.

ESAU (108)
Gen 25:25 a hairy mantle; so they called his name E
25:26 had taken hold of E's heel; so his name
25:27 the boys grew up, E was a skilful hunter,
25:28 Isaac loved E, because he ate of his game;
25:29 Jacob was boiling pottage, E came in from the
25:30 And E said to Jacob, "Let me eat some
25:32 E said, "I am about to die; of what
25:34 Then Jacob gave E bread and pottage of lentils,
25:34 Thus E despised his birthright.
26:34 When E was forty years old, he took to
27:1 not see, he called E his older son, and
27:5 was listening when Isaac spoke to his son E
27:5 So when E went to the field to hunt
27:6 speak to your brother E,
27:11 mother, "Behold, my brother E is a hairy man,
27:15 the best garments of E her older son, which
27:19 his father, "I am E your first-born.
27:21 are really my son E or not."
27:22 voice, but the hands are the hands of E
27:23 hairy like his brother E's hands; so he blessed
27:24 He said, "Are you really my son E
27:30 of Isaac his father, E his brother came in
27:32 He answered, "I am your son, your first-born, E
27:34 When E heard the words of his father, he
27:36 E said, "Is he not rightly named Jacob?
27:37 Isaac answered E, "Behold, I have made him your
27:38 E said to his father, "Have you but one
27:38 And E lifted up his voice and wept.
27:41 Now E hated Jacob because of the blessing with
27:41 had blessed him, and E said to himself, "The
27:42 But the words of E her older son were
27:42 him, "Behold, your brother E comforts himself by
28:5 of Rebekah, Jacob's and E's mother.
28:6 Now E saw that Isaac had blessed Jacob and
28:8 So when E saw that the Canaanite women did
28:9 please Isaac his father, E went to Ishmael and
32:3 messengers before him to E his brother in the
32:4 say to my lord E: Thus says your servant
32:6 came to your brother E, and he is coming
32:8 two companies, thinking, "If E comes to the one
32:11 from the hand of E, for I fear him,
32:13 present for his brother E,
32:17 instructed the foremost, "When E my brother meets
32:18 sent to my lord E; and moreover he is
32:19 the same thing to E when you meet him,
33:1 and looked, and behold, E was coming, and four
33:4 But E ran to meet him, and embraced him,
33:5 And when E raised his eyes and saw the
33:8 E said, "What do you mean by all this
33:9 But E said, "I have enough, my brother; keep
33:12 Then E said, "Let us journey on our way,
33:15 So E said, "Let me leave with you some
33:16 So E returned that day on his way to
35:1 to you when you fled from your brother E
35:29 days; and his sons E and Jacob buried him.
36:1 are the descendants of E (that is, Edom).
36:2 E took his wives from the Canaanites: Adah the
36:4 And Adah bore to E, Eliphaz; Basemath bore Reuel;
36:5 are the sons of E who were born to
36:6 Then E took his wives, his sons, his daughters,
36:8 So E dwelt in the hill country of Seir;
36:8 hill country of Seir; E is Edom.
36:9 are the descendants of E the father of the
36:10 are the names of E's sons: Eliphaz the son
36:10 Adah the wife of E, Reuel the son of
36:10 Reuel the son of Basemath the wife of E
36:12 a concubine of Eliphaz, E's son; she bore Amalek
36:12 the sons of Adah, E's wife.
36:13 the sons of Basemath, E's wife.
36:14 the son of Zibeon, E's wife: she bore to
36:14 wife: she bore to E Jeush, Jalam, and Korah.
36:15 These are the chiefs of the sons of E
36:15 Eliphaz the first-born of E: the chiefs Teman, Omar,
36:17 the sons of Reuel, E's son: the chiefs Nahath,
36:17 the sons of Basemath, E's wife.
36:18 the sons of Oholibamah, E's wife: the chiefs Jeush,
36:18 the daughter of Anah, E's wife.
36:19 are the sons of E (that is, Edom), and
36:40 of the chiefs of E, according to their families
36:43 of Edom (that is, E, the father of Edom),
Deut 2:4 brethren the sons of E, who live in Seir;
2:5 given Mount Seir to E as a possession.
2:8 brethren the sons of E who live in Seir,
2:12 but the sons of E dispossessed them, and destroyed
2:22 for the sons of E, who live in Seir,
2:29 as the sons of E who live in Seir
Josh 24:4 Isaac; and to Isaac I gave Jacob and E
24:4 And I gave E the hill country of Seir
1Chr 1:34 The sons of Isaac: E and Israel.
1:35 The sons of E: Eliphaz, Reuel, Jeush, Jalam, and
Jud 7:8 of the people of E and all the leaders
7:18 And the sons of E and the sons of
Jer 49:8 bring the calamity of E upon him, the time
49:10 But I have stripped E bare, I have uncovered
Obad 1:6 How E has been pillaged, his treasures sought out!
1:8 out of Edom, and understanding out of Mount E
1:9 every man from Mount E will be cut off
1:18 and the house of E stubble; they shall burn

	1:18	to the house of E; for the LORD has
	1:19	Negeb shall possess Mount E, and those of the
	1:21	Zion to rule Mount E; and the kingdom shall
Mal	1:2	"Is not E Jacob's brother?" says the LORD.
	1:3	but I have hated E; I have laid waste
1Mac	5:3	on the sons of E in Idumea, at Akrabattene,
	5:65	fought the sons of E in the land to
Rom	9:13	"Jacob I loved, but E I hated."
Heb	11:20	faith Isaac invoked future blessings on Jacob and E
	12:16	immoral or irreligious like E, who sold his birthright

ESCAPE (80)

Gen	7:7	into the ark, to E the waters of the
	19:20	Let me E there--is it not a little
	19:22	Make haste, E there; for I can do nothing
	32:8	it, then the company which is left will E
Ex	1:9	fight against us and E from the land."
Lev	26:37	another, as if to E a sword, though none
1Sam	23:28	therefore that place was called the Rock of E
	27:1	than that I should E to the land of
	27:1	Israel, and I shall E out of his hand."
2Sam	15:14	there will be no E for us from Absalom;
1Kgs	18:40	prophets of Baal; let not one of them E
2Kgs	10:24	into your hands to E shall forfeit his life."
	10:25	in and slay them; let not a man E
Ezra	9:14	there should be no remnant, nor any to E
Tob	13:2	no one who can E his hand.
Jud	7:19	was no way of E from them.
Esth	4:13	king's palace you will E any more than all
	16:4	suppose that they will E the evil-hating justice of
Job	11:20	fail; all way of E will be lost to
	15:30	earth; he will not E from darkness; the flame
Ps	68:20	GOD, the Lord, belongs E from death.
	88:8	so that I cannot E;
	141:10	together fall into their own nets, while I E
Prov	3:21	discretion; let them not E from your sight,
	4:22	Let them not E from your sight; keep them
	19:5	unpunished, and he who utters lies will not E
Wis	1:8	utters unrighteous things will E notice, and justice,
	16:15	To E from thy hand is impossible;
Sir	6:35	not let wise proverbs E you.
	11:10	not overtake, and by fleeing you will not E
	16:13	The sinner will not E with his plunder, and
	22:11	yourself from him to E trouble, and you will
	27:19	allow a bird to E from your hand, so
Is	15:9	those of Moab who E, for the remnant of
	20:6	And we, how shall we E
Jer	11:11	them which they cannot E; though they cry to
	25:35	for the shepherds, nor E for the lords of
	32:4	of Judah shall not E out of the hand
	34:3	You shall not E from his hand, but shall
	38:18	and you shall not E from their hand."
	38:23	you yourself shall not E from their hand, but
	44:14	land of Egypt shall E or survive or return
	44:28	And those who E the sword shall return from
	46:6	away, nor the warrior E; in the north by
	48:8	and no city shall E; the valley shall perish,
	50:28	they flee and E from the land of Babylon,
	50:29	Encamp round about her; let no one E
Lam	3:7	so that I cannot E; he has put heavy
Bar	6:55	priests will flee and E, but the gods will
Ezek	6:8	the nations some who E the sword, and when
	6:9	those of you who E will remember me among
	7:16	And if any survivors E, they will be on
	12:16	a few of them E from the sword, from
	15:7	against them; though they E from the fire, the
	17:15	Can a man E who does such things?
	17:15	Can he break the covenant and yet E
	17:18	yet did all these things, he shall not E
Dan	11:42	countries, and the land of Egypt shall not E
	13:22	not, I shall not E your hands.
Joel	2:32	shall be those who E, as the LORD has
Amos	9:1	shall flee away, not one of them shall E
Obad	1:17	shall be those that E, and it shall be
Zech	2:7	E to Zion, you who dwell with the daughter
Mal	3:15	when they put God to the test they E
1Mac	2:43	who became fugitives to E their troubles joined
2Mac	6:26	die I shall not E the hands of the
	7:31	Hebrews, will certainly not E the hands of God.
Mt	23:32	how are you to E being sentenced to hell?
Lk	21:36	may have strength to E all these things that
Acts	25:11	do not seek to E death; but if there
	27:30	sailors were seeking to E from the ship, and
	27:42	should swim away and E;
Rom	2:3	them yourself, you will E the judgment of God?
1Cor	10:13	provide the way of E, that you may be
1Thes	5:3	woman with child, and there will be no E
2Tim	2:26	truth, and they may E from the snare of
Heb	2:3	retribution, how shall we E if we neglect such
	12:25	if they did not E when they refused him
	12:25	much less shall we E if we reject him
2Pet	1:4	through these you may E from the corruption that

ESCAPED (62)

Gen	14:13	Then one who had E came, and told Abram
Deut	23:15	a slave who has E from his master to
Josh	8:22	until there was left none that survived or E
Judg	3:26	Ehud E while they delayed, and passed beyond the
	3:26	the sculptured stones, and E to Se-irah.
	3:29	Moabites, all strong, able-bodied men; not a man E
1Sam	14:41	Jonathan and Saul were taken, but the people E
	19:10	And David fled, and E
	19:12	through the window; and he fled away and E
	19:17	let my enemy go, so that he has E
	19:18	Now David fled and E, and he came to
	22:1	departed from there and E to the cave of
	22:20	of Ahitub, named Abiathar, E and fled after David.
	23:13	told that David had E from Keilah, he gave
	30:17	a man of them E, except four hundred young
2Sam	1:3	to him, "I have E from the camp of
1Kgs	20:20	Ben-hadad king of Syria E on a horse with
2Kgs	13:5	savior, so that they E from the hand of
	19:37	with the sword, and E into the land of
1Chr	4:43	the Amalekites that had E, and they have dwelt
2Chr	16:7	king of Syria has E you.
	20:24	dead bodies lying on the ground; none had E
	30:6	of you who have E from the hand of
	36:20	Babylon those who had E from the sword, and
Ezra	9:15	a remnant that has E, as at this day.
Neh	1:2	survived, who had E exile, and concerning
	1:3	in the province who E exile are in great
Tob	14:10	Ahikar gave alms and E the deathtrap which Nadab
Job	1:15	and I alone have E to tell you."
	1:16	and I alone have E to tell you."
	1:17	and I alone have E to tell you."
	1:19	and I alone have E to tell you."
	19:20	flesh, and I have E by the skin of
Ps	124:7	We have E as a bird from the snare
	124:7	fowlers; the snare is broken, and we have E
Wis	10:6	ungodly were perishing; he E the fire that descended
	15:19	them, but they have E both the praise of
Sir	27:20	too far-off, and has E like a gazelle from
	34:12	of death, but have E because of these experiences.
	40:6	like one who has E from the battle-front;
Is	37:38	with the sword, and E into the land of
Jer	26:21	afraid and fled and E to Egypt.
	41:15	the son of Nethaniah E from Johanan with eight
	51:50	"You that have E from the sword, go, stand
Lam	2:22	of the LORD none E or survived; those whom
Ezek	33:21	a man who had E from Jerusalem came to
1Mac	4:26	of the foreigners who E went and reported to
	6:21	some of the garrison E from the siege and
	15:37	on a ship and E to Orthosia.
2Mac	7:35	You have not yet E the judgment of the
	11:12	wounded, and Lysias himself E by disgraceful flight.
	12:35	his arm; so Gorgias E and reached Marisa.
Jn	10:39	arrest him, but he E from their hands.
Acts	16:27	to kill himself, supposing that the prisoners had E
	26:26	of these things has E his notice, for this
	27:44	it was that all E to land.
	28:1	After we had E, we then learned that the
	28:4	Though he has E from the sea, justice has
2Cor	11:33	in the wall, and E his hands.
Heb	11:34	lions, quenched raging fire, E the edge of the
2Pet	2:18	men who have barely E from those who live
	2:20	if, after they have E the defilements of the

ESCAPES (8)

1Kgs	19:17	And him who E from the sword of Hazael
	19:17	slay; and him who E from the sword of
Prov	12:13	lips, but the righteous E from trouble.
Eccl	7:26	he who pleases God E her, but the sinner
Sir	42:20	No thought E him, and not one word is
Jer	48:19	flees and her who E; say, 'What has happened?'
Joel	2:3	desolate wilderness, and nothing E them.
2Mac	3:38	thoroughly scourged, if he E at all, for there

ESCORT (4)

2Sam	19:31	to the Jordan, to E him over the Jordan.
Jud	10:15	some of us will E you and hand you
Ps	45:14	her virgin companions, her E, in her train.
1Mac	9:37	nobles of Canaan, from Nadabath with a large E

ESCORTED
Tob 8:1 had finished eating, they E Tobias in to her.

ESDRAELON (4)
Jud 1:8 the great Plain of E,
3:9 to the edge of E, near Dothan, fronting the
4:6 and Betomesthaim, which faces E opposite the plain
7:3 in length from Bethulia to Cyamon, which faces E

ESDRIS
2Mac 12:36 As E and his men had been fighting for

ESEK
Gen 26:20 name of the well E, because they contended with

ESHAN
Josh 15:52 Arab, Dumah, E,

ESHBAAL (2)
1Chr 8:33 Jonathan, Malchishua, Abinadab, and E;
9:39 Jonathan, Malchishua, Abinadab, and E;

ESHBAN (2)
Gen 36:26 sons of Dishon: Hemdan, E, Ithran, and Cheran.
1Chr 1:41 sons of Dishon: Hamran, E, Ithran, and Cheran.

ESHCOL (6)
Gen 14:13 the Amorite, brother of E and of Aner; these
14:24 with me; let Aner, E, and Mamre take their
Num 13:23 to the Valley of E, and cut down from
13:24 called the Valley of E, because of the cluster
32:9 to the Valley of E, and saw the land,
Deut 1:24 to the Valley of E and spied it out.

ESHEK
1Chr 8:39 The sons of E his brother: Ulam his first-born,

ESHTAOL (7)
Josh 15:33 And in the lowland, E, Zorah, Ashnah,
19:41 its inheritance included Zorah, E, Ir-shemesh,
Judg 13:25 to stir him in Mahaneh-dan, between Zorah and E
16:31 him between Zorah and E in the tomb of
18:2 from Zorah and from E, to spy out the
18:8 brethren at Zorah and E, their brethren said to
18:11 forth from Zorah and E,

ESHTAOLITES
1Chr 2:53 from these came the Zorathites and the E

ESHTEMOA (5)
Josh 21:14 with its pasture lands, E with its pasture lands,
1Sam 30:28 Aroer, in Siphmoth, in E,
1Chr 4:17 bore Miriam, Shammai, and Ishbah, the father of E
4:19 Keilah the Garmite and E the Ma-acathite.
6:57 its pasture lands, Jattir, E with its pasture lands,

ESHTEMOH
Josh 15:50 (that is, Debir), Anab, E, Anim,

ESHTON (2)
1Chr 4:11 father of Mehir, who was the father of E
4:12 E was the father of Bethrapha, Paseah, and

ESLI
Lk 3:25 Nah, the son of E, the son of Naggai,

ESPECIALLY (15)
Josh 2:1 "Go, view the land, E Jericho." And they went,
2Mac 7:20 The mother was E admirable and worthy of
10:32 a stronghold called Gazara, E well garrisoned, where
Acts 25:26 him before you, and, E before you, King Agrippa,
26:3 Jews, because you are E familiar with all customs
1Cor 14:1 desire the spiritual gifts, E that you may prophesy.
Gal 6:10 to all men, and E to those who are
Phil 4:22 the saints greet you, E those of Caesar's household.
1Tim 4:10 Savior of all men, E of those who believe.
5:8 for his relatives, and E for his own family,
5:17 worthy of double honor, E those who labor in
Tit 1:9 empty talkers and deceivers, E the circumcision
Philem 1:16 as a beloved brother, E to me but how
2Pet 2:10 day of judgment, and E those who indulge in
3Jn 1:5 service to the brethren, E to strangers,

ESSENTIAL
2Mac 4:23 complete the records of E business.

ESSENTIALS
Sir 29:21 The E for life are water and bread and

ESTABLISH (57)
Gen 6:18 But I will E my covenant with you; and
9:9 with him, "Behold, I E my covenant with you
9:11 I E my covenant with you, that never again
17:7 And I will E my covenant between me and
17:19 I will E my covenant with him as an
17:21 But I will E my covenant with Isaac, whom
Num 30:13 herself, her husband may E, or her husband may
Deut 28:9 The LORD will E you as a people holy
29:13 day; that he may E you this day as
1Sam 1:23 only, may the LORD E his word." So the
2Sam 7:12 body, and I will E his kingdom.
7:13 name, and I will E the throne of his
7:24 And thou didst E for thyself thy people Israel
1Kgs 2:4 that the LORD may E his word which he
6:12 them, then I will E my word with you,
9:5 ordinances, then I will E your royal throne over
20:34 restore; and you may E bazaars for yourself in
2Kgs 23:24 Jerusalem, that he might E the words of the
1Chr 17:11 sons, and I will E his kingdom.
17:12 me, and I will E his throne for ever.
22:10 father, and I will E his royal throne in
28:7 I will E his kingdom for ever if he
2Chr 7:18 ordinances, then I will E your royal throne, as
9:8 loved Israel and would E them for ever, he
Job 38:33 Can you E their rule on the earth?
Ps 7:9 to an end, but E thou the righteous, thou
76:9 when God arose to E judgment to save all
87:5 Most High himself will E her.
89:4 my servant: 'I will E your descendants for ever,
89:29 I will E his line for ever and his
90:17 be upon us, and E thou the work of
90:17 work of our hands E thou it.
107:36 hungry dwell, and they E a city to live
Sir 28:1 and he will firmly E his sins.
37:13 And E the counsel of your own heart, for
40:19 building of a city E a man's name, but
Is 9:7 over his kingdom, to E it, and to uphold
49:8 to the people, to E the land, to apportion
Jer 33:2 who formed it to E it—the LORD is
Ezek 16:60 youth, and I will E with you an everlasting
16:62 I will E my covenant with you, and you
Dan 6:7 that the king should E an ordinance and enforce
6:8 Now, O king, E the interdict and sign the
Amos 5:15 and love good, and E justice in the gate;
1Mac 8:17 them to Rome to E friendship and alliance,
8:20 us to you to E alliance and peace with
10:54 now therefore let us E friendship with one another;
2Mac 4:9 permission were given to E by his authority a
4:11 on the mission to E friendship and alliance with
Rom 10:3 God, and seeking to E their own, they did
1Thes 3:2 gospel of Christ, to E you in your faith
3:13 so that he may E your hearts unblamable in
2Thes 2:17 comfort your hearts and E them in every good
Heb 8:8 Lord, when I will E a new covenant with
10:9 first in order to E the second.
Jas 5:8 E your hearts, for the coming of the Lord
1Pet 5:10 Christ, will himself restore, E, and strengthen you.

ESTABLISHED (101)
Gen 9:17 covenant which I have E between me and all
Ex 6:4 I also E my covenant with them, to give
15:17 the sanctuary, O LORD, which thy hands have E
Num 21:27 be built, let the city of Sihon be E
30:14 upon her; he has E them, because he said
Deut 32:6 who made you and E you?
1Sam 3:20 knew that Samuel was E as a prophet of
13:13 the LORD would have E your kingdom over Israel
20:31 earth, neither you nor your kingdom shall be E
24:20 of Israel shall be E in your hand.
2Sam 5:12 that the LORD had E him king over Israel,
7:16 your throne shall be E for ever.'"
7:26 servant David will be E before thee.
1Kgs 2:12 David his father; and his kingdom was firmly E
2:24 LORD lives, who has E me, and placed me
2:45 of David shall be E before the LORD for
2:46 So the kingdom was E in the hand of
1Chr 9:22 and Samuel the seer E them in their office
14:2 that the LORD had E him king over Israel,
17:14 his throne shall be E for ever.'"
17:23 concerning his house be E for ever, and do
17:24 thy name will be E and magnified for ever,
17:24 servant David will be E before thee.

24:19 according to the procedure E for them by Aaron
2Chr 1:1 the son of David E himself in his kingdom,
12:1 rule of Rehoboam was E and was strong, he
12:13 So King Rehoboam E himself in Jerusalem and
17:5 Therefore the LORD E the kingdom in his hand;
20:20 and you will be E; believe his prophets, and
21:4 his father and was E, he slew all his
Neh 13:30 everything foreign, and I E the duties of the
Tob 1:4 High was consecrated and E for all generations for
Job 21:8 Their children are E in their presence, and their
22:28 and it will be E for you, and light
28:27 and declared it; he E it, and searched it
Ps 8:3 stars which thou hast E;
9:7 for ever, he has E his throne for judgment;
24:2 upon the seas, and E it upon the rivers.
30:7 O LORD, thou hadst E me as a strong
65:6 by thy strength hast E the mountains, being girded
74:16 the night; thou hast E the luminaries and the
76:2 His abode has been E in Salem, his dwelling
78:5 He E a testimony in Jacob, and appointed a
89:2 thy steadfast love was E for ever, thy faithfulness
89:37 moon it shall be E for ever; it shall
93:1 Yea, the world is E; it shall never be
93:2 moved; thy throne is E from of old; thou
96:10 Yea, the world is E, it shall never be
99:4 of justice, thou hast E equity; thou hast executed
102:28 their posterity shall be E before thee.
103:19 The LORD has E his throne in the heavens,
111:8 are trustworthy, they are E for ever and ever,
119:90 all generations; thou hast E the earth, and it
140:11 not the slanderer be E in the land; let
148:6 And he E them for ever and ever; he
Prov 3:19 earth; by understanding he E the heavens;
8:27 When he E the heavens, I was there, when
8:28 skies above, when he E the fountains of the
10:25 but the righteous is E for ever.
12:3 A man is not E by wickedness, but the
16:3 to the LORD, and your plans will be E
16:12 for the throne is E by righteousness.
19:21 the purpose of the LORD that will be E
20:18 Plans are E by counsel; by wise guidance wage
24:3 by understanding it is E;
25:5 his throne will be E in righteousness.
29:14 his throne will be E for ever.
30:4 Who has E all the ends of the earth?
Sir 17:10 He E with them an eternal covenant, and showed
24:10 and so I was E in Zion.
31:11 His prosperity will be E, and the assembly will
38:32 a city cannot be E, and men can neither
42:17 Lord the Almighty has E that the universe may
44:21 covenant with him; he E the covenant in his
45:24 covenant of peace was E with him, that he
45:25 A covenant was also E with David, the son
46:13 prophet of the Lord, E the kingdom and anointed
Is 2:2 the LORD shall be E as the highest of
7:9 will not believe, surely you shall not be E
16:5 a throne will be E in steadfast love and
42:4 discouraged till he has E justice in the earth;
45:18 and made it (he E it; he did not
54:14 righteousness you shall be E; you shall be far
Jer 10:12 by his power, who E the world by his
30:20 their congregation shall be E before me; and I
33:25 If I have not E my covenant with day
51:15 by his power, who E the world by his
Dan 4:36 me, and I was E in my kingdom, and
Mic 4:1 the LORD shall be E as the highest of
Hab 1:12 thou, O Rock, hast E them for chastisement.
1Mac 1:16 that his kingdom was E, he determined to become
10:52 of my fathers, and E my rule –
14:11 He E peace in the land, and Israel rejoiced
14:18 alliance which they had E with Judas and Jonathan
14:26 repulsed Israel's enemies and E its freedom."
2Mac 13:3 that he would be E in office.
14:15 prayed to him who E his own people for
1Cor 7:37 But whoever is firmly E in his heart, being
Col 2:7 up in him and E in the faith, just
Heb 9:16 of the one who made it must be E
2Pet 1:12 know them and are E in the truth that

ESTABLISHES (6)

Num 30:14 to day, then he E all her vows, or
Ps 37:23 the LORD, and he E him in whose way
48:8 our God, which God E for ever.
Is 62:7 no rest until he E Jerusalem and makes it
Dan 6:15 ordinance which the king E can be changed."
2Cor 1:21 it is God who E us with you in

ESTABLISHING (2)

1Kgs 15:4 son after him, and E Jerusalem;
Acts 3:21 until the time for E all that God spoke

ESTABLISHMENT

2Chr 36:20 his sons until the E of the kingdom of

ESTATE (13)

1Kgs 2:26 to Anathoth, to your E; for you deserve death.
Jud 8:7 and cattle, and fields; and she maintained this E
16:21 and remained on her E, and was honored in
Ps 62:9 [Selah] Men of low E are but a breath,
62:9 breath, men of high E are a delusion; in
136:23 us in our low E, for his steadfast love
Sir 11:12 out of his low E
Ezek 16:13 You grew exceedingly beautiful, and came to regal E
16:55 return to their former E, and Samaria and her
16:55 return to their former E; and you and your
16:55 and your daughters shall return to your former E
Lk 1:48 has regarded the low E of his handmaiden.
Gal 4:1 owner of all the E;

ESTEEM (3)

Neh 6:16 greatly in their own E; for they perceived that
2Mac 9:21 remember with affection your E and good will.
1Thes 5:13 admonish you, and to E them very highly in

ESTEEMED (8)

1Sam 2:30 and those who despise me shall be lightly E
18:30 of Saul; so that his name was highly E
2Sam 16:23 the counsel of Ahithophel E, both by David and
Sir 40:25 but good counsel is E more than both.
41:16 not everything is confidently E by every one.
Is 53:3 was despised, and we E him not.
53:4 our sorrows; yet we E him stricken, smitten by
1Cor 6:4 those who are least E by the church?

ESTEEMS (2)

Rom 14:5 One man E one day as better than another,
14:5 another, while another man E all days alike.

ESTHER (60)

Esth 2:7 up Hadassah, that is E, the daughter of his
2:8 in custody of Hegai, E also was taken into
2:10 E had not made known her people or kindred,
2:11 harem, to learn how E was and how she
2:15 the turn came for E the daughter of Abihail
2:15 Now E found favor in the eyes of all
2:16 And when E was taken to King Ahasuerus into
2:17 reign, the king loved E more than all the
2:18 and servants; it was E's banquet.
2:20 Now E had not made known her kindred or
2:20 had charged her; for E obeyed Mordecai just as
2:22 told it to Queen E, and E told the
4:4 When E's maids and her eunuchs came and told
4:5 Then E called for Hathach, one of the king's
4:8 might show it to E and explain it to
4:9 Hathach went and told E what Mordecai had said.
4:10 Then E spoke to Hathach and gave him a
4:12 they told Mordecai what E had said.
4:13 to return answer to E, "Think not that in
4:15 Then E told them to reply to Mordecai,
4:17 and did everything as E had ordered him.
5:1 On the third day E put on her royal
5:2 the king saw Queen E standing in the court,
5:2 he held out to E the golden scepter that
5:2 Then E approached and touched the top of the
5:3 king said to her, "What is it, Queen E
5:4 And E said, "If it please the king, let
5:5 we may do as E desires." So the king
5:5 to the dinner that E had prepared.
5:6 the king said to E, "What is your petition?
5:7 But E said, "My petition and my request is:
5:12 Haman added, "Even Queen E let no one come
6:14 to the banquet that E had prepared.
7:1 and Haman went in to feast with Queen E
7:2 said to E, "What is your petition, Queen E
7:3 Then Queen E answered, "If I have found favor
7:5 Ahasuerus said to Queen E, "Who is he, and
7:6 And E said, "A foe and enemy!
7:7 his life from Queen E, for he saw that
7:8 on the couch where E was; and the king
8:1 Ahasuerus gave to Queen E the house of Haman,
8:1 before the king, for E had told what he
8:2 And E set Mordecai over the house of Haman.
8:3 Then E spoke again to the king; she fell

E

8:4 the golden scepter to E,
8:5 scepter to Esther, and E rose and stood before
8:7 Ahasuerus said to Queen E and to Mordecai the
8:7 "Behold, I have given E the house of Haman,
9:12 king said to Queen E, "In Susa the capital
9:13 And E said, "If it please the king, let
9:25 destroy them; but when E came before the king,
9:29 Queen E, the daughter of Abihail, and Mordecai
9:31 the Jew and Queen E enjoined upon the Jews,
9:32 The command of Queen E fixed these practices of
10:6 _ the river is E, whom the king married
14:1 And E the queen, seized with deathly anxiety, fled
15:9 words, and said to her, "What is it, E
16:13 perpetual benefactor, and of E, the blameless

ESTRANGE

Sir 11:32 with commotion, and will E you from your family.

ESTRANGED (9)

Job 19:13 my acquaintances are wholly E from me.
Prov 18:1 He who is E seeks pretexts to break out
Is 1:4 the Holy One of Israel, they are utterly E
Ezek 14:5 Israel, who are all E from me through their
1Mac 11:12 He was E from Alexander, and their enmity became
11:53 promised; and he became E from Jonathan and did
12:10 we may not become E from you, for considerable
15:27 with Simon, and became E from him.
Col 1:21 you, who once were E and hostile in mind,

ETAM (5)

Judg 15:8 stayed in the cleft of the rock of E
15:11 of the rock of E, and said to Samson,
1Chr 4:3 were the sons of E: Jezreel, Ishma, and Idbash;
4:32 And their villages were E, Ain, Rimmon, Tochen, and
2Chr 11:6 He built Bethlehem, E, Tekoa,

ETERNAL (84)

Gen 49:26 the blessings of the E mountains, the bounties of
Deut 33:27 The E God is your dwelling place, and underneath
Tob 3:6 to go to the E abode; do not turn
Eccl 12:5 man goes to his E home, and the mourners
Wis 7:26 is a reflection of E light, a spotless mirror
17:2 their roofs, exiles from E providence.
Sir 1:13 made among men an E foundation, and among their
16:25 his works in an E order, and their dominion
17:10 established with them an E covenant, and showed
30:17 a miserable life, and E rest than chronic sickness.
46:19 the time of his E sleep, Samuel called men
Jer 20:11 Their E dishonor will never be forgotten.
Dan 13:42 voice, and said, "O E God, who dost discern
Hab 3:6 the nations; then the E mountains were scattered,
2Mac 1:25 just and almighty and E, who dost rescue Israel
Mt 18:8 be thrown into the E fire.
19:16 I do, to have E life?"
19:29 a hundredfold, and inherit E life.
25:41 you cursed, into the E fire prepared for the
25:46 will go away into E punishment, but the righteous
25:46 but the righteous into E life."
Mk 3:29 is guilty of an E sin"–
10:17 I do to inherit E life?"
10:30 the age to come E life.
Lk 10:25 I do to inherit E life?"
16:9 receive you into the E habitations.
18:18 I do to inherit E life?"
18:30 the age to come E life."
Jn 3:15 in him may have E life."
3:16 not perish but have E life.
3:36 in the Son has E life; he who does
4:14 water welling up to E life."
4:36 and gathers fruit for E life, so that sower
5:23 who sent me, has E life; he does not
5:38 in them you have E life; and it is
6:27 food which endures to E life, which the Son
6:40 in him should have E life; and I will
6:47 he who believes has E life.
6:54 drinks my blood has E life, and I will
6:68 have the words of E life;
10:28 and I give them E life, and they shall
12:25 will keep it for E life.
12:50 that his commandment is E life.
17:2 all flesh, to give E life to all whom
17:3 And this is E life, that they know thee
Acts 13:46 judge yourselves unworthy of E life, behold, we turn
13:48 as were ordained to E life believed.
Rom 1:20 invisible nature, namely, his E power and deity, has
2:7 immortality, he will give E life;
5:21 through righteousness to E life through Jesus Christ
6:22 sanctification and its end, E life.
6:23 gift of God is E life in Christ Jesus
16:25 the command of the E God, to bring about
2Cor 4:17 preparing for us an E weight of glory beyond
4:18 transient, but the things that are unseen are E
5:1 not made with hands, E in the heavens.
Gal 6:8 from the Spirit reap E life.
Eph 3:11 was according to the E purpose which he has
2Thes 1:9 suffer the punishment of E destruction and exclusion
2:16 us and gave us E comfort and good hope
1Tim 1:16 believe in him for E life.
6:12 take hold of the E life to which you
6:16 him be honor and E dominion.
2Tim 2:10 Christ Jesus with its E glory.
Tit 1:2 godliness, in hope of E life which God, who
3:7 heirs in hope of E life.
Heb 5:9 became the source of E salvation to all who
6:2 of the dead, and E judgment.
9:12 blood, thus securing an E redemption.
9:14 Christ, who through the E Spirit offered himself
9:15 may receive the promised E inheritance, since a
13:20 the blood of the E covenant,
1Pet 5:10 called you to his E glory in Christ, will
2Pet 1:11 an entrance into the E kingdom of our Lord
1Jn 1:2 proclaim to you the E life which was with
2:25 he has promised us, E life.
3:15 that no murderer has E life abiding in him.
5:11 that God gave us E life, and this life
5:13 know that you have E life.
5:20 the true God and E life.
Jude 1:6 kept by him in E chains in the nether
1:7 undergoing a punishment of E fire.
1:21 Lord Jesus Christ unto E life.
Rev 14:6 in midheaven, with an E gospel to proclaim to

ETERNITY (11)

Tob 6:17 afraid, for she was destined for you from E
Eccl 3:11 also he has put E into man's mind, yet
Wis 2:23 image of his own E,
Sir 1:2 and the days of E –who can count them?
1:4 before all things, and prudent understanding from E
18:9 are a few years in the day of E
24:9 receive your inheritance.' From E, in the beginning,
24:9 created me, and for E I shall not cease
Is 45:17 be put to shame or confounded to all E
57:15 lofty One who inhabits E, whose name is Holy:
2Pet 3:18 glory both now and to the day of E

ETH-KAZIN

Josh 19:13 sunrise to Gath-hepher, to E, and going on to

ETHAM (4)

Ex 13:20 Succoth, and encamped at E, on the edge of
Num 33:6 Succoth, and encamped at E, which is on the
33:7 they set out from E, and turned back to
33:8 in the wilderness of E, and encamped at Marah.

ETHAN (7)

1Kgs 4:31 other men, wiser than E the Ezrahite, and Heman,
1Chr 2:6 sons of Zerah: Zimri, E, Heman, Calcol, and Dara,
2:8 the devoted thing; and E's son was Azariah.
6:42 of Adaiah, son of E, son of Zimmah, son
6:44 the sons of Merari: E the son of Kishi,
15:17 of Merari, their brethren, E the son of Kushaiah;
15:19 singers, Heman, Asaph, and E, were to sound bronze

ETHANIM

1Kgs 8:2 feast in the month E, which is the seventh

ETHBAAL

1Kgs 16:31 Jezebel the daughter of E king of the Sidonians,

ETHER (2)

Josh 15:42 Libnah, E, Ashan,
19:7 with their villages; En-rimmon, E, and Ashan–four

ETHIOPIA (22)

2Kgs 19:9 concerning Tirhakah king of E, "Behold, he has set
Jud 1:10 in Egypt as far as the borders of E
Esth 1:1 reigned from India to E over one hundred and
8:9 provinces from India to E, a hundred and
13:1 provinces from India to E and to the governors
16:1 from India to E, one hundred and twenty-seven
Job 28:19 The topaz of E cannot compare with it, nor
Ps 68:31 brought from Egypt; let E hasten to stretch out

87:4 Philistia and Tyre, with E -- "This one was
Is 11:11 Egypt, from Pathros, from E, from Elam, from
18:1 beyond the rivers of E;
20:3 portent against Egypt and E,
20:5 and confounded because of E their hope and of
37:9 concerning Tirhakah king of E, "He has set out
43:3 Egypt as your ransom, E and Seba in exchange
45:14 and the merchandise of E, and the Sabeans, men
Jer 46:9 go forth: men of E and Put who handle
Ezek 29:10 to Syene, as far as the border of E
30:4 anguish shall be in E, when the slain fall
30:5 E, and Put, and Lud, and all Arabia, and
Nah 3:9 E was her strength, Egypt too, and that without
Zeph 3:10 beyond the rivers of E my suppliants, the daughter

ETHIOPIAN (7)

2Chr 14:9 Zerah the E came out against them with an
Jer 13:23 Can the E change his skin or the leopard
38:7 When Ebed-melech the E, a eunuch, who was in
38:10 king commanded Ebed-melech, the E, "Take three
38:12 Then Ebed-melech the E said to Jeremiah, "Put the
39:16 say to Ebed-melech the E, 'Thus says the LORD
Acts 8:27 And behold, an E, a eunuch, a minister of

ETHIOPIANS (12)

2Chr 12:3 with him from Egypt–Libyans, Sukki-im, and E
14:12 the LORD defeated the E before Asa and before
14:12 before Judah, and the E fled.
14:13 as Gerar, and the E fell until none remained
16:8 Were not the E and the Libyans a huge
21:16 who are near the E;
Is 20:4 Egyptians captives and the E exiles, both the young
Ezek 30:9 to terrify the unsuspecting E; and anguish shall come
Dan 11:43 the Libyans and the E shall follow in his
Amos 9:7 you not like the E to me, O people
Zeph 2:12 You also, O E, shall be slain by my
Acts 8:27 Candace, queen of the E, in charge of all

ETHNAN

1Chr 4:7 The sons of Helah: Zereth, Izhar, and E

ETHNARCH (3)

1Mac 14:47 to be commander and E of the Jews and
15:1 Simon, the priest and E of the Jews, and
15:2 the high priest and E and to the nation

ETHNI

1Chr 6:41 of Malchijah, son of E, son of Zerah, son

EU-ODIA

Phil 4:2 I entreat E and I entreat Syntyche to agree

EUBULUS

2Tim 4:21 E sends greetings to you, as do Pudens and

EUMENES

1Mac 8:8 him and gave to E the king.

EUNICE

2Tim 1:5 Lois and your mother E and now, I am

EUNUCH (15)

Jud 12:11 said to Bagoas, the E who had charge of
Esth 2:3 of Hegai the king's E who is in charge
2:14 of Sha-ashgaz the king's E who was in charge
2:15 what Hegai the king's E, who had charge of
Wis 3:14 Blessed also is the E whose hands have done
Sir 20:3 Like a E's desire to violate a maiden is
30:20 and groans, like a E who embraces a maiden
Is 56:3 and let not the E say, "Behold, I am
Jer 38:7 Ebed-melech the Ethiopian, a E, who was in the
Dan 1:3 commanded Ashpenaz, his chief E, to bring some of
Acts 8:27 behold, an Ethiopian, a E, a minister of the
8:34 And the E said to Philip, "About whom, pray,
8:36 some water, and the E said, "See, here is
8:37 water, Philip and the E, and he baptized him.
8:38 up Philip; and the E saw him no more,

EUNUCHS (30)

2Kgs 9:32 Two or three E looked out at him.
20:18 and they shall be E in the palace of
Esth 1:10 and Carkas, the seven E who served King Ahasuerus
1:12 come at the king's command conveyed by the E
1:15 the command of King Ahasuerus conveyed by the E
2:21 two of the king's E, who guarded the threshold,
4:4 Esther's maids and her E came and told her,
4:5 one of the king's E, who had been appointed
6:2 two of the king's E, who guarded the threshold,
6:14 with him, the king's E arrived and brought Haman
7:9 Harbona, one of the E in attendance on the
12:1 and Tharra, the two E of the king who
12:3 king examined the two E, and when they confessed
12:6 because of the two E of the king.
Is 39:7 and they shall be E in the palace of
56:4 the LORD: "To the E who keep my sabbaths,
Jer 29:2 the queen mother, the E, the princes of Judah
34:19 princes of Jerusalem, the E, the priests, and all
41:16 soldiers, women, children, and E, whom Johanan
Dan 1:7 the chief of the E gave them names: Daniel
1:8 the chief of the E to allow him not
1:9 the chief of the E;
1:10 the chief of the E said to Daniel, "I
1:11 the chief of the E had appointed over Daniel,
1:18 the chief of the E brought them in before
Mt 19:12 For there are E who have been so from
19:12 birth, and there are E who have been made
19:12 who have been made E by men, and there
19:12 men, and there are E who have made themselves
19:12 who have made themselves E for the sake of

EUPATOR (5)

1Mac 6:17 up as a boy, and he named him E
2Mac 2:20 Epiphanes and his son E,
10:10 took place under Antiochus E, who was the son
10:13 he was accused before E by the king's friends.
13:1 his men that Antiochus E was coming with a

EUPHRATES (40)

Gen 2:14 And the fourth river is the E
15:18 great river, the river E,
31:21 arose and crossed the E, and set his face
36:37 of Rehoboth on the E reigned in his stead.
Ex 23:31 the wilderness to the E; for I will deliver
Deut 1:7 as far as the great river, the river E
11:24 the River, the river E, to the western sea.
Josh 1:4 great river, the river E, all the land of
24:2 of old beyond the E, Terah, the father of
2Sam 8:3 went to restore his power at the river E
10:16 who were beyond the E; and they came to
1Kgs 4:21 the kingdoms from the E to the land of
4:24 region west of the E from Tiphsah to Gaza,
4:24 kings west of the E; and he had peace
14:15 scatter them beyond the E, because they have made
2Kgs 23:29 to the king of Assyria to the river E
24:7 from the Brook of Egypt to the river E
1Chr 1:48 of Rehoboth on the E reigned in his stead.
5:9 this side of the E, because their cattle had
18:3 to set up his monument at the river E
19:16 who were beyond the E, with Shophach the
2Chr 9:26 the kings from the E to the land of
35:20 at Carchemish on the E and Josiah went out
Jud 1:6 who lived along the E and the Tigris and
2:24 he followed the E and passed through Mesopotamia
Sir 24:24 of understanding, like the E, and like the Jordan
Is 27:12 day from the river E to the Brook of
Jer 2:18 to Assyria, to drink the waters of the E
13:4 arise, go to the E, and hide it there
13:5 hid it by the E, as the LORD commanded
13:6 "Arise, go to the E, and take from there
13:7 I went to the E, and dug, and I
46:2 was by the river E at Carchemish and which
46:6 north by the river E they have stumbled and
46:10 sacrifice in the north country by the river E
51:63 the midst of the E,
1Mac 3:32 affairs from the river E to the borders of
3:37 He crossed the E river and went through the
Rev 9:14 angels who are bound at the great river E
16:12 on the great river E, and its water was

EUPOLEMUS (2)

1Mac 8:17 So Judas chose E the son of John, son
2Mac 4:11 John the father of E, who went on the

EUTYCHUS

Acts 20:9 a young man named E was sitting in the

EVACUATED (2)

1Mac 6:49 of Bethzur, and they E the city, because they
6:61 these conditions the Jews E the stronghold.

EVADED

1Sam 18:11 But David E him twice.

EVANGELIST (2)
Acts 21:8 house of Philip the E, who was one of
2Tim 4:5 the work of an E, fulfil your ministry.

EVANGELISTS
Eph 4:11 apostles, some prophets, some E, some pastors and

EVE (5)
Gen 3:20 called his wife's name E, because she was the
4:1 Now Adam knew E his wife, and she conceived
Tob 8:6 Adam and gavest him E his wife as a
2Cor 11:3 as the serpent deceived E by his cunning, your
1Tim 2:13 was formed first, then E;

EVENING (155)
Gen 1:5 And there was E and there was morning, one
1:8 And there was E and there was morning, a
1:13 And there was E and there was morning, a
1:19 And there was E and there was morning, a
1:23 And there was E and there was morning, a
1:31 And there was E and there was morning, a
8:11 to him in the E, and lo, in her
19:1 to Sodom in the E; and Lot was sitting
24:11 at the time of E, the time when women
24:63 the field in the E; and he lifted up
29:23 But in the E he took his daughter Leah
30:16 the field in the E, Leah went out to
Ex 12:6 of Israel shall kill their lambs in the E
12:18 of the month at E, you shall eat unleavened
12:18 until the twenty-first day of the month at E
16:6 people of Israel, "At E you shall know that
16:8 gives you in the E flesh to eat and
16:13 In the E quails came up and covered the
18:13 the people stood about Moses from morning till E
18:14 the people stand about you from morning till E
27:21 shall tend it from E to morning before the
29:39 shall offer in the E;
29:41 shall offer in the E, and shall offer with
30:8 the lamps in the E, he shall burn it,
Lev 6:20 it in the morning and half in the E
11:24 be unclean until the E,
11:25 wash his clothes and be unclean until the E
11:27 be unclean until the E,
11:28 be unclean until the E; they are unclean to
11:31 they are dead shall be unclean until the E
11:32 be unclean until the E; then it shall be
11:39 be unclean until the E,
11:40 be unclean until the E; he also who carries
11:40 wash his clothes and be unclean until the E
14:46 be unclean until the E;
15:5 himself in water, and be unclean until the E
15:6 himself in water, and be unclean until the E
15:7 himself in water, and be unclean until the E
15:8 himself in water, and be unclean until the E
15:10 be unclean until the E; and he who carries
15:10 himself in water, and be unclean until the E
15:11 himself in water, and be unclean until the E
15:16 body in water, and be unclean until the E
15:17 washed with water, and be unclean until the E
15:18 themselves in water, and be unclean until the E
15:19 whoever touches her shall be unclean until the E
15:21 himself in water, and be unclean until the E
15:22 be unclean until the E;
15:23 touches it he shall be unclean until the E
15:27 himself in water, and be unclean until the E
17:15 be unclean until the E; then he shall be
22:6 be unclean until the E and shall not eat
23:5 the month in the E, is the LORD's passover.
23:32 the month beginning at E, from evening to evening
23:32 beginning at evening, from E to evening shall you
23:32 evening, from evening to E shall you keep your
24:3 it in order from E to morning before the
Num 9:3 this month, in the E, you shall keep it
9:5 the month, in the E, in the wilderness of
9:11 fourteenth day in the E they shall keep it;
9:15 the testimony; and at E it was over the
9:21 the cloud remained from E until morning; and when
19:7 camp; and the priest shall be unclean until E
19:8 body in water, and shall be unclean until E
19:10 shall wash his clothes, and be unclean until E
19:19 in water, and at E he shall be clean.
19:21 the water for impurity shall be unclean until E
19:22 one who touches it shall be unclean until E
28:4 shall offer in the E;
28:8 shall offer in the E; like the cereal offering
Deut 16:4 you sacrifice on the E of the first day
16:6 passover sacrifice, in the E at the going down
23:11 the camp; but when E comes on, he shall
28:67 say, 'Would it were E and at evening you
28:67 were evening!' and at E you shall say, 'Would
Josh 5:10 of the month at E in the plains of
7:6 the LORD until the E, he and the elders
8:29 on a tree until E; and at the going
10:26 upon the trees until E;
Judg 19:9 day has waned toward E; pray tarry all night.
19:16 in the field at E; the man was from
20:23 the LORD until the E; and they inquired of
20:26 fasted that day until E, and offered burnt offerings
21:2 and sat there till E before God, and they
Ruth 2:17 in the field until E; then she beat out
1Sam 14:24 food until it is E and I am avenged
17:16 came forward and took his stand, morning and E
20:5 in the field till the third day at E
30:17 from twilight until the E of the next day;
2Sam 1:12 wept and fasted until E for Saul and for
11:13 drunk; and in the E he went out to
1Kgs 17:6 and meat in the E; and he drank from
22:35 the Syrians, until at E he died; and the
2Kgs 16:15 burnt offering, and the E cereal offering, and the
1Chr 16:40 offering continually morning and E, according to all
23:30 LORD, and likewise at E,
2Chr 2:4 burnt offerings morning and E, on the sabbaths and
13:11 morning and every E burnt offerings and incense
13:11 lamps may burn every E; for we keep the
18:34 facing the Syrians until E; then at sunset he
31:3 offerings of morning and E, and the burnt offerings
Ezra 3:3 it to the LORD, burnt offerings morning and E
9:4 sat appalled until the E sacrifice.
9:5 And at the E sacrifice I rose from my
Tob 6:1 way they came at E to the Tigris river
Jud 9:1 very time when that E's incense was being offered
12:9 the tent until she ate her food toward E
13:1 When E came, his slaves quickly withdrew, and
Esth 2:14 In the E she went, and in the morning
Job 4:20 Between morning and E they are destroyed; they
Ps 55:17 E and morning and at noon I utter my
59:6 [Selah] Each E they come back, howling like dogs
59:14 [Selah] Each E they come back, howling like dogs
65:8 the morning and the E to shout for joy.
90:6 is renewed; in the E it fades and withers.
102:11 days are like an E shadow; I wither away
104:23 his work and to his labor until the E
109:23 like a shadow at E; I am shaken off
141:2 my hands as an E sacrifice!
Prov 7:9 the twilight, in the E, at the time of
Eccl 11:6 your seed, and at E withhold not your hand;
Sir 18:25 From morning to E conditions change, and all things
Is 5:11 tarry late into the E till wine inflames them!
17:14 At E time, behold, terror!
Jer 6:4 for the shadows of E lengthen!"
Ezek 12:4 go forth yourself at E in their sight, as
12:7 exile, and in the E I dug through the
24:18 the morning, and at E my wife died.
33:22 been upon me the E before the fugitive came;
46:2 but the gate shall not be shut until E
Dan 9:21 the time of the E sacrifice.
Hab 1:8 more fierce than the E wolves; their horsemen press
Zeph 2:7 houses of Ashkelon they shall lie down at E
3:3 lions; her judges are E wolves that leave nothing
Zech 14:7 not night, for at E time there shall be
1Mac 9:13 armies, and the battle raged from morning till E
Mt 8:16 That E they brought to him many who were
14:15 When it was E, the disciples came to him
14:23 When E came, he was there alone,
16:2 them, "When it is E, you say, 'It will
20:8 vineyard too.' And when E came, the owner of
26:20 When it was E, he sat at table with
27:57 When it was E, there came a rich man
Mk 1:32 That E, at sundown, they brought to him all
4:35 On that day, when E had come, he said
6:47 And when E came, the boat was out on
11:19 And when E came they went out of the
13:35 will come, in the E, or at midnight, or
14:17 And when it was E he came with the
15:41 And when E had come, since it was the
Lk 24:29 for it is toward E and the day is
Jn 6:16 When E came, his disciples went down to the
20:19 On the E of that day, the first day
Acts 4:3 custody until the morrow, for it was already E
28:23 them from morning till E, testifying to the kingdom

EVENINGS (2)
Dan 8:14 thousand and three hundred E and mornings; then
8:26 The vision of the E and the mornings which

EVENLY
1Kgs 6:35 overlaid them with gold E applied upon the carved

EVENTIDE
Is 24:11 joy has reached its E; the gladness of the

EVENTS (6)
Wis 11:14 the end of the E they marveled at him,
19:10 they still recalled the E of their sojourn, how
1Mac 7:33 After these E Nicanor went up to Mount Zion.
2Mac 4:17 a fact which later E will make clear.
Acts 19:21 Now after these E Paul resolved in the Spirit
Heb 11:7 warned by God concerning E as yet unseen, took

EVER (600)
Gen 3:22 eat, and live for E –
6:3 abide in man for E, for he is flesh,
8:21 youth; neither will I E again destroy every living
13:15 give to you and to your descendants for E
34:12 Ask of me E so much as marriage present
43:9 bear the blame for E;
Ex 3:15 is my name for E, and thus I am
5:22 Why didst thou E send me?
10:10 be with you, if E I let you and
10:14 never been before, nor E shall be again.
11:6 has never been, nor E shall be again.
12:14 you shall observe it as an ordinance for E
12:17 throughout your generations, as an ordinance for E
12:24 ordinance for you and for your sons for E
15:18 LORD will reign for E and ever."
15:18 The LORD will reign for ever and E
19:9 with you, and may also believe you for E
22:26 If E you take your neighbor's garment in pledge,
27:21 be a statute for E to be observed throughout
30:21 be a statute for E to them, even to
31:17 is a sign for E between me and the
32:13 your descendants, and they shall inherit it for E
Lev 6:18 it, as decreed for E throughout your generations,
6:22 LORD as decreed for E; the whole of it
10:9 be a statute for E throughout your generations.
10:15 as a due for E; as the LORD has
16:29 statute to you for E that in the seventh
16:31 shall afflict yourselves; it is a statute for E
17:7 be a statute for E to them throughout their
23:14 is a statute for E throughout your generations in
23:21 is a statute for E in all your dwellings
23:31 is a statute for E throughout your generations in
23:41 is a statute for E throughout your generations; you
24:3 be a statute for E throughout your generations.
24:8 the people of Israel as a covenant for E
25:46 as a possession for E; you may make slaves
Num 18:19 covenant of salt for E before the LORD for
22:30 Was I E accustomed to do so to you?"
Deut 4:32 thing as this has E happened or was ever
4:32 ever happened or was E heard of.
4:33 Did any people E hear the voice of a
4:34 Or has any god E attempted to go and
4:40 which the LORD your God gives you for E
5:29 well with them and with their children for E
12:28 children after you for E, when you do what
13:16 be a heap for E, it shall not be
15:17 door, and he shall be your bondman for E
18:5 of the LORD, him and his sons for E
19:9 God and by walking E in his ways–then
23:3 of the LORD for E;
23:6 peace or their prosperity all your days for E
28:46 and a wonder, and upon your descendants for E
29:29 to our children for E, that we may do
32:40 As I live for E,
Josh 4:7 to the people of Israel a memorial for E
4:24 you may fear the LORD your God for E
8:28 and made it for E a heap of ruins,
14:9 and your children for E, because you have wholly
Judg 11:25 Did he E strive against Israel, or did he
11:25 Israel, or did he E go to war with
1Sam 1:22 presence of the LORD, and abide there for E
2:30 out before me for E; but now the LORD
2:32 be an old man in your house for E
2:35 go in and out before my anointed for E
3:13 punish his house for E, for the iniquity which
3:14 not be expiated by sacrifice or offering for E
13:13 have established your kingdom over Israel for E
20:15 cut off your loyalty from my house for E
20:23 the LORD is between you and me for E
20:42 my descendants and your descendants, for E
2Sam 2:26 called to Joab, "Shall the sword devour for E
3:28 my kingdom are for E guiltless before the LORD
7:13 will establish the throne of his kingdom for E
7:16 be made sure for E before me; your throne
7:16 before me; your throne shall be established for E
7:24 be thy people for E; and thou, O LORD,
7:25 LORD God, confirm for E the word which thou
7:26 will be magnified for E, saying, 'The LORD of
7:29 it may continue for E before thee; for thou,
7:29 the house of thy servant be blessed for E
16:4 do obeisance; let me E find favor in your
22:51 his anointed, to David, and his descendants for E
1Kgs 1:31 said, "May my lord King David live for E
2:33 of his descendants for E; but to David, and
2:45 David shall be established before the LORD for E
8:13 a place for thee to dwell in for E
9:3 my name there for E; my eyes and my
9:5 throne over Israel for E, as I promised David
10:9 LORD loved Israel for E, he has made you
11:39 afflict the descendants of David, but not for E
12:7 them, then they will be your servants for E
2Kgs 5:27 cleave to you, and to your descendants for E
8:19 lamp to him and to his sons for E
18:33 gods of the nations E delivered his land out
21:7 put my name for E;
1Chr 15:2 the LORD and to minister to him for E
16:15 of his covenant for E, of the word that
16:34 is good; for his steadfast love endures for E
16:41 the LORD, for his steadfast love endures for E
17:12 me, and I will establish his throne for E
17:14 in my kingdom for E and his throne shall
17:14 ever and his throne shall be established for E
17:22 be thy people for E; and thou, O LORD,
17:23 house be established for E, and do as thou
17:24 established and magnified for E, saying, 'The LORD
17:27 it may continue for E before thee; for what
17:27 thou, O LORD, hast blessed is blessed for E
22:10 throne in Israel for E
23:13 and his sons for E should burn incense before
23:13 him and pronounce blessings in his name for E
23:25 his people; and he dwells in Jerusalem for E
28:4 king over Israel for E; for he chose Judah
28:7 establish his kingdom for E if he continues resolute
28:8 an inheritance to your children after you for E
28:9 forsake him, he will cast you off for E
29:10 Israel our father, for E and ever.
29:10 God of Israel our father, for ever and E
29:18 our fathers, keep for E such purposes and thoughts
2Chr 2:4 God, as ordained for E for Israel.
5:13 is good, for his steadfast love endures for E
6:2 a place for thee to dwell in for E
7:3 is good, for his steadfast love endures for E
7:6 love endures for E –whenever David offered
7:16 may be there for E; my eyes and my
9:8 would establish them for E, he has made you
10:7 them, then they will be your servants for E
13:5 kingship over Israel for E to David and his
20:7 and give it for E to the descendants of
20:21 the LORD, for his steadfast love endures for E
21:7 lamp to him and to his sons for E
30:8 he has sanctified for E, and serve the LORD
33:4 said, "In Jerusalem shall my name be for E
33:7 put my name for E;
Ezra 3:11 steadfast love endures for E toward Israel." And all
4:2 been sacrificing to him E since the days of
9:12 to your children for E
Neh 2:3 to the king, "Let the king live for E
13:1 Ammonite or Moabite should E enter the assembly
Tob 1:4 consecrated and established for all generations for E
3:2 thou dost render true and righteous judgment for E
3:11 blessed is thy holy and honored name for E
3:11 May all thy works praise thee for E
8:5 blessed by thy holy and glorious name for E
8:15 angels and thy chosen people bless thee for E
10:7 given up hope of E seeing me again."
11:14 is thy name for E, and blessed are all
12:17 But praise God for E
12:18 Therefore praise him for E
13:1 God who lives for E, and blessed is his
13:4 Lord and God, he is our Father for E
13:10 you who are distressed, to all generations for E
13:12 hate you; blessed for E will be all who
13:14 glory, and they will be made glad for E

13:18 'Blessed is God, who has exalted you for E
14:5 for all generations for E, just as the prophets
Jud 12:16 opportunity to deceive her, E since the day he
12:20 more than he had E drunk in any one
15:10 May the Almighty Lord bless you for E
16:16 who fears the Lord shall be great for E
16:17 their flesh; they shall weep in pain for E
16:25 And no one E again spread terror among the
Esth 10:13 to generation for E among his people Israel."
14:5 E since I was born I have heard in
14:10 and to magnify for E a mortal king.
Job 4:7 who that was innocent E perished?
4:20 destroyed; they perish for E without any regarding it.
7:16 loathe my life; I would not live for E
14:20 Thou prevailest for E against him, and he passes;
19:24 lead they were graven in the rock for E
20:7 he will perish for E like his own dung;
23:7 should be acquitted for E by my judge.
29:20 me, and my bow E new in my hand.'
36:7 he sets them for E, and they are exalted.
37:20 Did a man E wish that he would be
41:4 you to take him for your servant for E
Ps 5:11 thee rejoice, let them E sing for joy; and
9:5 out their name for E and ever.
9:5 hast blotted out their name for ever and E
9:7 LORD sits enthroned for E, he has established his
9:18 hope of the poor shall not perish for E
10:16 LORD is king for E and ever; the nations
10:16 king for ever and E; the nations shall perish
12:7 protect us, guard us E from this generation.
13:1 Wilt thou forget me for E
18:50 his anointed, to David and his descendants for E
19:9 is clean, enduring for E; the ordinances of the
21:4 length of days for E and ever.
21:4 to him, length of days for ever and E
21:6 him most blessed for E; thou dost make him
22:26 May your hearts live for E
23:6 dwell in the house of the LORD for E
25:15 My eyes are E toward the LORD, for he
28:9 be thou their shepherd, and carry them for E
29:10 flood; the LORD sits enthroned as king for E
30:12 God, I will give thanks to thee for E
33:11 the LORD stands for E, the thoughts of his
37:18 heritage will abide for E;
37:26 He is E giving liberally and lending, and his
37:27 and do good; so shall you abide for E
37:28 shall be preserved for E, but the children of
37:29 possess the land, and dwell upon it for E
38:17 and my pain is E with me.
40:11 love and thy faithfulness E preserve me!
41:12 integrity, and set me in thy presence for E
44:8 we will give thanks to thy name for E
44:23 Do not cast us off for E
45:2 your lips; therefore God has blessed you for E
45:6 divine throne endures for E and ever.
45:6 Your divine throne endures for ever and E
45:17 will praise you for E and ever.
45:17 the peoples will praise you for ever and E
48:8 city of our God, which God establishes for E
48:14 God, our God for E and ever.
48:14 this is God, our God for ever and E
48:14 He will be our guide for E
49:9 to live on for E, and never see the
49:11 are their homes for E, their dwelling places to
51:3 and my sin is E before me.
52:5 break you down for E; he will snatch and
52:8 love of God for E and ever.
52:8 the steadfast love of God for ever and E
52:9 will thank thee for E, because thou hast done
61:4 Let me dwell in thy tent for E
61:7 he be enthroned for E before God; bid steadfast
61:8 So will I E sing praises to thy name,
66:7 by his might for E, whose eyes keep watch
68:16 abode, yea, where the LORD will dwell for E
72:17 his name endure for E, his fame continue as
72:19 his glorious name for E; may his glory fill
73:26 strength of my heart and my portion for E
74:1 God, why dost thou cast us off for E
74:10 Is the enemy to revile thy name for E
74:19 not forget the life of thy poor for E
75:9 I will rejoice for E, I will sing praises
77:7 the Lord spurn for E, and never again be
77:8 his steadfast love for E ceased?
78:69 like the earth, which he has founded for E
79:5 Wilt thou be angry for E
79:13 thanks to thee for E; from generation to generation
81:15 toward him, and their fate would last for E
83:17 shame and dismayed for E; let them perish in
84:4 dwell in thy house, E singing thy praise!
85:5 Wilt thou be angry with us for E
86:12 heart, and I will glorify thy name for E
89:1 love, O LORD, for E; with my mouth I
89:2 love was established for E, thy faithfulness is firm
89:4 establish your descendants for E, and build your
89:21 that my hand shall E abide with him, my
89:28 keep for him for E, and my covenant will
89:29 establish his line for E and his throne as
89:36 line shall endure for E, his throne as long
89:37 shall be established for E; it shall stand firm
89:46 Wilt thou hide thyself for E
89:52 Blessed be the LORD for E
90:2 were brought forth, or E thou hadst formed the
92:7 doomed to destruction for E,
92:8 but thou, O LORD, art on high for E
92:14 old age, they are E full of sap and
100:5 steadfast love endures for E, and his faithfulness to
102:12 LORD, art enthroned for E; thy name endures to
103:9 chide, nor will he keep his anger for E
104:31 the LORD endure for E, may the LORD rejoice
105:8 of his covenant for E, of the word that
106:1 is good; for his steadfast love endures for E
106:31 righteousness from generation to generation for E
107:1 is good; for his steadfast love endures for E
110:4 are a priest for E after the order of
111:3 is his work, and his righteousness endures for E
111:5 fear him; he is E mindful of his covenant.
111:8 they are established for E and ever, to be
111:8 established for ever and E, to be performed with
111:9 his people; he has commanded his covenant for E
111:10 His praise endures for E
112:3 in his house; and his righteousness endures for E
112:6 never be moved; he will be remembered for E
112:9 his righteousness endures for E; his horn is exalted
117:2 and the faithfulness of the LORD endures for E
118:1 he is good; his steadfast love endures for E
118:2 Let Israel say, "His steadfast love endures for E
118:3 of Aaron say, "His steadfast love endures for E
118:4 the LORD say, "His steadfast love endures for E
118:29 is good; for his steadfast love endures for E
119:44 thy law continually, for E and ever;
119:44 continually, for ever and E;
119:89 For E, O LORD, thy word is firmly fixed
119:98 enemies, for it is E with me.
119:111 are my heritage for E; yea, they are the
119:112 perform thy statutes for E, to the end.
119:142 righteousness is righteous for E, and thy law is
119:144 testimonies are righteous for E; give me
119:152 thy testimonies that thou hast founded them for E
119:160 every one of thy righteous ordinances endures for E
125:1 Zion, which cannot be moved, but abides for E
132:12 their sons also for E shall sit upon your
132:14 my resting place for E; here I will dwell,
135:13 O LORD, endures for E, thy renown, O LORD,
136:1 is good, for his steadfast love endures for E
136:2 of gods, for his steadfast love endures for E
136:3 steadfast love endures for E;
136:4 steadfast love endures for E;
136:5 steadfast love endures for E;
136:6 steadfast love endures for E;
136:7 steadfast love endures for E;
136:8 steadfast love endures for E;
136:9 steadfast love endures for E;
136:10 steadfast love endures for E;
136:11 steadfast love endures for E;
136:12 steadfast love endures for E;
136:13 steadfast love endures for E;
136:14 steadfast love endures for E;
136:15 steadfast love endures for E;
136:16 steadfast love endures for E;
136:17 steadfast love endures for E;
136:18 steadfast love endures for E;
136:19 steadfast love endures for E;
136:20 steadfast love endures for E;
136:21 steadfast love endures for E;
136:22 his servant, for his steadfast love endures for E
136:23 steadfast love endures for E;
136:24 steadfast love endures for E;
136:25 all flesh, for his steadfast love endures for E
136:26 of heaven, for his steadfast love endures for E
138:8 me; thy steadfast love, O LORD, endures for E
145:1 bless thy name for E and ever.
145:1 King, and bless thy name for ever and E

145:2 praise thy name for E and ever.
145:2 thee, and praise thy name for ever and E
145:21 his holy name for E and ever.
145:21 flesh bless his holy name for ever and E
146:6 who keeps faith for E;
146:10 LORD will reign for E, thy God, O Zion,
148:6 he established them for E and ever; he fixed
148:6 them for ever and E; he fixed their bounds
Prov 10:25 no more, but the righteous is established for E
12:19 Truthful lips endure for E, but a lying tongue
27:24 do not last for E; and does a crown
29:14 with equity his throne will be established for E
30:16 barren womb, the earth E thirsty for water, and
Eccl 1:4 a generation comes, but the earth remains for E
3:14 God does endures for E; nothing can be added
9:6 have no more for E any share in all
Wis 3:1 and no torment will E touch them.
3:8 and the Lord will reign over them for E
4:18 among the dead for E;
5:15 the righteous live for E, and their reward is
6:21 peoples, honor wisdom, that you may reign for E
14:13 from the beginning nor will they exist for E
Sir 1:1 from the Lord and is with him for E
2:10 generations and see: who E trusted in the Lord
2:10 Or who E persevered in the fear of the
2:10 Or who E called upon him and was overlooked?
18:1 He who lives for E created the whole universe;
20:25 and his shame is E with him.
37:26 inherit confidence, and his name will live for E
40:12 blotted out, but good faith will stand for E
40:17 a garden of blessings, and almsgiving endures for E
41:13 are numbered, but a good name endures for E
42:23 live and remain for E for every need, and
44:14 posterity will continue for E, and their glory will
45:13 No outsider E put them on, but only his
45:24 should have the dignity of the priesthood for E
46:3 Who before him E stood so firm?
47:11 exalted his power for E; he gave him the
47:13 name and prepare a sanctuary to stand for E
Is 17:2 will be deserted for E; they will be for
25:8 swallow up death for E, and the Lord GOD
26:4 in the LORD for E, for the LORD GOD
28:28 not thresh it for E; when he drives his
30:8 the time to come as a witness for E
32:14 will become dens for E, a joy of wild
32:17 the result of righteousness, quietness and trust for E
34:10 be quenched; its smoke shall go up for E
34:10 pass through it for E and ever.
34:10 none shall pass through it for ever and E
34:17 shall possess it for E, from generation to generation
40:8 the word of our God will stand for E
47:7 You said, "I shall be mistress for E
51:6 salvation will be for E, and my deliverance will
51:8 deliverance will be for E, and my salvation to
57:16 will not contend for E, nor will I always
60:15 make you majestic for E, a joy from age
60:21 possess the land for E, the shoot of my
64:9 angry, O LORD, and remember not iniquity for E
65:18 glad and rejoice for E in that which I
Jer 3:5 he be angry for E, will he be indignant
3:12 the LORD; I will not be angry for E
6:7 sickness and wounds are E before me.
7:7 I gave of old to your fathers for E
15:14 a fire is kindled which shall burn for E
17:4 a fire is kindled which shall burn for E
17:25 Jerusalem; and this city shall be inhabited for E
18:16 horror, a thing to be hissed at for E
20:17 and her womb for E great.
25:5 of old and for E;
31:36 cease from being a nation before me for E
31:40 not be uprooted or overthrown any more for E
32:39 may fear me for E, for their own good
33:11 steadfast love endures for E For I will restore
33:18 burn cereal offerings, and to make sacrifices for E
35:6 nor your sons for E;
50:39 peopled no more for E, nor inhabited for all
51:62 shall be desolate for E
Lam 3:31 not cast off for E,
4:17 Our eyes failed, E watching vainly for help; in
5:19 LORD, dost reign for E; thy throne endures to
5:20 thou forget us for E, why dost thou so
Bar 3:3 thou art enthroned for E, and we are perishing
3:3 enthroned for ever, and we are perishing for E
3:13 God, you would be dwelling in peace for E
4:1 of God, and the law that endures for E
4:23 back to me with joy and gladness for E
5:1 and put on for E the beauty of the
5:4 your name will for E be called by God,
Ezek 15:5 is charred, can it E be used for anything!
16:16 has never been, nor E shall be.
27:32 over you: 'Who was E destroyed like Tyre in
27:36 dreadful end and shall be no more for E
28:19 dreadful end and shall be no more for E
36:11 good to you than E before.
37:25 shall dwell there for E; and David my servant
37:25 David my servant shall be their prince for E
43:7 the midst of the people of Israel for E
43:9 and I will dwell in their midst for E
Dan 2:4 said to the king, "O king, live for E
2:20 name of God for E and ever.
2:20 be the name of God for ever and E
2:44 it shall stand for E;
3:9 said to King Nebuchadnezzar, "O king, live for E
3:26 of praise; and thy name is glorified for E
3:52 and highly exalted for E;
3:53 and highly exalted for E;
3:54 and to be extolled and highly glorified for E
3:55 and to be praised and highly exalted for E
3:56 and to be extolled and highly exalted for E
3:57 heaven and to be sung and glorified for E
3:58 praise to him and highly exalt him for E
3:59 praise to him and highly exalt him for E
3:60 praise to him and highly exalt him for E
3:61 praise to him and highly exalt him for E
3:62 praise to him and highly exalt him for E
3:63 praise to him and highly exalt him for E
3:64 praise to him and highly exalt him for E
3:65 praise to him and highly exalt him for E
3:66 praise to him and highly exalt him for E
3:67 praise to him and highly exalt him for E
3:68 praise to him and highly exalt him for E
3:69 praise to him and highly exalt him for E
3:70 praise to him and highly exalt him for E
3:71 praise to him and highly exalt him for E
3:72 praise to him and highly exalt him for E
3:73 praise to him and highly exalt him for E
3:74 praise to him and highly exalt him for E
3:75 praise to him and highly exalt him for E
3:76 praise to him and highly exalt him for E
3:77 praise to him and highly exalt him for E
3:78 praise to him and highly exalt him for E
3:79 praise to him and highly exalt him for E
3:80 praise to him and highly exalt him for E
3:81 praise to him and highly exalt him for E
3:82 praise to him and highly exalt him for E
3:83 praise to him and highly exalt him for E
3:84 praise to him and highly exalt him for E
3:85 praise to him and highly exalt him for E
3:86 praise to him and highly exalt him for E
3:87 praise to him and highly exalt him for E
3:88 praise to him and highly exalt him for E
3:89 highly exalt him for E; for he has rescued
3:90 he is good, for his mercy endures for E
3:91 thanks to him, for his mercy endures for E
4:34 him who lives for E; for his dominion is
5:10 and the queen said, "O king, live for E
6:6 said to him, "O King Darius, live for E
6:21 said to the king, "O king, live for E
6:26 living God, enduring for E; his kingdom shall never
7:18 possess the kingdom for E, for ever and ever.'
7:18 kingdom for ever, for E and ever.'
7:18 ever, for ever and E
12:3 like the stars for E and ever.
12:3 to righteousness, like the stars for ever and E
12:7 him who lives for E that it would be
13:27 nothing like this had E been said about Susanna.
Hos 2:19 you to me for E; I will betroth you
Joel 3:20 shall be inhabited for E, and Jerusalem to all
Amos 1:11 tore perpetually, and he kept his wrath for E
Obad 1:10 you, and you shall be cut off for E
Jon 2:6 closed upon me for E; yet thou didst bring
Mic 2:9 young children you take away my glory for E
4:5 LORD our God for E and ever.
4:5 of the LORD our God for ever and E
7:18 retain his anger for E because he delights in
Hab 1:17 his net, and mercilessly slaying nations for E
Zeph 2:9 nettles and salt pits, and a waste for E
Zech 1:5 And the prophets, do they live for E
Mal 1:4 people with whom the LORD is angry for E
1Mac 2:57 merciful, inherited the throne of the kingdom for E
3:7 his deeds, and his memory is blessed for E
4:24 he is good, for his mercy endures for E

8:11 islands, as many as E opposed them, they destroyed
8:23 and on land for E, and may sword and
11:36 shall be canceled from this time forth for E
14:41 and high priest for E, until a trustworthy prophet
2Mac 8:14 ungodly Nicanor before he E met them,
10:4 that, if they should E sin, they might be
13:10 and night, now if E to help those who
14:15 his own people for E and always upholds his
14:36 holiness, keep undefiled for E this house that has
15:30 the man who was E in body and soul
Mt 21:19 it, "May no fruit E come from you again!"
Mk 11:2 which no one has E sat; untie it and
11:14 it, "May no one E eat fruit from you
Lk 1:33 house of Jacob for E; and of his kingdom
1:55 fathers, to Abraham and to his posterity for E
19:30 which no one has E yet sat; untie it
23:52 where no one had E yet been laid.
Jn 1:18 No one has E seen God; the only Son,
4:29 me all that I E did.
4:39 me all that I E did."
6:51 he will live for E; and the bread which
6:58 he who eats this bread will live for E
7:46 officers answered, "No man E spoke like this man!"
8:35 in the house for E; the son continues for
8:35 the house for ever; the son continues for E
12:34 from the law that the Christ remains for E
14:16 be with you for E,
19:41 where no one had E been laid.
Acts 5:14 And more than E believers were added to the
11:8 common or unclean has E entered my mouth.'
Rom 1:20 E since the creation of the world his invisible
1:25 rather than the Creator, who is blessed for E
9:5 God who is over all be blessed for E
11:10 they cannot see, and bend their backs for E
11:36 To him be glory for E
1Cor 12:3 the Spirit of God E says "Jesus be cursed!"
2Cor 8:22 now more earnest than E because of his great
9:9 gives to the poor; his righteousness endures for E
11:31 who is blessed for E, knows that I do
Gal 1:5 be the glory for E and ever.
1:5 to whom be the glory for ever and E
Eph 3:21 to all generations, for E and ever.
3:21 Christ Jesus to all generations, for ever and E
5:29 For no man E hates his own flesh, but
Phil 4:20 Father be glory for E and ever.
4:20 God and Father be glory for ever and E
1Tim 1:17 honor and glory for E and ever.
1:17 God, be honor and glory for ever and E
6:16 whom no man has E seen or can see.
2Tim 4:18 be the glory for E and ever.
4:18 To him be the glory for ever and E
Philem 1:15 have him back for E,
Heb 1:5 what angel did God E say, "Thou art my
1:8 O God, is for E and ever, the righteous
1:8 is for ever and E, the righteous scepter is
1:13 what angel has he E said, "Sit at my
5:6 art a priest for E, after the order of
6:20 a high priest for E after the order of
7:3 Son of God he continues a priest for E
7:13 which no one has E served at the altar.
7:17 art a priest for E, after the order of
7:21 change his mind, 'Thou art a priest for E
7:24 priesthood permanently, because he continues for E
7:28 a Son who has been made perfect for E
13:8 is the same yesterday and today and for E
13:21 whom be glory for E and ever.
13:21 Christ; to whom be glory for ever and E
1Pet 1:25 but the word of the Lord abides for E
4:11 glory and dominion for E and ever.
4:11 him belong glory and dominion for ever and E
5:11 be the dominion for E and ever.
5:11 To him be the dominion for ever and E
2Pet 1:21 interpretation, because no prophecy E came by
3:4 For E since the fathers fell asleep, all things
1Jn 2:17 who does the will of God abides for E
4:12 No man has E seen God; if we love
2Jn 1:2 be with us for E:
Jude 1:13 nether gloom of darkness has been reserved for E
1:25 authority, before all time and now and for E
Rev 1:6 glory and dominion for E and ever.
1:6 him be glory and dominion for ever and E
4:9 throne, who lives for E and ever,
4:9 lives for ever and E,
4:10 him who lives for E and ever; they cast
4:10 lives for ever and E; they cast their crowns
5:13 glory and might for E and ever!"
5:13 honor and glory and might for ever and E
7:12 to our God for E and ever!
7:12 might be to our God for ever and E
10:6 him who lives for E and ever, who created
10:6 lives for ever and E, who created heaven and
11:15 he shall reign for E and ever."
11:15 Christ, and he shall reign for ever and E
14:11 torment goes up for E and ever; and they
14:11 up for ever and E; and they have no
15:7 God who lives for E and ever;
15:7 lives for ever and E;
19:3 her goes up for E and ever."
19:3 smoke from her goes up for ever and E
20:10 day and night for E and ever.
20:10 be tormented day and night for ever and E
22:5 they shall reign for E and ever.
22:5 light, and they shall reign for ever and E

EVER-FLOWING (3)

Ps 74:15 thou didst dry up E streams.
Wis 11:6 the fountain of an E river, stirred up and
Amos 5:24 and righteousness like an E stream.

EVERFLOWING

2Mac 7:36 suffering have drunk of E life under God's covenant;

EVERGREEN (2)

Dan 13:58 He answered, "Under an E oak."
Hos 14:8 I am like an E cypress, from me comes

EVERLASTING (99)

Gen 9:16 it and remember the E covenant between God and
17:7 their generations for an E covenant, to be God
17:8 of Canaan, for an E possession; and I will
17:13 in your flesh an E covenant.
17:19 with him as an E covenant for his descendants
21:33 of the LORD, the E God.
48:4 after you for an E possession.'
49:26 the bounties of the E hills; may they be
Lev 16:34 this shall be an E statute for you, that
Deut 33:15 the abundance of the E hills,
33:27 and underneath are the E arms.
2Sam 23:5 made with me an E covenant, ordered in all
1Chr 16:17 to Jacob, as an E covenant to Israel,
16:36 God of Israel, from E to everlasting!" Then all
16:36 LORD, the God of Israel, from everlasting to E
Neh 9:5 LORD your God from E to everlasting.
9:5 bless the LORD your God from everlasting to E
Tob 1:6 all Israel by an E decree.
Esth 14:5 their ancestors, for an E inheritance, and that thou
Ps 9:6 enemy have vanished in E ruins; their cities thou
41:13 God of Israel, from E to everlasting!
41:13 LORD, the God of Israel, from everlasting to E
76:4 more majestic than the E mountains.
78:66 he put them to E shame.
90:2 and the world, from E to everlasting thou art
90:2 world, from everlasting to E thou art God.
93:2 is established from of old; thou art from E
103:17 the LORD is from E to everlasting upon those
103:17 is from everlasting to E upon those who fear
105:10 to Israel as an E covenant,
106:48 God of Israel, from E to everlasting!
106:48 LORD, the God of Israel, from everlasting to E
139:24 in me, and lead me in the way E
145:13 Thy kingdom is an E kingdom, and thy dominion
Wis 8:13 immortality, and leave an E remembrance to those
10:14 and she gave him E honor.
Sir 2:9 for good things, for E joy and mercy.
15:6 and will acquire an E name.
39:20 From E to everlasting he beholds them, and nothing
39:20 From everlasting to E he beholds them, and nothing
42:21 and he is from E and to everlasting.
42:21 wisdom, and he is from everlasting and to E
43:6 and to be an E sign.
44:19 E covenants were made with him that all flesh
45:7 He made an E covenant with him, and gave
45:15 oil; it was an E covenant for him and
49:12 the Lord, prepared for E glory.
Is 9:6 "Wonderful Counselor, Mighty God, E Father, Prince
24:5 the statutes, broken the E covenant.
26:4 LORD GOD is an E rock.
33:14 us can dwell with E burnings?"
35:10 to Zion with singing; E joy shall be upon
40:28 The LORD is the E God, the Creator of
45:17 by the LORD with E salvation; you shall not
51:11 to Zion with singing; E joy shall be upon

54:8 from you, but with E love I will have
55:3 make with you an E covenant, my steadfast, sure
55:13 a memorial, for an E sign which shall not
56:5 will give them an E name which shall not
60:19 LORD will be your E light, and your God
60:20 LORD will be your E light, and your days
61:7 portion; yours shall be E joy.
61:8 I will make an E covenant with them.
63:12 make for himself an E name,
Jer 10:10 living God and the E King.
23:40 will bring upon you E reproach and perpetual shame,
25:9 a hissing, and an E reproach.
25:12 making the land an E waste.
31:3 loved you with an E love; therefore I have
32:40 make with them an E covenant, that I will
49:33 haunt of jackals, an E waste; no man shall
50:5 the LORD in an E covenant which will never
Bar 2:35 I will make an E covenant with them to
4:8 You forgot the E God, who brought you up,
4:10 and daughters, which the E brought upon them.
4:14 and daughters, which the E brought upon them.
4:20 will cry to the E all my days.
4:22 my hope in the E to save you, and
4:22 to you from your E Savior.
4:24 great glory and with the splendor of the E
4:29 you will bring you E joy with your salvation."
4:35 upon her from the E for many days, and
5:2 head the diadem of the glory of the E
5:7 high mountain and the E hills be made low
Ezek 16:60 establish with you an E covenant.
37:26 it shall be an E covenant with them; and
Dan 4:3 His kingdom is an E kingdom, and his dominion
4:34 his dominion is an E dominion, and his kingdom
7:14 his dominion is an E dominion, which shall not
7:27 kingdom shall be an E kingdom, and all dominions
9:24 iniquity, to bring in E righteousness, to seal both
12:2 shall awake, some to E life, and some to
12:2 some to shame and E contempt.
Hab 1:12 Art thou not from E, O LORD my God,
3:6 mountains were scattered, the E hills sank low.
1Mac 2:51 great honor and an E name.
2:54 received the covenant of E priesthood.
6:44 win for himself an E name.
2Mac 7:9 us up to an E renewal of life, because

EVERMORE (18)

1Kgs 2:33 there shall be peace from the LORD for E
Ps 16:11 joy, in thy right hand are pleasures for E
35:27 be glad, and say E, "Great is the LORD,
70:4 love thy salvation say E, "God is great!"
93:5 sure; holiness befits thy house, O LORD, for E
113:2 the LORD from this time forth and for E
115:18 the LORD from this time forth and for E
121:8 coming in from this time forth and for E
125:2 his people, from this time forth and for E
131:3 the LORD from this time forth and for E
133:3 the LORD has commanded the blessing, life for E
Is 9:7 with righteousness from this time forth and for E
59:21 the LORD, from this time forth and for E
Ezek 37:26 my sanctuary in the midst of them for E
37:28 sanctuary is in the midst of them for E
Mic 4:7 Mount Zion from this time forth and for E
Rom 16:26 God be glory for E through Jesus Christ!
Rev 1:18 I am alive for E, and I have the

EVERY (1,121)

Gen 1:21 great sea monsters and E living creature that moves,
1:21 to their kinds, and E winged bird according to
1:26 the earth, and over E creeping thing that creeps
1:28 the air and over E living thing that moves
1:29 I have given you E plant yielding seed which
1:29 all the earth, and E tree with seed in
1:30 And to E beast of the earth, and to
1:30 the earth, and to E bird of the air,
1:30 life, I have given E green plant for food."
2:9 God made to grow E tree that is pleasant
2:16 may freely eat of E tree of the garden;
2:19 the LORD God formed E beast of the field
2:19 of the field and E bird of the air,
2:19 whatever the man called E living creature, that was
2:20 the air, and to E beast of the field;
3:24 flaming sword which turned E way, to guard the
6:5 the earth, and that E imagination of the thoughts
6:19 And of E living thing of all flesh, you
6:19 shall bring two of E sort into the ark,
6:20 to their kinds, of E creeping thing of the
6:20 its kind, two of E sort shall come in
6:21 Also take with you E sort of food that
7:4 and forty nights; and E living thing that I
7:14 the ark, they and E beast according to its
7:14 to their kinds, and E creeping thing that creeps
7:14 to its kind, and E bird according to its
7:14 according to its kind, E bird of every sort.
7:14 kind, every bird of E sort.
7:21 upon the earth, and E man;
7:23 He blotted out E living thing that was upon
8:17 Bring forth with you E living thing that is
8:17 birds and animals and E creeping thing that creeps
8:19 And E beast, every creeping thing, and every bird,
8:19 And every beast, E creeping thing, and every bird,
8:19 every creeping thing, and E bird, everything that
8:20 LORD, and took of E clean animal and of
8:20 clean animal and of E clean bird, and offered
8:21 I ever again destroy E living creature as I
9:2 you shall be upon E beast of the earth,
9:2 the earth, and upon E bird of the air,
9:3 E moving thing that lives shall be food for
9:5 require a reckoning; of E beast I will require
9:5 and of man; of E man's brother I will
9:10 after you, and with E living creature that is
9:10 birds, the cattle, and E beast of the earth
9:12 me and you and E living creature that is
9:15 me and you and E living creature of all
9:16 covenant between God and E living creature of all
16:12 man, his hand against E man and every man's
16:12 against every man and E man's hand against him;
17:10 your descendants after you: E male among you shall
17:12 you shall be circumcised; E male throughout your
17:23 bought with his money, E male among the men
20:13 must do me: at E place to which we
20:16 with you; and before E one you are righted."
21:6 made laughter for me; E one who hears will
27:29 Cursed be E one who curses you, and blessed
27:29 you, and blessed be E one who blesses you!"
30:32 removing from it E speckled and spotted sheep
30:32 and spotted sheep and E black lamb, and the
30:33 E one that is not speckled and spotted among
30:35 were speckled and spotted, E one that had white
30:35 white on it, and E lamb that was black,
32:16 hand of his servants, E drove by itself, and
34:15 as we are and E male of you be
34:22 become one people: that E male among us be
34:24 his son Shechem; and E male was circumcised, all
41:48 he stored up in E city the food from
42:25 grain, and to replace E man's money in his
42:35 emptied their sacks, behold, E man's bundle of
43:21 sacks, and there was E man's money in the
44:11 Then E man quickly lowered his sack to the
44:11 to the ground, and E man opened his sack.
44:13 rent their clothes, and E man loaded his ass,
45:1 and he cried, "Make E one go out from
46:34 land of Goshen; for E shepherd is an abomination
Ex 1:21 commanded all his people, E son that is born
1:21 but you shall let E daughter live."
7:12 For E man cast down his rod, and they
9:19 shall come down upon E man and beast that
9:22 man and beast and E plant of the field,
9:25 the hail struck down E plant of the field,
9:25 the field, and shattered E tree of the field.
10:5 and they shall eat E tree of yours which
10:12 of Egypt, and eat E plant in the land,
11:2 people, that they ask, E man of his neighbor
11:2 of his neighbor and E woman of her neighbor,
12:3 month they shall take E man a lamb according
12:16 those days; but what E one must eat, that
12:44 eat of it; but E slave that is bought
13:13 E firstling of an ass you shall redeem with
13:13 E first-born of man among your sons you shall
16:4 gather a day's portion E day, that I may
16:16 commanded: 'Gather of it, E man of you, as
16:29 for two days; remain E man of you in
18:22 people at all times; E great matter they shall
20:24 and your oxen; in E place where I cause
22:9 "For E breach of trust, whether it is for
25:2 me an offering; from E man whose heart makes
27:19 of the tabernacle for E use, and all its
29:36 you ordain them, and E day you shall offer
30:7 fragrant incense on it; E morning when he dresses
30:14 E one who is numbered in the census, from
31:5 wood, for work in E craft.
31:14 is holy for you; E one who profanes it
32:27 God of Israel, 'Put E man his sword on

32:27 the camp, and slay E man his brother, and
32:27 man his brother, and E man his companion, and
32:27 man his companion, and E man his neighbor.'"
33:7 And E one who sought the LORD would go
33:8 people rose up, and E man stood at his
33:10 rise up and worship, E man at his tent
35:10 "And let E able man among you come and
35:21 And they came, E one whose heart stirred him,
35:21 heart stirred him, and E one whose spirit moved
35:22 sorts of gold objects, E man dedicating an offering
35:23 And E man with whom was found blue or
35:24 E one who could make an offering of silver
35:24 the LORD's offering; and E man with whom was
35:33 wood, for work in E skilled craft.
35:35 with ability to do E sort of work done
36:1 Bezalel and Oholiab and E able man in whom
36:2 Bezalel and Oholiab and E able man in whose
36:2 LORD had put ability, E one whose heart stirred
36:3 bringing him freewill offerings E morning,
36:4 men who were doing E sort of task on
36:30 silver: sixteen bases, under E frame two bases.
38:26 of the sanctuary), for E one who was numbered
Lev 6:12 burn wood on it E morning, and he shall
6:18 E male among the children of Aaron may eat
6:23 E cereal offering of a priest shall be wholly
6:29 E male among the priests may eat of it;
7:6 E male among the priests may eat of it;
7:9 And E cereal offering baked in the oven and
7:10 And E cereal offering, mixed with oil or dry,
7:25 For E person who eats of the fat of
11:15 according to its kind, E raven according to its
11:26 E animal which parts the hoof but is not
11:26 is unclean to you; E one who touches them
11:34 may be drunk from E such vessel shall be
11:41 E swarming thing that swarms upon the earth is
11:46 beast and bird and E living creature that moves
11:46 through the waters and E creature that swarms upon
15:4 E bed on which he who has the discharge
15:12 shall be broken; and E vessel of wood shall
15:17 And E garment and every skin on which the
15:17 And every garment and E skin on which the
15:24 unclean seven days; and E bed on which he
15:26 E bed on which she lies, all the days
17:14 "For the life of E creature is the blood
17:14 for the life of E creature is its blood;
17:15 And E person that eats what dies of itself
19:3 E one of you shall revere his mother and
19:8 not be accepted, and E one who eats it
20:9 For E one who curses his father or his
24:8 E sabbath day Aaron shall set it in order
27:25 E valuation shall be according to the shekel of
27:28 be sold or redeemed; E devoted thing is most
27:32 of herds and flocks, E tenth animal of all
Num 1:2 the number of names, E male, head by head;
1:20 names, head by head, E male from twenty years
1:22 names, head by head, E male from twenty years
1:26 years old and upward, E man able to go
1:28 years old and upward, E man able to go
1:30 years old and upward, E man able to go
1:32 years old and upward, E man able to go
1:34 years old and upward, E man able to go
1:36 years old and upward, E man able to go
1:38 years old and upward, E man able to go
1:40 years old and upward, E man able to go
1:42 years old and upward, E man able to go
1:45 years old and upward, E man able to go
1:52 tents by their companies, E man by his own
1:52 his own camp and E man by his own
2:2 tent of meeting on E side.
2:34 so they set out, E one in his family,
3:12 of Israel instead of E first-born that opens the
3:15 houses and by families; E male from a month
4:30 you shall number them, E one that can enter
4:35 to fifty years old, E one that could enter
4:39 to fifty years old, E one that could enter
4:43 to fifty years old, E one that could enter
4:47 to fifty years old, E one that could enter
5:2 out of the camp E leper, and every one
5:2 camp every leper, and E one having a discharge,
5:2 having a discharge, and E one that is unclean
5:9 And E offering, all the holy things of the
5:10 shall be his; and E man's holy things shall
7:3 oxen, a wagon for E two of the leaders,
11:10 weeping throughout their families, E man at the
13:2 you send a man, E one a leader among
14:34 land, forty days, for E day a year, you
15:12 shall you do with E one according to their
16:3 the congregation are holy, E one of them, and
16:17 Aaron, tomorrow; and let E one of you take
16:17 incense upon it, and E one of you bring
16:18 So E man took his censer, and they put
17:13 E one who comes near, who comes near to
18:9 reserved from the fire; E offering of theirs, every
18:9 every offering of theirs, E cereal offering of theirs
18:9 offering of theirs and E sin offering of theirs
18:9 offering of theirs and E guilt offering of theirs,
18:10 you eat of it; E male may eat of
18:11 as a perpetual due; E one who is clean
18:13 LORD, shall be yours; E one who is clean
18:14 E devoted thing in Israel shall be yours.
18:21 Levites I have given E tithe in Israel for
18:29 you, you shall present E offering due to the
19:14 dies in a tent: E one who comes into
19:14 into the tent, and E one who is in
19:15 And E open vessel, which has no cover fastened
21:8 on a pole; and E one who is bitten,
24:9 Blessed be E one who blesses you, and cursed
24:9 you, and cursed be E one who curses you."
25:5 the judges of Israel, E one of you slay
26:54 give a small inheritance; E tribe shall be given
26:62 them were twenty-three thousand, E male from a
28:10 the burnt offering of E sabbath, besides the continual
28:13 a cereal offering for E lamb; for a burnt
30:4 vows shall stand, and E pledge by which she
30:11 vows shall stand, and E pledge by which she
31:7 commanded Moses, and slew E male.
31:17 Now therefore, kill E male among the little ones,
31:17 little ones, and kill E woman who has known
31:20 You shall purify E garment, every article of skin,
31:20 shall purify every garment, E article of skin, all
31:20 of goats' hair, and E article of wood."
31:30 one drawn out of E fifty, of the persons,
31:47 Moses took one of E fifty, both of persons
31:53 war had taken booty, E man for himself.)
32:21 for the war, and E armed man of you
32:27 servants will pass over, E man who is armed
32:29 the sons of Reuben, E man who is armed
34:18 take one leader of E tribe, to divide the
36:7 tribe to another; for E one of the people
36:8 And E daughter who possesses an inheritance in any
36:8 her father, so that E one of the people
Deut 1:41 God commanded us.' And E man of you girded
2:34 time and utterly destroyed E city, men, women, and
3:6 king of Heshbon, destroying E city, men, women, and
3:20 then you shall return E man to his possession
11:6 households, their tents, and E living thing that
11:24 E place on which the sole of your foot
12:2 the hills and under E green tree;
12:8 doing here this day, E man doing whatever is
12:13 your burnt offerings at E place that you see;
12:31 LORD your God; for E abominable thing which the
14:6 E animal that parts the hoof and has the
14:14 kite, after their kinds; E raven after its kind;
14:28 "At the end of E three years you shall
15:1 "At the end of E seven years you shall
15:2 manner of the release: E creditor shall release what
16:17 before the LORD empty-handed; E man shall give as
21:5 and by their word E dispute and every assault
21:5 word every dispute and E assault shall be settled.
23:9 shall keep yourself from E evil thing.
24:16 death for the fathers; E man shall be put
28:61 E sickness also, and every affliction which is not
28:61 Every sickness also, and E affliction which is not
31:10 "At the end of E seven years, at the
Josh 1:3 E place that the sole of your foot will
6:5 people shall go up E man straight before him."
6:20 up into the city, E man straight before him,
10:28 sword; he utterly destroyed E person in it, he
10:30 of the sword, and E person in it; he
10:32 of the sword, and E person in it, as
10:35 of the sword; and E person in it he
10:37 and its towns, and E person in it; he
10:37 utterly destroyed it with E person in it.
10:39 sword, and utterly destroyed E person in it; he
11:14 for their booty; but E man they smote with
21:44 gave them rest on E side just as he
22:14 tribal families of Israel, E one of them the
24:28 sent the people away, E man to his inheritance.
Judg 5:30 maiden or two for E man; spoil of dyed
7:5 LORD said to Gideon, E one that laps the
7:5 set by himself; likewise E one that kneels down
7:7 all the others go E man to his home."

7:8 the rest of Israel E man to his tent,
7:18 the trumpets also on E side of all the
7:21 They stood E man in his place round about
7:22 trumpets, the LORD set E man's sword against his
8:18 are, so were they, E one of them; they
8:24 of you; give me E man of you the
8:25 spread a garment, and E man cast in it
8:34 all their enemies on E side;
9:49 So E one of the people cut down his
9:55 was dead, they departed E man to his home.
17:6 no king in Israel; E man did what was
20:16 men who were left-handed; E one could sling a
21:11 what you shall do; E male and every woman
21:11 do; every male and E woman that has lain
21:24 there at that time, E man to his tribe
21:24 went out from there E man to his inheritance.
21:25 no king in Israel; E man did what was
1Sam 2:29 the choicest parts of E offering of my people
2:36 And E one who is left in your house
3:11 the two ears of E one that hears it
4:8 smote the Egyptians with E sort of plague in
4:10 defeated, and they fled, E man to his home;
8:22 men of Israel, "Go E man to his city."
12:11 of your enemies on E side; and you dwelt
13:2 people he sent home, E man to his tent.
13:20 swords or spears"; but E one of the Israelites
14:20 the battle; and behold, E man's sword was against
14:34 say to them, 'Let E man bring his ox
14:34 So E one of the people brought his ox
14:47 all his enemies on E side, against Moab, against
20:15 the LORD cuts off E one of the enemies
22:2 And E one who was in distress, and every
22:2 was in distress, and E one who was in
22:2 was in debt, and E one who was discontented,
22:7 son of Jesse give E one of you fields
23:14 And Saul sought him E day, but God did
25:13 said to his men, E man gird on his
25:13 And E man of them girded on his sword;
26:23 The LORD rewards E man for his righteousness and
27:3 he and his men, E man with his household,
2Sam 2:3 who were with him, E one with his household;
4:9 my life out of E adversity,
13:9 Amnon said, "Send out E one from me." So
13:9 So E one went out from him.
14:26 at the end of E year he used to
15:4 Then E man with a suit or cause might
18:17 and all Israel fled E one to his own
19:8 Now Israel had fled E man to his own
20:1 the son of Jesse; E man to his tents,
20:22 dispersed from the city, E man to his home.
1Kgs 1:29 my soul out of E adversity,
4:25 Dan even to Beer-sheba, E man under his vine
5:4 given me rest on E side; there is neither
10:22 Once E three years the fleet of ships of
10:25 E one of them brought his present, articles of
11:15 the slain, he slew E male in Edom
11:16 he had cut off E male in Edom);
12:24 Return E man to his home, for this thing
14:10 cut off from Jeroboam E male, both bond and
14:23 pillars, and Asherim on E high hill and under
14:23 high hill and under E green tree;
19:18 bowed to Baal, and E mouth that has not
21:21 cut off from Ahab E male, bond or free,
22:36 went through the army, E man to his city,
22:36 to his city, and E man to his country!"
22:53 Israel, to anger in E way that his father
2Kgs 3:19 and you shall conquer E fortified city, and every
3:19 every fortified city, and E choice city, and shall
3:19 city, and shall fell E good tree, and stop
3:19 of water, and ruin E good piece of land
3:25 the cities, and on E good piece of land
3:25 good piece of land E man threw a stone,
3:25 was covered; they stopped E spring of water, and
9:8 cut off from Ahab E male, bond or free,
9:13 Then in haste E man of them took his
11:11 and the guards stood, E man with his weapons
14:6 for the fathers; but E man shall die for
14:12 defeated by Israel, and E man fled to his
15:20 shekels of silver from E man, to give to
16:4 the hills, and under E green tree.
17:10 pillars and Asherim on E high hill and under
17:10 high hill and under E green tree;
17:13 Israel and Judah by E prophet and every seer,
17:13 by every prophet and E seer, saying, "Turn from
17:29 But E nation still made gods of its own,
17:29 the Samaritans had made, E nation in the cities
18:31 out to me; then E one of you will
18:31 his own vine, and E one of his own
18:31 own fig tree, and E one of you will
21:12 that the ears of E one who hears of
23:35 of the land, from E one according to his
25:9 the houses of Jerusalem; E great house he burned
25:29 And E day of his life he dined regularly
25:30 him by the king, E day a portion, as
1Chr 9:25 obliged to come in E seven days, from time
9:27 charge of opening it E morning.
9:32 showbread, to prepare it E sabbath.
13:1 and of hundreds, with E leader.
22:18 given you peace on E side?
23:30 And they shall stand E morning, thanking and
28:9 all hearts, and understands E plan and thought.
28:21 the work will be E willing man who has
2Chr 7:21 house, which is exalted, E one passing by will
9:21 servants of Huram; once E three years the ships
9:24 E one of them brought his present, articles of
11:4 Return E man to his home, for this thing
13:11 offer to the LORD E morning and every evening
13:11 LORD every morning and E evening burnt offerings
13:11 its lamps may burn E evening; for we keep
14:7 given us peace on E side." So they built
15:6 God troubled them with E sort of distress.
20:27 Then they returned, E man of Judah and Jerusalem,
23:10 guard for the king, E man with his weapon
25:4 for the fathers; but E man shall die for
25:22 defeated by Israel, and E man fled to his
28:4 the hills, and under E green tree.
28:24 made himself altars in E corner of Jerusalem.
28:25 In E city of Judah he made high places
30:17 the passover lamb for E one who was not
30:18 "The good LORD pardon E one
31:1 returned to their cities, E man to his possession.
31:19 to distribute portions to E male among the priests
31:19 the priests and to E one among the Levites
31:21 And E work that he undertook in the service
32:22 gave them rest on E side.
34:13 who did work in E kind of service; and
Ezra 1:5 priests and the Levites, E one whose spirit God
3:5 and the offerings of E one who made a
6:21 exile, and also by E one who had joined
10:14 elders and judges of E city, till the fierce
Neh 4:22 at that time, "Let E man and his servant
5:13 may God shake out E man from his house
5:18 prepared for me, and E ten days skins of
9:22 didst allot to them E corner; so they took
10:31 and the exaction of E debt.
10:35 of all fruit of E tree, year by year,
10:37 contributions, the fruit of E tree, the wine and
11:3 the towns of Judah E one lived on his
11:20 the towns of Judah, E one in his inheritance.
11:23 for the singers, as E day required.
Tob 4:18 Seek advice from E wise man, and do not
4:19 the Lord God on E occasion; ask him that
4:21 God and refrain from E sin and do what
8:15 thou, O God, with E pure and holy blessing.
10:7 And she went out E day to the road
12:9 it will purge away E sin.
Jud 1:12 and all Judea, and E one in Egypt, as
2:3 it was decided that E one who had not
2:8 fill their valleys, and E brook and river shall
2:18 plenty of food for E man, and a huge
2:25 of Cilicia, and killed E one who resisted him,
4:4 So they sent to E district of Samaria, and
4:9 And E man of Israel cried out to God
4:10 and their cattle and E resident alien and hired
7:4 were greatly terrified, and E one said to his
7:20 of water belonging to E inhabitant of Bethulia were
9:14 thy whole nation and E tribe to know and
10:19 them by her, and E one said to his
11:7 sent you to direct E living soul, not only
11:17 remain with you, and E night your servant will
13:3 out, as she did E day; for she said
13:4 So E one went out, and no one, either
14:2 the sun rises, let E valiant man take his
14:7 "Blessed are you in E tent of Judah!
14:7 In E nation those who hear your name will
14:11 on the wall, and E man took his weapons,
15:2 out and fled by E path across the plain
15:3 the men of Israel, E one that was a
16:16 For E sacrifice as a fragrant offering is a
16:21 After this E one returned home to his own
Esth 1:8 palace to do as E man desired.
1:22 the royal provinces, to E province in its own

1:22 own script and to E people in its own
1:22 its own language, that E man be lord in
2:11 And E day Mordecai walked in front of the
3:8 different from those of E other people, and they
3:12 all the peoples, to E province in its own
3:12 its own script and E people in its own
3:14 as a decree in E province by proclamation to
4:3 And in E province, wherever the king's command and
8:9 and twenty-seven provinces, to E province in its own
8:9 own script and to E people in its own
8:11 Jews who were in E city to gather and
8:13 as a decree in E province, and by proclamation
8:17 And in E province and in E city, wherever
9:27 at the time appointed E year,
9:28 throughout E generation, in E family, province,
11:7 And at their roaring E nation prepared for war,
11:12 to understand it in E detail.
13:4 contrary to those of E nation and continually
13:10 heaven and earth and E wonderful thing under
14:2 humbled her body, and E part that she loved
16:11 that we have for E nation that he was
16:19 this letter publicly in E place, and permit the
16:24 E city and country, without exception, which does not
Job 1:10 that he has, on E side?
7:18 him, dost visit him E morning, and test him
7:18 morning, and test him E moment?
12:10 is the life of E living thing and the
18:11 Terrors frighten him on E side, and chase him
19:10 breaks me down on E side, and I am
28:10 and his eye sees E precious thing.
37:7 up the hand of E man, that all men
39:8 and he searches after E green thing.
40:11 anger, and look on E one that is proud,
40:12 Look on E one that is proud, and bring
Ps 6:6 weary with my moaning; E night I flood my
7:11 God who has indignation E day.
12:2 E one utters lies to his neighbor; with flattering
12:8 On E side the wicked prowl, as vileness is
31:13 many-- terror on E side!-- as they
32:6 [Selah] Therefore let E one who is godly offer
39:5 Surely E man stands as a mere breath!
39:11 dear to him; surely E man is a mere
50:10 For E beast of the forest is mine, the
54:7 hast delivered me from E trouble, and my eye
73:14 been stricken, and chastened E morning.
77:17 thy arrows flashed on E side.
88:9 E day I call upon thee, O LORD; I
104:11 they give drink to E beast of the field;
105:16 the land, and broke E staff of bread,
118:11 me, surrounded me on E side; in the name
119:101 back my feet from E evil way, in order
119:104 understanding; therefore I hate E false way.
119:128 thy precepts; I hate E false way.
119:160 word is truth; and E one of thy righteous
128:1 Blessed is E one who fears the LORD, who
135:18 make them!-- yea, E one who trusts in
139:16 thy book were written, E one of them, the
145:2 E day I will bless thee, and praise thy
145:16 satisfiest the desire of E living thing.
Prov 2:9 and justice and equity, E good path;
7:12 the market, and at E corner she lies in
15:3 the LORD are in E place, keeping watch on
16:5 E one who is arrogant is an abomination to
19:6 a generous man, and E one is a friend
20:3 aloof from strife; but E fool will be quarreling.
21:2 E way of a man is right in his
21:5 surely to abundance, but E one who is hasty
30:5 E word of God proves true; he is a
Eccl 3:1 and a time for E matter under heaven:
3:13 gift to man that E one should eat and
3:17 appointed a time for E matter, and for every
3:17 every matter, and for E work.
5:19 E man also to whom God has given wealth
8:6 For E matter has its time and way, although
10:3 and he says to E one that he is
12:14 For God will bring E deed into judgment, with
12:14 deed into judgment, with E secret thing, whether
Wis 6:16 and meets them in E thought.
7:27 renews all things; in E generation she passes into
7:29 the sun, and excels E constellation of the stars.
13:14 surface red and covering E blemish in it with
14:4 thou canst save from E danger, so that even
14:27 cause and end of E evil.
16:8 thou who deliverest from E evil.
16:20 ready to eat, providing E pleasure and suited to
16:20 pleasure and suited to E taste.
16:21 was changed to suit E one's liking.
Sir 5:9 Do not winnow with E wind, nor follow every
5:9 every wind, nor follow E path: the double-tongued
6:35 ready to listen to E narrative, and do not
8:19 reveal your thoughts to E one, lest you drive
11:27 Do not bring E man into your home, for
13:14 E creature loves its like, and every person his
13:14 loves its like, and E person his neighbor;
14:19 E product decays and ceases to exist, and the
15:19 him, and he knows E deed of man.
16:14 will make room for E act of mercy; every
16:14 every act of mercy; E one will receive in
17:14 appointed a ruler for E nation, but Israel is
18:27 E intelligent man knows wisdom, and he praises the
22:1 a filthy stone, and E one hisses at his
24:6 whole earth, and in E people and nation I
26:12 sit in front of E post and open her
29:3 with him, and on E occasion you will find
30:7 will be troubled at E cry.
31:7 devoted to it, and E fool will be taken
31:13 it sheds tears from E face.
31:15 your own, and in E matter be thoughtful.
32:23 Guard yourself in E act, for this is the
33:6 friend; he neighs under E one who sits on
35:9 With E gift show a cheerful face, and dedicate
36:22 the countenance, and surpasses E human desire.
37:1 E friend will say, "I too am a friend";
37:7 E counselor praises counsel, but some give counsel in
37:16 is the beginning of E work, and counsel precedes
37:16 work, and counsel precedes E undertaking.
37:28 everything is good for E one, and not every
37:28 every one, and not E person enjoys everything.
38:27 So too is E craftsman and master workman who
39:33 and he will supply E need in its hour.
40:1 labor was created for E man, and a heavy
41:16 is good to retain E kind of shame, and
41:16 is confidently esteemed by E one.
41:23 will find favor with E man.
42:23 remain for ever for E need, and are all
43:20 water; it rests upon E pool of water, and
45:14 be wholly burned twice E day continually.
46:5 enemies pressed him on E side,
46:16 enemies pressed him on E side, and he offered
47:7 out his enemies on E side, and annihilated his
47:13 gave him rest on E side, that he might
47:25 For they sought out E sort of wickedness, till
49:1 sweet as honey to E mouth, and like music
49:16 men, and Adam above E living being in the
50:22 of all, who in E way does great things;
51:4 from choking fire on E side and from the
51:7 They surrounded me on E side, and there was
Is 1:23 E one loves a bribe and runs after gifts.
2:15 the lofty hills; against E high tower, and against
2:15 high tower, and against E fortified wall;
3:5 will oppress one another, E man his fellow and
3:5 man his fellow and E man his neighbor; the
4:3 will be called holy, E one who has been
7:22 will eat curds; for E one that is left
7:23 In that day E place where there used to
9:5 For E boot of the tramping warrior in battle
9:5 in battle tumult and E garment rolled in blood
9:17 fatherless and widows; for E one is godless and
9:17 and an evildoer, and E mouth speaks folly.
13:7 will be feeble, and E man's heart will melt,
13:14 none to gather them, E man will turn to
13:14 his own people, and E man will flee to
15:2 On E head is baldness, every beard is shorn;
15:2 every head is baldness, E beard is shorn;
15:3 and in the squares E one wails and melts
16:7 let Moab wail, let E one wail for Moab.
19:2 and they will fight, E man against his brother
19:2 against his brother and E man against his neighbor,
19:17 terror to the Egyptians; E one to whom it
22:24 the offspring and issue, E small vessel, from the
24:10 chaos is broken down, E house is shut up
27:3 LORD, am its keeper; E moment I water it.
30:5 his envoys reach Hanes, E one comes to shame
30:25 And upon E lofty mountain and every high hill
30:25 every lofty mountain and E high hill there will
30:32 And E stroke of the staff of punishment which
31:7 For in that day E one shall cast away
33:2 Be our arm E morning, our salvation in the
36:16 out to me; then E one of you will
36:16 his own vine, and E one of his own
36:16 own fig tree, and E one of you will
40:4 E valley shall be lifted up, and every mountain

	40:4	be lifted up, and E mountain and hill be
	41:2	whom victory meets at E step?
	41:6	E one helps his neighbor, and says to his
	43:7	end of the earth, E one who is called
	44:23	mountains, O forest, and E tree in it!
	45:23	not return: 'To me E knee shall bow, every
	45:23	every knee shall bow, E tongue shall swear.'
	51:20	at the head of E street like an antelope
	53:6	astray; we have turned E one to his own
	54:17	and you shall confute E tongue that rises against
	55:1	"Ho, E one who thirsts, come to the waters;
	56:6	to be his servants, E one who keeps the
	57:5	among the oaks, under E green tree; who slay
	57:14	prepare the way, remove E obstruction from my
	58:6	free, and to break E yoke?
Jer	1:15	they shall come and E one shall set his
	2:20	not serve.' Yea, upon E high hill and under
	2:20	high hill and under E green tree you bowed
	3:6	she went up on E high hill and under
	3:6	high hill and under E green tree, and there
	3:13	favors among strangers under E green tree, and that
	4:29	of horseman and archer E city takes to flight;
	5:6	watching against their cities, E one who goes out
	6:13	the greatest of them, E one is greedy for
	6:13	from prophet to priest, E one deals falsely.
	6:25	sword, terror is on E side.
	8:6	'What have I done?' E one turns to his
	8:10	least to the greatest E one is greedy for
	8:10	from prophet to priest E one deals falsely.
	9:4	Let E one beware of his neighbor, and put
	9:4	in any brother; for E brother is a supplanter,
	9:4	is a supplanter, and E neighbor goes about as
	9:5	E one deceives his neighbor, and no one speaks
	10:14	E man is stupid and without knowledge; every
	10:14	stupid and without knowledge; E goldsmith is put to
	11:8	incline their ear, but E one walked in the
	12:4	and the grass of E field wither?
	13:12	the God of Israel, E jar shall be filled
	13:12	not indeed know that E jar will be filled
	16:12	your fathers, for behold, E one of you follows
	16:16	shall hunt them from E mountain and every hill,
	16:16	from every mountain and E hill, and out of
	17:2	and their Asherim, beside E green tree, and on
	17:10	heart, to give to E man according to his
	18:11	Return, E one from his evil way, and amend
	18:12	own plans, and will E one act according to
	18:16	E one who passes by it is horrified and
	19:3	that the ears of E one who hears of
	19:8	to be hissed at; E one who passes by
	19:9	and their daughters, and E one shall eat the
	20:3	Pashhur, but Terror on E side.
	20:7	laughingstock all the day; E one mocks me.
	20:10	Terror is on E side!
	22:8	by this city, and E man will say to
	23:17	with you'; and to E one who stubbornly follows
	23:35	Thus shall you say, E one to his neighbor
	23:35	to his neighbor and E one to his brother,
	23:36	for the burden is E man's own word, and
	25:5	prophets, saying, 'Turn now, E one of you, from
	26:3	they will listen, and E one turn from his
	29:26	of the LORD over E madman who prophesies, to
	30:6	then do I see E man with his hands
	30:6	Why has E face turned pale?
	30:16	and all your foes, E one of them, shall
	31:25	the weary soul, and E languishing soul I will
	31:30	set on edge.' But E one shall die for
	32:19	ways of men, rewarding E man according to his
	34:9	liberty to them, that E one should set free
	34:10	into the covenant that E one would set free
	34:17	me by proclaiming liberty, E one to his brother
	35:15	persistently, saying, 'Turn now E one of you from
	36:3	to them, so that E one may turn from
	36:7	the LORD, and that E one will turn from
	37:10	them only wounded men, E man in his tent,
	43:6	the princesses, and E person whom Nebuzaradan
	46:5	not back—terror on E side!
	47:2	shall cry out, and E inhabitant of the land
	47:4	from Tyre and Sidon E helper that remains.
	48:8	destroyer shall come upon E city, and no city
	48:37	"For E head is shaved and every beard cut
	48:37	head is shaved and E beard cut off; upon
	49:5	shall be driven out, E man straight before him,
	49:17	shall become a horror; E one who passes by
	49:29	to them: 'Terror on E side!'
	49:32	I will scatter to E wind those who cut
	49:32	bring their calamity from E side of them, says
	50:13	be an utter desolation; E one who passes by
	50:16	sword of the oppressor, E one shall turn to
	50:16	his own people, and E one shall flee to
	50:26	against her from E quarter; open her granaries;
	51:2	come against her from E side on the day
	51:6	midst of Babylon, let E man save his life!
	51:17	E man is stupid and without knowledge; every
	51:17	stupid and without knowledge; E goldsmith is put to
	51:28	governors and deputies, and E land under their
	51:31	city is taken on E side;
	51:45	Let E man save his life from the fierce
	52:13	the houses of Jerusalem; E great house he burned
	52:33	And E day of his life he dined regularly
Lam	2:19	at the head of E street.
	2:22	feast my terrors on E side; and on the
	3:23	end; they are new E morning; great is thy
	4:1	at the head of E street.
Bar	5:7	God has ordered that E high mountain and the
	5:8	The woods and E fragrant tree have shaded Israel
	6:18	gates are shut on E side upon a man
	6:61	wind likewise blows in E land.
	6:71	a garden, on which E bird sits; or like
Ezek	1:9	one another; they went E one straight forward,
	6:13	about their altars, upon E high hill, on all
	6:13	the mountain tops, under E green tree, and under
	6:13	green tree, and under E leafy oak, wherever they
	7:16	all of them moaning, E one over his iniquity.
	8:12	doing in the dark, E man in his room
	9:2	gate, which faces north, E man with his weapon
	10:14	And E one had four faces: the first face
	10:22	They went E one straight forward.
	12:14	I will scatter toward E wind all who are
	12:22	days grow long, and E vision comes to nought?
	12:23	and the fulfilment of E vision.
	13:18	heads of persons of E stature, in the hunt
	16:24	a lofty place in E square;
	16:25	at the head of E street you built your
	16:31	at the head of E street, and making your
	16:31	your lofty place in E square.
	16:33	come to you from E side for your harlotries.
	16:37	them against you from E side, and will uncover
	16:44	Behold, E one who uses proverbs will use this
	17:21	shall be scattered to E wind; and you shall
	17:23	its branches birds of E sort will nest.
	18:30	O house of Israel, E one according to his
	19:8	against him snares on E side; they spread their
	20:7	your eyes feast on, E one of you, and
	20:8	me; they did not E man cast away the
	20:39	Lord GOD: Go serve E one of you his
	20:47	and it shall devour E green tree in you
	20:47	tree in you and E dry tree; the blazing
	21:7	When it comes, E heart will melt and all
	21:7	hands will be feeble, E spirit will faint and
	22:6	of Israel in you, E one according to his
	23:7	all the idols of E one on whom she
	23:22	them against you from E side:
	23:24	themselves against you on E side with buckler, shield,
	26:16	the ground and tremble E moment, and be appalled
	27:12	your great wealth of E kind; silver, iron, tin,
	27:18	your great wealth of E kind; wine of Helbon,
	28:13	the garden of God; E precious stone was your
	28:23	is against her on E side.
	29:18	labor hard against Tyre; E head was made bald
	29:18	was made bald and E shoulder was rubbed bare;
	32:10	them; they shall tremble E moment, every one for
	32:10	shall tremble every moment, E one for his own
	34:6	the mountains and on E high hill; my sheep
	38:20	cliffs shall fall, and E wall shall tumble to
	38:21	I will summon E kind of terror against Gog,
	38:21	says the Lord GOD; E man's sword will be
	39:4	birds of prey of E sort and to the
	39:17	to the birds of E sort and to all
	41:10	about the temple on E side.
	41:18	E cherub had two faces:
	44:29	the guilt offering; and E devoted thing in Israel
	44:30	of all kinds, and E offering of all kinds
	45:15	and one sheep from E flock of two hundred,
	47:9	the river goes E living creature which swarms
	47:12	will bear fresh fruit E month, because the water
Dan	1:20	And in E matter of wisdom and understanding
	3:5	trigon, harp, bagpipe, and E kind of music, you
	3:7	trigon, harp, bagpipe, and E kind of music, all
	3:10	made a decree, that E man who hears the
	3:10	trigon, harp, bagpipe, and E kind of music, shall
	3:15	trigon, harp, bagpipe, and E kind of music, to
	11:36	and magnify himself above E god, and shall speak

12:1 people shall be delivered, E one whose name shall
13:8 used to see her E day, going in and
13:22 am hemmed in on E side.
14:3 idol called Bel, and E day they spent on
14:4 revered it and went E day to worship it.
14:6 he eats and drinks E day?"
14:32 in the den, and E day they had been
Hos 9:15 E evil of theirs is in Gilgal; there I
13:15 strip his treasury of E precious thing.
Amos 2:8 lay themselves down beside E altar upon garments
4:3 out through the breaches, E one straight before her;
4:4 bring your sacrifices E morning, your tithes every
4:4 every morning, your tithes E three days;
8:3 shall be many; in E place they shall be
8:8 on this account, and E one mourn who dwells
8:10 loins, and baldness on E head; I will make
Obad 1:9 O Teman, so that E man from Mount Esau
Jon 3:8 to God; yea, let E one turn from his
Mic 4:4 but they shall sit E man under his vine
Nah 2:9 treasure, or wealth of E precious thing.
3:10 at the head of E street; for her honored
Hab 1:10 They laugh at E fortress, for they heap up
Zeph 1:9 day I will punish E one who leaps over
2:15 E one who passes by her hisses and shakes
3:5 he does no wrong; E morning he shows forth
Hag 2:14 LORD; and so with E work of their hands;
2:22 riders shall go down, E one by the sword
Zech 3:10 the LORD of hosts, E one of you will
5:3 the whole land; for E one who steals shall
5:3 according to it, and E one who swears falsely
8:10 in; for I set E man against his fellow.
8:23 from the nations of E tongue shall take hold
10:1 showers of rain, to E one the vegetation in
10:4 bow, out of them E ruler.
12:4 LORD, I will strike E horse with panic, and
12:4 eyes, when I strike E horse of the peoples
13:4 On that day E prophet will be ashamed of
14:16 Then E one that survives of all the nations
14:21 before the altar; and E pot in Jerusalem and
Mal 1:11 the nations, and in E place incense is offered
2:17 By saying, E one who does evil is good
1Mac 1:25 Israel mourned deeply in E community,
1:27 E bridegroom took up the lament; she who sat
1:37 On E side of the sanctuary they shed innocent
1:52 Many of the people, E one who forsook the
1:53 Israel into hiding in E place of refuge they
2:27 loud voice, saying: "Let E one who is zealous
2:41 "Let us fight against E man who comes to
2:42 mighty warriors of Israel, E one who offered himself
4:59 of Israel determined that E year at that season
5:28 the city, and killed E male by the edge
5:35 it; and he killed E male in it, plundered
5:51 He destroyed E male by the edge of the
6:18 They were trying in E way to harm them
8:4 rest paid them tribute E year.
8:15 a senate chamber, and E day three hundred and
10:33 And E one of the Jews taken as a
10:42 my officials have received E year from the income
12:4 to the people in E place, asking them to
12:11 remember you constantly on E occasion, both in our
13:10 he fortified it on E side.
13:20 along opposite him to E place he went.
13:52 And Simon decreed that E year they should
14:14 and did away with E lawless and wicked man.
14:35 He sought in E way to exalt his people.
15:8 E debt you owe to the royal treasury and
2Mac 1:17 Blessed in E way be our God, who has
1:23 the priests and E one.
1:25 dost rescue Israel from E evil, who didst choose
2:30 to discuss matters from E side and to take
5:12 to cut down relentlessly E one they met and
9:7 hard as to torture E limb of his body.
9:11 was tortured with pain E moment.
9:17 Jew and would visit E inhabited place to proclaim
10:8 should observe these days E year.
10:13 called a traitor at E turn, because he had
10:14 of mercenaries, and at E turn kept on warring
10:35 savage fury cut down E one they met.
11:3 the high-priesthood for sale E year.
11:15 For the king granted E request in behalf of
12:40 under the tunic of E one of the dead
15:35 and conspicuous sign to E one of the help
Mt 3:10 root of the trees; E tree therefore that does
4:4 bread alone, but by E word that proceeds from
4:23 the kingdom and healing E disease and every
4:23 healing every disease and E infirmity among the
5:22 say to you that E one who is angry
5:28 say to you that E one who looks at
5:32 say to you that E one who divorces his
7:8 For E one who asks receives, and he who
7:17 So, E sound tree bears good fruit, but the
7:19 E tree that does not bear good fruit is
7:21 "Not E one who says to me, 'Lord, Lord,'
7:24 from me, you evildoers.' E one then who hears
7:26 And E one who hears these words of mine
9:35 the kingdom, and healing E disease and every
9:35 healing every disease and E infirmity.
10:1 out, and to heal E disease and every infirmity.
10:1 heal every disease and E infirmity.
10:32 So E one who acknowledges me before men, I
12:25 he said to them, E kingdom divided against itself
12:31 Therefore I tell you, E sin and blasphemy will
12:36 will render account for E careless word they utter;
13:47 and gathered fish of E kind;
13:52 said to them, "Therefore E scribe who has been
15:13 He answered, E plant which my heavenly Father has
16:27 then he will repay E man for what he
18:15 along with you, that E word may be confirmed
18:34 Father will do to E one of you, if
19:29 And E one who has left houses or brothers
25:29 For to E one who has will more be
Mk 1:37 and said to him, E one is searching for
1:45 came to him from E quarter.
9:47 For E one will be salted with fire.
Lk 2:23 law of the Lord, E male that opens the
2:41 parents went to Jerusalem E year at the feast
3:5 E valley shall be filled, and every mountain and
3:5 shall be filled, and E mountain and hill shall
3:9 root of the trees; E tree therefore that does
4:13 the devil had ended E temptation, he departed from
4:37 him went out into E place in the surrounding
4:40 laid his hands on E one of them and
5:17 who had come from E village of Galilee and
6:30 Give to E one who begs from you; and
6:40 above his teacher, but E one when he is
6:47 E one who comes to me and hears my
10:1 two by two, into E town and place where
11:4 for we ourselves forgive E one who is indebted
11:10 For E one who asks receives, and he who
11:17 thoughts, said to them, E kingdom divided against
11:42 mint and rue and E herb, and neglect justice
12:8 "And I tell you, E one who acknowledges me
12:10 And E one who speaks a word against the
12:48 E one to whom much is given, of him
14:11 For E one who exalts himself will be humbled,
16:16 God is preached, and E one enters it violently.
16:18 E one who divorces his wife and marries another
16:19 and who feasted sumptuously E day.
18:14 than the other; for E one who exalts himself
19:26 tell you, that to E one who has will
19:43 hem you in on E side,
20:18 E one who falls on that stone will be
21:37 And E day he was teaching in the temple,
Jn 1:9 true light that enlightens E man was coming into
2:10 and said to him, E man serves the good
3:8 so it is with E one who is born
3:20 For E one who does evil hates the light,
4:13 Jesus said to her, E one who drinks of
6:40 of my Father, that E one who sees the
6:45 be taught by God.' E one who has heard
8:34 I say to you, E one who commits sin
11:48 him go on thus, E one will believe in
13:10 are clean, but not E one of you."
15:2 E branch of mine that bears no fruit, he
15:2 he takes away, and E branch that does bear
16:32 you will be scattered, E man to his home,
18:37 E one who is of the truth hears my
19:12 are not Caesar's friend; E one who makes himself
21:25 which Jesus did; were E one of them to
Acts 2:5 Jews, devout men from E nation under heaven.
2:38 "Repent, and be baptized E one of you in
2:39 all that are far-off, E one whom the Lord
2:43 And fear came upon E soul; and many wonders
3:23 it shall be that E soul that does not
3:26 bless you in turning E one of you from
5:42 And E day in the temple and at home
10:35 no partiality, but in E nation any one who
10:43 prophets bear witness that E one who believes in
11:29 And the disciples determined, E one according to his
13:27 prophets which are read E sabbath, fulfilled these by
13:39 you, and by him E one that believes is
14:23 elders for them in E church, with prayer and

15:21 Moses has had in E city those who preach
15:21 for he is read E sabbath in the synagogues."
15:35 visit the brethren in E city where we proclaimed
16:26 doors were opened and E one's fetters were
17:17 in the market place E day with those who
17:22 I perceive that in E way you are very
17:26 he made from one E nation of men to
18:4 in the synagogue E sabbath, and persuaded Jews
20:23 testifies to me in E city that imprisonment and
20:31 or day to admonish E one with tears.
21:26 the offering presented for E one of them.
22:19 themselves know that in E synagogue I imprisoned
24:3 of this nation, in E way and everywhere we
Rom 1:16 God for salvation to E one who has faith,
2:6 he will render to E man according to his
2:9 tribulation and distress for E human being who does
2:10 honor and peace for E one who does good,
3:2 Much in E way.
3:4 God be true though E man be false, as
3:19 the law, so that E mouth may be stopped,
10:4 of the law, that E one who has faith
10:13 For, E one who calls upon the name of
12:3 to me I bid E one among you not
13:1 Let E person be subject to the governing authorities.
14:5 Let E one be fully convinced in his own
14:11 live, says the Lord, E knee shall bow to
14:11 bow to me, and E tongue shall give praise
1Cor 1:2 all those who in E place call on the
1:5 Christ Jesus, that in E way you were enriched
4:5 E man will receive his commendation from God.
4:17 teach them everywhere in E church.
6:18 E other sin which a man commits is outside
7:17 Only, let E one lead the life which the
7:20 E one should remain in the state in which
9:25 E athlete exercises self-control in all things.
11:3 that the head of E man is Christ, the
12:6 inspires them all in E one.
15:24 the Father after destroying E rule and every
15:24 destroying every rule and E authority and power.
15:28 may be everything to E one.
15:30 am I in peril E hour?
15:31 our Lord, I die E day!
16:2 the first day of E week, each of you
16:16 such men and to E fellow worker and laborer.
2Cor 4:2 would commend ourselves to E man's conscience in
4:8 We are afflicted in E way, but not crushed;
4:16 nature is being renewed E day.
6:4 commend ourselves in E way: through great
7:1 us cleanse ourselves from E defilement of body and
7:5 we were afflicted at E turn--fighting without and
7:11 At E point you have proved yourselves guiltless in
9:8 to provide you with E blessing in abundance, so
9:8 provide in abundance for E good work.
9:11 will be enriched in E way for great generosity,
10:5 We destroy arguments and E proud obstacle to the
10:5 of God, and take E thought captive to obey
10:6 being ready to punish E disobedience, when your
11:6 not in knowledge; in E way we have made
Gal 3:10 is written, "Cursed be E one who does not
3:13 is written, "Cursed be E one who hangs on
5:3 I testify again to E man who receives circumcision
Eph 1:3 us in Christ with E spiritual blessing in the
1:21 and dominion, and above E name that is named,
3:15 the Father, from whom E family in heaven and
4:14 and carried about with E wind of doctrine, by
4:15 to grow up in E way into him who
4:16 and knit together by E joint with which it
4:19 licentiousness, greedy to practice E kind of
4:25 putting away falsehood, let E one speak the truth
Phil 1:4 of you, always in E prayer of mine for
1:18 Only that in E way, whether in pretense or
2:9 name which is above E name,
2:10 the name of Jesus E knee should bow, in
2:11 under the earth, and E tongue confess that Jesus
4:19 my God will supply E need of yours according
4:21 Greet E saint in Christ Jesus.
Col 1:10 him, bearing fruit in E good work and increasing
1:23 has been preached to E creature under heaven, and
1:28 Him we proclaim, warning E man and teaching
1:28 every man and teaching E man in all wisdom,
1:28 that we may present E man mature in Christ.
4:6 you ought to answer E one.
1Thes 5:22 is good, abstain from E form of evil.
2Thes 1:3 and the love of E one of you for
1:11 call, and may fulfil E good resolve and work
2:4 and exalts himself against E so-called god or object
2:17 and establish them in E good work and word.
3:17 is the mark in E letter of mine; it
1Tim 2:2 godly and respectful in E way.
2:8 desire then that in E place the men should
3:4 submissive and respectful in E way;
4:8 is of value in E way, as it holds
5:10 to doing good in E way.
2Tim 2:19 and, "Let E one who names the name of
2:24 quarrelsome but kindly to E one, an apt teacher,
3:17 be complete, equipped for E good work.
4:18 will rescue me from E evil and save me
Tit 1:4 and appoint elders in E town as I directed
2:9 to give satisfaction in E respect; they are not
Heb 2:2 angels was valid and E transgression or disobedience
2:9 might taste death for E one.
2:17 like his brethren in E respect, so that he
3:4 (For E house is built by some one, but
3:13 But exhort one another E day, as long as
4:15 but one who in E respect has been tempted
5:1 For E high priest chosen from among men is
5:13 not solid food; for E one who lives on
8:3 For E high priest is appointed to offer gifts
8:11 they shall not teach E one his fellow or
8:11 one his fellow or E one his brother, saying,
9:19 For when E commandment of the law had been
10:11 And E priest stands daily at his service, offering
12:1 us also lay aside E weight, and sin which
12:6 he loves, and chastises E son whom he receives."
Jas 1:16 E good endowment and every perfect gift is from
1:16 Every good endowment and E perfect gift is from
1:18 Let E man be quick to hear, slow to
3:7 For E kind of beast and bird, of reptile
3:16 will be disorder and E vile practice.
1Pet 2:13 the Lord's sake to E human institution, whether it
2Pet 1:5 this very reason make E effort to supplement your
1Jn 2:29 may be sure that E one who does right
3:3 And E one who thus hopes in him purifies
3:4 E one who commits sin is guilty of lawlessness;
4:1 Beloved, do not believe E spirit, but test the
4:2 the Spirit of God: E spirit which confesses that
4:3 is of God, and E spirit which does not
5:1 E one who believes that Jesus is the Christ
5:1 child of God, and E one who loves the
3Jn 1:12 Demetrius has testimony from E one, and from the
1:15 Greet the friends, E one of them.
Rev 1:7 with the clouds, and E eye will see him,
1:7 eye will see him, E one who pierced him;
5:9 men for God from E tribe and tongue and
5:13 And I heard E creature in heaven and on
6:14 is rolled up, and E mountain and island was
6:15 and the strong, and E one, slave and free,
7:4 thousand sealed, out of E tribe of the sons
7:9 man could number, from E nation, from all tribes
7:17 God will wipe away E tear from their eyes."
11:6 smite the earth with E plague, as often as
13:7 was given it over E tribe and people and
13:8 earth will worship it, E one whose name has
14:6 dwell on earth, to E nation and tribe and
16:3 a dead man, and E living thing died that
16:20 And E island fled away, and no mountains were
18:2 demons, a haunt of E foul spirit, a haunt
18:2 spirit, a haunt of E foul and hateful bird;
21:4 he will wipe away E tear from their eyes,
21:19 city were adorned with E jewel; the first was
22:12 my recompense, to repay E one for what he
22:15 murderers and idolaters, and E one who loves and
22:18 I warn E one who hears the words of

EVERYBODY

Prov 26:10 an archer who wounds E is he who hires

EVERYONE

1Kgs 9:8 a heap of ruins; E passing by it will

EVERYTHING (164)

Gen 1:25 to their kinds, and E that creeps upon the
1:30 the air, and to E that creeps on the
1:30 creeps on the earth, E that has the breath
1:31 And God saw E that he had made, and
6:17 life from under heaven; E that is on the
7:8 of birds, and of E that creeps on the
7:22 earth, and every man; E on the dry land
8:19 thing, and every bird, E that moves upon the
9:2 of the air, upon E that creeps on the
9:3 gave you the green plants, I give you E
14:20 And Abram gave him a tenth of E

32:23 the stream, and likewise E that he had.
39:8 and he has put E that he has in
Ex 9:25 The hail struck down E that was in the
Lev 11:9 E in the waters that has fins and scales,
11:12 E in the waters that has not fins and
11:35 And E upon which any part of their carcass
15:4 shall be unclean; and E on which he sits
15:20 And E upon which she lies during her impurity
15:20 impurity shall be unclean; E also upon which she
15:26 of her impurity; and E on which she sits
Num 18:15 E that opens the womb of all flesh, whether
29:40 the people of Israel E just as the LORD
31:23 tin, and the lead, E that can stand the
Deut 8:3 that man lives by E that proceeds out of
12:32 E that I command you, you shall be careful
20:14 ones, the cattle, and E else in the city,
Josh 4:10 of the Jordan, until E was finished that the
1Sam 3:18 So Samuel told him E and hid nothing from
2Sam 3:36 it pleased them; as E that the king did
15:36 shall send to me E you hear."
1Kgs 14:26 treasures of the king's house; he took away E
1Chr 16:32 the field exult, and E in it!
26:32 of the Manassites for E pertaining to God and
2Chr 12:9 treasures of the king's house; he took away E
31:5 and they brought in abundantly the tithe of E
Ezra 8:34 and the weight of E was recorded.
Neh 13:30 I cleansed them from E foreign, and I established
Tob 2:14 You seem to know E
4:14 yourself, my son, in E you do, and be
5:1 "Father, I will do E that you have commanded
12:20 Write in a book E that has happened."
Jud 4:1 in Judea heard of E that Holofernes, the general
8:25 In spite of E let us give thanks to
Esth 4:17 went away and did E as Esther had ordered
6:13 and all his friends E that had befallen him.
16:4 the evil-hating justice of God, who always sees E
Job 28:24 the earth, and sees E under the heavens.
41:34 He beholds E that is high; he is king
Ps 69:34 him, the seas and E that moves therein.
74:3 the enemy has destroyed E in the sanctuary!
96:12 the field exult, and E in it!
138:2 thou hast exalted above E thy name and thy
150:6 Let E that breathes praise the LORD!
Prov 13:16 In E a prudent man acts with knowledge, but
14:15 The simple believes E, but the prudent looks where
16:4 The LORD has made E for its purpose, even
24:27 your work outside, get E ready for you in
27:7 one who is hungry E bitter is sweet.
Eccl 1:14 I have seen E that is done under the
3:1 For E there is a season, and a time
3:11 with He has made E beautiful in its time;
7:15 life I have seen E; there is a righteous
9:1 E before them is vanity,
10:19 and wine gladdens life, and money answers E
11:5 not know the work of God who makes E
Wis 18:13 though they had disbelieved E because of their
19:22 For in E, O Lord, thou hast exalted and
Sir 10:26 has an abundance of E, than one who goes
15:18 in power and sees E;
18:26 man is cautious in E, and in days of
19:15 so do not believe E you hear.
25:11 of the Lord surpasses E; to whom shall be
31:14 out your hand for E you see, and do
37:28 For not E is good for every one, and
37:28 for every one, and not every person enjoys E
39:21 for E has been created for its use.
41:1 who is prosperous in E, and who still has
41:2 old and distracted over E; to one who is
41:16 of shame, and not E is confidently esteemed by
42:16 sun looks down on E with its light, and
Jer 1:17 and say to them E that I command you.
25:13 have uttered against it, E written in this book,
44:17 But we will do E that we have vowed,
44:18 her, we have lacked E and have been consumed
Ezek 21:10 rod, my son, with E of wood.
30:12 upon the land and E in it, by the
47:9 may become fresh; so E will live where the
Dan 14:15 were accustomed to do, and ate and drank E
Zeph 1:2 will utterly sweep away E from the face of
1Mac 1:48 make themselves abominable by E unclean and
2Mac 7:28 the earth and see E that is in them,
10:23 success at arms in E he undertook, he destroyed
11:14 persuaded them to settle E on just terms, promising
11:18 informed the king of E that needed to be
Mt 8:33 the city they told E, and what had happened
18:25 I will pay you E
19:27 "Lo, we have left E and followed you.
22:4 calves are killed, and E is ready; come to
23:19 by it and by E on it;
Mk 4:11 but for those outside E is in parables;
4:34 but privately to his own disciples he explained E
8:25 was restored, and saw E clearly.
10:28 "Lo, we have left E and followed you."
11:11 had looked round at E, as it was already
12:44 poverty has put in E she had, her whole
Lk 2:39 when they had performed E according to the law
5:11 to land, they left E and followed him.
5:28 And he left E, and rose and followed him.
9:43 were all marveling at E he did, he said
11:41 are within; and behold, E is clean for you.
15:14 when he had spent E, a great famine arose
18:31 up to Jerusalem, and E that is written of
24:44 still with you, that E written about me in
Jn 10:41 did no sign, but E that John said about
17:7 Now they know that E that thou hast given
21:17 him, "Lord, you know E; you know that I
Acts 4:24 and the sea and E in them,
4:32 own, but they had E in common.
10:8 him, and having related E to them, he sent
13:39 believes is freed from E from which you could
17:24 made the world and E in it, being Lord
17:25 gives to all men life and breath and E
24:7 learn from him about E of which we accuse
24:13 of our fathers, believing E laid down by the
Rom 8:28 We know that in E God works for good
14:20 E is indeed clean, but it is wrong for
1Cor 2:10 For the Spirit searches E, even the depths of
10:26 is the Lords, and E in it."
10:33 please all men in E I do, not seeking
11:2 you remember me in E and maintain the traditions
15:28 that God may be E to every one.
2Cor 2:9 you and know whether you are obedient in E
6:10 many rich; as having nothing, and yet possessing E
7:14 shame; but just as E we said to you
8:7 as you excel in E – in faith, in utterance,
9:8 always have enough of E and may provide in
Eph 5:20 heart, always and for E giving thanks in the
5:24 also be subject in E to their husbands.
6:21 faithful minister in the Lord will tell you E
Phil 3:8 Indeed I count E as loss because of the
4:6 about anything, but in E by prayer and supplication
Col 1:18 the dead, that in E he might be pre-eminent.
3:14 on love, which binds E together in perfect harmony.
3:17 word or deed, do E in the name of
3:20 obey your parents in E, for this pleases the
3:22 Slaves, obey in E those who are your earthly
4:9 will tell you of E that has taken place
1Thes 5:21 despise prophesying, but test E; hold fast what is
1Tim 4:4 For E created by God is good, and nothing
6:17 richly furnishes us with E to enjoy.
2Tim 2:7 for the Lord will grant you understanding in E
2:10 Therefore I endure E for the sake of the
Tit 2:10 fidelity, so that in E they may adorn the
Heb 2:8 glory and honor, putting E in subjection under his
2:8 Now in putting E in subjection to him, he
2:8 do not yet see E in subjection to him.
7:2 to him Abraham apportioned a tenth part of E
8:5 "See that you make E according to the pattern
9:22 under the law almost E is purified with blood,
13:21 covenant, equip you with E good that you may
1Pet 4:11 in order that in E God may be glorified
1Jn 2:27 anointing teaches you about E, and is true, and
3:20 is greater than our hearts, and he knows E

EVERYWHERE (15)

Gen 13:10 valley was well watered E like the garden of
Wis 2:9 share in our revelry, E let us leave signs
Bar 5:3 will show your splendor E under heaven.
2Mac 2:18 will gather us from E under heaven into his
8:7 And talk of his valor spread E
Mk 1:28 once his fame spread E throughout all the
16:20 went forth and preached E, while the Lord worked
Lk 9:6 the villages, preaching the gospel and healing E
Acts 17:30 he commands all men E to repent,
21:28 who is teaching men E against the people and
24:3 in every way and E we accept this with
28:22 sect we know that E it is spoken against."
1Cor 4:17 as I teach them E in every church.
2Cor 2:14 spreads the fragrance of the knowledge of him E
1Thes 1:8 God has gone forth E, so that we need

EVI (2)

Num 31:8 rest of their slain, E, Rekem, Zur, Hur, and
Josh 13:21 the leaders of Midian, E and Rekem and Zur

EVICTIONS

Ezek 45:9 and righteousness; cease your E of my people, says

EVIDENCE (14)

Ex 22:13 him bring it as E; he shall not make
Num 35:30 to death on the E of witnesses; but no
Deut 17:6 On the E of two witnesses or of three
17:6 to death on the E of one witness.
19:15 committed; only on the E of two witnesses, or
Prov 12:17 the truth gives honest E, but a false witness
Wis 5:11 through the air, no E of its passage is
10:7 E of their wickedness still remains: a continually
Bar 6:69 So we have no E whatever that they are
Mt 18:15 be confirmed by the E of two or three
2Cor 13:1 be sustained by the E of two or three
2Thes 1:5 This is E of the righteous judgment of God,
1Tim 5:19 elder except on the E of two or three
Jas 5:3 their rust will be E against you and will

EVIDENT (3)

Gal 3:11 Now it is E that no man is justified
Heb 7:14 For it is E that our Lord was descended
7:15 This becomes even more E when another priest

EVIDENTLY

Bar 6:16 Therefore they E are not gods; so do not

EVIL (647)

Gen 2:9 the tree of the knowledge of good and E
2:17 knowledge of good and E you shall not eat,
3:5 you will be like God, knowing good and E
3:22 us, knowing good and E; and now, lest he
6:5 his heart was only E continually.
8:21 of man's heart is E from his youth; neither
44:4 'Why have you returned E for good?
44:34 fear to see the E that would come upon
47:9 thirty years; few and E have been the days
48:16 redeemed me from all E, bless the lads; and
50:15 back for all the E which we did to
50:17 sin, because they did E to you.' And now,
50:20 for you, you meant E against me; but God
Ex 5:19 that they were in E plight, when they said,
5:22 why hast thou done E to this people?
5:23 name, he has done E to this people, and
10:10 Look, you have some E purpose in mind.
23:2 a multitude to do E; nor shall you bear
32:12 the Egyptians say, 'With E intent did he bring
32:12 and repent of this E against thy people.
32:14 LORD repented of the E which he thought to
32:22 know the people, that they are set on E
33:4 the people heard these E tidings, they mourned; and
Lev 5:4 rash oath to do E or to do good,
26:6 and I will remove E beasts from the land,
Num 13:32 people of Israel an E report of the land
14:36 by bringing up an E report against the land,
14:37 who brought up an E report of the land,
20:5 bring us to this E place?
22:34 therefore, if it is E in thy sight, I
32:13 generation that had done E in the sight of
Deut 1:35 these men of this E generation shall see the
1:39 knowledge of good or E, shall go in there,
4:25 by doing what is E in the sight of
7:15 and none of the E diseases of Egypt, which
9:18 in doing what was E in the sight of
13:5 you shall purge the E from the midst of
17:2 who does what is E in the sight of
17:5 who has done this E thing, and you shall
17:7 you shall purge the E from the midst of
17:12 you shall purge the E from Israel.
19:19 you shall purge the E from the midst of
19:20 again commit any such E among you.
21:21 you shall purge the E from your midst; and
22:14 conduct, and brings an E name upon her, saying,
22:19 he has brought an E name upon a virgin
22:21 you shall purge the E from the midst of
22:22 you shall purge the E from Israel.
22:24 you shall purge the E from the midst of
23:9 keep yourself from every E thing.
24:7 you shall purge the E from the midst of
28:20 on account of the E of your doings, because
30:15 you this day life and good, death and E
31:18 account of all the E which they have done,
31:29 the days to come E will befall you, because
31:29 will do what is E in the sight of
Josh 23:15 upon you all the E things, until he have
Judg 2:11 Israel did what was E in the sight of
2:15 was against them for E, as the LORD had
3:7 Israel did what was E in the sight of
3:12 again did what was E in the sight of
3:12 had done what was E in the sight of
4:1 again did what was E in the sight of
6:1 Israel did what was E in the sight of
9:23 And God sent an E spirit between Abimelech and
10:6 again did what was E in the sight of
13:1 again did what was E in the sight of
20:13 death, and put away E from Israel." But the
1Sam 2:23 I hear of your E dealings from all the
12:19 all our sins this E, to ask for ourselves
12:20 have done all this E, yet do not turn
15:19 and do what was E in the sight of
16:14 from Saul, and an E spirit from the LORD
16:15 him, "Behold now, an E spirit from God is
16:16 lyre; and when the E spirit from God is
16:23 And whenever the E spirit from God was upon
16:23 was well, and the E spirit departed from him.
17:28 your presumption, and the E of your heart; for
18:10 on the morrow an E spirit from God rushed
19:9 Then an E spirit from the LORD came upon
20:7 angry, then know that E is determined by him.
20:9 by my father that E should come upon you,
23:9 that Saul was plotting E against him; and he
24:17 repaid me good, whereas I have repaid you E
25:17 you should do; for E is determined against our
25:21 he has returned me E for good.
25:26 who seek to do E to my lord be
25:28 of the LORD; and E shall not be found
25:39 back his servant from E; the LORD has returned
2Sam 12:9 to do what is E in his sight?
12:11 I will raise up E against you out of
14:17 the angel of God to discern good and E
15:14 quickly, and bring down E upon us, and smite
17:14 the LORD might bring E upon Absalom.
18:32 up against you for E, be like that young
19:7 you than all the E that has come upon
24:16 LORD repented of the E, and said to the
1Kgs 2:44 own heart all the E that you did to
2:44 will bring back your E upon your own head.
3:9 discern between good and E; for who is able
9:9 has brought all this E upon them.'"
11:6 Solomon did what was E in the sight of
13:33 not turn from his E way, but made priests
14:9 but you have done E above all that were
14:10 behold, I will bring E upon the house of
14:22 Judah did what was E in the sight of
15:26 He did what was E in the sight of
15:34 He did what was E in the sight of
16:7 because of all the E that he did in
16:19 which he committed, doing E in the sight of
16:25 Omri did what was E in the sight of
16:25 LORD, and did more E than all who were
16:30 son of Omri did E in the sight of
21:20 to do what is E in the sight of
21:21 Behold, I will bring E upon you; I will
21:25 to do what was E in the sight of
21:29 will not bring the E in his days; but
21:29 I will bring the E upon his house."
22:8 for he never prophesies good concerning me, but E
22:18 he would not prophesy good concerning me, but E
22:23 the LORD has spoken E concerning you."
22:52 He did what was E in the sight of
2Kgs 3:2 He did what was E in the sight of
8:12 "Because I know the E that you will do
8:18 he did what was E in the sight of
8:27 and did what was E in the sight of
13:2 He did what was E in the sight of
13:11 also did what was E in the sight of
14:24 he did what was E in the sight of
15:9 he did what was E in the sight of
15:18 he did what was E in the sight of
15:24 he did what was E in the sight of
15:28 he did what was E in the sight of
17:2 he did what was E in the sight of
17:13 saying, "Turn from your E ways and keep my
17:17 sold themselves to do E in the sight of
21:2 he did what was E in the sight of
21:6 He did much E in the sight of the
21:9 them to do more E than the nations had
21:12 Jerusalem and Judah such E that the ears of

E

21:15 have done what is E in my sight and
21:16 they did what was E in the sight of
21:20 he did what was E in the sight of
22:16 Behold, I will bring E upon this place and
22:20 not see all the E which I will bring
23:32 he did what was E in the sight of
23:37 he did what was E in the sight of
24:9 he did what was E in the sight of
24:19 he did what was E in the sight of
1Chr 7:23 his name Beriah, because E had befallen his house.
21:15 he repented of the E; and he said to
2Chr 7:22 has brought all this E upon them'"
12:14 And he did E, for he did not set
18:7 never prophesies good concerning me, but always E
18:17 he would not prophesy good concerning me, but E
18:22 the LORD has spoken E concerning you."
20:9 thy name, saying, 'If E comes upon us, the
21:6 he did what was E in the sight of
22:4 He did what was E in the sight of
29:6 have done what was E in the sight of
33:2 He did what was E in the sight of
33:6 He did much E in the sight of the
33:9 that they did more E than the nations whom
33:22 He did what was E in the sight of
34:24 Behold, I will bring E upon this place and
34:28 not see all the E which I will bring
36:5 He did what was E in the sight of
36:9 He did what was E in the sight of
36:12 He did what was E in the sight of
Ezra 9:13 upon us for our E deeds and for our
Neh 6:13 could give me an E name, in order to
9:28 had rest they did E again before thee, and
13:7 I then discovered the E that Eliashib had done
13:17 them, "What is this E thing which you are
13:18 God bring all this E on us and on
13:27 do all this great E and act treacherously against
Tob 3:8 seven husbands, and the E demon Asmodeus had
3:17 to bind Asmodeus the E demon, because Tobias was
6:7 if a demon or E spirit gives trouble to
12:7 Do good, and E will not overtake you.
Jud 7:15 pay them back with E, because they rebelled and
Esth 7:7 for he saw that E was determined against him
8:3 tears to avert the E design of Haman the
16:6 false trickery of their E natures beguile the sincere
Job 1:1 one who feared God, and turned away from E
1:8 man, who fears God and turns away from E
2:3 man, who fears God and turns away from E
2:10 hand of God, and shall we not receive E
2:11 heard of all this E that had come upon
5:19 seven there shall no E touch you.
15:35 mischief and bring forth E and their heart prepares
28:28 and to depart from E is understanding.'"
30:26 I looked for good, E came; and when I
31:29 me, or exulted when E overtook him
35:12 of the pride of E men.
42:11 him for all the E that the LORD had
Ps 5:4 who delights in wickedness; E may not sojourn with
6:8 all you workers of E; for the LORD has
7:4 requited my friend with E or plundered my enemy
7:9 O let the E of the wicked come to
7:14 the wicked man conceives E, and is pregnant with
15:3 tongue, and does no E to his friend, nor
21:11 If they plan E against you, if they devise
23:4 death, I fear no E; for thou art with
26:10 in whose hands are E devices, and whose right
28:3 who are workers of E, who speak peace with
28:4 and according to the E of their deeds; requite
34:13 Keep your tongue from E, and your lips from
34:14 Depart from E, and do good; seek peace, and
34:21 E shall slay the wicked; and those who hate
35:4 and confounded who devise E against me!
35:12 They requite me E for good; my soul is
36:4 way that is not good; he spurns not E
37:7 man who carries out E devices!
37:8 Fret not yourself; it tends only to E
37:19 put to shame in E times, in the days
37:27 Depart from E, and do good; so shall you
38:20 Those who render me E for good are my
50:19 mouth free rein for E, and your tongue frames
51:4 done that which is E in thy sight, so
52:3 You love E more than good, and lying more
53:4 Have those who work E no understanding, who eat
54:5 requite my enemies with E; in thy faithfulness put
56:5 cause; all their thoughts are against me for E
59:2 from those who work E, and save me from
59:5 spare none of those who treacherously plot E
64:5 hold fast to their E purpose; they talk of
90:15 and as many years as we have seen E
91:10 High your habitation, no E shall befall you, no
92:11 the doom of my E assailants.
97:10 loves those who hate E; he preserves the lives
101:4 far from me; I will know nothing of E
107:26 melted away in their E plight;
109:5 So they reward me E for good, and hatred
109:20 of those who speak E against my life!
112:7 is not afraid of E tidings; his heart is
119:101 my feet from every E way, in order to
119:150 who persecute me with E purpose; they are far
121:7 keep you from all E; he will keep your
139:20 thee, who lift themselves up against thee for E
140:1 me, O LORD, from E men; preserve me from
140:2 violent men, who plan E things in their heart,
140:8 do not further his E plot!
140:11 in the land; let E hunt down the violent
141:4 my heart to any E, to busy myself with
Prov 1:16 their feet run to E, and they make haste
1:33 and will be at ease, without dread of E
2:12 from the way of E, from men of perverted
2:14 who rejoice in doing E and delight in the
2:14 in the perverseness of E;
3:7 eyes; fear the LORD, and turn away from E
3:29 Do not plan E against your neighbor who dwells
4:10 Good and E
4:15 in the way of E men.
4:28 to the left; turn your foot away from E
6:14 with perverted heart devises E, continually sowing
6:18 haste to run to E,
6:24 preserve you from the E woman, from the smooth
8:13 The fear of tQhe LORD is hatred of E
8:13 and the way of E and perverted speech I
11:19 but he who pursues E will die.
11:21 Be assured, an E man will not go unpunished,
11:27 good seeks favor, but E comes to him who
12:2 but a man of E devices he condemns.
12:13 An E man is ensnared by the transgression of
12:20 of those who devise E, but those who plan
12:26 man turns away from E, but the way of
13:19 to turn away from E is an abomination to
14:16 and turns away from E, but a fool throws
14:19 The E bow down before the good, the wicked
14:22 Do they not err that devise E
15:3 keeping watch on the E and the good.
15:15 of the afflicted are E, but a cheerful heart
15:28 the wicked pours out E things.
16:6 the fear of the LORD a man avoids E
16:12 to kings to do E, for the throne is
16:17 upright turns aside from E; he who guards his
16:27 A worthless man plots E, and his speech is
16:30 compresses his lips brings E to pass.
17:11 An E man seeks only rebellion, and a cruel
17:13 If a man returns E for good, evil will
17:13 returns evil for good, E will not depart from
20:8 of judgment winnows all E with his eyes.
20:22 say, "I will repay E; wait for the LORD,
20:30 that wound cleanse away E; strokes make clean the
21:10 of the wicked desires E; his neighbor finds no
21:27 he brings it with E intent.
24:1 Be not envious of E men, nor desire to
24:8 who plans to do E will be called a
24:20 the wicked; for the E man has no future;
26:23 smooth lips with an E heart.
28:5 E men do not understand justice, but those who
28:10 the upright into an E way will fall into
29:6 An E man is ensnared in his transgression, but
30:32 you have been devising E, put your hand on
Eccl 2:21 This also is vanity and a great E
4:3 has not seen the E deeds that are done
5:1 they do not know that they are doing E
5:13 There is a grievous E which I have seen
5:16 also is a grievous E: just as he came,
6:1 There is an E which I have seen under
8:11 Because sentence against an E deed is not executed
8:11 sons of men is fully set to do E
8:12 Though a sinner does E a hundred times and
9:2 the good and the E, to the clean and
9:3 This is an E in all that is done
9:3 men are full of E, and madness is in
9:12 are taken in an E net, and like birds
9:12 are snared at an E time, when it suddenly
10:1 ointment give off an E odor; so a little
10:5 There is an E which I have seen under
11:2 you know not what E may happen on earth.

	12:1	your youth, before the E days come, and the
	12:14	with every secret thing, whether good or E
Wis	3:12	foolish, and their children E;
	4:6	unions are witnesses of E against their parents when
	4:11	was caught up lest E change his understanding or
	7:30	night, but against wisdom E does not prevail.
	12:10	that their origin was E and their wickedness inborn,
	14:27	the beginning and cause and end of every E
	15:4	For neither has the E intent of human art
	15:6	Lovers of E things and fit for such objects
	16:8	that it is thou who deliverest from every E
Sir	4:20	time, and beware of E; and do not bring
	6:4	An E soul will destroy him who has it,
	7:1	Do no E, and evil will never befall you.
	7:1	Do no evil, and E will never befall you.
	9:1	not teach her an E lesson to your own
	11:29	wait, turning good into E, and to worthy actions
	11:31	scoundrel, for he devises E, lest he give you
	12:3	man who persists in E or to him who
	12:5	receive twice as much E for all the good
	13:23	sin, and poverty is E in the opinion of
	13:24	changes his countenance, either for good or for E
	14:8	E is the man with a grudging eye; he
	17:6	and understanding, and showed them good and E
	17:26	So flesh and blood devise E
	18:7	What is his good and what is his E
	18:11	their end will be E; therefore he grants them
	19:6	one who hates gossip E is lessened.
	19:25	sinning, he will do E when he finds an
	23:5	and remove from me E desire.
	25:15	than dwell with an E wife.
	25:22	are caused by an E wife.
	25:24	of speech in an E wife.
	26:7	An E wife is an ox yoke which chafes;
	27:22	winks his eye plans E deeds, and no one
	27:27	If a man does E, it will roll back
	28:21	its death is an E death, and Hades is
	31:10	transgress, and to do E and did not do
	33:1	No E will befall the man who fears the
	33:14	is the opposite of E, and life the opposite
	33:27	may not be idle, for idleness teaches much E
	37:3	O E imagination, why were you formed to cover
	37:18	fortune appear, good and E, life and death; and
	39:4	the good and the E among men.
	39:25	good people, just as E things for sinners.
	41:11	their bodies, but the E name of sinners will
	42:6	Where there is an E wife, a seal is
	51:12	rescue me from an E plight.
Is	1:16	yourselves clean; remove the E of your doings from
	1:16	eyes; cease to do E,
	3:9	For they have brought E upon themselves.
	5:20	to those who call E good and good evil,
	5:20	evil good and good E, who put darkness for
	7:5	of Remaliah, has devised E against you, saying,
	7:15	how to refuse the E and choose the good.
	7:16	how to refuse the E and choose the good,
	13:11	the world for its E, and the wicked for
	29:20	who watch to do E shall be cut off,
	32:7	of the knave are E; he devises wicked devices
	33:15	eyes from looking upon E,
	47:11	But E shall come upon you, for which you
	56:2	it, and keeps his hand from doing any E
	59:7	Their feet run to E, and they make haste
	59:15	he who departs from E makes himself a prey.
	65:12	you did what was E in my eyes, and
	66:4	they did what was E in my eyes, and
Jer	1:14	"Out of the north E shall break forth upon
	2:3	of it became guilty; E came upon them, says
	2:19	see that it is E and bitter for you
	3:5	have done all the E that you could."
	3:17	stubbornly follow their own E heart.
	4:4	it, because of the E of your doings."
	4:6	not, for I bring E from the north, and
	4:14	How long shall your E thoughts lodge within you?
	4:15	from Dan and proclaims E from Mount Ephraim.
	4:22	are skilled in doing E, but how to do
	5:12	will do nothing; no E will come upon us,
	6:1	signal on Beth-haccherem; for E looms out of the
	6:19	behold, I am bringing E upon this people, the
	7:24	the stubbornness of their E hearts, and went
	7:30	of Judah have done E in my sight, says
	8:3	that remains of this E family in all the
	9:3	for they proceed from E to evil, and they
	9:3	proceed from evil to E, and they do not
	10:5	for they cannot do E, neither is it in
	11:8	the stubbornness of his E heart.
	11:11	Behold, I am bringing E upon them which they
	11:17	planted you, has pronounced E against you, because
	11:17	you, because of the E which the house of
	11:18	didst show me their E deeds.
	11:23	For I will bring E upon the men of
	12:14	LORD concerning all my E neighbors who touch the
	13:10	This E people, who refuse to hear my words,
	13:23	can do good who are accustomed to do E
	16:10	pronounced all this great E against us?
	16:12	you follows his stubborn E will, refusing to listen
	17:16	pressed thee to send E, nor have I desired
	17:17	thou art my refuge in the day of E
	17:18	them the day of E; destroy them with double
	18:8	spoken, turns from its E, I will repent of
	18:8	will repent of the E that I intended to
	18:10	and if it does E in my sight, not
	18:11	Behold, I am shaping E against you and devising
	18:11	every one from his E way, and amend your
	18:12	the stubbornness of his E heart.'
	18:20	Is E a recompense for good?
	19:3	I am bringing such E upon this place that
	19:15	its towns all the E that I have pronounced
	21:10	against this city for E and not for good,
	23:10	Their course is E, and their might is not
	23:12	for I will bring E upon them in the
	23:17	heart, they say, 'No E shall come upon you.'"
	23:22	turned them from their E way, and from the
	23:22	way, and from the E of their doings.
	25:5	of you, from his E way and wrong doings,
	25:29	I begin to work E at the city which
	25:32	LORD of hosts: Behold, E is going forth from
	26:3	one turn from his E way, that I may
	26:3	may repent of the E which I intend to
	26:13	will repent of the E which he has pronounced
	26:19	LORD repent of the E which he had pronounced
	26:19	about to bring great E upon ourselves."
	29:11	welfare and not for E, to give you a
	31:28	overthrow, destroy, and bring E, so I will watch
	32:23	hast made all this E come upon them.
	32:30	have done nothing but E in my sight from
	32:32	because of all the E of the sons of
	32:42	brought all this great E upon this people, so
	35:15	of you from his E way, and amend your
	35:17	of Jerusalem all the E that I have pronounced
	36:3	will hear all the E which I intend to
	36:3	may turn from his E way, and that I
	36:7	will turn from his E way, for great is
	36:31	of Judah, all the E that I have pronounced
	38:9	these men have done E in all that they
	39:16	against this city for E and not for good,
	40:2	your God pronounced this E against this place;
	41:11	heard of all the E which Ishmael the son
	42:6	it is good or E, we will obey the
	42:10	I repent of the E which I did to
	42:17	or survivor from the E which I will bring
	44:2	have seen all the E that I brought upon
	44:7	you commit this great E against yourselves, to cut
	44:11	face against you for E, to cut off all
	44:17	plenty of food, and prospered, and saw no E
	44:23	his testimonies, that this E has befallen you, as
	44:27	watching over them for E and not for good;
	44:29	stand against you for E:
	45:5	behold, I am bringing E upon all flesh, says
	48:2	In Heshbon they planned E against her: 'Come, let
	49:23	for they have heard E tidings; they melt in
	49:37	life; I will bring E upon them, my fierce
	51:24	eyes for all the E that they have done
	51:60	a book all the E that should come upon
	51:64	more, because of the E that I am bringing
	52:2	he did what was E in the sight of
Lam	3:38	High that good and E come?
Bar	1:21	and doing what is E in the sight of
	6:34	Whether one does E to them or good, they
Ezek	6:10	I would do this E to them."
	6:11	because of all the E abominations of the house
	14:21	of judgment, sword, famine, E beasts, and pestilence,
	14:22	be consoled for the E that I have brought
	20:44	not according to your E ways, nor according to
	30:12	into the hand of E men; I will bring
	33:11	turn back from your E ways; for why will
	36:3	became the talk and E gossip of the people;
	36:31	you will remember your E ways, and your deeds
	38:10	you will devise an E scheme
Hos	7:3	I remember all their E works.
	7:16	arms, yet they devise E against me.
	9:15	Every E of theirs is in Gilgal; there I

Joel 2:13 and abounding in steadfast love, and repents of E
Amos 3:6 Does E befall a city, unless the LORD has
5:13 for it is an E time.
5:14 Seek good, and not E, that you may live;
5:15 Hate E, and love good, and establish justice in
6:3 put far away the E day, and bring near
9:4 eyes upon them for E and not for good."
9:10 the sword, who say, E shall not overtake or
Jon 1:7 on whose account this E has come upon us."
1:8 on whose account this E has come upon us?
3:8 one turn from his E way and from the
3:10 they turned from their E way, God repented of
3:10 God repented of the E which he had said
4:2 and abounding in steadfast love, and repentest of E
Mic 1:12 anxiously for good, because E has come down from
2:1 devise wickedness and work E upon their beds!
2:3 family I am devising E, from which you cannot
2:3 it will be an E time.
3:2 good and love the E, who tear the skin
3:4 that time, because they have made their deeds E
3:11 No E shall come upon us."
7:3 are upon what is E, to do it diligently;
7:3 great man utters the E desire of his soul;
Nah 1:11 from you, who plotted E against the LORD, and
3:19 For upon whom has not come your unceasing E
Hab 1:13 eyes than to behold E and canst not look
2:9 to him who gets E gain for his house,
Zeph 3:15 midst; you shall fear E no more.
Zech 1:4 hosts, Return from your E ways and from your
1:4 ways and from your E deeds.' But they did
7:10 none of you devise E against his brother in
8:14 I purposed to do E to you, when your
8:17 peace, do not devise E in your hearts against
Mal 1:8 offer blind animals in sacrifice, is that no E
1:8 that are lame or sick, is that no E
2:17 "Every one who does E is good in the
1Mac 1:15 with the Gentiles and sold themselves to do E
1:36 against the sanctuary, an E adversary of Israel
1:52 them, and they did E in the land;
7:23 Judas saw all the E that Alcimus and those
11:8 and he kept devising E designs against Alexander.
16:17 great treachery and returned E for good.
2Mac 1:5 may he not forsake you in time of E
1:25 rescue Israel from every E, who didst choose the
4:47 cause of all the E, he acquitted of the
6:3 Harsh and utterly grievous was the onslaught of E
7:31 contrived all sorts of E against the Hebrews, will
8:4 his name, and to show his hatred of E
Mt 5:11 utter all kinds of E against you falsely on
5:37 or 'No'; anything more than this comes from E
5:39 to you, Do not resist one who is E
5:45 sun rise on the E and on the good,
6:13 us not into temptation, But deliver us from E
7:11 you then, who are E, know how to give
7:17 the bad tree bears E fruit.
7:18 sound tree cannot bear E fruit, nor can a
9:4 "Why do you think E in your hearts?
12:34 how can you speak good, when you are E
12:35 forth good, and the E man out of his
12:35 man out of his E treasure brings forth evil.
12:35 man out of his evil treasure brings forth E
12:39 he answered them, "An E and adulterous generation
12:45 seven other spirits more E than himself, and they
12:45 be also with this E generation."
13:19 not understand it, the E one comes and snatches
13:38 the sons of the E one,
13:49 out and separate the E from the righteous,
15:4 and, 'He who speaks E of father or mother,
15:19 of the heart come E thoughts, murder, adultery,
16:4 An E and adulterous generation seeks for a sign,
27:23 he said, "Why, what E has he done?" But
Mk 7:10 and, 'He who speaks E of father or mother,
7:20 heart of man, come E thoughts, fornication, theft,
7:22 All these E things come from within, and they
9:39 soon after to speak E of me.
15:14 to them, "Why, what E has he done?" But
Lk 3:19 and for all the E things that Herod had
6:22 out your name as E, on account of the
6:45 produces good, and the E man out of his
6:45 man out of his E treasure produces evil; for
6:45 his evil treasure produces E; for out of the
7:21 diseases and plagues and E spirits, and on many
8:2 had been healed of E spirits and infirmities: Mary,
11:13 you then, who are E, know how to give
11:26 seven other spirits more E than himself, and they
11:29 "This generation is an E generation; it seeks a
16:25 Lazarus in like manner E things; but now he
23:21 to them, "Why, what E has he done?
Jn 3:19 rather than light, because their deeds were E
3:20 every one who does E hates the light, and
5:28 those who have done E, to the resurrection of
7:7 I testify of it that its works are E
17:15 keep them from the E one.
Acts 9:13 this man, how much E he has done to
19:9 stubborn and disbelieved, speaking E of the Way
19:12 left them and the E spirits came out of
19:13 over those who had E spirits, saying, "I adjure
19:15 But the E spirit answered them, "Jesus I know,
19:16 man in whom the E spirit was leaped on
23:5 'You shall not speak E of a ruler of
28:21 reported or spoken any E about you.
Rom 1:29 all manner of wickedness, E, covetousness, malice.
1:30 haughty, boastful, inventors of E, disobedient to
2:9 human being who does E, the Jew first and
3:8 And why not do E that good may come?--
7:19 I want, but the E I do not want
7:21 want to do right, E lies close at hand.
12:9 genuine; hate what is E, hold fast to what
12:17 Repay no one E for evil, but take thought
12:17 no one evil for E, but take thought for
12:21 not be overcome by E, but overcome evil with
12:21 by evil, but overcome E with good.
14:16 not let your good be spoken of as E
16:19 as to what is E;
1Cor 5:8 leaven of malice and E, but with the unleavened
10:6 us, not to desire E as they did.
14:20 thinking; be babes in E, but in thinking be
2Cor 5:10 may receive good or E, according to what he
Gal 1:4 us from the present E age, according to the
Eph 4:29 Let no E talk come out of your mouths,
5:16 most of the time, because the days are E
6:13 to withstand in the E day, and having done
6:16 flaming darts of the E one.
Col 1:21 hostile in mind, doing E deeds,
3:5 fornication, impurity, passion, E desire, and
1Thes 5:15 none of you repays E for evil, but always
5:15 you repays evil for E, but always seek to
5:22 what is good, abstain from every form of E
2Thes 3:2 delivered from wicked and E men; for not all
3:3 he will strengthen you and guard you from E
2Tim 3:13 will be persecuted, while E men and impostors will
4:18 rescue me from every E and save me for
Tit 1:11 "Cretans are always liars, E beasts, lazy gluttons."
2:8 to shame, having nothing E to say of us.
3:2 honest work, to speak E of no one, to
Heb 3:12 any of you an E, unbelieving heart, leading you
5:14 trained by practice to distinguish good from E
10:22 sprinkled clean from an E conscience and our bodies
Jas 1:12 cannot be tempted with E and he himself tempts
2:4 and become judges with E thoughts?
3:8 the tongue--a restless E, full of deadly poison.
4:11 Do not speak E against one another, brethren.
4:11 He that speaks E against a brother or judges
4:11 judges his brother, speaks E against the law and
4:16 All such boasting is E
1Pet 2:16 as a pretext for E; but live as servants
3:9 Do not return E for evil or reviling for
3:9 not return evil for E or reviling for reviling;
3:10 keep his tongue from E and his lips from
3:11 him turn away from E and do right; let
3:12 of the Lord is against those that do E
1Jn 2:13 you have overcome the E one.
2:14 you have overcome the E one.
3:12 who was of the E one and murdered his
3:12 his own deeds were E and his brother's righteous.
5:18 keeps him, and the E one does not touch
5:19 the power of the E one.
3Jn 1:10 prating against me with E words.
1:11 Beloved, do not imitate E but imitate good.
1:11 God; he who does E has not seen God.
Rev 2:2 how you cannot bear E men but have tested
16:2 earth, and foul and E sores came upon the
22:11 the evildoer still do E, and the filthy still

EVIL-DOING (5)

1Sam 25:39 LORD has returned the E of Nabal upon his
Prov 14:32 is overthrown through his E, but the righteous finds
Eccl 7:15 wicked man who prolongs his life in his E
Wis 5:23 the whole earth, and E will overturn the thrones
Lam 1:22 "Let all their E come before thee; and deal

EVIL-DOINGS (4)
Jer 21:12 with none to quench it, because of your E
23:2 to you for your E, says the LORD.
26:3 intend to do to them because of their E
44:22 no longer bear your E and the abominations which

EVIL-HATING
Esth 16:4 they will escape the E justice of God, who

EVIL-MERODACH (2)
2Kgs 25:27 day of the month, E king of Babylon, in
Jer 52:31 day of the month, E king of Babylon, in

EVIL-WORKERS
Phil 3:2 look out for the E, look out for those

EVILDOER (6)
2Sam 3:39 The LORD requite the E according to his
Ps 10:15 of the wicked and E; seek out his wickedness
Prov 17:4 An E listens to wicked lips; and a liar
Is 9:17 is godless and an E, and every mouth speaks
Jn 18:30 man were not an E, we would not have
Rev 22:11 Let the E still do evil, and the filthy

EVILDOERS (35)
Esth 14:19 despairing, and save us from the hands of E
16:15 thrice-accursed man, are not E but are governed by
Job 8:20 a blameless man, nor take the hand of E
34:8 goes in company with E and walks with wicked
34:22 or deep darkness where E may hide themselves.
Ps 5:5 not stand before thy eyes; thou hatest all E
14:4 no knowledge, all the E who eat up my
22:16 me; a company of E encircle me; they have
26:5 hate the company of E, and I will not
27:2 When E assail me, uttering slanders against me, my
34:16 the LORD is against E, to cut off the
36:12 There the E lie prostrate, they are thrust down,
64:2 from the scheming of E,
92:7 like grass and all E flourish, they are doomed
92:9 enemies shall perish; all E shall be scattered.
94:4 out their arrogant words, they boast, all the E
94:16 Who stands up for me against E
101:8 cutting off all the E from the city of
119:115 Depart from me, you E, that I may keep
125:5 crooked ways the LORD will lead away with E
141:9 laid for me, and from the snares of E
Prov 10:29 him whose way is upright, but destruction to E
21:15 a joy to the righteous, but dismay to E
24:19 not yourself because of E, and be not envious
Is 1:4 with iniquity, offspring of E, sons who deal corruptly!
14:20 "May the descendants of E nevermore be named!
31:2 the house of the E, and against the helpers
Jer 20:13 life of the needy from the hand of E
23:14 strengthen the hands of E, so that no one
Hos 6:8 is a city of E, tracked with blood.
Mal 3:15 deem the arrogant blessed; E not only prosper but
4:1 the arrogant and all E will be stubble; the
1Mac 3:6 of him; all the E were confounded; and deliverance
Mt 7:23 depart from me, you E
13:41 of sin and all E,

EVILS (20)
Deut 31:17 be devoured; and many E and troubles will come
31:17 day, 'Have not these E come upon us because
31:21 And when many E and troubles have come upon
32:23 "'And I will heap E upon them; I will
Esth 10:9 us from all these E; God has done great
11:9 troubled; they feared the E that threatened them,
Ps 40:12 For E have encompassed me without number; my
Wis 14:22 they call such great E peace.
Sir 39:27 as they turn into E for sinners.
Jer 2:13 people have committed two E: they have forsaken
Ezek 6:9 own sight for the E which they have committed,
20:43 yourselves for all the E that you have committed.
1Mac 1:9 and they caused many E on the earth.
1:11 separated from them many E have come upon us."
2:30 and their cattle, because E pressed heavily upon
6:12 now I remember the E I did in Jerusalem.
6:13 of this that these E have come upon me;
2Mac 2:18 rescued us from great E and has purified the
Acts 25:18 his case of such E as I supposed;
1Tim 6:10 the root of all E; it is through this

EWE (7)
Gen 21:28 Abraham set seven E lambs of the flock apart.
21:29 meaning of these seven E lambs which you have
21:30 He said, "These seven E lambs you will take
Lev 14:10 without blemish, and one E lamb a year old
22:28 a cow or a E, you shall not kill
Num 6:14 burnt offering, and one E lamb a year old
2Sam 12:3 nothing but one little E lamb, which he had

EWES (5)
Gen 31:38 been with you; your E and your she-goats have
32:14 twenty he-goats, two hundred E and twenty rams,
Ps 78:71 sheepfolds; from tending the E that had young he
Song 4:2 a flock of shorn E that have come up
6:6 like a flock of E, that have come up

EXACT (8)
Ex 22:25 and you shall not E interest from him.
Deut 15:2 neighbor; he shall not E it of his neighbor,
15:3 a foreigner you may E it; but whatever of
2Kgs 16:10 altar, and its pattern, E in all its details.
Jud 8:21 plundered; and he will E of us the penalty
Esth 4:7 to him, and the E sum of money that
1Mac 10:35 shall have authority to E anything from them or
2Mac 2:28 leaving the responsibility for E details to the

EXACTED (3)
2Kgs 15:20 Menahem E the money from Israel, that is, from
23:35 He E the silver and the gold of the
Job 22:6 For you have E pledges of your brothers for

EXACTING (3)
Neh 5:7 to them, "You are E interest, each from his
5:11 which you have been E of them."
Tob 3:5 judgments are true in E penalty from me for

EXACTION (2)
Neh 10:31 seventh year and the E of every debt.
2Cor 9:5 ready not as an E but as a willing

EXACTIONS
Amos 5:11 and take from him E of wheat, you have

EXACTLY (3)
2Mac 14:43 he did not hit E, and the crowd was
Acts 23:15 you were going to determine his case more E
27:25 that it will be E as I have been

EXACTOR
Dan 11:20 who shall send an E of tribute through the

EXACTS (3)
Job 11:6 Know then that God E of you less than
Prov 29:4 land, but one who E gifts ruins it.
Ezek 18:16 not wrong any one, E no pledge, commits no

EXAGGERATED
Wis 17:11 conscience, it has always E the difficulties.

EXALT (68)
Ex 15:2 God, and I will E him.
Num 16:3 why then do you E yourselves above the assembly
Josh 3:7 I will begin to E you in the sight
1Sam 2:10 to his king, and E the power of his
2Sam 22:49 my enemies; thou didst E me above my adversaries,
1Chr 25:5 promise of God to E him; for God had
Tob 12:6 give thanks to him; E him and give thanks
12:6 praise God and to E his name, worthily declaring
13:4 greatness known there, and E him in the presence
13:6 Lord of righteousness, and E the King of the
13:7 I E my God; my soul exalts the King
14:7 and the Lord will E his people.
Jud 16:2 him a new psalm; E him, and call upon
16:8 her widow's mourning to E the oppressed in Israel.
Ps 18:48 enemies; yea, thou didst E me above my adversaries;
34:3 me, and let us E his name together!
37:34 way, and he will E you to possess the
66:7 let not the rebellious E themselves.
Prov 4:9 highly, and she will E you; she will honor
Sir 1:27 Do not E yourself lest you fall, and thus
6:2 Do not E yourself through your soul's counsel, lest
11:4 wearing fine clothes, nor E yourself in the day
15:5 She will E him above his neighbors, and will
32:1 the feast, do not E yourself; be among them
43:30 you praise the Lord, E him as much as
43:30 When you E him, put forth all your strength,
44:22 of the earth, and E his posterity like the
47:5 mighty in war, to E the power of his
Is 25:1 my God; I will E thee, I will praise

Ezek 21:26 remain as they are; E that which is low,
29:15 kingdoms, and never again E itself above the nations;
Dan 3:58 to him and highly E him for ever.
3:59 to him and highly E him for ever.
3:60 to him and highly E him for ever.
3:61 to him and highly E him for ever.
3:62 to him and highly E him for ever.
3:63 to him and highly E him for ever.
3:64 to him and highly E him for ever.
3:65 to him and highly E him for ever.
3:66 to him and highly E him for ever.
3:67 to him and highly E him for ever.
3:68 to him and highly E him for ever.
3:69 to him and highly E him for ever.
3:70 to him and highly E him for ever.
3:71 to him and highly E him for ever.
3:72 to him and highly E him for ever.
3:73 to him and highly E him for ever.
3:74 to him and highly E him for ever.
3:75 to him and highly E him for ever.
3:76 to him and highly E him for ever.
3:77 to him and highly E him for ever.
3:78 to him and highly E him for ever.
3:79 to him and highly E him for ever.
3:80 to him and highly E him for ever.
3:81 to him and highly E him for ever.
3:82 to him and highly E him for ever.
3:83 to him and highly E him for ever.
3:84 to him and highly E him for ever.
3:85 to him and highly E him for ever.
3:86 to him and highly E him for ever.
3:87 to him and highly E him for ever.
3:88 to him and highly E him for ever.
3:89 to him and highly E him for ever; for
11:36 his will; he shall E himself and magnify himself
1Mac 14:35 in every way to E his people.
Heb 5:5 also Christ did not E himself to be made
Jas 4:10 Lord and he will E you.
1Pet 5:6 due time he may E you.

EXALTATION (4)

Jud 13:4 my hands for the E of Jerusalem.
15:9 her, "You are the E of Jerusalem, you are
1Mac 1:40 as her glory; her E was turned into mourning.
Jas 1:8 brother boast in his E,

EXALTED (84)

Num 24:7 higher than Agag, and his kingdom shall be E
Josh 4:14 that day the LORD E Joshua in the sight
1Sam 2:1 LORD; my strength is E in the LORD.
2Sam 5:12 and that he had E his kingdom for the
22:47 be my rock, and E be my God, the
1Kgs 1:5 the son of Haggith E himself, saying, "I will
8:13 have built thee an E house, a place for
14:7 of Israel: "Because I E you from among the
16:2 Baasha, saying, "Since I E you out of the
1Chr 14:2 his kingdom was highly E for the sake of
29:11 LORD, and thou art E as head above all.
2Chr 6:2 have built thee an E house, a place for
7:21 this house, which is E, every one passing by
32:23 so that he was E in the sight of
Neh 9:5 glorious name which is E above all blessing and
Tob 13:18 is God, who has E you for ever.'"
Jud 9:7 their might; they are E, with their horses and
10:8 of Israel may glory and Jerusalem may be E
Esth 11:11 and the lowly were E and consumed those held
Job 24:24 They are E a little while, and then are
36:7 he sets them for ever, and they are E
36:22 Behold, God is E in his power; who is
Ps 12:8 prowl, as vileness is E among the sons of
13:2 shall my enemy be E over me?
18:46 be my rock, and E be the God of
21:13 Be E, O LORD, in thy strength!
46:10 I am E among the nations, I am exalted
46:10 the nations, I am E in the earth!"
47:9 the earth belong to God; he is highly E
57:5 Be E, O God, above the heavens!
57:11 Be E, O God, above the heavens!
75:10 but the horns of the righteous shall be E
89:17 their strength; by thy favor our horn is E
89:19 is mighty, I have E one chosen from the
89:24 and in my name shall his horn be E
89:42 Thou hast E the right hand of his foes;
92:10 But thou hast E my horn like that of
97:9 the earth; thou art E far above all gods.
99:2 in Zion; he is E over all the peoples.
108:5 Be E, O God, above the heavens!
112:9 ever; his horn is E in honor.
118:16 of the LORD is E, the right hand of
138:2 faithfulness; for thou hast E above everything thy
148:13 his name alone is E; his glory is above
Prov 11:11 upright a city is E, but it is overthrown
Wis 19:22 O Lord, thou hast E and glorified thy people;
Sir 1:17 discerning comprehension, and he E the glory of
33:9 some of them he E and hallowed, and some
33:12 them he blessed and E, and some of them
45:6 He E Aaron, the brother of Moses, a holy
47:11 away his sins, and E his power for ever;
Is 2:11 LORD alone will be E in that day.
2:17 LORD alone will be E in that day.
5:16 LORD of hosts is E in justice, and the
12:4 among the nations, proclaim that his name is E
33:5 The LORD is E, for he dwells on high;
33:10 will lift myself up; now I will be E
52:13 prosper, he shall be E and lifted up, and
Lam 2:17 rejoice over you, and E the might of your
Dan 3:52 be praised and highly E for ever;
3:53 highly praised and highly E for ever;
3:55 be praised and highly E for ever.
3:56 be extolled and highly E for ever.
11:12 his heart shall be E, and he shall cast
Hos 13:1 men trembled; he was E in Israel; but he
Zech 12:7 Jerusalem may not be E over that of Judah.
1Mac 1:3 before him, he was E, and his heart was
2:63 Today he will be E, but tomorrow he will
8:13 wish they depose; and they have been greatly E
11:16 to find protection there, and King Ptolemy was E
11:26 had treated him; he E him in the presence
Mt 11:23 Caperna-um, will you be E to heaven?
23:12 be humbled, and whoever humbles himself will be E
Lk 1:52 from their thrones, and E those of low degree;
10:15 Caperna-um, will you be E to heaven?
14:11 humbled, and he who humbles himself will be E
16:15 hearts; for what is E among men is an
18:14 humbled, but he who humbles himself will be E
Acts 2:33 Being therefore E at the right hand of God,
5:31 God E him at his right hand as Leader
2Cor 11:7 that you might be E, because I preached God's
Phil 2:9 Therefore God has highly E him and bestowed on
Heb 7:26 unstained, separated from sinners, E above the
1Pet 1:8 rejoice with unutterable and E joy.

EXALTING (2)

Ex 9:17 You are still E yourself against my people, and
Prov 30:32 you have been foolish, E yourself, or if you

EXALTS (12)

1Sam 2:7 and makes rich; he brings low, he also E
Tob 13:7 my God; my soul E the King of heaven,
Prov 14:29 has a hasty temper E folly.
14:34 Righteousness E a nation, but sin is a reproach
Sir 4:11 Wisdom E her sons and gives help to those
7:11 soul, for there is One who abases and E
50:22 does great things; who E our days from birth,
Is 30:18 to you; therefore he E himself to show mercy
Mt 23:12 be your servant; whoever E himself will be humbled,
Lk 14:11 For every one who E himself will be humbled,
18:14 for every one who E himself will be humbled,
2Thes 2:4 perdition, who opposes and E himself against every

EXAMINATION (8)

Lev 13:8 priest shall make an E, and if the eruption
13:10 priest shall make an E, and if there is
13:13 priest shall make an E, and if the leprosy
13:20 priest shall make an E, and if it appears
13:39 priest shall make an E, and if the spots
14:3 the camp, and the priest shall make an E
14:48 comes and makes an E, and the disease has
Dan 13:48 daughter of Israel without E and without learning

EXAMINE (28)

Lev 13:3 and the priest shall E the diseased spot on
13:5 and the priest shall E him on the seventh
13:6 and the priest shall E him again on the
13:15 And the priest shall E the raw flesh, and
13:17 and the priest shall E him, and if the
13:25 white, the priest shall E it, and if the
13:27 and the priest shall E him the seventh day;
13:30 beard, the priest shall E the disease; and if
13:32 day the priest shall E the disease; and if
13:34 day the priest shall E the itch, and if
13:36 then the priest shall E him, and if the

13:43 Then the priest shall E him, and if the
13:50 And the priest shall E the disease, and shut
13:51 days; then he shall E the disease on the
13:55 and the priest shall E the diseased thing after
14:36 the priest goes to E the disease, lest all
14:37 And he shall E the disease; and if the
Ezra 10:16 they sat down to E the matter;
Wis 11:10 warning, but thou didst E the ungodly as a
Sir 18:19 Before judgment, E yourself, and in the hour of
Jer 2:10 send to Kedar and E with care; see if
Lam 3:40 Let us test and E our ways, and return
Dan 13:51 other, and I will E them."
Lk 14:19 and I go to E them; I pray you,
Acts 22:29 who were about to E him withdrew from him
1Cor 9:3 to those who would E me.
11:28 Let a man E himself, and so eat of
2Cor 13:5 E yourselves, to see whether you are holding to

EXAMINED (9)

Lev 13:3 when the priest has E him he shall pronounce
Jud 7:7 Israelites in Bethulia, and E the approaches to the
Esth 12:3 Then the king E the two eunuchs, and when
Sir 23:10 servant who is continually E under torture will not
Acts 4:9 if we are being E today concerning a good
12:19 not find him, he E the sentries and ordered
22:24 ordered him to be E by scourging, to find
25:26 that, after we have E him, I may have
28:18 When they had E me, they wished to set

EXAMINES (8)

Lev 13:21 But if the priest E it, and the hair
13:26 But if the priest E it, and the hair
13:31 And if the priest E the itching disease, and
13:53 "And if the priest E, and the disease has
13:56 "But if the priest E, and the disease is
Prov 18:17 the other comes and E him.
Wis 3:13 have fruit when God E souls.
4:6 their parents when God E them.

EXAMINING (5)

Eccl 9:1 I laid to heart, E it all, how the
Sir 13:11 smiles he will be E you.
Lk 23:14 the people; and after E him before you, behold,
Acts 17:11 word with all eagerness, E the scriptures daily to
24:7 By E him yourself you will be able to

EXAMPLE (20)

Jud 8:24 let us set an E to our brethren, for
Esth 14:11 themselves, and make an E of the man who
Eccl 9:13 have also seen this E of wisdom under the
Sir 44:17 up; he was an E of repentance to all
2Mac 6:10 For E, two women were brought in for having
6:28 the young a noble E of how to die
6:31 in his death an E of nobility and a
Jn 13:15 have given you an E, that you also should
Rom 4:12 but also follow the E of the faith which
Gal 3:15 To give a human E, brethren: no one annuls
Phil 3:17 as you have an E in us.
Col 2:15 and made a public E of them, triumphing over
1Thes 1:7 that you became an E to all the believers
2Thes 3:9 in our conduct an E to imitate.
1Tim 1:16 perfect patience for an E to those who were
4:12 set the believers an E in speech and conduct,
Jas 5:10 As an E of suffering and patience, brethren, take
1Pet 2:21 you, leaving you an E, that you should follow
2Pet 2:6 and made them an E to those who were
Jude 1:7 lust, serve as an E by undergoing a punishment

EXAMPLES

1Pet 5:3 your charge but being E to the flock.

EXASPERATED

2Mac 7:39 than the others, being E at his scorn.

EXCEED (2)

2Cor 3:9 of righteousness must far E it in splendor.
Rev 2:19 that your latter works E the first.

EXCEEDING (3)

Ps 43:4 God, to God my E joy; and I will
150:2 him according to his E greatness!
Dan 2:31 image, mighty and of E brightness, stood before you,

EXCEEDINGLY (46)

Gen 17:2 between me and you, and will multiply you E
17:6 I will make you E fruitful; and I will
17:20 fruitful and multiply him E; he shall be the
27:34 cried out with an E great and bitter cry,
30:43 Thus the man grew E rich, and had large
47:27 possessions in it, and were fruitful and multiplied E
Ex 1:6 they multiplied and grew E strong; so that the
Num 14:7 it out, is an E good land.
Ruth 1:13 daughters, for it is E bitter to me for
1Sam 26:21 I have played the fool, and have erred E
2Kgs 10:4 But they were E afraid, and said, "Behold, the
1Chr 22:5 the LORD must be E magnificent, of fame and
2Chr 1:1 him and made him E great.
16:8 a huge army with E many chariots and horsemen?
36:14 the people likewise were E unfaithful, following all
Jud 2:28 who lived in Azotus and Ascalon feared him E
Job 3:22 hid treasures; who rejoice E, and are glad, when
Ps 119:96 but thy commandment is E broad.
119:167 My soul keeps thy testimonies; I love them E
Prov 30:24 small, but they are E wise:
Sir 43:11 him who made it, E beautiful in its brightness.
47:24 Their sins became E many, so as to remove
Is 47:6 you made your yoke E heavy.
64:9 Be not E angry, O LORD, and remember not
Lam 5:22 Art thou E angry with us?
Ezek 9:9 Israel and Judah is E great; the land is
16:13 You grew E beautiful, and came to regal estate.
37:10 upon their feet, an E great host.
Dan 6:23 Then the king was E glad, and commanded that
7:7 terrible and dreadful and E strong; and it had
7:19 from all the rest, E terrible, with its teeth
8:8 the he-goat magnified himself E; but when he was
8:9 little horn, which grew E great toward the south,
11:25 wage war with an E great and mighty army;
Joel 2:11 for his host is E great; he that executes
Jon 1:10 Then the men were E afraid, and said to
1:16 men feared the LORD E, and they offered a
3:3 Now Nineveh was an E great city, three days'
4:1 But it displeased Jonah E, and he was angry.
4:6 So Jonah was E glad because of the plant.
Zech 1:14 of hosts: I am E jealous for Jerusalem and
2Mac 8:30 got possession of some E high strongholds, and they
Mt 2:10 the star, they rejoiced E with great joy;
Mk 6:26 And the king was E sorry; but because of
9:6 say, for they were E afraid.
10:26 And they were E astonished, and said to him,

EXCEEDS

Mt 5:20 you, unless your righteousness E that of the scribes

EXCEL (4)

Sir 33:22 E in all that you do; bring no stain
1Cor 14:12 the Spirit, strive to E in building up the
2Cor 8:7 Now as you E in everything--in faith, in
8:7 us--see that you E in this gracious work

EXCELLED (3)

1Kgs 10:23 Thus King Solomon E all the kings of the
2Chr 9:22 Thus King Solomon E all the kings of the
Sir 33:16 of the Lord I E, and like a grape-gatherer

EXCELLENCE (5)

Sir 6:15 faithful friend, and no scales can measure his E
31:23 their testimony to his E is trustworthy.
2Mac 15:12 all that belongs to E, was praying with outstretched
Phil 4:8 if there is any E, if there is anything
2Pet 1:3 his own glory and E,

EXCELLENCY

Acts 23:26 "Claudius Lysias to his E the governor Felix,

EXCELLENT (19)

Tob 4:11 it charity is an E offering in the presence
Esth 16:16 fathers in the most E order.
Sir 14:25 will lodge in an E lodging place;
32:2 a wreath for your E leadership.
Is 28:29 wonderful in counsel, and E in wisdom.
Dan 5:12 and astrologers, because an E spirit, knowledge, and
5:14 light and understanding and E wisdom are found in
6:3 and satraps, because an E spirit was in him;
2Mac 1:35 favored he exchanged many E gifts.
6:23 with distinction and his E life even from childhood,
Lk 1:3 account for you, most E Theophilus,
Acts 24:2 by your provision, most E Felix, reforms are
26:25 am not mad, most E Festus, but I am
Rom 2:18 and approve what is E, because you are instructed
1Cor 12:31 you a still more E way.
Phil 1:10 may approve what is E, and may be pure

E

Tit 3:8 good deeds; these are E and profitable to men.
Heb 1:4 has obtained is more E than theirs.
8:6 is as much more E than the old as

EXCELLENTLY

Prov 31:29 "Many women have done E, but you surpass them

EXCELS (4)

Esth 13:3 be accomplished, Haman who E among us in sound
Eccl 2:13 I saw that wisdom E folly as light excels
2:13 excels folly as light E darkness.
Wis 7:29 than the sun, and E every constellation of the

EXCEPTED

1Cor 15:27 plain that he is E who put all things

E

EXCEPTION

Esth 16:24 city and country, without E, which does not act

EXCESS (3)

Num 3:48 money by which the E number of them is
Tob 4:15 not drink wine to E or let drunkenness go
Sir 31:29 Wine drunk to E is bitterness of soul, with

EXCESSIVE

2Cor 2:7 may be overwhelmed by E sorrow.

EXCHANGE (12)

Gen 47:16 give you food in E for your cattle, if
47:17 gave them food in E for the horses, the
47:17 them with food in E for all their cattle
Lev 27:10 anything for it or E it, a good for
27:10 if he makes any E of beast for beast,
27:33 bad, neither shall he E it; and if he
Sir 7:18 Do not E a friend for money, or a
44:18 he was taken in E; therefore a remnant was
Is 43:3 Ethiopia and Seba in E for you.
43:4 for you, peoples in E for your life.
Ezek 48:14 shall not sell or E any of it; they
Rev 11:10 and make merry and E presents, because these two

EXCHANGED (15)

Lev 27:10 for which it is E shall be holy.
27:33 for which it is E shall be holy; it
Job 28:17 nor can it be E for jewels of fine
Ps 106:20 They E the glory of God for the image
Ezek 27:12 tin, and lead they E for your wares.
27:13 traded with you; they E the persons of men
27:14 Beth-togarmah E for your wares horses, war horses,
27:16 your abundant goods; they E for your wares
27:17 traded with you; they E for your merchandise wheat,
27:19 wine from Uzal they E for your wares; wrought
27:22 traded with you; they E for your wares the
2Mac 1:35 the king favored he E many excellent gifts.
Rom 1:23 they became fools, and E the glory of the
1:25 themselves, because they E the truth about God
1:26 Their women E natural relations for unnatural,

EXCHANGES

Lev 27:33 it; and if he E it, then both it

EXCHANGING

Ruth 4:7 Israel concerning redeeming and E: to confirm a

EXCITED (2)

2Mac 14:27 The king became E and, provoked by the false
2Thes 2:2 shaken in mind or E, either by spirit or

EXCITEMENT

Jud 10:18 There was great E in the whole camp, for

EXCLAIMED (2)

Tob 7:7 he blessed him and E, "Son of that good
Lk 1:42 Holy Spirit and she E with a loud cry,

EXCLUDE

Lk 6:22 you, and when they E you and revile you,

EXCLUDED (5)

2Chr 26:21 house, for he was E from the house of
Ezra 2:62 and so they were E from the priesthood as
Neh 7:64 there, so they were E from the priesthood as
Ezek 44:5 who are to be E from the sanctuary.
Rom 3:27 It is E

EXCLUSION

2Thes 1:9 of eternal destruction and E from the presence of

EXCREMENT

Deut 23:13 it, and turn back and cover up your E

EXCUSE (4)

Jn 15:22 now they have no E for their sin.
Rom 1:20 So they are without E;
2:1 Therefore you have no E, O man, whoever you
2:15 thoughts accuse or perhaps E them

EXCUSED (3)

Wis 13:8 they are to be E;
Lk 14:18 pray you, have me E
14:19 pray you, have me E

EXCUSES

Lk 14:18 ready.' But they all alike began to make E

EXECRATION (4)

Num 5:21 LORD make you an E and an oath among
5:27 woman shall become an E among her people.
Jer 42:18 You shall become an E, a horror, a curse,
44:12 they shall become an E, a horror, a curse,

EXECUTE (36)

Ex 12:12 of Egypt I will E judgments: I am the
Lev 26:25 upon you, that shall E vengeance for the covenant;
Num 5:30 and the priest shall E upon her all this
31:3 go against Midian, to E the LORD's vengeance on
1Kgs 10:9 king, that you may E justice and righteousness."
2Chr 2:14 sorts of engraving and E any design that may
9:8 them, that you may E justice and righteousness."
20:12 God, wilt thou not E judgment upon them?
Jud 2:12 kingdom, what I have spoken my hand will E
Ps 110:6 He will E judgment among the nations, filling them
149:9 fetters of iron, to E on them the judgment
Is 13:3 my mighty men to E my anger, my proudly
66:16 fire will the LORD E judgment, and by his
Jer 7:5 doings, if you truly E justice one with another,
21:12 Thus says the LORD: E justice in the morning,
23:5 deal wisely, and shall E justice and righteousness in
33:15 David; and he shall E justice and righteousness in
51:52 LORD, when I will E judgment upon her images,
Ezek 5:8 you; and I will E judgments in the midst
5:10 fathers; and I will E judgments on you, and
5:15 about you, when I E judgments on you in
11:9 hands of foreigners, and E judgments upon you.
16:41 burn your houses and E judgments upon you in
25:11 nations, and I will E judgments upon Moab.
25:17 I will E great vengeance upon them with wrathful
28:22 the LORD when I E judgments in her, and
28:26 dwell securely, when I E judgments upon all their
30:14 to Zoan, and will E acts of judgment upon
30:19 Thus I will E acts of judgment upon Egypt.
45:9 and oppression, and E justice and righteousness;
Hos 11:9 I will not E my fierce anger, I will
Mic 5:15 and wrath I will E vengeance upon the nations
Jn 5:26 given him authority to E judgment, because he is
Rom 9:28 for the Lord will E his sentence upon the
13:4 servant of God to E his wrath on the
Jude 1:15 his holy myriads, to E judgment on all, and

EXECUTED (15)

Num 33:4 gods also the LORD E judgments.
Deut 33:21 people, with Israel he E the commands and just
2Chr 24:24 Thus they E judgment on Joash.
Ezra 7:26 let judgment be strictly E upon him, whether for
Esth 9:1 were about to be E, on the very day
Ps 9:16 himself known, he has E judgment; the wicked are
99:4 established equity; thou hast E justice and
Eccl 8:11 evil deed is not E speedily, the heart of
Jer 23:20 back until he has E and accomplished the intents
30:24 back until he has E and accomplished the intents
Ezek 11:12 in my statutes, nor E my ordinances, but have
20:24 because they had not E my ordinances, but had
23:10 when judgment had been E upon her.
39:21 judgment which I have E, and my hand which
Dan 3:28 Thou hast E true judgments in all that thou

EXECUTES (9)

Deut 10:18 He E justice for the fatherless and the widow,
Ps 75:7 it is God who E judgment, putting down one
140:12 of the afflicted, and E justice for the needy.
146:7 faith for ever; who E justice for the oppressed;

Sir 20:3 is a man who E judgments by violence.
35:17 for the righteous, and E judgment.
Ezek 18:8 his hand from iniquity, E true justice between man
Joel 2:11 exceedingly great; he that E his word is powerful.
Mic 7:9 pleads my cause and E judgment for me.

EXECUTING
2Chr 22:8 And when Jehu was E judgment upon the house

EXECUTION (2)
Esth 12:3 they were led to E,
16:17 not to put in E the letters sent by

EXECUTIONER
2Mac 5:8 and abhorred as the E of his country and

EXECUTIONERS
Ezek 9:1 saying, "Draw near, you E of the city, each

EXEMPT (2)
1Kgs 15:22 all Judah, none was E, and they carried away
1Mac 10:29 I free you and E all the Jews from

EXERCISE (7)
Lev 25:33 the Levites does not E his right of redemption,
Esth 16:7 behavior of those who E authority unworthily, can be
Mt 20:25 and their great men E authority over them.
Mk 10:42 and their great men E authority over them.
Lk 22:25 kings of the Gentiles E lordship over them; and
1Cor 7:9 But if they cannot E self-control, they should marry.
Rev 13:5 it was allowed to E authority for forty-two months;

EXERCISED (2)
Num 24:19 Jacob shall dominion be E, and the survivors of
2Chr 8:10 hundred and fifty, who E authority over the people.

EXERCISES (2)
1Cor 9:25 Every athlete E self-control in all things.
Rev 13:12 It E all the authority of the first beast

EXERT
Sir 29:6 If the lender E pressure, he will hardly get

EXERTION
Rom 9:16 upon man's will or E, but upon God's mercy.

EXERTS
Wis 16:24 who hast made it, E itself to punish the

EXHAUSTED (6)
1Sam 30:10 behind, who were too E to cross the brook
30:21 who had been too E to follow David, and
Jud 11:12 their food supply is E and their water has
Is 40:30 young men shall fall E;
1Mac 3:29 in the treasury was E, and that the revenues
10:82 (for the cavalry was E; they were overwhelmed by

EXHAUSTIVE
2Mac 2:31 expression and to forego E treatment.

EXHIBIT
2Mac 14:39 Nicanor, wishing to E the enmity which he had

EXHIBITED
1Cor 4:9 think that God has E us apostles as last

EXHORT (10)
1Thes 3:2 your faith and to E you,
4:1 brethren, we beseech and E you in the Lord
4:10 But we E you, brethren, to do so more
5:14 And we E you, brethren, admonish the idlers,
2Thes 3:12 persons we command and E in the Lord Jesus
1Tim 5:1 an older man but E him as you would
2Tim 4:2 season, convince, rebuke, and E, be unfailing in
Tit 2:15 Declare these things; E and reprove with all.
Heb 3:13 But E one another every day, as long as
1Pet 5:1 So I E the elders among you, as a

EXHORTATION (5)
Acts 13:15 have any word of E for the people, say
15:31 when they read it, they rejoiced at the E
Rom 12:8 who exhorts, in his E; he who contributes, in
Heb 12:5 have you forgotten the E which addresses you as
13:22 with my word of E, for I have written

EXHORTATIONS
Lk 3:18 So, with many other E, he preached good news

EXHORTED (12)
2Mac 2:3 other similar words he E them that the law
8:16 number six thousand, and E them not to be
12:31 they thanked them and E them to be well-disposed
12:42 And the noble Judas E the people to keep
13:12 days without ceasing, Judas E them and ordered
15:8 And he E his men not to fear the
Acts 2:40 many other words and E them, saying, "Save
11:23 was glad; and he E them all to remain
15:32 who were themselves prophets, E the brethren with
16:40 seen the brethren, they E them and departed.
20:1 the disciples and having E them took leave of
1Thes 2:11 with his children, we E each one of you

EXHORTING (3)
2Mac 13:14 of the world and E his men to fight
Acts 14:22 souls of the disciples, E them to continue in
1Pet 5:12 written briefly to you, E and declaring that this

EXHORTS
Rom 12:8 his teaching; he who E, in his exhortation; he

EXILE (68)
2Sam 15:19 foreigner, and also an E from your home.
2Kgs 25:11 Nebuzaradan the captain of the guard carried into E
25:21 Judah was taken into E out of its land.
25:27 thirty-seventh year of the E of Jehoiachin king of
1Chr 5:6 Assyria carried away into E; he was a chieftain
5:22 And they dwelt in their place until the E
6:15 and Jehozadak went into E when the LORD sent
6:15 Judah and Jerusalem into E by the hand of
8:6 they were carried into E to Manahath):
9:1 Judah was taken into E in Babylon because of
2Chr 36:20 He took into E in Babylon those who had
Ezra 6:21 who had returned from E, and also by every
Neh 1:2 who had escaped E, and concerning Jerusalem.
1:3 the province who escaped E are in great trouble
7:6 Babylon had carried into E; they returned to
Sir 29:18 men of power into E, and they have wandered
Is 5:13 my people go into E for want of knowledge;
27:8 Measure by measure, by E thou didst contend with
Jer 13:19 Judah is taken into E, wholly taken into exile.
13:19 Judah is taken into exile, wholly taken into E
24:1 Babylon had taken into E from Jerusalem Jeconiah
27:20 when he took into E from Jerusalem to Babylon
29:1 had taken into E from Jerusalem to Babylon.
29:4 I have sent into E from Jerusalem to Babylon:
29:7 have sent you into E, and pray to the
29:14 the place from which I sent you into E
29:16 out with you into E:
29:28 in Babylon, saying, "Your E will be long; build
39:9 the guard, carried into E to Babylon the rest
40:7 not been taken into E to Babylon,
43:3 or take us into E in Babylon."
46:19 Prepare yourselves baggage for E, O inhabitants of
48:7 shall go forth into E, with his priests and
48:11 has he gone into E; so his taste remains
49:3 Milcom shall go into E, with his priests and
Lam 1:3 Judah has gone into E because of affliction and
4:22 will keep you in E no longer; but your
Bar 2:14 have carried us into E;
2:30 the land of their E they will come to
2:32 the land of their E, and will remember my
3:7 praise thee in our E, for we have put
3:8 are today in our E where thou hast scattered
Ezek 1:2 fifth year of the E of King Jehoiachin),
12:3 prepare for yourself an E's baggage, and go into
12:3 baggage, and go into E by day in their
12:3 shall go like an E from your place to
12:4 sight, as baggage for E; and you shall go
12:4 sight, as men do who must go into E
12:7 day, as baggage for E, and in the evening
12:11 they shall go into E, into captivity.'
25:3 when it went into E;
33:21 twelfth year of our E, in the tenth month,
39:28 I sent them into E among the nations, and
40:1 twenty-fifth year of our E, at the beginning of
Amos 1:5 Syria shall go into E to Kir," says the
1:6 because they carried into E a whole people to
1:15 king shall go into E, he and his princes
5:5 shall surely go into E, and Bethel shall come
5:27 will take you into E beyond Damascus," says the
6:7 those to go into E, and the revelry of

7:11 Israel must go into E away from his land.'"
7:17 shall surely go into E away from its land.'"
Mic 1:16 eagle, for they shall go from you into E
Zech 14:2 city shall go into E, but the rest of
2Mac 5:9 their own country into E died in exile, having
5:9 into exile died in E, having embarked to go
Acts 7:29 fled, and became an E in the land of
1Pet 1:17 yourselves with fear throughout the time of your E

EXILED (4)
2Kgs 17:23 So Israel was E from their own land to
Is 49:21 was bereaved and barren, E and put away, but
Jer 40:1 Judah who were being E to Babylon.
2Mac 1:33 the place where the E priests had hidden the

EXILES (39)
Ezra 1:11 bring up, when the E were brought up from
2:1 the captivity of those E whom Nebuchadnezzar the
4:1 heard that the returned E were building a temple
6:16 rest of the returned E, celebrated the dedication of
6:19 first month the returned E kept the passover.
6:20 for all the returned E, for their fellow priests,
8:35 captivity, the returned E, offered burnt offerings to
9:4 faithlessness of the returned E, gathered round me
10:6 he was mourning over the faithlessness of the E
10:7 to all the returned E that they should assemble
10:8 he himself banned from the congregation of the E
10:16 Then the returned E did so.
Neh 7:6 the captivity of those E whom Nebuchadnezzar the
Wis 17:2 in under their roofs, E from eternal providence.
Is 20:4 captives and the Ethiopians E, both the young and
45:13 city and set my E free, not for price
Jer 24:5 regard as good the E from Judah, whom I
28:4 Judah, and all the E from Judah who went
28:6 the house of the LORD, and all the E
29:1 the elders of the E, and to the priests,
29:4 Israel, to all the E whom I have sent
29:20 the LORD, all you E whom I sent away
29:22 used by all the E from Judah in Babylon:
29:31 "Send to all the E, saying, 'Thus says the
Ezek 1:1 I was among the E by the river Chebar,
3:11 get you to the E, to your people, and
3:15 I came to the E at Tel-abib, who dwelt
11:15 your brethren, your fellow E, the whole house of
11:24 the Spirit of God into Chaldea, to the E
11:25 And I told the E all the things that
Dan 2:25 have found among the E from Judah a man
5:13 Daniel, one of the E of Judah, whom the
6:13 is one of the E from Judah, pays no
Obad 1:20 The E in Halah who are of the people
1:20 as Zarephath; and the E of Jerusalem who are
Zech 6:10 me: "Take from the E Heldai, Tobijah, and Jedaiah,
Heb 11:13 they were strangers and E on the earth.
1Pet 1:1 Jesus Christ, to the E of the dispersion in
2:11 you as aliens and E to abstain from the

EXIST (14)
Wis 1:14 things that they might E, and the generative forces
2:6 the good things that E, and make use of
11:24 lovest all things that E, and hast loathing for
14:13 beginning nor will they E for ever.
Sir 14:19 decays and ceases to E, and the man who
17:23 one who does not E, thanksgiving has ceased; he
24:9 and for eternity I shall not cease to E
Rom 4:17 calls into existence the things that do not E
13:1 God, and those that E have been instituted by
1Cor 8:6 and for whom we E, and one Lord, Jesus
8:6 whom are all things and through whom we E
Heb 2:10 by whom all things E, in bringing many sons
Jas 3:16 jealousy and selfish ambition E, there will be
2Pet 3:7 and earth that now E have been stored up

EXISTED (7)
Wis 14:13 for neither have they E from the beginning nor
Sir 16:24 of the Lord have E from the beginning by
1Mac 3:29 the laws that had E from the earliest days.
2Mac 7:28 did not make them out of things that E
2Pet 3:5 word of God heavens E long ago, and an
3:6 the world that then E was deluged with water
Rev 4:11 by thy will they E and were created."

EXISTENCE (5)
Wis 7:5 a different beginning of E;
15:12 But he considered our E an idle game, and
Sir 40:29 table of another, his E cannot be considered as
Rom 4:17 dead and calls into E the things that do

1Cor 8:4 we know that "an idol has no real E

EXISTING
2Mac 4:11 He set aside the E royal concessions to the

EXISTS (4)
Wis 7:17 unerring knowledge of what E, to know the structure
8:6 who more than she is fashioner of what E
13:1 to know him who E, nor did they recognize
Heb 11:6 must believe that he E and that he rewards

EXITS (3)
Ezek 42:11 breadth, with the same E and arrangements and
43:11 temple, its arrangement, its E and its entrances, and
48:30 "These shall be the E of the city: On

EXODUS
Heb 11:22 made mention of the E of the Israelites and

EXORCISTS
Acts 19:13 of the itinerant Jewish E undertook to pronounce

EXPANSE
Job 38:18 Have you comprehended the E of the earth?

EXPECT (7)
Jud 8:14 thinking; how do you E to search out God,
Wis 12:22 are judged we may E mercy.
14:29 swear wicked oaths and E to suffer no harm.
Ezek 13:6 them, and yet they E him to fulfil their
Mt 24:44 is coming at an hour you do not E
24:50 when he does not E him and at an
Lk 12:46 when he does not E him and at an

EXPECTATION (7)
Prov 10:28 in gladness, but the E of the wicked comes
11:7 hope perishes, and the E of the godless comes
11:23 only in good; the E of the wicked in
Wis 17:13 reason; and the inner E of help, being weak,
Lam 3:18 my glory, and my E from the LORD."
Lk 3:15 the people were in E, and all men questioned
Phil 1:20 it is my eager E and hope that I

EXPECTED (4)
1Kgs 2:15 that all Israel fully E me to reign; however
Tob 8:16 to me as I E; but thou hast treated
Wis 18:7 of their enemies were E by thy people.
2Cor 8:5 this, not as we E, but first they gave

EXPECTING (9)
2Mac 8:11 for a talent, not E the judgment from the
12:37 when they were not E it, and put them
12:44 if he were not E that those who had
Lk 6:35 do good, and lend, E nothing in return; and
Acts 3:5 his attention upon them, E to receive something
10:24 Cornelius was E them and had called together his
12:11 and from all that the Jewish people were E
28:6 They waited, E him to swell up or suddenly
1Cor 16:11 me; for I am E him with the brethren.

EXPEDIENT (3)
Mt 19:10 wife, it is not E to marry."
Jn 11:50 understand that it is E for you that one
18:14 Jews that it was E that one man should

EXPEDITION (3)
1Sam 21:5 I go on an E; the vessels of the
23:13 had escaped from Keilah, he gave up the E
1Mac 9:68 his plan and his E had been in vain.

EXPEDITIONS
2Mac 9:23 occasions when he made E into the upper country,

EXPELLED (3)
1Kgs 2:27 So Solomon E Abiathar from being priest to the
1Mac 13:47 But he E them from the city and cleansed
13:50 But he E them from there and cleansed the

EXPEND
2Mac 4:19 was inappropriate, but to E it for another purpose.

EXPENSE (4)
2Sam 19:42 Have we eaten at all at the king's E
Sir 18:31 great luxury, lest you become impoverished by its E
Acts 28:29 years at his own E, and welcomed all who
1Cor 9:7 Who serves as a soldier at his own E

EXPENSES (6)
Tob 5:14 drachma a day, and E for yourself as for
1Mac 3:30 had before for his E and for the gifts
10:39 to meet the necessary E of the sanctuary.
2Mac 3:3 own revenues all the E connected with the service
9:16 times over; and the E incurred for the sacrifices
Acts 21:24 them and pay their E, so that they may

EXPENSIVE
Mt 26:7 alabaster flask of very E ointment, and she poured

EXPERIENCE (16)
Judg 3:1 Israel who had no E of any war in
Eccl 1:16 mind has had great E of wisdom and knowledge."
Wis 2:24 belong to his party E it.
8:8 one longs for wide E, she knows the things
8:18 wealth, and in the E of her company, understanding,
12:26 of light rebukes will E the deserved judgment of
18:20 The E of death touched also the righteous, and
19:5 that thy people might E an incredible journey, but
Sir 21:22 but a man of E stands respectfully before it.
25:6 Rich E is the crown of the aged, and
34:9 and one with much E will speak with understanding.
36:20 but a man of E will pay him back.
2Mac 8:9 and a man of E in military service.
2Cor 1:6 your comfort, which you E when you patiently
Gal 3:4 Did you E so many things in vain?–if
1Pet 5:9 knowing that the same E of suffering is required

EXPERIENCED (4)
Deut 1:13 Choose wise, understanding, and E men, according to
1:15 your tribes, wise and E men, and set them
1Chr 12:8 the wilderness mighty and E warriors, expert with
2Cor 1:8 of the affliction we E in Asia; for we

EXPERIENCES
Sir 34:12 of death, but have escaped because of these E

EXPERT (8)
Gen 21:20 wilderness, and became an E with the bow.
2Sam 17:8 Besides, your father is E in war; he will
1Chr 5:18 and drew the bow, E in war, forty-four thousand
12:8 mighty and experienced warriors, E with shield and
Song 3:8 girt with swords and E in war, each with
Sir 45:12 the work of an E, the delight of the
Is 3:3 skilful magician and the E in charms.
Bar 3:26 old, great in stature, E in war.

EXPIATE
Is 47:11 not be able to E; and ruin shall come

EXPIATED (2)
1Sam 3:14 house shall not be E by sacrifice or offering
Is 27:9 of Jacob will be E, and this will be

EXPIATION (9)
Num 8:7 sprinkle the water of E upon them, and let
35:33 the land, and no E can be made for
Deut 32:43 his adversaries, and makes E for the land of
2Sam 21:3 how shall I make E, that you may bless
Sir 28:5 wrath, who will make E for his sins?
Rom 3:25 put forward as an E by his blood, to
Heb 2:17 of God, to make E for the sins of
1Jn 2:2 and he is the E for our sins, and
4:10 Son to be the E for our sins.

EXPIRE
Job 3:11 at birth, come forth from the womb and E

EXPIRED (3)
1Sam 18:26 Before the time had E,
Tob 10:1 for the journey had E and they did not
10:7 the wedding feast had E which Raguel had sworn

EXPLAIN (14)
Gen 41:24 no one who could E it to me."
Deut 1:5 Moab, Moses undertook to E this law, saying,
Josh 20:4 of the city, and E his case to the
1Kgs 10:3 which he could not E to her.
2Chr 9:2 which he could not E to her.
Tob 4:2 so that I may E to him about the
4:20 And now let me E to you about the
7:10 But let me E the true situation to you.
Esth 4:8 it to Esther and E it to her and
Is 28:9 to whom will he E the message?
Dan 5:12 to interpret dreams, E riddles, and solve problems
Mt 13:36 came to him, saying, E to us the parable
15:15 Peter said to him, E the parable to us."
Heb 5:11 which is hard to E, since you have become

EXPLAINED (3)
2Mac 3:10 The high priest E that there were some deposits
Mk 4:34 his own disciples he E everything.
Acts 11:4 But Peter began and E to them in order:

EXPLAINING
Acts 17:3 them from the scriptures, E and proving that it

EXPLOIT (2)
Sir 13:4 A rich man will E you if you can
2Pet 2:3 their greed they will E you with false words;

EXPLORE (3)
Deut 1:22 us, that they may E the land for us,
Judg 18:2 the land and to E it; and they said
18:2 to them, "Go and E the land." And they

EXPLORED
Jer 31:37 earth below can be E, then I will cast

EXPORTED (2)
1Kgs 10:29 king's traders they were E to all the kings
2Chr 1:17 through them these were E to all the kings

EXPOSE (2)
Acts 7:19 forced our fathers to E their infants, that they
Eph 5:11 of darkness, but instead E them.

EXPOSED (14)
Ex 20:26 your nakedness be not E on it.'
Prov 26:26 his wickedness will be E in the assembly.
Wis 11:14 been cast out and E, at the end of
18:5 one child had been E and rescued, thou didst
Sir 28:19 who has not been E to its anger, who
Lam 2:14 visions; they have not E your iniquity to restore
Ezek 28:17 to the ground; I E you before kings, to
1Mac 14:29 Joarib, and his brothers, E themselves to danger and
2Mac 4:33 these acts he publicly E them, having first withdrawn
Jn 3:20 to the light, lest his deeds should be E
Acts 7:21 and when he was E, Pharaoh's daughter adopted
Eph 5:13 but when anything is E by the light it
Heb 10:33 sufferings, sometimes being publicly E to abuse and,
Rev 16:15 naked and be seen E

EXPOSING
Gen 30:37 white streaks in them, E the white of the

EXPOSURE
2Cor 11:27 and thirst, often without food, in cold and E

EXPOUND
Sir 38:33 of judgment; they cannot E discipline or judgment,

EXPOUNDED (2)
Acts 18:26 they took him and E to him the way
28:23 And he E the matter to them from morning

EXPRESS
Sir 34:11 travels, and I understand more than I can E

EXPRESSED
2Cor 7:14 For if I have E to him some pride

EXPRESSES (2)
Num 30:5 But if her father E disapproval to her on
30:8 hear of it, he E disapproval, then he shall

EXPRESSING
Prov 18:2 understanding, but only in E his opinion.

EXPRESSION (4)
Sir 12:18 his hands, and whisper much, and change his E
27:6 a tree; so the E of a thought discloses
Dan 3:19 of fury, and the E of his face was
2Mac 2:31 strive for brevity of E and to forego exhaustive

EXPRESSLY (3)
1Chr 12:31 eighteen thousand, who were E named to come and
16:41 of those chosen and E named to give thanks
1Tim 4:1 Now the Spirit E says that in later times

EXTEND (6)

Ex	27:5	that the net shall E halfway down the altar.
Num	34:9	then the boundary shall E to Ziphron, and its
Ps	109:12	there be none to E kindness to him, nor
Is	11:11	day the Lord will E his hand yet a
	66:12	LORD: "Behold, I will E prosperity to her like
Jer	25:33	on that day shall E from one end of

EXTENDED (11)

Gen	10:19	territory of the Canaanites E from Sidon, in the
	10:30	in which they lived E from Mesha in the
Josh	13:30	Their region E from Mahanaim, through all Bashan,
2Chr	3:11	of the cherubim together E twenty cubits: one wing
	3:13	wings of these cherubim E twenty cubits; the
Ezra	7:28	in Jerusalem, and who E to me his steadfast
	9:9	our bondage, but has E to us his steadfast
Sir	4:31	not your hand be E to receive, but withdrawn
Mic	7:11	In that day the boundary shall be far E
1Mac	3:3	He E the glory of his people.
	14:6	He E the borders of his nation, and gained

EXTENDING (4)

Ex	38:4	bronze, under its ledge, E halfway down.
Ezek	45:7	the tribal portions, and E from the western to
	48:1	over against Hamath), and E from the east side
	48:21	E from the twenty-five thousand cubits of the holy

EXTENDS (5)

Num	21:13	in the wilderness, that E from the boundary of
	21:15	of the valleys that E to the seat of
Josh	15:9	Rephaim; then the boundary E from the top of
Ps	36:5	steadfast love, O LORD, E to the heavens, thy
2Cor	4:15	so that as grace E to more and more

EXTENT (4)

Num	34:2	Canaan in its full E,
Esth	13:2	travel throughout all its E, to re-establish the peace
Ezek	45:1	broad; it shall be holy throughout its whole E
2Mac	3:11	To such an E the impious Simon had misrepresented

EXTERMINATE (2)

Wis	11:19	only could their damage E men, but the mere
Dan	11:44	with great fury to E and utterly destroy many.

EXTERMINATED (3)

Josh	11:20	no mercy but be E, as the LORD commanded
1Kgs	22:46	his father Asa, he E from the land.
1Chr	4:41	were found there, and E them to this day,

EXTERNAL

Rom	2:28	is true circumcision something E and physical.

EXTINCT

Job	17:1	broken, my days are E, the grave is ready

EXTINCTION

2Pet	2:6	he condemned them to E and made them an

EXTINGUISHED (3)

Wis	2:3	When it is E, the body will turn to
Sir	10:17	destroyed them, and has E the memory of them
Is	43:17	cannot rise, they are E, quenched like a wick:

EXTINGUISHES

Sir	3:28	Water E a blazing fire: so almsgiving atones for

EXTOL (15)

2Sam	22:50	"For this I will E thee, O LORD, among
Job	36:24	"Remember to E his work, of which men have
Ps	18:49	For this I will E thee, O LORD, among
	30:1	I will E thee, O LORD, for thou hast
	89:16	all the day, and E thy righteousness.
	99:5	E the LORD our God; worship at his footstool!
	99:9	E the LORD our God, and worship at his
	107:32	Let them E him in the congregation of the
	117:1	E him, all peoples!
	118:28	my God, I will E thee.
	145:1	I will E thee, my God and King, and
Song	1:4	in you; we will E your love more than
Sir	13:22	are silent, and they E to the clouds what
	43:31	Or who can E him as he is?
Dan	4:37	I, Nebuchadnezzar, praise and E and honor the King

EXTOLLED (5)

Ps	66:17	him, and he was E with my tongue.
Dan	3:54	glory and to be E and highly glorified for
	3:56	kingdom and to be E and highly exalted for
2Mac	4:24	presented to the king, E him with an air
Acts	19:17	and the name of the Lord Jesus was E

EXTOLLING

Acts	10:46	speaking in tongues and E God.

EXTORTED

Ezek	22:29	and needy, and have E from the sojourner without

EXTORTION (7)

Ps	62:10	Put no confidence in E, set no vain hopes
Ezek	18:18	father, because he practiced E, robbed his brother,
	22:7	you; the sojourner suffers E in your midst; the
	22:12	of your neighbors by E; and you have forgotten
	22:29	the land have practiced E and committed robbery;
Mt	23:24	they are full of E and rapacity.
Lk	11:39	you are full of E and wickedness.

EXTORTIONERS

Lk	18:11	not like other men, E, unjust, adulterers, or even

EXTRAORDINARY (3)

Deut	28:59	you and your offspring E afflictions, afflictions severe
Sir	10:13	Lord brought upon them E afflictions, and destroyed
Acts	19:11	And God did E miracles by the hands of

EXTREME (5)

Josh	15:21	of Judah in the E South, toward the boundary
Ezek	46:19	a place at the E western end of them.
2Mac	4:13	There was such an E of Hellenization and increase
	7:42	of sacrifices and the E tortures.
2Cor	8:2	of joy and their E poverty have overflowed in

EXTREMELY

Gal	1:14	among my people, so E zealous was I for

EXTREMITY

Num	22:36	the Arnon, at the E of the boundary.

EXULT (24)

2Sam	1:20	rejoice, lest the daughters of the uncircumcised E
1Chr	16:32	it, let the field E, and everything in it!
Job	6:10	consolation; I would even E in pain unsparing; for
Ps	5:11	love thy name may E in thee.
	9:2	will be glad and E in thee, I will
	25:2	let not my enemies E over me.
	68:3	be joyful; let them E before God; let them
	68:4	name is the LORD, E before him!
	89:16	of thy countenance, who E in thy name all
	94:3	shall the wicked, how long shall the wicked E
	96:12	it; let the field E, and everything in it!
	149:5	Let the faithful E in glory; let them sing
Song	1:4	We will E and rejoice in you; we will
Is	23:12	"You will no more E, O oppressed virgin daughter
	29:19	poor among men shall E in the Holy One
	49:13	joy, O heavens, and E, O earth; break forth,
	61:10	LORD, my soul shall E in my God; for
Jer	11:15	Can you then E
	50:11	you rejoice, though you E, O plunderers of my
Hos	9:1	E not like the peoples; for you have played
Zeph	3:14	Rejoice and E with all your heart, O daughter
	3:17	his love; he will E over you with loud
Zech	10:7	rejoice, their hearts shall E in the LORD.
Rev	19:7	Let us rejoice and E and give him the

EXULTANT (4)

Is	22:2	of shoutings, tumultuous city, E town?
	23:7	Is this your E city whose origin is from
Zeph	2:15	This is the E city that dwelt secure, that
	3:11	your midst your proudly E ones, and you shall

EXULTATION (4)

Ps	60:6	in his sanctuary: "With E I will divide up
	108:7	in his sanctuary: "With E I will divide up
Wis	14:28	worshippers either rave in E, or prophesy lies, or
Sir	1:9	Lord is glory and E, and gladness and a

EXULTED

Job	31:29	that hated me, or E when evil overtook him

EXULTING (3)

Job	20:5	upon earth, that the E of the wicked is
Ps	35:9	rejoice in the LORD, E in his deliverance.
Is	13:3	my anger, my proudly E ones.

EXULTS (6)
1Sam 2:1 and said, "My heart E in the LORD; my
Job 39:21 in the valley, and E in his strength; he
Ps 21:1 LORD; and in thy help how greatly he E
28:7 helped, and my heart E, and with my song
Is 5:14 throng and he who E in her.
Hab 1:15 them in his seine; so he rejoices and E

EYE (119)
Ex 21:24 give life for life, E for eye, tooth for
21:24 for life, eye for E, tooth for tooth, hand
21:26 a man strikes the E of his slave, male
21:26 go free for the E's sake.
Lev 24:20 him, fracture for fracture, E for eye, tooth for
24:20 for fracture, eye for E, tooth for tooth; as
Num 24:3 of the man whose E is opened,
24:15 of the man whose E is opened,
Deut 7:16 over to you, your E shall not pity them;
13:8 him, nor shall your E pity him, nor shall
15:9 is near,' and your E be hostile to your
19:13 Your E shall not pity him, but you shall
19:21 Your E shall not pity; it shall be life
19:21 be life for life, E for eye, tooth for
19:21 for life, eye for E, tooth for tooth, hand
25:12 off her hand; your E shall have no pity.
32:10 he kept him as the apple of his E
34:7 when he died; his E was not dim, nor
Judg 18:6 go is under the E of the LORD."
1Sam 2:29 then look with greedy E at my sacrifices and
2:32 will look with envious E on all the prosperity
Ezra 5:5 But the E of their God was upon the
Tob 4:7 do not let your E begrudge the gift when
4:16 do not let your E begrudge the gift when
Jud 2:11 if they refuse, your E shall not spare and
Job 7:7 is a breath; my E will never again see
7:8 The E of him who sees me will behold
10:18 had died before any E had seen me,
13:1 "Lo, my E has seen all this, my ear
16:20 friends scorn me; my E pours out tears to
17:2 about me, and my E dwells on their provocation.
17:7 My E has grown dim from grief, and all
20:9 The E which saw him will see him no
24:15 The E of the adulterer also waits for the
24:15 the twilight, saying, 'No E will see me'; and
28:7 knows, and the falcon's E has not seen it.
28:10 the rocks, and his E sees every precious thing.
29:11 blessed, and when the E saw, it approved;
42:5 ear, but now my E sees thee;
Ps 6:7 My E wastes away because of grief, it grows
17:8 the apple of the E; hide me in the
31:9 am in distress; my E is wasted from grief,
32:8 counsel you with my E upon you.
33:18 Behold, the E of the LORD is on those
35:19 not those wink the E who hate me without
54:7 every trouble, and my E has looked in triumph
88:9 I cannot escape; my E grows dim through sorrow.
94:9 He who formed the E, does he not see?
Prov 7:2 the apple of your E;
10:10 He who winks the E causes trouble, but he
20:12 ear and the seeing E, the LORD has made
22:9 who has a bountiful E will be blessed, for
30:17 The E that mocks a father and scorns to
Eccl 1:8 cannot utter it; the E is not satisfied with
Sir 4:5 Do not avert your E from the needy, nor
14:8 man with a grudging E; he averts his face
14:9 A greedy man's E is not satisfied with a
14:10 A stingy man's E begrudges bread, and it is
16:5 Many such things my E has seen, and my
17:7 He set his E upon their hearts to show
17:17 a person's kindness like the apple of his E
22:17 man who pricks an E will make tears fall,
26:11 guard against her impudent E, and do not wonder
27:22 Whoever winks his E plans evil deeds, and no
31:13 Remember that a greedy E is a bad thing.
31:13 What has been created more greedy than the E
40:22 The E desires grace and beauty, but the green
43:18 The E marvels at the beauty of its whiteness,
Is 52:8 sing for joy; for E to eye they see
52:8 joy; for eye to E they see the return
64:4 by the ear, no E has seen a God
Jer 32:4 face and see him E to eye;
32:4 see him eye to E;
34:3 the king of Babylon E to eye and speak
34:3 of Babylon eye to E and speak with him
Ezek 5:11 cut you down; my E will not spare, and
7:4 And my E will not spare you, nor will
7:9 And my E will not spare, nor will I
8:18 deal in wrath; my E will not spare, nor
9:5 him, and smite; your E shall not spare, and
9:10 As for me, my E will not spare, nor
16:5 No E pitied you, to do any of these
20:17 Nevertheless my E spared them, and I did not
Zech 2:8 the apple of his E:
11:17 the sword smite his arm and his right E
11:17 wholly withered, his right E utterly blinded!"
Mt 5:29 If your right E causes you to sin, pluck
5:38 it was said, 'An E for an eye and
5:38 'An eye for an E and a tooth for
6:22 "The E is the lamp of the body.
6:22 So, if your E is sound, your whole body
6:23 light; but if your E is not sound, your
7:3 is in your brother's E, but do not notice
7:3 notice the log that is in your own E
7:4 speck out of your E when there is the
7:4 when there is the log in your own E
7:5 out of your own E, and then you will
7:5 to take the speck out of your brother's E
18:9 And if your E causes you to sin, pluck
18:9 enter life with one E than with two eyes
19:24 to go through the E of a needle than
Mk 9:45 And if your E causes you to sin, pluck
9:45 of God with one E than with two eyes
10:25 to go through the E of a needle than
Lk 6:41 is in your brother's E, but do not notice
6:41 notice the log that is in your own E
6:42 that is in your E when you yourself do
6:42 see the log that is in your own E
6:42 out of your own E, and then you will
6:42 out the speck that is in your brother's E
11:34 Your E is the lamp of your body; when
11:34 your body; when your E is sound, your whole
18:25 to go through the E of a needle than
1Cor 2:9 is written, "What no E has seen, nor ear
12:16 I am not an E, I do not belong
12:17 whole body were an E, where would be the
12:21 The E cannot say to the hand, "I have
15:52 the twinkling of an E, at the last trumpet.
Rev 1:7 the clouds, and every E will see him, every

EYE-SERVICE (2)
Eph 6:6 in the way of E, as men-pleasers, but as
Col 3:22 earthly masters, not with E, as men-pleasers, but in

EYEBROWS
Lev 14:9 his beard and his E, all his hair.

EYED
1Sam 18:9 And Saul E David from that day on.

EYELASHES
Prov 6:25 capture you with her E;

EYELIDS (10)
Job 3:9 none, nor see the E of the morning;
16:16 weeping, and on my E is deep darkness;
41:18 eyes are like the E of the dawn.
Ps 11:4 his eyes behold, his E test, the children of
77:4 Thou dost hold my E from closing; I am
132:4 or slumber to my E,
Prov 6:4 no sleep and your E no slumber;
30:13 eyes, how high their E lift!
Sir 26:9 lustful eyes, and she is known by her E
Jer 9:18 with tears, and our E gush with water.

EYES (568)
Gen 3:5 eat of it your E will be opened, and
3:6 a delight to the E, and that the tree
3:7 Then the E of both were opened, and they
6:8 found favor in the E of the LORD.
13:10 Lot lifted up his E, and saw that the
13:14 him, "Lift up your E, and look from the
18:2 He lifted up his E and looked, and behold,
20:16 your vindication in the E of all who are
21:19 Then God opened her E, and she saw a
22:4 Abraham lifted up his E and saw the place
22:13 Abraham lifted up his E and looked, and behold,
24:63 he lifted up his E and looked, and behold,
24:64 Rebekah lifted up her E, and when she saw
27:1 was old and his E were dim so that
29:17 Leah's E were weak, but Rachel was beautiful and
30:41 the runnels before the E of the flock, that
31:10 I lifted up my E, and saw in a

E

31:12 said, 'Lift up your E and see, all the
31:40 by night, and my sleep fled from my E
33:1 Jacob lifted up his E and looked, and behold,
33:5 when Esau raised his E and saw the women
34:11 find favor in your E, and whatever you say
39:7 master's wife cast her E upon Joseph, and said,
42:24 Simeon from them and bound him before their E
43:29 he lifted up his E, and saw his brother
44:21 I may set my E upon him.'
45:12 poverty.' And now your E see, and the eyes
45:12 eyes see, and the E of my brother Benjamin
46:4 up again; and Joseph's hand shall close your E
47:15 us food; why should we die before your E
47:19 we die before your E, both we and our
48:10 Now the E of Israel were dim with age,
49:12 blood of grapes; his E shall be red with
50:4 found favor in your E, speak, I pray you,
Ex 8:26 the Egyptians before their E, will they not stone
13:9 a memorial between your E, that the law of
13:16 or frontlets between your E; for by a strong
14:10 Israel lifted up their E, and behold, the Egyptians
15:26 is right in his E, and give heed to
20:20 may be before your E, that you may not
Lev 4:13 is hidden from the E of the assembly, and
13:5 and if in his E the disease is checked
13:37 But if in his E the itch is checked,
20:4 at all hide their E from that man, when
26:16 fever that waste the E and cause life to
Num 5:13 is hidden from the E of her husband, and
10:31 you will serve as E for us.
15:39 heart and your own E, which you are inclined
16:14 you put out the E of these men?
20:8 the rock before their E to yield its water;
20:12 sanctify me in the E of the people of
22:31 the LORD opened the E of Balaam, and he
24:2 Balaam lifted up his E, and saw Israel encamping
24:4 down, but having his E uncovered:
24:16 down, but having his E uncovered:
27:14 to sanctify me at the waters before their E
33:55 as pricks in your E and thorns in your
Deut 1:30 in Egypt before your E,
3:21 at that time, 'Your E have seen all that
3:27 and lift up your E westward and northward and
3:27 behold it with your E; for you shall not
4:3 Your E have seen what the LORD did at
4:9 the things which your E have seen, and lest
4:19 you lift up your E to heaven, and when
4:34 God did for you in Egypt before your E
6:8 and they shall be as frontlets between your E
6:22 his household, before our E;
7:19 great trials which your E saw, the signs, the
9:17 my two hands, and broke them before your E
10:21 terrible things which your E have seen.
11:7 all Israel; for your E have seen all the
11:12 God cares for; the E of the LORD your
11:18 and they shall be as frontlets between your E
12:8 right in his own E;
16:19 a bribe blinds the E of the wise and
21:7 blood, neither did our E see it shed.
24:1 no favor in his E because he has found
28:31 be slain before your E, and you shall not
28:32 another people, while your E look on and fail
28:34 the sight which your E shall see.
28:65 heart, and failing E, and a languishing soul;
28:67 the sights which your E shall see.
29:2 LORD did before your E in the land of
29:3 great trials which your E saw, the signs, and
29:4 mind to understand, or E to see, or ears
34:4 see it with your E, but you shall not
Josh 5:13 he lifted up his E and looked, and behold,
23:13 and thorns in your E, till you perish from
24:7 cover them; and your E saw what I did
Judg 16:21 and gouged out his E, and brought him down
16:28 upon the Philistines for one of my two E
17:6 man did what was right in his own E
19:17 he lifted up his E, and saw the wayfarer
21:25 man did what was right in his own E
Ruth 2:9 Let your E be upon the field which they
2:10 found favor in your E, that you should take
1Sam 1:18 said, "Let your maidservant find favor in your E
2:33 to weep out his E and grieve his heart;
4:15 years old and his E were set, so that
6:13 they lifted up their E and saw the ark,
11:2 out all your right E, and thus put disgrace
12:3 bribe to blind my E with it?
12:16 thing, which the LORD will do before your E
14:27 his mouth; and his E became bright.
14:29 land; see how my E have become bright, because
15:17 little in your own E, are you not the
16:12 ruddy, and had beautiful E, and was handsome.
20:3 found favor in your E; and he thinks, 'Let
20:29 found favor in your E, let me get away,
24:10 Lo, this day your E have seen how the
25:8 find favor in your E; for we come on
26:21 was precious in your E this day; behold, I
27:5 found favor in your E, let a place be
2Sam 6:20 himself today before the E of his servants' maids,
6:22 be abased in your E; but by the maids
7:19 small thing in thy E, O Lord GOD; thou
12:11 your wives before your E, and give them to
13:34 watch lifted up his E, and looked, and behold,
15:25 find favor in the E of the LORD, he
18:24 he lifted up his E and looked, he saw
22:28 humble people, but thy E are upon the haughty
24:3 they are, while the E of my lord the
1Kgs 1:20 lord the king, the E of all Israel are
1:48 this day, my own E seeing it.'"
8:29 this day; that thy E may be open night
8:52 Let thy E be open to the supplication of
9:3 there for ever; my E and my heart will
10:7 came and my own E had seen it; and,
11:38 is right in my E by keeping my statutes
14:4 not see, for his E were dim because of
14:8 was right in my E,
15:5 was right in the E of the LORD, and
15:11 was right in the E of the LORD, as
20:38 way, disguising himself with a bandage over his E
20:41 bandage away from his E; and the king of
2Kgs 4:34 upon his mouth, his E upon his eyes, and
4:34 his eyes upon his E, and his hands upon
4:35 sneezed seven times, and the child opened his E
6:17 pray thee, open his E that he may see."
6:17 the LORD opened the E of the young man,
6:20 "O LORD, open the E of these men, that
6:20 the LORD opened their E, and they saw; and
7:2 it with your own E, but you shall not
7:19 it with your own E, but you shall not
9:30 and she painted her E, and adorned her head,
10:5 one king; do whatever is good in your E
10:30 is right in my E, and have done to
12:2 was right in the E of the LORD all
14:3 was right in the E of the LORD, yet
15:3 was right in the E of the LORD, according
15:34 was right in the E of the LORD, according
16:2 was right in the E of the LORD his
18:3 was right in the E of the LORD, according
19:16 and hear; open thy E, O LORD, and see;
19:22 you raised your voice and haughtily lifted your E
22:2 was right in the E of the LORD, and
22:20 in peace, and your E shall not see all
25:7 of Zedekiah before his E, and put out the
25:7 and put out the E of Zedekiah, and bound
1Chr 13:4 was right in the E of all the people.
17:17 small thing in thy E, O God; thou hast
21:16 And David lifted his E and saw the angel
2Chr 6:20 before thee; that thy E may be open day
6:40 my God, let thy E be open and thy
7:15 Now my E will be open and my ears
7:16 there for ever; my E and my heart will
9:6 came and my own E had seen it; and
14:2 and right in the E of the LORD his
16:9 For the E of the LORD run to and
20:12 to do, but our E are upon thee."
24:2 was right in the E of the LORD all
25:2 was right in the E of the LORD, yet
26:4 was right in the E of the LORD, according
27:2 was right in the E of the LORD according
28:1 was right in the E of the LORD, like
29:2 was right in the E of the LORD, according
29:8 of hissing, as you see with your own E
34:2 was right in the E of the LORD, and
34:28 in peace, and your E shall not see all
Ezra 9:8 God may brighten our E and grant us a
Neh 1:6 be attentive, and thy E open, to hear the
Tob 2:10 fell into my open E and white films formed
2:10 open eyes and white films formed on my E
3:12 I have turned my E and my face toward
3:17 white films of Tobit's E; to give Sarah the
5:20 and sound, and your E will see him.
6:8 white films in his E, and he will be
10:5 go, you who are the light of my E
11:7 know, Tobias, that your father will open his E

11:8 therefore must anoint his E with the gall; and
11:11 gall upon his father's E, saying, "Be of good
11:12 And when his E began to smart he rubbed
11:13 films scaled off from the corners of his E
Jud 7:28 our babes before our E, or see our wives
8:22 a reproach in the E of those who acquire
10:4 beautiful, to entice the E of all men who
10:14 she was in their E marvelously beautiful–they said
16:9 Her sandal ravished his E, her beauty captivated his
Esth 2:15 found favor in the E of all who saw
8:5 be pleasing in his E, let an order be
13:15 thy people; for the E of our foes are
13:18 out mightily, for their death was before their E
16:9 what comes before our E with more equitable
Job 3:10 my mother's womb, nor hide trouble from my E
4:16 form was before my E; there was silence, then
7:8 no more; while thy E are upon me, I
10:4 Hast thou E of flesh?
11:4 am clean in God's E
11:20 But the E of the wicked will fail; all
14:3 dost thou open thy E upon such a one
15:12 and why do your E flash,
16:9 my adversary sharpens his E against me.
17:5 of their property, the E of his children will
19:15 stranger; I have become an alien in their E
19:27 my side, and my E shall behold, and not
21:8 in their presence, and their offspring before their E
21:20 Let their own E see their destruction, and let
24:23 are supported; and his E are upon their ways.
27:19 more; he opens his E, and his wealth is
28:21 is hid from the E of all living, and
29:15 I was E to the blind, and feet to
31:1 a covenant with my E; how then could I
31:7 has gone after my E, and if any spot
31:16 or have caused the E of the widow to
32:1 Job, because he was righteous in his own E
34:21 "For his E are upon the ways of a
36:7 does not withdraw his E from the righteous, but
39:29 out the prey; his E behold it afar off.
41:18 forth light, and his E are like the eyelids
Ps 5:5 not stand before thy E; thou hatest all evildoers.
10:8 His E stealthily watch for the hapless,
11:4 is in heaven; his E behold, his eyelids test,
13:3 my God; lighten my E, lest I sleep the
15:4 his neighbor; in whose E a reprobate is despised,
17:2 Let thy E see the right!
17:11 me; they set their E to cast me to
18:27 people; but the haughty E thou dost bring down.
19:8 is pure, enlightening the E;
25:15 My E are ever toward the LORD, for he
26:3 love is before my E, and I walk in
34:15 The E of the LORD are toward the righteous,
35:21 our E have seen it!"
36:1 there is no fear of God before his E
36:2 himself in his own E that his iniquity cannot
38:10 the light of my E –it also has gone
66:7 might for ever, whose E keep watch on the
69:3 My E grow dim with waiting for my God.
69:23 Let their E be darkened, so that they cannot
73:7 Their E swell out with fatness, their hearts overflow
79:10 servants be known among the nations before our E
91:8 only look with your E and see the recompense
92:11 My E have seen the downfall of my enemies,
101:3 not set before my E anything that is base.
115:5 but do not speak; E, but do not see.
116:8 soul from death, my E from tears, my feet
118:23 the LORD's doing; it is marvelous in our E
119:6 to shame, having my E fixed on all thy
119:15 precepts, and fix my E on thy ways.
119:18 Open my E, that I may behold wondrous things
119:37 Turn my E from looking at vanities; and give
119:82 My E fail with watching for thy promise; I
119:123 My E fail with watching for thy salvation, and
119:136 My E shed streams of tears, because men do
119:148 My E are awake before the watches of the
121:1 I lift up my E to the hills.
123:1 I lift up my E, O thou who art
123:2 Behold, as the E of servants look to the
123:2 their master, as the E of a maid to
123:2 her mistress, so our E look to the LORD
131:1 not lifted up, my E are not raised too
132:4 give sleep to my E or slumber to my
135:16 speak not, they have E, but they see not,
139:16 Thy E beheld my unformed substance; in thy book
141:8 But my E are toward thee, O LORD God;
145:15 The E of all look to thee, and thou
146:8 the LORD opens the E of the blind.
Prov 3:7 wise in your own E; fear the LORD, and
4:26 Let your E look directly forward, and your gaze
5:21 ways are before the E of the LORD, and
6:4 Give your E no sleep and your eyelids no
6:13 speech, winks with his E, scrapes with his feet,
6:17 abomination to him: haughty E, a lying tongue, and
10:26 and smoke to the E, so is the sluggard
12:15 right in his own E, but a wise man
15:3 The E of the LORD are in every place,
15:30 The light of the E rejoices the heart, and
16:2 pure in his own E, but the LORD weighs
16:30 He who winks his E plans perverse things, he
17:8 magic stone in the E of him who gives
17:24 toward wisdom, but the E of a fool are
20:8 throne of judgment winnows all evil with his E
20:13 to poverty; open your E, and you will have
21:2 right in his own E, but the LORD weighs
21:4 Haughty E and a proud heart, the lamp of
21:10 evil; his neighbor finds no mercy in his E
22:12 The E of the LORD keep watch over knowledge,
23:5 When your E light upon it, it is gone;
23:26 heart, and let your E observe my ways.
23:29 Who has redness of E
23:33 Your E will see strange things, and your mind
25:7 What your E have seen
26:5 folly, lest he be wise in his own E
26:12 a man who is wise in his own E
26:16 wiser in his own E than seven men who
27:20 never satisfied are the E of man.
28:11 wise in his own E, but a poor man
28:27 he who hides his E will get many a
29:13 gives light to the E of both.
30:12 pure in their own E but are not cleansed
30:13 how lofty are their E, how high their eyelids
Eccl 2:10 And whatever my E desired I did not keep
2:14 wise man has his E in his head, but
4:8 his toil, and his E are never satisfied with
5:11 their owner but to see them with his E
6:9 the sight of the E than the wandering of
8:16 day nor night one's E see sleep;
11:7 is pleasant for the E to behold the sun.
11:9 of your heart and the sight of your E
Song 1:15 you are beautiful; your E are doves.
4:1 Your E are doves behind your veil.
4:9 a glance of your E, with one jewel of
5:12 His E are like doves beside springs of water,
6:5 Turn away your E from me, for they disturb
7:4 Your E are pools in Heshbon, by the gate
8:10 I was in his E as one who brings
Wis 3:2 In the E of the foolish they seemed to
11:18 terrible sparks from their E;
15:15 the use of their E to see with, nor
Sir 4:1 do not keep needy E waiting.
9:8 Turn away your E from a shapely woman, and
10:20 the Lord are worthy of honor in his E
11:12 in poverty; but the E of the Lord look
12:16 will weep with his E, but if he finds
15:19 and sees everything; his E are on those who
17:5 for them tongue and E; he gave them ears
17:11 Their E saw his glorious majesty, and their ears
17:13 him, they will not be hid from his E
17:15 before him, and his E are continually upon their
18:17 grudging man makes the E dim.
20:13 for he has many E instead of one.
20:28 and gifts blind the E of the wise; like
23:4 not give me haughty E,
23:19 is confined to the E of men, and he
23:19 not realize that the E of the Lord are
26:9 shows in her lustful E, and she is known
27:1 whoever seeks to get rich will avert his E
30:20 he sees with his E and groans, like a
34:16 The E of the Lord are upon those who
34:17 gives light to the E; he grants healing, life,
34:20 son before his father's E is the man who
38:28 the hammer, and his E are on the pattern
39:19 him, and nothing can be hid from his E
43:4 vapors, and with bright beams it blinds the E
45:12 the delight of the E, richly adorned.
51:27 See with your E that I have labored little
Is 1:15 I will hide my E from you; even though
1:16 doings from before my E; cease to do evil,
3:16 glancing wantonly with their E, mincing along as
5:15 brought low, and the E of the haughty are
5:21 wise in their own E, and shrewd in their
6:5 unclean lips; for my E have seen the King,

6:10 heavy, and shut their E; lest they see with
6:10 they see with their E, and hear with their
11:3 judge by what his E see, or decide by
13:16 in pieces before their E; their houses will be
13:18 of the womb; their E will not pity children.
17:7 their Maker, and their E will look to the
29:10 and has closed your E, the prophets, and covered
29:18 gloom and darkness the E of the blind shall
30:20 any more, but your E shall see your Teacher.
32:3 Then the E of those who see will not
33:15 bloodshed and shuts his E from looking upon evil,
33:17 Your E will see the king in his beauty;
33:20 Your E will see Jerusalem, a quiet habitation, an
35:5 Then the E of the blind shall be opened,
37:17 and hear; open thy E, O LORD, and see;
37:23 you raised your voice and haughtily lifted your E
38:14 My E are weary with looking upward.
40:26 Lift up your E on high and see: who
42:7 nations, to open the E that are blind, to
43:4 are precious in my E, and honored, and I
43:8 are blind, yet have E, who are deaf, yet
44:18 he has shut their E, so that they cannot
49:5 am honored in the E of the LORD, and
49:18 Lift up your E round about and see; they
51:6 Lift up your E to the heavens, and look
52:10 holy arm before the E of all the nations;
59:10 those who have no E; we stumble at noon
60:4 Lift up your E round about, and see; they
65:12 was evil in my E, and chose what I
65:16 troubles are forgotten and are hid from my E
66:4 was evil in my E, and chose that in
Jer 3:2 Lift up your E to the bare heights, and
4:30 that you enlarge your E with paint?
5:3 LORD, do not thy E look for truth?
5:21 senseless people, who have E, but see not, who
7:11 name, become a den of robbers in your E
9:1 were waters, and my E a fountain of tears,
9:18 over us, that our E may run down with
13:17 for your pride; my E will weep bitterly and
13:20 "Lift up your E and see those who come
14:6 air like jackals; their E fail because there is
14:17 this word: 'Let my E run down with tears
16:9 this place, before your E and in your days,
16:17 For my E are upon all their ways; they
16:17 me, nor is their iniquity concealed from my E
22:17 But you have E and heart only for your
24:6 I will set my E upon them for good,
29:21 Babylon, and he shall slay them before your E
31:16 from weeping, and your E from tears; for your
32:19 mighty in deed; whose E are open to all
34:15 was right in my E by proclaiming liberty, each
39:6 at Riblah before his E; and the king of
39:7 He put out the E of Zedekiah, and bound
42:2 of many, as your E see us),
51:24 Chaldea before your very E for all the evil
52:10 of Zedekiah before his E, and also slew all
52:11 He put out the E of Zedekiah, and bound
Lam 1:16 things I weep; my E flow with tears; for
2:4 the pride of our E in the tent of
2:11 My E are spent with weeping; my soul is
2:18 yourself no rest, your E no respite!
3:48 devastation and destruction; my E flow with rivers of
3:49 "My E will flow without ceasing, without respite,
3:51 down and sees; my E cause me grief at
4:17 Our E failed, ever watching vainly for help; in
5:17 for these things our E have grown dim,
Bar 1:12 give light to our E, and we shall live
2:17 and hear; open thy E, O Lord, and see;
2:18 and feeble, and the E that are failing, and
3:14 is light for the E, and peace.
6:17 Their E are full of the dust raised by
Ezek 1:18 rims were full of E round about.
6:9 me, and blinded their E which turn wantonly after
8:5 man, lift up your E now in the direction
8:5 I lifted up my E toward the north, and
10:2 And he went in before my E
10:12 wheels were full of E round about--the wheels
12:2 rebellious house, who have E to see, but see
12:12 he may not see the land with his E
18:6 or lift up his E to the idols of
18:12 pledge, lifts up his E to the idols, commits
18:15 or lift up his E to the idols of
20:7 the detestable things your E feast on, every one
20:8 the detestable things their E feasted on, nor did
20:24 my sabbaths, and their E were set on their
21:6 with breaking heart and bitter grief before their E
23:27 not lift up your E to the Egyptians or
23:40 bathed yourself, painted your E, and decked yourself
24:16 the delight of your E away from you at
24:21 the delight of your E, and the desire of
24:25 the delight of their E and their heart's desire,
28:17 kings, to feast their E on you.
33:25 and lift up your E to your idols, and
36:23 through you I vindicate my holiness before their E
37:20 your hand before their E,
38:16 O Gog, I vindicate my holiness before their E
38:23 myself known in the E of many nations.
40:4 man, look with your E, and hear with your
44:5 well, see with your E, and hear with your
Dan 4:34 I, Nebuchadnezzar, lifted my E to heaven, and my
7:8 in this horn were E like the eyes of
7:8 were eyes like the E of a man, and
7:20 the horn which had E and a mouth that
8:3 I raised my E and saw, and behold, a
8:5 the goat had a conspicuous horn between his E
8:21 great horn between his E is the first king.
9:18 and hear; open thy E and behold our desolations,
10:5 I lifted up my E and looked, and behold,
10:6 appearance of lightning, his E like flaming torches,
13:9 and turned away their E from looking to Heaven
14:42 and they were devoured immediately before his E
Hos 13:14 Compassion is hid from my E
Joel 1:15 cut off before our E, joy and gladness from
Amos 9:4 I will set my E upon them for evil
9:8 Behold, the E of the Lord GOD are upon
Mic 4:11 profaned, and let our E gaze upon Zion."
7:10 My E will gloat over her; now she will
Hab 1:13 who art of purer E than to behold evil
Zech 1:18 And I lifted my E and saw, and behold,
2:1 And I lifted my E and saw, and behold,
4:10 "These seven are the E of the LORD, which
5:1 Again I lifted my E and saw, and behold,
5:5 to me, "Lift your E, and see what this
5:9 Then I lifted my E and saw, and behold,
6:1 again I lifted my E and saw, and behold,
9:8 them, for now I see with my own E
12:4 I will open my E, when I strike every
14:12 on their feet, their E shall rot in their
Mal 1:5 Your own E shall see this, and you shall
1Mac 6:10 "Sleep departs from my E and I am downhearted
9:39 They raised their E and looked, and saw a
11:51 gained glory in the E of the king and
2Mac 3:36 God, which he had seen with his own E
8:17 nobly, keeping before their E the lawless outrage
12:42 seen with their own E what had happened because
Mt 9:29 Then he touched their E, saying, "According to your
9:30 And their E were opened.
13:15 of hearing, and their E they have closed, lest
13:15 should perceive with their E, and hear with their
13:16 But blessed are your E, for they see, and
17:8 they lifted up their E, they saw no one
18:9 eye than with two E to be thrown into
20:33 him, "Lord, let our E be opened."
20:34 in pity touched their E, and immediately they
21:42 Lord's doing, and it is marvelous in our E
26:43 them sleeping, for their E were heavy.
Mk 8:18 Having E do you not see, and having ears
8:23 had spit on his E and laid his hands
8:25 his hands upon his E; and he looked intently
9:45 eye than with two E to be thrown into
12:11 Lord's doing, and it is marvelous in our E
14:40 them sleeping, for their E were very heavy; and
Lk 2:30 thy word; for mine E have seen thy salvation
4:20 sat down; and the E of all in the
6:20 he lifted up his E on his disciples, and
10:23 privately, "Blessed are the E which see what you
16:23 he lifted up his E, and saw Abraham far-off
18:13 even lift up his E to heaven, but beat
19:42 But now they are hid from your E
24:16 But their E were kept from recognizing him.
24:31 And their E were opened and they recognized him;
Jn 4:35 you, lift up your E, and see how the
6:5 Lifting up his E, then, and seeing that a
9:6 and anointed the man's E with the clay,
9:10 "Then how were your E opened?"
9:11 clay and anointed my E and said to me,
9:14 when Jesus made the clay and opened his E
9:15 put clay on my E, and I washed, and
9:17 say about him, since he has opened your E
9:21 know, nor do we know who opened his E
9:26 How did he open your E
9:30 he comes from, and yet he opened my E

9:32 any one opened the E of a man born
10:21 a demon open the E of the blind?"
11:37 he who opened the E of the blind man
11:41 Jesus lifted up his E and said, "Father, I
12:40 "He has blinded their E and hardened their heart,
12:40 should see with their E and perceive with their
17:1 he lifted up his E to heaven and said,
Acts 9:8 ground; and when his E were opened, he could
9:18 scales fell from his E and he regained his
9:40 And she opened her E, and when she saw
26:18 you to open their E, that they may turn
28:27 of hearing, and their E they have closed; lest
28:27 should perceive with their E, and hear with their
Rom 3:18 "There is no fear of God before their E
11:8 a spirit of stupor, E that should not see
11:10 for them; let their E be darkened so that
2Cor 10:7 Look at what is before your E
Gal 3:1 bewitched you, before whose E Jesus Christ was
4:15 have plucked out your E and given them to
Eph 1:18 of him, having the E of your hearts enlightened,
Heb 4:13 laid bare to the E of him with whom
1Pet 3:12 For the E of the Lord are upon the
2Pet 2:14 They have E full of adultery, insatiable for sin.
1Jn 1:1 have seen with our E, which we have looked
2:11 is going, because the darkness has blinded his E
2:16 the lust of the E and the pride of
Rev 1:14 white as snow; his E were like a flame
2:18 of God, who has E like a flame of
3:18 salve to anoint your E, that you may see.
4:6 living creatures, full of E in front and behind:
4:8 wings, are full of E all round and within,
5:6 horns and with seven E, which are the seven
7:17 God will wipe away every tear from their E
19:12 His E are like a flame of fire, and
21:4 every tear from their E, and death shall be

EYESIGHT

1Sam 3:2 that time Eli, whose E had begun to grow

EYEWITNESSES (2)

Lk 1:2 from the beginning were E and ministers of the
2Pet 1:16 Christ, but we were E of his majesty.

EZBAI

1Chr 11:37 Naarai the son of E,

EZBON (2)

Gen 46:16 Gad: Ziphion, Haggi, Shuni, E, Eri, Arodi, and Areli.
1Chr 7:7 The sons of Bela: E, Uzzi, Uzziel, Jerimoth, and

EZEKIEL (3)

Sir 49:8 It was E who saw the vision of glory
Ezek 1:3 the LORD came to E the priest, the son
24:24 Thus shall E be to you a sign; according

EZEM (3)

Josh 15:29 Beer-sheba, Biziothiah, Baalah, Iim, E,
19:3 Sheba, Moladah, Hazar-shual, Balah, E,
1Chr 4:29 Beer-sheba, Moladah, Hazar-shual, Bilhah, E, Tolad,

EZER (10)

Gen 36:21 Shobal, Zibeon, Anah, Dishon, E, and Dishan; these
36:27 are the sons of E: Bilhan, Zaavan, and Akan.
36:30 Shobal, Zibeon, Anah, Dishon, E, and Dishan; these
1Chr 1:38 Shobal, Zibeon, Anah, Dishon, E, and Dishan.
1:42 The sons of E: Bilhan, Zaavan, and Jaakan.
4:4 father of Gedor, and E the father of Hushah.
7:21 Shuthelah his son, and E and Ele-ad, whom the
12:9 gazelles upon the mountains: E the chief, Obadiah
Neh 3:19 Keilah; next to him E the son of Jeshua,
12:42 Ma-aseiah, Shemaiah, Eleazar, Uzzi, Jehohanan,

EZION-GEBER (7)

Num 33:35 they set out from Abronah, and encamped at E
33:36 they set out from E, and encamped in the
Deut 2:8 away from the Arabah road from Elath and E
1Kgs 9:26 fleet of ships at E, which is near Eloth
22:48 not go, for the ships were wrecked at E
2Chr 8:17 Then Solomon went to E and Eloth on the
20:36 to Tarshish, and they built the ships in E

EZRA (26)

Ezra 7:1 Artaxerxes king of Persia, E the son of Seraiah,
7:6 chief priest– this E went up from Babylonia.
7:10 For E had set his heart to study the
7:11 King Artaxerxes gave to E the priest, the scribe,
7:12 king of kings, to E the priest, the scribe
7:21 Beyond the River: Whatever E the priest, the scribe
7:25 "And you, E, according to the wisdom of your
10:1 While E prayed and made confession, weeping and
10:2 sons of Elam, addressed E: "We have broken faith
10:5 Then E arose and made the leading priests and
10:6 Then E withdrew from before the house of God,
10:10 And E the priest stood up and said to
10:16 E the priest selected men, heads of fathers' houses,
Neh 8:1 Gate; and they told E the scribe to bring
8:2 And E the priest brought the law before the
8:4 And E the scribe stood on a wooden pulpit
8:5 And E opened the book in the sight of
8:6 And E blessed the LORD, the great God; and
8:9 was the governor, and E the priest and scribe,
8:13 Levites, came together to E the scribe in order
9:6 And E said: "Thou art the LORD, thou alone;
12:1 and Jeshua: Seraiah, Jeremiah, E,
12:13 Jeremiah, Hananiah; of E, Meshullam; of Amariah,
12:26 the governor and of E the priest the scribe.
12:33 of Judah, and Azariah, E, Meshullam,
12:36 man of God; and E the scribe went before

EZRAH

1Chr 4:17 The sons of E: Jether, Mered, Epher, and Jalon.

EZRAHITE

1Kgs 4:31 wiser than Ethan the E, and Heman, Calcol, and

EZRI

1Chr 27:26 tilling the soil was E the son of Chelub;

F

FABRIC

Sir 38:34 they keep stable the F of the world, and

FABRICS (3)

2Chr 2:7 purple, crimson, and blue F, trained also in engraving,
2:14 purple, blue, and crimson F and fine linen, and
3:14 and purple and crimson F and fine linen, and

FACE (416)

Gen 1:2 darkness was upon the F of the deep; and
1:2 was moving over the F of the waters.
1:29 which is upon the F of all the earth,
2:6 and watered the whole F of the ground–
3:19 the sweat of your F you shall eat bread
4:14 ground; and from thy F I shall be hidden;
6:1 to multiply on the F of the ground, and
6:7 have created from the F of the ground, man
7:3 kind alive upon the F of all the earth.
7:4 blot out from the F of the ground."
7:18 ark floated on the F of the waters.
7:23 that was upon the F of the ground, man
8:8 had subsided from the F of the ground;
8:9 were still on the F of the whole earth.
8:13 looked, and behold, the F of the ground was
11:4 scattered abroad upon the F of the whole earth.
11:8 from there over the F of all the earth,
11:9 them abroad over the F of all the earth.
17:3 Abram fell on his F; and God said to
17:17 Abraham fell on his F and laughed, and said
19:1 bowed himself with his F to the earth,
31:21 Euphrates, and set his F toward the hill country
32:20 I shall see his F; perhaps he will accept
32:30 I have seen God F to face, and yet
32:30 seen God face to F, and yet my life
33:10 truly to see your F is like seeing the
33:10 is like seeing the F of God, with such
38:15 be a harlot, for she had covered her F
43:3 shall not see my F, unless your brother is
43:5 shall not see my F, unless your brother is
43:31 Then he washed his F and came out; and
44:23 you shall see my F no more.'
44:26 cannot see the man's F unless our youngest brother
46:30 I have seen your F and know that you
48:11 thought to see your F; and lo, God has
48:12 bowed himself with his F to the earth.
50:1 fell on his father's F, and wept over him,
Ex 3:6 And Moses hid his F, for he was afraid
10:5 they shall cover the F of the land, so
10:15 For they covered the F of the whole land,
10:28 yourself; never see my F again; for in the

10:28 day you see my F you shall die."
10:29 will not see your F again."
16:14 there was on the F of the wilderness a
32:12 consume them from the F of the earth?
33:11 to speak to Moses F to face, as a
33:11 to Moses face to F, as a man speaks
33:16 that are upon the F of the earth?"
33:20 "you cannot see my F; for man shall not
33:23 my back; but my F shall not be seen."
34:29 the skin of his F shone because he had
34:30 the skin of his F shone, and they were
34:33 a veil on his F;
34:35 of Israel saw the F of Moses, that the
34:35 the skin of Moses' F shone; and Moses would
34:35 the veil upon his F again, until he went
Lev 17:10 I will set my F against that person who
19:32 head, and honor the F of an old man,
20:3 myself will set my F against that man, and
20:5 I will set my F against that man and
20:6 I will set my F against that person, and
21:18 who has a mutilated F or a limb too
26:17 I will set my F against you, and you
Num 6:25 The LORD make his F to shine upon you,
11:31 two cubits above the F of the earth.
12:3 that were on the F of the earth.
12:14 but spit in her F, should she not be
14:14 O LORD, art seen F to face, and thy
14:14 art seen face to F, and thy cloud stands
16:4 he fell on his F;
22:5 Egypt; they cover the F of the earth, and
22:11 and it covers the F of the earth; now
22:31 he bowed his head, and fell on his F
24:1 omens, but set his F toward the wilderness.
Deut 1:17 be afraid of the F of man, for the
5:4 LORD spoke with you F to face at the
5:4 with you face to F at the mountain, out
6:15 you from off the F of the earth.
7:6 that are on the F of the earth.
7:10 and requites to their F those who hate him,
7:10 hates him, he will requite him to his F
14:2 that are on the F of the earth.
25:9 and spit in his F; and she shall answer
28:31 taken away before your F, and shall not be
31:17 them and hide my F from them, and they
31:18 will surely hide my F in that day on
32:20 'I will hide my F from them, I will
34:10 whom the LORD knew F to face,
34:10 LORD knew face to F,
Josh 5:14 Joshua fell on his F to the earth, and
7:6 the earth upon his F before the ark of
7:10 "Arise, why have you thus fallen upon your F
Judg 6:22 angel of the LORD F to face."
6:22 seen the angel of the LORD face to F
Ruth 2:10 she fell on her F, bowing to the ground,
1Sam 5:3 behold, Dagon had fallen F downward on the ground
5:4 behold, Dagon had fallen F downward on the ground
17:49 he fell on his F to the ground.
20:15 of David from the F of the earth,
20:41 and fell on his F to the ground, and
24:8 David bowed with his F to the earth, and
25:23 before David on her F, and bowed to the
25:41 and bowed with her F to the ground, and
28:14 he bowed with his F to the ground, and
2Sam 2:22 I lift up my F to your brother Joab?"
3:13 shall not see my F, unless you first bring
3:13 Saul's daughter, when you come to see my F
9:6 and fell on his F and did obeisance.
14:4 she fell on her F to the ground, and
14:7 nor remnant upon the F of the earth."
14:22 Joab fell on his F to the ground, and
14:33 bowed himself on his F to the ground before
18:8 battle spread over the F of all the country;
18:28 the king with his F to the earth, and
19:4 The king covered his F, and the king cried
21:1 and David sought the F of the LORD.
24:20 the king with his F to the ground.
1Kgs 1:23 the king, with his F to the ground.
1:31 Bathsheba bowed with her F to the ground, and
13:34 destroy it from the F of the earth.
18:7 and fell on his F, and said, "Is it
18:42 earth, and put his F between his knees.
19:13 it, he wrapped his F in his mantle and
21:4 and turned away his F, and would eat no
2Kgs 4:29 my staff upon the F of the child."
4:31 the staff upon the F of the child, but
8:15 spread it over his F, till he died.
9:32 he lifted up his F to the window, and
9:37 as dung upon the F of the field in
12:17 when Hazael set his F to go up against
14:8 "Come, let us look one another in the F
20:2 Then Hezekiah turned his F to the wall, and
1Chr 21:21 to David with his F to the ground.
2Chr 6:42 not turn away the F of thy anointed one!
7:14 pray and seek my F, and turn from their
20:18 his head with his F to the ground, and
25:17 "Come, let us look one another in the F
30:9 not turn away his F from you, if you
32:21 returned with shame of F to his own land.
Ezra 9:6 blush to lift my F to thee, my God,
Neh 2:2 me, "Why is your F sad, seeing you are
2:3 Why should not my F be sad, when the
Tob 2:9 the courtyard, and my F was uncovered.
3:6 do not turn thy F away from me."
3:12 my eyes and my F toward thee.
4:7 Do not turn your F away from any poor
4:7 poor man, and the F of God will not
13:6 will not hide his F from you.
Jud 2:7 will cover the whole F of the earth with
2:19 to cover the whole F of the earth to
6:3 destroy them from the F of the earth, and
6:5 shall not see my F again from this day
7:4 now lick up the F of the whole land;
7:18 and covered the whole F of the land, and
8:7 had a very lovely F; and her husband Manasseh
9:1 Judith fell upon her F, and put ashes on
10:7 and noted how her F was altered and her
10:14 words, and observed her F --she was in their
10:23 the beauty of her F; and she prostrated herself
11:21 either for beauty of F or wisdom of speech!"
13:16 went, it was my F that tricked him to
14:6 fell down on his F and his spirit failed
16:8 She anointed her F with ointment and fastened her
Esth 1:14 who saw the king's F, and sat first in
7:8 the mouth of the king, they covered Haman's F
15:7 Lifting his F, flushed with splendor, he looked at
Job 1:11 has, and he will curse thee to thy F
2:5 flesh, and he will curse thee to thy F
4:15 spirit glided past my F; the hair of my
6:28 me; for I will not lie to your F
11:15 will lift up your F without blemish; you will
13:15 yet I will defend my ways to his F
13:20 hide myself from thy F:
13:24 dost thou hide thy F, and count me as
15:27 he has covered his F with his fat, and
16:8 risen up against me, it testifies to my F
16:16 My F is red with weeping, and on my
21:31 his way to his F, and who requites him
22:26 and lift up your F to God.
23:17 in by darkness, and thick darkness covers my F
24:15 eye will see me'; and he disguises his F
24:18 carried away upon the F of the waters; their
26:9 He covers the F of the moon, and spreads
26:10 a circle upon the F of the waters at
34:29 When he hides his F, who can behold him,
37:12 commands them on the F of the habitable world.
38:30 like stone, and the F of the deep is
41:14 Who can open the doors of his F
Ps 10:11 he has hidden his F, he will never see
11:7 loves righteous deeds; the upright shall behold his F
13:1 wilt thou hide thy F from me?
17:15 I shall behold thy F in righteousness; when I
22:24 has not hid his F from him, but has
24:6 him, who seek the F of the God of
27:8 Thou hast said, "Seek ye my F
27:8 says to thee, "Thy F, LORD, do I seek."
27:9 Hide not thy F from me.
30:7 thou didst hide thy F, I was dismayed.
31:16 Let thy F shine on thy servant; save me
34:16 The F of the LORD is against evildoers, to
42:2 come and behold the F of God?
44:15 shame has covered my F,
44:24 Why dost thou hide thy F
51:9 Hide thy F from my sins, and blot out
67:1 us and make his F to shine upon us,
69:7 have borne reproach, that shame has covered my F
69:17 Hide not thy F from thy servant; for I
80:3 O God; let thy F shine, that we may
80:7 of hosts; let thy F shine, that we may
80:19 let thy F shine, that we may be saved!
84:9 God; look upon the F of thine anointed!
88:14 dost thou hide thy F from me?
102:2 Do not hide thy F from me in the

104:15 oil to make his F shine, and bread to
104:29 When thou hidest thy F, they are dismayed; when
104:30 and thou renewest the F of the ground.
119:135 Make thy F shine upon thy servant, and teach
132:10 not turn away the F of thy anointed one.
143:7 Hide not thy F from me, lest I be
Prov 7:13 him, and with impudent F she says to him:
8:27 a circle on the F of the deep,
16:15 light of a king's F there is life, and
17:24 of understanding sets his F toward wisdom, but the
21:29 puts on a bold F, but an upright man
27:19 As in water F answers to face, so the
27:19 water face answers to F, so the mind of
Eccl 8:1 man's wisdom makes his F shine, and the hardness
Song 2:14 let me see your F, let me hear your
2:14 is sweet, and your F is comely.
Wis 4:20 their lawless deeds will convict them to their F
10:5 him strong in the F of his compassion for
Sir 4:4 suppliant, nor turn your F away from the poor.
13:25 heart is a cheerful F, but to devise proverbs
14:8 eye; he averts his F and disregards people.
18:23 moment of vengeance when he turns away his F
19:24 He hides his F and pretends not to hear;
19:26 is known by his F, when you meet him.
25:16 appearance, and darkens her F like that of a
25:22 dejected mind, a gloomy F, and a wounded heart
26:4 at all times his F is cheerful.
26:17 so is a beautiful F on a stately figure.
31:6 destruction has met them F to face.
31:6 and their destruction has met them face to F
31:13 Therefore it sheds tears from every F
34:3 the likeness of a F confronting a face.
34:3 that, the likeness of a face confronting a F
35:9 gift show a cheerful F, and dedicate your tithe
37:5 sake, and in the F of battle take up
38:8 health is upon the F of the earth.
45:5 gave him the commandments F to face, the law
45:5 the commandments face to F, the law of life
Is 3:15 people, by grinding the F of the poor?" says
6:2 two he covered his F, and with two he
8:17 who is hiding his F from the house of
14:21 earth, and fill the F of the world with
23:17 the world upon the F of the earth.
29:22 no more shall his F grow pale.
38:2 Then Hezekiah turned his F to the wall, and
50:6 I hid not my F from shame and spitting.
50:7 I have set my F like a flint, and
54:8 moment I hid my F from you, but with
57:17 him, I hid my F and was angry; but
59:2 sins have hid his F from you so that
64:7 thou hast hid thy F from us, and hast
65:3 provoke me to my F continually, sacrificing in
Jer 2:27 turned their back to me, and not their F
13:26 your skirts over your F, and your shame will
17:16 came out of my lips was before thy F
18:17 my back, not my F, in the day of
21:10 I have set my F against this city for
25:26 which are on the F of the earth.
28:16 remove you from the F of the earth.
30:6 Why has every F turned pale?
32:4 shall speak with him F to face and see
32:4 with him face to F and see him eye
32:33 back and not their F; and though I have
33:5 I have hidden my F from this city because
34:3 and speak with him F to face; and you
34:3 with him face to F; and you shall go
44:11 I will set my F against you for evil,
51:51 dishonor has covered our F, for aliens have come
Lam 1:8 groans, and turns her F away.
2:3 right hand in the F of the enemy; he
Bar 1:15 God, but confusion of F, as at this day,
2:6 God, but confusion of F to us and our
Ezek 1:10 faces, each had the F of a man in
1:10 the four had the F of a lion on
1:10 the four had the F of an ox on
1:10 the four had the F of an eagle at
1:28 I fell upon my F, and I heard the
3:8 I have made your F hard against their faces,
3:23 the river Chebar; and I fell on my F
4:3 city; and set your F toward it, and let
4:7 you shall set your F toward the siege of
6:2 of man, set your F toward the mountains of
7:22 I will turn my F from them, that they
9:8 I fell upon my F, and cried, "Ah Lord
10:14 four faces: the first F was the face of
10:14 first face was the F of the cherub, and
10:14 cherub, and the second F was the face of
10:14 second face was the F of a man, and
10:14 and the third the F of a lion, and
10:14 and the fourth the F of an eagle.
11:13 fell down upon my F, and cried with a
12:6 you shall cover your F, that you may not
12:12 he shall cover his F, that he may not
13:17 of man, set your F against the daughters of
14:4 his iniquity before his F, and yet comes to
14:7 his iniquity before his F, and yet comes to
14:8 I will set my F against that man, I
15:7 I will set my F against them; though they
15:7 when I set my F against them.
20:35 into judgment with you F to face.
20:35 will enter into judgment with you face to F
20:46 of man, set your F toward the south, preach
21:2 of man, set your F toward Jerusalem and preach
25:2 of man, set your F toward the Ammonites, and
28:21 of man, set your F toward Sidon, and prophesy
29:2 of man, set your F against Pharaoh king of
34:6 scattered over all the F of the earth, with
35:2 of man, set your F against Mount Seir, and
38:2 of man, set your F toward Gog, of the
38:20 that are upon the F of the earth, shall
39:14 those remaining upon the F of the land, so
39:23 that I hid my F from them and gave
39:24 transgressions, and hid my F from them.
39:29 will not hide my F any more from them,
41:19 had two faces: the F of a man toward
41:19 one side, and the F of a young lion
43:3 the river Chebar; and I fell upon my F
43:17 of the altar shall F east."
44:4 of the LORD; and I fell upon my F
Dan 2:46 Nebuchadnezzar fell upon his F, and did homage to
3:19 expression of his F was changed against Shadrach,
3:41 follow thee, we fear thee and seek thy F
8:5 the west across the F of the whole earth,
8:17 came, I was frightened and fell upon my F
8:18 deep sleep with my F to the ground; but
9:3 Then I turned my F to the Lord God,
9:7 to us confusion of F, as at this day,
9:8 Lord, belongs confusion of F, to our kings, to
9:17 O Lord, cause thy F to shine upon thy
10:6 was like beryl, his F like the appearance of
10:9 I fell on my F in a deep sleep
10:9 deep sleep with my F to the ground.
10:15 words, I turned my F toward the ground and
11:17 He shall set his F to come with the
11:18 he shall turn his F to the coastlands, and
11:19 he shall turn his F back toward the fortresses
Hos 2:2 her harlotry from her F, and her adultery from
5:5 Israel testifies to his F; Ephraim shall stumble in
5:15 guilt and seek my F, and in their distress
7:3 their deeds encompass them, they are before my F
10:7 a chip on the F of the waters.
Mic 3:4 he will hide his F from them at that
Nah 3:5 your skirts over your F; and I will let
Zeph 1:2 away everything from the F of the earth," says
1:3 off mankind from the F of the earth," says
Zech 5:3 goes out over the F of the whole land;
1Mac 4:40 They fell F down on the ground, and sounded
7:28 men to see you F to face in peace."
7:28 see you face to F in peace."
11:68 they themselves met him F to face.
11:68 mountains, but they themselves met him face to F
2Mac 3:16 at heart, for his F and the change in
Mt 6:17 head and wash your F,
11:10 my messenger before thy F, who shall prepare thy
17:2 before them, and his F shone like the sun,
18:10 angels always behold the F of my Father who
26:39 he fell on his F and prayed, "My Father,
26:67 they spat in his F, and struck him; and
Mk 1:2 my messenger before thy F, who shall prepare thy
14:65 and to cover his F, and to strike him,
Lk 5:12 he fell on his F and besought him, "Lord,
7:27 my messenger before thy F, who shall prepare thy
9:51 up, he set his F to go to Jerusalem.
9:53 him, because his F was set toward Jerusalem.
17:16 he fell on his F at Jesus' feet, giving
21:35 who dwell upon the F of the whole earth.
Jn 11:44 with bandages, and his F wrapped with a cloth.
Acts 6:15 council saw that his F was like the face
6:15 face was like the F of an angel.
17:26 live on all the F of the earth, having
20:25 kingdom will see my F no more.
20:38 they should see his F no more.

25:16 accused met the accusers F to face, and had
25:16 the accusers face to F, and had opportunity to
27:15 caught and could not F the wind, we gave
1Cor 13:12 mirror dimly, but then F to face.
13:12 in a mirror dimly, but then face to F
14:25 so, falling on his F, he will worship God
2Cor 3:7 not look at Moses' F because of its brightness,
3:13 a veil over his F so that the Israelites
3:18 we all, with unveiled F, beholding the glory of
4:6 of God in the F of Christ.
10:1 who am humble when F to face with you,
10:1 humble when face to F with you, but bold
11:20 puts on airs, or strikes you in the F
Gal 2:11 opposed him to his F, because he stood condemned.
Col 2:1 have not seen my F,
1Thes 2:2 of God in the F of great opposition.
2:17 desire to see you F to face;
2:17 see you face to F;
3:10 we may see you F to face and supply
3:10 see you face to F and supply what is
Jas 1:22 who observes his natural F in a mirror;
1Pet 3:12 But the F of the Lord is against those
2Jn 1:12 and talk with you F to face, so that
1:12 with you face to F, so that our joy
3Jn 1:14 we will talk together F to face.
1:14 soon, and we will talk together face to F
Rev 1:16 two-edged sword, and his F was like the sun
4:7 living creature with the F of a man, and
6:16 hide us from the F of him who is
10:1 his head, and his F was like the sun,
22:4 they shall see his F, and his name shall

FACED (16)

1Kgs 8:14 Then the king F about, and blessed all the
2Kgs 14:11 Amaziah king of Judah F one another in battle
2Chr 6:3 Then the king F about, and blessed all the
25:21 Amaziah king of Judah F one another in battle
Tob 4:4 my son, that she F many dangers for you
Esth 9:26 of what they had F in this matter, and
Job 31:23 I could not have F his majesty.
Ezek 10:11 direction the front wheel F the others followed
40:20 was a gate which F toward the north, belonging
40:22 of the gate which F toward the east; and
40:31 Its vestibule F the outer court, and palm trees
40:34 Its vestibule F the outer court, and it had
40:37 Its vestibule F the outer court, and it had
42:15 by the gate which F east, and measured the
47:1 east (for the temple F east); and the water
1Mac 4:61 have a stronghold that F Idumea.

FACES (83)

Gen 9:23 of their father; their F were turned away, and
30:40 lambs, and set the F of the flocks toward
40:7 house, "Why are your F downcast today?"
42:6 before him with their F to the ground.
Ex 25:20 with their wings, their F one to another; toward
25:20 mercy seat shall the F of the cherubim be.
37:9 their wings, with their F one to another; toward
37:9 mercy seat were the F of the cherubim.
Lev 9:24 saw it, they shouted, and fell on their F
Num 14:5 Aaron fell on their F before all the assembly
16:22 they fell on their F, and said, "O God,
16:45 And they fell on their F
20:6 the tent of meeting, and fell on their F
Josh 15:2 from the bay that F southward;
Judg 13:20 they fell on their F to the ground.
2Sam 19:5 covered with shame the F of all your servants,
1Kgs 18:39 they fell on their F; and they said, "The
1Chr 12:8 shield and spear, whose F were like the faces
12:8 faces were like the F of lions, and who
21:16 the elders, clothed in sackcloth, fell upon their F
2Chr 7:3 bowed down with their F to the earth on
29:6 have turned away their F from the habitation of
Neh 8:6 the LORD with their F to the ground.
Tob 12:16 they fell upon their F, for they were afraid.
Jud 4:6 Betomesthaim, which F Esdraelon opposite the plain
6:19 this day upon the F of those who are
7:3 Bethulia to Cyamon, which F Esdraelon.
Job 9:24 wicked; he covers the F of its judges--
40:13 dust together; bind their F in the world below.
Ps 21:12 will aim at their F with your bows.
34:5 be radiant; so your F shall never be ashamed.
83:16 Fill their F with shame, that they may seek
Wis 17:4 dismal phantoms with gloomy F appeared.
Sir 50:17 the ground upon their F to worship their Lord,
Is 8:21 God, and turn their F upward;
13:8 at one another; their F will be aflame.
25:8 away tears from all F, and the reproach of
49:23 With their F to the ground they shall bow
53:3 whom men hide their F he was despised, and
Jer 5:3 They have made their F harder than rock; they
42:15 If you set your F to enter Egypt and
42:17 men who set their F to go to Egypt
44:12 who have set their F to come to the
50:5 way to Zion, with F turned toward it, saying,
Bar 6:13 in purple robes, their F are wiped because of
6:21 not notice when their F have been blackened by
Ezek 1:6 but each had four F, and each of them
1:8 the four had their F and their wings thus:
1:10 the likeness of their F, each had the face
1:11 Such were their F
3:8 face hard against their F, and your forehead hard
7:18 shame is upon all F, and baldness on all
8:3 the inner court that F north, where was the
8:16 the LORD, and their F toward the east, worshiping
9:2 the upper gate, which F north, every man with
10:14 every one had four F: the first face was
10:21 Each had four F, and each four wings, and
10:22 the likeness of their F, they were the very
10:22 they were the very F whose appearance I had
11:1 of the LORD, which F east.
14:3 their iniquity before their F; should I let myself
14:6 and turn away your F from all your abominations.
20:47 be quenched, and all F from south to north
27:35 are horribly afraid, their F are convulsed.
40:45 me, This chamber which F south is for the
40:46 and the chamber which F north is for the
41:18 Every cherub had two F:
44:1 of the sanctuary, which F east; and it was
46:1 the inner court that F east shall be shut
47:2 the outer gate, that F toward the east; and
Joel 2:6 are in anguish, all F grow pale.
Nah 2:10 on all loins, all F grow pale!
Mal 2:3 spread dung upon your F, the dung of your
1Mac 4:55 people fell on their F and worshiped and blessed
7:3 he said, "Do not let me see their F
2Mac 7:6 the people to their F, when he said, ïAnd
Mt 6:16 for they disfigure their F that their fasting may
17:6 they fell on their F, and were filled with
Lk 24:5 frightened and bowed their F to the ground, the
Rev 7:11 they fell on their F before the throne and
9:7 crowns of gold; their F were like human faces,
9:7 faces were like human F,
11:16 God fell on their F and worshiped God,

FACETS

Zech 3:9 single stone with seven F, I will engrave its

FACING (26)

Num 2:2 houses; they shall encamp F the tent of meeting
1Kgs 7:25 upon twelve oxen, three F north, three facing west,
7:25 three facing north, three F west, three facing south,
7:25 three facing west, three F south, and three facing
7:25 facing south, and three F east; the sea was
22:35 up in his chariot F the Syrians, until at
2Chr 3:13 stood on their feet, F the nave.
4:4 upon twelve oxen, three F north, three facing west,
4:4 three facing north, three F west, three facing south,
4:4 three facing west, three F south, and three facing
4:4 facing south, and three F east; the sea was
18:34 up in his chariot F the Syrians until evening;
Neh 8:3 he read from it F the square before the
Jer 1:13 see a boiling pot, F away from the north."
Ezek 40:6 went into the gateway F east, going up its
40:44 of the north gate F south, the other at
40:44 of the south gate F north.
41:12 The building that was F the temple yard on
41:15 length of the building F the yard which was
42:3 the inner court, and F the pavement which belonged
43:1 the gate, the gate F east.
43:4 temple by the gate F east,
46:12 the LORD, the gate F east shall be opened
1Mac 13:13 Simon encamped in Adida, F the plain.
Mk 15:38 the centurion, who stood F him, saw that he
Phil 4:12 learned the secret of F plenty and hunger, abundance

FACT (12)

1Sam 24:11 hand; for by the F that I cut off
2Mac 3:8 and Phoenicia, but in F to carry out the
4:17 laws -- a F which later events will
6:13 In F, not to let the impious alone for
13:25 over the treaty; in F they were so angry

FAINT (43)

Deut 20:3 let not your heart F; do not fear, or
25:18 way, when you were F and weary, and cut
Judg 8:4 who were with him, F yet pursuing.
8:5 me; for they are F, and I am pursuing
8:15 should give bread to your men who are F
1Sam 14:28 And the people were F
14:31 the people were very F;
2Sam 16:2 wine for those who F in the wilderness to
Jud 8:9 ruler, because they were F for lack of water,
8:31 our cisterns and we will no longer be F
Esth 15:7 and turned pale and F, and collapsed upon the
Job 23:16 has made my heart F; the Almighty has terrified
Ps 61:2 I call to thee, when my heart is F
142:3 When my spirit is F, thou knowest my way!
Prov 24:10 If you F in the day of adversity, your
Sir 2:13 Woe to the F heart, for it has no
Is 1:5 whole head is sick, and the whole heart F
7:4 let your heart be F because of these two
29:8 is drinking and awakes F, with his thirst not
40:28 He does not F or grow weary, his understanding
40:29 gives power to the F, and to him who
40:30 Even youths shall F and be weary, and young
40:31 not be weary, they shall walk and not F
44:12 strength fails, he drinks no water and is F
57:10 for your strength, and so you were not F
61:3 praise instead of a F spirit; that they may
Jer 51:46 Let not your heart F, and be not fearful
Lam 1:13 has left me stunned, F all the day long.
1:22 my groans are many and my heart is F
2:11 because infants and babes F in the streets of
2:12 as they F like wounded men in the streets
2:19 of your children, who F for hunger at the
Ezek 21:7 feeble, every spirit will F and all knees will
31:15 of the field shall F because of it.
Amos 8:13 the young men shall F for thirst.
Jon 4:8 so that he was F; and he asked that
Nah 2:10 Hearts F and knees tremble, anguish is on all
1Mac 1:26 and young men became F, the beauty of women
3:17 And we are F, for we have eaten nothing
9:8 He became F, but he said to those who
2Mac 3:24 of God, and became F with terror.
Mt 15:32 away hungry, lest they F on the way."
Mk 8:3 their homes, they will F on the way; and

FAINTED (5)

Gen 45:26 And his heart F, for he did not believe
Jud 7:23 women and young men F from thirst and fell
Ps 107:5 and thirsty, their soul F within them.
Is 51:20 Your sons have F, they lie at the head
Jon 2:7 When my soul F within me, I remembered the

FAINTHEARTED (7)

Deut 20:8 What man is there that is fearful and F
Josh 2:24 of the land are F because of us."
Sir 4:9 and do not be F in judging a case.
7:10 Do not be F in your prayer, nor neglect
1Mac 3:56 planting vineyards, or were F, that each should return
1Thes 5:14 the idlers, encourage the F, help the weak, be
Heb 12:3 so that you may not grow weary or F

FAINTING (3)

Esth 15:15 But as she was speaking, she fell F
Jer 4:31 I am F before murderers."
Lk 21:26 and the waves, men F with fear and with

FAINTNESS

Lev 26:36 left, I will send F into their hearts in

FAINTS (5)

Job 19:27 My heart F within me!
Ps 63:1 for thee; my flesh F for thee, as in
77:3 and I moan; I meditate, and my spirit F
84:2 My soul longs, yea, F for the courts of
143:4 Therefore my spirit F within me; my heart within

FAIR (29)

Gen 6:2 daughters of men were F; and they took to
24:16 The maiden was very F to look upon, a
26:7 Rebekah"; because she was F to look upon.
Num 24:5 his eyes uncovered: how F are your tents, O
Esth 1:11 beauty; for she was F to behold.
Job 26:13 the heavens were made F; his hand pierced the
42:15 were no women so F as Job's daughters; and
Prov 1:9 for they are a F garland for your head,
4:10 on your head a F garland; she will bestow
Song 2:10 "Arise, my love, my F one, and come away;
2:13 Arise, my love, my F one, and come away.
4:7 You are all F, my love; there is no
6:10 forth like the dawn, F as the moon, bright
7:6 How F and pleasant you are, O loved one,
Sir 3:15 favor; as frost in F weather, your sins will
Jer 11:16 'A green olive tree, F with goodly fruit'; but
12:6 not, though they speak F words to you."
Ezek 16:17 You also took your F jewels of my gold
16:39 clothes and take your F jewels, and leave you
31:3 cedar in Lebanon, with F branches and forest shade,
Dan 4:12 Its leaves were F and its fruit abundant, and
4:21 earth; whose leaves were F and its fruit abundant,
Hos 10:11 and I spared her F neck; but I will
Amos 8:13 "In that day the F virgins and the young
Zech 9:17 how good and how F it shall be!
Mt 15:26 answered, "It is not F to take the children's
16:2 say, 'It will be F weather; for the sky
Acts 27:8 to a place called F Havens, near which was
Rom 16:18 own appetites, and by F and flattering words they

FAIRER

Judg 15:2 not her younger sister F than she?

FAIREST (5)

1Kgs 20:3 gold are mine; your F wives and children also
Ps 45:2 You are the F of the sons of men;
Song 1:8 do not know, O F among women, follow in
5:9 than another beloved, O F among women?
6:1 your beloved gone, O F among women?

FAIRLY

Col 4:1 your slaves justly and F, knowing that you also

FAITH (274)

Lev 5:15 commits a breach of F and sins unwittingly in
6:2 commits a breach of F against the LORD by
Num 5:6 men commit by breaking F with the LORD, and
Deut 32:51 people; because you broke F with me in the
Josh 7:1 people of Israel broke F in regard to the
22:20 son of Zerah break F in the matter of
22:22 or in breach of F toward the LORD, spare
Judg 9:15 trees, 'If in good F you are anointing me
9:16 you acted in good F and honor when you
9:19 have acted in good F and honor with Jerubbaal
Ezra 10:2 Ezra: "We have broken F with our God and
Job 39:12 Do you have F in him that he will
Ps 78:22 because they had no F in God, and did
106:24 pleasant land, having no F in his promise.
116:10 I kept my F, even when I said, "I
146:6 in them; who keeps F for ever;
Sir 4:16 If he has F in her he will obtain
27:17 your friend and keep F with him; but if
29:3 your word and keep F with him, and on
40:12 blotted out, but good F will stand for ever.
Is 26:2 righteous nation which keeps F may enter in.
Hab 2:4 fail, but the righteous shall live by his F
1Mac 10:27 continue still to keep F with us, and we
2Mac 8:1 continued in the Jewish F, and so they gathered
Mt 6:30 much more clothe you, O men of little F
8:10 not even in Israel have I found such F
8:26 "Why are you afraid, O men of little F
9:2 when Jesus saw their F he said to the
9:22 "Take heart, daughter; your F has made you well."
9:29 saying, "According to your F be it done to
14:31 "O man of little F, why did you doubt?"
15:28 Jesus answered her, "O woman, great is your F
16:8 "O men of little F, why do you discuss
17:20 He said to them, "Because of your little F
17:20 you, if you have F as a grain of
21:21 you, if you have F and never doubt, you
21:22 in prayer, you will receive, if you have F
23:22 justice and mercy and F; these you ought to
Mk 2:5 when Jesus saw their F, he said to the
4:40 Have you no F
5:34 to her, "Daughter, your F has made you well;
10:52 "Go your way; your F has made you well."
11:22 Jesus answered them, "Have F in God.
Lk 5:20 when he saw their F he said, "Man, your
7:9 not even in Israel have I found such F
7:50 to the woman, "Your F has saved you; go
8:25 He said to them, "Where is your F
8:48 to her, "Daughter, your F has made you well;
12:28 will he clothe you, O men of little F
17:5 The apostles said to the Lord, "Increase our F
17:6 said, "If you had F as a grain of

	17:19	go your way; your F has made you well."
	18:8	comes, will he find F on earth?"
	18:42	"Receive your sight; your F has made you well."
	22:32	for you that your F may not fail; and
Acts	3:16	And his name, by F in his name, has
	3:16	and know; and the F which is through Jesus
	6:5	a man full of F and of the Holy
	6:7	many of the priests were obedient to the F
	11:24	man, full of the Holy Spirit and of F
	13:8	seeking to turn away the proconsul from the F
	14:9	seeing that he had F to be made well,
	14:22	to continue in the F, and saying that through
	14:27	opened a door of F to the Gentiles.
	15:9	us and them, but cleansed their hearts by F
	16:5	were strengthened in the F, and they increased in
	20:21	to God and of F in our Lord Jesus
	24:23	heard him speak upon F in Christ Jesus.
	26:18	who are sanctified by F in me.'
	27:25	men, for I have F in God that it
Rom	1:5	about the obedience of F for the sake of
	1:8	of you, because your F is proclaimed in all
	1:12	encouraged by each other's F, both yours and mine.
	1:16	every one who has F, to the Jew first
	1:17	God is revealed through F for faith; as it
	1:17	revealed through faith for F; as it is written,
	1:17	written, "He who through F is righteous shall live."
	3:22	righteousness of God through F in Jesus Christ for
	3:25	expiation by his blood, to be received by F
	3:26	justifies him who has F in Jesus.
	3:27	No, but on the principle of F
	3:28	man is justified by F apart from works of
	3:30	the ground of their F and the uncircumcised through
	3:30	of their faith and the uncircumcised through their F
	3:31	Do we then overthrow the law by this F
	4:5	justifies the ungodly, his F is reckoned as
	4:9	We say that F was reckoned to Abraham as
	4:11	which he had by F while he was still
	4:12	the example of the F which our father Abraham
	4:13	through the law but through the righteousness of F
	4:14	to be the heirs, F is null and the
	4:16	why it depends on F, in order that the
	4:16	those who share the F of Abraham, for he
	4:19	did not weaken in F when he considered his
	4:20	grew strong in his F as he gave glory
	4:22	That is why his F was "reckoned to him
	5:1	we are justified by F, we have peace with
	9:30	that is, righteousness through F;
	9:32	not pursue it through F, but as if it
	10:4	every one who has F may be justified.
	10:6	the righteousness based on F says, Do not say
	10:8	is, the word of F which we preach);
	10:17	So F comes from what is heard, and what
	11:20	their unbelief, but you stand fast only through F
	12:3	to the measure of F which God has assigned
	12:6	in proportion to our F;
	14:1	who is weak in F, welcome him, but not
	14:22	The F that you have, keep between yourself and
	14:23	does not act from F; for whatever does not
	14:23	does not proceed from F is sin.
	16:25	about the obedience of F --
1Cor	2:5	of power, that your F might not rest in
	12:9	same Spirit, to another F by the same Spirit,
	13:2	if I have all F, so as to remove
	13:13	So F, hope, love abide, these three; but the
	15:14	in vain and your F is in vain.
	15:17	not been raised, your F is futile and you
	16:13	stand firm in your F, be courageous, be strong.
2Cor	1:24	lord it over your F; we work with you
	1:24	your joy, for you stand firm in your F
	4:13	the same spirit of F as he had who
	5:7	for we walk by F, not by sight.
	8:7	excel in everything--in F, in utterance, in knowledge,
	10:15	is that as your F increases, our field among
	13:5	to see whether you are holding to your F
Gal	1:23	is now preaching the F he once tried to
	2:16	the law but through F in Jesus Christ, even
	2:16	to be justified by F in Christ, and not
	2:20	flesh I live by F in the Son of
	3:2	works of the law, or by hearing with F
	3:5	works of the law, or by hearing with F
	3:7	it is men of F who are the sons
	3:8	justify the Gentiles by F, preached the gospel
	3:9	who are men of F are blessed with Abraham
	3:9	of faith are blessed with Abraham who had F
	3:11	for "He who through F is righteous shall live";
	3:12	does not rest on F, for "He who does
	3:14	might receive the promise of the Spirit through F
	3:22	what was promised to F in Jesus Christ might
	3:23	Now before F came, we were confined under the
	3:23	kept under restraint until F should be revealed.
	3:24	Christ came, that we might be justified by F
	3:25	But now that F has come, we are no
	3:26	Jesus you are all sons of God, through F
	5:5	through the Spirit, by F, we wait for the
	5:6	of any avail, but F working through love.
	6:10	to those who are of the household of F
Eph	1:15	have heard of your F in the Lord Jesus
	2:8	have been saved through F; and this is not
	3:12	of access through our F in him.
	3:17	in your hearts through F; that you, being rooted
	4:5	call, one Lord, one F, one baptism,
	4:13	the unity of the F and of the knowledge
	6:16	taking the shield of F, with which you can
	6:23	brethren, and love with F, from God the Father
Phil	1:25	and joy in the F,
	1:27	by side for the F of the gospel,
	2:17	sacrificial offering of your F, I am glad and
	3:9	that which is through F in Christ, the righteousness
	3:9	God that depends on F;
Col	1:4	have heard of your F in Christ Jesus and
	1:23	you continue in the F, stable and steadfast, not
	2:5	the firmness of your F in Christ.
	2:7	and established in the F, just as you were
	2:12	raised with him through F in the working of
1Thes	1:3	Father your work of F and labor of love
	1:8	and Achaia, but your F in God has gone
	3:2	establish you in your F and to exhort you,
	3:5	I might know your F, for fear that somehow
	3:6	good news of your F and love and reported
	3:7	about you through your F;
	3:10	face and supply what is lacking in your F
	5:8	on the breastplate of F and love, and for
2Thes	1:3	is fitting, because your F is growing abundantly, and
	1:4	for your steadfastness and F in all your persecutions
	1:11	resolve and work of F by his power,
	3:2	wicked and evil men; for not all have F
1Tim	1:2	true child in the F: Grace, mercy, and peace
	1:4	training that is in F;
	1:5	pure heart and a good conscience and sincere F
	1:14	for me with the F and love that are
	1:19	the good warfare, holding F and a good conscience.
	1:19	made shipwreck of their F,
	2:7	of the Gentiles in F and truth.
	2:15	if she continues in F and love and holiness,
	3:9	the mystery of the F with a clear conscience.
	3:13	great confidence in the F which is in Christ
	4:1	will depart from the F by giving heed to
	4:6	the words of the F and of the good
	4:12	conduct, in love, in F, in purity.
	5:8	he has disowned the F and is worse than
	6:10	wandered away from the F and pierced their hearts
	6:11	aim at righteousness, godliness, F, love, steadfastness,
	6:12	good fight of the F; take hold of the
	6:21	some have missed the mark as regards the F
2Tim	1:5	reminded of your sincere F, a faith that dwelt
	1:5	your sincere faith, a F that dwelt first in
	1:13	from me, in the F and love which are
	2:18	They are upsetting the F of some.
	2:22	and aim at righteousness, F, love, and peace, along
	3:8	corrupt mind and counterfeit F;
	3:10	aim in life, my F, my patience, my love,
	3:15	you for salvation through F in Christ Jesus.
	4:7	have finished the race, I have kept the F
Tit	1:1	Christ, to further the F of God's elect and
	1:3	child in a common F: Grace and peace from
	1:12	be sound in the F,
	2:2	serious, sensible, sound in F, in love, and in
	3:15	Greet those who love us in the F
Philem	1:5	love and of the F which you have toward
	1:6	the sharing of your F may promote the knowledge
Heb	4:2	did not meet with F in the hearers.
	6:1	dead works and of F toward God,
	6:12	of those who through F and patience inherit the
	10:22	in full assurance of F, with our hearts sprinkled
	10:38	one shall live by F, and if he shrinks
	10:39	of those who have F and keep their souls.
	11:1	Now F is the assurance of things hoped for,
	11:3	By F we understand that the world was created
	11:4	By F Abel offered to God a more acceptable
	11:4	died, but through his F he is still speaking.
	11:5	By F Enoch was taken up so that he
	11:6	And without F it is impossible to please him.

	11:7	By F Noah, being warned by God concerning events
	11:7	an heir of the righteousness which comes by F
	11:8	By F Abraham obeyed when he was called to
	11:9	By F he sojourned in the land of promise,
	11:11	By F Sarah herself received power to conceive, even
	11:13	These all died in F, not having received what
	11:17	By F Abraham, when he was tested, offered up
	11:20	By F Isaac invoked future blessings on Jacob and
	11:21	By F Jacob, when dying, blessed each of the
	11:22	By F Joseph, at the end of his life,
	11:23	By F Moses, when he was born, was hid
	11:24	By F Moses, when he was grown up, refused
	11:27	By F he left Egypt, not being afraid of
	11:28	By F he kept the Passover and sprinkled the
	11:29	By F the people crossed the Red Sea as
	11:30	By F the walls of Jericho fell down after
	11:31	By F Rahab the harlot did not perish with
	11:33	who through F conquered kingdoms, enforced
	11:39	well attested by their F, did not receive what
	12:2	and perfecter of our F, who for the joy
	13:7	the outcome of their life, and imitate their F
Jas	1:3	the testing of your F produces steadfastness.
	1:6	let him ask in F, with no doubting, for
	2:1	as you hold the F of our Lord Jesus
	2:5	to be rich in F and heirs of the
	2:14	man says he has F but has not works?
	2:14	Can his F save him?
	2:17	So F by itself, if it has no works,
	2:18	will say, "You have F and I have works."
	2:18	Show me your F apart from your works, and
	2:18	I by my works will show you my F
	2:20	you shallow man, that F apart from works is
	2:22	You see that F was active along with his
	2:22	with his works, and F was completed by works,
	2:24	works and not by F alone.
	2:26	spirit is dead, so F apart from works is
	5:15	and the prayer of F will save the sick
1Pet	1:5	power are guarded through F for a salvation ready
	1:7	the genuineness of your F, more precious than gold
	1:9	the outcome of your F you obtain the salvation
	1:21	glory, so that your F and hope are in
	5:9	him, firm in your F, knowing that the same
2Pet	1:1	who have obtained a F of equal standing with
	1:5	effort to supplement your F with virtue, and virtue
1Jn	5:4	is the victory that overcomes the world, our F
Jude	1:3	to contend for the F which was once for
	1:20	on your most holy F; pray in the Holy
Rev	2:13	did not deny my F even in the days
	2:19	works, your love and F and service and patient
	13:10	for the endurance and F of the saints.
	14:12	of God and the F of Jesus.

FAITHFUL (95)

Deut	7:9	God is God, the F God who keeps covenant
Judg	5:15	with Deborah, and Issachar F to Barak; into the
1Sam	2:9	the feet of his F ones; but the wicked
	2:35	up for myself a F priest, who shall do
	22:14	your servants is so F as David, who is
2Sam	20:19	who are peaceable and F in Israel; you seek
2Chr	31:18	multitude; for they were F in keeping themselves
	31:20	good and right and F before the LORD his
Neh	7:2	he was a more F and God-fearing man than
	9:8	didst find his heart F before thee, and didst
	13:13	for they were counted F; and their duty was
Ps	12:1	is godly; for the F have vanished from among
	31:5	redeemed me, O LORD, F God.
	31:23	The LORD preserves the F, but abundantly requites
	50:5	"Gather to me my F ones, who made a
	69:13	With thy F help
	78:8	whose spirit was not F to God.
	89:19	a vision to thy F one, and say: "I
	101:6	with favor on the F in the land, that
	111:7	of his hands are F and just; all his
	145:13	The LORD is F in all his words, and
	149:1	song, his praise in the assembly of the F
	149:5	Let the F exult in glory; let them sing
	149:9	glory for all his F ones.
Prov	13:17	into trouble, but a F envoy brings healing.
	14:5	A F witness does not lie, but a false
	20:6	own loyalty, but a F man who can find?
	25:13	of harvest is a F messenger to those who
	27:6	F are the wounds of a friend; profuse are
	28:20	A F man will abound with blessings, but he
Wis	3:9	understand truth, and the F will abide with him
Sir	1:12	is created with the F in the womb.
	6:14	A F friend is a sturdy shelter: he that
	6:15	so precious as a F friend, and no scales
	6:16	A F friend is an elixir of life; and
	37:13	no one is more F to you than it
	44:21	and when he was tested he was found F
	48:22	who was great and F in his vision.
Is	1:21	How the F city has become a harlot, she
	1:26	city of righteousness, the F city."
	25:1	plans formed of old, F and sure.
	49:7	the LORD, who is F, the Holy One of
Jer	42:5	be a true and F witness against us if
Dan	6:4	fault, because he was F, and no error or
Hos	11:12	by God, and is F to the Holy One.
Zech	8:3	shall be called the F city, and the mountain
1Mac	2:52	Was not Abraham found F when tested, and it
	3:13	including a body of F men who stayed with
	7:8	the kingdom and was F to the king.
2Mac	1:2	Isaac and Jacob, his F servants.
Mt	24:45	"Who then is the F and wise servant, whom
	25:21	'Well done, good and F servant; you have been
	25:21	servant; you have been F over a little, I
	25:23	'Well done, good and F servant; you have been
	25:23	servant; you have been F over a little, I
Lk	12:42	"Who then is the F and wise steward, whom
	16:10	"He who is F in a very little is
	16:10	a very little is F also in much; and
	16:11	you have not been F in the unrighteous mammon,
	16:12	you have not been F in that which is
	19:17	Because you have been F in a very little,
Acts	11:23	them all to remain F to the Lord with
	16:15	judged me to be F to the Lord, come
1Cor	1:9	God is F, by whom you were called into
	4:17	Timothy, my beloved and F child in the Lord,
	10:13	God is F, and he will not let you
2Cor	1:18	surely as God is F, our word to you
Eph	1:1	saints who are also F in Christ Jesus:
	6:21	the beloved brother and F minister in the Lord
Col	1:2	To the saints and F brethren in Christ at
	1:7	He is a F minister of Christ on our
	4:7	a beloved brother and F minister and fellow servant
	4:9	with him Onesimus, the F and beloved brother, who
1Thes	5:24	who calls you is F, and he will do
2Thes	3:3	But the Lord is F; he will strengthen you
1Tim	1:12	because he judged me F by appointing me to
	3:11	no slanderers, but temperate, F in all things.
2Tim	2:2	many witnesses entrust to F men who will be
	2:13	are faithless, he remains F -- for he cannot
Heb	2:17	become a merciful and F high priest in the
	3:2	He was F to him who appointed him, just
	3:2	as Moses also was F in God's house.
	3:5	God.) Now Moses was F in all God's house
	3:6	later, but Christ was F over God's house as
	10:23	he who promised is F;
	11:11	since she considered him F who had promised.
1Pet	4:19	their souls to a F Creator.
	5:12	By Silvanus, a F brother as I regard him,
1Jn	1:9	our sins, he is F and just, and will
Rev	1:5	from Jesus Christ the F witness, the first-born of
	2:10	Be F unto death, and I will give you
	2:13	Antipas my witness, my F one, who was killed
	3:14	of the Amen, the F and true witness, the
	17:14	those with him are called and chosen and F
	19:11	upon it is called F and True, and in

FAITHFULLY (12)

Josh	2:14	will deal kindly and F with you when the
1Sam	12:24	LORD, and serve him F with all your heart;
2Chr	31:12	And they F brought in the contributions, the tithes
	31:15	Amariah, and Shecaniah were F assisting him in the
	34:12	And the men did the work F
Neh	9:33	for thou hast dealt F and we have acted
Prov	12:22	but those who act F are his delight.
Sir	7:20	who performs his work F, or a hired laborer
	15:15	commandments, and to act F is a matter of
Is	42:3	not quench; he will F bring forth justice.
	61:8	and wrong; I will F give them their recompense,
Jer	23:28	him who has my word speak my word F

FAITHFULNESS (75)

Gen	24:27	steadfast love and his F toward my master.
	32:10	love and all the F which thou hast shown
Ex	34:6	in steadfast love and F,
Deut	32:4	A God of F and without iniquity, just and
	32:20	a perverse generation, children in whom is no F
Josh	24:14	in sincerity and in F; put away the gods
1Sam	26:23	his righteousness and his F; for the LORD gave
2Sam	2:6	show steadfast love and F to you!

15:20 show steadfast love and F to you."
1Kgs 2:4 walk before me in F with all their heart
3:6 walked before thee in F, in righteousness, and in
2Kgs 20:3 walked before thee in F and with a whole
2Chr 19:9 of the LORD, in F, and with your whole
32:1 and these acts of F Sennacherib king of Assyria
Ps 25:10 are steadfast love and F, for those who keep
26:3 and I walk in F to thee.
30:9 Will it tell of thy F
33:4 upright; and all his work is done in F
36:5 to the heavens, thy F to the clouds.
40:10 have spoken of thy F and thy salvation; I
40:10 steadfast love and thy F from the great congregation.
40:11 steadfast love and thy F ever preserve me!
54:5 with evil; in thy F put an end to
57:3 will send forth his steadfast love and his F
57:10 to the heavens, thy F to the clouds.
61:7 bid steadfast love and F watch over him!
71:22 the harp for thy F, O my God; I
85:10 Steadfast love and F will meet; righteousness and
85:11 F will spring up from the ground, and righteousness
86:15 to anger and abounding in steadfast love and F
88:11 the grave, or thy F in Abaddon?
89:1 I will proclaim thy F to all generations.
89:2 established for ever, thy F is firm as the
89:5 wonders, O LORD, thy F in the assembly of
89:8 O LORD, with thy F round about thee?
89:14 throne; steadfast love and F go before thee.
89:24 My F and my steadfast love shall be with
89:33 my steadfast love, or be false to my F
89:49 old, which by thy F thou didst swear to
91:4 will find refuge; his F is a shield and
92:2 the morning, and thy F by night,
98:3 his steadfast love and F to the house of
100:5 for ever, and his F to all generations.
108:4 above the heavens, thy F reaches to the clouds.
111:8 to be performed with F and uprightness.
115:1 the sake of thy steadfast love and thy F
117:2 toward us; and the F of the LORD endures
119:30 chosen the way of F, I set thy ordinances
119:75 right, and that in F thou hast afflicted me.
119:90 Thy F endures to all generations; thou hast
119:138 thy testimonies in righteousness and in all F
138:2 steadfast love and thy F; for thou hast exalted
143:1 In thy F answer me, in thy righteousness!
Prov 3:3 Let not loyalty and F forsake you; bind them
14:22 Those who devise good meet loyalty and F
16:6 By loyalty and F iniquity is atoned for, and
20:28 Loyalty and F preserve the king, and his throne
Wis 3:14 shown him for his F, and a place of
Sir 45:4 He sanctified him through F and meekness; he chose
46:15 By his F he was proved to be a
Is 11:5 of his waist, and F the girdle of his
16:5 it will sit in F in the tent of
38:3 walked before thee in F and with a whole
38:18 down to the pit cannot hope for thy F
38:19 the father makes known to the children thy F
Jer 31:3 I have continued my F to you.
32:41 in this land in F, with all my heart
Lam 3:23 they are new every morning; great is thy F
Hos 2:20 you to me in F; and you shall know
4:1 There is no F or kindness, and no knowledge
Mic 7:20 Thou wilt show F to Jacob and steadfast love
Zech 8:8 be their God, in F and in righteousness."
1Mac 14:35 "The people saw Simon's F and the glory which
Rom 3:3 their faithlessness nullify the F of God?
Gal 5:22 peace, patience, kindness, goodness, F,

FAITHLESS (35)

2Chr 28:19 Judah and had been F to the LORD.
28:22 he became yet more F to the LORD—this
29:19 reign when he was F, we have made ready
30:7 your brethren, who were F to the LORD God
Ps 119:158 I look at the F with disgust, because they
Prov 13:15 the way of the F is their ruin.
21:18 the righteous, and the F for the upright.
22:12 knowledge, but he overthrows the words of the F
23:28 robber and increases the F among men.
25:19 Trust in a F man in time of trouble
Jer 3:6 what she did, that F one, Israel, how she
3:8 the adulteries of that F one, Israel, I had
3:11 LORD said to me, F Israel has shown herself
3:12 north, and say, 'Return, F Israel, says the LORD.
3:14 Return, O F children, says the LORD; for I
3:20 Surely, as a F wife leaves her husband, so
3:20 so have you been F to me, O house
3:22 "Return, O F sons, I will heal your faithlessness."
5:11 Judah have been utterly F to me, says the
31:22 will you waver, O F daughter?
49:4 of your valleys, O F daughter, who trusted in
Hab 1:13 dost thou look on F men, and art silent
Zeph 3:4 Her prophets are wanton, F men; her priests profane
Mal 2:10 Why then are we F to one another, profaning
2:11 Judah has been F, and abomination has been
2:14 whom you have been F, though she is your
2:15 and let none be F to the wife of
2:16 take heed to yourselves and do not be F
Mt 17:17 And Jesus answered, "O F and perverse generation,
Mk 9:19 he answered them, "O F generation, how long am
Lk 9:41 Jesus answered, "O F and perverse generation, how
Jn 20:27 side; do not be F, but believing."
Rom 1:31 disobedient to parents, foolish, F, heartless, ruthless.
2Tim 2:13 us; if we are F, he remains faithful—
Rev 21:8 for the cowardly, the F, the polluted, as for

FAITHLESSLY (5)

Ex 21:8 since he has dealt F with her.
Ezek 14:13 against me by acting F, and I stretch out
15:8 because they have acted F, says the Lord GOD."
Hos 5:7 They have dealt F with the LORD; for they
6:7 covenant; there they dealt F with me.

FAITHLESSNESS (9)

Num 14:33 shall suffer for your F, until the last of
2Chr 33:19 his sin and his F, and the sites on
Ezra 9:2 And in this F the hand of the officials
9:4 Israel, because of the F of the returned exiles,
10:6 was mourning over the F of the exiles.
Wis 14:25 theft and deceit, corruption, F, tumult, perjury,
Jer 3:22 "Return, O faithless sons, I will heal your F
Hos 14:4 I will heal their F; I will love them
Rom 3:3 Does their F nullify the faithfulness of God?

FALCON (2)

Lev 11:14 osprey, the kite, the F according to its kind,
Job 28:7 prey knows, and the F's eye has not seen

FALL (275)

Gen 2:21 a deep sleep to F upon the man, and
43:18 occasion against us and F upon us, to make
Ex 5:3 our God, lest he F upon us with pestilence
9:3 of the LORD will F with a very severe
9:18 very heavy hail to F, such as never has
12:13 and no plague shall F upon you to destroy
15:16 Terror and dread F upon them; because of the
21:13 but God let him F into his hand, then
Lev 19:29 harlot, lest the land F into harlotry and the
26:7 enemies, and they shall F before you by the
26:8 and your enemies shall F before you by the
26:36 sword, and they shall F when none pursues.
Num 5:21 LORD makes your thigh F away and your body
5:22 swell and your thigh F away.' And the woman
5:27 and her thigh shall F away, and the woman
11:31 sea, and let them F beside the camp, about
14:3 into this land, to F by the sword?
14:29 your dead bodies shall F in this wilderness; and
14:32 your dead bodies shall F in this wilderness.
14:43 you, and you shall F by the sword; because
34:2 the land that shall F to you for an
Deut 22:8 house, if any one F from it.
Josh 6:5 of the city will F down flat, and the
10:19 yourselves, pursue your enemies, F upon their rear,
Judg 8:21 said, "Rise yourself, and F upon us; for as
9:57 the men of Shechem F back upon their heads,
15:12 that you will not F upon me yourselves."
15:18 die of thirst, and F into the hands of
18:25 us, lest angry fellows F upon you, and you
1Sam 3:19 none of his words F to the ground.
14:45 hair of his head F to the ground; for
18:25 thought to make David F by the hand of
22:17 forth their hand to F upon the priests of
22:18 Doeg, "You turn and F upon the priests." And
26:20 let not my blood F to the earth away
2Sam 1:15 men and said, "Go, F upon him." And he
3:29 May it F upon the head of Joab, and
14:11 of your son shall F to the ground."
17:9 some of the people F at the first attack,
24:14 great distress; let us F into the hand of
24:14 but let me not F into the hand of
1Kgs 1:52 of his hairs shall F to the earth; but
22:20 may go up and F at Ramoth-gilead?' And one
2Kgs 6:6 the man of God said, "Where did it F

F

10:10 then that there shall F to the earth nothing
14:10 trouble so that you F, you and Judah with
19:7 will cause him to F by the sword in
1Chr 21:13 great distress; let me F into the hand of
21:13 but let me not F into the hand of
2Chr 18:19 may go up and F at Ramoth-gilead?' And one
25:19 trouble so that you F, you and Judah with
Tob 11:8 the white films to F away, and he will
Jud 6:6 sides, and you shall F among their wounded, when
7:11 and not a man of your army will F
11:11 purpose frustrated, death will F upon them, for a
16:7 mighty one did not F by the hands of
Esth 6:13 you have begun to F, is of the Jewish
6:13 him but will surely F before him."
9:28 of Purim should never F into disuse among the
Job 13:11 the dread of him F upon you?
31:22 let my shoulder blade F from my shoulder, and
37:6 the snow he says, F on the earth'; and
Ps 5:10 O God; let them F by their own counsels;
20:8 They will collapse and F; but we shall rise
27:2 my adversaries and foes, they shall stumble and F
35:8 ensnare them; let them F therein to ruin!
37:24 he delights; though he F, he shall not be
38:17 I am ready to F, and my pain is
45:5 king's enemies; the peoples F under you.
72:11 May all kings F down before him, all nations
73:18 thou dost make them F to ruin.
78:28 seas; he let them F in the midst of
82:7 die like men, and F like any prince."
91:7 A thousand may F at your side, ten thousand
101:3 work of those who F away; it shall not
106:26 he would make them F in the wilderness,
140:10 Let burning coals F upon them!
141:10 Let the wicked together F into their own nets,
144:15 Happy the people to whom such blessings F
Prov 16:18 before destruction, and a haughty spirit before a F
22:14 LORD is angry will F into it.
26:27 digs a pit will F into it, and a
28:10 an evil way will F into his own pit;
28:14 hardens his heart will F into calamity.
28:18 in his ways will F into a pit.
Eccl 4:10 For if they F, one will lift up his
10:8 digs a pit will F into it; and a
Wis 11:20 from these, men could F at a single breath
13:16 that it may not F, because he knows that
16:11 delivered, lest they should F into deep forgetfulness
Sir 1:27 exalt yourself lest you F, and thus bring dishonor
2:7 his mercy; and turn not aside, lest you F
2:18 Let us F into the hands of the Lord,
8:1 powerful man, lest you F into his hands.
9:3 loose woman, lest you F into her snares.
15:4 her and will not F, and he will rely
18:18 learn, and before you F ill, take care of
22:17 eye will make tears F, and one who pricks
23:1 and let me not F because of them!
23:3 then I will not F before my adversaries, and
23:24 assembly, and punishment will F on her children.
27:26 digs a pit will F into it, and he
27:29 who rejoice in the F of the godly will
28:23 forsake the Lord will F into its power; it
28:26 your tongue, lest you F before him who lies
29:19 and pursues gain will F into lawsuits.
29:20 ability, but take heed to yourself lest you F
35:15 out against him who has caused them to F
36:2 fear of thee to F upon all the nations.
38:15 his Maker, may he F into the care of
38:16 son, let your tears F for the dead, and
46:11 whose hearts did not F into idolatry and who
Is 3:25 Your men shall F by the sword and your
8:15 stumble thereon; they shall F and be broken; they
10:4 among the prisoners or F among the slain.
10:34 axe, and Lebanon with its majestic trees will F
13:15 whoever is caught will F by the sword.
22:25 be cut down and F, and the burden that
24:18 of the terror shall F into the pit; and
26:19 land of the shades thou wilt let it F
28:13 they may go, and F backward, and be broken,
30:25 day of the great slaughter, when the towers F
31:3 who is helped will F, and they will all
31:8 "And the Assyrian shall F by a sword, not
34:4 All their host shall F, as leaves fall from
34:4 shall fall, as leaves F from the vine, like
34:7 Wild oxen shall F with them, and young steers
37:7 I will make him F by the sword in
40:30 and young men shall F exhausted;
44:19 Shall I F down before a block of wood?"
46:6 a god; then they F down and worship!
47:11 cannot atone; disaster shall F upon you, which you
54:15 strife with you shall F because of you.
Jer 6:15 Therefore they shall F among those who fall; at
6:15 fall among those who F; at the time that
6:24 of it, our hands F helpless; anguish has taken
8:4 the LORD: When men F, do they not rise
8:12 Therefore they shall F among the fallen; when I
9:22 bodies of men shall F like dung upon the
12:5 a safe land you F down, how will you
15:8 made anguish and terror F upon them suddenly.
19:7 cause their people to F by the sword before
20:4 They shall F by the sword of their enemies
20:10 say all my familiar friends, watching for my F
23:12 shall be driven and F; for I will bring
25:27 be drunk and vomit, F and rise no more,
25:34 come, and you shall F like choice rams.
39:18 and you shall not F by the sword; but
44:12 of Egypt they shall F; by the sword and
48:44 from the terror shall F into the pit, and
49:21 the sound of their F the earth shall tremble;
49:26 her young men shall F in her squares, and
50:30 her young men shall F in her squares, and
50:32 one shall stumble and F, with none to raise
51:4 They shall F down slain in the land of
51:47 all her slain shall F in the midst of
51:49 Babylon must F for the slain of Israel, as
Lam 1:9 her doom; therefore her F is terrible, she has
Bar 4:31 those who afflicted you and rejoiced at your F
4:33 she rejoiced at your F and was glad for
6:27 to stand, lest they F to the ground.
Ezek 5:12 a third part shall F by the sword round
6:7 And the slain shall F in the midst of
6:11 Israel; for they shall F by the sword, by
6:12 that is near shall F by the sword; and
11:10 You shall F by the sword; I will judge
13:11 who daub it with whitewash that it shall F
13:11 rain, great hailstones will F, and a stormy wind
17:21 of his troops shall F by the sword, and
21:15 may melt, and many F at all their gates.
23:25 and your survivors shall F by the sword.
24:21 you left behind shall F by the sword.
25:13 to Dedan they shall F by the sword.
26:11 your mighty pillars will F to the ground.
26:15 the sound of your F, when the wounded groan,
26:18 the day of your F; yea, the isles that
28:23 and the slain shall F in the midst of
29:5 your streams; you shall F upon the open field,
30:4 Ethiopia, when the slain F in Egypt, and her
30:5 is in league, shall F with them by the
30:6 who support Egypt shall F, and her proud might
30:6 to Syene they shall F within her by the
30:17 and of Pibeseth shall F by the sword; and
30:22 will make the sword F from his hand.
30:25 arms of Pharaoh shall F; and they shall know
31:12 valleys its branches will F, and its boughs will
31:16 the sound of its F, when I cast it
32:12 cause your multitude to F by the swords of
32:20 the uncircumcised.' They shall F amid those who are
33:12 wicked, he shall not F by it when he
33:27 the waste places shall F by the sword; and
35:8 your ravines those slain with the sword shall F
38:11 unwalled villages; I will F upon the quiet people
38:20 and the cliffs shall F, and every wall shall
39:4 You shall F upon the mountains of Israel, you
39:5 You shall F in the open field; for I
47:14 and this land shall F to you as your
Dan 3:5 music, you are to F down and worship the
3:6 and whoever does not F down and worship shall
3:10 kind of music, shall F down and worship the
3:11 and whoever does not F down and worship shall
3:15 kind of music, to F down and worship the
11:19 he shall stumble and F, and shall not be
11:26 away, and many shall F down slain.
11:33 understand, though they shall F by sword and flame,
11:34 When they F, they shall receive a little help.
11:35 who are wise shall F, to refine and to
11:41 tens of thousands shall F, but these shall be
13:23 do it and to F into your hands, rather
Hos 7:17 bow, their princes shall F by the sword because
10:8 and to the hills, F upon us.
13:8 I will F upon them like a bear robbed
13:16 her God; they shall F by the sword, their
Amos 3:5 Does a bird F in a snare on the
3:14 be cut off and F to the ground.
7:17 and your daughters shall F by the sword, and

8:14 Beer-sheba lives,' they shall F, and never rise again."
9:9 but no pebble shall F upon the earth.
Mic 7:8 my enemy; when I F, I shall rise; when
Nah 3:12 figs--if shaken they F into the mouth of
Zech 11:6 will cause men to F each into the hand
14:13 from the LORD shall F on them, so that
14:15 like this plague shall F on the horses, the
1Mac 4:2 out by night to F upon the camp of
7:38 army, and let them F by the sword; remember
7:43 was the first to F in the battle.
12:26 up in formation to F upon the Jews by
2Mac 3:6 possible for them to F under the control of
9:7 rushing along, and the F was so hard as
10:4 they might never again F into such misfortunes, but
12:45 up for those who F asleep in godliness, it
13:11 just begun to revive F into the hands of
14:42 nobly rather than to F into the hands of
Mt 4:9 you, if you will F down and worship me."
7:25 but it did not F, because it had been
7:27 and great was the F of it."
10:29 one of them will F to the ground without
15:14 blind man, both will F into a pit."
15:27 eat the crumbs that F from their masters' table."
24:10 And then many will F away, and betray one
24:29 and the stars will F from heaven, and the
26:31 them, "You will all F away because of me
26:33 him, "Though they all F away because of you,
26:33 you, I will never F away."
Mk 4:17 the word, immediately they F away.
14:27 them, "You will all F away; for it is
14:29 "Even though they all F away, I will not."
Lk 2:34 is set for the F and rising of many
6:39 Will they not both F into a pit?
8:13 in time of temptation F away.
10:18 them, "I saw Satan F like lightning from heaven.
21:24 this people; they will F by the edge of
23:29 say to the mountains, F on us'; and to
Acts 5:15 least his shadow might F on some of them.
28:6 swell up or suddenly F down dead; but when
Rom 3:23 all have sinned and F short of the glory
8:15 spirit of slavery to F back into fear, but
9:33 that will make them F; and he who believes
11:11 I ask, have they stumbled so as to F
14:20 one to make others F by what he eats;
1Cor 8:13 eat meat, lest I cause my brother to F
10:12 thinks that he stands take heed lest he F
2Cor 11:29 Who is made to F, and I am not
1Tim 3:6 up with conceit and F into the condemnation of
3:7 outsiders, or he may F into reproach and the
6:9 desire to be rich F into temptation, into a
Heb 3:12 heart, leading you to F away from the living
4:11 rest, that no one F by the same sort
10:31 a fearful thing to F into the hands of
Jas 5:12 that you may not F under condemnation.
1Pet 2:8 that will make them F; for they stumble because
2Pet 1:10 this you will never F;
Rev 4:10 ever, the twenty-four elders F down before him who
6:16 the mountains and rocks, F on us and hide
11:6 that no rain may F during the days of

FALLEN (105)

Gen 4:6 are you angry, and why has your countenance F
Lev 13:40 a man's hair has F from his head, he
13:41 a man's hair has F from his forehead and
19:10 shall you gather the F grapes of your vineyard;
Deut 22:4 ass or his ox F down by the way,
Josh 2:9 fear of you has F upon us, and that
7:10 why have you thus F upon your face?
8:24 the very last had F by the edge of
Judg 8:10 East; for there had F a hundred and twenty
18:1 tribes of Israel had F to them.
1Sam 5:3 day, behold, Dagon had F face downward on the
5:4 morning, behold, Dagon had F face downward on the
26:12 from the LORD had F upon them.
31:8 and his three sons F on Mount Gilboa.
2Sam 1:4 the people also have F and are dead; and
1:10 live after he had F; and I took the
1:12 Israel, because they had F by the sword.
1:19 How are the mighty F
1:25 "How are the mighty F in the midst of
1:27 "How are the mighty F, and the weapons of
2:23 place where Asahel had F and died, stood still.
3:34 as one falls before the wicked you have F
3:38 a great man has F this day in Israel?
23:20 a pit on a day when snow had F
2Kgs 2:13 of Elijah that had F from him, and went
2:14 of Elijah that had F from him, and struck
13:14 Now when Elisha had F sick with the illness
1Chr 10:8 Saul and his sons F on Mount Gilboa.
11:22 a pit on a day when snow had F
2Chr 29:9 lo, our fathers have F by the sword and
Esth 8:17 of the Jews had F upon them.
9:2 fear of them had F upon all peoples.
9:3 fear of Mordecai had F upon them.
Ps 16:6 The lines have F for me in pleasant places;
53:3 They have all F away; they are all alike
55:4 terrors of death have F upon me.
57:6 way, but they have F into it themselves.
69:9 who insult thee have F on me.
105:38 dread of them had F upon it.
119:56 This blessing has F to me, that I have
Wis 18:23 the dead had already F on one another in
Sir 28:18 Many have F by the edge of the sword,
28:18 so many as have F because of the tongue.
29:19 The sinner who has F into suretyship and pursues
46:20 Even after he had F asleep he prophesied and
49:13 the walls that had F, and set up the
Is 3:8 stumbled, and Judah has F; because their speech and
9:10 heart: "The bricks have F, but we will build
14:12 "How you are F from heaven, O Day Star,
16:9 fruit and your harvest the battle shout has F
21:9 And he answered, F, fallen is Babylon; and all
21:9 And he answered, "Fallen, F is Babylon; and all
26:18 and the inhabitants of the world have not F
59:14 off; for truth has F in the public squares,
Jer 8:12 shall fall among the F; when I punish them,
46:6 by the river Euphrates they have stumbled and F
46:12 warrior; they have both F together."
48:32 summer fruits and your vintage the destroyer has F
50:15 surrendered; her bulwarks have F, her walls are
51:8 Suddenly Babylon has F and been broken; wail for
51:44 flow to him; the wall of Babylon has F
51:49 as for Babylon have F the slain of all
Lam 2:21 my young men have F by the sword; in
5:16 The crown has F from our head; woe to
Ezek 32:22 all of them slain, F by the sword;
32:23 all of them slain, F by the sword, who
32:24 all of them slain, F by the sword, who
32:27 not lie with the F mighty men of old
33:21 came to me and said, "The city has F
Hos 7:8 All their kings have F; and none of them
Amos 5:2 O house of Israel: F, no more to rise,
9:11 of David that is F and repair its breaches,
Zech 11:2 for the cedar has F, for the glorious trees
1Mac 5:12 many of us have F,
5:54 one of them had F before they returned in
7:44 saw that Nicanor had F, they threw down their
9:1 and his army had F in battle, he sent
9:21 "How is the mighty F, the savior of Israel!"
12:37 to the east had F, and he repaired the
2Mac 7:38 Almighty which has justly F on our whole nation."
12:39 the bodies of the F and to bring them
12:40 all that this was why these men had F
12:42 because of the sin of those who had F
12:44 that those who had F would rise again, it
Mt 27:52 the saints who had F asleep were raised,
Lk 14:5 an ox that has F into a well, will
Jn 11:11 "Our friend Lazarus has F asleep, but I go
11:12 "Lord, if he has F asleep, he will recover."
Acts 8:16 it had not yet F on any of them,
15:16 of David, which has F; I will rebuild its
26:14 when we had all F to the ground, I
Rom 11:22 toward those who have F, but God's kindness to
1Cor 15:6 alive, though some have F asleep.
15:18 those also who have F asleep in Christ have
15:20 of those who have F asleep.
Gal 5:4 the law; you have F away from grace.
1Thes 4:14 him those who have F asleep.
4:15 precede those who have F asleep.
Rev 2:5 from what you have F, repent and do the
9:1 I saw a star F from heaven to earth,
14:8 a second, followed, saying, F, fallen is Babylon the
14:8 second, followed, saying, "Fallen, F is Babylon the
17:10 five of whom have F, one is, the other
18:2 with a mighty voice, F, fallen is Babylon the
18:2 a mighty voice, "Fallen, F is Babylon the great!

FALLING (21)

Num 24:4 vision of the Almighty, F down, but having his
24:16 vision of the Almighty, F down, but having his
Esth 7:8 wine, as Haman was F on the couch where
Ps 56:13 yea, my feet from F, that I may walk

118:13 so that I was F, but the LORD helped
145:14 upholds all who are F, and raises up all
Sir 3:29 the moment of his F he will find support.
18:20 Before F ill, humble yourself, and when you are
22:25 may keep me from F, so that my tongue
34:16 a guard against stumbling and a defense against F
43:18 whiteness, and the mind is amazed at its F
Is 34:4 the vine, like leaves F from the fig tree.
2Mac 10:26 F upon the steps before the altar, they besought
Mk 13:25 the stars will be F from heaven, and the
Lk 8:41 of the synagogue; and F at Jesus' feet he
8:47 she came trembling, and F down before him
Jn 16:1 to keep you from F away.
Acts 1:18 of his wickedness; and F headlong he burst open
1Cor 8:13 cause of my brother's F, I will never eat
14:25 are disclosed; and so, F on his face, he
Jude 1:24 to keep you from F and to present you

FALLOW (4)

Ex 23:11 it rest and lie F, that the poor of
Prov 13:23 The F ground of the poor yields much food,
Jer 4:3 Jerusalem: "Break up your F ground, and sow not
Hos 10:12 love; break up your F ground, for it is

FALLS (52)

Gen 49:17 so that his rider F backward.
Ex 21:33 ox or an ass F into it,
Lev 11:32 which any of them F when they are dead
11:33 if any of them F into any earthen vessel,
11:35 part of their carcass F shall be unclean; whether
11:37 part of their carcass F upon any seed for
11:38 part of their carcass F on it, it is
Num 33:54 inheritance; wherever the lot F to any man, that
Deut 20:20 city that makes war with you, until it F
2Sam 3:34 not fettered; as one F before the wicked you
17:12 him as the dew F on the ground; and
Job 4:13 night, when deep sleep F on men,
14:18 "But the mountain F and crumbles away, and the
30:30 skin turns black and F from me, and my
33:15 night, when deep sleep F upon men, while they
Ps 7:15 digging it out, and F into the hole which
10:10 crushed, sinks down, and F by his might.
72:6 be like rain that F on the mown grass,
133:3 dew of Hermon, which F on the mountains of
Prov 11:5 straight, but the wicked F by his own wickedness.
11:14 no guidance, a people F; but in an abundance
14:35 favor, but his wrath F on one who acts
17:20 with a perverse tongue F into calamity.
24:16 for a righteous man F seven times, and rises
24:17 rejoice when your enemy F, and let not your
Eccl 4:10 is alone when he F and has not another
9:12 time, when it suddenly F upon them.
11:3 and if a tree F to the south or
11:3 place where the tree F, there it will lie.
Wis 6:5 swiftly, because severe judgment F on those in high
11:22 of morning dew that F upon the ground.
Sir 13:20 when a humble man F, he is even pushed
Is 24:20 upon it, and it F, and will not rise
44:15 a graven image and F down before it.
44:17 god, his idol; and F down to it and
Ezek 13:12 and when the wall F, will it not be
13:14 laid bare; when it F, you shall perish in
Mt 12:11 one sheep and it F into a pit on
13:21 the word, immediately he F away.
17:15 terribly; for often he F into the fire, and
21:44 And he who F on this stone will be
21:44 pieces; but when it F on any one, it
Lk 11:17 itself is laid waste, and a divided household F
15:12 share of property that F to me.' And he
20:18 Every one who F on that stone will be
20:18 pieces; but when it F on any one it
Jn 12:24 a grain of wheat F into the earth and
Rom 2:2 judgment of God rightly F upon those who do
14:4 before his own master that he stands or F
Heb 6:7 the rain that often F upon it, and brings
Jas 1:10 the grass; its flower F, and its beauty perishes.
1Pet 1:24 withers, and the flower F,

FALSE (107)

Ex 20:16 "You shall not bear F witness against your neighbor.
23:1 shall not utter a F report.
23:7 Keep far from a F charge, and do not
Deut 5:20 "Neither shall you bear F witness against your
19:18 the witness is a F witness and has accused
2Kgs 17:15 They went after F idols, and became false, and
17:15 false idols, and became F, and they followed the
2Chr 26:16 For he was F to the LORD his God,
Tob 3:6 because I have heard F reproaches, and great is
Jud 11:5 I will tell nothing F to my lord this
Esth 16:6 these men by the F trickery of their evil
Job 31:28 I should have been F to God above.
36:4 my words are not F; one who is perfect
Ps 24:4 soul to what is F, and does not swear
26:4 do not sit with F men, nor do I
27:12 of my adversaries; for F witnesses have risen against
40:4 who go astray after F gods!
44:17 forgotten thee, or been F to thy covenant.
73:27 to those who are F to thee.
89:33 steadfast love, or be F to my faithfulness.
119:29 Put F ways far from me; and graciously teach
119:104 therefore I hate every F way.
119:128 precepts; I hate every F way.
Prov 6:19 run to evil, a F witness who breathes out
11:1 A F balance is an abomination to the LORD,
12:17 honest evidence, but a F witness utters deceit.
14:5 not lie, but a F witness breathes out lies.
17:7 fool; still less is F speech to a prince.
19:5 A F witness will not go unpunished, and he
19:9 A F witness will not go unpunished, and he
20:23 to the LORD, and F scales are not good.
21:28 A F witness will perish, but the word of
25:18 A man who bears F witness against his neighbor
Wis 10:14 she showed to be F, and she gave him
Sir 26:5 of a mob, and F accusation--all these are
34:1 understanding has vain and F hopes, and dreams
34:4 And from something F what will be true?
36:19 an intelligent mind detects F words.
Is 16:6 pride, and his insolence-- his boasts are F
Jer 3:7 not return, and her F sister Judah saw it.
3:8 of divorce; yet her F sister Judah did not
3:10 for all this her F sister Judah did not
3:11 herself less guilty than F Judah.
8:8 But, behold, the F pen of the scribes has
10:3 them, for the customs of the peoples are F
10:14 for his images are F, and there is no
14:22 there any among the F gods of the nations
18:15 they burn incense to F gods; they have stumbled
37:14 Jeremiah said, "It is F; I am not deserting
48:30 LORD; his boasts are F, his deeds are false.
48:30 LORD; his boasts are false, his deeds are F
51:17 for his images are F, and there is no
Lam 2:14 have seen for you F and deceptive visions; they
2:14 seen for you oracles F and misleading.
Bar 6:8 silver; but they are F and cannot speak.
6:44 Whatever is done for them is F
6:50 it will afterward be known that they are F
6:59 than to be these F gods; better even the
6:59 its contents, than these F gods; better also a
6:59 a palace, than these F gods.
Ezek 12:24 be no more any F vision or flattering divination
21:23 will seem like a F divination; they have sworn
21:29 they see for you F visions, while they divine
22:28 them with whitewash, seeing F visions and divining
Dan 13:43 these men have borne F witness against me.
13:49 these men have borne F witness against her."
13:61 convicted them of bearing F witness;
Hos 10:2 Their heart is F; now they must bear their
12:7 in whose hands are F balances, he loves to
Amos 8:5 and deal deceitfully with F balances,
Zech 8:17 another, and love no F oath, for all these
10:2 lies; the dreamers tell F dreams, and give empty
2Mac 5:5 When a F rumor arose that Antiochus was dead,
14:27 and, provoked by the F accusations of that depraved
Mt 7:15 "Beware of F prophets, who come to you in
15:19 murder, adultery, fornication, theft, F witness,
19:18 You shall not bear F witness,
24:11 And many F prophets will arise and lead many
24:24 For F Christs and false prophets will arise and
24:24 For false Christs and F prophets will arise and
26:59 the whole council sought F testimony against Jesus
26:60 found none, though many F witnesses came forward.
Mk 10:19 steal, Do not bear F witness, Do not defraud,
13:22 F Christs and false prophets will arise and show
13:22 False Christs and F prophets will arise and show
14:56 For many bore F witness against him, and their
14:57 stood up and bore F witness against him, saying,
Lk 3:14 by violence or by F accusation, and be content
6:26 fathers did to the F prophets.
18:20 steal, Do not bear F witness, Honor your father
Acts 6:13 council, and set up F witnesses who said, "This
13:6 magician, a Jewish F prophet, named Bar-Jesus.
Rom 3:4 though every man be F, as it is written,

2Cor 11:13 For such men are F apostles, deceitful workmen,
11:26 at sea, danger from F brethren;
Gal 2:4 But because of F brethren secretly brought in, who
2Thes 2:11 them believe what is F,
Heb 6:18 that God should prove F, we who have fled
Jas 3:14 not boast and be F to the truth.
2Pet 2:1 But F prophets also arose among the people, just
2:1 as there will be F teachers among you, who
2:3 will exploit you with F words; from of old
1Jn 4:1 of God; for many F prophets have gone out
Rev 2:2 found them to be F;
16:13 the mouth of the F prophet, three foul spirits
19:20 and with it the F prophet who in its
20:10 the beast and the F prophet were, and they

FALSEHOOD (22)

Jud 5:5 No F shall come from your servant's mouth.
Job 21:34 There is nothing left of your answers but F
27:4 lips will not speak F, and my tongue will
31:5 I have walked with F, and my foot has
Ps 62:4 They take pleasure in F
119:86 they persecute me with F; help me!
119:163 I hate and abhor F, but I love thy
144:8 whose right hand is a right hand of F
144:11 whose right hand is a right hand of F
Prov 13:5 A righteous man hates F, but a wicked man
29:12 a ruler listens to F, all his officials will
30:8 Remove far from me F and lying; give me
Is 5:18 iniquity with cords of F, who draw sin as
28:15 our refuge, and in F we have taken shelter";
Jer 9:3 tongue like a bow; F and not truth has
Ezek 13:6 They have spoken F and divined a lie; they
Hos 12:1 day long; they multiply F and violence; they make
Jn 7:18 is true, and in him there is no F
Rom 3:7 But if through my F God's truthfulness abounds to
Eph 4:25 Therefore, putting away F, let every one speak the
Rev 21:27 who practices abomination or F, but only those who
22:15 idolaters, and every one who loves and practices F

FALSELY (27)

Gen 21:23 you will not deal F with me or with
Ex 8:29 let not Pharaoh deal F again by not letting
Lev 6:3 lied about it, swearing F—in any of all
6:5 which he has sworn F; he shall restore it
19:11 not steal, nor deal F, nor lie to one
19:12 swear by my name F, and so profane the
Deut 19:18 has accused his brother F,
Josh 24:27 you, lest you deal F with your God."
Job 13:7 Will you speak F for God, and speak deceitfully
Is 63:8 who will not deal F; and he became their
Jer 5:2 yet they swear F
5:12 They have spoken F of the LORD, and have
5:31 land: the prophets prophesy F, and the priests rule
6:13 and from prophet to priest, every one deals F
7:9 murder, commit adultery, swear F, burn incense to
8:10 gain; from prophet to priest every one deals F
20:6 all your friends, to whom you have prophesied F
27:15 but they are prophesying F in my name, with
40:16 for you are speaking F of Ishmael."
Ezek 13:22 have disheartened the righteous F, although I have
Hos 7:2 Samaria; for they deal F, the thief breaks in,
Zech 5:3 every one who swears F shall be cut off
5:4 of him who swears F by my name; and
Mal 3:5 against those who swear F, against those who
Mt 5:11 of evil against you F on my account.
5:33 'You shall not swear F, but shall perform to
1Tim 6:20 contradictions of what is F called knowledge,

FALTER

Sir 12:15 time, but if you F, he will not stand

FALTERED

Esth 15:7 And the queen F, and turned pale and faint,

FAME (21)

Num 14:15 who have heard thy F will say,
Deut 26:19 in praise and in F and in honor, and
Josh 6:27 with Joshua; and his F was in all the
1Kgs 4:31 of Mahol; and his F was in all the
10:1 Sheba heard of the F of Solomon concerning the
1Chr 14:17 And the F of David went out into all
22:5 exceedingly magnificent, of F and glory throughout
2Chr 9:1 Sheba heard of the F of Solomon she came
26:8 to Uzziah, and his F spread even to the
26:15 And his F spread far, for he was marvelously
Esth 9:4 king's house, and his F spread throughout all the
Ps 72:17 endure for ever, his F continue as long as
145:7 shall pour forth the F of thy abundant goodness,
Is 66:19 have not heard my F or seen my glory;
1Mac 3:26 His F reached the king, and the Gentiles talked
8:1 Judas heard of the F of the Romans, that
8:12 have heard of their F have feared them.
Mt 4:24 So his F spread throughout all Syria, and they
9:31 away and spread his F through all that district.
14:1 tetrarch heard about the F of Jesus;
Mk 1:28 And at once his F spread everywhere throughout all

FAMED

1Mac 6:1 Persia was a city F for its wealth in

FAMILIAR (7)

1Kgs 9:27 servants, seamen who were F with the sea, together
2Kgs 10:11 great men, and his F friends, and his priests,
2Chr 8:18 servants ships and servants F with the sea, and
Tob 5:6 with you; I am F with the way, and
Ps 55:13 equal, my companion, my F friend.
Jer 20:10 say all my F friends, watching for my fall.
Acts 26:3 because you are especially F with all customs and

FAMILIES (178)

Gen 8:19 earth, went forth by F out of the ark.
10:5 own language, by their F, in their nations.
10:18 Afterward the F of the Canaanites spread abroad.
10:20 of Ham, by their F, their languages, their lands,
10:31 of Shem, by their F, their languages, their lands,
10:32 These are the F of the sons of Noah,
12:3 by you all the F of the earth shall
28:14 descendants shall all the F of the earth bless
36:40 Esau, according to their F and their dwelling places,
Ex 1:20 because the midwives feared God he gave them F
6:14 Carmi; these are the F of Reuben.
6:15 woman; these are the F of Simeon.
6:17 sons of Gershon: Libni and Shimei, by their F
6:19 These are the F of the Levites according to
6:24 Abiasaph; these are the F of the Korahites.
6:25 the fathers' houses of the Levites by their F
12:21 yourselves according to your F, and kill the passover
Lev 25:45 with you and their F that are with you,
Num 1:2 people of Israel, by F, by fathers' houses, according
1:18 who registered themselves by F, by fathers' houses,
1:20 their generations, by their F, by their fathers' houses,
1:22 their generations, by their F, by their fathers' houses,
1:24 their generations, by their F, by their fathers' houses,
1:26 their generations, by their F, by their fathers' houses,
1:28 their generations, by their F, by their fathers' houses,
1:30 their generations, by their F, by their fathers' houses,
1:32 their generations, by their F, by their fathers' houses,
1:34 their generations, by their F, by their fathers' houses,
1:36 their generations, by their F, by their fathers' houses,
1:38 their generations, by their F, by their fathers' houses,
1:40 their generations, by their F, by their fathers' houses,
1:42 their generations, by their F, by their fathers' houses,
3:15 fathers' houses and by F; every male from a
3:18 of Gershon by their F: Libni and Shimei.
3:19 of Kohath by their F: Amram, Izhar, Hebron, and
3:20 of Merari by their F: Mahli and Mushi.
3:20 These are the F of the Levites, by their
3:21 Shimeites; these were the F of the Gershonites.
3:23 The F of the Gershonites were to encamp behind
3:27 Uzzielites; these are the F of the Kohathites.
3:29 The F of the sons of Kohath were to
3:30 fathers' house of the F of the Kohathites.
3:33 Mushites: these are the F of Merari.
3:35 fathers' house of the F of Merari was Zuriel
3:39 of the LORD, by F, all the males from
4:2 of Levi, by their F and their fathers' houses,
4:18 the tribe of the F of the Kohathites be
4:22 Gershon also, by their F and their fathers' houses;
4:24 the service of the F of the Gershonites, in
4:28 the service of the F of the sons of
4:29 number them by their F and their fathers' houses;
4:33 the service of the F of the sons of
4:34 the Kohathites, by their F and their fathers' houses,
4:36 and their number by F was two thousand seven
4:37 the number of the F of the Kohathites, all
4:38 of Gershon, by their F and their fathers' houses,
4:40 their number by their F and their fathers' houses
4:41 the number of the F of the sons of
4:42 The number of the F of the sons of
4:42 of Merari, by their F and their fathers' houses,
4:44 their number by F was three thousand two
4:45 were numbered of the F of the sons of

F

4:46 Israel numbered, by their F and their fathers' houses,
11:10 people weeping throughout their F, every man at the
26:7 These are the F of the Reubenites; and their
26:12 Simeon according to their F: of Nemuel, the family
26:14 These are the F of the Simeonites, twenty-two
26:15 Gad according to their F: of Zephon, the family
26:18 These are the F of the sons of Gad
26:20 Judah according to their F were: of Shelah, the
26:22 These are the F of Judah according to their
26:23 Issachar according to their F: of Tola, the family
26:25 These are the F of Issachar according to their
26:26 Zebulun, according to their F: of Sered, the family
26:27 These are the F of the Zebulunites according to
26:28 Joseph according to their F: Manasseh and Ephraim.
26:34 These are the F of Manasseh; and their number
26:35 Ephraim according to their F: of Shuthelah, the
26:37 These are the F of the sons of Ephraim
26:37 are the sons of Joseph according to their F
26:38 Benjamin according to their F: of Bela, the family
26:41 Benjamin according to their F; and their number
26:42 Dan according to their F: of Shuham, the family
26:42 These are the F of Dan according to their
26:42 are the families of Dan according to their F
26:43 All the F of the Shuhamites, according to their
26:44 Asher according to their F: of Imnah, the family
26:47 These are the F of the sons of Asher
26:48 Naphtali according to their F: of Jahzeel, the family
26:50 These are the F of Naphtali according to their
26:50 Naphtali according to their F; and their number was
26:57 numbered according to their F: of Gershon, the
26:58 These are the F of Levi: the family of
27:1 of Manasseh, from the F of Manasseh the son
33:54 lot according to your F; to a large tribe
36:1 fathers' houses of the F of the sons of
36:12 were married into the F of the sons of
Josh 7:14 shall come near by F; and the family which
7:17 he brought near the F of Judah, and the
13:15 the tribe of the Reubenites according to their F
13:23 Reubenites, according to their F with their cities and
13:24 the tribe of the Gadites, according to their F
13:28 Gadites according to their F, with their cities and
13:29 the half-tribe of the Manassites according to their F
13:31 the half of the Machirites according to their F
15:1 Judah according to their F reached southward to the
15:12 about the people of Judah according to their F
15:20 of the people of Judah according to their F
16:5 the Ephraimites by their F was as follows: the
16:8 the Ephraimites by their F,
17:2 of Manasseh, by their F, Abi-ezer, Helek, Asriel,
17:2 of Manasseh the son of Joseph, by their F
18:11 Benjamin according to its F came up, and the
18:20 Benjamin, according to its F, boundary by boundary
18:21 according to their F were Jericho, Beth-hoglah,
18:28 of the tribe of Benjamin according to its F
19:1 Simeon, according to its F; and its inheritance was
19:8 of the tribe of Simeon according to its F
19:10 for the tribe of Zebulun, according to its F
19:16 Zebulun, according to its F --these cities with their
19:17 for the tribe of Issachar, according to its F
19:23 Issachar, according to its F --the cities with their
19:24 for the tribe of Asher according to its F
19:31 Asher according to its F --these cities with their
19:32 for the tribe of Naphtali, according to its F
19:39 Naphtali according to its F --the cities with their
19:40 for the tribe of Dan, according to its F
19:48 Dan, according to their F --these cities with their
21:4 came out for the F of the Kohathites.
21:5 by lot from the F of the tribe of
21:6 by lot from the F of the tribe of
21:7 Merarites according to their F received from the
21:10 Aaron, one of the F of the Kohathites who
21:20 belonging to the Kohathite F of the Levites, the
21:26 The cities of the F of the rest of
21:27 Gershonites, one of the F of the Levites, were
21:33 cities of the several F of the Gershonites were
21:34 the Levites, the Merarite F, were given out of
21:40 of the several Merarite F, that is, the remainder
21:40 the remainder of the F of the Levites, those
22:14 each of the tribal F of Israel, every one
22:21 the heads of the F of Israel,
22:30 the heads of the F of Israel who were
1Sam 9:21 humblest of all the F of the tribe of
10:21 Benjamin near by its F, and the family of
1Chr 2:53 And the F of Kiriath-jearim: the Ithrites, the
2:55 The F also of the scribes that dwelt at
4:2 These were the F of the Zorathites.
4:8 Anub, Zobebah, and the F of Aharhel the son
4:21 of Mareshah, and the F of the house of
4:38 were princes in their F, and their fathers' houses
5:7 his kinsmen by their F, when the genealogy of
6:19 These are the F of the Levites according to
6:54 of Aaron of the F of Kohathites, for theirs
6:60 their cities throughout their F were thirteen.
6:62 Gershomites according to their F were allotted
6:63 Merarites according to their F were allotted twelve
6:66 And some of the F of the sons of
6:70 the rest of the F of the Kohathites.
7:5 belonging to all the F of Issachar were in
16:28 to the LORD, O F of the peoples, ascribe
2Chr 19:8 priests and heads of F of Israel, to give
Ezra 2:68 of the heads of F, when they came to
Neh 4:13 people according to their F, with their swords, their
Job 31:34 and the contempt of F terrified me, so that
Ps 22:27 LORD; and all the F of the nations shall
96:7 to the LORD, O F of the peoples, ascribe
107:41 affliction, and makes their F like flocks.
Jer 2:4 Jacob, and all the F of the house of
31:1 God of all the F of Israel, and they
33:24 has rejected the two F which he chose?
Ezek 45:15 two hundred, from the F of Israel.
Amos 3:2 known of all the F of the earth; therefore
Zech 12:14 themselves; and all the F that are left, each
14:17 if any of the F of the earth do
1Mac 1:61 children circumcised, and their F and those who
Acts 3:25 posterity shall all the F of the earth be
Tit 1:10 they are upsetting whole F by teaching for base

FAMILY (155)

Gen 34:19 he was the most honored of all his F
37:2 the history of the F of Jacob.
Lev 20:5 man and against his F, and will cut them
25:10 and each of you shall return to his F
25:41 back to his own F, and return to the
25:47 member of the stranger's F,
25:49 kinsman belonging to his F may redeem him; or
Num 2:34 every one in his F, according to his fathers'
3:21 Of Gershon were the F of the Libnites and
3:21 the Libnites and the F of the Shimeites; these
3:27 Of Kohath were the F of the Amramites, and
3:27 the Amramites, and the F of the Izharites, and
3:27 the Izharites, and the F of the Hebronites, and
3:27 the Hebronites, and the F of the Uzzielites; these
3:33 Of Merari were the F of the Mahlites and
3:33 the Mahlites and the F of the Mushites: these
25:6 Midianite woman to his F, in the sight of
26:5 Reuben: of Hanoch, the F of the Hanochites; of
26:5 Hanochites; of Pallu, the F of the Palluites;
26:6 Palluites; of Hezron, the F of the Hezronites; of
26:6 Hezronites; of Carmi, the F of the Carmites.
26:12 families: of Nemuel, the F of the Nemuelites; of
26:12 Nemuelites; of Jamin, the F of the Jaminites; of
26:12 Jaminites; of Jachin, the F of the Jachinites;
26:13 Jachinites; of Zerah, the F of the Zerahites; of
26:13 Zerahites; of Shaul, the F of the Shaulites.
26:15 families: of Zephon, the F of the Zephonites; of
26:15 Zephonites; of Haggi, the F of the Haggites; of
26:15 Haggites; of Shuni, the F of the Shunites;
26:16 Shunites; of Ozni, the F of the Oznites; of
26:16 Oznites; of Eri, the F of the Erites;
26:17 Erites; of Arod, the F of the Arodites; of
26:17 Arodites; of Areli, the F of the Arelites.
26:20 were: of Shelah, the F of the Shelanites; of
26:20 Shelanites; of Perez, the F of the Perezites; of
26:20 Perezites; of Zerah, the F of the Zerahites.
26:21 were: of Hezron, the F of the Hezronites; of
26:21 Hezronites; of Hamul, the F of the Hamulites.
26:23 families: of Tola, the F of the Tolaites; of
26:23 Tolaites; of Puvah, the F of the Punites;
26:24 Punites; of Jashub, the F of the Jashubites; of
26:24 Jashubites; of Shimron, the F of the Shimronites.
26:26 families: of Sered, the F of the Seredites; of
26:26 Seredites; of Elon, the F of the Elonites; of
26:26 Elonites; of Jahleel, the F of the Jahleelites.
26:29 Manasseh: of Machir, the F of the Machirites; and
26:29 Gilead; of Gilead, the F of the Gileadites.
26:30 Gilead: of Iezer, the F of the Iezerites; of
26:30 Iezerites; of Helek, the F of the Helekites;
26:31 and of Asriel, the F of the Asrielites; and
26:31 and of Shechem, the F of the Shechemites;
26:32 and of Shemida, the F of the Shemidaites; and
26:32 and of Hepher, the F of the Hepherites.
26:35 families: of Shuthelah, the F of the Shuthelahites; of

	26:35	Shuthelahites; of Becher, the F of the Becherites; of
	26:35	Becherites; of Tahan, the F of the Tahanites.
	26:36	Shuthelah: of Eran, the F of the Eranites.
	26:38	families: of Bela, the F of the Bela-ites; of
	26:38	Bela-ites; of Ashbel, the F of the Ashbelites; of
	26:38	Ashbelites; of Ahiram, the F of the Ahiramites;
	26:39	f Shephupham, the F of the Shuphamites; of
	26:39	Shuphamites; of Hupham, the F of the Huphamites.
	26:40	Naaman: of Ard, the F of the Ardites; of
	26:40	Ardites; of Naaman, the F of the Naamites.
	26:42	families: of Shuham, the F of the Shuhamites.
	26:44	families: of Imnah, the F of the Imnites; of
	26:44	Imnites; of Ishvi, the F of the Ishvites; of
	26:44	Ishvites; of Beriah, the F of the Beriites.
	26:45	Beriah: of Heber, the F of the Heberites; of
	26:45	Heberites; of Malchi-el, the F of the Malchi-elites.
	26:48	families: of Jahzeel, the F of the Jahzeelites; of
	26:48	Jahzeelites; of Guni, the F of the Gunites;
	26:49	Gunites; of Jezer, the F of the Jezerites; of
	26:49	Jezerites; of Shillem, the F of the Shillemites.
	26:57	families: of Gershon, the F of the Gershonites; of
	26:57	Gershonites; of Kohath, the F of the Kohathites; of
	26:57	Kohathites; of Merari, the F of the Merarites.
	26:58	families of Levi: the F of the Libnites, the
	26:58	of the Libnites, the F of the Hebronites, the
	26:58	of the Hebronites, the F of the Mahlites, the
	26:58	of the Mahlites, the F of the Mushites, the
	26:58	of the Mushites, the F of the Korahites.
	27:4	taken away from his F, because he had no
	27:11	to him of his F, and he shall possess
	36:6	shall marry within the F of the tribe of
	36:8	to one of the F of the tribe of
	36:12	the tribe of the F of their father.
Deut	25:5	be married outside the F to a stranger; her
	29:18	man or woman or F or tribe, whose heart
Josh	7:14	by families; and the F which the LORD takes
	7:17	of Judah, and the F of the Zerahites was
	7:17	he brought near the F of the Zerahites man
	22:14	the head of a F among the clans of
Judg	1:25	man and all his F go.
	6:15	Manasseh, and I am the least in my F
	6:27	too afraid of his F and the men of
	8:27	became a snare to Gideon and to his F
	8:35	show kindness to the F of Jerubbaal (that is,
	9:1	clan of his mother's F,
	16:31	brothers and all his F came down and took
	17:7	in Judah, of the F of Judah, who was
	18:19	to a tribe and F in Israel?"
	21:24	to his tribe and F, and they went out
Ruth	2:1	of wealth, of the F of Elimelech, whose name
	2:3	who was of the F of Elimelech.
1Sam	9:21	And is not my F the humblest of all
	10:21	its families, and the F of the Matrites was
	10:21	finally he brought the F of the Matrites near
	18:18	my kinsfolk, my father's F in Israel, that I
	20:6	there for all the F
	20:29	me go; for our F holds a sacrifice in
2Sam	14:7	And now the whole F has risen against your
	16:5	a man of the F of the house of
2Kgs	11:1	dead, she arose and destroyed all the royal F
	25:25	Elishama, of the royal F, came with ten men,
1Chr	4:27	nor did all their F multiply like the men
	6:61	lot out of the F of the tribe, out
2Chr	22:10	destroyed all the royal F of house of Judah.
Tob	1:9	a member of our F, and by her I
	5:10	to what tribe and F do you belong?
	5:11	a tribe and a F or for a man
	5:13	because I tried to learn your tribe and F
Jud	8:2	to her tribe and F, had died during the
	8:18	been any tribe or F or people or city
Esth	9:28	every generation, in every F, province, and city, and
	14:5	the tribe of my F that thou, O Lord,
Job	32:2	the Buzite, of the F of Ram, became angry.
Sir	11:32	with commotion, and will estrange you from your F
Jer	3:14	and two from a F, and I will bring
	8:3	remains of this evil F in all the places
	41:1	Elishama, of the royal F, one of the chief
Ezek	43:19	Levitical priests of the F of Zadok, who draw
Dan	1:3	both of the royal F and of the nobility,
	13:33	But her F and friends and all who saw
Amos	3:1	Israel, against the whole F which I brought up
Mic	2:3	LORD: Behold, against this F I am devising evil,
Zech	12:12	land shall mourn, each F by itself; the family
	12:12	family by itself; the F of the house of
	12:12	wives by themselves; the F of the house of
	12:13	wives by themselves; the F of the house of
	12:13	wives by themselves; the F of the Shimeites by
	14:18	And if the F of Egypt do not go
1Mac	5:62	not belong to the F of those men through
	12:21	and are of the F of Abraham.
2Mac	1:10	who is of the F of the anointed priests,
Mk	3:21	And when his F heard it, they went out
Acts	4:6	Alexander, and all who were of the high-priestly F
	7:13	brothers, and Joseph's F became known to Pharaoh.
	13:26	"Brethren, sons of the F of Abraham, and those
	16:33	he was baptized at once, with all his F
Rom	16:10	who belong to the F of Aristobulus.
	16:11	who belong to the F of Narcissus.
Eph	3:15	Father, from whom every F in heaven and on
1Tim	5:4	duty to their own F and make some return
	5:8	especially for his own F, he has disowned the

FAMINE (114)

Gen	12:10	Now there was a F in the land.
	12:10	sojourn there, for the F was severe in the
	26:1	Now there was a F in the land, besides
	26:1	land, besides the former F that was in the
	41:27	the east wind are also seven years of F
	41:30	arise seven years of F, and all the plenty
	41:30	land of Egypt; the F will consume the land,
	41:31	by reason of that F which will follow, for
	41:36	the seven years of F which are to befall
	41:36	that the land may not perish through the F
	41:50	Before the year of F came, Joseph had two
	41:54	the seven years of F began to come, as
	41:54	There was F in all lands; but in all
	41:56	So when the F had spread over all the
	41:56	the Egyptians, for the F was severe in the
	41:57	buy grain, because the F was severe over all
	42:5	who came, for the F was in the land
	42:19	carry grain for the F of your households,
	42:33	take grain for the F of your households, and
	43:1	Now the F was severe in the land.
	45:6	For the F has been in the land these
	45:11	yet five years of F to come; lest you
	47:4	servants' flocks, for the F is severe in the
	47:13	the land; for the F was very severe, so
	47:13	land of Canaan languished by reason of the F
	47:20	their fields, because the F was severe upon them.
Ruth	1:1	ruled there was a F in the land, and
2Sam	21:1	Now there was a F in the days of
	24:13	"Shall three years of F come to you in
1Kgs	8:37	"If there is F in the land, if there
	18:2	Now the F was severe in Samaria.
2Kgs	4:38	when there was a F in the land.
	6:25	there was a great F in Samaria, as they
	7:4	enter the city,' the F is in the city,
	8:1	has called for a F, and it will come
	25:3	the fourth month the F was so severe in
1Chr	21:12	either three years of F; or three months of
2Chr	6:28	"If there is F in the land, if there
	20:9	judgment, or pestilence, or F, we will stand before
	32:11	over to die by F and by thirst, when
Neh	5:3	our houses to get grain because of the F
Tob	4:13	great want, because shiftlessness is the mother of F
Jud	5:10	When a F spread over Canaan they went down
	7:14	will waste away with F, and before the sword
Job	5:20	In F he will redeem you from death, and
	5:22	At destruction and F you shall laugh, and shall
Ps	33:19	soul from death, and keep them alive in F
	37:19	in the days of F they have abundance.
	105:16	When he summoned a F on the land, and
Sir	39:29	Fire and hail and F and pestilence, all these
	40:9	strife and sword, calamities, F and affliction and
	48:2	He brought a F upon them, and by his
Is	14:30	kill your root with F, and your remnant I
	51:19	devastation and destruction, F and sword; who will
Jer	5:12	upon us, nor shall we see sword or F
	11:22	daughters shall die by F;
	14:12	by the sword, by F, and by pestilence."
	14:13	nor shall you have F, but I will give
	14:15	who say, 'Sword and F shall not come on
	14:15	land: By sword and F those prophets shall be
	14:16	of Jerusalem, victims of F and sword, with none
	14:18	I enter the city, behold, the diseases of F
	15:2	those who are for F, to famine, and those
	15:2	are for famine, to F, and those who are
	16:4	the sword and by F, and their dead bodies
	18:21	up their children to F; give them over to
	21:7	the pestilence, sword, and F, into the hand of
	21:9	by the sword, by F, and by pestilence; but
	24:10	I will send sword, F, and pestilence upon them,

27:8 with the sword, with F, and with pestilence, says
27:13 by the sword, by F, and by pestilence, as
28:8 ancient times prophesied war, F, and pestilence
29:17 sending on them sword, F, and pestilence, and I
29:18 pursue them with sword, F, and pestilence, and will
32:24 because of sword and F and pestilence the city
32:36 Babylon by sword, by F, and by pestilence:
34:17 to pestilence, and to F, says the LORD.
38:2 by the sword, by F, and by pestilence; but
42:16 of Egypt; and the F of which you are
42:17 by the sword, by F, and by pestilence; they
42:22 by the sword, by F, and by pestilence in
44:12 the sword and by F they shall be consumed;
44:12 the sword and by F; and they shall become
44:13 with the sword, with F, and with pestilence,
44:18 have been consumed by the sword and by F
44:27 the sword and by F, until there is an
52:6 the fourth month the F was so severe in
Lam 5:10 as an oven with the burning heat of F
Bar 2:25 in great misery, by F and sword and pestilence.
Ezek 5:12 and be consumed with F in the midst of
5:16 my deadly arrows of F, arrows for destruction, which
5:16 bring more and more F upon you, and break
5:17 I will send F and wild beasts against you,
6:11 by the sword, by F, and by pestilence.
6:12 is left and is preserved shall die of F
7:15 is without, pestilence and F are within; he that
7:15 is in the city F and pestilence devour.
12:16 from the sword, from F and pestilence, that they
14:13 of bread and send F upon it, and cut
14:21 acts of judgment, sword, F, evil beasts, and
36:29 abundant and lay no F upon you.
36:30 suffer the disgrace of F among the nations.
Amos 8:11 I will send a F on the land; not
8:11 the land; not a F of bread, nor a
1Mac 6:54 in the sanctuary, because F had prevailed over the
9:24 days a very great F occurred, and the country
13:49 very hungry, and many of them perished from F
Lk 4:25 there came a great F over all the land;
15:14 spent everything, a great F arose in that country,
Acts 7:11 Now there came a F throughout all Egypt and
11:28 would be a great F over all the world;
Rom 8:35 distress, or persecution, or F, or nakedness, or peril,
Rev 6:8 with sword and with F and with pestilence and
18:8 pestilence and mourning and F, and she shall be

FAMINES (3)

Mt 24:7 and there will be F and earthquakes in various
Mk 13:8 places, there will be F; this is but the
Lk 21:11 and in various places F and pestilences; and there

FAMISH

Zeph 2:11 them; yea, he will F all the gods of

FAMISHED (3)

Gen 25:29 came in from the field, and he was F
25:30 some of that red pottage, for I am F
41:55 land of Egypt was F, the people cried to

FAMOUS (11)

1Kgs 1:47 name of Solomon more F than yours, and make
1Chr 5:24 and Jahdi-el, mighty warriors, F men, heads of their
12:30 mighty men of valor, F men in their fathers'
Jud 16:23 became more and more F, and grew old in
Ps 136:18 for ever; and slew F kings, for his steadfast
Sir 44:1 Let us now praise F men, and our fathers
48:6 down to destruction, and F men from their beds;
Jer 49:25 How the F city is forsaken, the joyful city!
Bar 3:26 born there, who were F of old, great in
2Mac 2:22 and recovered the temple F throughout the world
2Cor 8:18 the brother who is F among all the churches

FANCIES (2)

Sir 34:5 like a woman in travail the mind has F
Dan 4:5 lay in bed the F and the visions of

FANCY

Song 6:12 I was aware, my F set me in a

FANGS (3)

Job 29:17 I broke the F of the unrighteous, and made
Ps 58:6 mouths; tear out the F of the young lions,
Joel 1:6 and it has the F of a lioness.

FAR (281)

Gen 10:19 direction of Gerar, as F as Gaza, and in
10:19 Admah, and Zeboiim, as F as Lasha.
13:3 from the Negeb as F as Bethel, to the
13:12 moved his tent as F as Sodom.
14:6 their Mount Seir as F as El-paran on the
14:14 went in pursuit as F as Dan.
18:25 F be it from thee to do such a
18:25 F be that from thee!
44:7 F be it from your servants that they should
44:17 But he said, F be it from me that
Ex 8:28 shall not go very F away.
23:7 Keep F from a false charge, and do not
Lev 13:12 head to foot, so F as the priest can
Num 16:3 and said to them, "You have gone too F
16:7 You have gone too F, sons of Levi!"
16:37 then scatter the fire F and wide.
21:24 to the Jabbok, as F as to the Ammonites;
21:26 of his hand, as F as the Arnon.
21:30 perished from Heshbon, as F as Dibon, and we
33:49 Jordan from Beth-jeshimoth as F as Abel-shittim in
Deut 1:7 Canaanites, and Lebanon, as F as the great river,
1:44 down in Seir as F as Hormah.
2:23 lived in villages as F as Gaza, the Caphtorim,
2:36 in the valley, as F as Gilead, there was
3:10 and all Bashan, as F as Salecah and Edre-i,
3:14 that is, Bashan, as F as the border of
3:16 territory from Gilead as F as the valley of
3:16 as a boundary, as F over as the river
3:17 boundary, from Chinnereth as F as the sea of
4:48 of the Arnon, as F as Mount Sirion (that
4:49 of the Jordan as F as the Sea of
12:21 name there is too F from you, then you
14:24 the place is too F from you, which the
20:15 cities which are very F from you, which are
29:22 who comes from a F land, would say, when
34:1 the land, Gilead as F as Dan,
34:2 land of Judah as F as the Western Sea,
34:3 of palm trees, as F as Zoar.
Josh 1:4 and this Lebanon as F as the great river,
2:7 to the Jordan as F as the fords; and
7:5 before the gate as F as Shebarim, and slew
8:4 do not go very F from the city, but
9:6 have come from a F country; so now make
9:9 him, "From a very F country your servants have
9:22 saying, 'We are very F from you,' when you
10:10 and smote them as F as Azekah and Makkedah.
10:11 heaven upon them as F as Azekah, and they
10:41 country of Goshen, as F as Gibeon.
11:8 and chased them as F as Great Sidon and
11:8 Misrephoth-maim, and eastward as F as the valley
11:17 rises toward Seir, as F as Baal-gad in the
12:2 of the valley as F as the river Jabbok,
13:9 tableland of Medeba as F as Dibon;
13:10 reigned in Heshbon, as F as the boundary of
16:3 of the Japhletites, as F as the territory of
16:5 east was Ataroth-addar as F as Upper Beth-horon,
19:8 about these cities as F as Baalath-beer, Ramah of
19:10 its inheritance reached as F as Sarid;
19:28 Rehob, Hammon, Kanah, as F as Sidon the Great;
19:33 Adami-nekeb, and Jabneel, as F as Lakkum; and it
22:29 between us and you.' F be it from us
24:16 Then the people answered, F be it from us
Judg 3:3 from Mount Baal-hermon as F as the entrance of
4:11 pitched his tent as F away as the oak
6:4 of the land, as F as the neighborhood of
7:22 the army fled as F as Beth-shittah toward Zererah,
7:22 Beth-shittah toward Zererah, as F as the border of
7:24 waters against them, as F as Beth-barah, and also
7:24 seized the waters as F as Beth-barah, and also
11:33 twenty cities, and as F as Abel-keramim, with a
18:7 and how they were F from the Sidonians and
18:28 deliverer because it was F from Sidon, and they
19:11 Jebus, the day was F spent, and the servant
20:43 down from Nohah as F as opposite Gibe-ah on
1Sam 2:30 now the LORD declares: F be it from me;
6:12 went after them as F as the border of
7:11 and smote them, as F as below Beth-car.
12:23 Moreover as for me, F be it from me
14:45 F from it!
15:7 Amalekites, from Havilah as F as Shur, which is
17:52 pursued the Philistines as F as Gath and the
17:52 way from Sha-araim as F as Gath and Ekron.
20:2 he said to him, F from it!
20:9 And Jonathan said, F be it from you!
27:8 from of old, as F as Shur, to the
2Sam 7:18 my house, that thou hast brought me thus F
20:20 Joab answered, F be it from me, far be

20:20 be it from me, F be it, that I
23:17 the LORD, and said, F be it from me,
1Kgs 4:12 Beth-shean to Abel-meholah, as F as the other side
8:41 Israel, comes from a F country for thy name's
12:30 to the other as F as Dan.
2Kgs 2:2 has sent me as F as Bethel." But Elisha
7:15 went after them as F as the Jordan; and,
14:25 entrance of Hamath as F as the Sea of
18:8 smote the Philistines as F as Gaza and its
19:23 the mountains, to the F recesses of Lebanon; I
20:14 have come from a F country, from Babylon."
1Chr 4:33 about these cities as F as Baal.
5:8 dwelt in Aroer, as F as Nebo and Baal-meon.
5:9 to the east as F as the entrance of
5:11 land of Bashan as F as Salecah:
11:19 the LORD, and said, F be it from me
12:40 their neighbors, from as F as Issachar and Zebulun
17:16 my house, that thou hast brought me thus F
29:2 of my God, so F as I was able,
2Chr 6:32 Israel, comes from a F country for the sake
6:36 captive to a land F or near;
12:4 Judah and came as F as Jerusalem.
14:9 chariots, and came as F as Mareshah.
14:13 him pursued them as F as Gerar, and the
26:15 And his fame spread F, for he was marvelously
30:10 and Manasseh, and as F as Zebulun; but they
34:6 and Simeon, and as F as Naphtali, in their
Neh 3:1 they consecrated it as F as the Tower of
3:1 of the Hundred, as F as the Tower of
3:8 they restored Jerusalem as F as the Broad Wall.
3:13 of the wall, as F as the Dung Gate.
3:15 the king's garden, as F as the stairs that
3:27 great projecting tower as F as the wall of
3:31 the goldsmiths, repaired as F as the house of
4:19 separated on the wall, F from one another.
5:8 to them, "We, as F as we are able,
Jud 1:9 beyond the Jordan as F as Jerusalem and Bethany
1:10 lived in Egypt as F as the borders of
1:12 one in Egypt, as F as the coasts of
2:24 the brook Abron, as F as the sea.
7:3 breadth over Dothan as F as Balbaim and in
15:5 cut them down as F as Choba.
Esth 9:20 Ahasuerus, both near and F,
16:11 become our guest, so F enjoyed the good will
Job 5:4 His sons are F from safety, they are crushed
11:14 your hand, put it F away, and let not
13:21 face: withdraw thy hand F from me, and let
19:13 has put my brethren F from me, and my
21:16 of the wicked is F from me.
22:18 of the wicked is F from me.
22:23 if you remove unrighteousness F from your tents,
27:5 F be it from me to say that you
34:10 you men of understanding, F be it from God
38:11 doors, and said, 'Thus F shall you come, and
Ps 22:1 Why art thou so F from helping me, from
22:11 Be not F from me, for trouble is near
31:22 alarm, "I am driven F from thy sight." But
35:22 O Lord, be not F from me!
38:21 my God, be not F from me!
48:2 Mount Zion, in the F north, the city of
71:12 O God, be not F from me; O my
73:27 lo, those who are F from thee shall perish;
97:9 earth; thou art exalted F above all gods.
101:4 of heart shall be F from me; I will
103:12 who fear him; as F as the east is
103:12 from the west, so F does he remove our
109:17 blessing; may it be F from him!
113:6 on high, who looks F down upon the heavens
119:29 Put false ways F from me; and graciously teach
119:150 evil purpose; they are F from thy law.
119:155 Salvation is F from the wicked, for they do
Prov 4:25 and put devious talk F from you.
5:8 Keep your way F from her, and do not
15:29 The LORD is F from the wicked, but he
19:7 do his friends go F from him!
22:5 guards himself will keep F from them.
22:15 of discipline drives it F from him.
25:25 good news from a F country.
27:10 a brother who is F away.
30:8 before I die: Remove F from me falsehood and
31:10 She is F more precious than jewels.
Eccl 7:23 wise"; but it was F from me.
Wis 12:24 For they went F astray on the paths of
14:17 they imagined their appearance F away, and made a
Sir 6:13 Keep yourself F from your enemies, and be on
9:13 Keep F from a man who has the power
15:8 She is F from men of pride, and liars
23:12 these errors will be F from the godly, and
30:23 heart, and remove sorrow F from you, for sorrow
Is 6:12 the LORD removes men F away, and the forsaken
8:9 give ear, all you F countries; gird yourselves and
14:13 of assembly in the F north;
15:4 voice is heard as F as Jahaz; therefore the
17:13 and they will flee F away, chased like chaff
18:2 people feared near and F, a nation mighty and
18:7 people feared near and F, a nation mighty and
22:3 though they had fled F away.
29:13 while their hearts are F from me, and their
30:27 the LORD comes from F, burning with his anger,
37:24 the mountains, to the F recesses of Lebanon; I
39:3 to me from a F country, from Babylon."
46:11 my counsel from a F country.
46:12 heart, you who are F from deliverance:
49:19 you up will be F away.
54:14 established; you shall be F from oppression, for you
57:19 Peace, peace, to the F and to the near,
59:9 Therefore justice is F from us, and righteousness
59:11 salvation, but it is F from us.
60:4 sons shall come from F, and your daughters shall
60:9 bring your sons from F, their silver and gold
Jer 2:5 me that they went F from me, and went
12:2 in their mouth and F from their heart.
25:26 kings of the north, F and near, one after
27:10 you will be removed F from your land, and
31:40 all the fields as F as the brook Kidron,
48:4 cry is heard as F as Zoar.
48:24 the land of Moab, F and near.
48:32 the sea, reached as F as Jazer, upon your
48:34 Ele-aleh cry out; as F as Jahaz they utter
48:47 Thus F is the judgment on Moab.
49:30 every side!' Flee, wander F away, dwell in the
51:64 Thus F are the words of Jeremiah.
Lam 1:16 for a comforter is F from me, one to
Bar 3:21 Their sons have strayed F from her way.
6:73 for he will be F from reproach.
Ezek 8:6 here, to drive me F from my sanctuary?
10:5 cherubim was heard as F as the outer court,
11:15 said, 'They have gone F from the LORD; to
22:5 and those who are F from you will mock
23:40 men to come from F, to whom a messenger
29:10 Migdol to Syene, as F as the border of
43:9 bodies of their kings F from me, and I
44:10 the Levites who went F from me, going astray
47:16 Damascus and Hamath), as F as Hazer-hatticon,
47:18 eastern sea and as F as Tamar.
47:19 run from Tamar as F as the waters of
48:1 entrance of Hamath, as F as Hazar-enon (which is
Dan 9:7 and those that are F away, in all the
11:2 a fourth shall be F richer than all of
11:10 carry the war as F as his fortress.
13:51 to them, "Separate them F from each other, and
Joel 2:20 will remove the northerner F from you, and drive
3:6 the Greeks, removing them F from their own border.
Amos 6:3 O you who put F away the evil day,
Obad 1:20 shall possess Phoenicia as F as Zarephath; and the
Mic 7:11 the boundary shall be F extended.
Zech 10:9 the nations, yet in F countries they shall remember
1Mac 2:21 F be it from us to desert the law
7:45 journey, from Adasa as F as Gazara, and as
8:4 though the place was F distant from them.
8:12 They have subdued kings F and near, and as
8:23 sword and enemy be F from them.
9:10 But Judas said, F be it from us to
9:15 he pursued them as F as Mount Azotus.
11:7 with the king as F as the river called
11:8 the coastal cities as F as Seleucia by the
11:62 through the country as F as Damascus.
11:73 in the pursuit as F as Kadesh, to their
12:33 through the country as F as Askalon and the
13:5 And now, F be it from me to spare
14:16 in Rome, and as F away as Sparta, that
2Mac 13:9 show the Jews things F worse than those that
Mt 15:8 but their heart is F from me;
24:27 east and shines as F as the west, so
26:58 at a distance, as F as the courtyard of
Mk 7:6 but their heart is F from me;
12:34 him, "You are not F from the kingdom of
Lk 7:6 When he was not F from the house, the
15:13 his journey into a F country, and there he
19:12 nobleman went into a F country to receive a
24:29 the day is now F spent." So he went
24:50 led them out as F as Bethany, and lifting

F

Jn	21:8	for they were not F from the land, but
Acts	11:19	over Stephen traveled as F as Phoenicia and Cyprus
	13:6	the whole island as F as Paphos, they came
	17:15	Paul brought him as F as Athens; and receiving
	17:27	Yet he is not F from each one of
	22:21	I will send you F away to the Gentiles.'"
	23:23	spearmen to go as F as Caesarea.
	28:15	of us, came as F as the Forum of
Rom	1:13	to you (but thus F have been prevented), in
	12:18	If possible, so F as it depends upon you,
	13:12	believed; the night is F gone, the day is
	15:19	from Jerusalem and as F round as Illyricum I
2Cor	3:9	dispensation of righteousness must F exceed it in
	11:23	like a madman--with F greater labors, far more
	11:23	with far greater labors, F more imprisonments, with
Gal	6:14	But F be it from me to glory except
Eph	1:21	in the heavenly places, F above all rule and
	3:20	is able to do F more abundantly than all
	4:10	he who also ascended F above all the heavens,
Phil	1:23	Christ, for that is F better.
2Tim	3:9	will not get very F, for their folly will
1Pet	4:13	But rejoice in so F as you share Christ's

FAR-OFF (26)

Ex	33:7	it outside the camp, F from the camp; and
Deut	13:7	whether near you or F from you, from the
	30:11	not too hard for you, neither is it F
Josh	3:16	up in a heap F, at Adam, the city
1Kgs	8:46	land of the enemy, F or near;
Ps	22:19	But thou, O LORD, be not F
Eccl	7:24	That which is, is F, and deep, very deep;
Sir	16:20	For the covenant is F
	27:20	for he is too F, and has escaped like
	47:16	Your name reached to F islands, and you were
Is	33:13	Hear, you who are F, what I have done;
	46:13	deliverance, it is not F, and my salvation will
	57:9	you sent your envoys F, and sent down even
Ezek	6:12	He that is F shall die of pestilence; and
	11:16	Though I removed them F among the nations, and
	12:27	he prophesies of times F
Joel	3:8	Sabeans, to a nation F; for the LORD has
Zech	6:15	"And those who are F shall come and help
Lk	16:23	eyes, and saw Abraham F and Lazarus in his
	18:13	the tax collector, standing F, would not even lift
Acts	2:39	to all that are F, every one whom the
Eph	2:13	you who once were F have been brought near
	2:17	to you who were F and peace to those
Rev	18:10	burning; they will stand F, in fear of her
	18:15	from her, will stand F, in fear of her
	18:17	on the sea, stood F

FARE (8)

Gen	18:25	so that the righteous F as the wicked!
Ruth	3:16	said, "How did you F, my daughter?" Then she
1Sam	17:18	See how your brothers F, and bring some token
1Kgs	22:27	feed him with scant F of bread and water,
2Kgs	7:13	are left here will F like the whole multitude
2Chr	18:26	feed him with scant F of bread and water,
Jon	1:3	so he paid the F, and went on board,
Hag	2:16	the temple of the LORD, how did you F

FARED (7)

Gen	30:29	how your cattle have F with me.
2Sam	11:7	and how the people F, and how the war
Esth	2:11	to learn how Esther was and how she F
Sir	47:12	a wise son who F amply because of him;
Hag	1:5	the LORD of hosts: Consider how you have F
	1:7	the LORD of hosts: Consider how you have F
Rom	9:29	children, we would have F like Sodom and been

FARES (2)

Deut	15:16	your household, since he F well with you,
Sir	6:1	shame and reproach: so F the double-tongued sinner.

FAREWELL (9)

Gen	31:28	me to kiss my sons and my daughters F
2Mac	3:35	and having bidden Onias F, he marched off with
	11:21	and my representatives to confer with you. F
	11:33	to encourage you. F
	11:38	so thatwe may have your judgement. F
Lk	9:61	let me first say F to those at my
Acts	15:29	keep yourselves from these, you will do well. F
	21:5	the beach we prayed and bade one another F
2Cor	13:11	Finally, brethren, F

FARM (2)

Sir	7:15	hate toilsome labor, or F work, which were created
Mt	22:5	off, one to his F, another to his business,

FARMER (4)

Wis	17:17	whether he was a F or a shepherd or
Jer	51:23	break in pieces the F and his team; with
2Tim	2:6	It is the hard-working F who ought to have
Jas	5:7	Behold, the F waits for the precious fruit of

FARMERS (4)

2Chr	26:10	plain, and he had F and vinedressers in the
Jer	14:4	on the land, the F are ashamed, they cover
	31:24	there together, and the F and those who wander
Amos	5:16	They shall call the F to mourning and to

FARMING

2Mac	12:1	the king, and the Jews went about their F

FARTHER (7)

Job	38:11	you come, and no F, and here shall your
Jer	31:39	line shall go out F, straight to the hill
1Mac	10:77	went to Azotus as though he were going F
Mt	26:39	And going a little F he fell on his
Mk	1:19	going on a little F, he saw James the
	14:35	And going a little F, he fell on the
Acts	27:28	twenty fathoms; a little F on they sounded again

FARTHEST (12)

Josh	15:1	of Zin at the F south.
	17:18	possess it to its F borders; for you shall
2Kgs	19:23	cypresses; I entered its F retreat, its densest forest.
Neh	1:9	dispersed be under the F skies, I will gather
Job	28:3	search out to the F bound the ore in
Ps	65:5	earth, and of the F seas;
	65:8	who dwell at earth's F bounds are afraid at
Is	41:9	and called from its F corners, saying to you,
Jer	6:22	is stirring from the F parts of the earth.
	25:32	is stirring from the F parts of the earth!
	31:8	gather them from the F parts of the earth,
	50:41	are stirring from the F parts of the earth.

FASCINATION

Wis	4:12	For the F of wickedness obscures what is good,

FASHION (3)

2Chr	32:15	mislead you in this F, and do not believe
Job	31:15	And did not one F us in the womb?
2Cor	10:2	some who suspect us of acting in worldly F

FASHIONED (6)

Ex	32:4	at their hand, and F it with a graving
Job	10:8	Thy hands F and made me; and now thou
Ps	119:73	hands have made and F me; give me understanding
Wis	13:10	hands, gold and silver F with skill, and likenesses
	19:6	in its nature was F anew, complying with thy
Is	54:17	no weapon that is F against you shall prosper,

FASHIONER (2)

Wis	7:22	manifest, for wisdom, the F of all things, taught
	8:6	more than she is F of what exists?

FASHIONS (6)

Ps	33:15	the earth, he who F the hearts of them
Wis	15:7	for our service, he F out of the same
Is	44:10	Who F a god or casts an image, that
	44:12	The ironsmith F it and works it over the
	44:13	with a pencil; he F it with planes, and
	45:9	say to him who F it, 'What are you

FAST (89)

Gen	21:18	lad, and hold him F with your hand; for
Deut	4:4	but you who held F to the LORD your
Judg	4:21	as he was lying F asleep from weariness.
2Sam	12:23	But now he is dead; why should I F
	18:9	and his head caught F in the oak, and
1Kgs	21:9	the letters, "Proclaim a F, and set Naboth on
	21:12	them, they proclaimed a F, and set Naboth on
2Kgs	6:32	and hold the door F against him.
	18:6	For he held F to the LORD; he did
2Chr	20:3	LORD, and proclaimed a F throughout all Judah.
Ezra	8:21	Then I proclaimed a F there, at the river
Esth	4:16	Susa, and hold a F on my behalf, and
	4:16	my maids will also F as you do.
Job	2:3	He still holds F his integrity, although you moved
	2:9	"Do you still hold F your integrity?

23:11 My foot has held F to his steps; I
27:6 I hold F my righteousness, and will not let
37:10 is given, and the broad waters are frozen F
38:38 and the clods cleave F together?
Ps 17:5 My steps have held F to thy paths, my
64:5 They hold F to their evil purpose; they talk
119:90 thou hast established the earth, and it stands F
Prov 3:18 those who hold her F are called happy.
4:5 "Let your heart hold F my words; keep my
7:22 a stag is caught F
Sir 1:17 exalted the glory of those who held her F
4:13 Whoever holds her F will obtain glory, and the
25:11 shall be likened the one who holds it F
45:23 the Lord, and stood F, when the people turned
Is 47:12 Stand F in your enchantments and your many
56:2 man who holds it F, who keeps the sabbath,
56:4 please me and hold F my covenant,
56:6 profane it, and holds F my covenant--
58:3 the day of your F you seek your own
58:4 Behold, you F only to quarrel and to fight
58:5 Is such the F that I choose, a day
58:5 you call this a F, and a day acceptable
58:6 "Is not this the F that I choose: to
Jer 8:5 They hold F to deceit, they refuse to return.
14:12 Though they F, I will not hear their cry,
36:6 go, and on a F day in the hearing
36:9 to Jerusalem proclaimed a F before the LORD.
50:33 captive have held them F, they refuse to let
Bar 4:1 All who hold her F will live, and those
Dan 6:12 answered, "The thing stands F, according to the law
Hos 12:6 your God, return, hold F to love and justice,
Joel 1:13 Sanctify a F, call a solemn assembly.
2:15 in Zion; sanctify a F; call a solemn assembly;
Jon 1:5 lain down, and was F asleep.
3:5 God; they proclaimed a F, and put on sackcloth,
Zeph 1:14 near, near and hastening F; the sound of the
Zech 7:3 "Should I mourn and F in the fifth month,
8:19 LORD of hosts: The F of the fourth month,
8:19 fourth month, and the F of the fifth, and
8:19 the fifth, and the F of the seventh, and
8:19 the seventh, and the F of the tenth, shall
1Mac 10:81 But his men stood F, as Jonathan commanded, and
Mt 6:16 "And when you F, do not look dismal, like
6:17 But when you F, anoint your head and wash
9:14 we and the Pharisees F, but your disciples do
9:14 the Pharisees fast, but your disciples do not F
9:15 taken away from them, and then they will F
Mk 2:18 disciples of the Pharisees F, but your disciples do
2:18 the Pharisees fast, but your disciples do not F
2:19 "Can the wedding guests F while the bridegroom is
2:19 they have the bridegroom with them, they cannot F
2:20 and then they will F in that day.
7:8 of God, and hold F the tradition of men."
Lk 5:33 "The disciples of John F often and offer prayers,
5:34 you make wedding guests F while the bridegroom is
5:35 and then they will F in those days."
8:15 the word, hold it F in an honest and
18:12 I F twice a week, I give tithes of
Acts 27:9 already dangerous because the F had already gone
Rom 11:20 unbelief, but you stand F only through faith.
12:9 what is evil, hold F to what is good;
1Cor 15:2 if you hold it F --unless you believed in
Gal 5:1 set us free; stand F therefore, and do not
Phil 2:16 in the world, holding F the word of life,
Col 2:19 mind, and not holding F to the Head, from
1Thes 3:8 live, if you stand F in the Lord.
5:21 but test everything; hold F what is good,
Heb 3:6 house if we hold F our confidence and pride
4:14 God, let us hold F our confession.
10:23 Let us hold F the confession of our hope
1Pet 5:12 grace of God; stand F in it.
Rev 2:13 throne is; you hold F my name and you
2:25 other burden; only hold F what you have, until
3:11 am coming soon; hold F what you have, so

FASTED (18)

Judg 20:26 before the LORD, and F that day until evening,
1Sam 7:6 before the LORD, and F on that day, and
31:13 tree in Jabesh, and F seven days.
2Sam 1:12 mourned and wept and F until evening for Saul
12:16 the child; and David F, and went in and
12:21 You F and wept for the child while it
12:22 was still alive, I F and wept; for I
1Kgs 21:27 upon his flesh, and F and lay in sackcloth,
1Chr 10:12 oak in Jabesh, and F seven days.
Ezra 8:23 So we F and besought our God for this,
Jud 4:13 for the people F many days throughout Judea
8:6 She F all the days of her widowhood, except
Is 58:3 'Why have we F, and thou seest it not?
Bar 1:5 Then they wept, and F, and prayed before the
Zech 7:5 the priests, When you F and mourned in the
7:5 seventy years, was it for me that you F
1Mac 3:47 They F that day, put on sackcloth and sprinkled
Mt 4:2 And he F forty days and forty nights, and

FASTEN (7)

Ex 25:26 rings of gold, and F the rings to the
28:37 LORD.' And you shall F it on the turban
39:31 lace of blue, to F it on the turban
Sir 14:24 her house will also F his tent peg to
Is 22:23 And I will F him like a peg in
41:7 is good"; and they F it with nails so
Jer 10:4 silver and gold; they F it with hammer and

FASTENED (14)

Ex 37:13 rings of gold, and F the rings to the
Num 19:15 which has no cover F upon it, is unclean.
1Sam 31:10 of Ashtaroth; and they F his body to the
2Sam 20:8 sword in its sheath F upon his loins, and
1Chr 10:10 of their gods, and F his head in the
Jud 16:8 face with ointment and F her hair with a
Ps 41:8 "A deadly thing has F upon him; he will
Is 22:25 the peg that was F in a sure place
Lam 1:14 his hand they were F together; they were set
Ezek 40:43 a handbreadth long, were F round about within.
1Mac 6:37 and covered; they were F upon each beast by
Mt 18:6 have a great millstone F round his neck and
Acts 16:24 the inner prison and F their feet in the
28:3 of the heat and F on his hand.

FASTENS

Wis 13:15 in the wall, and F it there with iron.

FASTING (22)

Ezra 9:5 I rose from my F, with my garments and
Neh 1:4 days; and I continued F and praying before the
9:1 Israel were assembled with F and in sackcloth, and
Tob 12:8 good when accompanied by F, almsgiving, and
Jud 4:9 fervor, and they humbled themselves with much F
Esth 4:3 among the Jews, with F and weeping and lamenting,
Ps 35:13 I wore sackcloth, I afflicted myself with F
69:10 humbled my soul with F, it became my reproach.
109:24 knees are weak through F; my body has become
Is 58:4 F like yours this day will not make your
Dan 6:18 and spent the night F; no diversions were brought
9:3 prayer and supplications with F and sackcloth and
Joel 2:12 all your heart, with F, with weeping, and with
2Mac 13:12 Lord with weeping and F and lying prostrate for
Mt 6:16 their faces that their F may be seen by
6:18 your face, that your F may not be seen
Mk 2:18 and the Pharisees were F; and people came and
9:29 be driven out by anything but prayer and F
Lk 2:37 the temple, worshiping with F and prayer night and
Acts 13:2 worshiping the Lord and F, the Holy Spirit said,
13:3 Then after F and praying they laid their hands
14:23 church, with prayer and F they committed them to

FASTNESS

Job 39:28 his home in the F of the rocky crag.

FASTNESSES (2)

2Sam 22:46 lost heart, and came trembling out of their F
Ps 18:45 lost heart, and came trembling out of their F

FASTS (2)

Esth 9:31 with regard to their F and their lamenting.
Sir 34:26 So if a man F for his sins, and

FAT (118)

Gen 4:4 flock and of their F portions.
41:2 seven cows sleek and F, and they fed in
41:4 the seven sleek and F cows.
41:18 Nile; and seven cows, F and sleek, came up
41:20 up the first seven F cows,
45:18 you shall eat the F of the land.'
Ex 23:18 bread, or let the F of my feast remain
29:13 shall take all the F that covers the entrails,
29:13 two kidneys with the F that is on them,
29:22 shall also take the F of the ram, and
29:22 the ram, and the F tail, and the fat
29:22 fat tail, and the F that covers the entrails,
29:22 two kidneys with the F that is on them,

F

Lev 1:8 the head, and the F, in order upon the
1:12 its head and its F, and the priest shall
3:3 he shall offer the F covering the entrails and
3:3 entrails and all the F that is on the
3:4 two kidneys with the F that is on them
3:9 he shall offer its F, the fat tail entire,
3:9 offer its fat, the F tail entire, taking it
3:9 the backbone, and the F that covers the entrails,
3:9 entrails, and all the F that is on the
3:10 two kidneys with the F that is on them
3:14 to the LORD, the F covering the entrails, and
3:14 entrails, and all the F that is on the
3:15 two kidneys with the F that is on them
3:16 All F is the LORDs.
3:17 that you eat neither F nor blood."
4:8 And all the F of the bull of the
4:8 take from it, the F that covers the entrails
4:8 entrails and all the F that is on the
4:9 two kidneys with the F that is on them
4:19 And all its F he shall take from it
4:26 And all its F he shall burn on the
4:26 the altar, like the F of the sacrifice of
4:31 And all its F he shall remove, as the
4:31 shall remove, as the F is removed from the
4:35 And all its F he shall remove as the
4:35 shall remove as the F of the lamb is
6:12 burn on it the F of the peace offerings.
7:3 And all its F shall be offered, the fat
7:3 shall be offered, the F tail, the fat that
7:3 the fat tail, the F that covers the entrails,
7:4 two kidneys with the F that is on them
7:23 You shall eat no F, of ox, or sheep,
7:24 The F of an animal that dies of itself,
7:24 of itself, and the F of one that is
7:25 who eats of the F of an animal of
7:30 he shall bring the F with the breast, that
7:31 priest shall burn the F on the altar, but
7:33 peace offerings and the F shall have the right
8:16 he took all the F that was on the
8:16 two kidneys with their F, and Moses burned them
8:20 burned the head and the pieces and the F
8:25 Then he took the F, and the fat tail,
8:25 the fat, and the F tail, and all the
8:25 tail, and all the F that was on the
8:25 two kidneys with their F, and the right thigh;
8:26 placed them on the F and on the right
9:10 the altar; but the F and the kidneys and
9:19 round about, and the F of the ox and
9:19 of the ram, the F tail, and that which
9:20 and they put the F upon the breasts, and
9:20 and he burned the F upon the altar,
9:24 burnt offering and the F upon the altar; and
10:15 by fire of the F, to wave for a
16:25 And the F of the sin offering he shall
17:6 meeting, and burn the F for a pleasing odor
Num 18:17 and shall burn their F as an offering by
Deut 31:20 are full and grown F, they will turn to
32:14 from the flock, with F of lambs and rams,
32:15 "But Jeshurun waxed F, and kicked; you waxed fat,
32:15 and kicked; you waxed F, you grew thick, you
32:38 refuge, who ate the F of their sacrifices, and
Judg 3:17 Eglon was a very F man.
3:22 the blade, and the F closed over the blade,
1Sam 2:15 Moreover, before the F was burned, the priest's
2:16 "Let them burn the F first, and then take
15:22 to hearken than the F of rams.
2Sam 1:22 the slain, from the F of the mighty, the
1Kgs 4:23 cors of meal, ten F oxen, and twenty pasture-fed
8:64 cereal offering and the F pieces of the peace
8:64 cereal offering and the F pieces of the peace
2Chr 7:7 burnt offering and the F of the peace offerings,
7:7 burnt offering and the cereal offering and the F
29:35 offerings there was the F of the peace offerings,
35:14 burnt offerings and the F parts until night; so
Neh 8:10 your way, eat the F and drink sweet wine
9:25 were filled and became F, and delighted themselves
Jud 16:16 small thing, and all F for burnt offerings to
Job 15:27 his face with his F, and gathered fat upon
15:27 his fat, and gathered F upon his loins,
21:24 his body full of F and the marrow of
Ps 63:5 as with marrow and F, and my mouth praises
119:70 heart is gross like F, but I delight in
Sir 26:13 and her skill puts F on his bones.
47:2 As the F is selected from the peace offering,
Is 1:11 of rams and the F of fed beasts; I
6:10 heart of this people F, and their ears heavy,
17:4 brought low, and the F of his flesh will
25:6 peoples a feast of F things, a feast of
25:6 on the lees, of F things full of marrow,
34:6 it is gorged with F, with the blood of
34:6 and goats, with the F of the kidneys of
34:7 with blood, and their soil made rich with F
43:24 satisfied me with the F of your sacrifices.
Jer 5:28 rich, they have grown F and sleek.
Ezek 34:3 You eat the F, you clothe yourselves with the
34:14 grazing land, and on F pasture they shall feed
34:16 the weak, and the F and the strong I
34:20 will judge between the F sheep and the lean
39:19 And you shall eat F till you are filled,
44:7 me my food, the F and the blood.
44:15 to offer me the F and the blood, says
Dan 3:39 tens of thousands of F lambs;
14:27 Then Daniel took pitch, F, and hair, and boiled
Zech 11:16 the flesh of the F ones, tearing off even
Mt 22:4 my oxen and my F calves are killed, and

FATE (15)

Num 16:29 are visited by the F of all men, then
Ps 49:13 This is the F of those who have foolish
81:15 toward him, and their F would last for ever.
Eccl 2:14 I perceived that one F comes to all of
3:19 For the F of the sons of men and
3:19 of men and the F of beasts is the
9:2 is vanity, since one F comes to all, to
9:3 the sun, that one F comes to all; also
Wis 17:17 and endured the inescapable F; for with one chain
19:4 For the F they deserved drew them on to
Jer 49:20 surely their fold shall be appalled at their F
50:45 surely their fold shall be appalled at their F
Lam 3:51 me grief at the F of all the maidens
2Mac 9:28 by a most pitiable F, among the mountains in
13:7 By such a F it came about that Menelaus

FATHER (1,301)

Gen 2:24 a man leaves his F and his mother and
4:18 and Irad was the F of Me-huja-el, and Me-huja-el
4:18 Me-huja-el the F of Me-thusha-el, and Me-thusha-el
4:18 Me-thusha-el, and Me-thusha-el the F of Lamech.
4:20 Jabal; he was the F of those who dwell
4:21 Jubal; he was the F of all those who
5:3 years, he became the F of a son in
5:4 after he became the F of Seth were eight
5:6 years, he became the F of Enosh.
5:9 years, he became the F of Kenan.
5:12 years, he became the F of Mahalalel.
5:15 years, he became the F of Jared.
5:18 years he became the F of Enoch.
5:21 years, he became the F of Methuselah.
5:25 years, he became the F of Lamech.
5:28 years, he became the F of a son,
5:32 old, Noah became the F of Shem, Ham, and
9:18 Ham was the F of Canaan.
9:22 And Ham, the F of Canaan, saw the nakedness
9:22 the nakedness of his F, and told his two
9:23 the nakedness of their F; their faces were turned
9:23 did not see their F's nakedness.
10:8 Cush became the F of Nimrod; he was the
10:13 Egypt became the F of Ludim, Anamim, Lehabim,
10:15 Canaan became the F of Sidon his first-born, and
10:21 To Shem also, the F of all the children
10:24 Arpachshad became the F of Shelah; and Shelah
10:24 and Shelah became the F of Eber.
10:26 Joktan became the F of Almodad, Sheleph,
11:10 old, he became the F of Arpachshad two years
11:12 years, he became the F of Shelah;
11:14 years, he became the F of Eber;
11:16 years, he became the F of Peleg;
11:18 years, he became the F of Reu;
11:20 years, he became the F of Serug;
11:22 years, he became the F of Nahor;
11:24 years, he became the F of Terah;
11:26 years, he became the F of Abram, Nahor, and
11:27 Terah was the F of Abram, Nahor, and Haran;
11:27 and Haran was the F of Lot.
11:28 Haran died before his F Terah in the land
11:29 daughter of Haran the F of Milcah and Iscah.
12:1 your kindred and your F's house to the land
17:4 you shall be the F of a multitude of
17:5 have made you the F of a multitude of
17:20 he shall be the F of twelve princes, and
19:31 to the younger, "Our F is old, and there
19:32 let us make our F drink wine, and we

FATHER

19:32 him, that we may preserve offspring through our F
19:33 So they made their F drink wine that night;
19:33 and lay with her F; he did not know
19:34 last night with my F; let us make him
19:34 him, that we may preserve offspring through our F
19:35 So they made their F drink wine that night
19:36 daughters of Lot were with child by their F
19:37 Moab; he is the F of the Moabites to
19:38 Ben-ammi; he is the F of the Ammonites to
20:12 the daughter of my F but not the daughter
20:13 to wander from my F's house, I said to
22:7 Isaac said to his F Abraham, "My father!" And
22:7 And Isaac said to his father Abraham, "My F
22:21 his brother, Kemuel the F of Aram,
22:23 Bethuel became the F of Rebekah.
24:7 took me from my F's house and from the
24:23 there room in your F's house for us to
24:38 shall go to my F's house and to my
24:40 kindred and from my F's house;
25:3 Jokshan was the F of Sheba and Dedan.
25:19 son: Abraham was the F of Isaac,
26:3 the oath which I swore to Abraham your F
26:15 the wells which his F's servants had dug in
26:15 days of Abraham his F
26:18 days of Abraham his F; for the Philistines had
26:18 the names which his F had given them.
26:24 God of Abraham your F; fear not, for I
27:6 Jacob, "I heard your F speak to your brother
27:9 savory food for your F, such as he loves;
27:10 bring it to your F to eat, so that
27:12 Perhaps my F will feel me, and I shall
27:14 food, such as his F loved.
27:18 went in to his F, and said, "My father";
27:18 father, and said, "My F; and he said, "Here
27:19 Jacob said to his F, "I am Esau your
27:22 near to Isaac his F, who felt him and
27:26 Then his F Isaac said to him, "Come near
27:30 presence of Isaac his F, Esau his brother came
27:31 prepared savory food, and brought it to his F
27:31 he said to his F, "Let my father arise,
27:31 his father, "Let my F arise, and eat of
27:32 His F Isaac said to him, "Who are you?"
27:34 the words of his F, he cried out with
27:34 and said to his F, "Bless me, even me
27:34 father, "Bless me, even me also, O my F
27:38 Esau said to his F, "Have you but one
27:38 his father, "Have you but one blessing, my F
27:38 Bless me, even me also, O my F
27:39 Then Isaac his F answered him: "Behold, away from
27:41 blessing with which his F had blessed him, and
27:41 of mourning for my F are approaching; then I
28:2 of Bethuel your mother's F; and take as wife
28:7 Jacob had obeyed his F and his mother and
28:8 not please Isaac his F,
28:13 God of Abraham your F and the God of
28:21 come again to my F's house in peace, then
29:9 Rachel came with her F's sheep; for she kept
29:12 that he was her F's kinsman, and that he
29:12 Rebekah's son; and she ran and told her F
31:1 from what was our F's he has gained all
31:5 "I see that your F does not regard me
31:5 the God of my F has been with me.
31:6 I have served your F with all my strength;
31:7 my strength; yet your F has cheated me and
31:9 the cattle of your F, and given them to
31:14 to us in our F's house?
31:16 taken away from our F belongs to us and
31:18 of Canaan to his F Isaac.
31:19 and Rachel stole her F's household gods.
31:29 the God of your F spoke to me last
31:30 longed greatly for your F's house, but why did
31:35 she said to her F, "Let not my lord
31:42 the God of my F, the God of Abraham
31:53 the God of their F, judge between us." So
31:53 the Fear of his F Isaac,
32:9 "O God of my F Abraham and God of
32:9 and God of my F Isaac, O LORD who
33:19 sons of Hamor, Shechem's F, he bought for a
34:4 Shechem spoke to his F Hamor, saying, "Get me
34:6 And Hamor the F of Shechem went out to
34:11 also said to her F and to her brothers,
34:13 answered Shechem and his F Hamor deceitfully,
35:18 name Ben-oni; but his F called his name Benjamin.
35:22 lay with Bilhah his F's concubine; and Israel heard
35:27 Jacob came to his F Isaac at Mamre, or
36:9 descendants of Esau the F of the Edomites in
36:24 as he pastured the asses of Zibeon his F
36:43 (that is, Esau, the F of Edom), according to
37:1 the land of his F's sojournings, in the land
37:2 Bilhah and Zilpah, his F's wives; and Joseph brought
37:2 brought an ill report of them to their F
37:4 brothers saw that their F loved him more than
37:10 told it to his F and to his brothers,
37:10 to his brothers, his F rebuked him, and said
37:11 of him, but his F kept the saying in
37:12 went to pasture their F's flock near Shechem.
37:22 of their hand, to restore him to his F
37:32 brought it to their F, and said, "This we
37:35 Thus his F wept for him.
38:11 a widow in your F's house, till Shelah my
38:11 and dwelt in her F's house.
41:51 hardship and all my F's house."
42:13 this day with our F, and one is no
42:29 came to Jacob their F in the land of
42:32 brothers, sons of our F; one is no more,
42:32 this day with our F in the land of
42:35 when they and their F saw their bundles of
42:36 And Jacob their F said to them, "You have
42:37 Reuben said to his F, "Slay my two sons
43:2 brought from Egypt, their F said to them, "Go
43:7 kindred, saying, 'Is your F still alive?
43:8 said to Israel his F, "Send the lad with
43:11 Then their F Israel said to them, "If it
43:23 the God of your F must have put treasure
43:27 and said, "Is your F well, the old man
43:28 said, "Your servant our F is well, he is
44:17 for you, go up in peace to your F
44:19 saying, 'Have you a F, or a brother?'
44:20 lord, 'We have a F, an old man, and
44:20 mother's children; and his F loves him.'
44:22 lad cannot leave his F, for if he should
44:22 he should leave his F, his father would die.'
44:22 leave his father, his F would die.'
44:24 to your servant my F we told him the
44:25 And when our F said, 'Go again, buy us
44:27 Then your servant my F said to us, 'You
44:30 to your servant my F, and the lad is
44:31 of your servant our F with sorrow to Sheol.
44:32 the lad to my F, saying, 'If I do
44:32 the sight of my F all my life.'
44:34 go back to my F if the lad is
44:34 see the evil that would come upon my F
45:3 am Joseph; is my F still alive?" But his
45:8 has made me a F to Pharaoh, and lord
45:9 go up to my F and say to him,
45:13 You must tell my F of all my splendor
45:13 haste and bring my F down here."
45:18 Canaan; and take your F and your households, and
45:19 wives, and bring your F, and come.
45:23 To his F he sent as follows: ten asses
45:23 and provision for his F on the journey.
45:25 of Canaan to their F Jacob.
45:27 the spirit of their F Jacob revived;
46:1 the God of his F Isaac.
46:3 the God of your F; do not be afraid
46:5 Israel carried Jacob their F, their little ones, and
46:29 to meet Israel his F in Goshen; and he
46:31 brothers and to his F's household, "I will go
46:31 'My brothers and my F's household, who were in
47:1 and told Pharaoh, "My F and my brothers, with
47:5 said to Joseph, "Your F and your brothers have
47:6 before you; settle your F and your brothers in
47:7 brought in Jacob his F, and set him before
47:11 Then Joseph settled his F and his brothers, and
47:12 And Joseph provided his F, his brothers, and all
47:12 brothers, and all his F's household with food,
48:1 was told, "Behold, your F is ill"; so he
48:9 Joseph said to his F, "They are my sons,
48:17 Joseph saw that his F laid his right hand
48:17 and he took his F's hand, to remove it
48:18 Joseph said to his F, "Not so, my father;
48:18 father, "Not so, my F; for this one is
48:19 But his F refused, and said, "I know, my
49:2 sons of Jacob, and hearken to Israel your F
49:4 went up to your F's bed; then you defiled
49:8 of your enemies; your F's sons shall bow down
49:25 the God of your F who will help you,
49:26 The blessings of your F are mighty beyond the
49:28 this is what their F said to them as
50:1 Joseph fell on his F's face, and wept over
50:2 his servants the physicians to embalm his F
50:5 of Pharaoh, saying, My F made me swear, saying,

F

50:5 you, and bury my F; then I will return."
50:6 up, and bury your F, as he made you
50:7 up to bury his F; and with him went
50:8 his brothers, and his F's household; only their
50:10 a mourning for his F seven days.
50:14 he had buried his F, Joseph returned to Egypt
50:14 had gone up with him to bury his F
50:15 brothers saw that their F was dead, they said,
50:16 to Joseph, saying, "Your F gave this command before
50:17 of the servants of the God of your F
50:22 Egypt, he and his F's house; and Joseph lived
Ex 2:16 troughs to water their F's flock.
2:18 they came to their F Reuel, he said, "How
3:6 the God of your F, the God of Abraham,
6:20 to wife Jochebed his F's sister and she bore
15:2 will praise him, my F's God, and I will
18:4 "The God of my F was my help, and
20:12 "Honor your F and your mother, that your days
21:15 "Whoever strikes his F or his mother shall be
21:17 "Whoever curses his F or his mother shall be
22:17 If her F utterly refuses to give her to
Lev 16:32 as priest in his F's place shall make atonement,
18:7 the nakedness of your F, which is the nakedness
18:8 the nakedness of your F's wife; it is your
18:8 wife; it is your F's nakedness.
18:9 the daughter of your F or the daughter of
18:11 the nakedness of your F's wife's daughter, begotten
18:11 daughter, begotten by your F, since she is your
18:12 the nakedness of your F's sister; she is your
18:12 sister; she is your F's near kinswoman.
18:14 the nakedness of your F's brother, that is, you
19:3 his mother and his F, and you shall keep
20:9 one who curses his F or his mother shall
20:9 he has cursed his F or his mother, his
20:11 who lies with his F's wife has uncovered his
20:11 wife has uncovered his F's nakedness; both of them
20:17 a daughter of his F or a daughter of
20:19 sister or of your F's sister, for that is
21:2 kin, his mother, his F, his son, his daughter,
21:9 the harlot, profanes her F; she shall be burned
21:11 himself, even for his F or for his mother;
22:13 and returns to her F's house, as in her
22:13 may eat of her F's food; yet no outsider
24:10 Israelite woman's son, whose F was an Egyptian,
Num 3:4 as priests in the lifetime of Aaron their F
6:7 Neither for his F nor for his mother, nor
12:14 to Moses, "If her F had but spit in
18:2 the tribe of your F, that they may join
26:29 and Machir was the F of Gilead; of Gilead,
26:58 And Kohath was the F of Amram.
27:3 of meeting, saying, "Our F died in the wilderness;
27:4 the name of our F be taken away from
27:4 a possession among our F's brethren."
27:7 an inheritance among their F's brethren and cause
27:7 the inheritance of their F to pass to them.
27:10 his inheritance to his F's brothers.
27:11 And if his F has no brothers, then you
30:3 pledge, while within her F's house, in her youth,
30:4 her youth, and her F hears of her vow
30:5 But if her F expresses disapproval to her on
30:5 forgive her, because her F opposed her.
30:16 wife, and between a F and his daughter, while
30:16 her youth, within her F's house.
36:6 within the family of the tribe of their F
36:8 the tribe of her F, so that every one
36:11 to sons of their F's brothers.
36:12 in the tribe of the family of their F
Deut 5:16 "Honor your F and your mother, as the LORD
21:13 house and bewail her F and her mother a
21:18 the voice of his F or the voice of
21:19 to them, then his F and his mother shall
22:15 of virginity,' then the F of the young woman
22:16 the gate; and the F of the young woman
22:19 give them to the F of the young woman,
22:21 the door of her F's house, and the men
22:21 the harlot in her F's house; so you shall
22:29 shall give to the F of the young woman
22:30 shall not take his F's wife, nor shall he
26:5 wandering Aramean was my F; and he went down
27:16 he who dishonors his F or his mother.' And
27:20 who lies with his F's wife, because he has
27:20 because he has uncovered her who is his F's.
27:22 the daughter of his F or the daughter of
32:6 Is not he your F, who created you, who
32:7 many generations; ask your F, and he will show
33:9 who said of his F and mother, 'I regard

Josh 2:12 deal kindly with my F's house, and give me
2:13 and save alive my F and mother, my brothers
2:18 into your house your F and mother, your brothers,
2:18 brothers, and all your F's household.
6:23 out Rahab, and her F and mother and brothers
6:25 the harlot, and her F's household, and all who
15:13 Hebron (Arba was the F of Anak).
15:18 him to ask her F for a field; and
17:1 first-born of Manasseh, the F of Gilead, were
17:4 them an inheritance among the brethren of their F
21:11 Kiriath-arba (Arba being the F of Anak), that is
24:2 the Euphrates, Terah, the F of Abraham and of
24:3 Then I took your F Abraham from beyond the
24:32 sons of Hamor the F of Shechem for a
Judg 1:14 him to ask her F for a field; and
6:25 to him, "Take your F's bull, the second bull
6:25 of Baal which your F has, and cut down
8:32 tomb of Joash his F, at Ophrah of the
9:5 he went to his F's house at Ophrah, and
9:17 deserved-- for my F fought for you, and
9:18 risen up against my F's house this day, and
9:28 men of Hamor the F of Shechem?
9:56 he committed against his F in killing his seventy
11:1 Gilead was the F of Jephthah.
11:2 not inherit in our F's house; for you are
11:7 me out of my F's house?
11:36 said to him, "My F, if you have opened
11:37 she said to her F, "Let this thing be
11:39 she returned to her F, who did with her
14:2 up, and told his F and mother, "I saw
14:3 But his F and mother said to him, "Is
14:3 Samson said to his F, "Get her for me;
14:4 His F and mother did not know that it
14:5 went down with his F and mother to Timnah,
14:6 did not tell his F or his mother what
14:9 he came to his F and mother, and gave
14:10 And his F went down to the woman, and
14:15 burn you and your F's house with fire.
14:16 have not told my F nor my mother, and
14:19 went back to his F's house.
15:1 But her F would not allow him to go
15:2 And her F said, "I really thought that you
15:6 burned her and her F with fire.
16:31 and Eshtaol in the tomb of Manoah his F
17:10 be to me a F and a priest, and
18:19 be to us a F and a priest.
19:2 from him to her F's house at Bethlehem in
19:3 he came to her F's house; and when the
19:3 and when the girl's F saw him, he came
19:4 his father-in-law, the girl's F, made him stay, and
19:5 go; but the girl's F said to his son-in-law,
19:6 together; and the girl's F said to the man,
19:8 depart; and the girl's F said, "Strengthen your heart,
19:9 his father-in-law, the girl's F, said to him, "Behold,
Ruth 2:11 how you left your F and mother and your
4:17 Obed; he was the F of Jesse, the father
4:17 father of Jesse, the F of David.
4:18 Perez: Perez was the F of Hezron,
1Sam 2:25 the voice of their F; for it was the
2:27 the house of your F when they were in
2:28 the house of your F all my offerings by
2:30 the house of your F should go in and
2:31 the strength of your F's house, so that there
9:3 asses of Kish, Saul's F, were lost.
9:5 go back, lest my F cease to care about
9:20 and for all your F's house?"
10:2 found, and now your F has ceased to care
10:12 of the place answered, "And who is their F
14:1 But he did not tell his F
14:27 had not heard his F charge the people with
14:28 the people said, "Your F strictly charged the people
14:29 Then Jonathan said, "My F has troubled the land;
14:51 uncle; Kish was the F of Saul, and Ner
14:51 Saul, and Ner the F of Abner was the
17:15 Saul to feed his F's sheep at Bethlehem.
17:25 daughter, and make his F's house free in Israel."
17:34 keep sheep for his F; and when there came
18:2 him return to his F's house.
18:18 are my kinsfolk, my F's family in Israel, that
19:2 told David, "Saul my F seeks to kill you;
19:3 and stand beside my F in the field where
19:3 will speak to my F about you; and if
19:4 David to Saul his F, and said to him,
20:1 my sin before your F, that he seeks my
20:2 Behold, my F does nothing either great or small
20:2 and why should my F hide this from me?

20:3 But David replied, "Your F knows well that I
20:6 If your F misses me at all, then say,
20:8 for why should you bring me to your F
20:9 was determined by my F that evil should come
20:10 tell me if your F answers you roughly?"
20:12 I have sounded my F, about this time tomorrow,
20:13 should it please my F to do you harm,
20:13 with you, as he has been with my F
20:32 Jonathan answered Saul his F, "Why should he be
20:33 Jonathan knew that his F was determined to put
20:34 for David, because his F had disgraced him.
22:1 brothers and all his F's house heard it, they
22:3 Moab, "Pray let my F and my mother stay
22:11 Ahitub, and all his F's house, the priests who
22:15 the house of my F; for your servant has
22:16 you and all your F's house."
22:22 the persons of your F's house.
23:17 hand of Saul my F shall not find you;
23:17 to you; Saul my F also knows this."
24:11 LORD's anointed.' See, my F, see the skirt of
24:21 name out of my F's house."
2Sam 2:32 the tomb of his F, which was at Bethlehem.
3:7 gone in to my F's concubine?"
3:8 house of Saul your F, to his brothers, and
3:29 and upon all his F's house; and may the
6:21 chose me above your F, and above all his
7:14 I will be his F, and he shall be
9:7 the sake of your F Jonathan, and I will
9:7 land of Saul your F; and you shall eat
10:2 of Nahash, as his F dealt loyally with me."
10:2 by his servants to console him concerning his F
10:3 comforters to you, that he is honoring your F
13:5 ill; and when your F comes to see you,
14:9 king, and on my F's house; let the king
15:34 I have been your F's servant in time past,
16:3 will give me back the kingdom of my F
16:19 I have served your F, so I will serve
16:21 "Go in to your F's concubines, whom he has
16:21 yourself odious to your F, and the hands of
16:22 went in to his F's concubines in the sight
17:8 "You know that your F and his men are
17:8 Besides, your F is expert in war; he will
17:10 Israel knows that your F is a mighty man,
17:23 and was buried in the tomb of his F
19:28 For all my F's house were but men doomed
19:37 the grave of my F and my mother.
21:14 tomb of Kish his F; and they did all
24:17 me and against my F's house."
1Kgs 1:6 His F had never at any time displeased him
2:12 throne of David his F; and his kingdom was
2:24 throne of David my F, and who has made
2:26 GOD before David my F, and because you shared
2:26 you shared in all the affliction of my F
2:31 me and from my F's house the guilt for
2:32 the knowledge of my F David, he attacked and
2:44 did to David my F; so the LORD will
3:3 statutes of David his F; only, he sacrificed and
3:6 thy servant David my F, because he walked before
3:7 place of David my F, although I am but
3:14 my commandments, as your F David walked, then I
5:1 in place of his F; for Hiram always loved
5:3 know that David my F could not build a
5:5 said to David my F, 'Your son, whom I
6:12 with you, which I spoke to David your F
7:14 of Naphtali, and his F was a man of
7:51 things which David his F had dedicated, the silver,
8:15 mouth to David my F, saying,
8:17 heart of David my F to build a house
8:18 said to David my F, 'Whereas it was in
8:20 place of David my F, and sit on the
8:24 thy servant David my F what thou didst declare
8:25 thy servant David my F what thou hast promised
8:26 thou hast spoken to thy servant David my F
9:4 me, as David your F walked, with integrity of
9:5 I promised David your F, saying, 'There shall not
11:4 God, as was the heart of David his F
11:6 LORD, as David his F had done.
11:12 sake of David your F I will not do
11:17 certain Edomites of his F's servants, Hadad being yet
11:27 the breach of the city of David his F
11:33 ordinances, as David his F did.
11:43 city of David his F; and Rehoboam his son
12:4 said to Rehoboam, "Your F made our yoke heavy.
12:4 hard service of your F and his heavy yoke
12:6 stood before Solomon his F while he was yet
12:9 the yoke that your F put upon us'?"
12:10 said to you, 'Your F made our yoke heavy,
12:10 is thicker than my F's loins.
12:11 And now, whereas my F laid upon you a
12:11 My F chastised you with whips, but I will
12:14 young men, saying, "My F made your yoke heavy,
12:14 to your yoke; my F chastised you with whips,
13:11 spoken to the king, they told to their F
13:12 And their F said to them, "Which way did
15:3 the sins which his F did before him; and
15:3 his God, as the heart of David his F
15:11 LORD, as David his F had done.
15:15 votive gifts of his F and his own votive
15:19 you, as between my F and your father: behold,
15:19 my father and your F: behold, I am sending
15:24 city of David his F; and Jehoshaphat his son
15:26 the way of his F, and in his sin
18:18 you have, and your F's house, because you have
19:20 "Let me kiss my F and my mother, and
20:34 "The cities which my F took from your father
20:34 father took from your F I will restore; and
20:34 in Damascus, as my F did in Samaria." And
22:43 way of Asa his F; he did not turn
22:46 the days of his F Asa, he exterminated from
22:50 city of David his F; and Jehoram his son
22:52 the way of his F, and in the way
22:53 every way that his F had done.
2Kgs 2:12 and he cried, "My F, my father!
2:12 saw it and he cried, "My father, my F
3:2 though not like his F and mother, for he
3:2 of Baal which his F had made.
3:13 the prophets of your F and the prophets of
4:18 one day to his F among the reapers.
4:19 he said to his F, "Oh, my head, my
4:19 The F said to his servant, "Carry him to
5:13 said to him, "My F, if the prophet had
6:21 said to Elisha, "My F, shall I slay them?
9:25 side behind Ahab his F, how the LORD uttered
10:3 set him on his F's throne, and fight for
13:14 before him, crying, "My F, my father!
13:14 and wept before him, crying, "My father, my F
13:25 taken from Jehoahaz his F in war.
14:3 not like David his F; he did in all
14:3 things as Joash his F had done.
14:5 his servants who had slain the king his F
14:21 king instead of his F Amaziah.
15:3 to all that his F Amaziah had done.
15:34 to all that his F Uzziah had done.
15:38 city of David his F; and Ahaz his son
16:2 his God, as his F David had done,
18:3 all that David his F had done.
20:5 God of David your F: I have heard your
21:3 places which Hezekiah his F had destroyed; and he
21:20 LORD, as Manasseh his F had done.
21:21 way in which his F walked, and served the
21:21 the idols that his F served, and worshiped them;
22:2 way of David his F, and he did not
23:30 him king in his F's stead.
23:34 place of Josiah his F, and changed his name
24:9 to all that his F had done.
1Chr 1:10 Cush was the F of Nimrod; he began to
1:11 Egypt was the F of Ludim, Anamim, Lehabim,
1:13 Canaan was the F of Sidon his first-born, and
1:18 Arpachshad was the F of Shelah; and Shelah was
1:18 and Shelah was the F of Eber.
1:20 Joktan was the F of Almodad, Sheleph,
1:34 Abraham was the F of Isaac.
2:10 Ram was the F of Amminadab, and Amminadab was
2:10 and Amminadab was the F of Nahshon, prince of
2:11 Nahshon was the F of Salma, Salma of Boaz,
2:13 Jesse was the F of Eliab his first-born, Abinadab
2:17 bore Amasa, and the F of Amasa was Jether
2:20 Hur was the F of Uri, and Uri was
2:20 and Uri was the F of Bezalel.
2:21 daughter of Machir the F of Gilead, whom he
2:22 and Segub was the F of Jair, who had
2:23 descendants of Machir, the F of Gilead.
2:24 wife of Hezron his F, and she bore him
2:24 bore him Ashhur, the F of Tekoa.
2:36 Attai was the F of Nathan and Nathan of
2:37 Zabad was the F of Ephlal, and Ephlal of
2:38 Obed was the F of Jehu, and Jehu of
2:39 Azariah was the F of Helez, and Helez of
2:40 Ele-asah was the F of Sismai, and Sismai of
2:41 Shallum was the F of Jekamiah, and Jekamiah of
2:42 first-born, who was the F of Ziph.
2:44 Shema was the F of Raham, the father of

2:44 father of Raham, the F of Jorke-am; and Rekem
2:44 and Rekem was the F of Shammai.
2:45 and Maon was the F of Bethzur.
2:46 and Haran was the F of Gazez.
2:49 also bore Shaaph the F of Madmannah, Sheva the
2:49 of Madmannah, Sheva the F of Machbenah and the
2:49 of Machbenah and the F of Gibe-a; and the
2:50 of Ephrathah: Shobal the F of Kiriath-jearim,
2:51 of Kiriath-jearim, Salma, the F of Bethelem, and
2:51 Bethelem, and Hareph the F of Beth-gader.
2:52 Shobal the F of Kiriath-jearim had other sons:
2:55 came from Hammath, the F of the house of
4:2 of Shobal was the F of Jahath, and Jahath
4:2 and Jahath was the F of Ahumai and Lahad.
4:4 and Penuel was the F of Gedor, and Ezer
4:4 Gedor, and Ezer the F of Hushah.
4:4 first-born of Ephrathah, the F of Bethlehem.
4:5 Ashhur, the F of Tekoa, had two wives, Helah
4:8 Koz was the F of Anub, Zobebah, and the
4:11 of Shuhah, was the F of Mehir, who was
4:11 Mehir, who was the F of Eshton.
4:12 Eshton was the F of Bethrapha, Paseah, and
4:12 Paseah, and Tehinnah the F of Irnahash.
4:14 Meonothai was the F of Ophrah; and Seraiah was
4:14 and Seraiah was the F of Joab the father
4:14 father of Joab the F of Ge-harashim, so-called
4:17 Shammai, and Ishbah, the F of Eshtemoa.
4:18 wife bore Jered the F of Gedor, Heber the
4:18 of Gedor, Heber the F of Soco, and Jekuthiel
4:18 Soco, and Jekuthiel the F of Zanoah.
4:21 of Judah: Er the F of Lecah, Laadah the
4:21 of Lecah, Laadah the F of Mareshah, and the
5:1 because he polluted his F's couch, his birthright was
6:4 Eleazar was the F of Phinehas, Phinehas of Abishua,
6:11 Azariah was the F of Amariah, Amariah of Ahitub,
7:14 she bore Machir the F of Gilead.
7:22 And Ephraim their F mourned many days, and his
7:31 Malchi-el, who was the F of Birzaith.
7:32 Heber was the F of Japhlet, Shomer, Hotham, and
8:1 Benjamin was the F of Bela his first-born, Ashbel
8:7 Heglam, who was the F of Uzza and Ahihud.
8:29 Je-iel the F of Gibeon dwelt in Gibeon, and
8:32 Mikloth (he was the F of Shimeah).
8:33 Ner was the F of Kish, Kish of Saul,
8:34 and Merib-baal was the F of Micah.
8:36 Ahaz was the F of Jehoaddah; and Jehoaddah was
8:36 and Jehoaddah was the F of Alemeth, Azmaveth, and
8:36 Zimri; Zimri was the F of Moza.
8:37 Moza was the F of Bine-a; Raphah was his
9:35 In Gibeon dwelt the F of Gibeon, Je-iel, and
9:38 and Mikloth was the F of Shimeam; and these
9:39 Ner was the F of Kish, Kish of Saul,
9:40 and Merib-baal was the F of Micah.
9:42 and Ahaz was the F of Jarah, and Jarah
9:42 and Zimri was the F of Moza.
9:43 Moza was the F of Bine-a; and Rephaiah was
12:28 commanders from his own F's house.
17:13 I will be his F, and he shall be
19:2 of Nahash, for his F dealt loyally with me."
19:2 sent messengers to console him concerning his F
19:3 comforters to you, that he is honoring your F
21:17 me and against my F's house; but let not
22:10 I will be his F, and I will establish
23:11 therefore they became a F's house in one reckoning.
24:2 Abihu died before their F, and had no children,
24:6 of the Levites; one F's house being chosen for
24:19 them by Aaron their F, as the LORD God
24:31 the head of each F's house and his younger
25:3 the direction of their F Jeduthun, who prophesied
25:6 the direction of their F in the music in
26:10 not the first-born, his F made him chief),
28:4 me from all my F's house to be king
28:4 house of Judah my F's house, and among my
28:4 house, and among my F's sons he took pleasure
28:6 be my son, and I will be his F
28:9 the God of your F, and serve him with
29:10 God of Israel our F, for ever and ever.
29:23 instead of David his F; and he prospered, and
2Chr 1:8 love to David my F, and hast made me
1:9 promise to David my F be now fulfilled, for
2:3 dealt with David my F and sent him cedar
2:7 Jerusalem, whom David my F provided.
2:14 of Dan, and his F was a man of
2:14 craftsmen, the craftsmen of my lord, David your F
2:17 them which David his F had taken; and there
3:1 appeared to David his F, at the place that
5:1 things which David his F had dedicated, and stored
6:4 mouth to David my F, saying,
6:7 heart of David my F to build a house
6:8 said to David my F, 'Whereas it was in
6:10 place of David my F, and sit on the
6:15 thy servant David my F what thou didst declare
6:16 thy servant David my F what thou hast promised
7:17 me, as David your F walked, doing according to
7:18 covenanted with David your F, saying, 'There shall
8:14 ordinance of David his F, he appointed the divisions
9:31 city of David his F; and Rehoboam his son
10:4 said to Rehoboam, "Your F made our yoke heavy.
10:4 hard service of your F and his heavy yoke
10:6 stood before Solomon his F while he was yet
10:9 the yoke that your F put upon us'?"
10:10 said to you, 'Your F made our yoke heavy,
10:10 is thicker than my F's loins.
10:11 And now, whereas my F laid upon you a
10:11 My F chastised you with whips, but I will
10:14 young men, saying, "My F made your yoke heavy,
10:14 add to it; my F chastised you with whips,
15:18 votive gifts of his F and his own votive
16:3 you, as between my F and your father; behold,
16:3 my father and your F; behold, I am sending
17:2 Ephraim which Asa his F had taken.
17:3 earlier ways of his F; he did not seek
17:4 the God of his F and walked in his
20:32 way of Asa his F and did not turn
21:3 Their F gave them great gifts, of silver, gold,
21:4 the throne of his F and was established, he
21:12 God of David your F, 'Because you have not
21:12 ways of Jehoshaphat your F, or in the ways
21:13 your brothers, of your F's house, who were better
22:4 the death of his F they were his counselors,
24:22 kindness which Jehoiada, Zechariah's F, had shown
25:3 his servants who had slain the king his F
26:1 king instead of his F Amaziah.
26:4 to all that his F Amaziah had done.
27:2 to all that his F Uzziah had done--only
28:1 the LORD, like his F David,
29:2 all that David his F had done.
33:3 high places which his F Hezekiah had broken down,
33:22 LORD, as Manasseh his F had done.
33:22 images that Manasseh his F had made, and served
33:23 LORD, as Manasseh his F had humbled himself, but
34:2 ways of David his F; and he did not
34:3 God of David his F; and in the twelfth
35:5 a part of a F's house of the Levites.
36:1 him king in his F's stead in Jerusalem.
Neh 1:6 Yea, I and my F's house have sinned.
12:10 And Jeshua was the F of Joiakim, Joiakim the
12:10 of Joiakim, Joiakim the F of Eliashib, Eliashib the
12:10 of Eliashib, Eliashib the F of Joiada,
12:11 of Joiada, Joiada the F of Jonathan, and Jonathan
12:11 Jonathan, and Jonathan the F of Jaddu-a.
Tob 1:8 duty, as Deborah my F's mother had commanded me,
1:8 for I was left an orphan by my F
1:9 her I became the F of Tobias.
2:3 came back and said, F, one of our people
3:7 was reproached by her F's maids,
3:10 only child of my F; if I do this,
3:15 the name of my F in the land of
3:15 I am my F's only child, and he has
4:12 is not of your F's tribe; for we are
5:1 Then Tobias answered him, F, I will do everything
5:7 "Wait for me, and I shall tell my F
5:8 and said to his F, "I have found some
5:16 And his F said to him, "Go with this
6:12 will speak to her F, and as soon as
6:14 the only son my F has, and I am
6:14 the lives of my F and mother to the
6:15 words with which your F commanded you to take
7:5 And Tobias said, "He is my F
7:13 Moses, and take her with you to your F
8:21 in safety to his F, and that the rest
9:4 not leave; but my F is counting the days,
10:1 Now his F Tobit was counting each day, and
10:7 me back, for my F and mother have given
10:8 send messengers to your F, and they will inform
10:9 Tobias replied, "No, send me back to my F
11:2 not aware, brother, of how you left your F
11:6 and said to his F, "Behold, your son is
11:7 know, Tobias, that your F will open his eyes.
11:11 took hold of his F, and he sprinkled the
11:11 the gall upon his F's eyes, saying, "Be of
11:11 his father's eyes, saying, "Be of good cheer, F

11:15 he reported to his F the great things that
11:17 and blessed are your F and your mother." So
12:2 He replied, F, it would do me no harm
13:4 God, he is our F for ever.
14:12 when Anna died he buried her with his F
14:13 and that of his F Tobit.
Jud 9:2 Lord God of my F Simeon, to whom thou
9:12 me, God of my F, God of the inheritance
Esth 2:7 for she had neither F nor mother; the maiden
2:7 lovely, and when her F and her mother died,
4:14 but you and your F's house will perish.
13:6 and is our second F, shall all, with their
16:11 he was called our F and was continually bowed
Job 15:10 the aged are among us, older than your F
17:14 pit, 'You are my F and to the worm,
29:16 I was a F to the poor, and I
31:18 reared him as a F, and from his mother's
38:28 "Has the rain a F, or who has begotten
42:15 Job's daughters; and their F gave them inheritance
Ps 27:10 For my F and my mother have forsaken me,
45:10 your people and your F's house;
68:5 F of the fatherless and protector of widows is
89:26 me, 'Thou art my F, my God, and the
103:13 As a F pities his children, so the LORD
Prov 1:8 Hear, my son, your F's instruction, and reject not
3:12 he loves, as a F the son in whom
4:2 Hear, O sons, a F's instruction, and be attentive,
4:4 a son with my F, tender, the only one
6:20 My son, keep your F's commandment, and forsake
10:1 son makes a glad F, but a foolish son
13:1 wise son hears his F's instruction, but a scoffer
15:5 A fool despises his F's instruction, but he who
15:20 son makes a glad F, but a foolish man
17:21 a grief to a F; and the father of
17:21 a father; and the F of a fool has
17:25 a grief to his F and bitterness to her
19:13 is ruin to his F, and a wife's quarreling
19:26 does violence to his F and chases away his
20:20 If one curses his F or his mother, his
23:22 Hearken to your F who begot you, and do
23:24 The F of the righteous will greatly rejoice; he
23:25 Let your F and mother be glad, let her
27:10 Your friend, and your F's friend, do not forsake;
28:7 son, but a companion of gluttons shames his F
28:24 He who robs his F or his mother and
29:3 loves wisdom makes his F glad, but one who
30:17 eye that mocks a F and scorns to obey
Eccl 5:14 venture; and he is F of a son, but
Wis 2:16 righteous happy, and boasts that God is his F
9:12 shall be worthy of the throne of my F
10:1 Wisdom protected the first-formed F of the world,
11:10 test them as a F does in warning, but
14:3 is thy providence, O F, that steers its course,
14:15 For a F, consumed with grief at an untimely
Sir 3:1 Listen to me your F, O children; and act
3:2 the Lord honored the F above the children, and
3:3 Whoever honors his F atones for sins,
3:5 Whoever honors his F will be gladdened by his
3:6 Whoever glorifies his F will have long life, and
3:8 Honor your F by word and deed, that a
3:9 For a F's blessing strengthens the houses of the
3:10 yourself by dishonoring your F, for your father's
3:10 your father, for your F's dishonor is no glory
3:11 comes from honoring his F, and it is a
3:12 O son, help your F in his old age,
3:14 For kindness to a F will not be forgotten,
3:16 Whoever forsakes his F is like a blasphemer, and
4:10 Be like a F to orphans, and instead of
7:27 your heart honor your F, and do not forget
22:3 disgrace to be the F of an undisciplined son,
22:4 one who acts shamefully brings grief to her F
22:5 An impudent daughter disgraces F and husband, and
23:1 O Lord, F and Ruler of my life, do
23:4 O Lord, F and God of my life, do
23:14 Remember your F and mother when you sit among
30:4 The F may die, and yet he is not
34:20 a son before his F's eyes is the man
41:7 will blame an ungodly F, for they suffer reproach
41:17 of immorality, before your F or mother; and of
42:9 A daughter keeps her F secretly wakeful, and worry
42:10 become pregnant in her F's house; or having a
44:20 Abraham was the great F of a multitude of
44:23 same assurance for the sake of Abraham his F
48:10 the heart of the F to the son, and
48:22 ways of David his F, which Isaiah the prophet
51:10 to the Lord, the F of my lord, not
Is 3:6 the house of his F, saying: "You have a
7:17 people and upon your F's house such days as
8:4 how to cry 'My F or 'My mother,' the
9:6 Counselor, Mighty God, Everlasting F, Prince of
22:21 he shall be a F to the inhabitants of
22:23 of honor to his F's house.
22:24 whole weight of his F's house, the offspring and
38:5 God of David your F: I have heard your
38:19 do this day; the F makes known to the
43:27 Your first F sinned, and your mediators transgressed
45:10 who says to a F, 'What are you begetting?'
51:2 Look to Abraham your F and to Sarah who
58:14 heritage of Jacob your F, for the mouth of
63:16 For thou art our F, though Abraham does not
63:16 O LORD, art our F, our Redeemer from of
64:8 LORD, thou art our F; we are the clay,
Jer 2:27 tree, 'You are my F and to a stone,
3:4 called to me, 'My F, thou art the friend
3:19 would call me, My F, and would not turn
12:6 the house of your F, even they have dealt
16:7 to drink for his F or his mother.
20:15 the news to my F, "A son is born
22:11 instead of Josiah his F, and who went away
22:15 Did not your F eat and drink and do
31:9 for I am a F to Israel, and Ephraim
35:6 son of Rechab, our F, commanded us, 'You shall
35:8 son of Rechab, our F, in all that he
35:10 all that Jonadab our F commanded us.
35:14 they have obeyed their F's command.
35:16 the command which their F gave them, but this
35:18 command of Jonadab your F, and kept all his
Ezek 16:3 of the Canaanites; your F was an Amorite, and
16:45 a Hittite and your F an Amorite.
18:4 the soul of the F as well as the
18:14 the sins which his F has done, and fears,
18:17 not die for his F's iniquity; he shall surely
18:18 As for his F, because he practiced extortion, robbed
18:19 the iniquity of the F When the son has
18:20 the iniquity of the F, nor the father suffer
18:20 the father, nor the F suffer for the iniquity
22:7 F and mother are treated with contempt in you;
22:11 defiles his sister, his F's daughter.
44:25 dead person; however, for F or mother, for son
Dan 5:2 silver which Nebuchadnezzar his F had taken out of
5:11 the days of your F light and understanding and
5:11 and King Nebuchadnezzar, your F, made him chief of
5:13 whom the king my F brought from Judah.
5:18 God gave Nebuchadnezzar your F kingship and
Amos 2:7 a man and his F go in to the
Mic 7:6 the son treats the F with contempt, the daughter
Zech 13:3 as a prophet, his F and mother who bore
13:3 the LORD'; and his F and mother who bore
Mal 1:6 "A son honors his F, and a servant his
1:6 then I am a F, where is my honor?
2:10 Have we not all one F
1Mac 2:54 Phinehas our F, because he was deeply zealous,
2:65 always listen to him; he shall be your F
3:2 who had joined his F helped him; they gladly
6:23 happy to serve your F, to live by what
11:9 shall reign over your F's kingdom.
11:32 Demetrius to Lasthenes his F, greeting.
11:40 him, to become king in place of his F
13:3 the house of my F have done for the
13:27 the tomb of his F and his brothers; he
13:28 one another, for his F and mother and four
14:26 the house of his F have stood firm; they
16:1 reported to Simon his F what Cendebeus had done.
16:2 the house of my F have fought the wars
16:21 at Gazara that his F and brothers had perished,
16:24 time that he became high priest after his F
2Mac 4:11 secured through John the F of Eupolemus, who went
9:23 I observed that my F, on the occasions when
11:23 Now that our F has gone on to the
11:24 not consent to our F's change to Greek customs
13:9 been done in his F's time.
14:37 good will was called F of the Jews.
Mt 1:2 Abraham was the F of Isaac, and Isaac the
1:2 Isaac, and Isaac the F of Jacob, and Jacob
1:2 Jacob, and Jacob the F of Judah and his
1:3 brothers, and Judah the F of Perez and Zerah
1:3 Tamar, and Perez the F of Hezron, and Hezron
1:3 Hezron, and Hezron the F of Ram,
1:4 and Ram the F of Amminadab, and Amminadab
1:4 Amminadab, and Amminadab the F of Nahshon, and
1:4 Nahshon, and Nahshon the F of Salmon,
1:5 Salmon, and Salmon the F of Boaz by Rahab,

F

1:5 Rahab, and Boaz the F of Obed by Ruth,
1:5 Ruth, and Obed the F of Jesse,
1:6 Jesse, and Jesse the F of David the king.
1:6 And David was the F of Solomon by the
1:7 Uriah, and Solomon the F of Rehoboam, and
1:7 Rehoboam, and Rehoboam the F of Abijah, and
1:7 Abijah, and Abijah the F of Asa,
1:8 Asa, and Asa the F of Jehoshaphat, and Jehoshaphat
1:8 Jehoshaphat, and Jehoshaphat the F of Joram, and
1:8 Joram, and Joram the F of Uzziah,
1:9 Uzziah, and Uzziah the F of Jotham, and Jotham
1:9 Jotham, and Jotham the F of Ahaz, and Ahaz
1:9 Ahaz, and Ahaz the F of Hezekiah,
1:10 Hezekiah, and Hezekiah the F of Manasseh, and
1:10 Manasseh, and Manasseh the F of Amos, and Amos
1:10 Amos, and Amos the F of Josiah,
1:11 Josiah, and Josiah the F of Jechoniah and his
1:12 Babylon: Jechoniah was the F of Shealtiel, and
1:12 Shealtiel, and Shealtiel the F of Zerubbabel,
1:13 Zerubbabel, and Zerubbabel the F of Abiud, and
1:13 Abiud, and Abiud the F of Eliakim, and Eliakim
1:13 Eliakim, and Eliakim the F of Azor,
1:14 Azor, and Azor the F of Zadok, and Zadok
1:14 Zadok, and Zadok the F of Achim, and Achim
1:14 Achim, and Achim the F of Eliud,
1:15 Eliud, and Eliud the F of Eleazar, and Eleazar
1:15 Eleazar, and Eleazar the F of Matthan, and Matthan
1:15 Matthan, and Matthan the F of Jacob,
1:16 Jacob, and Jacob the F of Joseph the husband
2:22 in place of his F Herod, he was afraid
3:9 have Abraham as our F; for I tell you,
4:21 boat with Zebedee their F, mending their nets, and
4:22 the boat and their F, and followed him.
5:16 give glory to your F who is in heaven.
5:45 be sons of your F who is in heaven;
5:48 perfect, as your heavenly F is perfect.
6:1 no reward from your F who is in heaven.
6:4 in secret; and your F who sees in secret
6:6 and pray to your F who is in secret;
6:6 in secret; and your F who sees in secret
6:8 like them, for your F knows what you need
6:9 then like this: Our F who art in heaven,
6:14 their trespasses, your heavenly F also will forgive
6:15 trespasses, neither will your F forgive your
6:18 men but by your F who is in secret;
6:18 in secret; and your F who sees in secret
6:26 and yet your heavenly F feeds them.
6:32 things; and your heavenly F knows that you need
7:11 much more will your F who is in heaven
7:21 the will of my F who is in heaven.
8:21 "Lord, let me first go and bury my F
10:20 the Spirit of your F speaking through you.
10:21 to death, and the F his child, and children
10:29 the ground without your F's will.
10:32 will acknowledge before my F who is in heaven;
10:33 will deny before my F who is in heaven.
10:35 a man against his F, and a daughter against
10:37 He who loves F or mother more than me
11:25 declared, "I thank thee, F, Lord of heaven and
11:26 them to babes; yea, F, for such was thy
11:27 to me by my F; and no one knows
11:27 the Son except the F, and no one knows
11:27 no one knows the F except the Son and
12:49 the will of my F in heaven is my
13:43 like the sun in the kingdom of their F
15:4 God commanded, 'Honor your F and your mother,'
15:4 who speaks evil of F or mother, let him
15:5 any one tells his F or his mother, What
15:5 need not honor his F
15:13 plant which my heavenly F has not planted will
16:17 to you, but my F who is in heaven.
16:27 the glory of his F, and then he will
18:10 the face of my F who is in heaven.
18:13 the will of my F who is in heaven
18:18 for them by my F in heaven.
18:34 So also my heavenly F will do to every
19:5 man shall leave his F and mother and be
19:19 false witness, Honor your F and mother, and, You
19:29 brothers or sisters or F or mother or children
20:23 for whom it has been prepared by my F
21:31 of the two did the will of his F
23:9 call no man your F on earth, for you
23:9 for you have one F, who is in heaven.
24:36 the Son, but the F only.
25:34 O blessed of my F, inherit the kingdom prepared
26:29 with you in my F's kingdom."
26:39 face and prayed, "My F, if it be possible,
26:42 away and prayed, "My F, if this cannot pass
26:53 cannot appeal to my F, and he will at
28:19 the name of the F and of the Son
Mk 1:20 and they left their F Zebedee in the boat
5:40 and took the child's F and mother and those
7:10 Moses said, 'Honor your F and your mother'; and,
7:10 who speaks evil of F or mother, let him
7:11 a man tells his F or his mother, What
7:12 do anything for his F or mother,
8:38 the glory of his F with the holy angels."
9:21 And Jesus asked his F, "How long has he
9:24 Immediately the F of the child cried out and
10:7 man shall leave his F and mother and be
10:19 not defraud, Honor your F and mother.'"
10:29 sisters or mother or F or children or lands,
11:10 the kingdom of our F David that is coming!
11:25 one; so that your F also who is in
13:12 to death, and the F his child, and children
13:32 in heaven, nor the Son, but only the F
14:36 And he said, "Abba, F, all things are possible
15:21 from the country, the F of Alexander and Rufus,
Lk 1:32 the throne of his F David,
1:59 him Zechariah after his F,
1:62 made signs to his F, inquiring what he would
1:67 And his F Zechariah was filled with the Holy
1:73 he swore to our F Abraham,
2:33 And his F and his mother marveled at what
2:48 Behold, your F and I have been looking for
2:49 must be in my F's house?"
3:8 have Abraham as our F; for I tell you,
6:36 merciful, even as your F is merciful.
8:51 and James, and the F and mother of the
9:26 the glory of the F and of the holy
9:42 the boy, and gave him back to his F
9:59 "Lord, let me first go and bury my F
10:21 said, "I thank thee, F, Lord of heaven and
10:21 them to babes; yea, F, for such was thy
10:22 to me by my F; and no one knows
10:22 Son is except the F, or who the Father
10:22 Father, or who the F is except the Son
11:2 "When you pray, say: F, hallowed be thy name.
11:11 What F among you, if his son asks for
11:13 more will the heavenly F give the Holy Spirit
12:30 these things; and your F knows that you need
12:32 for it is your F's good pleasure to give
12:53 they will be divided, F against son and son
12:53 son and son against F, mother against daughter and
14:26 not hate his own F and mother and wife
15:12 them said to his F, 'Father, give me the
15:12 said to his father, F, give me the share
15:17 'How many of my F's hired servants have bread
15:18 and go to my F, and I will say
15:18 will say to him, F, I have sinned against
15:20 servants.'" And he arose and came to his F
15:20 at a distance, his F saw him and had
15:21 son said to him, F, I have sinned against
15:22 your son.' But the F said to his servants,
15:27 has come, and your F has killed the fatted
15:28 His F came out and entreated him,
15:29 but he answered his F, 'Lo, these many years
16:24 And he called out, F Abraham, have mercy upon
16:27 'Then I beg you, F, to send him to
16:27 send him to my F's house,
16:30 And he said, 'No, F Abraham; but if some
18:20 false witness, Honor your F and mother.'"
22:29 to you, as my F assigned to me, a
22:42 knelt down and prayed, F, if thou art willing,
23:33 And Jesus said, F, forgive them; for they know
23:45 a loud voice, said, F, into thy hands I
24:49 the promise of my F upon you; but stay
Jn 1:14 glory as of the only Son from the F
1:18 the bosom of the F, he has made him
2:16 shall not make my F's house a house of
3:35 gives the Spirit; the F loves the Son, and
4:12 you greater than our F Jacob, who gave us
4:21 mountain nor in Jerusalem will you worship the F
4:23 worshipers will worship the F in spirit and truth,
4:23 truth, for such the F seeks to worship him.
4:53 The F knew that was the hour when Jesus
5:16 Jesus answered them, "My F is working still, and
5:17 also called God his F, making himself equal with
5:18 what he sees the F doing; for whatever he
5:19 For the F loves the Son, and shows him
5:20 For as the F raises the dead and gives
5:21 The F judges no one, but has given all

FATHER

5:22 honor the Son, even as they honor the F
5:22 does not honor the F who sent him.
5:25 For as the F has life in himself, so
5:35 the works which the F has granted me to
5:35 me witness that the F has sent me.
5:36 And the F who sent me has himself borne
5:42 have come in my F's name, and you do
5:44 accuse you to the F; it is Moses who
6:27 him has God the F set his seal."
6:32 bread from heaven; my F gives you the true
6:37 All that the F gives me will come to
6:40 the will of my F, that every one who
6:42 son of Joseph, whose F and mother we know?
6:44 to me unless the F who sent me draws
6:45 and learned from the F comes to me.
6:46 one has seen the F except him who is
6:46 who is from God; he has seen the F
6:57 As the living F sent me, and I live
6:57 live because of the F, so he who eats
6:65 me unless it is granted him by the F
8:18 to myself, and the F who sent me bears
8:19 They said to him therefore, "Where is your F
8:19 neither me nor my F; if you knew me,
8:19 you would know my F also."
8:27 understand that he spoke to them of the F
8:28 speak thus as the F taught me.
8:38 have seen with my F, and you do what
8:38 you do what you have heard from your F
8:39 They answered him, "Abraham is our F
8:41 You do what your F did." They said to
8:41 fornication; we have one F, even God."
8:42 "If God were your F, you would love me,
8:44 You are of your F the devil, and your
8:44 is to do your F's desires.
8:44 a liar and the F of lies.
8:49 but I honor my F, and you dishonor me.
8:53 you greater than our F Abraham, who died?
8:54 nothing; it is my F who glorifies me, of
8:56 Your F Abraham rejoiced that he was to see
10:15 know me, as the F knows me and I
10:15 and I know the F; and I lay down
10:17 For this reason the F loves me, because I
10:18 again; this charge I have received from my F
10:25 I do in my F's name, they bear witness
10:29 My F, who has given them to me, is
10:29 them out of the F's hand.
10:30 I and the F are one."
10:32 good works from the F; for which of these
10:36 of him whom the F consecrated and sent into
10:37 the works of my F, then do not believe
10:38 and understand that the F is in me and
10:38 is in me and I am in the F
11:41 his eyes and said, F, I thank thee that
12:26 one serves me, the F will honor him.
12:27 F, save me from this hour?
12:28 F, glorify thy name." Then a voice came from
12:49 my own authority; the F who sent me has
12:50 I say as the F has bidden me."
13:1 this world to the F, having loved his own
13:3 Jesus, knowing that the F had given all things
14:2 In my F's house are many rooms; if it
14:6 one comes to the F, but by me.
14:7 would have known my F also; henceforth you know
14:8 "Lord, show us the F, and we shall be
14:9 me has seen the F; how can you say,
14:9 Father; how can you say, 'Show us the F
14:10 I am in the F and the Father in
14:10 the Father and the F in me?
14:10 own authority; but the F who dwells in me
14:11 I am in the F and the Father in
14:11 the Father and the F in me; or else
14:12 will he do, because I go to the F
14:13 do it, that the F may be glorified in
14:16 I will pray the F, and he will give
14:20 I am in my F, and you in me,
14:21 be loved by my F, and I will love
14:23 my word, and my F will love him, and
14:24 not mine but the F's who sent me.
14:26 Holy Spirit, whom the F will send in my
14:28 I go to the F; for the Father is
14:28 the Father; for the F is greater than I.
14:31 I do as the F has commanded me, so
14:31 the world may know that I love the F
15:1 true vine, and my F is the vinedresser.
15:8 By this my F is glorified, that you bear
15:9 As the F has loved me, so have I
15:10 I have kept my F's commandments and abide in
15:15 have heard from my F I have made known
15:16 whatever you ask the F in my name, he
15:23 hates me hates my F also.
15:24 have seen and hated both me and my F
15:26 to you from the F, even the Spirit of
15:26 who proceeds from the F, he will bear witness
16:3 have not known the F, nor me.
16:10 I go to the F, and you will see
16:15 All that the F has is mine; therefore I
16:17 see me'; and, 'because I go to the F
16:23 ask anything of the F, he will give it
16:25 in figures but tell you plainly of the F
16:26 I shall pray the F for you;
16:27 for you; for the F himself loves you, because
16:27 and have believed that I came from the F
16:28 I came from the F and have come into
16:28 am leaving the world and going to the F
16:32 not alone, for the F is with me.
17:1 to heaven and said, F, the hour has come;
17:5 to do; and now, F, glorify thou me in
17:11 Holy F, keep them in thy name, which thou
17:21 one; even as thou, F, art in me, and
17:24 F, I desire that they also, whom thou hast
17:25 O righteous F, the world has not known thee,
18:11 the cup which the F has given me?"
20:17 yet ascended to the F; but go to my
20:17 am ascending to my F and your Father, to
20:17 my Father and your F, to my God and
20:21 As the F has sent me, even so I

Acts 1:4 the promise of the F, which, he said, "you
1:7 or seasons which the F has fixed by his
2:33 having received from the F the promise of the
4:25 the mouth of our F David, thy servant, didst
7:2 glory appeared to our F Abraham, when he was
7:4 And after his F died, God removed him from
7:8 so Abraham became the F of Isaac, and circumcised
7:8 and Isaac became the F of Jacob, and Jacob
7:14 to him Jacob his F and all his kindred,
7:20 three months in his F's house;
7:29 where he became the F of two sons.
16:1 a believer; but his F was a Greek.
16:3 all knew that his F was a Greek
28:8 It happened that the F of Publius lay sick

Rom 1:7 peace from God our F and the Lord Jesus
4:11 to make him the F of all who believe
4:12 them, and likewise the F of the circumcised who
4:12 the faith which our F Abraham had before he
4:16 for he is the F of us all,
4:17 have made you the F of many nations" –
4:18 he should become the F of many nations; as
6:4 the glory of the F, we too might walk
8:15 F
15:6 glorify the God and F of our Lord Jesus

1Cor 1:3 peace from God our F and the Lord Jesus
4:15 For I became your F in Christ Jesus through
5:1 is living with his F's wife.
8:6 is one God, the F, from whom are all
15:24 kingdom to God the F after destroying every rule

2Cor 1:2 peace from God our F and the Lord Jesus
1:3 be the God and F of our Lord Jesus
1:3 Lord Jesus Christ, the F of mercies and God
6:18 I will be a F to you, and you
11:31 The God and F of the Lord Jesus, he

Gal 1:1 Christ and God the F, who raised him from
1:3 peace from God the F and our Lord Jesus
1:4 of our God and F;
4:2 and trustees until the date set by the F
4:6 F

Eph 1:2 peace from God our F and the Lord Jesus
1:3 be the God and F of our Lord Jesus
1:17 Lord Jesus Christ, the F of glory, may give
2:18 both have access in one Spirit to the F
3:14 my knees before the F,
4:6 baptism, one God and F of us all, who
5:20 of our Lord Jesus Christ to God the F
5:31 man shall leave his F and mother and be
6:2 "Honor your F and mother" (this is the first
6:23 faith, from God the F and the Lord Jesus

Phil 1:2 peace from God our F and the Lord Jesus
2:11 is Lord, to the glory of God the F
2:22 a son with a F he has served with
4:20 To our God and F be glory for ever

Col 1:2 Grace to you and peace from God our F
1:3 always thank God, the F of our Lord Jesus
1:12 giving thanks to the F, who has qualified us

3:17 thanks to God the F through him.
1Thes 1:1 Thessalonians in God the F and the Lord Jesus
1:3 before our God and F your work of faith
2:11 know how, like a F with his children, we
3:11 may our God and F himself, and our Lord
3:13 before our God and F, at the coming of
2Thes 1:1 Thessalonians in God our F and the Lord Jesus
1:2 peace from God the F and the Lord Jesus
2:16 himself, and God our F, who loved us and
1Tim 1:2 peace from God the F and Christ Jesus our
5:1 as you would a F; treat younger men like
2Tim 1:2 peace from God the F and Christ Jesus our
Tit 1:3 peace from God the F and Christ Jesus our
Philem 1:3 peace from God our F and the Lord Jesus
1:10 my child, Onesimus, whose F I have become in
Heb 1:5 be to him a F, and he shall be
7:3 He is without F or mother or genealogy, and
12:7 is there whom his F does not discipline?
12:9 be subject to the F of spirits and live?
Jas 1:16 coming down from the F of lights with whom
1:26 before God and the F is this: to visit
2:21 Was not Abraham our F justified by works, when
3:9 bless the Lord and F, and with it we
1Pet 1:2 destined by God the F and sanctified by the
1:3 be the God and F of our Lord Jesus
1:17 if you invoke as F him who judges each
2Pet 1:17 glory from God the F and the voice was
1Jn 1:2 which was with the F and was made manifest
1:3 fellowship is with the F and with his Son
2:1 an advocate with the F, Jesus Christ the righteous;
2:13 write to you, children, because you know the F
2:15 world, love for the F is not in him.
2:16 is not of the F but is of the
2:22 he who denies the F and the Son.
2:23 No one who denies the Son has the F
2:23 the Son has the F also.
2:24 will abide in the Son and in the F
3:1 See what love the F has given us, that
4:14 and testify that the F has sent his Son
2Jn 1:3 us, from God the F and from Jesus Christ
1:3 from Jesus Christ the F's Son, in truth and
1:4 just as we have been commanded by the F
1:9 doctrine has both the F and the Son.
Jude 1:1 beloved in God the F and kept for Jesus
Rev 1:6 to his God and F, to him be glory
2:27 received power from my F;
3:5 his name before my F and before his angels.
3:21 sat down with my F on his throne.
14:1 his name and his F's name written on their

FATHER-IN-LAW (32)

Gen 38:13 Tamar was told, "Your F is going up to
38:25 sent word to her F, "By the man to
Ex 3:1 the flock of his F, Jethro, the priest of
4:18 back to Jethro his F and said to him,
18:1 priest of Midian, Moses' F, heard of all that
18:2 Jethro, Moses' F, had taken Zipporah, Moses' wife,
18:5 And Jethro, Moses' F, came with his sons and
18:6 told Moses, "Lo, your F Jethro is coming to
18:7 out to meet his F, and did obeisance and
18:8 Then Moses told his F all that the LORD
18:12 And Jethro, Moses' F, offered a burnt offering and
18:12 eat bread with Moses' F before God.
18:14 When Moses' F saw all that he was doing
18:15 Moses said to his F, "Because the people come
18:17 Moses' F said to him, "What you are doing
18:24 the voice of his F and did all that
18:27 Then Moses let his F depart, and he went
Num 10:29 Reuel the Midianite, Moses' F, "We are setting out
Judg 1:16 of the Kenite, Moses' F, went up with the
4:11 descendants of Hobab the F of Moses, and had
19:4 And his F, the girl's father, made him stay,
19:7 up to go, his F urged him, till he
19:9 up to depart, his F, the girl's father, said
1Sam 4:19 captured, and that her F and her husband were
4:21 and because of her F and her husband.
Tob 10:8 But his F said to him, "Stay with me,
10:12 his daughter, "Honor your F and your mother-in-law;
14:12 and his sons to Ecbatana, to Raguel his F
14:13 gave his F and mother-in-law magnificent funerals.
1Mac 10:56 I will become your F, as you have said."
11:2 them to meet him, since he was Alexander's F
Jn 18:13 for he was the F of Caiaphas, who was

FATHERLESS (41)

Ex 22:24 your wives shall become widows and your children F
Deut 10:18 executes justice for the F and the widow, and
14:29 and the sojourner, the F, and the widow, who
16:11 towns, the sojourner, the F, and the widow who
16:14 Levite, the sojourner, the F, and the widow who
24:17 sojourner or to the F, or take a widow's
24:19 for the sojourner, the F, and the widow; that
24:20 for the sojourner, the F, and the widow.
24:21 for the sojourner, the F, and the widow.
26:12 Levite, the sojourner, the F, and the widow, that
26:13 Levite, the sojourner, the F, and the widow, according
27:19 to the sojourner, the F, and the widow.' And
Job 5:15 But he saves the F from their mouth, the
6:27 cast lots over the F, and bargain over your
22:9 the arms of the F were crushed.
24:3 the ass of the F; they take the widow's
24:9 those who snatch the F child from the breast,
29:12 who cried, and the F who had none to
31:17 morsel alone, and the F has not eaten of
31:21 my hand against the F, because I saw help
Ps 10:14 thee; thou hast been the helper of the F
10:18 do justice to the F and the oppressed, so
68:5 Father of the F and protector of widows is
82:3 the weak and the F; maintain the right of
94:6 sojourner, and murder the F;
109:9 May his children be F, and his wife a
109:12 any to pity his F children!
146:9 the widow and the F; but the way of
Prov 23:10 the fields of the F;
Sir 35:14 the supplication of the F, nor the widow when
Is 1:17 oppression; defend the F, plead for the widow.
1:23 do not defend the F, and the widow's cause
9:17 no compassion on their F and widows; for every
10:2 they may make the F their prey!
Jer 5:28 the cause of the F, to make it prosper,
7:6 oppress the alien, the F or the widow, or
22:3 to the alien, the F, and the widow, nor
49:11 Leave your F children, I will keep them alive;
Lam 5:3 We have become orphans, F; our mothers are like
Ezek 22:7 in your midst; the F and the widow are
Zech 7:10 oppress the widow, the F, the sojourner, or the

FATHERS (631)

Gen 15:15 shall go to your F in peace; you shall
31:1 all that was our F; and from what was
31:3 the land of your F and to your kindred,
46:34 both we and our F in order that you
47:3 are shepherds, as our F were."
47:9 the life of my F in the days of
47:30 me lie with my F; carry me out of
48:15 God before whom my F Abraham and Isaac walked,
48:16 the name of my F Abraham and Isaac; and
48:21 bring you again to the land of your F
49:29 bury me with my F in the cave that
Ex 3:13 'The God of your F has sent me to
3:15 the God of your F, the God of Abraham,
3:16 the God of your F, the God of Abraham,
4:5 the God of their F, the God of Abraham,
6:14 the heads of their F houses: the sons of
6:25 the heads of the F houses of the Levites
10:6 Egyptians; as neither your F nor your grandfathers
12:3 lamb according to their F houses, a lamb for
13:5 he swore to your F to give you, a
13:11 to you and your F, and shall give it
20:5 the iniquity of the F upon the children to
34:7 the iniquity of the F upon the children and
Lev 25:41 family, and return to the possession of his F
26:39 the iniquities of their F they shall pine away
26:40 the iniquity of their F in their treachery which
Num 1:2 Israel, by families, by F houses, according to the
1:4 being the head of the house of his F
1:18 themselves by families, by F houses, according to the
1:20 their families, by their F houses, according to the
1:22 their families, by their F houses, those of them
1:24 their families, by their F houses, according to the
1:26 their families, by their F houses, according to the
1:28 their families, by their F houses, according to the
1:30 their families, by their F houses, according to the
1:32 their families, by their F houses, according to the
1:34 their families, by their F houses, according to the
1:36 their families, by their F houses, according to the
1:38 their families, by their F houses, according to the
1:40 their families, by their F houses, according to the
1:42 their families, by their F houses, according to the
1:44 men, each representing his F house.
1:45 of Israel, by their F houses, from twenty years
2:2 the ensigns of their F houses; they shall encamp

2:32 as numbered by their F houses; all in the
2:34 family, according to his F house.
3:15 sons of Levi, by F houses and by families;
3:20 the Levites, by their F houses.
3:24 as head of the F house of the Gershonites.
3:30 as head of the F house of the families
3:35 the head of the F house of the families
4:2 their families and their F houses,
4:22 their families and their F houses;
4:29 their families and their F houses;
4:34 their families and their F houses,
4:38 their families and their F houses,
4:40 their families and their F houses was two thousand
4:42 their families and their F houses,
4:46 their families and their F houses,
7:2 Israel, heads of their F houses, the leaders of
11:12 swear to give their F
13:2 each tribe of their F shall you send a
14:18 visiting the iniquity of F upon children, upon the
14:23 to give to their F; and none of those
17:2 rods, one for each F house, from all their
17:2 leaders according to their F houses, twelve rods.
17:3 the head of each F house.
17:6 leader, according to their F houses, twelve rods; and
18:1 your sons and your F house with you shall
20:15 befallen us: how our F went down to Egypt,
20:15 with us and our F;
25:14 Salu, head of a F house belonging to the
25:15 the people of a F house in Midian.
26:2 and upward, by their F houses, all in Israel
26:55 the tribes of their F they shall inherit.
31:26 the heads of the F houses of the congregation;
32:8 Thus did your F, when I sent them from
32:14 have risen in your F stead, a brood of
32:28 the heads of the F houses of the tribes
33:54 the tribes of your F you shall inherit.
34:14 sons of Reuben by F houses and the tribe
34:14 of Gad by their F houses have received their
36:1 The heads of the F houses of the families
36:1 of Manasseh, of the F houses of the sons
36:1 the heads of the F houses of the people
36:3 the inheritance of our F, and added to the
36:4 from the inheritance of the tribe of our F
36:7 to the inheritance of the tribe of his F
36:8 of Israel may possess the inheritance of his F
Deut 1:8 LORD swore to your F, to Abraham, to Isaac,
1:11 the God of your F, make you a thousand
1:21 the God of your F, has told you; do
1:35 to give to your F,
4:1 the God of your F, gives you.
4:31 the covenant with your F which he swore to
4:37 because he loved your F and chose their descendants
5:3 Not with our F did the LORD make this
5:9 the iniquity of the F upon the children to
6:3 the God of your F, has promised you, in
6:10 he swore to your F, to Abraham, to Isaac,
6:18 to give to your F
6:23 land which he swore to give to our F
7:8 he swore to your F, that the LORD has
7:12 he swore to your F to keep;
7:13 he swore to your F to give you.
8:1 which the LORD swore to give to your F
8:3 know, nor did your F know; that he might
8:16 with manna which your F did not know, that
8:18 he swore to your F, as at this day.
9:5 LORD swore to your F, to Abraham, to Isaac,
10:11 I swore to their F to give them.'
10:15 in love upon your F and chose their descendants
10:22 Your F went down to Egypt seventy persons; and
11:9 LORD swore to your F to give to them
11:21 LORD swore to your F to give them, as
12:1 the God of your F, has given you to
13:6 neither you nor your F have known,
13:17 he swore to your F,
19:8 has sworn to your F, and gives you all
19:8 to give to your F —
22:30 nor shall he uncover her who is his F
24:16 "The F shall not be put to death for
24:16 to death for the F; every man shall be
26:3 LORD swore to our F to give us.'
26:7 the God of our F, and the LORD heard
26:15 didst swear to our F, a land flowing with
27:3 the God of your F, has promised you.
28:11 LORD swore to your F to give you.
28:36 neither you nor your F have known; and there
28:64 neither you nor your F have known.
29:13 he swore to your F, to Abraham, to Isaac,
29:25 the God of their F, which he made with
30:5 the land which your F possessed, that you may
30:5 you more prosperous and numerous than your F
30:9 took delight in your F,
30:20 LORD swore to your F, to Abraham, to Isaac,
31:7 has sworn to their F to give them; and
31:16 to sleep with your F; then this people will
31:20 to give to their F, and they have eaten
32:17 of late, whom your F had never dreaded.
Josh 1:6 I swore to their F to give them.
4:21 your children ask their F in time to come,
5:6 had sworn to their F to give us, a
14:1 the heads of the F houses of the tribes
18:3 the God of your F, has given you?
19:51 the heads of the F houses of the tribes
21:1 the heads of the F houses of the Levites
21:1 the heads of the F houses of the tribes
21:43 to give to their F; and having taken possession
21:44 had sworn to their F; not one of all
22:28 the LORD, which our F made, not for burnt
24:2 God of Israel, 'Your F lived of old beyond
24:6 Then I brought your F out of Egypt, and
24:6 Egyptians pursued your F with chariots and
24:14 the gods which your F served beyond the River,
24:15 whether the gods your F served in the region
24:17 brought us and our F up from the land
Judg 2:1 land which I swore to give to your F
2:10 were gathered to their F; and there arose another
2:12 the God of their F, who had brought them
2:17 way in which their F had walked, who had
2:19 behaved worse than their F, going after other gods,
2:20 which I commanded their F, and have not obeyed
2:22 the LORD as their F did, or not."
3:4 which he commanded their F by Moses.
6:13 wonderful deeds which our F recounted to us, saying,
21:22 And when their F or their brothers come to
1Sam 12:6 Aaron and brought your F up out of the
12:7 which he performed for you and for your F
12:8 oppressed them, then your F cried to the LORD
12:8 who brought forth your F out of Egypt, and
2Sam 7:12 lie down with your F, I will raise up
1Kgs 1:21 king sleeps with his F, that I and my
2:10 David slept with his F, and was buried in
8:1 the leaders of the F houses of the people
8:21 he made with our F, when he brought them
8:34 to the land which thou gavest to their F
8:40 in the land which thou gavest to our F
8:48 thou gavest to their F, the city which thou
8:53 thou didst bring our F out of Egypt, O
8:57 he was with our F; may he not leave
8:58 and his ordinances, which he commanded our F
9:9 God who brought their F out of the land
11:21 David slept with his F and that Joab the
11:43 Solomon slept with his F, and was buried in
13:22 shall not come to the tomb of your F
14:15 he gave to their F, and scatter them beyond
14:20 he slept with his F, and Nadab his son
14:22 than all that their F had done.
14:31 Rehoboam slept with his F and was buried with
14:31 was buried with his F in the city of
15:8 Abijam slept with his F; and they buried him
15:12 the idols that his F had made.
15:24 Asa slept with his F, and was buried with
15:24 was buried with his F in the city of
16:6 Baasha slept with his F, and was buried at
16:28 Omri slept with his F, and was buried in
19:4 life; for I am no better than my F
21:3 I should give you the inheritance of my F
21:4 will not give you the inheritance of my F
22:40 Ahab slept with his F; and Ahaziah his son
22:50 Jehoshaphat slept with his F, and was buried with
22:50 was buried with his F in the city of
2Kgs 8:24 Joram slept with his F, and was buried with
8:24 was buried with his F in the city of
9:28 his tomb with his F in the city of
10:35 Jehu slept with his F, and they buried him
12:18 Jehoram and Ahaziah, his F, the kings of Judah,
12:21 buried him with his F in the city of
13:9 Jehoahaz slept with his F, and they buried him
13:13 Joash slept with his F, and Jeroboam sat upon
14:6 the LORD commanded, "The F shall not be put
14:6 to death for the F; but every man shall
14:16 Jehoash slept with his F, and was buried in
14:20 in Jerusalem with his F in the city of
14:22 to Judah, after the king slept with his F

14:29 Jeroboam slept with his F, the kings of Israel,
15:7 Azariah slept with his F, and they buried him
15:7 buried him with his F in the city of
15:9 the LORD, as his F had done.
15:22 Menahem slept with his F, and Pekahiah his son
15:38 Jotham slept with his F, and was buried with
15:38 was buried with his F in the city of
16:20 Ahaz slept with his F, and was buried with
16:20 was buried with his F in the city of
17:13 which I commanded your F, and which I sent
17:14 were stubborn, as their F had been, who did
17:15 he made with their F, and the warnings which
17:41 children's children--as their F did, so they do
19:12 nations which my F destroyed, Gozan, Haran,
20:17 and that which your F have stored up till
20:21 Hezekiah slept with his F; and Manasseh his son
21:8 I gave to their F, if only they will
21:15 since the day their F came out of Egypt,
21:18 Manasseh slept with his F, and was buried in
21:22 the God of his F, and did not walk
22:13 against us, because our F have not obeyed the
22:20 gather you to your F, and you shall be
23:32 to all that his F had done.
23:37 to all that his F had done.
24:6 Jehoiakim slept with his F, and Jehoiachin his son
1Chr 4:19 of Naham, were the F of Keilah the Garmite
4:38 their families, and their F houses increased greatly.
5:13 kinsmen according to their F houses: Michael,
5:15 was chief in their F houses;
5:24 the heads of their F houses: Epher, Ishi, Eliel,
5:24 men, heads of their F houses.
5:25 the God of their F, and played the harlot
6:19 the families of the Levites according to their F
7:2 Shemuel, heads of their F houses, namely of Tola,
7:4 generations, according to their F houses, were units
7:7 Iri, five, heads of F houses, mighty warriors; and
7:9 as heads of their F houses, mighty warriors, was
7:11 the heads of their F houses, mighty warriors,
7:40 of Asher, heads of F houses, approved, mighty
8:6 (they were heads of F houses of the inhabitants
8:10 his sons, heads of F houses.
8:13 (they were heads of F houses of the inhabitants
8:28 were the heads of F houses, according to their
9:9 these were heads of F houses according to their
9:9 houses according to their F houses.
9:13 kinsmen, heads of their F houses, one thousand seven
9:19 his kinsmen of his F house, the Korahites, were
9:19 the tent, as their F had been in charge
9:33 singers, the heads of F houses of the Levites,
9:34 These were heads of F houses of the Levites,
12:17 the God of our F see and rebuke you."
12:30 famous men in their F houses.
15:12 the heads of the F houses of the Levites;
17:11 to be with your F, I will raise up
23:9 the heads of the F houses of Ladan.
23:24 of Levi by their F houses, the heads of
23:24 houses, the heads of F houses as they were
24:4 under sixteen heads of F houses of the sons
24:6 the heads of the F houses of the priests
24:30 Levites according to their F houses.
24:31 and the heads of F houses of the priests
26:6 were rulers in their F houses, for they were
26:13 they cast lots by F houses, small and great
26:21 the heads of the F houses belonging to Ladan
26:26 the heads of the F houses, and the officers
26:31 of whatever genealogy or F houses.
26:32 of ability, heads of F houses, to have the
27:1 Israel, the heads of F houses, the commanders of
29:6 Then the heads of F houses made their freewill
29:15 sojourners, as all our F were; our days on
29:18 Isaac, and Israel, our F, keep for ever such
29:20 the God of their F, and bowed their heads,
2Chr 1:2 Israel, the heads of F houses.
5:2 the leaders of the F houses of the people
6:25 which thou gavest to them and to their F
6:31 in the land which thou gavest to our F
6:38 thou gavest to their F, the city which thou
7:22 the God of their F who brought them out
9:31 Solomon slept with his F, and was buried in
11:16 sacrifice to the LORD, the God of their F
12:16 Rehoboam slept with his F, and was buried in
13:12 the God of your F; for you cannot succeed."
13:18 relied upon the LORD, the God of their F
14:1 Abijah slept with his F, and they buried him
14:4 the God of their F, and to keep the
15:12 the God of their F, with all their heart
16:13 Asa slept with his F, dying in the forty-first
17:14 muster of them by F houses: Of Judah, the
19:4 back to the LORD, the God of their F
20:6 LORD, God of our F, art thou not God
20:33 set their hearts upon the God of their F
21:1 Jehoshaphat slept with his F, and was buried with
21:1 was buried with his F in the city of
21:10 had forsaken the LORD, the God of his F
21:19 his honor, like the fires made for his F
23:2 and the heads of F houses of Israel, and
24:18 the God of their F, and served the Asherim
24:24 had forsaken the LORD, the God of their F
25:4 the LORD commanded, "The F shall not be put
25:4 to death for the F; but every man shall
25:5 and set them by F houses under commanders of
25:28 was buried with his F in the city of
26:2 to Judah, after the king slept with his F
26:12 of the heads of F houses of mighty men
26:23 Uzziah slept with his F, and they buried him
26:23 buried him with his F in the burial field
27:9 Jotham slept with his F, and they buried him
28:6 had forsaken the LORD, the God of their F
28:9 the God of your F, was angry with Judah,
28:25 to anger the LORD, the God of his F
28:27 Ahaz slept with his F, and they buried him
29:5 the God of your F, and carry out the
29:6 For our F have been unfaithful and have done
29:9 For lo, our F have fallen by the sword
30:7 not be like your F and your brethren, who
30:7 LORD God of their F, so that he made
30:8 be stiff-necked as your F were, but yield yourselves
30:19 the God of his F, even though not according
30:22 thanks to the LORD the God of their F
31:17 was according to their F houses; that of the
32:13 what I and my F have done to all
32:14 those nations which my F utterly destroyed was able
32:15 my hand or from the hand of my F
32:33 Hezekiah slept with his F, and they buried him
33:8 I appointed for your F, if only they will
33:12 humbled himself greatly before the God of his F
33:20 Manasseh slept with his F, and they buried him
34:21 on us, because our F have not kept the
34:28 gather you to your F, and you shall be
34:32 the covenant of God, the God of their F
34:33 from following the LORD the God of their F
35:4 yourselves according to your F houses by your
35:5 the groupings of the F houses of your brethren
35:12 the groupings of the F houses of the lay
35:24 and was buried in the tombs of his F
36:15 the God of their F, sent persistently to them
Ezra 1:5 the heads of the F houses of Judah and
2:59 could not prove their F houses or their descent,
3:12 Levites and heads of F houses, old men who
4:2 and the heads of F houses and said to
4:3 of the heads of F houses in Israel said
4:15 in the book of the records of your F
5:12 But because our F had angered the God of
7:27 the God of our F, who put such a
8:1 the heads of their F houses, and this is
8:28 offering to the LORD, the God of your F
8:29 and the heads of F houses in Israel at
9:7 the days of our F to this day we
10:11 the God of your F, and do his will;
10:16 selected men, heads of F houses, according to their
10:16 houses, according to their F houses, each of them
Neh 2:3 the place of my F sepulchres, lies waste, and
2:5 the city of my F sepulchres, that I may
7:61 could not prove their F houses nor their descent,
7:70 of the heads of F houses gave to the
7:71 of the heads of F houses gave into the
8:13 day the heads of F houses of all the
9:2 confessed their sins and the iniquities of their F
9:9 the affliction of our F in Egypt and hear
9:10 acted insolently against our F; and thou didst get
9:16 "But they and our F acted presumptuously and
9:23 thou hadst told their F to enter and possess.
9:32 priests, our prophets, our F, and all thy people,
9:34 our priests, and our F have not kept thy
9:36 thou gavest to our F to enjoy its fruit
10:34 God, according to our F houses, at times appointed,
11:13 his brethren, heads of F houses, two hundred and
12:12 were priests, heads of F houses: of Seraiah,
12:22 recorded the heads of F houses; also the priests
12:23 of Levi, heads of F houses, were written in
13:18 Did not your F act in this way, and
Tob 3:3 and those which my F committed before thee.

3:5 and those of my F, because we did not
4:12 the descendants of your F and do not marry
4:12 Isaac, and Jacob, our F of old, all took
8:5 O God of our F, and blessed by thy
Jud 5:7 the gods of their F who were in Chaldea.
7:29 the Lord of our F, who punishes us according
7:29 to our sins and the sins of our F
8:3 buried him with his F in the field between
8:19 that was why our F were handed over to
10:8 the God of our F grant you favor and
Esth 14:5 the nations, and our F from among all their
16:16 us an for our F in the most excellent
Job 8:8 and consider what the F have found;
15:18 have told, and their F have not hidden,
30:1 younger than I, whose F I would have disdained
Ps 22:4 In thee our F trusted; they trusted, and thou
39:12 thy passing guest, a sojourner, like all my F
44:1 ears, O God, our F have told us, what
45:16 Instead of your F shall be your sons; you
49:19 the generation of his F, who will never more
78:3 and known, that our F have told us.
78:5 which he commanded our F to teach to their
78:8 not be like their F, a stubborn and rebellious
78:12 the sight of their F he wrought marvels in
78:57 acted treacherously like their F; they twisted like a
95:9 the wilderness, when your F tested me, and put
106:6 Both we and our F have sinned; we have
106:7 Our F, when they were in Egypt, did not
109:14 the iniquity of his F be remembered before the
Prov 17:6 aged, and the glory of sons is their F
19:14 wealth are inherited from F, but a prudent wife
22:28 ancient landmark which your F have set.
30:11 those who curse their F and do not bless
Wis 9:1 "O God of my F and Lord of mercy,
12:6 the hands of our F,
12:21 thy sons, to whose F thou gavest oaths and
18:6 known beforehand to our F, so that they might
18:9 already they were singing the praises of the F
18:22 to the oaths and covenants given to our F
18:24 the glories of the F were engraved on the
Sir 8:9 themselves learned from their F; because from them
44:1 famous men, and our F in their generations.
47:23 Solomon rested with his F, and left behind him
Is 14:21 the guilt of their F, lest they rise and
37:12 the nations which my F destroyed, Gozan, Haran,
39:6 and that which your F have stored up till
49:23 shall be your foster F, and their queens your
64:11 beautiful house, where our F praised thee, has been
65:7 their iniquities and their F iniquities together, says
Jer 2:5 "What wrong did your F find in me that
3:18 that I gave your F for a heritage.
3:24 all for which our F labored, their flocks and
3:25 God, we and our F, from our youth even
6:21 which they shall stumble; F and sons together,
7:7 of old to your F for ever.
7:14 you and to your F, as I did to
7:18 children gather wood, the F kindle fire, and the
7:22 not speak to your F or command them concerning
7:25 the day that your F came out of the
7:26 They did worse than their F
9:14 the Baals, as their F taught them.
9:16 neither they nor their F have known; and I
11:4 which I commanded your F when I brought them
11:5 I swore to your F, to give them a
11:7 I solemnly warned your F when I brought them
11:10 broken my covenant which I made with their F
13:14 them one against another, F and sons together, says
14:20 the iniquity of our F, for we have sinned
16:3 bore them and the F who begot them in
16:11 to them: 'Because your F have forsaken me, says
16:12 done worse than your F, for behold, every one
16:13 neither you nor your F have known, and there
16:15 their own land which I gave to their F
16:19 earth and say: "Our F have inherited nought but
17:22 the sabbath day holy, as I commanded your F
19:4 neither they nor their F nor the kings of
23:27 another, even as their F forgot my name for
23:39 city which I gave to you and your F
24:10 land which I gave to them and their F
25:5 to you and your F from of old and
30:3 I gave to their F, and they shall take
31:29 no longer say: 'The F have eaten sour grapes,
31:32 I made with their F when I took them
32:18 requite the guilt of F to their children after
32:22 didst swear to their F to give them, a
34:5 were burned for your F, the former kings who
34:13 a covenant with your F when I brought them
34:14 your service.' But your F did not listen to
35:15 to you and your F But you did not
44:3 knew not, neither they, nor you, nor your F
44:9 the wickedness of your F, the wickedness of the
44:10 which I set before you and before your F
44:17 both we and our F, our kings and our
44:21 Jerusalem, you and your F, your kings and your
47:3 of their wheels, the F look not back to
50:7 the hope of their F
Lam 5:7 Our F sinned, and are no more; and we
Bar 1:16 our prophets and our F,
1:19 the Lord brought our F out of the land
1:20 when he brought our F out of the land
2:6 to us and our F, as at this day.
2:19 righteous deeds of our F or our kings that
2:21 in the land which I gave to your F
2:24 the bones of our F would be brought out
2:33 the ways of their F, who sinned before the
2:34 to give to their F, to Abraham and to
3:5 the iniquities of our F, but in this crisis
3:7 the iniquity of our F who sinned before thee.
3:8 the iniquities of our F who forsook the Lord
Ezek 2:3 me; they and their F have transgressed against me
5:10 Therefore F shall eat their sons in the midst
5:10 sons shall eat their F; and I will execute
18:2 land of Israel, 'The F have eaten sour grapes,
20:4 the abominations of their F,
20:18 the statutes of your F, nor observe their ordinances,
20:24 were set on their F idols.
20:27 In this again your F blasphemed me, by dealing
20:30 the manner of your F and go astray after
20:36 into judgment with your F in the wilderness of
20:42 country which I swore to give to your F
22:10 you men uncover their F nakedness; in you they
36:28 I gave to your F; and you shall be
37:25 the land where your F dwelt that I gave
47:14 give it to your F, and this land shall
Dan 2:23 O God of my F, I give thanks and
3:26 Lord, God of our F, and worthy of praise;
3:28 holy city of our F, for in truth and
3:52 Lord, God of our F, and to be praised
9:6 our princes, and our F, and to all the
9:8 princes, and to our F, because we have sinned
9:16 the iniquities of our F, Jerusalem and thy people
11:24 do what neither his F nor his fathers' fathers
11:24 his fathers nor his F fathers have done, scattering
11:24 fathers nor his fathers' F have done, scattering
11:37 the gods of his F, or to the one
11:38 a god whom his F did not know he
14:1 was laid with his F, Cyrus the Persian received
Hos 9:10 tree, in its first season, I saw your F
Joel 1:2 your days, or in the days of your F
Amos 2:4 astray, after which their F walked.
Mic 7:20 hast sworn to our F from the days of
Zech 1:2 saying, "The LORD was very angry with your F
1:4 Be not like your F, to whom the former
1:5 Your F, where are they?
1:6 servants the prophets, did they not overtake your F
8:14 to you, when your F provoked me to wrath,
Mal 2:10 to one another, profaning the covenant of our F
3:7 the days of your F you have turned aside
4:6 turn the hearts of F to their children and
4:6 of children to their F, lest I come and
1Mac 2:19 the religion of his F,
2:20 brothers will live by the covenant of our F
2:50 give your lives for the covenant of our F
2:51 the deeds of the F, which they did in
2:69 he blessed them, and was gathered to his F
2:70 the tomb of his F at Modein.
4:9 Remember how our F were saved at the Red
4:10 his covenant with our F and crush this army
7:2 royal palace of his F, the army seized Antiochus
9:19 the tomb of their F at Modein,
10:52 the throne of my F, and established my rule
10:55 the land of your F and took your seat
10:67 came from Crete to the land of his F
10:72 before us, for your F were twice put to
11:38 who had served his F hated him.
13:25 buried him in Modein, the city of his F
15:3 the kingdom of our F, and I intend to
15:10 set out and invaded the land of his F
15:33 the inheritance of our F, which at one time
15:34 we are firmly holding the inheritance of our F
2Mac 1:19 For when our F were being led captive to
1:25 who didst choose the F and consecrate them,

4:15 honors prized by their F and putting the highest
5:10 and no place in the tomb of his F
6:1 the laws of their F and cease to live
6:6 the feasts of his F, nor so much as
7:2 die rather than transgress the laws of our F
7:8 the language of his F, and said to them,
7:21 each of them in the language of their F
7:24 the ways of his F, and that he would
7:30 was given to our F through Moses.
7:37 the laws of our F, appealing to God to
8:15 covenants made with their F, and because he had
8:33 the city of their F, they burned those who
12:37 the language of their F he raised the battle
12:39 with their kinsmen in the sepulchres of their F
15:29 the Sovereign Lord in the language of their F
Mt 23:29 the days of our F, we would not have
23:31 Fill up, then, the measure of your F
Lk 1:17 the hearts of the F to the children, and
1:55 he spoke to our F, to Abraham and to
1:72 mercy promised to our F, and to remember his
6:23 heaven; for so their F did to the prophets.
6:26 you, for so their F did to the false
11:47 the prophets whom your F killed.
11:48 the deeds of your F; for they killed them,
Jn 4:20 Our F worshiped on this mountain; and you say
6:31 Our F ate the manna in the wilderness; as
6:49 Your F ate the manna in the wilderness, and
6:58 not such as the F ate and died; he
7:22 Moses, but from the F, and you circumcise a
Acts 3:13 the God of our F, glorified his servant Jesus,
3:25 God gave to your F, saying to Abraham, 'And
5:30 The God of our F raised Jesus whom you
7:2 Stephen said: "Brethren and F, hear me.
7:11 great affliction, and our F could find no food.
7:12 he sent forth our F the first time.
7:15 died, himself and our F,
7:19 race and forced our F to expose their infants,
7:32 the God of your F, the God of Abraham
7:38 Sinai, and with our F; and he received living
7:39 Our F refused to obey him, but thrust him
7:44 you beyond Babylon.' "Our F had the tent of
7:45 Our F in turn brought it in with Joshua
7:45 the nations which God thrust out before our F
7:51 As your F did, so do you.
7:52 prophets did not your F persecute?
13:17 people Israel chose our F and made the people
13:32 God promised to the F,
13:36 was laid with his F, and saw corruption;
15:10 disciples which neither our F nor we have been
22:1 language, saying: "Brethren and F, hear the defense
22:3 the law of our F, being zealous for God
22:14 'The God of our F appointed you to know
24:13 the God of our F, believing everything laid down
26:6 by God to our F,
28:17 the customs of our F, yet I was delivered
28:25 in saying to your F through Isaiah the prophet:
1Cor 4:15 guides in Christ, you do not have many F
10:1 know, brethren, that our F were all under the
Gal 1:14 zealous was I for the traditions of my F
Eph 6:4 F, do not provoke your children to anger, but
Col 3:21 F, do not provoke your children, lest they become
1Tim 1:9 for murderers of F and murderers of mothers,
2Tim 1:3 conscience, as did my F, when I remember you
Heb 1:1 of old to our F by the prophets,
3:9 the wilderness, where your F put me to the
8:9 I made with their F on the day when
12:9 we have had earthly F to discipline us and
1Pet 1:18 ways inherited from your F, not with perishable
2Pet 3:4 For ever since the F fell asleep, all things
1Jn 2:13 am writing to you, F, because you know him
2:14 I write to you, F, because you know him

FATHOMED
Sir 24:26 last one has not F her;

FATHOMS (2)
Acts 27:28 sounded and found twenty F; a little farther on
27:28 farther on they sounded again and found fifteen F

FATLING (2)
2Sam 6:13 six paces, he sacrificed an ox and a F
Is 11:6 the lion and the F together, and a little

FATLINGS (8)
1Sam 15:9 oxen and of the F, and the lambs, and
1Kgs 1:9 sacrificed sheep, oxen, and F by the Serpent's Stone,
1:19 He has sacrificed oxen, F, and sheep in abundance,
1:25 and has sacrificed oxen, F, and sheep in abundance,
Ps 66:15 thee burnt offerings of F, with the smoke of
Is 5:17 as in their pasture, F and kids shall feed
Ezek 34:3 wool, you slaughter the F; but you do not
39:18 bulls, all of them F of Bashan.

FATNESS (7)
Gen 27:28 heaven, and of the F of the earth, and
27:39 "Behold, away from the F of the earth shall
Judg 9:9 'Shall I leave my F, by which gods and
Job 36:16 was set on your table was full of F
Ps 65:11 bounty; the tracks of thy chariot drip with F
73:7 eyes swell out with F, their hearts overflow with
Is 55:2 eat what is good, and delight yourselves in F

FATTED (8)
1Sam 28:24 the woman had a F calf in the house,
1Kgs 4:23 harts, gazelles, roebucks, and F fowl.
Prov 15:17 love is than a F ox and hatred with
Jer 46:21 her midst are like F calves; yea, they have
Amos 5:22 peace offerings of your F beasts I will not
Lk 15:23 feet; and bring the F calf and kill it,
15:27 father has killed the F calf, because he has
15:30 killed for him the F calf!'

FATTENED
Jas 5:5 in pleasure; you have F your hearts in a

FATTENING
1Sam 2:29 sons above me by F yourselves upon the choicest

FATTER
Dan 1:15 better in appearance and F in flesh than all

FAULT (16)
Ex 5:16 are beaten; but the F is in your own
17:2 Therefore the people found F with Moses, and said,
17:2 "Why do you find F with me?
1Sam 29:3 I have found no F in him to this
2Sam 3:8 me today with a F concerning a woman.
Ps 59:4 O LORD, for no F of mine, they run
73:10 them; and find no F in them.
Sir 11:7 Do not find F before you investigate; first consider,
20:2 one who confesses his F will be kept from
29:5 unconcern, and will find F with the time.
Dan 6:4 for complaint or any F, because he was faithful,
6:4 and no error or F was found in him.
Mt 18:14 and tell him his F, between you and him
Rom 9:19 to me then, "Why does he still find F
2Cor 6:3 way, so that no F may be found with
Heb 8:8 For he finds F with them when he says:

FAULTFINDER (2)
Job 40:2 to Job: "Shall a F contend with the Almighty?
Sir 4:30 home, nor be a F with your servants.

FAULTFINDING
Ex 17:7 Meribah, because of the F of the children of

FAULTLESS
Heb 8:7 first covenant had been F, there would have been

FAULTS (3)
Gen 41:9 Pharaoh, "I remember my F today.
Ps 19:12 Clear thou me from hidden F
Sir 38:10 Give up your F and direct your hands aright,

FAVOR (144)
Gen 6:8 But Noah found F in the eyes of the
18:3 if I have found F in your sight, do
19:19 your servant has found F in your sight, and
19:21 I grant you this F also, that I will
31:2 not regard him with F as before.
31:5 not regard me with F as he did before.
32:5 that I may find F in your sight.'"
33:8 Jacob answered, "To find F in the sight of
33:10 if I have found F in your sight, then
33:10 of God, with such F have you received me.
33:15 Let me find F in the sight of my
34:11 brothers, "Let me find F in your eyes, and
39:4 So Joseph found F in his sight and attended
39:21 love, and gave him F in the sight of
47:29 now I have found F in your sight, put
50:4 now I have found F in your eyes, speak,
Ex 3:21 will give this people F in the sight of

11:3 LORD gave the people F in the sight of
12:36 had given the people F in the sight of
33:12 you have also found F in my sight.'
33:13 if I have found F in thy sight, show
33:13 know thee and find F in thy sight.
33:16 that I have found F in thy sight, I
33:17 for you have found F in my sight, and
34:9 now I have found F in thy sight, O
Num 11:11 have I not found F in thy sight, that
11:15 once, if I find F in thy sight, that
32:5 "If we have found F in your sight, let
Deut 24:1 then she finds no F in his eyes because
28:50 the old or show F to the young,
33:16 its fulness, and the F of him that dwelt
33:23 "O Naphtali, satisfied with F, and full of the
Judg 6:17 now I have found F with thee, then show
Ruth 2:2 after him in whose sight I shall find F
2:10 "Why have I found F in your eyes, that
1Sam 1:18 "Let your maidservant find F in your eyes." Then
2:26 in stature and in F with the LORD and
13:12 have not entreated the F of the LORD'; so
16:22 for he has found F in my sight."
20:3 that I have found F in your eyes; and
20:29 if I have found F in your eyes, let
25:8 my young men find F in your eyes; for
27:5 "If I have found F in your eyes, let
2Sam 14:22 that I have found F in your sight, my
15:25 If I find F in the eyes of the
16:4 let me ever find F in your sight, my
1Kgs 11:19 And Hadad found great F in the sight of
13:6 God, "Entreat now the F of the LORD your
2Kgs 5:1 master and in high F, because by him the
2Chr 33:12 distress he entreated the F of the LORD his
Ezra 9:8 for a brief moment F has been shown by
Neh 2:5 your servant has found F in your sight, that
13:22 this also in my F, O my God, and
Tob 1:13 Most High gave me F and good appearance in
12:18 not come as a F on my part, but
Jud 4:15 might to look with F upon the whole house
8:23 not bring us into F, but the Lord our
10:8 our fathers grant you F and fulfill your plans,
Esth 2:9 him and won his F; and he quickly provided
2:15 Now Esther found F in the eyes of all
2:17 she found grace and F in his sight more
5:2 the court, she found F in his sight and
5:8 If I have found F in the sight of
7:3 "If I have found F in your sight, O
8:5 if I have found F in his sight, and
Job 10:3 of thy hands and F the designs of the
11:19 will make you afraid; many will entreat your F
20:10 children will seek the F of the poor, and
Ps 5:12 dost cover him with F as with a shield.
20:3 offerings, and regard with F your burnt sacrifices!
30:5 a moment, and his F is for a lifetime.
30:7 By thy F, O LORD, thou hadst established me
45:12 Tyre will sue your F with gifts, the richest
84:11 and shield; he bestows F and honor.
86:17 a sign of thy F, that those who hate
89:17 their strength; by thy F our horn is exalted.
90:17 Let the F of the Lord our God be
101:6 I will look with F on the faithful in
102:13 is the time to F her; the appointed time
106:4 LORD, when thou showest F to thy people; help
119:58 I entreat thy F with all my heart; be
132:1 O LORD, in David's F, all the hardships he
Prov 3:4 So you will find F and good repute in
3:34 is scornful, but to the humble he shows F
8:35 finds life and obtains F from the LORD;
11:27 diligently seeks good seeks F, but evil comes to
12:2 A good man obtains F from the LORD, but
13:15 Good sense wins F, but the way of the
14:9 scorns the wicked, but the upright enjoy his F
14:35 wisely has the king's F, but his wrath falls
16:15 is life, and his F is like the clouds
18:22 good thing, and obtains F from the LORD.
19:6 Many seek the F of a generous man, and
19:12 a lion, but his F is like dew upon
22:1 than great riches, and F is better than silver
28:23 will afterward find more F than he who flatters
29:26 Many seek the F of a ruler, but from
Eccl 9:11 to the intelligent, nor F to the men of
10:12 man's mouth win him F, but the lips of
Wis 3:14 the Lord; for special F will be shown him
Sir 3:15 be remembered in your F; as frost in fair
3:18 so you will find F in the sight of
4:21 there is a shame which is glory and F
8:14 for the decision will F him because of his
32:14 who rise early to seek him will find F
41:23 shame, and will find F with every man.
45:1 of mercy, who found F in the sight of
Is 26:10 If F is shown to the wicked, he does
27:11 he that formed them will show them no F
49:8 "In a time of F I have answered you,
60:10 you, but in my F I have had mercy
61:2 year of the LORD's F, and the day of
Jer 16:13 will show you no F
26:19 LORD and entreat the F of the LORD, and
Lam 4:16 to the priests, no F to the elders.
Bar 1:12 many days and find F in their sight.
2:8 have not entreated the F of the Lord by
2:14 us, and grant us F in the sight of
Dan 1:9 And God gave Daniel F and compassion in the
9:13 have not entreated the F of the LORD our
Hos 12:4 angel and prevailed, he wept and sought his F
Zech 7:2 men, to entreat the F of the LORD,
8:21 once to entreat the F of the LORD, and
8:22 and to entreat the F of the LORD.
Mal 1:8 he be pleased with you or show you F
1:9 And now entreat the F of God, that he
1:9 hand, will he show F to any of you?
2:13 or accepts it with F at your hand.
1Mac 4:10 see whether he will F us and remember his
10:60 many gifts, and found F with them.
11:24 And he won his F
Lk 1:30 for you have found F with God.
2:40 with wisdom; and the F of God was upon
2:52 in stature, and in F with God and man.
Acts 2:47 praising God and having F with all the people.
7:10 and gave him F and wisdom before Pharaoh,
7:46 of David, who found F in the sight of
24:26 do the Jews a F, Felix left Paul in
25:3 him, asking as a F to have the man
25:9 do the Jews a F, said to Paul, "Do
1Cor 4:6 be puffed up in F of one against another.
2Cor 8:4 us earnestly for the F of taking part in
Gal 1:10 I now seeking the F of men, or of
1Tim 5:21 keep these rules without F, doing nothing from

FAVORABLE (9)

Gen 40:16 that the interpretation was F, he said to Joseph,
41:16 will give Pharaoh a F answer."
1Kgs 22:13 with one accord are F to the king; let
2Chr 18:12 with one accord are F to the king; let
Ps 77:7 Lord spurn for ever, and never again be F
85:1 LORD, thou wast F to thy land; thou didst
Ezek 16:52 you have made judgment F to your sisters; because
1Mac 12:1 that the time was F for him, he chose
13:35 king sent him a F reply to this request,

FAVORABLY (3)

1Kgs 22:13 the word of one of them, and speak F
2Chr 18:12 the word of one of them, and speak F
Tob 3:3 Remember me and look F upon me; do not

FAVORED (5)

Job 22:8 the land, and the F man dwelt in it.
Ezek 27:21 of Kedar were your F dealers in lambs, rams,
1Mac 10:47 They F Alexander, because he had been the first
2Mac 1:35 persons whom the king F he exchanged many
2Cor 12:13 what were you less F than the rest of

FAVORITE

Deut 33:24 let him be the F of his brothers, and

FAVORS (5)

2Sam 20:11 Amasa, and said, "Whoever F Joab, and whoever is
Wis 14:26 is good, forgetfulness of F, pollution of souls, sex
Sir 3:29 Whoever requites F gives thought to the future; at
Jer 3:13 God and scattered your F among strangers under
1Mac 11:53 did not repay the F which Jonathan had done

FAWNING

Deut 33:29 Your enemies shall come F to you; and you

FAWNS (3)

Gen 49:21 is a hind let loose, that bears comely F
Song 4:5 breasts are like two F, twins of a gazelle,
7:3 breasts are like two F, twins of a gazelle.

FEAR (456)

Gen 9:2 The F of you and the dread of you
15:1 Abram in a vision, F not, Abram, I am

20:11 thought, There is no F of God at all
21:17 F not; for God has heard the voice of
22:12 I know that you F God, seeing you have
26:24 of Abraham your father; F not, for I am
31:42 of Abraham and the F of Isaac, had not
31:53 Jacob swore by the F of his father Isaac,
32:11 of Esau, for I F him, lest he come
35:17 midwife said to her, F not; for now you
42:18 will live, for I F God:
44:34 I F to see the evil that would come
50:19 Joseph said to them, F not, for am I
50:21 So do not F; I will provide for you
Ex 9:30 you do not yet F the LORD God."
14:10 marching after them; and they were in great F
14:13 said to the people, F not, stand firm, and
18:21 the people, such as F God, men who are
20:20 the people, "Do not F; for God has come
20:20 you, and that the F of him may be
Lev 19:14 blind, but you shall F your God: I am
19:32 man, and you shall F your God: I am
25:17 another, but you shall F your God; for I
25:36 him or increase, but F your God; that your
25:43 with harshness, but shall F your God.
Num 14:9 LORD; and do not F the people of the
14:9 with us; do not F them."
21:34 to Moses, "Do not F him; for I have
22:3 Moab was overcome with F of the people of
Deut 1:21 told you; do not F or be dismayed.'
2:25 put the dread and F of you upon the
3:2 to me, 'Do not F him; for I have
3:22 You shall not F them; for it is the
4:10 they may learn to F me all the days
5:29 as this always, to F me and to keep
6:2 it; that you may F the LORD your God,
6:13 You shall F the LORD your God; you shall
6:24 all these statutes, to F the LORD our God,
10:12 of you, but to F the LORD your God,
10:20 You shall F the LORD your God; you shall
11:25 God will lay the F of you and the
13:4 LORD your God and F him, and keep his
13:11 Israel shall hear, and F, and never again do
14:23 you may learn to F the LORD your God
17:13 people shall hear, and F, and not act presumptuously
17:19 he may learn to F the LORD his God,
19:20 rest shall hear, and F, and shall never again
20:3 heart faint; do not F, or tremble, or be
21:21 your midst; and all Israel shall hear, and F
25:18 and he did not F God.
28:58 book, that you may F this glorious and awful
28:67 which your heart shall F, and the sights which
31:6 good courage, do not F or be in dread
31:8 forsake you; do not F or be dismayed."
31:12 hear and learn to F the LORD your God,
31:13 hear and learn to F the LORD your God,
Josh 2:9 land, and that the F of you has fallen
4:24 mighty; that you may F the LORD your God
8:1 to Joshua, "Do not F or be dismayed; take
10:8 to Joshua, "Do not F them, for I have
22:24 we did it from F that in time to
24:14 not plant.' "Now therefore F the LORD, and serve
Judg 4:18 my lord, turn aside to me; have no F
6:23 to you; do not F, you shall not die."
7:10 But if you F to go down, go down
9:21 and dwelt there, for F of Abimelech his brother.
Ruth 3:11 my daughter, do not F, I will do for
1Sam 4:20 her said to her, F not, for you have
12:14 If you will F the LORD and serve him
12:20 said to the people, F not; you have done
12:24 Only F the LORD, and serve him faithfully with
22:23 Stay with me, F not; for he that seeks
23:17 he said to him, F not; for the hand
28:13 to her, "Have no F; what do you see?"
28:20 the ground, filled with F because of the words
2Sam 9:7 to him, "Do not F; for I will show
13:28 F not; have I not commanded you?
17:10 will utterly melt with F; for all Israel knows
23:3 men, ruling in the F of God,
1Kgs 8:40 men); that they may F thee all the days
8:43 know thy name and F thee, as do thy
17:13 Elijah said to her, F not; go and do
2Kgs 6:16 He said, F not, for those who are with
17:25 there, they did not F the LORD; therefore the
17:28 them how they should F the LORD.
17:34 They do not F the LORD, and they do
17:35 them, "You shall not F other gods or bow
17:36 them; but you shall F the LORD, who brought
17:37 You shall not F other gods,
17:38 You shall not F other gods,
17:39 gods, but you shall F the LORD your God,
1Chr 14:17 the LORD brought the F of him upon all
22:13 F not; be not dismayed.
28:20 F not, be not dismayed; for the LORD God,
2Chr 6:31 men); that they may F thee and walk in
6:33 know thy name and F thee, as do thy
14:14 about Gerar, for the F of the LORD was
17:10 And the F of the LORD fell upon all
19:7 Now then, let the F of the LORD be
19:9 shall do in the F of the LORD, in
20:15 the LORD to you, F not, and be not
20:17 O Judah and Jerusalem.' F not, and be not
20:29 And the F of God came on all the
26:5 instructed him in the F of God; and as
Ezra 3:3 in its place, for F was upon them because
Neh 1:11 servants who delight to F thy name; and give
5:9 to walk in the F of our God to
5:15 so, because of the F of God.
Tob 1:19 be put to death, I left home in F
4:21 great wealth if you F God and refrain from
6:14 So now I F that I may die and
14:2 and he continued to F the Lord God and
14:6 Gentiles will turn to F the Lord God in
Jud 2:28 So F and terror of him fell upon all
14:3 Then F will come over them, and they will
15:2 F and trembling came over them, so that they
16:15 but to those who F thee thou wilt continue
Esth 8:17 themselves Jews, for the F of the Jews had
9:2 against them, for the F of them had fallen
9:3 the Jews, for the F of Mordecai had fallen
14:19 And save me from my F
15:5 if beloved, but her heart was frozen with F
15:13 heart was shaken with F at your glory.
Job 1:9 the LORD, "Does Job F God for nought?
3:25 the thing that I F comes upon me, and
4:6 Is not your F of God your confidence, and
5:21 tongue, and shall not F destruction when it comes.
5:22 laugh, and shall not F the beasts of the
6:14 a friend forsakes the F of the Almighty.
9:35 I would speak without F of him, for I
11:15 blemish; you will be secure, and will not F
15:4 doing away with the F of God, and hindering
21:9 houses are safe from F, and no rod of
22:4 Is it for your F of him that he
25:2 Shuhite answered: "Dominion and F are with God;
28:28 to man, 'Behold, the F of the Lord, that
31:34 I stood in great F of the multitude, and
33:7 Behold, no F of me need terrify you; my
37:24 Therefore men F him; he does not regard any
39:16 yet she has no F;
39:22 He laughs at F, and is not dismayed; he
41:33 there is not his like, a creature without F
Ps 2:11 Serve the LORD with F, with trembling
5:7 holy temple in the F of thee.
9:20 Put them in F, O LORD!
15:4 who honors those who F the LORD; who swears
19:9 enlightening the eyes; the F of the LORD is
22:23 praise thee: You who F the LORD, praise him!
22:25 pay before those who F him.
23:4 shadow of death, I F no evil; for thou
25:14 is for those who F him, and he makes
27:1 my light and my salvation; whom shall I F
27:3 my heart shall not F; though war arise against
31:19 up for those who F thee, and wrought for
33:8 Let all the earth F the LORD, let all
33:18 is on those who F him, on those who
34:7 encamps around those who F him, and delivers them.
34:9 O F the LORD, you his saints, for those
34:9 saints, for those who F him have no want!
34:11 will teach you the F of the LORD.
36:1 heart; there is no F of God before his
40:3 Many will see and F, and put their trust
46:2 Therefore we will not F though the earth should
49:5 Why should I F in times of trouble, when
52:6 righteous shall see, and F, and shall laugh at
55:5 F and trembling come upon me, and horror
55:19 law, and do not F God.
56:4 I praise, in God I trust without a F
56:11 I praise, in God I trust without a F
60:4 banner for those who F thee, to rally to
61:5 heritage of those who F thy name.
64:4 blameless, shooting at him suddenly and without F
64:9 Then all men will F; they will tell what
66:16 hear, all you who F God, and I will

67:7 ends of the earth F him!
85:9 hand for those who F him, that glory may
86:11 unite my heart to F thy name.
90:11 wrath according to the F of thee?
91:5 You will not F the terror of the night,
102:15 The nations will F the name of the LORD,
103:11 love toward those who F him;
103:13 LORD pities those who F him.
103:17 everlasting upon those who F him, and his
111:5 food for those who F him; he is ever
111:10 The F of the LORD is the beginning of
115:11 You who F the LORD, trust in the LORD!
115:13 will bless those who F the LORD, both small
118:4 Let those who F the LORD say, "His steadfast
118:6 the LORD on my side I do not F
119:38 is for those who F thee.
119:63 companion of all who F thee, of those who
119:74 Those who F thee shall see me and rejoice,
119:79 Let those who F thee turn to me, that
119:120 My flesh trembles for F of thee, and I
135:20 You that F the LORD, bless the LORD!
145:19 desire of all who F him, he also hears
147:11 pleasure in those who F him, in those who
Prov 1:7 The F of the LORD is the beginning of
1:29 did not choose the F of the LORD,
2:5 you will understand the F of the LORD and
3:7 in your own eyes; F the LORD, and turn
8:13 The F of tQhe LORD is hatred of evil.
9:10 The F of the LORD is the beginning of
10:27 The F of the LORD prolongs life, but the
14:26 In the F of the LORD one has strong
14:27 The F of the LORD is a fountain of
15:16 a little with the F of the LORD than
15:33 The F of the LORD is instruction in wisdom,
16:6 for, and by the F of the LORD a
19:23 The F of the LORD leads to life; and
22:4 reward for humility and F of the LORD is
23:17 but continue in the F of the LORD all
24:21 My son, F the LORD and the king, and
29:25 The F of man lays a snare, but he
Eccl 3:14 order that men should F before him.
5:7 many: but do you F God.
8:12 well with those who F God, because they fear
8:12 fear God, because they F before him;
8:13 because he does not F before God.
12:13 F God, and keep his commandments; for this is
Wis 5:2 be shaken with dreadful F, and they will be
12:11 it was not through F of any one that
17:4 them protected them from F, but terrifying sounds
17:8 a sick soul were sick themselves with ridiculous F
17:10 they perished in trembling F, refusing to look even
17:12 For F is nothing but surrender of the helps
17:15 for sudden and unexpected F overwhelmed them.
Sir 1:9 The F of the Lord is glory and exultation,
1:10 The F of the Lord delights the heart, and
1:12 To F the Lord is the beginning of wisdom
1:14 To F the Lord is wisdom's full measure; she
1:16 The F of the Lord is the crown of
1:18 To F the Lord is the root of wisdom,
1:24 For the F of the Lord is wisdom and
1:25 Do not disobey the F of the Lord; do
1:27 not come in the F of the Lord, and
2:7 You who F the Lord, wait for his mercy;
2:8 You who F the Lord, trust in him, and
2:9 not fail; you who F the Lord, hope for
2:10 ever persevered in the F of the Lord and
2:15 Those who F the Lord will not disobey his
2:16 Those who F the Lord will seek his approval,
2:17 Those who F the Lord will prepare their hearts,
4:17 paths, she will bring F and cowardice upon him,
6:16 life; and those who F the Lord will find
7:29 With all your soul F the Lord, and honor
7:31 F the Lord and honor the priest, and give
9:13 be worried by the F of death.
9:16 glorying be in the F of the Lord.
10:19 Those who F the Lord.
10:20 honor, and those who F the Lord are worthy
10:21 their glory is the F of the Lord.
15:13 loved by those who F him.
15:19 are on those who F him, and he knows
16:2 in them, unless the F of the Lord is
17:4 He placed the F of them in all living
19:18 All wisdom is the F of the Lord, and
21:11 the fulfilment of the F of the Lord.
22:16 fool's purpose will not stand firm against any F
23:18 Why should I F
23:19 His F is confined to the eyes of men,
23:27 is better than the F of the Lord, and
25:6 their boast is the F of the Lord.
25:11 The F of the Lord surpasses everything; to whom
27:3 and zealous in the F of the Lord, his
32:16 Those who F the Lord will form true judgments,
32:18 insolent and proud man will not cower in F
34:13 spirit of those who F the Lord will live,
36:2 us, and cause the F of thee to fall
40:2 Their perplexities and F of heart-- their anxious
40:5 trouble and unrest, and F of death, and fury
40:7 and wonders that his F came to nothing.
40:26 the heart, but the F of the Lord is
40:26 no loss in the F of the Lord, and
40:27 The F of the Lord is like a garden
41:3 Do not F the sentence of death; remember your
45:23 was zealous in the F of the Lord, and
Is 7:4 be quiet, do not F, and do not let
7:25 not come there for F of briers and thorns;
8:6 gently, and melt in F before Rezin and the
8:12 conspiracy, and do not F what they fear, nor
8:12 not fear what they F, nor be in dread.
8:13 let him be your F, and let him be
11:2 of knowledge and the F of the LORD.
11:3 shall be in the F of the LORD.
14:31 O city; melt in F, O Philistia, all of
19:16 women, and tremble with F before the hand which
19:17 it is mentioned will F because of the purpose
25:3 of ruthless nations will F thee.
29:13 from me, and their F of me is a
33:6 wisdom, and knowledge; the F of the LORD is
35:4 fearful heart, "Be strong, F not!
40:9 tidings, lift it up, F not; say to the
41:10 not cast you off"; F not, for I am
41:13 who say to you, F not, I will help
41:14 F not, you worm Jacob, you men of Israel!
43:1 formed you, O Israel: F not, for I have
43:5 F not, for I am with you; I will
44:2 and will help you: F not, O Jacob my
44:8 F not, nor be afraid; have I not told
51:7 heart is my law; F not the reproach of
51:13 of the earth, and F continually all the day
54:4 F not, for you will not be ashamed; be
54:14 for you shall not F; and from terror, for
57:11 did you dread and F, so that you lied,
57:11 so you do not F me?
59:19 So they shall F the name of the LORD
63:17 heart, so that we F thee not?
Jer 2:19 LORD your God; the F of me is not
3:8 sister Judah did not F, but she too went
5:22 Do you not F me?
5:24 their hearts, 'Let us F the LORD our God,
10:7 Who would not F thee, O King of the
17:8 stream, and does not F when heat comes, for
23:4 them, and they shall F no more, nor be
26:19 Did he not F the LORD and entreat the
30:10 "Then F not, O Jacob my servant, says the
32:39 way, that they may F me for ever, for
32:40 I will put the F of me in their
33:9 for them; they shall F and tremble because of
35:11 go to Jerusalem for F of the army of
36:16 one to another in F; and they said to
42:11 Do not F the king of Babylon, of whom
42:11 are afraid; do not F him, says the LORD,
42:16 the sword which you F shall overtake you there
46:27 "But F not, O Jacob my servant, nor be
46:28 F not, O Jacob my servant, says the LORD,
49:23 tidings; they melt in F, they are troubled like
Lam 3:57 didst say, 'Do not F
Bar 3:7 thou hast put the F of thee in our
3:33 it obeyed him in F;
6:4 men's shoulders and inspire F in the heathen.
6:5 foreigners or to let F for these gods possess
6:16 gods; so do not F them.
6:23 gods; so do not F them.
6:29 not gods, do not F them.
6:65 not gods, do not F them.
6:69 gods; therefore do not F them.
Ezek 3:9 I made your forehead; F them not, nor be
30:13 so I will put F in the land of
Dan 1:10 said to Daniel, "I F lest my lord the
3:41 we follow thee, we F thee and seek thy
6:26 dominion men tremble and F before the God of
10:12 he said to me, F not, Daniel, for from
10:19 "O man greatly beloved, F not, peace be with
13:57 intimate with you through F; but a daughter of

F

Hos 3:5 they shall come in F to the LORD and
10:3 no king, for we F not the LORD, and
Joel 2:21 F not, O land; be glad and rejoice, for
2:22 F not, you beasts of the field, for the
Amos 3:8 The lion has roared; who will not F
Jon 1:9 a Hebrew; and I F the LORD, the God
Mic 6:9 is sound wisdom to F thy name: "Hear, O
7:17 God, and they shall F because of thee.
Hab 3:2 thee, and thy work, O LORD, do I F
Zeph 3:7 said, 'Surely she will F me, she will accept
3:15 your midst; you shall F evil no more.
3:16 to Jerusalem: "Do not F, O Zion; let not
Hag 2:5 Spirit abides among you; F not.
Zech 8:13 F not, but let your hands be strong."
8:15 the house of Judah; F not.
Mal 1:6 if I am a master, where is my F
2:5 him, that he might F; and he feared me,
3:5 sojourner, and do not F me, says the LORD
4:2 But for you who F my name the sun
1Mac 2:62 Do not F the words of a sinner, for
3:6 men shrank back for F of him; all the
4:8 with him, "Do not F their numbers or be
5:41 But if he shows F and camps on the
7:18 Then the F and dread of them fell upon
12:52 and were in great F; and all Israel mourned
2Mac 3:30 before was full of F and disturbance, was filled
6:30 these things because I F him."
7:29 Do not F this butcher, but prove worthy of
8:16 enemy and not to F the great multitude of
12:22 division appeared, terror and F came over the enemy
15:8 his men not to F the attack of the
15:18 their greatest and first F was for the consecrated
Mt 1:20 of David, do not F to take Mary your
10:26 "So have no F of them; for nothing is
10:28 And do not F those who kill the body
10:28 kill the soul; rather F him who can destroy
10:31 F not, therefore; you are of more value than
14:26 And they cried out for F
14:27 saying, "Take heart, it is I; have no F
17:7 and touched them, saying, "Rise, and have no F
28:4 And for F of him the guards trembled and
28:8 from the tomb with F and great joy, and
Mk 5:33 to her, came in F and trembling and fell
5:36 the synagogue, "Do not F, only believe."
6:50 said, "Take heart, it is I; have no F
Lk 1:12 he saw him, and F fell upon him.
1:50 is on those who F him from generation to
1:65 And F came on all their neighbors.
1:74 might serve him without F,
2:9 shone around them, and they were filled with F
7:16 F seized them all; and they glorified God, saying,
8:37 were seized with great F; so he got into
8:50 answered him, "Do not F; only believe, and she
12:4 my friends, do not F those who kill the
12:5 warn you whom to F: fear him who, after
12:5 you whom to fear: F him who, after he
12:5 yes, I tell you, F him!
12:7 F not; you are of more value than many
12:32 F not, little flock, for it is your Father's
18:4 himself, 'Though I neither F God nor regard man,
21:26 waves, men fainting with F and with foreboding of
23:39 saying, "Do you not F God, since you are
Jn 7:13 Yet for F of the Jews no one spoke
12:15 as it is written, F not, daughter of Zion;
12:42 in him, but for F of the Pharisees they
19:38 Jesus, but secretly, for F of the Jews, asked
20:19 the disciples were, for F of the Jews, Jesus
Acts 2:43 And F came upon every soul; and many wonders
5:5 And great F came upon all who heard of
5:11 And great F came upon the whole church, and
9:31 and walking in the F of the Lord and
13:16 Israel, and you that F God, listen.
13:26 those among you that F God, to us has
16:29 in, and trembling with F he fell down before
19:17 Jews and Greeks; and F fell upon them all;
Rom 3:18 "There is no F of God before their eyes."
8:15 to fall back into F, but you have received
13:3 Would you have no F of him who is
1Cor 2:3 weakness and in much F and trembling;
2Cor 5:11 Therefore, knowing the F of the Lord, we persuade
7:1 holiness perfect in the F of God.
7:5 turn—fighting without and F within.
7:15 you all, and the F and trembling with which
12:20 For I F that perhaps I may come and
12:21 I F that when I come again my God
Eph 6:5 your earthly masters, with F and trembling, in
Phil 1:14 bold to speak the word of God without F
2:12 your own salvation with F and trembling;
1Thes 3:5 know your faith, for F that somehow the tempter
1Tim 5:20 all, so that the rest may stand in F
Heb 2:15 all those who through F of death were subject
4:1 rest remains, let us F lest any of you
5:7 death, and he was heard for his godly F
12:21 the sight that Moses said, "I tremble with F
1Pet 1:17 conduct yourselves with F throughout the time of
2:17 F God.
3:14 Have no F of them, nor be troubled,
1Jn 4:18 There is no F in love, but perfect love
4:18 fear in love, but perfect love casts out F
4:18 For F has to do with punishment, and he
Jude 1:23 some have mercy with F, hating even the garment
Rev 1:17 hand upon me, saying, F not, I am the
2:10 Do not F what you are about to suffer.
11:11 their feet, and great F fell on those who
11:18 saints, and those who F thy name, both small
14:7 with a loud voice, F God and give him
15:4 Who shall not F and glorify thy name, O
18:10 will stand far-off, in F of her torment, and
18:15 will stand far-off, in F of her torment, weeping
19:5 his servants, you who F him, small and great."

FEARED (63)

Gen 26:7 my sister"; for he F to say, "My wife,"
38:11 grows up"—for he F that he would die,
42:4 his brothers, for he F that harm might befall
Ex 1:16 But the midwives F God, and did not do
1:20 And because the midwives F God he gave them
9:20 Then he who F the word of the LORD
14:31 Egyptians, and the people F the LORD; and they
Deut 32:27 had I not F provocation by the enemy, lest
Josh 9:24 before you; so we F greatly for our lives
10:2 were among them, he F greatly, because Gibeon was
1Sam 12:18 all the people greatly F the LORD and Samuel.
14:26 mouth; for the people F the oath.
15:24 your words, because I F the people and obeyed
31:4 would not; for he F greatly.
2Sam 3:11 another word, because he F him.
10:19 So the Syrians F to help the Ammonites any
12:18 the servants of David F to tell him that
1Kgs 1:50 And Adonijah F Solomon; and he arose, and went,
2Kgs 4:1 know that your servant F the LORD, but the
17:7 of Egypt, and had F other gods
17:32 They also F the LORD, and appointed from among
17:33 So they F the LORD but also served their
17:41 So these nations F the LORD, and also served
1Chr 10:4 would not; for he F greatly.
2Chr 20:3 Then Jehoshaphat F, and set himself to seek the
Jud 2:28 in Azotus and Ascalon F him exceedingly.
8:8 of her, for she F God with great devotion.
Esth 11:9 nation was troubled; they F the evils that threatened
Job 1:1 and upright, one who F God, and turned away
Ps 76:8 utter judgment; the earth F and was still,
76:11 who is to be F,
89:7 the LORD, a God F in the council of
96:4 he is to be F above all gods.
130:4 is forgiveness with thee, that thou mayest be F
Wis 18:25 destroyer yielded, these he F; for merely to test
Sir 1:6 wise, greatly to be F, sitting upon his throne.
9:18 A babbler is F in his city, and the
Is 18:2 smooth, to a people F near and far, a
18:7 smooth, from a people F near and far, a
Jer 44:10 day, nor have they F, nor walked in my
Ezek 11:8 You have F the sword; and I will bring
Dan 5:19 and languages trembled and F before him; whom he
13:2 woman and one who F the Lord.
Jon 1:16 Then the men F the LORD exceedingly, and they
Hag 1:12 him; and the people F before the LORD.
Mal 1:14 and my name is F among the nations.
2:5 might fear; and he F me, he stood in
3:16 Then those who F the LORD spoke with one
3:16 him of those who F the LORD and thought
1Mac 3:25 brothers began to be F, and terror fell upon
3:30 He F that he might not have such funds
8:12 of their fame have F them.
12:40 He F that Jonathan might not permit him to
Mt 14:5 him to death, he F the people, because they
21:46 to arrest him, they F the multitudes, because they
Mk 6:20 could not, for Herod F John, knowing that he
11:18 destroy him; for they F him, because all the
12:12 to arrest him, but F the multitude, for they
Lk 18:2 a judge who neither F God nor regarded man;
20:19 very hour, but they F the people; for they

22:2 to death; for they F the people.
Jn 9:22 said this because they F the Jews, for the
Acts 10:2 a devout man who F God with all his

FEARFUL (10)

Deut 20:8 is there that is F and fainthearted?
Judg 7:3 people, saying, 'Whoever is F and trembling, let him
Ps 139:14 thee, for thou art F and wonderful.
Is 35:4 who are of a F heart, "Be strong, fear
Jer 51:46 faint, and be not F at the report heard
Dan 8:24 and he shall cause F destruction, and shall succeed
1Mac 13:2 he saw that the people were trembling and F
Heb 10:27 for sins, but a F prospect of judgment, and
10:31 It is a F thing to fall into the
Rev 16:21 of the hail, so F was that plague.

FEARFULLY

Dan 10:8 my radiant appearance was F changed, and I

FEARFULNESS (3)

Ezek 4:16 by weight and with F; and they shall drink
12:18 with trembling and with F;
12:19 eat their bread with F, and drink water in

FEARING (7)

Deut 8:6 his ways and by F him.
2Mac 3:32 And the high priest, F that the king might
9:29 his body home; then, F the son of Antiochus,
Acts 27:17 undergird the ship; then, F that they should run
27:29 And F that we might run on the rocks,
Gal 2:12 back and separated himself, F the circumcision party.
Col 3:22 in singleness of heart, F the Lord.

FEARS (32)

1Kgs 1:51 Solomon, "Behold, Adonijah F King Solomon; for, lo,
Jud 16:16 thing, but he who F the Lord shall be
Job 1:8 and upright man, who F God and turns away
2:3 and upright man, who F God and turns away
Ps 25:12 is the man that F the LORD?
34:4 answered me, and delivered me from all my F
112:1 is the man who F the LORD, who greatly
128:1 is every one who F the LORD, who walks
128:4 man be blessed who F the LORD.
Prov 14:2 who walks in uprightness F the LORD, but he
28:14 is the man who F the LORD always; but
31:30 but a woman who F the LORD is to
Eccl 7:18 hand; for he who F God shall come forth
Wis 17:8 to drive off the F and disorders of a
18:17 troubled them, and unexpected F assailed them;
Sir 1:11 With him who F the Lord it will go
6:17 Whoever F the Lord directs his friendship aright, for
10:23 than the man who F the Lord.
15:1 The man who F the Lord will do this,
21:6 sinner, but he that F the Lord will repent
25:10 superior to him who F the Lord.
26:3 of the man who F the Lord.
32:14 He who F the Lord will accept his discipline,
33:1 befall the man who F the Lord, but in
34:14 He who F the Lord will not be timid,
34:15 of the man who F the Lord!
45:2 him great in the F of his enemies.
Is 50:10 Who among you F the LORD and obeys the
66:4 them, and bring their F upon them; because, when
Ezek 18:14 father has done, and F, and does not do
Acts 10:35 nation any one who F him and does what
1Jn 4:18 punishment, and he who F is not perfected in

FEAST (158)

Gen 19:3 he made them a F, and baked unleavened bread,
21:8 Abraham made a great F on the day that
26:30 he made them a F, and they ate and
29:22 the men of the place, and made a F
40:20 birthday, he made a F for all his servants,
Ex 5:1 they may hold a F to me in the
10:9 we must hold a F to the LORD."
12:14 keep it as a F to the LORD; throughout
12:17 you shall observe the F of unleavened bread, for
13:6 there shall be a F to the LORD.
23:14 you shall keep a F to me.
23:15 You shall keep the F of unleavened bread; as
23:16 You shall keep the F of harvest, of the
23:16 You shall keep the F of ingathering at the
23:18 the fat of my F remain until the morning.
32:5 "Tomorrow shall be a F to the LORD."
34:18 he F of unleavened bread you shall keep.
34:22 you shall observe the F of weeks, the first
34:22 wheat harvest, and the F of ingathering at the
34:25 the sacrifice of the F of the passover be
Lev 23:6 same month is the F of unleavened bread to
23:34 seven days is the F of booths to the
23:39 you shall keep the F of the LORD seven
23:41 keep it as a F to the LORD seven
Num 28:17 this month is a F; seven days shall unleavened
28:26 the LORD at your F of weeks, you shall
29:12 you shall keep a F to the LORD seven
Deut 16:10 you shall keep the F of weeks to the
16:13 "You shall keep the F of booths seven days,
16:14 shall rejoice in your F, you and your son
16:15 you shall keep the F to the LORD your
16:16 will choose: at the F of unleavened bread, at
16:16 unleavened bread, at the F of weeks, and at
16:16 weeks, and at the F of booths.
31:10 of release, at the F of booths,
Judg 14:10 and Samson made a F there; for so the
14:12 seven days of the F, and find it out,
14:17 seven days that their F lasted; and on the
21:19 there is the yearly F of the LORD at
1Sam 25:8 we come on a F day.
25:36 he was holding a F in his house, like
25:36 his house, like the F of a king.
2Sam 3:20 Hebron, David made a F for Abner and the
1Kgs 3:15 offerings, and made a F for all his servants.
8:2 King Solomon at the F in the month Ethanim,
8:65 So Solomon held the F at that time, and
12:32 And Jeroboam appointed a F on the fifteenth day
12:32 eighth month like the F that was in Judah,
12:33 and he ordained a F for the people of
2Kgs 6:23 for them a great F; and when they had
1Chr 23:31 sabbaths, new moons, and F days, according to the
2Chr 5:3 the king at the F which is in the
7:8 time Solomon held the F for seven days, and
7:9 seven days and the F seven days.
8:13 three annual feasts–the F of unleavened bread, the
8:13 of unleavened bread, the F of weeks, and the
8:13 of weeks, and the F of tabernacles.
30:13 Jerusalem to keep the F of unleavened bread in
30:21 at Jerusalem kept the F of unleavened bread seven
30:23 together to keep the F for another seven days;
35:17 that time, and the F of unleavened bread seven
Ezra 3:4 And they kept the F of booths, as it
6:22 And they kept the F of unleavened bread seven
Neh 8:14 in booths during the F of the seventh month,
8:18 They kept the F seven days; and on the
Tob 2:1 to me, at the F of Pentecost, which is
8:19 he gave a wedding F for them which lasted
8:20 the days of the F were over, Raguel declared
8:20 days of the wedding F were ended,
9:2 for me; and bring him to the wedding F
9:6 got up early and came to the wedding F
10:7 days of the wedding F had expired which Raguel
Jud 10:2 sabbaths and on her F days;
Esth 7:1 Haman went in to F with Queen Esther
7:7 king rose from the F in wrath and went
8:17 among the Jews, a F and a holiday.
14:17 not honored the king's F or drunk the wine
Job 1:4 go and hold a F in the house of
1:5 the days of the F had run their course,
Ps 36:8 They F on the abundance of thy house, and
81:3 full moon, on our F day.
Prov 15:15 evil, but a cheerful heart has a continual F
Eccl 10:16 child, and your princes F in the morning!
10:17 men, and your princes F at the proper time,
Sir 32:1 you master of the F, do not exalt yourself;
43:7 comes the sign for F days, a light that
Is 25:6 for all peoples a F of fat things, a
25:6 of fat things, a F of wine on the
30:29 night when a holy F is kept; and gladness
Jer 31:14 I will F the soul of the priests with
51:39 will prepare them a F and make them drunk,
Lam 2:6 end in Zion appointed F and sabbath, and in
2:7 LORD as on the day of an appointed F
2:22 day of an appointed F my terrors on every
Bar 6:32 do at a funeral F for a man who
Ezek 20:7 detestable things your eyes F on, every one of
28:17 you before kings, to F their eyes on you.
39:17 sides to the sacrificial F which I am preparing
39:17 you, a great sacrificial F upon the mountains of
39:19 drunk, at the sacrificial F which I am preparing
45:21 you shall celebrate the F of the passover, and
45:25 seven days of the F, he shall make the
Dan 5:1 Belshazzar made a great F for a thousand of
Hos 2:13 punish her for the F days of the Baals

F

9:5 the day of the F of the LORD?
12:9 tents, as in the days of the appointed F
Zech 14:16 and to keep the F of booths.
14:18 up to keep the F of booths.
14:19 up to keep the F of booths.
1Mac 10:21 sixtieth year, at the F of tabernacles, and he
10:34 three days before a F and the three after
10:34 the three after a F – let them
2Mac 1:9 that you keep the F of booths in the
1:18 also may celebrate the F of booths and the
1:18 of booths and the F of the fire given
6:7 sacrifices; and when the F of Dionysus came, they
10:6 the manner of the F of booths, remembering how
10:6 long before, during the F of booths, they had
12:31 to Jerusalem, as the F of weeks was close
12:32 After the F called Pentecost, they hastened against
Mt 22:2 who gave a marriage F for his son,
22:3 invited to the marriage F; but they would not
22:4 come to the marriage F
22:9 invite to the marriage F as many as you
25:10 him to the marriage F; and the door was
26:5 said, "Not during the F, lest there be a
27:15 Now at the F the governor was accustomed to
Mk 14:1 the Passover and the F of Unleavened Bread.
14:2 said, "Not during the F, lest there be a
15:6 Now at the F he used to release for
Lk 2:41 every year at the F of the Passover.
2:43 custom; and when the F was ended, as they
5:29 made him a great F in his house; and
12:36 home from the marriage F, so that they may
14:8 one to a marriage F, do not sit down
14:13 when you give a F, invite the poor, the
22:1 Now the F of Unleavened Bread drew near, which
Jn 2:8 and take it to the steward of the F
2:9 the steward of the F tasted the water now
2:9 the steward of the F called the bridegroom
2:23 Jerusalem at the Passover F, many believed in his
4:45 in Jerusalem at the F, for they too had
4:45 feast, for they too had gone to the F
5:1 this there was a F of the Jews, and
6:4 Now the Passover, the F of the Jews, was
7:2 Now the Jews' F of Tabernacles was at hand.
7:8 Go to the F yourselves; I am not going
7:8 going up to this F, for my time has
7:10 gone up to the F, then he also went
7:11 for him at the F, and saying, "Where is
7:14 the middle of the F Jesus went up into
7:37 last day of the F, the great day, Jesus
10:22 It was the F of the Dedication at Jerusalem;
11:56 That he will not come to the F
12:12 had come to the F heard that Jesus was
12:20 to worship at the F were some Greeks.
13:1 Now before the F of the Passover, when Jesus
13:29 we need for the F; or, that he should

FEASTED (5)

Jud 1:16 his forces rested and F for one hundred and
Ps 63:5 My soul is F as with marrow and fat,
Lam 4:5 Those who F on dainties perish in the streets;
Ezek 20:8 detestable things their eyes F on, nor did they
Lk 16:19 fine linen and who F sumptuously every day.

FEASTING (13)

1Kgs 1:41 were with him heard it as they finished F
Jud 16:20 So the people continued F in Jerusalem before the
Esth 9:17 that a day of F and gladness.
9:18 that a day of F and gladness.
9:19 day for gladness and F and holiday-making, and a
9:22 make them days of F and gladness, days for
13:17 turn our mourning into F, that we may live
Prov 17:1 a house full of F with strife.
Eccl 7:2 to the house of F; for this is the
Wis 12:5 children, and their sacrificial F on human flesh and
Sir 13:8 astray, and not to be humiliated in your F
18:32 become a beggar by F with borrowed money, when
Jer 16:8 into the house of F to sit with them,

FEASTS (47)

Lev 23:2 of Israel, The appointed F of the LORD which
23:2 holy convocations, my appointed F, are these.
23:4 "These are the appointed F of the LORD, the
23:37 "These are the appointed F of the LORD, which
23:44 of Israel the appointed F of the LORD.
Num 10:10 and at your appointed F, and at the beginnings
15:3 or at your appointed F, to make a pleasing
29:39 LORD at your appointed F, in addition to your
2Chr 2:4 moons and the appointed F of the LORD our
8:13 and the three annual F –the feast of unleavened
31:3 moons, and the appointed F, as it is written
Ezra 3:5 at all the appointed F of the LORD, and
Neh 10:33 new moons, the appointed F, the holy things, and
Tob 1:6 to Jerusalem for the F, as it is ordained
2:6 how he said, "Your F shall be turned into
Jud 8:6 new moon, and the F and days of rejoicing
Ps 69:22 snare; let their sacrificial F be a trap.
Sir 33:8 the different seasons and F;
47:10 gave beauty to the F, and arranged their times
Is 1:14 moons and your appointed F my soul hates; they
5:12 and wine at their F; but they do not
29:1 to year; let the F run their round.
33:20 Look upon Zion, the city of our appointed F
Lam 1:4 come to the appointed F; all her gates are
2:6 place of his appointed F; the LORD has brought
Bar 1:14 the days of the F and at appointed seasons.
Ezek 36:38 Jerusalem during her appointed F, so shall the waste
44:24 in all my appointed F, and they shall keep
45:17 drink offerings, at the F, the new moons, and
45:17 sabbaths, all the appointed F of the house of
46:9 LORD at the appointed F, he who enters by
46:11 "At the F and the appointed seasons the cereal
Hos 2:11 all her mirth, her F, her new moons, her
2:11 new moons, her sabbaths, and all her appointed F
Amos 5:21 hate, I despise your F, and I take no
8:10 I will turn your F into mourning, and all
Nah 1:15 Keep your F, O Judah, fulfil your vows, for
Zech 8:19 and gladness, and cheerful F; therefore love truth
1Mac 1:39 as a desert; her F were turned into mourning,
1:45 to profane sabbaths and F,
10:34 "And all the F and sabbaths and new moons
12:11 occasion, both in our F and on other appropriate
2Mac 6:6 sabbath, nor observe the F of his fathers, nor
Mt 23:6 place of honor at F and the best seats
Mk 12:39 places of honor at F,
Lk 20:46 places of honor at F,
Jude 1:12 blemishes on your love F, as they boldly carouse

FEATHERS (2)

Lev 1:16 its crop with the F, and cast it beside
Dan 4:33 as long as eagles' F, and his nails were

FED (24)

Gen 30:36 and Jacob; and Jacob F the rest of Laban's
41:2 and fat, and they F in the reed grass.
41:18 of the Nile and F in the reed grass;
Ex 16:32 bread with which I F you in the wilderness,
Deut 8:3 let you hunger and F you with manna, which
8:16 the flinty rock, who F you in the wilderness
1Kgs 18:4 in a cave, and F them with bread and
18:13 in a cave, and F them with bread and
Ps 80:5 Thou hast F them with the bread of tears,
Wis 16:23 the righteous might be F, even forgot its native
Is 1:11 and the fat of F beasts; I do not
Jer 5:7 When I F them to the full, they committed
Ezek 16:19 I gave you–I F you with fine flour
34:8 but the shepherds have F themselves, and have not
34:8 themselves, and have not F my sheep;
Dan 4:12 and all flesh was F from it.
5:21 wild asses; he was F grass like an ox,
14:27 made cakes, which he F to the dragon.
Hos 11:4 down to them and F them.
13:6 but when they had F to the full, they
Mk 7:26 the children first be F, for it is not
Lk 15:16 he would gladly have F on the pods that
16:21 who desired to be F with what fell from
1Cor 3:2 I F you with milk, not solid food; for

FEEBLE (12)

1Sam 2:4 are broken, but the F gird on strength.
2Chr 28:15 and carrying all the F among them on asses,
Neh 4:2 Samaria, "What are these F Jews doing?
Job 4:4 have made firm the F knees.
Is 13:7 all hands will be F, and every man's heart
16:14 those who survive will be very few and F
35:3 and make firm the F knees.
Jer 47:3 to their children, so F are their hands,
49:24 Damascus has become F, she turned to flee, and
Bar 2:18 about bent over and F, and the eyes that
Ezek 7:17 All hands are F, and all knees weak as
21:7 all hands will be F, every spirit will faint

FEEBLER (2)

Gen 30:42 rods, but for the F of the flock he

	30:42	them there; so the F were Labans, and the

FEEBLEST

Zech	12:8	Jerusalem so that the F among them on that

FEED (51)

Gen	30:31	me, I will again F your flock and keep
Ex	34:3	no flocks or herds F before that mountain."
1Sam	17:15	forth from Saul to F his father's sheep at
1Kgs	17:4	commanded the ravens to F you there."
	17:9	a widow there to F you."
	22:27	fellow in prison, and F him with scant fare
2Chr	18:26	fellow in prison, and F him with scant fare
Job	24:21	like a tree.' "They F on the barren childless
Ps	80:13	move in the field F on it.
	81:16	I would F you with the finest of the
Prov	10:21	lips of the righteous F many, but fools die
	15:14	the mouths of fools F on folly.
	30:8	neither poverty nor riches; F me with the food
Song	4:5	of a gazelle, that F among the lilies.
Sir	15:3	She will F him with the bread of understanding,
Is	5:17	fatlings and kids shall F among the ruins.
	11:7	and the bear shall F; their young shall lie
	14:30	of the poor will F, and the needy lie
	40:11	He will F his flock like a shepherd, he
	49:9	darkness, 'Appear.' They shall F along the ways, on
	58:14	the earth; I will F you with the heritage
	61:5	Aliens shall stand and F your flocks, foreigners shall
	65:25	and the lamb shall F together, the lion shall
Jer	3:15	own heart, who will F you with knowledge and
	9:15	Israel: Behold, I will F this people with wormwood,
	23:15	prophets: "Behold, I will F them with wormwood,
	50:19	pasture, and he shall F on Carmel and in
Ezek	34:2	Should not shepherds F the sheep?
	34:3	but you do not F the sheep.
	34:10	longer shall the shepherds F themselves.
	34:13	land; and I will F them on the mountains
	34:14	I will F them with good pasture, and upon
	34:14	fat pasture they shall F on the mountains of
	34:16	watch over; I will F them in justice.
	34:18	enough for you to F on the good pasture,
	34:23	David, and he shall F them: he shall feed
	34:23	feed them: he shall F them and be their
Dan	13:32	unveiled, that they might F upon her beauty.
Hos	4:8	They F on the sin of my people; they
	4:16	can the LORD now F them like a lamb
	9:2	and winevat shall not F them, and the new
Jon	3:7	anything; let them not F, or drink water,
Mic	5:4	he shall stand and F his flock in the
	7:14	garden land; let them F in Bashan and Gilead
Mt	15:33	in the desert to F so great a crowd?"
	25:37	see thee hungry and F thee, or thirsty and
Mk	8:4	him, "How can one F these men with bread
Lk	15:15	into his fields to F swine.
Jn	21:15	He said to him, F my lambs."
	21:17	Jesus said to him, F my sheep.
Rom	12:20	your enemy is hungry, F him; if he is

FEEDING (7)

Job	1:14	plowing and the asses F beside them;
Ezek	34:2	Israel who have been F yourselves!
	34:10	a stop to their F the sheep; no longer
Dan	3:46	in did not cease F the furnace fires with
Mt	8:30	of many swine was F at some distance from
Mk	5:11	herd of swine was F there on the hillside;
Lk	8:32	herd of swine was F there on the hillside;

FEEDS (5)

Ex	22:5	beast loose and it F in another man's field,
Wis	16:26	production of crops that F man, but that thy
Is	44:20	He F on ashes; a deluded mind has led
Mt	6:26	yet your heavenly Father F them.
Lk	12:24	barn, and yet God F them.

FEEL (15)

Gen	27:12	Perhaps my father will F me, and I shall
	27:21	near, that I may F you, my son, to
Judg	16:26	the hand, "Let me F the pillars on which
Ps	58:9	than your pots can F the heat of thorns,
	115:7	hands, but do not F; feet, but do not
Prov	23:35	but I did not F it.
Wis	15:15	hear, nor fingers to F with, and their feet
Sir	29:17	one who does not F grateful will abandon his
Jer	10:18	them, that they may F it."
Amos	6:1	and to those who F secure on the mountain
Acts	17:27	hope that they might F after him and find
2Cor	11:2	I F a divine jealousy for you, for I
Phil	1:7	right for me to F thus about you all,
1Thes	3:9	the joy which we F for your sake before
Heb	6:9	your case, beloved, we F sure of better things

FEELING (3)

Sir	22:17	one who pricks the heart makes it show F
	29:28	a man who has F: scolding about lodging and
Bar	6:24	when they were being cast, they had no F

FEELINGS (3)

Wis	1:6	witness of his inmost F, and a true observer
Sir	30:7	his wounds, and his F will be troubled at
	31:15	Judge your neighbor's F by your own, and in

FEELS (3)

Job	14:22	He F only the pain of his own body,
Sir	20:20	when he rests he F no remorse.
	31:20	he rises early, and F fit.

FEES

Num	22:7	Midian departed with the F for divination in their

FEET (260)

Gen	18:4	brought, and wash your F, and rest yourselves under
	19:2	night, and wash your F; then you may rise
	24:32	water to wash his F and the feet of
	24:32	his feet and the F of the men who
	43:24	they had washed their F, and when he had
	49:10	staff from between his F, until he comes to
	49:33	he drew up his F into the bed, and
Ex	3:5	your shoes from your F, for the place on
	4:25	foreskin, and touched Moses' F with it, and said,
	12:11	your sandals on your F, and your staff in
	24:10	there was under his F as it were a
	25:12	them on its four F, two rings on the
	29:20	toes of their right F, and throw the rest
	30:19	his sons shall wash their hands and their F
	30:21	their hands and their F, lest they die: it
Lev	8:24	toes of their right F; and Moses threw the
	11:21	have legs above their F, with which to leap
	11:23	insects which have four F are an abomination to
	11:42	or whatever has many F, all the swarming things
Deut	11:10	watered it with your F, like a garden of
	28:57	out from between her F and her children whom
	29:5	not worn off your F;
Josh	3:13	the soles of the F of the priests who
	3:15	the Jordan, and the F of the priests bearing
	4:3	place where the priests' F stood, and carry them
	4:9	the place where the F of the priests bearing
	4:18	soles of the priests' F were lifted up on
	5:15	your shoes from your F; for the place where
	9:5	patched sandals on their F, and worn-out clothes; and
	10:24	"Come near, put your F upon the necks of
	10:24	near, and put their F on their necks.
Judg	5:27	lay still at her F; at her feet he
	5:27	her feet; at her F he sank, he fell;
	19:21	and they washed their F, and ate and drank.
Ruth	3:4	go and uncover his F and lie down; and
	3:7	softly, and uncovered his F, and lay down.
	3:8	over, and behold, a woman lay at his F
	3:14	she lay at his F until the morning, but
1Sam	2:9	"He will guard the F of his faithful ones;
	14:13	on his hands and F, and his armor-bearer after
	25:24	She fell at his F and said, "Upon me
	25:41	servant to wash the F of the servants of
2Sam	3:34	were not bound, your F were not fettered; as
	4:4	had a son who was crippled in his F
	4:12	off their hands and F, and hanged them beside
	9:3	son of Jonathan; he is crippled in his F
	9:13	Now he was lame in both his F
	11:8	"Go down to your house, and wash your F
	19:24	had neither dressed his F, nor trimmed his beard,
	22:10	and came down; thick darkness was under his F
	22:34	He made my F like hinds' feet, and set
	22:34	my feet like hinds' F, and set me secure
	22:37	under me, and my F did not slip;
	22:39	they did not rise; they fell under my F
1Kgs	2:5	my loins, and upon the sandals on my F
	5:3	LORD put them under the soles of his F
	14:6	the sound of her F, as she came in
	14:12	When your F enter the city, the child shall
	15:23	his old age he was diseased in his F
2Kgs	4:27	man of God, she caught hold of his F
	4:37	and fell at his F, bowing to the ground;
	6:32	sound of his master's F behind him?"

F

	9:35	the skull and the F and the palms of
	13:21	of Elisha, he revived, and stood on his F
	21:8	will not cause the F of Israel to wander
1Chr	28:2	David rose to his F and said: "Hear me,
2Chr	3:13	cherubim stood on their F, facing the nave.
	16:12	was diseased in his F, and his disease became
Neh	9:21	wear out and their F did not swell.
Jud	2:7	the earth with the F of my armies, and
	10:4	put sandals on her F, and put on her
	14:7	he fell at Judith's F, and knelt before her,
Esth	8:3	she fell at his F and besought him with
	13:13	the soles of his F, to save Israel!
Job	12:5	ready for those whose F slip.
	13:27	Thou puttest my F in the stocks, and watchest
	13:27	settest a bound to the soles of my F
	18:8	net by his own F, and he walks on
	29:15	to the blind, and F to the lame.
	33:11	enemy; he puts my F in the stocks, and
Ps	2:12	with trembling kiss his F, lest he be angry,
	8:6	all things under his F,
	17:5	to thy paths, my F have not slipped.
	18:9	and came down; thick darkness was under his F
	18:33	He made my F like hinds' feet, and set
	18:33	my feet like hinds' F, and set me secure
	18:36	under me, and my F did not slip.
	18:38	not able to rise; they fell under my F
	22:16	pierced my hands and F --
	25:15	he will pluck my F out of the net.
	31:8	thou hast set my F in a broad place.
	40:2	bog, and set my F upon a rock, making
	47:3	subdued peoples under us, and nations under our F
	56:13	from death, yea, my F from falling, that I
	58:10	he will bathe his F in the blood of
	66:9	has not let our F slip.
	68:23	you may bathe your F in blood, that the
	73:2	as for me, my F had almost stumbled, my
	105:18	His F were hurt with fetters, his neck was
	115:7	but do not feel; F, but do not walk;
	116:8	eyes from tears, my F from stumbling;
	119:59	ways, I turn my F to thy testimonies;
	119:101	I hold back my F from every evil way,
	119:105	a lamp to my F and a light to
	122:2	Our F have been standing within your gates, O
	140:4	men, who have planned to trip up my F
Prov	1:16	their paths; for their F run to evil, and
	4:27	the path of your F, then all your ways
	5:5	Her F go down to death; her steps follow
	6:13	eyes, scrapes with his F, points with his finger,
	6:18	that devises wicked plans, F that make haste to
	6:28	hot coals and his F not be scorched?
	7:11	loud and wayward, her F do not stay at
	19:2	makes haste with his F misses his way.
	26:6	cuts off his own F and drinks violence.
	29:5	flatters his neighbor spreads a net for his F
Song	5:3	I had bathed my F, how could I soil
	7:1	How graceful are your F in sandals, O queenly
Wis	14:11	a snare to the F of the foolish.
	15:15	feel with, and their F are of no use
Sir	6:24	Put your F into her fetters, and your neck
	21:19	is fetters on his F, and like manacles on
	25:19	sandy ascent for the F of the aged--
	26:18	silver, so are beautiful F with a steadfast heart.
	38:29	the wheel with his F; he is always deeply
	38:30	it pliable with his F; he sets his heart
Is	3:16	go, tinkling with their F;
	6:2	two he covered his F, and with two he
	7:20	the hair of the F, and it will sweep
	20:2	loins and take off your shoes from your F
	23:7	days of old, whose F carried her to settle
	26:6	foot tramples it, the F of the poor, the
	32:20	waters, who let the F of the ox and
	41:3	safely, by paths his F have not trod.
	49:23	to you, and lick the dust of your F
	52:7	the mountains are the F of him who brings
	59:7	Their F run to evil, and they make haste
	60:13	the place of my F glorious.
	60:14	bow down at your F; they shall call you
Jer	2:25	Keep your F from going unshod and your throat
	13:16	brings darkness, before your F stumble on the
	14:10	have not restrained their F; therefore the LORD
	18:22	to take me, and laid snares for my F
	38:22	you; now that your F are sunk in the
Lam	1:13	a net for my F; he turned me back;
Bar	6:17	dust raised by the F of those who enter.
	6:26	Having no F, they are carried on men's shoulders,
Ezek	1:7	the soles of their F were like the sole
	2:1	man, stand upon your F, and I will speak
	2:2	set me upon my F; and I heard him
	3:24	set me upon my F; and he spoke with
	24:17	your shoes on your F; do not cover your
	24:23	your shoes on your F; you shall not mourn
	25:6	hands and stamped your F and rejoiced with all
	32:2	the waters with your F, and foul their rivers.
	34:18	tread down with your F the rest of your
	34:18	that you must foul the rest with your F
	34:19	have trodden with your F, and drink what you
	34:19	and drink what you have fouled with your F
	37:10	and stood upon their F, an exceedingly great host.
	43:7	the soles of my F, where I will dwell
Dan	2:33	legs of iron, its F partly of iron and
	2:34	the image on its F of iron and clay,
	2:41	as you saw the F and toes partly of
	2:42	the toes of the F were partly iron and
	7:4	to stand upon two F like a man; and
	7:7	in pieces, and stamped the residue with its F
	7:19	the residue with its F;
	8:18	he touched me and set me on my F
Nah	1:3	and the clouds are the dust of his F
	1:15	on the mountains the F of him who brings
Hab	3:19	strength; he makes my F like hinds' feet, he
	3:19	my feet like hinds' F, he makes me tread
Zech	14:4	On that day his F shall stand on the
	14:12	are still on their F, their eyes shall rot
Mal	4:3	the soles of your F, on the day when
2Mac	7:4	off his hands and F, while the rest of
Mt	10:14	the dust from your F as you leave that
	15:30	put them at his F, and he healed them,
	18:8	two hands or two F to be thrown into
	22:44	hand, till I put thy enemies under thy F
	28:9	took hold of his F and worshipped him.
Mk	5:22	he fell at his F,
	6:11	that is on your F for a testimony against
	7:24	him, and came and fell down at his F
	9:44	lame than with two F to be thrown into
	12:36	thy enemies under thy F
Lk	1:79	death, to guide our F into the way of
	7:38	behind him at his F, weeping, she began to
	7:38	began to wet his F with her tears, and
	7:38	head, and kissed his F, and anointed them with
	7:44	no water for my F, but she has wet
	7:44	she has wet my F with her tears and
	7:45	in she has not ceased to kiss my F
	7:46	she has anointed my F with ointment.
	8:35	gone, sitting at the F of Jesus, clothed and
	8:41	and falling at Jesus' F he besought him to
	9:5	the dust from your F as a testimony against
	10:11	that clings to our F, we wipe off against
	10:39	sat at the Lord's F and listened to his
	15:22	and shoes on his F;
	17:16	his face at Jesus' F, giving him thanks.
	20:43	a stool for thy F
	24:39	my hands and my F, that it is I
	24:40	this, he showed them his hands and his F
Jn	11:2	ointment and wiped his F with her hair, whose
	11:32	him, fell at his F, saying to him, "Lord,
	11:44	out, his hands and F bound with bandages, and
	12:3	nard and anointed the F of Jesus and wiped
	12:3	Jesus and wiped his F with her hair; and
	13:5	to wash the disciples' F, and to wipe them
	13:6	said to him, "Lord, do you wash my F
	13:8	said to him, "You shall never wash my F
	13:9	him, "Lord, not my F only but also my
	13:10	wash, except for his F, but he is clean
	13:12	he had washed their F, and taken his garments,
	13:14	Teacher, have washed your F, you also ought to
	13:14	feet, you also ought to wash one another's F
	20:12	one at the head and one at the F
Acts	2:35	a stool for thy F
	3:7	up; and immediately his F and ankles were made
	4:35	it at the apostles' F; and distribution was made
	4:37	the money and laid it at the apostles' F
	5:2	a part and laid it at the apostles' F
	5:9	Hark, the F of those that have buried your
	5:10	fell down at his F and died.
	7:33	the shoes from your F, for the place where
	7:58	their garments at the F of a young man
	10:25	fell down at his F and worshiped him.
	13:25	the sandals of whose F I am not worthy
	13:51	the dust from their F against them, and went
	14:8	could not use his F; he was a cripple
	14:10	in a loud voice, "Stand upright on your F
	16:24	prison and fastened their F in the stocks.

21:11 and bound his own F and hands, and said,
22:3 this city at the F of Gamali-el, educated according
26:16 and stand upon your F; for I have appeared
Rom 3:15 "Their F are swift to shed blood,
10:15 "How beautiful are the F of those who preach
16:20 of peace will soon crush Satan under your F
1Cor 12:21 the head to the F, "I have no need
15:25 he has put all his enemies under his F
15:27 has put all things in subjection under his F
Eph 1:22 all things under his F and has made him
6:15 and having shod your F with the equipment of
1Tim 5:10 shown hospitality, washed the F of the saints,
Heb 1:13 I make thy enemies a stool for thy F
2:8 honor, putting everything in subjection under his F
10:13 enemies should be made a stool for his F
12:13 straight paths for your F, so that what is
Jas 2:3 or, "Sit at my F
Rev 1:15 flame of fire, his F were like burnished bronze,
1:17 I fell at his F as though dead.
2:18 of fire, and whose F are like burnished bronze.
3:9 bow down before your F, and learn that I
11:11 stood up on their F, and great fear fell
12:1 the moon under her F, and on her head
13:2 like a leopard, its F were like a bears,
19:10 fell down at his F to worship him, but
22:8 to worship at the F of the angel who

FEIGNED

1Sam 21:13 behavior before them, and F himself mad in their

FELIX (9)

Acts 23:24 bring him safely to F the governor."
23:26 his Excellency the governor F, greeting.
24:2 provision, most excellent F, reforms are introduced
24:21 But F, having a rather accurate knowledge of the
24:23 After some days F came with his wife Drusilla,
24:24 self-control and future judgment, F was alarmed and
24:26 two years had elapsed, F was succeeded by Porcius
24:26 the Jews a favor, F left Paul in prison.
25:14 man left prisoner by F;

FELL (277)

Gen 4:5 So Cain was very angry, and his countenance F
7:12 And rain F upon the earth forty days and
14:10 and Gomorrah fled, some F into them, and the
15:12 down, a deep sleep F on Abram; and lo,
15:12 dread and great darkness F upon him.
17:3 Then Abram F on his face; and God said
17:17 Then Abraham F on his face and laughed, and
33:4 and embraced him, and F on his neck and
35:5 a terror from God F upon the cities that
41:5 And he F asleep and dreamed a second time;
44:14 still there; and they F before him to the
45:14 Then he F upon his brother Benjamin's neck and
46:29 himself to him, and F on his neck, and
50:1 Then Joseph F on his father's face, and wept
50:18 brothers also came and F down before him, and
Ex 32:28 of Moses; and there F of the people that
Lev 9:24 it, they shouted, and F on their faces.
16:9 on which the lot F for the LORD, and
16:10 on which the lot F for Azazel shall be
Num 11:9 When the dew F upon the camp in the
11:9 the night, the manna F with it.
14:5 Then Moses and Aaron F on their faces before
16:4 Moses heard it, he F on his face;
16:22 And they F on their faces, and said, "O
16:45 And they F on their faces.
20:6 tent of meeting, and F on their faces.
22:31 bowed his head, and F on his face.
Josh 5:14 And Joshua F on his face to the earth,
6:20 shout, and the wall F down flat, so that
7:6 rent his clothes, and F to the earth upon
8:25 And all who F that day, both men and
11:7 waters of Merom, and F upon them.
17:5 Thus there F to Manasseh ten portions, besides the
18:11 territory allotted to it F between the tribe of
21:10 Levites; since the lot F to them first.
22:20 devoted things, and wrath F upon all the
Judg 4:16 the army of Sisera F by the edge of
5:27 He sank, he F, he lay still at her
5:27 feet he sank, he F; where he sank, there
5:27 he sank, there he F dead.
7:13 it so that it F, and turned it upside
9:40 before him; and many F wounded, up to the
12:6 And there F at that time forty-two thousand of
13:20 looked on; and they F on their faces to
16:30 might; and the house F upon the lords and
19:26 the woman came and F down at the door
20:44 thousand men of Benjamin F, all of them men
20:46 So all who F that day of Benjamin were
Ruth 2:10 Then she F on her face, bowing to the
1Sam 4:10 great slaughter, for there F of Israel thirty thousand
4:18 ark of God, Eli F over backward from his
11:7 dread of the LORD F upon the people, and
14:13 And they F before Jonathan, and his armor-bearer
17:49 his forehead, and he F on his face to
17:52 that the wounded Philistines F on the way from
20:41 the stone heap and F on his face to
22:18 the Edomite turned and F upon the priests, and
25:23 from the ass, and F before David on her
25:24 She F at his feet and said, "Upon me
28:20 Then Saul F at once full length upon the
30:13 me behind because I F sick three days ago.
31:1 before the Philistines, and F slain on Mount Gilboa.
31:4 his own sword, and F upon it.
31:5 was dead, he also F upon his sword, and
2Sam 1:2 came to David, he F to the ground and
2:16 opponent's side; so they F down together.
2:23 his back; and he F there, and died where
4:4 in her haste, he F, and became lame.
9:6 came to David, and F on his face and
11:17 of the servants of David among the people F
14:4 to the king, she F on her face to
14:22 And Joab F on his face to the ground,
19:18 the son of Gera F down before the king,
20:8 he went forward it F out.
21:10 of harvest until rain F upon them from the
21:22 in Gath; and they F by the hand of
22:39 did not rise; they F under my feet.
1Kgs 14:1 the son of Jeroboam F sick.
18:7 Obadiah recognized him, and F on his face, and
18:38 fire of the LORD F, and consumed the burnt
18:39 people saw it, they F on their faces; and
20:30 Aphek; and the wall F upon twenty-seven thousand
2Kgs 1:2 Now Ahaziah F through the lattice in his upper
1:13 up, and came and F on his knees before
3:19 choice city, and shall F every good tree, and
4:37 She came and F at his feet, bowing to
6:5 log, his axe head F into the water; and
1Chr 5:10 on the Hagrites, who F by their hand; and
5:22 For many F slain, because the war was of
10:1 before the Philistines, and F slain on Mount Gilboa.
10:4 his own sword, and F upon it.
10:5 was dead, he also F upon his sword, and
20:8 in Gath; and they F by the hand of
21:14 upon Israel; and there F seventy thousand men of
21:16 elders, clothed in sackcloth, F upon their faces.
24:7 The first lot F to Jehoiarib, the second to
25:9 The first lot F for Asaph to Joseph; the
26:14 lot for the east F to Shelemiah.
2Chr 13:17 great slaughter; so there F slain of Israel five
14:13 Gerar, and the Ethiopians F until none remained
17:10 fear of the LORD F upon all the kingdoms
20:18 inhabitants of Jerusalem F down before the LORD,
25:13 with him to battle, F upon the cities of
Ezra 9:5 my mantle rent, and F upon my knees and
Neh 6:16 us were afraid and F greatly in their own
Tob 2:10 and their fresh droppings F into my open eyes
6:17 heard these things, he F in love with her
12:16 both alarmed; and they F upon their faces, for
14:10 for him; but Nadab F into the trap and
Jud 2:28 and terror of him F upon all the people
6:18 Then the people F down and worshiped God, and
7:23 fainted from thirst and F down in the streets
9:1 Then Judith F upon her face, and put ashes
14:6 of the people, he F down on his face
14:7 raised him up he F at Judith's feet, and
15:5 with one accord they F upon the enemy, and
15:6 the people of Bethulia F upon the Assyrian camp
Esth 8:3 to the king; she F at his feet and
15:15 she was speaking, she F fainting.
Job 1:15 them; and the Sabeans F upon them and took
1:16 "The fire of God F from heaven and burned
1:19 the house, and it F upon the young people,
1:20 shaved his head, and F upon the ground, and
Ps 18:38 able to rise; they F under my feet.
68:14 scattered kings there, snow F on Zalmon.
78:64 Their priests F by the sword, and their widows
107:12 with hard labor; they F down, with none to
Wis 7:3 the common air, and F upon the kindred earth,
8:19 and a good soul F to my lot;
17:16 And whoever was there F down, and thus was

F

Sir 50:17 together made haste and F to the ground upon
Jer 46:16 Your multitude stumbled and F, and they said one
46:22 axes, like those who F trees.
50:43 them, and his hands F helpless; anguish seized him,
Lam 1:7 When her people F into the hand of the
Ezek 1:28 I saw it, I F upon my face, and
3:23 river Chebar; and I F on my face.
8:1 of the Lord GOD F there upon me.
9:8 was left alone, I F upon my face, and
11:5 Spirit of the LORD F upon me, and he
11:13 Then I F down upon my face, and cried
39:23 adversaries, and they all F by the sword.
43:3 river Chebar; and I F upon my face.
44:4 the LORD; and I F upon my face.
Dan 2:46 Then King Nebuchadnezzar F upon his face, and did
3:7 nations, and languages F down and worshiped the
3:23 Shadrach, Meshach, and Abednego, F bound into the
4:31 the king's mouth, there F a voice from heaven,
7:20 which three of them F, the horn which had
8:17 I was frightened and F upon my face.
8:18 speaking to me, I F into a deep sleep
10:7 but a great trembling F upon them, and they
10:9 of his words, I F on my face in
Jon 1:7 lots, and the lot F upon Jonah.
1Mac 1:5 After this he F sick and perceived that he
1:18 fled before him, and many were wounded and F
1:30 him; but he suddenly F upon the city, dealt
3:11 Many were wounded and F, and the rest fled.
3:24 eight hundred of them F, and the rest fled
3:25 be feared, and terror F upon the Gentiles round
4:15 those in the rear F by the sword.
4:15 Azotus and Jamnia; and three thousand of them F
4:34 sides attacked, and there F of the army of
4:34 five thousand men; they F in action.
4:40 They F face down on the ground, and sounded
4:55 All the people F on their faces and worshiped
5:22 thousand of the Gentiles F, and he despoiled them.
5:34 eight thousand of them F that day.
5:60 the people of Israel F that day.
5:67 do a brave deed, F in battle, for they
6:42 and six hundred men of the king's army F
6:46 killed it; but it F to the ground upon
7:18 and dread of them F upon all the people,
7:32 the army of Nicanor F, and the rest fled
7:46 so that they all F by the sword; not
8:10 them were wounded and F, and the Romans took
9:17 and many on both sides were wounded and F
9:18 Judas also F, and the rest fled.
9:40 Many were wounded and F, and the rest fled
9:49 thousand of Bacchides' men F that day.
10:50 sun set, and Demetrius F on that day.
10:85 number of those who F by the sword, with
11:74 thousand of the foreigners F that day.
13:22 a very heavy snow F, and he did not
16:8 them were wounded and F; the rest fled into
16:10 with fire, and about two thousand of them F
2Mac 3:27 When he suddenly F to the ground and deep
7:3 The king F into a rage, and gave orders
7:39 The king F into a rage, and handled him
9:7 came about that he F out of his chariot
10:4 had done this, they F prostrate and besought the
12:24 Timothy himself F into the hands of Dositheus and
12:34 it happened that a few of the Jews F
14:41 Being surrounded, Razis F upon his own sword,
14:44 space opened and he F in the middle of
Mt 2:11 his mother, and they F down and worshiped him.
7:25 rock; and the rain F, and the floods came,
7:27 sand; and the rain F, and the floods came,
7:27 that house, and it F; and great was the
13:4 he sowed, some seeds F along the path, and
13:5 Other seeds F on rocky ground, where they had
13:7 Other seeds F upon thorns, and the thorns grew
13:8 Other seeds F on good soil and brought forth
17:6 disciples heard this, they F on their faces, and
18:25 So the servant F on his knees, imploring him,
18:28 So his fellow servant F down and besought him,
26:39 a little farther he F on his face and
Mk 3:11 spirits beheld him, they F down before him and
4:4 he sowed, some seed F along the path, and
4:5 Other seed F on rocky ground, where it had
4:7 Other seed F among thorns and the thorns grew
4:8 And other seeds F into good soil and brought
5:22 and seeing him, he F at his feet,
5:33 fear and trembling and F down before him, and
7:24 him, and came and F down at his feet.
9:20 the boy, and he F on the ground and
10:22 that saying his countenance F, and he went away
14:35 a little farther, he F on the ground and
Lk 1:9 of the priesthood, it F to him by lot
1:12 saw him, and fear F upon him.
5:8 Peter saw it, he F down at Jesus' knees,
5:12 he saw Jesus, he F on his face and
6:49 broke, and immediately it F, and the ruin of
8:5 as he sowed, some F along the path, and
8:6 And some F on the rock; and as it
8:7 And some F among thorns; and the thorns grew
8:8 And some F into good soil and grew, and
8:14 And as for what F among the thorns, they
8:23 as they sailed he F asleep.
8:28 he cried out and F down before him, and
10:30 to Jericho, and he F among robbers, who stripped
10:36 to the man who F among the robbers?"
13:4 the tower in Siloam F and killed them, do
16:21 be fed with what F from the rich man's
17:16 loud voice; and he F on his face at
Jn 11:32 was and saw him, F at his feet, saying
18:6 they drew back and F to the ground.
Acts 1:26 them, and the lot F on Matthias; and he
5:5 heard these words, he F down and died.
5:10 Immediately she F down at his feet and died.
7:60 had said this, he F asleep.
9:4 And he F to the ground and heard a
9:18 immediately something like scales F from his eyes
9:37 In those days she F sick and died; and
10:10 were preparing it, he F into a trance
10:25 Cornelius met him and F down at his feet
10:44 this, the Holy Spirit F on all who heard
11:15 speak, the Holy Spirit F on them just as
12:7 And the chains F off his hands.
13:11 Immediately mist and darkness F upon him and he
13:36 in his own generation, F asleep, and was laid
16:29 trembling with fear he F down before Paul and
19:17 and Greeks; and fear F upon them all; and
19:35 the sacred stone that F from the sky?
20:9 overcome by sleep, he F down from the third
22:7 And I F to the ground and heard a
22:17 in the temple, I F into a trance
Rom 15:3 those who reproached thee F on me."
1Cor 10:8 did, and twenty-three thousand F in a single day.
Heb 3:17 who sinned, whose bodies F in the wilderness?
11:30 the walls of Jericho F down after they had
2Pet 3:4 ever since the fathers F asleep, all things have
Rev 1:17 I saw him, I F at his feet as
5:8 and the twenty-four elders F down before the Lamb,
5:14 and the elders F down and worshiped.
6:13 stars of the sky F to the earth as
7:11 living creatures, and they F on their faces before
8:7 mixed with blood, which F on the earth; and
8:10 and a great star F from heaven, blazing like
8:10 a torch, and it F on a third of
11:11 feet, and great fear F on those who saw
11:13 tenth of the city F; seven thousand people were
11:16 their thrones before God F on their faces and
16:19 cities of the nations F, and God remembered great
19:4 the four living creatures F down and worshiped God
19:10 Then I F down at his feet to worship
22:8 and saw them, I F down to worship at

FELLED (7)

Judg 20:21 out of Gibe-ah, and F to the ground on
20:25 the second day, and F to the ground eighteen
2Kgs 3:25 spring of water, and F all the good trees;
19:23 recesses of Lebanon; I F its tallest cedars, its
Is 6:13 oak, whose stump remains standing when it is F
37:24 recesses of Lebanon; I F its tallest cedars, its
Zech 11:2 of Bashan, for the thick forest has been F

FELLING

2Kgs 6:5 But as one was F a log, his axe

FELLOW (81)

Gen 19:9 And they said, "This F came to sojourn, and
Ex 2:13 did the wrong, "Why do you strike your F
Judg 7:22 man's sword against his F and against all the
Ruth 3:11 ask, for all my F townsmen know that you
1Sam 14:20 sword was against his F, and there was very
21:15 you have brought this F to play the madman
21:15 Shall this F come into my house?"
25:21 guarded all that this F has in the wilderness,
25:25 lord regard this ill-natured F, Nabal; for as his
29:4 For how could this F reconcile himself to his
2Sam 16:7 "Begone, begone, you man of blood, you worthless F

	20:1	be there a worthless F, whose name was Sheba,
1Kgs	20:35	prophets said to his F at the command of
	22:27	the king, "Put this F in prison, and feed
2Kgs	9:11	Why did this mad F come to you?" And
	9:11	them, "You know the F and his talk."
2Chr	18:26	the king, Put this F in prison, and feed
Ezra	3:2	of Jozadak, with his F priests, and Zerubbabel the
	6:20	exiles, for their F priests, and for themselves;
Eccl	4:10	will lift up his F; but woe to him
Sir	4:27	yourself to a foolish F, nor show partiality to
	8:11	and leave an insolent F, lest he lie in
	8:15	road with a foolhardy F, lest he be burdensome
	13:22	poor man speaks they say, "Who is this F
Is	3:5	another, every man his F and every man his
	3:5	elder, and the base F to the honorable.
	34:14	shall cry to his F; yea, there shall the
Jer	34:14	must set free the F Hebrew who has been
Ezek	11:15	even your brethren, your F exiles, the whole house
Hag	2:22	down, every one by the sword of his F
Zech	8:10	in; for I set every man against his F
	14:13	the hand of his F, and the hand of
2Mac	4:2	the protector of his F countrymen, and a zealot
	4:5	king, not accusing his F citizens but having in
	4:38	Onias, and there he dispatched the bloodthirsty F
	4:50	chief plotter against his F citizens.
	5:6	kept relentlessly slaughtering his F citizens, not
	5:6	enemies and not over F countrymen.
	5:8	his country and his F citizens, he was cast
	5:23	lorded it over his F citizens worse than the
	9:13	Then the abominable F made a vow to the
	14:8	regard also for my F citizens.
	14:37	man who loved his F citizens and was very
	15:30	the defender of his F citizens, the man who
Mt	18:27	upon one of his F servants who owed him
	18:28	you owe.' So his F servant fell down and
	18:30	When his F servants saw what had taken place,
	18:32	had mercy on your F servant, as I had
	24:49	begins to beat his F servants, and eats and
	26:61	forward and said, "This F said, 'I am able
Jn	11:16	Twin, said to his F disciples, "Let us also
Acts	22:22	"Away with such a F from the earth!
	24:5	this man a pestilent F, an agitator among all
Rom	8:17	heirs of God and F heirs with Christ, provided
	11:14	order to make my F Jews jealous, and thus
	16:3	Prisca and Aquila, my F workers in Christ Jesus,
	16:7	my kinsmen and my F prisoners; they are men
	16:9	Greet Urbanus, our F worker in Christ, and my
	16:21	Timothy, my F worker, greets you; so do Lucius
1Cor	3:9	For we are God's F workers; you are God's
	16:16	men and to every F worker and laborer.
2Cor	8:23	is my partner and F worker in your service;
Eph	2:19	sojourners, but you are F citizens with the saints
	3:6	how the Gentiles are F heirs, members of the
Phil	2:25	Epaphroditus my brother and F worker and fellow
	2:25	and fellow worker and F soldier, and your messenger
	4:3	the rest of my F workers, whose names are
Col	1:7	from Epaphras our beloved F servant.
	4:7	and faithful minister and F servant in the Lord.
	4:10	Aristarchus my F prisoner greets you, and Mark the
	4:11	circumcision among my F workers for the kingdom
Philem	1:1	To Philemon our beloved F worker
	1:2	sister and Archippus our F soldier, and the church
	1:23	Epaphras, my F prisoner in Christ Jesus, sends
	1:24	Demas, and Luke, my F workers.
Heb	8:11	teach every one his F or every one his
1Pet	5:1	among you, as a F elder and a witness
3Jn	1:8	that we may be F workers in the truth.
Rev	6:11	the number of their F servants and their brethren
	19:10	I am a F servant with you and your
	22:9	I am a F servant with you and your

FELLOW-LEVITES

Deut	18:7	God, like all his F who stand to minister

FELLOWS (18)

Deut	13:13	there, that certain base F have gone out among
	20:8	the heart of his F melt as his heart.'
Judg	9:4	hired worthless and reckless F, who followed him.
	11:3	of Tob; and worthless F collected round Jephthah,
	18:25	among us, lest angry F fall upon you, and
	19:22	of the city, base F, beset the house round
	20:13	the men, the base F in Gibe-ah, that we
1Sam	10:27	But some worthless F said, "How can this man
	30:22	the wicked and base F among the men who
2Sam	6:20	one of the vulgar F shamelessly uncovers himself!"
1Kgs	21:10	and set two base F opposite him, and let
	21:13	And the two base F came in and sat
	21:13	him; and the base F brought a charge against
2Kgs	9:2	rise from among his F, and lead him to
Ps	45:7	of gladness above your F;
Is	44:11	Behold, all his F shall be put to shame,
Dan	7:20	great things, and which seemed greater than its F
Acts	17:5	and taking some wicked F of the rabble, they

FELLOWSHIP (11)

Ps	55:14	together; within God's house we walked in F
Sir	13:16	What F has a wolf with a lamb?
Acts	2:42	the apostles' teaching and F, to the breaking of
1Cor	1:9	were called into the F of his Son, Jesus
2Cor	6:14	Or what F has light with darkness?
	13:14	of God and the F of the Holy Spirit
Gal	2:9	the right hand of F, that we should go
1Jn	1:3	that you may have F with us; and our
	1:3	with us; and our F is with the Father
	1:6	we say we have F with him while we
	1:7	the light, we have F with one another, and

FELT (14)

Gen	27:22	Isaac his father, who F him and said, "The
	31:34	Laban F all about the tent, but did not
	31:37	Although you have F through all my goods, what
Ex	10:21	the land of Egypt, a darkness to be F
2Sam	18:12	Joab, "Even if I F in my hand the
Is	47:10	You F secure in your wickedness, you said, "No
Jer	5:3	smitten them, but they F no anguish; thou hast
2Mac	7:24	Antiochus F that he was being treated with
	9:9	stench the whole army F revulsion at his decay.
Mk	5:29	hemorrhage ceased; and she F in her body that
2Cor	1:9	Why, we F that we had received the sentence
	2:3	me rejoice, for I F sure of all of
	7:9	into repenting; for you F a godly grief, so
Gal	4:15	What has become of the satisfaction you F

FEMALE (44)

Gen	1:27	created him; male and F he created them.
	5:2	Male and F he created them, and he blessed
	6:19	alive with you; they shall be male and F
	7:3	air also, male and F, to keep their kind
	7:9	and two, male and F, went into the ark
	7:16	that entered, male and F of all flesh, went
	20:14	oxen, and male and F slaves, and gave them
	20:17	healed his wife and F slaves so that they
Ex	21:20	his slave, male or F, with a rod and
	21:26	his slave, male or F, and destroys it, he
	21:27	his slave, male or F, he shall let the
	21:32	a slave, male or F, the owner shall give
Lev	3:1	the herd, male or F, he shall offer it
	3:6	the flock, male or F, he shall offer it
	4:28	offering a goat, a F without blemish, for his
	4:32	he shall bring a F without blemish,
	5:6	he has committed, a F from the flock, a
	12:5	if she bears a F child, then she shall
	12:7	her who bears a child, either male or F
	15:33	any one, male or F, who has a discharge,
	25:6	for your male and F slaves and for your
	25:44	for your male and F slaves whom you may
	25:44	may buy male and F slaves from among the
	27:4	the person is a F, your valuation shall be
	27:5	shekels, and for a F ten shekels.
	27:6	silver, and for a F your valuation shall be
	27:7	shekels, and for a F ten shekels.
Num	5:3	out both male and F, putting them outside the
	15:27	he shall offer a F goat a year old
Deut	4:16	likeness of male or F,
	7:14	not be male or F barren among you, or
	28:68	enemies as male and F slaves, but no man
2Chr	28:10	and Jerusalem, male and F, as your slaves.
Ezra	2:65	two hundred male and F singers.
Neh	7:67	had two hundred and forty-five singers, male and F
Eccl	2:7	I bought male and F slaves, and had slaves
Is	14:2	land as male and F slaves; they will take
Jer	34:9	Hebrew slaves, male and F, so that no one
	34:10	his slave, male or F, so that they would
	34:11	back the male and F slaves they had set
	34:16	back his male and F slaves, whom you had
Mt	19:4	made them male and F,
Mk	10:6	made them male and F
Gal	3:28	is neither male nor F; for you are all

FENCE (3)

Ps	62:3	of you, like a leaning wall, a tottering F
Sir	28:24	See that you F in your property with thorns,

36:25 Where there is no F, the property will be

FENCES (2)
Sir 22:16 F set on a high place will not stand
Nah 3:17 locusts settling on the F in a day of

FERTILE (4)
Judg 18:9 seen the land, and behold, it is very F
2Chr 26:10 hills and in the F lands, for he loved
Is 5:1 vineyard on a very F hill.
Ezek 17:5 and planted it in F soil; he placed it

FERVENT (2)
Sir 38:17 bitter and your wailing F; observe the mourning
Acts 18:25 the Lord; and being F in spirit, he spoke

FERVENTLY
Jas 5:17 ourselves and he prayed F that it might not

F

FERVOR
Jud 4:9 to God with great F, and they humbled themselves

FESTAL (13)
Gen 45:22 of them he gave F garments; but to Benjamin
45:22 of silver and five F garments.
Judg 14:12 linen garments and thirty F garments;
14:13 linen garments and thirty F garments." And they said
14:19 spoil and gave the F garments to those who
2Kgs 5:5 of gold, and ten F garments.
5:22 of silver and two F garments.'"
5:23 two bags, with two F garments, and laid them
Ps 89:15 people who know the F shout, who walk, O
118:27 Bind the F procession with branches, up to the
Wis 19:16 receiving them with F celebrations, afflicted with
Is 3:22 and nose rings; the F robes, the mantles, the
Heb 12:22 to innumerable angels in F gathering,

FESTER
Ps 38:5 wounds grow foul and F because of my foolishness,

FESTIVAL (10)
Judg 9:27 trod them, and held F, and went into the
2Chr 30:22 the food of the F for seven days, sacrificing
Tob 2:1 which is the sacred F of the seven weeks,
Ps 42:4 songs of thanksgiving, a multitude keeping F
Wis 15:12 game, and life a F held for profit, for
Ezek 45:23 seven days of the F he shall provide as
Hos 9:5 the day of appointed F, and on the day
Zeph 3:18 with loud singing as on a day of F
1Cor 5:8 us, therefore, celebrate the F, not with the old
Col 2:16 with regard to a F or a new moon

FESTIVALS
Esth 16:22 day among your commemorative F,

FESTIVITIES
Tob 2:6 mourning, and all your F into lamentation." And I

FESTIVITY
Tob 11:19 marriage was celebrated for seven days with great F

FESTUS (13)
Acts 24:26 was succeeded by Porcius F; and desiring to do
25:1 Now when F had come into his province, after
25:4 F replied that Paul was being kept at Caesarea,
25:9 But F, wishing to do the Jews a favor,
25:12 Then F, when he had conferred with his council,
25:13 king and Bernice arrived at Caesarea to welcome F
25:14 stayed there many days, F laid Paul's case before
25:22 And Agrippa said to F, "I should like to
25:23 Then by command of F Paul was brought in.
25:24 And F said, "King Agrippa and all who are
26:24 thus made his defense, F said with a loud
26:25 not mad, most excellent F, but I am speaking
26:32 And Agrippa said to F, "This man could have

FETCH (12)
Gen 18:5 the tree, while I F a morsel of bread,
27:9 to the flock, and F me two good kids,
27:13 my word, and go, F them to me."
27:45 I will send, and F you from there.
Ex 2:5 sent her maid to F it.
Deut 19:12 city shall send and F him from there, and
24:10 into his house to F his pledge.
30:4 from there he will F you;
1Sam 16:11 to Jesse, "Send and F him; for we will
20:31 Therefore send and F him to me, for he
26:22 men come over and F it.
Job 36:3 I will F my knowledge from afar, and ascribe

FETCHED (5)
1Sam 10:23 Then they ran and F him from there; and
2Sam 14:2 sent to Tekoa, and F from there a wise
2Chr 8:18 servants of Solomon, and F from there four hundred
Esth 5:10 and he sent and F his friends and his
Jer 26:23 with him, and they F Uriah from Egypt and

FETTERED (2)
2Sam 3:34 your feet were not F; as one falls before
2Tim 2:9 But the word of God is not F

FETTERS (24)
Judg 16:21 bound him with bronze F; and he ground at
2Kgs 25:7 and bound him in F, and took him to
2Chr 33:11 and bound him with F of bronze and brought
36:6 and bound him in F to take him to
Job 36:8 they are bound in F and caught in the
Ps 105:18 feet were hurt with F, his neck was put
149:8 and their nobles with F of iron,
Eccl 7:26 and whose hands are F; he who pleases God
Sir 6:24 your feet into her F, and your neck into
6:29 Then her F will become for you a strong
21:19 senseless man education is F on his feet, and
28:19 been bound with its F;
28:20 of iron, and its F are fetters of bronze;
28:20 and its fetters are F of bronze;
33:28 not obey, make his F heavy.
Jer 39:7 and bound him in F to take him to
52:11 and bound him in F, and the king of
1Mac 3:41 in immense amounts, and F, and went to the
Mk 5:4 often been bound with F and chains, but the
5:4 wrenched apart, and the F he broke in pieces;
Lk 8:29 bound with chains and F, but he broke the
Acts 16:26 opened and every one's F were unfastened.
Col 4:18 Remember my F.
2Tim 2:9 am suffering and wearing F like a criminal.

FEUD
Judg 12:2 people had a great F with the Ammonites; and

FEVER (10)
Lev 26:16 sudden terror, consumption, and F that waste the
Deut 28:22 consumption, and with F, inflammation, and fiery
Mt 8:14 lying sick with a F;
8:15 her hand, and the F left her, and she
Mk 1:30 lay sick with a F, and immediately they told
1:31 her up, and the F left her; and she
Lk 4:38 ill with a high F, and they besought him
4:39 her and rebuked the F, and it left her;
Jn 4:52 the seventh hour the F left him."
Acts 28:8 Publius lay sick with F and dysentery; and Paul

FEW (87)
Gen 11:1 had one language and F words.
29:20 to him but a F days because of the
34:30 Perizzites; my numbers are F, and if they gather
47:9 hundred and thirty years; F and evil have been
Lev 25:16 if the years are F you shall diminish the
25:52 there remain but a F years until the year
26:22 cattle, and make you F in number, so that
Num 9:20 the cloud was a F days over the tabernacle,
13:18 weak, whether they are F or many,
35:8 tribes you shall take F; each, in proportion to
Deut 4:27 you will be left F in number among the
26:5 Egypt and sojourned there, F in number; and there
28:62 you shall be left F in number; because you
33:6 and not die, nor let his men be F
Josh 7:3 people toil up there, for they are but F
1Sam 14:6 the LORD from saving by many or by F
17:28 have you left those F sheep in the wilderness?
2Kgs 4:3 all your neighbors, empty vessels and not too F
1Chr 16:19 When they were F in number, and of little
2Chr 24:24 Syrians had come with F men, the LORD delivered
29:34 the priests were too F and could not flay
30:11 Only a F men of Asher, of Manasseh, and
Neh 2:12 night, I and a F men with me; and
7:4 people within it were F and no houses had
Tob 4:8 them in proportion; if F, do not be afraid
Job 10:20 Are not the days of my life F
14:1 a woman is of F days, and full of
16:22 For when a F years have come I shall
Ps 39:5 made my days a F handbreadths, and my lifetime

105:12 When they were F in number, of little account,
109:8 May his days be F; may another seize his
Eccl 2:3 under heaven during the F days of their life.
5:2 you upon earth; therefore let your words be F
5:18 under the sun the F days of his life
6:12 while he lives the F days of his vain
9:14 a little city with F men in it; and
12:3 cease because they are F, and those that look
Sir 17:2 He gave to men F days, a limited time,
18:9 sand so are a F years in the day
32:8 concisely, say much in F words; be as one
34:10 that is inexperienced knows F things, but he that
43:32 we have seen but F of his works.
48:2 zeal he made them F in number.
48:15 people were left very F in number, but with
Is 1:9 not left us a F survivors, we should have
10:7 off nations not a F;
10:19 forest will be so F that a child can
16:14 survive will be very F and feeble."
21:17 of Kedar will be F; for the LORD, the
24:6 earth are scorched, and F men are left.
65:20 that lives but a F days, or an old
Jer 30:19 they shall not be F; I will make them
42:2 are left but a F of many, as your
44:28 the land of Judah, F in number; and all
Bar 2:13 for we are left, F in number, among the
Ezek 12:16 I will let a F of them escape from
Dan 11:20 kingdom; but within a F days he shall be
1Mac 3:17 Judas, "How can we, F as we are, fight
3:18 be hemmed in by F, for in the sight
3:18 no difference between saving by many or by F
6:54 F men were left in the sanctuary, because famine
7:1 Rome, sailed with a F men to a city
7:28 shall come with a F men to see you
7:50 had rest for a F days.
9:9 our brethren and fight them; we are too F
9:65 went with only a F men.
12:45 choose for yourself a F men to stay with
15:10 so that there were F with Trypho.
2Mac 1:15 had come with a F men inside the wall
2:21 Judaism, so that though F in number they seized
8:6 to flight not a F of the enemy.
12:34 it happened that a F of the Jews fell.
14:30 he gathered not a F of his men, and
Mt 7:14 to life, and those who find it are F
9:37 but the laborers are F;
15:34 said, "Seven, and a F small fish."
22:14 many are called, but F are chosen."
Mk 6:5 his hands upon a F sick people and healed
8:7 And they had a F small fish; and having
Lk 10:2 but the laborers are F; pray therefore the Lord
13:23 him, "Lord, will those who are saved be F
Jn 2:12 they stayed for a F days.
Acts 17:4 Greeks and not a F of the leading women.
17:12 believed, with not a F Greek women of high
1Pet 3:20 ark, in which a F, that is, eight persons,
Rev 2:14 But I have a F things against you: you
3:4 you have still a F names in Sardis, people

FEWER (3)
Dan 3:37 O Lord, have become F than any nation, and
2Mac 8:9 in command of no F than twenty thousand Gentiles
10:17 they encountered, killing no F than twenty thousand.

FEWEST
Deut 7:7 for you were the F of all peoples;

FIDELITY (3)
Esth 13:3 good will and steadfast F, and has attained the
Sir 1:24 and he delights in F and meekness.
Tit 2:10 show entire and true F, so that in everything

FIELD (263)
Gen 2:5 no plant of the F was yet in the
2:5 no herb of the F had yet sprung up–
2:19 every beast of the F and every bird of
2:20 every beast of the F; but for the man
3:18 and you shall eat the plants of the F
4:8 his brother, "Let us go out to the F
4:8 they were in the F, Cain rose up against
23:9 owns; it is at the end of his F
23:11 I give you the F, and I give you
23:13 the price of the F; accept it from me,
23:17 So the F of Ephron in Mach-pelah, which was
23:17 east of Mamre, the F with the cave which
23:17 that were in the F, throughout its whole area,
23:19 the cave of the F of Mach-pelah east of
23:20 The F and the cave that is in it
24:63 to meditate in the F in the evening; and
24:65 yonder, walking in the F to meet us?" The
25:9 of Mach-pelah, in the F of Ephron the son
25:10 east of Mamre, the F which Abraham purchased
25:27 a man of the F, while Jacob was a
25:29 came in from the F, and he was famished.
27:3 go out to the F, and hunt game for
27:5 Esau went to the F to hunt for game
27:27 the smell of a F which the LORD has
29:2 a well in the F, and lo, three flocks
30:14 found mandrakes in the F, and brought them to
30:16 Jacob came from the F in the evening, Leah
31:4 and Leah into the F where his flock was,
34:5 his cattle in the F, so Jacob held his
34:7 came in from the F when they heard of
34:28 city and in the F;
37:7 binding sheaves in the F, and lo, my sheaf
39:5 upon all that he had, in house and F
47:24 as seed for the F and as food for
49:29 that is in the F of Ephron the Hittite,
49:30 that is in the F at Mach-pelah, to the
49:30 Abraham bought with the F from Ephron the Hittite
49:32 buried Leah– the F and the cave that
50:13 the cave of the F at Mach-pelah, to the
50:13 Abraham bought with the F from Ephron the Hittite,
Ex 1:13 of work in the F; in all their work
9:3 which are in the F, the horses, the asses,
9:19 you have in the F into safe shelter; for
9:19 that is in the F and is not brought
9:21 left his slaves and his cattle in the F
9:22 every plant of the F, throughout the land of
9:25 that was in the F throughout all the land
9:25 every plant of the F, and shattered every tree
9:25 the field, and shattered every tree of the F
10:5 which grows in the F,
10:15 nor plant of the F, through all the land
16:25 today you will not find it in the F
22:5 a man causes a F or vineyard to be
22:5 feeds in another man's F, he shall make restitution
22:5 best in his own F and in his own
22:6 standing grain or the F is consumed, he that
22:31 by beasts in the F; you shall cast it
23:16 your labor, of what you sow in the F
23:16 gather in from the F the fruit of your
Lev 14:7 let the living bird go into the open F
14:53 city into the open F; so he shall make
17:5 slay in the open F, that they may bring
19:9 shall not reap your F to its very border,
19:19 shall not sow your F with two kinds of
23:22 shall not reap your F to its very border,
25:3 you shall sow your F, and six years you
25:4 shall not sow your F or prune your vineyard.
25:12 shall eat what it yields out of the F
26:4 the trees of the F shall yield their fruit.
27:17 If he dedicates his F from the year of
27:18 if he dedicates his F after the jubilee, then
27:19 he who dedicates the F wishes to redeem it,
27:20 wish to redeem the F, or if he has
27:20 he has sold the F to another man, it
27:21 any more; but the F, when it is released
27:21 the LORD, as a F that has been devoted;
27:22 to the LORD a F which he has bought,
27:24 year of jubilee the F shall return to him
27:28 or of his inherited F, shall be sold or
Num 19:16 Whoever in the open F touches one who is
20:17 will not pass through F or vineyard, neither will
21:22 not turn aside into F or vineyard; we will
22:4 the ox licks up the grass of the F
22:23 and went into the F; and Balaam struck the
23:14 took him to the F of Zophim, to the
Deut 5:21 your neighbor's house, his F, or his manservant, or
14:22 comes forth from the F year by year.
20:19 the trees in the F men that they should
24:19 your harvest in your F, and have forgotten a
24:19 a sheaf in the F, you shall not go
28:3 city, and blessed shall you be in the F
28:16 city, and cursed shall you be in the F
28:38 much seed into the F, and shall gather little
32:13 the produce of the F; and he made him
Josh 15:18 her father for a F; and she alighted from
Judg 1:14 her father for a F; and she alighted from
5:18 death; Naphtali too, on the heights of the F
9:27 went out into the F, and gathered the grapes
13:9 she sat in the F; but Manoah her husband

19:16 his work in the F at evening; the man
Ruth 2:2 me go to the F, and glean among the
2:3 and gleaned in the F after the reapers; and
2:3 the part of the F belonging to Boaz, who
2:8 to glean in another F or leave this one,
2:9 eyes be upon the F which they are reaping,
2:17 she gleaned in the F until evening; then she
2:22 maidens, lest in another F you be molested."
4:5 day you buy the F from the hand of
1Sam 4:2 thousand men on the F of battle.
6:14 cart came into the F of Joshua of Beth-shemesh,
6:18 this day in the F of Joshua of Beth-shemesh.
11:5 was coming from the F behind the oxen; and
14:15 the camp, in the F, and among all the
17:44 the air and to the beasts of the F
19:3 my father in the F where you are, and
20:5 hide myself in the F till the third day
20:11 David, "Come, let us go out into the F
20:11 So they both went out into the F
20:24 hid himself in the F; and when the new
20:35 went out into the F to the appointment with
2Sam 11:11 camping in the open F; shall I then go
11:23 against us in the F; but we drove them
14:6 one another in the F; there was no one
14:30 his servants, "See, Joab's F is next to mine,
14:30 Absalom's servants set the F on fire.
14:31 your servants set my F on fire?"
17:8 a bear robbed of her cubs in the F
18:6 went out into the F against Israel; and the
20:12 the highway into the F, and threw a garment
21:10 the beasts of the F by night.
1Kgs 16:4 who dies in the F the birds of the
2Kgs 4:39 went out into the F to gather herbs, and
9:37 the face of the F in the territory of
18:17 which is on the highway to the Fuller's F
19:26 like plants of the F, and like tender grass,
1Chr 16:32 fills it, let the F exult, and everything in
27:26 the work of the F for tilling the soil
2Chr 26:23 fathers in the burial F which belonged to the
31:5 the produce of the F; and they brought in
Neh 13:10 did the work, had fled each to his F
Jud 8:3 binding sheaves in the F, he was overcome by
8:3 his fathers in the F between Dothan and Balamon.
11:7 the beasts of the F and the cattle and
Job 5:23 the stones of the F, and the beasts of
5:23 the beasts of the F shall be at peace
24:6 their fodder in the F and they glean the
Ps 8:7 the beasts of the F,
50:11 that moves in the F is mine.
72:16 from the cities like the grass of the F
80:13 that move in the F feed on it.
96:12 fills it; let the F exult, and everything in
103:15 a flower of the F;
104:11 every beast of the F; the wild asses quench
Prov 24:27 for you in the F; and after that build
24:30 I passed by the F of a sluggard, by
27:26 the price of a F;
31:16 She considers a F and buys it; with the
Song 2:7 the hinds of the F, that you stir not
3:5 the hinds of the F, that you stir not
Sir 24:14 olive tree in the F, and like a plane
Is 1:8 lodge in a cucumber F, like a besieged city.
5:8 to house, who add F to field, until there
5:8 who add field to F, until there is no
7:3 highway to the Fuller's F,
16:10 away from the fruitful F; and in the vineyards
29:17 turned into a fruitful F, and the fruitful field
29:17 field, and the fruitful F shall be regarded as
32:15 wilderness becomes a fruitful F, and the fruitful field
32:15 field, and the fruitful F is deemed a forest.
32:16 wilderness, and righteousness abide in the fruitful F
36:2 upper pool on the highway to the Fuller's F
37:27 like plants of the F and like tender grass,
40:6 its beauty is like the flower of the F
55:12 the trees of the F shall clap their hands.
56:9 you beasts of the F, come to devour—
Jer 4:17 Like keepers of a F are they against her
6:25 not forth into the F, nor walk on the
7:20 the trees of the F and the fruit of
9:22 dung upon the open F, like sheaves after the
10:5 scarecrows in a cucumber F, and they cannot speak;
12:4 the grass of every F wither?
13:27 your lewd harlotries, on the hills in the F
14:5 the hind in the F forsakes her newborn calf
14:18 go out into the F, behold, those slain by
26:18 be plowed as a F; Jerusalem shall become a
27:6 the beasts of the F to serve him.
28:14 given to him even the beasts of the F
32:7 and say, 'Buy my F which is at Anathoth,
32:8 to me, 'Buy my F which is at Anathoth
32:9 "And I bought the F at Anathoth from Hanamel
32:25 to me, "Buy the F for money and get
35:9 have no vineyard or F or seed;
Lam 4:9 stricken by want of the fruits of the F
Ezek 7:15 that is in the F dies by the sword;
16:5 out on the open F, for you were abhorred,
16:7 a plant of the F And you grew up
17:24 the trees of the F shall know that I
29:5 fall upon the open F, and not be gathered
31:6 the beasts of the F brought forth their young;
31:13 branches will be all the beasts of the F
31:15 the trees of the F shall faint because of
32:4 ground, on the open F I will fling you,
33:27 is in the open F I will give to
34:27 the trees of the F shall yield their fruit,
36:30 the increase of the F abundant, that you may
38:20 the beasts of the F, and all creeping things
39:5 fall in the open F; for I have spoken,
39:10 wood out of the F or cut down any
39:17 all beasts of the F, 'Assemble and come, gather
Dan 2:38 the beasts of the F, and the birds of
4:12 The beasts of the F found shade under it,
4:15 and bronze, amid the tender grass of the F
4:21 which beasts of the F found shade, and in
4:23 tender grass of the F; and let him be
4:23 the beasts of the F, till seven times pass
4:25 the beasts of the F; you shall be made
4:32 the beasts of the F; and you shall be
14:33 was going into the F to take it to
Hos 2:12 the beasts of the F shall devour them.
2:18 the beasts of the F, the birds of the
4:3 the beasts of the F, and the birds of
10:4 like poisonous weeds in the furrows of the F
12:11 like stone heaps on the furrows of the F
Joel 1:10 the harvest of the F has perished.
1:11 the trees of the F are withered; and gladness
1:18 flame has burned all the trees of the F
2:22 you beasts of the F, for the pastures of
Amos 4:7 upon another city; one F would be rained upon,
4:7 rained upon, and the F on which it did
Mic 3:12 be plowed as a F; Jerusalem shall become a
Zeph 2:14 the beasts of the F; the vulture and the
Zech 10:1 rain, to every one the vegetation in the F
Mal 3:11 your vine in the F shall not fail to
Mt 6:28 the lilies of the F, how they grow; they
6:30 the grass of the F, which today is alive
13:24 good seed in his F;
13:27 did you not sow good seed in your F
13:31 and sowed in his F;
13:36 us the parable of the weeds of the F
13:38 Son of man; the F is the world, and
13:44 treasure hidden in a F, which a man found
13:44 sells all that he has and buys that F
24:18 who is in the F not turn back to
24:40 will be in the F; one is taken and
27:7 with them the potter's F, to bury strangers in.
27:8 Therefore that F has been called the Field of
27:8 has been called the F of Blood to this
27:10 them for the potter's F, as the Lord directed
Mk 13:16 who is in the F not turn back to
Lk 2:8 shepherds out in the F, keeping watch over their
12:28 is alive in the F today and tomorrow is
14:18 'I have bought a F, and I must go
15:25 son was in the F; and as he came
17:7 come in from the F, 'Come at once and
17:31 who is in the F not turn back.
Jn 4:5 called Sychar, near the F that Jacob gave to
Acts 1:18 this man bought a F with the reward of
1:19 Jerusalem, so that the F was called in their
1:19 language Akeldama, that is, F of Blood.)
4:37 of Cyprus, sold a F which belonged to him,
1Cor 3:9 workers; you are God's F, God's building.
2Cor 10:15 your faith increases, our F among you may be
10:16 without boasting of work already done in another's F

FIELDS (63)

Gen 37:15 him wandering in the F; and the man asked
41:48 the food from the F around it.
47:20 the Egyptians sold their F, because the famine was
Ex 8:13 the houses and courtyards and out of the F
Lev 25:31 be reckoned with the F of the country; they
25:34 But the F of common land belonging to their

Num 16:14 given us inheritance of F and vineyards.
Deut 11:15 give grass in your F for your cattle, and
32:32 Sodom, and from the F of Gomorrah; their grapes
Josh 21:12 But the F of the city and its villages
Judg 9:32 with you, and lie in wait in the F
9:42 following day the men went out into the F
9:43 laid wait in the F; and he looked and
9:44 who were in the F and slew them.
1Sam 8:14 the best of your F and vineyards and olive
22:7 every one of you F and vineyards, will he
25:15 we were in the F, as long as we
2Kgs 8:6 the produce of the F from the day that
23:4 outside Jerusalem in the F of the Kidron, and
1Chr 6:56 pasture lands, but the F of the city and
2Chr 31:19 who were in the F of common land belonging
Neh 5:3 "We are mortgaging our F, our vineyards, and our
5:4 king's tax upon our F and our vineyards.
5:5 other men have our F and our vineyards."
5:11 this very day their F, their vineyards, their olive
11:25 the villages, with their F, some of the people
11:30 villages, Lachish and its F, and Azekah and its
12:44 Levites according to the F of the towns; for
Jud 2:27 and burned all their F and destroyed their flocks
3:3 and all our wheat F, and our flocks and
4:5 for war--since their F had recently been harvested.
6:4 their blood, and their F will be full of
8:7 slaves, and cattle, and F; and she maintained this
Job 5:10 sends waters upon the F;
Ps 78:12 of Egypt, in the F of Zoan.
78:43 his miracles in the F of Zoan.
107:37 live in; they sow F, and plant vineyards, and
132:6 found it in the F of Jaar.
144:13 ten thousands in our F;
Prov 8:26 the earth with its F, or the first of
23:10 landmark or enter the F of the fatherless;
Eccl 5:9 is an advantage to a land with cultivated F
Song 7:11 go forth into the F, and lodge in the
Is 16:8 For the F of Heshbon languish, and the vine
32:12 breasts for the pleasant F, for the fruitful vine,
Jer 6:12 over to others, their F and wives together; for
8:10 to others and their F to conquerors, because from
31:40 ashes, and all the F as far as the
32:15 of Israel: Houses and F and vineyards shall again
32:43 F shall be bought in this land of which
32:44 F shall be bought for money, and deeds shall
39:10 gave them vineyards and F at the same time.
41:8 wheat, barley, oil, and honey hidden in the F
Hos 5:7 the new moon shall devour them with their F
Joel 1:10 The F are laid waste, the ground mourns; because
Mic 2:2 They covet F, and seize them; and houses, and
2:4 Among our captors he divides our F
Hab 3:17 olive fail and the F yield no food, the
1Mac 16:10 that were in the F of Azotus, and John
Mk 11:8 leafy branches which they had cut from the F
Lk 15:15 sent him into his F to feed swine.
Jn 4:35 and see how the F are already white for
Jas 5:4 laborers who mowed your F, which you kept back

FIERCE (46)

Gen 49:7 anger, for it is F; and their wrath, for
Ex 32:12 Turn from thy F wrath, and repent of this
Num 25:4 the LORD, that the F anger of the LORD
32:14 increase still more the F anger of the LORD
1Sam 20:34 from the table in F anger and ate no
28:18 not carry out his F wrath against Amalek, therefore
2Sam 2:17 the battle was very F that day; and Abner
2Chr 25:10 and returned home in F anger.
28:11 have taken, for the F wrath of the LORD
28:13 great, and there is F wrath against Israel."
29:10 of Israel, that his F anger may turn away
30:8 your God, that his F anger may turn away
Ezra 10:14 every city, till the F wrath of our God
Esth 15:7 looked at her in F anger.
Job 4:10 the voice of the F lion, the teeth of
20:23 God will send his F anger into him, and
41:10 No one is so F that he dares to
Ps 59:3 wait for my life; F men band themselves against
78:49 loose on them his F anger, wrath, indignation, and
Sir 10:18 created for men, nor F anger for those born
Is 7:4 of firebrands, at the F anger of Rezin and
13:9 cruel, with wrath and F anger, to make the
13:13 the day of his F anger.
19:4 hard master; and a F king will rule over
27:8 removed them with his F blast in the day
Jer 4:8 and wail; for the F anger of the LORD
4:26 the LORD, before his F anger.
12:13 harvests because of the F anger of the LORD."
25:37 devastated, because of the F anger of the LORD.
25:38 and because of his F anger."
30:24 The F anger of the LORD will not turn
49:37 evil upon them, my F anger, says the LORD.
51:45 his life from the F anger of the LORD!
Lam 1:12 the day of his F anger.
2:3 has cut down in F anger all the might
2:6 sabbath, and in his F indignation has spurned king
Hos 11:9 will not execute my F anger, I will not
Jon 3:9 and turn from his F anger, so that we
Hab 1:8 swifter than leopards, more F than the evening
Zeph 2:2 comes upon you the F anger of the LORD,
1Mac 6:47 royal might and the F attack of the forces,
2Mac 10:29 When the battle became F, there appeared to the
Mt 8:28 of the tombs, so F that no one could
Acts 20:29 that after my departure F wolves will come in
2Tim 3:3 implacable, slanderers, profligates, F, haters of good,
Rev 16:9 were scorched by the F heat, and they cursed

FIERCELY (2)

Gen 49:23 The archers F attacked him, shot at him, and
Jer 6:29 The bellows blow F, the lead is consumed by

FIERCENESS (3)

Deut 13:17 may turn from the F of his anger, and
2Kgs 23:26 not turn from the F of his great wrath,
Job 39:24 With F and rage he swallows the ground; he

FIERCER

2Sam 19:43 men of Judah were F than the words of

FIERY (21)

Num 21:6 Then the LORD sent F serpents among the people,
21:8 to Moses, "Make a F serpent, and set it
Deut 8:15 terrible wilderness, with its F serpents and scorpions
28:22 with fever, inflammation, and F heat, and with
Ps 7:13 weapons, making his arrows F shafts.
78:14 the night with a F light.
Wis 11:18 such as breathe out F breath, or belch forth
Sir 36:9 be consumed in the F wrath, and may those
43:4 much; it breathes out F vapors, and with bright
Dan 3:6 cast into a burning F furnace."
3:11 cast into a burning F furnace.
3:15 cast into a burning F furnace; and who is
3:17 us from the burning F furnace; and he will
3:20 them into the burning F furnace.
3:21 cast into the burning F furnace.
3:23 bound into the burning F furnace.
3:49 companions, and drove the F flame out of the
3:89 midst of the burning F furnace; from the midst
3:94 door of the burning F furnace and said, "Shadrach,
7:9 wool; his throne was F flames, its wheels were
1Pet 4:12 be surprised at the F ordeal which comes upon

FIFTEEN (20)

Gen 5:10 Kenan eight hundred and F years, and had other
7:20 the mountains, covering them F cubits deep.
Ex 27:14 the gate shall be F cubits, with three pillars
27:15 the hangings shall be F cubits, with three pillars
38:14 of the gate were F cubits, with three pillars
38:15 court were hangings of F cubits, with three pillars
Lev 27:7 a male shall be F shekels, and for a
Judg 8:10 with their army, about F thousand men, all who
2Sam 9:10 Now Ziba had F sons and twenty servants.
19:17 of Saul, with his F sons and his twenty
1Kgs 7:3 upon the forty-five pillars, F in each row.
2Kgs 14:17 king of Judah, lived F years after the death
20:6 And I will add F years to your life.
2Chr 25:25 king of Judah lived F years after the death
Is 38:5 behold, I will add F years to your life.
Hos 3:2 I bought her for F shekels of silver and
1Mac 10:40 I also grant F thousand shekels of silver yearly
2Mac 8:22 command a division, putting F hundred men under
Acts 27:28 sounded again and found F fathoms.
Gal 1:18 and remained with him F days.

FIFTEENTH (22)

Ex 16:1 and Sinai, on the F day of the second
Lev 23:6 And on the F day of the same month
23:34 of Israel, On the F day of this seventh
23:39 "On the F day of the seventh month, when
Num 28:17 And on the F day of this month is
29:12 "On the F day of the seventh month you
33:3 first month, on the F day of the first
1Kgs 12:32 a feast on the F day of the eighth

12:33 in Bethel on the F day in the eighth
2Kgs 14:23 In the F year of Amaziah the son of
1Chr 24:14 fourteenth to Jeshebe-ab, the F to Bilgah, the
25:22 brethren, twelve; to the F, to Jeremoth, his sons
2Chr 15:10 third month of the F year of the reign
Esth 9:18 and rested on the F day, making that a
9:21 Adar and also the F day of the same,
10:13 on the fourteenth and F of that month, with
Ezek 32:17 first month, on the F day of the month,
45:25 seventh month, on the F day of the month
1Mac 1:54 Now on the F day of Chislev, in the
2Mac 11:33 The one hundred and forty-eighth year, Xanthicus F
11:38 The one hundred and forty-eighth year, Xanthicus F
Lk 3:1 In the F year of the reign of Tiberi-us

FIFTH (58)

Gen 1:23 there was morning, a F day.
30:17 and bore Jacob a F son.
41:34 land, and take the F part of the produce
47:24 you shall give a F to Pharaoh, and four
47:26 Pharaoh should have the F; the land of the
Lev 5:16 and shall add a F to it and give
6:5 and shall add a F to it, and give
19:25 But in the F year you may eat of
22:14 he shall add the F of its value to
27:13 he shall add a F to the valuation.
27:15 he shall add a F of the valuation in
27:19 he shall add a F of the valuation in
27:27 valuation, and add a F to it; or, if
27:31 he shall add a F to it.
Num 5:7 his wrong, adding a F to it, and giving
7:36 On the F day Shelumi-el the son of Zurishaddai,
29:26 "On the F day nine bulls, two rams, fourteen
33:38 first day of the F month.
Josh 19:24 The F lot came out for the tribe of
Judg 19:8 And on the F day he arose early in
2Sam 3:4 of Haggith; and the F, Shephatiah the son of
1Kgs 14:25 In the F year of King Rehoboam, Shishak king
2Kgs 8:16 In the F year of Joram the son of
25:8 In the F month, on the seventh day of
1Chr 2:14 the fourth, Raddai the F,
3:3 mother was Haggith; the F Shephatiah, by Abital;
8:2 the third, Nohah the fourth, and Rapha the F
12:10 third, Mishmannah fourth, Jeremiah F,
24:9 fourth to Se-orim, the F to Malchijah, the sixth
25:12 his brethren, twelve; the F to Nethaniah, his sons
26:3 Elam the F, Jehohanan the sixth, Eli-e-ho-enai
26:4 the fourth, Nethanel the F,
27:8 The F commander, for the fifth month, was
27:8 fifth commander, for the F month, was Shamhuth,
2Chr 12:2 In the F year of King Rehoboam, because they
Ezra 7:8 to Jerusalem in the F month, which was in
7:9 first day of the F month he came to
Neh 6:5 way Sanballat for the F time sent his servant
Jer 1:3 of Jerusalem in the F month.
28:1 of Judah, in the F month of the fourth
36:9 In the F year of Jehoiakim the son of
52:12 In the F month, on the tenth day of
Bar 1:2 in Babylon, in the F year, on the seventh
Ezek 1:1 fourth month, on the F day of the in
1:2 On the F day of the month (it was
1:2 month (it was the F year of the exile
8:1 sixth month, on the F day of the month,
20:1 seventh year, in the F month, on the tenth
33:21 tenth month, on the F day of the month,
Zech 7:3 and fast in the F month, as I have
7:5 and mourned in the F month and in the
8:19 the fast of the F, and the fast of
2Mac 7:15 they brought forward the F and maltreated him.
10:35 at dawn of the F day, twenty young men
Rev 6:9 When he opened the F seal, I saw under
9:1 And the F angel blew his trumpet, and I
16:10 The F angel poured his bowl on the throne
21:20 the fourth emerald, the F onyx, the sixth carnelian,

FIFTHS

Gen 47:24 to Pharaoh, and four F shall be your own,

FIFTIES (9)

Ex 18:21 thousands, of hundreds, of F, and of tens.
18:25 thousands, of hundreds, of F, and of tens.
Deut 1:15 of hundreds, commanders of F, commanders of tens,
1Sam 8:12 thousands and commanders of F, and some to plow
1Kgs 18:4 and hid them by F in a cave, and
18:13 the LORD's prophets by F in a cave, and
2Kgs 1:14 fifty men with their F; but now let my
1Mac 3:55 thousands and hundreds and F and tens.
Mk 6:40 sat down in groups, by hundreds and by F

FIFTIETH (4)

Lev 25:10 you shall hallow the F year, and proclaim liberty
25:11 A jubilee shall that F year be to you;
2Kgs 15:23 In the F year of Azariah king of Judah
1Mac 6:20 the one hundred and F year; and he built

FIFTY (128)

Gen 6:15 hundred cubits, its breadth F cubits, and its height
7:24 earth a hundred and F days.
8:3 of a hundred and F days the waters had
9:28 lived three hundred and F years.
9:29 were nine hundred and F years; and he died.
18:24 Suppose there are F righteous within the city; wilt
18:24 spare it for the F righteous who are in
18:26 I find at Sodom F righteous in the city,
18:28 Suppose five of the F righteous are lacking?
Ex 26:5 F loops you shall make on the one curtain,
26:5 the one curtain, and F loops you shall make
26:6 And you shall make F clasps of gold, and
26:10 And you shall make F loops on the edge
26:10 in one set, and F loops on the edge
26:11 "And you shall make F clasps of bronze, and
27:12 shall be hangings for F cubits, with ten pillars
27:13 the east shall be F cubits.
27:18 hundred cubits, the breadth F, and the height five
30:23 is, two hundred and F, and of aromatic cane
30:23 cane two hundred and F,
36:12 second set; he made F loops on the one
36:12 curtain, and he made F loops on the edge
36:13 And he made F clasps of gold, and coupled
36:17 And he made F loops on the edge of
36:17 the one set, and F loops on the edge
36:18 And he made F clasps of bronze to couple
38:12 side were hangings of F cubits, their pillars ten,
38:13 front to the east, F cubits.
38:26 thousand, five hundred and F men.
Lev 23:16 shall they be, counting F days to the morrow
27:3 years old shall be F shekels of silver, according
27:16 shall be valued at F shekels of silver.
Num 1:25 of Gad was forty-five thousand six hundred and F
1:46 six hundred and three thousand five hundred and F
2:15 being forty-five thousand six hundred and F
2:16 a hundred and fifty-one thousand four hundred and F
2:32 six hundred and three thousand five hundred and F
4:3 years old up to F years old, all who
4:23 years old up to F years old, you shall
4:30 years old up to F years old, you shall
4:35 years old up to F years old, every one
4:36 by families was two thousand seven hundred and F
4:39 years old up to F years old, every one
4:43 years old up to F years old, every one
4:47 years old up to F years old, every one
8:25 from the age of F years they shall withdraw
16:2 Israel, two hundred and F leaders of the
16:17 censer, two hundred and F censers; you also, and
16:35 the two hundred and F men offering the incense.
26:10 devoured two hundred and F men; and they became
31:30 drawn out of every F, of the persons, of
31:47 took one of every F, both of persons and
31:52 thousand seven hundred and F shekels.
Deut 22:29 of the young woman F shekels of silver, and
Josh 7:21 bar of gold weighing F shekels, then I coveted
2Sam 15:1 chariot and horses, and F men to run before
24:24 and the oxen for F shekels of silver.
1Kgs 1:5 chariots and horsemen, and F men to run before
7:2 cubits, and its breadth F cubits, and its height
7:6 Pillars; its length was F cubits, and its breadth
9:23 work: five hundred and F, who had charge of
10:29 for a hundred and F; and so through the
18:19 the four hundred and F prophets of Baal and
18:22 are four hundred and F men.
2Kgs 1:9 him a captain of F men with his fifty.
1:9 him a captain of fifty men with his F
1:10 answered the captain of F, "If I am a
1:10 down from heaven and consume you and your F
1:10 down from heaven, and consumed him and his F
1:11 him another captain of F men with his fifty.
1:11 him another captain of fifty men with his F
1:12 down from heaven and consume you and your F
1:12 down from heaven and consumed him and his F
1:13 captain of a third F with his fifty.
1:13 the captain of a third fifty with his F
1:13 the third captain of F went up, and came

1:13 the life of these F servants of yours, be
1:14 two former captains of F men with their fifties;
2:7 F men of the sons of the prophets also
2:16 are with your servants F strong men; pray, let
2:17 They sent therefore F men; and for three days
13:7 army of more than F horsemen and ten chariots
15:20 all the wealthy men, F shekels of silver from
15:25 conspired against him with F men of the Gileadites,
1Chr 5:21 carried off their livestock: F thousand of their
5:21 camels, two hundred and F thousand sheep, two
8:40 having many sons and grandsons, one hundred and F
12:33 Of Zebulun F thousand seasoned troops, equipped for
2Chr 1:17 for a hundred and F; likewise through them these
3:9 was one shekel to F shekels of gold.
8:10 Solomon, two hundred and F, who exercised
8:18 there four hundred and F talents of gold and
Ezra 8:3 registered one hundred and F men.
8:6 Jonathan, and with him F men.
8:26 hand six hundred and F talents of silver, and
Neh 5:17 table a hundred and F men, Jews and officials,
7:70 thousand darics of gold, F basins, five hundred and
Tob 1:21 But not F days passed before two of Sennacherib's
Jud 1:2 seventy cubits high and F cubits wide;
Esth 5:14 him, "Let a gallows F cubits high be made,
7:9 standing in Haman's house, F cubits high."
Is 3:3 elder, the captain of F and the man of
Ezek 40:15 of the gate was F cubits.
40:21 gate; its length was F cubits, and its breadth
40:25 others; its length was F cubits, and its breadth
40:29 vestibule; its length was F cubits, and its breadth
40:33 vestibule; its length was F cubits, and its breadth
40:36 about; its length was F cubits, and its breadth
42:2 cubits, and the breadth F cubits.
42:7 court, opposite the chambers, F cubits long.
42:8 the outer court were F cubits long, while those
45:2 for the sanctuary, with F cubits for an open
45:12 your mina shall be F shekels.
48:17 north two hundred and F cubits, on the south
48:17 south two hundred and F, on the east two
48:17 east two hundred and F, and on the west
48:17 fifty, and on the west two hundred and F
Dan 14:3 and forty sheep and F gallons of wine.
Hag 2:16 the winevat to draw F measures, there were but
1Mac 9:61 Jonathan's men seized about F of the men of
2Mac 4:9 pay one hundred and F more if permission were
13:5 tower in that place, F cubits high, full of
Lk 7:41 one owed five hundred denarii, and the other F
9:14 down in companies, about F each."
16:6 down quickly and write F
Jn 8:57 "You are not yet F years old, and have
Acts 13:19 about four hundred and F years.
19:19 found it came to F thousand pieces of silver.

FIFTY-EIGHT (2)
Tob 14:2 He was F years old when he lost his
14:11 was a hundred and F years old; and Tobias

FIFTY-FIRST (2)
1Mac 7:1 the one hundred and F year Demetrius the son
2Mac 14:4 the one hundred and F year, presenting to him

FIFTY-FIVE (3)
2Kgs 21:1 reign, and he reigned F years in Jerusalem.
2Chr 33:1 reign, and he reigned F years in Jerusalem.
Neh 7:20 The sons of Adin, six hundred and F

FIFTY-FOUR (7)
Num 1:29 tribe of Issachar was F thousand four hundred.
2:6 host as numbered being F thousand four hundred.
Ezra 2:7 sons of Elam, one thousand two hundred and F
2:15 The sons of Adin, four hundred and F
2:31 the other Elam, one thousand two hundred and F
Neh 7:12 sons of Elam, a thousand two hundred and F
7:34 the other Elam, a thousand two hundred and F

FIFTY-NINE (2)
Num 1:23 tribe of Simeon was F thousand three hundred.
2:13 host as numbered being F thousand three hundred.

FIFTY-ONE
Num 2:16 is a hundred and F thousand four hundred and

FIFTY-SECOND (2)
2Kgs 15:27 In the F year of Azariah king of Judah
1Mac 9:3 the one hundred and F year they encamped against

FIFTY-SEVEN (3)
Num 1:31 tribe of Zebulun was F thousand four hundred.
2:8 host as numbered being F thousand four hundred.
2:31 is a hundred and F thousand six hundred.

FIFTY-SIX (4)
1Chr 9:9 according to their generations, nine hundred and F
Ezra 2:14 The sons of Bigvai, two thousand and F
2:22 The men of Netophah, F
2:30 The sons of Magbish, one hundred and F

FIFTY-THIRD
1Mac 9:54 the one hundred and F year, in the second

FIFTY-THREE (5)
Num 1:43 tribe of Naphtali was F thousand four hundred.
2:30 host as numbered being F thousand four hundred.
26:47 according to their number, F thousand four hundred.
2Chr 2:17 found a hundred and F thousand six hundred.
Jn 21:11 fish, a hundred and F of them; and although

FIFTY-TWO (10)
Num 26:34 and their number was F thousand seven hundred.
2Kgs 15:2 reign, and he reigned F years in Jerusalem.
2Chr 26:3 reign, and he reigned F years in Jerusalem.
Ezra 2:29 The sons of Nebo, F
2:37 The sons of Immer, one thousand and F
2:60 and the sons of Nekoda, six hundred and F
Neh 6:15 the month Elul, in F days.
7:10 The sons of Arah, six hundred and F
7:33 The men of the other Nebo, F
7:40 The sons of Immer, a thousand and F

FIG (43)
Gen 3:7 naked; and they sewed F leaves together and made
Deut 8:8 barley, of vines and F trees and pomegranates, a
Judg 9:10 trees said to the F tree, 'Come you, and
9:11 over us.' But the F tree said to them,
1Kgs 4:25 vine and under his F tree, all the days
2Kgs 18:31 one of his own F tree, and every one
Ps 105:33 smote their vines and F trees, and shattered the
Prov 27:18 He who tends a F tree will eat its
Song 2:13 The F tree puts forth its figs, and the
Is 28:4 be like a first-ripe F before the summer: when
34:4 leaves falling from the F tree.
36:16 one of his own F tree, and every one
Jer 5:17 your vines and your F trees; your fortified cities
8:13 nor figs on the F tree; even the leaves
Hos 2:12 her vines and her F trees, of which she
9:10 first fruit on the F tree, in its first
Joel 1:7 vines, and splintered my F trees; it has stripped
1:11 The vine withers, the F tree languishes.
2:22 bears its fruit, the F tree and vine give
Amos 4:9 and your vineyards; your F trees and your olive
Mic 4:4 vine and under his F tree, and none shall
7:1 to eat, no first-ripe F which my soul desires.
Nah 3:12 your fortresses are like F trees with first-ripe figs—
Hab 3:17 Though the F tree do not blossom, nor fruit
Hag 2:19 Do the vine, the F tree, the pomegranate, and
Zech 3:10 vine and under his F tree."
1Mac 14:12 his vine and his F tree, and there was
Mt 21:19 And seeing a F tree by the wayside he
21:19 And the F tree withered at once.
21:20 saying, "How did the F tree wither at once?"
21:21 been done to the F tree, but even if
24:32 "From the F tree learn its lesson: as soon
Mk 11:13 in the distance a F tree in leaf, he
11:20 morning, they saw the F tree withered away to
11:21 The F tree which you cursed has withered."
13:28 "From the F tree learn its lesson: as soon
Lk 13:6 "A man had a F tree planted in his
13:7 seeking fruit on this F tree, and I find
21:29 parable: "Look at the F tree, and all the
Jn 1:48 you were under the F tree, I saw you."
1:50 saw you under the F tree, do you believe?
Jas 3:12 Can a F tree, my brethren, yield olives, or
Rev 6:13 the earth as the F tree sheds its winter

FIGHT (132)
Ex 1:9 join our enemies and F against us and escape
14:14 The LORD will F for you, and you have
17:9 men, and go out, F with Amalek; tomorrow I
Num 22:11 shall be able to F against them and drive
Deut 1:30 before you will himself F for you, just as
1:41 will go up and F, just as the LORD
1:42 not go up or F, for I am not

F

20:4 goes with you, to F for you against your
20:10 to a city to F against it, offer terms
25:11 "When men F with one another, and the wife
Josh 9:2 with one accord to F Joshua and Israel.
10:25 do to all your enemies against whom you F
11:5 waters of Merom, to F with Israel.
Judg 1:1 against the Canaanites, to F against them?"
1:3 me, that we may F against the Canaanites; and
1:9 Judah went down to F against the Canaanites who
8:1 when you went to F with Midian?" And they
9:38 Go out now and F with them."
10:9 crossed the Jordan to F also against Judah and
10:18 that will begin to F against the Ammonites?
11:6 leader, that we may F with the Ammonites."
11:8 go with us and F with the Ammonites, and
11:9 me home again to F with the Ammonites, and
11:12 come to me to F against my land?"
11:32 to the Ammonites to F against them; and the
12:1 you cross over to F against the Ammonites, and
12:3 me this day, to F against me?"
1Sam 4:9 been to you; acquit yourselves like men and F
8:20 out before us and F our battles."
13:5 the Philistines mustered to F with Israel, thirty
15:18 sinners, the Amalekites, and F against them until
17:9 he is able to F with me and kill
17:10 man, that we may F together."
17:32 servant will go and F with this Philistine."
17:33 against this Philistine to F with him; for you
18:17 valiant for me and F the LORD's battles." For
28:1 forces for war, to F against Israel.
29:8 may not go and F against the enemies of
2Sam 2:28 more, nor did they F any more.
11:20 did you go so near the city to F
1Kgs 12:21 thousand chosen warriors, to F against the house of
12:24 not go up or F against your kinsmen the
20:23 we; but let us F against them in the
20:25 chariot; then we will F against them in the
20:26 up to Aphek, to F against Israel.
22:31 captains of his chariots, F with neither small nor
22:32 So they turned to F against him; and Jehoshaphat
2Kgs 3:21 had come up to F against them, all who
10:3 his father's throne, and F for your master's house."
13:17 For you shall F the Syrians in Aphek until
19:9 has set out to F against you," he sent
2Chr 11:1 thousand chosen warriors, to F against Israel, to
11:4 not go up or F against your brethren.
13:12 of Israel, do not F against the LORD, the
18:30 captains of his chariots, F with neither small nor
18:31 So they turned to F against him; and Jehoshaphat
20:17 will not need to F in this battle; take
32:2 come and intended to F against Jerusalem,
32:8 help us and to F our battles." And the
35:20 Egypt went up to F at Carchemish on the
35:22 himself in order to F with him.
Neh 4:8 together to come and F against Jerusalem and to
4:14 great and terrible, and F for your brethren, your
4:20 Our God will F for us."
Jud 7:11 my lord, do not F against them in battle
Esth 11:6 forward, both ready to F, and they roared terribly.
11:7 prepared for war, to F against the nation of
Ps 35:1 who contend with me; F against those who fight
35:1 fight against those who F against me!
56:2 day long, for many F against me proudly.
Wis 5:20 join with him to F against the madmen.
Sir 4:28 the Lord God will F for you.
8:16 Do not F with a wrathful man, and do
29:13 heavy spear, it will F on your behalf against
Is 19:2 Egyptians, and they will F, every man against his
29:7 all the nations that F against Ariel, all that
29:7 against Ariel, all that F against her and her
29:8 the nations be that F against Mount Zion.
30:32 brandished arm he will F with them.
31:4 will come down to F upon Mount Zion and
37:9 has set out to F against you." And when
58:4 to quarrel and to F and to hit with
Jer 1:19 They will F against you; but they shall not
15:20 of bronze; they will F against you, but they
21:5 I myself will F against you with outstretched hand
32:5 the LORD; though you F against the Chaldeans, you
33:5 are coming in to F and to fill them
34:22 city; and they will F against it, and take
37:8 shall come back and F against this city; they
41:12 men and went to F against Ishmael the son
Dan 10:20 I will return to F against the prince of
11:11 shall come out and F with the king of
Zech 10:5 the streets; they shall F because the LORD is
14:3 will go forth and F against those nations as
14:14 other; even Judah will F against Jerusalem.
1Mac 2:40 done and refuse to F with the Gentiles for
2:41 that day: "Let us F against every man who
2:66 army for you and F the battle against the
3:10 force from Samaria to F against Israel.
3:17 few as we are, F against so great and
3:21 despoil us; but we F for our lives and
3:43 of our people, and F for our people and
3:58 in the morning to F with these Gentiles who
4:18 against our enemies and F them, and afterward
4:41 Judas detailed men to F against those in the
5:32 men of his forces, F today for your brethren!"
5:39 ready to come and F against you." And Judas
8:6 Asia, who went to F against them with a
8:32 defend their rights and F you on sea and
9:8 may be able to F them."
9:9 with our brethren and F them; we are too
9:30 ruler and leader, to F our battle."
9:44 rise up now and F for our lives, for
11:46 main streets of the city and began to F
12:51 saw that they would F for their lives, they
13:9 F our battles, and all that you say to
14:13 in the land to F them, and the kings
15:26 thousand picked men, to F for him, and silver
16:3 and go out and F for our nation, and
2Mac 7:19 for having tried to F against God!"
8:16 against them, but to F nobly,
10:16 and beseeching God to F on their side, rushed
10:21 their enemies free to F against them.
10:28 the other made rage their leader in the F
12:11 After a hard F Judas and his men won
13:14 exhorting his men to F nobly to the death
Jn 18:36 world, my servants would F, that I might not
1Tim 6:12 F the good fight of the faith; take hold
6:12 Fight the good F of the faith; take hold
2Tim 4:7 have fought the good F, I have finished the
Jas 4:2 cannot obtain; so you F and wage war.
Rev 13:4 beast, and who can F against it?"

FIGHTING (34)

Josh 8:1 dismayed; take all the F men with you, and
8:3 arose, and all the F men, to go up
8:11 And all the F men who were with him
1Sam 14:52 There was hard F against the Philistines all the
17:19 the valley of Elah, F with the Philistines.
23:1 "Behold, the Philistines are F against Keilah, and
25:28 because my lord is F the battles of the
2Sam 10:14 Then Joab returned from F against the Ammonites,
11:15 forefront of the hardest F, and then draw back
11:18 the news about the F;
11:19 the news about the F to the king,
2Kgs 19:8 the king of Assyria F against Libnah; for he
Esth 14:13 the man who is F against us, so that
Sir 46:6 armament, that he was F in the sight of
Is 37:8 the king of Assyria F against Libnah; for he
Jer 21:4 with which you are F against the king of
32:24 the Chaldeans who are F against it.
32:29 The Chaldeans who are F against this city shall
34:1 all the peoples were F against Jerusalem and all
34:7 king of Babylon was F against Jerusalem and
37:10 of Chaldeans who are F against you, and there
51:30 of Babylon have ceased F, they remain in their
1Mac 6:57 against which we are F is strong, and the
7:28 "Let there be no F between me and you;
11:41 strongholds; for they kept F against Israel.
11:50 make the Jews stop F against us and our
12:41 with forty thousand picked F men, and he came
13:47 with them and stopped F against them.
2Mac 5:14 forty thousand in hand-to-hand F; and as many were
12:36 his men had been F for a long time
15:17 decide the matter, by F hand-to-hand with all
15:27 So, F with their hands and praying to God
2Cor 7:5 afflicted at every turn– F without and fear within.
Rev 12:7 Michael and his angels F against the dragon; and

FIGHTINGS

Jas 4:1 wars, and what causes F among you?

FIGHTS (4)

Ex 14:25 Israel; for the LORD F for them against the
Deut 3:22 LORD your God who F for you.'
Josh 23:10 LORD your God who F for you, as he
Zech 14:3 nations as when he F on a day of

FIGS (26)

Num	13:23	them; they brought also some pomegranates and F
	20:5	place for grain, or F, or vines, or pomegranates;
1Sam	25:18	two hundred cakes of F, and laid them on
	30:12	of a cake of F and two clusters of
2Kgs	20:7	And Isaiah said, "Bring a cake of F
1Chr	12:40	of meal, cakes of F, clusters of raisins, and
Neh	13:15	and also wine, grapes, F, and all kinds of
Song	2:13	tree puts forth its F, and the vines are
Is	38:21	take a cake of F, and apply it to
Jer	8:13	on the vine, nor F on the fig tree;
	24:1	Behold, two baskets of F placed before the temple
	24:2	basket had very good F, like first-ripe figs, but
	24:2	good figs, like first-ripe F, but the other basket
	24:2	basket had very bad F, so bad that they
	24:3	I said, F, the good figs very good, and
	24:3	said, "Figs, the good F very good, and the
	24:3	good, and the bad F very bad, so bad
	24:5	Israel: Like these good F, so I will regard
	24:8	LORD: Like the bad F which are so bad
	29:17	make them like vile F which are so bad
Ezek	27:17	wheat, olives and early F, honey, oil, and balm.
Nah	3:12	fig trees with first-ripe F --if shaken they fall
Mt	7:16	gathered from thorns, or F from thistles?
Mk	11:13	leaves, for it was not the season for F
Lk	6:44	For F are not gathered from thorns, nor are
Jas	3:12	tree, my brethren, yield olives, or a grapevine F

FIGURATIVELY

Heb	11:19	from the dead; hence, F speaking, he did receive

FIGURE (7)

Deut	4:16	the form of any F, the likeness of male
Prov	1:6	a proverb and a F, the words of the
Wis	15:4	toil of painters, a F stained with varied colors,
Sir	26:17	so is a beautiful face on a stately F
Is	44:13	shapes it into the F of a man, with
Jn	10:6	This F Jesus used with them, but they did
	16:29	now you are speaking plainly, not in any F

FIGURED (2)

Lev	26:1	not set up a F stone in your land,
Num	33:52	and destroy all their F stones, and destroy all

FIGUREHEAD

Acts	28:11	ship of Alexandria, with the Twin Brothers as F

FIGURES (7)

1Sam	6:8	at its side the F of gold, which you
	6:15	which were the golden F, and set them upon
1Kgs	6:29	round about with carved F of cherubim and palm
2Chr	4:3	Under it were F of gourds, for thirty cubits,
Jn	16:25	this to you in F; the hour is coming
	16:25	speak to you in F but tell you plainly
Acts	7:43	the god Rephan, the F which you made to

FILIGREE (8)

Ex	28:11	you shall enclose them in settings of gold F
	28:13	make settings of gold F,
	28:20	a jasper; they shall be set in gold F
	28:25	the two settings of F, and so attach it
	39:6	in settings of gold F and engraved like the
	39:13	jasper; they were enclosed in settings of gold F
	39:16	two settings of gold F and two gold rings,
	39:18	the two settings of F; thus they attached it

FILL (71)

Gen	1:22	fruitful and multiply and F the waters in the
	1:28	fruitful and multiply, and F the earth and subdue
	9:1	fruitful and multiply, and F the earth.
	42:25	Joseph gave orders to F their bags with grain,
	44:1	steward of his house, F the men's sacks with
Ex	10:6	field, and they shall F your houses, and the
	15:9	desire shall have its F of them.
Lev	25:19	you will eat your F, and dwell in it
Deut	6:11	which you did not F, and cisterns hewn out,
	23:24	you may eat your F of grapes, as many
Judg	6:38	from the fleece to F a bowl with water.
1Sam	16:1	F your horn with oil, and go; I will
1Kgs	18:33	And he said, F four jars with water, and
Tob	8:18	ordered his servants to F in the grave.
Jud	2:8	till their wounded shall F their valleys, and every
	7:21	water to drink their F for a single day,
	8:31	send us rain to F our cisterns and we
Job	8:21	He will yet F your mouth with laughter, and
	15:2	with windy knowledge, and F himself with the east
	20:23	To F his belly to the full God will
	23:4	case before him and F my mouth with arguments.
	41:7	Can you F his skin with harpoons, or his
Ps	51:8	F me with joy and gladness; let the bones
	59:15	and growl if they do not get their F
	72:19	ever; may his glory F the whole earth!
	81:10	wide, and I will F it.
	83:16	F their faces with shame, that they may seek
	129:7	the reaper does not F his hand or the
Prov	1:13	precious goods, we shall F our houses with spoil;
	5:10	lest strangers take their F of your strength, and
	5:19	Let her affection F you at all times with
	7:18	let us take our F of love till morning;
Wis	2:7	Let us take our F of costly wine and
	5:7	We took our F of the paths of lawlessness
	13:12	work to prepare his food, and eat his F
	19:4	order that they might F up the punishment which
Sir	24:18	me, and eat your F of my produce.
	36:14	F Zion with the celebration of thy wondrous deeds,
Is	8:8	its outspread wings will F the breadth of your
	14:21	possess the earth, and F the face of the
	27:6	put forth shoots, and F the whole world with
	33:5	on high; he will F Zion with justice and
	34:5	sword has drunk its F in the heavens; behold,
	56:12	get wine, let us F ourselves with strong drink;
	65:11	table for Fortune and F cups of mixed wine
	65:20	man who does not F out his days, for
Jer	13:13	LORD: Behold, I will F with drunkenness all the
	23:24	Do I not F heaven and earth?
	33:5	to fight and to F them with the dead
	46:10	sated, and drink its F of their blood.
	51:14	himself: Surely I will F you with men, as
Ezek	3:3	I give you and F your stomach with it."
	7:19	satisfy their hunger or F their stomachs with it.
	8:17	here, that they should F the land with violence,
	9:7	"Defile the house, and F the courts with the
	10:2	wheels underneath the cherubim; F your hands with
	24:4	thigh and the shoulder; F it with choice bones.
	30:11	swords against Egypt, and F the land with the
	32:5	upon the mountains, and F the valleys with your
	35:8	And I will F your mountains with the slain;
Zeph	1:9	threshold, and those who F their master's house with
Hag	1:6	you never have your F; you clothe yourselves, but
	2:7	in, and I will F this house with splendor,
1Mac	4:32	F them with cowardice; melt the boldness of their
Mt	23:31	F up, then, the measure of your fathers.
Jn	2:7	Jesus said to them, F the jars with water."
	6:12	they had eaten their F, he told his disciples,
	6:26	because you ate your F of the loaves.
Rom	15:13	the God of hope F you with all joy
Eph	4:10	heavens, that he might F all things.)
1Thes	2:16	so as always to F up the measure of

FILLED (163)

Gen	6:11	and the earth was F with violence.
	6:13	for the earth is F with violence through them;
	21:19	and she went, and F the skin with water,
	24:16	to the spring, and F her jar, and came
	26:15	Philistines had stopped and F with earth all the
Ex	1:6	that the land was F with them.
	2:16	and drew water, and F the troughs to water
	8:21	the Egyptians shall be F with swarms of flies,
	16:12	morning you shall be F with bread; then you
	31:3	Judah: and I have F him with the Spirit
	35:31	Judah; and he has F him with the Spirit
	35:35	He has F them with ability to do every
Lev	9:17	the cereal offering, and F his hand from it,
Num	14:21	the earth shall be F with the glory of
Deut	14:29	and eat and be F; that the LORD your
	26:12	your towns and be F,
Josh	9:13	were new when we F them, and behold, they
1Sam	28:20	length upon the ground, F with fear because of
1Kgs	8:10	holy place, a cloud F the house of the
	8:11	glory of the LORD F the house of the
	18:35	about the altar, and F the trench also with
	20:27	goats, but the Syrians F the country.
2Kgs	3:17	that stream-bed shall be F with water, so that
	3:20	till the country was F with water.
	10:21	house of Baal was F from one end to
	21:16	blood, till he had F Jerusalem from one end
	23:14	down the Asherim, and F their places with the
	24:4	had shed; for he F Jerusalem with innocent blood,
2Chr	5:13	of the LORD, was F with a cloud,
	5:14	glory of the LORD F the house of God.
	7:1	glory of the LORD F the temple.
	7:2	glory of the LORD F the LORD's house.

	16:14	bier which had been F with various kinds of
Ezra	9:11	their abominations which have F it from end to
Neh	9:25	they ate, and were F and became fat, and
Jud	2:8	and river shall be F with their dead, and
	10:5	flask of oil, and F a bag with parched
Esth	3:5	to him, Haman was F with fury.
	5:9	before him, he was F with wrath against Mordecai.
Job	3:15	who had gold, who F their houses with silver.
	10:15	head, for I am F with disgrace and look
	22:18	to us?' Yet he F their houses with good
	31:31	that has not been F with his meat?'
Ps	10:7	His mouth is F with cursing and deceit and
	17:14	May their belly be F with what thou hast
	38:7	For my loins are F with burning, and there
	48:10	Thy right hand is F with victory;
	71:8	My mouth is F with thy praise, and with
	78:29	ate and were well F, for he gave them
	80:9	took deep root and F the land.
	104:28	thy hand, they are F with good things.
	126:2	Then our mouth was F with laughter, and our
Prov	3:10	your barns will be F with plenty, and your
	12:21	but the wicked are F with trouble.
	14:14	perverse man will be F with the fruit of
	24:4	knowledge the rooms are F with all precious and
	30:22	fool when he is F with food;
Eccl	1:8	seeing, nor the ear F with hearing.
Wis	1:7	of the Lord has F the world, and that
	12:19	kind, and thou hast F thy sons with good
	18:16	command, and stood and F all things with death,
Sir	2:16	love him will be F with the law.
	4:12	her early will be F with joy.
	16:4	a city will be F with people, but through
	16:27	upon the earth, and F it with his good
	17:6	He F them with knowledge and understanding, and
	23:11	many oaths will be F with iniquity, and the
	23:11	his house will be F with calamities.
	32:15	the law will be F with it, but the
	33:16	like a grape-gatherer I F my wine press.
	39:6	willing, he will be F with the spirit of
	39:12	upon, and I am F, like the moon at
	47:15	the earth, and you F it with parables and
	48:12	whirlwind, and Elisha was F with his spirit; in
Is	2:7	Their land is F with silver and gold, and
	2:7	treasures; their land is F with horses, and there
	2:8	Their land is F with idols; they bow down
	6:1	up; and his train F the temple.
	6:4	and the house was F with smoke.
	21:3	Therefore my loins are F with anguish; pangs have
Jer	13:12	"Every jar shall be F with wine."' And they
	13:12	every jar will be F with wine?'
	15:17	me, for thou hadst F me with indignation.
	16:18	detestable idols, and have F my inheritance with
	19:4	and because they have F this place with the
	41:9	the son of Nethaniah F it with the slain.
	51:34	a monster; he has F his belly with my
Lam	3:15	He has F me with bitterness, he has sated
	3:30	the smiter, and be F with insults.
Bar	3:32	earth for all time F it with four-footed creatures;
	5:7	low and the valleys F up, to make level
Ezek	10:3	in; and a cloud F the inner court.
	10:4	and the house was F with the cloud, and
	11:6	this city, and have F its streets with the
	23:33	much; you will be F with drunkenness and sorrow.
	27:25	"So you were F and heavily laden in the
	28:16	your trade you were F with violence, and you
	36:38	the waste cities be F with flocks of men.
	39:19	fat till you are F, and drink blood till
	39:20	And you shall be F at my table with
	43:5	glory of the LORD F the temple.
	44:4	glory of the LORD F the temple of the
Dan	2:35	a great mountain and F the whole earth.
Hos	13:6	the full, they were F, and their heart was
Mic	3:8	for me, I am F with power, with the
Nah	2:12	for his lionesses; he F his caves with prey
Hab	2:14	the earth will be F with the knowledge of
2Mac	3:30	fear and disturbance, was F with joy and gladness,
	4:37	grieved at heart and F with pity, and wept
	4:40	becoming aroused and F with anger, Lysimachus
	6:4	For the temple was F with debauchery and reveling
	7:21	F with a noble spirit, she fired her woman's
	8:21	With these words he F them with good courage
	9:7	but was even more F with arrogance, breathing fire
	13:16	In the end they F the camp with terror
Mt	17:6	their faces, and were F with awe.
	22:10	the wedding hall was F with guests.
	27:48	and took a sponge, F it with vinegar, and
	27:54	took place, they were F with awe, and said,
Mk	4:41	And they were F with awe, and said to
Lk	1:15	and he will be F with the Holy Spirit,
	1:41	womb; and Elizabeth was F with the Holy Spirit
	1:53	low degree; he has F the hungry with good
	1:67	his father Zechariah was F with the Holy Spirit,
	2:9	them, and they were F with fear.
	2:40	grew and became strong, F with wisdom; and the
	3:5	Every valley shall be F, and every mountain and
	4:28	in the synagogue were F with wrath.
	5:7	And they came and F both the boats, so
	5:26	glorified God and were F with awe, saying, "We
	6:11	But they were F with fury and discussed with
	14:23	to come in, that my house may be F
Jn	2:7	And they F them up to the brim.
	6:13	gathered them up and F twelve baskets with
	12:3	and the house was F with the fragrance of
	16:6	to you, sorrow has F your hearts.
Acts	2:2	mighty wind, and it F all the house where
	2:4	And they were all F with the Holy Spirit
	2:13	mocking said, "They are F with new wine."
	3:10	temple; and they were F with wonder and
	4:8	Then Peter, F with the Holy Spirit, said to
	4:31	and they were all F with the Holy Spirit
	5:3	"Ananias, why has Satan F your heart to lie
	5:17	of the Sadducees, and F with jealousy
	5:28	yet here you have F Jerusalem with your teaching
	9:17	your sight and be F with the Holy Spirit."
	13:9	is also called Paul, F with the Holy Spirit,
	13:45	the multitudes, they were F with jealousy, and
	13:52	And the disciples were F with joy and with
	19:29	So the city was F with the confusion; and
Rom	1:29	They were F with all manner of wickedness, evil,
	15:14	are full of goodness, F with all knowledge, and
1Cor	4:8	Already you are F
2Cor	7:4	in you; I am F with comfort.
Eph	3:19	that you may be F with all the fulness
	5:18	is debauchery; but be F with the Spirit,
Phil	1:11	the day of Christ, F with the fruits of
	4:18	more; I am F, having received from Epaphroditus
Col	1:9	that you may be F with the knowledge of
2Tim	1:4	that I may be F with joy.
Jas	2:16	to them, "Go in peace, be warmed and F
Rev	8:5	took the censer and F it with fire from
	15:8	and the temple was F with smoke from the

FILLETED (2)

Ex	27:17	the court shall be F with silver; their hooks
	38:17	of the court were F with silver.

FILLETS (9)

Ex	27:10	the pillars and their F shall be of silver.
	27:11	the pillars and their F shall be of silver.
	36:38	their capitals, and their F were of gold, but
	38:10	the pillars and their F were of silver.
	38:11	the pillars and their F were of silver.
	38:12	the pillars and their F were of silver.
	38:17	the pillars and their F were of silver; the
	38:19	their capitals and their F of silver.
	38:28	their capitals and made F for them.

FILLING (6)

Ps	110:6	judgment among the nations, F them with corpses;
Prov	8:21	who love me, and F their treasuries.
Jer	23:16	who prophesy to you, F you with vain hopes;
Mk	4:37	the boat, so that the boat was already F
	15:35	And one ran and, F a sponge full of
Lk	8:23	lake, and they were F with water, and were

FILLS (15)

1Chr	16:32	roar, and all that F it, let the field
Job	9:18	get my breath, but F me with bitterness.
Ps	96:11	roar, and all that F it;
	98:7	roar, and all that F it; the world and
	107:9	and the hungry he F with good things.
	147:14	in your borders; he F you with the finest
Sir	1:15	with her fruits; she F their whole house with
	24:23	It F men with wisdom, like the Pishon, and
	31:3	when he rests he F himself with his dainties.
Is	34:1	listen, and all that F it; the world, and
	42:10	roar and all that F it, the coastlands and
Jer	8:16	land and all that F it, the city and
	47:2	land and all that F it, the city and
Ezek	32:15	stripped of all that F it, when I smite
Eph	1:23	fulness of him who F all in all.

FILMS (5)
Tob 2:10 open eyes and white F formed on my eyes.
3:17 scale away the white F of Tobit's eyes; to
6:8 man who has white F in his eyes, and
11:8 will cause the white F to fall away, and
11:13 them, and the white F scaled off from the

FILTH (6)
2Chr 29:5 and carry out the F from the holy place.
Prov 30:12 own eyes but are not cleansed of their F
Sir 22:2 be compared to the F of dunghills; any one
27:4 remains; so a man's F remains in his thoughts.
Is 4:4 have washed away the F of the daughters of
Nah 3:6 I will throw F at you and treat you

FILTHINESS (6)
Is 28:8 are full of vomit, no place is without F
Ezek 22:15 I will consume your F out of you.
24:11 may burn, that its F may be melted in
24:13 not cleansed from your F, you shall not be
Eph 5:4 Let there be no F, nor silly talk, nor
Jas 1:20 Therefore put away all F and rank growth of

FILTHY (8)
Sir 22:1 be compared to a F stone, and every one
Lam 1:8 grievously, therefore she became F; all who honored
1:17 Jerusalem has become a F thing among them.
Ezek 24:13 Its rust is your F lewdness.
Zech 3:3 the angel, clothed with F garments.
3:4 before him, "Remove the F garments from him." And
Rev 22:11 do evil, and the F still be filthy, and
22:11 the filthy still be F, and the righteous still

FINAL (5)
Ezek 21:25 the time of your F punishment,
21:29 the time of their F punishment.
35:5 the time of their F punishment;
1Mac 3:42 people to cause their F destruction.
Heb 6:16 disputes an oath is F for confirmation.

FINALLY (13)
1Sam 10:21 was taken by lot; F he brought the family
Wis 3:17 of no account, and F their old age will
Sir 13:7 or three times; and F he will deride you.
Bar 6:72 gods; and they will F themselves be consumed, and
2Mac 5:8 F he met a miserable end.
Mk 12:6 other, a beloved son; F he sent him to
2Cor 13:11 F, brethren, farewell.
Eph 6:10 F, be strong in the Lord and in the
Phil 3:1 F, my brethren, rejoice in the Lord.
4:8 F, brethren, whatever is true, whatever is honorable,
1Thes 4:1 F, brethren, we beseech and exhort you in the
2Thes 3:1 F, brethren, pray for us, that the word of
1Pet 3:8 F, all of you, have unity of spirit, sympathy,

FIND (223)
Gen 18:26 LORD said, "If I F at Sodom fifty righteous
18:28 destroy it if I F forty-five there."
18:30 do it, if I F thirty there."
31:32 one with whom you F your gods shall not
31:33 but he did not F them.
31:34 tent, but did not F them.
31:35 searched, but did not F the household gods.
32:5 order that I may F favor in your sight.'"
33:8 Jacob answered, "To F favor in the sight of
33:15 Let me F favor in the sight of my
34:11 her brothers, "Let me F favor in your eyes,
38:20 hand, he could not F her.
38:23 and you could not F her."
41:38 his servants, "Can we F such a man as
Ex 5:11 straw wherever you can F it; but your work
16:25 today you will not F it in the field.
17:2 them, "Why do you F fault with me?
33:13 may know thee and F favor in thy sight.
Lev 23:11 LORD, that you may F acceptance; on the morrow
Num 11:15 at once, if I F favor in thy sight,
32:23 sure your sin will F you out.
Deut 4:29 God, and you will F him, if you search
22:3 he loses and you F; you may not withhold
22:14 her, I did not F in her the tokens
22:17 saying, "I did not F in your daughter the
28:65 these nations you shall F no ease, and there
Judg 14:12 of the feast, and F it out, then I
17:8 live where he could F a place; and as
17:9 sojourn where I may F a place."
Ruth 1:9 grant that you may F a home, each of
2:2 whose sight I shall F favor." And she said
1Sam 1:18 said, "Let your maidservant F favor in your eyes."
9:4 but they did not F them.
9:4 Benjamin, but did not F them.
9:13 the city, you will F him, before he goes
20:21 the lad, saying, 'Go, F the arrows.' If I
20:36 his lad, "Run and F the arrows which I
23:17 my father shall not F you; you shall be
25:8 let my young men F favor in your eyes;
2Sam 15:25 If I F favor in the eyes of the
16:4 obeisance; let me ever F favor in your sight,
17:20 sought and could not F them, they returned to
1Kgs 18:5 valleys; perhaps we may F grass and save the
18:12 Ahab and he cannot F you, he will kill
2Kgs 2:17 him but did not F him.
2Chr 20:16 of Ziz; you will F them at the end
30:9 and your children will F compassion with their
32:4 of Assyria come and F much water?"
Ezra 4:15 You will F in the book of the records
7:16 gold which you shall F in the whole province
Neh 5:8 silent, and could not F a word to say.
9:8 Abraham; and thou didst F his heart faithful before
Tob 2:2 our brethren you may F who is mindful of
5:3 and said to him, F a man to go
8:7 Grant that I may F mercy and may grow
Jud 5:20 their God and we F out their offense, then
8:14 the human heart, nor F out what a man
8:14 all these things, and F out his mind or
8:34 do not try to F out what I plan;
14:3 Holofernes, and will not F him.
14:17 when he did not F her he rushed out
Esth 16:14 this way he would F us undefended and would
16:15 "But we F that the Jews, who were consigned
Job 3:22 are glad, when they F the grave?
10:20 alone, that I may F a little comfort
11:7 "Can you F out the deep things of God?
11:7 Can you F out the limit of the Almighty?
16:18 and let my cry F no resting place.
17:10 and I shall not F a wise man among
23:3 knew where I might F him, that I might
32:20 speak, that I may F relief; I must open
37:23 The Almighty—we cannot F him; he is great
Ps 10:15 his wickedness till thou F none.
17:3 testest me, thou wilt F no wickedness in me;
21:8 Your hand will F out all your enemies; your
21:8 your right hand will F out those who hate
22:2 and by night, but F no rest.
55:8 I would haste to F me a shelter from
73:10 and praise them; and F no fault in them.
91:4 his wings you will F refuge; his faithfulness is
119:47 to shame; for I F my delight in thy
132:5 my eyelids, until I F a place for the
Prov 1:13 the Pit; we shall F all precious goods, we
1:28 diligently but will not F me.
2:5 of the LORD and F the knowledge of God.
3:4 So you will F favor and good repute in
8:9 right to those who F knowledge.
8:12 in prudence, and I F knowledge and discretion.
8:17 who seek me diligently F me.
20:6 own loyalty, but a faithful man who can F
21:21 righteousness and kindness will F life and honor.
24:14 your soul; if you F it, there will be
28:11 who has understanding will F him out.
28:23 a man will afterward F more favor than he
29:21 will in the end F him his heir.
31:10 A good wife who can F
Eccl 2:24 eat and drink, and F enjoyment in his toil.
3:11 so that he cannot F out what God has
5:18 eat and drink and F enjoyment in all the
5:19 accept his lot and F enjoyment in his toil—
7:14 that man may not F out anything that will
7:24 very deep; who can F it out?
7:27 thing to another to F the sum,
8:17 God, that man cannot F out the work that
8:17 seeking, he will not F it out; even though
8:17 to know, he cannot F it out.
11:1 waters, for you will F it after many days.
12:10 The Preacher sought to F pleasing words, and
Song 5:8 of Jerusalem, if you F my beloved, that you
Wis 2:19 torture, that we may F out how gentle he
6:10 been taught them will F a defense.
6:14 difficulty, for he will F her sitting at his
8:16 my house, I shall F rest with her, for
9:16 is at hand we F with labor; but who
13:6 God and desiring to F him.
13:9 did they fail to F sooner the Lord of

F

19:17 darkness, each tried to F the way through his
Sir 3:18 yourself; so you will F favor in the sight
3:29 his falling he will F support.
6:16 fear the Lord will F him.
6:28 at last you will F the rest she gives,
11:7 Do not F fault before you investigate; first consider,
12:17 befalls you, you will F him there ahead of
15:6 He will F gladness and a crown of rejoicing,
18:19 of visitation you will F forgiveness.
22:11 him and you will F rest, and you will
25:3 how then can you F anything in your old
27:16 and he will never F a congenial friend.
28:16 to slander will not F rest, nor will he
29:3 every occasion you will F what you need.
29:5 of unconcern, and will F fault with the time.
32:14 to seek him will F favor.
32:17 shun reproof, and will F a decision according to
33:25 work, and you will F rest; leave his hands
41:23 proper shame, and will F favor with every man.
43:28 Where shall we F strength to praise him?
Is 14:32 afflicted of his people F refuge."
34:14 night hag alight, and F for herself a resting
41:12 but you shall not F them; those who war
Jer 2:5 wrong did your fathers F in me that they
2:24 her month they will F her.
2:34 poor; you did not F them breaking in.
5:1 see if you can F a man, one who
6:16 walk in it, and F rest for your souls.
14:3 to the cisterns, they F no water, they return
29:7 its welfare you will F your welfare.
29:13 will seek me and F me; when you seek
45:3 my groaning, and I F no rest.'
Lam 1:6 become like harts that F no pasture; they fled
Bar 1:12 them many days and F favor in their sight.
Dan 3:38 before thee or to F mercy.
6:4 the satraps sought to F a ground for complaint
6:4 kingdom; but they could F no ground for complaint
6:5 said, "We shall not F any ground for complaint
6:5 this Daniel unless we F it in connection with
13:14 time when they could F her alone.
14:12 if you do not F that Bel has eaten
Hos 2:6 so that she cannot F her paths.
2:7 them, but shall not F them.
5:6 but they will not F him; he has withdrawn
Amos 8:12 but they shall not F it.
1Mac 10:16 he said, "Shall we F another such man?
11:16 fled into Arabia to F protection there, and King
11:42 your nation, if I F an opportunity.
2Mac 2:6 way, but could not F it.
12:18 They did not F Timothy in that region, for
14:10 for the government to F peace."
Mt 7:7 seek, and you will F; knock, and it will
7:14 life, and those who F it are few.
10:11 or village you enter, F out who is worthy
10:39 for my sake will F it.
11:29 heart, and you will F rest for your souls.
16:25 for my sake will F it.
17:26 its mouth you will F a shekel; take that
21:2 and immediately you will F an ass tied, and
22:9 as many as you F
24:46 when he comes will F so doing.
Mk 11:2 enter it you will F a colt tied, on
11:13 see if he could F anything on it.
13:36 he come suddenly and F you asleep.
Lk 2:12 for you: you will F a babe wrapped in
2:45 when they did not F him, they returned to
6:7 so that they might F an accusation against him.
11:9 seek, and you will F; knock, and it will
12:43 when he comes will F so doing.
13:7 fig tree, and I F none.
18:8 man comes, will he F faith on earth?"
19:30 on entering you will F a colt tied, on
19:48 but they did not F anything they could do,
23:4 and the multitudes, "I F no crime in this
23:14 behold, I did not F this man guilty of
24:3 in they did not F the body.
24:23 morning and did not F his body; and they
Jn 7:34 and you will not F me; where I am
7:35 that we shall not F him?
7:36 and you will not F me,' and, 'Where I
10:9 in and out and F pasture.
18:38 and told them, "I F no crime in him.
19:4 may know that I F no crime in him."
19:6 crucify him, for I F no crime in him."
21:6 boat, and you will F some." So they cast
Acts 5:22 came, they did not F them in the prison,
7:11 and our fathers could F no food.
7:46 and asked leave to F a habitation for the
12:19 him and could not F him, he examined the
17:6 when they could not F them, they dragged Jason
17:27 feel after him and F him.
22:24 examined by scourging, to F out why they shouted
23:9 up and contended, "We F nothing wrong in this
24:11 and they did not F me disputing with any
Rom 7:21 So I F it to be a law that
9:19 "Why does he still F fault?
1Cor 4:19 wills, and I will F out not the talk
2Cor 1:20 the promises of God F their Yes in him.
2:13 because I did not F my brother Titus there.
9:4 come with me and F that you are not
12:20 I may come and F you not what I
12:20 and that you may F me not what you
13:6 I hope you will F out that we have
2Tim 1:18 Lord grant him to F mercy from the Lord
Heb 4:16 may receive mercy and F grace to help in
2Jn 1:4 I rejoiced greatly to F some of your children
Rev 9:6 death and will not F it; they will long

FINDING (11)

Judg 5:30 herself, 'Are they not F and dividing the spoil?–
Ps 107:4 wandered in desert wastes, F no way to a
Sir 6:18 old you will keep F wisdom.
2Mac 5:9 Lacedaemonians in hope of F protection because of
5:25 holy sabbath day; then, F the Jews not at
Mt 13:46 fine pearls, who, on F one pearl of great
Lk 5:19 him before Jesus; but F no way to bring
11:24 places seeking rest; and F none he says, 'I
Acts 4:21 they let them go, F no way to punish
Rom 7:8 But sin, F opportunity in the commandment, wrought
7:11 sin, F opportunity in the commandment, deceived

FINDS (42)

Gen 4:14 the earth, and whoever F me will slay me."
Lev 25:26 prosperous and F sufficient means to redeem
Num 35:27 the avenger of blood F him outside the bounds
Deut 24:1 her, if then she F no favor in his
1Sam 10:7 do whatever your hand F to do, for God
24:19 For if a man F his enemy, will he
Job 33:10 Behold, he F occasions against me, he counts me
Ps 84:3 Even the sparrow F a home, and the swallow
119:162 word like one who F great spoil.
Prov 3:13 is the man who F wisdom, and the man
4:23 life to him who F them, and healing to
8:35 For he who F me finds life and obtains
8:35 he who finds me F life and obtains favor
14:32 evil-doing, but the righteous F refuge through his
18:22 He who F a wife finds a good thing,
18:22 who finds a wife F a good thing, and
21:10 desires evil; his neighbor F no mercy in his
Eccl 6:5 known anything; yet it F rest rather than he.
9:10 Whatever your hand F to do, do it with
Sir 12:16 eyes, but if he F an opportunity his thirst
18:27 praises the one who F her.
19:25 do evil when he F an opportunity.
26:10 daughter, lest, when she F liberty, she use it
36:26 and lodges wherever night F him?
40:18 worker, but he who F treasure is better off
43:26 of him his messenger F the way, and by
Lam 1:3 among the nations, but F no resting place; her
Hos 14:3 In thee the orphan F mercy."
2Mac 2:1 One F in the records that Jeremiah the prophet
Mt 7:8 and he who seeks F, and to him who
10:39 He who F his life will lose it, and
12:43 seeking rest, but he F none.
12:44 when he comes he F it empty, swept, and
18:12 And if he F it, truly, I say to
Lk 11:10 and he who seeks F, and to him who
11:25 when he comes he F it swept and put
12:37 servants whom the master F awake when he comes;
12:38 in the third, and F them so, blessed are
15:4 is lost, until he F it?
15:8 seek diligently until she F it?
Jn 8:37 me, because my word F no place in you.
Heb 8:8 For he F fault with them when he says:

FINE (138)

Gen 18:6 quickly three measures of F meal, knead it, and
41:42 him in garments of F linen, and put a
Ex 9:9 And it shall become F dust over all the
16:14 of the wilderness a F, flake-like thing, fine as
16:14 a fine, flake-like thing, F as hoarfrost on the
25:4 and scarlet stuff and F twined linen, goats' hair,

26:1 with ten curtains of F twined linen and blue
26:31 and scarlet stuff and F twined linen; in skilled
26:36 and scarlet stuff and F twined linen, embroidered
27:9 shall have hangings of F twined linen a hundred
27:16 and scarlet stuff and F twined linen, embroidered
27:18 cubits, with hangings of F twined linen and bases
28:5 and scarlet stuff, and F twined linen.
28:6 scarlet stuff, and of F twined linen, skilfully worked.
28:8 and scarlet stuff, and F twined linen.
28:15 and scarlet stuff, and F twined linen shall you
28:39 in checker work of F linen, and you shall
28:39 make a turban of F linen, and you shall
29:2 shall make them of F wheat flour.
29:40 a tenth measure of F flour mingled with a
35:6 and scarlet stuff and F twined linen; goats' hair,
35:23 or scarlet stuff or F linen or goats' hair
35:25 and scarlet stuff and F twined linen;
35:35 and scarlet stuff and F twined linen, or by
36:8 they were made of F twined linen and blue
36:35 and scarlet stuff and F twined linen; with cherubim
36:37 and scarlet stuff and F twined linen, embroidered
38:9 the court were of F twined linen, a hundred
38:16 the court were of F twined linen.
38:18 and scarlet stuff and F twined linen; it was
38:23 and scarlet stuff and F twined linen.
39:2 and scarlet stuff, and F twined linen.
39:3 stuff, and into the F twined linen, in skilled
39:5 and scarlet stuff, and F twined linen; as the
39:8 and scarlet stuff, and F twined linen.
39:24 and scarlet stuff and F twined linen.
39:27 the coats, woven of F linen, for Aaron and
39:28 and the turban of F linen, and the caps
39:28 and the caps of F linen, and the linen
39:28 the linen breeches of F twined linen,
39:29 and the girdle of F twined linen and of
Lev 2:1 offering shall be of F flour; he shall pour
2:2 a handful of the F flour and oil, with
2:4 be unleavened cakes of F flour mixed with oil,
2:5 it shall be of F flour unleavened, mixed with
2:7 shall be made of F flour with oil.
5:11 of an ephah of F flour for a sin
6:15 a handful of the F flour of the cereal
6:20 of an ephah of F flour as a regular
7:12 oil, and cakes of F flour well mixed with
14:10 of an ephah of F flour mixed with oil,
14:21 of an ephah of F flour mixed with oil
23:13 of an ephah of F flour mixed with oil,
23:17 they shall be of F flour, they shall be
24:5 "And you shall take F flour, and bake twelve
Num 6:15 unleavened bread, cakes of F flour mixed with oil,
7:13 of them full of F flour mixed with oil
7:19 of them full of F flour mixed with oil
7:25 of them full of F flour mixed with oil
7:31 of them full of F flour mixed with oil
7:37 of them full of F flour mixed with oil
7:43 of them full of F flour mixed with oil
7:49 of them full of F flour mixed with oil
7:55 of them full of F flour mixed with oil
7:61 of them full of F flour mixed with oil
7:67 of them full of F flour mixed with oil
7:73 of them full of F flour mixed with oil
7:79 of them full of F flour mixed with oil
8:8 its cereal offering of F flour mixed with oil,
15:4 of an ephah of F flour, mixed with a
15:6 of an ephah of F flour mixed with a
15:9 of an ephah of F flour, mixed with half
28:5 of an ephah of F flour for a cereal
28:9 of an ephah of F flour for a cereal
28:12 of an ephah of F flour for a cereal
28:12 and two tenths of F flour for a cereal
28:13 and a tenth of F flour mixed with oil
28:20 their cereal offering of F flour mixed with oil;
28:28 their cereal offering of F flour mixed with oil,
29:3 their cereal offering of F flour mixed with oil,
29:9 their cereal offering of F flour mixed with oil,
29:14 their cereal offering of F flour mixed with oil,
Deut 9:21 until it was as F as dust; and I
22:19 him; and they shall F him a hundred shekels
2Sam 22:43 I beat them F as the dust of the
1Kgs 4:22 was thirty cors of F flour, and sixty cors
2Kgs 7:1 time a measure of F meal shall be sold
7:16 So a measure of F meal was sold for
7:18 and a measure of F meal for a shekel,
1Chr 9:29 utensils, also over the F flour, the wine, the
15:27 with a robe of F linen, as also were
2Chr 2:14 and crimson fabrics and F linen, and to do
3:5 and covered it with F gold, and made palms
3:8 six hundred talents of F gold.
3:14 and crimson fabrics and F linen, and worked
5:12 and kinsmen, arrayed in F linen, with cymbals, harps,
Ezra 8:27 and two vessels of F bright bronze as precious
Jud 10:5 of dried fruit and F bread; and she wrapped
Esth 1:6 up with cords of F linen and purple to
8:15 and a mantle of F linen and purple, while
Job 28:17 exchanged for jewels of F gold.
31:24 my trust, or called F gold my confidence;
Ps 18:42 I beat them F as dust before the wind;
19:10 than gold, even much F gold; sweeter also than
21:3 set a crown of F gold upon his head.
119:127 commandments above gold, above F gold.
Prov 8:19 better than gold, even F gold, and my yield
17:7 F speech is not becoming to a fool; still
17:26 To impose a F on a righteous man is
31:22 coverings; her clothing is F linen and purple.
Sir 11:4 not boast about wearing F clothes, nor exalt yourself
35:2 returns a kindness offers F flour, and he who
38:11 a memorial portion of F flour, and pour oil
Is 13:12 men more rare than F gold, and mankind than
23:18 supply abundant food and F clothing for those who
40:15 up the isles like F dust.
Lam 4:2 worth their weight in F gold, how they are
Ezek 16:10 I swathed you in F linen and covered you
16:13 your raiment was of F linen, and silk, and
16:13 embroidered cloth; you ate F flour and honey and
16:19 I fed you with F flour and oil and
23:26 and take away your F jewels.
27:7 Of F embroidered linen from Egypt was your sail,
27:16 emeralds, purple, embroidered work, F linen, coral,
Dan 2:32 this image was of F gold, its breast and
14:3 it twelve bushels of F flour and forty sheep
Mt 13:45 merchant in search of F pearls,
Mk 7:9 them, "You have a F way of rejecting the
Lk 16:19 clothed in purple and F linen and who feasted
Jas 2:2 gold rings and in F clothing comes into your
2:3 one who wears the F clothing and say, "Have
1Pet 3:3 gold, and wearing of F clothing,
Rev 18:12 silver, jewels and pearls, F linen, purple, silk and
18:13 myrrh, frankincense, wine, oil, F flour and wheat,
18:16 that was clothed in F linen, in purple and
19:8 to be clothed with F linen, bright and pure"–
19:8 pure"– for the F linen is the righteous
19:14 of heaven, arrayed in F linen, white and pure,

FINED (2)
Ex 21:22 hurt her shall be F, according as the woman's
Amos 2:8 drink the wine of those who have been F

FINELY (4)
Ex 31:10 its base, and the F worked garments, the holy
35:19 and their cords; the F wrought garments for
39:1 scarlet stuff they made F wrought garments, for
39:41 tent of meeting; the F worked garments for

FINERY (2)
Jud 12:15 in all her woman's F, and her maid went
Is 3:18 will take away the F of the anklets, the

FINEST (10)
Ex 30:23 to Moses, "Take the F spices: of liquid myrrh
Deut 32:14 and goats, with the F of the wheat–and
33:15 the months, with the F produce of the ancient
1Kgs 10:18 overlaid it with the F gold.
Ps 81:16 feed you with the F of the wheat, and
147:14 fills you with the F of the wheat.
Song 5:11 His head is the F gold; his locks are
Amos 6:6 anoint themselves with the F oils, but are not
2Mac 3:2 the temple with the F presents,
9:16 would adorn with the F offerings; and the holy

FINGER (29)
Ex 8:19 Pharaoh, "This is the F of God." But Pharaoh's
29:12 the altar with your F, and the rest of
31:18 stone, written with the F of God.
Lev 4:6 priest shall dip his F in the blood and
4:17 priest shall dip his F in the blood and
4:25 sin offering with his F and put it on
4:30 its blood with his F and put it on
4:34 sin offering with his F and put it on
8:15 blood, and with his F put it on the
9:9 and he dipped his F in the blood and
14:16 and dip his right F in the oil that
14:16 some oil with his F seven times before the

F

14:27 sprinkle with his right F some of the oil
16:14 sprinkle it with his F on the front of
16:14 the blood with his F seven times.
16:19 upon it with his F seven times, and cleanse
Num 19:4 her blood with his F, and sprinkle some of
Deut 9:10 stone written with the F of God; and on
1Kgs 12:10 to them, 'My little F is thicker than my
2Chr 10:10 to them, 'My little F is thicker than my
Prov 6:13 feet, points with his F,
Is 58:9 the pointing of the F, and speaking wickedness,
Mt 23:4 they themselves will not move them with their F
Lk 11:20 it is by the F of God that I
16:24 the end of his F in water and cool
Jn 8:6 and wrote with his F on the ground.
8:8 and wrote with his F on the ground.
20:25 nails, and place my F in the mark of
20:27 to Thomas, "Put your F here, and see my

FINGERS (15)

2Sam 21:20 stature, who had six F on each hand, and
1Kgs 7:15 its thickness was four F; the second pillar was
1Chr 20:6 stature, who had six F on each hand, and
Ps 8:3 the work of thy F, the moon and the
144:1 for war, and my F for battle;
Prov 7:3 bind them on your F, write them on the
Song 5:5 dripped with myrrh, my F with liquid myrrh, upon
Wis 15:15 which to hear, nor F to feel with, and
Is 2:8 to what their own F have made.
17:8 to what their own F have made, either the
59:3 with blood and your F with iniquity; your lips
Jer 52:21 its thickness was four F, and it was hollow.
Dan 5:5 Immediately the F of a man's hand appeared and
Mk 7:32 privately, he put his F into his ears, and
Lk 11:46 not touch the burdens with one of your F

FINISH (13)

Gen 6:16 for the ark, and F it to a cubit
1Chr 27:24 number, but did not F; yet wrath came upon
Ezra 5:3 this house and to F this structure?"
5:9 this house and to F this structure?'
Neh 4:2 Will they F up in a day?
Sir 38:27 he is careful to F his work.
38:30 sets his heart to F the glazing, and he
Jer 51:63 for ever.' When you F reading this book, bind
Dan 9:24 your holy city, to F the transgression, to put
2Mac 15:5 take up arms and F the king's business."
Lk 13:32 the third day I F my course.
14:29 is not able to F, all who see it
14:30 was not able to F

FINISHED (101)

Gen 2:1 and the earth were F, and all the host
2:2 the seventh day God F his work which he
17:22 When he had F talking with him, God went
18:33 way, when he had F speaking to Abraham; and
24:19 When she had F giving him a drink, she
27:30 soon as Isaac had F blessing Jacob, when Jacob
49:33 When Jacob F charging his sons, he drew up
Ex 34:33 And when Moses had F speaking with them, he
39:32 tent of meeting was F; and the people of
Num 4:15 and his sons have F covering the sanctuary and
7:1 day when Moses had F setting up the tabernacle,
16:31 And as he F speaking all these words, the
Deut 26:12 "When you have F paying all the tithe of
31:24 When Moses had F writing the words of this
31:30 song until they were F, in the ears of
32:45 And when Moses had F speaking all these words
Josh 3:17 until all the nation F passing over the Jordan.
4:1 all the nation had F passing over the Jordan,
4:10 Jordan, until everything was F that the LORD
4:11 all the people had F passing over, the ark
8:24 When Israel had F slaughtering all the inhabitants of
10:20 men of Israel had F slaying them with a
19:49 When they had F distributing the several territories
19:51 So they F dividing the land.
Judg 3:18 And when Ehud had F presenting the tribute, he
15:17 When he had F speaking, he threw away the
Ruth 2:21 servants, till they have F all my harvest.'"
3:3 man until he has F eating and drinking.
1Sam 10:13 When he had F prophesying, he came to the
13:10 soon as he had F offering the burnt offering,
18:1 When he had F speaking to Saul, the soul
24:16 When David had F speaking these words to Saul,
2Sam 6:18 And when David had F offering the burnt offerings
11:19 messenger, "When you have F telling all the news
13:36 soon as he had F speaking, behold, the king's
1Kgs 1:41 heard it as they F feasting.
3:1 David, until he had F building his own house
6:9 built the house, and F it; and he made
6:14 built the house, and F it.
6:22 house with gold, until all the house was F
6:38 month, the house was F in all its parts,
7:1 thirteen years, and he F his entire house.
7:7 of Judgment; it was F with cedar from floor
7:22 Thus the work of the pillars was F
7:40 So Hiram F all the work that he did
7:51 did on the house of the LORD was F
8:54 Now as Solomon F offering all this prayer and
9:1 When Solomon had F building the house of the
9:25 So he F the house.
1Chr 16:2 And when David had F offering the burnt offerings
28:20 service of the house of the LORD is F
2Chr 4:11 So Huram F the work that he did for
5:1 did for the house of the LORD was F
7:11 Thus Solomon F the house of the LORD and
8:16 of the LORD was laid until it was F
24:10 dropped it into the chest until they had F
24:14 And when they had F, they brought the rest
29:17 the sixteenth day of the first month they F
29:28 all this continued until the burnt offering was F
29:29 When the offering was F, the king and all
29:34 until the work was F —for the Levites were
31:1 when all this was F, all Israel who were
31:7 up the heaps, and F them in the seventh
Ezra 4:13 rebuilt and the walls F, they will not pay
4:16 rebuilt and its walls F, you will then have
5:11 which a great king of Israel built and F
5:16 it is not yet F
6:14 They F their building by command of the God
6:15 and this house was F on the third day
Neh 6:15 So the wall was F on the twenty-fifth day
Tob 8:1 When they had F eating, they escorted Tobias in
Jud 2:4 When he had F setting forth his plan,
5:22 When Achior had F saying this, all the men
8:34 you until I have F what I am about
14:9 And when she had F, the people raised a
Sir 7:25 marriage; you will have F a great task.
18:6 When a man has F, he is just beginning,
23:20 him; so it was also after it was F
38:8 works will never be F; and from him health
Is 10:12 When the Lord has F all his work on
Jer 26:8 And when Jeremiah had F speaking all that the
43:1 When Jeremiah F speaking to all the people all
Ezek 42:15 Now when he had F measuring the interior of
43:23 When you have F cleansing it, you shall offer
Amos 7:2 When they had F eating the grass of the
1Mac 2:23 When he had F speaking these words, a Jew
3:23 When he F speaking, he rushed suddenly against
4:51 Thus they F all the work they had undertaken.
Mt 7:28 And when Jesus F these sayings, the crowds were
11:1 And when Jesus had F instructing his twelve
13:53 And when Jesus had F these parables, he went
19:1 Now when Jesus had F these sayings, he went
26:1 When Jesus had F all these sayings, he said
Jn 19:28 that all was now F, said (to fulfill the
19:30 he said, "It is F; and he bowed his
21:15 When they had F breakfast, Jesus said to Simon
Acts 15:13 After they F speaking, James replied, "Brethren,
21:7 When we had F the voyage from Tyre, we
2Tim 4:7 good fight, I have F the race, I have
Heb 4:3 although his works were F from the foundation of
Rev 11:7 And when they have F their testimony, the beast

FINISHING (5)

Ezra 4:12 wicked city; they are F the walls and repairing
Sir 38:28 sets his heart on F his handiwork, and he
50:14 F the service at the altars, and arranging the
1Mac 4:19 Just as Judas was F this speech, a detachment
Acts 13:25 And as John was F his course, he said,

FINS (5)

Lev 11:9 the waters that has F and scales, whether in
11:10 rivers that has not F and scales, of the
11:12 waters that has not F and scales is an
Deut 14:9 eat these: whatever has F and scales you may
14:10 whatever does not have F and scales you shall

FIR (3)

Ps 104:17 her home in the F trees.
Ezek 27:5 all your planks of F trees from Senir; they
31:8 rival it, nor the F trees equal its boughs;

FIRE (607)

Gen 15:17 dark, behold, a smoking F pot and a flaming
19:24 and Gomorrah brimstone and F from the LORD out
22:6 in his hand the F and the knife.
22:7 He said, "Behold, the F and the wood; but
Ex 3:2 in a flame of F out of the midst
9:23 thunder and hail, and F ran down to the
9:24 there was hail, and F flashing continually in the
13:21 in a pillar of F to give them light,
13:22 and the pillar of F by night did not
14:24 in the pillar of F and of cloud looked
19:18 descended upon it in F; and the smoke of
22:6 "When F breaks out and catches in thorns so
22:6 he that kindled the F shall make full restitution.
24:17 was like a devouring F on the top of
29:14 you shall burn with F outside the camp; it
29:18 odor, an offering by F to the LORD.
29:25 is an offering by F to the LORD.
29:34 burn the remainder with F; it shall not be
29:41 odor, an offering by F to the LORD.
30:20 burn an offering by F to the LORD, they
32:20 and burnt it with F, and ground it to
32:24 threw it into the F, and there came out
35:3 you shall kindle no F in all your habitations
Lev 1:7 the priest shall put F on the altar, and
1:7 in order upon the F;
1:8 that is on the F upon the altar;
1:9 offering, an offering by F, a pleasing odor to
1:12 that is on the F upon the altar;
1:13 offering, an offering by F, a pleasing odor to
1:17 that is on the F; it is a burnt
1:17 offering, an offering by F, a pleasing odor to
2:2 altar, an offering by F, a pleasing odor to
2:3 of the offerings by F to the LORD.
2:9 altar, an offering by F, a pleasing odor to
2:10 of the offerings by F to the LORD.
2:11 as an offering by F to the LORD.
2:14 crushed new grain from fresh ears, parched with F
2:16 is an offering by F to the LORD.
3:3 as an offering by F to the LORD, he
3:5 the wood on the F; it is an offering
3:5 is an offering by F, a pleasing odor to
3:9 as an offering by F to the LORD he
3:11 as food offered by F to the LORD.
3:14 for an offering by F to the LORD, the
3:16 as food offered by F for a pleasing odor.
4:12 burn it on a F of wood; where the
4:35 upon the offerings by F to the LORD; and
5:12 upon the offerings by F to the LORD; it
6:9 the morning, and the F of the altar shall
6:10 ashes to which the F has consumed the burnt
6:12 The F on the altar shall be kept burning
6:13 F shall be kept burning upon the altar continually;
6:17 of my offerings by F; it is a thing
6:18 the LORD's offerings by F; whoever touches them
6:30 the holy place; it shall be burned with F
7:5 as an offering by F to the LORD; it
7:17 on the third day shall be burned with F
7:19 not be eaten; it shall be burned with F
7:25 which an offering by F is made to the
7:30 hands the offerings by F to the LORD; he
7:35 the offerings made by F to the LORD, consecrated
8:17 dung, he burned with F outside the camp, as
8:21 odor, an offering by F to the LORD, as
8:28 odor, an offering by F to the LORD.
8:32 flesh and the bread you shall burn with F
9:11 skin he burned with F outside the camp.
9:24 And F came forth from before the LORD and
10:1 his censer, and put F in it, and laid
10:1 it, and offered unholy F before the LORD, such
10:2 And F came forth from the presence of the
10:12 of the offerings by F to the LORD, and
10:13 from the offerings by F to the LORD; for
10:15 with the offerings by F of the fat, to
13:52 malignant leprosy; it shall be burned in the F
13:55 burn it in the F, whether the leprous spot
13:57 you shall burn with F that in which is
16:12 full of coals of F from the altar before
16:13 the incense on the F before the LORD, that
16:27 flesh and their dung shall be burned with F
18:21 to devote them by F to Molech, and so
19:6 until the third day shall be burned with F
20:14 shall be burned with F, both he and they,
21:6 offer the offerings by F to the LORD, the
21:9 profanes her father; she shall be burned with F
21:21 the LORD's offerings by F; since he has a
22:22 them an offering by F upon the altar to
22:27 as an offering by F to the LORD.
23:8 present an offering by F to the LORD seven
23:13 to be offered by F to the LORD, a
23:18 offerings, an offering by F, a pleasing odor to
23:25 present an offering by F to the LORD."
23:27 present an offering by F to the LORD.
23:36 shall present offerings by F to the LORD; on
23:36 present an offering by F to the LORD; it
23:37 the LORD offerings by F, burnt offerings and cereal
24:7 to be offered by F to the LORD.
24:9 of the offerings by F to the LORD, a
Num 3:4 when they offered unholy F before the LORD in
6:18 put it on the F which is under the
9:15 like the appearance of F until morning.
9:16 and the appearance of F by night.
11:1 was kindled, and the F of the LORD burned
11:2 the LORD, and the F abated.
11:3 called Taberah, because the F of the LORD burned
14:14 in a pillar of F by night.
15:3 flock an offering by F or a burnt offering
15:10 as an offering by F, a pleasing odor to
15:13 offering an offering by F, a pleasing odor to
15:14 offer an offering by F, a pleasing odor to
15:25 offering, an offering by F to the LORD, and
16:7 all his company; put F in them and put
16:18 censer, and they put F in them and laid
16:35 And F came forth from the LORD, and consumed
16:37 blaze; then scatter the F far and wide.
16:46 your censer, and put F therein from off the
18:9 things, reserved from the F; every offering of theirs,
18:17 as an offering by F, a pleasing odor to
21:28 For F went forth from Heshbon, flame from the
21:30 we laid waste until F spread to Medeba."
26:10 company died, when the F devoured two hundred
26:61 when they offered unholy F before the LORD.
28:2 for my offerings by F, my pleasing odor, you
28:3 is the offering by F which you shall offer
28:6 odor, an offering by F to the LORD.
28:8 as an offering by F, a pleasing odor to
28:13 odor, an offering by F to the LORD.
28:19 offer an offering by F, a burnt offering to
28:24 of an offering by F, a pleasing odor to
29:6 odor, an offering by F to the LORD.
29:13 offering, an offering by F, a pleasing odor to
29:36 offering, an offering by F, a pleasing odor to
31:10 encampments, they burned with F,
31:23 that can stand the F, you shall pass through
31:23 shall pass through the F, and it shall be
31:23 whatever cannot stand the F, you shall pass through
Deut 1:33 pitch your tents, in F by night, to show
4:11 the mountain burned with F to the heart of
4:12 the midst of the F; you heard the sound
4:15 the midst of the F,
4:24 God is a devouring F, a jealous God.
4:33 the midst of the F, as you have heard,
4:36 you see his great F, and you heard his
4:36 his words out of the midst of the F
5:4 the midst of the F,
5:5 afraid because of the F, and you did not
5:22 the midst of the F, the cloud, and the
5:23 mountain was burning with F, you came near to
5:24 the midst of the F; we have this day
5:25 For this great F will consume us; if we
5:26 of the midst of F, as we have, and
7:5 their Asherim, and burn their graven images with F
7:25 you shall burn with F; you shall not covet
9:3 you as a devouring F is the LORD your
9:10 the midst of the F on the day of
9:15 mountain was burning with F; and the two tables
9:21 and burned it with F and crushed it, grinding
10:4 the midst of the F on the day of
12:3 burn their Asherim with F; you shall hew down
12:31 their daughters in the F to their gods.
13:16 all its spoil with F, as a whole burnt
18:1 eat the offerings by F to the LORD, and
18:16 or see this great F any more, lest I
32:22 For a F is kindled by my anger, and
32:22 increase, and sets on F the foundations of the
33:2 holy ones, with flaming F at his right hand.
Josh 6:24 burned the city with F, and all within it;
7:15 shall be burned with F, he and all that
7:25 they burned them with F, and stoned them with
8:8 set the city on F, doing as the LORD
8:19 they made haste to set the city on F
11:6 their horses, and burn their chariots with F

F

11:9 horses, and burned their chariots with F
11:11 left that breathed, and he burned Hazor with F
13:14 inheritance; the offerings by F to the LORD God
Judg 1:8 of the sword, and set the city on F
6:21 and there sprang up F from the rock and
9:15 but if not, let F come out of the
9:20 but if not, let F come out from Abimelech,
9:20 and Beth-millo; and let F come out from the
9:49 set the stronghold on F over them, so that
9:52 door of the tower to burn it with F
12:1 We will burn your house over you with F
14:15 we burn you and your father's house with F
15:5 when he had set F to the torches, he
15:6 up, and burned her and her father with F
15:14 flax that has caught F, and his bonds melted
16:9 string of tow snaps when it touches the F
18:27 of the sword, and burned the city with F
20:48 the towns which they found they set on F
1Sam 2:28 all my offerings by F from the people of
30:1 and burned it with F,
30:3 found it burned with F, and their wives and
30:14 Negeb of Caleb; and we burned Ziklag with F
2Sam 14:30 has barley there; go and set it on F
14:30 So Absalom's servants set the field on F
14:31 "Why have your servants set my field on F
22:9 his nostrils, and devouring F from his mouth; glowing
22:13 before him coals of F flamed forth.
23:7 a spear, and they are utterly consumed with F
1Kgs 9:16 and burnt it with F, and had slain the
16:18 house over him with F, and died,
18:23 wood, but put no F to it; and I
18:23 wood, and put no F to it.
18:24 God who answers by F, he is God." And
18:25 god, but put no F to it."
18:38 Then the F of the LORD fell, and consumed
19:12 after the earthquake a F, but the LORD was
19:12 was not in the F; and after the fire
19:12 fire; and after the F a still small voice.
2Kgs 1:10 man of God, let F come down from heaven
1:10 Then F came down from heaven, and consumed him
1:12 man of God, let F come down from heaven
1:12 Then the F of God came down from heaven
1:14 Lo, F came down from heaven, and consumed the
2:11 behold, a chariot of F and horses of fire
2:11 fire and horses of F separated the two of
6:17 horses and chariots of F round about Elisha.
8:12 you will set on F their fortresses, and you
17:31 children in the F to Adrammelech and Anammelech,
19:18 their gods into the F; for they were no
23:11 he burned the chariots of the sun with F
1Chr 21:26 he answered him with F from heaven upon the
2Chr 7:1 had ended his prayer, F came down from heaven
7:3 of Israel saw the F come down and the
16:14 made a very great F in his honor.
21:19 His people made no F in his honor, like
35:13 the passover lamb with F according to the ordinance;
36:19 all its palaces with F, and destroyed all its
Neh 1:3 broken down, and its gates are destroyed by F
2:3 waste, and its gates have been destroyed by F
2:13 and its gates which had been destroyed by F
9:12 by a pillar of F in the night to
9:19 nor the pillar of F by night which lighted
Jud 8:27 not tried us with F, as he did them,
13:13 and they kindled a F for light, and gathered
16:17 the day of judgment; F and worms he will
Esth 16:24 shall be destroyed in wrath with spear and F
Job 1:16 another, and said, "The F of God fell from
15:34 godless is barren, and F consumes the tents of
18:5 the flame of his F does not shine.
20:26 for his treasures; a F not blown upon will
22:20 what they left the F has consumed.'
28:5 but underneath it is turned up as by F
31:12 that would be a F which consumes unto Abaddon,
41:19 flaming torches; sparks of F leap forth.
Ps 11:6 will rain coals of F and brimstone; a scorching
18:8 his nostrils, and devouring F from his mouth; glowing
18:12 broke through his clouds hailstones and coals of F
18:13 High uttered his voice, hailstones and coals of F
21:9 in his wrath; and F will consume them.
29:7 voice of the LORD flashes forth flames of F
39:3 As I mused, the F burned; then I spoke
46:9 shatters the spear, he burns the chariots with F
50:3 him is a devouring F, round about him a
66:12 heads; we went through F and through water; yet
68:2 as wax melts before F, let the wicked perish
74:7 set thy sanctuary on F; to the ground they
78:21 full of wrath; a F was kindled against Jacob,
78:63 F devoured their young men, and their maidens had
79:5 Will thy jealous wrath burn like F
80:16 have burned it with F, they have cut it
83:14 As F consumes the forest, as the flame sets
89:46 How long will thy wrath burn like F
97:3 F goes before him, and burns up his adversaries
104:4 the winds thy messengers, F and flame thy ministers.
105:39 for a covering, and F to give light by
106:18 F also broke out in their company; the flame
118:12 they blazed like a F of thorns; in the
148:8 monsters and all deeps, F and hail, snow and
Prov 6:27 Can a man carry F in his bosom and
16:27 evil, and his speech is like a scorching F
25:22 will heap coals of F on his head, and
26:20 lack of wood the F goes out; and where
26:21 embers and wood to F, so is a quarrelsome
30:16 for water, and the F which never says, "Enough."
Song 8:6 flashes are flashes of F, a most vehement flame.
Wis 10:6 perishing; he escaped the F that descended on the
13:2 they supposed that either F or wind or swift
16:16 hail and relentless storms, and utterly consumed by F
16:17 quenches all things, the F had still greater effect,
16:19 burned more intensely than F, to destroy the crops
16:22 Snow and ice withstood F without melting, so that
16:22 being destroyed by the F that blazed in the
16:23 of rain; whereas the F, in order that the
16:27 was not destroyed by F was melted when simply
17:5 And no power of F was able to give
17:6 except a dreadful, self-kindled F, and in terror they
18:3 a flaming pillar of F as a guide for
19:20 F even in water retained its normal power, and
Sir 2:5 is tested in the F, and acceptable men in
3:28 Water extinguishes a blazing F: so almsgiving atones
7:17 of the ungodly is F and worms.
8:3 with a chatterer, nor heap wood on his F
8:10 sinner, lest you be burned in his flaming F
9:8 and by it passion is kindled like a F
11:30 From a spark of F come many burning coals,
15:16 has placed before you F and water: stretch out
16:6 assembly of sinners a F will be kindled, and
21:9 together, and their end is a flame of F
22:22 the furnace precede the F; so insults precede
23:16 heated like a burning F will not be quenched
23:16 never cease until the F burns him up.
28:10 the fuel for the F, so will be the
28:11 A hasty quarrel kindles F, and urgent strife sheds
31:26 F and water prove the temper of steel, so
38:28 the breath of the F melts his flesh, and
39:26 life are water and F and iron and salt
39:29 F and hail and famine and pestilence, all these
40:30 in his stomach a F is kindled.
43:21 the wilderness, and withers the tender grass like F
45:19 wonders against them to consume them in flaming F
48:1 Elijah arose like a F, and his word burned
48:3 the heavens, and also three times brought down F
48:9 by a whirlwind of F, in a chariot with
48:9 chariot with horses of F;
49:6 foreign nation, who set F to the chosen city
50:9 a summer day; like F and incense in the
51:4 I endured, from choking F on every side and
51:4 from the midst of F which I did not
Is 1:7 cities are burned with F; in your very presence
4:5 shining of a flaming F by night; for over
5:24 as the tongue of F devours the stubble, and
9:5 blood will be burned as fuel for the F
9:18 wickedness burns like a F, it consumes briers and
9:19 like fuel for the F; no man spares his
10:16 burning will be kindled, like the burning of F
10:17 Israel will become a F, and his Holy One
26:11 Let the F for thy adversaries consume them.
27:11 come and make a F of them.
29:6 and tempest, and the flame of a devouring F
30:14 with which to take F from the hearth, or
30:27 is like a devouring F;
30:30 a flame of devouring F, with a cloudburst and
30:33 deep and wide, with F and wood in abundance;
31:9 says the LORD, whose F is in Zion, and
33:11 your breath is a F that will consume you.
33:12 thorns cut down, that are burned in the F
33:14 "Who among us can dwell with the devouring F
37:19 their gods into the F; for they were no
42:25 it set him on F round about, but he
43:2 when you walk through F you shall not be
44:15 himself, he kindles a F and bakes bread; also
44:16 he burns in the F; over the half he

44:16 "Aha, I am warm, I have seen the F
44:19 I burned in the F, I also baked bread
47:14 are like stubble, the F consumes them; they cannot
47:14 oneself is this, no F to sit before!
50:11 you who kindle a F, who set brands alight.
50:11 the light of your F, and by the brands
54:16 smith who blows the F of coals, and produces
64:2 presence-- as when F kindles brushwood and the
64:2 kindles brushwood and the F causes water to boil--
64:11 has been burned by F, and all our pleasant
65:5 in my nostrils, a F that burns all the
66:15 LORD will come in F, and his chariots like
66:15 in fury, and his rebuke with flames of F
66:16 For by F will the LORD execute judgment, and
66:24 shall not die, their F shall not be quenched,
Jer 4:4 wrath go forth like F, and burn with none
5:14 in your mouth a F, and this people wood,
5:14 people wood, and the F shall devour them.
6:29 is consumed by the F; in vain the refining
7:18 wood, the fathers kindle F, and the women knead
7:31 their daughters in the F; which I did not
11:16 tempest he will set F to it, and its
15:14 in my anger a F is kindled which shall
17:4 in my anger a F is kindled which shall
17:27 I will kindle a F in its gates, and
19:5 their sons in the F as burnt offerings to
20:9 it were a burning F shut up in my
21:10 shall burn it with F
21:12 wrath go forth like F, and burn with none
21:14 I will kindle a F in her forest, and
22:7 your choicest cedars, and cast them into the F
23:29 not my word like F, says the LORD, and
29:22 whom the king of Babylon roasted in the F
32:29 set this city on F, and burn it, with
34:2 of Babylon, and he shall burn it with F
34:22 it, and take it, and burn it with F
36:22 and there was a F burning in the brazier
36:23 throw them into the F in the brazier, until
36:23 was consumed in the F that was in the
36:32 had burned in the F; and many similar words
37:8 they shall take it and burn it with F
37:10 would rise up and burn this city with F
38:17 not be burned with F, and you and your
38:18 shall burn it with F, and you shall not
38:23 Babylon; and this city shall be burned with F
43:12 He shall kindle a F in the temples of
43:13 the gods of Egypt he shall burn with F
48:45 without strength; for a F has gone forth from
49:2 shall be burned with F; then Israel shall dispossess
49:27 I will kindle a F in the wall of
50:32 I will kindle a F in his cities, and
51:30 her dwellings are on F, her bars are broken.
51:32 bulwarks are burned with F, and the soldiers are
51:58 and her high gates shall be burned with F
51:58 nought, and the nations weary themselves only for F
Lam 1:13 on high he sent F; into my bones he
2:3 burned like a flaming F in Jacob, consuming all
2:4 Zion; he has poured out his fury like F
4:11 and he kindled a F in Zion, which consumed
Bar 1:2 the Chaldeans took Jerusalem and burned it with F
4:35 For F will come upon her from the Everlasting
6:55 When F breaks out in a temple of wooden
6:63 And the F sent from above to consume mountains
Ezek 1:4 round about it, and F flashing forth continually, and
1:4 the midst of the F, as it were gleaming
1:13 like burning coals of F, like torches moving to
1:13 living creatures; and the F was bright, and out
1:13 and out of the F went forth lightning.
1:27 like the appearance of F enclosed round about; and
1:27 were the appearance of F, and there was brightness
5:2 shall burn in the F in the midst of
5:4 cast them into the F, and burn them in
5:4 burn them in the F; from there a fire
5:4 fire; from there a F will come forth into
8:2 his loins it was F, and above his loins
10:6 clothed in linen, "Take F from between the whirling
10:7 the cherubim to the F that was between the
15:4 is given to the F for fuel; when the
15:4 for fuel; when the F has consumed both ends
15:5 much less, when the F has consumed it and
15:6 have given to the F for fuel, so will
15:7 they escape from the F, the fire shall yet
15:7 from the fire, the F shall yet consume them;
16:21 as an offering by F to them?
19:12 stem was withered; the F consumed it.
19:14 And F has gone out from its stem, has
20:26 making them offer by F all their first-born, that
20:31 sacrifice your sons by F, you defile yourselves with
20:47 I will kindle a F in you, and it
21:31 upon you with the F of my wrath; and
21:32 be fuel for the F; your blood shall be
22:20 furnace, to blow the F upon it in order
22:21 upon you with the F of my wrath, and
22:31 consumed them with the F of my wrath; their
23:25 daughters, and your survivors shall be devoured by F
24:10 the logs, kindle the F, boil well the flesh,
24:12 rust does not go out of it by F
28:14 of the stones of F you walked.
28:16 out from the midst of the stones of F
28:18 so I brought forth F from the midst of
30:8 when I have set F to Egypt, and all
30:14 desolation, and will set F to Zoan, and will
30:16 And I will set F to Egypt; Pelusium shall
38:22 torrential rains and hailstones, F and brimstone.
39:6 I will send F on Magog and on those
Dan 3:22 the flame of the F slew those men who
3:25 the midst of the F he opened his mouth
3:50 wind, so that the F did not touch them
3:67 Bless the Lord, F and heat, sing praise to
3:89 the midst of the F he has delivered us.
3:92 we not cast three men bound into the F
3:93 the midst of the F, and they are not
3:94 Meshach, and Abednego came out from the F
3:95 and saw that the F had not had any
3:95 and no smell of F had come upon them.
7:9 throne was fiery flames, its wheels were burning F
7:10 A stream of F issued and came forth from
7:11 destroyed and given over to be burned with F
Hos 7:5 ceases to stir the F, from the kneading of
7:7 in the morning it blazes like a flaming F
8:14 I will send a F upon his cities, and
Joel 1:18 For F has devoured the pastures of the wilderness,
1:19 are dried up, and F has devoured the pastures
2:3 F devours before them, and behind them a flame
2:5 of a flame of F devouring the stubble, like
2:30 the earth, blood and F and columns of smoke.
Amos 1:4 I will send a F upon the house of
1:7 I will send a F upon the wall of
1:10 I will send a F upon the wall of
1:12 I will send a F upon Teman, and it
1:14 I will kindle a F in the wall of
2:2 I will send a F upon Moab, and it
2:5 I will send a F upon Judah, and it
5:6 he break out like F in the house of
7:4 for a judgment by F, and it devoured the
Obad 1:18 Jacob shall be a F, and the house of
Mic 1:4 like wax before the F, like waters poured down
1:7 shall be burned with F, and all her idols
Nah 1:6 is poured out like F, and the rocks are
3:13 open to your foes; F has devoured your bars.
3:15 There will the F devour you, the sword will
Hab 2:13 peoples labor only for F, and nations weary
Zeph 1:18 In the F of his jealous wrath, all the
3:8 anger; for in the F of my jealous wrath
Zech 2:5 her a wall of F round about, says the
3:2 Is not this a brand plucked from the F
9:4 the sea, and she shall be devoured by F
11:1 O Lebanon, that the F may devour your cedars!
13:9 this third into the F, and refine them as
Mal 1:10 you might not kindle F upon my altar in
3:2 is like a refiner's F and like fullers' soap;
1Mac 1:31 city, burned it with F, and tore down its
1:56 found they tore to pieces and burned with F
5:5 destruction, and burned with F their towers and all
5:28 seized all its spoils and burned it with F
5:35 in it, plundered it, and burned it with F
5:44 the sacred precincts with F, together with all who
5:68 gods he burned with F; he plundered the cities
6:31 and burned these with F, and fought manfully.
6:51 of war to throw F and stones, machines to
9:67 the city and set F to the machines of
10:84 had taken refuge in it he burned with F
11:48 They set F to the city and seized much
11:61 burned its suburbs with F and plundered them.
16:10 John burned it with F, and about two thousand
2Mac 1:18 the feast of the F given when Nehemiah, who
1:19 took some of the F of the altar and
1:20 who had hidden the F to get it.
1:20 they had not found F but thick liquid, he
1:22 shone out, a great F blazed up, so that
1:33 priests had hidden the F, the liquid had appeared
2:1 take some of the F, as has been told,

2:10 to the Lord, and F came down from heaven
2:10 Solomon prayed, and the F came down and
7:5 take him to the F, still breathing, and to
8:6 warning, he would set F to towns and villages.
8:33 those who had set F to the sacred gates,
9:7 filled with arrogance, breathing F in his rage against
10:3 of sacrifice; then, striking F out of flint, they
10:36 the defenders and set F to the towers; they
12:6 He set F to the harbor by night, and
12:9 by night and set F to the harbor and
13:8 against the altar whose F and ashes were holy,
14:41 courtyard, they ordered that F be brought and the
Mt 3:10 fruit is cut down and thrown into the F
3:11 baptize you with the Holy Spirit and with F
3:12 but the chaff he will burn with unquenchable F
5:22 fool!' shall be liable to the hell of F
7:19 fruit is cut down and thrown into the F
13:40 gathered and burned with F, so will it be
13:42 into the furnace of F; there men will weep
13:50 into the furnace of F; there men will weep
17:15 he falls into the F, and often into the
18:8 two feet to be thrown into the eternal F
18:9 eyes to be thrown into the hell of F
25:41 cursed, into the eternal F prepared for the devil
Mk 9:22 cast him into the F and into the water,
9:43 hands to go to hell, to the unquenchable F
9:46 not die, and the F is not quenched.
9:47 For every one will be salted with F
14:54 with the guards, and warming himself at the F
Lk 3:9 fruit is cut down and thrown into the F
3:16 baptize you with the Holy Spirit and with F
3:17 but the chaff he will burn with unquenchable F
9:54 want us to bid F come down from heaven
12:49 "I came to cast F upon the earth; and
17:29 went out from Sodom F and sulphur rained from
22:53 they had kindled a F in the middle of
Jn 15:6 gathered, thrown into the F and burned.
18:18 had made a charcoal F, because it was cold,
21:9 they saw a charcoal F there, with fish lying
Acts 2:3 them tongues as of F, distributed and resting on
2:19 earth beneath, blood, and F, and vapor of smoke;
7:30 in a flame of F in a bush.
28:2 for they kindled a F and welcomed us all,
28:3 put them on the F, when a viper came
28:5 the creature into the F and suffered no harm.
1Cor 3:13 will be revealed with F, and the fire will
3:13 with fire, and the F will test what sort
3:15 himself will be saved, but only as through F
2Thes 1:7 mighty angels in flaming F,
Heb 1:7 his angels winds, and his servants flames of F
10:27 and a fury of F which will consume the
11:34 of lions, quenched raging F, escaped the edge of
12:18 be touched, a blazing F, and darkness, and gloom,
12:29 and awe; for our God is a consuming F
Jas 3:5 a forest is set ablaze by a small F
3:6 And the tongue is a F
3:6 whole body, setting on F the cycle of nature,
3:6 nature, and set on F by hell.
5:3 against you and will eat your flesh like F
1Pet 1:7 perishable is tested by F, may redound to praise
2Pet 3:7 been stored up for F, being kept until the
3:10 will be dissolved with F, and the earth and
3:12 and dissolved, and the elements will melt with F
Jude 1:7 an example by undergoing a punishment of eternal F
1:23 them out of the F; on some have mercy
Rev 1:14 like a flame of F,
2:18 like a flame of F, and whose feet are
3:18 me gold refined by F, that you may be
4:5 burn seven torches of F, which are the seven
8:5 and filled it with F from the altar and
8:7 there followed hail and F, mixed with blood, which
8:8 great mountain, burning with F, was thrown into the
9:17 breastplates the color of F and of sapphire and
9:17 like lions' heads, and F and smoke and sulphur
9:18 was killed, by the F and smoke and sulphur
10:1 the sun, and his legs like pillars of F
11:5 one would harm them, F pours out from their
13:13 great signs, even making F come down from heaven
14:10 shall be tormented with F and sulphur in the
14:18 who has power over F, and he called with
15:2 of glass mingled with F, and those who had
16:8 to scorch men with F;
17:16 burn her up with F,
18:8 shall be burned with F; for mighty is the
19:12 like a flame of F, and on his head
19:20 into the lake of F that burns with sulphur.
20:9 the beloved city; but F came down from heaven
20:10 into the lake of F and sulphur where the
20:14 and Hades were thrown into the lake of F
20:14 death, the lake of F;
20:15 life, he was thrown into the lake of F
21:8 lake that burns with F and sulphur, which is

FIRE-QUENCHING

Wis 19:20 and water forgot its F nature.

FIREBRANDS (2)

Prov 26:18 a madman who throws F, arrows, and death,
Is 7:4 two smoldering stumps of F, at the fierce anger

FIRED (2)

2Mac 7:21 a noble spirit, she F her woman's reasoning with
10:35 the army of Maccabeus, F with anger because of

FIREPANS (7)

Ex 27:3 basins and forks and F; all its utensils you
38:3 the forks, and the F: all its utensils he
Num 4:14 the service there, the F, the forks, the shovels,
1Kgs 7:50 dishes for incense, and F, of pure gold; and
2Kgs 25:15 the temple service, the F also, and the bowls.
2Chr 4:22 dishes for incense, and F, of pure gold; and
Jer 52:19 small bowls, and the F, and the basins, and

FIRES (9)

2Chr 21:19 his honor, like the F made for his fathers.
Jud 7:5 when they had kindled F on their towers they
Ezek 39:9 go forth and make F of the weapons and
39:9 and they will make F of them for seven
39:10 they will make their F of the weapons; they
Dan 3:46 cease feeding the furnace F with naphtha, pitch, tow,
1Mac 12:28 heart; so they kindled F in their camp and
12:29 for they saw the F burning.
2Mac 10:36 towers; they kindled F and burned the blasphemers

FIRM (30)

Ex 14:13 people, "Fear not, stand F, and see the salvation
1Chr 16:30 yea, the world stands F, never to be moved.
Neh 9:38 this we make a F covenant and write it,
Job 4:4 and you have made F the feeble knees.
Ps 89:2 ever, thy faithfulness is F as the heavens.
89:28 my covenant will stand F for him.
89:37 ever; it shall stand F while the skies endure.
112:7 tidings; his heart is F, trusting in the LORD.
Prov 8:28 deep, when he made F the skies above, when
12:12 ruin, but the root of the righteous stands F
Wis 4:3 root or take a F hold.
Sir 22:16 place will not stand F against the wind; so
22:16 purpose will not stand F against any fear.
42:17 the universe may stand F in his glory.
46:3 Who before him ever stood so F
Is 22:17 He will seize F hold on you,
33:23 cannot hold the mast F in its place, or
35:3 weak hands, and make F the feeble knees.
Dan 11:32 their God shall stand F and take action.
1Mac 1:62 many in Israel stood F and were resolved in
14:26 his father have stood F; they have fought and
1Cor 16:13 Be watchful, stand F in your faith, be courageous,
2Cor 1:24 joy, for you stand F in your faith.
Phil 1:27 you that you stand F in one spirit, with
4:1 joy and crown, stand F thus in the Lord,
2Thes 2:15 So then, brethren, stand F and hold to the
2Tim 2:19 But God's F foundation stands, bearing this seal:
Tit 1:8 self-controlled; he must hold F to the sure word
Heb 3:14 hold our first confidence F to the end,
1Pet 5:9 Resist him, F in your faith, knowing that the

FIRMAMENT (20)

Gen 1:6 "Let there be a F in the midst of
1:7 And God made the F and separated the waters
1:7 which were under the F from the waters which
1:7 firmament from the waters which were above the F
1:8 And God called the F Heaven.
1:14 be lights in the F of the heavens to
1:15 be lights in the F of the heavens to
1:17 set them in the F of the heavens to
1:20 the earth across the F of the heavens."
Ps 19:1 of God; and the F proclaims his handiwork.
150:1 in his sanctuary; praise him in his mighty F
Sir 43:1 heights is the clear F, the appearance of heaven
43:8 shining forth in the F of heaven.
Ezek 1:22 the likeness of a F, shining like crystal, spread
1:23 And under the F their wings were stretched out

1:25 voice from above the F over their heads; when
1:26 And above the F over their heads there was
10:1 and behold, on the F that was over the
Dan 3:57 art thou in the F of heaven and to
12:3 the brightness of the F; and those who turn

FIRMLY (15)

1Kgs 2:12 and his kingdom was F established.
2Kgs 14:5 the royal power was F in his hand he
2Chr 25:3 the royal power was F in his hand he
Jud 14:10 had done, he believed F in God, and was
Job 41:23 his flesh cleave together, F cast upon him and
Ps 119:89 LORD, thy word is F fixed in the heavens.
122:3 city which is bound F together,
Eccl 12:11 goads, and like nails F fixed are the collected
Sir 22:14 A wooden beam F bonded into a building will
22:14 earthquake; so the mind F fixed on a reasonable
27:2 a stake is driven F into a fissure between
28:1 Lord, and he will F establish his sins.
1Mac 15:34 the opportunity, we are F holding the inheritance of
1Cor 7:37 But whoever is F established in his heart, being
2Tim 3:14 have learned and have F believed, knowing from

FIRMNESS (2)

Dan 2:41 but some of the F of iron shall be
Col 2:5 good order and the F of your faith in

FIRST (450)

Gen 2:11 The name of the F is Pishon; it is
8:5 tenth month, on the F day of the month,
8:13 the six hundred and F year, in the first
8:13 first year, in the F month, the first day
8:13 the first month, the F day of the month,
9:20 Noah was the F tiller of the soil.
10:8 Nimrod; he was the F on earth to be
13:4 an altar at the F; and there Abram called
25:25 The F came forth red, all his body like
25:31) Jacob said, F sell me your birthright."
25:33 Jacob said, "Swear to me F
28:19 name of the city was Luz at the F
38:28 hand a scarlet thread, saying, "This came out F
41:20 cows ate up the F seven fat cows,
43:18 in our sacks the F time, that we are
43:20 we came down the F time to buy food;
49:3 my might, and the F fruits of my strength,
Ex 4:8 said, "or heed the F sign, they may believe
12:2 it shall be the F month of the year
12:15 unleavened bread; on the F day you shall put
12:15 is leavened, from the F day until the seventh
12:16 On the F day you shall hold a holy
12:18 In the F month, on the fourteenth day of
13:2 first-born; whatever is the F to open the womb
13:12 the LORD all that F opens the womb.
13:15 all the males that F open the womb; but
23:16 of harvest, of the F fruits of your labor,
23:19 "The F of the first fruits of your ground
23:19 "The first of the F fruits of your ground
26:4 outmost curtain in the F set; and likewise you
26:24 the top, at the F ring; thus shall it
28:17 carbuncle shall be the F row;
29:40 evening; and with the F lamb a tenth measure
34:1 of stone like the F; and I will write
34:1 that were on the F tables, which you broke.
34:4 of stone like the F; and he rose early
34:22 feast of weeks, the F fruits of wheat harvest,
34:26 The F of the first fruits of your ground
34:26 The first of the F fruits of your ground
36:11 outmost curtain of the F set; likewise he made
36:29 the top, at the F ring; he made two
39:10 and carbuncle was the F row;
Lev 2:12 As an offering of F fruits you may bring
2:14 a cereal offering of F fruits to the LORD,
2:14 cereal offering of your F fruits crushed new grain
4:21 as he burned the F bull; it is the
5:8 priest, who shall offer F the one for the
9:15 for sin, like the F sin offering.
23:5 In the F month, on the fourteenth day of
23:7 On the F day you shall have a holy
23:10 the sheaf of the F fruits of your harvest
23:17 baked with leaven, as F fruits to the LORD.
23:20 the bread of the F fruits as a wave
23:24 seventh month, on the F day of the month,
23:35 On the F day shall be a holy convocation;
23:39 seven days; on the F day shall be a
23:40 shall take on the F day the fruit of
Num 1:1 of meeting, on the F day of the second
1:18 named, and on the F day of the second
2:9 They shall set out F on the march.
7:12 offered his offering the F day was Nahshon the
9:1 of Sinai, in the F month of the second
9:5 the passover in the F month, on the fourteenth
10:13 set out for the F time at the command
10:14 of Judah set out F by their companies; and
15:20 Of the F of your coarse meal you shall
15:21 Of the F of your coarse meal you shall
18:12 of the grain, the F fruits of what they
20:1 of Zin in the F month, and the people
24:20 said, "Amalek was the F of the nations, but
28:16 fourteenth day of the F month is the LORD's
28:18 On the F day there shall be a holy
28:26 the day of the F fruits, when you offer
29:1 "On the F day of the seventh month you
33:3 from Rameses in the F month, on the fifteenth
33:3 fifteenth day of the F month; on the day
33:38 of Egypt, on the F day of the fifth
Deut 1:3 fortieth year, on the F day of the eleventh
10:1 of stone like the F, and come up to
10:2 that were on the F tables which you broke,
10:3 of stone like the F, and went up the
10:4 tables, as at the F writing, the ten commandments
10:10 mountain, as at the F time, forty days and
13:9 your hand shall be F against him to put
16:4 the evening of the F day remain all night
16:9 from the time you F put the sickle to
17:7 the witnesses shall be F against him to put
18:4 The F fruits of your grain, of your wine
18:4 your oil, and the F of the fleece of
21:17 for he is the F issue of his strength;
25:6 And the F son whom she bears shall succeed
26:2 take some of the F of all the fruit
26:10 now I bring the F of the fruit of
Josh 4:19 tenth day of the F month, and they encamped
8:33 had commanded at the F, that they should bless
21:10 the Levites; since the lot fell to them F
Judg 1:1 "Who shall go up F for us against the
18:29 name of the city was Laish at the F
20:18 us shall go up F to battle against the
20:18 And the LORD said, "Judah shall go up F
20:22 formed it on the F day.
20:32 "They are routed before us, as at the F
20:39 us, as in the F battle."
Ruth 3:10 kindness greater than the F, in that you have
1Sam 2:16 them burn the fat F, and then take as
14:14 after him; and that F slaughter, which Jonathan and
14:35 LORD; it was the F altar that he built
22:15 Is today the F time that I have inquired
2Sam 3:13 my face, unless you F bring Michal, Saul's daughter,
17:9 people fall at the F attack, whoever hears it
19:20 come this day, the F of all the house
19:43 Were we not the F to speak of bringing
21:9 to death in the F days of harvest, at
1Kgs 1:51 Solomon swear to me F that he will not
3:22 The F said, "No, the dead child is yours,
3:27 living child to the F woman, and by no
17:13 you have said; but F make me a little
18:25 bull and prepare it F, for you are many;
20:9 king, 'All that you F demanded of your servant
20:17 of the governors of the districts went out F
22:5 king of Israel, "Inquire F for the word of
2Kgs 4:42 God bread of the F fruits, twenty loaves of
1Chr 9:2 Now the F to dwell again in their possessions
11:6 shall smite the Jebusites F shall be chief and
11:6 of Zeruiah went up F, so he became chief.
12:15 the Jordan in the F month, when it was
15:13 not carry it the F time, the LORD our
16:7 on that day David F appointed that thanksgiving be
24:7 The F lot fell to Jehoiarib, the second to
25:9 The F lot fell for Asaph to Joseph; the
27:2 in charge of the F division in the first
27:2 first division in the F month; in his division
27:3 the army for the F month.
29:29 of King David, from F to last, are written
2Chr 3:12 the wing of the F cherub.
9:29 acts of Solomon, from F to last, are they
12:15 acts of Rehoboam, from F to last, are they
16:11 acts of Asa, from F to last, are written
18:4 king of Israel, "Inquire F for the word of
20:34 acts of Jehoshaphat, from F to last, are written
25:26 deeds of Amaziah, from F to last, are they
26:22 acts of Uzziah, from F to last, Isaiah the
28:26 all his ways, from F to last, behold, they
29:3 In the F year of his reign, in the

F

29:3 his reign, in the F month, he opened the
29:17 to sanctify on the F day of the first
29:17 first day of the F month, and on the
29:17 sixteenth day of the F month they finished.
31:5 gave in abundance the F fruits of grain, wine,
35:1 fourteenth day of the F month.
35:27 LORD, and his acts, F and last, behold, they
36:22 Now in the F year of Cyrus king of
Ezra 1:1 In the F year of Cyrus King
3:6 From the F day of the seventh month they
3:12 who had seen the F house, wept with a
5:13 However in the F year of Cyrus king of
6:3 In the F year of Cyrus the king, Cyrus
6:19 fourteenth day of the F month the returned exiles
7:9 king; for on the F day of the first
7:9 first day of the F month he began to
7:9 Babylonia, and on the F day of the fifth
8:31 twelfth day of the F month, to go to
10:16 On the F day of the tenth month they
10:17 matter; and by the F day of the first
10:17 first day of the F month they had come
Neh 7:5 came up at the F, and I found written
8:2 with understanding, on the F day of the seventh
8:18 by day, from the F day to the last
10:35 ourselves to bring the F fruits of our ground
10:35 our ground and the F fruits of all fruit
10:37 and to bring the F of our coarse meal,
12:44 stores, the contributions, the F fruits, and the tithes,
13:31 times, and for the F fruits.
Tob 1:6 Taking the F fruits and the tithes of my
1:6 my produce and the F shearings, I would give
4:12 F of all take a wife from among the
Jud 2:1 twenty-second day of the F month, there was talk
8:29 Today is not the F time your wisdom has
11:13 decided to consume the F fruits of the grain
12:16 since the day he F saw her.
Esth 1:14 king's face, and sat F in the kingdom--:
3:7 In the F month, which is the month of
3:12 thirteenth day of the F month, and an edict,
11:2 the Great, on the F day of Nisan, Mordecai
Job 15:7 "Are you the F man that was born?
40:19 "He is the F of the works of God;
42:14 the name of the F Jemimah; and the name
Ps 78:51 first-born in Egypt, the F issue of their strength
105:36 in their land, the F issue of all their
Prov 3:9 substance and with the F fruits of all your
8:22 of his work, the F of his acts of
8:23 set up, at the F, before the beginning of
8:26 its fields, or the F of the dust of
18:17 who states his case F seems right, until the
Wis 7:3 kindred earth, and my F sound was a cry,
Sir 4:17 For at F she will walk with him on
7:31 is commanded you: the F fruits, the guilt offering,
7:31 of sanctification, and the F fruits of the holy
11:7 fault before you investigate; F consider, and then
23:23 For F of all, she has disobeyed the law
24:23 the time of the F fruits.
24:26 Just as the F man did not know her
31:17 Be the F to stop eating, for the sake
35:8 do not stint the F fruits of your hands.
37:8 a counselor, and learn F what is his interest--
45:20 allotted to him the F of the first fruits,
45:20 the first of the F fruits, he prepared bread
45:20 he prepared bread of F fruits in abundance;
50:8 the days of the F fruits, like lilies by
51:20 with her from the F, therefore I will not
Is 1:26 judges as at the F, and your counselors as
41:4 I, the LORD, the F, and with the last;
41:27 I F have declared it to Zion, and I
43:27 Your F father sinned, and your mediators
44:6 hosts: "I am the F and I am the
48:12 He, I am the F, and I am the
52:4 went down at the F into Egypt to sojourn
60:9 the ships of Tarshish F, to bring your sons
Jer 2:3 to the LORD, the F fruits of his harvest.
4:31 one bringing forth her F child, the cry of
7:12 my name dwell at F, and see what I
25:1 Judah (that was the F year of Nebuchadrezzar king
33:7 Israel, and rebuild them as they were at F
33:11 the land as at F, says the LORD.
36:28 that were in the F scroll, which Jehoiakim the
50:17 F the king of Assyria devoured him, and now
Ezek 10:14 had four faces: the F face was the face
26:1 eleventh year, on the F day of the month,
29:17 twenty-seventh year, in the F month, on the first
29:17 first month, on the F day of the month,
30:20 eleventh year, in the F month, on the seventh
31:1 third month, on the F day of the month,
32:1 twelfth month, on the F day of the month,
32:17 twelfth year, in the F month, on the fifteenth
40:21 as those of the F gate; its length was
44:30 And the F of all the first fruits of
44:30 first of all the F fruits of all kinds,
44:30 to the priests the F of your coarse meal,
45:18 Lord GOD: In the F month, on the first
45:18 first month, on the F day of the month,
45:21 "In the F month, on the fourteenth day of
Dan 1:21 Daniel continued until the F year of King Cyrus.
7:1 In the F year of Belshazzar king of Babylon,
7:4 The F was like a lion and had eagles'
7:8 which three of the F horns were plucked up
8:1 after that which appeared to me at the F
8:21 his eyes is the F king.
9:1 In the F year of Darius the son of
9:2 Chaldeans-- in the F year of his reign,
9:21 the vision at the F, came to me in
10:4 twenty-fourth day of the F month, as I was
10:12 Daniel, for from the F day that you set
11:1 for me, in the F year of Darius the
Hos 1:2 When the LORD F spoke through Hosea, the LORD
2:7 and return to my F husband, for it was
9:10 Like the F fruit on the fig tree, in
9:10 fig tree, in its F season, I saw your
Amos 6:1 notable men of the F of the nations, to
6:7 shall now be the F of those to go
Hag 1:1 sixth month, on the F day of the month,
Zech 6:2 The F chariot had red horses, the second black
12:7 the tents of Judah F, that the glory of
1Mac 2:18 Now be the F to come and do what
3:49 the priesthood and the F fruits and the tithes,
5:40 crosses over to us F, we will not be
5:43 crossed over against them F, and the whole army
6:2 Macedonian king who F reigned over the Greeks.
6:6 that Lysias had gone F with a strong force,
7:13 The Hasideans were F among the sons of Israel
7:43 he himself was the F to fall in the
8:24 If war comes F to Rome or to any
8:27 way, if war comes F to the nation of
9:3 In the F month of the one hundred and
10:4 said, "Let us act F to make peace with
10:41 they did in the F years, they shall give
10:47 he had been the F to speak peaceable words
13:42 and contracts, "In the F year of Simon the
16:6 so he crossed over F; and when his men
2Mac 4:33 publicly exposed them, having F withdrawn to a
7:7 After the F brother had died in this way,
7:8 underwent tortures as the F brother had done.
8:23 help"; then, leading the F division himself, he joined
11:7 Maccabeus himself was the F to take up arms,
12:22 But when Judas' F division appeared, terror and fear
14:8 have now come here, F because I am genuinely
15:18 heavily; their greatest and F fear was for the
Mt 5:24 the altar and go; F be reconciled to your
6:33 But seek F his kingdom and his righteousness, and
7:5 You hypocrite, F take the log out of your
8:21 him, "Lord, let me F go and bury my
10:2 twelve apostles are these: F, Simon, who is called
12:29 his goods, unless he F binds the strong man?
12:45 state of that man becomes worse than the F
13:30 reapers, Gather the weeds F and bind them in
17:10 the scribes say that F Elijah must come?"
17:24 Jesus spoke to him F, saying, "What do you
17:26 hook, and take the F fish that comes up,
19:30 But many that are F will be last, and
19:30 are first will be last, and the last F
20:8 last, up to the F
20:10 Now when the F came, they thought they would
20:16 the last will be F, and the first last."
20:16 be first, and the F last."
20:27 and whoever would be F among you must be
21:28 he went to the F and said, 'Son, go
21:31 They said, "The F
21:36 servants, more than the F; and they did the
22:25 brothers among us; the F married, and died, and
22:38 is the great and F commandment.
23:25 F cleanse the inside of the cup and of
26:17 Now on the F day of Unleavened Bread the
27:64 the last fraud will be worse than the F
28:1 the dawn of the F day of the week,
Mk 3:27 his goods, unless he F binds the strong man;
4:28 earth produces of itself, F the blade, then the
7:26 her, "Let the children F be fed, for it

9:11 the scribes say that F Elijah must come?"
9:12 them, "Elijah does come F to restore all things;
9:35 any one would be F, he must be last
10:31 But many that are F will be last, and
10:31 are first will be last, and the last F
10:44 and whoever would be F among you must be
12:20 were seven brothers; the F took a wife, and
12:28 "Which commandment is the F of all?"
12:29 Jesus answered, "The F is, 'Hear, O Israel: The
13:10 And the gospel must F be preached to all
14:12 And on the F day of Unleavened Bread, when
16:2 very early on the F day of the week
16:9 rose early on the F day of the week,
16:9 the week, he appeared F to Mary Magdalene, from
Lk 2:2 This was the F enrollment, when Quirinius was
6:42 You hypocrite, F take the log out of your
9:59 said, "Lord, let me F go and bury my
9:61 Lord; but let me F say farewell to those
10:5 Whatever house you enter, F say, 'Peace be to
11:26 state of that man becomes worse than the F
11:38 that he did not F wash before dinner.
12:1 say to his disciples F, "Beware of the leaven
13:30 last who will be F, and some are first
13:30 first, and some are F who will be last."
14:18 The F said to him, 'I have bought a
14:28 a tower, does not F sit down and count
14:31 will not sit down F and take counsel whether
16:5 he said to the F, 'How much do you
17:25 But F he must suffer many things and be
19:16 The F came before him, saying, 'Lord, your pound
20:29 were seven brothers; the F took a wife, and
21:9 terrified; for this must F take place, but the
24:1 But on the F day of the week, at
Jn 1:41 He F found his brother Simon, and said to
2:10 serves the good wine F; and when men have
2:11 This, the F of his signs, Jesus did at
6:64 Jesus knew from the F who those were that
7:51 judge a man without F giving him a hearing
8:7 among you be the F to throw a stone
10:40 place where John at F baptized, and there he
12:16 not understand this at F; but when Jesus was
18:13 F they led him to Annas; for he was
19:32 the legs of the F, and of the other
19:39 also, who had at F come to him by
20:1 Now on the F day of the week Mary
20:4 and reached the tomb F;
20:8 who reached the tomb F, also went in, and
20:19 of that day, the F day of the week,
Acts 1:1 In the F book, O Theophilus, I
3:26 sent him to you F, to bless you in
7:12 forth our fathers the F time.
11:26 disciples were for the F time called Christians.
12:10 they had passed the F and the second guard,
13:46 God should be spoken F to you.
15:14 has related how God F visited the Gentiles, to
20:7 On the F day of the week, when we
20:18 the time from the F day that I set
26:20 heavenly vision, but declared F to those at Damascus,
26:23 that, by being the F to rise from the
27:43 to throw themselves overboard F and make for the
Rom 1:8 F, I thank my God through Jesus Christ for
1:16 faith, to the Jew F and also to the
2:9 does evil, the Jew F and also the Greek,
2:10 does good, the Jew F and also the Greek.
8:23 ourselves, who have the F fruits of the Spirit,
10:19 F Moses says, "I will make you jealous of
11:16 the dough offered as F fruits is holy, so
13:11 now than when we F believed;
16:5 Epaenetus, who was the F convert in Asia for
1Cor 11:18 For, in the F place, when you assemble as
12:28 appointed in the church F apostles, second prophets,
14:30 sitting by, let the F be silent.
15:3 to you as of F importance what I also
15:20 from the dead, the F fruits of those who
15:23 own order: Christ the F fruits, then at his
15:45 it is written, "The F man Adam became a
15:46 the spiritual which is F but the physical, and
15:47 The F man was from the earth, a man
16:2 On the F day of every week, each of
16:15 of Stephanas were the F converts in Achaia, and
2Cor 1:15 to come to you F, so that you might
8:5 as we expected, but F they gave themselves to
10:14 you; we were the F to come all the
Gal 4:13 gospel to you at F;
Eph 1:12 his will, we who F hoped in Christ have
6:2 (this is the F commandment with a promise),
Phil 1:5 the gospel from the F day until now.
1Thes 4:16 in Christ will rise F;
2Thes 2:3 unless the rebellion comes F, and the man of
1Tim 2:1 F of all, then, I urge that supplications, prayers,
2:13 For Adam was formed F, then Eve;
3:10 them also be tested F; then if they prove
5:4 or grandchildren, let them F learn their religious
5:12 for having violated their F pledge.
2Tim 1:5 a faith that dwelt F in your grandmother Lois
2:6 ought to have the F share of the crops.
4:16 At my F defense no one took my part;
Heb 2:3 It was declared at F by the Lord, and
3:14 only we hold our F confidence firm to the
5:12 teach you again the F principles of God's word.
7:2 He is F, by translation of his name, king
7:27 to offer sacrifices daily, F for his own sins
8:7 For if that F covenant had been faultless, there
8:13 covenant he treats the F as obsolete.
9:1 Now even the F covenant had regulations for
9:15 the transgressions under the F covenant.
9:18 Hence even the F covenant was not ratified without
10:9 He abolishes the F in order to establish the
Jas 1:17 be a kind of F fruits of his creatures.
3:17 wisdom from above is F pure, then peaceable, gentle,
2Pet 1:20 F of all you must understand this, that no
2:20 state has become worse for them than the F
3:3 F of all you must understand this, that scoffers
1Jn 4:19 We love, because he F loved us.
3Jn 1:9 likes to put himself F, does not acknowledge my
Rev 1:17 not, I am the F and the last,
2:4 you have abandoned the love you had at F
2:5 repent and do the works you did at F
2:8 'The words of the F and the last, who
2:19 endurance, and that your latter works exceed the F
4:1 And the F voice, which I had heard speaking
4:7 front and behind: the F living creature like a
8:7 The F angel blew his trumpet, and there followed
9:12 The F woe has passed; behold, two woes are
13:12 the authority of the F beast in its presence,
13:12 its inhabitants worship the F beast, whose mortal
14:4 redeemed from mankind as F fruits for God and
16:2 So the F angel went and poured his bowl
20:5 This is the F resurrection.
20:6 who shares in the F resurrection!
21:1 new earth; for the F heaven and the first
21:1 first heaven and the F earth had passed away,
21:19 with every jewel; the F was jasper, the second
22:13 and the Omega, the F and the last, the

FIRST-BORN (123)

Gen 10:15 father of Sidon his F, and Heth,
19:31 And the F said to the younger, "Our father
19:33 that night; and the F went in, and lay
19:34 the next day, the F said to the younger,
19:37 The F bore a son, and called his name
22:21 brother Nahor: Uz the F, Buz his brother, Kemuel
25:13 their birth: Nebaioth, the F of Ishmael; and Kedar,
27:19 said to his father, "I am Esau your F
27:32 am your son, your F, Esau."
29:26 our country, to give the younger before the F
35:23 Reuben (Jacob's F, Simeon, Levi, Judah, Issachar,
36:15 sons of Eliphaz the F of Esau: the chiefs
38:6 wife for Er his F, and her name was
38:7 But Er, Judah's F, was wicked in the sight
41:51 the name of the F Manasseh, "For," he said,
43:33 sat before him, the F according to his birthright
46:8 Reuben, Jacob's F,
48:14 crossing his hands, for Manasseh was the F
48:18 this one is the F; put your right hand
49:3 Reuben, you are my F, my might, and the
Ex 4:22 LORD, Israel is my F son,
4:23 I will slay your F son.'"
6:14 sons of Reuben, the F of Israel: Hanoch, Pallu,
11:5 Egypt; and all the F in the land of
11:5 shall die, from the F of Pharaoh who sits
11:5 throne, even to the F of the maidservant who
11:5 mill; and all the F of the cattle.
12:12 will smite all the F in the land of
12:29 LORD smote all the F in the land of
12:29 of Egypt, from the F of Pharaoh who sat
12:29 his throne to the F of the captive who
12:29 dungeon, and all the F of the cattle.
13:2 to me all the F; whatever is the first
13:13 Every F of man among your sons you shall
13:15 LORD slew all the F in the land of
13:15 of Egypt, both the F of man and the

13:15 of man and the F of cattle.
13:15 womb; but all the F of my sons I
22:29 "The F of your sons you shall give to
34:20 All the F of your sons you shall redeem.
Num 1:20 people of Reuben, Israel's F, their generations, by
3:2 of Aaron: Nadab the F, and Abihu, Eleazar, and
3:12 Israel instead of every F that opens the womb
3:13 mine, for all the F are mine; on the
3:13 I slew all the F in the land of
3:13 my own all the F in Israel, both of
3:40 Moses, "Number all the F males of the people
3:41 instead of all the F among the people of
3:42 Moses numbered all the F among the people of
3:43 And all the F males, according to the number
3:45 instead of all the F among the people of
3:46 and seventy-three of the F of the people of
3:50 the Levites; from the F of the people of
8:16 open the womb, the F of all the people
8:17 For all the F among the people of Israel
8:17 I slew all the F in the land of
8:18 instead of all the F among the people of
18:15 be yours; nevertheless the F of man you shall
26:5 Egypt, were: Reuben, the F of Israel; the sons
33:4 were burying all their F, whom the LORD had
Deut 21:15 disliked, and if the F son is hers that
21:16 the loved as the F in preference to the
21:16 disliked, who is the F,
21:17 he shall acknowledge the F, the son of the
21:17 the right of the F is his.
Josh 6:26 the cost of his F shall he lay its
17:1 for he was the F of Joseph.
17:1 To Machir the F of Manasseh, the father of
Judg 8:20 said to Jether his F, "Rise, and slay them."
1Sam 8:2 The name of his F son was Joel, and
14:49 the name of the F was Merab, and the
17:13 battle were Eliab the F, and next to him
2Sam 3:2 David at Hebron: his F was Amnon, of Ahino-am
1Kgs 16:34 cost of Abiram his F, and set up its
1Chr 1:13 father of Sidon his F, and Heth,
1:29 are their genealogies: the F of Ishmael, Nebaioth;
2:3 Now Er, Judah's F, was wicked in the sight
2:13 father of Eliab his F, Abinadab the second, Shimea
2:25 sons of Jerahmeel, the F of Hezron: Ram, his
2:25 of Hezron: Ram, his F, Bunah, Oren, Ozem, and
2:27 sons of Ram, the F of Jerahmeel: Maaz, Jamin,
2:42 of Jerahmeel: Mareshah his F, who was the father
2:50 sons of Hur the F of Ephrathah: Shobal the
3:1 him in Hebron: the F Amnon, by Ahino-am the
3:15 of Josiah: Johanan the F, the second Jehoiakim, the
4:4 sons of Hur, the F of Ephrathah, the father
5:1 sons of Reuben the F of Israel (for he
5:1 (for he was the F; but because he polluted
5:3 sons of Reuben, the F of Israel: Hanoch, Pallu,
6:28 of Samuel: Joel his F, the second Abijah.
8:1 father of Bela his F, Ashbel the second, Aharah
8:30 His F son: Abdon, then Zur, Kish, Baal, Nadab,
8:39 his brother: Ulam his F, Jeush the second, and
9:5 the Shilonites: Asaiah the F, and his sons.
9:31 of the Levites, the F of Shallum the Korahite,
9:36 was Maacah, and his F son Abdon, then Zur,
26:2 had sons: Zechariah the F, Jedia-el the second,
26:4 had sons: Shemaiah the F, Jehozabad the second,
26:10 he was not the F, his father made him
2Chr 21:3 the kingdom to Jehoram, because he was the F
Neh 10:36 of our God, the F of our sons and
Tob 5:13 worship and offered the F of our flocks and
Job 18:13 skin is consumed, the F of death consumes his
Ps 78:51 He smote all the F in Egypt, the first
89:27 will make him the F, the highest of the
105:36 He smote all the F in their land, the
135:8 was who smote the F of Egypt, both of
136:10 him who smote the F of Egypt, for his
Wis 18:13 when their F were destroyed, they acknowledged
Sir 36:12 hast likened to a F son.
Is 14:30 And the F of the poor will feed, and
Jer 31:9 a father to Israel, and Ephraim is my F
Ezek 20:26 by fire all their F, that I might horrify
Mic 6:7 Shall I give my F for my transgression, the
Zech 12:10 bitterly over him, as one weeps over a F
Lk 2:7 gave birth to her F son and wrapped him
Rom 8:29 he might be the F among many brethren.
Col 1:15 the invisible God, the F of all creation;
1:18 is the beginning, the F from the dead, that
Heb 1:6 when he brings the F into the world, he
11:28 the Destroyer of the F might not touch them.
12:23 the assembly of the F who are enrolled in

Rev 1:5 the faithful witness, the F of the dead, and

FIRST-FORMED (2)

Wis 7:1 a descendant of the F child of earth; and
10:1 Wisdom protected the F father of the world, when

FIRST-RIPE (6)

Num 13:20 the season of the F grapes.
18:13 The F fruits of all that is in their
Is 28:4 will be like a F fig before the summer:
Jer 24:2 very good figs, like F figs, but the other
Mic 7:1 cluster to eat, no F fig which my soul
Nah 3:12 like fig trees with F figs—if shaken they

FIRSTLING (12)

Ex 13:13 Every F of an ass you shall redeem with
34:20 The F of an ass you shall redeem with
Lev 27:26 "But a F of animals, which as a firstling
27:26 animals, which as a F belongs to the LORD,
Num 18:15 shall redeem, and the F of unclean beasts you
18:17 But the F of a cow, or the firstling
18:17 a cow, or the F of a sheep, or
18:17 a sheep, or the F of a goat, you
Deut 15:19 "All the F males that are born of your
15:19 no work with the F of your herd, nor
15:19 herd, nor shear the F of your flock.
33:17 His F bull has majesty, and his horns are

FIRSTLINGS (8)

Gen 4:4 Abel brought of the F of his flock and
Ex 13:12 All the F of your cattle that are males
34:19 your male cattle, the F of cow and sheep.
Num 3:41 instead of all the F among the cattle of
Deut 12:6 freewill offerings, and the F of your herd and
12:17 your oil, or the F of your herd or
14:23 your oil, and the F of your herd and
Neh 10:36 the law, and the F of our herds and

FISH (72)

Gen 1:26 have dominion over the F of the sea, and
1:28 have dominion over the F of the sea and
9:2 ground and all the F of the sea; into
Ex 7:18 to blood, and the F in the Nile shall
7:21 And the F in the Nile died; and the
Num 11:5 We remember the F we ate in Egypt for
11:22 Or shall all the F of the sea be
Deut 4:18 the likeness of any F that is in the
1Kgs 4:33 and of birds, and of reptiles, and of F
2Chr 33:14 the entrance into the F Gate, and carried it
Neh 3:3 of Hassenaah built the F Gate; they laid its
12:39 Gate, and by the F Gate and the Tower
13:16 the city, brought in F and all kinds of
Tob 6:2 A F leaped up from the river and would
6:3 and the angel said to him, "Catch the F
6:3 young man seized the F and threw it up
6:4 him, "Cut open the F and take the heart
6:5 told him; and they roasted and ate the F
6:6 the liver and heart and gall of the F
6:16 and liver of the F so as to make
8:2 and liver of the F upon them and made
11:4 the gall of the F with you." So they
Job 12:8 teach you; and the F of the sea will
Ps 8:8 the air, and the F of the sea, whatever
105:29 blood, and caused their F to die.
Eccl 9:12 Like F which are taken in an evil net,
Wis 19:10 gnats, and instead of F the river spewed out
Is 50:2 rivers a desert; their F stink for lack of
Ezek 29:4 jaws, and make the F of your streams stick
29:4 streams, with all the F of your streams which
29:5 you and all the F of your streams; you
38:20 land of Israel; the F of the sea, and
47:9 will be very many F; for this water goes
47:10 spreading of nets; its F will be of very
47:10 many kinds, like the F of the Great Sea.
Hos 4:3 air; and even the F of the sea are
Jon 1:17 LORD appointed a great F to swallow up Jonah;
1:17 the belly of the F three days and three
2:1 the belly of the F,
2:10 LORD spoke to the F, and it vomited out
Hab 1:14 makest men like the F of the sea, like
Zeph 1:3 the air and the F of the sea.
1:10 be heard from the F Gate, a wail from
Mt 7:10 he asks for a F, will give him a
13:47 the sea and gathered F of every kind;
14:17 "We have only five loaves here and two F
14:19 loaves and the two F he looked up to

15:34 They said, "Seven, and a few small F
15:36 seven loaves and the F, and having given thanks
17:26 and take the first F that comes up, and
Mk 6:38 had found out, they said, "Five, and two F
6:41 loaves and the two F he looked up to
6:41 he divided the two F among them all.
6:43 baskets full of broken pieces and of the F
8:7 had a few small F; and having blessed them,
Lk 5:6 a great shoal of F; and as their nets
5:9 at the catch of F which they had taken;
9:13 five loaves and two F –unless we are to
9:16 loaves and the two F he looked up to
11:11 son asks for a F, will instead of a
11:11 will instead of a F give him a serpent;
24:42 a piece of broiled F,
Jn 6:9 barley loaves and two F; but what are they
6:11 seated; so also the F, as much as they
21:5 Jesus said to them, "Children, have you any F
21:6 to haul it in, for the quantity of F
21:8 the net full of F, for they were not
21:9 charcoal fire there, with F lying on it, and
21:10 "Bring some of the F that you have just
21:11 ashore, full of large F, a hundred and fifty-three
21:13 gave it to them, and so with the F
1Cor 15:39 for animals, another for birds, and another for F

FISHERMEN (5)
Is 19:8 The F will mourn and lament, all who cast
Ezek 47:10 F will stand beside the sea; from Engedi to
Mt 4:18 a net into the sea; for they were F
Mk 1:16 a net in the sea; for they were F
Lk 5:2 the lake; but the F had gone out of

FISHERS (3)
Jer 16:16 am sending for many F, says the LORD, and
Mt 4:19 I will make you F of men."
Mk 1:17 will make you become F of men."

FISHHOOK
Job 41:1 out Leviathan with a F, or press down his

FISHHOOKS
Amos 4:2 with hooks, even the last of you with F

FISHING (2)
Job 41:7 or his head with F spears?
Jn 21:3 Simon Peter said to them, "I am going F

FISSURE
Sir 27:2 driven firmly into a F between stones, so sin

FIST (4)
Ex 21:18 stone or with his F and the man does
Is 10:32 he will shake his F at the mount of
58:4 and to fight and to hit with wicked F
Zeph 2:15 who passes by her hisses and shakes his F

FISTS
Prov 30:4 Who has gathered the wind in his F

FIT (12)
Gen 2:18 make him a helper F for him."
2:20 not found a helper F for him.
2Kgs 24:16 of them strong and F for war.
2Chr 25:5 hundred thousand picked men, F for war, able to
26:11 an army of soldiers, F for war, in divisions
Wis 1:16 him, because they are F to belong to his
15:6 of evil things and F for such objects of
Sir 31:20 on moderate eating; he rises early, and feels F
36:24 best possession, a helper F for him and a
Lk 9:62 and looks back is F for the kingdom of
14:35 It is F neither for the land nor for
Rom 1:28 they did not see F to acknowledge God, God

FITLY (2)
Prov 25:11 A word F spoken is like apples of gold
Song 5:12 water, bathed in milk, F set.

FITS
Eph 4:29 good for edifying, as F the occasion, that it

FITTED
Ps 11:2 the bow, they have F their arrow to the

FITTEST
2Kgs 10:3 select the best and F of your master's sons

FITTING (17)
Ex 26:17 in each frame, for F together; so shall you
36:22 had two tenons, for F together; he did this
Ezra 4:14 and it is not F for us to witness
Prov 19:10 It is not F for a fool to live
26:1 so honor is not F for a fool.
Eccl 5:18 good and to be F is to eat and
Sir 15:9 of praise is not F on the lips of
32:3 older, for it is F that you should, but
33:28 to work, as is F for him, and if
Mt 3:15 for thus it is F for us to fulfil
Lk 15:32 It was F to make merry and be glad,
Eph 5:3 among you, as is F among saints.
5:4 levity, which are not F; but instead let there
Col 3:18 your husbands, as is F in the Lord.
2Thes 1:3 you, brethren, as is F, because your faith is
Heb 2:10 For it was F that he, for whom and
7:26 For it was F that we should have such

FITTINGLY
2Mac 15:12 manner, one who spoke F and had been trained

FIVE (282)
Gen 5:6 lived a hundred and F years, he became the
5:11 were nine hundred and F years; and he died.
5:30 the birth of Noah F hundred and ninety-five years,
5:32 After Noah was F hundred years old, Noah became
11:11 the birth of Arpachshad F hundred years, and had
11:32 were two hundred and F years; and Terah died
14:9 and Arioch king of Ellasar, four kings against F
18:28 Suppose F of the fifty righteous are lacking?
18:28 thou destroy the whole city for lack of F
43:34 but Benjamin's portion was F times as much as
45:6 and there are yet F years in which there
45:11 for there are yet F years of famine to
45:22 shekels of silver and F festal garments.
47:2 his brothers he took F men and presented them
Ex 22:1 it, he shall pay F oxen for an ox,
26:3 F curtains shall be coupled to one another; and
26:3 another; and the other F curtains shall be coupled
26:9 And you shall couple F curtains by themselves, and
26:26 bars of acacia wood, F for the frames of
26:27 of the tabernacle, and F bars for the frames
26:27 of the tabernacle, and F bars for the frames
26:37 make for the screen F pillars of acacia, and
26:37 and you shall cast F bases of bronze for
27:1 altar of acacia wood, F cubits long and five
27:1 five cubits long and F cubits broad; the altar
27:18 fifty, and the height F cubits, with hangings of
30:23 spices: of liquid myrrh F hundred shekels, and of
30:24 fifty, and of cassia F hundred, according to the
36:10 And he coupled F curtains to one another, and
36:10 another, and the other F curtains he coupled to
36:16 He coupled F curtains by themselves, and six
36:31 bars of acacia wood, F for the frames of
36:32 of the tabernacle, and F bars for the frames
36:32 of the tabernacle, and F bars for the frames
36:38 with needlework; and its F pillars with their hooks.
36:38 of gold, but their F bases were of bronze.
38:1 also of acacia wood; F cubits was its length,
38:1 was its length, and F cubits its breadth; it
38:18 twenty cubits long and F cubits high in its
38:26 hundred and three thousand, F hundred and fifty
Lev 26:8 F of you shall chase a hundred, and a
27:5 the person is from F years old up to
27:6 month old up to F years old, your valuation
27:6 be for a male F shekels of silver, and
Num 1:21 Reuben was forty-six thousand F hundred.
1:33 Ephraim was forty thousand F hundred.
1:41 Asher was forty-one thousand F hundred.
1:46 hundred and three thousand F hundred and fifty.
2:11 numbered being forty-six thousand F hundred.
2:19 numbered being forty thousand F hundred.
2:28 numbered being forty-one thousand F hundred.
2:32 hundred and three thousand F hundred and fifty.
3:22 upward was seven thousand F hundred.
3:47 Levites, you shall take F shekels apiece; reckoning
4:48 them were eight thousand F hundred and eighty.
7:17 peace offerings, two oxen, F rams, five male goats,
7:17 two oxen, five rams, F male goats, and five
7:17 five male goats, and F male lambs a year
7:23 peace offerings, two oxen, F rams, five male goats,
7:23 two oxen, five rams, F male goats, and five
7:23 five male goats, and F male lambs a year
7:29 peace offerings, two oxen, F rams, five male goats,
7:29 two oxen, five rams, F male goats, and five

F

7:29 five male goats, and F male lambs a year
7:35 peace offerings, two oxen, F rams, five male goats,
7:35 two oxen, five rams, F male goats, and five
7:35 five male goats, and F male lambs a year
7:41 peace offerings, two oxen, F rams, five male goats,
7:41 two oxen, five rams, F male goats, and five
7:41 five male goats, and F male lambs a year
7:47 peace offerings, two oxen, F rams, five male goats,
7:47 two oxen, five rams, F male goats, and five
7:47 five male goats, and F male lambs a year
7:53 peace offerings, two oxen, F rams, five male goats,
7:53 two oxen, five rams, F male goats, and five
7:53 five male goats, and F male lambs a year
7:59 peace offerings, two oxen, F rams, five male goats,
7:59 two oxen, five rams, F male goats, and five
7:59 five male goats, and F male lambs a year
7:65 peace offerings, two oxen, F rams, five male goats,
7:65 two oxen, five rams, F male goats, and five
7:65 five male goats, and F male lambs a year
7:71 peace offerings, two oxen, F rams, five male goats,
7:71 two oxen, five rams, F male goats, and five
7:71 five male goats, and F male lambs a year
7:77 peace offerings, two oxen, F rams, five male goats,
7:77 two oxen, five rams, F male goats, and five
7:77 five male goats, and F male lambs a year
7:83 peace offerings, two oxen, F rams, five male goats,
7:83 two oxen, five rams, F male goats, and five
7:83 five male goats, and F male lambs a year
11:19 or two days, or F days, or ten days,
18:16 you shall fix at F shekels in silver, according
26:18 their number, forty thousand F hundred.
26:22 their number, seventy-six thousand F hundred.
26:27 their number, sixty thousand F hundred.
26:37 their number, thirty-two thousand F hundred.
31:8 Hur, and Reba, the F kings of Midian; and
31:28 battle, one out of F hundred, of the persons
31:36 hundred and thirty-seven thousand F hundred sheep,
31:39 asses were thirty thousand F hundred, of which the
31:43 hundred and thirty-seven thousand F hundred sheep,
31:45 cattle, and thirty thousand F hundred asses,
Josh 8:12 And he took about F thousand men, and set
10:5 Then the F kings of the Amorites, the king
10:16 These F kings fled, and hid themselves in the
10:17 was told Joshua, "The F kings have been found,
10:22 cave, and bring those F kings out to me
10:23 so, and brought those F kings out to him
10:26 he hung them on F trees.
13:3 as Canaanite; there are F rulers of the Philistines,
Judg 3:3 are the nations: the F lords of the Philistines,
18:2 So the Danites sent F able men from the
18:7 Then the F men departed, and came to Laish,
18:14 Then the F men who had gone to spy
18:17 the gate; and the F men who had gone
20:45 the rock of Rimmon; F thousand men of them
1Sam 6:4 They answered, F golden tumors and five golden
6:4 "Five golden tumors and F golden mice, according to
6:16 And when the F lords of the Philistines saw
6:18 Philistines belonging to the F lords, both fortified
17:5 of the coat was F thousand shekels of bronze.
17:40 his hand, and chose F smooth stones from the
21:3 Give me F loaves of bread, or whatever is
25:18 skins of wine, and F sheep ready dressed, and
25:18 sheep ready dressed, and F measures of parched
25:42 an ass, and her F maidens attended her; she
2Sam 4:4 He was F years old when the news about
21:8 and Mephibosheth; and the F sons of Merab the
24:9 men of Judah were F hundred thousand.
1Kgs 4:32 proverbs; and his songs were a thousand and F
6:6 The lowest story was F cubits broad, the middle
6:10 whole house, each story F cubits high, and it
6:24 F cubits was the length of one wing of
6:24 of the cherub, and F cubits the length of
7:16 the one capital was F cubits, and the height
7:16 the other capital was F cubits.
7:23 brim to brim, and F cubits high, and a
7:39 he set the stands, F on the south side
7:39 of the house, and F on the north side
7:49 lampstands of pure gold, F on the south side
7:49 the south side and F on the north, before
9:23 were over Solomon's work: F hundred and fifty, who
2Kgs 6:25 of dove's dung for F shekels of silver.
7:13 "Let some men take F of the remaining horses,
13:19 "You should have struck F or six times; then
25:19 men of war, and F men of the king's
1Chr 2:4 Judah had F sons in all.
2:6 Heman, Calcol, and Dara, F in all.
3:20 Ohel, Berechiah, Hasadiah, and Jushab-hesed, F
4:32 Rimmon, Tochen, and Ashan, F cities,
4:42 And some of them, F hundred men of the
7:3 Obadiah, Joel, and Isshiah, F, all of them chief
7:7 Uzziel, Jerimoth, and Iri, F, heads of fathers' houses,
11:23 man of great stature, F cubits tall.
29:7 the house of God F thousand talents and ten
2Chr 3:11 of the one, of F cubits, touched the wall
3:11 its other wing, of F cubits, touched the wing
3:12 cherub, one wing, of F cubits, touched the wall
3:12 other wing, also of F cubits, was joined to
3:15 with a capital of F cubits on the top
4:2 brim to brim, and F cubits high, and a
4:6 to wash, and set F on the south side,
4:6 the south side, and F on the north side.
4:7 them in the temple, F on the south side
4:7 the south side and F on the north.
4:8 them in the temple, F on the south side
4:8 the south side and F on the north.
6:13 made a bronze platform F cubits long, five cubits
6:13 platform five cubits long, F cubits wide, and three
13:17 fell slain of Israel F hundred thousand picked men.
26:13 hundred and seven thousand F hundred, who could
35:9 for the passover offerings F thousand lambs and kids
35:9 lambs and kids and F hundred bulls.
Ezra 1:11 and of silver were F thousand four hundred and
2:69 thousand darics of gold, F thousand minas of silver,
Neh 7:70 of gold, fifty basins, F hundred and thirty priests'
Jud 7:17 moved forward, together with F thousand Assyrians,
7:31 us hold out for F more days; by that
8:9 to the Assyrians after F days,
8:15 help us within these F days, he has power
16:23 was one hundred and F years old.
Esth 9:6 Jews slew and destroyed F hundred men,
9:12 the Jews have slain F hundred men and also
Job 1:3 sheep, three thousand camels, F hundred yoke of
1:3 yoke of oxen, and F hundred she-asses, and very
Wis 10:6 that descended on the F Cities.
Is 17:6 highest bough, four or F on the branches of
19:18 day there will be F cities in the land
30:17 at the threat of F you shall flee, till
Jer 52:22 the one capital was F cubits; a network and
Ezek 40:7 between the side rooms, F cubits; and the threshold
40:13 other, a breadth of F and twenty cubits, from
40:30 twenty-five cubits long and F cubits broad.
40:48 jambs of the vestibule, F cubits on either side;
41:2 of the entrance were F cubits on either side;
41:9 the side chambers was F cubits; and the part
41:9 was left free was F cubits.
41:11 was left free was F cubits round about.
41:12 of the building was F cubits thick round about,
42:16 with the measuring reed, F hundred cubits by the
42:17 measured the north side, F hundred cubits by the
42:18 measured the south side, F hundred cubits by the
42:19 west side and measured, F hundred cubits by the
42:20 a wall around it, F hundred cubits long and
42:20 hundred cubits long and F hundred cubits broad, to
45:2 a square plot of F hundred by five hundred
45:2 of five hundred by F hundred cubits shall be
45:6 the city an area F thousand cubits broad, and
45:12 shall be twenty gerahs; F shekels shall be five
45:12 five shekels shall be F shekels, and ten shekels
48:15 F thousand cubits in breadth and twenty-five
48:16 north side four thousand F hundred cubits, the south
48:16 south side four thousand F hundred, the east side
48:16 east side four thousand F hundred, and the west
48:16 side four thousand and F hundred.
48:30 to be four thousand F hundred cubits by measure,
48:32 to be four thousand F hundred cubits, three gates,
48:33 to be four thousand F hundred cubits by measure,
48:34 to be four thousand F hundred cubits, three gates,
1Mac 2:2 He had F sons, John surnamed Gaddi,
4:1 Now Gorgias took F thousand infantry and a
4:28 infantrymen and F thousand cavalry to subdue
4:34 the army of Lysias F thousand men; they fell
6:35 on their heads; and F hundred picked horsemen
7:32 About F hundred men of the army of Nicanor
10:42 Moreover, the F thousand shekels of silver which my
15:31 give me for them F hundred talents of silver,
15:31 money of the cities, F hundred talents more.
2Mac 2:23 Jason of Cyrene in F volumes, we shall attempt
10:29 the enemy from heaven F resplendent men on horses
10:31 Twenty thousand F hundred were slaughtered,
11:5 a fortified place about F leagues from Jerusalem,
12:10 Timothy, not less than F thousand Arabs with five
12:10 five thousand Arabs with F hundred horsemen

12:20 infantry and two thousand F hundred cavalry.
13:2 and ten thousand infantry, F thousand three hundred
14:39 Jews, sent more than F hundred soldiers to arrest
Mt 14:17 him, "We have only F loaves here and two
14:19 grass; and taking the F loaves and the two
14:21 who ate were about F thousand men, besides women
16:9 you not remember the F loaves of the five
16:9 five loaves of the F thousand, and how many
25:2 F of them were foolish, and five were wise.
25:2 them were foolish, and F were wise.
25:15 to one he gave F talents, to another two,
25:16 who had received the F talents went at once
25:16 them; and he made F talents more.
25:20 who had received the F talents came forward,
25:20 forward, bringing F talents more, saying, 'Master,
25:20 you delivered to me F talents; here I have
25:20 here I have made F talents more.'
Mk 6:38 found out, they said, F, and two fish."
6:41 And taking the F loaves and the two fish
6:44 ate the loaves were F thousand men.
8:19 When I broke the F loaves for the five
8:19 five loaves for the F thousand, how many baskets
Lk 1:24 Elizabeth conceived, and for F months she hid
7:41 two debtors; one owed F hundred denarii, and the
9:13 have no more than F loaves and two fish—
9:14 For there were about F thousand men.
9:16 And taking the F loaves and the two fish
12:6 Are not F sparrows sold for two pennies?
12:52 house there will be F divided, three against two
14:19 said, 'I have bought F yoke of oxen, and
16:28 house, for I have F brothers, so that he
19:18 your pound has made F pounds.'
19:19 are to be over F cities.'
Jn 4:18 for you have had F husbands, and he whom
5:2 called Beth-zatha, which has F porticoes.
6:9 lad here who has F barley loaves and two
6:10 down, in number about F thousand.
6:13 with fragments from the F barley loaves, left by
Acts 4:4 men came to about F thousand.
20:6 Unleavened Bread, and in F days we came to
24:1 And after F days the high priest Ananias came
1Cor 14:19 I would rather speak F words with my mind,
15:6 appeared to more than F hundred brethren at one
2Cor 11:24 F times I have received at the hands of
Rev 9:5 to torture them for F months, but not to
9:10 of hurting men for F months lies in their
17:10 are also seven kings, F of whom have fallen,

FIX (3)
Num 18:16 redeem them) you shall F at five shekels in
Ps 119:15 on thy precepts, and F my eyes on thy
Wis 6:15 To F one's thought on her is perfect understanding,

FIXED (19)
Gen 41:32 that the thing is F by God, and God
47:22 the priests had a F allowance from Pharaoh, and
Deut 32:8 sons of men, he F the bounds of the
2Kgs 8:11 And he F his gaze and stared at him,
Esth 9:32 of Queen Esther F these practices of Purim,
Ps 74:17 Thou hast F all the bounds of the earth;
119:6 shame, having my eyes F on all thy commandments.
119:89 thy word is firmly F in the heavens.
148:6 ever and ever; he F their bounds which cannot
Eccl 12:11 and like nails firmly F are the collected sayings
Sir 22:14 so the mind firmly F on a reasonable counsel
Jer 31:35 by day and the F order of the moon
31:36 his name: "If this F order departs from before
Ezek 45:14 barley, and as the F portion of oil, one
Lk 4:20 in the synagogue were F on him.
16:26 great chasm has been F, in order that those
Acts 1:7 which the Father has F by his own authority.
3:5 And he F his attention upon them, expecting to
17:31 repent, because he has F a day on which

FLAG
Rom 12:11 Never F in zeal, be aglow with the Spirit,

FLAGONS (4)
Ex 25:29 for incense, and its F and bowls with which
37:16 and its bowls and F with which to pour
Num 4:7 the bowls, and the F for the drink offering;
Is 22:24 small vessel, from the cups to all the F

FLAGRANT (2)
Jer 30:14 your guilt is great, because your sins are F
30:15 because your sins are F, I have done these

FLAGSTAFF
Is 30:17 are left like a F on the top of

FLAIL
Judg 8:7 my hand, I will F your flesh with the

FLAKE-LIKE
Ex 16:14 the wilderness a fine, F thing, fine as hoarfrost

FLAME (39)
Ex 3:2 to him in a F of fire out of
Num 21:28 went forth from Heshbon, F from the city of
Judg 13:20 And when the F went up toward heaven from
13:20 LORD ascended in the F of the altar while
Job 15:30 escape from darkness; the F will dry up his
18:5 put out, and the F of his fire does
41:21 kindles coals, and a F comes forth from his
Ps 83:14 the forest, as the F sets the mountains ablaze,
104:4 thy messengers, fire and F thy ministers.
106:18 in their company; the F burned up the wicked.
Song 8:6 flashes are flashes of fire, a most vehement F
Wis 10:17 day, and a starry F through the night.
16:18 At one time the F was restrained, so that
Sir 21:9 their end is a F of fire.
28:22 and they will not be burned in its F
Is 5:24 sinks down in the F, so their root will
10:17 his Holy One a F; and it will burn
29:6 and tempest, and the F of a devouring fire.
30:30 furious anger and a F of devouring fire, with
43:2 be burned, and the F shall not consume you.
47:14 cannot deliver themselves from the power of the F
Jer 48:45 forth from Heshbon, a F from the house of
Ezek 20:47 dry tree; the blazing F shall not be quenched,
Dan 3:22 furnace very hot, the F of the fire slew
3:47 And the F streamed out above the furnace forty-nine
3:49 and drove the fiery F out of the furnace,
11:33 fall by sword and F, by captivity and plunder,
Joel 1:18 of the wilderness, and F has burned all the
2:3 and behind them a F burns.
2:5 the crackling of a F of fire devouring the
Obad 1:18 house of Joseph a F, and the house of
Nah 2:3 The chariots flash like F when mustered in array;
1Mac 2:59 and Mishael believed and were saved from the F
2Mac 1:32 this was done, a F blazed up; but when
Lk 16:24 in anguish in this F
Acts 7:30 Mount Sinai, in a F of fire in a
Rev 1:14 eyes were like a F of fire,
2:18 has eyes like a F of fire, and whose
19:12 eyes are like a F of fire, and on

FLAMED (3)
2Sam 22:9 his mouth; glowing coals F forth from him.
22:13 him coals of fire F forth.
Ps 18:8 his mouth; glowing coals F forth from him.

FLAMES (7)
Ps 29:7 the LORD flashes forth F of fire.
Wis 17:5 nor did the brilliant F of the stars avail
19:21 F, on the contrary, failed to consume the flesh
Is 66:15 and his rebuke with F of fire.
Dan 3:24 the midst of the F, singing hymns to God
7:9 his throne was fiery F, its wheels were burning
Heb 1:7 winds, and his servants F of fire."

FLAMING (15)
Gen 3:24 the cherubim, and a F sword which turned every
15:17 fire pot and a F torch passed between these
Deut 33:2 of holy ones, with F fire at his right
Job 41:19 of his mouth go F torches; sparks of fire
Wis 18:3 thou didst provide a F pillar of fire as
Sir 8:10 be burned in his F fire.
45:19 to consume them in F fire.
Is 4:5 the shining of a F fire by night; for
Lam 2:3 has burned like a F fire in Jacob, consuming
Dan 10:6 lightning, his eyes like F torches, his arms and
Hos 7:7 it blazes like a F fire.
Zech 12:6 of wood, like a F torch among sheaves; and
1Mac 6:39 them and gleamed like F torches.
Eph 6:16 can quench all the F darts of the evil
2Thes 1:7 his mighty angels in F fire,

FLANK
Ezek 25:9 will lay open the F of Moab from the

FLANKED
1Mac 9:12 F by the two companies, the phalanx advanced to

FLANKS (2)
1Mac 6:38 side, on the two F of the army, to
2Mac 15:20 cavalry deployed on the F,

FLASH (11)
Job 15:12 why do your eyes F,
41:18 His sneezings F forth light, and his eyes are
Ps 144:6 F forth the lightning and scatter them, send out
Wis 11:18 pall of smoke, or F terrible sparks from their
Ezek 1:14 and fro, like a F of lightning.
21:10 for slaughter, polished to F like lightning!
21:28 to glitter and to F like lightning—
Amos 5:9 name, who makes destruction F forth against the
Nah 2:3 The chariots F like flame when mustered in array;
Hab 3:11 they sped, at the F of thy glittering spear.
2Mac 5:3 hurling of missiles, the F of golden trappings, and

FLASHED (6)
Ps 18:14 and scattered them; he F forth lightnings, and routed
77:17 forth thunder; thy arrows F on every side.
105:32 rain, and lightning that F through their land.
Wis 16:22 in the hail and F in the showers of
Hab 3:4 like the light, rays F from his hand; and
Acts 9:3 a light from heaven F about him.

FLASHES (9)
Ps 29:7 voice of the LORD F forth flames of fire.
Song 8:6 Its F are flashes of fire, a most vehement
8:6 Its flashes are F of fire, a most vehement
Bar 6:61 the lightning, when it F, is widely seen; and
Lk 17:24 For as the lightning F and lights up the
Rev 4:5 From the throne issue F of lightning, and voices
8:5 peals of thunder, voices, F of lightning, and an
11:19 temple; and there were F of lightning, voices, peals
16:18 And there were F of lightning, voices, peals of

FLASHING (5)
Ex 9:24 was hail, and fire F continually in the midst
Job 39:23 rattle the quiver, the F spear and the javelin.
Ps 76:3 There he broke the F arrows, the shield, the
Ezek 1:4 about it, and fire F forth continually, and in
Nah 3:3 Horsemen charging, F sword and glittering spear,

FLASK (9)
2Kgs 9:1 loins, and take this F of oil in your
9:3 Then take the F of oil, and pour it
Jud 10:5 of wine and a F of oil, and filled
Jer 19:1 buy a potter's earthen F, and take some of
19:10 you shall break the F in the sight of
Mt 26:7 him with an alabaster F of very expensive ointment,
Mk 14:3 came with an alabaster F of ointment of pure
14:3 and she broke the F and poured it over
Lk 7:37 house, brought an alabaster F of ointment,

FLASKS
Mt 25:4 but the wise took F of oil with their

FLAT (4)
Josh 6:5 city will fall down F, and the people shall
6:20 the wall fell down F, so that the people
Judg 7:13 it upside down, so that the tent lay F
1Chr 9:31 charge of making the F cakes.

FLATTER (3)
Job 32:22 not know how to F, else would my Maker
Ps 5:9 an open sepulchre, they F with their tongue.
Wis 14:17 their zeal they might F the absent one as

FLATTERED
Ps 78:36 But they F him with their mouths; they lied

FLATTERIES
Dan 11:21 in without warning and obtain the kingdom by F

FLATTERING (6)
Ps 12:2 to his neighbor; with F lips and a double
12:3 LORD cut off all F lips, the tongue that
Prov 26:28 its victims, and a F mouth works ruin.
Ezek 12:24 any false vision or F divination within the house
Rom 16:18 and by fair and F words they deceive the
Jude 1:16 passions, loud-mouthed boasters, F people to gain

FLATTERS (3)
Ps 36:2 For he F himself in his own eyes that
Prov 28:23 favor than he who F with his tongue.
29:5 A man who F his neighbor spreads a net

FLATTERY (4)
Job 32:21 any person or use F toward any man.
Dan 11:32 He shall seduce with F those who violate the
11:34 themselves to them with F;
1Thes 2:5 used either words of F, as you know, or

FLAUNTED
Ezek 23:18 harlotry so openly and F her nakedness, I turned

FLAUNTS
Prov 13:16 knowledge, but a fool F his folly.

FLAW
Song 4:7 love; there is no F in you.

FLAWLESS
Song 6:9 darling of her mother, F to her that bore

FLAX (9)
Ex 9:31 (The F and the barley were ruined, for the
9:31 the ear and the F was in bud.
Josh 2:6 with the stalks of F which she had laid
Judg 15:14 his arms became as F that has caught fire,
Prov 31:13 She seeks wool and F, and works with willing
Is 19:9 The workers in combed F will be in despair,
Ezek 40:3 with a line of F and a measuring reed
Hos 2:5 my wool and my F, my oil and my
2:9 my wool and my F, which were to cover

FLAY (3)
Lev 1:6 And he shall F the burnt offering and cut
2Chr 29:34 few and could not F all the burnt offerings,
Mic 3:3 of my people, and F their skin from off

FLAYED
2Chr 35:11 them while the Levites F the victims.

FLEA
1Sam 24:14 After a F

FLED (188)
Gen 14:10 of Sodom and Gomorrah F, some fell into them,
14:10 them, and the rest F to the mountain.
16:6 with her, and she F from her.
31:21 He F with all that he had, and arose
31:22 day that Jacob had F,
31:40 night, and my sleep F from my eyes.
35:1 to you when you F from your brother Esau."
35:7 to him when he F from his brother.
39:12 in her hand, and F and got out of
39:13 her hand, and had F out of the house,
39:15 garment with me, and F and got out of
39:18 garment with me, and F out of the house."
Ex 2:15 But Moses F from Pharaoh, and stayed in the
4:3 a serpent; and Moses F from it.
14:5 that the people had F, the mind of Pharaoh
14:27 appeared; and the Egyptians F into it, and the
Num 16:34 were round about them F at their cry; for
35:25 to which he had F, and he shall live
35:26 refuge to which he F,
35:32 for him who has F to his city of
Josh 7:4 the people; and they F before the men of
8:15 beaten before them, and F in the direction of
8:20 for the people that F to the wilderness turned
10:11 And as they F before Israel, while they were
10:16 These five kings F, and hid themselves in the
20:6 own home, to the town from which he F
Judg 1:6 Adoni-bezek F; but they pursued him, and caught
4:15 from his chariot and F away on foot.
4:17 But Sisera F away on foot to the tent
7:21 all the army ran; they cried out and F
7:22 army; and the army F as far as Beth-shittah
8:12 And Zebah and Zalmunna F; and he pursued them
9:21 Jotham ran away and F, and went to Beer
9:40 chased him, and he F before him; and many
9:51 people of the city F to it, all the
11:3 Then Jephthah F from his brothers, and dwelt in
20:45 And they turned and F toward the wilderness to
20:47 hundred men turned and F toward the wilderness to
1Sam 4:10 was defeated, and they F, every man to his
4:16 from the battle; I F from the battle today."
4:17 and said, "Israel has F before the Philistines, and
17:24 they saw the man, F from him, and were
17:51 Philistines saw that their champion was dead, they F
19:8 them, so that they F before him.
19:10 And David F, and escaped.

19:12 the window; and he F away and escaped.
19:18 Now David F and escaped, and he came to
20:1 Then David F from Naioth in Ramah, and came
21:10 And David rose and F that day from Saul,
22:17 they knew that he F, and did not disclose
22:20 named Abiathar, escaped and F after David.
23:6 the son of Ahimelech F to David to Keilah,
27:4 Saul that David had F to Gath, he sought
30:17 four hundred young men, who mounted camels and F
31:1 the men of Israel F before the Philistines, and
31:7 men of Israel had F and that Saul and
31:7 forsook their cities and F; and the Philistines came
2Sam 1:4 answered, "The people have F from the battle, and
4:3 to Benjamin; the Be-erothites F to Gittaim, and have
4:4 took him up, and F; and, as she fled
4:4 fled; and, as she F in her haste, he
10:13 the Syrians; and they F before him.
10:14 saw that the Syrians F, they likewise fled before
10:14 Syrians fled, they likewise F before Abishai, and
10:18 And the Syrians F before Israel; and David slew
13:29 sons arose, and each mounted his mule and F
13:34 But Absalom F
13:37 But Absalom F, and went to Talmai the son
13:38 So Absalom F, and went to Geshur, and was
18:17 stones; and all Israel F every one to his
19:8 Now Israel had F every man to his own
19:9 and now he has F out of the land
23:11 lentils; and the men F from the Philistines.
1Kgs 2:7 met me when I F from Absalom your brother.
2:28 supported Absalom-- Joab F to the tent of
2:29 King Solomon, "Joab has F to the tent of
11:17 in Edom); but Hadad F to Egypt, together with
11:23 of Eliada, who had F from his master Hadadezer
11:40 but Jeroboam arose, and F into Egypt, to Shishak
12:2 Egypt, whither he had F from King Solomon), then
20:20 his man; the Syrians F and Israel pursued them,
20:30 And the rest F into the city of Aphek;
20:30 Ben-hadad also F, and entered an inner chamber in
2Kgs 3:24 the Moabites, till they F before them; and they
7:7 So they F away in the twilight and forsook
7:7 as it was, and F for their lives.
8:21 him; but his army F home.
9:10 Then he opened the door, and F
9:23 reined about and F, saying to Ahaziah, "Treachery,
9:27 Judah saw this, he F in the direction of
9:27 And he F to Megiddo, and died there.
14:12 Israel, and every man F to his home.
14:19 in Jerusalem, and he F to Lachish.
25:4 the men of war F by night by the
1Chr 10:1 the men of Israel F before the Philistines, and
10:7 that the army had F and that Saul and
10:7 forsook their cities and F; and the Philistines came
11:13 barley, and the men F from the Philistines.
19:14 for battle; and they F before him.
19:15 saw that the Syrians F, they likewise fled before
19:15 Syrians fled, they likewise F before Abishai, Joab's
19:18 And the Syrians F before Israel; and David slew
2Chr 10:2 Egypt, whither he had F from King Solomon), then
13:16 The men of Israel F before Judah, and God
14:12 before Asa and before Judah, and the Ethiopians F
25:22 Israel, and every man F to his home.
25:27 in Jerusalem, and he F to Lachish.
Neh 13:10 did the work, had F each to his field.
Tob 1:21 killed him, and they F to the mountains of
8:3 smelled the odor he F to the remotest parts
Jud 5:8 their gods; and they F to Mesopotamia, and lived
11:3 me why you have F from them and have
11:16 learned all this, I F from them; and God
15:2 all rushed out and F by every path across
Esth 14:1 seized with deathly anxiety, F to the Lord;
Ps 104:7 At thy rebuke they F; at the sound of
114:3 The sea looked and F, Jordan turned back.
143:9 I have F to thee for refuge!
Wis 10:10 When a righteous man F from his brother's wrath,
Is 10:29 the night; Ramah trembles, Gibe-ah of Saul has F
20:6 and to whom we F for help to be
21:15 For they have F from the swords, from the
22:3 All your rulers have F together, without the bow
22:3 captured, though they had F far away.
38:15 All my sleep has F because of the bitterness
Jer 4:25 and all the birds of the air had F
9:10 and the beasts have F and are gone.
26:21 he was afraid and F and escaped to Egypt.
39:4 soldiers saw them, they F, going out of the
46:5 beaten down, and have F in haste; they look
46:15 shall devour round about you.' Why has Apis F
46:21 they have turned and F together, they did not
52:7 the men of war F and went out from
Lam 1:6 find no pasture; they F without strength before the
Dan 6:18 to him, and sleep F from him.
10:7 upon them, and they F to hide themselves.
Hos 12:12 (Jacob F to the land of Aram, there Israel
Amos 5:19 as if a man F from a lion, and
Zech 14:5 shall flee as you F from the earthquake in
1Mac 1:18 and Ptolemy turned and F before him, and many
1:38 the residents of Jerusalem F; she became a dwelling
2:28 he and his sons F to the hills and
2:44 their wrath; the survivors F to the Gentiles for
3:11 Many were wounded and fell, and the rest F
3:24 fell, and the rest F into the land of
4:14 Gentiles were crushed and F into the plain,
4:22 for battle, they all F into the land of
5:9 But they F to the stronghold of Dathema,
5:11 to which we have F, and Timothy is leading
5:34 it was Maccabeus, they F before him, and he
5:43 away their arms and F into the sacred precincts
6:4 So he F and in great grief departed from
6:6 but had turned and F before the Jews; that
7:32 fell, and the rest F into the city of
7:44 had fallen, they threw down their arms and F
9:18 Judas also fell, and the rest F
9:33 of it, and they F into the wilderness of
9:40 fell, and the rest F to the mountain; and
10:12 that Bacchides had built F;
10:49 the army of Demetrius F, and Alexander pursued him
10:64 and saw him clothed in purple, they all F
10:82 overwhelmed by him and F,
10:83 They F to Azotus and entered Beth-dagon, the
11:16 So Alexander F into Arabia to find protection there,
11:46 But the king F into the palace.
11:55 against Demetrius, and he F and was routed.
11:70 the men with Jonathan F; not one of them
11:72 against the enemy and routed them, and they F
15:21 any pestilent men have F to you from their
16:8 and fell; the rest F into the stronghold.
16:10 They also F into the towers that were in
2Mac 5:7 from his conspiracy, and F again into the country
8:33 some others, who had F into one little house;
10:32 Timothy himself F to a stronghold called Gazara,
14:14 throughout Judea, who had F before Judas, flocked t
Mt 8:33 The herdsmen F, and going into the city they
26:56 Then all the disciples forsook him and F
Mk 5:14 The herdsmen F, and told it in the city
14:50 And they all forsook him, and F
16:8 they went out and F from the tomb; for
Lk 8:34 what had happened, they F, and told it in
Acts 7:29 At this retort Moses F, and became an exile
14:6 learned of it and F to Lystra and Derbe,
19:16 them, so that they F out of that house
Heb 6:18 false, we who have F for refuge might have
Rev 12:6 throne, and the woman F into the wilderness, where
16:20 And every island F away, and no mountains were
20:11 presence earth and sky F away, and no place

FLEE (106)

Gen 19:17 them forth, they said, F for your life; do
19:17 anywhere in the valley; F to the hills, lest
19:19 life; but I cannot F to the hills, lest
19:20 is near enough to F to, and it is
27:43 obey my voice; arise, F to Laban my brother
31:20 did not tell him that he intended to F
31:27 Why did you F secretly, and cheat me, and
Ex 9:20 slaves and his cattle F into the houses;
14:25 Egyptians said, "Let us F from before Israel; for
21:13 for you a place to which he may F
Lev 26:17 you, and you shall F when none pursues you.
26:36 flight, and they shall F as one flees from
Num 10:35 them that hate thee F before thee."
24:11 Therefore now F to your place; I said, 'I
35:6 permit the manslayer to F, and in addition to
35:11 person without intent may F there.
35:15 person without intent may F there.
Deut 4:42 that the manslayer might F there, who kills his
19:3 that any manslayer can F to them.
19:5 he dies--he may F to one of these
28:7 you one way, and F before you seven ways.
28:25 way against them, and F seven ways before them;
Josh 8:5 as before, we shall F before them;
8:6 before.' So we will F from them;
8:20 had no power to F this way or that,
20:3 intent or unwittingly may F there; they shall be
20:4 He shall F to one of these cities and

20:9 person without intent could F there, so that he
Judg 20:32 Israel said, "Let us F, and draw them away
2Sam 15:14 "Arise, and let us F; or else there will
17:2 all the people who are with him will F
18:3 For if we F, they will not care about
19:3 are ashamed when they F in battle.
24:13 Or will you F three months before your foes
1Kgs 12:18 mount his chariot, to F to Jerusalem.
2Kgs 9:3 open the door and F; do not tarry."
2Chr 10:18 mount his chariot, to F to Jerusalem.
Neh 6:11 I said, "Should such a man as I F
Tob 6:17 will smell it and F away, and will never
Jud 14:3 them, and they will F before you,
14:4 pursue them and cut them down as they F
Job 9:25 than a runner; they F away, they see no
20:24 He will F from an iron weapon; a bronze
39:18 she rouses herself to F, she laughs at the
41:28 arrow cannot make him F; for him slingstones are
Ps 11:1 you say to me, F like a bird to
31:11 me in the street F from me.
68:1 those who hate him F before him!
68:12 of the armies, they F, they flee!" The women
68:12 "The kings of the armies, they flee, they F
114:5 What ails you, O sea, that you F
139:7 Or whither shall I F from thy presence?
Prov 28:1 The wicked F when no one pursues, but the
Song 2:17 breathes and the shadows F, turn, my beloved, be
4:6 breathes and the shadows F, I will hie me
Wis 1:5 and disciplined spirit will F from deceit, and will
Sir 21:2 F from sin as from a snake; for if
22:20 blow-- in these cases any friend will F
Is 10:3 To whom will you F for help, and where
10:31 the inhabitants of Gebim F for safety.
13:14 and every man will F to his own land.
15:5 for Moab; his fugitives F to Zoar, to
17:11 yet the harvest will F away in a day
17:13 them, and they will F far away, chased like
30:17 A thousand shall F at the threat of one,
30:17 of five you shall F, till you are left
31:8 him; and he shall F from the sword, and
33:3 the thunderous noise peoples F, at the lifting up
35:10 sorrow and sighing shall F away.
48:20 Go forth from Babylon, F from Chaldea, declare this
51:11 sorrow and sighing shall F away.
Jer 4:6 a standard toward Zion, F for safety, stay not,
6:1 F for safety, O people of Benjamin, from the
46:6 The swift cannot F away, nor the warrior escape;
48:6 F
49:8 F, turn back, dwell in the depths, O inhabitants
49:24 feeble, she turned to F, and panic seized her;
49:30 'Terror on every side!' F, wander far away, dwell
50:3 man and beast shall F away.
50:8 hope of their fathers.' F from the midst of
50:16 and every one shall F to his own land.
50:28 they F and escape from the land of Babylon,
51:6 F from the midst of Babylon, let every man
Bar 6:55 silver, their priests will F and escape, but the
6:68 are, for they can F to cover and help
Dan 4:14 fruit; let the beasts F from under it and
Amos 2:16 among the mighty shall F away naked in that
7:12 Amos, "O seer, go, F away to the land
9:1 one of them shall F away, not one of
Jon 1:3 But Jonah rose to F to Tarshish from the
4:2 I made haste to F to Tarshish; for I
Zech 2:6 F from the land of the north, says the
14:5 it; and you shall F as you fled from
1Mac 9:10 a thing as to F from them.
10:73 is no stone or pebble, or place to F
2Mac 8:24 of Nicanor's army, and forced them all to F
11:11 hundred horsemen, and forced all the rest to F
Mt 2:13 and his mother, and F to Egypt, and remain
3:7 Who warned you to F from the wrath to
10:23 you in one town, F to the next; for
24:16 who are in Judea F to the mountains;
Mk 13:14 who are in Judea F to the mountains;
Lk 3:7 Who warned you to F from the wrath to
21:21 who are in Judea F to the mountains, and
Jn 10:5 follow, but they will F from him, for they
Jas 4:7 devil and he will F from you.

FLEECE (9)

Deut 18:4 the first of the F of your sheep, you
Judg 6:37 I am laying a F of wool on the
6:37 is dew on the F alone, and it is
6:38 morning and squeezed the F, he wrung enough dew
6:38 enough dew from the F to fill a bowl
6:39 this once with the F; pray, let it be
6:39 dry only on the F, and on all the
6:40 was dry on the F only, and on all
Job 31:20 not warmed with the F of my sheep;

FLEECES

Jud 12:15 before Holofernes the soft F which she had received

FLEEING (14)

Gen 16:8 She said, "I am F from my mistress Sarai."
Deut 4:42 past, and that by F to one of these
19:4 the manslayer, who by F there may save his
Josh 8:6 will say, 'They are F from us, as before.'
1Sam 14:22 that the Philistines were F, they too followed hard
Tob 1:18 death any who came F from Judea, I buried
Jud 10:12 Hebrews, but I am F from them, for they
Job 26:13 his hand pierced the F serpent.
Sir 11:10 not overtake, and by F you will not escape.
Is 27:1 will punish Leviathan the F serpent, Leviathan the
Jon 1:10 knew that he was F from the presence of
1Mac 4:5 said, "These men are F from us."
11:73 his men who were F saw this, they returned
2Mac 5:8 ruler of the Arabs, F from city to city,

FLEES (9)

Lev 26:36 shall flee as one F from the sword, and
Deut 19:11 dies, and the man F into one of these
Job 14:2 flower, and withers; he F like a shadow, and
27:22 him without pity; he F from its power in
Is 24:18 He who F at the sound of the terror
Jer 48:19 Ask him who F and her who escapes; say,
48:44 He who F from the terror shall fall into
Jn 10:12 leaves the sheep and F; and the wolf snatches
10:13 He F because he is a hireling and cares

FLEET (9)

1Kgs 9:26 King Solomon built a F of ships at Ezion-geber,
9:27 Hiram sent with the F his servants, seamen who
10:11 Moreover the F of Hiram, which brought gold from
10:22 the king had a F of ships of Tarshish
10:22 at sea with the F of Hiram.
10:22 every three years the F of ships of Tarshish
1Mac 1:17 and elephants and cavalry and with a large F
2Mac 12:9 the harbor and the F, so that the glow
14:1 strong army and a F,

FLEETING (4)

Ps 39:4 let me know how F my life is!
Prov 21:6 lying tongue is a F vapor and a snare
Wis 16:27 simply warmed by a F ray of the sun,
Heb 11:25 than to enjoy the F pleasures of sin.

FLESH (344)

Gen 2:21 up its place with F;
2:23 of my bones and F of my flesh; she
2:23 and flesh of my F; she shall be called
2:24 cleaves to his wife, and they become one F
6:3 ever, for he is F, but his days shall
6:12 was corrupt; for all F had corrupted their way
6:13 an end of all F; for the earth is
6:17 earth, to destroy all F in which is the
6:19 living thing of all F, you shall bring two
7:15 and two of all F in which there was
7:16 and female of all F, went in as God
7:21 And all F died that moved upon the earth,
8:17 with you of all F --birds and animals and
9:4 you shall not eat F with its life, that
9:11 never again shall all F be cut off by
9:15 living creature of all F; and the waters shall
9:15 never again become a flood to destroy all F
9:16 living creature of all F that is upon the
9:17 between me and all F that is upon the
17:11 be circumcised in the F of your foreskins, and
17:13 covenant be in your F an everlasting covenant.
17:14 not circumcised in the F of his foreskin shall
17:23 and he circumcised the F of their foreskins that
17:24 was circumcised in the F of his foreskin.
17:25 was circumcised in the F of his foreskin.
29:14 him, "Surely you are my bone and my F
37:27 him, for he is our brother, our own F
40:19 birds will eat the F from you."
Ex 4:7 it was restored like the rest of his F
12:8 They shall eat the F that night, roasted; with
12:46 forth any of the F outside the house; and
16:8 you in the evening F to eat and in
16:12 twilight you shall eat F, and in the morning

21:28 be stoned, and its F shall not be eaten;
22:31 shall not eat any F that is torn by
28:42 to cover their naked F; from the loins to
29:14 But the F of the bull, and its skin,
29:31 ordination, and boil its F in a holy place;
29:32 sons shall eat the F of the ram and
29:34 if any of the F for the ordination, or
Lev 4:11 bull and all its F, with its head, its
6:27 Whatever touches its F shall be holy; and when
7:15 And the F of the sacrifice of his peace
7:17 what remains of the F of the sacrifice on
7:18 If any of the F of the sacrifice of
7:19 F that touches any unclean thing shall not be
7:19 are clean may eat F,
7:20 who eats of the F of the sacrifice of
7:21 then eats of the F of the sacrifice of
8:17 its skin, and its F, and its dung, he
8:31 his sons, "Boil the F at the door of
8:32 what remains of the F and the bread you
9:11 The F and the skin he burned with fire
11:8 Of their F you shall not eat, and their
11:11 to you; of their F you shall not eat,
12:3 the eighth day the F of his foreskin shall
13:10 there is quick raw F in the swelling,
13:14 But when raw F appears on him, he shall
13:15 shall examine the raw F, and pronounce him unclean;
13:15 pronounce him unclean; raw F is unclean, for it
13:16 But if the raw F turns again and is
13:24 skin and the raw F of the burn becomes
16:27 their skin and their F and their dung shall
17:11 the life of the F is in the blood;
17:16 them or bathe his F, he shall bear his
19:26 shall not eat any F with the blood in
19:28 any cuttings in your F on account of the
21:5 their beards, nor make any cuttings in their F
26:29 You shall eat the F of your sons, and
26:29 you shall eat the F of your daughters.
Num 12:12 dead, of whom the F is half consumed when
16:22 the spirits of all F, shall one man sin,
18:15 the womb of all F, whether man or beast,
18:18 the LORD; but their F shall be yours, as
19:5 sight; her skin, her F, and her blood, with
27:16 the spirits of all F, appoint a man over
Deut 5:26 is there of all F, that has heard the
12:15 may slaughter and eat F within any of your
12:20 say, 'I will eat F because you crave flesh,
12:20 flesh,' because you crave F, you may eat as
12:20 may eat as much F as you desire.
12:23 you shall not eat the life with the F
12:27 your burnt offerings, the F and the blood, on
12:27 your God, but the F you may eat.
14:8 Their F you shall not eat, and their carcasses
16:4 shall any of the F which you sacrifice on
28:53 your own body, the F of your sons and
28:55 them any of the F of his children whom
32:42 my sword shall devour F --with the blood of
Judg 6:21 rock and consumed the F and the unleavened cakes;
8:7 I will flail your F with the thorns of
9:2 also that I am your bone and your F
1Sam 17:44 I will give your F to the birds of
2Sam 5:1 and said, "Behold, we are your bone and F
19:12 my bone and my F; why then should you
19:13 Amasa, 'Are you not my bone and my F
1Kgs 19:21 them, and boiled their F with the yokes of
21:27 put sackcloth upon his F, and fasted and lay
2Kgs 4:34 himself upon him, the F of the child became
5:10 seven times, and your F shall be restored, and
5:14 of God; and his F was restored like the
5:14 was restored like the F of a little child,
9:36 dogs shall eat the F of Jezebel;
1Chr 11:1 and said, "Behold, we are your bone and F
2Chr 32:8 is an arm of F; but with us is
Neh 5:5 Now our F is as the flesh of our
5:5 flesh is as the F of our brethren, our
Jud 16:17 will give to their F; they shall weep in
Job 2:5 his bone and his F, and he will curse
4:15 the hair of my F stood up.
6:12 stones, or is my F bronze?
7:5 My F is clothed with worms and dirt; my
10:4 Hast thou eyes of F
10:11 me with skin and F, and knit me together
13:14 I will take my F in my teeth, and
19:20 skin and to my F, and I have escaped
19:22 Why are you not satisfied with my F
19:26 destroyed, then from my F I shall see God,
21:6 it I am dismayed, and shuddering seizes my F
33:21 His F is so wasted away that it cannot
33:25 a ransom; let his F become fresh with youth;
34:15 himself his breath, all F would perish together, and
41:23 The folds of his F cleave together, firmly cast
Ps 38:3 no soundness in my F because of thy indignation;
38:7 burning, and there is no soundness in my F
50:13 Do I eat the F of bulls, or drink
56:4 What can F do to me?
63:1 thirsts for thee; my F faints for thee, as
65:2 To thee shall all F come
73:26 My F and my heart may fail, but God
78:27 south wind; he rained F upon them like dust,
78:39 that they were but F, a wind that passes
79:2 air for food, the F of thy saints to
84:2 LORD; my heart and F sing for joy to
102:5 my loud groaning my bones cleave to my F
119:120 My F trembles for fear of thee, and I
136:25 gives food to all F, for his steadfast love
145:21 LORD, and let all F bless his holy name
Prov 3:8 be healing to your F and refreshment to your
4:23 who finds them, and healing to all his F
5:11 you groan, when your F and body are consumed,
14:30 gives life to the F, but passion makes the
Eccl 4:5 fool folds his hands, and eats his own F
12:12 and much study is a weariness of the F
Wis 7:1 I was molded into F,
12:5 sacrificial feasting on human F and blood.
19:21 failed to consume the F of perishable creatures that
Sir 1:8 She dwells with all F according to his gift,
14:18 are the generations of F and blood: one dies
17:26 So F and blood devise evil.
19:12 arrow stuck in the F of the thigh, so
28:5 If he himself, being F, maintains wrath, who will
31:1 wealth wastes away one's F, and anxiety about it
38:28 the fire melts his F, and he wastes away
39:19 The works of all F are before him, and
40:8 With all F, both man and beast, and upon
41:3 the Lord for all F,
44:19 with him that all F should not be blotted
44:21 the covenant in his F, and when he was
45:1 the sight of all F and was beloved by
Is 9:20 each devours his neighbor's F,
17:4 the fat of his F will grow lean.
22:13 and killing sheep, eating F and drinking wine.
31:3 and their horses are F, and not spirit.
40:5 be revealed, and all F shall see it together,
40:6 All F is grass, and all its beauty is
44:16 the half he eats F, he roasts meat and
44:19 its coals, I roasted F and have eaten; and
49:26 oppressors eat their own F, and they shall be
49:26 Then all F shall know that I am the
58:7 and not to hide yourself from your own F
65:4 places; who eat swine's F, and broth of abominable
66:16 his sword, upon all F; and those slain by
66:17 the midst, eating swine's F and the abomination and
66:23 sabbath to sabbath, all F shall come to worship
66:24 and they shall be an abhorrence to all F
Jer 7:21 burnt offerings to your sacrifices, and eat the F
11:15 Can vows and sacrificial F avert your doom?
12:12 to the other; no F has peace.
17:5 in man and makes F his arm, whose heart
19:9 make them eat the F of their sons and
19:9 one shall eat the F of his neighbor in
25:31 into judgment with all F, and the wicked he
32:27 the God of all F; is anything too hard
45:5 bringing evil upon all F, says the LORD; but
Lam 3:4 He has made my F and my skin waste
Bar 2:3 should eat, one the F of his son and
2:3 son and another the F of his daughter.
Ezek 4:14 beasts, nor has foul F come into my mouth."
11:3 and we are the F
11:7 it, they are the F, and this city is
11:11 shall you be the F in the midst of
11:19 heart out of their F and give them a
11:19 them a heart of F,
20:48 All F shall see that I the LORD have
21:4 its sheath against all F from south to north;
21:5 to north; and all F shall know that I
24:4 it the pieces of F, all the good pieces,
24:10 fire, boil well the F, and empty out the
32:5 I will strew your F upon the mountains, and
33:25 Lord GOD: You eat F with the blood, and
36:26 take out of your F the heart of stone
36:26 of stone and give you a heart of F
37:6 you, and will cause F to come upon you,
37:8 sinews on them, and F had come upon them,

39:17 and you shall eat F and drink blood.
39:18 You shall eat the F of the mighty, and
40:43 on the tables the F of the offering was
44:7 uncircumcised in heart and F, to be in my
44:9 uncircumcised in heart and F, of all the foreigners
Dan 1:15 appearance and fatter in F than all the youths
2:11 except the gods, whose dwelling is not with F
4:12 its branches, and all F was fed from it.
7:5 told, 'Arise, devour much F
14:5 heaven and earth and has dominion over all F
Hos 8:13 love sacrifice; they sacrifice F and eat it; but
Joel 2:28 my spirit on all F; your sons and your
Mic 3:2 my people, and their F from off their bones;
3:3 bones; who eat the F of my people, and
3:3 in a kettle, like F in a caldron.
Nah 2:12 caves with prey and his dens with torn F
Zeph 1:17 like dust, and their F like dung.
Hag 2:12 'If one carries holy F in the skirt of
Zech 2:13 Be silent, all F, before the LORD; for he
11:9 are left devour the F of one another."
11:16 sound, but devours the F of the fat ones,
14:12 war against Jerusalem: their F shall rot while they
14:21 them and boil the F of the sacrifice in
1Mac 7:17 which was written, "The F of thy saints and
2Mac 6:18 forced to open his mouth to eat swine's F
6:19 accord, spitting out the F,
6:21 he was eating the F of the sacrificial meal
7:1 whips and cords, to partake of unlawful swine's F
9:9 anguish and pain, his F rotted away, and because
Mt 16:17 For F and blood has not revealed this to
26:41 is willing, but the F is weak."
Mk 14:38 is willing, but the F is weak."
Lk 3:6 made smooth; and all F shall see the salvation
24:39 a spirit has not F and bones as you
Jn 1:13 the will of the F nor of the will
1:14 And the Word became F and dwelt among us,
3:6 is born of the F is flesh, and that
3:6 of the flesh is F, and that which is
6:51 for the life of the world is my F
6:52 man give us his F to eat?"
6:53 unless you eat the F of the Son of
6:54 he who eats my F and drinks my blood
6:55 For my F is food indeed, and my blood
6:56 He who eats my F and drinks my blood
6:63 that gives life, the F is of no avail;
8:15 judge according to the F, I judge no one.
17:2 him power over all F, to give eternal life
Acts 2:17 my Spirit upon all F, and your sons and
2:26 tongue rejoiced; moreover my F will dwell in hope.
2:31 Hades, nor did his F see corruption.
Rom 1:3 David according to the F
4:1 about Abraham, our forefather according to the F
7:5 were living in the F, our sinful passions, aroused
7:18 good dwells within me, that is, in my F
7:25 mind, but with my F I serve the law
8:3 law, weakened by the F, could not do: sending
8:3 the likeness of sinful F and for sin, he
8:3 condemned sin in the F,
8:4 not according to the F but according to the
8:5 live according to the F set their minds on
8:5 the things of the F, but those who live
8:6 the mind on the F is death, but to
8:7 is set on the F is hostile to God;
8:8 who are in the F cannot please God.
8:9 are not in the F, you are in the
8:12 debtors, not to the F, to live according to
8:12 live according to the F –
8:13 live according to the F you will die, but
9:5 race, according to the F, is the Christ.
9:8 the children of the F who are the children
13:14 no provision for the F, to gratify its desires.
1Cor 3:1 as men of the F, as babes in Christ.
3:3 not ready, for you are still of the F
3:3 you not of the F, and behaving like ordinary
5:5 the destruction of the F, that his spirit may
15:39 For not all F is alike, but there is
15:50 tell you this, brethren: F and blood cannot inherit
2Cor 4:11 of Jesus may be manifested in our mortal F
12:7 given me in the F, a messenger of Satan,
Gal 1:16 did not confer with F and blood,
2:20 now live in the F I live by faith
3:3 the Spirit, are you now ending with the F
4:23 born according to the F, the son of the
4:29 born according to the F persecuted him who was
5:13 an opportunity for the F, but through love be
5:16 and do not gratify the desires of the F
5:17 the desires of the F are against the Spirit,
5:17 Spirit are against the F; for these are opposed
5:19 the works of the F are plain: fornication, impurity,
5:24 Jesus have crucified the F with its passions and
6:8 sows to his own F will from the flesh
6:8 flesh will from the F reap corruption; but he
6:12 good showing in the F that would compel you
6:13 you circumcised that they may glory in your F
Eph 2:3 the passions of our F, following the desires of
2:11 you Gentiles in the F, called the uncircumcision by
2:11 is made in the F by hands–
2:15 by abolishing in his F the law of commandments
5:29 ever hates his own F, but nourishes and cherishes
5:31 his wife, and the two shall become one F
6:12 are not contending against F and blood, but against
Phil 1:22 be life in the F, that means fruitful labor
1:24 to remain in the F is more necessary on
3:2 evil-workers, look out for those who mutilate the F
3:3 Christ Jesus, and put no confidence in the F
3:4 for confidence in the F also.
3:4 for confidence in the F, I have more:
Col 1:22 in his body of F by his death, in
1:24 sake, and in my F I complete what is
2:11 off the body of F in the circumcision of
2:13 the uncircumcision of your F, God made alive
2:23 no value in checking the indulgence of the F
1Tim 3:16 was manifested in the F, vindicated in the Spirit,
Philem 1:16 you, both in the F and in the Lord.
Heb 2:14 the children share in F and blood, he himself
5:7 the days of his F, Jesus offered up prayers
9:13 the purification of the F,
10:20 that is, through his F,
Jas 5:3 and will eat your F like fire.
1Pet 1:24 of God; for "All F is like grass and
2:11 the passions of the F that wage war against
3:18 to death in the F but made alive in
4:1 Christ suffered in the F, arm yourselves with the
4:1 has suffered in the F has ceased from sin,
4:2 the time in the F no longer by human
4:6 though judged in the F like men, they might
2Pet 2:18 licentious passions of the F men who have barely
1Jn 2:16 the lust of the F and the lust of
4:2 has come in the F is of God,
2Jn 1:7 Jesus Christ in the F; such a one is
Jude 1:8 their dreamings defile the F, reject authority, and
1:23 fear, hating even the garment spotted by the F
Rev 17:16 naked, and devour her F and burn her up
19:18 God, to eat the F of kings, the flesh
19:18 flesh of kings, the F of captains, the flesh
19:18 flesh of captains, the F of mighty men, the
19:18 of mighty men, the F of horses and their
19:18 their riders, and the F of all men, both
19:21 and all the birds were gorged with their F

FLESHPOTS

Ex 16:3 we sat by the F and ate bread to

FLEW (6)

1Sam 14:32 very faint; the people F upon the spoil, and
2Sam 22:11 on a cherub, and F; he was seen upon
Ps 18:10 on a cherub, and F; he came swiftly upon
Is 6:2 he covered his feet, and with two he F
6:6 Then F one of the seraphim to me, having
Rev 8:13 loud voice, as it F in midheaven, "Woe, woe,

FLIES (16)

Ex 8:21 will send swarms of F on you and your
8:21 filled with swarms of F, and also the ground
8:22 that no swarms of F shall be there; that
8:24 came great swarms of F into the house of
8:24 the land was ruined by reason of the F
8:29 that the swarms of F may depart from Pharaoh,
8:31 removed the swarms of F from Pharaoh, from his
Deut 4:17 any winged bird that F in the air,
28:49 swift as the eagle F, a nation whose language
Ps 78:45 among them swarms of F, which devoured them, and
91:5 nor the arrow that F by day,
105:31 there came swarms of F, and gnats throughout their
Eccl 10:1 Dead F make the perfumer's ointment give off an
Wis 5:11 as, when a bird F through the air, no
16:9 bites of locusts and F, and no healing was
Nah 3:16 spreads its wings and F away.

FLIGHT (32)

Lev 26:36 shall put them to F, and they shall flee
Deut 16:3 of Egypt in hurried F –that all the days

32:30 put ten thousand to F, unless their Rock had
Josh 23:10 of you puts to F a thousand, since it
1Chr 8:13 Aijalon, who put to F the inhabitants of Gath);
12:15 banks, and put to F all those in the
Jud 15:3 in the hills around Bethulia also took to F
Job 27:22 pity; he flees from its power in headlong F
Ps 21:12 will put them to F; you will aim at
48:5 panic, they took to F;
104:7 the sound of thy thunder they took to F
Wis 5:11 force of its rushing F, is traversed by the
Is 10:31 Madmenah is in F, the inhabitants of Gebim flee
52:12 shall not go in F, for the LORD will
Jer 4:29 every city takes to F; they enter thickets; they
Dan 9:21 to me in swift F at the time of
Amos 2:14 F shall perish from the swift, and the strong
1Mac 4:20 had been put to F, and that the Jews
6:47 attack of the forces, they turned away in F
10:72 were twice put to F in their own land.
11:15 with a strong force, and put him to F
15:11 he came in his F to Dor, which is
16:8 army were put to F, and many of them
2Mac 4:42 put them all to F; and the temple robber
8:6 positions and put to F not a few of
9:2 Antiochus was put to F by the inhabitants and
9:4 had put him to F; so he ordered his
11:12 and Lysias himself escaped by disgraceful F
12:22 they rushed off in F and were swept on,
12:37 were not expecting it, and put them to F
Mt 24:20 Pray that your F may not be in winter
Heb 11:34 became mighty in war, put foreign armies to F

FLING

Ezek 32:4 open field I will F you, and will cause

FLINT (8)

Ex 4:25 Then Zipporah took a F and cut off her
Josh 5:2 said to Joshua, "Make F knives and circumcise the
5:3 So Joshua made F knives, and circumcised the
Ps 114:8 pool of water, the F into a spring of
Is 5:28 horses' hoofs seem like F, and their wheels like
50:7 my face like a F, and I know that
Ezek 3:9 Like adamant harder than F have I made your
2Mac 10:3 striking fire out of F, they offered sacrifices, after

FLINTY (4)

Deut 8:15 water out of the F rock,
32:13 oil out of the F rock.
Job 28:9 his hand to the F rock, and overturns mountains
Wis 11:4 given them out of F rock, and slaking of

FLITTING

Prov 26:2 a sparrow in its F, like a swallow in

FLOAT

2Kgs 6:6 threw it in there, and made the iron F

FLOATED

Gen 7:18 earth; and the ark F on the face of

FLOCK (127)

Gen 4:4 the firstlings of his F and of their fat
21:28 ewe lambs of the F apart.
27:9 Go to the F, and fetch me two good
29:10 mouth, and watered the F of Laban his mother's
30:31 will again feed your F and keep it:
30:32 pass through all your F today, removing from it
30:36 Jacob; and Jacob fed the rest of Laban's F
30:40 the black in the F of Laban; and he
30:40 apart, and did not put them with Laban's F
30:41 the stronger of the F were breeding Jacob laid
30:41 the eyes of the F, that they might breed
30:42 the feebler of the F he did not lay
31:4 the field where his F was,
31:8 wages,' then all the F bore spotted; and if
31:8 wages,' then all the F bore striped.
31:10 mating season of the F I lifted up my
31:10 which leaped upon the F were striped, spotted, and
31:12 that leap upon the F are striped, spotted, and
31:41 six years for your F, and you have changed
37:2 old, was shepherding the F with his brothers; he
37:12 to pasture their father's F near Shechem.
37:13 your brothers pasturing the F at Shechem?
37:14 brothers, and with the F; and bring me word
37:16 I pray you, where they are pasturing the F
38:17 "I will send you a kid from the F
Ex 2:16 and filled the troughs to water their father's F
2:17 stood up and helped them, and watered their F
2:19 even drew water for us and watered the F
3:1 Moses was keeping the F of his father-in-law, Jethro,
3:1 and he led his F to the west side
Lev 1:2 of cattle from the herd or from the F
1:10 offering is from the F, from the sheep or
3:6 an animal from the F, male or female, he
5:6 a female from the F, a lamb or a
5:15 blemish out of the F, valued by you in
5:18 blemish out of the F, valued by you at
6:6 blemish out of the F, valued by you at
22:21 herd or from the F, to be accepted it
Num 15:3 herd or from the F an offering by fire
Deut 7:13 the young of your F, in the land which
12:6 herd and of your F;
12:17 herd or of your F, or any of your
12:21 your herd or your F, which the LORD has
14:23 of your herd and F; that you may learn
15:14 liberally out of your F, out of your threshing
15:19 of your herd and F you shall consecrate to
15:19 your herd, nor shear the firstling of your F
16:2 your God, from the F or the herd, at
28:4 of your cattle, and the young of your F
28:18 of your cattle, and the young of your F
28:51 the young of your F, until they have caused
32:14 and milk from the F, with fat of lambs
1Sam 17:34 a lamb from the F,
2Sam 12:4 one of his own F or herd to prepare
2Chr 35:7 and kids from the F to the number of
Ezra 10:19 a ram of the F for their guilt.
Tob 7:8 a ram from the F and set large servings
Job 21:11 little ones like a F, and their children dance.
30:1 disdained to set with the dogs of my F
Ps 68:10 as it languished; thy F found a dwelling in
77:20 thy people like a F by the hand of
78:52 and guided them in the wilderness like a F
79:13 we thy people, the F of thy pasture, will
80:1 of Israel, thou who leadest Joseph like a F
Song 1:7 where you pasture your F, where you make it
1:8 the tracks of the F, and pasture your kids
2:16 his, he pastures his F among the lilies.
4:1 hair is like a F of goats, moving down
4:2 teeth are like a F of shorn ewes that
6:2 spices, to pasture his F in the gardens, and
6:3 mine; he pastures his F among the lilies.
6:5 hair is like a F of goats, moving down
6:6 teeth are like a F of ewes, that have
Sir 18:12 and turns them back, as a shepherd his F
27:9 Birds F with their kind; so truth returns to
47:3 and with bears as with lambs of the F
Is 40:11 He will feed his F like a shepherd, he
63:11 out of the sea the shepherds of his F
Jer 10:21 prospered, and all their F is scattered.
13:17 tears, because the LORD's F has been taken captive.
13:20 Where is the F that was given you, your
13:20 the flock that was given you, your beautiful F
23:2 "You have scattered my F, and have driven them
23:3 the remnant of my F out of all the
25:34 you lords of the F, for the days of
25:35 shepherds, nor escape for the lords of the F
25:36 and the wail of the lords of the F
31:10 a shepherd keeps his F
31:12 the young of the F and the herd; their
49:20 little ones of the F shall be dragged away;
50:8 the Chaldeans, and be as he-goats before the F
50:45 little ones of their F shall be dragged away;
51:23 the shepherd and his F; with you I break
Bar 4:26 taken away like a F carried off by the
Ezek 24:5 choicest one of the F, pile the logs under
34:12 shepherd seeks out his F when some of his
34:17 "As for you, my F, thus says the Lord
34:22 I will save my F, they shall no longer
36:37 for them: to increase their men like a F
36:38 Like the F for sacrifices, like the flock at
36:38 for sacrifices, like the F at Jerusalem during her
43:23 a ram from the F without blemish.
43:25 a ram from the F, without blemish, shall be
45:15 one sheep from every F of two hundred, from
Amos 6:4 eat lambs from the F, and calves from the
7:15 me from following the F, and the LORD said
Jon 3:7 nor beast, herd nor F, taste anything; let them
Mic 2:12 a fold, like a F in its pasture, a
4:8 O tower of the F, hill of the daughter
5:4 stand and feed his F in the strength of
7:14 with thy staff, the F of thy inheritance, who
Hab 3:17 yield no food, the F be cut off from

Zech 9:16 for they are the F of his people; for
10:3 hosts cares for his F, the house of Judah,
11:4 "Become shepherd of the F doomed to slaughter.
11:7 the shepherd of the F doomed to be slain
11:17 Woe to my worthless shepherd, who deserts the F
Mal 1:14 a male in his F, and vows it, and
Mt 26:31 the sheep of the F will be scattered.'
Lk 2:8 keeping watch over their F by night.
12:32 "Fear not, little F, for it is your Father's
Jn 10:16 there shall be one F, one shepherd.
Acts 20:28 and to all the F, in which the Holy
20:29 you, not sparing the F;
1Cor 9:7 Who tends a F without getting some of the
1Pet 5:2 Tend the F of God that is your charge,
5:3 in your charge but being examples to the F

FLOCKED

2Mac 14:14 had fled before Judas, F to join Nicanor, thinking

FLOCKS (81)

Gen 13:5 with Abram, also had F and herds and tents,
24:35 he has given him F and herds, silver and
26:14 He had possessions of F and herds, and a
29:2 field, and lo, three F of sheep lying beside
29:2 of that well the F were watered.
29:3 and when all the F were gathered there, the
29:8 cannot until all the F are gathered together, and
30:38 in front of the F in the runnels, that
30:38 watering troughs, where the F came to drink.
30:39 came to drink, the F bred in front of
30:39 rods and so the F brought forth striped, speckled,
30:40 the faces of the F toward the striped and
30:43 rich, and had large F, maidservants and menservants,
31:38 I have not eaten the rams of your F
31:43 are my children, the F are my flocks, and
31:43 the flocks are my F, and all that you
32:5 I have oxen, asses, F, menservants, and maidservants;
32:7 with him, and the F and herds and camels,
33:13 frail, and that the F and herds giving suck
33:13 one day, all the F will die.
34:28 defiled; they took their F and their herds, their
45:10 children's children, and your F, your herds, and all
46:32 they have brought their F, and their herds, and
47:1 my brothers, with their F and herds and all
47:4 pasture for your servants' F, for the famine is
47:17 for the horses, the F, the herds, and the
50:8 only their children, their F, and their herds were
Ex 9:3 the asses, the camels, the herds, and the F
10:9 daughters and with our F and herds, for we
10:24 you; only let your F and your herds remain
12:32 Take your F and your herds, as you have
12:38 very many cattle, both F and herds.
34:3 the mountain; let no F or herds feed before
Lev 27:32 tithe of herds and F, every tenth animal of
Num 11:22 a whole month!' Shall F and herds be slaughtered
31:9 all their cattle, their F, and all their goods.
31:28 asses and of the F;
31:30 asses, and of the F, of all the cattle,
32:16 sheepfolds here for our F, and cities for our
32:26 ones, our wives, our F, and all our cattle,
Deut 8:13 when your herds and F multiply, and your silver
Judg 5:16 the sheepfolds, to hear the piping for the F
1Sam 8:17 the tenth of your F, and you shall be
30:20 also captured all the F and herds; and the
2Sam 12:2 man had very many F and herds;
1Kgs 20:27 them like two little F of goats, but the
1Chr 4:39 seek pasture for their F,
4:41 place, because there was pasture there for their F
27:30 Over the F was Jaziz the Hagrite.
2Chr 32:29 cities for himself, and F and herds in abundance;
Neh 10:36 herds and of our F;
Tob 5:13 the first-born of our F and the tithes of
Jud 2:27 fields and destroyed their F and herds and sacked
3:3 wheat fields, and our F and herds, and all
Job 24:2 remove landmarks; they seize F and pasture them.
Ps 65:13 meadows clothe themselves with F, the valleys deck
78:48 the hail, and their F to thunderbolts.
107:41 out of affliction, and makes their families like F
Prov 27:23 the condition of your F, and give attention to
Eccl 2:7 possessions of herds and F, more than any who
Song 1:7 who wanders beside the F of your companions?
Is 13:20 shepherds will make their F lie down there.
17:2 they will be for F, which will lie down,
32:14 asses, a pasture of F;
60:7 All the F of Kedar shall be gathered to
61:5 stand and feed your F, foreigners shall be your
65:10 become a pasture for F, and the Valley of
Jer 3:24 our fathers labored, their F and their herds, their
5:17 shall eat up your F and your herds; they
6:3 Shepherds with their F shall come against her; they
31:24 the farmers and those who wander with their F
33:12 again be habitations of shepherds resting their F
33:13 the cities of Judah, F shall again pass under
49:29 Their tents and their F shall be taken, their
Ezek 25:5 the cities of the Ammonites a fold for F
36:38 cities be filled with F of men.
Hos 5:6 With their F and herds they shall go to
Joel 1:17 for them; even the F of sheep are dismayed.
Mic 5:8 young lion among the F of sheep, which, when
Zeph 2:6 be pastures, meadows for shepherds and folds for F
2Mac 14:23 way, but dismissed the F of people that had

FLOG (2)

Prov 17:26 is not good; to F noble men is wrong.
Mt 10:17 up to councils, and F you in their synagogues,

FLOGGING (2)

Prov 18:6 lips bring strife, and his mouth invites a F
19:29 ready for scoffers, and F for the backs of

FLOOD (40)

Gen 6:17 I will bring a F of waters upon the
7:6 years old when the F of waters came upon
7:7 the ark, to escape the waters of the F
7:10 the waters of the F came upon the earth.
7:17 The F continued forty days upon the earth; and
9:11 the waters of a F, and never again shall
9:11 shall there be a F to destroy the earth."
9:15 never again become a F to destroy all flesh.
9:28 After the F Noah lived three hundred and fifty
10:1 Japheth; sons were born to them after the F
10:32 nations spread abroad on the earth after the F
11:10 two years after the F;
2Sam 5:20 through my enemies before me, like a bursting F
1Chr 14:11 my enemies by my hand, like a bursting F
Job 22:11 cannot see, and a F of water covers you.
27:20 overtake him like a F; in the night a
38:34 the clouds, that a F of waters may cover
Ps 6:6 moaning; every night I F my bed with tears;
29:10 sits enthroned over the F; the LORD sits enthroned
69:2 deep waters, and the F sweeps over me.
69:15 Let not the F sweep over me, or the
88:17 surround me like a F all day long; they
124:4 against us; then the F would have swept us
Wis 18:5 didst destroy them all together by a mighty F
Sir 21:13 will increase like a F, and his counsel like
39:22 like a river, and drenches it like a F
40:10 on their account the F came.
44:18 the earth when the F came.
44:19 flesh should not be blotted out by a F
Dan 9:26 shall come with a F, and to the end
Jon 2:3 the seas, and the F was round about me;
Nah 1:8 But with an overflowing F he will make a
1Mac 6:11 into what a great F I now am plunged!
2Mac 2:24 For considering the F of numbers involved and the
Mt 24:38 those days before the F they were eating and
24:39 not know until the F came and swept them
Lk 6:48 rock; and when a F arose, the stream broke
17:27 the ark, and the F came and destroyed them
2Pet 2:5 when he brought a F upon the world of
Rev 12:15 the woman, to sweep her away with the F

FLOODED

Wis 10:4 When the earth was F because of him, wisdom

FLOODS (9)

Ex 15:5 The F cover them; they went down into the
15:8 waters piled up, the F stood up in a
Ps 93:3 The F have lifted up, O LORD, the floods
93:3 up, O LORD, the F have lifted up their
93:3 up their voice, the F lift up their roaring.
98:8 Let the F clap their hands; let the hills
Song 8:7 quench love, neither can F drown it.
Mt 7:25 rain fell, and the F came, and the winds
7:27 rain fell, and the F came, and the winds

FLOOR (45)

Gen 50:10 came to the threshing F of Atad, which is
50:11 mourning on the threshing F of Atad, they said,
Num 5:17 that is on the F of the tabernacle and
15:20 offering from the threshing F, so shall you present
18:27 grain of the threshing F, and as the fulness

18:30 produce of the threshing F, and as produce of
Deut 15:14 out of your threshing F, and out of your
16:13 ingathering from your threshing F and your wine
Judg 3:25 and there lay their lord dead on the F
6:37 wool on the threshing F; if there is dew
Ruth 3:2 he is winnowing barley tonight at the threshing F
3:3 down to the threshing F; but do not make
3:6 down to the threshing F and did just as
3:14 known that the woman came to the threshing F
2Sam 6:6 came to the threshing F of Nacon, Uzzah put
24:16 was by the threshing F of Araunah the Jebusite.
24:18 LORD on the threshing F of Araunah the Jebusite."
24:21 "To buy the threshing F of you, in order
24:24 David bought the threshing F and the oxen for
1Kgs 6:15 of cedar; from the F of the house to
6:15 and he covered the F of the house with
6:16 of cedar from the F to the rafters, and
6:30 The F of the house he overlaid with gold
7:7 finished with cedar from F to rafters.
22:10 robes, at the threshing F at the entrance of
2Kgs 6:27 From the threshing F, or from the wine press?"
1Chr 13:9 came to the threshing F of Chidon, Uzzah put
21:15 standing by the threshing F of Ornan the Jebusite.
21:18 LORD on the threshing F of Ornan the Jebusite.
21:21 forth from the threshing F, and did obeisance to
21:22 site of the threshing F that I may build
21:28 him at the threshing F of Ornan the Jebusite,
2Chr 3:1 appointed, on the threshing F of Ornan the Jebusite.
18:9 sitting at the threshing F at the entrance of
Job 5:26 up to the threshing F in its season.
39:12 return, and bring your grain to your threshing F
Jer 51:33 is like a threshing F at the time when
Ezek 41:16 round about, from the F up to the windows
41:20 round about; from the F to above the door
Dan 14:19 said, "Look at the F, and notice whose footsteps
Hos 9:2 Threshing F and winevat shall not feed them, and
13:3 swirls from the threshing F or like smoke from
Mic 4:12 has gathered them as sheaves to the threshing F
Mt 3:12 will clear his threshing F and gather his wheat
Lk 3:17 to clear his threshing F, and to gather the

FLOORS (4)

1Sam 23:1 against Keilah, and are robbing the threshing F
Dan 2:35 of the summer threshing F; and the wind carried
Hos 9:1 have loved a harlot's hire upon all threshing F
Joel 2:24 "The threshing F shall be full of grain, the

FLOUR (59)

Ex 29:2 You shall make them of fine wheat F
29:40 tenth measure of fine F mingled with a fourth
Lev 2:1 shall be of fine F; he shall pour oil
2:2 handful of the fine F and oil, with all
2:4 unleavened cakes of fine F mixed with oil, or
2:5 shall be of fine F unleavened, mixed with oil;
2:7 be made of fine F with oil.
5:11 an ephah of fine F for a sin offering;
6:15 handful of fine F of the cereal offering
6:20 an ephah of fine F as a regular cereal
7:12 and cakes of fine F well mixed with oil.
14:10 an ephah of fine F mixed with oil, and
14:21 an ephah of fine F mixed with oil for
23:13 an ephah of fine F mixed with oil, to
23:17 shall be of fine F, they shall be baked
24:5 you shall take fine F, and bake twelve cakes
Num 6:15 bread, cakes of fine F mixed with oil, and
7:13 them full of fine F mixed with oil for
7:19 them full of fine F mixed with oil for
7:25 them full of fine F mixed with oil for
7:31 them full of fine F mixed with oil for
7:37 them full of fine F mixed with oil for
7:43 them full of fine F mixed with oil for
7:49 them full of fine F mixed with oil for
7:55 them full of fine F mixed with oil for
7:61 them full of fine F mixed with oil for
7:67 them full of fine F mixed with oil for
7:73 them full of fine F mixed with oil for
7:79 them full of fine F mixed with oil for
8:8 cereal offering of fine F mixed with oil, and
15:4 an ephah of fine F, mixed with a fourth
15:6 an ephah of fine F mixed with a third
15:9 an ephah of fine F, mixed with half a
28:5 an ephah of fine F for a cereal offering,
28:9 an ephah of fine F for a cereal offering,
28:12 an ephah of fine F for a cereal offering,
28:12 two tenths of fine F for a cereal offering,
28:13 a tenth of fine F mixed with oil as
28:20 cereal offering of fine F mixed with oil; three
28:28 cereal offering of fine F mixed with oil, three
29:3 cereal offering of fine F mixed with oil, three
29:9 cereal offering of fine F mixed with oil, three
29:14 cereal offering of fine F mixed with oil, three
Judg 6:19 from an ephah of F; the meat he put
1Sam 1:24 bull, an ephah of F, and a skin of
28:24 it, and she took F, and kneaded it and
1Kgs 4:22 thirty cors of fine F, and sixty cors of
1Chr 9:29 also over the fine F, the wine, the oil,
23:29 with the showbread, the F for the cereal offering,
Sir 35:2 a kindness offers fine F, and he who gives
38:11 memorial portion of fine F, and pour oil on
39:26 and salt and wheat F and milk and honey,
Ezek 16:13 cloth; you ate fine F and honey and oil.
16:19 fed you with fine F and oil and honey—
46:14 oil to moisten the F, as a cereal offering
Dan 14:3 twelve bushels of fine F and forty sheep and
Mt 13:33 in three measures of F, till it was all
Lk 13:21 in three measures of F, till it was all
Rev 18:13 frankincense, wine, oil, fine F and wheat, cattle and

FLOURISH (14)

Job 8:11 Can reeds F where there is no water?
Ps 72:7 his days may righteousness F, and peace abound, till
92:7 grass and all evildoers F, they are doomed to
92:12 The righteous F like the palm tree, and grow
92:13 of the LORD, they F in the courts of
Prov 11:28 but the righteous will F like a green leaf.
14:11 destroyed, but the tent of the upright will F
Sir 1:16 of wisdom, making peace and perfect health to F
11:20 godly, and quickly God causes his blessing to F
Is 66:14 rejoice; your bones shall F like the grass; and
Ezek 17:24 the green tree, and make the dry tree F
Hos 13:15 Though he may F as the reed plant, the
14:7 my shadow, they shall F as a garden; they
Zech 9:17 make the young men F, and new wine the

FLOURISHES (2)

Ps 90:6 in the morning it F and is renewed; in
103:15 are like grass; he F like a flower of

FLOURISHING

Sir 14:18 Like F leaves on a spreading tree which sheds

FLOUTED

Lam 1:15 "The LORD F all my mighty men in the

FLOW (28)

Ex 14:27 returned to its wonted F when the morning
Lev 12:7 be clean from the F of her blood.
Num 24:7 Water shall F from his buckets, and his seed
Ps 78:16 and caused waters to F down like rivers.
104:10 in the valleys; they F between the hills,
147:18 he makes his wind blow, and the waters F
Prov 4:24 vigilance; for from it F the springs of life.
Eccl 1:7 place where the streams F, there they flow again.
1:7 streams flow, there they F again.
Wis 16:29 like wintry frost, and F away like waste water.
Is 2:2 all the nations shall F to it,
8:6 waters of Shiloah that F gently, and melt in
34:3 rise; the mountains shall F with their blood.
48:21 deserts; he made water F for them from the
Jer 51:44 nations shall no longer F to him; the wall
Lam 1:16 I weep; my eyes F with tears; for a
3:48 and destruction; my eyes F with rivers of tears
3:49 "My eyes will F without ceasing, without respite,
Ezek 31:4 tall, making its rivers F round the place of
Joel 3:18 and the hills shall F with milk, and all
3:18 beds of Judah shall F with water; and a
Amos 9:13 all the hills shall F with it.
Mic 4:1 hills; and peoples shall F to it,
Zech 14:8 day living waters shall F out from Jerusalem, half
Mk 5:25 who had had a F of blood for twelve
Lk 8:43 who had had a F of blood for twelve
8:44 garment; and immediately her F of blood ceased.
Jn 7:38 of his heart shall F rivers of living water.'"

FLOWED (5)

Gen 2:10 A river F out of Eden to water the
1Kgs 22:35 blood of the wound F into the bottom of
2Chr 32:4 and the brook that F through the land, saying,
Ps 105:41 water gushed forth; it F through the desert like
Rev 14:20 the city, and blood F from the wine press,

FLOWER (20)

Ex 25:33 each with capital and F, on one branch, and
25:33 each with capital and F, on the other branch--
37:19 each with capital and F, on one branch, and
37:19 each with capital and F, on the other branch
1Kgs 7:26 a cup, like the F of a lily; it
2Chr 4:5 a cup, like the F of a lily; it
Job 8:12 While yet in F and not cut down, they
14:2 comes forth like a F, and withers; he flees
Ps 103:15 he flourishes like a F of the field;
Wis 2:7 perfumes, and let no F of spring pass by
Is 18:5 is over, and the F becomes a ripening grape,
28:1 and to the fading F of its glorious beauty,
28:4 foot; and the fading F of its glorious beauty,
40:6 beauty is like the F of the field.
40:7 The grass withers, the F fades, when the breath
40:8 The grass withers, the F fades; but the word
Jas 1:9 humiliation, because like the F of the grass he
1:10 withers the grass; its F falls, and its beauty
1Pet 1:24 its glory like the F of grass.
1:24 grass withers, and the F falls,

FLOWERS (12)

Ex 25:31 its capitals, and its F shall be of one
25:34 with their capitals and F,
37:17 its capitals, and its F were of one piece
37:20 with their capitals and F,
Num 8:4 its base to its F, it was hammered work;
1Kgs 6:18 of gourds and open F; all was cedar, no
6:29 palm trees and open F, in the inner and
6:32 palm trees, and open F; he overlaid them with
6:35 palm trees and open F; and he overlaid them
7:49 the inner sanctuary; the F, the lamps, and the
2Chr 4:21 sanctuary, as prescribed; the F, the lamps, and the
Song 2:12 The F appear on the earth, the time of

FLOWING (36)

Ex 3:8 broad land, a land F with milk and honey,
3:17 the Jebusites, a land F with milk and honey.'"
13:5 give you, a land F with milk and honey,
33:3 up to a land F with milk and honey;
Lev 20:24 to possess, a land F with milk and honey.'
Num 16:13 out of a land F with milk and honey,
16:14 us into a land F with milk and honey,
Deut 6:3 you, in a land F with milk and honey.
8:7 of fountains and springs, F forth in valleys and
11:9 their descendants, a land F with milk and honey.
26:9 this land, a land F with milk and honey.
26:15 our fathers, a land F with milk and honey.'
27:3 gives you, a land F with milk and honey,
31:20 them into the land F with milk and honey,
Josh 3:13 shall be stopped from F, and the waters coming
3:16 beside Zarethan, and those F down toward the sea
5:6 give us, a land F with milk and honey.
2Kgs 4:6 Then the oil stopped F
Job 20:17 the rivers, the streams F with honey and curds.
Ps 42:1 a hart longs for F streams, so longs my
Prov 5:15 from your own cistern, F water from your own
Song 4:15 of living water, and F streams from Lebanon.
7:5 like Carmel, and your F locks are like purple;
Sir 21:13 his counsel like a F spring.
46:8 inheritance, into a land F with milk and honey.
Is 44:4 waters, like willows by F streams.
Jer 11:5 give them a land F with milk and honey,
18:14 run dry, the cold F streams?
32:22 give them, a land F with milk and honey;
Bar 1:20 to us a land F with milk and honey.
Ezek 20:6 for them, a land F with milk and honey,
20:15 given them, a land F with milk and honey,
23:15 on their loins, with F turbans on their heads,
32:6 the mountains with your F blood; and the
47:1 and the water was F down from below the
Rev 22:1 life, bright as crystal, F from the throne of

FLOWS (8)

Gen 2:11 is the one which F around the whole land
2:13 is the one which F around the whole land
2:14 river is Tigris, which F east of Assyria.
Num 13:27 you sent us; it F with milk and honey,
14:8 us, a land which F with milk and honey.
Jud 7:12 spring of water that F from the foot of
Ezek 47:8 to me, "This water F toward the eastern region
47:12 the water for them F from the sanctuary.

FLUNG (2)

2Sam 16:13 stones at him and F dust.
Lam 3:53 enemies without cause; they F me alive into the

FLUSHED

Esth 15:7 Lifting his face, F with splendor, he looked at

FLUTE (10)

1Sam 10:5 place with harp, tambourine, F, and lyre before them,
Sir 40:21 The F and the harp make pleasant melody, but
Is 5:12 and harp, timbrel and F and wine at their
30:29 the sound of the F to go to the
Jer 48:36 for Moab like a F, and my heart moans
48:36 heart moans like a F for the men of
1Mac 3:45 taken from Jacob; the F and the harp ceased
Mt 9:23 house, and saw the F players, and the crowd
1Cor 14:7 instruments, such as the F or the harp, do
Rev 18:22 harpers and minstrels, of F players and trumpeters,

FLUTTERING

Is 16:2 Like F birds, like scattered nestlings, so are the

FLUTTERS

Deut 32:11 up its nest, that F over its young, spreading

FLY (18)

Gen 1:20 creatures, and let birds F above the earth across
Job 5:7 trouble as the sparks F upward.
20:8 is he?' He will F away like a dream,
Ps 55:6 I would F away and be at rest;
90:10 soon gone, and we F away.
Wis 5:21 Shafts of lightning will F with true aim, and
Sir 43:14 opened, and the clouds F forth like birds.
Is 7:18 will whistle for the F which is at the
60:8 Who are these that F like a cloud, and
Jer 48:9 Moab, for she would F away; her cities shall
48:40 LORD: "Behold, one shall F swiftly like an eagle,
49:22 shall mount up and F swiftly like an eagle,
Hos 9:11 Ephraim's glory shall F away like a bird--no
Nah 3:17 the sun rises, they F away; no one knows
Hab 1:8 come from afar; they F like an eagle swift
Rev 9:6 die, and death will F from them.
12:14 eagle that she might F from the serpent into
19:17 all the birds that F in midheaven, "Come, gather

FLYING (11)

Ps 148:10 cattle, creeping things and F birds!
Prov 23:5 takes to itself wings, F like an eagle toward
26:2 a swallow in its F, a curse that is
Sir 11:3 bee is small among F creatures, but her product
43:17 the snow like birds F down, and its descent
Is 14:29 fruit will be a F serpent.
30:6 the viper and the F serpent, they carry their
Zech 5:1 saw, and behold, a F scroll!
5:2 answered, "I see a F scroll; its length is
Rev 4:7 living creature like a F eagle.
14:6 I saw another angel F in midheaven, with an

FOAL (3)

Gen 49:11 Binding his F to the vine and his ass's
Zech 9:9 on a colt the F of an ass.
Mt 21:5 on a colt, the F of an ass."

FOAM (2)

Ps 46:3 its waters roar and F, though the mountains tremble
Jude 1:13 sea, casting up the F of their own shame;

FOAMING (2)

Ps 75:8 is a cup, with F wine, well mixed; and
Mk 9:20 ground and rolled about, F at the mouth.

FOAMS (2)

Mk 9:18 him down; and he F and grinds his teeth
Lk 9:39 convulses him till he F, and shatters him, and

FODDER (4)

Job 6:5 has grass, or the ox low over his F
24:6 They gather their F in the field and they
Sir 33:24 F and a stick and burdens for an ass;
38:26 he is careful about F for the heifers.

FOE (19)

Esth 7:6 And Esther said, "A F and enemy!
Ps 44:10 turn back from the F; and our enemies have
60:11 us help against the F, for vain is the
68:23 your dogs may have their portion from the F
74:10 O God, is the F to scoff?
78:42 redeemed them from the F;

	78:61	captivity, his glory to the hand of the F
	106:10	the hand of the F, and delivered them from
	108:12	us help against the F, for vain is the
Sir	19:8	With friend or F do not report it, and
Jer	30:14	punishment of a merciless F, because your guilt is
Lam	1:5	her children have gone away, captives before the F
	1:7	the hand of the F, and there was none
	1:7	to help her, the F gloated over her, mocking
	2:4	hand set like a F; and he has slain
	4:12	of the world, that F or enemy could enter
Zech	8:10	any safety from the F for him who went
	10:5	in battle, trampling the F in the mud of
1Mac	2:9	streets, her youths by the sword of the F

FOEMEN

Ps	56:1	me; all day long F oppress me;

FOES (45)

Deut	30:7	these curses upon your F and enemies who
2Sam	24:13	three months before your F while they pursue you?
1Chr	21:12	of devastation by your F, while the sword of
Esth	9:1	the mastery over their F,
	13:15	the eyes of our F are upon us to
Ps	3:1	O LORD, how many are my F
	6:7	grief, it grows weak because of all my F
	8:2	bulwark because of thy F, to still the enemy
	10:5	as for all his F, he puffs at them.
	13:4	over him"; lest my F rejoice because I am
	25:19	how many are my F, and with what violent
	27:2	me, my adversaries and F, they shall stumble and
	30:1	hast not let my F rejoice over me.
	35:19	who are wrongfully my F, and let not those
	38:19	Those who are my F without cause are mighty,
	44:5	we push down our F; through thy name we
	44:7	saved us from our F, and hast put to
	60:12	it is he who will tread down our F
	69:19	and my dishonor; my F are all known to
	72:9	May his F bow down before him, and his
	74:4	Thy F have roared in the midst of thy
	74:23	the clamor of thy F, the uproar of thy
	81:14	their enemies, and turn my hand against their F
	89:23	I will crush his F before him and strike
	89:42	right hand of his F; thou hast made all
	105:24	very fruitful, and made them stronger than their F
	108:13	it is he who will tread down our F
	110:2	Rule in the midst of your F
	119:139	consumes me, because my F forget thy words.
	136:24	rescued us from our F, for his steadfast love
Wis	11:3	They withstood their enemies and fought off their F
Sir	25:7	the downfall of his F;
Is	1:24	on my enemies, and avenge myself on my F
	29:5	the multitude of your F shall be like small
	42:13	shouts aloud, he shows himself mighty against his F
Jer	30:16	devoured, and all your F, every one of them,
	46:10	day of vengeance, to avenge himself on his F
Lam	1:5	Her F have become the head, her enemies prosper,
	1:17	neighbors should be his F; Jerusalem has become a
	2:17	over you, and exalted the might of your F
Nah	1:9	he will not take vengeance twice on his F
	3:13	wide open to your F; fire has devoured your
Mt	10:36	mother-in-law; and a man's F will be those of
Rev	11:5	mouth and consumes their F; if any one would
	11:12	the sight of their F they went up to

FOILED

Jud	16:6	the Lord Almighty has F them by the hand

FOLD (10)

Job	5:24	you shall inspect your F and miss nothing.
Jer	23:3	them back to their F, and they shall be
	25:30	roar mightily against his F, and shout, like those
	49:20	dragged away; surely their F shall be appalled at
	50:6	hill they have gone, they have forgotten their F
	50:45	dragged away; surely their F shall be appalled at
Ezek	25:5	of the Ammonites a F for flocks.
Mic	2:12	like sheep in a F, like a flock in
Hab	3:17	cut off from the F and there be no
Jn	10:16	are not of this F; I must bring them

FOLDING (4)

1Kgs	6:34	the one door were F, and the two leaves
	6:34	the two leaves of the other door were F
Prov	6:10	little slumber, a little F of the hands to
	24:33	little slumber, a little F of the hands to

FOLDS (7)

Num	32:24	your little ones, and F for your sheep; and
	32:36	Beth-haran, fortified cities, and F for sheep.
Job	41:23	The F of his flesh cleave together, firmly cast
Ps	50:9	bull from your house, nor he-goat from your F
Eccl	4:5	The fool F his hands, and eats his own
Jer	25:37	pasture, and the peaceful F are devastated, because
Zeph	2:6	meadows for shepherds and F for flocks.

FOLIAGE

Ezek	17:6	vine, and brought forth branches and put forth F

FOLK (2)

Jer	6:11	be taken, the old F and the very aged.
	25:20	and all the foreign F among them; all the

FOLLIES

Ps	73:7	swell out with fatness, their hearts overflow with F

FOLLOW (103)

Gen	24:5	not be willing to F me to this land;
	24:8	is not willing to F you, then you will
	24:39	the woman will not F me.'
	41:31	that famine which will F, for it will be
	44:4	to his steward, "Up, F after the men; and
Ex	11:8	all the people who F you.' And after that
	23:2	You shall not F a multitude to do evil;
Lev	20:5	him and all who F him in playing the
Num	15:39	do them, not to F after your own heart
Deut	12:30	be not ensnared to F them, after they have
	16:20	only justice, you shall F, that you may live
	18:9	shall not learn to F the abominable practices of
Josh	3:3	from your place and F it,
Judg	3:28	he said to them, F after me; for the
	6:34	were called out to F him.
	6:35	were called out to F him.
	8:5	to the people who F me; for they are
	9:3	their hearts inclined to F Abimelech, for they said,
1Sam	12:14	reigns over you will F the LORD your God,
	25:27	the young men who F my lord.
	30:21	been too exhausted to F David, and who had
2Sam	17:9	among the people who F Absalom.'
	20:11	for David, let him F Joab."
1Kgs	11:6	and did not wholly F the LORD, as David
	18:21	the LORD is God, F him; but if Baal,
	18:21	but if Baal, then F him." And the people
	19:20	and then I will F you." And he said
	20:10	all the people who F me."
2Kgs	6:19	is not the city; F me, and I will
	17:34	and they do not F the statutes or the
Jud	5:7	because they would not F the gods of their
	11:6	And if you F out the words of your
Job	21:33	to him; all men F after him, and those
Ps	23:6	goodness and mercy shall F me all the days
	38:20	my adversaries because I F after good.
	81:12	their stubborn hearts, to F their own counsels.
	94:15	upright in heart will F it.
Prov	5:5	to death; her steps F the path to Sheol;
Song	1:8	O fairest among women, F in the tracks of
Sir	5:2	Do not F your inclination and strength, walking
	5:9	every wind, nor F every path: the double-tongued
	18:29	Do not F your base desires, but restrain your
	46:10	it is good to F the Lord.
Is	45:14	be yours, they shall F you; they shall come
Jer	3:17	shall no more stubbornly F their own evil heart.
	13:10	my words, who stubbornly F their own heart and
	18:12	We will F our own plans, and will every
	42:16	you are afraid shall F hard after you to
Ezek	13:3	the foolish prophets who F their own spirit, and
	37:24	They shall F my ordinances and be careful to
Dan	3:40	and may we wholly F thee, for there will
	3:41	all our heart we F thee, we fear thee
	11:43	and the Ethiopians shall F in his train.
1Mac	1:44	he directed them to F customs strange to the
	6:23	he said and to F his commands.
2Mac	2:4	and the ark should F with him, and that
	9:27	sure that he will F my policy and will
	15:2	who were compelled to F him said, "Do not
Mt	4:19	he said to them, F me, and I will
	8:19	him, "Teacher, I will F you wherever you go."
	8:22	Jesus said to him, F me, and leave the
	9:9	he said to him, F me." And he rose
	10:38	take his cross and F me is not worthy
	16:24	up his cross and F me.
	19:21	in heaven; and come, F me."
Mk	1:17	Jesus said to them, F me and I will

2:14 he said to him, F me." And he rose
5:37 allowed no one to F him except Peter and
8:34 up his cross and F me.
10:21 in heaven; and come, F me."
14:13 water will meet you; F him,
Lk 5:27 he said to him, F me."
9:23 his cross daily and F me.
9:49 because he does not F with us."
9:57 to him, "I will F you wherever you go."
9:59 To another he said, F me." But he said,
9:61 Another said, "I will F you, Lord; but let
17:23 not go, do not F them.
18:22 in heaven; and come, F me."
22:10 water will meet you; F him into the house
22:47 him saw what would F, they said, "Lord, shall
Jn 1:43 and said to him, F me."
10:4 them, and the sheep F him, for they know
10:5 stranger they will not F, but they will flee
10:27 know them, and they F me;
12:26 serves me, he must F me; and where I
13:36 am going you cannot F me now; but you
13:36 now; but you shall F afterward."
13:37 "Lord, why cannot I F you now?
21:19 he said to him, F me."
21:22 F me!"
Acts 12:8 mantle around you and F me."
Rom 4:12 merely circumcised but also F the example of the
2Tim 1:13 F the pattern of the sound words which you
1Pet 2:21 example, that you should F in his steps.
2Pet 1:16 For we did not F cleverly devised myths when
2:2 And many will F their licentiousness, and because of
2Jn 1:6 is love, that we F his commandments; this is
1:6 the beginning, that you F love.
3Jn 1:3 as indeed you do F the truth.
1:4 hear that my children F the truth.
Rev 14:4 it is these who F the Lamb wherever he
14:13 labors, for their deeds F them!"

FOLLOWED (127)

Gen 24:61 upon the camels and F the man; thus the
31:23 for seven days and F close after him into
32:19 third and all who F the droves, "You shall
Ex 14:28 of Pharaoh that had F them into the sea;
Num 14:24 different spirit and has F me fully, I will
16:25 the elders of Israel F him.
32:11 they have not wholly F me;
32:12 for they have wholly F the LORD.'
Deut 1:36 because he has wholly F the LORD!'
4:3 all the men who F the Baal of Peor;
11:6 every living thing that F them, in the midst
33:3 his hand; so they F in thy steps, receiving
Josh 14:8 melt; yet I wholly F the LORD my God.
14:9 because you have wholly F the LORD my God.'
14:14 day, because he wholly F the LORD, the God
Judg 9:4 and reckless fellows, who F him.
1Sam 13:7 and all the people F him trembling.
14:22 were fleeing, they too F hard after them in
17:13 sons of Jesse had F Saul to the battle;
17:14 youngest; the three eldest F Saul,
2Sam 2:10 the house of Judah F David.
3:31 And King David F the bier.
11:8 king's house, and there F him a present from
15:18 hundred Gittites who had F him from Gath, passed
17:23 his counsel was not F, he saddled his ass,
20:2 withdrew from David, and F Sheba the son of
20:2 the men of Judah F their king steadfastly from
20:14 the Bichrites assembled, and F him in.
1Kgs 1:7 the priest; and they F Adonijah and helped him.
12:20 There was none that F the house of David,
14:8 kept my commandments, and F me with all his
16:21 half of the people F Tibni the son of
16:21 him king, and half F Omri.
16:22 But the people who F Omri overcame the people
16:22 overcame the people who F Tibni the son of
18:18 of the LORD and F the Baals.
20:19 and the army which F them.
2Kgs 3:9 for the beasts which F them.
4:30 So he arose and F her.
5:21 So Gehazi F Naaman.
13:2 of the LORD, and F the sins of Jeroboam
17:15 became false, and they F the nations that were
2Chr 22:5 He even F their counsel, and went with Jehoram
27:2 But the people still F corrupt practices.
Neh 4:23 of the guard who F me, none of us
12:38 the left, and I F them with half of
Jud 2:24 Then he F the Euphrates and passed through
9:5 before and those that F; thou hast designed the
15:13 the men of Israel F, bearing their arms and
Esth 15:4 one, while the other F carrying her train.
Sir 46:6 Lord; for he wholly F the Mighty One.
51:15 from my youth I F her steps.
Jer 2:2 a bride, how you F me in the wilderness,
9:14 it, but have stubbornly F their own hearts and
Bar 1:21 us, but we each F the intent of his
Ezek 10:11 wheel faced the others F without turning as they
Hab 3:5 went pestilence, and plague F close behind.
1Mac 5:43 and the whole army F him.
7:45 Gazara, and as they F kept sounding the battle
9:16 crushed, they turned and F close behind Judas and
2Mac 2:6 Some of those who F him came up to
8:36 were invulnerable, because they F the laws ordained
Mt 4:20 left their nets and F him.
4:22 and their father, and F him.
4:25 And great crowds F him from Galilee and the
8:1 the mountain, great crowds F him;
8:10 said to those who F him, "Truly, I say
8:23 the boat, his disciples F him.
9:9 And he rose and F him.
9:19 And Jesus rose and F him, with his disciples.
9:27 there, two blind men F him, crying aloud, "Have
12:15 And many F him, and he healed them all,
14:13 crowds heard it, they F him on foot from
19:2 Jordan; and large crowds F him, and he healed
19:27 have left everything and F you.
19:28 throne, you who have F me will also sit
20:29 Jericho, a great crowd F him.
20:34 received their sight and F him.
21:9 before him and that F him shouted, "Hosanna to
26:58 But Peter F him at a distance, as far
27:55 from afar, who had F Jesus from Galilee, ministering
Mk 1:18 left their nets and F him.
1:20 the hired servants, and F him.
2:14 And he rose and F him.
2:15 there were many who F him.
3:7 great multitude from Galilee F; also from Judea
5:24 And a great crowd F him and thronged about
6:1 country; and his disciples F him.
10:28 have left everything and F you."
10:32 amazed, and those who F were afraid.
10:52 received his sight and F him on the way.
11:9 before and those who F cried out, "Hosanna!
14:51 And a young man F him, with nothing but
14:54 And Peter had F him at a distance, right
15:40 he was in Galilee, F him, and ministered to
Lk 1:3 to me also, having F all things closely for
5:11 they left everything and F him.
5:28 everything, and rose and F him.
7:9 to the multitude that F him, "I tell you,
9:11 crowds learned it, they F him; and he welcomed
18:28 left our homes and F you."
18:43 received his sight and F him, glorifying God; and
22:39 Olives; and the disciples F him.
22:52 Peter F at a distance;
23:26 And there F him a great multitude of the
23:48 the women who had F him from Galilee stood
23:54 with him from Galilee F, and saw the tomb,
Jn 1:37 say this, and they F Jesus.
1:40 heard John speak, and F him, was Andrew, Simon
6:2 And a multitude F him, because they saw the
11:31 and go out, they F her, supposing that she
18:15 Simon Peter F Jesus, and so did another disciple.
Acts 5:36 slain and all who F him were dispersed and
5:37 perished, and all who F him were scattered.
12:9 he went out and F him; he did not
13:43 devout converts to Judaism F Paul and Barnabas,
16:17 She F Paul and us, crying, "These men are
21:36 mob of the people F, crying, "Away with him!"
1Cor 10:4 the supernatural Rock which F them, and the Rock
1Tim 4:6 and of the good doctrine which you have F
2Pet 2:15 gone astray; they have F the way of Balaam,
Rev 6:8 was Death, and Hades F him; and they were
8:7 his trumpet, and there F hail and fire, mixed
13:3 and the whole earth F the beast with wonder.
14:8 Another angel, a second, F, saying, "Fallen, fallen is
14:9 another angel, a third, F them, saying with a
19:14 linen, white and pure, F him on white horses.

FOLLOWERS

2Mac 10:1 Now Maccabeus and his F, the Lord leading them

FOLLOWING (75)

Gen 47:18 came to him the F year, and said to

Num 14:43 have turned back from F the LORD, the LORD
32:15 you turn away from F him, he will again
Deut 7:4 away your sons from F me, to serve other
Josh 6:8 covenant of the LORD F them.
21:3 to the Levites the F cities and pasture lands
21:9 Simeon they gave the F cities mentioned by name,
22:16 away this day from F the LORD, by building
22:18 away this day from F the LORD?
22:23 to turn away from F the LORD; or if
22:29 away this day from F the LORD by building
Judg 4:14 with ten thousand men F him.
5:14 thither into the valley, F you, Benjamin, with your
9:42 On the F day the men went out into
9:49 down his bundle and F Abimelech put it against
Ruth 1:16 or to return from F you; for where you
1Sam 12:20 not turn aside from F the LORD, but serve
15:11 has turned back from F me, and has not
24:1 When Saul returned from F the Philistines, he was
2Sam 2:19 to the left from F Abner.
2:21 not turn aside from F him.
2:22 Asahel, "Turn aside from F me; why should I
7:8 from the pasture, from F the sheep, that you
1Kgs 9:6 you turn aside from F me, you or your
19:21 And he returned from F him, and took the
2Kgs 4:17 about that time the F spring, as Elisha had
17:21 Jeroboam drove Israel from F the LORD and made
18:6 did not depart from F him, but kept the
1Chr 17:7 from the pasture, from F the sheep, that you
2Chr 34:33 not turn away from F the LORD the God
35:4 houses by your divisions, F the directions of David
36:14 were exceedingly unfaithful, F all the abominations
Ezra 2:59 The F were those who came up from Tel-melah,
Neh 7:61 The F were those who came up from Tel-melah,
Esth 13:5 to all men, perversely F a strange manner of
16:1 The F is a copy of this letter: "The
Job 34:27 they turned aside from F him, and had no
Sir 42:1 Of the F things do not be ashamed, and
Is 59:13 and turning away from F our God, speaking
65:2 that is not good, F their own devices;
66:17 go into the gardens, F one in the midst,
Jer 3:19 would not turn from F me.
Dan 9:10 LORD our God by F his laws, which he
Amos 7:15 LORD took me from F the flock, and the
Zeph 1:6 have turned back from F the LORD, who do
1Mac 10:17 to him, in the F words:
10:25 to them in the F words: "King Demetrius to
10:51 of Egypt with the F message:
10:69 Then he sent the F message to Jonathan the
14:28 of the country, the F was proclaimed to us:
15:15 countries, in which the F was written:
2Mac 9:18 to the Jews the F letter, in the form
Mk 9:38 because he was not F us."
11:12 On the F day, when they came from Bethany,
Lk 13:33 tomorrow and the day F; for it cannot be
Jn 1:38 turned, and saw them F, and said to them,
20:6 Then Simon Peter came, F him, and went into
21:20 Peter turned and saw F them the disciple whom
Acts 7:26 And on the F day he appeared to them
10:24 And on the F day they entered Caesarea.
15:23 the brethren, with the F letter: "The brethren, both
16:11 to Samothrace, and the F day to Ne-apolis,
20:15 there we came the F day opposite Chios; the
21:18 On the F day Paul went in with us
23:11 The F night the Lord stood by him and
Rom 5:16 the judgment F one trespass brought condemnation,
5:16 the free gift F many trespasses brings justification.
1Cor 11:17 But in the F instructions I do not commend
Eph 2:2 which you once walked, F the course of this
2:2 course of this world, F the prince of the
2:3 passions of our flesh, F the desires of body
2Pet 3:3 last days with scoffing, F their own passions
2Jn 1:4 some of your children F the truth, just as
Jude 1:16 are grumblers, malcontents, F their own passions,
1:18 there will be scoffers, F their own ungodly passions."

FOLLOWS (26)

Gen 45:23 father he sent as F: ten asses loaded with
Ex 21:22 and yet no harm F, the one who hurt
21:23 If any harm F, then you shall give life
Josh 16:5 their families was as F: the boundary of their
2Kgs 11:15 sword any one who F her." For the priest
2Chr 23:14 ranks; any one who F her is to be
Ezra 4:8 Artaxerxes the king as F --
5:7 which was written as F: "To Darius the king,
Prov 7:22 All at once he F her, as an ox
12:11 bread, but he who F worthless pursuits has no
28:19 bread, but he who F worthless pursuits will have
Jer 4:20 Disaster F hard on disaster, the whole land is
16:12 every one of you F his stubborn evil will,
23:17 every one who stubbornly F his own heart, they
Ezek 7:26 comes upon disaster, rumor F rumor; they seek a
Hos 4:2 all bounds and murder F murder.
1Mac 2:17 spoke to Mattathias as F: "You are a leader,
8:19 chamber and spoke as F:
8:31 written to him as F, 'Why have you made
11:29 its contents were as F:
13:35 him a letter as F,
14:22 our public decrees, as F, 'Numenius the son of
15:2 its contents were as F: "King Antiochus to Simon
2Mac 7:27 their native tongue as F, deriding the cruel tyrant:
11:27 king's letter was as F: "King Antiochus to the
Jn 8:12 the world; he who F me will not walk

FOLLY (57)

Gen 34:7 because he had wrought F in Israel by lying
Deut 22:21 because she has wrought F in Israel by playing
1Sam 25:25 is his name, and F is with him; but
2Sam 13:12 done in Israel; do not do this wanton F
Job 42:8 you according to your F; for you have not
Ps 69:5 God, thou knowest my F; the wrongs I have
Prov 5:23 because of his great F he is lost.
12:23 conceals his knowledge, but fools proclaim their F
13:16 acts with knowledge, but a fool flaunts his F
14:1 builds her house, but F with her own hands
14:8 his way, but the F of fools is deceiving.
14:18 The simple acquire F, but the prudent are crowned
14:24 is their wisdom, but F is the garland of
14:29 but he who has a hasty temper exalts F
15:2 knowledge, but the mouths of fools pour out F
15:14 knowledge, but the mouths of fools feed on F
15:21 F is a joy to him who has no
16:22 who has it, but F is the chastisement of
17:12 her cubs, rather than a fool in his F
18:13 hears, it is his F and shame.
19:3 When a man's F brings his way to ruin,
22:15 F is bound up in the heart of a
24:9 The devising of F is sin, and the scoffer
26:4 fool according to his F, lest you be like
26:5 fool according to his F, lest he be wise
26:11 his vomit is a fool that repeats his F
27:22 crushed grain, yet his F will not depart from
Eccl 1:17 to know wisdom and to know madness and F
2:3 to lay hold on F, till I might see
2:12 wisdom and madness and F; for what can the
2:13 saw that wisdom excels F as light excels darkness.
7:25 know the wickedness of F and the foolishness which
10:1 odor; so a little F outweighs wisdom and honor.
10:6 proceeding from the ruler: F is set in many
Wis 10:8 a reminder of their F, so that their failures
12:23 Therefore those who in F of life lived unrighteously
Sir 8:15 pleases, and through his F you will perish with
20:30 man who hides his F than the man who
34:5 omens and dreams are F, and like a woman
41:15 man who hides his F than the man who
47:20 were grieved at your F,
47:23 his sons, ample in F and lacking in understanding,
Is 9:17 godless and an evildoer, and every mouth speaks F
32:6 For the fool speaks F, and his mind plots
Jer 29:23 because they have committed F in Israel, they have
Bar 3:28 they had no wisdom, they perished through their F
2Mac 4:6 settlement, and that Simon would not stop his F
4:40 advanced in years and no less advanced in F
14:8 For through the F of those whom I have
15:33 these rewards of his F opposite the sanctuary.
1Cor 1:18 of the cross is F to those who are
1:21 pleased God through the F of what we preach
1:23 block to Jews and F to Gentiles,
2:14 God, for they are F to him, and he
3:19 of this world is F with God.
2Tim 3:9 very far, for their F will be plain to
2Pet 2:18 uttering loud boasts of F, they entice with licentious

FONDLING

Gen 26:8 window and saw Isaac F Rebekah his wife.

FOOD (279)

Gen 1:29 in its fruit; you shall have them for F
1:30 life, I have given every green plant for F
2:9 sight and good for F, the tree of life
3:6 tree was good for F, and that it was
6:21 you every sort of F that is eaten, and
6:21 it shall serve as F for you and for

9:3 that lives shall be F for you; and as
24:33 Then F was set before him to eat; but
27:4 prepare for me savory F, such as I love,
27:7 prepare for me savory F, that I may eat
27:9 prepare from them savory F for your father, such
27:14 his mother prepared savory F, such as his father
27:17 she gave the savory F and the bread, which
27:31 He also prepared savory F, and brought it to
39:6 for anything but the F which he ate.
40:17 all sorts of baked F for Pharaoh, but the
41:35 them gather all the F of these good years
41:35 authority of Pharaoh for F in the cities, and
41:36 That F shall be a reserve for the land
41:48 gathered up all the F of the seven years
41:48 Egypt, and stored up F in the cities; he
41:48 in every city the F from the fields around
42:7 said, "From the land of Canaan, to buy F
42:10 lord, but to buy F have your servants come.
43:2 to them, "Go again, buy us a little F
43:4 down and buy you F;
43:20 first time to buy F;
43:22 other money down in our hand to buy F
43:31 himself he said, "Let F be served."
44:1 the men's sacks with F, as much as they
44:25 buy us a little F
47:12 his father's household with F, according to the
47:13 Now there was no F in all the land;
47:15 and said, "Give us F; why should we die
47:16 I will give you F in exchange for your
47:17 and Joseph gave them F in exchange for the
47:17 he supplied them with F in exchange for all
47:19 and our land for F, and we with our
47:24 the field and as F for yourselves and your
47:24 your households, and as F for your little ones."
49:20 Asher's F shall be rich, and he shall yield
Ex 21:10 shall not diminish her F, her clothing, or her
Lev 3:11 on the altar as F offered by fire to
3:16 on the altar as F offered by fire for
11:34 Any F in it which may be eaten, upon
19:23 kinds of trees for F, then you shall count
22:7 of the holy things, because such are his F
22:11 born in his house may eat of his F
22:13 eat of her father's F; yet no outsider shall
25:6 the land shall provide F for you, for yourself
25:7 your land all its yield shall be for F
25:37 nor give him your F for profit.
Num 15:19 you eat of the F of the land, you
21:5 For there is no F and no water, and
21:5 and no water, and we loathe this worthless F
28:2 them, 'My offering, my F for my offerings by
28:24 for seven days, the F of an offering by
Deut 2:6 You shall purchase F from them for money, that
2:28 You shall sell me F for money, that I
10:18 the sojourner, giving him F and clothing.
20:20 are not trees for F you may destroy and
28:26 dead body shall be F for all birds of
28:54 among you will grudge F to his brother, to
Josh 9:12 our houses as our F for the journey, on
Judg 13:16 not eat of your F; but if you make
Ruth 1:6 LORD had visited his people and given them F
2:18 and gave her what F she had left over
1Sam 14:24 the man who eats F until it is evening
14:24 So none of the people tasted F
14:28 the man who eats F this day.'" And the
20:24 moon came, the king sat down to eat F
20:34 anger and ate no F the second day of
2Sam 12:17 nor did he eat F with them.
12:20 he asked, they set F before him, and he
12:21 when the child died, you arose and ate F
13:5 eat, and prepare the F in my sight, that
13:7 Amnon's house, and prepare F for him."
13:10 to Tamar, "Bring the F into the chamber, that
19:32 provided the king with F while he stayed at
1Kgs 4:7 all Israel, who provided F for the king and
5:9 my wishes by providing F for my household."
5:11 cors of wheat as F for his household, and
10:5 he had built, the F of his table, the
11:18 him an allowance of F, and gave him land.
19:8 the strength of that F forty days and forty
21:4 turned away his face, and would eat no F
21:5 your spirit so vexed that you eat no F
2Kgs 4:8 woman lived, who urged him to eat some F
4:8 way, he would turn in there to eat F
25:3 that there was no F for the people of
1Chr 12:40 and Naphtali, came bringing F on asses and on
2Chr 9:4 he had built, the F of his table, the
11:11 them, and stores of F, oil, and wine.
28:15 sandals, provided them with F and drink, and
30:22 the people ate the F of the festival for
Ezra 2:63 of the most holy F, until there should be
3:7 and the carpenters, and F, drink, and oil to
Neh 5:14 my brethren ate the F allowance of the governor.
5:15 and took from them F and wine, besides forty
5:18 did not demand the F allowance of the governor,
7:65 of the most holy F, until a priest with
13:15 warned them on the day when they sold F
Tob 1:10 my relatives ate the F of the Gentiles;
2:2 seeing the abundance of F I said to my
2:5 myself and ate my F in sorrow.
7:8 set large servings of F before them.
Jud 2:18 provision; also plenty of F for every man, and
4:5 them and stored up F in preparation for war–
5:10 long as they had F; and there they became
11:12 Since their F supply is exhausted and their water
12:1 some of his own F and to serve her
12:9 until she ate her F toward evening.
13:10 placed it in her F bag.
Esth 2:9 and her portion of F, and with seven chosen
Job 6:7 them; they are as F that is loathsome to
12:11 the ear try words as the palate tastes F
20:14 his mouth, yet his F is turned in his
20:23 him, and rain it upon him as his F
24:5 in the wilderness as F for their children.
33:20 his life loathes bread, and his appetite dainty F
34:3 the ear tests words as the palate tastes F
36:31 judges peoples; he gives F in abundance.
38:41 to God, and wander about for lack of F
40:20 For the mountains yield F for him where all
Ps 42:3 tears have been my F day and night, while
59:15 They roam about for F, and growl if they
69:21 gave me poison for F, and for my thirst
74:14 didst give him as F for the creatures of
78:18 heart by demanding the F they craved.
78:25 angels; he sent them F in abundance.
78:30 their craving, while the F was still in their
79:2 of the air for F, the flesh of thy
104:14 he may bring forth F from the earth,
104:21 their prey, seeking their F from God.
104:27 to give them their F in due season.
107:18 loathed any kind of F, and they drew near
111:5 He provides F for those who fear him; he
136:25 ever; he who gives F to all flesh, for
145:15 thou givest them their F in due season.
146:7 the oppressed; who gives F to the hungry.
147:9 to the beasts their F, and to the young
Prov 6:8 ruler, she prepares her F in summer, and gathers
13:23 the poor yields much F, but it is swept
23:3 not desire his delicacies, for they are deceptive F
27:27 goats' milk for your F, for the food of
27:27 your food, for the F of your household and
28:3 poor is a beating rain that leaves no F
30:8 feed me with the F that is needful for
30:22 he is filled with F;
30:25 yet they provide their F in the summer;
31:14 merchant, she brings her F from afar.
31:15 yet night and provides F for her household and
Wis 13:12 work to prepare his F, and eat his fill.
16:3 men, when they desired F, might lose the least
16:20 didst give thy people F of angels, and without
19:11 to ask for luxurious F;
19:21 melt the crystalline, easily melted kind of heavenly F
Sir 29:22 his roof than sumptuous F in another man's house.
30:18 are like offerings of F placed upon a grave.
30:25 give heed to the F he eats.
31:21 you are overstuffed with F, get up in the
31:23 who is liberal with F, and their testimony to
31:24 who is niggardly with F, and their testimony to
36:18 stomach will take any F, yet one food is
36:18 any food, yet one F is better than another.
37:20 be destitute of all F,
37:29 give yourself up to F;
40:29 himself with another man's F, but a man who
41:1 who still has the vigor to enjoy his F
Is 23:18 merchandise will supply abundant F and fine clothing
62:8 your grain to be F for your enemies, and
65:25 the ox; and dust shall be the serpent's F
Jer 5:17 your harvest and your F; they shall eat up
7:33 this people will be F for the birds of
16:4 dead bodies shall be F for the birds of
19:7 their dead bodies for F to the birds of
34:20 dead bodies shall be F for the birds of
40:5 him an allowance of F and a present, and

Lam 1:11 trade their treasures for F to revive their strength.
44:17 we had plenty of F, and prospered, and saw
52:6 that there was no F for the people of
Lam 1:11 trade their treasures for F to revive their strength.
1:19 city, while they sought F to revive their strength.
4:4 the children beg for F, but no one gives
4:10 children; they became their F in the destruction of
Ezek 4:10 And the F which you eat shall be by
16:49 had pride, surfeit of F, and prosperous ease, but
23:37 up to them for F the sons whom they
29:5 of the air I have given you as F
34:5 shepherd; and they became F for all the wild
34:8 my sheep have become F for all the wild
34:10 they may not be F for them.
44:7 offer to me my F, the fat and the
47:12 there will grow all kinds of trees for F
47:12 fruit will be for F, and their leaves for
48:18 Its produce shall be F for the workers of
Dan 1:5 portion of the rich F which the king ate,
1:8 with the king's rich F, or with the wine
1:10 king, who appointed your F and your drink, should
1:13 eat the king's rich F be observed by you,
1:15 all the youths who ate the king's rich F
1:16 took away their rich F and the wine they
4:12 and in it was F for all.
4:21 and in which was F for all; under which
11:26 who eat his rich F shall be his undoing;
14:11 shall set forth the F and mix and place
14:14 king set forth the F for Bel.
Hos 9:3 they shall eat unclean F in Assyria.
Joel 1:15 Is not the F cut off before our eyes,
Hab 1:16 in luxury, and his F is rich.
3:17 the fields yield no F, the flock be cut
Hag 2:12 or any kind of F, does it become holy?"
Mal 1:7 name?' By offering polluted F upon my altar.
1:12 is polluted, and the F for it may be
3:10 that there may be F in my house; and
1Mac 1:35 stored up arms and F, and collecting the spoils
1:62 resolved in their hearts not to eat unclean F
1:63 to be defiled by F or to profane the
6:53 But they had no F in storage, because it
6:57 daily grow weaker, our F supply is scant, the
9:52 in them he put troops and stores of F
13:21 way of the wilderness and to send them F
13:33 bolts, and he stored F in the strongholds.
14:10 supplied the cities with F, and furnished them with
2Mac 11:31 to enjoy their own F and laws, just as
Mt 3:4 his waist; and his F was locusts and wild
6:25 not life more than F, and the body more
10:10 nor a staff; for the laborer deserves his F
14:15 the villages and buy F for themselves."
24:45 to give them their F at the proper time?
25:35 and you gave me F, I was thirsty and
25:42 you gave me no F, I was thirsty and
Lk 3:11 and he who has F, let him do likewise."
9:13 to go and buy F for all these people."
12:23 life is more than F, and the body more
12:42 them their portion of F at the proper time?
Jn 4:8 had gone away into the city to buy F
4:32 to them, "I have F to eat of which
4:33 to one another, "Has any one brought him F
4:34 said to them, "My F is to do the
6:27 not labor for the F which perishes, but for
6:27 perishes, but for the F which endures to eternal
6:55 For my flesh is F indeed, and my blood
Acts 2:46 homes, they partook of F with glad and generous
7:11 great affliction, and our fathers could find no F
9:19 was baptized, and took F and was strengthened.
12:20 their country depended on the king's country for F
14:17 satisfying your hearts with F and gladness."
16:34 his house, and set F before them; and he
23:14 oath to taste no F till we have killed
27:21 had been long without F, Paul then came forward
27:33 all to take some F, saying, "Today is the
27:33 in suspense and without F, having taken nothing.
27:34 you to take some F; it will give you
27:36 encouraged and ate some F themselves.
Rom 14:17 of God is not F and drink but righteousness
14:20 for the sake of F, destroy the work of
1Cor 3:2 with milk, not solid F; for you were not
6:13 F is meant for the stomach and the stomach
6:13 and the stomach for F —and God will destroy
8:1 Now concerning F offered to idols: we know that
8:4 to the eating of F offered to idols, we
8:7 accustomed to idols, eat F as really offered to
8:8 F will not commend us to God.
8:10 is weak, to eat F offered to idols?
8:13 Therefore, if F is a cause of my brother's
9:4 the right to our F and drink?
9:13 temple service get their F from the temple, and
10:3 ate the same supernatural F
10:19 That F offered to idols is anything, or that
2Cor 9:10 sower and bread for F will supply and multiply
11:27 and thirst, often without F, in cold and exposure.
Col 2:16 you in questions of F and drink or with
1Tim 6:8 but if we have F and clothing, with these
Heb 5:12 need milk, not solid F;
5:14 But solid F is for the mature, for those
9:10 but deal only with F and drink and various
Jas 2:15 in lack of daily F,
Rev 2:14 that they might eat F sacrificed to idols and
2:20 immorality and to eat F sacrificed to idols.

FOODS (4)

Sir 13:7 shame you with his F, until he has drained
Mk 7:18 (Thus he declared all F clean.)
1Tim 4:3 and enjoin abstinence from F which God created to
Heb 13:9 by grace, not by F, which have not benefited

FOOL (104)

1Sam 26:21 I have played the F, and have erred exceedingly."
2Sam 3:33 Abner die as a F dies?
Job 5:2 Surely vexation kills the F, and jealousy slays the
5:3 I have seen the F taking root, but suddenly
Ps 14:1 The F says in his heart, "There is no
39:8 Make me not the scorn of the F
49:10 the wise die, the F and the stupid alike
53:1 The F says in his heart, "There is no
Prov 10:8 commandments, but a prating F will come to ruin.
10:14 the babbling of a F brings ruin near.
10:18 lips, and he who utters slander is a F
10:23 like sport to a F to do wrong, but
11:29 inherit wind, and the F will be servant to
12:15 The way of a F is right in his
12:16 The vexation of a F is known at once,
13:16 with knowledge, but a F flaunts his folly.
14:3 The talk of a F is a rod for
14:7 the presence of a F, for there you do
14:16 from evil, but a F throws off restraint and
15:5 A F despises his father's instruction, but he who
17:7 not becoming to a F; still less is false
17:10 of understanding than a hundred blows into a F
17:12 cubs, rather than a F in his folly.
17:16 Why should a F have a price in his
17:21 the father of a F has no joy.
17:24 the eyes of a F are on the ends
17:28 Even a F who keeps silent is considered wise;
18:2 A F takes no pleasure in understanding, but only
18:6 A F's lips bring strife, and his mouth invites
18:7 A F's mouth is his ruin, and his lips
19:1 who is perverse in speech, and is a F
19:10 not fitting for a F to live in luxury,
20:3 from strife; but every F will be quarreling.
23:9 the hearing of a F, for he will despise
24:7 too high for a F; in the gate he
26:1 harvest, so honor is not fitting for a F
26:4 Answer not a F according to his folly, lest
26:5 Answer a F according to his folly, lest he
26:6 the hand of a F cuts off his own
26:8 sling is he who gives honor to a F
26:10 who hires a passing F or drunkard.
26:11 his vomit is a F that repeats his folly.
26:12 more hope for a F than for him.
27:3 is weighty, but a F's provocation is heavier than
27:22 Crush a F in a mortar with a pestle
28:26 own mind is a F; but he who walks
29:9 an argument with a F, the fool only rages
29:9 with a fool, the F only rages and laughs,
29:11 A F gives full vent to his anger, but
29:20 more hope for a F than for him.
30:22 becomes king, and a F when he is filled
Eccl 2:14 his head, but the F walks in darkness; and
2:15 myself, "What befalls the F will befall me also;
2:16 man as of the F there is no enduring
2:16 How the wise man dies just like the F
2:19 he will be a wise man or a F
4:5 The F folds his hands, and eats his own
5:3 much business, and a F's voice with many words.
6:8 what advantage has the wise man over the F
7:17 overmuch, neither be a F; why should you die
10:2 the right, but a F's heart toward the left.
10:3 Even when the F walks on the road, he
10:3 says to every one that he is a F

10:12 the lips of a F consume him.
10:14 A F multiplies words, though no man knows what
10:15 The toil of a F wearies him, so that
Sir 8:17 not consult with a F, for he will not
18:17 A F is ungracious and abusive, and the gift
19:11 such a word a F will suffer pangs like
19:12 the thigh, so is a word inside a F.
19:20 but there is a F who merely lacks wisdom.
20:6 but a braggart and F goes beyond the right
20:13 A F's gift will profit you nothing, for he
20:15 A F will say, "I have no friend, and
20:19 A proverb from a F's lips will be rejected,
21:14 The mind of a F is like a broken
21:16 A F's narration is like a burden on a
21:18 is wisdom to a F; and the knowledge of
21:20 A F raises his voice when he laughs, but
21:22 The foot of a F rushes into a house,
22:7 He who teaches a F is like one who
22:8 a story to a F tells it to a
22:9 and weep for the F, for he lacks intelligence;
22:9 the life of the F is worse than death.
22:10 days, but for a F or an ungodly man
22:12 And what is its name except F
22:16 timid heart with a F's purpose will not stand
23:14 and be deemed a F on account of your
27:11 always wise, but the F changes like the moon.
31:7 to it, and every F will be taken captive
31:30 the anger of a F to his injury, reducing
33:5 The heart of a F is like a cart
Is 32:5 The F will no more be called noble, nor
32:6 For the F speaks folly, and his mind plots
Jer 17:11 and at his end he will be a F
Hos 9:7 The prophet is a F, the man of the
Mt 5:22 and whoever says, 'You F shall be liable to
Lk 12:20 drink, be merry.' But God said to him, F
1Cor 3:18 let him become a F that he may become
2Cor 11:16 accept me as a F, so that I too
11:17 authority but as a F, in this boastful confidence;
11:21 am speaking as a F --I also dare to
12:6 shall not be a F, for I shall be
12:11 I have been a F

FOOLHARDY

Sir 8:15 the road with a F fellow, lest he be

FOOLISH (56)

Deut 32:6 requite the LORD, you F and senseless people?
32:21 provoke them with a F nation.
Job 2:10 as one of the F women would speak.
Ps 49:13 of those who have F confidence, the end of
Prov 8:5 ones, learn prudence; O F men, pay attention.
9:13 A F woman is noisy; she is wanton and
10:1 glad father, but a F son is a sorrow
15:20 glad father, but a F man despises his mother.
17:25 A F son is a grief to his father
19:13 A F son is ruin to his father, and
21:20 man's dwelling, but a F man devours it.
30:32 If you have been F, exalting yourself, or if
Eccl 4:13 than an old and F king, who will no
7:7 makes the wise man F, and a bribe corrupts
Wis 1:3 tested, it convicts the F;
1:5 rise and depart from F thoughts, and will be
3:2 the eyes of the F they seemed to have
3:12 Their wives are F, and their children evil;
11:15 In return for their F and wicked thoughts, which
12:24 they were deceived like F babes.
13:1 ignorant of God were F by nature; and they
14:11 and a snare to the feet of the F
15:14 But most F, and more miserable than an infant,
19:3 dead, they reached another F decision, and pursued
Sir 4:27 subject yourself to a F fellow, nor show partiality
15:7 F men will not obtain her, and sinful men
20:21 it because of his F look.
22:11 talk much with a F man, and do not
42:8 instruct the stupid or F or the aged man
50:26 the Philistines, and the F people that dwell in
Is 19:11 of Zoan are utterly F; the wise counselors of
44:25 and makes their knowledge F;
Jer 4:22 "For my people are F, they know me not;
5:21 Judah: "Hear this, O F and senseless people, who
10:8 are both stupid and F; the instruction of idols
Ezek 13:3 GOD, Woe to the F prophets who follow their
2Mac 2:32 said; for it is F to lengthen the preface
12:44 have been superfluous and F to pray for the
Mt 7:26 will be like a F man who built his
25:2 Five of them were F, and five were wise.
25:3 For when the F took their lamps, they took
25:8 And the F said to the wise, 'Give us
Lk 24:25 said to them, "O F men, and slow of
Rom 1:14 wise and to the F:
1:31 evil, disobedient to parents, F, faithless, heartless,
2:20 a corrector of the F, a teacher of children,
10:19 a nation; with a F nation I will make
1Cor 1:20 Has not God made F the wisdom of the
1:27 God chose what is F in the world to
15:36 You F man!
2Cor 11:16 no one think me F; but even if you
Gal 3:1 O F Galatians!
3:3 Are you so F
Eph 5:17 Therefore do not be F, but understand what the
Tit 3:3 we ourselves were once F, disobedient, led astray,
1Pet 2:15 silence the ignorance of F men.

FOOLISHLY (9)

Gen 31:28 Now you have done F
Num 12:11 because we have done F and have sinned.
1Sam 13:13 Saul, "You have done F; you have not kept
2Sam 24:10 of thy servant; for I have done very F
1Chr 21:8 of thy servant; for I have done very F
2Chr 16:9 You have done F in this; for from now
Prov 14:17 of quick temper acts F, but a man of
20:19 therefore do not associate with one who speaks F
Sir 16:21 thinks; a senseless and misguided man thinks F

FOOLISHNESS (7)

2Sam 15:31 pray thee, turn the counsel of Ahithophel into F
Ps 38:5 fester because of my F,
Eccl 7:25 of folly and the F which is madness.
10:13 of his mouth is F, and the end of
Mk 7:21 coveting, wickedness, deceit, licentiousness, envy,
1Cor 1:25 For the F of God is wiser than men,
2Cor 11:1 you would bear with me in a little F

FOOLS (45)

2Sam 13:13 one of the wanton F in Israel.
Job 12:17 counselors away stripped, and judges he makes F
Ps 94:8 F, when will you be wise?
Prov 1:7 the beginning of knowledge; F despise wisdom and
1:22 in their scoffing and F hate knowledge?
1:32 and the complacence of F destroys them;
3:35 will inherit honor, but F get disgrace.
10:21 righteous feed many, but F die for lack of
12:23 conceals his knowledge, but F proclaim their folly.
13:19 turn away from evil is an abomination to F
13:20 but the companion of F will suffer harm.
14:8 but the folly of F is deceiving.
14:24 their wisdom, but folly is the garland of F
14:33 it is not known in the heart of F
15:2 but the mouths of F pour out folly.
15:7 wise spread knowledge; not so the minds of F
15:14 but the mouths of F feed on folly.
16:22 has it, but folly is the chastisement of F
19:29 for scoffers, and flogging for the backs of F
26:3 ass, and a rod for the back of F
26:7 useless, is a proverb in the mouth of F
26:9 drunkard is a proverb in the mouth of F
Eccl 5:1 offer the sacrifice of F; for they do not
5:4 paying it; for he has no pleasure in F
7:4 but the heart of F is in the house
7:5 the wise than to hear the song of F
7:6 the laughter of the F; this also is vanity.
7:9 anger, for anger lodges in the bosom of F
9:17 better than the shouting of a ruler among F
Wis 5:4 derision and made a byword of reproach--we F
15:5 appearance arouses yearning in F, so that they desire
Sir 20:12 but the courtesies of F are wasted.
21:26 The mind of F is in their mouth, but
27:13 The talk of F is offensive, and their laughter
34:1 and false hopes, and dreams give wings to F
Is 19:13 of Zoan have become F, and the princes of
35:8 pass over it, and F shall not err therein.
44:25 of liars, and makes F of diviners; who turns
Jer 50:36 sword upon the diviners, that they may become F
Dan 13:48 said, "Are you such F, you sons of Israel?
Mt 23:16 he is bound by his oath.' You blind F
Lk 11:40 You F
Rom 1:22 be wise, they became F,
1Cor 4:10 We are F for Christ's sake, but you are
2Cor 11:19 you gladly bear with F, being wise yourselves!

FOOT (121)

Gen 8:9 place to set her F, and she returned to

	41:44	lift up hand or F in all the land
Ex	12:37	hundred thousand men on F, besides women and
	19:17	their stand at the F of the mountain.
	21:24	tooth, hand for hand, F for foot,
	21:24	for hand, foot for F,
	24:4	an altar at the F of the mountain, and
	32:19	broke them at the F of the mountain.
Lev	8:23	and on the great toe of his right F
	13:12	person from head to F, so far as the
	14:14	and on the great toe of his right F
	14:17	toe of his right F, upon the blood of
	14:25	and on the great toe of his right F
	14:28	toe of his right F, in the place where
	21:19	who has an injured F or an injured hand,
Num	11:21	six hundred thousand on F; and thou hast said,
	20:19	only pass through on F, nothing more."
	22:25	wall, and pressed Balaam's F against the wall; so
Deut	2:5	the sole of the F to tread on, because
	2:28	me pass through on F,
	4:11	and stood at the F of the mountain, while
	8:4	upon you, and your F did not swell, these
	11:24	the sole of your F treads shall be yours;
	19:21	tooth, hand for hand, F for foot.
	19:21	tooth for tooth, hand for hand, foot for F
	25:9	his sandal off his F, and spit in his
	28:35	the sole of your F to the crown of
	28:56	the sole of her F upon the ground because
	28:65	the sole of your F; but the LORD will
	32:35	the time when their F shall slip; for the
	33:24	let him dip his F in oil.
Josh	1:3	the sole of your F will tread upon I
	12:3	Sea, southward to the F of the slopes of
	14:9	land on which your F has trodden shall be
Judg	4:15	alighted from his chariot and fled away on F
	4:17	Sisera fled away on F to the tent of
	20:2	hundred thousand men on F that drew the sword.
1Sam	4:10	of Israel thirty thousand F soldiers.
	15:4	hundred thousand men on F, and ten thousand men
2Sam	2:18	was as swift of F as a wild gazelle;
	8:4	twenty thousand F soldiers; and David hamstrung
	10:6	of Zobah, twenty thousand F soldiers, and the king
	14:25	the sole of his F to the crown of
	21:20	six toes on each F, twenty-four in number; and
1Kgs	20:29	Syrians a hundred thousand F soldiers in one day.
2Kgs	19:24	the sole of my F all the streams of
1Chr	18:4	horsemen, and twenty thousand F soldiers; and David
	19:18	chariots, and forty thousand F soldiers, and killed
	20:6	six toes on each F, twenty-four in number; and
2Chr	33:8	no more remove the F of Israel from the
Jud	2:5	hundred and twenty thousand F soldiers and twelve
	6:13	him lying at the F of the hill, and
	7:2	the baggage and the F soldiers handling it, a
	7:12	that flows from the F of the mountain–
	9:7	the strength of their F soldiers; they trust in
Job	2:7	the sole of his F to the crown of
	23:11	My F has held fast to his steps; I
	31:5	with falsehood, and my F has hastened to deceit;
	39:15	ground, forgetting that a F may crush them, and
Ps	9:15	hid has their own F been caught.
	26:12	My F stands on level ground; in the great
	36:11	Let not the F of arrogance come upon me,
	38:16	against me when my F slips!"
	66:6	dry land; men passed through the river on F
	68:30	Trample under F those who lust after tribute; scatter
	91:12	lest you dash your F against a stone.
	91:13	lion and the serpent you will trample under F
	94:18	When I thought, "My F slips," thy steadfast love,
	121:3	will not let your F be moved, he who
Prov	1:15	them, hold back your F from their paths;
	3:23	way securely and your F will not stumble.
	3:26	and will keep your F from being caught.
	4:28	the left; turn your F away from evil.
	25:17	Let your F be seldom in your neighbor's house,
	25:19	bad tooth or a F that slips.
Eccl	10:7	and princes walking on F like slaves.
Sir	6:36	him early; let your F wear out his doorstep.
	16:10	thousand men on F, who rebelliously assembled in
	21:22	The F of a fool rushes into a house,
	40:25	and silver make the F stand sure, but good
	46:8	hundred thousand people on F, to bring them into
	50:15	it out at the F of the altar, a
	51:15	delighted in her; my F entered upon the straight
Is	1:6	the sole of the F even to the head,
	14:19	the Pit, like a dead body trodden under F
	14:25	mountains trample him under F; and his yoke shall
	16:4	he who tramples under F has vanished from the
	26:6	The F tramples it, the feet of the poor,
	28:3	will be trodden under F;
	37:25	the sole of my F all the streams of
	41:2	he tramples kings under F; he makes them like
	58:13	you turn back your F from the sabbath, from
Jer	12:5	raced with men on F, and they have wearied
Lam	3:34	To crush under F all the prisoners of the
Bar	5:6	forth from you on F, led away by their
Ezek	1:7	sole of a calf's F; and they sparkled like
	6:11	hands, and stamp your F, and say, Alas!
	29:11	No F of man shall pass through it, and
	29:11	through it, and no F of beast shall pass
	32:13	many waters; and no F of man shall trouble
Dan	8:13	the sanctuary and host to be trampled under F
Amos	2:15	who is swift of F shall not save himself,
Mic	7:19	upon us, he will tread our iniquities under F
1Mac	5:48	you harm; we will simply pass by on F
	6:30	was a hundred thousand F soldiers, twenty thousand
	9:4	Berea with twenty thousand F soldiers and two
Mt	4:6	lest you strike your F against a stone.'"
	5:13	out and trodden under F by men.
	7:6	they trample them under F and turn to attack
	14:13	they followed him on F from the towns.
	18:8	your hand or your F causes you to sin,
	22:13	'Bind him hand and F, and cast him into
Mk	6:33	they ran there on F from all the towns,
	9:44	And if your F causes you to sin, cut
Lk	4:11	lest you strike your F against a stone.'"
	8:5	and was trodden under F, and the birds of
Acts	7:5	it, not even a F's length, but promised to
	20:18	day that I set F in Asia,
1Cor	12:15	If the F should say, "Because I am not
Rev	10:2	he set his right F on the sea, and
	10:2	sea, and his left F on the land,

FOOTHOLD

Ps	69:2	where there is no F; I have come into

FOOTMEN

2Kgs	13:7	chariots and ten thousand F; for the king of

FOOTPRINTS

Ps	77:19	great waters; yet thy F were unseen.

FOOTSTEPS (4)

Ps	85:13	him, and make his F a way.
	89:51	which they mock the F of thy anointed.
Dan	14:19	floor, and notice whose F these are."
	14:20	said, "I see the F of men and women

FOOTSTOOL (9)

1Chr	28:2	LORD, and for the F of our God; and
2Chr	9:18	six steps and a F of gold, which were
Ps	99:5	Extol the LORD our God; worship at his F
	110:1	right hand, till I make your enemies your F
	132:7	his dwelling place; let us worship at his F
Is	66:1	the earth is my F; what is the house
Lam	2:1	has not remembered his F in the day of
Mt	5:35	for it is his F, or by Jerusalem, for
Acts	7:49	says, 'Heaven is my throne, and earth my F

FORASMUCH

1Sam	20:42	David, "Go in peace, F as we have sworn

FORBADE (3)

Deut	2:37	the LORD our God F us.
Mk	9:38	your name, and we F him, because he was
Lk	9:49	your name, and we F him, because he does

FORBEAR (6)

1Kgs	22:6	go to battle against Ramoth-gilead, or shall I F
	22:15	go to Ramoth-gilead to battle, or shall we F
2Chr	18:5	go to battle against Ramoth-gilead, or shall I F
	18:14	go to Ramoth-gilead to battle, or shall I F
Job	16:6	assuaged, and if I F, how much of it
Eph	6:9	same to them, and F threatening, knowing that he

FORBEARANCE (11)

Wis	2:19	gentle he is, and make trial of his F
	12:18	mildness, and with great F thou dost govern us;
Sir	3:13	lacking in understanding, show F; in all your strength
Jer	15:15	In thy F take me not away; know that
Dan	3:42	with us in thy F and in thy abundant
2Mac	10:4	disciplined by him with F and not be handed
Rom	2:4	of his kindness and F and patience?
	3:25	because in his divine F he had passed over

2Cor 6:6 by purity, knowledge, F, kindness, the Holy Spirit,
Phil 4:5 Let all men know your F
2Pet 3:15 And count the F of our Lord as salvation.

FORBEARING (4)

Eph 4:2 and meekness, with patience, F one another in love,
Col 3:13 meekness, and patience, F one another and, if
2Tim 2:24 one, an apt teacher, F,
2Pet 3:9 count slowness, but is F toward you, not wishing

FORBID (13)

Num 11:28 said, "My lord Moses, F them."
1Sam 24:6 his men, "The LORD F that I should do
26:11 The LORD F that I should put forth my
1Kgs 21:3 to Ahab, "The LORD F that I should give
Lam 1:10 those whom thou didst F to enter thy congregation.
1Mac 1:45 to the land, to F burnt offerings and sacrifices
Mt 16:22 rebuke him, saying, "God F, Lord!
Mk 9:39 Jesus said, "Do not F him; for no one
Lk 9:50 to him, "Do not F him; for he that
20:16 When they heard this, they said, "God F
Acts 10:47 declared, "Can any one F water for baptizing these
1Cor 14:39 prophesy, and do not F speaking in tongues;
1Tim 4:3 consciences are seared, who F marriage and enjoin

FORBIDDEN (7)

Lev 19:23 count their fruit as F; three years it shall
19:23 years it shall be F to you, it must
Deut 4:23 LORD your God has F you.
17:3 heaven, which I have F,
Jud 11:12 by his laws has F them to eat.
2Mac 6:5 abominable offerings which were F by the laws.
Acts 16:6 and Galatia, having been F by the Holy Spirit

FORBIDDING

Lk 23:2 perverting our nation, and F us to give tribute

FORBIDS

2Mac 12:40 Jamnia, which the law F the Jews to wear.

FORCE (50)

Gen 31:31 you would take your daughters from me by F
Num 20:20 them with many men, and with a strong F
Deut 34:7 dim, nor his natural F abated.
1Sam 2:16 and if not, I will take it by F
2Sam 13:12 my brother, do not F me; for such a
2Kgs 11:7 come on duty in F on the sabbath and
Ezra 4:23 at Jerusalem and by F and power made them
Jud 1:4 could march out in F and his infantry form
7:2 camp that day; their F of men of war
Esth 8:11 to annihilate any armed F of any people or
Job 20:22 in straits; all the F of misery will come
36:19 distress, or all the F of your strength?
Wis 5:11 and pierced by the F of its rushing flight,
18:22 body, and not by F of arms, but by
Jer 46:22 her enemies march in F, and come against her
Ezek 34:4 not sought, and with F and harshness you have
1Mac 1:17 Egypt with a strong F, with chariots and elephants
1:20 Israel and came to Jerusalem with a strong F
1:29 and he came to Jerusalem with a large F
3:10 Gentiles and a large F from Samaria to fight
3:35 was to send a F against them to wipe
3:40 departed with their entire F, and when they arrived
4:3 to attack the king's F in Emmaus
4:16 Then Judas and his F turned back from pursuing
4:18 us; Gorgias and his F are near us in
5:38 gathered to him; it is a very large F
6:6 first with a strong F, but had turned and
6:63 fought against him, and took the city by F
7:10 came with a large F into the land of
7:11 saw that they had come with a large F
7:20 left with him a F to help him; then
7:27 Jerusalem with a large F, and treacherously sent to
9:43 came with a large F on the sabbath day
9:60 come with a large F, and secretly sent letters
10:69 assembled a large F and encamped against Jamnia.
10:82 Simon brought forward his F and engaged the
11:15 him with a strong F, and put him to
12:24 returned, with a larger F than before, to wage
16:5 and behold, a large F of infantry and horsemen
2Mac 1:13 reached Persia with a F that seemed irresistible,
10:14 region, he maintained a F of mercenaries, and at
10:19 and his men, a F sufficient to besiege them;
10:24 before, gathered a tremendous F of mercenaries and
10:36 the rest of the F, and they occupied the
13:2 them had a Greek F of one hundred and
13:15 and with a picked F of the bravest young
Mt 11:12 violence, and men of violence take it by F
Jn 6:15 and take him by F to make him king,
Acts 23:10 and take him by F from among them and
Heb 9:17 it is not in F as long as the

FORCED (32)

Gen 49:15 became a slave at F labor.
Deut 20:11 in it shall do F labor for you and
Josh 16:10 become slaves to do F labor.
17:13 put the Canaanites to F labor, and did not
Judg 1:28 put the Canaanites to F labor, but did not
1:30 and became subject to F labor.
1:33 Beth-anath became subject to F labor for them.
1:35 they became subject to F labor.
1Sam 13:12 the LORD'; so I F myself, and offered the
2Sam 13:14 stronger than she, he F her, and lay with
13:22 Amnon, because he had F his sister Tamar.
13:32 from the day he F his sister Tamar.
20:24 in charge of the F labor; and Jehoshaphat the
1Kgs 4:6 in charge of the F labor.
5:13 raised a levy of F labor out of all
9:15 the account of the F labor which King Solomon
9:21 these Solomon made a F levy of slaves, and
11:28 charge over all the F labor of the house
12:18 was taskmaster over the F labor, and all Israel
2Chr 8:8 these Solomon made a F levy and so they
10:18 was taskmaster over the F labor, and the people
Prov 12:24 will be put to F labor.
Wis 14:19 please his ruler, skilfully F the likeness to take
Is 31:8 shall be put to F labor.
1Mac 6:33 his army by a F march along the road
8:2 had defeated them and F them to pay tribute,
2Mac 5:5 the wall had been F back and at last
6:18 noble presence, was being F to open his mouth
8:24 of Nicanor's army, and F them all to flee.
11:11 sixteen hundred horsemen, and F all the rest to
Acts 7:19 with our race and F our fathers to expose
2Cor 12:11 You F me to it, for I ought to

FORCEFUL

Job 6:25 How F are honest words!

FORCES (69)

Gen 14:3 And all these joined F in the Valley of
14:15 And he divided his F against them by night,
Josh 8:13 So they stationed the F, the main encampment which
10:5 of Eglon, gathered their F, and went up with
11:5 these kings joined their F, and came and encamped
1Sam 28:1 the Philistines gathered their F for war, to fight
29:1 Philistines gathered all their F at Aphek; and the
2Kgs 25:23 the captains of the F in the open country
25:26 the captains of the F arose, and went to
1Chr 19:17 and drew up his F against them.
2Chr 17:2 He placed F in all the fortified cities of
32:9 Lachish with all his F, sent his servants to
Jud 1:6 Many nations joined the F of the Chaldeans.
1:13 year he led his F against King Arphaxad, and
1:16 and all his combined F, a vast body of
1:16 there he and his F rested and feasted for
6:3 He will send his F and will destroy them
7:12 the men in your F with you; only let
7:27 and to all his F, to be plundered.
Wis 1:14 exist, and the generative F of the world are
Jer 40:7 the captains of the F in the open country
40:13 the leaders of the F in the open country
41:11 the leaders of the F with him heard of
41:13 the leaders of the F with him, they rejoiced.
41:16 the leaders of the F with him took all
42:1 the commanders of the F, and Johanan the son
42:8 the commanders of the F who were with him,
43:4 the commanders of the F and all the people
43:5 the commanders of the F took all the remnant
Dan 11:10 a multitude of great F, which shall come on
11:15 And the F of the south shall not stand,
11:31 F from him shall appear and profane the temple
1Mac 3:27 and gathered all the F of his kingdom, a
3:28 year's pay to his F, and ordered them to
3:41 And F from Syria and the land of the
3:42 increased and that the F were encamped in their
4:9 when Pharaoh with his F pursued them.
5:11 we have fled, and Timothy is leading their F
5:18 the rest of the F, in Judea to guard
5:32 the men of his F, "Fight today for your
5:40 the officers of his F, "If he crosses over
5:50 the men of the F encamped, and he fought

5:56 the commanders of the F, heard of their brave
5:58 the men of the F that were with them,
6:28 the commanders of his F and those in authority.
6:29 And mercenary F came to him from other kingdoms
6:30 The number of his F was a hundred thousand
6:47 fierce attack of the F, they turned away in
6:56 and Media with the F that had gone with
6:57 the commanders of the F, and to the men,
9:6 number of the enemy F, they were greatly
9:63 he assembled all his F, and sent orders to
9:67 into battle with his F; and Simon and his
10:36 enrolled in the king's F to the number of
10:36 due to all the F of the king.
10:48 large F and encamped opposite Demetrius.
10:71 have confidence in your F, come down to the
11:1 of Egypt gathered great F, like the sand by
11:3 the cities he stationed F as a garrison in
11:70 Chalphi, commanders of the F of the army.
13:53 commander of all the F, and he dwelt in
14:1 the king assembled his F and marched into Media
14:32 men of his nation's F and paid them wages.
15:25 anew, continually throwing his F against it and
2Mac 3:35 marched off with his F to the king.
8:30 In encounters with the F of Timothy and Bacchides
8:32 the commander of Timothy's F, a most unholy man,
9:3 to Nicanor and the F of Timothy.
Mt 5:41 and if any one F you to go one

FORCIBLY

1Mac 2:46 the altars; they F circumcised all the uncircumcised

FORCING (3)

Neh 5:5 children; yet we are F our sons and our
1Mac 2:25 king's officer who was F them to sacrifice, and
2Mac 14:41 the tower and were F the door of the

FORD (2)

Gen 32:22 children, and crossed the F of the Jabbok.
2Sam 19:18 and they crossed the F to bring over the

FORDS (9)

Josh 2:7 as far as the F; and as soon as
Judg 3:28 him, and seized the F of the Jordan against
12:5 the Gileadites took the F of the Jordan against
12:6 slew him at the F of the Jordan.
1Sam 13:7 cisterns, or crossed the F of the Jordan to
2Sam 15:28 will wait at the F of the wilderness, until
17:16 lodge tonight at the F of the wilderness, but
Is 16:2 of Moab at the F of the Arnon.
Jer 51:32 on every side; the F have been seized, the

FOREBODING

Lk 21:26 with fear and with F of what is coming

FOREFATHER (4)

Tob 1:4 tribe of Naphtali my F deserted the house of
1:5 and so did the house of Naphtali my F
Rom 4:1 say about Abraham, our F according to the flesh?
9:10 by one man, our F Isaac,

FOREFATHERS (5)

Lev 26:45 the covenant with their F, whom I brought forth
Jud 8:25 us to the test as he did our F
Ps 79:8 the iniquities of our F; let thy compassion come
Jer 11:10 the iniquities of their F, who refused to hear
Rom 11:28 they are beloved for the sake of their F

FOREFRONT

2Sam 11:15 "Set Uriah in the F of the hardest fighting,

FOREGO (2)

Neh 10:31 day; and we will F the crops of the
2Mac 2:31 of expression and to F exhaustive treatment.

FOREHEAD (20)

Ex 28:38 shall be upon Aaron's F, and Aaron shall take
28:38 always be upon his F, that they may be
Lev 13:41 has fallen from his F and temples, he has
13:41 has baldness of the F but he is clean.
13:42 head or the bald F a reddish-white diseased spot,
13:42 out on his bald head or his bald F
13:43 or on his bald F, like the appearance of
Num 24:17 it shall crush the F of Moab, and break
1Sam 17:49 the Philistine on his F; the stone sank into
17:49 stone sank into his F, and he fell on
2Chr 26:19 broke out on his F, in the presence of
26:20 him, and behold, he was leprous in his F
Is 48:4 iron sinew and your F brass,
Jer 48:45 it has destroyed the F of Moab, the crown
Ezek 3:7 are of a hard F and of a stubborn
3:8 their faces, and your F hard against their foreheads.
3:9 have I made your F; fear them not, nor
Rev 13:16 right hand or the F,
14:9 a mark on his F or on his hand,
17:5 fornication; and on her F was written a name

FOREHEADS (8)

Deut 14:1 any baldness on your F for the dead.
Ezek 3:8 their faces, and your forehead hard against their F
9:4 a mark upon the F of the men who
Rev 7:3 sealed the servants of our God upon their F
9:4 of God upon their F;
14:1 name and his Father's name written on their F
20:4 its mark on their F or their hands.
22:4 face, and his name shall be on their F

FOREIGN (53)

Gen 35:2 him, "Put away the F gods that are among
35:4 to Jacob all the F gods that they had,
Ex 2:22 a sojourner in a F land."
18:3 a sojourner in a F land"),
21:8 sell her to a F people, since he has
Deut 32:12 and there was no F god with him.
Josh 24:20 the LORD and serve F gods, then he will
24:23 "Then put away the F gods which are among
Judg 10:16 they put away the F gods from among them
1Sam 7:3 then put away the F gods and the Ashtaroth
1Kgs 11:1 King Solomon loved many F women: the daughter of
11:8 did for all his F wives, who burned incense
2Kgs 19:24 dug wells and drank F waters, and I dried
2Chr 14:3 He took away the F altars and the high
33:15 he took away the F gods and the idol
Ezra 10:2 God and have married F women from the peoples
10:10 have trespassed and married F women, and so
10:11 land and from the F wives."
10:14 cities who have taken F wives come at appointed
10:17 men who had married F women.
10:18 who had married F women were found Ma-aseiah,
10:44 All these had married F women, and they put
Neh 13:3 Israel all those of F descent.
13:26 over all Israel; nevertheless F women made even
13:27 our God by marrying F women?"
13:30 cleansed them from everything F, and I established
Tob 4:12 do not marry a F woman, who is not
Jud 5:18 away captive to a F country; the temple of
6:1 presence of all the F contingents:
Ps 81:9 bow down to a F god.
137:4 LORD's song in a F land?
Sir 29:18 they have wandered among F nations.
36:3 up thy hand against F nations and let them
39:4 through the lands of F nations, for he tests
49:5 their glory to a F nation,
Jer 5:19 forsaken me and served F gods in your land,
8:19 images, and with their F idols?"
25:20 people, and all the F folk among them; all
50:37 and upon all the F troops in her midst,
Bar 3:10 growing old in a F country, that you are
Ezek 3:5 to a people of F speech and a hard
3:6 to many peoples of F speech and a hard
Dan 11:39 the help of a F god; those who acknowledge
Zeph 1:8 who array themselves in F attire.
Mal 2:11 the daughter of a F god.
1Mac 11:38 own place, except the F troops which he had
15:33 "We have neither taken F land nor seized foreign
15:33 foreign land nor seized F property, but only the
2Mac 4:13 in the adoption of F ways because of the
Acts 17:18 be a preacher of F divinities"—because he preached
26:11 persecuted them even to F cities.
Heb 11:9 promise, as in a F land, living in tents
11:34 mighty in war, put F armies to flight.

FOREIGNER (20)

Gen 17:12 your money from any F who is not of
17:27 with money from a F, were circumcised with him.
Ex 12:43 of the passover: no F shall eat of it;
Lev 22:25 your God any such animals gotten from a F
Deut 14:21 sell it to a F; for you are a
15:3 Of a F you may exact it; but whatever
17:15 may not put a F over you, who is
23:20 To a F you may lend upon interest, but
29:22 after you, and the F who comes from a
Ruth 2:10 take notice of me, when I am a F

2Sam 15:19 for you are a F, and also an exile
1Kgs 8:41 "Likewise when a F, who is not of thy
8:43 all for which the F calls to thee; in
2Chr 6:32 "Likewise when a F, who is not of thy
6:33 all for which the F calls to thee; in
Is 56:3 Let not the F who has joined himself to
Ezek 44:9 the Lord GOD: No F, uncircumcised in heart and
Lk 17:18 return and give praise to God except this F
1Cor 14:11 I shall be a F to the speaker and
14:11 and the speaker a F to me.

FOREIGNERS (33)
Gen 31:15 Are we not regarded by him as F
Judg 19:12 into the city of F, who do not belong
2Sam 22:45 F came cringing to me; as soon as they
22:46 F lost heart, and came trembling out of their
Neh 9:2 separated themselves from all F, and stood and
Ps 18:44 me they obeyed me; F came cringing to me.
18:45 F lost heart, and came trembling out of their
Prov 20:16 him in pledge when he gives surety for F
27:13 him in pledge when he gives surety for F
Is 2:6 like the Philistines, and they strike hands with F
56:6 "And the F who join themselves to the LORD,
60:10 F shall build up your walls, and their kings
61:5 and feed your flocks, F shall be your plowmen
62:8 for your enemies, and F shall not drink your
Bar 6:5 at all like the F or to let fear
Ezek 7:21 into the hands of F for a prey, and
11:9 into the hands of F, and execute judgments upon
28:10 by the hand of F; for I have spoken,
30:12 by the hand of F; I, the LORD, have
31:12 F, the most terrible of the nations, will cut
44:7 abominations, in admitting F, uncircumcised in heart
44:8 but you have set F to keep my charge
44:9 flesh, of all the F who are among the
Obad 1:11 off his wealth, and F entered his gates and
1Mac 4:12 When the F looked up and saw them coming
4:26 Those of the F who escaped went and reported
10:12 Then the F who were in the strongholds that
11:68 the army of the F met him in the
11:74 three thousand of the F fell that day.
2Mac 10:2 public square by the F, and also destroyed the
10:5 been profaned by the F, the purification of the
Acts 17:21 the Athenians and the F who lived there spent
1Cor 14:21 by the lips of F will I speak to

FOREKNEW (2)
Rom 8:29 For those whom he F he also predestined to
11:2 God has not rejected his people whom he F

FOREKNOWLEDGE (4)
Jud 9:6 prepared in advance, and thy judgment is with F
11:19 told me, by my F; it was announced to
Wis 8:8 of riddles; she has F of signs and wonders
Acts 2:23 the definite plan and F of God, you crucified

FOREMEN (5)
Ex 5:6 the people and their F,
5:10 the taskmasters and the F of the people went
5:14 And the F of the people of Israel, whom
5:15 Then the F of the people of Israel came
5:19 The F of the people of Israel saw that

FOREMOST (5)
Gen 32:17 He instructed the F, "When Esau my brother meets
2Sam 18:27 the running of the F is like the running
Ezra 9:2 of the officials and chief men has been F
1Tim 1:15 And I am the F of sinners;
1:16 in me, as the F, Jesus Christ might display

FORENOON
2Sam 2:29 and marching the whole F they came to Mahanaim.

FORERUNNER
Heb 6:20 has gone as a F on our behalf, having

FORERUNNERS
Wis 12:8 didst send wasps as F of thy army, to

FORESAIL
Acts 27:40 rudders; then hoisting the F to the wind they

FORESAW
Acts 2:31 upon his throne, he F and spoke of the

FORESEEING
Gal 3:8 And the scripture, F that God would justify the

FORESEEN
Heb 11:40 promised, since God had F something better for us,

FORESKIN (7)
Gen 17:14 the flesh of his F shall be cut off
17:24 he was circumcised in the flesh of his F
17:25 he was circumcised in the flesh of his F
Ex 4:25 cut off her son's F, and touched Moses' feet
Lev 12:3 the flesh of his F shall be circumcised.
Deut 10:16 Circumcise therefore the F of your heart, and be
Jer 4:4 the LORD, remove the F of your hearts, O

FORESKINS (5)
Gen 17:11 the flesh of your F, and it shall be
17:23 the flesh of their F that very day, as
1Sam 18:25 present except a hundred F of the Philistines, that
18:27 and David brought their F, which were given in
2Sam 3:14 price of a hundred F of the Philistines."

FOREST (52)
Deut 19:5 man goes into the F with his neighbor to
Josh 17:15 go up to the F, and there clear ground
17:18 though it is a F, you shall clear it
1Sam 14:25 people came into the F; and there was honey
14:26 the people entered the F, behold, the honey was
22:5 and went into the F of Hereth.
2Sam 18:6 was fought in the F of Ephraim.
18:8 the country; and the F devoured more people that
18:17 great pit in the F, and raised over him
1Kgs 7:2 the House of the F of Lebanon; its length
10:17 the House of the F of Lebanon.
10:21 the House of the F of Lebanon were of
2Kgs 19:23 cypresses; I entered its farthest retreat, its densest F
2Chr 9:16 the House of the F of Lebanon.
9:20 the House of the F of Lebanon were of
Neh 2:8 keeper of the king's F, that he may give
Ps 50:10 every beast of the F is mine, the cattle
80:13 The boar from the F ravages it, and all
83:14 As fire consumes the F, as the flame sets
104:20 the beasts of the F creep forth.
Eccl 2:6 which to water the F of growing trees.
Is 7:2 the trees of the F shake before the wind.
9:18 the thickets of the F, and they roll upward
10:18 The glory of his F and of his fruitful
10:19 the trees of his F will be so few
10:34 the thickets of the F with an axe, and
22:8 the House of the F,
29:17 the fruitful field shall be regarded as a F
32:15 field, and the fruitful field is deemed a F
32:19 And the F will utterly go down, and the
37:24 I came to its remotest height, its densest F
44:14 the trees of the F; he plants a cedar
44:23 singing, O mountains, O F, and every tree in
56:9 to devour-- all you beasts in the F
Jer 5:6 a lion from the F shall slay them, a
10:3 A tree from the F is cut down, and
12:8 a lion in the F, she has lifted up
21:14 a fire in her F, and it shall devour
46:23 shall cut down her F, says the LORD, though
Ezek 15:2 branch which is among the trees of the F
15:6 the trees of the F, which I have given
20:46 and prophesy against the F land in the Negeb;
20:47 Negeb; say to the F of the Negeb, Hear
31:3 with fair branches and F shade, and of great
31:4 its streams to all the trees of the F
31:5 the trees of the F; its boughs grew large
Hos 2:12 will make them a F, and the beasts of
Amos 3:4 lion roar in the F, when he has no
Mic 5:8 the beasts of the F, like a young lion
7:14 dwell alone in a F in the midst of
Zech 11:2 Bashan, for the thick F has been felled!
Jas 3:5 How great a F is set ablaze by a

FORESTALL
Sir 19:24 one notices, he will F you.

FORESTS (2)
Ps 29:9 whirl, and strips the F bare; and in his
Ezek 39:10 any out of the F, for they will make

FORETOLD (3)
2Kgs 24:13 of Israel had made, as the LORD had F
Acts 3:18 But what God F by the mouth of all

F

11:28 Agabus stood up and F by the Spirit that

FOREWARNED (2)

Wis 18:19 dreams which disturbed them F them of this, so
1Thes 4:6 things, as we solemnly F you.

FORFEIT (2)

2Kgs 10:24 hands to escape shall F his life."
Mk 8:36 the whole world and F his life?

FORFEITED (3)

Deut 22:9 the whole yield be F to the sanctuary, the
Ezra 10:8 his property should be F, and he himself banned
Hab 2:10 many peoples; you have F your life.

FORFEITS (3)

Prov 20:2 provokes him to anger F his life.
Mt 16:26 the whole world and F his life?
Lk 9:25 world and loses or F himself?

FORGAVE (6)

Ps 78:38 Yet he, being compassionate, F their iniquity, and did
Mt 18:26 servant released him and F him the debt.
18:31 I F you all that debt because you besought
Lk 7:42 could not pay, he F them both.
7:43 suppose, to whom he F more." And he said
Eph 4:32 as God in Christ F you.

FORGER

Gen 4:22 Tubal-cain; he was the F of all instruments of

FORGES

Is 44:12 it with hammers, and F it with his strong

FORGET (64)

Gen 41:51 "God has made me F all my hardship and
Deut 4:9 soul diligently, lest you F the things which your
4:23 to yourselves, lest you F the covenant of the
4:31 or destroy you or F the covenant with your
6:12 take heed lest you F the LORD, who brought
8:11 "Take heed lest you F the LORD your God,
8:14 lifted up, and you F the LORD your God,
8:19 And if you F the LORD your God and
9:7 Remember and do not F how you provoked the
25:19 of Amalek from under heaven; you shall not F
1Sam 1:11 remember me, and not F thy maidservant, but wilt
2Kgs 17:38 and you shall not F the covenant that I
Job 8:13 paths of all who F God; the hope of
9:27 I say, 'I will F my complaint, I will
11:16 You will F your misery; you will remember it
24:20 squares of the town F them; their name is
39:17 God has made her F wisdom, and given her
Ps 9:12 them; he does not F the cry of the
9:17 all the nations that F God.
10:12 lift up thy hand; F not the afflicted.
13:1 Wilt thou F me for ever?
44:24 Why dost thou F our affliction and oppression?
45:10 and incline your ear; F your people and your
50:22 this, then, you who F God, lest I rend,
59:11 not, lest my people F; make them totter by
74:19 wild beasts; do not F the life of thy
74:23 Do not F the clamor of thy foes, the
78:7 in God, and not F the works of God,
102:4 grass, and withered; I F to eat my bread.
103:2 O my soul, and F not all his benefits,
119:16 statutes; I will not F thy word.
119:61 me, I do not F thy law.
119:93 I will never F thy precepts; for by them
119:109 but I do not F thy law.
119:139 me, because my foes F thy words.
119:141 yet I do not F thy precepts.
119:153 for I do not F thy law.
119:176 for I do not F thy commandments.
137:5 If I F you, O Jerusalem, let my right
Prov 3:1 My son, do not F my teaching, but let
4:6 do not F, and do not turn away from
31:5 lest they drink and F what has been decreed,
31:7 let them drink and F their poverty, and remember
Wis 19:4 end, and made them F what had happened, in
Sir 7:27 father, and do not F the birth-pangs of your
11:25 an hour makes one F luxury, and at the
29:15 Do not F all the kindness of your surety,
37:6 Do not F a friend in your heart, and
38:21 Do not F, there is no coming back; you
Is 49:15 "Can a woman F her sucking child, that she
49:15 Even these may F, yet I will not forget
49:15 yet I will not F you.
54:4 shame; for you will F the shame of your
65:11 forsake the LORD, who F my holy mountain, who
Jer 2:32 Can a maiden F her ornaments, or a bride
23:27 to make my people F my name by their
Lam 5:20 Why dost thou F us for ever, why dost
Ezek 39:26 They shall F their shame, and all the treachery
Hos 4:6 God, I also will F your children.
Amos 8:7 "Surely I will never F any of their deeds.
Mic 6:10 Can I F the treasures of wickedness in the
1Mac 1:49 so that they should F the law and change
2Mac 2:2 being deported not to F the commandments of the
7:23 again, since you now F yourselves for the sake

FORGETFUL

Sir 23:14 men; lest you be F in their presence, and

FORGETFULNESS (4)

Ps 88:12 or thy saving help in the land of F
Wis 14:26 over what is good, F of favors, pollution of
16:11 should fall into deep F and become unresponsive to
17:3 a dark curtain of F, they were scattered, terribly

FORGETS (4)

Gen 27:45 turns away, and he F what you have done
Prov 2:17 of her youth and F the covenant of her
Jas 1:23 away and at once F what he was like.
1:24 being no hearer that F but a doer that

FORGETTING (3)

Judg 3:7 sight of the LORD, F the LORD their God,
Job 39:15 warmed on the ground, F that a foot may
Phil 3:13 one thing I do, F what lies behind and

FORGIVE (66)

Gen 50:17 died, 'Say to Joseph, F, I pray you, the
50:17 now, we pray you, F the transgression of the
Ex 10:17 Now therefore, F my sin, I pray you, only
32:32 now, if thou wilt F their sin--and if
Num 30:5 and the LORD will F her, because her father
30:8 and the LORD will F her.
30:12 and the LORD will F her.
Deut 21:8 F, O LORD, thy people Israel, whom thou hast
Josh 24:19 God; he will not F your transgressions or your
1Sam 25:28 Pray F the trespass of your handmaid; for the
1Kgs 8:30 heaven thy dwelling place; and when thou hearest, F
8:34 thou in heaven, and F the sin of thy
8:36 thou in heaven, and F the sin of thy
8:39 thy dwelling place, and F, and act, and render
8:50 maintain their cause and F thy people who have
2Chr 6:21 heaven thy dwelling place; and when thou hearest, F
6:25 thou from heaven, and F the sin of thy
6:27 thou in heaven, and F the sin of thy
6:30 thy dwelling place, and F, and render to each
6:39 maintain their cause and F thy people who have
7:14 from heaven, and will F their sin and heal
Neh 9:17 a God ready to F, gracious and merciful, slow
Ps 25:18 and my trouble, and F all my sins.
32:5 LORD"; then thou didst F the guilt of my
65:3 over us, thou dost F them.
79:9 name; deliver us, and F our sins, for thy
85:2 Thou didst F the iniquity of thy people; thou
Sir 5:6 is great, he will F the multitude of my
16:11 he is mighty to F, and he pours out
28:2 F your neighbor the wrong he has done, and
Is 2:9 are brought low-- F them not!
Jer 18:23 F not their iniquity, nor blot out their sin
31:34 LORD; for I will F their iniquity, and I
33:8 me, and I will F all the guilt of
36:3 and that I may F their iniquity and their
Ezek 16:63 your shame, when I F you all that you
Dan 9:19 LORD, hear; O LORD, F; O LORD, give heed
Hos 1:6 house of Israel, to F them at all.
Amos 7:2 said, "O Lord GOD, F, I beseech thee!
Mt 6:12 our daily bread; And F us our debts, As
6:14 For if you F men their trespasses, your heavenly
6:14 heavenly Father also will F you;
6:15 if you do not F men their trespasses, neither
6:15 neither will your Father F your trespasses.
9:6 authority on earth to F sins"--he then said
18:20 against me, and I F him?
18:34 if you do not F your brother from your
Mk 2:7 Who can F sins but God alone?"
2:10 authority on earth to F sins"--he said to
11:25 whenever you stand praying, F, if you have anything
11:25 is in heaven may F you your trespasses."

Lk 5:21 Who can F sins but God only?"
5:24 authority on earth to F sins"--he said to
6:37 will not be condemned; F, and you will be
11:4 our daily bread; and F us our sins, for
11:4 sins, for we ourselves F every one who is
17:3 and if he repents, F him;
17:4 'I repent,' you must F him."
23:33 And Jesus said, "Father, F them; for they know
Jn 20:23 If you F the sins of any, they are
2Cor 2:7 should rather turn to F and comfort him, or
2:10 Any one whom you F, I also forgive.
2:10 Any one whom you forgive, I also F
12:13 F me this wrong!
Col 3:13 Lord has forgiven you, so you also must F
1Jn 1:9 and just, and will F our sins and cleanse

FORGIVEN (48)

Lev 4:20 make atonement for them, and they shall be F
4:26 him for his sin, and he shall be F
4:31 make atonement for him, and he shall be F
4:35 which he has committed, and he shall be F
5:10 which he has committed, and he shall be F
5:13 one of these things, and he shall be F
5:16 of the guilt offering, and he shall be F
5:18 which he committed unwittingly, and he shall be F
6:7 and he shall be F for any of the
19:22 has committed shall be F him.
Num 14:19 according as thou hast F this people, from Egypt
15:25 and they shall be F; because it was an
15:26 of Israel shall be F, and the stranger who
15:28 make atonement for him; and he shall be F
Deut 21:8 guilt of blood be F them.'
Ps 32:1 he whose transgression is F, whose sin is covered.
Is 6:7 your guilt is taken away, and your sin F
22:14 iniquity will not be F you till you die,"
33:24 dwell there will be F their iniquity.
Lam 3:42 have transgressed and rebelled, and thou hast not F
Mt 6:12 As we also have F our debtors;
9:2 paralytic, "Take heart, my son; your sins are F
9:5 say, 'Your sins are F or to say, 'Rise
12:31 and blasphemy will be F men, but the blasphemy
12:31 the blasphemy against the Spirit will not be F
12:32 of man will be F; but whoever speaks against
12:32 Spirit will not be F, either in this age
Mk 2:5 to the paralytic, "My son, your sins are F
2:9 paralytic, 'Your sins are F or to say,' Rise,
3:28 all sins will be F the sons of men,
4:12 understand; lest they should turn again, and be F
Lk 5:20 "Man, your sins are F you."
5:23 say, 'Your sins are F you,' or to say,
6:37 and you will be F;
7:47 which are many, are F, for she loved much;
7:47 but he who is F little, loves little."
7:48 And he said to her, "Your sins are F
12:10 of man will be F; but he who blasphemes
12:10 blasphemes against the Holy Spirit will not be F
Jn 20:23 of any, they are F; if you retain the
Acts 8:22 your heart may be F you.
Rom 4:7 those whose iniquities are F, and whose sins are
2Cor 2:10 What I have F, if I have forgiven anything,
2:10 forgiven, if I have F anything, has been for
Col 2:13 together with him, having F us all our trespasses,
3:13 as the Lord has F you, so you also
Jas 5:15 if he has committed sins, he will be F
1Jn 2:12 because your sins are F for his sake.

FORGIVENESS (20)

Ps 130:4 But there is F with thee, that thou mayest
Sir 17:24 the Lord, and his F for those who turn
18:11 therefore he grants them F in abundance.
18:19 in the hour of visitation you will find F
Dan 9:9 God belong mercy and F; because we have rebelled
Mt 26:28 for many for the F of sins.
Mk 1:4 of repentance for the F of sins.
3:29 Holy Spirit never has F, but is guilty of
Lk 1:77 his people in the F of their sins,
3:3 of repentance for the F of sins.
24:47 and that repentance and F of sins should be
Acts 2:38 Jesus Christ for the F of your sins; and
5:31 repentance to Israel and F of sins.
10:43 believes in him receives F of sins through his
13:38 that through this man F of sins is proclaimed
26:18 that they may receive F of sins and a
Eph 1:7 through his blood, the F of our trespasses, according
Col 1:14 we have redemption, the F of sins.
Heb 9:22 blood there is no F of sins.

10:18 Where there is F of these, there is no

FORGIVES (4)

Ps 103:3 all his benefits, who F all your iniquity, who
Prov 17:9 He who F an offense seeks love, but he
Sir 2:11 compassionate and merciful; he F sins and saves in
Lk 7:49 is this, who even F sins?"

FORGIVING (6)

Ex 34:7 steadfast love for thousands, F iniquity and
Num 14:18 abounding in steadfast love, F iniquity and
Ps 86:5 Lord, art good and F, abounding in steadfast love
99:8 them; thou wast a F God to them, but
Eph 4:32 to one another, tenderhearted, F one another, as God
Col 3:13 a complaint against another, F each other; as the

FORGOT (12)

Gen 40:23 not remember Joseph, but F him.
Deut 32:18 begot you, and you F the God who gave
1Sam 12:9 But they F the LORD their God; and he
Ps 78:11 They F what he had done, and the miracles
106:13 But they soon F his works; they did not
106:21 They F God, their Savior, who had done great
Wis 16:23 might be fed, even F its native power.
19:20 normal power, and water F its fire-quenching nature.
Jer 23:27 even as their fathers F my name for Baal?
Bar 4:8 You F the everlasting God, who brought you up,
Hos 2:13 after her lovers, and F me, says the LORD.
13:6 lifted up; therefore they F me.

FORGOTTEN (46)

Gen 41:30 the plenty will be F in the land of
Deut 24:19 your field, and have F a sheaf in the
26:13 commandments, neither have I F them;
Job 19:15 in my house have F me; my maidservants count
28:4 men live; they are F by travelers, they hang
Ps 9:18 shall not always be F, and the hope of
10:11 his heart, "God has F, he has hidden his
42:9 rock: "Why hast thou F me?
44:17 though we have not F thee, or been false
44:20 If we had F the name of our God,
77:9 Has God F to be gracious?
119:83 yet I have not F thy statutes.
Eccl 2:16 days to come all will have been long F
Wis 2:4 Our name will be F in time and no
Sir 3:14 father will not be F, and against your sins
11:23 of prosperity, adversity is F, and in the day
13:10 not remain at a distance, lest you be F
35:7 and the memory of it will not be F
44:11 deeds have not been F;
Is 17:10 For you have F the God of your salvation,
23:15 day Tyre will be F for seventy years, like
23:16 about the city, O F harlot!
44:21 you will not be F by me.
49:14 me, my Lord has F me."
51:13 like grass, and have F the LORD, your Maker,
65:16 the former troubles are F and are hid from
Jer 2:32 Yet my people have F me days without number.
3:21 their way, they have F the LORD their God.
13:25 LORD, because you have F me and trusted in
18:15 But my people have F me, they burn incense
20:11 Their eternal dishonor will never be F
23:40 reproach and perpetual shame, which shall not be F
30:14 All your lovers have F you; they care nothing
44:9 Have you F the wickedness of your fathers, the
50:5 which will never be F
50:6 have gone, they have F their fold.
Lam 3:17 of peace, I have F what happiness is;
Ezek 22:12 extortion; and you have F me, says the Lord
23:35 GOD: Because you have F me and cast me
Hos 4:6 And since you have F the law of your
8:14 For Israel has F his Maker, and built palaces;
Mt 16:5 other side, they had F to bring any bread.
Mk 8:14 Now they had F to bring bread; and they
Lk 12:6 one of them is F before God.
Heb 12:5 And have you F the exhortation which addresses you
2Pet 1:9 and shortsighted and has F that he was cleansed

FORK (6)

1Sam 2:13 boiling, with a three-pronged F in his hand,
2:14 pot; all that the F brought up the priest
Is 30:24 which has been winnowed with shovel and F
Jer 15:7 them with a winnowing F in the gates of
Mt 3:12 His winnowing F is in his hand, and he
Lk 3:17 His winnowing F is in his hand, to clear

FORKS (5)
Ex 27:3 shovels and basins and F and firepans; all its
38:3 shovels, the basins, the F, and the firepans: all
Num 4:14 there, the firepans, the F, the shovels, and the
1Chr 28:17 pure gold for the F, the basins, and the
2Chr 4:16 pots, the shovels, the F, and all the equipment

FORLORN (3)
1Sam 2:5 seven, but she who has many children is F
Jud 9:11 weak, protector of the F, savior of those without
Ps 35:12 requite me evil for good; my soul is F

FORM (45)
Gen 1:2 The earth was without F and void, and darkness
Ex 26:24 of them; they shall F the two corners.
Num 12:8 and he beholds the F of the LORD.
Deut 4:12 words, but saw no F; there was only a
4:15 Since you saw no F on the day that
4:16 for yourselves, in the F of any figure, the
4:23 graven image in the F of anything which the
4:25 graven image in the F of anything, and by
1Kgs 6:18 was carved in the F of gourds and open
6:25 cherubim had the same measure and the same F
6:33 of olivewood, in the F of a square,
7:37 alike, of the same measure and the same F
Jud 1:4 force and his infantry F their ranks--
Job 4:16 A F was before my eyes; there was silence,
Ps 17:15 awake, I shall be satisfied with beholding thy F
49:14 they descend, and their F shall waste away; Sheol
104:26 Leviathan which thou didst F to sport in it.
139:13 For thou didst F my inward parts, thou didst
Wis 14:19 to take more beautiful F,
15:5 they desire the lifeless F of a dead image.
15:16 for no man can F a god which is
18:12 together, by the one F of death, had corpses
Sir 32:16 fear the Lord will F true judgments, and like
Is 45:7 I F light and create darkness, I make weal
52:14 human semblance, and his F beyond that of the
53:2 ground; he had no F or comeliness that we
Lam 4:7 the beauty of their F was like sapphire.
Ezek 1:5 appearance: they had the F of men,
1:26 a likeness as it were of a human F
8:2 beheld, and, lo, a F that had the appearance
8:3 He put forth the F of a hand, and
10:1 like a sapphire, in F resembling a throne.
10:8 appeared to have the F of a human hand
43:11 entrances, and its whole F; and make known to
2Mac 9:18 following letter, in the F of a supplication.
Mk 16:12 he appeared in another F to two of them,
Lk 3:22 upon him in bodily F, as a dove, and
Jn 5:36 have never heard, his F you have never seen;
1Cor 7:31 For the F of this world is passing away.
Phil 2:6 he was in the F of God, did not
2:7 emptied himself, taking the F of a servant, being
2:8 being found in human F he humbled himself and
1Thes 5:22 good, abstain from every F of evil.
2Tim 3:5 of God, holding the F of religion but denying
Heb 10:1 instead of the true F of these realities, it

FORMATION (2)
1Mac 12:26 being drawn up in F to fall upon the
12:50 kept marching in close F, ready for battle.

FORMED (48)
Gen 2:7 then the LORD God F man of dust from
2:8 there he put the man whom he had F
2:19 ground the LORD God F every beast of the
Num 22:36 Moab, on the boundary F by the Arnon, at
Josh 19:9 the tribe of Simeon F part of the territory
Judg 20:22 took courage, and again F the battle line in
20:22 place where they had F it on the first
1Kgs 6:31 lintel and the doorposts F a pentagon.
Tob 2:10 eyes and white films F on my eyes.
Jud 7:18 great number, and they F a vast multitude.
16:14 thy Spirit, and it F them; there is none
Job 1:17 and said, "The Chaldeans F three companies, and
33:6 are; I too was F from a piece of
Ps 90:2 or ever thou hadst F the earth and the
94:9 He who F the eye, does he not see?
95:5 it; for his hands F the dry land.
139:16 the days that were F for me, when as
Wis 9:2 by thy wisdom hast F man, to have dominion
13:4 powerful is he who F them.
15:11 know the one who F him and inspired him
15:16 whose spirit is borrowed F them; for no man
Sir 37:3 imagination, why were you F to cover the land
Is 25:1 done wonderful things, plans F of old, faithful and
27:11 on them, he that F them will show them
29:16 me"; or the thing F say of him who
29:16 say of him who F it, "He has no
43:1 O Jacob, he who F you, O Israel: "Fear
43:7 my glory, whom I F and made."
43:10 me no god was F, nor shall there be
43:21 the people whom I F for myself that they
44:2 who made you, who F you from the womb
44:21 are my servant; I F you, you are my
44:24 LORD, your Redeemer, who F you from the womb:
45:18 (he is God!), who F the earth and made
45:18 it a chaos, he F it to be inhabited!):
49:5 the LORD says, who F me from the womb
Jer 1:5 me saying, "Before I F you in the womb
10:16 is the one who F all things, and Israel
33:2 earth, the LORD who F it to establish it--
49:20 purposes which he has F against the inhabitants of
49:30 plan against you, and F a purpose against you.
50:45 purposes which he has F against the land of
51:19 is the one who F all things, and Israel
Ezek 16:7 maidenhood; your breasts were F, and your hair had
Zech 12:1 founded the earth and F the spirit of man
Gal 4:19 travail until Christ be F in you!
1Tim 2:13 For Adam was F first, then Eve;
2Pet 3:5 ago, and an earth F out of water and

FORMER (60)
Gen 26:1 the land, besides the F famine that was in
Num 6:12 guilt offering; but the F time shall be void,
21:26 had fought against the F king of Moab and
Deut 24:4 his wife, then her F husband, who sent her
Ruth 4:7 was the custom in F times in Israel concerning
2Kgs 1:14 and consumed the two F captains of fifty men
17:34 do according to the F manner.
17:40 did according to their F manner.
1Chr 4:40 and peaceful; for the F inhabitants there belonged to
Neh 5:15 The F governors who were before me laid heavy
Tob 14:5 not be like the F one until the times
Eccl 1:11 is no remembrance of F things, nor will there
7:10 not, "Why were the F days better than these?"
Wis 19:15 will come upon the F for their hostile reception
Sir 21:1 but pray about your F sins.
41:3 of death; remember your F days and the end
Is 9:1 In the F time he brought into contempt the
41:22 Tell us the F things, what they are, that
42:9 Behold, the F things have come to pass, and
43:9 and show us the F things?
43:18 wick: "Remember not the F things, nor consider the
46:9 you transgressors, remember the F things of old; for
48:3 "The F things I declared of old, they went
61:4 shall raise up the F devastations; they shall repair
65:7 bosom payment for their F doings."
65:16 of truth; because the F troubles are forgotten and
65:17 new earth; and the F things shall not be
Jer 34:5 for your fathers, the F kings who were before
36:28 on it all the F words that were in
Ezek 16:55 shall return to their F estate, and Samaria and
16:55 shall return to their F estate; and you and
16:55 shall return to your F estate.
36:11 inhabited as in your F times, and will do
38:17 whom I spoke in F days by my servants
Dan 7:24 be different from the F ones, and shall put
11:13 multitude, greater than the F; and after some years
Mic 4:8 shall it come, the F dominion shall come, the
Hag 2:3 this house in its F glory?
2:9 be greater than the F, says the LORD of
Zech 1:4 fathers, to whom the F prophets cried out, 'Thus
7:7 LORD proclaimed by the F prophets?"
7:12 his Spirit through the F prophets.
8:11 people as in the F days, says the LORD
14:10 the place of the F gate, to the Corner
Mal 3:4 old and as in F years.
1Mac 4:47 new altar like the F one.
12:3 us to renew the F friendship and alliance with
12:16 Rome to renew our F friendship and alliance with
2Mac 14:38 For in F times, when there was no mingling
15:8 keep in mind the F times when help had
Rom 3:25 he had passed over F sins;
15:4 whatever was written in F days was written for
Gal 1:13 have heard of my F life in Judaism, how
Eph 4:22 which belongs to your F manner of life and
Phil 1:17 of the gospel; the F proclaim Christ out of
Heb 7:18 the one hand, a F commandment is set aside
7:23 The F priests were many in number, because they
10:32 But recall the F days, when, after you were

F

1Pet 1:14 the passions of your F ignorance,
Rev 21:4 any more, for the F things have passed away."

FORMERLY (34)

Gen 40:13 in his hand as F, when you were his
Deut 2:10 a possession.' (The Emim F lived there, a people
2:12 also lived in Seir F, but the sons of
2:20 land of Rephaim; Rephaim F lived there, but the
Josh 11:10 the sword; for Hazor F was the head of
14:15 the name of Hebron F was Kiriath-arba; this Arba
15:15 the name of Debir F was Kiriath-sepher.
Judg 1:10 name of Hebron was F Kiriath-arba); and they
1:11 name of Debir was F Kiriath-sepher.
1:23 of the city was F Luz.)
1Sam 9:9 F in Israel, when a man went to inquire
9:9 called a prophet was F called a seer.)
2Sam 7:10 them no more, as F,
2Kgs 13:5 people of Israel dwelt in their homes as F
1Chr 17:9 them no more, as F,
1Mac 3:46 opposite Jerusalem, because Israel F had a place of
9:72 captives whom he had F taken from the land
11:27 honors as he had F had, and made him
11:34 taxes which the king F received from them each
11:39 Now Trypho had F been one of Alexander's
14:33 borders of Judea, where F the arms of the
14:34 Azotus, where the enemy F dwelt.
15:3 restore it as it F was, and have recruited
15:27 all the agreements he F had made with Simon,
2Mac 9:16 sanctuary, which he had F plundered, he would adorn
11:31 and laws, just as F, and none of them
14:3 certain Alcimus, who had F been high priest but
Jn 9:13 the man who had F been blind.
Gal 4:8 F, when you did not know God, you were
1Tim 1:13 his service, though I F blasphemed and persecuted
Philem 1:11 F he was useless to you, but now he
Heb 4:6 it, and those who F received the good news
7:21 Those who F became priests took their office
1Pet 3:20 spirits in prison, who F did not obey, when

FORMING (4)

Deut 31:21 which they are already F, before I have brought
Josh 17:10 Manassehs, with the sea F its boundary; on the
Amos 7:1 me: behold, he was F locusts in the beginning
1Mac 10:23 ahead of us in F a friendship with the

FORMLESS

Wis 11:17 the world out of F matter, did not lack

FORMS (8)

Josh 18:14 This F the western side.
18:20 The Jordan F its boundary on the eastern side.
Wis 13:13 gained in idleness; he F it like the image
15:8 With misspent toil, he F a futile god from
16:25 also, changed into all F, it served thy all-nourishing
18:1 did not see their F, and counted them happy
Amos 4:13 For lo, he who F the mountains, and creates
2Mac 4:15 highest value upon Greek F of prestige.

FORNICATION (14)

Wis 14:12 was the beginning of F, and the invention of
Sir 23:16 a man who commits F with his near of
Mt 15:19 evil thoughts, murder, adultery, F, theft, false witness,
Mk 7:20 man, come evil thoughts, F, theft, murder, adultery,
Jn 8:41 were not born of F; we have one Father,
Gal 5:19 the flesh are plain: F, impurity, licentiousness,
Eph 5:3 But F and all impurity or covetousness must not
Col 3:5 is earthly in you: F, impurity, passion, evil desire,
Rev 17:2 the earth have committed F, and with the wine
17:2 the wine of whose F the dwellers on earth
17:4 the impurities of her F;
18:3 the earth have committed F with her, and the
18:9 the earth, who committed F and were wanton with
19:2 the earth with her F, and he has avenged

FORNICATOR (2)

Sir 23:17 To a F all bread tastes sweet; he will
Eph 5:5 of this, that no F or impure man, or

FORNICATORS (2)

Rev 21:8 polluted, as for murderers, F, sorcerers, idolaters, and
22:15 dogs and sorcerers and F and murderers and

FORSAKE (68)

Deut 12:19 that you do not F the Levite as long
14:27 And you shall not F the Levite who is
31:6 not fail you or F you."
31:8 not fail you or F you; do not fear
31:16 them, and they will F me and break my
31:17 day, and I will F them and hide my
Josh 1:5 not fail you or F you.
24:16 us that we should F the LORD, to serve
24:20 If you F the LORD and serve foreign gods,
1Kgs 6:13 Israel, and will not F my people Israel."
8:57 not leave us or F us;
1Chr 28:9 you; but if you F him, he will cast
28:20 not fail you or F you, until all the
2Chr 7:19 you turn aside and F my statutes and my
15:2 you, but if you F him, he will forsake
15:2 forsake him, he will F you.
Ezra 8:22 is against all that F him."
Neh 9:17 love, and didst not F them.
9:19 great mercies didst not F them in the wilderness;
9:31 end of them or F them; for thou art
Jud 7:31 for he will not F us utterly.
Ps 27:9 Cast me not off, F me not, O God
37:8 Refrain from anger, and F wrath!
37:28 justice; he will not F his saints.
38:21 Do not F me, O LORD!
71:9 time of old age; F me not when my
71:18 O God, do not F me, till I proclaim
89:30 If his children F my law and do not
94:14 the LORD will not F his people; he will
119:8 observe thy statutes; O F me not utterly!
119:53 of the wicked, who F thy law.
138:8 Do not F the work of thy hands.
Prov 2:13 of perverted speech, who F the paths of uprightness
3:3 not loyalty and faithfulness F you; bind them about
4:3 good precepts: do not F my teaching.
4:7 Do not F her, and she will keep you,
6:20 your father's commandment, and F not your mother's
27:10 father's friend, do not F; and do not go
28:4 Those who F the law praise the wicked, but
Sir 4:19 goes astray she will F him, and hand him
7:30 Maker, and do not F his ministers.
9:10 F not an old friend, for a new one
13:4 in need he will F you.
13:7 you afterwards, he will F you, and shake his
17:20 to the Lord and F your sins; pray in
28:23 Those who F the Lord will fall into its
35:3 the Lord, and to F unrighteousness is atonement.
48:15 and they did not F their sins, till they
51:10 my lord, not to F me in the days
Is 1:28 together, and those who F the LORD shall be
41:17 of Israel will not F them.
42:16 and I will not F them.
55:7 near; let the wicked F his way, and the
58:2 righteousness and did not F the ordinance of their
65:11 But you who F the LORD, who forget my
Jer 2:19 bitter for you to F the LORD your God;
17:13 of Israel, all who F thee shall be put
51:9 F her, and let us go each to his
Lam 5:20 dost thou so long F us?
Bar 4:1 live, and those who F her will die.
Ezek 20:8 on, nor did they F the idols of Egypt.
Dan 11:30 heed to those who F the holy covenant.
Jon 2:8 regard to vain idols F their true loyalty.
2Mac 1:5 and may he not F you in time of
6:1 compel the Jews to F the laws of their
6:16 calamities, he does not F his own people.
Acts 21:21 among the Gentiles to F Moses, telling them not
Heb 13:5 never fail you nor F you."

FORSAKEN (73)

Gen 24:27 Abraham, who has not F his steadfast love and
Deut 28:20 doings, because you have F me.
Josh 22:3 you; you have not F your brethren these many
Judg 10:10 thee, because we have F our God and have
10:13 Yet you have F me and served other gods;
Ruth 2:20 whose kindness has not F the living or the
1Sam 12:10 sinned, because we have F the LORD, and have
1Kgs 11:33 Israel), because he has F me, and worshiped
18:18 house, because you have F the commandments of the
19:10 people of Israel have F thy covenant, thrown down
19:14 people of Israel have F thy covenant, thrown down
2Kgs 22:17 Because they have F me and have burned incense
2Chr 13:10 and we have not F him.
13:11 God, but you have F him.
21:10 rule, because he had F the LORD, the God
24:20 Because you have F the LORD, he has forsaken
24:20 the LORD, he has F you.'"
24:24 army, because they had F the LORD, the God
28:6 valor, because they had F the LORD, the God

	29:6	our God; they have F him, and have turned
	34:25	Because they have F me and have burned incense
Ezra	9:9	our God has not F us in our bondage,
	9:10	For we have F thy commandments,
Neh	13:11	and said, "Why is the house of God F
Job	18:4	shall the earth be F for you, or the
Ps	9:10	O LORD, hast not F those who seek thee.
	22:1	God, why hast thou F me?
	27:10	and my mother have F me, but the LORD
	37:25	not seen the righteous F or his children begging
	71:11	and say, "God has F him; pursue and seize
	88:5	no strength, like one F among the dead, like
	119:87	but I have not F thy precepts.
Sir	2:10	in the fear of the Lord and was F
	10:12	Lord; his heart has F his Maker.
	41:8	ungodly men, who have F the law of the
	51:20	from the first, therefore I will not be F
Is	1:4	They have F the LORD, they have despised the
	6:12	far away, and the F places are many in
	10:14	eggs that have been F so I have gathered
	27:10	a habitation deserted and F, like the wilderness; thee
	32:14	the palace will be F, the populous city deserted;
	49:14	said, "The LORD has F me, my Lord has
	54:6	you like a wife F and grieved in spirit,
	60:15	Whereas you have been F and hated, with no
	62:4	no more be termed F, and your land shall
	62:12	shall be called Sought out, a city not F
Jer	2:13	two evils: they have F me, the fountain of
	4:29	all the cities are F, and no man dwells
	5:7	Your children have F me, and have sworn by
	5:19	them, 'As you have F me and served foreign
	7:29	LORD has rejected and F the generation of his
	9:13	says: "Because they have F my law which I
	12:7	"I have F my house, I have abandoned my
	16:11	'Because your fathers have F me, says the LORD,
	16:11	worshiped them, and have F me and have not
	17:13	earth, for they have F the LORD, the fountain
	19:4	Because the people have F me, and have profaned
	49:25	the famous city is F, the joyful city!
	51:5	Judah have not been F by their God, the
Bar	3:12	You have F the fountain of wisdom.
Ezek	8:12	us, the LORD has F the land.'"
	9:9	say, 'The LORD has F the land, and the
Dan	14:38	God, and hast not F those who love thee."
Hos	4:10	multiply; because they have F the LORD to cherish
Amos	5:2	is the virgin Israel; F on her land, with
1Mac	10:14	some remain who had F the law and the
2Mac	5:20	benefits; and what was F in the wrath of
	7:16	think that God has F our people.
Mt	23:37	Behold, your house is F and desolate.
	27:46	God, why hast thou F me?"
Mk	15:33	God, why hast thou F me?"
Lk	13:35	Behold, your house is F
2Cor	4:9	despair; persecuted, but not F; struck down, but not

FORSAKES (6)

Job	6:14	kindness from a friend F the fear of the
Prov	2:17	her smooth words, who F the companion of her
	15:10	discipline for him who F the way; he who
	28:13	he who confesses and F them will obtain mercy.
Sir	3:16	Whoever F his father is like a blasphemer, and
Jer	14:5	hind in the field F her newborn calf because

FORSAKING (8)

1Sam	8:8	even to this day, F me and serving other
1Kgs	12:13	the people harshly, and F the counsel which the
2Chr	10:13	answered them harshly, and F the counsel of the
Jer	1:16	all their wickedness in F me; they have burned
	2:17	this upon yourself by F the LORD your God,
Hos	1:2	commits great harlotry by F the LORD."
	9:1	have played the harlot, F your God.
2Pet	2:15	F the right way they have gone astray; they

FORSOOK (25)

Deut	29:25	'It is because they F the covenant of the
	32:15	became sleek; then he F God who made him,
Judg	2:12	the Baals; and they F the LORD, the God
	2:13	They F the LORD, and served the Baals and
	10:6	the Philistines; and they F the LORD, and did
1Sam	31:7	sons were dead, they F their cities and fled;
1Kgs	9:9	will say, 'Because they F the LORD their God
	12:8	But he F the counsel which the old men
2Kgs	7:7	in the twilight and F their tents, their horses,
	17:16	And they F all the commandments of the LORD
	21:22	and worshiped them; he F the LORD, the God
1Chr	10:7	sons were dead, they F their cities and fled;
2Chr	7:22	will say, 'Because they F the LORD the God
	10:8	But he F the counsel which the old men
	12:1	and was strong, he F the law of the
	24:18	And they F the house of the LORD, the
Ps	78:60	He F his dwelling at Shiloh, the tent where
Sir	49:4	sinned greatly, for they F the law of the
Is	54:7	a brief moment I F you, but with great
Jer	22:9	will answer, "Because they F the covenant of the
Bar	3:8	of our fathers who F the Lord our God.'"
1Mac	1:38	offspring, and her children F her.
	1:52	people, every one who F the law, joined them,
Mt	26:56	Then all the disciples F him and fled.
Mk	14:50	And they all F him, and fled.

FORT

2Mac	10:33	and they besieged the F for four days.

FORTH (549)

Gen	1:11	"Let the earth put F vegetation, plants yielding seed,
	1:12	The earth brought F vegetation, plants yielding seed
	1:20	"Let the waters bring F swarms of living creatures,
	1:24	"Let the earth bring F living creatures according to
	3:16	pain you shall bring F children, yet your desire
	3:18	thistles it shall bring F to you; and you
	3:22	now, lest he put F his hand and take
	3:23	LORD God sent him F from the garden of
	7:11	the great deep burst F, and the windows of
	8:7	had made, and sent F a raven; and it
	8:8	Then he sent F a dove from him, to
	8:9	So he put F his hand and took her
	8:10	and again he sent F the dove out of
	8:12	seven days, and sent F the dove; and she
	8:16	said to Noah, "Go F from the ark, you
	8:17	Bring F with you every living thing that is
	8:18	So Noah went F, and his sons and his
	8:19	upon the earth, went F by families out of
	9:7	fruitful and multiply, bring F abundantly on the earth
	9:18	of Noah who went F from the ark were
	11:31	wife, and they went F together from Ur of
	12:5	Haran; and they set F to go to the
	14:14	taken captive, he led F his trained men, born
	17:6	and kings shall come F from you.
	19:10	But the men put F their hands and brought
	19:16	and they brought him F and set him outside
	19:17	they had brought them F, they said, "Flee for
	22:10	Then Abraham put F his hand, and took the
	24:53	And the servant brought F jewelry of silver and
	25:25	The first came F red, all his body like
	25:26	Afterward his brother came F, and his hand had
	30:39	so the flocks brought F striped, speckled, and
	31:13	Now arise, go F from this land, and return
	40:10	budded, its blossoms shot F, and the clusters ripened
	41:47	years the earth brought F abundantly,
Ex	3:10	that you may bring F my people, the sons
	3:12	when you have brought F the people out of
	5:20	them, as they came F from Pharaoh;
	7:4	upon Egypt and bring F my hosts, my people
	7:5	LORD, when I stretch F my hand upon Egypt
	8:18	secret arts to bring F gnats, but they could
	9:15	I could have put F my hand and struck
	9:22	said to Moses, "Stretch F your hand toward heaven,
	9:23	Then Moses stretched F his rod toward heaven; and
	10:13	So Moses stretched F his rod over the land
	11:4	midnight I will go F in the midst of
	12:31	said, "Rise up, go F from among my people,
	12:46	you shall not carry F any of the flesh
	13:4	you are to go F, in the month of
	14:8	Israel as they went F defiantly.
	14:27	So Moses stretched F his hand over the sea,
	15:7	thy adversaries; thou sendest F thy fury, it consumes
	19:1	of Israel had gone F out of the land
	29:46	God, who brought them F out of the land
	32:11	whom thou hast brought F out of the land
	32:12	did he bring them F, to slay them in
Lev	4:12	bull he shall carry F outside the camp to
	4:21	And he shall carry F the bull outside the
	6:11	other garments, and carry F the ashes outside the
	9:24	And fire came F from before the LORD and
	10:2	And fire came F from the presence of the
	14:45	he shall carry them F out of the city
	16:24	his garments, and come F, and offer his burnt
	16:27	place, shall be carried F outside the camp; their
	19:16	you shall not stand F against the life of
	25:21	that it will bring F fruit for three years.
	25:38	God, who brought you F out of the land
	25:42	servants, whom I brought F out of the land

57:3 [Selah] God will send F his steadfast love and
60:10 Thou dost not go F, O God, with our
66:12 thou hast brought us F to a spacious place.
68:7 when thou didst go F before thy people, when
68:33 heavens; lo, he sends F his voice, his mighty
72:16 and may men blossom F from the cities like
77:17 water; the skies gave F thunder; thy arrows flashed
78:52 Then he led F his people like sheep, and
80:1 upon the cherubim, shine F
89:34 the word that went F from my lips.
90:2 the mountains were brought F, or ever thou hadst
92:14 They still bring F fruit in old age, they
94:1 God of vengeance, thou God of vengeance, shine F
98:4 all the earth; break F into joyous song and
104:10 Thou makest springs gush F in the valleys; they
104:14 that he may bring F food from the earth,
104:20 when all the beasts of the forest creep F
104:23 Man goes F to his work and to his
104:30 When thou sendest F thy Spirit, they are created;
105:37 Then he led F Israel with silver and gold,
105:41 rock, and water gushed F; it flowed through the
105:43 So he led F his people with joy, his
106:2 the LORD, or show F all his praise?
107:20 their distress; he sent F his word, and healed
108:11 Thou dost not go F, O God, with our
109:7 tried, let him come F guilty; let his prayer
110:2 The LORD sends F from Zion your mighty scepter.
113:2 LORD from this time F and for evermore!
114:1 When Israel went F from Egypt, the house of
115:18 LORD from this time F and for evermore.
119:171 My lips will pour F praise that thou dost
121:8 in from this time F and for evermore.
125:2 people, from this time F and for evermore.
125:3 lest the righteous put F their hands to do
126:6 He that goes F weeping, bearing the seed for
131:3 LORD from this time F and for evermore.
135:7 the rain and brings F the wind from his
144:6 Flash F the lightning and scatter them, send out
144:7 Stretch F thy hand from on high, rescue me
144:13 may our sheep bring F thousands and ten thousands
145:7 They shall pour F the fame of thy abundant
147:15 He sends F his command to the earth; his
147:17 He casts F his ice like morsels; who can
147:18 He sends F his word, and melts them; he
Prov 3:20 knowledge the deeps broke F, and the clouds drop
8:24 depths I was brought F, when there were no
8:25 hills, I was brought F;
10:31 of the righteous brings F wisdom, but the perverse
25:23 The north wind brings F rain; and a backbiting
27:1 do not know what a day may bring F
Eccl 7:18 fears God shall come F from them all.
10:10 edge, he must put F more strength; but wisdom
Song 1:12 couch, my nard gave F its fragrance.
2:13 The fig tree puts F its figs, and the
2:13 in blossom; they give F fragrance.
3:11 Go F, O daughters of Zion, and behold King
6:10 is this that looks F like the dawn, fair
7:11 beloved, let us go F into the fields, and
7:13 The mandrakes give F fragrance, and over our doors
Wis 3:7 visitation they will shine F, and will run like
4:4 even if they put F boughs for a while,
9:10 Send her F from the holy heavens, and from
11:18 fiery breath, or belch F a thick pall of
11:25 would anything not called F by thee have been
19:2 and hastily sent them F, they would change their
19:10 animals the earth brought F gnats, and instead of
Sir 1:20 then joy will burst F for him.
5:7 the Lord will go F, and at the time
7:32 Stretch F your hand to the poor, so that
14:18 sheds some and puts F others, so are the
18:28 skilled themselves, and pour F apt proverbs.
23:23 through harlotry and brought F children by another
24:3 will glory: "I came F from the mouth of
24:15 camel's thorn I gave F the aroma of spices,
24:25 It makes instruction shine F like light, like the
24:28 I went F like a canal from a river
24:30 again make instruction shine F like the dawn, and
39:6 understanding; he will pour F words of wisdom and
39:14 stream of water; send F fragrance like frankincense,
39:14 like frankincense, and put F blossoms like a lily.
40:1 the day they come F from their mother's womb
40:15 ungodly will not put F many branches; they are
43:2 proclamation as it goes F, is a marvelous instrument,
43:8 hosts on high shining F in the firmament of
43:14 and the clouds fly F like birds.
43:30 you exalt him, put F all your strength, and
44:5 musical tunes, and set F verses in writing;
45:1 descendants the Lord brought F a man of mercy,
45:9 round about, to send F a sound as he
48:20 who is merciful, spreading F their hands toward him;
50:10 an olive tree putting F its fruit, and like
50:27 of his heart poured F wisdom.
Is 1:15 When you spread F your hands, I will hide
2:3 of Zion shall go F the law, and the
2:20 day men will cast F their idols of silver
7:3 said to Isaiah, "Go F to meet Ahaz, you
9:7 righteousness from this time F and for evermore.
11:1 There shall come F a shoot from the stump
11:14 They shall put F their hand against Edom and
14:7 and quiet; they break F into singing.
14:29 serpent's root will come F an adder, and its
26:18 as it were brought F wind.
26:21 the LORD is coming F out of his place
27:6 shall blossom and put F shoots, and fill the
31:4 of shepherds is called F against him is not
33:11 conceive chaff, you bring F stubble; your breath is
35:6 For waters shall break F in the wilderness, and
37:3 and there is no strength to bring them F
37:32 of Jerusalem shall go F a remnant, and out
37:36 of the LORD went F, and slew a hundred
41:21 Set F your case, says the LORD; bring your
42:1 him, he will bring F justice to the nations.
42:3 he will faithfully bring F justice.
42:5 them out, who spread F the earth and what
42:9 declare; before they spring F I tell you of
42:13 The LORD goes F like a mighty man, like
43:8 Bring F the people who are blind, yet have
43:17 mighty waters, who brings F chariot and horse, army
43:19 thing; now it springs F, do you not perceive
43:26 us argue together; set F your case, that you
44:7 declare and set it F before me.
44:11 assemble, let them stand F, they shall be terrified,
44:23 of the earth; break F into singing, O mountains,
45:8 that salvation may sprout F, and let it cause
45:23 my mouth has gone F in righteousness a word
47:13 counsels; let them stand F and save you, those
48:1 Israel, and who came F from the loins of
48:3 of old, they went F from my mouth and
48:6 From this time F I make you hear new
48:13 to them, they stand F together.
48:20 Go F from Babylon, flee from Chaldea, declare this
48:20 proclaim it, send it F to the end of
49:9 to the prisoners, 'Come F to those who are
49:13 exult, O earth; break F, O mountains, into singing!
49:17 laid you waste go F from you.
51:4 a law will go F from me, and my
51:5 my salvation has gone F, and my arms will
52:9 Break F together into singing, you waste places of
54:1 did not bear; break F into singing and cry
55:10 earth, making it bring F and sprout, giving seed
55:11 word be that goes F from my mouth; it
55:12 joy, and be led F in peace; the mountains
55:12 before you shall break F into singing, and all
58:8 shall your light break F like the dawn, and
59:4 conceive mischief and bring F iniquity.
59:21 LORD, from this time F and for evermore."
61:11 as the earth brings F its shoots, and as
61:11 and praise to spring F before all the nations.
62:1 until her vindication goes F as brightness, and her
65:9 I will bring F descendants from Jacob, and from
66:8 a nation be brought F in one moment?
66:8 in labor she brought F her sons.
66:9 to the birth and not cause to bring F
66:9 who cause to bring F, shut the womb?
66:24 "And they shall go F and look on the
Jer 1:9 Then the LORD put F his hand and touched
1:14 north evil shall break F upon all the inhabitants
4:4 lest my wrath go F like fire, and burn
4:7 out; he has gone F from his place to
4:31 as of one bringing F her first child, the
6:25 Go not F into the field, nor walk on
10:13 rain, and he brings F the wind from his
12:2 they grow and bring F fruit; thou art near
20:18 Why did I come F from the womb to
21:12 lest my wrath go F like fire, and burn
22:19 buried, dragged and cast F beyond the gates of
23:15 Jerusalem ungodliness has gone F into all the land."
23:19 Wrath has gone F, a whirling tempest; it will
25:32 Behold, evil is going F from nation to nation,
30:21 their ruler shall come F from their midst; I
30:23 Wrath has gone F, a whirling tempest; it will
31:4 timbrels, and shall go F in the dance of

F

33:15 righteous Branch to spring F for David; and he
44:6 my anger were poured F and kindled in the
46:9 Let the warriors go F: men of Ethiopia and
48:7 and Chemosh shall go F into exile, with his
48:45 a fire has gone F from Heshbon, a flame
51:10 The LORD has brought F our vindication; come, let
51:16 rain, and he brings F the wind from his
Bar 3:33 creatures; he who sends F the light, and it
5:6 For they went F from you on foot, led
6:60 stars, shining and sent F for service, are obedient.
Ezek 1:4 it, and fire flashing F continually, and in the
1:13 of the fire went F lightning.
3:22 to me, "Arise, go F into the plain, and
3:23 I arose and went F into the plain; and,
5:4 a fire will come F into all the house
8:3 He put F the form of a hand, and
9:7 Go F
9:7 So they went F, and smote in the city.
10:7 And a cherub stretched F his hand from between
10:18 of the LORD went F from the threshold of
10:19 sight as they went F, with the wheels beside
11:7 you shall be brought F out of the midst
11:9 I will bring you F out of the midst
12:4 and you shall go F yourself at evening in
12:7 own hands; I went F in the dark, carrying
12:12 dark, and shall go F; he shall dig through
14:22 daughters, when they come F to you, and you
16:14 And your renown went F among the nations because
17:6 a vine, and brought F branches and put forth
17:6 forth branches and put F foliage.
17:7 toward him, and shot F its branches toward him
17:8 that it might bring F branches, and bear fruit,
17:23 that it may bring F boughs and bear fruit,
21:3 you, and will draw F my sword out of
21:19 of them shall come F from the same land.
28:18 sanctuaries; so I brought F fire from the midst
29:5 I will cast you F into the wilderness, you
29:21 a horn to spring F to the house of
30:9 swift messengers shall go F from me to terrify
31:4 of its planting, sending F its streams to all
31:6 of the field brought F their young; and under
32:2 the seas; you burst F in your rivers, trouble
33:30 word is that comes F from the LORD.'
36:8 of Israel, shall shoot F your branches, and yield
38:4 I will bring you F, and all your army,
39:9 of Israel will go F and make fires of
46:21 Then he brought me F to the outer court,
Dan 2:13 So the decree went F that the wise men
3:94 Most High God, come F, and come here!" Then
7:10 fire issued and came F from before him; a
8:9 one of them came F a little horn, which
9:23 supplications a word went F, and I have come
9:25 that from the going F of the word to
11:44 and he shall go F with great fury to
13:5 said: "Iniquity came F from Babylon, from elders
14:11 O king, shall set F the food and mix
14:14 out, the king set F the food for Bel.
Hos 6:3 the LORD; his going F is sure as the
6:5 and my judgment goes F as the light.
9:13 prey; Ephraim must lead F his sons to slaughter.
9:16 Even though they bring F, I will slay their
Joel 3:18 a fountain shall come F from the house of
Amos 4:3 you shall be cast F into Harmon," says the
5:3 "The city that went F a thousand shall have
5:3 and that which went F a hundred shall have
5:9 who makes destruction flash F against the strong, so
Mic 1:3 the LORD is coming F out of his place,
1:11 Zaanan do not come F; the wailing of Beth-ezel
4:2 of Zion shall go F the law, and the
4:7 Zion from this time F and for evermore.
4:10 now you shall go F from the city and
5:2 from you shall come F for me one who
5:3 in travail has brought F; then the rest of
7:9 He will bring me F to the light; I
Hab 1:4 the law is slacked and justice never goes F
1:4 righteous, so justice goes F perverted.
2:1 the tower, and look F to see what he
3:10 on; the deep gave F its voice, it lifted
3:13 Thou wentest F for the salvation of thy people,
Zeph 3:5 every morning he shows F his justice, each dawn
Hag 1:11 what the ground brings F, upon men and cattle,
Zech 5:4 I will send it F, says the LORD of
5:5 eyes, and see what this is that goes F
5:6 He said, "This is the ephah that goes F
6:5 me, "These are going F to the four winds
9:14 and his arrow go F like lightning; the Lord
9:14 the trumpet, and march F in the whirlwinds of
14:3 the LORD will go F and fight against those
Mal 4:2 You shall go F leaping like calves from the
1Mac 1:10 them came F a sinful root, Antiochus Epiphanes,
1:11 days lawless men came F from Israel, and misled
4:13 against them, they went F from their camp to
5:65 and his brothers went F and fought the sons
7:1 son of Seleucus set F from Rome, sailed with
7:41 blasphemy, thy angel went F and struck down one
10:63 to his officers, "Go F with him into the
11:36 canceled from this time F for ever.
11:60 Then Jonathan set F and traveled beyond the river
12:33 Simon also went F and marched through the country
12:40 him, and he marched F and came to Beth-shan.
14:36 they used to sally F and defile the environs
2Mac 2:23 which has been set F by Jason of Cyrene
7:10 tongue and courageously stretched F his hands,
14:34 Then the priests stretched F their hands toward
14:45 though his blood gushed F and his wounds were
Mt 12:35 his good treasure brings F good, and the evil
12:35 his evil treasure brings F evil.
13:8 good soil and brought F grain, some a hundredfold,
24:32 becomes tender and puts F its leaves, you know
Mk 4:8 good soil and brought F grain, growing up and
4:32 all shrubs, and puts F large branches, so that
5:30 that power had gone F from him, immediately
13:28 becomes tender and puts F its leaves, you know
16:20 And they went F and preached everywhere, while
Lk 6:19 him, for power came F from him and healed
8:15 good heart, and bring F fruit with patience.
8:46 that power has gone F from me."
12:16 a rich man brought F plentifully;
Jn 5:28 his voice and come F, those who have done
8:42 I proceeded and came F from God; I came
15:6 me, he is cast F as a branch and
18:1 these words, he went F with his disciples across
Acts 7:12 in Egypt, he sent F our fathers the first
Gal 4:4 fully come, God sent F his Son, born of
4:27 does not bear; break F and shout, you who
Eph 1:9 purpose which he set F in Christ
1Thes 1:8 of the Lord sounded F from you in Macedonia
1:8 in God has gone F everywhere, so that we
Heb 1:14 all ministering spirits sent F to serve, for the
6:7 upon it, and brings F vegetation useful to those
13:13 Therefore let us go F to him outside the
Jas 1:14 it is full-grown brings F death.
1:17 will he brought us F by the word of
3:11 Does a spring pour F from the same opening
5:18 and the earth brought F its fruit.
Rev 12:4 when she brought it F;
12:5 it forth; she brought F a male child, one

FORTIETH (3)

Num 33:38 died there, in the F year after the people
Deut 1:3 And in the F year, on the first day
1Chr 26:31 (In the F year of David's reign search was

FORTIFICATION

1Mac 10:11 squared stones, for better F; and they did so.

FORTIFICATIONS (3)

Is 25:12 And the high F of his walls he will
1Mac 13:48 He also strengthened its F and built in it
13:52 He strengthened the F of the temple hill alongside

FORTIFIED (71)

Num 13:28 and the cities are F and very large; and
32:17 shall live in the F cities because of the
32:36 Beth-nimrah and Beth-haran, F cities, and folds for
Deut 1:28 cities are great and F up to heaven; and
3:5 All these were cities F with high walls, gates,
9:1 yourselves, cities great and F up to heaven,
28:52 until your high and F walls, in which you
Josh 10:20 had entered into the F cities,
14:12 were there, with great F cities: it may be
19:29 Ramah, reaching to the F city of Tyre; then
19:35 The F cities are Ziddim, Zer, Hammath, Rakkath,
1Sam 6:18 the five lords, both F cities and unwalled villages.
2Sam 20:6 lest he get himself F cities, and cause us
1Kgs 16:24 of silver; and he F the hill, and called
2Kgs 3:19 you shall conquer every F city, and every choice
10:2 you chariots and horses, F cities also, and weapons,
17:9 towns, from watchtower to F city;
18:8 territory, from watchtower to F city.
18:13 up against all the F cities of Judah and
19:25 that you should turn F cities into heaps of

2Chr	8:5	Beth-horon and Lower Beth-horon, F cities with
	11:10	Zorah, Aijalon, and Hebron, F cities which are in
	11:23	Benjamin, in all the F cities; and he gave
	12:4	And he took the F cities of Judah and
	14:6	He built F cities in Judah, for the land
	17:2	forces in all the F cities of Judah, and
	17:19	had placed in the F cities throughout all Judah.
	19:5	land in all the F cities of Judah, city
	21:3	valuable possessions, together with F cities in Judah;
	26:9	at the Angle, and F them.
	32:1	and encamped against the F cities, thinking to win
	33:14	army in all the F cities in Judah.
Neh	9:25	And they captured F cities and a rich land,
Jud	4:5	the high hilltops and F the villages on them
	5:1	in the hills and F all the high hilltops
Ps	60:9	bring me to the F city?
	108:10	bring me to the F city?
Sir	48:17	Hezekiah F his city, and brought water into the
	50:1	and in his time F the temple.
	50:4	people from ruin, and F the city to withstand
Is	2:15	tower, and against every F wall;
	25:2	city a heap, the F city a ruin; the
	27:10	For the F city is solitary, a habitation deserted
	36:1	up against all the F cities of Judah and
	37:26	that you should make F cities crash into heaps
Jer	1:18	you this day a F city, an iron pillar,
	4:5	us go into the F cities!'
	5:17	your fig trees; your F cities in which you
	8:14	us go into the F cities and perish there;
	15:20	to this people a F wall of bronze; they
	34:7	these were the only F cities of Judah that
Ezek	21:20	Ammonites and to Judah and to Jerusalem the F
	36:35	are now inhabited and F
Hos	8:14	and Judah has multiplied F cities; but I will
Zeph	1:16	battle cry against the F cities and against the
1Mac	1:19	And they captured the F cities in the land
	1:33	Then they F the city of David with a
	4:7	the Gentiles, strong and F, with cavalry round about
	4:60	At that time they F Mount Zion with high
	4:61	He also F Bethzur, so that the people might
	6:26	take it; they have F both the sanctuary and
	9:52	He also F the city of Bethzur, and Gazara,
	9:62	been demolished, and they F it.
	12:38	in the Shephelah; he F it and installed gates
	13:10	of Jerusalem, and he F it on every side.
	14:33	He F the cities of Judea, and Bethzur on
	14:34	He also F Joppa, which is by the sea,
	14:37	Jews in it, and F it for the safety
2Mac	11:5	Bethzur, which was a F place about five leagues
	12:13	city which was strongly F with earthworks and walls,
	12:27	also against Ephron, a F city where Lysias dwelt

FORTIFY (3)

Is	22:10	down the houses to F the wall.
Jer	51:53	and though she should F her strong height, yet
1Mac	15:39	build up Kedron and F its gates, and to

FORTIFYING

1Mac	10:45	walls of Jerusalem and F it round about, and

FORTRESS (25)

2Sam	22:2	my rock, and my F, and my deliverer,
	24:7	and came to the F of Tyre and to
Neh	2:8	the gates of the F of the temple, and
Ps	18:2	my rock, and my F, and my deliverer, my
	31:2	for me, a strong F to save me!
	31:3	my rock and my F; for thy name's sake
	59:9	to thee; for thou, O God, art my F
	59:16	been to me a F and a refuge in
	59:17	O God, art my F, the God who shows
	62:2	and my salvation, my F; I shall not be
	62:6	and my salvation, my F; I shall not be
	71:3	of refuge, a strong F, to save me, for
	71:3	me, for thou art my rock and my F
	91:2	"My refuge and my F; my God, in whom
	144:2	my rock and my F, my stronghold and my
Is	17:3	The F will disappear from Ephraim, and the
Jer	48:1	it is taken; the F is put to shame
Dan	11:7	army and enter the F of the king of
	11:10	shall carry the war as far as his F
	11:31	profane the temple and F, and shall take away
Amos	5:9	the strong, so that destruction comes upon the F
Hab	1:10	They laugh at every F, for they heap up
1Mac	6:62	saw what a strong F the place was, he
	9:50	cities in Judea: the F in Jericho, and Emmaus,
2Mac	13:19	against Bethzur, a strong F of the Jews, was

FORTRESSES (11)

2Kgs	8:12	set on fire their F, and you will slay
2Chr	11:11	He made the F strong, and put commanders in
	17:12	He built in Judah F and store-cities,
Is	33:16	defense will be the F of rocks; his bread
	34:13	over its strongholds, nettles and thistles in its F
Dan	11:19	face back toward the F of his own land;
	11:38	honor the god of F instead of these; a
	11:39	deal with the strongest F by the help of
Hos	10:14	people, and all your F shall be destroyed, as
	11:6	of their gates, and devour them in their F
Nah	3:12	All your F are like fig trees with first-ripe

FORTS (2)

2Chr	27:4	country of Judah, and F and towers on the
Nah	3:14	the siege, strengthen your F; go into the clay,

FORTUNATE (2)

Eccl	4:2	are already dead more F than the living who
Acts	26:2	defense: "I think myself F that it is before

FORTUNATUS

1Cor	16:17	coming of Stephanas and F and Achaicus, because

FORTUNE (4)

Gen	30:11	And Leah said, "Good F
Sir	20:8	There may be good F for a man in
	37:18	heart four turns of F appear, good and evil,
Is	65:11	set a table for F and fill cups of

FORTUNES (30)

Deut	30:3	God will restore your F, and have compassion upon
Job	42:10	the LORD restored the F of Job, when he
Ps	14:7	the LORD restores the F of his people, Jacob
	53:6	When God restores the F of his people, Jacob
	85:1	thou didst restore the F of Jacob.
	126:1	the LORD restored the F of Zion, we were
	126:4	Restore our F, O LORD, like the watercourses in
Jer	29:14	I will restore your F and gather you from
	30:3	I will restore the F of my people, Israel
	30:18	I will restore the F of the tents of
	31:23	when I restore their F: 'The LORD bless you,
	32:44	I will restore their F, says the LORD."
	33:7	I will restore the F of Judah and the
	33:7	of Judah and the F of Israel, and rebuild
	33:11	I will restore the F of the land as
	33:26	I will restore their F, and will have mercy
	48:47	I will restore the F of Moab in the
	49:6	I will restore the F of the Ammonites, says
	49:39	I will restore the F of Elam, says the
Lam	2:14	iniquity to restore your F, but have seen for
Ezek	16:53	"I will restore their F, both the fortunes of
	16:53	their fortunes, both the F of Sodom and her
	16:53	her daughters, and the F of Samaria and her
	16:53	will restore your own F in the midst of
	29:14	I will restore the F of Egypt, and bring
	39:25	I will restore the F of Jacob, and have
Hos	7:1	I would restore the F of my people,
Joel	3:1	when I restore the F of Judah and Jerusalem,
Amos	9:14	I will restore the F of my people Israel,
Zeph	2:7	will be mindful of them and restore their F

FORTY (109)

Gen	5:13	Mahalalel eight hundred and F years, and had other
	7:4	rain upon the earth F days and forty nights;
	7:4	earth forty days and F nights; and every living
	7:12	fell upon the earth F days and forty nights.
	7:12	earth forty days and F nights.
	7:17	The flood continued F days upon the earth; and
	8:6	At the end of F days Noah opened the
	18:29	him, and said, "Suppose F are found there." He
	18:29	"For the sake of F I will not do
	25:20	Isaac, and Isaac was F years old when he
	26:34	When Esau was F years old, he took to
	32:15	camels and their colts, F cows and ten bulls,
	50:3	the physicians embalmed Israel; F days were
Ex	16:35	Israel ate the manna F years, till they came
	24:18	was on the mountain F days and forty nights.
	24:18	mountain forty days and F nights.
	26:19	the south side; and F bases of silver you
	26:21	twenty frames, and their F bases of silver, two
	34:28	there with the LORD F days and forty nights;
	34:28	LORD forty days and F nights; he neither ate
	36:24	side; and he made F bases of silver under
	36:26	twenty frames and their F bases of silver, two
Num	1:33	tribe of Ephraim was F thousand five hundred.

F

2:19 host as numbered being F thousand five hundred.
13:25 At the end of F days they returned from
14:33 shepherds in the wilderness F years, and shall suffer
14:34 spied out the land, F days, for every day
14:34 shall bear your iniquity, F years, and you shall
26:18 according to their number, F thousand five hundred.
32:13 wander in the wilderness F years, until all the
Deut 2:7 this great wilderness; these F years the LORD your
8:2 has led you these F years in the wilderness,
8:4 did not swell, these F years.
9:9 remained on the mountain F days and forty nights;
9:9 mountain forty days and F nights; I neither ate
9:11 at the end of F days and forty nights
9:11 of forty days and F nights the LORD gave
9:18 the LORD as before, F days and forty nights;
9:18 before, forty days and F nights; I neither ate
9:25 the LORD for these F days and forty nights,
9:25 these forty days and F nights, because the LORD
10:10 at the first time, F days and forty nights,
10:10 time, forty days and F nights, and the LORD
25:3 F stripes may be given him, but not more;
29:5 I have led you F years in the wilderness;
Josh 4:13 had bidden them; about F thousand ready armed for
5:6 people of Israel walked F years in the wilderness,
14:7 I was F years old when Moses the servant
Judg 3:11 the land had rest F years.
5:8 to be seen among F thousand in Israel?
5:31 land had rest for F years.
8:28 the land had rest F years in the days
12:14 He had F sons and thirty grandsons, who rode
13:1 of the Philistines for F years.
1Sam 4:18 He had judged Israel F years.
17:16 For F days the Philistine came forward and took
2Sam 2:10 Ish-bosheth, Saul's son, was F years old when he
5:4 reign, and he reigned F years.
10:18 seven hundred chariots, and F thousand horsemen,
1Kgs 2:11 reigned over Israel was F years; he reigned seven
4:26 Solomon also had F thousand stalls of horses for
6:17 the inner sanctuary, was F cubits long.
7:38 bronze; each laver held F baths, each laver measured
11:42 over all Israel was F years.
19:8 strength of that food F days and forty nights
19:8 food forty days and F nights to Horeb the
2Kgs 8:9 of goods of Damascus, F camel loads.
12:1 reign, and he reigned F years in Jerusalem.
1Chr 12:36 Of Asher F thousand seasoned troops ready for
19:18 thousand chariots, and F thousand foot soldiers, and
29:27 reigned over Israel was F years; he reigned seven
2Chr 9:30 Jerusalem over all Israel F years.
24:1 reign, and he reigned F years in Jerusalem; his
Neh 5:15 food and wine, besides F shekels of silver.
9:21 F years didst thou sustain them in the wilderness,
Jud 1:4 seventy cubits high and F cubits wide, so that
Job 42:16 lived a hundred and F years, and saw his
Ps 95:10 For F years I loathed that generation and said,
Ezek 4:6 the house of Judah; F days I assign you,
29:11 it shall be uninhabited F years.
29:12 shall be a desolation F years among cities that
29:13 At the end of F years I will gather
41:2 length of the nave F cubits, and its breadth,
46:22 court were small courts, F cubits long and thirty
Dan 14:3 of fine flour and F sheep and fifty gallons
Amos 2:10 Egypt, and led you F years in the wilderness,
5:25 sacrifices and offerings the F years in the wilderness,
Jon 3:4 And he cried, "Yet F days, and Nineveh shall
1Mac 3:39 and sent with them F thousand infantry and seven
12:41 to meet him with F thousand picked fighting men,
2Mac 5:2 for almost F days, there appeared golden-clad
5:14 were destroyed, F thousand in hand-to-hand fighti
Mt 4:2 And he fasted F days and forty nights, and
4:2 fasted forty days and F nights, and afterward he
Mk 1:13 was in the wilderness F days, tempted by Satan;
Lk 4:2 by the Spirit for F days in the wilderness,
Acts 1:3 appearing to them during F days, and speaking of
4:22 performed was more than F years old.
7:23 "When he was F years old, it came into
7:30 "Now when F years had passed, an angel appeared
7:36 in the wilderness for F years.
7:42 slain beasts and sacrifices, F years in the wilderness,
13:18 And for about F years he bore with them
13:21 tribe of Benjamin, for F years.
23:13 There were more than F who made this conspiracy.
23:21 them; for more than F of their men lie
2Cor 11:24 of the Jews the F lashes less one.
Heb 3:9 saw my works for F years.
3:17 whom was he provoked F years?

FORTY-EIGHT (4)

Num 35:7 the Levites shall be F, with their pasture lands.
Josh 21:41 Israel were in all F cities with their pasture
Neh 7:15 The sons of Binnui, six hundred and F
7:44 singers: the sons of Asaph, a hundred and F

FORTY-EIGHTH (4)

1Mac 4:52 the one hundred and F year,
2Mac 11:21 The one hundred and F year, Dioscorinthius
11:33 The one hundred and F year, Xanthicus fifteenth."
11:38 The one hundred and F year, Xanthicus fifteenth."

FORTY-FIFTH

1Mac 1:54 the one hundred and F year, they erected a

FORTY-FIRST

2Chr 16:13 fathers, dying in the F year of his reign.

FORTY-FIVE (15)

Gen 18:28 it if I find F there."
Num 1:25 tribe of Gad was F thousand six hundred and
2:15 host as numbered being F thousand six hundred and
26:41 and their number was F thousand six hundred.
26:50 and their number was F thousand four hundred.
Josh 14:10 as he said, these F years since the time
1Kgs 7:3 that were upon the F pillars, fifteen in each
Ezra 2:8 The sons of Zattu, nine hundred and F
2:34 The sons of Jericho, three hundred and F
2:66 were two hundred and F,
Neh 7:13 The sons of Zattu, eight hundred and F
7:36 The sons of Jericho, three hundred and F
7:67 had two hundred and F singers, male and female.
7:68 mules two hundred and F,
Jer 52:30 Jews seven hundred and F persons; all the persons

FORTY-FOUR (5)

1Chr 5:18 bow, expert in war, F thousand seven hundred and
Rev 7:4 sealed, a hundred and F thousand sealed, out of
14:1 him a hundred and F thousand who had his
14:3 except the hundred and F thousand who had been
21:17 wall, a hundred and F cubits by a man's

FORTY-NINE (2)

Lev 25:8 shall be to you F years.
Dan 3:47 out above the furnace F cubits,

FORTY-NINTH (2)

1Mac 6:16 the one hundred and F year.
2Mac 13:1 the one hundred and F year word came to

FORTY-ONE (6)

Num 1:41 tribe of Asher was F thousand five hundred.
2:28 host as numbered being F thousand five hundred.
1Kgs 14:21 Rehoboam was F years old when he began to
15:10 Judah, and he reigned F years in Jerusalem.
2Kgs 14:23 Samaria, and he reigned F years.
2Chr 12:13 Rehoboam was F years old when he began to

FORTY-SEVEN (3)

Gen 47:28 were a hundred and F years.
Ezra 2:38 sons of Pashhur, one thousand two hundred and F
Neh 7:41 sons of Pashhur, a thousand two hundred and F

FORTY-SEVENTH

1Mac 3:37 the one hundred and F year.

FORTY-SIX (3)

Num 1:21 tribe of Reuben was F thousand five hundred.
2:11 host as numbered being F thousand five hundred.
Jn 2:20 said, "It has taken F years to build this

FORTY-SIXTH

1Mac 2:70 the one hundred and F year and was buried

FORTY-THIRD

1Mac 1:20 the one hundred and F year.

FORTY-THREE (3)

Num 26:7 and their number was F thousand seven hundred and
Ezra 2:25 Chephirah, and Be-eroth, seven hundred and F
Neh 7:29 Chephirah, and Be-eroth, seven hundred and F

FORTY-TWO (14)

Num 35:6 them you shall give F cities.
Judg 12:6 fell at that time F thousand of the Ephraimites.
2Kgs 2:24 the woods and tore F of the boys.

	10:14	the pit of Beth-eked, F persons, and he spared
2Chr	22:2	Ahaziah was F years old when he began to
Ezra	2:10	The sons of Bani, six hundred and F
	2:24	The sons of Azmaveth, F
	2:64	assembly together was F thousand three hundred
Neh	7:28	The men of Beth-azmaveth, F
	7:62	Tobiah, the sons of Nekoda, six hundred and F
	7:66	whole assembly together was F thousand three
	11:13	houses, two hundred and F; and Amashsai, the son
Rev	11:2	the holy city for F months.
	13:5	to exercise authority for F months;

FORUM

Acts	28:15	as far as the F of Appius and Three

FORWARD (61)

Ex	14:15	Tell the people of Israel to go F
Num	12:5	called Aaron and Miriam; and they both came F
Deut	20:2	the priest shall come F and speak to the
	21:5	of Levi shall come F, for the LORD your
Josh	6:7	to the people, "Go F; march around the city,
	6:8	before the LORD went F, blowing the trumpets, with
Judg	9:44	was with him rushed F and stood at the
1Sam	16:13	LORD came mightily upon David from that day F
	17:16	days the Philistine came F and took his stand,
	30:25	And from that day F he made it a
2Sam	20:8	and as he went F it fell out.
1Kgs	22:21	Then a spirit came F and stood before the
2Kgs	3:24	them; and they went F, slaughtering the Moabites as
	20:9	shall the shadow go F ten steps, or go
2Chr	18:20	Then a spirit came F and stood before the
	24:13	and the repairing went F in their hands, and
Ezra	3:10	in their vestments came F with trumpets, and the
Neh	4:7	of Jerusalem was going F and that the breaches
Jud	7:17	of the Ammonites moved F, together with five
	10:22	of her he came F to the front of
Esth	11:6	two great dragons came F, both ready to fight,
Job	23:8	"Behold, I go F, but he is not there;
Prov	4:26	your eyes look directly F, and your gaze be
	25:6	Do not put yourself F in the king's presence
Wis	18:21	their champion; he brought F the shield of his
Sir	2:1	son, if you come F to serve the Lord,
	13:10	Do not push F, lest you be repulsed; and
Jer	7:24	their evil hearts, and went backward and not F
Ezek	1:9	went every one straight F, without turning as they
	1:12	And each went straight F; wherever the spirit would
	10:22	They went every one straight F
	39:2	about and drive you F, and bring you up
	39:22	am the LORD their God, from that day F
Dan	3:8	certain Chaldeans came F and maliciously accused
Zech	2:3	talked with me came F, and another angel came
	2:3	and another angel came F to meet him,
	4:7	and he shall bring F the top stone amid
	5:5	talked with me came F and said to me,
	5:9	eyes and saw, and behold, two women coming F
1Mac	2:23	words, a Jew came F in the sight of
	10:82	Then Simon brought F his force and engaged the
2Mac	5:18	soon as he came F, just as Heliodorus was,
	7:7	this way, they brought F the second for their
	7:15	Next they brought F the fifth and maltreated him.
	7:18	After him they brought F the sixth.
	14:21	A chariot came F from each army; seats of
	15:20	all were now looking F to the coming decision,
Mt	8:5	Caperna-um, a centurion came F to him, beseeching
	25:20	the five talents came F, bringing five talents more,
	25:22	the two talents came F, saying, 'Master, you delivered
	25:24	the one talent came F, saying, 'Master, I knew
	26:60	found none, though many false witnesses came F
	26:60	At last two came F
Mk	10:35	sons of Zebedee, came F to him, and said
Jn	18:4	to befall him, came F and said to them,
Acts	1:23	And they put F two, Joseph called Barsabbas, who
	19:33	prompted Alexander, whom the Jews had put F
	27:21	food, Paul then came F among them and said,
Rom	3:25	Jesus, whom God put F as an expiation by
Phil	3:13	lies behind and straining F to what lies ahead,
Heb	11:10	For he looked F to the city which has

FOSTER

Is	49:23	Kings shall be your F fathers, and their queens

FOUGHT (83)

Ex	17:8	Then came Amalek and F with Israel at Rephidim.
	17:10	Moses told him, and F with Amalek; and Moses,
Num	21:1	way of Atharim, he F against Israel, and took
	21:23	came to Jahaz, and F against Israel.
	21:26	the Amorites, who had F against the former king
Josh	10:14	man; for the LORD F for Israel.
	10:29	him, to Libnah, and F against Libnah;
	10:42	LORD God of Israel F for Israel.
	19:47	Danites went up and F against Leshem, and after
	23:3	your God who has F for you.
	24:8	of the Jordan; they F with you, and I
	24:9	of Moab, arose and F against Israel; and he
	24:11	the men of Jericho F against you, and also
Judg	1:5	Adoni-bezek at Bezek, and F against him, and
	1:8	the men of Judah F against Jerusalem, and took
	5:19	"The kings came, they F; then fought the kings
	5:19	came, they fought; then F the kings of Canaan,
	5:20	From heaven F the stars, from their courses they
	5:20	from their courses they F against Sisera.
	9:17	for my father F for you, and risked
	9:39	men of Shechem, and F with Abimelech.
	9:45	And Abimelech F against the city all that day;
	9:52	to the tower, and F against it, and drew
	11:20	encamped at Jahaz, and F with Israel.
	12:4	men of Gilead and F with Ephraim; and the
1Sam	4:10	So the Philistines F, and Israel was defeated, and
	12:9	of Moab; and they F against them.
	14:47	kingship over Israel, he F against all his enemies
	19:8	David went out and F with the Philistines, and
	23:5	went to Keilah, and F with the Philistines, and
	31:1	Now the Philistines F against Israel; and the men
2Sam	8:10	because he had F against Hadadezer and defeated
	10:17	themselves against David, and F with him.
	11:17	city came out and F with Joab; and some
	12:26	Now Joab F against Rabbah of the Ammonites, and
	12:27	and said, "I have F against Rabbah; moreover, I
	12:29	went to Rabbah, and F against it and took
	18:6	and the battle was F in the forest of
	21:15	his servants, and they F against the Philistines; and
1Kgs	20:1	and besieged Samaria, and F against it.
2Kgs	3:23	the kings have surely F together, and slain one
	8:29	at Ramah, when he F against Hazael king of
	9:15	given him, when he F with Hazael king of
	12:17	Syria went up and F against Gath, and took
	13:12	might with which he F against Amaziah king of
	14:15	might, and how he F with Amaziah king of
	14:28	his might, how he F, and how he recovered
1Chr	10:1	Now the Philistines F against Israel; and the men
	18:10	him because he had F against Hadadezer and
	19:17	against the Syrians, they F with him.
2Chr	20:29	that the LORD had F against the enemies of
	22:6	at Ramah, when he F against Hazael king of
	27:5	He F with the king of the Ammonites and
Wis	11:3	withstood their enemies and F off their foes.
Is	20:1	came to Ashdod and F against it and took
	63:10	their enemy, and himself F against them.
1Mac	1:2	king of Greece.) He F many battles, conquered
	3:2	helped him; they gladly F for Israel.
	5:21	went to Galilee and F many battles against the
	5:35	aside to Alema, and F against it and took
	5:50	forces encamped, and he F against the city all
	5:56	deeds and of the heroic war they had F
	5:65	brothers went forth and F the sons of Esau
	6:31	for many days they F and built engines of
	6:31	these with fire, and F manfully.
	6:37	four armed men who F from there, and also
	6:52	to match theirs, and F for many days.
	6:63	the city, but he F against him, and took
	9:64	encamped against Bethbasi; he F against it for many
	9:68	They F with Bacchides, and he was crushed by
	10:15	and his brothers had F, of the brave deeds
	10:76	So they F against it, and the men of
	11:55	around him, and they F against Demetrius, and he
	11:65	encamped before Bethzur and F against it for many
	14:26	stood firm; they have F and repulsed Israel's enemies
	14:32	Simon rose up and F for his nation.
	16:2	of my father have F the wars of Israel
2Mac	1:12	drove out those who F against the holy city.
	10:17	beat off all who F upon the wall, and
	11:13	because the mighty God F on their side.
1Cor	15:32	if, humanly speaking, I F with beasts at Ephesus?
2Tim	4:7	I have F the good fight, I have finished
Rev	12:7	dragon and his angels F,

FOUL (17)

Ex	7:18	the Nile shall become F, and the Egyptians will
	7:21	and the Nile became F, so that the Egyptians
	16:20	bred worms and became F; and Moses was angry
	16:24	it did not become F, and there were no
Job	31:40	instead of wheat, and F weeds instead of barley."

Ps 38:5 My wounds grow F and fester because of my
Is 19:6 its canals will become F, and the branches of
Ezek 4:14 by beasts, nor has F flesh come into my
32:2 with your feet, and F their rivers.
34:18 water, that you must F the rest with your
Joel 2:20 sea; the stench and F smell of him will
2Mac 3:32 the notion that some F play had been perpetrated
Col 3:8 wrath, malice, slander, and F talk from your mouth.
Rev 16:2 on the earth, and F and evil sores came
16:13 the false prophet, three F spirits like frogs;
18:2 a haunt of every F spirit, a haunt of
18:2 a haunt of every F and hateful bird;

FOULED

Ezek 34:19 drink what you have F with your feet?

FOUND (427)

Gen 2:20 man there was not F a helper fit for
6:8 But Noah F favor in the eyes of the
8:9 ground; but the dove F no place to set
11:2 from the east, they F a plain in the
16:7 angel of the LORD F her by a spring
18:3 lord, if I have F favor in your sight,
18:29 said, "Suppose forty are F there." He answered, "For
18:30 Suppose thirty are F there." He answered, "I will
18:31 Suppose twenty are F there." He answered, "For the
18:32 Suppose ten are F there." He answered, "For the
19:19 behold, your servant has F favor in your sight,
26:19 in the valley and F there a well of
26:32 to him, "We have F water."
27:20 it that you have F it so quickly, my
30:14 harvest Reuben went and F mandrakes in the field,
30:33 among the lambs, if F with me, shall be
31:37 goods, what have you F of all your household
33:10 you, if I have F favor in your sight,
36:24 is the Anah who F the hot springs in
37:15 And a man F him wandering in the fields;
37:17 after his brothers, and F them at Dothan.
37:32 said, "This we have F; see now whether it
38:22 said, "I have not F her; and also the
39:4 So Joseph F favor in his sight and attended
44:8 the money which we F in the mouth of
44:9 your servants it be F, let him die, and
44:10 with whom it is F shall be my slave,
44:12 and the cup was F in Benjamin's sack.
44:16 God has F out the guilt of your servants;
44:16 also in whose hand the cup has been F
44:17 hand the cup was F shall be my slave;
47:14 the money that was F in the land of
47:29 "If now I have F favor in your sight,
50:4 "If now I have F favor in your eyes,
Ex 12:19 no leaven shall be F in your houses; for
15:22 in the wilderness and F no water.
16:27 to gather, and they F none.
17:2 Therefore the people F fault with Moses, and said,
21:16 sells him or is F in possession of him,
22:2 the stolen beast is F alive in his possession,
22:3 "If a thief is F breaking in, and is
22:7 if the thief is F, he shall pay double.
22:8 the thief is not F, the owner of the
33:12 and you have also F favor in my sight.'
33:13 thee, if I have F favor in thy sight,
33:16 known that I have F favor in thy sight,
33:17 do; for you have F favor in my sight,
34:9 "If now I have F favor in thy sight,
35:23 man with whom was F blue or purple or
35:24 man with whom was F acacia wood of any
Lev 6:3 his neighbor or has F what was lost and
6:4 lost thing which he F,
Num 11:11 why have I not F favor in thy sight,
15:32 in the wilderness, they F a man gathering sticks
15:33 And those who F him gathering sticks brought him
31:50 offering, what each man F, articles of gold, armlets
32:5 said, "If we have F favor in your sight,
Deut 17:2 "If there is F among you, within any of
18:10 There shall not be F among you any one
20:11 the people who are F in it shall do
21:1 possess, any one is F slain, lying in the
22:20 of virginity were not F in the young woman,
22:22 "If a man is F lying with the wife
22:28 her, and they are F,
24:1 eyes because he has F some indecency in her,
24:7 "If a man is F stealing one of his
32:10 "He F him in a desert land, and in
Josh 2:22 along the way and F nothing.
10:17 five kings have been F, hidden in the cave

Judg 6:17 "If now I have F favor with thee, then
14:18 you would not have F out my riddle."
15:15 And he F a fresh jawbone of an ass,
20:48 sword, men and beasts and all that they F
20:48 the towns which they F they set on fire.
21:12 And they F among the inhabitants of Jabesh-gilead
Ruth 2:10 him, "Why have I F favor in your eyes,
1Sam 9:20 your mind on them, for they have been F
10:2 went to seek are F, and now your father
10:14 were not to be F, we went to Samuel."
10:16 told us plainly that the asses had been F
10:21 when they sought him, he could not be F
12:5 that you have not F anything in my hand."
13:19 no smith to be F throughout all the land
13:22 neither sword nor spear F in the hand of
14:30 their enemies which they F; for now the slaughter
16:22 service, for he has F favor in my sight."
20:3 well that I have F favor in your eyes;
20:29 now, if I have F favor in your eyes,
25:28 evil shall not be F in you so long
27:5 Achish, "If I have F favor in your eyes,
29:3 to me I have F no fault in him
29:6 campaign; for I have F nothing wrong in you
29:8 What have you F in your servant from the
30:3 to the city, they F it burned with fire,
30:11 They F an Egyptian in the open country, and
31:3 Saul, and the archers F him; and he was
31:8 strip the slain, they F Saul and his three
2Sam 7:27 therefore thy servant has F courage to pray this
14:22 knows that I have F favor in your sight,
17:12 he is to be F, and we shall light
17:13 pebble is to be F there."
1Kgs 1:3 territory of Israel, and F Abishag the Shunammite,
1:52 but if wickedness is F in him, he shall
7:47 the bronze was not F out.
11:19 And Hadad F great favor in the sight of
11:29 prophet Ahijah the Shilonite F him on the road.
13:14 man of God, and F him sitting under an
13:28 And he went and F his body thrown in
14:13 in him there is F something pleasing to the
18:10 that they had not F you.
19:19 departed from there, and F Elisha the son of
20:37 Then he F another man, and said, "Strike me,
21:20 to Elijah, "Have you F me, O my enemy?"
21:20 He answered, "I have F you, because you have
2Kgs 4:39 to gather herbs, and F a wild vine and
9:35 to bury her, they F no more of her
12:10 the money that was F in the house of
12:18 the gold that was F in the treasuries of
14:14 the vessels that were F in the house of
16:8 and gold that was F in the house of
17:4 the king of Assyria F treachery in Hoshea; for
18:15 the silver that was F in the house of
19:8 The Rabshakeh returned, and F the king of Assyria
20:13 armory, all that was F in his storehouses; there
22:8 the secretary, "I have F the book of the
22:9 the money that was F in the house, and
22:13 book that has been F; for great is the
23:2 covenant which had been F in the house of
23:24 that Hilkiah the priest F in the house of
25:19 king's council who were F in the city; and
25:19 the land who were F in the city.
1Chr 4:40 their flocks, where they F rich, good pasture, and
4:41 the Me-unim who were F there, and exterminated
10:3 Saul, and the archers F him; and he was
10:8 strip the slain, they F Saul and his sons
17:25 therefore thy servant has F courage to pray before
20:2 from his head; he F that it weighed a
24:4 more chief men were F among the sons of
26:31 ability among them were F at Jazer in Gilead.)
28:9 him, he will be F by you; but if
2Chr 2:17 taken; and there were F a hundred and fifty-three
15:2 him, he will be F by you, but if
15:4 sought him, he was F by them.
15:15 desire, and he was F by them, and the
19:3 Nevertheless some good is F in you, for you
20:25 spoil from them, they F cattle in great numbers,
21:17 all the possessions they F that belonged to the
25:5 old and upward, and F that they were three
25:24 the vessels that were F in the house of
29:16 the uncleanness that they F in the temple of
34:14 LORD, Hilkiah the priest F the book of the
34:15 the secretary, "I have F the book of the
34:17 the money that was F in the house of
34:21 book that has been F; for great is the
34:30 covenant which had been F in the house of

36:8 did, and what was F against him, behold, they
Ezra 2:62 but they were not F there, and so they
4:19 and it has been F that this city from
6:2 Media, a scroll was F on which this was
8:15 and the priests, I F there none of the
10:18 married foreign women were F Ma-aseiah, Eliezer,
Neh 2:5 if your servant has F favor in your sight,
7:5 And I F the book of the genealogy of
7:5 the first, and I F written in it:
7:64 but it was not F there, so they were
8:14 And they F it written in the law that
13:1 and in it was F written that no Ammonite
13:10 I also F out that the portions of the
Tob 1:18 were sought by the king, they were not F
5:4 a man; and he F Raphael, who was an
5:8 his father, "I have F some one to go
8:13 and went in, and F them both asleep.
Jud 6:14 from their city and F him; and they untied
10:6 gate of Bethulia, and F Uzziah standing there with
14:15 into the bedchamber and F him thrown down on
Esth 2:15 Now Esther F favor in the eyes of all
2:17 the women, and she F grace and favor in
2:23 affair was investigated and F to be so, the
4:16 the Jews to be F in Susa, and hold
5:2 in the court, she F favor in his sight
5:8 is: If I have F favor in the sight
6:2 And it was F written how Mordecai had told
7:3 answered, "If I have F favor in your sight,
8:5 and if I have F favor in his sight,
Job 8:8 what the fathers have F;
19:28 of the matter is F in him';
20:8 dream, and not be F; he will be chased
28:12 "But where shall wisdom be F
28:13 and it is not F in the land of
32:3 friends because they had F no answer, although they
32:13 you say, 'We have F wisdom; God may vanquish
33:24 the Pit, I have F a ransom;
Ps 36:2 his iniquity cannot be F out and hated.
37:36 though I sought him, he could not be F
68:10 it languished; thy flock F a dwelling in it;
69:20 for comforters, but I F none.
89:20 I have F David, my servant; with my holy
132:6 it in Ephrathah, we F it in the fields
Prov 7:15 eagerly, and I have F you.
10:9 his ways will be F out.
10:13 has understanding wisdom is F, but a rod is
25:16 If you have F honey, eat only enough for
30:6 you, and you be F a liar.
Eccl 2:10 pleasure, for my heart F pleasure in all my
7:26 And I F more bitter than death the woman
7:27 this is what I F, says the Preacher, adding
7:28 mind has sought repeatedly, but I have not F
7:28 among a thousand I F, but a woman among
7:28 a woman among all these I have not F
7:29 Behold, this alone I F, that God made man
9:15 But there was F in it a poor wise
Song 3:1 I sought him, but F him not; I called
3:2 I sought him, but F him not.
3:3 The watchmen F me, as they went about in
3:4 passed them, when I F him whom my soul
5:6 I sought him, but F him not; I called
5:7 The watchmen F me, as they went about in
Wis 1:2 heart; because he is F by those who do
3:5 God tested them and F them worthy of himself;
5:10 no trace can be F, nor track of its
5:11 of its passage is F; the light air, lashed
5:11 of its coming is F there;
6:12 love her, and is F by those who seek
7:29 the light she is F to be superior,
8:11 I shall be F keen in judgment, and in
16:9 and no healing was F for them, because they
Sir 6:14 shelter: he that has F one has found a
6:14 has found one has F a treasure.
11:17 he says, "I have F rest, and now I
18:16 Both are to be F in a gracious man.
20:4 by keeping silent is F wise, while another is
21:16 but delight will be F in the speech of
23:12 may it never be F in the inheritance of
31:8 rich man who is F blameless, and who does
31:10 by it and been F perfect?
35:10 given, and as generously as your hand has F
36:16 let thy prophets be F trustworthy.
38:33 and they are not F using proverbs.
44:18 Noah was F perfect and righteous; in the time
44:20 no one has been F like him in glory;
44:21 was tested he was F faithful.
45:1 man of mercy, who F favor in the sight
51:16 received her, and I F for myself much instruction.
51:20 and through purification I F her.
51:26 it is to be F close by.
51:27 have labored little and F myself much rest.
Is 10:14 My hand has F like a nest the wealth
13:15 Whoever is F will be thrust through, and whoever
22:3 of you who were F were captured, though they
30:14 not a sherd is F with which to take
35:9 they shall not be F there, but the redeemed
37:8 The Rabshakeh returned, and F the king of Assyria
39:2 armory, all that was F in his storehouses.
51:3 and gladness will be F in her, thanksgiving and
55:6 while he may be F, call upon him while
57:10 "It is hopeless"; you F new life for your
65:1 was ready to be F by those who did
65:8 "As the wine is F in the cluster, and
Jer 2:34 on your skirts is F the lifeblood of guiltless
5:26 For wicked men are F among my people; they
15:16 Thy words were F, and I ate them, and
23:11 my house I have F their wickedness, says the
29:14 heart, I will be F by you, says the
31:2 who survived the sword F grace in the wilderness;
48:27 Was he F among thieves, that whenever you spoke
50:7 All who F them have devoured them, and their
50:20 and none shall be F; for I will pardon
50:24 know it; you were F and caught, because you
52:25 king's council, who were F in the city; and
52:25 the land, who were F in the midst of
Bar 3:15 Who has F her place?
3:30 over the sea, and F her, and will buy
3:32 things knows her, he F her by his understanding.
3:36 He F the whole way to knowledge, and gave
Ezek 22:30 destroy it; but I F none.
26:21 you will never be F again, says the Lord
28:15 created, till iniquity was F in you.
Dan 1:19 them all none was F like Daniel, Hananiah, Mishael,
1:20 inquired of them, he F them ten times better
2:25 to him: "I have F among the exiles from
2:35 that not a trace of them could be F
4:12 beasts of the field F shade under it, and
4:21 beasts of the field F shade, and in whose
5:11 of the gods, were F in him, and King
5:12 and solve problems were F in this Daniel, whom
5:14 and excellent wisdom are F in you.
5:27 in the balances and F wanting;
6:4 error or fault was F in him.
6:11 came by agreement and F Daniel making petition
6:22 me, because I was F blameless before him; and
6:23 kind of hurt was F upon him, because he
11:19 shall stumble and fall, and shall not be F
12:1 whose name shall be F written in the book.
13:63 because nothing shameful was F in her.
Hos 9:10 in the wilderness, I F Israel.
Jon 1:3 down to Joppa and F a ship going to
Mic 1:13 for in you were F the transgressions of Israel.
Zeph 3:13 nor shall there be F in their mouth a
Mal 2:6 and no wrong was F on his lips.
1Mac 1:23 he took also the hidden treasures which he F
1:56 the law which they F they tore to pieces
1:57 of the covenant was F in the possession of
1:58 against Israel, against those F month after month in
2:46 uncircumcised boys that they F within the borders of
2:52 Was not Abraham F faithful when tested, and it
2:63 he will not be F, because he has returned
4:5 Judas by night, he F no one there, so
5:6 the Ammonites, where he F a strong band and
6:53 seventh year; those who F safety in Judea from
6:63 He F Philip in control of the city, but
9:34 Bacchides F this out on the sabbath day, and
10:60 and many gifts, and F favor with them.
12:21 It has been F in writing concerning the Spartans
16:22 them, for he had F out that they were
2Mac 1:20 that they had not F fire but thick liquid,
2:5 And Jeremiah came and F a cave, and he
8:7 He F the nights most advantageous for such attacks.
12:40 of the dead they F sacred tokens of the
14:5 But he F an opportunity that furthered his mad
Mt 1:18 came together she was F to be with child
2:8 and when you have F him bring me word,
8:10 in Israel have I F such faith.
13:44 field, which a man F and covered up; then
20:6 he went out and F others standing; and he
21:19 went to it, and F nothing on it but
22:10 gathered all whom they F, both bad and good;
26:40 to the disciples and F them sleeping; and he

26:43 again he came and F them sleeping, for their
26:60 to death, but they F none, though many false
Mk 1:37 pursued him, and they F him and said to
6:38 And when they had F out, they said, "Five,
7:29 she went home, and F the child lying in
11:4 they went away, and F a colt tied at
11:13 came to it, he F nothing but leaves, for
14:16 to the city, and F it as he had
14:37 And he came and F them sleeping, and he
14:40 again he came and F them sleeping, for their
14:55 to death; but they F none.
Lk 1:30 Mary, for you have F favor with God.
2:16 went with haste, and F Mary and Joseph, and
2:46 After three days they F him in the temple,
4:17 opened the book and F the place where it
7:9 in Israel have I F such faith."
7:10 to the house, they F the slave well.
8:35 came to Jesus, and F the man from whom
9:36 had spoken, Jesus was F alone.
13:6 fruit on it and F none.
15:5 And when he has F it, he lays it
15:6 me, for I have F my sheep which was
15:9 And when she has F it, she calls together
15:9 me, for I have F the coin which I
15:24 was lost, and is F And they began to
15:32 and is alive; he was lost, and is F
17:18 Was no one F to return and give praise
19:32 sent went away and F it as he had
22:13 And they went, and F it as he had
22:43 to the disciples and F them sleeping for sorrow,
23:2 accuse him, saying, "We F this man perverting our
23:21 I have F in him no crime deserving death;
24:2 And they F the stone rolled away from the
24:24 to the tomb, and F it just as the
24:33 to Jerusalem; and they F the eleven gathered
Jn 1:41 He first F his brother Simon, and said to
1:41 to him, "We have F the Messiah" (which means
1:43 And he F Philip and said to him, "Follow
1:45 Philip F Nathanael, and said to him, "We have
1:45 to him, "We have F him of whom Moses
2:14 In the temple he F those who were selling
5:13 Afterward, Jesus F him in the temple, and said
6:25 When they F him on the other side of
9:35 him out, and having F him he said, "Do
11:17 when Jesus came, he F that Lazarus had already
12:14 And Jesus F a young ass and sat upon
Acts 5:10 men came in they F her dead, and they
5:23 returned and reported, "We F the prison securely
5:23 we opened it we F no one inside."
5:39 You might even be F opposing God!"
7:46 days of David, who F favor in the sight
8:39 But Philip was F at Azotus, and passing on
9:2 so that if he F any belonging to the
9:33 There he F a man named Aeneas, who had
10:27 he went in and F many persons gathered;
11:26 and when he had F him, he brought him
13:22 and said, 'I have F in David the son
17:23 of your worship, I F also an altar with
18:2 And he F a Jew named Aquila, a native
19:1 There he F some disciples.
19:19 value of them and F it came to fifty
21:2 And having F a ship crossing to Phoenicia, we
23:29 I F that he was accused about questions of
24:5 For we have F this man a pestilent fellow,
24:17 was doing this, they F me purified in the
24:19 say what wrongdoing they F when I stood before
25:25 But I F that he had done nothing deserving
27:6 There the centurion F a ship of Alexandria sailing
27:28 So they sounded and F twenty fathoms; a little
27:28 they sounded again and F fifteen fathoms.
28:14 There we F brethren, and were invited to stay
Rom 10:20 say, "I have been F by those who did
1Cor 4:2 stewards that they be F trustworthy.
5:1 kind that is not F even among pagans; for
15:15 We are even F to be misrepresenting God, because
2Cor 5:3 we may not be F naked.
6:3 no fault may be F with our ministry,
8:22 have often tested and F earnest in many matters,
Gal 2:17 Christ, we ourselves were F to be sinners, is
Eph 5:9 fruit of light is F in all that is
Phil 2:8 And being F in human form he humbled himself
3:9 gain Christ and be F in him, not having
2Tim 1:17 for me eagerly and F me—
Heb 1:10 And, "Thou, Lord, didst F the earth in the
11:5 and he was not F, because God had taken
12:17 was rejected, for he F no chance to repent,
1Pet 2:22 sin; no guile was F on his lips.
2Pet 3:14 be zealous to be F by him without spot
Jude 1:3 our common salvation, I F it necessary to write
Rev 2:2 but are not, and F them to be false;
3:2 for I have not F your works perfect in
5:4 that no one was F worthy to open the
14:5 mouth no lie was F, for they are spotless.
16:20 mountains were to be F;
18:14 thee, never to be F again!"
18:21 violence, and shall be F no more;
18:22 any craft shall be F in thee no more;
18:24 And in her was F the blood of prophets
20:11 and no place was F for them.
20:15 one's name was not F written in the book

FOUNDATION (50)

Josh 6:26 shall he lay its F, and at the cost
1Kgs 5:17 order to lay the F of the house with
6:37 the fourth year the F of the house of
7:9 front, even from the F to the coping, and
7:10 The F was of costly stones, huge stones, stones
16:34 Jericho; he laid its F at the cost of
2Chr 8:16 from the day the F of the house of
23:5 the Gate of the F; and all the people
Ezra 3:6 But the F of the temple of the LORD
3:10 the builders laid the F of the temple of
3:11 the LORD, because the F of the house of
3:12 when they saw the F of this house being
Job 4:19 houses of clay, whose F is in the dust,
22:16 before their time; their F was washed away.
38:4 when I laid the F of the earth?
Ps 89:14 and justice are the F of thy throne; steadfast
97:2 and justice are the F of his throne.
102:25 thou didst lay the F of the earth, and
Sir 1:13 among men an eternal F, and among their
Is 28:16 in Zion for a F a stone, a tested
28:16 cornerstone, of a sure F: 'He who believes will
44:28 of the temple, 'Your F shall be laid.'"
48:13 My hand laid the F of the earth, and
Jer 51:26 no stone for a F, but you shall be
Ezek 13:14 ground, so that its F will be laid bare;
Hag 2:18 the day that the F of the LORD's temple
Zech 4:9 Zerubbabel have laid the F of this house; his
8:9 the day that the F of the house of
Mt 13:35 been hidden since the F of the world."
25:34 for you from the F of the world;
Lk 6:48 deep, and laid the F upon rock; and when
6:49 the ground without a F; against which the stream
11:50 prophets, shed from the F of the world, may
14:29 he has laid a F, and is not able
Jn 17:24 for me before the F of the world.
Rom 15:20 build on another man's F,
1Cor 3:10 builder I laid a F, and another man is
3:11 For no other F can any one lay than
3:12 one builds on the F with gold, silver, precious
3:14 has built on the F survives, he will receive
Eph 1:4 in him before the F of the world, that
2:20 God, built upon the F of the apostles and
1Tim 6:19 for themselves a good F for the future, so
2Tim 2:19 But God's firm F stands, bearing this seal: "The
Heb 4:3 were finished from the F of the world.
6:1 not laying again a F of repentance from dead
9:26 suffer repeatedly since the F of the world.
1Pet 1:20 was destined before the F of the world but
Rev 13:8 been written before the F of the world in
17:8 of life from the F of the world, will

FOUNDATIONS (36)

Deut 32:22 sets on fire the F of the mountains.
2Sam 22:8 reeled and rocked; the F of the heavens trembled
22:16 sea were seen, the F of the world were
Ezra 4:12 they are finishing the walls and repairing the F
5:16 came and laid the F of the house of
Jud 1:3 cubits wide at the F;
16:15 be shaken to their F with the waters; at
Ps 11:3 in heart; if the F are destroyed, what can
18:7 reeled and rocked; the F also of the mountains
18:15 were seen, and the F of the world were
82:5 in darkness; all the F of the earth are
104:5 the earth on its F, so that it should
137:7 Down to its F
Prov 8:29 he marked out the F of the earth,
Wis 4:19 shake them from the F; they will be left
Sir 3:9 the children, but a mother's curse uproots their F
10:16 destroyed them to the F of the earth.
16:17 mountains also and the F of the earth shake

50:2 He laid the F for the high double walls,
Is 6:4 And the F of the thresholds shook at the
24:18 are opened, and the F of the earth tremble.
40:21 not understood from the F of the earth?
51:13 heavens and laid the F of the earth, and
51:16 heavens and laying the F of the earth, and
54:11 antimony, and lay your F with sapphires.
58:12 shall raise up the F of many generations; you
Jer 31:37 be measured, and the F of the earth below
Lam 4:11 kindled a fire in Zion, which consumed its F
Ezek 30:4 carried away, and her F are torn down.
41:8 platform round about; the F of the side chambers
Mic 1:6 her stones into the valley, and uncover her F
6:2 LORD, and you enduring F of the earth; for
Acts 16:26 earthquake, so that the F of the prison were
Heb 11:10 the city which has F, whose builder and maker
Rev 21:14 the city had twelve F, and on them the
21:19 The F of the wall of the city were

FOUNDED (13)

Ex 9:18 the day it was F until now.
Ps 8:2 and infants, thou hast F a bulwark because of
24:2 therein; for he has F it upon the seas,
78:69 earth, which he has F for ever.
87:1 stands the city he F;
89:11 in it, thou hast F them.
119:152 testimonies that thou hast F them for ever.
Prov 3:19 The LORD by wisdom F the earth; by understanding
Is 14:32 "The LORD has F Zion, and in her the
Zech 12:1 out the heavens and F the earth and formed
2Mac 2:13 and also that he F a library and collected
4:12 For with alacrity he F a gymnasium right under
Mt 7:25 because it had been F on the rock.

FOUNDS (2)

Amos 9:6 in the heavens, and F his vault upon the
Hab 2:12 town with blood, and F a city on iniquity!

FOUNTAIN (29)

Lev 20:18 has made naked her F, and she has uncovered
20:18 she has uncovered the F of her blood; both
Deut 33:28 dwelt in safety, the F of Jacob alone, in
1Sam 29:1 were encamped by the F which is in Jezreel.
Neh 2:14 went on to the F Gate and to the
3:15 of Mizpah, repaired the F Gate; he rebuilt it
12:37 At the F Gate they went up straight before
Ps 36:9 with thee is the F of life; in thy
68:26 the LORD, O you who are of Israel's F
Prov 5:18 Let your F be blessed, and rejoice in the
10:11 the righteous is a F of life, but the
13:14 the wise is a F of life, that one
14:27 the LORD is a F of life, that one
16:22 Wisdom is a F of life to him who
18:4 are deep waters; the F of wisdom is a
25:26 spring or a polluted F is a righteous man
Eccl 12:6 is broken at the F, or the wheel broken
Song 4:12 a garden locked, a F sealed.
4:15 spices-- a garden F, a well of living
Wis 11:6 Instead of the F of an ever-flowing river, stirred
Jer 2:13 have forsaken me, the F of living waters, and
9:1 and my eyes a F of tears, that I
17:13 forsaken the LORD, the F of living water.
51:36 sea and make her F dry;
Bar 3:12 You have forsaken the F of wisdom.
Hos 13:15 the wilderness; and his F shall dry up, his
Joel 3:18 with water; and a F shall come forth from
Zech 13:1 there shall be a F opened for the house
Rev 21:6 will give from the F of the water of

FOUNTAINS (9)

Gen 7:11 that day all the F of the great deep
8:2 the waters subsided; the F of the deep and
Deut 8:7 brooks of water, of F and springs, flowing forth
Prov 8:28 when he established the F of the deep,
Is 41:18 the bare heights, and F in the midst of
Ezek 34:13 of Israel, by the F, and in all the
Rev 8:10 rivers and on the F of water.
14:7 the sea and the F of water."
16:4 the rivers and the F of water, and they

FOUR (278)

Gen 2:10 it divided and became F rivers.
11:13 the birth of Shelah F hundred and three years,
11:15 the birth of Eber F hundred and three years,
11:17 the birth of Peleg F hundred and thirty years,
14:9 Arioch king of Ellasar, F kings against five.
15:13 will be oppressed for F hundred years;
23:15 piece of land worth F hundred shekels of silver,
23:16 hearing of the Hittites, F hundred shekels of silver,
32:6 to meet you, and F hundred men with him."
33:1 Esau was coming, and F hundred men with him.
47:24 fifth to Pharaoh, and F fifths shall be your
Ex 12:40 dwelt in Egypt was F hundred and thirty years.
12:41 at the end of F hundred and thirty years,
22:1 for an ox, and F sheep for a sheep.
25:12 And you shall cast F rings of gold for
25:12 put them on its F feet, two rings on
25:26 shall make for it F rings of gold, and
25:26 the rings to the F corners at its four
25:26 four corners at its F legs.
25:34 on the lampstand itself F cups made like almonds,
26:2 breadth of each curtain F cubits; all the curtains
26:8 breadth of each curtain F cubits; the eleven curtains
26:32 shall hang it upon F pillars of acacia overlaid
26:32 hooks of gold, upon F bases of silver.
27:2 for it on its F corners; its horns shall
27:4 net you shall make F bronze rings at its
27:4 bronze rings at its F corners.
27:16 needlework; it shall have F pillars and with them
27:16 pillars and with them F bases.
28:17 shall set in it F rows of stones.
36:9 breadth of each curtain F cubits; all the curtains
36:15 breadth of each curtain F cubits; the eleven curtains
36:36 for it he made F pillars of acacia, and
36:36 he cast for them F bases of silver.
37:3 he cast for it F rings of gold for
37:3 of gold for its F corners, two rings on
37:13 He cast for it F rings of gold, and
37:13 the rings to the F corners at its four
37:13 four corners at its F legs.
37:20 the lampstand itself were F cups made like almonds,
38:2 for it on its F corners; its horns were
38:5 He cast F rings on the four corners of
38:5 four rings on the F corners of the bronze
38:19 And their pillars were F; their four bases were
38:19 pillars were four; their F bases were of bronze,
38:29 and two thousand and F hundred shekels;
39:10 they set in it F rows of stones.
Lev 11:23 winged insects which have F feet are an abomination
Num 1:29 Issachar was fifty-four thousand F hundred.
1:31 Zebulun was fifty-seven thousand F hundred.
1:37 Benjamin was thirty-five thousand F hundred.
1:43 Naphtali was fifty-three thousand F hundred.
2:6 numbered being fifty-four thousand F hundred.
2:8 numbered being fifty-seven thousand F hundred.
2:9 hundred and eighty-six thousand F hundred.
2:16 hundred and fifty-one thousand F hundred and fifty.
2:23 numbered being thirty-five thousand F hundred.
2:30 numbered being fifty-three thousand F hundred.
7:7 Two wagons and F oxen he gave to the
7:8 to their service; and F wagons and eight oxen
7:85 vessels two thousand F hundred shekels according to
26:43 number, were sixty-four thousand F hundred.
26:47 their number, fifty-three thousand F hundred.
26:50 number was forty-five thousand F hundred.
Deut 3:11 was its length, and F cubits its breadth, according
22:12 yourself tassels on the F corners of your cloak
Josh 19:7 En-rimmon, Ether, and Ashan-- F cities with their
21:18 with its pasture lands-- F cities.
21:22 with its pasture lands-- F cities;
21:24 with its pasture lands-- F cities;
21:29 with its pasture lands-- F cities;
21:31 with its pasture lands-- F cities;
21:35 with its pasture lands-- F cities;
21:37 with its pasture lands-- F cities;
21:39 with its pasture lands-- F cities in all.
Judg 9:34 wait against Shechem in F companies.
11:40 of Jephthah the Gileadite F days in the year.
19:2 and was there some F months.
20:2 the people of God, F hundred thousand men on
20:17 apart from Benjamin, mustered F hundred thousand
20:47 the rock of Rimmon F months.
21:12 inhabitants of Jabesh-gilead F hundred young virgins
1Sam 4:2 Philistines, who slew about F thousand men on the
22:2 were with him about F hundred men.
25:13 his sword; and about F hundred men went up
27:7 was a year and F months.
30:10 the pursuit, he and F hundred men; two hundred
30:17 of them escaped, except F hundred young men, who
2Sam 15:7 at the end of F years Absalom said to
21:22 These F were descended from the giants in Gath;
1Kgs 6:1 In the F hundred and eightieth year after the

F

7:15 and its thickness was F fingers; the second pillar
7:19 vestibule were of lily-work, F cubits.
7:27 bronze; each stand was F cubits long, four cubits
7:27 was four cubits long, F cubits wide, and three
7:30 Moreover each stand had F bronze wheels and axles
7:30 bronze; and at the F corners were supports for
7:32 And the F wheels were underneath the panels; the
7:34 There were F supports at the four corners of
7:34 four supports at the F corners of each stand;
7:38 baths, each laver measured F cubits, and there was
7:42 the pillars; and the F hundred pomegranates for the
9:28 to the amount of F hundred and twenty talents;
18:19 Mount Carmel, and the F hundred and fifty prophets
18:19 of Baal and the F hundred prophets of Asherah,
18:22 but Baal's prophets are F hundred and fifty men.
18:33 And he said, "Fill F jars with water, and
22:6 the prophets together, about F hundred men, and
2Kgs 7:3 Now there were F men who were lepers at
14:13 wall of Jerusalem for F hundred cubits, from the
1Chr 3:5 Nathan and Solomon, F by Bath-shua, the daughter
7:1 sons of Issachar: Tola, Puah, Jashub, and Shimron, F
9:24 gatekeepers were on the F sides, east, west, north,
9:26 with these; for the F chief gatekeepers, who were
12:26 Of the Levites F thousand six hundred.
21:5 sword, and in Judah F hundred and seventy thousand
21:20 the angel, and his F sons who were with
23:5 be officers and judges, F thousand gatekeepers, and
23:5 four thousand gatekeepers, and F thousand shall
23:10 These F were the sons of Shimei.
23:12 sons of Kohath: Amram, Izhar, Hebron, and Uzziel, F
26:17 day, on the north F each day, on the
26:17 day, on the south F each day, as well
26:18 the west there were F at the road and
2Chr 4:13 the pillars; and the F hundred pomegranates for the
8:18 and fetched from there F hundred and fifty talents
9:25 And Solomon had F thousand stalls for horses and
13:3 valiant men of war, F hundred thousand picked men;
18:5 gathered the prophets together, F hundred men, and
25:23 wall of Jerusalem for F hundred cubits, from the
Ezra 1:10 of gold, two thousand F hundred and ten bowls
1:11 silver were five thousand F hundred and sixty-nine.
2:15 The sons of Adin, F hundred and fifty-four.
2:67 their camels were F hundred and thirty-five, and
6:17 bulls, two hundred rams, F hundred lambs, and as
Neh 6:4 they sent to me F times in this way
7:69 and forty-five, their camels F hundred and thirty-five,
11:6 lived in Jerusalem were F hundred and sixty-eight
Jud 8:4 for three years and F months.
Job 1:19 wilderness, and struck the F corners of the house,
42:16 and his sons' sons, F generations.
Prov 30:15 things are never satisfied; F never say, "Enough":
30:18 too wonderful for me; F I do not understand:
30:21 the earth trembles; under F it cannot bear up:
30:24 F things on earth are small, but they are
30:29 stately in their tread; F are stately in their
Wis 18:24 were engraved on the F rows of stones, and
Sir 37:18 to changes of heart F turns of fortune appear,
Is 11:12 of Judah from the F corners of the earth.
17:6 of the highest bough, F or five on the
Jer 15:3 will appoint over them F kinds of destroyers, says
36:23 Jehudi read three or F columns, the king would
49:36 bring upon Elam the F winds from the four
49:36 four winds from the F quarters of heaven; and
52:21 and its thickness was F fingers, and it was
52:30 all the persons were F thousand and six hundred.
Ezek 1:5 came the likeness of F living creatures.
1:6 men, but each had F faces, and each of
1:6 each of them had F wings.
1:8 their wings on their F sides they had human
1:8 And the F had their faces and their wings
1:10 man in front; the F had the face of
1:10 the right side, the F had the face of
1:10 left side, and the F had the face of
1:15 for each of the F of them.
1:16 a chrysolite; and the F had the same likeness,
1:17 in any of their F directions without turning as
1:18 The F wheels had rims and they had spokes;
7:2 has come upon the F corners of the land.
10:9 behold, there were F wheels beside the cherubim,
10:10 for their appearance, the F had the same likeness,
10:11 in any of their F directions without turning as
10:12 the wheels that the F of them had.
10:14 And every one had F faces: the first face
10:21 Each had F faces, and each four wings, and
10:21 four faces, and each F wings, and underneath their
14:21 send upon Jerusalem my F sore acts of judgment,
37:9 GOD: Come from the F winds, O breath, and
40:41 F tables were on the inside, and four tables
40:41 on the inside, and F tables on the outside
40:42 And there were also F tables of hewn stone
41:5 of the side chambers, F cubits, round about the
42:20 measured it on the F sides.
43:14 to the larger ledge, F cubits, with a breadth
43:15 and the altar hearth, F cubits; and from the
43:15 altar hearth projecting upward, F horns, one cubit
43:20 put it on the F horns of the altar,
43:20 altar, and on the F corners of the ledge,
45:19 of the temple, the F corners of the ledge
46:21 led me to the F corners of the court;
46:22 court-- in the F corners of the court
46:22 and thirty broad; the F were of the same
46:23 around each of the F courts was a row
48:16 dimensions: the north side F thousand five hundred
48:16 cubits, the south side F thousand five hundred, the
48:16 hundred, the east side F thousand five hundred, and
48:16 and the west side F thousand and five hundred.
48:30 which is to be F thousand five hundred cubits
48:32 which is to be F thousand five hundred cubits,
48:33 which is to be F thousand five hundred cubits
48:34 which is to be F thousand five hundred cubits,
Dan 1:17 As for these F youths, God gave them learning
3:93 answered, "But I see F men loose, walking in
7:2 night, and behold, the F winds of heaven were
7:3 And F great beasts came up out of the
7:6 like a leopard, with F wings of a bird
7:6 and the beast had F heads; and dominion was
7:17 'These F great beasts are four kings who shall
7:17 four great beasts are F kings who shall arise
8:8 it there came up F conspicuous horns toward the
8:8 conspicuous horns toward the F winds of heaven.
8:22 in place of which F others arose, four kingdoms
8:22 which four others arose, F kingdoms shall arise from
11:4 and divided toward the F winds of heaven, but
Amos 1:3 of Damascus, and for F, I will not revoke
1:6 of Gaza, and for F, I will not revoke
1:9 of Tyre, and for F, I will not revoke
1:11 of Edom, and for F, I will not revoke
1:13 the Ammonites, and for F, I will not revoke
2:1 of Moab, and for F, I will not revoke
2:4 of Judah, and for F, I will not revoke
2:6 of Israel, and for F, I will not revoke
Zech 1:18 and saw, and behold, F horns!
1:20 the LORD showed me F smiths.
2:6 you abroad as the F winds of the heavens,
6:1 and saw, and behold, F chariots came out from
6:5 going forth to the F winds of heaven, after
1Mac 6:37 and upon each were F armed men who fought
11:57 set you over the F districts and make you
13:28 father and mother and F brothers.
2Mac 3:11 it totaled in all F hundred talents of silver
8:20 into the affair, with F thousand Macedonians; and
8:21 divided his army into F parts.
10:33 besieged the fort for F days.
12:33 three thousand infantry and F hundred cavalry.
Mt 15:38 Those who ate were F thousand men, besides
16:10 seven loaves of the F thousand, and how many
24:31 his elect from the F winds, from one end
Mk 2:3 a paralytic carried by F men.
8:9 And there were about F thousand people.
8:20 the seven for the F thousand, how many baskets
13:27 his elect from the F winds, from the ends
Jn 4:35 say, 'There are yet F months, then comes the
6:19 rowed about three or F miles, they saw Jesus
11:17 been in the tomb F days.
11:39 he has been dead F days."
19:23 his garments and made F parts, one for each
Acts 5:36 number of men, about F hundred, joined him; but
7:6 them and ill-treat them F hundred years.
10:11 sheet, let down by F corners upon the earth.
10:30 And Cornelius said, F days ago, about this hour,
11:5 down from heaven by F corners; and it came
12:4 and delivered him to F squads of soldiers to
13:19 an inheritance, for about F hundred and fifty years.
21:9 And he had F unmarried daughters, who prophesied.
21:23 We have F men who are under a vow;
21:38 revolt and led the F thousand men of the
27:29 rocks, they let out F anchors from the stern,
Gal 3:17 the law, which came F hundred and thirty years
Rev 4:6 of the throne, are F living creatures, full of
4:8 And the F living creatures, each of them with
5:6 the throne and the F living creatures and among
5:8 taken the scroll, the F living creatures and the

5:14 And the F living creatures said, "Amen!" and the
6:1 heard one of the F living creatures say, as
6:6 the midst of the F living creatures saying, "A
7:1 After this I saw F angels standing at the
7:1 angels standing at the F corners of the earth,
7:1 earth, holding back the F winds of the earth,
7:2 loud voice to the F angels who had been
7:11 the elders and the F living creatures, and they
9:13 a voice from the F horns of the golden
9:14 the trumpet, "Release the F angels who are bound
9:15 So the F angels were released, who had been
14:3 throne and before the F living creatures and before
15:7 And one of the F living creatures gave the
19:4 twenty-four elders and the F living creatures fell
20:8 which are at the F corners of the earth,

FOUR-FOOTED

Bar 3:32 time filled it with F creatures;

FOURFOLD (2)

2Sam 12:6 shall restore the lamb F, because he did this
Lk 19:8 defrauded any one of anything, I restore it F

FOURS (4)

Lev 11:20 that go upon all F are an abomination to
11:21 that go on all F you may eat those
11:27 that go on all F, are unclean to you;
11:42 whatever goes on all F, or whatever has many

FOURSCORE

Ps 90:10 by reason of strength F; yet their span is

FOURSQUARE (2)

Ezek 40:47 a hundred cubits broad, F; and the altar was
Rev 21:16 The city lies F, its length the same as

FOURTEEN (29)

Gen 31:41 house; I served you F years for your two
46:22 were born to Jacob-- F persons in all).
Num 16:49 by the plague were F thousand seven hundred,
29:13 young bulls, two rams, F male lambs a year
29:15 for each of the F lambs;
29:17 young bulls, two rams, F male lambs a year
29:20 eleven bulls, two rams, F male lambs a year
29:23 ten bulls, two rams, F male lambs a year
29:26 nine bulls, two rams, F male lambs a year
29:29 eight bulls, two rams, F male lambs a year
29:32 seven bulls, two rams, F male lambs a year
Josh 15:36 Adithaim, Gederah, Gederothaim: F cities with their
18:28 Jerusalem), Gibe-ah and Kiriath-jearim-- F cities
1Kgs 10:26 and horsemen; he had F hundred chariots and twelve
1Chr 25:5 God had given Heman F sons and three daughters.
2Chr 1:14 and horsemen; he had F hundred chariots and twelve
13:21 And he took F wives, and had twenty-two sons
Tob 8:19 for them which lasted F days.
8:20 not leave until the F days of the wedding
10:7 son Tobias, until the F days of the wedding
Job 42:12 beginning; and he had F thousand sheep, six
Ezek 40:48 of the gate was F cubits; and the sidewalls
43:17 also shall be square, F cubits long by fourteen
43:17 fourteen cubits long by F broad, with a rim
Mt 1:17 Abraham to David were F generations, and from
1:17 the deportation to Babylon F generations, and from
1:17 Babylon to the Christ F generations.
2Cor 12:2 man in Christ who F years ago was caught
Gal 2:1 Then after F years I went up again to

FOURTEENTH (27)

Gen 14:5 In the F year Ched-or-laomer and the kings who
Ex 12:6 keep it until the F day of this month,
12:18 first month, on the F day of the month
Lev 23:5 first month, on the F day of the month
Num 9:3 On the F day of this month, in the
9:5 first month, on the F day of the month,
9:11 second month on the F day in the evening
28:16 "On the F day of the first month is
Josh 5:10 the passover on the F day of the month
2Kgs 18:13 In the F year of King Hezekiah Sennacherib king
1Chr 24:13 thirteenth to Huppah, the F to Jeshebe-ab,
25:21 brethren, twelve; to the F, Mattithiah, his sons and
2Chr 30:15 passover lamb on the F day of the second
35:1 passover lamb on the F day of the first
Ezra 6:19 On the F day of the first month the
Esth 9:15 gathered also on the F day of the month
9:17 Adar, and on the F day they rested and
9:18 day and on the F, and rested on the
9:19 open towns, hold the F day of the month
9:21 they should keep the F day of the month
10:13 of Adar, on the F and fifteenth of that
13:6 or mercy, on the F day of the twelfth
Is 36:1 In the F year of King Hezekiah, Sennacherib king
Ezek 40:1 the month, in the F year after the city
45:21 first month, on the F day of the month,
Acts 27:27 When the F night had come, as we were
27:33 saying, "Today is the F day that you have

FOURTH (87)

Gen 1:19 there was morning, a F day.
2:14 And the F river is the Euphrates.
15:16 back here in the F generation; for the iniquity
Ex 20:5 the third and the F generation of those who
28:20 an amethyst; and the F row a beryl, an
29:40 flour mingled with a F of a hin of
29:40 beaten oil, and a F of a hin of
34:7 the third and the F generation."
39:13 an amethyst; and the F row, a beryl, an
Lev 19:24 And in the F year all their fruit shall
23:13 be of wine, a F of a hin.
Num 7:30 On the F day Elizur the son of Shedeur,
14:18 third and upon the F generation.'
15:4 flour, mixed with a F of a hin of
15:5 the drink offering, a F of a hin, you
23:10 Jacob, or number the F part of Israel?
28:5 offering, mixed with a F of a hin of
28:7 offering shall be a F of a hin for
28:14 a ram, and a F of a hin for
29:23 "On the F day ten bulls, two rams, fourteen
Deut 5:9 to the third and F generation of those who
Josh 19:17 The F lot came out for Issachar, for the
Judg 14:15 On the F day they said to Samson's wife,
19:5 And on the F day they arose early in
1Sam 9:8 have with me the F part of a shekel
2Sam 3:4 of Geshur; and the F, Adonijah the son of
1Kgs 6:1 of Egypt, in the F year of Solomon's reign
6:37 In the F year the foundation of the house
22:41 over Judah in the F year of Ahab king
2Kgs 6:25 of silver, and the F part of a kab
10:30 your sons of the F generation shall sit on
15:12 of Israel to the F generation." And so it
18:9 In the F year of King Hezekiah, which was
25:3 ninth day of the F month the famine was
1Chr 2:14 the third, Nethanel the F, Raddai the fifth,
3:2 king of Geshur; the F Adonijah, whose mother was
3:15 the third Zedekiah, the F Shallum.
8:2 the third, Nohah the F, and Rapha the fifth.
12:10 second, Eliab third, Mishmannah F, Jeremiah fifth,
23:19 the second, Jahaziel the third, and Jekameam the F
24:8 third to Harim, the F to Se-orim,
24:23 the second, Jahaziel the third, Jekameam the F
25:11 his brethren, twelve; the F to Izri, his sons
26:2 the third, Jathni-el the F,
26:4 the third, Sachar the F, Nethanel the fifth,
26:11 the third, Zechariah the F: all the sons and
27:7 brother of Joab was F, for the fourth month,
27:7 was fourth, for the F month, and his son
2Chr 3:2 second month of the F year of his reign.
20:26 On the F day they assembled in the Valley
Ezra 8:33 On the F day, within the house of our
Neh 9:3 their God for a F of the day; for
9:3 the day; for another F of it they made
Jud 12:10 On the F day Holofernes held a banquet for
Esth 11:1 In the F year of the reign of Ptolemy
Sir 26:5 afraid, and of a F I am frightened: The
Jer 25:1 of Judah, in the F year of Jehoiakim the
28:1 fifth month of the F year, Hananiah the son
36:1 In the F year of Jehoiakim the son of
39:2 of Zedekiah, in the F month, on the ninth
45:1 of Jeremiah, in the F year of Jehoiakim the
46:2 Babylon defeated in the F year of Jehoiakim the
51:59 to Babylon, in the F year of his reign.
52:6 ninth day of the F month the famine was
Ezek 1:1 thirtieth year, in the F month, on the fifth
10:14 a lion, and the F the face of an
Dan 2:40 there shall be a F kingdom, strong as iron,
3:93 the appearance of the F is like a son
7:7 visions, and behold, a F beast, terrible and dreadful
7:19 the truth concerning the F beast, which was different
7:23 said: 'As for the F beast, there shall be
7:23 there shall be a F kingdom on earth, which
11:2 in Persia; and a F shall be far richer
Zech 6:3 white horses, and the F chariot dappled gray horses.
7:1 In the F year of King Darius, the word

7:1 to Zechariah in the F day of the ninth
8:19 The fast of the F month, and the fast
2Mac 7:13 maltreated and tortured the F in the same way.
Mt 14:25 And in the F watch of the night he
Mk 6:48 And about the F watch of the night he
Rev 4:7 a man, and the F living creature like a
6:7 When he opened the F seal, I heard the
6:7 the voice of the F living creature say, "Come!"
6:8 given power over a F of the earth, to
8:12 The F angel blew his trumpet, and a third
16:8 The F angel poured his bowl on the sun,
21:19 the third agate, the F emerald,

FOWL (2)
Lev 7:26 blood whatever, whether of F or of animal, in
1Kgs 4:23 sheep, besides harts, gazelles, roebucks, and fatted F

FOWLER (3)
Ps 91:3 the snare of the F and from the deadly
Prov 6:5 like a bird from the hand of the F
Hos 9:8 my God, yet a F's snare is on all

FOWLERS (2)
Ps 124:7 the snare of the F; the snare is broken,
Jer 5:26 people; they lurk like F lying in wait.

FOWLS
Neh 5:18 and six choice sheep; F likewise were prepared for

FOX (2)
Neh 4:3 building– if a F goes up on it
Lk 13:32 "Go and tell that F, 'Behold, I cast out

FOXES (7)
Judg 15:4 and caught three hundred F, and took torches; and
15:5 torches, he let the F go into the standing
Song 2:15 Catch us the F, the little foxes, that spoil
2:15 the foxes, the little F, that spoil the vineyards,
Ezek 13:4 prophets have been like F among ruins, O Israel.
Mt 8:20 Jesus said to him, F have holes, and birds
Lk 9:58 Jesus said to him, F have holes, and birds

FRACTURE (2)
Lev 24:20 be done to him, F for fracture, eye for
24:20 to him, fracture for F, eye for eye, tooth

FRAGILE (2)
Wis 14:1 piece of wood more F than the ship which
15:13 makes from earthy matter F vessels and graven

FRAGMENTS (4)
Is 30:14 ruthlessly that among its F not a sherd is
Amos 6:11 shall be smitten into F, and the little house
Jn 6:12 disciples, "Gather up the F left over, that nothing
6:13 filled twelve baskets with F from the five barley

FRAGRANCE (15)
Song 1:12 on his couch, my nard gave forth its F
2:13 the vines are in blossom; they give forth F
4:10 than wine, and the F of your oils than
4:16 my garden, let its F be wafted abroad.
5:13 His cheeks are like beds of spices, yielding F
7:13 The mandrakes give forth F, and over our doors
Sir 24:15 stacte, and like the F of frankincense in the
39:14 of water; send forth F like frankincense, and put
39:14 Scatter the F, and sing a hymn of praise;
Hos 14:6 the olive, and his F like Lebanon.
14:7 as the vine, their F shall be like the
Jn 12:3 was filled with the F of the ointment.
2Cor 2:14 through us spreads the F of the knowledge of
2:16 perishing, to one a F from death to death,
2:16 to the other a F from life to life.

FRAGRANT (17)
Ex 25:6 oil and for the F incense,
30:7 And Aaron shall burn F incense on it; every
31:11 anointing oil and the F incense for the holy
35:8 oil and for the F incense,
35:15 anointing oil and the F incense, and the screen
35:28 oil, and for the F incense.
37:29 also, and the pure F incense, blended as by
39:38 anointing oil and the F incense, and the screen
Lev 4:7 of the altar of F incense before the LORD
Num 4:16 for the light, the F incense, the continual cereal
Jud 16:16 every sacrifice as a F offering is a small
Ps 45:8 your robes are all F with myrrh and aloes
Song 1:3 your anointing oils are F, your name is oil
3:6 frankincense, with all the F powders of the
Bar 5:8 The woods and every F tree have shaded Israel
Eph 5:2 up for us, a F offering and sacrifice to
Phil 4:18 gifts you sent, a F offering, a sacrifice acceptable

FRAIL
Gen 33:13 that the children are F, and that the flocks

FRAME (29)
Ex 25:25 make around it a F a handbreadth wide, and
25:25 wide, and a molding of gold around the F
25:27 Close to the F the rings shall lie, as
26:16 the length of a F, and a cubit and
26:16 cubit and a half the breadth of each F
26:17 two tenons in each F, for fitting together; so
26:19 two bases under one F for its two tenons,
26:19 two bases under another F for its two tenons;
26:21 two bases under one F, and two bases under
26:21 two bases under another F;
26:25 two bases under one F, and two bases under
26:25 under one frame, and two bases under another F
36:21 the length of a F, and a cubit and
36:21 cubit and a half the breadth of each F
36:22 Each F had two tenons, for fitting together; he
36:24 two bases under one F for its two tenons,
36:24 two bases under another F for its two tenons.
36:26 two bases under one F and two bases under
36:26 under one frame and two bases under another F
36:30 sixteen bases, under every F two bases.
37:12 made around it a F a handbreadth wide, and
37:12 and made a molding of gold around the F
37:14 Close to the F were the rings, as holders
Num 4:10 of goatskin and put it upon the carrying F
4:12 of goatskin, and put them on the carrying F
Job 41:12 limbs, or his mighty strength, or his goodly F
Ps 94:20 allied with thee, who F mischief by statute?
103:14 For he knows our F; he remembers that we
139:15 me right well; my F was not hidden from

FRAMES (41)
Ex 26:15 you shall make upright F for the tabernacle of
26:17 do for all the F of the tabernacle.
26:18 You shall make the F for the tabernacle: twenty
26:18 for the tabernacle: twenty F for the south side;
26:19 make under the twenty F, two bases under one
26:20 the north side twenty F,
26:22 of the tabernacle westward you shall make six F
26:23 you shall make two F for corners of the
26:25 there shall be eight F, with their bases of
26:26 wood, five for the F of the one side
26:27 five bars for the F of the other side
26:27 five bars for the F of the side of
26:28 bar, halfway up the F, shall pass through from
26:29 You shall overlay the F with gold, and shall
35:11 its hooks and its F, its bars, its pillars,
36:20 he made the upright F for the tabernacle of
36:22 this for all the F of the tabernacle.
36:23 The F for the tabernacle he made thus: twenty
36:23 he made thus: twenty F for the south side;
36:24 silver under the twenty F, two bases under one
36:25 side, he made twenty F
36:27 rear of the tabernacle westward he made six F
36:28 And he made two F for corners of the
36:30 There were eight F with their bases of silver:
36:31 wood, five for the F of the one side
36:32 five bars for the F of the other side
36:32 five bars for the F of the tabernacle at
36:33 through from end to end halfway up the F
36:34 And he overlaid the F with gold, and made
39:33 utensils, its hooks, its F, its bars, its pillars,
Num 3:36 was to be the F of the tabernacle, the
4:31 tent of meeting: the F of the tabernacle, with
1Kgs 6:4 he made for the house windows with recessed F
7:4 There were window F in three rows, and window
7:5 and windows had square F, and window was opposite
7:28 were set in the F
7:29 were set in the F were lions, oxen, and
7:29 Upon the F, both above and below the lions
2Kgs 16:17 Ahaz cut off the F of the stands, and
Ps 50:19 evil, and your tongue F deceit.
Ezek 41:16 round about all three had windows with recessed F

FRANKINCENSE (23)
Ex 30:34 sweet spices with pure F (of each shall there
Lev 2:1 upon it, and put F on it,

2:2 with all of its F; and the priest shall
2:15 upon it, and lay F on it; it is
2:16 with all of its F; it is an offering
5:11 and shall put no F on it, for it
6:15 oil and all the F which is on the
24:7 you shall put pure F with each row, that
Num 5:15 it and put no F on it, for it
Neh 13:5 the cereal offering, the F, the vessels, and the
13:9 of God, with the cereal offering and the F
Song 3:6 perfumed with myrrh and F, with all the fragrant
4:6 the mountain of myrrh and the hill of F
4:14 with all trees of F, myrrh and aloes, with
Sir 24:15 like the fragrance of F in the tabernacle.
39:14 send forth fragrance like F, and put forth blossoms
Is 43:23 burdened you with offerings, or wearied you with F
60:6 shall bring gold and F, and shall proclaim the
66:3 a memorial offering of F, like him who blesses
Jer 6:20 To what purpose does F come to me from
17:26 sacrifices, cereal offerings and F, and bringing thank
Mt 2:11 him gifts, gold and F and myrrh.
Rev 18:13 cinnamon, spice, incense, myrrh, F, wine, oil, fine

FRAUD (4)

Ps 55:11 its midst; oppression and F do not depart from
Zeph 1:9 who fill their master's house with violence and F
Mt 27:64 dead,' and the last F will be worse than
Jas 5:4 you kept back by F, cry out; and the

FREE (115)

Gen 24:8 then you will be F from this oath of
24:41 then you will be F from my oath, when
24:41 you, you will be F from my oath.'
Ex 21:2 he shall go out F, for nothing.
21:5 will not go out F
21:26 let the slave go F for the eye's sake.
21:27 let the slave go F for the tooth's sake.
Lev 19:20 because she was not F;
Num 5:19 your husband's authority, be F from this water of
5:28 then she shall be F and shall conceive children.
5:31 The man shall be F from iniquity, but the
32:22 shall return and be F of obligation to the
Deut 15:12 shall let him go F from you.
15:13 you let him go F from you, you shall
15:18 you let him go F from you; for at
24:5 business; he shall be F at home one year,
32:36 gone, and there is none remaining, bond or F
Judg 16:20 out as at other times, and shake myself F
1Sam 17:25 make his father's house F in Israel."
1Kgs 14:10 male, both bond and F in Israel, and will
21:21 every male, bond or F, in Israel;
2Kgs 9:8 every male, bond or F, in Israel.
14:26 none left, bond or F, and there was none
1Chr 9:33 chambers of the temple F from other service, for
Jud 16:23 She set her maid F
Job 3:19 and the slave is F from his master.
10:1 life; I will give F utterance to my complaint;
39:5 "Who has let the wild ass go F
Ps 17:1 my prayer from lips F of deceit!
44:2 them thou didst set F;
50:19 "You give your mouth F rein for evil, and
69:18 redeem me, set me F because of my enemies!
102:20 the prisoners, to set F those who were doomed
105:20 the peoples set him F;
118:5 LORD; the LORD answered me and set me F
146:7 LORD sets the prisoners F;
Eccl 10:17 is the son of F men, and your princes
Wis 1:6 spirit and will not F a blasphemer from the
6:15 account will soon be F from care,
7:23 humane, steadfast, sure, F from anxiety, all-powerful,
16:14 departed spirit, nor set F the imprisoned soul.
Sir 10:24 F men will be at the service of a
13:23 good if they are F from sin, and poverty
Is 32:20 feet of the ox and the ass range F
45:13 and set my exiles F, not for price or
58:6 let the oppressed go F, and to break every
Jer 2:31 people say, 'We are F, we will come no
34:9 every one should set F his Hebrew slaves, male
34:10 every one would set F his slave, male or
34:10 be enslaved again; they obeyed and set them F
34:11 slaves they had set F, and brought them into
34:14 of you must set F the fellow Hebrew who
34:14 you must set him F from your service.' But
34:16 whom you had set F according to their desire,
Ezek 13:20 that you hunt go F like birds.
41:9 platform which was left F was five cubits.
41:11 platform that was left F, one door toward the
41:11 part that was left F was five cubits round
Dan 13:53 letting the guilty go F, though the Lord said,
Zech 9:11 will set your captives F from the waterless pit.
1Mac 2:11 taken away; no longer F, she has become a
8:18 and alliance, and to F themselves from the yoke;
10:29 "And now I F you and exempt all the
10:31 revenues, be holy and F from tax.
10:33 my kingdom, I set F without payment; and let
11:28 asked the king to F Judea and the three
2Mac 1:27 our scattered people, set F those who are slaves
9:14 now declaring to be F;
10:21 by setting their enemies F to fight against them.
11:25 this nation also be F from disturbance, our decision
12:42 people to keep themselves F from sin, for they
Mt 17:25 Jesus said to him, "Then the sons are F
Jn 8:32 the truth, and the truth will make you F
8:33 it that you say, 'You will be made F
8:36 the Son makes you F, you will be free
8:36 free, you will be F indeed.
Acts 26:32 could have been set F if he had not
Rom 5:15 But the F gift is not like the trespass.
5:15 of God and the F gift in the grace
5:16 And the F gift is not like the effect
5:16 brought condemnation, but the F gift following many
5:17 of grace and the F gift of righteousness reign
6:18 and, having been set F from sin, have become
6:20 of sin, you were F in regard to righteousness.
6:22 you have been set F from sin and have
6:23 is death, but the F gift of God is
7:3 husband dies she is F from that law, and
8:2 Jesus has set me F from the law of
8:21 itself will be set F from its bondage to
1Cor 7:22 Likewise he who was F when called is a
7:27 Do not seek to be F
7:27 Are you F from a wife?
7:32 want you to be F from anxieties.
7:39 husband dies, she is F to be married to
9:1 Am I not F
9:18 may make the gospel F of charge, not making
9:19 For though I am F from all men, I
12:13 or Greeks, slaves or F—and all were made
2Cor 8:3 means, of their own F will,
Gal 3:28 is neither slave nor F, there is neither male
4:22 and one by a F woman.
4:23 the son of the F woman through promise.
4:26 the Jerusalem above is F, and she is our
4:30 the son of the F woman."
4:31 slave but of the F woman.
5:1 Christ has set us F; stand fast therefore, and
Eph 6:8 the Lord, whether he is a slave or F
Col 3:11 barbarian, Scythian, slave, F man, but Christ is
1Tim 6:14 commandment unstained and F from reproach until
Philem 1:14 but of your own F will.
Heb 13:5 Keep your life F from love of money, and
1Pet 2:16 Live as F men, yet without using your freedom
Rev 6:15 every one, slave and F, hid in the caves
13:16 rich and poor, both F and slave, to be
19:18 of all men, both F and slave, both small

FREED (10)

2Kgs 25:27 to reign, graciously F Jehoiachin king of Judah
Ps 81:6 burden; your hands were F from the basket.
Wis 12:2 that they may be F from wickedness and put
2Mac 2:22 throughout the world and F the city and restored
4:47 who would have been F uncondemned if they had
Lk 13:12 her, "Woman, you are F from your infirmity."
Acts 13:39 one that believes is F from everything from which
13:39 you could not be F by the law of
Rom 6:7 who has died is F from sin.
Rev 1:5 loves us and has F us from our sins

FREEDMAN

1Cor 7:22 a slave is a F of the Lord.

FREEDMEN

Acts 6:9 the synagogue of the F (as it was called),

FREEDOM (12)

Lev 19:20 ransomed or given her F, an inquiry shall be
Sir 7:21 intelligent servant; do not withhold from him his F
1Mac 14:26 and repulsed Israel's enemies and established its F
15:7 country, and I grant F to Jerusalem and the
1Cor 7:21 you can gain your F, avail yourself of the
2Cor 3:17 the Spirit of the Lord is, there is F
Gal 2:4 to spy out our F which we have in
5:1 For F Christ has set us free; stand fast

5:13 you were called to F, brethren; only do not
5:13 do not use your F as an opportunity for
1Pet 2:16 yet without using your F as a pretext for
2Pet 2:19 They promise them F, but they themselves are slaves

FREELY (18)

Gen 2:16 man, saying, "You may F eat of every tree
Deut 15:10 shall give to him F, and your heart shall
1Sam 14:30 the people had eaten F today of the spoil
1Chr 12:1 could not move about F because of Saul the
29:9 heart they had offered F to the LORD; David
29:17 my heart I have F offered all these things,
29:17 are present here, offering F and joyously to thee.
Ezra 1:6 besides all that was F offered.
7:13 in my kingdom, who F offers to go to
7:15 and his counselors have F offered to the God
Ps 110:3 people will offer themselves F on the day you
112:9 He has distributed F, he has given to the
Prov 11:24 One man gives F, yet grows all the richer;
Hos 14:4 I will love them F, for my anger has
Mk 1:45 and began to talk F about it, and to
Jn 2:10 when men have drunk F, then the poor wine;
Acts 26:26 to him I speak F; for I am persuaded
Eph 1:6 glorious grace which he F bestowed on us in

FREEWILL (26)

Ex 35:29 brought it as their F offering to the LORD.
36:3 from Moses all the F offering which the people
36:3 still kept bringing him F offerings every morning,
Lev 7:16 votive offering or a F offering, it shall be
22:18 vow or as a F offering which is offered
22:21 vow or as a F offering, from the herd
22:23 may present for a F offering; but for a
23:38 and besides all your F offerings, which you give
Num 15:3 vow or as a F offering or at your
29:39 votive offerings and your F offerings, for your burnt
Deut 12:6 votive offerings, your F offerings, and the firstlings
12:17 you vow, or your F offerings, or the offering
16:10 the tribute of a F offering from your hand,
1Chr 29:6 fathers' houses made their F offerings, as did also
2Chr 31:14 gate, was over the F offerings to God, to
Ezra 1:4 and with beasts, besides F offerings for the house
2:68 is in Jerusalem, made F offerings for the house
3:5 one who made a F offering to the LORD.
7:16 Babylonia, and with the F offerings of the people
8:28 the gold are a F offering to the LORD,
Jud 4:14 and the vows and F offerings of the people.
16:18 their burnt offerings, their F offerings, and their gifts.
Ps 54:6 With a F offering I will sacrifice to thee;
Ezek 46:12 the prince provides a F offering, either a burnt
46:12 peace offerings as a F offering to the LORD,
Amos 4:5 is leavened, and proclaim F offerings, publish them;

FREEZES (2)

Sir 43:19 salt, and when it F, it becomes pointed thorns.
43:20 wind blows, and ice F over the water; it

FRENZIED

Wis 14:23 secret mysteries, or hold F revels with strange

FREQUENT (5)

1Sam 3:1 days; there was no F vision.
Sir 41:5 abominable children, and they F the haunts of the
2Mac 8:8 pushing ahead with more F successes, he wrote to
2Cor 11:26 adrift at sea; on F journeys, in danger from
1Tim 5:23 your stomach and your F ailments.

FREQUENTLY

Dan 13:6 These men were F at Joakim's house, and all

FRESH (27)

Gen 30:37 Then Jacob took F rods of poplar and almond
Lev 2:14 crushed new grain from F ears, parched with fire.
23:14 nor grain parched or F until this same day,
Num 6:3 grapes or eat grapes, F or dried.
Judg 15:15 And he found a F jawbone of an ass,
16:7 bind me with seven F bowstrings which have not
16:8 Philistines brought her seven F bowstrings which
2Kgs 4:42 loaves of barley, and F ears of grain in
Tob 2:10 the wall and their F droppings fell into my
Job 10:17 me; thou dost bring F hosts against me.
29:20 my branches, my glory F with me, and my
33:25 let his flesh become F with youth; let him
Ps 92:10 hast poured over me F oil.
Sir 39:23 just as he turns F water into salt.
Is 29:19 The meek shall obtain F joy in the LORD,
Jer 6:7 well keeps its water F, so she keeps fresh
6:7 fresh, so she keeps F her wickedness; violence and
Ezek 17:9 so that all its F sprouting leaves wither?
47:8 waters of the sea, the water will become F
47:9 the sea may become F; so everything will live
47:11 marshes will not become F; they are to be
47:12 but they will bear F fruit every month, because
Mt 9:17 wine is put into F wineskins, and so both
Mk 2:22 new wine is for F skins."
Lk 5:38 must be put into F wineskins.
Jas 3:11 from the same opening F water and brackish?
3:12 No more can salt water yield F

FRESHETS

Job 6:15 as a torrent-bed, as F that pass away,

FRESHLY

Gen 8:11 in her mouth a F plucked olive leaf; so

FRET (5)

Ps 37:1 F not yourself because of the wicked, be not
37:7 wait patiently for him; F not yourself over him
37:8 F not yourself; it tends only to evil.
Prov 24:19 F not yourself because of evildoers, and be not
Sir 6:25 her, and do not F under her bonds.

FRETFUL

Prov 21:19 with a contentious and F woman.

FRIEND (99)

Gen 38:12 sheepshearers, he and his F Hirah the Adullamite.
38:20 the kid by his F the Adullamite, to receive
Ex 33:11 to face, as a man speaks to his F
Deut 13:6 your bosom, or your F who is as your
Ruth 4:1 Boaz said, "Turn aside, F; sit down here"; and
2Sam 13:3 But Amnon had a F, whose name was Jonadab,
15:37 So Hushai, David's F, came into the city, just
16:16 Hushai the Archite, David's F, came to Absalom,
16:17 to Hushai, "Is this your loyalty to your F
16:17 Why did you not go with your F
1Kgs 4:5 was priest and king's F;
1Chr 27:33 counselor, and Hushai the Archite was the king's F
2Chr 20:7 for ever to the descendants of Abraham thy F
Job 6:14 withholds kindness from a F forsakes the fear of
6:27 lots over the fatherless, and bargain over your F
Ps 7:4 I have requited my F with evil or plundered
15:3 no evil to his F, nor takes up a
35:14 I grieved for my F or my brother; I
41:9 Even my bosom F in whom I trusted, who
50:18 thief, you are a F of his; and you
55:13 is you, my equal, my companion, my familiar F
88:18 hast caused lover and F to shun me; my
Prov 7:4 call insight your intimate F;
17:9 but he who repeats a matter alienates a F
17:17 A F loves at all times, and a brother
18:24 but there is a F who sticks closer than
19:4 but a poor man is deserted by his F
19:6 every one is a F to a man who
22:11 is gracious, will have the king as his F
27:6 the wounds of a F; profuse are the kisses
27:10 Your F, and your father's friend, do not forsake;
27:10 friend, and your father's F, do not forsake; and
Song 5:16 and this is my F, O daughters of Jerusalem.
Wis 1:16 death; considering him a F, they pined away, and
Sir 5:15 do not become an enemy instead of a F
6:7 When you gain a F, gain him through testing,
6:8 For there is a F who is such at
6:9 And there is a F who changes into an
6:10 And there is a F who is a table
6:14 A faithful F is a sturdy shelter: he that
6:15 precious as a faithful F, and no scales can
6:16 A faithful F is an elixir of life; and
7:12 your brother, nor do the like to a F
7:18 Do not exchange a F for money, or a
9:10 Forsake not an old F, for a new one
9:10 A new F is like new wine; when it
12:8 A F will not be known in prosperity, nor
12:9 his adversity even his F will separate from him.
14:13 Do good to a F before you die, and
19:8 With F or foe do not report it, and
19:13 Question a F, perhaps he did not do it;
19:15 Question a F, for often it is slander; so
20:15 say, "I have no F, and there is no
20:22 make promises to a F, and needlessly make him
22:18 one who reviles a F will break off the
22:19 your sword against a F, do not despair, for

22:20 your mouth against your F, do not worry, for
22:20 in these cases any F will flee.
22:23 ashamed to protect a F, and I will not
27:16 confidence, and he will never find a congenial F
27:17 Love your F and keep faith with him; but
29:10 a brother or a F, and do not let
33:6 is like a mocking F; he neighs under every
33:19 wife, to brother or F, do not give power
37:1 Every F will say, "I too am a friend";
37:1 "I too am a F; but some friends are
37:2 when a companion and F turns to enmity?
37:4 the happiness of a F, but in time of
37:5 Some companions help a F for their stomach's sake,
37:6 Do not forget a F in your heart, and
40:23 A F or a companion never meets one amiss,
41:18 before your partner or F;
Is 41:8 offspring of Abraham, my F;
Jer 3:4 father, thou art the F of my youth–
6:21 sons together, neighbor and F shall perish.'"
Mic 7:5 no confidence in a F; guard the doors of
1Mac 10:16 will make him our F and ally."
10:19 a mighty warrior and worthy to be our F
10:20 nation; you are to be called the king's F
13:36 the high priest and F of kings, and to
15:32 So Athenobius the F of the king came to
2Mac 6:2 temple of Zeus the F of Strangers, as did
7:24 take him for his F and entrust him with
11:14 persuade the king, constraining him to be their F
Mt 11:19 and a drunkard, a F of tax collectors and
20:13 to one of them, F, I am doing you
22:12 he said to him, F, how did you get
26:50 Jesus said to him, F, why are you here?"
Lk 7:34 and a drunkard, a F of tax collectors and
11:5 you who has a F will go to him
11:5 and say to him, F, lend me three loaves;
11:6 three loaves; for a F of mine has arrived
11:8 because he is his F, yet because of his
14:10 may say to you, F, go up higher'; then
Jn 3:29 is the bridegroom; the F of the bridegroom, who
11:11 said to them, "Our F Lazarus has fallen asleep,
19:12 you are not Caesar's F; every one who makes
Jas 2:23 he was called the F of God.
4:4 wishes to be a F of the world makes

FRIENDLY (3)

Gen 34:21 saying, "These men are F with us; let them
1Mac 5:48 Judas sent them this F message, "Let us pass
Heb 11:31 because she had given F welcome to the spies.

FRIENDS (109)

Judg 5:31 But thy F be like the sun as he
1Sam 30:26 the spoil to his F, the elders of Judah,
2Sam 3:8 brothers, and to his F, and have not given
1Kgs 16:11 a single male of his kinsmen or his F
2Kgs 10:11 men, and his familiar F, and his priests, until
Esth 5:10 sent and fetched his F and his wife Zeresh.
5:14 Zeresh and all his F said to him, "Let
6:13 Zeresh and all his F everything that had befallen
16:5 by the persuasion of F who have been entrusted
Job 2:11 Now when Job's three F heard of all this
12:4 a laughingstock to my F; I, who called upon
16:20 My F scorn me; my eye pours out tears
17:5 who informs against his F to get a share
19:14 kinsfolk and my close F have failed me;
19:19 All my intimate F abhor me, and those whom
19:21 me, O you my F, for the hand of
24:17 them; for they are F with the terrors of
32:3 also at Job's three F because they had found
35:4 answer you and your F with you.
42:7 and against your two F; for you have not
42:10 had prayed for his F; and the LORD gave
Ps 38:11 My F and companions stand aloof from my plague,
55:20 his hand against his F, he violated his covenant.
Prov 14:20 by his neighbor, but the rich has many F
16:28 spreads strife, and a whisperer separates close F
18:24 There are F who pretend to be friends, but
18:24 who pretend to be F, but there is a
19:4 Wealth brings many new F, but a poor man
19:7 much more do his F go far from him!
Song 5:1 Eat, O F, and drink: drink deeply, O lovers!
Wis 7:27 souls and makes them F of God, and prophets;
Sir 6:5 A pleasant voice multiplies F, and a gracious tongue
6:13 your enemies, and be on guard toward your F
13:20 he is steadied by F, but when a humble
13:20 man falls, he is even pushed away by F
28:9 sinful man will disturb F and inject enmity among
30:3 will glory in him in the presence of F
30:6 and one to repay the kindness of his F
37:1 a friend"; but some F are friends only in
37:1 but some friends are F only in name.
41:22 of abusive words, before F -- and do not
42:3 dividing the inheritance of F;
Jer 13:21 have taught to be F to you?
20:4 a terror to yourself and to all your F
20:6 you and all your F, to whom you have
20:10 say all my familiar F, watching for my fall.
38:22 were saying, 'Your trusted F have deceived you and
Lam 1:2 comfort her; all her F have dealt treacherously with
Dan 13:33 But her family and F and all who saw
14:2 king, and was the most honored of his F
Obad 1:7 against you; your trusted F have set a trap
Zech 3:8 priest, you and your F who sit before you,
13:6 wounds I received in the house of my F
1Mac 2:18 be numbered among the F of the king, and
2:39 When Mattathias and his F learned of it, they
2:45 And Mattathias and his F went about and tore
3:38 mighty men among the F of the king,
6:10 he called all his F and said to them,
6:14 Philip, one of his F, and made him ruler
6:28 He assembled all his F, the commanders of his
7:6 have destroyed all your F, and have driven us
7:8 one of the king's F, governor of the province
7:15 will not seek to injure you or your F
8:12 enslaved; but with their F and those who rely
8:20 we may be enrolled as your allies and F
8:31 yoke heavy upon our F and allies the Jews?
9:26 and searched for the F of Judas, and brought
9:28 Then all the F of Judas assembled and said
9:35 Nabateans, who were his F, for permission to store
9:39 came out with his F and his brothers to
10:60 gave them and their F silver and gold and
10:65 him among his chief F, and made him general
11:26 exalted him in the presence of all his F
11:27 to be regarded as one of his chief F
11:33 Jews, who are our F and fulfil their obligations
11:57 you one of the F of the king."
12:14 our other allies and F with these wars,
12:43 him to all his F, and he gave him
12:43 gifts and commanded his F and his troops to
14:39 one of the king's F and paid him high
14:40 by the Romans as F and allies and brethren,
15:17 to us as our F and allies to renew
15:28 Athenobius, one of his F, to confer with him,
2Mac 1:14 place together with his F, to secure most of
3:31 Quickly some of Heliodorus' F asked Onias to call
8:9 of the king's chief F, and sent him, in
10:13 he was accused before Eupator by the king's F
14:11 rest of the king's F, who were hostile to
Mt 5:25 Make F quickly with your accuser, while you are
Mk 5:19 "Go home to your F, and tell them how
Lk 7:6 house, the centurion sent F to him, saying to
12:4 "I tell you, my F, do not fear those
14:12 do not invite your F or your brothers or
15:6 he calls together his F and his neighbors, saying
15:9 calls together her F and neighbors, saying, 'Rejoice
15:29 kid, that I might make merry with my F
16:9 I tell you, make F for yourselves by means
21:16 brothers and kinsmen and F, and some of you
23:12 Herod and Pilate became F with each other that
Jn 15:13 a man lay down his life for his F
15:14 You are my F if you do what I
15:15 I have called you F, for all that I
Acts 4:23 they went to their F and reported what the
10:24 and had called together his kinsmen and close F
19:31 Asi-archs also, who were F of his, sent to
24:22 that none of his F should be prevented from
27:3 to go to his F and be cared for.
3Jn 1:15 The F greet you.
1:15 Greet the F, every one of them.

FRIENDSHIP (33)

1Chr 12:17 come to me in F to help me, my
Job 29:4 autumn days, when the F of God was upon
Ps 25:14 The F of the LORD is for those who
Prov 22:24 Make no F with a man given to anger,
Wis 7:14 who get it obtain F with God, commended for
8:18 is immortality, and in F with her, pure delight,
Sir 6:17 the Lord directs his F aright, for as he
22:18 who reviles a friend will break off the F
22:19 for a renewal of F is possible.
25:1 agreement between brothers, F between neighbors,
27:18 you have destroyed the F of your neighbor.

1Mac 8:1 them, that they pledged F to those who came
8:12 those who rely on them they have kept F
8:17 to Rome to establish F and alliance,
10:20 our side and keep F with us."
10:23 us in forming a F with the Jews to
10:26 and have continued your F with us, and have
10:54 therefore let us establish F with one another; give
12:1 confirm and renew the F with them.
12:3 to renew the former F and alliance with them."
12:8 contained a clear declaration of alliance and F
12:10 renew our brotherhood and F with you, so that
12:16 to renew our former F and alliance with them.
14:18 renew with him the F and alliance which they
14:22 us to renew their F with us.
15:17 to renew our ancient F and alliance.
2Mac 4:11 the mission to establish F and alliance with the
6:22 account of his old F with them.
11:26 give them pledges of F, so that they may
11:30 have our pledge of F and full permission
12:11 grant them pledges of F, promising to give him
14:19 and Mattathias to give and receive pledges of F
Jas 4:4 you not know that F with the world is

FRIGHT

Wis 11:19 the mere sight of them could kill by F

FRIGHTEN (7)

Deut 28:26 be no one to F them away.
2Chr 32:18 upon the wall, to F and terrify them, in
Neh 6:9 they all wanted to F us, thinking, "Their hands
Job 13:25 Wilt thou F a driven leaf and pursue dry
18:11 Terrors F him on every side, and chase him
Sir 30:9 child, and he will F you; play with him,
Jer 7:33 earth; and none will F them away.

FRIGHTENED (12)

Josh 1:9 good courage; be not F, neither be dismayed; for
Job 40:23 turbulent he is not F; he is confident though
Wis 17:9 even if nothing disturbing F them, yet, scared by
Sir 26:5 a fourth I am F: The slander of a
Dan 8:17 he came, I was F and fell upon my
1Mac 4:21 this they were greatly F, and when they also
9:6 forces, they were greatly F, and many slipped away
2Mac 8:16 them not to be F by the enemy and
Lk 24:5 and as they were F and bowed their faces
24:37 they were startled and F, and supposed that they
Jn 6:19 They were F,
Phil 1:28 the gospel, and not F in anything by your

FRIGHTENING (3)

Dan 2:31 stood before you, and its appearance was F
2Mac 3:25 with a rider of F mien, and it rushed
2Cor 10:9 not seem to be F you with letters.

FRINGE (4)

Mt 9:20 him and touched the F of his garment;
14:36 might only touch the F of his garment; and
Mk 6:56 might touch even the F of his garment; and
Lk 8:44 him, and touched the F of his garment; and

FRINGES

Mt 23:5 phylacteries broad and their F long,

FRO (18)

Gen 8:7 it went to and F until the waters were
Ex 32:27 and go to and F from gate to gate
2Kgs 4:35 walked once to and F in the house, and
2Chr 16:9 LORD run to and F throughout the whole earth,
Job 1:7 "From going to and F on the earth, and
2:2 "From going to and F on the earth, and
28:4 hang afar from men, they swing to and F
Jer 4:24 quaking, and all the hills moved to and F
5:1 Run to and F through the streets of Jerusalem,
49:3 and run to and F among the hedges!
Ezek 1:13 torches moving to and F among the living creatures;
1:14 creatures darted to and F, like a flash of
Dan 12:4 shall run to and F, and knowledge shall increase."
Amos 8:12 shall run to and F, to seek the word
Nah 2:4 they rush to and F through the squares; they
Zech 7:14 one went to and F, and the pleasant land
9:8 shall march to and F; no oppressor shall again
Eph 4:14 children, tossed to and F and carried about with

FROGS (15)

Ex 8:2 all your country with F;
8:3 Nile shall swarm with F which shall come up
8:4 your kneading bowls; the F shall come up on
8:5 the pools, and cause F to come upon the
8:6 of Egypt; and the F came up and covered
8:7 secret arts, and brought F upon the land of
8:8 to take away the F from me and from
8:9 your people, that the F be destroyed from you
8:11 The F shall depart from you and your houses
8:12 the LORD concerning the F, as he had agreed
8:13 word of Moses; the F died out of the
Ps 78:45 which devoured them, and F, which destroyed them.
105:30 Their land swarmed with F, even in the chambers
Wis 19:10 fish the river spewed out vast numbers of F
Rev 16:13 three foul spirits like F;

FRONDS

2Mac 10:7 beautiful branches and also F of palm, they offered

FRONT (76)

Gen 18:2 three men stood in F of him.
30:38 he had peeled in F of the flocks in
30:39 the flocks bred in F of the rods and
33:2 with their children in F, then Leah with her
Ex 14:2 and encamp in F of Pi-ha-hiroth, between Migdol
14:2 and the sea, in F of Baal-zephon; you shall
14:9 sea, by Pi-ha-hiroth, in F of Baal-zephon.
25:37 upon the space in F of it.
26:9 double over at the F of the tent.
27:13 the court on the F to the east shall
28:25 so attach it in F to the shoulder-pieces of
28:27 and attach them in F to the lower part
28:37 shall be on the F of the turban.
38:13 And for the F to the east, fifty cubits.
39:18 they attached it in F to the shoulder-pieces of
39:20 and attached them in F to the lower part
Lev 4:6 before the LORD in F of the veil of
4:17 before the LORD in F of the veil.
6:14 before the LORD, in F of the altar.
8:9 on the turban, in F, he set the golden
13:55 spot is on the back or on the F
16:14 his finger on the F of the mercy seat,
Num 8:2 shall give light in F of the lampstand."
8:3 to give light in F of the lampstand, as
16:43 Aaron came to the F of the tent of
19:4 her blood toward the F of the tent of
Josh 8:33 half of them in F of Mount Gerizim and
8:33 half of them in F of Mount Ebal, as
Judg 18:21 and the goods in F of them.
1Sam 14:5 on the north in F of Michmash, and the
14:5 on the south in F of Geba.
17:41 with his shield-bearer in F of him.
24:2 and his men in F of the Wildgoats' Rocks.
2Sam 10:9 against him both in F and in the rear,
1Kgs 6:3 The vestibule in F of the nave of the
6:3 ten cubits deep in F of the house.
6:17 is, the nave in F of the inner sanctuary,
6:21 of gold across, in F of the inner sanctuary,
7:6 was a porch in F with pillars, and a
7:9 with saws, back and F, even from the foundation
2Kgs 16:14 he removed from the F of the house, from
1Chr 19:10 against him both in F and in the rear,
2Chr 3:4 The vestibule in F of the nave of the
3:15 In F of the house he made two pillars
3:17 up the pillars in F of the temple, one
13:13 his troops were in F of Judah, and the
15:8 LORD that was in F of the vestibule of
Jud 10:22 came forward to the F of the tent, with
Esth 2:11 day Mordecai walked in F of the court of
4:6 of the city in F of the king's gate,
Ps 68:25 the singers in F, the minstrels last, between
Prov 8:3 beside the gates in F of the town, at
Sir 26:12 will she sit in F of every post and
Ezek 1:10 of a man in F; the four had the
2:10 had writing on the F and on the back,
10:11 in whatever direction the F wheel faced the others
40:15 From the F of the gate at the entrance
40:19 distance from the inner F of the lower gate
40:19 gate to the outer F of the inner court,
40:47 the altar was in F of the temple.
41:14 breadth of the east F of the temple and
41:21 were squared; and in F of the holy place
41:25 canopy of wood in F of the vestibule outside.
42:11 with a passage in F of them; they were
44:4 north gate to the F of the temple; and
Dan 5:1 and drank wine in F of the thousand.
Joel 2:20 and desolate land, his F into the eastern sea,
1Mac 1:22 gold decoration on the F of the temple; he

4:57 They decorated the F of the temple with golden
9:45 the battle is in F of us and behind
13:27 polished stone at the F and back.
2Mac 3:25 at him with its F hoofs.
Lk 18:39 those who were in F rebuked him, telling him
Acts 14:13 whose temple was in F of the city, brought
18:17 and beat him in F of the tribunal.
Rev 4:6 full of eyes in F and behind:

FRONTED
Ezek 40:17 the court; thirty chambers F on the pavement.

FRONTIER (4)
Deut 2:19 when you approach the F of the sons of
Josh 22:11 an altar at the F of the land of
2Kgs 3:21 called out, and were drawn up at the F
Ezek 25:9 the cities on its F, the glory of the

FRONTIERS
Jud 15:4 and to all the F of Israel, to tell

FRONTING (2)
Jud 2:25 southern borders of Japheth, F toward Arabia.
3:9 of Esdraelon, near Dothan, F the great ridge of

FRONTLETS (3)
Ex 13:16 on your hand or F between your eyes; for
Deut 6:8 they shall be as F between your eyes.
11:18 they shall be as F between your eyes.

FROST (7)
Ps 78:47 their vines with hail, and their sycamores with F
148:8 and hail, snow and F, stormy wind fulfilling his
Wis 16:29 will melt like wintry F, and flow away like
Sir 3:15 in your favor; as F in fair weather, your
Jer 36:30 by day and the F by night.
Bar 2:25 of day and the F of night.
Zech 14:6 that day there shall be neither cold nor F

FROSTS
Dan 3:73 Bless the Lord, F and snows, sing praise to

FROZEN (3)
Esth 15:5 but her heart was F with fear.
Job 37:10 the broad waters are F fast.
38:30 stone, and the face of the deep is F

FRUIT (217)
Gen 1:11 plants yielding seed, and F trees bearing fruit in
1:11 and fruit trees bearing F in which is their
1:12 kinds, and trees bearing F in which is their
1:29 with seed in its F; you shall have them
3:2 may eat of the F of the trees of
3:3 not eat of the F of the tree which
3:6 she took of its F and ate; and she
3:12 me, she gave me F of the tree, and
4:3 an offering of the F of the ground,
30:2 withheld from you the F of the womb?"
Ex 10:15 land and all the F of the trees which
23:16 from the field the F of your labor.
Lev 19:23 you shall count their F as forbidden; three years
19:24 fourth year all their F shall be holy, an
19:25 may eat of their F, that they may yield
23:40 the first day the F of goodly trees, branches
25:19 land will yield its F, and you will eat
25:21 it will bring forth F for three years.
26:4 the trees of the field shall yield their F
26:20 trees of the land shall not yield their F
27:30 land or of the F of the trees, is
Num 13:20 bring some of the F of the land." Now
13:26 and showed them the F of the land.
13:27 with milk and honey, and this is its F
Deut 1:25 hands some of the F of the land and
7:13 will also bless the F of your body and
7:13 your body and the F of your ground, your
11:17 the land yield no F, and you perish quickly
20:6 planted a vineyard and has not enjoyed its F
20:6 in the battle and another man enjoy its F
26:2 first of all the F of the ground, which
26:10 the first of the F of the ground, which
28:4 Blessed shall be the F of your body, and
28:4 your body, and the F of your ground, and
28:4 your ground, and the F of your beasts, the
28:11 in prosperity, in the F of your body, and
28:11 body, and in the F of your cattle, and
28:11 cattle, and in the F of your ground, within
28:18 Cursed shall be the F of your body, and
28:18 your body, and the F of your ground, the
28:30 shall not use the F of it.
28:33 shall eat up the F of your ground and
28:42 your trees and the F of your ground the
28:51 your cattle and the F of your ground, until
29:18 bearing poisonous and bitter F,
30:9 your hand, in the F of your body, and
30:9 body, and in the F of your cattle, and
30:9 cattle, and in the F of your ground; for
Josh 5:12 but ate of the F of the land of
24:13 therein; you eat the F of vineyards and oliveyards
Judg 9:11 sweetness and my good F, and go to sway
2Sam 16:2 the bread and summer F for the young men
2Kgs 19:29 and reap, and plant vineyards, and eat their F
19:30 root downward, and bear F upward;
Neh 9:25 vineyards, olive orchards and F trees in abundance;
9:36 fathers to enjoy its F and its good gifts,
10:35 first fruits of all F of every tree, year
10:37 and our contributions, the F of every tree, the
Jud 10:5 a cake of dried F and fine bread; and
Job 20:18 will give back the F of his toil, and
Ps 1:3 water, that yields its F in its season, and
72:16 it wave; may its F be like Lebanon; and
78:46 the caterpillar, and the F of their labor to
80:12 all who pass along the way pluck its F
92:14 They still bring forth F in old age, they
104:13 is satisfied with the F of thy work.
105:35 and ate up the F of their ground.
105:44 took possession of the F of the peoples' toil,
127:3 from the LORD, the F of the womb a
128:2 You shall eat the F of the labor of
148:9 Mountains and all hills, F trees and all cedars!
Prov 1:31 they shall eat the F of their way and
8:19 My F is better than gold, even fine gold,
11:30 The F of the righteous is a tree of
12:14 From the F of his words a man is
13:2 From the F of his mouth a good man
14:14 be filled with the F of his ways, and
14:14 good man with the F of his deeds.
18:20 From the F of his mouth a man is
27:18 tree will eat its F, and he who guards
31:16 buys it; with the F of her hands she
31:31 Give her of the F of her hands, and
Eccl 2:5 them all kinds of F trees.
Song 2:3 his shadow, and his F was sweet to my
8:11 to bring for its F a thousand pieces of
8:12 the keepers of the F two hundred.
Wis 3:13 union; she will have F when God examines souls.
3:15 For the F of good labors is renowned, and
4:5 to maturity, and their F will be useless, not
10:7 smoking wasteland, plants bearing F that does not
10:10 labors, and increased the F of his toil.
Sir 6:3 leaves and destroy your F, and will be left
14:15 you not leave the F of your labors to
23:25 take root, and her branches will not bear F
24:17 and my blossoms became glorious and abundant F
27:6 The F discloses the cultivation of a tree; so
28:15 deprived them of the F of their toil.
30:19 use to an idol is an offering of F
50:10 tree putting forth its F, and like a cypress
Is 3:10 they shall eat the F of their deeds.
4:2 and glorious, and the F of the land shall
13:18 no mercy on the F of the womb; their
14:29 an adder, and its F will be a flying
16:9 Ele-aleh; for upon your F and your harvest the
17:6 the branches of a F tree, says the LORD
27:6 forth shoots, and fill the whole world with F
27:9 will be the full F of the removal of
32:10 vintage will fail, the F harvest will not come.
37:30 and reap, and plant vineyards, and eat their F
37:31 root downward, and bear F upward;
53:11 he shall see the F of the travail of
57:18 for his mourners the F of the lips.
65:21 them; they shall plant vineyards and eat their F
Jer 6:19 upon this people, the F of their devices, because
7:20 the field and the F of the ground; it
11:16 tree, fair with goodly F; but with the roar
11:19 the tree with its F, let us cut him
12:2 grow and bring forth F; thou art near in
17:8 drought, for it does not cease to bear F
17:10 ways, according to the F of his doings."
21:14 you according to the F of your doings, says
31:5 the planters shall plant, and shall enjoy the F
32:19 and according to the F of his doings;
Ezek 17:8 forth branches, and bear F, and become a noble

F

17:23 forth boughs and bear F, and become a noble
19:12 dried it up; its F was stripped off, its
19:14 consumed its branches and F, so that there remains
23:29 take away all the F of your labor, and
25:4 they shall eat your F, and they shall drink
34:27 field shall yield their F, and the earth shall
36:8 branches, and yield your F to my people Israel;
36:30 I will make the F of the tree and
47:12 not wither nor their F fail, but they will
47:12 they will bear fresh F every month, because the
47:12 Their F will be for food, and their leaves
Dan 4:12 were fair and its F abundant, and in it
4:14 leaves and scatter its F; let the beasts flee
4:21 were fair and its F abundant, and in which
Hos 9:10 Like the first F on the fig tree, in
9:16 root is dried up, they shall bear no F
10:1 Israel is a luxuriant vine that yields its F
10:1 The more his F increased the more altars he
10:12 righteousness, reap the F of steadfast love; break
10:13 you have eaten the F of lies.
14:2 we will render the F of our lips.
14:8 like an evergreen cypress, from me comes your F
Joel 2:22 the tree bears its F, the fig tree and
Amos 2:9 oaks; I destroyed his F above, and his roots
6:12 poison and the F of righteousness into wormwood--
8:1 GOD showed me: behold, a basket of summer F
8:2 And I said, "A basket of summer F
9:14 and they shall make gardens and eat their F
Mic 6:7 for my transgression, the F of my body for
7:1 as when the summer F has been gathered, as
7:13 its inhabitants, for the F of their doings.
Hab 3:17 do not blossom, nor F be on the vines,
Zech 8:12 vine shall yield its F, and the ground shall
1Mac 10:30 the half of the F of the trees that
11:34 the land and the F of the trees.
14:8 increase, and the trees of the plains their F
Mt 3:8 Bear F that befits repentance,
3:10 does not bear good F is cut down and
7:17 sound tree bears good F, but the bad tree
7:17 good fruit, but the bad tree bears evil F
7:18 tree cannot bear evil F, nor can a bad
7:18 fruit, nor can a bad tree bear good F
7:19 does not bear good F is cut down and
12:33 tree good, and its F good; or make the
12:33 tree bad, and its F bad; for the tree
12:33 bad; for the tree is known by its F
13:23 it; he indeed bears F, and yields, in one
21:19 to it, "May no F ever come from you
21:34 When the season of F drew near, he sent
21:34 tenants, to get his F;
26:29 drink again of this F of the vine until
Mk 4:20 accept it and bear F, thirtyfold and sixtyfold and
11:14 no one ever eat F from you again." And
12:2 them some of the F of the vineyard.
14:25 drink again of the F of the vine until
Lk 1:42 and blessed is the F of your womb!
3:9 does not bear good F is cut down and
6:43 good tree bears bad F, nor again does a
6:43 bad tree bear good F;
6:44 for each tree is known by its own F
8:14 of life, and their F does not mature.
8:15 heart, and bring forth F with patience.
13:6 and he came seeking F on it and found
13:7 I have come seeking F on this fig tree,
13:9 And if it bears F next year, well and
20:10 him some of the F of the vineyard; but
22:18 not drink of the F of the vine until
Jn 4:36 receives wages, and gathers F for eternal life, so
12:24 alone; but if it dies, it bears much F
15:2 mine that bears no F, he takes away, and
15:2 branch that does bear F he prunes, that it
15:2 fruit he prunes, that it may bear more F
15:4 the branch cannot bear F by itself, unless it
15:5 is that bears much F, for apart from me
15:8 that you bear much F, and so prove to
15:16 should go and bear F and that your fruit
15:16 fruit and that your F should abide; so that
Rom 7:4 that we may bear F for God.
7:5 our members to bear F for death.
1Cor 9:7 plants a vineyard without eating any of its F
Gal 5:22 But the F of the Spirit is love, joy,
Eph 5:9 of light (for the F of light is found
Phil 4:17 but I seek the F which increases to your
Col 1:6 world it is bearing F and growing--so among
1:10 pleasing to him, bearing F in every good work
Heb 12:11 it yields the peaceful F of righteousness to those
13:15 God, that is, the F of lips that acknowledge
Jas 5:7 waits for the precious F of the earth, being
5:18 gave rain, and the earth brought forth its F
Rev 6:13 tree sheds its winter F when shaken by a
18:14 "The F for which thy soul longed has gone
22:2 its twelve kinds of F, yielding its fruit each
22:2 of fruit, yielding its F each month; and the

FRUITFUL (36)

Gen 1:22 blessed them, saying, "Be F and multiply and fill
1:28 said to them, "Be F and multiply, and fill
8:17 the earth, and be F and multiply upon the
9:1 said to them, "Be F and multiply, and fill
9:7 And you, be F and multiply, bring forth abundantly
17:6 will make you exceedingly F; and I will make
17:20 him and make him F and multiply him exceedingly;
26:22 and we shall be F in the land."
28:3 you and make you F and multiply you, that
35:11 am God Almighty: be F and multiply; a nation
41:52 God has made me F in the land of
47:27 in it, and were F and multiplied exceedingly.
48:4 I will make you F, and multiply you, and
49:22 Joseph is a F bough, a fruitful bough by
49:22 a fruitful bough, a F bough by a spring;
Ex 1:6 descendants of Israel were F and increased greatly;
Lev 26:9 you and make you F and multiply you, and
Ps 105:24 made his people very F, and made them stronger
107:34 into thirsty ground, a F land into a salty
107:37 vineyards, and get a F yield.
128:3 will be like a F vine within your house;
Is 10:18 forest and of his F land the LORD will
16:10 taken away from the F field; and in the
29:17 be turned into a F field, and the fruitful
29:17 fruitful field, and the F field shall be regarded
32:12 pleasant fields, for the F vine,
32:15 the wilderness becomes a F field, and the fruitful
32:15 fruitful field, and the F field is deemed a
32:16 righteousness abide in the F field.
Jer 4:26 looked, and lo, the F land was a desert,
23:3 and they shall be F and multiply.
48:33 taken away from the F land of Moab; I
Ezek 19:10 transplanted by the water, F and full of branches
36:11 shall increase and be F; and I will cause
Acts 14:17 heaven rains and F seasons, satisfying your hearts
Phil 1:22 the flesh, that means F labor for me.

FRUITLESS (2)

Wis 15:4 misled us, nor the F toil of painters, a
Jude 1:12 carried along by winds; F trees in late autumn,

FRUITS (65)

Gen 43:11 some of the choice F of the land in
49:3 might, and the first F of my strength, pre-eminent
Ex 23:16 harvest, of the first F of your labor, of
23:19 first of the first F of your ground you
34:22 of weeks, the first F of wheat harvest, and
34:26 first of the first F of your ground you
Lev 2:12 an offering of first F you may bring them
2:14 cereal offering of first F to the LORD, you
2:14 offering of your first F crushed new grain from
23:10 sheaf of the first F of your harvest to
23:17 with leaven, as first F to the LORD.
23:20 bread of the first F as a wave offering
25:3 and gather in its F;
Num 18:12 the grain, the first F of what they give
18:13 The first-ripe F of all that is in their
28:26 day of the first F, when you offer a
Deut 18:4 The first F of your grain, of your wine
33:14 beneath, with the choicest F of the sun, and
2Sam 16:1 a hundred of summer F, and a skin of
2Kgs 4:42 bread of the first F, twenty loaves of barley,
2Chr 31:5 in abundance the first F of grain, wine, oil,
Neh 10:35 to bring the first F of our ground and
10:35 ground and the first F of all fruit of
12:44 the contributions, the first F, and the tithes, to
13:31 offering, at appointed times, and for the first F
Tob 1:6 Taking the first F and the tithes of my
Jud 11:13 to consume the first F of the grain and
Ps 109:11 may strangers plunder the F of his toil!
Prov 3:9 and with the first F of all your produce;
18:21 and those who love it will eat its F
Song 4:13 pomegranates with all choicest F, henna with nard,
4:16 come to his garden, and eat its choicest F
7:13 doors are all choice F, new as well as
Sir 1:14 satisfies men with her F;
7:31 commanded you: the first F, the guilt offering, the

	7:31	sanctification, and the first F of the holy things.
	24:23	the Tigris at the time of the first F
	35:8	not stint the first F of your hands.
	37:22	own advantage, and the F of his understanding may
	37:23	own people, and the F of his understanding will
	45:20	first of the first F, he prepared bread of
	45:20	prepared bread of first F in abundance;
	50:8	days of the first F, like lilies by a
Jer	2:3	the LORD, the first F of his harvest.
	2:7	land to enjoy its F and its good things.
	40:10	gather wine and summer F and oil, and store
	40:12	gathered wine and summer F in great abundance.
	48:32	Jazer, upon your summer F and your vintage the
Lam	4:9	by want of the F of the field.
Ezek	44:30	of all the first F of all kinds, and
Mal	3:11	will not destroy the F of your soil; and
1Mac	3:49	priesthood and the first F and the tithes, and
Mt	7:16	You will know them by their F
	7:20	Thus you will know them by their F
	21:41	will give him the F in their seasons."
	21:43	a nation producing the F of it.
Lk	3:8	Bear F that befit repentance, and do not begin
Rom	8:23	who have the first F of the Spirit, groan
	11:16	dough offered as first F is holy, so is
1Cor	15:20	the dead, the first F of those who have
	15:23	order: Christ the first F, then at his coming
Phil	1:11	Christ, filled with the F of righteousness which come
Jas	1:17	a kind of first F of his creatures.
	3:17	of mercy and good F, without uncertainty or
Rev	14:4	from mankind as first F for God and the

FRUSTRATE

Ezra	4:5	counselors against them to F their purpose, all the

FRUSTRATED (3)

Neh	4:15	and that God had F their plan, we all
Jud	11:11	defeated and his purpose F, death will fall upon
Sir	16:13	the patience of the godly will not be F

FRUSTRATES (3)

Job	5:12	He F the devices of the crafty, so that
Ps	33:10	nations to nought; he F the plans of the
Is	44:25	-- who F the omens of liars, and

FRUSTRATION

Deut	28:20	you curses, confusion, and F, in all that you

FRY

2Mac	7:5	still breathing, and to F him in a pan.

FUEL (8)

Sir	28:10	In proportion to the F for the fire, so
Is	9:5	will be burned as F for the fire.
	9:19	the people are like F for the fire; no
	40:16	would not suffice for F, nor are its beasts
	44:15	Then it becomes F for a man; he takes
Ezek	15:4	to the fire for F; when the fire has
	15:6	to the fire for F, so will I give
	21:32	You shall be F for the fire; your blood

FUGITIVE (9)

Gen	4:12	you shall be a F and a wanderer on
	4:14	I shall be a F and a wanderer on
Prov	28:17	let him be a F until death; let no
Is	16:3	outcasts, betray not the F;
	21:14	bring water, meet the F with bread, O inhabitants
Ezek	24:26	on that day a F will come to you
	24:27	be opened to the F, and you shall speak
	33:22	the evening before the F came; and he had
2Mac	4:26	was driven as a F into the land of

FUGITIVES (12)

Num	21:29	has made his sons F, and his daughters captives,
Judg	12:4	they said, "You are F of Ephraim, you Gileadites,
	12:5	when any of the F of Ephraim said, "Let
Jud	16:12	like the children of F, they perished before the
Wis	19:3	decision, and pursued as F those whom they had
Is	15:5	out for Moab; his F flee to Zoar, to
Jer	44:14	there; for they shall not return, except some F
	48:45	the shadow of Heshbon F stop without strength; for
	49:5	straight before him, with none to gather the F
Lam	4:15	So they became F and wanderers; men said among
Obad	1:14	to cut off his F; you should not have
1Mac	2:43	And all who became F to escape their troubles

FULFIL (39)

Gen	26:3	lands, and I will F the oath which I
Ex	23:26	your land; I will F the number of your
Lev	22:21	to the LORD, to F a vow or as
Num	15:3	or a sacrifice, to F a vow or as
	15:8	for a sacrifice, to F a vow, or for
	23:19	and will he not F it?
1Sam	3:12	that day I will F against Eli all that
1Kgs	12:15	LORD that he might F his word, which the
2Chr	10:15	that the LORD might F his word, which he
	36:21	kingdom of Persia, to F the word of the
	36:21	it kept sabbath, to F seventy years.
Esth	5:8	grant my petition and F my request, let the
Job	39:2	the months that they F, and do you know
Ps	20:4	your heart's desire, and F all your plans!
	20:5	May the LORD F all your petitions!
	138:8	The LORD will F his purpose for me; thy
Sir	36:15	in the beginning, and F the prophecies spoken in
Is	44:28	shepherd, and he shall F all my purpose'; saying
Jer	29:10	you, and I will F to you my promise
	33:14	LORD, when I will F the promise I made
	39:16	Israel: Behold, I will F my words against this
Ezek	13:6	they expect him to F their word.
Dan	11:14	up in order to F the vision; but they
Nah	1:15	your feasts, O Judah, F your vows, for never
1Mac	11:33	are our friends and F their obligations to us,
Mt	1:22	this took place to F what the Lord had
	2:15	This was to F what the Lord had spoken
	3:15	fitting for us to F all righteousness." Then he
	5:17	abolish them but to F them.
	8:17	This was to F what was spoken by the
	12:17	This was to F what was spoken by the
	13:35	This was to F what was spoken by the
	21:4	This took place to F what was spoken by
Lk	21:22	days of vengeance, to F all that is written.
Gal	6:2	another's burdens, and so F the law of Christ.
Col	4:17	Archippus, "See that you F the ministry which you
2Thes	1:11	his call, and may F every good resolve and
2Tim	4:5	work of an evangelist, F your ministry.
Jas	2:8	If you really F the royal law, according to

FULFILL (6)

Jud	10:8	grant you favor and F your plans, that the
Jn	15:25	It is to F the word that is written
	18:9	This was to F the word which he had
	18:32	This was to F the word which Jesus had
	19:24	This was to F the scripture, "They parted my
	19:28	now finished, said (to F the scripture), "I thirst."

FULFILLED (59)

Gen	25:24	to be delivered were F, behold, there were twins
Josh	23:15	concerning you have been F for you, so the
2Sam	7:12	When your days are F and you lie down
1Kgs	8:15	with his hand has F what he promised with
	8:20	Now the LORD has F his promise which he
	8:24	with thy hand hast F it this day.
1Chr	17:11	When your days are F to go to be
2Chr	1:9	my father be now F, for thou hast made
	6:4	with his hand has F what he promised with
	6:10	Now the LORD has F his promise which he
	6:15	with thy hand hast F it this day.
Neh	9:8	Girgashite; and thou hast F thy promise, for thou
Esth	5:6	the half of my kingdom, it shall be F
	7:2	the half of my kingdom, it shall be F
	9:12	It shall be F
	10:5	and none of them has failed to be F
Prov	13:12	sick, but a desire F is a tree of
	13:19	A desire F is sweet to the soul; but
Wis	4:13	a short time, he F long years;
Sir	32:2	seated; when you have F your duties, take your
	34:8	the law will be F, and wisdom is made
Jer	44:25	your mouths, and have F it with your hands,
Ezek	21:7	Behold, it comes and it will be F
Dan	4:33	Immediately the word was F upon Nebuchadnezzar.
1Mac	2:55	Joshua, because he F the command, became a judge
Mt	2:17	Then was F what was spoken by the prophet
	2:23	the prophets might be F, "He shall be called
	4:14	prophet Isaiah might be F:
	13:14	With them indeed is F the prophecy of Isaiah
	26:54	should the scriptures be F, that it must be
	26:56	that the scriptures of the prophets might be F
	27:9	Then was F what had been spoken by the
Mk	1:15	saying, "The time is F, and the kingdom of
	14:49	But let the scriptures be F
Lk	1:20	words, which will be F in their time."
	4:21	this scripture has been F in your hearing."

F

21:24 Gentiles, until the times of the Gentiles are F
22:16 it until it is F in the kingdom of
22:37 this scripture must be F in me, 'And he
24:44 and the prophets and the psalms must be F
Jn 12:38 prophet Isaiah might be F: "Lord, who has believed
13:18 the scripture may be F, 'He who ate my
17:12 son of perdition, that the scripture might be F
17:13 may have my joy F in themselves.
19:36 the scripture might be F, "Not a bone of
Acts 1:16 scripture had to be F, which the Holy Spirit
3:18 prophets, that his Christ should suffer, he thus F
12:25 Jerusalem when they had F their mission, bringing
13:27 are read every sabbath, F these by condemning him.
13:29 And when they had F all that was written
13:33 fathers, this he has F to us their children
14:26 of God for the work which they had F
21:26 of purification would be F and the offering presented
Rom 8:4 the law might be F in us, who walk
13:8 loves his neighbor has F the law.
Gal 5:14 the whole law is F in one word, "You
Jas 2:23 the scripture was F which says, "Abraham believed
Rev 10:7 announced to his servants the prophets, should be F
17:17 beast, until the words of God shall be F

FULFILLING (4)

1Kgs 2:27 to the LORD, thus F the word of the
Ps 148:8 and frost, stormy wind F his command!
Rom 9:31 did not succeed in F that law.
13:10 therefore love is the F of the law.

FULFILMENT (7)

Tob 8:17 bring their lives to F in health and happiness
Ps 119:123 salvation, and for the F of thy righteous promise.
Sir 19:18 wisdom there is the F of the law.
21:11 and wisdom is the F of the fear of
Ezek 12:23 at hand, and the F of every vision.
Lk 1:45 there would be a F of what was spoken
22:37 for what is written about me has its F

FULFILS (2)

Ps 57:2 High, to God who F his purpose for me.
145:19 He F the desire of all who fear him,

FULL (301)

Gen 14:10 Valley of Siddim was F of bitumen pits; and
23:9 For the F price let him give it to
25:8 an old man and F of years, and was
35:29 his people, old and F of days; and his
41:7 the seven plump and F ears.
41:22 growing on one stalk, F and good;
43:21 sack, our money in F weight; so we have
Ex 16:3 ate bread to the F; for you have brought
16:8 morning bread to the F, because the LORD has
22:6 the fire shall make F restitution.
22:14 it, he shall make F restitution.
Lev 6:5 shall restore it in F, and shall add a
16:12 shall take a censer F of coals of fire
19:29 and the land become F of wickedness.
23:15 the wave offering; seven F weeks shall they be,
25:29 its sale; for a F year he shall have
25:30 not redeemed within a F year, then the house
26:5 your bread to the F, and dwell in your
27:17 shall stand at your F valuation;
Num 5:7 and he shall make F restitution for his wrong,
7:13 sanctuary, both of them F of fine flour mixed
7:14 dish of ten shekels, F of incense;
7:19 sanctuary, both of them F of fine flour mixed
7:20 dish of ten shekels, F of incense;
7:25 sanctuary, both of them F of fine flour mixed
7:26 dish of ten shekels, F of incense;
7:31 sanctuary, both of them F of fine flour mixed
7:32 dish of ten shekels, F of incense;
7:37 sanctuary, both of them F of fine flour mixed
7:38 dish of ten shekels, F of incense;
7:43 sanctuary, both of them F of fine flour mixed
7:44 dish of ten shekels, F of incense;
7:49 sanctuary, both of them F of fine flour mixed
7:50 dish of ten shekels, F of incense;
7:55 sanctuary, both of them F of fine flour mixed
7:56 dish of ten shekels, F of incense;
7:61 sanctuary, both of them F of fine flour mixed
7:62 dish of ten shekels, F of incense;
7:67 sanctuary, both of them F of fine flour mixed
7:68 dish of ten shekels, F of incense;
7:73 sanctuary, both of them F of fine flour mixed
7:74 dish of ten shekels, F of incense;
7:79 sanctuary, both of them F of fine flour mixed
7:80 dish of ten shekels, F of incense;
7:86 the twelve golden dishes, F of incense, weighing ten
14:35 shall come to a F end, and there they
22:18 give me his house F of silver and gold,
24:13 give me his house F of silver and gold,
34:2 of Canaan in its F extent),
Deut 6:11 not build, and houses F of all good things,
6:11 you eat and are F,
8:10 shall eat and be F, and you shall bless
8:12 have eaten and are F, and have built goodly
11:15 your cattle, and you shall eat and be F
21:13 and her mother a F month; after that you
25:15 A F and just weight you shall have, a
25:15 you shall have, a F and just measure you
31:20 have eaten and are F and grown fat, they
33:23 satisfied with favor, and F of the blessing of
34:9 son of Nun was F of the spirit of
Judg 16:27 Now the house was F of men and women;
Ruth 1:21 I went away F, and the LORD has brought
2:12 have done, and a F reward be given you
1Sam 2:5 Those who were F have hired themselves out for
18:27 which were given in F number to the king,
28:20 Saul fell at once F length upon the ground,
2Sam 8:2 to death, and one F line to be spared.
13:23 After two F years Absalom had sheepshearers at
14:28 So Absalom dwelt two F years in Jerusalem, without
23:11 a plot of ground F of lentils; and the
1Kgs 7:14 bronze; and he was F of wisdom, understanding, and
2Kgs 3:16 make this dry stream-bed F of pools.'
4:4 and when one is F, set it aside."
4:6 When the vessels were F, she said to her
4:39 from it his lap F of wild gourds, and
6:17 behold, the mountain was F of horses and chariots
9:24 his bow with his F strength, and shot Joram
1Chr 11:13 a plot of ground F of barley, and the
12:38 came to Hebron with F intent to make David
21:22 to me at its F price--that the plague
21:24 buy it for the F price; I will not
23:1 David was old and F of days, he made
29:28 a good old age, F of days, riches, and
2Chr 24:15 Jehoiada grew old and F of days, and died;
Ezra 6:8 to these men in F and without delay from
7:23 it be done in F for the house of
Neh 9:25 took possession of houses F of all good things,
Tob 13:6 to him with your F voice.
Jud 6:4 their fields will be F of their dead.
7:6 all his cavalry in F view of the Israelites
Esth 9:29 Mordecai the Jew gave F written authority,
10:2 and might, and the F account of the high
15:6 throne, clothed in the F array of his majesty,
15:14 and your countenance is F of grace."
Job 7:4 long, and I am F of tossing till the
11:2 unanswered, and a man F of talk be vindicated?
14:1 of few days, and F of trouble.
15:32 will be paid in F before his time, and
20:11 His bones are F of youthful vigor, but it
20:23 his belly to the F God will send his
21:23 One dies in F prosperity, being wholly at ease
21:24 and secure, his body F of fat and the
32:18 For I am F of words, the spirit within
36:16 on your table was F of fatness.
36:17 "But you are F of the judgment on the
42:17 an old man, and F of days.
Ps 26:10 whose right hands are F of bribes.
29:4 of the LORD is F of majesty.
33:5 justice; the earth is F of the steadfast love
65:9 river of God is F of water; thou providest
74:20 of the land are F of the habitations of
78:21 LORD heard, he was F of wrath; a fire
78:59 God heard, he was F of wrath, and he
80:5 tears to drink in F measure.
81:3 new moon, at the F moon, on our feast
88:3 For my soul is F of troubles, and my
89:38 and rejected, thou art F of wrath against thy
92:14 age, they are ever F of sap and green,
104:24 all; the earth is F of thy creatures.
111:3 F of honor and majesty is his work, and
119:64 earth, O LORD, is F of thy steadfast love;
127:5 who has his quiver F of them!
144:13 may our garners be F, providing all manner of
Prov 4:19 brighter and brighter until F day.
7:20 money with him; at F moon he will come
17:1 quiet than a house F of feasting with strife.
20:17 his mouth will be F of gravel.
29:11 A fool gives F vent to his anger, but

30:9 me, lest I be F, and deny thee, and
Eccl 1:7 the sea is not F; to the place where
1:8 All things are F of weariness; a man cannot
2:23 all his days are F of pain, and his
4:6 quietness than two hands F of toil and a
9:3 hearts of men are F of evil, and madness
11:3 If the clouds are F of rain, they empty
Wis 2:6 the creation to the F as in youth.
3:4 punished, their hope is F of immortality.
5:22 of clouds, and hailstones F of wrath will be
11:18 newly created unknown beasts F of rage, or such
12:21 gavest oaths and covenants F of good promises!
13:13 a stick crooked and F of knots, he takes
Sir 1:14 the Lord is wisdom's F measure; she satisfies men
1:27 and your heart was F of deceit.
19:23 but inwardly he is F of deceit.
24:24 makes them F of understanding, like the Euphrates,
32:20 go on a path F of hazards, and do
39:12 I am filled, like the moon at the F
42:16 of the Lord is F of his glory.
43:7 light that wanes when it has reached the F
50:6 moon when it is F;
Is 1:15 listen; your hands are F of blood.
1:21 harlot, she that was F of justice!
2:6 Jacob, because they are F of diviners from the
6:3 the whole earth is F of his glory."
10:23 hosts, will make a F end, as decreed, in
11:9 the earth shall be F of the knowledge of
13:21 its houses will be F of howling creatures; there
15:9 waters of Dibon are F of blood; yet I
22:2 housetops, you who are F of shoutings, tumultuous
22:7 Your choicest valleys were F of chariots, and the
25:6 lees, of fat things F of marrow, of wine
27:9 this will be the F fruit of the removal
28:8 For all tables are F of vomit, no place
30:27 smoke; his lips are F of indignation, and his
47:9 come upon you in F measure, in spite of
51:20 a net; they are F of the wrath of
59:10 twilight, among those in F vigor we are like
Jer 4:12 cleanse, a wind too F for this comes for
4:27 will not make a F end.
5:7 fed them to the F, they committed adultery and
5:10 but make not a F end; strip away her
5:18 will not make a F end of you.
5:27 Like a basket F of birds, their houses are
5:27 birds, their houses are F of treachery; therefore they
6:11 Therefore I am F of the wrath of the
12:6 you; they are in F cry after you; believe
23:10 For the land is F of adulterers; because of
30:11 I will make a F end of all the
30:11 will not make a F end.
35:5 before the Rechabites pitchers F of wine, and cups;
46:12 and the earth is F of your cry; for
46:28 I will make a F end of all the
46:28 will not make a F end.
51:5 of the Chaldeans is F of guilt against the
Lam 1:1 the city that was F of people!
4:11 The LORD gave F vent to his wrath, he
Bar 6:17 Their eyes are F of the dust raised by
Ezek 1:18 and their rims were F of eyes round about.
7:23 "Because the land is F of bloody crimes and
7:23 and the city is F of violence,
9:9 great; the land is F of blood, and the
9:9 blood, and the city F of injustice; for they
10:4 and the court was F of the brightness of
10:12 and the wheels were F of eyes round about--
11:13 wilt thou make a F end of the remnant
16:7 tall and arrived at F maidenhood; your breasts were
19:10 the water, fruitful and F of branches by reason
20:13 wilderness, to make a F end of them.
20:17 them or make a F end of them in
22:5 you, you infamous one, F of tumult.
23:12 warriors clothed in F armor, horsemen riding on
28:12 the signet of perfection, F of wisdom and perfect
32:6 the watercourses will be F of you.
37:1 the valley; it was F of bones.
38:4 of them clothed in F armor, a great company,
41:8 side chambers measured a F reed of six long
Dan 3:19 Then Nebuchadnezzar was F of fury, and the
8:23 transgressors have reached their F measure, a king
10:3 at all, for the F three weeks.
13:28 the two elders came, F of their wicked plot
Hos 13:6 had fed to the F, they were filled, and
Joel 2:22 and vine give their F yield.
2:24 threshing floors shall be F of grain, the vats
3:13 Go in, tread, for the wine press is F
Amos 2:13 place, as a cart F of sheaves presses down.
Mic 6:12 Your rich men are F of violence; your inhabitants
Nah 1:8 he will make a F end of his adversaries,
1:9 He will make a F end; he will not
3:1 the bloody city, all F of lies and booty--
Hab 3:3 and the earth was F of his praise.
Zeph 1:18 be consumed; for a F, yea, sudden end he
Zech 8:5 the city shall be F of boys and girls
9:15 like wine, and be F like a bowl, drenched
Mal 3:10 Bring the F tithes into the storehouse, that there
1Mac 2:68 back the Gentiles in F, and heed what the
14:6 his nation, and gained F control of the country.
2Mac 3:6 treasury in Jerusalem was F of untold sums of
3:30 little while before was F of fear and disturbance,
6:14 they have reached the F measure of their sins;
11:30 pledge of friendship and F permission
13:5 place, fifty cubits high, F of ashes, and it
15:28 Nicanor, lying dead, in F armor.
Mt 6:22 whole body will be F of light;
6:23 whole body will be F of darkness.
13:48 kind; when it was F, men drew it ashore
14:20 took up twelve baskets F of the broken pieces
15:37 took up seven baskets F of the broken pieces
23:24 but inside they are F of extortion and rapacity.
23:26 but within they are F of dead men's bones
23:27 but within you are F of hypocrisy and iniquity.
Mk 4:28 the ear, then the F grain in the ear.
6:43 took up twelve baskets F of broken pieces and
8:8 up the broken pieces left over, seven baskets F
8:19 thousand, how many baskets F of broken pieces did
8:20 thousand, how many baskets F of broken pieces did
15:35 and, filling a sponge F of vinegar, put it
Lk 1:28 her and said, "Hail, F of grace, the Lord
4:1 And Jesus, F of the Holy Spirit, returned from
5:12 there came a man F of leprosy; and when
6:25 to you that are F now, for you shall
11:34 your whole body is F of light; but when
11:34 sound, your body is F of darkness.
11:36 your whole body is F of light, having no
11:39 but inside you are F of extortion and wickedness.
16:20 poor man named Lazarus, F of sores,
Jn 1:14 and dwelt among us, F of grace and truth;
3:29 voice; therefore this joy of mine is now F
15:11 in you, and that your joy may be F
16:24 you will receive, that your joy may be F
19:29 A bowl F of vinegar stood there; so they
19:29 they put a sponge F of the vinegar on
21:8 boat, dragging the net F of fish, for they
21:11 hauled the net ashore, F of large fish, a
Acts 2:28 thou wilt make me F of gladness with thy
6:3 men of good repute, F of the Spirit and
6:5 chose Stephen, a man F of faith and of
6:8 And Stephen, F of grace and power, did great
7:55 But he, F of the Holy Spirit, gazed into
9:36 She was F of good works and acts of
11:24 was a good man, F of the Holy Spirit
13:10 enemy of all righteousness, F of all deceit and
17:16 that the city was F of idols.
Rom 1:29 F of envy, murder, strife, deceit, malignity, they are
3:14 "Their mouth is F of curses and bitterness."
11:12 much more will their F inclusion mean!
11:25 of Israel, until the F number of the Gentiles
13:11 is, how it is F time now for you
15:14 that you yourselves are F of goodness, filled with
1Cor 9:18 of charge, not making F use of my right
Phil 1:20 ashamed, but that with F courage now as always
2:2 same love, being in F accord and of one
4:18 I have received F payment, and more; I am
1Thes 1:5 Holy Spirit and with F conviction.
1Tim 1:15 sure and worthy of F acceptance, that Christ Jesus
4:9 sure and worthy of F acceptance.
Heb 6:11 earnestness in realizing the F assurance of hope
10:22 a true heart in F assurance of faith, with
Jas 1:4 let steadfastness have its F effect, that you may
3:8 tongue--a restless evil, F of deadly poison.
3:17 gentle, open to reason, F of mercy and good
2Pet 2:14 They have eyes F of adultery, insatiable for sin.
2Jn 1:8 but may win a F reward.
Rev 1:16 the sun shining in F strength.
4:6 are four living creatures, F of eyes in front
4:8 with six wings, are F of eyes all round
5:8 and with golden bowls F of incense, which are
6:12 black as sackcloth, the F moon became like blood,
15:7 angels seven golden bowls F of the wrath of
17:3 scarlet beast which was F of blasphemous names,
17:4 hand a golden cup F of abominations and the

F

21:9 had the seven bowls F of the seven last

FULL-GROWN (2)

Ps 144:12 youth be like plants F, our daughters like corner
Jas 1:14 sin when it is F brings forth death.

FULL-TONED

Sir 50:18 voices in sweet and F melody.

FULLER (4)

2Kgs 18:17 the highway to the F's Field.
Is 7:3 the highway to the F's Field,
36:2 the highway to the F's Field.
Mk 9:3 intensely white, as no F on earth could bleach

FULLERS

Mal 3:2 refiner's fire and like F soap;

F

FULLNESS

Eph 1:10 a plan for the F of time, to unite

FULLY (30)

Num 14:24 and has followed me F, I will bring into
Ruth 2:11 your husband has been F told me, and how
1Kgs 2:15 and that all Israel F expected me to reign;
Tob 14:4 my son, for I F believe what Jonah the
Jud 2:2 secret plan and recounted F, with his own lips,
Eccl 8:11 sons of men is F set to do evil.
Sir 18:4 And who can F recount his mercies?
1Mac 9:42 And when they had F avenged the blood of
2Mac 4:33 When Onias became F aware of these acts he
5:2 the air, in companies F armed with lances and
14:20 the terms had been F considered, and the leader
15:22 Judea, and he slew F a hundred and eighty-five
Lk 6:40 one when he is F taught will be like
11:21 When a strong man, F armed, guards his own
13:11 over and could not F straighten herself.
Jn 7:8 time has not yet F come."
Rom 4:21 gave glory to God, F convinced that God was
14:5 Let every one be F convinced in his own
15:19 as Illyricum I have F preached the gospel of
1Cor 13:12 then I shall understand F, even as I have
13:12 as I have been F understood.
2Cor 1:13 hope you will understand F,
Gal 4:4 when the time had F come, God sent forth
Col 1:10 worthy of the Lord, F pleasing to him, bearing
1:25 the word of God F known,
4:12 may stand mature and F assured in all the
2Tim 4:17 to proclaim the message F, that all the Gentiles
1Pet 1:13 sober, set your hope F upon the grace that
Jude 1:5 were once for all F informed, that he who
Rev 14:15 of the earth is F ripe."

FULNESS (16)

Ex 22:29 to offer from the F of your harvest and
Num 18:27 floor, and as the F of the wine press.
Deut 33:16 the earth and its F, and the favor of
Tob 12:9 of righteousness will have F of life;
Job 20:22 In the F of his sufficiency he will be
Ps 16:11 thy presence there is F of joy, in thy
24:1 the LORD's and the F thereof, the world and
Sir 33:11 In the F of his knowledge the Lord distinguished
Jn 1:16 me.'") And from his F have we all received,
Rom 15:29 shall come in the F of the blessing of
Eph 1:23 is his body, the F of him who fills
3:19 filled with all the F of God.
4:13 the stature of the F of Christ;
Col 1:19 in him all the F of God was pleased
2:9 in him the whole F of deity dwells bodily,
2:10 you have come to F of life in him,

FUNCTION

Rom 12:4 not have the same F,

FUND

1Mac 3:31 revenues from those regions and raise a large F

FUNDS (4)

1Mac 3:30 might not have such F as he had before
10:41 And all the additional F which the government
2Mac 3:6 the amount of the F could not be reckoned,
3:14 went in to direct the inspection of these F

FUNERAL (5)

Tob 14:11 years old; and Tobias gave him a magnificent F
Bar 6:32 some do at a F feast for a man
1Mac 9:41 their musicians into a F dirge.
2Mac 4:49 of the crime, provided magnificently for their F
5:10 him; he had no F of any sort and

FUNERALS

Tob 14:13 his father-in-law and mother-in-law magnificent F

FURIOUS (8)

Prov 6:34 jealousy makes a man F, and he will not
Is 30:30 to be seen, in F anger and a flame
34:2 all the nations, and F against all their host,
Ezek 5:15 and fury, and with F chastisements--I, the LORD,
Dan 2:12 was angry and very F, and commanded that all
3:13 Then Nebuchadnezzar in F rage commanded that
1Mac 2:49 time of ruin and F anger.
Mt 2:16 men, was in a F rage, and he sent

FURIOUSLY (3)

2Kgs 9:20 Jehu the son of Nimshi; for he drives F
2Mac 3:25 mien, and it rushed F at Heliodorus and struck
12:15 days of Joshua, rushed F upon the walls.

FURLONGS

Mt 14:24 this time was many F distant from the land,

FURNACE (41)

Gen 19:28 land went up like the smoke of a F
Deut 4:20 out of the iron F, out of Egypt, to
1Kgs 8:51 of Egypt, from the midst of the iron F
Ps 12:6 silver refined in a F on the ground, purified
102:3 like smoke, and my bones burn like a F
Prov 17:3 for silver, and the F is for gold, and
27:21 for silver, and the F is for gold, and
Wis 3:6 like gold in the F he tried them, and
Sir 2:5 acceptable men in the F of humiliation.
22:22 and smoke of the F precede the fire; so
38:28 the heat of the F; he inclines his ear
38:30 glazing, and he is careful to clean the F
43:4 A man tending a F works in burning heat,
Is 31:9 in Zion, and whose F is in Jerusalem.
48:10 tried you in the F of affliction.
Jer 11:4 Egypt, from the iron F, saying, Listen to my
Ezek 22:18 and lead in the F, have become dross.
22:20 and tin into a F, to blow the fire
22:22 is melted in a F, so you shall be
Dan 3:6 shall immediately be cast into a burning fiery F
3:11 worship shall be cast into a burning fiery F
3:15 into a burning fiery F; and who is the
3:17 from the burning fiery F; and he will deliver
3:19 He ordered the F heated seven times more than
3:20 and to cast them into the burning fiery F
3:21 and they were cast into the burning fiery F
3:22 was strict and the F very hot, the flame
3:23 and Abednego, fell bound into the burning fiery F
3:46 not cease feeding the F fires with naphtha, pitch,
3:47 streamed out above the F forty-nine cubits,
3:48 of the Chaldeans whom it caught about the F
3:49 came down into the F to be with Azariah
3:49 flame out of the F,
3:50 the midst of the F like a moist whistling
3:51 blessed God in the F, saying:
3:89 of the burning fiery F; from the midst of
3:94 of the burning fiery F and said, "Shadrach, Meshach,
Mt 13:42 throw them into the F of fire; there men
13:50 throw them into the F of fire; there men
Rev 1:15 refined as in a F, and his voice was
9:2 smoke of a great F, and the sun and

FURNISH (2)

Deut 15:14 go empty-handed; you shall F him liberally out of
Ezek 45:17 the prince's duty to F the burnt offerings, cereal

FURNISHED (5)

Sir 44:6 in writing; rich men F with resources,
1Mac 4:57 for the priests, and F them with doors.
14:10 cities with food, and F them with the means
Mk 14:15 a large upper room F and ready; there prepare
Lk 22:12 a large upper room F; there make ready."

FURNISHES

1Tim 6:17 on God who richly F us with everything to

FURNISHINGS (7)

Ex 31:7 thereon, and all the F of the tent,
Num 1:50 and over all its F, and over all that
1:50 tabernacle and all its F, and they shall tend

	3:8	charge of all the F of the tent of
	4:15	sanctuary and all the F of the sanctuary, as
	7:1	it with all its F, and had anointed and
	19:18	and upon all the F, and upon the persons

FURNITURE (4)

Ex	25:9	and of all its F, so you shall make
1Chr	9:29	were appointed over the F, and over all the
Neh	13:8	threw all the household F of Tobiah out of
Jud	15:11	bowls and all his F; and she took them

FURROW (2)

1Sam	14:14	it were half a F's length in an acre
Job	39:10	bind him in the F with ropes, or will

FURROWS (7)

Job	31:38	against me, and its F have wept together;
Ps	65:10	Thou waterest its F abundantly, settling its ridges,
	129:3	plowed upon my back; they made long their F
Sir	7:3	do not sow the F of injustice, and you
	38:26	his heart on plowing F, and he is careful
Hos	10:4	poisonous weeds in the F of the field.
	12:11	stone heaps on the F of the field.

FURTHER (24)

Deut	20:8	the officers shall speak F to the people, and
1Sam	10:3	go on from there F and come to the
2Sam	19:28	What F right have I, then, to cry to
2Chr	34:16	to the king, and F reported to the king,
Esth	9:12	And what F is your request?
Job	40:5	not answer; twice, but I will proceed no F
Ps	140:8	the wicked; do not F his evil plot!
Sir	36:6	signs anew, and work F wonders; make thy hand
Ezek	8:17	violence, and provoke me F to anger?
	23:14	she carried her harlotry F; she saw men portrayed
2Mac	2:20	of the altar, and F the wars against Antiochus
Mk	5:35	Why trouble the Teacher any F
	15:5	But Jesus made no F answer, so that Pilate
Lk	22:69	And they said, "What F testimony do we need?
	24:28	appeared to be going F,
Acts	4:17	it may spread no F among the people, let
	4:21	And when they had F threatened them, they let
	19:39	if you seek anything F, it shall be settled
	24:4	to detain you no F, I beg you in
Rom	15:12	peoples praise him"; and F Isaiah says, "The root
2Cor	5:4	that we would be F clothed, so that what
Tit	1:1	of Jesus Christ, to F the faith of God's
Heb	7:11	received the law), what F need would there have
	12:19	hearers entreat that no F messages be spoken to

FURTHERED (2)

Zech	1:15	but a little they F the disaster.
2Mac	14:5	found an opportunity that F his mad purpose when

FURTHERMORE (3)

Deut	4:21	F the LORD was angry with me on your
	9:13	themselves a molten image.' F the LORD said to
2Chr	17:6	of the LORD; and F he took the high

FURY (38)

Gen	27:44	while, until your brother's F turns away;
Ex	15:7	thou sendest forth thy F, it consumes them like
Lev	26:28	contrary to you in F, and chastise you myself
Deut	29:28	land in anger and F and great wrath, and
Esth	3:5	do obeisance to him, Haman was filled with F
Ps	2:5	terrify them in his F, saying,
	7:6	thyself up against the F of my enemies; awake,
Prov	22:8	the rod of his F will fail.
Sir	40:5	fear of death, and F and strife.
	48:10	it breaks out in F, to turn the heart
Is	10:5	rod of my anger, the staff of my F
	14:4	has ceased, the insolent F ceased!
	42:13	he stirs up his F; he cries out, he
	51:13	day because of the F of the oppressor, when
	51:13	And where is the F of the oppressor?
	59:17	and wrapped himself in F as a mantle.
	66:15	render his anger in F, and his rebuke with
Jer	21:5	in anger, and in F, and in great wrath.
Lam	2:4	has poured out his F like fire.
Ezek	5:13	I will vent my F upon them and satisfy
	5:13	when I spend my F upon them.
	5:15	you in anger and F, and with furious chastisements--
	6:12	I will spend my F upon them.
	16:42	will I satisfy my F on you, and my
	19:12	was plucked up in F, cast down to the
	21:17	I will satisfy my F; I the LORD have
	23:25	you, that they may deal with you in F
	24:13	I have satisfied my F upon you.
Dan	3:19	Nebuchadnezzar was full of F, and the expression of
	11:44	go forth with great F to exterminate and utterly
Hab	3:12	bestride the earth in F, thou didst trample the
2Mac	10:35	wall and with savage F cut down every one
Lk	6:11	they were filled with F and discussed with one
Acts	26:11	blaspheme; and in raging F against them, I
Rom	2:8	but obey wickedness, there will be wrath and F
Heb	10:27	of judgment, and a F of fire which will
Rev	16:19	the cup of the F of his wrath.
	19:15	wine press of the F of the wrath of

FUTILE (6)

Wis	15:8	toil, he forms a F god from the same
Rom	1:21	him, but they became F in their thinking and
1Cor	3:20	knows that the thoughts of the wise are F
	15:17	raised, your faith is F and you are still
Tit	3:9	over the law, for they are unprofitable and F
1Pet	1:18	were ransomed from the F ways inherited from your

FUTILITY (2)

Rom	8:20	creation was subjected to F, not of its own
Eph	4:17	Gentiles do, in the F of their minds;

FUTURE (22)

Gen	9:12	with you, for all F generations:
2Sam	7:19	and hast shown me F generations, O Lord GOD!
1Chr	17:17	and hast shown me F generations, O LORD God!
Esth	16:8	For the F we will take care to render
Prov	19:20	instruction, that you may gain wisdom for the F
	23:18	Surely there is a F, and your hope will
	24:14	there will be a F, and your hope will
	24:20	evil man has no F; the lamp of the
Wis	19:1	in advance even their F actions,
Sir	3:29	gives thought to the F; at the moment of
	11:21	and what prosperity could be mine in the F
	11:22	what calamity could happen to me in the F
	24:31	leave it to all F generations.
Jer	29:11	to give you a F and a hope.
	31:17	is hope for your F, says the LORD, and
1Mac	15:8	treasury and any such F debts shall be canceled
2Mac	11:19	will endeavor for the F to help promote your
	12:31	their race in the F also.
Acts	24:24	justice and self-control and F judgment, Felix was
1Cor	3:22	the present or the F, all are yours;
1Tim	6:19	good foundation for the F, so that they may
Heb	11:20	By faith Isaac invoked F blessings on Jacob and

G

GAAL (9)

Judg	9:26	And G the son of Ebed moved into Shechem
	9:28	And G the son of Ebed said, "Who is
	9:30	heard the words of G the son of Ebed,
	9:31	at Arumah, saying, "Behold, G the son of Ebed
	9:35	And G the son of Ebed went out and
	9:36	And when G saw the men, he said to
	9:37	G spoke again and said, "Look, men are coming
	9:39	And G went out at the head of the
	9:41	and Zebul drove out G and his kinsmen, so

GAASH (4)

Josh	24:30	country of Ephraim, north of the mountain of G
Judg	2:9	country of Ephraim, north of the mountain of G
2Sam	23:30	of the brooks of G,
1Chr	11:32	of the brooks of G, Abiel the Arbathite,

GABAEL (10)

Tob	1:1	of Aduel, son of G, of the descendants of
	1:14	silver in trust with G, the brother of Gabrias.
	4:1	left in trust with G at Rages in Media,
	4:20	left in trust with G the son of Gabrias
	5:6	way, and I have stayed with our brother G
	9:2	you and go to G at Rages in Media
	9:5	made the journey and stayed over night with G
	9:5	him the receipt, and G brought out the money
	9:6	And G blessed Tobias and his wife.
	10:2	is it possible that G has died and there

GABATHA

Esth	12:1	in the courtyard with G and Tharra, the two

F G

GABBAI
Neh 11:8 after him G, Sallai, nine hundred and twenty-eight.

GABBATHA
Jn 19:13 a place called The Pavement, and in Hebrew, G

GABRIAS (2)
Tob 1:14 silver in trust with Gabael, the brother of G
4:20 Gabael the son of G at Rages in Media.

GABRIEL (4)
Dan 8:16 Ulai, and it called, G, make this man understand
9:21 in prayer, the man G, whom I had seen
Lk 1:19 answered him, "I am G, who stand in the
1:26 sixth month the angel G was sent from God

GAD (58)
Gen 30:11 so she called his name G
35:26 of Zilpah, Leah's maid: G and Asher.
46:16 The sons of G: Ziphion, Haggi, Shuni, Ezbon, Eri,
49:19 Raiders shall raid G, but he shall raid at
Ex 1:3 Benjamin, Dan and Naphtali, G and Asher.
Num 1:14 son of Ochran; from G, Eliasaph the son of
1:24 Of the people of G, their generations, by their
1:25 of the tribe of G was forty-five thousand six
2:14 Then the tribe of G, the leader of the
2:14 of the people of G being Eliasaph the son
7:42 of the men of G:
10:20 of the men of G was Eliasaph the son
13:15 from the tribe of G, Geuel the son of
26:15 The sons of G according to their families: of
26:18 of the sons of G according to their number,
32:1 and the sons of G had a very great
32:2 So the sons of G and the sons of
32:6 to the sons of G and to the sons
32:25 And the sons of G and the sons of
32:29 "If the sons of G and the sons of
32:31 And the sons of G and the sons of
32:33 to the sons of G and to the sons
32:34 And the sons of G built Dibon, Ataroth, Aroer,
34:14 of the sons of G by their fathers' houses
Deut 27:13 for the curse: Reuben, G, Asher, Zebulun, Dan, and
33:20 And of G he said, "Blessed be he who
33:20 Gad he said, "Blessed be he who enlarges G
33:20 G couches like a lion, he tears the arm,
Josh 4:12 and the sons of G and the half-tribe of
18:7 is their heritage; and G and Reuben and half
20:8 from the tribe of G, and Golan in Bashan,
21:7 Reuben, the tribe of G, and the tribe of
21:38 of the tribe of G, Ramoth in Gilead with
1Sam 13:7 to the land of G and Gilead.
22:5 Then the prophet G said to David, "Do not
2Sam 24:5 of the valley, toward G and on to Jazer.
24:11 came to the prophet G, David's seer, saying,
24:13 So G came to David and told him, and
24:14 Then David said to G, "I am in great
24:18 And G came that day to David, and said
24:19 David went up at G's word, as the LORD
1Chr 2:2 Dan, Joseph, Benjamin, Naphtali, G, and Asher.
5:11 The sons of G dwelt over against them in
6:63 the tribes of Reuben, G, and Zebulun.
6:80 of the tribe of G: Ramoth in Gilead with
21:9 the LORD spoke to G, David's seer, saying,
21:11 So G came to David and said to him,
21:13 Then David said to G, "I am in great
21:18 of the LORD commanded G to say to David
21:19 David went up at G's word, which he had
29:29 in the Chronicles of G the seer,
2Chr 29:25 of David and of G the king's seer and
Jer 2:36 sinned.' How lightly you G about, changing your way!
49:1 then has Milcom dispossessed G, and his people
Ezek 48:27 side to the west, G, one portion.
48:28 adjoining the territory of G to the south, the
48:34 gates, the gate of G, the gate of Asher,
Rev 7:5 of the tribe of G,

GADARENES
Mt 8:28 the country of the G, two demoniacs met him,

GADDI (2)
Num 13:11 the tribe of Manasseh), G the son of Susi;
1Mac 2:2 five sons, John surnamed G,

GADDIEL
Num 13:10 the tribe of Zebulun, G the son of Sodi;

GADDING
1Tim 5:13 learn to be idlers, G about from house to

GADFLY
Jer 46:20 is Egypt, but a G from the north has

GADI (2)
2Kgs 15:14 Menahem the son of G came up from Tirzah
15:17 Menahem the son of G began to reign over

GADITE
2Sam 23:36 of Zobah, Bani the G,

GADITES (29)
Deut 3:12 the Reubenites and the G the territory beginning at
3:16 the Reubenites and the G I gave the territory
4:43 in Gilead for the G, and Golan in Bashan
29:8 to the Reubenites, the G, and the half-tribe of
Josh 1:12 to the Reubenites, the G, and the half-tribe of
12:6 the Reubenites and the G and the half-tribe of
13:8 the Reubenites and the G received their inheritance,
13:24 the tribe of the G, according to their families.
13:28 the inheritance of the G according to their families,
22:1 the Reubenites, and the G, and the half-tribe of
22:9 the Reubenites and the G and the half-tribe of
22:10 the Reubenites and the G and the half-tribe of
22:11 the Reubenites and the G and the half-tribe of
22:13 the Reubenites and the G and the half-tribe of
22:15 to the Reubenites, the G, and the half-tribe of
22:21 Then the Reubenites, the G, and the half-tribe of
22:25 you, you Reubenites and G; you have no portion
22:30 the Reubenites and the G and the Manassites spoke,
22:31 Reubenites and the G and the Manassites, "Today
22:32 the Reubenites and the G in the land of
22:33 the Reubenites and the G were settled.
22:34 The Reubenites and the G called the altar Witness;
2Kgs 10:33 land of Gilead, the G, and the Reubenites, and
1Chr 5:18 The Reubenites, the G, and the half-tribe of
5:26 namely, the Reubenites, the G, and the half-tribe of
12:8 From the G there went over to David at
12:14 These G were officers of the army, the lesser
12:37 Of the Reubenites and G and the half-tribe of
26:32 of the Reubenites, the G, and the half-tribe of

GAHAM
Gen 22:24 was Reumah, bore Tebah, G, Tahash, and Maacah.

GAHAR (2)
Ezra 2:47 Giddel, the sons of G, the sons of Re-aiah,
Neh 7:49 Giddel, the sons of G,

GAILY
Ezek 16:16 and made for yourself G decked shrines, and on

GAIN (71)
1Sam 8:3 but turned aside after G; they took bribes and
Job 22:3 righteous, or is it G to him if you
30:2 What could I G from the strength of their
Ps 10:3 the man greedy for G curses and renounces the
119:36 my heart to thy testimonies, and not to G
Prov 1:19 of all who get G by violence; it takes
3:14 gets understanding, for the G from it is better
3:14 it is better than G from silver and its
4:2 attentive, that you may G insight;
10:16 leads to life, the G of the wicked to
15:27 is greedy for unjust G makes trouble for his
19:20 instruction, that you may G wisdom for the future.
19:25 understanding, and he will G knowledge.
28:16 he who hates unjust G will prolong his days.
31:11 her, and he will have no lack of G
Eccl 1:3 What does man G by all the toil at
3:9 What G has the worker from his toil?
5:10 who loves wealth, with G: this also is vanity.
5:11 eat them; and what G has their owner but
5:16 he go; and what G has he that he
Wis 14:2 it was desire for G that planned that vessel,
Sir 6:7 When you G a friend, gain him through testing,
6:7 you gain a friend, G him through testing, and
6:33 to listen you will G knowledge, and if you
8:8 from them you will G instruction and learn how
8:9 from them you will G understanding and learn how
19:22 who distort kindness to G a verdict.
22:21 G the trust of your neighbor in his poverty,
29:19 into suretyship and pursues G will fall into lawsuits.
34:23 down, what do they G but toil?
51:28 silver, and you will G by it much gold.

Is 33:15 uprightly, who despises the G of oppressions, who
56:11 each to his own G, one and all.
Jer 2:18 now what do you G by going to Egypt,
2:18 Or what do you G by going to Assyria,
6:13 is greedy for unjust G; and from prophet to
8:10 is greedy for unjust G; from prophet to priest
22:17 only for your dishonest G, for shedding innocent
Ezek 22:12 and increase and make G of your neighbors by
22:13 together at the dishonest G which you have made,
22:27 shedding blood, destroying lives to get dishonest G
33:31 love, but their heart is set on their G
Dan 2:8 you are trying to G time, because you see
Mic 4:13 and shall devote their G to the LORD, their
Hab 2:9 him who gets evil G for his house, to
1Mac 2:48 never let the sinner G the upper hand.
2:64 by it you will G honor.
15:9 When we G control of our kingdom, we will
2Mac 5:7 He did not G control of the government, however;
Mk 8:36 profit a man, to G the whole world and
Lk 17:33 Whoever seeks to G his life will lose it,
21:19 your endurance you will G your lives.
Acts 16:16 brought her owners much G by soothsaying.
16:19 that their hope of G was gone, they seized
1Cor 7:21 But if you can G your freedom, avail yourself
13:3 have not love, I G nothing.
15:32 What do I G if, humanly speaking, I fought
Phil 1:21 to live is Christ, and to die is G
3:7 But whatever G I had, I counted as loss
3:8 order that I may G Christ
1Tim 3:8 wine, not greedy for G;
3:13 serve well as deacons G a good standing for
6:5 truth, imagining that godliness is a means of G
6:6 There is great G in godliness with contentment;
Tit 1:6 violent or greedy for G,
1:10 by teaching for base G what they have no
Jas 4:13 and trade and get G;
1Pet 5:2 willingly, not for shameful G but eagerly,
2Pet 2:15 of Beor, who loved G from wrongdoing,
Jude 1:11 for the sake of G to Balaam's error, and
1:16 boasters, flattering people to G advantage.

GAINED (39)

Gen 26:13 man became rich, and G more and more until
31:1 our father's he has G all this wealth."
31:18 livestock which he had G, the cattle in his
46:6 goods, which they had G in the land of
47:27 of Goshen; and they G possessions in it, and
2Sam 11:23 to David, "The men G an advantage over us,
Prov 10:2 Treasures G by wickedness do not profit, but
16:31 of glory; it is G in a righteous life.
20:17 Bread G by deceit is sweet to a man,
Eccl 2:11 was nothing to be G under the sun.
Wis 13:13 shapes it with skill G in idleness; he forms
Sir 25:9 is he who has G good sense, and he
25:10 is he who has G wisdom!
34:25 again, what has he G by his washing?
34:26 And what has he G by humbling himself?
51:20 I G understanding with her from the first, therefore
51:21 her, therefore I have G a good possession.
Is 15:7 the abundance they have G and what they have
Jer 48:36 therefore the riches they G have perished.
Hos 12:8 am rich, I have G wealth for myself": but
1Mac 7:22 They G control of the land of Judah and
8:4 and how they had G control of the whole
10:52 I crushed Demetrius and G control of our country;
10:76 the gates, and Jonathan G possession of Joppa.
11:8 So King Ptolemy G control of the coastal cities
11:49 that the Jews had G control of the city
11:51 So the Jews G glory in the eyes of
11:56 captured the elephants and G control of Antioch.
14:6 of his nation, and G full control of the
15:3 certain pestilent men have G control of the kingdom
2Mac 10:17 Attacking them vigorously, they G possession of the
13:26 convinced them, appeased them, G their good will,
Mt 15:5 What you would have G from me is given
18:14 to you, you have G your brother.
Mk 7:11 What you would have G from me is Corban'
Lk 19:15 know what they had G by trading.
2Cor 12:1 is nothing to be G by it, but I
Jude 1:4 admission has been secretly G by some who long
Rev 18:15 of these wares, who G wealth from her, will

GAINING (3)

2Mac 8:8 that the man was G ground little by little,
Mt 27:24 saw that he was G nothing, but rather that
2Cor 2:11 to keep Satan from G the advantage over us;

GAINS (8)

Prov 15:32 he who heeds admonition G understanding.
21:11 man is instructed, he G knowledge.
Wis 7:25 Almighty; therefore nothing defiled G entrance into
Sir 9:2 woman so that she G mastery over your strength.
Jer 20:5 the city, all its G, all its prized belongings,
2Mac 15:21 Lord decides, that he G the victory for those
Mt 16:26 a man, if he G the whole world and
Lk 9:25 a man if he G the whole world and

GAIUS (5)

Acts 19:29 dragging with them G and Aristarchus, Macedonians
20:4 Aristarchus and Secundus; and G of Derbe, and
Rom 16:23 G, who is host to me and to the
1Cor 1:14 you except Crispus and G;
3Jn 1:1 elder to the beloved G, whom I love in

GALAL (3)

1Chr 9:15 Merari; and Bakbakkar, Heresh, G, and Mattaniah
9:16 of Shemaiah, son of G, son of Jeduthun, and
Neh 11:17 of Shammua, son of G, son of Jeduthun.

GALATIA (6)

Acts 16:6 region of Phrygia and G, having been forbidden by
18:23 through the region of G and Phrygia, strengthening
1Cor 16:1 directed the churches of G, so you also are
Gal 1:2 To the churches of G:
2Tim 4:10 Crescens has gone to G, Titus to Dalmatia.
1Pet 1:1 the dispersion in Pontus, G, Cappadocia, Asia, and

GALATIANS (2)

2Mac 8:20 the battle with the G that took place in
Gal 3:1 O foolish G

GALBANUM (2)

Ex 30:34 stacte, and onycha, and G, sweet spices with pure
Sir 24:15 a pleasant odor, like G, onycha, and stacte, and

GALE

Rev 6:13 when shaken by a G;

GALEED (2)

Gen 31:47 called it Jegar-sahadutha: but Jacob called it G
31:48 Therefore he named it G,

GALILEAN (5)

Mt 26:69 and said, "You also were with Jesus the G
Mk 14:70 are one of them; for you are a G
Lk 22:57 also was with him; for he is a G
23:6 this, he asked whether the man was a G
Acts 5:37 After him Judas the G arose in the days

GALILEANS (5)

Lk 13:1 told him of the G whose blood Pilate had
13:2 you think that these G were worse sinners than
13:2 than all the other G, because they suffered thus?
Jn 4:45 came to Galilee, the G welcomed him, having seen
Acts 2:7 saying, "Are not all these who are speaking G

GALILEE (83)

Josh 12:23 king of Goiim in G, one;
20:7 set apart Kedesh in G in the hill country
21:32 of Naphtali, Kedesh in G with its pasture lands,
1Kgs 9:11 to Hiram twenty cities in the land of G
2Kgs 15:29 Kedesh, Hazor, Gilead, and G, all the land of
1Chr 6:76 of Naphtali: Kedesh in G with its pasture lands,
Tob 1:2 of Kedesh Naphtali in G above Asher.
Jud 1:8 and Gilead, and Upper G and the great Plain
15:5 in Gilead and in G out-flanked them with great
Is 9:1 land beyond the Jordan, G of the nations.
1Mac 5:14 garments rent, came from G and made a similar
5:15 and Sidon, and all G of the Gentiles, "to
5:17 rescue your brethren in G; I and Jonathan my
5:20 Simon to go to G, and eight thousand to
5:21 So Simon went to G and fought many battles
5:23 took the Jews of G and Arbatta, with their
5:55 his brother was in G before Ptolemais,
10:30 it from Samaria and G, from this day and
11:63 come to Kadesh in G with a large army,
12:47 whom he left in G, while a thousand accompanied
12:49 troops and cavalry into G and the Great Plain
Mt 2:22 a dream he withdrew to the district of G
3:13 Then Jesus came from G to the Jordan to
4:12 arrested, he withdrew into G;
4:15 sea, across the Jordan, G of the Gentiles—
4:18 by the Sea of G, he saw two brothers,

4:23 he went about all G, teaching in their synagogues
4:25 crowds followed him from G and the Decapolis and
15:29 from there and passed along the Sea of G
17:21 they were gathering in G, Jesus said to them,
19:1 he went away from G and entered the region
21:11 "This is the prophet Jesus from Nazareth of G
26:32 raised up, I will go before you to G
27:55 had followed Jesus from G, ministering to him;
28:7 going before you to G; there you will see
28:10 brethren to go to G, and there they will
28:16 eleven disciples went to G, to the mountain to
Mk 1:9 came from Nazareth of G and was baptized by
1:14 arrested, Jesus came into G, preaching the gospel of
1:16 by the Sea of G, he saw Simon and
1:28 throughout all the surrounding region of G
1:39 throughout all G, preaching in their synagogues
3:7 a great multitude from G followed; also from Judea
6:21 courtiers and officers and the leading men of G
7:30 to the Sea of G, through the region of
9:30 They went on from there and passed through G
14:28 raised up, I will go before you to G
15:40 when he was in G, followed him, and ministered
16:7 going before you to G; there you will see
Lk 1:26 to a city of G named Nazareth,
2:4 also went up from G, from the city of
2:39 Lord, they returned into G, to their own city,
3:1 Herod being tetrarch of G, and his brother Philip
4:14 of the Spirit into G, and a report concerning
4:31 he went down to Caperna-um, a city of G
5:17 from every village of G and Judea and from
8:26 the country of the Gerasenes, which is opposite G
17:11 he was passing along between Samaria and G
23:5 throughout all Judea, from G even to this place."
23:48 had followed him from G stood at a distance
23:54 come with him from G followed, and saw the
24:6 he was still in G,
Jn 1:43 The next day Jesus decided to go to G
2:1 marriage at Cana in G, and the mother of
2:11 did at Cana in G, and manifested his glory;
4:3 disciples), he left Judea and departed again to G
4:43 After the two days he departed to G
4:45 when he came to G, the Galileans welcomed him,
4:46 again to Cana in G, where he had made
4:47 come from Judea to G, he went and begged
4:54 did when he had come from Judea to G
6:1 of the Sea of G, which is the Sea
7:1 Jesus went about in G; he would not go
7:9 So saying, he remained in G
7:41 some said, "Is the Christ to come from G
7:52 replied, "Are you from G too?
7:52 see that no prophet is to rise from G
12:21 was from Beth-saida in G, and said to him,
21:2 Nathanael of Cana in G, the sons of Zebedee,
Acts 1:11 and said, "Men of G, why do you stand
9:31 throughout all Judea and G and Samaria had peace
10:37 all Judea, beginning from G after the baptism which
13:31 up with him from G to Jerusalem, who are

GALL (12)
Tob 6:4 heart and liver and G and put them away
6:6 liver and heart and G of the fish?"
6:8 And as for the G, anoint with it a
11:4 And take the G of the fish with you."
11:8 his eyes with the G; and when they smart
11:11 and he sprinkled the G upon his father's eyes,
Job 16:13 he pours out my G on the ground.
20:14 stomach; it is the G of asps within him.
20:25 comes out of his G; terrors come upon him.
Lam 3:19 and my bitterness, the wormwood and the G
Mt 27:34 to drink, mingled with G; but when he tasted
Acts 8:23 you are in the G of bitterness and in

GALLERIES
Ezek 42:5 were narrower, for the G took more away from

GALLERY (2)
Ezek 42:3 the outer court, was G against gallery in three
42:3 court, was gallery against G in three stories.

GALLEY
Is 33:21 and streams, where no G with oars can go,

GALLIM (2)
1Sam 25:44 Palti the son of Laish, who was of G
Is 10:30 Cry aloud, O daughter of G

GALLIO (3)
Acts 18:12 But when G was proconsul of Achaia, the Jews
18:14 to open his mouth, G said to the Jews,
18:17 But G paid no attention to this.

GALLONS (2)
Dan 14:3 forty sheep and fifty G of wine.
Jn 2:6 rites of purification, each holding twenty or thirty G

GALLOPING (3)
Judg 5:22 horses' hoofs with the G, galloping of his steeds.
5:22 hoofs with the galloping, G of his steeds.
Nah 3:2 and rumble of wheel, G horse and bounding chariot!

GALLOWS (9)
Esth 2:23 so, the men were both hanged on the G
5:14 to him, "Let a G fifty cubits high be
5:14 and he had the G made.
6:4 Mordecai hanged on the G that he had prepared
7:9 the king, "Moreover, the G which Haman has
7:10 hanged Haman on the G which he had prepared
8:7 hanged him on the G, because he would lay
9:13 ten sons of Haman be hanged on the G
9:25 and his sons should be hanged on the G

GAMAD
Ezek 27:11 about, and men of G were in your towers;

GAMALI-EL (2)
Acts 5:34 in the council named G, a teacher of the
22:3 at the feet of G, educated according to the

GAMALIEL (5)
Num 1:10 Ammihud, and from Manasseh, G the son of
2:20 people of Manasseh being G the son of Pedahzur,
7:54 On the eighth day G the son of Pedahzur,
7:59 was the offering of G the son of Pedahzur.
10:23 men of Manasseh was G the son of Pedahzur.

GAME (10)
Gen 25:28 he ate of his G; but Rebekah loved Jacob.
27:3 the field, and hunt G for me,
27:5 field to hunt for G and bring it,
27:7 brother Esau, 'Bring me G, and prepare for me
27:19 and eat of my G, that you may bless
27:25 eat of my son's G and bless you." So
27:31 eat of his son's G, that you may bless
27:33 it then that hunted G and brought it to
Wis 15:12 our existence an idle G, and life a festival
Sir 36:19 tastes the kinds of G, so an intelligent mind

GAMES
2Mac 4:18 When the quadrennial G were being held at Tyre

GAMUL
1Chr 24:17 Jachin, the twenty-second to G,

GANGRENE
2Tim 2:17 and their talk will eat its way like G

GAPED
Job 16:10 Men have G at me with their mouth, they

GARB
Deut 21:13 put off her captive's G, and shall remain in

GARDEN (69)
Gen 2:8 LORD God planted a G in Eden, in the
2:9 the midst of the G, and the tree of
2:10 Eden to water the G, and there it divided
2:15 put him in the G of Eden to till
2:16 every tree of the G;
3:1 shall not eat of any tree of the G
3:2 the trees of the G;
3:3 the midst of the G, neither shall you touch
3:8 God walking in the G in the cool of
3:8 the LORD God among the trees of the G
3:10 of thee in the G, and I was afraid,
3:23 him forth from the G of Eden, to till
3:24 the east of the G of Eden he placed
13:10 watered everywhere like the G of the LORD, like
Deut 11:10 your feet, like a G of vegetables;
1Kgs 21:2 it for a vegetable G, because it is near
2Kgs 21:18 was buried in the G of his house, in
21:18 his house, in the G of Uzza; and Amon
21:26 his tomb in the G of Uzza; and Josiah

	25:4	walls, by the king's G, though the Chaldeans were
Neh	3:15	Shelah of the king's G, as far as the
Esth	1:5	the court of the G of the king's palace.
	7:7	went into the palace G; but Haman stayed to
	7:8	returned from the palace G to the place where
Job	8:16	the sun, and his shoots spread over his G
Song	4:12	A G locked is my sister, my bride, a
	4:12	sister, my bride, a G locked, a fountain sealed.
	4:15	chief spices-- a G fountain, a well of
	4:16	Blow upon my G, let its fragrance be wafted
	4:16	beloved come to his G, and eat its choicest
	5:1	I come to my G, my sister, my bride,
	6:2	gone down to his G, to the beds of
Sir	24:28	river and like a water channel into a G
	24:29	orchard and drench my G plot"; and lo, my
	40:17	Kindness is like a G of blessings, and almsgiving
	40:27	Lord is like a G of blessing, and covers
Is	1:30	withers, and like a G without water.
	51:3	her desert like the G of the LORD; joy
	58:11	be like a watered G, like a spring of
	61:11	shoots, and as a G causes what is sown
Jer	31:12	be like a watered G, and they shall languish
	39:4	way of the king's G through the gate between
	52:7	walls, by the king's G, while the Chaldeans were
Lam	2:6	like that of a G, laid in ruins the
Bar	6:71	thorn bush in a G, on which every bird
Ezek	28:13	were in Eden, the G of God; every precious
	31:8	The cedars in the G of God could not
	31:8	no tree in the G of God was like
	31:9	that were in the G of God.
	36:35	has become like the G of Eden; and the
Dan	13:4	and had a spacious G adjoining his house; and
	13:7	go into her husband's G to walk.
	13:15	to bathe in the G, for it was very
	13:17	ointments, and shut the G doors so that I
	13:18	she said, shut the G doors, and went out
	13:20	and said: "Look, the G doors are shut, no
	13:25	ran and opened the G doors.
	13:26	the shouting in the G, they rushed in at
	13:36	were walking in the G alone, this woman came
	13:36	two maids, shut the G doors, and dismissed the
	13:38	a corner of the G, and when we saw
Hos	14:7	shall flourish as a G; they shall blossom as
Joel	2:3	land is like the G of Eden before them,
Mic	7:14	the midst of a G land; let them feed
Lk	13:19	and sowed in his G; and it grew and
Jn	18:1	where there was a G, which he and his
	18:26	see you in the G with him?"
	19:41	crucified there was a G, and in the garden
	19:41	garden, and in the G a new tomb where

GARDENER

Jn	20:15	him to be the G, she said to him,

GARDENS (11)

Num	24:6	that stretch afar, like G beside a river, like
Eccl	2:5	myself; I made myself G and parks, and planted
Song	6:2	his flock in the G, and to gather lilies.
	8:13	who dwell in the G, my companions are listening
Is	1:29	shall blush for the G which you have chosen.
	65:3	face continually, sacrificing in G and burning incense
	66:17	to go into the G, following one in the
Jer	29:5	live in them; plant G and eat their produce.
	29:28	in them, and plant G and eat their produce."'''
Amos	4:9	I laid waste your G and your vineyards; your
	9:14	and they shall make G and eat their fruit.

GAREB (3)

2Sam	23:38	Zeruiah, Ira the Ithrite, G the Ithrite,
1Chr	11:40	Zeruiah, Ira the Ithrite, G the Ithrite,
Jer	31:39	straight to the hill G, and shall then turn

GARLAND (6)

Prov	1:9	they are a fair G for your head, and
	4:10	your head a fair G; she will bestow on
	14:24	but folly is the G of fools.
Sir	50:12	the altar with a G of brethren around him,
Is	61:3	to give them a G instead of ashes, the
	61:10	decks himself with a G, and as a bride

GARLANDS (3)

Jud	3:7	welcomed him with G and dances and tambourines.
	15:13	their arms and wearing G and with songs on
Acts	14:13	city, brought oxen and G to the gates and

GARLIC

Num	11:5	the onions, and the G;

GARMENT (81)

Gen	9:23	and Japheth took a G, laid it upon both
	39:12	caught him by his G, saying, "Lie with me."
	39:12	But he left his G in her hand, and
	39:13	he had left his G in her hand, and
	39:15	cried, he left his G with me, and fled
	39:16	she laid up his G by her until his
	39:18	cried, he left his G with me, and fled
Ex	22:26	you take your neighbor's G in pledge, you shall
	28:32	the opening in a G, that it may not
	39:23	the opening in a G, with a binding around
Lev	6:10	put on his linen G, and put his linen
	6:27	is sprinkled on a G, you shall wash that
	11:32	of wood or a G or a skin or
	13:47	leprous disease in a G, whether a woolen or
	13:47	woolen or a linen G,
	13:49	or reddish in the G, whether in warp or
	13:51	has spread in the G, in warp or woof,
	13:52	he shall burn the G, whether diseased in warp
	13:53	not spread in the G in warp or woof
	13:56	spot out of the G or the skin or
	13:57	appears again in the G, in warp or woof,
	13:58	But the G, warp or woof, or anything of
	13:59	leprous disease in a G of wool or linen,
	14:55	for leprosy in a G or in a house,
	15:17	And every G and every skin on which the
	19:19	come upon you a G of cloth made of
Num	31:20	You shall purify every G, every article of skin,
Deut	22:3	shall do with his G; so you shall do
	22:5	put on a woman's G; for whoever does these
	22:17	they shall spread the G before the elders of
	24:17	or take a widow's G in pledge;
Judg	8:25	And they spread a G, and every man cast
2Sam	20:8	was wearing a soldier's G, and over it was
	20:12	field, and threw a G over him.
1Kgs	11:29	himself with a new G; and the two of
	11:30	hold of the new G that was on him,
2Kgs	1:8	him, "He wore a G of haircloth, with a
	9:13	of them took his G, and put it under
Job	13:28	rotten thing, like a G that is moth-eaten.
	30:18	violence it seizes my G; it binds me about
	38:9	I made clouds its G, and thick darkness its
	38:14	the seal, and it is dyed like a G
	41:13	Who can strip off his outer G
Ps	73:6	is their necklace; violence covers them as a G
	102:26	endure; they will all wear out like a G
	104:2	light as with a G, who hast stretched out
	104:6	deep as with a G; the waters stood above
	109:19	it be like a G which he wraps round
Prov	20:16	Take a man's G when he has given surety
	25:20	who takes off a G on a cold day,
	27:13	Take a man's G when he has given surety
	30:4	Who has wrapped up the waters in a G
Song	5:3	had put off my G, how could I put
Sir	14:17	become old like a G, for the decree from
	45:10	people; with a holy G, of gold and blue
Is	9:5	battle tumult and every G rolled in blood will
	50:9	wear out like a G; the moth will eat
	51:6	wear out like a G, and they who dwell
	51:8	them up like a G, and the worm will
	64:6	all our righteous deeds are like a polluted G
Bar	5:1	Take off the G of your sorrow and affliction,
Ezek	18:7	the naked with a G,
	18:16	the naked with a G,
Hag	2:12	the skirt of his G, and touches with his
Mal	2:16	Israel, and covering one's G with violence, says the
Mt	3:4	Now John wore a G of camel's hair, and
	9:16	cloth on an old G, for the patch tears
	9:16	tears away from the G, and a worse tear
	9:20	the fringe of his G;
	9:21	I only touch his G, I shall be made
	14:36	the fringe of his G; and as many as
	22:11	who had no wedding G;
	22:12	here without a wedding G And he was speechless.
Mk	2:21	cloth on an old G; if he does, the
	5:27	behind him in the crowd and touched his G
	6:56	the fringe of his G; and as many as
Lk	5:36	piece from a new G and puts it upon
	5:36	it upon an old G; if he does, he
	8:44	the fringe of his G; and immediately her flow
Heb	1:11	grow old like a G,
Jude	1:23	fear, hating even the G spotted by the flesh.

G

GARMENTS (157)

Gen 3:21 and for his wife G of skins, and clothed
27:15 Rebekah took the best G of Esau her older
27:27 the smell of his G, and blessed him, and
35:2 yourselves, and change your G;
37:34 Then Jacob rent his G, and put sackcloth upon
38:14 put off her widow's G, and put on a
38:19 she put on the G of her widowhood.
41:42 and arrayed him in G of fine linen, and
45:22 them he gave festal G; but to Benjamin he
45:22 three hundred shekels of silver and five festal G
49:11 vine, he washes his G in wine and his
Ex 19:10 let them wash their G,
19:14 and consecrated the people; and they washed their G
28:2 you shall make holy G for Aaron your brother,
28:3 that they make Aaron's G to consecrate him for
28:4 These are the G which they shall make: a
28:4 they shall make holy G for Aaron your brother
29:5 you shall take the G, and put on Aaron
29:21 upon Aaron and his G, and upon his sons
29:21 sons and his sons' G with him; and he
29:21 and he and his G shall be holy, and
29:21 sons and his sons' G with him.
29:29 "The holy G of Aaron shall be for his
31:10 and the finely worked G, the holy garments for
31:10 worked garments, the holy G for Aaron the priest
31:10 the priest and the G of his sons, for
35:19 cords; the finely wrought G for ministering in the
35:19 holy place, the holy G for Aaron the priest,
35:19 the priest, and the G of his sons, for
35:21 for all its service, and for the holy G
39:1 they made finely wrought G, for ministering in the
39:1 they made the holy G for Aaron; as the
39:41 meeting; the finely worked G for ministering in the
39:41 holy place, the holy G for Aaron the priest,
39:41 the priest, and the G of his sons to
Lev 6:11 shall put off his G, and put on other
6:11 and put on other G, and carry forth the
8:2 with him, and the G, and the anointing oil,
8:30 upon Aaron and his G, and also upon his
8:30 sons and his sons' G; so he consecrated Aaron
8:30 consecrated Aaron and his G, and his sons and
8:30 sons and his sons' G with him.
16:4 wear the linen turban; these are the holy G
16:23 put off the linen G which he put on
16:24 and put on his G, and come forth, and
16:32 wearing the holy linen G;
21:10 consecrated to wear the G, shall not let the
Num 15:38 the corners of their G throughout their generations,
20:26 strip Aaron of his G, and put them upon
20:28 stripped Aaron of his G, and put them upon
Josh 9:13 are burst; and these G and shoes of ours
Judg 8:26 pendants and the purple G worn by the kings
14:12 give you thirty linen G and thirty festal garments;
14:12 garments and thirty festal G;
14:13 give me thirty linen G and thirty festal garments."
14:13 give me thirty linen garments and thirty festal G
14:19 and gave the festal G to those who had
1Sam 27:9 the camels, and the G, and came back to
28:8 and put on other G, and went, he and
2Sam 10:4 and cut off their G in the middle, at
13:31 arose, and rent his G, and lay on the
13:31 his servants who were standing by rent their G
14:2 and put on mourning G; do not anoint yourself
1Kgs 10:25 of silver and gold, G, myrrh, spices, horses, and
2Kgs 5:5 six thousand shekels of gold, and ten festal G
5:22 them a talent of silver and two festal G
5:23 bags, with two festal G, and laid them upon
5:26 to accept money and G, olive orchards and vineyards,
7:15 way was littered with G and equipment which the
25:29 So Jehoiachin put off his prison G
1Chr 19:4 and cut off their G in the middle, at
2Chr 9:24 silver and of gold, G, myrrh, spices, horses, and
Ezra 2:69 thousand minas of silver, and one hundred priests' G
9:3 this, I rent my G and my mantle, and
9:5 my fasting, with my G and my mantle rent,
Neh 7:70 gold, fifty basins, five hundred and thirty priests' G
7:72 thousand minas of silver, and sixty-seven priests' G
Jud 8:5 loins and wore the G of her widowhood.
10:3 took off her widow's G, and bathed her body
14:16 wept and groaned and shouted, and rent his G
Esth 4:4 deeply distressed; she sent G to clothe Mordecai, so
14:2 and put on the G of distress and mourning,
15:1 she took off the G in which she had
Job 37:17 in knowledge, you whose G are hot when the
Ps 22:18 me; they divide my G among them, and for
Prov 31:24 She makes linen G and sells them; she delivers
Eccl 9:8 Let your G be always white; let not oil
Song 4:11 the scent of your G is like the scent
Sir 42:13 of women; for from G comes the moth, and
Is 3:23 and the handbags; the G of gauze, the linen
3:23 of gauze, the linen G, the turbans, and the
52:1 put on your beautiful G, O Jerusalem, the holy
59:17 head; he put on G of vengeance for clothing,
61:10 clothed me with the G of salvation, he has
63:1 from Edom, in crimsoned G from Bozrah, he that
63:2 apparel red, and thy G like his that treads
63:3 is sprinkled upon my G, and I have stained
Jer 36:24 words, was afraid, nor did they rend their G
52:33 So Jehoiachin put off his prison G
Lam 4:14 defiled with blood that none could touch their G
Bar 6:11 their gods out with G like men—these gods
Ezek 16:16 took some of your G, and made for yourself
16:18 you took your embroidered G to cover them, and
26:16 strip off their embroidered G; they will clothe
27:24 with you in choice G, in clothes of blue
42:14 without laying there the G in which they minister,
42:14 shall put on other G before they go near
44:17 they shall wear linen G; they shall have nothing
44:19 shall put off the G in which they have
44:19 shall put on other G, lest they communicate holiness
44:19 communicate holiness to the people with their G
Dan 3:21 hats, and their other G, and they were cast
Joel 2:13 mourning; and rend your hearts and not your G
Amos 2:8 beside every altar upon G taken in pledge; and
Zech 3:3 was standing before the angel, clothed with filthy G
3:4 him, "Remove the filthy G from him." And to
3:5 and clothed him with G; and the angel of
14:14 collected, gold, silver, and G in great abundance.
1Mac 3:49 They also brought the G of the priesthood and
5:14 messengers, with their G rent, came from Galilee
10:21 put on the holy G in the seventh month
10:62 to take off Jonathan's G and to clothe him
11:71 Jonathan rent his G and put dust on his
14:9 donned the glories and G of war.
2Mac 3:15 altar in their priestly G and called toward heaven
4:38 Andronicus, tore off his G, and led him about
Mt 17:2 the sun, and his G became white as light.
21:7 colt, and put their G on them, and he
21:8 the crowd spread their G on the road, and
27:35 him, they divided his G among them by casting
Mk 5:28 I touch even his G, I shall be made
5:30 in the crowd, and said, "Who touched my G
9:3 before them, and his G became glistening, intensely
11:7 Jesus, and threw their G on it; and he
11:8 And many spread their G on the road, and
14:63 high priest tore his G, and said, "Why do
15:24 him, and divided his G among them, casting lots
Lk 19:35 Jesus, and throwing their G on the colt they
19:36 along, they spread their G on the road.
23:33 And they cast lots to divide his G
Jn 13:4 supper, laid aside his G, and girded himself with
13:12 feet, and taken his G, and resumed his place,
19:23 Jesus they took his G and made four parts,
19:24 scripture, "They parted my G among them, and for
Acts 7:58 witnesses laid down their G at the feet of
9:39 showing tunics and other G which Dorcas made
14:14 it, they tore their G and rushed out among
16:22 the magistrates tore the G off them and gave
18:6 he shook out his G and said to them,
22:20 approving, and keeping the G of those who killed
22:23 out and waved their G and threw dust into
Jas 5:2 have rotted and your G are moth-eaten.
Rev 3:4 have not soiled their G; and they shall walk
3:5 clad thus in white G, and I will not
3:18 be rich, and white G to clothe you and
4:4 elders, clad in white G, with golden crowns upon
16:15 is awake, keeping his G that he may not

GARMITE

1Chr 4:19 of Keilah the G and Eshtemoa the Ma-acathite.

GARNER

Is 62:9 labored; but those who G it shall eat it

GARNERS

Ps 144:13 a palace; may our G be full, providing all

GARRISON (22)

1Sam 10:5 where there is a G of the Philistines; and
13:3 Jonathan defeated the G of the Philistines which
13:4 Saul had defeated the G of the Philistines, and

13:23 And the G of the Philistines went out to
14:1 over to the Philistine G on yonder side." But
14:4 over to the Philistine G, there was a rocky
14:6 go over to the G of these uncircumcised; it
14:11 showed themselves to the G of the Philistines; and
14:12 the men of the G hailed Jonathan and his
14:15 all the people; the G and even the raiders
2Sam 23:14 the stronghold; and the G of the Philistines was
1Chr 11:16 the stronghold; and the G of the Philistines was
1Mac 4:61 And he stationed a G there to hold it.
6:21 But some of the G escaped from the siege
10:75 for Apollonius had a G in Joppa.
11:3 stationed forces as a G in each city.
11:66 city, and set a G over it.
12:34 And he stationed a G there to guard it.
12:36 it so that its G could neither buy nor
14:33 he placed there a G of Jews.
2Mac 12:18 one place he had left a very strong G
13:20 sent in to the G whatever was necessary.

GARRISONED

2Mac 10:32 especially well G, where Chaereas was command

GARRISONS (8)

2Sam 8:6 Then David put G in Aram of Damascus; and
8:14 And he put G in Edom; throughout all Edom
8:14 all Edom he put G, and all the Edomites
1Chr 18:6 Then David put G in Syria of Damascus; and
18:13 And he put G in Edom; and all the
2Chr 17:2 of Judah, and set G in the land of
Jud 3:6 his army and stationed G in the hilltop cities
1Mac 9:51 And he placed G in them to harass Israel.

GARRULOUS

Sir 25:19 such is a G wife for a quiet

GASH (2)

Jer 47:5 how long will you G yourselves?
Hos 7:15 grain and wine they G themselves, they rebel against

GASHED

Jer 41:5 torn, and their bodies G, bringing cereal offerings

GASHES

Jer 48:37 all the hands are G, and on the loins

GASP

Is 42:14 in travail, I will G and pant.

GASPING

Jer 4:31 the daughter of Zion G for breath, stretching out

GATAM (3)

Gen 36:11 were Teman, Omar, Zepho, G, and Kenaz.
36:16 Omar, Zepho, Kenaz, Korah, G, and Amalek; these
1Chr 1:36 Eliphaz: Teman, Omar, Zephi, G, Kenaz, Timna, and

GATE (271)

Gen 19:1 was sitting in the G of Sodom.
22:17 descendants shall possess the G of their enemies,
23:10 went in at the G of his city,
23:18 went in at the G of his city.
24:60 your descendants possess the G of those who hate
28:17 and this is the G of heaven."
34:20 Shechem came to the G of their city and
34:24 went out of the G of his city hearkened
34:24 went out of the G of his city.
Ex 27:14 one side of the G shall be fifteen cubits,
27:16 For the G of the court there shall be
32:26 Moses stood in the G of the camp, and
32:27 to and fro from G to gate throughout the
32:27 fro from gate to G throughout the camp, and
35:17 the screen for the G of the court;
38:14 one side of the G were fifteen cubits, with
38:15 that hand by the G of the court were
38:18 the screen for the G of the court was
38:31 the bases of the G of the court, all
39:40 the screen for the G of the court, its
Num 4:26 the entrance of the G of the court which
Deut 21:19 his city at the G of the place where
22:15 the city in the G;
22:24 both out to the G of that city, and
25:7 go up to the G to the elders, and
Josh 2:5 from; and when the G was to be closed,
2:7 had gone out, the G was shut.
7:5 chased them before the G as far as Shebarim,
8:29 the entrance of the G of the city, and
20:4 the entrance of the G of the city, and
Judg 9:35 the entrance of the G of the city; and
9:40 fell wounded, up to the entrance of the G
9:44 the entrance of the G of the city, while
16:2 all night at the G of the city.
16:3 the doors of the G of the city and
18:16 the entrance of the G;
18:17 the entrance of the G with the six hundred
Ruth 4:1 went up to the G and sat down there;
4:10 brethren and from the G of his native place;
4:11 who were at the G, and the elders, said,
1Sam 4:18 the side of the G; and his neck was
9:18 approached Samuel in the G, and said, "Tell me
21:13 the doors of the G, and let his spittle
2Sam 3:27 the midst of the G to speak with him
10:8 the entrance of the G; and the Syrians of
11:23 drove them back to the entrance of the G
15:2 the way of the G; and when any man
18:4 the side of the G, while all the army
18:24 the roof of the G by the wall, and
18:26 watchman called to the G and said, "See, another
18:33 the chamber over the G, and wept; and as
19:8 king arose, and took his seat in the G
19:8 is sitting in the G; and all the people
23:15 the well of Bethlehem which is by the G
23:16 which was by the G, and took and brought
1Kgs 17:10 he came to the G of the city, behold,
22:10 the entrance of the G of Samaria; and all
2Kgs 7:1 a shekel, at the G of Samaria."
7:3 the entrance to the G; and they said to
7:17 have charge of the G; and the people trod
7:17 upon him in the G, so that he died,
7:18 time tomorrow in the G of Samaria,"
7:20 upon him in the G and he died.
9:31 as Jehu entered the G, she said, "Is it
10:8 the entrance of the G until the morning."
11:6 third being at the G Sur and a third
11:6 a third at the G behind the guards), shall
11:19 LORD, marching through the G of the guards to
14:13 cubits, from the Ephraim G to the Corner Gate.
14:13 cubits, from the Ephraim Gate to the Corner G
15:35 He built the upper G of the house of
23:8 the entrance of the G of Joshua the governor
23:8 one's left at the G of the city.
25:4 the way of the G between the two walls,
1Chr 9:18 hitherto in the king's G on the east side.
11:17 the well of Bethlehem which is by the G
11:18 which was by the G, and took and brought
16:42 The sons of Jeduthun were appointed to the G
26:16 the west, at the G of Shallecheth on the
2Chr 18:9 the entrance of the G of Samaria; and all
23:5 one third at the G of the Foundation; and
23:15 entrance of the horse G of the king's house,
23:20 marching through the upper G to the king's house.
24:8 set it outside the G of the house of
25:23 cubits, from the Ephraim G to the Corner Gate.
25:23 cubits, from the Ephraim Gate to the Corner G
26:9 Jerusalem at the Corner G and at the Valley
26:9 and at the Valley G and at the Angle,
27:3 He built the upper G of the house of
31:14 keeper of the east G, was over the freewill
32:6 the square at the G of the city and
33:14 entrance into the Fish G, and carried it round
35:15 gatekeepers were at each G; they did not need
Neh 2:13 night by the Valley G to the Jackal's Well
2:13 and to the Dung G, and I inspected the
2:14 on to the Fountain G and to the King's
2:15 entered by the Valley G, and so returned.
3:1 brethren the priests and they built the Sheep G
3:3 Hassenaah built the Fish G; they laid its beams
3:6 Besodeiah repaired the Old G; they laid its beams
3:13 Zanoah repaired the Valley G; they rebuilt it and
3:13 of the wall, as far as the Dung G
3:14 Beth-haccherem, repaired the Dung G; he rebuilt it
3:15 Mizpah, repaired the Fountain G; he rebuilt it and
3:26 point opposite the Water G on the east and
3:28 Above the Horse G the priests repaired, each one
3:29 keeper of the East G, repaired.
3:31 merchants, opposite the Muster G, and to the upper
3:32 corner and the Sheep G the goldsmiths and the
8:1 square before the Water G; and they told Ezra
8:3 square before the Water G from early morning until
8:16 square at the Water G and in the square
8:16 the square at the G of Ephraim.
12:31 wall to the Dung G;

12:37 At the Fountain G they went up straight before
12:37 David, to the Water G on the east.
12:39 Wall, and above the G of Ephraim, and by
12:39 and by the Old G, and by the Fish
12:39 and by the Fish G and the Tower of
12:39 Hundred, to the Sheep G; and they came to
12:39 a halt at the G of the Guard.
Tob 11:16 his daughter-in-law at the G of Nineveh, rejoicing
Jud 8:33 Stand at the city G tonight, and I will
10:6 out to the city G of Bethulia, and found
10:9 to them, "Order the G of the city to
10:9 men to open the G for her, as she
13:11 the watchmen at the gates, "Open, open the G
13:12 down to the city G and called together the
13:13 returned; they opened the G and admitted them, and
Esth 2:19 second time, Mordecai was sitting at the king's G
2:21 sitting at the king's G, Bigthan and Teresh, two
3:2 were at the king's G bowed down and did
3:3 were at the king's G said to Mordecai, "Why
4:2 entrance of the king's G, for no one might
4:2 might enter the king's G clothed with sackcloth.
4:6 front of the king's G,
5:9 Mordecai in the king's G, that he neither rose
5:13 see Mordecai the Jew sitting at the king's G
6:10 Mordecai the Jew who sits at the king's G
6:12 Then Mordecai returned to the king's G
16:18 been hanged at the G of Susa, with all
Job 5:4 are crushed in the G, and there is no
29:7 went out to the G of the city, when
31:21 saw help in the G;
Ps 69:12 who sit in the G, and the drunkards make
118:20 This is the G of the LORD; the righteous
127:5 when he speaks with his enemies in the G
Prov 22:22 the afflicted at the G;
24:7 a fool; in the G he does not open
Song 7:4 in Heshbon, by the G of Bath-rabbim.
Is 14:31 Wail, O G; cry, O city; melt in fear,
28:6 those who turn back the battle at the G
29:21 who reproves in the G, and with an empty
Jer 7:2 LORD: "Stand in the G of the LORD's house,
17:19 stand in the Benjamin G, by which the kings
19:2 entry of the Potsherd G, and proclaim there the
20:2 in the upper Benjamin G of the house of
26:10 entry of the New G of the house of
31:38 from the tower of Hananel to the Corner G
31:40 corner of the Horse G toward the east, shall
36:10 entry of the New G of the LORD's house.
37:13 was at the Benjamin G, a sentry there named
38:7 sitting in the Benjamin G --
39:3 middle G: Nergal-sharezer, Samgar-nebo, Sarsechim
39:4 king's garden through the G between the two walls;
52:7 the way of a G between the two walls,
Lam 5:14 have quit the city G, the young men their
Ezek 8:5 north of the altar G, in the entrance, was
8:14 entrance of the north G of the house of
9:2 direction of the upper G, which faces north, every
10:19 door of the east G of the house of
11:1 me to the east G of the house of
26:2 concerning Jerusalem, 'Aha, the G of the peoples is
40:6 the threshold of the G, one reed deep;
40:7 the threshold of the G by the vestibule of
40:7 the vestibule of the G at the inner end,
40:9 the vestibule of the G was at the inner
40:10 side of the east G; the three were of
40:13 Then he measured the G from the back of
40:15 the front of the G at the entrance to
40:15 inner vestibule of the G was fifty cubits.
40:19 front of the lower G to the outer front
40:20 behold, there was a G which faced toward the
40:21 those of the first G; its length was fifty
40:22 as those of the G which faced toward the
40:23 And opposite the G on the north, as on
40:23 the east, was a G to the inner court;
40:23 and he measured from G to gate, a hundred
40:23 measured from gate to G, a hundred cubits.
40:24 behold, there was a G on the south; and
40:27 And there was a G on the south of
40:27 and he measured from G to gate toward the
40:27 measured from gate to G toward the south, a
40:28 court by the south G, and he measured the
40:28 he measured the south G; it was of the
40:32 and he measured the G; it was of the
40:35 me to the north G, and he measured it;
40:38 the vestibule of the G, where the burnt offering
40:39 the vestibule of the G were two tables on
40:40 entrance of the north G were two tables; and
40:40 the vestibule of the G were two tables.
40:41 the side of the G, eight tables, on which
40:44 side of the north G facing south, the other
40:44 side of the south G facing north.
40:48 the breadth of the G was fourteen cubits; and
40:48 the sidewalls of the G were three cubits on
42:15 me out by the G which faced east, and
43:1 brought me to the G, the gate facing east.
43:1 to the gate, the G facing east.
43:4 the temple by the G facing east,
44:1 back to the outer G of the sanctuary, which
44:2 said to me, "This G shall remain shut; it
44:3 the vestibule of the G, and shall go out
44:4 way of the north G to the front of
45:19 the posts of the G of the inner court.
46:1 the Lord GOD: The G of the inner court
46:2 the vestibule of the G from without, and shall
46:2 take his stand by the post of the G
46:2 he shall worship at the threshold of the G
46:2 go out, but the G shall not be shut
46:3 the entrance of that G before the LORD on
46:8 the vestibule of the G, and he shall go
46:9 enters by the north G to worship shall go
46:9 out by the south G; and he who enters
46:9 enters by the south G shall go out by
46:9 out by the north G: no one shall return
46:9 by way of the G by which he entered,
46:12 to the LORD, the G facing east shall be
46:12 has gone out the G shall be shut.
46:19 the side of the G, to the north row
47:2 way of the north G, and led me round
47:2 outside to the outer G, that faces toward the
48:31 measure, three gates, the G of Reuben, the gate
48:31 gate of Reuben, the G of Judah, and the
48:31 of Judah, and the G of Levi, the gates
48:32 cubits, three gates, the G of Joseph, the gate
48:32 gate of Joseph, the G of Benjamin, and the
48:32 of Benjamin, and the G of Dan.
48:33 measure, three gates, the G of Simeon, the gate
48:33 gate of Simeon, the G of Issachar, and the
48:33 of Issachar, and the G of Zebulun.
48:34 cubits, three gates, the G of Gad, the gate
48:34 gate of Gad, the G of Asher, and the
48:34 of Asher, and the G of Naphtali.
Amos 5:10 who reproves in the G, and they abhor him
5:12 bribe, and turn aside the needy in the G
5:15 establish justice in the G; it may be that
Obad 1:13 not have entered the G of my people in
Mic 1:9 has reached to the G of my people, to
1:12 the LORD to the G of Jerusalem.
2:13 through and pass the G, going out by it.
Zeph 1:10 heard from the Fish G, a wail from the
Zech 14:10 its site from the G of Benjamin to the
14:10 place of the former G, to the Corner Gate,
14:10 gate, to the Corner G, and from the Tower
1Mac 5:22 pursued them to the G of Ptolemais, and as
2Mac 1:8 kingdom and burned the G and shed innocent blood.
Mt 7:13 "Enter by the narrow G; for the gate is
7:13 narrow gate; for the G is wide and the
7:14 For the G is narrow and the way is
Lk 7:12 drew near to the G of the city, behold,
16:20 And at his G lay a poor man named
Jn 5:2 Jerusalem by the Sheep G a pool, in Hebrew
Acts 3:2 laid daily at that G of the temple which
3:10 alms at the Beautiful G of the temple; and
10:17 house, stood before the G
12:10 came to the iron G leading into the city.
12:14 did not open the G but ran in and
12:14 and told that Peter was standing at the G
16:13 we went outside the G to the riverside, where
Heb 13:12 also suffered outside the G in order to sanctify

GATEKEEPER (2)

1Chr 9:21 son of Meshelemiah was G at the entrance of
Jn 10:3 To him the G opens; the sheep hear his

GATEKEEPERS (34)

2Kgs 7:10 and called to the G of the city, and
7:11 Then the G called out, and it was told
1Chr 9:17 The G were: Shallum, Akkub, Talmon, Ahiman, and
9:18 These were the G of the camp of the
9:22 who were chosen as G at the thresholds, were
9:24 The G were on the four sides, east, west,
9:26 for the four chief G, who were Levites, were
15:18 and Mikneiah, and the G Obed-edom and Je-iel.
15:23 Elkanah were to be G for the ark.

	15:24	also were to be G for the ark.
	16:38	son of Jeduthun, and Hosah were to be G
	23:5	and judges, four thousand G, and four thousand shall
	26:1	the divisions of the G: of the Korahites, Meshelemiah
	26:12	These divisions of the G, corresponding to their chief
	26:19	the divisions of the G among the Korahites and
2Chr	8:14	day required, and the G in their divisions for
	23:4	one third shall be G,
	23:19	He stationed the G at the gates of the
	34:13	of the Levites were scribes, and officials, and G
	35:15	king's seer; and the G were at each gate;
Ezra	2:42	The sons of the G: the sons of Shallum,
	2:70	and the singers, the G, and the temple servants
	7:7	Levites, the singers and G, and the temple servants.
	10:24	Of the G: Shallum, Telem, and Uri.
Neh	7:1	the doors, and the G, the singers, and the
	7:45	The G: the sons of Shallum, the sons of
	7:73	priests, the Levites, the G, the singers, some of
	10:28	priests, the Levites, the G, the singers, the temple
	10:39	that minister, and the G and the singers.
	11:19	The G, Akkub, Talmon and their brethren, who kept
	12:25	Talmon, and Akkub were G standing guard at the
	12:45	the singers and the G, according to the command
	12:47	the singers and the G; and they set apart
	13:5	the Levites, singers, and G, and the contributions for

GATES (143)

Ex	20:10	who is within your G;
Deut	3:5	fortified with high walls, G, and bars, besides very
	5:14	who is within your G, that your manservant and
	6:9	the doorposts of your house and on your G
	11:20	house and upon your G,
	17:5	bring forth to your G that man or woman
Josh	6:26	his youngest son shall he set up its G
Judg	5:8	gods were chosen, then war was in the G
	5:11	Israel."Then down to the G marched the people of
1Sam	17:52	as Gath and the G of Ekron, so that
	23:7	a town that has G and bars."
2Sam	18:24	sitting between the two G; and the watchman went
1Kgs	16:34	and set up its G at the cost of
2Kgs	23:8	high places of the G that were at the
1Chr	9:23	in charge of the G of the house of
	22:3	the doors of the G and for clamps, as
	26:13	fathers' houses, small and great alike, for their G
2Chr	8:5	fortified cities with walls, G, and bars,
	8:14	divisions for the several G; for so David the
	14:7	with walls and towers, G and bars; the land
	23:19	the gatekeepers at the G of the house of
	31:2	to minister in the G of the camp of
Neh	1:3	broken down, and its G are destroyed by fire."
	2:3	lies waste, and its G have been destroyed by
	2:8	make beams for the G of the fortress of
	2:13	broken down and its G which had been destroyed
	2:17	in ruins with its G burned.
	6:1	the doors in the G,
	7:3	them, "Let not the G of Jerusalem be opened
	11:19	kept watch at the G, were a hundred and
	12:25	standing guard at the storehouses of the G
	12:30	the people and the G and the wall.
	13:19	be dark at the G of Jerusalem before the
	13:19	my servants over the G, that no burden might
	13:22	come and guard the G, to keep the sabbath
Jud	1:3	cubits wide; at the G he built towers a
	1:4	and he made its G, which were seventy cubits
	7:23	the passages through the G; there was no strength
	13:10	the mountain to Bethulia and came to its G
	13:11	the watchmen at the G, "Open, open the gate!
Job	38:17	Have the G of death been revealed to you,
	38:17	have you seen the G of deep darkness?
Ps	9:13	me up from the G of death,
	9:14	praises, that in the G of the daughter of
	24:7	[Selah] Lift up your heads, O G
	24:9	Lift up your heads, O G
	87:2	the LORD loves the G of Zion more than
	100:4	Enter his G with thanksgiving, and his courts with
	107:18	drew near to the G of death.
	118:19	Open to me the G of righteousness, that I
	122:2	been standing within your G, O Jerusalem!
	147:13	the bars of your G; he blesses your sons
Prov	1:21	entrance of the city G she speaks:
	8:3	her stand; beside the G in front of the
	8:34	watching daily at my G, waiting beside my doors.
	14:19	the wicked at the G of the righteous.
	31:23	is known in the G, when he sits among
	31:31	and let her works praise her in the G
Wis	6:14	for he will find her sitting at his G
	16:13	men down to the G of Hades and back
Sir	49:13	and set up the G and bars and rebuilt
Is	3:26	And her G shall lament and mourn; ravaged, she
	13:2	them to enter the G of the nobles.
	22:7	and the horsemen took their stand at the G
	24:12	in the city, the G are battered into ruins.
	26:2	Open the G, that the righteous nation which keeps
	38:10	am consigned to the G of Sheol for the
	45:1	doors before him that G may not be closed:
	54:12	pinnacles of agate, your G of carbuncles, and all
	60:11	Your G shall be open continually; day and night
	60:18	walls Salvation, and your G Praise.
	62:10	through, go through the G, prepare the way for
Jer	1:15	the entrance of the G of Jerusalem, against all
	7:2	Judah who enter these G to worship the LORD.
	14:2	"Judah mourns and her G languish; her people
	15:7	winnowing fork in the G of the land; I
	17:19	and in all the G of Jerusalem,
	17:20	the inhabitants of Jerusalem, who enter by these G
	17:21	it in by the G of Jerusalem.
	17:24	no burden by the G of this city on
	17:25	shall enter by the G of this city kings
	17:27	and enter by the G of Jerusalem on the
	17:27	a fire in its G, and it shall devour
	22:2	your servants, and your people who enter these G
	22:4	there shall enter the G of this house kings
	22:19	cast forth beyond the G of Jerusalem."
	49:31	LORD, that has no G or bars, that dwells
	51:58	ground and her high G shall be burned with
Lam	1:4	appointed feasts; all her G are desolate, her priests
	2:9	Her G have sunk into the ground; he has
	4:12	enemy could enter the G of Jerusalem.
Bar	6:18	And just as the G are shut on every
Ezek	21:15	may melt, and many fall at all their G
	21:22	set battering-rams against the G, to cast up mounds,
	26:10	when he enters your G as one enters a
	38:11	having no bars or G;
	40:18	the side of the G, corresponding to the length
	40:18	the length of the G; this was the lower
	44:11	having oversight at the G of the temple, and
	44:17	When they enter the G of the inner court,
	44:17	they minister at the G of the inner court,
	48:31	cubits by measure, three G, the gate of Reuben,
	48:31	gate of Levi, the G of the city being
	48:32	five hundred cubits, three G, the gate of Joseph,
	48:33	cubits by measure, three G, the gate of Simeon,
	48:34	five hundred cubits, three G, the gate of Gad,
Hos	11:6	the bars of their G, and devour them in
Obad	1:11	and foreigners entered his G and cast lots for
Nah	2:6	The river G are opened, the palace is in
	3:13	The G of your land are wide open to
Zech	8:16	another, render in your G judgments that are true
1Mac	4:38	altar profaned, and the G burned.
	4:57	shields; they restored the G and the chambers for
	5:47	and blocked up the G with stones.
	9:50	with high walls and G and bars.
	10:75	the city closed its G, for Apollonius had a
	10:76	afraid and opened the G, and Jonathan gained
	11:2	the cities opened their G to him and went
	12:38	fortified it and installed G with bolts.
	12:48	of Ptolemais closed the G and seized him, and
	13:33	and great walls and G and bolts, and he
	15:39	Kedron and fortify its G, and to make war
2Mac	3:19	ran together to the G, and some to the
	8:33	fire to the sacred G, Callisthenes and some others,
	10:36	Others broke open the G and let in the
	12:7	Then, because the city's G were closed, he withdrew,
Mt	24:33	know that he is near, at the very G
Mk	13:29	know that he is near, at the very G
Acts	9:24	They were watching the G day and night, to
	14:13	and garlands to the G and wanted to offer
	21:30	and at once the G were shut.
Rev	21:12	high wall, with twelve G, and at the gates
	21:12	gates, and at the G twelve angels, and on
	21:12	angels, and on the G the names of the
	21:13	on the east three G, on the north three
	21:13	on the north three G, on the south three
	21:13	on the south three G, and on the west
	21:13	south three gates, and on the west three G
	21:15	the city and its G and walls.
	21:21	And the twelve G were twelve pearls, each of
	21:21	pearls, each of the G made of a single
	21:25	into it, and its G shall never be shut
	22:14	that they may enter the city by the G

GATEWAY (11)
Ezek 8:3 the entrance of the G of the inner court
11:1 the door of the G there were twenty-five men;
40:3 his hand; and he was standing in the G
40:6 he went into the G facing east, going up
40:8 the vestibule of the G, eight cubits;
40:11 the opening of the G, ten cubits; and the
40:11 the breadth of the G, thirteen cubits.
40:14 the vestibule of the G was the court.
40:16 And the G had windows round about, narrowing
Mk 14:68 And he went out into the G
Acts 12:13 the door of the G, a maid named Rhoda

GATH (34)
Josh 11:22 only in Gaza, in G, and in Ashdod, did
13:3 of Gaza, Ashdod, Ashkelon, G, and Ekron), and those
1Sam 5:8 the God of Israel be brought around to G
6:17 for Ashkelon, one for G, one for Ekron;
7:14 Israel, from Ekron to G; and Israel rescued their
17:4 champion named Goliath, of G, whose height was six
17:23 champion, the Philistine of G, Goliath by name, came
17:52 Philistines as far as G and the gates of
17:52 Sha-araim as far as G and Ekron.
21:10 Saul, and went to Achish the king of G
21:12 was much afraid of Achish the king of G
27:2 to Achish the son of Maoch, king of G
27:3 dwelt with Achish at G, he and his men,
27:4 David had fled to G, he sought for him
27:11 to bring tidings to G, thinking, "Lest they should
2Sam 1:20 Tell it not in G, publish it not in
15:18 had followed him from G, passed on before the
21:20 was again war at G, where there was a
21:22 from the giants in G; and they fell by
1Kgs 2:39 away to Achish, son of Maacah, king of G
2:39 was told Shimei, "Behold, your slaves are in G
2:40 ass, and went to G to Achish, to seek
2:40 slaves; Shimei went and brought his slaves from G
2:41 gone from Jerusalem to G and returned,
2Kgs 12:17 up and fought against G, and took it.
1Chr 7:21 whom the men of G who were born in
8:13 flight the inhabitants of G;
18:1 them, and he took G and its villages out
20:6 was again war at G, where there was a
20:8 from the giants in G; and they fell by
2Chr 11:8 Bethzur, Soco, Adullam, G, Mareshah, Ziph,
26:6 down the wall of G and the wall of
Amos 6:2 then go down to G of the Philistines.
Mic 1:10 Tell it not in G, weep not at all;

GATH-HEPHER (2)
Josh 19:13 toward the sunrise to G, to Eth-kazin, and going
2Kgs 14:25 son of Amittai, the prophet, who was from G

GATH-RIMMON (4)
Josh 19:45 Gibbethon, Baalath, Jehud, Bene-berak, G,
21:24 with its pasture lands, G with its pasture lands—
21:25 its pasture lands, and G with its pasture lands—
1Chr 6:69 with its pasture lands, G with its pasture lands,

GATHER (144)
Gen 31:46 said to his kinsmen, G stones," and they took
34:30 few, and if they G themselves against me and
41:35 And let them G all the food of these
49:1 his sons, and said, G yourselves together, that I
Ex 3:16 Go and G the elders of Israel together, and
5:7 let them go and G straw for themselves.
5:12 land of Egypt, to G stubble for straw.
16:4 shall go out and G a day's portion every
16:5 as much as they G daily."
16:16 the LORD has commanded: G of it, every man
16:26 Six days you shall G it; but on the
16:27 people went out to G, and they found none.
23:10 sow your land and G in its yield;
23:16 the year, when you G in from the field
Lev 19:9 border, neither shall you G the gleanings after your
19:10 bare, neither shall you G the fallen grapes of
23:22 border, nor shall you G the gleanings after your
25:3 prune your vineyard, and G in its fruits;
25:5 vine you shall not G; it shall be a
25:11 grows of itself, nor G the grapes from the
25:20 may not sow or G in our crop?'
26:25 covenant; and if you G within your cities I
Num 10:3 all the congregation shall G themselves to you at
10:4 tribes of Israel, shall G themselves to you.
11:16 LORD said to Moses, G for me seventy men
19:9 who is clean shall G up the ashes of
21:16 LORD said to Moses, G the people together, and
Deut 4:10 LORD said to me, G the people to me,
11:14 rain, that you may G in your grain and
13:16 You shall G all its spoil into the midst
24:21 When you G the grapes of your vineyard, you
28:38 the field, and shall G little in; for the
28:39 of the wine nor G the grapes; for the
30:3 you, and he will G you again from all
30:4 LORD your God will G you, and from there
Josh 2:18 down; and you shall G into your house your
Judg 4:6 Israel, commands you, 'Go, G your men at Mount
Ruth 2:7 let me glean and G among the sheaves after
1Sam 7:5 Then Samuel said, G all Israel at Mizpah, and
2Sam 3:21 and go, and will G all Israel to my
12:28 Now, then, G the rest of the people together,
1Kgs 18:19 Now therefore send and G all Israel to me
2Kgs 4:39 into the field to G herbs, and found a
22:20 Therefore, behold, I will G you to your fathers,
1Chr 16:35 of our salvation, and G and save us from
22:2 David commanded to G together the aliens who
2Chr 24:5 cities of Judah, and G from all Israel money
34:28 Behold, I will G you to your fathers, and
Neh 1:9 farthest skies, I will G them thence and bring
12:44 and the tithes, to G into them the portions
Tob 13:5 show mercy, and will G us from all the
Esth 2:3 of his kingdom to G all the beautiful young
4:16 reply to Mordecai, "Go, G all the Jews to
8:11 in every city to G and defend their lives,
Job 24:6 They G their fodder in the field and they
34:14 spirit to himself, and G to himself his breath,
Ps 39:6 man heaps up, and knows not who will G
47:9 princes of the peoples G as the people of
50:5 may judge his people: G to me my faithful
102:22 his praise, when peoples G together, and kingdoms,
104:28 givest to them, they G it up; when thou
106:47 LORD our God, and G us from among the
Eccl 3:5 and a time to G stones together; a time
Song 5:1 sister, my bride, I G my myrrh with my
6:2 the gardens, and to G lilies.
Sir 36:11 G all the tribes of Jacob, and give them
Is 10:14 peoples; and as men G eggs that have been
11:12 outcasts of Israel, and G the dispersed of Judah
13:14 sheep with none to G them, every man will
34:15 lay and hatch and G her young in her
40:11 a shepherd, he will G the lambs in his
43:5 the west I will G you;
43:9 Let all the nations G together, and let the
49:18 and see; they all G, they come to you.
54:7 great compassion I will G you.
56:8 of Israel, I will G yet others to him
60:4 and see; they all G together, they come to
62:9 LORD, and those who G it shall drink it
66:18 I am coming to G all nations and tongues;
Jer 3:17 and all nations shall G to it, to the
7:18 The children G wood, the fathers kindle fire, and
8:13 When I would G them, says the LORD, there
8:14 G together, let us go into the fortified cities
9:22 reaper, and none shall G them.'"
10:17 G up your bundle from the ground, O you
23:3 Then I will G the remnant of my flock
29:14 restore your fortunes and G you from all the
31:8 the north country, and G them from the farthest
31:10 who scattered Israel will G him, and will keep
32:37 pestilence: Behold, I will G them from all the
40:10 but as for you, G wine and summer fruits
49:5 him, with none to G the fugitives.
49:14 sent among the nations: G yourselves together and
Ezek 11:17 Lord GOD: I will G you from the peoples,
16:37 therefore, behold, I will G all your lovers, with
16:37 you loathed; I will G them against you from
20:34 from the peoples and G you out of the
20:41 from the peoples, and G you out of the
22:19 therefore, behold, I will G you into the midst
22:20 As men G silver and bronze and iron and
22:20 it; so I will G you in my anger
22:21 I will G you and blow upon you with
28:25 Lord GOD: When I G the house of Israel
29:13 forty years I will G the Egyptians from the
34:13 from the peoples, and G them from the countries,
36:24 from the nations, and G you from all the
37:21 have gone, and will G them from all sides,
39:17 field, 'Assemble and come, G from all sides to
Hos 8:10 nations, I will soon G them up.
9:6 to Assyria; Egypt shall G them, Memphis shall bury
Joel 1:13 G the elders and all the inhabitants of the
2:16 call a solemn assembly; G the people.

	2:16	assemble the elders; G the children, even nursing
	3:2	and Jerusalem, I will G all the nations and
	3:11	you nations round about, G yourselves there.
Mic	2:12	I will surely G all of you, O Jacob,
	2:12	O Jacob, I will G the remnant of Israel;
	4:6	assemble the lame and G those who have been
Nah	3:18	mountains with none to G them.
Hab	1:9	They G captives like sand.
Zeph	3:8	my decision is to G nations, to assemble kingdoms,
	3:19	save the lame and G the outcast, and I
Zech	10:8	signal for them and G them in, for I
	10:10	land of Egypt, and G them from Assyria; and
	14:2	For I will G all the nations against Jerusalem
2Mac	1:27	G together our scattered people, set free those who
	2:18	upon us and will G us from everywhere under
Mt	3:12	his threshing floor and G his wheat into the
	6:26	sow nor reap nor G into barns, and yet
	12:30	he who does not G with me scatters.
	13:28	us to go and G them?'
	13:30	will tell the reapers, G the weeds first and
	13:30	to be burned, but G the wheat into my
	13:41	angels, and they will G out of his kingdom
	24:31	call, and they will G his elect from the
	25:26	have not sowed, and G where I have not
Mk	13:27	out the angels, and G his elect from the
Lk	3:17	threshing floor, and to G the wheat into his
	11:23	he who does not G with me scatters.
Jn	6:12	he told his disciples, G up the fragments left
	11:52	nation only, but to G into one the children
Rev	14:18	in your sickle, and G the clusters of the
	19:17	fly in midheaven, "Come, G for the great supper
	20:8	Gog and Magog, to G them for battle; their

GATHERED (263)

Gen	1:9	under the heavens be G together into one place,
	1:10	the waters that were G together he called Seas.
	12:5	possessions which they had G, and the persons that
	25:8	of years, and was G to his people.
	25:17	and died, and was G to his kindred.)
	29:3	all the flocks were G there, the shepherds would
	29:7	the animals to be G together; water the sheep,
	29:8	all the flocks are G together, and the stone
	29:22	So Laban G together all the men of the
	35:29	he died and was G to his people, old
	37:7	and behold, your sheaves G round it, and bowed
	41:48	forth abundantly, and he G up all the food
	47:14	And Joseph G up all the money that was
	49:29	"I am to be G to my people; bury
	49:33	his last, and was G to his people.
Ex	4:29	and Aaron went and G together all the elders
	8:14	And they G them together in heaps, and the
	16:17	Israel did so; they G, some more, some less.
	16:18	an omer, he that G much had nothing over,
	16:18	over, and he that G little had no lack;
	16:18	had no lack; each G according to what he
	16:21	Morning by morning they G it, each as much
	16:22	the sixth day they G twice as much bread,
	32:1	the people G themselves together to Aaron,
	32:26	the sons of Levi G themselves together to him.
Lev	23:39	month, when you have G in the produce of
Num	10:7	assembly is to be G together, you shall blow,
	11:8	people went about and G it, and ground it
	11:22	of the sea be G together for them, to
	11:24	the LORD; and he G seventy men of the
	11:32	the next day, and G the quails; he who
	11:32	the quails; he who G least gathered ten homers;
	11:32	he who gathered least G ten homers; and they
	14:35	wicked congregation that are G together against me:
	16:11	all your company have G together; what is Aaron
	20:10	And Moses and Aaron G the assembly together
	20:24	Edom, "Aaron shall be G to his people; for
	20:26	and Aaron shall be G to his people, and
	21:23	He G all his men together, and went out
	27:3	company of those who G themselves together
	27:13	you also shall be G to your people, as
	27:13	your brother Aaron was G,
	31:2	afterward you shall be G to your people."
Deut	32:50	you ascend, and be G to your people, as
	32:50	Mount Hor and was G to his people;
	33:5	of the people were G, all the tribes of
Josh	9:2	heard of this, they G together with one accord
	10:5	the king of Eglon, G their forces, and went
	10:6	the hill country are G against us."
	22:12	the people of Israel G at Shiloh, to make
	24:1	Then Joshua G all the tribes of Israel to
Judg	2:10	that generation also were G to their fathers; and
	3:13	He G to himself the Ammonites and the Amalekites,
	9:27	into the field, and G the grapes from their
	9:47	Tower of Shechem were G together.
	11:20	his territory; so Sihon G all his people together,
	12:4	Then Jephthah G all the men of Gilead and
	16:23	lords of the Philistines G to offer a great
	20:11	the men of Israel G against the city, united
1Sam	5:8	So they sent and G together all the lords
	5:11	They sent therefore and G together all the lords
	7:6	So they G at Mizpah, and drew water and
	7:7	people of Israel had G at Mizpah, the lords
	8:4	the elders of Israel G together and came to
	17:1	Now the Philistines G their armies for battle; and
	17:1	battle; and they were G at Socoh, which belongs
	17:2	men of Israel were G, and encamped in the
	20:38	So Jonathan's lad G up the arrows, and came
	22:2	one who was discontented, G to him; and he
	28:1	those days the Philistines G their forces for war,
	28:4	at Shunem; and Saul G all Israel, and they
	29:1	Now the Philistines G all their forces at Aphek;
2Sam	2:25	Benjaminites G themselves together behind Abner,
	2:30	and when he had G all the people together,
	6:1	David again G all the chosen men of Israel,
	10:15	defeated by Israel, they G themselves together.
	10:17	was told David, he G all Israel together, and
	12:29	So David G all the people together and went
	14:14	ground, which cannot be G up again; but God
	17:11	that all Israel be G to you, from Dan
	21:13	son Jonathan; and they G the bones of those
	23:9	the Philistines who were G there for battle, and
	23:11	The Philistines G together at Lehi, where there was
1Kgs	10:26	And Solomon G together chariots and horsemen; he
	11:24	And he G men about him and became leader
	18:20	people of Israel, and G the prophets together at
	20:1	the king of Syria G all his army together;
	22:6	the king of Israel G the prophets together, about
2Kgs	4:39	a wild vine and G from it his lap
	22:20	and you shall be G to your grave in
	23:1	Judah and Jerusalem were G to him.
1Chr	11:1	Then all Israel G together to David at Hebron,
	11:13	when the Philistines were G there for battle.
	15:4	And David G together the sons of Aaron and
	19:17	was told David, he G all Israel together, and
2Chr	1:14	Solomon G together chariots and horsemen; he had
	12:5	of Judah, who had G at Jerusalem because of
	13:7	certain worthless scoundrels G about him and defied
	15:9	And he G all Judah and Benjamin, and those
	15:10	They were G at Jerusalem in the third month
	18:5	the king of Israel G the prophets together, four
	23:2	about through Judah and G the Levites from all
	24:5	And he G the priests and the Levites, and
	28:24	And Ahaz G together the vessels of the house
	29:15	They G their brethren, and sanctified themselves,
	29:20	king rose early and G the officials of the
	32:4	great many people were G, and they stopped all
	32:6	over the people, and G them together to him
	34:28	and you shall be G to your grave in
	34:29	the king sent and G together all the elders
Ezra	3:1	the towns, the people G as one man to
	7:28	upon me, and I G leading men from Israel
	8:15	I G them to the river that runs to
	9:4	of the returned exiles, G round me while I
	10:1	men, women, and children, G to him out of
Neh	5:16	all my servants were G there for the work.
	8:1	And all the people G as one man into
	12:28	sons of the singers G together from the circuit
	13:11	And I G them together and set them in
Tob	13:13	for they will be G together, and will praise
Jud	4:3	of Judea were newly G together, and the sacred
	7:24	women, and the children, G about Uzziah and the
	13:13	fire for light, and G around them.
	15:12	the women of Israel G to see her, and
	16:22	husband died and was G to his people.
Esth	2:8	when many maidens were G in Susa the capital
	2:19	When the virgins were G together the second time,
	9:2	their foes, the Jews G in their cities throughout
	9:15	who were in Susa G also on the fourteenth
	9:16	the king's provinces also G to defend their lives,
	9:18	who were in Susa G on the thirteenth day
	10:8	nations are those that G to destroy the name
Job	15:27	with his fat, and G fat upon his loins,
Ps	7:7	of the peoples be G about thee; and over
	33:7	He G the waters of the sea as in
	35:15	at my stumbling they G in glee, they gathered
	35:15	gathered in glee, they G together against me;
	107:3	redeemed from trouble and G in from the lands,

Prov	27:25	of the mountains is G,
	30:4	Who has G the wind in his fists?
Eccl	2:8	I also G for myself silver and gold and
Sir	21:9	wicked is like tow G together, and their end
	25:3	You have G nothing in your youth; how then
	47:18	God of Israel, you G gold like tin and
	50:5	was when the people G round him as he
Is	10:14	forsaken so I have G all the earth; and
	24:22	They will be G together as prisoners in a
	27:12	and you will be G one by one, O
	33:4	scattered; and spoil is G as the caterpillar gathers;
	34:15	shall the kites be G, each one with her
	34:16	and his Spirit has G them.
	49:5	that Israel might be G to him, for I
	56:8	gather yet others to him besides those already G
	60:7	of Kedar shall be G to you, the rams
Jer	8:2	they shall not be G or buried; they shall
	25:33	not be lamented, or G, or buried; they shall
	26:9	And all the people G about Jeremiah in the
	40:12	at Mizpah; and they G wine and summer fruits
	40:15	the Jews who are G about you would be
Bar	4:37	away; they are coming, G from east and west,
	5:5	and see your children G from west and east,
Ezek	28:4	for yourself, and have G gold and silver into
	29:5	field, and not be G and buried.
	38:8	land where people were G from many nations upon
	38:12	the people who were G from the nations, who
	39:27	from the peoples and G them from their enemies'
	39:28	the nations, and then G them into their own
Dan	3:95	and the king's counselors G together and saw that
	13:28	day, when the people G at the house of
Hos	1:11	of Israel shall be G together, and they shall
	10:10	and nations shall be G against them when they
Mic	1:7	of a harlot she G them, and to the
	4:12	plan, that he has G them as sheaves to
	7:1	summer fruit has been G, as when the vintage
1Mac	1:4	He G a very strong army and ruled over
	2:69	blessed them, and was G to his fathers.
	3:9	of the earth; he G in those who were
	3:10	But Apollonius G together Gentiles and a large force
	3:13	heard that Judas had G a large company, including
	3:27	and he sent and G all the forces of
	5:9	Gentiles in Gilead G together against the Israelites
	5:10	Gentiles around us have G together against us to
	5:15	that against them had G together men of Ptolemais
	5:37	these things Timothy G another army and encamped
	5:38	Gentiles around us have G to him; it is
	5:45	Then Judas G together all the Israelites in Gilead,
	5:64	Men G to them and praised them.
	6:20	They G together and besieged the citadel in the
	10:61	from Israel, lawless men, G together against him to
	11:1	the king of Egypt G great forces, like the
	11:55	Demetrius had cast off G around him, and they
	11:60	the army of Syria G to him as allies.
	12:37	So they G together to build up the city;
	13:6	all the nations have G together out of hatred
	14:7	He G a host of captives; he ruled over
	14:30	high priest, and was G to his people.
2Mac	4:39	spread abroad, the populace G against Lysimachus,
	8:1	faith, and so they G about six thousand men.
	8:16	But Maccabeus G his men together, to the number
	10:21	came to Maccabeus, he G the leaders of the
	10:24	by the Jews before, G a tremendous force of
	11:2	at what had happened, G about eighty thousand men
	14:23	but dismissed the flocks of people that had G
	14:30	So he G not a few of his men,
Mt	7:16	Are grapes G from thorns, or figs from thistles?
	13:2	And great crowds G about him, so that he
	13:40	as the weeds are G and burned with fire,
	13:47	into the sea and G fish of every kind;
	16:9	the five thousand, and how many baskets you G
	16:10	the four thousand, and how many baskets you G
	18:19	two or three are G in my name, there
	22:10	into the streets and G all whom they found,
	22:41	while the Pharisees were G together, Jesus asked
	23:36	often would I have G your children together as
	24:28	the eagles will be G together.
	25:32	Before him will be G all the nations, and
	26:3	elders of the people G in the palace of
	26:57	priest, where the scribes and the elders had G
	27:17	So when they had G, Pilate said to them,
	27:27	the praetorium, and they G the whole battalion befre
	27:62	priests and the Pharisees G before Pilate
Mk	1:33	the whole city was G together about the door.
	2:2	And many were G together, so that there was
	2:13	and all the crowd G about him, and he
	4:1	a very large crowd G about him, so that
	5:21	side, a great crowd G about him; and he
	7:1	Now when the Pharisees G together to him, with
	8:1	a great crowd had G, and they had nothing
	10:1	the Jordan, and crowds G to him again; and
Lk	5:15	him; and great multitudes G to hear and to
	6:44	For figs are not G from thorns, nor are
	12:1	of the multitude had G together that they trod
	13:34	often would I have G your children together as
	15:13	later, the younger son G all he had and
	17:36	the eagles will be G together."
	22:64	elders of the people G together, both chief priests
	24:33	they found the eleven G together and those who
Jn	6:13	So they G them up and filled twelve baskets
	10:24	So the Jews G round him and said to
	11:47	priests and the Pharisees G the council, and said,
	15:6	and the branches are G, thrown into the fire
Acts	4:5	elders and scribes were G together in Jerusalem,
	4:26	and the rulers were G together, against the Lord
	4:27	this city there were G together against thy holy
	4:31	in which they were G together was shaken; and
	5:16	The people also G from the towns around Jerusalem,
	10:27	and found many persons G;
	12:12	Mark, where many were G together and were
	13:44	almost the whole city G together to hear the
	14:20	But when the disciples G about him, he rose
	14:27	when they arrived, they G the church together and
	15:6	and the elders were G together to consider this
	15:30	to Antioch; and having G the congregation together,
	17:5	of the rabble, they G a crowd, set the
	19:25	These he G together, with the workmen of like
	20:7	week, when we were G together to break bread,
	20:8	lights in the upper chamber where we were G
	28:3	Paul had G a bundle of sticks and put
	28:17	and when they had G, he said to them,
2Cor	8:15	is written, "He who G much had nothing over,
	8:15	over, and he who G little had no lack."
Rev	14:19	on the earth and G the vintage of the
	19:19	earth with their armies G to make war against

GATHERING (15)

Num	15:32	they found a man G sticks on the sabbath
	15:33	those who found him G sticks brought him to
2Sam	22:12	canopy, thick clouds, a G of water.
1Kgs	17:10	a widow was there G sticks; and he called
	17:12	and now, I am G a couple of sticks,
Jud	14:6	the men at the G of the people, he
Eccl	2:26	gives the work of G and heaping, only to
Sir	26:5	of a city, the G of a mob, and
Is	13:4	of kingdoms, of nations G together!
1Mac	13:2	up to Jerusalem, and G the people together
2Mac	14:15	Nicanor's coming and the G of the Gentiles, they
Mt	13:29	said, 'No; lest in G the weeds you root
	17:21	As they were G in Galilee, Jesus said to
	25:24	did not sow, and G where you did not
Heb	12:22	innumerable angels in festal G,

GATHERINGS

Jer	6:11	street, and upon the G of young men, also;

GATHERS (18)

Num	19:10	And he who G the ashes of the heifer
Ps	41:6	words, while his heart G mischief; when he goes
	147:2	builds up Jerusalem; he G the outcasts of Israel.
Prov	6:8	food in summer, and G her sustenance in harvest.
	10:5	A son who G in summer is prudent, but
	13:11	dwindle, but he who G little by little will
	28:8	by interest and increase G it for him who
Sir	21:8	is like one who G stones for his burial
Is	17:5	as when the reaper G standing grain and his
	33:4	gathered as the caterpillar G; as locusts leap, men
	56:8	the Lord GOD, who G the outcasts of Israel,
Jer	17:11	Like the partridge that G a brood which she
Hab	1:15	with his net, he G them in his seine;
	2:5	He G for himself all nations, and collects as
2Mac	2:7	be unknown until God G his people together again
Mt	23:36	together as a hen G her brood under her
Lk	13:34	together as a hen G her brood under her
Jn	4:36	reaps receives wages, and G fruit for eternal life,

GAULS

1Mac	8:2	were doing among the G, how they had defeated

GAUNT (7)

Gen	41:3	behold, seven other cows, G and thin, came up
	41:4	And the G and thin cows ate up the

41:19 them, poor and very G and thin, such as
41:20 And the thin and G cows ate up the
41:21 they were still as G as at the beginning.
41:27 The seven lean and G cows that came up
Ps 109:24 are weak through fasting; my body has become G

GAUZE

Is 3:23 handbags; the garments of G, the linen garments, the

GAVE (629)

Gen 2:20 The man G names to all cattle, and to
3:6 ate; and she also G some to her husband,
3:12 be with me, she G me fruit of the
9:3 you; and as I G you the green plants,
12:20 And Pharaoh G men orders concerning him; and
14:20 And Abram G him a tenth of everything.
16:3 Egyptian, her maid, and G her to Abram her
16:5 I G my maid to your embrace, and when
18:7 tender and good, and G it to the servant,
20:14 and female slaves, and G them to Abraham, and
21:14 skin of water, and G it to Hagar, putting
21:19 skin with water, and G the lad a drink.
21:27 sheep and oxen and G them to Abimelech, and
24:18 upon her hand, and G him a drink.
24:32 ungirded the camels, and G him straw and provender
24:46 I drank, and she G the camels drink also.
24:53 gold, and raiment, and G them to Rebekah; he
24:53 to Rebekah; he also G to her brother and
25:5 Abraham G all he had to Isaac.
25:6 of his concubines Abraham G gifts, and while he
25:34 Then Jacob G Esau bread and pottage of lentils,
26:18 of Abraham; and he G them the names which
27:17 his neck; and she G the savory food and
28:4 your sojournings which God G to Abraham!"
29:24 (Laban G his maid Zilpah to his daughter Leah
29:28 her week; then Laban G him his daughter Rachel
29:29 (Laban G his maid Bilhah to his daughter Rachel
30:4 So she G him her maid Bilhah as a
30:9 her maid Zilpah and G her to Jacob as
30:18 my hire because I G my maid to my
35:4 So they G to Jacob all the foreign gods
35:12 The land which I G to Abraham and Isaac
38:18 So he G them to her, and went in
39:21 him steadfast love, and G him favor in the
41:45 name Zaphenath-paneah; and he G him in marriage
42:25 And Joseph G orders to fill their bags with
45:21 did so; and Joseph G them wagons, according to
45:21 command of Pharaoh, and G them provisions for the
45:22 all of them he G festal garments; but to
45:22 but to Benjamin he G three hundred shekels of
46:18 of Zilpah, whom Laban G to Leah his daughter;
46:25 of Bilhah, whom Laban G to Rachel his daughter,
47:11 and his brothers, and G them a possession in
47:17 to Joseph; and Joseph G them food in exchange
47:22 the allowance which Pharaoh G them; therefore they
50:16 Joseph, saying, "Your father G this command before
Ex 1:20 midwives feared God he G them families.
2:21 the man, and he G Moses his daughter Zipporah.
6:13 Moses and Aaron, and G them a charge to
11:3 And the LORD G the people favor in the
18:24 So Moses G heed to the voice of his
31:18 And he G to Moses, when he had made
32:24 it off'; so they G it to me, and
34:32 came near, and he G them in commandment all
36:6 So Moses G command, and word was proclaimed
Num 3:51 the sanctuary; and Moses G the redemption money
7:6 and the oxen, and G them to the Levites.
7:7 and four oxen he G to the sons of
7:8 and eight oxen he G to the sons of
7:9 sons of Kohath he G none, because they were
15:23 day that the LORD G commandment, and onward
17:6 and all their leaders G him rods, one for
21:3 voice of Israel, and G over the Canaanites; and
22:7 came to Balaam, and G him Balak's message.
31:41 And Moses G the tribute, which was the offering
31:47 and of beasts, and G them to the Levites
32:28 So Moses G command concerning them to Eleazar
32:33 And Moses G to them, to the sons of
32:38 and Sibmah; and they G other names to the
32:40 And Moses G Gilead to Machir the son of
Deut 2:12 possession, which the LORD G to them.)
2:33 the LORD our God G him over to us;
2:36 the LORD our God G all into our hands.
3:3 the LORD our God G into our hand Og
3:12 at that time, I G to the Reubenites and
3:13 region of Argob, I G to the half-tribe of
3:15 day.) To Machir I G Gilead,
3:16 and the Gadites I G the territory from Gilead
5:22 tables of stone, and G them to me.
9:10 And the LORD G me the two tables of
9:11 forty nights the LORD G me the two tables
10:4 assembly; and the LORD G them to me.
22:16 to the elders, 'I G my daughter to this
26:9 into this place and G us this land, a
29:8 took their land, and G it for an inheritance
31:9 wrote this law, and G it to the priests
32:8 When the Most High G to the nations their
32:18 forgot the God who G you birth.
Josh 1:14 the land which Moses G you beyond the Jordan;
1:15 servant of the LORD G you beyond the Jordan
10:12 day when the LORD G the Amorites over to
10:30 Libnah; and the LORD G it also and its
10:32 it: and the LORD G Lachish into the hand
11:8 And the LORD G them into the hand of
11:23 to Moses; and Joshua G it for an inheritance
12:6 servant of the LORD G their land for a
12:7 toward Seir (and Joshua G their land to the
13:8 inheritance, which Moses G them, beyond the Jordan
13:8 servant of the LORD G them:
13:14 of Levi alone Moses G no inheritance; the offerings
13:15 And Moses G an inheritance to the tribe of
13:24 And Moses G an inheritance also to the tribe
13:29 And Moses G an inheritance to the half-tribe of
13:33 tribe of Levi Moses G no inheritance; the LORD
14:3 to the Levites he G no inheritance among them.
14:13 blessed him; and he G Hebron to Caleb the
15:13 LORD to Joshua, he G to Caleb the son
15:17 took it; and he G him Achsah his daughter
15:19 And Caleb G her the upper springs and the
17:4 of the LORD he G them an inheritance among
18:7 servant of the LORD G them."
19:49 the people of Israel G an inheritance among them
19:50 of the LORD they G him the city which
21:3 the people of Israel G to the Levites the
21:8 the people of Israel G by lot to the
21:9 tribe of Simeon they G the following cities
21:11 They G them Kiriath-arba (Arba being the father of
21:13 Aaron the priest they G Hebron, the city of
21:43 Thus the LORD G to Israel all the land
21:44 And the LORD G them rest on every side
22:4 servant of the LORD G you on the other
24:3 I G him Isaac;
24:4 and to Isaac I G Jacob and Esau.
24:4 And I G Esau the hill country of Seir
24:8 with you, and I G them into your hand,
24:11 the Jebusites; and I G them into your hand.
24:13 I G you a land on which you had
Judg 1:4 up and the LORD G the Canaanites and the
1:13 took it; and he G him Achsah his daughter
1:15 And Caleb G her the upper springs and the
2:14 against Israel, and he G them over to plunderers,
3:6 their own daughters they G to their sons; and
3:10 LORD G Cushan-rishathaim king of Mesopotamia
4:19 skin of milk and G him a drink and
5:25 asked water and she G him milk, she brought
6:1 LORD; and the LORD G them into the hand
6:9 out before you, and G you their land;
9:4 And they G him seventy pieces of silver out
11:21 the God of Israel, G Sihon and all his
11:32 them; and the LORD G them into his hand.
12:3 Ammonites, and the LORD G them into my hand;
12:9 and thirty daughters he G in marriage outside his
13:1 LORD; and the LORD G them into the hand
14:9 father and mother, and G some to them, and
14:19 took their spoil and G the festal garments to
15:2 hated her; so I G her to your companion.
17:4 pieces of silver, and G it to the silversmith,
19:21 into his house, and G the asses provender; and
20:36 The men of Israel G ground to Benjamin, because
21:14 that time; and they G them the women whom
Ruth 2:18 also brought out and G her what food she
3:17 measures of barley he G to me, for he
4:7 off his sandal and G it to the other,
4:13 her, and the LORD G her conception, and she
4:17 women of the neighborhood G him a name, saying,
1Sam 2:28 before me; and I G to the house of
4:5 the camp, all Israel G a mighty shout, so
4:19 dead, she bowed and G birth; for her pains
9:22 into the hall and G them a place at
9:23 "Bring the portion I G you, of which I
10:9 to leave Samuel, God G him another heart; and
18:4 was upon him, and G it to David, and

G

18:27 And Saul G him his daughter Michal for a
20:40 And Jonathan G his weapons to his lad, and
21:6 So the priest G him the holy bread; for
22:10 LORD for him, and G him provisions, and gave
22:10 gave him provisions, and G him the sword of
23:13 escaped from Keilah, he G up the expedition.
24:10 seen how the LORD G you today into my
26:23 faithfulness; for the LORD G you into my hand
27:6 So that day Achish G him Ziklag; therefore Ziklag
30:11 to David; and they G him bread and he
30:11 and he ate, they G him water to drink,
30:12 to drink, and they G him a piece of
2Sam 4:10 was the reward I G him for his news.
8:6 And the LORD G victory to David wherever he
8:14 And the LORD G victory to David wherever he
12:8 of Saul; and I G you your master's house,
12:8 into your bosom, and G you the house of
13:25 would not go but G him his blessing.
16:23 the counsel which Ahithophel G was as if one
18:5 heard when the king G orders to all the
19:23 And the king G him his oath.
21:9 the Meholathite; and he G them into the hands
22:48 salvation, the God who G me vengeance and brought
24:9 And Joab G the sum of the numbering of
1Kgs 3:17 same house; and I G birth to a child
3:18 delivered, this woman also G birth; and we were
4:29 God G Solomon wisdom and understanding beyond
5:11 he desired, while Solomon G Hiram twenty thousand
5:11 Solomon G this to Hiram year by year.
5:12 And the LORD G Solomon wisdom, as he promised
9:11 he desired, King Solomon G to Hiram twenty cities
10:10 Then she G the king a hundred and twenty
10:10 the queen of Sheba G to King Solomon.
10:13 And King Solomon G to the queen of Sheba
11:18 king of Egypt, who G him a house, and
11:18 allowance of food, and G him land.
11:19 Pharaoh, so that he G him in marriage the
11:28 man was industrious he G him charge over all
12:8 which the old men G him, and took counsel
13:3 And he G a sign the same day, saying,
14:8 house of David and G it to you; and
14:15 good land which he G to their fathers, and
15:4 the LORD his God G him a lamp in
15:18 the king's house, and G them into the hands
19:21 of the oxen, and G it to the people,
2Kgs 10:15 So he G him his hand.
11:12 crown upon him, and G him the testimony; and
13:3 against Israel, and he G them continually into the
13:5 (Therefore the LORD G Israel a savior, so that
15:12 the LORD which he G to Jehu, "Your sons
15:19 the land; and Menahem G Pul a thousand talents
17:15 the warnings which he G them.
17:20 and afflicted them, and G them into the hand
18:15 And Hezekiah G him all the silver that was
18:16 Judah had overlaid and G it to the king
21:8 the land which I G to their fathers, if
22:8 And Hilkiah G the book to Shaphan, and he
23:35 And Jehoiakim G the silver and the gold to
24:12 the king of Judah G himself up to the
25:28 kindly to him, and G him a seat above
1Chr 2:35 So Sheshan G his daughter in marriage to Jarha
6:55 lot, to them they G Hebron in the land
6:56 and its villages they G to Caleb the son
6:57 sons of Aaron they G the cities of refuge:
6:64 the people of Israel G the Levites the cities
6:65 They also G them by lot out of the
11:10 David's mighty men, who G him strong support in
14:12 gods there, and David G command, and they were
18:6 And the LORD G victory to David wherever he
18:13 And the LORD G victory to David wherever he
21:5 And Joab G the sum of the numbering of
21:17 it not I who G command to number the
28:11 Then David G Solomon his son the plan of
29:7 They G for the service of the house of
29:8 whoever had precious stones G them to the treasury
29:25 And the LORD G Solomon great repute in the
2Chr 7:3 pavement, and worshiped and G thanks to the LORD,
9:9 Then she G the king a hundred and twenty
9:9 the queen of Sheba G to King Solomon.
9:12 And King Solomon G to the queen of Sheba
10:8 which the old men G him, and took counsel
11:23 fortified cities; and he G them abundant provisions,
13:5 LORD God of Israel G the kingship over Israel
13:16 before Judah, and God G them into their hand.
14:6 years, for the LORD G him peace.
15:15 them, and the LORD G them rest round about.
16:8 on the LORD, he G them into your hand.
20:30 quiet, for his God G him rest round about.
21:3 Their father G them great gifts, of silver, gold,
21:3 in Judah; but he G the kingdom to Jehoram,
23:11 crown upon him, and G him the testimony; and
24:12 the king and Jehoiada G it to those who
27:5 And the Ammonites G him that year a hundred
28:5 the LORD his God G him into the hand
28:9 angry with Judah, he G them into your hand,
28:15 them; they clothed them, G them sandals, provided
28:21 of the princes, and G tribute to the king
30:24 Hezekiah king of Judah G the assembly a thousand
30:24 offerings, and the princes G the assembly a thousand
31:5 the people of Israel G in abundance the first
32:22 his enemies; and he G them rest on every
32:24 he answered him and G him a sign.
33:10 his people, but they G no heed.
34:10 house of the LORD G it for repairing and
34:11 They G it to the carpenters and the builders
34:15 the LORD"; and Hilkiah G the book to Shaphan.
35:8 the house of God, G to the priests for
35:9 chiefs of the Levites, G to the Levites for
36:17 man or aged; he G them all into his
Ezra 2:69 to their ability they G to the treasury of
3:7 So they G money to the masons and the
5:3 to them thus, "Who G you a decree to
5:9 to them thus, 'Who G you a decree to
5:12 God of heaven, he G them into the hand
7:11 letter which King Artaxerxes G to Ezra the priest,
Neh 2:1 up the wine and G it to the king.
2:9 Beyond the River, and G them the king's letters.
7:2 had been appointed, I G my brother Hanani and
7:70 heads of fathers' houses G to the work.
7:70 The governor G to the treasury a thousand darics
7:71 heads of fathers' houses G into the treasury of
7:72 rest of the people G was twenty thousand darics
8:8 God, clearly; and they G the sense, so that
12:31 two great companies which G thanks and went in
12:38 company of those who G thanks went to the
12:40 companies of those who G thanks stood in the
12:47 the days of Nehemiah G the daily portions for
13:9 Then I G orders and they cleansed the chambers;
13:19 should be shut and G orders that they should
Tob 1:13 Then the Most High G me favor and good
2:12 her wages, they also G her a kid;
5:3 Then Tobit G him the receipt, and said to
7:13 by the hand he G her to Tobias to
8:19 After this he G a wedding feast for them
9:5 He G him the receipt, and Gabael brought out
9:5 their seals intact and G them to him.
10:10 So Raguel arose and G him his wife Sarah
11:17 And Tobit G thanks before them that God had
14:2 He G alms, and he continued to fear the
14:10 Ahikar G alms and escaped the deathtrap which
14:11 years old; and Tobias G him a magnificent funeral.
14:13 honor, and he G his father-in-law and mother-in-law
Jud 6:21 his own house and G a banquet for the
7:16 his servants, and he G orders to do as
10:5 And she G her maid a bottle of wine
10:5 all her vessels and G them to her to
13:9 she went out, and G Holofernes' head to her
15:11 They G Judith the tent of Holofernes and all
15:12 in her hands and G them to the women
16:19 from his bedchamber she G as a votive offering
Esth 1:3 of his reign he G a banquet for all
1:5 were completed, the king G for all the people
1:9 Queen Vashti also G a banquet for the women
2:18 Then the king G a great banquet to all
2:18 to the provinces, and G gifts with royal liberality.
3:10 from his hand and G it to Haman the
4:8 Mordecai also G him a copy of the written
4:10 spoke to Hathach and G him a message for
6:1 not sleep; and he G orders to bring the
8:1 that day King Ahasuerus G to Queen Esther the
8:2 taken from Haman, and G it to Mordecai.
9:25 before the king, he G orders in writing that
9:29 and Mordecai the Jew G full written authority,
Job 1:21 I return; the LORD G, and the LORD has
28:25 When he G to the wind its weight, and
32:12 I G you my attention, and, behold, there was
34:13 Who G him charge over the earth and who
42:10 friends; and the LORD G Job twice as much
42:11 and each of them G him a piece of
42:15 daughters; and their father G them inheritance
Ps 18:47 salvation, the God who G me vengeance and subdued
69:21 They G me poison for food, and for my

	69:21	for my thirst they G me vinegar to drink.
	77:17	out water; the skies G forth thunder; thy arrows
	78:15	in the wilderness, and G them drink abundantly as
	78:24	manna to eat, and G them the grain of
	78:29	well filled, for he G them what they craved.
	78:46	He G their crops to the caterpillar, and the
	78:48	He G over their cattle to the hail, and
	78:50	them from death, but G their lives over to
	78:62	He G his people over to the sword, and
	81:12	So I G them over to their stubborn hearts,
	99:7	the statutes that he G them.
	105:32	He G them hail for rain, and lightning that
	105:40	he brought quails, and G them bread from heaven
	105:44	And he G them the lands of the nations;
	106:15	in the desert; he G them what they asked,
	106:41	abhorred his heritage; he G them into the hand
	135:12	kingdoms of Canaan, and G their land as a
	136:21	endures for ever; and G their land as a
Eccl	2:20	I turned about and G my heart up to
	12:7	returns to God who G it.
Song	1:12	his couch, my nard G forth its fragrance.
	3:1	called him, but he G no answer.
	5:6	called him, but he G no answer.
Wis	7:17	it is he who G me unerring knowledge of
	8:21	possess wisdom unless God G her to me–
	10:2	from his transgression, and G him strength to rule
	10:10	kingdom of God, and G him knowledge of angels;
	10:12	his arduous contest she G him the victory, so
	10:14	be false, and she G him everlasting honor.
	10:17	She G holy men the reward of their labors;
Sir	17:2	He G to men few days, a limited time,
	17:5	tongue and eyes; he G them ears and a
	17:12	And he G commandment to each of them concerning
	24:8	Creator of all things G me a commandment, and
	24:11	beloved city likewise he G me a resting place,
	24:15	and camel's thorn I G forth the aroma of
	38:6	And he G skill to men that he might
	44:23	To Isaac also he G the same assurance for
	44:24	with his blessings, and G him his inheritance; he
	45:3	He G him commands for his people, and showed
	45:5	the thick darkness, and G him the commandments
	45:7	covenant with him, and G him the priesthood of
	45:17	In his commandments he G him authority and
	45:20	glory to Aaron and G him a heritage; he
	45:21	the Lord, which he G to him and his
	46:9	And the Lord G Caleb strength, which remained with
	47:5	Most High, and he G him strength in his
	47:8	that he did he G thanks to the Holy
	47:10	He G beauty to the feasts, and arranged their
	47:11	power for ever; he G him the covenant of
	47:13	of peace, and God G him rest on every
	47:22	loved him; so he G a remnant to Jacob,
	47:23	Israel to sin and G Ephraim a sinful way.
	49:5	an end; for they G their power to others,
	51:22	The Lord G me a tongue as my reward,
Is	42:24	Who G up Jacob to the spoiler, and Israel
	47:6	profaned my heritage; I G them into your hand,
	50:6	I G my back to the smiters, and my
	63:14	Spirit of the LORD G them rest.
	66:7	was in labor she G birth; before her pain
Jer	2:27	to a stone, 'You G me birth.' For they
	3:18	the land that I G your fathers for a
	7:7	the land that I G of old to your
	7:14	the place which I G to you and to
	7:23	But this command I G them, 'Obey my voice,
	8:13	withered, and what I G them has passed away
	16:15	own land which I G to their fathers.
	17:4	your heritage which I G to you, and I
	23:39	the city which I G to you and your
	24:10	the land which I G to them and their
	30:3	the land which I G to their fathers, and
	32:12	open copy; and I G the deed of purchase
	35:14	the son of Rechab G to his sons, to
	35:15	the land which I G to you and your
	35:16	command which their father G them, but this people
	36:32	took another scroll and G it to Baruch the
	37:21	So King Zedekiah G orders, and they committed
	39:10	who owned nothing, and G them vineyards and fields
	39:11	king of Babylon G command concerning Jeremiah
	40:5	captain of the guard G him an allowance of
	44:30	his life, as I G Zedekiah king of Judah
	52:32	kindly to him, and G him a seat above
Lam	1:14	to fail; the Lord G me into the hands
	4:11	The LORD G full vent to his wrath, he
Bar	2:4	And he G them into subjection to all the
	2:21	the land which I G to your fathers.

	3:36	way to knowledge, and G her to Jacob his
Ezek	3:2	my mouth, and he G me the scroll to
	16:19	my bread which I G you–I fed you
	16:33	all harlots; but you G your gifts to all
	16:34	the harlot; and you G hire, while no hire
	16:36	your children that you G to them,
	17:18	the covenant, because he G his hand and yet
	20:11	I G them my statutes and showed them my
	20:12	Moreover I G them my sabbaths, as a sign
	20:25	Moreover I G them statutes that were not good
	27:10	helmet in you; they G you splendor.
	28:25	own land which I G to my servant Jacob.
	35:5	cherished perpetual enmity, and G over the people of
	36:5	against all Edom, who G my land to themselves
	36:28	the land which I G to your fathers; and
	37:25	fathers dwelt that I G to my servant Jacob;
	39:23	face from them and G them into the hand
Dan	1:2	And the Lord G Jehoiakim king of Judah into
	1:7	chief of the eunuchs G them names: Daniel he
	1:9	And God G Daniel favor and compassion in the
	1:16	were to drink, and G them vegetables.
	1:17	these four youths, God G them learning and skill
	2:48	Then the king G Daniel high honors and many
	5:6	alarmed him; his limbs G way, and his knees
	5:18	the Most High God G Nebuchadnezzar your father
	5:19	the greatness that he G him, all peoples, nations,
	6:10	day and prayed and G thanks before his God,
	14:22	them to death, and G Bel over to Daniel,
Hos	2:8	it was I who G her the grain, the
	12:10	and through the prophets G parables.
Amos	4:6	"I G you cleanness of teeth in all your
Hab	3:10	swept on; the deep G forth its voice, it
Mal	2:5	and peace, and I G them to him, that
1Mac	2:24	He G vent to righteous anger; he ran and
	3:28	opened his coffers and G a year's pay to
	3:34	and the elephants, and G him orders about all
	3:54	sounded the trumpets and G a loud shout.
	4:50	the lampstand, and these G light in the temple.
	5:19	guard it; and he G them this command, "Take
	5:42	at the stream and G them this command, "Permit
	6:15	He G him the crown and his robe and
	6:44	So he G his life to save his people
	6:57	So he quickly G orders to depart, and said
	6:61	king and the commanders G them their oath.
	6:62	he had sworn and G orders to tear down
	8:8	took from him and G to Eumenes the king.
	9:54	the second month, Alcimus G orders to tear down
	10:6	So Demetrius G him authority to recruit troops, to
	10:58	met him, and Ptolemy G him Cleopatra his daughter
	10:60	the two kings; he G them and their friends
	10:62	The king G orders to take off Jonathan's garments
	10:89	He also G him Ekron and all its environs
	11:10	now regret that I G him my daughter, for
	11:12	away from him and G her to Demetrius.
	11:23	Jonathan heard this, he G orders to continue the
	12:4	And the Romans G them letters to the people
	12:25	of Hamath, for he G them no opportunity to
	12:43	his friends, and he G him gifts and commanded
	14:8	in peace; the ground G its increase, and the
	14:48	And they G orders to inscribe this decree upon
	15:33	the king, but Simon G him this reply: "We
	15:38	the coastal country, and G him troops of infantry
	16:15	he had built; he G them a great banquet,
2Mac	4:32	of the temple and G them to Andronicus; other
	4:34	him sworn pledges and G him his right hand,
	7:3	into a rage, and G orders that pans and
	7:22	was not I who G you life and breath,
	8:23	the holy book, and G the watchword, "God's help";
	8:28	After the sabbath they G some of the spoils
	9:18	come upon him, he G up all hope for
	12:5	on his countrymen, he G orders to his men
	13:15	He G his men the watchword, "God's victory," and
	13:21	ranks of the Jews, G secret information to the
	13:22	the people in Bethzur, G pledges, received theirs,
	15:10	aroused their courage, he G his orders, at the
	15:15	his right hand and G to Judas a golden
	15:15	sword, and as he G it he addressed him
Mt	8:18	crowds around him, he G orders to go over
	10:1	his twelve disciples and G them authority over
	14:19	blessed, and broke and G the loaves to the
	14:19	disciples, and the disciples G them to the crowds.
	15:36	he broke them and G them to the disciples,
	15:36	disciples, and the disciples G them to the crowds.
	21:23	these things, and who G you this authority?"
	22:2	to a king who G a marriage feast for
	25:15	property; to one he G five talents, to another

	25:35	was hungry and you G me food, I was
	25:35	was thirsty and you G me drink, I was
	25:42	was hungry and you G me no food, I
	25:42	was thirsty and you G me no drink,
	26:26	and broke it, and G it to the disciples
	26:27	had given thanks he G it to them, saying,
	27:10	of Israel, and they G them for the potter's
	27:14	But he G him no answer, not even to
	27:48	on a reed, and G it to him to
	28:12	and taken counsel, they G a sum of money
Mk	2:26	to eat, and also G it to those who
	5:13	So he G them leave.
	6:7	two by two, and G them authority over the
	6:21	Herod on his birthday G a banquet for his
	6:27	of the guard and G orders to bring his
	6:28	on a platter, and G it to the girl;
	6:28	girl; and the girl G it to her mother.
	6:41	broke the loaves, and G them to the disciples
	8:6	he broke them and G them to his disciples
	11:27	these things, or who G you this authority to
	14:22	and broke it, and G it to them, and
	14:23	had given thanks he G it to them, and
	15:35	on a reed and G it to him to
Lk	1:57	be delivered, and she G birth to a son.
	2:7	And she G birth to her first-born son and
	2:38	that very hour she G thanks to God, and
	4:20	closed the book, and G it back to the
	6:4	to eat, and also G it to those with
	7:15	And he G him to his mother.
	7:44	entered your house, you G me no water for
	7:45	You G me no kiss, but from the time
	8:32	So he G them leave.
	9:1	the twelve together and G them power and authority
	9:16	and broke them, and G them to the disciples
	9:42	healed the boy, and G him back to his
	10:35	out two denarii and G them to the innkeeper,
	14:16	him, "A man once G a great banquet, and
	15:16	ate; and no one G him anything.
	15:29	command; yet you never G me a kid, that
	18:43	when they saw it, G praise to God.
	19:13	of his servants, he G them ten pounds, and
	20:2	who it is that G you this authority."
	22:19	he broke it and G it to them, saying,
	23:23	So Pilate G sentence that their demand should be
	23:28	the breasts that never G suck!'
	24:30	and broke it, and G it to them.
	24:42	They G him a piece of broiled fish,
Jn	1:12	in his name, he G power to become children
	3:16	the world that he G his only Son, that
	4:5	the field that Jacob G to his son Joseph.
	4:12	our father Jacob, who G us the well, and
	6:31	it is written, 'He G them bread from heaven
	6:32	was not Moses who G you the bread from
	7:22	Moses G you circumcision (not that it is from
	13:26	dipped the morsel, he G it to Judas, the
	19:9	But Jesus G no answer.
	19:30	bowed his head and G up his spirit.
	19:38	of Jesus, and Pilate G him leave.
	21:13	took the bread and G it to them, and
Acts	2:4	tongues, as the Spirit G them utterance.
	3:25	the covenant which God G to your fathers, saying
	4:33	great power the apostles G their testimony to the
	7:5	now living; yet he G him no inheritance in
	7:8	this place.' And he G him the covenant of
	7:10	all his afflictions, and G him favor and wisdom
	7:42	But God turned and G them over to worship
	8:6	multitudes with one accord G heed to what was
	8:10	They all G heed to him, from the least
	8:11	And they G heed to him, because for a
	9:41	And he G her his hand and lifted her
	10:2	with all his household, G alms liberally to the
	11:17	Spirit.' If then God G the same gift to
	11:17	to them as he G to us when we
	13:19	land of Canaan, he G them their land as
	13:20	And after that he G them judges until Samuel
	13:21	a king; and God G them Saul the son
	14:17	he did good and G you from heaven rains
	15:3	the Gentiles, and they G great joy to all
	15:24	your minds, although we G them no instructions,
	16:22	garments off them and G orders to beat them
	24:22	Then he G orders to the centurion that he
	25:15	elders of the Jews G information about him, asking
	27:3	treated Paul kindly, and G him leave to go
	27:15	face the wind, we G way to it and
Rom	1:24	Therefore God G them up in the lusts of
	1:26	For this reason God G them up to dishonorable
	1:27	and the men likewise G up natural relations with
	1:28	to acknowledge God, God G them up to a
	4:20	his faith as he G glory to God,
	8:32	his own Son but G him up for us
	11:8	it is written, "God G them a spirit of
1Cor	3:6	Apollos watered, but God G the growth.
	13:11	became a man, I G up childish ways.
2Cor	5:18	us to himself and G us the ministry of
	8:3	For they G according to their means, as I
	8:5	expected, but first they G themselves to the Lord
	10:8	authority, which the Lord G for building you up
Gal	1:4	Lord Jesus Christ, who G himself for our sins
	2:9	reputed to be pillars, G to me and Barnabas
	2:20	who loved me and G himself for me.
	3:18	by promise; but God G it to Abraham by
Eph	4:8	of captives, and he G gifts to men."
	5:2	Christ loved us and G himself up for us,
	5:25	loved the church and G himself up for her,
1Thes	4:2	know what instructions we G you through the Lord
2Thes	2:16	who loved us and G us eternal comfort and
	3:10	were with you, we G you this command: If
1Tim	2:6	man Christ Jesus, who G himself as a ransom
2Tim	1:9	the grace which he G us in Christ Jesus
	4:17	stood by me and G me strength to proclaim
Tit	2:14	Savior Jesus Christ, who G himself for us to
Heb	7:4	Abraham the patriarch G him a tithe of the
	11:22	of the Israelites and G directions concerning his
Jas	5:18	again and the heaven G rain, and the earth
1Pet	1:21	from the dead and G him glory, so that
1Jn	5:11	the testimony, that God G us eternal life, and
Rev	1:1	Jesus Christ, which God G him to show to
	2:21	I G her time to repent, but she refuses
	11:13	rest were terrified and G glory to the God
	13:2	to it the dragon G his power and his
	15:7	the four living creatures G the seven angels seven
	20:13	And the sea G up the dead in it,
	20:13	it, Death and Hades G up the dead in

GAVEST (26)

Gen	3:12	"The woman whom thou G to be with me,
1Kgs	8:34	the land which thou G to their fathers.
	8:40	the land which thou G to our fathers.
	8:48	their land, which thou G to their fathers, the
2Chr	6:25	the land which thou G to them and to
	6:31	the land which thou G to our fathers.
	6:38	their land, which thou G to their fathers, the
Neh	9:20	Thou G thy good Spirit to instruct them, and
	9:20	from their mouth, and G them water for their
	9:35	great goodness which thou G them, and in the
	9:36	the land that thou G to our fathers to
Tob	3:4	thy commandments, and thou G us over to plunder,
	8:6	Thou madest Adam and G him Eve his wife
Jud	9:2	Simeon, to whom thou G a sword to take
	9:3	So thou G up their rulers to be slain,
	9:4	their thrones; and thou G their wives for a
Ps	21:4	life of thee; thou G it to him, length
Wis	11:7	slay the infants, thou G them abundant water
	12:10	little by little thou G them a chance to
	12:21	to whose fathers thou G oaths and covenants full
Jer	32:22	great terror; and thou G them this land, which
Jn	17:4	the work which thou G me to do;
	17:6	the men whom thou G me out of the
	17:6	they were, and thou G them to me, and
	17:8	the words which thou G me, and they have
	18:9	"Of those whom thou G me I lost not

GAYEST

Jud	10:3	arrayed herself in her G apparel, which she used

GAZA (25)

Gen	10:19	Gerar, as far as G, and in the direction
Deut	2:23	villages as far as G, the Caphtorim, who came
Josh	10:41	them from Kadesh-barnea to G, and all the country
	11:22	of Israel; only in G, in Gath, and in
	13:3	the Philistines, those of G, Ashdod, Ashkelon, Gath,
	15:47	towns and its villages; G, its towns and its
Judg	1:18	Judah also took G with its territory, and Ashkelon
	6:4	as the neighborhood of G, and leave no sustenance
	16:1	Samson went to G, and there he saw a
	16:21	brought him down to G, and bound him with
1Sam	6:17	for Ashdod, one for G, one for Ashkelon, one
1Kgs	4:24	Euphrates from Tiphsah to G, over all the kings
2Kgs	18:8	Philistines as far as G and its territory, from
Jer	25:20	of the Philistines (Ashkelon, G, Ekron, and the
	47:1	concerning the Philistines, before Pharaoh smote G
	47:5	Baldness has come upon G, Ashkelon has perished.

Amos 1:6 "For three transgressions of G, and for four, I
1:7 upon the wall of G, and it shall devour
Zeph 2:4 For G shall be deserted, and Ashkelon shall become
Zech 9:5 it, and be afraid; G too, and shall writhe
9:5 king shall perish from G; Ashkelon shall be
1Mac 11:61 there he departed to G, but the men of
11:61 but the men of G shut him out.
11:62 Then the people of G pleaded with Jonathan, and
Acts 8:26 the road that goes down from Jerusalem to G

GAZARA (13)

1Mac 4:15 They pursued them to G, and to the plains
7:45 Adasa as far as G, and as they followed
9:52 city of Bethzur, and G, and the citadel, and
13:43 days Simon encamped against G and surrounded it
13:53 of all the forces, and he dwelt in G
14:7 captives; he ruled over G and Bethzur and the
14:34 by the sea, and G, which is on the
15:28 control of Joppa and G and the citadel in
15:35 As for Joppa and G, which you demand, they
16:1 John went up from G and reported to Simon
16:19 sent other men to G to do away with
16:21 reported to John at G that his father and
2Mac 10:32 to a stronghold called G, especially well garrisoned,

GAZE (9)

Ex 19:21 to the LORD to G and many of them
2Kgs 8:11 And he fixed his G and stared at him,
Prov 4:26 directly forward, and your G be straight before you.
Song 1:6 Do not G at me because I am swarthy,
Is 47:13 divide the heavens, who G at the stars, who
Mic 4:11 and let our eyes G upon Zion."
Hab 2:15 makes them drunk, to G on their shame!
Acts 3:4 And Peter directed his G at him, with John,
Rev 11:9 and tongues and nations G at their dead bodies

GAZED (3)

Gen 24:21 The man G at her in silence to learn
Judg 5:28 the mother of Sisera G through the lattice: 'Why
Acts 7:55 of the Holy Spirit, G into heaven and saw

GAZELLE (13)

Deut 12:15 it, as of the G and as of the
12:22 Just as the G or the hart is eaten,
14:5 goat, the hart, the G, the roebuck, the wild
15:22 though it were a G or a hart.
2Sam 2:18 foot as a wild G;
Prov 6:5 save yourself like a G from the hunter, like
Song 2:9 beloved is like a G, or a young stag.
2:17 beloved, be like a G, or a young stag
4:5 fawns, twins of a G, that feed among the
7:3 breasts are like two fawns, twins of a G
8:14 and be like a G or a young stag
Sir 27:20 has escaped like a G from a snare.
Is 13:14 And like a hunted G, or like sheep with

GAZELLES (4)

1Kgs 4:23 hundred sheep, besides harts, G, roebucks, and fatted
1Chr 12:8 who were swift as G upon the mountains:
Song 2:7 of Jerusalem, by the G or the hinds of
3:5 of Jerusalem, by the G or the hinds of

GAZEZ (2)

1Chr 2:46 bore Haran, Moza, and G; and Haran was the
2:46 and Gazez; and Haran was the father of G

GAZING (6)

Song 2:9 stands behind our wall, G in at the windows,
Wis 19:8 as one nation, after G on marvelous wonders.
Sir 41:21 or gift, and of G at another man's wife;
Lk 22:54 in the light and G at him, said, "This
Acts 1:10 And while they were G into heaven as he
6:15 And G at him, all who sat in the

GAZINGSTOCK

Nah 3:6 treat you with contempt, and make you a G

GAZITES

Judg 16:2 The G were told, "Samson has come here," and

GAZZAM (2)

Ezra 2:48 Nekoda, the sons of G,
Neh 7:51 Nekoda, the sons of G, the sons of Uzza,

GE-HARASHIM

1Chr 4:14 Joab the father of G, so-called because they were

GEAR

Acts 27:17 Syrtis, they lowered the G, and so were driven.

GEBA (19)

Josh 18:24 Ophrah, Chephar-ammoni, Ophni, G -- twelve cities
21:17 with its pasture lands, G with its pasture lands,
Judg 20:33 ambush rushed out of their place west of G
1Sam 13:3 Philistines which was at G; and the Philistines heard
13:16 with them, stayed in G of Benjamin; but the
14:5 the other on the south in front of G
2Sam 5:25 smote the Philistines from G to Gezer.
1Kgs 15:22 them King Asa built G of Benjamin and Mizpah.
2Kgs 23:8 had burned incense, from G to Beer-sheba; and he
1Chr 6:60 the tribe of Benjamin, G with its pasture lands,
8:6 of the inhabitants of G, and they were carried
2Chr 16:6 with them he built G and Mizpah.
Ezra 2:26 sons of Ramah and G, six hundred and twenty-one.
Neh 7:30 men of Ramah and G, six hundred and twenty-one.
11:31 Benjamin also lived from G onward, at Michmash,
12:29 from the region of G and Azmaveth; for the
Jud 3:10 here he camped between G and Scythopolis, and
Is 10:29 over the pass, at G they lodge for the
Zech 14:10 into a plain from G to Rimmon south of

GEBAL (3)

1Kgs 5:18 and the men of G did the hewing and
Ps 83:7 Moab and the Hagrites, G and Ammon and Amalek,
Ezek 27:9 The elders of G and her skilled men were

GEBALITES

Josh 13:5 the land of the G, and all Lebanon, toward

GEBER

1Kgs 4:19 of Ela, in Benjamin; G the son of Uri,

GEBIM

Is 10:31 flight, the inhabitants of G flee for safety.

GECKO

Lev 11:30 to its kind, the G, the land crocodile, the

GEDALIAH (31)

2Kgs 25:22 had left, he appointed G the son of Ahikam,
25:23 of Babylon had appointed G governor, they came
25:23 with their men to G at Mizpah, namely, Ishmael
25:24 And G swore to them and their men, saying,
25:25 and attacked and killed G and the Jews and
1Chr 25:3 the sons of Jeduthun: G, Zeri, Jeshaiah, Shimei,
25:9 Joseph; the second to G, to him and his
Ezra 10:18 Ma-aseiah, Eliezer, Jarib, and G, of the sons of
Jer 38:1 the son of Mattan, G the son of Pashhur,
39:14 They entrusted him to G the son of Ahikam,
40:5 remain, then return to G the son of Ahikam,
40:6 Then Jeremiah went to G the son of Ahikam,
40:7 of Babylon had appointed G the son of Ahikam
40:8 Babylon, they went to G at Mizpah--Ishmael the
40:9 G the son of Ahikam, son of Shaphan, swore
40:11 Judah and had appointed G the son of Ahikam,
40:12 land of Judah, to G at Mizpah; and they
40:13 open country came to G at Mizpah
40:14 But G the son of Ahikam would not believe
40:15 Kareah spoke secretly to G at Mizpah, "Let me
40:16 But G the son of Ahikam said to Johanan
41:1 with ten men to G the son of Ahikam,
41:2 up and struck down G the son of Ahikam,
41:3 Jews who were with G at Mizpah, and the
41:4 after the murder of G, before any one knew
41:6 them, "Come in to G the son of Ahikam."
41:10 guard, had committed to G the son of Ahikam.
41:16 after he had slain G the son of Ahikam--
41:18 of Nethaniah had slain G the son of Ahikam,
43:6 guard had left with G the son of Ahikam,
Zeph 1:1 of Cushi, son of G, son of Amariah, son

GEDER

Josh 12:13 one; the king of G, one;

GEDERAH (3)

Josh 15:36 Azekah, Shaaraim, Adithaim, G, Gederothaim:
1Chr 4:23 inhabitants of Netaim and G; they dwelt there with
12:4 Jahaziel, Johanan, Jozabad of G,

GEDERITE

1Chr 27:28 Shephelah was Baal-hanan the G; and over the

G

GEDEROTH (2)

Josh 15:41 Cabbon, Lahmam, Chitlish, G, Beth-dagon, Naamah,
2Chr 28:18 had taken Beth-shemesh, Aijalon, G, Soco with its

GEDEROTHAIM

Josh 15:36 Azekah, Shaaraim, Adithaim, Gederah, G: fourteen

GEDOR (7)

Josh 15:58 Halhul, Bethzur, G,
1Chr 4:4 was the father of G, and Ezer the father
4:18 Jered the father of G, Heber the father of
4:39 to the entrance of G, to the east side
8:31 Zur, Kish, Baal, Nadab, G, Ahio, Zecher,
9:37 Kish, Baal, Ner, Nadab, G, Ahio, Zechariah and
12:7 Joelah and Zebadiah, the sons of Jeroham of G

GEHAZI (13)

2Kgs 4:12 And he said to G his servant, "Call this
4:14 G answered, "Well, she has no son, and her
4:25 coming, he said to G his servant, "Look, yonder
4:27 And G came to thrust her away.
4:29 He said to G, "Gird up your loins, and
4:31 G went on ahead and laid the staff upon
4:36 he summoned G and said, "Call this Shunammite."
5:20 him a short distance, G, the servant of Elisha
5:21 So G followed Naaman.
5:23 of his servants; and they carried them before G
5:25 Elisha said to him, "Where have you been, G
8:4 king was talking with G the servant of the
8:5 And G said, "My lord, O king, here is

GELILOTH

Josh 18:17 and thence goes to G, which is opposite the

GEM

Wis 7:9 to her any priceless G, because all gold is

GEMALLI

Num 13:12 Ammiel the son of G;

GEMARIAH (5)

Jer 29:3 son of Shaphan and G the son of Hilkiah,
36:10 in the chamber of G the son of Shaphan
36:11 Micaiah the son of G, son of Shaphan, heard
36:12 the son of Achbor, G the son of Shaphan,
36:25 Elnathan and Delaiah and G urged the king not

GENEALOGICAL

1Chr 4:33 and they kept a G record.

GENEALOGIES (12)

Gen 10:32 Noah, according to their G, in their nations; and
1Chr 1:29 These are their G: the first-born of Ishmael,
5:17 these were enrolled by G in the days of
7:7 and their enrollment by G was twenty-two thousand
7:9 and their enrollment by G, according to their
7:40 Their number enrolled by G, for service in war,
9:1 Israel was enrolled by G; and these are written
9:22 They were enrolled by G in their villages.
Ezra 2:62 those enrolled in the G, but they were not
Neh 7:64 those enrolled in the G, but it was not
1Tim 1:4 with myths and endless G which promote
Tit 3:9 But avoid stupid controversies, G, dissensions, and

GENEALOGY (11)

1Chr 5:1 not enrolled in the G according to the birthright;
5:7 their families, when the G of their generations was
7:5 eighty-seven thousand mighty warriors, enrolled by G
26:31 the Hebronites of whatever G or fathers' houses.
2Chr 31:16 except those enrolled by G, males from three years
Ezra 8:1 and this is the G of those who went
Neh 7:5 officials and the people to be enrolled by G
7:5 the book of the G of those who came
Mt 1:1 THE book of the G of Jesus Christ, the
Heb 7:3 father or mother or G, and has neither beginning
7:6 who has not their G received tithes from Abraham

GENERAL (12)

Judg 4:7 draw out Sisera, the G of Jabin's army, to
Jud 2:4 called Holofernes, the chief G of his army, second
4:1 that Holofernes, the G of Nebuchadnezzar the king
5:1 When Holofernes, the G of the Assyrian army, heard
7:30 Then great and G lamentation arose throughout the
1Mac 8:10 and they sent a G against the Greeks and
10:65 friends, and made him G and governor of the
13:37 ready to make a G peace with you and
2Mac 3:18 crowds to make a G supplication because the holy
8:9 with him Gorgias, a G and a man of
9:19 Antiochus their king and G sends hearty greetings
9:21 take thought for the G security of all.

GENERALS (3)

Jud 2:14 together all the commanders, G, and officers of the
14:12 they went to the G and the captains and
Rev 6:15 great men and the G and the rich and

GENERATION (101)

Gen 6:9 man, blameless in his G; Noah walked with God.
7:1 that you are righteous before me in this G
15:16 here in the fourth G; for the iniquity of
50:23 children of the third G; the children also of
Ex 1:5 died, and all his brothers, and all that G
17:16 will have war with Amalek from G to G
20:5 third and the fourth G of those who hate
34:7 children's children, to the third and the fourth G
Num 14:18 and upon the fourth G
32:13 years, until all the G that had done evil
Deut 1:35 men of this evil G shall see the good
2:14 years, until the entire G, that is, the men
5:9 the third and fourth G of those who hate
23:2 even to the tenth G none of his descendants
23:3 even to the tenth G none belonging to them
23:8 children of the third G that are born to
29:22 And the G to come, your children who rise
32:5 their blemish; they are a perverse and crooked G
32:20 they are a perverse G, children in whom is
Judg 2:10 And all that G also were gathered to their
2:10 and there arose another G after them, who did
2Kgs 10:30 sons of the fourth G shall sit on the
15:12 upon the throne of Israel to the fourth G
Jud 8:18 "For never in our G, nor in these present
Esth 9:28 and kept throughout every G, in every family,
10:13 gladness before God, from G to generation for ever
10:13 God, from generation to G for ever among his
Ps 12:7 LORD, protect us, guard us ever from this G
14:5 God is with the G of the righteous.
22:30 Lord to the coming G,
24:6 Such is the G of those who seek him,
48:13 may tell the next G
49:19 will go to the G of his fathers, who
73:15 been untrue to the G of thy children.
78:4 tell to the coming G the glorious deeds of
78:6 children; that the next G might know them, the
78:8 stubborn and rebellious G, a G whose heart
79:13 thee for ever; from G to G we will
95:10 years I loathed that G and said, "They are
102:18 be recorded for a G to come, so that
106:31 him as righteousness from G to generation for ever.
106:31 righteousness from generation to G for ever.
109:13 his name be blotted out in the second G
112:2 in the land; the G of the upright will
145:4 One G shall laud thy works to another, and
Eccl 1:4 A G goes, and a generation comes, but the
1:4 generation goes, and a G comes, but the earth
Wis 3:19 end of an unrighteous G is grievous.
7:27 all things; in every G she passes into holy
14:6 to the world the seed of a new G
Is 34:10 From G to generation it shall lie waste; none
34:10 From generation to G it shall lie waste; none
34:17 it for ever, from G to generation they shall
34:17 ever, from generation to G they shall dwell in
53:8 and as for his G, who considered that he
Jer 2:31 And you, O G, heed the word of the
7:29 rejected and forsaken the G of his wrath.'
Dan 4:3 his dominion is from G to generation.
4:3 kingdom, and his dominion is from generation to G
4:34 his kingdom endures from G to generation;
4:34 endures from generation to G;
Joel 1:3 tell their children, and their children another G
1Mac 2:61 "And so observe, from G to generation, that none
2:61 observe, from generation to G, that none who put
Mt 11:16 "But to what shall I compare this G
12:39 "An evil and adulterous G seeks for a sign;
12:41 the judgment with this G and condemn it; for
12:42 the judgment with this G and condemn it; for
12:45 So shall it be also with this evil G
16:4 An evil and adulterous G seeks for a sign,
17:17 "O faithless and perverse G, how long am I
23:35 to you, all this will come upon this G
24:34 say to you, this G will not pass away
Mk 8:12 said, "Why does this G seek a sign?
8:12 you, no sign shall be given to this G

	8:38	this adulterous and sinful G, of him will the
	9:19	answered them, "O faithless G, how long am I
	13:30	say to you, this G will not pass away
Lk	1:50	who fear him from G to generation.
	1:50	on those who fear him from generation to G
	7:31	the men of this G, and what are they
	9:41	"O faithless and perverse G, how long am I
	11:29	began to say, "This G is an evil generation;
	11:29	generation is an evil G; it seeks a sign,
	11:30	will the Son of man be to this G
	11:31	the men of this G and condemn them; for
	11:32	the judgment with this G and condemn it; for
	11:50	be required of this G,
	11:51	tell you, it shall be required of this G
	16:8	dealing with their own G than the sons of
	17:25	suffer many things and be rejected by this G
	21:32	say to you, this G will not pass away
Acts	2:40	them, saying, "Save yourselves from this crooked G
	8:33	Who can describe his G
	13:36	God in his own G, fell asleep, and was
Phil	2:15	a crooked and perverse G, among whom you shine
Heb	3:10	was provoked with that G, and said, 'They always
Jude	1:14	Enoch in the seventh G from Adam prophesied,

GENERATIONS (131)

Gen	2:4	These are the G of the heavens and the
	5:1	the book of the G of Adam.
	6:9	These are the G of Noah.
	9:12	you, for all future G:
	10:1	These are the G of the sons of Noah,
	17:7	you throughout their G for an everlasting covenant,
	17:9	and your descendants after you throughout their G
	17:12	every male throughout your G, whether born in your
Ex	3:15	thus I am to be remembered throughout all G
	6:16	Levi according to their G: Gershon, Kohath, and
	6:19	the families of the Levites according to their G
	12:14	the LORD; throughout your G you shall observe it
	12:17	this day, throughout your G, as an ordinance for
	12:42	by all the people of Israel throughout their G
	16:32	be kept throughout your G, that they may see
	16:33	before the LORD, to be kept throughout your G
	27:21	be observed throughout their G by the people of
	29:42	burnt offering throughout your G at the door of
	30:8	incense before the LORD throughout your G
	30:10	the year throughout your G; it is most holy
	30:21	to him and to his descendants throughout their G
	30:31	shall be my holy anointing oil throughout your G
	31:13	and you throughout your G, that you may know
	31:16	sabbath throughout their G, as a perpetual covenant.
Lev	3:17	perpetual statute throughout your G, in all your
	6:18	for ever throughout your G, from the LORD's
	7:36	anointed; it is a perpetual due throughout their G
	10:9	shall be a statute for ever throughout your G
	17:7	a statute for ever to them throughout their G
	21:17	descendants throughout their G who has a blemish
	22:3	throughout your G approaches the holy things,
	23:14	for ever throughout your G in all your dwellings.
	23:21	for ever in all your dwellings throughout your G
	23:31	for ever throughout your G in all your dwellings.
	23:41	for ever throughout your G; you shall keep it
	23:43	in booths, that your G may know that I
	24:3	shall be a statute for ever throughout your G
	25:30	bought it, throughout his G; it shall not be
Num	1:20	Reuben, Israel's first-born, their G, by their families,
	1:22	people of Simeon, their G, by their families, by
	1:24	people of Gad, their G, by their families, by
	1:26	people of Judah, their G, by their families, by
	1:28	people of Issachar, their G, by their families, by
	1:30	people of Zebulun, their G, by their families, by
	1:32	people of Ephraim, their G, by their families, by
	1:34	people of Manasseh, their G, by their families, by
	1:36	people of Benjamin, their G, by their families, by
	1:38	people of Dan, their G, by their families, by
	1:40	people of Asher, their G, by their families, by
	1:42	people of Naphtali, their G, by their families, by
	3:1	These are the G of Aaron and Moses at
	10:8	to you for a perpetual statute throughout your G
	15:14	among you throughout your G, and he wishes to
	15:15	perpetual statute throughout your G; as you are, so
	15:21	give to the LORD an offering throughout your G
	15:23	and onward throughout your G,
	15:38	their garments throughout their G, and to put upon
	18:23	perpetual statute throughout your G; and among the
	35:29	to you throughout your G in all your dwellings.
Deut	7:9	commandments, to a thousand G,
	32:7	the years of many G; ask your father, and
Josh	22:27	you, and between the G after us, that we
Judg	3:2	was only that the G of the people of
2Sam	7:19	hast shown me future G, O Lord GOD!
1Chr	5:7	the genealogy of their G was reckoned: the chief,
	7:2	mighty warriors of their G, their number in the
	7:4	with them, by their G, according to their fathers'
	7:9	genealogies, according to their G, as heads of their
	8:28	houses, according to their G, chief men.
	9:9	according to their G, nine hundred and fifty-six.
	9:34	Levites, according to their G, leaders, who lived in
	16:15	commanded, for a thousand G,
	17:17	hast shown me future G, O LORD God!
Tob	1:4	and established for all G for ever.
	13:10	are distressed, to all G for ever.
	13:11	G of generations will give you joyful praise.
	13:11	Generations of G will give you joyful praise.
	14:5	glorious building for all G for ever, just as
Jud	8:32	go down through all G of our descendants.
Job	42:16	saw his sons, and his sons' sons, four G
Ps	10:6	be moved; throughout all G I shall not meet
	33:11	ever, the thoughts of his heart to all G
	45:17	be celebrated in all G; therefore the peoples will
	49:11	dwelling places to all G, though they named lands
	61:6	the king; may his years endure to all G
	71:18	might to all the G to come.
	72:5	and as long as the moon, throughout all G
	85:5	Wilt thou prolong thy anger to all G
	89:1	mouth I will proclaim thy faithfulness to all G
	89:4	for ever, and build your throne for all G
	90:1	thou hast been our dwelling place in all G
	100:5	endures for ever, and his faithfulness to all G
	102:12	enthroned for ever; thy name endures to all G
	102:24	my days, thou whose years endure throughout all G
	105:8	commanded, for a thousand G,
	119:90	faithfulness endures to all G; thou hast established
	145:13	kingdom, and thy dominion endures throughout all G
	146:10	for ever, thy God, O Zion, to all G
Prov	27:24	ever; and does a crown endure to all G
Sir	2:10	Consider the ancient G and see: who ever trusted
	14:18	others, so are the G of flesh and blood:
	16:25	their dominion for all G; they neither hunger nor
	24:31	like prophecy, and leave it to all future G
	39:9	disappear, and his name will live through all G
	44:1	praise famous men, and our fathers in their G
	44:8	were honored in their G, and were the glory
	44:15	in peace, and their name lives to all G
	44:17	he was an example of repentance to all G
	45:26	and that their glory may endure throughout their G
Is	13:20	dwelt in for all G; no Arab will pitch
	41:4	done this, calling the G from the beginning?
	51:8	be for ever, and my salvation to all G
	51:9	days of old, the G of long ago.
	58:12	the foundations of many G; you shall be called
	61:4	repair the ruined cities, the devastations of many G
Jer	50:39	no more for ever, nor inhabited for all G
Lam	5:19	reign for ever; thy throne endures to all G
Bar	6:3	time, up to seven G; after that I will
Joel	2:2	again after them through the years of all G
	3:20	be inhabited for ever, and Jerusalem to all G
1Mac	2:51	they did in their G; and receive great honor
Mt	1:17	So all the G from Abraham to David were
	1:17	to David were fourteen G, and from David to
	1:17	deportation to Babylon fourteen G, and from the
	1:17	the deportation to Babylon to the Christ fourteen G
Lk	1:48	For behold, henceforth all G will call me blessed;
Acts	14:16	In past G he allowed all the nations to
	15:21	For from early G Moses has had in every
Eph	3:5	of men in other G as it has now
	3:21	Christ Jesus to all G, for ever and ever.
Col	1:26	hidden for ages and G but now made manifest

GENERATIVE

Wis	1:14	might exist, and the G forces of the world

GENEROSITY (4)

2Mac	13:23	the sanctuary and showed G to the holy place.
Mt	20:15	do you begrudge my G
2Cor	9:11	every way for great G, which through us will
	9:13	Christ, and by the G of your contribution for

GENEROUS (7)

Ex	35:5	whoever is of a G heart, let him bring
Ps	37:21	but the righteous is G and gives;
Prov	19:6	the favor of a G man, and every one
Sir	14:5	mean to himself, to whom will he be G
	40:14	A G man will be made glad; likewise transgressors

Acts 2:46 food with glad and G hearts,
1Tim 6:18 good deeds, liberal and G,

GENEROUSLY (4)

Ps 112:5 the man who deals G and lends, who conducts
Sir 35:8 Glorify the Lord G, and do not stint the
35:10 has given, and as G as your hand has
Jas 1:5 gives to all men G and without reproaching, and

GENNAEUS

2Mac 12:2 Apollonius the son of G, as well as Hieronymus

GENNESARET (4)

1Mac 11:67 and his army encamped by the waters of G
Mt 14:34 had crossed over, they came to land at G
Mk 6:53 came to land at G, and moored to the
Lk 5:1 God, he was standing by the lake of G

GENTILE (4)

1Mac 1:14 in Jerusalem, according to G custom,
Mt 18:16 to you as a G and a tax collector.
Gal 2:14 Jew, live like a G and not like a
2:15 by birth and not G sinners,

G

GENTILES (150)

Tob 1:10 the food of the G;
14:6 Then all the G will turn to fear the
14:7 All the G will praise the Lord, and his
Jud 4:12 and desecrated to the malicious joy of the G
8:22 our heads among the G, wherever we serve as
1Mac 1:11 a covenant with the G round about us, for
1:13 authorized them to observe the ordinances of the G
1:15 They joined with the G and sold themselves to
1:43 All the G accepted the command of the king.
2:12 been laid waste; the G have profaned it.
2:18 commands, as all the G and the men of
2:40 to fight with the G for our lives and
2:44 survivors fled to the G for safety.
2:48 the hands of the G and kings, and they
2:68 Pay back the G in full, and heed what
3:10 But Apollonius gathered together G and a large
3:25 terror fell upon the G round about them.
3:26 the king, and the G talked of the battles
3:45 citadel; it was a lodging place for the G
3:48 matters about which the G were consulting the
3:52 And behold, the G are assembled against us to
3:58 to fight with these G who have assembled against
4:7 the camp of the G, strong and fortified, with
4:11 Then all the G will know that there is
4:14 The G were crushed and fled into the plain,
4:45 upon them, for the G had defiled it.
4:54 very day that the G had profaned it, it
4:58 the reproach of the G was removed.
4:60 about, to keep the G from coming and trampling
5:1 When the G round about heard that the altar
5:9 Now the G in Gilead gathered together against the
5:10 letter which said, "The G around us have gathered
5:15 all Galilee of the G, "to annihilate us."
5:19 in battle with the G until we return."
5:21 many battles against the G, and the Gentiles were
5:21 the Gentiles, and the G were crushed before him.
5:22 three thousand of the G fell, and he despoiled
5:38 to him, "All the G around us have gathered
5:43 All the G were defeated before him, and they
5:57 make war on the G around us."
5:63 and among all the G, wherever their name was
6:18 every way to harm them and strengthen the G
6:53 in Judea from the G had consumed the last
7:23 was more than the G had done.
13:41 the yoke of the G was removed from Israel,
14:36 hands, so that the G were put out of
2Mac 1:27 are slaves among the G, look upon those who
1:27 despised, and let the G know that thou art
6:4 and reveling by the G, who dallied with harlots
8:5 his army organized, the G could not withstand him,
8:9 fewer than twenty thousand G of all nations, to
8:16 the great multitude of G who were wickedly coming
8:17 lawless outrage which the G had committed against
12:13 and walls, and inhabited by all sorts of G
13:11 revive fall into the hands of the blasphemous G
14:14 And the G throughout Judea, who had fled before
14:15 the gathering of the G, they sprinkled dust upon
14:38 no mingling with the G, he had been accused
15:8 the attack of the G, but to keep in
15:10 the perfidy of the G and their violation of
Mt 4:15 Jordan, Galilee of the G --
5:47 Do not even the G do the same?
6:7 empty phrases as the G do; for they think
6:32 we wear?' For the G seek all these things;
10:5 "Go nowhere among the G, and enter no town
10:18 sake, to bear testimony before them and the G
12:18 him, and he shall proclaim justice to the G
12:21 his name will the G hope."
20:19 deliver him to the G to be mocked and
20:25 the rulers of the G lord it over them,
Mk 10:33 deliver him to the G;
10:42 to rule over the G lord it over them,
Lk 2:32 for revelation to the G, and for glory to
18:32 be delivered to the G, and will be mocked
21:24 trodden down by the G, until the times of
21:24 the times of the G are fulfilled.
22:25 "The kings of the G exercise lordship over them;
Acts 4:25 Spirit, 'Why did the G rage, and the peoples
4:27 Pontius Pilate, with the G and the peoples of
9:15 my name before the G and kings and the
10:45 Spirit had been poured out even on the G
11:1 Judea heard that the G also had received the
11:18 saying, "Then to the G also God has granted
13:46 of eternal life, behold, we turn to the G
13:47 a light for the G, that you may bring
13:48 And when the G heard this, they were glad
14:2 Jews stirred up the G and poisoned their minds
14:5 was made by both G and Jews, with their
14:27 had opened a door of faith to the G
15:3 the conversion of the G, and they gave great
15:7 by my mouth the G should hear the word
15:12 wonders God had done through them among the G
15:14 God first visited the G, to take out of
15:17 Lord, and all the G who are called by
15:19 trouble those of the G who turn to God,
15:23 who are of the G in Antioch and Syria
18:6 From now on I will go to the G
21:11 and deliver him into the hands of the G
21:19 had done among the G through his ministry.
21:21 who are among the G to forsake Moses, telling
21:25 But as for the G who have believed, we
22:21 I will send you far away to the G
26:17 people and from the G --to whom I send
26:20 and also to the G, that they should repent
26:23 light both to the people and to the G
28:28 been sent to the G; they will listen."
Rom 1:13 as well as among the rest of the G
2:14 When G who have not the law do by
2:24 is blasphemed among the G because of you."
3:29 not the God of G also?
3:29 Yes, of G also,
9:24 from the Jews only but also from the G
9:30 That G who did not pursue righteousness have
11:11 has come to the G, so as to make
11:12 means riches for the G, how much more will
11:13 Now I am speaking to you G
11:13 an apostle to the G, I magnify my ministry
11:25 full number of the G come in,
15:9 in order that the G might glorify God for
15:9 praise thee among the G, and sing to thy
15:10 is said, "Rejoice, O G, with his people";
15:11 "Praise the Lord, all G, and let all the
15:12 rises to rule the G; in him shall the
15:12 in him shall the G hope."
15:16 Christ Jesus to the G in the priestly service
15:16 the offering of the G may be acceptable, sanctified
15:18 win obedience from the G, by word and deed,
15:27 them, for if the G have come to share
16:4 the churches of the G give thanks;
1Cor 1:23 Jews and folly to G,
2Cor 11:26 own people, danger from G, danger in the city,
Gal 1:16 preach him among the G, I did not confer
2:2 I preach among the G, lest somehow I should
2:8 me also for the G,
2:9 should go to the G and they to the
2:12 he ate with the G; but when they came
2:14 can you compel the G to live like Jews?"
3:8 God would justify the G by faith, preached the
3:14 might come upon the G, that we might receive
Eph 2:11 at one time you G in the flesh, called
3:1 on behalf of you G --
3:6 that is, how the G are fellow heirs, members
3:8 to preach to the G the unsearchable riches of
4:17 longer live as the G do, in the futility
Col 1:27 how great among the G are the riches of
1Thes 2:16 from speaking to the G that they may be
1Tim 2:7 a teacher of the G in faith and truth.

2Tim	4:17	fully, that all the G might hear it.
1Pet	2:12	good conduct among the G, so that in case
	4:3	for doing what the G like to do, living

GENTLE (13)

Deut	32:2	the dew, as the G rain upon the tender
Prov	15:4	A G tongue is a tree of life, but
Wis	2:19	may find out how G he is, and make
	18:14	For while G silence enveloped all things, and night
Jer	11:19	I was like a G lamb led to the
2Mac	15:12	of modest bearing and G manner, one who spoke
Mt	11:29	me; for I am G and lowly in heart,
1Thes	2:7	But we were G among you, like a nurse
1Tim	3:3	drunkard, not violent but G, not quarrelsome, and no
Tit	3:2	avoid quarreling, to be G, and to show perfect
Jas	3:17	first pure, then peaceable, G, open to reason, full
1Pet	2:18	to the kind and G but also to the
	3:4	imperishable jewel of a G and quiet spirit, which

GENTLENESS (8)

Esth	15:8	of the king to G, and in alarm he
1Cor	4:21	rod, or with love in a spirit of G
2Cor	10:1	by the meekness and G of Christ--I who
Gal	5:23	kindness, goodness, faithfulness, G, self-control;
	6:1	spiritual should restore him in a spirit of G
1Tim	6:11	righteousness, godliness, faith, love, steadfastness, G
2Tim	2:25	teacher, forbearing, correcting his opponents with G
1Pet	3:15	yet do it with G and reverence;

GENTLY (7)

2Sam	18:5	Abishai and Ittai, "Deal G for my sake with
Job	15:11	the word that deals G with you?
Sir	4:8	to the poor, and answer him peaceably and G
Is	8:6	of Shiloah that flow G, and melt in fear
	40:11	in his bosom, and G lead those that are
Acts	27:13	the south wind blew G, supposing that they had
Heb	5:2	He can deal G with the ignorant and wayward,

GENUBATH (2)

1Kgs	11:20	of Tahpenes bore him G his son, whom Tahpenes
	11:20	in Pharaoh's house; and G was in Pharaoh's house

GENUINE (5)

Esth	11:1	which they said was G and had been translated
Rom	12:9	Let love be G; hate what is evil, hold
1Cor	11:19	that those who are G among you may be
2Cor	6:6	kindness, the Holy Spirit, G love,
	8:8	earnestness of others that your love also is G

GENUINELY (2)

2Mac	14:8	first because I am G concerned for the interests
Phil	2:20	him, who will be G anxious for your welfare.

GENUINENESS

1Pet	1:7	trials, so that the G of your faith, more

GERA (9)

Gen	46:21	Benjamin: Bela, Becher, Ashbel, G, Naaman, Ehi,
Judg	3:15	Ehud, the son of G, the Benjaminite, a left-handed
2Sam	16:5	Shimei, the son of G; and as he came
	19:16	Shimei the son of G, the Benjaminite, from Bahurim,
	19:18	Shimei the son of G fell down before the
1Kgs	2:8	Shimei the son of G, the Benjaminite from Bahurim,
1Chr	8:3	Bela had sons: Addar, G, Abihud,
	8:5	Abishua, Naaman, Ahoah, G, Shephuphan, and
	8:7	Manahath): Naaman, Ahijah, and G, that is, Heglam,

GERAHS (5)

Ex	30:13	(the shekel is twenty G, half a shekel as
Lev	27:25	of the sanctuary: twenty G shall make a shekel.
Num	3:47	the shekel of twenty G, you shall take them,
	18:16	the shekel of the sanctuary, which is twenty G
Ezek	45:12	shekel shall be twenty G; five shekels shall be

GERAR (11)

Gen	10:19	in the direction of G, as far as Gaza,
	20:1	between Kadesh and Shur; and he sojourned in G
	20:2	And Abimelech king of G sent and took Sarah.
	26:1	And Isaac went to G, to Abimelech king of
	26:6	So Isaac dwelt in G
	26:17	in the valley of G and dwelt there.
	26:20	water, the herdsmen of G quarreled with Isaac's
	26:26	went to him from G with Ahuzzath his adviser
2Chr	14:13	them as far as G, and the Ethiopians fell
	14:14	the cities round about G, for the fear of
2Mac	13:24	governor from Ptolemais to G,

GERASENES (3)

Mk	5:1	of the sea, to the country of the G
Lk	8:26	the country of the G, which is opposite Galilee.
	8:37	surrounding country of the G asked him to depart

GERGESITES

Jud	5:16	Shechemites and all the G, and lived there a

GERIZIM (6)

Deut	11:29	the blessing on Mount G and the curse on
	27:12	shall stand upon Mount G to bless the people:
Josh	8:33	in front of Mount G and half of them
Judg	9:7	the top of Mount G, and cried aloud and
2Mac	5:23	appointed him; and at G, Andronicus; and besides
	6:2	call the one in G the temple of Zeus

GERSHOM (15)

Ex	2:22	he called his name G; for he said, "I
	18:3	of the one was G (for he said, "I
Judg	18:30	Jonathan the son of G, son of Moses, and
1Chr	6:1	The sons of Levi: G, Kohath, and Merari.
	6:16	The sons of Levi: G, Kohath, and Merari.
	6:17	of the sons of G: Libni and Shimei.
	6:20	Of G: Libni his son, Jahath his son, Zimmah
	6:43	of Jahath, son of G, son of Levi.
	15:7	of the sons of G, Joel the chief, with
	23:6	the sons of Levi: G, Kohath, and Merari.
	23:7	The sons of G were Ladan and Shimei.
	23:15	The sons of Moses: G and Eliezer.
	23:16	The sons of G: Shebuel the chief.
	26:24	Shebuel the son of G, son of Moses, was
Ezra	8:2	Artaxerxes the king: Of the sons of Phinehas, G

GERSHOMITES (2)

1Chr	6:62	To the G according to their families were allotted
	6:71	To the G were given out of the half-tribe

GERSHON (13)

Gen	46:11	The sons of Levi: G, Kohath, and Merari.
Ex	6:16	to their generations: G, Kohath, and Merari, the
	6:17	The sons of G: Libni and Shimei, by their
Num	3:17	Levi by their names: G and Kohath and Merari.
	3:18	of the sons of G by their families: Libni
	3:21	Of G were the family of the Libnites and
	3:25	of the sons of G in the tent of
	4:22	of the sons of G also, by their families
	4:38	of the sons of G, by their families and
	4:41	of the sons of G, all who served in
	7:7	to the sons of G, according to their service;
	10:17	down, the sons of G and the sons of
	26:57	to their families: of G, the family of the

GERSHONITE (2)

1Chr	26:21	belonging to Ladan the G: Jehieli.
	29:8	the LORD, in the care of Jehiel the G

GERSHONITES (11)

Num	3:21	the Shimeites; these were the families of the G
	3:23	The families of the G were to encamp behind
	3:24	as head of the fathers' house of the G
	4:24	the families of the G, in serving and bearing
	4:27	the sons of the G shall be at the
	4:28	the sons of the G in the tent of
	26:57	the family of the G; of Kohath, the family
Josh	21:27	And to the G, one of the families of
	21:33	several families of the G were in all thirteen
1Chr	26:21	the sons of the G belonging to Ladan, the
2Chr	29:12	Jehallelel; and of the G, Joah the son of

GERSONITES

Josh	21:6	The G received by lot from the families of

GERUTH

Jer	41:17	went and stayed at G Chimham near Bethlehem,

GESHAN

1Chr	2:47	of Jahdai: Regem, Jotham, G, Pelet, Ephah, and

GESHEM (4)

Neh	2:19	servant, the Ammonite, and G the Arab heard of
	6:1	and Tobiah and to G the Arab and to
	6:2	the gates), Sanballat and G sent to me, saying,
	6:6	among the nations, and G also says it, that

GESHUR (9)

Josh	13:13	or the Ma-acathites; but G and Maacath dwell in

2Sam 3:3 of Talmai king of G;
13:37 to Talmai the son of Ammihud, king of G
13:38 fled, and went to G, and was there three
14:23 arose and went to G, and brought Absalom to
14:32 king, to ask, "Why have I come from G
15:8 while I dwelt at G in Aram, saying, 'If
1Chr 2:23 But G and Aram took from them Havvoth-jair,
3:2 of Talmai, king of G; the fourth Adonijah, whose

GESHURITES (6)

Deut 3:14 the border of the G and the Ma-acathites, and
Josh 12:5 the boundary of the G and the Ma-acathites, and
13:2 all those of the G
13:11 the region of the G and Ma-acathites, and all
13:13 not drive out the G or the Ma-acathites; but
1Sam 27:8 made raids upon the G, the Girzites, and the

GET (143)

Gen 19:14 marry his daughters, "Up, G out of this place;
34:4 his father Hamor, saying, G me this maiden for
34:10 trade in it, and G property in it."
40:14 to Pharaoh, and so G me out of this
Ex 5:4 G to your burdens."
5:11 Go yourselves, G your straw wherever you can find
9:19 Now therefore send, G your cattle and all that
10:28 Pharaoh said to him, G away from me; take
11:8 down to me, saying, G you out, and all
14:4 them and I will G glory over Pharaoh and
14:17 them, and I will G glory over Pharaoh and
Lev 25:28 not sufficient means to G it back for himself,
Num 11:13 Where am I to G meat to give to
16:24 "Say to the congregation, G away from about the
16:45 LORD said to Moses, G away from the midst
17:2 people of Israel, and G from them rods, one
Deut 8:18 gives you power to G wealth; that he may
24:19 not go back to G it; it shall be
Judg 14:2 Philistines at Timnah; now G her for me as
14:3 said to his father, G her for me; for
19:28 He said to her, G up, let us be
1Sam 20:29 your eyes, let me G away, and see my
23:26 was making haste to G away from Saul, as
2Sam 5:8 the Jebusites, let him G up the water shaft
20:6 pursue him, lest he G himself fortified cities, and
1Kgs 1:1 clothes, he could not G warm.
2Kgs 5:20 run after him, and G something from him."
6:2 and each of us G there a log, and
7:12 take them alive and G into the city.'"
Neh 5:2 are many; let us G grain, that we may
5:3 and our houses to G grain because of the
9:10 fathers; and thou didst G thee a name, as
Tob 2:13 her, "Where did you G the kid?
5:3 live; and go and G the money."
5:16 he said to Tobias, G ready for the journey,
8:4 bed and said, "Sister, G up, and let us
9:2 Rages in Media and G the money for me;
Jud 7:13 the people of Bethulia G their water.
12:3 out, where can we G more like it for
Esth 9:1 the Jews hoped to G the mastery over them,
9:1 when the Jews should G the mastery over their
Job 9:18 will not let me G my breath, but fills
11:12 a stupid man will G understanding, when a wild
17:5 against his friends to G a share of their
20:18 his trading he will G no enjoyment.
21:15 what profit do we G if we pray to
Ps 59:15 if they do not G their fill.
90:12 days that we may G a heart of wisdom.
104:22 the sun rises, they G them away and lie
107:37 and plant vineyards, and G a fruitful yield.
119:104 Through thy precepts I G understanding; therefore I
119:133 and let no iniquity G dominion over me.
132:3 enter my house or G into my bed;
Prov 1:19 ways of all who G gain by violence; it
3:35 inherit honor, but fools G disgrace.
4:6 and live; G Wisdom, G understanding!" do
4:8 of wisdom is this: G wisdom, and whatever you
4:8 wisdom, and whatever you G, G insight.
6:33 and dishonor will he G, and his disgrace will
11:16 honor, and violent men G riches.
12:27 the diligent man will G precious wealth.
16:16 To G wisdom is better than gold; to G
24:27 Prepare your work outside, G everything ready for
28:27 hides his eyes will G many a curse.
Wis 7:14 for men; those who G it obtain friendship with
8:18 about seeking how to G her for myself.
15:12 he says one must G money however one can,
Sir 6:27 you; and when you G hold of her, do
8:11 Do not G up and leave an insolent fellow,
27:1 and whoever seeks to G rich will avert his
29:6 pressure, he will hardly G back half, and will
31:21 are overstuffed with food, G up in the middle
51:25 my mouth and said, G these things for yourselves
51:28 G instruction with a large sum of silver, and
Is 40:9 G you up to a high mountain, O Zion,
56:12 they say, "let us G wine, let us fill
Jer 32:25 field for money and G witnesses"—though the city
36:21 king sent Jehudi to G the scroll, and he
Lam 5:4 drink, the wood we G must be bought.
5:6 and to Assyria, to G bread enough.
5:9 We G our bread at the peril of our
Bar 3:18 those who scheme to G silver, and are anxious,
Ezek 3:4 "Son of man, go, G you to the house
3:11 And go, G you to the exiles, to your
18:31 committed against me, and G yourselves a new heart
22:27 blood, destroying lives to G dishonest gain.
Zech 6:7 they were impatient to G off and patrol the
1Mac 3:41 to the camp to G the sons of Israel
5:48 through your land to G to our land.
8:3 land of Spain to G control of the silver
11:1 and he tried to G possession of Alexander's kingdom
13:17 but he sent to G the money and the
16:13 up; he determined to G control of the country,
2Mac 1:20 hidden the fire to G it.
2:15 them, send people to G them for you.
3:32 that the king might G the notion that some
3:38 there, for you will G him back thoroughly scourged,
7:11 him I hope to G them back again."
7:29 God's mercy I may G you back again with
9:4 he said, "When I G there I will make
13:13 could enter Judea and G possession of the city.
15:7 confidence that he would G help from the Lord.
Mt 5:26 you, you will never G out till you have
7:2 measure you give will be the measure you G
13:54 "Where did this man G this wisdom and these
13:56 then did this man G all this?"
14:22 he made the disciples G into the boat and
15:33 "Where are we to G bread enough in the
16:23 and said to Peter, G behind me, Satan!
21:34 to the tenants, to G his fruit;
22:12 'Friend, how did you G in here without a
Mk 2:4 when they could not G near him because of
4:24 be the measure you G, and still more will
6:2 "Where did this man G all this?
6:45 he made his disciples G into the boat and
8:33 rebuked Peter, and said, G behind me, Satan!
12:2 to the tenants, to G from them some of
Lk 6:38 be the measure you G back."
9:12 about, to lodge and G provisions; for we are
11:7 in bed; I cannot G up and give you
11:8 though he will not G up and give him
12:45 eat and drink and G drunk,
12:59 you, you will never G out till you have
13:31 and said to him, G away from here, for
18:12 of all that I G
Jn 4:11 deep; where do you G that living water?
6:7 each of them to G a little."
Acts 12:7 and woke him, saying, G up quickly." And the
22:18 me, 'Make haste and G quickly out of Jerusalem,
23:23 hour of the night G ready two hundred soldiers
Rom 6:21 what return did you G from the things of
6:22 God, the return you G is sanctification and its
1Cor 9:13 in the temple service G their food from the
9:14 proclaim the gospel should G their living by the
14:8 indistinct sound, who will G ready for battle?
Eph 5:18 And do not G drunk with wine, for that
1Thes 5:7 night, and those who G drunk are drunk at
2Tim 3:9 but they will not G very far, for their
4:11 G Mark and bring him with you; for he
Jas 4:13 there and trade and G gain";

GETHER (2)

Gen 10:23 of Aram: Uz, Hul, G, and Mash.
1Chr 1:17 Lud, Aram, Uz, Hul, G, and Meshech.

GETHSEMANE (2)

Mt 26:36 to a place called G, and he said to
Mk 14:32 place which was called G; and he said to

GETS (17)

Jud 7:13 that not a man G out of the city.
Ps 49:18 and though a man G praise when he does
Prov 3:13 and the man who G understanding,
9:7 who corrects a scoffer G himself abuse, and he

11:8 trouble, and the wicked G into it instead.
11:16 A gracious woman G honor, and violent men get
11:18 one who sows righteousness G a sure reward.
13:4 the sluggard craves, and G nothing, while the soul
19:8 He who G wisdom loves himself; he who keeps
29:26 the LORD a man G justice.
30:23 unloved woman when she G a husband, and a
Sir 29:5 another's hands until he G a loan, and will
36:24 who acquires a wife G his best possession, a
40:6 He G little or no rest, and afterward in
Jer 17:11 so is he who G riches but not by
Hab 2:9 Woe to him who G evil gain for his
2Tim 2:4 No soldier on service G entangled in civilian pursuits,

GETTING (8)

Prov 21:6 The G of treasures by a lying tongue is
Bar 3:17 no end to their G;
1Mac 5:27 Gilead; the enemy are G ready to attack the
Mt 9:1 And G into a boat he crossed over and
Mk 5:18 And as he was G into the boat, the
8:13 he left them, and G into the boat again
Lk 5:3 G into one of the boats, which was Simons,
1Cor 9:7 tends a flock without G some of the milk?

GEUEL

Num 13:15 the tribe of Gad, G the son of Machi.

GEZER (15)

Josh 10:33 Then Horam king of G came up to help
12:12 one; the king of G, one;
16:3 Lower Beth-horon, then to G, and it ends at
16:10 Canaanites that dwelt in G: so the Canaanites have
21:21 hill country of Ephraim, G with its pasture lands,
Judg 1:29 Canaanites who dwelt in G; but the Canaanites dwelt
1:29 the Canaanites dwelt in G among them.
2Sam 5:25 him, and smote the Philistines from Geba to G
1Kgs 9:15 Hazor and Megiddo and G
9:16 gone up and captured G and burnt it with
9:17 wife; so Solomon rebuilt G and Lower Beth-horon
1Chr 6:67 hill country of Ephraim, G with its pasture lands,
7:28 eastward Naaran, and westward G and its towns,
14:16 they smote the Philistine army from Gibeon to G
20:4 with the Philistines at G; then Sibbecai the

GHOST (3)

Is 29:4 the voice of a G, and your speech shall
Mt 14:26 sea, they were terrified, saying, "It is a G
Mk 6:49 thought it was a G, and cried out;

GIAH

2Sam 2:24 Ammah, which lies before G on the way to

GIANT (2)

Sir 47:4 he not kill a G, and take away reproach
1Mac 3:3 Like a G he put on his breastplate; he

GIANTS (11)

2Sam 21:16 the descendants of the G, whose spear weighed three
21:18 who was one of the descendants of the G
21:20 number; and he also was descended from the G
21:22 were descended from the G in Gath; and they
1Chr 20:4 the descendants of the G; and the Philistines were
20:6 number; and he also was descended from the G
20:8 were descended from the G in Gath; and they
Jud 16:7 him, nor did tall G set upon him; but
Wis 14:6 the beginning, when arrogant G were perishing, the
Sir 16:7 propitiated for the ancient G who revolted in their
Bar 3:26 The G were born there, who were famous of

GIBBAR

Ezra 2:20 The sons of G, ninety-five.

GIBBETHON (6)

Josh 19:44 Elon, Timnah, Ekron, Eltekeh, G, Baalath,
21:23 with its pasture lands, G with its pasture lands,
1Kgs 15:27 struck him down at G, which belonged to the
15:27 Nadab and all Israel were laying siege to G
16:15 troops were encamped against G, which belonged to
16:17 Omri went up from G, and all Israel with

GIBE-A

1Chr 2:49 and the father of G; and the daughter of

GIBE-AH (46)

Josh 15:57 Jezreel, Jokde-am, Zanoah, Kain, G, and Timnah: ten
18:28 Jebus (that is, Jerusalem), G and Kiriath-jearim—
24:33 they buried him at G, the town of Phinehas
Judg 19:12 of Israel; but we will pass on to G
19:13 spend the night at G or at Ramah."
19:14 down on them near G, which belongs to Benjamin,
19:15 to go in and spend the night at G
19:16 he was sojourning in G; the men of the
20:4 said, "I came to G that belongs to Benjamin,
20:5 And the men of G rose against me, and
20:9 we will do to G: we will go up
20:10 come they may requite G of Benjamin, for all
20:13 the base fellows in G, that we may put
20:14 of the cities to G, to go out to
20:15 besides the inhabitants of G, who mustered seven
20:19 Israel rose in the morning, and encamped against G
20:20 drew up the battle line against them at G
20:21 Benjaminites came out of G, and felled to the
20:25 against them out of G the second day, and
20:29 So Israel set men in ambush round about G
20:30 themselves in array against G, as at other times.
20:31 and the other to G, and in the open
20:34 And there came against G ten thousand picked men
20:36 men in ambush whom they had set against G
20:37 haste and rushed upon G; the men in ambush
20:43 as far as opposite G on the east.
1Sam 10:10 When they came to G, behold, a band of
10:26 to his home at G, and with him went
11:4 the messengers came to G of Saul, they reported
13:2 were with Jonathan in G of Benjamin; the rest
13:15 up from Gilgal to G of Benjamin.
14:2 in the outskirts of G under the pomegranate tree
14:16 watchmen of Saul in G of Benjamin looked; and
15:34 to his house in G of Saul.
22:6 Saul was sitting at G, under the tamarisk tree
23:19 up to Saul at G, saying, "Does not David
26:1 came to Saul at G, saying, "Is not David
2Sam 23:29 son of Ribai of G of the Benjaminites,
1Chr 11:31 son of Ribai of G of the Benjaminites, Benaiah
12:3 sons of Shemaah of G; also Jezi-el and Pelet
2Chr 13:2 name was Micaiah the daughter of Uriel of G
Is 10:29 the night; Ramah trembles, G of Saul has fled.
Hos 5:8 Blow the horn in G, the trumpet in Ramah.
9:9 in the days of G: he will remember their
10:9 From the days of G, you have sinned, O
10:9 Shall not war overtake them in G

GIBE-ATH-ELOHIM

1Sam 10:5 you shall come to G, where there is a

GIBEATH-HAARALOTH

Josh 5:3 knives, and circumcised the people of Israel at G

GIBEON (39)

Josh 9:3 when the inhabitants of G heard what Joshua had
9:17 Now their cities were G, Chephirah, Be-eroth, and
10:1 how the inhabitants of G had made peace with
10:2 he feared greatly, because G was a great city,
10:4 and let us smite G; for it has made
10:5 armies and encamped against G, and made war
10:6 And the men of G sent to Joshua at
10:10 a great slaughter at G, and chased them by
10:12 stand thou still at G, and thou Moon in
10:41 all the country of Goshen, as far as G
11:19 Hivites, the inhabitants of G; they took all in
18:25 cities with their villages: G, Ramah, Be-eroth,
21:17 the tribe of Benjamin, G with its pasture lands,
2Sam 2:12 son of Saul, went out from Mahanaim to G
2:13 at the pool of G; and they sat down,
2:16 place was called Helkath-hazzurim, which is at G
2:24 Giah on the way to the wilderness of G
3:30 killed their brother Asahel in the battle at G
20:8 stone which is in G, Amasa came to meet
21:6 before the LORD at G on the mountain of
1Kgs 3:4 the king went to G to sacrifice there, for
3:5 At G the LORD appeared to Solomon in a
9:2 time, as he had appeared to him at G
1Chr 8:29 Je-iel the father of G dwelt in Gibeon, and
8:29 of Gibeon dwelt in G, and the name of
9:35 In G dwelt the father of Gibeon, Je-iel, and
9:35 dwelt the father of G, Je-iel, and the name
12:4 of Anathoth, Ishmaiah of G, a mighty man among
14:16 the Philistine army from G to Gezer.
16:39 place that was at G,
21:29 the high place at G;
2Chr 1:3 place that was at G; for the tent of
1:13 the high place at G, from before the tent
Neh 3:7 Meronothite, the men of G and of Mizpah, who

7:25 The sons of G, ninety-five.
Is 28:21 in the valley of G; to do his deed--
Jer 28:1 Azzur, the prophet from G, spoke to me in
41:12 him at the great pool which is in G
41:16 and eunuchs, whom Johanan brought back from G

GIBEONITE

Neh 3:7 repaired Melatiah the G and Jadon the Meronothite,

GIBEONITES (6)

2Sam 21:1 because he put the G to death."
21:2 So the king called the G
21:2 Now the G were not of the people of
21:3 David said to the G, "What shall I do
21:4 The G said to him, "It is not a
21:9 the hands of the G, and they hanged them

GIDDALTI (2)

1Chr 25:4 Hananiah, Hanani, Eliathah, G, and Romamti-eze
25:29 to the twenty-second, to G, his sons and his

GIDDEL (4)

Ezra 2:47 Hanan, the sons of G, the sons of Gahar,
2:56 Darkon, the sons of G,
Neh 7:49 Hanan, the sons of G, the sons of Gahar,
7:58 Darkon, the sons of G,

GIDEON (42)

Judg 6:11 Abiezrite, as his son G was beating out wheat
6:13 And G said to him, "Pray, sir, if the
6:19 So G went into his house and prepared a
6:22 Then G perceived that he was the angel of
6:22 of the LORD; and G said, "Alas, O Lord
6:24 Then G built an altar there to the LORD,
6:27 So G took ten men of his servants, and
6:29 and inquired, they said, G the son of Joash
6:34 LORD took possession of G; and he sounded the
6:36 Then G said to God, "If thou wilt deliver
6:39 Then G said to God, "Let not thy anger
7:1 Then Jerubbaal (that is, G and all the people
7:2 The LORD said to G, "The people with you
7:3 And G tested them; twenty-two thousand returned,
7:4 the LORD said to G, "The people are still
7:5 the LORD said to G, "Every one that laps
7:7 the LORD said to G, "With the three hundred
7:13 When G came, behold, a man was telling a
7:14 than the sword of G the son of Joash,
7:15 When G heard the telling of the dream and
7:18 camp, and shout, 'For the LORD and for G
7:19 So G and the hundred men who were with
7:20 cried, "A sword for the LORD and for G
7:24 And G sent messengers throughout all the hill
7:25 Oreb and Zeeb to G beyond the Jordan.
8:4 And G came to the Jordan and passed over,
8:7 And G said, "Well then, when the LORD has
8:11 And G went up by the caravan route east
8:13 Then G the son of Joash returned from the
8:21 And G arose and slew Zebah and Zalmunna; and
8:22 of Israel said to G, "Rule over us, you
8:23 G said to them, "I will not rule over
8:24 And G said to them, "Let me make a
8:27 And G made an ephod of it and put
8:27 became a snare to G and to his family.
8:28 had rest forty years in the days of G
8:30 Now G had seventy sons, his own offspring, for
8:32 And G the son of Joash died in a
8:33 As soon as G died, the people of Israel
8:35 of Jerubbaal (that is, G in return for all
Jud 8:1 of Ananias, son of G, son of Raphaim, son
Heb 11:32 me to tell of G, Barak, Samson, Jephthah, of

GIDEONI (5)

Num 1:11 Abidan the son of G;
2:22 Abidan the son of G,
7:60 Abidan the son of G, the leader of the
7:65 was the offering of Abidan the son of G
10:24 men of Benjamin was Abidan the son of G

GIDOM

Judg 20:45 were pursued hard to G, and two thousand men

GIFT (83)

Gen 33:11 I pray you, my G that is brought to
34:12 as marriage present and G, and I will give
Lev 1:10 "If his G for a burnt offering is from
17:4 offer it as a G to the LORD before
Num 6:14 he shall offer his G to the LORD, one
8:19 the Levites as a G to Aaron and his
18:6 Israel; they are a G to you, given to
18:7 your priesthood as a G, and any one else
18:11 the offering of their G, all the wave offerings
2Sam 19:42 Or has he given us any G
Tob 2:14 to me as a G in addition to my
4:7 your eye begrudge the G when you make it.
4:8 many possessions, make your G from them in
4:16 your eye begrudge the G when you made it.
Job 6:22 Have I said, 'Make me a G
Prov 18:16 A man's G makes room for him and brings
21:14 A G in secret averts anger; and a bribe
25:14 who boasts of a G he does not give.
Eccl 3:13 that it is God's G to man that every
5:19 toil--this is the G of God.
Wis 8:21 insight to know whose G she was-- so
Sir 1:8 flesh according to his G, and he supplied her
4:3 mind, nor delay your G to a beggar.
7:28 them that equals their G to you?
7:31 the guilt offering, the G of the shoulders, the
11:15 The G of the Lord endures for those who
18:14 grief by your words when you present a G
18:15 So a word is better than a G
18:16 Indeed, does not a word surpass a good G
18:17 and abusive, and the G of a grudging man
20:9 There is a G that profits you nothing, and
20:9 and there is a G that brings a double
20:13 A fool's G will profit you nothing, for he
26:14 silent wife is a G of the Lord, and
35:9 With every G show a cheerful face, and dedicate
38:2 he will receive a G from the king.
41:21 some one's portion or G, and of gazing at
41:22 upbraid after making a G;
Ezek 46:16 the prince makes a G to any of his
46:17 if he makes a G out of his inheritance
46:17 sons may keep a G from his inheritance.
Mal 1:9 With such a G from your hand, will he
1Mac 10:39 have given as a G to the sanctuary in
2Mac 15:16 this holy sword, a G from God, with which
Mt 5:23 you are offering your G at the altar, and
5:24 against you, leave your G there before the altar
5:24 your brother, and then come and offer your G
8:4 priest, and offer the G that Moses commanded, for
23:17 one swears by the G that is on the
23:18 which is greater, the G or the altar that
23:18 altar that makes the G sacred?
Jn 4:10 "If you knew the G of God, and who
Acts 2:38 you shall receive the G of the Holy Spirit.
8:20 you could obtain the G of God with money!
10:45 were amazed, because the G of the Holy Spirit
11:17 God gave the same G to them as he
Rom 1:11 to you some spiritual G to strengthen you,
3:24 his grace as a G, through the redemption which
4:4 not reckoned as a G but as his due.
5:15 But the free G is not like the trespass.
5:15 God and the free G in the grace of
5:16 And the free G is not like the effect
5:16 condemnation, but the free G following many
5:17 grace and the free G of righteousness reign in
6:23 death, but the free G of God is eternal
11:35 who has given a G to him that he
1Cor 1:7 lacking in any spiritual G, as you wait for
4:7 you boast as if it were not a G
7:7 has his own special G from God, one of
16:3 letter to carry your G to Jerusalem.
2Cor 8:20 us about this liberal G which we are administering,
9:5 in advance for this G you have promised, so
9:5 not as an exaction but as a willing G
9:15 Thanks be to God for his inexpressible G
Eph 2:8 doing, it is the G of God --
3:7 minister according to the G of God's grace which
4:7 of us according to the measure of Christ's G
Phil 4:17 that I seek the G; but I seek the
1Tim 4:14 Do not neglect the G you have, which was
2Tim 1:6 you to rekindle the G of God that is
Heb 6:4 have tasted the heavenly G, and have become
Jas 1:16 endowment and every perfect G is from above,
1Pet 4:10 each has received a G, employ it for one

GIFTS (87)

Gen 24:10 all sorts of choice G from his master; and
25:6 his concubines Abraham gave G, and while he was
Ex 28:38 hallow as their holy G; it shall always be
Lev 23:38 LORD, and besides your G, and besides all your
Num 18:29 Out of all the G to you, you shall

Deut 33:13 land, with the choicest G of heaven above, and
33:16 hills, with the best G of the earth and
1Kgs 15:15 the LORD the votive G of his father and
15:15 and his own votive G, silver, and gold, and
2Kgs 12:18 took all the votive G that Jehoshaphat and Jehoram
12:18 and his own votive G, and all the gold
1Chr 26:20 of God and the treasuries of the dedicated G
26:26 treasuries of the dedicated G which David the king,
26:27 in battles they dedicated G for the maintenance of
26:28 had dedicated--all dedicated G were in the care
28:12 the treasuries for dedicated G;
2Chr 15:18 of God the votive G of his father and
15:18 and his own votive G, silver, and gold, and
21:3 father gave them great G, of silver, gold, and
32:23 And many brought G to the LORD to Jerusalem
Neh 9:36 fruit and its good G, behold, we are slaves.
Tob 13:11 the Lord God, bearing G in their hands, gifts
13:11 gifts in their hands, G for the King of
Jud 16:18 burnt offerings, their freewill offerings, and their G
Esth 2:18 the provinces, and gave G with royal liberality.
9:22 to one another and G to the poor.
Ps 45:12 sue your favor with G, the richest of the
68:18 thy train, and receiving G among men, even among
68:29 at Jerusalem kings bear G to thee.
72:10 may the kings of Sheba and Seba bring G
76:11 all around him bring G to him who is
Prov 6:35 nor be appeased though you multiply G
19:6 is a friend to a man who gives G
29:4 but one who exacts G ruins it.
Wis 7:14 God, commended for the G that come from
Sir 7:9 the multitude of my G, and when I make
20:28 Presents and G blind the eyes of the wise;
32:13 made you and satisfies you with his good G
34:18 offering is blemished; the G of the lawless are
Is 1:23 Every one loves a bribe and runs after G
18:7 At that time G will be brought to the
Bar 6:27 cannot straighten itself; but G are placed before
Ezek 16:33 Men give G to all harlots; but you gave
16:33 but you gave your G to all your lovers,
20:26 them through their very G in making them offer
20:31 When you offer your G and sacrifice your sons
20:39 more profane with your G and your idols.
20:40 the choicest of your G, with all your sacred
Dan 2:6 shall receive from me G and rewards and great
2:48 honors and many great G, and made him ruler
5:17 the king, "Let your G be for yourself, and
11:38 gold and silver, with precious stones and costly G
Mic 1:14 you shall give parting G to Moresheth-gath; the
1Mac 2:18 be honored with silver and gold and many G
3:30 expenses and for the G which he used to
10:24 promise them honor and G, that I may have
10:28 will grant you many immunities and give you G
10:54 son-in-law, and will make G to you and to
10:60 and gold and many G, and found favor with
11:24 silver and gold and clothing and numerous other G
12:43 and he gave him G and commanded his friends
16:19 silver and gold and G;
2Mac 1:35 the king favored he exchanged many excellent G
Mt 2:11 treasures, they offered him G, gold and frankincense
7:11 how to give good G to your children, how
Lk 11:13 how to give good G to your children, how
21:1 the rich putting their G into the treasury;
Acts 28:10 They presented many G to us; and when we
Rom 11:29 For the G and the call of God are
12:6 Having G that differ according to the grace given
1Cor 2:12 we might understand the G bestowed on us by
2:14 does not receive the G of the Spirit of
12:1 Now concerning spiritual G, brethren, I do not want
12:4 there are varieties of G, but the same Spirit;
12:9 same Spirit, to another G of healing by the
12:30 Do all possess G of healing?
12:31 But earnestly desire the higher G
14:1 earnestly desire the spiritual G, especially that you
Eph 4:8 captives, and he gave G to men."
4:11 all things.) And his G were that some should
Phil 4:18 received from Epaphroditus the G you sent, a
Heb 2:4 various miracles and by G of the Holy Spirit
5:1 to God, to offer G and sacrifices for sins.
8:3 is appointed to offer G and sacrifices; hence it
8:4 are priests who offer G according to the law.
9:9 According to this arrangement, G and sacrifices are
11:4 witness by accepting his G; he died, but through

GIHON (7)

Gen 2:13 the second river is G; it is the one
1Kgs 1:33 bring him down to G;
1:38 on King David's mule, and brought him to G
1:45 anointed him king at G; and they have gone
2Chr 32:30 of the waters of G and directed them down
33:14 of David west of G, in the valley, and
Sir 24:25 like light, like the G at the time of

GILALAI

Neh 12:36 kinsmen, Shemaiah, Azarel, Milalai, G, Maai,

GILBOA (8)

1Sam 28:4 Saul gathered all Israel, and they encamped at G
31:1 before the Philistines, and fell slain on Mount G
31:8 Saul and his three sons fallen on Mount G
2Sam 1:6 to be on Mount G; and there was Saul
1:21 "Ye mountains of G, let there be no dew
21:12 Philistines killed Saul on G;
1Chr 10:1 before the Philistines, and fell slain on Mount G
10:8 found Saul and his sons fallen on Mount G

GILEAD (110)

Gen 31:21 set his face toward the hill country of G
31:23 close after him into the hill country of G
31:25 his kinsmen encamped in the hill country of G
37:25 of Ishmaelites coming from G, with their camels
Num 26:29 was the father of G; of Gilead, the family
26:29 father of Gilead; of G, the family of the
26:30 are the sons of G: of Iezer, the family
27:1 of Hepher, son of G, son of Machir, son
32:1 and the land of G, and behold, the place
32:26 in the cities of G;
32:29 them the land of G for a possession;
32:39 of Manasseh went to G and took it, and
32:40 And Moses gave G to Machir the son of
36:1 of the sons of G the son of Machir,
Deut 2:36 valley, as far as G, there was not a
3:10 the tableland and all G and all Bashan, as
3:12 the hill country of G with its cities;
3:13 cities; the rest of G, and all Bashan, the
3:15 To Machir I gave G,
3:16 gave the territory from G as far as the
4:43 Reubenites, and Ramoth in G for the Gadites, and
34:1 him all the land, G as far as Dan,
Josh 12:2 that is, half of G,
12:5 and over half of G to the boundary of
13:11 of the Ammonites; and G, and the region of
13:25 all the cities of G, and half the land
13:31 sixty cities, and half G, and Ashtaroth, and Edre-i,
17:1 Manasseh, the father of G, were allotted Gilead and
17:1 of Gilead, were allotted G and Bashan, because he
17:3 of Hepher, son of G, son of Machir, son
17:5 besides the land of G and Bashan, which is
17:6 The land of G was allotted to the rest
20:8 Reuben, and Ramoth in G, from the tribe of
21:38 of Gad, Ramoth in G with its pasture lands,
22:9 to the land of G, their own land of
22:13 in the land of G, Phinehas the son of
22:15 in the land of G, and they said to
22:32 in the land of G to the land of
Judg 5:17 G stayed beyond the Jordan; and Dan, why did
10:4 this day, which are in the land of G
10:8 the land of the Amorites, which is in G
10:17 and they encamped in G; and the people of
10:18 people, the leaders of G, said one to another,
10:18 shall be head over all the inhabitants of G
11:1 G was the father of Jephthah.
11:2 And G's wife also bore him sons; and when
11:5 Israel, the elders of G went to bring Jephthah
11:7 to the elders of G, "Did you not hate
11:8 And the elders of G said to Jephthah, "That
11:8 be our head over all the inhabitants of G
11:9 to the elders of G, "If you bring me
11:10 And the elders of G said to Jephthah, "The
11:11 with the elders of G, and the people made
11:29 and he passed through G and Manasseh, and passed
11:29 on to Mizpah of G, and from Mizpah of
11:29 and from Mizpah of G he passed on to
12:4 all the men of G and fought with Ephraim;
12:4 and the men of G smote Ephraim, because they
12:5 the men of G said to him, "Are you
12:7 died, and was buried in his city in G
20:1 including the land of G, and the congregation
1Sam 13:7 the Jordan to the land of Gad and G
2Sam 2:9 made him king over G and the Ashurites and
17:26 Israel and Absalom encamped in the land of G
24:6 Then they came to G, and to Kadesh in
1Kgs 4:13 Manasseh, which are in G, and he had the

4:19 in the land of G, the country of Sihon
17:1 Tishbite, of Tishbe in G, said to Ahab, "As
2Kgs 10:33 all the land of G, the Gadites, and the
10:33 the Arnon, that is, G and Bashan.
15:29 Abel-beth-maacah, Jan-oah, Kedesh, Hazor, G, and,
1Chr 2:21 Machir the father of G, whom he married when
2:22 who had twenty-three cities in the land of G
2:23 these were descendants of Machir, the father of G
5:9 their cattle had multiplied in the land of G
5:10 their tents throughout all the region east of G
5:14 of Jaroah, son of G, son of Michael, son
5:16 and they dwelt in G, in Bashan and in
6:80 of Gad: Ramoth in G with its pasture lands,
7:14 concubine bore; she bore Machir the father of G
7:17 were the sons of G the son of Machir,
26:31 found at Jazer in G
27:21 half-tribe of Manasseh in G, Iddo the son of
Jud 1:8 nations of Carmel and G, and Upper Galilee and
15:5 enemy; and those in G and in Galilee out-flanked
Ps 60:7 G is mine; Manasseh is mine; Ephraim is my
108:8 G is mine; Manasseh is mine; Ephraim is my
Song 4:1 flock of goats, moving down the slopes of G
6:5 flock of goats, moving down the slopes of G
Jer 8:22 Is there no balm in G
22:6 Judah: "You are as G to me, as the
46:11 Go up to G, and take balm, O virgin
50:19 satisfied on the hills of Ephraim and in G
Ezek 47:18 along the Jordan between G and the land of
Hos 6:8 G is a city of evildoers, tracked with blood.
12:11 there is iniquity in G they shall surely come
Amos 1:3 because they have threshed G with threshing sledges
1:13 women with child in G, that they might enlarge
Obad 1:19 the land of Samaria and Benjamin shall possess G
Mic 7:14 feed in Bashan and G as in the days
Zech 10:10 to the land of G and to Lebanon, till
1Mac 5:9 Now the Gentiles in G gathered together against the
5:17 I and Jonathan my brother will go to G
5:20 to Galilee, and eight thousand to Judas for G
5:25 to their brethren in G:
5:27 the other cities of G; the enemy are getting
5:36 Maked, and Bosor, and the other cities of G
5:45 all the Israelites in G, the small and the
5:55 and Jonathan were in G and Simon his brother
13:22 marched off and went into the land of G

GILEADITE (9)

Judg 10:3 him arose Jair the G, who judged Israel twenty-two
11:1 Now Jephthah the G was a mighty warrior, but
11:40 daughter of Jephthah the G four days in the
12:7 Then Jephthah the G died, and was buried in
2Sam 17:27 Lo-debar, and Barzillai the G from Rogelim,
19:31 Now Barzillai the G had come down from Rogelim;
1Kgs 2:7 sons of Barzillai the G, and let them be
Ezra 2:61 daughters of Barzillai the G, and was called by
Neh 7:63 daughters of Barzillai the G and was called by

GILEADITES (4)

Num 26:29 of Gilead; of Gilead, the family of the G
Judg 12:4 fugitives of Ephraim, you G, in the midst of
12:5 And the G took the fords of the Jordan
2Kgs 15:25 fifty men of the G, and slew him in

GILGAL (40)

Deut 11:30 the Arabah, over against G, beside the oak of
Josh 4:19 and they encamped in G on the east border
4:20 out of the Jordan, Joshua set up in G
5:9 that place is called G to this day.
5:10 Israel were encamped in G they kept the passover
9:6 in the camp at G, and said to him
10:6 at the camp in G, saying, "Do not relax
10:7 Joshua went up from G, he and all the
10:9 them suddenly, having marched up all night from G
10:15 all Israel with him, to the camp at G
10:43 all Israel with him, to the camp at G
14:6 came to Joshua at G; and Caleb the son
15:7 so northward, turning toward G, which is opposite
Judg 2:1 LORD went up from G to Bochim.
3:19 the sculptured stones near G, and said, "I have
1Sam 7:16 by year to Bethel, G, and Mizpah; and he
10:8 down before me to G; and behold, I am
11:14 let us go to G and there renew the
11:15 the people went to G, and there they made
11:15 they made Saul king before the LORD in G
13:4 people were called out to join Saul at G
13:7 Saul was still at G, and all the people
13:8 did not come to G, and the people were
13:12 down upon me at G, and I have not
13:15 and went up from G to Gibe-ah of Benjamin.
15:12 turned, and passed on, and went down to G
15:21 to sacrifice to the LORD your God in G
15:33 hewed Agag in pieces before the LORD in G
2Sam 19:15 and Judah came to G to meet the king
19:40 king went on to G, and Chimham went on
2Kgs 2:1 Elijah and Elisha were on their way from G
4:38 Elisha came again to G when there was a
Hos 4:15 Enter not into G, nor go up to Beth-aven,
9:15 of theirs is in G; there I began to
12:11 to nought; if in G they sacrifice bulls, their
Amos 4:4 transgress; to G, and multiply transgression; bring
5:5 do not enter into G or cross over to
5:5 over to Beer-sheba; for G shall surely go into
Mic 6:5 happened from Shittim to G, that you may know
1Mac 9:2 road which leads to G and encamped against

GILO

2Sam 23:34 son of Ahithophel of G,

GILOH (2)

Josh 15:51 Anim, Goshen, Holon, and G: eleven cities with their
2Sam 15:12 the Gilonite, David's counselor, from his city G

GILONITE

2Sam 15:12 sent for Ahithophel the G, David's counselor, from his

GIMZO

2Chr 28:18 with its villages, and G with its villages; and

GINATH (2)

1Kgs 16:21 Tibni the son of G, to make him king,
16:22 Tibni the son of G; so Tibni died, and

GINNETHOI

Neh 12:4 Shecaniah, Rehum, Meremoth, Iddo, G, Abijah,

GINNETHON (2)

Neh 10:6 Harim, Meremoth, Obadiah, Daniel, G, Baruch,
12:16 of Iddo, Zechariah; of G, Meshullam;

GIRD (35)

Ex 28:8 band upon it, to G it on, shall be
29:5 and the breastpiece, and G him with the skilfully
29:9 them, and you shall G them with girdles and
39:5 band upon it, to G it on, was of
1Sam 2:4 broken, but the feeble G on strength.
25:13 his men, "Every man G on his sword!" And
2Sam 3:31 "Rend your clothes, and G on sackcloth, and mourn
22:40 For thou didst G me with strength for the
2Kgs 4:29 He said to Gehazi, G up your loins, and
9:1 and said to him, G up your loins, and
Job 38:3 G up your loins like a man, I will
40:7 out of the whirlwind: G up your loins like
Ps 18:39 For thou didst G me with strength for the
45:3 G your sword upon your thigh, O mighty one,
65:12 wilderness drip, the hills G themselves with joy,
76:10 of wrath thou wilt G upon thee.
Is 8:9 all you far countries; G yourselves and be dismayed;
8:9 yourselves and be dismayed; G yourselves and be
15:3 in the streets they G on sackcloth; on the
32:11 yourselves bare, and G sackcloth upon your loins.
45:5 is no God; I G you, though you do
Jer 1:17 But you, G up your loins; arise, and say
4:8 For this G you with sackcloth, lament and wail;
6:26 daughter of my people, G on sackcloth, and roll
49:3 G yourselves with sackcloth, lament, and run to and
Ezek 7:18 They G themselves with sackcloth, and horror covers
27:31 bald for you, and G themselves with sackcloth, and
44:18 loins; they shall not G themselves with anything that
Joel 1:12 G on sackcloth and lament, O priests, wail, O
Nah 2:1 ramparts; watch the road; G your loins; collect all
1Mac 3:58 And Judas said, G yourselves and be valiant.
Lk 12:37 to you, he will G himself and have them
17:8 supper for me, and G yourself and serve me,
Jn 21:18 hands, and another will G you and carry you
1Pet 1:13 Therefore G up your minds, be sober, set your

GIRDED (35)

Ex 12:11 eat it: your loins G, your sandals on your
Lev 8:7 him the coat, and G him with the girdle,
8:7 ephod upon him, and G him with the skilfully
8:13 them with coats, and G them with girdles, and
16:4 on his body, be G with the linen girdle,
Deut 1:41 every man of you G on his weapons of

Judg 3:16 in length; and he G it on his right
1Sam 2:18 the LORD, a boy G with a linen ephod.
17:39 And David G his sword over his armor, and
25:13 every man of them G on his sword; David
25:13 his sword; David also G on his sword; and
2Sam 6:14 might; and David was G with a linen ephod.
21:16 bronze, and who was G with a new sword,
1Kgs 18:46 on Elijah; and he G up his loins and
20:32 So they G sackcloth on their loins, and put
Neh 4:18 builders had his sword G at his side while
Jud 4:10 purchased slave--they all G themselves with
4:14 Lord, with their loins G with sackcloth, offered the
8:5 of her house, and G sackcloth about her loins
Ps 18:32 the God who G me with strength, and
30:11 loosed my sackcloth and G me with gladness,
65:6 established the mountains, being G with might;
93:1 is robed, he is G with strength.
Ezek 23:15 Chaldeans portrayed in vermilion, G with belts on
Dan 10:5 linen, whose loins were G with gold of Uphaz.
Joel 1:8 Lament like a virgin G with sackcloth for the
1Mac 3:3 on his breastplate; he G on his armor of
2Mac 3:19 Women, G with sackcloth under their breasts,
10:25 upon their heads and G their loins with sackcloth,
Lk 12:35 "Let your loins be G and your lamps burning,
Jn 13:4 aside his garments, and G himself with a towel.
13:5 them with the towel with which he was G
21:18 you were young, you G yourself and walked where
Eph 6:14 Stand therefore, having G your loins with truth, and
Rev 15:6 linen, and their breasts G with golden girdles.

GIRDING (2)

Is 3:24 a rich robe, a G of sackcloth; instead of
22:12 mourning, to baldness and G with sackcloth;

GIRDLE (20)

Ex 28:4 a turban, and a G; they shall make holy
28:39 you shall make a G embroidered with needlework.
39:29 twined linen, and the G of fine twined linen
Lev 8:7 girded him with the G, and clothed him with
16:4 girded with the linen G, and wear the linen
1Sam 18:4 even his sword and his bow and his G
2Sam 18:11 give you ten pieces of silver and a G
20:8 over it was a G with a sword in
1Kgs 2:5 innocent blood upon the G about my loins, and
2Kgs 1:8 of haircloth, with a G of leather about his
Jud 9:2 who had loosed the G of a virgin to
Is 3:24 and instead of a G, a rope; and instead
11:5 Righteousness shall be the G of his waist, and
11:5 waist, and faithfulness the G of his loins.
22:21 and will bind your G on him, and will
Mt 3:4 hair, and a leather G around his waist; and
Mk 1:6 and had a leather G around his waist, and
Acts 21:11 us he took Paul's G and bound his own
21:11 man who owns this G and deliver him into
Rev 1:13 and with a golden G round his breast;

GIRDLES (5)

Ex 28:40 shall make coats and G and caps; you shall
29:9 shall gird them with G and bind caps on
Lev 8:13 and girded them with G, and bound caps on
Prov 31:24 sells them; she delivers G to the merchant.
Rev 15:6 bright linen, and their breasts girded with golden G

GIRDS (3)

1Kgs 20:11 'Let not him that G on his armor boast
Ps 109:19 with which he daily G himself!
Prov 31:17 She G her loins with strength and makes her

GIRGASHITE

Neh 9:8 the Jebusite, and the G; and thou hast fulfilled

GIRGASHITES (6)

Gen 10:16 Jebusites, the Amorites, the G,
15:21 Amorites, the Canaanites, the G and the Jebusites."
Deut 7:1 you, the Hittites, the G, the Amorites, the Canaanites,
Josh 3:10 Hivites, the Perizzites, the G, the Amorites, and the
24:11 Canaanites, the Hittites, the G, the Hivites, and the
1Chr 1:14 Jebusites, the Amorites, the G,

GIRL (23)

Ex 2:8 So the G went and called the child's mother.
Judg 19:3 house; and when the G's father saw him, he
19:4 And his father-in-law, the G's father, made him stay,
19:5 to go; but the G's father said to his
19:6 drank together; and the G's father said to the
19:8 to depart; and the G's father said, "Strengthen your
19:9 depart, his father-in-law, the G's father, said to him,
Tob 6:12 The G is also beautiful and sensible.
6:13 have heard that the G has been given to
7:17 her there; and the G began to weep.
Bar 6:9 they would for a G who loves ornaments;
Joel 3:3 and have sold a G for wine, and have
Mt 9:24 said, "Depart; for the G is not dead but
9:25 the hand, and the G arose.
14:11 and given to the G, and she brought it
Mk 5:41 cumi"; which means, "Little G, I say to you,
5:42 And immediately the G got up and walked (she
6:22 king said to the G, "Ask me for whatever
6:28 gave it to the G; and the girl gave
6:28 the girl; and the G gave it to her
Acts 16:16 met by a slave G who had a spirit
1Cor 7:28 sin, and if a G marries she does not
7:34 the unmarried woman or G is anxious about the

GIRLS (2)

Num 31:18 But all the young G who have not known
Zech 8:5 full of boys and G playing in its streets.

GIRT

Song 3:8 men of Israel, all G with swords and expert

GIRZITES

1Sam 27:8 upon the Geshurites, the G, and the Amalekites; for

GISHPA

Neh 11:21 Ophel; and Ziha and G were over the temple

GITTAIM (2)

2Sam 4:3 the Be-erothites fled to G, and have been sojourners
Neh 11:33 Nob, Ananiah, Hazor, Ramah, G,

GITTITE (8)

2Sam 6:10 it aside to the house of Obed-edom the G
6:11 house of Obed-edom the G three months; and the
15:19 said to Ittai the G, "Why do you also
15:22 So Ittai the G passed on, with all his
18:2 one third under the command of Ittai the G
21:19 Bethlehemite, slew Goliath the G, the shaft of whose
1Chr 13:13 it aside to the house of Obed-edom the G
20:5 brother of Goliath the G, the shaft of whose

GITTITES

2Sam 15:18 all the six hundred G who had followed him

GIVE (1,123)

Gen 1:15 of the heavens to G light upon the earth."
1:17 of the heavens to G light upon the earth,
9:3 the green plants, I G you everything.
12:7 your descendants I will G this land." So he
13:15 you see I will G to you and to
13:17 land, for I will G it to you."
14:21 Sodom said to Abram, G me the persons, but
15:2 GOD, what wilt thou G me, for I continue
15:7 of the Chaldeans, to G you this land to
15:18 "To your descendants I G this land, from the
17:8 And I will G to you, and to your
17:16 and moreover I will G you a son by
23:4 a sojourner among you; G me property among you
23:9 Zohar, that he may G me the cave of
23:9 full price let him G it to me in
23:11 lord, hear me; I G you the field, and
23:11 the field, and I G you the cave that
23:11 of my people I G it to you; bury
23:13 hear me; I will G the price of the
24:7 your descendants I will G this land,' he will
24:17 her, and said, "Pray G me a little water
24:41 if they will not G her to you, you
24:43 I shall say, "Pray G me a little water
24:46 'Drink, and I will G your camels drink also.'
26:3 your descendants I will G all these lands, and
26:4 of heaven, and will G to your descendants all
27:28 May God G you of the dew of heaven,
28:4 May he G the blessing of Abraham to you
28:13 you lie I will G to you and to
28:20 I go, and will G me bread to eat
28:22 givest me I will G the tenth to thee."
29:19 is better that I G her to you than
29:19 than that I should G her to any other
29:21 Jacob said to Laban, G me my wife that
29:26 in our country, to G the younger before the
29:27 one, and we will G you the other also
30:1 she said to Jacob, G me children, or I

G

30:14 Rachel said to Leah, G me, I pray, some
30:26 G me my wives and my children for whom
30:28 wages, and I will G it."
30:31 said, "What shall I G you?" Jacob said, "You
30:31 said, "You shall not G me anything; if you
34:8 daughter; I pray you, G her to him in
34:9 Make marriages with us; G your daughters to us,
34:11 and whatever you say to me I will G
34:12 gift, and I will G according as you say
34:12 say to me; only G me the maiden to
34:14 do this thing, to G our sister to one
34:16 Then we will G our daughters to you, and
34:21 marriage, and let us G them our daughters.
35:12 and Isaac I will G to you, and I
35:12 you, and I will G the land to your
38:9 ground, lest he should G offspring to his brother.
38:16 said, "What will you G me, that you may
38:17 she said, "Will you G me a pledge, till
38:18 "What pledge shall I G you?" She replied, "Your
38:26 as I did not G her to my son
41:16 in me; God will G Pharaoh a favorable answer."
42:25 his sack, and to G them provisions for the
42:27 opened his sack to G his ass provender at
45:18 me, and I will G you the best of
45:20 G no thought to your goods, for the best
47:15 to Joseph, and said, G us food; why should
47:16 And Joseph answered, G your cattle, and I will
47:16 cattle, and I will G you food in exchange
47:19 slaves to Pharaoh; and G us seed, that we
47:24 the harvests you shall G a fifth to Pharaoh,
48:4 of peoples, and will G this land to your
Ex 2:9 me, and I will G you your wages." So
3:21 And I will G this people favor in the
5:7 "You shall no longer G the people straw to
5:10 Pharaoh, 'I will not G you straw.
6:4 covenant with them, to G them the land of
6:8 which I swore to G to Abraham, to Isaac,
6:8 to Jacob; I will G it to you for
12:25 which the LORD will G you, as he has
13:5 to your fathers to G you, a land flowing
13:11 your fathers, and shall G it to you,
13:21 pillar of fire to G them light, that they
15:26 in his eyes, and G heed to his commandments
17:2 with Moses, and said, G us water to drink."
18:19 my voice; I will G you counsel, and God
21:23 follows, then you shall G life for life,
21:30 him, then he shall G for the redemption of
21:32 female, the owner shall G to their master thirty
21:34 it good; he shall G money to its owner,
22:16 with her, he shall G the marriage present for
22:17 father utterly refuses to G her to him, he
22:29 your sons you shall G to me.
22:30 eighth day you shall G it to me.
23:21 G heed to him and hearken to his voice,
24:12 there; and I will G you the tables of
25:16 testimony which I shall G you.
25:21 testimony that I shall G you.
25:22 all that I will G you in commandment for
25:37 up so as to G light upon the space
30:12 Israel, then each shall G a ransom for himself
30:13 in the census shall G this: half a shekel
30:14 old and upward, shall G the LORD's offering.
30:15 The rich shall not G more, and the poor
30:15 the poor shall not G less, than the half-shekel,
30:15 the half-shekel, when you G the LORD's offering to
32:13 have promised I will G to your descendants, and
33:1 your descendants I will G it.'
33:14 you, and I will G you rest."
Lev 5:16 fifth to it and G it to the priest;
6:5 fifth to it, and G it to him to
7:32 right thigh you shall G to the priest as
14:34 of Canaan, which I G you for a possession,
15:14 tent of meeting, and G them to the priest;
18:21 You shall not G any of your children to
18:23 neither shall any woman G herself to a beast
20:24 land, and I will G it to you to
22:14 value to it, and G the holy thing to
23:10 the land which I G you and reap its
23:38 freewill offerings, which you G to the LORD.
25:2 the land which I G you, the land shall
25:37 money at interest, nor G him your food for
25:38 land of Egypt to G you the land of
26:4 them, then I will G you your rains in
26:6 And I will G peace in the land, and
27:23 and the man shall G the amount of the
Num 3:9 And you shall G the Levites to Aaron and
3:48 shall take them, and G the money by which
6:26 countenance upon you, and G you peace.
7:5 tent of meeting, and G them to the Levites,
8:2 the seven lamps shall G light in front of
8:3 up its lamps to G light in front of
10:29 LORD said, 'I will G it to you'; come
11:12 thou didst swear to G their fathers?'
11:13 to get meat to G to all this people?
11:13 before me and say, G us meat, that we
11:18 LORD, saying, "Who will G us meat to eat?
11:18 Therefore the LORD will G you meat, and you
11:21 hast said, 'I will G them meat, that they
13:2 of Canaan, which I G to the people of
14:8 into this land and G it to us, a
14:16 which he swore to G to them, therefore he
14:23 which I swore to G to their fathers; and
15:2 to inhabit, which I G you,
15:21 coarse meal you shall G to the LORD an
18:7 I G your priesthood as a gift, and any
18:12 fruits of what they G to the LORD, I
18:12 to the LORD, I G to you.
18:19 to the LORD I G to you, and to
18:28 from it you shall G the LORD's offering to
19:3 And you shall G her to Eleazar the priest,
20:8 them; so you shall G drink to the congregation
20:21 Thus Edom refused to G Israel passage through his
21:2 "If thou wilt indeed G this people into my
21:16 together, and I will G them water."
22:18 "Though Balak were to G me his house full
24:13 me, 'If Balak should G me his house full
25:12 Therefore say, 'Behold, I G to him my covenant
26:54 large tribe you shall G a large inheritance, and
26:54 small tribe you shall G a small inheritance; every
27:4 G to us a possession among our father's brethren."
27:7 are right; you shall G them possession of an
27:9 daughter, then you shall G his inheritance to his
27:10 brothers, then you shall G his inheritance to his
27:11 brothers, then you shall G his inheritance to his
31:29 from their half, and G it to Eleazar the
31:30 all the cattle, and G them to the Levites
32:11 which I swore to G to Abraham, to Isaac,
32:29 you, then you shall G them the land of
33:54 large tribe you shall G a large inheritance, and
33:54 small tribe you shall G a small inheritance; wherever
34:13 LORD has commanded to G to the nine tribes
35:2 of Israel, that they G to the Levites, from
35:2 in; and you shall G to the Levites pasture
35:4 cities, which you shall G to the Levites, shall
35:6 The cities which you G to the Levites shall
35:6 to them you shall G forty-two cities.
35:7 the cities which you G to the Levites shall
35:8 cities which you shall G from the possession of
35:8 which it inherits, shall G of its cities to
35:13 the cities which you G shall be your six
35:14 You shall G three cities beyond the Jordan, and
36:2 commanded my lord to G the land for inheritance
36:2 by the LORD to G the inheritance of Zelophehad
Deut 1:8 and to Jacob, to G to them and to
1:27 land of Egypt, to G us into the hand
1:35 which I swore to G to your fathers,
1:36 his children I will G the land upon which
1:39 to them I will G it, and they shall
1:45 to your voice or G ear to you.
2:5 for I will not G you any of their
2:9 for I will not G you any of their
2:19 for I will not G you any of the
2:28 I may eat, and G me water for money,
2:30 obstinate, that he might G him into your hand,
2:31 I have begun to G Sihon and his land
4:1 "And now, O Israel, G heed to the statutes
4:38 bring you in, to G you their land for
5:31 the land which I G them to possess.'
6:10 and to Jacob, to G you, with great and
6:18 the LORD swore to G to your fathers
6:23 bring us in and G us the land which
6:23 which he swore to G to our fathers.
7:13 to your fathers to G you.
7:16 LORD your God will G over to you, your
7:23 LORD your God will G them over to you,
7:24 And he will G their kings into your hand,
8:1 the LORD swore to G to your fathers.
10:11 to their fathers to G them.'
11:9 to your fathers to G to them and to
11:14 your soul, he will G the rain for your
11:15 And he will G grass in your fields for
11:21 to your fathers to G them, as long as

14:21 of itself; you may G it to the alien
15:9 poor brother, and you G him nothing, and he
15:10 You shall G to him freely, and your heart
15:10 be grudging when you G to him; because for
15:14 blessed you, you shall G to him.
16:10 hand, which you shall G as the LORD your
16:17 empty-handed; every man shall G as he is able,
17:11 the instructions which they G you, and according to
18:3 or sheep: they shall G to the priest the
18:4 your sheep, you shall G him.
18:14 are about to dispossess, G heed to soothsayers and
18:19 And whoever will not G heed to my words
19:8 which he promised to G to your fathers--
20:4 against your enemies, to G you the victory.'
21:18 chastise him, will not G heed to them,
22:19 shekels of silver, and G them to the father
22:29 lay with her shall G to the father of
23:14 save you and to G up your enemies before
23:15 "You shall not G up to his master a
24:15 your towns; you shall G him his hire on
26:3 to our fathers to G us.'
28:11 to your fathers to G you.
28:12 treasury the heavens, to G the rain of your
28:55 that he will not G to any of them
28:65 but the LORD will G you there a trembling
30:20 and to Jacob, to G them."
31:5 And the LORD will G them over to you,
31:7 to their fathers to G them; and you shall
31:20 which I swore to G to their fathers, and
31:21 them into the land that I swore to G
31:23 which I swore to G them: I will be
32:1 G ear, O heavens, and I will speak; and
32:49 of Canaan, which I G to the people of
32:52 the land which I G to the people of
33:8 of Levi he said, G to Levi thy Thummim,
34:4 to Jacob, 'I will G it to your descendants.'
Josh 1:6 to their fathers to G them.
1:13 of rest, and will G you this land.'
2:12 my father's house, and G me a sure sign,
5:6 to their fathers to G us, a land flowing
7:7 Jordan at all, to G us into the hands
7:19 to Achan, "My son, G glory to the LORD
8:7 LORD your God will G it into your hand.
8:18 Ai; for I will G it into your hand."
9:24 his servant Moses to G you all the land,
11:6 this time I will G over all of them,
14:12 So now G me this hill country of which
15:16 to him will I G Achsah my daughter as
15:19 She said to him, G me a present; since
15:19 land of the Negeb, G me also springs of
17:4 LORD commanded Moses to G us an inheritance
20:4 into the city, and G him a place, and
20:5 him, they shall not G up the slayer into
21:43 which he swore to G to their fathers; and
Judg 1:12 takes it, I will G him Achsah my daughter
1:15 She said to him, G me a present; since
1:15 land of the Negeb, G me also springs of
2:1 which I swore to G to your fathers.
2:23 and he did not G them into the power
4:7 troops; and I will G him into your hand.'"
4:19 said to her, "Pray, G me a little water
5:3 "Hear, O kings; G ear, O princes; to the
7:2 many for me to G the Midianites into their
7:7 will deliver you, and G the Midianites into your
8:5 men of Succoth, "Pray, G loaves of bread to
8:6 hand, that we should G bread to your army?"
8:15 hand, that we should G bread to your men
8:24 a request of you; G me every man of
8:25 answered, "We will willingly G them." And they
11:30 said, "If thou wilt G the Ammonites into my
14:12 out, then I will G you thirty linen garments
14:13 is, then you shall G me thirty linen garments
15:12 you, that we may G you into the hands
15:13 only bind you and G you into their hands;
16:5 and we will each G you eleven hundred pieces
17:10 priest, and I will G you ten pieces of
20:7 Israel, all of you, G your advice and counsel
20:13 Now therefore G up the men, the base fellows
20:28 for tomorrow I will G them into your hand."
21:1 one of us shall G his daughter in marriage
21:7 that we will not G them any of our
21:18 Yet we cannot G them wives of our daughters."
21:22 battle, neither did you G them to them, else
Ruth 4:12 that the LORD will G you by this young
1Sam 1:4 Elkanah sacrificed, he would G portions to Peninnah
1:5 loved Hannah, he would G Hannah only one portion,
1:11 thy maidservant, but wilt G to thy maidservant a
1:11 son, then I will G him to the LORD
2:10 the earth; he will G strength to his king,
2:15 man who was sacrificing, G meat for the priest
2:16 say, "No, you must G it now; and if
2:20 and say, "The LORD G you children by this
4:19 with child, about to G birth.
4:20 did not answer or G heed.
6:5 ravage the land, and G glory to the God
8:6 Samuel when they said, G us a king to
8:14 and olive orchards and G them to his servants.
8:15 of your vineyards and G it to his officers
9:8 silver, and I will G it to the man
10:4 will greet you and G you two loaves of
11:3 Jabesh said to him, G us seven days respite
11:3 save us, we will G ourselves up to you."
11:10 said, "Tomorrow we will G ourselves up to you,
14:37 Wilt thou G them into the hand of Israel?"
14:41 LORD, God of Israel, G Urim; but if this
14:41 in thy people Israel, G Thummim." And Jonathan and
17:10 of Israel this day; G me a man, that
17:25 great riches, and will G him his daughter, and
17:44 me, and I will G your flesh to the
17:46 head; and I will G the dead bodies of
17:47 LORD's and he will G you into our hand."
18:17 daughter Merab; I will G her to you for
18:21 Saul thought, "Let me G her to him, that
21:3 G me five loaves of bread, or whatever is
21:9 is none like that; G it to me."
22:7 the son of Jesse G every one of you
23:4 Keilah; for I will G the Philistines into your
23:14 but God did not G him into his hand.
24:4 you, 'Behold, I will G your enemy into your
24:15 therefore be judge, and G sentence between me and
25:8 Pray, G whatever you have at hand to your
25:11 for my shearers, and G it to men who
28:19 Moreover the LORD will G Israel also with you
28:19 me; the LORD will G the army of Israel
30:22 us, we will not G them any of the
2Sam 3:14 Ish-bosheth Saul's son, saying, G me my wife Michal,
5:19 Wilt thou G them into my hand?" And the
5:19 for I will certainly G the Philistines into your
7:11 Israel; and I will G you rest from all
12:11 before your eyes, and G them to your neighbor,
13:5 sister Tamar come and G me bread to eat,
14:7 handmaid, and they say, G up the man who
14:8 house, and I will G orders concerning you."
15:4 me, and I would G him justice."
16:3 house of Israel will G me back the kingdom
16:20 Absalom said to Ahithophel, G your counsel; what
18:11 have been glad to G you ten pieces of
20:21 hand against King David; G up him alone, and
21:6 king said, "I will G them."
22:37 Thou didst G a wide place for my steps
23:15 that some one would G me water to drink
1Kgs 1:12 therefore come, let me G you counsel, that you
2:17 not refuse you--to G me Abishag the Shunammite
3:5 "Ask what I shall G you."
3:9 G thy servant therefore an understanding mind to
3:12 Behold, I G you a wise and discerning mind,
3:13 I G you also what you have not asked,
3:25 child in two, and G half to the one,
3:26 son, "Oh, my lord, G her the living child,
3:27 king answered and said, G the living child to
8:46 with them, and dost G them to an enemy,
11:11 from you and will G it to your servant.
11:13 kingdom; but I will G one tribe to your
11:31 of Solomon, and will G you ten tribes
11:35 son's hand, and will G it to you, ten
11:36 his son I will G one tribe, that David
11:38 David, and I will G Israel to you.
13:7 yourself, and I will G you a reward."
13:8 the king, "If you G me half your house,
14:16 And he will G Israel up because of the
17:19 he said to her, G me your son." And
18:9 sinned, that you would G your servant into the
20:13 Behold, I will G it into your hand this
20:28 therefore I will G all this great multitude into
21:2 Ahab said to Naboth, G me your vineyard, that
21:2 house; and I will G you a better vineyard
21:2 to you, I will G you its value in
21:3 forbid that I should G you the inheritance of
21:4 said, "I will not G you the inheritance of
21:6 and said to him, G me your vineyard for
21:6 please you, I will G you another vineyard for
21:6 answered, 'I will not G you my vineyard.'"

G

21:7 be cheerful; I will G you the vineyard of
21:15 which he refused to G you for money; for
22:6 for the Lord will G it into the hand
22:12 triumph; the LORD will G it into the hand
22:15 triumph; the LORD will G it into the hand
2Kgs 3:10 these three kings to G them into the hand
3:13 these three kings to G them into the hand
3:18 LORD; he will also G the Moabites into your
4:42 And Elisha said, G to the men, that they
4:43 So he repeated, G them to the men, that
5:22 of the prophets; pray, G them a talent of
6:28 woman said to me, G your son, that we
6:29 I said to her, G your son, that we
8:19 since he promised to G a lamp to him
10:15 said, "If it is, G me your hand." So
10:24 of those whom I G into your hands to
12:11 Then they would G the money that was weighed
14:9 cedar on Lebanon, saying, G your daughter to my
15:20 from every man, to G to the king of
18:23 of Assyria: I will G you two thousand horses,
21:14 of my heritage, and G them into the hand
22:5 LORD; and let them G it to the workmen
23:35 taxed the land to G the money according to
23:35 to his assessment, to G it to Pharaoh Neco.
1Chr 11:17 that some one would G me water to drink
14:10 Wilt thou G them into my hand?" And the
14:10 up, and I will G them into your hand."
16:8 O G thanks to the LORD, call on his
16:18 "To you I will G the land of Canaan,
16:34 O G thanks to the LORD, for he is
16:35 nations, that we may G thanks to thy holy
16:41 and expressly named to G thanks to the LORD,
21:22 David said to Ornan, G me the site of
21:22 altar to the LORD– G it to me at
21:23 to him; see, I G the oxen for burnt
21:23 I G it all."
22:9 I will G him peace from all his enemies
22:9 Solomon, and I will G peace and quiet to
29:3 of my God I G it to the house
29:12 make great and to G strength to all.
2Chr 1:7 "Ask what I shall G you."
1:10 G me now wisdom and knowledge to go out
1:12 I will also G you riches, possessions, and honor,
2:10 I will G for your servants, the hewers who
6:36 with them, and dost G them to an enemy,
18:5 up; for God will G it into the hand
18:11 triumph; the LORD will G it into the hand
19:8 families of Israel, to G judgment for the LORD
20:7 thy people Israel, and G it for ever to
20:21 the army, and say, G thanks to the LORD,
21:7 he had promised to G a lamp to him
24:19 but they would not G heed.
25:9 LORD is able to G you much more than
25:18 cedar on Lebanon, saying, G your daughter to my
25:20 order that he might G them into the hand
30:12 also upon Judah to G them one heart to
31:2 the LORD and to G thanks and praise.
31:4 lived in Jerusalem to G the portion due to
31:4 Levites, that they might G themselves to the law
32:11 you, that he may G you over to die
Ezra 9:8 a remnant, and to G us a secure hold
9:9 its ruins, and to G us protection in Judea
9:12 Therefore G not your daughters to their sons, neither
Neh 1:11 fear thy name; and G success to thy servant
2:8 forest, that he may G me timber to make
4:4 their own heads, and G them up to be
6:13 and so they could G me an evil name,
9:7 of the Chaldeans and G him the name Abraham;
9:8 him the covenant to G to his descendants the
9:13 them from heaven and G them right ordinances and
9:15 Thou didst G them bread from heaven for their
9:15 thou hadst sworn to G them.
9:22 And thou didst G them kingdoms and peoples, and
9:24 the Canaanites, and didst G them into their hands,
9:27 Therefore thou didst G them into the hand of
9:27 great mercies thou didst G them saviors who saved
9:30 yet they would not G ear.
9:30 Therefore thou didst G them into the hand of
9:34 warnings which thou didst G them.
10:30 We will not G our daughters to the peoples
12:24 to praise and to G thanks, according to the
13:25 saying, "You shall not G your daughters to their
Tob 1:6 first shearings, I would G these to the priests,
1:7 my produce I would G a tenth to the
1:8 third tenth I would G to those to whom
1:17 I would G my bread to the hungry and

3:17 of Tobit's eyes; to G Sarah the daughter of
4:7 G alms from your possessions to all who live
4:8 not be afraid to G according to the little
4:16 G of your bread to the hungry, and of
4:16 G all your surplus to charity, and do not
4:17 of the righteous, but G none to sinners.
6:12 law of Moses, cannot G her to another man
10:2 is no one to G him the money?"
12:2 me no harm to G him half of what
12:6 them: "Praise God and G thanks to him; exalt
12:6 him; exalt him and G thanks to him in
12:6 not be slow to G him thanks.
12:8 It is better to G alms than to treasure
12:20 And now G thanks to God, for I am
13:6 will do with you; G thanks to him with
13:6 I G him thanks in the land of my
13:8 all men speak, and G him thanks in Jerusalem.
13:10 G thanks worthily to the Lord, and praise the
13:11 Generations of generations will G you joyful praise.
13:18 cry 'Hallelujah!' and will G praise, saying, 'Blessed is
14:7 and his people will G thanks to God, and
Jud 4:12 of Israel not to G up their infants as
7:13 them, and they will G up their city.
8:25 of everything let us G thanks to the Lord
9:9 wrath upon their heads; G to me, a widow,
10:13 of your army, to G him a true report;
13:7 his head, and said, G me strength this day,
14:13 down against us to G battle, in order to
16:17 and worms he will G to their flesh; they
Esth 1:19 and let the king G her royal position to
1:20 is, all women will G honor to their husbands,
14:12 of our affliction, and G me courage, O King
16:20 And G them reinforcements, so that on the thirteenth
Job 2:4 man has he will G for his life.
10:1 my life; I will G free utterance to my
17:3 is there that will G surety for me?
20:10 and his hands will G back his wealth.
20:18 He will G back the fruit of his toil,
23:6 No; he would G heed to me.
31:37 a crown; I would G him an account of
32:17 I also will G my answer; I also will
33:31 G heed, O Job, listen to me; be silent,
34:2 you wise men, and G ear to me, you
35:7 righteous, what do you G to him; or what
39:19 "Do you G the horse his might?
40:14 own right hand can G you victory.
Ps 5:1 G ear to my words, O LORD; give heed
5:1 my words, O LORD; G heed to my groaning.
6:5 in Sheol who can G thee praise?
7:17 I will G to the LORD the thanks due
9:1 I will G thanks to the LORD with my
16:10 For thou dost not G me up to Sheol,
17:1 G ear to my prayer from lips free of
18:36 Thou didst G a wide place for my steps
20:2 from the sanctuary, and G you support from Zion!
20:9 G victory to the king, O LORD; answer us
27:12 G me not up to the will of my
28:7 with my song I G thanks to him.
29:11 May the LORD G strength to his people!
30:4 you his saints, and G thanks to his holy
30:12 my God, I will G thanks to thee for
37:4 LORD, and he will G you the desires of
39:12 prayer, O LORD, and G ear to my cry;
41:2 land; thou dost not G him up to the
44:3 did their own arm G them victory; but thy
44:8 continually, and we will G thanks to thy name
49:1 G ear, all inhabitants of the world,
49:7 can ransom himself, or G to God the price
50:19 "You G your mouth free rein for evil, and
51:16 sacrifice; were I to G a burnt offering, thou
54:2 my prayer, O God; G ear to the words
54:6 to thee; I will G thanks to thy name,
55:1 G ear to my prayer, O God; and hide
55:19 God will G ear, and humble them, he who
57:9 I will G thanks to thee, O Lord, among
60:5 beloved may be delivered, G victory by thy right
66:2 glory of his name; G to him glorious praise!
72:1 G the king thy justice, O God, and thy
72:4 poor of the people, G deliverance to the needy,
74:14 of Leviathan, thou didst G him as food for
75:1 We G thanks to thee, O God; we give
75:1 thee, O God; we G thanks; we call on
78:1 G ear, O my people, to my teaching; incline
78:20 Can he also G bread, or provide meat for
79:13 of thy pasture, will G thanks to thee for
80:1 G ear, O Shepherd of Israel, thou who leadest

80:18 turn back from thee; G us life, and we
82:3 [Selah] G justice to the weak and the fatherless;
84:8 hosts, hear my prayer; G ear, O God of
85:12 Yea, the LORD will G what is good, and
86:6 G ear, O LORD, to my prayer; hearken to
86:12 I G thanks to thee, O Lord my God,
86:16 take pity on me; G thy strength to thy
91:11 For he will G his angels charge of you
92:1 It is good to G thanks to the LORD,
94:13 of thy law to G him respite from days
97:12 O you righteous, and G thanks to his holy
100:4 G thanks to him, bless his name!
101:2 I will G heed to the way that is
104:11 between the hills, they G drink to every beast
104:27 look to thee, to G them their food in
105:1 O G thanks to the LORD, call on his
105:11 "To you I will G the land of Canaan
105:39 covering, and fire to G light by night.
106:1 O G thanks to the LORD, for he is
106:47 nations, that we may G thanks to thy holy
107:1 O G thanks to the LORD, for he is
107:43 is wise, let him G heed to these things;
108:3 I will G thanks to thee, O LORD, among
108:6 beloved may be delivered, G help by thy right
109:30 my mouth I will G great thanks to the
111:1 I will G thanks to the LORD with my
115:1 but to thy name G glory, for the sake
115:14 May the LORD G you increase, you and your
118:1 O G thanks to the LORD, for he is
118:19 enter through them and G thanks to the LORD.
118:25 LORD, we beseech thee, G us success!
118:28 God, and I will G thanks to thee; thou
118:29 O G thanks to the LORD, for he is
119:34 G me understanding, that I may keep thy law
119:37 looking at vanities; and G me life in thy
119:40 precepts; in thy righteousness G me life!
119:73 made and fashioned me; G me understanding that I
119:107 I am sorely afflicted; G me life, O LORD,
119:125 I am thy servant; G me understanding, that I
119:144 are righteous for ever; G me understanding that I
119:154 cause and redeem me; G me life according to
119:156 thy mercy, O LORD; G me life according to
119:169 before thee, O LORD; G me understanding according
122:4 decreed for Israel, to G thanks to the name
132:4 bed; I will not G sleep to my eyes
135:1 name of the LORD, G praise, O servants of
136:1 O G thanks to the LORD, for he is
136:2 O G thanks to the God of gods, for
136:3 O G thanks to the Lord of lords, for
136:26 O G thanks to the God of heaven, for
138:1 I G thee thanks, O LORD, with my whole
138:2 thy holy temple and G thanks to thy name
140:6 Thou art my God; G ear to the voice
140:13 Surely the righteous shall G thanks to thy name;
141:1 G ear to my voice, when I call to
142:6 G heed to my cry; for I am brought
142:7 prison, that I may G thanks to thy name!
143:1 my prayer, O LORD; G ear to my supplications!
145:10 All thy works shall G thanks to thee, O
Prov 1:23 G heed to my reproof; behold, I will pour
3:2 abundant welfare will they G you.
3:28 again, tomorrow I will G it"—when you have
4:3 gain insight; for I G you good precepts: do
5:9 her house; lest you G your honor to others
6:4 G your eyes no sleep and your eyelids no
6:31 pay sevenfold; he will G all the goods of
9:9 G instruction to a wise man, and he will
11:24 withholds what he should G, and only suffers want.
22:21 true, that you may G a true answer to
22:26 one of those who G pledges, who become surety
23:26 My son, G me your heart, and let your
25:14 who boasts of a gift he does not G
25:21 your enemy is hungry, G him bread to eat;
25:21 if he is thirsty, G him water to drink;
27:23 of your flocks, and G attention to your herds;
29:15 The rod and reproof G wisdom, but a child
29:17 son, and he will G you rest; he will
29:17 you rest; he will G delight to your heart.
29:19 understands, he will not G heed.
30:8 me falsehood and lying; G me neither poverty nor
30:15 leech has two daughters; G, give," they cry.
30:15 The leech has two daughters; "Give, G
31:3 G not your strength to women, your ways to
31:6 G strong drink to him who is perishing, and
31:31 G her of the fruit of her hands, and
Eccl 2:26 and heaping, only to G to one who pleases
6:2 yet God does not G him power to enjoy
7:21 Do not G heed to all the things that
10:1 make the perfumer's ointment G off an evil odor;
11:2 G a portion to seven, or even to eight,
Song 2:13 are in blossom; they G forth fragrance.
7:12 There I will G you my love.
7:13 The mandrakes G forth fragrance, and over our
8:2 I would G you spiced wine to drink, the
Wis 6:2 G ear, you that rule over multitudes, and boast
8:9 knowing that she would G me good counsel and
8:12 I speak they will G heed; and when I
9:4 in uprightness of soul, G me the wisdom that
12:9 wast not unable to G the ungodly into the
12:20 time and opportunity to G up their wickedness,
13:10 are the men who G the name "gods" to
16:20 these things thou didst G thy people food of
16:28 before the sun to G thee thanks, and must
17:5 fire was able to G light, nor did the
19:12 luxurious food; for, to G them relief, quails came
Sir 4:5 from the needy, nor G a man occasion to
6:37 is he who will G insight to your mind,
7:10 prayer, nor neglect to G alms.
7:25 G a daughter in marriage; you will have finished
7:25 But G her to a man of understanding.
7:28 and what can you G back to them that
7:31 honor the priest, and G him his portion, as
7:33 G graciously to all the living, and withhold not
8:9 and learn how to G an answer in time
8:13 Do not G surety beyond your means, but if
8:13 means, but if you G surety, be concerned as
9:2 Do not G yourself to a woman so that
9:6 Do not G yourself to harlots lest you lose
11:31 devises evil, lest he G you a lasting blemish.
12:3 him who does not G alms.
12:4 G to the godly man, but do not help
12:5 humble, but do not G to the ungodly; hold
12:5 bread, and do not G it to him, lest
12:7 G to the good man, but do not help
13:6 smile at you and G you hope.
14:13 and reach out and G to him as much
14:16 G, and take, and beguile yourself, because in Hades
15:3 bread of understanding, and G him the water of
17:22 who are alive and G thanks?
23:4 my life, do not G me haughty eyes,
27:23 own words he will G offense.
29:27 G place, stranger, to an honored person; my brother
30:9 him, and he will G you grief.
30:11 G him no authority in his youth, and do
30:21 Do not G yourself over to sorrow, and do
30:25 and good heart will G heed to the food
31:17 be insatiable, lest you G offense.
32:22 a smooth way, and G good heed to your
33:13 who made them, to G them as he decides.
33:19 or friend, do not G power over yourself, as
33:19 live; and do not G your property to another,
34:1 false hopes, and dreams G wings to fools.
34:6 a visitation, do not G your mind to them.
35:10 G to the Most High as he has given,
36:11 tribes of Jacob, and G them their inheritance, as
37:7 praises counsel, but some G counsel in their own
37:27 it and do not G it that.
37:29 luxury, and do not G yourself up to food;
38:10 G up your faults and direct your hands aright,
38:12 And G the physician his place, for the Lord
38:20 Do not G your heart to sorrow; drive it
39:6 words of wisdom and G thanks to the Lord
39:15 to his name and G thanks to him with
42:7 of all that you G out or take in.
46:1 so that he might G Israel its inheritance.
47:22 the Lord will never G up his mercy, nor
50:23 May he G us gladness of heart, and grant
51:1 I will G thanks to thee, O Lord and
51:1 I G thanks to thy name,
51:12 Therefore I will G thanks to thee and praise
51:17 gives wisdom I will G glory.
51:30 God's time he will G you your reward.
Is 1:2 Hear, O heavens, and G ear, O earth; for
1:10 G ear to the teaching of our God, you
7:14 the Lord himself will G you a sign.
7:22 of milk which they G, he will eat curds;
8:9 peoples, and be dismayed; G ear, all you far
12:1 that day: "I will G thanks to thee, O
12:4 say in that day: G thanks to the LORD,
13:10 their constellations will not G their light; the sun
16:3 G counsel, grant justice; make your shade like night
19:4 wizards; and I will G over the Egyptians into

19:11 wise counselors of Pharaoh G stupid counsel.
22:25 a sure place will G way; and it will
24:15 Therefore in the east G glory to the LORD;
28:12 said, "This is rest; G rest to the weary;
28:23 G ear, and hear my voice; hearken, and hear
29:11 When men G it to one who can read,
29:12 And when they G the book to one who
30:20 And though the Lord G you the bread of
30:23 And he will G rain for the seed with
32:9 voice; you complacent daughters, G ear to my
36:8 of Assyria: I will G you two thousand horses,
41:27 to Zion, and I G to Jerusalem a herald
42:8 name; my glory I G to no other, nor
42:12 Let them G glory to the LORD, and declare
42:23 Who among you will G ear to this, will
43:3 I G Egypt as your ransom, Ethiopia and Seba
43:4 I love you, I G men in return for
43:6 say to the north, G up, and to the
43:20 the ostriches; for I G water in the wilderness,
43:20 in the desert, to G drink to my chosen
45:3 of iron, I will G you the treasures of
48:11 glory I will not G to another.
49:6 of Israel; I will G you as a light
51:4 me, my people, and G ear to me, my
56:5 my covenant, I will G in my house and
56:5 and daughters; I will G them an everlasting name
57:11 remember me, did not G me a thought?
60:19 brightness shall the moon G light to you by
61:3 in Zion-- to G them a garland instead
61:8 wrong; I will faithfully G them their recompense, and
62:2 name which the mouth of the LORD will G
62:7 take no rest, and G him no rest until
62:8 "I will not again G your grain to be
Jer 3:15 "And I will G you shepherds after my own
3:19 among my sons, and G you a pleasant land,
6:10 shall I speak and G warning, that they may
6:17 watchmen over you, saying, G heed to the sound
6:17 said, 'We will not G heed.'
8:10 Therefore I will G their wives to others and
9:15 people with wormwood, and G them poisonous
11:5 to your fathers, to G them a land flowing
13:15 Hear and G ear; be not proud, for the
13:16 G glory to the LORD your God before he
14:13 famine, but I will G you assured peace in
14:22 Or can the heavens G showers?
15:9 of them I will G to the sword before
15:13 your treasures I will G as spoil, without price,
16:7 nor shall any one G him the cup of
17:3 your treasures I will G for spoil as the
17:10 try the heart, to G to every man according
18:19 G heed to me, O LORD, and hearken to
18:21 their children to famine; G them over to the
19:7 I will G their dead bodies for food to
20:4 And I will G all Judah into the hand
20:5 Moreover, I will G all the wealth of the
21:7 the LORD, I will G Zedekiah king of Judah,
22:13 nothing, and does not G him his wages;
22:25 tear you off and G you into the hand
23:15 them with wormwood, and G them poisoned water
24:7 I will G them a heart to know that
27:4 G them this charge for their masters: 'Thus says
27:5 the earth, and I G it to whomever it
27:22 the day when I G attention to them, says
29:6 for your sons, and G your daughters in marriage,
29:11 not for evil, to G you a future and
31:7 of the nations; proclaim, G praise, and say, 'The
31:13 will comfort them, and G them gladness for sorrow.
32:22 to their fathers to G them, a land flowing
32:39 I will G them one heart and one way,
33:11 house of the LORD: G thanks to the LORD
34:20 calf; and I will G them into the hand
34:21 his princes I will G into the hand of
38:15 And if I G you counsel, you will not
44:30 LORD, Behold, I will G Pharaoh Hophra king of
45:5 LORD; but I will G you your life as
48:9 G wings to Moab, for she would fly away;
50:34 cause, that he may G rest to the earth,
Lam 2:18 G yourself no rest, your eyes no respite!
3:30 be hope; let him G his cheek to the
3:65 Thou wilt G them dullness of heart; thy curse
4:3 Even the jackals G the breast and suckle their
Bar 1:12 And the Lord will G us strength, and he
1:12 strength, and he will G light to our eyes,
1:20 land of Egypt to G to us a land
2:31 I will G them a heart that obeys and
2:34 which I swore to G to their fathers, to

3:9 of life, O Israel; G ear, and learn wisdom!
3:27 not choose them, nor G them the way to
4:3 Do not G your glory to another, or your
4:23 weeping, but God will G you back to me
6:1 of the Babylonians, to G them the message which
6:11 upon themselves, and even G some of it to
6:28 some with salt, but G none to the poor
6:35 are not able to G either wealth or money;
6:53 over a country or G rain to men.
6:67 like the sun or G light like the moon.
Ezek 2:8 and eat what I G you."
3:3 this scroll that I G you and fill your
3:17 my mouth, you shall G them warning from me.
3:18 surely die,' and you G him no warning, nor
7:21 And I will G it into the hands of
11:2 devise iniquity and who G wicked counsel in this
11:9 midst of it, and G you into the hands
11:17 scattered, and I will G you the land of
11:19 And I will G them one heart, and put
11:19 of their flesh and G them a heart of
13:9 delusive visions and who G lying divinations; they
15:6 fuel, so will I G up the inhabitants of
16:33 Men G gifts to all harlots; but you gave
16:39 And I will G you into the hand of
16:41 and you shall also G hire no more.
16:61 and your younger, and G them to you as
17:15 Egypt, that they might G him horses and a
20:28 which I swore to G them, then wherever they
20:42 which I swore to G to your fathers.
21:27 to him I will G it.
23:8 She did not G up her harlotry which she
23:31 sister; therefore I will G her cup into your
25:10 I will G it along with the Ammonites to
29:19 GOD: Behold, I will G the land of Egypt
31:11 its height, I will G it into the hand
32:7 the moon shall not G its light.
33:7 my mouth, you shall G them warning from me.
33:27 open field I will G to the beasts to
36:26 new heart I will G you, and a new
36:26 heart of stone and G you a heart of
39:4 with you; I will G you to birds of
39:11 that day I will G to Gog a place
43:19 against it, you shall G to the Levitical priests
44:28 inheritance: and you shall G them no possession in
44:30 priests; you shall also G to the priests the
45:16 of the land shall G this offering to the
46:11 one is able to G, together with a hin
46:18 their property; he shall G his sons their inheritance
47:14 equally; I swore to G it to your fathers,
Dan 2:23 of my fathers, I G thanks and praise, for
3:34 name's sake do not G us up utterly, and
3:43 thy marvelous works, and G glory to thy name,
3:90 G thanks to the Lord, for he is good,
3:91 praise to him and G thanks to him, for
5:16 heard that you can G interpretations and solve
5:17 be for yourself, and G your rewards to another;
6:2 whom these satraps should G account, so that the
9:19 LORD, forgive; O LORD, G heed and act; delay
9:22 now come out to G you wisdom and understanding.
10:11 Daniel, man greatly beloved, G heed to the words
11:17 He shall G him the daughter of women to
11:30 shall turn back and G heed to those who
11:37 He shall G no heed to the gods of
11:37 women; he shall not G heed to any other
13:20 love with you; so G your consent, and lie
14:26 you, O king, will G me permission, I will
14:26 The king said, "I G you permission."
Hos 2:5 after my lovers, who G me my bread and
2:15 And there I will G her her vineyards, and
4:18 band of drunkards, they G themselves to harlotry;
5:1 G heed, O house of Israel!
9:14 G them, O LORD--what wilt thou give?
9:14 Give them, O LORD--what wilt thou G
9:14 G them a miscarrying womb and dry breasts.
11:8 How can I G you up, O Ephraim!
13:10 of whom you said, G me a king and
Joel 1:2 this, you aged men, G ear, all inhabitants of
2:22 fig tree and vine G their full yield.
2:30 "And I will G portents in the heavens and
Jon 1:6 Perhaps the god will G a thought to us,
Mic 1:14 you shall G parting gifts to Moresheth-gath; the
3:11 Its heads G judgment for a bribe, its priests
5:3 Therefore he shall G them up until the time
6:7 Shall I G my first-born for my transgression, the
6:14 you save I will G to the sword.
Hab 2:19 Can this G revelation?

Hag 2:9 this place I will G prosperity, says the LORD
Zech 3:7 courts, and I will G you the right of
8:12 and the ground shall G its increase, and the
8:12 and the heavens shall G their dew; and I
10:2 tell false dreams, and G empty consolation.
11:12 seems right to you, G me my wages; but
12:7 "And the LORD will G victory to the tents
Mal 2:2 it to heart to G glory to my name,
1Mac 1:42 and that each should G up his customs.
2:50 for the law, and G your lives for the
3:30 which he used to G more lavishly than preceding
4:30 servant David, and didst G the camp of the
8:7 a heavy tribute and G hostages and surrender some
8:26 war they shall not G or supply grain, arms,
9:55 say a word or G commands concerning his house.
10:28 you many immunities and G you gifts.
10:32 citadel in Jerusalem and G it to the high
10:41 first years, they shall G from now on for
10:54 friendship with one another; G me now your
10:89 is the custom to G to the kinsmen of
11:9 other, and I will G you in marriage my
15:31 of Judea; or else G me for them five
15:35 for them we will G you a hundred talents."
16:19 so that he might G them silver and gold
2Mac 1:3 May he G you all a heart to worship
7:23 will in his mercy G life and breath back
7:37 I, like my brothers, G up body and life
9:16 holy vessels he would G back, all of them,
10:10 ungodly man, and will G a brief summary of
11:26 word to them and G them pledges of friendship,
11:35 granted you, we also G consent.
12:11 of friendship, promising to G him cattle and to
14:19 Theodotus and Mattathias to G and receive pledges
14:46 life and spirit to G them back to him
15:8 which the Almighty would G them.
15:33 said that he would G it piecemeal to the
Mt 4:6 is written, 'He will G his angels charge of
4:9 "All these I will G you, if you will
5:16 your good works and G glory to your Father
5:31 his wife, let him G her a certificate of
5:42 G to him who begs from you, and do
6:2 "Thus, when you G alms, sound no trumpet before
6:3 But when you G alms, do not let your
6:11 G us this day our daily bread;
7:2 and the measure you G will be the measure
7:6 "Do not G dogs what is holy; and do
7:9 him for bread, will G him a stone?
7:10 for a fish, will G him a serpent?
7:11 evil, know how to G good gifts to your
7:11 who is in heaven G good things to those
10:8 You received without paying, G without pay.
11:28 laden, and I will G you rest.
14:7 with an oath to G her whatever she might
14:8 her mother, she said, G me the head of
14:16 not go away; you G them something to eat."
16:19 I will G you the keys of the kingdom
16:26 what shall a man G in return for his
17:26 However, not to G offense to them, go to
17:26 shekel; take that and G it to them for
19:7 Moses command one to G a certificate of divorce,
19:21 what you possess and G to the poor, and
20:4 is right I will G you.' So they went.
20:14 go; I choose to G to this last as
20:14 this last as I G to you.
20:28 to serve, and to G his life as a
21:41 other tenants who will G him the fruits in
24:19 and for those who G suck in those days!
24:29 the moon will not G its light, and the
24:45 over his household, to G them their food at
25:8 said to the wise, G us some of your
25:28 talent from him, and G it to him who
25:37 thee, or thirsty and G thee drink?
26:15 said, "What will you G me if I deliver
Mk 4:24 hear; the measure you G will be the measure
5:43 and told them to G her something to eat.
6:23 ask me, I will G you, even half of
6:25 "I want you to G me at once the
6:37 he answered them, "You G them something to eat."
6:37 worth of bread, and G it to them to
8:37 what can a man G in return for his
10:21 what you have, and G to the poor, and
10:45 to serve, and to G his life as a
12:9 destroy the tenants, and G the vineyard to others.
13:17 and for those who G suck in those days!
13:24 the moon will not G its light,
14:11 glad, and promised to G him money.
Lk 1:32 the Lord God will G to him the throne
1:77 prepare his ways, to G knowledge of salvation to
1:79 from on high to G light to those who
4:6 "To you I will G all this authority and
4:6 to me, and I G it to whom I
4:10 is written, 'He will G his angels charge of
6:30 G to every one who begs from you; and
6:38 you will be forgiven; G, and it will be
6:38 For the measure you G will be the measure
9:13 said to them, "You G them something to eat."
11:3 G us each day our daily bread;
11:7 cannot get up and G you anything?
11:8 not get up and G him anything because he
11:8 he will rise and G him whatever he needs.
11:11 instead of a fish G him a serpent;
11:12 for an egg, will G him a scorpion?
11:13 evil, know how to G good gifts to your
11:13 will the heavenly Father G the Holy Spirit to
11:41 But G for alms those things which are within;
12:32 Father's good pleasure to G you the kingdom.
12:33 Sell your possessions, and G alms; provide yourselves
12:42 over his household, to G them their portion of
12:51 I have come to G peace on earth?
14:9 and say to you, G place to this man,'
14:12 invited him, "When you G a dinner or a
14:13 But when you G a feast, invite the poor,
15:12 to his father, 'Father, G me the share of
16:12 is anothers, who will G you that which is
17:18 found to return and G praise to God except
18:12 twice a week, I G tithes of all that
19:8 of my goods I G to the poor; and
19:24 pound from him, and G it to him who
20:10 tenants, that they should G him some of the
20:16 destroy those tenants, and G the vineyard to others."
20:22 lawful for us to G tribute to Caesar, or
21:15 answer; for I will G you a mouth and
21:23 and for those who G suck in those days!
22:5 glad, and engaged to G him money.
23:2 and forbidding us to G tribute to Caesar, and
Jn 4:7 Jesus said to her, G me a drink."
4:10 is saying to you, G me a drink,' you
4:14 water that I shall G him will never thirst;
4:14 water that I shall G him will become in
4:15 said to him, "Sir, G me this water, that
6:27 Son of man will G to you; for on
6:34 said to him, "Lord, G us this bread always."
6:51 bread which I shall G for the life of
6:52 "How can this man G us his flesh to
7:19 Did not Moses G you the law?
9:24 and said to him, G God the praise; we
10:28 follow me; and I G them eternal life, and
11:22 from God, God will G you."
13:26 to whom I shall G this morsel when I
13:29 or, that he should G something to the poor.
13:34 A new commandment I G to you, that you
14:16 Father, and he will G you another Counselor, to
14:27 you; my peace I G to you; not as
14:27 world gives do I G to you.
15:16 my name, he may G it to you.
16:23 the Father, he will G it to you in
17:2 over all flesh, to G eternal life to all
Acts 2:14 known to you, and G ear to my words.
3:6 and gold, but I G you what I have;
5:31 Leader and Savior, to G repentance to Israel and
6:2 right that we should G up preaching the word
7:5 length, but promised to G it to him in
7:38 received living oracles to G to us.
8:19 offered them money, saying, G me also this power,
12:23 because he did not G God the glory; and
13:34 this way, 'I will G you the holy and
16:14 opened her heart to G heed to what was
19:40 cause that we can G to justify this commotion."
20:32 you up and to G you the inheritance among
20:35 is more blessed to G than to receive.'"
21:26 into the temple, to G notice when the days
23:15 along with the council, G notice now to the
25:11 me, no one can G me up to them.
25:16 of the Romans to G up any one before
27:34 some food; it will G you strength, since not
Rom 1:21 him as God or G thanks to him, but
2:7 and immortality, he will G eternal life;
8:11 from the dead will G life to your mortal
8:32 will he not also G us all things with
12:20 if he is thirsty, G him drink; for by
14:11 and every tongue shall G praise to God."
14:12 each of us shall G account of himself to

16:4 churches of the Gentiles G thanks;
1Cor 1:4 I G thanks to God always for you because
7:3 The husband should G to his wife her conjugal
7:10 To the married I G charge, not I but
7:25 the Lord, but I G my opinion as one
10:30 that for which I G thanks?
10:32 G no offense to Jews or to Greeks or
11:34 other things I will G directions when I come.
13:3 If I G away all I have, and if
14:7 the harp, do not G distinct notes, how will
14:17 For you may G thanks well enough, but the
16:18 G recognition to such men.
2Cor 1:11 so that many will G thanks on our behalf
4:6 in our hearts to G the light of the
8:10 in this matter I G my advice: it is
8:24 So G proof, before the churches, of your love
Gal 3:15 To G a human example, brethren: no one annuls
Eph 1:16 do not cease to G thanks for you, remembering
1:17 Father of glory, may G you a spirit of
4:27 on your anger, and G no opportunity to the
4:28 may be able to G to those in need.
5:14 dead, and Christ shall G you light."
Col 4:15 G my greetings to the brethren at La-odicea, and
1Thes 1:2 We G thanks to God always for you all,
5:18 pray constantly, G thanks in all circumstances;
2Thes 1:3 We are bound to G thanks to God always
2:13 we are bound to G thanks to God always
3:9 that right, but to G you in our conduct
3:16 Lord of peace himself G you peace at all
1Tim 5:14 rule their households, and G the enemy no occasion
2Tim 1:7 for God did not G us a spirit of
Tit 1:8 may be able to G instruction in sound doctrine
2:9 their masters and to G satisfaction in every respect;
Heb 13:17 who will have to G account.
1Pet 4:5 you; but they will G account to him who
1Jn 5:16 ask, and God will G him life for those
2Jn 1:10 into the house or G him any greeting;
Rev 2:10 death, and I will G you the crown of
2:17 who conquers I will G some of the hidden
2:17 manna, and I will G him a white stone,
2:23 heart, and I will G to each of you
2:26 the end, I will G him power over the
2:28 Father; and I will G him the morning star.
4:9 whenever the living creatures G glory and honor and
9:20 of their hands nor G up worshiping demons and
10:9 and told him to G me the little scroll;
11:17 worshiped God, saying, "We G thanks to thee, Lord
13:15 it was allowed to G breath to the image
14:7 voice, "Fear God and G him glory, for the
16:9 did not repent and G him glory.
17:13 of one mind and G over their power and
18:7 played the wanton, so G her a like measure
19:7 rejoice and exult and G him the glory, for
21:6 the thirsty I will G from the fountain of

GIVEN (546)

Gen 1:29 said, "Behold, I have G you every plant yielding
1:30 of life, I have G every green plant for
15:3 said, "Behold, thou hast G me no offspring; and
16:11 because the LORD has G heed to your affliction.
20:16 said, "Behold, I have G your brother a thousand
24:35 become great; he has G him flocks and herds,
24:36 to him he has G all that he has.
26:18 which his father had G them.
27:37 his brothers I have G to him for servants,
29:33 am hated, he has G me this son also";
30:6 heard my voice and G me a son"; therefore
30:18 Leah said, "God has G me my hire because
30:26 service which I have G you."
31:9 of your father, and G them to me.
31:15 using up the money G for us.
33:5 whom God has graciously G your servant."
38:14 she had not been G to him in marriage.
43:24 into Joseph's house, and G them water, and they
43:24 and when he had G their asses provender,
48:9 sons, whom God has G me here." And he
48:22 Moreover I have G to you rather than to
Ex 5:16 No straw is G to your servants, yet they
5:18 no straw shall be G you, yet you shall
12:36 and the LORD had G the people favor in
16:15 which the LORD has G you to eat.
16:29 The LORD has G you the sabbath, therefore on
31:6 Dan; and I have G to all able men
Lev 6:17 I have G it as their portion of my
7:34 peace offerings, and have G them to Aaron the
7:36 commanded this to be G them by the people
10:14 you; for they are G as your due and
10:17 holy and has been G to you that you
17:11 blood; and I have G it for you upon
19:20 not yet ransomed or G her freedom, an inquiry
20:3 people, because he has G one of his children
Num 3:9 sons; they are wholly G to him from among
8:16 For they are wholly G to me from among
8:19 And I have G the Levites as a gift
16:14 milk and honey, nor G us inheritance of fields
18:6 a gift to you, G to the LORD, to
18:8 "And behold, I have G you whatever is kept
18:8 of Israel; I have G them to you as
18:11 of Israel; I have G them to you, and
18:21 the Levites I have G every tithe in Israel
18:24 the LORD, I have G to the Levites for
18:26 tithe which I have G you from them for
20:12 land which I have G them."
20:24 land which I have G to the people of
21:34 him; for I have G him into your hand,
26:54 every tribe shall be G its inheritance according to
26:62 there was no inheritance G to them among the
27:12 land which I have G to the people of
32:5 let this land be G to your servants for
32:7 which the LORD has G them?
32:9 which the LORD had G them.
33:53 it, for I have G the land to you
Deut 1:3 that the LORD had G him in commandment to
2:5 on, because I have G Mount Seir to Esau
2:9 possession, because I have G Ar to the sons
2:19 possession, because I have G it to the sons
2:24 Arnon; behold, I have G into your hand Sihon
3:2 him; for I have G him and all his
3:18 LORD your God has G you this land to
3:19 cities which I have G you,
3:20 possession which I have G you.'
8:10 good land he has G you.
9:23 land which I have G you,' then you rebelled
12:1 of your fathers, has G you to possess, all
12:15 God which he has G you; the unclean and
12:21 which the LORD has G you, as I have
16:17 God which he has G you.
20:14 LORD your God has G you.
25:3 Forty stripes may be G him, but not more;
25:19 LORD your God has G you rest from all
26:10 thou, O LORD, hast G me.' And you shall
26:11 LORD your God has G to you and to
26:13 and moreover I have G it to the Levite,
26:15 ground which thou hast G us, as thou didst
28:31 your sheep shall be G to your enemies, and
28:32 your daughters shall be G to another people, while
28:52 LORD your God has G you.
28:53 LORD your God has G you, in the siege
29:4 the LORD has not G you a mind to
32:30 and the LORD had G them up?
Josh 1:3 tread upon I have G to you, as I
2:9 that the LORD has G you the land, and
2:24 "Truly the LORD has G all the land into
6:2 Joshua, "See, I have G into your hand Jericho,
6:16 for the LORD has G you the city.
8:1 Ai; see, I have G into your hand the
10:8 them, for I have G them into your hands;
10:19 LORD your God has G them into your hand."
14:3 For Moses had G an inheritance to the two
14:4 and no portion was G to the Levites in
17:14 saying, "Why have you G me but one lot
18:3 of your fathers, has G you?
21:2 Moses that we be G cities to dwell in,
21:12 its villages had been G to Caleb the son
21:21 To them were G Shechem, the city of refuge
21:27 of the Levites, were G out of the half-tribe
21:34 the Merarite families, were G out of the tribe
21:44 for the LORD had G all their enemies into
22:4 LORD your God has G rest to your brethren,
22:7 of Manasseh Moses had G a possession in Bashan;
22:7 other half Joshua had G a possession beside their
23:1 when the LORD had G rest to Israel from
23:13 LORD your God has G you.
23:15 LORD your God has G you,
23:16 land which he has G to you."
24:33 son, which had been G him in the hill
Judg 1:2 up; behold, I have G the land into his
1:20 And Hebron was G to Caleb, as Moses had
3:28 for the LORD has G your enemies the Moabites
4:14 which the LORD has G Sisera into your hand.
6:10 But you have not G heed to my voice."
6:13 cast us off, and G us into the hand

GIVEN

7:9 camp; for I have G it into your hand.
7:14 his hand God has G Midian and all the
7:15 for the LORD has G the host of Midian
8:3 God has G into your hands the princes of
8:7 when the LORD has G Zebah and Zalmunna into
14:20 And Samson's wife was G to his companion, who
15:6 taken his wife and G her to his companion."
16:23 said, "Our god has G Samson our enemy into
16:24 said, "Our god has G our enemy into our
18:10 broad; yea, God has G it into your hands,
Ruth 1:6 visited his people and G them food.
2:12 a full reward be G you by the LORD,
1Sam 14:10 for the LORD has G them into our hand.
14:12 for the LORD has G them into the hand
15:28 this day, and has G it to a neighbor
18:19 daughter, should have been G to David, she was
18:19 to David, she was G to Adriel the Meholathite
18:27 their foreskins, which were G in full number to
22:13 in that you have G him bread and a
23:7 Saul said, "God has G him into my hand;
25:27 to my lord be G to the young men
25:44 Saul had G Michal his daughter, David's wife, to
26:8 to David, "God has G your enemy into your
27:5 let a place be G me in one of
28:17 of your hand, and G it to your neighbor,
30:23 what the LORD has G us; he has preserved
30:23 has preserved us and G into our hand the
2Sam 2:27 the men would have G up the pursuit of
3:8 friends, and have not G you into the hand
7:1 and the LORD had G him rest from all
9:9 his house I have G to your master's son.
16:8 and the LORD has G the kingdom into the
17:7 counsel which Ahithophel has G is not good."
19:42 Or has he G us any gift?"
21:6 of his sons be G to us, so that
22:36 Thou hast G me the shield of thy salvation,
1Kgs 2:21 Abishag the Shunammite be G to Adonijah your
3:6 steadfast love, and hast G him a son to
5:4 LORD my God has G me rest on every
5:7 this day, who has G to David a wise
8:36 land, which thou hast G to thy people as
8:56 the LORD who has G rest to his people
9:7 land which I have G them; and the house
9:12 cities which Solomon had G him, they did not
9:13 these which you have G me, my brother?" So
9:16 the city, and had G it as dowry to
10:13 asked besides what was G her by the bounty
12:13 the old men had G him,
13:5 man of God had G by the word of
13:26 therefore the LORD has G him to the lion,
18:23 Let two bulls be G to us; and let
18:26 the bull which was G them, and they prepared
2Kgs 5:1 him the LORD had G victory to Syria.
5:17 you, let there be G to your servant two
8:29 which the Syrians had G him at Ramah, when
9:15 which the Syrians had G him, when he fought
12:14 LORD, for that was G to the workmen who
18:30 city will not be G into the hand of
19:10 Jerusalem will not be G into the hand of
22:5 and let it be G into the hand of
22:10 "Hilkiah the priest has G me a book." And
25:30 a regular allowance was G him by the king,
1Chr 5:1 couch, his birthright was G to the sons of
5:20 were with them were G into their hands, for
6:61 of the Kohathites were G by lot out of
6:67 They were G the cities of refuge: Shechem with
6:71 To the Gershomites were G out of the half-tribe
22:18 And has he not G you peace on every
23:25 God of Israel, has G peace to his people;
25:5 him; for God had G Heman fourteen sons and
28:5 (for the LORD has G me many sons) he
29:9 rejoiced because these had G willingly, for with a
29:14 thy own have we G thee.
2Chr 2:12 and earth, who has G King David a wise
6:27 land, which thou hast G to thy people as
7:20 land which I have G you; and this house,
8:2 cities which Huram had G to him, and settled
14:7 him, and he has G us peace on every
18:14 triumph; they will be G into your hand."
20:11 possession, which thou hast G us to inherit.
25:9 talents which I have G to the army of
28:5 He was also G into the hand of the
32:29 abundance; for God had G him very great
33:8 statutes, and the ordinances G through Moses."
34:14 law of the LORD G through Moses.
34:18 "Hilkiah the priest has G me a book." And
36:23 God of heaven, has G me all the kingdoms
Ezra 1:2 God of heaven, has G me all the kingdoms
6:9 let that be G to them day by
7:6 God of Israel had G; and the king granted
7:19 vessels that have been G you for the service
9:7 our priests have been G into the hand of
9:13 iniquities deserved and hast G us such a remnant
Neh 2:7 king, let letters be G me to the governors
8:1 which the LORD had G to Israel.
10:29 God's law which was G by Moses the servant
13:5 and oil, which were G by commandment to the
13:10 Levites had not been G to them; so that
Tob 2:14 she said, "It was G to me as a
3:8 because she had been G to seven husbands, and
5:19 the life that is G to us by the
6:10 suggest that she be G to you in marriage,
6:13 the girl has been G to seven husbands and
6:15 night she will be G to you in marriage.
7:11 I have G my daughter to seven husbands, and
10:7 father and mother have G up hope of ever
12:1 he must also be G more."
Jud 3:8 for it had been G to him to destroy
4:8 session at Jerusalem, had G order.
11:12 their water has almost G out, they have planned
16:19 which the people had G her; and the canopy
Esth 1:8 for the king had G orders to all the
2:3 let their ointments be G them.
2:13 this way she was G whatever she desired to
3:11 Haman, "The money is G to you, the people
5:3 It shall be G you, even to the half
7:3 let my life be G me at my petition,
8:7 Jew, "Behold, I have G Esther the house of
14:6 thee, and thou hast G us into the hands
Job 3:20 "Why is light G to him that is in
3:23 Why is light G to a man whose way
9:24 The earth is G into the hand of the
15:19 alone the land was G, and no stranger passed
22:7 You have G no water to the weary to
37:10 of God ice is G, and the broad waters
38:29 forth, and who has G birth to the hoarfrost
38:36 in the clouds, or G understanding to the mists?
39:6 to whom I have G the steppe for his
39:17 her forget wisdom, and G her no share in
41:11 Who has G to me, that I should repay
Ps 4:1 Thou hast G me room when I was in
8:6 Thou hast G him dominion over the works of
18:35 Thou hast G me the shield of thy salvation,
21:2 Thou hast G him his heart's desire, and hast
40:6 desire; but thou hast G me an open ear.
60:3 hard things; thou hast G us wine to drink
61:5 my vows, thou hast G me the heritage of
63:10 earth; they shall be G over to the power
66:19 has listened; he has G heed to the voice
72:15 gold of Sheba be G to him!
79:2 They have G the bodies of thy servants to
80:5 bread of tears, and G them tears to drink
112:9 distributed freely, he has G to the poor; his
115:16 the earth he has G to the sons of
118:18 but he has not G me over to death.
118:27 God, and he has G us light.
119:93 by them thou hast G me life.
120:3 What shall be G to you?
124:6 LORD, who has not G us as prey to
141:6 When they are G over to those who shall
Prov 1:4 that prudence may be G to the simple, knowledge
6:1 for your neighbor, have G your pledge for a
20:16 garment when he has G surety for a stranger,
22:24 friendship with a man G to anger, nor go
23:2 you are a man G to appetite.
27:13 garment when he has G surety for a stranger,
29:22 strife, and a man G to anger causes much
Eccl 1:13 business that God has G to the sons of
3:10 business that God has G to the sons of
5:18 life which God has G him, for this is
5:19 to whom God has G wealth and possessions and
8:8 deliver those who are G to it.
9:9 life which he has G you under the sun,
12:11 collected sayings which are G by one Shepherd.
Wis 6:3 For your dominion was G you from the Lord,
7:7 prayed, and understanding was G me; I called upon
9:8 Thou hast G command to build a temple on
9:17 counsel, unless thou hast G wisdom and sent thy
11:4 thee, and water was G them out of flinty
14:3 course, because thou hast G it a path in
18:4 law was to be G to the world.
18:22 the oaths and covenants G to our fathers.

G

Sir 14:2 and who has not G up his hope.
15:17 he chooses will be G to him.
15:20 and he has not G any one permission to
18:3 To none has he G power to proclaim his
27:14 The talk of men G to swearing makes one's
28:8 sins; for a man G to anger will kindle
29:15 surety, for he has G his life for you.
35:10 High as he has G, and as generously as
37:21 for grace was not G him by the Lord,
Is 8:18 whom the LORD has G me are signs and
9:6 us a son is G; and the government will
14:3 When the LORD has G you rest from your
23:4 have neither travailed nor G birth, I have neither
23:11 the LORD has G command concerning Canaan to
33:16 his bread will be G him, his water will
34:2 has doomed them, has G them over for slaughter.
35:2 of Lebanon shall be G to it, the majesty
36:15 city will not be G into the hand of
37:10 Jerusalem will not be G into the hand of
42:6 kept you; I have G you as a covenant
49:8 have kept you and G you as a covenant
50:4 The Lord GOD has G me the tongue of
Jer 6:19 because they have not G heed to my words;
8:6 I have G heed and listened, but they have
8:14 to perish, and has G us poisoned water to
12:7 my heritage; I have G the beloved of my
12:14 heritage which I have G my people Israel to
13:20 the flock that was G you, your beautiful flock?
21:10 LORD: it shall be G into the hand of
23:18 word, or who has G heed to his word
25:5 which the LORD has G to you and your
26:24 that he was not G over to the people
27:6 Now I have G all these lands into the
27:6 servant, and I have G him also the beasts
28:14 him, for I have G to him even the
32:4 but shall surely be G into the hand of
32:16 land.' "After I had G the deed of purchase
32:24 pestilence the city is G into the hands of
32:25 though the city is G into the hands of
32:36 you say, 'It is G into the hand of
32:43 or beast; it is G into the hands of
37:21 loaf of bread was G him daily from the
38:3 city shall surely be G into the hand of
38:18 this city shall be G into the hand of
38:20 "You shall not be G to them.
39:17 you shall not be G into the hand of
44:20 the people who had G him this answer:
47:7 when the LORD has G it a charge?
52:34 a regular allowance was G him by the king
Lam 5:5 are weary, we are G no rest.
5:6 We have G the hand to Egypt, and to
Bar 2:35 land which I have G them."
3:23 way to wisdom, nor G thought to her paths.
Ezek 11:15 us this land is G for a possession.'
15:4 Lo, it is G to the fire for fuel;
15:6 forest, which I have G to the fire for
16:17 silver, which I had G you, and made for
16:34 while no hire was G to you; therefore you
20:15 land which I had G them, a land flowing
21:11 So the sword is G to be polished, that
21:11 and polished to be G into the hand of
21:15 I have G the glittering sword; ah!
29:5 the air I have G you as food.
29:20 I have G him the land of Egypt as
31:14 for they are all G over to death, to
33:24 the land is surely G us to possess.'
35:12 laid desolate, they are G us to devour.'
Dan 1:12 days; let us be G vegetables to eat and
2:23 praise, for thou hast G me wisdom and strength,
2:37 God of heaven has G the kingdom, the power,
2:38 whose hand he has G, wherever they dwell, the
3:32 Thou hast G us into the hands of lawless
4:16 a beast's mind be G to him; and let
5:28 kingdom is divided and G to the Medes and
7:4 of a man was G to it.
7:6 heads; and dominion was G to it.
7:11 its body destroyed and G over to be burned
7:14 And to him was G dominion and glory and
7:22 came, and judgment was G for the saints of
7:25 and they shall be G into his hand for
7:27 whole heaven shall be G to the people of
8:12 And the host was G over to it together
11:6 but she shall be G up, and her attendants,
11:11 but it shall be G into his hand.
11:21 majesty has not been G; he shall come in
13:50 us, for God has G you that right."
14:32 day they had been G two human bodies and
14:32 but these were not G to them now, so
Hos 2:12 which my lovers have G me.' I will make
12:14 Ephraim has G bitter provocation; so his LORD will
13:11 I have G you kings in my anger, and
Joel 2:23 God; for he has G the early rain for
3:3 my people, and have G a boy for a
Amos 9:15 land which I have G them," says the LORD
Nah 1:14 The LORD has G commandment about you: "No
1Mac 2:7 there when it was G over to the enemy,
2:7 the enemy, the sanctuary G over to aliens?
5:62 through whom deliverance was G to Israel.
8:28 enemy allies shall be G no grain, arms, money,
10:8 that the king had G him authority to recruit
10:36 let the maintenance be G them that is due
10:39 adjoining it I have G as a gift to
11:37 and let it be G to Jonathan and put
2Mac 1:18 feast of the fire G when Nehemiah, who built
3:15 upon him who had G the law about deposits,
4:9 more if permission were G to establish by his
4:30 their cities had been G as a present to
7:30 the law that was G to our fathers through
10:7 to him who had G success to the purifying
Mt 7:7 and it will be G you; seek, and you
9:8 glorified God, who had G such authority to men.
10:19 to say will be G to you in that
12:39 no sign shall be G to it except the
13:11 you it has been G to know the secrets
13:11 heaven, but to them it has not been G
13:12 has will more be G, and he will have
14:9 commanded it to be G;
14:11 on a platter and G to the girl, and
15:5 gained from me is G to God, he need
15:36 the fish, and having G thanks he broke them
16:4 no sign shall be G to it except the
19:11 saying, but only those to whom it is G
21:43 away from you and G to a nation producing
22:30 neither marry nor are G in marriage, but are
25:29 has will more be G, and he will have
26:9 a large sum, and G to the poor."
26:27 and when he had G thanks he gave it
26:48 Now the betrayer had G them a sign, saying,
27:58 ordered it to be G to him.
28:18 on earth has been G to me.
Mk 4:11 "To you has been G the secret of the
4:24 still more will be G you.
4:25 has will more be G; and from him who
6:2 What is the wisdom G to him?
7:11 is Corban' (that is, G to God) –
8:6 seven loaves, and having G thanks he broke them
8:12 no sign shall be G to this generation."
12:25 neither marry nor are G in marriage, but are
13:11 but say whatever is G you in that hour,
14:5 three hundred denarii, and G to the poor." And
14:23 and when he had G thanks he gave it
14:44 Now the betrayer had G them a sign, saying,
Lk 2:21 called Jesus, the name G by the angel before
4:17 read; and there was G to him the book
6:38 and it will be G to you; good measure,
8:10 you it has been G to know the secrets
8:18 has will more be G, and from him who
8:55 that something should be G her to eat.
10:19 Behold, I have G you authority to tread upon
11:9 and it will be G you; seek, and you
11:29 no sign shall be G to it except the
12:48 to whom much is G, of him will much
17:27 they married, they were G in marriage, until the
19:15 to whom he had G the money, to be
19:26 has will more be G; but from him who
20:34 age marry and are G in marriage;
20:35 neither marry nor are G in marriage,
22:17 and when he had G thanks he said, "Take
22:19 and when he had G thanks he broke it
22:19 my body which is G for you.
Jn 1:17 For the law was G through Moses; grace and
3:27 anything except what is G him from heaven.
3:35 the Son, and has G all things into his
4:10 and he would have G you living water."
5:21 no one, but has G all judgment to the
5:26 in himself, and has G him authority to execute
6:11 and when he had G thanks, he distributed them
6:23 after the Lord had G thanks.
6:39 all that he has G me, but raise it
7:39 Spirit had not been G, because Jesus was not
10:29 My Father, who has G them to me, is
11:57 and the Pharisees had G orders that if any

12:5 three hundred denarii and G to the poor?"
12:49 sent me has himself G me commandment what to
13:3 that the Father had G all things into his
13:15 For I have G you an example, that you
17:2 thee, since thou hast G him power over all
17:2 all whom thou hast G him.
17:7 everything that thou hast G me is from thee;
17:8 thee; for I have G them the words which
17:9 those whom thou hast G me, for they are
17:11 name, which thou hast G me, that they may
17:12 name, which thou hast G me; I have guarded
17:14 I have G them thy word; and the world
17:22 glory which thou hast G me I have given
17:22 given me I have G to them, that they
17:24 also, whom thou hast G me, may be with
17:24 glory which thou hast G me in thy love
18:11 which the Father has G me?"
18:14 was Caiaphas who had G counsel to the Jews
19:11 unless it had been G you from above; therefore
Acts 1:2 up, after he had G commandment through the Holy
3:16 is through Jesus has G the man this perfect
4:12 other name under heaven G among men by which
5:32 Spirit whom God has G to those who obey
8:18 that the Spirit was G through the laying on
17:31 of this he has G assurance to all men
20:2 these parts and had G them much encouragement,
21:40 And when he had G him leave, Paul, standing
24:25 that money would be G him by Paul.
Rom 5:5 Spirit which has been G to us.
5:13 before the law was G, but sin is not
11:35 "Or who has G a gift to him that
12:3 For by the grace G to me I bid
12:6 according to the grace G to us, let us
15:8 to confirm the promises G to the patriarchs,
15:15 because of the grace G me by God
1Cor 1:4 of God which was G you in Christ Jesus,
3:10 the grace of God G to me, like a
11:15 For her hair is G to her for a
11:24 and when he had G thanks, he broke it,
12:7 To each is G the manifestation of the Spirit
12:8 To one is G through the Spirit the utterance
2Cor 1:22 seal upon us and G us his Spirit in
4:11 we are always being G up to death for
5:5 is God, who has G us the Spirit as
12:7 revelations, a thorn was G me in the flesh,
13:10 which the Lord has G me for building up
Gal 2:9 the grace that was G to me, James and
3:21 a law had been G which could make alive,
3:22 Jesus Christ might be G to those who believe.
4:15 out your eyes and G them to me.
Eph 3:2 God's grace that was G to me for you,
3:7 God's grace which was G me by the working
3:8 saints, this grace was G, to preach to the
4:7 But grace was G to each of us according
4:19 callous and have G themselves up to licentiousness,
6:19 that utterance may be G me in opening my
Col 1:25 divine office which was G to me for you,
1Tim 1:12 thank him who has G me strength for this,
4:14 you have, which was G you by prophetic utterance
Heb 2:13 the children God has G me."
4:8 For if Joshua had G them rest, God would
11:31 disobedient, because she had G friendly welcome to
12:20 the order that was G, "If even a beast
Jas 1:5 and it will be G him.
2Pet 3:15 according to the wisdom G him,
1Jn 3:1 love the Father has G us, that we should
3:24 Spirit which he has G us.
4:13 us, because he has G us of his own
5:20 has come and has G us understanding, to know
Rev 6:2 and a crown was G to him, and he
6:4 another; and he was G a great sword.
6:8 him; and they were G power over a fourth
6:11 Then they were each G a white robe and
7:2 angels who had been G power to harm earth
8:2 and seven trumpets were G to them.
8:3 censer; and he was G much incense to mingle
9:1 earth, and he was G the key of the
9:3 earth, and they were G power like the power
11:1 Then I was G a measuring rod like a
11:2 out, for it is G over to the nations,
12:14 But the woman was G the two wings of
13:4 dragon, for he had G his authority to the
13:5 And the beast was G a mouth uttering haughty
13:7 And authority was G it over every tribe and
16:6 prophets, and thou hast G them blood to drink.
18:20 prophets, for God has G judgment for you against

GIVER

2Cor 9:7 or under compulsion, for God loves a cheerful G

GIVES (176)

Ex 16:8 said, "When the LORD G you in the evening
16:29 the sixth day he G you bread for two
20:12 the LORD your God G you.
21:4 If his master G him a wife and she
Lev 20:2 sojourn in Israel, who G any of his children
20:4 that man, when he G one of his children
27:9 such that any man G to the LORD is
Num 5:10 his; whatever any man G to the priest shall
Deut 1:20 the LORD our God G us.
1:25 the LORD our God G us.'
2:29 the LORD our God G to us.'
3:20 you, until the LORD G rest to your brethren,
3:20 the LORD your God G them beyond the Jordan;
4:1 God of your fathers, G you.
4:21 the LORD your God G you for an inheritance.
4:40 the LORD your God G you for ever."
5:16 the LORD your God G you.
7:2 the LORD your God G them over to you,
8:18 it is he who G you power to get
11:17 land which the LORD G you.
11:31 the LORD your God G you; and when you
12:9 the LORD your God G you.
12:10 the LORD your God G you to inherit, and
12:10 inherit, and when he G you rest from all
13:1 dreamer of dreams, and G you a sign or
13:12 the LORD your God G you to dwell there,
15:4 the LORD your God G you for an inheritance
15:7 the LORD your God G you, you shall not
16:5 the LORD your God G you;
16:18 the LORD your God G you, according to your
16:20 the LORD your God G you.
17:2 the LORD your God G you, a man or
17:14 the LORD your God G you, and you possess
18:9 the LORD your God G you, you shall not
19:1 the LORD your God G you, and you dispossess
19:2 the LORD your God G you to possess.
19:3 the LORD your God G you as a possession,
19:8 to your fathers, and G you all the land
19:10 the LORD your God G you for an inheritance,
19:14 the LORD your God G you to possess, you
20:13 the LORD your God G it into your hand
20:16 the LORD your God G you for an inheritance,
21:1 the LORD your God G you to possess, any
21:10 the LORD your God G them into your hands,
21:23 the LORD your God G you for an inheritance.
24:4 the LORD your God G you for an inheritance.
25:15 the LORD your God G you.
25:19 the LORD your God G you for an inheritance
26:1 the LORD your God G you for an inheritance,
26:2 the LORD your God G you, and you shall
27:2 the LORD your God G you, you shall set
27:3 the LORD your God G you, a land flowing
28:8 the LORD your God G you.
Josh 1:11 the LORD your God G you to possess.'"
1:15 them, until the LORD G rest to your brethren
2:14 you when the LORD G us the land."
Judg 5:29 make answer, nay, she G answer to herself,
11:9 Ammonites, and the LORD G them over to me,
11:24 what Chemosh your god G you to possess?
21:18 "Cursed be he who G a wife to Benjamin."
2Sam 22:51 Great triumphs he G to his king, and shows
24:23 this, O king, Araunah G to the king." And
1Chr 22:12 understanding, that when he G you charge over
Tob 4:19 but the Lord himself G all good things, and
6:7 demon or evil spirit G trouble to any one,
Job 5:10 things without number: he G rain upon the earth
16:11 God G me up to the ungodly, and casts
19:16 my servant, but he G me no answer; I
24:23 He G them security, and they are supported; and
33:4 breath of the Almighty G me life.
35:10 God my Maker, who G songs in the night,
36:6 the wicked alive, but G the afflicted their right.
36:31 he judges peoples; he G food in abundance.
Ps 16:7 bless the LORD who G me counsel; in the
18:50 Great triumphs he G to his king, and shows
37:21 righteous is generous and G;
68:6 God G the desolate a home to dwell in;
68:11 The Lord G the command; great is the host
68:35 God of Israel, he G power and strength to
113:9 He G the barren woman a home, making her
119:50 affliction that thy promise G me life.
119:130 unfolding of thy words G light; it imparts

127:2 anxious toil; for he G to his beloved sleep.
136:25 for ever; he who G food to all flesh,
146:7 for the oppressed; who G food to the hungry.
147:4 of the stars, he G to all of them
147:9 He G to the beasts their food, and to
147:16 He G snow like wool; he scatters hoarfrost like
Prov 2:6 For the LORD G wisdom; from his mouth come
11:15 He who G surety for a stranger will smart
11:24 One man G freely, yet grows all the richer;
12:17 who speaks the truth G honest evidence, but a
14:30 A tranquil mind G life to the flesh, but
16:20 He who G heed to the word will prosper,
17:4 lips; and a liar G heed to a mischievous
17:8 eyes of him who G it; wherever he turns
17:18 A man without sense G a pledge, and becomes
18:13 If one G answer before he hears, it is
19:6 to a man who G gifts.
20:16 in pledge when he G surety for foreigners.
21:26 covets, but the righteous G and does not hold
22:16 his own wealth, or G to the rich, will
24:26 He who G a right answer kisses the lips.
25:26 a righteous man who G way before the wicked.
26:8 sling is he who G honor to a fool.
27:13 in pledge when he G surety for foreigners.
28:27 He who G to the poor will not want,
29:4 By justice a king G stability to the land,
29:11 A fool G full vent to his anger, but
29:13 meet together; the LORD G light to the eyes
Eccl 2:26 who pleases him God G wisdom and knowledge and
2:26 to the sinner he G the work of gathering
6:2 man to whom God G wealth, possessions, and honor,
7:19 Wisdom G strength to the wise man more than
8:15 of life which God G him under the sun.
Sir 1:10 delights the heart, and G gladness and joy and
3:29 Whoever requites favors G thought to the future; at
4:11 exalts her sons and G help to those who
4:15 the nations, and whoever G heed to her will
6:28 find the rest she G, and she will be
20:14 He G little and upbraids much, he opens his
32:24 who believes the law G heed to the commandments,
34:2 so is he who G heed to dreams.
34:17 up the soul and G light to the eyes;
35:2 flour, and he who G alms sacrifices a thank
51:17 therein; to him who G wisdom I will give
Is 40:29 He G power to the faint, and to him
41:2 He G up nations before him, so that he
41:28 who, when I ask, G an answer.
42:5 comes from it, who G breath to the people
Jer 5:24 LORD our God, who G the rain in its
31:35 says the LORD, who G the sun for light
Lam 4:4 food, but no one G to them.
Ezek 18:7 pledge, commits no robbery, G his bread to the
18:16 commits no robbery, but G his bread to the
33:15 wicked restores the pledge, G back what he has
Dan 2:21 sets up kings; he G wisdom to the wise
4:17 kingdom of men, and G it to whom he
4:25 kingdom of men, and G it to whom he
4:32 kingdom of men and G it to whom he
Hos 4:12 wood, and their staff G them oracles.
Zeph 3:17 midst, a warrior who G victory; he will rejoice
Zech 10:1 the storm clouds, who G men showers of rain,
2Mac 7:14 the hope that God G of being raised again
10:38 kindness to Israel and G them the victory.
Mt 5:15 a stand, and it G light to all in
10:42 And whoever G to one of these little ones
Mk 9:41 say to you, whoever G you a cup of
Lk 11:36 lamp with its rays G you light."
Jn 3:34 by measure that he G the Spirit;
5:20 raises the dead and G them life, so also
5:20 so also the Son G life to whom he
6:32 from heaven; my Father G you the true bread
6:33 down from heaven, and G life to the world."
6:37 All that the Father G me will come to
6:63 is the spirit that G life, the flesh is
14:27 not as the world G do I give to
Acts 17:25 anything, since he himself G to all men life
Rom 4:17 whom he believed, who G life to the dead
12:8 in liberality; he who G aid, with zeal; he
14:6 the Lord, since he G thanks to God; while
14:6 of the Lord and G thanks to God.
1Cor 3:7 but only God who G the growth.
9:16 preach the gospel, that G me no ground for
14:8 And if the bugle G an indistinct sound, who
15:38 But God G it a body as he has
15:57 be to God, who G us the victory through
2Cor 3:6 kills, but the Spirit G life.
9:9 "He scatters abroad, he G to the poor; his
1Thes 4:8 man but God, who G his Holy Spirit to
1Tim 6:13 presence of God who G life to all things,
Jas 1:5 him ask God, who G to all men generously
1:14 when it has conceived G birth to sin; and
4:6 But he G more grace; therefore it says, "God
4:6 opposes the proud, but G grace to the humble."
1Pet 5:5 opposes the proud, but G grace to the humble."

GIVEST (6)

Gen 28:22 of all that thou G me I will give
Ps 36:8 thy house, and thou G them drink from the
104:28 When thou G to them, they gather it up;
144:10 play to thee, who G victory to kings, who
145:15 to thee, and thou G them their food in
Wis 12:19 good hope, because thou G repentance for sins.

GIVING (57)

Gen 24:19 When she had finished G him a drink, she
33:13 the flocks and herds G suck are a care
41:12 our dreams to us, G an interpretation to each
Num 5:7 fifth to it, and G it to him to
18:29 the best of them, G the hallowed part from
Deut 7:3 make marriages with them, G your daughters to
9:6 your God is not G you this good land
10:18 and loves the sojourner, G him food and clothing.
21:17 of the disliked, by G him a double portion
26:12 the year of tithing, G it to the Levite,
Josh 1:2 land which I am G to them, to the
1:15 LORD your God is G them; then you shall
2Sam 14:13 For in G this decision the king convicts himself,
1Kgs 8:52 of thy people Israel, G ear to them whenever
2Chr 7:6 David had made for G thanks to the LORD--
19:6 is with you in G judgment.
30:22 sacrificing peace offerings and G thanks to the LORD
Ezra 3:11 responsively, praising and G thanks to the LORD,
Ps 9:4 sat on the throne G righteous judgment.
37:26 He is ever G liberally and lending, and his
111:6 of his works, in G them the heritage of
Wis 6:18 of her laws, and G heed to her laws
13:14 like some worthless animal, G it a coat of
Sir 41:19 surliness in receiving and G,
44:3 for their power, G counsel by their understanding,
Is 28:7 vision, they stumble in G judgment.
55:10 bring forth and sprout, G seed to the sower
Jer 32:3 LORD: Behold, I am G this city into the
32:28 LORD: Behold, I am G this city into the
34:2 LORD: Behold, I am G this city into the
43:11 the land of Egypt, G to the pestilence those
Bar 1:6 they collected money, each G what he could;
Dan 8:13 makes desolate, and the G over of the sanctuary
9:13 from our iniquities and G heed to thy truth.
2Mac 2:2 that the prophet after G them the law instructed
6:27 Therefore, by manfully G up my life now, I
8:27 they kept the sabbath, G great praise and thanks
8:30 divided very much plunder, G to those who had
9:7 against the Jews, and G orders to hasten the
Mt 24:38 and drinking, marrying and G in marriage, until the
Lk 17:16 face at Jesus' feet, G him thanks.
Jn 7:51 a man without first G him a hearing and
Acts 5:36 these days Theudas arose, G himself out to be
7:25 understood that God was G them deliverance by his
15:8 bore witness to them, G them the Holy Spirit
27:35 he took bread, and G thanks to God in
Rom 9:4 glory, the covenants, the G of the law, the
1Cor 12:24 so composed the body, G the greater honor to
2Cor 5:12 to you again but G you cause to be
Eph 5:20 always and for everything G thanks in the name
Phil 4:15 partnership with me in G and receiving except you
Col 1:12 and patience with joy, G thanks to the Father,
3:17 of the Lord Jesus, G thanks to God the
1Tim 4:1 from the faith by G heed to deceitful spirits
Tit 1:13 the faith, instead of G heed to Jewish myths
Jas 2:16 without G them the things needed for the body,
Rev 17:17 of one mind and G over their royal power

GIZONITE

1Chr 11:34 of Sha-albon, Hashem the G, Jonathan the son of

GLAD (102)

Ex 4:14 you he will be G in his heart.
Judg 18:20 the priest's heart was G; he took the ephod,
1Sam 11:9 and told the men of Jabesh, they were G
2Sam 18:11 I would have been G to give you ten
1Kgs 8:66 their homes joyful and G of heart for all
1Chr 16:31 Let the heavens be G, and let the earth

2Chr 7:10 their homes, joyful and G of heart for the
Tob 8:16 Blessed art thou, because thou hast made me G
13:13 Rejoice and be G for the sons of the
13:14 they will be made G for ever.
Esth 5:9 that day joyful and G of heart.
Job 3:22 rejoice exceedingly, and are G, when they find the
22:19 see it and are G; the innocent laugh them
Ps 9:2 I will be G and exult in thee, I
14:7 his people, Jacob shall rejoice, Israel shall be G
16:9 Therefore my heart is G, and my soul rejoices;
21:6 thou dost make him G with the joy of
31:7 will rejoice and be G for thy steadfast love,
32:11 Be G in the LORD, and rejoice, O righteous,
33:21 Yea, our heart is G in him, because we
34:2 the LORD; let the afflicted hear and be G
35:27 for joy and be G, and say evermore, "Great
40:9 I have told the G news of deliverance in
40:16 thee rejoice and be G in thee; may those
42:4 house of God, with G shouts and songs of
45:8 stringed instruments make you G;
46:4 river whose streams make G the city of God,
48:11 is filled with victory; let Mount Zion be G
53:6 his people, Jacob will rejoice and Israel be G
67:4 Let the nations be G and sing for joy,
69:32 see it and be G; you who seek God,
70:4 thee rejoice and be G in thee!
90:14 may rejoice and be G all our days.
90:15 Make us G as many days as thou hast
92:4 LORD, hast made me G by thy work; at
96:11 Let the heavens be G, and let the earth
97:1 the earth rejoice; let the many coastlands be G
97:8 Zion hears and is G, and the daughters of
105:38 Egypt was G when they departed, for dread of
107:30 Then they were G because they had quiet, and
107:42 see it and are G; and all wickedness stops
109:28 be put to shame; may thy servant be G
118:15 Hark, G songs of victory in the tents of
118:24 us rejoice and be G in it.
122:1 I was G when they said to me, "Let
126:3 has done great things for us; we are G
149:2 Let Israel be G in his Maker, let the
Prov 10:1 wise son makes a G father, but a foolish
12:25 him down, but a good word makes him G
15:13 A G heart makes a cheerful countenance, but by
15:20 wise son makes a G father, but a foolish
17:5 Maker; he who is G at calamity will not
23:15 heart is wise, my heart too will be G
23:24 wise son will be G in him.
23:25 father and mother be G, let her who bore
24:17 not your heart be G when he stumbles;
27:9 perfume make the heart G, but the soul is
27:11 and make my heart G, that I may answer
29:3 wisdom makes his father G, but one who keeps
Eccl 7:3 by sadness of countenance the heart is made G
Sir 26:4 poor, his heart is G, and at all times
31:27 It has been created to make men G
40:14 man will be made G; likewise transgressors will
Is 25:9 him; let us be G and rejoice in his
35:1 dry land shall be G, the desert shall rejoice
65:18 But be G and rejoice for ever in that
65:19 in Jerusalem, and be G in my people; no
66:10 with Jerusalem, and be G for her, all you
Jer 20:15 making him very G
Lam 1:21 my trouble; they are G that thou hast done
4:21 Rejoice and be G, O daughter of Edom, dweller
Bar 3:34 their watches, and were G; he called them, and
4:33 your fall and was G for your ruin, so
Dan 6:23 king was exceedingly G, and commanded that Daniel
Hos 7:4 they make the king G, and the princes by
Joel 2:21 not, O land; be G and rejoice, for the
2:23 "Be G, O sons of Zion, and rejoice in
Jon 4:6 So Jonah was exceedingly G because of the plant.
Zech 10:7 their hearts shall be G as with wine.
1Mac 3:7 but he made Jacob G by his deeds, and
2Mac 6:30 my soul I am G to suffer these things
9:20 your affairs are as you wish, I am G
10:33 and his men were G, and they besieged the
Mt 5:12 Rejoice and be G, for your reward is great
Mk 14:11 heard it they were G, and promised to give
Lk 15:32 make merry and be G, for this your brother
22:5 And they were G, and engaged to give him
23:8 Jesus, he was very G, for he had long
Jn 6:21 Then they were G to take him into the
8:56 see my day; he saw it and was G
11:15 your sake I am G that I was not
20:20 Then the disciples were G when they saw the
Acts 2:26 therefore my heart was G, and my tongue rejoiced;
2:46 partook of food with G and generous hearts,
11:23 of God, he was G; and he exhorted them
13:48 heard this, they were G and glorified the word
2Cor 2:2 there to make me G but the one whom
13:9 For we are G when we are weak and
Phil 2:17 your faith, I am G and rejoice with you
2:18 you also should be G and rejoice with me.
Philem 1:13 I would have been G to keep him with
1Pet 4:13 also rejoice and be G when his glory is

GLADDEN (4)

Ps 86:4 G the soul of thy servant, for to thee,
104:15 earth, and wine to G the heart of man,
Sir 4:18 back to him and G him, and will reveal
40:20 Wine and music G the heart, but the love

GLADDENED (3)

Sir 3:5 his father will be G by his own children,
25:7 nine thoughts I have G my heart, and a
2Mac 15:27 men, and were greatly G by God's manifestation.

GLADDENS (2)

Eccl 10:19 for laughter, and wine G life, and money answers
Sir 36:22 A woman's beauty G the countenance, and surpasses

GLADLY (10)

1Mac 1:43 Many even from Israel G adopted his religion; they
3:2 father helped him; they G fought for Israel.
2Mac 2:27 of many we will G endure the uncomfortable toil,
Mk 6:20 was much perplexed; and yet he heard him G
12:37 And the great throng heard him G
Lk 15:16 And he would G have fed on the pods
Acts 21:17 had come to Jerusalem, the brethren received us G
2Cor 11:19 will boast.) For you G bear with fools, being
12:9 will all the more G boast of my weaknesses,
12:15 I will most G spend and be spent for

GLADNESS (69)

Num 10:10 the day of your G also, and at your
Deut 28:47 God with joyfulness and G of heart, by reason
1Chr 29:22 before the LORD on that day with great G
2Chr 29:30 they sang praises with G, and they bowed down
30:21 seven days with great G; and the Levites and
30:23 they kept it for another seven days with G
Neh 12:27 celebrate the dedication with G, with thanksgivings
Esth 8:16 Jews had light and G and joy and honor.
8:17 edict came, there was G and joy among the
9:17 and made that a day of feasting and G
9:18 day, making that a day of feasting and G
9:19 as a day for G and feasting and holiday-making,
9:22 them from sorrow into G and from mourning into
9:22 days of feasting and G, days for sending choice
10:13 assembly and joy and G before God, from generation
Ps 30:11 and girded me with G,
39:13 that I may know G, before I depart and
45:7 with the oil of G above your fellows;
45:15 With joy and G they are led along as
51:8 me with joy and G; let the bones which
100:2 Serve the LORD with G
106:5 may rejoice in the G of thy nation, that
Prov 10:28 the righteous ends in G, but the expectation of
11:10 when the wicked perish there are shouts of G
Song 3:11 the day of the G of his heart.
Wis 8:16 has no pain, but G and joy.
Sir 1:9 glory and exultation, and G and a crown of
1:10 the heart, and gives G and joy and long
6:31 and put her on like a crown of G
15:6 He will find G and a crown of rejoicing,
30:16 and there is no G above joy of heart.
30:22 G of heart is the life of man, and
31:28 rejoicing of heart and G of soul.
35:9 a cheerful face, and dedicate your tithe with G
50:23 May he give us G of heart, and grant
Is 16:10 And joy and G are taken away from the
22:13 and behold, joy and G, slaying oxen and killing
24:11 reached its eventide; the G of the earth is
30:29 feast is kept; and G of heart, as when
35:10 shall obtain joy and G, and sorrow and sighing
51:3 the LORD; joy and G will be found in
51:11 shall obtain joy and G, and sorrow and sighing
61:3 ashes, the oil of G instead of mourning, the
65:14 servants shall sing for G of heart, but you
Jer 7:34 and the voice of G, the voice of the
16:9 and the voice of G, the voice of the
25:10 and the voice of G, the voice of the

G

	31:7	LORD: "Sing aloud with G for Jacob, and raise
	31:13	them, and give them G for sorrow.
	33:11	and the voice of G, the voice of the
	48:33	G and joy have been taken away from the
Bar	2:23	and the voice of G, the voice of the
	3:34	They shone with G for him who made them.
	4:23	me with joy and G for ever.
Joel	1:11	field are withered; and G fails from the sons
	1:15	our eyes, joy and G from the house of
Zeph	3:17	rejoice over you with G, he will renew you
Zech	8:19	seasons of joy and G, and cheerful feasts; therefore
1Mac	4:56	burnt offerings with G; they offered a sacrifice
	4:58	There was very great G among the people, and
	4:59	should be observed with G and joy for eight
	5:54	to Mount Zion with G and joy, and offered
	7:48	celebrated that day as a day of great G
	10:66	And Jonathan returned to Jerusalem in peace and G
2Mac	3:30	filled with joy and G, now that the Almighty
Lk	1:14	will have joy and G, and many will rejoice
Acts	2:28	make me full of G with thy presence.'
	14:17	seasons, satisfying your hearts with food and G
Heb	1:9	with the oil of G beyond thy comrades."

G

GLANCE

Song	4:9	my heart with a G of your eyes, with

GLANCING

Is	3:16	walk with outstretched necks, G wantonly with their

GLASS (6)

Job	28:17	Gold and G cannot equal it, nor can it
Rev	4:6	were a sea of G, like crystal.
	15:2	be a sea of G mingled with fire, and
	15:2	beside the sea of G with harps of God
	21:18	while the city was pure gold, clear as G
	21:21	of the city was pure gold, transparent as G

GLAZE

Prov	26:23	Like the G covering an earthen vessel are smooth

GLAZING

Sir	38:30	heart to finish the G, and he is careful

GLEAM (2)

Dan	10:6	and legs like the G of burnished bronze, and
Nah	2:4	through the squares; they G like torches, they dart

GLEAMED

1Mac	6:39	ablaze with them and G like flaming torches.

GLEAMING (6)

Sir	43:9	beauty of heaven, a G array in the heights
	50:7	and like the rainbow G in glorious clouds;
Ezek	1:4	fire, as it were G bronze.
	1:16	appearance was like the G of a chrysolite; and
	1:27	saw as it were G bronze, like the appearance
	8:2	appearance of brightness, like G bronze.

GLEAN (10)

Deut	24:21	vineyard, you shall not G it afterward; it shall
Ruth	2:2	to the field, and G among the ears of
	2:7	said, 'Pray, let me G and gather among the
	2:8	do not go to G in another field or
	2:15	When she rose to G, Boaz instructed his young
	2:15	men, saying, "Let her G even among the sheaves,
	2:16	it for her to G, and do not rebuke
	2:19	her, "Where did you G today?
Job	24:6	the field and they G the vineyard of the
Jer	6:9	the LORD of hosts: G thoroughly as a vine

GLEANED (5)

Ruth	2:3	forth and went and G in the field after
	2:17	So she G in the field until evening; then
	2:17	out what she had G, and it was about
	2:18	mother-in-law what she had G, and she also brought
Mic	7:1	the vintage has been G: there is no cluster

GLEANING (3)

Judg	8:2	Is not the G of the grapes of Ephraim
Ruth	2:23	the maidens of Boaz, G until the end of
Is	24:13	beaten, as at the G when the vintage is

GLEANINGS (5)

Lev	19:9	shall you gather the G after your harvest.
	23:22	shall you gather the G after your harvest; you
Is	17:6	G will be left in it, as when an
Jer	49:9	grape-gatherers came to you, would they not leave G
Obad	1:5	grape-gatherers came to you, would they not leave G

GLEANS (2)

Sir	33:16	was like one who G after the grape-gatherers; by
Is	17:5	and as when one G the ears of grain

GLEE

Ps	35:15	stumbling they gathered in G, they gathered together

GLEN

Zech	1:8	myrtle trees in the G; and behind him were

GLIDED

Job	4:15	A spirit G past my face; the hair of

GLIDING (2)

Song	7:9	that goes down smoothly, G over lips and teeth.
Jer	46:22	sound like a serpent G away; for her enemies

GLISTENING

Mk	9:3	and his garments became G, intensely white, as no

GLITTER

Ezek	21:28	it is polished to G and to flash like

GLITTERING (5)

Deut	32:41	if I whet my G sword, and my hand
Job	20:25	of his body, the G point comes out of
Ezek	21:15	I have given the G sword; ah!
Nah	3:3	charging, flashing sword and G spear, hosts of slain,
Hab	3:11	the flash of thy G spear.

GLOAT (2)

Ps	22:17	they stare and G over me;
Mic	7:10	My eyes will G over her; now she will

GLOATED (3)

Lam	1:7	help her, the foe G over her, mocking at
Obad	1:12	you should not have G over the day of
	1:13	you should not have G over his disaster in

GLOOM (24)

Deut	4:11	heart of heaven, wrapped in darkness, cloud, and G
Esth	11:8	day of darkness and G, tribulation and distress,
Job	3:5	Let G and deep darkness claim it.
	10:21	to the land of G and deep darkness,
	10:22	darkness, the land of G and chaos, where light
	28:3	bound the ore in G and deep darkness.
	34:22	There is no G or deep darkness where evildoers
Ps	107:10	in darkness and in G, prisoners in affliction and
	107:14	out of darkness and G, and broke their bonds
Is	8:22	distress and darkness, the G of anguish; and they
	9:1	there will be no G for her that was
	29:18	and out of their G and darkness the eyes
	58:10	the darkness and your G be as the noonday.
	59:9	darkness, and for brightness, but we walk in G
Jer	13:16	he turns it into G and makes it deep
Ezek	31:15	will clothe Lebanon in G for it, and all
Joel	2:2	day of darkness and G, a day of clouds
Amos	5:20	and not light, and G with no brightness in
Zeph	1:15	day of darkness and G, a day of clouds
Heb	12:18	fire, and darkness, and G, and a tempest,
2Pet	2:4	to pits of nether G to be kept until
	2:17	for them the nether G of darkness has been
Jude	1:6	chains in the nether G until the judgment of
	1:13	for whom the nether G of darkness has been

GLOOMY (2)

Wis	17:4	and dismal phantoms with G faces appeared.
Sir	25:22	A dejected mind, a G face, and a wounded

GLORIES (4)

Wis	18:24	was depicted, and the G of the fathers were
Sir	38:25	the plow, and who G in the shaft of
Jer	9:24	but let him who G glory in this, that
1Mac	14:9	the youths donned the G and garments of war.

GLORIFICATION

1Cor	2:7	which God decreed before the ages for our G

GLORIFIED (49)

Lev	10:3	and before all the people I will be G
Esth	14:7	our enemies, because we G their gods.
Wis	19:22	thou hast exalted and G thy people; and thou
Sir	3:19	the Lord; he is G by the humble.

38:6 that he might be G in his marvelous works.
45:3 to cease; the Lord G him in the presence
47:6 So they G him for his ten thousands, and
Is 26:15 the nation; thou art G; thou hast enlarged all
44:23 Jacob, and will be G in Israel.
49:3 my servant, Israel, in whom I will be G
55:5 Israel, for he has G you.
60:9 Israel, because he has G you.
60:21 work of my hands, that I might be G
61:3 planting of the LORD, that he may be G
66:5 'Let the LORD be G, that we may see
Dan 3:26 and thy name is G for ever.
3:51 one mouth, praised and G and blessed God in
3:54 be extolled and highly G for ever.
3:57 to be sung and G for ever.
2Mac 3:2 honored the place and G the temple with the
Mt 9:8 were afraid, and they G God, who had given
15:31 blind seeing; and they G the God of Israel.
Mk 2:12 were all amazed and G God, saying, "We never
Lk 4:15 in their synagogues, being G by all.
5:26 them all, and they G God and were filled
7:16 them all; and they G God, saying, "A great
Jn 7:39 not been given, because Jesus was not yet G
11:4 of God may be G by means of it."
12:16 but when Jesus was G, then they remembered that
12:23 come for the Son of man to be G
12:28 from heaven, "I have G it, and I will
13:31 the Son of man G, and in him God
13:31 in him God is G;
13:32 glorified; if God is G in him, God will
14:13 the Father may be G in the Son;
15:8 this my Father is G, that you bear much
17:4 I G thee on earth, having accomplished the work
17:10 mine, and I am G in them.
Acts 3:13 God of our fathers, G his servant Jesus, whom
11:18 And they G God, saying, "Then to the Gentiles
13:48 they were glad and G the word of God;
21:20 they heard it, they G God.
Rom 8:17 we may also be G with him.
8:30 justified; and those whom he justified he also G
Gal 1:24 And they G God because of me.
2Thes 1:10 that day to be G in his saints, and
1:12 Lord Jesus may be G in you, and you
1Pet 4:11 everything God may be G through Jesus Christ.
Rev 18:7 As she G herself and played the wanton, so

GLORIFIES (4)

Wis 8:3 She G her noble birth by living with God,
Sir 3:4 for sins, and whoever G his mother is like
3:6 Whoever G his father will have long life, and
Jn 8:54 is my Father who G me, of whom you

GLORIFY (28)

Ps 22:23 you sons of Jacob, G him, and stand in
50:15 you, and you shall G me."
86:9 O Lord, and shall G thy name.
86:12 heart, and I will G thy name for ever.
Wis 18:8 us to thyself and G us.
Sir 3:10 Do not G yourself by dishonoring your father, for
10:25 do your work, nor G yourself at a time
10:27 My son, G yourself with humility, and ascribe to
35:8 G the Lord generously, and do not stint the
Is 25:3 Therefore strong peoples will G thee; cities of
60:7 altar, and I will G my glorious house.
Jn 8:54 Jesus answered, "If I G myself, my glory is
12:28 Father, G thy name." Then a voice came from
12:28 it, and I will G it again."
13:32 him, God will also G him in himself, and
13:32 him in himself, and G him at once.
16:14 He will G me, for he will take what
17:1 the hour has come; G thy Son that the
17:1 that the Son may G thee,
17:5 do; and now, Father, G thou me in thy
21:19 death he was to G God.) And after this
Rom 15:6 may with one voice G the God and Father
15:9 that the Gentiles might G God for his mercy.
1Cor 6:20 So G God in your body.
2Cor 9:13 this service, you will G God by your obedience
1Pet 2:12 your good deeds and G God on the day
4:16 that name let him G God.
Rev 15:4 shall not fear and G thy name, O Lord?

GLORIFYING (3)

Lk 2:20 And the shepherds returned, G and praising God for
5:25 lay, and went home, G God.
18:43 sight and followed him, G God; and all the

GLORIOUS (74)

Ex 15:6 right hand, O LORD, G in power, thy right
15:11 in holiness, terrible in G deeds, doing wonders?
Deut 28:58 you may fear this G and awful name, the
1Chr 29:13 God, and praise thy G name.
Neh 9:5 Blessed be thy G name which is exalted above
Tob 8:5 by thy holy and G name for ever.
14:5 rebuilt there with a G building for all generations
Jud 9:8 the tabernacle where thy G name rests, and to
16:13 thou are great and G, wonderful in strength,
Ps 66:2 name; give to him G praise!
72:19 Blessed be his G name for ever; may his
76:4 [Selah] G art thou, more majestic than the
78:4 the coming generation the G deeds of the LORD,
87:3 G things are spoken of you, O city of
90:16 thy servants, and thy G power to their children.
145:5 On the G splendor of thy majesty, and on
145:12 mighty deeds, and the G splendor of thy kingdom.
Wis 5:16 they will receive a G crown and a beautiful
18:3 harmless sun for their G wandering.
Sir 6:29 and her collar a G robe.
6:31 wear her like a G robe, and put her
17:11 Their eyes saw his G majesty, and their ears
24:16 and my branches are G and graceful.
24:17 and my blossoms became G and abundant fruit.
27:8 wear it as a G robe.
36:6 wonders; make thy hand and thy right arm G
43:12 the heaven with its G arc; the hands of
45:7 vestments, and put a G robe upon him.
46:2 How G he was when he lifted his hands
47:6 the Lord, when the G diadem was bestowed upon
48:4 How G you were, O Elijah, in your wondrous
50:5 How G he was when the people gathered round
50:7 the rainbow gleaming in G clouds;
50:11 he put on his G robe and clothed himself
50:11 altar, he made the court of the sanctuary G
Is 3:8 the LORD, defying his G presence.
4:2 shall be beautiful and G, and the fruit of
9:1 time he will make G the way of the
11:10 the nations seek, and his dwellings shall be G
28:1 fading flower of its G beauty, which is on
28:4 fading flower of its G beauty, which is on
42:21 sake, to magnify his law and make it G
60:7 I will glorify my G house.
60:13 I will make the place of my feet G
63:1 Bozrah, he that is G in his apparel, marching
63:12 Spirit, who caused his G arm to go at
63:14 make for thyself a G name.
63:15 from thy holy and G habitation.
Jer 14:21 do not dishonor thy G throne; remember and do
17:12 A G throne set on high from the beginning
48:17 scepter is broken, the G staff.'
Ezek 20:6 and honey, the most G of all lands.
20:15 and honey, the most G of all lands,
Dan 3:45 Lord, the only God, G over the whole world."
3:53 And blessed is thy G, holy name and to
8:9 east, and toward the G land.
11:16 shall stand in the G land, and all of
11:41 shall come into the G land.
11:45 the sea and the G holy mountain; yet he
Zech 11:2 has fallen, for the G trees are ruined!
1Mac 2:9 man without honor; her G vessels have been carried
14:15 He made the sanctuary G, and added to the
2Mac 8:15 by his holy and G name.
Mt 19:28 shall sit on his G throne, you who have
25:31 will sit on his G throne.
Lk 13:17 rejoiced at all the G things that were done
Rom 8:21 decay and obtain the G liberty of the children
Eph 1:6 the praise of his G grace which he freely
1:18 the riches of his G inheritance in the saints,
Phil 3:21 to be like his G body, by the power
Col 1:11 power, according to his G might, for all endurance
1Tim 1:11 in accordance with the G gospel of the blessed
2Pet 2:10 afraid to revile the G ones,
Jude 1:8 authority, and revile the G ones.

GLORIOUSLY (6)

Ex 15:1 for he has triumphed G; the horse and his
15:21 for he has triumphed G; the horse and his
Tob 12:7 of a king, but G to reveal the works
12:11 of a king, but G to reveal the works
Is 12:5 for he has done G; let this be known
2Mac 3:26 to him, remarkably strong, G beautiful and splendidly

GLORY (431)

Ex 14:4 and I will get G over Pharaoh and all

G

14:17 and I will get G over Pharaoh and all
14:18 when I have gotten G over Pharaoh, his chariots,
16:7 you shall see the G of the LORD, because
16:10 wilderness, and behold, the G of the LORD appeared
24:16 The G of the LORD settled on Mount Sinai,
24:17 the appearance of the G of the LORD was
28:2 Aaron your brother, for G and for beauty.
28:40 shall make them for G and beauty.
29:43 be sanctified by my G;
33:18 Moses said, "I pray thee, show me thy G
33:22 rock; and while my G passes by I will
Lev 9:6 to do; and the G of the LORD will
9:23 the people, and the G of the LORD appeared
Num 14:10 Then the G of the LORD appeared at the
14:21 be filled with the G of the LORD,
14:22 who have seen my G and my signs which
16:19 And the G of the LORD appeared to all
16:42 covered it, and the G of the LORD appeared.
20:6 And the G of the LORD appeared to them,
Deut 5:24 has shown us his G and greatness, and we
Josh 7:19 Achan, "My son, give G to the LORD God
Judg 4:9 not lead to your G, for the LORD will
1Sam 4:21 child Ichabod, saying, "The G has departed from
4:22 And she said, "The G has departed from Israel,
6:5 the land, and give G to the God of
15:29 And also the G of Israel will not lie
2Sam 1:19 He said: "Thy G, O Israel, is slain upon
1Kgs 8:11 the cloud; for the G of the LORD filled
2Kgs 14:10 Be content with your G, and stay at home;
1Chr 16:10 G in his holy name; let the hearts of
16:24 Declare his G among the nations, his marvelous
16:28 ascribe to the LORD G and strength!
16:29 to the LORD the G due his name; bring
16:35 thy holy name, and G in thy praise.
22:5 magnificent, of fame and G throughout all lands; I
29:11 the power, and the G, and the victory, and
2Chr 5:14 the cloud; for the G of the LORD filled
7:1 the sacrifices, and the G of the LORD filled
7:2 the LORD, because the G of the LORD filled
7:3 come down and the G of the LORD upon
Tob 3:16 the presence of the G of the great God.
12:15 the presence of the G of the Holy One."
13:14 upon seeing all your G, and they will be
Jud 9:7 horses and riders; they G in the strength of
10:8 people of Israel may G and Jerusalem may be
15:9 you are the great G of Israel, you are
Esth 1:4 riches of his royal G and the splendor and
13:12 for any love of G that I did this,
13:14 might not set the G of man above the
13:14 of man above the G of God, and I
14:9 thy altar and the G of thy house,
15:13 my heart was shaken with fear at your G
Job 19:9 stripped from me my G, and taken the crown
29:20 on my branches, my G fresh with me, and
40:10 dignity; clothe yourself with G and splendor.
Ps 3:3 shield about me, my G, and the lifter of
8:1 Thou whose G above the heavens is chanted
8:5 dost crown him with G and honor.
19:1 heavens are telling the G of God; and the
21:5 His G is great through thy help; splendor and
24:7 that the King of G may come in.
24:8 Who is the King of G
24:9 that the King of G may come in.
24:10 Who is this King of G
24:10 LORD of hosts, he is the King of G
26:8 the place where thy G dwells.
29:1 ascribe to the LORD G and strength.
29:2 to the LORD the G of his name; worship
29:3 waters; the God of G thunders, the LORD, upon
29:9 forests bare; and in his temple all cry, G
37:20 LORD are like the G of the pastures, they
45:3 mighty one, in your G and majesty!
49:16 becomes rich, when the G of his house increases.
49:17 carry nothing away; his G will not go down
57:5 Let thy G be over all the earth!
57:11 Let thy G be over all the earth!
63:2 thee in the sanctuary, beholding thy power and G
63:11 swear by him shall G; for the mouths of
64:10 Let all the upright in heart G
66:2 the earth; sing the G of his name; give
71:8 praise, and with thy G all the day.
72:19 for ever; may his G fill the whole earth!
73:24 counsel, and afterward thou wilt receive me to G
78:61 power to captivity, his G to the hand of
79:9 our salvation, for the G of thy name; deliver
85:9 who fear him, that G may dwell in our
89:17 For thou art the G of their strength; by
96:3 Declare his G among the nations, his marvelous
96:7 ascribe to the LORD G and strength!
96:8 to the LORD the G due his name; bring
97:6 his righteousness; and all the peoples behold his G
102:15 and all the kings of the earth thy G
102:16 will appear in his G;
104:31 May the G of the LORD endure for ever,
105:3 G in his holy name; let the hearts of
106:5 nation, that I may G with thy heritage.
106:20 They exchanged the G of God for the image
106:47 thy holy name and G in thy praise.
108:5 Let thy G be over all the earth!
113:4 all nations, and his G above the heavens!
115:1 to thy name give G, for the sake of
138:5 for great is the G of the LORD.
145:11 shall speak of the G of thy kingdom, and
148:13 alone is exalted; his G is above earth and
149:5 the faithful exult in G; let them sing for
149:9 This is G for all his faithful ones.
Prov 14:28 of people is the G of a king, but
16:31 is a crown of G; it is gained in
17:6 the aged, and the G of sons is their
19:11 and it is his G to overlook an offense.
20:29 The G of young men is their strength, but
25:2 It is the G of God to conceal things,
25:2 conceal things, but the G of kings is to
28:12 triumph, there is great G; but when the wicked
Wis 7:25 pure emanation of the G of the Almighty; therefore
8:10 her I shall have G among the multitudes and
9:10 the throne of thy G send her, that she
9:11 in my actions and guard me with her G
15:9 he counts it his G that he molds counterfeit
Sir 1:9 of the Lord is G and exultation, and gladness
1:17 and he exalted the G of those who held
3:10 father's dishonor is no G to you.
3:11 For a man's G comes from honoring his father,
4:13 her fast will obtain G, and the Lord will
4:21 a shame which is G and favor.
5:13 G and dishonor come from speaking, and a man's
10:21 the poor— their G is the fear of
14:27 and will dwell in the midst of her G
17:11 their ears heard the G of his voice.
20:10 are losses because of G, and there are men
24:1 praise herself, and will G in the midst of
24:2 his host she will G:
29:6 reproaches, and instead of G will repay him with
30:3 enemies envious, and will G in him in the
36:14 thy wondrous deeds, and thy temple with thy G
39:8 his teaching, and will G in the law of
40:27 blessing, and covers a man better than any G
42:16 work of the Lord is full of his G
42:17 that the universe may stand firm in his G
42:25 and who can have enough of beholding his G
43:1 the appearance of heaven in a spectacle of G
43:9 The G of the stars is the beauty of
44:2 apportioned to them great G, his majesty from the
44:8 generations, and were the G of their times.
44:14 for ever, and their G will not be blotted
44:20 found like him in G;
45:2 made him equal in G to the holy ones,
45:3 his people, and showed him part of his G
45:20 He added G to Aaron and gave him a
45:23 is the third in G, for he was zealous
45:26 vanish, and that their G may endure throughout their
47:8 High, with ascriptions of G; he sang praise with
47:11 and a throne of G in Israel.
49:5 to others, and their G to a foreign nation,
49:8 saw the vision of G which God showed him
49:12 temple holy to the Lord, prepared for everlasting G
50:20 his lips, and to G in his name;
51:17 to him who gives wisdom I will give G
Is 2:10 LORD, and from the G of his majesty.
2:19 LORD, and from the G of his majesty, when
2:21 LORD, and from the G of his majesty, when
4:2 be the pride and G of the survivors of
4:5 for over all the G there will be a
6:3 hosts; the whole earth is full of his G
8:7 Assyria and all his G; and it will rise
10:16 warriors, and under his G a burning will be
10:18 The G of his forest and of his fruitful
13:19 And Babylon, the G of kingdoms, the splendor and
14:18 the nations lie in G, each in his own
16:14 of a hireling, the G of Moab will be
17:3 will be like the G of the children of
17:4 in that day the G of Jacob will be

21:16 a hireling, all the G of Kedar will come
23:9 the pride of all G, to dishonor all the
24:15 in the east give G to the LORD; in
24:16 songs of praise, of G to the Righteous One.
24:23 and before his elders he will manifest his G
28:5 be a crown of G, and a diadem of
35:2 The G of Lebanon shall be given to it,
35:2 They shall see the G of the LORD, the
40:5 And the G of the LORD shall be revealed,
41:16 in the Holy One of Israel you shall G
42:8 is my name; my G I give to no
42:12 Let them give G to the LORD, and declare
43:7 I created for my G, whom I formed and
45:25 all the offspring of Israel shall triumph and G
46:13 will put salvation in Zion, for Israel my G
48:11 My G I will not give to another.
58:8 go before you, the G of the LORD shall
59:19 the west, and his G from the rising of
60:1 has come, and the G of the LORD has
60:2 upon you, and his G will be seen upon
60:13 The G of Lebanon shall come to you, the
60:19 everlasting light, and your God will be your G
61:6 the nations, and in their riches you shall G
62:2 all the kings your G; and you shall be
66:11 deeply with delight from the abundance of her G
66:18 and shall see my G,
66:19 fame or seen my G; and they shall declare
66:19 they shall declare my G among the nations.
Jer 2:11 people have changed their G for that which does
4:2 themselves in him, and in him shall they G
9:23 not the wise man G in his wisdom, let
9:23 not the mighty man G in his might, let
9:23 not the rich man G in his riches;
9:24 let him who glories G in this, that he
13:11 a praise, and a G, but they would not
13:16 Give G to the LORD your God before he
33:9 a praise and a G before all the nations
48:18 "Come down from your G, and sit on the
Lam 3:18 say, "Gone is my G, and my expectation from
Bar 2:17 bodies, will not ascribe G or justice to the
2:18 will ascribe to thee G and righteousness, O Lord.
4:3 Do not give your G to another, or your
4:24 to you with great G and with the splendor
4:37 One, rejoicing in the G of God.
5:1 the beauty of the G from God.
5:2 the diadem of the G of the Everlasting.
5:4 "Peace of righteousness and G of godliness."
5:6 to you, carried in G, as on a royal
5:7 walk safely in the G of God.
5:9 the light of his G, with the mercy and
Ezek 1:28 the likeness of the G of the LORD.
3:12 up, and as the G of the LORD arose
3:23 plain; and, lo, the G of the LORD stood
3:23 stood there, like the G which I had seen
8:4 And behold, the G of the God of Israel
9:3 Now the G of the God of Israel had
10:4 And the G of the LORD went up from
10:4 the brightness of the G of the LORD.
10:18 Then the G of the LORD went forth from
10:19 the LORD; and the G of the God of
11:22 beside them; and the G of the God of
11:23 And the G of the LORD went up from
24:25 stronghold, their joy and G, the delight of their
25:9 on its frontier, the G of the country, Beth-jeshimoth,
28:22 I will manifest my G in the midst of
31:18 you thus like in G and in greatness among
39:13 that I show my G, says the Lord GOD.
39:21 I will set my G among the nations; and
43:2 And behold, the G of the God of Israel
43:2 many waters; and the earth shone with his G
43:4 As the G of the LORD entered the temple
43:5 court; and behold, the G of the LORD filled
44:4 looked, and behold, the G of the LORD filled
Dan 2:37 the might, and the G,
3:43 marvelous works, and give G to thy name, O
3:54 temple of thy holy G and to be extolled
4:30 residence and for the G of my majesty?"
4:36 me; and for the G of my kingdom, my
5:18 kingship and greatness and G and majesty;
5:20 kingly throne, and his G was taken from him;
7:14 was given dominion and G and kingdom, that all
11:20 of tribute through the G of the kingdom; but
Hos 4:7 I will change their G into shame.
4:18 to harlotry; they love shame more than their G
9:11 Ephraim's G shall fly away like a bird—no
10:5 over it, over its G which has departed from
Mic 1:15 inhabitants of Mareshah; the G of Israel shall come
2:9 you take away my G for ever.
Hab 2:14 the knowledge of the G of the LORD, as
2:16 You will be sated with contempt instead of G
2:16 to you, and shame will come upon your G
3:3 His G covered the heavens, and the earth was
Hag 1:8 may appear in my G, says the LORD.
2:3 you that saw this house in its former G
Zech 2:5 I will be the G within her.'"
2:8 of hosts, after his G sent me to the
10:12 LORD and they shall G in his name," says
11:3 the shepherds, for their G is despoiled!
12:7 Judah first, that the G of the house of
12:7 of David and the G of the inhabitants of
Mal 2:2 to heart to give G to my name, says
1Mac 1:40 as great as her G; her exaltation was turned
2:12 our beauty, and our G have been laid waste;
3:3 He extended the G of his people.
11:51 So the Jews gained G in the eyes of
12:12 And we rejoice in your G
14:21 told us about your G and honor, and we
14:29 and they brought great G to their nation.
14:35 Simon's faithfulness and the G which he had resolved
15:9 temple, so that your G will become manifest in
2Mac 2:8 these things, and the G of the Lord and
5:16 made to enhance the G and honor of the
5:20 again in all its G when the great Lord
14:7 laid aside my ancestral G – I mean
Mt 4:8 the world and the G of them;
5:16 good works and give G to your Father who
6:29 Solomon in all his G was not arrayed like
16:27 his angels in the G of his Father, and
24:30 with power and great G;
25:31 man comes in his G, and all the angels
Mk 8:38 he comes in the G of his Father with
10:37 hand and one at your left, in your G
13:26 man coming in clouds with great power and G
Lk 2:9 to them, and the G of the Lord shone
2:14 praising God and saying, G to God in the
2:32 the Gentiles, and for G to thy people Israel."
4:6 this authority and their G; for it has been
9:26 he comes in his G and the glory of
9:26 his glory and the G of the Father and
9:31 Elijah, who appeared in G and spoke of his
9:32 wakened they saw his G and the two men
12:27 Solomon in all his G was not arrayed like
19:38 Peace in heaven and G in the highest!"
21:27 coming in a cloud with power and great G
24:26 should suffer these things and enter into his G
Jn 1:14 we have beheld his G, glory as of the
1:14 have beheld his glory, G as of the only
2:11 Galilee, and manifested his G; and his disciples
5:40 I do not receive G from men.
5:43 you believe, who receive G from one another and
5:43 do not seek the G that comes from the
7:18 authority seeks his own G; but he who seeks
7:18 he who seeks the G of him who sent
8:50 not seek my own G; there is One who
8:54 I glorify myself, my G is nothing; it is
11:4 it is for the G of God, so that
11:40 you would see the G of God?"
12:41 because he saw his G and spoke of him.
17:5 own presence with the G which I had with
17:22 The G which thou hast given me I have
17:24 am, to behold my G which thou hast given
Acts 7:2 The God of G appeared to our father Abraham,
7:55 heaven and saw the G of God, and Jesus
12:23 not give God the G; and he was eaten
Rom 1:23 fools, and exchanged the G of the immortal God
2:7 in well-doing seek for G and honor and immortality,
2:10 also the Greek, but G and honor and peace
3:7 truthfulness abounds to his G, why am I still
3:23 fall short of the G of God,
4:20 faith as he gave G to God,
5:2 hope of sharing the G of God.
6:4 the dead by the G of the Father, we
8:18 worth comparing with the G that is to be
9:4 belong the sonship, the G, the covenants, the giving
9:23 the riches of his G for the vessels of
9:23 has prepared beforehand for G,
11:36 To him be G for ever.
15:7 welcomed you, for the G of God.
16:26 only wise God be G for evermore through Jesus
1Cor 2:8 they would not have crucified the Lord of G
10:31 do all to the G of God.
11:7 is the image and G of God; but woman

G

Eccl 12:11 the wise are like G, and like nails firmly
Acts 26:14 to kick against the G

GOAH
Jer 31:39 the hill Gareb, and shall then turn to G

GOAL
Phil 3:14 press on toward the G for the prize of

GOAT (56)
Gen 37:31 robe, and killed a G, and dipped the robe
Lev 3:12 his offering is a G, then he shall offer
4:23 as his offering a G, a male without blemish,
4:24 the head of the G, and kill it in
4:28 for his offering a G, a female without blemish,
5:6 a lamb or a G, for a sin offering;
7:23 eat no fat, of ox, or sheep, or G
9:3 Israel, 'Take a male G for a sin offering,
9:15 offering, and took the G of the sin offering
10:16 diligently inquired about the G of the sin offering,
16:9 Aaron shall present the G on which the lot
16:10 sin offering; but the G on which the lot
16:15 he shall kill the G of the sin offering
16:18 the blood of the G, and put it on
16:20 shall present the live G;
16:21 head of the live G, and confess over him
16:21 the head of the G, and send him away
16:22 The G shall bear all their iniquities upon him
16:22 he shall let the G go in the wilderness.
16:26 he who lets the G go to Azazel shall
16:27 sin offering and the G for the sin offering,
17:3 a lamb or a G in the camp, or
22:27 bull or sheep or G is born, it shall
23:19 shall offer one male G for a sin offering,
Num 7:16 burnt offering; one male G for a sin offering;
7:22 burnt offering; one male G for a sin offering;
7:28 burnt offering; one male G for a sin offering;
7:34 burnt offering; one male G for a sin offering;
7:40 burnt offering; one male G for a sin offering;
7:46 burnt offering; one male G for a sin offering;
7:52 burnt offering; one male G for a sin offering;
7:58 burnt offering; one male G for a sin offering;
7:64 burnt offering; one male G for a sin offering;
7:70 burnt offering; one male G for a sin offering;
7:76 burnt offering; one male G for a sin offering;
7:82 burnt offering; one male G for a sin offering;
15:24 ordinance, and one male G for a sin offering.
15:27 shall offer a female G a year old for
18:17 the firstling of a G, you shall not redeem;
28:15 Also one male G for a sin offering to
28:22 lambs; also one male G for a sin offering,
28:30 lambs; with one male G, to make atonement for
29:5 lambs; with one male G for a sin offering,
29:11 lambs: also one male G for a sin offering,
29:16 lambs; also one male G for a sin offering,
29:19 ordinance; also one male G for a sin offering,
29:22 ordinance; also one male G for a sin offering,
29:25 ordinance; also one male G for a sin offering,
29:28 ordinance; also one male G for a sin offering;
29:31 ordinance; also one male G for a sin offering;
29:34 ordinance; also one male G for a sin offering;
29:38 ordinance; also one male G for a sin offering;
Deut 14:4 ox, the sheep, the G,
14:5 the roebuck, the wild G, the ibex, the antelope,
Ezek 43:25 shall provide daily a G for a sin offering;
Dan 8:5 the ground; and the G had a conspicuous horn

GOATS (55)
Gen 30:32 and speckled among the G; and such shall be
30:33 and spotted among the G and black among the
31:12 and see, all the G that leap upon the
Ex 12:5 sheep or from the G;
25:4 and fine twined linen, G hair,
26:7 also make curtains of G hair for a tent
35:6 and fine twined linen; G hair,
35:23 or fine linen or G hair or tanned rams'
35:26 with ability spun the G hair.
36:14 also made curtains of G hair for a tent
Lev 1:10 from the sheep or G, he shall offer a
16:5 of Israel two male G for a sin offering,
16:7 shall take the two G, and set them before
16:8 lots upon the two G, one lot for the
22:19 of the bulls or the sheep or the G
Num 7:17 five rams, five male G, and five male lambs
7:23 five rams, five male G, and five male lambs
7:29 five rams, five male G, and five male lambs
7:35 five rams, five male G, and five male lambs
7:41 five rams, five male G, and five male lambs
7:47 five rams, five male G, and five male lambs
7:53 five rams, five male G, and five male lambs
7:59 five rams, five male G, and five male lambs
7:65 five rams, five male G, and five male lambs
7:71 five rams, five male G, and five male lambs
7:77 five rams, five male G, and five male lambs
7:83 five rams, five male G, and five male lambs
7:87 offering; and twelve male G for a sin offering;
7:88 rams sixty, the male G sixty, the male lambs
31:20 skin, all work of G hair, and every article
Deut 32:14 herds of Bashan and G, with the finest of
1Sam 19:13 put a pillow of G hair at its head,
19:16 with the pillow of G hair at its head.
25:2 he had three thousand sheep and a thousand G
1Kgs 20:27 two little flocks of G, but the Syrians filled
Jud 2:17 sheep and oxen and G for provision;
Job 39:1 know when the mountain G bring forth?
Ps 50:13 flesh of bulls, or drink the blood of G
66:15 I will make an offering of bulls and G
104:18 are for the wild G; the rocks are a
Prov 27:26 your clothing, and the G the price of a
27:27 there will be enough G milk for your food,
Song 4:1 like a flock of G, moving down the slopes
6:5 like a flock of G, moving down the slopes
Sir 47:3 lions as with young G, and with bears as
Is 34:6 blood of lambs and G, with the fat of
Ezek 27:21 in lambs, rams, and G; in these they trafficked
39:18 of lambs, and of G, of bulls, all of
Mt 25:32 the sheep from the G,
25:33 right hand, but the G at the left.
Heb 9:12 not the blood of G and calves but his
9:13 with the blood of G and bulls and with
9:19 blood of calves and G, with water and scarlet
10:4 blood of bulls and G should take away sins.
11:37 skins of sheep and G, destitute, afflicted, ill-treated--

GOATSKIN (7)
Num 4:6 it a covering of G, and spread over that
4:8 with a covering of G, and shall put in
4:10 in a covering of G and put it upon
4:11 with a covering of G, and shall put in
4:12 with a covering of G, and put them on
4:14 it a covering of G, and shall put in
4:25 and the covering of G that is on top

GOATSKINS (6)
Ex 25:5 hair, tanned rams' skins, G, acacia wood,
26:14 tent a covering of tanned rams' skins and G
35:7 tanned rams' skins, and G; acacia wood,
35:23 tanned rams' skins or G, brought them.
36:19 tent a covering of tanned rams' skins and G
39:34 tanned rams' skins and G, and the veil of

GOB (2)
2Sam 21:18 the Philistines at G; then Sibbecai the Hushathite
21:19 with the Philistines at G; and Elhanan the son

GOBLETS (2)
Esth 1:7 were served in golden G, goblets of different kinds,
1:7 served in golden goblets, G of different kinds, and

GOD (4,773)
Gen 1:1 IN the beginning G created the heavens and
1:2 and the Spirit of G was moving over the
1:3 And G said, "Let there be light"; and there
1:4 And G saw that the light was good; and
1:4 light was good; and G separated the light from
1:5 G called the light Day, and the darkness he
1:6 And G said, "Let there be a firmament in
1:7 G made the firmament and separated the waters
1:8 And G called the firmament Heaven.
1:9 And G said, "Let the waters under the heavens
1:10 G called the dry land Earth, and the waters
1:10 And G saw that it was good.
1:11 And G said, "Let the earth put forth vegetation,
1:12 And G saw that it was good.
1:14 And G said, "Let there be lights in the
1:16 And G made the two great lights, the greater
1:17 And G set them in the firmament of the
1:18 And G saw that it was good.
1:20 And G said, "Let the waters bring forth swarms
1:21 So G created the great sea monsters and every
1:21 And G saw that it was good.
1:22 And G blessed them, saying, "Be fruitful and multiply

1:24 And G said, "Let the earth bring forth living
1:25 And G made the beasts of the earth according
1:25 And G saw that it was good.
1:26 Then G said, "Let us make man in our
1:27 So G created man in his own image, in
1:27 in the image of G he created him; male
1:28 And G blessed them, and God said to them,
1:28 God blessed them, and G said to them, "Be
1:29 And G said, "Behold, I have given you every
1:31 And G saw everything that he had made, and
2:2 on the seventh day G finished his work which
2:3 So G blessed the seventh day and hallowed it,
2:3 it, because on it G rested from all his
2:4 day that the LORD G made the earth and
2:5 up—for the LORD G had not caused it
2:7 then the LORD G formed man of dust
2:8 And the LORD G planted a garden in Eden,
2:9 the ground the LORD G made to grow every
2:15 The LORD G took the man and put him
2:16 And the LORD G commanded the man, saying, "You
2:18 Then the LORD G said, "It is not good
2:19 the ground the LORD G formed every beast of
2:21 So the LORD G caused a deep sleep to
2:22 rib which the LORD G had taken from the
3:1 creature that the LORD G had made.
3:1 to the woman, "Did G say, 'You shall not
3:3 of the garden; but G said, 'You shall not
3:5 For G knows that when you eat of it
3:5 you will be like G, knowing good and evil."
3:8 sound of the LORD G walking in the garden
3:8 presence of the LORD G among the trees of
3:9 But the LORD G called to the man, and
3:13 Then the LORD G said to the woman, "What
3:14 The LORD G said to the serpent, "Because you
3:21 And the LORD G made for Adam and for
3:22 Then the LORD G said, "Behold, the man has
3:23 therefore the LORD G sent him forth from
4:25 Seth, for she said, G has appointed for me
5:1 When G created man, he made him in the
5:1 man, he made him in the likeness of G
5:22 Enoch walked with G after the birth of Methuselah
5:24 Enoch walked with G; and he was not, for
5:24 he was not, for G took him.
6:2 them, the sons of G saw that the daughters
6:4 when the sons of G came in to the
6:9 blameless in his generation; Noah walked with G
6:11 earth was corrupt in G's sight, and the earth
6:12 And G saw the earth, and behold, it was
6:13 And G said to Noah, "I have determined to
6:22 he did all that G commanded him.
7:9 ark with Noah, as G had commanded Noah.
7:16 flesh, went in as G had commanded him; and
8:1 But G remembered Noah and all the beasts and
8:1 And G made a wind blow over the earth,
8:15 Then G said to Noah,
9:1 And G blessed Noah and his sons, and said
9:6 blood be shed; for G made man in his
9:8 Then G said to Noah and to his sons
9:12 And G said, "This is the sign of the
9:16 everlasting covenant between G and every living
9:17 G said to Noah, "This is the sign of
9:26 by the LORD my G be Shem; and let
9:27 G enlarge Japheth, and let him dwell in the
14:18 he was priest of G Most High.
14:19 "Blessed be Abram by G Most High, maker of
14:20 earth; and blessed be G Most High, who has
14:22 sworn to the LORD G Most High, maker of
15:2 Abram said, "O Lord G, what wilt thou give
15:8 he said, "O Lord G, how am I to
16:13 her, "Thou art a G of seeing"; for she
16:13 "Have I really seen G and remained alive after
17:1 to him, "I am G Almighty; walk before me,
17:3 on his face; and G said to him,
17:7 everlasting covenant, to be G to you and to
17:8 an everlasting possession; and I will be their G
17:9 And G said to Abraham, "As for you, you
17:15 And G said to Abraham, "As for Sarai your
17:18 And Abraham said to G, "O that Ishmael might
17:19 G said, "No, but Sarah your wife shall bear
17:22 finished talking with him, G went up from Abraham.
17:23 that very day, as G had said to him.
19:29 it was that, when G destroyed the cities of
19:29 cities of the valley, G remembered Abraham, and
20:3 But G came to Abimelech in a dream by
20:6 Then G said to him in the dream, "Yes,
20:11 is no fear of G at all in this
20:13 And when G caused me to wander from my
20:17 Abraham prayed to G; and God healed Abimelech,
20:17 prayed to God; and G healed Abimelech, and also
21:2 the time of which G had spoken to him.
21:4 eight days old, as G had commanded him.
21:6 And Sarah said, G has made laughter for me;
21:12 But G said to Abraham, "Be not displeased because
21:17 And G heard the voice of the lad; and
21:17 and the angel of G called to Hagar from
21:17 Fear not; for G has heard the voice of
21:19 Then G opened her eyes, and she saw a
21:20 And G was with the lad, and he grew
21:22 army said to Abraham, G is with you in
21:23 to me here by G that you will not
21:33 on the name of the LORD, the Everlasting G
22:1 After these things G tested Abraham, and said to
22:3 the place of which G had told him.
22:8 Abraham said, G will provide himself the lamb for
22:9 the place of which G had told him, Abraham
22:12 know that you fear G, seeing you have not
24:3 by the LORD, the G of heaven and of
24:7 The LORD, the G of heaven, who took me
24:12 he said, "O LORD, G of my master Abraham,
24:27 be the LORD, the G of my master Abraham,
24:42 said, 'O LORD, the G of my master Abraham,
24:48 blessed the LORD, the G of my master Abraham,
25:11 the death of Abraham G blessed Isaac his son.
26:24 said, "I am the G of Abraham your father;
27:20 "Because the LORD your G granted me success."
27:28 May G give you of the dew of heaven,
28:3 G Almighty bless you and make you fruitful and
28:4 of your sojournings which G gave to Abraham!"
28:12 behold, the angels of G were ascending and
28:13 am the LORD, the G of Abraham your father
28:13 your father and the G of Isaac; the land
28:17 than the house of G, and this is the
28:20 a vow, saying, "If G will be with me,
28:21 LORD shall be my G,
28:22 a pillar, shall be G's house; and of all
30:2 in the place of G, who has withheld from
30:6 Then Rachel said, G has judged me, and has
30:17 And G hearkened to Leah, and she conceived and
30:18 Leah said, G has given me my hire because
30:20 Then Leah said, G has endowed me with a
30:22 Then G remembered Rachel, and God hearkened to
30:22 God remembered Rachel, and G hearkened to her
30:23 a son, and said, G has taken away my
31:5 But the G of my father has been with
31:7 wages ten times, but G did not permit him
31:9 Thus G has taken away the cattle of your
31:11 Then the angel of G said to me in
31:13 I am the G of Bethel, where you anointed
31:16 All the property which G has taken away from
31:16 children; now then, whatever G has said to you,
31:24 But G came to Laban the Aramean in a
31:29 you harm; but the G of your father spoke
31:42 If the G of my father, the God of
31:42 of my father, the G of Abraham and the
31:42 G saw my affliction and the labor of my
31:50 is with us, remember, G is witness between you
31:53 The G of Abraham and the God of Nahor,
31:53 of Abraham and the G of Nahor, the God
31:53 God of Nahor, the G of their father, judge
32:1 and the angels of G met him;
32:2 he said, "This is G's army!" So he called
32:9 And Jacob said, "O G of my father Abraham
32:9 my father Abraham and G of my father Isaac,
32:28 you have striven with G and with men, and
32:30 "For I have seen G face to face, and
33:5 said, "The children whom G has graciously given
33:10 seeing the face of G, with such favor have
33:11 brought to you, because G has dealt graciously with
35:1 G said to Jacob, "Arise, go up to Bethel,
35:1 an altar to the G who appeared to you
35:3 an altar to the G who answered me in
35:5 journeyed, a terror from G fell upon the cities
35:7 El-bethel, because there G had revealed himself to
35:9 G appeared to Jacob again, when he came from
35:10 And G said to him, "Your name is Jacob;
35:11 And G said to him, "I am God Almighty:
35:11 to him, "I am G Almighty: be fruitful and
35:13 Then G went up from him in the place
35:15 of the place where G had spoken with him,
39:9 I do this great wickedness, and sin against G
40:8 said to them, "Do not interpretations belong to G
41:16 is not in me; G will give Pharaoh a

41:25 of Pharaoh is one; G has revealed to Pharaoh
41:28 as I told Pharaoh, G has shown to Pharaoh
41:32 thing is fixed by G, and God will shortly
41:32 fixed by God, and G will shortly bring it
41:38 as this, in whom is the Spirit of G
41:39 said to Joseph, "Since G has shown you all
41:51 he said, G has made me forget all my
41:52 he called Ephraim, "For G has made me fruitful
42:18 live, for I fear G:
42:28 "What is this that G has done to us?"
43:14 to the man; may G Almighty grant you mercy
43:23 not be afraid; your G and the God of
43:23 your God and the G of your father must
43:29 G be gracious to you, my son!"
44:16 G has found out the guilt of your servants;
45:5 sold me here; for G sent me before you
45:7 And G sent me before you to preserve for
45:8 sent me here, but G; and he has made
45:9 says your son Joseph, G has made me lord
46:1 offered sacrifices to the G of his father Isaac.
46:2 And G spoke to Israel in visions of the
46:3 he said, "I am G, the God of your
46:3 "I am God, the G of your father; do
48:3 Jacob said to Joseph, G Almighty appeared to me
48:9 are my sons, whom G has given me here."
48:11 your face; and lo, G has let me see
48:15 Joseph, and said, "The G before whom my fathers
48:15 and Isaac walked, the G who has led me
48:20 pronounce blessings, saying, G make you as Ephraim
48:21 about to die, but G will be with you,
49:25 of Israel), by the G of your father who
49:25 will help you, by G Almighty who will bless
50:17 the servants of the G of your father." Joseph
50:19 not, for am I in the place of G
50:20 evil against me; but G meant it for good,
50:24 about to die; but G will visit you, and
50:25 sons of Israel, saying, G will visit you, and

Ex 1:16 But the midwives feared G, and did not do
1:19 So G dealt well with the midwives; and the
1:20 because the midwives feared G he gave them
2:23 and their cry under bondage came up to G
2:24 And G heard their groaning, and God remembered
2:24 their groaning, and G remembered his covenant with
2:25 And G saw the people of Israel, and God
2:25 people of Israel, and G knew their condition.
3:1 wilderness, and came to Horeb, the mountain of G
3:4 turned aside to see, G called to him out
3:6 said, "I am the G of your father, the
3:6 of your father, the G of Abraham, the God
3:6 God of Abraham, the G of Isaac, and the
3:6 of Isaac, and the G of Jacob." And Moses
3:6 face, for he was afraid to look at G
3:11 But Moses said to G, "Who am I that
3:12 Egypt, you shall serve G upon this mountain."
3:13 Then Moses said to G, "If I come to
3:13 say to them, 'The G of your fathers has
3:14 G said to Moses, "I AM WHO AM." And
3:15 G also said to Moses, "Say this to the
3:15 Israel, 'The LORD, the G of your fathers, the
3:15 of your fathers, the G of Abraham, the God
3:15 God of Abraham, the G of Isaac, and the
3:15 of Isaac, and the G of Jacob, has sent
3:16 them, 'The LORD, the G of your fathers, the
3:16 of your fathers, the G of Abraham, of Isaac,
3:18 him, 'The LORD, the G of the Hebrews, has
3:18 to the LORD our G
4:5 that the LORD, the G of their fathers, the
4:5 of their fathers, the G of Abraham, the God
4:5 God of Abraham, the G of Isaac, and the
4:5 of Isaac, and the G of Jacob, has appeared
4:7 Then G said, "Put your hand back into your
4:8 G said, "or heed the first sign, they may
4:16 you, and you shall be to him as G
4:20 in his hand Moses took the rod of G
4:27 at the mountain of G and kissed him.
5:1 says the LORD, the G of Israel, 'Let my
5:3 Then they said, "The G of the Hebrews has
5:3 to the LORD our G, lest he fall upon
5:8 offer sacrifice to our G
6:2 And G said to Moses, "I am the LORD.
6:3 and to Jacob, as G Almighty, but by my
6:7 I will be your G; and you shall know
6:7 am the LORD your G, who has brought you
7:1 I make you as G to Pharaoh; and Aaron
7:16 him, 'The LORD, the G of the Hebrews, sent
8:10 there is no one like the LORD our G
8:19 said to Pharaoh, "This is the finger of G
8:25 "Go, sacrifice to your G within the land."
8:26 to the LORD our G offerings abominable to the
8:27 to the LORD our G as he will command
8:28 to the LORD your G in the wilderness; only
9:1 says the LORD, the G of the Hebrews, "Let
9:13 says the LORD, the G of the Hebrews, "Let
9:30 that you do not yet fear the LORD G
10:3 says the LORD, the G of the Hebrews, 'How
10:7 serve the LORD their G; do you not yet
10:8 serve the LORD your G; but who are to
10:16 against the LORD your G, and against you.
10:17 entreat the LORD your G only to remove this
10:25 that we may sacrifice to the LORD our G
10:26 serve the LORD our G, and we do not
13:17 let the people go, G did not lead them
13:17 that was near; for G said, "Lest the people
13:18 But G led the people round by the way
13:19 people of Israel, saying, G will visit you; then
14:19 Then the angel of G who went before the
15:2 salvation; this is my G, and I will praise
15:2 praise him, my father's G, and I will exalt
15:26 of the LORD your G, and do that which
16:12 shall know that I am the LORD your G
17:9 with the rod of G in my hand."
18:1 heard of all that G had done for Moses
18:4 (for he said, "The G of my father was
18:5 where he was encamped at the mountain of G
18:12 offering and sacrifices to G; and Aaron came with
18:12 to eat bread with Moses' father-in-law before G
18:15 me to inquire of G;
18:16 know the statutes of G and his decisions."
18:19 give you counsel, and G be with you!
18:19 represent the people before G, and bring their cases
18:19 bring their cases to G;
18:21 people, such as fear G, men who are trustworthy
18:23 you do this, and G so commands you, then
19:3 Moses went up to G, and the LORD called
19:17 the camp to meet G; and they took their
19:19 louder, Moses spoke, and G answered him in thunder.
20:1 And G spoke all these words, saying,
20:2 am the LORD your G, who brought you out
20:5 I the LORD your G am a jealous God,
20:5 God am a jealous G, visiting the iniquity of
20:7 of the LORD your G in vain; for the
20:10 to the LORD your G; in it you shall
20:12 which the LORD your G gives you.
20:19 hear; but let not G speak to us, lest
20:20 "Do not fear; for G has come to prove
20:21 the thick darkness where G was.
21:6 shall bring him to G, and he shall bring
21:13 wait for him, but G let him fall into
22:8 shall come near to G, to show whether or
22:9 parties shall come before G; he whom God shall
22:9 before God; he whom G shall condemn shall pay
22:20 "Whoever sacrifices to any G, save to the LORD
22:28 "You shall not revile G, nor curse a ruler
23:17 shall all your males appear before the Lord G
23:19 bring into the house of the LORD your G
23:25 serve the LORD your G, and I will bless
24:10 and they saw the G of Israel; and there
24:11 of Israel; they beheld G, and ate and drank.
24:13 and Moses went up into the mountain of G
29:45 the people of Israel, and will be their G
29:46 am the LORD their G, who brought them forth
29:46 dwell among them; I am the LORD their G
31:3 with the Spirit of G, with ability and intelligence,
31:18 tables of stone, written with the finger of G
32:11 besought the LORD his G, and said, "O LORD,
32:16 were the work of G, and the writing was
32:16 was the writing of G, graven upon the tables.
32:27 "Thus says the LORD G of Israel, 'Put every
34:6 LORD, the LORD, a G merciful and gracious, slow
34:14 shall worship no other G, for the LORD, whose
34:14 Jealous, is a jealous G,
34:23 appear before the LORD G, the God of Israel.
34:23 the LORD God, the G of Israel.
34:24 before the LORD your G three times in the
34:26 bring to the house of the LORD your G .
34:29 face shone because he had been talking with G
35:31 with the Spirit of G, with ability, with intelligence,

Lev 2:13 the covenant with your G be lacking from your
4:22 which the LORD his G has commanded not to
11:44 am the LORD your G; consecrate yourselves
11:45 Egypt, to be your G; you shall therefore be
18:2 people of Israel, I am the LORD your G

18:4 I am the LORD your G
18:21 the name of your G: I am the LORD.
18:30 yourselves by them: I am the LORD your G
19:2 I the LORD your G am holy.
19:3 keep my sabbaths: I am the LORD your G
19:4 yourselves molten gods: I am the LORD your G
19:10 for the sojourner: I am the LORD your G
19:12 the name of your G: I am the LORD.
19:14 you shall fear your G: I am the LORD.
19:25 richly for you: I am the LORD your G
19:31 defiled by them: I am the LORD your G
19:32 you shall fear your G: I am the LORD.
19:34 land of Egypt: I am the LORD your G
19:36 am the LORD your G, who brought you out
20:7 be holy; for I am the LORD your G
20:24 am the LORD your G, who have separated you
21:6 be holy to their G, and not profane the
21:6 the name of their G; for they offer the
21:6 the bread of their G; therefore they shall be
21:7 husband; for the priest is holy to his G
21:8 the bread of your G; he shall be holy
21:12 the sanctuary of his G; for the consecration of
21:12 anointing oil of his G is upon him: I
21:17 may approach to offer the bread of his G
21:21 come near to offer the bread of his G
21:22 the bread of his G, both of the most
22:25 the bread of your G any such animals gotten
22:33 Egypt to be your G: I am the LORD."
23:14 the offering of your G: it is a statute
23:22 for the stranger: I am the LORD your G
23:28 make atonement for you before the LORD your G
23:40 before the LORD your G seven days.
23:43 land of Egypt: I am the LORD your G
24:15 Israel, Whoever curses his G shall bear his sin.
24:22 the native; for I am the LORD your G
25:17 you shall fear your G; for I am the
25:17 your God; for I am the LORD your G
25:36 increase, but fear your G; that your brother may
25:38 am the LORD your G, who brought you forth
25:38 the land of Canaan, and to be your G
25:43 over him with harshness, but shall fear your G
25:55 land of Egypt: I am the LORD your G
26:1 to them; for I am the LORD your G
26:12 and will be your G, and you shall be
26:13 am the LORD your G, who brought you forth
26:44 am the LORD their G;
26:45 I might be their G: I am the LORD."
Num 6:7 because his separation to G is upon his head.
10:9 before the LORD your G, and you shall be
10:10 for remembrance before your G: I am the LORD
10:10 before your God: I am the LORD your G
12:13 LORD, "Heal her, O G, I beseech thee."
15:40 all my commandments, and be holy to your G
15:41 am the LORD your G, who brought you out
15:41 Egypt, to be your G: I am the LORD
15:41 be your God: I am the LORD your G
16:9 for you that the G of Israel has separated
16:22 faces, and said, "O G, the God of the
16:22 said, "O God, the G of the spirits of
21:5 the people spoke against G and against Moses, "Why
22:9 And G came to Balaam and said, "Who are
22:10 And Balaam said to G, "Balak the son of
22:12 G said to Balaam, "You shall not go with
22:18 of the LORD my G, to do less or
22:20 And G came to Balaam at night and said
22:22 But G's anger was kindled because he went; and
22:38 The word that G puts in my mouth, that
23:4 And G met Balaam; and Balaam said to him,
23:8 can I curse whom G has not cursed?
23:19 O son of Zippor: G is not man, that
23:21 The LORD their G is with them, and the
23:22 G brings them out of Egypt; they have as
23:23 and Israel, 'What has G wrought!'
23:27 perhaps it will please G that you may curse
24:2 And the Spirit of G came upon him,
24:4 hears the words of G, who sees the vision
24:8 G brings him out of Egypt; he has as
24:16 hears the words of G, and knows the knowledge
24:23 who shall live when G does this?
25:13 was jealous for his G, and made atonement for
27:16 "Let the LORD, the G of the spirits of
Deut 1:6 saying, "The LORD our G said to us in
1:10 you; the LORD your G has multiplied you, and
1:11 May the LORD, the G of your fathers, make
1:19 as the LORD our G commanded us; and we
1:20 which the LORD our G gives us.
1:21 Behold, the LORD your G has set the land
1:21 as the LORD, the G of your fathers, has
1:25 which the LORD our G gives us.'
1:26 of the LORD your G;
1:30 The LORD your G who goes before you will
1:31 how the LORD your G bore you, as a
1:32 believe the LORD your G,
1:41 as the LORD our G commanded us.' And every
2:7 For the LORD your G has blessed you in
2:7 years the LORD your G has been with you;
2:29 which the LORD our G gives to us.'
2:30 for the LORD your G hardened his spirit and
2:33 And the LORD our G gave him over to
2:36 us; the LORD our G gave all into our
2:37 wherever the LORD our G forbade us.
3:3 So the LORD our G gave into our hand
3:18 saying, 'The LORD your G has given you this
3:20 which the LORD your G gives them beyond the
3:21 that the LORD your G has done to these
3:22 is the LORD your G who fights for you.'
3:24 time, saying, 'O Lord G, thou hast only begun
3:24 mighty hand; for what G is there in heaven
4:1 which the LORD, the G of your fathers, gives
4:2 of the LORD your G which I command you.
4:3 for the LORD your G destroyed from among you
4:4 to the LORD your G are all alive this
4:5 as the LORD my G commanded me, that you
4:7 there that has a G so near to it
4:7 as the LORD our G is to us, whenever
4:10 before the LORD your G at Horeb, the LORD
4:19 which the LORD your G has allotted to all
4:21 which the LORD your G gives you for an
4:23 of the LORD your G, which he made with
4:23 which the LORD your G has forbidden you.
4:24 For the LORD your G is a devouring fire,
4:24 your God is a devouring fire, a jealous G
4:25 of the LORD your G, so as to provoke
4:29 seek the LORD your G, and you will find
4:30 to the LORD your G and obey his voice,
4:31 for the LORD your G is a merciful God;
4:31 God is a merciful G; he will not fail
4:32 since the day that G created man upon the
4:33 the voice of a G speaking out of the
4:34 Or has any G ever attempted to go and
4:34 that the LORD your G did for you in
4:35 that the LORD is G; there is no other
4:39 that the LORD is G in heaven above and
4:40 which the LORD your G gives you for ever."
5:2 The LORD our G made a covenant with us
5:6 am the LORD your G, who brought you out
5:9 I the LORD your G am a jealous God,
5:9 God am a jealous G, visiting the iniquity of
5:11 of the LORD your G in vain: for the
5:12 as the LORD your G commanded you.
5:14 to the LORD your G; in it you shall
5:15 and the LORD your G brought you out thence
5:15 therefore the LORD your G commanded you to keep
5:16 as the LORD your G commanded you; that your
5:16 which the LORD your G gives you.
5:24 'Behold, the LORD our G has shown us his
5:24 have this day seen G speak with man and
5:25 of the LORD our G any more, we shall
5:26 voice of the living G speaking out of the
5:27 that the LORD our G will say; and speak
5:27 that the LORD our G will speak to you;
5:32 as the LORD your G has commanded you; you
5:33 which the LORD your G has commanded you, that
6:1 which the LORD your G commanded me to teach
6:2 fear the LORD your G, you and your son
6:3 as the LORD, the G of your fathers, has
6:4 Israel: The LORD our G is one LORD;
6:5 love the LORD your G with all your heart,
6:10 when the LORD your G brings you into the
6:13 fear the LORD your G; you shall serve him,
6:15 for the LORD your G in the midst of
6:15 you is a jealous G; lest the anger of
6:15 of the LORD your G be kindled against you,
6:16 put the LORD your G to the test, as
6:17 of the LORD your G, and his testimonies, and
6:20 which the LORD our G has commanded you?'
6:24 fear the LORD our G, for our good always,
6:25 before the LORD our G, as he has commanded
7:1 "When the LORD your G brings you into the
7:2 when the LORD your G gives them over to
7:6 to the LORD your G; the LORD your God
7:6 God; the LORD your G has chosen you to

7:9 that the LORD your G is God, the faithful
7:9 LORD your God is G, the faithful God who
7:9 is God, the faithful G who keeps covenant and
7:12 them, the LORD your G will keep with you
7:16 that the LORD your G will give over to
7:18 what the LORD your G did to Pharaoh and
7:19 which the LORD your G brought you out; so
7:19 will the LORD your G do to all the
7:20 Moreover the LORD your G will send hornets among
7:21 for the LORD your G is in the midst
7:21 the midst of you, a great and terrible G
7:22 The LORD your G will clear away these nations
7:23 But the LORD your G will give them over
7:25 it is an abomination to the LORD your G
8:2 which the LORD your G has led you these
8:5 son, the LORD your G disciplines you.
8:6 of the LORD your G, by walking in his
8:7 For the LORD your G is bringing you into
8:10 bless the LORD your G for the good land
8:11 forget the LORD your G, by not keeping his
8:14 forget the LORD your G, who brought you out
8:18 remember the LORD your G, for it is he
8:19 forget the LORD your G and go after other
8:20 not obey the voice of the LORD your G
9:3 is the LORD your G; he will destroy them
9:4 after the LORD your G has thrust them out
9:5 nations the LORD your G is driving them out
9:6 that the LORD your G is not giving you
9:7 provoked the LORD your G to wrath in the
9:10 with the finger of G; and on them were
9:16 against the LORD your G; you had made yourselves
9:23 of the LORD your G, and did not believe
9:26 the LORD, 'O Lord G, destroy not thy people
10:9 as the LORD your G said to him.)
10:12 does the LORD your G require of you, but
10:12 fear the LORD your G, to walk in all
10:12 serve the LORD your G with all your heart
10:14 to the LORD your G belong heaven and the
10:17 For the LORD your G is God of gods
10:17 LORD your God is G of gods and Lord
10:17 mighty, and the terrible G, who is not partial
10:20 fear the LORD your G; you shall serve him
10:21 praise; he is your G, who has done for
10:22 now the LORD your G has made you as
11:1 love the LORD your G, and keep his charge,
11:2 of the LORD your G, his greatness, his mighty
11:12 which the LORD your G cares for; the eyes
11:12 of the LORD your G are always upon it,
11:13 love the LORD your G, and to serve him
11:22 loving the LORD your G, walking in all his
11:25 you; the LORD your G will lay the fear
11:27 of the LORD your G, which I command you
11:28 of the LORD your G, but turn aside from
11:29 when the LORD your G brings you into the
11:31 which the LORD your G gives you; and when
12:1 which the LORD, the G of your fathers, has
12:4 shall not do so to the LORD your G
12:5 which the LORD your G will choose out of
12:7 before the LORD your G, and you shall rejoice,
12:7 which the LORD your G has blessed you.
12:9 which the LORD your G gives you.
12:10 which the LORD your G gives you to inherit,
12:11 which the LORD your G will choose, to make
12:12 before the LORD your G, you and your sons
12:15 of the LORD your G which he has given
12:18 before the LORD your G in the place which
12:18 which the LORD your G will choose, you and
12:18 before the LORD your G in all that you
12:20 "When the LORD your G enlarges your territory, as
12:21 which the LORD your G will choose to put
12:27 of the LORD your G; the blood of your
12:27 of the LORD your G, but the flesh you
12:28 right in the sight of the LORD your G
12:29 "When the LORD your G cuts off before you
12:31 to the LORD your G; for every abominable thing
13:3 for the LORD your G is testing you, to
13:3 love the LORD your G with all your heart
13:4 after the LORD your G and fear him, and
13:5 against the LORD your G, who brought you out
13:5 which the LORD your G commanded you to walk.
13:10 from the LORD your G, who brought you out
13:12 which the LORD your G gives you to dwell
13:16 to the LORD your G; it shall be a
13:18 of the LORD your G, keeping all his commandments
13:18 right in the sight of the LORD your G
14:1 of the LORD your G; you shall not cut
14:2 to the LORD your G, and the LORD has
14:21 are a people holy to the LORD your G
14:23 before the LORD your G, in the place which
14:23 fear the LORD your G always.
14:24 when the LORD your G blesses you, because the
14:24 which the LORD your G chooses, to set his
14:25 which the LORD your G chooses,
14:26 before the LORD your G and rejoice, you and
14:29 that the LORD your G may bless you in
15:4 which the LORD your G gives you for an
15:5 of the LORD your G, being careful to do
15:6 For the LORD your G will bless you, as
15:7 which the LORD your G gives you, you shall
15:10 this the LORD your G will bless you in
15:14 as the LORD your G has blessed you, you
15:15 and the LORD your G redeemed you; therefore I
15:18 So the LORD your G will bless you in
15:19 to the LORD your G; you shall do no
15:20 before the LORD your G year by year at
15:21 shall not sacrifice it to the LORD your G
16:1 to the LORD your G; for in the month
16:1 Abib the LORD your G brought you out of
16:2 to the LORD your G, from the flock or
16:5 which the LORD your G gives you;
16:6 which the LORD your G will choose, to make
16:7 which the LORD your G will choose; and in
16:8 to the LORD your G; you shall do no
16:10 to the LORD your G with the tribute of
16:10 as the LORD your G blesses you;
16:11 before the LORD your G, you and your son
16:11 which the LORD your G will choose, to make
16:15 to the LORD your G at the place which
16:15 because the LORD your G will bless you in
16:16 before the LORD your G at the place which
16:17 of the LORD your G which he has given
16:18 which the LORD your G gives you, according to
16:20 which the LORD your G gives you.
16:21 of the LORD your G which you shall make.
16:22 which the LORD your G hates.
17:1 to the LORD your G an ox or a
17:1 that is an abomination to the LORD your G
17:2 which the LORD your G gives you, a man
17:2 of the LORD your G, in transgressing his covenant,
17:8 which the LORD your G will choose,
17:12 before the LORD your G, or the judge, that
17:14 which the LORD your G gives you, and you
17:15 whom the LORD your G will choose.
17:19 fear the LORD his G, by keeping all the
18:5 For the LORD your G has chosen him out
18:7 of the LORD his G, like all his fellow-Levites
18:9 which the LORD your G gives you, you shall
18:12 practices the LORD your G is driving them out
18:13 You shall be blameless before the LORD your G
18:14 you, the LORD your G has not allowed you
18:15 "The LORD your G will raise up for you
18:16 of the LORD your G at Horeb on the
18:16 of the LORD my G, or see this great
19:1 "When the LORD your G cuts off the nations
19:1 land the LORD your G gives you, and you
19:2 which the LORD your G gives you to possess.
19:3 which the LORD your G gives you as a
19:8 if the LORD your G enlarges your border, as
19:9 loving the LORD your G and by walking ever
19:10 which the LORD your G gives you for an
19:14 that the LORD your G gives you to possess,
20:1 for the LORD your G is with you, who
20:4 for the LORD your G is he that goes
20:13 when the LORD your G gives it into your
20:14 which the LORD your G has given you.
20:16 that the LORD your G gives you for an
20:17 as the LORD your G has commanded;
20:18 and so to sin against the LORD your G
21:1 which the LORD your G gives you to possess,
21:5 for the LORD your G has chosen them to
21:10 and the LORD your G gives them into your
21:23 man is accursed by G; you shall not defile
21:23 which the LORD your G gives you for an
22:5 things is an abomination to the LORD your G
23:5 Nevertheless the LORD your G would not hearken to
23:5 but the LORD your G turned the curse into
23:5 because the LORD your G loved you.
23:14 Because the LORD your G walks in the midst
23:18 of the LORD your G in payment for any
23:18 these are an abomination to the LORD your G
23:20 that the LORD your G may bless you in
23:21 to the LORD your G, you shall not be

G

23:21 for the LORD your G will surely require it
23:23 to the LORD your G what you have promised
24:4 which the LORD your G gives you for an
24:9 what the LORD your G did to Miriam on
24:13 be righteousness to you before the LORD your G
24:18 and the LORD your G redeemed you from there;
24:19 that the LORD your G may bless you in
25:15 which the LORD your G gives you.
25:16 dishonestly, are an abomination to the LORD your G
25:18 lagged behind you; and he did not fear G
25:19 when the LORD your G has given you rest
25:19 which the LORD your G gives you for an
26:1 which the LORD your G gives you for an
26:2 that the LORD your G gives you, and you
26:2 which the LORD your G will choose, to make
26:3 to the LORD your G that I have come
26:4 down before the altar of the LORD your G
26:5 before the LORD your G, 'A wandering Aramean was
26:7 to the LORD the G of our fathers, and
26:10 before the LORD your G, and worship before the
26:10 before the LORD your G;
26:11 which the LORD your G has given to you
26:13 before the LORD your G, 'I have removed the
26:14 of the LORD my G, I have done according
26:16 day the LORD your G commands you to do
26:17 that he is your G, and that you will
26:19 to the LORD your G, as he has spoken."
27:2 which the LORD your G gives you, you shall
27:3 which the LORD your G gives you, a land
27:3 as the LORD, the G of your fathers, has
27:5 to the LORD your G, an altar of stones;
27:6 to the LORD your G of unhewn stones; and
27:6 to the LORD your G;
27:7 and you shall rejoice before the LORD your G
27:9 have become the people of the LORD your G
27:10 of the LORD your G, keeping his commandments and
28:1 of the LORD your G, being careful to do
28:1 day, the LORD your G will set you high
28:2 you obey the voice of the LORD your G
28:8 which the LORD your G gives you.
28:9 of the LORD your G, and walk in his
28:13 of the LORD your G, which I command you
28:15 of the LORD your G or be careful to
28:45 of the LORD your G, to keep his commandments
28:47 serve the LORD your G with joyfulness and gladness
28:52 which the LORD your G has given you.
28:53 whom the LORD your G has given you, in
28:58 name, the LORD your G,
28:62 not obey the voice of the LORD your G
29:6 may know that I am the LORD your G
29:10 before the LORD your G; the heads of your
29:12 of the LORD your G, which the LORD your
29:12 which the LORD your G makes with you this
29:13 he may be your G, as he promised you,
29:15 with us this day before the LORD our G
29:18 from the LORD our G to go and serve
29:25 of the LORD, the G of their fathers, which
29:29 to the LORD our G; but the things that
30:1 where the LORD your G has driven you,
30:2 to the LORD your G, you and your children,
30:3 then the LORD your G will restore your fortunes,
30:3 where the LORD your G has scattered you.
30:4 there the LORD your G will gather you, and
30:5 and the LORD your G will bring you into
30:6 And the LORD your G will circumcise your heart
30:6 love the LORD your G with all your heart
30:7 And the LORD your G will put all these
30:9 The LORD your G will make you abundantly
30:10 of the LORD your G, to keep his commandments
30:10 to the LORD your G with all your heart
30:16 of the LORD your G which I command you
30:16 loving the LORD your G, by walking in his
30:16 and the LORD your G will bless you in
30:20 loving the LORD your G, obeying his voice, and
31:3 Jordan.' The LORD your G himself will go over
31:6 is the LORD your G who goes with you;
31:11 before the LORD your G at the place which
31:12 fear the LORD your G, and be careful to
31:13 fear the LORD your G, as long as you
31:17 upon us because our G is not among us?'
31:26 of the LORD your G, that it may be
32:3 Ascribe greatness to our G
32:4 A G of faithfulness and without iniquity, just and
32:8 according to the number of the sons of G
32:12 there was no foreign G with him.
32:15 sleek; then he forsook G who made him, and
32:18 and you forgot the G who gave you birth.
32:21 with what is no G; they have provoked me
32:39 and there is no G beside me; I kill
33:1 Moses the man of G blessed the children of
33:26 "There is none like G, O Jeshurun, who rides
33:27 The eternal G is your dwelling place, and underneath

Josh 1:9 for the LORD your G is with you wherever
1:11 which the LORD your G gives you to possess.'"
1:13 saying, 'The LORD your G is providing you a
1:15 which the LORD your G is giving them; then
1:17 may the LORD your G be with you, as
2:11 for the LORD your G is he who is
2:11 is he who is G in heaven above and
3:3 of the LORD your G being carried by the
3:9 and hear the words of the LORD your G
3:10 know that the living G is among you, and
4:5 of the LORD your G into the midst of
4:23 For the LORD your G dried up the waters
4:23 as the LORD your G did to the Red
4:24 fear the LORD your G for ever."
7:7 said, "Alas, O Lord G, why hast thou brought
7:13 thus says the LORD, G of Israel, "There are
7:19 glory to the LORD G of Israel, and render
7:20 sinned against the LORD G of Israel, and this
8:7 for the LORD your G will give it into
8:30 to the LORD, the G of Israel,
9:9 of the LORD your G; for we have heard
9:18 by the LORD, the G of Israel.
9:19 by the LORD, the G of Israel, and now
9:23 drawers of water for the house of my G
9:24 that the LORD your G had commanded his servant
10:19 for the LORD your G has given them into
10:40 breathed, as the LORD G of Israel commanded.
10:42 time, because the LORD G of Israel fought for
13:14 fire to the LORD G of Israel are their
13:33 no inheritance; the LORD G of Israel is their
14:6 Moses the man of G in Kadesh-barnea concerning
14:8 melt; yet I wholly followed the LORD my G
14:9 followed the LORD my G
14:14 followed the LORD, the G of Israel.
18:3 which the LORD, the G of your fathers, has
18:6 lots for you here before the LORD our G
22:3 to keep the charge of the LORD your G
22:4 now the LORD your G has given rest to
22:5 love the LORD your G, and to walk in
22:16 have committed against the G of Israel in turning
22:19 other than the altar of the LORD our G
22:22 Israel, "The Mighty One, G, the LORD!
22:22 The Mighty One, G, the LORD!
22:24 with the LORD, the G of Israel?
22:29 of the LORD our G that stands before his
22:33 people of Israel blessed G and spoke no more
22:34 a witness between us that the LORD is G
23:3 that the LORD your G has done to all
23:3 is the LORD your G who has fought for
23:5 The LORD your G will push them back before
23:5 as the LORD your G promised you.
23:8 to the LORD your G as you have done
23:10 is the LORD your G who fights for you,
23:11 to yourselves, therefore, to love the LORD your G
23:13 that the LORD your G will not continue to
23:13 which the LORD your G has given you.
23:14 which the LORD your G promised concerning you;
23:15 which the LORD your G promised concerning you
23:15 which the LORD your G has given you,
23:16 of the LORD your G, which he commanded you,
24:1 of Israel; and they presented themselves before G
24:2 says the LORD, the G of Israel, 'Your fathers
24:17 is the LORD our G who brought us and
24:18 will serve the LORD, for he is our G
24:19 he is a holy G; he is a jealous
24:19 he is a jealous G; he will not forgive
24:23 to the LORD, the G of Israel."
24:24 Joshua, "The LORD our G we will serve, and
24:26 of the law of G; and he took a
24:27 against you, lest you deal falsely with your G

Judg 1:7 I have done, so G has requited me." And
2:12 forsook the LORD, the G of their fathers, who
3:7 forgetting the LORD their G, and serving the Baals
3:20 have a message from G for you." And he
4:6 him, "The LORD, the G of Israel, commands you,
4:23 So on that day G subdued Jabin the king
5:3 to the LORD, the G of Israel.
5:5 before the LORD, the G of Israel.
6:8 says the LORD, the G of Israel: I led
6:10 am the LORD your G; you shall not pay

6:20 And the angel of G said to him, "Take
6:22 the LORD; and Gideon said, "Alas, O Lord G
6:26 to the LORD your G on the top of
6:31 If he is a G, let him contend for
6:36 Then Gideon said to G, "If thou wilt deliver
6:39 Then Gideon said to G, "Let not thy anger
6:40 And G did so that night; for it was
7:14 Israel; into his hand G has given Midian and
8:3 G has given into your hands the princes of
8:33 harlot after the Baals, and made Baal-berith their G
8:34 remember the LORD their G, who had rescued them
9:7 men of Shechem, that G may listen to you.
9:23 And G sent an evil spirit between Abimelech and
9:27 the house of their G, and ate and drank
9:56 Thus G requited the crime of Abimelech, which he
9:57 his seventy brothers; and G also made all the
10:10 we have forsaken our G and have served the
11:21 And the LORD, the G of Israel, gave Sihon
11:23 then the LORD, the G of Israel, dispossessed the
11:24 possess what Chemosh your G gives you to possess?
11:24 that the LORD our G has dispossessed before us,
13:5 be a Nazirite to G from birth; and he
13:6 husband, "A man of G came to me, and
13:6 of the angel of G, very terrible; I did
13:7 be a Nazirite to G from birth to the
13:8 let the man of G whom thou didst send
13:9 And G listened to the voice of Manoah, and
13:9 and the angel of G came again to the
13:22 "We shall surely die, for we have seen G
15:19 And G split open the hollow place that is
16:17 been a Nazirite to G from my mother's womb.
16:23 sacrifice to Dagon their G, and to rejoice; for
16:23 for they said, "Our G has given Samson our
16:24 him, they praised their G; for they said, "Our
16:24 for they said, "Our G has given our enemy
16:28 and said, "O Lord G, remember me, I pray
16:28 only this once, O G, that I may be
18:5 to him, "Inquire of G, we pray thee, that
18:10 land is broad; yea, G has given it into
18:31 as the house of G was at Shiloh.
20:2 of the people of G, four hundred thousand men
20:18 Bethel, and inquired of G, "Which of us shall
20:27 of the covenant of G was there in those
21:2 there till evening before G, and they lifted up
21:3 said, "O LORD, the G of Israel, why has
Ruth 1:16 my people, and your G my God;
1:16 and your God my G;
2:12 by the LORD, the G of Israel, under whose
1Sam 1:17 in peace, and the G of Israel grant your
2:2 besides thee; there is no rock like our G
2:3 the LORD is a G of knowledge, and by
2:25 sins against a man, G will mediate for him;
2:27 came a man of G to Eli, and said
2:30 Therefore the LORD the G of Israel declares: 'I
3:3 place; the lamp of G had not yet gone
3:3 where the ark of G was.
3:13 his sons were blaspheming G, and he did not
3:17 May G do so to you and more also,
4:4 there with the ark of the covenant of G
4:7 for they said, "A G has come into the
4:11 And the ark of G was captured; and the
4:13 for his heart trembled for the ark of G
4:17 and the ark of G has been captured."
4:18 mentioned the ark of G, Eli fell over backward
4:19 that the ark of G was captured, and that
4:21 because the ark of G had been captured and
4:22 for the ark of G has been captured."
5:1 captured the ark of G, they carried it from
5:2 took the ark of G and brought it into
5:7 "The ark of the G of Israel must not
5:7 is heavy upon us and upon Dagon our G
5:8 the ark of the G of Israel?" They answered,
5:8 the ark of the G of Israel be brought
5:8 the ark of the G of Israel there.
5:10 sent the ark of G to Ekron.
5:10 when the ark of G came to Ekron, the
5:10 the ark of the G of Israel to slay
5:11 the ark of the G of Israel, and let
5:11 The hand of G was very heavy there;
6:3 the ark of the G of Israel, do not
6:5 give glory to the G of Israel; perhaps he
6:20 able to stand before the LORD, this holy G
7:8 to the LORD our G for us, that he
9:6 is a man of G in this city, and
9:7 no present to bring to the man of G
9:8 to the man of G, to tell us our
9:9 went to inquire of G, he said, "Come, let
9:10 where the man of G was.
9:27 may make known to you the word of G
10:3 men going up to G at Bethel will meet
10:7 finds to do, for G is with you.
10:9 back to leave Samuel, G gave him another heart;
10:10 and the spirit of G came mightily upon him,
10:18 says the LORD, the G of Israel, 'I brought
10:19 this day rejected your G, who saves you from
10:26 of valor whose hearts G had touched.
11:6 And the spirit of G came mightily upon Saul
12:9 forgot the LORD their G; and he sold them
12:12 when the LORD your G was your king.
12:14 follow the LORD your G, it will be well;
12:19 to the LORD your G, that we may not
13:13 of the LORD your G, which he commanded you;
14:18 said to Ahijah, "Bring hither the ark of G
14:18 For the ark of G went at that time
14:36 priest said, "Let us draw near hither to G
14:37 And Saul inquired of G, "Shall I go down
14:41 Saul said, "O LORD G of Israel, why hast
14:41 my son, O LORD, G of Israel, give Urim;
14:44 And Saul said, G do so to me and
14:45 he has wrought with G this day." So the
15:15 to the LORD your G; and the rest we
15:21 to the LORD your G in Gilgal."
15:30 me, that I may worship the LORD your G
16:15 an evil spirit from G is tormenting you.
16:16 the evil spirit from G is upon you, he
16:23 the evil spirit from G was upon Saul, David
17:26 he should defy the armies of the living G
17:36 he has defied the armies of the living G
17:45 LORD of hosts, the G of the armies of
17:46 that there is a G in Israel,
18:10 an evil spirit from G rushed upon Saul, and
19:20 them, the Spirit of G came upon the messengers
19:23 and the Spirit of G came upon him also,
20:12 David, "The LORD, the G of Israel, be witness!
22:3 till I know what G will do for me."
22:13 and have inquired of G for him, so that
22:15 I have inquired of G for him?
23:7 And Saul said, G has given him into my
23:10 David, "O LORD, the G of Israel, thy servant
23:11 O LORD, the G of Israel, I beseech thee,
23:14 him every day, but G did not give him
23:16 David at Horesh, and strengthened his hand in G
25:22 G do so to David and more also, if
25:29 of the LORD your G; and the lives of
25:32 be the LORD, the G of Israel, who sent
25:34 as the LORD the G of Israel lives, who
26:8 said Abishai to David, G has given your enemy
28:13 Saul, "I see a G coming up out of
28:15 warring against me, and G has turned away from
29:9 as an angel of G; nevertheless the commanders of
30:6 But David strengthened himself in the LORD his G
30:15 "Swear to me by G, that you will not
2Sam 2:27 And Joab said, "As G lives, if you had
3:9 G do so to Abner, and more also, if
3:35 but David swore, saying, G do so to me
5:10 for the LORD, the G of hosts, was with
6:2 there the ark of G, which is called by
6:3 carried the ark of G upon a new cart,
6:4 with the ark of G; and Ahio went before
6:6 to the ark of G and took hold of
6:7 kindled against Uzzah; and G smote him there
6:7 and he died there beside the ark of G
6:12 belongs to him, because of the ark of G
6:12 up the ark of G from the house of
7:2 but the ark of G dwells in a tent."
7:18 am I, O Lord G, and what is my
7:19 thy eyes, O Lord G; thou hast spoken also
7:19 and hast shown me future generations, O Lord G
7:20 For thou knowest thy servant, O Lord G
7:22 art great, O LORD G; for there is none
7:22 and there is no G besides thee, according to
7:23 thy people Israel, whom G went to redeem to
7:24 ever; and thou, O LORD, didst become their G
7:25 And now, O LORD G, confirm for ever the
7:26 LORD of hosts is G over Israel,' and the
7:27 LORD of hosts, the G of Israel, hast made
7:28 And now, O Lord G, thou art God, and
7:28 Lord GOD, thou art G, and thy words are
7:29 for thou, O Lord G, hast spoken, and with
9:3 show the kindness of G to him?" Ziba said
10:12 the cities of our G; and may the LORD
12:7 says the LORD, the G of Israel, 'I anointed

G

12:16 David therefore besought G for the child; and David
14:11 invoke the LORD your G, that the avenger of
14:13 planned such a thing against the people of G
14:14 gathered up again; but G will not take away
14:16 from the heritage of G
14:17 like the angel of G to discern good and
14:17 The LORD your G be with you!"
14:20 of the angel of G to know all things
15:24 of the covenant of G; and they set down
15:24 down the ark of G, until the people had
15:25 "Carry the ark of G back into the city.
15:29 carried the ark of G back to Jerusalem; and
15:32 the summit, where G was worshiped, behold, Hushai
16:23 consulted the oracle of G; so was all the
18:28 be the LORD your G, who has delivered up
19:13 G do so to me, and more also, if
19:27 like the angel of G; do therefore what seems
21:14 And after that G heeded supplications for the land.
22:3 and my deliverer, my G, my rock, in whom
22:7 the LORD; to my G I called.
22:22 LORD, and have not wickedly departed from my G
22:29 O LORD, and my G lightens my darkness.
22:30 troop, and by my G I can leap over
22:31 This G –his way is perfect; the promise of
22:32 "For who is G, but the LORD?
22:32 And who is a rock, except our G
22:33 This G is my strong refuge, and has made
22:47 and exalted be my G, the rock of my
22:48 of my salvation, the G who gave me vengeance
23:1 the anointed of the G of Jacob, the sweet
23:3 The G of Israel has spoken, the Rock of
23:3 in the fear of G,
23:5 Yea, does not my house stand so with G
24:3 "May the LORD your G add to the people
24:23 king, "The LORD your G accept you."
24:24 to the LORD my G which cost me nothing."

1Kgs 1:17 by the LORD your G, saying, 'Solomon your son
1:30 by the LORD, the G of Israel, saying, 'Solomon
1:36 May the LORD, the G of my lord the
1:47 King David, saying, 'Your G make the name of
1:48 be the LORD, the G of Israel, who has
2:3 of the LORD your G, walking in his ways
2:23 by the LORD, saying, G do so to me
2:26 ark of the Lord G before David my father,
3:5 dream by night; and G said, "Ask what I
3:7 now, O LORD my G, thou hast made thy
3:11 And G said to him, "Because you have asked
3:28 that the wisdom of G was in him, to
4:29 And G gave Solomon wisdom and understanding
5:3 of the LORD his G because of the warfare
5:4 now the LORD my G has given me rest
5:5 of the LORD my G, as the LORD said
8:15 be the LORD, the G of Israel, who with
8:17 of the LORD, the G of Israel.
8:20 of the LORD, the G of Israel.
8:23 and said, "O LORD, G of Israel, there is
8:23 Israel, there is no G like thee, in heaven
8:25 Now therefore, O LORD, G of Israel, keep with
8:26 me.' Now therefore, O G of Israel, let thy
8:27 "But will G indeed dwell on the earth?
8:28 supplication, O LORD my G, hearkening to the cry
8:53 bring our fathers out of Egypt, O Lord G
8:57 The LORD our G be with us, as he
8:59 to the LORD our G day and night, and
8:60 that the LORD is G; there is no other.
8:61 to the LORD our G, walking in his statutes
8:65 before the LORD our G, seven days.
9:9 forsook the LORD their G who brought their fathers
10:9 be the LORD your G, who has delighted in
10:24 hear his wisdom, which G had put into his
11:4 to the LORD his G, as was the heart
11:9 from the LORD, the G of Israel, who had
11:23 G also raised up as an adversary to him,
11:31 says the LORD, the G of Israel, 'Behold, I
11:33 the Sidonians, Chemosh the G of Moab, and Milcom
11:33 Moab, and Milcom the G of the Ammonites, and
12:22 But the word of G came to Shemaiah the
12:22 Shemaiah the man of G:
13:1 behold, a man of G came out of Judah
13:4 of the man of G, which he cried against
13:5 which the man of G had given by the
13:6 to the man of G, "Entreat now the favor
13:6 of the LORD your G, and pray for me,
13:6 And the man of G entreated the LORD; and
13:7 to the man of G, "Come home with me,
13:8 And the man of G said to the king,
13:11 that the man of G had done that day
13:12 which the man of G who came from Judah
13:14 after the man of G, and found him sitting
13:14 you the man of G who came from Judah?"
13:21 to the man of G who came from Judah,
13:21 which the LORD your G commanded you,
13:26 is the man of G, who disobeyed the word
13:29 of the man of G and laid it upon
13:31 which the man of G is buried; lay my
14:7 says the LORD, the G of Israel: "Because I
14:13 to the LORD, the G of Israel, in the
15:3 to the LORD his G, as the heart of
15:4 sake the LORD his G gave him a lamp
15:30 provoked the LORD, the G of Israel.
16:13 sin, provoking the LORD G of Israel to anger
16:26 provoking the LORD, the G of Israel, to anger
16:33 provoke the LORD, the G of Israel, to anger
17:1 "As the LORD the G of Israel lives, before
17:12 "As the LORD your G lives, I have nothing
17:14 says the LORD the G of Israel, 'The jar
17:18 "What have you against me, O man of G
17:20 LORD, "O LORD my G, hast thou brought calamity
17:21 LORD, "O LORD my G, let this child's soul
17:24 are a man of G, and that the word
18:10 As the LORD your G lives, there is no
18:21 If the LORD is G, follow him; but if
18:24 the name of your G and I will call
18:24 the LORD; and the G who answers by fire,
18:24 the God who answers by fire, he is G
18:25 the name of your G, but put no fire
18:27 for he is a G; either he is musing,
18:36 and said, "O LORD, G of Abraham, Isaac, and
18:36 day that thou art G in Israel, and that
18:37 thou, O LORD, art G, and that thou hast
18:39 "The LORD, he is G; the LORD, he is
18:39 LORD, he is God; the LORD, he is G
19:8 and forty nights to Horeb the mount of G
19:10 for the LORD, the G of hosts; for the
19:14 for the LORD, the G of hosts; for the
20:28 And a man of G came near and said
20:28 "The LORD is a G of the hills but
20:28 he is not a G of the valleys," therefore
21:10 saying, 'You have cursed G and the king.' Then
21:13 people, saying, "Naboth cursed G and the king." So
22:53 provoked the LORD, the G of Israel, to anger

2Kgs 1:2 inquire of Baal-zebub, the G of Ekron, whether I
1:3 because there is no G in Israel that you
1:3 inquire of Baal-zebub, the G of Ekron?'
1:6 because there is no G in Israel that you
1:6 inquire of Baal-zebub, the G of Ekron?
1:9 him, "O man of G, the king says, 'Come
1:10 am a man of G, let fire come down
1:11 him, "O man of G, this is the king's
1:12 am a man of G, let fire come down
1:12 Then the fire of G came down from heaven
1:13 him, "O man of G, I pray you, let
1:16 inquire of Baal-zebub, the G of Ekron,–is it
1:16 because there is no G in Israel to inquire
2:14 is the LORD, the G of Elijah?" And when
4:7 told the man of G, and he said, "Go,
4:9 a holy man of G, who is continually passing
4:16 lord, O man of G; do not lie to
4:21 of the man of G, and shut the door
4:22 to the man of G, and come back again."
4:25 to the man of G at Mount Carmel.
4:25 When the man of G saw her coming, he
4:27 to the man of G, she caught hold of
4:27 But the man of G said, "Let her alone,
4:40 out, "O man of G, there is death in
4:42 bringing the man of G bread of the first
5:7 and said, "Am I G, to kill and to
5:8 Elisha the man of G heard that the king
5:11 of the LORD his G, and wave his hand
5:14 of the man of G; and his flesh was
5:15 to the man of G, he and all his
5:15 that there is no G in all the earth
5:17 or sacrifice to any G but the LORD.
5:20 Elisha the man of G, said, "See, my master
6:6 Then the man of G said, "Where did it
6:9 But the man of G sent word to the
6:10 which the man of G told him.
6:15 of the man of G rose early in the
6:31 and he said, "May G do so to me,
7:2 to the man of G, "If the LORD himself
7:17 as the man of G had said when the
7:18 when the man of G had said to the

	7:19	answered the man of G, "If the LORD himself
	8:2	of the man of G; she went with her
	8:4	of the man of G, saying, "Tell me all
	8:7	him, "The man of G has come here,"
	8:8	meet the man of G, and inquire of the
	8:11	And the man of G wept.
	9:6	says the LORD the G of Israel, I anoint
	10:31	of the LORD the G of Israel with all
	13:19	Then the man of G was angry with him,
	14:25	of the LORD, the G of Israel, which he
	16:2	of the LORD his G, as his father David
	17:7	against the LORD their G, who had brought them
	17:9	against the LORD their G things that were not
	17:14	who did not believe in the LORD their G
	17:16	of the LORD their G, and made for themselves
	17:19	of the LORD their G, but walked in the
	17:26	the law of the G of the land; therefore
	17:26	the law of the G of the land."
	17:27	the law of the G of the land."
	17:39	fear the LORD your G, and he will deliver
	18:5	in the LORD the G of Israel; so that
	18:12	of the LORD their G but transgressed his covenant,
	18:22	to me, "We rely on the LORD our G
	19:4	that the LORD your G heard all the words
	19:4	to mock the living G, and will rebuke the
	19:4	which the LORD your G has heard; therefore lift
	19:10	'Do not let your G on whom you rely
	19:15	said: "O LORD the G of Israel, who art
	19:15	cherubim, thou art the G, thou alone, of all
	19:16	which he has sent to mock the living G
	19:19	now, O LORD our G, save us, I beseech
	19:19	thou, O LORD, art G alone."
	19:20	says the LORD, the G of Israel: Your prayer
	19:37	house of Nisroch his G, Adrammelech and Sharezer,
	20:5	says the LORD, the G of David your father:
	21:12	says the LORD, the G of Israel, Behold, I
	21:22	forsook the LORD, the G of his fathers, and
	22:15	says the LORD, the G of Israel: 'Tell the
	22:18	says the LORD, the G of Israel: Regarding the
	23:16	which the man of G proclaimed, who had predicted
	23:17	of the man of G who came from Judah
	23:21	to the LORD your G, as it is written
1Chr	4:10	Jabez called on the G of Israel, saying, "Oh
	4:10	And G granted what he asked.
	5:20	for they cried to G in the battle, and
	5:22	many fell slain, because the war was of G
	5:25	they transgressed against the G of their fathers, and
	5:25	of the land, whom G had destroyed before them.
	5:26	So the G of Israel stirred up the spirit
	6:48	service of the tabernacle of the house of G
	6:49	Moses the servant of G had commanded.
	9:11	of the house of G;
	9:13	work of the service of the house of G
	9:26	chambers and the treasures of the house of G
	9:27	about the house of G; for upon them lay
	11:2	and the LORD your G said to you, 'You
	11:19	from me before my G that I should do
	12:17	hands, then may the G of our fathers see
	12:18	For your G helps you." Then David received them,
	12:22	was a great army, like an army of G
	13:2	of the LORD our G, let us send abroad
	13:3	the ark of our G to us; for we
	13:5	bring the ark of G from Kiriath-jearim.
	13:6	there the ark of G, which is called by
	13:7	carried the ark of G upon a new cart,
	13:8	were making merry before G with all their might,
	13:10	to the ark; and he died there before G
	13:12	David was afraid of G that day; and he
	13:12	bring the ark of G home to me?"
	13:14	And the ark of G remained with the household
	14:10	And David inquired of G, "Shall I go up
	14:11	there; and David said, G has broken through my
	14:14	David again inquired of G, God said to him,
	14:14	again inquired of God, G said to him, "You
	14:15	out to battle; for G has gone out before
	14:16	And David did as G commanded him, and they
	15:1	for the ark of G, and pitched a tent
	15:2	carry the ark of G, for the LORD chose
	15:12	of the LORD, the G of Israel, to the
	15:13	time, the LORD our G broke forth upon us,
	15:14	of the LORD, the G of Israel.
	15:15	carried the ark of G upon their shoulders with
	15:24	should blow the trumpets before the ark of G
	15:26	because G helped the Levites who were carrying
	16:1	brought the ark of G, and set it inside
	16:1	offered burnt offerings and peace offerings before G
	16:4	praise the LORD, the G of Israel.
	16:6	continually, before the ark of the covenant of G
	16:14	is the LORD our G; his judgments are in
	16:35	also: "Deliver us, O G of our salvation, and
	16:36	be the LORD, the G of Israel, from everlasting
	17:2	in your heart, for G is with you."
	17:16	am I, O LORD G, and what is my
	17:17	in thy eyes, O G; thou hast also spoken
	17:17	and hast shown me future generations, O LORD G
	17:20	and there is no G besides thee, according to
	17:21	thy people Israel, whom G went to redeem to
	17:22	ever; and thou, O LORD, didst become their G
	17:24	LORD of hosts, the G of Israel, is Israel's
	17:24	of Israel, is Israel's G and the house of
	17:25	For thou, my G, hast revealed to thy servant
	17:26	O LORD, thou art G, and thou hast promised
	19:13	the cities of our G; and may the LORD
	21:7	But G was displeased with this thing, and he
	21:8	And David said to G, "I have sinned greatly
	21:15	And G sent the angel to Jerusalem to destroy
	21:17	And David said to G, "Was it not I
	21:17	thee, O LORD my G, be against me and
	21:30	it to inquire of G, for he was afraid
	22:1	house of the LORD G and here the altar
	22:2	prepare dressed stones for building the house of G
	22:6	for the LORD, the G of Israel.
	22:7	house to the name of the LORD my G
	22:11	of the LORD your G, as he has spoken
	22:12	may keep the law of the LORD your G
	22:18	not the LORD your G with you?
	22:19	mind and heart to seek the LORD your G
	22:19	sanctuary of the LORD G, so that the ark
	22:19	the holy vessels of G may be brought into
	23:14	Moses the man of G were named among the
	23:25	said, "The LORD, the G of Israel, has given
	23:28	of the house of G;
	24:5	sanctuary and officers of G among both the sons
	24:19	father, as the LORD G of Israel had commanded
	25:5	to the promise of G to exalt him; for
	25:5	to exalt him; for G had given Heman fourteen
	25:6	lyres for the service of the house of G
	26:5	Pe-ullethai the eighth; for G blessed him.
	26:20	of the house of G and the treasuries of
	26:32	for everything pertaining to G and for the affairs
	28:2	the footstool of our G; and I made preparations
	28:3	But G said to me, 'You may not build
	28:4	blood.' Yet the LORD G of Israel chose me
	28:8	the hearing of our G, observe and seek out
	28:8	of the LORD your G; that you may possess
	28:9	my son, know the G of your father, and
	28:12	of the house of G, and the treasuries for
	28:20	dismayed; for the LORD G, even my God, is
	28:20	LORD God, even my G, is with you.
	28:21	of the house of G; and with you in
	29:1	my son, whom alone G has chosen, is young
	29:1	not be for man but for the LORD G
	29:2	the house of my G, so far as I
	29:3	the house of my G I give it to
	29:3	the house of my G:
	29:7	of the house of G five thousand talents and
	29:10	thou, O LORD, the G of Israel our father,
	29:13	we thank thee, our G, and praise thy glorious
	29:16	O LORD our G, all this abundance that we
	29:17	I know, my G, that thou triest the heart,
	29:18	O LORD, the G of Abraham, Isaac, and Israel,
	29:20	to all the assembly, "Bless the LORD your G
	29:20	blessed the LORD, the G of their fathers, and
2Chr	1:1	and the LORD his G was with him and
	1:3	tent of meeting of G, which Moses the servant
	1:4	up the ark of G from Kiriath-jearim to the
	1:7	In that night G appeared to Solomon, and said
	1:8	And Solomon said to G, "Thou hast shown great
	1:9	O LORD G, let thy promise to David my
	1:11	G answered Solomon, "Because this was in your
	2:4	of the LORD my G and dedicate it to
	2:4	of the LORD our G, as ordained for ever
	2:5	be great, for our G is greater than all
	2:12	"Blessed be the LORD G of Israel, who made
	3:3	building the house of G: the length, in cubits
	4:11	on the house of G:
	4:19	in the house of G: the golden altar, the
	5:1	vessels in the treasuries of the house of G
	5:14	glory of the LORD filled the house of G
	6:4	be the LORD, the G of Israel, who with
	6:7	of the LORD, the G of Israel.
	6:10	of the LORD, the G of Israel.

6:14 and said, "O LORD, G of Israel, there is
6:14 Israel, there is no G like thee, in heaven
6:16 Now therefore, O LORD, G of Israel, keep with
6:17 Now therefore, O LORD, G of Israel, let thy
6:18 "But will G dwell indeed with man on the
6:19 supplication, O LORD my G, hearkening to the cry
6:40 Now, O my G, let thy eyes be open
6:41 now arise, O LORD G, and go to thy
6:41 thy priests, O LORD G, be clothed with salvation,
6:42 O LORD G, do not turn away the face
7:5 and all the people dedicated the house of G
7:22 forsook the LORD the G of their fathers who
8:14 David the man of G had commanded.
9:8 be the LORD your G, who has delighted in
9:8 his throne as king for the LORD your G
9:8 Because your G loved Israel and would establish
9:23 hear his wisdom, which G had put into his
10:15 affairs brought about by G that the LORD might
11:2 Shemaiah the man of G:
11:16 to seek the LORD G of Israel came after
11:16 to the LORD, the G of their fathers.
13:5 know that the LORD G of Israel gave the
13:10 the LORD is our G, and we have not
13:11 of the LORD our G, but you have forsaken
13:12 Behold, G is with us at our head, and
13:12 against the LORD, the G of your fathers; for
13:15 men of Judah shouted, G defeated Jeroboam and all
13:16 fled before Judah, and G gave them into their
13:18 upon the LORD, the G of their fathers.
14:2 right in the eyes of the LORD his G
14:4 seek the LORD, the G of their fathers, and
14:7 sought the LORD our G; we have sought him,
14:11 to the LORD his G, "O LORD, there is
14:11 us, O LORD our G, for we rely on
14:11 LORD, thou art our G; let not man prevail
15:1 The Spirit of G came upon Azariah the son
15:3 was without the true G, and without a teaching
15:4 to the LORD, the G of Israel, and sought
15:6 city against city, for G troubled them with every
15:9 that the LORD his G was with him.
15:12 seek the LORD, the G of their fathers, with
15:13 seek the LORD, the G of Israel, should be
15:18 into the house of G the votive gifts of
16:7 on the LORD your G, the army of the
17:4 Baals, but sought the G of his father and
18:5 said, "Go up; for G will give it into
18:13 LORD lives, what my G says, that I will
18:31 G drew them away from him,
19:3 land, and have set your heart to seek G
19:4 to the LORD, the G of their fathers.
19:7 with the LORD our G, or partiality, or taking
20:6 and said, "O LORD, G of our fathers, art
20:6 fathers, art thou not G in heaven?
20:7 thou not, O our G, drive out the inhabitants
20:12 O our G, wilt thou not execute judgment upon
20:19 praise the LORD, the G of Israel, with a
20:20 in the LORD your G, and you will be
20:29 And the fear of G came on all the
20:30 was quiet, for his G gave him rest round
20:33 their hearts upon the G of their fathers.
21:10 forsaken the LORD, the G of his fathers.
21:12 says the LORD, the G of David your father,
22:7 it was ordained by G that the downfall of
22:12 in the house of G, while Athaliah reigned over
23:3 covenant with the king in the house of G
23:9 in the house of G;
24:5 the house of your G from year to year;
24:7 into the house of G; and had also used
24:9 Moses the servant of G laid upon Israel in
24:13 restored the house of G to its proper condition
24:16 in Israel, and toward G and his house.
24:18 of the LORD, the G of their fathers, and
24:20 Then the Spirit of G took possession of Zechariah
24:20 to them, "Thus says G, 'Why do you transgress
24:24 forsaken the LORD, the G of their fathers.
24:27 of the house of G are written in the
25:7 But a man of G came to him and
25:8 be strong for war, G will cast you down
25:8 before the enemy; for G has power to help
25:9 to the man of G, "But what shall we
25:9 The man of G answered, "The LORD is able
25:16 said, "I know that G has determined to destroy
25:20 for it was of G, in order that he
25:24 in the house of G, and Obed-edom with them;
26:5 set himself to seek G in the days of
26:5 in the fear of G; and as long as
26:5 he sought the LORD, G made him prosper.
26:7 G helped him against the Philistines, and against the
26:16 to the LORD his G, and entered the temple
26:18 will bring you no honor from the LORD G
27:6 he ordered his ways before the LORD his G
28:5 Therefore the LORD his G gave him into the
28:6 forsaken the LORD, the G of their fathers.
28:9 because the LORD, the G of your fathers, was
28:10 sins of your own against the LORD your G
28:24 of the house of G and cut in pieces
28:24 of the house of G, and he shut up
28:25 anger the LORD, the G of his fathers.
29:5 of the LORD, the G of your fathers, and
29:6 of the LORD our G; they have forsaken him,
29:7 holy place to the G of Israel.
29:10 with the LORD, the G of Israel, that his
29:36 rejoiced because of what G had done for the
30:1 to the LORD the G of Israel.
30:5 to the LORD the G of Israel, at Jerusalem;
30:6 to the LORD, the G of Abraham, Isaac, and
30:7 faithless to the LORD G of their fathers, so
30:8 serve the LORD your G, that his fierce anger
30:9 For the LORD your G is gracious and merciful,
30:12 The hand of G was also upon Judah to
30:16 Moses the man of G; the priests sprinkled the
30:19 his heart to seek G, the LORD the God
30:19 God, the LORD the G of his fathers, even
30:22 to the LORD the G of their fathers.
31:6 to the LORD their G, and laid them in
31:13 Azariah the chief officer of the house of G
31:14 freewill offerings to G, to apportion the contribution
31:20 and right and faithful before the LORD his G
31:21 of the house of G and in accordance with
31:21 the commandments, seeking his G, he did with all
32:8 is the LORD our G, to help us and
32:11 you, "The LORD our G will deliver us from
32:14 my hand, that your G should be able to
32:15 believe him, for no G of any nation or
32:15 much less will your G deliver you out of
32:16 more against the Lord G and against his servant
32:17 on the LORD the G of Israel and to
32:17 my hands, so the G of Hezekiah will not
32:19 they spoke of the G of Jerusalem as they
32:21 the house of his G, some of his own
32:29 herds in abundance; for G had given him very
32:31 done in the land, G left him to himself,
33:7 in the house of G, of which God said
33:7 of God, of which G said to David and
33:12 of the LORD his G and humbled himself greatly
33:12 himself greatly before the G of his fathers.
33:13 prayed to him, and G received his entreaty and
33:13 Then Manasseh knew that the LORD was G
33:16 serve the LORD the G of Israel.
33:17 high places, but only to the LORD their G
33:18 his prayer to his G, and the words of
33:18 of the LORD the G of Israel, behold, they
33:19 his prayer, and how G received his entreaty, and
34:3 began to seek the G of David his father;
34:8 to repair the house of the LORD his G
34:9 into the house of G, which the Levites, the
34:23 says the LORD, the G of Israel: 'Tell the
34:26 says the LORD, the G of Israel: Regarding the
34:27 you humbled yourself before G when you heard his
34:32 to the covenant of G, the God of their
34:32 covenant of God, the G of their fathers.
34:33 who were in Israel serve the LORD their G
34:33 following the LORD the G of their fathers.
35:3 serve the LORD your G and his people Israel.
35:8 of the house of G, gave to the priests
35:21 am at war; and G has commanded me to
35:21 Cease opposing G, who is with me, lest he
35:22 from the mouth of G, but joined battle in
36:5 evil in the sight of the LORD his G
36:12 evil in the sight of the LORD his G
36:13 made him swear by G; he stiffened his neck
36:13 to the LORD, the G of Israel.
36:15 The LORD, the G of their fathers, sent persistently
36:16 mocking the messengers of G, despising his words,
36:18 of the house of G, great and small, and
36:19 burned the house of G, and broke down the
36:23 Persia, 'The LORD, the G of heaven, has given
36:23 may the LORD his G be with him.
Ezra 1:2 Persia: The LORD, the G of heaven, has given
1:3 his people, may his G be with him, and
1:3 of the LORD, the G of Israel– he
1:3 he is the G who is in Jerusalem;

1:4 for the house of G which is in Jerusalem."
1:5 every one whose spirit G had stirred to go
2:68 for the house of G, to erect it on
3:2 the altar of the G of Israel, to offer
3:2 in the law of Moses the man of G
3:8 to the house of G at Jerusalem, in the
3:9 in the house of G, along with the sons
4:1 to the LORD, the G of Israel,
4:2 for we worship your G as you do, and
4:3 a house to our G; but we alone will
4:3 to the LORD, the G of Israel, as King
4:24 on the house of G which is in Jerusalem
5:1 the name of the G of Israel who was
5:2 rebuild the house of G which is in Jerusalem;
5:2 were the prophets of G, helping them.
5:5 the eye of their G was upon the elders
5:8 of Judah, to the house of the great G
5:11 the servants of the G of heaven and earth,
5:12 fathers had angered the G of heaven, he gave
5:13 that this house of G should be rebuilt.
5:14 of the house of G, which Nebuchadnezzar had taken
5:15 let the house of G be rebuilt on its
5:16 of the house of G which is in Jerusalem;
5:17 of this house of G in Jerusalem.
6:3 Concerning the house of G at Jerusalem, let the
6:5 of the house of G, which Nebuchadnezzar took out
6:5 you shall put them in the house of G
6:7 on this house of G alone; let the governor
6:7 rebuild this house of G on its site.
6:8 of this house of G; the cost is to
6:9 burnt offerings to the G of heaven, wheat, salt,
6:10 pleasing sacrifices to the G of heaven, and pray
6:12 May the G who has caused his name to
6:12 destroy this house of G which is in Jerusalem.
6:14 by command of the G of Israel and by
6:16 of this house of G with joy.
6:17 of this house of G one hundred bulls, two
6:18 for the service of G at Jerusalem, as it
6:21 worship the LORD, the G of Israel.
6:22 of the house of G, the God of Israel.
6:22 house of God, the G of Israel.
7:6 which the LORD the G of Israel had given;
7:6 of the LORD his G was upon him.
7:9 good hand of his G was upon him.
7:12 the law of the G of heaven.
7:14 the law of your G, which is in your
7:15 freely offered to the G of Israel, whose dwelling
7:16 the house of their G which is in Jerusalem.
7:17 the house of your G which is in Jerusalem.
7:18 may do, according to the will of your G
7:19 the house of your G, you shall deliver before
7:19 shall deliver before the G of Jerusalem.
7:20 the house of your G, which you have occasion
7:21 the law of the G of heaven, requires of
7:23 is commanded by the G of heaven, let it
7:23 the house of the G of heaven, lest his
7:24 servants, or other servants of this house of G
7:25 the wisdom of your G which is in your
7:25 the laws of your G; and those who do
7:26 the law of your G and the law of
7:27 be the LORD, the G of our fathers, who
7:28 of the LORD my G was upon me, and
8:17 send us ministers for the house of our G
8:18 good hand of our G upon us, they brought
8:21 humble ourselves before our G, to seek from him
8:22 "The hand of our G is for good upon
8:23 fasted and besought our G for this, and he
8:25 the house of our G which the king and
8:28 to the LORD, the G of your fathers.
8:30 them to Jerusalem, to the house of our G
8:31 the hand of our G was upon us, and
8:33 the house of our G, the silver and the
8:35 burnt offerings to the G of Israel, twelve bulls
8:36 they aided the people and the house of G
9:4 the words of the G of Israel, because of
9:5 to the LORD my G,
9:6 God, saying: "O my G, I am ashamed and
9:6 face to thee, my G, for our iniquities have
9:8 by the LORD our G, to leave us a
9:8 holy place, that our G may brighten our eyes
9:9 are bondmen; yet our G has not forsaken us
9:9 the house of our G, to repair its ruins,
9:10 "And now, O our G, what shall we say
9:13 seeing that thou, our G, hast punished us less
9:15 O LORD the G of Israel, thou art just,
10:1 before the house of G, a very great assembly
10:2 broken faith with our G and have married foreign
10:3 a covenant with our G to put away all
10:3 the commandment of our G; and let it be
10:6 before the house of G, and went to the
10:9 before the house of G, trembling because of this
10:11 to the LORD the G of your fathers, and
10:14 fierce wrath of our G over this matter be
Neh 1:4 and praying before the G of heaven.
1:5 I said, "O LORD G of heaven, the great
1:5 the great and terrible G who keeps covenant and
2:4 I prayed to the G of heaven.
2:8 good hand of my G was upon me.
2:12 no one what my G had put into my
2:18 the hand of my G which had been upon
2:20 replied to them, "The G of heaven will make
4:4 Hear, O our G, for we are despised; turn
4:9 we prayed to our G, and set a guard
4:15 to us and that G had frustrated their plan,
4:20 Our G will fight for us."
5:9 the fear of our G to prevent the taunts
5:13 and said, "So may G shake out every man
5:15 not do so, because of the fear of G
5:19 my good, O my G, all that I have
6:9 But now, O G, strengthen thou my hands.
6:10 in the house of G, within the temple, and
6:12 understood, and saw that G had not sent him,
6:14 and Sanballat, O my G, according to these things
6:16 had been accomplished with the help of our G
7:5 Then G put it into my mind to assemble
8:6 the LORD, the great G; and all the people
8:8 from the law of G, clearly; and they gave
8:9 to the LORD your G; do not mourn or
8:16 of the house of G, and in the square
8:18 read from the book of the law of G
9:3 of the LORD their G for a fourth of
9:3 made confession and worshiped the LORD their G
9:4 with a loud voice to the LORD their G
9:5 bless the LORD your G from everlasting to
9:7 art the LORD, the G who didst choose Abram
9:17 But thou art a G ready to forgive, gracious
9:18 said, 'This is your G who brought you up
9:31 them; for thou art a gracious and merciful G
9:32 "Now therefore, our G, the great and mighty and
9:32 and mighty and terrible G, who keepest covenant
10:28 to the law of G, their wives, their sons,
10:29 oath to walk in G's law which was given
10:29 Moses the servant of G, and to observe and
10:32 the house of our G:
10:33 all the work of the house of our G
10:34 the house of our G, according to our fathers'
10:34 of the LORD our G, as it is written
10:36 the house of our G, to the priests who
10:36 the house of our G, the first-born of our
10:37 the house of our G; and to bring to
10:38 the house of our G, to the chambers, to
10:39 We will not neglect the house of our G
11:11 of the house of G,
11:16 of the house of G;
11:22 singers, over the work of the house of G
12:24 David the man of G, watch corresponding to watch.
12:36 David the man of G; and Ezra the scribe
12:40 in the house of G, and I and half
12:43 day and rejoiced, for G had made them rejoice
12:45 the service of their G and the service of
12:46 there were songs of praise and thanksgiving to G
13:1 enter the assembly of G;
13:2 them—yet our G turned the curse into
13:4 the house of our G, and who was connected
13:7 chamber in the courts of the house of G
13:9 of the house of G, with the cereal offering
13:11 is the house of G forsaken?" And I gathered
13:14 Remember me, O my G, concerning this, and wipe
13:14 the house of my G and for his service.
13:18 and did not our G bring all this evil
13:22 my favor, O my G, and spare me according
13:25 in the name of G, saying, "You shall not
13:26 was beloved by his G, and God made him
13:26 by his God, and G made him king over
13:27 act treacherously against our G by marrying foreign
13:29 Remember them, O my G, because they have defiled
13:31 Remember me, O my G, for good.
Tob 1:12 it, because I remembered G with all my heart.
3:11 thou, O Lord my G, and blessed is thy
3:16 the presence of the glory of the great G
4:5 "Remember the Lord our G all your days, my
4:7 and the face of G will not be turned

4:14 and if you serve G you will receive payment.
4:19 Bless the Lord G on every occasion; ask him
4:21 wealth if you fear G and refrain from every
5:16 "Go with this man; G who dwells in heaven
6:17 out to the merciful G, and he will save
7:12 The merciful G will guide you both for the
8:5 "Blessed art thou, O G of our fathers, and
8:15 Then Raguel blessed G and said, "Blessed art thou,
8:15 "Blessed art thou, O G, with every pure and
10:11 them away, saying, "The G of heaven will prosper
11:1 on his way, praising G because he had made
11:14 "Blessed art thou, O G, and blessed is thy
11:16 at the gate of Nineveh, rejoicing and praising G
11:17 thanks before them that G had been merciful to
11:17 Blessed is G who has brought you to us,
12:6 said to them: "Praise G and give thanks to
12:6 is good to praise G and to exalt his
12:6 exalt his name, worthily declaring the works of G
12:7 king, but gloriously to reveal the works of G
12:11 reveal the works of G
12:14 So now G sent me to heal you and
12:17 But praise G for ever.
12:18 my part, but by the will of our G
12:20 now give thanks to G, for I am ascending
12:22 and wonderful works of G, and acknowledged that
13:1 and said: "Blessed is G who lives for ever,
13:4 is our Lord and G, he is our Father
13:7 I exalt my G; my soul exalts the King
13:11 name of the Lord G, bearing gifts in their
13:15 Let my soul praise G the great King.
13:18 praise, saying, 'Blessed is G, who has exalted you
14:2 to fear the Lord G and to praise him.
14:4 The house of G in it will be burned
14:5 But G will again have mercy on them, and
14:5 rebuild the house of G, though it will not
14:5 And the house of G will be rebuilt there
14:6 to fear the Lord G in truth, and will
14:7 will give thanks to G, and the Lord will
14:7 who love the Lord G in truth and righteousness
Jud 3:8 tongues and tribes should call upon him as G
4:2 and for the temple of the Lord their G
4:9 Israel cried out to G with great fervor, and
4:12 praying earnestly to the G of Israel not to
5:8 and they worshiped the G of heaven, the God
5:8 God of heaven, the G they had come to
5:9 Then their G commanded them to leave the place
5:12 cried out to their G, and he afflicted the
5:13 Then G dried up the Red Sea before them,
5:17 not sin against their G they prospered, for the
5:17 they prospered, for the G who hates iniquity is
5:18 the temple of their G was razed to the
5:19 have returned to their G, and have come back
5:20 they sin against their G and we find out
5:21 defend them, and their G will protect them, and
6:2 of Israel because their G will defend them?
6:2 Who is G except Nebuchadnezzar?
6:3 the earth, and their G will not deliver them--
6:18 fell down and worshiped G, and cried out to
6:19 and said, "O Lord G of heaven, behold their
6:21 they called on the G of Israel for help.
7:19 to the Lord their G, for their courage failed,
7:25 before all the elders, G be judge between you
7:26 one to help us; G has sold us into
7:29 and earth and our G, the Lord of our
7:30 out to the Lord G with a loud voice.
7:31 time the Lord our G will restore to us
8:8 her, for she feared G with great devotion.
8:11 pronounced this oath between G and you, promising
8:12 you, that have put G to the test this
8:12 in the place of G among the sons of
8:14 expect to search out G, who made all these
8:14 provoke the Lord our G to anger.
8:16 of the Lord our G; for God is not
8:16 Lord our God; for G is not like man,
8:20 we know no other G but him, and therefore
8:23 but the Lord our G will turn it to
8:25 to the Lord our G, who is putting us
8:35 and may the Lord G go before you, to
9:1 in the house of G in Jerusalem, Judith cried
9:2 and said, "O Lord G of my father Simeon,
9:4 thee for help--O G, my God, hear me
9:4 help--O God, my G, hear me also, a
9:11 strength; for thou art G of the lowly, helper
9:12 Hear, O hear me, G of my father, God
9:12 God of my father, G of the inheritance of
9:14 understand that thou art G, the God of all
9:14 thou art God, the G of all power and
10:1 crying out to the G of Israel, and had
10:8 to her, "May the G of our fathers grant
10:8 And she worshipped G
11:6 words of your maidservant, G will accomplish
11:10 prevail against them, unless they sin against their G
11:11 about to provoke their G to anger when they
11:12 to use all that G by his laws has
11:13 the presence of our G at Jerusalem--although it
11:16 fled from them; and G has sent me to
11:17 religious, and serves the G of heaven day and
11:17 I will pray to G and he will tell
11:22 Holofernes said to her, G has done well to
11:23 you have said, your G shall be my God,
11:23 God shall be my G, and you shall live
12:8 she prayed the Lord G of Israel to direct
13:4 her heart, "O Lord G of all might, look
13:7 this day, O Lord G of Israel!"
13:11 G, our God, is still with us, to show
13:11 God, our G, is still with us, to show
13:14 a loud voice, "Praise G, O praise him!
13:14 Praise G, who has not withdrawn his mercy from
13:17 bowed down and worshipped G, and said with one
13:17 "Blessed art thou, our G, who hast brought into
13:18 by the Most High G above all women on
13:18 blessed be the Lord G, who created the heavens
13:19 of men, as they remember the power of G
13:20 May G grant this to be a perpetual honor
13:20 ruin, walking in the straight path before our G
14:10 saw all that the G of Israel had done,
14:10 he believed firmly in G, and was circumcised, and
15:10 good to Israel, and G is well pleased with
16:2 a song to my G with tambourines, sing to
16:3 For G is the Lord who crushes wars; for
16:13 will sing to my G a new song: O
16:18 When they arrived at Jerusalem they worshiped G
16:19 Judith also dedicated to G all the vessels of
Esth 10:4 And Mordecai said, "These things have come from G
10:9 who cried out to G and were saved.
10:9 from all these evils; G has done great signs
10:10 for the people of G and one for all
10:11 day of decision before G and among all the
10:12 And G remembered his people and vindicated his.
10:13 joy and gladness before G, from generation to
11:10 Then they cried to G; and from their cry,
11:12 in his dream what G had determined to do,
13:14 above the glory of G, and I will not
13:15 And now, O Lord G and King, God of
13:15 Lord God and King, G of Abraham, spare thy
14:3 prayed to the Lord G of Israel, and said:
14:18 in thee, O Lord G of Abraham.
14:19 O G, whose might is over all, hear the
15:2 aid of the all-seeing G and Savior, she took
15:8 Then G changed the spirit of the king to
15:13 like an angel of G, and my heart was
16:4 the evil-hating justice of G, who always sees
16:16 the most mighty living G, who has directed the
16:18 For G, who rules over all things, has speedily
16:21 For G, who rules over all things, has made
Job 1:1 upright, one who feared G, and turned away from
1:5 have sinned, and cursed G in their hearts." Thus
1:6 when the sons of G came to present themselves
1:8 upright man, who fears G and turns away from
1:9 LORD, "Does Job fear G for nought?
1:16 said, "The fire of G fell from heaven and
1:22 not sin or charge G with wrong.
2:1 when the sons of G came to present themselves
2:3 upright man, who fears G and turns away from
2:9 Curse G, and die."
2:10 at the hand of G, and shall we not
3:4 May G above not seek it, nor light shine
3:23 way is hid, whom G has hedged in?
4:6 not your fear of G your confidence, and the
4:9 By the breath of G they perish, and by
4:17 a voice: 'Can mortal man be righteous before G
5:8 me, I would seek G, and to God would
5:8 seek God, and to G would I commit my
5:17 is the man whom G reproves; therefore despise not
6:4 poison; the terrors of G are arrayed against me.
6:8 my request, and that G would grant my desire;
6:9 that it would please G to crush me, that
8:3 Does G pervert justice?
8:5 If you will seek G and make supplication to
8:13 of all who forget G; the hope of the
8:20 "Behold, G will not reject a blameless man, nor
9:2 But how can a man be just before G

9:13 G will not turn back his anger; beneath him
10:2 I will say to G, Do not condemn me;
11:4 I am clean in G's eyes.'
11:5 eyes.' But oh, that G would speak, and open
11:6 Know then that G exacts of you less than
11:7 "Can you find out the deep things of G
12:4 I, who called upon G and he answered me,
12:6 and those who provoke G are secure, who bring
12:6 secure, who bring their G in their hand.
12:13 "With G are wisdom and might; he has counsel
13:3 and I desire to argue my case with G
13:7 you speak falsely for G, and speak deceitfully for
13:8 toward him, will you plead the case for G
15:4 with the fear of G, and hindering meditation before
15:4 the fear of God, and hindering meditation before G
15:8 Have you listened in the council of G
15:11 Are the consolations of G too small for you,
15:13 turn your spirit against G, and let such words
15:15 Behold, G puts no trust in his holy ones,
15:25 forth his hand against G, and bids defiance to
16:7 Surely now G has worn me out; he has
16:11 G gives me up to the ungodly, and casts
16:20 pours out tears to G,
16:21 of a man with G, like that of a
18:21 is the place of him who knows not G
19:6 me, know then that G has put me in
19:21 for the hand of G has touched me!
19:22 Why do you, like G, pursue me?
19:26 flesh I shall see G,
20:15 vomits them up again; G casts them out of
20:23 belly to the full G will send his fierce
20:28 in the day of G's wrath.
20:29 wicked man's portion from G, the heritage decreed
20:29 from God, the heritage decreed for him by G
21:9 and no rod of G is upon them.
21:14 They say to G, 'Depart from us!
21:17 That G distributes pains in his anger?
21:19 You say, G stores up their iniquity for their
21:22 Will any teach G knowledge, seeing that he judges
22:2 Temanite answered: "Can a man be profitable to G
22:12 "Is not G high in the heavens?
22:13 you say, 'What does G know?
22:17 They said to G, 'Depart from us,' and 'What
22:21 has consumed.' "Agree with G, and be at peace;
22:26 the Almighty, and lift up your face to G
22:29 For G abases the proud, but he saves the
23:16 G has made my heart faint; the Almighty has
24:12 cries for help; yet G pays no attention to
24:22 Yet G prolongs the life of the mighty by
25:2 and fear are with G; he makes peace in
25:4 How then can man be righteous before G
26:6 Sheol is naked before G, and Abaddon has no
27:2 discourse, and said: "As G lives, who has taken
27:3 and the spirit of G is in my nostrils;
27:8 of the godless when G cuts him off, when
27:8 cuts him off, when G takes away his life?
27:9 Will G hear his cry, when trouble comes upon
27:10 Will he call upon G at all times?
27:11 concerning the hand of G; what is with the
27:13 a wicked man with G, and the heritage which
28:23 it with our ears.' G understands the way to
29:2 in the days when G watched over me;
29:4 when the friendship of G was upon my tent;
30:11 Because G has loosed my cord and humbled me,
30:19 G has cast me into the mire, and I
31:2 be my portion from G above, and my heritage
31:6 just balance, and let G know my integrity!)
31:14 shall I do when G rises up?
31:23 terror of calamity from G, and I could not
31:28 have been false to G above.
32:2 justified himself rather than G;
32:13 'We have found wisdom; G may vanquish him, not
33:4 The spirit of G has made me, and the
33:6 Behold, I am toward G as you are; I
33:12 G is greater than man.
33:14 For G speaks in one way, and in two,
33:26 then man prays to G, and he accepts him,
33:29 see the light.' "Behold, G does all these things,
34:5 'I am innocent, and G has taken away my
34:9 should take delight in G
34:10 far be it from G that he should do
34:12 Of a truth, G will not do wickedly, and
34:23 man to go before G in judgment.
34:31 any one said to G, 'I have borne chastisement;
34:37 hands among us, and multiplies his words against G
35:2 is my right before G
35:10 none says, 'Where is G my Maker, who gives
35:13 Surely G does not hear an empty cry, nor
36:2 something to say on G's behalf.
36:5 "Behold, G is mighty, and does not despise any;
36:22 Behold, G is exalted in his power; who is
36:26 Behold, G is great, and we know him not;
37:5 G thunders wondrously with his voice; he does great
37:10 By the breath of G ice is given, and
37:14 Job; stop and consider the wondrous works of G
37:15 Do you know how G lays his command upon
37:22 north comes golden splendor; G is clothed with
38:7 all the sons of G shouted for joy?
38:41 young ones cry to G, and wander about for
39:17 has no fear; because G has made her forget
40:2 He who argues with G, let him answer it."
40:9 you an arm like G, and can you thunder
40:19 of the works of G; let him who made
Ps 3:2 me, there is no help for him in G
3:7 Deliver me, O my G
4:1 when I call, O G of my right!
5:2 my King and my G, for to thee do
5:4 thou art not a G who delights in wickedness;
5:10 bear their guilt, O G; let them fall by
7:1 O LORD my G, in thee do I take
7:3 O LORD my G, if I have done this,
7:6 enemies; awake, O my G; thou hast appointed a
7:9 who triest the minds and hearts, thou righteous G
7:10 My shield is with G, who saves the upright
7:11 G is a righteous judge, and a God who
7:11 righteous judge, and a G who has indignation every
7:12 man does not repent, G will whet his sword;
8:5 him little less than G, and dost crown him
9:17 depart to Sheol, all the nations that forget G
10:4 him; all his thoughts are, "There is no G
10:11 thinks in his heart, G has forgotten, he has
10:12 Arise, O LORD; O G, lift up thy hand;
10:13 does the wicked renounce G, and say in his
13:3 me, O LORD my G; lighten my eyes, lest
14:1 fool says in his heart, "There is no G
14:2 are any that act wisely, that seek after G
14:5 in great terror, for G is with the generation
16:1 Preserve me, O G, for in thee I take
16:4 Those who choose another G multiply their sorrows;
17:6 wilt answer me, O G; incline thy ear to
18:2 and my deliverer, my G, my rock, in whom
18:6 the LORD; to my G I cried for help.
18:21 LORD, and have not wickedly departed from my G
18:28 lamp; the LORD my G lightens my darkness.
18:29 troop; and by my G I can leap over
18:30 This G --his way is perfect; the promise of
18:31 For who is G, but the LORD?
18:31 a rock, except our G --
18:32 our God?-- the G who girded me with
18:46 and exalted be the G of my salvation,
18:47 of my salvation, the G who gave me vengeance
19:1 telling the glory of G; and the firmament proclaims
20:1 The name of the G of Jacob protect you!
20:5 the name of our G set up our banners!
20:7 boast of the name of the LORD our G
22:1 My G, my God, why hast thou forsaken me?
22:1 My God, my G, why hast thou forsaken me?
22:2 O my G, I cry by day, but thou
22:10 my mother bore me thou hast been my G
24:5 and vindication from the G of his salvation.
24:6 the face of the G of Jacob.
25:2 O my G, in thee I trust, let me
25:5 for thou art the G of my salvation; for
25:22 Redeem Israel, O G, out of all his troubles.
27:9 forsake me not, O G of my salvation!
29:3 upon the waters; the G of glory thunders, the
30:2 O LORD my G, I cried to thee for
30:12 O LORD my G, I will give thanks to
31:5 spirit; thou hast redeemed me, O LORD, faithful G
31:14 thee, O LORD, I say, "Thou art my G
33:12 is the nation whose G is the LORD, the
35:23 for my cause, my G and my Lord!
35:24 me, O LORD, my G, according to thy righteousness;
36:1 is no fear of G before his eyes.
36:6 like the mountains of G, thy judgments are like
36:7 How precious is thy steadfast love, O G
37:31 The law of his G is in his heart;
38:15 thou, O LORD my G, who wilt answer.
38:21 O my G, be not far from me!
40:3 my mouth, a song of praise to our G
40:5 multiplied, O LORD my G, thy wondrous deeds and
40:8 thy will, O my G; thy law is within

40:17 and my deliverer; do not tarry, O my G
41:13 be the LORD, the G of Israel, from everlasting
42:1 streams, so longs my soul for thee, O G
42:2 My soul thirsts for G, for the living God.
42:2 My soul thirsts for God, for the living G
42:2 shall I come and behold the face of G
42:3 men say to me continually, "Where is your G
42:4 to the house of G, with glad shouts and
42:5 Hope in G; for I shall again praise him,
42:6 shall again praise him, my help and my G
42:8 a prayer to the G of my life.
42:9 I say to G, my rock: "Why hast thou
42:10 they say to me continually, "Where is your G
42:11 Hope in G; for I shall again praise him,
42:11 shall again praise him, my help and my G
43:1 Vindicate me, O G, and defend my cause against
43:2 For thou art the G in whom I take
43:4 to the altar of G, to God my exceeding
43:4 altar of God, to G my exceeding joy; and
43:4 with the lyre, O G, my God.
43:4 praise thee with the lyre, O God, my G
43:5 Hope in G; for I shall again praise him,
43:5 shall again praise him, my help and my G
44:1 with our ears, O G, our fathers have told
44:4 my King and my G, who ordainest victories for
44:8 In G we have boasted continually, and we will
44:20 the name of our G, or spread forth our
44:20 hands to a strange G,
44:21 strange god, would not G discover this?
45:2 upon your lips; therefore G has blessed you for
45:7 Therefore G, your God, has anointed you with the
45:7 Therefore God, your G, has anointed you with the
46:1 G is our refuge and strength, a very present
46:4 glad the city of G, the holy habitation of
46:5 G is in the midst of her, she shall
46:5 shall not be moved; G will help her right
46:7 is with us; the G of Jacob is our
46:10 "Be still, and know that I am G
46:11 is with us; the G of Jacob is our
47:1 Shout to G with loud songs of joy!
47:5 [Selah] G has gone up with a shout, the
47:6 Sing praises to G, sing praises!
47:7 For G is the king of all the earth;
47:8 G reigns over the nations; God sits on his
47:8 reigns over the nations; G sits on his holy
47:9 the people of the G of Abraham.
47:9 the earth belong to G; he is highly exalted!
48:1 to be praised in the city of our G
48:3 Within her citadels G has shown himself a sure
48:8 the city of our G, which God establishes for
48:8 of our God, which G establishes for ever.
48:9 thy steadfast love, O G, in the midst of
48:10 As thy name, O G, so thy praise reaches
48:14 generation that this is G, our God for ever
48:14 this is God, our G for ever and ever.
49:7 himself, or give to G the price of his
49:15 But G will ransom my soul from the power
50:1 The Mighty One, G the LORD, speaks and summons
50:2 the perfection of beauty, G shines forth.
50:3 Our G comes, he does not keep silence, before
50:6 declare his righteousness, for G himself is judge!
50:7 I am G, your God.
50:7 I am God, your G
50:14 Offer to G a sacrifice of thanksgiving, and pay
50:16 But to the wicked G says: "What right have
50:22 then, you who forget G, lest I rend, and
50:23 way aright I will show the salvation of G
51:1 mercy on me, O G, according to thy steadfast
51:10 a clean heart, O G, and put a new
51:14 me from bloodguiltiness, O G, thou God of my
51:14 bloodguiltiness, O God, thou G of my salvation, and
51:17 The sacrifice acceptable to G is a broken spirit;
51:17 and contrite heart, O G, thou wilt not despise.
52:5 But G will break you down for ever; he
52:7 who would not make G his refuge, but trusted
52:8 a green olive tree in the house of G
52:8 the steadfast love of G for ever and ever.
53:1 fool says in his heart, "There is no G
53:2 G looks down from heaven upon the sons of
53:2 are any that are wise, that seek after G
53:4 they eat bread, and do not call upon G
53:5 For G will scatter the bones of the ungodly;
53:5 put to shame, for G has rejected them.
53:6 When G restores the fortunes of his people, Jacob
54:1 Save me, O G, by thy name, and vindicate
54:2 Hear my prayer, O G; give ear to the
54:3 they do not set G before them.
54:4 [Selah] Behold, G is my helper; the Lord is
55:1 to my prayer, O G; and hide not thyself
55:14 sweet converse together; within G's house we
55:16 But I call upon G; and the LORD will
55:19 G will give ear, and humble them, he who
55:19 they keep no law, and do not fear G
55:23 But thou, O G, wilt cast them down into
56:1 gracious to me, O G, for men trample upon
56:4 In G, whose word I praise, in God I
56:4 word I praise, in G I trust without a
56:7 crime; in wrath cast down the peoples, O G
56:9 This I know, that G is for me.
56:10 In G, whose word I praise, in the LORD,
56:11 word I praise, in G I trust without a
56:12 I must perform, O G; I will render thank
56:13 I may walk before G in the light of
57:1 merciful to me, O G, be merciful to me,
57:2 I cry to G Most High, to God who
57:2 God Most High, to G who fulfils his purpose
57:3 [Selah] G will send forth his steadfast love and
57:5 Be exalted, O G, above the heavens!
57:7 heart is steadfast, O G, my heart is steadfast!
57:11 Be exalted, O G, above the heavens!
58:6 O G, break the teeth in their mouths; tear
58:11 surely there is a G who judges on earth."
59:1 my enemies, O my G, protect me from those
59:5 Thou, LORD G of hosts, art God of Israel.
59:5 God of hosts, art G of Israel.
59:9 thee; for thou, O G, art my fortress.
59:10 My G in his steadfast love will meet me;
59:10 will meet me; my G will let me look
59:13 men may know that G rules over Jacob to
59:17 thee, for thou, O G, art my fortress, the
59:17 art my fortress, the G who shows me steadfast
60:1 O G, thou hast rejected us, broken our defenses;
60:6 G has spoken in his sanctuary: "With exultation I
60:10 Hast thou not rejected us, O G
60:10 not go forth, O G, with our armies.
60:12 With G we shall do valiantly; it is he
61:1 Hear my cry, O G, listen to my prayer;
61:5 [Selah] For thou, O G, hast heard my vows,
61:7 enthroned for ever before G; bid steadfast love and
62:1 For G alone my soul waits in silence; from
62:5 [Selah] For G alone my soul waits in silence,
62:7 On G rests my deliverance and my honor; my
62:7 my honor; my mighty rock, my refuge is G
62:8 your heart before him; G is a refuge for
62:11 Once G has spoken; twice have I heard this:
62:11 that power belongs to G;
63:1 O G, thou art my God, I seek thee,
63:1 God, thou art my G, I seek thee, my
63:11 king shall rejoice in G; all who swear by
64:1 Hear my voice, O G, in my complaint; preserve
64:7 But G will shoot his arrow at them; they
64:9 they will tell what G has wrought, and ponder
65:1 due to thee, O G, in Zion; and to
65:5 us with deliverance, O G of our salvation, who
65:9 it; the river of G is full of water;
66:1 a joyful noise to G, all the earth;
66:3 Say to G, "How terrible are thy deeds!
66:5 Come and see what G has done: he is
66:8 [Selah] Bless our G, O peoples, let the sound
66:10 For thou, O G, hast tested us; thou hast
66:16 all you who fear G, and I will tell
66:19 But truly G has listened; he has given heed
66:20 Blessed be G, because he has not rejected my
67:1 May G be gracious to us and bless us
67:3 peoples praise thee, O G; let all the peoples
67:5 peoples praise thee, O G; let all the peoples
67:6 has yielded its increase; G, our God, has blessed
67:6 its increase; God, our G, has blessed us.
67:7 G has blessed us; let all the ends of
68:1 Let G arise, let his enemies be scattered; let
68:2 melts before fire, let the wicked perish before G
68:3 let them exult before G; let them be jubilant
68:4 Sing to G, sing praises to his name; lift
68:5 protector of widows is G in his holy habitation.
68:6 G gives the desolate a home to dwell in;
68:7 O G, when thou didst go forth before thy
68:8 at the presence of G; yon Sinai quaked at
68:8 at the presence of G, the God of Israel.
68:8 presence of God, the G of Israel.
68:9 Rain in abundance, O G, thou didst shed abroad;
68:10 in thy goodness, O G, thou didst provide for
68:16 at the mount which G desired for his abode,

68:18 rebellious, that the LORD G may dwell there.
68:19 daily bears us up; G is our salvation.
68:20 [Selah] Our G is a God of salvation; and
68:20 Our God is a G of salvation; and to
68:20 of salvation; and to G, the Lord, belongs escape
68:21 But G will shatter the heads of his enemies,
68:24 processions are seen, O G, the processions of my
68:24 the processions of my G, my King, into the
68:26 maidens playing timbrels: "Bless G in the great
68:28 Summon thy might, O G; show thy strength, O
68:28 show thy strength, O G, thou who hast wrought
68:31 Ethiopia hasten to stretch out her hands to G
68:32 Sing to G, O kingdoms of the earth; sing
68:34 Ascribe power to G, whose majesty is over Israel,
68:35 Terrible is G in his sanctuary, the God of
68:35 in his sanctuary, the G of Israel, he gives
68:35 Blessed be G
69:1 Save me, O G
69:3 My eyes grow dim with waiting for my G
69:5 O G, thou knowest my folly; the wrongs I
69:6 through me, O Lord G of hosts; let not
69:6 dishonor through me, O G of Israel.
69:13 an acceptable time, O G, in the abundance of
69:29 let thy salvation, O G, set me on high!
69:30 praise the name of G with a song; I
69:32 glad; you who seek G, let your hearts revive.
69:35 For G will save Zion and rebuild the cities
70:1 Be pleased, O G, to deliver me!
70:4 thy salvation say evermore, G is great!"
70:5 am poor and needy; hasten to me, O G
71:4 Rescue me, O my G, from the hand of
71:11 consult together, and say, G has forsaken him; pursue
71:12 O G, be not far from me; O my
71:12 from me; O my G, make haste to help
71:16 deeds of the Lord G I will come, I
71:17 O G, from my youth thou hast taught me,
71:18 and gray hairs, O G, do not forsake me,
71:19 and thy righteousness, O G, reach the high heavens.
71:19 done great things, O G, who is like thee?
71:22 thy faithfulness, O my G; I will sing praises
72:1 king thy justice, O G, and thy righteousness to
72:18 be the LORD, the G of Israel, who alone
73:1 Truly G is good to the upright, to those
73:11 they say, "How can G know?
73:17 into the sanctuary of G; then I perceived their
73:26 heart may fail, but G is the strength of
73:28 good to be near G; I have made the
73:28 have made the Lord G my refuge, that I
74:1 O G, why dost thou cast us off for
74:8 the meeting places of G in the land.
74:10 How long, O G, is the foe to scoff?
74:12 Yet G my King is from of old, working
74:22 Arise, O G, plead thy cause; remember how the
75:1 thanks to thee, O G; we give thanks; we
75:7 up; but it is G who executes judgment, putting
75:9 sing praises to the G of Jacob.
76:1 In Judah G is known, his name is great
76:6 At thy rebuke, O G of Jacob, both rider
76:9 and was still, when G arose to establish judgment
76:11 to the LORD your G, and perform them; let
77:1 I cry aloud to G, aloud to God, that
77:1 to God, aloud to G, that he may hear
77:3 I think of G, and I moan; I meditate,
77:9 Has G forgotten to be gracious?
77:13 Thy way, O G, is holy.
77:13 What G is great like our God?
77:13 What god is great like our G
77:14 Thou art the G who workest wonders, who hast
77:16 waters saw thee, O G, when the waters saw
78:7 set their hope in G, and not forget the
78:7 forget the works of G, but keep his commandments;
78:8 not steadfast, whose spirit was not faithful to G
78:10 They did not keep G's covenant, but refused to
78:18 They tested G in their heart by demanding the
78:19 They spoke against G, saying, "Can God spread a
78:19 against God, saying, "Can G spread a table in
78:22 had no faith in G, and did not trust
78:31 mouths, the anger of G rose against them and
78:34 they repented and sought G earnestly.
78:35 They remembered that G was their rock, the Most
78:35 rock, the Most High G their redeemer.
78:56 against the Most High G, and did not observe
78:59 When G heard, he was full of wrath, and
79:1 O G, the heathen have come into thy inheritance;
79:9 Help us, O G of our salvation, for the
79:10 Why should the nations say, "Where is their G
80:3 Restore us, O G; let thy face shine, that
80:4 O LORD G of hosts, how long wilt thou
80:7 Restore us, O G of hosts; let thy face
80:14 Turn again, O G of hosts!
80:19 Restore us, O LORD G of hosts!
81:1 Sing aloud to G our strength; shout for joy
81:1 for joy to the G of Jacob!
81:4 an ordinance of the G of Jacob.
81:9 shall be no strange G among you; you shall
81:9 you shall not bow down to a foreign G
81:10 am the LORD your G, who brought you up
82:1 G has taken his place in the divine council;
82:8 Arise, O G, judge the earth; for to thee
83:1 O G, do not keep silence; do not hold
83:1 not hold thy peace or be still, O G
83:12 take possession for ourselves of the pastures of G
83:13 O my G, make them like whirling dust, like
84:2 and flesh sing for joy to the living G
84:3 O LORD of hosts, my King and my G
84:7 strength to strength; the G of gods will be
84:8 O LORD G of hosts, hear my prayer; give
84:8 prayer; give ear, O G of Jacob!
84:9 Behold our shield, O G; look upon the face
84:10 the house of my G than dwell in the
84:11 For the LORD G is a sun and shield;
85:4 Restore us again, O G of our salvation, and
85:8 Let me hear what G the LORD will speak,
86:2 Thou art my G;
86:10 great and doest wondrous things, thou alone art G
86:12 thee, O Lord my G, with my whole heart,
86:14 O G, insolent men have risen up against me;
86:15 O Lord, art a G merciful and gracious, slow
87:3 things are spoken of you, O city of G
88:1 O LORD, my G, I call for help by
89:7 like the LORD, a G feared in the council
89:8 O LORD G of hosts, who is mighty as
89:26 art my Father, my G, and the Rock of
90:2 the world, from everlasting to everlasting thou art G
90:17 of the Lord our G be upon us, and
91:2 and my fortress; my G, in whom I trust."
92:13 LORD, they flourish in the courts of our G
94:1 O LORD, thou G of vengeance, thou God of
94:1 God of vengeance, thou G of vengeance, shine forth!
94:7 does not see; the G of Jacob does not
94:22 my stronghold, and my G the rock of my
94:23 wickedness; the LORD our G will wipe them out.
95:3 LORD is a great G, and a great King
95:7 For he is our G, and we are the
97:8 of Judah rejoice, because of thy judgments, O G
98:3 the earth have seen the victory of our G
99:5 Extol the LORD our G; worship at his footstool!
99:8 O LORD our G, thou didst answer them; thou
99:8 thou wast a forgiving G to them, but an
99:9 Extol the LORD our G, and worship at his
99:9 for the LORD our G is holy!
100:3 Know that the LORD is G
102:24 "O my G
104:1 O LORD my G, thou art very great!
104:21 roar for their prey, seeking their food from G
104:33 sing praise to my G while I have being.
105:7 is the LORD our G; his judgments are in
106:14 the wilderness, and put G to the test in
106:20 exchanged the glory of G for the image of
106:21 They forgot G, their Savior, who had done great
106:47 us, O LORD our G, and gather us from
106:48 be the LORD, the G of Israel, from everlasting
107:11 against the words of G, and spurned the counsel
108:1 heart is steadfast, O G, my heart is steadfast!
108:5 Be exalted, O G, above the heavens!
108:7 G has promised in his sanctuary: "With exultation I
108:11 Hast thou not rejected us, O G
108:11 not go forth, O G, with our armies.
108:13 With G we shall do valiantly; it is he
109:1 Be not silent, O G of my praise!
109:21 But thou, O G my Lord, deal on my
109:26 Help me, O LORD my G
113:5 like the LORD our G, who is seated on
114:7 the presence of the G of Jacob,
115:2 Why should the nations say, "Where is their G
115:3 Our G is in the heavens; he does whatever
116:5 LORD, and righteous; our G is merciful.
118:27 The LORD is G, and he has given us
118:28 Thou art my G, and I will give thanks
118:28 thee; thou art my G, I will extol thee.
119:115 that I may keep the commandments of my G
122:9 of the LORD our G, I will seek your

123:2 to the LORD our G, till he have mercy
135:2 in the courts of the house of our G
136:2 give thanks to the G of gods, for his
136:26 give thanks to the G of heaven, for his
139:17 How precious to me are thy thoughts, O G
139:19 slay the wicked, O G, and that men of
139:23 Search me, O G, and know my heart!
140:6 LORD, Thou art my G; give ear to the
141:8 toward thee, O LORD G; in thee I seek
143:10 to do thy will, for thou art my G
144:9 song to thee, O G; upon a ten-stringed harp
144:15 Happy the people whose G is the LORD!
145:1 will extol thee, my G and King, and bless
146:2 sing praises to my G while I have being.
146:5 whose help is the G of Jacob, whose hope
146:5 in the LORD his G,
146:10 reign for ever, thy G, O Zion, to all
147:1 sing praises to our G; for he is gracious,
147:7 make melody to our G upon the lyre!
147:12 Praise your G, O Zion!
149:6 the high praises of G be in their throats
150:1 Praise G in his sanctuary; praise him in his

G

Prov 2:5 of the LORD and find the knowledge of G
2:17 the covenant of her G;
3:4 in the sight of G and man.
14:9 G scorns the wicked, but the upright enjoy his
25:2 is the glory of G to conceal things, but
30:5 Every word of G proves true; he is a
30:9 and steal, and profane the name of my G
Eccl 1:13 an unhappy business that G has given to the
2:24 from the hand of G;
2:26 man who pleases him G gives wisdom and
2:26 heaping, only to give to one who pleases G
3:10 seen the business that G has given to the
3:11 cannot find out what G has done from the
3:13 also that it is G's gift to man that
3:14 I know that whatever G does endures for ever;
3:14 anything taken from it; G has made it so,
3:15 already has been; and G seeks what has been
3:17 said in my heart, G will judge the righteous
3:18 sons of men that G is testing them to
5:1 to the house of G; to draw near to
5:2 utter a word before G, for God is in
5:2 word before God, for G is in heaven, and
5:4 vow a vow to G, do not delay paying
5:6 a mistake; why should G be angry at your
5:7 empty words grow many: but do you fear G
5:18 of his life which G has given him, for
5:19 man also to whom G has given wealth and
5:19 in his toil—this is the gift of G
5:20 of his life because G keeps him occupied with
6:2 a man to whom G gives wealth, possessions, and
6:2 that he desires, yet G does not give him
7:13 Consider the work of G; who can make straight
7:14 day of adversity consider; G has made the one
7:18 for he who fears G shall come forth from
7:26 fetters; he who pleases G escapes her, but the
7:29 alone I found, that G made man upright, but
8:12 with those who fear G, because they fear before
8:13 a shadow, because he does not fear before G
8:15 days of life which G gives him under the
8:17 all the work of G, that man cannot find
9:1 in the hand of G; whether it is love
9:7 a merry heart; for G has already approved what
11:5 know the work of G who makes everything.
11:9 for all these things G will bring you into
12:7 the spirit returns to G who gave it.
12:13 Fear G, and keep his commandments; for this is
12:14 For G will bring every deed into judgment, with
Wis 1:3 thoughts separate men from G, and when his power
1:6 of his words; because G is witness of his
1:13 of your hands; because G did not make death,
2:13 to have knowledge of G, and calls himself a
2:16 happy, and boasts that G is his father.
2:18 the righteous man is G's son, he will help
2:22 the secret purposes of G, nor hope for the
2:23 blameless souls; for G created man for incorruption,
3:1 in the hand of G, and no torment will
3:5 receive great good, because G tested them and found
3:13 will have fruit when G examines souls.
4:1 is known both by G and by men.
4:6 against their parents when G examines them.
4:10 was one who pleased G and was loved by
4:15 thing to heart, that G's grace and mercy are
5:5 has he been numbered among the sons of G
6:4 to the purpose of G,
6:19 brings one near to G;
7:7 me; I called upon G, and the spirit of
7:14 it obtain friendship with G, commended for the gifts
7:15 May G grant that I speak with judgment and
7:25 of the power of G, and a pure emanation
7:26 of the working of G, and an image of
7:27 makes them friends of G, and prophets;
7:28 God, and prophets; for G loves nothing so much
8:3 birth by living with G, and the Lord of
8:4 in the knowledge of G, and an associate in
8:21 not possess wisdom unless G gave her to me—
9:1 heart I said: "O G of my fathers and
9:13 For what man can learn the counsel of G
10:5 preserved him blameless before G, and kept him
10:10 him the kingdom of G, and gave him knowledge
12:7 receive a worthy colony of the servants of G
12:13 neither is there any G besides thee, whose care
12:26 rebukes will experience the deserved judgment of G
12:27 recognized as the true G him whom they had
13:1 who were ignorant of G were foolish by nature;
13:6 go astray while seeking G and desiring to find
14:8 work, and the perishable thing was named a G
14:9 For equally hateful to G are the ungodly man
14:11 though part of what G created, they became an
14:15 now honored as a G what was once a
14:22 about the knowledge of G, but they live in
14:30 they thought wickedly of G in devoting themselves to
15:1 But thou, our G, art kind and true, patient,
15:8 he forms a futile G from the same clay—
15:16 man can form a G which is like himself.
15:19 both the praise of G and his blessing.
16:18 by the judgment of G;
18:13 thy people to be G's son.
19:1 by pitiless anger, for G knew in advance even
Sir 3:17 loved by those whom G accepts.
4:28 truth and the Lord G will fight for you.
7:9 to the Most High G he will accept it."
11:20 the godly, and quickly G causes his blessing to
21:5 to the ears of G, and his judgment comes
23:4 O Lord, Father and G of my life, do
24:22 of the Most High G, the law which Moses
36:1 us, O Lord, the G of all, and look
36:5 that there is not G but thee, O Lord.
36:17 art the Lord, the G of the ages.
39:17 for in G's time all things will be sought
41:8 have forsaken the law of the Most High G
41:19 before the truth of G and his covenant.
45:1 and was beloved by G and man, Moses, whose
46:1 a great savior of G's elect, to take vengeance
47:10 year, while they praised G's holy name, and the
47:13 days of peace, and G gave him rest on
47:18 name of the Lord G, who is called the
47:18 who is called the G of Israel, you gathered
48:10 calm the wrath of G before it breaks out
48:16 what was pleasing to G, but others multiplied sins.
49:8 vision of glory which G showed him above the
49:9 For G remembered his enemies with storm, and did
50:17 their Lord, the Almighty, G Most High.
50:22 And now bless the G of all, who in
51:1 will praise thee as G my Savior.
51:30 appointed time, and in G's time he will give
Is 1:10 the teaching of our G, you people of Gomorrah!
2:3 the house of the G of Jacob; that he
3:15 says the Lord G of hosts.
5:16 justice, and the Holy G shows himself holy in
7:7 thus says the Lord G: It shall not stand,
7:11 of the LORD your G; let it be deep
7:13 that you weary my G also?
8:10 will not stand, for G is with us.
8:19 should not a people consult their G
8:21 their king and their G, and turn their faces
9:6 "Wonderful Counselor, Mighty G, Everlasting Father,
10:21 return, the remnant of Jacob, to the mighty G
12:2 "Behold, G is my salvation; I will trust, and
12:2 afraid; for the LORD G is my strength and
13:19 Sodom and Gomorrah when G overthrew them.
14:13 above the stars of G I will set my
17:6 tree, says the LORD G of Israel.
17:10 you have forgotten the G of your salvation, and
17:10 slips of an alien G,
21:10 LORD of hosts, the G of Israel, I announce
21:17 for the LORD, the G of Israel, has spoken."
22:5 For the Lord G of hosts has a day
22:12 that day the Lord G of hosts called to
22:14 says the Lord G of hosts.
22:15 Thus says the Lord G of hosts, "Come, go

24:15 of the LORD, the G of Israel.
25:1 LORD, thou art my G; I will exalt thee,
25:8 ever, and the Lord G will wipe away tears
25:9 "Lo, this is our G; we have waited for
26:4 ever, for the LORD G is an everlasting rock.
26:13 O LORD our G, other lords besides thee have
28:16 thus says the Lord G, "Behold, I am laying
28:22 destruction from the Lord G of hosts upon the
28:26 is instructed aright; his G teaches him.
29:23 in awe of the G of Israel.
30:15 thus said the Lord G, the Holy One of
30:18 the LORD is a G of justice; blessed are
31:3 are men, and not G; and their horses are
35:2 glory of the LORD, the majesty of our G
35:4 Behold, your G will come with vengeance, with the
35:4 will come with vengeance, with the recompense of G
36:7 to me, "We rely on the LORD our G
37:4 that the LORD your G heard the words of
37:4 to mock the living G, and will rebuke the
37:4 which the LORD your G has heard; therefore lift
37:10 'Do not let your G on whom you rely
37:16 "O LORD of hosts, G of Israel, who art
37:16 cherubim, thou art the G, thou alone, of all
37:17 which he has sent to mock the living G
37:20 now, O LORD our G, save us from his
37:21 says the LORD, the G of Israel: Because you
37:38 house of Nisroch his G, Adrammelech and Sharezer,
38:5 says the LORD, the G of David your father:
40:1 Comfort, comfort my people, says your G
40:3 straight in the desert a highway for our G
40:8 the word of our G will stand for ever.
40:9 say to the cities of Judah, "Behold your G
40:10 Behold, the Lord G comes with might, and his
40:18 then will you liken G, or what likeness compare
40:27 LORD, and my right is disregarded by my G
40:28 LORD is the everlasting G, the Creator of the
41:10 for I am your G; I will strengthen you,
41:13 I, the LORD your G, hold your right hand;
41:17 answer them, I the G of Israel will not
42:5 Thus says G, the LORD, who created the heavens
43:3 am the LORD your G, the Holy One of
43:10 Before me no G was formed, nor shall there
43:12 there was no strange G among you; and you
43:13 "I am G, and also henceforth I am He;
44:6 am the last; besides me there is no G
44:8 Is there a G besides me?
44:10 Who fashions a G or casts an image, that
44:15 also he makes a G and worships it, he
44:17 he makes into a G, his idol; and falls
44:17 and says, "Deliver me, for thou art my G
45:3 I, the LORD, the G of Israel, who call
45:5 me there is no G; I gird you, though
45:14 supplication to you, saying: G is with you only,
45:14 is no other, no G besides him.'"
45:15 Truly, thou art a G who hidest thyself, O
45:15 who hidest thyself, O G of Israel, the Savior.
45:18 the heavens (he is G, who formed the earth
45:20 on praying to a G that cannot save.
45:21 there is no other G besides me, a righteous
45:21 besides me, a righteous G and a Savior; there
45:22 For I am G, and there is no other.
46:6 makes it into a G; then they fall down
46:9 old; for I am G, and there is no
46:9 no other; I am G, and there is none
48:1 LORD, and confess the G of Israel, but not
48:2 stay themselves on the G of Israel; the LORD
48:16 And now the Lord G has sent me and
48:17 am the LORD your G, who teaches you to
49:4 with the LORD, and my recompense with my G
49:5 the LORD, and my G has become my strength--
49:22 Thus says the Lord G: "Behold, I will lift
50:4 The Lord G has given me the tongue of
50:5 The Lord G has opened my ear, and I
50:7 For the Lord G helps me; therefore I have
50:9 Behold, the Lord G helps me; who will declare
50:10 name of the LORD and relies upon his G
51:15 am the LORD your G, who stirs up the
51:20 wrath of the LORD, the rebuke of your G
51:22 Lord, the LORD, your G who pleads the cause
52:4 thus says the Lord G: My people went down
52:7 says to Zion, "Your G reigns."
52:10 the earth shall see the salvation of our G
52:12 before you, and the G of Israel will be
53:4 him stricken, smitten by G, and afflicted.
54:5 is your Redeemer, the G of the whole earth
54:6 youth when she is cast off, says your G
55:5 of the LORD your G, and of the Holy
55:7 him, and to our G, for he will abundantly
56:8 Thus says the Lord G, who gathers the outcasts
57:21 no peace, says my G, for the wicked."
58:2 the ordinance of their G; they ask of me
58:2 righteous judgments, they delight to draw near to G
59:2 between you and your G, and your sins have
59:13 away from following our G, speaking oppression and
60:9 of the LORD your G, and for the Holy
60:19 everlasting light, and your G will be your glory.
61:1 Spirit of the Lord G is upon me, because
61:2 of vengeance of our G; to comfort all who
61:6 the ministers of our G; you shall eat the
61:10 shall exult in my G; for he has clothed
61:11 up, so the Lord G will cause righteousness and
62:3 a royal diadem in the hand of your G
62:5 bride, so shall your G rejoice over you.
64:4 eye has seen a G besides thee, who works
65:13 thus says the Lord G: "Behold, my servants shall
65:15 curse, and the Lord G will slay you; but
65:16 bless himself by the G of truth, and he
65:16 shall swear by the G of truth; because the
66:9 says your G

Jer 1:6 Then I said, "Ah, Lord G
2:17 forsaking the LORD your G, when he led you
2:19 forsake the LORD your G; the fear of me
2:19 you, says the Lord G of hosts.
2:22 guilt is still before me, says the Lord G
3:13 against the LORD your G and scattered your favors
3:21 their way, they have forgotten the LORD their G
3:22 to thee; for thou art the LORD our G
3:23 in the LORD our G is the salvation of
3:25 against the LORD our G, we and our fathers,
3:25 not obeyed the voice of the LORD our G
4:10 I said, "Ah, Lord G, surely thou hast utterly
5:4 way of the LORD, the law of their G
5:5 way of the LORD, the law of their G
5:14 says the LORD, the G of hosts: "Because they
5:19 has the LORD our G done all these things
5:24 fear the LORD our G, who gives the rain
7:3 LORD of hosts, the G of Israel, Amend your
7:20 thus says the Lord G: Behold, my anger and
7:21 LORD of hosts, the G of Israel: "Add your
7:23 I will be your G, and you shall be
7:28 of the LORD their G, and did not accept
8:14 for the LORD our G has doomed us to
9:15 LORD of hosts, the G of Israel: Behold, I
10:10 LORD is the true G; he is the living
10:10 he is the living G and the everlasting King.
11:3 says the LORD, the G of Israel: Cursed be
11:4 I will be your G,
13:12 says the LORD, the G of Israel, "Every jar
13:16 to the LORD your G before he brings darkness,
14:13 I said: "Ah, Lord G, behold, the prophets say
14:22 Art thou not he, O LORD our G
15:16 thy name, O LORD, G of hosts.
16:9 LORD of hosts, the G of Israel: Behold, I
16:10 against the LORD our G
19:3 LORD of hosts, the G of Israel, Behold, I
19:15 LORD of hosts, the G of Israel, Behold, I
21:4 says the LORD, the G of Israel: Behold, I
22:9 of the LORD their G, and worshiped other gods
23:2 says the LORD, the G of Israel, concerning the
23:23 "Am I a G at hand, says the LORD,
23:23 LORD, and not a G afar off?
23:36 words of the living G, the LORD of hosts,
23:36 the living God, the LORD of hosts, our G
24:5 says the LORD, the G of Israel: Like these
24:7 I will be their G, for they shall return
25:15 Thus the LORD, the G of Israel, said to
25:27 LORD of hosts, the G of Israel: Drink, be
26:13 of the LORD your G, and the LORD will
26:16 us in the name of the LORD our G
27:4 LORD of hosts, the G of Israel: This is
27:21 LORD of hosts, the G of Israel, concerning the
28:2 LORD of hosts, the G of Israel: I have
28:14 LORD of hosts, the G of Israel: I have
29:4 LORD of hosts, the G of Israel, to all
29:8 LORD of hosts, the G of Israel: Do not
29:21 LORD of hosts, the G of Israel, concerning Ahab
29:25 LORD of hosts, the G of Israel: You have
30:2 says the LORD, the G of Israel: Write in
30:9 serve the LORD their G and David their king,
30:22 be my people, and I will be your G
31:1 I will be the G of all the families
31:6 go up to Zion, to the LORD our G

31:18 be restored, for thou art the LORD my G
31:23 LORD of hosts, the G of Israel: "Once more
31:33 I will be their G, and they shall be
32:14 LORD of hosts, the G of Israel: Take these
32:15 LORD of hosts, the G of Israel: Houses and
32:17 I prayed to the LORD, saying: 'Ah Lord G
32:18 O great and mighty G whose name is the
32:25 Yet thou, O Lord G, hast said to me,
32:27 am the LORD, the G of all flesh; is
32:36 says the LORD, the G of Israel, concerning this
32:38 be my people, and I will be their G
33:4 says the LORD, the G of Israel, concerning the
34:2 says the LORD, the G of Israel: Go and
34:13 says the LORD, the G of Israel: I made
35:4 Igdaliah, the man of G, which was near the
35:13 LORD of hosts, the G of Israel: Go and
35:17 says the LORD, the G of hosts, the God
35:17 God of hosts, the G of Israel: Behold, I
35:18 LORD of hosts, the G of Israel: Because you
35:19 LORD of hosts, the G of Israel: Jonadab the
37:3 saying, "Pray for us to the LORD our G
37:7 "Thus says the LORD, G of Israel: Thus shall
38:17 says the LORD, the G of hosts, the God
38:17 God of hosts, the G of Israel, If you
39:16 LORD of hosts, the G of Israel: Behold, I
40:2 him, "The LORD your G pronounced this evil against
42:2 to the LORD your G for us, for all
42:3 that the LORD your G may show us the
42:4 to the LORD your G according to your request,
42:5 which the LORD your G sends you to us.
42:6 of the LORD our G to whom we are
42:6 we obey the voice of the LORD our G
42:9 says the LORD, the G of Israel, to whom
42:13 of the LORD your G
42:15 LORD of hosts, the G of Israel: If you
42:18 LORD of hosts, the G of Israel: As my
42:20 to the LORD your G, saying, 'Pray for us
42:20 to the LORD our G, and whatever the LORD
42:20 whatever the LORD our G says declare to us
42:21 of the LORD your G in anything that he
43:1 of the LORD their G, with which the LORD
43:1 which the LORD their G had sent him to
43:2 The LORD our G did not send you to
43:10 LORD of hosts, the G of Israel: Behold, I
44:2 LORD of hosts, the G of Israel: You have
44:7 thus says the LORD G of hosts, the God
44:7 God of hosts, the G of Israel: Why do
44:11 LORD of hosts, the G of Israel: Behold, I
44:25 LORD of hosts, the G of Israel: You and
44:26 saying, 'As the Lord G lives.'
45:2 says the LORD, the G of Israel, to you,
46:10 day of the Lord G of hosts, a day
46:10 For the Lord G of hosts holds a sacrifice
46:25 LORD of hosts, the G of Israel, said: "Behold,
48:1 LORD of hosts, the G of Israel: "Woe to
48:35 the high place and burns incense to his G
49:5 you, says the Lord G of hosts, from all
50:4 come; and they shall seek the LORD their G
50:18 LORD of hosts, the G of Israel: Behold, I
50:25 wrath, for the Lord G of hosts has a
50:28 of the LORD our G, vengeance for his temple.
50:31 one, says the Lord G of hosts; for your
50:40 As when G overthrew Sodom and Gomorrah and
51:5 been forsaken by their G, the LORD of hosts;
51:10 in Zion the work of the LORD our G
51:33 LORD of hosts, the G of Israel: The daughter
51:56 the LORD is a G of recompense, he will

Lam 3:41 hearts and hands to G in heaven:

Bar 1:10 of the Lord our G;
1:13 to the Lord our G, for we have sinned
1:13 against the Lord our G, and to this day
1:15 to the Lord our G, but confusion of face,
1:18 of the Lord our G, to walk in the
1:19 to the Lord our G, and we have been
1:21 of the Lord our G in all the words
1:21 evil in the sight of the Lord our G
2:5 against the Lord our G, in not heeding his
2:6 to the Lord our G, but confusion of face
2:11 "'And now, O Lord G of Israel, who didst
2:12 wrong, O Lord our G, against all thy ordinances.
2:15 art the Lord our G, for Israel and his
2:19 thee our prayer for mercy, O Lord our G
2:27 us, O Lord our G, in all thy kindness
2:31 will know that I am the Lord their G
2:35 them to be their G and they shall be
3:1 "'O Lord Almighty, G of Israel, the soul in
3:4 O Lord Almighty, G of Israel, hear now the
3:4 of the Lord their G, so that calamities have
3:6 art the Lord our G, and thee, O Lord,
3:8 of our fathers who forsook the Lord our G
3:13 in the way of G, you would be dwelling
3:24 O Israel, how great is the house of G
3:27 G did not choose them, nor give them the
3:35 This is our G; no other can be compared
4:1 of the commandments of G, and the law that
4:4 Israel, for we know what is pleasing to G
4:6 handed over to your enemies because you angered G
4:7 you, by sacrificing to demons and not to G
4:8 You forgot the everlasting G, who brought you up,
4:9 came upon you from G, and she said: "Hearken,
4:9 you neighbors of Zion, G has brought great sorrow
4:12 because they turned away from the law of G
4:13 in the ways of G's commandments, nor tread the
4:21 my children, cry to G, and he will deliver
4:23 sorrow and weeping, but G will give you back
4:24 see your salvation by G, which will come to
4:25 the wrath that has come upon you from G
4:27 children, and cry to G, for you will be
4:28 to go astray from G, return with tenfold zeal
4:36 the joy that is coming to you from G
4:37 the Holy One, rejoicing in the glory of G
5:1 for ever the beauty of the glory from G
5:2 of the righteousness from G; put on your head
5:3 For G will show your splendor everywhere under
5:4 ever be called by G, "Peace of righteousness and
5:5 Holy One, rejoicing that G has remembered them.
5:6 by their enemies; but G will bring them back
5:7 For G has ordered that every high mountain and
5:7 Israel may walk safely in the glory of G
5:8 have shaded Israel at G's command.
5:9 For G will lead Israel with joy, in the
6:1 them the message which G had commanded him.
6:2 you have committed before G, you will be taken
6:14 a local ruler the G holds a scepter, though
6:51 is no work of G in them.
6:62 When G commands the clouds to go over the

Ezek 1:1 heavens were opened, and I saw visions of G
2:4 'Thus says the Lord G
3:11 'Thus says the Lord G; whether they hear or
3:27 'Thus says the Lord G; he that will hear,
4:14 Then I said, "Ah Lord G
5:5 Thus says the Lord G: This is Jerusalem; I
5:7 thus says the Lord G: Because you are more
5:8 thus says the Lord G: Behold, I, even I,
5:11 live, says the Lord G, surely, because you have
6:3 of Israel, hear the word of the Lord G
6:3 Thus says the Lord G to the mountains and
6:11 Thus says the Lord G: "Clap your hands, and
7:2 thus says the Lord G to the land of
7:5 "Thus says the Lord G: Disaster after disaster!
8:1 hand of the Lord G fell there upon me.
8:3 me in visions of G to Jerusalem, to the
8:4 the glory of the G of Israel was there,
9:3 the glory of the G of Israel had gone
9:8 fell upon my face, and cried, "Ah Lord G
10:5 like the voice of G Almighty when he speaks.
10:19 the glory of the G of Israel was over
10:20 I saw underneath the G of Israel by the
11:7 thus says the Lord G: Your slain whom you
11:8 bring the sword upon you, says the Lord G
11:13 with a loud voice, and said, "Ah Lord G
11:16 'Thus says the Lord G: Though I removed them
11:17 'Thus says the Lord G: I will gather you
11:20 be my people, and I will be their G
11:21 deeds upon their own heads, says the Lord G
11:22 the glory of the G of Israel was over
11:24 by the Spirit of G into Chaldea, to the
12:10 'Thus says the Lord G: This oracle concerns the
12:19 Thus says the Lord G concerning the inhabitants of
12:23 'Thus says the Lord G: I will put an
12:25 the word and perform it, says the Lord G
12:28 Thus says the Lord G: None of my words
12:28 I speak will be performed, says the Lord G
13:3 Thus says the Lord G, Woe to the foolish
13:8 thus says the Lord G: "Because you have uttered
13:8 behold, I am against you, says the Lord G
13:9 you shall know that I am the Lord G
13:13 thus says the Lord G: I will make a
13:16 when there was no peace, says the Lord G
13:18 Thus says the Lord G: Woe to the women
13:20 thus says the Lord G: Behold, I am against
14:4 Thus says the Lord G: Any man of the

14:6 Thus says the Lord G: Repent and turn away
14:11 I may be their G, says the Lord GOD."
14:11 I may be their God, says the Lord G
14:14 own lives by their righteousness, says the Lord G
14:16 live, says the Lord G, they would deliver neither
14:18 live, says the Lord G, they would deliver neither
14:20 live, says the Lord G, they would deliver neither
14:21 thus says the Lord G: How much more when
14:23 I have done in it, says the Lord G
15:6 thus says the Lord G: Like the wood of
15:8 because they have acted faithlessly, says the Lord G
16:3 Thus says the Lord G to Jerusalem: Your origin
16:8 you, says the Lord G, and you became mine.
16:14 I had bestowed upon you, says the Lord G
16:19 them for a pleasing odor, says the Lord G
16:23 says the Lord G,
16:30 heart, says the Lord G, seeing you did all
16:36 Thus says the Lord G, Because your shame was
16:43 your deeds upon your head, says the Lord G
16:48 live, says the Lord G, your sister Sodom and
16:59 thus says the Lord G: I will deal with
16:63 all that you have done, says the Lord G
17:3 Thus says the Lord G: A great eagle with
17:9 Thus says the Lord G: Will it thrive?
17:16 live, says the Lord G, surely in the place
17:19 thus says the Lord G: As I live, surely
17:22 Thus says the Lord G: "I myself will take
18:3 live, says the Lord G, this proverb shall no
18:9 righteous, he shall surely live, says the Lord G
18:23 wicked, says the Lord G, and not rather that
18:30 one according to his ways, says the Lord G
18:32 one, says the Lord G; so turn, and live."
20:3 Thus says the Lord G, Is it to inquire
20:3 live, says the Lord G, I will not be
20:5 Thus says the Lord G: On the day when
20:5 to them, saying, I am the LORD your G
20:7 idols of Egypt; I am the LORD your G
20:19 the LORD am your G; walk in my statutes,
20:20 may know that I the LORD am your G
20:27 Thus says the Lord G: In this again your
20:30 Thus says the Lord G: Will you defile yourselves
20:31 live, says the Lord G, I will not be
20:33 live, says the Lord G, surely with a mighty
20:36 enter into judgment with you, says the Lord G
20:39 thus says the Lord G: Go serve every one
20:40 Israel, says the Lord G, there all the house
20:44 doings, O house of Israel, says the Lord G
20:47 Thus says the Lord G, Behold, I will kindle
20:49 Then I said, "Ah Lord G
21:7 says the Lord G
21:13 says the Lord G
21:24 thus says the Lord G: Because you have made
21:26 thus says the Lord G: Remove the turban, and
21:28 Thus says the Lord G concerning the Ammonites,
22:3 Thus says the Lord G: A city that sheds
22:12 and you have forgotten me, says the Lord G
22:19 thus says the Lord G: Because you have all
22:28 'Thus says the Lord G when the LORD has
22:31 I requited upon their heads, says the Lord G
23:22 thus says the Lord G: "Behold, I will rouse
23:28 thus says the Lord G: Behold, I will deliver
23:32 Thus says the Lord G: "You shall drink your
23:34 breasts; for I have spoken, says the Lord G
23:35 thus says the Lord G: Because you have forgotten
23:46 thus says the Lord G: "Bring up a host
23:49 you shall know that I am the Lord G
24:3 Thus says the Lord G: Set on the pot,
24:6 thus says the Lord G: Woe to the bloody
24:9 thus says the Lord G: Woe to the bloody
24:14 doings I will judge you, says the Lord G
24:21 Thus says the Lord G: Behold, I will profane
24:24 I am the Lord G
25:3 word of the Lord G: Thus says the Lord
25:3 Thus says the Lord G, Because you said, 'Aha!'
25:6 thus says the Lord G: Because you have clapped
25:8 "Thus says the Lord G: Because Moab said, Behold,
25:12 "Thus says the Lord G: Because Edom acted
25:13 thus says the Lord G, I will stretch out
25:14 they shall know my vengeance, says the Lord G
25:15 "Thus says the Lord G: Because the Philistines
25:16 thus says the Lord G, Behold, I will stretch
26:3 thus says the Lord G: Behold, I am against
26:5 spoken, says the Lord G; and she shall become
26:7 thus says the Lord G: Behold, I will bring
26:14 I the LORD have spoken, says the Lord G
26:15 "Thus says the Lord G to Tyre: Will not
26:19 thus says the Lord G: When I make you
26:21 will never be found again, says the Lord G
27:3 thus says the Lord G: "O Tyre, you have
28:2 Thus says the Lord G: "Because your heart is
28:2 said, 'I am a G, I sit in the
28:2 a man, and no G, though you consider yourself
28:2 as wise as a G –
28:6 thus says the Lord G: "Because you consider yourself
28:6 as wise as a G,
28:9 say, 'I am a G in the presence of
28:9 a man, and no G, in the hands of
28:10 foreigners; for I have spoken, says the Lord G
28:12 Thus says the Lord G: "You were the signet
28:13 Eden, the garden of G; every precious stone was
28:14 the holy mountain of G; in the midst of
28:16 from the mountain of G, and the guardian cherub
28:22 Thus says the Lord G: "Behold, I am against
28:24 they will know that I am the Lord G
28:25 "Thus says the Lord G: When I gather the
28:26 will know that I am the LORD their G
29:3 Thus says the Lord G: "Behold, I am against
29:8 thus says the Lord G: Behold, I will bring
29:13 thus says the Lord G: At the end of
29:16 they will know that I am the Lord G
29:19 thus says the Lord G: Behold, I will give
29:20 because they worked for me, says the Lord G
30:2 Thus says the Lord G: "Wail, 'Alas for the
30:6 within her by the sword, says the Lord G
30:10 "Thus says the Lord G: I will put an
30:13 "Thus says the Lord G: I will destroy the
30:22 thus says the Lord G: Behold, I am against
31:8 in the garden of G could not rival it,
31:8 in the garden of G was like it in
31:9 envied it, that were in the garden of G
31:10 thus says the Lord G: Because it towered high
31:15 "Thus says the Lord G: When it goes down
31:18 Pharaoh and all his multitude, says the Lord G
32:3 Thus says the Lord G: I will throw my
32:8 put darkness upon your land, says the Lord G
32:11 thus says the Lord G: The sword of the
32:14 rivers to run like oil, says the Lord G
32:16 multitude, shall they chant it, says the Lord G
32:31 army, slain by the sword, says the Lord G
32:32 Pharaoh and all his multitude, says the Lord G
33:11 live, says the Lord G, I have no pleasure
33:25 Thus says the Lord G: You eat flesh with
33:27 Thus says the Lord G: As I live, surely
34:2 Thus says the Lord G: Ho, shepherds of Israel
34:8 live, says the Lord G, because my sheep have
34:10 Thus says the Lord G, Behold, I am against
34:11 thus says the Lord G: Behold, I, I myself
34:15 will make them lie down, says the Lord G
34:17 thus says the Lord G: Behold, I judge between
34:20 thus says the Lord G to them: Behold, I,
34:24 LORD, will be their G, and my servant David
34:30 I, the LORD their G, am with them, and
34:30 of Israel, are my people, says the Lord G
34:31 and I am your G, says the Lord GOD."
34:31 and I am your God, says the Lord G
35:3 Thus says the Lord G: Behold, I am against
35:6 live, says the Lord G, I will prepare you
35:11 live, says the Lord G, I will deal with
35:14 Thus says the Lord G: For the rejoicing of
36:2 Thus says the Lord G: Because the enemy said
36:3 Thus says the Lord G: Because, yea, because they
36:4 word of the Lord G: Thus says the Lord
36:4 Thus says the Lord G to the mountains and
36:5 thus says the Lord G: I speak in my
36:6 Thus says the Lord G: Behold, I speak in
36:7 thus says the Lord G: I swear that the
36:13 Thus says the Lord G: Because men say to
36:14 children, says the Lord G;
36:15 cause your nation to stumble, says the Lord G
36:22 Thus says the Lord G: It is not for
36:23 LORD, says the Lord G, when through you I
36:28 be my people, and I will be your G
36:32 act, says the Lord G; let that be known
36:33 "Thus says the Lord G: On the day that
36:37 "Thus says the Lord G: This also I will
37:3 I answered, "O Lord G, thou knowest."
37:5 Thus says the Lord G to these bones: Behold,
37:9 Thus says the Lord G: Come from the four
37:12 Thus says the Lord G: Behold, I will open
37:19 Thus says the Lord G: Behold, I am about
37:21 Thus says the Lord G: Behold, I will take
37:23 be my people, and I will be their G

37:27 I will be their G, and they shall be
38:3 Thus says the Lord G: Behold, I am against
38:10 "Thus says the Lord G: On that day thoughts
38:14 Thus says the Lord G: On that day when
38:17 "Thus says the Lord G: Are you he of
38:18 Israel, says the Lord G, my wrath will be
38:21 Gog, says the Lord G; every man's sword will
39:1 Thus says the Lord G: Behold, I am against
39:5 field; for I have spoken, says the Lord G
39:8 it will be brought about, says the Lord G
39:10 plunder those who plundered them, says the Lord G
39:13 that I show my glory, says the Lord G
39:17 thus says the Lord G: Speak to the birds
39:20 and all kinds of warriors,' says the Lord G
39:22 am the LORD their G, from that day forward.
39:25 thus says the Lord G: Now I will restore
39:28 am the LORD their G because I sent them
39:29 upon the house of Israel, says the Lord G
40:2 in the visions of G into the land of
43:2 the glory of the G of Israel came from
43:18 thus says the Lord G: These are the ordinances
43:19 me, says the Lord G, a bull for a
43:27 and I will accept you, says the Lord G
44:2 for the LORD, the G of Israel, has entered
44:6 Thus says the Lord G: O house of Israel,
44:9 thus says the Lord G: No foreigner, uncircumcised in
44:12 them, says the Lord G, that they shall bear
44:15 blood, says the Lord G;
44:27 shall offer his sin offering, says the Lord G
45:9 "Thus says the Lord G: Enough, O princes of
45:9 your evictions of my people, says the Lord G
45:15 to make atonement for them, says the Lord G
45:18 "Thus says the Lord G: In the first month,
46:1 "Thus says the Lord G: The gate of the
46:16 "Thus says the Lord G: If the prince makes
47:13 Thus says the Lord G: "These are the boundaries
47:23 shall assign him his inheritance, says the Lord G
48:29 these are their several portions, says the Lord G
Dan 1:2 of the house of G; and he brought them
1:2 the house of his G, and placed the vessels
1:2 placed the vessels in the treasury of his G
1:9 And G gave Daniel favor and compassion in the
1:17 for these four youths, G gave them learning and
2:18 seek mercy of the G of heaven concerning this
2:19 Then Daniel blessed the G of heaven.
2:20 be the name of G for ever and ever.
2:23 To thee, O G of my fathers, I give
2:28 but there is a G in heaven who reveals
2:37 kings, to whom the G of heaven has given
2:44 of those kings the G of heaven will set
2:45 A great G has made known to the king
2:47 to Daniel, "Truly, your G is God of gods
2:47 "Truly, your God is G of gods and Lord
3:15 and who is the G that will deliver you
3:17 it be so, our G whom we serve is
3:24 flames, singing hymns to G and blessing the Lord.
3:26 art thou, O Lord, G of our fathers, and
3:45 the Lord, the only G, glorious over the whole
3:51 and glorified and blessed G in the furnace, saying:
3:52 art thou, O Lord, G of our fathers, and
3:91 worship the Lord, the G of gods, sing praise
3:94 of the Most High G, come forth, and come
3:96 said, "Blessed be the G of Shadrach, Meshach, and
3:96 serve and worship any G except their own God.
3:96 serve and worship any god except their own G
3:97 speaks anything against the G of Shadrach, Meshach,
3:97 there is no other G who is able to
4:2 that the Most High G has wrought toward me.
4:8 the name of my G, and in whom is
5:3 temple, the house of G in Jerusalem; and the
5:18 king, the Most High G gave Nebuchadnezzar your
5:21 that the Most High G rules the kingdom of
5:23 or know, but the G in whose hand is
5:26 of the matter: MENE, G has numbered the days
6:5 it in connection with the law of his G
6:7 makes petition to any G or man for thirty
6:10 gave thanks before his G, as he had done
6:11 Daniel making petition and supplication before his G
6:12 makes petition to any G or man within thirty
6:16 to Daniel, "May your G, whom you serve continually,
6:20 servant of the living G, has your God, whom
6:20 living God, has your G, whom you serve continually,
6:22 My G sent his angel and shut the lions'
6:23 upon him, because he had trusted in his G
6:26 and fear before the G of Daniel, for he
6:26 he is the living G, enduring for ever; his
9:3 face to the Lord G, seeking him by prayer
9:4 to the LORD my G and made confession, saying,
9:4 the great and terrible G, who keepest covenant and
9:9 To the Lord our G belong mercy and forgiveness;
9:10 of the LORD our G by following his laws,
9:11 Moses the servant of G have been poured out
9:13 of the LORD our G, turning from our iniquities
9:14 for the LORD our G is righteous in all
9:15 now, O Lord our G, who didst bring thy
9:17 Now therefore, O our G, hearken to the prayer
9:18 O my G, incline thy ear and hear; open
9:19 own sake, O my G, because thy city and
9:20 before the LORD my G for the holy hill
9:20 holy hill of my G;
10:12 humbled yourself before your G, your words have
11:32 people who know their G shall stand firm and
11:36 magnify himself above every G, and shall speak
11:36 astonishing things against the G of gods.
11:37 heed to any other G, for he shall magnify
11:38 He shall honor the G of fortresses instead of
11:38 instead of these; a G whom his fathers did
11:39 help of a foreign G; those who acknowledge him
13:42 and said, "O eternal G, who dost discern what
13:45 be put to death, G aroused the holy spirit
13:50 and inform us, for G has given you that
13:55 for the angel of G has received the sentence
13:55 received the sentence from G and will immediately
13:59 for the angel of G is waiting with his
13:60 shouted loudly and blessed G, who saves those who
13:63 and his wife praised G for their daughter Susanna,
14:4 But Daniel worshiped his own G
14:5 idols, but the living G, who created heaven and
14:6 you not think that Bel is a living G
14:24 this is a living G; so worship him."
14:25 worship the Lord my G, for he is the
14:25 Lord my God, for he is the living G
14:37 Take the dinner which G has sent you."
14:38 hast remembered me, O G, and hast not forsaken
14:39 And the angel of G immediately returned Habakkuk
14:41 art great, O Lord G of Daniel, and there
Hos 1:7 by the LORD their G; I will not deliver
1:9 not my people and I am not your G
1:10 be said to them, "Sons of the living G
2:23 people'; and he shall say 'Thou art my G
3:5 seek the LORD their G, and David their king;
4:1 and no knowledge of G in the land;
4:6 the law of your G, I also will forget
4:12 they have left their G to play the harlot.
5:4 do not permit them to return to their G
6:6 sacrifice, the knowledge of G, rather than burnt
7:11 to the LORD their G, nor seek him, for
8:2 me they cry, My G, we Israel know thee.
8:6 A workman made it; it is not G
9:1 for you have played the harlot, forsaking your G
9:8 the people of my G, yet a fowler's snare
9:8 ways, and hatred in the house of his G
9:17 My G will cast them off, because they have
11:9 Ephraim; for I am G and not man, the
11:12 is still known by G, and is faithful to
12:3 heel, and in his manhood he strove with G
12:4 He met G at Bethel, and there God spoke
12:4 at Bethel, and there G spoke with him –
12:5 the LORD the G of hosts, the LORD
12:6 the help of your G, return, hold fast to
12:6 love and justice, and wait continually for your G
12:9 am the LORD your G from the land of
13:4 am the LORD your G from the land of
13:4 Egypt; you know no G but me, and besides
13:16 has rebelled against her G; they shall fall by
14:1 to the LORD your G, for you have stumbled
14:3 say no more, 'Our G to the work of
Joel 1:12 the night in sackcloth, O ministers of my G
1:12 offering are withheld from the house of your G
1:13 of the LORD your G; and cry to the
1:15 joy and gladness from the house of our G
2:13 to the LORD, your G, for he is gracious
2:14 and a drink offering for the LORD, your G
2:17 they say among the peoples, 'Where is their G
2:23 in the LORD, your G; for he has given
2:26 of the LORD your G, who has dealt wondrously
2:27 the LORD, am your G and there is none
3:17 am the LORD your G, who dwell in Zion,
Amos 1:8 says the Lord G
2:8 the house of their G they drink the wine
3:7 Surely the Lord G does nothing, without revealing
3:8 The Lord G has spoken; who can but prophesy?"

GOD

3:11 thus says the Lord G: "An adversary shall surround
3:13 says the Lord G, the God of hosts,
3:13 the Lord GOD, the G of hosts,
4:2 may drink!' The Lord G has sworn by his
4:5 says the Lord G
4:11 of you, as when G overthrew Sodom and Gomorrah,
4:12 prepare to meet your G, O Israel!"
4:13 earth--the LORD, the G of hosts, is his
5:3 thus says the Lord G: "The city that went
5:14 so the LORD, the G of hosts, will be
5:15 that the LORD, the G of hosts, will be
5:16 says the LORD, the G of hosts, the Lord:
5:27 whose name is the G of hosts.
6:8 The Lord G has sworn by himself (says the
6:8 (says the LORD, the G of hosts): "I abhor
6:14 says the LORD, the G of hosts; "and they
7:1 Thus the Lord G showed me: behold, he was
7:2 I said, "O Lord G, forgive, I beseech thee!
7:4 Thus the Lord G showed me: behold, the Lord
7:4 me: behold, the Lord G was calling for a
7:5 I said, "O Lord G, cease, I beseech thee!
7:6 said the Lord G
8:1 Thus the Lord G showed me: behold, a basket
8:3 says the Lord G; "the dead bodies shall be
8:9 says the Lord G, "I will make the sun
8:11 says the Lord G, "when I will send a
8:14 and say, 'As thy G lives, O Dan,' and,
9:5 The Lord, G of hosts, he who touches the
9:8 eyes of the Lord G are upon the sinful
9:15 says the LORD your G
Obad 1:1 Thus says the Lord G concerning Edom: We have
Jon 1:5 each cried to his G; and they threw the
1:6 Arise, call upon your G
1:6 Perhaps the G will give a thought to us,
1:9 fear the LORD, the G of heaven, who made
2:1 to the LORD his G from the belly of
2:6 my life from the Pit, O LORD my G
3:5 people of Nineveh believed G; they proclaimed a
3:8 them cry mightily to G; yea, let every one
3:9 Who knows, G may yet repent and turn from
3:10 When G saw what they did, how they turned
3:10 from their evil way, G repented of the evil
4:2 thou art a gracious G and merciful, slow to
4:6 And the LORD G appointed a plant, and made
4:7 up the next day, G appointed a worm which
4:8 When the sun rose, G appointed a sultry east
4:9 But G said to Jonah, "Do you do well
Mic 1:2 and let the Lord G be a witness against
3:7 their lips, for there is no answer from G
4:2 the house of the G of Jacob; that he
4:5 the name of its G, but we will walk
4:5 of the LORD our G for ever and ever.
5:4 majesty of the name of the LORD his G
6:6 and bow myself before G on high?
6:8 love kindness, and to walk humbly with your G
7:7 will wait for the G of my salvation; my
7:7 of my salvation; my G will hear me.
7:10 said to me, "Where is the LORD your G
7:17 to the LORD our G, and they shall fear
7:18 Who is a G like thee, pardoning iniquity and
Nah 1:2 LORD is a jealous G and avenging, the LORD
Hab 1:1 The oracle of G which Habakkuk the prophet
1:11 on, guilty men, whose own might is their G
1:12 everlasting, O LORD my G, my Holy One?
3:3 G came from Teman, and the Holy One from
3:18 will joy in the G of my salvation.
3:19 G, the Lord, is my strength; he makes my
Zeph 1:7 Be silent before the Lord G
2:7 For the LORD their G will be mindful of
2:9 LORD of hosts, the G of Israel, "Moab shall
3:2 LORD, she does not draw near to her G
3:17 The LORD, your G, is in your midst, a
Hag 1:12 of the LORD their G, and the words of
1:12 as the LORD their G had sent him; and
1:14 LORD of hosts, their G,
Zech 6:15 diligently obey the voice of the LORD your G
8:8 I will be their G, in faithfulness and in
8:23 we have heard that G is with you.'"
9:7 a remnant for our G; it shall be like
9:14 like lightning; the Lord G will sound the trumpet,
9:16 day the LORD their G will save them for
10:6 am the LORD their G and I will answer
11:4 said the LORD my G: "Become shepherd of the
12:5 LORD of hosts, their G
12:8 David shall be like G, like the angel of
13:9 and they will say, 'The LORD is my G
14:5 Then the LORD your G will come, and all
Mal 1:9 entreat the favor of G, that he may be
2:10 Has not one G created us?
2:11 and has married the daughter of a foreign G
2:15 Has not the one G made and sustained for
2:16 says the LORD the G of Israel, and covering
2:17 asking, "Where is the G of justice?"
3:8 say, 'How shall we return?' Will man rob G
3:14 You have said, 'It is vain to serve G
3:15 but when they put G to the test they
3:18 between one who serves G and one who does
2Mac 1:2 May G do good to you, and may he
1:11 Having been saved by G out of grave dangers
1:17 every way be our G, who has brought judgment
1:20 passed, when it pleased G, Nehemiah, having been
1:24 effect: "O Lord, Lord G, Creator of all things,
1:27 let the Gentiles know that thou art our G
2:4 gone up and had seen the inheritance of G
2:7 shall be unknown until G gathers his people together
2:17 It is G who has saved all his people,
2:18 we have hope in G that he will soon
3:24 by the power of G, and became faint with
3:28 and they recognized clearly the sovereign power of G
3:34 report to all men the majestic power of G
3:36 deeds of the supreme G, which he had seen
3:38 certainly is about the place some power of G
6:1 by the laws of G,
7:6 nobly, saying, "The Lord G is watching over us
7:14 cherish the hope that G gives of being raised
7:16 do not think that G has forsaken our people.
7:18 account, because of our sins against our own G
7:19 go unpunished for having tried to fight against G
7:28 them, and recognize that G did not make them
7:29 death, so that in G's mercy I may get
7:31 Hebrews, will certainly not escape the hands of G
7:35 escaped the judgment of the almighty, all-seeing G
7:36 of everflowing life under G's covenant; but you, by
7:36 by the judgment of G, will receive just punishment
7:37 our fathers, appealing to G to show mercy soon
7:37 that he alone is G,
8:13 cowardly and distrustful of G's justice ran off and
8:18 trust in the Almighty G, who is able with
8:23 and gave the watchword, G's help"; then, leading the
9:5 the all-seeing Lord, the G of Israel, struck him
9:8 making the power of G manifest to all.
9:11 under the scourge of G, for he was tortured
9:12 to be subject to G, and no mortal should
9:12 mortal should think that he is equal to G
9:17 every inhabited place to proclaim the power of G
9:18 for the judgment of G had justly come upon
10:16 solemn supplication and beseeching G to fight on
10:25 girded their loins with sackcloth, in supplication to G
11:4 of the power of G, but was elated with
11:9 praised the merciful G, and were strengthened in
11:13 invincible because the mighty G fought on their side.
12:6 calling upon G the righteous Judge, attacked
12:11 men won the victory, by the help of G
12:16 by the will of G, and slaughtered untold numbers,
13:13 by the help of G before the king's army
13:15 his men the watchword, G's victory," and with a
14:33 level this precinct of G to the ground and
15:14 and the holy city, Jeremiah, the prophet of G
15:16 sword, a gift from G, with which you will
15:26 battle with invocation to G and prayers.
15:27 hands and praying to G in their hearts, they
15:27 were greatly gladdened by G's manifestation.
Mt 1:23 (which means, G with us).
3:9 for I tell you, G is able from these
3:16 saw the Spirit of G descending like a dove,
4:3 are the Son of G, command these stones to
4:4 every word that proceeds from the mouth of G
4:6 are the Son of G, throw yourself down; for
4:7 written, 'You shall not tempt the Lord your G
4:10 worship the Lord your G and him only shall
5:8 the pure in heart, for they shall see G
5:9 peacemakers, for they shall be called sons of G
5:34 is the throne of G,
6:24 You cannot serve G and mammon.
6:30 But if G so clothes the grass of the
8:29 you to do with us, O Son of G
9:8 afraid, and they glorified G, who had given such
12:4 entered the house of G and ate the bread
12:28 by the Spirit of G that I cast out
12:28 then the kingdom of G has come upon you.
14:33 him, saying, "Truly you are the Son of G
15:3 transgress the commandment of G for the sake of

15:4 For G commanded, 'Honor your father and your
15:5 me is given to G, he need not honor
15:6 tradition, you have made void the word of G
15:31 and they glorified the G of Israel.
16:16 are the Christ, the Son of the living G
16:22 to rebuke him, saying, G forbid, Lord!
16:23 on the side of G, but of men."
19:6 What therefore G has joined together, let not man
19:24 a rich man to enter the kingdom of G
19:26 is impossible, but with G all things are possible."
21:12 entered the temple of G and drove out all
21:31 into the kingdom of G before you.
21:43 you, the kingdom of G will be taken away
22:16 teach the way of G truthfully, and care for
22:21 are Caesars, and to G the things that are
22:29 know neither the scriptures nor the power of G
22:31 said to you by G,
22:32 God, 'I am the G of Abraham, and the
22:32 of Abraham, and the G of Isaac, and the
22:32 of Isaac, and the G of Jacob?
22:32 He is not G of the dead, but of
22:37 love the Lord your G with all your heart,
23:21 by the throne of G and by him who
26:61 destroy the temple of G, and to build it
26:63 you by the living G, tell us if you
26:63 if you are the Christ, the Son of G
27:40 are the Son of G, come down from the
27:43 He trusts in G; let God deliver him now,
27:43 trusts in God; let G deliver him now, if
27:43 for he said, 'I am the Son of G
27:46 that is, "My G, my God, why hast thou
27:46 is, "My God, my G, why hast thou forsaken
27:54 and said, "Truly this was the Son of G
Mk 1:1 the gospel of Jesus Christ, the Son of G
1:14 preaching the gospel of G,
1:15 and the kingdom of G is at hand; repent,
1:24 know who you are, the Holy One of G
2:7 can forgive sins but G alone?"
2:12 all amazed and glorified G, saying, "We never saw
2:26 entered the house of G, when Abiathar was high
3:11 and cried out, "You are the Son of G
3:35 does the will of G is my brother, and
4:11 of the kingdom of G, but for those outside
4:26 said, "The kingdom of G is as if a
4:30 compare the kingdom of G, or what parable shall
5:7 with me, Jesus, Son of the Most High G
5:7 I adjure you by G, do not torment me."
7:8 leave the commandment of G, and hold fast the
7:9 rejecting the commandment of G, in order to keep
7:11 (that is, given to G –
7:13 void the word of G through your tradition which
8:33 on the side of G, but of men."
9:1 that the kingdom of G has come with power."
9:45 enter the kingdom of G with one eye than
10:6 the beginning of creation, G made them male and
10:9 What therefore G has joined together, let not man
10:14 them; for to such belongs the kingdom of G
10:15 receive the kingdom of G like a child shall
10:18 one is good but G alone.
10:23 trust in riches to enter the kingdom of G
10:24 trust in riches to enter the kingdom of G
10:25 a rich man to enter the kingdom of G
10:27 impossible, but not with G; for all things are
10:27 with God; for all things are possible with G
11:22 And Jesus answered them, "Have faith in G
12:14 of men, but truly teach the way of G
12:17 are Caesars, and to G the things that are
12:24 know neither the scriptures nor the power of G
12:26 about the bush, how G said to him, 'I
12:26 him, 'I am the G of Abraham, and the
12:26 of Abraham, and the G of Isaac, and the
12:26 of Isaac, and the G of Jacob?
12:27 He is not G of the dead, but of
12:29 Israel: The Lord our G, the Lord is one;
12:30 love the Lord your G with all your heart,
12:34 "You are not far from the kingdom of G
13:19 of the creation which G created until now, and
14:25 I drink it new in the kingdom of G
15:33 which means, "My G, my God, why hast thou
15:33 means, "My God, my G, why hast thou forsaken
15:38 said, "Truly this man was the Son of G
15:42 for the kingdom of G, took courage and went
16:19 and sat down at the right hand of G
Lk 1:6 were both righteous before G, walking in all the
1:8 serving as priest before G when his division was
1:16 to the Lord their G,
1:19 in the presence of G; and I was sent
1:26 Gabriel was sent from G to a city of
1:30 afraid, Mary, for you have found favor with G
1:32 High; and the Lord G will give to him
1:35 born will be called holy, the Son of G
1:37 For with G nothing will be impossible."
1:47 my spirit rejoices in G my Savior,
1:64 and his tongue loosed, and he spoke, blessing G
1:68 "Blessed be the Lord G of Israel, for he
1:78 tender mercy of our G, when the day shall
2:13 the heavenly host praising G and saying,
2:14 and saying, "Glory to G in the highest, and
2:20 returned, glorifying and praising G for all they had
2:28 his arms and blessed G and said,
2:38 she gave thanks to G, and spoke of him
2:40 and the favor of G was upon him.
2:52 and in favor with G and man.
3:2 Caiaphas, the word of G came to John the
3:6 and all flesh shall see the salvation of G
3:8 for I tell you, G is able from these
3:38 Seth, the son of Adam, the son of G
4:3 are the Son of G, command this stone to
4:8 worship the Lord your G, and him only shall
4:9 are the Son of G, throw yourself down from
4:12 said, 'You shall not tempt the Lord your G
4:34 know who you are, the Holy One of G
4:41 of many, crying, "You are the Son of G
4:43 of the kingdom of G to the other cities
5:1 hear the word of G, he was standing by
5:21 can forgive sins but G only?"
5:25 on which he lay, and went home, glorifying G
5:26 all, and they glorified G and were filled with
6:4 entered the house of G, and took and ate
6:12 and all night he continued in prayer to G
6:20 you poor, for yours is the kingdom of G
7:16 all; and they glorified G, saying, "A great prophet
7:16 and G has visited his people!"
7:28 in the kingdom of G is greater than he."
7:29 the tax collectors justified G, having been baptized
7:30 rejected the purpose of G for themselves, not having
8:1 bringing the good news of the kingdom of G
8:10 of the kingdom of G; but for others they
8:11 is this: The seed is the word of G
8:21 hear the word of G and do it."
8:28 with me, Jesus, Son of the Most High G
8:39 and declare how much G has done for you."
9:2 preach the kingdom of G and to heal.
9:11 of the kingdom of G, and cured those who
9:20 And Peter answered, "The Christ of G
9:27 taste death before they see the kingdom of G
9:43 And all were astonished at the majesty of G
9:60 for you, go and proclaim the kingdom of G
9:62 looks back is fit for the kingdom of G
10:9 them, 'The kingdom of G has come near to
10:11 that the kingdom of G has come near.'
10:27 love the Lord your G with all your heart,
11:20 by the finger of G that I cast out
11:20 then the kingdom of G has come upon you.
11:28 hear the word of G and keep it!"
11:42 and the love of G; these you ought to
11:49 also the Wisdom of G said, 'I will send
12:6 And not one of them is forgotten before G
12:8 before the angels of G;
12:9 men will be denied before the angels of G
12:20 drink, be merry.' But G said to him, 'Fool!
12:21 treasure for himself, and is not rich toward G
12:24 nor barn, and yet G feeds them.
12:28 But if G so clothes the grass which is
13:13 she was made straight, and she praised G
13:18 is the kingdom of G like?
13:20 "To what shall I compare the kingdom of G
13:28 in the kingdom of G and you yourselves thrust
13:29 and sit at table in the kingdom of G
14:15 who shall eat bread in the kingdom of G
15:10 before the angels of G over one sinner who
16:13 You cannot serve G and mammon."
16:15 yourselves before men, but G knows your hearts; for
16:15 men is an abomination in the sight of G
16:16 of the kingdom of G is preached, and every
17:15 healed, turned back, praising G with a loud voice;
17:18 and give praise to G except this foreigner?"
17:20 when the kingdom of G was coming, he answered
17:20 them, "The kingdom of G is not coming with
17:21 behold, the kingdom of G is in the midst
18:2 judge who neither feared G nor regarded man;
18:4 'Though I neither fear G nor regard man,

18:7 And will not G vindicate his elect, who cry
18:11 prayed thus with himself, G, I thank thee that
18:13 beat his breast, saying, G, be merciful to me
18:16 them; for to such belongs the kingdom of G
18:17 receive the kingdom of G like a child shall
18:19 one is good but G alone.
18:24 who have riches to enter the kingdom of G
18:25 a rich man to enter the kingdom of G
18:27 "What is impossible with men is possible with G
18:29 of the kingdom of G,
18:43 and followed him, glorifying G; and all the people,
18:43 people, when they saw it, gave praise to G
19:11 that the kingdom of G was to appear immediately.
19:37 to rejoice and praise G with a loud voice
20:16 heard this, they said, G forbid!"
20:21 no partiality, but truly teach the way of G
20:25 are Caesars, and to G the things that are
20:36 and are sons of G, being sons of the
20:37 calls the Lord the G of Abraham and the
20:37 of Abraham and the G of Isaac and the
20:37 of Isaac and the G of Jacob.
20:38 Now he is not G of the dead, but
21:31 that the kingdom of G is near.
22:16 until it is fulfilled in the kingdom of G
22:18 until the kingdom of G comes."
22:67 at the right hand of the power of G
22:68 you the Son of G, then?" And he said
23:34 is the Christ of G, his Chosen One!"
23:39 "Do you not fear G, since you are under
23:46 taken place, he praised G, and said, "Certainly this
23:50 and he was looking for the kingdom of G
24:19 deed and word before G and all the people,
24:53 joy, and were continually in the temple blessing G
Jn 1:1 the Word was with G, and the Word was
1:1 Word was with God, and the Word was G
1:2 in the beginning with G;
1:6 a man sent from G, whose name was John.
1:12 to become children of G;
1:13 nor of the will of man, but of G
1:18 one has ever seen G; the only Son, who
1:29 "Behold, the Lamb of G, who takes away the
1:34 borne witness that this is the Son of G
1:36 he walked, and said, "Behold, the Lamb of G
1:49 answered him, "Rabbi, you are the Son of G
1:51 and the angels of G ascending and descending upon
3:2 a teacher come from G; for no one can
3:2 that you do, unless G is with him."
3:3 born anew, he cannot see the kingdom of G
3:5 the Spirit, he cannot enter the kingdom of G
3:16 For G so loved the world that he gave
3:17 For G sent the Son into the world, not
3:18 in the name of the only Son of G
3:21 seen that his deeds have been wrought in G
3:33 seal to this, that G is true.
3:34 For he whom G has sent utters the words
3:34 utters the words of G, for it is not
3:36 but the wrath of G rests upon him.
4:10 knew the gift of G, and who it is
4:24 G is spirit, and those who worship him must
5:17 sabbath but also called G his Father, making himself
5:17 called God his Father, making himself equal with G
5:24 of the Son of G, and those who hear
5:41 not the love of G within you.
5:43 seek the glory that comes from the only G
6:27 for on him has G the Father set his
6:28 we do, to be doing the works of G
6:29 is the work of G, that you believe in
6:33 For the bread of G is that which comes
6:45 all be taught by G Every one who has
6:46 him who is from G; he has seen the
6:69 know, that you are the Holy One of G
7:17 the teaching is from G or whether I am
8:40 which I heard from G; this is not what
8:41 born of fornication; we have one Father, even G
8:42 said to them, "If G were your Father, you
8:42 and came forth from G; I came not of
8:47 He who is of G hears the words of
8:47 hears the words of G; the reason why you
8:47 hear them is that you are not of G
8:54 of whom you say that he is your G
9:3 that the works of G might be made manifest
9:16 man is not from G, for he does not
9:24 said to him, "Give G the praise; we know
9:29 We know that G has spoken to Moses, but
9:31 We know that G does not listen to sinners,
9:31 is a worshiper of G and does his will,
9:31 and does his will, G listens to him.
9:33 man were not from G, he could do nothing."
10:33 because you, being a man, make yourself G
10:35 whom the word of G came (and scripture cannot
10:36 because I said, 'I am the Son of G
11:4 for the glory of G, so that the Son
11:4 that the Son of G may be glorified by
11:22 whatever you ask from G, God will give you."
11:22 you ask from God, G will give you."
11:27 Christ, the Son of G, he who is coming
11:40 would believe you would see the glory of G
11:52 one the children of G who are scattered abroad.
12:43 praise of men more than the praise of G
13:3 he had come from G and was going to
13:3 and was going to G,
13:31 glorified, and in him G is glorified;
13:32 God is glorified; if G is glorified in him,
13:32 is glorified in him, G will also glorify him
14:1 be troubled; believe in G, believe also in me.
16:2 you will think he is offering service to G
16:30 by this we believe that you came from G
17:3 thee the only true G, and Jesus Christ whom
19:7 because he has made himself the Son of G
20:17 your Father, to my G and your God."
20:17 and your Father, to my God and your G
20:28 Thomas answered him, "My Lord and my G
20:31 Christ, the Son of G, and that believing you
21:19 he was to glorify G And after this he
Acts 1:3 forty days, and speaking of the kingdom of G
2:11 in our own tongues the mighty works of G
2:17 days it shall be, G declares, that I will
2:22 attested to you by G with mighty works and
2:22 wonders and signs which G did through him in
2:23 plan and foreknowledge of G, you crucified and killed
2:24 But G raised him up, having loosed the pangs
2:30 prophet, and knowing that G had sworn with an
2:32 This Jesus G raised up, and of that we
2:33 the right hand of G, and having received from
2:36 therefore know assuredly that G has made him both
2:39 whom the Lord our G calls to him."
2:47 and generous hearts, praising G and having favor
3:8 with them, walking and leaping and praising G
3:9 him walking and praising G,
3:13 The G of Abraham and of Isaac and of
3:13 and of Jacob, the G of our fathers, glorified
3:15 Author of life, whom G raised from the dead.
3:18 But what G foretold by the mouth of all
3:21 for establishing all that G spoke by the mouth
3:22 Moses said, 'The Lord G will raise up for
3:25 of the covenant which G gave to your fathers,
3:26 the earth be blessed.' G, having raised up his
4:10 whom you crucified, whom G raised from the dead,
4:19 in the sight of G to listen to you
4:19 you rather than to G, you must judge;
4:21 for all men praised G for what had happened.
4:24 their voices together to G and said, "Sovereign Lord,
4:31 spoke the word of G with boldness.
5:4 You have not lied to men but to G
5:29 answered, "We must obey G rather than men.
5:30 The G of our fathers raised Jesus whom you
5:31 G exalted him at his right hand as Leader
5:32 the Holy Spirit whom G has given to those
5:39 if it is of G, you will not be
5:39 You might even be found opposing G
6:2 preaching the word of G to serve tables.
6:7 And the word of G increased; and the number
6:11 him speak blasphemous words against Moses and G
7:2 The G of glory appeared to our father Abraham,
7:4 after his father died, G removed him from there
7:6 And G spoke to this effect, that his posterity
7:7 which they serve,' said G, 'and after that they
7:9 him into Egypt; but G was with him,
7:17 drew near, which G had granted to Abraham,
7:20 time Moses was born, and was beautiful before G
7:25 his brethren understood that G was giving them
7:32 came, 'I am the G of your fathers, the
7:32 of your fathers, the G of Abraham and of
7:35 ruler and a judge?' G sent as both ruler
7:37 said to the Israelites, G will raise up for
7:42 But G turned and gave them over to worship
7:43 the star of the G Rephan, the figures which
7:45 dispossessed the nations which G thrust out before
7:46 in the sight of G and asked leave to
7:46 a habitation for the G of Jacob.
7:55 saw the glory of G, and Jesus standing at
7:55 the right hand of G;

7:56 of man standing at the right hand of G
8:10 is that power of G which is called Great."
8:12 about the kingdom of G and the name of
8:14 received the word of G, they sent to them
8:20 obtain the gift of G with money!
8:21 matter, for your heart is not right before G
9:20 proclaimed Jesus, saying, "He is the Son of G
10:2 devout man who feared G with all his household,
10:2 liberally to the people, and prayed constantly to G
10:3 vision an angel of G coming in and saying
10:4 your alms have ascended as a memorial before G
10:15 a second time, "What G has cleansed, you must
10:28 of another nation; but G has shown me that
10:31 and your alms have been remembered before G
10:33 in the sight of G, to hear all that
10:34 "Truly I perceive that G shows no partiality,
10:38 John preached: how G anointed Jesus of Nazareth
10:38 by the devil, for G was with him.
10:40 on a tree; but G raised him on the
10:41 who were chosen by G as witnesses, who ate
10:42 the one ordained by G to be judge of
10:46 they heard them speaking in tongues and extolling G
11:1 the Gentiles also had received the word of G
11:9 time from heaven, 'What G has cleansed you must
11:17 Holy Spirit.' If then G gave the same gift
11:17 Christ, who was I that I could withstand G
11:18 And they glorified G, saying, "Then to the Gentiles
11:18 to the Gentiles also G has granted repentance unto
11:23 saw the grace of G, he was glad; and
12:5 him was made to G by the church.
12:22 "The voice of a G, and not of man!"
12:23 he did not give G the glory; and he
12:24 But the word of G grew and multiplied.
13:5 proclaimed the word of G in the synagogues of
13:7 Saul and sought to hear the word of G
13:16 and you that fear G, listen.
13:17 The G of this people Israel chose our fathers
13:21 for a king; and G gave them Saul the
13:23 Of this man's posterity G has brought to Israel
13:26 among you that fear G, to us has been
13:30 But G raised him from the dead;
13:32 good news that what G promised to the fathers,
13:36 served the counsel of G in his own generation,
13:37 corruption; but he whom G raised up saw no
13:43 urged them to continue in the grace of G
13:44 city gathered together to hear the word of G
13:46 that the word of G should be spoken first
13:48 glorified the word of G; and as many as
14:15 things to a living G who made the heaven
14:22 many tribulations we must enter the kingdom of G
14:26 to the grace of G for the work which
14:27 and declared all that G had done with them,
15:4 they declared all that G had done with them.
15:7 in the early days G made choice among you,
15:8 And G who knows the heart bore witness to
15:10 you make trial of G by putting a yoke
15:12 what signs and wonders G had done through them
15:14 Simeon has related how G first visited the Gentiles,
15:19 Gentiles who turn to G,
16:10 into Macedonia, concluding that G had called us to
16:14 of purple goods, who was a worshiper of G
16:17 of the Most High G, who proclaim to you
16:25 and singing hymns to G, and the prisoners were
16:34 all his household that he had believed in G
17:13 that the word of G was proclaimed by Paul
17:23 inscription, 'To an unknown G. What therefore you
17:24 The G who made the world and everything in
17:27 that they should seek G, in the hope that
17:29 his offspring.' Being then G's offspring, we ought not
17:30 The times of ignorance G overlooked, but now he
18:7 Justus, a worshiper of G; his house was next
18:11 teaching the word of G among them.
18:13 persuading men to worship G contrary to the law."
18:21 return to you if G wills," and he set
18:26 him the way of G more accurately.
19:8 about the kingdom of G;
19:11 And G did extraordinary miracles by the hands of
20:21 Greeks of repentance to G and of faith in
20:24 testify to the gospel of the grace of G
20:27 from declaring to you the whole counsel of G
20:32 I commend you to G and to the word
21:19 one the things that G had done among the
21:20 And when they heard it, they glorified G
22:3 fathers, being zealous for G as you all are
22:14 And he said, 'The G of our fathers appointed
23:1 I have lived before G in all good conscience
23:3 Paul said to him, G shall strike you, you
23:4 said, "Would you revile G's high priest?"
24:13 sect, I worship the G of our fathers, believing
24:14 having a hope in G which these themselves accept,
24:15 a clear conscience toward G and toward men.
26:6 the promise made by G to our fathers,
26:8 any of you that G raises the dead?
26:18 power of Satan to G, that they may receive
26:20 repent and turn to G and perform deeds worthy
26:22 help that comes from G, and so I stand
26:29 long, I would to G that not only you
27:23 an angel of the G to whom I belong
27:24 before Caesar; and lo, G has granted you all
27:25 I have faith in G that it will be
27:35 and giving thanks to G in the presence of
28:6 their minds and said that he was a G
28:15 seeing them Paul thanked G and took courage.
28:23 to the kingdom of G and trying to convince
28:28 that this salvation of G has been sent to
28:30 preaching the kingdom of G and teaching about the

Rom 1:1 an apostle, set apart for the gospel of G
1:4 and designated Son of G in power according to
1:7 Jesus Christ; To all G's beloved in Rome, who
1:7 you and peace from G our Father and the
1:8 First, I thank my G through Jesus Christ for
1:9 For G is my witness, whom I serve with
1:10 asking that somehow by G's will I may now
1:16 is the power of G for salvation to every
1:17 it the righteousness of G is revealed through faith
1:18 For the wrath of G is revealed from heaven
1:19 can be known about G is plain to them,
1:19 plain to them, because G has shown it to
1:21 for although they knew G they did not honor
1:21 not honor him as G or give thanks to
1:23 glory of the immortal G for images resembling
1:24 Therefore G gave them up in the lusts of
1:25 exchanged the truth about G for a lie and
1:26 For this reason G gave them up to dishonorable
1:28 see fit to acknowledge G, God gave them up
1:28 fit to acknowledge God, G gave them up to
1:30 slanderers, haters of G, insolent, haughty, boastful,
1:32 Though they know G's decree that those who do
2:2 that the judgment of G rightly falls upon those
2:3 them yourself, you will escape the judgment of G
2:4 you not know that G's kindness is meant to
2:5 day of wrath when G's righteous judgment will be
2:11 For G shows no partiality.
2:13 who are righteous before G, but the doers of
2:16 according to my gospel, G judges the secrets of
2:17 of your relation to G
2:23 law, do you dishonor G by breaking the law?
2:24 written, "The name of G is blasphemed among the
2:29 His praise is not from men but from G
3:2 the Jews are entrusted with the oracles of G
3:3 Does their faithlessness nullify the faithfulness of G
3:4 Let G be true though every man be false,
3:5 show the justice of G, what shall we say?
3:5 That G is unjust to inflict wrath on us?
3:6 For then how could G judge the world?
3:7 if through my falsehood G's truthfulness abounds to
3:11 one; no one understands, no one seeks for G
3:18 is no fear of G before their eyes."
3:19 the whole world may be held accountable to G
3:21 now the righteousness of G has been manifested
3:22 it, the righteousness of G through faith in Jesus
3:23 of the glory of G,
3:25 in Christ Jesus, whom G put forward as an
3:25 This was to show G's righteousness, because in his
3:29 Or is G the God of Jews only?
3:29 Or is God the G of Jews only?
3:29 Is he not the G of Gentiles also?
3:30 of Gentiles also, since G is one; and he
4:2 has something to boast about, but not before G
4:3 "Abraham believed G, and it was reckoned to him
4:6 the man to whom G reckons righteousness apart
4:17 the presence of the G in whom he believed,
4:20 concerning the promise of G, but he grew strong
4:20 he gave glory to G,
4:21 God, fully convinced that G was able to do
5:1 we have peace with G through our Lord Jesus
5:2 in our hope of sharing the glory of G
5:5 not disappoint us, because G's love has been poured
5:8 But G shows his love for us in that
5:9 be saved by him from the wrath of G
5:10 we were reconciled to G by the death of
5:11 we also rejoice in G through our Lord Jesus

5:15 have the grace of G and the free gift
6:10 but the life he lives he lives to G
6:11 sin and alive to G in Christ Jesus.
6:13 but yield yourselves to G as men who have
6:13 your members to G as instruments of righteousness.
6:17 But thanks be to G, that you who were
6:22 have become slaves of G, the return you get
6:23 the free gift of G is eternal life in
7:4 in order that we may bear fruit for G
7:22 in the law of G, in my inmost self,
7:25 Thanks be to G through Jesus Christ our Lord!
7:25 serve the law of G with my mind, but
8:3 For G has done what the law, weakened by
8:7 flesh is hostile to G; it does not submit
8:7 does not submit to G's law, indeed it cannot;
8:8 those who are in the flesh cannot please G
8:9 fact the Spirit of G dwells in you.
8:14 by the Spirit of G are sons of God.
8:14 by the Spirit of God are sons of G
8:16 we are children of G,
8:17 then heirs, heirs of G and fellow heirs with
8:19 of the sons of G;
8:21 obtain the glorious liberty of the children of G
8:27 for the saints according to the will of G
8:28 know that in everything G works for good with
8:31 If G is for us, who is against us?
8:33 bring any charge against G's elect?
8:33 It is G who justifies;
8:34 the right hand of G, who indeed intercedes for
8:39 from the love of G in Christ Jesus our
9:5 G who is over all be blessed for ever.
9:6 though the word of G had failed.
9:8 are the children of G, but the children of
9:11 bad, in order that G's purpose of election might
9:14 Is there injustice on G's part?
9:16 or exertion, but upon G's mercy.
9:20 are you, a man, to answer back to G
9:22 What if G, desiring to show his wrath and
9:26 they will be called 'sons of the living G
10:1 desire and prayer to G for them is that
10:2 have a zeal for G, but it is not
10:3 righteousness that comes from G, and seeking to
10:3 did not submit to G's righteousness.
10:9 in your heart that G raised him from the
11:1 I ask, then, has G rejected his people?
11:2 G has not rejected his people whom he foreknew.
11:2 how he pleads with G against Israel?
11:4 But what is G's reply to him?
11:8 as it is written, G gave them a spirit
11:21 For if G did not spare the natural branches,
11:22 and the severity of G: severity toward those who
11:22 who have fallen, but G's kindness to you, provided
11:23 be grafted in, for G has the power to
11:28 they are enemies of G, for your sake; but
11:29 and the call of G are irrevocable.
11:30 were once disobedient to G but now have received
11:32 For G has consigned all men to disobedience, that
11:33 of the riches and wisdom and knowledge of G
12:1 by the mercies of G, to present your bodies
12:1 holy and acceptable to G, which is your spiritual
12:2 is the will of G, what is good and
12:3 measure of faith which G has assigned him.
12:19 to the wrath of G; for it is written,
13:1 no authority except from G, and those that exist
13:1 and those that exist have been instituted by G
13:2 the authorities resists what G has appointed, and
13:4 approval, for he is G's servant for your good.
13:4 is the servant of G to execute his wrath
13:5 not only to avoid G's wrath but also for
13:6 authorities are ministers of G, attending to this very
14:3 him who eats; for G has welcomed him.
14:6 he gives thanks to G; while he who abstains,
14:6 honor of the Lord and gives thanks to G
14:10 the judgment seat of G;
14:11 me, and every tongue shall give praise to G
14:12 of us shall give account of himself to G
14:17 For the kingdom of G is not food and
14:18 Christ is acceptable to G and approved by men.
14:20 the sake of food, destroy the work of G
14:22 keep between yourself and G; happy is he who
15:5 May the G of steadfastness and encouragement
15:6 one voice glorify the G and Father of our
15:7 Christ has welcomed you, for the glory of G
15:8 the circumcised to show G's truthfulness, in order to
15:9 the Gentiles might glorify G for his mercy.
15:13 May the G of hope fill you with all
15:15 grace given me by G
15:16 of the gospel of G, so that the offering
15:17 reason to be proud of my work for G
15:30 in your prayers to G on my behalf,
15:32 saints, so that by G's will I may come
15:33 The G of peace be with you all.
16:20 is evil; then the G of peace will soon
16:25 command of the eternal G, to bring about the
16:26 to the only wise G be glory for evermore

1Cor 1:1 by the will of G to be an apostle
1:2 To the church of G which is at Corinth,
1:3 you and peace from G our Father and the
1:4 I give thanks to G always for you because
1:4 of the grace of G which was given you
1:9 G is faithful, by whom you were called into
1:18 are being saved it is the power of G
1:20 Has not G made foolish the wisdom of the
1:21 in the wisdom of G, the world did not
1:21 world did not know G through wisdom, it pleased
1:21 through wisdom, it pleased G through the folly of
1:24 Christ the power of G and the wisdom of
1:24 the power of God and the wisdom of G
1:25 For the foolishness of G is wiser than men,
1:25 and the weakness of G is stronger than men.
1:27 of noble birth; but G chose what is foolish
1:27 to shame the wise, G chose what is weak
1:28 to shame the strong, G chose what is low
1:29 human being might boast in the presence of G
1:30 in Christ Jesus, whom G made our wisdom, our
2:1 you the testimony of G in lofty words or
2:5 wisdom of men but in the power of G
2:7 and hidden wisdom of G, which God decreed before
2:7 wisdom of God, which G decreed before the ages
2:9 of man conceived, what G has prepared for those
2:10 G has revealed to us through the Spirit.
2:10 the Spirit searches everything, even the depths of G
2:11 comprehends the thoughts of G except the Spirit of
2:11 the thoughts of God except the Spirit of G
2:12 Spirit which is from G, that we might understand
2:12 might understand the gifts bestowed on us by G
2:14 of the Spirit of G, for they are folly
3:6 planted, Apollos watered, but G gave the growth.
3:7 is anything, but only G who gives the growth.
3:9 For we are G's fellow workers; you are God's
3:9 fellow workers; you are G's field, God's building.
3:9 you are God's field, G's building.
3:10 to the grace of G given to me, like
3:16 know that you are G's temple and that God's
3:16 God's temple and that G's Spirit dwells in you?
3:17 If any one destroys G's temple, God will destroy
3:17 one destroys God's temple, G will destroy him.
3:17 For G's temple is holy, and that temple you
3:19 the wisdom of this world is folly with G
4:1 of Christ and stewards of the mysteries of G
4:5 every man will receive his commendation from G
4:9 For I think that G has exhibited us apostles
4:20 For the kingdom of G does not consist in
5:13 G judges those outside.
6:9 the unrighteous will not inherit the kingdom of G
6:10 revilers, nor robbers will inherit the kingdom of G
6:11 Jesus Christ and in the Spirit of our G
6:13 stomach for food"—and G will destroy both one
6:14 And G raised the Lord and will also raise
6:19 Holy Spirit within you, which you have from G
6:20 So glorify G in your body.
7:7 own special gift from G, one of one kind
7:15 For G has called us to peace.
7:17 him, and in which G has called him.
7:19 uncircumcision, but keeping the commandments of G
7:24 each was called, there let him remain with G
7:40 I think that I have the Spirit of G
8:3 But if one loves G, one is known by
8:4 that "there is no G but one."
8:6 us there is one G, the Father, from whom
8:8 Food will not commend us to G
9:9 it for oxen that G is concerned?
9:21 being without law toward G but under the law
10:5 with most of them G was not pleased; for
10:13 G is faithful, and he will not let you
10:20 sacrifice they offer to demons and not to G
10:31 you do, do all to the glory of G
10:32 to the church of G,
11:3 her husband, and the head of Christ is G
11:7 image and glory of G; but woman is the
11:12 all things are from G
11:13 woman to pray to G with her head uncovered?

11:16 no other practice, nor do the churches of G
11:22 despise the church of G and humiliate those who
12:3 by the Spirit of G ever says "Jesus be
12:6 it is the same G who inspires them all
12:18 But as it is, G arranged the organs in
12:24 But G has so composed the body, giving the
12:28 And G has appointed in the church first apostles,
14:2 to men but to G; for no one understands
14:18 I thank G that I speak in tongues more
14:25 face, he will worship G and declare that God
14:25 God and declare that G is really among you.
14:28 in church and speak to himself and to G
14:33 For G is not a God of confusion but
14:33 God is not a G of confusion but of
14:36 Did the word of G originate with you, or
15:9 an apostle, because I persecuted the church of G
15:10 by the grace of G I am what I
15:10 but the grace of G which is with me.
15:15 found to be misrepresenting G, because we testified
15:15 because we testified of G that he raised Christ,
15:24 delivers the kingdom to G the Father after
15:27 "For G has put all things in subjection under
15:28 things under him, that G may be everything to
15:34 For some have no knowledge of G
15:38 But G gives it a body as he has
15:50 inherit the kingdom of G, nor does the perishable
15:57 But thanks be to G, who gives us the
2Cor 1:1 by the will of G, and Timothy our brother.
1:1 To the church of G which is at Corinth,
1:2 you and peace from G our Father and the
1:3 Blessed be the G and Father of our Lord
1:3 Father of mercies and G of all comfort,
1:4 comfort with which we ourselves are comforted by G
1:9 on ourselves but on G who raises the dead;
1:12 by earthly wisdom but by the grace of G
1:18 As surely as G is faithful, our word to
1:19 For the Son of G, Jesus Christ, whom we
1:20 all the promises of G find their Yes in
1:20 the Amen through him, to the glory of G
1:21 But it is G who establishes us with you
1:23 But I call G to witness against me--it
2:14 But thanks be to G, who in Christ always
2:15 aroma of Christ to G among those who are
2:17 so many, peddlers of G's word; but as men
2:17 sincerity, as commissioned by G, in the sight of
2:17 in the sight of G we speak in Christ.
3:3 Spirit of the living G, not on tablets of
3:4 the confidence that we have through Christ toward G
3:5 our competence is from G,
4:1 by the mercy of G, we do not lose
4:2 or to tamper with G's word, but by the
4:2 to every man's conscience in the sight of G
4:4 In their case the G of this world has
4:4 glory of Christ, who is the likeness of G
4:6 For it is the G who said, "Let light
4:6 of the glory of G in the face of
4:7 transcendent power belongs to G and not to us.
4:15 it may increase thanksgiving, to the glory of G
5:1 have a building from G, a house not made
5:5 this very thing is G, who has given us
5:11 are is known to G, and I hope it
5:13 ourselves, it is for G; if we are in
5:18 All this is from G, who through Christ reconciled
5:19 that is, in Christ G was reconciling the world
5:20 are ambassadors for Christ, G making his appeal
5:20 you on behalf of Christ, be reconciled to G
5:21 in him we might become the righteousness of G
6:1 accept the grace of G in vain.
6:4 but as servants of G we commend ourselves in
6:7 and the power of G; with the weapons of
6:16 has the temple of G with idols?
6:16 temple of the living G; as God said, "I
6:16 the living God; as G said, "I will live
6:16 I will be their G, and they shall be
7:1 and make holiness perfect in the fear of G
7:6 But G, who comforts the downcast, comforted us by
7:12 be revealed to you in the sight of G
8:1 about the grace of G which has been shown
8:5 Lord and to us by the will of G
8:16 But thanks be to G who puts the same
9:7 or under compulsion, for G loves a cheerful giver.
9:8 And G is able to provide you with every
9:11 will produce thanksgiving to G;
9:12 saints but also overflows in many thanksgivings to G
9:13 service, you will glorify G by your obedience in
9:14 the surpassing grace of G in you.
9:15 Thanks be to G for his inexpressible gift!
10:5 to the knowledge of G, and take every thought
10:13 keep to the limits G has apportioned us, to
11:7 exalted, because I preached G's gospel without cost
11:11 G knows I do!
11:31 The G and Father of the Lord Jesus, he
12:2 I do not know, G knows.
12:3 I do not know, G knows--
12:19 in the sight of G that we have been
12:21 I come again my G may humble me before
13:4 in weakness, but lives by the power of G
13:4 shall live with him by the power of G
13:7 But we pray G that you may not do
13:11 in peace, and the G of love and peace
13:14 and the love of G and the fellowship of
Gal 1:1 through Jesus Christ and G the Father, who raised
1:3 you and peace from G the Father and our
1:4 the will of our G and Father;
1:10 now seeking the favor of men, or of G
1:13 persecuted the church of G violently and tried to
1:20 writing to you, before G, I do not lie!)
1:24 And they glorified G because of me.
2:6 no difference to me; G shows no partiality)--those,
2:19 to the law, that I might live to G
2:20 in the Son of G, who loved me and
2:21 nullify the grace of G; for if justification were
3:6 Thus Abraham "believed G, and it was reckoned to
3:8 scripture, foreseeing that G would justify the Gentiles
3:11 man is justified before G by the law; for
3:17 covenant previously ratified by G, so as to make
3:18 longer by promise; but G gave it to Abraham
3:20 more than one; but G is one.
3:21 Is the law then against the promises of G
3:26 are all sons of G, through faith.
4:4 time had fully come, G sent forth his Son,
4:6 because you are sons, G has sent the Spirit
4:7 So through G you are no longer a slave
4:8 you did not know G, you were in bondage
4:9 have come to know G, or rather to be
4:9 to be known by G, how can you turn
4:14 as an angel of G, as Christ Jesus.
5:21 such things shall not inherit the kingdom of G
6:7 Do not be deceived; G is not mocked, for
6:16 walk by this rule, upon the Israel of G
Eph 1:1 by the will of G, To the saints who
1:2 you and peace from G our Father and the
1:3 Blessed be the G and Father of our Lord
1:17 my prayers, that the G of our Lord Jesus
2:4 But G, who is rich in mercy, out of
2:8 is the gift of G --
2:10 for good works, which G prepared beforehand, that
2:12 no hope and without G in the world.
2:16 reconcile us both to G in one body through
2:19 of the household of G,
2:22 a dwelling place of G in the Spirit.
3:2 of the stewardship of G's grace that was given
3:7 to the gift of G's grace which was given
3:9 hidden for ages in G who created all things;
3:10 the manifold wisdom of G might now be made
3:19 may be filled with all the fulness of G
4:6 faith, one baptism, one G and Father of us
4:13 of the Son of G, to mature manhood, to
4:18 from the life of G because of the ignorance
4:24 after the likeness of G in true righteousness and
4:30 the Holy Spirit of G, in whom you were
4:32 forgiving one another, as G in Christ forgave you.
5:1 Therefore be imitators of G, as beloved children.
5:2 for us, a fragrant offering and sacrifice to G
5:5 inheritance in the kingdom of Christ and of G
5:6 that the wrath of G comes upon the sons
5:20 Lord Jesus Christ to G the Father.
6:6 doing the will of G from the heart,
6:11 the whole armor of G, that you may be
6:13 the whole armor of G, that you may be
6:17 of the Spirit, which is the word of G
6:23 love with faith, from G the Father and the
Phil 1:2 you and peace from G our Father and the
1:3 I thank my G in all my remembrance of
1:8 For G is my witness, how I yearn for
1:11 Jesus Christ, to the glory and praise of G
1:14 speak the word of G without fear.
1:28 destruction, but of your salvation, and that from G
2:6 in the form of G, did not count equality
2:6 not count equality with G a thing to be
2:9 Therefore G has highly exalted him and bestowed on
2:11 to the glory of G the Father.

GOD

2:13 fear and trembling; for G is at work in
2:15 and innocent, children of G without blemish in the
2:27 But G had mercy on him, and not only
3:3 true circumcision, who worship G in spirit, and glory
3:9 the righteousness from G that depends on faith;
3:14 the upward call of G in Christ Jesus.
3:15 you are otherwise minded, G will reveal that also
3:19 end is destruction, their G is the belly, and
4:6 thanksgiving let your requests be made known to G
4:7 And the peace of G, which passes all understanding,
4:9 me, do; and the G of peace will be
4:18 offering, a sacrifice acceptable and pleasing to G
4:19 And my G will supply every need of yours
4:20 To our G and Father be glory for ever
Col 1:1 by the will of G, and Timothy our brother,
1:2 you and peace from G our Father.
1:3 We always thank G, the Father of our Lord
1:6 understood the grace of G in truth,
1:10 good work and increasing in the knowledge of G
1:15 image of the invisible G, the first-born of all
1:19 all the fulness of G was pleased to dwell,
1:25 make the word of G fully known,
1:27 To them G chose to make known how great
2:2 and the knowledge of G's mystery, of Christ,
2:12 in the working of G, who raised him from
2:13 uncircumcision of your flesh, G made alive together
2:19 ligaments, grows with a growth that is from G
3:1 Christ is, seated at the right hand of G
3:3 and your life is hid with Christ in G
3:6 these the wrath of G is coming.
3:12 Put on then, as G's chosen ones, holy and
3:16 spiritual songs with thankfulness in your hearts to G
3:17 Jesus, giving thanks to G the Father through him.
4:3 for us also, that G may open to us
4:11 for the kingdom of G, and they have been
4:12 and fully assured in all the will of G
1Thes 1:1 of the Thessalonians in G the Father and the
1:2 We give thanks to G always for you all,
1:3 remembering before our G and Father your work of
1:4 know, brethren beloved by G, that he has chosen
1:8 but your faith in G has gone forth everywhere,
1:9 how you turned to G from idols, to serve
1:9 a living and true G,
2:2 had courage in our G to declare to you
2:2 you the gospel of G in the face of
2:4 have been approved by G to be entrusted with
2:4 men, but to please G who tests our hearts.
2:5 cloak for greed, as G is witness;
2:8 only the gospel of G but also our own
2:9 while we preached to you the gospel of G
2:10 You are witnesses, and G also, how holy and
2:12 a life worthy of G, who calls you into
2:13 And we also thank G constantly for this, that
2:13 received the word of G which you heard from
2:13 is, the word of G, which is at work
2:14 of the churches of G in Christ Jesus which
2:15 us out, and displease G and oppose all men
2:16 But G's wrath has come upon them at last!
3:2 Timothy, our brother and G's servant in the gospel
3:9 can we render to G for you, for all
3:9 your sake before our G,
3:11 Now may our G and Father himself, and our
3:13 in holiness before our G and Father, at the
4:1 live and to please G, just as you are
4:3 is the will of G, your sanctification: that you
4:5 who do not know G;
4:7 For G has not called us for uncleanness, but
4:8 disregards not man but G, who gives his Holy
4:9 have been taught by G to love one another;
4:14 even so, through Jesus, G will bring with him
4:16 and with the sound of the trumpet of G
5:9 For G has not destined us for wrath, but
5:18 is the will of G in Christ Jesus for
5:23 May the G of peace himself sanctify you wholly;
2Thes 1:1 of the Thessalonians in G our father and the
1:2 you and peace from G the Father and the
1:3 to give thanks to G always for you, brethren,
1:4 in the churches of G for your steadfastness and
1:5 the righteous judgment of G, that you may be
1:5 of the kingdom of G, for which you are
1:6 suffering– since indeed G deems it just to
1:8 who do not know G and upon those who
1:11 for you, that our G may make you worthy
1:12 the grace of our G and the Lord Jesus
2:4 against every so-called G or object of worship,
2:4 in the temple of G, proclaiming himself to be
2:4 the temple of God, proclaiming himself to be G
2:11 Therefore G sends upon them a strong delusion, to
2:13 to give thanks to G always for you, brethren
2:13 by the Lord, because G chose you from the
2:16 Jesus Christ himself, and G our Father, who loved
3:5 to the love of G and to the steadfastness
1Tim 1:1 Jesus by command of G our Savior and of
1:2 mercy, and peace from G the Father and Christ
1:11 gospel of the blessed G with which I have
1:17 immortal, invisible, the only G, be honor and glory
2:3 in the sight of G our Savior,
2:5 For there is one G, and there is one
2:5 is one mediator between G and men, the man
3:5 can he care for G's church?
3:15 in the household of G, which is the church
3:15 church of the living G, the pillar and bulwark
4:3 abstinence from foods which G created to be
4:4 For everything created by G is good, and nothing
4:5 by the word of G and prayer.
4:10 set on the living G, who is the Savior
5:4 for this is acceptable in the sight of G
5:5 set her hope on G and continues in supplications
5:21 In the presence of G and of Christ Jesus
6:1 that the name of G and the teaching may
6:11 for you, man of G, shun all this; aim
6:13 In the presence of G who gives life to
6:17 uncertain riches but on G who richly furnishes us
2Tim 1:1 by the will of G according to the promise
1:2 mercy, and peace from G the Father and Christ
1:3 I thank G whom I serve with a clear
1:6 rekindle the gift of G that is within you
1:7 of my hands; for G did not give us
1:8 in the power of G,
2:9 But the word of G is not fettered.
2:15 to present yourself to G as one approved, a
2:19 But G's firm foundation stands, bearing this seal:
2:25 G may perhaps grant that they will repent and
3:4 rather than lovers of G,
3:16 scripture is inspired by G and profitable for teaching,
3:17 that the man of G may be complete, equipped
4:1 in the presence of G and of Christ Jesus
Tit 1:1 Paul, a servant of G and an apostle of
1:1 further the faith of G's elect and their knowledge
1:2 of eternal life which G, who never lies, promised
1:3 entrusted by command of G our Savior; To Titus,
1:3 Grace and peace from G the Father and Christ
1:6 For a bishop, as G's steward, must be blameless;
1:15 They profess to know G, but they deny him
2:5 that the word of G may not be discredited.
2:10 adorn the doctrine of G our Savior.
2:11 For the grace of G has appeared for the
2:13 glory of our great G and Savior Jesus Christ,
3:4 and loving kindness of G our Savior appeared,
3:8 who have believed in G may be careful to
Philem 1:3 you and peace from G our Father and the
1:4 I thank my G always when I remember you
Heb 1:1 many and various ways G spoke of old to
1:3 reflects the glory of G and bears the very
1:5 to what angel did G ever say, "Thou art
1:6 he says, "Let all G's angels worship him."
1:8 says, "Thy throne, O G, is for ever and
1:9 hated lawlessness; therefore G, thy God, has anointed
1:9 lawlessness; therefore God, thy G, has anointed thee
2:4 who heard him, while G also bore witness by
2:5 not to angels that G subjected the world to
2:9 by the grace of G he might taste death
2:13 I, and the children G has given me."
2:17 in the service of G, to make expiation for
3:2 also was faithful in G's house.
3:4 of all things is G
3:5 was faithful in all G's house as a servant,
3:6 Christ was faithful over G's house as a son.
3:12 leading you to fall away from the living G
4:4 in this way, "And G rested on the seventh
4:8 had given them rest, G would not speak later
4:9 for the people of G;
4:10 God; for whoever enters G's rest also ceases from
4:10 from his labors as G did from his.
4:12 For the word of G is living and active,
4:14 Jesus, the Son of G, let us hold fast
5:1 men in relation to G, to offer gifts and
5:4 he is called by G, just as Aaron was.
5:10 him, being designated by G a high priest after
5:12 the first principles of G's word.
6:1 and of faith toward G,
6:3 we will do if G permits.

G

6:5 of the word of G and the powers of
6:6 crucify the Son of G on their own account
6:7 sake it is cultivated, receives a blessing from G
6:10 For G is not so unjust as to overlook
6:13 For when G made a promise to Abraham, since
6:17 So when G desired to show more convincingly to
6:18 it is impossible that G should prove false, we
7:1 of the Most High G, met Abraham returning from
7:3 resembling the Son of G he continues a priest
7:19 is introduced, through which we draw near to G
7:25 who draw near to G through him, since he
8:5 he was instructed by G, saying, "See that you
8:10 I will be their G, and they shall be
9:14 himself without blemish to G, purify your conscience
9:14 conscience from dead works to serve the living G
9:20 of the covenant which G commanded you."
9:24 in the presence of G on our behalf.
10:7 do thy will, O G as it is written
10:12 the right hand of G,
10:21 over the house of G,
10:29 spurned the Son of G, and profaned the blood
10:31 to fall into the hands of the living G
10:36 do the will of G and receive what is
11:3 by the word of G, so that what is
11:4 faith Abel offered to G a more acceptable sacrifice
11:4 received approval as righteous, G bearing witness by
11:5 was not found, because G had taken him.
11:5 was taken he was attested as having pleased G
11:6 would draw near to G must believe that he
11:7 Noah, being warned by G concerning events as yet
11:10 which has foundations, whose builder and maker is G
11:16 Therefore G is not ashamed to be called their
11:16 to be called their G, for he has prepared
11:19 He considered that G was able to raise men
11:25 with the people of G than to enjoy the
11:40 what was promised, since G had foreseen something
12:2 at the right hand of the throne of G
12:7 G is treating you as sons; for what son
12:15 obtain the grace of G; that no "root of
12:22 city of the living G, the heavenly Jerusalem, and
12:23 a judge who is G of all, and to
12:28 let us offer to G acceptable worship, with reverence
12:29 and awe; for our G is a consuming fire.
13:4 bed be undefiled; for G will judge the immoral
13:7 you the word of G; consider the outcome of
13:15 sacrifice of praise to G, that is, the fruit
13:16 you have, for such sacrifices are pleasing to G
13:20 Now may the G of peace who brought again
Jas 1:1 James, a servant of G and of the LORD
1:5 wisdom, let him ask G, who gives to all
1:11 crown of life which G has promised to those
1:12 "I am tempted by G; for God cannot be
1:12 tempted by God"; for G cannot be tempted with
1:19 of man does not work the righteousness of G
1:26 pure and undefiled before G and the Father is
2:5 Has not G chosen those who are poor in
2:19 You believe that G is one; you do well.
2:23 says, "Abraham believed G, and it was reckoned
2:23 righteousness"; and he was called the friend of G
3:9 men, who are made in the likeness of G
4:4 that friendship with the world is enmity with G
4:4 of the world makes himself an enemy of G
4:6 grace; therefore it says, G opposes the proud, but
4:7 Submit yourselves therefore to G
4:8 Draw near to G and he will draw near
1Pet 1:2 chosen and destined by G the Father and sanctified
1:3 Blessed be the G and Father of our Lord
1:5 for you, who by G's power are guarded through
1:21 you have confidence in G, who raised him from
1:21 so that your faith and hope are in G
1:23 and abiding word of G;
2:4 by men but in G's sight chosen and precious;
2:5 sacrifices acceptable to G through Jesus Christ.
2:9 priesthood, a holy nation, G's own people, that you
2:10 but now you are G's people; once you had
2:12 good deeds and glorify G on the day of
2:15 For it is G's will that by doing right
2:16 pretext for evil; but live as servants of G
2:17 Fear G
2:19 approved if, mindful of G, he endures pain while
2:20 it patiently, you have G's approval.
3:4 quiet spirit, which in G's sight is very precious.
3:5 women who hoped in G used to adorn themselves
3:17 if that should be G's will, than for doing
3:18 might bring us to G, being put to death
3:20 did not obey, when G's patience waited in the
3:21 as an appeal to G for a clear conscience,
3:22 the right hand of G, with angels, authorities, and
4:2 by human passions but by the will of G
4:6 men, they might live in the spirit like G
4:10 as good stewards of G's varied grace:
4:11 who utters oracles of G; whoever renders service, as
4:11 by the strength which G supplies; in order that
4:11 order that in everything G may be glorified through
4:14 of glory and of G rests upon you.
4:16 ashamed, but under that name let him glorify G
4:17 with the household of G; and if it begins
4:17 those who do not obey the gospel of G
4:19 who suffer according to G's will do right and
5:2 Tend the flock of G that is your charge,
5:5 toward one another, for G opposes the proud, but
5:6 the mighty hand of G, that in due time
5:10 a little while, the G of all grace, who
5:12 the true grace of G; stand fast in it.
2Pet 1:1 the righteousness of our G and Savior Jesus Christ:
1:2 in the knowledge of G and of Jesus our
1:17 honor and glory from G the Father and the
1:21 men moved by the Holy Spirit spoke from G
2:4 For if G did not spare the angels when
3:5 by the word of G heavens existed long ago,
3:12 of the day of G, because of which the
1Jn 1:5 proclaim to you, that G is light and in
2:5 him truly love for G is perfected.
2:14 and the word of G abides in you, and
2:17 does the will of G abides for ever.
3:1 be called children of G; and so we are.
3:2 Beloved, we are G's children now; it does not
3:8 reason the Son of G appeared was to destroy
3:9 No one born of G commits sin; for God's
3:9 God commits sin; for G's nature abides in him,
3:9 he cannot sin because he is born of G
3:10 are the children of G, and who are the
3:10 right is not of G, nor he who does
3:17 against him, how does G's love abide in him?
3:20 hearts condemn us; for G is greater than our
3:21 we have confidence before G;
4:1 whether they are of G; for many false prophets
4:2 know the Spirit of G: every spirit which confesses
4:2 the flesh is of G,
4:3 which does not confess Jesus is not of G
4:4 children, you are of G, and have overcome them;
4:6 We are of G
4:6 Whoever knows G listens to us, and he who
4:6 who is not of G does not listen to
4:7 for love is of G, and he who loves
4:7 loves is born of G and knows God.
4:7 who loves is born of God and knows G
4:8 love does not know G; for God is love.
4:8 not know God; for G is love.
4:9 this the love of G was made manifest among
4:9 manifest among us, that G sent his only Son
4:10 not that we loved G but that he loved
4:11 Beloved, if G so loved us, we also ought
4:12 man has ever seen G; if we love one
4:12 we love one another, G abides in us and
4:15 is the Son of G, God abides in him,
4:15 the Son of God, G abides in him, and
4:15 God, God abides in him, and he in G
4:16 and believe the love G has for us.
4:16 G is love, and he who abides in love
4:16 in love abides in G, and God abides in
4:16 abides in God, and G abides in him.
4:20 If any one says, "I love G
4:20 has seen, cannot love G whom he has not
4:21 that he who loves G should love his brother
5:1 is a child of G, and every one who
5:2 love the children of G, when we love God
5:2 God, when we love G and obey his commandments.
5:3 is the love of G, that we keep his
5:4 whatever is born of G overcomes the world; and
5:5 who believes that Jesus is the Son of G
5:9 men, the testimony of G is greater; for this
5:9 is the testimony of G that he has borne
5:10 in the Son of G has the testimony in
5:10 who does not believe G has made him a
5:10 in the testimony that G has borne to his
5:11 is the testimony, that G gave us eternal life,
5:12 not the Son of G has not life.
5:13 of the Son of G, that you may know
5:16 he will ask, and G will give him life
5:18 any one born of G does not sin, but
5:18 who was born of G keeps him, and the

	5:19	that we are of G, and the whole world
	5:20	that the Son of G has come and has
	5:20	This is the true G and eternal life.
2Jn	1:3	be with us, from G the Father and from
	1:9	Christ does not have G; he who abides in
3Jn	1:6	their journey as befits G's service.
	1:11	does good is of G; he who does evil
	1:11	God; he who does evil has not seen G
Jude	1:1	are called, beloved in G the Father and kept
	1:4	the grace of our G into licentiousness and deny
	1:21	in the love of G; wait for the mercy
	1:25	rejoicing, to the only G, our Savior through Jesus
Rev	1:1	of Jesus Christ, which G gave him to show
	1:2	to the word of G and to the testimony
	1:6	kingdom, priests to his G and Father, to him
	1:8	says the Lord G, who is and who was
	1:9	of the word of G and the testimony of
	2:7	in the paradise of G
	2:18	of the Son of G, who has eyes like
	3:1	the seven spirits of G and the seven stars.
	3:2	your works perfect in the sight of my G
	3:12	the temple of my G; never shall he go
	3:12	the name of my G, and the name of
	3:12	the city of my G, the new Jerusalem which
	3:12	comes down from my G out of heaven, and
	3:14	witness, the beginning of G's creation.
	4:5	the seven spirits of G;
	4:8	holy, is the Lord G Almighty, who was and
	4:11	thou, our Lord and G, to receive glory and
	5:6	the seven spirits of G sent out into all
	5:9	didst ransom men for G from every tribe and
	5:10	and priests to our G, and they shall reign
	6:9	for the word of G and for the witness
	7:2	seal of the living G, and he called with
	7:3	the servants of our G upon their foreheads."
	7:10	"Salvation belongs to our G who sits upon the
	7:11	the throne and worshiped G,
	7:12	might be to our G for ever and ever!
	7:15	before the throne of G, and serve him day
	7:17	of living water; and G will wipe away every
	8:2	angels who stand before G, and seven trumpets were
	8:4	saints from the hand of the angel before G
	9:4	not the seal of G upon their foreheads;
	9:13	the golden altar before G,
	10:7	angel, the mystery of G, as he announced to
	11:1	measure the temple of G and the altar and
	11:11	breath of life from G entered them, and they
	11:13	gave glory to the G of heaven.
	11:16	on their thrones before G fell on their faces
	11:16	their faces and worshiped G,
	11:17	thanks to thee, Lord G Almighty, who art and
	11:19	Then G's temple in heaven was opened, and the
	12:5	was caught up to G and to his throne,
	12:6	a place prepared by G, in which to be
	12:10	the kingdom of our G and the authority of
	12:10	who accuses them day and night before our G
	12:17	keep the commandments of G and bear testimony to
	13:6	to utter blasphemies against G, blaspheming his
	14:4	as first fruits for G and the Lamb,
	14:7	a loud voice, "Fear G and give him glory,
	14:10	drink the wine of G's wrath, poured unmixed into
	14:12	keep the commandments of G and the faith of
	14:19	of the wrath of G;
	15:1	them the wrath of G is ended.
	15:2	glass with harps of G in their hands.
	15:3	Moses, the servant of G, and the song of
	15:3	thy deeds, O Lord G the Almighty!
	15:7	of the wrath of G who lives for ever
	15:8	from the glory of G and from his power,
	16:1	earth the seven bowls of the wrath of G
	16:7	altar cry, "Yea, Lord G the Almighty, true and
	16:9	cursed the name of G who had power over
	16:11	anguish and cursed the G of heaven for their
	16:14	the great day of G the Almighty.
	16:19	the nations fell, and G remembered great Babylon,
	16:21	heaven, till men cursed G for the plague of
	17:17	up with fire, for G has put it into
	17:17	until the words of G shall be fulfilled.
	18:5	as heaven, and G has remembered her iniquities.
	18:8	mighty is the Lord G who judges her."
	18:20	apostles and prophets, for G has given judgment for
	19:1	power belong to our G,
	19:4	fell down and worshiped G who is seated on
	19:5	voice crying, "Praise our G, all you his servants,
	19:6	For the Lord our G the Almighty reigns.
	19:9	said to me, "These are true words of G
	19:10	Worship G
	19:13	which he is called is The Word of G
	19:15	of the wrath of G the Almighty.
	19:17	the great supper of G,
	20:4	for the word of G, and who had not
	20:6	shall be priests of G and of Christ, and
	21:2	out of heaven from G, prepared as a bride
	21:3	"Behold, the dwelling of G is with men.
	21:3	be his people, and G himself will be with
	21:7	I will be his G and he shall be
	21:10	out of heaven from G,
	21:11	having the glory of G, its radiance like a
	21:22	temple is the Lord G the Almighty and the
	21:23	for the glory of G is its light, and
	22:1	from the throne of G and of the Lamb
	22:3	but the throne of G and of the Lamb
	22:5	sun, for the Lord G will be their light,
	22:6	And the Lord, the G of the spirits of
	22:9	Worship G
	22:18	one adds to them, G will add to him
	22:19	book of this prophecy, G will take away his

GOD-FEARING (3)

Neh	7:2	a more faithful and G man than many.
Sir	19:21	Better is the G man who lacks intelligence, than
Acts	10:22	centurion, an upright and G man, who is well

GOD-GIVEN

2Mac	6:23	according to the holy G law, he declared himself

GODDESS (4)

1Kgs	11:5	went after Ashtoreth the G of the Sidonians, and
	11:33	and worshiped Ashtoreth the G of the Sidonians,
Acts	19:27	temple of the great G Artemis may count for
	19:37	are neither sacrilegious nor blasphemers of our G

GODLESS (22)

2Sam	23:6	But G men are all like thorns that are
Job	8:13	the hope of the G man shall perish.
	13:16	my salvation, that a G man shall not come
	15:34	the company of the G is barren, and fire
	17:8	and the innocent stirs himself up against the G
	20:5	the joy of the G but for a moment?
	27:8	the hope of the G when God cuts him
	34:30	man?– that a G man should not reign,
	36:13	"The G in heart cherish anger; they do not
Ps	119:51	G men utterly deride me, but I do not
	119:69	The G besmear me with lies, but with my
	119:78	Let the G be put to shame, because they
	119:85	G men have dug pitfalls for me, men who
	119:122	good; let not the G oppress me.
Prov	11:7	the expectation of the G comes to nought.
	11:9	With his mouth the G man would destroy his
Is	9:17	for every one is G and an evildoer, and
	10:6	Against a G nation I send him, and against
	33:14	trembling has seized the G: "Who among us can
1Tim	4:7	nothing to do with G and silly myths.
	6:20	Avoid the G chatter and contradictions of what is
2Tim	2:16	Avoid such G chatter, for it will lead people

GODLINESS (16)

Wis	10:12	he might learn that G is more powerful than
Sir	1:22	are wise sayings, but G is an abomination to
	49:3	in the days of wicked men he strengthened G
Bar	5:4	by God, "Peace of righteousness and glory of G
2Mac	12:45	who fall asleep in G, it was a holy
1Tim	4:7	Train yourself in G;
	4:8	is of some value, G is of value in
	6:3	teaching which accords with G,
	6:5	the truth, imagining that G is a means of
	6:6	is great gain in G with contentment;
	6:11	aim at righteousness, G, faith, love, steadfastness,
Tit	1:1	truth which accords with G,
2Pet	1:3	pertain to life and G, through the knowledge of
	1:6	steadfastness, and steadfastness with G,
	1:7	steadfastness with godliness, and G with brotherly
	3:11	lives of holiness and G,

GODLY (33)

Deut	33:8	thy Urim to thy G one, whom thou didst
Ps	4:3	has set apart the G for himself; the LORD
	12:1	longer any that is G; for the faithful have
	16:10	Sheol, or let thy G one see the Pit.
	32:6	every one who is G offer prayer to thee;
	52:1	O mighty man, of mischief done against the G
	52:9	it is good, in the presence of the G

86:2 life, for I am G; save thy servant who
Sir 11:15 for those who are G, and what he approves
11:20 the reward of the G, and quickly God causes
12:2 Do good to a G man, and you will
12:4 Give to the G man, but do not help
13:16 a sinner with a G man.
16:13 the patience of the G will not be frustrated.
23:12 be far from the G, and they will not
27:11 The talk of the G man is always wise,
27:29 the fall of the G will be caught in
28:22 be master over the G, and they will not
33:14 so the sinner is the opposite of the G
37:12 stay constantly with a G man whom you know
39:27 for good to the G, just as they turn
43:33 things, and to the G he has granted wisdom.
Mic 7:2 The G man has perished from the earth, and
Mal 2:15 G offspring.
2Cor 1:12 you, with holiness and G sincerity, not by earthly
7:9 for you felt a G grief, so that you
7:10 For G grief produces a repentance that leads to
7:11 see what earnestness this G grief has produced in
1Tim 2:2 quiet and peaceable life, G and respectful in every
2Tim 3:12 desire to live a G life in Christ Jesus
Tit 2:12 live sober, upright, and G lives in this world,
Heb 5:7 was heard for his G fear.
2Pet 2:9 how to rescue the G from trial, and to

GODS (309)

Gen 31:19 his sheep, and Rachel stole her father's household G
31:30 father's house, but why did you steal my G
31:32 whom you find your G shall not live.
31:34 had taken the household G and put them in
31:35 he searched, but did not find the household G
35:2 "Put away the foreign G that are among you,
35:4 Jacob all the foreign G that they had, and
Ex 12:12 and on all the G of Egypt I will
15:11 "Who is like thee, O LORD, among the G
18:11 is greater than all G, because he delivered the
20:3 shall have no other G before me.
20:23 You shall not make G of silver to be
20:23 you make for yourselves G of gold.
23:13 the names of other G, nor let such be
23:24 bow down to their G, nor serve them, nor
23:32 make no covenant with them or with their G
23:33 if you serve their G, it will surely be
32:1 him, "Up, make us G, who shall go before
32:4 said, "These are your G, O Israel, who brought
32:8 said, 'These are your G, O Israel, who brought
32:23 to me, 'Make us G, who shall go before
32:31 have made for themselves G of gold.
34:15 the harlot after their G and sacrifice to their
34:15 and sacrifice to their G and one invites you,
34:16 the harlot after their G and make your sons
34:16 make your sons play the harlot after their G
34:17 "You shall make for yourself no molten G
Lev 19:4 make for yourselves molten G: I am the LORD
Num 25:2 the sacrifices of their G, and the people ate,
25:2 the people ate, and bowed down to their G
33:4 among them; upon their G also the LORD executed
Deut 1:17 for the judgment is G; and the case that
4:28 there you will serve G of wood and stone,
5:7 shall have no other G before me.
6:14 not go after other G, of the gods of
6:14 other gods, of the G of the peoples who
7:4 me, to serve other G; then the anger of
7:16 shall you serve their G, for that would be
7:25 graven images of their G you shall burn with
8:19 and go after other G and serve them and
10:17 God is God of G and Lord of lords,
11:16 aside and serve other G and worship them,
11:28 to go after other G which you have not
12:2 dispossess served their G, upon the high mountains
12:3 graven images of their G, and destroy their name
12:30 not inquire about their G, saying, 'How did these
12:30 these nations serve their G —that I also may
12:31 have done for their G; for they even burn
12:31 and their daughters in the fire to their G
13:2 us go after other G which you have not
13:6 go and serve other G which neither you nor
13:7 known, some of the G of the peoples that
13:13 go and serve other G which you have not
17:3 gone and served other G and worshiped them, or
18:20 the name of other G, that same prophet shall
20:18 the service of their G, and so to sin
28:14 to go after other G to serve them.
28:36 you shall serve other G, of wood and stone.
28:64 you shall serve other G, of wood and stone,
29:18 go and serve the G of those nations; lest
29:26 went and served other G and worshiped them, gods
29:26 gods and worshiped them, G whom they had not
30:17 away to worship other G and serve them,
31:16 harlot after the strange G of the land, where
31:18 have done, because they have turned to other G
31:20 will turn to other G and serve them, and
32:16 jealousy with strange G; with abominable practices
32:17 demons which were no G, to gods they had
32:17 were no gods, to G they had never known,
32:17 never known, to new G that had come in
32:37 say, 'Where are their G, the rock in which
Josh 23:7 the names of their G, or swear by them,
23:16 go and serve other G and bow down to
24:2 Abraham and of Nahor; and they served other G
24:14 faithfulness; put away the G which your fathers
24:15 will serve, whether the G your fathers served in
24:15 the River, or the G of the Amorites in
24:16 LORD, to serve other G;
24:20 LORD and serve foreign G, then he will turn
24:23 put away the foreign G which are among you,
Judg 2:3 to you, and their G shall be a snare
2:12 they went after other G, from among the gods
2:12 gods, from among the G of the peoples who
2:17 the harlot after other G and bowed down to
2:19 fathers, going after other G, serving them and
3:6 gave to their sons; and they served their G
5:8 When new G were chosen, then war was in
6:10 pay reverence to the G of the Amorites, in
9:9 my fatness, by which G and men are honored,
9:13 my wine which cheers G and men, and go
10:6 and the Ashtaroth, the G of Syria, the gods
10:6 gods of Syria, the G of Sidon, the gods
10:6 gods of Sidon, the G of Moab, the gods
10:6 gods of Moab, the G of the Ammonites, and
10:6 the Ammonites, and the G of the Philistines; and
10:13 me and served other G; therefore I will deliver
10:14 and cry to the G whom you have chosen;
10:16 put away the foreign G from among them and
18:24 said, "You take my G which I made, and
Ruth 1:15 people and to her G; return after your sister-in-law."
1Sam 4:8 deliver us from the power of these mighty G
4:8 These are the G who smote the Egyptians with
6:5 off you and your G and your land.
7:3 put away the foreign G and the Ashtaroth from
8:8 me and serving other G, so they are also
17:43 And the Philistine cursed David by his G
26:19 saying, 'Go, serve other G
2Sam 7:23 out before his people a nation and its G
1Kgs 9:6 go and serve other G and worship them,
9:9 laid hold on other G, and worshipped them and
11:2 your heart after their G; Solomon clung to these
11:4 his heart after other G; and his heart was
11:8 wives, who burned incense and sacrificed to their G
11:10 not go after other G; but he did not
12:28 Behold your G, O Israel, who brought you up
14:9 for yourself other G, and molten images, provoking
19:2 saying, "So may the G do to me, and
20:10 him and said, "The G do so to me,
20:23 said to him, "Their G are gods of the
20:23 him, "Their gods are G of the hills, and
2Kgs 17:7 and had feared other G
17:29 every nation still made G of its own, and
17:31 and Anammelech, the G of Sepharvaim.
17:33 also served their own G, after the manner of
17:35 shall not fear other G or bow yourselves to
17:37 shall not fear other G,
17:38 shall not fear other G,
18:33 Has any of the G of the nations ever
18:34 Where are the G of Hamath and Arpad?
18:34 Where are the G of Sepharvaim, Hena, and Ivvah?
18:35 Who among all the G of the countries have
19:12 Have the G of the nations delivered them, the
19:18 and have cast their G into the fire; for
19:18 for they were no G, but the work of
22:17 burned incense to other G, that they might provoke
1Chr 5:25 the harlot after the G of the peoples of
10:10 the temple of their G, and fastened his head
14:12 And they left their G there, and David gave
16:25 is to be held in awe above all G
16:26 For all the G of the peoples are idols;
2Chr 2:5 great, for our God is greater than all G
7:19 go and serve other G and worship them,
7:22 laid hold on other G, and worshiped them and
13:8 the golden calves which Jeroboam made you for G

	13:9	rams becomes a priest of what are no G
	20:15	multitude; for the battle is not yours but G
	25:14	Edomites, he brought the G of the men of
	25:14	them up as his G, and worshiped them, making
	25:15	you resorted to the G of a people, which
	25:20	they had sought the G of Edom.
	28:23	he sacrificed to the G of Damascus which had
	28:23	and said, "Because the G of the kings of
	28:25	burn incense to other G, provoking to anger the
	32:13	Were the G of the nations of those lands
	32:14	Who among all the G of those nations which
	32:17	him, saying, "Like the G of the nations of
	32:19	they spoke of the G of the peoples of
	33:15	took away the foreign G and the idol from
	34:25	burned incense to other G, that they might provoke
Ezra	1:7	Jerusalem and placed in the house of his G
Jud	3:8	to destroy all the G of the land, so
	5:7	would not follow the G of their fathers who
	5:8	the presence of their G; and they fled to
	8:18	of ours which worshiped G made with hands, as
Esth	14:7	hands of our enemies, because we glorified their G
	14:12	O King of the G and Master of all
Ps	40:4	proud, to those who go astray after false G
	58:1	Do you indeed decree what is right, you G
	82:1	the midst of the G he holds judgment:
	82:6	I say, "You are G, sons of the Most
	84:7	strength; the God of G will be seen in
	86:8	like thee among the G, O Lord, nor are
	95:3	great God, and a great King above all G
	96:4	praised; he is to be feared above all G
	96:5	For all the G of the peoples are idols;
	97:7	in worthless idols; all G bow down before him.
	97:9	the earth; thou art exalted far above all G
	135:5	great, and that our Lord is above all G
	136:2	to the God of G, for his steadfast love
	138:1	whole heart; before the G I sing thy praise;
Wis	12:24	of error, accepting as G those animals which even
	12:27	had thought to be G, being punished by means
	13:2	of heaven were the G that rule the world.
	13:3	assumed them to be G, let them know how
	13:10	things, are the men who give the name G
	15:9	counts it his glory that he molds counterfeit G
	15:15	their heathen idols were G, though these have
Is	21:9	the images of her G he has shattered to
	36:18	Has any of the G of the nations delivered
	36:19	Where are the G of Hamath and Arpad?
	36:19	Where are the G of Sepharvaim?
	36:20	Who among all the G of these countries have
	37:12	Have the G of the nations delivered them, the
	37:19	and have cast their G into the fire; for
	37:19	for they were no G, but the work of
	41:23	know that you are G; do good, or do
	42:17	who say to molten images, "You are our G
Jer	1:16	burned incense to other G, and worshiped the works
	2:11	a nation changed its G, even though they are
	2:11	changed its gods, even though they are no G
	2:28	But where are your G that you made for
	2:28	your cities are your G, O Judah.
	5:7	and have sworn by those who are no G
	5:19	me and served foreign G in your land, so
	7:6	not go after other G to your own hurt,
	7:9	and go after other G that you have not
	7:18	drink offerings to other G, to provoke me to
	10:11	say to them: "The G who did not make
	11:10	have gone after other G to serve them; the
	11:12	and cry to the G to whom they burn
	11:13	For your G have become as many as your
	13:10	have gone after other G to serve them and
	14:22	any among the false G of the nations that
	16:11	have gone after other G and have served and
	16:13	you shall serve other G day and night, for
	16:20	Can man make for himself G
	16:20	Such are no G
	18:15	burn incense to false G; they have stumbled in
	19:4	in it to other G whom neither they nor
	19:13	poured out to other G --shall be defiled like
	22:9	God, and worshiped other G and served them.'""
	25:6	not go after other G to serve and worship
	32:29	poured out to other G, to provoke me to
	35:15	not go after other G to serve them, and
	43:12	the temples of the G of Egypt; and he
	43:13	the temples of the G of Egypt he shall
	44:3	incense and serve other G that they knew not,
	44:5	their wickedness and burn no incense to other G
	44:8	burning incense to other G in the land of
	44:15	offered incense to other G, and all the women
	46:25	and Egypt and her G and her kings, upon
Bar	1:21	heart by serving other G and doing what is
	6:4	Babylon you will see G made of silver and
	6:5	let fear for these G possess you, when you
	6:9	the heads of their G, as they would for
	6:10	and silver from their G and spend it upon
	6:11	They deck their G out with garments like men--
	6:11	garments like men--these G of silver and gold
	6:16	they evidently are not G; so do not fear
	6:17	broken, so are the G of the heathen, when
	6:19	for themselves, though their G can see none of
	6:23	that they are not G; so do not fear
	6:27	because through them these G are made to stand,
	6:28	are offered to these G and use the money;
	6:29	that they are not G, do not fear them.
	6:30	For why should they be called G
	6:30	Women serve meals for G of silver and gold
	6:32	and shout before their G as some do at
	6:33	the clothing of their G to clothe their wives
	6:40	think that they are G, or call them gods?
	6:40	think that they are gods, or call them G
	6:44	think that they are G, or call them gods?
	6:44	think that they are gods, or call them G
	6:46	the things that are made by them be G
	6:48	to where they can hide themselves and their G
	6:49	that these are not G, for they cannot save
	6:51	that they are not G but the work of
	6:52	can fail to know that they are not G
	6:55	a temple of wooden G overlaid with gold or
	6:55	and escape, but the G will be burnt in
	6:56	any one admit or think that they are G
	6:57	G made of wood and overlaid with silver and
	6:59	to be these false G; better even the door
	6:59	contents, than these false G; better also a wooden
	6:59	wooden pillar in a palace, than these false G
	6:64	think that they are G nor call them gods,
	6:64	gods nor call them G, for they are not
	6:65	that they are not G, do not fear them.
	6:69	whatever that they are G; therefore do not fear
	6:70	nothing, so are their G of wood, overlaid with
	6:71	the same way, their G of wood, overlaid with
	6:72	that they are not G; and they will finally
Ezek	28:2	the seat of the G, in the heart of
Dan	2:11	the king except the G, whose dwelling is not
	2:47	God is God of G and Lord of kings,
	3:12	do not serve your G or worship the golden
	3:14	do not serve my G or worship the golden
	3:18	will not serve your G or worship the golden
	3:91	Lord, the God of G, sing praise to him
	3:93	the fourth is like a son of the G
	4:8	spirit of the holy G --and I told
	4:9	spirit of the holy G is in you and
	4:18	spirit of the holy G is in you."
	5:4	wine, and praised the G of gold and silver,
	5:11	in whom is the spirit of the holy G
	5:11	the wisdom of the G, were found in him,
	5:14	spirit of the holy G is in you, and
	5:23	you have praised the G of silver and gold,
	11:8	off to Egypt their G with their molten images
	11:36	shall speak astonishing things against the God of G
	11:37	no heed to the G of his fathers, or
Hos	3:1	they turn to other G and love cakes of
Nah	1:14	the house of your G I will cut off
Zeph	2:11	will famish all the G of the earth, and
1Mac	5:68	graven images of their G he burned with fire;
2Mac	11:23	gone on to the G, we desire that the
Mt	22:21	Caesars, and to God the things that are G
Mk	12:17	Caesars, and to God the things that are G
Lk	20:25	Caesars, and to God the things that are G
Jn	10:34	written in your law, 'I said, you are G
	10:35	If he called them G to whom the word
Acts	7:40	Aaron, 'Make for us G to go before us;
	14:11	saying in Lycaonian, "The G have come down to
	19:26	of people, saying that G made with hands are
	19:26	saying that gods made with hands are not G
1Cor	3:23	yours; and you are Christs; and Christ is G
	8:5	there may be so-called G in heaven or on
	8:5	or on earth--as indeed there are many G
Gal	4:8	by nature are no G;

GOEST

Num	14:14	over them and thou G before them, in a

GOG (12)

1Chr	5:4	Joel: Shemaiah his son, G his son, Shimei his
Ezek	38:2	set your face toward G, of the land of

	38:3	am against you, O G, chief prince of Meshech
	38:14	prophesy, and say to G, Thus says the Lord
	38:16	when through you, O G, I vindicate my holiness
	38:18	on that day, when G shall come against the
	38:21	kind of terror against G, says the Lord GOD;
	39:1	of man, prophesy against G, and say, Thus says
	39:1	am against you, O G, chief prince of Meshech
	39:11	I will give to G a place for burial
	39:11	the travelers, for there G and all his multitude
Rev	20:8	the earth, that is, G and Magog, to gather

GOIIM (3)

Gen	14:1	and Tidal king of G,
	14:9	Elam, Tidal king of G, Amraphel king of Shinar,
Josh	12:23	one; the king of G in Galilee, one;

GOLAN (4)

Deut	4:43	for the Gadites, and G in Bashan for the
Josh	20:8	tribe of Gad, and G in Bashan, from the
	21:27	the half-tribe of Manasseh, G in Bashan with its
1Chr	6:71	the half-tribe of Manasseh: G in Bashan with its

G

GOLD (488)

Gen	2:11	Havilah, where there is G;
	2:12	is gold; and the G of that land is
	13:2	very rich in cattle, in silver, and in G
	24:22	the man took a G ring weighing a half-shekel,
	24:22	her arms weighing ten G shekels,
	24:35	herds, silver and G, menservants and maidservants,
	24:53	of silver and of G, and raiment, and gave
	41:42	linen, and put a G chain about his neck;
	44:8	we steal silver or G from your lord's house?
Ex	3:22	of silver and of G, and clothing, and you
	11:2	of her neighbor, jewelry of silver and of G
	12:35	of silver and of G, and clothing;
	20:23	nor shall you make for yourselves gods of G
	25:3	shall receive from them: G, silver, and bronze,
	25:11	overlay it with pure G, within and without shall
	25:11	it a molding of G round about.
	25:12	cast four rings of G for it and put
	25:13	poles of acacia wood, and overlay them with G
	25:17	mercy seat of pure G; two cubits and a
	25:18	make two cherubim of G; of hammered work shall
	25:24	overlay it with pure G, and make a molding
	25:24	make a molding of G around it.
	25:25	and a molding of G around the frame.
	25:26	it four rings of G, and fasten the rings
	25:28	and overlay them with G, and the table shall
	25:29	pour libations; of pure G you shall make them.
	25:31	"And you shall make a lampstand of pure G
	25:36	it one piece of hammered work of pure G
	25:38	snuffers and their trays shall be of pure G
	25:39	a talent of pure G shall it be made,
	26:6	make fifty clasps of G, and couple the curtains
	26:29	overlay the frames with G, and shall make their
	26:29	make their rings of G for holders for the
	26:29	bars; and you shall overlay the bars with G
	26:32	of acacia overlaid with G, with hooks of gold,
	26:32	gold, with hooks of G, upon four bases of
	26:37	and overlay them with G; their hooks shall be
	26:37	hooks shall be of G, and you shall cast
	28:5	"They shall receive G, blue and purple and scarlet
	28:6	make the ephod of G, of blue and purple
	28:8	workmanship and materials, of G, blue and purple
	28:11	them in settings of G filigree.
	28:13	shall make settings of G filigree,
	28:14	two chains of pure G, twisted like cords; and
	28:15	shall make it; of G, blue and purple and
	28:20	shall be set in G filigree.
	28:22	like cords, of pure G;
	28:23	breastpiece two rings of G, and put the two
	28:24	the two cords of G in the two rings
	28:26	make two rings of G, and put them at
	28:27	make two rings of G, and attach them in
	28:33	skirts, with bells of G between them,
	28:36	a plate of pure G, and engrave on it,
	30:3	overlay it with pure G, its top and its
	30:3	it a molding of G round about.
	30:5	poles of acacia wood, and overlay them with G
	31:4	designs, to work in G, silver, and bronze,
	32:2	off the rings of G which are in the
	32:3	off the rings of G which were in their
	32:4	And he received the G at their hand, and
	32:24	'Let any who have G take it off'; so
	32:31	sin; they have made for themselves gods of G
	35:5	bring the LORD's offering: G, silver, and bronze;
	35:22	armlets, all sorts of G objects, every man dedicating
	35:22	dedicating an offering of G to the LORD.
	35:32	designs, to work in G and silver and bronze,
	36:13	made fifty clasps of G, and coupled the curtains
	36:34	overlaid the frames with G, and made their rings
	36:34	made their rings of G for holders for the
	36:34	for the bars, and overlaid the bars with G
	36:36	and overlaid them with G; their hooks were of
	36:36	their hooks were of G, and he cast for
	36:38	their fillets were of G, but their five bases
	37:2	overlaid it with pure G within and without, and
	37:2	made a molding of G around it.
	37:3	it four rings of G for its four corners,
	37:4	and overlaid them with G,
	37:6	mercy seat of pure G; two cubits and a
	37:7	two cherubim of hammered G; on the two ends
	37:11	overlaid it with pure G, and made a molding
	37:11	made a molding of G around it.
	37:12	made a molding of G around the frame.
	37:13	it four rings of G, and fastened the rings
	37:15	to carry the table, and overlaid them with G
	37:16	the vessels of pure G which were to be
	37:17	He also made the lampstand of pure G
	37:22	was one piece of hammered work of pure G
	37:23	and its snuffers and its trays of pure G
	37:24	all its utensils of a talent of pure G
	37:26	overlaid it with pure G, its top, and its
	37:26	made a molding of G round about it,
	37:27	made two rings of G on it under its
	37:28	poles of acacia wood, and overlaid them with G
	38:24	All the G that was used for the work,
	38:24	of the sanctuary, the G from the offering, was
	39:2	made the ephod of G, blue and purple and
	39:3	And G leaf was hammered out and cut into
	39:5	materials and workmanship, of G, blue and purple
	39:6	enclosed in settings of G filigree and engraved like
	39:8	of the ephod, of G, blue and purple and
	39:13	enclosed in settings of G filigree.
	39:15	like cords, of pure G;
	39:16	made two settings of G filigree and two gold
	39:16	gold filigree and two G rings, and put the
	39:17	the two cords of G in the two rings
	39:19	made two rings of G, and put them at
	39:20	made two rings of G, and attached them in
	39:25	made bells of pure G, and put the bells
	39:30	holy crown of pure G, and wrote upon it
	39:37	the lampstand of pure G and its lamps with
Lev	24:4	the lampstand of pure G before the LORD
	24:6	in a row, upon the table of pure G
Num	7:86	the sanctuary, all the G of the dishes being
	8:4	lampstand, hammered work of G; from its base to
	22:18	full of silver and G, I could not go
	24:13	full of silver and G, I would not be
	31:22	commanded Moses: only the G, the silver, the bronze,
	31:50	found, articles of G, armlets and bracelets, signet
	31:51	received from them the G, all wrought articles.
	31:52	And all the G of the offering that they
	31:54	the priest received the G from the commanders of
Deut	7:25	the silver or the G that is on them,
	8:13	and your silver and G is multiplied, and all
	17:17	shall he greatly multiply for himself silver and G
	29:17	stone, of silver and G, which were among them.
Josh	6:19	But all silver and G, and vessels of bronze
	6:24	only the silver and G, and the vessels of
	7:21	and a bar of G weighing fifty shekels, then
	7:24	and the bar of G, and his sons and
	22:8	many cattle, with silver, G, bronze, and iron, and
Judg	8:26	seven hundred shekels of G; besides the crescents
1Sam	6:8	side the figures of G, which you are returning
2Sam	1:24	who put ornaments of G upon your apparel.
	8:7	took the shields of G which were carried by
	8:10	articles of silver, of G, and of bronze;
	8:11	with the silver and G which he dedicated from
	12:30	was a talent of G, and in it was
	21:4	matter of silver or G between us and Saul
1Kgs	6:20	cubits high; and he overlaid it with pure G
	6:21	the house with pure G, and he drew chains
	6:21	he drew chains of G across, in front of
	6:21	of the inner sanctuary, and overlaid it with G
	6:22	the whole house with G, until all the house
	6:22	belonged to the inner sanctuary he overlaid with G
	6:28	And he overlaid the cherubim with G
	6:30	house he overlaid with G in the inner and
	6:32	he overlaid them with G, and spread gold upon
	6:32	with gold, and spread G upon the cherubim and
	6:35	he overlaid them with G evenly applied upon the

7:49 the lampstands of pure G, five on the south
7:49 and the tongs, of G;
7:50 and firepans, of pure G; and the sockets of
7:50 and the sockets of G, for the doors of
7:51 dedicated, the silver, the G, and the vessels, and
9:11 and cypress timber and G, as much as he
9:14 the king one hundred and twenty talents of G
9:28 and brought from there G, to the amount of
10:2 spices, and very much G, and precious stones; and
10:10 and twenty talents of G, and a very great
10:11 of Hiram, which brought G from Ophir, brought from
10:14 Now the weight of G that came to Solomon
10:14 and sixty-six talents of G,
10:16 large shields of beaten G; six hundred shekels of
10:16 six hundred shekels of G went into each shield.
10:17 hundred shields of beaten G; three minas of gold
10:17 gold; three minas of G went into each shield;
10:18 ivory throne, and overlaid it with the finest G
10:21 drinking vessels were of G, and all the vessels
10:21 Lebanon were of pure G; none were of silver,
10:22 used to come bringing G, silver, ivory, apes, and
10:25 articles of silver and G, garments, myrrh, spices,
12:28 king took counsel, and made two calves of G
14:26 all the shields of G which Solomon had made;
15:15 votive gifts, silver, and G, and vessels.
15:18 the silver and the G that were left in
15:19 present of silver and G; go, break your league
20:3 'Your silver and your G are mine; your fairest
20:5 your silver and your G, your wives and your
20:7 my silver and my G, and I did not
22:48 go to Ophir for G; but they did not
2Kgs 5:5 six thousand shekels of G, and ten festal garments.
7:8 carried off silver and G and clothing, and went
12:13 or any vessels of G, or of silver, from
12:18 gifts, and all the G that was found in
14:14 he seized all the G and silver, and all
16:8 took the silver and G that was found in
18:14 hundred talents of silver and thirty talents of G
18:16 time Hezekiah stripped the G from the doors of
20:13 house, the silver, the G, the spices, the precious
23:33 hundred talents of silver and a talent of G
23:35 the silver and the G to Pharaoh, but he
23:35 the silver and the G of the people of
24:13 all the vessels of G in the temple of
25:15 What was of G the captain of the guard
25:15 guard took away as G, and what was of
1Chr 18:7 took the shields of G which were carried by
18:10 sorts of articles of G, of silver, and of
18:11 with the silver and G which he had carried
20:2 weighed a talent of G, and in it was
21:25 six hundred shekels of G by weight for the
22:14 hundred thousand talents of G, a million talents of
22:16 number, skilled in working G, silver, bronze, and iron.
28:14 LORD, the weight of G for all golden vessels
28:15 lamps, the weight of G for each lampstand and
28:16 service, the weight of G for each table for
28:17 silver tables, and pure G for the forks, the
28:18 incense made of refined G, and its weight; also
29:2 I was able, the G for the things of
29:2 for the things of G, the silver for the
29:3 of my own of G and silver, and because
29:4 three thousand talents of G, of the gold of
29:4 of gold, of the G of Ophir, and seven
29:5 be done by craftsmen, G for the things of
29:5 for the things of G and silver for the
29:7 ten thousand darics of G, ten thousand talents of
2Chr 1:15 king made silver and G as common in Jerusalem
2:7 skilled to work in G, silver, bronze, and iron,
2:14 trained to work in G, silver, bronze, iron, stone,
3:4 He overlaid it on the inside with pure G
3:5 covered it with fine G, and made palms and
3:6 The G was gold of Parvaim.
3:6 The gold was G of Parvaim.
3:7 lined the house with G --its beams, its thresholds,
3:8 overlaid it with six hundred talents of fine G
3:9 nails was one shekel to fifty shekels of G
3:9 And he overlaid the upper chambers with G
3:10 two cherubim of wood and overlaid them with G
4:8 And he made a hundred basins of G
4:20 their lamps of pure G to burn before the
4:21 the tongs, of purest G;
4:22 and firepans, of pure G; and the sockets of
4:22 of the nave of the temple were of G
5:1 stored the silver, the G, and all the vessels
8:18 and fifty talents of G and brought it to
9:1 spices and very much G and precious stones.
9:9 and twenty talents of G, and a very great
9:10 Solomon, who brought G from Ophir, brought algum
9:13 Now the weight of G that came to Solomon
9:13 and sixty-six talents of G,
9:14 of the land brought G and silver to Solomon.
9:15 large shields of beaten G; six hundred shekels of
9:15 hundred shekels of beaten G went into each shield.
9:16 hundred shields of beaten G; three hundred shekels
9:16 three hundred shekels of G went into each shield;
9:17 great ivory throne, and overlaid it with pure G
9:18 and a footstool of G, which were attached to
9:20 drinking vessels were of G, and all the vessels
9:20 Lebanon were of pure G; silver was not considered
9:21 used to come bringing G, silver, ivory, apes, and
9:24 of silver and of G, garments, myrrh, spices, horses,
12:9 away the shields of G which Solomon had made;
13:11 the table of pure G, and care for the
15:18 votive gifts, silver, and G, and vessels.
16:2 Asa took silver and G from the treasures of
16:3 to you silver and G; go, break your league
21:3 great gifts, of silver, G, and valuable possessions,
24:14 incense, and vessels of G and silver.
25:24 he seized all the G and silver, and all
32:27 treasuries for silver, for G, for precious stones, for
36:3 hundred talents of silver and a talent of G
Ezra 1:4 place with silver and G, with goods and with
1:6 vessels of silver, with G, with goods, with beasts,
1:9 a thousand basins of G, a thousand basins of
1:10 censers, thirty bowls of G, two thousand four hundred
1:11 all the vessels of G and of silver were
2:69 sixty-one thousand darics of G, five thousand minas
5:14 And the G and silver vessels of the house
6:5 And also let the G and silver vessels of
7:15 convey the silver and G which the king and
7:16 all the silver and G which you shall find
7:18 of the silver and G, you may do, according
8:25 the silver and the G and the vessels, the
8:26 a hundred talents of G,
8:27 gold, twenty bowls of G worth a thousand darics,
8:27 vessels of fine bright bronze as precious as G
8:28 the silver and the G are a freewill offering
8:30 the silver and the G and the vessels, to
8:33 the silver and the G and the vessels were
Neh 7:70 a thousand darics of G, fifty basins, five hundred
7:71 twenty thousand darics of G and two thousand two
7:72 twenty thousand darics of G, two thousand minas of
Tob 12:8 better to give alms than to treasure up G
13:16 stones, and her towers and battlements with pure G
Jud 2:18 a huge amount of G and silver from the
5:9 and prospered, with much G and silver and very
8:7 Manasseh had left her G and silver, and men
10:21 woven with purple and G and emeralds and precious
Esth 1:6 and also couches of G and silver on a
15:6 majesty, all covered with G and precious stones.
Job 3:15 with princes who had G, who filled their houses
22:24 tents, if you lay G in the dust, and
22:24 in the dust, and G of Ophir among the
22:25 the Almighty is your G, and your precious silver;
23:10 has tried me, I shall come forth as G
28:1 and a place for G which they refine.
28:6 place of sapphires, and it has dust of G
28:15 cannot be gotten for G, and silver cannot be
28:16 be valued in the G of Ophir, in precious
28:17 G and glass cannot equal it, nor can it
28:17 can it be exchanged for jewels of fine G
28:19 it, nor can it be valued in pure G
31:24 "If I have made G my trust, or called
31:24 trust, or called fine G my confidence;
42:11 a piece of money and a ring of G
Ps 19:10 desired are they than G, even much fine gold;
19:10 gold, even much fine G; sweeter also than honey
21:3 a crown of fine G upon his head.
45:9 stands the queen in G of Ophir.
68:13 dove covered with silver, its pinions with green G
72:15 may he live, may G of Sheba be given
105:37 Israel with silver and G, and there was none
115:4 idols are silver and G, the work of men's
119:72 me than thousands of G and silver pieces.
119:127 love thy commandments above G, above fine gold.
119:127 I love thy commandments above gold, above fine G
135:15 nations are silver and G, the work of men's
Prov 3:14 gain from silver and its profit better than G
8:10 knowledge rather than choice G;
8:19 fruit is better than G, even fine gold, and
8:19 than gold, even fine G, and my yield than
11:22 Like a G ring in a swine's snout is

16:16 wisdom is better than G; to get understanding is
17:3 the furnace is for G, and the LORD tries
20:15 There is G, and abundance of costly stones; but
22:1 riches, and favor is better than silver or G
25:11 is like apples of G in a setting of
25:12 Like a G ring or an ornament of gold
25:12 or an ornament of G is a wise reprover
27:21 the furnace is for G, and a man is
Eccl 2:8 for myself silver and G and the treasure of
Song 1:11 make you ornaments of G, studded with silver.
3:10 silver, its back of G, its seat of purple;
5:11 head is the finest G; his locks are wavy,
5:14 His arms are rounded G, set with jewels.
5:15 legs are alabaster columns, set upon bases of G
Wis 3:6 worthy of himself; like G in the furnace he
7:9 priceless gem, because all G is but a little
13:10 works of men's hands, G and silver fashioned with
15:9 competes with workers in G and silver, and imitates
Sir 2:5 For G is tested in the fire, and acceptable
7:18 real brother for the G of Ophir.
7:19 wife, for her charm is worth more than G
8:2 resources outweigh yours; for G has ruined many,
26:18 Like pillars of G on a base of silver,
28:24 up your silver and G,
29:11 High, and it will profit you more than G
30:15 are better than all G, and a robust body
31:5 He who loves G will not be justified, and
31:6 to ruin because of G, and their destruction has
31:8 found blameless, and who does not go after G
32:5 in a setting of G is a concert of
32:6 a rich setting of G is the melody of
40:25 G and silver make the foot stand sure, but
41:12 you longer than a thousand great stores of G
45:10 a holy garment, of G and blue and purple,
45:11 in a setting of G, the work of a
45:12 of Israel; with a G crown upon his turban,
47:18 of Israel, you gathered G like tin and amassed
50:9 a vessel of hammered G adorned with all kinds
51:28 silver, and you will gain by it much G
Is 2:7 filled with silver and G, and there is no
2:20 and their idols of G, which they made for
13:12 more rare than fine G, and mankind than the
13:12 and mankind than the G of Ophir.
13:17 regard for silver and do not delight in G
31:7 and his idols of G, which your hands have
39:2 house, the silver, the G, the spices, the precious
40:19 goldsmith overlays it with G, and casts for it
46:6 Those who lavish G from the purse, and weigh
60:6 They shall bring G and frankincense, and shall
60:9 far, their silver and G with them, for the
60:17 bronze I will bring G, and instead of iron
Jer 4:30 yourself with ornaments of G, that you enlarge your
10:4 it with silver and G; they fasten it with
10:9 brought from Tarshish, and G from Uphaz.
52:19 What was of G the captain of the guard
52:19 guard took away as G, and what was of
Lam 4:1 How the G has grown dim, how the pure
4:1 dim, how the pure G is changed!
4:2 their weight in fine G, how they are reckoned
Bar 3:17 hoard up silver and G, in which men trust,
3:30 found her, and will buy her for pure G
6:4 made of silver and G and wood, which are
6:8 themselves are overlaid with G and silver; but they
6:9 People take G and make crowns for the heads
6:10 the priests secretly take G and silver from their
6:11 gods of silver and G and wood,
6:24 As for the G which they wear for beauty--
6:30 gods of silver and G and wood;
6:39 wood and overlaid with G and silver are like
6:50 wood and overlaid with G and silver, it will
6:55 wooden gods overlaid with G or silver, their priests
6:57 overlaid with silver and G are not able to
6:58 strip them of their G and silver and of
6:70 of wood, overlaid with G and silver.
6:71 of wood, overlaid with G and silver, and like
Ezek 7:19 the streets, and their G is like an unclean
7:19 thing; their silver and G are not able to
16:13 you were decked with G and silver; and your
16:17 fair jewels of my G and of my silver,
27:22 kinds of spices, and all precious stones, and G
28:4 yourself, and have gathered G and silver into your
28:13 emerald; and wrought in G were your settings and
38:13 carry away silver and G, to take away cattle
Dan 2:32 image was of fine G, its breast and arms
2:35 the silver, and the G, all together were broken
2:38 over them all--you are the head of G
2:45 the bronze, the clay, the silver, and the G
3:1 made an image of G, whose height was sixty
5:2 that the vessels of G and of silver which
5:4 praised the gods of G and silver, bronze, iron,
5:7 have a chain of G about his neck, and
5:16 have a chain of G about your neck, and
5:23 gods of silver and G, of bronze, iron, wood,
5:29 purple, a chain of G was put about his
10:5 loins were girded with G of Uphaz.
11:8 of silver and of G; and for some years
11:38 he shall honor with G and silver, with precious
11:43 of the treasures of G and of silver, and
Hos 2:8 upon her silver and G which they used for
8:4 With their silver and G they made idols for
Joel 3:5 my silver and my G, and have carried my
Nah 2:9 Plunder the silver, plunder the G
Hab 2:19 it is overlaid with G and silver, and there
Zeph 1:18 their silver nor their G shall be able to
Hag 2:8 is mine, and the G is mine, says the
Zech 4:2 a lampstand all of G, with a bowl on
6:11 from them silver and G, and make a crown,
9:3 silver like dust, and G like the dirt of
13:9 and test them as G is tested.
14:14 about shall be collected, G, silver, and garments in
Mal 3:3 and refine them like G and silver, till they
1Mac 1:22 the crowns, and the G decoration on the front
1:23 the silver and the G, and the costly vessels;
2:18 honored with silver and G and many gifts."
3:41 they took silver and G in immense amounts, and
4:23 and they seized much G and silver, and cloth
6:1 city famed for its wealth in silver and G
6:12 vessels of silver and G; and I sent to
6:39 upon the shields of G and brass, the hills
8:3 of the silver and G mines there,
10:60 their friends silver and G and many gifts, and
11:24 Ptolemais, taking silver and G and clothing and
11:58 And he sent him G plate and a table
11:58 right to drink from G cups and dress in
11:58 purple and wear a G buckle.
13:37 We have received the G crown and the palm
14:24 Rome with a large G shield weighing a thousand
14:43 he should be clothed in purple and wear G
14:44 or put on a G buckle.
15:18 and have brought a G shield weighing a thousand
15:26 him, and silver and G and much military equipment.
15:32 the sideboard with its G and silver plate, and
16:11 had much silver and G,
16:19 give them silver and G and gifts;
2Mac 2:2 thoughts upon seeing the G and silver statues and
3:11 hundred talents of silver and two hundred of G
3:25 was seen to have armor and weapons of G
4:32 stole some of the G vessels of the temple
4:39 because many of the G vessels had already been
11:8 head, clothed in white and brandishing weapons of G
14:4 him a crown of G and a palm, and
Mt 2:11 offered him gifts, G and frankincense and myrrh.
10:9 Take no G, nor silver, nor copper in your
23:15 one swears by the G of the temple, he
23:16 which is greater, the G or the temple that
23:16 that has made the G sacred?
Acts 3:6 have no silver and G, but I give you
17:29 the Deity is like G, or silver, or stone,
20:33 no one's silver or G or apparel.
1Cor 3:12 the foundation with G, silver, precious stones, wood,
1Tim 2:9 with braided hair or G or pearls or costly
2Tim 2:20 not only vessels of G and silver but also
Heb 9:4 on all sides with G, which contained a golden
Jas 2:2 if a man with G rings and in fine
5:3 Your G and silver have rusted, and their rust
1Pet 1:7 faith, more precious than G which though perishable
1:18 such as silver or G,
3:3 of hair, decoration of G, and wearing of fine
Rev 3:18 to buy from me G refined by fire, that
9:7 looked like crowns of G; their faces were like
9:20 demons and idols of G and silver and bronze
17:4 scarlet, and bedecked with G and jewels and pearls,
18:12 any more, cargo of G, silver, jewels and pearls,
18:16 and scarlet, bedecked with G, with jewels, and with
21:15 a measuring rod of G to measure the city
21:18 the city was pure G, clear as glass.
21:21 the city was pure G, transparent as glass.

GOLD-PLATED

Is 30:22 graven images and your G molten images.

GOLD-WOVEN
Ps 45:13 in her chamber with G robes;

GOLDEN (83)
Ex 28:34 gold between them, a G bell and a pomegranate,
28:34 and a pomegranate, a G bell and a pomegranate,
30:4 And two G rings shall you make for it;
39:38 for the light; the G altar, the anointing oil
Lev 8:9 front, he set the G plate, the holy crown,
Num 4:11 And over the G altar they shall spread a
7:14 a cereal offering; one G dish of ten shekels,
7:20 a cereal offering; one G dish of ten shekels,
7:26 a cereal offering; one G dish of ten shekels,
7:32 a cereal offering; one G dish of ten shekels,
7:38 a cereal offering; one G dish of ten shekels,
7:44 a cereal offering; one G dish of ten shekels,
7:50 a cereal offering; one G dish of ten shekels,
7:56 a cereal offering; one G dish of ten shekels,
7:62 a cereal offering; one G dish of ten shekels,
7:68 a cereal offering; one G dish of ten shekels,
7:74 a cereal offering; one G dish of ten shekels,
7:80 a cereal offering; one G dish of ten shekels,
7:84 twelve silver basins, twelve G dishes,
7:86 the sanctuary, the twelve G dishes, full of incense,
Judg 8:24 they had G earrings, because they were Ishmaelites.)
8:26 the weight of the G earrings that he requested
1Sam 6:4 They answered, "Five G tumors and five golden mice,
6:4 golden tumors and five G mice, according to the
6:11 the box with the G mice and the images
6:15 in which were the G figures, and set them
6:17 These are the G tumors, which the Philistines
6:18 for Ekron; also the G mice, according to the
1Kgs 7:48 of the LORD: the G altar, the golden table
7:48 the golden altar, the G table for the bread
2Kgs 10:29 Israel to sin, the G calves that were in
1Chr 28:14 of gold for all G vessels for each service,
28:15 the weight of the G lampstands and their lamps,
28:17 the cups; for the G bowls and the weight
28:18 his plan for the G chariot of the cherubim
2Chr 4:7 And he made ten G lampstands as prescribed, and
4:19 house of God: the G altar, the tables for
13:8 have with you the G calves which Jeroboam made
13:11 and care for the G lampstand that its lamps
Esth 1:7 Drinks were served in G goblets, goblets of different
4:11 king holds out the G scepter that he may
5:2 out to Esther the G scepter that was in
8:4 king held out the G scepter to Esther,
8:15 white, with a great G crown and a mantle
15:11 Then he raised the G scepter and touched it
Job 37:22 of the north comes G splendor; God is clothed
Eccl 12:6 is snapped, or the G bowl is broken, or
Sir 6:30 Her yoke is a G ornament, and her bonds
21:21 education is like a G ornament, and like a
45:9 pomegranates, with very many G bells round about,
Jer 51:7 Babylon was a G cup in the LORD's hand,
Dan 3:5 and worship the G image that King Nebuchadnezzar
3:7 worshiped the G image which King Nebuchadnezzar
3:10 down and worship the G image;
3:12 gods or worship the G image which you have
3:14 gods or worship the G image which I have
3:18 gods or worship the G image which you have
5:3 they brought in the G and silver vessels which
Zech 4:12 are beside the two G pipes from which the
1Mac 1:21 sanctuary and took the G altar, the lampstand for
1:22 offerings, the bowls, the G censers, the curtain, the
4:57 of the temple with G crowns and small shields;
6:2 rich, containing G shields, breastplates, and weapons
10:20 purple robe and a G crown) "and you are
10:89 sent to him a G buckle, such as it
2Mac 5:3 missiles, the flash of G trappings, and armor of
10:29 men on horses with G bridles, and they were
15:15 gave to Judas a G sword, and as he
Heb 9:4 of Holies, having the G altar of incense and
9:4 gold, which contained a G urn holding the manna,
Rev 1:12 turning I saw seven G lampstands,
1:13 robe and with a G girdle round his breast;
1:20 hand, and the seven G lampstands, the seven stars
2:1 walks among the seven G lampstands.
4:4 in white garments, with G crowns upon their heads.
5:8 a harp, and with G bowls full of incense,
8:3 the altar with a G censer; and he was
8:3 the saints upon the G altar before the throne;
9:13 four horns of the G altar before God,
14:14 of man, with a G crown on his head,
15:6 their breasts girded with G girdles.
15:7 the seven angels seven G bowls full of the
17:4 in her hand a G cup full of abominations

GOLDEN-CLAD
2Mac 5:2 forty days, there appeared G horsemen charging

GOLDSMITH (6)
Is 40:19 casts it, and a G overlays it with gold,
41:7 craftsman encourages the G, and he who smooths
46:6 the scales, hire a G, and he makes it
Jer 10:9 the hands of the G; their clothing is violet
10:14 and without knowledge; every G is put to shame
51:17 and without knowledge; every G is put to shame

GOLDSMITHS (4)
Neh 3:8 the son of Harhaiah, G, repaired.
3:31 Malchijah, one of the G, repaired as far as
3:32 the Sheep Gate the G and the merchants repaired.
Bar 6:45 made by carpenters and G; they can be nothing

GOLGOTHA (3)
Mt 27:33 to a place called G (which means the place
Mk 15:22 to the place called G (which means the place
Jn 19:17 of a skull, which is called in Hebrew G

GOLIATH (7)
1Sam 17:4 Philistines a champion named G, of Gath, whose
17:23 the Philistine of Gath, G by name, came up
21:9 said, "The sword of G the Philistine, whom you
22:10 him the sword of G the Philistine."
2Sam 21:19 the Bethlehemite, slew G the Gittite, the shaft
1Chr 20:5 Lahmi the brother of G the Gittite, the shaft
Sir 47:4 the sling and struck down the boasting of G

GOMER (6)
Gen 10:2 The sons of Japheth: G, Magog, Madai, Javan, Tubal,
10:3 The sons of G: Ashkenaz, Riphath, and Togarmah.
1Chr 1:5 The sons of Japheth: G, Magog, Madai, Javan, Tubal,
1:6 The sons of G: Ashkenaz, Diphath, and Togarmah.
Ezek 38:6 with shield and helmet; G and all his hordes;
Hos 1:3 he went and took G the daughter of Diblaim,

GOMORRAH (23)
Gen 10:19 the direction of Sodom, G, Admah, and Zeboiim, as
13:10 this was before the LORD destroyed Sodom and G
14:2 Sodom, Birsha king of G, Shinab king of Admah,
14:8 Sodom, the king of G, the king of Admah,
14:10 kings of Sodom and G fled, some fell into
14:11 goods of Sodom and G, and all their provisions,
18:20 outcry against Sodom and G is great and their
19:24 rained on Sodom and G brimstone and fire from
19:28 down toward Sodom and G and toward all the
Deut 29:23 that of Sodom and G, Admah and Zeboiim, which
32:32 from the fields of G; their grapes are grapes
Is 1:9 should have been like Sodom, and become like G
1:10 the teaching of our God, you people of G
13:19 be like Sodom and G when God overthrew them.
Jer 23:14 like Sodom to me, and its inhabitants like G
49:18 As when Sodom and G and their neighbor cities
50:40 God overthrew Sodom and G and their neighbor
Amos 4:11 God overthrew Sodom and G, and you were as
Zeph 2:9 and the Ammonites like G, a land possessed by
Mt 10:15 land of Sodom and G than for that town.
Rom 9:29 have fared like Sodom and been made like G
2Pet 2:6 cities of Sodom and G to ashes he condemned
Jude 1:7 just as Sodom and G and the surrounding cities,

GONG
1Cor 13:1 I am a noisy G or a clanging cymbal.

GOOD (811)
Gen 1:4 that the light was G; and God separated the
1:10 And God saw that it was G
1:12 And God saw that it was G
1:18 And God saw that it was G
1:21 And God saw that it was G
1:25 And God saw that it was G
1:31 he had made, and behold, it was very G
2:9 to the sight and G for food, the tree
2:9 of the knowledge of G and evil.
2:12 of that land is G; bdellium and onyx stone
2:17 of the knowledge of G and evil you shall
2:18 said, "It is not G that the man should
3:5 be like God, knowing G and evil."
3:6 that the tree was G for food, and that
3:22 one of us, knowing G and evil; and now,
15:15 be buried in a G old age.

	18:7	a calf, tender and G, and gave it to
	21:16	over against him a G way off, about the
	24:50	LORD; we cannot speak to you bad or G
	25:8	and died in a G old age, an old
	26:29	to you nothing but G and have sent you
	27:9	and fetch me two G kids, that I may
	27:46	of the land, what G will my life be
	30:11	And Leah said, G fortune!" so she called his
	30:20	endowed me with a G dowry; now my husband
	30:34	Laban said, G
	31:24	word to Jacob, either G or bad."
	31:29	speak to Jacob neither G nor bad.'
	32:9	I will do you G
	32:12	'I will do you G, and make your descendants
	41:5	of grain, plump and G, were growing on one
	41:22	one stalk, full and G;
	41:24	swallowed up the seven G ears.
	41:26	The seven G cows are seven years, and the
	41:26	years, and the seven G ears are seven years;
	41:35	the food of these G years that are coming,
	41:37	This proposal seemed G to Pharaoh and to all
	44:4	to them, 'Why have you returned evil for G
	45:23	asses loaded with the G things of Egypt, and
	46:29	on his neck a G while.
	49:15	a resting place was G, and that the land
	50:20	God meant it for G, to bring it about
Ex	3:8	that land to a G and broad land, a
	18:9	rejoiced for all the G which the LORD had
	18:17	to him, "What you are doing is not G
	21:34	pit shall make it G; he shall give money
Lev	5:4	evil or to do G, any sort of rash
	24:18	beast shall make it G, life for life.
	24:21	beast shall make it G; and he who kills
	27:10	or exchange it, a G for a bad, or
	27:10	a bad for a G; and if he makes
	27:12	value it as either G or bad; as you,
	27:14	value it as either G or bad; as the
	27:33	inquire whether it is G or bad, neither shall
Num	10:29	we will do you G; for the LORD has
	10:29	the LORD has promised G to Israel."
	10:32	go with us, whatever G the LORD will do
	13:19	they dwell in is G or bad, and whether
	13:20	Be of G courage, and bring some of the
	14:7	out, is an exceedingly G land.
	24:13	LORD, to do either G or bad of my
Deut	1:14	you have spoken is G for us to do.'
	1:23	come.' The thing seemed G to me, and I
	1:25	said, 'It is a G land which the LORD
	1:35	generation shall see the G land which I swore
	1:39	have no knowledge of G or evil, shall go
	2:4	So take G heed;
	3:25	pray, and see the G land beyond the Jordan,
	4:15	"Therefore take G heed to yourselves.
	4:21	should not enter the G land which the LORD
	4:22	take possession of that G land.
	6:11	houses full of all G things, which you did
	6:18	what is right and G in the sight of
	6:18	take possession of the G land which the LORD
	6:24	our God, for our G always, that he might
	8:7	bringing you into a G land, a land of
	8:10	your God for the G land he has given
	8:16	you, to do you G in the end.
	9:6	not giving you this G land to possess because
	10:13	which I command you this day for your G
	11:17	perish quickly off the G land which the LORD
	12:28	you do what is G and right in the
	26:11	rejoice in all the G which the LORD your
	28:12	open to you his G treasury the heavens, to
	28:63	delight in doing you G and multiplying you, so
	30:15	this day life and G, death and evil.
	31:6	Be strong and of G courage, do not fear
	31:7	"Be strong and of G courage; for you shall
	31:23	"Be strong and of G courage; for you shall
Josh	1:6	Be strong and of G courage; for you shall
	1:7	that you may have G success wherever you go.
	1:8	then you shall have G success.
	1:9	Be strong and of G courage; be not frightened,
	1:18	be strong and of G courage."
	9:25	do as it seems G and right in your
	10:25	be strong and of G courage; for thus the
	21:45	one of all the G promises which the LORD
	22:5	Take G care to observe the commandment and the
	23:11	Take G heed to yourselves, therefore, to love the
	23:13	perish from off this G land which the LORD
	23:14	failed of all the G things which the LORD
	23:15	just as all the G things which the LORD
	23:15	you from off this G land which the LORD
	23:16	quickly from off the G land which he has
	24:20	harm, and consume you, after having done you G
Judg	8:32	Joash died in a G old age, and was
	8:35	return for all the G that he had done
	9:11	my sweetness and my G fruit, and go to
	9:15	the trees, 'If in G faith you are anointing
	9:16	if you acted in G faith and honor when
	9:19	then have acted in G faith and honor with
	10:15	to us whatever seems G to thee; only deliver
	18:22	When they were a G way from the home
	19:24	with them what seems G to you; but against
1Sam	2:24	sons; it is no G report that I hear
	3:18	him do what seems G to him."
	11:10	to us whatever seems G to you."
	12:23	instruct you in the G and the right way.
	14:36	said, "Do whatever seems G to you." But the
	14:40	Saul, "Do what seems G to you."
	15:9	and all that was G, and would not utterly
	16:18	and a man of G presence; and the LORD
	18:5	And this was G in the sight of all
	19:4	deeds have been of G service to you;
	20:7	family.' If he says, G it will be well
	24:4	as it shall seem G to you."' Then David
	24:17	you have repaid me G, whereas I have repaid
	24:19	LORD reward you with G for what you have
	25:3	The woman was of G understanding and beautiful,
	25:15	the men were very G to us, and we
	25:21	him; and he has returned me evil for G
	25:30	according to all the G that he has spoken
	26:16	This thing that you have done is not G
	31:9	Philistines, to carry the G news to their idols
2Sam	2:6	And I will do G to you because you
	3:13	And he said, G; I will make a covenant
	3:19	house of Benjamin thought G to do.
	4:10	thought he was bringing G news, I seized him
	7:28	thou hast promised this G thing to thy servant;
	10:12	Be of G courage, and let us play the
	10:12	LORD do what seems G to him."
	13:22	spoke to Amnon neither G nor bad; for Absalom
	14:17	of God to discern G and evil.
	15:3	"See, your claims are G and right; but there
	15:26	to me what seems G to him."
	16:12	will repay me with G for this cursing of
	17:7	the counsel which Ahithophel has given is not G
	17:14	ordained to defeat the G counsel of Ahithophel, so
	18:27	said, "He is a G man, and comes with
	18:27	man, and comes with G tidings."
	18:31	and the Cushite said, G tidings for my lord
	19:27	do therefore what seems G to you.
	19:37	for him whatever seems G to you."
	19:38	for him whatever seems G to you; and all
	24:22	offer up what seems G to him; here are
1Kgs	1:42	worthy man and bring G news."
	2:38	"What you say is G; as my lord the
	2:42	'What you say is G; I obey.'
	3:9	I may discern between G and evil; for who
	8:36	dost teach them the G way in which they
	8:56	failed of all his G promise, which he uttered
	12:7	serve them, and speak G words to them when
	14:15	Israel out of this G land which he gave
	21:2	or, if it seems G to you, I will
	22:8	for he never prophesies G concerning me, but evil."
	22:18	he would not prophesy G concerning me, but evil?"
2Kgs	3:19	and shall fell every G tree, and stop up
	3:19	water, and ruin every G piece of land with
	3:25	cities, and on every G piece of land every
	3:25	and felled all the G trees; till only its
	7:9	is a day of G news; if we are
	10:5	king; do whatever is G in your eyes."
	20:3	have done what is G in thy sight." And
	20:19	of the LORD which you have spoken is G
1Chr	4:40	where they found rich, G pasture, and the land
	10:9	Philistines, to carry the G news to their idols
	13:2	Israel, "If it seems G to you, and if
	16:34	LORD, for he is G; for his steadfast love
	17:26	thou hast promised this G thing to thy servant;
	19:13	Be of G courage, and let us play the
	19:13	LORD do what seems G to him."
	21:23	king do what seems G to him; see, I
	22:13	Be strong, and of G courage.
	28:8	you may possess this G land, and leave it
	28:20	"Be strong and of G courage, and do it.
	29:28	he died in a G old age, full of
2Chr	5:13	LORD, "For he is G, for his steadfast love
	6:27	dost teach them the G way in which they

7:3 saying, "For he is G, for his steadfast love
10:7 please them, and speak G words to them, then
12:12 destruction; moreover, conditions were G in Judah.
14:2 Asa did what was G and right in the
18:7 for he never prophesies G concerning me, but always
18:17 he would not prophesy G concerning me, but evil?"
19:3 Nevertheless some G is found in you, for you
24:16 because he had done G in Israel, and toward
30:18 for them, saying, "The G LORD pardon every one
30:22 the Levites who showed G skill in the service
31:20 he did what was G and right and faithful
32:7 "Be strong and of G courage.
32:32 of Hezekiah, and his G deeds, behold, they are
35:26 of Josiah, and his G deeds according to what
Ezra 3:11 LORD, "For he is G, for his steadfast love
5:17 Therefore, if it seem G to the king, let
7:9 to Jerusalem, for the G hand of his God
7:18 Whatever seems G to you and your brethren to
8:18 And by the G hand of our God upon
8:22 our God is for G upon all that seek
9:12 strong, and eat the G of the land, and
Neh 2:8 I asked, for the G hand of my God
2:18 been upon me for G, and also of the
2:18 their hands for the G work.
5:9 "The thing that you are doing is not G
5:19 Remember for my G, O my God, all that
6:19 they spoke of his G deeds in my presence,
9:13 and true laws, G statutes and commandments,
9:20 Thou gavest thy G Spirit to instruct them, and
9:25 houses full of all G things, cisterns hewn out,
9:36 its fruit and its G gifts, behold, we are
13:14 wipe not out my G deeds that I have
13:31 Remember me, O my God, for G
Tob 1:13 gave me favor and G appearance in the sight
2:1 the seven weeks, a G dinner was prepared for
4:9 be laying up a G treasure for yourself against
4:19 Lord himself gives all G things, and according to
5:13 of mine, of a G and noble lineage.
5:13 brother, you come of G stock.
5:16 for the journey, and G success to you both."
5:21 For a G angel will go with him; his
7:4 them, "Is he in G health?"
7:5 is alive and in G health." And Tobias said,
7:7 exclaimed, "Son of that G and noble man!" When
8:6 say, 'It is not G that the man should
10:12 Let me hear a G report of you.
11:11 eyes, saying, "Be of G cheer, father."
12:6 It is G to praise God and to exalt
12:7 It is G to guard the secret of a
12:7 Do G, and evil will not overtake you.
12:8 Prayer is G when accompanied by fasting,
12:11 have said, 'It is G to guard the secret
12:13 out the dead, your G deed was not hidden
14:4 the earth from the G land, and Jerusalem will
Jud 3:4 any way that seems G to you."
11:8 you are the one G man in the whole
15:8 came to witness the G things which the Lord
15:10 you have done great G to Israel, and God
Esth 3:11 them as it seems G to you."
5:13 this does me no G, so long as I
13:3 distinguished for his unchanging G will and steadfast
16:6 natures beguile the sincere G will of their sovereigns.
16:11 so far enjoyed the G will that we have
16:22 observe this with all G cheer as a notable
Job 2:10 Shall we receive G at the hand of God,
5:27 Hear, and know it for your G
7:7 a breath; my eye will never again see G
9:25 a runner; they flee away, they see no G
9:27 countenance, and be of G cheer,'
10:3 Does it seem G to thee to oppress, to
15:3 in words with which he can do no G
21:25 in bitterness of soul, never having tasted of G
22:18 filled their houses with G things-- but the
22:21 be at peace; thereby G will come to you.
24:21 woman, and do no G to the widow.
30:26 when I looked for G, evil came; and when
34:4 right; let us determine among ourselves what is G
Ps 4:6 who say, "O that we might see some G
14:1 do abominable deeds, there is none that does G
14:3 is none that does G, no, not one.
16:2 Lord; I have no G apart from thee."
25:8 G and upright is the LORD; therefore he instructs
34:8 O taste and see that the LORD is G
34:10 the LORD lack no G thing.
34:12 and covets many days, that he may enjoy G
34:14 from evil, and do G; seek peace, and pursue
35:12 requite me evil for G; my soul is forlorn.
36:3 he has ceased to act wisely and do G
36:4 way that is not G; he spurns not evil.
37:3 the LORD, and do G; so you will dwell
37:27 from evil, and do G; so shall you abide
38:20 render me evil for G are my adversaries because
38:20 good are my adversaries because I follow after G
51:18 Do G to Zion in thy good pleasure; rebuild
51:18 to Zion in thy G pleasure; rebuild the walls
52:3 love evil more than G, and lying more than
52:9 name, for it is G, in the presence of
53:1 doing abominable iniquity; there is none that does G
53:3 is none that does G, no, not one.
54:6 to thy name, O LORD, for it is G
69:16 thy steadfast love is G; according to thy abundant
73:1 Truly God is G to the upright, to those
73:28 for me it is G to be near God;
84:11 No G thing does the LORD withhold from those
85:12 will give what is G, and our land will
86:5 thou, O Lord, art G and forgiving, abounding in
92:1 It is G to give thanks to the LORD,
100:5 For the LORD is G; his steadfast love endures
103:5 who satisfies you with G as long as you
104:28 they are filled with G things.
106:1 LORD, for he is G; for his steadfast love
107:1 LORD, for he is G; for his steadfast love
107:9 hungry he fills with G things.
109:5 reward me evil for G, and hatred for my
109:21 thy steadfast love is G, deliver me!
111:10 beginning of wisdom; a G understanding have all
118:1 LORD, for he is G; his steadfast love endures
118:29 LORD, for he is G; for his steadfast love
119:39 reproach which I dread; for thy ordinances are G
119:66 Teach me G judgment and knowledge, for I believe
119:68 Thou art G and doest good; teach me thy
119:68 art good and doest G; teach me thy statutes.
119:71 It is G for me that I was afflicted,
119:122 for thy servant for G; let not the godless
122:9 the LORD our God, I will seek your G
125:4 Do G, O LORD, to those who are good,
125:4 to those who are G, and to those who
133:1 Behold, how G and pleasant it is when brothers
135:3 for the LORD is G; sing to his name,
136:1 LORD, for he is G, for his steadfast love
141:5 Let a G man strike or rebuke me in
143:10 Let thy G spirit lead me on a level
145:9 The LORD is G to all, and his compassion
147:1 For it is G to sing praises to our
Prov 2:9 justice and equity, every G path;
2:20 in the way of G men and keep to
3:4 will find favor and G repute in the sight
3:27 Do not withhold G from those to whom it
4:3 for I give you G precepts: do not forsake
4:10 G and Evil
11:23 righteous ends only in G; the expectation of the
11:27 He who diligently seeks G seeks favor, but evil
12:2 A G man obtains favor from the LORD, but
12:4 A G wife is the crown of her husband,
12:8 commended according to his G sense, but one of
12:14 man is satisfied with G, and the work of
12:20 but those who plan G have joy.
12:25 him down, but a G word makes him glad.
13:2 of his mouth a G man eats good, but
13:2 a good man eats G, but the desire of
13:15 G sense wins favor, but the way of the
13:22 A G man leaves an inheritance to his children's
14:14 his ways, and a G man with the fruit
14:19 bow down before the G, the wicked at the
14:22 Those who devise G meet loyalty and faithfulness.
15:3 place, keeping watch on the evil and the G
15:23 word in season, how G it is!
15:30 rejoices the heart, and G news refreshes the bones.
16:29 leads him in a way that is not G
17:13 man returns evil for G, evil will not depart
17:22 cheerful heart is a G medicine, but a downcast
17:26 righteous man is not G; to flog noble men
18:5 It is not G to be partial to a
18:22 a wife finds a G thing, and obtains favor
19:2 It is not G for a man to be
19:11 G sense makes a man slow to anger, and
20:23 to the LORD, and false scales are not G
22:1 A G name is to be chosen rather than
24:13 honey, for it is G, and the drippings of
24:23 Partiality in judging is not G
24:25 have delight, and a G blessing will be upon
25:25 thirsty soul, so is G news from a far

25:27 It is not G to eat much honey, so
28:21 show partiality is not G; but for a piece
31:10 A G wife who can find?
31:12 She does him G, and not harm, all the
Eccl 2:3 might see what was G for the sons of
4:9 because they have a G reward for their toil.
5:18 have seen to be G and to be fitting
6:3 does not enjoy life's G things, and also has
6:6 told, yet enjoy no G --do not all go
6:12 who knows what is G for man while he
7:1 A G name is better than precious ointment; and
7:11 Wisdom is G with an inheritance, an advantage to
7:18 It is G that you should take hold of
7:20 on earth who does G and never sins.
8:15 for man has no G thing under the sun
9:2 the wicked, to the G and the evil, to
9:2 As is the G man, so is the sinner;
9:18 weapons of war, but one sinner destroys much G
11:6 or that, or whether both alike will be G
12:14 every secret thing, whether G or evil.
Wis 2:6 let us enjoy the G things that exist, and
3:5 they will receive great G, because God tested them
3:15 For the fruit of G labors is renowned, and
4:5 enough to eat, and G for nothing.
4:12 wickedness obscures what is G, and roving desire
5:8 And what G has our boasted wealth brought us?
7:11 All G things came to me along with her,
7:22 distinct, invulnerable, loving the G, keen, irresistible,
8:9 she would give me G counsel and encouragement in
8:19 well endowed, and a G soul fell to my
8:20 lot; or rather, being G, I entered an undefiled
10:8 hindered from recognizing the G, but also left for
12:19 filled thy sons with G hope, because thou givest
12:21 and covenants full of G promises!
13:1 were unable from the G things that are seen
14:26 confusion over what is G, forgetfulness of favors,
18:9 the holy children of G men offered sacrifices, and
Sir 1:21 will tell of his G sense.
2:9 the Lord, hope for G things, for everlasting joy
6:19 and wait for her G harvest.
7:13 lie, for the habit of lying serves no G
7:19 of a wise and G wife, for her charm
8:19 you drive away your G luck.
11:2 a man for his G looks, nor loathe a
11:12 upon him for his G; he lifts him out
11:14 G things and bad, life and death, poverty and
11:29 lies in wait, turning G into evil, and to
12:1 be thanked for your G deeds.
12:2 Do G to a godly man, and you will
12:3 No G will come to the man who persists
12:5 Do G to the humble, but do not give
12:5 evil for all the G which you do to
12:7 Give to the G man, but do not help
13:23 Riches are G if they are free from sin,
13:24 his countenance, either for G or for evil.
14:7 even if he does G, he does it unintentionally,
14:13 Do G to a friend before you die, and
14:14 your share of desired G pass by you.
16:27 filled it with his G things;
17:6 understanding, and showed them G and evil.
18:7 What is his G and what is his evil?
18:14 mix reproach with your G deeds, nor cause grief
18:16 a word surpass a G gift?
20:8 There may be G fortune for a man in
20:15 no gratitude for my G deeds; those who eat
25:2 old man who lacks G sense.
25:4 the aged to possess G counsel!
25:9 he who has gained G sense, and he who
26:1 the husband of a G wife; the number of
26:3 A G wife is a great blessing; she will
26:16 the beauty of a G wife in her well-ordered
29:14 A G man will be surety for his neighbor,
30:18 G things poured out upon a mouth that is
30:25 man of cheerful and G heart will give heed
31:17 for the sake of G manners, and do not
32:1 one of them; take G care of them and
32:6 melody of music with G wine.
32:11 Leave in G time and do not be the
32:13 satisfies you with his G gifts.
32:22 smooth way, and give G heed to your paths.
33:14 G is the opposite of evil, and life the
37:9 against you and tell you, "Your way is G
37:18 turns of fortune appear, G and evil, life and
37:28 For not everything is G for every one, and
38:21 do the dead no G, and you injure yourself.
39:4 for he tests the G and the evil among
39:16 for they are very G, and whatever he commands
39:25 From the beginning G things were created for good
39:25 things were created for G people, just as evil
39:27 All these are for G to the godly, just
39:33 the Lord are all G, and he will supply
39:34 all things will prove G in their season.
40:12 be blotted out, but G faith will stand for
40:25 foot stand sure, but G counsel is esteemed more
41:4 can you reject the G pleasure of the Most
41:13 The days of a G life are numbered, but
41:13 are numbered, but a G name endures for ever.
41:16 words: For it is G to retain every kind
42:6 a seal is a G thing; and where there
42:14 a woman who does G; and it is a
42:25 One confirms the G things of the other, and
46:10 see that it is G to follow the Lord.
49:9 with storm, and did G to those who directed
51:18 was zealous for the G; and I shall never
51:21 I have gained a G possession.
Is 1:17 evil, learn to do G; seek justice, correct oppression;
1:19 you shall eat the G of the land;
5:20 those who call evil G and good evil, who
5:20 call evil good and G evil, who put darkness
7:15 how to refuse the evil and choose the G
7:16 evil and choose the G, the land before whose
32:4 the rash will have G judgment, and the tongue
38:3 have done what is G in thy sight." And
39:8 of the LORD which you have spoken is G
40:9 O Zion, herald of G tidings; lift up your
40:9 O Jerusalem, herald of G tidings, lift it up,
41:7 the soldering, "It is G; and they fasten it
41:23 you are gods; do G, or do harm, that
41:27 Jerusalem a herald of G tidings.
52:7 of him who brings G tidings, who publishes peace,
52:7 publishes peace, who brings G tidings of good, who
52:7 brings good tidings of G, who publishes salvation,
55:2 and eat what is G, and delight yourselves in
58:11 satisfy your desire with G things, and make your
61:1 anointed me to bring G tidings to the afflicted;
65:2 way that is not G, following their own devices;
Jer 2:7 its fruits and its G things.
4:22 but how to do G they know not."
5:25 your sins have kept G from you.
6:16 ancient paths, where the G way is; and walk
8:15 for peace, but no G came, for a time
10:5 evil, neither is it in them to do G
13:7 was spoiled; it was G for nothing.
13:10 this waistcloth, which is G for nothing.
13:23 also you can do G who are accustomed to
14:19 for peace, but no G came; for a time
15:11 entreated thee for their G, if I have not
17:6 shall not see any G come.
18:4 vessel, as it seemed G to the potter to
18:10 will repent of the G which I had intended
18:20 Is evil a recompense for G
18:20 before thee to speak G for them, to turn
21:10 evil and not for G, says the LORD: it
24:2 One basket had very G figs, like first-ripe figs,
24:3 I said, "Figs, the G figs very good, and
24:3 the good figs very G, and the bad figs
24:5 of Israel: Like these G figs, so I will
24:5 I will regard as G the exiles from Judah,
24:6 eyes upon them for G, and I will bring
26:14 with me as seems G and right to you.
29:32 people to see the G that I will do
32:39 ever, for their own G and the good of
32:39 own good and the G of their children after
32:40 turn away from doing G to them; and I
32:41 rejoice in doing them G, and I will plant
32:42 upon them all the G that I promise them.
33:9 hear of all the G that I do for
33:9 because of all the G and all the prosperity
33:11 for the LORD is G, for his steadfast love
39:16 evil and not for G, and they shall be
40:4 If it seems G to you to come with
40:4 wherever you think it G and right to go.
42:6 Whether it is G or evil, we will obey
44:27 evil and not for G; all the men of
Lam 3:25 The LORD is G to those who wait for
3:26 It is G that one should wait quietly for
3:27 It is G for a man that he bear
3:38 the Most High that G and evil come?
Bar 6:34 evil to them or G, they will not be
6:38 a widow or do G to an orphan.
6:64 case or to do G to men.
Ezek 17:8 he transplanted it to G soil by abundant waters,

18:18 did what is not G among his people, behold,
20:25 statutes that were not G and ordinances by which
24:4 of flesh, all the G pieces, the thigh and
34:14 will feed them with G pasture, and upon the
34:14 shall lie down in G grazing land, and on
34:18 to feed on the G pasture, that you must
36:11 and will do more G to you than ever
36:31 deeds that were not G; and you will loathe
Dan 3:15 have made, well and G; but if you do
3:90 Lord, for he is G, for his mercy endures
4:2 It has seemed G to me to show the
10:19 be strong and of G courage." And when he
Hos 4:13 oak, poplar, and terebinth, because their shade is G
8:3 Israel has spurned the G; the enemy shall pursue
14:2 accept that which is G and we will render
Amos 5:14 Seek G, and not evil, that you may live;
5:15 Hate evil, and love G, and establish justice in
9:4 eyes upon them for evil and not for G
Mic 1:12 Maroth wait anxiously for G, because evil has come
2:7 not my words do G to him who walks
3:2 you who hate the G and love the evil,
6:8 O man, what is G; and what does the
Nah 1:7 The LORD is G, a stronghold in the day
1:15 of him who brings G tidings, who proclaims peace!
Zeph 1:12 LORD will not do G, nor will he do
Zech 3:8 they are men of G omen: behold, I will
8:15 these days to do G to Jerusalem and to
9:17 Yea, how G and how fair it shall be!
Mal 2:17 who does evil is G in the sight of
3:14 What is the G of our keeping his charge
1Mac 4:24 Heaven, for he is G, for his mercy endures
6:12 inhabitants of Judah without G reason.
6:40 advanced steadily and in G order.
10:27 will repay you with G for what you do
11:33 have determined to do G, because of the good
11:33 good, because of the G will they show toward
14:4 He sought the G of his nation; his rule
14:9 all talked together of G things; and the youths
15:20 And it has seemed G to us to accept
16:17 act of great treachery and returned evil for G
2Mac 1:1 in Egypt, Greeting, and G peace.
1:2 May God do G to you, and may he
1:10 in Egypt, Greeting, and G health.
4:37 of the moderation and G conduct of the deceased;
4:45 But Menelaus, already as G as beaten, promised a
5:4 to have been a G omen.
6:28 how to die a G death willingly and nobly
6:29 acted toward him with G will now changed to
7:20 she bore it with G courage because of her
8:21 he filled them with G courage and made them
9:19 sends hearty greetings and G wishes for their health
9:21 affection your esteem and G will.
9:22 condition, for I have G hope of recovering from
9:26 to maintain your present G will, each of you,
11:6 Lord to send a G angel to save Israel.
11:15 regard for the common G, agreed to all that
11:19 will maintain your G will toward the government,
11:26 policy and be of G cheer and go on
11:28 We also are in G health.
12:30 bore witness to the G will which the people
13:26 appeased them, gained their G will, and set out
14:26 when Alcimus noticed their G will for one another,
14:37 of and for his G will was called father
15:12 priest, a noble and G man, of modest bearing
15:23 the heavens, send a G angel to carry terror
15:30 who maintained his youthful G will toward his
Mt 3:10 that does not bear G fruit is cut down
5:13 It is no longer G for anything except to
5:16 they may see your G works and give glory
5:45 evil and on the G, and sends rain on
7:11 know how to give G gifts to your children,
7:11 is in heaven give G things to those who
7:17 every sound tree bears G fruit, but the bad
7:18 a bad tree bear G fruit.
7:19 that does not bear G fruit is cut down
11:5 and the poor have G news preached to them.
12:12 is lawful to do G on the sabbath."
12:33 "Either make the tree G, and its fruit good;
12:33 good, and its fruit G; or make the tree
12:34 how can you speak G, when you are evil?
12:35 The G man out of his good treasure brings
12:35 man out of his G treasure brings forth good,
12:35 good treasure brings forth G, and the evil man
13:8 Other seeds fell on G soil and brought forth
13:23 what was sown on G soil, this is he
13:24 a man who sowed G seed in his field;
13:27 did you not sow G seed in your field?
13:37 "He who sows the G seed is the Son
13:38 the world, and the G seed means the sons
13:48 down and sorted the G into vessels but threw
19:16 him, saying, "Teacher, what G deed must I do,
19:17 "Why do you ask me about what is G
19:17 One there is who is G
22:10 found, both bad and G; so the wedding hall
25:21 to him, 'Well done, G and faithful servant; you
25:23 to him, 'Well done, G and faithful servant; you
Mk 3:4 the sabbath to do G or to do harm,
4:8 other seeds fell into G soil and brought forth
4:20 were sown upon the G soil are the ones
9:48 Salt is G; but if the salt has lost
10:17 him, and asked him, G Teacher, what must I
10:18 said to him, "Why do you call me G
10:18 No one is G but God alone.
14:7 will, you can do G to them; but you
Lk 1:3 the word, it seemed G to me also, having
1:19 to bring you this G news.
1:53 filled the hungry with G things, and the rich
2:10 behold, I bring you G news of a great
3:9 that does not bear G fruit is cut down
3:18 exhortations, he preached G news to the people.
4:18 anointed me to preach G news to the poor.
4:43 "I must preach the G news of the kingdom
5:39 desires new; for he says, 'The old is G
6:9 the sabbath to do G or to do harm,
6:27 Love your enemies, do G to those who hate
6:33 And if you do G to those who do
6:33 to those who do G to you, what credit
6:35 your enemies, and do G, and lend, expecting nothing
6:38 be given to you; G measure, pressed down, shaken
6:43 "For no G tree bears bad fruit, nor again
6:43 a bad tree bear G fruit;
6:45 The G man out of the good treasure of
6:45 man out of the G treasure of his heart
6:45 of his heart produces G, and the evil man
7:22 up, the poor have G news preached to them.
8:1 preaching and bringing the G news of the kingdom
8:8 And some fell into G soil and grew, and
8:15 for that in the G soil, they are those
8:15 in an honest and G heart, and bring forth
10:42 Mary has chosen the G portion, which shall not
11:13 know how to give G gifts to your children,
12:32 it is your Father's G pleasure to give you
13:9 next year, well and G; but if not, you
14:34 "Salt is G; but if salt has lost its
16:16 John; since then the G news of the kingdom
16:25 your lifetime received your G things, and Lazarus in
18:18 a ruler asked him, G Teacher, what shall I
18:19 said to him, "Why do you call me G
18:19 No one is G but God alone.
19:17 to him, 'Well done, G servant!
23:49 of the council, a G and righteous man,
Jn 1:46 to him, "Can anything G come out of Nazareth?"
2:10 "Every man serves the G wine first; and when
2:10 you have kept the G wine until now."
5:28 those who have done G, to the resurrection of
7:12 said, "He is a G man," others said, "No,
10:11 I am the G shepherd.
10:11 The G shepherd lays down his life for the
10:14 I am the G shepherd; I know my own
10:32 have shown you many G works from the Father;
10:33 is not for a G work that we stone
16:33 tribulation; but be of G cheer, I have overcome
Acts 4:9 examined today concerning a G deed done to a
6:3 you seven men of G repute, full of the
8:12 Philip as he preached G news about the kingdom
8:35 he told him the G news of Jesus.
9:36 She was full of G works and acts of
10:36 sent to Israel, preaching G news of peace by
10:38 he went about doing G and healing all that
11:24 for he was a G man, full of the
13:32 we bring you the G news that what God
14:15 you, and bring you G news, that you should
14:17 witness, for he did G and gave you from
15:22 Then it seemed G to the apostles and the
15:25 instructions, it has seemed G to us, having come
15:28 For it has seemed G to the Holy Spirit
23:1 before God in all G conscience up to this
Rom 2:10 every one who does G, the Jew first and
3:8 not do evil that G may come?—as some
3:12 wrong; no one does G, not even one."
4:19 body, which was as G as dead because he
5:7 though perhaps for a G man one will dare

G

	7:12	and the commandment is holy and just and G
	7:13	Did that which is G, then, bring death to
	7:13	me through what is G, in order that sin
	7:16	not want, I agree that the law is G
	7:18	I know that nothing G dwells within me, that
	7:19	do not do the G I want, but the
	8:28	everything God works for G with those who love
	9:11	had done nothing either G or bad, in order
	10:15	of those who preach G news!"
	12:2	of God, what is G and acceptable and perfect.
	12:9	fast to what is G;
	12:21	be overcome by evil, but overcome evil with G
	13:3	not a terror to G conduct, but to bad.
	13:3	Then do what is G, and you will receive
	13:4	approval, for he is God's servant for your G
	14:16	do not let your G be spoken of as
	15:2	his neighbor for his G, to edify him.
	16:19	as to what is G and guileless as to
1Cor	5:6	Your boasting is not G
	7:35	you, but to promote G order and to secure
	9:11	we have sown spiritual G among you, is it
	10:24	one seek his own G, but the good of
	10:24	own good, but the G of his neighbor.
	12:7	the manifestation of the Spirit for the common G
	15:33	deceived: "Bad company ruins G morals."
2Cor	5:6	we are always of G courage; we know that
	5:8	We are of G courage, and we would rather
	5:10	each one may receive G or evil, according to
	6:8	in ill repute and G repute.
	8:19	and to show our G will.
	9:8	in abundance for every G work.
Gal	4:17	you, but for no G purpose; they want to
	4:18	For a G purpose it is always good to
	4:18	purpose it is always G to be made much
	6:6	the word share all G things with him who
	6:10	opportunity, let us do G to all men, and
	6:12	want to make a G showing in the flesh
Eph	2:10	in Christ Jesus for G works, which God prepared
	4:29	only such as is G for edifying, as fits
	5:9	in all that is G and right and true),
	6:7	rendering service with a G will as to the
	6:8	men, knowing that whatever G any one does, he
Phil	1:6	he who began a G work in you will
	1:15	rivalry, but others from G will.
	2:13	to work for his G pleasure.
Col	1:10	bearing fruit in every G work and increasing in
	2:5	rejoicing to see your G order and the firmness
1Thes	3:6	has brought us the G news of your faith
	5:15	always seek to do G to one another and
	5:21	hold fast what is G,
2Thes	1:11	and may fulfil every G resolve and work of
	2:16	us eternal comfort and G hope through grace,
	2:17	establish them in every G work and word.
1Tim	1:5	pure heart and a G conscience and sincere faith.
	1:8	that the law is G, if any one uses
	1:18	you may wage the G warfare,
	1:19	holding faith and a G conscience.
	2:3	This is G, and it is acceptable in the
	2:10	costly attire but by G deeds, as befits women
	3:13	as deacons gain a G standing for themselves and
	4:4	created by God is G, and nothing is to
	4:6	you will be a G minister of Christ Jesus,
	4:6	faith and of the G doctrine which you have
	5:10	well attested for her G deeds, as one who
	5:10	devoted herself to doing G in every way.
	5:25	So also G deeds are conspicuous; and even when
	6:12	Fight the G fight of the faith; take hold
	6:12	when you made the G confession in the presence
	6:13	Pontius Pilate made the G confession,
	6:18	They are to do G, to be rich in
	6:18	to be rich in G deeds, liberal and generous,
	6:19	up for themselves a G foundation for the future,
2Tim	2:3	in suffering as a G soldier of Christ Jesus.
	2:14	words, which does no G, but only ruins the
	2:21	house, ready for any G work.
	3:3	profligates, fierce, haters of G,
	3:17	complete, equipped for every G work.
	4:7	I have fought the G fight, I have finished
Tit	1:15	disobedient, unfit for any G deed.
	2:3	to teach what is G,
	2:7	respects a model of G deeds, and in your
	2:14	who are zealous for G deeds.
	3:8	to apply themselves to G deeds; these are excellent
	3:14	to apply themselves to G deeds, so as to
Philem	1:6	knowledge of all the G that is ours in
Heb	4:2	For G news came to us just as to
	4:6	who formerly received the G news failed to enter
	5:14	by practice to distinguish G from evil.
	9:11	high priest of the G things that have come,
	10:1	a shadow of the G things to come instead
	10:24	another to love and G works,
	11:12	man, and him as G as dead, were born
	12:10	disciplines us for our G, that we may share
	13:16	not neglect to do G and to share what
	13:21	equip you with everything G that you may do
Jas	1:16	Every G endowment and every perfect gift is from
	3:13	By his G life let him show his works
	3:17	full of mercy and G fruits, without uncertainty or
1Pet	1:12	those who preached the G news to you through
	1:25	That word is the G news which was preached
	2:12	Maintain G conduct among the Gentiles, so that in
	2:12	they may see your G deeds and glorify God
	3:10	love life and see G days, let him keep
	3:16	those who revile your G behavior in Christ may
	4:10	for one another, as G stewards of God's varied
3Jn	1:11	Beloved, do not imitate evil but imitate G
	1:11	He who does G is of God; he who

GOOD-LOOKING

Gen	39:6	Now Joseph was handsome and G

GOODLY (11)

Ex	2:2	that he was a G child, she hid him
Lev	23:40	day the fruit of G trees, branches of palm
Deut	3:25	beyond the Jordan, that G hill country, and Lebanon.'
	6:10	you, with great and G cities, which you did
	8:12	full, and have built G houses and live in
Job	41:12	mighty strength, or his G frame.
Ps	16:6	yea, I have a G heritage.
	21:3	dost meet him with G blessings; thou dost set
	45:1	heart overflows with a G theme; I address my
Prov	28:10	blameless will have a G inheritance.
Jer	11:16	olive tree, fair with G fruit'; but with the

GOODNESS (27)

Ex	33:19	will make all my G pass before you, and
1Kgs	8:66	heart for all the G that the LORD had
2Chr	6:41	salvation, and let thy saints rejoice in thy G
	7:10	of heart for the G that the LORD had
Neh	9:25	became fat, and delighted themselves in thy great G
	9:35	and in thy great G which thou gavest them,
Esth	16:4	who know nothing of G they suppose that they
Ps	23:6	Surely G and mercy shall follow me all the
	25:7	remember me, for thy G sake, O LORD!
	27:13	I shall see the G of the LORD in
	31:19	how abundant is thy G, which thou hast laid
	65:4	be satisfied with the G of thy house, thy
	68:10	in it; in thy G, O God, thou didst
	145:7	fame of thy abundant G, and shall sing aloud
Wis	7:26	working of God, and an image of his G
	12:22	may meditate upon thy G when we judge, and
Sir	45:23	away, in the ready G of his soul, and
Is	63:7	us, and the great G to the house of
Jer	31:12	be radiant over the G of the LORD, over
	31:14	be satisfied with my G, says the LORD."
Hos	3:5	LORD and to his G in the latter days.
Rom	15:14	yourselves are full of G, filled with all knowledge,
Gal	5:22	joy, peace, patience, kindness, G, faithfulness,
Tit	1:7	hospitable, a lover of G, master of himself, upright,
	3:4	another; but when the G and loving kindness of
Philem	1:14	in order that your G might not be by
Heb	6:5	and have tasted the G of the word of

GOODS (53)

Gen	14:11	enemy took all the G of Sodom and Gomorrah,
	14:12	in Sodom, and his G, and departed.
	14:16	brought back all the G, and also brought back
	14:16	kinsman Lot with his G, and the women and
	14:21	persons, but take the G for yourself."
	31:37	felt through all my G, what have you found
	31:37	what have you found of all your household G
	45:20	no thought to your G, for the best of
	46:6	their cattle and their G, which they had gained
Ex	22:7	his neighbor money or G to keep, and it
	22:8	he has put his hand to his neighbor's G
Num	16:32	men that belonged to Korah and all their G
	31:9	all their cattle, their flocks, and all their G
Judg	18:21	the cattle and the G in front of them.
2Kgs	8:9	him, all kinds of G of Damascus, forty camel
2Chr	20:25	cattle in great numbers, G, clothing, and precious
Ezra	1:4	silver and gold, with G and with beasts, besides
	1:6	silver, with gold, with G, with beasts, and with

G

	7:26	for confiscation of his G or for imprisonment."
	8:21	way for ourselves, our children, and all our G
Esth	3:13	the month of Adar, and to plunder their G
	8:11	and to plunder their G,
Ps	109:8	his days be few; may another seize his G
Prov	1:13	shall find all precious G, we shall fill our
	6:31	will give all the G of his house.
Eccl	5:11	When G increase, they increase who eat them; and
Sir	1:15	whole house with desirable G, and their storehouses
	11:17	found rest, and now I shall enjoy my G
	14:4	and others will live in luxury on his G
Jer	49:29	curtains and all their G; their camels shall be
Ezek	27:16	because of your abundant G; they exchanged for your
	27:18	you for your abundant G, because of your great
	38:12	have gotten cattle and G, who dwell at the
	38:13	take away cattle and G, to seize great spoil?'
Dan	11:24	done, scattering among them plunder, spoil, and G
Obad	1:13	not have looted his G in the day of
Zeph	1:13	he do ill.' Their G shall be plundered, and
1Mac	5:13	wives and children and G, and have destroyed about
	5:45	wives and children and G, a very large company,
	9:40	to the mountain; and they took all their G
Mt	12:29	house and plunder his G, unless he first binds
Mk	3:27	house and plunder his G, unless he first binds
Lk	6:30	who takes away your G do not ask them
	11:21	his own palace, his G are in peace;
	12:18	I will store all my grain and my G
	12:19	Soul, you have ample G laid up for many
	16:1	to him that this man was wasting his G
	17:31	the housetop, with his G in the house, not
	19:8	the half of my G I give to the
Acts	2:45	sold their possessions and G and distributed them to
	16:14	a seller of purple G, who was a worshiper
1Cor	7:30	though they had no G,
1Jn	3:17	one has the world's G and sees his brother

GOPHER

Gen	6:14	yourself an ark of G wood; make rooms in

GORE (2)

Ex	21:29	has been accustomed to G in the past, and
	21:36	has been accustomed to G in the past, and

GORES (3)

Ex	21:28	"When an ox G a man or a woman
	21:31	If it G a man's son or daughter, he
	21:32	If the ox G a slave, male or female,

GORGE (2)

Jer	48:28	in the sides of the mouth of a G
Ezek	32:4	you, and I will G the beasts of the

GORGED (2)

Is	34:6	with blood, it is G with fat, with the
Rev	19:21	all the birds were G with their flesh.

GORGEOUS

Lk	23:11	then, arraying him in G apparel, he sent him

GORGEOUSLY

Lk	7:25	Behold, those who are G appareled and live in

GORGIAS (11)

1Mac	3:38	Dorymenes, and Nicanor and G, mighty men among
	4:1	Now G took five thousand infantry and a thousand
	4:5	When G entered the camp of Judas by night,
	4:18	a battle before us; G and his force are
	5:59	And G and his men came out of the
2Mac	8:9	He associated with him G, a general and a
	10:14	When G became governor of the region, he
	12:32	Pentecost, they hastened against G, the governor of
	12:35	man, caught hold of G, and grasping his cloak
	12:35	off his arm; so G escaped and reached Marisa.
	12:37	then he charged against G men when they were

GORTYNA

1Mac	15:23	and to Aradus and G and Cnidus and Cyprus

GOSHEN (16)

Gen	45:10	in the land of G, and you shall be
	46:28	appear before him in G; and they came into
	46:28	Goshen; and they came into the land of G
	46:29	Israel his father in G; and he presented himself
	46:34	in the land of G; for every shepherd is
	47:1	Canaan; they are now in the land of G
	47:4	let your servants dwell in the land of G
	47:6	in the land of G; and if you know
	47:27	in the land of G; and they gained possessions
	50:8	their herds were left in the land of G
Ex	8:22	apart the land of G, where my people dwell,
	9:26	in the land of G, where the people of
Josh	10:41	all the country of G, as far as Gibeon.
	11:16	all the land of G and the lowland and
	15:51	Anab, Eshtemoh, Anim, G, Holon, and Giloh: eleven
Jud	1:9	the whole land of G,

GOSPEL (101)

Mt	4:23	synagogues and preaching the G of the kingdom and
	9:35	synagogues and preaching the G of the kingdom, and
	24:14	And this G of the kingdom will be preached
	26:13	to you, wherever this G is preached in the
Mk	1:1	The beginning of the G of Jesus Christ, the
	1:14	into Galilee, preaching the G of God,
	1:15	is at hand; repent, and believe in the G
	8:35	my sake and the G's will save it.
	10:29	sake and for the G,
	13:10	And the G must first be preached to all
	14:9	to you, wherever the G is preached in the
	16:15	world and preach the G to the whole creation.
Lk	9:6	the villages, preaching the G and healing
	20:1	temple and preaching the G, the chief priests and
Acts	8:25	to Jerusalem, preaching the G to many villages of
	8:39	on he preached the G to all the towns
	14:7	surrounding country; and there they preached the G
	14:21	they had preached the G to that city and
	15:7	the word of the G and believe.
	16:10	us to preach the G to them.
	20:24	to testify to the G of the grace of
Rom	1:1	set apart for the G of God.
	1:3	the holy scriptures, the G concerning his Son, who
	1:9	my spirit in the G of his Son, that
	1:15	eager to preach the G to you also who
	1:16	not ashamed of the G: it is the power
	2:16	when, according to my G, God judges the secrets
	10:16	not all obeyed the G; for Isaiah says, "Lord,
	11:28	As regards the G they are enemies of God,
	15:16	priestly service of the G of God, so that
	15:19	have fully preached the G of Christ,
	15:20	ambition to preach the G, not where Christ has
	16:24	you according to my G and the preaching of
1Cor	1:17	but to preach the G, and not with eloquent
	4:15	became your father in Christ Jesus through the G
	9:12	the way of the G of Christ.
	9:14	those who proclaim the G should get their living
	9:14	the gospel should get their living by the G
	9:16	if I preach the G, that gives me no
	9:16	to me if I do not preach the G
	9:18	I may make the G free of charge, not
	9:18	making full use of my right in the G
	9:23	the sake of the G, that I may share
	15:1	preached to you the G, which you received, in
2Cor	2:12	Troas to preach the G of Christ, a door
	4:3	And even if our G is veiled, it is
	4:4	the light of the G of the glory of
	8:18	his preaching of the G;
	9:13	obedience in acknowledging the G of Christ, and by
	10:14	to you with the G of Christ.
	10:16	we may preach the G in lands beyond you,
	11:4	you accept a different G from the one you
	11:7	because I preached God's G without cost to you?
Gal	1:6	turning to a different G –
	1:7	that there is another G, but there are some
	1:7	want to pervert the G of Christ.
	1:8	preach to you a G contrary to that which
	1:9	preaching to you a G contrary to that which
	1:11	know, brethren, that the G which was preached by
	1:11	which was preached by me is not man's G
	2:2	were of repute) the G which I preach among
	2:5	the truth of the G might be preserved for
	2:7	been entrusted with the G to the uncircumcised, just
	2:7	been entrusted with the G to the circumcised
	2:14	the truth of the G, I said to Cephas
	3:8	by faith, preached the G beforehand to Abraham,
	4:13	that I preached the G to you at first;
Eph	1:13	word of truth, the G of your salvation, and
	3:6	of the promise in Christ Jesus through the G
	3:7	Of this G I was made a minister according
	6:15	the equipment of the G of peace;
	6:19	the mystery of the G,
Phil	1:5	your partnership in the G from the first day
	1:7	and in the defense and confirmation of the G
	1:12	served to advance the G,

1:16 the defense of the G;
1:27 be worthy of the G of Christ, so that
1:27 the faith of the G,
2:22 father he has served with me in the G
4:3 with me in the G together with Clement and
4:15 the beginning of the G, when I left Macedonia,
Col 1:5 of the truth, the G
1:23 the hope of the G which you heard, which
1Thes 1:5 chosen you; for our G came to you not
2:2 declare to you the G of God in the
2:4 be entrusted with the G, so we speak, not
2:8 you not only the G of God but also
2:9 preached to you the G of God.
3:2 God's servant in the G of Christ, to establish
2Thes 1:8 do not obey the G of our Lord Jesus.
2:14 called you through our G, so that you may
1Tim 1:11 accordance with the glorious G of the blessed God
2Tim 1:8 in suffering for the G in the power of
1:10 brought life and immortality to light through the G
1:11 For this G I was appointed a preacher and
2:8 as preached in my G,
2:9 in my gospel, the G for which I am
Philem 1:13 my imprisonment for the G;
1Pet 4:6 this is why the G was preached even to
4:17 do not obey the G of God?
Rev 14:6 midheaven, with an eternal G to proclaim to those

GOSSIP (3)
Sir 19:6 for one who hates G evil is lessened.
Ezek 36:3 the talk and evil G of the people;
2Cor 12:20 jealousy, anger, selfishness, slander, G, conceit, and

GOSSIPING
Prov 20:19 He who goes about G reveals secrets; therefore do

GOSSIPS (2)
Rom 1:29 deceit, malignity, they are G,
1Tim 5:13 not only idlers but G and busybodies, saying what

GOT (53)
Gen 39:12 hand, and fled and G out of the house.
39:15 me, and fled and G out of the house."
Lev 6:4 robbery, or what he G by oppression, or the
Num 16:27 So they G away from about the dwelling of
Judg 5:19 waters of Megiddo; they G no spoils of silver.
2Sam 15:1 After this Absalom G himself a chariot and horses,
2Kgs 4:35 Then he G up again, and walked once to
2Chr 24:3 Jehoiada G for him two wives, and he had
Tob 8:4 two were alone, Tobias G up from the bed
9:6 the morning they both G up early and came
Jud 6:13 However, they G under the shelter of the hill
12:15 So she G up and arrayed herself in all
15:7 and in the plain G a great amount of
Esth 9:16 defend their lives, and G relief from their enemies,
9:22 on which the Jews G relief from their enemies,
Eccl 2:8 kings and provinces; I G singers, both men and
Is 8:2 And I G reliable witnesses, Uriah the priest and
Jer 32:10 the deed, sealed it, G witnesses, and weighed the
Ezek 29:18 he nor his army G anything from Tyre to
33:24 one man, yet he G possession of the land;
Dan 6:10 toward Jerusalem; and he G down upon his knees
11:6 child, and he who G possession of her.
1Mac 6:46 He G under the elephant, stabbed it from beneath,
13:22 So Trypho G all his cavalry ready to go,
2Mac 5:7 and in the end G only disgrace from his
5:27 with about nine others, G away to the wilderness,
7:11 and said nobly, "I G these from Heaven, and
8:5 As soon as Maccabeus G his army organized, the
8:13 justice ran off and G away.
8:30 thousand of them and G possession of some
11:6 Maccabeus and his men G word that Lysias was
11:12 Most of them G away stripped and wounded, and
12:28 his enemies, and they G the city into their
13:23 men, was defeated he G word that Philip, who
Mt 8:23 And when he G into the boat, his disciples
13:2 him, so that he G into a boat and
14:29 So Peter G out of the boat and walked
14:32 And when they G into the boat, the wind
15:39 away the crowds, he G into the boat and
Mk 4:1 him, so that he G into a boat and
5:42 And immediately the girl G up and walked (she
6:33 all the towns, and G there ahead of them.
6:51 And he G into the boat with them and
6:54 And when they G out of the boat, immediately
8:10 away; and immediately he G into the boat with
Lk 8:22 One day he G into a boat with his
8:37 great fear; so he G into the boat and
8:55 spirit returned, and she G up at once; and
Jn 6:17 down to the sea, G into a boat, and
6:24 his disciples, they themselves G into the boats and
21:3 They went out and G into the boat; but
21:9 When they G out on land, they saw a
2Cor 12:16 crafty, you say, and G the better of you

GOTHONIEL
Jud 6:15 Chabris the son of G, and Charmis the son

GOTTEN (16)
Gen 4:1 Cain, saying, "I have G a man with the
12:5 persons that they had G in Haran; and they
Ex 14:18 LORD, when I have G glory over Pharaoh, his
Lev 22:25 God any such animals G from a foreigner.
Deut 8:17 of my hand have G me this wealth.'
Job 28:15 me.' It cannot be G for gold, and silver
31:25 because my hand had G much;
Ps 44:10 and our enemies have G spoil.
74:2 congregation, which thou hast G of old, which thou
98:1 his holy arm have G him victory.
Prov 13:11 Wealth hastily G will dwindle, but he who gathers
20:21 An inheritance G hastily in the beginning will in
Sir 24:6 and nation I have G a possession.
Ezek 28:4 your understanding you have G wealth for yourself,
38:12 the nations, who have G cattle and goods, who
1Mac 10:23 Alexander has G ahead of us in forming a

GOUGE
1Sam 11:2 with you, that I G out all your right

GOUGED
Judg 16:21 Philistines seized him and G out his eyes, and

GOURDS (6)
1Kgs 6:18 in the form of G and open flowers; all
7:24 Under its brim were G, for thirty cubits, compassing
7:24 sea round about; the G were in two rows,
2Kgs 4:39 lap full of wild G, and came and cut
2Chr 4:3 it were figures of G, for thirty cubits, compassing
4:3 sea round about; the G were in two rows,

GOVERN (14)
1Sam 8:5 us a king to G us like all the
8:6 us a king to G us." And Samuel prayed
8:20 that our king may G us and go out
1Kgs 3:9 an understanding mind to G thy people, that I
3:9 who is able to G this thy great people?"
21:7 him, "Do you now G Israel?
Job 34:17 Shall one who hates justice G
Prov 8:16 princes rule, and nobles G the earth.
Wis 3:8 They will G nations and rule over peoples, and
8:14 I shall G peoples, and nations will be subject
12:18 great forbearance thou dost G us; for thou hast
Dan 13:5 who were supposed to G the people."
1Mac 8:15 concerning the people, to G them well.
Mt 2:6 a ruler who will G my people Israel.'"

GOVERNED
Esth 16:15 not evildoers but are G by most righteous laws

GOVERNING (3)
2Kgs 15:5 was over the household, G the people of the
2Chr 26:21 over the king's household, G the people of the
Rom 13:1 be subject to the G authorities.

GOVERNMENT (21)
Esth 13:5 is ill-disposed to our G, doing all the harm
13:7 Hades, and leave our G completely secure and
16:1 are loyal to our G, greeting.
Sir 10:4 The G of the earth is in the hands
Is 9:6 is given; and the G will be upon his
9:7 the increase of his G and of peace there
1Mac 6:56 he was trying to seize control of the G
10:41 additional funds which the G officials have not paid
2Mac 3:38 or plotter against your G, send him there, for
4:2 a plotter against the G the man who was
4:21 become hostile to his G, and he took measures
5:7 gain control of the G, however; and in the
8:8 Coelesyria and Phoenicia, for aid to the king's G
9:24 know to whom the G was left.
10:11 have charge of the G and to be chief
11:1 in charge of the G, being vexed at what
11:19 good will toward the G, I will endeavor for
13:2 Lysias, his guardian, who had charge of the G

G

16:20 The G of our Lord Jesus Christ be with
1Cor 1:3 their Lord and ours: G to you and peace
1:4 you because of the G of God which was
3:10 According to the G of God given to me,
15:10 But by the G of God I am what
15:10 I am, and his G toward me was not
15:10 not I, but the G of God which is
16:23 The G of the Lord Jesus be with you.
2Cor 1:2 the whole of Achaia: G to you and peace
1:12 wisdom but by the G of God.
4:15 sake, so that as G extends to more and
6:1 not to accept the G of God in vain.
8:1 know, brethren, about the G of God which has
8:9 For you know the G of our Lord Jesus
9:14 because of the surpassing G of God in you.
12:9 said to me, "My G is sufficient for you,
13:14 The G of the Lord Jesus Christ and the
Gal 1:3 the churches of Galatia: G to you and peace
1:6 called you in the G of Christ and turning
1:15 called me through his G,
2:9 when they perceived the G that was given to
2:21 do not nullify the G of God; for if
5:4 by the law; you have fallen away from G
6:18 The G of our Lord Jesus Christ be with
Eph 1:2 faithful in Christ Jesus: G to you and peace
1:6 praise of his glorious G which he freely bestowed
1:7 the riches of his G
2:5 together with Christ (by G you have been saved),
2:7 immeasurable riches of his G in kindness toward us
2:8 For by G you have been saved through faith;
3:2 the stewardship of God's G that was given to
3:7 the gift of God's G which was given me
3:8 all the saints, this G was given, to preach
4:7 But G was given to each of us according
4:29 that it may impart G to those who hear.
6:24 G be with all who love our Lord Jesus
Phil 1:2 the bishops and deacons: G to you and peace
1:7 partakers with me of G, both in my imprisonment
4:23 The G of the Lord Jesus Christ be with
Col 1:2 in Christ at Colossae: G to you and peace
1:6 heard and understood the G of God in truth,
4:18 G be with you.
1Thes 1:1 the Lord Jesus Christ: G to you and peace.
5:28 The G of our Lord Jesus Christ be with
2Thes 1:2 the Lord Jesus Christ: G to you and peace
1:12 him, according to the G of our God and
2:16 and good hope through G,
3:18 The G of our Lord Jesus Christ be with
1Tim 1:2 child in the faith: G, mercy, and peace from
1:14 in unbelief, and the G of our Lord overflowed
6:21 G be with you.
2Tim 1:2 Timothy, my beloved child: G, mercy, and peace from
1:9 own purpose and the G which he gave us
2:1 be strong in the G that is in Christ
4:22 G be with you.
Tit 1:3 in a common faith: G and peace from God
2:11 For the G of God has appeared for the
3:7 be justified by his G and become heirs in
3:15 G be with you all.
Philem 1:3 church in your house: G to you and peace
1:25 The G of the Lord Jesus Christ be with
Heb 2:9 so that by the G of God he might
4:16 to the throne of G, that we may receive
4:16 receive mercy and find G to help in time
10:29 he was sanctified, and outraged the Spirit of G
12:15 fail to obtain the G of God; that no
13:9 heart be strengthened by G, not by foods, which
13:25 G be with all of you.
Jas 4:6 But he gives more G; therefore it says, "God
4:6 the proud, but gives G to the humble."
1Pet 1:2 with his blood: May G and peace be multiplied
1:10 who prophesied of the G that was to be
1:13 hope fully upon the G that is coming to
3:7 joint heirs of the G of life, in order
4:10 stewards of God's varied G:
5:5 the proud, but gives G to the humble."
5:10 the God of all G, who has called you
5:12 this is the true G of God; stand fast
2Pet 1:2 Savior Jesus Christ: May G and peace be multiplied
3:18 But grow in the G and knowledge of our
2Jn 1:3 with us for ever: G, mercy, and peace will
Jude 1:4 persons who pervert the G of our God into
Rev 1:4 that are in Asia: G to you and peace
22:21 The G of the Lord Jesus be with all

GRACEFUL (4)

Prov 5:19 a lovely hind, a G doe.
Song 7:1 How G are your feet in sandals, O queenly
Sir 24:16 my branches, and my branches are glorious and G
Nah 3:4 harlotries of the harlot, G and of deadly charms,

GRACIOUS (60)

Gen 43:29 God be G to you, my son!"
Ex 33:19 and I will be G to whom I will
33:19 whom I will be G, and will show mercy
34:6 a God merciful and G, slow to anger, and
Num 6:25 upon you, and be G to you:
Ruth 2:13 said, "You are most G to me, my lord,
2Sam 12:22 the LORD will be G to me, that the
2Kgs 13:23 But the LORD was G to them and had
2Chr 30:9 LORD your God is G and merciful, and will
Neh 9:17 God ready to forgive, G and merciful, slow to
9:31 for thou art a G and merciful God.
Job 33:24 him; and he is G to him, and says,
Ps 4:1 Be G to me, and hear my prayer.
6:2 Be G to me, O LORD, for I am
9:13 Be G to me, O LORD!
25:16 to me, and be G to me; for I
26:11 redeem me, and be G to me.
27:7 I cry aloud, be G to me and answer
30:10 O LORD, and be G to me!
31:9 Be G to me, O LORD, for I am
41:4 said, "O LORD, be G to me; heal me,
41:10 thou, O LORD, be G to me, and raise
56:1 Be G to me, O God, for men trample
67:1 May God be G to us and bless us
77:9 Has God forgotten to be G
86:3 art my God; be G to me, O Lord,
86:15 a God merciful and G, slow to anger and
103:8 LORD is merciful and G, slow to anger and
111:4 remembered; the LORD is G and merciful.
112:4 upright; the LORD is G, merciful, and righteous.
116:5 G is the LORD, and righteous; our God is
119:58 all my heart; be G to me according to
119:132 to me and be G to me, as is
135:3 good; sing to his name, for he is G
145:8 The LORD is G and merciful, slow to anger
145:13 all his words, and G in all his deeds.
147:1 God; for he is G, and a song of
Prov 11:16 A G woman gets honor, and violent men get
22:11 and whose speech is G, will have the king
Sir 6:5 multiplies friends, and a G tongue multiplies
18:16 be found in a G man.
Is 30:18 LORD waits to be G to you; therefore he
30:19 He will surely be G to you at the
33:2 O LORD, be G to us; we wait for
Joel 2:13 God, for he is G and merciful, slow to
Amos 5:15 of hosts, will be G to the remnant of
Jon 4:2 that thou art a G God and merciful, slow
Zech 1:13 And the LORD answered G and comforting words to
Mal 1:9 that he may be G to us.
2Mac 2:22 with great kindness became G to them—
10:26 besought him to be G to them and to
14:9 hard-pressed nation with the G kindness which you
Mt 11:26 for such was thy G will.
Lk 4:22 and wondered at the G words which proceeded out
10:21 for such was thy G will.
2Cor 8:6 complete among you this G work.
8:7 you excel in this G work also.
8:19 with us in this G work which we are
Phil 4:8 is lovely, whatever is G, if there is any
Col 4:6 your speech always be G, seasoned with salt, so

GRACIOUSLY (9)

Gen 33:5 children whom God has G given your servant."
33:11 because God has dealt G with me, and because
Judg 21:22 to them, 'Grant them G to us; because we
2Kgs 25:27 he began to reign, G freed Jehoiachin king of
Ps 119:29 far from me; and G teach me thy law!
Prov 26:25 heart; when he speaks G, believe him not, for
Wis 6:16 of her, and she G appears to them in
Sir 7:33 Give G to all the living, and withhold not
Heb 12:24 blood that speaks more G than the blood of

GRAFT

Rom 11:23 has the power to G them in again.

GRAFTED (5)

Rom 11:17 wild olive shoot, were G in their place to
11:19 that I might be G in."
11:23 their unbelief, will be G in, for God has

11:24 wild olive tree, and G, contrary to nature, into
11:24 these natural branches be G back into their own

GRAIN (124)

Gen 27:28 earth, and plenty of G and wine.
27:37 for servants, and with G and wine I have
41:5 behold, seven ears of G, plump and good, were
41:35 coming, and lay up G under the authority of
41:49 And Joseph stored up G in great abundance, like
41:57 to Joseph to buy G, because the famine was
42:1 learned that there was G in Egypt, he said
42:2 heard that there is G in Egypt; go down
42:2 go down and buy G for us there, that
42:3 went down to buy G in Egypt.
42:19 rest go and carry G for the famine of
42:25 fill their bags with G, and to replace every
42:26 their asses with their G, and departed.
42:33 with me, and take G for the famine of
43:2 they had eaten the G which they had brought
44:2 of the youngest, with his money for the G
45:23 ten she-asses loaded with G, bread, and provision for
47:14 of Canaan, for the G which they bought; and
Ex 22:6 so that the stacked G or the standing grain
22:6 grain or the standing G or the field is
Lev 2:14 first fruits crushed new G from fresh ears, parched
2:16 part of the crushed G and of the oil
23:14 eat neither bread nor G parched or fresh until
23:16 cereal offering of new G to the LORD.
Num 18:12 wine and of the G, the first fruits of
18:27 though it were the G of the threshing floor,
20:5 is no place for G, or figs, or vines,
28:26 cereal offering of new G to the LORD at
Deut 7:13 of your ground, your G and your wine and
11:14 may gather in your G and your wine and
12:17 the tithe of your G or of your wine
14:23 the tithe of your G, of your wine, and
16:9 you first put the sickle to the standing G
18:4 first fruits of your G, of your wine and
23:25 into your neighbor's standing G, you may pluck the
23:25 not put a sickle to your neighbor's standing G
25:4 muzzle an ox when it treads out the G
28:51 shall not leave you G, wine, or oil, the
33:28 in a land of G and wine; yea, his
Josh 5:11 of the land, unleavened cakes and parched G
Judg 15:5 go into the standing G of the Philistines, and
15:5 shocks and the standing G, as well as the
Ruth 2:2 among the ears of G after him in whose
2:14 passed to her parched G; and she ate until
3:7 down at the end of the heap of G
1Sam 8:15 the tenth of your G and of your vineyards
17:17 ephah of this parched G, and these ten loaves,
25:18 five measures of parched G, and a hundred clusters
2Sam 17:19 well's mouth, and scattered G upon it; and nothing
17:28 wheat, barley, meal, parched G, beans and lentils,
2Kgs 4:42 and fresh ears of G in his sack.
18:32 land, a land of G and wine, a land
2Chr 31:5 the first fruits of G, wine, oil, honey, and
32:28 for the yield of G, wine, and oil; and
Neh 5:2 many; let us get G, that we may eat
5:3 our houses to get G because of the famine."
5:10 and my servants are lending them money and G
5:11 the hundredth of money, G, wine, and oil which
10:31 in wares or any G on the sabbath day
10:39 bring the contribution of G, wine, and oil to
13:5 and the tithes of G, wine, and oil, which
13:12 the tithe of the G, wine, and oil into
13:15 bringing in heaps of G and loading them on
Jud 10:5 a bag with parched G and a cake of
11:13 first fruits of the G and the tithes of
Job 5:26 as a shock of G comes up to the
24:24 they are cut off like the heads of G
39:12 return, and bring your G to your threshing floor?
Ps 4:7 they have when their G and wine abound.
65:9 water; thou providest their G, for so thou hast
65:13 valleys deck themselves with G, they shout and sing
72:16 there be abundance of G in the land; on
78:24 and gave them the G of heaven.
Prov 11:26 him who holds back G, but a blessing is
14:4 oxen, there is no G; but abundant crops come
27:22 pestle along with crushed G, yet his folly will
Sir 18:9 the sea and a G of sand so are
40:22 the green shoots of G more than both.
Is 17:5 the reaper gathers standing G and his arm harvests
17:5 gleans the ears of G in the Valley of
23:3 your revenue was the G of Shihor, the harvest
27:12 will thresh out the G, and you will be
28:28 Does one crush bread G
30:23 sow the ground, and G, the produce of the
36:17 land, a land of G and wine, a land
62:8 not again give your G to be food for
Jer 31:12 the LORD, over the G, the wine, and the
50:26 up like heaps of G, and destroy her utterly;
Ezek 36:29 I will summon the G and make it abundant
Hos 2:8 who gave her the G, the wine, and the
2:9 will take back my G in its time, and
2:22 earth shall answer the G, the wine, and the
7:15 upon their beds; for G and wine they gash
8:7 The standing G has no heads, it shall yield
Joel 1:10 ground mourns; because the G is destroyed, the wine
1:16 are ruined because the G has failed.
2:19 am sending to you G, wine, and oil, and
2:24 shall be full of G, the vats shall overflow
Amos 8:5 new moon be over, that we may sell G
Hag 1:11 the hills, upon the G, the new wine, the
Zech 9:17 G shall make the young men flourish, and new
1Mac 8:26 not give or supply G, arms, money, or ships,
8:28 shall be given no G, arms, money, or ships,
10:30 the third of the G and the half of
Mt 12:1 to pluck heads of G and to eat.
13:8 soil and brought forth G, some a hundredfold, some
13:26 came up and bore G, then the weeds appeared
13:31 heaven is like a G of mustard seed which
17:20 have faith as a G of mustard seed, you
Mk 2:23 way his disciples began to pluck heads of G
4:7 up and choked it, and it yielded no G
4:8 soil and brought forth G, growing up and increasing
4:28 ear, then the full G in the ear.
4:29 But when the G is ripe, at once he
4:31 It is like a G of mustard seed, which,
Lk 6:1 ate some heads of G, rubbing them in their
12:18 will store all my G and my goods.
13:19 It is like a G of mustard seed which
17:6 had faith as a G of mustard seed, you
Jn 12:24 to you, unless a G of wheat falls into
Acts 7:12 heard that there was G in Egypt, he sent
1Cor 9:9 an ox when it is treading out the G
15:37 kernel, perhaps of wheat or of some other G
1Tim 5:18 an ox when it is treading out the G

GRAINFIELDS (3)

Mt 12:1 Jesus went through the G on the sabbath; his
Mk 2:23 was going through the G; and as they made
Lk 6:1 was going through the G, his disciples plucked and

GRAINS (2)

Is 48:19 your descendants like its G; their name would never
Heb 11:12 and as the innumerable G of sand by the

GRANARIES (2)

Jer 50:26 every quarter; open her G; pile her up like
Joel 1:16 storehouses are desolate; the G are ruined because

GRANARY (2)

Mt 3:12 his wheat into the G, but the chaff he
Lk 3:17 the wheat into his G, but the chaff he

GRANDCHILDREN (3)

Gen 31:55 arose, and kissed his G and his daughters and
Prov 17:6 G are the crown of the aged, and the
1Tim 5:4 widow has children or G, let them first learn

GRANDDAUGHTER (2)

2Kgs 8:26 Athaliah; she was a G of Omri king of
2Chr 22:2 name was Athaliah, the G of Omri.

GRANDEUR

Sir 17:8 name, to proclaim the G of his works.

GRANDFATHERS

Ex 10:6 your fathers nor your G have seen, from the

GRANDMOTHER

2Tim 1:5 dwelt first in your G Lois and your mother

GRANDSON (4)

Gen 11:31 son of Haran, his G, and Sarai his daughter-in-law,
Judg 8:22 your son and your G also; for you have
2Chr 22:9 said, "He is the G of Jehoshaphat, who sought
Jer 27:7 his son and his G, until the time of

GRANDSONS (3)

Judg 12:14 forty sons and thirty G, who rode on seventy

1Chr 8:40 having many sons and G, one hundred and fifty.
Tob 14:3 called his son and G, and said to him,

GRANT (67)

Gen 19:21 to him, "Behold, I G you this favor also,
24:12 of my master Abraham, G me success today, I
43:14 man; may God Almighty G you mercy before the
Lev 25:24 you possess, you shall G a redemption of the
Deut 15:1 seven years you shall G a release.
Judg 21:22 will say to them, G them graciously to us;
Ruth 1:9 The LORD G that you may find a home,
1Sam 1:17 the God of Israel G your petition which you
2Sam 14:21 Joab, "Behold now, I G this; go, bring back
1Kgs 8:36 they should walk; and G rain upon thy land,
8:50 committed against thee; and G them compassion in
1Chr 22:12 may the LORD G you discretion and understanding,
29:19 G to Solomon my son that with a whole
2Chr 6:27 they should walk; and G rain upon thy land,
12:7 them, but I will G them some deliverance, and
Ezra 3:7 Joppa, according to the G which they had from
9:8 brighten our eyes and G us a little reviving
9:9 kings of Persia, to G us some reviving to
Neh 1:11 thy servant today, and G him mercy in the
Tob 7:18 of heaven and earth G you joy in place
8:7 G that I may find mercy and may grow
10:12 safely, dear brother, and G me to see your
Jud 10:8 God of our fathers G you favor and fulfill
13:20 May God G this to be a perpetual honor
Esth 5:8 please the king to G my petition and fulfil
Job 6:8 and that God would G my desire;
13:20 Only G two things to me, then I will
Ps 20:4 [Selah] May he G you your heart's desire, and
60:11 O G us help against the foe, for vain
85:7 love, O LORD, and G us thy salvation.
108:12 O G us help against the foe, for vain
140:8 G not, O LORD, the desires of the wicked;
Wis 7:15 May God G that I speak with judgment and
Sir 38:14 Lord that he should G them success in diagnosis
45:26 May the Lord G you wisdom in your heart
50:23 gladness of heart, and G that peace may be
Is 16:3 "Give counsel, G justice; make your shade like night
61:3 all who mourn; to G to those who mourn
Jer 42:12 I will G you mercy, that he may have
Bar 2:14 sake deliver us, and G us favor in the
1Mac 10:28 We will G you many immunities and give you
10:40 I also G fifteen thousand shekels of silver yearly
11:35 all these we shall G them release.
11:50 king with this entreaty, G us peace, and make
11:66 they asked him to G them terms of peace,
13:34 with a request to G relief to the country,
13:37 to our officials to G you release from tribute.
14:46 the people agreed to G Simon the right to
15:7 your country, and I G freedom to Jerusalem and
2Mac 3:31 Most High and to G life to one who
12:11 nomads besought Judas to G them pledges of
Mt 20:23 is not mine to G, but it is for
Mk 6:22 wish, and I will G it."
10:37 they said to him, G us to sit, one
10:40 is not mine to G, but it is for
Lk 1:74 our father Abraham, to G us that we, being
Acts 4:29 upon their threats, and G to thy servants to
Rom 15:5 of steadfastness and encouragement G you to live in
Eph 3:16 his glory he may G you to be strengthened
2Thes 1:7 afflict you, and to G rest with us to
2Tim 1:16 May the Lord G mercy to the household of
1:18 may the Lord G him to find mercy
2:7 for the Lord will G you understanding in everything.
2:25 God may perhaps G that they will repent and
Rev 2:7 who conquers I will G to eat of the
3:21 who conquers, I will G him to sit with
11:3 And I will G my two witnesses power to

GRANTED (47)

Gen 25:21 barren; and the LORD G his prayer, and Rebekah
27:20 the LORD your God G me success."
Judg 15:18 and said, "Thou hast G this great deliverance by
1Sam 1:27 and the LORD has G me my petition which
25:35 voice, and I have G your petition."
2Sam 14:22 that the king has G the request of his
1Kgs 1:48 of Israel, who has G one of my offspring
1Chr 4:10 And God G what he asked.
5:20 the battle, and he G their entreaty because they
2Chr 1:12 wisdom and knowledge are G to you.
Ezra 7:6 given; and the king G him all that he
Neh 2:8 And the king G me what I asked, for
Esth 2:18 He also G a remission of taxes to the
5:6 It shall be G you.
7:2 It shall be G you.
9:12 It shall be G you.
Job 10:12 Thou hast G me life and steadfast love; and
Prov 10:24 but the desire of the righteous will be G
Sir 6:37 mind, and your desire for wisdom will be G
17:2 a limited time, but G them authority over the
17:4 all living beings, and G them dominion over beasts
26:3 blessing; she will be G among the blessings of
43:33 the godly he has G wisdom.
Is 63:7 that the LORD has G us, and the great
63:7 Israel which he has G them according to his
1Mac 11:34 in Jerusalem, we have G release from the royal
11:58 a table service, and G him the right to
15:5 kings before me have G you, and release from
2Mac 3:33 sake the Lord has G you your life.
11:15 For the king G every request in behalf of
11:35 of the king has G you, we also give
Mk 15:44 he was dead, he G the body to Joseph.
Lk 1:43 And why is this G me, that the mother
23:23 Pilate gave sentence that their demand should be G
Jn 5:25 himself, so he has G the Son also to
5:35 which the Father has G me to accomplish, these
6:65 me unless it is G him by the Father."
Acts 3:14 a murderer to be G to you,
7:17 near, which God had G to Abraham, the people
11:18 Gentiles also God has G repentance unto life."
27:24 and lo, God has G you all those who
2Cor 1:11 behalf for the blessing G us in answer to
Phil 1:29 For it has been G to you that for
Philem 1:22 your prayers to be G to you.
2Pet 1:3 His divine power has G to us all things
1:4 by which he has G to us his precious
Rev 19:8 herself ready; it was G her to be clothed

GRANTING (3)

Wis 12:20 deserving of death, G them time and opportunity
Acts 14:3 word of his grace, G signs and wonders to
2Cor 12:16 But G that I myself did not burden you,

GRANTS (5)

Sir 17:19 those who repent he G a return, and he
18:11 be evil; therefore he G them forgiveness in
34:17 to the eyes; he G healing, life, and blessing.
1Mac 11:36 not one of these G shall be canceled from
13:38 All the G that we have made to you

GRAPE (7)

Deut 32:14 the blood of the G you drank wine.
Job 15:33 shake off his unripe G, like the vine, and
Song 7:12 have budded, whether the G blossoms have opened
Sir 39:26 the blood of the G, and oil and clothing.
50:15 the blood of the G; he poured it out
51:15 From blossom to ripening G my heart delighted in
Is 18:5 flower becomes a ripening G, he will cut off

GRAPE-GATHERER (2)

Sir 33:16 excelled, and like a G I filled my wine
Jer 6:9 of Israel; like a G pass your hand again

GRAPE-GATHERERS (3)

Sir 33:16 who gleans after the G; by the blessing of
Jer 49:9 If G came to you, would they not leave
Obad 1:5 If G came to you, would they not leave

GRAPES (34)

Gen 40:10 blossoms shot forth, and the clusters ripened into G
40:11 and I took the G and pressed them into
49:11 in the blood of G;
Lev 19:10 you gather the fallen G of your vineyard; you
25:5 not reap, and the G of your undressed vine
25:11 itself, nor gather the G from the undressed vines.
Num 6:3 drink any juice of G or eat grapes, fresh
6:3 of grapes or eat G, fresh or dried.
13:20 the time was the season of the first-ripe G
13:23 a single cluster of G, and they carried it
Deut 23:24 eat your fill of G, as many as you
24:21 When you gather the G of your vineyard, you
28:39 wine nor gather the G; for the worm shall
32:32 fields of Gomorrah; their G are grapes of poison,
32:32 Gomorrah; their grapes are G of poison, their
Judg 8:2 the gleaning of the G of Ephraim better than
9:27 field, and gathered the G from their vineyards and
Neh 13:15 asses; and also wine, G, figs, and all kinds
Is 5:2 for it to yield G, but it yielded wild
5:2 it to yield grapes, but it yielded wild G

5:4 for it to yield G, why did it yield
5:4 to yield grapes, why did it yield wild G
Jer 8:13 LORD, there are no G on the vine, nor
25:30 like those who tread G, against all the inhabitants
31:29 fathers have eaten sour G, and the children's teeth
31:30 man who eats sour G, his teeth shall be
Ezek 18:2 fathers have eaten sour G, and the children's teeth
Hos 9:10 Like G in the wilderness, I found Israel.
Amos 9:13 and the treader of G him who sows the
Mic 6:15 oil; you shall tread G, but not drink wine.
1Mac 6:34 elephants the juice of G and mulberries, to arouse
Mt 7:16 Are G gathered from thorns, or figs from thistles?
Lk 6:44 from thorns, nor are G picked from a bramble
Rev 14:18 the earth, for its G are ripe."

GRAPEVINE (2)
Num 6:4 is produced by the G, not even the seeds
Jas 3:12 yield olives, or a G figs?

GRAPPLED
Sir 51:19 My soul G with wisdom, and in my conduct

GRASP (4)
Ps 71:4 the wicked, from the G of the unjust and
Prov 27:16 the wind or to G oil in his right
Jer 15:21 redeem you from the G of the ruthless."
Lk 18:34 and they did not G what was said.

GRASPED (4)
Judg 16:29 And Samson G the two middle pillars upon which
Is 45:1 right hand I have G, to subdue nations before
Ezek 29:7 of Israel; when they G you with the hand,
Phil 2:6 a thing to be G,

GRASPING (2)
Sir 26:7 of her is like G a scorpion.
2Mac 12:35 hold of Gorgias, and G his cloak was dragging

GRASS (67)
Gen 41:2 and fat, and they fed in the reed G
41:18 fed in the reed G;
Num 22:4 ox licks up the G of the field." So
Deut 11:15 And he will give G in your fields for
29:23 growing nothing, where no G can sprout, an
32:2 rain upon the tender G, and as the showers
2Sam 23:4 like rain that makes G to sprout from the
1Kgs 18:5 perhaps we may find G and save the horses
2Kgs 19:26 field, and like tender G, like grass on the
19:26 like tender grass, like G on the housetops; blighted
Job 5:25 your offspring as the G of the earth.
6:5 bray when he has G, or the ox low
38:27 land, and to make the ground put forth G
40:15 made you; he eats G like an ox.
Ps 37:2 soon fade like the G, and wither like the
58:7 that runs away; like G let them be trodden
72:6 falls on the mown G, like showers that water
72:16 the cities like the G of the field!
90:5 like a dream, like G which is renewed in
92:7 the wicked sprout like G and all evildoers flourish,
102:4 heart is smitten like G, and withered; I forget
102:11 like an evening shadow; I wither away like G
103:15 his days are like G; he flourishes like a
104:14 Thou dost cause the G to grow for the
106:20 for the image of an ox that eats G
129:6 them be like the G on the housetops, which
147:8 the earth, he makes G grow upon the hills.
Prov 19:12 but his favor is like dew upon the G
27:25 When the G is gone, and the new growth
Sir 40:16 river bank will be plucked up before any G
43:21 and withers the tender G like fire.
Is 5:24 stubble, and as dry G sinks down in the
15:6 are a desolation; the G is withered, the new
35:7 become a swamp, the G shall become reeds and
37:27 field and like tender G, like grass on the
37:27 like tender grass, like G on the housetops, blighted
40:6 All flesh is G, and all its beauty is
40:7 The G withers, the flower fades, when the breath
40:7 LORD blows upon it; surely the people is G
40:8 The G withers, the flower fades; but the word
44:4 shall spring up like G amid waters, like willows
51:12 who is made like G,
66:14 shall flourish like the G; and it shall be
Jer 12:4 land mourn, and the G of every field wither?
14:5 forsakes her newborn calf because there is no G
50:11 as a heifer at G, and neigh like stallions,
Dan 4:15 bronze, amid the tender G of the field.
4:15 the beasts in the G of the earth;
4:23 bronze, in the tender G of the field; and
4:25 be made to eat G like an ox, and
4:32 be made to eat G like an ox; and
4:33 among men, and ate G like an ox, and
5:21 asses; he was fed G like an ox, and
Amos 7:2 had finished eating the G of the land, I
Mic 5:7 like showers upon the G, which tarry not for
Mt 6:30 God so clothes the G of the field, which
14:19 sit down on the G; and taking the five
Mk 6:39 to sit down by companies upon the green G
Lk 12:28 God so clothes the G which is alive in
Jn 6:10 Now there was much G in the place; so
Jas 1:9 the flower of the G he will pass away.
1:10 heat and withers the G; its flower falls, and
1Pet 1:24 "All flesh is like G and all its glory
1:24 and all its glory like the flower of G
1:24 The G withers, and the flower falls,
Rev 8:7 up, and all green G was burnt up.
9:4 not to harm the G of the earth or

GRASSHOPPER (3)
Lev 11:22 its kind, and the G according to its kind.
Eccl 12:5 almond tree blossoms, the G drags itself along and
Nah 3:15 yourselves like the locust, multiply like the G

GRASSHOPPERS (3)
Num 13:33 seemed to ourselves like G, and so we seemed
Is 40:22 its inhabitants are like G; who stretches out the
Nah 3:17 Your princes are like G, your scribes like clouds

GRASSY
Wis 19:7 Red Sea, and a G plain out of the

GRATEFUL (3)
Sir 29:17 who does not feel G will abandon his rescuer.
2Mac 3:33 and said, "Be very G to Onias the high
Heb 12:28 Therefore let us be G for receiving a kingdom

GRATIFY (2)
Rom 13:14 for the flesh, to G its desires.
Gal 5:16 Spirit, and do not G the desires of the

GRATING (6)
Ex 27:4 make for it a G, a network of bronze;
35:16 burnt offering, with its G of bronze, its poles,
38:4 for the altar a G, a network of bronze,
38:5 corners of the bronze G as holders for the
38:30 altar and the bronze G for it and all
39:39 bronze altar, and its G of bronze, its poles,

GRATITUDE (4)
Sir 20:15 and there is no G for my good deeds;
37:11 a grudging man about G or with a merciless
2Mac 2:27 However, to secure the G of many we will
Acts 24:3 way and everywhere we accept this with all G

GRAVE (36)
Gen 18:20 their sin is very G,
35:20 a pillar upon her G; it is the pillar
Num 19:16 a man, or a G, shall be unclean seven
19:18 the dead, or the G;
2Sam 3:32 and wept at the G of Abner; and all
19:37 own city, near the G of my father and
1Kgs 13:30 body in his own G; and they mourned over
13:31 bury me in the G in which the man
14:13 shall come to the G, because in him there
2Kgs 13:21 was cast into the G of Elisha; and as
22:20 be gathered to your G in peace, and your
2Chr 34:28 be gathered to your G in peace, and your
Tob 2:7 went and dug a G and buried the body.
3:10 his old age down in sorrow to the G
4:4 dies bury her beside me in the same G
4:17 your bread on the G of the righteous, but
6:14 and mother to the G in sorrow on my
8:9 went and dug a G,
8:18 he ordered his servants to fill in the G
Job 3:22 exceedingly, and are glad, when they find the G
5:26 shall come to your G in ripe old age,
10:19 not been, carried from the womb to the G
17:1 days are extinct, the G is ready for me.
21:32 is borne to the G, watch is kept over
Ps 49:14 shepherd; straight to the G they descend, and their
88:5 that lie in the G, like those whom thou
88:11 love declared in the G, or thy faithfulness in
Song 8:6 strong as death, jealousy is cruel as the G

Sir 30:18 are like offerings of food placed upon a G
Is 53:9 And they made his G with the wicked and
Jer 20:17 would have been my G, and her womb for
Ezek 32:23 is round about her G; all of them slain,
32:24 her multitude about her G; all of them slain,
Nah 1:14 I will make your G, for you are vile."
2Mac 1:11 by God out of G dangers we thank him
Rom 3:13 throat is an open G, they use their tongues

GRAVEL (2)
Prov 20:17 but afterward his mouth will be full of G
Lam 3:16 my teeth grind on G, and made me cower

GRAVEN (37)
Ex 20:4 make for yourself a G image, or any likeness
32:16 the writing of God, G upon the tables.
Lev 26:1 idols and erect no G image or pillar, and
Deut 4:16 corruptly by making a G image for yourselves, in
4:23 you, and make a G image in the form
4:25 corruptly by making a G image in the form
5:8 make for yourself a G image, or any likeness
7:5 Asherim, and burn their G images with fire.
7:25 The G images of their gods you shall burn
12:3 shall hew down the G images of their gods,
27:15 man who makes a G or molten image, an
Judg 17:3 son, to make a G image and a molten
17:4 made it into a G image and a molten
18:14 an ephod, teraphim, a G image, and a molten
18:17 entered and took the G image, the ephod, the
18:18 house and took the G image, the ephod, the
18:20 the teraphim, and the G image, and went in
18:30 Danites set up the G image for themselves; and
18:31 they set up Micah's G image which he made,
2Kgs 17:41 and also served their G images; their children
21:7 And the G image of Asherah that he had
2Chr 34:3 the Asherim, and the G and the molten images.
34:4 the Asherim and the G and the molten images,
Job 19:24 and lead they were G in the rock for
Ps 78:58 to jealousy with their G images.
Wis 14:16 command of monarchs G images were worshiped.
15:13 matter fragile vessels and G images.
Is 10:10 of the idols whose G images were greater than
30:22 will defile your silver-covered G images and your
42:8 nor my praise to G images.
42:17 shame, who trust in G images, who say to
44:15 he makes it a G image and falls down
48:5 idol did them, my G image and my molten
49:16 Behold, I have G you on the palms of
Jer 8:19 to anger with their G images, and with their
Nah 1:14 will cut off the G image and the molten
1Mac 5:68 their altars, and the G images of their gods

GRAVES (16)
Ex 14:11 because there are no G in Egypt that you
2Kgs 23:6 of it upon the G of the common people.
2Chr 34:4 strewed it over the G of those who had
Ps 49:11 Their G are their homes for ever, their dwelling
55:15 let them go away in terror into their G
Wis 19:3 were lamenting at the G of their dead, they
Bar 2:24 brought out of their G;
Ezek 32:22 all her company, their G round about her, all
32:23 by the sword; whose G are set in the
32:25 all her multitude, their G round about her, all
32:26 all their multitude, their G round about them, all
37:12 I will open your G, and raise you from
37:12 raise you from your G, O my people; and
37:13 when I open your G, and raise you from
37:13 raise you from your G, O my people.
Lk 11:44 for you are like G which are not seen,

GRAVING
Ex 32:4 fashioned it with a G tool, and made a

GRAVITY
Tit 2:7 your teaching show integrity, G,

GRAY (16)
Gen 42:38 would bring down my G hairs with sorrow to
44:29 will bring down my G hairs in sorrow to
44:31 will bring down the G hairs of your servant
Deut 32:25 with the man of G hairs.
1Sam 12:2 I am old and G, and behold, my sons
1Kgs 2:6 do not let his G head go down to
2:9 you shall bring his G head down with blood
Ps 71:18 to old age and G hairs, O God, do
Prov 20:29 old men is their G hair.
Wis 2:10 widow nor regard the G hairs of the aged.
4:9 years; but understanding is G hair for men, and
Is 46:4 am He, and to G hairs I will carry
Hos 7:10 he knows it not; G hairs are sprinkled upon
Zech 6:3 the fourth chariot dappled G horses.
2Mac 6:23 old age and the G hairs which he had
15:13 appeared, distinguished by his G hair and dignity, and

GRAY-HAIRED (2)
Job 15:10 Both the G and the aged are among us,
Sir 25:4 thing is judgment in G men, and for the

GRAZE (2)
Is 5:17 Then shall the lambs G as in their pasture,
30:23 day your cattle will G in large pastures;

GRAZED
Ex 22:5 or vineyard to be G over, or lets his

GRAZES
Is 27:10 wilderness; there the calf G, there he lies down,

GRAZING
Ezek 34:14 lie down in good G land, and on fat

GREAT (1,075)
Gen 1:16 God made the two G lights, the greater light
1:21 So God created the G sea monsters and every
6:5 wickedness of man was G in the earth, and
7:11 the fountains of the G deep burst forth, and
10:12 Calah; that is the G city.
12:2 make of you a G nation, and I will
12:2 and make your name G, so that you will
12:17 and his house with G plagues because of Sarai,
13:6 their possessions were so G that they could not
13:13 of Sodom were wicked, G sinners against the LORD.
15:1 am your shield; your reward shall be very G
15:12 lo, a dread and G darkness fell upon him.
15:14 shall come out with G possessions.
15:18 of Egypt to the G river, the river Euphrates,
17:20 will make him a G nation.
18:18 Abraham shall become a G and mighty nation, and
18:20 Sodom and Gomorrah is G and their sin is
19:11 house, both small and G, so that they wearied
19:13 its people has become G before the LORD, and
19:19 you have shown me G kindness in saving my
20:9 and my kingdom a G sin?
21:8 and Abraham made a G feast on the day
21:18 will make him a G nation."
24:35 and he has become G; he has given him
26:14 and herds, and a G household, so that the
27:34 out with an exceedingly G and bitter cry, and
36:7 their possessions were too G for them to dwell
39:9 can I do this G wickedness, and sin against
41:29 come seven years of G plenty throughout all the
41:49 stored up grain in G abundance, like the sand
46:3 make of you a G nation.
48:19 he also shall be G; nevertheless his younger brother
50:9 it was a very G company.
50:10 there with a very G and sorrowful lamentation; and
Ex 3:3 aside and see this G sight, why the bush
6:6 outstretched arm and with G acts of judgment,
7:4 land of Egypt by G acts of judgment.
8:24 did so; there came G swarms of flies into
11:3 man Moses was very G in the land of
11:6 there shall be a G cry throughout all the
12:30 and there was a G cry in Egypt, for
14:10 and they were in G fear.
14:31 And Israel saw the G work which the LORD
18:22 at all times; every G matter they shall bring
29:20 hands, and upon the G toes of their right
32:10 I will make a G nation."
32:11 land of Egypt with G power and with a
32:21 you have brought a G sin upon them?"
32:30 "You have sinned a G sin.
32:31 people have sinned a G sin; they have made
Lev 8:23 hand and on the G toe of his right
8:24 hands and on the G toes of their right
11:29 weasel, the mouse, the G lizard according to its
14:14 hand, and on the G toe of his right
14:17 hand, and on the G toe of his right
14:25 hand, and on the G toe of his right
14:28 right hand, and the G toe of his right
19:15 or defer to the G, but in righteousness shall
Num 11:33 people with a very G plague.
13:32 it are men of G stature.

GREAT

14:17 of the LORD be G as thou hast promised,
22:3 And Moab was in G dread of the people,
22:17 will surely do you G honor, and whatever you
32:1 Gad had a very G multitude of cattle; and
34:6 you shall have the G Sea and its coast;
34:7 northern boundary: from the G Sea you shall mark
Deut 1:7 as far as the G river, the river Euphrates.
1:17 the small and the G alike; you shall not
1:19 went through all that G and terrible wilderness
1:28 we; the cities are G and fortified up to
2:7 going through this G wilderness; these forty yars
2:10 lived there, a people G and many, and tall
2:21 them Zamzummim, a people G and many, and tall
4:6 will say, 'Surely this G nation is a wise
4:7 understanding people.' For what G nation is there
4:8 And what G nation is there, that has statutes
4:32 other, whether such a G thing as this has
4:34 outstretched arm, and by G terrors, according to all
4:36 let you see his G fire, and you heard
4:37 own presence, by his G power,
5:25 For this G fire will consume us; if we
6:10 to give you, with G and goodly cities, which
6:22 signs and wonders, G and grievous, against Egypt
7:19 to all Egypt, the G trials which your eyes
7:21 midst of you, a G and terrible God.
7:23 and throw them into G confusion, until they are
8:15 led you through the G and terrible wilderness, with
9:1 mightier than yourselves, cities G and fortified up to
9:2 to heaven, a people G and tall, the sons
9:29 bring out by thy G power and by thy
10:17 Lord of lords, the G, the mighty, and the
10:21 done for you these G and terrible things which
11:7 have seen all the G work of the LORD
14:16 little owl and the G owl, the water hen
18:16 God, or see this G fire any more, lest
26:5 he became a nation, G, mighty, and populous.
26:8 an outstretched arm, with G terror, with signs and
29:3 all his land, the G trials which your eyes
29:3 the signs, and those G wonders;
29:24 the heat of this G anger?'
29:28 anger and fury and G wrath, and cast them
34:12 power and all the G and terrible deeds which
Josh 1:4 as far as the G river, the river Euphrates,
1:4 the Hittites to the G Sea toward the going
6:5 shall shout with a G shout; and the wall
6:20 the people raised a G shout, and the wall
7:9 thou do for thy G name?"
7:26 raised over him a G heap of stones that
8:29 raised over it a G heap of stones, which
9:1 the coast of the G Sea toward Lebanon, the
10:2 because Gibeon was a G city, like one of
10:10 slew them with a G slaughter at Gibeon, and
10:11 the LORD threw down G stones from heaven upon
10:18 And Joshua said, "Roll G stones against the mouth
10:20 them with a very G slaughter, until they were
10:27 themselves, and they set G stones against the mouth
11:4 all their troops, a G host, in number like
11:8 them as far as G Sidon and Misrephoth-maim, and
14:12 Anakim were there, with G fortified cities: it may
15:12 west boundary was the G Sea with its coast-line.
15:47 of Egypt, and the G Sea with its coast-line.
17:17 numerous people, and have G power; you shall not
19:28 far as Sidon the G;
22:10 Jordan, an altar of G size.
23:4 the Jordan to the G Sea in the west.
23:9 driven out before you G and strong nations; and
24:17 and who did those G signs in our sight,
24:26 and he took a G stone, and set it
Judg 1:6 his thumbs and his G toes.
1:7 their thumbs and their G toes cut off used
2:7 had seen all the G work which the LORD
5:15 of Reuben there were G searchings of heart.
5:16 of Reuben there were G searchings of heart.
11:33 Abel-keramim, with a very G slaughter.
11:35 become the cause of G trouble to me; for
12:2 my people had a G feud with the Ammonites;
15:8 hip and thigh with G slaughter; and he went
15:18 "Thou hast granted this G deliverance by the hand
16:5 and see wherein his G strength lies, and by
16:6 tell me wherein your G strength lies, and how
16:15 told me wherein your G strength lies."
16:23 gathered to offer a G sacrifice to Dagon their
20:38 when they made a G cloud of smoke rise
21:5 they had taken a G oath concerning him who
1Sam 1:16 speaking out of my G anxiety and vexation."
2:17 young men was very G in the sight of
4:6 said, "What does this G shouting in the camp
4:10 there was a very G slaughter, for there fell
4:17 has also been a G slaughter among the people;
5:9 city, causing a very G panic, and he afflicted
6:9 has done us this G harm; but if not,
6:14 A G stone was there; and they split up
6:15 set them upon the G stone; and the men
6:18 The G stone, beside which they set down the
6:19 LORD had made a G slaughter among the people.
12:16 still and see this G thing, which the LORD
12:17 that your wickedness is G, which you have done
12:22 his people, for his G name's sake, because it
12:24 heart; for consider what G things he has done
14:15 it became a very G panic.
14:20 and there was very G confusion.
14:30 the slaughter among the Philistines has not been G
14:33 dealt treacherously; roll a G stone to me here.
14:45 who has wrought this G victory in Israel?
15:22 "Has the LORD as G delight in burnt offerings
17:25 king will enrich with G riches, and will give
18:15 saw that he had G success, he stood in
19:5 the LORD wrought a G victory for all Israel.
19:8 Philistines, and made a G slaughter among them, so
19:22 and came to the G well that is in
20:2 father does nothing either G or small without
23:5 cattle, and made a G slaughter among them.
26:13 the mountain, with a G space between them;
28:15 answered, "I am in G distress; for the Philistines
30:2 it, both small and G; they killed no one,
30:16 because of all the G spoil they had taken
30:19 missing, whether small or G, sons or daughters, spoil
2Sam 3:38 a prince and a G man has fallen this
7:9 make for you a G name, like the name
7:9 the name of the G ones of the earth.
7:19 servant's house for a G while to come, and
7:22 Therefore thou art G, O LORD God; for there
7:23 and doing for them G and terrible things, by
12:30 the city, a very G amount.
13:15 hated her with very G hatred; so that the
18:7 the slaughter there was G on that day, twenty
18:9 thick branches of a G oak, and his head
18:17 threw him into a G pit in the forest,
18:17 over him a very G heap of stones; and
18:29 servant, I saw a G tumult, but I do
20:8 they were at the G stone which is in
21:20 was a man of G stature, who had six
22:36 of thy salvation, and thy help made me G
22:51 G triumphs he gives to his king, and shows
23:10 the LORD wrought a G victory that day; and
23:12 the LORD wrought a G victory.
23:20 Kabzeel, a doer of G deeds; he smote two
24:14 Gad, "I am in G distress; let us fall
24:14 for his mercy is G; but let me not
1Kgs 1:40 pipes, and rejoicing with G joy, so that the
3:4 for that was the G high place; Solomon used
3:6 said, "Thou hast shown G and steadfast love to
3:6 kept for him this G and steadfast love, and
3:8 thou hast chosen, a G people, that cannot be
3:9 to govern this thy G people?"
4:13 is in Bashan, sixty G cities with walls and
5:7 to be over this G people."
5:17 command, they quarried out G, costly stones in order
7:9 the LORD to the G court.
7:12 The G court had three courses of hewn stone
8:42 shall hear of thy G name, and thy mighty
8:65 Israel with him, a G assembly, from the entrance
10:2 Jerusalem with a very G retinue, with camels
10:10 gold, and a very G quantity of spices, and
10:11 from Ophir a very G amount of almug wood
10:18 king also made a G ivory throne, and overlaid
11:19 And Hadad found G favor in the sight of
18:32 about the altar, as G as would contain two
18:45 and there was a G rain.
19:7 journey will be too G for you."
19:11 passed by, and a G and strong wind rent
20:13 you seen all this G multitude?
20:21 the Syrians with a G slaughter.
20:28 will give all this G multitude into your hand,
22:31 with neither small nor G, but only with the
2Kgs 3:27 And there came G wrath upon Israel; and they
4:38 servant, "Set on the G pot, and boil pottage
5:1 of Syria, was a G man with his master
5:13 you to do some G thing, would you not
6:14 and chariots and a G army; and they came
6:23 prepared for them a G feast; and when they
6:25 And there was a G famine in Samaria, as

7:6 the sound of a G army, so that they
8:4 "Tell me all the G things that Elisha has
8:13 he should do this G thing?" Elisha answered, "The
10:6 persons, were with the G men of the city,
10:11 in Jezreel, all his G men, and his familiar
10:19 for I have a G sacrifice to offer to
16:15 priest, saying, "Upon the G altar burn the morning
17:21 and made them commit G sin.
17:36 land of Egypt with G power and with an
18:17 the Rabshakeh with a G army from Lachish to
18:19 Hezekiah, 'Thus says the G king, the king of
18:28 the word of the G king, the king of
22:13 has been found; for G is the wrath of
23:2 people, both small and G; and he read in
23:26 the fierceness of his G wrath, by which his
25:9 houses of Jerusalem; every G house he burned down.
25:26 people, both small and G, and the captains of
1Chr 11:14 saved them by a G victory.
11:22 Kabzeel, a doer of G deeds; he smote two
11:23 Egyptian, a man of G stature, five cubits tall.
12:22 until there was a G army, like an army
16:25 For G is the LORD, and greatly to be
17:8 the name of the G ones of the earth.
17:17 servant's house for a G while to come, and
17:19 making known all these G things.
17:21 thyself a name for G and terrible things, in
20:2 the city, a very G amount.
20:6 was a man of G stature, who had six
21:13 Gad, "I am in G distress; let me fall
21:13 his mercy is very G; but let me not
22:3 David also provided G stores of iron for nails
22:4 Sidonians and Tyrians brought G quantities of cedar
22:5 David provided materials in G quantity before his
22:8 blood and have waged G wars; you shall not
22:14 With G pains I have provided for the house
25:8 their duties, small and G, teacher and pupil alike.
26:6 they were men of G ability.
26:13 fathers' houses, small and G alike, for their gates.
26:31 made and men of G ability among them were
29:1 and the work is G; for the palace will
29:2 things of wood, besides G quantities of onyx and
29:12 it is to make G and to give strength
29:22 on that day with G gladness.
29:25 the LORD gave Solomon G repute in the sight
2Chr 1:1 God was with him and made him exceedingly G
1:8 God, "Thou hast shown G and steadfast love to
1:10 can rule this thy people, that is so G
2:5 to build will be G, for our God is
2:9 to build will be G and wonderful.
4:9 the priests, and the G court, and doors for
4:18 all these things in G quantities, so that the
6:32 the sake of thy G name, and thy mighty
7:8 with him, a very G congregation, from the entrance
9:1 questions, having a very G retinue and camels
9:9 gold, and a very G quantity of spices, and
9:17 king also made a G ivory throne, and overlaid
13:8 because you are a G multitude and have with
13:17 slew them with a G slaughter; so there fell
15:5 who came in, for G disturbances afflicted all the
15:9 sojourning with them, for G numbers had deserted to
16:14 they made a very G fire in his honor.
17:5 Jehoshaphat; and he had G riches and honor.
17:13 store-cities, and he had G stores in the cities
18:1 Now Jehoshaphat had G riches and honor; and he
18:30 with neither small nor G, but only with the
20:2 and told Jehoshaphat, "A G multitude is coming
20:12 are powerless against this G multitude that is coming
20:15 not dismayed at this G multitude; for the battle
20:25 they found cattle in G numbers, goods, clothing, and
21:3 Their father gave them G gifts, of silver, gold,
21:14 LORD will bring a G plague on your people,
21:19 and he died in G agony.
24:24 their hand a very G army, because they had
26:15 to shoot arrows and G stones.
28:5 and took captive a G number of his people
28:5 who defeated him with G slaughter.
28:13 our guilt is already G, and there is fierce
29:35 Besides the G number of burnt offerings there was
30:5 not kept it in G numbers as prescribed.
30:13 second month, a very G assembly.
30:21 bread seven days with G gladness; and the Levites
30:24 priests sanctified themselves in G numbers.
30:26 So there was G joy in Jerusalem, for since
31:10 that we have this G store left."
32:4 A G many people were gathered, and they stopped
32:27 And Hezekiah had very G riches and honor; and
32:29 had given him very G possessions.
33:14 it to a very G height; he also put
34:21 has been found; for G is the wrath of
34:30 all the people both G and small; and he
36:18 the house of God, G and small, and the
Ezra 3:11 people shouted with a G shout, when they praised
3:13 people shouted with a G shout, and the sound
4:10 nations whom the G and noble Osnappar deported
5:8 the house of the G God.
5:11 years ago, which a G king of Israel built
6:4 with three courses of G stones and one course
9:7 we have been in G guilt; and for our
9:13 deeds and for our G guilt, seeing that thou,
10:1 of God, a very G assembly of men, women,
Neh 1:3 escaped exile are in G trouble and shame; the
1:5 God of heaven, the G and terrible God who
1:10 hast redeemed by thy G power and by thy
3:27 another section opposite the G projecting tower as
4:14 the Lord, who is G and terrible, and fight
4:19 people, "The work is G and widely spread, and
5:1 Now there arose a G outcry of the people
5:7 And I held a G assembly against them,
6:3 "I am doing a G work and I cannot
8:6 blessed the LORD, the G God; and all the
8:12 portions and to make G rejoicing, because they had
8:17 And there was very G rejoicing.
9:18 Egypt,' and had committed G blasphemies,
9:19 blasphemies, thou in thy G mercies didst not forsake
9:25 delighted themselves in thy G goodness.
9:26 thee, and they committed G blasphemies.
9:27 and according to thy G mercies thou didst give
9:31 Nevertheless in thy G mercies thou didst not make
9:32 therefore, our God, the G and mighty and terrible
9:35 kingdom, and in thy G goodness which thou gavest
9:37 and we are in G distress."
12:31 wall, and appointed two G companies which gave
12:43 And they offered G sacrifices that day and rejoiced,
12:43 made them rejoice with G joy; the women and
13:27 and do all this G evil and act treacherously
Tob 3:6 heard false reproaches, and G is the sorrow within
3:16 the glory of the G God.
4:13 there is ruin and G confusion; and in shiftlessness
4:13 there is loss and G want, because shiftlessness is
4:21 You have G wealth if you fear God and
5:12 the son of the G Ananias, one of your
5:13 the sons of the G Shemaiah, when we went
8:16 us according to thy G mercy.
11:15 to his father the G things that had happened
11:19 for seven days with G festivity.
12:22 So they confessed the G and wonderful works of
13:15 soul praise God the G King.
Jud 1:1 the Assyrians in the G city of Nineveh, in
1:5 King Arphaxad in the G plain which is on
1:8 Upper Galilee and the G Plain of Esdraelon,
2:5 him, "Thus says the G King, the lord of
2:16 organized them as a G army is marshaled for
3:2 of Nebuchadnezzar, the G King, lie prostrate
3:9 near Dothan, fronting the G ridge of Judea;
4:9 out to God with G fervor, and they humbled
5:10 there they became a G multitude-- so great
5:10 great multitude-- so G that they could not
7:2 handling it, a very G multitude.
7:18 trains spread out in G number, and they formed
7:25 have done us a G injury in not making
7:30 Then G and general lamentation arose throughout
8:8 she feared God with G devotion.
8:19 so they suffered a G catastrophe before our enemies.
10:18 There was G excitement in the whole camp, for
12:16 he was moved with G desire to possess her;
12:20 her, and drank a G quantity of wine, much
13:4 one, either small or G, was left in the
13:13 together, both small and G, for it was unbelievable
14:9 the people raised a G shout and made a
15:5 Galilee out-flanked them with G slaughter, even
15:7 the plain got a G amount of booty, for
15:9 Jerusalem, you are the G glory of Israel, you
15:9 Israel, you are the G pride of our nation!
15:10 singlehanded; you have done G good to Israel, and
16:13 O Lord, thou are G and glorious, wonderful in
16:16 the Lord shall be G for ever.
Esth 1:5 Susa the capital, both G and small, a banquet
2:18 the king gave a G banquet to all his
4:3 came, there was G mourning among the Jews,
8:15 and white, with a G golden crown and a
9:4 For Mordecai was G in the king's house, and
10:3 Ahasuerus, and he was G among the Jews and

G

10:33 with terrifying power; the G in height will be
12:6 inhabitant of Zion, for G in your midst is
13:4 mountains as of a G multitude!
16:14 spite of all his G multitude, and those who
27:1 with his hard and G and strong sword will
27:13 in that day a G trumpet will be blown,
29:6 and with earthquake and G noise, with whirlwind
30:25 the day of the G slaughter, when the towers
32:2 the shade of a G rock in a weary
34:6 sacrifice in Bozrah, a G slaughter in the land
36:2 at Jerusalem, with a G army.
36:4 Hezekiah, 'Thus says the G king, the king of
36:13 the words of the G king, the king of
38:17 welfare that I had G bitterness; but thou hast
47:9 sorceries and the G power of your enchantments.
51:10 the waters of the G deep; that didst make
53:12 a portion with the G, and he shall divide
54:7 forsook you, but with G compassion I will gather
54:13 by the LORD, and G shall be the prosperity
56:12 be like this day, G beyond measure."
63:7 granted us, and the G goodness to the house
Jer 4:6 from the north, and G destruction.
5:5 will go to the G, and will speak to
5:6 transgressions are many, their apostasies are G
5:27 therefore they have become G and rich,
6:1 of the north, and G destruction.
6:22 the north country, a G nation is stirring from
10:6 O LORD; thou art G, and thy name is
10:6 and thy name is G in might.
10:22 Behold, it comes!--a G commotion out of the
11:16 the roar of a G tempest he will set
13:9 of Judah and the G pride of Jerusalem.
14:17 is smitten with a G wound, with a very
16:6 Both G and small shall die in this land;
16:10 LORD pronounced all this G evil against us?
20:17 been my grave, and her womb for ever G
21:5 in fury, and in G wrath.
21:6 shall die of a G pestilence.
22:8 dealt thus with this G city?"
22:14 will build myself a G house with spacious upper
25:14 For many nations and G kings shall make slaves
25:32 to nation, and a G tempest is stirring from
26:19 are about to bring G evil upon ourselves."
27:5 I who by my G power and my outstretched
27:7 then many nations and G kings shall make him
28:8 against many countries and G kingdoms.
30:7 that day is so G there is none like
30:14 because your guilt is G, because your sins are
30:15 Because your guilt is G, because your sins are
31:8 in travail, together; a G company, they shall return
32:17 the earth by thy G power and by thy
32:18 children after them, O G and mighty God whose
32:19 the LORD of hosts, G in counsel and mighty
32:21 outstretched arm, and with G terror;
32:37 my wrath and in G indignation; I will bring
32:42 have brought all this G evil upon this people,
33:3 and will tell you G and hidden things which
36:7 his evil way, for G is the anger and
40:12 and summer fruits in G abundance.
41:12 upon him at the G pool which is in
44:7 do you commit this G evil against yourselves, to
44:15 who stood by, a G assembly, all the people
44:26 have sworn by my G name, says the LORD,
45:5 And do you seek G things for yourself?
48:3 from Horonaim, 'Desolation and G destruction!'
50:9 Babylon a company of G nations, from the north
50:22 in the land, and G destruction!
51:54 The noise of G destruction from the land of
52:13 houses of Jerusalem; every G house he burned down.
Lam 1:1 become, she that was G among the nations!
3:23 are new every morning; G is thy faithfulness.
Bar 1:4 the people, small and G, all who dwelt in
2:11 wonders and with G power and outstretched arm,
2:25 They perished in G misery, by famine and sword
2:27 and in all thy G compassion,
2:29 my voice, this very G multitude will surely turn
3:24 O Israel, how G is the house of God!
3:25 It is G and has no bounds; it is
3:26 were famous of old, G in stature, expert in
4:9 Zion, God has brought G sorrow upon me;
4:24 come to you with G glory and with the
4:34 her pride in her G population, and her insolence
Ezek 1:4 the north, and a G cloud, with brightness round
3:12 the sound of a G earthquake;
3:13 that sounded like a G earthquake.
8:6 they are doing, the G abominations that the house
9:9 and Judah is exceedingly G; the land is full
13:11 a deluge of rain, G hailstones will fall, and
13:13 in my anger, and G hailstones in wrath to
17:3 the Lord GOD: A G eagle with great wings
17:3 A great eagle with G wings and long pinions,
17:7 "But there was another G eagle with great wings
17:7 great eagle with G wings and much plumage;
17:17 his mighty army and G company will not help
21:14 the sword for the G slaughter, which encompasses
24:9 I also will make the pile G
25:17 I will execute G vengeance upon them with wrathful
26:19 over you, and the G waters cover you,
27:12 you because of your G wealth of every kind;
27:18 goods, because of your G wealth of every kind;
28:5 your treasuries; by your G wisdom in trade you
29:3 king of Egypt, the G dragon that lies in
30:16 Pelusium shall be in G agony; Thebes shall be
31:3 forest shade, and of G height, its top among
31:6 its shadow dwelt all G nations.
36:23 the holiness of my G name, which has been
37:10 their feet, an exceedingly G host.
38:4 in full armor, a G company, all of them
38:13 and goods, to seize G spoil?'
38:15 riding on horses, a G host, a mighty army;
38:19 there shall be a G shaking in the land
39:17 preparing for you, a G sacrificial feast upon the
47:10 the fish of the G Sea.
47:15 north side, from the G Sea by way of
47:19 of Egypt to the G Sea.
47:20 the west side, the G Sea shall be the
48:28 of Egypt to the G Sea.
Dan 2:6 gifts and rewards and G honor.
2:10 king's demand; for no G and powerful king has
2:31 king, and behold, a G image.
2:35 the image became a G mountain and filled the
2:45 A G God has made known to the king
2:48 high honors and many G gifts, and made him
4:3 How G are his signs, how mighty his wonders!
4:10 midst of the earth; and its height was G
4:30 said, "Is not this G Babylon, which I have
5:1 King Belshazzar made a G feast for a thousand
7:2 were stirring up the G sea.
7:3 And four G beasts came up out of the
7:7 strong; and it had G iron teeth; it devoured
7:8 and a mouth speaking G things.
7:11 the sound of the G words which the horn
7:17 'These four G beasts are four kings who shall
7:20 a mouth that spoke G things, and which seemed
8:8 he was strong, the G horn was broken, and
8:9 horn, which grew exceedingly G toward the south,
8:10 It grew G, even to the host of heaven;
8:21 of Greece; and the G horn between his eyes
8:24 His power shall be G, and he shall cause
9:4 saying, "O Lord, the G and terrible God, who
9:12 bringing upon us a G calamity; for under the
9:18 the ground of thy G mercy.
10:1 and it was a G conflict.
10:4 the bank of the G river, that is, the
10:7 the vision, but a G trembling fell upon them,
10:8 alone and saw this G vision, and no strength
11:3 who shall rule with G dominion and do according
11:5 dominion shall be a G dominion.
11:10 assemble a multitude of G forces, which shall come
11:11 he shall raise a G multitude, but it shall
11:13 come on with a G army and abundant supplies.
11:25 the south with a G army; and the king
11:25 war with an exceedingly G and mighty army; but
11:28 to his land with G substance, but his heart
11:44 shall go forth with G fury to exterminate and
12:1 shall arise Michael, the G prince who has charge
13:31 was a woman of G refinement, and beautiful in
13:64 onward Daniel had a G reputation among the people.
14:18 loud voice, "You are G, O Bel; and with
14:23 There was also a G dragon, which the Babylonians
14:41 loud voice, "Thou art G, O Lord God of
Hos 1:2 for the land commits G harlotry by forsaking the
1:11 from the land, for G shall be the day
5:13 and sent to the G king.
9:7 mad, because of your G iniquity and great hatred.
9:7 your great iniquity and G hatred.
10:6 as tribute to the G king.
10:15 Israel, because of your G wickedness.
Joel 2:2 upon the mountains a G and powerful people; their
2:11 his host is exceedingly G; he that executes his
2:11 of the LORD is G and very terrible; who
2:20 for he has done G things.

2:21 the LORD has done G things!
2:25 and the cutter, my G army, which I sent
2:31 to blood, before the G and terrible day of
3:13 The vats overflow, for their wickedness is G
Amos 3:9 Samaria, and see the G tumults within her, and
3:15 shall perish, and the G houses shall come to
5:12 your transgressions, and how G are your sins--you
6:2 go to Hamath the G; then go down to
6:11 LORD commands, and the G house shall be smitten
7:4 and it devoured the G deep and was eating
8:5 small and the shekel G, and deal deceitfully with
Jon 1:2 go to Nineveh, that G city, and cry against
1:4 the LORD hurled a G wind upon the sea,
1:12 of me that this G tempest has come upon
1:17 the LORD appointed a G fish to swallow up
3:2 go to Nineveh, that G city, and proclaim to
3:3 Nineveh was an exceedingly G city, three days'
4:11 I pity Nineveh, that G city, in which there
Mic 5:4 now he shall be G to the ends of
7:3 a bribe, and the G man utters the evil
Nah 1:3 to anger and of G might, and the LORD
3:10 cast, and all her G men were bound in
Zeph 1:14 The G day of the LORD is near, near
Zech 4:7 What are you, O G mountain?
7:12 Therefore G wrath came from the LORD of hosts.
8:2 jealous for Zion with G jealousy, and I am
8:2 jealous for her with G wrath.
12:11 Jerusalem will be as G as the mourning for
14:13 on that day a G panic from the LORD
14:14 silver, and garments in G abundance.
Mal 1:5 and you shall say, G is the LORD, beyond
1:11 setting my name is G among the nations, and
1:11 for my name is G among the nations, says
1:14 for I am a G King, says the LORD
4:5 the prophet before the G and terrible day of
1Mac 1:24 murder, and spoke with G arrogance.
1:33 of David with a G strong wall and strong
1:35 there, and became a G snare.
1:40 dishonor now grew as G as her glory; her
1:64 And very G wrath came upon Israel.
2:17 a leader, honored and G in this city, and
2:51 generations; and receive G honor and an everlasting
2:58 Elijah because of G zeal for the law was
2:70 mourned for him with G lamentation.
3:17 are, fight against so G and strong a multitude?
3:20 come against us in G pride and lawlessness to
4:23 and sea purple, and G riches.
4:25 Thus Israel had a G deliverance that day.
4:39 and mourned with G lamentation, and sprinkled
4:58 There was very G gladness among the people, and
5:16 heard these messages, a G assembly was called to
5:23 them to Judea with G rejoicing.
5:45 the small and the G, with their wives and
5:61 the people suffered a G rout because, thinking to
6:4 he fled and in G grief departed from there
6:11 And into what a G flood I now am
7:8 River; he was a G man in the kingdom
7:19 threw them into a G pit.
7:22 of Judah and did G damage in Israel.
7:35 he went out in G anger.
7:48 as a day of G gladness.
8:4 crushed them and inflicted G disaster upon them; the
8:6 also defeated Antiochus the G, king of Asia, who
9:20 And all Israel made G lamentation for him; they
9:24 those days a very G famine occurred, and the
9:27 Thus there was G distress in Israel, such as
9:35 store with them the G amount of baggage which
9:37 Jambri are celebrating a G wedding, and are
9:37 of one of the G nobles of Canaan, from
9:56 at that time in G agony.
10:37 be stationed in the G strongholds of the king,
10:46 they remembered the G wrongs which Demetrius
10:58 wedding at Ptolemais with G pomp, as kings do.
10:86 to meet him with G pomp.
11:1 king of Egypt gathered G forces, like the sand
11:42 but I will confer G honor on you and
12:49 into Galilee and the G Plain to destroy all
12:52 companions and were in G fear; and all Israel
13:3 "You yourselves know what G things I and my
13:17 sons, lest he arouse G hostility among the people,
13:26 Israel bewailed him with G lamentation, and
13:29 setting, erecting about them G columns, and upon the
13:32 Asia; and he brought G calamity upon the land.
13:33 with high towers and G walls and gates and
13:42 year of Simon the G high priest and commander
13:44 the city, and a G tumult arose in the
13:51 and songs, because a G enemy had been crushed
14:11 and Israel rejoiced with G joy.
14:27 year of Simon the G high priest,
14:28 in Asaramel, in the G assembly of the priests
14:29 perserved; and they brought G glory to their nation.
14:32 He spent G sums of his own money; he
14:36 the sanctuary and do G damage to its purity.
15:9 kingdom, we will bestow G honor upon you and
15:29 territory, you have done G damage in the land,
15:32 silver plate, and his G magnificence, he was amazed.
15:35 they were causing G damage among the people
16:15 he gave them a G banquet, and hid men
16:17 committed an act of G treachery and returned evil
2Mac 1:22 over, shone out, a G fire blazed up, so
2:18 has rescued us from G evils and has purified
2:19 the purification of the G temple, and the dedication
2:22 while the Lord with G kindness became gracious to
3:21 high priest in his G anguish.
3:24 all authority caused so G a manifestation that all
3:28 aforesaid treasury with a G retinue and all his
3:35 Lord and made very G vows to the Savior
5:20 its glory when the G Lord became reconciled.
5:26 armed men and killed G numbers of people.
6:13 is a sign of G kindness.
6:31 young but to the G body of his nation.
8:16 not to fear the G multitude of Gentiles who
8:27 kept the sabbath, giving G praise and thanks to
10:38 the Lord who shows G kindness to Israel and
12:15 men, calling upon the G Sovereign of the world,
12:24 With G guile he besought them to let him
12:27 a vigorous defense; and G stores of war engines
13:1 was coming with a G army against Judea,
14:31 he went to the G and holy temple while
Mt 2:10 they rejoiced exceedingly with G joy;
4:16 darkness have seen a G light, and for those
4:25 And G crowds followed him from Galilee and the
5:12 for your reward is G in heaven, for so
5:19 them shall be called G in the kingdom of
5:35 the city of the G King.
6:23 you is darkness, how G is the darkness!
7:27 and it fell; and G was the fall of
8:1 down from the mountain, G crowds followed him;
8:18 Now when Jesus saw G crowds around him, he
8:24 behold, there arose a G storm on the sea,
8:26 and there was a G calm.
13:2 And G crowds gathered about him, so that he
13:46 finding one pearl of G value, went and sold
14:14 ashore he saw a G throng; and he had
15:28 answered her, "O woman, G is your faith!
15:30 And G crowds came to him, bringing with them
15:33 desert to feed so G a crowd?"
18:6 him to have a G millstone fastened round his
19:22 sorrowful; for he had G possessions.
20:25 over them, and their G men exercise authority over
20:26 but whoever would be G among you must be
20:29 out of Jericho, a G crowd followed him.
22:36 "Teacher, which is the G commandment in the law?"
22:38 This is the G and first commandment.
24:21 then there will be G tribulation, such as has
24:24 will arise and show G signs and wonders, so
24:30 heaven with power and G glory;
26:47 and with him a G crowd with swords and
27:60 and he rolled a G stone to the door
28:2 behold, there was a G earthquake; for an angel
28:8 tomb with fear and G joy, and ran to
Mk 1:35 in the morning, a G while before day, he
3:7 the sea, and a G multitude from Galilee followed;
3:8 Tyre and Sidon a G multitude, hearing all that
4:37 And a G storm of wind arose, and the
4:39 and there was a G calm.
5:11 Now a G herd of swine was feeding there
5:21 the other side, a G crowd gathered about him;
5:24 And a G crowd followed him and thronged about
6:34 ashore he saw a G throng, and he had
8:1 days, when again a G crowd had gathered, and
9:14 disciples, they saw a G crowd about them, and
9:42 for him if a G millstone were hung round
10:22 sorrowful; for he had G possessions.
10:42 over them, and their G men exercise authority over
10:43 but whoever would be G among you must be
10:46 his disciples and a G multitude, Bartimaeus, a blind
12:37 And the G throng heard him gladly.
13:2 "Do you see these G buildings?
13:26 coming in clouds with G power and glory.
Lk 1:15 for he will be G before the Lord, and
1:32 He will be G, and will be called the

1:49 is mighty has done G things for me, and
1:58 the Lord had shown G mercy to her, and
2:10 good news of a G joy which will come
2:36 she was of a G age, having lived with
4:25 when there came a G famine over all the
5:6 this, they enclosed a G shoal of fish; and
5:15 abroad concerning him; and G multitudes gathered
5:29 Levi made him a G feast in his house;
6:17 level place, with a G crowd of his disciples
6:17 his disciples and a G multitude of people from
6:23 behold, your reward is G in heaven; for so
6:35 your reward will be G, and you will be
6:49 fell, and the ruin of that house was G
7:11 his disciples and a G crowd went with him.
7:16 glorified God, saying, "A G prophet has arisen among
8:4 And when a G crowd came together and people
8:37 they were seized with G fear; so he got
9:37 from the mountain, a G crowd met him.
9:48 among you all is the one who is G
14:16 man once gave a G banquet, and invited many;
14:25 Now G multitudes accompanied him; and he turned
14:32 other is yet a G way off, he sends
15:14 had spent everything, a G famine arose in that
16:26 us and you a G chasm has been fixed,
21:11 kingdom; there will be G earthquakes, and in various
21:11 will be terrors and G signs from heaven.
21:23 For G distress shall be upon the earth and
21:27 cloud with power and G glory.
23:26 there followed him a G multitude of the people,
24:52 returned to Jerusalem with G joy,
Jn 7:37 of the feast, the G day, Jesus stood up
12:9 When the G crowd of the Jews learned that
12:12 The next day a G crowd who had come
Acts 2:20 the Lord comes, the G and manifest day.
4:33 And with G power the apostles gave their testimony
4:33 the Lord Jesus, and G grace was upon them
5:5 And G fear came upon all who heard of
5:11 And G fear came upon the whole church, and
6:7 in Jerusalem, and a G many of the priests
6:8 grace and power, did G wonders and signs among
7:11 Egypt and Canaan, and G affliction, and our fathers
8:1 on that day a G persecution arose against the
8:2 buried Stephen, and made G lamentation over him.
8:9 of Samaria, saying that he himself was somebody G
8:10 is that power of God which is called G
8:13 And seeing signs and G miracles performed, he was
10:11 something descending, like a G sheet, let down by
11:5 something descending, like a G sheet, let down from
11:21 with them, and a G number that believed turned
11:28 there would be a G famine over all the
13:17 and made the people G during their stay in
14:1 so spoke that a G company believed, both of
15:3 Gentiles, and they gave G joy to all the
16:26 suddenly there was a G earthquake, so that the
17:4 Silas; as did a G many of the devout
19:27 the temple of the G goddess Artemis may count
19:28 enraged, and cried out, G is Artemis of the
19:34 one voice cried out, G is Artemis of the
19:35 temple keeper of the G Artemis, and of the
21:40 when there was a G hush, he spoke to
22:6 Damascus, about noon a G light from heaven
23:9 Then a G clamor arose; and some of the
25:23 and Bernice came with G pomp, and they entered
26:22 both to small and G, saying nothing but what
26:24 you are mad; your G learning is turning you
28:23 at his lodging in G numbers.
Rom 9:2 Spirit, that I have G sorrow and unceasing anguish
2Cor 6:4 every way: through G endurance, in afflictions,
7:4 I have G confidence in you; I have great
7:4 in you; I have G pride in you; I
8:22 ever because of his G confidence in you.
9:11 in every way for G generosity, which through us
Eph 1:19 the working of his G might
2:4 mercy, out of the G love with which he
Col 1:27 to make known how G among the Gentiles are
1Thes 2:2 in the face of G opposition.
2:17 more eagerly and with G desire to see you
1Tim 3:13 for themselves and also G confidence in the faith
3:16 G indeed, we confess, is the mystery of our
6:6 There is G gain in godliness with contentment;
2Tim 2:20 In a G house there are not only vessels
4:14 the coppersmith did me G harm; the Lord will
Tit 2:13 the glory of our G God and Savior Jesus
Heb 2:3 we neglect such a G salvation?
4:14 then we have a G high priest who has
7:4 See how G he is!
10:21 since we have a G priest over the house
10:35 confidence, which has a G reward.
12:1 are surrounded by so G a cloud of witnesses,
13:20 our Lord Jesus, the G shepherd of the sheep,
Jas 3:4 though they are so G and are driven by
3:5 member and boasts of G things.
3:5 How G a forest is set ablaze by a
5:16 a righteous man has G power in its effects.
1Pet 1:3 By his G mercy we have been born anew
2Pet 1:4 his precious and very G promises, that through these
Jude 1:6 the judgment of the G day;
Rev 2:22 I will throw into G tribulation, unless they repent
6:4 he was given a G sword.
6:12 behold, there was a G earthquake; and the sun
6:15 the earth and the G men and the generals
6:17 the Lamb; for the G day of their wrath
7:9 looked, and behold, a G multitude which no man
7:14 come out of the G tribulation; they have washed
8:8 and something like a G mountain, burning with fire,
8:10 his trumpet, and a G star fell from heaven,
9:2 the smoke of a G furnace, and the sun
9:14 are bound at the G river Euphrates."
11:8 the street of the G city which is allegorically
11:11 on their feet, and G fear fell on those
11:13 hour there was a G earthquake, and a tenth
11:17 thou hast taken thy G power and begun to
11:18 name, both small and G, and for destroying the
12:1 And a G portent appeared in heaven, a woman
12:3 in heaven; behold, a G red dragon, with seven
12:9 And the G dragon was thrown down, that ancient
12:12 down to you in G wrath, because he knows
12:14 two wings of the G eagle that she might
13:2 and his throne and G authority.
13:13 It works G signs, even making fire come down
13:16 all, both small and G, both rich and poor,
14:8 fallen is Babylon the G, she who made all
14:19 threw it into the G wine press of the
15:1 portent in heaven, G and wonderful, seven angels
15:3 of the Lamb, saying, G and wonderful are thy
16:12 his bowl on the G river Euphrates, and its
16:14 for battle on the G day of God the
16:18 of thunder, and a G earthquake such as had
16:18 on the earth, so G was that earthquake.
16:19 The G city was split into three parts, and
16:19 fell, and God remembered G Babylon, to make her
16:21 to be found; and G hailstones, heavy as a
17:1 the judgment of the G harlot who is seated
17:5 of mystery: "Babylon the G, mother of harlots and
17:18 you saw is the G city which has dominion
18:1 down from heaven, having G authority; and the earth
18:2 a mighty voice, "Fallen, fallen is Babylon the G
18:10 thou G city, thou mighty city, Babylon!
18:16 "Alas, alas, for the G city that was clothed
18:18 city was like the G city?"
18:19 "Alas, alas, for the G city where all who
18:21 a stone like a G millstone and threw it
18:21 "So shall Babylon the G city be thrown down
18:23 thy merchants were the G men of the earth,
19:1 loud voice of a G multitude in heaven, crying,
19:2 he has judged the G harlot who corrupted the
19:5 his servants, you who fear him, small and G
19:6 the voice of a G multitude, like the sound
19:17 "Come, gather for the G supper of God,
19:18 men, both free and slave, both small and G
20:1 bottomless pit and a G chain.
20:11 Then I saw a G white throne and him
20:12 I saw the dead, G and small, standing before
21:10 me away to a G, high mountain, and showed
21:12 It had a G, high wall, with twelve gates,

GREATER (93)

Gen 1:16 two great lights, the G light to rule the
4:13 LORD, "My punishment is G than I can bear.
39:9 hand; he is not G in this house than
41:40 throne will I be G than you."
48:19 younger brother shall be G than he, and his
Ex 18:11 that the LORD is G than all gods, because
Num 14:12 of you a nation G and mightier than they."
Deut 1:28 saying, "The people are G and taller than we;
4:38 before you nations G and mightier than yourselves,
7:1 the Jebusites, seven nations G and mightier than
7:17 heart, 'These nations are G than I; how can
9:1 in to dispossess nations G and mightier than
9:14 a nation mightier and G than they.'
11:23 dispossess nations G and mightier than yourselves.
Josh 10:2 and because it was G than Ai, and all

Ruth 3:10 made this last kindness G than the first, in
2Sam 5:10 And David became G and greater, for the LORD,
5:10 David became greater and G, for the LORD, the
13:15 he hated her was G than the love with
13:16 sending me away is G than the other which
1Kgs 1:37 and make his throne G than the throne of
1:47 and make his throne G than your throne.' And
1Chr 11:9 And David became G and greater, for the LORD
11:9 David became greater and G, for the LORD of
12:14 a hundred and the G over a thousand.
2Chr 2:5 for our God is G than all gods.
17:12 And Jehoshaphat grew steadily G
32:7 for there is one G with us than with
Job 33:12 God is G than man.
Wis 8:12 when I speak at G length they will put
16:17 the fire had still G effect, for the universe
Sir 3:18 The G you are, the more you must humble
10:23 none of them is G than the man who
39:11 will leave a name G than a thousand, and
43:28 For he is G than all his works.
43:32 Many things G than these lie hidden, for we
Is 10:10 graven images were G than those of Jerusalem
Lam 4:6 my people has been G than the punishment of
Ezek 8:6 you will see still G abominations."
8:13 "You will see still G abominations which they
8:15 You will see still G abominations than these."
Dan 7:20 things, and which seemed G than its fellows.
11:13 again raise a multitude, G than the former; and
Amos 6:2 Or is their territory G than your territory,
Hag 2:9 this house shall be G than the former, says
1Mac 6:27 they will do still G things, and you will
Mt 11:11 has risen no one G than John the Baptist;
11:11 kingdom of heaven is G than he.
12:6 I tell you, something G than the temple is
12:41 Jonah, and behold, something G than Jonah is here.
12:42 and behold, something G than Solomon is here.
23:16 For which is G, the gold or the temple
23:18 For which is G, the gift or the altar
Mk 12:31 is no other commandment G than these."
12:40 They will receive the G condemnation."
Lk 7:28 of women none is G than John; yet he
7:28 kingdom of God is G than he."
11:31 Solomon, and behold, something G than Solomon is
11:32 Jonah, and behold, something G than Jonah is here.
20:47 They will receive the G condemnation."
22:27 For which is the G, one who sits at
Jn 1:50 You shall see G things than these."
4:12 Are you G than our father Jacob, who gave
5:19 himself is doing; and G works than these will
5:35 which I have is G than that of John;
8:53 taste death.' Are you G than our father Abraham,
10:29 them to me, is G than all, and no
13:16 a servant is not G than his master; nor
13:16 he who is sent G than he who sent
14:12 that I do; and G works than these will
14:28 for the Father is G than I.
15:13 G love has no man than this, that a
15:20 'A servant is not G than his master.' If
19:11 to you has the G sin."
Acts 15:28 lay upon you no G burden than these necessary
Rom 6:19 to impurity and to G and greater iniquity, so
6:19 and to greater and G iniquity, so now yield
1Cor 12:23 we invest with the G honor, and our unpresentable
12:23 parts are treated with G modesty,
12:24 the body, giving the G honor to the inferior
14:5 He who prophesies is G than he who speaks
2Cor 3:8 Spirit be attended with G splendor?
11:23 madman—with far G labors, far more imprisonments,
Heb 6:13 he had no one G by whom to swear,
6:16 indeed swear by a G than themselves, and in
9:11 come, then through the G and more perfect tent
11:26 suffered for the Christ G wealth than the treasures
Jas 3:1 shall be judged with G strictness.
2Pet 2:11 ones, whereas angels, though G in might and power,
1Jn 3:20 us; for God is G than our hearts, and
4:4 is in you is G than he who is
5:9 testimony of God is G; for this is the
3Jn 1:4 No G joy can I have than this, to

GREATEST (24)

Josh 14:15 this Arba was the G man among the Anakim.
Job 1:3 this man was the G of all the people
Jer 6:13 the least to the G of them, every one
8:10 the least to the G every one is greedy
31:34 of them to the G, says the LORD; for
42:1 the least to the G, came near
42:8 the least to the G,
44:12 the least to the G, they shall die by
Jon 3:5 on sackcloth, from the G of them to the
2Mac 5:6 one's kindred is the G misfortune, but imagining that
14:13 high priest of the G temple.
15:18 them less heavily; their G and first fear was
Mt 13:32 grown it is the G of shrubs and becomes
18:1 saying, "Who is the G in the kingdom of
18:4 child, he is the G in the kingdom of
23:11 He who is G among you shall be your
Mk 4:32 up and becomes the G of all shrubs, and
9:34 had discussed with one another who was the G
Lk 9:46 them as to which of them was the G
22:24 of them was to be regarded as the G
22:26 you; rather let the G among you become as
Acts 8:10 the least to the G, saying, "This man is
1Cor 13:13 these three; but the G of these is love.
Heb 8:11 me, from the least of them to the G

GREATLY (117)

Gen 3:16 he said, "I will G multiply your pain in
7:18 waters prevailed and increased G upon the earth;
16:10 her, "I will so G multiply your descendants that
24:35 The LORD has G blessed my master, and he
31:30 away because you longed G for your father's house,
32:7 Then Jacob was G afraid and distressed; and he
Ex 1:6 were fruitful and increased G; they multiplied and
19:18 of a kiln, and the whole mountain quaked G
Num 14:39 the people of Israel, and the people mourned G
Deut 6:3 that you may multiply G, as the LORD, the
17:17 away; nor shall he G multiply for himself silver
Josh 9:24 you; so we feared G for our lives because
10:2 among them, he feared G, because Gibeon was a
1Sam 11:6 and his anger was G kindled.
11:15 Saul and all the men of Israel rejoiced G
12:18 and all the people G feared the LORD and
16:21 And Saul loved him G, and he became his
17:11 they were dismayed and G afraid.
20:19 day you will be G missed; then go to
28:5 Philistines, he was afraid, and his heart trembled G
30:6 And David was G distressed; for the people spoke
31:4 But his armor-bearer would not; for he feared G
2Sam 10:5 for the men were G ashamed.
12:5 Then David's anger was G kindled against the man;
24:10 LORD, "I have sinned G in what I have
1Kgs 5:7 of Solomon, he rejoiced G, and said, "Blessed be
18:3 Obadiah revered the LORD G;
2Kgs 6:11 king of Syria was G troubled because of this
1Chr 4:38 their families, and their fathers' houses increased G
10:4 But his armor-bearer would not; for he feared G
16:25 is the LORD, and G to be praised, and
19:5 for the men were G ashamed.
21:8 God, "I have sinned G in that I have
29:9 to the LORD; David the king also rejoiced G
2Chr 33:12 God and humbled himself G before the God of
Ezra 10:13 two; for we have G transgressed in this matter.
Neh 2:10 this, it displeased them G that some one had
4:1 he was angry and G enraged, and he ridiculed
6:16 were afraid and fell G in their own esteem;
Tob 9:4 long he will be G distressed."
10:3 And he was G distressed.
Jud 4:2 they were therefore very G terrified at his approach,
6:20 Then they consoled Achior, and praised him G
7:4 vast numbers they were G terrified, and every one
7:33 And they were G depressed in the city.
10:7 her clothing changed, they G admired her beauty,
12:20 And Holofernes was G pleased with her, and drank
13:17 All the people were G astonished, and bowed down
14:19 their tunics and were G dismayed, and their loud
15:6 plundered it, and were G enriched.
Job 35:15 and he does not G heed transgression,
Ps 21:1 in thy help how G he exults!
48:1 is the LORD and G to be praised in
62:2 I shall not be G moved.
65:9 and waterest it, thou G enrichest it; the river
96:4 is the LORD, and G to be praised; he
107:38 his blessing they multiply G; and he does not
112:1 the LORD, who G delights in his commandments!
116:10 I said, "I am G afflicted";
145:3 is the LORD, and G to be praised, and
Prov 23:24 of the righteous will G rejoice; he who begets
Wis 18:17 apparitions in dreadful dreams G troubled them, and
Sir 1:6 One who is wise, G to be feared, sitting
7:17 Humble yourself G, for the punishment of the
11:6 rulers have been G disgraced, and illustrious men
25:2 men, and I am G offended at their life:

	42:22	How G to be desired are all his works,
	49:4	Josiah they all sinned G, for they forsook the
Is	8:21	pass through the land, G distressed and hungry; and
	61:10	I will G rejoice in the LORD, my soul
Jer	3:1	not that land be G polluted?
	20:11	They will be G shamed, for they will not
Bar	2:18	the person that is G distressed, that goes about
Ezek	20:13	and my sabbaths they G profaned.
Dan	5:9	Then King Belshazzar was G alarmed, and his color
	7:28	me, Daniel, my thoughts G alarmed me, and my
	9:23	you, for you are G beloved; therefore consider the
	10:11	me, "O Daniel, man G beloved, give heed to
	10:19	he said, "O man G beloved, fear not, peace
	13:27	tale, the servants were G ashamed, for nothing like
Zech	9:9	Rejoice G, O daughter of Zion!
1Mac	2:14	rent their clothes, put on sackcloth, and mourned G
	3:27	these reports, he was G angered; and he sent
	3:31	He was G perplexed in mind, and determined to
	4:21	perceived this they were G frightened, and when
	5:63	and his brothers were G honored in all Israel
	7:48	The people rejoiced G and celebrated that day as
	8:13	and they have been G exalted.
	9:6	enemy forces, they were G frightened, and many
	9:68	They distressed him G, for his plan and his
	9:69	So he was G enraged at the lawless men
	10:8	They were G alarmed when they heard that the
	10:46	and how he had G oppressed them.
	10:68	of it, he was G grieved and returned to
	11:53	which Jonathan had done him, but oppressed him G
	15:36	And the king was G angered.
	16:22	heard this, he was G shocked; and he seized
2Mac	1:11	dangers we thank him G for taking our side
	8:32	and one who had G troubled the Jews.
	15:27	thousand men, and were G gladdened by God's.
Mt	17:22	And they were G distressed.
	18:30	taken place, they were G distressed, and they went
	19:25	heard this they were G astonished, saying, "Who
	27:14	a single charge; so that the governor wondered G
Mk	9:15	they saw him, were G amazed, and ran up
	14:33	and began to be G distressed and troubled.
Lk	1:29	But she was G troubled at the saying, and
Jn	3:29	and hears him, rejoices G at the bridegroom's voice;
Acts	6:7	of the disciples multiplied G in Jerusalem, and a
	18:27	When he arrived, he G helped those who through
2Cor	10:15	among you may be G enlarged,
Phil	4:10	rejoice in the Lord G that now at length
Col	2:1	you to know how G I strive for you,
2Pet	2:7	rescued righteous Lot, G distressed by the
2Jn	1:4	I rejoiced G to find some of your children
3Jn	1:3	For I G rejoiced when some of the brethren
Rev	17:6	When I saw her I marveled G

GREATNESS (36)

Ex	15:7	In the G of thy majesty thou overthrowest thy
	15:16	them; because of the G of thy arm, they
Num	14:19	thee, according to the G of thy steadfast love,
Deut	3:24	show thy servant thy G and thy mighty hand;
	5:24	us his glory and G, and we have heard
	9:26	hast redeemed through thy G, whom thou hast
	11:2	LORD your God, his G, his mighty hand and
	32:3	Ascribe G to our God!
2Sam	7:21	hast wrought all this G, to make thy servant
1Chr	17:19	hast wrought all this G, in making known all
	29:11	O LORD, is the G, and the power, and
2Chr	9:6	and behold, half the G of your wisdom was
Neh	13:22	me according to the G of thy steadfast love.
Tob	13:4	Make his G known there, and exalt him in
Job	23:6	with me in the G of his power?
	36:18	and let not the G of the ransom turn
Ps	145:3	be praised, and his G is unsearchable.
	145:6	thy terrible acts, and I will declare thy G
	150:2	deeds; praise him according to his exceeding G
Wis	6:7	nor show deference to G; because he himself made
	13:5	For from the G and beauty of created things
Sir	51:3	deliver me, in the G of thy mercy and
Is	40:26	by name; by the G of his might, and
	63:1	apparel, marching in the G of his strength?
Jer	13:22	it is for the G of your iniquity that
Ezek	31:2	his multitude: "Whom are you like in your G
	31:7	was beautiful in its G, in the length of
	31:18	in glory and in G among the trees of
	38:23	I will show my G and my holiness and
Dan	4:22	Your G has grown and reaches to heaven, and
	4:36	kingdom, and still more G was added to me.
	5:18	your father kingship and G and glory and majesty;
	5:19	and because of the G that he gave him,
	7:27	the dominion and the G of the kingdoms under
1Mac	9:22	he did, and his G, have not been recorded,
Eph	1:19	what is the immeasurable G of his power in

GREAVES

1Sam	17:6	And he had G of bronze upon his legs,

GREECE (6)

Dan	8:21	is the king of G; and the great horn
	10:20	lo, the prince of G will come.
	11:2	shall stir up all against the kingdom of G
Zech	9:13	over your sons, O G, and wield you like
1Mac	1:1	previously become king of G
Acts	20:2	had given them much encouragement, he came to G

GREED (8)

Job	20:20	"Because his G knew no rest, he will not
Prov	1:7	of the Path of G and Violence
Ezek	16:27	delivered you to the G of your enemies, the
Hab	2:5	His G is as wide as Sheol; like death
1Cor	5:11	guilty of immorality or G, or is an idolater,
1Thes	2:5	or a cloak for G, as God is witness;
2Pet	2:3	And in their G they will exploit you with
	2:14	They have hearts trained in G

GREEDILY (2)

Ps	57:4	midst of lions that G devour the sons of
Sir	31:16	and do not chew G, lest you be hated.

GREEDY (17)

1Sam	2:29	Why then look with G eye at my sacrifices
Ps	10:3	heart, and the man G for gain curses and
Prov	15:27	He who is G for unjust gain makes trouble
	28:25	A G man stirs up strife, but he who
Sir	14:9	A G man's eye is not satisfied with a
	31:12	Do not be G at it, and do not
	31:13	Remember that a G eye is a bad thing.
	31:13	has been created more G than the eye?
Jer	6:13	them, every one is G for unjust gain; and
	8:10	greatest every one is G for unjust gain; from
Hos	4:8	my people; they are G for their iniquity.
1Mac	4:17	people, "Do not be G for plunder, for there
1Cor	5:10	this world, or the G and robbers, or idolaters,
	6:10	nor thieves, nor the G, nor drunkards, nor revilers,
Eph	4:19	themselves up to licentiousness, G to practice every
1Tim	3:8	to much wine, not G for gain;
Tit	1:6	drunkard or violent or G for gain,

GREEK (21)

2Mac	4:10	countrymen over to the G way of life.
	4:12	men to wear the G hat.
	4:15	the highest value upon G forms of prestige.
	6:8	issued to the neighboring G cities, that they should
	6:9	to change over to G customs.
	11:24	our father's change to G customs but prefer their
	13:2	of them had a G force of one hundred
Mk	7:25	the woman was a G, a Syrophoenician by birth.
Jn	19:20	was written in Hebrew, in Latin, and in G
Acts	16:1	was a believer; but his father was a G
	16:3	his father was a G
	17:12	with not a few G women of high standing
	21:37	And he said, "Do you know G
Rom	1:16	to the Jew first and also to the G
	2:9	first and also the G,
	2:10	does good, the Jew first and also the G
	10:12	distinction between Jew and G; the same Lord is
Gal	2:3	compelled to be circumcised, though he was a G
	3:28	is neither Jew nor G, there is neither slave
Col	3:11	Here there cannot be G and Jew, circumcised and
Rev	9:11	is Abaddon, and in G he is called Apollyon.

GREEKS (25)

Joel	3:6	and Jerusalem to the G, removing them far from
1Mac	1:10	and thirty-seventh year of the kingdom of the G
	6:2	the Macedonian king who first reigned over the G
	8:9	The G planned to come and destroy them,
	8:10	a general against the G and attacked them.
	8:18	kingdom of the G was completely enslaving Israel.
2Mac	4:36	of Onias, and the G shared their hatred of
	11:2	city a home for G,
Jn	7:35	the Dispersion among the G and teach the Greeks?
	7:35	the Dispersion among the Greeks and teach the G
	12:20	up to worship at the feast were some G
Acts	11:20	Antioch spoke to the G also, preaching the Lord
	14:1	great company believed, both of Jews and of G
	17:4	many of the devout G and not a few

18:4 synagogue every sabbath, and persuaded Jews and G
19:10 the word of the Lord, both Jews and G
19:17 Ephesus, both Jews and G; and fear fell upon
20:21 to Jews and to G of repentance to God
21:28 moreover he also brought G into the temple, and
Rom 1:14 under obligation both to G and to barbarians, both
3:9 men, both Jews and G, are under the power
1Cor 1:22 Jews demand signs and G seek wisdom,
1:24 called, both Jews and G, Christ the power of
10:32 to Jews or to G or to the church
12:13 one body–Jews or G, slaves or free–and

GREEN (35)

Gen 1:30 I have given every G plant for food." And
9:3 I gave you the G plants, I give you
Ex 10:15 had left; not a G thing remained, neither tree
Deut 12:2 hills and under every G tree;
1Kgs 14:23 hill and under every G tree;
2Kgs 16:4 hills, and under every G tree.
17:10 hill and under every G tree;
2Chr 28:4 hills, and under every G tree.
Job 15:32 his time, and his branch will not be G
39:8 he searches after every G thing.
Ps 23:2 me lie down in G pastures.
37:2 and wither like the G herb.
52:8 I am like a G olive tree in the
58:9 heat of thorns, whether G or ablaze, may he
68:13 silver, its pinions with G gold.
92:14 full of sap and G,
Prov 11:28 will flourish like a G leaf.
Song 1:16 Our couch is G;
Sir 40:22 and beauty, but the G shoots of grain more
50:8 of water, like a G shoot on Lebanon on
Is 57:5 the oaks, under every G tree; who slay your
Jer 2:20 hill and under every G tree you bowed down
3:6 hill and under every G tree, and there played
3:13 among strangers under every G tree, and that you
11:16 once called you, 'A G olive tree, fair with
17:2 their Asherim, beside every G tree, and on the
17:8 for its leaves remain G, and is not anxious
Ezek 6:13 mountain tops, under every G tree, and under every
17:24 tree, dry up the G tree, and make the
20:47 it shall devour every G tree in you and
Joel 2:22 of the wilderness are G; the tree bears its
Mk 6:39 by companies upon the G grass.
Lk 23:30 when the wood is G, what will happen when
Rev 8:7 burnt up, and all G grass was burnt up.
9:4 the earth or any G growth or any tree,

GREENISH (2)

Lev 13:49 if the disease shows G or reddish in the
14:37 of the house with G or reddish spots, and

GREET (44)

1Sam 10:4 And they will G you and give you two
25:5 go to Nabal, and G him in my name.
2Sam 8:10 to King David, to G him, and to congratulate
1Chr 18:10 to King David, to G him, and to congratulate
Jud 15:8 see Judith and to G her.
Sir 41:20 silence, before those who G you; of looking at
Is 14:9 rouses the shades to G you, all who were
1Mac 7:33 of the people, to G him peaceably and to
12:17 also to you and G you and deliver to
Rom 16:3 G Prisca and Aquila, my fellow workers in Christ
16:5 the Gentiles give thanks; G also the church in
16:5 G my beloved Epaenetus, who was the first convert
16:6 G Mary, who has worked hard among you.
16:7 G Andronicus and Junias, my kinsmen and my fellow
16:8 G Ampliatus, my beloved in the Lord.
16:9 G Urbanus, our fellow worker in Christ, and my
16:10 G Apelles, who is approved in Christ.
16:10 G those who belong to the family of Aristobulus.
16:11 G my kinsman Herodion.
16:11 G those in the Lord who belong to the
16:12 G those workers in the Lord, Tryphaena and
16:12 G the beloved Persis, who has worked hard in
16:13 G Rufus, eminent in the Lord, also his mother
16:14 G Asyncritus, Phlegon, Hermes, Patrobas, Hermas,
16:15 G Philologus, Julia, Nereus and his sister, and
16:16 G one another with a holy kiss.
16:16 the churches of Christ G you.
16:22 writer of this letter, G you in the Lord.
16:23 and our brother Quartus, G you.
1Cor 16:20 G one another with a holy kiss.
2Cor 13:12 G one another with a holy kiss.
13:13 All the saints G you.
Phil 4:21 G every saint in Christ Jesus.
4:21 who are with me G you.
4:22 All the saints G you, especially those of Caesar's
Col 4:14 beloved physician and Demas G you.
1Thes 5:26 G all the brethren with a holy kiss.
2Tim 4:19 G Prisca and Aquila, and the household of
Tit 3:15 G those who love us in the faith.
Heb 13:24 G all your leaders and all the saints.
1Pet 5:14 G one another with the kiss of love.
2Jn 1:13 of your elect sister G you.
3Jn 1:15 The friends G you.
1:15 G the friends, every one of them.

GREETED (11)

1Sam 17:22 ranks, and went and G his brothers.
2Kgs 10:15 meet him; and he G him, and said to
Tob 5:9 he entered and they G each other.
7:1 Sarah met them and G them.
1Mac 7:29 to Judas, and they G one another peaceably.
11:6 with pomp, and they G one another and spent
Mk 9:15 up to him and G him.
Lk 1:40 house of Zechariah and G Elizabeth.
Acts 18:22 he went up and G the church, and then
21:7 at Ptolemais; and we G the brethren and stayed
Heb 11:13 having seen it and G it from afar, and

GREETING (31)

Ezra 4:11 men of the province Beyond the River, send G
4:17 the rest of the province Beyond the River, G
Tob 7:1 They returned her G, and she brought them into
Esth 16:1 to those who are loyal to our government, G
1Mac 10:18 words: "King Alexander to his brother Jonathan, G
10:25 "King Demetrius to the nation of the Jews, G
11:30 brother and to the nation of the Jews, G
11:32 'King Demetrius to Lasthenes his father, G
12:6 the Jewish people to their brethren the Spartans, G
12:20 of the Spartans, to Onias the high priest, G
13:36 to the elders and nation of the Jews, G
14:20 the rest of the Jewish people, our brethren, G
15:2 ethnarch and to the nation of the Jews, G
15:16 "Lucius, consul of the Romans, to King Ptolemy, G
2Mac 1:1 Jewish brethren in Egypt, G, and good peace.
1:10 the Jews in Egypt, G, and good health.
11:16 effect: "Lysias to the people of the Jews, G
11:22 ran thus: "King Antiochus to his brother Lysias, G
11:27 of the Jews and to the other Jews, G
11:34 the Romans, to the people of the Jews, G
Lk 1:29 mind what sort of G this might be.
1:41 when Elizabeth heard the G of Mary, the babe
1:44 the voice of your G came to my ears,
Acts 15:23 the Gentiles in Antioch and Syria and Cilicia, G
21:19 After G them, he related one by one the
23:26 "Claudius Lysias to his Excellency the governor
1Cor 16:21 I, Paul, write this G with my own hand.
Col 4:18 I, Paul, write this G with my own hand.
2Thes 3:17 I, Paul, write this G with my own hand.
Jas 1:1 Christ, to the twelve tribes in the dispersion: G
2Jn 1:10 or give him any G;

GREETINGS (10)

2Mac 9:19 and general sends hearty G and good wishes for
1Cor 16:19 The churches of Asia send G
16:19 house, send you hearty G in the Lord.
16:20 All the brethren send G
Col 4:15 Give my G to the brethren at La-odicea, and
2Tim 4:21 Eubulus sends G to you, as do Pudens and
Tit 3:15 are with me send G to you.
Philem 1:23 in Christ Jesus, sends G to you,
Heb 13:24 Those who come from Italy send you G
1Pet 5:13 likewise chosen, sends you G; and so does my

GREETS (5)

Rom 16:21 Timothy, my fellow worker, G you; so do Lucius
16:23 to the whole church, G you.
Col 4:10 Aristarchus my fellow prisoner G you, and Mark the
4:12 servant of Christ Jesus, G you, always remembering
2Jn 1:11 greeting; for he who G him shares his wicked

GREW (67)

Gen 19:25 the cities, and what G on the ground.
21:8 And the child G, and was weaned; and Abraham
21:20 the lad, and he G up; he lived in
25:27 When the boys G up, Esau was a skilful
30:43 Thus the man G exceedingly rich, and had large
Ex 1:6 greatly; they multiplied and G exceedingly strong; so
1:19 the people multiplied and G very strong.

2:10 And the child G, and she brought him to
16:21 but when the sun G hot, it melted.
17:12 But Moses' hands G weary; so they took a
19:19 sound of the trumpet G louder and louder, Moses
Deut 32:15 you waxed fat, you G thick, you became sleek;
Josh 17:13 the people of Israel G strong, they put the
Judg 1:28 When Israel G strong, they put the Canaanites to
11:2 when his wife's sons G up, they thrust Jephthah
13:24 Samson; and the boy G, and the LORD blessed
1Sam 2:21 And the boy Samuel G in the presence of
3:19 And Samuel G, and the LORD was with him
2Sam 3:1 of David; and David G stronger and stronger, while
4:6 cleaning wheat, but she G drowsy and slept; so
12:3 it up, and it G up with him and
15:12 And the conspiracy G strong, and the people with
21:15 the Philistines; and David G weary.
1Kgs 18:45 little while the heavens G black with clouds and
22:35 And the battle G hot that day, and the
2Chr 13:21 But Abijah G mighty.
17:12 And Jehoshaphat G steadily greater.
18:34 And the battle G hot that day, and the
24:15 But Jehoiada G old and full of days, and
26:16 he was strong he G proud, to his destruction.
Tob 14:13 He G old with honor, and he gave his
Jud 16:23 and more famous, and G old in her husband's
Esth 9:4 for the man Mordecai G more and more powerful.
Ps 39:2 no avail; my distress G worse,
Sir 24:13 I G tall like a cedar in Lebanon, and
24:14 I G tall like a palm tree in En-ge'di,
24:14 a plane tree I G tall.
Is 53:2 For he G up before him like a young
Ezek 16:7 the field.' And you G up and became tall
16:13 You G exceedingly beautiful, and came to regal
17:10 it—wither away on the bed where it G
31:5 the forest; its boughs G large and its branches
Dan 4:11 The tree G and became strong, and its top
4:20 tree you saw, which G and became strong, so
4:33 heaven till his hair G as long as eagles'
8:9 a little horn, which G exceedingly great toward the
8:10 It G great, even to the host of heaven;
Jon 1:11 For the sea G more and more tempestuous.
1:13 not, for the sea G more and more tempestuous
1Mac 1:40 Her dishonor now G as great as her glory;
10:81 and the enemy's horses G tired.
2Mac 5:27 to live on what G wild, so that they
Mt 13:7 thorns, and the thorns G up and choked them.
Mk 4:7 thorns and the thorns G up and choked it,
5:26 no better but rather G worse.
6:35 And when it G late, his disciples came to
Lk 1:80 And the child G and became strong in spirit,
2:40 And the child G and became strong, filled with
8:6 rock; and as it G up, it withered away,
8:7 thorns; and the thorns G with it and choked
8:8 into good soil and G, and yielded a hundredfold."
13:19 his garden; and it G and became a tree,
Acts 7:17 to Abraham, the people G and multiplied in Egypt
12:24 the word of God G and multiplied.
19:20 word of the Lord G and prevailed mightily.
Rom 4:20 of God, but he G strong in his faith
Rev 18:19 had ships at sea G rich by her wealth!

GRIDDLE (3)

Lev 2:5 offering baked on a G, it shall be of
6:21 with oil on a G; you shall bring it
7:9 a pan or a G shall belong to the

GRIEF (38)

1Sam 25:31 have no cause of G, or pangs of conscience,
Tob 3:1 Then in my G I wept, and I prayed
7:7 he was stricken with G and wept.
Job 17:7 has grown dim from G, and all my members
Ps 6:7 wastes away because of G, it grows weak because
31:9 eye is wasted from G, my soul and my
77:10 say, "It is my G that the right hand
Prov 14:13 is sad, and the end of joy is G
17:21 stupid son is a G to a father; and
17:25 foolish son is a G to his father and
Eccl 5:17 days in darkness and G, in much vexation and
Wis 8:9 me good counsel and encouragement in cares and G
11:12 distressed, for a twofold G possessed them, and a
14:15 father, consumed with G at an untimely bereavement,
Sir 14:1 and need not suffer G for sin.
18:14 good deeds, nor cause G by your words when
22:4 who acts shamefully brings G to her father.
26:6 There is G of heart and sorrow when a
30:9 play with him, and he will give you G
36:20 perverse mind will cause G, but a man of
37:2 Is it not a G to the death when
Is 17:11 in a day of G and incurable pain.
53:3 sorrows, and acquainted with G; and as one from
53:10 has put him to G; when he makes himself
Jer 8:18 My G is beyond healing, my heart is sick
Lam 2:11 is poured out in G because of the destruction
3:32 but, though he cause G, he will have compassion
3:51 my eyes cause me G at the fate of
Bar 4:34 population, and her insolence will be turned to G
Ezek 21:6 breaking heart and bitter G before their eyes.
1Mac 6:4 fled and in great G departed from there to
6:8 and became sick from G, because things had not
6:9 many days, because deep G continually gripped him,
6:13 am perishing of deep G in a strange land."
2Cor 7:9 you felt a godly G, so that you suffered
7:10 For godly G produces a repentance that leads to
7:10 no regret, but worldly G produces death.
7:11 what earnestness this godly G has produced in you,

GRIEFS

Is 53:4 he has borne our G and carried our sorrows;

GRIEVANCE

1Cor 6:1 of you has a G against a brother, does

GRIEVE (10)

1Sam 2:33 out his eyes and G his heart; and all
16:1 "How long will you G over Saul, seeing I
Tob 4:3 her, and do not G her.
10:12 you; do nothing to G her."
Wis 14:24 kill one another, or G one another by adultery,
Sir 3:12 age, and do not G him as long as
4:2 Do not G the one who is hungry, nor
Lam 3:33 not willingly afflict or G the sons of men.
Eph 4:30 And do not G the Holy Spirit of God,
1Thes 4:13 that you may not G as others do who

GRIEVED (33)

Gen 6:6 the earth, and it G him to his heart.
1Sam 15:35 his death, but Samuel G over Saul.
20:3 this, lest he be G But truly, as the
20:34 month, for he was G for David, because his
Neh 8:10 and do not be G, for the joy of
8:11 for this day is holy; do not be G
Tob 3:10 things she was deeply G, even to the thought
13:14 Blessed are those who G over all your afflictions;
Job 30:25 Was not my soul G for the poor?
Ps 35:14 bosom, as though I G for my friend or
78:40 in the wilderness and G him in the desert!
Sir 12:9 A man's enemies are G when he prospers, and
21:24 a discreet man is G by the disgrace.
26:19 things my heart is G, and because of a
30:5 died he was not G;
47:20 children and they were G at your folly,
Is 19:10 and all who work for hire will be G
54:6 a wife forsaken and G in spirit, like a
63:10 But they rebelled and G his holy Spirit; therefore
Bar 4:8 you up, and you G Jerusalem, who reared you.
4:33 so she will be G at her own desolation.
Amos 6:6 oils, but are not G over the ruin of
1Mac 10:22 these things he was G and said,
10:68 it, he was greatly G and returned to Antioch.
14:16 that Jonathan had died, and they were deeply G
2Mac 4:35 of other nations, were G and displeased at the
4:37 Therefore Antiochus was G at heart and filled with
14:28 he was troubled and G that he had to
Mk 3:5 at them with anger, G at their hardness of
Jn 21:17 Peter was G because he said to him the
2Cor 7:8 see that that letter G you, though only for
7:9 not because you were G, but because you were
7:9 but because you were G into repenting; for you

GRIEVING

2Sam 19:2 day, "The king is G for his son."

GRIEVOUS (17)

Gen 41:31 which will follow, for it will be very G
50:11 said, "This is a G mourning to the Egyptians."
Deut 6:22 and wonders, great and G, against Egypt and against
28:35 on the legs with G boils of which you
28:59 and lasting, and sicknesses G and lasting.
1Kgs 2:8 cursed me with a G curse on the day
Eccl 2:17 under the sun was G to me; for all
5:13 There is a G evil which I have seen
5:16 This also is a G evil: just as he

G

	28:56	her foot upon the G because she is so
	30:9	the fruit of your G; for the LORD will
Josh	3:17	passing over on dry G, the priests who bore
	3:17	LORD stood on dry G in the midst of
	4:18	lifted up on dry G, the waters of the
	4:22	this Jordan on dry G
	17:15	forest, and there clear G for yourselves in the
	24:32	in the portion of G which Jacob bought from
Judg	4:21	went down into the G, as he was lying
	6:37	dry on all the G, then I shall know
	6:39	and on all the G let there be dew."
	6:40	and on all the G there was dew.
	13:20	and they fell on their faces to the G
	16:21	bronze fetters; and he G at the mill in
	20:21	and felled to the G on that day twenty-two
	20:25	and felled to the G eighteen thousand men of
	20:36	men of Israel gave G to Benjamin, because they
Ruth	2:10	face, bowing to the G, and said to him,
1Sam	3:19	let none of his words fall to the G
	5:3	face downward on the G before the ark of
	5:4	face downward on the G before the ark of
	8:12	some to plow his G and to reap his
	14:25	the forest; and there was honey on the G
	14:32	slew them on the G; and the people ate
	14:45	head fall to the G; for he has wrought
	17:49	and he fell on his face to the G
	20:41	his face to the G, and bowed three times;
	25:23	David on her face, and bowed to the G
	25:41	her face to the G, and said, "Behold, your
	26:7	spear stuck in the G at his head; and
	28:14	his face to the G, and did obeisance.
	28:20	full length upon the G, filled with fear because
2Sam	1:2	he fell to the G and did obeisance.
	2:22	me; why should I smite you to the G
	8:2	lie down on the G; two lines he measured
	12:16	went in and lay all night upon the G
	12:17	raise him from the G; but he would not,
	14:4	her face to the G, and did obeisance, and
	14:11	hair of your son shall fall to the G
	14:14	water spilt on the G, which cannot be gathered
	14:22	his face to the G, and did obeisance, and
	14:33	his face to the G before the king; and
	17:12	dew falls on the G; and of him and
	18:11	did you not strike him there to the G
	20:10	his bowels to the G, without striking a second
	23:11	was a plot of G full of lentils; and
	24:20	to the king with his face to the G
1Kgs	1:23	before the king, with his face to the G
	1:31	her face to the G, and did obeisance to
	7:46	them, in the clay G between Succoth and Zarethan.
2Kgs	2:8	two of them could go over on dry G
	2:15	and bowed to the G before him.
	4:37	feet, bowing to the G; then she took up
	9:25	on the plot of G belonging to Naboth the
	9:26	on this plot of G Now therefore take him
	9:26	on the plot of G, in accordance with the
	13:18	of Israel, "Strike the G with them"; and he
1Chr	11:13	was a plot of G full of barley, and
	21:21	obeisance to David with his face to the G
2Chr	4:17	them, in the clay G between Succoth and Zeredah.
	20:18	his face to the G, and all Judah and
	20:24	bodies lying on the G; none had escaped.
Neh	8:6	worshiped the LORD with their faces to the G
	10:35	first fruits of our G and the first fruits
	10:37	the tithes from our G, for it is the
Jud	5:18	was razed to the G, and their cities were
	7:26	strew us on the G before them with thirst
	12:15	and spread on the G for her before Holofernes
	14:18	Holofernes lying on the G, and his head is
	16:5	my infants to the G and seize my children
Job	1:20	and fell upon the G, and worshiped.
	2:13	with him on the G seven days and seven
	5:6	trouble sprout from the G;
	14:8	stump die in the G,
	16:13	spare; he pours out my gall on the G
	18:10	for him in the G, a trap for him
	30:3	the dry and desolate G;
	38:27	and to make the G put forth grass?
	39:14	be warmed on the G,
	39:24	rage he swallows the G; he cannot stand still
Ps	7:5	my life to the G, and lay my soul
	12:6	a furnace on the G, purified seven times.
	17:11	set their eyes to cast me to the G
	26:12	foot stands on level G; in the great congregation
	44:25	to the dust; our body cleaves to the G
	74:7	on fire; to the G they desecrated the dwelling
	80:9	Thou didst clear the G for it; it took
	83:10	destroyed at Endor, who became dung for the G
	85:11	spring up from the G, and righteousness will look
	89:44	his hand, and cast his throne to the G
	104:30	created; and thou renewest the face of the G
	105:35	land, and ate up the fruit of their G
	107:33	of water into thirsty G,
	143:3	my life to the G; he has made me
	147:6	the downtrodden, he casts the wicked to the G
Prov	13:23	The fallow G of the poor yields much food,
	24:31	overgrown with thorns; the G was covered with
Wis	4:19	them speechless to the G, and shake them from
	11:22	drop of morning dew that falls upon the G
Sir	11:5	to sit on the G, but one who was
	31:10	be for him a G for boasting.
	32:20	of hazards, and do not stumble over stony G
	33:10	men are from the G, and Adam was created
	50:17	and fell to the G upon their faces to
Is	2:19	the holes of the G, from before the terror
	3:26	and mourn; ravaged, she shall sit upon the G
	14:12	cut down to the G, you who laid the
	21:9	of her gods he has shattered to the G
	25:12	and cast to the G, even to the dust.
	26:5	it low to the G, casts it to the
	28:24	does he continually open and harrow his G
	29:4	shall come from the G like the voice of
	30:23	which you sow the G, and grain, the produce
	30:23	the produce of the G, which will be rich
	30:24	asses that till the G will eat salted provender,
	35:7	pool, and the thirsty G springs of water; the
	40:4	made low; the uneven G shall become level, and
	42:16	them into light, the rough places into level G
	44:3	streams on the dry G; I will pour my
	47:1	Babylon; sit on the G without a throne, O
	49:23	their faces to the G they shall bow down
	51:23	your back like the G and like the street
	53:2	root out of dry G; he had no form
Jer	4:3	"Break up your fallow G, and sow not among
	7:20	the fruit of the G; it will burn and
	8:2	be as dung on the surface of the G
	10:17	your bundle from the G, O you who dwell
	14:2	people lament on the G, and the cry of
	14:4	Because of the G which is dismayed, since there
	16:4	be as dung on the surface of the G
	25:33	shall be dung on the surface of the G
	48:18	sit on the parched G, O inhabitant of Dibon!
	51:58	be leveled to the G and her high gates
Lam	2:2	brought down to the G in dishonor the kingdom
	2:9	have sunk into the G; he has ruined and
	2:10	Zion sit on the G in silence; they have
	2:10	of Jerusalem have bowed their heads to the G
Bar	5:7	up, to make level G, so that Israel may
	6:27	made to stand, lest they fall to the G
Ezek	13:14	it down to the G, so that its foundation
	19:12	cast down to the G; the east wind dried
	24:7	pour it upon the G to cover it with
	26:11	and your mighty pillars will fall to the G
	26:16	will sit upon the G and tremble every moment,
	28:17	cast you to the G; I exposed you before
	32:4	cast you on the G, on the open field
	38:20	that creep on the G, and all the men
	38:20	fall, and every wall shall tumble to the G
	42:6	set back from the G more than the lower
	43:14	the base on the G to the lower ledge,
Dan	6:4	sought to find a G for complaint against Daniel
	6:4	they could find no G for complaint or any
	6:5	shall not find any G for complaint against this
	7:4	lifted up from the G and made to stand
	8:5	earth, without touching the G; and the goat had
	8:7	him down to the G and trampled upon him;
	8:10	cast down to the G, and trampled upon them.
	8:12	cast down to the G, and the horn acted
	8:18	my face to the G; but he touched me
	9:18	before thee on the G of our righteousness, but
	9:18	righteousness, but on the G of thy great mercy.
	10:9	a deep sleep with my face to the G
	10:15	my face toward the G and was dumb.
Hos	2:18	creeping things of the G; and I will abolish
	10:12	break up your fallow G, for it is the
Joel	1:10	are laid waste, the G mourns; because the grain
Amos	3:5	spring up from the G, when it has taken
	3:14	shall be cut off and fall to the G
	9:8	the surface of the G; except that I will
Obad	1:3	heart, "Who will bring me down to the G
Hag	1:11	oil, upon what the G brings forth, upon men
Zech	8:12	its fruit, and the G shall give its increase,

1Mac	4:40	face down on the G, and sounded the signal
	6:46	it fell to the G upon him and he
	14:8	land in peace; the G gave its increase, and
2Mac	2:30	historian to occupy the G and to discuss matters
	3:27	suddenly fell to the G and deep darkness came
	8:3	be leveled to the G, and to hearken to
	8:8	the man was gaining G little by little, and
	9:14	to level to the G and to make a
	14:33	of God to the G and tear down the
Mt	5:32	wife, except on the G of unchastity, makes her
	10:29	will fall to the G without your Father's will.
	13:5	seeds fell on rocky G, where they had not
	13:20	was sown on rocky G, this is he who
	15:35	sit down on the G,
	25:18	and dug in the G and hid his master's
	25:25	I went and hid your talent in the G
Mk	4:5	seed fell on rocky G, where it had not
	4:16	ones sown upon rocky G, who, when they hear
	4:26	scatter seed upon the G,
	4:31	when sown upon the G, is the smallest of
	8:6	sit down on the G; and he took the
	9:20	he fell on the G and rolled about, foaming
	14:35	he fell on the G and prayed that, if
Lk	6:49	a house on the G without a foundation; against
	13:7	it use up the G
	19:44	dash you to the G, you and your children
	24:5	their faces to the G, the men said to
Jn	8:6	down and wrote with his finger on the G
	8:8	down and wrote with his finger on the G
	9:6	he spat on the G and made clay of
	18:6	they drew back and fell to the G
Acts	7:33	the place where you are standing is holy G
	7:54	were enraged, and they G their teeth against him.
	9:4	he fell to the G and heard a voice
	9:8	Saul arose from the G; and when his eyes
	22:7	I fell to the G and heard a voice
	26:14	all fallen to the G, I heard a voice
Rom	3:30	the circumcised on the G of their faith and
1Cor	9:15	deprive me of my G for boasting.
	9:16	that gives me no G for boasting.
	10:25	any question on the G of conscience.
	10:27	any question on the G of conscience.
1Tim	6:2	be disrespectful on the G that they are brethren;

GROUNDED

Eph	3:17	you, being rooted and G in love,

GROUP (2)

1Mac	7:12	Then a G of scribes appeared in a body
	10:61	A G of pestilent men from Israel, lawless men,

GROUPINGS (2)

2Chr	35:5	place according to the G of the fathers' houses
	35:12	them according to the G of the fathers' houses

GROUPS

Mk	6:40	they sat down in G, by hundreds and by

GROVES

Jud	3:8	cut down their sacred G; for it had been

GROW (61)

Gen	2:9	LORD God made to G every tree that is
	48:16	Isaac; and let them G into a multitude in
Num	6:5	hair of his head G long.
Deut	7:22	lest the wild beasts G too numerous for you.
Judg	16:22	his head began to G again after it had
1Sam	2:26	boy Samuel continued to G both in stature and
	3:2	eyesight had begun to G dim, so that he
Ezra	4:22	matter; why should damage G to the hurt of
Tob	8:7	find mercy and may G old together with her."
Job	8:11	"Can papyrus G where there is no marsh?
	14:8	Though its root G old in the earth, and
	21:7	reach old age, and G mighty in power?
	31:40	its owners; let thorns G instead of wheat, and
	39:4	ones become strong, they G up in the open;
Ps	38:5	My wounds G foul and fester because of my
	69:3	My eyes G dim with waiting for my God.
	92:12	the palm tree, and G like a cedar in
	104:14	cause the grass to G for the cattle, and
	147:8	earth, he makes grass G upon the hills.
Eccl	5:7	dreams increase, empty words G many: but do you
Sir	10:3	but a city will G through the understanding of
	11:18	attend to it, and G old in your work.
	16:25	they neither hunger nor G weary, and they do
	43:30	strength, and do not G weary, for you cannot
Is	5:6	briers and thorns shall G up; I will also
	11:1	and a branch shall G out of his roots.
	17:4	of his flesh will G lean.
	17:11	though you make them G on the day that
	29:22	more shall his face G pale.
	34:13	shall G over its strongholds, nettles and thistles
	40:28	does not faint or G weary, his understanding is
	44:14	oak and lets it G strong among the trees
Jer	12:2	they take root; they G and bring forth fruit;
Ezek	12:22	Israel, saying, 'The days G long, and every vision
	16:7	your blood, 'Live, and G up like a plant
	31:4	the deep made it G tall, making its rivers
	31:14	by the waters may G to lofty height or
	44:20	or let their locks G long; they shall only
	47:12	the river, there will G all kinds of trees
Dan	3:77	Lord, all things that G on the earth, sing
Hos	10:8	Thorn and thistle shall G up on their altars;
Joel	2:6	in anguish, all faces G pale.
Jon	4:10	did you make it G, which came into being
Nah	2:10	all loins, all faces G pale!
Zeph	3:16	let not your hands G weak.
Zech	6:12	Branch: for he shall G up in his place,
1Mac	2:64	children, be courageous and G strong in the law,
	6:57	the men, "We daily G weaker, our food supply
Mt	6:28	the field, how they G; they neither toil nor
	13:30	Let both G together until the harvest; and at
	24:12	most men's love will G cold.
Mk	4:27	seed should sprout and G, he knows not how.
Lk	12:27	the lilies, how they G; they neither toil nor
	12:33	purses that do not G old, with a treasure
Gal	6:9	And let us not G weary in well-doing, for
Eph	4:15	love, we are to G up in every way
1Tim	5:11	widows; for when they G wanton against Christ they
Heb	1:11	remainest; they will all G old like a garment,
	12:3	that you may not G weary or fainthearted.
1Pet	2:2	by it you may G up to salvation;
2Pet	3:18	But G in the grace and knowledge of our

GROWING (13)

Gen	41:5	plump and good, were G on one stalk.
	41:22	my dream seven ears G on one stalk, full
Deut	29:23	burnt-out waste, unsown, and G nothing, where no
Eccl	2:6	water the forest of G trees.
Sir	8:6	some of us are G old.
	39:13	bud like a rose G by a stream of
Is	32:13	soil of my people G up in thorns and
Bar	3:10	enemies, that you are G old in a foreign
2Mac	4:50	power, remained in office, G in wickedness, having
Mk	4:8	and brought forth grain, G up and increasing and
Col	1:6	is bearing fruit and G --so among yourselves, from
2Thes	1:3	because your faith is G abundantly, and the love
Heb	8:13	is becoming obsolete and G old is ready to

GROWL (7)

Ex	11:7	not a dog shall G; that you may know
Jud	11:19	open its mouth to G at you.
Ps	59:15	about for food, and G if they do not
Is	5:29	lions they roar; they G and seize their prey,
	5:30	They will G over it on that day, like
	59:11	We all G like bears, we moan and moan
Jer	51:38	like lions; they shall G like lions' whelps.

GROWLING (2)

Prov	19:12	wrath is like the G of a lion, but
	20:2	king is like the G of a lion; he

GROWLS

Is	31:4	or a young lion G over his prey, and

GROWN (39)

Gen	18:12	saying, "After I have G old, and my husband
	38:14	saw that Shelah was G up, and she had
Ex	2:11	day, when Moses had G up, he went out
Lev	13:37	and black hair has G in it, the itch
Deut	4:25	children's children, and have G old in the land,
	31:20	and are full and G fat, they will turn
Ruth	1:13	sons, would you therefore wait till they were G
2Sam	10:5	until your beards have G, and then return."
1Kgs	12:8	young men who had G up with him and
	12:10	young men who had G up with him said
2Kgs	4:18	When the child had G, he went out one
	19:26	grass on the housetops; blighted before it is G
1Chr	19:5	until your beards have G, and then return."
2Chr	10:8	young men who had G up with him and
	10:10	young men who had G up with him said
Tob	14:3	When he had G very old he called his

G

	14:3	sons; behold, I have G old and am about
Job	17:7	My eye has G dim from grief, and all
Wis	14:16	Then the ungodly custom, G strong with time, was
Is	37:27	grass on the housetops, blighted before it is G
Jer	5:28	and rich, they have G fat and sleek.
	9:3	and not truth has G strong in the land;
Lam	4:1	How the gold has G dim, how the pure
	5:17	things our eyes have G dim,
Ezek	7:11	Violence has G up into a rod of wickedness;
	16:7	and your hair had G; yet you were naked
Dan	4:22	O king, who have G and become strong.
	4:22	Your greatness has G and reaches to heaven, and
1Mac	6:6	that the Jews had G strong from the arms,
	7:25	those with him had G strong, and realized that
	16:3	But now I have G old, and you by
2Mac	5:24	to slay all the G men and to sell
Mt	13:15	this people's heart has G dull, and their ears
	13:32	but when it has G it is the greatest
Acts	28:27	this people's heart has G dull, and their ears
1Cor	7:29	the appointed time has G very short; from now
Heb	11:24	Moses, when he was G up, refused to be
Rev	2:3	and you have not G weary.
	18:3	of the earth have G rich with the wealth

GROWS (18)

Gen	38:11	till Shelah my son G up"—for he feared
Ex	10:5	tree of yours which G in the field,
Lev	25:5	What G of itself in your harvest you shall
	25:11	sow, nor reap what G of itself, nor gather
	25:49	him; or if he G rich he may redeem
1Kgs	4:33	to the hyssop that G out of the wall;
2Kgs	19:29	you shall eat what G of itself, and in
Job	17:9	that has clean hands G stronger and stronger.
	31:8	eat; and let what G for me be rooted
Ps	6:7	because of grief, it G weak because of all
	88:9	cannot escape; my eye G dim through sorrow.
	129:6	which withers before it G up,
Prov	11:24	man gives freely, yet G all the richer; another
Is	37:30	this year eat what G of itself, and in
Hos	11:8	within me, my compassion G warm and tender.
Mk	4:32	it is sown it G up and becomes the
Eph	2:21	is joined together and G into a holy temple
Col	2:19	its joints and ligaments, G with a growth that

GROWTH (11)

Ps	65:10	ridges, softening it with showers, and blessing its G
Prov	27:25	gone, and the new G appears, and the herbage
Is	15:6	is withered, the new G fails, the verdure is
Amos	7:1	up of the latter G; and lo, it was
	7:1	it was the latter G after the king's mowings.
1Cor	3:6	I planted, Apollos watered, but God gave the G
	3:7	is anything, but only God who gives the G
Eph	4:16	working properly, makes bodily G and upbuilds itself
Col	2:19	ligaments, grows with a G that is from God.
Jas	1:20	all filthiness and rank G of wickedness and receive
Rev	9:4	earth or any green G or any tree, but

GRUDGE (4)

Lev	19:18	vengeance or bear any G against the sons of
Deut	28:54	bred among you will G food to his brother,
	28:56	delicate and tender, will G to the husband of
Mk	6:19	And Herodi-as had a G against him, and wanted

GRUDGING (6)

Deut	15:10	heart shall not be G when you give to
Wis	7:13	and I impart without G; I do not hide
Sir	14:6	the man who is G to himself, and this
	14:8	the man with a G eye; he averts his
	18:17	the gift of a G man makes the eyes
	37:11	about selling, with a G man about gratitude or

GRUMBLE (3)

Sir	10:24	servant, and a man of understanding will not G
1Cor	10:10	destroyed by serpents; nor G, as some of them
Jas	5:9	Do not G, brethren, against one another, that you

GRUMBLED

Mt	20:11	on receiving it they G at the householder,

GRUMBLERS

Jude	1:16	These are G, malcontents, following their own

GRUMBLING

Phil	2:14	Do all things without G or questioning,

GUARANTEE (3)

2Cor	1:22	us his Spirit in our hearts as a G
	5:5	who has given us the Spirit as a G
Eph	1:14	Spirit, which is the G of our inheritance until

GUARANTEED

Rom	4:16	on grace and be G to all his descendants—

GUARD (124)

Gen	3:24	turned every way, to G the way to the
	37:36	an officer of Pharaoh, the captain of the G
	39:1	the captain of the G, an Egyptian, bought him
	40:3	the captain of the G, in the prison where
	40:4	The captain of the G charged Joseph with them,
	41:10	the captain of the G,
	41:12	the captain of the G; and when we told
Ex	23:20	angel before you, to G you on the way
Num	10:25	acting as the rear G of all the camps,
Josh	6:9	trumpets, and the rear G came after the ark,
	6:13	them, and the rear G came after the ark
	8:13	city and its rear G west of the city.
	10:18	men by it to G them;
Judg	8:11	the army; for the army was off its G
1Sam	2:9	"He will G the feet of his faithful ones;
	22:17	king said to the G who stood about him,
2Sam	20:3	in a house under G, and provided for them,
1Kgs	14:27	the officers of the G, who kept the door
	14:28	of the LORD, the G bore them and brought
2Kgs	9:14	Israel had been on G at Ramoth-gilead against
	10:25	Jehu said to the G and to the officers,
	10:25	to the sword, the G and the officers cast
	11:5	on the sabbath and G the king's house
	11:6	behind the guards), shall G the palace;
	11:7	on the sabbath and G the house of the
	11:13	the noise of the G and of the people,
	25:10	the captain of the G, broke down the walls
	25:11	the captain of the G carried into exile.
	25:12	the captain of the G left some of the
	25:15	the captain of the G took away as gold,
	25:18	the captain of the G took Seraiah the chief
	25:20	the captain of the G took them, and brought
2Chr	12:10	the officers of the G, who kept the door
	12:11	of the LORD, the G came and bore them,
	23:10	the people as a G for the king, every
Ezra	8:29	G them and keep them until you weigh them
Neh	3:25	of the king at the court of the G
	4:9	God, and set a G as a protection against
	4:22	they may be a G for us by night
	4:23	the men of the G who followed me, none
	7:3	they are still standing G let them shut and
	12:25	were gatekeepers standing G at the storehouses of
	12:39	to a halt at the Gate of the G
	13:22	themselves and come and G the gates, to keep
Tob	12:7	It is good to G the secret of a
	12:11	'It is good to G the secret of a
Jud	7:5	towers they remained on G all that night.
Job	7:12	that thou settest a G over me?
Ps	12:7	O LORD, protect us, G us ever from this
	25:20	Oh G my life, and deliver me; let me
	39:1	I said, "I will G my ways, that I
	91:11	charge of you to G you in all your
	140:4	[Selah] G me, O LORD, from the hands of
	141:3	Set a G over my mouth, O LORD, keep
Prov	2:11	over you; understanding will G you;
	4:7	her, and she will G you.
	4:14	do not let go; G her, for she is
	5:2	and your lips may G knowledge.
Eccl	5:1	G your steps when you go to the house
Wis	9:11	in my actions and G me with her glory.
Sir	6:13	enemies, and be on G toward your friends.
	12:11	and be on your G against him; and you
	22:11	visit an unintelligent man; G yourself from him to
	22:25	O that a G were set over my mouth,
	26:11	Be on G against her impudent eye, and do
	32:23	G yourself in every act, for this is the
	34:16	from noonday sun, a G against stumbling and a
Is	27:3	one harm it, I G it night and day;
	52:12	the God of Israel will be your rear G
	58:8	glory of the LORD shall be your rear G
Jer	32:2	the court of the G which was in the
	32:8	the court of the G, in accordance with the
	32:12	who were sitting in the court of the G
	33:1	the court of the G:
	37:21	the court of the G; and a loaf of
	37:21	So Jeremiah remained in the court of the G
	38:6	the court of the G, letting Jeremiah down by

38:13 And Jeremiah remained in the court of the G
38:28 the court of the G until the day that
39:9 the captain of the G, carried into exile to
39:10 the captain of the G, left in the land
39:11 the captain of the G, saying,
39:13 the G, Nebushazban the Rabsaris, Nergal-sharezer
39:14 and took Jeremiah from the court of the G
39:15 the court of the G:
40:1 the captain of the G had let him go
40:2 The captain of the G took Jeremiah and said
40:5 the captain of the G gave him an allowance
41:10 the captain of the G, had committed to Gedaliah
43:6 the captain of the G had left with Gedaliah
52:14 the captain of the G, broke down all the
52:15 the captain of the G carried away captive some
52:16 the captain of the G left some of the
52:19 the captain of the G took away as gold,
52:24 the captain of the G took Seraiah the chief
52:26 the captain of the G took them, and brought
52:30 the captain of the G carried away captive of
Ezek 38:7 you, and be a G for them.
Dan 2:14 captain of the king's G, who had gone out
Mic 7:5 confidence in a friend; G the doors of your
Zech 9:8 my house as a G, so that none shall
Mal 2:7 of a priest should G knowledge, and men should
1Mac 5:18 forces, in Judea to G it;
6:50 Bethzur and stationed a G there to hold it.
9:53 and put them under G in the citadel at
10:32 his own choice to G it.
12:34 a garrison there to G it.
13:12 of Judah, and Jonathan was with him under G
14:3 took him to Arsaces, who put him under G
Mt 5:25 the judge to the G, and you be put
27:65 them, "You have a G of soldiers; go, make
27:66 secure by sealing the stone and setting a G
28:11 behold, some of the G went into the city
Mk 6:27 a soldier of the G and gave orders to
14:44 man; seize him and lead him away under G
Lk 4:10 charge of you, to G you,'
8:29 he was kept under G, and bound with chains
Acts 12:4 squads of soldiers to G him, intending after the
12:10 first and the second G, they came to the
Phil 1:13 throughout the whole praetorian G and to all the
2Thes 3:3 will strengthen you and G you from evil.
1Tim 6:20 O Timothy, G what has been entrusted to you.
2Tim 1:12 he is able to G until that Day what
1:14 are in Christ Jesus; G the truth that has

GUARDED (9)

1Sam 25:21 in vain have I G all that this fellow
2Kgs 12:9 and the priests who G the threshold put in
Esth 2:21 king's eunuchs, who G the threshold, became angry
6:2 the king's eunuchs, who G the threshold, and who
Jn 17:12 given me; I have G them, and none of
Acts 23:35 commanded him to be G in Herod's praetorium.
28:16 with the soldier that G him.
2Cor 11:32 governor under King Aretas G the city of Damascus
1Pet 1:5 by God's power are G through faith for a

GUARDIAN (6)

Ezek 28:14 With an anointed G cherub I placed you; you
28:16 of God, and the G cherub drove you out
2Mac 11:1 this, Lysias, the king's G and kinsman, who was
13:2 with him Lysias, his G, who had charge of
14:2 with Antiochus and his G Lysias.
1Pet 2:25 to the Shepherd and G of your souls.

GUARDIANS (3)

2Kgs 10:1 elders, and to the G of the sons of
10:5 the elders and the G, sent to Jehu, saying,
Gal 4:2 but he is under G and trustees until the

GUARDING (3)

Ps 119:9 By G it according to thy word.
Prov 2:8 who walk in integrity, G the paths of justice
Acts 12:6 before the door were G the prison;

GUARDROOM (2)

1Kgs 14:28 bore them and brought them back to the G
2Chr 12:11 bore them, and brought them back to the G

GUARDS (22)

2Kgs 11:4 Carites and of the G, and had them come
11:6 the gate behind the G, shall guard the palace;
11:11 the LORD; and the G stood, every man with
11:19 captains, the Carites, the G, and all the people
11:19 the gate of the G to the king's house.
1Chr 9:23 that is, the house of the tent, as G
Neh 7:3 Appoint G from among the inhabitants of Jerusalem,
Jud 7:7 seized them and set G of soldiers over them,
12:7 So Holofernes commanded his G not to hinder her.
Prov 13:3 He who G his mouth preserves his life; he
13:6 Righteousness G him whose way is upright, but sin
16:17 from evil; he who G his way preserves his
22:5 the perverse; he who G himself will keep far
27:18 fruit, and he who G his master will be
Sir 18:26 days of sin he G against wrongdoing.
40:29 intelligent and well instructed G against that.
Bar 6:70 a cucumber bed, that G nothing, so are their
Mt 26:58 he sat with the G to see the end.
28:4 fear of him the G trembled and became like
Mk 14:54 was sitting with the G, and warming himself at
14:65 And the G received him with blows.
Lk 11:21 strong man, fully armed, G his own palace, his

GUDGODAH (2)

Deut 10:7 there they journeyed to G, and from Gudgodah to
10:7 to Gudgodah, and from G to Jotbathah, a land

GUESS

Wis 9:16 We can hardly G at what is on earth,

GUEST (7)

Esth 16:10 kindliness), having become our G,
Ps 39:12 I am thy passing G, a sojourner, like all
Wis 5:14 the remembrance of a G who stays but a
Mk 14:14 says, Where is my G room, where I am
Lk 19:7 in to be the G of a man who
22:11 you, Where is the G room, where I am
Philem 1:22 same time, prepare a G room for me, for

GUESTS (17)

1Sam 9:24 hour appointed, that you might eat with the G
2Sam 15:11 Jerusalem who were invited G, and they went in
1Kgs 1:41 Adonijah and all the G who were with him
1:49 Then all the G of Adonijah trembled, and rose,
Job 19:15 have failed me; the G in my house have
Prov 9:18 are there, that her G are in the depths
Wis 19:14 these made slaves of G who were their benefactors.
Zeph 1:7 has prepared a sacrifice and consecrated his G
Mt 9:15 them, "Can the wedding G mourn as long as
14:9 his oaths and his G he commanded it to
22:10 good; so the wedding hall was filled with G
22:11 to look at the G, he saw there a
Mk 2:19 them, "Can the wedding G fast while the bridegroom
6:22 pleased Herod and his G; and the king said
6:26 his oaths and his G he did not want
Lk 5:34 "Can you make wedding G fast while the
Acts 10:23 So he called them in to be his G

GUIDANCE (7)

1Chr 10:13 consulted a medium, seeking G,
10:14 and did not seek G from the LORD.
Job 37:12 and round by his G, to accomplish all that
Prov 4:1 The Supreme G of Wisdom
11:14 Where there is no G, a people falls; but
20:18 by counsel; by wise G wage war.
24:6 strength; for by wise G you can wage your

GUIDE (20)

Tob 7:12 The merciful God will G you both for the
Job 38:32 season, or can you G the Bear with its
Ps 31:3 sake lead me and G me,
48:14 He will be our G for ever.
67:4 peoples with equity and G the nations upon earth.
73:24 Thou dost G me with thy counsel, and afterward
Wis 7:15 for he is the G even of wisdom and
9:11 things, and she will G me wisely in my
18:3 of fire as a G for thy people's unknown
Is 42:16 not known I will G them.
49:10 springs of water will G them.
51:18 There is none to G her among all the
58:11 And the LORD will G you continually, and satisfy
1Mac 6:15 signet, that he might G Antiochus his son and
Lk 1:79 shadow of death, to G our feet into the
Jn 16:13 truth comes, he will G you into all the
Acts 1:16 concerning Judas who was G to those who arrested
Rom 2:19 that you are a G to the blind, a
Jas 3:3 may obey us, we G their whole bodies.
Rev 7:17 shepherd, and he will G them to springs of

GUIDED (10)

Ex 15:13 hast redeemed, thou hast G them by thy strength
Jud 13:18 the earth, who has G you to strike the
Job 31:18 his mother's womb I G him);
Ps 78:52 people like sheep, and G them in the wilderness
78:72 he tended them, and G them with skilful hand.
Wis 10:10 his brother's wrath, she G him on straight paths;
10:17 of their labors; she G them along a marvelous
14:6 on a raft, and G by thy hand left
2Mac 5:15 in all the world, G by Menelaus, who had
Jas 3:4 strong winds, they are G by a very small

GUIDEPOSTS

Jer 31:21 yourself, make yourself G; consider well the highway,

GUIDES (7)

Prov 11:3 integrity of the upright G them, but the crookedness
1Mac 4:2 Men from the citadel were his G
Mt 15:14 Let them alone; they are blind G
23:15 "Woe to you, blind G, who say, 'If any
23:23 You blind G, straining out a gnat and swallowing
Acts 8:31 I, unless some one G me?" And he invited
1Cor 4:15 though you have countless G in Christ, you do

G

GUIDING

Eccl 2:3 wine—my mind still G me with wisdom—and

GUILE (12)

Gen 27:35 "Your brother came with G, and he has taken
Ps 119:78 have subverted me with G; as for me, I
Prov 26:26 hatred be covered with G, his wickedness will be
Wis 4:11 change his understanding or G deceive his soul.
7:13 I learned without G and I impart without grudging;
2Mac 12:24 With great G he besought them to let him
Jn 1:47 "Behold, an Israelite indeed, in whom is no G
2Cor 12:16 say, and got the better of you by G
1Thes 2:3 is it made with G;
1Pet 2:1 all malice and all G and insincerity and envy
2:22 committed no sin; no G was found on his
3:10 his lips from speaking G;

GUILELESS

Rom 16:19 what is good and G as to what is

GUILT (110)

Gen 26:10 you would have brought G upon us."
44:16 has found out the G of your servants; behold,
Ex 28:38 take upon himself any G incurred in the holy
28:43 place; lest they bring G upon themselves and die.
Lev 4:3 who sins, thus bringing G on the people, then
5:6 he shall bring his G offering to the LORD
5:7 shall bring, as his G offering to the LORD
5:15 shall bring, as his G offering to the LORD,
5:15 sanctuary; it is a G offering.
5:16 the ram of the G offering, and he shall
5:18 the price for a G offering, and the priest
5:19 It is a G offering; he is guilty before
6:5 the day of his G offering.
6:6 to the priest his G offering to the LORD,
6:6 the price for a G offering;
6:17 sin offering and the G offering.
7:1 the law of the G offering.
7:2 they shall kill the G offering, and its blood
7:5 LORD; it is a G offering.
7:7 The G offering is like the sin offering, there
7:37 sin offering, of the G offering, of the consecration,
14:12 offer it for a G offering, along with the
14:13 holy place; for the G offering, like the sin
14:14 the blood of the G offering, and the priest
14:17 the blood of the G offering;
14:21 male lamb for a G offering to be waved,
14:24 the lamb of the G offering, and the log
14:25 the lamb of the G offering; and the priest
14:25 the blood of the G offering, and put it
14:28 the blood of the G offering was put;
19:21 he shall bring a G offering for himself to
19:21 a ram for a G offering.
19:22 the ram of the G offering before the LORD
22:16 to bear iniquity and G, by eating their holy
Num 6:12 year old for a G offering; but the former
18:9 of theirs and every G offering of theirs, which
Deut 19:10 inheritance, and so the G of bloodshed be upon
19:13 you shall purge the G of innocent blood from
21:8 and set not the G of innocent blood in
21:8 Israel; but let the G of blood be forgiven
21:9 you shall purge the G of innocent blood from
22:8 may not bring the G of blood upon your
24:4 you shall not bring G upon the land which
1Sam 6:3 means return him a G offering.
6:4 said, "What is the G offering that we shall
6:8 to him as a G offering.
6:17 Philistines returned as a G offering to the LORD:
14:41 If this G is in me or in Jonathan
14:41 Urim; but if this G is in thy people
20:1 What is my G
20:8 But if there is G in me, slay me
25:24 my lord, be the G; pray let your handmaid
26:18 What G is on my hands?
2Sam 14:9 "On me be the G, my lord the king,
14:32 and if there is G in me, let him
22:24 blameless before him, and I kept myself from G
1Kgs 2:31 my father's house the G for the blood which
2Kgs 12:16 The money from the G offerings and the money
1Chr 21:3 Why should he bring G upon Israel?"
2Chr 19:10 they may not incur G before the LORD and
19:10 you shall do, and you will not incur G
24:18 came upon Judah and Jerusalem for this their G
28:13 to bring upon us G against the LORD in
28:13 LORD in addition to our present sins and G
28:13 For our G is already great, and there is
33:23 but this Amon incurred G more and more.
Ezra 9:6 our heads, and our G has mounted up to
9:7 have been in great G; and for our iniquities
9:13 and for our great G, seeing that thou, our
9:15 before thee in our G, for none can stand
10:10 and so increased the G of Israel.
10:19 their wives, and their G offering was a ram
10:19 was a ram of the flock for their G
Neh 4:5 Do not cover their G, and let not their
Job 11:6 you less than your G deserves.
Ps 5:10 Make them bear their G, O God; let them
18:23 blameless before him, and I kept myself from G
25:11 O LORD, pardon my G, for it is great.
32:5 thou didst forgive the G of my sin.
Wis 1:6 a blasphemer from the G of his words; because
Sir 7:31 the first fruits, the G offering, the gift of
Is 6:7 touched your lips; your G is taken away, and
14:21 sons because of the G of their fathers, lest
24:6 suffer for their G; therefore the inhabitants of
27:9 Therefore by this the G of Jacob will be
Jer 2:22 the stain of your G is still before me,
3:13 Only acknowledge your G, that you rebelled against
30:14 merciless foe, because your G is great, because your
30:15 Because your G is great, because your sins are
32:18 but dost requite the G of fathers to their
33:8 them from all the G of their sin against
33:8 will forgive all the G of their sin and
51:5 Chaldeans is full of G against the Holy One
Ezek 9:9 said to me, "The G of the house of
16:49 Behold, this was the G of your sister Sodom:
21:23 but he brings their G to remembrance, that they
21:24 you have made your G to be remembered, in
40:39 sin offering and the G offering were to be
42:13 sin offering, and the G offering, for the place
44:29 sin offering, and the G offering; and every devoted
46:20 priests shall boil the G offering and the sin
Hos 5:5 shall stumble in his G; Judah also shall stumble
5:15 until they acknowledge their G and seek my face,
10:2 heart is false; now they must bear their G
12:8 can never offset the G he has incurred.
13:1 Israel; but he incurred G through Baal and died.
13:16 Samaria shall bear her G, because she has rebelled
Zech 3:9 I will remove the G of this land in
Jn 9:41 you would have no G; but now that you
9:41 say, 'We see,' your G remains.

GUILTLESS (15)

Ex 20:7 will not hold him G who takes his name
Deut 5:11 will not hold him G who takes his name
Josh 2:17 her, "We will be G with respect to this
2:19 and we shall be G; but if a hand
2:20 then we shall be G with respect to your
1Sam 26:9 his hand against the LORD's anointed, and be G
2Sam 3:28 kingdom are for ever G before the LORD for
14:9 house; let the king and his throne be G
1Kgs 2:9 therefore hold him not G, for you are a
Sir 9:12 will not be held G as long as they
Jer 2:34 found the lifeblood of G poor; you did not
Mt 12:5 in the temple profane the sabbath, and are G
12:7 not sacrifice,' you would not have condemned the G
1Cor 1:8 you to the end, G in the day of
2Cor 7:11 you have proved yourselves G in the matter.

GUILTY (48)
Gen 42:21 "In truth we are G concerning our brother, in
Ex 34:7 no means clear the G, visiting the iniquity of
Lev 4:13 be done and are G;
4:22 be done, and is G,
4:27 be done, and is G,
5:2 and he has become unclean, he shall be G
5:3 he comes to know it he shall be G
5:4 it he shall in any of these be G
5:5 When a man is G in any of these,
5:17 it, yet he is G and shall bear his
5:19 guilt offering; he is G before the LORD."
6:4 has sinned and become G, he shall restore what
6:7 things which one may do and thereby become G
Num 5:6 and that person is G,
14:18 no means clear the G, visiting the iniquity of
35:27 he shall not be G of blood.
35:31 a murderer, who is G of death; but he
Deut 25:1 innocent and condemning the G,
25:2 guilty, then if the G man deserves to be
Judg 21:22 them to them, else you would now be G
2Sam 19:19 my lord hold me G or remember how your
1Kgs 8:32 servants, condemning the G by bringing his conduct
2Chr 6:23 thy servants, requiting the G by bringing his conduct
Job 10:7 that I am not G, and there is none
Ps 68:21 who walks in his G ways.
109:7 let him come forth G; let his prayer be
Prov 21:8 The way of the G is crooked, but the
30:10 lest he curse you, and you be held G
Is 5:23 drink, who acquit the G for a bribe, and
50:9 Lord GOD helps me; who will declare me G
Jer 2:3 ate of it became G; evil came upon them,
3:11 has shown herself less G than false Judah.
50:7 said, 'We are not G, for they have sinned
Ezek 18:24 of which he is G and the sin he
22:4 You have become G by the blood which you
35:6 you; because you are G of blood, therefore blood
Dan 13:53 innocent and letting the G go free, though the
Hos 4:15 the harlot, O Israel, let not Judah become G
Joel 3:21 will not clear the G, for the LORD dwells
Nah 1:3 the LORD will by no means clear the G
Hab 1:11 wind and go on, G men, whose own might
2Mac 13:6 to destruction any man G of sacrilege or notorious
Mk 3:29 has forgiveness, but is G of an eternal sin"--
Lk 23:14 not find this man G of any of your
1Cor 5:11 brother if he is G of immorality or greed,
11:27 unworthy manner will be G of profaning the body
Jas 2:10 one point has become G of all of it.
1Jn 3:4 who commits sin is G of lawlessness; sin is

GULL (2)
Lev 11:16 the nighthawk, the sea G, the hawk according to
Deut 14:15 the nighthawk, the sea G, the hawk, after their

GULLIES
Job 30:6 In the G of the torrents they must dwell,

GUM (2)
Gen 37:25 with their camels bearing G, balm, and myrrh, on
43:11 and a little honey, G, myrrh, pistachio nuts, and

GUNI (4)
Gen 46:24 sons of Naphtali: Jahzeel, G, Jezer, and Shillem
Num 26:48 of the Jahzeelites; of G, the family of the
1Chr 5:15 of Abdi-el, son of G, was chief in their
7:13 sons of Naphtali: Jahzi-el, G, Jezer, and Shallum, the

GUNITES
Num 26:48 the family of the G;

GUR
2Kgs 9:27 at the ascent of G, which is by Ibleam.

GURBAAL
2Chr 26:7 Arabs that dwelt in G, and against the Me-unites.

GUSH (2)
Ps 104:10 Thou makest springs G forth in the valleys; they
Jer 9:18 tears, and our eyelids G with water.

GUSHED (6)
1Kgs 18:28 lances, until the blood G out upon them.
Ps 78:20 rock so that water G out and streams overflowed.
105:41 the rock, and water G forth; it flowed through
Is 48:21 rock and the water G out.
2Mac 14:45 and though his blood G forth and his wounds
Acts 1:18 and all his bowels G out.

GUSHING
Prov 18:4 of wisdom is a G stream.

GYMNASIUM (3)
1Mac 1:14 So they built a G in Jerusalem, according to
2Mac 4:9 by his authority a G and a body of
4:12 alacrity he founded a G right under the citadel,

H

HA-AHASHTARI
1Chr 4:6 Naarah bore him Ahuzzam, Hepher, Temeni, and H

HA-ELEPH
Josh 18:28 Irpeel, Taralah, Zela, H, Jebus (that is, Jerusalem),

HABAIAH
Ezra 2:61 priests: the sons of H, the sons of Hakkoz,

HABAKKUK (7)
Dan 14:33 Now the prophet H was in Judea.
14:34 the Lord said to H, "Take the dinner which
14:35 H said, "Sir, I have never seen Babylon, and
14:37 Then H shouted, "Daniel, Daniel!
14:39 of God immediately returned H to his own place.
Hab 1:1 oracle of God which H the prophet saw.
3:1 A prayer of H the prophet, according to Shigionoth.

HABAZZINIAH
Jer 35:3 of Jeremiah, son of H, and his brothers, and

HABIT (2)
Sir 7:13 any lie, for the H of lying serves no
Heb 10:25 together, as is the H of some, but encouraging

HABITABLE (2)
Ex 16:35 they came to a H land; they ate the
Job 37:12 the face of the H world.

HABITATION (31)
Lev 13:46 dwell alone in a H outside the camp.
Deut 12:5 name and make his H there; thither you shall
26:15 down from thy holy H, from heaven, and bless
2Sam 15:25 both it and his H;
2Chr 29:6 their faces from the H of the LORD, and
30:27 came to his holy H in heaven.
Job 8:6 for you and reward you with a rightful H
18:15 none of his; brimstone is scattered upon his H
Ps 26:8 LORD, I love the H of thy house, and
46:4 of God, the holy H of the Most High.
68:5 protector of widows is God in his holy H
79:7 they have devoured Jacob, and laid waste his H
91:9 the Most High your H,
104:12 the air have their H; they sing among the
132:13 desired it for his H:
Wis 9:8 the city of thy H, a copy of the
Is 22:16 height, and carve a H for yourself in the
27:10 city is solitary, a H deserted and forsaken, like
32:18 abide in a peaceful H, in secure dwellings, and
33:20 see Jerusalem, a quiet H, an immovable tent, whose
63:15 heaven and see, from thy holy and glorious H
Jer 10:25 and consumed him, and have laid waste his H
25:30 and from his holy H utter his voice; he
31:23 LORD bless you, O H of righteousness, O holy
50:7 the LORD, their true H, the LORD, the hope
Bar 2:16 down from thy holy H, and consider us.
Hab 3:11 stood still in their H at the light of
2Mac 14:35 a temple for thy H among us;
Acts 1:20 of Psalms, 'Let his H become desolate, and let
7:46 leave to find a H for the God of
17:26 the boundaries of their H,

HABITATIONS (11)
Ex 35:3 fire in all your H on the sabbath day."
Ps 74:20 are full of the H of violence.
78:28 the midst of their camp, all around their H
Sir 44:7 living peaceably in their H --
Is 54:2 the curtains of your H be stretched out; hold
Jer 21:13 who shall enter our H
33:12 there shall again be H of shepherds resting their
Lam 2:2 without mercy all the H of Jacob; in his
Ezek 6:14 waste, throughout all their H, from the wilderness to

G H

Hab 1:6 the earth, to seize H not their own.
Lk 16:9 fails they may receive you into the eternal H

HABITS

Sir 23:14 on account of your H; then you will wish

HABITUAL

Sir 20:24 is preferable to a H liar, but the lot

HABITUALLY

Sir 23:9 oaths, and do not H utter the name of

HABOR (3)

2Kgs 17:6 Halah, and on the H, the river of Gozan,
18:11 Halah, and on the H, the river of Gozan,
1Chr 5:26 brought them to Halah, H, Hara, and the river

HACALIAH (2)

Neh 1:1 The words of Nehemiah the son of H
10:1 governor, the son of H, Zedekiah,

HACHILAH (3)

1Sam 23:19 on the hill of H, which is south of
26:1 on the hill of H, which is on the
26:3 on the hill of H, which is beside the

HACHMONI

1Chr 27:32 Jehiel the son of H attended the king's sons.

HACHMONITE

1Chr 11:11 mighty men: Jashobe-am, a H, was chief of the

HACKED

Ps 74:5 the upper entrance they H the wooden trellis with

HADAD (15)

Gen 25:15 Mishma, Dumah, Massa, H, Tema, Jetur, Naphish,
36:35 Husham died, and H the son of Bedad, who
36:36 H died, and Samlah of Masrekah reigned in his
1Kgs 11:14 an adversary against Solomon, H the Edomite; he
11:17 male in Edom); but H fled to Egypt, together
11:17 of his father's servants, H being yet a little
11:19 And H found great favor in the sight of
11:21 But when H heard in Egypt that David slept
11:21 the army was dead, H said to Pharaoh, "Let
11:25 Solomon, doing mischief as H did; and he abhorred
1Chr 1:30 Mibsam, Mishma, Dumah, Massa, H, Tema,
1:46 When Husham died, H the son of Bedad, who
1:47 When H died, Samlah of Masrekah reigned in his
1:50 When Baal-hanan died, H reigned in his stead; and
1:51 And H died.

HADADEZER (21)

2Sam 8:3 David also defeated H the son of Rehob, king
8:5 Damascus came to help H king of Zobah, David
8:7 by the servants of H, and brought them to
8:8 from Berothai, cities of H, King David took very
8:9 the whole army of H,
8:10 he had fought against H and defeated him; for
8:10 and defeated him; for H had often been at
8:12 from the spoil of H the son of Rehob,
10:16 And H sent, and brought out the Syrians who
10:16 of the army of H at their head.
10:19 who were servants of H saw that they had
1Kgs 11:23 fled from his master H king of Zobah.
1Chr 18:3 David also defeated H king of Zobah, toward
18:5 Damascus came to help H king of Zobah, David
18:7 by the servants of H, and brought them to
18:8 from Cun, cities of H, David took very much
18:9 the whole army of H, king of Zobah,
18:10 he had fought against H and defeated him; for
18:10 and defeated him; for H had often been at
19:16 of the army of H at their head.
19:19 when the servants of H saw that they had

HADADRIMMON

Zech 12:11 as the mourning for H in the plain of

HADAR

Gen 36:39 of Achbor died, and H reigned in his stead,

HADASHAH

Josh 15:37 Zenan, H, Migdal-gad,

HADASSAH

Esth 2:7 He had brought up H, that is Esther, the

HADES (29)

Tob 13:2 he leads down to H, and brings up again,
Esth 13:7 down in violence to H, and leave our government
Wis 1:14 and the dominion of H is not on earth.
2:1 no one has been known to return from H
16:13 to the gates of H and back again.
17:14 the recesses of powerless H, they all slept the
Sir 14:12 and the decree of H has not been shown
14:16 beguile yourself, because in H one cannot look for
17:22 the Most High in H, as do those who
21:10 but at its end is the pit of H
28:21 an evil death, and H is preferable to it.
41:4 years, there is no inquiry about it in H
48:5 from death and from H, by the word of
51:5 of the belly of H, from an unclean tongue
51:6 was very near to H beneath.
Bar 2:17 dead who are in H, whose spirit has been
3:11 dead, that you are counted among those in H
3:19 and gone down to H, and others have arisen
Dan 3:89 has rescued us from H and saved us from
2Mac 6:23 himself quickly, telling them to send him to H
Mt 11:23 You shall be brought down to H
Lk 10:15 You shall be brought down to H
16:23 was buried; and in H, being in torment, he
Acts 2:27 abandon my soul to H, nor let thy Holy
2:31 was not abandoned to H, nor did his flesh
Rev 1:18 and I have the keys of Death and H
6:8 name was Death, and H followed him; and they
20:13 in it, Death and H gave up the dead
20:14 Then Death and H were thrown into the lake

HADID (3)

Ezra 2:33 The sons of Lod, H, and Ono, seven hundred
Neh 7:37 The sons of Lod, H, and Ono, seven hundred
11:34 Hazor, Ramah, Gittaim, H, Zeboim, Neballat,

HADLAI

2Chr 28:12 Amasa the son of H, stood up against those

HADORAM (4)

Gen 10:27 Sheleph, Hazarmaveth, Jerah, H, Uzal, Diklah,
1Chr 1:21 Sheleph, Hazarmaveth, Jerah, H, Uzal, Diklah,
18:10 he sent his son H to King David, to
2Chr 10:18 Then King Rehoboam sent H, who was taskmaster

HADRACH

Zech 9:1 against the land of H and will rest upon

HADST (7)

Neh 9:15 the land which thou H sworn to give them.
9:23 the land which thou H told their fathers to
Ps 30:7 favor, O LORD, thou H established me as a
90:2 forth, or ever thou H formed the earth and
Wis 11:24 made anything if thou H hated it.
11:25 have endured if thou H not willed it?
Jer 15:17 upon me, for thou H filled me with indignation.

HAG

Is 34:14 there shall the night H alight, and find for

HAGAB

Ezra 2:46 Akkub, the sons of H, the sons of Shamlai,

HAGABA

Neh 7:48 Lebana, the sons of H, the sons of Shalmai,

HAGABAH

Ezra 2:45 Lebanah, the sons of H, the sons of Akkub,

HAGAR (15)

Gen 16:1 maid whose name was H;
16:3 Sarai, Abram's wife, took H the Egyptian, her maid,
16:4 he went in to H, and she conceived; and
16:8 And he said, H, maid of Sarai, where have
16:15 And H bore Abram a son; and Abram called
16:15 of his son, whom H bore, Ishmael.
16:16 eighty-six years old when H bore Ishmael to Abram.
21:9 saw the son of H the Egyptian, whom she
21:14 and gave it to H, putting it on her
21:17 of God called to H from heaven, and said
21:17 heaven, and said to her, "What troubles you, H
25:12 Abraham's son, whom H the Egyptian, Sarah's maid,
Bar 3:23 Teman; the sons of H, who seek for understanding
Gal 4:24 Mount Sinai, bearing children for slavery; she is H
4:25 Now H is Mount Sinai in Arabia; she corresponds

HAGGAI (11)
Ezra 5:1 Now the prophets, H and Zechariah the son of
6:14 the prophesying of H the prophet and Zechariah
Hag 1:1 the LORD came by H the prophet to Zerubbabel
1:3 the LORD came by H the prophet,
1:12 and the words of H the prophet, as the
1:13 Then H, the messenger of the LORD, spoke to
2:1 the LORD came by H the prophet,
2:10 the LORD came by H the prophet,
2:13 Then said H, "If one who is unclean by
2:14 Then H said, "So is it with this people,
2:20 a second time to H on the twenty-fourth day

HAGGARD
2Sam 13:4 why are you so H morning after morning?

HAGGEDOLIM
Neh 11:14 their overseer was Zabdiel the son of H

HAGGI (2)
Gen 46:16 sons of Gad: Ziphion, H, Shuni, Ezbon, Eri, Arodi,
Num 26:15 of the Zephonites; of H, the family of the

HAGGIAH
1Chr 6:30 son, Shimea his son, H his son, and Asaiah

HAGGITES
Num 26:15 the family of the H; of Shuni, the family

HAGGITH (5)
2Sam 3:4 Adonijah the son of H; and the fifth, Shephatiah
1Kgs 1:5 Adonijah the son of H exalted himself, saying, "I
1:11 Adonijah the son of H has become king and
2:13 Adonijah the son of H came to Bathsheba the
1Chr 3:2 Adonijah, whose mother was H;

HAGRI
1Chr 11:38 Mibhar the son of H,

HAGRITE
1Chr 27:30 Over the flocks was Jaziz the H

HAGRITES (4)
1Chr 5:10 made war on the H, who fell by their
5:19 made war upon the H, Jetur, Naphish, and Nodab;
5:20 help against them, the H and all who were
Ps 83:6 Ishmaelites, Moab and the H,

HAHIROTH
Num 33:8 set out from before H, and passed through the

HAIL (38)
Ex 9:18 will cause very heavy H to fall, such as
9:19 safe shelter; for the H shall come down upon
9:22 that there may be H in all the land
9:23 LORD sent thunder and H, and fire ran down
9:23 And the LORD rained H upon the land of
9:24 of Egypt; there was H, and fire flashing continually
9:24 the midst of the H, very heavy hail, such
9:24 the hail, very heavy H, such as had never
9:25 The H struck down everything that was in the
9:25 and beast; and the H struck down every plant
9:26 the people of Israel were, there was no H
9:28 of this thunder and H; I will let you
9:29 will be no more H, that you may know
9:33 the thunder and the H ceased, and the rain
9:34 the rain and the H and the thunder had
10:5 to you after the H, and they shall eat
10:12 land, all that the H has left."
10:15 the trees which the H had left; not a
Job 38:22 the storehouses of the H,
Ps 78:47 destroyed their vines with H, and their sycamores
78:48 their cattle to the H, and their flocks to
105:32 He gave them H for rain, and lightning that
148:8 all deeps, fire and H, snow and frost, stormy
Wis 16:16 by unusual rains and H and relentless storms, and
16:22 that blazed in the H and flashed in the
Sir 39:29 Fire and H and famine and pestilence, all these
Is 28:2 like a storm of H, a destroying tempest, like
28:17 righteousness the plummet; and H will sweep away
Hag 2:17 blight and mildew and H; yet you did not
Mt 26:49 at once and said, H, Master!" And he kissed
27:29 they mocked him, saying, H, King of the Jews!"
28:9 And behold, Jesus met them and said, H
Mk 15:18 began to salute him, H, King of the Jews!"
Lk 1:28 to her and said, H, full of grace, the
Jn 19:3 up to him, saying, H, King of the Jews!"
Rev 8:7 trumpet, and there followed H and fire, mixed with
11:19 voices, peals of thunder, an earthquake, and heavy H
16:21 the plague of the H, so fearful was that

HAILED
1Sam 14:12 of the garrison H Jonathan and his armor-bearer,

HAILSTONES (11)
Josh 10:11 died because of the H than the men of
Ps 18:12 broke through his clouds H and coals of fire.
18:13 High uttered his voice, H and coals of fire.
Wis 5:22 bow of clouds, and H full of wrath will
Sir 43:15 the clouds, and the H are broken in pieces.
46:6 Lord answered him with H of mighty power.
Is 30:30 devouring fire, with a cloudburst and tempest and H
Ezek 13:11 deluge of rain, great H will fall, and a
13:13 my anger, and great H in wrath to destroy
38:22 him, torrential rains and H, fire and brimstone.
Rev 16:21 be found; and great H, heavy as a hundred-weight,

HAIR (89)
Ex 25:4 fine twined linen, goats' H,
26:7 make curtains of goats' H for a tent over
35:6 fine twined linen; goats' H,
35:23 fine linen or goats' H or tanned rams' skins
35:26 hearts were moved with ability spun the goats' H
36:14 made curtains of goats' H for a tent over
Lev 10:6 "Do not let the H of your heads hang
13:3 body; and if the H in the diseased spot
13:4 the skin, and the H in it has not
13:10 which has turned the H white, and there is
13:20 the skin and its H has turned white, then
13:21 examines it, and the H on it is not
13:25 it, and if the H in the spot has
13:26 examines it, and the H in the spot is
13:30 the skin, and the H in it is yellow
13:31 there is no black H in it, then the
13:32 in it no yellow H, and the itch appears
13:36 seek for the yellow H; he is unclean.
13:37 is checked, and black H has grown in it,
13:40 "If a man's H has fallen from his head,
13:41 And if a man's H has fallen from his
13:45 clothes and let the H of his head hang
14:8 shave off all his H, and bathe himself in
14:9 shall shave all his H off his head; he
14:9 off his beard and his eyebrows, all his H
19:27 not round off the H on your temples or
21:10 shall not let the H of his head hang
Num 5:18 LORD, and unbind the H of the woman's head,
6:5 let the locks of H of his head grow
6:18 and shall take the H from his consecrated head
6:19 he has shaven the H of his consecration,
31:20 all work of goats' H, and every article of
Judg 16:22 But the H of his head began to grow
20:16 a stone at a H, and not miss.
1Sam 14:45 there shall not one H of his head fall
19:13 a pillow of goats' H at its head, and
19:16 the pillow of goats' H at its head.
2Sam 14:11 LORD lives, not one H of your son shall
14:26 when he cut the H of his head (for
14:26 it), he weighed the H of his head, two
Ezra 9:3 my mantle, and pulled H from my head and
Neh 13:25 and pulled out their H; and I made them
Jud 10:3 ointment, and combed her H and put on a
13:7 took hold of the H of his head, and
16:8 ointment and fastened her H with a tiara and
Esth 14:2 loved to adorn she covered with her tangled H
Job 4:15 past my face; the H of my flesh stood
Prov 20:29 the beauty of old men is their gray H
Song 4:1 Your H is like a flock of goats, moving
6:5 disturb me-- Your H is like a flock
Wis 4:9 but understanding is gray H for men, and a
Sir 27:14 to swearing makes one's H stand on end, and
Is 3:24 and instead of well-set H, baldness; and instead of
7:20 the head and the H of the feet, and
Jer 7:29 Cut off your H and cast it away; raise
9:26 the corners of their H; for all these nations
25:23 the corners of their H;
49:32 the corners of their H, and I will bring
Ezek 5:1 then take balances for weighing, and divide the H
16:7 were formed, and your H had grown; yet you
23:34 and pluck out your H, and tear your breasts;
44:20 shall only trim the H of their heads.
Dan 3:95 of those men; the H of their heads was
4:33 of heaven till his H grew as long as

H

7:9 as snow, and the H of his head like
14:27 took pitch, fat, and H, and boiled them together
14:36 lifted him by his H and set him down
Mic 1:16 and cut off your H, for the children of
2Mac 7:7 his head with the H, and asked him, "Will
15:13 distinguished by his gray H and dignity, and of
Mt 3:4 a garment of camel's H, and a leather girdle
5:36 you cannot make one H white or black.
Mk 1:6 was clothed with camel's H, and had a leather
Lk 7:38 wiped them with the H of her head, and
7:44 with her tears and wiped them with her H
21:18 But not a H of your head will perish.
Jn 11:2 his feet with her H, whose brother Lazarus was
12:3 his feet with her H; and the house was
Acts 18:18 Cenchre-ae he cut his H, for he had a
27:34 strength, since not a H is to perish from
1Cor 11:6 should cut off her H; but if it is
11:14 man to wear long H is degrading to him,
11:15 a woman has long H, it is her pride?
11:15 For her H is given to her for a
1Tim 2:9 apparel, not with braided H or gold or pearls
1Pet 3:3 adorning with braiding of H, decoration of gold, and
Rev 1:14 his head and his H were white as white
9:8 like human faces, their H like women's hair, and
9:8 their hair like women's H, and their teeth like

HAIRCLOTH

2Kgs 1:8 wore a garment of H, with a girdle of

HAIRS (14)

Gen 42:38 bring down my gray H with sorrow to Sheol."
44:29 bring down my gray H in sorrow to Sheol.'
44:31 bring down the gray H of your servant our
Deut 32:25 the sucking child with the man of gray H
1Kgs 1:52 not one of his H shall fall to the
Ps 40:12 are more than the H of my head; my
69:4 in number than the H of my head are
71:18 old age and gray H, O God, do not
Wis 2:10 nor regard the gray H of the aged.
Is 46:4 He, and to gray H I will carry you.
Hos 7:10 knows it not; gray H are sprinkled upon him,
2Mac 6:23 age and the gray H which he had reached
Mt 10:30 But even the H of your head are all
Lk 12:7 Why, even the H of your head are all

HAIRY (5)

Gen 25:25 his body like a H mantle; so they called
27:11 brother Esau is a H man, and I am
27:23 because his hands were H like his brother Esau's
Ps 68:21 of his enemies, the H crown of him who
Zech 13:4 not put on a H mantle in order to

HAKKATAN

Ezra 8:12 Johanan the son of H, and with him a

HAKKOZ (5)

1Chr 24:10 Mijamin, the seventh to H, the eighth to Abijah,
Ezra 2:61 Habaiah, the sons of H, and the sons of
Neh 3:4 of Uriah, son of H repaired.
3:21 of Uriah, son of H repaired another section from
7:63 Hobaiah, the sons of H, the sons of Barzillai

HAKUPHA (2)

Ezra 2:51 Bakbuk, the sons of H, the sons of Harhur,
Neh 7:53 Bakbuk, the sons of H, the sons of Harhur,

HALAH (4)

2Kgs 17:6 and placed them in H, and on the Habor,
18:11 and put them in H, and on the Habor,
1Chr 5:26 and brought them to H, Habor, Hara, and the
Obad 1:20 The exiles in H who are of the people

HALAK (2)

Josh 11:17 its lowland from Mount H, that rises toward Seir,
12:7 of Lebanon to Mount H, that rises toward Seir

HALF (115)

Gen 15:10 two, and laid each H over against the other;
Ex 24:6 And Moses took H of the blood and put
24:6 it in basins, and H of the blood he
25:10 two cubits and a H shall be its length,
25:10 a cubit and a H its breadth, and a
25:10 a cubit and a H its height.
25:17 two cubits and a H shall be its length,
25:17 a cubit and a H its breadth.
25:23 a cubit and a H its height.
26:12 of the tent, the H curtain that remains, shall
26:16 a cubit and a H the breadth of each
30:13 census shall give this: H a shekel according to
30:13 shekel is twenty gerahs), H a shekel as an
30:23 and of sweet-smelling cinnamon H as much, that is,
36:21 a cubit and a H the breadth of each
37:1 two cubits and a H was its length, a
37:1 a cubit and a H its breadth, and a
37:1 a cubit and a H its height.
37:6 two cubits and a H was its length, and
37:6 a cubit and a H its breadth.
37:10 a cubit and a H its height;
38:26 a head (that is, H a shekel, by the
Lev 6:20 a regular cereal offering, H of it in the
6:20 in the morning and H in the evening.
Num 12:12 whom the flesh is H consumed when he comes
15:9 fine flour, mixed with H a hin of oil,
15:10 for the drink offering H a hin of wine,
28:14 drink offerings shall be H a hin of wine
31:29 take it from their H, and give it to
31:30 the people of Israel's H you shall take one
31:36 And the H, the portion of those who had
31:42 the people of Israel's H, which Moses separated
31:43 now the congregation's H was three hundred and
31:47 the people of Israel's H Moses took one of
Deut 3:12 of the Arnon, and H the hill country of
15:18 from you; for at H the cost of a
Josh 8:33 covenant of the LORD, H of them in front
8:33 of Mount Gerizim and H of them in front
12:2 the Ammonites, that is, H of Gilead,
12:5 the Ma-acathites, and over H of Gilead to the
13:7 the nine tribes and H the tribe of Manasseh."
13:8 With the other H of the tribe of Manasseh
13:25 cities of Gilead, and H the land of the
13:31 Bashan, sixty cities, and H Gilead, and Ashtaroth, and
13:31 of Manasseh for the H of the Machirites according
18:7 Gad and Reuben and H the tribe of Manasseh
22:7 Now to the one H of the tribe of
22:7 but to the other H Joshua had given a
1Sam 14:14 within as it were H a furrow's length in
2Sam 10:4 servants, and shaved off H the beard of each,
18:3 If H of us die, they will not care
19:40 of Judah, and also H the people of Israel,
1Kgs 3:25 in two, and give H to the one, and
3:25 to the one, and H to the other."
7:31 a cubit and a H deep.
7:32 of a wheel was a cubit and a H
7:35 was a round band H a cubit high; and
10:7 it; and, behold, the H was not told me;
13:8 "If you give me H your house, I will
16:9 Zimri, commander of H his chariots, conspired
16:21 divided into two parts; H of the people followed
16:21 make him king, and H followed Omri.
1Chr 2:52 had other sons: Haroeh, H of the Menuhoth.
2:54 Atroth-beth-joab, and H of the Manahathites,
6:61 of the half-tribe, the H of Manasseh, ten cities.
2Chr 9:6 seen it; and behold, H the greatness of your
Neh 3:9 of Hur, ruler of H the district of Jerusalem,
3:12 of Hallohesh, ruler of H the district of Jerusalem,
3:16 of Azbuk, ruler of H the district of Bethzur,
3:17 him Hashabiah, ruler of H the district of Keilah,
3:18 of Henadad, ruler of H the district of Keilah;
4:6 was joined together to H its height.
4:16 From that day on, H of my servants worked
4:16 worked on construction, and H held the spears,
4:21 at the work, and H of them held the
12:32 them went Hoshaiah and H of the princes of
12:38 I followed them with H of the people, upon
12:40 God, and I and H of the officials with
13:24 Ammon, and Moab; and H of their children spoke
Tob 8:21 then he should take H of Raguel's property and
10:10 his wife Sarah and H of his property in
12:2 harm to give him H of what I have
12:5 said to him, "Take H of all that you
Esth 5:3 you, even to the H of my kingdom."
5:6 Even to the H of my kingdom, it shall
7:2 Even to the H of my kingdom, it shall
Ps 55:23 shall not live out H their days.
Wis 18:14 swift course was now H gone,
18:18 another there, hurled down H dead, made known
Sir 29:6 will hardly get back H, and will regard that
Is 44:16 H of it he burns in the fire; over
44:16 the fire; over the H he eats flesh, he
44:19 or discernment to say, H of it I burned
Ezek 16:51 Samaria has not committed H your sins; you have
40:42 a cubit and a H long, and a cubit

40:42 a cubit and a H broad, and one cubit
43:17 a rim around it H a cubit broad, and
Dan 7:25 time, two times, and H a time.
9:27 one week; and for H of the week he
12:7 time, two times, and H a time; and that
Zech 14:2 and the women ravished; H of the city shall
14:4 valley; so that one H of the Mount shall
14:4 northward, and the other H southward.
14:8 flow out from Jerusalem, H of them to the
14:8 the eastern sea and H of them to the
1Mac 3:34 turned over to Lysias H of his troops and
3:37 king took the remaining H of his troops and
10:30 the grain and the H of the fruit of
Mk 6:23 will give you, even H of my kingdom."
Lk 10:30 and departed, leaving him H dead.
19:8 Lord, "Behold, Lord, the H of my goods I
Rev 8:1 in heaven for about H an hour.
11:9 three days and a H men from the peoples
11:11 the three and a H days a breath of
12:14 time, and times, and H a time.

HALF-SHEKEL (3)

Gen 24:22 gold ring weighing a H, and two bracelets for
Ex 30:15 give less, than the H, when you give the
Mt 17:23 the collectors of the H tax went up to

HALF-TRIBE (33)

Num 32:33 Reuben and to the H of Manasseh the son
34:13 tribes and to the H;
34:14 inheritance, and also the H of Manasseh;
34:15 two tribes and the H have received their inheritance
Deut 3:13 I gave to the H of Manasseh.
29:8 the Gadites, and the H of the Manassites.
Josh 1:12 the Gadites, and the H of Manasseh Joshua said,
4:12 of Gad and the H of Manasseh passed over
12:6 the Gadites and the H of Manasseh.
13:29 an inheritance to the H of Manasseh; it was
13:29 was allotted to the H of the Manassites according
21:5 of Dan and the H of Manasseh, ten cities.
21:6 Naphtali, and from the H of Manasseh in Bashan,
21:25 and out of the H of Manasseh, Taanach with
21:27 given out of the H of Manasseh, Golan in
22:1 the Gadites, and the H of Manasseh,
22:9 the Gadites and the H of Manasseh returned home,
22:10 the Gadites and the H of Manasseh built there
22:11 the Gadites and the H of Manasseh have built
22:13 the Gadites, and the H of Manasseh, in the
22:15 the Gadites, and the H of Manasseh, in the
22:21 the Gadites, and the H of Manasseh said in
1Chr 5:18 the Gadites, and the H of Manasseh had valiant
5:23 The members of the H of Manasseh dwelt in
5:26 the Gadites, and the H of Manasseh, and brought
6:61 tribe, out of the H, the half of Manasseh,
6:70 and out of the H of Manasseh, Aner with
6:71 given out of the H of Manasseh: Golan in
12:31 Of the H of Manasseh eighteen thousand, who were
12:37 and Gadites and the H of Manasseh from beyond
26:32 the Gadites, and the H of the Manassites for
27:20 of Azaziah; for the H of Manasseh, Joel the
27:21 of Pedaiah; for the H of Manasseh in Gilead,

HALFWAY (4)

Ex 26:28 The middle bar, H up the frames, shall pass
27:5 the net shall extend H down the altar.
36:33 from end to end H up the frames.
38:4 under its ledge, extending H down.

HALHUL

Josh 15:58 H, Bethzur, Gedor,

HALI

Josh 19:25 Its territory included Helkath, H, Beten, Achshaph,

HALICARNASSUS

1Mac 15:23 to Lycia, and to H, and to Rhodes, and

HALL (12)

1Sam 9:22 brought them into the H and gave them a
1Kgs 7:6 And he made the H of Pillars; its length
7:7 And he made the H of the Throne where
7:7 pronounce judgment, even the H of Judgment; it was
7:8 court back of the H, was of like workmanship.
7:8 a house like this H for Pharaoh's daughter whom
Esth 5:1 court of the king's palace, opposite the king's H
Dan 5:10 came into the banqueting H; and the queen said,
1Mac 16:16 Simon in the banquet H, and they killed him
Mt 22:10 good; so the wedding H was filled with guests.
Acts 19:9 argued daily in the H of Tyrannus.
25:23 entered the audience H with the military tribunes

HALLELUJAH (5)

Tob 13:18 her lanes will cry H and will give praise,
Rev 19:1 voice of a great multitude in heaven, crying, H
19:3 Once more they cried, H
19:4 saying, "Amen. H!"
19:6 and like the sound of mighty thunderpeals, crying, H

HALLOHESH (2)

Neh 3:12 Shallum the son of H, ruler of half the
10:24 Hoshea, Hananiah, Hasshub, H, Pilha, Shobek,

HALLOW (4)

Ex 28:38 the people of Israel H as their holy gifts;
Lev 16:19 and cleanse it and H it from the uncleannesses
25:10 And you shall H the fiftieth year, and proclaim
Ezek 20:20 observe my ordinances, and H my sabbaths that they

HALLOWED (10)

Gen 2:3 the seventh day and H it, because on it
Ex 20:11 the sabbath day and H it.
Lev 12:4 shall not touch any H thing, nor come into
22:32 but I will be H among the people of
Num 18:29 of them, giving the H part from them.'
2Chr 36:14 LORD which he had H in Jerusalem.
Sir 33:9 them he exalted and H, and some of them
2Mac 15:2 things has honored and H above other days,"
Mt 6:9 who art in heaven, H be thy name.
Lk 11:2 you pray, say: "Father, H be thy name.

HALT (4)

Neh 12:39 they came to a H at the Gate of
Is 10:32 very day he will H at Nob, he will
Nah 2:8 H! H!" they cry; but none turns

HALTED (4)

2Sam 15:17 after him; and they H at the last house.
2Kgs 5:9 horses and chariots, and H at the door of
Joel 2:8 they burst through the weapons and are not H
2Mac 10:27 when they came near to the enemy they H

HALVES (2)

Song 4:3 Your cheeks are like H of a pomegranate behind
6:7 Your cheeks are like H of a pomegranate behind

HAM (17)

Gen 5:32 the father of Shem, H, and Japheth.
6:10 had three sons, Shem, H, and Japheth.
7:13 his sons, Shem and H and Japheth, and Noah's
9:18 the ark were Shem, H, and Japheth.
9:18 H was the father of Canaan.
9:22 And H, the father of Canaan, saw the nakedness
10:1 sons of Noah, Shem, H, and Japheth; sons were
10:6 The sons of H: Cush, Egypt, Put, and Canaan.
10:20 are the sons of H, by their families, their
14:5 the Zuzim in H, the Emim in Shaveh-kiriatha
1Chr 1:4 Thuselah, Lamech, Noah, Shem, H, and Japheth.
1:8 The sons of H: Cush, Egypt, Put, and Canaan.
4:40 for the former inhabitants there belonged to H
Ps 78:51 issue of their strength in the tents of H
105:23 to Egypt; Jacob sojourned in the land of H
105:27 among them, and miracles in the land of H
106:22 in the land of H, and terrible things by

HAMAN (62)

Esth 3:1 things King Ahasuerus promoted H the Agagite, the
3:2 and did obeisance to H; for the king had
3:4 to them, they told H, in order to see
3:5 And when H saw that Mordecai did not bow
3:5 do obeisance to him, H was filled with fury.
3:6 the people of Mordecai, H sought to destroy all
3:7 is the lot, before H day after day; and
3:8 Then H said to King Ahasuerus, "There is a
3:10 and gave it to H the Agagite, the son
3:11 the king said to H, "The money is given
3:12 according to all that H commanded, was written to
3:15 And the king and H sat down to drink;
4:7 sum of money that H had promised to pay
4:8 for by me, because H, who is next to
5:4 let the king and H come this day to
5:5 said the king, "Bring H quickly, that we may
5:5 So the king and H came to the dinner
5:8 let the king and H come tomorrow to the

H

HAMRAN

1Chr 1:41 The sons of Dishon: H, Eshban, Ithran, and Cheran.

HAMSTRING (2)

Gen 49:6 in their wantonness they H oxen.
Josh 11:6 to Israel; you shall H their horses, and burn

HAMSTRUNG (3)

Josh 11:9 LORD bade him; he H their horses, and burned
2Sam 8:4 foot soldiers; and David H all the chariot horses,
1Chr 18:4 foot soldiers; and David H all the chariot horses,

HAMUL (3)

Gen 46:12 and the sons of Perez were Hezron and H
Num 26:21 of the Hezronites; of H, the family of the
1Chr 2:5 The sons of Perez: Hezron and H

HAMULITES

Num 26:21 the Hezronites; of Hamul, the family of the H

HAMUTAL (3)

2Kgs 23:31 His mother's name was H the daughter of Jeremiah
24:18 His mother's name was H the daughter of Jeremiah
Jer 52:1 His mother's name was H the daughter of Jeremiah

HANAMEL (4)

Jer 32:7 came to me: Behold, H the son of Shallum
32:8 purchase is yours.' Then H my cousin came to
32:9 field at Anathoth from H my cousin, and weighed
32:12 in the presence of H my cousin, in the

HANAN (12)

1Chr 8:23 Eber, Eliel, Abdon, Zichri, H,
8:38 Bocheru, Ishmael, She-ariah, Obadiah, and H
9:44 She-ariah, Obadiah, and H; these were the sons
11:43 and thirty with him, H the son of Maacah,
Ezra 2:46 Shamlai, the sons of H,
Neh 7:49 Shalmai, the sons of H, the sons of Giddel,
8:7 Azariah, Jozabad, H, Pelaiah, the Levites, helped
10:10 Shebaniah, Hodiah, Kelita, Pelaiah, H,
10:22 Meshezabel, Zadok, Jaddu-a, Pelatiah, H, Anaiah,
10:26 Rehum, Hashabnah, Ma-aseiah, Ahiah, H, Anan,
13:13 and as their assistant H the son of Zaccur,
Jer 35:4 of the sons of H the son of Igdaliah,

HANANEL (4)

Neh 3:1 the Hundred, as far as the Tower of H
12:39 and the Tower of H and the Tower of
Jer 31:38 from the tower of H to the Corner Gate.
Zech 14:10 from the Tower of H to the king's wine

HANANI (11)

1Kgs 16:1 Jehu the son of H against Baasha, saying,
16:7 Jehu the son of H against Baasha and his
1Chr 25:4 Jerimoth, Hananiah, H, Eliathah, Giddalti, and R
25:25 to the eighteenth, to H, his sons and his
2Chr 16:7 At that time H the seer came to Asa
19:2 Jehu the son of H the seer went out
20:34 Jehu the son of H, which are recorded in
Ezra 10:20 the sons of Immer: H and Zebadiah.
Neh 1:2 Susa the capital, that H, one of my brethren,
7:2 I gave my brother H and Hananiah the governor
12:36 Judah, and H, with the musical instruments

HANANIAH (30)

1Chr 3:19 Zerubbabel: Meshullam and H, and Shelomith was
3:21 The sons of H: Pelatiah and Jeshaiah, his son
8:24 Abdon, Zichri, Hanan, H, Elam, Anthothijah,
25:4 and Jerimoth, H, Hanani, Eliathah, Giddalti, and
25:23 to the sixteenth, to H, his sons and his
2Chr 26:11 under the direction of H, one of the king's
Ezra 10:28 of Bebai were Jehohanan, H, Zabbai, and Athlai.
Neh 3:8 Next to him H, one of the perfumers, repaired;
3:30 After him H the son of Shelemiah and Hanun
7:2 my brother Hanani and H the governor of the
10:23 Pelatiah, Hanan, Anaiah, Hoshea, H, Hasshub,
12:12 Seraiah, Meraiah; of Jeremiah, H;
12:41 Eli-o-enai, Zechariah, and H, with trumpets;
Jer 28:1 of the fourth year, H the son of Azzur,
28:5 prophet Jeremiah spoke to H the prophet in the
28:10 Then the prophet H took the yoke-bars from the
28:11 And H spoke in the presence of all the
28:12 after the prophet H had broken the yoke-bars
28:13 to Jeremiah: "Go, tell H, 'Thus says the LORD:
28:15 said to the prophet H, "Listen, Hananiah, the LORD
28:15 the prophet Hananiah, "Listen, H, the LORD has not
28:17 seventh month, the prophet H died.
36:12 Zedekiah the son of H, and all the princes.
37:13 of Shelemiah, son of H, seized Jeremiah the prophet,
Dan 1:6 Among these were Daniel, H, Mishael, and Azariah
1:7 Daniel he called Belteshazzar, H he called Shadrach,
1:11 had appointed over Daniel, H, Mishael, and Azariah;
1:19 was found like Daniel, H, Mishael, and Azariah;
2:17 the matter known to H, Mishael, and Azariah, his
3:89 Bless the Lord, H, Azariah, and Mishael, sing praise

HAND (1,329)

Gen 3:22 he put forth his H and take also of
4:11 mouth to receive your brother's blood from your H
8:9 he put forth his H and took her and
9:2 the sea; into your H they are delivered.
13:9 you take the left H, then I will go
13:9 you take the right H, then I will go
14:20 High, who has delivered your enemies into your H
16:12 of a man, his H against every man and
16:12 man and every man's H against him; and he
19:16 two daughters by the H, the LORD being merciful
21:18 him fast with your H; for I will make
21:30 will take from my H, that you may be
22:6 he took in his H the fire and the
22:10 Abraham put forth his H, and took the knife
22:12 "Do not lay your H on the lad or
24:2 he had, "Put your H under my thigh,
24:9 the servant put his H under the thigh of
24:18 her jar upon her H, and gave him a
24:49 turn to the right H or to the left."
25:26 came forth, and his H had taken hold of
27:17 had prepared, into the H of her son Jacob.
31:39 it myself; of my H you required it, whether
32:11 pray thee, from the H of my brother, from
32:11 my brother, from the H of Esau, for I
32:16 he delivered into the H of his servants, every
33:10 my present from my H; for truly to see
37:22 wilderness, but lay no H upon him"—that he
37:22 him out of their H, to restore him to
37:27 and let not our H be upon him, for
38:18 cord, and your staff that is in your H
38:20 pledge from the woman's H, he could not find
38:28 one put out a H; and the midwife took
38:28 and bound on his H a scarlet thread, saying,
38:29 he drew back his H, behold, his brother came
38:30 scarlet thread upon his H; and his name was
39:8 he has in my H;
39:12 his garment in her H, and fled and got
39:13 his garment in her H, and had fled out
40:11 cup was in my H; and I took the
40:11 Pharaoh's cup, and placed the cup in Pharaoh's H
40:13 Pharaoh's cup in his H as formerly, when you
40:21 the cup in Pharaoh's H;
41:42 signet ring from his H and put it on
41:42 put it on Joseph's H, and arrayed him in
41:44 man shall lift up H or foot in all
43:9 for him; of my H you shall require him.
43:22 money down in our H to buy food.
44:16 he also in whose H the cup has been
44:17 the man in whose H the cup was found
46:4 up again; and Joseph's H shall close your eyes."
47:29 your sight, put your H under my thigh, and
48:13 Ephraim in his right H toward Israel's left hand,
48:13 hand toward Israel's left H, and Manasseh in his
48:13 Manasseh in his left H toward Israel's right hand,
48:13 hand toward Israel's right H, and brought them near
48:14 stretched out his right H and laid it upon
48:14 younger, and his left H upon the head of
48:17 father laid his right H upon the head of
48:17 he took his father's H, to remove it from
48:18 first-born; put your right H upon his head."
48:22 I took from the H of the Amorites with
49:8 shall praise you; your H shall be on the
Ex 2:19 us out of the H of the shepherds, and
3:8 them out of the H of the Egyptians, and
3:19 let you go unless compelled by a mighty H
3:20 will stretch out my H and smite Egypt with
4:2 said to him, "What is that in your H
4:4 Moses, "Put out your H, and take it by
4:4 he put out his H and caught it, and
4:4 a rod in his H —
4:6 to him, "Put your H into your bosom." And
4:6 And he put his H into his bosom; and
4:6 it out, behold, his H was leprous, as white
4:7 God said, "Put your H back into your bosom."
4:7 So he put his H back into his bosom;

4:17 shall take in your H this rod, with which
4:20 Egypt; and in his H Moses took the rod
5:21 a sword in their H to kill us."
6:1 for with a strong H he will send them
6:1 yea, with a strong H he will drive them
7:4 I will lay my H upon Egypt and bring
7:5 I stretch forth my H upon Egypt and bring
7:15 and take in your H the rod which was
7:17 that is in my H, and it shall be
7:19 and stretch out your H over the waters of
8:5 Aaron, 'Stretch out your H with your rod over
8:6 Aaron stretched out his H over the waters of
8:17 Aaron stretched out his H with his rod, and
9:3 hold them, behold, the H of the LORD will
9:15 have put forth my H and struck you and
9:22 Moses, "Stretch forth your H toward heaven, that
10:12 Moses, "Stretch out your H over the land of
10:21 Moses, "Stretch out your H toward heaven that
10:22 Moses stretched out his H toward heaven, and there
12:11 your staff in your H; and you shall eat
13:3 for by strength of H the LORD brought you
13:9 a sign on your H and as a memorial
13:9 for with a strong H the LORD has brought
13:14 him, 'By strength of H the LORD brought us
13:16 a mark on your H or frontlets between your
13:16 for by a strong H the LORD brought us
14:16 and stretch out your H over the sea and
14:21 Moses stretched out his H over the sea; and
14:22 them on their right H and on their left.
14:26 Moses, "Stretch out your H over the sea, that
14:27 Moses stretched forth his H over the sea, and
14:29 them on their right H and on their left.
14:30 that day from the H of the Egyptians; and
15:6 Thy right H, O LORD, glorious in power, thy
15:6 in power, thy right H, O LORD, shatters the
15:9 draw my sword, my H shall destroy them.'
15:12 stretch out thy right H, the earth swallowed them.
15:20 a timbrel in her H; and all the women
16:3 had died by the H of the LORD in
17:5 and take in your H the rod with which
17:9 hill with the rod of God in my H
17:11 Moses held up his H, Israel prevailed; and whenever
17:11 whenever he lowered his H, Amalek prevailed.
17:16 my banner, saying, "A H upon the banner of
18:9 them out of the H of the Egyptians.
18:10 you out of the H of the Egyptians and
18:10 and out of the H of Pharaoh.
18:11 people from under the H of the Egyptians, when
19:13 put to death; no H shall touch him, but
21:13 him fall into his H, then I will appoint
21:20 slave dies under his H, he shall be punished.
21:24 eye, tooth for tooth, H for hand, foot for
21:24 for tooth, hand for H, foot for foot,
22:8 he has put his H to his neighbor's goods.
22:11 has not put his H to his neighbor's property;
23:31 the land into your H, and you shall drive
24:11 did not lay his H on the chief men
32:4 the gold at their H, and fashioned it with
32:11 Egypt with great power and with a mighty H
33:22 cover you with my H until I have passed
33:23 will take away my H, and you shall see
34:4 and took in his H two tables of stone.
34:29 the testimony in his H as he came down
38:15 other side; on this H and that hand by
38:15 this hand and that H by the gate of
Lev 1:4 he shall lay his H upon the head of
3:2 he shall lay his H upon the head of
3:8 the LORD, laying his H upon the head of
3:13 LORD, and lay his H upon its head, and
4:4 LORD, and lay his H on the head of
4:24 and shall lay his H upon the head of
4:29 he shall lay his H on the head of
4:33 blemish, and lay his H upon the head of
8:23 thumb of his right H and on the great
9:17 offering, and filled his H from it, and burned
14:14 thumb of his right H, and on the great
14:15 of his own left H,
14:16 is in his left H, and sprinkle some oil
14:17 that remains in his H the priest shall put
14:17 thumb of his right H, and on the great
14:18 is in the priest's H he shall put on
14:25 thumb of his right H, and on the great
14:26 of his own left H;
14:27 is in his left H seven times before the
14:28 that is in his H on the tip of
14:28 thumb of his right H, and the great toe
14:29 is in the priest's H he shall put on
16:21 the wilderness by the H of a man who
21:19 foot or an injured H,
25:28 shall remain in the H of him who bought
26:25 be delivered into the H of the enemy.
Num 4:33 of meeting, under the H of Ithamar the son
5:18 And in his H the priest shall have the
5:25 out of the woman's H, and shall wave the
11:23 Moses, "Is the LORD's H shortened?
15:30 anything with a high H, whether he is native
20:11 Moses lifted up his H and struck the rock
20:17 aside to the right H or to the left,
21:2 this people into my H, then I will utterly
21:26 land out of his H, as far as the
21:34 given him into your H, and all his people,
22:7 for divination in their H; and they came to
22:23 drawn sword in his H; and the ass turned
22:29 a sword in my H, for then I would
22:31 drawn sword in his H; and he bowed his
25:7 a spear in his H
27:18 spirit, and lay your H upon him;
31:6 and the trumpets for the alarm in his H
35:17 a stone in the H, by which a man
35:18 of wood in the H, by which a man
35:21 him down with his H, so that he died,
35:25 the manslayer from the H of the avenger of
Deut 1:27 give us into the H of the Amorites, to
2:15 For indeed the H of the LORD was against
2:24 have given into your H Sihon the Amorite, king
2:30 give him into your H, as at this day.
3:2 his land into your H; and you shall do
3:3 God gave into our H Og also, the king
3:8 time out of the H of the two kings
3:24 greatness and thy mighty H; for what god is
4:34 war, by a mighty H and an outstretched arm,
5:15 thence with a mighty H and an outstretched arm;
5:32 aside to the right H or to the left.
6:8 a sign upon your H, and they shall be
6:21 Egypt with a mighty H;
7:8 out with a mighty H, and redeemed you from
7:8 of bondage, from the H of Pharaoh king of
7:19 wonders, the mighty H, and the outstretched arm,
7:24 their kings into your H, and you shall make
8:17 the might of my H have gotten me this
9:26 hast brought out of Egypt with a mighty H
10:3 the mountain with the two tables in my H
11:2 his greatness, his mighty H and his outstretched arm,
11:18 a sign upon your H, and they shall be
13:9 shall kill him; your H shall be first against
13:9 death, and afterwards the H of all the people.
13:17 shall cleave to your H; that the LORD may
14:25 the money in your H, and go to the
15:3 with your brother your H shall release.
15:7 heart or shut your H against your poor brother,
15:8 you shall open your H to him, and lend
15:11 shall open wide your H to your brother, to
16:10 freewill offering from your H, which you shall give
17:7 The H of the witnesses shall be first against
17:7 death, and afterward the H of all the people.
17:11 either to the right H or to the left.
17:20 either to the right H or to the left;
19:5 cut wood, and his H swings the axe to
19:12 him from there, and H him over to the
19:21 eye, tooth for tooth, H for hand, foot for
19:21 for tooth, hand for H, foot for foot.
20:13 gives it into your H you shall put all
23:25 the ears with your H, but you shall not
24:1 puts it in her H and sends her out
24:3 puts it in her H and sends her out
25:11 her husband from the H of him who is
25:11 and puts out her H and seizes him by
25:12 shall cut off her H; your eye shall have
26:4 the basket from your H, and set it down
26:8 Egypt with a mighty H and an outstretched arm,
28:14 day, to the right H or to the left,
28:32 the power of your H to prevent it.
30:9 the work of your H, in the fruit of
32:27 they should say, "Our H is triumphant, the LORD
32:35 their calamity is at H, and their doom comes
32:39 is none that can deliver out of my H
32:40 I lift up my H to heaven, and swear,
32:41 glittering sword, and my H takes hold on judgment,
33:2 holy ones, with flaming fire at his right H
33:3 him were in his H; so they followed in
Josh 1:7 it to the right H or to the left,
2:19 guiltless; but if a H is laid upon any

	4:24	may know that the H of the LORD is
	5:13	drawn sword in his H; and Joshua went to
	6:2	have given into your H Jericho, with its king
	8:1	have given into your H the king of Ai,
	8:7	LORD your God will give it into your H
	8:18	that is in your H toward Ai; for I
	8:18	Ai; for I will give it into your H
	8:18	that was in his H toward the city.
	8:19	had stretched out his H, they ran and entered
	8:26	not draw back his H, with which he stretched
	9:11	'Take provisions in your H for the journey, and
	9:25	we are in your H: do as it seems
	9:26	them out of the H of the people of
	10:6	"Do not relax your H from your servants; come
	10:19	LORD your God has given them into your H
	10:30	its king into the H of Israel; and he
	10:32	gave Lachish into the H of Israel, and he
	11:8	gave them into the H of Israel, who smote
	20:5	the slayer into his H; because he killed his
	20:9	not die by the H of the avenger of
	22:31	of Israel from the H of the LORD."
	23:6	neither to the right H nor to the left,
	24:8	gave them into your H, and you took possession
	24:10	you; so I delivered you out of his H
	24:11	the Jebusites; and I gave them into your H
Judg	1:2	behold, I have given the land into his H
	1:4	the Perizzites into their H; and they defeated ten
	1:35	in Sha-albim, but the H of the house of
	2:15	they marched out, the H of the LORD was
	2:18	saved them from the H of their enemies all
	3:8	sold them into the H of Cushan-rishathaim king of
	3:10	of Mesopotamia into his H; and his hand prevailed
	3:10	hand; and his H prevailed over Cushan-rishathaim.
	3:21	reached with his left H, took the sword from
	3:28	has given your enemies the Moabites into your H
	3:30	that day under the H of Israel.
	4:2	sold them into the H of Jabin king of
	4:7	troops; and I will give him into your H
	4:9	sell Sisera into the H of a woman." Then
	4:14	which the LORD has given Sisera into your H
	4:21	a hammer in her H, and went softly to
	4:24	And the H of the people of Israel bore
	5:26	She put her H to the tent peg and
	5:26	peg and her right H to the workmen's mallet;
	6:1	gave them into the H of Midian seven years.
	6:2	And the H of Midian prevailed over Israel; and
	6:9	delivered you from the H of the Egyptians, and
	6:9	Egyptians, and from the H of all who oppressed
	6:13	given us into the H of Midian."
	6:14	deliver Israel from the H of Midian; do not
	6:21	that was in his H, and touched the meat
	6:36	deliver Israel by my H, as thou hast said,
	6:37	deliver Israel by my H, as thou hast said."
	7:2	the Midianites into their H, lest Israel vaunt
	7:2	me, saying, 'My own H has delivered me.'
	7:7	the Midianites into your H; and let all the
	7:9	camp; for I have given it into your H
	7:14	of Israel; into his H God has given Midian
	7:15	has given the host of Midian into your H
	8:6	Zalmunna already in your H, that we should give
	8:7	and Zalmunna into my H, I will flail your
	8:15	Zalmunna already in your H, that we should give
	8:22	us out of the H of Midian."
	8:34	rescued them from the H of all their enemies
	9:17	rescued you from the H of Midian;
	9:29	Would that this people were under my H
	9:48	an axe in his H, and cut down a
	10:7	sold them into the H of the Philistines and
	10:7	Philistines and into the H of the Ammonites,
	10:12	me, and I delivered you out of their H
	11:21	his people into the H of Israel, and they
	11:30	the Ammonites into my H,
	11:32	them; and the LORD gave them into his H
	12:2	you, you did not deliver me from their H
	12:3	my life in my H, and crossed over against
	12:3	gave them into my H; why then have you
	13:1	gave them into the H of the Philistines for
	13:5	deliver Israel from the H of the Philistines."
	14:6	a kid; and he had nothing in his H
	15:15	and put out his H and seized it, and
	15:17	jawbone out of his H; and that place was
	15:18	great deliverance by the H of thy servant; and
	16:23	god has given Samson our enemy into our H
	16:24	our enemy into our H, the ravager of our
	16:26	held him by the H, "Let me feel the
	16:29	upon them, his right H on the one and
	16:29	one and his left H on the other.
	17:3	the LORD from my H for my son, to
	18:19	"Keep quiet, put your H upon your mouth, and
	20:28	for tomorrow I will give them into your H
Ruth	1:13	your sake that the H of the LORD has
	4:5	the field from the H of Naomi, you are
	4:9	have bought from the H of Naomi all that
1Sam	2:13	three-pronged fork in his H,
	5:6	The H of the LORD was heavy upon the
	5:7	with us; for his H is heavy upon us
	5:9	brought it around, the H of the LORD was
	5:11	The H of God was very heavy there;
	6:3	to you why his H does not turn away
	6:5	he will lighten his H from off you and
	6:9	it is not his H that struck us, it
	7:3	you out of the H of the Philistines."
	7:8	save us from the H of the Philistines."
	7:13	And the H of the LORD was against the
	7:14	their territory from the H of the Philistines.
	9:16	my people from the H of the Philistines; for
	10:1	save them from the H of their enemies round
	10:4	of bread, which you shall accept from their H
	10:7	you, do whatever your H finds to do, for
	10:18	delivered you from the H of the Egyptians and
	10:18	Egyptians and from the H of all the kingdoms
	11:7	of Israel by the H of messengers, saying, "Whoever
	12:3	Or from whose H have I taken a bribe
	12:4	oppressed us or taken anything from any man's H
	12:5	that you have not found anything in my H
	12:9	sold them into the H of Sisera, commander of
	12:9	Hazor, and into the H of the Philistines, and
	12:9	Philistines, and into the H of the king of
	12:10	us out of the H of our enemies, and
	12:11	you out of the H of your enemies on
	12:15	the LORD, then the H of the LORD will
	13:22	spear found in the H of any of the
	14:10	for the LORD has given them into our H
	14:12	given them into the H of Israel."
	14:19	and Saul said to the priest, "Withdraw your H
	14:26	no man put his H to his mouth; for
	14:27	that was in his H, and dipped it in
	14:27	honeycomb, and put his H to his mouth; and
	14:37	give them into the H of Israel?" But he
	14:43	that was in my H; here I am, I
	16:23	played it with his H; so Saul was refreshed,
	17:37	deliver me from the H of this Philistine." And
	17:40	his staff in his H, and chose five smooth
	17:40	sling was in his H, and he drew near
	17:46	deliver you into my H, and I will strike
	17:47	LORD's and he will give you into our H
	17:49	And David put his H in his bag and
	17:50	no sword in the H of David.
	17:57	with the head of the Philistine in his H
	18:10	his spear in his H;
	18:17	thought, "Let not my H be upon him, but
	18:17	him, but let the H of the Philistines be
	18:21	him, and that the H of the Philistines may
	18:25	David fall by the H of the Philistines.
	19:5	his life in his H and he slew the
	19:9	his spear in his H; and David was playing
	20:19	the matter was in H, and remain beside yonder
	21:3	Now then, what have you at H
	21:4	no common bread at H, but there is holy
	21:8	not here a spear or a sword at H
	22:6	his spear in his H, and all his servants
	22:17	the LORD; because their H also is with David,
	22:17	not put forth their H to fall upon the
	23:4	for I will give the Philistines into your H
	23:6	he came down with an ephod in his H
	23:7	given him into my H; for he has shut
	23:11	the men of Keilah surrender me into his H
	23:12	my men into the H of Saul?" And the
	23:14	but God did not give him into his H
	23:16	Horesh, and strengthened his H in God.
	23:17	"Fear not; for the H of Saul my father
	23:20	shall be to surrender him into the king's H
	24:4	your enemy into your H, and you shall do
	24:6	to put forth my H against him, seeing he
	24:10	you today into my H in the cave; and
	24:10	not put forth my H against my lord; for
	24:11	your robe in my H; for by the fact
	24:12	upon you; but my H shall not be against
	24:13	forth wickedness'; but my H shall not be against
	24:15	plead my cause, and deliver me from your H
	24:20	kingdom of Israel shall be established in your H
	25:8	whatever you have at H to your servants and

25:26 vengeance with your own H, now then let your
25:33 bloodguilt and from avenging myself with my own H
25:35 David received from her H what she had brought
25:39 I received at the H of Nabal, and has
26:8 your enemy into your H this day; now therefore
26:9 can put forth his H against the LORD's anointed,
26:11 should put forth my H against the LORD's anointed;
26:23 gave you into my H today, and I would
26:23 not put forth my H against the LORD's anointed.
27:1 one day by the H of Saul; there is
27:1 Israel, and I shall escape out of his H
28:17 kingdom out of your H, and given it to
28:19 with you into the H of the Philistines; and
28:19 Israel also into the H of the Philistines."
28:21 my life in my H, and have hearkened to
30:23 and given into our H the band that came
2Sam 1:14 to put forth your H to destroy the LORD's
2:19 neither to the right H nor to the left
2:21 aside to your right H or to your left,
3:8 given you into the H of David; and yet
3:12 me, and behold, my H shall be with you
3:18 David, saying, 'By the H of my servant David
3:18 people Israel from the H of the Philistines, and
3:18 Philistines, and from the H of all their enemies.'"
4:11 his blood at your H, and destroy you from
5:19 Wilt thou give them into my H
5:19 I will certainly give the Philistines into your H
6:6 Uzzah put out his H to the ark of
6:7 he put forth his H to the ark; and
8:1 Metheg-ammah out of the H of the Philistines.
11:14 sent it by the H of Uriah.
12:7 you out of the H of Saul;
13:5 may see it, and eat it from her H
13:6 my sight, that I may eat from her H
13:10 the chamber, that I may eat from your H
13:19 and she laid her H on her head, and
14:16 his servant from the H of the man who
14:19 king said, "Is the H of Joab with you
14:19 turn to the right H or to the left
15:5 would put out his H, and take hold of
16:6 were on his right H and on his left.
16:8 the kingdom into the H of your son Absalom.
18:12 I felt in my H the weight of a
18:12 not put forth my H against the king's son;
18:13 Absalom.' On the other H, if I had dealt
18:14 three darts in his H, and thrust them into
18:28 men who raised their H against my lord the
19:9 delivered us from the H of our enemies, and
19:9 saved us from the H of the Philistines; and
20:9 beard with his right H to kiss him.
20:10 which was in Joab's H; so Joab struck him
20:21 has lifted up his H against King David; give
21:20 six fingers on each H, and six toes on
21:22 they fell by the H of David and by
21:22 David and by the H of his servants.
22:1 delivered him from the H of all his enemies,
22:1 enemies, and from the H of Saul.
23:6 be taken with the H;
23:10 the Philistines until his H was weary, and his
23:10 was weary, and his H cleaved to the sword;
23:21 a spear in his H; but Benaiah went down
23:21 out of the Egyptian's H, and slew him with
24:14 us fall into the H of the LORD, for
24:14 not fall into the H of man."
24:16 angel stretched forth his H toward Jerusalem to
24:16 the people, "It is enough; now stay your H
24:17 Let thy H, I pray thee, be against me
1Kgs 2:46 was established in the H of Solomon.
8:15 Israel, who with his H has fulfilled what he
8:24 mouth, and with thy H hast fulfilled it this
8:42 name, and thy mighty H, and of thy outstretched
11:12 it out of the H of your son.
11:26 also lifted up his H against the king.
11:27 he lifted up his H against the king.
11:31 the kingdom from the H of Solomon, and will
11:34 kingdom out of his H; but I will make
11:35 out of his son's H, and will give it
13:4 Jeroboam stretched out his H from the altar, saying,
13:4 And his H, which he stretched out against him,
13:6 for me, that my H may be restored to
13:6 LORD; and the king's H was restored to him,
17:11 "Bring me a morsel of bread in your H
18:9 your servant into the H of Ahab, to kill
18:44 cloud like a man's H is rising out of
18:46 And the H of the LORD was on Elijah;
20:13 give it into your H this day; and you
20:28 great multitude into your H, and you shall know
20:42 go out of your H the man whom I
22:3 it out of the H of the king of
22:6 give it into the H of the king."
22:12 give it into the H of the king."
22:15 give it into the H of the king."
22:19 him on his right H and on his left;
2Kgs 3:10 give them into the H of Moab."
3:13 give them into the H of Moab."
3:18 the Moabites into your H,
4:29 my staff in your H, and go.
5:11 God, and wave his H over the place, and
5:20 not accepting from his H what he brought.
5:24 took them from their H, and put them in
6:7 he reached out his H and took it.
7:2 the captain on whose H the king leaned said
7:17 the captain on whose H he leaned to have
9:1 of oil in your H, and go to Ramoth-gilead.
10:15 Jehu said, "If it is, give me your H
10:15 So he gave him his H
11:8 his weapons in his H; and whoever approaches the
11:11 his weapons in his H, from the south side
12:7 from your acquaintances, but H it over for the
12:15 the men into whose H they delivered the money
13:3 them continually into the H of Hazael king of
13:3 Syria and into the H of Ben-hadad the son
13:5 they escaped from the H of the Syrians; and
14:5 was firmly in his H he killed his servants
14:27 saved them by the H of Jeroboam the son
16:7 rescue me from the H of the king of
16:7 Syria and from the H of the king of
17:7 Egypt from under the H of Pharaoh king of
17:20 gave them into the H of spoilers, until he
17:39 you out of the H of all your enemies."
18:21 which will pierce the H of any man who
18:29 be able to deliver you out of my H
18:30 be given into the H of the king of
18:33 land out of the H of the king of
18:34 Have they delivered Samaria out of my H
18:35 countries out of my H, that the LORD should
18:35 the LORD should deliver Jerusalem out of my H
19:10 be given into the H of the king of
19:14 the letter from the H of the messengers, and
19:19 beseech thee, from his H, that all the kingdoms
20:6 city out of the H of the king of
21:14 give them into the H of their enemies, and
22:2 aside to the right H or to the left.
22:5 be given into the H of the workmen who
22:7 is delivered into their H, for they deal honestly."
22:9 delivered it into the H of the workmen who
1Chr 4:10 border, and that thy H might be with me,
5:10 who fell by their H; and they dwelt in
6:15 into exile by the H of Nebuchadnezzar.
6:39 stood on his right H, namely, Asaph the son
6:44 On the left H were their brethren the sons
11:23 Egyptian had in his H a spear like a
11:23 out of the Egyptian's H, and slew him with
12:2 right or the left H; they were Benjaminites, Saul's
13:9 Uzzah put out his H to hold the ark,
13:10 he put forth his H to the ark; and
14:10 Wilt thou give them into my H
14:10 up, and I will give them into your H
14:11 my enemies by my H, like a bursting flood."
18:1 villages out of the H of the Philistines.
20:6 six fingers on each H, and six toes on
20:8 they fell by the H of David and by
20:8 David and by the H of his servants.
21:13 me fall into the H of the LORD, for
21:13 not fall into the H of man."
21:15 destroying angel, "It is enough; now stay your H
21:16 heaven, and in his H a drawn sword stretched
21:17 Let thy H, I pray thee, O LORD my
22:18 the land into my H; and the land is
28:19 the writing from the H of the LORD concerning
29:12 In thy H are power and might; and in
29:12 might; and in thy H it is to make
29:16 name comes from thy H and is all thy
2Chr 6:4 Israel, who with his H has fulfilled what he
6:15 mouth, and with thy H hast fulfilled it this
6:32 name, and thy mighty H, and thy outstretched arm,
12:5 abandoned you to the H of Shishak.'"
12:7 upon Jerusalem by the H of Shishak.
13:8 the LORD in the H of the sons of
13:16 before Judah, and God gave them into their H
16:8 on the LORD, he gave them into your H
17:5 the kingdom in his H; and all Judah brought

18:5 give it into the H of the king."
18:11 give it into the H of the king."
18:14 and triumph; they will be given into your H
18:18 standing on his right H and on his left;
20:6 In thy H are power and might, so that
23:7 his weapons in his H; and whoever enters the
23:10 his weapon in his H, from the south side
24:24 LORD delivered into their H a very great army,
25:3 was firmly in his H he killed his servants
25:15 did not deliver their own people from your H
25:20 give them into the H of their enemies, because
26:19 a censer in his H to burn incense, and
28:5 gave him into the H of the king of
28:5 also given into the H of the king of
28:9 gave them into your H, but you have slain
30:6 have escaped from the H of the kings of
30:12 The H of God was also upon Judah to
30:16 they received from the H of the Levites.
32:11 deliver us from the H of the king of
32:13 able to deliver their lands out of my H
32:14 his people from my H, that your God should
32:14 should be able to deliver you from my H
32:15 his people from my H or from the hand
32:15 hand or from the H of my fathers.
32:15 will your God deliver you out of my H
32:17 Hezekiah will not deliver his people from my H
32:22 of Jerusalem from the H of Sennacherib king of
32:22 Assyria and from the H of all his enemies;
34:17 delivered it into the H of the overseers and
36:17 or aged; he gave them all into his H
Ezra 5:12 gave them into the H of Nebuchadnezzar king of
6:12 shall put forth a H to alter this, or
7:6 he asked, for the H of the LORD his
7:9 Jerusalem, for the good H of his God was
7:14 which is in your H,
7:25 which is in your H, appoint magistrates and judges
7:28 took courage, for the H of the LORD my
8:18 And by the good H of our God upon
8:22 told the king, "The H of our God is
8:26 weighed out into their H six hundred and fifty
8:31 go to Jerusalem; the H of our God was
8:31 delivered us from the H of the enemy and
9:2 in this faithlessness the H of the officials and
9:7 been given into the H of the kings of
Neh 1:10 by thy great power and by thy strong H
2:8 asked, for the good H of my God was
2:18 told them of the H of my God which
4:17 that each with one H labored on the work
4:23 our clothes; each kept his weapon in his H
6:5 to me with an open letter in his H
8:4 Ma-aseiah on his right H; and Pedaiah, Mishael,
8:4 Zechariah, and Meshullam on his left H
9:27 give them into the H of their enemies, who
9:27 saved them from the H of their enemies.
9:28 abandon them to the H of their enemies, so
9:30 give them into the H of the peoples of
11:24 was at the king's H in all matters concerning
Tob 7:13 taking her by the H he gave her to
13:2 there is no one who can escape his H
Jud 2:7 my armies, and will H them over to be
2:11 spare and you shall H them over to slaughter
2:12 I have spoken my H will execute.
6:10 him to Bethulia and H him over to the
8:33 enemies, the Lord will deliver Israel by my H
9:10 their arrogance by the H of a woman.
10:15 will escort you and H you over to him.
12:4 carries out by my H what he has determined
13:14 our enemies by my H this very night!"
13:15 him down by the H of a woman.
14:6 of Holofernes in the H of one of the
16:6 foiled them by the H of a woman.
Esth 3:10 signet ring from his H and gave it to
5:2 Esther the golden scepter that was in his H
9:10 but they laid no H on the plunder.
14:4 but thee, for my danger is in my H
14:14 save us by thy H, and help me, who
16:7 ancient records which we H on as from investigation
16:7 on as from investigation of matters close at H
Job 1:11 But put forth thy H now, and touch all
1:12 only upon himself do not put forth your H
2:5 But put forth thy H now, and touch his
2:10 receive good at the H of God, and shall
5:15 the needy from the H of the mighty.
6:9 would let loose his H and cut me off!
6:23 Or, 'Deliver me from the adversary's H
6:23 'Ransom me from the H of oppressors?
8:20 man, nor take the H of evildoers.
9:24 is given into the H of the wicked; he
9:33 who might lay his H upon us both.
10:7 there is none to deliver out of thy H
11:14 iniquity is in your H, put it far away,
12:6 are secure, who bring their god in their H
12:9 not know that the H of the LORD has
12:10 In his H is the life of every living
13:14 my teeth, and put my life in my H
13:21 thy face: withdraw thy H far from me, and
15:23 is ready at his H;
15:25 has stretched forth his H against God, and bids
19:21 my friends, for the H of God has touched
21:5 appalled, and lay your H upon your mouth.
21:16 him?' Behold, is not their prosperity in their H
23:2 complaint is bitter, his H is heavy in spite
23:9 him; on the left H I seek him, but
23:9 turn to the right H, but I cannot see
26:13 were made fair; his H pierced the fleeing serpent.
27:11 teach you concerning the H of God; what is
28:9 "Man puts his H to the flinty rock, and
29:9 talking, and laid their H on their mouth;
29:20 ever new in my H
30:12 On my right H the rabble rise, they drive
30:21 the might of thy H thou dost persecute me.
30:24 ruins stretch out his H, and in his disaster
31:21 I have raised my H against the fatherless, because
31:25 great, or because my H had gotten much;
31:27 mouth has kissed my H;
34:20 the mighty are taken away by no human H
35:7 him; or what does he receive from your H
37:7 He seals up the H of every man, that
40:4 I lay my H on my mouth.
40:14 that your own right H can give you victory.
Ps 10:12 God, lift up thy H; forget not the afflicted.
16:8 is at my right H, I shall not be
16:11 joy, in thy right H are pleasures for evermore.
17:7 seek refuge from their adversaries at thy right H
17:14 from men by thy H, O LORD, from men
18:35 salvation, and thy right H supported me, and thy
20:6 holy heaven with mighty victories by his right H
21:8 Your H will find out all your enemies; your
21:8 your enemies; your right H will find out those
31:5 Into thy H I commit my spirit; thou hast
31:8 delivered me into the H of the enemy; thou
31:15 times are in thy H; deliver me from the
31:15 deliver me from the H of my enemies and
32:4 day and night thy H was heavy upon me;
36:11 upon me, nor the H of the wicked drive
37:24 for the LORD is the stay of his H
38:2 into me, and thy H has come down on
39:10 I am spent by the blows of thy H
44:2 thou with thy own H didst drive out the
44:3 victory; but thy right H, and thy arm, and
45:4 right; let your right H teach you dread deeds!
45:9 honor; at your right H stands the queen in
48:10 Thy right H is filled with victory;
55:20 companion stretched out his H against his friends, he
60:5 victory by thy right H and answer us!
63:8 to thee; thy right H upholds me.
71:4 my God, from the H of the wicked, from
73:23 continually with thee; thou dost hold my right H
74:11 thou hold back thy H, why dost thou keep
74:11 thou keep thy right H in thy bosom?
75:8 For in the H of the LORD there is
77:2 in the night my H is stretched out without
77:10 grief that the right H of the Most High
77:20 a flock by the H of Moses and Aaron.
78:54 mountain which his right H had won.
78:61 his glory to the H of the foe.
78:72 he tended them, and guided them with skilful H
80:15 stock which thy right H planted.
80:17 But let thy H be upon the man of
80:17 man of thy right H, the son of man
81:14 enemies, and turn my H against their foes.
82:4 deliver them from the H of the wicked."
85:9 his salvation is at H for those who fear
88:5 more, for they are cut off from thy H
89:13 arm; strong is thy H, high thy right hand.
89:13 arm; strong is thy hand, high thy right H
89:21 him; so that my H shall ever abide with
89:25 I will set his H on the sea and
89:25 sea and his right H on the rivers.
89:42 hast exalted the right H of his foes; thou
89:44 the scepter from his H, and cast his throne
91:7 thousand at your right H; but it will not

H

95:4 In his H are the depths of the earth;
95:7 of his pasture, and the sheep of his H
97:10 delivers them from the H of the wicked.
98:1 His right H and his holy arm have gotten
104:28 when thou openest thy H, they are filled with
106:10 saved them from the H of the foe, and
106:26 Therefore he raised his H and swore to them
106:41 gave them into the H of the nations, so
108:6 help by thy right H, and answer me!
109:27 that this is thy H; thou, O LORD, hast
109:31 stands at the right H of the needy, to
110:1 "Sit at my right H, till I make your
110:5 is at your right H; he will shatter kings
118:15 the righteous: "The right H of the LORD does
118:16 does valiantly, the right H of the LORD is
118:16 is exalted, the right H of the LORD does
119:109 my life in my H continually, but I do
119:173 Let thy H be ready to help me, for
121:5 the LORD is your shade on your right H
123:2 servants look to the H of their master, as
123:2 a maid to the H of her mistress, so
127:4 Like arrows in the H of a warrior are
129:7 does not fill his H or the binder of
136:12 ever; with a strong H and an outstretched arm,
137:5 Jerusalem, let my right H wither!
138:7 dost stretch out thy H against the wrath of
138:7 enemies, and thy right H delivers me.
139:5 before, and layest thy H upon me.
139:10 sea, even there thy H shall lead me, and
139:10 me, and thy right H shall hold me.
144:7 Stretch forth thy H from on high, rescue me
144:7 many waters, from the H of aliens,
144:8 lies, and whose right H is a right hand
144:8 hand is a right H of falsehood.
144:11 deliver me from the H of aliens, whose mouths
144:11 lies, and whose right H is a right hand
144:11 hand is a right H of falsehood.
145:16 Thou openest thy H, thou satisfiest the desire of

Prov 1:24 have stretched out my H and no one has
3:16 is in her right H; in her left hand
3:16 hand; in her left H are riches and honor.
6:5 a bird from the H of the fowler.
10:4 A slack H causes poverty, but the hand of
10:4 causes poverty, but the H of the diligent makes
12:14 work of a man's H comes back to him.
12:24 The H of the diligent will rule, while the
17:16 a price in his H to buy wisdom, when
19:24 The sluggard buries his H in the dish, and
21:1 of water in the H of the LORD; he
26:6 a message by the H of a fool cuts
26:9 goes up into the H of a drunkard is
26:15 The sluggard buries his H in the dish; it
27:16 wind or to grasp oil in his right H
30:32 devising evil, put your H on your mouth.
31:20 She opens her H to the poor, and reaches

Eccl 2:24 saw, is from the H of God;
5:14 a son, but he has nothing in his H
5:15 toil, which he may carry away in his H
7:18 that withhold not your H; for he who fears
9:1 deeds are in the H of God; whether it
9:10 Whatever your H finds to do, do it with
11:6 evening withhold not your H; for you do not

Song 2:6 O that his left H were under my head,
2:6 and that his right H embraced me!
5:4 My beloved put his H to the latch, and
7:1 are like jewels, the work of a master H
8:3 O that his left H were under my head,
8:3 and that his right H embraced me!

Wis 2:18 deliver him from the H of his adversaries.
3:1 righteous are in the H of God, and no
5:16 beautiful diadem from the H of the Lord, because
5:16 because with his right H he will cover them,
7:16 words are in his H, as are all understanding
9:16 and what is at H we find with labor;
10:20 one accord thy defending H,
11:1 their works by the H of a holy prophet.
11:17 For thy all-powerful H, which created the world out
13:10 a useless stone, the work of an ancient H
14:6 and guided by thy H left to the world
16:15 To escape from thy H is impossible;
19:8 those protected by thy H passed through as one

Sir 4:9 is wronged from the H of the wrongdoer; and
4:19 will forsake him, and H him over to his
4:31 Let not your H be extended to receive, but
5:12 if not, put your H on your mouth.
7:32 Stretch forth your H to the poor, so that
8:16 no help is at H, he will strike you
15:16 water: stretch out your H for whichever you wish.
21:19 his feet, and like manacles on his right H
22:2 picks it up will shake it off his H
27:19 to escape from your H, so you have let
29:1 him with his H keeps the commandments.
29:26 you have anything at H, let me have it
31:14 not reach out your H for everything you see,
31:18 not reach out your H before they do.
33:13 As clay in the H of the potter—
33:13 men are in the H of him who made
33:21 should look to the H of you sons.
35:10 as generously as your H has found.
36:3 Lift up thy H against foreign nations and let
36:6 further wonders; make thy H and thy right arm
39:1 On the other H he who devotes himself to
46:4 Was not the sun held back by his H
47:4 when he lifted his H with a stone in
47:5 strength in his right H to slay a man
48:18 he lifted up his H against Zion and made
48:20 delivered them by the H of Isaiah.
49:11 signet on the right H,
50:15 he reached out his H to the cup and
51:3 devour me, from the H of those who sought
51:8 save them from the H of their enemies.

Is 1:25 I will turn my H against you and will
5:25 he stretched out his H against them and smote
5:25 turned away and his H is stretched out still.
6:6 me, having in his H a burning coal which
8:11 me with his strong H upon me, and warned
9:12 turned away and his H is stretched out still.
9:17 turned away and his H is stretched out still.
9:21 turned away and his H is stretched out still.
10:4 turned away and his H is stretched out still.
10:10 As my H has reached to the kingdoms of
10:13 the strength of my H I have done it,
10:14 My H has found like a nest the wealth
11:8 child shall put his H on the adder's den.
11:11 Lord will extend his H yet a second time
11:14 shall put forth their H against Edom and Moab,
11:15 and will wave his H over the River with
13:2 to them; wave the H for them to enter
13:22 time is close at H and its days will
14:26 and this is the H that is stretched out
14:27 His H is stretched out, and who will turn
19:4 the Egyptians into the H of a hard master;
19:16 with fear before the H which the LORD of
22:21 your authority to his H; and he shall be
23:11 has stretched out his H over the sea, he
25:10 For the H of the LORD will rest on
26:11 O LORD, thy H is lifted up, but they
28:4 up as soon as it is in his H
31:3 LORD stretches out his H, the helper will stumble,
34:17 lot for them, his H has portioned it out
36:6 which will pierce the H of any man who
36:15 be given into the H of the king of
36:18 land out of the H of the king of
36:19 Have they delivered Samaria out of my H
36:20 countries out of my H, that the LORD should
36:20 the LORD should deliver Jerusalem out of my H
37:10 be given into the H of the king of
37:14 the letter from the H of the messengers, and
37:20 save us from his H, that all the kingdoms
38:6 city out of the H of the king of
40:2 received from the LORD's H double for all her
40:12 the hollow of his H and marked off the
41:10 I will uphold you with my victorious right H
41:13 God, hold your right H; it is I who
41:20 understand together, that the H of the LORD has
42:6 taken you by the H and kept you; I
43:13 can deliver from my H; I work and who
44:5 will write on his H, 'The LORDs,' and surname
44:20 "Is there not a lie in my right H
45:1 to Cyrus, whose right H I have grasped, to
47:6 gave them into your H, you showed them no
48:13 My H laid the foundation of the earth, and
48:13 earth, and my right H spread out the heavens;
49:2 the shadow of his H he hid me; he
49:22 will lift up my H to the nations, and
50:2 Is my H shortened, that it cannot redeem?
50:11 you have from my H: you shall lie down
51:16 the shadow of my H, stretching out the heavens
51:17 have drunk at the H of the LORD the
51:18 take her by the H among all the sons
51:22 have taken from your H the cup of staggering;
51:23 put it into the H of your tormentors, who

	53:10	shall prosper in his H;
	56:2	it, and keeps his H from doing any evil."
	59:1	Behold, the LORD's H is not shortened, that it
	62:3	of beauty in the H of the LORD, and
	62:3	royal diadem in the H of your God.
	62:8	sworn by his right H and by his mighty
	63:12	go at the right H of Moses, who divided
	64:7	delivered us into the H of our iniquities.
	64:8	potter; we are all the work of thy H
	66:2	All these things my H has made, and so
	66:14	be known that the H of the LORD is
Jer	1:9	LORD put forth his H and touched my mouth;
	6:9	a grape-gatherer pass your H again over its
	6:12	will stretch out my H against the inhabitants of
	11:21	will die by our H –
	15:6	have stretched out my H against you and destroyed
	15:17	sat alone, because thy H was upon me, for
	15:21	you out of the H of the wicked, and
	17:4	You shall loosen your H from your heritage which
	18:4	spoiled in the potter's H, and he reworked it
	18:6	clay in the potter's H, so are you in
	18:6	are you in my H, O house of Israel.
	19:7	enemies, and by the H of those who seek
	20:4	all Judah into the H of the king of
	20:5	of Judah into the H of their enemies, who
	20:13	the needy from the H of evildoers.
	21:5	against you with outstretched H and strong arm, in
	21:7	and famine, into the H of Nebuchadrezzar king of
	21:7	Babylon and into the H of their enemies, into
	21:7	their enemies, into the H of those who seek
	21:10	be given into the H of the king of
	21:12	and deliver from the H of the oppressor him
	22:3	and deliver from the H of the oppressor him
	22:24	ring on my right H, yet I would tear
	22:25	give you into the H of those who seek
	22:25	your life, into the H of those of whom
	22:25	afraid, even into the H of Nebuchadrezzar king of
	22:25	Babylon and into the H of the Chaldeans.
	23:23	I a God at H, says the LORD, and
	25:15	me: "Take from my H this cup of the
	25:17	cup from the LORD's H, and made all the
	25:28	the cup from your H to drink, then you
	26:24	But the H of Ahikam the son of Shaphan
	27:3	of Sidon by the H of the envoys who
	27:6	these lands into the H of Nebuchadnezzar, the king
	27:8	LORD, until I have consumed it by his H
	29:3	was sent by the H of Elasah the son
	29:21	deliver them into the H of Nebuchadrezzar king of
	31:32	took them by the H to bring them out
	32:3	this city into the H of the king of
	32:4	escape out of the H of the Chaldeans, but
	32:4	be given into the H of the king of
	32:21	wonders, with a strong H and outstretched arm, and
	32:28	Chaldeans and into the H of Nebuchadrezzar king of
	32:36	is given into the H of the king of
	34:2	this city into the H of the king of
	34:3	not escape from his H, but shall surely be
	34:3	and delivered into his H; you shall see the
	34:20	give them into the H of their enemies and
	34:20	enemies and into the H of those who seek
	34:21	will give into the H of their enemies and
	34:21	enemies and into the H of those who seek
	34:21	their lives, into the H of the army of
	36:14	Baruch, "Take in your H the scroll that you
	36:14	the scroll in his H and came to them.
	37:17	be delivered into the H of the king of
	38:3	be given into the H of the army of
	38:16	deliver you into the H of these men who
	38:18	be given into the H of the Chaldeans, and
	38:18	fire, and you shall not escape from their H
	38:23	not escape from their H, but shall be seized
	39:17	be given into the H of the men of
	42:11	save you and to deliver you from his H
	43:3	deliver us into the H of the Chaldeans, that
	44:30	of Egypt into the H of his enemies and
	44:30	enemies and into the H of those who seek
	44:30	of Judah into the H of Nebuchadrezzar king of
	46:24	be delivered into the H of a people from
	46:26	deliver them into the H of those who seek
	46:26	their life, into the H of Nebuchadrezzar king of
	48:16	Moab is near at H and his affliction hastens
	51:7	cup in the LORD's H, making all the earth
	51:25	will stretch out my H against you, and roll
Lam	1:7	people fell into the H of the foe, and
	1:14	a yoke; by his H they were fastened together;
	2:3	from them his right H in the face of
	2:4	enemy, with his right H set like a foe;
	2:7	has delivered into the H of the enemy the
	2:8	he restrained not his H from destroying; he caused
	3:3	me he turns his H again and again the
	4:6	in a moment, no H being laid on it.
	5:6	We have given the H to Egypt, and to
	5:8	there is none to deliver us from their H
Bar	2:11	Egypt with a mighty H and with signs and
	4:18	deliver you from the H of your enemies.
	4:21	from the power and H of the enemy.
	6:15	dagger in its right H, and has an axe;
Ezek	1:3	river Chebar; and the H of the LORD was
	2:9	I looked, behold, a H was stretched out to
	3:14	of my spirit, the H of the LORD being
	3:18	but his blood I will require at your H
	3:20	but his blood I will require at your H
	3:22	And the H of the LORD was there upon
	6:14	will stretch out my H against them, and make
	8:1	sitting before me, the H of the Lord GOD
	8:3	the form of a H, and took me by
	8:11	his censer in his H, and the smoke of
	9:1	city, each with his destroying weapon in his H
	9:2	for slaughter in his H, and with them was
	10:7	stretched forth his H from between the cherubim
	10:8	form of a human H under their wings.
	12:23	The days are at H, and the fulfilment of
	13:9	My H will be against the prophets who see
	13:21	people out of your H, and they shall be
	13:21	no more in your H as prey; and you
	13:23	I will deliver my people out of your H
	14:9	will stretch out my H against him, and will
	14:13	I stretch out my H against it, and break
	16:27	I stretched out my H against you, and diminished
	16:39	give you into the H of your lovers, and
	17:18	because he gave his H and yet did all
	18:8	increase, withholds his H from iniquity, executes true
	18:17	a garment, withholds his H from iniquity, takes no
	20:22	But I withheld my H, and acted for the
	20:33	surely with a mighty H and an outstretched arm,
	20:34	scattered, with a mighty H and an outstretched arm,
	21:11	be given into the H of the slayer.
	21:22	Into his right H comes the lot for Jerusalem,
	23:31	therefore I will give her cup into your H
	25:7	have stretched out my H against you, and will
	25:7	against you, and will H you over as spoil
	25:13	will stretch out my H against Edom, and cut
	25:14	upon Edom by the H of my people Israel;
	25:16	will stretch out my H against the Philistines, and
	28:10	the uncircumcised by the H of foreigners; for I
	29:7	grasped you with the H, you broke, and tore
	30:10	of Egypt, by the H of Nebuchadrezzar king of
	30:12	the land into the H of evil men; I
	30:12	in it, by the H of foreigners; I, the
	30:22	I will make the sword fall from his H
	30:24	my sword in his H; but I will break
	30:25	my sword into the H of the king of
	31:11	give it into the H of a mighty one
	33:6	his blood I will require at the watchman's H
	33:8	but his blood I will require at your H
	33:22	Now the H of the LORD had been upon
	34:10	my sheep at their H, and put a stop
	34:27	deliver them from the H of those who enslaved
	35:3	will stretch out my H against you, and I
	37:1	The H of the LORD was upon me, and
	37:17	stick, that they may become one in your H
	37:19	(which is in the H of Ephraim) and the
	37:19	stick, that they may be one in my H
	37:20	write are in your H before their eyes,
	39:3	bow from your left H, and will make your
	39:3	make your arrows drop out of your right H
	39:21	have executed, and my H which I have laid
	39:23	gave them into the H of their adversaries, and
	40:1	that very day, the H of the LORD was
	40:3	measuring reed in his H; and he was standing
	40:5	reed in the man's H was six long cubits,
	47:3	a line in his H, the man measured a
Dan	1:2	of Judah into his H, with some of the
	2:34	out by no human H, and it smote the
	2:38	glory, and into whose H he has given, wherever
	2:45	mountain by no human H, and that it broke
	3:17	us out of your H, O king.
	3:89	saved us from the H of death, and delivered
	4:35	none can stay his H or say to him,
	5:5	fingers of a man's H appeared and wrote on
	5:5	the king saw the H as it wrote.
	5:23	the God in whose H is your breath, and

5:24 from his presence the H was sent, and this
7:25 be given into his H for a time, two
8:25 deceit prosper under his H, and in his own
8:25 but, by no human H, he shall be broken.
9:15 Egypt with a mighty H, and hast made thee
10:10 And behold, a H touched me and set me
11:11 multitude, but it shall be given into his H
11:41 delivered out of his H: Edom and Moab and
11:42 shall stretch out his H against the countries, and
12:7 stream, raised his right H and his left hand
12:7 hand and his left H toward heaven; and I
14:29 the king, they said, H Daniel over to us,
Hos 2:10 no one shall rescue her out of my H
7:6 he stretched out his H with mockers.
11:8 How can I H you over, O Israel!
Joel 3:8 your daughters into the H of the sons of
Amos 1:8 I will turn my H against Ekron; and the
5:19 and leaned with his H against the wall, and
7:7 plumb line, with a plumb line in his H
9:2 from there shall my H take them; though they
Jon 4:11 not know their right H from their left, and
Mic 2:1 because it is in the power of their H
4:10 redeem you from the H of your enemies.
5:9 Your H shall be lifted up over your adversaries,
5:12 off sorceries from your H, and you shall have
7:4 punishment, has come; now their confusion is at H
Hab 2:16 in the LORD's right H will come around to
3:4 rays flashed from his H; and there he veiled
Zeph 1:4 will stretch out my H against Judah, and against
1:7 the LORD is at H; the LORD has prepared
2:13 will stretch out his H against the north, and
Zech 2:1 a man with a measuring line in his H
2:9 I will shake my H over them, and they
3:1 standing at his right H to accuse him.
4:10 the plummet in the H of Zerubbabel.
8:4 each with staff in H for very age.
11:6 fall each into the H of his shepherd, and
11:6 and each into the H of his king; and
11:6 earth, and I will deliver none from their H
13:7 I will turn my H against the little ones.
14:13 lay hold on the H of his fellow, and
14:13 his fellow, and the H of the one will
14:13 be raised against the H of the other;
Mal 1:9 a gift from your H, will he show favor
1:10 I will not accept an offering from your H
1:13 Shall I accept that from your H
2:13 offering or accepts it with favor at your H
1Mac 2:22 religion to the right H or to the left."
2:48 they never let the sinner gain the upper H
3:6 confounded; and deliverance prospered by his H
4:30 mighty warrior by the H of thy servant David,
4:31 this army by the H of thy people Israel,
7:47 head and the right H which he so arrogantly
9:47 Jonathan stretched out his H to strike Bacchides, but
11:40 insistently urged him to H Antiochus over to him,
12:27 keep their arms at H so as to be
12:34 they were ready to H over the stronghold to
12:39 and to raise his H against Antiochus the king.
12:42 afraid to raise his H against him.
12:45 I will H it over to you as well
15:21 you from their country, H them over to Simon
15:30 Now then, H over the cities which you have
2Mac 4:34 gave him his right H, and in spite of
7:34 when you raise your H against the children of
8:11 slaves and promising to H over ninety slaves for
12:31 as the feast of weeks was close at H
14:31 and commanded them to H the man over.
14:33 stretched out his right H toward the sanctuary, and
14:33 "If you do not H Judas over to me
15:15 stretched out his right H and gave to Judas
15:20 was already close at H with their army drawn
Mt 3:2 "Repent, for the kingdom of heaven is at H
3:12 fork is in his H, and he will clear
4:17 "Repent, for the kingdom of heaven is at H
5:25 court, lest your accuser H you over to the
5:30 And if your right H causes you to sin,
6:3 not let your left H know what your right
6:3 know what your right H is doing,
8:3 he stretched out his H and touched him, saying,
8:15 fever; he touched her H, and the fever left
9:18 come and lay your H on her, and she
9:25 took her by the H, and the girl arose.
10:7 of heaven is at H
12:10 behold, there was a man with a withered H
12:13 he said to the man, "Stretch out your H
12:48 And stretching out his H toward his disciples, he
14:31 immediately reached out his H and caught him,
18:8 And if your H or your foot causes you
20:21 one at your right H and one at your
20:23 sit at my right H and at my left
22:13 the attendants, 'Bind him H and foot, and cast
22:44 Sit at my right H, till I put thy
25:33 sheep at his right H, but the goats at
25:34 those at his right H, 'Come, O blessed of
25:41 those at his left H, 'Depart from me, you
26:18 My time is at H; I will keep the
26:23 who has dipped his H in the dish with
26:45 the hour is at H, and the Son of
26:46 us be going; see, my betrayer is at H
26:51 Jesus stretched out his H and drew his sword,
26:64 seated at the right H of Power, and coming
27:29 head, and put a reed in his right H
Mk 1:15 of God is at H; repent, and believe in
1:31 took her by the H and lifted her up,
1:41 he stretched out his H and touched him, and
3:1 a man was there who had a withered H
3:3 who had the withered H, "Come here."
3:5 and said to the man, "Stretch out your H
3:5 it out, and his H was restored.
5:41 Taking her by the H he said to her,
7:13 your tradition which you H on.
7:31 him to lay his H upon him.
8:23 blind man by the H, and led him out
9:27 took him by the H and lifted him up,
9:43 And if your H causes you to sin, cut
10:37 one at your right H and one at your
10:40 sit at my right H or at my left
12:36 Sit at my right H, till I put thy
14:42 us be going; see, my betrayer is at H
14:62 seated at the right H of Power, and coming
16:19 down at the right H of God.
Lk 1:66 For the H of the Lord was with him.
1:71 enemies, and from the H of all who hate
1:74 being delivered from the H of our enemies, might
3:17 fork is in his H, to clear his threshing
5:13 he stretched out his H, and touched him, saying,
6:6 was there whose right H was withered.
6:8 who had the withered H, "Come and stand here."
6:10 all, and said to him, "Stretch out your H
6:10 did so, and his H was restored.
8:54 taking her by the H he called, saying, "Child,
9:62 one who puts his H to the plow and
12:58 judge, and the judge H you over to the
15:22 a ring on his H, and shoes on his
20:42 Sit at my right H,
21:8 'The time is at H Do not go after
22:21 But behold the H of him who betrays me
22:67 seated at the right H of the power of
Jn 2:13 the Jews was at H, and Jesus went up
3:35 Son, and has given all things into his H
6:4 Passover, the feast of the Jews, was at H
7:2 Now the Jews' feast of Tabernacles was at H
10:28 no one shall snatch them out of my H
10:29 able to snatch them out of the Father's H
11:55 the Jews was at H, and many went up
18:22 struck Jesus with his H, saying, "Is that how
19:42 tomb was close at H, they laid Jesus there.
20:25 nails, and place my H in his side, I
20:27 and put out your H, and place it in
Acts 2:25 is at my right H that I may not
2:33 exalted at the right H of God, and having
2:34 Sit at my right H,
3:7 him by the right H and raised him up;
4:28 to do whatever thy H and thy plan had
4:30 thou stretchest out thy H to heal, and signs
5:31 him at his right H as Leader and Savior,
7:25 them deliverance by his H, but they did not
7:35 and deliverer by the H of the angel that
7:50 Did not my H make all these things?'
7:55 standing at the right H of God;
7:56 standing at the right H of God."
9:8 led him by the H and brought him into
9:41 he gave her his H and lifted her up.
11:21 And the H of the Lord was with them,
11:30 the elders by the H of Barnabas and Saul.
12:11 rescued me from the H of Herod and from
12:17 to them with his H to be silent, he
13:11 And now, behold, the H of the Lord is
13:11 about seeking people to lead him by the H
13:16 and motioning with his H said: "Men of Israel,
19:33 Alexander motioned with his H, wishing to make a
21:40 steps, motioned with his H to the people; and

	22:11	was led by the H by those who were
	23:19	took him by the H, and going aside asked
	26:1	Paul stretched out his H and made his defense:
	28:3	because of the heat and fastened on his H
	28:4	creature hanging from his H, they said to one
Rom	7:21	want to do right, evil lies close at H
	8:34	is at the right H of God, who indeed
	13:12	night is far gone, the day is at H
1Cor	12:15	I am not a H, I do not belong
	12:21	cannot say to the H, "I have no need
	14:3	On the other H, he who prophesies speaks to
	16:21	I, Paul, write this greeting with my own H
2Cor	6:7	righteousness for the right H and for the left;
Gal	2:9	and Barnabas the right H of fellowship, that we
	6:11	I am writing to you with my own H
Eph	1:20	sit at his right H in the heavenly places,
Phil	4:5	The Lord is at H
Col	3:1	seated at the right H of God.
	4:18	I, Paul, write this greeting with my own H
2Thes	3:17	I, Paul, write this greeting with my own H
Philem	1:19	this with my own H, I will repay it—
Heb	1:3	down at the right H of the Majesty on
	1:13	"Sit at my right H, till I make thy
	7:18	On the one H, a former commandment is set
	7:19	perfect); on the other H, a better hope is
	8:1	seated at the right H of the throne of
	8:9	took them by the H to lead them out
	10:12	down at the right H of God,
	12:2	seated at the right H of the throne of
Jas	5:8	for the coming of the Lord is at H
1Pet	3:22	is at the right H of God, with angels,
	4:7	all things is at H; therefore keep sane and
	5:6	therefore under the mighty H of God, that in
Rev	1:16	waters; in his right H he held seven stars,
	1:17	he laid his right H upon me, saying, "Fear
	1:20	saw in my right H, and the seven golden
	2:1	stars in his right H, who walks among the
	5:1	saw in the right H of him who was
	5:7	scroll from the right H of him who was
	6:5	a balance in his H;
	8:4	the saints from the H of the angel before
	10:2	He had a little scroll open in his H
	10:5	lifted up his right H to heaven
	10:8	is open in the H of the angel who
	10:10	little scroll from the H of the angel and
	13:16	marked on the right H or the forehead,
	14:9	forehead or on his H,
	14:14	his head, and a sharp sickle in his H
	17:4	pearls, holding in her H a golden cup full
	20:1	heaven, holding in his H the key of the

HAND-TO-HAND (2)

2Mac	5:14	destroyed, forty thousand in H fighting; and as many
	15:17	the matter, by fighting H with all courage, because

HANDBAGS

Is	3:22	the cloaks, and the H;

HANDBREADTH (7)

Ex	25:25	it a frame a H wide, and a molding
	37:12	it a frame a H wide, and made a
1Kgs	7:26	Its thickness was a H; and its brim was
2Chr	4:5	Its thickness was a H; and its brim was
Ezek	40:5	a cubit and a H in length; so he
	40:43	And hooks, a H long, were fastened round about
	43:13	a cubit and a H: its base shall be

HANDBREADTHS

Ps	39:5	my days a few H, and my lifetime is

HANDED (14)

Jud	8:19	why our fathers were H over to the sword,
	10:12	are about to be H over to you to
	11:15	day they will be H over to you to
Esth	6:9	and the horse be H over to one of
Wis	14:15	dead human being, and H on to his dependents
Sir	11:6	illustrious men have been H over to others.
Jer	38:19	Chaldeans, lest I be H over to them and
Bar	4:6	nations, but you were H over to your enemies
Dan	14:30	and under compulsion he H Daniel over to them.
2Mac	10:4	forbearance and not be H over to blasphemous and
Jn	18:30	we would not have H him over."
	18:35	the chief priests have H you over to me;
	18:36	I might not be H over to the Jews;
	19:16	Then he H him over to them to be

HANDFUL (6)

Lev	2:2	take from it a H of the fine flour
	5:12	priest shall take a H of it as its
	6:15	take from it a H of the fine flour
Num	5:26	priest shall take a H of the cereal offering,
1Kgs	17:12	nothing baked, only a H of meal in a
Eccl	4:6	Better is a H of quietness than two hands

HANDFULS (5)

Ex	9:8	Moses and Aaron, "Take H of ashes from the
Lev	16:12	the LORD, and two H of sweet incense beaten
1Kgs	20:10	Samaria shall suffice for H for all the people
Ezek	13:19	among my people for H of barley and for
2Mac	4:41	wood, and others took H of the ashes that

HANDING

Ezek	25:4	exile; therefore I am H you over to the

HANDIWORK (3)

Ps	19:1	glory of God; and the firmament proclaims his H
Sir	38:28	anvil, intent upon his H in iron; the breath
	38:28	heart on finishing his H, and he is careful

HANDKERCHIEFS

Acts	19:12	of Paul, so that H or aprons were carried

HANDLE (8)

Deut	19:5	head slips from the H and strikes his neighbor
2Chr	25:5	for war, able to H spear and shield.
Wis	13:11	a tree easy to H and skilfully strip off
Jer	2:8	the LORD?' Those who H the law did not
	46:9	Ethiopia and Put who H the shield, men of
Ezek	27:29	ships come all that H the oar.
Lk	24:39	it is I myself; H me, and see; for
Col	2:21	to regulations, "Do not H, Do not taste, Do

HANDLED (5)

Ezek	21:11	that it may be H; it is sharpened and
	23:3	their breasts were pressed and their virgin bosoms H
	23:8	lain with her and H her virgin bosom and
	23:21	youth, when the Egyptians H your bosom and
2Mac	7:39	into a rage, and H him worse than the

HANDLES (5)

Song	5:5	liquid myrrh, upon the H of the bolt.
Sir	38:25	he become wise who H the plow, and who
Is	45:9	or 'Your work has no H
Jer	50:16	and the one who H the sickle in time
Amos	2:15	his life; he who H the bow shall not

HANDLING (3)

Jud	7:2	and the foot soldiers H it, a very great
Jer	46:9	of Lud, skilled in H the bow.
2Tim	2:15	to be ashamed, rightly H the word of truth.

HANDMAID (17)

1Sam	25:24	guilt; pray let your H speak in your ears,
	25:24	your ears, and hear the words of your H
	25:25	him; but I your H did not see the
	25:28	the trespass of your H; for the LORD will
	25:31	dealt well with my lord, then remember your H
	25:41	and said, "Behold, your H is a servant to
	28:21	to him, "Behold, your H has hearkened to you;
	28:22	also hearken to your H; let me set a
2Sam	14:6	And your H had two sons, and they quarreled
	14:7	has risen against your H, and they say, 'Give
	14:12	said, "Pray let your H speak a word to
	14:15	me afraid; and your H thought, 'I will speak
	14:17	of God.' And your H thought, 'The word of
	14:19	all these words in the mouth of your H
Ps	86:16	thy servant, and save the son of thy H
	116:16	I am thy servant, the son of thy H
Lk	1:38	"Behold, I am the H of the Lord; let

HANDMAIDEN

Lk	1:48	he has regarded the low estate of his H

HANDPIKES

Ezek	39:9	bucklers, bows and arrows, H and spears, and they

HANDS (532)

Gen	5:29	our work and from the toil of our H
	19:10	men put forth their H and brought Lot into
	20:5	the innocence of my H I have done this."
	27:16	she put upon his H and upon the smooth
	27:22	Jacob's voice, but the H are the hands of

H

27:22 the hands are the H of Esau."
27:23 recognize him, because his H were hairy like his
27:23 like his brother Esau's H; so he blessed him.
31:42 the labor of my H, and rebuked you last
37:21 him out of their H, saying, "Let us not
39:3 all that he did to prosper in his H
42:37 put him in my H, and I will bring
48:14 of Manasseh, crossing his H, for Manasseh was the
49:24 made agile by the H of the Mighty One
Ex 9:29 will stretch out my H to the LORD; the
9:33 and stretched out his H to the LORD; and
15:17 O LORD, which thy H have established.
17:12 But Moses' H grew weary; so they took a
17:12 Hur held up his H, one on one side,
17:12 other side; so his H were steady until the
23:1 You shall not join H with a wicked man,
29:10 sons shall lay their H upon the head of
29:15 sons shall lay their H upon the head of
29:19 sons shall lay their H upon the head of
29:20 thumbs of their right H, and upon the great
29:24 all these in the H of Aaron and in
29:24 Aaron and in the H of his sons, and
29:25 take them from their H, and burn them on
30:19 sons shall wash their H and their feet.
30:21 They shall wash their H and their feet, lest
32:15 the testimony in his H, tables that were written
32:19 tables out of his H and broke them at
35:25 ability spun with their H, and brought what they
Lev 4:15 congregation shall lay their H upon the head of
7:30 bring with his own H the offerings by fire
8:14 his sons laid their H upon the head of
8:18 his sons laid their H on the head of
8:22 his sons laid their H on the head of
8:24 thumbs of their right H and on the great
8:27 all these in the H of Aaron and in
8:27 Aaron and in the H of his sons, and
8:28 took them from their H, and burned them on
9:22 Aaron lifted up his H toward the people and
15:11 without having rinsed his H in water shall wash
16:21 shall lay both his H upon the head of
24:14 heard him lay their H upon his head, and
Num 5:18 and place in her H the cereal offering of
6:19 put them upon the H of the Nazirite, after
8:10 Israel shall lay their H upon the Levites,
8:12 Levites shall lay their H upon the heads of
24:10 and he struck his H together; and Balak said
27:23 and he laid his H upon him, and commissioned
Deut 1:25 they took in their H some of the fruit
2:7 the work of your H; he knows your going
2:36 the LORD our God gave all into our H
4:28 the work of men's H, that neither see, nor
9:15 tables of the covenant were in my two H
9:17 out of my two H, and broke them before
14:29 the work of your H that you do.
16:15 the work of your H, so that you will
21:6 man shall wash their H over the heifer whose
21:7 they shall testify, 'Our H did not shed this
21:10 gives them into your H, and you take them
24:19 bless you in all the work of your H
27:15 thing made by the H of a craftsman, and
28:12 the work of your H; and you shall lend
31:29 him to anger through the work of your H
33:7 With thy H contend for him, and be a
33:11 the work of his H; crush the loins of
34:9 Moses had laid his H upon him; so the
Josh 2:24 the land into our H; and moreover all the
7:7 give us into the H of the Amorites, to
10:8 given them into your H; there shall not a
21:44 LORD had given all their enemies into their H
Judg 7:6 that lapped, putting their H to their mouths, was
7:8 the people from their H, and their trumpets; and
7:11 say, and afterward your H shall be strengthened to
7:16 put trumpets into the H of all of them
7:19 and smashed the jars that were in their H
7:20 holding in their left H the torches, and in
7:20 and in their right H the trumpets to blow;
8:3 has given into your H the princes of Midian,
9:24 Shechem, who strengthened his H to slay his
13:23 cereal offering at our H, or shown us all
14:9 it out into his H, and went on, eating
15:12 give you into the H of the Philistines." And
15:13 give you into their H; we will not kill
15:14 caught fire, and his bonds melted off his H
15:18 and fall into the H of the uncircumcised?"
16:18 to her, and brought the money in their H
18:10 given it into your H, a place where there

19:27 the house, with her H on the threshold.
1Sam 5:4 Dagon and both his H were lying cut off
14:13 climbed up on his H and feet, and his
14:48 Israel out of the H of those who plundered
21:13 himself mad in their H, and made marks on
24:11 there is no wrong or treason in my H
24:18 me when the LORD put me into your H
26:18 What guilt is on my H
30:15 deliver me into the H of my master, and
2Sam 2:7 Now therefore let your H be strong, and be
3:34 Your H were not bound, your feet were not
4:12 and cut off their H and feet, and hanged
16:21 your father, and the H of all who are
21:9 gave them into the H of the Gibeonites, and
22:21 the cleanness of my H he recompensed me.
22:35 He trains my H for war, so that my
1Kgs 8:22 and spread forth his H toward heaven;
8:38 and stretching out his H toward this house;
8:54 he had knelt with H outstretched toward heaven;
14:27 committed them to the H of the officers of
15:18 gave them into the H of his servants; and
16:7 the work of his H, in being like the
20:6 your servants, and lay H on whatever pleases them,
2Kgs 3:11 poured water on the H of Elijah."
4:34 his eyes, and his H upon his hands; and
4:34 his hands upon his H; and as he stretched
9:35 and the feet and the palms of her H
10:24 I give into your H to escape shall forfeit
11:12 and they clapped their H, and said, "Long live
11:16 So they laid H on her; and she went
12:11 weighed out into the H of the workmen who
13:16 And Elisha laid his H upon the king's hands.
13:16 And Elisha laid his hands upon the king's H
19:18 the work of men's H, wood and stone; therefore
22:17 the work of their H, therefore my wrath will
1Chr 5:20 were given into their H, for they cried to
12:17 no wrong in my H, then may the God
2Chr 6:12 the assembly of Israel, and spread forth his H
6:13 and spread forth his H toward heaven;
6:29 and stretching out his H toward this house;
12:10 committed them to the H of the officers of
15:7 Do not let your H be weak, for your
23:15 So they laid H on her; and she went
24:13 went forward in their H, and they restored the
29:23 and they laid their H upon them,
32:17 their people from my H, so the God of
32:19 the earth, which are the work of men's H
34:25 the works of their H, therefore my wrath will
Ezra 5:8 work goes on diligently and prospers in their H
8:33 were weighed into the H of Meremoth the priest,
9:5 and spread out my H to the LORD my
Neh 2:18 So they strengthened their H for the good work.
6:9 frighten us, thinking, "Their H will drop from the
6:9 But now, O God, strengthen thou my H
8:6 lifting up their H; and they bowed their heads
9:24 give them into their H, with their kings and
13:21 again I will lay H on you." From that
Tob 5:17 the staff of our H as he goes in
13:11 bearing gifts in their H, gifts for the King
Jud 7:26 sold us into their H, to strew us on
8:18 worshiped gods made with H, as was done in
11:13 much as to touch these things with their H
11:22 lend strength to our H and to bring destruction
13:4 the work of my H for the exaltation of
15:12 took branches in her H and gave them to
16:3 me out of the H of my pursuers, and
16:7 not fall by the H of the young men,
Esth 2:21 and sought to lay H on King Ahasuerus.
3:6 he disdained to lay H on Mordecai alone.
3:9 of silver into the H of those who have
6:2 had sought to lay H upon King Ahasuerus.
8:7 because he would lay H on the Jews.
9:2 King Ahasuerus to lay H on such as sought
9:15 but they laid no H on the plunder.
9:16 but they laid no H on the plunder.
12:2 were preparing to lay H upon Artaxerxes the king;
14:6 given us into the H of our enemies,
14:19 save us from the H of evildoers.
Job 1:10 the work of his H, and his possessions have
4:3 many, and you have strengthened the weak H
5:12 crafty, so that their H achieve no success.
5:18 he smites, but his H heal.
9:30 snow, and cleanse my H with lye,
10:3 the work of thy H and favor the designs
10:8 Thy H fashioned and made me; and now thou
11:13 will stretch out your H toward him.

HANDS

	14:15	thou wouldest long for the work of thy H
	16:11	casts me into the H of the wicked.
	16:17	no violence in my H, and my prayer is
	17:9	he that has clean H grows stronger and stronger.
	20:10	the poor, and his H will give back his
	22:30	will be delivered through the cleanness of your H
	27:23	It claps its H at him, and hisses at
	30:2	the strength of their H, men whose vigor is
	31:7	has cleaved to my H;
	34:19	for they are all the work of his H
	34:37	sin; he claps his H among us, and multiplies
	36:32	He covers his H with the lightning, and commands
	41:8	Lay H on him; think of the battle; you
Ps	7:3	is wrong in my H,
	8:6	the works of thy H; thou hast put all
	9:16	are snared in the work of their own H
	10:14	take it into thy H; the hapless commits himself
	18:20	the cleanness of my H he recompensed me.
	18:24	the cleanness of my H in his sight.
	18:34	He trains my H for war, so that my
	22:16	they have pierced my H and feet--
	24:4	He who has clean H and a pure heart,
	26:6	I wash my H in innocence, and go about
	26:10	men, men in whose H are evil devices, and
	26:10	devices, and whose right H are full of bribes.
	28:2	I lift up my H toward thy most holy
	28:4	the work of their H; render them their due
	28:5	the work of his H, he will break them
	44:20	or spread forth our H to a strange god,
	47:1	[Selah] Clap your H, all peoples!
	58:2	you devise wrongs; your H deal out violence on
	63:4	will lift up my H and call on thy
	68:31	to stretch out her H to God.
	73:13	clean and washed my H in innocence.
	76:5	men of war were unable to use their H
	81:6	of the burden; your H were freed from the
	88:9	I spread out my H to thee.
	90:17	the work of our H upon us, yea, the
	90:17	the work of our H establish thou it.
	91:12	On their H they will bear you up, lest
	92:4	the works of thy H I sing for joy.
	95:5	made it; for his H formed the dry land.
	98:8	the floods clap their H; let the hills sing
	102:25	and the heavens are the work of thy H
	111:7	The works of his H are faithful and just;
	115:4	are silver and gold, the work of men's H
	115:7	They have H, but do not feel; feet, but
	119:73	Thy H have made and fashioned me; give me
	125:3	righteous put forth their H to do wrong.
	128:2	the labor of your H; you shall be happy,
	134:2	Lift up your H to the holy place, and
	135:15	are silver and gold, the work of men's H
	138:8	Do not forsake the work of thy H
	140:4	O LORD, from the H of the wicked; preserve
	141:2	lifting up of my H as an evening sacrifice!
	143:5	muse on what thy H have wrought.
	143:6	I stretch out my H to thee; my soul
	144:1	rock, who trains my H for war, and my
	149:6	two-edged swords in their H,
Prov	6:10	little folding of the H to rest,
	6:17	a lying tongue, and H that shed innocent blood,
	14:1	folly with her own H tears it down.
	21:25	kills him for his H refuse to labor.
	24:33	little folding of the H to rest,
	30:28	can take in your H, yet it is in
	31:13	seeks wool and flax, and works with willing H
	31:16	the fruit of her H she plants a vineyard.
	31:19	She puts her H to the distaff, and her
	31:19	the distaff, and her H hold the spindle.
	31:20	and reaches out her H to the needy.
	31:31	the fruit of her H, and let her works
Eccl	2:11	considered all that my H had done and the
	4:5	The fool folds his H, and eats his own
	4:6	of quietness than two H full of toil and
	5:6	your voice, and destroy the work of your H
	7:26	and nets, and whose H are fetters; he who
Song	5:5	my beloved, and my H dripped with myrrh, my
Wis	1:12	the works of your H;
	3:14	is the eunuch whose H have done no lawless
	7:11	her, and in her H uncounted wealth.
	8:12	they will put their H on their mouths.
	8:18	the labors of her H, unfailing wealth, and in
	12:6	to destroy by the H of our fathers,
	12:9	the ungodly into the H of the righteous in
	13:10	the works of men's H, gold and silver fashioned
	13:19	and success with his H he asks strength of
	13:19	of a thing whose H have no strength.
	14:8	the idol made with H is accursed, and so
	15:17	he makes with lawless H is dead, for he
Sir	2:12	hearts and to slack H, and to the sinner
	2:18	us fall into the H of the Lord, but
	2:18	but not into the H of men; for as
	8:1	a powerful man, lest you fall into his H
	10:4	earth is in the H of the Lord, and
	10:5	man is in the H of the Lord, and
	12:18	head, and clap his H, and whisper much, and
	25:22	Drooping H and weak knees are caused by the
	29:5	man will kiss another's H until he gets a
	33:25	find rest; leave his H idle, and he will
	35:8	do not stint the first fruits of your H
	38:10	faults and direct your H aright, and cleanse your
	38:13	success lies in the H of physicians,
	38:31	these rely upon their H, and each is skilful
	42:6	where there are many H, lock things up.
	43:12	its glorious arc; the H of the Most High
	46:2	when he lifted his H and stretched out his
	48:19	were shaken and their H trembled, and they were
	48:20	merciful, spreading forth their H toward him; and
	50:12	the portions from the H of the priests, as
	50:13	Lord's offering in their H, before the whole
	50:20	and lifted up his H over the whole congregation
	51:19	I spread out my H to the heavens, and
Is	1:15	you spread forth your H, I will hide my
	1:15	will not listen; your H are full of blood.
	2:6	Philistines, and they strike H with foreigners.
	2:8	the work of their H, to what their own
	3:11	him, for what his H have done shall be
	5:12	the LORD, or see the work of his H
	13:7	Therefore all H will be feeble, and every man's
	17:8	the work of their H, and they will not
	19:25	the work of my H, and Israel my heritage."
	25:11	will spread out his H in the midst of
	25:11	a swimmer spreads his H out to swim; but
	25:11	his pride together with the skill of his H
	29:23	the work of my H, in his midst, they
	31:7	of gold, which your H have sinfully made for
	33:15	oppressions, who shakes his H, lest they hold a
	35:3	Strengthen the weak H, and make firm the feeble
	37:19	the work of men's H, wood and stone; therefore
	45:11	or command me concerning the work of my H
	45:12	it; it was my H that stretched out the
	49:16	the palms of my H; your walls are continually
	55:12	the trees of the field shall clap their H
	59:3	For your H are defiled with blood and your
	59:6	iniquity, and deeds of violence are in their H
	60:21	the work of my H, that I might be
	65:2	I spread out my H all the day to
	65:22	chosen shall long enjoy the work of their H
Jer	1:16	gods, and worshiped the works of their own H
	2:37	come away with your H upon your head, for
	4:31	breath, stretching out her H, "Woe is me!
	6:24	report of it, our H fall helpless; anguish has
	10:3	an axe by the H of a craftsman.
	10:9	craftsman and of the H of the goldsmith; their
	12:7	my soul into the H of her enemies.
	21:4	which are in your H and with which you
	23:14	lies; they strengthen the H of evildoers, so that
	25:6	me to anger with the work of your H
	25:7	the work of your H to your own harm.
	25:14	to their deeds and the work of their H
	26:14	as for me, behold, I am in your H
	30:6	every man with his H on his loins like
	31:11	has redeemed him from H too strong for him.
	32:24	is given into the H of the Chaldeans who
	32:25	is given into the H of the Chaldeans.'"
	32:28	this city into the H of the Chaldeans and
	32:30	the work of their H, says the LORD.
	32:43	is given into the H of the Chaldeans.
	33:13	again pass under the H of the one who
	38:4	he is weakening the H of the soldiers who
	38:4	this city, and the H of all the people,
	38:5	he is in your H; for the king can
	40:4	release you today from the chains on your H
	43:9	Tahpanhes: "Take in your H large stones, and hide
	44:8	the works of your H, burning incense to other
	44:25	fulfilled it with your H, saying, 'We will surely
	47:3	so feeble are their H,
	48:37	off; upon all the H are gashes, and on
	50:43	of them, and his H fell helpless; anguish seized
Lam	1:10	has stretched out his H over all her precious
	1:14	gave me into the H of those whom I
	1:17	Zion stretches out her H, but there is none

2:15 the way clap their H at you; they hiss
2:19 Lift your H to him for the lives of
3:41 up our hearts and H to God in heaven:
3:64 O LORD, according to the work of their H
4:2 as earthen pots, the work of a potter's H
4:10 The H of compassionate women have boiled their
5:12 hung up by their H; no respect is shown
Bar 6:51 the work of men's H, and that there is
Ezek 1:8 wings on their four sides they had human H
6:11 Lord GOD: "Clap your H, and stamp your foot,
7:17 All H are feeble, and all knees weak as
7:21 give it into the H of foreigners for a
7:27 in despair, and the H of the people of
10:2 the cherubim; fill your H with burning coals from
10:7 put it into the H of the man clothed
10:21 underneath their wings the semblance of human H
11:9 give you into the H of foreigners, and execute
12:7 wall with my own H; I went forth in
21:7 will melt and all H will be feeble, every
21:14 of man; clap your H and let the sword
21:17 also will clap my H, and I will satisfy
21:31 deliver you into the H of brutal men, skilful
22:13 therefore, I strike my H together at the dishonest
22:14 endure, or can your H be strong, in the
23:9 delivered her into the H of her lovers, into
23:9 her lovers, into the H of the Assyrians, upon
23:28 deliver you into the H of those whom you
23:28 you hate, into the H of those from whom
23:37 blood is upon their H; with their idols they
23:42 put bracelets upon the H of the women, and
23:45 they are adulteresses, and blood is upon their H
25:6 you have clapped your H and stamped your feet
28:9 no god, in the H of those who wound
Dan 3:15 god that will deliver you out of my H
3:32 given us into the H of lawless enemies, most
10:10 me trembling on my H and knees.
13:22 I do not, I shall not escape your H
13:23 to fall into your H, rather than to sin
13:34 people, and laid their H upon her head.
Hos 12:7 A trader, in whose H are false balances, he
14:3 more, 'Our God,' to the work of our H
Jon 3:8 and from the violence which is in his H
Mic 5:13 the work of your H;
7:3 Their H are upon what is evil, to do
7:16 they shall lay their H on their mouths; their
Nah 3:19 of you clap their H over you.
Hab 3:10 voice, it lifted its H on high.
Zeph 3:16 Zion; let not your H grow weak.
Hag 2:14 every work of their H; and what they offer
Zech 4:9 to me, saying, "The H of Zerubbabel have laid
4:9 of this house; his H shall also complete it.
8:9 of hosts: "Let your H be strong, you who
8:13 not, but let your H be strong."
1Mac 2:47 arrogant men, and the work prospered in their H
2:48 law out of the H of the Gentiles and
4:30 the Philistines into the H of Jonathan, the son
5:12 rescue us from their H, for many of us
5:50 night, and the city was delivered into his H
6:25 they stretched out their H, but also against all
7:35 are delivered into my H this time, then if
9:46 be delivered from the H of our enemies."
12:9 which are in our H,
14:31 their country and lay H on their sanctuary,
14:36 things prospered in his H, so that the Gentiles
16:2 have prospered in our H so that we have
2Mac 3:20 And holding up their H to heaven, they all
5:16 vessels with his polluted H, and swept away with
5:16 swept away with profane H the votive offerings
6:26 shall not escape the H of the Almighty.
7:4 and cut off his H and feet, while the
7:10 courageously stretched forth his H,
7:14 to die at the H of men and to
7:31 certainly not escape the H of God.
12:24 himself fell into the H of Dositheus and Sosipater
12:28 the city into their H, and killed as many
13:11 revive fall into the H of the blasphemous Gentiles.
14:34 priests stretched forth their H toward heaven and
14:42 to fall into the H of sinners and suffer
14:46 took them with both H and hurled them at
15:12 was praying with outstretched H for the whole body
15:21 elephants, stretched out his H toward heaven and
15:27 So, fighting with their H and praying to God
Mt 4:6 you,' and 'On their H they will bear you
15:2 do not wash their H when they eat."
15:20 to eat with unwashed H does not defile a
17:12 the Son of man will suffer at their H
17:21 be delivered into the H of men,
18:8 lame than with two H or two feet to
19:13 he might lay his H on them and pray.
19:15 And he laid his H on them and went
26:45 is betrayed into the H of sinners.
26:50 came up and laid H on Jesus and seized
27:24 water and washed his H before the crowd, saying,
Mk 5:23 Come and lay your H on her, so that
6:2 What mighty works are wrought by his H
6:5 that he laid his H upon a few sick
7:2 his disciples ate with H defiled, that is, unwashed.
7:3 unless they wash their H, observing the tradition of
7:5 elders, but eat with H defiled?"
8:23 eyes and laid his H upon him, he asked
8:25 again he laid his H upon his eyes; and
9:31 be delivered into the H of men, and they
9:43 maimed than with two H to go to hell,
10:16 blessed them, laying his H upon them.
14:41 is betrayed into the H of sinners.
14:46 And they laid H on him and seized him.
14:58 that is made with H, and in three days
14:58 days I will build another, not made with H
16:18 they will lay their H on the sick, and
Lk 4:11 you,' and 'On their H they will bear you
4:40 and he laid his H on every one of
6:1 some heads of grain, rubbing them in their H
9:44 be delivered into the H of men."
13:13 And he laid his H upon her, and immediately
20:19 priests tried to lay H on him at that
21:12 they will lay their H on you and persecute
22:51 you did not lay H on me.
23:45 said, "Father, into thy H I commit my spirit!"
24:7 be delivered into the H of sinful men, and
24:39 See my H and my feet, that it is
24:40 he showed them his H and his feet.
24:50 and lifting up his H he blessed them.
Jn 7:30 but no one laid H on him, because his
7:44 but no one laid H on him.
10:39 to arrest him, but he escaped from their H
11:44 man came out, his H and feet bound with
13:3 all things into his H, and that he had
13:9 only but also my H and my head!"
19:3 and struck him with their H
20:20 he showed them his H and his side.
20:25 I see in his H the print of the
20:27 here, and see my H; and put out your
21:18 will stretch out your H, and another will gird
Acts 2:23 and killed by the H of lawless men.
5:12 the people by the H of the apostles.
6:6 prayed and laid their H upon them.
7:41 idol and rejoiced in the works of their H
7:48 in houses made with H; as the prophet says,
8:17 Then they laid their H on them and they
8:18 on of the apostles' H, he offered them money,
8:19 whom I lay my H may receive the Holy
9:12 in and lay his H on him so that
9:17 And laying his H on him he said, "Brother
12:1 the king laid violent H upon some who belonged
12:7 And the chains fell off his H
13:3 praying they laid their H on them and sent
14:3 signs and wonders to be done by their H
17:25 he served by human H, as though he needed
19:6 Paul had laid his H upon them, the Holy
19:11 extraordinary miracles by the H of Paul,
19:26 that gods made with H are not gods.
20:34 know that these H ministered to my necessities,
21:11 his own feet and H, and said, "Thus says
21:11 deliver him into the H of the Gentiles.'"
21:27 the crowd, and laid H on him,
27:19 out with their own H the tackle of the
28:8 prayed, and putting his H on him healed him.
28:17 from Jerusalem into the H of the Romans.
Rom 10:21 have held out my H to a disobedient and
1Cor 4:12 homeless, and we labor, working with our own H
2Cor 5:1 house not made with H, eternal in the heavens.
11:24 have received at the H of the Jews the
11:33 a window in the wall, and escaped his H
Eph 2:11 in the flesh by H --
4:28 honest work with his H, so that he may
Col 2:11 a circumcision made without H, by putting off the
1Thes 4:11 to work with your H, as we charged you;
1Tim 2:8 pray, lifting holy H without anger or quarreling;
4:14 of elders laid their H upon you.
5:22 the laying on of H, nor participate in another
2Tim 1:6 laying on of my H;
Heb 1:10 the work of thy H;

H

6:2 the laying on of H, the resurrection of the
9:11 tent (not made with H, that is, not of
9:24 a sanctuary made with H, a copy of the
10:31 to fall into the H of the living God.
12:12 Therefore lift your drooping H and strengthen your
Jas 4:8 Cleanse your H, you sinners, and purify your hearts,
1Jn 1:1 and touched with our H, concerning the word of
Rev 7:9 palm branches in their H,
9:20 the works of their H nor give up worshiping
15:2 of glass with harps of God in their H
20:4 received its mark on their foreheads or their H

HANDSOME (7)

Gen 39:6 Now Joseph was H and good-looking.
1Sam 9:2 name was Saul, a H young man.
9:2 people of Israel more H than he; from his
16:12 was ruddy, and had beautiful eyes, and was H
2Sam 23:21 slew an Egyptian, a H man.
1Kgs 1:6 was also a very H man; and he was
Dan 1:4 nobility, youths without blemish, H and skillful in all

HANES

Is 30:4 and his envoys reach H,

HANG (20)

Gen 40:19 head--from you!--and H you on a tree;
Ex 26:12 curtain that remains, shall H over the back of
26:13 of the tent shall H over the sides of
26:32 cherubim; and you shall H it upon four pillars
26:33 And you shall H the veil from the clasps,
Lev 10:6 hair of your heads H loose, and do not
13:45 hair of his head H loose, and he shall
21:10 hair of his head H loose, nor rend his
Num 25:4 of the people, and H them in the sun
Deut 21:22 to death, and you H him on a tree,
28:66 soul; your life shall H in doubt before you;
2Sam 21:6 so that we may H them up before the
Jud 14:1 take this head and H it upon the parapet
Esth 7:10 And the king said, H him on that." So
Job 28:4 forgotten by travelers, they H afar from men, they
Prov 26:7 lame man's legs, which H useless, is a proverb
Song 4:4 for an arsenal, whereon H a thousand bucklers, all
Is 22:24 And they will H on him the whole weight
Ezek 15:3 peg from it to H any vessel on?
2Mac 15:33 to the birds and H up these rewards of

HANGED (20)

Gen 40:22 Pharaoh's hand; but he H the chief baker, as
41:13 restored to my office, and the baker was H
Deut 21:23 same day, for a H man is accursed by
Josh 8:29 And he H the king of Ai on a
2Sam 4:12 hands and feet, and H them beside the pool
17:23 house in order, and H himself; and he died,
21:9 the Gibeonites, and they H them on the mountain
21:12 where the Philistines had H them, on the day
21:13 they gathered the bones of those who were H
Esth 2:23 the men were both H on the gallows.
5:14 king to have Mordecai H upon it; then go
6:4 king about having Mordecai H on the gallows that
7:10 So they H Haman on the gallows which he
8:7 Haman, and they have H him on the gallows,
9:13 sons of Haman be H on the gallows."
9:14 Susa, and the ten sons of Haman were H
9:25 his sons should be H on the gallows.
16:18 these things has been H at the gate of
Mt 27:5 and he went and H himself.
Lk 23:38 the criminals who were H railed at him, saying,

HANGING (6)

2Sam 18:9 and he was left H between heaven and earth,
18:10 "Behold, I saw Absalom H in an oak."
Tob 3:10 to the thought of H herself.
Acts 5:30 whom you killed by H him on a tree.
10:39 him to death by H him on a tree;
28:4 natives saw the creature H from his hand, they

HANGINGS (18)

Ex 27:9 the court shall have H of fine twined linen
27:11 side there shall be H a hundred cubits long,
27:12 side there shall be H for fifty cubits, with
27:14 The H for the one side of the gate
27:15 the other side the H shall be fifteen cubits,
27:18 height five cubits, with H of fine twined linen
35:17 and its base; the H of the court, its
38:9 the south side the H of the court were
38:12 the west side were H of fifty cubits, their
38:14 The H for one side of the gate were
38:15 of the court were H of fifteen cubits, with
38:16 All the H round about the court were of
38:18 breadth, corresponding to the H of the court.
39:40 and its base; the H of the court, its
Num 3:26 tent of meeting, the H of the court, the
4:26 of meeting, and the H of the court, and
2Kgs 23:7 where the women wove H for the Asherah.
Esth 1:6 cotton curtains and blue H caught up with cords

HANGS (3)

Job 26:7 over the void, and H the earth upon nothing.
Is 33:23 Your tackle H loose; it cannot hold the mast
Gal 3:13 be every one who H on a tree"--

HANNAH (14)

1Sam 1:2 of the one was H, and the name of
1:2 Peninnah had children, but H had no children.
1:5 and, although he loved H, he would give Hannah
1:5 Hannah, he would give H only one portion, because
1:7 Therefore H wept and would not eat.
1:8 husband, said to her, H, why do you weep?
1:9 and drunk in Shiloh, H rose.
1:13 H was speaking in her heart; only her lips
1:15 But H answered, "No, my lord, I am a
1:19 And Elkanah knew H his wife, and the LORD
1:20 and in due time H conceived and bore a
1:22 But H did not go up, for she said
2:1 H also prayed and said, "My heart exults in
2:21 And the LORD visited H, and she conceived and

HANNANIAH

1Mac 2:59 H, Azariah, and Mishael believed and were saved

HANNATHON

Josh 19:14 boundary turns about to H, and it ends at

HANNIEL (2)

Num 34:23 of Manasseh a leader, H the son of Ephod.
1Chr 7:39 sons of Ulla: Arah, H, and Rizia.

HANOCH (6)

Gen 25:4 Midian were Ephah, Epher, H, Abida, and Eldaah.
46:9 the sons of Reuben: H, Pallu, Hezron, and Carmi.
Ex 6:14 the first-born of Israel: H, Pallu, Hezron, and Carmi;
Num 26:5 sons of Reuben: of H, the family of the
1Chr 1:33 of Midian: Ephah, Epher, H, Abida, and Eldaah.
5:3 the first-born of Israel: H, Pallu, Hezron, and Carmi.

HANOCHITES

Num 26:5 the family of the H; of Pallu, the family

HANUN (11)

2Sam 10:1 the Ammonites died, and H his son reigned in
10:2 will deal loyally with H the son of Nahash,
10:3 the Ammonites said to H their lord, "Do you
10:4 So H took David's servants, and shaved off half
1Chr 19:2 will deal loyally with H the son of Nahash,
19:2 David's servants came to H in the land of
19:3 the Ammonites said to H, "Do you think, because
19:4 So H took David's servants, and shaved them, and
19:6 themselves odious to David, H and the Ammonites
Neh 3:13 H and the inhabitants of Zanoah repaired the Valley
3:30 son of Shelemiah and H the sixth son of

HAPHARA-IM

Josh 19:19 included Jezreel, Chesulloth, Shunem, H, Shion,

HAPLESS (3)

Ps 10:8 stealthily watch for the H,
10:10 The H is crushed, sinks down, and falls by
10:14 into thy hands; the H commits himself to thee;

HAPPEN (19)

1Kgs 14:3 tell you what shall H to the child."
Tob 14:8 because what the prophet Jonah said will surely H
Job 37:13 land, or for love, he causes it to H
Eccl 1:11 later things yet to H among those who come
9:11 but time and chance H to them all.
11:2 not what evil may H on earth.
Wis 2:17 us test what will H at the end of
Sir 11:22 and what calamity could H to me in the
22:24 if some harm should H to me because of
37:9 to see what will H to you.
Is 23:15 seventy years, it will H to Tyre as in
41:22 bring them, and tell us what is to H

H

Jer 6:18 O congregation, what will H to them.
Ezek 20:32 your mind shall never H --the thought, 'Let us
2Mac 9:25 for opportunities and waiting to see what will H
Mt 16:22 This shall never H to you."
Mk 10:32 them what was to H to him,
13:18 that it may not H in winter.
Lk 23:30 is green, what will H when it is dry?"

HAPPENED (72)

Gen 38:1 It H at that time that Judah went down
Deut 4:32 as this has ever H or was ever heard
Judg 19:30 a thing has never H or been seen from
Ruth 2:3 the reapers; and she H to come to the
1Sam 4:7 nothing like this has H before.
6:9 that struck us, it H to us by chance."
2Sam 1:6 said, "By chance I H to be on Mount
11:2 It H, late one afternoon, when David arose from
20:1 Now there H to be there a worthless fellow,
1Kgs 2:39 But it H at the end of three years
2Kgs 7:20 And so it H to him, for the people
Neh 1:1 Now it H in the month of Chislev, in
Tob 3:7 in Media, it also H that Sarah, the daughter
8:16 It has not H to me as I expected;
11:15 great things that had H to him in Media.
12:20 Write in a book everything that has H
Jud 6:16 their people, and Uzziah asked him what had H
8:26 tested Isaac, and what H to Jacob in Mesopotamia
15:1 heard it, they were amazed at what had H
15:5 were told what had H in the camp of
Esth 4:7 him all that had H to him, and the
Wis 19:4 them forget what had H, in order that they
Sir 5:4 "I sinned, and what H to me?" for the
Is 20:6 this is what has H to those in whom
Jer 5:30 and horrible thing has H in the land:
41:3 the Chaldean soldiers who H to be there.
48:19 escapes; say, 'What has H
Dan 13:26 to see what had H to her.
Joel 1:2 Has such a thing H in your days, or
Mic 6:5 answered him, and what H from Shittim to Gilgal,
1Mac 4:20 the smoke that was seen showed what had H
4:26 went and reported to Lysias all that had H
4:27 for things had not H to Israel as he
5:25 them all that had H to their brethren in
2Mac 4:30 state of affairs, it H that the people of
4:32 other vessels, as it H, he had sold to
5:2 And it H that over all the city, for
5:11 news of what had H reached the king, he
5:18 if it had not H that they were involved
7:1 It H also that seven brothers and their mother
7:18 Therefore astounding things have H
9:1 that time, as it H, Antiochus had retreated in
9:3 him of what had H to Nicanor and the
9:24 if anything unexpected H or any unwelcome news
10:5 It H that on the same day on which
10:21 word of what had H came to Maccabeus, he
11:1 vexed at what had H,
12:34 they joined battle, it H that a few of
12:42 own eyes what had H because of the sin
13:17 This H, just as day was dawning, because the
Mt 8:33 everything, and what had H to the demoniacs.
Mk 5:14 came to see what it was that had H
5:16 it told what had H to the demoniac and
Lk 2:15 this thing that has H, which the Lord has
8:34 herdsmen saw what had H, they fled, and told
8:35 to see what had H, and they came to
8:56 charged them to tell no one what had H
9:18 Now it H that as he was praying alone
24:12 and he went home wondering at what had H
24:14 each other about all these things that had H
24:18 the things that have H there in these days?"
24:21 it is now the third day since this H
24:35 they told what had H on the road, and
Acts 3:10 amazement at what had H to him.
4:21 for all men praised God for what had H
5:7 his wife came in, not knowing what had H
10:16 This H three times, and the thing was taken
11:10 not call common.' This H three times, and all
28:8 It H that the father of Publius lay sick
1Cor 10:11 Now these things H to them as a warning,
Phil 1:12 brethren, that what has H to me has really
2Pet 2:22 It has H to them according to the true

HAPPENING

1Pet 4:12 though something strange were H to you.

HAPPENS (4)

Eccl 8:14 men to whom it H according to the deeds
8:14 men to whom it H according to the deeds
Lk 12:54 once, 'A shower is coming'; and so it H
12:55 say, 'There will be scorching heat'; and it H

HAPPIER (2)

Lam 4:9 H were the victims of the sword than the
1Cor 7:40 my judgment she is H if she remains as

HAPPILY

2Mac 11:26 cheer and go on H in the conduct of

HAPPINESS (3)

Tob 8:17 fulfilment in health and H and mercy."
Sir 37:4 companions rejoice in the H of a friend, but
Lam 3:17 I have forgotten what H is;

HAPPIZZEZ

1Chr 24:15 Hezir, the eighteenth to H,

HAPPY (46)

Gen 30:13 And Leah said, H am I!
30:13 women will call me H; so she called his
Deut 24:5 one year, to be H with his wife whom
33:29 H are you, O Israel!
1Kgs 4:20 the sea; they ate and drank and were H
10:8 H are your wives!
10:8 H are these your servants, who continually stand
2Chr 9:7 H are your wives!
9:7 H are these your servants, who continually stand
Esth 15:5 beauty, and she looked H, as if beloved, but
Job 5:17 "Behold, H is the man whom God reproves;
Ps 34:8 H is the man who takes refuge in him!
49:18 lives, he counts himself H, and though a man
127:5 H is the man who has his quiver full
128:2 hands; you shall be H, and it shall be
137:8 H shall he be who requites you with what
137:9 H shall he be who takes your little ones
144:15 H the people to whom such blessings fall!
144:15 H the people whose God is the LORD!
146:5 H is he whose help is the God of
Prov 3:13 Wisdom's Value H is the man who finds wisdom,
3:18 her; those who hold her fast are called H
8:32 sons, listen to me: H are those who keep
8:34 H is the man who listens to me, watching
14:21 is a sinner, but H is he who is
16:20 word will prosper, and H is he who trusts
Eccl 3:12 them than to be H and enjoy themselves as
10:17 H are you, O land, when your king is
Song 6:9 her and called her H; the queens and concubines
Wis 2:16 end of the righteous H, and boasts that God
18:1 forms, and counted them H for not having suffered,
Sir 11:26 Call no one H before his death; a man
13:25 The mark of a H heart is a cheerful
14:14 deprive yourself of a H day; let not your
25:8 downfall of his foes; H is he who lives
25:9 man inferior to himself; H is he who has
25:22 the wife who does not make her husband H
26:1 H is the husband of a good wife; the
28:19 H is the man who is protected from it,
37:24 and all who see him will call him H
Is 32:20 H are you who sow beside all waters, who
Bar 4:4 H are we, O Israel, for we know what
1Mac 6:23 We were H to serve your father, to live
10:55 king replied and said, H was the day on
Rom 14:22 between yourself and God; H is he who has
Jas 5:11 Behold, we call those H who were steadfast.

HAR-HERES

Judg 1:35 persisted in dwelling in H, in Aijalon, and in

HARA

1Chr 5:26 them to Halah, Habor, H, and the river Gozan,

HARADAH (2)

Num 33:24 set out from Mount Shepher, and encamped at H
33:25 they set out from H, and encamped at Makheloth.

HARAN (21)

Gen 11:26 he became the father of Abram, Nahor, and H
11:27 of Abram, Nahor, and H; and Haran was the
11:27 Nahor, and Haran; and H was the father of
11:28 H died before his father Terah in the land
11:29 Milcah, the daughter of H the father of Milcah
11:31 Lot the son of H, his grandson, and Sarai

H

11:31 when they came to H, they settled there.
11:32 hundred and five years; and Terah died in H
12:4 was seventy-five years old when he departed from H
12:5 they had gotten in H; and they set forth
27:43 Laban my brother in H,
28:10 Jacob left Beer-sheba, and went toward H
29:4 They said, "We are from H
2Kgs 19:12 fathers destroyed, Gozan, H, Rezeph, and the people
1Chr 2:46 also, Caleb's concubine, bore H, Moza, and Gazez;
2:46 Moza, and Gazez; and H was the father of
23:9 Shimei: Shelomoth, Hazi-el, and H, three.
Is 37:12 fathers destroyed, Gozan, H, Rezeph, and the people
Ezek 27:23 H, Canneh, Eden, Asshur, and Chilmad traded with
Acts 7:2 before he lived in H,
7:4 the land of the Chaldeans, and lived in H

HARARITE (5)

2Sam 23:11 him was Shammah, the son of Agee the H
23:33 Jashen, Jonathan, Shammah the H, Ahiam the son of
23:33 son of Sharar the H,
1Chr 11:34 son of Shagee the H,
11:35 son of Sachar the H, Eliphal the son of

HARASS (8)

Num 25:17 LORD said to Moses, H the Midianites, and smite
Deut 2:9 to me, 'Do not H Moab or contend with
2:19 of Ammon, do not H them or contend with
Is 11:13 depart, and those who H Judah shall be cut
11:13 and Judah shall not H Ephraim.
1Mac 6:38 of the army, to H the enemy while being
9:51 garrisons in them to H Israel.
2Cor 12:7 messenger of Satan, to H me, to keep me

HARASSED (3)

Gen 49:23 shot at him, and H him sorely;
Num 25:18 them; for they have H you with their wiles,
Mt 9:36 them, because they were H and helpless, like sheep

HARASSING

2Mac 10:15 of important strongholds, were H the Jews; they

HARBONA (2)

Esth 1:10 he commanded Mehuman, Biztha, H, Bigtha and
7:9 Then said H, one of the eunuchs in attendance

HARBOR (7)

Sir 28:3 Does a man H anger against another, and yet
1Mac 14:5 took Joppa for a H, and opened a way
2Mac 12:6 set fire to the H by night, and burned
12:9 set fire to the H and the fleet, so
14:1 had sailed into the H of Tripolis with a
Acts 27:12 And because the H was not suitable to winter
27:12 could reach Phoenix, a H of Crete, looking northeast

HARBORS

Prov 26:24 with his lips and H deceit in his heart;

HARD (77)

Gen 18:14 old?' Is anything too H for the LORD?
19:9 Then they pressed H against the man Lot, and
35:16 travailed, and she had H labor.
35:17 she was in her H labor, the midwife said
Ex 1:13 their lives bitter with H service, in mortar and
18:26 people at all times; H cases they brought to
Deut 1:17 case that is too H for you, you shall
15:18 It shall not seem H to you, when you
26:6 and laid upon us H bondage.
30:11 day is not too H for you, neither is
Judg 14:17 day he told her, because she pressed him H
16:16 when she pressed him H with her words day
20:34 and the battle was H; but the Benjaminites did
20:45 and they were pursued H to Gidom, and two
1Sam 14:22 fleeing, they too followed H after them in the
14:52 There was H fighting against the Philistines all the
31:3 The battle pressed H upon Saul, and the archers
2Sam 3:39 of Zeruiah are too H for me.
1Kgs 10:1 to test him with H questions.
12:4 Now therefore lighten the H service of your father
2Kgs 2:10 "You have asked a H thing; yet, if you
1Chr 10:3 The battle pressed H upon Saul, and the archers
2Chr 9:1 to test him with H questions, having a very
10:4 Now therefore lighten the H service of your father
Job 7:1 "Has not man a H service upon earth, and
30:3 Through want and H hunger they gnaw the dry
30:25 not I weep for him whose day was H
37:18 spread out the skies, H as a molten mirror?
38:30 The waters become H like stone, and the face
41:24 His heart is H as a stone, hard as
41:24 hard as a stone, H as the nether millstone.
Ps 60:3 made thy people suffer H things; thou hast given
107:12 were bowed down with H labor; they fell down,
118:13 I was pushed H, so that I was falling,
Wis 11:4 slaking of thirst from H stone.
17:1 are thy judgments and H to describe; therefore
Sir 29:28 These things are H to bear for a man
48:13 Nothing was too H for him, and when he
Is 14:3 and turmoil and the H service with which you
19:4 the hand of a H master; and a fierce
27:1 the LORD with his H and great and strong
Jer 4:20 Disaster follows H on disaster, the whole land is
32:17 Nothing is too H for thee,
32:27 flesh; is anything too H for me?
42:16 are afraid shall follow H after you to Egypt;
Lam 1:3 because of affliction and H servitude; she dwells now
5:5 our necks we are H driven; we are weary,
Ezek 3:5 foreign speech and a H language, but to the
3:6 foreign speech and a H language, whose words you
3:7 Israel are of a H forehead and of a
3:8 have made your face H against their faces, and
3:8 faces, and your forehead H against their foreheads.
29:18 made his army labor H against Tyre; every head
Dan 14:30 they were pressing him H, and under compulsion he
Jon 1:13 Nevertheless the men rowed H to bring the ship
1Mac 15:14 he pressed the city H from land and sea,
2Mac 9:7 the fall was so H as to torture every
11:5 about five leagues from Jerusalem, and pressed it H
12:11 After a H fight Judas and his men won
12:21 for that place was H to besiege and difficult
Mt 7:14 and the way is H, that leads to life,
19:23 you, it will be H for a rich man
23:4 They bind heavy burdens, H to bear, and lay
25:24 you to be a H man, reaping where you
Mk 10:23 to his disciples, "How H it will be for
10:24 them again, "Children, how H it is for those
Lk 11:46 load men with burdens H to bear, and you
11:53 began to press him H, and to provoke him
18:24 at him said, "How H it is for those
Jn 6:60 said, "This is a H saying; who can listen
Rom 2:5 But by your H and impenitent heart you are
16:6 Mary, who has worked H among you.
16:12 Persis, who has worked H in the Lord.
Col 4:13 that he has worked H for you and for
Heb 5:11 to say which is H to explain, since you
10:32 enlightened, you endured a H struggle with
2Pet 3:16 some things in them H to understand, which the

HARD-PRESSED (4)

1Sam 13:6 (for the people were H, the people hid themselves
2Mac 8:20 when the Macedonians were H, the eight thousand,
14:9 our country and our H nation with the gracious
Phil 1:23 I am H between the two.

HARD-WORKING

2Tim 2:6 It is the H farmer who ought to have

HARDEN (12)

Ex 4:21 power; but I will H his heart, so that
7:3 But I will H Pharaoh's heart, and though I
14:4 in.' And I will H Pharaoh's heart, and he
14:17 And I will H the hearts of the Egyptians
Deut 15:7 you, you shall not H your heart or shut
Josh 11:20 the LORD's doing to H their hearts that they
1Sam 6:6 Why should you H your hearts as the Egyptians
Ps 95:8 H not your hearts, as at Meribah, as on
Is 63:17 from thy ways and H our heart, so that
Heb 3:8 his voice, do not H your hearts as in
3:15 his voice, do not H your hearts as in
4:7 his voice, do not H your hearts."

HARDENED (26)

Ex 7:13 Still Pharaoh's heart was H, and he would not
7:14 Moses, "Pharaoh's heart is H, he refuses to let
7:22 so Pharaoh's heart remained H, and he would not
8:15 was a respite, he H his heart, and would
8:19 But Pharaoh's heart was H, and he would not
8:32 But Pharaoh H his heart this time also, and
9:7 heart of Pharaoh was H, and he did not
9:12 But the LORD H the heart of Pharaoh, and
9:34 sinned yet again, and H his heart, he and
9:35 heart of Pharaoh was H, and he did not
10:1 Pharaoh; for I have H his heart and the
10:20 But the LORD H Pharaoh's heart, and he did

10:27 But the LORD H Pharaoh's heart, and he would
11:10 Pharaoh; and the LORD H Pharaoh's heart, and he
14:8 And the LORD H the heart of Pharaoh king
Deut 2:30 the LORD your God H his spirit and made
1Sam 6:6 the Egyptians and Pharaoh H their hearts?
2Chr 36:13 stiffened his neck and H his heart against turning
Job 9:4 strength --who has H himself against him, and
Dan 5:20 and his spirit was H so that he dealt
Mk 6:52 understand about the loaves, but their hearts were H
8:17 Are your hearts H
Jn 12:40 blinded their eyes and H their heart, lest they
Rom 11:7 but the rest were H,
2Cor 3:14 But their minds were H; for to this day,
Heb 3:13 of you may be H by the deceitfulness of

HARDENING
Rom 11:25 this mystery, brethren: a H has come upon part

HARDENS (3)
Job 7:5 and dirt; my skin H, then breaks out afresh.
Prov 28:14 always; but he who H his heart will fall
Rom 9:18 he wills, and he H the heart of whomever

HARDER (5)
Judg 4:24 people of Israel bore H and harder on Jabin
4:24 Israel bore harder and H on Jabin the king
Jer 5:3 have made their faces H than rock; they have
Ezek 3:9 Like adamant H than flint have I made your
1Cor 15:10 the contrary, I worked H than any of them,

HARDEST
2Sam 11:15 the forefront of the H fighting, and then draw

HARDLY (5)
Wis 9:16 We can H guess at what is on earth,
Sir 26:20 A merchant can H keep from wrongdoing, and a
29:6 exert pressure, he will H get back half, and
Lk 9:39 shatters him, and will H leave him.
Rom 5:7 Why, one will H die for a righteous man--

HARDNESS (6)
Eccl 8:1 face shine, and the H of his countenance is
Mt 19:8 to them, "For your H of heart Moses allowed
Mk 3:5 anger, grieved at their H of heart, and said
10:5 to them, "For your H of heart he wrote
16:14 for their unbelief and H of heart, because they
Eph 4:18 them, due to their H of heart;

HARDSHIP (4)
Gen 41:51 me forget all my H and all my father's
Ex 18:8 Israel's sake, all the H that had come upon
Neh 9:32 let not all the H seem little to thee
2Cor 11:27 brethren; in toil and H, through many a sleepless

HARDSHIPS (3)
Ps 132:1 David's favor, all the H he endured;
2Cor 6:4 great endurance, in afflictions, H, calamities,
12:10 content with weaknesses, insults, H, persecutions,

HARE (2)
Lev 11:6 And the H, because it chews the cud but
Deut 14:7 these: the camel, the H, and the rock badger,

HAREM (5)
Esth 2:3 young virgins to the H in Susa the capital,
2:9 her maids to the best place in the H
2:11 the court of the H, to learn how Esther
2:13 with her from the H to the king's palace.
2:14 back to the second H in custody of Sha-ashgaz

HAREPH
1Chr 2:51 father of Bethelem, and H the father of Beth-gader.

HARHAIAH
Neh 3:8 Uzziel the son of H, goldsmiths, repaired.

HARHAS
2Kgs 22:14 of Tikvah, son of H, keeper of the wardrobe

HARHUR (2)
Ezra 2:51 Hakupha, the sons of H,
Neh 7:53 Hakupha, the sons of H,

HARIM (11)
1Chr 24:8 Jedaiah, the third to H, the fourth to Se-orim,
Ezra 2:32 The sons of H, three hundred and twenty.
2:39 The sons of H, one thousand and seventeen.
10:21 Of the sons of H: Ma-aseiah, Elijah, Shemaiah,
10:31 Of the sons of H: Eliezer, Isshijah, Malchijah,
Neh 3:11 Malchijah the son of H and Hasshub the son
7:35 The sons of H, three hundred and twenty.
7:42 The sons of H, a thousand and seventeen.
10:5 Hattush, Shebaniah, Malluch, H, Meremoth,
10:27 Ahiah, Hanan, Anan, Malluch, H, Baanah.
12:15 of Shebaniah, Joseph; of H, Adna; of Meraioth,

HARIPH (2)
Neh 7:24 The sons of H, a hundred and twelve.
10:19 Hodiah, Hashum, Bezai, H, Anathoth, Nebai,

HARK (15)
Ps 118:15 H, glad songs of victory in the tents of
Song 5:2 H! My beloved is knocking.
Is 13:4 H, a tumult on the mountains as of a
13:4 H, an uproar of kingdoms, of nations gathering
52:8 H, your watchmen lift up their voice, together they
66:6 H, an uproar from the city!
Jer 8:19 H, the cry of the daughter of my people
10:22 H, a rumor!
25:36 H, the cry of the shepherds, and the wail
48:3 H! a cry from Horonaim.
50:28 H! they flee and escape
51:54 H! a cry from Babylon!
Zech 11:3 H, the wail of the shepherds, for their glory
11:3 H, the roar of the lions, for the jungle
Acts 5:9 H, the feet of those that have buried your

HARLOT (83)
Gen 34:31 said, "Should he treat our sister as a H
38:15 her to be a H, for she had covered
38:21 place, "Where is the H who was at Enaim
38:21 And they said, "No H has been here."
38:22 the place said, 'No H has been here.'"
38:24 daughter-in-law has played the H; and moreover she
Ex 34:15 when they play the H after their gods and
34:16 their daughters play the H after their gods and
34:16 your sons play the H after their gods.
Lev 17:7 sacrifices for satyrs, after whom they play the H
19:29 by making her a H, lest the land fall
20:5 him in playing the H after Molech.
20:6 and wizards, playing the H after them, I will
21:7 shall not marry a H or a woman who
21:9 herself by playing the H, profanes her father; she
21:14 been defiled, or a H, these he shall not
Num 25:1 began to play the H with the daughters of
Deut 22:21 Israel by playing the H in her father's house;
23:18 the hire of a H, or the wages of
31:16 rise and play the H after the strange gods
Josh 2:1 the house of a H whose name was Rahab,
6:17 destruction; only Rahab the H and all who are
6:22 land, "Go into the H's house, and bring out
6:25 But Rahab the H, and her father's household, and
Judg 2:17 for they played the H after other gods and
8:27 all Israel played the H after it there, and
8:33 again and played the H after the Baals, and
11:1 warrior, but he was the son of a H
16:1 there he saw a H, and he went in
1Chr 5:25 fathers, and played the H after the gods of
Ps 106:39 acts, and played the H in their doings.
Prov 6:26 her eyelashes; for a H may be hired for
7:10 him, dressed as a H, wily of heart.
23:27 For a H is a deep pit; an adventures
Sir 41:20 woman who is a H,
Is 1:21 city has become a H, she that was full
23:15 the song of the H:
23:16 a harp, go about the city, O forgotten H
23:17 and will play the H with all the kingdoms
57:3 the sorceress, offspring of the adulterer and the H
Jer 2:20 every green tree you bowed down as a H
3:1 You have played the H with many lovers; and
3:3 yet you have a H's brow, you refuse to
3:6 under every green tree, and there played the H
3:8 fear, but she too went and played the H
Ezek 16:15 beauty, and played the H because of your renown,
16:16 on them played the H; the like has never
16:17 with them played the H;
16:26 You also played the H with the Egyptians, your
16:28 You played the H also with the Assyrians, because
16:28 yea, you played the H with them, and still
16:30 deeds of a brazen H;
16:31 were not like a H, because you scorned hire.
16:34 you to play the H; and you gave hire,

16:35 "Wherefore, O H, hear the word of the LORD:
16:41 you stop playing the H, and you shall also
23:3 mother; they played the H in Egypt; they played
23:3 Egypt; they played the H in their youth; there
23:5 "Oholah played the H while she was mine; and
23:19 when she played the H in the land of
23:30 because you played the H with the nations, and
23:44 to her, as men go in to a H
Hos 2:5 mother has played the H; she that conceived them
3:3 shall not play the H, or belong to another
4:10 they shall play the H, but not multiply; because
4:12 they have left their God to play the H
4:13 your daughters play the H, and your brides commit
4:14 when they play the H, nor your brides when
4:15 Though you play the H, O Israel, let not
5:3 you have played the H, Israel is defiled.
9:1 you have played the H, forsaking your God.
9:1 You have loved a H's hire upon all threshing
Joel 3:3 a boy for a H, and have sold a
Amos 7:17 wife shall be a H in the city, and
Mic 1:7 the hire of a H she gathered them, and
1:7 the hire of a H they shall return.
Nah 3:4 countless harlotries of the H, graceful and of deadly
Heb 11:31 By faith Rahab the H did not perish with
Jas 2:25 not also Rahab the H justified by works when
Rev 17:1 judgment of the great H who is seated upon
17:15 you saw, where the H is seated, are peoples
17:16 beast will hate the H; they will make her
19:2 has judged the great H who corrupted the earth

HARLOTRIES (11)

2Kgs 9:22 so long as the H and the sorceries of
Jer 13:27 and neighings, your lewd H, on the hills in
Ezek 16:15 renown, and lavished your H on any passer-by.
16:20 Were your H so small a matter
16:22 your abominations and your H you did not remember
16:33 come to you from every side for your H
16:34 other women in your H: none solicited you to
16:36 nakedness uncovered in your H with your lovers, and
23:7 She bestowed her H upon them, the choicest men
Nah 3:4 all for the countless H of the harlot, graceful
3:4 betrays nations with her H, and peoples with her

HARLOTRY (30)

Gen 38:24 harlot; and moreover she is with child by H
Lev 19:29 the land fall into H and the land become
Sir 23:23 has committed adultery through H and brought forth
26:9 A wife's H shows in her lustful eyes, and
Jer 3:2 You have polluted the land with your vile H
3:9 Because H was so light to her, she polluted
Ezek 16:25 yourself to any passer-by, and multiplying your H
16:26 lustful neighbors, multiplying your H, to provoke me
16:29 You multiplied your H also with the trading land
23:8 not give up her H which she had practiced
23:11 doting and in her H, which was worse than
23:14 But she carried her H further; she saw men
23:18 she carried on her H so openly and flaunted
23:19 Yet she increased her H, remembering the days of
23:27 your lewdness and your H brought from the land
23:29 the nakedness of your H shall be uncovered.
23:29 Your lewdness and your H
23:35 bear the consequences of your lewdness and H
23:43 adultery when they practice H with her?
43:7 their kings, by their H, and by the dead
Hos 1:2 yourself a wife of H and have children of
1:2 and have children of H, for the land commits
1:2 the land commits great H by forsaking the LORD."
2:2 she put away her H from her face, and
2:4 have no pity, because they are children of H
4:10 because they have forsaken the LORD to cherish H
4:12 For a spirit of H has led them astray,
4:18 they give themselves to H; they love shame more
5:4 For the spirit of H is within them, and
6:10 a horrible thing; Ephraim's H is there, Israel is

HARLOTS (14)

1Kgs 3:16 Then two H came to the king, and stood
22:38 his blood, and the H washed themselves in it,
Prov 29:3 who keeps company with H squanders his substance.
Sir 9:6 not give yourself to H lest you lose your
19:2 man who consorts with H is very reckless.
Jer 5:7 committed adultery and trooped to the houses of H
Bar 6:11 of it to the H in the brothel.
Ezek 16:33 give gifts to all H; but you gave your
Hos 4:14 themselves go aside with H, and sacrifice with cult
2Mac 6:4 Gentiles, who dallied with H and had intercourse

Mt 21:31 tax collectors and the H go into the kingdom
21:32 tax collectors and the H believed him; and even
Lk 15:30 devoured your living with H, you killed for him
Rev 17:5 the great, mother of H and of earth's abominations."

HARM (61)

Gen 26:29 will do us no H, just as we have
31:7 not permit him to H me.
31:29 power to do you H; but the God of
31:52 this heap and this pillar to me, for H
42:4 for he feared that H might befall him.
42:38 If H should befall him on the journey that
44:29 also from me, and H befalls him, you will
Ex 21:22 miscarriage, and yet no H follows, the one who
21:23 If any H follows, then you shall give life
Num 35:23 did not seek his H;
Josh 24:20 turn and do you H, and consume you, after
1Sam 6:9 done us this great H; but if not, then
20:13 father to do you H, the LORD do so
25:7 we did them no H, and they missed nothing,
25:15 and we suffered no H, and we did not
26:21 no more do you H, because my life was
2Sam 12:18 He may do himself some H
20:6 will do us more H than Absalom; take your
2Kgs 4:41 And there was no H in the pot.
1Chr 4:10 wouldst keep me from H so that it might
16:22 not my anointed ones, do my prophets no H
Neh 6:2 But they intended to do me H
Tob 12:2 would do me no H to give him half
Esth 13:5 government, doing all the H they can so that
Ps 105:15 not my anointed ones, do my prophets no H
Prov 3:30 no reason, when he has done you no H
13:20 wise, but the companion of fools will suffer H
19:23 rests satisfied; he will not be visited by H
31:12 him good, and not H, all the days of
Eccl 8:5 command will meet no H, and the mind of
Wis 14:29 swear wicked oaths and expect to suffer no H
Sir 4:22 partiality, to your own H, or deference, to your
22:24 him; but if some H should happen to me
36:9 and may those who H thy people meet destruction.
Is 27:3 Lest any one H it, I guard it night
41:23 do good, or do H, that we may be
Jer 25:6 will do you no H
25:7 the work of your hands to your own H
38:4 seeking the welfare of this people, but their H
39:12 and do him no H, but deal with him
Dan 3:43 Let all who do H to thy servants be
Hab 2:9 high, to be safe from the reach of H
1Mac 5:48 one will do you H; we will simply pass
6:18 in every way to H them and strengthen the
7:14 and he will not H us."
9:71 would not try to H him as long as
15:19 should not seek their H or make war against
Mk 3:4 good or to do H, to save life or
Lk 4:35 came out of him, having done him no H
6:9 good or to do H, to save life or
Acts 16:28 loud voice, "Do not H yourself, for we are
18:10 shall attack you to H you; for I have
28:5 the creature into the fire and suffered no H
2Tim 4:14 coppersmith did me great H; the Lord will requite
1Pet 3:13 who is there to H you if you are
Rev 6:6 denarius; but do not H oil and wine!"
7:2 been given power to H earth and sea,
7:3 sea, saying, "Do not H the earth or the
9:4 were told not to H the grass of the
11:5 if any one would H them, fire pours out
11:5 if any one would H them, thus he is

HARMED (2)

Num 16:15 and I have not H one of them."
Dan 3:95 their mantles were not H, and no smell of

HARMFUL

2Mac 15:39 just as it is H to drink wine alone,

HARMLESS

Wis 18:3 unknown journey, and a H sun for their glorious

HARMON

Amos 4:3 her; and you shall be cast forth into H

HARMONY (4)

Sir 25:1 a wife and a husband who live in H
Rom 12:16 Live in H with one another; do not be
15:5 to live in such H with one another, in
Col 3:14 on love, which binds everything together in perfect H

HARMS
Tob 6:14 with her, and he H no one except those

HARNEPHER
1Chr 7:36 sons of Zophah: Suah, H, Shual, Beri, Imrah,

HARNESS (3)
Jer 46:4 H the horses; mount, O horsemen!
Mic 1:13 H the steeds to the chariots, inhabitants of Lachish;
1Mac 6:37 each beast by special H, and upon each were

HAROD (4)
Judg 7:1 beside the spring of H; and the camp of
2Sam 23:25 of Bethlehem, Shammah of H, Elika of Harod,
23:25 of Harod, Elika of H,
1Chr 11:27 of Bethlehem, Shammoth of H, Helez the Pelonite,

HAROEH
1Chr 2:52 Kiriath-jearim had other sons: H, half of the

HAROSHETH-HA-GOIIM (3)
Judg 4:2 of his army was Sisera, who dwelt in H
4:13 were with him, from H to the river Kishon.
4:16 and the army to H, and all the army

HARP (21)
1Sam 10:5 the high place with H, tambourine, flute, and lyre
Ps 33:2 to him with the H of ten strings!
57:8 Awake, O H and lyre!
71:22 praise thee with the H for thy faithfulness, O
81:2 sound the timbrel, the sweet lyre with the H
92:3 the lute and the H, to the melody of
108:2 Awake, O H and lyre!
144:9 God; upon a ten-stringed H I will play to
150:3 with trumpet sound; praise him with lute and H
Wis 19:18 another, as on a H the notes vary the
Sir 40:21 The flute and the H make pleasant melody, but
Is 5:12 They have lyre and H, timbrel and flute and
23:16 the harlot: "Take a H, go about the city,
Dan 3:5 horn, pipe, lyre, trigon, H, bagpipe, and every kind
3:7 horn, pipe, lyre, trigon, H, bagpipe, and every kind
3:10 horn, pipe, lyre, trigon, H, bagpipe, and every kind
3:15 horn, pipe, lyre, trigon, H, bagpipe, and every kind
Amos 6:5 the sound of the H, and like David invent
1Mac 3:45 the flute and the H ceased to play.
1Cor 14:7 the flute or the H, do not give distinct
Rev 5:8 Lamb, each holding a H, and with golden bowls

HARPERS (2)
Rev 14:2 like the sound of H playing on their harps,
18:22 and the sound of H and minstrels, of flute

HARPOONS
Job 41:7 fill his skin with H, or his head with

HARPS (20)
2Sam 6:5 and lyres and H and tambourines and castanets
1Kgs 10:12 house, lyres also and H for the singers; no
1Chr 13:8 song and lyres and H and tambourines and cymbals
15:16 on musical instruments, on H and lyres and cymbals,
15:20 Benaiah were to play H according to Alamoth;
15:28 made loud music on H and lyres.
16:5 who were to play H and lyres; Asaph was
25:1 prophesy with lyres, with H, and with cymbals.
25:6 the LORD with cymbals, H, and lyres for the
2Chr 5:12 fine linen, with cymbals, H, and lyres, stood east
9:11 house, lyres also and H for the singers; there
20:28 came to Jerusalem, with H and lyres and trumpets,
29:25 the LORD with cymbals, H, and lyres, according to
Neh 12:27 with singing, with cymbals, H, and lyres.
Is 14:11 the sound of your H; maggots are the bed
Amos 5:23 the melody of your H I will not listen.
1Mac 4:54 dedicated with songs and H and lutes and cymbals.
13:51 palm branches, and with H and cymbals and stringed
Rev 14:2 harpers playing on their H,
15:2 sea of glass with H of God in their

HARROW (3)
Job 39:10 ropes, or will he H the valleys after you?
Is 28:24 he continually open and H his ground?
Hos 10:11 must plow, Jacob must H for himself.

HARSH (6)
Prov 15:1 away wrath, but a H word stirs up anger.
Wis 17:19 rushing water, or the H crash of rocks hurled
Sir 6:20 She seems very H to the uninstructed; a weakling
2Mac 6:3 H and utterly grievous was the onslaught of evil.
Col 3:19 and do not be H with them.
Jude 1:15 and of all the H things which ungodly sinners

HARSHA (2)
Ezra 2:52 Mehida, the sons of H,
Neh 7:54 Mehida, the sons of H,

HARSHLY (5)
Gen 16:6 Then Sarai dealt H with her, and she fled
Num 20:15 and the Egyptians dealt H with us and our
Deut 26:6 the Egyptians treated us H, and afflicted us, and
1Kgs 12:13 king answered the people H, and forsaking the
2Chr 10:13 the king answered them H, and forsaking the counsel

HARSHNESS (4)
Lev 25:43 rule over him with H, but shall fear your
25:46 you shall not rule, one over another, with H
25:53 shall not rule with H over him in your
Ezek 34:4 and with force and H you have ruled them.

HART (6)
Deut 12:15 as of the gazelle and as of the H
12:22 the gazelle or the H is eaten, so you
14:5 sheep, the goat, the H, the gazelle, the roebuck,
15:22 as though it were a gazelle or a H
Ps 42:1 As a H longs for flowing streams, so longs
Is 35:6 man leap like a H, and the tongue of

HARTS (2)
1Kgs 4:23 a hundred sheep, besides H, gazelles, roebucks, and
Lam 1:6 princes have become like H that find no pasture;

HARUM
1Chr 4:8 and the families of Aharhel the son of H

HARUMAPH
Neh 3:10 Jedaiah the son of H repaired opposite his house;

HARUPHITE
1Chr 12:5 Bealiah, Shemariah, Shephatiah the H;

HARUZ
2Kgs 21:19 Meshullemeth the daughter of H of Jotbah.

HARVEST (71)
Gen 8:22 earth remains, seedtime and H, cold and heat,
30:14 the days of wheat H Reuben went and found
45:6 in which there will be neither plowing nor H
Ex 22:29 the fulness of your H and from the outflow
23:16 keep the feast of H, of the first fruits
34:21 plowing time and in H you shall rest.
34:22 first fruits of wheat H, and the feast of
Lev 19:9 "When you reap the H of your land, you
19:9 neither shall you gather the gleanings after your H
23:10 you and reap its H, you shall bring the
23:10 first fruits of your H to the priest;
23:22 when you reap the H of your land, you
23:22 the gleanings after your H; you shall leave them
25:5 of itself in your H you shall not reap,
Deut 24:19 "When you reap your H in your field, and
26:2 the ground, which you H from your land that
Josh 3:15 throughout the time of H,
Judg 15:1 the time of wheat H, Samson went to visit
Ruth 1:22 came to Bethlehem at the beginning of barley H
2:21 my servants, till they have finished all my H
1Sam 6:13 were reaping their wheat H in the valley; and
8:12 and to reap his H, and to make his
12:17 Is it not wheat H today?
2Sam 21:9 the first days of H, at the beginning of
21:9 days of harvest, at the beginning of barley H
21:10 from the beginning of H until rain fell upon
23:13 down, and came about H time to David at
Jud 2:27 Damascus during the wheat H, and burned all their
8:2 tribe and family, had died during the barley H
Job 5:5 His H the hungry eat, and he takes it
Prov 6:8 food in summer, and gathers her sustenance in H
10:5 son who sleeps in H brings shame.
20:4 he will seek at H and have nothing.
25:13 in the time of H is a faithful messenger
26:1 summer or rain in H, so honor is not
Sir 6:19 plows and sows, and wait for her good H
20:27 will heap up his H, and whoever pleases great
24:24 like the Jordan at H time.
Is 9:3 with joy at the H, as men rejoice when
16:9 your fruit and your H the battle shout has

17:11 you sow; yet the H will flee away in
18:4 a cloud of dew in the heat of H
18:5 For before the H, when the blossom is over,
23:3 grain of Shihor, the H of the Nile; you
32:10 will fail, the fruit H will not come.
Jer 2:3 to the LORD, the first fruits of his H
5:17 shall eat up your H and your food; they
5:24 weeks appointed for the H
8:20 "The H is past, the summer is ended, and
50:16 sickle in time of H; because of the sword
51:33 the time of her H will come."
Hos 6:11 also, O Judah, a H is appointed.
Joel 1:10 the barley; because the H of the field has
3:13 the sickle, for the H is ripe.
Amos 4:7 three months to the H; I would send rain
Mt 9:37 to his disciples, "The H is plentiful, but the
9:38 the Lord of the H to send out laborers
9:38 the harvest to send out laborers into his H
13:30 grow together until the H; and at harvest time
13:30 the harvest; and at H time I will tell
13:39 is the devil; the H is the close of
Mk 4:29 the sickle, because the H has come."
Lk 10:2 said to them, "The H is plentiful, but the
10:2 the Lord of the H to send out laborers
10:2 the harvest to send out laborers into his H
Jn 4:35 'There are yet four months, then comes the H
4:35 see how the fields are already white for H
Rom 1:13 I may reap some H among you as well
2Cor 9:10 resources and increase the H of your righteousness.
Jas 3:18 And the H of righteousness is sown in peace
Rev 14:15 has come, for the H of the earth is

HARVESTED (2)
Jud 4:5 for war--since their fields had recently been H
Hag 1:6 have sown much, and H little; you eat, but

HARVESTERS
Jas 5:4 the cries of the H have reached the ears

HARVESTS (4)
Gen 47:24 And at the H you shall give a fifth
Ruth 2:23 the barley and wheat H; and she lived with
Is 17:5 grain and his arm H the ears, and as
Jer 12:13 be ashamed of their H because of the fierce

HASADIAH (2)
1Chr 3:20 Hashubah, Ohel, Berechiah, H, and Jushab-hesed,
Bar 1:1 of Zedekiah, son of H, son of Hilkiah, wrote

HASH-BADDANAH
Neh 8:4 Mishael, Malchijah, Hashum, H, Zechariah, and

HASHABIAH (16)
1Chr 6:45 of Malluch, son of H, son of Amaziah, son
9:14 of Azrikam, son of H, of the sons of
25:3 Zeri, Jeshaiah, Shimei, H, and Mattithiah, six,
25:19 twelve; the twelfth to H, his sons and his
26:30 Of the Hebronites, H and his brethren, one thousand
27:17 of Maacah; for Levi, H the son of Kemuel;
2Chr 35:9 Nethanel his brothers, and H and Je-iel and Jozabad,
Ezra 8:19 and kinsmen, eighteen; also H and with him Jeshaiah
8:24 the leading priests: Sherebiah, H, and ten of their
10:25 Izziah, Malchijah, Mijamin, Eleazar, H, and Benaiah.
Neh 3:17 Bani; next to him H, ruler of half the
10:11 Pelaiah, Hanan, Mica, Rehob, H,
11:15 of Azrikam, son of H, son of Bunni;
11:22 of Bani, son of H, son of Mattaniah, son
12:21 Amok, Eber; of Hilkiah, H; of Jedaiah, Nethanel.
12:24 chiefs of the Levites: H, Sherebiah, and Jeshua the

HASHABNAH
Neh 10:25 Hallohesh, Pilha, Shobek, Rehum, H, Ma-aseiah,

HASHABNEIAH (2)
Neh 3:10 Hattush the son of H repaired.
9:5 Levites, Jeshua, Kadmi-el, Bani, H, Sherebiah,

HASHEM
1Chr 11:34 Baharum, Eliahba of Sha-albon, H the Gizonite,

HASHMONAH (2)
Num 33:29 they set out from Mithkah, and encamped at H
33:30 they set out from H, and encamped at Moseroth.

HASHUBAH
1Chr 3:20 was their sister; and H, Ohel, Berechiah, Hasadiah,

HASHUM (5)
Ezra 2:19 The sons of H, two hundred and twenty-three.
10:33 sons of H: Mattenai, Mattattah, Zabad, Eliphelet,
Neh 7:22 The sons of H, three hundred and twenty-eight.
8:4 Malchijah, H, Hash-baddanah, Zechariah, and M
10:18 Ater, Hezekiah, Azzur, Hodiah, H, Bezai,

HASIDEANS (3)
1Mac 2:42 them a company of H, mighty warriors of Israel,
7:13 The H were first among the sons of Israel
2Mac 14:6 Jews who are called H, whose leader is Judas

HASRAH
2Chr 34:22 of Tokhath, son of H, keeper of the wardrobe

HASSENAAH
Neh 3:3 And the sons of H built the Fish Gate;

HASSENUAH (2)
1Chr 9:7 of Hodaviah, son of H,
Neh 11:9 Judah the son of H was second over the

HASSHUB (5)
1Chr 9:14 Shemaiah the son of H, son of Azrikam, son
Neh 3:11 son of Harim and H the son of Pahath-moab
3:23 them Benjamin and H repaired opposite their house.
10:23 Hanan, Anaiah, Hoshea, Hananiah, H,
11:15 Shemaiah the son of H, son of Azrikam, son

HASSOPHERETH
Ezra 2:55 Sotai, the sons of H, the sons of Peruda,

HAST (399)
Gen 4:14 Behold, thou H driven me this day away from
15:3 Abram said, "Behold, thou H given me no offspring;
24:14 the one whom thou H appointed for thy servant
24:14 shall know that thou H shown steadfast love to
32:10 the faithfulness which thou H shown to thy servant,
Ex 4:10 heretofore or since thou H spoken to thy servant;
5:22 said, "O LORD, why H thou done evil to
5:23 this people, and thou H not delivered thy people
15:13 "Thou H led in thy steadfast love the people
15:13 the people whom thou H redeemed, thou hast guided
15:13 thou hast redeemed, thou H guided them by thy
15:16 pass by whom thou H purchased.
15:17 O LORD, which thou H made for thy abode,
32:11 thy people, whom thou H brought forth out of
32:32 thy book which thou H written."
33:12 this people'; but thou H not let me know
33:12 Yet thou H said, 'I know you by name,
Num 11:11 to the LORD, "Why H thou dealt ill with
11:21 on foot; and thou H said, 'I will give
14:17 be great as thou H promised, saying,
14:19 and according as thou H forgiven this people, from
Deut 3:24 'O Lord GOD, thou H only begun to show
9:26 thy heritage, whom thou H redeemed through thy
9:26 thy greatness, whom thou H brought out of Egypt
21:8 people Israel, whom thou H redeemed, and set not
26:10 which thou, O LORD, H given me.' And you
26:13 thy commandment which thou H commanded me; I
26:14 to all that thou H commanded me.
26:15 the ground which thou H given us, as thou
Josh 7:7 O Lord GOD, why H thou brought this people
Judg 6:36 my hand, as thou H said,
6:37 my hand, as thou H said."
15:18 LORD and said, "Thou H granted this great
1Sam 14:41 God of Israel, why H thou not answered thy
2Sam 7:18 my house, that thou H brought me thus far?
7:19 O Lord GOD; thou H spoken also of thy
7:19 while to come, and H shown me future generations,
7:21 thy own heart, thou H wrought all this greatness,
7:25 word which thou H spoken concerning thy servant
7:25 and do as thou H spoken;
7:27 the God of Israel, H made this revelation to
7:28 are true, and thou H promised this good thing
7:29 thou, O Lord GOD, H spoken, and with thy
22:36 Thou H given me the shield of thy salvation,
1Kgs 3:6 Solomon said, "Thou H shown great and steadfast
3:6 toward thee; and thou H kept for him this
3:6 and steadfast love, and H given him a son
3:7 LORD my God, thou H made thy servant king
3:8 thy people whom thou H chosen, a great people,
8:24 all their heart; who H kept with thy servant
8:24 and with thy hand H fulfilled it this day.
8:25 my father what thou H promised him, saying, 'There
8:26 be confirmed, which thou H spoken to thy servant

8:29 place of which thou H said, 'My name shall
8:36 thy land, which thou H given to thy people
8:44 the city which thou H chosen and the house
8:48 the city which thou H chosen, and the house
17:20 "O LORD my God, H thou brought calamity even
18:37 God, and that thou H turned their hearts back."
2Kgs 19:15 of the earth; thou H made heaven and earth.
1Chr 17:16 my house, that thou H brought me thus far?
17:17 eyes, O God; thou H also spoken of thy
17:17 while to come, and H shown me future generations,
17:19 thy own heart, thou H wrought all this greatness,
17:23 word which thou H spoken concerning thy servant
17:23 and do as thou H spoken;
17:25 For thou, my God, H revealed to thy servant
17:26 art God, and thou H promised this good thing
17:27 what thou, O LORD, H blessed is blessed for
29:17 triest the heart, and H pleasure in uprightness; in
2Chr 1:8 said to God, "Thou H shown great and steadfast
1:8 David my father, and H made me king in
1:9 now fulfilled, for thou H made me king over
6:15 all their heart; who H kept with thy servant
6:15 and with thy hand H fulfilled it this day.
6:16 my father what thou H promised him, saying, 'There
6:17 be confirmed, which thou H spoken to thy servant
6:20 the place where thou H promised to set thy
6:27 thy land, which thou H given to thy people
6:34 this city which thou H chosen and the house
6:38 the city which thou H chosen, and the house
20:11 thy possession, which thou H given us to inherit.
Ezra 9:13 that thou, our God, H punished us less than
9:13 our iniquities deserved and H given us such a
Neh 1:10 thy people, whom thou H redeemed by thy great
9:6 LORD, thou alone; thou H made heaven, the heaven
9:8 the Girgashite; and thou H fulfilled thy promise, for
9:33 Yet thou H been just in all that has
9:33 upon us, for thou H dealt faithfully and we
9:37 the kings whom thou H set over us because
Tob 8:16 art thou, because thou H made me glad.
8:16 I expected; but thou H treated us according to
8:17 art thou, because thou H had compassion on two
11:15 For thou H afflicted me, but thou hast had
11:15 afflicted me, but thou H had mercy upon me;
Jud 9:2 disgrace her; for thou H said, 'It shall not
9:5 "For thou H done these things and those that
9:5 those that followed; thou H designed the things that
13:17 thou, our God, who H brought into contempt this
Esth 13:10 For thou H made heaven and earth and every
14:6 before thee, and thou H given us into the
14:15 Thou H knowledge of all things; and thou knowest
Job 1:10 H thou not put a hedge about him and
1:10 Thou H blessed the work of his hands, and
7:20 Why H thou made me thy mark?
10:4 H thou eyes of flesh?
10:9 Remember that thou H made me of clay; and
10:12 Thou H granted me life and steadfast love; and
14:5 with thee, and thou H appointed his bounds that
17:4 Since thou H closed their minds to understanding,
30:21 Thou H turned cruel to me; with the might
36:23 who can say, 'Thou H done wrong?
Ps 4:1 Thou H given me room when I was in
4:7 Thou H put more joy in my heart than
7:6 O my God; thou H appointed a judgment.
8:2 babes and infants, thou H founded a bulwark because
8:3 the stars which thou H established;
8:5 Yet thou H made him little less than God,
8:6 Thou H given him dominion over the works of
8:6 of thy hands; thou H put all things under
9:4 For thou H maintained my just cause; thou hast
9:4 my just cause; thou H sat on the throne
9:5 Thou H rebuked the nations, thou hast destroyed the
9:5 rebuked the nations, thou H destroyed the wicked;
9:5 destroyed the wicked; thou H blotted out their name
9:6 ruins; their cities thou H rooted out; the very
9:10 for thou, O LORD, H not forsaken those who
10:14 himself to thee; thou H been the helper of
17:14 filled with what thou H stored up for them;
18:35 Thou H given me the shield of thy salvation,
21:2 Thou H given him his heart's desire, and hast
21:2 his heart's desire, and H not withheld the request
22:1 God, my God, why H thou forsaken me?
22:10 mother bore me thou H been my God.
27:8 Thou H said, "Seek ye my face." My heart
27:9 in anger, thou who H been my help.
30:1 O LORD, for thou H drawn me up, and
30:1 drawn me up, and H not let my foes
30:2 for help, and thou H healed me.
30:3 O LORD, thou H brought up my soul from
30:11 Thou H turned for me my mourning into dancing;
30:11 mourning into dancing; thou H loosed my sackcloth
31:5 commit my spirit; thou H redeemed me, O LORD,
31:7 steadfast love, because thou H seen my affliction,
31:7 seen my affliction, thou H taken heed of my
31:8 of my adversities, and H not delivered me into
31:8 of the enemy; thou H set my feet in
31:19 thy goodness, which thou H laid up for those
35:22 Thou H seen, O LORD; be not silent!
39:5 Behold, thou H made my days a few handbreadths,
39:9 it is thou who H done it.
40:5 Thou H multiplied, O LORD my God, thy wondrous
40:6 not desire; but thou H given me an open
40:6 and sin offering thou H not required.
41:12 But thou H upheld me because of my integrity,
42:9 God, my rock: "Why H thou forgotten me?
43:2 I take refuge; why H thou cast me off?
44:7 But thou H saved us from our foes, and
44:7 from our foes, and H put to confusion those
44:9 [Selah] Yet thou H cast us off and abased
44:9 and abased us, and H not gone out with
44:10 Thou H made us turn back from the foe;
44:11 Thou H made us like sheep for slaughter, and
44:11 sheep for slaughter, and H scattered us among the
44:12 Thou H sold thy people for a trifle, demanding
44:13 Thou H made us the taunt of our neighbors,
44:14 Thou H made us a byword among the nations,
51:8 the bones which thou H broken rejoice.
51:16 For thou H no delight in sacrifice; were I
52:9 for ever, because thou H done it.
54:7 For thou H delivered me from every trouble, and
56:8 Thou H kept count of my tossings; put thou
56:13 For thou H delivered my soul from death, yea,
59:16 For thou H been to me a fortress and
60:1 O God, thou H rejected us, broken our defenses;
60:1 broken our defenses; thou H been angry; oh, restore
60:2 Thou H made the land to quake, thou hast
60:2 land to quake, thou H rent it open; repair
60:3 Thou H made thy people suffer hard things; thou
60:3 suffer hard things; thou H given us wine to
60:4 Thou H set up a banner for those who
60:10 H thou not rejected us, O God?
61:5 For thou, O God, H heard my vows, thou
61:5 heard my vows, thou H given me the heritage
63:7 the night; for thou H been my help, and
65:6 who by thy strength H established the mountains,
65:9 grain, for so thou H prepared it.
66:10 For thou, O God, H tested us; thou hast
66:10 hast tested us; thou H tried us as silver
66:12 through water; yet thou H brought us forth to
68:28 O God, thou who H wrought for us.
69:26 persecute him whom thou H smitten, and him whom
69:26 and him whom thou H wounded, they afflict still
71:17 from my youth thou H taught me, and I
71:19 Thou who H done great things, O God, who
71:20 Thou who H made me see many sore troubles
71:23 soul also, which thou H rescued.
74:2 thy congregation, which thou H gotten of old, which
74:2 of old, which thou H redeemed to be the
74:2 Mount Zion, where thou H dwelt.
74:16 also the night; thou H established the luminaries and
74:17 Thou H fixed all the bounds of the earth;
74:17 of the earth; thou H made summer and winter.
77:14 who workest wonders, who H manifested thy might
80:5 Thou H fed them with the bread of tears,
80:12 Why then H thou broken down its walls, so
80:17 of man whom thou H made strong for thyself!
86:9 All the nations thou H made shall come and
86:13 love toward me; thou H delivered my soul from
86:17 shame because thou, LORD, H helped me and
88:6 Thou H put me in the depths of the
88:8 [Selah] Thou H caused my companions to shun me;
88:8 to shun me; thou H made me a thing
88:18 Thou H caused lover and friend to shun me;
89:3 Thou H said, "I have made a covenant with
89:11 is in it, thou H founded them.
89:12 and the south, thou H created them; Tabor and
89:13 Thou H a mighty arm; strong is thy hand,
89:38 [Selah] But now thou H cast off and rejected,
89:39 Thou H renounced the covenant with thy servant;
89:39 with thy servant; thou H defiled his crown in
89:40 Thou H breached all his walls; thou hast laid
89:40 all his walls; thou H laid his strongholds in
89:42 Thou H exalted the right hand of his foes;
89:42 of his foes; thou H made all his enemies

89:43 Yea, thou H turned back the edge of his
89:43 his sword, and thou H not made him stand
89:44 Thou H removed the scepter from his hand, and
89:45 Thou H cut short the days of his youth;
89:45 of his youth; thou H covered him with shame.
89:47 for what vanity thou H created all the sons
90:1 LORD, thou H been our dwelling place in all
90:8 Thou H set our iniquities before thee, our secret
90:15 many days as thou H afflicted us, and as
92:4 For thou, O LORD, H made me glad by
92:10 But thou H exalted my horn like that of
92:10 the wild ox; thou H poured over me fresh
99:4 lover of justice, thou H established equity; thou hast
99:4 hast established equity; thou H executed justice and
102:10 and anger; for thou H taken me up and
104:2 with a garment, who H stretched out the heavens
104:3 like a tent, who H laid the beams of
104:19 Thou H made the moon to mark the seasons;
104:24 In wisdom H thou made them all; the earth
108:11 H thou not rejected us, O God?
109:27 hand; thou, O LORD, H done it!
116:8 For thou H delivered my soul from death, my
116:16 Thou H loosed my bonds.
118:21 thank thee that thou H answered me and hast
118:21 hast answered me and H become my salvation.
119:4 Thou H commanded thy precepts to be kept.
119:49 servant, in which thou H made me hope.
119:65 Thou H dealt well with thy servant, O LORD,
119:75 that in faithfulness thou H afflicted me.
119:90 to all generations; thou H established the earth, and
119:93 for by them thou H given me life.
119:102 thy ordinances, for thou H taught me.
119:138 Thou H appointed thy testimonies in righteousness
119:152 thy testimonies that thou H founded them for ever.
138:2 thy faithfulness; for thou H exalted above everything
139:1 O LORD, thou H searched me and known me!
140:7 my strong deliverer, thou H covered my head in
143:5 on all that thou H done; I muse on
Wis 9:1 Lord of mercy, who H made all things by
9:2 and by thy wisdom H formed man, to have
9:2 over the creatures thou H made,
9:7 Thou H chosen me to be king of thy
9:8 Thou H given command to build a temple on
9:17 thy counsel, unless thou H given wisdom and sent
11:20 But thou H arranged all things by measure and
11:24 things that exist, and H loathing for none of
11:24 the things which thou H made, for thou wouldst
12:12 who will say, "What H thou done?" Or will
12:13 shouldst prove that thou H not judged unjustly;
12:14 about those whom thou H punished.
12:18 govern us; for thou H power to act whenever
12:19 be kind, and thou H filled thy sons with
12:21 with what strictness thou H judged thy sons, to
14:3 its course, because thou H given it a path
16:13 For thou H power over life and death; thou
16:24 creation, serving thee who H made it, exerts itself
19:22 everything, O Lord, thou H exalted and glorified thy
19:22 thy people; and thou H not neglected to help
Sir 36:4 As in us thou H been sanctified before them,
36:12 upon Israel, whom thou H likened to a first-born
51:2 thy name, for thou H been my protector and
51:2 protector and helper and H delivered my body from
Is 2:6 For thou H rejected thy people, the house of
9:3 Thou H multiplied the nation, thou hast increased its
9:3 multiplied the nation, thou H increased its joy; they
9:4 of his oppressor, thou H broken as on the
25:1 thy name; for thou H done wonderful things, plans
25:2 For thou H made the city a heap, the
25:4 For thou H been a stronghold to the poor,
26:12 peace for us, thou H wrought for us all
26:14 to that end thou H visited them with destruction
26:15 But thou H increased the nation, O LORD, thou
26:15 nation, O LORD, thou H increased the nation; thou
26:15 thou art glorified; thou H enlarged all the borders
37:16 of the earth; thou H made heaven and earth.
38:17 great bitterness; but thou H held back my life
38:17 of destruction, for thou H cast all my sins
63:19 those over whom thou H never ruled, like those
64:7 of thee; for thou H hid thy face from
64:7 face from us, and H delivered us into the
Jer 4:10 Lord GOD, surely thou H utterly deceived this people
5:3 Thou H smitten them, but they felt no anguish;
5:3 felt no anguish; thou H consumed them, but they
14:19 H thou utterly rejected Judah?
14:19 Why H thou smitten us so that there is
20:7 O LORD, thou H deceived me, and I was
20:7 than I, and thou H prevailed.
31:18 Ephraim bemoaning, 'Thou H chastened me, and I
32:17 It is thou who H made the heavens and
32:20 of his doings; who H shown signs and wonders
32:20 among all mankind, and H made thee a name,
32:23 Therefore thou H made all this evil come upon
32:25 thou, O Lord GOD, H said to me, "Buy
51:62 say, 'O LORD, thou H said concerning this place
Lam 1:21 are glad that thou H done it.
1:21 thou the day thou H announced, and let them
1:22 with them as thou H dealt with me because
2:20 With whom H thou dealt thus?
2:21 of thy anger thou H slain them, slaughtering without
3:42 and rebelled, and thou H not forgiven.
3:43 "Thou H wrapped thyself with anger and pursued us,
3:44 slaying without pity; thou H wrapped thyself with a
3:45 Thou H made us offscouring and refuse among the
3:58 'Do not fear!' "Thou H taken up my cause,
3:58 cause, O Lord, thou H redeemed my life.
3:59 Thou H seen the wrong done to me, O
3:60 Thou H seen all their vengeance, all their devices
3:61 "Thou H heard their taunts, O LORD, all their
5:22 Or H thou utterly rejected us?
Bar 2:11 and outstretched arm, and H made thee a name,
2:13 the nations where thou H scattered us.
2:20 For thou H sent thy anger and thy wrath
2:24 of Babylon; and thou H confirmed thy words, which
2:26 by thy name thou H made as it is
2:27 "Yet thou H dealt with us, O Lord our
3:7 For thou H put the fear of thee in
3:8 our exile where thou H scattered us, to be
Dan 2:23 and praise, for thou H given me wisdom and
2:23 wisdom and strength, and H now made known to
2:23 of thee, for thou H made known to us
3:27 in all that thou H done to us, and
3:28 Thou H executed true judgments in all that thou
3:28 in all that thou H brought upon us and
3:28 truth and justice thou H brought all this upon
3:30 done them, as thou H commanded us that it
3:31 So all that thou H brought upon us, and
3:31 and all that thou H done to us, thou
3:31 done to us, thou H done in true judgment.
3:32 Thou H given us into the hands of lawless
9:7 lands to which thou H driven them, because of
9:15 a mighty hand, and H made thee a name,
14:38 And Daniel said, "Thou H remembered me, O God,
14:38 me, O God, and H not forsaken those who
Jon 1:14 for thou, O LORD, H done as it pleased
Mic 7:20 to Abraham, as thou H sworn to our fathers
Hab 1:12 O LORD, thou H ordained them as a judgment;
1:12 thou, O Rock, H established them for chastisement.
Zech 1:12 Judah, against which thou H had indignation these
Mal 1:2 But you say, "How H thou loved us?" "Is
2Mac 14:35 Lord of all, who H need of nothing, thou
Mt 11:25 and earth, that thou H hidden these things from
21:16 babes and sucklings thou H brought perfect praise'?"
27:46 God, my God, why H thou forsaken me?"
Mk 15:33 God, my God, why H thou forsaken me?"
Lk 2:31 thy salvation which thou H prepared in the presence
10:21 and earth, that thou H hidden these things from
Jn 11:41 thank thee that thou H heard me.
17:2 glorify thee, since thou H given him power over
17:2 to all whom thou H given him.
17:3 Jesus Christ whom thou H sent.
17:7 that everything that thou H given me is from
17:9 for those whom thou H given me, for they
17:11 thy name, which thou H given me, that they
17:12 thy name, which thou H given me; I have
17:21 may believe that thou H sent me.
17:22 The glory which thou H given me I have
17:23 may know that thou H sent me and hast
17:23 hast sent me and H loved them even as
17:23 them even as thou H loved me.
17:24 they also, whom thou H given me, may be
17:24 my glory which thou H given me in thy
17:25 these know that thou H sent me.
17:26 love with which thou H loved me may be
Acts 1:24 of these two thou H chosen
2:28 Thou H made known to me the ways of
Heb 1:9 Thou H loved righteousness and hated lawlessness;
2:7 than the angels, thou H crowned him with glory
10:5 "Sacrifices and offerings thou H not desired, but a
10:5 desired, but a body H thou prepared for me;
10:6 and sin offerings thou H taken no pleasure.
10:8 he said above, "Thou H neither desired nor taken
Rev 5:10 people and nation, and H made them a kingdom

11:17 who wast, that thou H taken thy great power
16:6 and prophets, and thou H given them blood to

HASTE (71)

Gen 19:22 Make H, escape there; for I can do nothing
43:30 Then Joseph made H, for his heart yearned for
45:9 Make H and go up to my father and
45:13 Make H and bring my father down here."
Ex 10:16 Moses and Aaron in H, and said, "I have
12:11 your hand; and you shall eat it in H
12:33 of the land in H; for they said, "We
34:8 And Moses made H to bow his head toward
Josh 4:10 people passed over in H;
8:14 of the city, made H and went out early
8:19 it; and they made H to set the city
Judg 9:48 seen me do, make H to do, as I
13:10 the woman ran in H and told her husband,
20:37 men in ambush made H and rushed upon Gibe-ah;
1Sam 9:12 Make H; he has come just now to the
20:38 the lad, "Hurry, make H, stay not." So Jonathan's
21:8 with me, because the king's business required H
23:26 and David was making H to get away from
23:27 to Saul, saying, "Make H and come; for the
25:18 Then Abigail made H, and took two hundred loaves,
25:23 saw David, she made H, and alighted from the
25:34 unless you had made H and come to meet
25:42 And Abigail made H and rose and mounted on
2Sam 4:4 she fled in her H, he fell, and became
15:14 from Absalom; go in H, lest he overtake us
19:16 Benjaminite, from Bahurim, made H to come down
1Kgs 12:18 And King Rehoboam made H to mount his chariot,
20:41 Then he made H to take the bandage away
2Kgs 7:15 which the Syrians had thrown away in their H
9:13 Then in H every man of them took his
2Chr 10:18 And King Rehoboam made H to mount his chariot,
35:21 war; and God has commanded me to make H
Ezra 4:23 associates, they went in H to the Jews at
Esth 3:15 The couriers went in H by order of the
6:10 said to Haman, "Make H, take the robes and
6:14 and brought Haman in H to the banquet that
8:14 service, rode out in H, urged by the king's
Job 20:2 me, because of my H within me.
Ps 38:22 Make H to help me, O Lord, my salvation!
40:13 O LORD, make H to help me!
55:8 wilderness, [Selah] I would H to find me a
69:17 am in distress, make H to answer me.
70:1 O LORD, make H to help me!
71:12 O my God, make H to help me!
141:1 thee, O LORD; make H to me!
143:7 [Selah] Make H to answer me, O LORD!
Prov 1:16 evil, and they make H to shed blood.
6:18 plans, feet that make H to run to evil,
19:2 and he who makes H with his feet misses
Song 1:4 Draw me after you, let us make H
8:14 Make H, my beloved, and be like a gazelle
Sir 50:17 the people together made H and fell to the
Is 5:19 say: "Let him make H, let him speed his
28:16 will not be in H
52:12 not go out in H, and you shall not
59:7 evil, and they make H to shed innocent blood;
Jer 9:18 come; let them make H and raise a wailing
46:5 and have fled in H; they look not back—
Dan 2:25 before the king in H, and said thus to
3:92 Nebuchadnezzar was astonished and rose up in H
6:19 arose and went in H to the den of
13:50 Then all the people returned in H
Jon 4:2 is why I made H to flee to Tarshish;
1Mac 6:63 Then he departed with H and returned to Antioch.
2Mac 11:37 Therefore make H and send some men, so that
Mk 6:25 came in immediately with H to the king, and
Lk 1:39 arose and went with H into the hill country,
2:16 And they went with H, and found Mary and
19:5 to him, "Zacchaeus, make H and come down; for
19:6 So he made H and came down, and received
Acts 22:18 saying to me, 'Make H and get quickly out

HASTEN (13)

Josh 10:13 heaven, and did not H to go down for
2Chr 24:5 and see that you H the matter." But the
24:5 the Levites did not H it.
Ps 22:19 O thou my help, H to my aid!
68:31 from Egypt; let Ethiopia H to stretch out her
70:5 am poor and needy; H to me, O God!
119:60 to thy testimonies; I H and do not delay
Prov 6:3 your neighbor's power: go, H, and importune your
Sir 36:8 H the day, and remember the appointed time, and
Is 60:22 its time I will H it.
Joel 3:11 H and come, all you nations round about, gather
Nah 2:5 as they go, they H to the wall, the
2Mac 9:7 and giving orders to H the journey.

HASTENED (12)

Gen 18:6 And Abraham H into the tent to Sarah, and
18:7 to the servant, who H to prepare it.
1Sam 4:14 Then the man H and came and told Eli.
2Chr 26:20 quickly, and he himself H to go out, because
Job 31:5 and my foot has H to deceit;
1Mac 2:35 Then the enemy H to attack them.
13:10 all the warriors and H to complete the walls
2Mac 4:14 neglecting the sacrifices, they H to take part in
9:25 of you when I H off to the upper
12:20 of the divisions, and H after Timothy, who had
12:29 out from there, they H to Scythopolis, which is
12:32 called Pentecost, they H against Gorgias, the

HASTENING (4)

Zeph 1:14 is near, near and H fast; the sound of
2Mac 9:14 city, which he was H to level to the
Acts 20:16 Asia; for he was H to be at Jerusalem,
2Pet 3:12 godliness, waiting for and H the coming of the

HASTENS (7)

Prov 28:20 blessings, but he who H to be rich will
28:22 A miserly man H after wealth, and does not
Eccl 1:5 sun goes down, and H to the place where
Wis 6:13 She H to make herself known to those who
Sir 43:5 at his command it H on its course.
Jer 48:16 hand and his affliction H apace.
Hab 2:3 awaits its time; it H to the end—it

HASTILY (8)

Gen 41:14 and they brought him H out of the dungeon;
Judg 9:54 Then he called H to the young man his
Prov 13:11 Wealth H gotten will dwindle, but he who gathers
20:21 An inheritance gotten H in the beginning will in
25:8 have seen do not H bring into court; for
Wis 19:2 people to depart and H sent them forth, they
Sir 6:7 him through testing, and do not trust him H
2Mac 4:31 So the king went H to settle the trouble,

HASTY (9)

Prov 14:29 he who has a H temper exalts folly.
21:5 every one who is H comes only to want.
29:20 a man who is H in his words?
Eccl 5:2 let your heart be H to utter a word
Sir 2:2 and do not be H in time of calamity.
3:23 For their H judgment has led many astray, and
28:11 A H quarrel kindles fire, and urgent strife sheds
Hab 1:6 Chaldeans, that bitter and H nation, who march
1Tim 5:22 Do not be H in the laying on of

HASUPHA (2)

Ezra 2:43 Ziha, the sons of H, the sons of Tabbaoth,
Neh 7:46 Ziha, the sons of H, the sons of Tabbaoth,

HAT

2Mac 4:12 of the young men to wear the Greek H

HATCH (3)

Is 34:15 nest and lay and H and gather her young
59:5 They H adders' eggs, they weave the spider's web;
Jer 17:11 which she did not H, so is he who

HATCHED

Is 59:5 from one which is crushed a viper is H

HATCHETS

Ps 74:6 they broke down with H and hammers.

HATE (103)

Gen 24:60 gate of those who H them!"
26:27 me, seeing that you H me and have sent
50:15 be that Joseph will H us and pay us
Ex 18:21 are trustworthy and who H a bribe; and place
20:5 generation of those who H me,
Lev 19:17 "You shall not H your brother in your heart,
26:17 your enemies; those who H you shall rule over
Num 10:35 and let them that H thee flee before thee."
Deut 5:9 generation of those who H me,
7:10 their face those who H him, by destroying them;
7:15 them upon all who H you.
32:41 will requite those who H me.

33:11 adversaries, of those that H him, that they rise
Judg 11:7 Gilead, "Did you not H me, and drive me
14:16 and said, "You only H me, you do not
2Sam 19:6 you love those who H you and hate those
19:6 who hate you and H those who love you.
1Kgs 22:8 of Imlah; but I H him, for he never
2Chr 1:11 life of those who H you, and have not
18:7 of Imlah; but I H him, for he never
19:2 and love those who H the LORD?
Tob 4:15 And what you H, do not do to any
13:12 Cursed are all who H you; blessed for ever
Esth 14:13 turn his heart to H the man who is
14:15 thou knowest that I H the splendor of the
Job 8:22 Those who H you will be clothed with shame,
Ps 9:13 suffer from those who H me, O thou who
21:8 find out those who H you.
25:19 what violent hatred they H me.
26:5 consort with dissemblers; I H the company of
34:21 wicked; and those who H the righteous will be
35:19 wink the eye who H me without cause.
38:19 many are those who H me wrongfully.
41:7 All who H me whisper together about me; they
44:7 to confusion those who H us.
45:7 you love righteousness and H wickedness.
50:17 For you H discipline, and you cast my words
68:1 scattered; let those who H him flee before him!
69:4 head are those who H me without cause; mighty
81:15 Those who H the LORD would cringe toward him,
83:2 in tumult; those who H thee have raised their
86:17 favor, that those who H me may see and
89:23 strike down those who H him.
97:10 LORD loves those who H evil; he preserves the
101:3 I H the work of those who fall away;
105:25 turned their hearts to H his people, to deal
109:3 me with words of H, and attack me without
118:7 triumph on those who H me.
119:104 get understanding; therefore I H every false way.
119:113 I H double-minded men, but I love thy law.
119:128 all thy precepts; I H every false way.
119:163 I H and abhor falsehood, but I love thy
120:6 dwelling among those who H peace.
129:5 May all who H Zion be put to shame
139:21 Do I not H them that hate thee, O
139:21 not hate them that H thee, O LORD?
139:22 I H them with perfect hatred; I count them
Prov 1:22 their scoffing and fools H knowledge?
8:13 the way of evil and perverted speech I H
8:36 injures himself; all who H me love death."
9:8 scoffer, or he will H you; reprove a wise
19:7 a poor man's brothers H him; how much more
25:17 weary of you and H you.
29:10 Bloodthirsty men H one who is blameless, and the
Eccl 3:8 and a time to H; a time for war,
9:1 it is love or H man does not know.
9:6 Their love and their H and their envy have
Wis 12:4 holy land thou didst H for their detestable practices,
Sir 7:15 Do not H toilsome labor, or farm work, which
17:21 away from iniquity, and H abominations intensely.
19:9 time comes he will H you.
25:13 attack, but not an attack from those who H
27:24 even the Lord will H him.
33:2 wise man will not H the law, but he
Is 61:8 LORD love justice, I H robbery and wrong; I
66:5 word: "Your brethren who H you and cast you
Jer 12:8 against me; therefore I H her.
44:4 abominable thing that I H
Ezek 23:28 of those whom you H, into the hands of
Dan 4:19 be for those who H you and its interpretation
Hos 9:15 there I began to H them.
Amos 5:10 They H him who reproves in the gate, and
5:15 H evil, and love good, and establish justice in
5:21 "I H, I despise your feasts, and I take
6:8 pride of Jacob, and H his strongholds; and I
Mic 3:2 justice?—you who H the good and love
Zech 8:17 all these things I H, says the LORD."
Mal 2:16 "For I H divorce, says the LORD the God
1Mac 9:29 of our nation who H us.
Mt 5:43 love your neighbor and H your enemy.'
6:24 for either he will H the one and love
24:10 betray one another, and H one another.
Lk 1:71 hand of all who H us;
6:22 are you when men H you, and when they
6:27 good to those who H you,
14:26 me and does not H his own father and
16:13 for either he will H the one and love
Jn 7:7 The world cannot H you, but it hates me

Rom 7:15 want, but I do the very thing I H
12:9 Let love be genuine; H what is evil, hold
Rev 2:6 this you have, you H the works of the
2:6 the works of the Nicolaitans, which I also H
17:16 and the beast will H the harlot; they will

HATED (54)

Gen 27:41 Now Esau H Jacob because of the blessing with
29:31 saw that Leah was H, he opened her womb;
29:33 heard that I am H, he has given me
37:4 all his brothers, they H him, and could not
37:5 his brothers they only H him the more.
37:8 So they H him yet more for his dreams
Deut 1:27 said, 'Because the LORD H us he has brought
9:28 them, and because he H them, he has brought
Judg 15:2 thought that you utterly H her; so I gave
2Sam 5:8 the blind, who are H by David's soul." Therefore
13:15 Then Amnon H her with very great hatred; so
13:15 hatred with which he H her was greater than
13:22 nor bad; for Absalom H Amnon, because he had
22:18 enemy, from those who H me; for they were
22:41 to me, those who H me, and I destroyed
Esth 9:5 pleased to those who H them.
9:16 thousand of those who H them; but they laid
Job 16:9 in his wrath, and H me; he has gnashed
31:29 ruin of him that H me, or exulted when
Ps 18:17 and from those who H me; for they were
18:40 me, and those who H me I destroyed.
36:2 that his iniquity cannot be found out and H
106:41 so that those who H them ruled over them.
Prov 1:29 Because they H knowledge and did not choose the
5:12 you say, "How I H discipline, and my heart
Eccl 2:17 So I H life, because what is done under
2:18 I H all my toil in which I had
Wis 11:24 anything if thou hadst H it.
Sir 9:18 man who is reckless in speech will be H
20:7 whoever usurps the right to speak will be H
21:28 own soul and is H in his neighborhood.
27:24 I have H many things, but none to be
31:16 and do not chew greedily, lest you be H
37:20 in words may be H; he will be destitute
42:9 married, lest she be H;
Is 60:15 have been forsaken and H, with no one passing
Mal 1:3 Jacob but I have H Esau; I have laid
1Mac 7:26 his honored princes, who H and detested Israel, and
11:21 certain lawless men who H their nation went to
11:38 had served his fathers H him.
2Mac 5:8 pursued by all men, H as a rebel against
Mt 10:22 and you will be H by all for my
24:9 and you will be H by all nations for
Mk 13:13 and you will be H by all for my
Lk 19:14 come.' But his citizens H him and sent an
21:17 death; you will be H by all for my
Jn 15:18 know that it has H me before it hated
15:18 hated me before it H you.
15:24 they have seen and H both me and my
15:25 in their law, 'They H me without a cause.'
17:14 and the world has H them because they are
Rom 9:13 is written, "Jacob I loved, but Esau I H
Tit 3:3 in malice and envy, H by men and hating
Heb 1:9 righteousness and H lawlessness; therefore God,

HATEFUL (8)

Esth 16:24 men, but also most H for all time to
Wis 14:9 For equally H to God are the ungodly man
15:18 worship even the most H animals, which are worse
17:5 avail to illumine that H night.
Sir 10:7 Arrogance is H before the Lord and before men,
20:14 a one is a H man.
Dan 3:32 of lawless enemies, most H rebels, and to an
Rev 18:2 of every foul and H bird;

HATERS (2)

Rom 1:30 they are gossips, slanderers, H of God, insolent,
2Tim 3:3 implacable, slanderers, profligates, fierce, H of good,

HATES (39)

Ex 23:5 ass of one who H you lying under its
Deut 7:10 slack with him who H him, he will requite
12:31 thing which the LORD H they have done for
16:22 up a pillar, which the LORD your God H
19:11 "But if any man H his neighbor, and lies
Jud 5:17 for the God who H iniquity is with them.
Job 34:17 Shall one who H justice govern?
Ps 11:5 wicked, and his soul H him that loves violence.
Prov 6:16 things which the LORD H, seven which are an

	11:15	it, but he who H suretyship is secure.
	12:1	knowledge, but he who H reproof is stupid.
	13:5	A righteous man H falsehood, but a wicked man
	13:24	who spares the rod H his son, but he
	15:10	the way; he who H reproof will die.
	15:27	household, but he who H bribes will live.
	26:24	He who H, dissembles with his lips and harbors
	26:28	A lying tongue H its victims, and a flattering
	28:16	oppressor; but he who H unjust gain will prolong
	29:24	partner of a thief H his own life; he
Sir	12:6	the Most High also H sinners and will inflict
	15:11	way"; for he will not do what he H
	15:13	The Lord H all abominations, and they are not
	19:6	and for one who H gossip evil is lessened.
	21:6	Whoever H reproof walks in the steps of the
	25:2	My soul H three kinds of men, and I
Is	1:14	appointed feasts my soul H; they have become a
Jn	3:20	one who does evil H the light, and does
	7:7	hate you, but it H me because I testify
	12:25	it, and he who H his life in this
	15:18	"If the world H you, know that it has
	15:19	world, therefore the world H you.
	15:23	He who H me hates my Father also.
	15:23	He who hates me H my Father also.
Eph	5:29	For no man ever H his own flesh, but
1Jn	2:9	in the light and H his brother is in
	2:11	But he who H his brother is in the
	3:13	brethren, that the world H you.
	3:15	Any one who H his brother is a murderer,
	4:20	and H his brother, he is a liar; for

HATEST (2)

Ps	5:5	before thy eyes; thou H all evildoers.
	31:6	Thou H those who pay regard to vain idols;

HATHACH (4)

Esth	4:5	Then Esther called for H, one of the king's
	4:6	H went out to Mordecai in the open square
	4:9	And H went and told Esther what Mordecai had
	4:10	Then Esther spoke to H and gave him a

HATHATH

1Chr	4:13	the sons of Othni-el: H and Meonothai.

HATING (2)

Tit	3:3	hated by men and H one another;
Jude	1:23	have mercy with fear, H even the garment spotted

HATIPHA (2)

Ezra	2:54	the sons of Neziah, and the sons of H
Neh	7:56	Temah, the sons of Neziah, the sons of H

HATITA (2)

Ezra	2:42	Akkub, the sons of H, and the sons of
Neh	7:45	Akkub, the sons of H, the sons of Shobai,

HATRED (23)

Num	35:20	he stabbed him from H, or hurled at him,
2Sam	13:15	her with very great H; so that the hatred
	13:15	hatred; so that the H with which he hated
Ps	25:19	and with what violent H they hate me.
	109:5	evil for good, and H for my love.
	139:22	hate them with perfect H; I count them my
Prov	8:13	of tQhe LORD is H of evil.
	10:12	H stirs up strife, but love covers all offenses.
	10:18	He who conceals H has lying lips, and he
	15:17	a fatted ox and H with it.
	26:26	his heart; though his H be covered with guile,
Wis	19:13	practiced a more bitter H of strangers.
Ezek	23:29	deal with you in H, and take away all
	35:11	showed because of your H against them; and I
Hos	9:7	mad, because of your great iniquity and great H
	9:8	all his ways, and H in the house of
1Mac	11:40	and told of the H which the troops of
	13:6	gathered together out of H to destroy us."
2Mac	3:1	priest Onias and his H of wickedness,
	4:3	When his H progressed to such a degree that
	4:36	the Greeks shared their H of the crime.
	4:49	the Tyrians, showing their H of the crime, provided
	8:4	and to show his H of evil.

HATS

Dan	3:21	mantles, their tunics, their H, and their other

HATTIL (2)

Ezra	2:57	the sons of H, the sons of Pochereth-hazzebaim,
Neh	7:59	Shephatiah, the sons of H, the sons of

HATTUSH (5)

1Chr	3:22	the sons of Shemaiah: H, Igal, Bariah, Neariah, and
Ezra	8:2	the sons of David, H,
Neh	3:10	and next to him H the son of Hashabneiah
	10:4	Amariah, Malchijah, H, Shebaniah, Malluch,
	12:2	Jeremiah, Ezra, Amariah, Malluch, H,

HAUGHTILY (4)

2Kgs	19:22	raised your voice and H lifted your eyes?
Ps	31:23	the faithful, but abundantly requites him who acts H
Is	37:23	raised your voice and H lifted your eyes?
Mic	2:3	you shall not walk H, for it will be

HAUGHTINESS (3)

Is	2:17	And the H of man shall be humbled, and
	13:11	and lay low the H of the ruthless.
Jer	48:29	his arrogance, and the H of his heart.

HAUGHTY (20)

2Sam	22:28	eyes are upon the H to bring them down.
Ps	18:27	humble people; but the H eyes thou dost bring
	101:5	The man of H looks and arrogant heart I
	138:6	the lowly; but the H he knows from afar.
Prov	6:17	an abomination to him: H eyes, a lying tongue,
	16:18	before destruction, and a H spirit before a fall.
	18:12	a man's heart is H, but humility goes before
	21:4	H eyes and a proud heart, the lamp of
	21:24	name of the proud, H man who acts with
Sir	23:4	do not give me H eyes,
Is	2:11	The H looks of man shall be brought low,
	3:16	daughters of Zion are H and walk with outstretched
	5:15	the eyes of the H are humbled.
	10:12	of Assyria and his H pride.
Ezek	16:50	They were H, and did abominable things before me;
Zeph	3:11	shall no longer be H in my holy mountain.
Rom	1:30	haters of God, insolent, H, boastful, inventors of evil,
	12:16	another; do not be H, but associate with the
1Tim	6:17	them not to be H, nor to set their
Rev	13:5	given a mouth uttering H and blasphemous words,

HAUL (2)

Ezek	32:3	peoples; and I will H you up in my
Jn	21:6	were not able to H it in, for the

HAULED

Jn	21:11	Peter went aboard and H the net ashore, full

HAUNT (7)

1Sam	23:22	the place where his H is, and who has
Is	34:13	It shall be the H of jackals, an abode
	35:7	springs of water; the H of jackals shall become
Jer	49:33	Hazor shall become a H of jackals, an everlasting
	51:37	heap of ruins, the H of jackals, a horror
Rev	18:2	place of demons, a H of every foul spirit,
	18:2	every foul spirit, a H of every foul and

HAUNTS

Sir	41:5	and they frequent the H of the ungodly.

HAURAN (2)

Ezek	47:16	as Hazer-hatticon, which is on the border of H
	47:18	from Hazar-enon between H and Damascus; along

HAVEN (3)

Gen	49:13	he shall become a H for ships, and his
Ps	107:30	quiet, and he brought them to their desired H
Is	23:1	for Tyre is laid waste, without house or H

HAVENS

Acts	27:8	a place called Fair H, near which was the

HAVILAH (7)

Gen	2:11	the whole land of H, where there is gold;
	10:7	sons of Cush: Seba, H, Sabtah, Raamah, and
	10:29	Obal, Abima-el, Sheba, Ophir, H, and Jobab; all these
	25:18	kindred.) They dwelt from H to Shur, which is
1Sam	15:7	defeated the Amalekites, from H as far as Shur,
1Chr	1:9	sons of Cush: Seba, H, Sabta, Raama, and Sabteca.
	1:23	Ebal, Abima-el, Sheba, Ophir, H, and Jobab; all these

HAVOC

Acts	9:21	the man who made H in Jerusalem of those

HAVVOTH-JAIR (4)
Num 32:41 went and took their villages, and called them H
Deut 3:14 after his own name, H, as it is to
Judg 10:4 had thirty cities, called H to this day, which
1Chr 2:23 Aram took from them H, Kenath and its villages,

HAWK (4)
Lev 11:16 the sea gull, the H according to its kind,
Deut 14:15 the sea gull, the H, after their kinds;
Job 39:26 your wisdom that the H soars, and spreads his
Is 34:11 But the H and the porcupine shall possess it,

HAY
1Cor 3:12 silver, precious stones, wood, H, straw--

HAZAEL (24)
1Kgs 19:15 arrive, you shall anoint H to be king over
19:17 from the sword of H shall Jehu slay; and
2Kgs 8:8 the king said to H, "Take a present with
8:9 So H went to meet him, and took a
8:12 And H said, "Why does my lord weep?" He
8:13 And H said, "What is your servant, who is
8:15 And H became king in his stead.
8:28 to make war against H king of Syria at
8:29 when he fought against H king of Syria.
9:14 guard at Ramoth-gilead against H king of Syria;
9:15 when he fought with H king of Syria.) So
10:32 H defeated them throughout the territory of Israel:
12:17 At that time H king of Syria went up
12:17 But when H set his face to go up
12:18 and sent these to H king of Syria.
12:18 Then H went away from Jerusalem.
13:3 into the hand of H king of Syria and
13:3 into the hand of Ben-hadad the son of H
13:22 Now H king of Syria oppressed Israel all the
13:24 When H king of Syria died, Ben-hadad his son
13:25 Ben-hadad the son of H the cities which he
2Chr 22:5 to make war against H king of Syria at
22:6 when he fought against H king of Syria.
Amos 1:4 upon the house of H, and it shall devour

HAZAIAH
Neh 11:5 of Colhozeh, son of H, son of Adaiah, son

HAZAR-ADDAR
Num 34:4 shall go on to H, and pass along to

HAZAR-ENAN (2)
Num 34:9 end shall be at H; this shall be your
34:10 your eastern boundary from H to Shepham;

HAZAR-ENON (3)
Ezek 47:17 from the sea to H, which is on the
47:18 shall run from H between Hauran and Damascus;
48:1 Hamath, as far as H (which is on the

HAZAR-GADDAH
Josh 15:27 Amam, Shema, Moladah, H, Heshmon, Beth-pelet,

HAZAR-SHUAL (4)
Josh 15:28 Hazar-gaddah, Heshmon, Beth-pelet, H, Beer-sheba,
19:3 inheritance Beer-sheba, Sheba, Moladah, H, Balah,
1Chr 4:28 dwelt in Beer-sheba, Moladah, H,
Neh 11:27 Moladah and Beth-pelet, in H, in Beer-sheba and its

HAZAR-SUSAH
Josh 19:5 Bethul, Hormah, Ziklag, Beth-marcaboth, H,

HAZAR-SUSIM
1Chr 4:31 Hormah, Ziklag, Beth-marcaboth, H, Beth-biri,

HAZARDS
Sir 32:20 a path full of H, and do not stumble

HAZARMAVETH (2)
Gen 10:26 father of Almodad, Sheleph, H, Jerah,
1Chr 1:20 father of Almodad, Sheleph, H, Jerah,

HAZAZON-TAMAR (2)
Gen 14:7 Amalekites, and also the Amorites who dwelt in H
2Chr 20:2 beyond the sea; and, behold, they are in H

HAZER-HATTICON
Ezek 47:16 Hamath), as far as H, which is on the

HAZEROTH (6)
Num 11:35 the people journeyed to H; and they remained at
11:35 journeyed to Hazeroth; and they remained at H
12:16 people set out from H, and encamped in the
33:17 set out from Kibroth-hattaavah, and encamped at H
33:18 they set out from H, and encamped at Rithmah.
Deut 1:1 Paran and Tophel, Laban, H, and Dizahab.

HAZI-EL
1Chr 23:9 sons of Shimei: Shelomoth, H, and Haran, three.

HAZO
Gen 22:22 father of Aram, Chesed, H, Pildash, Jidlaph, and

HAZOR (19)
Josh 11:1 When Jabin king of H heard of this, he
11:10 that time, and took H, and smote its king
11:10 with the sword; for H formerly was the head
11:11 breathed, and he burned H with fire.
11:13 did Israel burn, except H only; that Joshua burned.
12:19 one; the king of H, one;
15:23 Kinah, Dimonah, Adadah, Kedesh, H, Ithnan,
15:25 Hazor-hadattah, Kerioth-hezron (that is, H,
19:36 Rakkath, Chinnereth, Adamah, Ramah, H,
Judg 4:2 Canaan, who reigned in H; the commander of his
4:17 Jabin the king of H and the house of
1Sam 12:9 of Jabin king of H, and into the hand
1Kgs 9:15 wall of Jerusalem and H and Megiddo and Gezer
2Kgs 15:29 Ijon, Abel-beth-maacah, Jan-oah, Kedesh, H, Gilead,
Neh 11:33 Anathoth, Nob, Ananiah, H, Ramah, Gittaim,
Jer 49:28 and the kingdoms of H which Nebuchadrezzar king
49:30 away, dwell in the depths, O inhabitants of H
49:33 H shall become a haunt of jackals, an everlasting
1Mac 11:67 to the plain of H,

HAZOR-HADATTAH
Josh 15:25 Ziph, Telem, Bealoth, H, Kerioth-hezron (that is,

HAZZELELPONI
1Chr 4:3 of their sister was H,

HE-ASSES (2)
Gen 12:16 had sheep, oxen, H, menservants, maidservants,
32:15 cows and ten bulls, twenty she-asses and ten H

HE-GOAT (7)
Ps 50:9 from your house, nor H from your folds.
Prov 30:31 the strutting cock, the H, and a king striding
Ezek 43:22 you shall offer a H without blemish for a
45:23 seven days; and a H daily for a sin
Dan 8:5 was considering, behold, a H came from the west
8:8 Then the H magnified himself exceedingly; but when
8:21 And the H is the king of Greece; and

HE-GOATS (12)
Gen 30:35 day Laban removed the H that were striped and
31:10 a dream that the H which leaped upon the
32:14 hundred she-goats and twenty H, two hundred ewes
2Chr 17:11 hundred rams and seven thousand seven hundred H
29:21 seven lambs, and seven H for a sin offering
29:23 Then the H for the sin offering were brought
Ezra 6:17 for all Israel twelve H, according to the number
8:35 a sin offering twelve H; all this was a
Is 1:11 blood of bulls, or of lambs, or of H
Jer 50:8 Chaldeans, and be as H before the flock.
51:40 like lambs to the slaughter, like rams and H
Ezek 34:17 I judge between sheep and sheep, rams and H

HEAD (416)
Gen 3:15 he shall bruise your H, and you shall bruise
24:26 The man bowed his H and worshiped the LORD,
24:48 Then I bowed my H and worshiped the LORD,
28:11 put it under his H and lay down in
28:18 had put under his H and set it up
40:13 will lift up your H and restore you to
40:16 cake baskets on my H,
40:17 eating it out of the basket on my H
40:19 will lift up your H --from you!--and hang
40:20 and lifted up the H of the chief butler
40:20 chief butler and the H of the chief baker
47:31 bowed himself upon the H of his bed.
48:14 laid it upon the H of Ephraim, who was
48:14 left hand upon the H of Manasseh, crossing his
48:17 right hand upon the H of Ephraim, it displeased
48:17 remove it from Ephraim's H to Manasseh's head.
48:17 to remove it from Ephraim's head to Manasseh's H

H

48:18 the first-born; put your right hand upon his H
49:26 they be on the H of Joseph, and on
Ex 12:9 water, but roasted, its H with its legs and
28:32 an opening for the H, with a woven binding
29:6 the turban on his H, and put the holy
29:7 pour it on his H and anoint him.
29:10 their hands upon the H of the bull,
29:15 their hands upon the H of the ram,
29:17 its pieces and its H,
29:19 their hands upon the H of the ram,
34:8 haste to bow his H toward the earth, and
38:26 sanctuary: a beka a H (that is, half a
Lev 1:4 his hand upon the H of the burnt offering,
1:8 lay the pieces, the H, and the fat, in
1:12 into pieces, with its H and its fat, and
1:15 and wring off its H, and burn it on
3:2 his hand upon the H of his offering and
3:8 his hand upon the H of his offering and
3:13 his hand upon its H, and kill it before
4:4 his hand on the H of the bull, and
4:11 its flesh, with its H, its legs, its entrails,
4:15 their hands upon the H of the bull before
4:24 his hand upon the H of the goat, and
4:29 his hand on the H of the sin offering,
4:33 his hand upon the H of the sin offering,
5:8 he shall wring its H from its neck, but
8:9 the turban upon his H, and on the turban,
8:12 anointing oil on Aaron's H, and anointed him, to
8:14 their hands upon the H of the bull of
8:18 their hands on the H of the ram.
8:20 pieces, Moses burned the H and the pieces and
8:22 their hands on the H of the ram.
9:13 by piece, and the H; and he burned them
13:12 the diseased person from H to foot, so far
13:29 a disease on the H or the beard,
13:30 a leprosy of the H or the beard.
13:40 has fallen from his H, he is bald but
13:42 is on the bald H or the bald forehead
13:42 out on his bald H or his bald forehead.
13:43 reddish-white on his bald H or on his bald
13:44 pronounce him unclean; his disease is on his H
13:45 the hair of his H hang loose, and he
14:9 his hair off his H; he shall shave off
14:18 shall put on the H of him who is
14:29 shall put on the H of him who is
16:21 his hands upon the H of the live goat,
16:21 put them upon the H of the goat, and
19:32 up before the hoary H, and honor the face
21:10 his brethren, upon whose H the anointing oil is
21:10 the hair of his H hang loose, nor rend
24:14 their hands upon his H, and let all the
Num 1:2 of names, every male, H by head;
1:2 every male, head by H;
1:4 each man being the H of the house of
1:18 years old and upward, H by head,
1:18 and upward, head by H,
1:20 the number of names, H by head, every male
1:20 of names, head by H, every male from twenty
1:22 the number of names, H by head, every male
1:22 of names, head by H, every male from twenty
3:24 son of Lael as H of the fathers' house
3:30 son of Uzziel as H of the fathers' house
3:35 And the H of the fathers' house of the
5:18 hair of the woman's H, and place in her
6:5 shall come upon his H; until the time is
6:5 of hair of his H grow long.
6:7 because his separation to God is upon his H
6:9 he defiles his consecrated H, then he shall shave
6:9 he shall shave his H on the day of
6:11 he shall consecrate his H that same day,
6:18 shall shave his consecrated H at the door of
6:18 hair from his consecrated H and put it on
17:3 one rod for the H of each fathers' house.
22:31 and he bowed his H, and fell on his
25:14 the son of Salu, H of a fathers' house
25:15 Zur, who was the H of the people of
Deut 3:28 go over at the H of this people, and
10:11 your journey at the H of the people, that
19:5 a tree, and the H slips from the handle
20:9 be appointed at the H of the people.
21:12 she shall shave her H and pare her nails.
28:13 will make you the H, and not the tail;
28:23 the heavens over your H shall be brass, and
28:35 of your foot to the crown of your H
28:44 he shall be the H, and you shall be
31:3 go over at your H, as the LORD has
33:16 these come upon the H of Joseph, and upon
33:16 the crown of the H of him that is
33:20 tears the arm, and the crown of the H
Josh 2:19 shall be upon his H, and we shall be
2:19 the house, his blood shall be on our H
11:10 Hazor formerly was the H of all those kingdoms.
22:14 one of them the H of a family among
Judg 3:27 from the hill country, having him at their H
5:26 blow, she crushed his H, she shattered and pierced
9:39 went out at the H of the men of
9:53 upper millstone upon Abimelech's H, and crushed his
10:18 He shall be H over all the inhabitants of
11:8 Ammonites, and be our H over all the inhabitants
11:9 them over to me, I will be your H
11:11 the people made him H and leader over them;
13:5 shall come upon his H, for the boy shall
16:13 seven locks of my H with the web and
16:14 seven locks of his H and wove them into
16:17 never come upon my H; for I have been
16:19 him shave off the seven locks of his H
16:22 the hair of his H began to grow again
1Sam 1:11 his life, and no razor shall touch his H
4:12 his clothes rent and with earth upon his H
5:4 the LORD, and the H of Dagon and both
9:22 a place at the H of those who had
10:1 poured it on his H, and kissed him and
14:45 one hair of his H fall to the ground;
15:17 are you not the H of the tribes of
17:5 of bronze on his H, and he was armed
17:7 beam, and his spear's H weighed six hundred shekels
17:38 of bronze on his H, and clothed him with
17:46 and cut off your H; and I will give
17:51 and cut off his H with it.
17:54 And David took the H of the Philistine and
17:57 before Saul with the H of the Philistine in
19:13 goats' hair at its H, and covered it with
19:16 with the pillow of goats' hair at its H
19:20 and Samuel standing as H over them, the Spirit
25:39 returned the evil-doing of Nabal upon his own H
26:7 the ground at his H; and Abner and the
26:11 that is at his H, and the jar of
26:12 of water from Saul's H; and they went away.
26:16 the jar of water that was at his H
31:9 they cut off his H, and stripped off his
2Sam 1:2 with his clothes rent and earth upon his H
1:10 which was on his H and the armlet which
1:16 blood be upon your H; for your own mouth
2:16 his opponent by the H, and thrust his sword
3:8 "Am I a dog's H of Judah?
3:29 it fall upon the H of Joab, and upon
4:7 They took his H, and went by the way
4:8 night, and brought the H of Ish-bosheth to David
4:8 king, "Here is the H of Ish-bosheth, the son
4:12 But they took the H of Ish-bosheth, and buried
10:16 commander of the army of Hadadezer at their H
12:30 their king from his H; the weight of it
12:30 precious stone; and it was placed on David's H
13:19 put ashes on her H, and rent the long
13:19 her hand on her H, and went away, crying
14:25 the crown of his H there was no blemish
14:26 the hair of his H (for at the end
14:26 the hair of his H, two hundred shekels by
15:30 barefoot and with his H covered; and all the
15:32 with his coat rent and earth upon his H
16:9 Let me go over and take off his H
18:9 great oak, and his H caught fast in the
20:21 to Joab, "Behold, his H shall be thrown to
20:22 they cut off the H of Sheba the son
22:44 keep me as the H of the nations; people
1Kgs 2:6 not let his gray H go down to Sheol
2:9 shall bring his gray H down with blood to
2:32 deeds upon his own H, because, without the
2:33 come back upon the H of Joab and upon
2:33 Joab and upon the H of his descendants for
2:37 die; your blood shall be upon your own H
2:44 will bring back your evil upon your own H
8:32 conduct upon his own H, and vindicating the
10:19 throne was a calf's H, and on each side
19:6 there was at his H a cake baked on
2Kgs 4:19 his father, "Oh, my H, my head!" The father
4:19 said to his father, "Oh, my head, my H
6:5 a log, his axe H fell into the water;
6:25 it, until an ass's H was sold for eighty
6:31 more also, if the H of Elisha the son
6:32 this murderer has sent to take off my H
9:3 pour it on his H, and say, 'Thus says

9:6 the oil on his H, saying to him, "Thus
9:30 eyes, and adorned her H, and looked out of
19:21 Zion; she wags her H behind you--the daughter
1Chr 10:9 him and took his H and his armor, and
10:10 gods, and fastened his H in the temple of
19:16 commander of the army of Hadadezer at their H
20:2 their king from his H; he found that it
20:2 precious stone; and it was placed on David's H
24:31 These also, the H of each father's house and
29:11 thou art exalted as H above all.
2Chr 6:23 conduct upon his own H, and vindicating the
13:12 with us at our H, and his priests with
20:18 Then Jehoshaphat bowed his H with his face to
20:27 and Jehoshaphat at their H, returning to Jerusalem
Ezra 5:10 down the names of the men at their H
9:3 pulled hair from my H and beard, and sat
Jud 9:1 put ashes on her H, and uncovered the sackcloth
13:6 the bed, above Holofernes' H, and took down his
13:7 the hair of his H, and said, "Give me
13:9 out, and gave Holofernes' H to her maid,
13:15 Then she took the H out of the bag
13:15 "See, here is the H of Holofernes, the commander
13:18 you to strike the H of the leader of
14:1 brethren, and take this H and hang it upon
14:6 came and saw the H of Holofernes in the
14:11 dawn they hung the H of Holofernes on the
14:15 platform dead, with his H cut off and missing.
14:18 the ground, and his H is not on him!"
Esth 2:17 royal crown on her H and made her queen
6:8 ridden, and on whose H a royal crown is
6:12 mourning and with his H covered.
9:25 come upon his own H, and that he and
14:2 perfumes she covered her H with ashes and dung,
14:16 which is upon my H on the days when
15:7 and collapsed upon the H of the maid who
Job 1:20 robe, and shaved his H, and fell upon the
2:7 of his foot to the crown of his H
10:15 cannot lift up my H, for I am filled
16:4 you, and shake my H at you.
19:9 my glory, and taken the crown from my H
20:6 the heavens, and his H reach to the clouds,
29:3 lamp shone upon my H, and by his light
41:7 with harpoons, or his H with fishing spears?
Ps 3:3 me, my glory, and the lifter of my H
7:16 returns upon his own H, and on his own
18:43 didst make me the H of the nations; people
21:3 set a crown of fine gold upon his H
23:5 enemies; thou anointest my H with oil, my cup
27:6 And now my H shall be lifted up above
35:13 I prayed with H bowed on my bosom,
38:4 have gone over my H; they weigh like a
40:12 the hairs of my H; my heart fails me.
69:4 the hairs of my H are those who hate
110:7 the way; therefore he will lift up his H
118:22 rejected has become the H of the corner.
133:2 precious oil upon the H, running down upon the
140:7 thou hast covered my H in the day of
140:9 me lift up their H, let the mischief of
141:5 wicked never anoint my H; for my prayer is
Prov 1:9 fair garland for your H, and pendants for your
4:10 will place on your H a fair garland; she
10:6 Blessings are on the H of the righteous, but
11:26 blessing is on the H of him who sells
16:31 A hoary H is a crown of glory; it
25:22 of fire on his H, and the LORD will
Eccl 2:14 his eyes in his H, but the fool walks
9:8 white; let not oil be lacking on your H
Song 2:6 hand were under my H, and that his right
5:2 perfect one; for my H is wet with dew,
5:11 His H is the finest gold; his locks are
7:5 Your H crowns you like Carmel, and your flowing
8:3 hand were under my H, and that his right
Wis 18:24 and thy majesty on the diadem upon his H
Sir 4:7 the congregation; bow your H low to a great
11:1 will lift up his H, and will seat him
11:13 and raises up his H, so that many are
12:18 he will shake his H, and clap his hands,
13:7 you, and shake his H at you.
27:25 it on his own H; and a treacherous blow
38:3 physician lifts up his H, and in the presence
44:24 to rest upon the H of Jacob; he acknowledged
Is 1:5 The whole H is sick, and the whole heart
1:6 foot even to the H, there is no soundness
7:8 For the H of Syria is Damascus, and the
7:8 is Damascus, and the H of Damascus is Rezin.
7:9 a people.) And the H of Ephraim is Samaria,
7:9 is Samaria, and the H of Samaria is the
7:20 of Assyria-- the H and the hair of
9:14 cut off from Israel H and tail, palm branch
9:15 honored man is the H, and the prophet who
15:2 On every H is baldness, every beard is shorn;
19:15 nothing for Egypt which H or tail, palm branch
28:1 which is on the H of the rich valley
28:4 which is on the H of the rich valley,
37:22 Zion; she wags her H behind you-- the
51:20 they lie at the H of every street like
58:5 to bow down his H like a rush, and
59:17 of salvation upon his H; he put on garments
Jer 2:16 and Tahpanhes have broken the crown of your H
2:37 your hands upon your H, for the LORD has
9:1 O that my H were waters, and my eyes
13:18 your beautiful crown has come down from your H
13:21 when they set as H over you those whom
18:16 passes by it is horrified and shakes his H
23:19 will burst upon the H of the wicked.
30:23 will burst upon the H of the wicked.
48:27 whenever you spoke of him you wagged your H
48:37 "For every H is shaved and every beard cut
52:31 king, lifted up the H of Jehoiachin king of
Lam 1:5 foes have become the H, her enemies prosper,
2:19 for hunger at the H of every street.
3:54 water closed over my H; 'I said, I am
4:1 lie scattered at the H of every street.
5:16 has fallen from our H; woe to us, for
Bar 5:2 God; put on your H the diadem of the
Ezek 5:1 pass it over your H and your beard; then
8:3 a lock of my H; and the Spirit lifted
16:12 your ears, and a beautiful crown upon your H
16:25 every square; at the H of every street you
16:31 vaulted chamber at the H of every street, and
16:43 your deeds upon your H, says the Lord GOD.
17:19 which he broke, I will requite upon his H
21:19 make it at the H of the way to
21:21 the way, at the H of the two ways,
29:18 hard against Tyre; every H was made bald and
33:4 away, his blood shall be upon his own H
Dan 1:10 you would endanger my H with the king."
2:28 the visions of your H as you lay in
2:32 The H of this image was of fine gold,
2:38 all--you are the H of gold.
4:5 the visions of my H alarmed me.
4:10 The visions of my H as I lay in
4:13 the visions of my H as I lay in
7:1 and visions of his H as he lay in
7:9 the hair of his H like pure wool; his
7:15 the visions of my H alarmed me.
7:20 that were on its H, and the other horn
13:34 the people, and laid their hands upon her H
13:55 lied against your own H, for the angel of
13:59 lied against your own H, for the angel of
14:36 the crown of his H, and lifted him by
Hos 1:11 appoint for themselves one H; and they shall go
Joel 3:4 deed upon your own H swiftly and speedily.
3:7 I will requite your deed upon your own H
Amos 2:7 they that trample the H of the poor into
8:10 and baldness on every H; I will make it
Obad 1:15 you, your deeds shall return on your own H
Jon 2:5 were wrapped about my H
4:6 a shade over his H, to save him from
4:8 sun beat upon the H of Jonah so that
Mic 2:13 pass on before them, the LORD at their H
Nah 3:10 in pieces at the H of every street; for
Hab 3:13 Thou didst crush the H of the wicked, laying
3:14 with thy shafts the H of his warriors, who
Zech 1:21 no man raised his H; and these have come
3:5 "Let them put a clean turban on his H
3:5 clean turban on his H and clothed him with
6:11 set it upon the H of Joshua, the son
12:8 like the angel of the LORD, at their H
1Mac 7:47 they cut off Nicanor's H and the right hand
11:13 two crowns upon his H, the crown of Egypt
11:17 Arab cut off the H of Alexander and sent
11:71 put dust on his H, and prayed.
2Mac 7:7 the skin of his H with the hair, and
11:8 horseman appeared at their H, clothed in white and
15:30 to cut off Nicanor's H and arm and carry
15:32 them the vile Nicanor's H and that profane man's
15:35 And he hung Nicanor's H from the citadel, a
Mt 5:36 not swear by your H, for you cannot make
6:17 you fast, anoint your H and wash your face,
8:20 Son of man has nowhere to lay his H
10:30 the hairs of your H are all numbered.

14:8 said, "Give me the H of John the Baptist
14:11 the prison, and his H was brought on a
21:42 rejected has become the H of the corner; this
26:7 poured it on his H, as he sat at
27:29 put it on his H, and put a reed
27:30 took the reed and struck him on the H
27:37 And over his H they put the charge against
Mk 6:24 And she said, "The H of John the baptizer."
6:25 me at once the H of John the Baptist
6:27 the guard and gave orders to bring his H
6:28 prison, and brought his H on a platter, and
12:4 wounded him in the H, and treated him shamefully.
12:10 rejected has become the H of the corner;
14:3 broke the flask and poured it over his H
15:19 And they struck his H with a reed, and
Lk 7:38 the hair of her H, and kissed his feet,
7:46 did not anoint my H with oil, but she
9:58 Son of man has nowhere to lay his H
12:7 the hairs of your H are all numbered.
20:17 rejected has become the H of the corner?
21:18 a hair of your H will perish.
Jn 13:9 feet only but also my hands and my H
19:2 put it on his H, and arrayed him in
19:30 and he bowed his H and gave up his
20:7 had been on his H, not lying with the
20:12 lain, one at the H and one at the
Acts 4:11 which has become the H of the corner.
27:34 to perish from the H of any of you."
Rom 12:20 doing you will heap burning coals upon his H
1Cor 11:3 to understand that the H of every man is
11:3 man is Christ, the H of a woman is
11:3 her husband, and the H of Christ is God.
11:4 or prophesies with his H covered dishonors his head,
11:4 head covered dishonors his H,
11:5 prophesies with her H unveiled dishonors her head
11:5 head unveiled dishonors her H—it is the same
11:5 same as if her H were shaven.
11:7 not to cover his H, since he is the
11:10 a veil on her H, because of the angels.
11:13 to God with her H uncovered?
12:21 nor again the H to the feet, "I have
Eph 1:22 has made him the H over all things for
4:15 him who is the H, into Christ,
5:23 the husband is the H of the wife as
5:23 as Christ is the H of the church, his
Col 1:18 He is the H of the body, the church;
2:10 him, who is the H of all rule and
2:19 holding fast to the H, from whom the whole
Heb 11:21 in worship over the H of his staff.
1Pet 2:7 rejected has become the H of the corner,"
Rev 1:14 round his breast; his H and his hair were
10:1 a rainbow over his H, and his face was
12:1 feet, and on her H a crown of twelve
14:14 golden crown on his H, and a sharp sickle
19:12 fire, and on his H are many diadems; and

HEADBANDS

Is 3:18 of the anklets, the H, and the crescents;

HEADDRESSES

Is 3:20 and the scarfs; the H, the armlets, the sashes,

HEADLONG (6)

Job 27:22 from its power in H flight.
Ps 37:24 shall not be cast H, for the LORD is
Jer 8:6 like a horse plunging H into battle.
2Mac 6:10 then hurled them down H from the wall.
Lk 4:29 was built, that they might throw him down H
Acts 1:18 his wickedness; and falling H he burst open in

HEADS (181)

Gen 43:28 And they bowed their H and made obeisance.
Ex 4:31 affliction, they bowed their H and worshiped.
6:14 These are the H of their fathers' houses: the
6:25 These are the H of the fathers' houses of
12:27 the people bowed their H and worshiped.
18:25 Israel, and made them H over the people, rulers
Lev 10:6 the hair of your H hang loose, and do
21:5 make tonsures upon their H, nor shave off the
Num 1:16 their ancestral tribes, the H of the clans of
7:2 the leaders of Israel, H of their fathers' houses,
8:12 their hands upon the H of the bulls; and
10:4 then the leaders, the H of the tribes of
13:3 them men who were H of the people of
30:1 Moses said to the H of the tribes of
31:26 the priest and the H of the fathers' houses
32:28 Nun, and to the H of the fathers' houses
36:1 The H of the fathers' houses of the families
36:1 before the leaders, the H of the fathers' houses
Deut 1:13 appoint them as your H
1:15 So I took the H of your tribes, wise
1:15 and set them as H over you, commanders of
5:23 to me, all the H of your tribes, and
29:10 LORD your God; the H of your tribes, your
32:42 captives, from the long-haired H of the enemy.'
33:5 in Jeshurun, when the H of the people were
33:21 he came to the H of the people, with
Josh 7:6 of Israel; and they put dust upon their H
14:1 of Nun, and the H of the fathers' houses
19:51 of Nun and the H of the fathers' houses
21:1 Then the H of the fathers' houses of the
21:1 Nun and to the H of the fathers' houses
22:21 in answer to the H of the families of
22:30 of the congregation, the H of the families of
23:2 Israel, their elders and H, their judges and officers,
24:1 summoned the elders, the H, the judges, and the
Judg 7:25 and they brought the H of Oreb and Zeeb
8:28 they lifted up their H no more.
9:57 fall back upon their H, and upon them came
1Sam 29:4 not be with the H of the men here?
2Sam 15:30 with him covered their H, and they went up,
1Kgs 8:1 Israel and all the H of the tribes, the
20:31 and ropes upon our H, and go out to
20:32 put ropes on their H, and went to the
2Kgs 10:6 obey me, take the H of your master's sons,
10:7 persons, and put their H in baskets, and sent
10:8 "They have brought the H of the king's sons,"
1Chr 5:24 These were the H of their fathers' houses: Epher,
5:24 mighty warriors, famous men, H of their fathers'
7:2 Jahmai, Ibsam, and Shemuel, H of their fathers'
7:7 Jerimoth, and Iri, five, H of fathers' houses, mighty
7:9 to their generations, as H of their fathers' houses,
7:11 Jedia-el according to the H of their fathers' houses,
7:40 were men of Asher, H of fathers' houses, approved,
8:6 of Ehud (they were H of fathers' houses of
8:10 These were his sons, H of fathers' houses.
8:13 and Shema (they were H of fathers' houses of
8:28 These were the H of fathers' houses, according to
9:9 All these were H of fathers' houses according to
9:13 Immer; besides their kinsmen, H of their fathers'
9:33 are the singers, the H of fathers' houses of
9:34 These were H of fathers' houses of the Levites,
12:19 "At peril to our H he will desert to
15:12 them, "You are the H of the fathers' houses
23:9 These were the H of the fathers' houses of
23:24 their fathers' houses, the H of fathers' houses as
24:4 organized them under sixteen H of fathers' houses of
24:6 of Abiathar, and the H of the fathers' houses
24:31 Zadok, Ahimelech, and the H of fathers' houses of
26:21 belonging to Ladan, the H of the fathers' houses
26:26 the king, and the H of the fathers' houses,
26:32 hundred men of ability, H of fathers' houses, to
27:1 people of Israel, the H of fathers' houses, the
29:6 Then the H of fathers' houses made their freewill
29:20 and bowed their H, and worshiped the LORD,
2Chr 1:2 in all Israel, the H of fathers' houses.
5:2 Israel and all the H of the tribes, the
19:8 Levites and priests and H of families of Israel,
23:2 of Judah, and the H of fathers' houses of
26:12 whole number of the H of fathers' houses of
Ezra 1:5 Then rose up the H of the fathers' houses
2:68 Some of the H of families, when they came
3:12 priests and Levites and H of fathers' houses, old
4:2 approached Zerubbabel and the H of fathers' houses
4:3 the rest of the H of fathers' houses in
8:1 These are the H of their fathers' houses, and
8:29 the Levites and the H of fathers' houses in
9:6 risen higher than our H, and our guilt has
10:16 the priest selected men, H of fathers' houses,
Neh 4:4 taunt upon their own H, and give them up
7:70 Now some of the H of fathers' houses gave
7:71 And some of the H of fathers' houses gave
8:6 and they bowed their H and worshiped the LORD
8:13 the second day the H of fathers' houses of
9:1 and in sackcloth, and with earth upon their H
11:13 Malchijah, and his brethren, H of fathers' houses,
12:12 of Joiakim were priests, H of fathers' houses: of
12:22 there were recorded the H of fathers' houses; also
12:23 The sons of Levi, H of fathers' houses, were
Jud 4:11 put ashes on their H and spread out their
8:22 will bring upon our H among the Gentiles, wherever

9:9 thy wrath upon their H; give to me, a
Job 2:12 sprinkled dust upon their H toward heaven.
24:24 cut off like the H of grain.
Ps 22:7 me, they wag their H;
24:7 [Selah] Lift up your H, O gates!
24:9 Lift up your H, O gates!
64:8 ruin; all who see them will wag their H
66:12 men ride over our H; we went through fire
68:21 God will shatter the H of his enemies, the
74:13 thou didst break the H of the dragons on
74:14 Thou didst crush the H of Leviathan, thou didst
83:2 tumult; those who hate thee have raised their H
109:25 accusers; when they see me, they wag their H
Sir 17:18 and he will bring their recompense on their H
20:10 who have raised their H from humble circumstances.
36:10 Crush the H of the rulers of the enemy,
Is 3:17 with a scab the H of the daughters of
29:10 prophets, and covered your H, the seers.
35:10 shall be upon their H; they shall obtain joy
51:11 shall be upon their H; they shall obtain joy
Jer 14:3 they are ashamed and confounded and cover their H
14:4 land, the farmers are ashamed, they cover their H
Lam 2:10 cast dust on their H and put on sackcloth;
2:10 Jerusalem have bowed their H to the ground.
2:15 hiss and wag their H at the daughter of
Bar 6:9 make crowns for the H of their gods, as
6:22 on their bodies and H; and so do cats.
6:31 their clothes rent, their H and beards shaved, and
6:31 beards shaved, and their H uncovered.
Ezek 1:22 Over the H of the living creatures there was
1:22 shining like crystal, spread out above their H
1:25 the firmament over their H; when they stood still,
1:26 the firmament over their H there was the likeness
7:18 upon all faces, and baldness on all their H
9:10 but I will requite their deeds upon their H
10:1 that was over the H of the cherubim there
11:21 deeds upon their own H, says the Lord GOD."
13:18 make veils for the H of persons of every
22:31 I requited upon their H, says the Lord GOD."
23:15 flowing turbans on their H, all of them looking
23:42 of the women, and beautiful crowns upon their H
24:23 shall be on your H and your shoes on
27:30 cast dust on their H and wallow in ashes;
32:27 were laid under their H, and whose shields are
44:18 linen turbans upon their H, and linen breeches upon
44:20 shall not shave their H or let their locks
44:20 they shall only trim the hair of their H
Dan 3:95 the hair of their H was not singed, their
7:6 the beast had four H; and dominion was given
Hos 8:7 standing grain has no H, it shall yield no
Amos 9:1 shatter them on the H of all the people;
Mic 3:1 I said: Hear, you H of Jacob and rulers
3:9 Hear this, you H of the house of Jacob
3:11 Its H give judgment for a bribe, its priests
1Mac 3:47 sprinkled ashes on their H, and rent their clothes.
6:35 brass helmets on their H; and five hundred picked
2Mac 1:16 and cut off their H and threw them to
10:25 sprinkled dust upon their H and girded their loins
14:15 sprinkled dust upon their H and prayed to him
Mt 12:1 they began to pluck H of grain and to
27:39 derided him, wagging their H
Mk 2:23 disciples began to pluck H of grain.
15:28 derided him, wagging their H, and saying, "Aha!
Lk 6:1 plucked and ate some H of grain, rubbing them
21:28 up and raise your H, because your redemption is
Acts 18:6 said to them, "Your blood be upon your H
21:24 their expenses, so that they may shave their H
Rev 4:4 in white garments, with golden crowns upon their H
9:7 for battle; on their H were what looked like
9:17 of sulphur, and the H of the horses were
9:17 horses were like lions' H, and fire and smoke
9:19 are like serpents, with H, and by means of
12:3 red dragon, with seven H and ten horns, and
12:3 and ten horns, and seven diadems upon his H
13:1 ten horns and seven H, with ten diadems upon
13:1 its horns and a blasphemous name upon its H
13:3 One of its H seemed to have a mortal
17:3 and it had seven H and ten horns.
17:7 the beast with seven H and ten horns that
17:9 with wisdom: the seven H are seven mountains on
18:19 threw dust on their H, as they wept and

HEADSTRONG (2)

Sir 26:10 strict watch over a H daughter, lest, when she
42:11 strict watch over a H daughter, lest she make

HEADWAY

Mk 6:48 that they were making H painfully, for the wind

HEAL (43)

Num 12:13 cried to the LORD, H her, O God, I
Deut 32:39 I wound and I H; and there is none
2Kgs 20:5 tears; behold, I will H you; on the third
20:8 that the LORD will H me, and that I
2Chr 7:14 forgive their sin and H their land.
Tob 3:17 Raphael was sent to H the two of them:
12:14 God sent me to H you and your daughter-in-law
Job 5:18 he binds up; he smites, but his hands H
Ps 6:2 am languishing; O LORD, H me, for my bones
41:4 be gracious to me; H me, for I have
Eccl 3:3 and a time to H; a time to break
Sir 38:9 Lord, and he will H you.
Is 19:22 heed their supplications and H them.
57:18 ways, but I will H him; I will lead
57:19 LORD; and I will H him.
Jer 3:22 faithless sons, I will H your faithlessness." "Behold,
17:14 H me, O LORD, and I shall be healed;
30:17 your wounds I will H, says the LORD, because
33:6 healing, and I will H them and reveal to
Ezek 30:21 been bound up, to H it by binding it
Hos 5:13 to cure you or H your wound.
6:1 torn, that he may H us; he has stricken,
7:2 people, when I would H Israel, the corruption of
14:4 I will H their faithlessness; I will love them
Zech 11:16 seek the wandering, or H the maimed, or nourish
Mt 8:7 "I will come and H him."
10:1 them out, and to H every disease and every
10:8 heaven is at hand.' H the sick, raise the
12:10 "Is it lawful to H on the sabbath?" so
13:15 turn for me to H them.'
17:16 and they could not H him."
Mk 3:2 see whether he would H him on the sabbath,
Lk 4:23 me this proverb, 'Physician, H yourself; what we have
5:17 power of the Lord was with him to H
6:7 see whether he would H on the sabbath, so
7:3 him to come and H his slave.
9:2 to preach the kingdom of God and to H
10:9 is set before you; H the sick in it
14:3 "Is it lawful to H on the sabbath, or
Jn 4:47 to come down and H his son, for he
12:40 turn for me to H them."
Acts 4:30 out thy hand to H, and signs and wonders
28:27 turn for me to H them.'

HEALED (77)

Gen 20:17 to God; and God H Abimelech, and also healed
20:17 healed Abimelech, and also H his wife and female
Ex 21:19 of his time, and shall have him thoroughly H
Lev 13:18 a boil that has H,
13:37 it, the itch is H, he is clean; and
14:3 the leprous disease is H in the leper,
14:48 pronounce the house clean, for the disease is H
Deut 28:27 and the itch, of which you cannot be H
28:35 which you cannot be H, from the sole of
Josh 5:8 their places in the camp till they were H
1Sam 6:3 Then you will be H, and it will be
2Kgs 8:29 Joram returned to be H in Jezreel of the
9:15 had returned to be H in Jezreel of the
2Chr 22:6 he returned to be H in Jezreel of the
30:20 LORD heard Hezekiah, and H the people.
Tob 12:3 me, and he also H you."
Ps 30:2 help, and thou hast H me.
107:20 forth his word, and H them, and delivered them
Wis 16:10 to their help and H them.
Is 6:10 understand with their hearts, and turn and be H
53:5 us whole, and with his stripes we are H
Jer 6:14 They have H the wound of my people lightly,
8:11 They have H the wound of my people lightly,
15:18 unceasing, my wound incurable, refusing to be H
17:14 and I shall be H; save me, and I
51:8 balm for her pain; perhaps she may be H
51:9 We would have H Babylon, but she was not
51:9 would have healed Babylon, but she was not H
Ezek 34:4 sick you have not H, the crippled you have
Hos 11:3 not know that I H them.
Mt 4:24 and paralytics, and he H them.
8:8 say the word, and my servant will be H
8:13 And the servant was H at that very moment.
8:16 with a word, and H all who were sick.
12:15 followed him, and he H them all,
12:22 to him, and he H him, so that the
14:14 compassion on them, and H their sick.

H

15:28 And her daughter was H instantly.
15:30 his feet, and he H them,
19:2 followed him, and he H them there.
21:14 the temple, and he H them.
Mk 1:34 And he H many who were sick with various
3:10 him; for he had H many, so that all
5:29 body that she was H of her disease.
5:34 in peace, and be H of your disease."
6:5 few sick people and H them.
6:13 that were sick and H them.
Lk 4:40 one of them and H them.
5:15 hear and to be H of their infirmities.
6:17 him and to be H of their diseases;
6:19 forth from him and H them all.
7:7 say the word, and let my servant be H
8:2 women who had been H of evil spirits and
8:36 he who had been possessed with demons was H
8:43 and could not be H by anyone
8:47 touched him, and how she had been immediately H
9:42 the unclean spirit, and H the boy, and gave
13:14 indignant because Jesus had H on the sabbath, said
13:14 those days and be H, and not on the
14:4 he took him and H him, and let him
17:15 saw that he was H, turned back, praising God
22:49 touched his ear and H him.
Jn 5:5 said to him, "Do you want to be H
5:8 once the man was H, and he took up
5:10 them, "The man who H me said to me,
5:12 man who had been H did not know who
5:14 was Jesus who had H him.
Acts 4:9 this man has been H,
4:14 man that had been H standing beside them, they
5:16 afflicted with unclean spirits, and they were all H
8:7 and many who were paralyzed or lame were H
28:8 his hands on him H him.
Heb 12:13 be put out of joint but rather be H
Jas 5:16 pray for one another, that you may be H
1Pet 2:24 By his wounds you have been H
Rev 13:3 its mortal wound was H, and the whole earth
13:12 worship the first beast, whose mortal wound was H

HEALER (2)
Ex 15:26 the Egyptians; for I am the LORD, your H
Is 3:7 will not be a H; in my house there

HEALERS
1Cor 12:28 workers of miracles, then H, helpers, administrators,

HEALEST
Ps 41:3 in his illness thou H all his infirmities.

HEALING (33)
Prov 3:8 It will be H to your flesh and refreshment
4:23 who finds them, and H to all his flesh.
6:15 in a moment he will be broken beyond H
12:18 thrusts, but the tongue of the wise brings H
13:17 men into trouble, but a faithful envoy brings H
29:1 stiffens his neck will suddenly be broken beyond H
Wis 16:9 and flies, and no H was found for them,
Sir 3:26 the proud has no H, for a plant of
21:3 sword; there is no H for its wound.
28:3 and yet seek for H from the Lord?
34:17 the eyes; he grants H, life, and blessing.
38:2 Lord created him; for H comes from the Most
38:14 in diagnosis and in H, for the sake of
Is 19:22 smite Egypt, smiting and H, and they will return
58:8 the dawn, and your H shall spring up speedily;
Jer 8:15 for a time of H, but behold, terror.
8:18 My grief is beyond H, my heart is sick
14:19 that there is no H for us?
14:19 for a time of H, but behold, terror.
30:13 for your wound, no H for you.
33:6 to it health and H, and I will heal
46:11 medicines; there is no H for you.
Ezek 47:12 will be for food, and their leaves for H
Mal 4:2 righteousness shall rise, with H in its wings.
Mt 4:23 of the kingdom and H every disease and every
9:35 of the kingdom, and H every disease and every
Lk 9:6 preaching the gospel and H everywhere.
9:11 God, and cured those who had need of H
Acts 4:22 whom this sign of H was performed was more
10:38 about doing good and H all that were oppressed
1Cor 12:9 to another gifts of H by the one Spirit,
12:30 Do all possess gifts of H
Rev 22:2 tree were for the H of the nations.

HEALS (7)
Ps 103:3 all your iniquity, who H all your diseases,
147:3 He H the brokenhearted, and binds up their wounds.
Wis 16:12 word, O Lord, which H all men.
Sir 38:7 By them he H and takes away pain;
43:22 A mist quickly H all things; when the dew
Is 30:26 of his people, and H the wounds inflicted by
Acts 9:34 him, "Aeneas, Jesus Christ H you; rise and make

HEALTH (21)
Tob 7:4 And he asked them, "Is he in good H
7:5 They replied, "He is alive and in good H
8:17 lives to fulfilment in H and happiness and mercy."
Ps 38:3 indignation; there is no H in my bones because
Prov 16:24 to the soul and H to the body.
Wis 7:10 loved her more than H and beauty, and I
13:18 For H he appeals to a thing that is
Sir 1:16 making peace and perfect H to flourish.
18:18 before you fall ill, take care of your H
30:15 H and soundness are better than all gold, and
30:16 no wealth better than H of body, and there
38:8 finished; and from him H is upon the face
Is 38:16 Oh, restore me to H and make me live!
Jer 8:22 Why then has the H of the daughter of
30:17 For I will restore H to you, and your
33:6 will bring to it H and healing, and I
2Mac 1:10 to the Jews in Egypt, Greeting, and good H
9:19 good wishes for their H and prosperity.
11:28 We also are in good H
Acts 3:16 the man this perfect H in the presence of
3Jn 1:2 you may be in H; I know that it

HEALTHY
Sir 31:20 H sleep depends on moderate eating; he rises early,

HEAP (44)
Gen 31:46 stones, and made a H; and they ate there
31:46 a heap; and they ate there by the H
31:48 Laban said, "This H is a witness between you
31:51 to Jacob, "See this H and the pillar, which
31:52 This H is a witness, and the pillar is
31:52 not pass over this H to you, and you
31:52 not pass over this H and this pillar to
Ex 15:8 stood up in a H; the deeps congealed in
Deut 13:16 it shall be a H for ever, it shall
32:23 "And I will H evils upon them; I will
Josh 3:13 coming down from above shall stand in one H
3:16 rose up in a H far-off, at Adam, the
7:26 over him a great H of stones that remains
8:28 it for ever a H of ruins, as it
8:29 over it a great H of stones, which stands
Ruth 3:7 the end of the H of grain.
1Sam 2:8 needy from the ash H, to make them sit
20:19 was in hand, and remain beside yonder stone H
20:41 from beside the stone H and fell on his
2Sam 18:17 him a very great H of stones; and all
1Kgs 9:8 house will become a H of ruins; everyone passing
Job 27:16 Though he H up silver like dust, and pile
30:24 not one in a H of ruins stretch out
Ps 78:13 it, and made the waters stand like a H
113:7 needy from the ash H,
Prov 25:22 drink; for you will H coals of fire on
Song 7:2 Your belly is a H of wheat, encircled with
Sir 3:25 and the sinner will H sin upon sin.
8:3 with a chatterer, nor H wood on his fire.
20:27 cultivates the soil will H up his harvest, and
39:17 waters stood in a H, and the reservoirs of
Is 3:6 our leader, and this H of ruins shall be
17:1 and will become a H of ruins.
25:2 made the city a H, the fortified city a
Jer 9:11 will make Jerusalem a H of ruins, a lair
26:18 Jerusalem shall become a H of ruins, and the
51:37 Babylon shall become a H of ruins, the haunt
Ezek 24:10 H on the logs, kindle the fire, boil well
Mic 1:6 will make Samaria a H in the open country,
3:12 Jerusalem shall become a H of ruins, and the
Hab 1:10 every fortress, for they H up earth and take
Hag 2:16 one came to a H of twenty measures, there
Mt 6:7 in praying do not H up empty phrases as
Rom 12:20 so doing you will H burning coals upon his

HEAPED (3)
Sir 37:24 man will have praise H upon him, and all
Zech 9:3 herself a rampart, and H up silver like dust,
Rev 18:5 for her sins are H high as heaven, and

H

13:6 H now my reasoning, and listen to the pleadings
15:17 "I will show you, H me; and what I
20:3 I H censure which insults me, and out of
22:27 him, and he will H you; and you will
26:14 a whisper do we H of him!
27:9 Will God H his cry, when trouble comes upon
31:35 I had one to H me!
33:1 "But now, H my speech, O Job, and listen
34:2 Then Elihu said: H my words, you wise
34:10 delight in God.' "Therefore, H me, you men of
34:16 "If you have understanding, H this; listen to what
35:13 Surely God does not H an empty cry, nor
37:14 H this, O Job; stop and consider the wondrous
42:4 H, and I will speak; I will question you,
Ps 4:1 gracious to me, and H my prayer.
5:3 the morning thou dost H my voice; in the
10:17 O LORD, thou wilt H the desire of the
17:1 H a just cause, O LORD; attend to my
17:6 thy ear to me, H my words.
27:7 H, O LORD, when I cry aloud, be gracious
28:2 H the voice of my supplication, as I cry
30:10 H, O LORD, and be gracious to me!
31:13 Yea, I H the whispering of many-- terror
31:22 But thou didst H my supplications, when I cried
34:2 LORD; let the afflicted H and be glad.
38:13 man, I do not H, like a dumb man
38:14 man who does not H, and in whose mouth
39:12 [Selah] H my prayer, O LORD, and give ear
45:10 H, O daughter, consider, and incline your ear; forget
49:1 H this, all peoples!
50:7 [Selah] H, O my people, and I will speak,
54:2 H my prayer, O God; give ear to the
55:17 moan, and he will H my voice.
58:5 that it does not H the voice of charmers
59:7 they think, "will H us?"
61:1 H my cry, O God, listen to my prayer;
64:1 H my voice, O God, in my complaint; preserve
66:16 [Selah] Come and H, all you who fear God,
77:1 God, that he may H me.
81:5 I H a voice I had not known:
81:8 [Selah] H, O my people, while I admonish you!
84:8 LORD God of hosts, H my prayer; give ear,
85:8 Let me H what God the LORD will speak,
94:9 He who planted the ear, does he not H
102:1 H my prayer, O LORD; let my cry come
102:20 at the earth, to H the groans of the
115:6 ears, but do not H; noses, but do not
119:149 H my voice in thy steadfast love; O LORD,
130:2 Lord, H my voice!
135:17 have ears, but they H not, nor is there
143:1 H my prayer, O LORD; give ear to my
143:8 Let me H in the morning of thy steadfast
Prov 1:5 wise man also may H and increase in learning,
1:8 of Greed and Violence H, my son, your father's
4:2 Supreme Guidance of Wisdom H, O sons, a father's
4:11 Good and Evil H, my son, and accept my
8:6 H, for I will speak noble things, and from
8:33 H instruction and be wise, and do not neglect
19:27 Cease, my son, to H instruction only to stray
22:17 Incline your ear, and H the words of the
23:19 H, my son, and be wise, and direct your
Eccl 7:5 for a man to H the rebuke of the
7:5 the wise than to H the song of fools.
7:21 men say, lest you H your servant cursing you;
Song 2:14 your face, let me H your voice, for your
8:13 your voice; let me H it.
Wis 8:15 of me when they H of me; among the
15:15 ears with which to H, nor fingers to feel
Sir 4:6 you, his Creator will H his prayer.
5:11 Be quick to H, and be deliberate in answering.
19:15 is slander; so do not believe everything you H
19:24 and pretends not to H; but where no one
27:7 a man before you H him reason, for this
27:15 to bloodshed, and their abuse is grievous to H
29:25 besides this you will H bitter words:
33:18 H me, you who are great among the people,
41:23 and telling what you H, and of revealing secrets.
43:24 its dangers, and we marvel at what we H
45:5 He made him H his voice, and led him
Is 1:2 H, O heavens, and give ear, O earth; for
1:10 H the word of the LORD, you rulers of
6:9 say to this people: H and hear, but do
6:9 this people: 'Hear and H, but do not understand;
6:10 with their eyes, and H with their ears, and
7:13 And he said, H then, O house of David!
11:3 by what his ears H;
18:3 When a trumpet is blown, H
21:3 so that I cannot H, I am dismayed so
24:16 of the earth we H songs of praise, of
28:12 and this is repose"; yet they would not H
28:14 Therefore H the word of the LORD, you scoffers,
28:23 Give ear, and H my voice; hearken, and hear
28:23 my voice; hearken, and H my speech.
29:18 day the deaf shall H the words of a
30:9 sons who will not H the instruction of the
30:11 the path, let us H no more of the
30:21 And your ears shall H a word behind you,
32:3 ears of those who H will hearken.
32:9 who are at ease, H my voice; you complacent
33:13 H, you who are far-off, what I have done;
34:1 near, O nations, to H, and hearken, O peoples!
36:13 the language of Judah: H the words of the
37:7 so that he shall H a rumor, and return
37:17 ear, O LORD, and H; open thy eyes, O
37:17 LORD, and see; and H all the words of
39:5 Isaiah said to Hezekiah, H the word of the
42:18 H, you deaf; and look, you blind, that you
42:20 his ears are open, but he does not H
43:9 them, and let them H and say, It is
44:1 "But now H, O Jacob my servant, Israel whom
47:8 Now therefore H this, you lover of pleasures, who
48:1 H this, O house of Jacob, who are called
48:6 forth I make you H new things, hidden things
48:14 "Assemble, all of you, and H
48:16 Draw near to me, H this: from the beginning
50:4 wakens my ear to H as those who are
51:21 Therefore H this, you who are afflicted, who are
55:3 and come to me; H, that your soul may
59:1 dull, that it cannot H;
59:2 face from you so that he does not H
65:24 answer, while they are yet speaking I will H
66:5 H the word of the LORD, you who tremble
Jer 2:4 H the word of the LORD, O house of
4:19 keep silent; for I H the sound of the
4:21 see the standard, and H the sound of the
5:21 proclaim it in Judah: H this, O foolish and
5:21 who have ears, but H not.
6:10 I speak and give warning, that they may H
6:18 not give heed.' Therefore H, O nations, and know,
6:19 H, O earth; behold, I am bringing evil upon
7:2 this word, and say, H the word of the
7:16 for I do not H you.
9:20 H, O women, the word of the LORD, and
10:1 H the word which the LORD speaks to you,
11:2 Jeremiah from the LORD: H the words of this
11:6 the streets of Jerusalem: H the words of this
11:10 forefathers, who refused to H my words; they have
13:10 people, who refuse to H my words, who stubbornly
13:15 H and give ear; be not proud, for the
14:12 fast, I will not H their cry, and though
17:20 of Jerusalem, and say: H the word of the
17:23 that they might not H and receive instruction.
18:2 I will let you H my words."
19:3 You shall say, H the word of the LORD,
19:15 their neck, refusing to H my words."
20:10 For I H many whispering.
20:16 without pity; let him H a cry in the
21:11 king of Judah say, H the word of the
22:2 this word, and say, H the word of the
22:29 O land, land, land, H the word of the
23:18 to perceive and to H his word, or who
25:4 inclined your ears to H, although the LORD
28:7 Yet H now this word which I speak in
29:12 me, and I will H you.
29:20 says the LORD.-- H the word of the
31:10 H the word of the LORD, O nations, and
33:9 the earth who shall H of all the good
34:4 go to Babylon.' Yet H the word of the
36:3 house of Judah will H all the evil which
36:31 have pronounced against them, but they would not H
37:20 Now H, I pray you, O my lord the
38:25 If the princes H that I have spoken with
42:14 not see war, or H the sound of the
42:15 will dwell there,' then H the word of the
44:24 and all the women, H the word of the
44:26 Therefore H the word of the LORD, all you
49:20 Therefore H the plan which the LORD has made
50:45 Therefore H the plan which the LORD has made
Lam 1:18 against his word; but H, all you peoples, and
1:21 H how I groan; there is none to comfort
3:56 the pit; thou didst H my plea, 'Do not
Bar 1:3 people who came to H the book,

2:14 H, O Lord, our prayer and our supplication, and
2:16 ear, O Lord, and H;
2:31 obeys and ears that H;
3:2 H, O Lord, and have mercy, for we have
3:4 Almighty, God of Israel, H now the prayer of
3:9 H the commandments of life, O Israel; give ear,
Ezek 2:5 GOD.' And whether they H or refuse to hear
2:5 hear or refuse to H (for they are a
2:7 to them, whether they H or refuse to hear;
2:7 hear or refuse to H; for they are a
2:8 you, son of man, H what I say to
3:10 in your heart, and H with your ears.
3:11 Lord GOD'; whether they H or refuse to hear."
3:11 Lord GOD'; whether they hear or refuse to H
3:17 of Israel; whenever you H a word from my
3:27 GOD'; he that will H, let him hear; and
3:27 will hear, let him H; and he that will
3:27 that will refuse to H, let him refuse; for
6:3 You mountains of Israel, H the word of the
8:18 voice, I will not H them."
12:2 who have ears to H, but hear not;
12:2 ears to hear, but H not;
13:2 of their own minds: H the word of the
16:35 "Wherefore, O harlot, H the word of the LORD:
18:25 Lord is not just.' H now, O house of
20:47 forest of the Negeb, H the word of the
25:3 Say to the Ammonites, H the word of the
33:7 of Israel; whenever you H a word from my
33:30 his brother, 'Come, and H what the word is
33:31 my people, and they H what you say but
33:32 an instrument, for they H what you say, but
34:7 "Therefore, you shepherds, H the word of the LORD:
34:9 sheep; therefore, you shepherds, H the word of the
36:1 O mountains of Israel, H the word of the
36:4 O mountains of Israel, H the word of the
36:15 will not let you H any more the reproach
37:4 them, O dry bones, H the word of the
40:4 with your eyes, and H with your ears, and
44:5 with your eyes, and H with your ears all
Dan 3:5 languages, that when you H the sound of the
3:15 are ready when you H the sound of the
5:23 do not see or H or know, but the
9:18 incline thy ear and H; open thy eyes and
9:19 O LORD, H; O LORD, forgive; O LORD, give
Hos 4:1 H the word of the LORD, O people of
5:1 H this, O priests!
Joel 1:2 the son of Pethuel: H this, you aged men,
Amos 3:1 H this word that the LORD has spoken against
3:13 H, and testify against the house of Jacob," says
4:1 H this word, you cows of Bashan, who are
5:1 H this word which I take up over you
7:16 people Israel.' "Now therefore H the word of the
8:4 H this, you who trample upon the needy, and
Jon 2:2 cried, and thou didst H my voice.
Mic 1:2 H, you peoples, all of you; hearken, O earth,
3:1 And I said: H, you heads of Jacob and
3:9 H this, you heads of the house of Jacob
6:1 H what the LORD says: Arise, plead your case
6:1 and let the hills H your voice.
6:2 H, you mountains, the controversy of the LORD, and
6:9 to fear thy name: H, O tribe and assembly
7:7 salvation; my God will H me.
Nah 3:19 All who H the news of you clap their
Hab 1:2 I cry for help, and thou wilt not H
3:16 I H, and my body trembles, my lips quiver
Zech 1:4 But they did not H or heed me, says
3:8 H now, O Joshua the high priest, you and
7:11 and stopped their ears that they might not H
7:12 adamant lest they should H the law and the
7:13 and they would not H, so they called, and
7:13 hear, so they called, and I would not H
2Mac 1:5 May he H your prayers and be reconciled to
Mt 10:27 light; and what you H whispered, proclaim upon the
11:4 tell John what you H and see:
11:5 cleansed and the deaf H, and the dead are
11:15 who has ears to H, let him hear.
11:15 He who has ears to hear, let him H
12:19 nor will any one H his voice in the
12:42 of the earth to H the wisdom of Solomon,
13:9 He who has ears, let him H
13:13 hearing they do not H, nor do they understand.
13:14 says: 'You shall indeed H but never understand, and
13:15 with their eyes, and H with their ears, and
13:16 for they see, and your ears, for they H
13:17 see it, and to H what you hear, and
13:17 to hear what you H, and did not hear
13:17 hear, and did not H it.
13:18 H then the parable of the sower.
13:43 He who has ears, let him H
15:10 and said to them, H and understand:
21:16 to him, "Do you H what these are saying?"
21:33 H another parable.
24:6 And you will H of wars and rumors of
27:13 him, "Do you not H how many things they
Mk 4:9 who has ears to H, let him hear."
4:9 "He who has ears to hear, let him H
4:12 perceive, and may indeed H but not understand; lest
4:15 is sown; when they H, Satan immediately comes and
4:16 ground, who, when they H the word, immediately
4:18 they are those who H the word,
4:20 are the ones who H the word and accept
4:23 man has ears to H, let him hear."
4:23 any man has ears to hear, let him H
4:24 "Take heed what you H; the measure you give
4:33 they were able to H it;
6:11 and they refuse to H you, when you leave,
7:14 and said to them, H me, all of you,
7:36 even makes the deaf H and the dumb speak."
8:18 not see, and having ears do you not H
12:29 answered, "The first is, H, O Israel: The Lord
13:7 And when you H of wars and rumors of
Lk 5:1 pressed upon him to H the word of God,
5:15 great multitudes gathered to H and to be healed
6:17 Sidon, who came to H him and to be
6:27 say to you that H, Love your enemies, do
7:22 cleansed, and the deaf H, the dead are raised
8:8 who has ears to H, let him hear."
8:8 "He who has ears to hear, let him H
8:13 those who, when they H the word, receive it
8:14 they are those who H, but as they go
8:18 heed then how you H; for to him who
8:21 brethren are those who H the word of God
9:9 this about whom I H such things?" And he
10:24 see it, and to H what you hear, and
10:24 to hear what you H, and did not hear
10:24 hear, and did not H it."
11:28 rather are those who H the word of God
11:31 of the earth to H the wisdom of Solomon,
14:35 who has ears to H, let him hear."
14:35 He who has ears to hear, let him H
15:1 all drawing near to H him.
16:2 is this that I H about you?
16:29 the prophets; let them H them.'
16:31 'If they do not H Moses and the prophets,
18:6 And the Lord said, H what the unrighteous judge
21:9 And when you H of wars and tumults, do
21:38 in the temple to H him.
Jn 3:8 it wills, and you H the sound of it,
5:24 when the dead will H the voice of the
5:24 God, and those who H will live.
5:27 in the tombs will H his voice
5:29 own authority; as I H, I judge; and my
8:43 you cannot bear to H my word.
8:47 why you do not H them is that you
9:27 do you want to H it again?
10:3 gatekeeper opens; the sheep H his voice, and he
10:27 My sheep H my voice, and I know them,
14:24 the word which you H is not mine but
Acts 2:8 is it that we H, each of us in
2:11 Cretans and Arabians, we H them telling in our
2:22 saved.' "Men of Israel, H these words: Jesus of
2:33 has poured out this which you see and H
7:2 said: "Brethren and fathers, H me.
10:22 his house, and to H what you have to
10:33 sight of God, to H all that you have
13:7 Saul and sought to H the word of God.
13:44 city gathered together to H the word of God.
15:7 mouth the Gentiles should H the word of the
17:32 others said, "We will H you again about this."
19:26 And you see and H that not only at
21:22 They will certainly H that you have come.
22:1 saying: "Brethren and fathers, H the defense which I
22:9 light but did not H the voice of the
22:14 Just One and to H a voice from his
23:35 he said, "I will H you when your accusers
24:4 in your kindness to H us briefly.
25:22 "I should like to H the man myself." "Tomorrow,"
25:22 said he, "you shall H him."
26:29 but also all who H me this day might
28:22 But we desire to H from you what your
28:26 say, You shall indeed H but never understand, and
28:27 with their eyes, and H with their ears, and

Rom 10:14 how are they to H without a preacher?
11:8 ears that should not H, down to this very
1Cor 11:18 as a church, I H that there are divisions
Gal 4:21 law, do you not H the law?
Eph 4:29 that it may impart grace to those who H
Phil 1:27 am absent, I may H of you that you
1:30 you saw and now H to be mine.
2Thes 3:11 For we H that some of you are living
2Tim 4:17 all the Gentiles might H it.
Philem 1:5 my prayers, because I H of your love and
Heb 3:7 says, "Today, when you H his voice,
3:15 said, "Today, when you H his voice, do not
4:7 quoted, "Today, when you H his voice, do not
Jas 1:18 man be quick to H, slow to speak, slow
3Jn 1:4 have than this, to H that my children follow
Rev 1:3 blessed are those who H, and who keep what
2:7 an ear, let him H what the Spirit says
2:11 an ear, let him H what the Spirit says
2:17 an ear, let him H what the Spirit says
2:29 an ear, let him H what the Spirit says
3:6 an ear, let him H what the Spirit says
3:13 an ear, let him H what the Spirit says
3:22 an ear, let him H what the Spirit says
9:20 cannot either see or H or walk;
13:9 an ear, let him H:

HEARD (692)

Gen 3:8 And they H the sound of the LORD God
3:10 And he said, "I H the sound of thee
14:14 When Abram H that his kinsman had been taken
17:20 for Ishmael, I have H you; behold, I will
21:17 And God H the voice of the lad; and
21:17 not; for God has H the voice of the
21:26 and I have not H of it until today."
24:30 arms, and when he H the words of Rebekah
24:52 When Abraham's servant H their words, he bowed
27:6 her son Jacob, "I H your father speak to
27:34 When Esau H the words of his father, he
29:13 When Laban H the tidings of Jacob his sister's
29:33 "Because the LORD has H that I am hated,
30:6 me, and has also H my voice and given
31:1 Now Jacob H that the sons of Laban were
34:5 Now Jacob H that he had defiled his daughter
34:7 the field when they H of it; and the
35:22 father's concubine; and Israel H of it.
37:17 gone away, for I H them say, 'Let us
37:21 But when Reuben H it, he delivered him out
39:15 voice; and when he H that I lifted up
39:19 When his master H the words which his wife
41:15 it; and I have H it said of you
42:2 said, "Behold, I have H that there is grain
43:25 at noon, for they H that they should eat
45:2 so that the Egyptians H it, and the household
45:2 the household of Pharaoh H it.
45:16 the report was H in Pharaoh's house, "Joseph's
Ex 2:15 When Pharaoh H of it, he sought to kill
2:24 And God H their groaning, and God remembered his
3:7 in Egypt, and have H their cry because of
4:31 believed; and when they H that the LORD had
6:5 Moreover I have H the groaning of the people
15:14 The peoples have H, they tremble; pangs have seized
16:7 LORD, because he has H your murmurings against
16:8 because the LORD has H your murmurings which
16:9 LORD, for he has H your murmurings.'"
16:12 to Moses, "I have H the murmurings of the
18:1 of Midian, Moses' father-in-law, H of all that God
23:13 nor let such be H out of your mouth.
28:35 its sound shall be H when he goes into
32:17 When Joshua H the noise of the people as
33:4 When the people H these evil tidings, they mourned;
Lev 10:20 And when Moses H that, he was content.
24:14 and let all who H him lay their hands
Num 7:89 with the LORD, he H the voice speaking to
11:1 and when the LORD H it, his anger was
11:10 Moses H the people weeping throughout their
12:2 And the LORD H it.
14:14 They have H that thou, O LORD, art in
14:15 the nations who have H thy fame will say,
14:27 I have H the murmurings of the people of
16:4 When Moses H it, he fell on his face;
20:16 to the LORD, he H our voice, and sent
21:1 dwelt in the Negeb, H that Israel was coming
22:36 When Balak H that Balaam had come, he went
30:11 oath, and her husband H of it, and said
30:14 the day that he H of them.
30:15 void after he has H of them, then he
33:40 the land of Canaan, H of the coming of
Deut 1:34 "And the LORD H your words, and was angered,
4:12 of the fire; you H the sound of words,
4:32 happened or was ever H of.
4:33 fire, as you have H, and still live?
4:36 great fire, and you H his words out of
5:23 And when you H the voice out of the
5:24 greatness, and we have H his voice out of
5:26 all flesh, that has H the voice of the
5:28 it.' "And the LORD H your words, when you
5:28 to me, 'I have H the words of this
9:2 of whom you have H it said, 'Who can
26:7 fathers, and the LORD H our voice, and saw
Josh 2:10 For we have H how the LORD dried up
2:11 as soon as we H it, our hearts melted,
5:1 were by the sea, H that the LORD had
6:10 let your voice be H, neither shall any word
6:20 soon as the people H the sound of the
9:1 Hivites, and the Jebusites, H of this,
9:3 the inhabitants of Gibeon H what Joshua had done
9:9 God; for we have H a report of him,
9:16 covenant with them, they H that they were their
10:1 Adoni-zedek king of Jerusalem H how Joshua had
11:1 Jabin king of Hazor H of this, he sent
14:12 that day; for you H on that day how
22:11 the people of Israel H say, "Behold, the Reubenites
22:12 the people of Israel H of it, the whole
22:30 who were with him, H the words that the
24:27 us; for it has H all the words of
Judg 7:15 When Gideon H the telling of the dream and
9:30 ruler of the city H the words of Gaal
9:46 the Tower of Shechem H of it, they entered
18:25 let your voice be H among us, lest angry
20:3 (Now the Benjaminites H that the people of Israel
Ruth 1:6 Moab, for she had H in the country of
1Sam 1:13 her voice was not H; therefore Eli took her
2:22 very old, and he H all that his sons
4:6 And when the Philistines H the noise of the
4:14 When Eli H the sound of the outcry, he
4:19 And when she H the tidings that the ark
7:7 Now when the Philistines H that the people of
7:7 the people of Israel H of it they were
8:21 And when Samuel had H all the words of
11:6 upon Saul when he H these words, and his
13:3 Geba; and the Philistines H of it.
13:4 And all Israel H it said that Saul had
14:22 hill country of Ephraim H that the Philistines were
14:27 But Jonathan had not H his father charge the
17:11 Saul and all Israel H these words of the
17:23 And David H him.
17:28 Eliab his eldest brother H when he spoke to
17:31 which David spoke were H, they repeated them
22:1 all his father's house H it, they went down
22:6 Now Saul H that David was discovered, and the
23:10 thy servant has surely H that Saul seeks to
23:11 Will Saul come down, as thy servant has H
23:25 And when Saul H that, he pursued after David
25:4 David H in the wilderness that Nabal was shearing
25:39 When David H that Nabal was dead, he said,
31:11 inhabitants of Jabesh-gilead H what the Philistines
2Sam 3:28 Afterward, when David H of it, he said, "I
4:1 When Ish-bosheth, Saul's son, H that Abner had died
5:17 the Philistines H that David had been anointed
5:17 of David; but David H of it and went
7:22 all that we have H with our ears.
8:9 Toi king of Hamath H that David had defeated
10:7 And when David H of it, he sent Joab
11:26 the wife of Uriah H that Uriah her husband
13:21 When King David H of all these things, he
18:5 And all the people H when the king gave
19:2 people; for the people H that day, "The king
22:7 From his temple he H my voice, and my
22:45 as soon as they H of me, they obeyed
1Kgs 1:11 Solomon, "Have you not H that Adonijah the son
1:41 who were with him H it as they finished
1:41 And when Joab H the sound of the trumpet,
1:45 This is the noise that you have H
3:28 And all Israel H of the judgment which the
4:34 the earth, who had H of his wisdom.
5:1 to Solomon, when he H that they had anointed
5:7 When Hiram H the words of Solomon, he rejoiced
5:8 Solomon, saying, "I have H the message which you
6:7 tool of iron was H in the temple, while
9:3 to him, "I have H your prayer and your
10:1 the queen of Sheba H of the fame of
10:6 was true which I H in my own land

	10:7	wisdom and prosperity surpass the report which I H
	11:21	But when Hadad H in Egypt that David slept
	12:2	the son of Nebat H of it (for he
	12:20	And when all Israel H that Jeroboam had returned,
	13:4	And when the king H the saying of the
	13:26	back from the way H of it, he said,
	14:6	But when Ahijah H the sound of her feet,
	15:21	And when Baasha H of it, he stopped building
	16:16	troops who were encamped H it said, "Zimri has
	19:13	And when Elijah H it, he wrapped his face
	20:12	When Ben-hadad H this message as he was drinking
	20:31	"Behold now, we have H that the kings of
	21:15	As soon as Jezebel H that Naboth had been
	21:16	as soon as Ahab H that Naboth was dead,
	21:27	Israel.) And when Ahab H those words, he rent
2Kgs	3:21	When all the Moabites H that the kings had
	5:8	the man of God H that the king of
	6:30	When the king H the words of the woman
	7:10	to be seen or H there, nothing but the
	9:30	came to Jezreel, Jezebel H of it; and she
	11:13	When Athaliah H the noise of the guard and
	19:1	When King Hezekiah H it, he rent his clothes,
	19:4	the LORD your God H all the words of
	19:4	LORD your God has H; therefore lift up your
	19:6	words that you have H, with which the servants
	19:8	against Libnah; for he H that the king had
	19:9	And when the king H concerning Tirhakah king of
	19:11	Behold, you have H what the kings of Assyria
	19:20	me about Sennacherib king of Assyria I have H
	19:25	Egypt.' "Have you not H that I determined it
	20:5	your father: I have H your prayer, I have
	20:12	to Hezekiah; for he H that Hezekiah had been
	22:11	And when the king H the words of the
	22:18	words which you have H,
	22:19	the LORD, when you H how I spoke against
	22:19	me, I also have H you, says the LORD.
	25:23	country and their men H that the king of
1Chr	10:11	But when all Jabesh-gilead H all that the Philistines
	14:8	When the Philistines H that David had been
	14:8	of David; and David H of it and went
	17:20	all that we have H with our ears.
	18:9	Tou king of Hamath H that David had defeated
	19:8	When David H of it, he sent Joab and
2Chr	5:13	singers to make themselves H in unison in praise
	7:12	to him: "I have H your prayer, and have
	9:1	the queen of Sheba H of the fame of
	9:5	was true which I H in my own land
	9:6	told me; you surpass the report which I H
	10:2	the son of Nebat H of it (for he
	15:8	When Asa H these words, the prophecy of Azariah
	16:5	And when Baasha H of it, he stopped building
	20:29	the countries when they H that the LORD had
	23:12	When Athaliah H the noise of the people running
	30:20	And the LORD H Hezekiah, and healed the people.
	30:27	and their voice was H, and their prayer came
	33:13	received his entreaty and H his supplication and
	34:19	When the king H the words of the law
	34:26	words which you have H,
	34:27	before God when you H his words against this
	34:27	me, I also have H you, says the LORD.
Ezra	3:13	and the sound was H afar.
	4:1	of Judah and Benjamin H that the returned exiles
	9:3	When I H this, I rent my garments and
Neh	1:4	When I H these words I sat down and
	2:10	the servant, the Ammonite, H this, it displeased them
	2:19	and Geshem the Arab H of it, they derided
	4:1	Now when Sanballat H that we were building the
	4:7	Ammonites and the Ashdodites H that the repairing
	4:15	When our enemies H that it was known to
	5:6	very angry when I H their outcry and these
	6:16	when all our enemies H of it, all the
	8:9	people wept when they H the words of the
	12:43	joy of Jerusalem was H afar off.
	13:3	When the people H the law, they separated from
Tob	3:6	live, because I have H false reproaches, and great
	3:10	When she H these things she was deeply grieved,
	3:16	prayer of both was H in the presence of
	6:13	"Brother Azarias, I have H that the girl has
	6:17	When Tobias H these things, he fell in love
	7:7	When he H that Tobit had lost his sight,
	14:15	before he died he H of the destruction of
Jud	4:1	living in Judea H of everything that Holofernes,
	4:13	So the Lord H their prayers and looked upon
	5:1	of the Assyrian army, H that the people of
	8:1	At that time Judith H about these things: she
	8:9	When Judith H the wicked words spoken by the
	8:9	water, and when she H all that Uzziah said
	10:14	When the men H her words, and observed her
	11:8	For we have H of your wisdom and skill,
	11:9	your council, we have H his words, for the
	13:12	men of her city H her voice, they hurried
	14:19	of the Assyrian army H this, they rent their
	15:1	men in the tents H it, they were amazed
	15:5	And when the Israelites H it, with one accord
Esth	1:18	and Media who have H of the queen's behavior
	14:5	was born I have H in the tribe of
Job	2:11	when Job's three friends H of all this evil
	3:7	no joyful cry be H in it.
	4:16	was silence, then I H a voice:
	13:1	this, my ear has H and understood it.
	16:2	Job answered: "I have H many such things;
	28:22	Death say, 'We have H a rumor of it
	29:11	When the ear H, it called me blessed, and
	33:8	hearing, and I have H the sound of your
	34:28	to him, and he H the cry of the
	37:4	not restrain the lightnings when his voice is H
	42:5	to me.' I had H of thee by the
Ps	6:8	for the LORD has H the sound of my
	6:9	The LORD has H my supplication; the LORD accepts
	18:6	From his temple he H my voice, and my
	18:44	As soon as they H of me they obeyed
	19:3	their voice is not H;
	22:24	from him, but has H, when he cried to
	28:6	for he has H the voice of my supplications.
	34:6	cried, and the LORD H him, and saved him
	40:1	inclined to me and H my cry.
	44:1	We have H with our ears, O God, our
	48:8	As we have H, so have we seen in
	61:5	thou, O God, hast H my vows, thou hast
	62:11	spoken; twice have I H this: that power belongs
	66:8	of his praise be H,
	78:3	things that we have H and known, that our
	78:21	Therefore, when the LORD H, he was full of
	78:59	When God H, he was full of wrath, and
	92:11	enemies, my ears have H the doom of my
	106:44	their distress, when he H their cry.
	116:1	LORD, because he has H my voice and my
	132:6	Lo, we H of it in Ephrathah, we found
	138:4	LORD, for they have H the words of thy
Prov	21:13	poor will himself cry out and not be H
Eccl	9:17	words of the wise H in quiet are better
	12:13	The end of the matter; all has been H
Song	2:12	of the turtledove is H in our land.
Wis	11:13	For when they H that through their own punishments
	18:1	Their enemies H their voices but did not see
Sir	3:5	children, and when he prays he will be H
	11:8	answer before you have H, nor interrupt a speaker
	16:5	and my ear has H things more striking than
	17:11	majesty, and their ears H the glory of his
	19:9	for some one has H you and watched you,
	19:10	Have you H a word?
	33:4	thus you will be H; bind together your instruction,
	45:9	to make their ringing H in the temple as
	46:17	and made his voice H with a mighty sound;
	48:7	from their beds; who H rebuke at Sinai and
	48:20	the Holy One quickly H them from heaven, and
	50:16	great noise to be H for remembrance before the
	51:11	My prayer was H,
Is	6:8	And I H the voice of the Lord saying,
	15:4	out, their voice is H as far as Jahaz;
	16:6	We have H of the pride of Moab, how
	21:10	one, what I have H from the LORD of
	28:22	strong; for I have H a decree of destruction
	30:30	majestic voice to be H and the descending blow
	37:1	When King Hezekiah H it, he rent his clothes,
	37:4	the LORD your God H the words of the
	37:4	LORD your God has H; therefore lift up your
	37:6	words that you have H, with which the servants
	37:8	Libnah; for he had H that the king had
	37:9	the king H concerning Tirhakah king of Ethiopia,
	37:9	And when he H it, he sent messengers to
	37:11	Behold, you have H what the kings of Assyria
	37:26	'Have you not H that I determined it long
	38:5	your father: I have H your prayer, I have
	39:1	to Hezekiah, for he H that he had been
	40:21	Have you not H
	40:28	Have you not H
	41:26	who proclaimed, none who H your words.
	42:2	voice, or make it H in the street;
	48:6	commanded them.' "You have H; now see all this;
	48:7	today you have never H of them, lest you
	48:8	them.' You have never H, you have never known,

52:15 which they have not H they shall understand.
53:1 Who has believed what we have H
58:4 your voice to be H on high.
60:18 shall no more be H in your land, devastation
64:4 old no one has H or perceived by the
65:19 no more shall be H in it the sound
66:8 Who has H such a thing?
66:19 off, that have not H my fame or seen
Jer 3:21 the bare heights is H, the weeping and pleading
4:31 For I H a cry as of a woman
6:7 violence and destruction are H within her; sickness
6:24 We have H the report of it, our hands
8:16 of their horses is H from Dan; at the
9:10 of cattle is not H; both the birds of
9:19 sound of wailing is H from Zion: 'How we
18:13 the nations, who has H the like of this?
18:22 May a cry be H from their houses, when
20:1 house of the LORD, H Jeremiah prophesying these
23:25 I have H what the prophets have said who
26:7 and all the people H Jeremiah speaking these words
26:10 the princes of Judah H these things, they came
26:11 city, as you have H with your own ears."
26:12 and this city all the words you have H
26:21 and all the princes, H his words, the king
26:21 death; but when Uriah H of it, he was
30:5 the LORD: We have H a cry of panic,
31:15 LORD: "A voice is H in Ramah, lamentation and
31:18 I have H Ephraim bemoaning, 'Thou hast chastened
33:10 beast, there shall be H again
36:11 Gemariah, son of Shaphan, H all the words of
36:13 words that he had H, when Baruch read the
36:16 When they H all the words, they turned one
36:24 of his servants who H all these words, was
37:5 who were besieging Jerusalem H news of them, they
38:1 the son of Malchiah H the words that Jeremiah
38:7 in the king's house, H that they had put
40:7 country and their men H that the king of
40:11 and in other lands H that the king of
41:11 the forces with him H of all the evil
42:4 to them, "I have H you; behold, I will
46:12 The nations have H of your shame, and the
48:4 destroyed; a cry is H as far as Zoar.
48:5 of Horonaim they have H the cry of destruction.
48:29 We have H of the pride of Moab--he
49:2 battle cry to be H against Rabbah of the
49:14 I have H tidings from the LORD, and a
49:21 their cry shall be H at the Red Sea.
49:23 confounded, for they have H evil tidings; they melt
50:43 "The king of Babylon H the report of them,
50:46 her cry shall be H among the nations."
51:46 fearful at the report H in the land, when
51:51 shame, for we have H reproach; dishonor has
Lam 1:21 All my enemies have H of my trouble; they
3:61 "Thou hast H their taunts, O LORD, all their
Bar 3:22 She has not been H of in Canaan, nor
Ezek 1:24 when they went, I H the sound of their
1:28 my face, and I H the voice of one
2:2 my feet; and I H him speaking to me.
3:12 from its place, I H behind me the sound
10:5 of the cherubim was H as far as the
19:9 should no more be H upon the mountains of
26:13 your lyres shall be H no more.
33:5 He H the sound of the trumpet, and did
35:12 I, the LORD, have H all the revilings which
35:13 words against me; I H it.
43:6 standing beside me, I H one speaking to me
Dan 3:7 as all the peoples H the sound of the
5:14 I have H of you that the spirit of
5:16 But I have H that you can give interpretations
6:14 the king, when he H these words, was much
8:13 Then I H a holy one speaking; and another
8:16 And I H a man's voice between the banks
10:9 Then I H the sound of his words; and
10:9 words; and when I H the sound of his
10:12 your words have been H, and I have come
12:7 toward heaven; and I H him swear by him
12:8 I H, but I did not understand.
13:26 When the household servants H the shouting in the
13:44 The Lord H her cry.
14:28 When the Babylonians H it, they were very indignant
Obad 1:1 Edom: We have H tidings from the LORD,
Nah 2:13 voice of your messengers shall no more be H
Hab 3:2 O LORD, I have H the report of thee,
Zeph 1:10 "a cry will be H from the Fish Gate,
2:8 "I have H the taunts of Moab and the
Zech 8:23 you, for we have H that God is with
Mal 3:16 the LORD heeded and H them, and a book
1Mac 3:13 of the Syrian army, H that Judas had gathered
3:27 When king Antiochus H these reports, he was greatly
3:41 traders of the region H what was said to
4:3 But Judas H of it, and he and his
4:27 When he H it, he was perplexed and discouraged,
5:1 the Gentiles round about H that the altar had
5:16 Judas and the people H these messages, a great
5:56 commanders of the forces, H of their brave deeds
5:63 among all the Gentiles, wherever their name was H
6:1 upper provinces when he H that Elymais in Persia
6:8 When the king H this news, he was astounded
6:28 was enraged when he H this.
6:41 All who H the noise made by their multitude,
6:55 Then Lysias H that Philip, whom King Antiochus
8:1 Now Judas H of the fame of the Romans,
8:12 as many as have H of their fame have
9:1 When Demetrius H that Nicanor and his army had
9:33 who were with him H of it, and they
9:43 When Bacchides H of this, he came with a
10:2 When Demetrius the king H of it, he assembled
10:8 greatly alarmed when they H that the king had
10:15 Now Alexander the king H of all the promises
10:19 We have H about you, that you are a
10:22 When Demetrius H of these things he was grieved
10:26 our enemies, we have H of it and rejoiced.
10:46 Jonathan and the people H these words, they did
10:68 When Alexander the king H of it, he was
10:74 When Jonathan H the words of Apollonius, his spirit
10:77 When Apollonius H of it, he mustered three thousand
10:88 When Alexander the king H of these things, he
11:15 And Alexander H of it and came against him
11:22 When he H this he was angry, and as
11:22 as soon as he H it he set out
11:23 When Jonathan H this, he gave orders to continue
11:63 Then Jonathan H that the officers of Demetrius had
12:24 Now Jonathan H that the commanders of Demetrius
12:28 When the enemy H that Jonathan and his men
12:34 surprise, for he had H that they were ready
13:1 Simon H that Trypho had assembled a large army
13:7 was rekindled when they H these words,
14:2 of Persia and Media H that Demetrius had invaded
14:16 It was H in Rome, and as far away
14:17 When they H that Simon his brother had become
14:25 When the people H these things they said, "How
14:40 For he had H that the Jews were addressed
16:22 When he H this, he was greatly shocked; and
2Mac 1:8 Lord and we were H, and we offered sacrifice
10:13 He H himself called a traitor at every turn,
11:24 We have H that the Jews do not consent
12:5 When Judas H of the cruelty visited on his
13:10 But when Judas H of this, he ordered the
14:15 When the Jews H of Nicanor's coming and the
15:1 When Nicanor H that Judas and his men were
Mt 2:3 When Herod the king H this, he was troubled,
2:9 When they had H the king they went their
2:18 Jeremiah: "A voice was H in Ramah, wailing and
2:22 But when he H that Archelaus reigned over Judea
4:12 Now when he H that John had been arrested,
5:21 "You have H that it was said to the
5:27 "You have H that it was said, 'You shall
5:33 "Again you have H that it was said to
5:38 "You have H that it was said, 'An eye
5:43 "You have H that it was said, 'You shall
6:7 that they will be H for their many words.
8:10 When Jesus H him, he marveled, and said to
9:12 But when he H it, he said, "Those who
11:2 Now when John H in prison about the deeds
12:24 But when the Pharisees H it they said, "It
14:1 time Herod the tetrarch H about the fame of
14:13 Now when Jesus H this, he withdrew from there
14:13 But when the crowds H it, they followed him
15:12 were offended when they H this saying?"
17:6 When the disciples H this, they fell on their
19:22 When the young man H this he went away
19:25 the disciples H this they were greatly astonished,
20:24 And when the ten H it, they were indignant
20:30 the roadside, when they H that Jesus was passing
21:45 and the Pharisees H his parables, they perceived
22:22 When they H it, they marveled; and they left
22:33 And when the crowd H it, they were astonished
22:34 But when the Pharisees H that he had silenced
26:65 You have now H his blasphemy.
Mk 2:17 And when Jesus H it, he said to them,
3:21 And when his family H it, they went out
5:27 She had H the reports about Jesus, and came

H

6:2 synagogue; and many who H him were astonished,
6:14 King Herod H of it; for Jesus' name had
6:16 But when Herod H of it he said, "John,
6:20 When he H him, he was much perplexed; and
6:20 perplexed; and yet he H him gladly.
6:29 When his disciples H of it, they came and
6:55 any place where they H he was.
7:24 by an unclean spirit, H of him, and came
10:41 And when the ten H it, they began to
10:47 And when he H that it was Jesus of
11:14 And his disciples H it.
11:18 priests and the scribes H it and sought a
12:28 scribes came up and H them disputing with one
12:37 And the great throng H him gladly.
14:11 And when they H it they were glad, and
14:58 against him, saying, "We H him say, 'I will
14:64 You have H his blasphemy.
16:11 But when they H that he was alive and
Lk 1:13 for your prayer is H, and your wife Elizabeth
1:41 And when Elizabeth H the greeting of Mary, the
1:58 her neighbors and kinsfolk H that the Lord had
1:66 Judea; and all who H them laid them up
2:18 child; and all who H it wondered at what
2:20 for all they had H and seen, as it
2:47 questions; and all who H him were amazed at
4:23 yourself; what we have H you did at Caperna-um,
4:28 When they H this, all in the synagogue were
7:3 When he H of Jesus, he sent to him
7:9 When Jesus H this he marveled at him, and
7:22 you have seen and H: the blind receive their
7:29 (When they H this all the people and the
8:12 are those who have H; then the devil comes
9:7 Now Herod the tetrarch H of all that was
12:3 the dark shall be H in the light, and
14:15 at table with him H this, he said to
15:25 to the house, he H music and dancing.
16:14 were lovers of money, H all this, and they
18:22 And when Jesus H it, he said to him,
18:23 But when he H this he became sad, for
18:26 Those who H it said, "Then who can be
19:11 As they H these things, he proceeded to tell
20:16 When they H this, they said, "God forbid!"
22:69 We have H it ourselves from his own lips."
23:6 When Pilate H this, he asked whether the man
23:8 him, because he had H about him, and he
Jn 1:37 The two disciples H him say this, and they
1:40 of the two who H John speak, and followed
3:32 he has seen and H, yet no one receives
4:1 that the Pharisees had H that Jesus was making
4:42 believe, for we have H for ourselves, and we
4:47 When he H that Jesus had come from Judea
5:36 voice you have never H, his form you have
6:45 Every one who has H and learned from the
6:60 his disciples, when they H it, said, "This is
7:32 The Pharisees H the crowd thus muttering about
7:40 When they H these words, some of the people
8:9 But when they H it, they went away, one
8:26 world what I have H from him."
8:38 do what you have H from your father."
8:40 the truth which I H from God; this is
9:32 began has it been H that any one opened
9:35 Jesus H that they had cast him out, and
9:40 the Pharisees near him H this, and they said
11:4 But when Jesus H it he said, "This illness
11:6 So when he H that he was ill, he
11:20 When Martha H that Jesus was coming, she went
11:29 And when she H it, she rose quickly and
11:41 thee that thou hast H me.
12:12 come to the feast H that Jesus was coming
12:18 him was that they H he had done this
12:29 The crowd standing by H it and said that
12:34 answered him, "We have H from the law that
14:28 You H me say to you, 'I go away,
15:15 all that I have H from my Father I
18:21 Ask those who have H me, what I said
19:8 When Pilate H these words, he was the more
19:13 When Pilate H these words, he brought Jesus out
21:7 When Simon Peter H that it was the Lord,
Acts 1:4 which, he said, "you H from me,
2:6 bewildered, because each one H them speaking in
2:37 Now when they H this they were cut to
4:4 many of those who H the word believed; and
4:20 but speak of what we have seen and H
4:24 And when they H it, they lifted their voices
5:5 When Ananias H these words, he fell down and
5:5 came upon all who H of it.
5:11 and upon all who H of these things.
5:21 And when they H this, they entered the temple
5:24 and the chief priests H these words, they were
5:33 When they H this they were enraged and wanted
6:11 who said, "We have H him speak blasphemous words
6:14 law; for we have H him say that this
7:12 But when Jacob H that there was grain in
7:34 are in Egypt and H their groaning, and I
7:54 Now when they H these things they were enraged,
8:6 by Philip, when they H him and saw the
8:14 apostles at Jerusalem H that Samaria had received
8:30 ran to him, and H him reading Isaiah the
9:4 to the ground and H a voice saying to
9:13 answered, "Lord, I have H from many about this
9:21 And all who H him were amazed, and said,
10:31 your prayer has been H and your alms have
10:44 fell on all who H the word.
10:46 For they H them speaking in tongues and extolling
11:1 who were in Judea H that the Gentiles also
11:7 And I H a voice saying to me, 'Rise,
11:18 When they H this they were silenced.
13:48 And when the Gentiles H this, they were glad
14:14 apostles Barnabas and Paul H of it, they tore
15:24 Since we have H that some persons from us
16:14 One who H us was a woman named Lydia,
16:38 were afraid when they H that they were Roman
17:8 were disturbed when they H this.
17:32 Now when they H of the resurrection of the
18:26 when Priscilla and Aquila H him, they took him
19:2 we have never even H that there is a
19:10 the residents of Asia H the word of the
19:28 When they H this they were enraged, and cried
21:12 When we H this, we and the people there
21:20 And when they H it, they glorified God.
22:2 And when they H that he addressed them in
22:7 to the ground and H a voice saying to
22:15 all men of what you have seen and H
22:26 When the centurion H that, he went to the
23:16 son of Paul's sister H of their ambush; so
24:23 sent for Paul and H him speak upon faith
26:14 to the ground, I H a voice saying to
28:15 brethren there, when they H of us, came as
Rom 10:14 believe in him of whom they have never H
10:16 believed what he has H from us?"
10:17 comes from what is H, and what is heard
10:17 heard, and what is H comes by the preaching
10:18 But I ask, have they not H
15:21 understand who have never H of him."
1Cor 2:9 has seen, nor ear H, nor the heart of
2Cor 12:4 knows— and he H things that cannot be
Gal 1:13 For you have H of my former life in
1:23 in Judea; they only H it said, "He who
Eph 1:13 you also, who have H the word of truth,
1:15 reason, because I have H of your faith in
3:2 assuming that you have H of the stewardship of
4:21 assuming that you have H about him and were
Phil 2:26 been distressed because you H that he was ill.
4:9 learned and received and H and seen in me,
Col 1:4 you, because we have H of your faith in
1:5 Of this you have H before in the word
1:6 from the day you H and understood the grace
1:9 from the day we H of it, we have
1:23 the gospel which you H, which has been preached
1Thes 2:13 of God which you H from us, you accepted
2Tim 1:13 words which you have H from me, in the
2:2 and what you have H from me before many
Heb 2:1 to what we have H, lest we drift away
2:3 us by those who H him,
3:16 Who were they that H and yet were rebellious?
4:2 the message which they H did not benefit them,
5:7 death, and he was H for his godly fear.
Jas 5:11 You have H of the steadfastness of Job, and
2Pet 1:18 we H this voice borne from heaven, for we
2:8 righteous man saw and H as he lived among
1Jn 1:1 beginning, which we have H, which we have seen
1:3 we have seen and H we proclaim also to
1:5 the message we have H from him and proclaim
2:7 old commandment is the word which you have H
2:18 and as you have H that antichrist is coming,
2:24 Let what you H from the beginning abide in
2:24 If what you H from the beginning abides in
3:11 message which you have H from the beginning, that
4:3 antichrist, of which you H that it was coming,
2Jn 1:6 commandment, as you have H from the beginning,
Rev 1:10 Lord's day, and I H behind me a loud
3:3 what you received and H; keep that, and repent.

4:1 voice, which I had H speaking to me like
5:11 I looked, and I H around the throne and
5:13 And I H every creature in heaven and on
6:1 seven seals, and I H one of the four
6:3 the second seal, I H the second living creature
6:5 the third seal, I H the third living creature
6:6 his hand; and I H what seemed to be
6:7 the fourth seal, I H the voice of the
7:4 And I H the number of the sealed, a
8:13 I looked, and I H an eagle crying with
9:13 his trumpet, and I H a voice from the
9:16 times ten thousand; I H their number.
10:4 to write, but I H a voice from heaven
10:8 voice which I had H from heaven spoke to
11:12 Then they H a loud voice from heaven saying
12:10 And I H a loud voice in heaven, saying,
14:2 And I H a voice from heaven like the
14:2 thunder; the voice I H was like the sound
14:13 And I H a voice from heaven saying, "Write
16:1 Then I H a loud voice from the temple
16:5 And I H the angel of water say, "Just
16:7 And I H the altar cry, "Yea, Lord God
18:4 Then I H another voice from heaven saying, "Come
18:22 and trumpeters, shall be H in thee no more;
18:22 the millstone shall be H in thee no more;
18:23 and bride shall be H in thee no more;
19:1 After this I H what seemed to be the
19:6 Then I H what seemed to be the voice
21:3 her husband; and I H a loud voice from
22:8 John am he who H and saw these things.
22:8 And when I H and saw them, I fell

HEARER (3)

Wis 1:6 his heart, and a H of his tongue.
Jas 1:22 any one is a H of the word and
1:24 and perseveres, being no H that forgets but a

HEARERS (6)

Rom 2:13 it is not the H of the law who
1Tim 4:16 doing you will save both yourself and your H
2Tim 2:14 which does no good, but only ruins the H
Heb 4:2 it did not meet with faith in the H
12:19 whose words made the H entreat that no further
Jas 1:21 the word, and not H only, deceiving yourselves.

HEAREST (4)

1Kgs 8:30 place; and when thou H, forgive.
2Chr 6:21 place; and when thou H, forgive.
Ps 65:2 performed, O thou who H prayer!
Jn 11:42 I knew that thou H me always, but I

HEARING (70)

Gen 23:10 answered Abraham in the H of the Hittites, of
23:13 to Ephron in the H of the people of
23:16 had named in the H of the Hittites, four
Ex 10:2 may tell in the H of your son and
11:2 Speak now in the H of the people, that
24:7 read it in the H of the people; and
Num 11:1 people complained in the H of the LORD about
11:18 have wept in the H of the LORD, saying,
14:28 have said in my H I will do to
Deut 5:1 I speak in your H this day, and you
31:11 read this law before all Israel in their H
32:44 this song in the H of the people, he
2Sam 18:12 son; for in our H the king commanded you
2Kgs 18:26 of Judah within the H of the people who
23:2 he read in their H all the words of
1Chr 28:8 LORD, and in the H of our God, observe
2Chr 34:30 he read in their H all the words of
Neh 13:1 of Moses in the H of the people; and
Job 33:8 have spoken in my H, and I have heard
42:5 of thee by the H of the ear, but
Prov 20:12 The H ear and the seeing eye, the LORD
23:9 not speak in the H of a fool, for
28:9 away his ear from H the law, even his
Eccl 1:8 satisfied with seeing, nor the ear filled with H
Is 5:9 has sworn in my H: "Surely many houses shall
33:15 stops his ears from H of bloodshed and shuts
36:11 of Judah within the H of the people who
Jer 2:2 and proclaim in the H of Jerusalem, Thus says
28:7 I speak in your H and in the hearing
28:7 hearing and in the H of all the people.
29:29 this letter in the H of Jeremiah the prophet.
36:6 fast day in the H of all the people
36:6 them also in the H of all the men
36:10 Then, in the H of all the people, Baruch
36:13 the scroll in the H of the people.
36:14 you read in the H of the people, and
Bar 1:3 this book in the H of Jeconiah the son
1:3 Judah, and in the H of all the people
1:4 book, and in the H of the mighty men
1:4 princes, and in the H of the elders, and
1:4 elders, and in the H of all the people,
Ezek 9:5 he said in my H, "Pass through the city
10:13 were called in my H the whirling wheels.
Amos 8:11 for water, but of H the words of the
Zech 8:9 these days have been H these words from the
1Mac 10:7 the letter in the H of all the people
2Mac 14:18 Nevertheless Nicanor, H of the valor of Judas and
Mt 13:13 do not see, and H they do not hear,
13:15 ears are heavy of H, and their eyes they
27:47 some of the bystanders H it said, "This man
Mk 3:8 Sidon a great multitude, H all that he did,
15:34 some of the bystanders H it said, "Behold, he
Lk 4:21 "Today this scripture has been fulfilled in your H
7:1 his sayings in the H of the people he
8:10 may not see, and H they may not understand.
8:15 they are those who, H the word, hold it
8:50 But Jesus on H this answered him, "Do not
18:36 the roadside begging and H a multitude going by,
20:45 And in the H of all the people he
Jn 7:51 first giving him a H and learning what he
Acts 9:7 with him stood speechless, H the voice but seeing
9:38 near Joppa, the disciples, H that Peter was there,
17:21 nothing except telling or H something new.
18:8 many of the Corinthians H Paul believed and were
19:5 On H this, they were baptized in the name
28:27 ears are heavy of H, and their eyes they
1Cor 12:17 body were an eye, where would be the H
Gal 3:2 the law, or by H with faith?
3:5 the law, or by H with faith?
Heb 5:11 to explain, since you have become dull of H

HEARKEN (62)

Gen 4:23 you wives of Lamech, H to what I say:
49:2 sons of Jacob, and H to Israel your father.
Ex 3:18 honey.'" And they will H to your voice; and
15:26 "If you will diligently H to the voice of
23:21 heed to him and H to his voice, do
23:22 "But if you H attentively to his voice and
Lev 26:14 if you will not H to me, and will
26:18 this you will not H to me, then I
26:21 me, and will not H to me, I will
26:27 this you will not H to me, but walk
Num 23:18 "Rise, Balak, and hear; H to me, O son
Deut 1:43 and you would not H; but you rebelled against
1:45 the LORD did not H to your voice or
3:26 account, and would not H to me; and the
7:12 "And because you H to these ordinances, and keep
23:5 your God would not H to Balaam; but the
Josh 5:6 because they did not H to the voice of
1Sam 8:7 LORD said to Samuel, H to the voice of
8:9 Now then, H to their voice; only, you shall
8:22 LORD said to Samuel, H to their voice, and
12:14 and serve him and H to his voice and
12:15 if you will not H to the voice of
15:1 people Israel; now therefore H to the words of
15:22 than sacrifice, and to H than the fat of
28:22 Now therefore, you also H to your handmaid; let
1Kgs 8:29 there,' that thou mayest H to the prayer which
8:30 And H thou to the supplication of thy servant
11:38 And if you will H to all that I
12:15 the king did not H to the people; for
12:16 the king did not H to them, the people
2Chr 6:20 name, that thou mayest H to the prayer which
6:21 And H thou to the supplications of thy servant
10:15 the king did not H to the people; for
10:16 the king did not H to them, the people
20:15 And he said, H, all Judah and inhabitants of
Job 36:11 If they H and serve him, they complete their
36:12 if they do not H, they perish by the
37:2 H to the thunder of his voice and the
Ps 5:2 H to the sound of my cry, my King
86:6 LORD, to my prayer; H to my cry of
95:7 that today you would H to his voice!
Prov 23:22 H to your father who begot you, and do
Sir 33:18 the people, and you leaders of the congregation, H
36:17 H, O Lord, to the prayer of thy servants,
Is 10:30 H, O Laishah!
28:23 and hear my voice; H, and hear my speech.
32:3 and the ears of those who hear will H
34:1 nations, to hear, and H, O peoples!

46:3 H to me, O house of Jacob, all the
46:12 H to me, you stubborn of heart, you who
48:12 H to me, O Jacob, and Israel, whom I
49:1 me, O coastlands, and H, you peoples from afar.
51:1 H to me, you who pursue deliverance, you who
51:7 H to me, you who know righteousness, the people
55:2 H diligently to me, and eat what is good,
Jer 18:19 me, O LORD, and H to my plea.
Bar 4:9 God, and she said: H, you neighbors of Zion,
Dan 9:17 therefore, O our God, H to the prayer of
Hos 5:1 H, O house of the king!
Mic 1:2 peoples, all of you; H, O earth, and all
Zech 7:11 But they refused to H, and turned a stubborn
2Mac 8:3 the ground, and to H to the blood that

HEARKENED (27)

Gen 16:2 And Abram H to the voice of Sarai.
30:17 And God H to Leah, and she conceived and
30:22 remembered Rachel, and God H to her and opened
34:24 gate of his city H to Hamor and his
Num 14:22 times and have not H to my voice,
21:3 And the LORD H to the voice of Israel,
Deut 9:19 But the LORD H to me that time also.
10:10 nights, and the LORD H to me that time
Josh 10:14 since, when the LORD H to the voice of
1Sam 12:1 Israel, "Behold, I have H to your voice in
19:6 And Saul H to the voice of Jonathan; Saul
25:35 house; see, I have H to your voice, and
28:21 "Behold, your handmaid has H to you; I have
28:21 my hand, and have H to what you have
28:23 urged him; and he H to their words.
1Kgs 12:24 So they H to the word of the LORD,
15:20 And Ben-hadad H to King Asa, and sent the
17:22 And the LORD H to the voice of Elijah;
20:25 And he H to their voice, and did so.
2Kgs 13:4 LORD, and the LORD H to him; for he
16:9 the king of Assyria H to him; the king
2Chr 11:4 So they H to the word of the LORD,
16:4 And Ben-hadad H to King Asa, and sent the
24:17 king; then the king H to them.
Is 48:18 O that you had H to my commandments!
Dan 1:14 So he H to them in this matter, and
Hos 9:17 because they have not H to him; they shall

HEARKENING (3)

1Kgs 8:28 O LORD my God, H to the cry and
2Chr 6:19 O LORD my God, H to the cry and
Ps 103:20 who do his word, H to the voice of

HEARS (59)

Gen 21:6 me; every one who H will laugh over me."
Lev 5:1 sins in that he H a public adjuration to
Num 24:4 oracle of him who H the words of God,
24:16 oracle of him who H the words of God,
30:4 youth, and her father H of her vow and
30:5 the day that he H of it, no vow
30:7 herself, and her husband H of it, and says
30:7 the day that he H; then her vows shall
30:12 the day that he H them, then whatever proceeds
Deut 29:19 one who, when he H the words of this
1Sam 3:9 you shall say, 'Speak, LORD, for thy servant H
3:10 And Samuel said, "Speak, for thy servant H
3:11 of every one that H it will tingle.
16:2 If Saul H it, he will kill me." And
2Sam 17:9 the first attack, whoever H it will say, 'There
2Kgs 21:12 of every one who H of it will tingle.
Job 34:34 the wise man who H me will say:
39:7 of the city; he H not the shouts of
Ps 4:3 for himself; the LORD H when I call to
34:17 for help, the LORD H, and delivers them out
69:33 For the LORD H the needy, and does not
97:8 Zion H and is glad, and the daughters of
145:19 fear him, he also H their cry, and saves
Prov 13:1 A wise son H his father's instruction, but a
15:29 the wicked, but he H the prayer of the
18:13 gives answer before he H, it is his folly
21:28 of a man who H will endure.
25:10 secret; lest he who H you bring shame upon
29:24 his own life; he H the curse, but discloses
Wis 1:10 because a jealous ear H all things, and the
Sir 21:15 a man of understanding H a wise saying, he
21:15 it; when a reveler H it, he dislikes it
22:24 because of him, whoever H of it will beware
Is 30:19 your cry; when he H it, he will answer
Jer 19:3 of every one who H of it will tingle.
Ezek 33:4 if any one who H the sound of the
Dan 3:10 that every man who H the sound of the
Mt 7:24 "Every one then who H these words of mine
7:26 And every one who H these words of mine
13:19 When any one H the word of the kingdom
13:20 this is he who H the word and immediately
13:22 this is he who H the word, but the
13:23 this is he who H the word and understands
Lk 6:47 comes to me and H my words and does
6:49 But he who H and does not do them
10:16 "He who H you hears me, and he who
10:16 "He who hears you H me, and he who
Jn 3:29 bridegroom, who stands and H him, rejoices greatly
5:23 to you, he who H my word and believes
8:47 who is of God H the words of God;
12:47 If any one H my sayings and does not
16:13 authority, but whatever he H he will speak, and
18:37 is of the truth H my voice."
2Cor 12:6 sees in me or H from me.
1Jn 5:14 to his will he H us.
5:15 we know that he H us in whatever we
Rev 3:20 knock; if any one H my voice and opens
22:17 And let him who H say, "Come." And let
22:18 warn every one who H the words of the

HEART (798)

Gen 6:5 the thoughts of his H was only evil continually.
6:6 the earth, and it grieved him to his H
8:21 LORD said in his H, "I will never again
8:21 the imagination of man's H is evil from his
20:5 the integrity of my H and the innocence of
20:6 the integrity of your H, and it was I
24:45 done speaking in my H, behold, Rebekah came out
43:30 made haste, for his H yearned for his brother,
45:26 And his H fainted, for he did not believe
Ex 4:14 sees you he will be glad in his H
4:21 I will harden his H, so that he will
7:3 I will harden Pharaoh's H, and though I multiply
7:13 Still Pharaoh's H was hardened, and he would not
7:14 said to Moses, "Pharaoh's H is hardened, he refuses
7:22 secret arts; so Pharaoh's H remained hardened, and
7:23 and he did not lay even this to H
8:15 respite, he hardened his H, and would not listen
8:19 But Pharaoh's H was hardened, and he would not
8:32 But Pharaoh hardened his H this time also, and
9:7 But the H of Pharaoh was hardened, and he
9:12 the LORD hardened the H of Pharaoh, and he
9:14 my plagues upon your H, and upon your servants
9:34 again, and hardened his H, he and his servants.
9:35 So the H of Pharaoh was hardened, and he
10:1 I have hardened his H and the heart of
10:1 his heart and the H of his servants, that
10:20 the LORD hardened Pharaoh's H, and he did not
10:27 the LORD hardened Pharaoh's H, and he would not
11:10 the LORD hardened Pharaoh's H, and he did not
14:4 I will harden Pharaoh's H, and he will pursue
14:8 the LORD hardened the H of Pharaoh king of
15:8 deeps congealed in the H of the sea.
23:9 stranger; you know the H of a stranger, for
25:2 from every man whose H makes him willing you
28:29 of judgment upon his H, when he goes into
28:30 shall be upon Aaron's H, when he goes in
28:30 of Israel upon his H before the LORD continually.
35:5 is of a generous H, let him bring the
35:21 came, every one whose H stirred him, and every
35:22 were of a willing H brought brooches and earrings
35:29 people of Israel, whose H moved them to bring
36:2 ability, every one whose H stirred him up to
Lev 19:17 your brother in your H, but you shall reason
26:41 if then their uncircumcised H is humbled and they
Num 15:39 follow after your own H and your own eyes,
32:7 will you discourage the H of the people of
32:9 land, they discouraged the H of the people of
Deut 2:30 spirit and made his H obstinate, that he might
4:9 they depart from your H all the days of
4:11 with fire to the H of heaven, wrapped in
4:29 him with all your H and with all your
4:39 lay it to your H, that the LORD is
6:5 God with all your H, and with all your
6:6 shall be upon your H;
7:17 you say in your H, 'These nations are greater
8:2 what was in your H, whether you would keep
8:5 Know then in your H that, as a man
8:14 is multiplied, then your H be lifted up, and
8:17 you say in your H, 'My power and the
9:4 not say in your H, after the LORD your
9:5 the uprightness of your H are you going in

H

10:12 God with all your H and with all your
10:15 the LORD set his H in love upon your
10:16 the foreskin of your H, and be no longer
11:13 him with all your H and with all your
11:16 Take heed lest your H be deceived, and you
11:18 of mine in your H and in your soul;
13:3 God with all your H and with all your
15:7 shall not harden your H or shut your hand
15:9 base thought in your H, and you say, 'The
15:10 him freely, and your H shall not be grudging
17:17 for himself, lest his H turn away; nor shall
17:20 doing them; that his H may not be lifted
18:21 you say in your H, 'How may we know
20:3 enemies: let not your H faint; do not fear,
20:8 his house, lest the H of his fellows melt
20:8 fellows melt as his H
24:15 poor, and sets his H upon it); lest he
26:16 them with all your H and with all your
28:47 joyfulness and gladness of H, by reason of the
28:65 you there a trembling H, and failing eyes, and
28:67 the dread which your H shall fear, and the
29:18 family or tribe, whose H turns away this day
29:19 blesses himself in his H, saying, 'I shall be
29:19 the stubbornness of my H This would lead to
30:2 day, with all your H and with all your
30:6 God will circumcise your H and the heart of
30:6 your heart and the H of your offspring, so
30:6 God with all your H and with all your
30:10 God with all your H and with all your
30:14 mouth and in your H, so that you can
30:17 But if your H turns away, and you will
32:46 to them, "Lay to H all the words which
Josh 5:1 had crossed over, their H melted, and there was
14:7 him word again as it was in my H
14:8 with me made the H of the people melt;
22:5 him with all your H and with all your
24:23 you, and incline your H to the LORD, the
Judg 5:9 My H goes out to the commanders of Israel
5:15 clans of Reuben there were great searchings of H
5:16 clans of Reuben there were great searchings of H
16:15 love you,' when your H is not with me?
18:20 And the priest's H was glad; he took the
19:5 his son-in-law, "Strengthen your H with a morsel of
19:6 night, and let your H be merry."
19:8 father said, "Strengthen your H, and tarry until the
19:9 here and let your H be merry; and tomorrow
Ruth 3:7 and drunk, and his H was merry, he went
1Sam 1:8 And why is your H sad?
1:13 was speaking in her H; only her lips moved,
2:1 prayed and said, "My H exults in the LORD;
2:33 eyes and grieve his H; and all the increase
2:35 what is in my H and in my mind;
4:13 road watching, for his H trembled for the ark
7:3 LORD with all your H, then put away the
7:3 you, and direct your H to the LORD, and
10:9 God gave him another H; and all these signs
12:20 LORD with all your H;
12:24 faithfully with all your H; for consider what great
13:14 man after his own H; and the LORD has
16:7 outward appearance, but the LORD looks on the H
17:28 the evil of your H; for you have come
17:32 Saul, "Let no man's H fail because of him;
21:12 took these words to H, and was much afraid
23:20 according to all your H's desire to come down;
24:5 And afterward David's H smote him, because he had
25:36 And Nabal's H was merry within him, for he
25:37 these things, and his H died within him, and
27:1 David said in his H, "I shall now perish
28:5 was afraid, and his H trembled greatly.
2Sam 3:21 over all that your H desires." So David sent
6:16 the LORD; and she despised him in her H
7:3 that is in your H; for the LORD is
7:21 according to thy own H, thou hast wrought all
13:20 is your brother; do not take this to H
13:28 servants, "Mark when Amnon's H is merry with
13:33 so take it to H as to suppose that
14:1 perceived that the king's H went out to Absalom.
17:10 the valiant man, whose H is like the heart
17:10 heart is like the H of a lion, will
18:14 thrust them into the H of Absalom, while he
19:14 And he swayed the H of all the men
22:46 Foreigners lost H, and came trembling out of their
24:10 But David's H smote him after he had numbered
1Kgs 2:4 faithfulness with all their H and with all their
2:44 know in your own H all the evil that
3:6 and in uprightness of H toward thee; and thou
3:26 the king, because her H yearned for her son,
8:17 it was in the H of David my father
8:18 it was in your H to build a house
8:18 it was in your H;
8:23 thee with all their H;
8:38 affliction of his own H and stretching out his
8:39 render to each whose H thou knowest, according to
8:47 they lay it to H in the land to
8:48 and with all their H in the land of
8:61 Let your H therefore be wholly true to the
8:66 joyful and glad of H for all the goodness
9:3 my eyes and my H will be there for
9:4 walked, with integrity of H and uprightness, doing
11:2 will turn away your H after their gods"; Solomon
11:3 hundred concubines; and his wives turned away his H
11:4 wives turned away his H after other gods; and
11:4 other gods; and his H was not wholly true
11:4 God, as was the H of David his father.
11:9 with Solomon, because his H had turned away from
12:26 Jeroboam said in his H, "Now the kingdom will
12:27 at Jerusalem, then the H of this people will
12:33 devised of his own H; and he ordained a
14:8 me with all his H, doing only that which
15:3 before him; and his H was not wholly true
15:3 his God, as the H of David his father.
15:14 Nevertheless the H of Asa was wholly true to
21:7 bread, and let your H be cheerful; I will
2Kgs 9:24 the arrow pierced his H, and he sank in
10:15 to him, "Is your H true to my heart
10:15 heart true to my H as mine is to
10:30 that was in my H, your sons of the
10:31 Israel with all his H; he did not turn
12:4 money which a man's H prompts him to bring
14:10 smitten Edom, and your H has lifted you up.
20:3 and with a whole H, and have done what
22:19 have heard, because your H was penitent, and you
23:3 statutes, with all his H and all his soul,
23:25 LORD with all his H and with all his
1Chr 12:17 to help me, my H will be knit to
15:29 making merry; and she despised him in her H
17:2 that is in your H, for God is with
17:19 according to thy own H, thou hast wrought all
22:7 had it in my H to build a house
22:19 set your mind and H to seek the LORD
28:2 had it in my H to build a house
28:9 him with a whole H and with a willing
29:9 for with a whole H they had offered freely
29:17 that thou triest the H, and hast pleasure in
29:17 the uprightness of my H I have freely offered
29:19 that with a whole H he may keep thy
2Chr 1:11 this was in your H, and you have not
6:7 it was in the H of David my father
6:8 it was in your H to build a house
6:8 it was in your H;
6:14 thee with all their H;
6:30 render to each whose H thou knowest, according to
6:37 they lay it to H in the land to
6:38 and with all their H in the land of
7:10 joyful and glad of H for the goodness that
7:16 my eyes and my H will be there for
12:14 did not set his H to seek the LORD.
15:12 fathers, with all their H and with all their
15:15 sworn with all their H, and had sought him
15:17 Nevertheless the H of Asa was blameless all his
16:9 behalf of those whose H is blameless toward him.
17:6 His H was courageous in the ways of the
19:3 and have set your H to seek God."
19:9 and with your whole H:
22:9 Jehoshaphat, who sought the LORD with all his H
25:2 of the LORD, yet not with a blameless H
25:19 smitten Edom,' and your H has lifted you up
29:10 it is in my H to make a covenant
29:31 were of a willing H brought burnt offerings.
29:34 were more upright in H than the priests in
30:12 to give them one H to do what the
30:19 one who sets his H to seek God, the
31:21 did with all his H, and prospered.
32:25 to him, for his H was proud.
32:26 the pride of his H, both he and the
32:31 and to know all that was in his H
34:27 have heard, because your H was penitent and you
34:31 statutes, with all his H and all his soul,
36:13 neck and hardened his H against turning to the
Ezra 6:22 and had turned the H of the king of
7:10 Ezra had set his H to study the law
7:27 as this into the H of the king, to

Neh	2:2	This is nothing else but sadness of the H
	2:12	had put into my H to do for Jerusalem.
	9:8	thou didst find his H faithful before thee, and
Tob	1:12	it, because I remembered God with all my H
	4:13	brethren, and in your H do not disdain your
	6:4	fish and take the H and liver and gall
	6:6	is the liver and H and gall of the
	6:7	replied, "As for the H and liver, if a
	6:16	them some of the H and liver of the
	8:2	incense and put the H and liver of the
	13:6	him with all your H and with all your
Jud	6:9	really hope in your H that they will not
	7:23	Their children lost H, and the women and
	8:14	depths of the human H, nor find out what
	8:28	out of a true H, and there is no
	8:29	your understanding, for your H's disposition is right.
	10:16	be afraid in your H, but tell him just
	11:1	be afraid in your H, for I have never
	12:16	lay down, and Holofernes' H was ravished with her
	13:4	bed, said in her H, "O Lord God of
Esth	1:10	seventh day, when the H of the king was
	5:9	went out that day joyful and glad of H
	14:13	lion, and turn his H to hate the man
	15:5	if beloved, but her H was frozen with fear.
	15:13	of God, and my H was shaken with fear
Job	9:4	He is wise in H, and mighty in strength
	10:13	didst hide in thy H; I know that this
	11:13	"If you set your H aright, you will stretch
	15:12	Why does your H carry you away, and why
	15:35	forth evil and their H prepares deceit."
	17:11	plans are broken off, the desires of my H
	19:27	My H faints within me!
	22:22	mouth, and lay up his words in your H
	23:16	God has made my H faint; the Almighty has
	27:6	let it go; my H does not reproach me
	29:13	I caused the widow's H to sing for joy.
	30:27	My H is in turmoil, and is never still;
	31:7	the way, and my H has gone after my
	31:9	"If my H has been enticed to a woman,
	31:27	in splendor, and my H has been secretly enticed,
	32:19	Behold, my H is like wine that has no
	33:3	the uprightness of my H, and what my lips
	36:13	"The godless in H cherish anger; they do not
	37:1	"At this also my H trembles, and leaps out
	41:24	His H is hard as a stone, hard as
Ps	4:7	more joy in my H than they have when
	5:9	in their mouth; their H is destruction, their throat
	7:10	is with God, who saves the upright in H
	9:1	LORD with my whole H; I will tell of
	10:3	the desires of his H, and the man greedy
	10:6	He thinks in his H, "I shall not be
	10:11	He thinks in his H, "God has forgotten, he
	10:13	and say in his H, "Thou wilt not call
	10:17	thou wilt strengthen their H, thou wilt incline thy
	11:2	at the upright in H;
	12:2	lips and a double H they speak.
	13:2	have sorrow in my H all the day?
	13:5	thy steadfast love; my H shall rejoice in thy
	14:1	fool says in his H, "There is no God."
	15:2	speaks truth from his H;
	16:7	the night also my H instructs me.
	16:9	Therefore my H is glad, and my soul rejoices;
	17:3	If thou triest my H, if thou visitest me
	18:45	Foreigners lost H, and came trembling out of their
	19:8	are right, rejoicing the H; the commandment of the
	19:14	the meditation of my H be acceptable in thy
	20:4	he grant you your H's desire, and fulfil all
	21:2	hast given him his H's desire, and hast not
	22:14	out of joint; my H is like wax, it
	24:4	hands and a pure H, who does not lift
	25:17	the troubles of my H, and bring me out
	26:2	try me; test my H and my mind.
	27:3	encamp against me, my H shall not fear; though
	27:8	My H says to thee, "Thy face, LORD, do
	27:14	strong, and let your H take courage; yea, wait
	28:7	shield; in him my H trusts; so I am
	28:7	am helped, and my H exults, and with my
	31:24	strong, and let your H take courage, all you
	32:11	and shout for joy, all you upright in H
	33:11	the thoughts of his H to all generations.
	33:21	Yea, our H is glad in him, because we
	35:25	"Aha, we have our H's desire!" Let them not
	36:1	wicked deep in his H; there is no fear
	36:10	thee, and thy salvation to the upright of H
	37:4	he will give you the desires of your H
	37:15	shall enter their own H, and their bows shall
	37:31	God is in his H; his steps do not
	38:8	I groan because of the tumult of my H
	38:10	My H throbs, my strength fails me; and the
	39:3	distress grew worse, my H became hot within me.
	40:8	O my God; thy law is within my H
	40:10	saving help within my H, I have spoken of
	40:12	of my head; my H fails me.
	41:6	empty words, while his H gathers mischief; when he
	44:18	Our H has not turned back, nor have our
	44:21	For he knows the secrets of the H
	45:1	My H overflows with a goodly theme; I address
	45:5	are sharp in the H of the king's enemies;
	46:2	mountains shake in the H of the sea;
	49:3	the meditation of my H shall be understanding.
	51:6	being; therefore teach me wisdom in my secret H
	51:10	in me a clean H, O God, and put
	51:17	a broken and contrite H, O God, thou wilt
	53:1	fool says in his H, "There is no God."
	55:4	My H is in anguish within me, the terrors
	55:21	war was in his H; his words were softer
	57:7	[Selah] My H is steadfast, O God, my heart
	57:7	steadfast, O God, my H is steadfast!
	61:2	to thee, when my H is faint.
	62:8	people; pour out your H before him; God is
	62:10	increase, set not your H on them.
	64:6	the inward mind and H of a man are
	64:10	all the upright in H glory!
	66:18	cherished iniquity in my H, the Lord would not
	69:20	Insults have broken my H, so that I am
	73:1	the upright, to those who are pure in H
	73:13	have I kept my H clean and washed my
	73:21	I was pricked in H,
	73:26	My flesh and my H may fail, but God
	73:26	the strength of my H and my portion for
	77:6	I commune with my H in the night; I
	78:8	generation, a generation whose H was not steadfast,
	78:18	tested God in their H by demanding the food
	78:37	Their H was not steadfast toward him; they were
	78:72	With upright H he tended them, and guided them
	84:2	of the LORD; my H and flesh sing for
	84:5	in thee, in whose H are the highways to
	86:11	thy truth; unite my H to fear thy name.
	86:12	God, with my whole H, and I will glorify
	90:12	we may get a H of wisdom.
	94:15	all the upright in H will follow it.
	94:19	the cares of my H are many, thy consolations
	95:10	people who err in H, and they do not
	97:11	the righteous, and joy for the upright in H
	101:2	walk with integrity of H within my house;
	101:4	Perverseness of H shall be far from me; I
	101:5	haughty looks and arrogant H I will not endure.
	102:4	My H is smitten like grass, and withered; I
	104:15	wine to gladden the H of man, oil to
	104:15	his face shine, and bread to strengthen man's H
	108:1	My H is steadfast, O God, my heart is
	108:1	steadfast, O God, my H is steadfast!
	109:22	and needy, and my H is stricken within me.
	111:1	LORD with my whole H, in the company of
	112:7	of evil tidings; his H is firm, trusting in
	112:8	His H is steady, he will not be afraid,
	119:2	him with their whole H,
	119:7	thee with an upright H, when I learn thy
	119:10	With my whole H I seek thee; let me
	119:11	thy word in my H, that I might not
	119:34	thy law and observe it with my whole H
	119:36	Incline my H to thy testimonies, and not to
	119:58	favor with all my H; be gracious to me
	119:69	but with my whole H I keep thy precepts;
	119:70	keep thy precepts; their H is gross like fat,
	119:80	May my H be blameless in thy statutes, that
	119:111	ever; yea, they are the joy of my H
	119:112	I incline my H to perform thy statutes for
	119:145	With my whole H I cry; answer me, O
	119:161	without cause, but my H stands in awe of
	131:1	O LORD, my H is not lifted up, my
	138:1	LORD, with my whole H; before the gods I
	139:23	Search me, O God, and know my H
	140:2	evil things in their H, and stir up wars
	141:4	Incline not my H to any evil, to busy
	143:4	faints within me; my H within me is appalled.
Prov	2:2	wisdom and inclining your H to understanding;
	2:10	will come into your H, and knowledge will be
	3:1	teaching, but let your H keep my commandments;
	3:3	neck, write them on the tablet of your H
	3:5	LORD with all your H, and do not rely
	4:5	to me, "Let your H hold fast my words;

4:22 escape from your sight; keep them within your H
4:24 Keep your H with all vigilance; for from it
5:12 hated discipline, and my H despised reproof!
6:14 his finger, with perverted H devises evil, continually
6:18 shed innocent blood, a H that devises wicked plans,
6:21 Bind them upon your H always; tie them about
6:25 her beauty in your H, and do not let
7:3 fingers, write them on the tablet of your H
7:10 meets him, dressed as a harlot, wily of H
7:25 Let not your H turn aside to her ways,
10:8 The wise of H will heed commandments, but a
12:20 Deceit is in the H of those who devise
12:25 Anxiety in a man's H weighs him down, but
13:12 Hope deferred makes the H sick, but a desire
14:10 The H knows its own bitterness, and no stranger
14:13 Even in laughter the H is sad, and the
14:33 not known in the H of fools.
15:13 A glad H makes a cheerful countenance, but by
15:13 but by sorrow of H the spirit is broken.
15:15 evil, but a cheerful H has a continual feast.
15:30 the eyes rejoices the H, and good news refreshes
16:21 The wise of H is called a man of
17:22 A cheerful H is a good medicine, but a
18:12 Before destruction a man's H is haughty, but humility
19:3 way to ruin, his H rages against the LORD.
19:18 o not set your H on his destruction.
20:9 "I have made my H clean; I am pure
21:1 The king's H is a stream of water in
21:2 his own eyes, but the LORD weighs the H
21:4 eyes and a proud H, the lamp of the
22:11 who loves purity of H, and whose speech is
22:15 bound up in the H of a child, but
23:7 to you; but his H is not with you.
23:15 My son, if your H is wise, my heart
23:15 heart is wise, my H too will be glad.
23:17 Let not your H envy sinners, but continue in
23:26 son, give me your H, and let your eyes
24:12 he who weighs the H perceive it?
24:17 and let not your H be glad when he
25:20 songs to a heavy H is like one who
26:23 earthen vessel are smooth lips with an evil H
26:24 harbors deceit in his H;
26:25 seven abominations in his H;
27:9 and perfume make the H glad, but the soul
27:11 son, and make my H glad, that I may
28:14 he who hardens his H will fall into calamity.
29:17 you rest; he will give delight to your H
31:11 The H of her husband trusts in her, and

Eccl 2:10 them; I kept my H from no pleasure, for
2:10 no pleasure, for my H found pleasure in all
2:20 about and gave my H up to despair over
3:17 I said in my H, God will judge the
3:18 I said in my H with regard to the
5:2 mouth, nor let your H be hasty to utter
5:20 God keeps him occupied with joy in his H
7:2 men, and the living will lay it to H
7:3 sadness of countenance the H is made glad.
7:4 The H of the wise is in the house
7:4 of mourning; but the H of fools is in
7:22 servant cursing you; your H knows that many times
7:26 death the woman whose H is snares and nets,
8:11 not executed speedily, the H of the sons of
9:1 this I laid to H, examining it all, how
9:7 wine with a merry H; for God has already
10:2 A wise man's H inclines him toward the right,
10:2 right, but a fool's H toward the left.
11:9 youth, and let your H cheer you in the
11:9 the ways of your H and the sight of

Song 3:11 on the day of the gladness of his H
4:9 You have ravished my H, my sister, my bride,
4:9 you have ravished my H with a glance of
5:2 I slept, but my H was awake.
5:4 the latch, and my H was thrilled within me.
8:6 a seal upon your H, as a seal upon

Wis 1:1 him with sincerity of H;
1:6 true observer of his H, and a hearer of
4:15 such a thing to H, that God's grace and
8:21 and with my whole H I said:
15:10 His H is ashes, his hope is cheaper than

Sir 1:10 the Lord delights the H, and gives gladness and
1:27 the Lord, and your H was full of deceit.
2:2 Set your H right and be steadfast, and do
2:13 Woe to the faint H, for it has no
5:1 Do not set your H on your wealth, nor
5:2 strength, walking according to the desires of your H
7:27 With all your H honor your father, and do
9:9 at wine; lest your H turn aside to her,
10:12 from the Lord; his H has forsaken his Maker.
13:24 A man's H changes his countenance, either for good
13:25 mark of a happy H is a cheerful face,
14:2 Blessed is he whose H does not condemn him,
21:6 that fears the Lord will repent in his H
22:16 wind; so a timid H with a fool's purpose
22:17 one who pricks the H makes it show feeling.
25:7 I have gladdened my H, and a tenth I
25:12 Any wound, but not a wound of the H
25:22 face, and a wounded H are caused by an
26:4 rich or poor, his H is glad, and at
26:5 Of three things my H is afraid, and of
26:6 There is grief of H and sorrow when a
26:18 silver, so are beautiful feet with a steadfast H
26:19 At two things my H is grieved, and because
30:16 and there is no gladness above joy of H
30:22 Gladness of H is the life of man, and
30:23 soul and comfort your H, and remove sorrow far
30:25 of cheerful and good H will give heed to
31:28 temperately is rejoicing of H and gladness of soul.
33:5 The H of a fool is like a cart
37:6 a friend in your H, and be not unmindful
37:13 counsel of your own H, for no one is
37:17 clue to changes of H
38:10 aright, and cleanse your H from all sin.
38:18 death, and sorrow of H saps one's strength.
38:19 life of the poor man weighs down his H
38:20 Do not give your H to sorrow; drive it
38:26 He sets his H on plowing furrows, and he
38:27 variety; he sets his H on painting a lifelike
38:28 He sets his H on finishing his handiwork, and
38:30 feet; he sets his H to finish the glazing,
39:5 He will set his H to rise early to
39:35 praise with all your H and voice, and bless
40:2 perplexities and fear of H -- their anxious thought
40:20 and music gladden the H, but the love of
40:26 strength lift up the H, but the fear of
45:26 you wisdom in your H to judge his people
47:8 praise with all his H, and he loved his
48:10 fury, to turn the H of the father to
49:3 He set his H upon the Lord; in the
50:23 give us gladness of H, and grant that peace
50:27 who out of his H poured forth wisdom.
50:28 who lays them to H will become wise.
51:15 to ripening grape my H delighted in her; my
51:21 My H was stirred to seek her, therefore I

Is 1:5 sick, and the whole H faint.
6:10 not perceive.' Make the H of this people fat,
7:2 his H and the heart of his people shook
7:2 his heart and the H of his people shook
7:4 do not let your H be faint because of
9:9 and in arrogance of H:
13:7 feeble, and every man's H will melt,
14:13 You said in your H, 'I will ascend to
15:5 My H cries out for Moab; his fugitives flee
16:11 for Moab, and my H for Kir-heres.
19:1 his presence, and the H of the Egyptians will
30:29 kept; and gladness of H, as when one sets
35:4 are of a fearful H, "Be strong, fear not!
38:3 and with a whole H, and have done what
42:25 him, but he did not take it to H
46:12 me, you stubborn of H, you who are far
47:7 lay these things to H or remember their end.
47:8 who say in your H, "I am, and there
47:10 you said in your H, "I am, and there
49:21 will say in your H: 'Who has borne me
51:7 the people in whose H is my law; fear
57:1 one lays it to H; devout men are taken
57:15 and to revive the H of the contrite.
57:17 on backsliding in the way of his own H
59:13 and uttering from the H lying words.
60:5 and be radiant, your H shall thrill and rejoice;
63:4 vengeance was in my H, and my year of
63:15 The yearning of thy H and thy compassion are
63:17 ways and harden our H, so that we fear
65:14 sing for gladness of H, but you shall cry
65:14 out for pain of H, and shall wail for
66:14 shall see, and your H shall rejoice; your bones

Jer 3:10 me with her whole H, but in pretense, says
3:15 shepherds after my own H, who will feed you
3:17 shall no more stubbornly follow their own evil H
4:14 O Jerusalem, wash your H from wickedness, that you
4:18 it is bitter; it has reached your very H
4:19 Oh, the walls of my H
4:19 My H is beating wildly; I cannot keep silent;

5:23 a stubborn and rebellious H; they have turned aside
8:18 is beyond healing, my H is sick within me.
8:21 my people is my H wounded, I mourn, and
9:8 neighbor, but in his H he plans an ambush
9:26 all the house of Israel is uncircumcised in H
11:8 one walked in the stubbornness of his evil H
11:20 righteously, who triest the H and the mind, let
12:2 near in their mouth and far from their H
12:11 made desolate, but no man lays it to H
13:10 stubbornly follow their own H and have gone after
13:22 you say in your H, 'Why have these things
15:1 before me, yet my H would not turn toward
15:16 the delight of my H; for I am called
17:1 the tablet of their H, and on the horns
17:5 flesh his arm, whose H turns away from the
17:9 The H is deceitful above all things, and desperately
17:10 mind and try the H, to give to every
18:12 stubbornness of his evil H
20:9 there is in my H as it were a
20:12 righteous, who seest the H and the mind, let
22:17 you have eyes and H only for your dishonest
23:9 Concerning the prophets: My H is broken within me,
23:17 stubbornly follows his own H, they say, 'No evil
23:26 be lies in the H of the prophets who
23:26 deceit of their own H,
24:7 will give them a H to know that I
24:7 they shall return to me with their whole H
29:13 me with all your H,
31:20 Therefore my H yearns for him; I will surely
32:39 will give them one H and one way, that
32:41 faithfulness, with all my H and all my soul.
48:29 and his arrogance, and the haughtiness of his H
48:36 Therefore my H moans for Moab like a flute,
48:36 a flute, and my H moans like a flute
48:41 The H of the warriors of Moab shall be
48:41 that day like the H of a woman in
49:16 the pride of your H, you who live in
49:22 against Bozrah, and the H of the warriors of
49:22 that day like the H of a woman in
51:46 Let not your H faint, and be not fearful

Lam 1:20 is in tumult, my H is wrung within me,
1:22 are many and my H is faint."
2:11 is in tumult; my H is poured out in
2:19 Pour out your H like water before the presence
3:13 He drove into my H the arrows of his
3:65 give them dullness of H; thy curse will be
5:17 For this our H has become sick, for these

Bar 1:21 of his own wicked H by serving other gods
2:8 of us, from the thoughts of his wicked H
2:31 will give them a H that obeys and ears
6:6 But say in your H, "It is thou, O

Ezek 3:7 of a hard forehead and of a stubborn H
3:10 you receive in your H, and hear with your
6:9 have broken their wanton H which has departed
11:19 will give them one H, and put a new
11:19 will take the stony H out of their flesh
11:19 and give them a H of flesh,
11:21 as for those whose H goes after their detestable
14:4 his idols into his H and sets the stumbling
14:7 his idols into his H and putting the stumbling
16:30 "How lovesick is your H, says the Lord GOD,
18:31 get yourselves a new H and a new spirit!
20:16 my sabbaths; for their H went after their idols.
21:6 man; sigh with breaking H and bitter grief before
21:7 When it comes, every H will melt and all
24:25 their eyes and their H's desire, and also their
25:15 vengeance with malice of H to destroy in
27:4 borders are in the H of the seas; your
27:25 heavily laden in the H of the seas.
27:26 wrecked you in the H of the seas.
27:27 midst, sink into the H of the seas on
28:2 Lord GOD: "Because your H is proud, and you
28:2 the gods, in the H of the seas,' yet
28:5 your wealth, and your H has become proud in
28:8 the slain in the H of the seas.
28:17 Your H was proud because of your beauty; you
31:10 the clouds, and its H was proud of its
33:31 much love, but their H is set on their
36:26 A new H I will give you, and a
36:26 of your flesh the H of stone and give
36:26 and give you a H of flesh.
44:7 admitting foreigners, uncircumcised in H and flesh,
44:9 No foreigner, uncircumcised in H and flesh, of all

Dan 3:39 Yet with a contrite H and a humble spirit
3:41 now with all our H we follow thee, we
3:88 holy and humble in H, sing praise to him
5:20 But when his H was lifted up and his
5:22 have not humbled your H, though you knew all
11:12 multitude is taken, his H shall be exalted, and
11:28 great substance, but his H shall be set against
13:35 toward heaven, for her H trusted in the Lord.
13:56 has deceived you and lust has perverted your H

Hos 7:15 to me from the H, but they wail upon
10:2 Their H is false; now they must bear their
11:8 My H recoils within me, my compassion grows warm
13:6 were filled, and their H was lifted up; therefore

Joel 2:12 me with all your H, with fasting, with weeping,

Amos 2:16 who is stout of H among the mighty shall

Obad 1:3 The pride of your H has deceived you, you
1:3 who say in your H, "Who will bring me

Jon 2:3 the deep, into the H of the seas, and

Zeph 3:14 exult with all your H, O daughter of Jerusalem!

Zech 7:10 you devise evil against his brother in your H

Mal 2:2 not lay it to H to give glory to
2:2 them, because you do not lay it to H

1Mac 1:3 was exalted, and his H was lifted up.
2:24 with zeal and his H was stirred.
12:28 and were terrified at H; so they kindled fires
16:13 His H was lifted up; he determined to get

2Mac 1:3 give you all a H to worship him and
1:3 will with a strong H and a willing spirit.
1:4 May he open your H to his law and
3:16 to be wounded at H, for his face and
3:17 looked at him the pain lodged in his H
4:37 Antiochus was grieved at H and filled with pity,
11:9 and were strengthened in H, ready to assail not

Mt 5:8 are the pure in H, for they shall see
5:28 has already committed adultery with her in his H
6:21 is, there will your H be also.
9:2 to the paralytic, "Take H, my son; your sins
9:22 her he said, "Take H, daughter; your faith has
11:29 gentle and lowly in H, and you will find
12:34 the abundance of the H the mouth speaks.
12:40 three nights in the H of the earth.
13:15 For this people's H has grown dull, and their
13:15 and understand with their H, and turn for me
13:19 is sown in his H; this is what was
14:27 to them, saying, "Take H, it is I; have
15:8 their lips, but their H is far from me;
15:18 mouth proceeds from the H, and this defiles a
15:19 For out of the H come evil thoughts, murder,
18:34 you do not forgive your brother from your H
19:8 "For your hardness of H Moses allowed you to
22:37 God with all your H, and with all your

Mk 3:5 at their hardness of H, and said to the
6:50 them and said, "Take H, it is I; have
7:6 their lips, but their H is far from me;
7:18 it enters, not his H but his stomach, and
7:20 within, out of the H of man, come evil
10:5 "For your hardness of H he wrote you this
10:49 saying to him, "Take H; rise, he is calling
11:23 not doubt in his H, but believes that what
12:30 God with all your H, and with all your
12:33 him with all the H, and with all the
16:14 unbelief and hardness of H, because they had not

Lk 2:19 kept all these things, pondering them in her H
2:51 his mother kept all these things in her H
6:45 good treasure of his H produces good, and the
6:45 the abundance of the H his mouth speaks.
8:15 an honest and good H, and bring forth fruit
10:27 God with all your H, and with all your
12:34 is, there will your H be also.
18:1 they ought always to pray and not lose H
24:25 men, and slow of H to believe all that

Jn 7:38 said, 'Out of his H shall flow rivers of
12:40 eyes and hardened their H, lest they should see
12:40 and perceive with their H, and turn for me
13:2 put it into the H of Judas Iscariot, Simon's

Acts 2:26 be shaken; therefore my H was glad, and my
2:37 were cut to the H, and said to Peter
4:32 believed were of one H and soul, and no
5:3 has Satan filled your H to lie to the
5:4 that you have contrived this deed in your H
7:23 it came into his H to visit his brethren,
7:51 stiff-necked people, uncircumcised in H and ears, you
8:21 this matter, for your H is not right before
8:22 the intent of your H may be forgiven you.
13:22 a man after my H, who will do all
15:8 God who knows the H bore witness to them,
16:14 The Lord opened her H to give heed to
21:13 "What are you doing, weeping and breaking my H
27:22 now bid you take H; for there will be

27:25 with you.' So take H, men, for I have
28:27 For this people's H has grown dull, and their
28:27 and understand with their H, and turn for me
Rom 2:5 your hard and impenitent H you are storing up
2:29 a matter of the H, spiritual and not literal.
6:17 become obedient from the H to the standard of
9:2 have great sorrow and unceasing anguish in my H
9:18 and he hardens the H of whomever he wills.
10:1 Brethren, my H's desire and prayer to God for
10:6 not say in your H, "Who will ascend into
10:8 lips and in your H (that is, the word
10:9 and believe in your H that God raised him
10:10 man believes with his H and so is justified,
1Cor 2:9 ear heard, nor the H of man conceived, what
4:5 darkness and will disclose the purposes of the H
7:37 firmly established in his H, being under no necessity
7:37 determined this in his H, to keep her as
14:25 the secrets of his H are disclosed; and so,
2Cor 2:4 affliction and anguish of H and with many tears,
4:1 the mercy of God, we do not lose H
4:16 So we do not lose H
5:12 on a man's position and not on his H
6:11 to you, Corinthians; our H is wide.
7:15 And his H goes out all the more to
8:16 for you into the H of Titus.
Gal 6:9 we shall reap, if we do not lose H
Eph 3:13 you not to lose H over what I am
4:18 to their hardness of H;
5:19 Lord with all your H,
6:5 trembling, in singleness of H, as to Christ;
6:6 of God from the H,
Phil 1:7 hold you in my H, for you are all
Col 3:22 but in singleness of H, fearing the Lord.
1Thes 2:17 in person not in H, we endeavored the more
1Tim 1:5 issues from a pure H and a good conscience
2Tim 2:22 who call upon the Lord from a pure H
Philem 1:12 sending him back to you, sending my very H
1:20 Refresh my H in Christ.
Heb 3:12 you an evil, unbelieving H, leading you to fall
4:12 and discerning the thoughts and intentions of the H
10:22 near with a true H in full assurance of
13:9 is well that the H be strengthened by grace,
Jas 1:25 tongue but deceives his H, this man's religion is
1Pet 1:22 the brethren, love one another earnestly from the H
3:4 hidden person of the H with the imperishable jewel
3:8 the brethren, a tender H and a humble mind.
1Jn 3:17 need, yet closes his H against him, how does
Rev 2:23 who searches mind and H, and I will give
18:7 Since in her H she says, 'A queen I

HEARTH (6)
Lev 6:9 shall be on the H upon the altar all
Sir 50:12 he stood by the H of the altar with
Is 30:14 take fire from the H, or to dip up
Ezek 43:15 cubit; and the altar H, four cubits; and from
43:15 and from the altar H projecting upward, four horns,
43:16 The altar H shall be square, twelve cubits long

HEARTHS
Ezek 46:23 row of masonry, with H made at the bottom

HEARTILY
Col 3:23 Whatever your task, work H, as serving the Lord

HEARTLESS
Rom 1:31 to parents, foolish, faithless, H, ruthless.

HEARTS (160)
Gen 42:28 At this their H failed them, and they turned
Ex 14:17 I will harden the H of the Egyptians so
35:26 all the women whose H were moved with ability
Lev 26:36 send faintness into their H in the lands of
Deut 1:28 brethren have made our H melt, saying, "The people
Josh 2:11 we heard it, our H melted, and there was
7:5 And the H of the people melted, and became
11:20 doing to harden their H that they should come
23:14 you know in your H and souls, all of
Judg 9:3 of Shechem; and their H inclined to follow
16:25 And when their H were merry, they said, "Call
19:22 they were making their H merry, behold, the men
1Sam 6:6 should you harden your H as the Egyptians and
6:6 as the Egyptians and Pharaoh hardened their H
10:26 men of valor whose H God had touched.
2Sam 15:6 so Absalom stole the H of the men of
15:13 to David, saying, "The H of the men of
1Kgs 8:39 thou only, knowest the H of all the children
8:58 he may incline our H to him, to walk
18:37 thou hast turned their H back."
1Chr 16:10 holy name; let the H of those who seek
28:9 the LORD searches all H, and understands every
29:18 and thoughts in the H of thy people, and
29:18 people, and direct their H toward thee.
2Chr 6:30 thou only, knowest the H of the children of
11:16 who had set their H to seek the LORD
20:33 not yet set their H upon the God of
Jud 8:27 them, to search their H, nor has he taken
13:19 never depart from the H of men, as they
Job 1:5 sons have sinned, and cursed God in their H
Ps 4:4 commune with your own H on your beds, and
7:9 triest the minds and H, thou righteous God.
17:10 They close their H to pity; with their mouths
22:26 May your H live for ever!
28:3 with their neighbors, while mischief is in their H
33:15 he who fashions the H of them all, and
58:2 Nay, in your H you devise wrongs; your hands
69:32 seek God, let your H revive.
73:7 out with fatness, their H overflow with follies.
81:12 over to their stubborn H, to follow their own
85:8 to those who turn to him in their H
95:8 Harden not your H, as at Meribah, as on
105:3 holy name; let the H of those who seek
105:25 He turned their H to hate his people, to
107:12 Their H were bowed down with hard labor; they
125:4 and to those who are upright in their H
Prov 15:11 how much more the H of men!
17:3 furnace is for gold, and the LORD tries H
Eccl 9:3 to all; also the H of men are full
9:3 madness is in their H while they live, and
Wis 2:2 a spark kindled by the beating of our H
Sir 2:12 Woe to timid H and to slack hands, and
2:17 Lord will prepare their H, and will humble
17:7 his eye upon their H to show them the
31:26 steel, so wine tests H in the strife of
42:18 the abyss, and the H of men, and considers
46:11 respective names, those whose H did not fall into
48:19 Then their H were shaken and their hands trembled,
Is 6:10 and understand with their H, and turn and be
29:13 their lips, while their H are far from me,
Jer 4:4 the foreskin of your H, O men of Judah
5:24 not say in their H, 'Let us fear the
7:24 stubbornness of their evil H, and went backward and
9:14 stubbornly followed their own H and have gone after
31:33 write it upon their H; and I will be
32:40 of me in their H, that they may not
Lam 3:41 us lift up our H and hands to God
5:15 The joy of our H has ceased; our dancing
Bar 3:7 of thee in our H in order that we
3:7 put away from our H all the iniquity of
6:20 but men say their H have melted, when worms
Ezek 14:3 their idols into their H, and set the stumbling
14:5 lay hold of the H of the house of
21:15 encompasses them, that their H may melt, and many
32:9 "I will trouble the H of many peoples, when
Hos 7:7 like an oven their H burn with intrigue; all
Joel 2:13 mourning; and rend your H and not your garments."
Nah 2:10 H faint and knees tremble, anguish is on all
Zeph 1:12 who say in their H, 'The LORD will not
Zech 7:12 They made their H like adamant lest they should
8:17 devise evil in your H against one another, and
10:7 mighty warrior, and their H shall be glad as
10:7 it and rejoice, their H shall exult in the
Mal 4:6 he will turn the H of fathers to their
4:6 their children and the H of children to their
1Mac 1:62 were resolved in their H not to eat unclean
2Mac 2:3 that the law should not depart from their H
15:27 to God in their H, they laid low no
Mt 9:4 said, "Why do you think evil in your H
Mk 2:6 there, questioning in their H,
2:8 them, "Why do you question thus in your H
6:52 the loaves, but their H were hardened.
8:17 Are your H hardened?
Lk 1:17 Elijah, to turn the H of the fathers to
1:51 the imagination of their H,
1:66 them up in their H, saying, "What then will
2:35 thoughts out of many H may be revealed."
3:15 men questioned in their H concerning John, whether
5:22 answered them, "Why do you question in your H
8:12 the word from their H, that they may not
9:47 the thought of their H, he took a child
16:15 but God knows your H; for what is exalted
21:34 to yourselves lest your H be weighed down with
24:32 other, "Did not our H burn within us while

24:38 troubled, and why do questionings rise in your H
Jn 14:1 "Let not your H be troubled; believe in God,
14:27 Let not your H be troubled, neither let them
16:6 these things to you, sorrow has filled your H
16:22 you again and your H will rejoice, and no
Acts 1:24 "Lord, who knowest the H of all men, show
2:46 with glad and generous H,
7:39 aside, and in their H they turned to Egypt,
14:17 fruitful seasons, satisfying your H with food and
15:9 them, but cleansed their H by faith.
Rom 1:24 the lusts of their H to impurity, to the
2:15 is written on their H, while their conscience also
5:5 been poured into our H through the Holy Spirit
8:27 he who searches the H of men knows what
16:18 words they deceive the H of the simple-minded.
2Cor 1:22 his Spirit in our H as a guarantee.
3:2 recommendation, written on your H, to be known
3:3 tablets of stone but on tablets of human H
4:6 has shone in our H to give the light
6:13 to children—widen your H also.
7:2 Open your H to us; we have wronged no
7:3 you are in our H, to die together and
Gal 4:6 his Son into our H, crying, "Abba!
Eph 1:18 the eyes of your H enlightened, that you may
3:17 may dwell in your H through faith; that you,
6:22 we are, and that he may encourage your H
Phil 4:7 understanding, will keep your H and your minds in
Col 2:2 my face, that their H may be encouraged as
3:15 Christ rule in your H, to which indeed you
3:16 with thankfulness in your H to God.
4:8 he may encourage your H,
1Thes 2:4 men, but to please God who tests our H
3:13 he may establish your H unblamable in holiness
2Thes 2:17 through grace, comfort your H and establish them in
3:5 the Lord direct your H to the love of
1Tim 6:10 faith and pierced their H with many pangs.
Philem 1:7 my brother, because the H of the saints have
Heb 3:8 do not harden your H as in the rebellion,
3:10 go astray in their H; they have not known
3:15 do not harden your H as in the rebellion."
4:7 you hear his voice, do not harden your H
8:10 write them on their H, and I will be
10:16 my laws on their H, and write them on
10:22 of faith, with our H sprinkled clean from an
Jas 3:14 selfish ambition in your H, do not boast and
4:8 sinners, and purify your H, you men of double
5:5 you have fattened your H in a day of
5:8 Establish your H, for the coming of the Lord
1Pet 3:15 troubled, but in your H reverence Christ as Lord.
2Pet 1:19 dawns and the morning star rises in your H
2:14 They have H trained in greed.
1Jn 3:19 truth, and reassure our H before him
3:20 before him whenever our H condemn us; for God
3:20 is greater than our H, and he knows everything.
3:21 Beloved, if our H do not condemn us, we
Rev 17:17 put it into their H to carry out his

HEARTY (2)

2Mac 9:19 king and general sends H greetings and good wishes
1Cor 16:19 their house, send you H greetings in the Lord.

HEAT (47)

Gen 8:22 and harvest, cold and H, summer and winter, day
18:1 his tent in the H of the day.
31:40 was; by day the H consumed me, and the
Deut 28:22 fever, inflammation, and fiery H, and with drought,
29:24 What means the H of this great anger?'
32:24 devoured with burning H and poisonous pestilence;
1Sam 11:11 the Ammonites until the H of the day; and
2Sam 4:5 out, and about the H of the day they
Jud 8:3 overcome by the burning H, and took to his
Job 6:17 In time of H they disappear; when it is
24:19 Drought and H snatch away the snow waters; so
30:30 falls from me, and my bones burn with H
Ps 19:6 them; and there is nothing hid from its H
32:4 up as by the H of summer.
58:9 pots can feel the H of thorns, whether green
Wis 2:4 rays of the sun and overcome by its H
Sir 14:27 by her from the H, and will dwell in
18:15 Does not the dew assuage the scorching H
38:28 wastes away in the H of the furnace; he
43:3 the land; and who can withstand its burning H
43:4 furnace works in burning H, but the sun burns
43:22 when the dew appears, it refreshes from the H
Is 4:6 by day from the H, and for a refuge
18:4 my dwelling like clear H in sunshine, like a
18:4 of dew in the H of harvest."
25:4 a shade from the H; for the blast of
25:5 against a wall, like H in a dry place.
25:5 of the aliens; as H by the shade of
42:25 poured upon him the H of his anger and
Jer 2:24 the wilderness, in her H sniffing the wind!
17:8 does not fear when H comes, for its leaves
36:30 cast out to the H by day and the
Lam 5:10 oven with the burning H of famine.
Bar 2:25 cast out to the H of day and the
Ezek 3:14 in bitterness in the H of my spirit, the
Dan 3:67 the Lord, fire and H, sing praise to him
3:68 winter cold and summer H, sing praise to him
Hos 7:6 became sick with the H of wine; he stretched
Nah 1:6 Who can endure the H of his anger?
Zeph 3:8 my indignation, all the H of my anger; for
2Mac 14:43 But in the H of the struggle he did
Mt 20:12 day and the scorching H
Lk 12:55 'There will be scorching H; and it happens.
Acts 28:3 out because of the H and fastened on his
Jas 1:10 rises with its scorching H and withers the grass;
Rev 7:16 sun shall not strike them, nor any scorching H
16:9 scorched by the fierce H, and they cursed the

HEATED (6)

Sir 23:16 The soul H like a burning fire will not
Dan 3:19 He ordered the furnace H seven times more than
3:19 times more than it was wont to be H
Hos 7:5 they are like a H oven, whose baker ceases
2Mac 7:3 and gave orders that pans and caldrons be H
7:4 These were H immediately, and he commanded that

HEATHEN (9)

Ps 79:1 O God, the H have come into thy inheritance;
Wis 12:5 the midst of a H cult,
14:11 visitation also upon the H idols, because, though part
15:15 thought that all their H idols were gods, though
Bar 6:4 on men's shoulders and inspire fear in the H
6:17 the gods of the H, when they have been
1Cor 12:2 that when you were H, you were led astray
1Thes 4:5 passion of lust like H who do not know
3Jn 1:7 his sake and have accepted nothing from the H

HEAVEN (575)

Gen 1:8 And God called the firmament H
6:17 of life from under H; everything that is on
7:19 mountains under the whole H were covered;
14:19 Most High, maker of H and earth;
14:22 Most High, maker of H and earth,
15:5 and said, "Look toward H, and number the stars,
19:24 the LORD out of H;
21:17 called to Hagar from H, and said to her,
22:11 to him from H, and said, "Abraham, Abraham!"
22:15 a second time from H,
22:17 as the stars of H and as the sand
24:3 LORD, the God of H and of the earth,
24:7 LORD, the God of H, who took me from
26:4 as the stars of H, and will give to
27:28 of the dew of H, and of the fatness
27:39 from the dew of H on high.
28:12 of it reached to H; and behold, the angels
28:17 of God, and this is the gate of H
49:25 you with blessings of H above, blessings of the
Ex 9:8 Moses throw them toward H in the sight of
9:10 Moses threw them toward H, and it became boils
9:22 forth your hand toward H, that there may be
9:23 forth his rod toward H; and the LORD sent
10:21 out your hand toward H that there may be
10:22 out his hand toward H, and there was thick
16:4 will rain bread from H for you; and the
17:14 blot out the remembrance of Amalek from under H
20:4 anything that is in H above, or that is
20:11 days the LORD made H and earth, the sea,
20:22 yourselves that I have talked with you from H
24:10 stone, like the very H for clearness.
31:17 days the LORD made H and earth, and on
32:13 as the stars of H, and all this land
Deut 1:10 as the stars of H for multitude.
1:28 and fortified up to H; and moreover we have
2:25 are under the whole H, who shall hear the
3:24 god is there in H or on earth who
4:11 to the heart of H, wrapped in darkness, cloud,
4:19 up your eyes to H, and when you see
4:19 all the host of H, you be drawn away
4:19 allotted to all the peoples under the whole H
4:26 to anger, I call H and earth to witness

4:32 from one end of H to the other, whether
4:36 Out of H he let you hear his voice,
4:39 LORD is God in H above and on the
5:8 anything that is in H above, or that is
7:24 name perish from under H; not a man shall
9:1 and fortified up to H,
9:14 their name from under H; and I will make
10:14 LORD your God belong H and the heaven of
10:14 belong heaven and the H of heavens, the earth
10:22 as the stars of H for multitude.
11:11 by the rain from H,
17:3 of the host of H, which I have forbidden,
25:19 of Amalek from under H; you shall not forget.
26:15 thy holy habitation, from H, and bless thy people
28:24 powder and dust; from H it shall come down
28:62 as the stars of H for multitude, you shall
29:20 LORD would blot out his name from under H
30:4 the uttermost parts of H, from there the LORD
30:12 It is not in H, that you should say,
30:12 up for us to H, and bring it to
30:19 I call H and earth to witness against you
31:28 their ears and call H and earth to witness
32:40 up my hand to H, and swear, As I
33:13 the choicest gifts of H above, and of the
Josh 2:11 who is God in H above and on earth
8:20 city went up to H; and they had no
10:11 down great stones from H upon them as far
10:13 in the midst of H, and did not hasten
Judg 5:20 From H fought the stars, from their courses they
13:20 flame went up toward H from the altar, the
20:40 of the city went up in smoke to H
1Sam 2:10 to pieces; against them he will thunder in H
5:12 the cry of the city went up to H
2Sam 18:9 was left hanging between H and earth, while the
22:14 The LORD thundered from H, and the Most High
1Kgs 8:22 forth his hands toward H;
8:23 God like thee, in H above or on earth
8:27 Behold, H and the highest heaven cannot contain
8:27 heaven and the highest H cannot contain thee; how
8:30 yea, hear thou in H thy dwelling place; and
8:32 then hear thou in H, and act, and judge
8:34 then hear thou in H, and forgive the sin
8:35 "When H is shut up and there is no
8:36 then hear thou in H, and forgive the sin
8:39 then hear thou in H thy dwelling place, and
8:43 house, hear thou in H thy dwelling place, and
8:45 then hear thou in H their prayer and their
8:49 then hear thou in H thy dwelling place their
8:54 with hands outstretched toward H;
22:19 all the host of H standing beside him on
2Kgs 1:10 fire come down from H and consume you and
1:10 fire came down from H, and consumed him and
1:12 fire come down from H and consume you and
1:12 God came down from H and consumed him and
1:14 fire came down from H, and consumed the two
2:1 take Elijah up to H by a whirlwind, Elijah
2:11 And Elijah went up by a whirlwind into H
7:2 should make windows in H, could this thing be?"
7:19 should make windows in H, could such a thing
14:27 of Israel from under H, so he saved them
17:16 all the host of H, and served Baal.
19:15 earth; thou hast made H and earth.
21:3 all the host of H, and served them.
21:5 all the host of H in the two courts
23:4 all the host of H; he burned them outside
1Chr 21:16 standing between earth and H, and in his hand
21:26 him with fire from H upon the altar of
27:23 make Israel as many as the stars of H
2Chr 2:6 him a house, since H, even highest heaven, cannot
2:6 since heaven, even highest H, cannot contain him?
2:12 of Israel, who made H and earth, who has
6:13 forth his hands toward H;
6:14 God like thee, in H or on earth, keeping
6:18 Behold, H and the highest H heaven cannot contain
6:18 heaven and the highest H cannot contain thee; how
6:21 yea, hear thou from H thy dwelling place; and
6:23 then hear thou from H, and act, and judge
6:25 then hear thou from H, and forgive the sin
6:26 "When H is shut up and there is no
6:27 then hear thou in H, and forgive the sin
6:30 then hear thou from H thy dwelling place, and
6:33 house, hear thou from H thy dwelling place, and
6:35 then hear thou from H their prayer and their
6:39 then hear thou from H thy dwelling place their
7:1 fire came down from H and consumed the burnt
7:14 I will hear from H, and will forgive their
18:18 all the host of H standing on his right
20:6 of our fathers, art thou not God in H
28:9 in a rage which has reached up to H
30:27 their prayer came to his holy habitation in H
32:20 Amoz, prayed because of this and cried to H
33:3 all the host of H, and served them.
33:5 all the host of H in the two courts
36:23 LORD, the God of H, has given me all
Ezra 1:2 LORD, the God of H, has given me all
5:11 of the God of H and earth, and we
5:12 angered the God of H, he gave them into
6:9 to the God of H, wheat, salt, wine, or
6:10 to the God of H, and pray for the
7:12 scribe of the law of the God of H
7:21 of the God of H, requires of you, be
7:23 by the God of H, let it be done
7:23 of the God of H, lest his wrath be
Neh 1:4 continued fasting and praying before the God of H
1:5 "O LORD God of H, the great and terrible
2:4 So I prayed to the God of H
2:20 them, "The God of H will make us prosper,
9:6 alone; thou hast made H, the heaven of heavens,
9:6 hast made heaven, the H of heavens, with all
9:6 and the host of H worships thee.
9:13 speak with them from H and give them right
9:15 give them bread from H for their hunger and
9:23 as the stars of H, and thou didst bring
9:27 didst hear them from H; and according to thy
9:28 thou didst hear from H, and many times thou
Tob 5:16 God who dwells in H will prosper your way,
7:18 child; the Lord of H and earth grant you
10:11 saying, "The God of H will prosper you, my
10:12 Tobias, "The Lord of H bring you back safely,
13:7 exalts the King of H, and will rejoice in
13:11 in their hands, gifts for the King of H
Jud 5:8 worshiped the God of H, the God they had
6:19 "O Lord God of H, behold their arrogance, and
7:29 to witness against you H and earth and our
9:12 of Israel, Lord of H and earth, Creator of
11:17 serves the God of H day and night; therefore,
Esth 13:10 For thou hast made H and earth and every
13:10 every wonderful thing under H,
Job 1:16 of God fell from H and burned up the
2:12 robes and sprinkled dust upon their heads toward H
11:8 It is higher than H—what can you
16:19 my witness is in H, and he that vouches
22:14 on the vault of H
25:2 with God; he makes peace in his high H
26:11 The pillars of H tremble, and are astounded at
37:3 Under the whole H he lets it go, and
38:29 who has given birth to the hoarfrost of H
41:11 is under the whole H is mine.
Ps 11:4 LORD's throne is in H; his eyes behold, his
14:2 LORD looks down from H upon the children of
20:6 him from his holy H with mighty victories by
33:13 LORD looks down from H, he sees all the
53:2 God looks down from H upon the sons of
57:3 He will send from H and save me, he
69:34 Let H and earth praise him, the seas and
73:25 Whom have I in H but thee?
78:23 opened the doors of H;
78:24 to eat, and gave them the grain of H
80:14 Look down from H, and see; have regard for
102:19 his holy height, from H the LORD looked at
105:40 gave them bread from H in abundance.
107:26 They mounted up to H, they went down to
115:15 the LORD, who made H and earth!
121:2 the LORD, who made H and earth.
124:8 the LORD, who made H and earth.
134:3 Zion, he who made H and earth!
135:6 pleases he does, in H and on earth, in
136:26 to the God of H, for his steadfast love
139:8 If I ascend to H, thou art there!
146:6 his God, who made H and earth, the sea,
148:13 is exalted; his glory is above earth and H
Prov 23:5 to itself wings, flying like an eagle toward H
30:4 Who has ascended to H and come down?
Eccl 1:13 that is done under H; it is an unhappy
2:3 men to do under H during the few days
3:1 for every matter under H:
5:2 for God is in H, and you upon earth;
Wis 13:2 of the luminaries of H were the gods that
16:20 didst supply them from H with bread ready to
18:15 all-powerful word leaped from H, from the royal
18:16 with death, and touched H while standing on the
Sir 1:3 The height of H, the breadth of the earth,

16:16 Behold, H and the highest heaven, the abyss and
16:16 heaven and the highest H, the abyss and the
17:27 of the height of H; but all men are
24:5 of the vault of H and have walked in
43:1 firmament, the appearance of H in a spectacle of
43:8 on high shining forth in the firmament of H
43:9 is the beauty of H, a gleaming array in
43:12 It encircles the H with its glorious arc; the
45:15 all the days of H, to minister to the
46:17 the Lord thundered from H, and made his voice
48:20 quickly heard them from H, and delivered them by
Is 7:11 it be deep as Sheol or high as H
14:12 you are fallen from H, O Day Star, son
14:13 'I will ascend to H; above the stars of
24:18 For the windows of H are opened, and the
24:21 punish the host of H, in heaven, and the
24:21 host of heaven, in H, and the kings of
34:4 All the host of H shall rot away, and
37:16 earth; thou hast made H and earth.
55:10 snow come down from H, and return not thither
63:15 Look down from H and see, from thy holy
66:1 Thus says the LORD: H is my throne and
Jer 7:18 for the queen of H; and they pour out
8:2 all the host of H, which they have loved
19:13 all the host of H, and drink offerings have
23:24 Do I not fill H and earth?
33:22 As the host of H cannot be numbered and
33:25 and the ordinances of H and earth,
44:17 to the queen of H and pour out libations
44:18 to the queen of H and pouring out libations
44:19 to the queen of H and poured out libations
44:25 to the queen of H and to pour out
49:36 the four quarters of H; and I will scatter
51:9 has reached up to H and has been lifted
51:53 should mount up to H, and though she should
Lam 2:1 has cast down from H to earth the splendor
3:41 hands to God in H:
3:50 until the LORD from H looks down and sees;
Bar 1:11 on earth may be like the days of H
2:2 Under the whole H there has not been done
3:29 has gone up into H, and taken her, and
5:3 God will show your splendor everywhere under H
6:54 are like crows between H and earth.
Ezek 8:3 up between earth and H, and brought me in
32:8 the bright lights of H will I make dark
Dan 2:18 of the God of H concerning this mystery, so
2:19 Then Daniel blessed the God of H
2:28 is a God in H who reveals mysteries, and
2:37 whom the God of H has given the kingdom,
2:44 kings the God of H will set up a
3:36 as the stars of H and as the sand
3:57 in the firmament of H and to be sung
3:61 all waters above the H, sing praise to him
3:64 the Lord, stars of H, sing praise to him
4:11 its top reached to H, and it was visible
4:13 a watcher, a holy one, came down from H
4:15 with the dew of H; let his lot be
4:20 its top reached to H, and it was visible
4:22 grown and reaches to H, and your dominion to
4:23 one, coming down from H and saying, 'Hew down
4:23 with the dew of H; and let his lot
4:25 with the dew of H, and seven times shall
4:26 that you know that H rules.
4:31 fell a voice from H, "O King Nebuchadnezzar, to
4:33 with the dew of H till his hair grew
4:34 lifted my eyes to H, and my reason returned
4:35 in the host of H and among the inhabitants
4:37 honor the King of H; for all his works
5:21 with the dew of H, until he knew that
5:23 against the Lord of H; and the vessels of
6:27 signs and wonders in H and on earth, he
7:2 the four winds of H were stirring up the
7:13 with the clouds of H there came one like
7:27 kingdoms under the whole H shall be given to
8:8 four conspicuous horns toward the four winds of H
8:10 to the host of H; and some of the
9:12 for under the whole H there has not been
11:4 the four winds of H, but not to his
12:7 his left hand toward H; and I heard him
13:9 eyes from looking to H or remembering righteous
13:35 weeping, looked up toward H, for her heart trusted
14:5 living God, who created H and earth and has
Amos 9:2 they climb up to H, from there I will
Jon 1:9 LORD, the God of H, who made the sea
Zech 5:9 they lifted up the ephah between earth and H
6:5 the four winds of H, after presenting themselves
Mal 3:10 open the windows of H for you and pour
1Mac 2:37 die in our innocence; H and earth testify for
2:58 zeal for the law was taken up into H
3:18 in the sight of H there is no difference
3:19 victory in battle depends, but strength comes from H
3:50 they cried aloud to H, saying, "What shall we
3:60 as his will in H may be, so he
4:10 let us cry to H, to see whether he
4:24 hymns and praises to H, for he is good,
4:40 signal on the trumpets, and cried out to H
4:55 and worshiped and blessed H, who had prospered
5:31 city went up to H with trumpets and loud
9:46 Cry out now to H that you may be
12:15 help which comes from H for our aid; and
16:3 help which comes from H be with you."
2Mac 2:10 fire came down from H and devoured the sacrifices,
2:18 us from everywhere under H into his holy place,
2:21 appearances which came from H to those who strove
3:15 garments and called toward H upon him who had
3:20 up their hands to H, they all made entreaty.
3:34 have been scourged by H, report to all men
3:39 has his dwelling in H watches over that place
7:11 "I got these from H, and because of his
7:28 to look at the H and the earth and
7:34 you raise your hand against the children of H
8:20 came to them from H, destroyed one hundred and
9:4 But the judgment of H rode with him!
9:10 thought that he could touch the stars of H
9:20 my hope is in H,
10:29 to the enemy from H five resplendent men on
14:34 forth their hands toward H and called upon the
15:3 were a sovereign in H who had commanded the
15:4 himself, the Sovereign in H, who ordered us to
15:8 come to them from H, and now to look
15:21 out his hands toward H and called upon the
15:34 they all, looking to H, blessed the Lord who
Mt 3:2 for the kingdom of H is at hand."
3:17 lo, a voice from H, saying, "This is my
4:17 for the kingdom of H is at hand."
5:3 in spirit, for theirs is the kingdom of H
5:10 righteousness' sake, for theirs is the kingdom of H
5:12 reward is great in H, for so men persecuted
5:16 give glory to your Father who is in H
5:18 say to you, till H and earth pass away,
5:19 in the kingdom of H; but he who does
5:19 shall be called great in the kingdom of H
5:20 Pharisees, you will never enter the kingdom of H
5:34 at all, either by H, for it is the
5:45 Father who is in H; for he makes his
6:1 no reward from your Father who is in H
6:9 Father who art in H, Hallowed be thy name.
6:10 be done, On earth as it is in H
6:20 for yourselves treasures in H, where neither moth
7:11 Father who is in H give good things to
7:21 enter the kingdom of H, but he who does
7:21 the will of my Father who is in H
8:11 in the kingdom of H,
10:7 saying, 'The kingdom of H is at hand.'
10:32 Father who is in H;
10:33 will deny before my Father who is in H
11:11 in the kingdom of H is greater than he.
11:12 now the kingdom of H has suffered violence, and
11:23 And you, Caperna-um, will you be exalted to H
11:25 thee, Father, Lord of H and earth, that thou
12:49 of my Father in H is my brother, and
13:11 of the kingdom of H, but to them it
13:24 saying, "The kingdom of H may be compared to
13:31 saying, "The kingdom of H is like a grain
13:33 "The kingdom of H is like leaven which a
13:44 "The kingdom of H is like treasure hidden in
13:45 "Again, the kingdom of H is like a merchant
13:47 "Again, the kingdom of H is like a net
13:52 for the kingdom of H is like a householder
14:19 he looked up to H, and blessed, and broke
16:1 asked him to show them a sign from H
16:17 to you, but my Father who is in H
16:19 of the kingdom of H, and whatever you bind
16:19 shall be bound in H, and whatever you loose
16:19 you loose on earth shall be loosed in H
18:1 "Who is the greatest in the kingdom of H
18:3 children, you will never enter the kingdom of H
18:4 he is the greatest in the kingdom of H
18:10 tell you that in H their angels always behold
18:10 the face of my Father who is in H
18:13 Father who is in H that one of these
18:17 shall be bound in H, and whatever you loose

18:17 you loose on earth shall be loosed in H
18:18 be done for them by my Father in H
18:22 "Therefore the kingdom of H may be compared to
19:12 eunuchs for the sake of the kingdom of H
19:14 them; for to such belongs the kingdom of H
19:21 will have treasure in H; and come, follow me."
19:23 a rich man to enter the kingdom of H
20:1 "For the kingdom of H is like a householder
21:25 From H or from men?" And they argued with
21:25 "If we say, 'From H he will say to
22:2 saying, "The kingdom of H may be compared to
22:30 given in marriage, but are like angels in H
23:9 for you have one Father, who is in H
23:13 shut the kingdom of H against men; for you
23:21 he who swears by H, swears by the throne
24:29 stars will fall from H, and the powers of
24:30 Son of man in H, and then all the
24:30 on the clouds of H with power and great
24:31 from one end of H to the other.
24:35 H and earth will pass away, but my words
24:36 even the angels of H, nor the Son, but
25:1 "Then the kingdom of H shall be compared to
26:64 of Power, and coming on the clouds of H
28:2 the Lord descended from H and came and rolled
28:18 them, "All authority in H and on earth has
Mk 1:11 a voice came from H, "Thou art my beloved
6:41 he looked up to H, and blessed, and broke
7:33 and looking up to H, he sighed, and said
8:11 him a sign from H, to test him.
10:21 will have treasure in H; and come, follow me."
11:25 also who is in H may forgive you your
11:29 baptism of John from H or from men?
11:30 "If we say, 'From H he will say, 'Why
12:25 given in marriage, but are like angels in H
13:25 will be falling from H, and the powers in
13:27 ends of the earth to the ends of H
13:31 H and earth will pass away, but my words
13:32 even the angels in H, nor the Son, but
14:62 of Power, and coming with the clouds of H
16:19 was taken up into H, and sat down at
Lk 2:15 away from them into H, the shepherds said to
3:21 and was praying, the H was opened,
3:22 a voice came from H, "Thou art my beloved
4:25 of Elijah, when the H was shut up three
6:23 reward is great in H; for so their fathers
9:16 he looked up to H, and blessed and broke
9:54 fire come down from H and consume them?"
10:15 And you, Caperna-um, will you be exalted to H
10:18 them, "I saw Satan fall like lightning from H
10:20 but rejoice that your names are written in H
10:21 thee, Father, Lord of H and earth, that thou
11:16 test him, sought from him a sign from H
15:7 be more joy in H over one sinner who
15:18 I have sinned against H and before you;
15:21 I have sinned against H and before you; I
16:17 it is easier for H and earth to pass
17:29 and sulphur rained from H and destroyed them all—
18:13 up his eyes to H, but beat his breast,
18:22 will have treasure in H; and come, follow me."
19:38 Peace in H and glory in the highest!"
20:4 baptism of John from H or from men?"
20:5 "If we say, 'From H he will say, 'Why
21:11 there will be terrors and great signs from H
21:33 H and earth will pass away, but my words
24:51 parted from them, and was carried up into H
Jn 1:32 as a dove from H, and it remained on
1:51 you, you will see H opened, and the angels
3:13 one has ascended into H but he who descended
3:13 he who descended from H, the Son of man.
3:27 receive anything except what is given him from H
3:31 he who comes from H is above all.
6:31 gave them bread from H to eat.'"
6:32 you the bread from H; my Father gives you
6:32 my Father gives you the true bread from H
6:33 which comes down from H, and gives life to
6:38 have come down from H, not to do my
6:41 "I am the bread which came down from H
6:42 he now say, 'I have come down from H
6:50 which comes down from H, that a man may
6:51 which came down from H; if any one eats
6:58 which came down from H, not such as the
12:28 a voice came from H, "I have glorified it,
17:1 up his eyes to H and said, "Father, the
Acts 1:10 they were gazing into H as he went, behold,
1:11 of Galilee, why do you stand looking into H
1:11 up from you into H, will come in the
1:11 same way as you saw him go into H
2:2 a sound came from H like the rush of
2:5 Jews, devout men from every nation under H
2:19 show wonders in the H above and signs on
3:21 for you, Jesus, whom H must receive until the
4:12 no other name under H given among men by
4:24 who didst make the H and the earth and
7:42 worship the host of H, as it is written
7:49 as the prophet says, H is my throne, and
7:55 Holy Spirit, gazed into H and saw the glory
9:3 suddenly a light from H flashed about him.
10:11 and saw the H opened, and something descending,
10:16 the thing was taken up at once to H
11:5 sheet, let down from H by four corners; and
11:9 a second time from H, 'What God has cleansed
11:10 times, and all was drawn up again into H
14:15 God who made the H and the earth and
14:17 and gave you from H rains and fruitful seasons,
17:24 it, being Lord of H and earth, does not
22:6 a great light from H suddenly shone about me.
26:13 way a light from H, brighter than the sun,
Rom 1:18 God is revealed from H against all ungodliness and
10:6 say in your heart, "Who will ascend into H
1Cor 8:5 be so-called gods in H or on earth—as
15:47 man of dust; the second man is from H
15:48 is the man of H, so are those who
15:48 of heaven, so are those who are of H
15:49 also bear the image of the man of H
2Cor 12:2 up to the third H —whether in the body
Gal 1:8 or an angel from H, should preach to you
Eph 1:10 in him, things in H and things on earth.
3:15 whom every family in H and on earth is
6:9 and yours is in H, and that there is
Phil 2:10 knee should bow, in H and on earth and
3:20 our commonwealth is in H, and from it we
Col 1:5 of the hope laid up for you in H
1:16 things were created, in H and on earth, visible
1:20 on earth or in H, making peace by the
1:23 to every creature under H, and of which I,
4:1 knowing that you also have a Master in H
1Thes 1:10 for his Son from H, whom he raised from
4:16 himself will descend from H with a cry of
2Thes 1:7 Jesus is revealed from H with his mighty angels
Heb 8:1 of the Majesty in H,
9:24 true one, but into H itself, now to appear
11:12 as the stars of H and as the innumerable
12:23 who are enrolled in H, and to a judge
12:25 escape if we reject him who warns from H
12:26 shake not only the earth but also the H
Jas 5:12 not swear, either by H or by earth or
5:18 prayed again and the H gave rain, and the
1Pet 1:4 and unfading, kept in H for you,
1:12 Holy Spirit sent from H, things into which angels
3:22 who has gone into H and is at the
2Pet 1:18 this voice borne from H, for we were with
Rev 3:12 my God out of H, and my own new
4:1 looked, and lo, in H an open door!
4:2 a throne stood in H, with one seated on
5:3 And no one in H or on earth or
5:13 heard every creature in H and on earth and
8:1 there was silence in H for about half an
8:10 great star fell from H, blazing like a torch,
9:1 a star fallen from H to earth, and he
10:1 angel coming down from H, wrapped in a cloud,
10:4 heard a voice from H saying, "Seal up what
10:5 his right hand to H
10:6 and ever, who created H and what is in
10:8 I had heard from H spoke to me again,
11:12 a loud voice from H saying to them, "Come
11:12 they went up to H in a cloud.
11:13 terrified and gave glory to the God of H
11:15 were loud voices in H, saying, "The kingdom of
11:19 Then God's temple in H was opened, and the
12:1 great portent appeared in H, a woman clothed with
12:3 another portent appeared in H; behold, a great red
12:4 of the stars of H, and cast them to
12:7 Now war arose in H, Michael and his angels
12:8 was no longer any place for them in H
12:10 a loud voice in H, saying, "Now the salvation
12:12 Rejoice then, O H and you that dwell therein!
13:6 his dwelling, that is, those who dwell in H
13:13 fire come down from H to earth in the
14:2 heard a voice from H like the sound of
14:7 worship him who made H and earth, the sea
14:13 heard a voice from H saying, "Write this: Blessed
14:17 of the temple in H, and he too had

15:1 saw another portent in H, great and wonderful, seven
15:5 tent of witness in H was opened,
16:11 cursed the God of H for their pain and
16:21 dropped on men from H, till men cursed God
18:1 angel coming down from H, having great authority;
18:4 heard another voice from H saying, "Come out of
18:5 are heaped high as H, and God has remembered
18:20 Rejoice over her, O H, O saints and apostles
19:1 a great multitude in H, crying, "Hallelujah!
19:11 Then I saw H opened, and behold, a white
19:14 And the armies of H, arrayed in fine linen,
20:1 angel coming down from H, holding in his hand
20:9 fire came down from H and consumed them,
21:1 I saw a new H and a new earth;
21:1 earth; for the first H and the first earth
21:2 coming down out of H from God, prepared as
21:10 coming down out of H from God,

HEAVENLY (29)

Ps 29:1 to the LORD, O H beings, ascribe to the
89:6 Who among the H beings is like the LORD,
Wis 19:21 easily melted kind of H food.
Sir 43:1 The pride of the H heights is the clear
2Mac 11:10 battle order, having their H ally, for the Lord
Mt 5:48 be perfect, as your H Father is perfect.
6:14 men their trespasses, your H Father also will forgive
6:26 barns, and yet your H Father feeds them.
6:32 these things; and your H Father knows that you
15:13 "Every plant which my H Father has not planted
18:34 So also my H Father will do to every
Lk 2:13 a multitude of the H host praising God and
11:13 much more will the H Father give the Holy
Jn 3:12 if I tell you H things?
Acts 26:19 not disobedient to the H vision,
2Cor 5:2 to put on our H dwelling,
Eph 1:3 spiritual blessing in the H places,
1:20 right hand in the H places,
2:6 with him in the H places in Christ Jesus,
3:10 and powers in the H places.
6:12 of wickedness in the H places.
2Tim 4:18 save me for his H kingdom.
Heb 3:1 who share in a H call, consider Jesus, the
6:4 who have tasted the H gift, and have become
8:5 and shadow of the H sanctuary; for when Moses
9:23 the copies of the H things to be purified
9:23 these rites, but the H things themselves with better
11:16 country, that is, a H one.
12:22 the living God, the H Jerusalem, and to innumerable

HEAVENS (183)

Gen 1:1 beginning God created the H and the earth.
1:9 the waters under the H be gathered together into
1:14 the firmament of the H to separate the day
1:15 the firmament of the H to give light upon
1:17 the firmament of the H to give light upon
1:20 above the earth across the firmament of the H
2:1 Thus the H and the earth were finished, and
2:4 the generations of the H and the earth when
2:4 the earth and the H,
7:11 the windows of the H were opened.
8:2 the windows of the H were closed, the rain
8:2 the rain from the H was restrained,
11:4 its top in the H, and let us make
Lev 26:19 I will make your H like iron and your
Deut 10:14 and the heaven of H, the earth with all
11:17 he shut up the H, so that there be
11:21 as long as the H are above the earth.
28:12 his good treasury the H, to give the rain
28:23 And the H over your head shall be brass,
32:1 "Give ear, O H, and I will speak; and
33:26 who rides through the H to your help, and
33:28 and wine; yea, his H drop down dew.
Judg 5:4 earth trembled, and the H dropped, yea, the clouds
2Sam 21:10 upon them from the H; and she did not
22:8 the foundations of the H trembled and quaked,
22:10 He bowed the H, and came down; thick darkness
1Kgs 8:12 the sun in the H, but has said that
18:45 a little while the H grew black with clouds
2Kgs 23:5 the constellations, and all the host of the H
1Chr 16:26 peoples are idols; but the LORD made the H
16:31 Let the H be glad, and let the earth
29:11 that is in the H and in the earth
2Chr 7:13 I shut up the H so that there is
Ezra 9:6 and our guilt has mounted up to the H
Neh 9:6 heaven, the heaven of H, with all their host,
Tob 8:5 Let the H and all thy creatures bless thee.
Jud 13:18 God, who created the H and the earth, who
Job 9:8 alone stretched out the H, and trampled the waves
14:12 not again; till the H are no more he
15:15 holy ones, and the H are not clean in
20:6 mount up to the H, and his head reach
20:27 The H will reveal his iniquity, and the earth
22:12 "Is not God high in the H
26:13 By his wind the H were made fair; his
28:24 of the earth, and sees everything under the H
35:5 Look at the H, and see; and behold the
38:33 Do you know the ordinances of the H
38:37 the waterskins of the H,
Ps 2:4 who sits in the H laughs; the LORD has
8:1 whose glory above the H is chanted
8:3 I look at thy H, the work of thy
18:9 He bowed the H, and came down; thick darkness
18:13 also thundered in the H, and the Most High
19:1 The H are telling the glory of God; and
19:6 the end of the H, and its circuit to
33:6 of the LORD the H were made, and all
36:5 LORD, extends to the H, thy faithfulness to the
50:4 He calls to the H above and to the
50:6 The H declare his righteousness, for God himself is
57:5 Be exalted, O God, above the H
57:10 is great to the H, thy faithfulness to the
57:11 Be exalted, O God, above the H
68:8 the earth quaked, the H poured down rain, at
68:33 who rides in the H, the ancient heavens; lo,
68:33 the heavens, the ancient H; lo, he sends forth
71:19 and thy righteousness, O God, reach the high H
73:9 their mouths against the H, and their tongue struts
76:8 From the H thou didst utter judgment; the earth
78:26 to blow in the H, and by his power
78:69 sanctuary like the high H, like the earth, which
89:2 for ever, thy faithfulness is firm as the H
89:5 [Selah] Let the H praise thy wonders, O LORD,
89:11 The H are thine, the earth also is thine;
89:29 and his throne as the days of the H
96:5 peoples are idols; but the LORD made the H
96:11 Let the H be glad, and let the earth
97:6 The H proclaim his righteousness; and all the
102:25 the earth, and the H are the work of
103:11 For as the H are high above the earth,
103:19 his throne in the H, and his kingdom rules
104:2 hast stretched out the H like a tent,
108:4 is great above the H, thy faithfulness reaches to
108:5 Be exalted, O God, above the H
113:4 above all nations, and his glory above the H
113:6 far down upon the H and the earth?
115:3 God is in the H; he does whatever he
115:16 The H are the LORD's heavens, but the earth
115:16 heavens are the LORD's H, but the earth he
119:89 LORD, thy word is firmly fixed in the H
123:1 eyes, O thou who art enthroned in the H
136:5 by understanding made the H, for his steadfast love
144:5 Bow thy H, O LORD, and come down!
147:8 He covers the H with clouds, he prepares rain
148:1 the LORD from the H, praise him in the
148:4 Praise him, you highest H, and you waters above
148:4 you highest heavens, and you waters above the H
Prov 3:19 understanding he established the H;
8:27 When he established the H, I was there, when
25:3 As the H for height, and the earth for
Wis 9:10 forth from the holy H, and from the throne
9:16 who has traced out what is in the H
Sir 48:3 he shut up the H, and also three times
51:19 my hands to the H, and lamented my ignorance
Is 1:2 Hear, O H, and give ear, O earth; for
13:5 the end of the H, the LORD and the
13:10 the stars of the H and their constellations will
13:13 I will make the H tremble, and the earth
24:4 languishes and withers; the H languish together with
34:5 its fill in the H; behold, it descends for
40:12 and marked off the H with a span, enclosed
40:22 who stretches out the H like a curtain, and
42:5 LORD, who created the H and stretched them out,
44:23 Sing, O H, for the LORD has done it;
44:24 who stretched out the H alone, who spread out
45:8 "Shower, O H, from above, and let the skies
45:12 that stretched out the H, and I commanded all
45:18 LORD, who created the H (he is God!), who
47:13 those who divide the H, who gaze at the
48:13 hand spread out the H; when I call to
49:13 Sing for joy, O H, and exult, O earth;
50:3 I clothe the H with blackness, and make sackcloth
51:6 your eyes to the H, and look at the

51:6 earth beneath; for the H will vanish like smoke,
51:13 who stretched out the H and laid the foundations
51:16 hand, stretching out the H and laying the foundations
55:9 For as the H are higher than the earth,
64:1 thou wouldst rend the H and come down, that
65:17 behold, I create new H and a new earth;
66:22 "For as the new H and the new earth
Jer 2:12 Be appalled, O H, at this, be shocked, be
4:23 void; and to the H, and they had no
4:28 shall mourn, and the H above be black; for
8:7 the stork in the H knows her times; and
10:2 the signs of the H because the nations are
10:11 did not make the H and the earth shall
10:11 perish from the earth and from under the H
10:12 and by his understanding stretched out the H
10:13 of waters in the H, and he makes the
14:22 Or can the H give showers?
31:37 the LORD: "If the H above can be measured,
32:17 who hast made the H and the earth by
51:15 and by his understanding stretched out the H
51:16 of waters in the H, and he makes the
51:48 Then the H and the earth, and all that
Lam 3:66 them from under thy H, O LORD."
4:19 the vultures in the H; they chased us on
Bar 6:67 show signs in the H and among the nations,
Ezek 1:1 the river Chebar, the H were opened, and I
32:7 I will cover the H, and make their stars
Dan 3:59 Bless the Lord, you H, sing praise to him
Hos 2:21 I will answer the H and they shall answer
Joel 2:10 quakes before them, the H tremble.
2:30 give portents in the H and on the earth,
3:16 from Jerusalem, and the H and the earth shake.
Amos 9:6 upper chambers in the H, and founds his vault
Nah 3:16 your merchants more than the stars of the H
Hab 3:3 His glory covered the H, and the earth was
Zeph 1:5 the host of the H; those who bow down
Hag 1:10 Therefore the H above you have withheld the dew,
2:6 I will shake the H and the earth and
2:21 about to shake the H and the earth,
Zech 2:6 four winds of the H, says the LORD.
8:12 its increase, and the H shall give their dew;
12:1 who stretched out the H and founded the earth
2Mac 15:23 O Sovereign of the H, send a good angel
Mt 3:16 water, and behold, the H were opened and he
24:29 the powers of the H will be shaken;
Mk 1:10 immediately he saw the H opened and the Spirit
13:25 the powers in the H will be shaken.
Lk 12:33 a treasure in the H that does not fail,
21:26 the powers of the H will be shaken.
Acts 2:34 not ascend into the H; but he himself says,
7:56 "Behold, I see the H opened, and the Son
2Cor 5:1 house not made with hands, eternal in the H
Eph 4:10 far above all the H, that he might fill
Heb 1:10 the beginning, and the H are the work of
4:14 has passed through the H, Jesus, the Son of
7:26 separated from sinners, exalted above the H
2Pet 3:5 the word of God H existed long ago, and
3:7 the same word the H and earth that now
3:10 thief, and then the H will pass away with
3:12 because of which the H will be kindled and
3:13 we wait for new H and a new earth

HEAVIER (5)

Ex 5:9 to our God.' Let H work be laid upon
Job 6:3 then it would be H than the sand of
Prov 27:3 a fool's provocation is H than both.
Wis 17:21 receive them; but still H than darkness were they
Sir 22:12 What is H than lead?

HEAVILY (7)

Ex 14:25 so that they drove H; and the Egyptians said,
Judg 1:35 house of Joseph rested H upon them, and they
Sir 31:19 He does not breathe H upon his bed.
39:28 their anger they scourge H; in the time of
Ezek 27:25 you were filled and H laden in the heart
1Mac 2:30 cattle, because evils pressed H upon them.
2Mac 15:18 lay upon them less H; their greatest and first

HEAVY (60)

Ex 1:10 to afflict them with H burdens; and they built
9:18 I will cause very H hail to fall, such
9:24 of the hail, very H hail, such as had
18:18 the thing is too H for you; you are
Num 11:14 the burden is too H for me.
1Sam 4:18 died, for he was an old man, and H
5:6 of the LORD was H upon the people of
5:7 for his hand is H upon us and upon
5:11 of God was very H there;
2Sam 14:26 it; when it was H on him, he cut
1Kgs 12:4 said to Rehoboam, "Your father made our yoke H
12:4 your father and his H yoke upon us, and
12:10 father made our yoke H, but do you lighten
12:11 laid upon you a H yoke, I will add
12:14 father made your yoke H, but I will add
14:6 I am charged with H tidings for you.
2Chr 10:4 said to Rehoboam, "Your father made our yoke H
10:4 your father and his H yoke upon us, and
10:10 father made our yoke H, but do you lighten
10:11 laid upon you a H yoke, I will add
10:14 father made your yoke H, but I will add
Ezra 10:9 and because of the H rain.
10:13 is a time of H rain; we cannot stand
Neh 5:15 were before me laid H burdens upon the people,
5:18 because the servitude was H upon this people.
Job 23:2 bitter, his hand is H in spite of my
33:7 pressure will not be H upon you.
Ps 32:4 night thy hand was H upon me; my strength
38:4 like a burden too H for me.
88:7 Thy wrath lies H upon me, and thou dost
144:14 may our cattle be H with young, suffering no
Prov 25:20 sings songs to a H heart is like one
27:3 stone is H, and sand is weighty, but a
Eccl 6:1 sun, and it lies H upon men:
8:6 although man's trouble lies H upon him.
Wis 17:21 over those men alone H night was spread, an
Sir 6:21 him down like a H testing stone, and he
29:13 and more than a H spear, it will fight
33:28 if he does not obey, make his fetters H
40:1 every man, and a H yoke is upon the
Is 6:10 fat, and their ears H, and shut their eyes;
24:20 hut; its transgression lies H upon it, and it
47:6 on the aged you made your yoke exceedingly H
Lam 3:7 escape; he has put H chains on me;
Zech 12:3 will make Jerusalem a H stone for all the
1Mac 5:3 He dealt them a H blow and humbled them
5:34 he dealt them a H blow.
8:7 him should pay a H tribute and give hostages
8:31 you made your yoke H upon our friends and
13:22 that night a very H snow fell, and he
2Mac 4:16 For this reason H disaster overtook them, and those
Mt 11:28 who labor and are H laden, and I will
13:15 and their ears are H of hearing, and their
23:4 They bind H burdens, hard to bear, and lay
26:43 and found them sleeping, for their eyes were H
Mk 14:40 their eyes were very H; and they did not
Lk 9:32 were with him were H with sleep, and when
Acts 28:27 and their ears are H of hearing, and their
Rev 11:19 thunder, an earthquake, and H hail.
16:21 great hailstones, H as a hundred-weight, dropped

HEBER (11)

Gen 46:17 the sons of Beriah: H and Malchi-el
Num 26:45 sons of Beriah: of H, the family of the
Judg 4:11 Now H the Kenite had separated from the Kenites,
4:17 Jael, the wife of H the Kenite; for there
4:17 and the house of H the Kenite.
4:21 Jael the wife of H took a tent peg,
5:24 Jael, the wife of H the Kenite, of tent-dwelling
1Chr 4:18 the father of Gedor, H the father of Soco,
7:31 The sons of Beriah: H and Malchi-el, who was
7:32 H was the father of Japhlet, Shomer, Hotham, and
8:17 Zebadiah, Meshullam, Hizki, H,

HEBERITES

Num 26:45 the family of the H; of Malchi-el, the family

HEBREW (28)

Gen 14:13 and told Abram the H, who was living by
39:14 brought among us a H to insult us; he
39:17 same story, saying, "The H servant, whom you have
41:12 A young H was there with us, a servant
Ex 1:14 Egypt said to the H midwives, one of whom
1:15 as midwife to the H women, and see them
1:18 to Pharaoh, "Because the H women are not like
2:7 a nurse from the H women to nurse the
2:11 an Egyptian beating a H, one of his people.
21:2 When you buy a H slave, he shall serve
Deut 15:12 "If your brother, a H man, or a Hebrew
15:12 Hebrew man, or a H woman, is sold to
Jud 12:11 now and persuade the H woman who is in
14:18 One H woman has brought disgrace upon the house
Jer 34:9 should set free his H slaves, male and female,

34:14 set free the fellow H who has been sold
Jon 1:9 them, "I am a H; and I fear the
Jn 5:2 Gate a pool, in H called Beth-zatha, which has
19:13 The Pavement, and in H, Gabbatha.
19:17 which is called in H Golgotha.
19:20 it was written in H, in Latin, and in
20:16 to him in H, "Rab-boni!" (which means Teacher).
Acts 21:40 to them in the H language, saying:
22:2 addressed them in the H language, they were the
26:14 to me in the H language, 'Saul, Saul, why
Phil 3:5 tribe of Benjamin, a H born of Hebrews; as
Rev 9:11 pit; his name in H is Abaddon, and in
16:16 which is called in H Armageddon.

HEBREWS (25)

Gen 40:15 the land of the H; and here also I
43:32 eat bread with the H, for that is an
Ex 1:21 is born to the H you shall cast into
2:6 is one of the H children."
2:13 next day, behold, two H were struggling together;
3:18 the God of the H, has met with us;
5:3 "The God of the H has met with us;
7:16 the God of the H, sent me to you,
9:1 the God of the H, "Let my people go,
9:13 the God of the H, "Let my people go,
10:3 the God of the H, 'How long will you
1Sam 4:6 the camp of the H mean?" And when they
4:9 become slaves to the H as they have been
13:3 land, saying, "Let the H hear."
13:19 Philistines said, "Lest the H make themselves
14:11 the Philistines said, "Look, H are coming out of
14:21 Now the H who had been with the Philistines
29:3 said, "What are these H doing here?" And Achish
Jud 10:12 a daughter of the H, but I am fleeing
2Mac 7:31 of evil against the H, will certainly not escape
11:13 and realized that the H were invincible because the
15:37 city has been in the possession of the H
Acts 6:1 Hellenists murmured against the H because their
2Cor 11:22 Are they H
Phil 3:5 a Hebrew born of H; as to the law

HEBRON (74)

Gen 13:18 Mamre, which are at H; and there he built
23:2 at Kiriath-arba (that is, H in the land of
23:19 of Mamre (that is, H in the land of
35:27 or Kiriath-arba (that is, H, where Abraham and Isaac
37:14 from the valley of H, and he came to
Ex 6:18 of Kohath: Amram, Izhar, H, and Uzziel, the years
Num 3:19 their families: Amram, Izhar, H, and Uzziel.
13:22 Negeb, and came to H; and Ahiman, Sheshai, and
13:22 H was built seven years before Zoan in Egypt.)
Josh 10:3 to Hoham king of H, to Piram king of
10:5 Jerusalem, the king of H, the king of Jarmuth,
10:23 Jerusalem, the king of H, the king of Jarmuth,
10:36 Israel from Eglon to H; and they assaulted it,
10:39 he had done to H and to Libnah and
11:21 the hill country, from H, from Debir, from Anab,
12:10 one; the king of H, one;
14:13 him; and he gave H to Caleb the son
14:14 So H became the inheritance of Caleb the son
14:15 Now the name of H formerly was Kiriath-arba; this
15:13 Judah, Kiriath-arba, that is, H (Arba was the father
15:54 Kiriath-arba (that is, H, and Zior: nine cities
20:7 and Kiriath-arba (that is, H in the hill country
21:11 of Anak), that is H, in the hill country
21:13 the priest they gave H, the city of refuge
Judg 1:10 Canaanites who dwelt in H (now the name of
1:10 (now the name of H was formerly Kiriath-arba); and
1:20 And H was given to Caleb, as Moses had
16:3 the top of the hill that is before H
1Sam 30:31 Borashan, in Athach, in H, for all the places
2Sam 2:1 And he said, "To H
2:3 household; and they dwelt in the towns of H
2:11 David was king in H over the house of
2:32 night, and the day broke upon them at H
3:2 born to David at H: his first-born was Amnon,
3:5 These were born to David in H
3:12 messengers to David at H, saying, "To whom does
3:19 to tell David at H all that Israel and
3:20 men to David at H, David made a feast
3:22 not with David at H, for he had sent
3:27 when Abner returned to H, Joab took him aside
3:32 They buried Abner at H; and the king lifted
4:1 Abner had died at H, his courage failed, and
4:8 brought the head of Ish-bosheth to David at H
4:12 feet, and hanged them beside the pool at H
4:12 buried it in the tomb of Abner at H
5:1 came to David at H, and said, "Behold, we
5:3 to the king at H; and King David made
5:3 covenant with them at H before the LORD, and
5:5 At H he reigned over Judah seven years and
5:13 after he came from H; and more sons and
15:7 which I have vowed to the LORD, in H
15:9 So he arose, and went to H
15:10 the trumpet, then say, 'Absalom is king at H
1Kgs 2:11 reigned seven years in H, and thirty-three years in
1Chr 2:42 The sons of Mareshah: H
2:43 The sons of H: Korah, Tappuah, Rekem, and Shema.
3:1 born to him in H: the first-born Amnon, by
3:4 born to him in H, where he reigned for
6:2 of Kohath: Amram, Izhar, H, and Uzziel.
6:18 of Kohath: Amram, Izhar, H, and Uzziel.
6:55 to them they gave H in the land of
6:57 the cities of refuge: H, Libnah with its pasture
11:1 together to David at H, and said, "Behold, we
11:3 to the king at H; and David made a
11:3 covenant with them at H before the LORD, and
12:23 came to David in H, to turn the kingdom
12:38 battle order, came to H with full intent to
15:9 of the sons of H, Eliel the chief, with
23:12 of Kohath: Amram, Izhar, H, and Uzziel, four.
23:19 The sons of H: Jeriah the chief, Amariah the
24:23 The sons of H: Jeriah the chief, Amariah the
29:27 reigned seven years in H, and thirty-three years in
2Chr 11:10 Azekah, Zorah, Aijalon, and H, fortified cities which
1Mac 5:65 He struck H and its villages and tore down

HEBRONITES (6)

Num 3:27 the family of the H, and the family of
26:58 the family of the H, the family of the
1Chr 26:23 Amramites, the Izharites, the H, and the Uzzielites--
26:30 Of the H, Hashabiah and his brethren, one thousand
26:31 Of the H, Jerijah was chief of the Hebronites
26:31 was chief of the H of whatever genealogy or

HEDGE (6)

Job 1:10 thou not put a H about him and his
Is 5:5 I will remove its H, and it shall be
Hos 2:6 drink.' Therefore I will H up her way with
Mic 7:4 brier, the most upright of them a thorn H
Mt 21:33 vineyard, and set a H around it, and dug
Mk 12:1 vineyard, and set a H around it, and dug

HEDGED

Job 3:23 hid, whom God has H in?

HEDGEHOG (2)

Is 14:23 a possession of the H, and pools of water,
Zeph 2:14 the vulture and the H shall lodge in her

HEDGES (2)

Jer 49:3 lament, and run to and fro among the H
Lk 14:23 to the highways and H, and compel people to

HEED (136)

Gen 16:11 the LORD has given H to your affliction.
31:24 said to him, "Take H that you say not
31:29 last night, saying, 'Take H that you speak to
39:23 the prison paid no H to anything that was
Ex 4:8 God said, "or H the first sign, they may
4:9 these two signs or H your voice, you shall
5:2 LORD, that I should H his voice and let
10:28 away from me; take H to yourself; never see
15:26 his eyes, and give H to his commandments and
18:24 So Moses gave H to the voice of his
19:12 round about, saying, 'Take H that you do not
23:13 Take H to all that I have said to
23:21 Give H to him and hearken to his voice,
34:12 Take H to yourself, lest you make a covenant
Num 23:12 "Must I not take H to speak what the
28:2 odor, you shall take H to offer to me
Deut 2:4 So take good H;
4:1 now, O Israel, give H to the statutes and
4:9 "Only take H, and keep your soul diligently, lest
4:15 "Therefore take good H to yourselves.
4:23 Take H to yourselves, lest you forget the covenant
6:12 are full, then take H lest you forget the
8:11 "Take H lest you forget the LORD your God,
11:16 Take H lest your heart be deceived, and you
12:13 Take H that you do not offer your burnt
12:19 Take H that you do not forsake the Levite
12:28 Be careful to H all these words which I

H

HEEDED (11)

HEEDING (2)

HEEDLESS

HEEDS (6)

HEEL (7)

HEELS (5)

HEGAI (4)

HEGEMONIDES

HEGLAM

HEIFER (18)

19:9 the ashes of the H, and deposit them outside
19:10 the ashes of the H shall wash his clothes,
Deut 21:3 man shall take a H which has never been
21:4 city shall bring the H down to a valley
21:4 and shall break the H's neck there in the
21:6 their hands over the H whose neck was broken
Judg 14:18 not plowed with my H, you would not have
1Sam 16:2 LORD said, "Take a H with you, and say,
Jer 46:20 "A beautiful H is Egypt, but a gadfly from
50:11 are wanton as a H at grass, and neigh
Hos 4:16 Like a stubborn H, Israel is stubborn; can the
10:11 Ephraim was a trained H that loved to thresh,
Heb 9:13 the ashes of a H sanctifies for the purification

HEIFERS

Sir 38:26 and he is careful about fodder for the H

HEIGHT (62)

Gen 6:15 fifty cubits, and its H thirty cubits.
Ex 25:10 breadth, and a cubit and a half its H
25:23 breadth, and a cubit and a half its H
27:1 be square, and its H shall be three cubits.
27:18 breadth fifty, and the H five cubits, with hangings
30:2 cubits shall be its H; its horns shall be
37:1 breadth, and a cubit and a half its H
37:10 and a half its H;
37:25 two cubits was its H; its horns were of
38:1 it was square, and three cubits was its H
Num 23:3 And he went to a bare H
1Sam 16:7 appearance or on the H of his stature, because
17:4 Goliath, of Gath, whose H was six cubits and
22:6 tamarisk tree on the H, with his spear in
1Kgs 6:26 The H of one cherub was ten cubits, and
7:2 fifty cubits, and its H thirty cubits, and it
7:15 Eighteen cubits was the H of one pillar, and
7:16 of the pillars; the H of the one capital
7:16 five cubits, and the H of the other capital
7:32 the stands; and the H of a wheel was
2Kgs 25:17 The H of the one pillar was eighteen cubits,
25:17 capital of bronze; the H of the capital was
2Chr 3:4 the house; and its H was a hundred and
33:14 to a very great H; he also put commanders
Ezra 6:3 offerings are brought; its H shall be sixty cubits
Neh 4:6 the wall was joined together to half its H
Jud 7:10 spears but on the H of the mountains where
Job 20:6 Though his H mount up to the heavens, and
Ps 102:19 down from his holy H, from heaven the LORD
Prov 25:3 As the heavens for H, and the earth for
Sir 1:3 The H of heaven, the breadth of the earth,
17:27 the host of the H of heaven; but all
Is 10:33 power; the great in H will be hewn down,
16:3 like night at the H of noon; hide the
22:16 a tomb on the H, and carve a habitation
26:5 the inhabitants of the H, the lofty city.
37:24 came to its remotest H, its densest forest.
Jer 26:18 the house a wooded H
31:12 sing aloud on the H of Zion, and they
49:16 rock, who hold the H of the hill.
51:53 should fortify her strong H, yet destroyers would
52:21 for the pillars, the H of the one pillar
52:22 capital of bronze; the H of the one capital
Bar 5:5 Jerusalem, stand upon the H and look toward the
Ezek 17:23 mountain; on the mountain H of Israel will I
19:11 was seen in its H with the mass of
20:40 holy mountain, the mountain H of Israel, says the
31:3 shade, and of great H, its top among the
31:10 was proud of its H,
31:14 may grow to lofty H or set their tops
31:14 up to them in H; for they are all
40:5 one reed; and the H, one reed.
43:13 this shall be the H of the altar:
Dan 3:1 image of gold, whose H was sixty cubits and
4:10 the earth; and its H was great.
Amos 2:9 Amorite before them, whose H was like the height
2:9 height was like the H of the cedars, and
Mic 3:12 and the mountain of the house a wooded H
2Mac 6:15 us afterward when our sins have reached their H
Rom 8:39 come, nor powers, nor H, nor depth, nor anything
Eph 3:18 breadth and length and H and depth,
Rev 21:16 length and breadth and H are equal.

HEIGHTEN

Sir 28:10 his wealth he will H his wrath.

HEIGHTS (29)

Num 14:40 went up to the H of the hill country,
14:44 go up to the H of the hill country,
21:28 the lords of the H of the Arnon.
Judg 5:18 Naphtali too, on the H of the field.
2Sam 22:34 hinds' feet, and set me secure on the H
2Kgs 19:23 have gone up the H of the mountains, to
Ps 18:33 hinds' feet, and set me secure on the H
95:4 of the earth; the H of the mountains are
148:1 LORD from the heavens, praise him in the H
Prov 8:2 On the H beside the way, in the paths
Sir 24:13 a cypress on the H of Hermon.
26:16 sun rising in the H of the Lord, so
43:1 pride of the heavenly H is the clear firmament,
43:9 gleaming array in the H of the Lord.
Is 14:14 will ascend above the H of the clouds, I
33:16 will dwell on the H; his place of defense
37:24 have gone up the H of the mountains, to
41:18 rivers on the bare H, and fountains in the
49:9 ways, on all bare H shall be their pasture;
58:14 you ride upon the H of the earth; I
Jer 3:2 eyes to the bare H, and see!
3:21 voice on the bare H is heard, the weeping
4:11 wind from the bare H in the desert toward
7:29 lamentation on the bare H, for the LORD has
12:12 Upon all the bare H in the desert destroyers
14:6 stand on the bare H, they pant for air
Ezek 34:14 and upon the mountain H of Israel shall be
36:2 'Aha!' and, 'The ancient H have become our
Amos 4:13 and treads on the H of the earth--the

HEINOUS

Job 31:11 that would be a H crime; that would be

HEIR (17)

Gen 15:2 continue childless, and the H of my house is
15:3 slave born in my house will be my H
15:4 shall not be your H; your own son shall
15:4 your heir; your own son shall be your H
21:10 woman shall not be H with my son Isaac."
2Sam 14:7 they would destroy the H also.
Tob 3:15 child to be his H, no near kinsman or
Prov 29:21 childhood, will in the end find him his H
Sir 23:22 husband and provides an H by a stranger.
Jer 49:1 Has he no H
Mt 21:38 themselves, 'This is the H; come, let us kill
Mk 12:7 another, 'This is the H; come, let us kill
Lk 20:14 themselves, 'This is the H; let us kill him,
Gal 4:1 I mean that the H, as long as he
4:7 a son, and if a son then an H
Heb 1:2 whom he appointed the H of all things, through
11:7 world and became an H of the righteousness which

HEIRS (11)

Rom 4:14 are to be the H, faith is null and
8:17 and if children, then H, heirs of God and
8:17 if children, then heirs, H of God and fellow
8:17 of God and fellow H with Christ, provided we
Gal 3:29 you are Abraham's offspring, H according to promise.
Eph 3:6 the Gentiles are fellow H, members of the same
Tit 3:7 his grace and become H in hope of eternal
Heb 6:17 more convincingly to the H of the promise the
11:9 with Isaac and Jacob, H with him of the
Jas 2:5 rich in faith and H of the kingdom which
1Pet 3:7 since you are joint H of the grace of

HELAH (2)

1Chr 4:5 Tekoa, had two wives, H and Naarah;
4:7 The sons of H: Zereth, Izhar, and Ethnan.

HELAM (2)

2Sam 10:16 and they came to H, with Shobach the commander
10:17 together, and crossed the Jordan, and came to H

HELBAH

Judg 1:31 of Achzib, or of H, or of Aphik, or

HELBON

Ezek 27:18 every kind; wine of H, and white wool,

HELD (79)

Gen 34:5 the field, so Jacob H his peace until they
Ex 17:11 Whenever Moses H up his hand, Israel prevailed;
17:12 and Aaron and Hur H up his hands, one
Lev 10:3 And Aaron H his peace.
19:20 or given her freedom, an inquiry shall be H
Num 24:11 but the LORD has H you back from honor."
Deut 4:4 Peor; but you who H fast to the LORD

H

Judg 9:27 and trod them, and H festival, and went into
16:26 to the lad who H him by the hand,
Ruth 3:15 So she H it, and he measured out six
1Sam 9:6 a man that is H in honor; all that
10:27 But he H his peace.
2Sam 6:22 them I shall be H in honor."
1Kgs 7:26 of a lily; it H two thousand baths.
7:38 of bronze; each laver H forty baths, each laver
8:65 So Solomon H the feast at that time, and
2Kgs 18:6 For he H fast to the LORD; he did
1Chr 16:25 he is to be H in awe above all
2Chr 4:5 of a lily; it H over three thousand baths.
7:8 At that time Solomon H the feast for seven
7:9 the eighth day they H a solemn assembly; for
11:12 So he H Judah and Benjamin.
Neh 4:16 on construction, and half H the spears, shields, bows,
4:17 and with the other H his weapon.
4:21 and half of them H the spears from the
5:7 And I H a great assembly against them,
5:16 I also H to the work on this wall,
Jud 12:10 the fourth day Holofernes H a banquet for his
Esth 5:2 his sight and he H out to Esther the
7:4 women, I would have H my peace; for our
8:4 And the king H out the golden scepter to
11:11 exalted and consumed those H in honor.
Job 23:11 My foot has H fast to his steps; I
Ps 17:5 My steps have H fast to thy paths, my
39:2 dumb and silent, I H my peace to no
94:18 steadfast love, O LORD, H me up.
106:46 by all those who H them captive.
Prov 30:10 you, and you be H guilty.
Song 3:4 I H him, and would not let him go
7:5 purple; a king is H captive in the tresses.
Wis 3:17 long they will be H of no account, and
5:4 man whom we once H in derision and made
15:12 and life a festival H for profit, for he
17:2 men supposed that they H the holy nation in
17:4 the inner chamber that H them protected them from
18:23 heaps, he intervened and H back the wrath, and
Sir 1:17 glory of those who H her fast.
9:12 they will not be H guiltless as long as
46:4 Was not the sun H back by his hand?
48:22 the Lord, and he H strongly to the ways
Is 38:17 bitterness; but thou hast H back my life from
42:14 long time I have H my peace, I have
57:11 Have I not H my peace, even for a
Jer 48:26 he too shall be H in derision.
50:33 took them captive have H them fast, they refuse
Ezek 23:32 be laughed at and H in derision, for it
1Mac 3:45 the sons of aliens H the citadel; it was
13:15 with the offices he H, that we are detaining
2Mac 4:18 quadrennial games were being H at Tyre and the
4:27 And Menelaus H the office, but he did not
12:24 in safety, because he H the parents of most
14:22 of the enemy; they H the proper conference.
Mt 14:5 the people, because they H him to be a
21:46 the multitudes, because they H him to be a
Mk 3:6 and immediately H counsel with the Herodi-ans
11:31 the people, for all H that John was a
15:1 and the whole council H a consultation; and they
Jn 19:29 vinegar on hyssop and H it to his mouth.
Acts 2:24 for him to be H by it.
5:13 them, but the people H them in high honor.
5:34 teacher of the law, H in honor by all
25:21 commanded him to be H until I could send
Rom 3:19 whole world may be H accountable to God.
7:6 dead to that which H us captive, so that
10:21 day long I have H out my hands to
1Cor 4:10 You are H in honor, but we in disrepute.
Heb 13:4 Let marriage be H in honor among all, and
Rev 1:16 his right hand he H seven stars, from his
9:15 released, who had been H ready for the hour,

HELDAI (3)

1Chr 27:15 twelfth month, was H the Netophathite, of Othni-el;
Zech 6:10 "Take from the exiles H, Tobijah, and Jedaiah, who
6:14 as a reminder to H, Tobijah, Jedaiah, and Josiah

HELEB

2Sam 23:29 Ahohite, Maharai of Netophah, H the son of Baanah

HELECH

Ezek 27:11 men of Arvad and H were upon your walls

HELED

1Chr 11:30 Ahohite, Maharai of Netophah, H the son of Baanah

HELEK (2)

Num 26:30 of the Iezerites; of H, the family of the
Josh 17:2 by their families, Abi-ezer, H, Asriel, Shechem,

HELEKITES

Num 26:30 the family of the H;

HELEM

1Chr 7:35 The sons of H his brother: Zophah, Imna, Shelesh,

HELEPH

Josh 19:33 its boundary ran from H, from the oak in

HELEZ (5)

2Sam 23:26 Harod, Elika of Harod, H the Paltite, Ira the
1Chr 2:39 was the father of H, and Helez of Ele-asah.
2:39 father of Helez, and H of Ele-asah.
11:27 Bethlehem, Shammoth of Harod, H the Pelonite,
27:10 the seventh month, was H the Pelonite, of the

HELI

Lk 3:23 Joseph, the son of H,

HELIODORUS (13)

2Mac 3:7 The king chose H, who was in charge of
3:8 H at once set out on his journey, ostensibly
3:13 But H, because of the king's commands which he
3:23 who had entrusted it, H went on with what
3:25 it rushed furiously at H and struck at him
3:31 Quickly some of H friends asked Onias to call
3:32 Jews with regard to H, offered sacrifice for the
3:33 men appeared again to H dressed in the same
3:35 Then H offered sacrifice to the Lord and made
3:37 When the king asked H what sort of person
3:40 of the episode of H and the protection of
4:1 he who had incited H and had been the
5:18 came forward, just as H was, whom Seleucus the

HELIOPOLIS

Jer 43:13 break the obelisks of H which is in the

HELKAI

Neh 12:15 Harim, Adna; of Meraioth, H;

HELKATH (2)

Josh 19:25 Its territory included H, Hali, Beten, Achshaph,
21:31 with its pasture lands, H with its pasture lands,

HELKATH-HAZZURIM

2Sam 2:16 that place was called H, which is at Gibeon.

HELL (13)

Mt 5:22 be liable to the H of fire.
5:29 than that your whole body be thrown into H
5:30 members than that your whole body go into H
10:28 who can destroy both soul and body in H
18:9 be thrown into the H of fire.
23:14 much a child of H as yourselves.
23:32 how are you to escape being sentenced to H
Mk 9:43 hands to go to H, to the unquenchable fire.
9:44 than with two feet to be thrown into H
9:45 to be thrown into H,
Lk 12:5 power to cast into H; yes, I tell you,
Jas 3:6 cycle of nature, and set on fire by H
2Pet 2:4 but cast them into H and committed them to

HELLENISTS (2)

Acts 6:1 in number, the H murmured against the Hebrews
9:29 and disputed against the H; but they were seeking

HELLENIZATION

2Mac 4:13 such an extreme of H and increase in the

HELMET (11)

1Sam 17:5 He had a H of bronze on his head,
17:38 armor; he put a H of bronze on his
Ps 60:7 mine; Ephraim is my H; Judah is my scepter.
108:8 mine; Ephraim is my H; Judah my scepter.
Wis 5:18 impartial justice as a H;
Is 59:17 a breastplate, and a H of salvation upon his
Ezek 23:24 with buckler, shield, and H, and I will commit
27:10 hung the shield and H in you; they gave
38:5 them with shield and H;
Eph 6:17 And take the H of salvation, and the sword
1Thes 5:8 love, and for a H the hope of salvation.

HELMETS (3)

2Chr 26:14 the army shields, spears, H, coats of mail, bows,
Jer 46:4 your stations with your H, polish your spears, put
1Mac 6:35 mail, and with brass H on their heads; and

HELON (5)

Num 1:9 Eliab the son of H;
2:7 Eliab the son of H,
7:24 Eliab the son of H, the leader of the
7:29 was the offering of Eliab the son of H
10:16 men of Zebulun was Eliab the son of H

HELP (242)

Gen 4:1 a man with the H of the LORD."
49:25 your father who will H you, by God Almighty
Ex 2:23 and cried out for H, and their cry under
18:4 my father was my H, and delivered me from
23:5 with it, you shall H him to lift it
Num 1:44 Aaron numbered with the H of the leaders of
Deut 22:1 astray, and withhold your H from them; you shall
22:3 and you find; you may not withhold your H
22:4 way, and withhold your H from them; you shall
22:4 from them; you shall H him to lift them
22:24 did not cry for H though she was in
22:27 young woman cried for H there was no one
28:29 be no one to H you.
28:31 be no one to H you.
32:38 them rise up and H you, let them be
33:7 him, and be a H against his adversaries."
33:26 the heavens to your H, and in his majesty
33:29 the shield of your H, and the sword of
Josh 1:14 your brethren and shall H them,
10:4 up to me, and H me, and let us
10:6 and save us, and H us; for all the
10:33 Gezer came up to H Lachish; and Joshua smote
Judg 4:3 to the LORD for H; for he had nine
5:23 came not to the H of the LORD, to
5:23 the LORD, to the H of the LORD against
6:6 of Israel cried for H to the LORD.
2Sam 8:5 of Damascus came to H Hadadezer king of Zobah,
10:11 me, then you shall H me; but if the
10:11 I will come and H you.
10:19 the Syrians feared to H the Ammonites any more.
14:4 did obeisance, and said, H, O king."
18:3 that you send us H from the city."
22:36 thy salvation, and thy H made me great.
23:5 to prosper all my H and my desire?
2Kgs 6:26 out to him, saying, H, my lord, O king!"
6:27 the LORD will not H you, whence shall I
6:27 you, whence shall I H you?
14:26 there was none to H Israel.
15:19 silver, that he might H him to confirm his
1Chr 5:20 and when they received H against them, the Hagrites
12:17 me in friendship to H me, my heart will
12:19 (Yet he did not H them, for the rulers
12:22 coming to David to H him, until there was
12:33 weapons of war, to H David with singleness of
18:5 of Damascus came to H Hadadezer king of Zobah,
19:12 me, then you shall H me; but if the
19:12 you, then I will H you.
19:19 were not willing to H the Ammonites any more.
22:17 leaders of Israel to H Solomon his son, saying,
24:3 With the H of Zadok of the sons of
2Chr 14:11 none like thee to H, between the mighty and
14:11 H us, O LORD our God, for we rely
16:12 the LORD, but sought H from physicians.
19:2 Jehoshaphat, "Should you H the wicked and love
20:4 Judah assembled to seek H from the LORD; from
25:8 God has power to H or to cast down."
26:13 with mighty power, to H the king against the
28:16 Ahaz sent to the king of Assyria for H
28:21 but it did not H him.
28:23 them that they may H me." But they were
32:8 LORD our God, to H us and to fight
Neh 5:5 in our power to H it, for other men
6:16 been accomplished with the H of our God.
Tob 2:10 but they did not H me.
Jud 6:21 they called on the God of Israel for H
7:26 have no one to H us; God has sold
7:32 pass by, and no H comes for us, I
8:15 does not choose to H us within these five
8:17 call upon him to H us, and he will
9:4 called on thee for H—O God, my God,
13:5 is the time to H thy inheritance, and to
Esth 14:3 only art our King; H me, who am alone
14:14 by thy hand, and H me, who am alone
Job 6:13 truth I have no H in me, and any
24:12 the wounded cries for H; yet God pays no
26:4 With whose H have you uttered words, and whose
29:12 who had none to H him.
30:24 his hand, and in his disaster cry for H
30:28 stand up in the assembly, and cry for H
31:21 fatherless, because I saw H in the gate;
35:9 out; they call for H because of the arm
36:13 do not cry for H when he binds them.
Ps 3:2 me, there is no H for him in God.
12:1 H, LORD; for there is no longer any that
18:6 the LORD; to my God I cried for H
18:35 supported me, and thy H made me great.
18:41 They cried for H, but there was none to
20:2 May he send you H from the sanctuary, and
20:6 that the LORD will H his anointed; he will
21:1 LORD; and in thy H how greatly he exults!
21:5 is great through thy H; splendor and majesty thou
22:11 trouble is near and there is none to H
22:19 O thou my H, hasten to my aid!
27:9 away in anger, thou who hast been my H
28:2 cry to thee for H, as I lift up
30:2 cried to thee for H, and thou hast healed
31:22 my supplications, when I cried to thee for H
33:20 LORD; he is our H and shield.
34:17 the righteous cry for H, the LORD hears, and
35:2 of shield and buckler, and rise for my H
38:22 Make haste to H me, O Lord, my salvation!
40:10 not hid thy saving H within my heart, I
40:13 LORD, make haste to H me!
40:17 Thou art my H and my deliverer; do not
42:5 again praise him, my H
42:11 again praise him, my H and my God.
43:5 again praise him, my H and my God.
44:26 Rise up, come to our H
46:1 strength, a very present H in trouble.
46:5 be moved; God will H her right early.
59:4 thyself, come to my H, and see!
60:11 O grant us H against the foe, for vain
60:11 for vain is the H of man!
63:7 thou hast been my H, and in the shadow
69:13 With thy faithful H
70:1 LORD, make haste to H me!
70:5 Thou art my H and my deliverer; O LORD,
71:12 God, make haste to H me!
71:24 talk of thy righteous H all the day long,
79:9 H us, O God of our salvation, for the
88:1 God, I call for H by day; I cry
88:12 darkness, or thy saving H in the land of
94:17 had not been my H, my soul would soon
106:4 favor to thy people; H me when thou deliverest
107:12 hard labor; they fell down, with none to H
108:6 may be delivered, give H by thy right hand,
108:12 O grant us H against the foe, for vain
108:12 for vain is the H of man!
109:26 H me, O LORD my God!
115:9 He is their H and their shield.
115:10 He is their H and their shield.
115:11 He is their H and their shield.
118:7 on my side to H me; I shall look
119:86 persecute me with falsehood; H me!
119:147 dawn and cry for H; I hope in thy
119:173 hand be ready to H me, for I have
119:175 and let thy ordinances H me.
121:1 From whence does my H come?
121:2 My H comes from the LORD, who made heaven
124:8 Our H is in the name of the LORD,
146:3 son of man, in whom there is no H
146:5 Happy is he whose H is the God of
Prov 20:22 LORD, and he will H you.
28:17 death; let no one H him.
Wis 2:18 God's son, he will H him, and will deliver
13:16 knows that it cannot H itself, for it is
13:16 is only an image and has need of H
16:10 mercy came to their H and healed them.
17:13 expectation of H, being weak, prefers ignorance
19:22 hast not neglected to H them at all times
Sir 2:6 him, and he will H you; make your ways
3:12 O son, H your father in his old age,
4:11 her sons and gives H to those who seek
8:16 sight, and where no H is at hand, he
11:12 is slow and needs H, who lacks strength and
12:4 man, but do not H the sinner.
12:7 man, but do not H the sinner.
12:17 and while pretending to H you, he will trip
24:21 who work with my H will not sin."

HELPED (27)

HELPER (19)

HELPERS (10)

HELPFUL (2)

HELPING (3)

HELPLESS (7)

HELPS (9)

8:31 us away into the H of swine."
8:32 and behold, the whole H rushed down the steep
Mk 5:11 Now a great H of swine was feeding there
5:13 the swine; and the H, numbering about two
Lk 8:32 Now a large H of swine was feeding there
8:33 the swine, and the H rushed down the steep

HERDED

Hos 12:12 for a wife he H sheep.)

HERDS (41)

Gen 13:5 also had flocks and H and tents,
24:35 given him flocks and H, silver and gold, menservants
26:14 possessions of flocks and H, and a great household,
32:7 and the flocks and H and camels, into two
33:13 that the flocks and H giving suck are a
34:28 their flocks and their H, their asses, and whatever
45:10 and your flocks, your H, and all that you
46:32 their flocks, and their H, and all that they
47:1 with their flocks and H and all that they
47:17 horses, the flocks, the H, and the asses: and
47:18 all spent; and the H of cattle are my
50:8 their flocks, and their H were left in the
Ex 9:3 asses, the camels, the H, and the flocks.
10:9 with our flocks and H, for we must hold
10:24 your flocks and your H remain behind."
12:32 your flocks and your H, as you have said,
12:38 them, and very many cattle, both flocks and H
34:3 let no flocks or H feed before that mountain."
Lev 27:32 all the tithe of H and flocks, every tenth
Num 11:22 month!' Shall flocks and H be slaughtered for them,
Deut 8:13 them, and when your H and flocks multiply, and
32:14 of lambs and rams, H of Bashan and goats,
1Sam 30:20 all the flocks and H; and the people drove
2Sam 12:2 very many flocks and H;
1Chr 27:29 Over the H that pastured in Sharon was Shitrai
27:29 the Sharonite; over the H in the valleys was
2Chr 26:10 for he had large H, both in the Shephelah
32:29 himself, and flocks and H in abundance; for God
Neh 10:36 the firstlings of our H and of our flocks;
Jud 2:27 destroyed their flocks and H and sacked their cities
3:3 and our flocks and H, and all our sheepfolds
Prov 27:23 give attention to your H;
Eccl 2:7 also great possessions of H and flocks, more than
Is 65:10 Achor a place for H to lie down, for
Jer 3:24 their flocks and their H, their sons and their
5:17 your flocks and your H; they shall eat up
49:32 shall become booty, their H of cattle a spoil.
Hos 5:6 With their flocks and H they shall go to
12:1 Ephraim H the wind, and pursues the east wind
Joel 1:17 The H of cattle are perplexed because there is
Zeph 2:14 H shall lie down in the midst of her,

HERDSMAN (2)

Lev 27:32 that pass under the H's staff, shall be holy
Amos 7:14 but I am a H, and a dresser of

HERDSMEN (10)

Gen 13:7 was strife between the H of Abram's cattle and
13:7 Abram's cattle and the H of Lot's cattle.
13:8 me, and between your H and my herdsmen; for
13:8 your herdsmen and my H; for we are kinsmen.
26:20 of springing water, the H of Gerar quarreled with
26:20 Gerar quarreled with Isaac's H, saying, "The water
1Sam 21:7 was Doeg the Edomite, the chief of Saul's H
Mt 8:33 The H fled, and going into the city they
Mk 5:14 The H fled, and told it in the city
Lk 8:34 When the H saw what had happened, they fled,

HERE (300)

Gen 12:19 Now then, H is your wife, take her, and
15:16 they shall come back H in the fourth generation;
19:12 said to Lot, "Have you any one else H
19:15 two daughters who are H, lest you be consumed
21:23 therefore swear to me H by God that you
22:1 And he said, H am I."
22:5 his young men, "Stay H with the ass; I
22:7 And he said, H am I, my son." He
22:11 And he said, H am I."
27:1 son"; and he answered, H I am."
27:18 father"; and he said, H I am; who are
30:3 Then she said, H is my maid Bilhah; go
31:11 'Jacob,' and I said, H I am!'
31:37 Set it H before my kinsmen and your kinsmen,
37:13 he said to him, H I am."
37:19 said to one another, H comes this dreamer.
37:22 him into this pit H in the wilderness, but
38:21 And they said, "No harlot has been H
38:22 of the place said, 'No harlot has been H
40:15 of the Hebrews; and H also I have done
42:15 this place unless your youngest brother comes H
42:28 has been put back; H it is in the
45:5 because you sold me H; for God sent me
45:8 you who sent me H, but God; and he
45:13 Make haste and bring my father down H
46:2 And he said, H am I."
47:23 Now H is seed for you, and you shall
48:9 are my sons, whom God has given me H
50:25 and you shall carry up my bones from H
Ex 3:4 And he said, H am I."
13:19 you must carry my bones with you from H
24:14 to the elders, "Tarry H for us, until we
33:15 with me, do not carry us up from H
Num 14:40 saying, "See, we are H, we will go up
20:4 that we should die H, both we and our
20:16 out of Egypt; and H we are in Kadesh,
22:8 said to them, "Lodge H this night, and I
22:19 Pray, now, tarry H this night also, that I
23:1 Balak, "Build for me H seven altars, and provide
23:1 and provide for me H seven bulls and seven
23:15 said to Balak, "Stand H beside your burnt offering,
23:29 Balak, "Build for me H seven altars, and provide
23:29 and provide for me H seven bulls and seven
32:6 brethren go to the war while you sit H
32:16 "We will build sheepfolds H for our flocks, and
Deut 5:3 are all of us H alive this day.
5:31 But you, stand H by me, and I will
9:12 go down quickly from H; for your people whom
12:8 that we are doing H this day, every man
20:15 you, which are not cities of the nations H
29:15 him who is not H with us this day
29:15 with him who stands H with us this day
Josh 2:2 of Israel have come H tonight to search out
4:3 'Take twelve stones from H out of the midst
9:12 a covenant with us."' H is our bread; it
17:9 The cities H, to the south of the brook,
18:6 and bring the description H to me; and I
18:6 cast lots for you H before the LORD our
18:8 cast lots for you H before the LORD in
23:7 with these nations left H among you, or make
23:12 of these nations left H among you, and make
Judg 4:20 you, 'Is any one H say, No.'
6:18 Do not depart from H, I pray thee, until
6:26 top of the stronghold H, with stones laid in
14:15 Have you invited us H to impoverish us?"
16:2 The Gazites were told, "Samson has come H
18:3 aside and said to him, "Who brought you H
18:3 What is your business H
19:9 to its close; lodge H and let your heart
19:24 Behold, H are my virgin daughter and his concubine;
20:7 all of you, give your advice and counsel H
Ruth 2:14 said to her, "Come H, and eat some bread,
4:1 aside, friend; sit down H; and he turned aside
4:2 and said, "Sit down H; so they sat down.
4:4 presence of those sitting H, and in the presence
1Sam 1:26 woman who was standing H in your presence,
3:4 and he said, H I am!"
3:5 to Eli, and said, H I am, for you
3:6 to Eli, and said, H I am, for you
3:8 to Eli, and said, H I am, for you
3:16 And he said, H I am."
4:3 covenant of the LORD H from Shiloh, that he
9:8 servant answered Saul again, H, I have with me
9:11 water, and said to them, "Is the seer H
9:17 the LORD told him, H is the man of
9:27 has passed on stop H yourself for a while,
12:3 H I am; testify against me before the LORD
13:9 "Bring the burnt offering H to me, and the
14:33 dealt treacherously; roll a great stone to me H
14:34 sheep, and slay them H, and eat; and do
14:43 was in my hand; H I am, I will
15:32 Then Samuel said, "Bring H to me Agag the
16:11 Samuel said to Jesse, "Are all your sons H
16:11 we will not sit down till he comes H
18:17 Saul said to David, H is my elder daughter
21:3 me five loaves of bread, or whatever is H
21:8 "And have you not H a spear or a
21:9 Elah, behold, it is H wrapped in a cloth
21:9 take it, for there is none but that H
22:12 And he answered, H I am, my lord."
23:3 "Behold, we are afraid H in Judah; how much
23:9 said to Abiathar the priest, "Bring the ephod H

24:4 David said to him, H is the day of
26:22 And David made answer, H is the spear, O
29:3 Philistines said, "What are these Hebrews doing H
29:4 not be with the heads of the men H
30:26 elders of Judah, saying, H is a present for
2Sam 1:7 And I answered, H I am.'
1:10 I have brought them H to my lord."
4:8 said to the king, H is the head of
5:6 will not come in H, but the blind and
5:6 ward you off"--thinking, "David cannot come in H
11:12 said to Uriah, "Remain H today also, and tomorrow
14:32 word to you, 'Come H, that I may send
15:26 pleasure in you,' behold, H I am, let him
18:30 And the king said, "Turn aside, and stand H
19:37 But H is your servant Chimham; let him go
20:4 three days, and be H yourself."
20:16 Tell Joab, 'Come H, that I may speak to
24:22 seems good to him; H are the oxen for
1Kgs 1:23 they told the king, H is Nathan the prophet."
2:30 But he said, "No, I will die H
17:3 to him, "Depart from H and turn eastward, and
18:8 Go, tell your lord, 'Behold, Elijah is H
18:10 say, 'He is not H he would take an
18:11 lord, "Behold, Elijah is H
18:14 lord, "Behold, Elijah is H; and he will kill
19:9 "What are you doing H, Elijah?"
19:13 "What are you doing H, Elijah?"
20:40 your servant was busy H and there, he was
22:7 said, "Is there not H another prophet of the
2Kgs 2:2 said to Elisha, "Tarry H, I pray you; for
2:4 to him, "Elisha, tarry H, I pray you; for
2:6 said to him, "Tarry H, I pray you; for
3:11 prophet of the LORD H, through whom we may
3:11 son of Shaphat is H, who poured water on
7:3 "Why do we sit H till we die?
7:4 and if we sit H, we die also.
7:13 those who are left H will fare like the
8:5 "My lord, O king, H is the woman, and
8:5 is the woman, and H is her son whom
8:7 told him, "The man of God has come H
10:23 servant of the LORD H among you, but only
1Chr 11:5 said to David, "You will not come in H
22:1 Then David said, H shall be the house of
22:1 the LORD God and H the altar of burnt
29:17 who are present H, offering freely and joyously
2Chr 18:6 said, "Is there not H another prophet of the
28:13 bring the captives in H, for you propose to
Ezra 4:2 of Esarhaddon king of Assyria who brought us H
Tob 2:8 once ran away, and H he is burying the
7:11 "I will eat nothing H until you make a
7:13 be his wife, saying, H she is; take her
11:15 had mercy upon me; H I see my son
14:1 H Tobit ended his words of praise.
Jud 3:10 great ridge of Judea; H he camped between Geba
9:6 said, 'Lo, we are H; for all they ways
12:3 of your people is H with us."
13:15 them, and said, "See, H is the head of
13:15 the Assyrian army, and H is the canopy beneath
14:18 For look, H is Holofernes lying on the ground,
Esth 14:18 that I was brought H until now, except in
Job 31:35 H is my signature!
38:11 and no farther, and H shall your proud waves
38:35 and say to you, H we are?
Ps 132:14 resting place for ever; H I will dwell, for
Prov 9:4 town, "Whoever is simple, let him turn in H
9:16 way, "Whoever is simple, let him turn in H
25:7 it is better to be told, "Come up H
Wis 18:18 assailed them; and one H and another there, hurled
Sir 29:26 bitter words: "Come H, stranger, prepare the table,
Is 6:8 Then I said, H am I!
21:9 And, behold, H come riders, horsemen in pairs!" And
22:16 have you to do H and whom have you
22:16 and whom have you H, that you have hewn
22:16 that you have hewn H a tomb for yourself,
28:10 line, line upon line, H a little, there a
28:13 line, line upon line, H a little, there a
52:5 therefore what have I H, says the LORD, seeing
52:6 is I who speak; H am I."
58:9 and he will say, H I am.
65:1 I said, H am I, here am I," to
65:1 said, "Here am I, H am I," to a
Jer 22:11 place: "He shall return H no more,
31:8 together; a great company, they shall return H
38:10 men with you from H, and lift Jeremiah the
Bar 3:34 them, and they said, H we are!" They shone
Ezek 8:6 of Israel are committing H, to drive me far
8:9 the vile abominations that they are committing H
8:17 abominations which they commit H, that they should
40:4 for you were brought H in order that I
Dan 3:94 the Most High God, come forth, and come H
4:9 is difficult for you, H is the dream which
7:28 serve and obey them.' H is the end of
Zech 3:7 right of access among those who are standing H
1Mac 12:45 For that is why I am H
2Mac 1:6 We are now praying for you H
9:25 I have written to him what is written H
14:7 and have now come H,
14:33 and I will build H a splendid temple to
15:37 So I too will H end my story.
15:39 And H will be the end.
Mt 8:29 Have you come H to torment us before the
12:6 tell you, something greater than the temple is H
12:41 and behold, something greater than Jonah is H
12:42 and behold, something greater than Solomon is H
12:48 his disciples, he said, H are my mother and
14:8 of John the Baptist H on a platter."
14:17 have only five loaves H and two fish."
14:18 he said, "Bring them H to me."
16:28 there are some standing H who will not taste
17:4 well that we are H; if you wish, I
17:4 will make three booths H, one for you and
17:17 Bring him H to me."
17:20 this mountain, 'Move from H to there,' and it
20:6 'Why do you stand H idle all day?'
22:12 did you get in H without a wedding garment?'
24:2 will not be left H one stone upon another,
24:23 says to you, 'Lo, H is the Christ!' or
25:20 to me five talents; H I have made five
25:22 to me two talents; H I have made two
25:25 H you have what is yours.'
26:36 to his disciples, "Sit H, while I go yonder
26:38 even to death; remain H, and watch with me."
26:50 Jesus said to him, "Friend, why are you H
28:6 He is not H; for he has risen, as
Mk 3:3 the man who had the withered hand, "Come H
3:34 about him, he said, H are my mother and
6:3 are not his sisters H with us?" And they
8:4 these men with bread H in the desert?"
9:1 there are some standing H who will not taste
9:5 well that we are H; let us make three
11:3 will send it back H immediately.'"
13:2 will not be left H one stone upon another,
13:21 says to you, 'Look, H is the Christ!' or
14:32 to his disciples, "Sit H, while I pray."
14:34 even to death; remain H, and watch."
16:6 risen, he is not H; see the place where
Lk 4:9 throw yourself down from H;
4:23 did at Caperna-um, do H also in your own
6:8 who had the withered hand, "Come and stand H
9:12 provisions; for we are H in a lonely place."
9:27 there are some standing H who will not taste
9:33 well that we are H; let us make three
9:41 Bring your son H
11:31 and behold, something greater than Solomon is H
11:32 and behold, something greater than Jonah is H
13:31 him, "Get away from H, for Herod wants to
15:17 spare, but I perish H with hunger!
16:25 now he is comforted H, and you are in
16:26 who would pass from H to you may not
17:21 will they say, 'Lo, H it is!' or 'There!'
17:23 'Lo, there!' or 'Lo, H Do not go, do
19:20 another came, saying, 'Lord, H is your pound, which
19:27 over them, bring them H and slay them before
19:30 ever yet sat; untie it and bring it H
21:6 shall not be left H one stone upon another
22:38 they said, "Look, Lord, H are two swords." And
24:5 He is not H, but has risen."
24:41 them, "Have you anything H to eat?"
Jn 3:26 whom you bore witness, H he is, baptizing, and
4:15 not thirst, nor come H to draw."
4:16 to her, "Go, call your husband, and come H
4:37 For H the saying holds true, 'One sows and
6:9 "There is a lad H who has five barley
6:25 said to him, "Rabbi, when did you come H
7:3 said to him, "Leave H and go to Judea,
7:6 not yet come, but your time is always H
7:26 And H he is, speaking openly, and they say
11:21 if you had been H, my brother would not
11:28 quietly, "The Teacher is H and is calling for
11:32 if you had been H, my brother would not
20:27 Thomas, "Put your finger H, and see my hands;
Acts 5:28 in this name, yet H you have filled Jerusalem

H

8:36 the eunuch said, "See, H is water!
9:10 And he said, H I am, Lord."
9:14 saints at Jerusalem; and H he has authority from
9:21 And he has come H for this purpose, to
9:32 Now as Peter went H and there among them
10:33 therefore we are all H present in the sight
16:28 "Do not harm yourself, for we are all H
17:6 upside down have come H also,
19:37 brought these men H who are neither sacrilegious
24:18 they ought to be H before you and to
25:17 therefore they came together H, I made no delay,
25:24 both at Jerusalem and H, shouting that he ought
26:6 And now I stand H on trial for hope
26:22 and so I stand H testifying both to small
28:21 of the brethren coming H has reported or spoken
2Cor 5:2 H indeed we groan, and long to put on
12:14 H for the third time I am ready to
Phil 1:16 that I am put H for the defense of
Col 3:11 H there cannot be Greek and Jew, circumcised and
4:9 tell you of everything that has taken place H
Heb 2:13 And again, H am I, and the children God
7:8 H tithes are received by mortal men; there, by
13:14 For H we have no lasting city, but we
Jas 2:3 say, "Have a seat H, please," while you say
Rev 13:10 H is a call for the endurance and faith
14:12 H is a call for the endurance of the

HEREAFTER (9)

Esth 13:7 our government completely secure and untroubled H
16:23 that both now and H it may mean salvation
Wis 2:2 by mere chance, and H we shall be as
Is 41:23 what is to come H, that we may know
Ezek 20:39 his idols, now and H, if you will not
Dan 2:29 of what would be H, and he who reveals
2:45 made known to the king what shall be H
Mt 26:64 But I tell you, H you will see the
Rev 1:19 what is and what is to take place H

HEREBY (2)

Num 16:28 And Moses said, H you shall know that the
Josh 3:10 And Joshua said, H you shall know that the

HERES

Judg 8:13 returned from the battle by the ascent of H

HERESH

1Chr 9:15 of Merari; and Bakbakkar, H, Galal, and Mattaniah

HERESIES

2Pet 2:1 bring in destructive H, even denying the Master

HERETH

1Sam 22:5 David departed, and went into the forest of H

HERETOFORE (3)

Ex 4:10 am not eloquent, either H or since thou hast
5:7 to make bricks, as H; let them go and
5:8 bricks which they made H you shall lay upon

HEREWITH

Bar 1:10 And they said: H we send you money; so

HERITAGE (59)

Deut 9:26 thy people and thy H, whom thou hast redeemed
9:29 thy people and thy H, whom thou didst bring
32:9 LORD's portion is his people, Jacob his allotted H
Josh 18:7 the LORD is their H; and Gad and Reuben
1Sam 10:1 has anointed you to be prince over his H
26:19 no share in the H of the LORD, saying,
2Sam 14:16 son together from the H of God.'
20:19 you swallow up the H of the LORD?"
21:3 you may bless the H of the LORD?"
1Kgs 8:51 thy people, and thy H, which thou didst bring
8:53 earth, to be thy H, as thou didst declare
2Kgs 21:14 the remnant of my H, and give them into
Job 20:29 portion from God, the H decreed for him by
27:13 with God, and the H which oppressors receive from
31:2 God above, and my H from the Almighty on
Ps 2:8 make the nations your H, and the ends of
16:6 in pleasant places; yea, I have a goodly H
28:9 people, and bless thy H; be thou their shepherd,
33:12 the people whom he has chosen as his H
37:18 the blameless, and their H will abide for ever;
47:4 He chose our H for us, the pride of
61:5 hast given me the H of those who fear
68:9 thou didst restore thy H as it languished;
74:2 hast redeemed to be the tribe of thy H
78:62 the sword, and vented his wrath on his H
94:5 crush thy people, O LORD, and afflict thy H
94:14 will not abandon his H;
106:5 thy nation, that I may glory with thy H
106:40 and he abhorred his H;
111:6 in giving them the H of the nations.
119:111 Thy testimonies are my H for ever; yea, they
127:3 Lo, sons are a H from the LORD, the
135:12 their land as a H, a heritage to his
135:12 as a heritage, a H to his people Israel.
136:21 their land as a H, for his steadfast love
136:22 endures for ever; a H to Israel his servant,
Sir 45:20 and gave him a H; he allotted to him
45:25 tribe of Judah: the H of the king is
45:25 son only; so the H of Aaron is for
Is 19:25 the work of my hands, and Israel my H
47:6 people, I profaned my H; I gave them into
54:17 This is the H of the servants of the
58:14 feed you with the H of Jacob your father,
63:17 sake of thy servants, the tribes of thy H
Jer 2:7 land, and made my H an abomination.
3:18 land that I gave your fathers for a H
3:19 a pleasant land, a H most beauteous of all
12:7 I have abandoned my H; I have given the
12:8 My H has become to me like a lion
12:9 Is my H to me like a speckled bird
12:14 neighbors who touch the H which I have given
12:15 again each to his H and each to his
17:4 your hand from your H which I gave to
50:11 O plunderers of my H, though you are wanton
Joel 2:17 and make not thy H a reproach, a byword
3:2 my people and my H Israel, because they have
Mal 1:3 country and left his H to jackals of the
2Mac 14:15 always upholds his own H by manifesting himself.
Rev 21:7 conquers shall have this H, and I will be

HERITAGES

Is 49:8 to apportion the desolate H;

HERMAS

Rom 16:14 Phlegon, Hermes, Patrobas, H, and the brethren

HERMES (2)

Acts 14:12 because he was the chief speaker, they called H
Rom 16:14 Greet Asyncritus, Phlegon, H, Patrobas, Hermas,

HERMOGENES

2Tim 1:15 away from me, and among them Phygelus and H

HERMON (15)

Deut 3:8 the Arnon to Mount H
3:9 Hermon (the Sidonians call H Sirion, while the
4:48 Mount Sirion (that is, H,
Josh 11:3 and the Hivites under H in the land of
11:17 Baal-gad in the valley of Lebanon below Mount H
12:1 the Arnon to Mount H, with all the Arabah
12:5 and ruled over Mount H and Salecah and all
13:5 from Baal-gad below Mount H to the entrance of
13:11 Ma-acathites, and all Mount H, and all Bashan to
1Chr 5:23 from Bashan to Baal-hermon, Senir, and Mount H
Ps 42:6 of Jordan and of H, from Mount Mizar.
89:12 created them; Tabor and H joyously praise thy name.
133:3 like the dew of H, which falls on the
Song 4:8 peak of Senir and H, from the dens of
Sir 24:13 and like a cypress on the heights of H

HEROD (44)

Mt 2:1 in the days of H the king, behold, wise
2:3 When H the king heard this, he was troubled,
2:7 Then H summoned the wise men secretly and
2:12 not to return to H, they departed to their
2:13 I tell you; for H is about to search
2:15 Egypt, and remained there until the death of H
2:16 Then H, when he saw that he had been
2:19 But when H died, behold, an angel of the
2:22 place of his father H, he was afraid to
14:1 At that time H the tetrarch heard about the
14:3 For H had seized John and bound him and
14:6 when H's birthday came, the daughter of Herodi-as
14:6 the company, and pleased H,
Mk 6:14 King H heard of it; for Jesus' name had
6:16 But when H heard of it he said, "John,
6:17 For H had sent and seized John, and bound
6:18 For John said to H, "It is not lawful
6:20 she could not, for H feared John, knowing that

	6:21	an opportunity came when H on his birthday gave
	6:22	and danced, she pleased H and his guests; and
	8:15	leaven of the Pharisees and the leaven of H
Lk	1:5	In the days of H, king of Judea, there
	3:1	governor of Judea, and H being tetrarch of Galilee,
	3:19	But H the tetrarch, who had been reproved by
	3:19	the evil things that H had done,
	8:3	the wife of Chuza, H's steward, and Susanna, and
	9:7	Now H the tetrarch heard of all that was
	9:9	H said, "John I beheaded; but who is this
	13:31	away from here, for H wants to kill you."
	23:7	that he belonged to H's jurisdiction, he sent him
	23:7	sent him over to H, who was himself in
	23:8	When H saw Jesus, he was very glad, for
	23:11	And H with his soldiers treated him with contempt
	23:12	And H and Pilate became friends with each other
	23:15	against him; neither did H, for he sent him
Acts	4:27	thou didst anoint, both H and Pontius Pilate, with
	12:1	About that time H the king laid violent hands
	12:6	The very night when H was about to bring
	12:11	from the hand of H and from all that
	12:19	And when H had sought for him and could
	12:20	Now H was angry with the people of Tyre
	12:21	On an appointed day H put on his royal
	13:1	of the court of H the tetrarch, and Saul.
	23:35	to be guarded in H's praetorium.

HERODI-ANS (3)

Mt	22:16	him, along with the H, saying, "Teacher, we know
Mk	3:6	held counsel with the H against him, how to
	12:13	and some of the H, to entrap him in

HERODI-AS (6)

Mt	14:3	for the sake of H, his brother Philip's wife;
	14:6	came, the daughter of H danced before the company,
Mk	6:17	for the sake of H, his brother Philip's wife;
	6:19	And H had a grudge against him, and wanted
	6:22	For when H daughter came in and danced, she
Lk	3:19	reproved by him for H, his brother's wife, and

HERODION

Rom	16:11	Greet my kinsman H

HEROES (2)

Is	5:22	to those who are H at drinking wine, and
Jer	48:14	you say, 'We are H and mighty men of

HEROIC

1Mac	5:56	deeds and of the H war they had fought.

HERON (2)

Lev	11:19	vulture, the stork, the H according to its kind,
Deut	14:18	cormorant, the stork, the H, after their kinds; the

HERSELF (67)

Gen	18:12	So Sarah laughed to H, saying, "After I have
	20:5	And she H said, 'He is my brother.' In
	24:65	So she took her veil and covered H
	38:14	on a veil, wrapping H up, and sat at
Lev	15:28	she shall count for H seven days, and after
	18:23	shall any woman give H to a beast to
	21:9	priest, if she profanes H by playing the harlot,
Num	5:13	though she has defiled H, and there is no
	5:14	wife who has defiled H; or if the spirit
	5:14	she has not defiled H;
	5:27	if she has defiled H and has acted unfaithfully
	5:28	woman has not defiled H and is clean, then
	5:29	goes astray and defiles H,
	30:3	the LORD, and binds H by a pledge, while
	30:4	which she has bound H, and says nothing to
	30:4	which she has bound H shall stand.
	30:5	which she has bound H, shall stand; and the
	30:6	which she has bound H,
	30:7	which she has bound H shall stand.
	30:8	by which she bound H; and the LORD will
	30:9	which she has bound H, shall stand against her.
	30:10	husband's house, or bound H by a pledge with
	30:11	by which she bound H shall stand.
	30:12	concerning her pledge of H, shall not stand: her
	30:13	binding oath to afflict H, her husband may establish,
Judg	5:29	she gives answer to H,
2Sam	11:4	(Now she was purifying H from her uncleanness.)
	21:10	and spread it for H on the rock, from
2Kgs	4:5	shut the door upon H and her sons; and
Tob	3:10	deeply grieved, even to the thought of hanging H
Jud	8:5	up a tent for H on the roof of
	10:3	with water, and anointed H with precious ointment,
	10:3	a tiara, and arrayed H in her gayest apparel,
	10:4	her ornaments, and made H very beautiful, to entice
	10:23	face; and she prostrated H and made obeisance to
	12:15	got up and arrayed H in all her woman's
	16:19	which she took for H from his bedchamber she
Esth	15:1	had worshipped, and arrayed H in splendid attire.
	15:8	her in his arms until she came to H
Job	39:18	When she rouses H to flee, she laughs at
Ps	84:3	swallow a nest for H, where she may lay
Prov	31:22	She makes H coverings; her clothing is fine linen
Wis	6:13	She hastens to make H known to those who
	7:27	and while remaining in H, she renews all things;
Sir	23:24	She H will be brought before the assembly, and
	24:1	Wisdom will praise H, and will glory in the
Is	34:14	alight, and find for H a resting place.
	61:10	as a bride adorns H with her jewels.
Jer	3:11	"Faithless Israel has shown H less guilty than false
Lam	1:4	dragged away, and she H suffers bitterly.
	1:8	her nakedness; yea, she H groans, and turns her
Bar	6:43	not as attractive as H and her cord was
Ezek	22:3	may come, and that makes idols to defile H
	23:7	them; and she defiled H with all the idols
Hos	2:13	to them and decked H with her ring and
Zeph	2:15	secure, that said to H, "I am and there
Zech	9:3	Tyre has built H a rampart, and heaped up
Mt	9:21	for she said to H, "If I only touch
Lk	1:24	five months she hid H, saying,
	13:11	was bent over and could not fully straighten H
1Cor	11:6	woman will not veil H, then she should cut
1Tim	5:10	the afflicted, and devoted H to doing good in
Heb	11:11	By faith Sarah H received power to conceive, even
Rev	2:20	woman Jezebel, who calls H a prophetess and is
	18:6	to her as she H has rendered, and repay
	18:7	As she glorified H and played the wanton, so
	19:7	his Bride has made H ready;

HESHBON (39)

Num	21:25	of the Amorites, in H, and in all its
	21:26	For H was the city of Sihon the king
	21:27	singers say, "Come to H, let it be built,
	21:28	fire went forth from H, flame from the city
	21:30	their posterity perished from H, as far as Dibon,
	21:34	Sihon king of the Amorites, who dwelt at H
	32:3	Dibon, Jazer, Nimrah, H, Elealeh, Sebam, Nebo,
	32:37	sons of Reuben built H, Elealeh, Kiriathaim,
Deut	1:4	Amorites, who lived in H, and Og the king
	2:24	the Amorite, king of H, and his land; begin
	2:26	Sihon the king of H, with words of peace,
	2:30	Sihon the king of H would not let us
	3:2	Amorites, who dwelt at H
	3:6	Sihon the king of H, destroying every city, men,
	4:46	Amorites, who lived at H, whom Moses and the
	29:7	Sihon the king of H and Og the king
Josh	9:10	Sihon the king of H, and Og king of
	12:2	Amorites who dwelt at H, and ruled from Aroer,
	12:5	Gilead to the boundary of Sihon king of H
	13:10	Amorites, who reigned in H, as far as the
	13:17	tableland by Medeba; with H, and all its cities
	13:21	Amorites, who reigned in H, whom Moses defeated
	13:26	of Rabbah, and from H to Ramath-mizpeh and,
	13:27	of Sihon king of H, having the Jordan as
	21:39	with its pasture lands, H with its pasture lands,
Judg	11:19	the Amorites, king of H; and Israel said to
	11:26	While Israel dwelt in H and its villages, and
1Chr	6:81	with its pasture lands, H with its pasture lands,
Neh	9:22	of Sihon king of H and the land of
Jud	5:15	all the inhabitants of H; and crossing over the
Song	7:4	eyes are pools in H, by the gate of
Is	15:4	H and Ele-aleh cry out, their voice is heard
	16:8	For the fields of H languish, and the vine
	16:9	with my tears, O H and Ele-aleh; for upon
Jer	48:2	In H they planned evil against her: 'Come, let
	48:34	H and Ele-aleh cry out; as far as Jahaz
	48:45	"In the shadow of H fugitives stop without strength;
	48:45	has gone forth from H, a flame from the
	49:3	"Wail, O H, for Ai is laid waste!

HESHMON

Josh	15:27	Shema, Moladah, Hazar-gaddah, H, Beth-pelet,

HESITATE (3)

Tob	12:13	When you did not H to rise and leave
Job	30:10	me; they do not H to spit at the
Sir	13:12	himself; he will not H to injure or to

HESITATION
Acts 10:20 and accompany them without H; for I have sent

HETH (2)
Gen 10:15 Sidon his first-born, and H,
1Chr 1:13 Sidon his first-born, and H,

HETHLON (2)
Ezek 47:15 Sea by way of H to the entrance of
48:1 sea by way of H to the entrance of

HEW (9)
Deut 6:11 which you did not H, and vineyards and olive
7:5 pieces their pillars, and H down their Asherim, and
10:1 LORD said to me, H two tables of stone
12:3 with fire; you shall H down the graven images
Is 18:5 spreading branches he will H away.
22:16 for yourself, you who H a tomb on the
Jer 6:6 the LORD of hosts: H down her trees; cast
Dan 4:14 aloud and said thus, H down the tree and
4:23 from heaven and saying, H down the tree and

HEWED (10)
Gen 50:5 my tomb which I H out for myself in
Deut 10:3 of acacia wood, and H two tables of stone
1Sam 15:33 And Samuel H Agag in pieces before the LORD
2Chr 14:3 down the pillars and H down the Asherim,
26:10 in the wilderness, and H out many cisterns, for
31:1 pieces the pillars and H down the Asherim and
34:4 his presence; and he H down the incense altars
34:7 images into powder, and H down all the incense
Is 5:2 midst of it, and H out a wine vat
Jer 2:13 of living waters, and H out cisterns for themselves,

HEWER
Is 14:8 were laid low, no H comes up against us.'

HEWERS (5)
Josh 9:21 So they became H of wood and drawers of
9:23 shall always be slaves, H of wood and drawers
9:27 made them that day H of wood and drawers
1Kgs 5:15 burden-bearers and eighty thousand H of stone in
2Chr 2:10 for your servants, the H who cut timber, twenty

HEWING
1Kgs 5:18 of Gebal did the H and prepared the timber

HEWN (18)
Ex 20:25 not build it of H stones; for if you
Deut 6:11 not fill, and cisterns H out, which you did
1Kgs 6:36 with three courses of H stone and one course
7:9 of costly stones, H according to measure, sawed
7:11 above were costly stones, H according to
7:12 had three courses of H stone round about, and
2Chr 16:14 tomb which he had H out for himself in
Neh 9:25 good things, cisterns H out, vineyards, olive orchards
Jud 1:2 walls about Ecbatana with H stones three cubits
Is 10:33 in height will be H down, and the lofty
22:16 here, that you have H here a tomb for
51:1 from which you were H, and to the quarry
Lam 3:9 blocked my ways with H stones, he has made
Ezek 40:42 also four tables of H stone for the burnt
Hos 6:5 Therefore I have H them by the prophets, I
Amos 5:11 have built houses of H stone, but you shall
Mt 27:60 tomb, which he had H in the rock; and
Mk 15:45 tomb which had been H out of the rock;

HEWS (2)
Deut 29:11 camp, both he who H your wood and he
Is 10:15 itself over him who H with it, or the

HEZEKIAH (136)
2Kgs 16:20 city of David; and H his son reigned in
18:1 Elah, king of Israel, H the son of Ahaz,
18:9 fourth year of King H, which was the seventh
18:10 the sixth year of H, which was the ninth
18:13 year of King H Sennacherib king of Assyria
18:14 And H king of Judah sent to the king
18:14 of Assyria required of H king of Judah three
18:15 And H gave him all the silver that was
18:16 At that time H stripped the gold from the
18:16 from the doorposts which H king of Judah had
18:17 from Lachish to King H at Jerusalem.
18:19 to them, "Say to H, 'Thus says the great
18:22 high places and altars H has removed, saying to
18:29 king: 'Do not let H deceive you, for he
18:30 Do not let H make you to rely on
18:31 Do not listen to H; for thus says the
18:32 do not listen to H when he misleads you
18:37 the recorder, came to H with their clothes rent,
19:1 When King H heard it, he rent his clothes,
19:3 to him, "Thus says H, This day is a
19:5 the servants of King H came to Isaiah,
19:9 sent messengers again to H, saying,
19:10 shall you speak to H king of Judah: 'Do
19:14 H received the letter from the hand of the
19:14 and read it; and H went up to the
19:15 And H prayed before the LORD, and said: "O
19:20 of Amoz sent to H, saying, "Thus says the
20:1 In those days H became sick and was at
20:2 Then H turned his face to the wall, and
20:3 And H wept bitterly.
20:5 back, and say to H the prince of my
20:8 And H said to Isaiah, "What shall be the
20:10 And H answered, "It is an easy thing for
20:12 and a present to H; for he heard that
20:12 for he heard that H had been sick.
20:13 And H welcomed them, and he showed them all
20:13 all his realm that H did not show them.
20:14 prophet came to King H, and said to him,
20:14 And H said, "They have come from a far
20:15 And H answered, "They have seen all that is
20:16 Then Isaiah said to H, "Hear the word of
20:19 Then said H to Isaiah, "The word of the
20:20 of the deeds of H, and all his might,
20:21 And H slept with his fathers; and Manasseh his
21:3 the high places which H his father had destroyed;
1Chr 3:13 son, Ahaz his son, H his son, Manasseh his
4:41 in the days of H, king of Judah, and
2Chr 28:27 And H his son reigned in his stead.
29:1 H began to reign when he was twenty-five years
29:18 they went in to H the king and said,
29:20 Then H the king rose early and gathered the
29:27 Then H commanded that the burnt offering be
29:30 And H the king and the princes commanded the
29:31 Then H said, "You have now consecrated yourselves
29:36 And H and all the people rejoiced because of
30:1 H sent to all Israel and Judah, and wrote
30:18 For H had prayed for them, saying, "The good
30:20 And the LORD heard H, and healed the people.
30:22 And H spoke encouragingly to all the Levites who
30:24 For H king of Judah gave the assembly a
31:2 And H appointed the divisions of the priests and
31:8 When H and the princes came and saw the
31:9 And H questioned the priests and the Levites about
31:11 Then H commanded them to prepare chambers in
31:13 by the appointment of H the king and Azariah
31:20 Thus H did throughout all Judah; and he did
32:2 And when H saw that Sennacherib had come and
32:8 from the words of H king of Judah.
32:9 servants to Jerusalem to H king of Judah and
32:11 Is not H misleading you, that he may give
32:12 Has not this same H taken away his high
32:15 therefore do not let H deceive you or mislead
32:16 against the Lord GOD and against his servant H
32:17 so the God of H will not deliver his
32:20 Then H the king and Isaiah the prophet, the
32:22 So the LORD saved H and the inhabitants of
32:23 and precious things to H king of Judah, so
32:24 In those days H became sick and was at
32:25 But H did not make return according to the
32:26 But H humbled himself for the pride of his
32:26 not come upon them in the days of H
32:27 And H had very great riches and honor; and
32:30 This same H closed the upper outlet of the
32:30 And H prospered in all his works.
32:32 of the acts of H, and his good deeds,
32:33 And H slept with his fathers, and they buried
33:3 places which his father H had broken down, and
Ezra 2:16 of Ater, namely of H, ninety-eight.
Neh 7:21 of Ater, namely of H, ninety-eight.
10:17 Adonijah, Bigvai, Adin, Ater, H, Azzur,
Prov 25:1 which the men of H king of Judah copied.
Sir 48:17 H fortified his city, and brought water into the
48:22 For H did what was pleasing to the Lord,
49:4 Except David and H and Josiah they all sinned
Is 1:1 Uzziah, Jotham, Ahaz, and H, kings of Judah.
36:1 year of King H, Sennacherib king of Assyria
36:2 from Lachish to King H at Jerusalem, with a
36:4 to them, "Say to H, 'Thus says the great
36:7 high places and altars H has removed, saying to
36:14 king: 'Do not let H deceive you, for he

36:15 Do not let H make you rely on the
36:16 Do not listen to H; for thus says the
36:18 Beware lest H mislead you by saying, "The LORD
36:22 the recorder, came to H with their clothes rent,
37:1 When King H heard it, he rent his clothes,
37:3 to him, "Thus says H, 'This day is a
37:5 the servants of King H came to Isaiah,
37:9 he sent messengers to H, saying,
37:10 shall you speak to H king of Judah: 'Do
37:14 H received the letter from the hand of the
37:14 and read it; and H went up to the
37:15 And H prayed to the LORD:
37:21 of Amoz sent to H, saying, "Thus says the
38:1 In those days H became sick and was at
38:2 Then H turned his face to the wall, and
38:3 And H wept bitterly.
38:5 "Go and say to H, Thus says the LORD,
38:9 A writing of H king of Judah, after he
38:22 H also had said, "What is the sign that
39:1 and a present to H, for he heard that
39:2 And H welcomed them; and he showed them his
39:2 all his realm that H did not show them.
39:3 prophet came to King H, and said to him,
39:3 H said, "They have come to me from a
39:4 H answered, "They have seen all that is in
39:5 Then Isaiah said to H, "Hear the word of
39:8 Then said H to Isaiah, "The word of the
Jer 15:4 Manasseh the son of H, king of Judah, did
26:18 in the days of H king of Judah, and
26:19 a wooded height.' Did H king of Judah and
Hos 1:1 Uzziah, Jotham, Ahaz, and H, kings of Judah, and
Mic 1:1 of Jotham, Ahaz, and H, kings of Judah, which
Zeph 1:1 of Amariah, son of H, in the days of
2Mac 15:22 in the time of H king of Judea, and
Mt 1:9 Ahaz the father of H,
1:10 father of Hezekiah, and H the father of Manasseh,

HEZI-ON

1Kgs 15:18 Tabrimmon, the son of H, king of Syria, who

HEZIR (2)

1Chr 24:15 Immer, the seventeenth to H, the eighteenth to
Neh 10:20 Anathoth, Nebai, Magpiash, Meshullam, H,

HEZRO (2)

2Sam 23:35 of Ahithophel of Gilo, H of Carmel, Paarai the
1Chr 11:37 Mecherathite, Ahijah the Pelonite, H of Carmel,

HEZRON (20)

Gen 46:9 of Reuben: Hanoch, Pallu, H, and Carmi.
46:12 sons of Perez were H and Hamul.
Ex 6:14 of Israel: Hanoch, Pallu, H, and Carmi; these are
Num 26:6 of the Palluites; of H, the family of the
26:21 of Perez were: of H, the family of the
Josh 15:3 of Kadesh-barnea, along by H, up to Addar, turns
Ruth 4:18 was the father of H,
4:19 the father of Hezron, H of Ram, Ram of
1Chr 2:5 The sons of Perez: H and Hamul.
2:9 The sons of H, that were born to him:
2:18 Caleb the son of H had children by his
2:21 Afterward H went in to the daughter of Machir
2:24 After the death of H, Caleb went in to
2:24 Ephrathah, the wife of H his father, and she
2:25 Jerahmeel, the first-born of H: Ram, his first-born,
4:1 sons of Judah: Perez, H, Carmi, Hur, and Shobal.
5:3 of Israel: Hanoch, Pallu, H, and Carmi.
Mt 1:3 Perez the father of H, and Hezron the father
1:3 father of Hezron, and H the father of Ram,
Lk 3:33 Arni, the son of H, the son of Perez,

HEZRONITES (2)

Num 26:6 the family of the H; of Carmi, the family
26:21 the family of the H; of Hamul, the family

HI-ERAPOLIS

Col 4:13 you and for those in La-odicea and in H

HID (81)

Gen 3:8 man and his wife H themselves from the presence
3:10 was naked; and I H myself."
35:4 their ears; and Jacob H them under the oak
Ex 2:2 a goodly child, she H him three months.
2:12 killed the Egyptian and H him in the sand.
3:6 And Moses H his face, for he was afraid
Josh 2:6 to the roof, and H them with the stalks
6:17 shall live, because she H the messengers that we
6:25 day, because she H the messengers whom Joshua
10:16 five kings fled, and H themselves in the cave
Judg 9:5 was left, for he H himself.
1Sam 3:18 told him everything and H nothing from him.
13:6 hard-pressed), the people H themselves in caves and
14:11 holes where they have H themselves."
14:22 of Israel who had H themselves in the hill
20:19 the place where you H yourself when the matter
20:24 So David H himself in the field; and when
1Kgs 18:4 a hundred prophets and H them by fifties in
18:13 the LORD, how I H a hundred men of
2Kgs 7:8 clothing, and went and H them; then they came
7:8 it, and went and H them.
11:2 Thus she H him from Athaliah, so that he
11:3 with her six years, H in the house of
1Chr 21:20 who were with him H themselves.
2Chr 22:11 a sister of Ahaziah, H him from Athaliah, so
22:12 with them six years, H in the house of
Tob 1:19 burying them; so I H myself.
Job 3:21 it more than for H treasures;
3:23 man whose way is H, whom God has hedged
5:21 You shall be H from the scourge of the
18:10 A rope is H for him in the ground,
28:11 the thing that is H he brings forth to
28:21 It is H from the eyes of all living,
Ps 9:15 the net which they H has their own foot
19:6 and there is nothing H from its heat.
22:24 and he has not H his face from him,
35:7 For without cause they H their net for me;
35:8 the net which they H ensnare them; let them
40:10 I have not H thy saving help within my
Sir 17:13 they will not be H from his eyes.
39:19 and nothing can be H from his eyes.
Is 29:14 the discernment of their discerning men shall be H
40:27 Israel, "My way is H from the LORD, and
49:2 of his hand he H me; he made me
49:2 in his quiver he H me away.
50:6 out the beard; I H not my face from
51:16 in your mouth, and H you in the shadow
54:8 for a moment I H my face from you,
57:17 I smote him, I H my face and was
59:2 and your sins have H his face from you
64:7 thee; for thou hast H thy face from us,
65:16 are forgotten and are H from my eyes.
Jer 13:5 So I went, and H it by the Euphrates,
16:17 ways; they are not H from me, nor is
36:26 prophet, but the LORD H them.
43:10 stones which I have H, and he will spread
Ezek 39:23 with me that I H my face from them
39:24 and their transgressions, and H my face from them.
Dan 13:16 two elders, who had H themselves and were
Hos 5:3 and Israel is not H from me; for now,
13:14 Compassion is H from my eyes.
1Mac 9:38 and went up and H under cover of the
16:15 a great banquet, and H men there.
2Mac 1:19 the altar and secretly H it in the hollow
Mt 5:14 A city set on a hill cannot be H
13:33 a woman took and H in three measures of
25:18 in the ground and H his master's money.
25:25 and I went and H your talent in the
Mk 4:22 For there is nothing H, except to be made
7:23 one know it; yet he could not be H
Lk 1:24 for five months she H herself, saying,
8:17 For nothing is H that shall not be made
13:21 a woman took and H in three measures of
18:34 things; this saying was H from them, and they
19:42 But now they are H from your eyes.
Jn 8:59 at him; but Jesus H himself, and went out
12:36 this, he departed and H himself from them.
Col 2:3 Christ, in whom are H all the treasures of
3:3 and your life is H with Christ in God.
Heb 11:23 he was born, was H for three months by
Rev 6:15 one, slave and free, H in the caves and

HIDDAI

2Sam 23:30 Benjaminites, Benaiah of Pirathon, H of the brooks

HIDDEN (77)

Gen 4:14 face I shall be H; and I shall be
Lev 4:13 and the thing is H from the eyes of
5:2 things, and it is H from him, and he
5:3 unclean, and it is H from him, when he
5:4 swear, and it is H from him, when he
Num 5:13 carnally, and it is H from the eyes of
Deut 33:19 the seas and the H treasures of the sand."
Josh 2:4 the two men and H them; and she said,

7:21 and behold, they are H in the earth inside
7:22 and behold, it was H in his tent with
10:17 kings have been found, H in the cave at
10:27 cave where they had H themselves, and they set
1Sam 10:22 said, "Behold, he has H himself among the baggage."
2Sam 17:9 even now he has H himself in one of
18:13 (and there is nothing H from the king), then
1Kgs 10:3 questions; there was nothing H from the king which
2Kgs 4:27 and the LORD has H it from me, and
6:29 him'; but she has H her son."
2Chr 9:2 questions; there was nothing H from Solomon which
Tob 12:13 good deed was not H from me, but I
Job 3:16 I not as a H untimely birth, as infants
15:18 their fathers have not H,
Ps 10:11 has forgotten, he has H his face, he will
19:12 Clear thou me from H faults.
31:4 the net which is H for me, for thou
38:9 my sighing is not H from thee.
69:5 have done are not H from thee.
139:15 my frame was not H from thee, when I
140:5 Arrogant men have H a trap for me, and
142:3 I walk they have H a trap for me.
Prov 2:4 for it as for H treasures;
11:13 who is trustworthy in spirit keeps a thing H
27:5 is open rebuke than H love.
Wis 14:21 And this became a H trap for mankind, because
Sir 3:21 you, for you do not need what is H
12:8 will an enemy be H in adversity.
16:15 say, "I shall be H from the Lord, and
17:16 Their iniquities are not H from him, and all
20:29 H wisdom and unseen treasure, what advantage is
23:19 and perceive even the H places.
39:3 will seek out the H meanings of proverbs and
41:14 and be at peace; H wisdom and unseen treasure,
42:19 reveals the tracks of H things.
42:20 not one word is H from him.
43:32 greater than these lie H, for we have seen
48:25 of time, and the H things before they came
Is 42:22 trapped in holes and H in prisons; they have
48:6 you hear new things, H things which you have
Jer 13:7 place where I had H it.
33:3 tell you great and H things which you have
33:5 wrath, for I have H my face from this
41:8 barley, oil, and honey H in the fields." So
Ezek 28:3 Daniel; no secret is H from you;
Dan 13:18 did not see the elders, because they were H
13:37 man, who had been H, came to her and
14:13 they had made a H entrance, through which they
Zeph 2:3 perhaps you may be H on the day of
1Mac 1:23 he took also the H treasures which he found.
2Mac 1:20 the priests who had H the fire to get
1:33 the exiled priests had H the fire, the liquid
10:37 killed Timothy, who was H in a cistern, and
12:41 the things that are H;
Mt 10:26 not be revealed, or H that will not be
11:25 earth, that thou hast H these things from the
13:35 utter what has been H since the foundation of
13:44 heaven is like treasure H in a field, which
Lk 8:47 that she was not H, she came trembling, and
10:21 earth, that thou hast H these things from the
12:2 not be revealed, or H that will not be
1Cor 2:7 impart a secret and H wisdom of God, which
4:5 light the things now H in darkness and will
Eph 3:9 plan of the mystery H for ages in God
Col 1:26 fully known, the mystery H for ages and generations
1Tim 5:25 even when they are not, they cannot remain H
Heb 4:13 him no creature is H, but all are open
1Pet 3:4 let it be the H person of the heart
Rev 2:17 give some of the H manna, and I will

HIDE (84)

Gen 18:17 LORD said, "Shall I H from Abraham what I
47:18 him, "We will not H from my lord that
Ex 2:3 And when she could H him no longer she
Lev 20:4 land do at all H their eyes from that
Deut 7:20 who are left and H themselves from you are
31:17 will forsake them and H my face from them,
31:18 And I will surely H my face in that
32:20 he said, 'I will H my face from them,
Josh 2:16 pursuers meet you; and H yourselves there three
7:19 have done; do not H it from me."
Judg 6:11 the wine press, to H it from the Midianites.
1Sam 3:17 Do not H it from me.
3:17 more also, if you H anything from me of
19:2 a secret place and H yourself;
20:2 why should my father H this from me?
20:5 go, that I may H myself in the field
23:19 saying, "Does not David H among us in the
2Sam 14:18 the woman, "Do not H from me anything I
1Kgs 17:3 and turn eastward, and H yourself by the brook
22:25 an inner chamber to H yourself."
2Kgs 7:12 of the camp to H themselves in the open
2Chr 18:24 an inner chamber to H yourself."
Tob 13:6 you and will not H his face from you.
Job 3:10 my mother's womb, nor H trouble from my eyes.
10:13 these things thou didst H in thy heart; I
13:20 then I will not H myself from thy face:
13:24 Why dost thou H thy face, and count me
14:13 Oh that thou wouldest H me in Sheol, that
24:4 of the earth all H themselves.
34:22 darkness where evildoers may H themselves.
40:13 H them all in the dust together; bind their
Ps 10:1 Why dost thou H thyself in times of trouble?
13:1 How long wilt thou H thy face from me?
17:8 apple of the eye; H me in the shadow
27:5 For he will H me in his shelter in
27:9 H not thy face from me.
30:7 strong mountain; thou didst H thy face, I was
32:5 and I did not H my iniquity; I said,
44:24 Why dost thou H thy face?
51:9 H thy face from my sins, and blot out
55:1 prayer, O God; and H not thyself from my
55:12 then I could H from him.
64:2 dread of the enemy, H me from the secret
69:17 H not thy face from thy servant; for I
78:4 We will not H them from their children, but
88:14 Why dost thou H thy face from me?
89:46 Wilt thou H thyself for ever?
102:2 Do not H thy face from me in the
119:19 a sojourner on earth; H not thy commandments from
143:7 H not thy face from me, lest I be
Prov 28:12 the wicked rise, men H themselves.
28:28 the wicked rise, men H themselves, but when they
Wis 6:22 be, and I will H no secrets from you,
7:13 grudging; I do not H her wealth,
Sir 1:21 He will H his words until the right moment,
4:23 time, and do not H your wisdom.
6:12 against you, and will H himself from your presence.
22:23 and I will not H from him;
23:18 me, and the walls H me, and no one
26:8 drunken; she will not H her shame.
37:10 looks at you suspiciously; H your counsel from those
Is 1:15 your hands, I will H my eyes from you;
2:10 into the rock, and H in the dust from
3:9 Sodom, they do not H it.
16:3 the height of noon; H the outcasts, betray not
26:20 your doors behind you; H yourselves for a little
29:15 Woe to those who H deep from the LORD
30:20 your Teacher will not H himself any more, but
53:3 one from whom men H their faces he was
58:7 him, and not to H yourself from your own
Jer 13:4 to the Euphrates, and H it there in a
13:6 I commanded you to H there."
23:24 Can a man H himself in secret places so
36:19 to Baruch, "Go and H, you and Jeremiah, and
38:14 ask you a question; H nothing from me."
38:25 king said to you; H nothing from us and
43:9 hands large stones, and H them in the mortar
Bar 6:48 to where they can H themselves and their gods.
Ezek 39:29 and I will not H my face any more
Dan 10:7 and they fled to H themselves.
Amos 9:3 Though they H themselves on the top of Carmel,
9:3 them; and though they H from my sight at
Mic 3:4 answer them; he will H his face from them
Rev 6:16 "Fall on us and H us from the face

HIDES (13)

1Sam 23:23 lurking places where he H, and come back to
Job 6:16 and where the snow H itself.
20:12 his mouth, though he H it under his tongue,
34:29 When he H his face, who can behold him,
42:3 'Who is this that H counsel without knowledge?'
Prov 22:3 man sees danger and H himself; but the simple
27:12 man sees danger and H himself; but the simple
28:27 want, but he who H his eyes will get
Sir 19:24 He H his face and pretends not to hear;
20:30 is the man who H his folly than the
20:30 than the man who H his wisdom.
41:15 is the man who H his folly than the
41:15 than the man who H his wisdom.

HIDEST (3)
Ps 31:20 of thy presence thou H them from the plots
104:29 When thou H thy face, they are dismayed; when
Is 45:15 art a God who H thyself, O God of

HIDING (15)
1Sam 26:1 saying, "Is not David H himself on the hill
2Chr 22:9 he was captured while H in Samaria, and he
Job 31:33 transgressions from men, by H my iniquity in my
Ps 10:8 in the villages; in H places he murders the
32:7 Thou art a H place for me, thou preservest
119:114 Thou art my H place and my shield; I
Is 8:17 the LORD, who is H his face from the
32:2 will be like a H place from the wind,
Jer 49:10 I have uncovered his H places, and he is
Lam 3:10 like a lion in H;
1Mac 1:53 they drove Israel into H in every place of
2:31 gone down to the H places in the wilderness.
2:36 or block up their H places,
2:41 brethren died in their H places."
2Mac 14:30 men, and went into H from Nicanor.

HIE
Song 4:6 shadows flee, I will H me to the mountain

HIEL
1Kgs 16:34 In his days H of Bethel built Jericho; he

HIERONYMUS
2Mac 12:2 Gennaeus, as well as H and Demophon, and in

HIGGAION
Ps 9:16 H. Selah

HIGH (489)
Gen 7:17 ark, and it rose H above the earth.
7:19 earth that all the H mountains under the whole
14:18 and wine; he was priest of God Most H
14:19 Abram by God Most H, maker of heaven and
14:20 blessed be God Most H, who has delivered your
14:22 the LORD God Most H, maker of heaven and
27:39 and away from the dew of heaven on H
29:7 "Behold, it is still H day, it is not
Ex 38:18 long and five cubits H in its breadth, corresponding
Lev 26:30 I will destroy your H places, and cut down
Num 15:30 does anything with a H hand, whether he is
24:16 knowledge of the Most H, who sees the vision
33:52 and demolish all their H places;
35:25 the death of the H priest who was anointed
35:28 the death of the H priest; but after the
35:28 the death of the H priest the manslayer may
35:32 the death of the H priest.
Deut 2:36 not a city too H for us; the LORD
3:5 were cities fortified with H walls, gates, and bars,
12:2 their gods, upon the H mountains and upon the
26:19 he will set you H above all nations that
28:1 God will set you H above all the nations
28:52 your towns, until your H and fortified walls, in
32:8 When the Most H gave to the nations their
32:13 him ride on the H places of the earth,
33:29 shall tread upon their H places."
Josh 20:6 of him who is H priest at the time:
1Sam 9:12 sacrifice today on the H place.
9:13 goes up to the H place to eat; for
9:14 way up to the H place.
9:19 before me to the H place, for today you
9:25 came down from the H place into the city,
10:5 down from the H place with harp, tambourine,
10:13 he came to the H place.
2Sam 1:19 is slain upon thy H places!
1:25 lies slain upon thy H places.
22:14 heaven, and the Most H uttered his voice.
22:17 "He reached from on H, he took me, he
23:1 who was raised on H, the anointed of the
1Kgs 3:2 were sacrificing at the H places, however, because no
3:3 burnt incense at the H places.
3:4 that was the great H place; Solomon used to
4:2 and these were his H officials: Azariah the son
6:2 cubits long, twenty cubits wide, and thirty cubits H
6:10 each story five cubits H, and it was joined
6:20 wide, and twenty cubits H; and he overlaid it
6:23 made two cherubim of olivewood, each ten cubits H
7:23 brim, and five cubits H, and a line of
7:27 cubits long, four cubits wide, and three cubits H
7:35 band half a cubit H; and on the top
11:7 Then Solomon built a H place for Chemosh the
12:31 also made houses on H places, and appointed priests
12:32 the priests of the H places that he had
13:2 the priests of the H places who burn incense
13:32 the houses of the H places which are in
13:33 made priests for the H places again from among
13:33 be priests of the H places.
14:23 also built for themselves H places, and pillars, and
14:23 and Asherim on every H hill and under every
15:14 But the H places were not taken away.
21:9 and set Naboth on H among the people;
21:12 and set Naboth on H among the people.
22:43 the LORD; yet the H places were not taken
22:43 burned incense on the H places.
2Kgs 5:1 his master and in H favor, because by him
12:3 Nevertheless the H places were not taken away; the
12:3 burn incense on the H places.
12:10 king's secretary and the H priest came up and
14:4 But the H places were not removed; the people
14:4 burned incense on the H places.
15:4 Nevertheless the H places were not taken away; the
15:4 burned incense on the H places.
15:35 Nevertheless the H places were not removed; the
15:35 burned incense on the H places.
16:4 burned incense on the H places, and on the
17:9 They built for themselves H places at all their
17:10 and Asherim on every H hill and under every
17:11 incense on all the H places, as the nations
17:29 the shrines of the H places which the Samaritans
17:32 as priests of the H places, who sacrificed for
17:32 the shrines of the H places.
18:4 He removed the H places, and broke the pillars,
18:22 it not he whose H places and altars Hezekiah
21:3 For he rebuilt the H places which Hezekiah his
22:4 up to Hilkiah the H priest, that he may
22:8 And Hilkiah the H priest said to Shaphan the
23:4 king commanded Hilkiah, the H priest, and the
23:5 burn incense in the H places at the cities
23:8 Judah, and defiled the H places where the priests
23:8 he broke down the H places of the gates
23:9 the priests of the H places did not come
23:13 the king defiled the H places that were east
23:15 altar at Bethel, the H place erected by Jeroboam
23:15 that altar with the H place he pulled down
23:19 shrines also of the H places that were in
23:20 the priests of the H places who were there,
1Chr 16:39 the LORD in the H place that was at
21:29 that time in the H place at Gibeon;
2Chr 1:3 him, went to the H place that was at
1:13 Solomon came from the H place at Gibeon, from
3:15 two pillars thirty-five cubits H, with a capital of
4:1 long, and twenty cubits wide, and ten cubits H
4:2 brim, and five cubits H, and a line of
6:13 wide, and three cubits H, and had set it
11:15 own priests for the H places, and for the
14:3 foreign altars and the H places, and broke down
14:5 cities of Judah the H places and the incense
15:17 But the H places were not taken out of
17:6 furthermore he took the H places and the Asherim
20:33 The H places, however, were not taken away; the
21:11 Moreover he made H places in the hill country
28:4 burned incense on the H places, and on the
28:25 of Judah he made H places to burn incense
31:1 and broke down the H places and the altars
32:12 Hezekiah taken away his H places and his altars
33:3 For he rebuilt the H places which his father
33:17 still sacrificed at the H places, but only to
33:19 on which he built H places and set up
34:3 and Jerusalem of the H places, the Asherim, and
34:9 came to Hilkiah the H priest and delivered the
Neh 3:1 Then Eliashib the H priest rose up with his
3:20 house of Eliashib the H priest.
13:28 son of Eliashib the H priest, was the son-in-law
Tob 1:4 dwelling of the Most H was consecrated and
1:13 Then the Most H gave me favor and good
4:11 excellent offering in the presence of the Most H
Jud 1:2 the walls seventy cubits H and fifty cubits wide;
1:3 towers a hundred cubits H and sixty cubits wide
1:4 which were seventy cubits H and forty cubits wide,
4:5 immediately seized all the H hilltops and fortified
4:6 And Joakim, the H priest, who was in Jerusalem
4:8 did as Joakim the H priest and the senate
4:14 And Joakim the H priest and all the priests
5:1 and fortified all the H hilltops and set up
7:4 whole land; neither the H mountains nor the valleys
13:18 blessed by the Most H God above all women
15:8 Then Joakim the H priest, and the senate of

H

Esth 1:20 honor to their husbands, H and low."
5:14 a gallows fifty cubits H be made, and in
7:9 king, is standing in Haman's house, fifty cubits H
10:2 full account of the H honor of Mordecai, to
16:16 sons of the Most H, the most mighty living
Job 5:11 fields; he sets on H those who are lowly,
16:19 and he that vouches for me is on H
21:22 seeing that he judges those that are on H
22:12 "Is not God H in the heavens?
25:2 makes peace in his H heaven.
31:2 above, and my heritage from the Almighty on H
39:27 eagle mounts up and makes his nest on H
41:34 beholds everything that is H; he is king over
Ps 7:7 thee; and over it take thy seat on H
7:17 to the name of the LORD, the Most H
9:2 will sing praise to thy name, O Most H
10:5 thy judgments are on H, out of his sight;
18:13 heavens, and the Most H uttered his voice, hailstones
18:16 He reached from on H, he took me, he
21:7 love of the Most H he shall not be
27:5 he will set me H upon a rock.
44:12 a trifle, demanding no H price for them.
46:4 of God, the holy habitation of the Most H
47:2 the LORD, the Most H, is terrible, a great
49:2 world, both low and H, rich and poor together!
50:14 vows to the Most H;
57:2 cry to God Most H, to God who fulfils
62:9 a breath, men of H estate are a delusion;
68:18 Thou didst ascend the H mount, leading captives in
69:29 let thy salvation, O God, set me on H
71:19 O God, reach the H heavens.
73:11 Is there knowledge in the Most H
75:5 up your horn on H, or speak with insolent
77:10 hand of the Most H has changed."
78:17 rebelling against the Most H in the desert.
78:35 their rock, the Most H God their redeemer.
78:56 rebelled against the Most H God, and did not
78:58 to anger with their H places; they moved him
78:69 his sanctuary like the H heavens, like the earth,
82:6 sons of the Most H, all of you;
83:18 LORD, art the Most H over all the earth.
87:5 her"; for the Most H himself will establish her.
89:13 strong is thy hand, H thy right hand.
91:1 shelter of the Most H, who abides in the
91:9 your refuge, the Most H your habitation,
92:1 thy name, O Most H;
92:8 O LORD, art on H for ever.
93:4 sea, the LORD on H is mighty!
97:9 O LORD, art most H over all the earth;
103:11 as the heavens are H above the earth, so
104:18 The H mountains are for the wild goats; the
106:7 rebelled against the Most H at the Red Sea.
107:11 God, and spurned the counsel of the Most H
113:4 The LORD is H above all nations, and his
113:5 who is seated on H,
131:1 are not raised too H; I do not occupy
138:6 though the LORD is H, he regards the lowly;
139:6 for me; it is H, I cannot attain it.
144:7 thy hand from on H, rescue me and deliver
149:6 Let the H praises of God be in their
Prov 9:14 a seat on the H places of the town,
17:19 who makes his door H seeks destruction.
18:11 city, and like a H wall protecting him.
24:7 Wisdom is too H for a fool; in the
30:13 are their eyes, how H their eyelids lift!
30:19 a ship on the H seas, and the way
Eccl 5:8 the matter; for the H official is watched by
10:6 is set in many H places, and the rich
12:5 also of what is H, and terrors are in
Wis 5:15 the Lord; the Most H takes care of them.
6:3 sovereignty from the Most H, who will search out
6:5 falls on those in H places.
9:17 wisdom and sent thy holy Spirit from on H
Sir 4:10 son of the Most H, and he will love
7:9 offering to the Most H God he will accept
7:15 farm work, which were created by the Most H
9:15 discussion be about the law of the Most H
12:2 if not by him, certainly by the Most H
12:6 For the Most H also hates sinners and will
16:15 and who from on H will remember me?
17:21 Return to the Most H and turn away from
17:22 praises to the Most H in Hades, as do
19:17 law of the Most H take its course.
22:16 Fences set on a H place will not stand
23:18 The Most H will not take notice of my
23:23 law of the Most H; second, she has committed
24:2 assembly of the Most H she will open her
24:3 mouth of the Most H, and covered the earth
24:4 I dwelt in H places, and my throne was
24:22 covenant of the Most H God, the law which
28:7 covenant of the Most H, and overlook ignorance.
29:11 commandments of the Most H, and it will profit
33:15 works of the Most H; they likewise are in
34:6 sent from the Most H as a visitation, do
34:19 The Most H is not pleased with the offerings
35:6 and its pleasing odor rises before the Most H
35:10 Give to the Most H as he has given,
35:17 desist until the Most H visits him, and does
37:14 than seven watchmen sitting H on a watchtower.
37:15 pray to the Most H that he may direct
38:2 comes from the Most H, and he will receive
39:1 law of the Most H will seek out the
39:5 supplication before the Most H; he will open his
41:4 you reject the good pleasure of the Most H
41:8 law of the Most H God!
42:2 law of the Most H and his covenant, and
42:18 For the Most H knows all that may be
43:2 a marvelous instrument, the work of the Most H
43:8 of the hosts on H shining forth in the
43:12 hands of the Most H have stretched it out.
44:21 law of the Most H, and was taken into
46:5 called upon the Most H, the Mighty One, when
47:5 the Lord, the Most H, and he gave him
47:8 Holy One, the Most H, with ascriptions of glory;
48:5 word of the Most H;
49:4 law of the Most H; the kings of Judah
50:1 people was Simon the H priest, son of Onias,
50:2 the foundations for the H double walls, the high
50:2 high double walls, the H retaining walls for the
50:7 temple of the Most H, and like the rainbow
50:14 offering to the Most H, the Almighty,
50:15 odor to the Most H, the King of all.
50:16 to be heard for remembrance before the Most H
50:17 to worship their Lord, the Almighty, God Most H
50:19 besought the Lord Most H in prayer before him
50:21 time, to receive the blessing from the Most H
Is 2:12 is lifted up and H;
2:14 Bashan; against all the H mountains, and against all
2:15 lofty hills; against every H tower, and against every
6:1 sitting upon a throne, H and lifted up; and
7:11 deep as Sheol or H as heaven."
14:13 set my throne on H; I will sit on
14:14 myself like the Most H
15:2 gone up to the H places to weep; over
16:12 wearies himself upon the H place, when he comes
25:12 And the H fortifications of his walls he will
30:13 a break in a H wall, bulging out, and
30:25 lofty mountain and every H hill there will be
32:15 upon us from on H, and the wilderness becomes
33:5 for he dwells on H; he will fill Zion
36:7 it not he whose H places and altars Hezekiah
40:9 you up to a H mountain, O Zion, herald
40:26 up your eyes on H and see: who created
52:13 exalted and lifted up, and shall be very H
57:7 Upon a H and lofty mountain you have set
57:15 For thus says the H and lofty One who
57:15 "I dwell in the H and holy place, and
58:4 not make your voice to be heard on H
Jer 2:20 serve.' Yea, upon every H hill and under every
3:6 went up on every H hill and under every
7:31 they have built the H place of Topheth, which
17:2 tree, and on the H hills,
17:12 glorious throne set on H from the beginning is
19:5 and have built the H places of Baal to
25:30 will roar from on H, and from his holy
32:35 They built the H places of Baal in the
48:35 offers sacrifice in the H place and burns incense
49:16 make your nest as H as the eagles, I
51:58 the ground and her H gates shall be burned
Lam 1:13 "From on H he sent fire; into my bones
3:35 presence of the Most H,
3:38 mouth of the Most H that good and evil
Bar 1:7 Jerusalem to Jehoiakim the H priest, the son of
3:25 no bounds; it is H and immeasurable.
5:7 ordered that every H mountain and the everlasting
Ezek 6:3 I will destroy your H places.
6:6 be waste and your H places ruined, so that
6:13 their altars, upon every H hill, on all the
17:22 plant it upon a H and lofty mountain;
17:24 LORD bring low the H tree, and make high
17:24 high tree, and make H the low tree, dry
20:28 wherever they saw any H hill or any leafy

20:29 them, What is the H place to which you
21:26 which is low, and abase that which is H
27:26 you out into the H seas.
31:5 So it towered H above all the trees of
31:10 GOD: Because it towered H and set its top
34:6 mountains and on every H hill; my sheep were
40:2 down upon a very H mountain, on which was
40:42 broad, and one cubit H, on which the instruments
41:22 of wood, three cubits H, two cubits long, and
43:13 shall be one cubit H, and one cubit broad,
43:15 hearth projecting upward, four horns, one cubit H
Dan 2:48 the king gave Daniel H honors and many great
3:94 servants of the Most H God, come forth, and
4:2 wonders that the Most H God has wrought toward
4:17 know that the Most H rules the kingdom of
4:24 decree of the Most H, which has come upon
4:25 know that the Most H rules the kingdom of
4:32 learned that the Most H rules the kingdom of
4:34 I blessed the Most H, and praised and honored
5:18 O king, the Most H God gave Nebuchadnezzar your
5:21 knew that the Most H God rules the kingdom
7:18 saints of the Most H shall receive the kingdom,
7:22 saints of the Most H, and the time came
7:25 words against the Most H, and shall wear out
7:25 saints of the Most H, and shall think to
7:27 saints of the Most H; their kingdom shall be
8:3 and both horns were H, but one was higher
Hos 10:8 The H places of Aven, the sin of Israel,
Amos 7:9 pass by them; the H places of Isaac shall
Obad 1:3 rock, whose dwelling is H, who say in your
Mic 1:3 and tread upon the H places of the earth.
6:6 the LORD, and bow myself before God on H
Hab 2:9 set his nest on H, to be safe from
3:10 forth its voice, it lifted its hands on H
3:19 me tread upon my H places.
Hag 1:1 son of Jehozadak, the H priest,
1:12 son of Jehozadak, the H priest, with all the
1:14 son of Jehozadak, the H priest, and the spirit
2:2 son of Jehozadak, the H priest, and to all
2:4 son of Jehozadak, the H priest; take courage, all
Zech 3:1 showed me Joshua the H priest standing before the
3:8 now, O Joshua the H priest, you and your
6:11 son of Jehozadak, the H priest;
1Mac 4:60 fortified Mount Zion with H walls and strong towers
6:7 surrounded the sanctuary with H walls as before, and
6:40 spread out on the H hills, and some troops
7:5 who wanted to be H priest.
7:9 Alcimus, whom he made H priest; and he
9:50 Pharathon, and Tephon, with H walls and gates and
10:20 today to be the H priest of your nation;
10:32 give it to the H priest, that he may
10:38 other authority but the H priest.
10:69 message to Jonathan the H priest:
12:3 and said, "Jonathan the H priest and the Jewish
12:6 the Spartans: "Jonathan the H priest, the senate of
12:7 sent to Onias the H priest from Arius, who
12:20 Spartans, to Onias the H priest, greeting.
12:36 and to erect a H barrier between the citadel
13:27 brothers; he made it H that it might be
13:33 them all around, with H towers and great walls
13:36 Demetrius to Simon, the H priest and friend of
13:42 of Simon the great H priest and commander and
14:17 his brother had become H priest in his place,
14:20 Spartans to Simon the H priest and to the
14:23 this to Simon the H priest.'"
14:27 of Simon the great H priest,
14:30 nation, and became their H priest, and was gathered
14:35 him their leader and H priest, because he had
14:39 friends and paid him H honors.
14:41 be their leader and H priest for ever, until
14:47 and agreed to be H priest, to be commander
15:2 Antiochus to Simon the H priest and ethnarch and
15:17 sent by Simon the H priest and by the
15:21 over to Simon the H priest, that he may
15:24 things to Simon the H priest.
16:12 was son-in-law of the H priest.
16:24 time that he became H priest after his father.
2Mac 3:1 the piety of the H priest Onias and his
3:4 a disagreement with the H priest about the
3:9 kindly welcomed by the H priest of the city,
3:10 The H priest explained that there were some
3:16 the appearance of the H priest was to be
3:21 the anxiety of the H priest in his great
3:31 call upon the Most H and to grant life
3:32 And the H priest, fearing that the king might
3:33 While the H priest was making the offering of
3:33 grateful to Onias the H priest, since for his
4:13 was ungodly and no H priest,
4:31 Andronicus, a man of H rank, to act as
6:18 of the scribes in H position, a man now
6:23 But making a H resolve, worthy of his years
8:30 of some exceedingly H strongholds, and they divided
9:8 he could weigh the H mountains in a balance,
13:5 that place, fifty cubits H, full of ashes, and
14:3 who had formerly been H priest but had wilfully
14:13 set up Alcimus as H priest of the greatest
15:12 Onias, who had been H priest, a noble and
Mt 4:8 him to a very H mountain, and showed him
17:1 led them up a H mountain apart.
26:3 the palace of the H priest, who was called
26:51 the slave of the H priest, and cut off
26:57 him to Caiaphas the H priest, where the scribes
26:58 the courtyard of the H priest, and going inside
26:62 And the H priest stood up and said, "Have
26:63 And the H priest said to him, "I adjure
26:65 Then the H priest tore his robes, and said,
Mk 2:26 God, when Abiathar was H priest, and ate the
5:7 Son of the Most H God?
9:2 led them up a H mountain apart by themselves;
14:47 the slave of the H priest and cut off
14:53 led Jesus to the H priest; and all the
14:54 the courtyard of the H priest; and he was
14:60 And the H priest stood up in the midst,
14:61 Again the H priest asked him, "Are you the
14:63 And the H priest tore his garments, and said,
14:66 the maids of the H priest came;
Lk 1:32 Son of the Most H; and the Lord God
1:35 power of the Most H will overshadow you; therefore
1:76 prophet of the Most H; for you will go
1:78 upon us from on H
4:38 was ill with a H fever, and they besought
6:35 sons of the Most H; for he is kind
8:28 Son of the Most H God?
22:48 the slave of the H priest and cut off
22:52 bringing him into the H priest's house.
24:49 until you are clothed with power from on H
Jn 11:49 them, Caiaphas, who was H priest that year, said
11:51 own accord, but being H priest that year he
18:10 it and struck the H priest's slave and cut
18:13 of Caiaphas, who was H priest that year.
18:15 was known to the H priest, he entered the
18:15 the court of the H priest along with Jesus,
18:16 was known to the H priest, went out and
18:19 The H priest then questioned Jesus about his
18:22 how you answer the H priest?"
18:24 bound to Caiaphas the H priest.
18:26 the servants of the H priest, a kinsman of
19:31 that sabbath was a H day), the Jews asked
Acts 4:6 Jerusalem, with Annas the H priest and Caiaphas
5:13 people held them in H honor.
5:17 But the H priest rose up and all who
5:21 Now the H priest came and those who were
5:27 And the H priest questioned them,
7:1 And the H priest said, "Is this so?"
7:48 Yet the Most H does not dwell in houses
9:1 Lord, went to the H priest
13:50 the devout women of H standing and the leading
16:17 servants of the Most H God, who proclaim to
17:12 few Greek women of H standing as well as
19:14 sons of a Jewish H priest named Sceva were
22:5 and women, as the H priest and the whole
23:2 And the H priest Ananias commanded those who
23:4 "Would you revile God's H priest?"
23:5 that he was the H priest; for it is
24:1 after five days the H priest Ananias came down
Eph 4:8 "When he ascended on H he led a host
1Tim 2:2 all who are in H positions, that we may
Heb 1:3 of the Majesty on H,
2:17 a merciful and faithful H priest in the service
3:1 Jesus, the apostle and H priest of our confession.
4:14 we have a great H priest who has passed
4:15 we have not a H priest who is unable
5:1 For every H priest chosen from among men is
5:5 to be made a H priest, but was appointed
5:10 designated by God a H priest after the order
6:20 behalf, having become a H priest for ever after
7:1 priest of the Most H God, met Abraham returning
7:26 have such a H priest, holy, blameless, unstained,
7:27 no need, like those H priests, to offer sacrifices
7:28 in their weakness as H priests, but the word
8:1 we have such a H priest, one who is
8:3 For every H priest is appointed to offer gifts

9:7 the second only the H priest goes, and he
9:11 Christ appeared as a H priest of the good
9:25 himself repeatedly, as the H priest enters the Holy
13:11 the sanctuary by the H priest as a sacrifice
Rev 14:20 the wine press, as H as a horse's bridle,
18:5 her sins are heaped H as heaven, and God
21:10 away to a great, H mountain, and showed me
21:12 It had a great, H wall, with twelve gates,

HIGH-PRIESTHOOD (12)

1Mac 7:21 Alcimus strove for the H,
11:27 confirmed him in the H and in as many
11:57 confirm you in the H and set you over
14:38 confirmed him in the H,
16:24 the chronicles of his H, from the time that
2Mac 4:7 of Onias obtained the H by corruption,
4:24 and secured the H for himself, outbidding Jason
4:25 no qualification for the H, but having the hot
4:29 as deputy in the H, while Sostratus left Crates,
11:3 to put up the H for sale every year.
14:7 I mean the H -- and have
Lk 3:2 of Abilene, in the H of Annas and Caiaphas,

HIGH-PRIESTLY

Acts 4:6 who were of the H family.

HIGHER (17)

Num 24:7 his king shall be H than Agag, and his
Deut 28:43 shall mount above you H and higher; and you
28:43 above you higher and H; and you shall come
Ezra 9:6 our iniquities have risen H than our heads, and
Job 11:8 It is H than heaven --what can you
35:5 the clouds, which are H than you.
Ps 61:2 the rock that is H than I;
Eccl 5:8 is watched by a H, and there are yet
5:8 and there are yet H ones over them.
Is 55:9 as the heavens are H than the earth, so
55:9 so are my ways H than your ways and
Dan 8:3 high, but one was H than the other, and
8:3 the other, and the H one came up last.
1Mac 12:36 walls of Jerusalem still H, and to erect a
14:37 the city, and built the walls of Jerusalem H
Lk 14:10 you, 'Friend, go up H; then you will be
1Cor 12:31 But earnestly desire the H gifts.

HIGHEST (18)

1Kgs 8:27 Behold, heaven and the H heaven cannot contain
2Chr 2:6 since heaven, even H heaven, cannot contain him?
6:18 heaven and the H heaven cannot contain thee;
Job 22:12 See the H stars, how lofty they are!
Ps 89:27 him the first-born, the H of the kings of
137:6 set Jerusalem above my H joy!
148:4 Praise him, you H heavens, and you waters above
Prov 9:3 to call from the H places in the town,
Sir 7:4 from the Lord the H office, nor the seat
16:16 Behold, heaven and the H heaven, the abyss and
Is 2:2 be established as the H of the mountains, and
17:6 the top of the H bough, four or five
Mic 4:1 be established as the H of the mountains, and
2Mac 4:15 fathers and putting the H value upon Greek forms
Mt 21:9 Hosanna in the H
Mk 11:10 Hosanna in the H
Lk 2:14 to God in the H, and on earth peace
19:38 Peace in heaven and glory in the H

HIGHLY (46)

1Sam 18:30 that his name was H esteemed.
1Chr 14:2 that his kingdom was H exalted for the sake
Ps 47:9 to God; he is H exalted!
Prov 4:9 Prize her H, and she will exalt you; she
Sir 19:21 lacks intelligence, than the H prudent man who
Dan 3:52 to be praised and H exalted for ever;
3:53 name and to be H praised and highly exalted
3:53 be highly praised and H exalted for ever;
3:54 to be extolled and H glorified for ever.
3:55 to be praised and H exalted for ever.
3:56 to be extolled and H exalted for ever.
3:58 praise to him and H exalt him for ever.
3:59 praise to him and H exalt him for ever.
3:60 praise to him and H exalt him for ever.
3:61 praise to him and H exalt him for ever.
3:62 praise to him and H exalt him for ever.
3:63 praise to him and H exalt him for ever.
3:64 praise to him and H exalt him for ever.
3:65 praise to him and H exalt him for ever.
3:66 praise to him and H exalt him for ever.
3:67 praise to him and H exalt him for ever.
3:68 praise to him and H exalt him for ever.
3:69 praise to him and H exalt him for ever.
3:70 praise to him and H exalt him for ever.
3:71 praise to him and H exalt him for ever.
3:72 praise to him and H exalt him for ever.
3:73 praise to him and H exalt him for ever.
3:74 praise to him and H exalt him for ever.
3:75 praise to him and H exalt him for ever.
3:76 praise to him and H exalt him for ever.
3:77 praise to him and H exalt him for ever.
3:78 praise to him and H exalt him for ever.
3:79 praise to him and H exalt him for ever.
3:80 praise to him and H exalt him for ever.
3:81 praise to him and H exalt him for ever.
3:82 praise to him and H exalt him for ever.
3:83 praise to him and H exalt him for ever.
3:84 praise to him and H exalt him for ever.
3:85 praise to him and H exalt him for ever.
3:86 praise to him and H exalt him for ever.
3:87 praise to him and H exalt him for ever.
3:88 praise to him and H exalt him for ever.
3:89 praise to him and H exalt him for ever;
Rom 12:3 think of himself more H than he ought to
Phil 2:9 Therefore God has H exalted him and bestowed on
1Thes 5:13 to esteem them very H in love because of

HIGHWAY (20)

Num 20:17 go along the King's H, we will not turn
20:19 go up by the H; and if we drink
21:22 go by the King's H, until we have passed
Judg 21:19 the east of the H that goes up from
1Sam 6:12 of Beth-shemesh along one H, lowing as they went;
2Sam 20:12 Amasa lay wallowing in his blood in the H
20:12 Amasa out of the H into the field, and
20:13 taken out of the H, all the people went
2Kgs 18:17 which is on the H to the Fuller's Field.
Prov 15:19 the path of the upright is a level H
16:17 The H of the upright turns aside from evil;
Is 7:3 upper pool on the H to the Fuller's Field,
11:16 there will be a H from Assyria for the
19:23 there will be a H from Egypt to Assyria,
35:8 And a H shall be there, and it shall
36:2 upper pool on the H to the Fuller's Field.
40:3 in the desert a H for our God.
62:10 up, build up the H, clear it of stones,
Jer 18:15 into bypaths, not the H,
31:21 guideposts; consider well the H, the road by which

HIGHWAYS (11)

Judg 20:31 the people, in the H, one of which goes
20:32 draw them away from the city to the H
20:45 cut down in the H, and they were pursued
Tob 1:15 and under him the H were unsafe, so that
Ps 84:5 whose heart are the H to Zion.
Is 33:8 The H lie waste, the wayfaring man ceases.
49:11 a way, and my H shall be raised up.
59:7 of iniquity, desolation and destruction are in their H
1Mac 5:4 to the people and ambushed them on the H
15:41 make raids along the H of Judea, as the
Lk 14:23 'Go out to the H and hedges, and compel

HILEN

1Chr 6:58 with its pasture lands, H with its pasture lands,

HILKIAH (40)

2Kgs 18:18 Eliakim the son of H, who was over the
18:26 Eliakim the son of H, and Shebnah, and Joah,
18:37 Eliakim the son of H, who was over the
22:4 saying, "Go up to H the high priest, that
22:8 And H the high priest said to Shaphan the
22:8 And H gave the book to Shaphan, and he
22:10 secretary told the king, H the priest has given
22:12 And the king commanded H the priest, and Ahikam
22:14 So H the priest, and Ahikam, and Achbor, and
23:4 And the king commanded H, the high priest, and
23:24 in the book that H the priest found in
1Chr 6:13 of Shallum, Shallum of H, Hilkiah of Azariah,
6:13 Shallum, Shallum of Hilkiah, H of Azariah,
6:45 of Amaziah, son of H,
9:11 Azariah the son of H, son of Meshullam, son
26:11 father made him chief), H the second, Tebaliah the
2Chr 34:9 They came to H the high priest and delivered
34:14 house of the LORD, H the priest found the
34:15 Then H said to Shaphan the secretary, "I have
34:15 of the LORD"; and H gave the book to

34:18 secretary told the king, H the priest has given
34:20 And the king commanded H, Ahikam the son of
34:22 So H and those whom the king had sent
35:8 H, Zechariah, and Jehiel, the chief officers of the
Ezra 7:1 of Azariah, son of H,
Neh 8:4 Mattithiah, Shema, Anaiah, Uriah, H, and Ma-aseiah
11:11 Seraiah the son of H, son of Meshullam, son
12:7 Joiarib, Jedaiah, Sallu, Amok, H, Jedaiah.
12:21 Amok, Eber; of H, Hashabiah; of Jedaiah, Nethanel.
Jud 8:1 of Elijah, son of H, son of Eliab, son
Is 22:20 Eliakim the son of H,
36:3 Eliakim the son of H, who was over the
36:22 Eliakim the son of H, who was over the
Jer 1:1 Jeremiah, the son of H, of the priests who
29:3 Gemariah the son of H, whom Zedekiah king of
Bar 1:1 of Hasadiah, son of H, wrote in Babylon,
1:7 priest, the son of H, son of Shallum, and
Dan 13:2 Susanna, the daughter of H, a very beautiful woman
13:29 Susanna, the daughter of H, who is the wife
13:63 And H and his wife praised God for their

HILL (167)

Gen 10:30 of Sephar to the H country of the east.
31:21 his face toward the H country of Gilead.
31:23 after him into the H country of Gilead.
31:25 his tent in the H country, and Laban with
31:25 kinsmen encamped in the H country of Gilead.
36:8 Esau dwelt in the H country of Seir; Esau
36:9 the Edomites in the H country of Seir.
Ex 17:9 the top of the H with the rod of
17:10 Hur went up to the top of the H
Num 13:17 go up into the H country,
13:29 Amorites dwell in the H country; and the Canaanites
14:40 the heights of the H country, saying, "See, we
14:44 the heights of the H country, although neither the
14:45 who dwelt in that H country came down, and
Deut 1:7 and go to the H country of the Amorites,
1:7 the Arabah, in the H country and in the
1:19 the way to the H country of the Amorites,
1:20 have come to the H country of the Amorites,
1:24 went up into the H country, and came to
1:41 go up into the H country.
1:43 went up into the H country.
1:44 who lived in that H country came out against
2:37 the cities of the H country, and wherever the
3:12 Arnon, and half the H country of Gilead with
3:25 the Jordan, that goodly H country, and Lebanon.'
Josh 9:1 the Jordan in the H country and in the
10:6 that dwell in the H country are gathered against
10:40 the whole land, the H country and the Negeb
11:2 were in the northern H country, and in the
11:3 the Jebusites in the H country, and the Hivites
11:16 all that land, the H country and all the
11:16 the Arabah and the H country of Israel and
11:21 the Anakim from the H country, from Hebron, from
11:21 and from all the H country of Judah, and
11:21 and from all the H country of Israel; Joshua
12:8 their allotments, in the H country, in the lowland,
13:6 the inhabitants of the H country from Lebanon to
13:19 and Zereth-shahar on the H of the valley,
14:12 now give me this H country of which the
15:11 the shoulder of the H north of Ekron, then
15:48 And in the H country, Shamir, Jattir, Socoh,
16:1 from Jericho into the H country to Bethel;
17:15 the Rephaim, since the H country of Ephraim is
17:16 of Joseph said, "The H country is not enough
17:18 lot only, but the H country shall be yours,
18:12 then up through the H country westward; and it
19:50 asked, Timnath-serah in the H country of Ephraim;
20:7 in Galilee in the H country of Naphtali, and
20:7 and Shechem in the H country of Ephraim, and
20:7 is, Hebron) in the H country of Judah.
21:11 is Hebron, in the H country of Judah, along
21:21 pasture lands in the H country of Ephraim, Gezer
24:4 I gave Esau the H country of Seir to
24:30 which is in the H country of Ephraim, north
24:33 given him in the H country of Ephraim.
Judg 1:9 who dwelt in the H country, in the Negeb,
1:19 took possession of the H country, but he could
1:34 Danites back into the H country, for they did
2:9 in Timnath-heres, in the H country of Ephraim, north
3:27 the trumpet in the H country of Ephraim; and
3:27 with him from the H country, having him at
4:5 and Bethel in the H country of Ephraim; and
7:1 of them, by the H of Moreh, in the
7:24 messengers throughout all the H country of Ephraim,
10:1 at Shamir in the H country of Ephraim.
12:15 of Ephraim, in the H country of the Amalekites.
16:3 the top of the H that is before Hebron.
17:1 a man of the H country of Ephraim, whose
17:8 he came to the H country of Ephraim to
18:2 they came to the H country of Ephraim, to
18:13 from there to the H country of Ephraim, and
19:1 remote parts of the H country of Ephraim, who
19:16 man was from the H country of Ephraim, and
19:18 remote parts of the H country of Ephraim, from
1Sam 1:1 of Ramathaim-zophim of the H country of Ephraim,
7:1 of Abinadab on the H; and they consecrated his
9:4 they passed through the H country of Ephraim and
9:11 they went up the H to the city, they
13:2 in Michmash and the H country of Bethel, and
14:22 hid themselves in the H country of Ephraim heard
23:14 the wilderness, in the H country of the Wilderness
23:19 at Horesh, on the H of Hachilah, which is
26:1 hiding himself on the H of Hachilah, which is
26:3 Saul encamped on the H of Hachilah, which is
2Sam 2:24 they came to the H of Ammah, which lies
2:25 took their stand on the top of a H
6:3 which was on the H; and Uzzah and Ahio,
20:21 a man of the H country of Ephraim, called
1Kgs 4:8 names: Ben-hur, in the H country of Ephraim;
5:15 of stone in the H country,
12:25 built Shechem in the H country of Ephraim, and
14:23 Asherim on every high H and under every green
16:24 He bought the H of Samaria from Shemer for
16:24 and he fortified the H, and called the name
16:24 the name of Shemer, the owner of the H
2Kgs 1:9 the top of a H, and said to him,
5:22 to me from the H country of Ephraim two
5:24 he came to the H, he took them from
17:10 Asherim on every high H and under every green
1Chr 6:67 pasture lands in the H country of Ephraim, Gezer
2Chr 2:2 to quarry in the H country, and three thousand
2:18 to quarry in the H country, and three thousand
13:4 which is in the H country of Ephraim, and
15:8 had taken in the H country of Ephraim, and
19:4 from Beer-sheba to the H country of Ephraim, and
21:11 high places in the H country of Judah, and
27:4 built cities in the H country of Judah, and
Jud 1:6 the people of the H country and all those
2:22 went up into the H country
5:3 that lives in the H country?
5:15 possession of all the H country.
5:19 have settled in the H country, because it was
6:7 you back into the H country and put you
6:11 went up into the H country and came to
6:12 the top of the H, and all the slingers
6:13 the shelter of the H and they bound Achior
6:13 the foot of the H, and returned to their
7:1 passes up into the H country and make war
7:18 and encamped in the H country opposite Dothan; and
10:13 and capture all the H country without losing one
11:2 who live in the H country had not slighted
15:2 plain and through the H country.
15:5 Jerusalem and all the H country also came, for
15:7 and towns in the H country and in the
Ps 2:6 have set my king on Zion, my holy H
3:4 LORD, and he answers me from his holy H
15:1 Who shall dwell on thy holy H
24:3 Who shall ascend the H of the LORD?
43:3 me to thy holy H and to thy dwelling!
Song 4:6 of myrrh and the H of frankincense.
Sir 46:9 went up to the H country, and his children
Is 5:1 beloved had a vineyard on a very fertile H
10:32 daughter of Zion, the H of Jerusalem.
13:2 On a bare H raise a signal, cry aloud
30:17 of a mountain, like a signal on a H
30:25 mountain and every high H there will be brooks
31:4 to fight upon Mount Zion and upon its H
32:14 populous city deserted; the H and the watchtower
40:4 and every mountain and H be made low; the
Jer 2:20 Yea, upon every high H and under every green
3:6 up on every high H and under every green
16:16 every mountain and every H, and out of the
17:26 the Shephelah, from the H country, and from the
31:6 will call in the H country of Ephraim: 'Arise,
31:23 of righteousness, O holy H
31:39 farther, straight to the H Gareb, and shall then
32:44 the cities of the H country, in the cities
33:13 the cities of the H country, in the cities
49:16 the rock, who hold the height of the H
50:6 mountains; from mountain to H they have gone, they

H

Ezek 6:13 altars, upon every high H, on all the mountain
20:28 they saw any high H or any leafy tree,
34:6 and on every high H; my sheep were scattered
34:26 places round about my H a blessing; and I
Dan 9:16 city Jerusalem, thy holy H; because for our sins,
9:20 God for the holy H of my God;
Mic 4:8 tower of the flock, H of the daughter of
Mal 1:3 have laid waste his H country and left his
1Mac 4:46 place on the temple H until there should come
10:70 against us in the H country?
13:52 fortifications of the temple H alongside the citadel,
16:20 to take possession of Jerusalem and the temple H
Mt 5:14 city set on a H cannot be hid.
Lk 1:39 with haste into the H country, to a city
1:65 about through all the H country of Judea;
3:5 and every mountain and H shall be brought low,
4:29 the brow of the H on which their city

HILLEL (2)

Judg 12:13 Abdon the son of H the Pirathonite judged Israel.
12:15 Abdon the son of H the Pirathonite died, and

HILLS (76)

Gen 19:17 valley; flee to the H, lest you be consumed."
19:19 cannot flee to the H, lest the disaster overtake
19:30 and dwelt in the H with his two daughters,
49:26 bounties of the everlasting H; may they be on
Num 23:9 see him, from the H I behold him; lo,
Deut 8:7 forth in valleys and H,
8:9 and out of whose H you can dig copper.
11:11 is a land of H and valleys, which drinks
12:2 mountains and upon the H and under every green
33:15 abundance of the everlasting H,
Josh 2:16 them, "Go into the H, lest the pursuers meet
2:22 and went into the H, and remained there three
2:23 down again from the H, and passed over and
1Kgs 20:23 are gods of the H, and so they were
20:28 a god of the H but he is not
2Kgs 16:4 places, and on the H, and under every green
2Chr 26:10 and vinedressers in the H and in the fertile
27:4 Judah, and forts and towers on the wooded H
28:4 places, and on the H, and under every green
Neh 8:15 "Go out to the H and bring branches of
Jud 4:7 passes up into the H, since by them Judea
5:1 the passes in the H and fortified all the
7:4 the valleys nor the H will bear their weight."
15:3 had camped in the H around Bethulia also took
16:4 blocked up the valleys, their cavalry covered the H
Job 15:7 Or were you brought forth before the H
Ps 50:10 forest is mine, the cattle on a thousand H
65:12 the wilderness drip, the H gird themselves with joy,
72:3 the people, and the H, in righteousness!
98:8 their hands; let the H sing for joy together
104:10 they flow between the H,
114:4 skipped like rams, the H like lambs.
114:6 O H, like lambs?
121:1 I lift up my eyes to the H
147:8 the earth, he makes grass grow upon the H
148:9 Mountains and all H, fruit trees and all cedars!
Prov 8:25 been shaped, before the H, I was brought forth;
Song 2:8 leaping upon the mountains, bounding over the H
Is 2:2 be raised above the H; and all the nations
2:14 against all the lofty H;
7:25 as for all the H which used to be
40:12 in scales and the H in a balance?
41:15 you shall make the H like chaff;
42:15 lay waste mountains and H, and dry up all
54:10 may depart and the H be removed, but my
55:12 the mountains and the H before you shall break
65:7 reviled me upon the H, I will measure into
Jer 3:23 Truly the H are a delusion, the orgies on
4:24 quaking, and all the H moved to and fro.
13:27 lewd harlotries, on the H in the field.
17:2 and on the high H,
50:19 be satisfied on the H of Ephraim and in
Bar 5:7 mountain and the everlasting H be made low and
Ezek 6:3 the mountains and the H, to the ravines and
35:8 the slain; on your H and in your valleys
36:4 the mountains and the H, the ravines and the
36:6 to the mountains and H, to the ravines and
Dan 3:76 the Lord, mountains and H, sing praise to him
Hos 4:13 make offerings upon the H, under oak, poplar, and
10:8 us, and to the H, Fall upon us.
Joel 3:18 sweet wine, and the H shall flow with milk,
Amos 9:13 wine, and all the H shall flow with it.
Mic 4:1 raised up above the H; and peoples shall flow
6:1 mountains, and let the H hear your voice.
Nah 1:5 quake before him, the H melt; the earth is
Hab 3:6 were scattered, the everlasting H sank low.
Zeph 1:10 the Second Quarter, a loud crash from the H
Hag 1:8 Go up to the H and bring wood and
1:11 the land and the H, upon the grain, the
1Mac 2:28 sons fled to the H and left all that
4:5 for them in the H, because he said, "These
4:18 and his force are near us in the H
4:19 speech, a detachment appeared, coming out of the H
6:39 gold and brass, the H were ablaze with them
6:40 out on the high H, and some troops were
Lk 23:29 us'; and to the H, 'Cover us.'

HILLSIDE (3)

2Sam 16:13 went along on the H opposite him and cursed
Mk 5:11 feeding there on the H;
Lk 8:32 feeding there on the H; and they begged him

HILLTOP (2)

Jud 2:24 and destroyed all the H cities along the brook
3:6 stationed garrisons in the H cities and took picked

HILLTOPS (2)

Jud 4:5 seized all the high H and fortified the villages
5:1 fortified all the high H and set up barricades

HILT

Judg 3:22 his belly; and the H also went in after

HIMSELF (583)

Gen 13:11 So Lot chose for H all the Jordan valley,
17:17 laughed, and said to H, "Shall a child be
18:2 meet them, and bowed H to the earth,
19:1 meet them, and bowed H with his face to
20:5 Did he not H say to me, 'She is
22:8 said, "God will provide H the lamb for a
24:52 their words, he bowed H to the earth before
27:41 and Esau said to H, "The days of mourning
27:42 your brother Esau comforts H by planning to kill
30:36 three days' journey between H and Jacob; and Jacob
32:21 before him; and he H lodged that night in
33:3 He H went on before them, bowing himself to
33:3 on before them, bowing H to the ground seven
33:17 to Succoth, and built H a house, and made
35:7 there God had revealed H to him when he
41:14 when he had shaved H and changed his clothes,
43:31 came out; and controlling H he said, "Let food
43:32 They served him by H, and them by themselves,
44:18 against your servant; for you are like Pharaoh H
45:1 Joseph could not control H before all those who
45:1 him when Joseph made H known to his brothers.
46:29 Goshen; and he presented H to him, and fell
47:31 Then Israel bowed H upon the head of his
48:12 knees, and he bowed H with his face to
Ex 21:8 has designated her for H, then he shall let
21:10 takes another wife to H, he shall not diminish
28:38 Aaron shall take upon H any guilt incurred in
30:12 give a ransom for H to the LORD when
Lev 7:8 offering shall have for H the skin of the
9:8 calf of the sin offering, which was for H
13:7 after he has shown H to the priest for
13:33 then he shall shave H, but the itch he
14:8 his hair, and bathe H in water, and he
15:5 his clothes, and bathe H in water, and be
15:6 his clothes, and bathe H in water, and be
15:7 his clothes, and bathe H in water, and be
15:8 his clothes, and bathe H in water, and be
15:10 his clothes, and bathe H in water, and be
15:11 his clothes, and bathe H in water, and be
15:13 he shall count for H seven days for his
15:21 his clothes, and bathe H in water, and be
15:22 his clothes, and bathe H in water, and be
15:27 his clothes, and bathe H in water, and be
16:6 a sin offering for H, and shall make atonement
16:6 shall make atonement for H and for his house.
16:11 a sin offering for H, and shall make atonement
16:11 shall make atonement for H and for his house;
16:11 kill the bull as a sin offering for H
16:17 has made atonement for H and for his house
16:24 and make atonement for H and for the people.
17:15 his clothes, and bathe H in water, and be
19:21 a guilt offering for H to the LORD, to
21:1 of them shall defile H for the dead among
21:3 had no husband; for her he may defile H
21:4 He shall not defile H as a husband among

	21:4	a husband among his people and so profane H
	21:11	dead body, nor defile H, even for his father
	22:8	shall not eat, defiling H by it: I am
	25:26	redeem it, and then H becomes prosperous and finds
	25:28	get it back for H, then what he sold
	25:35	poor, and cannot maintain H with you, you shall
	25:39	beside you, and sells H to you, you shall
	25:47	becomes poor and sells H to the stranger or
	25:49	or if he grows rich he may redeem H
	25:50	year when he sold H to him until the
Num	6:2	a Nazirite, to separate H to the LORD,
	6:3	LORD, he shall separate H from wine and strong
	6:5	for which he separates H to the LORD, he
	6:6	days that he separates H to the LORD he
	6:7	die, shall he make H unclean; because his separation
	6:12	same day, and separate H to the LORD for
	16:9	bring you near to H, to do service in
	19:12	days; he shall cleanse H with the water on
	19:12	he does not cleanse H on the third day
	19:13	and does not cleanse H, defiles the tabernacle of
	19:19	his clothes and bathe H in water, and at
	19:20	and does not cleanse H, that person shall be
	20:13	LORD, and he showed H holy among them.
	25:3	So Israel yoked H to Baal of Peor.
	30:2	an oath to bind H by a pledge, he
	31:53	booty, every man for H
	35:19	avenger of blood shall H put the murderer to
Deut	1:30	goes before you will H fight for you, just
	4:34	take a nation for H from the midst of
	17:16	not multiply horses for H, or cause the people
	17:17	not multiply wives for H, lest his heart turn
	17:17	he greatly multiply for H silver and gold.
	17:18	he shall write for H in a book a
	23:11	on, he shall bathe H in water, and when
	28:9	a people holy to H, as he has sworn
	29:19	this sworn covenant, blesses H in his heart, saying,
	31:3	The LORD your God H will go over before
	33:21	of the land for H, for there a commander's
Josh	22:23	it, may the LORD H take vengeance.
Judg	3:13	He gathered to H the Ammonites and the
	3:16	And Ehud made for H a sword with two
	3:19	But he H turned back at the sculptured stones
	3:24	"He is only relieving H in the closet of
	6:31	let him contend for H, because his altar has
	7:5	you shall set by H; likewise every one that
	9:5	son of Jerubbaal was left, for he hid H
	19:1	Ephraim, who took to H a concubine from
1Sam	2:14	fork brought up the priest would take for H
	3:21	for the LORD revealed H to Samuel at Shiloh
	8:12	he will appoint for H commanders of thousands and
	10:22	"Behold, he has hidden H among the baggage."
	12:22	the LORD to make you a people for H
	14:52	or any valiant man, he attached him to H
	15:12	up a monument for H and turned, and passed
	18:4	And Jonathan stripped H of the robe that was
	19:22	Then he H went to Ramah, and came to
	20:24	So David hid H in the field; and when
	20:41	and wept with one another, until David recovered H
	21:13	before them, and feigned H mad in their hands,
	23:7	for he has shut H in by entering a
	24:3	a cave; and Saul went in to relieve H
	25:31	without cause or for my lord taking vengeance H
	26:1	"Is not David hiding H on the hill of
	27:12	thinking, "He has made H utterly abhorred by his
	28:8	So Saul disguised H and put on other garments,
	29:4	could this fellow reconcile H to his lord?
	30:6	But David strengthened H in the LORD his God.
2Sam	3:6	David, Abner was making H strong in the house
	6:20	king of Israel honored H today, uncovering himself
	6:20	honored himself today, uncovering H today before
	6:20	as one of the vulgar fellows shamelessly uncovers H
	7:23	be his people, making H a name, and doing
	8:13	And David won a name for H
	12:18	He may do H some harm."
	12:20	washed, and anointed H, and changed his clothes;
	13:2	tormented that he made H ill because of his
	14:13	decision the king convicts H, inasmuch as the king
	14:33	the king, and bowed H on his face to
	15:1	After this Absalom got H a chariot and horses,
	16:14	weary at the Jordan; and there he refreshed H
	17:9	now he has hidden H in one of the
	17:23	in order, and hanged H; and he died, and
	18:18	and set up for H the pillar which is
	20:6	him, lest he get H fortified cities, and cause
	23:7	who touches them arms H with iron and the
1Kgs	1:5	son of Haggith exalted H, saying, "I will be
	1:5	and he prepared for H chariots and horsemen, and
	1:47	And the king bowed H upon the bed.
	2:32	righteous and better than H, Abner the son of
	11:29	Now Ahijah had clad H with a new garment;
	13:4	that he could not draw it back to H
	14:14	will raise up for H a king over Israel,
	16:9	was at Tirzah, drinking H drunk in the house
	16:11	as he had seated H on his throne, he
	17:21	Then he stretched H upon the child three times,
	18:2	Elijah went to show H to Ahab.
	18:6	in one direction by H, and Obadiah went in
	18:6	himself, and Obadiah went in another direction by H
	18:42	Carmel; and he bowed H down upon the earth,
	19:4	But he H went a day's journey into the
	20:11	on his armor boast H as he that puts
	20:16	while Ben-hadad was drinking H drunk in the booths,
	20:38	by the way, disguising H with a bandage over
	21:25	was none who sold H to do what was
	21:29	how Ahab has humbled H before me?
	21:29	Because he has humbled H before me, I will
	22:11	of Chenaanah made for H horns of iron, and
	22:30	king of Israel disguised H and went into battle.
2Kgs	4:34	and as he stretched H upon him, the flesh
	4:35	went up, and stretched H upon him; the child
	5:14	went down and dipped H seven times in the
	6:10	so that he saved H there more than once
	7:2	God, "If the LORD H should make windows in
	7:19	God, "If the LORD H should make windows in
	19:1	his clothes, and covered H with sackcloth, and went
	24:12	king of Judah gave H up to the king
	24:12	the king of Babylon, H, and his mother, and
1Chr	15:1	David built houses for H in the city of
	29:5	offer willingly, consecrating H today to the LORD?"
2Chr	1:1	son of David established H in his kingdom, and
	2:1	of the LORD, and a royal palace for H
	2:3	him cedar to build H a house to dwell
	2:12	for the LORD, and a royal palace for H
	12:12	And when he humbled H the wrath of the
	12:13	So King Rehoboam established H in Jerusalem and
	13:9	Whoever comes to consecrate H with a young bull
	16:14	had hewn out for H in the city of
	17:1	his stead, and strengthened H against Israel.
	18:10	of Chenaanah made for H horns of iron, and
	18:29	king of Israel disguised H; and they went into
	18:34	king of Israel propped H up in his chariot
	20:3	Jehoshaphat feared, and set H to seek the LORD,
	23:16	made a covenant between H and all the people
	26:5	He set H to seek God in the days
	26:20	out quickly, and he H hastened to go out,
	28:24	LORD; and he made H altars in every corner
	32:1	the fortified cities, thinking to win them for H
	32:26	But Hezekiah humbled H for the pride of his
	32:27	and he made for H treasuries for silver, for
	32:29	likewise provided cities for H, and flocks and herds
	32:31	God left him to H, in order to try
	33:12	his God and humbled H greatly before the God
	33:19	before he humbled H, behold, they are written
	33:23	he did not humble H before the LORD, as
	33:23	his father had humbled H, but this Amon incurred
	35:22	from him, but disguised H in order to fight
	36:12	He did not humble H before Jeremiah the prophet,
Ezra	6:21	joined them and separated H from the pollutions of
	10:1	confession, weeping and casting H down before the
	10:8	be forfeited, and he H banned from the congregation
Tob	1:22	for Esarhaddon had appointed him second to H
	4:1	and he said to H;
	4:19	understanding; but the Lord H gives all good things,
	6:2	Then the young man went down to wash H
	8:6	helper for him like H
	14:10	received repayment as he H went down into the
Jud	2:4	army, second only to H, and said to him,
Esth	5:10	Nevertheless Haman restrained H, and went home;
	6:6	And Haman said to H, "Whom would the king
	16:18	Hammedatha, because the man H who did these
Job	1:12	your power; only upon H do not put forth
	2:1	among them to present H before the LORD.
	2:8	with which to scrape H, and sat among the
	8:6	then he will rouse H for you and reward
	9:4	—who has hardened H against him, and succeeded?—
	14:22	his own body, and he mourns only for H
	15:2	windy knowledge, and fill H with the east wind?
	15:31	trust in emptiness, deceiving H; for emptiness will be
	17:8	and the innocent stirs H up against the godless.
	22:2	Surely he who is wise is profitable to H
	32:2	Job because he justified H rather than God;
	34:14	back his spirit to H, and gather to himself

34:14 himself, and gather to H his breath,
41:25 When he raises H up the mighty are afraid;
41:30 sharp potsherds; he spreads H like a threshing sledge
Ps 4:3 apart the godly for H; the LORD hears when
9:16 The LORD has made H known, he has executed
10:14 hands; the hapless commits H to thee; thou hast
22:29 he who cannot keep H alive.
25:13 He H shall abide in prosperity, and his children
36:2 For he flatters H in his own eyes that
36:4 his bed; he sets H in a way that
48:3 citadels God has shown H a sure defense.
49:7 no man can ransom H, or give to God
49:18 he lives, he counts H happy, and though a
49:18 he does well for H,
50:6 his righteousness, for God H is judge!
87:5 for the Most High H will establish her.
109:18 He clothed H with cursing as his coat, may
109:19 like a belt with which he daily girds H
132:18 with shame, but upon H his crown will shed
135:4 has chosen Jacob for H, Israel as his own
Prov 6:32 has no sense; he who does it destroys H
8:36 who misses me injures H; all who hate me
9:7 corrects a scoffer gets H abuse, and he who
11:17 who is kind benefits H, but a cruel man
11:17 kind benefits himself, but a cruel man hurts H
11:25 one who waters will H be watered.
12:9 standing who works for H than one who plays
13:13 word brings destruction on H, but he who respects
15:32 who ignores instruction despises H, but he who heeds
18:7 ruin, and his lips are a snare to H
19:8 gets wisdom loves H; he who keeps understanding
20:11 Even a child makes H known by his acts,
21:13 of the poor will H cry out and not
21:23 and his tongue keeps H out of trouble.
22:3 sees danger and hides H; but the simple go
22:5 perverse; he who guards H will keep far from
25:9 case with your neighbor H, and do not disclose
27:12 sees danger and hides H; but the simple go
29:15 a child left to H brings shame to his
Eccl 6:8 knows how to conduct H before the living?
8:15 and drink, and enjoy H, for this will go
Song 3:9 King Solomon made H a palanquin from the wood
Wis 1:2 the test, and manifests H to those who do
2:13 of God, and calls H a child of the
3:5 found them worthy of H;
6:7 to greatness; because he H made both small and
15:16 man can form a god which is like H
Sir 1:7 The Lord H created wisdom; he saw her and
6:11 prosperity he will make H your equal, and be
6:12 you, and will hide H from your presence.
7:20 hired laborer who devotes H to you.
10:28 Who will justify the man that sins against H
12:11 Even if he humbles H and goes about cringing,
13:12 not keep words to H; he will not hesitate
13:15 species, and a man clings to one like H
14:4 accumulates by depriving H, accumulates for others;
14:5 man is mean to H, to whom will he
14:6 who is grudging to H, and this is the
19:4 lightminded, and one who sins does wrong to H
20:12 The wise man makes H beloved through his words,
20:26 speaks wisely will advance H, and a sensible man
22:11 soiled when he shakes H off; avoid him and
23:18 marriage vows says to H, "Who sees me?
25:8 a man inferior to H;
28:4 toward a man like H, and yet pray for
28:5 If he H, being flesh, maintains wrath, who will
30:4 behind him one like H;
31:3 he rests he fills H with his dainties.
33:12 and brought near to H; but some of them
34:26 And what has he gained by humbling H
37:8 will take thought for H -- lest he cast
37:19 teacher of many, and yet be unprofitable to H
39:1 hand he who devotes H to the study of
40:29 He pollutes H with another man's food, but a
45:22 people; for the Lord H is his portion and
50:11 glorious robe and clothed H with superb perfection
50:28 is he who concerns H with these things, and
Is 5:16 the Holy God shows H holy in righteousness.
7:14 Therefore the Lord H will give you a sign.
16:12 And when Moab presents H, when he wearies
16:12 himself, when he wearies H upon the high place,
19:21 the LORD will make H known to the Egyptians;
22:14 of hosts has revealed H in my ears: "Surely
30:18 you; therefore he exalts H to show mercy to
30:20 Teacher will not hide H any more, but your
37:1 his clothes, and covered H with sackcloth, and went
38:15 to me, and he H has done it.
42:13 shouts aloud, he shows H mighty against his foes.
44:5 LORDs,' another will call H by the name of
44:5 'The LORDs,' and surname H by the name of
44:15 of it and warms H, he kindles a fire
44:16 satisfied; also he warms H and says, "Aha, I
44:20 and he cannot deliver H or say, "Is there
51:13 oppressor, when he sets H to destroy?
53:10 grief; when he makes H an offering for sin,
56:3 foreigner who has joined H to the LORD say,
58:5 choose, a day for a man to humble H
59:15 departs from evil makes H a prey.
59:17 for clothing, and wrapped H in fury as a
61:10 as a bridegroom decks H with a garland, and
63:10 be their enemy, and H fought against them.
63:12 them to make for H an everlasting name,
64:7 thy name, that bestirs H to take hold of
65:16 that he who blesses H in the land shall
65:16 the land shall bless H by the God of
Jer 10:23 man is not in H, that it is not
16:6 for them or cut H or make himself bald
16:6 cut himself or make H bald for them.
16:20 Can man make for H gods?
23:24 Can a man hide H in secret places so
30:21 who would dare of H to approach me?
46:10 of vengeance, to avenge H on his foes.
48:26 drunk, because he magnified H against the LORD; so
48:42 people, because he magnified H against the LORD.
49:10 places, and he is not able to conceal H
51:14 hosts has sworn by H: Surely I will fill
Lam 4:16 The LORD H has scattered them, he will regard
Ezek 14:7 in Israel, who separates H from me, taking his
14:7 prophet to inquire for H of me, I the
18:13 shall surely die; his blood shall be upon H
18:20 righteous shall be upon H, and the wickedness of
18:20 the wickedness of the wicked shall be upon H
32:31 them, he will comfort H for all his multitude,
33:5 not take warning; his blood shall be upon H
44:26 he shall count for H seven days, and then
45:22 prince shall provide for H and all the people
Dan 1:8 he would not defile H with the king's rich
1:8 the eunuchs to allow him not to defile H
8:4 power; he did as he pleased and magnified H
8:8 Then the he-goat magnified H exceedingly; but when
8:25 and in his own mind he shall magnify H
11:36 will; he shall exalt H and magnify himself above
11:36 exalt himself and magnify H above every god, and
11:37 for he shall magnify H above all.
Hos 7:9 Ephraim mixes H with the peoples; Ephraim is a
10:11 yoke, Judah must plow, Jacob must harrow for H
13:13 he does not present H at the mouth of
Amos 2:15 foot shall not save H, nor shall he who
6:8 GOD has sworn by H (says the LORD, the
Jon 3:6 his robe, and covered H with sackcloth, and sat
4:5 made a booth for H there.
Hab 2:5 He gathers for H all nations, and collects as
2:6 how long?--and loads H with pledges!"
Zech 2:13 for he has roused H from his holy dwelling.
1Mac 2:42 every one who offered H willingly for the law.
3:22 He H will crush them before us; as for
6:44 and to win for H an everlasting name.
7:43 was crushed, and he H was the first to
10:23 forming a friendship with the Jews to strengthen H
11:23 the priests, and put H in danger,
12:43 his troops to obey him as they would H
12:47 He kept with H three thousand men, two thousand
13:48 fortifications and built in it a house for H
2Mac 3:28 now unable to help H; and they recognized clearly
3:39 watches over that place H and brings it aid,
4:5 So he betook H to the king, not accusing
4:24 secured the high-priesthood for H, outbidding Jason
4:42 and the temple robber H they killed close by
5:27 the wilderness, and kept H and his companions alive
6:6 so much as confess H to be a Jew.
6:23 God-given law, he declared H quickly, telling them to
7:12 a result the king H and those with him
7:25 urged her to advise the youth to save H
8:23 leading the first division H, he joined battle with
9:18 up all hope for H and wrote to the
9:29 of Antiochus, he betook H to Ptolemy Philometor in
10:13 He heard H called a traitor at every turn,
10:19 besiege them; and he H set off for places
10:32 Timothy H fled to a stronghold called Gazara,
11:7 Maccabeus H was the first to take up arms,
11:12 wounded, and Lysias H escaped by disgraceful flight.
12:24 Timothy H fell into the hands of Dositheus and

HIMSELF

12:36 the Lord to show H their ally and leader
14:3 but had wilfully defiled H in the times of
14:15 always upholds his own heritage by manifesting H
14:43 wall, and manfully threw H down into the crowd.
15:4 is the living Lord H, the Sovereign in heaven,
15:34 Lord who had manifested H, saying, "Blessed is he
Mt 12:26 he is divided against H; how then will his
12:45 spirits more evil than H, and they enter and
13:21 has no root in H, but endures for a
14:23 on the mountain by H to pray.
16:24 me, let him deny H and take up his
18:4 Whoever humbles H like this child, he is the
23:12 your servant; whoever exalts H will be humbled, and
23:12 humbled, and whoever humbles H will be exalted.
24:48 wicked servant says to H, 'My master is delayed,'
26:74 invoke a curse on H and to swear, "I
27:5 temple, he departed; and he went and hanged H
27:42 him, saying, "He saved others; he cannot save H
Mk 3:21 him, for people were saying, "He is beside H
3:26 has risen up against H and is divided, he
5:5 crying out, and bruising H with stones.
5:30 And Jesus, perceiving in H that power had gone
8:34 me, let him deny H and take up his
12:36 David H, inspired by the Holy Spirit, declared, 'The
12:37 under thy feet.' David H calls him Lord; so
14:54 the guards, and warming H at the fire.
14:67 and seeing Peter warming H, she looked at him,
14:71 invoke a curse on H and to swear, "I
15:30 scribes, saying, "He saved others; he cannot save H
15:42 council, who was also H looking for the kingdom
Lk 7:39 it, he said to H, "If this man were
9:23 me, let him deny H and take up his
9:25 gains the whole world and loses or forfeits H
10:1 and place where he H was about to come.
10:29 he, desiring to justify H, said to Jesus, "And
11:18 also is divided against H, how will his kingdom
11:26 spirits more evil than H, and they enter and
12:17 and he thought to H, 'What shall I do,
12:21 lays up treasure for H, and is not rich
12:37 you, he will gird H and have them sit
12:45 that servant says to H, 'My master is delayed
14:11 every one who exalts H will be humbled, and
14:11 and he who humbles H will be exalted."
15:15 he went and joined H to one of the
15:17 when he came to H he said, 'How many
16:3 the steward said to H, 'What shall I do,
18:4 afterward he said to H, 'Though I neither fear
18:11 and prayed thus with H, 'God, I thank thee
18:14 every one who exalts H will be humbled, but
18:14 but he who humbles H will be exalted."
20:42 For David H says in the Book of Psalms,
23:2 and saying that he H is Christ a king."
23:7 to Herod, who was H in Jerusalem at that
23:34 others; let him save H, if he is the
24:15 and discussing together, Jesus H drew near and went
24:27 them in all the scriptures the things concerning H
24:36 were saying this, Jesus H stood among them, and
Jn 2:24 Jesus did not trust H to them,
2:25 of man; for he H knew what was in
4:2 than John (although Jesus H did not baptize, but
4:12 and drank from it H, and his sons, and
4:44 For Jesus H testified that a prophet has no
4:53 will live"; and he H believed, and all his
5:17 God his Father, making H equal with God.
5:19 him all that he H is doing; and greater
5:25 Father has life in H, so he has granted
5:25 to have life in H,
5:36 who sent me has H borne witness to me.
6:6 test him, for he H knew what he would
6:15 king, Jesus withdrew again to the mountain by H
6:61 But Jesus, knowing in H that his disciples murmured
8:22 Jews, "Will he kill H, since he says, 'Where
8:59 him; but Jesus hid H, and went out of
9:21 he is of age, he will speak for H
12:36 he departed and hid H from them.
12:49 who sent me has H given me commandment what
13:4 his garments, and girded H with a towel.
13:32 also glorify him in H, and glorify him at
16:27 you; for the Father H loves you, because you
18:18 Peter also was with them, standing and warming H
18:25 Now Simon Peter was standing and warming H
19:7 because he has made H the Son of God."
19:12 every one who makes H a king sets himself
19:12 himself a king sets H against Caesar."
21:1 After this Jesus revealed H again to the disciples
21:1 Tiberi-as; and he revealed H in this way.
Acts 1:3 To them he presented H alive after his passion
2:34 the heavens; but he H says, 'The Lord said
5:36 days Theudas arose, giving H out to be somebody,
7:13 second visit Joseph made H known to his brothers,
7:15 And he died, H and our fathers,
8:9 Samaria, saying that he H was somebody great.
8:13 Even Simon H believed, and after being baptized he
8:34 prophet say this, about H or about some one
12:11 And Peter came to H, and said, "Now I
14:17 he did not leave H without witness, for he
16:27 was about to kill H, supposing that the prisoners
17:25 needed anything, since he H gives to all men
18:19 them there; but he H went into the synagogue
19:22 Timothy and Erastus, he H stayed in Asia for
20:13 he had arranged, intending H to go by land.
21:26 next day he purified H with them and went
25:4 Caesarea, and that he H intended to go there
25:25 death; and as he H appealed to the emperor,
28:16 allowed to stay by H, with the soldier that
Rom 3:26 present time that he H is righteous and that
8:16 it is the Spirit H bearing witness with our
8:26 ought, but the Spirit H intercedes for us with
12:3 not to think of H more highly than he
14:7 of us lives to H, and none of us
14:7 to himself, and none of us dies to H
14:12 shall give account of H to God.
14:22 no reason to judge H for what he approves.
15:3 Christ did not please H; but, as it is
1Cor 2:15 all things, but is H to be judged by
3:15 suffer loss, though he H will be saved, but
3:18 Let no one deceive H
6:16 that he who joins H to a prostitute becomes
11:28 Let a man examine H, and so eat of
11:29 discerning the body eats and drinks judgment upon H
14:4 in a tongue edifies H, but he who prophesies
14:28 church and speak to H and to God.
15:28 him, then the Son H will also be subjected
2Cor 5:18 Christ reconciled us to H and gave us the
5:19 reconciling the world to H, not counting their
8:17 our appeal, but being H very earnest he is
10:7 Christs, let him remind H that as he is
10:18 the man who commends H that is accepted, but
11:14 for even Satan disguises H as an angel of
Gal 1:4 Jesus Christ, who gave H for our sins to
2:12 drew back and separated H, fearing the circumcision
2:20 loved me and gave H for me.
6:3 is something, when he is nothing, he deceives H
6:4 boast will be in H alone and not in
Eph 2:15 he might create in H one new man in
2:20 and prophets, Christ Jesus H being the cornerstone,
5:2 loved us and gave H up for us, a
5:23 his body, and is H its Savior.
5:25 the church and gave H up for her,
5:27 present the church to H in splendor, without spot
5:28 He who loves his wife loves H
5:33 love his wife as H, and let the wife
Phil 2:7 be grasped, but emptied H, taking the form of
2:8 human form he humbled H and became obedient
3:21 enables him even to subject all things to H
Col 1:20 him to reconcile to H all things, whether on
1Thes 3:11 our God and Father H, and our Lord Jesus,
4:4 take a wife for H in holiness and honor,
4:16 For the Lord H will descend from heaven with
5:23 the God of peace H sanctify you wholly; and
2Thes 2:4 opposes and exalts H against every so-called god
2:4 temple of God, proclaiming H to be God.
2:16 our Lord Jesus Christ H, and God our Father,
3:16 the Lord of peace H give you peace at
1Tim 2:6 Christ Jesus, who gave H as a ransom for
2Tim 2:13 he remains faithful– for he cannot deny H
2:21 If any one purifies H from what is ignoble,
Tit 1:7 master of H, upright, holy, and self-controlled;
2:14 Jesus Christ, who gave H for us to redeem
2:14 and to purify for H a people of his
Heb 2:14 flesh and blood, he H likewise partook of the
2:18 For because he H has suffered and been tempted,
5:2 and wayward, since he H is beset with weakness.
5:4 take the honor upon H, but he is called
5:5 Christ did not exalt H to be made a
6:13 swear, he swore by H,
7:9 even say that Levi H, who receives tithes, paid
7:27 this once for all when he offered up H
9:7 which he offers for H and for the errors
9:14 the eternal Spirit offered H without blemish to God,
9:25 was it to offer H repeatedly, as the high
9:26 to put away sin by the sacrifice of H

12:3 sinners such hostility against H, so that you may
Jas 1:12 with evil and he H tempts no one;
1:23 mirror; for he observes H and goes away and
4:4 of the world makes H an enemy of God.
1Pet 2:24 He H bore our sins in his body on
5:10 glory in Christ, will H restore, establish, and
1Jn 3:3 hopes in him purifies H as he is pure.
5:10 the Son of God has the testimony in H
3Jn 1:9 who likes to put H first, does not acknowledge
1:10 with that, he refuses H to welcome the brethren,
Rev 19:12 a name inscribed which no one knows but H
21:3 his people, and God H will be with them;

HIN (22)
Ex 29:40 a fourth of a H of beaten oil, and
29:40 a fourth of a H of wine for a
30:24 of olive oil a H;
Lev 19:36 ephah, and a just H: I am the LORD
23:13 shall be of wine, a fourth of a H
Num 15:4 a fourth of a H of oil;
15:5 a fourth of a H, you shall prepare with
15:6 a third of a H of oil;
15:7 a third of a H of wine, a pleasing
15:9 mixed with half a H of oil,
15:10 drink offering half a H of wine, as an
28:5 a fourth of a H of beaten oil.
28:7 a fourth of a H for each lamb; in
28:14 shall be half a H of wine for a
28:14 a third of a H for a ram, and
28:14 a fourth of a H for a lamb; this
Ezek 4:11 sixth part of a H; once a day you
45:24 each ram, and a H of oil to each
46:5 able, together with a H of oil to each
46:7 able, together with a H of oil to each
46:11 give, together with a H of oil to an
46:14 one third of a H of oil to moisten

HIND (3)
Gen 49:21 Naphtali is a H let loose, that bears comely
Prov 5:19 your youth, a lovely H, a graceful doe.
Jer 14:5 Even the H in the field forsakes her newborn

HINDER (13)
Gen 23:6 you his sepulchre, or H you from burying your
Num 22:16 of Zippor: 'Let nothing H you from coming to
1Sam 14:6 us; for nothing can H the LORD from saving
1Kgs 7:25 them, and all their H parts were inward.
2Chr 4:4 them, and all their H parts were inward.
Jud 12:7 his guards not to H her.
Job 9:12 snatches away; who can H him?
11:10 to judgment, who can H him?
Sir 18:21 Let nothing H you from paying a vow promptly,
Is 43:13 work and who can H it?"
Mt 19:14 me, and do not H them; for to such
Mk 10:14 to me, do not H them; for to such
Lk 18:16 me, and do not H them; for to such

HINDERED (7)
Wis 10:8 they not only were H from recognizing the good,
1Mac 9:55 and his work was H; his mouth was stopped
Lk 11:52 enter yourselves, and you H those who were
Rom 15:22 have so often been H from coming to you.
Gal 5:7 were running well; who H you from obeying the
1Thes 2:18 and again--but Satan H us.
1Pet 3:7 in order that your prayers may not be H

HINDERING (2)
Job 15:4 fear of God, and H meditation before God.
1Thes 2:16 oppose all men by H us from speaking to

HINDRANCE (2)
Mt 16:23 You are a H to me; for you are
Rom 14:13 a stumbling block or H in the way of

HINDS (6)
2Sam 22:34 made my feet like H feet, and set me
Job 39:1 Do you observe the calving of the H
Ps 18:33 made my feet like H feet, and set me
Song 2:7 the gazelles or the H of the field, that
3:5 the gazelles or the H of the field, that
Hab 3:19 makes my feet like H feet, he makes me

HINGES
Prov 26:14 door turns on its H, so does a sluggard

HINNOM (13)
Josh 15:8 of the son of H at the southern shoulder
15:8 against the valley of H, on the west, at
18:16 of the son of H, which is at the
18:16 down the valley of H, south of the shoulder
2Kgs 23:10 of the sons of H, that no one might
2Chr 28:3 of the son of H, and burned his sons
33:6 of the son of H, and practiced soothsaying and
Neh 11:30 they encamped from Beer-sheba to the valley of H
Jer 7:31 of the son of H, to burn their sons
7:32 of the son of H, but the valley of
19:2 of the son of H at the entry of
19:6 of the son of H, but the valley of
32:35 of the son of H, to offer up their

HIP (4)
Gen 32:32 the sinew of the H which is upon the
32:32 of Jacob's thigh on the sinew of the H
Judg 15:8 And he smote them H and thigh with great
Is 66:12 be carried upon her H, and dandled upon her

HIPS (2)
2Sam 10:4 the middle, at their H, and sent them away.
1Chr 19:4 the middle, at their H, and sent them away;

HIRAH (2)
Gen 38:1 in to a certain Adullamite, whose name was H
38:12 he and his friend H the Adullamite.

HIRAM (23)
2Sam 5:11 And H king of Tyre sent messengers to David,
1Kgs 5:1 Now H king of Tyre sent his servants to
5:1 of his father; for H always loved David.
5:2 Solomon sent word to H,
5:7 When H heard the words of Solomon, he rejoiced
5:8 And H sent to Solomon, saying, "I have heard
5:10 So H supplied Solomon with all the timber of
5:11 desired, while Solomon gave H twenty thousand cors
5:11 Solomon gave this to H year by year.
5:12 there was peace between H and Solomon; and the
5:18 So Solomon's builders and H's builders and the men
7:13 Solomon sent and brought H from Tyre.
7:40 H also made the pots, the shovels, and the
7:40 So H finished all the work that he did
7:45 of the LORD, which H made for King Solomon,
9:11 the king's house, and H king of Tyre had
9:11 King Solomon gave to H twenty cities in the
9:12 But when H came from Tyre to see the
9:14 H had sent to the king one hundred and
9:27 And H sent with the fleet his servants, seamen
10:11 Moreover the fleet of H, which brought gold from
10:22 of Tarshish at sea with the fleet of H
1Chr 14:1 And H king of Tyre sent messengers to David,

HIRE (20)
Gen 30:18 has given me my H because I gave my
Ex 22:15 if it was hired, it came for its H
Deut 23:18 shall not bring the H of a harlot, or
24:15 shall give him his H on the day he
1Chr 19:6 talents of silver to H chariots and horsemen from
Is 19:10 all who work for H will be grieved.
23:17 will return to her H, and will play the
23:18 Her merchandise and her H will be dedicated to
46:6 silver in the scales, H a goldsmith, and he
Ezek 16:31 were not like a harlot, because you scorned H
16:34 harlot; and you gave H, while no hire was
16:34 gave hire, while no H was given to you;
16:41 you shall also give H no more.
Hos 2:12 said, 'These are my H, which my lovers have
8:10 Though they H allies among the nations, I will
9:1 have loved a harlot's H upon all threshing floors.
Mic 1:7 waste; for from the H of a harlot she
1:7 them, and to the H of a harlot they
3:11 its priests teach for H, its prophets divine for
Mt 20:1 in the morning to H laborers for his vineyard.

HIRED (37)
Gen 30:16 me; for I have H you with my son's
Ex 12:45 No sojourner or H servant may eat of it.
22:15 restitution; if it was H, it came for its
Lev 19:13 The wages of a H servant shall not remain
22:10 the priest's or a H servant shall not eat
25:6 slaves and for your H servant and the sojourner
25:40 with you as a H servant and as a
25:50 the time of a H servant.
25:53 As a servant H year by year shall he

Deut 15:18 the cost of a H servant he has served
23:4 Egypt, and because they H against you Balaam the
24:14 shall not oppress a H servant who is poor
Judg 9:4 Baal-berith with which Abimelech H worthless and
18:4 with me: he has H me, and I have
1Sam 2:5 who were full have H themselves out for bread,
2Sam 10:6 the Ammonites sent and H the Syrians of
2Kgs 7:6 king of Israel has H against us the kings
1Chr 19:7 They H thirty-two thousand chariots and the king of
2Chr 24:12 the LORD, and they H masons and carpenters to
25:6 He H also a hundred thousand mighty men of
Ezra 4:5 afraid to build, and H counselors against them to
Neh 6:12 Tobiah and Sanballat had H him.
6:13 this purpose he was H, that I should be
13:2 bread and water, but H Balaam against them to
Jud 4:10 resident alien and H laborer and purchased slave--
Prov 6:26 a harlot may be H for a loaf of
Sir 7:20 work faithfully, or a H laborer who devotes himself
37:11 or with a man H for a year about
Is 7:20 a razor which is H beyond the River--
Jer 46:21 Even her H soldiers in her midst are like
Hos 8:9 wandering alone; Ephraim has H lovers.
1Mac 5:39 They also have H Arabs to help them, and
Mt 20:7 'Because no one has H us.' He said to
20:9 first.' And when those H about the eleventh hour
Mk 1:20 the boat with the H servants, and followed him.
Lk 15:17 many of my father's H servants have bread enough
15:19 as one of your H servants.'"

HIRELING (9)

Jud 6:5 you, Achior, you Ammonite H, who have said these
Job 7:1 not his days like the days of a H
7:2 shadow, and like a H who looks for his
14:6 may enjoy, like a H, his day.
Is 16:14 the years of a H, the glory of Moab
21:16 the years of a H, all the glory of
Mal 3:5 those who oppress the H in his wages, the
Jn 10:12 He who is a H and not a shepherd,
10:13 because he is a H and cares nothing for

HIRELINGS

Jud 6:2 you, Achior, and you H of Ephraim, to prophesy

HIRES (2)

Prov 26:10 everybody is he who H a passing fool or
Mic 1:7 to pieces, all her H shall be burned with

HISS (7)

1Kgs 9:8 be astonished, and will H; and they will say,
Jer 19:8 be horrified and will H because of all its
49:17 be horrified and will H because of all its
50:13 shall be appalled, and H because of all her
Lam 2:15 hands at you; they H and wag their heads
2:16 rail against you; they H, they gnash their teeth,
Ezek 27:36 merchants among the peoples H at you; you have

HISSED (2)

Jer 18:16 a thing to be H at for ever.
19:8 a thing to be H at; every one who

HISSES (3)

Job 27:23 hands at him, and H at him from its
Sir 22:1 stone, and every one H at his disgrace.
Zeph 2:15 who passes by her H and shakes his fist.

HISSING (7)

2Chr 29:8 of astonishment, and of H, as you see with
Wis 17:9 of beasts and the H of serpents,
Jer 25:9 them a horror, a H, and an everlasting reproach.
25:18 and a waste, a H and a curse, as
29:18 curse, a terror, a H, and a reproach among
51:37 a horror and a H, without inhabitant.
Mic 6:16 and your inhabitants a H; so you shall bear

HISTORIAN

2Mac 2:30 duty of the original H to occupy the ground

HISTORY (4)

Gen 37:2 This is the H of the family of Jacob.
2Chr 9:29 not written in the H of Nathan the prophet,
2Mac 2:24 upon the narratives of H because of the mass
2:32 while cutting short the H itself.

HIT (2)

Is 58:4 to fight and to H with wicked fist.
2Mac 14:43 struggle he did not H exactly, and the crowd

HITCHED

Jud 15:11 loaded her mule and H up her carts and

HITHER (9)

Josh 3:9 people of Israel, "Come H, and hear the words
1Sam 10:22 again of the LORD, "Did the man come H
14:16 the multitude was surging H and thither.
14:18 said to Ahijah, "Bring H the ark of God."
14:36 "Let us draw near H to God."
14:38 And Saul said, "Come H, all you leaders of
Is 57:3 But you, draw near H, sons of the sorceress,
Rev 4:1 trumpet, said, "Come up H, and I will show
11:12 voice from heaven saying to them, "Come up H

HITHERTO (7)

Ex 5:14 all your task of making bricks today, as H
Josh 17:14 a numerous people, since H the LORD has blessed
1Sam 7:12 Ebenezer; for he said, H the LORD has helped
1Chr 9:18 being the chief), stationed H in the king's gate
12:29 whom the majority had H kept their allegiance to
Jn 16:24 H you have asked nothing in my name; ask,
1Cor 8:7 But some, through being H accustomed to idols, eat

HITTITE (26)

Gen 23:10 Hittites; and Ephron the H answered Abraham in the
25:9 son of Zohar the H, east of Mamre,
26:34 daughter of Be-eri the H, and Basemath the
26:34 daughter of Elon the H;
27:46 life because of the H women.
27:46 marries one of the H women such as these,
36:2 daughter of Elon the H, Oholibamah the daughter of
49:29 field of Ephron the H,
49:30 field from Ephron the H to possess as a
50:13 field from Ephron the H, to possess as a
Ex 23:28 out Hivite, Canaanite, and H from before you.
1Sam 26:6 said to Ahimelech the H, and to Joab's brother
2Sam 11:3 daughter of Eliam, the wife of Uriah the H
11:6 sent word to Joab, "Send me Uriah the H
11:17 Uriah the H was slain also.
11:21 'Your servant Uriah the H is dead also.'"
11:24 your servant Uriah the H is dead also."
12:9 have smitten Uriah the H with the sword, and
12:10 wife of Uriah the H to be your wife.'
23:39 the Ithrite, Uriah the H: thirty-seven in all.
1Kgs 11:1 Ammonite, Edomite, Sidonian, and H women,
15:5 life, except in the matter of Uriah the H
1Chr 11:41 the Ithrite, Uriah the H, Zabad the son of
Neh 9:8 of the Canaanite, the H, the Amorite, the Perizzite,
Ezek 16:3 father was an Amorite, and your mother a H
16:45 Your mother was a H and your father an

HITTITES (35)

Gen 15:20 Kenizzites, the Kadmonites, the H, the Perizzites, the
23:3 and said to the H,
23:5 The H answered Abraham,
23:7 and bowed to the H, the people of the
23:10 was sitting among the H; and Ephron the Hittite
23:10 the hearing of the H, of all who went
23:16 the hearing of the H, four hundred shekels of
23:18 the presence of the H, before all who went
23:20 a possession for a burying place by the H
25:10 the field which Abraham purchased from the H
49:32 that is in it were purchased from the H
Ex 3:8 of the Canaanites, the H, the Amorites, the
3:17 of the Canaanites, the H, the Amorites, the
13:5 of the Canaanites, the H, the Amorites, the Hivites,
23:23 the Amorites, and the H, and the Perizzites, and
33:2 Canaanites, the Amorites, the H, the Perizzites, the
34:11 the Canaanites, the H, the Perizzites, the Hivites,
Num 13:29 of the Negeb; the H, the Jebusites, and the
Deut 7:1 nations before you, the H, the Girgashites, the
20:17 utterly destroy them, the H and the Amorites, the
Josh 1:4 the land of the H to the Great Sea
3:10 you the Canaanites, the H, the Hivites, the Perizzites,
9:1 Sea toward Lebanon, the H, the Amorites, the
11:3 west, the Amorites, the H, the Perizzites, and the
12:8 the land of the H, the Amorites, the Canaanites,
24:11 the Canaanites, the H, the Girgashites, the Hivites,
Judg 1:26 the land of the H and built a city,
3:5 among the Canaanites, the H, the Amorites, the
2Sam 24:6 the land of the H; and they came to
1Kgs 9:20 of the Amorites, the H, the Perizzites, the Hivites,
10:29 the kings of the H and the kings of
2Kgs 7:6 the kings of the H and the kings of
2Chr 1:17 the kings of the H and the kings of
8:7 were left of the H, the Amorites, the Perizzites,

Ezra 9:1 from the Canaanites, the H, the Perizzites, the

HIVITE (3)
Gen 34:2 son of Hamor the H, the prince of the
36:2 son of Zibeon the H,
Ex 23:28 which shall drive out H, Canaanite, and Hittite from

HIVITES (23)
Gen 10:17 Amorites, the Girgashites, the H, the Arkites, the
Ex 3:8 Amorites, the Perizzites, the H, and the Jebusites.
3:17 Amorites, the Perizzites, the H, and the Jebusites, a
13:5 Hittites, the Amorites, the H, and the Jebusites,
23:23 and the Canaanites, the H, and the Jebusites, and
33:2 Hittites, the Perizzites, the H, and the Jebusites.
34:11 Hittites, the Perizzites, the H, and the Jebusites.
Deut 7:1 Canaanites, the Perizzites, the H, and the Jebusites,
20:17 and the Perizzites, the H and the Jebusites, as
Josh 3:10 Canaanites, the Hittites, the H, the Perizzites, the
9:1 Canaanites, the Perizzites, the H, and the Jebusites,
9:7 Israel said to the H, "Perhaps you live among
11:3 hill country, and the H under Hermon in the
11:19 of Israel, except the H, the inhabitants of Gibeon;
12:8 Canaanites, the Perizzites, the H, and the Jebusites):
24:11 Hittites, the Girgashites, the H, and the Jebusites;
Judg 3:3 the Sidonians, and the H who dwelt on Mount
3:5 Amorites, the Perizzites, the H, and the Jebusites;
2Sam 24:7 the cities of the H and Canaanites; and they
1Kgs 9:20 Hittites, the Perizzites, the H, and the Jebusites, who
1Chr 1:15 Amorites, the Girgashites, the H, the Arkites, the
2Chr 8:7 Amorites, the Perizzites, the H, and the Jebusites,
Is 17:9 deserted places of the H and the Amorites, which

HIZKI
1Chr 8:17 Zebadiah, Meshullam, H, Heber,

HIZKIAH
1Chr 3:23 sons of Neariah: Eli-o-enai, H, and Azrikam, three.

HO (6)
Is 29:1 H Ariel, Ariel, the city where David encamped!
55:1 H, every one who thirsts, come to the waters;
Ezek 34:2 says the Lord GOD: H, shepherds of Israel who
Zech 2:6 H
2:6 H
2:7 H

HOARD
Bar 3:17 the air, and who H up silver and gold,

HOARDED
Is 23:18 not be stored or H, but her merchandise will

HOARDS
Is 45:3 of darkness and the H in secret places, that

HOARFROST (5)
Ex 16:14 flake-like thing, fine as H on the ground.
Job 38:29 given birth to the H of heaven?
Ps 147:16 like wool; he scatters H like ashes.
Wis 5:14 and like a light H driven away by a
Sir 43:19 He pours the H upon the earth like salt,

HOARY (3)
Lev 19:32 rise up before the H head, and honor the
Job 41:32 wake; one would think the deep to be H
Prov 16:31 A H head is a crown of glory; it

HOBAB (2)
Num 10:29 And Moses said to H the son of Reuel
Judg 4:11 the descendants of H the father-in-law of Moses,

HOBAH
Gen 14:15 and pursued them to H, north of Damascus.

HOBAIAH
Neh 7:63 priests: the sons of H, the sons of Hakkoz,

HOD
1Chr 7:37 Beri, Imrah, Bezer, H, Shamma, Shilshah, Ithran,

HODAVIAH (4)
1Chr 3:24 The sons of Eli-o-enai: H, Eliashib, Pelaiah, Akkub,
5:24 Azriel, Jeremiah, H, and Jahdi-el, mighty warriors,
9:7 of Meshullam, son of H, son of Hassenuah,
Ezra 2:40 of the sons of H, seventy-four.

HODESH
1Chr 8:9 He had sons by H his wife: Jobab, Zibi-a,

HODEVAH
Neh 7:43 of the sons of H, seventy-four.

HODIAH (6)
1Chr 4:19 of the wife of H, the sister of Naham,
Neh 8:7 Sherebiah, Jamin, Akkub, Shabbethai, H, Ma-aseiah,
9:5 Bani, Hashabneiah, Sherebiah, H, Shebaniah, and
10:10 and their brethren, Shebaniah, H, Kelita, Pelaiah,
10:13 Zaccur, Sherebiah, Shebaniah, H, Bani, Beninu.
10:18 Ater, Hezekiah, Azzur, H, Hashum, Bezai,

HOE
Is 7:25 be hoed with a H, you will not come

HOED (2)
Is 5:6 not be pruned or H, and briers and thorns
7:25 which used to be H with a hoe, you

HOGLAH (4)
Num 26:33 Zelophehad were Mahlah, Noah, H, Milcah, and
27:1 daughters were: Mahlah, Noah, H, Milcah, and
36:11 Moses; for Mahlah, Tirzah, H, Milcah, and Noah, the
Josh 17:3 his daughters: Mahlah, Noah, H, Milcah, and Tirzah.

HOHAM
Josh 10:3 of Jerusalem sent to H king of Hebron, to

HOISTING (2)
Acts 27:17 secure the boat; after H it up, they took
27:40 tied the rudders; then H the foresail to the

HOLD (168)
Gen 21:18 up the lad, and H him fast with your
25:26 his hand had taken H of Esau's heel; so
Ex 5:1 go, that they may H a feast to me
6:5 Israel whom the Egyptians H in bondage and I
9:2 them go and still H them,
10:9 herds, for we must H a feast to the
12:16 first day you shall H a holy assembly, and
20:7 the LORD will not H him guiltless who takes
Lev 20:25 apart for you to H unclean.
23:21 same day; you shall H a holy convocation; you
23:36 eighth day you shall H a holy convocation and
Deut 5:11 the LORD will not H him guiltless who takes
9:17 So I took H of the two tables, and
19:14 inheritance which you will H in the land that
21:19 his mother shall take H of him and bring
32:41 and my hand takes H on judgment, I will
Josh 8:4 from the city, but H yourselves all in readiness;
Judg 16:3 he arose and took H of the doors of
19:29 a knife, and laying H of his concubine he
Ruth 3:15 you are wearing and H it out." So she
1Sam 15:27 go away, Saul laid H upon the skirt of
2Sam 1:11 Then David took H of his clothes, and rent
6:6 of God and took H of it, for the
13:11 to eat, he took H of her, and said
13:20 Now H your peace, my sister; he is your
15:5 his hand, and take H of him, and kiss
19:19 "Let not my lord H me guilty or remember
1Kgs 1:50 and went, and caught H of the horns of
1:51 lo, he has laid H of the horns of
2:9 the sword.' Now therefore H him not guiltless, for
2:28 the LORD and caught H of the horns of
9:9 of Egypt, and laid H on other gods, and
11:30 Then Ahijah laid H of the new garment that
13:4 the altar, saying, "Lay H of him." And his
2Kgs 2:3 "Yes, I know it; H your peace."
2:5 "Yes, I know it; H your peace."
2:12 Then he took H of his own clothes and
4:27 of God, she caught H of his feet.
6:32 shut the door, and H the door fast against
15:19 him to confirm his H of the royal power.
1Chr 13:9 out his hand to H the ark, for the
2Chr 7:7 had made could not H the burnt offering and
7:22 of Egypt, and laid H on other gods, and
Ezra 9:8 give us a secure H within his holy place,
Tob 4:14 Do not H over till the next day the
11:11 to him and took H of his father, and
Jud 2:10 you, and you shall H them for me till
7:31 Let us H out for five more days; by
13:7 his bed and took H of the hair of
Esth 4:16 found in Susa, and H a fast on my
9:19 in the open towns, H the fourteenth day of

Job 1:4 used to go and H a feast in the
2:9 him, "Do you still H fast your integrity?
8:15 not stand; he lays H of it, but it
9:28 know thou wilt not H me innocent.
18:9 heel, a snare lays H of him.
27:6 I H fast my righteousness, and will not let
30:16 of affliction have taken H of me.
38:13 that it might take H of the skirts of
Ps 35:2 Take H of shield and buckler, and rise for
39:12 ear to my cry; H not thy peace at
48:6 to flight; trembling took H of them there, anguish
55:14 We used to H sweet converse together; within God's
59:8 at them; thou dost H all the nations in
64:5 They H fast to their evil purpose; they talk
73:23 with thee; thou dost H my right hand.
74:11 Why dost thou H back thy hand, why dost
77:4 [Selah] Thou dost H my eyelids from closing; I
83:1 keep silence; do not H thy peace or be
102:14 For thy servants H her stones dear, and have
116:3 pangs of Sheol laid H on me; I suffered
119:101 I H back my feet from every evil way,
119:109 I H my life in my hand continually, but
119:117 H me up, that I may be safe and
139:10 thy right hand shall H me.
Prov 1:15 the way with them, H back your foot from
3:18 to those who lay H of her; those who
3:18 of her; those who H her fast are called
4:5 me, "Let your heart H fast my words; keep
4:14 Keep H of instruction, do not let go; guard
20:16 for a stranger, and H him in pledge when
21:26 gives and does not H back.
24:11 taken away to death; H back those who are
27:13 for a stranger, and H him in pledge when
31:19 distaff, and her hands H the spindle.
Eccl 2:3 and how to lay H on folly, till I
7:18 that you should take H of this, and from
Song 7:8 palm tree and lay H of its branches.
Wis 4:3 strike a deep root or take a firm H
14:23 celebrate secret mysteries, or H frenzied revels with
Sir 6:27 and when you get H of her, do not
12:5 give to the ungodly; H back his bread, and
21:14 broken jar; it will H no knowledge.
26:7 yoke which chafes; taking H of her is like
43:26 his word all things H together.
Is 3:6 When a man takes H of his brother in
4:1 seven women shall take H of one man in
22:17 He will seize firm H on you,
27:5 Or let them lay H of my protection, let
33:15 his hands, lest they H a bribe, who stops
33:23 hangs loose; it cannot H the mast firm in
41:13 the LORD your God, H your right hand; it
54:2 habitations be stretched out; H not back, lengthen
56:4 that please me and H fast my covenant,
64:7 bestirs himself to take H of thee; for thou
Jer 2:13 broken cisterns, that can H no water.
6:23 They lay H on bow and spear, they are
6:24 helpless; anguish has taken H of us, pain as
8:5 They H fast to deceit, they refuse to return.
8:21 and dismay has taken H on me.
13:21 Will not pangs take H of you, like those
26:2 to them; do not H back a word.
26:8 all the people laid H of him, saying, "You
49:16 of the rock, who H the height of the
49:24 and sorrows have taken H of her, as of
50:42 They lay H of bow and spear; they are
Bar 3:20 her paths, nor laid H of her.
4:1 All who H her fast will live, and those
Ezek 14:5 that I may lay H of the hearts of
Dan 2:43 but they will not H together, just as iron
13:39 but we could not H the man, for he
Hos 12:6 of your God, return, H fast to love and
Nah 3:14 tread the mortar, take H of the brick mold!
Zeph 2:1 Come together and H assembly, O shameless nation,
Zech 8:23 every tongue shall take H of the robe of
14:13 that each will lay H on the hand of
Mal 2:4 covenant with Levi may H, says the LORD of
1Mac 4:61 a garrison there to H it.
6:50 a guard there to H it.
15:7 have built and now H shall remain yours.
15:28 with him, saying, "You H control of Joppa and
2Mac 12:35 a strong man, caught H of Gorgias, and grasping
Mt 12:11 sabbath, will not lay H of it and lift
21:26 the multitude; for all H that John was a
28:9 came up and took H of his feet and
Mk 7:8 commandment of God, and H fast the tradition of
Lk 8:15 who, hearing the word, H it fast in an
20:20 that they might take H of what he said,
Jn 20:17 to her, "Do not H me, for I have
Acts 7:60 voice, "Lord, do not H this sin against them."
17:19 And they took H of him and brought him
Rom 3:28 For we H that a man is justified by
12:9 hate what is evil, H fast to what is
1Cor 15:2 are saved, if you H it fast--unless you
Phil 1:7 you all, because I H you in my heart,
3:16 Only let us H true to what we have
Col 1:17 in him all things H together.
1Thes 5:21 prophesying, but test everything; H fast what is good,
2Thes 2:15 brethren, stand firm and H to the traditions which
1Tim 3:9 for gain; they must H the mystery of the
4:16 and to your teaching; H to that, for by
6:12 of the faith; take H of the eternal life
6:19 that they may take H of the life which
Tit 1:8 and self-controlled; he must H firm to the sure
Heb 3:6 his house if we H fast our confidence and
3:14 Christ, if only we H our first confidence firm
4:14 of God, let us H fast our confession.
6:6 their own account and H him up to contempt.
10:23 Let us H fast the confession of our hope
Jas 2:1 no partiality as you H the faith of our
1Pet 4:8 Above all H unfailing your love for one another,
Rev 2:13 Satan's throne is; you H fast my name and
2:14 have some there who H the teaching of Balaam,
2:15 also have some who H the teaching of the
2:24 Thyatira, who do not H this teaching, who have
2:25 any other burden; only H fast what you have,
3:11 I am coming soon; H fast what you have,
19:10 and your brethren who H the testimony of Jesus.

HOLDERS (7)

Ex 25:27 rings shall lie, as H for the poles to
26:29 rings of gold for H for the bars; and
30:4 and they shall be H for poles with which
36:34 rings of gold for H for the bars, and
37:14 were the rings, as H for the poles to
37:27 sides of it, as H for the poles with
38:5 the bronze grating as H for the poles;

HOLDEST (2)

Ps 16:5 and my cup; thou H my lot.
31:20 plots of men; thou H them safe under thy

HOLDING (21)

Lev 11:36 spring or a cistern H water shall be clean;
Judg 7:20 and broke the jars, H in their left hands
1Sam 25:36 and, lo, he was H a feast in his
Jer 6:11 I am weary of H it in.
20:9 I am weary with H it in, and I
1Mac 15:34 opportunity, we are firmly H the inheritance of our
2Mac 3:20 And H up their hands to heaven, they all
Lk 22:61 the men who were H Jesus mocked him and
24:17 conversation which you are H with each other as
Jn 2:6 rites of purification, each H twenty or thirty gallons.
2Cor 13:5 see whether you are H to your faith.
Phil 2:16 lights in the world, H fast the word of
Col 2:19 sensuous mind, and not H fast to the Head,
1Tim 1:19 wage the good warfare, H faith and a good
2Tim 2:18 from the truth by H that the resurrection is
3:5 than lovers of God, H the form of religion
Heb 9:4 contained a golden urn H the manna, and Aaron's
Rev 5:8 before the Lamb, each H a harp, and with
7:1 corners of the earth, H back the four winds
17:4 and jewels and pearls, H in her hand a
20:1 coming down from heaven, H in his hand the

HOLDINGS

2Chr 11:14 common lands and their H and came to Judah

HOLDS (24)

1Sam 20:29 go; for our family H a sacrifice in the
2Sam 3:29 is leprous, or who H a spindle, or who
Esth 4:11 to whom the king H out the golden scepter
Job 2:3 He still H fast his integrity, although you moved
17:9 Yet the righteous H to his way, and he
20:13 let it go, and H it in his mouth,
Ps 82:1 of the gods he H judgment:
Prov 11:26 people curse him who H back grain, but a
29:11 a wise man quietly H it back.
Wis 1:7 world, and that which H all things together knows
Sir 4:13 Whoever H her fast will obtain glory, and the
15:1 this, and he who H to the law will
25:11 likened the one who H it fast?
32:8 who knows and yet H his tongue.

H

Is 56:2 son of man who H it fast, who keeps
56:6 not profane it, and H fast my covenant--
Jer 46:10 Lord GOD of hosts H a sacrifice in the
Bar 6:14 local ruler the god H a scepter, though unable
Amos 1:5 Aven, and him that H the scepter from Beth-eden;
1:8 Ashdod, and him that H the scepter from Ashkelon;
Jn 4:37 For here the saying H true, 'One sows and
1Tim 4:8 every way, as it H promise for the present
Heb 7:24 in office; but he H his priesthood permanently,
Rev 2:1 words of him who H the seven stars in

HOLE (5)
Deut 23:13 you shall dig a H with it, and turn
2Kgs 12:9 chest, and bored a H in the lid of
Ps 7:15 and falls into the H which he has made.
Is 11:8 shall play over the H of the asp, and
Ezek 8:7 behold, there was a H in the wall.

HOLES (8)
1Sam 13:6 in caves and in H and in rocks and
14:11 coming out of the H where they have hid
Job 30:6 they must dwell, in H of the earth and
Is 2:19 the rocks and the H of the ground, from
42:22 of them trapped in H and hidden in prisons;
Hag 1:6 wages to put them into a bag with H
Mt 8:20 to him, "Foxes have H, and birds of the
Lk 9:58 to him, "Foxes have H, and birds of the

HOLIDAY (2)
Esth 8:17 joy among the Jews, a feast and a H
9:22 from mourning into a H; that they should make

HOLIDAY-MAKING
Esth 9:19 gladness and feasting and H, and a day on

HOLIES
Heb 9:3 called the Holy of H,

HOLINESS (34)
Ex 15:11 like thee, majestic in H, terrible in glorious deeds,
Ps 89:35 have sworn by my H; I will not lie
93:5 decrees are very sure; H befits thy house, O
Wis 2:22 for the wages of H, nor discern the prize
5:19 helmet; he will take H as an invincible shield,
6:10 observe holy things in H, and those who have
9:3 rule the world in H and righteousness, and
14:30 rhey swore unrighteously through contempt for H
Sir 45:12 upon his turban, inscribed like a signet with H
Ezek 20:41 I will manifest my H among you in the
28:22 her, and manifest my H in her;
28:25 scattered, and manifest my H in them in the
36:23 I will vindicate the H of my great name,
36:23 you I vindicate my H before their eyes.
38:16 Gog, I vindicate my H before their eyes.
38:23 my greatness and my H and make myself known
39:27 them have vindicated my H in the sight of
44:19 garments, lest they communicate H to the people
46:20 court and so communicate H to the people."
Amos 4:2 has sworn by his H that, behold, the days
2Mac 3:12 had trusted in the H of the place and
14:36 One, Lord of all H, keep undefiled for ever
Lk 1:75 him without fear, in H and righteousness before him
Rom 1:4 to the Spirit of H by his resurrection from
2Cor 1:12 more toward you, with H and godly sincerity, not
7:1 and spirit, and make H perfect in the fear
Eph 4:24 the likeness of God in true righteousness and H
1Thes 3:13 your hearts unblamable in H before our God and
4:4 wife for himself in H and honor,
4:7 has not called us for uncleanness, but in H
1Tim 2:15 faith and love and H, with modesty.
Heb 12:10 for our good, that we may share his H
12:14 men, and for the H without which no one
2Pet 3:11 be in lives of H and godliness,

HOLLOW (12)
Gen 32:25 Jacob, he touched the H of his thigh; and
32:32 which is upon the H of the thigh, because
32:32 because he touched the H of Jacob's thigh on
Ex 27:8 You shall make it H, with boards; as it
38:7 them; he made it H, with boards.
Judg 15:19 God split open the H place that is at
1Sam 25:29 out as from the H of a sling.
1Kgs 7:15 its circumference; it was H, and its thickness was
Wis 17:19 thrown back from a H of the mountains, it
Is 40:12 the waters in the H of his hand and
Jer 52:21 its thickness was four fingers, and it was H

2Mac 1:19 hid it in the H of a dry cistern,

HOLM
Is 44:14 or he chooses a H tree or an oak

HOLOFERNES (46)
Jud 2:4 of the Assyrians called H, the chief general of
2:14 So H left the presence of his master, and
2:22 From there H took his whole army, his infantry,
3:5 The men came to H and told him all
4:1 heard of everything that H, the general of
5:1 When H, the general of the Assyrian army, heard
5:22 tent began to complain; H officers and all the
5:24 us go up, Lord H, and they will be
6:1 the council died down, H, the commander of the
6:10 Then H ordered his slaves, who waited on him
6:17 at the council of H, and all that he
6:17 leaders, and all that H had said so boastfully
7:1 The next day H ordered his whole army, and
7:6 On the second day H led out all his
7:16 These words pleased H and all his servants, and
7:27 to the army of H and to all his
10:13 to the presence of H the commander of your
10:17 and they brought them to the tent of H
10:18 outside the tent of H while they told him
10:20 Then H companions and all his servants came out
10:21 H was resting on his bed, under a canopy
10:23 into the presence of H and his servants, they
11:1 Then H said to her, "Take courage, woman, and
11:20 Her words pleased H and all his servants, and
11:22 And H said to her, "God has done well
12:3 H said to her, "If your supply runs out,
12:5 Then the servants of H brought her into the
12:6 arose and sent to H and said, "Let my
12:7 So H commanded his guards not to hinder her.
12:10 On the fourth day H held a banquet for
12:13 from the presence of H, and approached her and
12:15 ground for her before H the soft fleeces which
12:16 and lay down, and H heart was ravished with
12:17 So H said to her.
12:20 And H was greatly pleased with her, and drank
13:2 the tent, with H stretched out on his
13:6 of the bed, above H head, and took down
13:9 went out, and gave H head to her maid,
13:15 is the head of H, the commander of the
14:3 into the tent of H, and will not find
14:6 saw the head of H in the hand of
14:11 hung the head of H on the wall, and
14:13 So they came to H tent and said to
14:18 For look, here is H lying on the ground,
15:11 Judith the tent of H and all his silver
16:19 all the vessels of H, which the people had

HOLON (3)
Josh 15:51 Eshtemoh, Anim, Goshen, H, and Giloh: eleven cities
21:15 with its pasture lands, H with its pasture lands,
Jer 48:21 upon the tableland, upon H, and Jahzah, and

HOLY (752)
Ex 3:5 you are standing is H ground."
12:16 you shall hold a H assembly, and on the
12:16 the seventh day a H assembly; no work shall
15:13 thy strength to thy H abode.
16:23 of solemn rest, a H sabbath to the LORD;
19:6 of priests and a H nation.
20:8 "Remember the sabbath day, to keep it H
26:33 separate for you the H place from the most
26:33 for you the holy place from the most H
26:34 testimony in the most H place.
28:2 And you shall make H garments for Aaron your
28:4 girdle; they shall make H garments for Aaron your
28:29 he goes into the H place, to bring them
28:35 he goes into the H place before the LORD,
28:36 engraving of a signet, H to the LORD.'
28:38 guilt incurred in the H offering which the people
28:38 Israel hallow as their H gifts; it shall always
28:43 to minister in the H place; lest they bring
29:6 head, and put the H crown upon the turban.
29:21 his garments shall be H, and his sons and
29:29 "The H garments of Aaron shall be for his
29:30 to minister in the H place.
29:31 its flesh in a H place;
29:33 shall not eat of them, because they are H
29:34 it shall not be eaten, because it is H
29:37 altar shall be most H; whatever touches the altar
29:37 holy; whatever touches the altar shall become H

	30:10	generations; it is most H to the LORD."
	30:25	by the perfumer; a H anointing oil it shall
	30:29	they may be most H; whatever touches them will
	30:29	be most holy; whatever touches them will become H
	30:31	'This shall be my H anointing oil throughout your
	30:32	in composition; it is H, and it shall be
	30:32	and it shall be H to you.
	30:35	with salt, pure and H;
	30:36	with you; it shall be for you most H
	30:37	shall be for you H to the LORD.
	31:10	finely worked garments, the H garments for Aaron
	31:11	fragrant incense for the H place.
	31:14	sabbath, because it is H for you; every one
	31:15	sabbath of solemn rest, H to the LORD; whoever
	35:2	you shall have a H sabbath of solemn rest
	35:19	for ministering in the H place, the holy garments
	35:19	the holy place, the H garments for Aaron the
	35:21	service, and for the H garments.
	37:29	He made the H anointing oil also, and the
	39:1	for ministering in the H place; they made the
	39:1	place; they made the H garments for Aaron; as
	39:30	the plate of the H crown of pure gold,
	39:30	engraving of a signet, H to the LORD."
	39:41	for ministering in the H place, the holy garments
	39:41	the holy place, the H garments for Aaron the
Lev	2:3	it is a most H part of the offerings
	2:10	it is a most H part of the offerings
	5:15	in any of the H things of the LORD,
	5:16	done amiss in the H thing, and shall add
	6:16	eaten unleavened in a H place; in the court
	6:17	is a thing most H, like the sin offering
	6:18	by fire; whoever touches them shall become H
	6:25	be killed before the LORD; it is most H
	6:26	eat it; in a H place it shall be
	6:27	its flesh shall be H; and when any of
	6:27	was sprinkled in a H place.
	6:29	priests may eat of it; it is most H
	6:30	make atonement in the H place; it shall be
	7:1	It is most H;
	7:6	be eaten in a H place; it is most
	7:6	eaten in a holy place; it is most H
	8:9	the golden plate, the H crown, as the LORD
	10:3	'I will show myself H among those who are
	10:10	to distinguish between the H and the common, and
	10:12	for it is most H;
	10:13	eat it in a H place, because it is
	10:17	is a thing most H and has been given
	11:44	yourselves therefore, and be H, for I am holy.
	11:44	yourselves therefore, and be holy, for I am H
	11:45	you shall therefore be H, for I am holy."
	11:45	you shall therefore be holy, for I am H
	14:13	burnt offering, in the H place; for the guilt
	14:13	offering, belongs to the priest; it is most H
	16:2	all times into the H place within the veil,
	16:3	Aaron come into the H place: with a young
	16:4	shall put on the H linen coat, and shall
	16:4	turban; these are the H garments.
	16:16	make atonement for the H place, because of the
	16:17	make atonement in the H place until he comes
	16:20	of atoning for the H place and the tent
	16:23	he went into the H place, and shall leave
	16:24	in water in a H place, and put on
	16:27	make atonement in the H place, shall be carried
	16:32	make atonement, wearing the H linen garments;
	19:2	Israel, You shall be H; for I the LORD
	19:2	holy; for I the LORD your God am H
	19:8	he has profaned a H thing of the LORD;
	19:24	their fruit shall be H, an offering of praise
	20:3	sanctuary and profaning my H name.
	20:7	yourselves therefore, and be H; for I am the
	20:26	You shall be H to me; for I the
	20:26	I the LORD am H, and have separated you
	21:6	They shall be H to their God, and not
	21:6	bread of their God; therefore they shall be H
	21:7	for the priest is H to his God.
	21:8	God; he shall be H to you; for I
	21:8	for I the LORD, who sanctify you, am H
	21:22	both of the most H and of the holy
	21:22	holy and of the H things,
	22:2	keep away from the H things of the people
	22:2	may not profane my H name; I am the
	22:3	your generations approaches the H things, which the
	22:4	may eat of the H things until he is
	22:6	not eat of the H things unless he has
	22:7	may eat of the H things, because such are
	22:10	not eat of a H thing.
	22:10	not eat of a H thing;
	22:12	the offering of the H things.
	22:14	man eats of a H thing unwittingly, he shall
	22:14	it, and give the H thing to the priest.
	22:15	shall not profane the H things of the people
	22:16	guilt, by eating their H things: for I am
	22:32	shall not profane my H name, but I will
	23:2	proclaim as H convocations, my appointed feasts,
	23:3	of solemn rest, a H convocation; you shall do
	23:4	of the LORD, the H convocations, which you shall
	23:7	you shall have a H convocation; you shall do
	23:8	seventh day is a H convocation; you shall do
	23:20	lambs; they shall be H to the LORD for
	23:21	you shall hold a H convocation; you shall do
	23:24	blast of trumpets, a H convocation.
	23:27	you a time of H convocation, and you shall
	23:35	day shall be a H convocation; you shall do
	23:36	you shall hold a H convocation and present an
	23:37	proclaim as times of H convocation, for presenting to
	24:9	eat it in a H place, since it is
	24:9	for him a most H portion out of the
	25:12	jubilee; it shall be H to you; you shall
	27:9	that any man gives to the LORD is H
	27:10	that for which it is exchanged shall be H
	27:14	his house to be H to the LORD, the
	27:21	the jubilee, shall be H to the LORD, as
	27:23	that day as a H thing to the LORD.
	27:28	devoted thing is most H to the LORD.
	27:30	the LORDs; it is H to the LORD.
	27:32	herdsman's staff, shall be H to the LORD.
	27:33	is exchanged shall be H; it shall not be
Num	4:4	of meeting: the most H things.
	4:15	must not touch the H things, lest they die.
	4:19	near to the most H things: Aaron and his
	4:20	to look upon the H things even for a
	5:9	every offering, all the H things of the people
	5:10	his; and every man's H things shall be his;
	5:17	the priest shall take H water in an earthen
	6:5	LORD, he shall be H; he shall let the
	6:8	his separation he is H to the LORD.
	6:20	LORD; they are a H portion for the priest,
	7:9	the care of the H things which had to
	10:21	set out, carrying the H things, and the tabernacle
	15:40	my commandments, and be H to your God.
	16:3	all the congregation are H, every one of them,
	16:5	his, and who is H, and will cause him
	16:7	chooses shall be the H one.
	16:37	For they are H,
	16:38	offered them before the LORD; therefore they are H
	18:9	yours of the most H things, reserved from the
	18:9	me, shall be most H to you and to
	18:10	In a most H place shall you eat of
	18:10	of it; it is H to you.
	18:17	a goat, you shall not redeem; they are H
	18:19	All the H offerings which the people of Israel
	18:32	shall not profane the H things of the people
	20:13	and he showed himself H among them.
	28:7	each lamb; in the H place you shall pour
	28:18	there shall be a H convocation: you shall do
	28:25	you shall have a H convocation; you shall do
	28:26	you shall have a H convocation; you shall do
	29:1	you shall have a H convocation; you shall do
	29:7	shall have a H convocation, and afflict yourselves;
	29:12	you shall have a H convocation; you shall do
	35:25	was anointed with the H oil.
Deut	5:12	day, to keep it H, as the LORD your
	7:6	you are a people H to the LORD your
	12:26	But the H things which are due from you,
	14:2	you are a people H to the LORD your
	14:21	you are a people H to the LORD your
	23:14	your camp must be H, that he may not
	26:15	Look down from thy H habitation, from heaven, and
	26:19	shall be a people H to the LORD your
	28:9	you as a people H to himself, as he
	32:51	not revere me as H in the midst of
	33:2	the ten thousands of H ones, with flaming fire
Josh	5:15	feet; for the place where you stand is H
	24:19	for he is a H God; he is a
1Sam	2:2	"There is none H like the LORD, there is
	6:20	before the LORD, this H God?
	21:4	hand, but there is H bread; if only the
	21:5	the young men are H, even when it is
	21:5	how much more today will their vessels be H
	21:6	priest gave him the H bread; for there was
1Kgs	6:16	sanctuary, as the most H place.
	7:50	the house, the most H place, and for the

8:4 meeting, and all the H vessels that were in
8:6 house, in the most H place, underneath the wings
8:8 were seen from the H place before the inner
8:10 came out of the H place, a cloud filled
2Kgs 4:9 that this is a H man of God, who
12:4 the money of the H things which is brought
19:22 Against the H One of Israel!
1Chr 6:49 work of the most H place, and to make
9:29 and over all the H utensils, also over the
16:10 Glory in his H name; let the hearts of
16:29 Worship the LORD in H array;
16:35 give thanks to thy H name, and glory in
22:19 the LORD and the H vessels of God may
23:13 to consecrate the most H things, that he and
23:28 of all that is H, and any work for
29:3 have provided for the H house, I have a
29:16 a house for thy H name comes from thy
2Chr 3:8 he made the most H place; its length, corresponding
3:10 In the most H place he made two cherubim
4:22 doors to the most H place and for the
5:5 meeting, and all the H vessels that were in
5:7 house, in the most H place, underneath the wings
5:9 were seen from the H place before the inner
5:11 came out of the H place (for all the
8:11 the ark of the LORD has come are H
20:21 and praise him in H array, as they went
23:6 enter, for they are H, but all the people
29:5 the filth from the H place.
29:7 burnt offerings in the H place to the God
30:17 clean, to make it H to the LORD.
30:27 prayer came to his H habitation in heaven.
31:14 LORD and the most H offerings.
31:18 for they were faithful in keeping themselves H
35:3 Israel and who were H to the LORD, "Put
35:3 the LORD, "Put the H ark in the house
35:5 And stand in the H place according to the
35:13 and they boiled the H offerings in pots, in
Ezra 2:63 partake of the most H food, until there should
8:28 to them, "You are H to the LORD, and
8:28 and the vessels are H; and the silver and
9:2 sons; so that the H race has mixed itself
9:8 secure hold within his H place, that our God
Neh 7:65 partake of the most H food, until a priest
8:9 people, "This day is H to the LORD your
8:10 for this day is H to our Lord; and
8:11 for this day is H; do not be grieved."
9:14 known to them thy H sabbath and command them
10:31 sabbath or on a H day; and we will
10:33 the appointed feasts, the H things, and the sin
11:1 live in Jerusalem the H city, while nine tenths
11:18 the Levites in the H city were two hundred
13:22 guard the gates, to keep the sabbath day H
Tob 3:11 and blessed is thy H and honored name for
8:5 and blessed by thy H and glorious name for
8:15 with every pure and H blessing.
11:14 blessed are all thy H angels.
12:12 your prayer before the H One; and when you
12:15 one of the seven H angels who present the
12:15 the glory of the H One."
13:9 O Jerusalem, the H city, he will afflict you
Job 5:1 To which of the H ones will you turn?
6:10 the words of the H One.
15:15 no trust in his H ones, and the heavens
Ps 2:6 king on Zion, my H hill."
3:4 answers me from his H hill.
5:7 will worship toward thy H temple in the fear
11:4 LORD is in his H temple, the LORD's throne
15:1 shall dwell on thy H hill?
20:6 answer him from his H heaven with mighty victories
22:3 Yet thou art H, enthroned on the praises of
24:3 shall stand in his H place?
28:2 hands toward thy most H sanctuary.
29:2 worship the LORD in H array.
30:4 give thanks to his H name.
33:21 we trust in his H name.
43:3 bring me to thy H hill and to thy
46:4 city of God, the H habitation of the Most
47:8 God sits on his H throne.
48:1 His H mountain,
51:11 and take not thy H Spirit from me.
65:4 of thy house, thy H temple!
68:5 is God in his H habitation.
68:17 from Sinai into the H place.
71:22 with the lyre, O H One of Israel.
74:4 the midst of thy H place; they set up
77:13 Thy way, O God, is H
78:41 again, and provoked the H One of Israel.
78:54 brought them to his H land, to the mountain
79:1 they have defiled thy H temple; they have laid
87:1 On the H mount stands the city he founded;
89:5 the assembly of the H ones!
89:7 the council of the H ones, great and terrible
89:18 our king to the H One of Israel.
89:20 my servant; with my H oil I have anointed
96:9 Worship the LORD in H array; tremble before him,
97:12 give thanks to his H name!
98:1 right hand and his H arm have gotten him
99:3 H is he!
99:5 H is he!
99:9 and worship at his H mountain; for the LORD
99:9 holy mountain; for the LORD our God is H
102:19 looked down from his H height, from heaven the
103:1 within me, bless his H name!
105:3 Glory in his H name; let the hearts of
105:42 For he remembered his H promise, and Abraham his
106:16 Moses and Aaron, the H one of the LORD,
106:47 give thanks to thy H name and glory in
110:3 your host upon the H mountains.
111:9 H and terrible is his name!
134:2 your hands to the H place, and bless the
138:2 bow down toward thy H temple and give thanks
145:21 all flesh bless his H name for ever and
Prov 9:10 the knowledge of the H One is insight.
20:25 for a man to say rashly, "It is H
30:3 I knowledge of the H One.
Eccl 8:10 and out of the H place, and were praised
Wis 1:5 For a H and disciplined spirit will flee from
3:9 he watches over his H ones.
4:15 he watches over his H ones.
6:10 they will be made H who observe holy things
6:10 made holy who observe H things in holiness, and
7:22 spirit that is intelligent, H, unique, manifold, subtle,
7:27 generation she passes into H souls and makes them
9:8 a temple on thy H mountain, and an altar
9:8 a copy of the H tent which thou didst
9:10 her forth from the H heavens, and from the
9:17 wisdom and sent thy H Spirit from on high?
10:15 A H people and blameless race wisdom delivered
10:17 She gave H men the reward of their labors;
10:20 O Lord, to thy H name, and praised with
11:1 the hand of a H prophet.
12:3 of old in thy H land
17:2 that they held the H nation in their power
18:1 But for thy H ones there was very great
18:2 thankful that thy H ones, though previously wronged,
18:5 the babes of thy H ones, and one child
18:9 For in secret the H children of good men
Sir 4:14 will minister to the H One; the Lord loves
7:31 first fruits of the H things.
17:8 they will praise his H name, to proclaim the
23:9 the name of the H One;
24:10 In the H tabernacle I ministered before him, and
26:17 shining lamp on the H lampstand, so is a
33:12 of them he made H and brought near to
39:13 to me, O you H sons, and bud like
39:24 To the H his ways are straight, just as
42:17 has not enabled his H ones to recount all
43:10 the command of the H One they stand as
45:2 in glory to the H ones, and made him
45:6 brother of Moses, a H man like him, of
45:10 his people; with a H garment, of gold and
45:15 and anointed him with H oil; it was an
47:8 gave thanks to the H One, the Most High,
47:10 while they praised God's H name, and the sanctuary
48:20 toward him; and the H One quickly heard them
49:12 and raised a temple H to the Lord, prepared
50:11 went up to the H altar, he made the
Is 1:4 they have despised the H One of Israel, they
4:3 Jerusalem will be called H, every one who has
5:16 in justice, and the H God shows himself holy
5:16 Holy God shows himself H in righteousness.
5:19 the purpose of the H One of Israel draw
5:24 the word of the H One of Israel.
6:3 to another and said: H, holy, holy is the
6:3 another and said: "Holy, H, holy is the LORD
6:3 and said: "Holy, holy, H is the LORD of
6:13 The H seed is its stump.
8:13 you shall regard as H; let him be your
10:17 a fire, and his H One a flame; and
10:20 upon the LORD, the H One of Israel, in
11:9 destroy in all my H mountain; for the earth
12:6 your midst is the H One of Israel."

17:7 will look to the H One of Israel;
27:13 the LORD on the H mountain at Jerusalem.
29:19 shall exult in the H One of Israel.
29:23 they will sanctify the H One of Jacob, and
30:11 no more of the H One of Israel."
30:12 Therefore thus says the H One of Israel, "Because
30:15 the Lord GOD, the H One of Israel, "In
30:29 the night when a H feast is kept; and
31:1 not look to the H One of Israel or
35:8 shall be called the H Way; the unclean shall
37:23 Against the H One of Israel!
40:25 says the H One.
41:14 your Redeemer is the H One of Israel.
41:16 the LORD; in the H One of Israel you
41:20 has done this, the H One of Israel has
43:3 LORD your God, the H One of Israel, your
43:14 LORD, your Redeemer, the H One of Israel: "For
43:15 am the LORD, your H One, the Creator of
45:11 says the LORD, the H One of Israel, and
47:4 name-- is the H One of Israel.
48:2 call themselves after the H city, and stay themselves
48:17 LORD, your Redeemer, the H One of Israel: "I
49:7 of Israel and his H One, to one deeply
49:7 who is faithful, the H One of Israel, who
52:1 garments, O Jerusalem, the H city; for there shall
52:10 LORD has bared his H arm before the eyes
54:5 his name; and the H One of Israel is
55:5 God, and of the H One of Israel, for
56:7 will bring to my H mountain, and make them
57:13 and shall inherit my H mountain.
57:15 eternity, whose name is H: "I dwell in the
57:15 in the high and H place, and also with
58:13 your pleasure on my H day, and call the
58:13 a delight and the H day of the LORD
60:9 God, and for the H One of Israel, because
60:14 the Zion of the H One of Israel.
62:12 shall be called The H people, The redeemed of
63:10 rebelled and grieved his H Spirit; therefore he
63:11 midst of them his H Spirit,
63:15 and see, from thy H and glorious habitation.
63:18 Thy H people possessed thy sanctuary a little while;
64:10 Thy H cities have become a wilderness, Zion has
64:11 Our H and beautiful house, where our fathers praised
65:11 LORD, who forget my H mountain, who set a
65:25 destroy in all my H mountain, says the LORD."
66:20 upon dromedaries, to my H mountain Jerusalem,
Jer 2:3 Israel was H to the LORD, the first fruits
17:22 keep the sabbath day H, as I commanded your
17:24 keep the sabbath day H and do no work
17:27 keep the sabbath day H, and not to bear
23:9 and because of his H words.
25:30 high, and from his H habitation utter his voice;
31:23 habitation of righteousness, O H hill!'
50:29 defied the LORD, the H One of Israel.
51:5 of guilt against the H One of Israel.
51:51 have come into the H places of the LORD's
Lam 4:1 The H stones lie scattered at the head of
Bar 2:16 look down from thy H habitation, and consider us.
4:22 to me from the H One, because of the
4:37 the word of the H One, rejoicing in the
5:5 the word of the H One, rejoicing that God
Ezek 7:24 proud might, and their H places shall be profaned.
20:39 to me; but my H name you shall no
20:40 "For on my H mountain, the mountain height of
22:8 You have despised my H things, and profaned my
22:26 and have profaned my H things; they have made
22:26 no distinction between the H and the common,
28:14 you were on the H mountain of God; in
36:20 came, they profaned my H name, in that men
36:21 had concern for my H name, which the house
36:22 the sake of my H name, which you have
39:7 "And my H name I will make known in
39:7 will not let my H name be profaned any
39:7 am the LORD, the H One in Israel.
39:25 be jealous for my H name.
41:4 This is the most H place.
41:21 in front of the H place was something resembling
41:23 The nave and the H place had each a
42:13 the yard are the H chambers, where the priests
42:13 shall eat the most H offerings; there they shall
42:13 shall put the most H offerings--the cereal offering,
42:13 and the guilt offering, for the place is H
42:14 the priests enter the H place, they shall not
42:14 minister, for these are H; they shall put on
42:20 a separation between the H and the common.
43:7 no more defile my H name, neither they, nor
43:8 They have defiled my H name by their abominations
43:12 the top of the mountain shall be most H
44:8 kept charge of my H things; but you have
44:19 lay them in the H chambers; and they shall
44:23 the difference between the H and the common, and
44:24 appointed feasts, and they shall keep my sabbaths H
44:27 he goes into the H place, into the inner
44:27 to minister in the H place, he shall offer
45:1 the land as a H district, twenty-five thousand cubits
45:1 broad; it shall be H throughout its whole extent.
45:3 And in the H district you shall measure off
45:3 the sanctuary, the most H place.
45:4 It shall be the H portion of the land;
45:4 their houses and a H place for the sanctuary.
45:6 set apart as the H district you shall assign
45:7 both sides of the H district and the property
45:7 the city, alongside the H district and the property
46:19 north row of the H chambers for the priests;
48:10 the allotments of the H portion: the priests shall
48:12 special portion from the H portion of the land,
48:12 the land, a most H place, adjoining the territory
48:14 land, for it is H to the LORD.
48:18 the length alongside the H portion shall be ten
48:18 shall be alongside the H portion.
48:20 square, that is, the H portion together with the
48:21 both sides of the H portion and of the
48:21 thousand cubits of the H portion to the east
48:21 The H portion with the sanctuary of the temple
Dan 3:28 and upon Jerusalem, the H city of our fathers,
3:35 servant and Israel thy H one,
3:53 blessed is thy glorious, H name and to be
3:54 the temple of thy H glory and to be
3:88 Lord, you who are H and humble in heart,
4:8 the spirit of the H gods --and I
4:9 the spirit of the H gods is in you
4:13 behold, a watcher, a H one, came down from
4:17 the word of the H ones, to the end
4:18 the spirit of the H gods is in you."
4:23 saw a watcher, a H one, coming down from
5:11 the spirit of the H gods.
5:14 the spirit of the H gods is in you,
8:13 Then I heard a H one speaking; and another
8:13 one speaking; and another H one said to the
9:16 thy city Jerusalem, thy H hill; because for our
9:20 my God for the H hill of my God;
9:24 your people and your H city, to finish the
9:24 to anoint a most H place.
11:28 be set against the H covenant.
11:30 take action against the H covenant.
11:30 those who forsake the H covenant.
11:45 sea and the glorious H mountain; yet he shall
12:7 the power of the H people comes to an
13:45 death, God aroused the H spirit of a young
Hos 11:9 and not man, the H One in your midst,
11:12 is faithful to the H One.
Joel 2:1 the alarm on my H mountain!
3:17 dwell in Zion, my H mountain.
3:17 And Jerusalem shall be H and strangers shall never
Amos 2:7 maiden, so that my H name is profaned;
Obad 1:16 have drunk upon my H mountain, all the nations
1:17 and it shall be H; and the house of
Jon 2:4 again look upon thy H temple?'
2:7 to thee, into thy H temple.
Mic 1:2 the Lord from his H temple.
Hab 1:12 LORD my God, my H One?
2:20 LORD is in his H temple; let all the
3:3 from Teman, and the H One from Mount Paran.
Zeph 3:11 be haughty in my H mountain.
Hag 2:12 question, 'If one carries H flesh in the skirt
2:12 or any kind of food, does it become H
Zech 2:12 his portion in the H land, and will again
2:13 roused himself from his H dwelling.
8:3 LORD of hosts, the H mountain.
14:5 come, and all the H ones with him.
14:20 bells of the horses, H to the LORD." And
1Mac 1:15 circumcision, and abandoned the H covenant.
1:63 or to profane the H covenant; and they did
2:7 the ruin of the H city, and to dwell
2:12 And behold, our H place, our beauty, and our
4:49 made new H vessels, and brought the lampstand,
10:21 Jonathan put on the H garments in the seventh
10:31 and her revenues, be H and free from tax.
11:37 conspicuous place on the H mountain.'"
12:9 have as encouragement the H books which are in
2Mac 1:7 company revolted from the H land and the kingdom
1:12 who fought against the H city.

H

1:26 Israel and preserve thy portion and make it H
1:29 thy people in thy H place, as Moses said.
2:18 under heaven into his H place, for he has
3:1 While the H city was inhabited in unbroken peace
3:18 general supplication because the H place was about
4:48 the villages and the H vessels quickly suffered the
5:15 to enter the most H temple in all the
5:16 He took the H vessels with his polluted hands,
5:17 he was disregarding the H place.
5:19 the sake of the H place, but the place
5:25 and waited until the H sabbath day; then, finding
6:11 regard for that most H day.
6:23 according to the H God-given law, he declared
6:28 for the revered and H laws." When he had
6:30 the Lord in his H knowledge that, though I
8:15 called them by his H and glorious name.
8:17 had committed against the H place, and the torture
8:23 read aloud from the H book, and gave the
9:14 him, stating that the H city, which he was
9:16 of Athens; and the H sanctuary, which he had
9:16 finest offerings; and the H vessels he would give
10:7 purifying of his own H place.
12:45 godliness, it was a H and pious thought.
13:8 fire and ashes were H, he met his death
13:10 their country and the H temple,
13:23 showed generosity to the H place.
14:3 access again to the H altar,
14:31 to the great and H temple while the priests
14:36 us; so now, O H One, Lord of all
15:14 the people and the H city, Jeremiah, the prophet
15:16 him thus: "Take this H sword, a gift from
15:24 who come against thy H people be struck down."
15:32 stretched out against the H house of the Almighty;
Mt 1:18 with child of the H Spirit;
1:20 her is of the H Spirit;
3:11 baptize you with the H Spirit and with fire.
4:5 took him to the H city, and set him
7:6 give dogs what is H; and do not throw
12:32 whoever speaks against the H Spirit will not be
24:15 Daniel, standing in the H place (let the reader
27:53 they went into the H city and appeared to
28:19 Son and of the H Spirit,
Mk 1:8 baptize you with the H Spirit."
1:24 who you are, the H One of God."
3:29 whoever blasphemes against the H Spirit never has
6:20 was a righteous and H man, and kept him
8:38 his Father with the H angels."
12:36 himself, inspired by the H Spirit, declared, 'The Lord
13:11 who speak, but the H Spirit.
Lk 1:15 be filled with the H Spirit, even from his
1:35 said to her, "The H Spirit will come upon
1:35 born will be called H, the Son of God.
1:41 was filled with the H Spirit
1:49 things for me, and H is his name.
1:67 was filled with the H Spirit, and prophesied, saying,
1:70 the mouth of his H prophets from of old,
1:72 and to remember his H covenant,
2:23 womb shall be called H to the Lord")
2:25 of Israel, and the H Spirit was upon him.
2:26 to him by the H Spirit that he should
3:16 baptize you with the H Spirit and with fire.
3:22 was opened, and the H Spirit descended upon him
4:1 Jesus, full of the H Spirit, returned from the
4:34 who you are, the H One of God."
9:26 Father and of the H angels.
10:21 he rejoiced in the H Spirit and said, "I
11:13 heavenly Father give the H Spirit to those who
12:10 who blasphemes against the H Spirit will not be
12:12 to say; for the H Spirit will teach you
Jn 1:33 who baptizes with the H Spirit.'
6:69 that you are the H One of God."
11:48 and destroy both our H place and our nation."
14:26 But the Counselor, the H Spirit, whom the Father
17:11 H Father, keep them in thy name, which thou
20:22 to them, "Receive the H Spirit.
Acts 1:2 commandment through the H Spirit to the apostles
1:5 be baptized with the H Spirit."
1:8 receive power when the H Spirit has come upon
1:16 be fulfilled, which the H Spirit spoke beforehand by
2:4 all filled with the H Spirit and began to
2:27 Hades, nor let thy H One see corruption.
2:33 the promise of the H Spirit, he has poured
2:38 the gift of the H Spirit.
3:14 But you denied the H and Righteous One, and
3:21 the mouth of his H prophets from of old.
4:8 Peter, filled with the H Spirit, said to them,
4:25 didst say by the H Spirit, 'Why did the
4:27 together against thy H servant Jesus, whom thou
4:30 the name of thy H servant Jesus."
4:31 all filled with the H Spirit and spoke the
5:3 to lie to the H Spirit and to keep
5:32 and so is the H Spirit whom God has
6:5 faith and of the H Spirit, and Philip, and
6:13 speak words against this H place and the law;
7:33 you are standing is H ground.
7:51 you always resist the H Spirit.
7:55 he, full of the H Spirit, gazed into heaven
8:15 they might receive the H Spirit;
8:17 and they received the H Spirit.
8:19 hands may receive the H Spirit."
9:17 be filled with the H Spirit."
9:31 the comfort of the H Spirit it was multiplied.
10:22 was directed by a H angel to send for
10:38 of Nazareth with the H Spirit and with power;
10:44 still saying this, the H Spirit fell on all
10:45 the gift of the H Spirit had been poured
10:47 who have received the H Spirit just as we
11:15 began to speak, the H Spirit fell on them
11:16 be baptized with the H Spirit.'
11:24 man, full of the H Spirit and of faith.
13:2 Lord and fasting, the H Spirit said, "Set apart
13:4 sent out by the H Spirit, they went down
13:9 Paul, filled with the H Spirit, looked intently at
13:34 will give you the H and sure blessings of
13:35 wilt not let thy H One see corruption.'
13:52 joy and with the H Spirit.
15:8 them, giving them the H Spirit just as he
15:28 seemed good to the H Spirit and to us
16:6 been forbidden by the H Spirit to speak the
19:2 "Did you receive the H Spirit when you believed?"
19:2 that there is a H Spirit."
19:6 hands upon them, the H Spirit came on them;
20:23 there; except that the H Spirit testifies to me
20:28 flock, in which the H Spirit has made you
21:11 said, "Thus says the H Spirit, 'So shall the
21:28 he has defiled this H place."
28:25 made one statement: "The H Spirit was right in
Rom 1:2 his prophets in the H scriptures,
5:5 our hearts through the H Spirit which has been
7:12 So the law is H, and the commandment is
7:12 and the commandment is H and just and good.
9:1 me witness in the H Spirit,
11:16 as first fruits is H, so is the whole
11:16 if the root is H, so are the branches.
12:1 as a living sacrifice, H and acceptable to God,
14:17 and joy in the H Spirit;
15:13 the power of the H Spirit you may abound
15:16 acceptable, sanctified by the H Spirit.
15:19 the power of the H Spirit, so that from
16:16 one another with a H kiss.
1Cor 3:17 For God's temple is H, and that temple you
6:19 a temple of the H Spirit within you, which
7:14 be unclean, but as it is they are H
7:34 Lord, how to be H in body and spirit;
12:3 except by the H Spirit.
16:20 one another with a H kiss.
2Cor 6:6 forbearance, kindness, the H Spirit, genuine love,
13:12 one another with a H kiss.
13:14 the fellowship of the H Spirit be with you
Eph 1:4 that we should be H and blameless before him.
1:13 sealed with the promised H Spirit,
2:21 and grows into a H temple in the Lord;
3:5 been revealed to his H apostles and prophets by
4:30 do not grieve the H Spirit of God, in
5:27 that she might be H and without blemish.
Col 1:22 order to present you H and blameless and
3:12 as God's chosen ones, H and beloved, compassion,
1Thes 1:5 power and in the H Spirit and with full
1:6 joy inspired by the H Spirit;
2:10 and God also, how H and righteous and blameless
4:8 God, who gives his H Spirit to you.
5:26 the brethren with a H kiss.
1Tim 2:8 men should pray, lifting H hands without anger or
2Tim 1:9 called us with a H calling, not in virtue
1:14 to you by the H Spirit who dwells within
Tit 1:7 master of himself, upright, H, and self-controlled;
3:5 and renewal in the H Spirit,
Heb 2:4 by gifts of the H Spirit distributed according to
3:1 Therefore, H brethren, who share in a heavenly call,
3:7 Therefore, as the H Spirit says, "Today, when you
6:4 become partakers of the H Spirit,
7:26 such a high priest, H, blameless, unstained, separated

	9:2	it is called the H Place.
	9:3	a tent called the H of Holies,
	9:8	By this the H Spirit indicates that the way
	9:12	for all into the H Place, taking not the
	9:25	high priest enters the H Place yearly with blood
	10:15	And the H Spirit also bears witness to us;
1Pet	1:12	to you through the H Spirit sent from heaven,
	1:15	who called you is H, be holy yourselves in
	1:15	you is holy, be H yourselves in all your
	1:16	written, "You shall be H, for I am holy."
	1:16	written, "You shall be holy, for I am H
	2:5	house, to be a H priesthood, to offer spiritual
	2:9	a royal priesthood, a H nation, God's own people,
	3:5	So once the H women who hoped in God
2Pet	1:18	with him on the H mountain.
	1:21	men moved by the H Spirit spoke from God.
	2:21	turn back from the H commandment delivered to
	3:2	the predictions of the H prophets and the
1Jn	2:20	been anointed by the H One, and you all
Jude	1:14	Lord came with his H myriads,
	1:20	up on your most H faith; pray in the
	1:20	faith; pray in the H Spirit;
Rev	3:7	'The words of the H one, the true one,
	4:8	never cease to sing, H, holy, holy, is the
	4:8	cease to sing, "Holy, H, holy, is the Lord
	4:8	to sing, "Holy, holy, H, is the Lord God
	6:10	voice, "O Sovereign Lord, H and true, how long
	11:2	will trample over the H city for forty-two months.
	14:10	the presence of the H angels and in the
	15:4	For thou alone art H
	16:5	art and wast, O H One.
	20:6	Blessed and H is he who shares in the
	21:2	And I saw the H city, new Jerusalem, coming
	21:10	and showed me the H city Jerusalem coming down
	22:11	do right, and the H still be holy."
	22:11	still do right, and the holy still be H
	22:19	life and in the H city, which are described

HOMAGE (2)

Dan	2:46	his face, and did H to Daniel, and commanded
Mk	15:19	they knelt down in H to him.

HOMAM

1Chr	1:39	of Lotan: Hori and H; and Lotan's sister was

HOME (142)

Gen	30:25	go to my own H and country.
	31:55	and blessed them; then he departed and returned H
	39:16	until his master came H,
	43:26	When Joseph came H, they brought into the house
Ex	9:19	and is not brought H, and they shall die."'
Lev	18:9	mother, whether born at H or born abroad.
Deut	21:12	you shall bring her H to your house, and
	22:2	you shall bring it H to your house, and
	24:5	shall be free at H one year, to be
Josh	20:6	town and his own H, to the town from
	22:4	and go to your H in the land where
	22:9	half-tribe of Manasseh returned H, parting from the
Judg	7:3	'Whoever is fearful and trembling, let him return H
	7:7	all the others go every man to his H
	9:55	was dead, they departed every man to his H
	11:9	"If you bring me H again to fight with
	11:34	Jephthah came to his H at Mizpah; and behold,
	18:15	young Levite, at the H of Micah, and asked
	18:22	good way from the H of Micah, the men
	18:26	him, he turned and went back to his H
	19:9	in the morning for your journey, and go H
	19:18	am going to my H; and nobody takes me
	19:28	man rose up and went away to his H
Ruth	1:9	you may find a H, each of you in
	3:1	I not seek a H for you, that it
1Sam	2:11	Then Elkanah went H to Ramah.
	2:20	LORD"; so then they would return to their H
	4:10	every man to his H; and there was a
	6:7	but take their calves H, away from them.
	6:10	the cart, and shut up their calves at H
	7:17	to Ramah, for his H was there, and there
	10:25	all the people away, each one to his H
	10:26	also went to his H at Gibe-ah, and with
	13:2	the people he sent H, every man to his
	18:6	As they were coming H, when David returned from
	23:18	David remained at Horesh, and Jonathan went H
	24:22	Then Saul went H; but David and his men
2Sam	13:7	Then David sent H to Tamar, saying, "Go to
	14:13	bring his banished one H again.
	15:19	a foreigner, and also an exile from your H
	17:3	as a bride comes H to her husband.
	17:23	ass, and went off H to his own city.
	18:17	all Israel fled every one to his own H
	19:8	Israel had fled every man to his own H
	19:30	since my lord the king has come safely H
	19:39	blessed him, and he returned to his own H
	20:22	dispersed from the city, every man to his H
1Kgs	5:14	and two months at H; Adoniram was in charge
	12:24	every man to his H, for this thing is
	12:24	the LORD, and went H again, according to the
	13:7	man of God, "Come H with me, and refresh
	13:15	said to him, "Come H with me and eat
	22:17	each return to his H in peace."'
2Kgs	8:21	who had surrounded him; but his army fled H
	14:10	glory, and stay at H; for why should you
	14:12	by Israel, and every man fled to his H
	19:36	Assyria departed, and went H, and dwelt at Nineveh.
1Chr	13:12	the ark of God H to me?"
	13:13	not take the ark H into the city of
	16:43	house, and David went H to bless his household.
2Chr	11:4	every man to his H, for this thing is
	18:16	each return to his H in peace."'
	25:10	from Ephraim, to go H again.
	25:10	with Judah, and returned H in fierce anger.
	25:19	But now stay at H; why should you provoke
	25:22	by Israel, and every man fled to his H
Tob	1:19	to death, I left H in fear.
	2:1	When I arrived H and my wife Anna and
Jud	7:33	The women and children he sent H
	8:4	Judith had lived at H as a widow for
	16:21	this every one returned H to his own inheritance,
Esth	5:10	restrained himself, and went H; and he sent and
Job	38:20	that you may discern the paths to its H
	39:6	the steppe for his H, and the salt land
	39:28	dwells and makes his H in the fastness of
Ps	49:14	form shall waste away; Sheol shall be their H
	68:6	gives the desolate a H to dwell in; he
	68:12	The women at H divide the spoil,
	84:3	the sparrow finds a H, and the swallow a
	104:17	the stork has her H in the fir trees.
	113:9	the barren woman a H, making her the joyous
	126:6	for sowing, shall come H with shouts of joy,
Prov	7:11	do not stay at H;
	7:19	husband is not at H; he has gone on
	7:20	with him; at full moon he will come H
	24:15	not violence to his H;
	27:8	nest, is a man who strays from his H
Eccl	12:5	goes to his eternal H, and the mourners go
Sir	4:30	a lion in your H, nor be a faultfinder
	11:27	every man into your H, for many are the
	11:32	a stranger into your H and he will upset
	26:16	beauty of a good wife in her well-ordered H
	32:11	be the last; go H quickly and do not
	36:26	man that has no H, and lodges wherever night
	39:3	proverbs and be at H with the obscurities of
Is	14:17	let his prisoners go H
	37:37	Assyria departed, and went H and dwelt at Nineveh.
Jer	39:14	son of Shaphan, that he should take him H
Ezek	36:8	my people Israel; for they will soon come H
	37:12	I will bring you H into the land of
Dan	13:13	other, "Let us go H, for it is mealtime."
	13:52	sins have now come H, which you have committed
Hag	1:9	when you brought it H, I blew it away.
Zech	10:10	I will bring them H from the land of
1Mac	3:56	should return to his H, according to the law.
	12:45	the officials, and will turn round and go H
2Mac	9:29	courtiers, took his body H; then, fearing the son
	11:2	make the city a H for Greeks,
	11:29	you wish to return H and look after your
	11:30	Therefore those who go H by the thirtieth day
Mt	8:6	is lying paralyzed at H, in terrible distress."
	9:6	paralytic—"Rise, take up your bed and go H
	9:7	And he rose and went H
	17:24	And when he came H, Jesus spoke to him
Mk	2:1	days, it was reported that he was at H
	2:11	you, rise, take up your pallet and go H
	3:19	Then he went H;
	5:19	said to him, "Go H to your friends, and
	7:29	And she went H, and found the child lying
	8:26	him away to his H, saying, "Do not even
	13:34	journey, when he leaves H and puts his servants
Lk	1:23	of service was ended, he went to his H
	1:56	her about three months, and returned to her H
	5:24	you, rise, take up your bed and go H
	5:25	he lay, and went H, glorifying God.
	8:39	saying, "Return to your H, and declare how much

9:61 me first say farewell to those at my H
12:36 their master to come H from the marriage feast,
15:6 And when he comes H, he calls together his
23:47 had taken place, returned H beating their breasts.
24:12 themselves; and he went H wondering at what had
Jn 1:11 came to his own H, and his own people
14:23 him and make our H with him.
16:32 every man to his H, and will leave me
19:27 hour the disciple took her to his own H
Acts 5:42 the temple and at H they did not cease
21:6 went on board the ship, and they returned H
1Cor 11:34 let him eat at H --lest you come together
14:35 to know, let them ask their husbands at H
2Cor 5:6 while we are at H in the body we
5:8 the body and at H with the Lord.
5:9 whether we are at H or away, we make

HOMEBORN (2)
Josh 8:33 sojourner as well as H, with their elders and
Jer 2:14 Is he a H servant?

HOMELAND
Heb 11:14 make it clear that they are seeking a H

HOMELESS (2)
Is 58:7 hungry, and bring the H poor into your house;
1Cor 4:11 ill-clad and buffeted and H,

HOMER (9)
Lev 27:16 a sowing of a H of barley shall be
Is 5:10 one bath, and a H of seed shall yield
Ezek 45:11 one tenth of a H, and the ephah one
45:11 one tenth of a H; the homer shall be
45:11 of a homer; the H shall be the standard
45:13 an ephah from each H of wheat, and one
45:13 an ephah from each H of barley,
45:14 (the cor, like the H, contains ten baths);
Hos 3:2 of silver and a H and a lethech of

HOMERS
Num 11:32 gathered least gathered ten H; and they spread them

HOMES (17)
Num 32:18 not return to our H until the people of
Josh 22:6 sent them away; and they went to their H
22:7 them away to their H and blessed them,
22:8 "Go back to your H with much wealth, and
1Kgs 8:66 and went to their H joyful and glad of
2Kgs 13:5 Israel dwelt in their H as formerly.
2Chr 7:10 people away to their H, joyful and glad of
Neh 4:14 your sons, your daughters, your wives, and your H
Ps 49:11 Their graves are their H for ever, their dwelling
Prov 30:26 yet they make their H in the rocks;
Lam 5:2 over to strangers, our H to aliens.
Hos 11:11 return them to their H, says the LORD.
1Mac 12:45 them now to their H and choose for yourself
Mk 8:3 away hungry to their H, they will faint on
Lk 18:28 we have left our H and followed you."
Jn 20:10 Then the disciples went back to their H
Acts 2:46 breaking bread in their H, they partook of food

HOMICIDE
Deut 17:8 between one kind of H and another, one kind

HOMOSEXUALS
1Cor 6:9 idolaters, nor adulterers, nor H,

HONEST (11)
Gen 42:11 one man, we are H men, your servants are
42:19 God: if you are H men, let one of
42:31 to him, 'We are H men, we are not
42:33 know that you are H men: leave one of
42:34 are not spies but H men, and I will
1Sam 29:6 lives, you have been H, and to me it
Job 6:25 How forceful are H words!
Prov 12:17 speaks the truth gives H evidence, but a false
Lk 8:15 it fast in an H and good heart, and
Eph 4:28 let him labor, doing H work with his hands,
Tit 3:1 be ready for any H work,

HONESTLY (3)
2Kgs 12:15 pay out to the workmen, for they dealt H
22:7 is delivered into their hand, for they deal H
Is 59:4 one goes to law H; they rely on empty

HONESTY
Gen 30:33 So my H will answer for me later, when

HONEY (63)
Gen 43:11 balm and a little H, gum, myrrh, pistachio nuts,
Ex 3:8 flowing with milk and H, to the place of
3:17 flowing with milk and H
13:5 flowing with milk and H, you shall keep this
16:31 taste of it was like wafers made with H
33:3 flowing with milk and H; but I will not
Lev 2:11 no leaven nor any H as an offering by
20:24 flowing with milk and H I am the LORD
Num 13:27 flows with milk and H, and this is its
14:8 us, a land which flows with milk and H
16:13 flowing with milk and H, to kill us in
16:14 flowing with milk and H, nor given us inheritance
Deut 6:3 you, in a land flowing with milk and H
8:8 of olive trees and H,
11:9 their descendants, a land flowing with milk and H
26:9 this land, a land flowing with milk and H
26:15 flowing with milk and H
27:3 flowing with milk and H, as the LORD, the
31:20 flowing with milk and H, which I swore to
32:13 he made him suck H out of the rock,
Josh 5:6 give us, a land flowing with milk and H
Judg 14:8 bees in the body of the lion, and H
14:9 he had taken the H from the carcass of
14:18 the sun went down, "What is sweeter than H
1Sam 14:25 forest; and there was H on the ground.
14:26 the forest, behold, the H was dropping, but no
14:29 bright, because I tasted a little of this H
14:43 "I tasted a little H with the tip of
2Sam 17:29 grain, beans and lentils, H and curds and sheep
1Kgs 14:3 and a jar of H, and go to him;
2Kgs 18:32 of olive trees and H, that you may live,
2Chr 31:5 of grain, wine, oil, H, and of all the
Job 20:17 the streams flowing with H and curds.
Ps 19:10 gold; sweeter also than H and drippings of the
81:16 the wheat, and with H from the rock I
119:103 my taste, sweeter than H to my mouth!
Prov 5:3 a loose woman drip H, and her speech is
24:13 My son, eat H, for it is good, and
25:16 If you have found H, eat only enough for
25:27 good to eat much H, so be sparing of
27:7 who is sated loathes H, but to one who
Song 4:11 distil nectar, my bride; H and milk are under
5:1 my honeycomb with my H, I drink my wine
Sir 24:19 me is sweeter than H, and my inheritance sweeter
39:26 flour and milk and H, the blood of the
46:8 inheritance, into a land flowing with milk and H
49:1 it is sweet as H to every mouth, and
Is 7:15 shall eat curds and H when he knows how
7:22 left in the land will eat curds and H
Jer 11:5 flowing with milk and H, as at this day."
32:22 flowing with milk and H;
41:8 wheat, barley, oil, and H hidden in the fields."
Bar 1:20 to us a land flowing with milk and H
Ezek 3:3 it was in my mouth as sweet as H
16:13 ate fine flour and H and oil.
16:19 flour and oil and H --you set before them
20:6 flowing with milk and H, the most glorious of
20:15 flowing with milk and H, the most glorious of
27:17 olives and early figs, H, oil, and balm.
Mt 3:4 waist; and his food was locusts and wild H
Mk 1:6 around his waist, and ate locusts and wild H
Rev 10:9 stomach, but sweet as H in your mouth."
10:10 it was sweet as H in my mouth, but

HONEYCOMB (6)
1Sam 14:27 dipped it in the H, and put his hand
Ps 19:10 sweeter also than honey and drippings of the H
Prov 16:24 words are like a H, sweetness to the soul
24:13 the drippings of the H are sweet to your
Song 5:1 spice, I eat my H with my honey, I
Sir 24:19 than honey, and my inheritance sweeter than the H

HONOR (199)
Gen 30:20 now my husband will H me, because I have
Ex 20:12 H your father and your mother, that your days
Lev 19:32 the hoary head, and H the face of an
Num 22:17 surely do you great H, and whatever you say
22:37 I not able to H you?"
24:11 said, 'I will certainly H you,' but the LORD
24:11 but the LORD has held you back from H
Deut 5:16 H your father and your mother, as the LORD
26:19 in fame and in H, and that you shall

Judg 9:16 in good faith and H when you made Abimelech
9:19 in good faith and H with Jerubbaal and with
13:17 come true, we may H you?"
1Sam 2:8 sit with princes and inherit a seat of H
2:29 which I commanded, and H your sons above me
2:30 me; for those who H me I will honor,
2:30 honor me I will H, and those who despise
9:6 that is held in H; all that he says
15:30 "I have sinned; yet H me now before the
2Sam 6:22 spoken, by them I shall be held in H
1Kgs 3:13 asked, both riches and H, so that no other
1Chr 16:27 H and majesty are before him; strength and joy
29:12 Both riches and H come from thee, and thou
29:28 of days, riches, and H; and Solomon his son
2Chr 1:11 not asked possessions, wealth, H, or the life of
1:12 you riches, possessions, and H, such as none of
16:14 they made a very great fire in his H
17:5 to Jehoshaphat; and he had great riches and H
18:1 had great riches and H; and he made a
21:19 no fire in his H, like the fires made
26:18 will bring you no H from the LORD God."
32:27 very great riches and H; and he made for
32:33 of Jerusalem did him H at his death.
Tob 4:3 H her all the days of your life; do
10:12 also to his daughter, H your father-in-law and your
14:13 He grew old with H, and he gave his
Jud 13:20 to be a perpetual H to you, and may
Esth 1:20 all women will give H to their husbands, high
6:3 the king said, "What H or dignity has been
6:6 to the man whom the king delights to H
6:6 the king delight to H more than me?"
6:7 the king delights to H,
6:9 the king delights to H, and let him conduct
6:9 to the man whom the king delights to H
6:11 to the man whom the king delights to H
8:16 Jews had light and gladness and joy and H
10:2 account of the high H of Mordecai, to which
11:11 lowly were exalted and consumed those held in H
12:6 Bougaean, was in great H with the king, and
Job 14:21 His sons come to H, and he does not
30:15 turned upon me; my H is pursued as by
Ps 4:2 how long shall my H suffer shame?
8:5 God, and dost crown him with glory and H
45:9 among your ladies of H; at your right hand
62:7 my deliverance and my H; my mighty rock, my
71:21 Thou wilt increase my H, and comfort me again.
84:11 a sun and shield; he bestows favor and H
91:15 will rescue him and H him.
96:6 H and majesty are before him; strength and beauty
104:1 Thou art clothed with H and majesty,
111:3 Full of H and majesty is his work, and
112:9 endures for ever; his horn is exalted in H
Prov 3:9 H the LORD with your substance and with the
3:16 hand; in her left hand are riches and H
3:35 The wise will inherit H, but fools get disgrace.
4:9 exalt you; she will H you if you embrace
5:9 lest you give your H to others and your
8:18 Riches and H are with me, enduring wealth and
11:16 A gracious woman gets H, and violent men get
15:33 is instruction in wisdom, and humility goes before H
18:12 man's heart is haughty, but humility goes before H
20:3 It is an H for a man to keep
21:21 righteousness and kindness will find life and H
22:4 LORD is riches and H and life.
26:1 rain in harvest, so H is not fitting for
26:8 is he who gives H to a fool.
29:23 he who is lowly in spirit will obtain H
Eccl 6:2 gives wealth, possessions, and H, so that he lacks
10:1 odor; so a little folly outweighs wisdom and H
Wis 3:17 and finally their old age will be without H
5:4 was madness and that his end was without H
6:21 monarchs over the peoples, H wisdom, that you may
8:10 among the multitudes and H in the presence of
10:14 to be false, and she gave him everlasting H
14:17 When men could not H monarchs in their presence,
Sir 3:8 H your father by word and deed, that a
7:4 nor the seat of H from the king.
7:27 With all your heart H your father, and do
7:29 fear the Lord, and H his priests.
7:31 Fear the Lord and H the priest, and give
10:5 and he confers his H upon the person of
10:19 What race is worthy of H
10:19 What race is worthy of H
10:19 What race is unworthy of H
10:19 What race is unworthy of H
10:20 leader is worthy of H, and those who fear
10:20 Lord are worthy of H in his eyes.
10:22 is it proper to H a sinful man.
10:27 and ascribe to yourself H according to your worth.
10:28 And who will H the man that dishonors his
12:12 take your seat of H, and at last you
33:22 that you do; bring no stain upon your H
38:1 H the physician with the honor due him, according
38:1 the physician with the H due him, according to
38:16 his body with the H due him, and do
47:20 put stain upon your H, and defiled your posterity,
Is 22:23 become a throne of H to his father's house.
29:13 with their mouth and H me with their lips,
43:20 The wild beasts will H me, the jackals and
58:13 LORD honorable; if you H it, not going your
Lam 4:16 them no more; no H was shown to the
Ezek 39:13 will redound to their H on the day that
Dan 2:6 receive from me gifts and rewards and great H
4:37 praise and extol and H the King of heaven;
11:38 He shall H the god of fortresses instead of
11:38 not know he shall H with gold and silver,
11:39 those who acknowledge him he shall magnify with H
Zech 6:13 and shall bear royal H, and shall sit and
Mal 1:6 then I am a father, where is my H
1Mac 1:39 into a reproach, her H into contempt.
2:8 like a man without H;
2:51 generations; and receive great H and an everlasting
2:64 the law, for by it you will gain H
3:14 for myself and win H in the kingdom.
9:10 brethren, and leave no cause to question our H
10:3 in peaceable words to H him;
10:24 encouragement and promise them H and gifts, that I
10:64 his accusers saw the H that was paid him,
11:42 I will confer great H on you and your
11:60 of the city met him and paid him H
12:8 welcomed the envoy with H, and received the letter,
12:43 he received him with H and commended him to
14:4 them, as was the H shown him, all his
14:21 about your glory and H, and we rejoiced at
14:23 receive these men with H and to put a
14:40 Romans had received the envoys of Simon with H
15:9 we will bestow great H upon you and your
2Mac 5:16 enhance the glory and H of the place.
6:7 in the procession in H of Dionysus, wearing wreaths
6:19 he, welcoming death with H rather than life with
14:21 each army; seats of H were set in place;
Mt 13:57 prophet is not without H except in his own
15:4 God commanded, H your father and your mother,'
15:5 God, he need not H his father.'
19:19 not bear false witness, H your father and mother,
23:6 love the place of H at feasts and the
Mk 6:4 prophet is not without H, except in his own
7:10 For Moses said, H your father and your mother';
10:19 witness, Do not defraud, H your father and mother.'"
12:39 and the places of H at feasts,
Lk 14:7 chose the places of H, saying to them,
14:8 in a place of H, lest a more eminent
18:20 not bear false witness, H your father and mother.'"
20:46 and the places of H at feasts,
Jn 4:44 a prophet has no H in his own country.
5:22 Son, that all may H the Son, even as
5:22 Son, even as they H the Father.
5:22 He who does not H the Son does not
5:22 the Son does not H the Father who sent
8:49 a demon; but I H my Father, and you
12:26 me, the Father will H him.
Acts 5:13 them, but the people held them in high H
5:34 the law, held in H by all the people,
Rom 1:21 God they did not H him as God or
2:7 seek for glory and H and immortality, he will
2:10 Greek, but glory and H and peace for every
12:10 brotherly affection; outdo one another in showing H
13:7 whom respect is due, H to whom honor is
13:7 due, honor to whom H is due.
14:6 day, observes it in H of the Lord.
14:6 who eats, eats in H of the Lord, since
14:6 who abstains, abstains in H of the Lord and
1Cor 4:10 You are held in H, but we in disrepute.
12:23 invest with the greater H, and our unpresentable
12:24 body, giving the greater H to the inferior part,
2Cor 6:8 for the left; in H and dishonor, in ill
Eph 6:2 H your father and mother" (this is the first
Phil 2:29 with all joy; and H such men,
1Thes 4:4 himself in holiness and H,
1Tim 1:17 the only God, be H and glory for ever
5:3 H widows who are real widows.
5:17 considered worthy of double H, especially those who

	6:1	as worthy of all H, so that the name
	6:16	To him be H and eternal dominion.
Heb	2:7	him with glory and H,
	2:9	crowned with glory and H because of the suffering
	3:3	a house has more H than the house.
	5:4	does not take the H upon himself, but he
	13:4	marriage be held in H among all, and let
1Pet	1:7	praise and glory and H at the revelation of
	2:17	H all men.
	2:17	H the emperor.
	3:7	with your wives, bestowing H on the woman as
2Pet	1:17	For when he received H and glory from God
Rev	4:9	creatures give glory and H and thanks to him
	4:11	to receive glory and H and power, for thou
	5:12	wisdom and might and H and glory and blessing!"
	5:13	Lamb be blessing and H and glory and might
	7:12	wisdom and thanksgiving and H and power and
	21:26	the glory and the H of the nations.

HONORABLE (11)

Num	22:15	in number and more H than they.
1Chr	4:9	Jabez was more H than his brothers; and his
Sir	25:5	understanding and counsel in H men!
Is	3:5	the elder, and the base fellow to the H
	32:5	called noble, nor the knave said to be H
	58:13	day of the LORD H; if you honor it,
2Mac	7:20	admirable and worthy of H memory.
1Cor	12:23	which we think less H we invest with the
2Cor	8:21	aim at what is H not only in the
Phil	4:8	is true, whatever is H, whatever is just, whatever
Jas	2:7	they who blaspheme that H name which was invoked

HONORABLY (3)

Esth	13:4	the kingdom which we H intend cannot be brought
2Mac	12:43	acted very well and H, taking account of the
Heb	13:18	conscience, desiring to act H in all things.

HONORED (56)

Gen	34:19	he was the most H of all his family.
Judg	9:9	gods and men are H, and go to sway
1Sam	22:14	over your bodyguard, and H in your house?
2Sam	6:20	the king of Israel H himself today, uncovering
Tob	3:11	is thy holy and H name for ever.
Jud	12:13	my lord and be H in his presence, and
	16:21	her estate, and was H in her time throughout
Esth	5:11	which the king had H him, and how he
	14:17	and I have not H the king's feast or
	16:2	more often they are H by the too great
Prov	13:18	ignores instruction, but he who heeds reproof is H
	27:18	and he who guards his master will be H
Wis	4:8	old age is not H for length of time,
	14:15	him; and he now H as a god what
	14:17	the king whom they H, so that by their
	14:20	shortly before they had H as a man.
Sir	2:3	that you may be H at the end of
	3:2	For the Lord H the father above the children,
	10:23	the ruler will be H, but none of them
	10:29	A poor man is H for his knowledge, while
	10:29	a rich man is H for his wealth.
	10:30	A man H in poverty, how much more in
	11:4	day that you are H; for the works of
	24:12	took root in an H people, in the portion
	29:27	place, stranger, to an H person; my brother has
	44:8	all these were H in their generations, and
	46:12	those who have been H live again in their
	49:16	Shem and Seth were H among men, and Adam
Is	5:13	want of knowledge; their H men are dying of
	9:15	the elder and H man is the head,
	23:8	whose traders were the H of the earth?
	23:9	to dishonor all the H of the earth.
	43:4	in my eyes, and H, and I love you,
	43:23	for burnt offerings, or H me with your sacrifices.
	49:5	him, for I am H in the eyes of
Jer	30:19	I will make them H, and they shall not
Lam	1:8	became filthy; all who H her despise her, for
Dan	4:34	High, and praised and H him who lives for
	5:23	whose are all your ways, you have not H
	13:4	he was the most H of them all.
	14:2	and was the most H of his friends.
Nah	3:10	every street; for her H men lots were cast,
1Mac	1:6	he summoned his most H officers, who had been
	2:17	"You are a leader, H and great in this
	2:18	your sons will be H with silver and gold
	5:63	his brothers were greatly H in all Israel and
	7:26	Nicanor, one of his H princes, who hated and
	10:65	Thus the king H him and enrolled him among
	10:88	of these things, he H Jonathan still more;
2Mac	3:2	that the kings themselves H the place and glorified
	3:12	the temple which is H throughout the whole world.
	13:23	them and offered sacrifice, H the sanctuary and
	15:2	sees all things has H and hallowed above other
Lk	14:10	then you will be H in the presence of
1Cor	12:26	if one member is H, all rejoice together.
Phil	1:20	always Christ will be H in my body, whether

HONORING (4)

2Sam	10:3	you, that he is H your father?
1Chr	17:18	say to thee for H thy servant?
	19:3	you, that he is H your father?
Sir	3:11	man's glory comes from H his father, and it

HONORS (14)

Ps	15:4	is despised, but who H those who fear the
	50:23	thanksgiving as his sacrifice H me; to him who
Prov	14:31	kind to the needy H him.
Sir	3:3	Whoever H his father atones for sins,
	3:5	Whoever H his father will be gladdened by his
	9:11	Do not envy the H of a sinner, for
Dan	2:48	king gave Daniel high H and many great gifts,
Mal	1:6	"A son H his father, and a servant his
1Mac	11:27	in as many other H as he had formerly
	14:5	To crown all his H he took Joppa for
	14:39	of the king's friends and paid him high H
2Mac	4:15	the discus, disdaining the H prized by their fathers
Mt	15:8	he said: 'This people H me with their lips,
Mk	7:6	is written, 'This people H me with their lips,

HOOF (13)

Ex	10:26	with us; not a H shall be left behind,
Lev	11:3	Whatever parts the H and is cloven-footed and
	11:4	cud or part the H, you shall not eat
	11:4	does not part the H, is unclean to you.
	11:5	does not part the H, is unclean to you.
	11:6	does not part the H, is unclean to you.
	11:7	because it parts the H and is cloven-footed but
	11:26	animal which parts the H but is not cloven-footed
Deut	14:6	animal that parts the H and has the hoof
	14:6	hoof and has the H cloven in two, and
	14:7	cud or have the H cloven you shall not
	14:7	do not part the H, are unclean for you.
	14:8	because it parts the H but does not chew

HOOFBEATS

Judg	5:28	Why tarry the H of his chariots?'

HOOFS (9)

Judg	5:22	loud beat the horses' H with the galloping, galloping
Ps	69:31	an ox or a bull with horns and H
Is	5:28	bows bent, their horses' H seem like flint, and
Jer	47:3	the stamping of the H of his stallions, at
Ezek	26:11	With the H of his horses he will trample
	32:13	more, nor shall the H of beasts trouble them.
Mic	4:13	horn iron and your H bronze; you shall beat
Zech	11:16	of the fat ones, tearing off even their H
2Mac	3:25	Heliodorus and struck at him with its front H

HOOK (6)

2Kgs	19:28	I will put my H in your nose and
Job	41:2	his nose, or pierce his jaw with a H
Is	19:8	lament, all who cast H in the Nile; and
	37:29	I will put my H in your nose and
Hab	1:15	them up with a H, he drags them out
Mt	17:26	sea and cast a H, and take the first

HOOKS (27)

Ex	26:32	overlaid with gold, with H of gold, upon four
	26:37	them with gold; their H shall be of gold,
	27:10	of bronze, but the H of the pillars and
	27:11	of bronze, but the H of the pillars and
	27:17	filleted with silver; their H shall be of silver,
	35:11	and its covering, its H and its frames, its
	36:36	them with gold; their H were of gold, and
	36:38	with needlework; and its five pillars with their H
	38:10	of bronze, but the H of the pillars and
	38:11	of bronze, but the H of the pillars and
	38:12	their sockets ten; the H of the pillars and
	38:17	of bronze, but the H of the pillars and
	38:19	were of bronze, their H of silver, and the
	38:28	seventy-five shekels he made H for the pillars, and
	39:33	all its utensils, its H, its frames, its bars,
2Chr	33:11	who took Manasseh with H and bound him with
Job	40:24	one take him with H, or pierce his nose

Is	2:4	their spears into pruning H; nation shall not lift
	18:5	the shoots with pruning H, and the spreading
Ezek	19:4	they brought him with H to the land of
	19:9	With H they put him in a cage, and
	29:4	it.' I will put H in your jaws, and
	38:4	you about, and put H into your jaws, and
	40:43	And H, a handbreadth long, were fastened round
Joel	3:10	swords, and your pruning H into spears; let the
Amos	4:2	take you away with H, even the last of
Mic	4:3	their spears into pruning H; nation shall not lift

HOOPOE (2)

Lev	11:19	to its kind, the H, and the bat.
Deut	14:18	after their kinds; the H and the bat.

HOOT

Zeph	2:14	capitals; the owl shall H in the window, the

HOPE (180)

Ruth	1:12	should say I have H, even if I should
Ezra	10:2	even now there is H for Israel in spite
Tob	10:7	mother have given up H of ever seeing me
Jud	6:9	If you really H in your heart that they
	8:20	him, and therefore we H that he will not
	9:11	protector of the forlorn, savior of those without H
	13:19	Your H will never depart from the hearts of
Job	3:9	be dark; let it H for light, but have
	4:6	confidence, and the integrity of your ways your H
	5:16	So the poor have H, and injustice shuts her
	6:19	caravans of Tema look, the travelers of Sheba H
	7:6	weaver's shuttle, and come to their end without H
	8:13	who forget God; the H of the godless man
	11:18	confidence, because there is H; you will be protected
	11:20	to them, and their H is to breathe their
	13:15	me; I have no H; yet I will defend
	14:7	"For there is H for a tree, if it
	14:19	so thou destroyest the H of man.
	17:15	mother,' or 'My sister,' where then is my H
	17:15	Who will see my H
	19:10	am gone, and my H has he pulled up
	27:8	For what is the H of the godless when
	41:9	Behold, the H of a man is disappointed; he
Ps	9:18	be forgotten, and the H of the poor shall
	33:17	horse is a vain H for victory, and by
	33:18	him, on those who H in his steadfast love,
	33:22	us, even as we H in thee.
	39:7	My H is in thee.
	42:5	H in God; for I shall again praise him,
	42:11	H in God; for I shall again praise him,
	43:5	H in God; for I shall again praise him,
	62:5	in silence, for my H is from him.
	65:5	salvation, who art the H of all the ends
	69:6	Let not those who H in thee be put
	71:5	O Lord, art my H, my trust, O LORD,
	71:14	But I will H continually, and will praise thee
	78:7	they should set their H in God, and not
	116:11	in my consternation, "Men are all a vain H
	119:43	my mouth, for my H is in thy ordinances.
	119:49	thy servant, in which thou hast made me H
	119:81	for thy salvation; I H in thy word.
	119:114	and my shield; I H in thy word.
	119:116	me not be put to shame in my H
	119:147	cry for help; I H in thy words.
	119:166	I H for thy salvation, O LORD, and I
	130:5	in his word I H;
	130:7	O Israel, H in the LORD!
	131:3	O Israel, H in the LORD from this time
	146:5	God of Jacob, whose H is in the LORD
	147:11	him, in those who H in his steadfast love.
Prov	10:28	The H of the righteous ends in gladness, but
	11:7	the wicked dies, his H perishes, and the expectation
	13:12	H deferred makes the heart sick, but a desire
	19:18	son while there is H; d o not set
	23:18	a future, and your H will not be cut
	24:14	a future, and your H will not be cut
	26:12	There is more H for a fool than for
	29:20	There is more H for a fool than for
Eccl	9:4	all the living has H, for a living dog
Wis	2:22	purposes of God, nor H for the wages of
	3:4	they were punished, their H is full of immortality.
	3:11	Their H is vain, their labors are unprofitable, and
	3:18	they will have no H and no consolation in
	5:14	Because the H of the ungodly man is like
	12:19	thy sons with good H, because thou givest
	14:6	giants were perishing, the H of the world took
	15:6	for such objects of H are those who either
	15:10	heart is ashes, his H is cheaper than dirt,
	16:29	the light; for the H of an ungrateful man
Sir	2:6	your ways straight, and H in him.
	2:9	who fear the Lord, H for good things, for
	13:6	he will smile at you and give you H
	14:2	him, and who has not given up his H
	27:21	abuse, but whoever has betrayed secrets is without H
	34:7	those who put their H in them have failed.
	34:13	will live, for their H is in him who
	34:14	nor play the coward, for he is his H
	49:10	people of Jacob and delivered them with confident H
Is	8:17	Jacob, and I will H in him.
	20:5	because of Ethiopia their H and of Egypt their
	38:18	to the pit cannot H for thy faithfulness.
	51:5	wait for me, and for my arm they H
Jer	14:8	O thou H of Israel, its savior in time
	14:22	We set our H on thee, for thou doest
	17:13	O LORD, the H of Israel, all who forsake
	29:11	evil, to give you a future and a H
	31:17	There is H for your future, says the LORD,
	50:7	habitation, the LORD, the H of their fathers.'
Lam	3:21	and therefore I have H:
	3:24	soul, "therefore I will H in him."
	3:29	there may yet be H;
Bar	4:22	I have put my H in the Everlasting to
Ezek	19:5	was baffled, that her H was lost, she took
	37:11	dried up, and our H is lost; we are
Dan	13:60	who saves those who H in him.
Hos	2:15	make the Valley of Achor a door of H
Zech	9:12	stronghold, O prisoners of H; today I declare that
2Mac	2:18	For we have H in God that he will
	3:29	and deprived of any H of recovery,
	5:9	to the Lacedaemonians in H of finding protection
	7:11	and from him I H to get them back
	7:14	and to cherish the H that God gives of
	7:20	courage because of her H in the Lord.
	9:18	he gave up all H for himself and wrote
	9:20	As my H is in heaven,
	9:22	for I have good H of recovering from my
Mt	12:21	victory; and in his name will the Gentiles H
Lk	6:34	those from whom you H to receive, what credit
Jn	5:44	who accuses you, on whom you set your H
Acts	2:26	tongue rejoiced; moreover my flesh will dwell in H
	16:19	owners saw that their H of gain was gone,
	17:27	seek God, in the H that they might feel
	23:6	with respect to the H and the resurrection of
	24:14	the prophets, having a H in God which these
	26:6	here on trial for H in the promise made
	26:7	which our twelve tribes H to attain, as they
	26:7	And for this H I am accused by Jews,
	27:20	lay on us, all H of our being saved
	28:20	is because of the H of Israel that I
Rom	4:18	In H he believed against hope, that he should
	4:18	hope he believed against H, that he should become
	5:2	we rejoice in our H of sharing the glory
	5:4	character, and character produces H,
	5:5	character produces hope, and H does not disappoint,
	8:20	who subjected it in H;
	8:24	For in this H we were saved.
	8:24	Now H that is seen is not hope.
	8:24	Now hope that is seen is not H
	8:25	But if we H for what we do not
	12:12	Rejoice in your H, be patient in tribulation, be
	15:4	encouragement of the scriptures we might have H
	15:12	rule the Gentiles; in him shall the Gentiles H
	15:13	May the God of H fill you with all
	15:13	of the Holy Spirit you may abound in H
	15:24	come to you, I H to see you in
1Cor	9:10	plowman should plow in H and the thresher thresh
	9:10	the thresher thresh in H of a share in
	13:13	So faith, H, love abide, these three; but the
	16:7	just in passing; I H to spend some time
2Cor	1:7	Our H for you is unshaken; for we know
	1:10	we have set our H that he will deliver
	1:13	read and understand; I H you will understand fully,
	3:12	we have such a H, we are very bold,
	5:11	to God, and I H it is known also
	10:15	men's labors; but our H is that as your
	13:6	I H you will find out that we have
Gal	5:5	we wait for the H of righteousness.
Eph	1:18	know what is the H to which he has
	2:12	of promise, having no H and without God in
	4:4	called to the one H that belongs to your
Phil	1:20	my eager expectation and H that I shall not
	2:19	I H in the Lord Jesus to send Timothy
	2:23	I H therefore to send him just as soon

H

Col 1:5 saints, because of the H laid up for you
1:23 not shifting from the H of the gospel which
1:27 Christ in you, the H of glory.
1Thes 1:3 love and steadfastness of H in our Lord Jesus
2:19 For what is our H or joy or crown
4:13 not grieve as others do who have no H
5:8 for a helmet the H of salvation.
2Thes 2:16 eternal comfort and good H through grace,
1Tim 1:1 of Christ Jesus our H,
3:14 I H to come to you soon, but I
4:10 because we have our H set on the living
5:5 alone, has set her H on God and continues
Tit 1:2 accords with godliness, in H of eternal life which
2:13 world, awaiting our blessed H, the appearing of the
3:7 and become heirs in H of eternal life.
Heb 3:6 hold fast our confidence and pride in our H
6:11 the full assurance of H until the end,
6:18 encouragement to seize the H set before us.
6:19 of the soul, a H that enters into the
7:19 other hand, a better H is introduced, through which
10:23 the confession of our H without wavering, for he
1Pet 1:3 anew to a living H through the resurrection of
1:13 be sober, set your H fully upon the grace
1:21 that your faith and H are in God.
3:15 to account for the H that is in you,
2Jn 1:12 and ink, but I H to come to see
3Jn 1:14 pen and ink I H to see you soon,

HOPED (9)

Esth 9:1 enemies of the Jews H to get the mastery
Ps 119:74 rejoice, because I have H in thy word.
Is 20:6 those in whom we H and to whom we
Lk 24:21 But we had H that he was the one
Acts 24:25 the same time he H that money would be
1Cor 15:19 life only we have H in Christ, we are
Eph 1:12 will, we who first H in Christ have been
Heb 11:1 the assurance of things H for, the conviction of
1Pet 3:5 the holy women who H in God used to

HOPELESS (2)

Is 57:10 not say, "It is H; you found new life
Jer 2:25 you said, 'It is H, for I have loved

HOPELESSLY

Sir 12:11 that it was not H tarnished.

HOPES (10)

Ps 62:10 extortion, set no vain H on robbery; if riches
Wis 13:10 But miserable, with their H set on dead things,
Sir 34:1 has vain and false H, and dreams give wings
Jer 23:16 filling you with vain H; they speak visions of
Zech 9:5 Ekron also, because its H are confounded.
2Mac 7:34 puffed up by uncertain H, when you raise your
Rom 8:24 For who H for what he sees?
1Cor 13:7 things, believes all things, H all things, endures all
1Tim 6:17 nor to set their H on uncertain riches but
1Jn 3:3 every one who thus H in him purifies himself

HOPHNI (5)

1Sam 1:3 two sons of Eli, H and Phinehas, were priests
2:34 befall your two sons, H and Phinehas, shall be
4:4 two sons of Eli, H and Phinehas, were there
4:11 two sons of Eli, H and Phinehas, were slain.
4:17 your two sons also, H and Phinehas, are dead,

HOPHRA

Jer 44:30 I will give Pharaoh H king of Egypt into

HOPING (2)

Lk 23:8 him, and he was H to see some sign
Philem 1:22 me, for I am H through your prayers to

HOPPER

Joel 2:25 locust has eaten, the H, the destroyer, and the

HOPPING (2)

Joel 1:4 swarming locust left, the H locust has eaten, and
1:4 eaten, and what the H locust left, the destroying

HOR (12)

Num 20:22 of Israel, the whole congregation, came to Mount H
20:23 and Aaron at Mount H, on the border of
20:25 them up to Mount H;
20:27 they went up Mount H in the sight of
21:4 From Mount H they set out by the way
33:37 and encamped at Mount H, on the edge of
33:38 priest went up Mount H at the command of
33:39 twenty-three years old when he died on Mount H
33:41 set out from Mount H, and encamped at Zalmonah.
34:7 your line to Mount H;
34:8 Mount Hor; from Mount H you shall mark it
Deut 32:50 brother died in Mount H and was gathered to

HOR-HAGGIDGAD (2)

Num 33:32 they set out from Bene-jaakan, and encamped at H
33:33 they set out from H, and encamped at Jotbathah.

HORAM

Josh 10:33 Then H king of Gezer came up to help

HORDE (2)

Num 22:4 elders of Midian, "This H will now lick up
2Chr 32:7 Assyria and all the H that is with him;

HORDES (6)

Ezek 38:6 Gomer and all his H; Beth-togarmah from the
38:6 north with all his H—many peoples are with
38:9 you and all your H, and many peoples with
38:22 upon him and his H and the many peoples
39:4 you and all your H and the peoples that
2Mac 2:21 and pursued the barbarian H,

HOREB (18)

Ex 3:1 wilderness, and came to H, the mountain of God.
17:6 on the rock at H; and you shall strike
33:6 their ornaments, from Mount H onward.
Deut 1:2 eleven days' journey from H by the way of
1:6 said to us in H, 'You have stayed long
1:19 we set out from H, and went through all
4:10 LORD your God at H, the LORD said to
4:15 spoke to you at H out of the midst
5:2 our God made a covenant with us in H
9:8 Even at H you provoked the LORD to wrath,
18:16 LORD your God at H on the day of
29:1 covenant which he had made with them at H
1Kgs 8:9 Moses put there at H, where the LORD made
19:8 and forty nights to H the mount of God.
2Chr 5:10 Moses put there at H, where the LORD made
Ps 106:19 made a calf in H and worshiped a molten
Sir 48:7 judgments of vengeance at H;
Mal 4:4 I commanded him at H for all Israel.

HOREM

Josh 19:38 Edre-i, En-hazor, Yiron, Migdal-el, H, Beth-anath,

HORESH (4)

1Sam 23:15 David was in the Wilderness of Ziph at H
23:16 went to David at H, and strengthened his hand
23:18 LORD; David remained at H, and Jonathan went
23:19 in the strongholds at H, on the hill of

HORI (3)

Gen 36:22 sons of Lotan were H and Heman; and Lotan's
Num 13:5 Shaphat the son of H;
1Chr 1:39 The sons of Lotan: H and Homam; and Lotan's

HORITE

Gen 36:20 sons of Seir the H, the inhabitants of the

HORITES (6)

Gen 14:6 in Shaveh-kiriathaim, and the H in their Mount Seir
36:21 the chiefs of the H, the sons of Seir
36:29 the chiefs of the H: the chiefs Lotan, Shobal,
36:30 the chiefs of the H, according to their clans
Deut 2:12 The H also lived in Seir formerly, but the
2:22 when he destroyed the H before them, and they

HORMAH (9)

Num 14:45 and defeated them and pursued them, even to H
21:3 so the name of the place was called H
Deut 1:44 beat you down in Seir as far as H
Josh 12:14 one; the king of H, one; the king of
15:30 Iim, Ezem, Eltolad, Chesil, H,
19:4 Balah, Ezem, Eltolad, Bethul, H,
Judg 1:17 So the name of the city was called H
1Sam 30:30 of the Kenites, in H, in Borashan, in Athach,
1Chr 4:30 Bilhah, Ezem, Tolad, Bethuel, H, Ziklag,

HORN (39)

Josh 6:5 blast with the ram's H, as soon as you
1Sam 16:1 Fill your H with oil, and go; I will
16:13 Then Samuel took the H of oil, and anointed

2Sam 6:15 with shouting, and with the sound of the H
22:3 my shield and the H of my salvation, my
1Kgs 1:39 the priest took the H of oil from the
1Chr 15:28 the sound of the H, trumpets, and cymbals, and
Jud 9:8 to cast down the H of thy altar with
Ps 18:2 my shield, and the H of my salvation, my
75:4 not lift up your H;
75:5 not lift up your H on high, or speak
89:17 by thy favor our H is exalted.
89:24 my name shall his H be exalted.
92:10 thou hast exalted my H like that of the
98:6 the sound of the H make a joyful noise
112:9 endures for ever; his H is exalted in honor.
132:17 I will make a H to sprout for David;
148:14 has raised up a H for his people, praise
Jer 48:25 The H of Moab is cut off, and his
Ezek 29:21 I will cause a H to spring forth to
Dan 3:5 the sound of the H, pipe, lyre, trigon, harp,
3:7 the sound of the H, pipe, lyre, trigon, harp,
3:10 the sound of the H, pipe, lyre, trigon, harp,
3:15 the sound of the H, pipe, lyre, trigon, harp,
7:8 up among them another H, a little one, before
7:8 and behold, in this H were eyes like the
7:11 great words which the H was speaking.
7:20 head, and the other H which came up and
7:20 of them fell, the H which had eyes and
7:21 As I looked, this H made war with the
8:5 goat had a conspicuous H between his eyes.
8:8 was strong, the great H was broken, and instead
8:9 came forth a little H, which grew exceedingly great
8:12 the ground, and the H acted and prospered.
8:21 Greece; and the great H between his eyes is
8:22 As for the H that was broken, in place
Hos 5:8 Blow the H in Gibe-ah, the trumpet in Ramah.
Mic 4:13 I will make your H iron and your hoofs
Lk 1:69 has raised up a H of salvation for us

HORNET

Josh 24:12 And I sent the H before you, which drove

HORNETS (2)

Ex 23:28 And I will send H before you, which shall
Deut 7:20 your God will send H among them, until those

HORNS (69)

Gen 22:13 a thicket by his H; and Abraham went and
Ex 27:2 And you shall make H for it on its
27:2 its four corners; its H shall be of one
29:12 put it upon the H of the altar with
30:2 be its height; its H shall be of one
30:3 round about and its H; and you shall make
30:10 make atonement upon its H once a year; with
37:25 was its height; its H were of one piece
37:26 round about, and its H; and he made a
38:2 He made H for it on its four corners;
38:2 its four corners; its H were of one piece
Lev 4:7 the blood on the H of the altar of
4:18 the blood on the H of the altar which
4:25 put it on the H of the altar of
4:30 put it on the H of the altar of
4:34 put it on the H of the altar of
8:15 put it on the H of the altar round
9:9 put it on the H of the altar, and
16:18 put it on the H of the altar round
Num 23:22 as it were the H of the wild ox.
24:8 as it were the H of the wild ox,
Deut 33:17 has majesty, and his H are the horns of
33:17 his horns are the H of a wild ox;
Josh 6:4 seven trumpets of rams' H before the ark; and
6:6 seven trumpets of rams' H before the ark of
6:8 seven trumpets of rams' H before the LORD went
6:13 seven trumpets of rams' H before the ark of
1Kgs 1:50 caught hold of the H of the altar.
1:51 laid hold of the H of the altar, saying,
2:28 caught hold of the H of the altar.
22:11 Chenaanah made for himself H of iron, and said,
2Chr 15:14 and with shouting, and with trumpets, and with H
18:10 Chenaanah made for himself H of iron, and said,
Ps 22:21 afflicted soul from the H of the wild oxen!
69:31 or a bull with H and hoofs.
75:10 All the H of the wicked he will cut
75:10 cut off, but the H of the righteous shall
118:27 branches, up to the H of the altar!
Jer 17:1 heart, and on the H of their altars,
Ezek 34:21 the weak with your H, till you have scattered
43:15 hearth projecting upward, four H, one cubit high.
43:20 it on the four H of the altar, and
Dan 7:7 that were before it; and it had ten H
7:8 I considered the H, and behold, there came up
7:8 three of the first H were plucked up by
7:20 and concerning the ten H that were on its
7:24 As for the ten H, out of this kingdom
8:3 It had two H; and both horns were high,
8:3 two horns; and both H were high, but one
8:6 ram with the two H, which I had seen
8:7 and broke his two H; and the ram had
8:8 came up four conspicuous H toward the four winds
8:20 saw with the two H, these are the kings
Amos 3:14 of Bethel, and the H of the altar shall
Zech 1:18 lifted my eyes and saw, and behold, four H
1:19 me, "These are the H which have scattered Judah,
1:21 answered, "These are the H which scattered Judah,
1:21 to cast down the H of the nations who
1:21 who lifted up their H against the land of
Rev 5:6 been slain, with seven H and with seven eyes,
9:13 voice from the four H of the golden altar
12:3 seven heads and ten H, and seven diadems upon
13:1 the sea, with ten H and seven heads, with
13:1 ten diadems upon its H and a blasphemous name
13:11 earth; it had two H like a lamb and
17:3 names, and it had seven heads and ten H
17:7 seven heads and ten H that carries her.
17:12 And the ten H that you saw are ten
17:16 And the ten H that you saw, they and

HORONAIM (5)

2Sam 13:34 were coming from the H road by the side
Is 15:5 on the road to H they raise a cry
Jer 48:3 a cry from H, 'Desolation and great destruction!'
48:5 at the descent of H they have heard the
48:34 voice, from Zoar to H and Eglath-shelishiyah.

HORONITE (3)

Neh 2:10 But when Sanballat the H and Tobiah the servant,
2:19 But when Sanballat the H and Tobiah the servant,
13:28 son-in-law of Sanballat the H; therefore I chased

HORRIBLE (4)

Jer 5:30 An appalling and H thing has happened in the
18:13 has done a very H thing.
23:14 I have seen a H thing: they commit adultery
Hos 6:10 I have seen a H thing; Ephraim's harlotry is

HORRIBLY

Ezek 27:35 and their kings are H afraid, their faces are

HORRIFIED (3)

Jer 18:16 passes by it is H and shakes his head.
19:8 by it will be H and will hiss because
49:17 by it will be H and will hiss because

HORRIFY

Ezek 20:26 first-born, that I might H them; I did it

HORROR (28)

Deut 28:25 you shall be a H to all the kingdoms
28:37 you shall become a H, a proverb, and a
2Chr 29:8 them an object of H, of astonishment, and of
Job 18:20 at his day, and H seizes them of the
Ps 31:11 all my adversaries, a H to my neighbors, an
55:5 come upon me, and H overwhelms me.
88:8 me a thing of H to them.
Is 21:4 My mind reels, H has appalled me; the twilight
Jer 15:4 will make them a H to all the kingdoms
18:16 making their land a H, a thing to be
19:8 make this city a H, a thing to be
24:9 will make them a H to all the kingdoms
25:9 and make them a H, a hissing, and an
29:18 will make them a H to all the kingdoms
34:17 will make you a H to all the kingdoms
42:18 become an execration, a H, a curse, and a
44:12 become an execration, a H, a curse, and a
48:39 a derision and a H to all that are
49:13 Bozrah shall become a H, a taunt, a waste,
49:16 The H you inspire has deceived you, and the
49:17 "Edom shall become a H; every one who passes
50:23 Babylon has become a H among the nations!
51:37 haunt of jackals, a H and a hissing, without
51:41 Babylon has become a H among the nations!
51:43 cities have become a H, a land of drought
Ezek 5:15 a warning and a H, to the nations round
7:18 with sackcloth, and H covers them; shame is

23:33 A cup of H and desolation, is the cup

HORSE (43)

Gen 49:17 path, that bites the H's heels so that his
Ex 15:1 has triumphed gloriously; the H and his rider he
15:21 has triumphed gloriously; the H and his rider he
1Kgs 10:29 of silver, and a H for a hundred and
20:20 Syria escaped on a H with horsemen.
20:25 that you have lost, H for horse, and chariot
20:25 have lost, horse for H, and chariot for chariot;
2Chr 1:17 of silver, and a H for a hundred and
23:15 the entrance of the H gate of the king's
Neh 3:28 Above the H Gate the priests repaired, each one
Esth 6:8 has worn, and the H which the king has
6:9 the robes and the H be handed over to
6:10 the robes and the H, as you have said,
6:11 the robes and the H, and he arrayed Mordecai
Job 39:18 she laughs at the H and his rider.
39:19 "Do you give the H his might?
Ps 32:9 Be not like a H or a mule, without
33:17 The war H is a vain hope for victory,
76:6 Jacob, both rider and H lay stunned.
147:10 the strength of the H, nor his pleasure in
Prov 21:31 The H is made ready for the day of
26:3 A whip for the H, a bridle for the
Sir 30:8 A H that is untamed turns out to be
Is 43:17 brings forth chariot and H, army and warrior; they
63:13 Like a H in the desert, they did not
Jer 8:6 own course, like a H plunging headlong into battle.
31:40 the corner of the H Gate toward the east,
51:21 break in pieces the H and his rider; with
Amos 2:15 he who rides the H save his life;
Nah 3:2 rumble of wheel, galloping H and bounding chariot!
Zech 1:8 and behold, a man riding upon a red H
9:10 Ephraim and the war H from Jerusalem; and the
12:4 I will strike every H with panic, and its
12:4 when I strike every H of the peoples with
2Mac 3:25 them a magnificently caparisoned H, with a rider of
Rev 6:2 and behold, a white H, and its rider had
6:4 And out came another H, bright red; its rider
6:5 and behold, a black H, and its rider had
6:8 and behold, a pale H, and its rider's name
14:20 as high as a H's bridle, for one thousand
19:11 I saw heaven opened, and behold, a white H
19:19 who sits upon the H and against his army.
19:21 who sits upon the H, the sword that issues

HORSEBACK (4)

2Kgs 9:18 So a man on H went to meet him,
Jud 2:15 twelve thousand archers on H,
Esth 6:9 conduct the man on H through the open square
2Mac 12:35 men, who was on H and was a strong

HORSEMAN (4)

2Kgs 9:17 Joram said, "Take a H, and send to meet
9:19 sent out a second H, who came to them,
Jer 4:29 At the noise of H and archer every city
2Mac 11:8 still near Jerusalem, a H appeared at their head,

HORSEMEN (69)

Gen 50:9 him both chariots and H; it was a very
Ex 14:9 and chariots and his H and his army, and
14:17 and all his host, his chariots, and his H
14:18 gotten glory over Pharaoh, his chariots, and his H
14:23 sea, all Pharaoh's horses, his chariots, and his H
14:26 the Egyptians, upon their chariots, and upon their H
14:28 the chariots and the H and all the host
15:19 his chariots and his H went into the sea,
Josh 24:6 fathers with chariots and H to the Red Sea.
1Sam 8:11 and to be his H, and to run before
13:5 chariots, and six thousand H, and troops like the
2Sam 1:6 the chariots and the H were close upon him.
8:4 thousand and seven hundred H, and twenty thousand
10:18 chariots, and forty thousand H, and wounded
1Kgs 1:5 for himself chariots and H, and fifty men to
4:26 of horses for his chariots, and twelve thousand H
9:19 the cities for his H, and whatever Solomon desired
9:22 his captains, his chariot commanders and his H
10:26 gathered together chariots and H; he had fourteen
10:26 chariots and twelve thousand H, whom he stationed
20:20 king of Syria escaped on a horse with H
2Kgs 2:12 the chariots of Israel and its H
13:7 of more than fifty H and ten chariots and
13:14 The chariots of Israel and its H
18:24 you rely on Egypt for chariots and for H
1Chr 18:4 chariots, seven thousand H, and twenty thousand
19:6 to hire chariots and H from Mesopotamia, from
2Chr 1:14 gathered together chariots and H; he had fourteen
1:14 chariots and twelve thousand H, whom he stationed
8:6 the cities for his H, and whatever Solomon desired
8:9 officers, the commanders of his chariots, and his H
9:25 chariots, and twelve thousand H, whom he stationed
12:3 with twelve hundred chariots and sixty thousand H
16:8 a huge army with exceedingly many chariots and H
Ezra 8:22 band of soldiers and H to protect us against
Neh 2:9 sent with me officers of the army and H
Jud 2:19 with their chariots and H and picked troops of
Is 21:7 When he sees riders, H in pairs, riders on
21:9 behold, here come riders, H in pairs!" And he
22:6 quiver with chariots and H, and Kir uncovered the
22:7 of chariots, and the H took their stand at
31:1 are many and in H because they are very
36:9 you rely on Egypt for chariots and for H
Jer 46:4 Harness the horses; mount, O H
Ezek 23:6 them desirable young men, H riding on horses.
23:12 clothed in full armor, H riding on horses, all
26:7 and chariots, and with H and a host of
26:10 the noise of the H and wagons and chariots,
38:4 your army, horses and H, all of them clothed
Dan 11:40 whirlwind, with chariots and H, and with many ships;
Hos 1:7 nor by war, nor by horses, nor by H
Nah 3:3 H charging, flashing sword and glittering spear, hosts
Hab 1:8 the evening wolves; their H press proudly on.
1:8 Yea, their H come from afar; they fly like
1Mac 6:30 foot soldiers, twenty thousand H, and thirty-two
6:35 and five hundred picked H were assigned to each
6:38 The rest of the H were stationed on either
15:41 Kedron and stationed there H and troops, so that
16:4 twenty thousand warriors and H, and they marched
16:5 force of infantry and H was coming to meet
16:7 army and placed the H in the midst of
2Mac 5:2 appeared golden-clad H charging through the air,
5:3 swords— troops of H drawn up, attacks and
10:31 hundred were slaughtered, besides six hundred H
11:11 them and sixteen hundred H, and forced all the
12:10 Arabs with five hundred H attacked them.
12:35 one of the Thracian H bore down upon him
Acts 23:23 soldiers with seventy H and two hundred spearmen
23:32 the barracks, leaving the H to go on with

HORSES (119)

Gen 47:17 in exchange for the H, the flocks, the herds,
Ex 9:3 in the field, the H, the asses, the camels,
14:9 pursued them, all Pharaoh's H and chariots and his
14:23 the sea, all Pharaoh's H, his chariots, and his
15:19 For when the H of Pharaoh with his chariots
Deut 11:4 of Egypt, to their H and to their chariots;
17:16 he must not multiply H for himself, or cause
17:16 in order to multiply H, since the LORD has
20:1 your enemies, and see H and chariots and an
Josh 11:4 seashore, with very many H and chariots.
11:6 you shall hamstring their H, and burn their chariots
11:9 him; he hamstrung their H, and burned their chariots
Judg 5:22 "Then loud beat the H hoofs with the galloping,
2Sam 8:4 hamstrung all the chariot H, but left enough for
15:1 himself a chariot and H, and fifty men to
1Kgs 4:26 forty thousand stalls of H for his chariots, and
4:28 and straw for the H and swift steeds they
10:25 gold, garments, myrrh, spices, H, and mules, so much
10:28 And Solomon's import of H was from Egypt and
18:5 grass and save the H and mules alive, and
20:1 were with him, and H and chariots; and he
20:21 out, and captured the H and chariots, and killed
22:4 as your people, my H as your horses."
22:4 people as your people, my horses as your H
2Kgs 2:11 chariot of fire and H of fire separated the
3:7 as your people, my H as your horses."
3:7 people as your people, my horses as your H
5:9 Naaman came with his H and chariots, and halted
6:14 So he sent there H and chariots and a
6:15 behold, an army with H and chariots was round
6:17 mountain was full of H and chariots of fire
7:6 of chariots, and of H, the sound of a
7:7 forsook their tents, their H, and their asses, leaving
7:10 there, nothing but the H tied, and the asses
7:13 five of the remaining H, seeing that those who
9:33 wall and on the H, and they trampled on
10:2 with you chariots and H, fortified cities also, and
11:16 she went through the H entrance to the king's
14:20 they brought him upon H; and he was buried
18:23 give you two thousand H, if you are able
23:11 And he removed the H that the kings of

1Chr	18:4	hamstrung all the chariot H, but left enough for
2Chr	1:16	And Solomon's import of H was from Egypt and
	9:24	gold, garments, myrrh, spices, H, and mules, so much
	9:25	four thousand stalls for H and chariots, and twelve
	9:28	And H were imported for Solomon from Egypt and
	25:28	they brought him upon H; and he was buried
Ezra	2:66	Their H were seven hundred and thirty-six, their
Neh	7:68	Their H were seven hundred and thirty-six, their
Jud	9:7	are exalted, with their H and riders; they glory
Esth	8:10	couriers riding on swift H that were used in
	8:14	mounted on their swift H that were used in
Ps	20:7	chariots, and some of H; but we boast of
Eccl	10:7	have seen slaves on H, and princes walking on
Wis	19:9	For they ranged like H, and leaped like lambs,
Sir	48:9	in a chariot with H of fire;
Is	2:7	land is filled with H, and there is no
	5:28	their bows bent, their H hoofs seem like flint,
	28:28	over it with his H, he does not crush
	30:16	We will speed upon H
	31:1	help and rely on H, who trust in chariots
	31:3	not God; and their H are flesh, and not
	36:8	give you two thousand H, if you are able
	66:20	to the LORD, upon H, and in chariots, and
Jer	4:13	like the whirlwind; his H are swifter than eagles—
	6:23	sea; they ride upon H, set in array as
	8:16	"The snorting of their H is heard from Dan;
	12:5	have wearied you, how will you compete with H
	17:25	in chariots and on H, they and their princes,
	22:4	in chariots and on H, they, and their servants,
	46:4	Harness the H; mount, O horsemen!
	46:9	Advance, O H, and rage, O chariots!
	50:37	A sword upon her H and upon her chariots,
	50:42	sea; they ride upon H, arrayed as a man
	51:27	against her, bring up H like bristling locusts.
Ezek	17:15	they might give him H and a large army.
	23:6	of them desirable young men, horsemen riding on H
	23:12	armor, horsemen riding on H, all of them desirable
	23:20	asses, and whose issue was like that of H
	23:23	officers and warriors, all of them riding on H
	26:7	king of kings, with H and chariots, and with
	26:10	His H will be so many that their dust
	26:11	the hoofs of his H he will trample all
	27:14	exchanged for your wares H, war horses, and mules.
	27:14	your wares horses, war H, and mules.
	38:4	and all your army, H and horsemen, all of
	38:15	of them riding on H, a great host, a
	39:20	at my table with H and riders, with mighty
Hos	1:7	by war, nor by H, nor by horsemen."
	14:3	will not ride upon H; and we will say
Joel	2:4	like the appearance of H, and like war horses
	2:4	horses, and like war H they run.
Amos	4:10	I carried away your H; and I made the
	6:12	Do H run upon rocks?
Mic	5:10	will cut off your H from among you and
Hab	1:8	Their H are swifter than leopards, more fierce than
	3:8	didst ride upon thy H, upon thy chariot of
	3:15	the sea with thy H, the surging of mighty
Hag	2:22	their riders; and the H and their riders shall
Zech	1:8	and behind him were red, sorrel, and white H
	6:2	first chariot had red H, the second black horses,
	6:2	horses, the second black H,
	6:3	horses, the third white H, and the fourth chariot
	6:3	white horses, and the fourth chariot dappled gray H
	6:6	chariot with the black H goes toward the north
	10:5	them, and they shall confound the riders on H
	14:15	shall fall on the H, the mules, the camels,
	14:20	the bells of the H, "Holy to the LORD."
1Mac	10:81	commanded, and the enemy's H grew tired.
2Mac	10:29	five resplendent men on H with golden bridles, and
Jas	3:3	into the mouths of H that they may obey
Rev	9:7	the locusts were like H arrayed for battle; on
	9:9	of many chariots with H rushing into battle.
	9:17	how I saw the H in my vision: the
	9:17	the heads of the H were like lions' heads,
	9:19	the power of the H is in their mouths
	18:13	wheat, cattle and sheep, H and chariots, and slaves,
	19:14	linen, white and pure, followed him on white H
	19:18	men, the flesh of H and their riders, and

HOSAH (5)

Josh	19:29	the boundary turns to H, and it ends at
1Chr	16:38	son of Jeduthun, and H were to be gatekeepers.
	26:10	And H, of the sons of Merari, had sons:
	26:11	sons and brethren of H were thirteen.
	26:16	For Shuppim and H it came out for the

HOSANNA (6)

Mt	21:9	that followed him shouted, H to the Son of
	21:9	H in the highest!"
	21:15	out in the temple, H to the Son of
Mk	11:9	went before and those who followed cried out, H
	11:10	H in the highest!"
Jn	12:13	trees and went out to meet him, crying, H

HOSEA (4)

Hos	1:1	LORD that came to H the son of Be-eri,
	1:2	LORD first spoke through H, the LORD said to
	1:2	the LORD said to H, "Go, take to yourself
Rom	9:25	indeed he says in H, "Those who were not

HOSHAIAH (3)

Neh	12:32	and after them went H and half of the
Jer	42:1	Azariah the son of H, and all the people
	43:2	Azariah the son of H and Johanan the son

HOSHAMA

1Chr	3:18	Malchiram, Pedaiah, Shenazzar, Jekamiah, H, and

HOSHEA (12)

Num	13:8	the tribe of Ephraim, H the son of Nun;
	13:16	And Moses called H the son of Nun Joshua.
2Kgs	15:30	Then H the son of Elah made a conspiracy
	17:1	Ahaz king of Judah H the son of Elah
	17:3	king of Assyria; and H became his vassal, and
	17:4	Assyria found treachery in H; for he had sent
	17:6	the ninth year of H the king of Assyria
	18:1	the third year of H son of Elah, king
	18:9	the seventh year of H son of Elah, king
	18:10	the ninth year of H king of Israel, Samaria
1Chr	27:20	Azriel; for the Ephraimites, H the son of Azaziah;
Neh	10:23	Pelatiah, Hanan, Anaiah, H, Hananiah, Hasshub,

HOSPITABLE (2)

1Tim	3:2	wife, temperate, sensible, dignified, H, an apt teacher,
Tit	1:7	greedy for gain, but H, a lover of goodness,

HOSPITABLY

Acts	28:7	us and entertained us H for three days.

HOSPITALITY (4)

Rom	12:13	Contribute to the needs of the saints, practice H
1Tim	5:10	brought up children, shown H, washed the feet of
Heb	13:2	not neglect to show H to strangers, for thereby
1Pet	4:9	Practice H ungrudgingly to one another.

HOST (99)

Gen	2:1	finished, and all the H of them.
Ex	14:4	Pharaoh and all his H; and the Egyptians shall
	14:17	Pharaoh and all his H, his chariots, and his
	14:19	who went before the H of Israel moved and
	14:20	them, coming between the H of Egypt and the
	14:20	of Egypt and the H of Israel.
	14:24	looked down upon the H of the Egyptians, and
	14:24	Egyptians, and discomfited the H of the Egyptians,
	14:28	horsemen and all the H of Pharaoh that had
	15:4	"Pharaoh's chariots and his H he cast into the
Num	2:4	son of Amminadab, his H as numbered being
	2:6	son of Zuar, his H as numbered being fifty-four
	2:8	son of Helon, his H as numbered being fifty-seven
	2:11	son of Shedeur, his H as numbered being forty-six
	2:13	of Zurishaddai, his H as numbered being fifty-nine
	2:15	son of Reuel, his H as numbered being forty-five
	2:19	son of Ammihud, his H as numbered being forty
	2:21	son of Pedahzur, his H as numbered being thirty-two
	2:23	son of Gideoni, his H as numbered being thirty-five
	2:26	of Ammishaddai, his H as numbered being sixty-two
	2:28	son of Ochran, his H as numbered being forty-one
	2:30	son of Enan, his H as numbered being fifty-three
	10:14	companies; and over their H was Nahshon the son
	10:15	And over the H of the tribe of the
	10:16	And over the H of the tribe of the
	10:18	companies; and over their H was Elizur the son
	10:19	And over the H of the tribe of the
	10:20	And over the H of the tribe of the
	10:22	companies; and over their H was Elishama the son
	10:23	And over the H of the tribe of the
	10:24	And over the H of the tribe of the
	10:25	companies; and over their H was Ahiezer the son
	10:26	And over the H of the tribe of the
	10:27	And over the H of the tribe of the
Deut	4:19	the stars, all the H of heaven, you be
	17:3	or any of the H of heaven, which I

H

Josh 11:4 their troops, a great H, in number like the
Judg 7:14 hand God has given Midian and all the H
7:15 LORD has given the H of Midian into your
1Sam 17:20 the encampment as the H was going forth to
17:46 dead bodies of the H of the Philistines this
2Sam 10:7 Joab and all the H of the mighty men.
1Kgs 22:19 throne, and all the H of heaven standing beside
2Kgs 17:16 and worshiped all the H of heaven, and served
21:3 and worshiped all the H of heaven, and served
21:5 altars for all the H of heaven in the
23:4 and for all the H of heaven; he burned
23:5 constellations, and all the H of the heavens.
2Chr 18:18 throne, and all the H of heaven standing on
33:3 and worshiped all the H of heaven, and served
33:5 altars for all the H of heaven in the
Neh 9:6 heavens, with all their H, the earth and all
9:6 of them; and the H of heaven worships thee.
Ps 27:3 Though a H encamp against me, my heart shall
33:6 made, and all their H by the breath of
68:11 command; great is the H of those who bore
110:3 day you lead your H upon the holy mountains.
136:15 overthrew Pharaoh and his H in the Red Sea,
148:2 him, all his angels, praise him, all his H
Prov 7:26 low; yea, all her slain are a mighty H
Sir 17:27 He marshals the H of the height of heaven;
24:2 the presence of his H she will glory:
29:25 you will play the H and provide drink without
Is 13:4 hosts is mustering a H for battle.
24:21 LORD will punish the H of heaven, in heaven,
34:2 furious against all their H, he has doomed them,
34:4 All the H of heaven shall rot away, and
34:4 All their H shall fall, as leaves fall from
40:26 who brings out their H by number, calling them
45:12 out the heavens, and I commanded all their H
Jer 8:2 moon and all the H of heaven, which they
19:13 burned to all the H of heaven, and drink
33:22 As the H of heaven cannot be numbered and
51:3 not her young men; utterly destroy all her H
Ezek 1:24 the sound of a H; when they stood still,
16:40 shall bring up a H against you, and they
23:24 and wagons and a H of peoples; they shall
23:46 GOD: "Bring up a H against them, and make
23:47 And the H shall stone them and dispatch them
26:7 with horsemen and a H of many soldiers.
32:3 over you with a H of many peoples; and
37:10 and stood upon their feet, an exceedingly great H
38:15 on horses, a great H, a mighty army;
Dan 4:35 his will in the H of heaven and among
8:10 great, even to the H of heaven; and some
8:10 and some of the H of the stars it
8:11 the Prince of the H; and the continual burnt
8:12 And the H was given over to it together
8:13 of the sanctuary and H to be trampled under
Joel 2:11 his army, for his H is exceedingly great; he
Zeph 1:5 the roofs to the H of the heavens; those
1Mac 3:3 waged battles, protecting the H by his sword.
14:7 He gathered a H of captives; he ruled over
15:3 and have recruited a H of mercenary troops and
Lk 2:13 multitude of the heavenly H praising God and saying,
14:10 so that when your H comes he may say
Acts 7:42 over to worship the H of heaven, as it
Rom 16:23 Gaius, who is H to me and to the
Eph 4:8 high he led a H of captives, and he

HOSTAGE

1Mac 1:10 he had been a H in Rome.

HOSTAGES (8)

2Kgs 14:14 the king's house, also H, and he returned to
2Chr 25:24 the king's house, and H, and he returned to
1Mac 8:7 heavy tribute and give H and surrender some of
9:53 of the land as H and put them under
10:6 he commanded that the H in the citadel should
10:9 the citadel released the H to Jonathan, and he
11:62 of their rulers as H and sent them to
13:16 of his sons as H, so that when released

HOSTILE (10)

Deut 15:9 and your eye be H to your poor brother,
Jud 5:11 king of Egypt became H to them; he took
Esth 13:4 is scattered a certain H people, who have laws
13:7 been and are now H may in one day
Wis 19:15 the former for their H reception of the aliens;
1Mac 6:24 the citadel and became H to us; moreover, they
2Mac 4:21 that Philometor had become H to his government,
14:11 king's friends, who were H to Judas, quickly inflamed

Rom 8:7 on the flesh is H to God; it does
Col 1:21 once were estranged and H in mind, doing evil

HOSTILITY (4)

1Mac 13:17 lest he arouse great H among the people, who
Eph 2:14 the dividing wall of H,
2:16 cross, thereby bringing the H to an end.
Heb 12:3 endured from sinners such H against himself, so that

HOSTS (301)

Ex 6:26 Israel from the land of Egypt by their H
7:4 and bring forth my H, my people the sons
12:17 day I brought your H out of the land
12:41 very day, all the H of the LORD went
12:51 out of the land of Egypt by their H
Num 10:28 Israel according to their H, when they set out.
33:1 of Egypt by their H under the leadership of
1Sam 1:3 to the LORD of H at Shiloh, where the
1:11 said, "O LORD of H, if thou wilt indeed
4:4 of the LORD of H, who is enthroned on
15:2 says the LORD of H, 'I will punish what
17:45 of the LORD of H, the God of the
2Sam 5:10 LORD, the God of H, was with him.
6:2 of the LORD of H who sits enthroned on
6:18 of the LORD of H,
7:8 says the LORD of H, I took you from
7:26 saying, 'The LORD of H is God over Israel,'
7:27 thou, O LORD of H, the God of Israel,
1Kgs 18:15 "As the LORD of H lives, before whom I
19:10 LORD, the God of H; for the people of
19:14 LORD, the God of H; for the people of
2Kgs 3:14 "As the LORD of H lives, whom I serve,
1Chr 11:9 for the LORD of H was with him.
17:7 says the LORD of H, I took you from
17:24 saying, 'The LORD of H, the God of Israel,
Job 10:17 thou dost bring fresh H against me.
Ps 24:10 The LORD of H, he is the King of
46:7 The LORD of H is with us; the God
46:11 The LORD of H is with us; the God
48:8 of the LORD of H, in the city of
59:5 Thou, LORD God of H, art God of Israel.
69:6 O Lord GOD of H; let not those who
80:4 O LORD God of H, how long wilt thou
80:7 us, O God of H; let thy face shine,
80:14 Turn again, O God of H
80:19 Restore us, O LORD God of H
84:1 lovely is thy dwelling place, O LORD of H
84:3 altars, O LORD of H, my King and my
84:8 O LORD God of H, hear my prayer; give
84:12 O LORD of H, blessed is the man who
89:8 O LORD God of H, who is mighty as
103:21 the LORD, all his H, his ministers that do
Sir 43:8 an instrument of the H on high shining forth
Is 1:9 If the LORD of H had not left us
1:24 says, the LORD of H, the Mighty One of
2:12 For the LORD of H has a day against
3:1 Lord, the LORD of H, is taking away from
3:15 says the Lord GOD of H
5:7 of the LORD of H is the house of
5:9 The LORD of H has sworn in my hearing:
5:16 But the LORD of H is exalted in justice,
5:24 of the LORD of H, and have despised the
6:3 is the LORD of H; the whole earth is
6:5 eyes have seen the King, the LORD of H
8:13 But the LORD of H, him you shall regard
8:18 from the LORD of H, who dwells on Mount
9:7 of the LORD of H will do this.
9:13 who smote them, nor seek the LORD of H
9:19 of the LORD of H the land is burned,
10:16 Lord, the LORD of H, will send wasting sickness
10:23 Lord, the LORD of H, will make a full
10:24 Lord, the LORD of H: "O my people, who
10:26 And the LORD of H will wield against them
10:33 Lord, the LORD of H will lop the boughs
13:4 The LORD of H is mustering a host for
13:13 of the LORD of H in the day of
14:22 says the LORD of H, "and will cut off
14:23 the broom of destruction, says the LORD of H
14:24 The LORD of H has sworn: "As I have
14:27 For the LORD of H has purposed, and who
17:3 the children of Israel, says the LORD of H
18:7 to the LORD of H from a people tall
18:7 place of the name of the LORD of H
19:4 over them, says the Lord, the LORD of H
19:12 what the LORD of H has purposed against Egypt.
19:16 which the LORD of H shakes over them.

19:17 which the LORD of H has purposed against them.
19:18 Canaan and swear allegiance to the LORD of H
19:20 to the LORD of H in the land of
19:25 whom the LORD of H has blessed, saying, "Blessed
21:10 from the LORD of H, the God of Israel,
22:5 the Lord GOD of H has a day of
22:12 the Lord GOD of H called to weeping and
22:14 The LORD of H has revealed himself in my
22:14 says the Lord GOD of H
22:15 the Lord GOD of H, "Come, go to this
22:25 says the LORD of H, the peg that was
23:9 The LORD of H has purposed it, to defile
24:23 for the LORD of H will reign on Mount
25:6 mountain the LORD of H will make for all
28:5 day the LORD of H will be a crown
28:22 the Lord GOD of H upon the whole land.
28:29 from the LORD of H; he is wonderful in
29:6 by the LORD of H with thunder and with
31:4 so the LORD of H will come down to
31:5 so the LORD of H will protect Jerusalem; he
37:16 LORD: "O LORD of H, God of Israel, who
37:32 of the LORD of H will accomplish this.
39:5 of the LORD of H:
44:6 Redeemer, the LORD of H: "I am the first
45:13 says the LORD of H
47:4 the LORD of H is his name–
48:2 Israel; the LORD of H is his name.
51:15 the LORD of H is his name.
54:5 husband, the LORD of H is his name; and
Jer 2:19 not in you, says the Lord GOD of H
5:14 LORD, the God of H: "Because they have spoken
6:6 says the LORD of H: "Hew down her trees;
6:9 says the LORD of H: "Glean thoroughly as a
7:3 says the LORD of H, the God of Israel,
7:21 says the LORD of H, the God of Israel:
8:3 I have driven them, says the LORD of H
9:7 says the LORD of H: "Behold, I will refine
9:15 says the LORD of H, the God of Israel:
9:17 says the LORD of H: "Consider, and call for
10:16 inheritance; the LORD of H is his name.
11:17 The LORD of H, who planted you, has pronounced
11:20 But, O LORD of H, who judgest righteously, who
11:22 says the LORD of H: "Behold, I will punish
15:16 called by thy name, O LORD, God of H
16:9 says the LORD of H, the God of Israel:
19:3 says the LORD of H, the God of Israel,
19:11 says the LORD of H: So will I break
19:15 says the LORD of H, the God of Israel,
20:12 O LORD of H, who triest the righteous, who
23:15 the LORD of H concerning the prophets: "Behold,
23:16 says the LORD of H: "Do not listen to
23:36 God, the LORD of H, our God.
25:8 says the LORD of H: Because you have not
25:27 says the LORD of H, the God of Israel:
25:28 says the LORD of H: You must drink!
25:29 says the LORD of H
25:32 says the LORD of H: Behold, evil is going
26:18 says the LORD of H, Zion shall be plowed
27:4 says the LORD of H, the God of Israel:
27:18 with the LORD of H, that the vessels which
27:19 says the LORD of H concerning the pillars, the
27:21 says the LORD of H, the God of Israel,
28:2 says the LORD of H, the God of Israel:
28:14 says the LORD of H, the God of Israel:
29:4 says the LORD of H, the God of Israel,
29:8 says the LORD of H, the God of Israel:
29:17 says the LORD of H, Behold, I am sending
29:21 says the LORD of H, the God of Israel,
29:25 says the LORD of H, the God of Israel:
30:8 says the LORD of H, that I will break
31:23 says the LORD of H, the God of Israel:
31:35 roar–the LORD of H is his name:
32:14 says the LORD of H, the God of Israel:
32:15 says the LORD of H, the God of Israel:
32:18 is the LORD of H,
33:11 to the LORD of H, for the LORD is
33:12 says the LORD of H: In this place which
35:13 says the LORD of H, the God of Israel:
35:17 LORD, the God of H, the God of Israel:
35:18 says the LORD of H, the God of Israel:
35:19 says the LORD of H, the God of Israel:
38:17 LORD, the God of H, the God of Israel,
39:16 says the LORD of H, the God of Israel:
42:15 says the LORD of H, the God of Israel:
42:18 says the LORD of H, the God of Israel:
43:10 says the LORD of H, the God of Israel:
44:2 says the LORD of H, the God of Israel:
44:7 the LORD God of H, the God of Israel:
44:11 says the LORD of H, the God of Israel:
44:25 says the LORD of H, the God of Israel:
46:10 the Lord GOD of H, a day of vengeance,
46:10 the Lord GOD of H holds a sacrifice in
46:18 is the LORD of H, like Tabor among the
46:25 The LORD of H, the God of Israel, said:
48:1 says the LORD of H, the God of Israel:
48:15 the King, whose name is the LORD of H
49:5 the Lord GOD of H, from all who are
49:7 says the LORD of H: "Is wisdom no more
49:26 destroyed in that day, says the LORD of H
49:35 says the LORD of H: "Behold, I will break
50:18 says the LORD of H, the God of Israel:
50:25 the Lord GOD of H has a work to
50:31 the Lord GOD of H; for your day has
50:33 says the LORD of H: The people of Israel
50:34 strong; the LORD of H is his name.
51:5 God, the LORD of H; but the land of
51:14 The LORD of H has sworn by himself: Surely
51:19 inheritance; the LORD of H is his name.
51:33 says the LORD of H, the God of Israel:
51:57 the King, whose name is the LORD of H
51:58 says the LORD of H: The broad wall of
Ezek 38:7 you and all the H that are assembled about
38:13 Have you assembled your H to carry off plunder,
Hos 12:5 LORD the God of H, the LORD is his
Amos 3:13 GOD, the God of H,
4:13 LORD, the God of H, is his name!
5:14 LORD, the God of H, will be with you,
5:15 LORD, the God of H, will be gracious to
5:16 LORD, the God of H, the Lord: "In all
5:27 the LORD, whose name is the God of H
6:8 LORD, the God of H: "I abhor the pride
6:14 LORD, the God of H; "and they shall oppress
9:5 The Lord, GOD of H, he who touches the
Mic 4:4 of the LORD of H has spoken.
Nah 2:13 says the LORD of H, and I will burn
3:3 sword and glittering spear, H of slain, heaps of
3:5 says the LORD of H, and will lift up
Hab 2:13 from the LORD of H that peoples labor only
Zeph 2:9 says the LORD of H, the God of Israel,
2:10 boasted against the people of the LORD of H
Hag 1:2 says the LORD of H: This people say the
1:5 says the LORD of H: Consider how you have
1:7 says the LORD of H: Consider how you have
1:9 says the LORD of H
1:14 of the LORD of H, their God,
2:4 says the LORD of H,
2:6 says the LORD of H: Once again, in a
2:7 this house with splendor, says the LORD of H
2:8 the gold is mine, says the LORD of H
2:9 says the LORD of H; and in this place
2:9 I will give prosperity, says the LORD of H
2:11 says the LORD of H: Ask the priests to
2:23 says the LORD of H, I will take you,
2:23 I have chosen you, says the LORD of H
Zech 1:3 says the LORD of H: Return to me, says
1:3 says the LORD of H, and I will return
1:3 will return to you, says the LORD of H
1:4 says the LORD of H, Return from your evil
1:6 As the LORD of H purposed to deal with
1:12 said, 'O LORD of H, how long wilt thou
1:14 says the LORD of H: I am exceedingly jealous
1:16 says the LORD of H, and the measuring line
1:17 says the LORD of H: My cities shall again
2:8 said the LORD of H, after his glory sent
2:9 that the LORD of H has sent me.
2:11 that the LORD of H has sent me to
3:7 says the LORD of H: If you will walk
3:9 says the LORD of H, and I will remove
3:10 says the LORD of H, every one of you
4:6 but by my Spirit, says the LORD of H
4:9 that the LORD of H has sent me to
5:4 says the LORD of H, and it shall enter
6:12 says the LORD of H, "Behold, the man whose
6:15 that the LORD of H has sent me to
7:3 of the LORD of H and the prophets, "Should
7:4 of the LORD of H came to me;
7:9 says the LORD of H, Render true judgments, show
7:12 which the LORD of H had sent by his
7:12 Therefore great wrath came from the LORD of H
7:13 says the LORD of H,
8:1 of the LORD of H came to me, saying,
8:2 says the LORD of H: I am jealous for

H

8:3 of the LORD of H, the holy mountain.
8:4 says the LORD of H: Old men and old
8:6 says the LORD of H: If it is marvelous
8:6 marvelous in my sight, says the LORD of H
8:7 says the LORD of H: Behold, I will save
8:9 says the LORD of H: "Let your hands be
8:9 of the LORD of H was laid, that the
8:11 in the former days, says the LORD of H
8:14 says the LORD of H: "As I purposed to
8:14 says the LORD of H,
8:18 of the LORD of H came to me, saying,
8:19 says the LORD of H: The fast of the
8:20 says the LORD of H: Peoples shall yet come,
8:21 seek the LORD of H; I am going.'
8:22 seek the LORD of H in Jerusalem, and to
8:23 says the LORD of H: In those days ten
9:15 The LORD of H will protect them, and they
10:3 for the LORD of H cares for his flock,
12:5 through the LORD of H, their God.'
13:2 says the LORD of H, I will cut off
13:7 says the LORD of H
14:16 King, the LORD of H, and to keep the
14:17 King, the LORD of H, there will be no
14:21 to the LORD of H, so that all who
14:21 of the LORD of H on that day.
Mal 1:4 the LORD of H says, "They may build, but
1:6 says the LORD of H to you, O priests,
1:8 says the LORD of H
1:9 says the LORD of H
1:10 says the LORD of H, and I will not
1:11 great among the nations, says the LORD of H
1:13 you sniff at me, says the LORD of H
1:14 says the LORD of H, and my name is
2:2 says the LORD of H, then I will send
2:4 with Levi may hold, says the LORD of H
2:7 he is the messenger of the LORD of H
2:8 says the LORD of H,
2:12 to bring an offering to the LORD of H
2:16 one's garment with violence, says the LORD of H
3:1 behold, he is coming, says the LORD of H
3:5 do not fear me, says the LORD of H
3:7 will return to you, says the LORD of H
3:10 says the LORD of H, if I will not
3:11 not fail to bear, says the LORD of H
3:12 a land of delight, says the LORD of H
3:14 walking as in mourning before the LORD of H
3:17 says the LORD of H, my special possession on
4:1 says the LORD of H, so that it will
4:3 day when I act, says the LORD of H
2Mac 15:21 Maccabeus, perceiving the H that were before him
Rom 9:29 "If the Lord of H had not left us
Eph 6:12 darkness, against the spiritual H of wickedness in the
Jas 5:4 have reached the ears of the Lord of H

HOT (37)

Gen 36:24 Anah who found the H springs in the wilderness,
Ex 11:8 out from Pharaoh in H anger.
16:21 when the sun grew H, it melted.
32:10 my wrath may burn H against them and I
32:11 does thy wrath burn H against thy people, whom
32:19 dancing, Moses' anger burned H, and he threw the
32:22 of my lord burn H; you know the people,
Deut 9:19 of the anger and H displeasure which the LORD
19:6 avenger of blood in H anger pursue the manslayer
Judg 14:19 In H anger he went back to his father's
1Sam 11:9 time the sun is H, you shall have deliverance.'"
21:6 to be replaced by H bread on the day
1Kgs 19:6 a cake baked on H stones and a jar
22:35 And the battle grew H that day, and the
2Chr 18:34 And the battle grew H that day, and the
Neh 7:3 until the sun is H; and while they are
Job 6:17 disappear; when it is H, they vanish from their
37:17 you whose garments are H when the earth is
Ps 39:3 worse, my heart became H within me.
85:3 didst turn from thy H anger.
119:53 H indignation seizes me because of the wicked, who
Prov 6:28 can one walk upon H coals and his feet
26:21 As charcoal to H embers and wood to fire,
Sir 34:16 a shelter from the H wind and a shade
Jer 4:11 and to Jerusalem, "A H wind from the bare
Lam 4:11 he poured out his H anger; and he kindled
5:10 Our skin is H as an oven with the
Ezek 24:11 that it may become H, and its copper may
36:5 I speak in my H jealousy against the rest
Dan 3:22 and the furnace very H, the flame of the
13:15 bathe in the garden, for it was very H

Hos 7:8 All of them are H as an oven, and
Zech 10:3 "My anger is H against the shepherds, and I
2Mac 4:25 high-priesthood, but having the H temper of a cruel
Rev 3:15 know your works: you are neither cold nor H
3:15 Would that you were cold or H
3:16 and neither cold nor H, I will spew you

HOT-TEMPERED

Prov 15:18 A H man stirs up strife, but he who

HOTHAM (2)

1Chr 7:32 father of Japhlet, Shomer, H, and their sister Shua.
11:44 Je-iel the sons of H the Aroerite,

HOTHIR (2)

1Chr 25:4 Joshbekashah, Mallothi, H, Mahazi-oth.
25:28 to the twenty-first, to H, his sons and his

HOTLY (3)

Gen 31:36 sin, that you have H pursued me?
Num 11:10 of the LORD blazed H, and Moses was displeased.
Ps 10:2 In arrogance the wicked H pursue the poor; let

HOUR (103)

1Sam 9:24 for you until the H appointed, that you might
Jud 13:4 might, look in this H upon the work of
Esth 10:11 lots came to the H and moment and day
Sir 11:25 The misery of an H makes one forget luxury,
18:19 yourself, and in the H of visitation you will
33:23 your life, in the H of death, distribute your
39:33 and he will supply every need in its H
Jer 46:17 one who lets the H go by.'
2Mac 8:25 to return because the H was late.
Mt 10:19 to you in that H;
20:3 out about the third H he saw others standing
20:5 again about the sixth H and the ninth hour,
20:5 hour and the ninth H, he did the same.
20:6 And about the eleventh H he went out and
20:9 hired about the eleventh H came, each of them
20:12 last worked only one H, and you have made
24:36 of that day and H no one knows, not
24:44 is coming at an H you do not expect.
24:50 him and at an H he does not know,
25:13 for you know neither the day nor the H
26:40 "So, could you not watch with me one H
26:45 Behold, the H is at hand, and the Son
26:55 At that H Jesus said to the crowds, "Have
27:45 Now from the sixth H there was darkness over
27:45 darkness over all the land until the ninth H
27:46 And about the ninth H Jesus cried with a
Mk 6:35 lonely place, and the H is now late;
13:11 given you in that H, for it is not
13:32 that day or that H no one knows, not
14:35 it were possible, the H might pass from him.
14:37 Could you not watch one H
14:41 It is enough; the H has come; the Son
15:25 it was the third H, when they crucified him.
15:32 And when the sixth H had come, there was
15:32 darkness over the whole land until the ninth H
15:33 And at the ninth H Jesus cried with a
Lk 1:10 praying outside at the H of incense.
2:38 up at that very H she gave thanks to
7:21 In that H he cured many of diseases and
10:21 In that same H he rejoiced in the Holy
12:12 you in that very H what you ought to
12:39 had known at what H the thief was coming,
12:40 Son of man is coming at an unexpected H
12:46 him and at an H he does not know,
13:31 At that very H some Pharisees came, and said
20:19 him at that very H, but they feared the
22:14 And when the H came, he sat at table,
22:51 But this is your H, and the power of
22:57 interval of about an H still another insisted, saying,
23:43 now about the sixth H, and there was darkness
23:43 land until the ninth H,
24:33 they rose that same H and returned to Jerusalem;
Jn 1:39 that day, for it was about the tenth H
2:4 My H has not yet come."
4:6 It was about the sixth H
4:21 "Woman, believe me, the H is coming when neither
4:23 But the H is coming, and now is, when
4:52 he asked them the H when he began to
4:52 "Yesterday at the seventh H the fever left him."
4:53 knew that was the H when Jesus had said
5:24 say to you, the H is coming, and now
5:27 at this; for the H is coming when all

7:30 on him, because his H had not yet come.
8:20 arrested him, because his H had not yet come.
12:23 Jesus answered them, "The H has come for the
12:27 'Father, save me from this H
12:27 for this purpose I have come to this H
13:1 Jesus knew that his H had come to depart
16:2 the synagogues; indeed, the H is coming when
16:4 you, that when their H comes you may remember
16:21 has sorrow, because her H has come; but when
16:25 you in figures; the H is coming when I
16:32 The H is coming, indeed it has come, when
17:1 and said, "Father, the H has come; glorify thy
19:14 of the Passover; it was about the sixth H
19:27 And from that H the disciple took her to
Acts 2:15 is only the third H of the day;
3:1 the temple at the H of prayer, the ninth
3:1 temple at the hour of prayer, the ninth H
10:3 About the ninth H of the day he saw
10:9 on the housetop to pray, about the sixth H
10:30 days ago, about this H, I was keeping the
10:30 was keeping the ninth H of prayer in my
16:18 And it came out that very H
16:33 took them the same H of the night, and
22:13 And in that very H I received my sight
23:23 said, "At the third H of the night get
Rom 13:11 this you know what H it is, how it
1Cor 4:11 To the present H we hunger and thirst, we
15:30 Why am I in peril every H
1Jn 2:18 it is the last H; and as you have
2:18 therefore we know that it is the last H
Rev 3:3 not know at what H I will come upon
3:10 keep you from the H of trial which is
8:1 was silence in heaven for about half an H
9:15 held ready for the H, the day, the month,
11:13 And at that H there was a great earthquake,
14:7 him glory, for the H of his judgment has
14:15 and reap, for the H to reap has come,
17:12 as kings for one H, together with the beast.
18:10 In one H has thy judgment come."
18:17 In one H all this wealth has been laid
18:19 In one H she has been laid waste.

HOURS (3)

Jn 11:9 "Are there not twelve H in the day?
Acts 5:7 interval of about three H his wife came in,
19:34 Jew, for about two H they all with one

HOUSE (1,845)

Gen 12:1 kindred and your father's H to the land that
12:15 And the woman was taken into Pharaoh's H
12:17 afflicted Pharaoh and his H with great plagues
14:14 men, born in his H, three hundred and eighteen
15:2 the heir of my H is Eliezer of Damascus?"
15:3 slave born in my H will be my heir."
17:12 whether born in your H, or bought with your
17:13 is born in your H and he that is
17:23 slaves born in his H or bought with his
17:23 the men of Abraham's H, and he circumcised the
17:27 the men of his H, those born in the
17:27 those born in the H and those bought with
19:2 you, to your servant's H and spend the night,
19:3 him and entered his H; and he made them
19:4 last man, surrounded the H;
19:10 brought Lot into the H to them, and shut
19:11 the door of the H, both small and great,
20:13 wander from my father's H, I said to her,
20:18 the wombs of the H of Abimelech because of
24:2 the oldest of his H, who had charge of
24:7 me from my father's H and from the land
24:23 room in your father's H for us to lodge
24:27 the way to the H of my master's kinsmen."
24:31 I have prepared the H and a place for
24:32 man came into the H; and Laban ungirded the
24:38 go to my father's H and to my kindred,
24:40 and from my father's H;
27:15 with her in the H, and put them on
28:2 to Paddan-aram to the H of Bethuel your mother's
28:17 none other than the H of God, and this
28:21 again to my father's H in peace, then the
28:22 pillar, shall be God's H; and of all that
29:13 and kissed him, and brought him to his H
31:14 or inheritance left to us in our father's H
31:30 greatly for your father's H, but why did you
31:41 have been in your H; I served you fourteen
33:17 and built himself a H, and made booths for
34:26 Dinah out of Shechem's H, and went away.
38:11 widow in your father's H, till Shelah my son
38:11 So Tamar went and dwelt in her father's H
39:2 he was in the H of his master the
39:4 him overseer of his H and put him in
39:5 him overseer in his H and over all that
39:5 LORD blessed the Egyptian's H for Joseph's sake;
39:5 that he had, in H and field.
39:8 about anything in the H, and he has put
39:9 not greater in this H than I am; nor
39:11 he went into the H to do his work
39:11 the men of the H was there in the
39:11 was there in the H,
39:12 hand, and fled and got out of the H
39:13 fled out of the H,
39:15 me, and fled and got out of the H
39:18 garment with me, and fled out of the H
40:3 in custody in the H of the captain of
40:7 custody in his master's H, "Why are your faces
40:14 Pharaoh, and so get me out of this H
41:10 in custody in the H of the captain of
41:40 shall be over my H, and all my people
41:51 forget all my hardship and all my father's H
43:16 the steward of his H, "Bring the men into
43:16 the men into the H, and slaughter an animal
43:17 bade him, and brought the men to Joseph's H
43:18 were brought to Joseph's H, and they said, "It
43:19 the steward of Joseph's H, and spoke with him
43:19 the door of the H,
43:24 the men into Joseph's H, and given them water,
43:26 they brought into the H to him the present
44:1 the steward of his H, "Fill the men's sacks
44:8 we steal silver or gold from your lord's H
44:14 brothers came to Joseph's H, he was still there;
45:8 lord of all his H and ruler over all
45:16 was heard in Pharaoh's H, "Joseph's brothers have
46:27 the persons of the H of Jacob, that came
47:14 and Joseph brought the money into Pharaoh's H
50:22 he and his father's H; and Joseph lived a
Ex 2:1 a man from the H of Levi went and
3:22 who sojourns in her H, jewelry of silver and
7:23 and went into his H, and he did not
8:3 come up into your H, and into your bedchamber
8:24 of flies into the H of Pharaoh and into
12:4 neighbor next to his H shall take according to
12:22 the door of his H until the morning.
12:30 there was not a H where one was not
12:46 In one H shall it be eaten; you shall
12:46 the flesh outside the H; and you shall not
13:3 Egypt, out of the H of bondage, for by
13:14 of Egypt, from the H of bondage.
16:31 Now the H of Israel called its name manna;
19:3 shall say to the H of Jacob, and tell
20:2 Egypt, out of the H of bondage.
20:17 not covet your neighbor's H; you shall not covet
22:7 out of the man's H, then, if the thief
22:8 the owner of the H shall come near to
23:19 shall bring into the H of the LORD your
34:26 shall bring to the H of the LORD your
Lev 10:6 your brethren, the whole H of Israel, may bewail
14:34 leprous disease in a H in the land of
14:35 he who owns the H shall come and tell
14:35 of disease in my H
14:36 that they empty the H before the priest goes
14:36 that is in the H be declared unclean; and
14:36 the priest shall go in to see the H
14:37 the walls of the H with greenish or reddish
14:38 go out of the H to the door of
14:38 the door of the H, and shut up the
14:38 and shut up the H seven days.
14:39 the walls of the H,
14:41 the inside of the H to be scraped round
14:42 he shall take other plaster and plaster the H
14:43 out again in the H, after he has taken
14:43 stones and scraped the H and plastered it,
14:44 has spread in the H, it is a malignant
14:44 malignant leprosy in the H; it is unclean.
14:45 shall break down the H, its stones and timber
14:45 the plaster of the H; and he shall carry
14:46 he who enters the H while it is shut
14:47 lies down in the H shall wash his clothes;
14:47 who eats in the H shall wash his clothes.
14:48 not spread in the H after the house was
14:48 the house after the H was plastered, then the
14:48 priest shall pronounce the H clean, for the disease
14:49 the cleansing of the H he shall take two
14:51 water, and sprinkle the H seven times.

	14:52	he shall cleanse the H with the blood of
	14:53	make atonement for the H, and it shall be
	14:55	garment or in a H,
	16:6	shall make atonement for himself and for his H
	16:11	himself and for his H; he shall kill the
	16:17	himself and for his H and for all the
	17:3	any man of the H of Israel kills an
	17:8	Any man of the H of Israel, or of
	17:10	any man of the H of Israel or of
	22:11	are born in his H may eat of his
	22:13	returns to her father's H, as in her youth,
	22:18	any one of the H of Israel or of
	25:29	man sells a dwelling H in a walled city,
	25:30	full year, then the H that is in the
	25:33	of redemption, then the H that was sold in
	27:14	a man dedicates his H to be holy to
	27:15	wishes to redeem his H, he shall add a
Num	1:4	the head of the H of his fathers.
	1:44	Israel, twelve men, each representing his fathers' H
	2:34	one in his family, according to his fathers' H
	3:24	head of the fathers' H of the Gershonites.
	3:30	head of the fathers' H of the families of
	3:35	head of the fathers' H of the families of
	12:7	servant Moses; he is entrusted with all my H
	17:2	one for each fathers' H, from all their leaders
	17:3	one rod for the head of each fathers' H
	17:8	of Aaron for the H of Levi had sprouted
	18:1	sons and your fathers' H with you shall bear
	18:11	is clean in your H may eat of it.
	18:13	is clean in your H may eat of it.
	20:29	was dead, all the H of Israel wept for
	22:18	to give me his H full of silver and
	24:13	should give me his H full of silver and
	25:14	head of a fathers' H belonging to the Simeonites.
	25:15	people of a fathers' H in Midian.
	30:3	while within her father's H, in her youth,
	30:10	vowed in her husband's H, or bound herself by
	30:16	daughter, while in her youth, within her father's H
Deut	5:6	Egypt, out of the H of bondage.
	5:21	not desire your neighbor's H, his field, or his
	6:7	you sit in your H, and when you walk
	6:9	the doorposts of your H and on your gates.
	6:12	Egypt, out of the H of bondage.
	7:8	redeemed you from the H of bondage, from the
	7:26	abominable thing into your H, and become accursed
	8:14	Egypt, out of the H of bondage,
	11:19	are sitting in your H, and when you are
	11:20	the doorposts of your H and upon your gates,
	13:5	you out of the H of bondage, to make
	13:10	Egypt, out of the H of bondage.
	20:5	has built a new H and has not dedicated
	20:5	go back to his H, lest he die in
	20:6	go back to his H, lest he die in
	20:7	go back to his H, lest he die in
	20:8	go back to his H, lest the heart of
	21:12	her home to your H, and she shall shave
	21:13	shall remain in your H and bewail her father
	22:2	it home to your H, and it shall be
	22:8	you build a new H, you shall make a
	22:8	of blood upon your H, if any one fall
	22:21	door of her father's H, and the men of
	22:21	harlot in her father's H; so you shall purge
	23:18	a dog, into the H of the LORD your
	24:1	her out of his H, and she departs out
	24:1	departs out of his H,
	24:3	her out of his H, or if the latter
	24:10	not go into his H to fetch his pledge.
	25:9	build up his brother's H
	25:10	the name of his H shall be called in
	25:10	called in Israel, The H of him that had
	25:14	not have in your H two kinds of measures,
	26:11	you and to your H, you, and the Levite,
	26:13	portion out of my H, and moreover I have
	28:30	you shall build a H, and you shall not
Josh	2:1	and came into the H of a harlot whose
	2:3	you, who entered your H; for they have come
	2:12	kindly with my father's H, and give me a
	2:15	the window, for her H was built into the
	2:18	shall gather into your H your father and mother,
	2:19	the doors of your H into the street, his
	2:19	with you in the H, his blood shall be
	6:17	with her in her H shall live, because she
	6:22	"Go into the harlot's H, and bring out from
	6:24	the treasury of the H of the LORD.
	9:23	of water for the H of my God."
	17:17	Joshua said to the H of Joseph, to Ephraim
	18:5	the south, and the H of Joseph in their
	21:45	had made to the H of Israel had failed;
	24:15	for me and my H, we will serve the
	24:17	Egypt, out of the H of bondage, and who
Judg	1:22	The H of Joseph also went up against Bethel;
	1:23	And the H of Joseph sent to spy out
	1:35	the hand of the H of Joseph rested heavily
	4:17	of Hazor and the H of Heber the Kenite.
	6:8	you out of the H of bondage;
	6:19	Gideon went into his H and prepared a kid,
	8:29	of Joash went and dwelt in his own H
	9:4	silver out of the H of Baal-berith with which
	9:5	went to his father's H at Ophrah, and slew
	9:16	with Jerubbaal and his H, and have done to
	9:18	up against my father's H this day, and have
	9:19	Jerubbaal and with his H this day, then rejoice
	9:27	and went into the H of their god, and
	9:46	the stronghold of the H of El-berith.
	10:9	Benjamin and against the H of Ephraim; so that
	11:2	inherit in our father's H; for you are the
	11:7	me, and drive me out of my father's H
	11:31	the doors of my H to meet me, when
	12:1	We will burn your H over you with fire."
	14:15	you and your father's H with fire.
	14:19	hot anger he went back to his father's H
	16:26	pillars on which the H rests, that I may
	16:27	Now the H was full of men and women;
	16:29	pillars upon which the H rested, and he leaned
	16:30	his might; and the H fell upon the lords
	17:4	it was in the H of Micah.
	17:8	of Ephraim to the H of Micah.
	17:12	and was in the H of Micah.
	18:2	of Ephraim, to the H of Micah, and lodged
	18:3	they were by the H of Micah, they recognized
	18:13	and came to the H of Micah.
	18:15	and came to the H of the young Levite,
	18:18	these went into Micah's H and took the graven
	18:19	be priest to the H of one man, or
	18:22	the houses near Micah's H were called out, and
	18:31	as long as the H of God was at
	19:2	him to her father's H at Bethlehem in Judah,
	19:3	came to her father's H; and when the girl's
	19:15	took them into his H to spend the night.
	19:18	my home; and nobody takes me into his H
	19:21	brought him into his H, and gave the asses
	19:22	base fellows, beset the H round about, beating on
	19:22	the master of the H, "Bring out the man
	19:22	who came into your H, that we may know
	19:23	the master of the H, went out to them
	19:23	has come into my H, do not do this
	19:26	door of the man's H where her master was,
	19:27	the doors of the H and went out to
	19:27	the door of the H, with her hands on
	19:29	when he entered his H, he took a knife,
	20:5	me, and beset the H round about me by
	20:8	and none of us will return to his H
Ruth	1:8	"Go, return each of you to her mother's H
	1:9	of you in the H of her husband!" Then
	4:11	is coming into your H, like Rachel and Leah,
	4:11	together built up the H of Israel.
	4:12	Bethlehem; and may your H be like the house
	4:12	house be like the H of Perez, whom Tamar
1Sam	1:7	went up to the H of the LORD, she
	1:19	went back to their H at Ramah.
	1:21	Elkanah and all his H went up to offer
	1:24	brought him to the H of the LORD at
	2:27	revealed myself to the H of your father when
	2:27	Egypt subject to the H of Pharaoh.
	2:28	I gave to the H of your father all
	2:30	'I promised that your H and the house of
	2:30	your house and the H of your father should
	2:31	strength of your father's H, so that there will
	2:31	will not be an old man in your H
	2:32	old man in your H for ever.
	2:33	the increase of your H shall die by the
	2:35	build him a sure H, and he shall go
	2:36	is left in your H shall come to implore
	3:12	spoken concerning his H, from beginning to end.
	3:13	about to punish his H for ever, for the
	3:14	I swear to the H of Eli that the
	3:14	the iniquity of Eli's H shall not be expiated
	3:15	the doors of the H of the LORD.
	5:2	brought it into the H of Dagon and set
	5:5	all who enter the H of Dagon do not
	7:1	brought it to the H of Abinadab on the
	7:2	years, and all the H of Israel lamented after

7:3 said to all the H of Israel, "If you
9:18 me where is the H of the seer?"
9:20 not for you and for all your father's H
15:34 went up to his H in Gibe-ah of Saul.
17:25 and make his father's H free in Israel."
18:2 would not let him return to his father's H
18:10 he raved within his H, while David was playing
19:9 he sat in his H with his spear in
19:11 sent messengers to David's H to watch him, that
20:15 your loyalty from my H for ever.
20:16 cut off from the H of David.
21:15 Shall this fellow come into my H
22:1 and all his father's H heard it, they went
22:11 and all his father's H, the priests who were
22:14 captain over your bodyguard, and honored in your H
22:15 or to all the H of my father; for
22:16 surely die, Ahimelech, you and all your father's H
22:22 death of all the persons of your father's H
24:21 not destroy my name out of my father's H
25:1 buried him in his H at Ramah.
25:6 peace be to your H, and peace be to
25:17 and against all his H, and he is so
25:28 my lord a sure H, because my lord is
25:35 in peace to your H; see, I have hearkened
25:36 a feast in his H, like the feast of
28:24 fatted calf in the H, and she quickly killed
2Sam 1:12 LORD and for the H of Israel, because they
2:4 David king over the H of Judah.
2:7 is dead, and the H of Judah has anointed
2:10 But the H of Judah followed David.
2:11 in Hebron over the H of Judah was seven
3:1 long war between the H of Saul and the
3:1 of Saul and the H of David; and David
3:1 and stronger, while the H of Saul became weaker
3:6 was war between the H of Saul and the
3:6 of Saul and the H of David, Abner was
3:6 himself strong in the H of Saul.
3:8 showing loyalty to the H of Saul your father,
3:10 the kingdom from the H of Saul, and set
3:19 Israel and the whole H of Benjamin thought good
3:29 upon all his father's H; and may the house
3:29 house; and may the H of Joab never be
4:5 they came to the H of Ish-bosheth, as he
4:6 the doorkeeper of the H had been cleaning wheat,
4:7 they came into the H, as he lay on
4:11 man in his own H upon his bed, shall
5:8 and the lame shall not come into the H
5:11 also carpenters and masons who built David a H
6:3 it out of the H of Abinadab which was
6:5 David and all the H of Israel were making
6:10 it aside to the H of Obed-edom the Gittite.
6:11 LORD remained in the H of Obed-edom the Gittite
6:12 of God from the H of Obed-edom to the
6:15 David and all the H of Israel brought up
6:19 Then all the people departed, each to his H
6:21 and above all his H, to appoint me as
7:1 king dwelt in his H, and the LORD had
7:2 I dwell in a H of cedar, but the
7:5 you build me a H to dwell in?
7:6 not dwelt in a H since the day I
7:7 not built me a H of cedar?'"
7:11 you that the LORD will make you a H
7:13 He shall build a H for my name, and
7:16 And your H and your kingdom shall be made
7:18 and what is my H, that thou hast brought
7:19 also of thy servant's H for a great while
7:25 servant and concerning his H, and do as thou
7:26 over Israel,' and the H of thy servant David
7:27 will build you a H; therefore thy servant has
7:29 thee to bless the H of thy servant, that
7:29 thy blessing shall the H of thy servant be
9:1 one left of the H of Saul, that I
9:2 a servant of the H of Saul whose name
9:3 some one of the H of Saul, that I
9:4 "He is in the H of Machir the son
9:5 brought him from the H of Machir the son
9:9 and to all his H I have given to
9:12 dwelt in Ziba's H became Mephibosheth's servants.
11:2 roof of the king's H, that he saw from
11:4 from her uncleanness.) Then she returned to her H
11:8 "Go down to your H, and wash your feet."
11:8 out of the king's H, and there followed him
11:9 door of the king's H with all the servants
11:9 lord, and did not go down to his H
11:10 David, "Uriah did not go down to his H
11:10 Why did you not go down to your H
11:11 then go to my H, to eat and to
11:13 but he did not go down to his H
11:27 brought her to his H, and she became his
12:8 gave you your master's H, and your master's wives
12:8 and gave you the H of Israel and of
12:10 never depart from your H, because you have
12:11 out of your own H; and I will take
12:15 Then Nathan went to his H
12:17 the elders of his H stood beside him, to
12:20 he went into the H of the LORD, and
12:20 went to his own H; and when he asked,
13:7 to your brother Amnon's H, and prepare food for
13:8 to her brother Amnon's H, where he was lying
13:20 dwelt, a desolate woman, in her brother Absalom's H
14:8 woman, "Go to your H, and I will give
14:9 and on my father's H; let the king and
14:24 apart in his own H; he is not to
14:24 apart in his own H, and did not come
14:31 to Absalom at his H, and said to him,
15:16 the king left ten concubines to keep the H
15:17 after him; and they halted at the last H
15:35 hear from the king's H, tell it to Zadok
16:3 he said, 'Today the H of Israel will give
16:5 the family of the H of Saul, whose name
16:8 the blood of the H of Saul, in whose
16:21 left to keep the H; and all Israel will
17:18 and came to the H of a man at
17:20 the woman at the H, they said, "Where are
17:23 And he set his H in order, and hanged
19:5 Joab came into the H to the king, and
19:11 king back to his H, when the word of
19:17 the servant of the H of Saul, with his
19:20 first of all the H of Joseph to come
19:28 For all my father's H were but men doomed
20:3 David came to his H at Jerusalem; and the
20:3 to care for the H, and put them in
20:3 put them in a H under guard, and provided
21:1 Saul and on his H, because he put the
21:4 and Saul or his H; neither is it for
23:5 Yea, does not my H stand so with God?
24:17 thee, be against me and against my father's H
1Kgs 1:53 and Solomon said to him, "Go to your H
2:24 has made me a H, as he promised, Adonijah
2:27 had spoken concerning the H of Eli in Shiloh.
2:31 and from my father's H the guilt for the
2:33 descendants, and to his H, and to his throne,
2:34 buried in his own H in the wilderness.
2:36 him, "Build yourself a H in Jerusalem, and dwell
3:1 finished building his own H and the house of
3:1 own house and the H of the LORD and
3:2 places, however, because no H had yet been built
3:17 dwell in the same H; and I gave birth
3:17 to a child while she was in the H
3:18 with us in the H, only we two were
3:18 the house, only we two were in the H
5:3 could not build a H for the name of
5:5 purpose to build a H for the name of
5:5 place, shall build the H for my name.'
5:17 the foundation of the H with dressed stones.
5:18 the timber and the stone to build the H
6:1 began to build the H of the LORD.
6:2 The H which King Solomon built for the LORD
6:3 the nave of the H was twenty cubits long,
6:3 the width of the H, and ten cubits deep
6:3 and ten cubits deep in front of the H
6:4 he made for the H windows with recessed frames.
6:5 the wall of the H, running round the walls
6:5 the walls of the H, both the nave and
6:6 the outside of the H he made offsets on
6:6 not be inserted into the walls of the H
6:7 When the H was built, it was with stone
6:8 south side of the H; and one went up
6:9 So he built the H, and finished it; and
6:9 the ceiling of the H of beams and planks
6:10 structure against the whole H, each story five cubits
6:10 was joined to the H with timbers of cedar.
6:12 Solomon, "Concerning this H which you are building,
6:14 So Solomon built the H, and finished it.
6:15 the walls of the H on the inside with
6:15 the floor of the H to the rafters of
6:15 the floor of the H with boards of cypress.
6:16 the rear of the H with boards of cedar
6:17 The H, that is, the nave in front of
6:18 The cedar within the H was carved in the
6:19 innermost part of the H, to set there the
6:21 the inside of the H with pure gold, and

6:22 he overlaid the whole H with gold, until all
6:22 gold, until all the H was finished.
6:27 innermost part of the H; and the wings of
6:27 touched each other in the middle of the H
6:29 the walls of the H round about with carved
6:30 The floor of the H he overlaid with gold
6:37 the foundation of the H of the LORD was
6:38 the eighth month, the H was finished in all
7:1 was building his own H thirteen years, and he
7:1 house thirteen years, and he finished his entire H
7:2 He built the H of the Forest of Lebanon;
7:8 His own H where he was to dwell, in
7:8 Solomon also made a H like this hall for
7:9 the court of the H of the LORD to
7:12 inner court of the H of the LORD, and
7:12 of the LORD, and the vestibule of the H
7:39 south side of the H, and five on the
7:39 north side of the H; and he set the
7:39 the sea on the southeast corner of the H
7:40 King Solomon on the H of the LORD:
7:45 these vessels in the H of the LORD, which
7:48 that were in the H of the LORD: the
7:50 innermost part of the H, the most holy place,
7:51 Solomon did on the H of the LORD was
7:51 the treasuries of the H of the LORD.
8:6 inner sanctuary of the H, in the most holy
8:10 a cloud filled the H of the LORD,
8:11 the LORD filled the H of the LORD.
8:13 built thee an exalted H, a place for thee
8:16 which to build a H, that my name might
8:17 father to build a H for the name of
8:18 heart to build a H for my name, you
8:19 shall not build the H, but your son who
8:19 you shall build the H for my name.'
8:20 I have built the H for the name of
8:27 how much less this H which I have built!
8:29 and day toward this H, the place of which
8:31 thine altar in this H,
8:33 to thee in this H;
8:38 his hands toward this H;
8:42 and prays toward this H,
8:43 may know that this H which I have built
8:44 hast chosen and the H which I have built
8:48 hast chosen, and the H which I have built
8:63 of Israel dedicated the H of the LORD.
8:64 that was before the H of the LORD; for
9:1 had finished building the H of the LORD and
9:1 LORD and the king's H and all that Solomon
9:3 I have consecrated this H which you have built,
9:7 given them; and the H which I have consecrated
9:8 And this H will become a heap of ruins;
9:8 land and to this H
9:10 the two houses, the H of the LORD and
9:10 LORD and the king's H,
9:15 levied to build the H of the LORD and
9:15 LORD and his own H and the Millo and
9:24 David to her own H which Solomon had built
9:25 So he finished the H
10:4 wisdom of Solomon, the H that he had built,
10:5 he offered at the H of the LORD, there
10:12 wood supports for the H of the LORD, and
10:12 and for the king's H, lyres also and harps
10:17 put them in the H of the Forest of
10:21 the vessels of the H of the Forest of
11:14 was of the royal H in Edom.
11:18 who gave him a H, and assigned him an
11:20 Tahpenes weaned in Pharaoh's H; and Genubath was
11:20 Genubath was in Pharaoh's H among the sons of
11:28 forced labor of the H of Joseph.
11:38 build you a sure H, as I built for
12:16 now to your own H, David." So Israel departed
12:19 in rebellion against the H of David to this
12:20 none that followed the H of David, but the
12:21 he assembled all the H of Judah, and the
12:21 to fight against the H of Israel, to restore
12:23 and to all the H of Judah and Benjamin,
12:26 turn back to the H of David;
12:27 offer sacrifices in the H of the LORD at
13:2 be born to the H of David, Josiah by
13:8 give me half your H, I will not go
13:18 with you into your H that he may eat
13:19 ate bread in his H, and drank water.
13:34 became sin to the H of Jeroboam, so as
14:4 and came to the H of Ahijah.
14:8 kingdom away from the H of David and gave
14:10 bring evil upon the H of Jeroboam, and will
14:10 will utterly consume the H of Jeroboam, as a
14:12 has spoken it.''' Arise therefore, go to your H
14:13 of Israel, in the H of Jeroboam.
14:14 shall cut off the H of Jeroboam today.
14:17 the threshold of the H, the child died.
14:26 the treasures of the H of the LORD and
14:26 treasures of the king's H; he took away everything.
14:27 guard, who kept the door of the king's H
14:28 king went into the H of the LORD, the
15:15 he brought into the H of the LORD the
15:18 the treasures of the H of the LORD and
15:18 treasures of the king's H, and gave them into
15:27 of Ahijah, of the H of Issachar, conspired against
15:29 he killed all the H of Jeroboam; he left
15:29 he left to the H of Jeroboam not one
16:3 away Baasha and his H, and I will make
16:3 I will make your H like the house of
16:3 your house like the H of Jeroboam the son
16:7 against Baasha and his H, both because of all
16:7 in being like the H of Jeroboam, and also
16:9 himself drunk in the H of Arza, who was
16:11 he killed all the H of Baasha; he did
16:12 Zimri destroyed all the H of Baasha, according to
16:18 citadel of the king's H, and burned the king's
16:18 and burned the king's H over him with fire,
16:32 for Baal in the H of Baal, which he
17:17 the mistress of the H, became ill; and his
17:23 upper chamber into the H, and delivered him to
18:18 have, and your father's H, because you have forsaken
20:6 they shall search your H and the houses of
20:31 the kings of the H of Israel are merciful
20:43 Israel went to his H resentful and sullen, and
21:2 it is near my H; and I will give
21:4 Ahab went into his H vexed and sullen because
21:22 I will make your H like the house of
21:22 your house like the H of Jeroboam the son
21:22 Nebat, and like the H of Baasha the son
21:29 days I will bring the evil upon his H
22:39 did, and the ivory H which he built, and
2Kgs 4:2 Tell me; what have you in the H
4:2 has nothing in the H, except a jar of
4:32 Elisha came into the H, he saw the child
4:35 and fro in the H, and went up, and
5:9 chariots, and halted at the door of Elisha's H
5:18 master goes into the H of Rimmon to worship
5:18 bow myself in the H of Rimmon, when I
5:18 bow myself in the H of Rimmon, the LORD
5:24 put them in the H; and he sent the
6:32 was sitting in his H, and the elders were
8:3 the king for her H and her land.
8:5 the king for her H and her land.
8:18 of Israel, as the H of Ahab had done,
8:27 the way of the H of Ahab, and did
8:27 the LORD, as the H of Ahab had done,
8:27 was son-in-law to the H of Ahab.
9:6 and went into the H; and the young man
9:7 shall strike down the H of Ahab your master,
9:8 For the whole H of Ahab shall perish; and
9:9 I will make the H of Ahab like the
9:9 of Ahab like the H of Jeroboam the son
9:9 Nebat, and like the H of Baasha the son
10:3 his father's throne, and fight for your master's H
10:10 LORD spoke concerning the H of Ahab; for the
10:11 that remained of the H of Ahab in Jezreel,
10:21 And they entered the H of Baal, and the
10:21 of Baal, and the H of Baal was filled
10:23 Jehu went into the H of Baal with Jehonadab
10:25 inner room of the H of Baal
10:26 that was in the H of Baal, and burned
10:27 Baal, and demolished the H of Baal, and made
10:30 have done to the H of Ahab according to
11:3 years, hid in the H of the LORD, while
11:4 to him in the H of the LORD; and
11:4 under oath in the H of the LORD, and
11:5 and guard the king's H
11:7 sabbath and guard the H of the LORD,
11:10 which were in the H of the LORD;
11:11 south side of the H to the north side
11:11 north side of the H, around the altar and
11:11 of the house, around the altar and the H
11:13 she went into the H of the LORD to
11:15 be slain in the H of the LORD."
11:16 entrance to the king's H, and there she was
11:18 land went to the H of Baal, and tore
11:18 posted watchmen over the H of the LORD.
11:19 king down from the H of the LORD, marching

11:19 the gate of the guards to the king's H
11:20 been slain with the sword at the king's H
12:4 is brought into the H of the LORD, the
12:4 to bring into the H of the LORD,
12:5 let them repair the H wherever any need of
12:6 the priests had made no repairs on the H
12:7 to them, "Why are you not repairing the H
12:7 hand it over for the repair of the H
12:8 people, and that they should not repair the H
12:9 as one entered the H of the LORD; and
12:9 was brought into the H of the LORD.
12:10 was found in the H of the LORD.
12:11 the oversight of the H of the LORD; and
12:11 who worked upon the H of the LORD,
12:12 making repairs on the H of the LORD, and
12:12 for any outlay upon the repairs of the H
12:13 not made for the H of the LORD basins
12:13 was brought into the H of the LORD,
12:14 who were repairing the H of the LORD with
12:16 not brought into the H of the LORD; it
12:18 the treasuries of the H of the LORD and
12:18 and of the king's H, and sent these to
12:20 slew Joash in the H of Millo, on the
13:6 the sins of the H of Jeroboam, which he
14:14 were found in the H of the LORD and
14:14 treasuries of the king's H, also hostages, and he
15:5 his death, and he dwelt in a separate H
15:25 citadel of the king's H; he slew him, and
15:35 upper gate of the H of the LORD.
16:8 was found in the H of the LORD and
16:8 treasures of the king's H, and sent a present
16:14 the front of the H, from the place between
16:14 his altar and the H of the LORD, and
16:18 he removed from the H of the LORD, because
17:21 torn Israel from the H of David they made
18:15 was found in the H of the LORD, and
18:15 LORD, and in the treasuries of the king's H
19:1 and went into the H of the LORD.
19:14 went up to the H of the LORD, and
19:30 surviving remnant of the H of Judah shall again
19:37 was worshiping in the H of Nisroch his god,
20:1 the LORD, 'Set your H in order; for you
20:5 go up to the H of the LORD.
20:8 go up to the H of the LORD on
20:13 them all his treasure H, the silver, the gold,
20:13 was nothing in his H or in all his
20:15 He said, "What have they seen in your H
20:15 that is in my H; there is nothing in
20:17 that is in your H, and that which your
21:4 built altars in the H of the LORD, of
21:5 two courts of the H of the LORD.
21:7 he set in the H of which the LORD
21:7 his son, "In this H, and in Jerusalem, which
21:13 the plummet of the H of Ahab; and I
21:18 the garden of his H, in the garden of
21:23 against him, and killed the king in his H
22:3 the secretary, to the H of the LORD, saying,
22:4 been brought into the H of the LORD, which
22:5 the oversight of the H of the LORD; and
22:5 who are at the H of the LORD, repairing
22:5 the LORD, repairing the H,
22:6 buying timber and quarried stone to repair the H
22:8 the law in the H of the LORD." And
22:9 was found in the H, and have delivered it
22:9 the oversight of the H of the LORD."
23:2 went up to the H of the LORD, and
23:2 been found in the H of the LORD.
23:6 the Asherah from the H of the LORD, outside
23:7 which were in the H of the LORD, where
23:11 the entrance to the H of the LORD, by
23:12 two courts of the H of the LORD, he
23:24 priest found in the H of the LORD.
23:27 chosen, Jerusalem, and the H of which I said,
24:13 the treasures of the H of the LORD, and
24:13 treasures of the king's H, and cut in pieces
25:9 And he burned the H of the LORD, and
25:9 LORD, and the king's H and all the houses
25:9 of Jerusalem; every great H he burned down.
25:13 that were in the H of the LORD, and
25:13 that were in the H of the LORD, the
25:16 had made for the H of the LORD, the
1Chr 2:55 the father of the H of Rechab.
4:21 the families of the H of linen workers at
6:10 as priest in the H that Solomon built in
6:31 of song in the H of the LORD, after
6:32 Solomon had built the H of the LORD in
6:48 the tabernacle of the H of God.
7:23 his name Beriah, because evil had befallen his H
9:11 chief officer of the H of God;
9:13 the service of the H of God.
9:19 kinsmen of his fathers' H, the Korahites, were in
9:23 the gates of the H of the LORD, that
9:23 LORD, that is, the H of the tent, as
9:26 the treasures of the H of God.
9:27 lodged round about the H of God; for upon
10:6 sons and all his H died together.
12:27 prince Jehoiada, of the H of Aaron, and with
12:28 and twenty-two commanders from his own father's H
12:29 their allegiance to the H of Saul.
13:7 new cart, from the H of Abinadab, and Uzzah
13:13 it aside to the H of Obed-edom the Gittite.
13:14 of Obed-edom in his H three months; and the
14:1 carpenters to build a H for him.
15:25 the LORD from the H of Obed-edom with rejoicing.
16:43 departed each to his H, and David went home
17:1 David dwelt in his H, David said to Nathan
17:1 I dwell in a H of cedar, but the
17:4 not build me a H to dwell in.
17:5 not dwelt in a H since the day I
17:6 not built me a H of cedar?'"
17:10 you that the LORD will build you a H
17:12 He shall build a H for me, and I
17:14 confirm him in my H and in my kingdom
17:16 and what is my H, that thou hast brought
17:17 spoken of thy servant's H for a great while
17:23 servant and concerning his H be established for ever,
17:24 Israel's God,' and the H of thy servant David
17:25 thou wilt build a H for him; therefore thy
17:27 thee to bless the H of thy servant, that
21:17 and against my father's H; but let not the
22:1 "Here shall be the H of the LORD God
22:2 stones for building the H of God.
22:5 and inexperienced, and the H that is to be
22:6 him to build a H for the LORD, the
22:7 heart to build a H to the name of
22:8 shall not build a H to my name, because
22:10 He shall build a H for my name.
22:11 succeed in building the H of the LORD your
22:14 have provided for the H of the LORD a
22:19 be brought into a H built for the name
23:4 the work in the H of the LORD, six
23:11 they became a father's H in one reckoning.
23:24 the service of the H of the LORD.
23:28 the service of the H of the LORD, having
23:28 the service of the H of God;
23:32 the service of the H of the LORD."
24:6 the Levites; one father's H being chosen for Eleazar
24:19 to come into the H of the LORD according
24:31 head of each father's H and his younger brother
25:6 the music in the H of the LORD with
25:6 the service of the H of God.
26:12 did, ministering in the H of the LORD;
26:20 the treasuries of the H of God and the
26:22 the treasuries of the H of the LORD.
26:27 the maintenance of the H of the LORD.
28:2 heart to build a H of rest for the
28:3 may not build a H for my name, for
28:4 from all my father's H to be king over
28:4 leader, and in the H of Judah my father's
28:4 of Judah my father's H, and among my father's
28:6 who shall build my H and my courts, for
28:10 you to build a H for the sanctuary; be
28:12 the courts of the H of the LORD, all
28:12 the treasuries of the H of God, and the
28:13 the service in the H of the LORD; for
28:13 the service in the H of the LORD,
28:20 the service of the H of the LORD is
28:21 the service of the H of God; and with
29:2 have provided for the H of my God, so
29:3 provided for the holy H, I have a treasure
29:3 my devotion to the H of my God I
29:3 give it to the H of my God:
29:4 the walls of the H,
29:7 the service of the H of God five thousand
29:8 the treasury of the H of the LORD, in
29:16 for building thee a H for thy holy name
2Chr 2:3 to build himself a H to dwell in, so
2:4 about to build a H for the name of
2:5 The H which I am to build will be
2:6 to build him a H, since heaven, even highest
2:6 I to build a H for him, except as
2:9 in abundance, for the H I am to build

3:1 began to build the H of the LORD in
3:3 measurements for building the H of God: the length,
3:4 the nave of the H was twenty cubits long,
3:4 the width of the H; and its height was
3:6 He adorned the H with settings of precious stones.
3:7 So he lined the H with gold--its beams,
3:8 the breadth of the H, was twenty cubits, and
3:11 the wall of the H, and its other wing,
3:12 the wall of the H, and the other wing,
3:15 In front of the H he made two pillars
4:10 the sea at the southeast corner of the H
4:11 King Solomon on the H of God:
4:16 King Solomon for the H of the LORD.
4:19 that were in the H of God: the golden
5:1 Solomon did for the H of the LORD was
5:1 the treasuries of the H of God.
5:7 inner sanctuary of the H, in the most holy
5:13 the H, the house of the LORD, was filled
5:13 the house, the H of the LORD, was filled
5:14 the LORD filled the H of God.
6:2 built thee an exalted H, a place for thee
6:5 which to build a H, that my name might
6:7 father to build a H for the name of
6:8 heart to build a H for my name, you
6:9 shall not build the H, but your son who
6:9 you shall build the H for my name.'
6:10 I have built the H for the name of
6:18 how much less this H which I have built!
6:20 and night toward this H, the place where thou
6:22 thy altar in this H,
6:24 to thee in this H,
6:29 his hands toward this H;
6:32 and prays toward this H,
6:33 may know that this H which I have built
6:34 hast chosen and the H which I have built
6:38 hast chosen, and the H which I have built
7:2 could not enter the H of the LORD, because
7:2 the glory of the LORD filled the LORD's H
7:5 the people dedicated the H of God.
7:7 that was before the H of the LORD; for
7:11 Thus Solomon finished the H of the LORD and
7:11 LORD and the king's H; all that Solomon had
7:11 to do in the H of the LORD and
7:11 and in his own H he successfully accomplished.
7:12 for myself as a H of sacrifice.
7:16 chosen and consecrated this H that my name may
7:20 given you; and this H, which I have consecrated
7:21 And at this H, which is exalted, every one
7:21 done thus to this land and to this H
8:1 Solomon had built the H of the LORD and
8:1 LORD and his own H,
8:11 of David to the H which he had built
8:11 not live in the H of David king of
8:16 the foundation of the H of the LORD was
8:16 So the H of the LORD was completed.
9:3 wisdom of Solomon, the H that he had built,
9:4 he offered at the H of the LORD, there
9:11 wood steps for the H of the LORD and
9:11 and for the king's H, lyres also and harps
9:16 put them in the H of the Forest of
9:20 the vessels of the H of the Forest of
10:16 now to your own H, David." So all Israel
10:19 in rebellion against the H of David to this
11:1 Jerusalem, he assembled the H of Judah, and
12:9 the treasures of the H of the LORD and
12:9 treasures of the king's H; he took away everything.
12:10 guard, who kept the door of the king's H
12:11 king went into the H of the LORD, the
15:8 the vestibule of the H of the LORD.
15:18 he brought into the H of God the votive
16:2 the treasures of the H of the LORD and
16:2 LORD and the king's H, and sent them to
19:1 in safety to his H in Jerusalem.
19:11 the governor of the H of Judah, in all
20:5 and Jerusalem, in the H of the LORD, before
20:9 will stand before this H, and before thee, for
20:9 name is in this H, and cry to thee
20:28 and trumpets, to the H of the LORD.
21:6 of Israel, as the H of Ahab had done;
21:7 would not destroy the H of David, because of
21:13 into unfaithfulness, as the H of Ahab led Israel
21:13 brothers, of your father's H, who were better than
21:17 belonged to the king's H, and also his sons
22:3 the ways of the H of Ahab, for his
22:4 the LORD, as the H of Ahab had done;
22:7 anointed to destroy the H of Ahab.
22:8 executing judgment upon the H of Ahab, he met
22:9 And the H of Ahaziah had no one able
22:10 the royal family of H of Judah.
22:12 years, hid in the H of God, while Athaliah
23:3 the king in the H of God.
23:5 be at the king's H and one third at
23:5 the courts of the H of the LORD.
23:6 no one enter the H of the LORD except
23:7 and whoever enters the H shall be slain.
23:9 which were in the H of God;
23:10 south side of the H to the north side
23:10 north side of the H, around the altar and
23:10 of the house, around the altar and the H
23:12 she went into the H of the LORD to
23:14 slay her in the H of the LORD."
23:15 gate of the king's H, and they slew her
23:17 people went to the H of Baal, and tore
23:18 posted watchmen for the H of the LORD under
23:18 in charge of the H of the LORD, to
23:19 the gates of the H of the LORD so
23:20 king down from the H of the LORD, marching
23:20 marching through the upper gate to the king's H
24:4 decided to restore the H of the LORD.
24:5 money to repair the H of your God from
24:7 had broken into the H of God; and had
24:7 dedicated things of the H of the LORD for
24:8 the gate of the H of the LORD.
24:12 the work of the H of the LORD, and
24:12 carpenters to restore the H of the LORD, and
24:12 bronze to repair the H of the LORD.
24:13 and they restored the H of God to its
24:14 made utensils for the H of the LORD, both
24:14 burnt offerings in the H of the LORD continually
24:16 good in Israel, and toward God and his H
24:18 And they forsook the H of the LORD, the
24:21 the court of the H of the LORD.
24:27 the rebuilding of the H of God are written
25:24 were found in the H of God, and Obed-edom
25:24 treasuries of the king's H, and hostages, and he
26:19 the priests in the H of the LORD, by
26:21 dwelt in a separate H, for he was excluded
26:21 was excluded from the H of the LORD.
27:3 upper gate of the H of the LORD, and
28:21 Ahaz took from the H of the LORD and
28:21 the LORD and the H of the king and
28:24 the vessels of the H of God and cut
28:24 the vessels of the H of God, and he
28:24 the doors of the H of the LORD; and
29:3 the doors of the H of the LORD, and
29:5 yourselves, and sanctify the H of the LORD, the
29:15 LORD, to cleanse the H of the LORD.
29:16 inner part of the H of the LORD to
29:16 the court of the H of the LORD; and
29:17 days they sanctified the H of the LORD, and
29:18 have cleansed all the H of the LORD, the
29:20 went up to the H of the LORD.
29:25 the Levites in the H of the LORD with
29:31 thank offerings to the H of the LORD." And
29:35 the service of the H of the LORD was
30:1 should come to the H of the LORD at
30:15 burnt offerings into the H of the LORD.
31:10 who was of the H of Zadok, answered him,
31:10 the contributions into the H of the LORD we
31:11 prepare chambers in the H of the LORD; and
31:13 chief officer of the H of God.
31:16 all who entered the H of the LORD as
31:21 the service of the H of God and in
32:21 he came into the H of his god, some
33:4 built altars in the H of the LORD, of
33:5 two courts of the H of the LORD.
33:7 he set in the H of God, of which
33:7 his son, "In this H, and in Jerusalem, which
33:15 the idol from the H of the LORD, and
33:15 the mountain of the H of the LORD and
33:20 buried him in his H; and Amon his son
33:24 conspired against him and killed him in his H
34:8 the land and the H, he sent Shaphan the
34:8 recorder, to repair the H of the LORD his
34:9 been brought into the H of God, which the
34:10 the oversight of the H of the LORD; and
34:10 were working in the H of the LORD gave
34:10 LORD gave it for repairing and restoring the H
34:14 been brought into the H of the LORD, Hilkiah
34:15 the law in the H of the LORD"; and
34:17 was found in the H of the LORD and
34:30 went up to the H of the LORD, with

	34:30	been found in the H of the LORD.
	35:2	the service of the H of the LORD.
	35:3	holy ark in the H which Solomon the son
	35:5	part of a father's H of the Levites.
	35:8	chief officers of the H of God, gave to
	35:21	day, but against the H with which I am
	36:7	the vessels of the H of the LORD to
	36:10	precious vessels of the H of the LORD, and
	36:14	and they polluted the H of the LORD which
	36:17	the sword in the H of their sanctuary, and
	36:18	the vessels of the H of God, great and
	36:18	the treasures of the H of the LORD, and
	36:19	And they burned the H of God, and broke
	36:23	to build him a H at Jerusalem, which is
Ezra	1:2	to build him a H at Jerusalem, which is
	1:3	Judah, and rebuild the H of the LORD, the
	1:4	freewill offerings for the H of God which is
	1:5	up to rebuild the H of the LORD which
	1:7	the vessels of the H of the LORD which
	1:7	and placed in the H of his gods.
	2:36	of Jedaiah, of the H of Jeshua, nine hundred
	2:68	they came to the H of the LORD which
	2:68	freewill offerings for the H of God, to erect
	3:8	their coming to the H of God at Jerusalem,
	3:8	the work of the H of the LORD.
	3:9	the workmen in the H of God, along with
	3:11	the foundation of the H of the LORD was
	3:12	had seen the first H, wept with a loud
	3:12	the foundation of this H being laid, though many
	4:3	us in building a H to our God; but
	4:24	the work on the H of God which is
	5:2	began to rebuild the H of God which is
	5:3	decree to build this H and to finish this
	5:8	of Judah, to the H of the great God.
	5:9	decree to build this H and to finish this
	5:11	we are rebuilding the H that was built many
	5:12	Chaldean, who destroyed this H and carried away
	5:13	a decree that this H of God should be
	5:14	silver vessels of the H of God, which
	5:15	Jerusalem, and let the H of God be rebuilt
	5:16	the foundations of the H of God which is
	5:17	the rebuilding of this H of God in Jerusalem.
	6:1	in Babylonia, in the H of the archives where
	6:3	a decree: Concerning the H of God at Jerusalem,
	6:3	at Jerusalem, let the H be rebuilt, the place
	6:5	vessels of the H of God, which Nebuchadnezzar
	6:5	put them in the H of God."
	6:7	the work on this H of God alone; let
	6:7	the Jews rebuild this H of God on its
	6:8	the rebuilding of this H of God; the cost
	6:11	pulled out of his H, and he shall be
	6:11	upon it, and his H shall be made a
	6:12	or to destroy this H of God which is
	6:15	of Persia; and this H was finished on the
	6:16	the dedication of this H of God with joy.
	6:17	the dedication of this H of God one hundred
	6:22	the work of the H of God, the God
	7:16	vowed willingly for the H of their God which
	7:17	the altar of the H of your God which
	7:19	the service of the H of your God, you
	7:20	is required for the H of your God, which
	7:23	in full for the H of the God of
	7:24	other servants of this H of God.
	7:27	king, to beautify the H of the LORD which
	8:17	us ministers for the H of our God.
	8:25	the offering for the H of our God which
	8:29	the chambers of the H of the LORD."
	8:30	to Jerusalem, to the H of our God.
	8:33	fourth day, within the H of our God, the
	8:36	the people and the H of God.
	9:9	to set up the H of our God, to
	10:1	himself down before the H of God, a very
	10:6	withdrew from before the H of God, and went
	10:9	open square before the H of God, trembling because
Neh	1:6	I and my father's H have sinned.
	2:8	city, and for the H which I shall occupy."
	3:10	Harumaph repaired opposite his H; and next to him
	3:16	pool, and to the H of the mighty men.
	3:20	the door of the H of Eliashib the high
	3:21	the door of the H of Eliashib to the
	3:21	the end of the H of Eliashib.
	3:23	Benjamin and Hasshub repaired opposite their H
	3:23	son of Ananiah repaired beside his own H
	3:24	another section, from the H of Azariah to the
	3:25	projecting from the upper H of the king at
	3:28	the priests repaired, each one opposite his own H

	3:29	the son of Immer repaired opposite his own H
	3:31	as far as the H of the temple servants
	4:16	stood behind all the H of Judah,
	5:13	every man from his H and from his labor
	6:10	I went into the H of Shemaiah the son
	6:10	meet together in the H of God, within the
	7:3	to his station and each opposite his own H
	7:39	of Jedaiah, namely the H of Jeshua, nine hundred
	8:16	the courts of the H of God, and in
	10:32	the service of the H of our God:
	10:33	the work of the H of our God.
	10:34	bring it into the H of our God, according
	10:35	by year, to the H of the LORD;
	10:36	to bring to the H of our God, to
	10:36	who minister in the H of our God, the
	10:37	the chambers of the H of our God; and
	10:38	the tithes to the H of our God, to
	10:39	will not neglect the H of our God.
	11:11	Ahitub, ruler of the H of God,
	11:12	the work of the H, eight hundred and twenty-two;
	11:16	outside work of the H of God;
	11:22	the work of the H of God.
	12:37	the wall, above the H of David, to the
	12:40	thanks stood in the H of God, and I
	13:4	the chambers of the H of our God, and
	13:7	the courts of the H of God.
	13:9	the vessels of the H of God, with the
	13:11	said, "Why is the H of God forsaken?" And
	13:14	have done for the H of my God and
Tob	1:4	my forefather deserted the H of Jerusalem.
	1:5	and so did the H of Naphtali my forefather.
	3:17	returned and entered his H and Sarah the daughter
	7:1	and arrived at the H of Raguel, Sarah met
	7:1	her greeting, and she brought them into the H
	8:11	Raguel went into his H
	11:3	run ahead of your wife and prepare the H
	14:4	The H of God in it will be burned
	14:5	they will rebuild the H of God, though it
	14:5	And the H of God will be rebuilt there
Jud	4:15	favor upon the whole H of Israel.
	6:17	so boastfully against the H of Israel.
	6:21	assembly to his own H and gave a banquet
	8:5	the roof of her H, and girded sackcloth about
	8:6	of rejoicing of the H of Israel.
	9:1	being offered in the H of God in Jerusalem,
	9:13	and against thy consecrated H, and against the top
	9:13	Zion, and against the H possessed by thy children.
	10:2	went down into the H where she lived on
	11:7	by your power under Nebuchadnezzar and all his H
	11:23	shall live in the H of King Nebuchadnezzar and
	12:13	who serve in the H of Nebuchadnezzar."
	13:14	his mercy from the H of Israel, but has
	14:5	man who despised the H of Israel and sent
	14:6	summoned Achior from the H of Uzziah.
	14:10	circumcised, and joined the H of Israel, remaining so
	14:18	disgrace upon the H of King Nebuchadnezzar!
	16:23	old in her husband's H, until she was one
	16:24	husband Manasseh, and the H of Israel mourned for
Esth	1:22	lord in his own H and speak according to
	4:14	you and your father's H will perish.
	6:12	Haman hurried to his H, mourning and with his
	7:8	the queen in my presence, in my own H
	7:9	is standing in Haman's H, fifty cubits high."
	8:1	to Queen Esther the H of Haman, the enemy
	8:2	set Mordecai over the H of Haman.
	8:7	have given Esther the H of Haman, and they
	9:4	great in the king's H, and his fame spread
	14:9	the glory of thy H,
Job	1:4	a feast in the H of each on his
	1:10	about him and his H and all that he
	1:13	in their eldest brother's H;
	1:18	in their eldest brother's H;
	1:19	four corners of the H, and it fell upon
	7:10	no more to his H, nor does his place
	8:15	He leans against his H, but it does not
	17:13	for Sheol as my H, if I spread my
	19:15	the guests in my H have forgotten me; my
	20:19	he has seized a H which he did not
	20:28	The possessions of his H will be carried away,
	21:28	say, 'Where is the H of the prince?
	27:18	The H which he builds is like a spider's
	30:23	death, and to the H appointed for all living.
	42:11	with him in his H; and they showed him
Ps	5:7	love will enter thy H, I will worship toward
	23:6	shall dwell in the H of the LORD for
	26:8	the habitation of thy H, and the place where

27:4 may dwell in the H of the LORD all
36:8 the abundance of thy H, and thou givest them
42:4 in procession to the H of God, with glad
45:10 people and your father's H;
49:16 the glory of his H increases.
50:9 no bull from your H, nor he-goat from your
52:8 olive tree in the H of God.
55:14 converse together; within God's H we walked in
65:4 the goodness of thy H, thy holy temple!
66:13 will come into thy H with burnt offerings; I
69:9 For zeal for thy H has consumed me, and
84:4 who dwell in thy H, ever singing thy praise!
84:10 a doorkeeper in the H of my God than
92:13 are planted in the H of the LORD, they
93:5 sure; holiness befits thy H, O LORD, for evermore.
98:3 and faithfulness to the H of Israel.
101:2 of heart within my H;
101:7 shall dwell in my H; no man who utters
105:21 him lord of his H, and ruler of all
112:3 riches are in his H; and his righteousness endures
114:1 forth from Egypt, the H of Jacob from a
115:10 O H of Aaron, put your trust in the
115:12 he will bless the H of Israel; he will
115:12 he will bless the H of Aaron;
116:19 the courts of the H of the LORD, in
118:3 Let the H of Aaron say, "His steadfast love
118:26 bless you from the H of the LORD.
119:54 my songs in the H of my pilgrimage.
122:1 us go to the H of the LORD!"
122:5 the thrones of the H of David.
122:9 the sake of the H of the LORD our
127:1 the LORD builds the H, those who build it
128:3 fruitful vine within your H; your children will be
132:3 will not enter my H or get into my
134:1 by night in the H of the LORD!
135:2 that stand in the H of the LORD, in
135:2 the courts of the H of our God!
135:19 O H of Israel, bless the LORD!
135:19 O H of Aaron, bless the LORD!
135:20 O H of Levi, bless the LORD!
Prov 2:18 her God; for her H sinks down to death,
3:33 curse is on the H of the wicked, but
5:8 the door of her H;
5:10 labors go to the H of an alien;
6:31 he will give all the goods of his H
7:6 the window of my H I have looked out
7:8 the road to her H
7:27 Her H is the way to Sheol, going down
9:1 Wisdom has built her H, she has set up
9:14 the door of her H, she takes a seat
12:7 no more, but the H of the righteous will
14:1 Wisdom builds her H, but folly with her own
14:11 The H of the wicked will be destroyed, but
15:6 In the H of the righteous there is much
15:25 LORD tears down the H of the proud, but
17:1 with quiet than a H full of feasting with
17:13 for good, evil will not depart from his H
19:14 H and wealth are inherited from fathers, but a
21:9 housetop than in a H shared with a contentious
21:12 The righteous observes the H of the wicked; the
24:3 By wisdom a H is built, and by understanding
24:27 in the field; and after that build your H
25:17 seldom in your neighbor's H, lest he become weary
25:24 housetop than in a H shared with a contentious
27:10 go to your brother's H in the day of
Eccl 2:7 were born in my H; I had also great
5:1 you go to the H of God; to draw
7:2 to go to the H of mourning than to
7:2 to go to the H of feasting; for this
7:4 wise is in the H of mourning; but the
7:4 fools is in the H of mirth.
10:18 and through indolence the H leaks.
12:3 the keepers of the H tremble, and the strong
Song 1:17 the beams of our H are cedar, our rafters
2:4 me to the banqueting H, and his banner over
3:4 him into my mother's H, and into the chamber
8:2 bring you into the H of my mother, and
8:7 the wealth of his H, it would be utterly
Wis 8:16 When I enter my H, I shall find rest
Sir 1:15 she fills their whole H with desirable goods, and
14:24 who encamps near her H will also fasten his
21:4 waste riches; thus the H of the proud will
21:8 man who builds his H with other people's money
21:18 Like a H that has vanished, so is wisdom
21:22 fool rushes into a H, but a man of
21:23 boor peers into the H from the door, but
23:11 will not leave his H; if he offends, his
23:11 be justified, for his H will be filled with
27:3 of the Lord, his H will be quickly overthrown.
29:21 and clothing and a H to cover one's nakedness.
29:22 his roof than sumptuous food in another man's H
29:24 life to go from H to house, and where
29:24 go from house to H, and where you are
29:27 come to stay with me; I need my H
42:10 pregnant in her father's H; or having a husband,
47:13 he might build a H for his name and
48:15 with rulers from the H of David.
49:12 days they built the H and raised a temple
50:1 his life repaired the H, and in his time
Is 2:2 the mountain of the H of the LORD shall
2:3 the LORD, to the H of the God of
2:5 O H of Jacob, come, let us walk in
2:6 rejected thy people, the H of Jacob, because they
3:6 his brother in the H of his father, saying:
3:7 a healer; in my H there is neither bread
5:7 of hosts is the H of Israel, and the
5:8 to those who join H to house, who add
5:8 who join house to H, who add field to
6:4 who called, and the H was filled with smoke.
7:2 When the H of David was told, "Syria is
7:13 said, "Hear then, O H of David!
7:17 and upon your father's H such days as have
8:17 his face from the H of Jacob, and I
10:20 the survivors of the H of Jacob will no
14:1 will cleave to the H of Jacob.
14:2 their place, and the H of Israel will possess
22:8 the weapons of the H of the Forest,
22:18 your splendid chariots, you shame of your master's H
22:21 Jerusalem and to the H of Judah.
22:22 the key of the H of David; he shall
22:23 become a throne of honor to his father's H
22:24 weight of his father's H, the offspring and issue,
23:1 is laid waste, without H or haven!
24:10 is broken down, every H is shut up so
29:22 Abraham, concerning the H of Jacob: "Jacob shall
31:2 will arise against the H of the evildoers, and
37:1 and went into the H of the LORD.
37:14 went up to the H of the LORD, and
37:31 surviving remnant of the H of Judah shall again
37:38 was worshiping in the H of Nisroch his god,
38:1 the LORD: Set your H in order; for you
38:20 our life, at the H of the LORD.
38:22 go up to the H of the LORD?"
39:2 showed them his treasure H, the silver, the gold,
39:2 was nothing in his H or in all his
39:4 He said, "What have they seen in your H
39:4 that is in my H; there is nothing in
39:6 that is in your H, and that which your
44:13 beauty of a man, to dwell in a H
46:3 "Hearken to me, O H of Jacob, all the
46:3 the remnant of the H of Israel, who have
48:1 Hear this, O H of Jacob, who are called
56:5 will give in my H and within my walls
56:7 them joyful in my H of prayer; their burnt
56:7 my altar; for my H shall be called a
56:7 shall be called a H of prayer for all
58:1 their transgression, to the H of Jacob their sins.
58:7 homeless poor into your H; when you see the
60:7 my altar, and I will glorify my glorious H
63:7 great goodness to the H of Israel which he
64:11 Our holy and beautiful H, where our fathers praised
66:1 footstool; what is the H which you would build
66:20 clean vessel to the H of the LORD.
Jer 2:4 of the LORD, O H of Jacob, and all
2:4 the families of the H of Israel.
2:26 when caught, so the H of Israel shall be
3:18 In those days the H of Judah shall join
3:18 Judah shall join the H of Israel, and together
3:20 faithless to me, O H of Israel, says the
5:11 For the H of Israel and the house of
5:11 of Israel and the H of Judah have been
5:15 nation from afar, O H of Israel, says the
5:20 Declare this in the H of Jacob, proclaim it
7:2 gate of the LORD's H, and proclaim there this
7:10 before me in this H, which is called by
7:11 Has this H, which is called by my name,
7:14 will do to the H which is called by
7:30 their abominations in the H which is called by
9:26 uncircumcised, and all the H of Israel is
10:1 speaks to you, O H of Israel.
11:10 to serve them; the H of Israel and the
11:10 of Israel and the H of Judah have broken

11:15 my beloved in my H, when she has done
11:17 the evil which the H of Israel and the
11:17 of Israel and the H of Judah have done,
12:6 your brothers and the H of your father, even
12:7 "I have forsaken my H, I have abandoned my
12:14 will pluck up the H of Judah from among
13:11 I made the whole H of Israel and the
13:11 Israel and the whole H of Judah cling to
16:5 Do not enter the H of mourning, or go
16:8 not go into the H of feasting to sit
17:26 thank offerings to the H of the LORD.
18:2 down to the potter's H, and there I will
18:3 down to the potter's H, and there he was
18:6 came to me: "O H of Israel, can I
18:6 in my hand, O H of Israel.
19:14 court of the LORD's H, and said to all
20:1 chief officer in the H of the LORD, heard
20:2 Benjamin Gate of the H of the LORD.
20:6 who dwell in your H, shall go into captivity;
21:11 fire.' "And to the H of the king of
21:12 of the LORD, O H of David!
22:1 "Go down to the H of the king of
22:4 the gates of this H kings who sit on
22:5 the LORD, that this H shall become a desolation.
22:6 the LORD concerning the H of the king of
22:13 him who builds his H by unrighteousness, and his
22:14 build myself a great H with spacious upper rooms,'
23:8 the descendants of the H of Israel out of
23:11 ungodly; even in my H I have found their
26:2 court of the LORD's H, and speak to all
26:2 to worship in the H of the LORD all
26:6 I will make this H like Shiloh, and I
26:7 these words in the H of the LORD.
26:9 the LORD, saying, 'This H shall be like Shiloh,
26:9 about Jeremiah in the H of the LORD.
26:10 up from the king's H to the house of
26:10 king's house to the H of the LORD and
26:10 New Gate of the H of the LORD.
26:12 to prophesy against this H and this city all
26:18 the mountain of the H a wooded height.'
27:16 vessels of the LORD's H will now shortly be
27:18 are left in the H of the LORD, in
27:18 the LORD, in the H of the king of
27:21 are left in the H of the LORD, in
27:21 the LORD, in the H of the king of
28:1 to me in the H of the LORD, in
28:3 vessels of the LORD's H, which Nebuchadnezzar
28:5 were standing in the H of the LORD;
28:6 the vessels of the H of the LORD, and
29:26 have charge in the H of the LORD over
31:27 I will sow the H of Israel and the
31:27 of Israel and the H of Judah with the
31:31 new covenant with the H of Israel and the
31:31 of Israel and the H of Judah,
31:33 will make with the H of Israel after those
32:34 their abominations in the H which is called by
33:11 thank offerings to the H of the LORD: 'Give
33:14 I made to the H of Israel and the
33:14 of Israel and the H of Judah.
33:17 the throne of the H of Israel,
34:13 Egypt, out of the H of bondage, saying,
34:15 before me in the H which is called by
35:2 Judah: "Go to the H of the Rechabites, and
35:2 bring them to the H of the LORD, into
35:3 sons, and the whole H of the Rechabites.
35:4 brought them to the H of the LORD into
35:7 shall not build a H; you shall not sow
35:18 But to the H of the Rechabites Jeremiah said,
36:3 may be that the H of Judah will hear
36:5 from going to the H of the LORD;
36:6 people in the LORD's H you shall read the
36:8 the words of the LORD in the LORD's H
36:10 the scroll, in the H of the LORD, in
36:10 entry of the New Gate of the LORD's H
36:12 down to the king's H, into the secretary's chamber;
36:22 sitting in the winter H and there was a
37:15 imprisoned him in the H of Jonathan the secretary,
37:17 him secretly in his H, and said, "Is there
37:20 me back to the H of Jonathan the secretary,
38:7 was in the king's H, heard that they had
38:8 went from the king's H and said to the
38:11 and went to the H of the king, to
38:17 and you and your H shall live.
38:22 women left in the H of the king of
38:26 me back to the H of Jonathan to die
39:8 Chaldeans burned the king's H and the house of
39:8 king's house and the H of the people, and
48:13 of Chemosh, as the H of Israel was ashamed
48:45 a flame from the H of Sihon; it has
51:51 places of the LORD's H
52:13 And he burned the H of the LORD, and
52:13 LORD, and the king's H and all the houses
52:13 of Jerusalem; every great H he burned down.
52:17 that were in the H of the LORD, and
52:17 that were in the H of the LORD, the
52:20 had made for the H of the LORD, the
Lam 1:20 sword bereaves; in the H it is like death.
2:7 was raised in the H of the LORD as
Bar 1:8 the vessels of the H of the Lord, which
1:14 your confession in the H of the Lord on
2:26 And the H which is called by thy name
2:26 the wickedness of the H of Israel and the
2:26 of Israel and the H of Judah.
3:24 how great is the H of God!
6:59 the door of a H that protects its contents,
Ezek 2:5 they are a rebellious H they will know that
2:6 at their looks, for they are a rebellious H
2:7 refuse to hear; for they are a rebellious H
2:8 rebellious like that rebellious H; open your mouth,
3:1 go, speak to the H of Israel."
3:4 get you to the H of Israel, and speak
3:5 language, but to the H of Israel--
3:7 But the H of Israel will not listen to
3:7 me; because all the H of Israel are of
3:9 at their looks, for they are a rebellious H
3:17 a watchman for the H of Israel; whenever you
3:24 said to me, "Go, shut yourself within your H
3:26 to reprove them; for they are a rebellious H
3:27 let him refuse; for they are a rebellious H
4:3 a sign for the H of Israel.
4:4 the punishment of the H of Israel upon you;
4:5 the punishment of the H of Israel.
4:6 the punishment of the H of Judah; forty days
5:4 forth into all the H of Israel.
6:11 evil abominations of the H of Israel; for they
8:1 I sat in my H, with the elders of
8:6 abominations that the H of Israel are committing
8:10 the idols of the H of Israel.
8:11 the elders of the H of Israel, with Ja-azaniah
8:12 the elders of the H of Israel are doing
8:14 north gate of the H of the LORD; and
8:16 inner court of the H of the LORD; and
8:17 a thing for the H of Judah to commit
9:3 the threshold of the H; and he called to
9:6 began with the elders who were before the H
9:7 to them, "Defile the H, and fill the courts
9:9 "The guilt of the H of Israel and Judah
10:3 south side of the H, when the man went
10:4 the threshold of the H; and the house was
10:4 the house; and the H was filled with the
10:18 the threshold of the H, and stood over the
10:19 east gate of the H of the LORD; and
11:1 east gate of the H of the LORD, which
11:5 So you think, O H of Israel; for I
11:15 fellow exiles, the whole H of Israel, all of
12:2 midst of a rebellious H, who have eyes to
12:3 but hear not; for they are a rebellious H
12:3 they will understand, though they are a rebellious H
12:6 a sign for the H of Israel."
12:9 man, has not the H of Israel, the rebellious
12:9 of Israel, the rebellious H, said to you, 'What
12:10 Jerusalem and all the H of Israel who are
12:24 flattering divination within the H of Israel.
12:25 your days, O rebellious H, I will speak the
12:27 behold, they of the H of Israel say, 'The
13:5 a wall for the H of Israel, that it
13:9 the register of the H of Israel, nor shall
14:4 Any man of the H of Israel who takes
14:5 the hearts of the H of Israel, who are
14:6 "Therefore say to the H of Israel, Thus says
14:7 any one of the H of Israel, or of
14:11 alike-- that the H of Israel may go
17:2 an allegory to the H of Israel;
17:12 now to the rebellious H, Do you not know
18:6 the idols of the H of Israel, does not
18:15 the idols of the H of Israel, does not
18:25 just.' Hear now, O H of Israel: Is my
18:29 Yet the H of Israel says, 'The way of
18:29 is not just.' O H of Israel, are my
18:30 will judge you, O H of Israel, every one
18:31 will you die, O H of Israel?
20:5 the seed of the H of Jacob, making myself

H

20:13 But the H of Israel rebelled against me in
20:27 man, speak to the H of Israel and say
20:30 Wherefore say to the H of Israel, Thus says
20:31 of by you, O H of Israel?
20:39 "As for you, O H of Israel, thus says
20:40 GOD, there all the H of Israel, all of
20:44 your corrupt doings, O H of Israel, says the
22:18 "Son of man, the H of Israel has become
23:39 lo, this is what they did in my H
24:3 allegory to the rebellious H and say to them,
24:21 me: 'Say to the H of Israel, Thus says
25:3 desolate, and over the H of Judah when it
25:8 Moab said, Behold, the H of Judah is like
25:12 acted revengefully against the H of Judah and has
28:24 "And for the H of Israel there shall be
28:25 When I gather the H of Israel from the
29:6 of reed to the H of Israel;
29:16 the reliance of the H of Israel, recalling their
29:21 spring forth to the H of Israel, and I
33:7 a watchman for the H of Israel; whenever you
33:10 man, say to the H of Israel, Thus have
33:11 will you die, O H of Israel?
33:20 is not just.' O H of Israel, I will
34:30 and that they, the H of Israel, are my
35:15 the inheritance of the H of Israel, because it
36:10 upon you, the whole H of Israel, all of
36:17 of man, when the H of Israel dwelt in
36:21 holy name, which the H of Israel caused to
36:22 "Therefore say to the H of Israel, Thus says
36:22 for your sake, O H of Israel, that I
36:32 for your ways, O H of Israel.
36:37 I will let the H of Israel ask me
37:11 bones are the whole H of Israel.
37:16 Ephraim) and all the H of Israel associated with
39:12 For seven months the H of Israel will be
39:22 The H of Israel shall know that I am
39:23 shall know that the H of Israel went into
39:25 mercy upon the whole H of Israel; and I
39:29 my Spirit upon the H of Israel, says the
40:4 you see to the H of Israel."
43:7 And the H of Israel shall no more defile
43:10 man, describe to the H of Israel the temple
44:6 say to the rebellious H, to the house of
44:6 rebellious house, to the H of Israel, Thus says
44:6 the Lord GOD: O H of Israel, let there
44:12 of iniquity to the H of Israel, therefore I
44:22 the stock of the H of Israel, or a
44:30 meal, that a blessing may rest on your H
45:6 belong to the whole H of Israel.
45:8 they shall let the H of Israel have the
45:17 appointed feasts of the H of Israel: he shall
45:17 make atonement for the H of Israel.
Dan 1:2 the vessels of the H of God; and he
1:2 of Shinar, to the H of his god, and
2:17 Daniel went to his H and made the matter
4:4 at ease in my H and prospering in my
5:3 of the temple, the H of God in Jerusalem;
5:23 the vessels of his H have been brought in
6:10 he went to his H where he had windows
13:4 spacious garden adjoining his H; and the Jews used
13:6 were frequently at Joakim's H, and all who had
13:28 people gathered at the H of her husband Joakim,
Hos 1:4 I will punish the H of Jehu for the
1:4 the kingdom of the H of Israel.
1:6 have pity on the H of Israel, to forgive
1:7 have pity on the H of Judah, and I
5:1 Give heed, O H of Israel!
5:1 Hearken, O H of the king!
5:12 dry rot to the H of Judah.
5:14 young lion to the H of Judah.
6:10 In the H of Israel I have seen a
8:1 vulture is over the H of the LORD, because
9:4 not come to the H of the LORD.
9:8 and hatred in the H of his God.
9:15 deeds I will drive them out of my H
10:15 done to you, O H of Israel, because of
11:12 with lies, and the H of Israel with deceit;
Joel 1:9 cut off from the H of the LORD.
1:12 are withheld from the H of your God.
1:13 the land to the H of the LORD your
1:15 and gladness from the H of our God?
3:18 come forth from the H of the LORD and
Amos 1:4 a fire upon the H of Hazael, and it
2:8 pledge; and in the H of their God they
3:13 and testify against the H of Jacob," says the
3:15 will smite the winter H with the summer house;
3:15 house with the summer H; and the houses of
5:1 you in lamentation, O H of Israel:
5:3 ten left to the H of Israel."
5:4 the LORD to the H of Israel: "Seek me
5:6 like fire in the H of Joseph, and it
5:19 or went into the H and leaned with his
5:25 in the wilderness, O H of Israel?
6:1 nations, to whom the H of Israel come!
6:9 men remain in one H, they shall die.
6:10 bones out of the H, and shall say to
6:10 innermost parts of the H, "Is there still any
6:11 commands, and the great H shall be smitten into
6:11 fragments, and the little H into bits.
6:14 you a nation, O H of Israel," says the
7:9 will rise against the H of Jeroboam with the
7:10 the midst of the H of Israel; the land
7:16 not preach against the H of Isaac.'
9:8 not utterly destroy the H of Jacob," says the
9:9 command, and shake the H of Israel among all
Obad 1:17 be holy; and the H of Jacob shall possess
1:18 The H of Jacob shall be a fire, and
1:18 a fire, and the H of Joseph a flame,
1:18 a flame, and the H of Esau stubble; they
1:18 no survivor to the H of Esau; for the
Mic 1:5 the sins of the H of Israel.
1:5 the sin of the H of Judah?
2:2 a man and his H, a man and his
2:7 this be said, O H of Jacob?
3:1 and rulers of the H of Israel!
3:9 you heads of the H of Jacob and rulers
3:9 and rulers of the H of Israel, who abhor
3:12 the mountain of the H a wooded height.
4:1 the mountain of the H of the LORD shall
4:2 the LORD, to the H of the God of
6:4 redeemed you from the H of bondage; and I
6:10 of wickedness in the H of the wicked, and
6:16 the works of the H of Ahab; and you
7:6 man's enemies are the men of his own H
Nah 1:14 be perpetuated; from the H of your gods I
Hab 2:9 evil gain for his H, to set his nest
2:10 devised shame to your H by cutting off many
Zeph 1:9 who fill their master's H with violence and fraud."
2:7 the remnant of the H of Judah, on which
Hag 1:2 come to rebuild the H of the LORD."
1:4 paneled houses, while this H lies in ruins?
1:8 wood and build the H, that I may take
1:9 Because of my H that lies in ruins, while
1:9 while you busy yourselves each with his own H
1:14 and worked on the H of the LORD of
2:3 you that saw this H in its former glory?
2:7 I will fill this H with splendor, says the
2:9 latter splendor of this H shall be greater than
Zech 1:16 Jerusalem with compassion; my H shall be built in
3:7 you shall rule my H and have charge of
4:9 the foundation of this H; his hands shall also
5:4 it shall enter the H of the thief, and
5:4 the thief, and the H of him who swears
5:4 shall abide in his H and consume it, both
5:11 Shinar, to build a H for it; and when
6:10 same day to the H of Josiah, the son
7:3 the priests of the H of the LORD of
8:9 the foundation of the H of the LORD of
8:13 among the nations, O H of Judah and house
8:13 house of Judah and H of Israel, so will
8:15 Jerusalem and to the H of Judah; fear not.
8:19 shall be to the H of Judah seasons of
9:8 will encamp at my H as a guard, so
10:3 for his flock, the H of Judah, and will
10:6 "I will strengthen the H of Judah, and I
10:6 I will save the H of Joseph.
11:13 the treasury in the H of the LORD.
12:4 But upon the H of Judah I will open
12:7 the glory of the H of David and the
12:8 like David, and the H of David shall be
12:10 pour out on the H of David and the
12:12 the family of the H of David by itself,
12:12 the family of the H of Nathan by itself,
12:13 the family of the H of Levi by itself,
13:1 fountain opened for the H of David and the
13:6 I received in the H of my friends.'"
14:20 the pots in the H of the LORD shall
14:21 a trader in the H of the LORD of
Mal 3:10 be food in my H; and thereby put me
1Mac 1:28 inhabitants, and all the H of Jacob was clothed
7:35 I return safely I will burn up this H
7:37 "Thou didst choose this H to be called by

7:37 for thy people a H of prayer and supplication.
9:55 say a word or give commands concerning his H
13:3 my brothers and the H of my father have
13:48 built in it a H for himself.
14:26 his brothers and the H of his father have
16:2 my brothers and the H of my father have
2Mac 2:29 builder of a new H must be concerned with
8:33 fled into one little H; so these received the
14:36 undefiled for ever this H that has been so
15:32 out against the holy H of the Almighty;
Mt 2:11 and going into the H they saw the child
5:15 and it gives light to all in the H
7:24 man who built his H upon the rock;
7:25 and beat upon that H, but it did not
7:26 man who built his H upon the sand;
7:27 and beat against that H, and it fell; and
8:14 Jesus entered Peter's H, he saw his mother-in-law
9:10 at table in the H, behold, many tax collectors
9:23 came to the ruler's H, and saw the flute
9:28 When he entered the H, the blind men came
10:6 lost sheep of the H of Israel.
10:12 As you enter the H, salute it.
10:13 And if the H is worthy, let your peace
10:14 as you leave that H or town.
10:25 the master of the H Be-elzebul, how much more
12:4 how he entered the H of God and ate
12:25 and no city or H divided against itself will
12:29 enter a strong man's H and plunder his goods,
12:29 Then indeed he may plunder his H
12:44 will return to my H from which I came.'
13:1 went out of the H and sat beside the
13:36 he left the crowds and went into the H
13:57 in his own country and in his own H
15:24 lost sheep of the H of Israel."
21:13 "It is written, 'My H shall be called a
21:13 shall be called a H of prayer'; but you
23:37 Behold, your H is forsaken and desolate.
24:17 what is in his H;
24:43 not have let his H be broken into.
26:6 at Bethany in the H of Simon the leper,
26:18 the passover at your H with my disciples.'"
Mk 1:29 synagogue, and entered the H of Simon and Andrew,
2:15 at table in his H, many tax collectors and
2:26 how he entered the H of God, when Abiathar
3:25 And if a H is divided against itself, that
3:25 divided against itself, that H will not be able
3:27 enter a strong man's H and plunder his goods,
3:27 strong man; then indeed he may plunder his H
5:35 came from the ruler's H some who said, "Your
5:38 they came to the H of the ruler of
6:4 among his own kin, and in his own H
6:10 "Where you enter a H, stay there until you
7:16 he had entered the H, and left the people,
7:23 And he entered a H, and would not have
9:28 he had entered the H, his disciples asked him
9:33 he was in the H he asked them, "What
10:10 And in the H the disciples asked him again
10:29 one who has left H or brothers or sisters
11:17 it not written, 'My H shall be called a
11:17 shall be called a H of prayer for all
13:15 down, nor enter his H, to take anything away;
13:35 the master of the H will come, in the
14:3 at Bethany in the H of Simon the leper,
Lk 1:27 was Joseph, of the H of David; and the
1:33 will reign over the H of Jacob for ever;
1:40 and she entered the H of Zechariah and greeted
1:69 for us in the H of his servant David,
2:4 he was of the H and lineage of David,
2:49 know that I must be in my Father's H
4:38 arose and left the synagogue, and entered Simon's H
5:29 great feast in his H; and there was a
6:4 how he entered the H of God, and took
6:48 a man building a H, who dug deep, and
6:48 stream broke against that H, and could not shake
6:49 man who built a H on the ground without
6:49 the ruin of that H was great."
7:6 not far from the H, the centurion sent friends
7:10 sent returned to the H, they found the slave
7:36 went into the Pharisee's H, and took his place
7:37 table in the Pharisee's H, brought an alabaster flask
7:44 I entered your H, you gave me no water
8:27 lived not in a H but among the tombs.
8:41 to come to his H,
8:49 man from the ruler's H came and said, "Your
8:51 he came to the H, he permitted no one
9:4 And whatever H you enter, stay there, and from
10:5 Whatever H you enter, first say, 'Peace be to
10:5 'Peace be to this H
10:7 remain in the same H, eating and drinking what
10:7 do not go from H to house.
10:7 his wages; do not go from house to H
10:38 a woman named Martha received him into her H
11:24 will return to my H from which I came.'
12:39 not have left his H to be broken into.
12:52 for henceforth in one H there will be five
13:35 Behold, your H is forsaken.
14:1 to dine at the H of a ruler who
14:23 come in, that my H may be filled.
15:8 lamp and sweep the H and seek diligently until
15:25 drew near to the H, he heard music and
16:27 him to my father's H,
17:31 his goods in the H, not come down to
18:14 went down to his H justified rather than the
18:29 man who has left H or wife or brothers
19:5 must stay at your H today."
19:9 has come to this H, since he also is
19:46 "It is written, 'My H shall be a house
19:46 house shall be a H of prayer'; but you
22:10 follow him into the H which he enters,
22:52 him away, bringing him into the high priest's H
Jn 2:16 not make my Father's H a house of trade."
2:16 my Father's house a H of trade."
2:17 written, "Zeal for thy H will consume me."
7:53 They went each to his own H
8:35 not continue in the H for ever; the son
11:20 and met him, while Mary sat in the H
11:31 with her in the H, consoling her, saw Mary
12:3 her hair; and the H was filled with the
14:2 In my Father's H are many rooms; if it
18:28 led Jesus from the H of Caiaphas to the
20:26 were again in the H, and Thomas was with
Acts 2:2 it filled all the H where they were sitting.
2:36 feet.' Let all the H of Israel therefore know
7:20 months in his father's H;
7:42 in the wilderness, O H of Israel?
7:47 Solomon who built a H for him.
7:49 What H will you build for me, says the
8:3 the church, and entering H after house, he dragged
8:3 and entering house after H, he dragged off men
9:11 and inquire in the H of Judas for a
9:17 So Ananias departed and entered the H
10:6 Simon, a tanner, whose H is by the seaside."
10:17 made inquiry for Simon's H, stood before the gate
10:22 to come to his H, and to hear what
10:30 of prayer in my H; and behold, a man
10:32 is lodging in the H of Simon, a tanner,
11:11 men arrived at the H in which we were,
11:12 also accompanied me, and we entered the man's H
11:13 angel standing in his H and saying, 'Send to
12:12 he went to the H of Mary, the mother
16:15 Lord, come to my H and stay." And she
16:32 him and to all that were in his H
16:34 them up into his H, and set food before
17:5 uproar, and attacked the H of Jason, seeking to
18:7 and went to the H of a man named
18:7 worshiper of God; his H was next door to
19:16 fled out of that H naked and wounded.
20:20 in public and from H to house,
20:20 and from house to H,
21:8 and we entered the H of Philip the evangelist,
21:16 bringing us to the H of Mnason of Cyprus,
Rom 16:5 give thanks; greet also the church in their H
1Cor 16:19 the church in their H, send you hearty greetings
2Cor 5:1 building from God, a H not made with hands,
Col 4:15 and to Nympha and the church in her H
1Tim 5:13 idlers, gadding about from H to house, and not
5:13 about from house to H, and not only idlers
2Tim 2:20 In a great H there are not only vessels
2:21 the master of the H, ready for any good
Philem 1:2 the church in your H:
Heb 3:2 just as Moses also was faithful in God's H
3:3 the builder of a H has more honor than
3:3 of a house has more honor than the H
3:4 (For every H is built by some one, but
3:5 faithful in all God's H as a servant, to
3:6 was faithful over God's H as a son.
3:6 And we are his H if we hold fast
8:8 new covenant with the H of Israel and with
8:8 Israel and with the H of Judah;
8:10 will make with the H of Israel after those
10:21 great priest over the H of God,
1Pet 2:5 built into a spiritual H, to be a holy

2Jn	1:10	receive him into the H or give him any

HOUSEHOLD (103)

Gen	7:1	you and all your H, for I have seen
	18:19	his children and his H after him to keep
	24:28	and told her mother's H about these things.
	26:14	herds, and a great H, so that the Philistines
	30:30	provide for my own H also?"
	31:19	Rachel stole her father's H gods.
	31:34	Rachel had taken the H gods and put them
	31:35	did not find the H gods.
	31:37	found of all your H goods?
	34:30	I shall be destroyed, both I and my H
	35:2	Jacob said to his H and to all who
	36:6	the members of his H, his cattle, all his
	39:14	the men of her H and said to them,
	45:2	heard it, and the H of Pharaoh heard it.
	45:11	lest you and your H, and all that you
	46:31	and to his father's H, "I will go up
	46:31	brothers and my father's H, who were in the
	47:12	and all his father's H with food, according to
	50:4	Joseph spoke to the H of Pharaoh, saying, "If
	50:7	the elders of his H, and all the elders
	50:8	well as all the H of Joseph, his brothers,
	50:8	brothers, and his father's H; only their children, their
Ex	1:1	Jacob, each with his H:
	12:3	a lamb for a H;
	12:4	household; and if the H is too small for
Deut	6:22	Pharaoh and all his H, before our eyes;
	14:26	LORD your God and rejoice, you and your H
	15:16	loves you and your H, since he fares well
	15:20	it, you and your H, before the LORD your
Josh	2:18	and mother, your brothers, and all your father's H
	6:25	harlot, and her father's H, and all who belonged
	7:14	by households; and the H which the LORD takes
	7:18	he brought near his H man by man, and
Judg	18:25	lose your life with the lives of your H
1Sam	27:3	every man with his H, and David with his
2Sam	2:3	every one with his H; and they dwelt in
	6:11	and the LORD blessed Obed-edom and all his H
	6:12	LORD has blessed the H of Obed-edom and all
	6:20	And David returned to bless his H
	15:16	forth, and all his H after him.
	16:2	are for the king's H to ride on, the
	19:18	bring over the king's H, and to do his
	19:41	the king and his H over the Jordan, and
1Kgs	4:7	the king and his H; each man had to
	5:9	meet my wishes by providing food for my H
	5:11	as food for his H, and twenty thousand cors
	16:9	who was over the H in Tirzah,
	17:15	and he, and her H ate for many days.
	18:3	And Ahab called Obadiah, who was over the H
2Kgs	7:9	come, let us go and tell the king's H
	7:11	out, and it was told within the king's H
	8:1	and depart with your H, and sojourn wherever you
	8:2	she went with her H and sojourned in the
	15:5	son was over the H, governing the people of
	18:18	who was over the H, and Shebnah the secretary,
	18:37	who was over the H, and Shebna the secretary,
	19:2	who was over the H, and Shebna the secretary,
1Chr	13:14	God remained with the H of Obed-edom in his
	13:14	the LORD blessed the H of Obed-edom and all
	16:43	house, and David went home to bless his H
2Chr	26:21	was over the king's H, governing the people of
Neh	13:8	I threw all the H furniture of Tobiah out
Esth	16:18	at the gate of Susa, with all his H
Prov	11:29	He who troubles his H will inherit wind, and
	15:27	makes trouble for his H, but he who hates
	27:27	the food of your H and maintenance for your
	31:15	provides food for her H and tasks for her
	31:21	of snow for her H, for all her household
	31:21	household, for all her H are clothed in scarlet.
	31:27	the ways of her H, and does not eat
Is	22:15	who is over the H, and say to him:
	36:3	who was over the H, and Shebna the secretary,
	36:22	who was over the H, and Shebna the secretary,
	37:2	who was over the H, and Shebna the secretary,
Jer	23:34	LORD,' I will punish that man and his H
Bar	6:59	his courage, or a H utensil that serves its
Dan	13:26	When the H servants heard the shouting in the
	14:29	or else we will kill you and your H
Mt	10:25	much more will they malign those of his H
	10:36	man's foes will be those of his own H
	24:45	has set over his H, to give them their
Lk	11:17	waste, and a divided H falls.
	12:42	will set over his H, to give them their
Jn	4:53	live"; and he himself believed, and all his H
Acts	7:10	him governor over Egypt and over all his H
	10:2	God with all his H, gave alms liberally to
	11:14	you and all your H
	16:15	was baptized, with her H, she besought us, saying,
	16:31	and you will be saved, you and your H
	16:34	rejoiced with all his H that he had believed
	18:8	together with all his H; and many of the
1Cor	1:16	did baptize also the H of Stephanas.
	16:15	you know that the H of Stephanas were the
Gal	6:10	who are of the H of faith.
Eph	2:19	and members of the H of God,
Phil	4:22	the saints greet you, especially those of Caesar's H
1Tim	3:4	must manage his own H well, keeping his children
	3:5	to manage his own H, how can he care
	3:15	to behave in the H of God, which is
2Tim	1:16	grant mercy to the H of Onesiphorus, for he
	4:19	and Aquila, and the H of Onesiphorus.
Heb	11:7	the saving of his H; by this he condemned
1Pet	4:17	to begin with the H of God; and if

HOUSEHOLDER (11)

Mt	13:27	the servants of the H came and said to
	13:52	heaven is like a H who brings out of
	20:1	heaven is like a H who went out early
	20:11	they grumbled at the H,
	21:33	There was a H who planted a vineyard, and
	24:43	this, that if the H had known in what
Mk	14:14	enters, say to the H, 'The Teacher says, Where
Lk	12:39	this, that if the H had known at what
	13:25	When once the H has risen up and shut
	14:21	Then the H in anger said to his servant,
	22:11	enters, and tell the H, 'The Teacher says to

HOUSEHOLDS (12)

Gen	42:19	the famine of your H,
	42:33	the famine of your H, and go your way.
	45:18	your father and your H, and come to me,
	47:24	for yourselves and your H, and as food for
Num	16:32	them up, with their H and all the men
	18:31	place, you and your H; for it is your
Deut	11:6	them up, with their H, their tents, and every
	12:7	rejoice, you and your H, in all that you
Josh	7:14	shall come near by H; and the household which
1Tim	3:12	their children and their H well;
	5:14	bear children, rule their H, and give the enemy
2Tim	3:6	make their way into H and capture weak women,

HOUSES (226)

Gen	34:29	that was in the H, they captured and made
Ex	6:14	heads of their fathers' H: the sons of Reuben,
	6:25	heads of the fathers' H of the Levites by
	8:3	bed, and into the H of your servants and
	8:9	from you and your H and be left only
	8:11	from you and your H and your servants and
	8:13	died out of the H and courtyards and out
	8:21	people, and into your H; and the houses of
	8:21	your houses; and the H of the Egyptians shall
	8:24	and into his servants' H, and in all the
	9:20	cattle flee into the H;
	10:6	they shall fill your H, and the houses of
	10:6	your houses, and the H of all your servants
	12:3	according to their fathers' H, a lamb for a
	12:7	the lintel of the H in which they eat
	12:13	for you, upon the H where you are; and
	12:15	leaven out of your H, for if any one
	12:19	be found in your H; for if any one
	12:23	destroyer to enter your H to slay you.
	12:27	he passed over the H of the people of
	12:27	when he slew the Egyptians but spared our H
Lev	25:31	But the H of the villages which have no
	25:32	of the Levites, the H in the cities of
	25:33	the jubilee; for the H in the cities of
Num	1:2	by families, by fathers' H, according to the number
	1:18	by families, by fathers' H, according to the number
	1:20	families, by their fathers' H, according to the number
	1:22	families, by their fathers' H, those of them that
	1:24	families, by their fathers' H, according to the number
	1:26	families, by their fathers' H, according to the number
	1:28	families, by their fathers' H, according to the number
	1:30	families, by their fathers' H, according to the number
	1:32	families, by their fathers' H, according to the number
	1:34	families, by their fathers' H, according to the number
	1:36	families, by their fathers' H, according to the number
	1:38	families, by their fathers' H, according to the number
	1:40	families, by their fathers' H, according to the number

	1:42	families, by their fathers' H, according to the number
	1:45	Israel, by their fathers' H, from twenty years old
	2:2	ensigns of their fathers' H; they shall encamp facing
	2:32	numbered by their fathers' H; all in the camps
	3:15	of Levi, by fathers' H and by families; every
	3:20	the families of the Levites, by their fathers' H
	4:2	families and their fathers' H,
	4:22	families and their fathers' H;
	4:29	families and their fathers' H;
	4:34	families and their fathers' H,
	4:38	families and their fathers' H,
	4:40	families and their fathers' H was two thousand six
	4:42	families and their fathers' H,
	4:46	families and their fathers' H,
	7:2	heads of their fathers' H, the leaders of the
	17:2	according to their fathers' H, twelve rods.
	17:6	according to their fathers' H, twelve rods; and the
	26:2	upward, by their fathers' H, all in Israel who
	31:26	heads of the fathers' H of the congregation;
	32:28	heads of the fathers' H of the tribes of
	34:14	of Reuben by fathers' H and the tribe of
	34:14	Gad by their fathers' H have received their
	36:1	heads of the fathers' H of the families of
	36:1	Manasseh, of the fathers' H of the sons of
	36:1	heads of the fathers' H of the people of
Deut	6:11	did not build, and H full of all good
	8:12	and have built goodly H and live in them,
	19:1	cities and in their H,
Josh	9:12	took it from our H as our food for
	14:1	heads of the fathers' H of the tribes of
	19:51	heads of the fathers' H of the tribes of
	21:1	heads of the fathers' H of the Levites came
	21:1	heads of the fathers' H of the tribes of
Judg	18:14	know that in these H there are an ephod,
	18:22	who were in the H near Micah's house were
1Kgs	8:1	leaders of the fathers' H of the people of
	9:10	had built the two H, the house of the
	12:31	He also made H on high places, and appointed
	13:32	and against all the H of the high places
	20:6	your house and the H of your servants, and
2Kgs	23:7	he broke down the H of the male cult
	25:9	house and all the H of Jerusalem; every great
1Chr	4:38	families, and their fathers' H increased greatly.
	5:13	to their fathers' H: Michael, Meshullam, Sheba,
	5:15	chief in their fathers' H;
	5:24	heads of their fathers' H: Epher, Ishi, Eliel, Azriel,
	5:24	warriors, famous men, heads of their fathers' H
	7:2	heads of their fathers' H, namely of Tola, mighty
	7:4	according to their fathers' H, were units of the
	7:7	five, heads of fathers' H, mighty warriors; and their
	7:9	heads of their fathers' H, mighty warriors, was
	7:11	heads of their fathers' H, mighty warriors, seventeen
	7:40	heads of fathers' H, approved, mighty warriors,
	8:6	were heads of fathers' H of the inhabitants of
	8:10	These were his sons, heads of fathers' H
	8:13	were heads of fathers' H of the inhabitants of
	8:28	heads of fathers' H, according to their generations,
	9:9	were heads of fathers' H according to their fathers'
	9:9	heads of fathers' houses according to their fathers' H
	9:13	of their fathers' H, one thousand seven hundred
	9:33	the heads of fathers' H of the Levites, dwelling
	9:34	were heads of fathers' H of the Levites, according
	12:30	men of valor, famous men in their fathers' H
	15:1	David built H for himself in the city of
	15:12	heads of the fathers' H of the Levites; sanctify
	23:9	heads of the fathers' H of Ladan.
	23:24	Levi by their fathers' H, the heads of fathers'
	23:24	the heads of fathers' H as they were registered
	24:4	sixteen heads of fathers' H of the sons of
	24:6	heads of the fathers' H of the priests and
	24:30	sons of the Levites according to their fathers' H
	24:31	the heads of fathers' H of the priests and
	26:6	rulers in their fathers' H, for they were men
	26:13	cast lots by fathers' H, small and great alike,
	26:21	heads of the fathers' H belonging to Ladan the
	26:26	heads of the fathers' H, and the officers of
	26:31	the Hebronites of whatever genealogy or fathers' H
	26:32	ability, heads of fathers' H, to have the oversight
	27:1	heads of fathers' H, the commanders of thousands
	28:11	temple, and of its H, its treasuries, its upper
	29:6	the heads of fathers' H made their freewill offerings,
2Chr	1:2	leaders in all Israel, the heads of fathers' H
	5:2	leaders of the fathers' H of the people of
	17:14	of them by fathers' H: Of Judah, the commanders
	23:2	the heads of fathers' H of Israel, and they
	25:5	set them by fathers' H under commanders of
	26:12	the heads of fathers' H of mighty men of
	31:17	according to their fathers' H; that of the Levites
	35:4	according to your fathers' H by your divisions,
	35:5	groupings of the fathers' H of your brethren the
	35:12	groupings of the fathers' H of the lay people,
Ezra	1:5	heads of the fathers' H of Judah and Benjamin,
	2:59	not prove their fathers' H or their descent, whether
	3:12	and heads of fathers' H, old men who had
	4:2	the heads of fathers' H and said to them,
	4:3	the heads of fathers' H in Israel said to
	8:1	heads of their fathers' H, and this is the
	8:29	the heads of fathers' H in Israel at Jerusalem,
	10:16	men, heads of fathers' H, according to their fathers'
	10:16	according to their fathers' H, each of them
Neh	5:3	our vineyards, and our H to get grain because
	5:11	olive orchards, and their H, and the hundredth of
	7:4	were few and no H had been built.
	7:61	not prove their fathers' H nor their descent, whether
	7:70	the heads of fathers' H gave to the work.
	7:71	the heads of fathers' H gave into the treasury
	8:13	the heads of fathers' H of all the people,
	9:25	and took possession of H full of all good
	10:34	according to our fathers' H, at times appointed, year
	11:13	heads of fathers' H, two hundred and forty-two;
	12:12	priests, heads of fathers' H: of Seraiah, Meraiah; of
	12:22	the heads of fathers' H; also the priests until
	12:23	Levi, heads of fathers' H, were written in the
Job	3:15	gold, who filled their H with silver.
	4:19	those who dwell in H of clay, whose foundation
	15:28	in desolate cities, in H which no man should
	21:9	Their H are safe from fear, and no rod
	21:21	they care for their H after them, when the
	22:18	Yet he filled their H with good things--
	24:16	dark they dig through H; by day they shut
Prov	1:13	we shall fill our H with spoil;
Eccl	2:4	great works; I built H and planted vineyards for
Sir	3:9	father's blessing strengthens the H of the children,
	28:14	cities, and overturned the H of great men.
	49:13	the gates and bars and rebuilt our ruined H
Is	3:14	the spoil of the poor is in your H
	5:9	my hearing: "Surely many H shall be desolate, large
	5:9	desolate, large and beautiful H, without inhabitant.
	6:11	waste without inhabitant, and H without men, and
	8:14	of stumbling to both H of Israel, a trap
	13:16	before their eyes; their H will be plundered and
	13:21	down there, and its H will be full of
	22:10	and you counted the H of Jerusalem, and you
	22:10	you broke down the H to fortify the wall.
	32:13	for all the joyous H in the joyful city.
	65:21	They shall build H and inhabit them; they shall
Jer	5:7	and trooped to the H of harlots.
	5:27	full of birds, their H are full of treachery;
	6:12	Their H shall be turned over to others, their
	17:22	burden out of your H on the sabbath or
	18:22	be heard from their H, when thou bringest the
	19:13	The H of Jerusalem and the houses of the
	19:13	of Jerusalem and the H of the kings of
	19:13	of Judah--all the H upon whose roofs incense
	29:5	Jerusalem to Babylon: Build H and live in them;
	29:28	will be long; build H and live in them,
	32:15	the God of Israel: H and fields and vineyards
	32:29	burn it, with the H on whose roofs incense
	33:4	of Israel, concerning the H of this city and
	33:4	this city and the H of the kings of
	35:9	and not to build H to dwell in.
	52:13	house and all the H of Jerusalem; every great
Ezek	7:24	take possession of their H; I will put an
	11:3	not near to build H; this city is the
	16:41	they shall burn your H and execute judgments upon
	23:47	sons and their daughters, and burn up their H
	26:12	and destroy your pleasant H; your stones and timber
	28:26	and they shall build H and plant vineyards.
	33:30	the doors of the H, say to one another,
	45:4	a place for their H and a holy place
Dan	2:5	from limb, and your H shall be laid in
	3:97	from limb, and their H laid in ruins; for
Joel	2:9	climb up into the H, they enter through the
Amos	3:15	summer house; and the H of ivory shall perish,
	3:15	perish, and the great H shall come to an
	5:11	wheat, you have built H of hewn stone, but
Mic	1:14	gifts to Moresheth-gath; the H of Achzib shall be
	2:2	and seize them; and H, and take them away;
	2:9	out from their pleasant H; from their young children
Zeph	1:13	be plundered, and their H laid waste.
	1:13	Though they build H, they shall not inhabit them;
	2:7	pasture, and in the H of Ashkelon they shall

Hag	1:4	dwell in your paneled H, while this house lies
Zech	14:2	be taken and the H plundered and the women
1Mac	1:31	and tore down its H and its surrounding walls.
	1:55	the doors of the H and in the streets.
	3:56	those who were building H, or were betrothed, or
	13:47	city and cleansed the H in which the idols
2Mac	3:18	hurried out of their H in crowds to make
	5:12	and to slay those who went into the H
Mt	11:8	those who wear soft raiment are in kings' H
	19:29	one who has left H or brothers or sisters
Mk	10:30	now in this time, H and brothers and sisters
	12:40	feasts, who devour widows' H and for a pretense
Lk	16:4	receive me into their H when I am put
	20:47	feasts, who devour widows' H and for a pretense
Acts	4:34	possessors of lands or H sold them, and brought
	7:48	does not dwell in H made with hands; as
1Cor	11:22	Do you not have H to eat and drink

HOUSETOP (7)

Ps	102:7	I am like a lonely bird on the H
Prov	21:9	a corner of the H than in a house
	25:24	a corner of the H than in a house
Mt	24:17	who is on the H not go down to
Mk	13:15	who is on the H not go down, nor
Lk	17:31	who is on the H, with his goods in
Acts	10:9	went up on the H to pray, about the

HOUSETOPS (8)

2Kgs	19:26	like grass on the H; blighted before it is
Ps	129:6	the grass on the H, which withers before it
Is	15:3	on sackcloth; on the H and in the squares
	22:1	of you, to the H,
	37:27	like grass on the H, blighted before it is
Jer	48:38	On all the H of Moab and in the
Mt	10:27	and what you hear whispered, proclaim upon the H
Lk	12:3	in private rooms shall be proclaimed upon the H

HOVERING

Is	31:5	Like birds H, so the LORD of hosts will

HOWL (2)

Bar	6:32	They H and shout before their gods as some
Jas	5:1	you rich, weep and H for the miseries that

HOWLING (4)

Deut	32:10	land, and in the H waste of the wilderness;
Ps	59:6	evening they come back, H like dogs and prowling
	59:14	evening they come back, H like dogs and prowling
Is	13:21	will be full of H creatures; there ostriches will

HUBS

1Kgs	7:33	their spokes, and their H, were all cast.

HUDDLE

Job	30:7	under the nettles they H together.

HUGE (6)

1Kgs	7:10	was of costly stones, H stones, stones of eight
2Chr	16:8	and the Libyans a H army with exceedingly many
Ezra	5:8	is being built with H stones, and timber is
Jud	2:18	every man, and a H amount of gold and
Sir	43:25	of living things, and H creatures of the sea.
1Mac	9:6	When they saw the H number of the enemy

HUKKOK

Josh	19:34	goes from there to H, touching Zebulun at the

HUKOK

1Chr	6:75	with its pasture lands, H with its pasture lands,

HUL (2)

Gen	10:23	sons of Aram: Uz, H, Gether, and Mash.
1Chr	1:17	Arpachshad, Lud, Aram, Uz, H, Gether, and Meshech.

HULDAH (2)

2Kgs	22:14	and Asaiah went to H the prophetess, the wife
2Chr	34:22	had sent went to H the prophetess, the wife

HUMAN (49)

Lev	5:3	Or if he touches H uncleanness, of whatever sort
Jud	8:14	the depths of the H heart, nor find out
	8:16	threatened, nor like a H being, to be won
Job	34:20	taken away by no H hand.
Wis	12:5	their sacrificial feasting on H flesh and blood.
	14:15	was once a dead H being, and handed on
	15:4	the evil intent of H art misled us, nor
Sir	3:22	matters too great for H understanding have been
	10:19	The H race.
	10:19	The H race.
	31:16	Eat like a H being what is set before
	36:22	countenance, and surpasses every H desire.
Is	52:14	was so marred, beyond H semblance, and his form
Ezek	1:8	four sides they had H hands.
	1:26	it were of a H form.
	4:12	in their sight on H dung."
	4:15	cow's dung instead of H dung, on which you
	10:8	the form of a H hand under their wings.
	10:21	wings the semblance of H hands.
	22:25	prey; they have devoured H lives; they have taken
Dan	2:34	cut out by no H hand, and it smote
	2:45	a mountain by no H hand, and that it
	8:25	princes; but, by no H hand, he shall be
	14:32	had been given two H bodies and two sheep;
Mt	24:22	not been shortened, no H being would be saved;
Mk	13:20	shortened the days, no H being would be saved;
Acts	17:25	is he served by H hands, as though he
Rom	2:9	and distress for every H being who does evil,
	3:5	(I speak in a H way.)
	3:20	For no H being will be justified in his
	6:19	I am speaking in H terms, because of your
1Cor	1:29	are, so that no H being might boast in
	2:13	words not taught by H wisdom but taught by
	4:3	you or by any H court.
	9:8	I say this on H authority?
2Cor	3:3	but on tablets of H hearts.
	5:16	no one from a H point of view; even
	5:16	regarded Christ from a H point of view, we
Gal	3:15	To give a H example, brethren: no one annuls
Phil	2:8	And being found in H form he humbled himself
Col	2:8	empty deceit, according to H tradition, according to
	2:22	are used), according to H precepts and doctrines?
Jas	3:8	by humankind, but no H being can tame the
1Pet	2:13	Lord's sake to every H institution, whether it be
	4:2	flesh no longer by H passions but by the
2Pet	2:16	dumb ass spoke with H voice and restrained the
Rev	9:7	their faces were like H faces,
	13:18	for it is a H number, its number is
	18:13	and slaves, that is, H souls.

HUMANE

Wis	7:23	keen, irresistible, beneficent, H, steadfast, sure, free

HUMANKIND

Jas	3:7	has been tamed by H,

HUMANLY

1Cor	15:32	do I gain if, H speaking, I fought with

HUMBLE (54)

Ex	10:3	will you refuse to H yourself before me?
Deut	8:2	wilderness, that he might H you, testing you to
	8:16	know, that he might H you and test you,
2Sam	22:28	Thou dost deliver a H people, but thy eyes
2Chr	7:14	called by my name H themselves, and pray and
	33:23	And he did not H himself before the LORD,
	36:12	He did not H himself before Jeremiah the prophet,
Ezra	8:21	Ahava, that we might H ourselves before our God,
Job	22:23	to the Almighty and H yourself, if you remove
Ps	18:27	thou dost deliver a H people; but the haughty
	25:9	He leads the H in what is right, and
	25:9	right, and teaches the H his way.
	55:19	will give ear, and H them, he who is
	89:22	the wicked shall not H him.
	149:4	people; he adorns the H with victory.
Prov	3:34	scornful, but to the H he shows favor.
	11:2	disgrace; but with the H is wisdom.
	12:9	is a man of H standing who works for
Sir	2:4	and in changes that H you be patient.
	2:17	their hearts, and will H themselves before him.
	3:18	the more you must H yourself; so you will
	3:19	of the Lord; he is glorified by the H
	7:17	H yourself greatly, for the punishment of the ungodly
	10:15	and has planted the H in their place.
	11:1	The wisdom of a H man will lift up
	12:5	Do good to the H, but do not give
	13:20	friends, but when a H man falls, he is
	13:21	If a H man slips, they even reproach him;
	18:20	Before falling ill, H yourself, and when you are
	20:10	raised their heads from H circumstances.
	29:8	with a man in H circumstances, and do not
	35:17	The prayer of the H pierces the clouds, and
Is	57:15	of a contrite and H spirit, to revive the

57:15 the spirit of the H, and to revive the
58:5 for a man to H himself?
66:2 look, he that is H and contrite in spirit,
Jer 37:20 the king: my H plea come before you,
38:26 them, 'I made a H plea to the king
Ezek 17:14 the kingdom might be H and not lift itself
22:10 nakedness; in you they H women who are unclean
Dan 3:39 contrite heart and a H spirit may we be
3:88 who are holy and H in heart, sing praise
Zeph 2:3 the LORD, all you H of the land, who
3:12 of you a people H and lowly.
Zech 9:9 and victorious is he, H and riding on an
1Mac 14:14 He strengthened all the H of his people; he
Mt 21:5 is coming to you, H, and mounted on an
2Cor 10:1 Christ--I who am H when face to face
12:21 again my God may H me before you, and
Jas 4:6 opposes the proud, but gives grace to the H
4:10 H yourselves before the Lord and he will exalt
1Pet 3:8 tender heart and a H mind.
5:5 opposes the proud, but gives grace to the H
5:6 H yourselves therefore under the mighty hand of

HUMBLED (39)

Gen 34:2 lay with her and H her.
Lev 26:41 uncircumcised heart is H and they make amends
Deut 8:3 And he H you and let you hunger and
1Kgs 21:29 seen how Ahab has H himself before me?
21:29 Because he has H himself before me, I will
2Kgs 22:19 was penitent, and you H yourself before the LORD,
2Chr 12:6 Israel and the king H themselves and said, "The
12:7 LORD saw that they H themselves, the word of
12:7 to Shemaiah: "They have H themselves; I will not
12:12 And when he H himself the wrath of the
30:11 Manasseh, and of Zebulun H themselves and came
32:26 But Hezekiah H himself for the pride of his
33:12 LORD his God and H himself greatly before the
33:19 the images, before he H himself, behold, they are
33:23 Manasseh his father had H himself, but this Amon
34:27 was penitent and you H yourself before God when
34:27 inhabitants, and you have H yourself before me, and
Jud 4:9 fervor, and they H themselves with much fasting.
5:11 to making bricks, and H them and made slaves
Esth 14:2 dung, and she utterly H her body, and every
Job 30:11 loosed my cord and H me, they have cast
Ps 69:10 When I H my soul with fasting, it became
Wis 17:7 their magic art lay H, and their boasted wisdom
Sir 40:3 the one who is H in dust and ashes,
Is 2:9 So man is H, and men are brought low--
2:11 of men shall be H; and the LORD alone
2:17 of man shall be H, and the pride of
5:15 low, and the eyes of the haughty are H
58:3 Why have we H ourselves, and thou takest no
Jer 44:10 They have not H themselves even to this day,
Dan 5:22 son, Belshazzar, have not H your heart, though you
10:12 mind to understand and H yourself before your God,
1Mac 5:3 a heavy blow and H them and despoiled them.
12:15 delivered from our enemies and our enemies were H
2Mac 8:35 the Jews, having been H with the help of
Mt 23:12 exalts himself will be H, and whoever humbles
Lk 14:11 exalts himself will be H, and he who humbles
18:14 exalts himself will be H, but he who humbles
Phil 2:8 in human form he H himself and became obedient

HUMBLES (6)

Tob 4:19 to his will he H whomever he wishes.
Sir 12:11 Even if he H himself and goes about cringing,
Mt 18:4 Whoever H himself like this child, he is the
23:12 be humbled, and whoever H himself will be exalted.
Lk 14:11 humbled, and he who H himself will be exalted."
18:14 humbled, but he who H himself will be exalted."

HUMBLEST

1Sam 9:21 not my family the H of all the families

HUMBLING

Sir 34:26 has he gained by H himself?

HUMBLY

Mic 6:8 kindness, and to walk H with your God?

HUMILIATE

1Cor 11:22 church of God and H those who have nothing?

HUMILIATED (3)

Deut 21:14 slave, since you have H her.
Sir 13:8 and not to be H in your feasting.
2Cor 9:4 not ready, we be H --to say nothing of

HUMILIATION (7)

Jud 6:19 have pity on the H of our people, and
Job 19:5 me, and make my H an argument against me,
Sir 2:5 fire, and acceptable men in the furnace of H
Is 30:3 shelter in the shadow of Egypt to your H
1Mac 3:51 down and profaned, and thy priests mourn in H
Acts 8:33 In his H justice was denied him.
Jas 1:9 the rich in his H, because like the flower

HUMILITY (10)

Prov 15:33 instruction in wisdom, and H goes before honor.
18:12 heart is haughty, but H goes before honor.
22:4 The reward for H and fear of the LORD
Sir 10:27 son, glorify yourself with H, and ascribe to yourself
13:19 H is an abomination to a proud man; likewise
36:23 If kindness and H mark her speech, her husband
Zeph 2:3 commands; seek righteousness, seek H; perhaps you
Acts 20:19 the Lord with all H and with tears and
Phil 2:3 or conceit, but in H count others better than
1Pet 5:5 all of you, with H toward one another, for

HUMPS

Is 30:6 their treasures on the H of camels, to a

HUMTAH

Josh 15:54 Janim, Beth-tappuah, Aphekah, H, Kiriath-arba

HUNCHBACK

Lev 21:20 injured hand, or a H, or a dwarf, or

HUNDRED (679)

Gen 5:3 Adam had lived a H and thirty years, he
5:4 of Seth were eight H years; and he had
5:5 Adam lived were nine H and thirty years; and
5:6 Seth had lived a H and five years, he
5:7 birth of Enosh eight H and seven years, and
5:8 of Seth were nine H and twelve years; and
5:10 birth of Kenan eight H and fifteen years, and
5:11 of Enosh were nine H and five years; and
5:13 birth of Mahalalel eight H and forty years, and
5:14 of Kenan were nine H and ten years; and
5:16 birth of Jared eight H and thirty years, and
5:17 of Mahalalel were eight H and ninety-five years; and
5:18 Jared had lived a H and sixty-two years he
5:19 birth of Enoch eight H years, and had other
5:20 of Jared were nine H and sixty-two years; and
5:22 birth of Methuselah three H years, and had other
5:23 of Enoch were three H and sixty-five years.
5:25 Methuselah had lived a H and eighty-seven years, he
5:26 birth of Lamech seven H and eighty-two years, and
5:27 of Methuselah were nine H and sixty-nine years; and
5:28 Lamech had lived a H and eighty-two years, he
5:30 birth of Noah five H and ninety-five years, and
5:31 of Lamech were seven H and seventy-seven years;
5:32 After Noah was five H years old, Noah became
6:3 days shall be a H and twenty years."
6:15 of the ark three H cubits, its breadth fifty
7:6 Noah was six H years old when the flood
7:24 upon the earth a H and fifty days.
8:3 the end of a H and fifty days the
8:13 In the six H and first year, in the
9:28 flood Noah lived three H and fifty years.
9:29 of Noah were nine H and fifty years; and
11:10 When Shem was a H years old, he became
11:11 birth of Arpachshad five H years, and had other
11:13 birth of Shelah four H and three years, and
11:15 birth of Eber four H and three years, and
11:17 birth of Peleg four H and thirty years, and
11:19 birth of Reu two H and nine years, and
11:21 birth of Serug two H and seven years, and
11:23 birth of Nahor two H years, and had other
11:25 birth of Terah a H and nineteen years, and
11:32 of Terah were two H and five years; and
14:14 in his house, three H and eighteen of them,
15:13 be oppressed for four H years;
17:17 man who is a H years old?
21:5 Abraham was a H years old when his son
23:1 Sarah lived a H and twenty-seven years; these were
23:15 of land worth four H shekels of silver, what
23:16 of the Hittites, four H shekels of silver, according
25:7 of Abraham's life, a H and seventy-five years.
25:17 life of Ishmael, a H and thirty-seven years; he
32:6 meet you, and four H men with him."
32:14 brother Esau, two H she-goats and twenty he-goats,

H

32:14 and twenty he-goats, two H ewes and twenty rams,
33:1 was coming, and four H men with him.
33:19 he bought for a H pieces of money the
35:28 of Isaac were a H and eighty years.
45:22 Benjamin he gave three H shekels of silver and
47:9 my sojourning are a H and thirty years; few
47:28 his life, were a H and forty-seven years.
50:22 and Joseph lived a H and ten years.
50:26 Joseph died, being a H and ten years old;
Ex 6:16 of Levi being a H and thirty-seven years.
6:18 of Kohath being a H and thirty-three years.
6:20 of Amram being one H and thirty-seven years.
12:37 to Succoth, about six H thousand men on foot,
12:40 in Egypt was four H and thirty years.
12:41 the end of four H and thirty years, on
14:7 him, and took six H picked chariots and all
27:9 fine twined linen a H cubits long for one
27:11 shall be hangings a H cubits long, their pillars
27:18 court shall be a H cubits, the breadth fifty,
30:23 of liquid myrrh five H shekels, and of sweet-smelling
30:23 much, that is, two H and fifty, and of
30:23 of aromatic cane two H and fifty,
30:24 and of cassia five H, according to the shekel
38:9 fine twined linen, a H cubits;
38:11 the north side a H cubits, their pillars twenty,
38:24 twenty-nine talents and seven H and thirty shekels,
38:25 were numbered was a H talents and a thousand
38:25 and a thousand seven H and seventy-five shekels, by
38:26 and upward, for six H and three thousand, five
38:26 and three thousand, five H and fifty men.
38:27 The H talents of silver were for casting the
38:27 of the veil; a H bases for the hundred
38:27 hundred bases for the H talents, a talent for
38:28 of the thousand seven H and seventy-five shekels he
38:29 two thousand and four H shekels;
Lev 26:8 you shall chase a H, and a hundred of
26:8 a hundred, and a H of you shall chase
Num 1:21 the tribe of Reuben was forty-six thousand five H
1:23 the tribe of Simeon was fifty-nine thousand three H
1:25 was forty-five thousand six H and fifty.
1:27 the tribe of Judah was seventy-four thousand six H
1:29 the tribe of Issachar was fifty-four thousand four H
1:31 the tribe of Zebulun was fifty-seven thousand four H
1:33 the tribe of Ephraim was forty thousand five H
1:35 tribe of Manasseh was thirty-two thousand two H
1:37 the tribe of Benjamin was thirty-five thousand four H
1:39 the tribe of Dan was sixty-two thousand seven H
1:41 the tribe of Asher was forty-one thousand five H
1:43 the tribe of Naphtali was fifty-three thousand four H
1:46 whole number was six H and three thousand five
1:46 and three thousand five H and fifty.
2:4 host as numbered being seventy-four thousand six H
2:6 his host as numbered being fifty-four thousand four H
2:8 host as numbered being fifty-seven thousand four H
2:9 their companies, is a H and eighty-six thousand four
2:9 is a hundred and eighty-six thousand four H
2:11 his host as numbered being forty-six thousand five H
2:13 host as numbered being fifty-nine thousand three H
2:15 being forty-five thousand six H and fifty.
2:16 their companies, is a H and fifty-one thousand four
2:16 and fifty-one thousand four H and fifty.
2:19 his host as numbered being forty thousand five H
2:21 host as numbered being thirty-two thousand two H
2:23 host as numbered being thirty-five thousand four H
2:24 their companies, is a H and eight thousand one
2:24 companies, is a hundred and eight thousand one H
2:26 host as numbered being sixty-two thousand seven H
2:28 his host as numbered being forty-one thousand five H
2:30 host as numbered being fifty-three thousand four H
2:31 of Dan is a H and fifty-seven thousand six
2:31 Dan is a hundred and fifty-seven thousand six H
2:32 their companies were six H and three thousand five
2:32 and three thousand five H and fifty.
3:22 month old and upward was seven thousand five H
3:28 were eight thousand six H, attending to the duties
3:34 month old and upward was six thousand two H
3:43 were twenty-two thousand two H and seventy-three.
3:46 redemption of the two H and seventy-three of the
3:50 thousand three H and sixty-five shekels, reckoned
4:36 was two thousand seven H and fifty.
4:40 was two thousand six H and thirty.
4:44 their number by families was three thousand two H
4:48 were eight thousand five H and eighty.
7:13 whose weight was a H and thirty shekels, one
7:19 whose weight was a H and thirty shekels, one
7:25 whose weight was a H and thirty shekels, one
7:31 whose weight was a H and thirty shekels, one
7:37 whose weight was a H and thirty shekels, one
7:43 whose weight was a H and thirty shekels, one
7:49 whose weight was a H and thirty shekels, one
7:55 whose weight was a H and thirty shekels, one
7:61 whose weight was a H and thirty shekels, one
7:67 whose weight was a H and thirty shekels, one
7:73 whose weight was a H and thirty shekels, one
7:79 whose weight was a H and thirty shekels, one
7:85 silver plate weighing a H and thirty shekels and
7:85 vessels two thousand four H shekels according to the
7:86 the dishes being a H and twenty shekels;
11:21 I am number six H thousand on foot; and
16:2 people of Israel, two H and fifty leaders of
16:17 LORD his censer, two H and fifty censers; you
16:35 and consumed the two H and fifty men offering
16:49 fourteen thousand seven H, besides those who died
26:7 was forty-three thousand seven H and thirty.
26:10 the fire devoured two H and fifty men; and
26:14 of the Simeonites, twenty-two thousand two H
26:18 Gad according to their number, forty thousand five H
26:22 to their number, seventy-six thousand five H
26:25 to their number, sixty-four thousand three H
26:27 according to their number, sixty thousand five H
26:34 and their number was fifty-two thousand seven H
26:37 according to their number, thirty-two thousand five H
26:41 and their number was forty-five thousand six H
26:43 to their number, were sixty-four thousand four H
26:47 to their number, fifty-three thousand four H
26:50 and their number was forty-five thousand four H
26:51 people of Israel, six H and one thousand seven
26:51 and one thousand seven H and thirty.
31:28 one out of five H, of the persons and
31:32 war took was: six H and seventy-five thousand sheep,
31:36 in number three H and thirty-seven thousand five
31:36 and thirty-seven thousand five H sheep,
31:37 of sheep was six H and seventy-five.
31:39 were thirty thousand five H, of which the LORD's
31:43 half was three H and thirty-seven thousand five
31:43 and thirty-seven thousand five H sheep,
31:45 and thirty thousand five H asses,
31:52 was sixteen thousand seven H and fifty shekels.
33:39 And Aaron was a H and twenty-three years old
Deut 22:19 shall fine him a H shekels of silver, and
31:2 them, "I am a H and twenty years old
34:7 Moses was a H and twenty years old when
Josh 7:21 from Shinar, and two H shekels of silver, and
24:29 LORD, died, being a H and ten years old.
24:32 of Shechem for a H pieces of money; it
Judg 2:8 the age of one H and ten years.
3:31 Anath, who killed six H of the Philistines with
4:3 for he had nine H chariots of iron, and
4:13 all his chariots, nine H chariots of iron, and
7:6 their mouths, was three H men; but all the
7:7 Gideon, "With the three H men that lapped I
7:8 but retained the three H men; and the camp
7:16 he divided the three H men into three companies,
7:19 So Gideon and the H men who were with
7:22 they blew the three H trumpets, the LORD set
8:4 he and the three H men who were with
8:10 there had fallen a H and twenty thousand men
8:26 was one thousand seven H shekels of gold; besides
11:26 of the Arnon, three H years, why did you
15:4 went and caught three H foxes, and took torches;
16:5 each give you eleven H pieces of silver."
17:2 his mother, "The eleven H pieces of silver which
17:3 he restored the eleven H pieces of silver to
17:4 his mother took two H pieces of silver, and
18:11 And six H men of the tribe of Dan,
18:16 Now the six H men of the Danites, armed
18:17 gate with the six H men armed with weapons
20:2 people of God, four H thousand men on foot
20:10 ten men of a H throughout all the tribes
20:10 of Israel, and a H of a thousand, and
20:15 Gibe-ah, who mustered seven H picked men.
20:16 all these were seven H picked men who were
20:17 Benjamin, mustered four H thousand men that drew
20:35 destroyed twenty-five thousand one H men of
20:47 But six H men turned and fled toward the
21:12 inhabitants of Jabesh-gilead four H young virgins
1Sam 11:8 of Israel were three H thousand, and the men
13:15 with him, about six H men.
14:2 him were about six H men,
15:4 them in Telaim, two H thousand men on foot,
17:7 spear's head weighed six H shekels of iron; and
18:25 marriage present except a H foreskins of the

18:27 men, and killed two H of the Philistines; and
22:2 with him about four H men.
23:13 who were about six H, arose and departed from
25:13 sword; and about four H men went up after
25:13 after David, while two H remained with the
25:18 haste, and took two H loaves, and two skins
25:18 parched grain, and a H clusters of raisins, and
25:18 of raisins, and two H cakes of figs, and
27:2 he and the six H men who were with
30:9 out, and the six H men who were with
30:10 pursuit, he and four H men; two hundred stayed
30:10 four hundred men; two H stayed behind, who were
30:17 them escaped, except four H young men, who
30:21 came to the two H men, who had been
2Sam 2:31 slain of Benjamin three H and sixty of Abner's
3:14 the price of a H foreskins of the Philistines."
8:4 a thousand and seven H horsemen, and twenty
8:4 left enough for a H chariots.
10:18 the men of seven H chariots, and forty thousand
14:26 of his head, two H shekels by the king's
15:11 With Absalom went two H men from Jerusalem who
15:18 and all the six H Gittites who had followed
16:1 asses saddled, bearing two H loaves of bread, a
16:1 loaves of bread, a H bunches of raisins, a
16:1 bunches of raisins, a H of summer fruits, and
21:16 whose spear weighed three H shekels of bronze, and
23:8 his spear against eight H whom he slew at
23:18 his spear against three H men and slew them,
24:3 to the people a H times as many as
24:9 Israel there were eight H thousand valiant men who
24:9 of Judah were five H thousand.
1Kgs 4:23 pasture-fed cattle, a H sheep, besides harts, gazelles,
5:16 Solomon's three thousand three H chief officers who
6:1 In the four H and eightieth year after the
7:2 its length was a H cubits, and its breadth
7:20 network; there were two H pomegranates, in two
7:42 pillars; and the four H pomegranates for the two
8:63 thousand oxen and a H and twenty thousand sheep.
9:14 to the king one H and twenty talents of
9:23 over Solomon's work: five H and fifty, who had
9:28 the amount of four H and twenty talents; and
10:10 gave the king a H and twenty talents of
10:14 one year was six H and sixty-six talents of
10:16 King Solomon made two H large shields of beaten
10:16 of beaten gold; six H shekels of gold went
10:17 And he made three H shields of beaten gold;
10:26 horsemen; he had fourteen H chariots and twelve
10:29 from Egypt for six H shekels of silver, and
10:29 a horse for a H and fifty; and so
11:3 He had seven H wives, princesses, and three hundred
11:3 wives, princesses, and three H concubines; and his
12:21 tribe of Benjamin, a H and eighty thousand chosen
18:4 LORD, Obadiah took a H prophets and hid them
18:13 how I hid a H men of the LORD's
18:19 Carmel, and the four H and fifty prophets of
18:19 Baal and the four H prophets of Asherah, who
18:22 Baal's prophets are four H and fifty men.
20:15 and they were two H and thirty-two; and after
20:29 of the Syrians a H thousand foot soldiers in
22:6 prophets together, about four H men, and said to
2Kgs 3:4 king of Israel a H thousand lambs, and the
3:4 the wool of a H thousand rams.
3:26 took with him seven H swordsmen to break through,
4:43 set this before a H men?" So he repeated,
14:13 of Jerusalem for four H cubits, from the Ephraim
18:14 king of Judah three H talents of silver and
19:35 forth, and slew a H and eighty-five thousand in
23:33 a tribute of a H talents of silver and
1Chr 4:42 some of them, five H men of the Simeonites,
5:18 war, forty-four thousand seven H and sixty, ready for
5:21 of their camels, two H and fifty thousand sheep,
5:21 thousand asses, and a H thousand men alive.
7:2 the days of David being twenty-two thousand six H
7:9 houses, mighty warriors, was twenty thousand two H
7:11 seventeen thousand and two H, ready for service in
8:40 sons and grandsons, one H and fifty.
9:6 and their kinsmen, six H and ninety.
9:9 to their generations, nine H and fifty-six.
9:13 houses, one thousand seven H and sixty, very able
9:22 the thresholds, were two H and twelve.
11:11 his spear against three H whom he slew at
11:20 his spear against three H men and slew them,
12:14 the lesser over a H and the greater over
12:24 were six thousand eight H armed troops.
12:25 men of valor for war, seven thousand one H
12:26 Of the Levites four thousand six H
12:27 of Aaron, and with him three thousand seven H
12:30 Ephraimites twenty thousand eight H, mighty men of
12:32 ought to do, two H chiefs, and all their
12:35 Danites twenty-eight thousand six H men equipped
12:37 beyond the Jordan, one H and twenty thousand men
15:5 the chief, with a H and twenty of his
15:6 the chief, with two H and twenty of his
15:7 the chief, with a H and thirty of his
15:8 the chief, with two H of his brethren;
15:10 the chief, with a H and twelve of his
18:4 left enough for a H chariots.
21:3 to his people a H times as many as
21:5 were one million one H thousand men who drew
21:5 and in Judah four H and seventy thousand who
21:25 David paid Ornan six H shekels of gold by
22:14 of the LORD a H thousand talents of gold,
25:7 were skilful, was two H and eighty-eight.
26:30 brethren, one thousand seven H men of ability, had
26:32 brethren, two thousand seven H men of ability, heads
29:7 of bronze, and a H thousand talents of iron.
2Chr 1:14 horsemen; he had fourteen H chariots and twelve
1:17 from Egypt for six H shekels of silver, and
1:17 a horse for a H and fifty; likewise through
2:2 and three thousand six H to oversee them.
2:17 there were found a H and fifty-three thousand six
2:17 were found a hundred and fifty-three thousand six H
2:18 and three thousand six H as overseers to make
3:4 its height was a H and twenty cubits.
3:8 overlaid it with six H talents of fine gold.
3:16 and he made a H pomegranates, and put them
4:8 And he made a H basins of gold.
4:13 pillars; and the four H pomegranates for the two
5:12 the altar with a H and twenty priests who
7:5 thousand oxen and a H and twenty thousand sheep.
8:10 of King Solomon, two H and fifty, who exercised
8:18 fetched from there four H and fifty talents of
9:9 gave the king a H and twenty talents of
9:13 one year was six H and sixty-six talents of
9:15 King Solomon made two H large shields of beaten
9:15 of beaten gold; six H shekels of beaten gold
9:16 And he made three H shields of beaten gold;
9:16 of beaten gold; three H shekels of gold went
11:1 and Benjamin, a H and eighty thousand chosen
12:3 against Jerusalem with twelve H chariots and sixty
13:3 men of war, four H thousand picked men; and
13:3 him with eight H thousand picked mighty warriors.
13:17 slain of Israel five H thousand picked men.
14:8 an army of three H thousand from Judah, armed
14:8 and spears, and two H and eighty thousand men
14:9 million men and three H chariots, and came as
15:11 they had brought, seven H oxen and seven thousand
17:11 him seven thousand seven H rams and seven
17:11 and seven thousand seven H he-goats.
17:14 the commander, with three H thousand mighty men
17:15 the commander, with two H and eighty thousand,
17:16 the LORD, with two H thousand mighty men of
17:17 of valor, with two H thousand men armed with
17:18 him Jehozabad with a H and eighty thousand armed
18:5 the prophets together, four H men, and said to
24:15 died; he was a H and thirty years old
25:5 that they were three H thousand picked men, fit
25:6 He hired also a H thousand mighty men of
25:6 from Israel for a H talents of silver.
25:9 we do about the H talents which I have
25:23 of Jerusalem for four H cubits, from the Ephraim
26:12 mighty men of valor was two thousand six H
26:13 an army of three H and seven thousand five
26:13 and seven thousand five H, who could make war
27:5 him that year a H talents of silver, and
28:6 of Remaliah slew a H and twenty thousand in
28:8 Israel took captive two H thousand of their kinsfolk,
29:32 was seventy bulls, a H rams, and two hundred
29:32 hundred rams, and two H lambs; all these were
29:33 consecrated offerings were six H bulls and three
35:8 offerings two thousand six H lambs and kids and
35:8 and kids and three H bulls.
35:9 and kids and five H bulls.
36:3 a tribute of a H talents of silver and
Ezra 1:10 gold, two thousand four H and ten bowls of
1:11 were five thousand four H and sixty-nine.
2:3 Parosh, two thousand one H and seventy-two.
2:4 sons of Shephatiah, three H and seventy-two.
2:5 sons of Arah, seven H and seventy-five.
2:6 Joab, two thousand eight H and twelve.
2:7 Elam, one thousand two H and fifty-four.
2:8 sons of Zattu, nine H and forty-five.

HUNDRED

2:9 sons of Zaccai, seven H and sixty.
2:10 sons of Bani, six H and forty-two.
2:11 sons of Bebai, six H and twenty-three.
2:12 Azgad, one thousand two H and twenty-two.
2:13 sons of Adonikam, six H and sixty-six.
2:15 sons of Adin, four H and fifty-four.
2:17 sons of Bezai, three H and twenty-three.
2:18 sons of Jorah, one H and twelve.
2:19 sons of Hashum, two H and twenty-three.
2:21 sons of Bethlehem, one H and twenty-three.
2:23 men of Anathoth, one H and twenty-eight.
2:25 Chephirah, and Be-eroth, seven H and forty-three.
2:26 Ramah and Geba, six H and twenty-one.
2:27 men of Michmas, one H and twenty-two.
2:28 Bethel and Ai, two H and twenty-three.
2:30 sons of Magbish, one H and fifty-six.
2:31 Elam, one thousand two H and fifty-four.
2:32 sons of Harim, three H and twenty.
2:33 Hadid, and Ono, seven H and twenty-five.
2:34 sons of Jericho, three H and forty-five.
2:35 Senaah, three thousand six H and thirty.
2:36 house of Jeshua, nine H and seventy-three.
2:38 Pashhur, one thousand two H and forty-seven.
2:41 sons of Asaph, one H and twenty-eight.
2:42 Shobai, in all one H and thirty-nine.
2:58 Solomon's servants were three H and ninety-two.
2:60 sons of Nekoda, six H and fifty-two.
2:64 was forty-two thousand three H and sixty,
2:65 were seven thousand three H and thirty-seven; and
2:65 and they had two H male and female singers.
2:66 Their horses were seven H and thirty-six, their mules
2:66 their mules were two H and forty-five,
2:67 their camels were four H and thirty-five, and their
2:67 were six thousand seven H and twenty.
2:69 of silver, and one H priests' garments.
6:17 house of God one H bulls, two hundred rams,
6:17 one hundred bulls, two H rams, four hundred lambs,
6:17 two hundred rams, four H lambs, and as a
7:22 diligence, up to a H talents of silver, a
7:22 talents of silver, a H cors of wheat, a
7:22 cors of wheat, a H baths of wine, a
7:22 baths of wine, a H baths of oil, and
8:3 whom were registered one H and fifty men.
8:4 and with him two H men.
8:5 and with him three H men.
8:9 and with him two H and eighteen men.
8:10 and with him a H and sixty men.
8:12 and with him a H and ten men.
8:20 sons, twenty; besides two H and twenty of the
8:26 into their hand six H and fifty talents of
8:26 silver vessels worth a H talents, and a hundred
8:26 hundred talents, and a H talents of gold,
Neh 3:1 the Tower of the H, as far as the
5:17 at my table a H and fifty men, Jews
7:8 Parosh, two thousand a H and seventy-two.
7:9 sons of Shephatiah, three H and seventy-two.
7:10 sons of Arah, six H and fifty-two.
7:11 Joab, two thousand eight H and eighteen.
7:12 Elam, a thousand two H and fifty-four.
7:13 sons of Zattu, eight H and forty-five.
7:14 sons of Zaccai, seven H and sixty.
7:15 sons of Binnui, six H and forty-eight.
7:16 sons of Bebai, six H and twenty-eight.
7:17 Azgad, two thousand three H and twenty-two.
7:18 sons of Adonikam, six H and sixty-seven.
7:20 sons of Adin, six H and fifty-five.
7:22 sons of Hashum, three H and twenty-eight.
7:23 sons of Bezai, three H and twenty-four.
7:24 sons of Hariph, a H and twelve.
7:26 Bethlehem and Netophah, a H and eighty-eight.
7:27 men of Anathoth, a H and twenty-eight.
7:29 Chephirah, and Be-eroth, seven H and forty-three.
7:30 Ramah and Geba, six H and twenty-one.
7:31 men of Michmas, a H and twenty-two.
7:32 Bethel and Ai, a H and twenty-three.
7:34 Elam, a thousand two H and fifty-four.
7:35 sons of Harim, three H and twenty.
7:36 sons of Jericho, three H and forty-five.
7:37 Hadid, and Ono, seven H and twenty-one.
7:38 Senaah, three thousand nine H and thirty.
7:39 house of Jeshua, nine H and seventy-three.
7:41 Pashhur, a thousand two H and forty-seven.
7:44 sons of Asaph, a H and forty-eight.
7:45 sons of Shobai, a H and thirty-eight.
7:60 Solomon's servants were three H and ninety-two.
7:62 sons of Nekoda, six H and forty-two.
7:66 was forty-two thousand three H and sixty,
7:67 were seven thousand three H and thirty-seven; and
7:67 and they had two H and forty-five singers, male
7:68 Their horses were seven H and thirty-six, their mules
7:68 thirty-six, their mules two H and forty-five,
7:69 forty-five, their camels four H and thirty-five, and
7:69 asses six thousand seven H and twenty.
7:70 gold, fifty basins, five H and thirty priests' garments.
7:71 and two thousand two H minas of silver.
11:6 Jerusalem were four H and sixty-eight valiant men.
11:8 him Gabbai, Sallai, nine H and twenty-eight.
11:12 of the house, eight H and twenty-two; and Adaiah
11:13 fathers' houses, two H and forty-two; and Amashsai,
11:14 men of valor, a H and twenty-eight; their overseer
11:18 holy city were two H and eighty-four.
11:19 the gates, were a H and seventy-two.
12:39 the Tower of the H, to the Sheep Gate;
Tob 14:11 He was a H and fifty-eight years old; and
14:14 the age of a H and twenty-seven years.
Jud 1:3 he built towers a H cubits high and sixty
1:16 and feasted for one H and twenty days.
2:5 the number of one H and twenty thousand foot
2:15 him to do, one H and twenty thousand of
7:2 of war was one H and seventy thousand infantry
10:17 from their number a H men to accompany her
16:23 until she was one H and five years old.
Esth 1:1 to Ethiopia over one H and twenty-seven provinces,
1:4 for many days, a H and eighty days.
8:9 India to Ethiopia, a H and twenty-seven provinces, to
9:6 slew and destroyed five H men,
9:12 Jews have slain five H men and also the
9:15 and they slew three H men in Susa; but
9:30 the Jews, to the H and twenty-seven provinces of
13:1 the rulers of the H and twenty-seven provinces from
16:1 India to Ethiopia, one H and twenty-seven satrapies,
Job 1:3 three thousand camels, five H yoke of oxen, and
1:3 of oxen, and five H she-asses, and very many
42:16 this Job lived a H and forty years, and
Prov 17:10 of understanding than a H blows into a fool.
Eccl 6:3 a man begets a H children, and lives many
8:12 sinner does evil a H times and prolongs his
Song 8:12 thousand, and the keepers of the fruit two H
Sir 16:10 nor for the six H thousand men on foot,
18:8 if he reaches a H years.
41:4 for ten or a H or a thousand years,
46:8 preserved out of six H thousand people on foot,
Is 37:36 forth, and slew a H and eighty-five thousand in
65:20 child shall die a H years old, and the
65:20 and the sinner a H years old shall be
Jer 52:23 the pomegranates were a H upon the network round
52:29 captive from Jerusalem eight H and thirty-two
52:30 of the Jews seven H and forty-five persons; all
52:30 all the persons were four thousand and six H
Ezek 4:5 number of days, three H and ninety days, equal
4:9 upon your side, three H and ninety days, you
40:19 the inner court, a H cubits.
40:23 gate to gate, a H cubits.
40:27 toward the south, a H cubits.
40:47 measured the court, a H cubits long, and a
40:47 cubits long, and a H cubits broad, foursquare; and
41:13 measured the temple, a H cubits long; and the
41:13 with its walls, a H cubits long;
41:14 and the yard, a H cubits.
41:15 on either side, a H cubits.
42:2 north side was a H cubits, and the breadth
42:4 cubits wide and a H cubits long, and their
42:8 the temple were a H cubits long.
42:16 the measuring reed, five H cubits by the measuring
42:17 the north side, five H cubits by the measuring
42:18 the south side, five H cubits by the measuring
42:19 side and measured, five H cubits by the measuring
42:20 wall around it, five H cubits long and five
42:20 cubits long and five H cubits broad, to make
45:2 square plot of five H by five hundred cubits
45:2 five hundred by five H cubits shall be for
45:15 every flock of two H, from the families of
48:16 side four thousand five H cubits, the south side
48:16 side four thousand five H, the east side four
48:16 side four thousand five H, and the west side
48:16 and the west side four thousand and five H
48:17 on the north two H and fifty cubits, on
48:17 on the south two H and fifty, on the
48:17 on the east two H and fifty, and on
48:17 on the west two H and fifty.
48:30 be four thousand five H cubits by measure,
48:32 be four thousand five H cubits, three gates, the

	48:33	be four thousand five H cubits by measure, three
	48:34	be four thousand five H cubits, three gates, the
Dan	6:1	over the kingdom a H and twenty satraps, to
	8:14	two thousand and three H evenings and mornings;
	12:11	be a thousand two H and ninety days.
	12:12	to the thousand three H and thirty-five days.
Amos	5:3	thousand shall have a H left, and that which
	5:3	which went forth a H shall have ten left
Jon	4:11	are more than a H and twenty thousand persons
1Mac	1:10	reign in the one H and thirty-seventh year of
	1:20	returned in the one H and forty-third year.
	1:54	Chislev, in the one H and forty-fifth year, they
	2:70	died in the one H and forty-sixth year and
	3:24	to the plain; eight H of them fell, and
	3:37	capital in the one H and forty-seventh year.
	4:52	Chislev, in the one H and forty-eighth year,
	6:16	there in the one H and forty-ninth year.
	6:20	citadel in the one H and fiftieth year; and
	6:30	his forces was a H thousand foot soldiers, twenty
	6:35	their heads; and five H picked horsemen were
	6:42	the battle, and six H men of the king's
	7:1	In the one H and fifty-first year Demetrius the
	7:32	About five H men of the army of Nicanor
	7:41	and struck down one H and eighty-five thousand of
	8:6	against them with a H and twenty elephants and
	8:15	and every day three H and twenty senators
	9:3	month of the one H and fifty-second year they
	9:6	no more than eight H of them were left.
	9:54	In the one H and fifty-third year, in the
	10:1	In the one H and sixtieth year Alexander Epiphanes,
	10:21	month of the one H and sixtieth year, at
	10:57	Ptolemais in the one H and sixty-second year.
	10:67	In the one H and sixty-fifth year Demetrius the
	11:19	king in the one H and sixty-seventh year.
	11:28	and promised him three H talents.
	11:45	the number of a H and twenty thousand, and
	11:47	as many as a H thousand men.
	13:16	Send now a H talents of silver and two
	13:19	the sons and the H talents, but Trypho broke
	13:41	In the one H and seventieth year the yoke
	13:51	month, in the one H and seventy-first year, the
	14:1	In the one H and seventy-second year Demetrius the
	14:27	Elul, in the one H and seventy-second year, which
	15:10	In the one H and seventy-fourth year Antiochus set
	15:13	with him were a H and twenty thousand warriors
	15:31	me for them five H talents of silver, and
	15:31	of the cities, five H talents more.
	15:35	will give you a H talents." Athenobius did not
	16:14	sons, in the one H and seventy-seventh year, in
2Mac	1:7	Demetrius, in the one H and sixty-ninth year, we
	1:9	Chislev, in the one H and eighty-eighth year.
	3:11	totaled in all four H talents of silver and
	3:11	of silver and two H of gold.
	4:8	at an interview three H and sixty talents of
	4:9	promised to pay one H and fifty more if
	4:19	Jerusalem, to carry three H silver drachmas for the
	4:24	outbidding Jason by three H talents of silver.
	5:21	Antiochus carried off eighteen H talents from the
	8:19	when one H and eighty-five thousand perished,
	8:20	from heaven, destroyed one H and twenty thousand
	8:22	a division, putting fifteen H men under each.
	10:31	Twenty thousand five H were slaughtered, besides
	10:31	were slaughtered, besides six H horsemen.
	11:11	of them and sixteen H horsemen, and forced all
	11:21	The one H and forty-eighth year, Dioscorinthius
	11:33	The one H and forty-eighth year, Xanthicus
	11:38	The one H and forty-eighth year, Xanthicus
	12:4	sea and drowned them, not less than two H
	12:10	thousand Arabs with five H horsemen attacked them.
	12:20	had with him a H and twenty thousand infantry
	12:20	and two thousand five H cavalry.
	12:33	thousand infantry and four H cavalry.
	13:1	In the one H and forty-ninth year word came
	13:2	Greek force of one H and ten thousand infantry,
	13:2	five thousand three H cavalry, twenty-two elephants,
	13:2	twenty-two elephants, and three H chariots armed.
	14:4	in about the one H and fifty-first year, presenting
	14:39	sent more than five H soldiers to arrest him;
	15:22	he slew fully a H and eighty-five thousand in
Mt	18:11	a man has a H sheep, and one of
	18:27	who owed him a H denarii; and seizing him
Mk	6:37	go and buy two H denarii worth of bread,
	14:5	for more than three H denarii, and given to
Lk	7:41	debtors; one owed five H denarii, and the other
	15:4	of you, having a H sheep, if he has
	16:6	master?' He said, 'A H measures of oil.' And
	16:7	owe?' He said, 'A H measures of wheat.' He
Jn	6:7	Philip answered him, "Two H denarii would not buy
	12:5	not sold for three H denarii and given to
	19:39	and aloes, about a H pounds' weight.
	21:8	land, but about a H yards off.
	21:11	of large fish, a H and fifty-three of them;
Acts	1:15	in all about a H and twenty), and said,
	5:36	of men, about four H, joined him; but he
	7:6	and ill-treat them four H years.
	13:19	inheritance, for about four H and fifty years.
	23:23	get ready two H soldiers with seventy horsemen
	23:23	seventy horsemen and two H spearmen to go as
	27:37	were in all two H and seventy-six persons in
Rom	4:19	he was about a H years old, or when
1Cor	15:6	to more than five H brethren at one time,
Gal	3:17	law, which came four H and thirty years afterward,
Rev	7:4	of the sealed, a H and forty-four thousand sealed,
	11:3	for one thousand two H and sixty days, clothed
	12:6	for one thousand two H and sixty days.
	13:18	its number is six H and sixty-six.
	14:1	and with him a H and forty-four thousand who
	14:3	that song except the H and forty-four thousand who
	14:20	for one thousand six H stadia.
	21:17	measured its wall, a H and forty-four cubits by

HUNDRED-WEIGHT

Rev	16:21	hailstones, heavy as a H, dropped on men from

HUNDREDFOLD (8)

Gen	26:12	land, and reaped in the same year a H
Mt	13:8	forth grain, some a H, some sixty, some thirty.
	13:23	in one case a H, in another sixty, and
	19:29	sake, will receive a H, and inherit eternal life.
Mk	4:8	and yielding thirtyfold and sixtyfold and a H
	4:20	and bear fruit, thirtyfold and sixtyfold and a H
	10:30	will not receive a H now in this time,
Lk	8:8	into good soil and grew, and yielded a H

HUNDREDS (21)

Ex	18:21	rulers of thousands, of H, of fifties, and of
	18:25	rulers of thousands, of H, of fifties, and of
Num	31:14	and the commanders of H, who had come from
	31:48	and the captains of H, came near to Moses,
	31:52	the commanders of H, was sixteen thousand seven
	31:54	of thousands and of H, and brought it into
Deut	1:15	of thousands, commanders of H, commanders of
1Sam	22:7	thousands and commanders of H,
	29:2	were passing on by H and by thousands, and
2Sam	18:1	commanders of thousands and commanders of H
	18:4	army marched out by H and by thousands.
1Chr	13:1	of thousands and of H, with every leader.
	26:26	the thousands and the H, and the commanders of
	27:1	commanders of thousands and H, and their officers
	28:1	thousands, the commanders of H, the stewards of all
	29:6	of thousands and of H, and the officers over
2Chr	1:2	of thousands and of H, to the judges, and
	23:1	with the commanders of H, Azariah the son of
	25:5	of thousands and of H for all Judah and
1Mac	3:55	charge of thousands and H and fifties and tens.
Mk	6:40	down in groups, by H and by fifties.

HUNDREDTH (2)

Gen	7:11	In the six H year of Noah's life, in
Neh	5:11	their houses, and the H of money, grain, wine,

HUNG (15)

Josh	10:26	to death, and he H them on five trees.
	10:26	And they H upon the trees until evening;
Jud	13:6	down his sword that H there.
	14:11	it was dawn they H the head of Holofernes
Ps	137:2	the willows there we H up our lyres.
Lam	5:12	Princes are H up by their hands; no respect
Ezek	27:10	men of war; they H the shield and helmet
	27:11	in your towers; they H their shields upon your
1Mac	1:61	circumcised them; and they H the infants from their
	4:51	on the table and H up the curtains.
2Mac	6:10	city, with their babies H at their breasts, then
	15:35	And he H Nicanor's head from the citadel, a
Mk	9:42	a great millstone were H round his neck and
Lk	17:2	if a millstone were H round his neck and
	19:48	for all the people H upon his words.

HUNGER (32)

Ex	16:3	this wilderness to kill this whole assembly with H
Deut	8:3	you and let you H and fed you with
	28:48	send against you, in H and thirst, in nakedness,

32:24 shall be wasted with H, and devoured with burning
1Sam 2:5 but those who were hungry have ceased to H
Neh 9:15 from heaven for their H and bring forth water
Job 30:3 Through want and hard H they gnaw the dry
Ps 34:10 lions suffer want and H; but those who seek
Prov 19:15 deep sleep, and an idle person will suffer H
Sir 16:25 all generations; they neither H nor grow weary, and
18:24 of the time of H; in the days of
24:20 who eat me will H for more, and those
Is 5:13 men are dying of H, and their multitude is
29:8 and awakes with his H not satisfied, or as
49:10 pasture; they shall not H or thirst, neither scorching
Jer 38:9 will die there of H, for there is no
Lam 2:19 children, who faint for H at the head of
4:9 than the victims of H, who pined away, stricken
Ezek 7:19 they cannot satisfy their H or fill their stomachs
34:29 more be consumed with H in the land, and
Hos 9:4 shall be for their H only; it shall not
Mic 6:14 and there shall be H in your inward parts;
Mt 5:6 "Blessed are those who H and thirst for
Lk 6:21 "Blessed are you that H now, for you shall
6:25 you that are full now, for you shall H
15:17 and to spare, but I perish here with H
Jn 6:35 to me shall not H, and he who believes
1Cor 4:11 the present hour we H and thirst, we are
2Cor 6:5 imprisonments, tumults, labors, watching, H;
11:27 a sleepless night, in H and thirst, often without
Phil 4:12 of facing plenty and H, abundance and want.
Rev 7:16 They shall H no more, neither thirst any more;

HUNGER-BITTEN
Job 18:12 His strength is H, and calamity is ready for

HUNGERS
Bar 2:18 and the person that H, will ascribe to thee

HUNGRY (50)
1Sam 2:5 but those who were H have ceased to hunger.
2Sam 17:29 said, "The people are H and weary and thirsty
2Kgs 7:12 know that we are H; therefore they have gone
Tob 1:17 my bread to the H and my clothing to
4:16 your bread to the H, and of your clothing
Job 5:5 His harvest the H eat, and he takes it
22:7 drink, and you have withheld bread from the H
24:10 naked, without clothing; H, they carry the sheaves;
Ps 50:12 "If I were H, I would not tell you;
107:5 city to dwell in; H and thirsty, their soul
107:9 is thirsty, and the H he fills with good
107:36 there he lets the H dwell, and they establish
146:7 for the oppressed; who gives food to the H
Prov 6:30 steals to satisfy his appetite when he is H
10:3 let the righteous go H, but he thwarts the
25:21 If your enemy is H, give him bread to
27:7 to one who is H everything bitter is sweet.
Sir 4:2 the one who is H, nor anger a man
Is 8:21 land, greatly distressed and H; and when they are
8:21 and when they are H, they will be enraged
9:20 right, but are still H, and they devour on
29:8 As when a H man dreams he is eating
32:6 the craving of the H unsatisfied, and to deprive
44:12 strong arm; he becomes H and his strength fails,
58:7 your bread with the H, and bring the homeless
58:10 yourself out for the H and satisfy the desire
65:13 but you shall be H; behold, my servants shall
Jer 42:14 the trumpet, or be H for bread, and we
Ezek 18:7 his bread to the H and covers the naked
18:16 his bread to the H and covers the naked
1Mac 13:49 So they were very H, and many of them
Mt 4:2 days and forty nights, and afterward he was H
12:1 sabbath; his disciples were H, and they began to
12:3 did, when he was H, and those who were
15:32 to send them away H, lest they faint on
21:18 he was returning to the city, he was H
25:35 world; for I was H and you gave me
25:37 did we see thee H and feed thee, or
25:42 angels; for I was H and you gave me
25:44 did we see thee H or thirsty or a
Mk 2:25 in need and was H, he and those who
8:3 I send them away H to their homes, they
11:12 day, when they came from Bethany, he was H
Lk 1:53 he has filled the H with good things, and
4:2 days; and when they were ended, he was H
6:3 did when he was H, he and those who
Acts 10:10 And he became H and desired something to eat;
Rom 12:20 "if your enemy is H, feed him; if he
1Cor 11:21 meal, and one is H and another is drunk.
11:34 if any one is H, let him eat at

HUNT (12)
Gen 27:3 to the field, and H game for me,
27:5 to the field to H for game and bring
1Sam 24:11 against you, though you H my life to take
Job 10:16 myself up, thou dost H me like a lion,
18:2 "How long will you H for words?
38:39 "Can you H the prey for the lion, or
Ps 140:11 the land; let evil H down the violent man
Jer 16:16 hunters, and they shall H them from every mountain
Ezek 13:18 every stature, in the H for souls!
13:18 Will you H down souls belonging to my people,
13:20 bands with which you H the souls, and I
13:20 the souls that you H go free like birds.

HUNTED (5)
Gen 27:33 was it then that H game and brought it
Is 13:14 And like a H gazelle, or like sheep with
Jer 50:17 "Israel is a H sheep driven away by lions.
Lam 3:52 "I have been H like a bird by those
1Mac 2:47 They H down the arrogant men, and the work

HUNTER (5)
Gen 10:9 He was a mighty H before the LORD; therefore
10:9 "Like Nimrod a mighty H before the LORD."
25:27 Esau was a skilful H, a man of the
Prov 6:5 a gazelle from the H, like a bird from
Sir 14:22 Pursue wisdom like a H, and lie in wait

HUNTERS
Jer 16:16 will send for many H, and they shall hunt

HUNTING (3)
Gen 27:30 father, Esau his brother came in from his H
Lev 17:13 them, who takes in H any beast or bird
Jud 1:15 struck him down with H spears; and he utterly

HUNTS (2)
1Sam 26:20 life, like one who H a partridge in the
Mic 7:2 for blood, and each H his brother with a

HUPHAM
Num 26:39 of the Shuphamites; of H, the family of the

HUPHAMITES
Num 26:39 the Shuphamites; of Hupham, the family of the H

HUPPAH
1Chr 24:13 the thirteenth to H, the fourteenth to Jeshebe-ab,

HUPPIM (3)
Gen 46:21 Naaman, Ehi, Rosh, Muppim, H, and Ard
1Chr 7:12 And Shuppim and H were the sons of Ir,
7:15 took a wife for H and for Shuppim.

HUR (15)
Ex 17:10 and Moses, Aaron, and H went up to the
17:12 it, and Aaron and H held up his hands,
24:14 and, behold, Aaron and H are with you; whoever
31:2 of Uri, son of H, of the tribe of
35:30 of Uri, son of H, of the tribe of
38:22 of Uri, son of H, of the tribe of
Num 31:8 slain, Evi, Rekem, Zur, H, and Reba, the five
Josh 13:21 Rekem and Zur and H and Reba, the princes
1Chr 2:19 died, Caleb married Ephrath, who bore him H
2:20 H was the father of Uri, and Uri was
2:50 The sons of H the first-born of Ephrathah: Shobal
4:1 Judah: Perez, Hezron, Carmi, H, and Shobal.
4:4 were the sons of H, the first-born of Ephrathah,
2Chr 1:5 of Uri, son of H, had made, was there
Neh 3:9 Rephaiah the son of H, ruler of half the

HURAI
1Chr 11:32 Benjaminites, Benaiah of Pirathon, H of the brooks

HURAM (10)
1Chr 8:5 Abishua, Naaman, Ahoah, Gera, Shephuphan, and H
2Chr 2:3 Solomon sent word to H the king of Tyre:
2:11 Then H the king of Tyre answered in a
2:12 H also said, "Blessed be the LORD God of
4:11 H also made the pots, the shovels, and the
4:11 So H finished the work that he did for
8:2 rebuilt the cities which H had given to him,
8:18 And H sent him by his servants ships and
9:10 Moreover the servants of H and the servants of

9:21 with the servants of H; once every three years

HURAM-ABI (2)

2Chr 2:13 man, endued with understanding, H,
4:16 the equipment for these H made of burnished bronze

HURI

1Chr 5:14 Abihail the son of H, son of Jaroah, son

HURL (5)

Is 22:17 Behold, the LORD will H you away violently, O
Jer 16:13 me; therefore I will H you out of this
22:26 I will H you and the mother who bore
Zech 9:4 of her possessions and H her wealth into the
1Mac 2:36 not answer them or H a stone at them

HURLED (12)

Num 35:20 him from hatred, or H at him, lying in
35:22 suddenly without enmity, or H anything on him
Wis 5:22 of wrath will be H as from a catapult;
17:19 harsh crash of rocks H down, or the unseen
18:18 here and another there, H down half dead, made
Sir 46:6 He H down war upon that nation, and at
Jer 22:28 he and his children H and cast into a
Jon 1:4 But the LORD H a great wind upon the
2Mac 6:10 at their breasts, then H them down headlong from
10:34 place, blasphemed terribly and H out wicked words.
11:11 They H themselves like lions against the enemy, and
14:46 with both hands and H them at the crowd,

HURLING

2Mac 5:3 shields, massing of spears, H of missiles, the flash

HURLS

Job 27:22 It H at him without pity; he flees from

HURRICANE

Ps 83:15 with thy tempest and terrify them with thy H

HURRIED (5)

Deut 16:3 land of Egypt in H flight—that all the
Jud 13:12 heard her voice, they H down to the city
Esth 6:12 But Haman H to his house, mourning and with
2Mac 3:18 People also H out of their houses in crowds
5:21 from the temple, and H away to Antioch, thinking

HURRY

1Sam 20:38 called after the lad, H, make haste, stay not."

HURRYING

Jud 10:15 saved your life by H down to the presence

HURT (40)

Ex 21:22 men strive together, and H a woman with child,
21:22 follows, the one who H her shall be fined,
22:10 it dies or is H or is driven away,
22:14 neighbor, and it is H or dies, the owner
1Sam 24:9 of men who say, 'Behold, David seeks your H
1Chr 4:10 that it might not H me!" And God granted
Ezra 4:22 damage grow to the H of the king?"
Jud 11:1 for I have never H any one who chose
11:4 No one will H you, but all will treat
Esth 9:2 to lay hands on such as sought their H
Ps 15:4 swears to his own H and does not change;
38:12 those who seek my H speak of ruin, and
40:14 back and brought to dishonor who desire my H
70:2 back and brought to dishonor who desire my H
71:13 disgrace may they be covered who seek my H
71:24 shame and disgraced who sought to do me H
105:18 His feet were H with fetters, his neck was
Prov 23:35 "but I was not H; they beat me, but
Eccl 5:13 their owner to his H,
8:9 while man lords it over man to his H
10:9 who quarries stones is H by them; and he
Sir 9:1 teach her an evil lesson to your own H
26:10 she finds liberty, she use it to her H
Is 11:9 They shall not H or destroy in all my
30:26 LORD binds up the H of his people, and
65:25 They shall not H or destroy in all my
Jer 7:6 gods to your own H,
10:19 Woe is me because of my H
30:12 says the LORD: Your H is incurable, and your
30:15 Why do you cry out over your H
Ezek 28:24 or a thorn to H them among all their
Dan 3:50 them at all or H or trouble them.
3:93 and they are not H; and the appearance of
6:22 and they have not H me, because I was
6:23 and no kind of H was found upon him,
Nah 3:19 is no assuaging your H, your wound is grievous.
Zech 12:3 lift it shall grievously H themselves.
Mk 16:18 thing, it will not H them; they will lay
Lk 10:19 enemy; and nothing shall H you.
Rev 2:11 conquers shall not be H by the second death.'

HURTFUL (2)

Ezra 4:15 is a rebellious city, H to kings and provinces,
1Tim 6:9 into many senseless and H desires that plunge men

HURTING (2)

1Sam 25:34 has restrained me from H you, unless you had
Rev 9:10 and their power of H men for five months

HURTS (3)

Ex 21:35 "When one man's ox H anothers, so that it
Prov 11:17 but a cruel man H himself.
Acts 26:14 It H you to kick against the goads.'

HUSBAND (153)

Gen 3:6 gave some to her H, and he ate.
3:16 shall be for your H, and he shall rule
16:3 her to Abram her H as a wife.
18:12 grown old, and my H is old, shall I
29:32 affliction; surely now my H will love me."
29:34 "Now this time my H will be joined to
30:15 small matter that you have taken away my H
30:18 my maid to my H; so she called his
30:20 good dowry; now my H will honor me, because
Ex 21:22 according as the woman's H shall lay upon him;
Lev 21:3 she has had no H; for her he may
21:4 defile himself as a H among his people and
21:7 woman divorced from her H; for the priest is
Num 5:13 the eyes of her H, and she is undetected
5:19 you were under your H's authority, be free from
5:20 you are under your H's authority, and if you
5:20 man other than your H has lain with you,
5:27 acted unfaithfully against her H, the water that
5:29 wife, though under her H's authority, goes astray and
30:6 is married to a H, while under her vows
30:7 bound herself, and her H hears of it, and
30:8 the day that her H comes to hear of
30:10 she vowed in her H's house, or bound herself
30:11 an oath, and her H heard of it, and
30:12 But if her H makes them null and void
30:12 shall not stand: her H has made them void,
30:13 to afflict herself, her H may establish, or her
30:13 may establish, or her H may make void.
30:14 But if her H says nothing to her from
Deut 21:13 her, and be her H, and she shall be
24:3 wife, and the latter H dislikes her and writes
24:3 or if the latter H dies, who took her
24:4 wife, then her former H, who sent her away,
25:5 to a stranger; her H's brother shall go in
25:5 the duty of a H's brother to her.
25:7 elders, and say, 'My H's brother refuses to perpetuate
25:7 the duty of a H's brother to me.'
25:11 near to rescue her H from the hand of
28:56 will grudge to the H of her bosom, to
Judg 13:6 came and told her H, "A man of God
13:9 field; but Manoah her H was not with her.
13:10 haste and told her H, "Behold, the man who
14:15 Samson's wife, "Entice your H to tell us what
19:3 Then her H arose and went after her, to
20:4 And the Levite, the H of the woman who
Ruth 1:3 But Elimelech, the H of Naomi, died, and she
1:5 was bereft of her two sons and her H
1:9 each of you in the house of her H
1:12 for I am too old to have a H
1:12 I should have a H this night and should
2:11 the death of your H has been fully told
1Sam 1:8 And Elkanah, her H, said to her, "Hannah, why
1:22 she said to her H, "As soon as the
1:23 Elkanah her H said to her, "Do what seems
2:19 went up with her H to offer the yearly
4:19 her father-in-law and her H were dead, she bowed
4:21 captured and because of her father-in-law and her H
25:19 did not tell her H Nabal.
2Sam 3:15 took her from her H Paltiel the son of
3:16 But her H went with her, weeping after her
11:26 heard that Uriah her H was dead, she made
11:26 husband was dead, she made lamentation for her H
14:5 am a widow; my H is dead.
14:7 and leave to my H neither name nor remnant

17:3 you as a bride comes home to her H
2Kgs 4:1 Elisha, "Your servant my H is dead; and you
4:9 she said to her H, "Behold now, I perceive
4:14 no son, and her H is old."
4:22 she called to her H, and said, "Send me
4:26 Is it well with your H
Jud 8:2 Her H Manasseh, who belonged to her tribe and
8:7 lovely face; and her H Manasseh had left her
10:3 to wear while her H Manasseh was living.
16:22 life after Manasseh her H died and was gathered
16:23 grew old in her H's house, until she was
16:23 the cave of her H Manasseh,
16:24 of kin to her H Manasseh, and to her
Prov 7:19 For my H is not at home; he has
12:4 the crown of her H, but she who brings
30:23 when she gets a H, and a maid when
31:11 The heart of her H trusts in her, and
31:23 Her H is known in the gates, when he
31:28 call her blessed; her H also, and he praises
Sir 4:10 and instead of a H to their mother; you
22:4 sensible daughter obtains her H, but one who acts
22:5 daughter disgraces father and H, and will be
23:22 woman who leaves her H and provides an heir
23:23 an offense against her H; and third, she has
25:1 a wife and a H who live in harmony.
25:17 Her H takes his meals among the neighbors, and
25:19 such is a garrulous wife for a quiet H
25:21 and great disgrace when a wife supports her H
25:22 does not make her H happy.
26:1 Happy is the H of a good wife; the
26:2 loyal wife rejoices her H, and he will complete
26:13 wife's charm delights her H, and her skill puts
36:23 mark her speech, her H is not like other
40:23 a wife with her H is better than both.
42:10 house; or having a H, lest she prove unfaithful,
Is 54:5 your Maker is your H, the LORD of hosts
Jer 3:20 faithless wife leaves her H, so have you been
6:11 young men, also; both H and wife shall be
31:32 though I was their H, says the LORD.
Ezek 16:32 wife, who receives strangers instead of her H
16:45 mother, who loathed her H and her children; and
Dan 13:7 would go into her H's garden to walk.
13:28 the house of her H Joakim, the two elders
13:63 so did Joakim her H and all her kindred,
Hos 2:2 I am not her H --that she put away
2:7 return to my first H, for it was better
2:16 will call me, 'My H and no longer will
Mt 1:16 father of Joseph the H of Mary, of whom
1:19 Holy Spirit; and her H Joseph, being a just
Mk 10:12 if she divorces her H and marries another, she
Lk 1:34 "How shall this be, since I have no H
2:36 having lived with her H seven years from her
16:18 woman divorced from her H commits adultery.
Jn 4:16 her, "Go, call your H, and come here."
4:17 The woman answered him, "I have no H
4:17 saying, 'I have no H;
4:18 have is not your H; this you said truly."
Acts 5:9 that have buried your H are at the door,
5:10 carried her out and buried her beside her H
Rom 7:2 by law to her H as long as he lives; but if her H dies
7:2 she is discharged from the law concerning the H
7:3 man while her H is alive. But if her H dies she is free
7:3 But if her H dies she is free from
1Cor 7:2 his own wife and each woman her own H
7:3 The H should give to his wife her conjugal
7:3 conjugal rights, and likewise the wife to her H
7:4 body, but the H does; likewise the H does not rule
7:10 not separate from her H
7:11 be reconciled to her H --and that the H should not
7:13 any woman has a H who is an unbeliever,
7:14 the unbelieving H is consecrated through his wife,
7:14 the unbelieving wife is consecrated through her H
7:16 do you know whether you will save your H
7:16 H, how do you know whether you will save
7:34 anxious about worldly affairs, how to please her H
7:39 is bound to her H as long as he
7:39 If the H dies, she is free to be
11:3 a woman is her H, and the head of
2Cor 11:2 you as a pure bride to her one H
Eph 5:23 For the H is the head of the wife
5:33 let the wife see that she respects her H
1Tim 3:2 be above reproach, the H of one wife, temperate,
3:12 Let deacons be the H of one wife, and
5:9 the wife of one H;
Tit 1:5 man is blameless, the H of one wife, and
Rev 21:2 bride adorned for her H;

HUSBANDS (25)
Ruth 1:11 in my womb that they may become your H
2:1 a kinsman of her H, a man of wealth,
Tob 3:8 been given to seven H, and the evil demon
3:8 "Do you not know that you strangle your H
3:15 Already seven H of mine are dead.
6:13 been given to seven H and that each died
7:11 my daughter to seven H, and when each came
Esth 1:17 with contempt upon their H, since they will say,
1:20 give honor to their H, high and low."
Jer 44:19 was it without our H approval that we made
Ezek 16:45 sisters, who loathed their H and their children.
Amos 4:1 who say to their H, 'Bring, that we may
Jn 4:18 you have had five H, and he whom you
1Cor 14:35 let them ask their H at home.
Eph 5:22 be subject to your H, as to the Lord.
5:24 wives also be subject in everything to their H
5:25 H, love your wives, as Christ loved the church
5:28 Even so H should love their wives as their
Col 3:18 be subject to your H, as is fitting in
3:19 H, love your wives, and do not be harsh
Tit 2:4 women to love their H and children,
2:5 and submissive to their H, that the word of
1Pet 3:1 be submissive to your H, so that some, though
3:5 were submissive to their H,
3:7 you H, live considerately with your wives, bestowing

HUSH (2)
Amos 6:10 he shall say, "No"; and he shall say, H
Acts 21:40 there was a great H, he spoke to them

HUSHAH
1Chr 4:4 father of Gedor, and Ezer the father of H

HUSHAI (14)
2Sam 15:32 God was worshiped, behold, H the Archite came to
15:37 So H, David's friend, came into the city, just
16:16 And when H the Archite, David's friend, came to
16:16 friend, came to Absalom, H said to Absalom, "Long
16:17 And Absalom said to H, "Is this your loyalty
16:18 And H said to Absalom, "No; for whom the
17:5 Then Absalom said, "Call H the Archite also, and
17:6 And when H came to Absalom, Absalom said to
17:7 Then H said to Absalom, "This time the counsel
17:8 H said moreover, "You know that your father and
17:14 said, "The counsel of H the Archite is better
17:15 Then H said to Zadok and Abiathar the priests,
1Kgs 4:16 Baana the son of H, in Asher and Bealoth;
1Chr 27:33 the king's counselor, and H the Archite was the

HUSHAM (4)
Gen 36:34 Jobab died, and H of the land of the
36:35 H died, and Hadad the son of Bedad, who
1Chr 1:45 When Jobab died, H of the land of the
1:46 When H died, Hadad the son of Bedad, who

HUSHATHITE (5)
2Sam 21:18 Gob; then Sibbecai the H slew Saph, who was
23:27 of Anathoth, Mebunnai the H,
1Chr 11:29 of Anathoth, Sibbecai the H, Ilai the Ahohite,
20:4 Gezer; then Sibbecai the H slew Sippai, who was
27:11 month, was Sibbecai the H, of the Zerahites; in

HUSHED (3)
Job 29:10 of the nobles was H, and their tongue cleaved
Ps 107:29 still, and the waves of the sea were H
Is 16:10 wine in the presses; the vintage shout is H

HUSHIM (4)
Gen 46:23 The sons of Dan: H
1Chr 7:12 the sons of Ir, H the sons of Aher.
8:8 he had sent away H and Baara his wives.
8:11 also had sons by H: Abitub and Elpaal.

HUT
Is 24:20 it sways like a H; its transgression lies heavy

HYDASPES
Jud 1:6 the Tigris and the H and in the plain

HYENA
Sir 13:17 is there between a H and a dog?

HYENAS (3)
Is 13:22 H will cry in its towers, and jackals in
34:14 beasts shall meet with H, the satyr shall cry

Jer 50:39 beasts shall dwell with H in Babylon, and ostriches

HYMENAEUS (2)

1Tim 1:20 their faith, among them H and Alexander, whom I
2Tim 2:17 Among them are H and Philetus,

HYMN (6)

Sir 15:9 A H of praise is not fitting on the
15:10 For a H of praise should be uttered in
39:14 fragrance, and sing a H of praise; bless the
Mt 26:30 they had sung a H, they went out to
Mk 14:26 they had sung a H, they went out to
1Cor 14:26 each one has a H, a lesson, a revelation,

HYMNS (13)

Wis 10:20 the ungodly; they sang H, O Lord, to thy
Dan 3:24 of the flames, singing H to God and blessing
1Mac 4:24 their return they sang H and praises to Heaven,
4:33 all who know thy name praise thee with H
13:47 then entered it with H and praise.
13:51 stringed instruments, and with H and songs, because
2Mac 1:30 Then the priests sang the H
10:7 of palm, they offered H of thanksgiving to him
10:38 these things, with H and thanksgivings they blessed
12:37 the battle cry, with H; then he charged against
Acts 16:25 were praying and singing H to God, and the
Eph 5:19 another in psalms and H and spiritual songs, singing
Col 3:16 and sing psalms and H and spiritual songs with

HYPOCRISY (4)

2Mac 13:3 them and with utter H urged Antiochus on, not
Mt 23:27 you are full of H and iniquity.
Mk 12:15 But knowing their H, he said to them, "Why
Lk 12:1 of the leaven of the Pharisees, which is H

HYPOCRITE (4)

Sir 1:26 Be not a H in men's sight, and keep
32:15 with it, but the H will stumble at it.
Mt 7:5 You H, first take the log out of your
Lk 6:42 You H, first take the log out of your

HYPOCRITES (15)

Mt 6:2 before you, as the H do in the synagogues
6:5 not be like the H; for they love to
6:16 look dismal, like the H, for they disfigure their
15:7 You H
22:18 said, "Why put me to the test, you H
23:13 "But woe to you, scribes and Pharisees, H
23:14 Woe to you, scribes and Pharisees, H
23:22 "Woe to you, scribes and Pharisees, H
23:24 "Woe to you, scribes and Pharisees, H
23:26 "Woe to you, scribes and Pharisees, H
23:28 "Woe to you, scribes and Pharisees, H
24:51 put him with the H; there men will weep
Mk 7:6 Isaiah prophesy of you H, as it is written,
Lk 12:56 You H
13:15 Then the Lord answered him, "You H

HYPOCRITICAL

Sir 33:2 but he who is H about it is like

HYRCANUS

2Mac 3:11 also some money of H, son of Tobias, a

HYSSOP (12)

Ex 12:22 Take a bunch of H and dip it in
Lev 14:4 and scarlet stuff and H;
14:6 scarlet stuff and the H, and dip them and
14:49 and scarlet stuff and H,
14:51 the cedarwood and the H and the scarlet stuff,
14:52 with the cedarwood and H and scarlet stuff;
Num 19:6 shall take cedarwood and H and scarlet stuff, and
19:18 clean person shall take H, and dip it in
1Kgs 4:33 in Lebanon to the H that grows out of
Ps 51:7 Purge me with H, and I shall be clean;
Jn 19:29 of the vinegar on H and held it to
Heb 9:19 and scarlet wool and H, and sprinkled both the

I

ÏAND

2Mac 7:6 faces, when he said, Ï he will have compassion

IBEX

Deut 14:5 the wild goat, the I, the antelope, and the

IBHAR (3)

2Sam 5:15 Shammua, Shobab, Nathan, Solomon, I, Elishu-a,
1Chr 3:6 daughter of Ammiel; then I, Elishama, Eliphelet,
14:5 Shammua, Shobab, Nathan, Solomon, I, Elishu-a,

IBIS

Lev 11:17 owl, the cormorant, the I,

IBLEAM (4)

Josh 17:11 and its villages, and I and its villages, and
Judg 1:27 or the inhabitants of I and its villages, or
2Kgs 9:27 at the ascent of Gur, which is by I
15:10 struck him down at I, and killed him, and

IBNEIAH

1Chr 9:8 Hodaviah, son of Hassenuah, I the son of Jeroham,

IBNIJAH

1Chr 9:8 of Reuel, son of I;

IBRI

1Chr 24:27 of Merari: of Ja-aziah, Beno, Shoham, Zaccur, and I

IBSAM

1Chr 7:2 Rephaiah, Jeri-el, Jahmai, I, and Shemuel, heads of

IBZAN (2)

Judg 12:8 After him I of Bethlehem judged Israel.
12:10 Then I died, and was buried at Bethlehem.

ICE (7)

Job 6:16 which are dark with I, and where the snow
37:10 the breath of God I is given, and the
38:29 whose womb did the I come forth, and who
Ps 147:17 He casts forth his I like morsels; who can
Wis 16:22 Snow and I withstood fire without melting, so that
Sir 43:20 north wind blows, and I freezes over the water;
Dan 3:72 Bless the Lord, I and cold, sing praise to

ICHABOD (2)

1Sam 4:21 she named the child I, saying, "The glory has
14:3 the son of Ahitub, I's brother, son of Phinehas,

ICONIUM (6)

Acts 13:51 from their feet against them, and went to I
14:1 Now at I they entered together into the Jewish
14:19 there from Antioch and I; and having persuaded the
14:21 to Lystra and to I and to Antioch,
16:2 spoken of by the brethren at Lystra and I
2Tim 3:11 me at Antioch, at I, and at Lystra, what

IDALAH

Josh 19:15 Nahalal, Shimron, I, and Bethlehem—twelve cities

IDBASH

1Chr 4:3 Etam: Jezreel, Ishma, and I; and the name of

IDDO (14)

1Kgs 4:14 Ahinadab the son of I, in Mahanaim;
1Chr 6:21 son, Joah his son, I his son, Zerah his
27:21 of Manasseh in Gilead, I the son of Zechariah;
2Chr 9:29 in the visions of I the seer concerning Jeroboam
12:15 the prophet and of I the seer?
13:22 are written in the story of the prophet I
Ezra 5:1 Zechariah the son of I, prophesied to the Jews
6:14 Haggai the prophet and Zechariah the son of I
8:17 and sent them to I, the leading man at
8:17 what to say to I and his brethren the
Neh 12:4 Shecaniah, Rehum, Meremoth, I, Ginnethoi, Abijah,
12:16 of Meraioth, Helkai; of I, Zechariah; of Ginnethon,
Zech 1:1 of Berechiah, son of I, the prophet, saying,
1:7 of Berechiah, son of I, the prophet; and Zechariah

IDEA (3)

Wis 14:12 For the I of making idols was the beginning
Sir 32:18 will not overlook an I, and an insolent and
2Mac 9:4 rage, he conceived the I of turning upon the

IDLE (13)

Ex 5:8 it; for they are I; therefore they cry, 'Let
5:17 he said, "You are I, you are idle; therefore
5:17 are idle, you are I; therefore you say, 'Let
Prov 19:15 deep sleep, and an I person will suffer hunger.

Wis	15:12	considered our existence an I game, and life a
Sir	33:25	rest; leave his hands I, and he will seek
	33:27	he may not be I, for idleness teaches much
Amos	6:5	the stall; who sing I songs to the sound
Mt	20:3	he saw others standing I in the market place;
	20:6	do you stand here I all day?'
Lk	24:11	seemed to them an I tale, and they did
2Thes	3:7	us; we were not I when we were with
2Pet	2:3	condemnation has not been I, and their destruction

IDLENESS (5)

Prov	31:27	household, and does not eat the bread of I
Wis	13:13	with skill gained in I; he forms it like
Sir	33:27	not be idle, for I teaches much evil.
2Thes	3:6	who is living in I and not in accord
	3:11	you are living in I, mere busybodies, not doing

IDLER

Sir	37:11	about kindness, with an I about any work or

IDLERS (3)

1Thes	5:14	brethren, admonish the I, encourage the,
1Tim	5:13	they learn to be I, gadding about from house
	5:13	house, and not only I but gossips and busybodies,

IDLY

Is	58:13	own pleasure, or talking I;

IDOL (17)

2Chr	33:7	the image of the I which he had made
	33:15	foreign gods and the I from the house of
Wis	14:8	But the I made with hands is accursed, and
Sir	30:19	what use to an I is an offering of
Is	40:19	The I
	44:17	into a god, his I; and falls down to
	48:5	you should say, 'My I did them, my graven
	66:3	offering of frankincense, like him who blesses an I
Dan	14:3	the Babylonians had an I called Bel, and every
Hos	10:6	shame, and Israel shall be ashamed of his I
Hab	2:18	What profit is an I when its maker has
1Mac	10:83	the temple of their I, for safety.
Acts	7:41	a sacrifice to the I and rejoiced in the
1Cor	8:4	we know that "an I has no real existence,"
	8:7	really offered to an I; and their conscience, being
	8:10	at table in an I's temple, might he not
	10:19	anything, or that an I is anything?

IDOLATER (2)

1Cor	5:11	greed, or is an I, reviler, drunkard, or robber–
Eph	5:5	covetous (that is, an I, has any inheritance in

IDOLATERS (5)

1Cor	5:10	greedy and robbers, or I, since then you would
	6:9	the immoral, nor I, nor adulterers, nor homosexuals,
	10:7	Do not be I as some of them were;
Rev	21:8	for murderers, fornicators, sorcerers, I, and all liars,
	22:15	fornicators and murderers and I, and every one who

IDOLATROUS (3)

2Kgs	23:5	And he deposed the I priests whom the kings
Hos	10:5	for it, and its I priests shall wail over
Zeph	1:4	the name of the I priests;

IDOLATRY (7)

1Sam	15:23	of divination, and stubbornness is as iniquity and I
Sir	46:11	did not fall into I and who did not
Ezek	23:49	penalty for your sinful I; and you shall know
	43:9	them put away their I and the dead bodies
Gal	5:20	plain: fornication, impurity, licentiousness, I, sorcery,
Col	3:5	passion, evil desire, and covetousness, which is I
1Pet	4:3	passions, drunkenness, revels, carousing, and

IDOLS (132)

Lev	19:4	Do not turn to I or make for yourselves
	26:1	make for yourselves no I and erect no graven
	26:30	dead bodies of your I; and my soul will
Deut	29:17	their detestable things, their I of wood and stone,
	32:21	no god; they have provoked me with their I
1Sam	31:9	good news to their I and to the people.
2Sam	5:21	the Philistines left their I there, and David and
1Kgs	15:12	and removed all the I that his fathers had
	16:13	LORD God of Israel to anger with their I
	16:26	the God of Israel, to anger by their I
	21:26	abominably in going after I, as the Amorites had
2Kgs	17:12	anger, and they served I, of which the LORD
	17:15	They went after false I, and became false, and
	21:11	to sin with his I;
	21:21	walked, and served the I that his father served,
	23:24	the teraphim and the I and all the abominations
1Chr	10:9	good news to their I and to the people.
	16:26	of the peoples are I; but the LORD made
2Chr	15:8	put away the abominable I from all the land
	24:18	their fathers, and served the Asherim and the I
Tob	14:6	Lord God in truth, and will bury their I
Esth	14:8	have covenanted with their I
	14:10	the praise of vain I, and to magnify for
Ps	31:6	pay regard to vain I; but I trust in
	96:5	of the peoples are I; but the LORD made
	97:7	their boast in worthless I; all gods bow down
	106:36	They served their I, which became a snare to
	106:38	they sacrificed to the I of Canaan; and the
	115:4	Their I are silver and gold, the work of
	135:15	The I of the nations are silver and gold,
Wis	14:11	also upon the heathen I, because, though part of
	14:12	the idea of making I was the beginning of
	14:27	For the worship of I not to be named
	14:29	they trust in lifeless I they swear wicked oaths
	14:30	in devoting themselves to I, and because in deceit
	15:15	that all their heathen I were gods, though these
Is	2:8	land is filled with I; they bow down to
	2:18	And the I shall utterly pass away.
	2:20	will cast forth their I of silver and their I of gold
	10:10	the kingdoms of the I whose graven images were
	10:11	to Jerusalem and her I as I have done
	19:1	to Egypt; and the I of Egypt will tremble
	19:3	they will consult the I and the sorcerers, and
	31:7	shall cast away his I of silver and his I of gold
	44:9	All who make I are nothing, and the things
	45:16	confounded, the makers of I go in confusion together.
	45:20	carry about their wooden I, and keep on praying
	46:1	down, Nebo stoops, their I are on beasts and
	57:13	let your collection of I deliver you!
Jer	8:19	with their graven images, and with their foreign I
	10:5	Their I are like scarecrows in a cucumber field,
	10:8	foolish; the instruction of I is but wood!
	10:14	to shame by his I; for his images are
	16:18	carcasses of their detestable I, and have filled my
	50:2	put to shame, her I are dismayed.'
	50:38	land of images, and they are mad over I
	51:17	to shame by his I; for his images are
Bar	6:63	But these I are not to be compared with
	6:73	man who has no I, for he will be
Ezek	6:4	I will cast down your slain before your I
	6:5	of Israel before their I; and I will scatter
	6:6	waste and ruined, your I broken and destroyed, your
	6:9	turn wantonly after their I; and they will be
	6:13	slain lie among their I round about their altars,
	6:13	wherever they offered pleasing odor to all their I
	8:10	beasts, and all the I of the house of
	14:3	men have taken their I into their hearts, and
	14:4	Israel who takes his I into his heart and
	14:4	the multitude of his I,
	14:5	who are all estranged from me through their I
	14:6	turn away from your I; and turn away your
	14:7	from me, taking his I into his heart and
	16:36	because of all your I, and because of the
	18:6	his eyes to the I of the house of
	18:12	his eyes to the I, commits abomination,
	18:15	his eyes to the I of the house of
	20:7	defile yourselves with the I of Egypt; I am
	20:8	did they forsake the I of Egypt.
	20:16	my sabbaths; for their heart went after their I
	20:18	their ordinances, nor defile yourselves with their I
	20:24	and their eyes were set on their fathers' I
	20:31	yourselves with all your I to this day.
	20:39	one of you his I, now and hereafter, if
	20:39	no more profane with your gifts and your I
	22:3	come, and that makes I to defile herself!
	22:4	and defiled by the I which you have made;
	23:7	herself with all the I of every one on
	23:30	with the nations, and polluted yourself with their I
	23:37	hands; with their I they have committed adultery;
	23:39	in sacrifice to their I, on the same day
	30:13	I will destroy the I, and put an end
	33:25	your eyes to your I, and shed blood; shall
	36:18	the land, for the I with which they had
	36:25	and from all your I I will cleanse you.
	37:23	any more with their I and their detestable things,
	44:10	from me after their I when Israel went astray,
	44:12	to them before their I and became a stumbling
Dan	14:5	do not revere man-made I, but the living God,
Hos	4:17	Ephraim is joined to I, let him alone.

8:4 and gold they made I for their own destruction.
11:2 sacrificing to the Baals, and burning incense to I
13:2 for themselves molten images, I skilfully made of
14:8 O Ephraim, what have I to do with I
Jon 2:8 pay regard to vain I forsake their true loyalty.
Mic 1:7 fire, and all her I I will lay waste;
Hab 2:18 in his own creation when he makes dumb I
Zech 13:2 the names of the I from the land, so
1Mac 1:43 they sacrificed to I and profaned the sabbath.
1:47 precincts and shrines for I, to sacrifice swine and
3:48 the Gentiles were consulting the images of their I
13:47 houses in which the I were, and then entered
2Mac 12:40 sacred tokens of the I of Jamnia, which the
Acts 15:20 from the pollutions of I and from unchastity and
15:29 has been sacrificed to I and from blood and
17:16 he saw that the city was full of I
21:25 has been sacrificed to I and from blood and
Rom 2:22 You who abhor I, do you rob temples?
1Cor 8:1 concerning food offered to I: we know that "all
8:4 of food offered to I, we know that "an
8:7 being hitherto accustomed to I, eat food as really
8:10 conscience is weak, to eat food offered to I
10:14 Therefore, my beloved, shun the worship of I
10:19 That food offered to I is anything, or that
12:2 led astray to dumb I, however you may have
2Cor 6:16 What agreement has the temple of God with I
1Thes 1:9 turned to God from I, to serve a living
1Jn 5:21 Little children, keep yourselves from I
Rev 2:14 eat food sacrificed to I and practice immorality.
2:20 practice immorality and to eat food sacrificed to I
9:20 up worshiping demons and I of gold and silver

IDUMEA (7)

1Mac 4:15 to the plains of I, and to Azotus and
4:29 They came into I and encamped at Bethzur, and
4:61 the people might have a stronghold that faced I
5:3 sons of Esau in I, at Akrabattene, because they
6:31 They came through I and encamped against Bethzur,
2Mac 12:32 they hastened against Gorgias, the governor of I
Mk 3:8 Judea and Jerusalem and I and from beyond the

IDUMEANS (2)

2Mac 10:15 Besides this, the I, who had control of important
10:16 their side, rushed to the strongholds of the I

IEZER

Num 26:30 sons of Gilead: of I, the family of the

IEZERITES

Num 26:30 the family of the I; of Helek, the family

IGAL (3)

Num 13:7 the tribe of Issachar, I the son of Joseph;
2Sam 23:36 Carmel, Paarai the Arbite, I the son of Nathan
1Chr 3:22 sons of Shemaiah: Hattush, I, Bariah, Neariah, and

IGDALIAH

Jer 35:4 Hanan the son of I, the man of God,

IGNOBLE (2)

2Tim 2:20 earthenware, and some for noble use, some for I
2:21 himself from what is I, then he will be

IGNORANCE (12)

Wis 14:22 great strife due to I, and they call such
17:13 help, being weak, prefers I of what causes the
Sir 4:25 against the truth, but be mindful of your I
28:7 the covenant of the Most High, and overlook I
51:19 heavens, and lamented my I of her.
Ezek 45:20 sinned through error or I; so you shall make
2Mac 11:31 way for what he may have done in I
Acts 3:17 that you acted in I, as did also your
17:30 The times of I God overlooked, but now he
Eph 4:18 God because of the I that is in them,
1Pet 1:14 passions of your former I,
2:15 put to silence the I of foolish men.

IGNORANT (12)

Ps 73:22 I was stupid and I, I was like a
Wis 13:1 all men who were I of God were foolish
Sir 20:18 which is continually on the lips of the I
20:23 it is continually on the lips of the I
21:18 the knowledge of the I is unexamined talk.
Rom 10:3 For, being I of the righteousness that comes from
2Cor 1:8 want you to be I, brethren, of the affliction
2:11 for we are not I of his designs.
1Thes 4:13 would not have you I, brethren, concerning those
Heb 5:2 deal gently with the I and wayward, since he
2Pet 2:12 of which they are I, will be destroyed in
3:16 to understand, which the I and unstable twist to

IGNORANTLY

1Tim 1:13 because I had acted I in unbelief,

IGNORE (4)

Sir 30:11 youth, and do not I his errors.
35:14 He will not I the supplication of the fatherless,
2Pet 3:5 They deliberately I this fact, that by the word
3:8 But do not I this one fact, beloved, that

IGNORED (2)

Deut 33:9 disowned his brothers, and I his children.
Prov 1:25 heeded, and you have I all my counsel and

IGNORES (3)

Prov 12:16 but the prudent man I an insult.
13:18 come to him who I instruction, but he who
15:32 He who I instruction despises himself, but he who

IGNORING

Mk 5:36 But I what they said, Jesus said to the

IIM

Josh 15:29 Hazar-shual, Beer-sheba, Biziothiah, Baalah, I,

I

IJON (3)

1Kgs 15:20 Israel, and conquered I, Dan, Abel-beth-maacah, and
2Kgs 15:29 Assyria came and captured I, Abel-beth-maacah,
2Chr 16:4 Israel, and they conquered I, Dan, Abel-maim, and

IKKESH (3)

2Sam 23:26 Ira the son of I of Tekoa,
1Chr 11:28 Ira the son of I of Tekoa, Abi-ezer of
27:9 Ira, the son of I the Tekoite; in his

ILAI

1Chr 11:29 Anathoth, Sibbecai the Hushathite, I the Ahohite,

ILL (30)

Gen 37:2 and Joseph brought an I report of them to
43:6 you treat me so I as to tell the
48:1 "Behold, your father is I; so he took with
Num 11:11 "Why hast thou dealt I with thy servant?
2Sam 13:2 that he made himself I because of his sister
13:5 and pretend to be I; and when your father
13:6 and pretended to be I; and when the king
1Kgs 17:17 of the house, became I; and his illness was
Jud 8:8 No one spoke I of her, for she feared
Ps 106:32 Meribah, and it went I with Moses on their
Prov 12:21 No I befalls the righteous, but the wicked are
25:10 upon you, and your I repute have no end.
Sir 18:18 and before you fall I, take care of your
18:20 Before falling I, humble yourself, and when you are
Is 3:11 It shall be I with him, for what his
Zeph 1:12 nor will he do I
2Mac 6:29 will now changed to I will, because the words
12:3 though there were no I will to the Jews;
Lk 4:38 Now Simon's mother-in-law was I with a high fever,
Jn 4:46 Caperna-um there was an official whose son was I
5:4 there, who had been I for thirty-eight years.
11:1 a certain man was I, Lazarus of Bethany, the
11:2 feet with her hair, whose brother Lazarus was I
11:3 him, saying, "Lord, he whom you love is I
11:6 heard that he was I, he stayed two days
1Cor 11:30 you are weak and I, and some have died.
2Cor 6:8 honor and dishonor, in I repute and good repute.
Phil 2:26 been distressed because you heard that he was I
2:27 Indeed he was I, near to death.
2Tim 4:20 Corinth; Trophimus I left I at Miletus.

ILL-BEHAVED

1Sam 25:3 man was churlish and I; he was a Calebite.

ILL-BRED

Sir 8:4 not jest with an I person, lest your ancestors

ILL-CLAD (2)

1Cor 4:11 and thirst, we are I and buffeted and homeless,
Jas 2:15 brother or sister is I and in lack of

ILL-DISPOSED

Esth 13:5 and laws, and is I to our government, doing

ILL-MANNERED

Sir 21:24 It is I for a man to listen at

ILL-NATURED (2)

1Sam 25:17 and he is so I that one cannot speak
25:25 my lord regard this I fellow, Nabal; for as

ILL-TREAT (3)

Gen 31:50 If you I my daughters, or if you take
Sir 33:31 If you I him, and he leaves and runs
Acts 7:6 would enslave them and I them four hundred years.

ILL-TREATED (2)

Heb 11:37 and goats, destitute, afflicted, I –
13:3 and those who are I, since you also are

ILL-TREATMENT (2)

Acts 7:34 have surely seen the I of my people that
Heb 11:25 choosing rather to share I with the people of

ILLEGITIMATE (2)

Wis 4:3 and none of their I seedlings will strike a
Heb 12:8 participated, then you are I children and not sons.

ILLNESS (8)

1Kgs 17:17 became ill; and his I was so severe that
2Kgs 13:14 fallen sick with the I of which he was
Ps 41:3 his sickbed; in his I thou healest all his
Sir 10:10 A long I baffles the physician; the king of
31:2 slumber, and a severe I carries off sleep.
2Mac 9:21 I suffered an annoying I, and I have deemed
9:22 of recovering from my I,
Jn 11:4 it he said, "This I is not unto death;

ILLUMINE

Wis 17:5 the stars avail to I that hateful night.

ILLUMINED

Wis 17:20 the whole world was I with brilliant light, and

ILLUSIONS

Is 30:10 us smooth things, prophesy I,

ILLUSTRIOUS

Sir 11:6 been greatly disgraced, and I men have been handed

ILLYRICUM

Rom 15:19 as far round as I I have fully preached

IMAGE (89)

Gen 1:26 make man in our I, after our likeness; and
1:27 man in his own I, in the image of
1:27 own image, in the I of God he created
5:3 own likeness, after his I, and named him Seth.
9:6 shed; for God made man in his own I
Ex 20:4 for yourself a graven I, or any likeness of
Lev 26:1 and erect no graven I or pillar, and you
Deut 4:16 by making a graven I for yourselves, in the
4:23 and make a graven I in the form of
4:25 by making a graven I in the form of
5:8 for yourself a graven I, or any likeness of
9:12 made themselves a molten I
27:15 a graven or molten I, an abomination to the
Judg 17:3 to make a graven I and a molten image;
17:3 image and a molten I; now therefore I will
17:4 it into a graven I and a molten image;
17:4 image and a molten I; and it was in
18:14 ephod, teraphim, a graven I, and a molten image?
18:14 ephod, teraphim, a graven image, and a molten I
18:17 and took the graven I, the ephod, the teraphim,
18:17 teraphim, and the molten I, while the priest stood
18:18 and took the graven I, the ephod, the teraphim,
18:18 teraphim, and the molten I, the priest said to
18:20 teraphim, and the graven I, and went in the
18:30 set up the graven I for themselves; and Jonathan
18:31 set up Micah's graven I which he made, as
1Sam 19:13 Michal took an I and laid it on the
19:16 came in, behold, the I was in the bed,
1Kgs 15:13 she had an abominable I made for Asherah; and
15:13 Asa cut down her I and burned it at
2Kgs 21:7 And the graven I of Asherah that he had
2Chr 15:16 had made an abominable I for Asherah.
15:16 Asa cut down her I, crushed it, and burned
33:7 And the I of the idol which he had
Ps 106:19 a calf in Horeb and worshiped a molten I
106:20 of God for the I of an ox that
Wis 2:23 made him in the I of his own eternity,
7:26 of God, and an I of his goodness.
13:13 forms it like the I of a man,
13:16 it is only an I and has need of
14:15 untimely bereavement, made an I of his child, who
14:17 and made a visible I of the king whom
15:5 they desire the lifeless form of a dead I
17:21 night was spread, an I of the darkness that
Sir 17:3 his own, and made them in his own I
38:27 on painting a lifelike I, and he is careful
Is 40:20 to set up an I that will not move.
44:10 god or casts an I, that is profitable for
44:15 makes it a graven I and falls down before
48:5 did them, my graven I and my molten image
48:5 image and my molten I commanded them.'
Jer 44:19 for her bearing her I and poured out libations
Ezek 8:3 the seat of the I of jealousy, which provokes
8:5 the entrance, was this I of jealousy.
Dan 2:31 "You saw, O king, and behold, a great I
2:31 This I, mighty and of exceeding brightness, stood
2:32 The head of this I was of fine gold,
2:34 and it smote the I on its feet of
2:35 stone that struck the I became a great mountain
3:1 Nebuchadnezzar made an I of gold, whose height
3:2 the dedication of the I which King Nebuchadnezzar
3:3 the dedication of the I that King Nebuchadnezzar
3:3 they stood before the I that Nebuchadnezzar had set
3:5 and worship the golden I that King Nebuchadnezzar
3:7 the golden I which King Nebuchadnezzar had
3:10 and worship the golden I;
3:12 or worship the golden I which you have set
3:14 or worship the golden I which I have set
3:15 down and worship the I which I have made,
3:18 or worship the golden I which you have set
Nah 1:14 cut off the graven I and the molten image.
1:14 cut off the graven image and the molten I
Hab 2:18 shaped it, a metal I, a teacher of lies?
Rom 8:29 be conformed to the I of his Son, in
1Cor 11:7 since he is the I and glory of God;
15:49 we have borne the I of the man of
15:49 shall also bear the I of the man of
Col 1:15 He is the I of the invisible God, the
3:10 in knowledge after the I of its creator.
Rev 13:14 bidding them make an I for the beast which
13:15 give breath to the I of the beast so
13:15 beast so that the I of the beast should
13:15 would not worship the I of the beast to
14:9 the beast and its I, and receives a mark
14:11 the beast and its I, and whoever receives the
15:2 the beast and its I and the number of
16:2 the mark of the beast and worshiped its I
19:20 of the beast and those who worshiped its I
20:4 the beast or its I and had not received

IMAGES (50)

Num 33:52 destroy all their molten I, and demolish all their
Deut 7:5 and burn their graven I with fire.
7:25 The graven I of their gods you shall burn
12:3 hew down the graven I of their gods, and
1Sam 6:5 So you must make I of your tumors and
6:5 of your tumors and I of your mice that
6:11 golden mice and the I of their tumors.
1Kgs 14:9 other gods, and molten I, provoking me to anger,
2Kgs 11:18 his altars and his I they broke in pieces,
17:16 made for themselves molten I of two calves; and
17:41 also served their graven I; their children likewise,
2Chr 23:17 his altars and his I they broke in pieces,
28:2 He even made molten I for the Baals;
33:19 the Asherim and the I, before he humbled himself,
33:22 sacrificed to all the I that Manasseh his father
34:3 the Asherim, and the graven and the molten I
34:4 graven and the molten I, and he made dust
34:7 the Asherim and the I into powder, and hewed
Ps 78:58 they moved him to jealousy with their graven I
97:7 All worshipers of I are put to shame, who
Wis 14:16 command of monarchs graven I were worshiped.
15:13 from earthy matter fragile vessels and graven I
Is 10:10 the idols whose graven I were greater than those
10:11 as I have done to Samaria and her I
21:9 Babylon; and all the I of her gods he
30:22 your silver-covered graven I and your gold-plated
30:22 graven images and your gold-plated molten I
41:29 are nothing; their molten I are empty wind.
42:8 to no other, nor my praise to graven I
42:17 who trust in graven I, who say to molten
42:17 who say to molten I, "You are our gods."

Jer 8:19 anger with their graven I, and with their foreign
10:14 his idols; for his I are false, and there
50:2 Her I are put to shame, her idols are
50:38 is a land of I, and they are mad
51:17 his idols; for his I are false, and there
51:47 I will punish the I of Babylon; her whole
51:52 execute judgment upon her I, and through all her
Ezek 7:20 they made their abominable I and their detestable
16:17 and made for yourself I of men, and with
23:14 upon the wall, the I of the Chaldeans portrayed
30:13 an end to the I, in Memphis; there shall
Dan 11:8 gods with their molten I and with their precious
Hos 13:2 make for themselves molten I, idols skilfully made of
Amos 5:26 Kaiwan your star-god, your I, which you made for
Mic 1:7 All her I shall be beaten to pieces, all
5:13 will cut off your I and your pillars from
1Mac 3:48 Gentiles were consulting the I of their idols.
5:68 altars, and the graven I of their gods he
Rom 1:23 the immortal God for I resembling mortal man or

IMAGINATION (5)

Gen 6:5 earth, and that every I of the thoughts of
8:21 of man, for the I of man's heart is
Sir 37:3 O evil I, why were you formed to cover
Lk 1:51 the proud in the I of their hearts,
Acts 17:29 by the art and I of man.

IMAGINE (2)

Ps 41:7 together about me; they I the worst for me.
Acts 4:25 rage, and the peoples I vain things?

IMAGINED

Wis 14:17 at a distance, they I their appearance far away,

IMAGINES

1Cor 8:2 If any one I that he knows something, he

IMAGINING (3)

2Mac 5:6 the greatest misfortune, but I that he was setting
9:8 his superhuman arrogance, and I that he could weigh
1Tim 6:5 bereft of the truth, I that godliness is a

IMALKUE (2)

1Mac 11:39 So he went to I the Arab, who was
11:40 He also reported to I what Demetrius had done

IMITATE (7)

Wis 4:2 it is present, men I it, and they long
2Mac 4:16 admired and wished to I completely became their
2Thes 3:7 how you ought to I us; we were not
3:9 give you in our conduct an example to I
Heb 13:7 of their life, and I their faith.
3Jn 1:11 Beloved, do not I evil but imitate good.
1:11 not imitate evil but I good.

IMITATES

Wis 15:9 gold and silver, and I workers in copper; and

IMITATING

Phil 3:17 Brethren, join in I me, and mark those who

IMITATORS (6)

1Cor 4:16 urge you, then, be I of me.
11:1 Be I of me, as I am of Christ.
Eph 5:1 Therefore be I of God, as beloved children.
1Thes 1:6 And you became I of us and of the
2:14 For you, brethren, became I of the churches of
Heb 6:12 not be sluggish, but I of those who through

IMLAH (4)

1Kgs 22:8 Micaiah the son of I; but I hate him,
22:9 and said, "Bring quickly Micaiah the son of I
2Chr 18:7 Micaiah the son of I; but I hate him,
18:8 and said, "Bring quickly Micaiah the son of I

IMMANU-EL (2)

Is 7:14 bear a son, and shall call his name I
8:8 will fill the breadth of your land, O I

IMMEASURABLE (3)

Bar 3:25 and has no bounds; it is high and I
Eph 1:19 and what is the I greatness of his power
2:7 he might show the I riches of his grace

IMMEDIATELY (92)

1Sam 9:13 Now go up, for you will meet him I
Jud 4:5 valley of Salem, and I seized all the high
Dan 3:6 down and worship shall I be cast into a
3:15 not worship, you shall I be cast into a
4:33 I the word was fulfilled upon Nebuchadnezzar.
5:5 I the fingers of a man's hand appeared and
13:55 from God and will I cut you in two."
14:39 the angel of God I returned Habakkuk to his
14:42 and they were devoured I before his eyes.
2Mac 4:34 regard for justice, he I put him out of
4:38 inflamed with anger, he I stripped off the purple
6:13 but to punish them I, is a sign of
7:4 These were heated I, and he commanded that the
8:11 And he I sent to the cities on the
10:22 had turned traitor, and I captured the two towers.
14:12 And he I chose Nicanor, who had been in
14:16 set out from there I and engaged them in
Mt 3:16 baptized, he went up I from the water, and
4:20 I they left their nets and followed him.
4:22 I they left the boat and their father, and
8:3 And I his leprosy was cleansed.
13:5 not much soil, and I they sprang up, since
13:20 hears the word and I receives it with joy;
13:21 account of the word, I he falls away.
14:27 But I he spoke to them, saying, "Take heart,
14:31 Jesus I reached out his hand and caught him,
20:34 touched their eyes, and I they received their sight
21:2 village opposite you, and I you will find an
21:3 need of them,' and he will send them I
24:29 I after the tribulation of those days the sun
26:74 And I the cock crowed.
Mk 1:10 out of the water, I he saw the heavens
1:12 The Spirit I drove him out into the wilderness.
1:18 And I they left their nets and followed him.
1:20 And I he called them; and they left their
1:21 went into Caperna-um; and I on the sabbath he
1:23 And I there was in their synagogue a man
1:29 And I he left the synagogue, and entered the
1:30 with a fever, and I they told him of
1:42 And I the leprosy left him, and he was
2:8 And I Jesus, perceiving in his spirit that they
2:12 And he rose, and I took up the pallet
3:6 Pharisees went out, and I held counsel with the
4:5 not much soil, and I it sprang up, since
4:15 when they hear, Satan I comes and takes away
4:16 they hear the word, I receive it with joy;
4:17 account of the word, I they fall away.
5:29 And I the hemorrhage ceased; and she felt in
5:30 gone forth from him, I turned about in the
5:42 And I the girl got up and walked (she
5:42 age), and they were I overcome with amazement.
6:25 And she came in I with haste to the
6:27 And I the king sent a soldier of the
6:45 I he made his disciples get into the boat
6:50 But I he spoke to them and said, "Take
6:54 out of the boat, I the people recognized him,
7:24 But I a woman, whose little daughter was possessed
8:10 sent them away; and I he got into the
9:15 And I all the crowd, when they saw him,
9:20 the spirit saw him, I it convulsed the boy,
9:24 I the father of the child cried out and
10:52 And I he received his sight and followed him
11:2 village opposite you, and I as you enter it
11:3 of it and will send it back here I
14:43 And I, while he was still speaking, Judas came,
14:72 And I the cock crowed a second time.
Lk 1:64 And I his mouth was opened and his tongue
4:39 it left her; and I she rose and served
5:13 And I the leprosy left him.
5:25 And I he rose before them, and took up
6:49 the stream broke, and I it fell, and the
8:44 of his garment; and I her flow of blood
8:47 how she had been I healed.
13:13 hands upon her, and I she was made straight,
14:5 a well, will not I pull him out on
18:43 And I he received his sight and followed him,
19:11 that the kingdom of God was to appear I
22:58 And I, while he was still speaking, the cock
Jn 6:21 into the boat, and I the boat was at
13:30 receiving the morsel, he I went out; and it
Acts 3:7 raised him up; and I his feet and ankles
5:10 I she fell down at his feet and died.
9:18 And I something like scales fell from his eyes
9:20 And in the synagogues I he proclaimed Jesus, saying,
9:34 And I he rose.
12:10 through one street; and I the angel left him.
12:23 I an angel of the Lord smote him, because

13:11 I mist and darkness fell upon him and he
16:10 had seen the vision, I we sought to go
16:26 prison were shaken; and I all the doors were
17:10 The brethren I sent Paul and Silas away by
17:14 Then the brethren I sent Paul off on his

IMMENSE
1Mac 3:41 silver and gold in I amounts, and fetters, and

IMMER (10)
1Chr 9:12 of Meshillemith, son of I;
24:14 Bilgah, the sixteenth to I,
Ezra 2:37 The sons of I, one thousand and fifty-two.
2:59 Tel-harsha, Cherub, Addan, and I, though they could
10:20 Of the sons of I: Hanani and Zebadiah.
Neh 3:29 Zadok the son of I repaired opposite his own
7:40 The sons of I, a thousand and fifty-two.
7:61 Tel-harsha, Cherub, Addon, and I, but they could not
11:13 of Meshillemoth, son of I,
Jer 20:1 priest, the son of I, who was chief officer

IMMINENT
1Mac 9:7 and the battle was I, he was crushed in

IMMODERATELY
Sir 33:29 Do not act I toward anybody, and do nothing

IMMORAL (7)
1Cor 5:9 not to associate with I men;
5:10 at all meaning the I of this world, or
6:9 be deceived; neither the I, nor idolaters, nor
6:18 the body; but the I man sins against his
1Tim 1:10 mothers, for manslayers, I persons, sodomites,
Heb 12:16 that no one be I or irreligious like Esau,
13:4 God will judge the I and adulterous.

IMMORALITY (13)
Tob 4:12 "Beware, my son, of all I
Sir 41:17 Be ashamed of I, before your father or mother;
1Cor 5:1 reported that there is I among you, and of
5:11 he is guilty of I or greed, or is
6:13 is not meant for I, but for the Lord,
6:18 Shun I
7:2 of the temptation to I, each man should have
10:8 must not indulge in I as some of them
2Cor 12:21 repented of the impurity, I, and licentiousness which
Rev 2:14 might eat food sacrificed to idols and practice I
2:20 my servants to practice I and to eat food
2:21 repent, but she refuses to repent of her I
9:21 their sorceries or their I or their thefts.

IMMORALLY
Jude 1:7 cities, which likewise acted I and indulged in

IMMORTAL (5)
Wis 1:15 For righteousness is I
12:1 For thy I spirit is in all things.
Sir 17:25 men, since a son of man is not I
Rom 1:23 the glory of the I God for images resembling
1Tim 1:17 the King of ages, I, invisible, the only God,

IMMORTALITY (12)
Wis 3:4 they were punished, their hope is full of I
4:1 memory of virtue is I, because it is known
6:18 laws is assurance of I,
6:19 assurance of immortality, and I brings one near to
8:13 her I shall have I, and leave an everlasting
8:17 with wisdom there is I,
15:3 to know thy power is the root of I
Rom 2:7 glory and honor and I, he will give eternal
1Cor 15:53 imperishable, and this mortal nature must put on I
15:54 the mortal puts on I, then shall come to
1Tim 6:16 lords, who alone has I and dwells in unapproachable
2Tim 1:10 and brought life and I to light through the

IMMOVABLE (4)
Job 41:23 flesh cleave together, firmly cast upon him and I
Is 33:20 a quiet habitation, an I tent, whose stakes will
Acts 27:41 bow stuck and remained I, and the stern was
1Cor 15:58 beloved brethren, be steadfast, I, always abounding

IMMUNITIES
1Mac 10:28 will grant you many I and give you gifts.

IMMUNITY
1Mac 10:34 all be days of I and release for all

IMNA
1Chr 7:35 Helem his brother: Zophah, I, Shelesh, and Amal.

IMNAH (4)
Gen 46:17 The sons of Asher: I, Ishvah, Ishvi, Beriah, with
Num 26:44 to their families: of I, the family of the
1Chr 7:30 The sons of Asher: I, Ishvah, Ishvi, Beriah, and
2Chr 31:14 Kore the son of I the Levite, keeper of

IMNITES
Num 26:44 the family of the I; of Ishvi, the family

IMPAIR
Ruth 4:6 for myself, lest I I my own inheritance.

IMPAIRED
Ezra 4:13 or toll, and the royal revenue will be I

IMPALED
Ezra 6:11 and he shall be I upon it, and his

IMPART (7)
Wis 7:13 without guile and I I without grudging; I do
Sir 16:23 I will I instruction by weight, and declare knowledge
Rom 1:11 you, that I may I to you some spiritual
1Cor 2:6 the mature we do I wisdom, although it is
2:7 But we I a secret and hidden wisdom of
2:13 And we I this in words not taught by
Eph 4:29 occasion, that it may I grace to those who

IMPARTIAL
Wis 5:18 a breastplate, and wear I justice as a helmet;

IMPARTIALLY
1Pet 1:17 who judges each one I according to his deeds,

IMPARTS
Ps 119:130 words gives light; it I understanding to the simple.

IMPASSABLE
Esth 16:24 be made not only I for men, but also

IMPATIENT (6)
Num 21:4 and the people became I on the way.
Job 4:5 you, and you are I; it touches you, and
21:4 Why should I not be I
Mic 2:7 Is the Spirit of the LORD I
Zech 6:7 came out, they were I to get off and
11:8 But I became I with them, and they also

IMPEDIMENT
Mk 7:31 deaf and had an I in his speech; and

IMPELLED
Wis 14:18 ambition of the craftsman I even those who did

IMPENETRABLE
Jer 46:23 LORD, though it is I, because they are more

IMPENITENT
Rom 2:5 by your hard and I heart you are storing

IMPERFECT (3)
1Cor 13:9 For our knowledge is I and our prophecy is
13:9 and our prophecy is I;
13:10 the perfect comes, the I will pass away.

IMPERISHABLE (10)
Wis 18:4 imprisoned, through whom the I light of the law
1Cor 9:25 to receive a perishable wreath, but we an I
15:42 is sown is perishable, what is raised is I
15:50 of God, nor does the perishable inherit the I
15:52 dead will be raised I, and we shall be
15:53 must put on the I, and this mortal nature
15:54 perishable puts on the I, and the mortal puts
1Pet 1:4 an inheritance which is I, undefiled, and unfading,
1:23 perishable seed but of I, through the living and
3:4 the heart with the I jewel of a gentle

IMPIETY
2Mac 8:33 so these received the proper recompense for their I

IMPIOUS (5)
Ps 74:18 enemy scoffs, and an I people reviles thy name.
74:22 cause; remember how the I scoff at thee all
2Mac 3:11 such an extent the I Simon had misrepresented the

6:13 not to let the I alone for long, but
1Pet 4:18 saved, where will the I and sinner appear?"

IMPIOUSLY (2)
Ps 35:16 me without ceasing; they I mocked more and more,
2Mac 1:17 brought judgment upon those who have behaved I

IMPLACABLE
2Tim 3:3 parents, ungrateful, unholy, inhuman, I, slanderers,

IMPLANTED
Jas 1:20 receive with meekness the I word, which is able

IMPLEMENTS (2)
1Sam 8:12 and to make his I of war and the
Zech 11:15 "Take once more the I of a worthless shepherd.

IMPLIES
Gal 3:20 Now an intermediary I more than one; but God

IMPLORE
1Sam 2:36 house shall come to I him for a piece

IMPLORING
Mt 18:25 fell on his knees, I him, 'Lord, have patience

IMPLY (2)
1Cor 10:19 What do I I then?
10:20 No, I I that what pagans sacrifice they offer

IMPORT (2)
1Kgs 10:28 And Solomon's I of horses was from Egypt and
2Chr 1:16 And Solomon's I of horses was from Egypt and

IMPORTANCE
1Cor 15:3 you as of first I what I also received,

IMPORTANT
2Mac 10:15 who had control of I strongholds, were harassing the

IMPORTED (3)
1Kgs 10:29 A chariot could be I from Egypt for six
2Chr 1:17 They I a chariot from Egypt for six hundred
9:28 And horses were I for Solomon from Egypt and

IMPORTUNE
Prov 6:3 power: go, hasten, and I your neighbor.

IMPORTUNITY
Lk 11:8 yet because of his I he will rise and

IMPOSE (3)
2Kgs 18:14 from me; whatever you I on me I will
Ezra 7:24 not be lawful to I tribute, custom, or toll
Prov 17:26 To I a fine on a righteous man is

IMPOSED (2)
Ezek 26:17 and your inhabitants, who I your terror on all
Heb 9:10 regulations for the body I until the time of

IMPOSSIBLE (14)
Gen 11:6 do will now be I for them.
2Sam 13:2 virgin, and it seemed I to Amnon to do
Wis 16:15 from thy hand is I;
2Mac 3:12 that it was utterly I that wrong should be
14:10 Judas lives, it is I for the government to
Mt 17:20 and nothing will be I to you."
19:26 "With men this is I, but with God all
Mk 10:27 "With men it is I, but not with God;
Lk 1:37 For with God nothing will be I
18:27 he said, "What is I with men is possible
Heb 6:4 For it is I to restore again to repentance
6:18 in which it is I that God should prove
10:4 For it is I that the blood of bulls
11:6 without faith it is I to please him.

IMPOSTOR
Mt 27:63 we remember how that I said, while he was

IMPOSTORS (2)
2Cor 6:8 We are treated as I, and yet are true;
2Tim 3:13 while evil men and I will go on from

IMPOVERISH
Judg 14:15 invited us here to I us?"

IMPOVERISHED (2)
Sir 18:31 luxury, lest you become I by its expense.
Is 40:20 He who is I chooses for an offering wood

IMPRISON
Sir 13:12 he will not hesitate to injure or to I

IMPRISONED (7)
Wis 16:14 nor set free the I soul.
18:4 deprived of light and I in darkness, those who
18:4 had kept thy sons I, through whom the imperishable
Jer 32:3 king of Judah had I him, saying, "Why do
37:15 they beat him and I him in the house
Acts 21:13 not only to be I but even to die
22:19 in every synagogue I I and beat those who

IMPRISONMENT (11)
Ezra 7:26 or for confiscation of his goods or for I
Acts 20:23 in every city that I and afflictions await me.
23:29 law, but charged with nothing deserving death or I
26:31 man is doing nothing to deserve death or I
Phil 1:7 grace, both in my I and in the defense
1:13 the rest that my I is for Christ;
1:14 Lord because of my I, and are much more
1:17 sincerely but thinking to afflict me in my I
Philem 1:10 Onesimus, whose father I have become in my I
1:13 your behalf during my I for the gospel;
Heb 11:36 mocking and scourging, and even chains and I

IMPRISONMENTS (2)
2Cor 6:5 afflictions, hardships, calamities, beatings, I, tumults,
11:23 greater labors, far more I, with countless beatings,

IMPRISONS
Job 11:10 he passes through, and I, and calls to judgment,

IMPROPER
Rom 1:28 base mind and to I conduct.

IMPROVED (2)
Hos 10:1 built; as his country I he improved his pillars.
10:1 his country improved he I his pillars.

IMPROVEMENT
2Cor 13:9 What we pray for is your I

IMPUDENCE
Sir 25:21 There is wrath and I and great disgrace when

IMPUDENT (4)
Prov 7:13 kisses him, and with I face she says to
Sir 22:5 An I daughter disgraces father and husband, and will
26:11 on guard against her I eye, and do not
Ezek 2:4 The people also are I and stubborn: I send

IMPULSE (2)
Jud 15:2 another, but with one I all rushed out and
2Pet 1:21 ever came by the I of man, but men

IMPULSES
2Tim 3:6 and swayed by various I,

IMPURE (3)
Eph 5:5 that no fornicator or I man, or one who
Rev 14:8 the wine of her I passion."
18:3 the wine of her I passion, and the kings

IMPURITIES
Rev 17:4 of abominations and the I of her fornication;

IMPURITY (25)
Lev 15:19 shall be in her I for seven days, and
15:20 she lies during her I shall be unclean; everything
15:24 with her, and her I is on him, he
15:25 the time of her I, or if she has
15:25 the time of her I, all the days of
15:25 the days of her I, she shall be unclean.
15:26 the bed of her I; and everything on which
15:26 be unclean, as in the uncleanness of her I
15:33 is sick with her I; that is, for any
20:21 brother's wife, it is I; he has uncovered his
Num 19:9 for the water for I, for the removal of
19:13 because the water for I was not thrown upon
19:20 because the water for I has not been thrown
19:21 sprinkles the water for I shall wash his clothes;
19:21 touches the water for I shall be unclean until

31:23 with the water of I; and whatever cannot stand
Ezek 18:6 in her time of I,
22:10 they humble women who are unclean in their I
36:17 like the uncleanness of a woman in her I
Rom 1:24 of their hearts to I, to the dishonoring of
6:19 yielded your members to I and to greater and
2Cor 12:21 not repented of the I, immorality, and licentiousness
Gal 5:19 flesh are plain: fornication, I, licentiousness,
Eph 5:3 But fornication and all I or covetousness must not
Col 3:5 earthly in you: fornication, I, passion, evil desire, and

IMPUTE
1Sam 22:15 Let not the king I anything to his servant

IMPUTED
Lev 17:4 LORD, bloodguilt shall be I to that man; he

IMPUTES
Ps 32:2 to whom the LORD I no iniquity, and in

IMRAH
1Chr 7:36 Suah, Harnepher, Shual, Beri, I,

IMRI (2)
1Chr 9:4 of Omri, son of I, son of Bani, from
Neh 3:2 Zaccur the son of I built.

I

INABILITY
Esth 16:3 subjects, but in their I to stand prosperity they

INAPPROPRIATE
2Mac 4:19 sacrifice, because that was I, but to expend it

INASMUCH (5)
Gen 38:26 more righteous than I, I as I did not
2Sam 14:13 the king convicts himself, I as the king does
Mal 2:9 before all the people, I as you have not
Lk 1:1 I as many have undertaken
Rom 11:13 I then as I am an apostle to the

INBORN
Wis 12:10 evil and their wickedness I, and that their way

INCENSE (156)
Ex 25:6 and for the fragrant I,
25:29 plates and dishes for I, and its flagons and
30:1 an altar to burn I upon; of acacia wood
30:7 Aaron shall burn fragrant I on it; every morning
30:8 burn it, a perpetual I before the LORD throughout
30:9 shall offer no unholy I thereon, nor burnt offering,
30:27 and the altar of I,
30:35 part), and make an I blended as by the
30:37 And the I which you shall make according to
31:8 and the altar of I,
31:11 oil and the fragrant I for the holy place.
35:8 and for the fragrant I,
35:15 and the altar of I, with its poles, and
35:15 oil and the fragrant I, and the screen for
35:28 for the anointing oil, and for the fragrant I
37:16 plates and dishes for I, and its bowls and
37:25 made the altar of I of acacia wood; its
37:29 and the pure fragrant I, blended as by the
39:38 oil and the fragrant I, and the screen for
Lev 4:7 the altar of fragrant I before the LORD which
10:1 in it, and laid I on it, and offered
16:12 two handfuls of sweet I beaten small; and he
16:13 veil and put the I on the fire before
16:13 the cloud of the I may cover the mercy
26:30 and cut down your I altars, and cast your
Num 4:7 plates, the dishes for I, the bowls, and the
4:16 the light, the fragrant I, the continual cereal offering,
7:14 ten shekels, full of I;
7:20 ten shekels, full of I;
7:26 ten shekels, full of I;
7:32 ten shekels, full of I;
7:38 ten shekels, full of I;
7:44 ten shekels, full of I;
7:50 ten shekels, full of I;
7:56 ten shekels, full of I;
7:62 ten shekels, full of I;
7:68 ten shekels, full of I;
7:74 ten shekels, full of I;
7:80 ten shekels, full of I;
7:86 golden dishes, full of I, weighing ten shekels apiece
16:7 in them and put I upon them before the
16:17 his censer, and put I upon it, and every
16:18 in them and laid I upon them, and they
16:35 the two hundred and fifty men offering the I
16:40 draw near to burn I before the LORD, lest
16:46 the altar, and lay I on it, and carry
16:47 he put on the I, and made atonement for
Deut 33:10 law; they shall put I before thee, and whole
1Sam 2:28 my altar, to burn I, to wear an ephod
1Kgs 3:3 he sacrificed and burnt I at the high places.
7:50 snuffers, basins, dishes for I, and firepans, of pure
9:25 to the LORD, burning I before the LORD.
11:8 foreign wives, who burned I and sacrificed to their
12:33 and went up to the altar to burn I
13:1 Jeroboam was standing by the altar to burn I
13:2 high places who burn I upon you, and men's
22:43 still sacrificed and burned I on the high places.
2Kgs 12:3 to sacrifice and burn I on the high places.
14:4 still sacrificed and burned I on the high places.
15:4 still sacrificed and burned I on the high places.
15:35 still sacrificed and burned I on the high places.
16:4 he sacrificed and burned I on the high places,
17:11 and there they burned I on all the high
18:4 of Israel had burned I to it; it was
22:17 me and have burned I to other gods, that
23:5 had ordained to burn I in the high places
23:5 those also who burned I to Baal, to the
23:8 the priests had burned I, from Geba to Beer-sheba;
25:14 and the dishes for I and all the vessels
1Chr 6:49 upon the altar of I for all the work
9:29 wine, the oil, the I, and the spices.
23:13 for ever should burn I before the LORD, and
28:18 for the altar of I made of refined gold,
2Chr 2:4 for the burning of I of sweet spices before
2:6 a place to burn I before him?
4:22 snuffers, basins, dishes for I, and firepans, of pure
13:11 evening burnt offerings and I of sweet spices, set
14:5 high places and the I altars.
24:14 offerings, and dishes for I, and vessels of gold
26:16 the LORD to burn I on the altar of
26:16 LORD to burn incense on the altar of I
26:18 you, Uzziah, to burn I to the LORD, but
26:18 sons of Aaron, who are consecrated to burn I
26:19 his hand to burn I, and when he became
26:19 house of the LORD, by the altar of I
28:3 Baals; and he burned I in the valley of
28:4 he sacrificed and burned I on the high places,
28:25 high places to burn I to other gods, provoking
29:7 and have not burned I or offered burnt offerings
29:11 his ministers and burn I to him."
30:14 the altars for burning I they took away and
34:4 he hewed down the I altars which stood above
34:7 hewed down all the I altars throughout all the
34:25 me and have burned I to other gods, that
Tob 6:16 take live ashes of I and lay upon them
8:2 the live ashes of I and put the heart
Jud 9:1 time when that evening's I was being offered in
Ps 141:2 prayer be counted as I before thee, and the
Wis 18:21 prayer and propitiation by I; he withstood the anger
Sir 45:16 sacrifice to the Lord, I and a pleasing odor
49:1 like a blending of I prepared by the art
50:9 day; like fire and I in the censer, like
Is 1:13 no more vain offerings; I is an abomination to
17:8 made, either the Asherim or the altars of I
27:9 pieces, no Asherim or I altars will remain standing.
65:3 in gardens and burning I upon bricks;
65:7 LORD; because they burned I upon the mountains
Jer 1:16 me; they have burned I to other gods, and
7:9 adultery, swear falsely, burn I to Baal, and go
11:12 to whom they burn I, but they cannot save
11:13 shame, altars to burn I to Baal.
11:17 to anger by burning I to Baal."
18:15 forgotten me, they burn I to false gods; they
19:4 this place by burning I in it to other
19:13 houses upon whose roofs I has been burned to
32:29 houses on whose roofs I has been offered to
41:5 bringing cereal offerings and I to present at the
44:3 they went to burn I and serve other gods
44:5 wickedness and burn no I to other gods.
44:8 of your hands, burning I to other gods in
44:15 their wives had offered I to other gods, and
44:17 we have vowed, burn I to the queen of
44:18 we left off burning I to the queen of
44:19 said, "When we burned I to the queen of
44:21 answer: "As for the I that you burned in
44:23 is because you burned I, and because you sinned
44:25 have made, to burn I to the queen of
48:35 high place and burns I to his god.

	52:18	and the dishes for I, and all the vessels
	52:19	and the dishes for I, and the bowls for
Bar	1:10	and sin offerings and I, and prepare a cereal
	6:43	passageways, burning bran for I; and when one of
Ezek	6:4	become desolate, and your I altars shall be broken;
	6:6	broken and destroyed, your I altars cut down, and
	8:11	of the cloud of I went up.
	16:18	my oil and my I before them.
	23:41	you had placed my I and my oil.
Dan	2:46	that an offering and I be offered up to
	3:38	sacrifice, or oblation, or I, no place to make
Hos	2:13	Baals when she burned I to them and decked
	11:2	the Baals, and burning I to idols.
Hab	1:16	his net and burns I to his seine; for
Mal	1:11	and in every place I is offered to my
1Mac	1:55	of Judah, and burned I at the doors of
	4:49	lampstand, the altar of I, and the table into
	4:50	Then they burned I on the altar and lighted
2Mac	2:5	and the altar of I, and he sealed up
	10:3	years, and they burned I and lighted lamps and
Lk	1:9	enter the temple of the Lord and burn I
	1:10	people were praying outside at the hour of I
	1:11	on the right side of the altar of I
Heb	9:4	the golden altar of I and the ark of
Rev	5:8	golden bowls full of I, which are the prayers
	8:3	he was given much I to mingle with the
	8:4	the smoke of the I rose with the prayers
	18:13	and marble, cinnamon, spice, I, myrrh, frankincense,

INCENSED (3)

Wis	12:27	their suffering they became I at those creatures
Is	41:11	Behold, all who are I against you shall be
	45:24	ashamed, all who were I against him.

INCENTIVE

Phil	2:1	encouragement in Christ, any I of love, any

INCEST

Lev	20:12	death; they have committed I, their blood is upon

INCIDENT

2Mac	4:43	Charges were brought against Menelaus about this I

INCITED (5)

2Sam	24:1	against Israel, and he I David against them, saying,
1Kgs	21:25	the LORD like Ahab, whom Jezebel his wife I
1Chr	21:1	up against Israel, and I David to number Israel.
2Mac	4:1	was he who had I Heliodorus and had been
Acts	13:50	But the Jews I the devout women of high

INCITING

Acts	17:13	too, stirring up and I the crowds.

INCLINATION (2)

Sir	5:2	Do not follow your I and strength, walking according
	15:14	left him in the power of his own I

INCLINE (33)

Josh	24:23	are among you, and I your heart to the
1Kgs	8:58	us; that he may I our hearts to him,
2Kgs	19:16	I thy ear, O LORD, and hear; open thy
Ps	10:17	their heart, thou wilt I thy ear
	17:6	answer me, O God; I thy ear to me,
	31:2	I thy ear to me, rescue me speedily!
	45:10	O daughter, consider, and I your ear; forget your
	49:4	I will I my ear to a proverb; I
	71:2	me and rescue me; I thy ear to me,
	78:1	people, to my teaching; I your ears to the
	86:1	I thy ear, O LORD, and answer me, for
	88:2	prayer come before thee, I thy ear to my
	102:2	I thy ear to me; answer me speedily in
	119:36	I my heart to thy testimonies, and not to
	119:112	I I my heart to perform thy statutes for
	141:4	I not my heart to any evil, to busy
Prov	4:21	attentive to my words; I your ear to my
	5:1	attentive to my wisdom, I your ear to my
	5:13	of my teachers or I my ear to my
	22:17	I your ear, and hear the words of the
Sir	4:8	I your ear to the poor, and answer him
	6:33	knowledge, and if you I your ear you will
Is	37:17	I thy ear, O LORD, and hear; open thy
	55:3	I your ear, and come to me; hear, that
Jer	7:24	did not obey or I their ear, but walked
	7:26	listen to me, or I their ear, but stiffened
	11:8	did not obey or I their ear, but every
	17:23	did not listen or I their ear, but stiffened
	34:14	listen to me or I their ears to me.
	35:15	But you did not I your ear or listen
	44:5	did not listen or I their ear, to turn
Bar	2:16	I thy ear, O Lord, and hear;
Dan	9:18	O my God, I thy ear and hear; open

INCLINED (7)

Num	15:39	eyes, which you are I to go after wantonly.
Judg	9:3	Shechem; and their hearts I to follow Abimelech, for
Ps	40:1	for the LORD; he I to me and heard
	116:2	Because he I his ear to me, therefore I
Sir	51:16	I I my ear a little and received her,
Jer	25:4	have neither listened nor I your ears to hear,
2Mac	2:25	for those who are I to memorize, and to

INCLINES (4)

1Sam	14:7	all that your mind I to; behold, I am
Eccl	10:2	A wise man's heart I him toward the right,
Sir	38:28	of the furnace; he I his ear to the
2Mac	13:5	which on all sides I precipitously into the ashes.

INCLINING

Prov	2:2	attentive to wisdom and I your heart to

INCLUDE

1Chr	21:6	But he did not I Levi and Benjamin in

INCLUDED (3)

Josh	19:18	Its territory I Jezreel, Chesulloth, Shunem,
	19:25	Its territory I Helkath, Hali, Beten, Achshaph,
	19:41	of its inheritance I Zorah, Eshtaol, Ir-shemesh,

INCLUDING (4)

Gen	46:26	his own offspring, not I Jacob's sons' wives, were
Judg	20:1	from Dan to Beer-sheba, I the land of Gilead,
1Mac	3:13	gathered a large company, I a body of faithful
Rom	1:6	among all the nations, I yourselves who are called

INCLUSION

Rom	11:12	more will their full I mean!

INCOME (2)

Prov	15:6	but trouble befalls the I of the wicked.
1Mac	10:42	every year from the I of the services of

INCOMPETENT

1Cor	6:2	by you, are you I to try trivial cases?

INCOMPLETE

Sir	42:24	opposite the other, and he has made nothing I

INCONVENIENT

Wis	2:12	man, because he is I to us and opposes

INCORRUPTION

Wis	2:23	God created man for I, and made him in

INCREASE (52)

Lev	25:16	are many you shall I the price, and if
	25:36	interest from him or I, but fear your God;
	26:4	land shall yield its I, and the trees of
	26:20	shall not yield its I, and the trees of
Num	32:14	of sinful men, to I still more the fierce
Deut	7:13	and your oil, the I of your cattle and
	28:4	of your beasts, the I of your cattle, and
	28:18	of your ground, the I of your cattle, and
	28:51	wine, or oil, the I of your cattle or
	32:22	the earth and its I, and sets on fire
Judg	9:29	would say to Abimelech, I your army, and come
1Sam	2:33	heart; and all the I of your house shall
Job	10:17	witnesses against me, and I thy vexation toward me;
	31:12	it would burn to the root all my I
Ps	62:10	on robbery; if riches I, set not your heart
	67:6	earth has yielded its I; God, our God, has
	71:21	Thou wilt I my honor, and comfort me again.
	73:12	always at ease, they I in riches.
	85:12	is good, and our land will yield its I
	115:14	the LORD give you I, you and your children!
	138:3	answer me, my strength of soul thou didst I
Prov	1:5	also may hear and I in learning, and the
	9:9	man and he will I in learning.
	13:11	little by little will I it.
	22:16	oppresses the poor to I his own wealth, or
	28:8	wealth by interest and I gathers it for him
	28:28	themselves, but when they perish, the righteous I
Eccl	5:7	For when dreams I, empty words grow many: but

I

	5:11	When goods I, they increase who eat them; and
	5:11	When goods increase, they I who eat them; and
Sir	18:5	possible to diminish or I them, nor is it
	21:13	a wise man will I like a flood, and
Is	9:7	Of the I of his government and of peace
Bar	2:34	it; and I will I them, and they will
Ezek	18:8	interest or take any I, withholds his hand from
	18:13	at interest, and takes I; shall he then live?
	18:17	takes no interest or I, observes my ordinances, and
	22:12	you take interest and I and make gain of
	34:27	earth shall yield its I, and they shall be
	36:11	beast; and they shall I and be fruitful; and
	36:30	the tree and the I of the field abundant,
	36:37	do for them: to I their men like a
Dan	12:4	shall run to and fro, and knowledge shall I
Zech	8:12	ground shall give its I, and the heavens shall
1Mac	14:8	the ground gave its I, and the trees of
2Mac	4:13	extreme of Hellenization and I in the adoption of
Lk	17:5	said to the Lord, I our faith!"
Jn	3:30	He must I, but I must decrease."
Rom	5:20	Law came in, to I the trespass; but where
2Cor	4:15	more people it may I thanksgiving, to the glory
	9:10	multiply your resources and I the harvest of your
1Thes	3:12	the Lord make you I and abound in love

INCREASED (26)

Gen	7:17	earth; and the waters I, and bore up the
	7:18	The waters prevailed and I greatly upon the earth;
	30:30	came, and it has I abundantly; and the LORD
Ex	1:6	Israel were fruitful and I greatly; they multiplied and
	23:30	you, until you are I and possess the land.
1Sam	14:19	camp of the Philistines I more and more; and
1Chr	4:38	and their fathers' houses I greatly.
Ezra	10:10	foreign women, and so I the guilt of Israel.
Jud	9:7	now, the Assyrians are I in their might; they
Job	1:10	and his possessions have I in the land.
Wis	10:10	in his labors, and I the fruit of his
Is	9:3	the nation, thou hast I its joy; they rejoice
	26:15	But thou hast I the nation, O LORD, thou
	26:15	O LORD, thou hast I the nation; thou art
Jer	3:16	you have multiplied and I in the land, in
Ezek	23:19	Yet she I her harlotry, remembering the days of
	28:5	in trade you have I your wealth, and your
Hos	4:7	The more they I, the more they sinned against
	10:1	The more his fruit I the more altars he
Nah	3:16	You I your merchants more than the stars of
1Mac	3:42	saw that misfortunes had I and that the forces
Lk	2:52	And Jesus I in wisdom and in stature, and
Acts	6:7	the word of God I; and the number of
	9:22	But Saul I all the more in strength, and
	16:5	the faith, and they I in numbers daily.
Rom	5:20	trespass; but where sin I, grace abounded all the

INCREASES (11)

Ps	49:16	becomes rich, when the glory of his house I
Prov	16:21	discernment, and pleasant speech I persuasiveness.
	23:28	like a robber and I the faithless among men.
	29:16	are in authority, transgression I; but the righteous
Eccl	1:18	vexation, and he who I knowledge increases sorrow.
	1:18	he who increases knowledge I sorrow.
Sir	21:12	is a cleverness which I bitterness.
	31:30	Drunkenness I the anger of a fool to his
Is	40:29	has no might he I strength.
2Cor	10:15	that as your faith I, our field among you
Phil	4:17	seek the fruit which I to your credit.

INCREASING (7)

2Sam	15:12	grew strong, and the people with Absalom kept I
Sir	43:8	named for the moon, I marvelously in its phases,
Mk	4:8	grain, growing up and I and yielding thirtyfold and
Lk	11:29	When the crowds were I, he began to say,
Acts	6:1	when the disciples were I in number, the Hellenists
Col	1:10	every good work and I in the knowledge of
2Thes	1:3	every one of you for one another is I

INCREDIBLE (3)

Wis	16:17	For—most I of all—in the water, which
	19:5	people might experience an I journey, but they
Acts	26:8	Why is it thought I by any of you

INCUR (6)

2Chr	19:10	that they may not I guilt before the LORD
	19:10	and you will not I guilt.
Sir	9:5	lest you stumble and I penalties for her.
	39:23	The nations will I his wrath, just as he
Rom	13:2	those who resist will I judgment.
1Tim	5:12	marry, and so they I condemnation for having

INCURABLE (9)

2Chr	21:18	his bowels with an I disease.
Jud	5:12	land of Egypt with I plagues; and so the
Job	34:6	liar; my wound is I, though I am without
Is	17:11	day of grief and I pain.
Jer	15:18	pain unceasing, my wound I, refusing to be healed?
	30:12	LORD: Your hurt is I, and your wound is
	30:15	Your pain is I
Mic	1:9	For her wound is I; and it has come
2Mac	9:5	Israel, struck him an I and unseen blow.

INCURRED (6)

Ex	28:38	upon himself any guilt I in the holy offering
2Chr	33:23	himself, but this Amon I guilt more and more.
Hos	12:8	riches can never offset the guilt he has I
	13:1	in Israel; but he I guilt through Baal and
2Mac	9:16	over; and the expenses I for the sacrifices he
Acts	27:21	sail from Crete and I this injury and loss.

INCURRING

Tob	6:12	to another man without I the penalty of death,

INCURS (3)

Prov	9:7	reproves a wicked man I injury.
Sir	6:1	for a bad name I shame and reproach: so
	23:16	sins, and a third I wrath.

INDEBTED

Lk	11:4	every one who is I to us; and lead

INDECENCY

Deut	24:1	he has found some I in her, and he

INDECENT

Deut	23:14	may not see anything I among you, and turn

INDEED (83)

Gen	18:13	and say, 'Shall I I bear a child, now
	18:23	and said, "Wilt thou I destroy the righteous with
	20:12	Besides she is I my sister, the daughter of
	22:17	only son, I will I bless you, and I
	37:8	to him, "Are you I to reign over us?
	37:8	Or are you I to have dominion over us?"
	37:10	mother and your brothers I come to bow ourselves
	40:15	For I was I stolen out of the land
	44:15	man as I can I divine?"
Num	12:2	said, "Has the LORD I spoken only through Moses?
	21:2	said, "If thou wilt I give this people into
Deut	2:15	For I the hand of the LORD was against
	17:15	about me'; you may I set as king over
1Sam	1:11	hosts, if thou wilt I look on the affliction
2Sam	15:8	'If the LORD will I bring me back to
1Kgs	8:27	"But will God I dwell on the earth?
2Kgs	14:10	You have I smitten Edom, and your heart has
2Chr	6:18	"But will God dwell I with man on the
Job	19:5	If I you magnify yourselves against me, and make
Ps	58:1	Do you I decree what is right, you gods?
Sir	18:16	I, does not a word surpass a good gift?
Jer	13:12	you, 'Do we not I know that every jar
	22:4	For if you will I obey this word, then
Ezek	28:3	god— you are I wiser than Daniel; no
Dan	11:18	end to his insolence; I he shall turn his
Amos	2:11	Is it not I so, O people of Israel?"
Mal	2:2	will curse your blessings; I I have already cursed
Mt	12:29	Then I he may plunder his house.
	13:14	With them I is fulfilled the prophecy of Isaiah
	13:14	which says: 'You shall I hear but never understand,
	13:14	understand, and you shall I see but never perceive.
	13:23	and understands it; he I bears fruit, and yields,
	13:34	the crowds in parables; I he said nothing to
	26:41	into temptation; the spirit I is willing, but the
Mk	3:27	the strong man; then I he may plunder his
	4:12	so that they may I see but not perceive,
	4:12	not perceive, and may I hear but not understand;
	14:38	into temptation; the spirit I is willing, but the
Lk	23:40	And we I justly; for we are receiving the
	24:34	"The Lord has risen I, and has appeared to
Jn	1:47	him, "Behold, an Israelite I, in whom is no
	4:42	know that this is I the Savior of the
	6:14	they said, "This is I the prophet who is
	6:55	my flesh is food I, and my blood is
	6:55	is food indeed, and my blood is drink I
	8:36	Son makes you free, you will be free I
	16:2	out of the synagogues; I, the hour is coming

	16:32	The hour is coming, I it has come, when
Acts	17:28	said, 'For we are I his offspring.'
	28:26	and say, You shall I hear but never understand,
	28:26	understand, and you shall I see but never perceive.
Rom	2:25	Circumcision I is of value if you obey the
	5:13	men sinned-- sin I was in the world
	8:7	submit to God's law, I it cannot;
	8:34	hand of God, who I intercedes for us?
	9:25	As I he says in Hosea, "Those who were
	10:18	I they have; for "Their voice has gone out
	14:20	Everything is I clean, but it is wrong for
	15:27	to do it, and I they are in debt
1Cor	8:5	or on earth--as I there are many "gods"
2Cor	3:10	I, in this case, what once had splendor has
	5:2	Here I we groan, and long to put on
	13:5	is in you?--unless I you fail to meet
Gal	3:21	alive, then righteousness would I be by the law.
Phil	1:15	Some I preach Christ from envy and rivalry, but
	2:27	I he was ill, near to death.
	3:8	I I count everything as loss because of the
	4:10	for me; you were I concerned for me, but
Col	1:6	come to you, as I in the whole world
	2:23	These have I an appearance of wisdom in promoting
	3:15	your hearts, to which I you were called in
1Thes	4:10	love one another; and I you do love all
2Thes	1:6	are suffering-- since I God deems it just
1Tim	3:16	Great I, we confess, is the mystery of our
	6:19	take hold of the life which is life I
2Tim	3:12	I all who desire to live a godly life
Philem	1:11	but now he is I useful to you and
Heb	6:16	Men I swear by a greater than themselves, and
	7:28	I, the law appoints men in their weakness as
	9:22	I, under the law almost everything is purified with
	12:21	I, so terrifying was the sight that Moses said,
3Jn	1:3	of your life, as I you do follow the
Rev	14:13	"Blessed I

INDEPENDENT

1Cor	11:11	Lord woman is not I of man nor man

INDESTRUCTIBLE

Heb	7:16	the power of an I life.

INDIA (5)

Esth	1:1	Ahasuerus who reigned from I to Ethiopia over one
	8:9	of the provinces from I to Ethiopia, a hundred
	13:1	and twenty-seven provinces from I to Ethiopia and to
	16:1	of the provinces from I to Ethiopia, one hundred
1Mac	8:8	provinces, the country of I and Media and Lydia.

INDIAN

1Mac	6:37	there, and also its I driver.

INDICATE (3)

1Mac	8:25	as the occasion may I to them.
	8:27	as the occasion may I to them.
Acts	25:27	a prisoner, not to I the charges against him."

INDICATED (3)

Esth	13:6	have decreed that those I to you in the
2Mac	11:17	asked about the matters I therein.
1Pet	1:11	person or time was I by the Spirit of

INDICATES (2)

Heb	9:8	this the Holy Spirit I that the way into
	12:27	I the removal of what is shaken, as of

INDICTMENT (3)

Job	31:35	that I had the I written by my adversary!
Jer	25:31	the LORD has an I against the nations; he
Hos	12:2	The LORD has an I against Judah, and will

INDIGNANT (12)

Gen	34:7	and the men were I and very angry, because
Judg	10:16	LORD; and he became I over the misery of
Jer	3:5	ever, will he be I to the end?' Behold,
Dan	14:28	it, they were very I and conspired against the
2Mac	13:25	people of Ptolemais were I over the treaty; in
Mt	20:24	heard it, they were I at the two brothers.
	21:15	they were I;
	26:8	saw it, they were I, saying, "Why this waste?
Mk	10:14	saw it he was I, and said to them,
	10:41	they began to be I at James and John.
Lk	13:14	ruler of the synagogue, I because Jesus had healed
2Cor	11:29	is made to fall, and I am not I

INDIGNANTLY

Mk	14:4	who said to themselves I, "Why was the ointment

INDIGNATION (27)

Ps	7:11	a God who has I every day.
	38:3	flesh because of thy I; there is no health
	69:24	Pour out thy I upon them, and let thy
	78:49	his fierce anger, wrath, I, and distress, a company
	85:4	and put away thy I toward us!
	102:10	drink, because of thy I and anger; for thou
	119:53	Hot I seizes me because of the wicked, who
Is	10:25	very little while my I will come to an
	13:5	the weapons of his I, to destroy the whole
	30:27	lips are full of I, and his tongue is
	66:14	his servants, and his I is against his enemies.
Jer	10:10	earth quakes, and the nations cannot endure his I
	15:17	upon me, for thou hadst filled me with I
	32:37	wrath and in great I; I will bring them
Lam	2:6	and in his fierce I has spurned king and
Ezek	21:31	will pour out my I upon you; I will
	22:24	cleansed, or rained upon in the day of I
	22:31	have poured out my I upon them; I have
	23:25	I will direct my I against you, that they
Dan	8:19	latter end of the I; for it pertains to
	11:36	shall prosper till the I is accomplished; for what
Mic	7:9	I will bear the I of the LORD because
Nah	1:6	Who can stand before his I
Hab	3:8	the rivers, or thy I against the sea, when
Zeph	3:8	out upon them my I, all the heat of
Zech	1:12	which thou hast had I these seventy years?'
2Cor	7:11	to clear yourselves, what I, what alarm, what

INDISPENSABLE

1Cor	12:22	to be weaker are I,

INDISTINCT

1Cor	14:8	the bugle gives an I sound, who will get

INDIVIDUALLY (3)

Rom	12:5	body in Christ, and I members one of another.
1Cor	12:11	apportions to each one I as he wills.
	12:27	body of Christ and I members of it.

INDIVIDUALS

1Chr	23:24	the names of the I from twenty years old

INDOLENCE

Eccl	10:18	sinks in, and through I the house leaks.

INDOLENT (2)

Sir	22:1	The I may be compared to a filthy stone,
	22:2	The I may be compared to the filth of

INDOORS

2Mac	3:19	maidens who were kept I ran together to the

INDUCED (3)

2Chr	18:2	were with him, and I him to go up
2Mac	4:12	the citadel, and he I the noblest of the
	4:46	as if for refreshment, I the king to change

INDULGE (2)

1Cor	10:8	We must not I in immorality as some of
2Pet	2:10	and especially those who I in the lust of

INDULGED

Jude	1:7	likewise acted immorally and I in unnatural lust,

INDULGENCE (2)

Wis	12:20	such great care and I the enemies of thy
Col	2:23	value in checking the I of the flesh.

INDULGENT

Sir	7:24	not show yourself too I with them.

INDUSTRIOUS (2)

1Kgs	11:28	the young man was I he gave him charge
Sir	31:22	all your work be I, and no sickness will

INEFFECTIVE

2Pet	1:8	keep you from being I or unfruitful in the

INESCAPABLE

Wis	17:17	seized, and endured the I fate; for with one

INEXORABLE
Wis 16:4 that upon those oppressors I want should come,

INEXPERIENCED (4)
1Chr 22:5 son is young and I, and the house that
29:1 chosen, is young and I, and the work is
Wis 13:18 thing that is utterly I; for a prosperous journey,
Sir 34:10 He that is I knows few things, but he

INEXPRESSIBLE
2Cor 9:15 to God for his I gift!

INFAMOUS
Ezek 22:5 will mock you, you I one, full of tumult.

INFANT (5)
1Sam 15:3 both man and woman, I and suckling, ox and
Job 24:9 take in pledge the I of the poor.)
Wis 15:14 more miserable than an I, are all the enemies
Is 65:20 be in it an I that lives but a
Jer 44:7 you man and woman, I and child, from the

INFANTRY (14)
Jud 1:4 in force and his I form their ranks—
2:19 their chariots and horsemen and picked troops of I
2:22 his whole army, his I, cavalry, and chariots, and
7:2 hundred and seventy thousand I and twelve thousand
7:20 whole Assyrian army, their I, chariots, and cavalry,
1Mac 3:39 with them forty thousand I and seven thousand
4:1 Gorgias took five thousand I and a thousand picked
15:38 gave him troops of I and cavalry.
16:5 a large force of I and horsemen was coming
16:7 the midst of the I, for the cavalry of
2Mac 11:4 his ten thousands of I, and his thousands of
12:20 hundred and twenty thousand I and two thousand
12:33 out with three thousand I and four hundred cavalry.
13:2 hundred and ten thousand I, five thousand three

INFANTRYMEN
1Mac 4:28 mustered sixty thousand picked I and five thousand

INFANTS (12)
Jud 4:12 to give up their I as prey and their
16:5 sword, and dash my I to the ground and
Job 3:16 hidden untimely birth, as I that never see the
Ps 8:2 mouth of babes and I, thou hast founded a
Wis 11:7 decree to slay the I, thou gavest them abundant
Is 13:16 Their I will be dashed in pieces before their
Lam 2:11 of my people, because I and babes faint in
Joel 2:16 the elders; gather the children, even nursing I
1Mac 1:61 and they hung the I from their mothers' necks.
2Mac 5:13 women, and children, and slaughter of virgins and I
Lk 18:15 they were bringing even I to him that he
Acts 7:19 fathers to expose their I, that they might not

INFATUATED (2)
Prov 5:19 times with delight, be I always with her love.
5:20 Why should you be I, my son, with a

INFERIOR (8)
Job 12:3 you; I am not I to you.
13:2 know; I am not I to you.
Sir 25:8 not served a man I to himself;
Dan 2:39 shall arise another kingdom I to you, and yet
1Cor 12:24 greater honor to the I part,
2Cor 11:5 not in the least I to these superlative apostles.
12:11 was not at all I to these superlative apostles,
Heb 7:7 beyond dispute that the I is blessed by the

INFERRED
Wis 19:18 This may be clearly I from the sight of

INFERS
Wis 8:8 things of old, and I the things to come;

INFIRMITIES (4)
Ps 41:3 sickbed; in his illness thou healest all his I
Mt 8:17 Isaiah, "He took our I and bore our diseases."
Lk 5:15 to hear and to be healed of their I
8:2 of evil spirits and I: Mary, called Magdalene, from

INFIRMITY (5)
Mt 4:23 every disease and every I among the people.
9:35 the kingdom, and healing every disease and every I
10:1 out, and to heal every disease and every I
Lk 13:11 had a spirit of I for eighteen years; she
13:12 to her, "Woman, you are freed from your I

INFLAMED (3)
Jer 51:39 While they are I I will prepare them a
2Mac 4:38 of the deceased; and I with anger, he immediately
14:11 hostile to Judas, quickly I Demetrius still more.

INFLAMES
Is 5:11 the evening till wine I them!

INFLAMMATION
Deut 28:22 consumption, and with fever, I, and fiery heat, and

INFLICT (4)
Deut 7:15 you knew, will he I upon you, but he
Sir 12:6 hates sinners and will I punishment on the ungodly.
48:8 who anointed kings to I retribution, and prophets to
Rom 3:5 God is unjust to I wrath on us?

INFLICTED (7)
2Chr 16:10 And Asa I cruelties upon some of the people
Esth 16:18 all things, has speedily I on him the punishment
Is 30:26 and heals the wounds I by his blow.
Lam 1:12 me, which the LORD I on the day of
1Mac 8:4 they crushed them and I great disaster upon them;
2Mac 9:28 such as he had I on others, came to
Acts 16:23 And when they had I many blows upon them,

INFLICTING (2)
2Mac 3:26 and scourged him continuously, I many blows on him.
2Thes 1:8 angels in flaming fire, I vengeance upon those who

INFLICTIONS
2Mac 9:6 the bowels of others with many and strange I

INFORM (4)
2Sam 15:28 comes from you to I me."
Ezra 4:14 therefore we send and I the king,
Tob 10:8 father, and they will I him how things are
Dan 13:50 sit among us and I us, for God has

INFORMATION (4)
1Sam 23:23 hides, and come back to me with sure I
Ezra 5:10 their names, for your I, that we might write
2Mac 13:21 the Jews, gave secret I to the enemy; he
Acts 25:15 of the Jews gave I about him, asking for

INFORMED (15)
Tob 1:19 of Nineveh went and I the king about me,
Jud 11:8 kingdom, thoroughly I and marvelous in military
Esth 12:2 the king; and he I the king concerning them.
Sir 37:14 sometimes keeps him better I than seven watchmen
2Mac 3:7 of the money about which he had been I
4:1 mentioned Simon, who had I about the money
11:18 I have I the king of everything that needed
11:29 Menelaus has I us that you wish to return
13:4 scoundrel; and when Lysias I him that this man
14:20 and the leader had I the people, and it
Lk 1:4 concerning the things of which you have been I
Acts 23:22 one that you have I me of this."
25:2 men of the Jews I him against Paul; and
1Cor 10:28 for the man who I you, and for conscience'
Jude 1:5 once for all fully I, that he who saved

INFORMS
Job 17:5 He who I against his friends to get a

INGATHERING (3)
Ex 23:16 keep the feast of I at the end of
34:22 and the feast of I at the year's end.
Deut 16:13 when you make your I from your threshing floor

INHABIT (9)
Num 15:2 land you are to I, which I give you,
Jud 5:3 What cities do they I
Job 15:28 which no man should I, which were destined to
Ps 109:10 they be driven out of the ruins they I
Prov 2:21 For the upright will I the land, and men
Is 65:21 shall build houses and I them; they shall plant
65:22 not build and another I; they shall not plant
Amos 9:14 the ruined cities and I them; they shall plant
Zeph 1:13 houses, they shall not I them; though they plant

INHABITANT (27)
Jud 7:20 water belonging to every I of Bethulia were empty;
Is 5:9 be desolate, large and beautiful houses, without I

6:11 cities lie waste without I, and houses without men,
12:6 sing for joy, O I of Zion, for great
24:17 are upon you, O I of the earth!
33:24 And no I will say, "I am sick"; the
Jer 2:15 a waste; his cities are in ruins, without I
4:7 a waste; your cities will be ruins without I
9:11 make the cities of Judah a desolation, without I
21:13 am against you, O I of the valley, O
22:23 O I of Lebanon, nested among the cedars, how
26:9 Shiloh, and this city shall be desolate, without I
33:10 desolate, without man or I or beast, there shall
34:22 make the cities of Judah a desolation without I
44:22 and a curse, without I, as it is this
46:19 Memphis shall become a waste, a ruin, without I
47:2 cry out, and every I of the land shall
48:9 a desolation, with no I in them.
48:18 the parched ground, O I of Dibon!
48:19 way and watch, O I of Aroer!
48:43 are before you, O I of Moab!
51:29 make the land of Babylon a desolation, without I
51:35 let the I of Zion say.
51:37 of jackals, a horror and a hissing, without I
Ezek 7:7 come to you, O I of the land; the
Zeph 2:5 destroy you till no I is left.
3:6 been made desolate, without a man, without an I

INHABITANTS (225)

Gen 19:25 valley, and all the I of the cities, and
34:30 me odious to the I of the land, the
36:20 Seir the Horite, the I of the land: Lotan,
50:11 When the I of the land, the Canaanites, saw
Ex 15:14 have seized on the I of Philistia.
15:15 seizes them; all the I of Canaan have melted
23:31 I will deliver the I of the land into
34:12 a covenant with the I of the land whither
34:15 a covenant with the I of the land, and
Lev 18:25 its iniquity, and the land vomited out its I
25:10 land to all its I; it shall be a
Num 13:32 land that devours its I; and all the people
14:14 they will tell the I of this land.
32:17 cities because of the I of the land.
33:52 drive out all the I of the land from
33:55 not drive out the I of the land from
Deut 13:13 have drawn away the I of the city, saying,
13:15 shall surely put the I of that city to
Josh 2:9 and that all the I of the land melt
2:24 and moreover all the I of the land are
7:9 Canaanites and all the I of the land will
8:24 finished slaughtering all the I of Ai in the
8:26 utterly destroyed all the I of Ai.
9:3 But when the I of Gibeon heard what Joshua
9:11 elders and all the I of our country said
9:24 to destroy all the I of the land from
10:1 king, and how the I of Gibeon had made
11:19 except the Hivites, the I of Gibeon; they took
13:6 of Hamath, all the I of the hill country
15:15 from there against the I of Debir; now the
15:63 But the Jebusites, the I of Jerusalem, the people
17:7 along southward to the I of En-tappuah.
17:11 its villages, and the I of Dor and its
17:11 its villages, and the I of Endor and its
17:11 its villages, and the I of Taanach and its
17:11 its villages, and the I of Megiddo and its
Judg 1:11 they went against the I of Debir.
1:19 not drive out the I of the plain, because
1:27 not drive out the I of Beth-shean and its
1:27 its villages, or the I of Dor and its
1:27 its villages, or the I of Ibleam and its
1:27 its villages, or the I of Megiddo and its
1:30 not drive out the I of Kitron, or the
1:30 of Kitron, or the I of Nahalol; but the
1:31 not drive out the I of Acco, or the
1:31 of Acco, or the I of Sidon, or of
1:32 among the Canaanites, the I of the land; for
1:33 not drive out the I of Beth-shemesh, or the
1:33 of Beth-shemesh, or the I of Beth-anath, but dwelt
1:33 among the Canaanites, the I of the land;
1:33 the land; nevertheless the I of Beth-shemesh and of
2:2 no covenant with the I of this land; you
5:23 LORD, curse bitterly its I, because they came not
10:18 head over all the I of Gilead."
11:8 head over all the I of Gilead."
20:15 the sword, besides the I of Gibe-ah, who mustered
21:9 not one of the I of Jabesh-gilead was there.
21:10 "Go and smite the I of Jabesh-gilead with the
21:12 they found among the I of Jabesh-gilead four
1Sam 6:21 sent messengers to the I of Kiriath-jearim, saying,
23:5 So David delivered the I of Keilah.
27:8 for these were the I of the land from
31:11 But when the I of Jabesh-gilead heard what the
2Sam 5:6 against the Jebusites, the I of the land, who
2Kgs 19:26 of ruins, while their I, shorn of strength, are
22:16 place and upon its I, all the words of
22:19 place, and against its I, that they should become
23:2 Judah and all the I of Jerusalem, and the
1Chr 4:23 were the potters and I of Netaim and Gederah;
4:40 peaceful; for the former I there belonged to Ham.
8:6 fathers' houses of the I of Geba, and they
8:13 fathers' houses of the I of Aijalon, who put
8:13 put to flight the I of Gath);
11:4 the Jebusites were, the I of the land.
11:5 The I of Jebus said to David, "You will
22:18 he has delivered the I of the land into
2Chr 15:5 disturbances afflicted all the I of the lands.
20:7 God, drive out the I of this land before
20:15 "Hearken, all Judah and I of Jerusalem, and King
20:18 all Judah and the I of Jerusalem fell down
20:20 "Hear me, Judah and I of Jerusalem!
20:23 Moab rose against the I of Mount Seir, destroying
20:23 an end of the I of Seir, they all
21:11 Judah, and led the I of Jerusalem into unfaithfulness,
21:13 led Judah and the I of Jerusalem into unfaithfulness,
22:1 And the I of Jerusalem made Ahaziah his youngest
32:22 saved Hezekiah and the I of Jerusalem from the
32:26 both he and the I of Jerusalem, so that
32:33 all Judah and the I of Jerusalem did him
33:9 seduced Judah and the I of Jerusalem, so that
34:9 Benjamin and from the I of Jerusalem.
34:24 place and upon its I, all the curses that
34:27 this place and its I, and you have humbled
34:28 I will bring upon this place and its I
34:30 of Judah and the I of Jerusalem and the
34:32 And the I of Jerusalem did according to the
35:18 were present, and the I of Jerusalem.
Ezra 4:6 an accusation against the I of Judah and Jerusalem.
Neh 3:13 Hanun and the I of Zanoah repaired the Valley
7:3 guards from among the I of Jerusalem, each to
9:24 subdue before them the I of the land, the
Jud 1:12 and also all the I of the land of
3:4 cities also and their I are your slaves; come
5:15 might destroyed all the I of Heshbon; and crossing
Job 26:5 The shades below tremble, the waters and their I
Ps 33:8 LORD, let all the I of the world stand
33:14 forth on all the I of the earth,
49:1 Give ear, all I of the world,
75:3 totters, and all its I, it is I who
83:7 Amalek, Philistia with the I of Tyre;
107:34 salty waste, because of the wickedness of its I
Sir 10:2 ruler of the city, so are all its I
Is 5:3 And now, O I of Jerusalem and men of
8:14 a snare to the I of Jerusalem.
9:9 know, Ephraim and the I of Samaria, who say
10:31 is in flight, the I of Gebim flee for
18:3 All you I of the world, you who dwell
20:6 And the I of this coastland will say in
21:14 fugitive with bread, O I of the land of
22:21 a father to the I of Jerusalem and to
23:2 Be still, O I of the coast, O merchants
23:6 to Tarshish, wail, O I of the coast!
24:1 he will twist its surface and scatter its I
24:5 lies polluted under its I; for they have transgressed
24:6 the earth, and its I suffer for their guilt;
24:6 their guilt; therefore the I of the earth are
26:5 has brought low the I of the height, the
26:9 in the earth, the I of the world learn
26:18 the earth, and the I of the world have
26:21 place to punish the I of the earth for
37:27 of ruins, while their I, shorn of strength, are
38:11 no more among the I of the world.
40:22 the earth, and its I are like grasshoppers; who
42:10 all that fills it, the coastlands and their I
42:11 Kedar inhabits; let the I of Sela sing for
49:19 too narrow for your I, and those who swallowed
Jer 1:14 forth upon all the I of the land.
4:3 Judah and to the I of Jerusalem: "Break up
4:4 men of Judah and I of Jerusalem; lest my
6:12 my hand against the I of the land," says
8:1 the bones of the I of Jerusalem shall be
10:18 am slinging out the I of the land at
11:2 of Judah and the I of Jerusalem.
11:9 of Judah and the I of Jerusalem.
11:12 of Judah and the I of Jerusalem will go

13:13 with drunkenness all the I of this land: the
13:13 prophets, and all the I of Jerusalem.
17:20 Judah, and all the I of Jerusalem, who enter
17:25 of Judah and the I of Jerusalem; and this
18:11 of Judah and the I of Jerusalem: 'Thus says
19:3 kings of Judah and I of Jerusalem.
19:12 LORD, and to its I, making this city like
21:6 I will smite the I of this city, both
23:14 to me, and its I like Gomorrah."
25:2 Judah and all the I of Jerusalem:
25:9 this land and its I, and against all these
25:29 sword against all the I of the earth, says
25:30 grapes, against all the I of the earth.
26:15 this city and its I, for in truth the
32:32 of Judah and the I of Jerusalem.
35:13 of Judah and the I of Jerusalem, Will you
35:17 Judah and all the I of Jerusalem all the
36:31 them, and upon the I of Jerusalem, and upon
42:18 poured out on the I of Jerusalem, so my
46:8 the earth, I will destroy cities and their I
46:19 baggage for exile, O I of Egypt!
48:28 in the rock, O I of Moab!
49:8 in the depths, O I of Dedan!
49:20 has formed against the I of Teman: Even the
49:30 in the depths, O I of Hazor!
50:21 Merathaim, and against the I of Pekod.
50:34 but unrest to the I of Babylon.
50:35 LORD, and upon the I of Babylon, and upon
51:1 against Babylon, against the I of Chaldea;
51:12 he spoke concerning the I of Babylon.
51:24 Babylon and all the I of Chaldea before your
51:35 blood be upon the I of Chaldea," let Jerusalem
Lam 4:12 or any of the I of the world, that
Bar 1:15 of Judah, to the I of Jerusalem,
2:23 the whole land will be a desolation without I
Ezek 11:15 those of whom the I of Jerusalem have said,
12:19 Lord GOD concerning the I of Jerusalem in the
15:6 I give up the I of Jerusalem.
26:17 sea, you and your I, who imposed your terror
27:8 The I of Sidon and Arvad were your rowers;
27:35 All the I of the coastlands are appalled at
29:6 "Then all the I of Egypt shall know that
33:24 "Son of man, the I of these waste places
Dan 4:35 to generation; all the I of the earth are
4:35 heaven and among the I of the earth; and
9:7 of Judah, to the I of Jerusalem, and to
Hos 4:1 a controversy with the I of the land.
10:5 The I of Samaria tremble for the calf of
Joel 1:2 men, give ear, all I of the land!
1:13 elders and all the I of the land to
2:1 Let all the I of the land tremble, for
Amos 1:5 and cut off the I from the Valley of
1:8 will cut off the I from Ashdod, and him
Mic 1:11 Pass on your way, I of Shaphir, in nakedness
1:11 nakedness and shame; the I of Zaanan do not
1:12 For the I of Maroth wait anxiously for good,
1:13 steeds to the chariots, I of Lachish; you were
1:15 a conqueror upon you, I of Mareshah; the glory
6:12 full of violence; your I speak lies, and their
6:16 a desolation, and your I a hissing; so you
7:13 desolate because of its I, for the fruit of
Zeph 1:4 and against all the I of Jerusalem; and I
1:11 Wail, O I of the Mortar!
1:18 make of all the I of the earth.
2:5 Woe to you I of the seacoast, you nation
Zech 8:20 yet come, even the I of many cities;
8:21 of many cities; the I of one city shall
11:6 have pity on the I of this land, says
12:5 say to themselves, 'The I of Jerusalem have strength
12:7 the glory of the I of Jerusalem may not
12:8 a shield about the I of Jerusalem so that
12:10 of David and the I of Jerusalem a spirit
13:1 of David and the I of Jerusalem to cleanse
1Mac 1:28 land shook for its I, and all the house
6:12 sent to destroy the I of Judah without good
11:18 were killed by the I of the strongholds.
2Mac 9:2 to flight by the I and beat a shameful
Acts 1:19 known to all the I of Jerusalem, so that
4:16 manifest to all the I of Jerusalem, and we
Rev 13:12 the earth and its I worship the first beast,

INHABITED (30)

Judg 1:17 defeated the Canaanites who I Zephath, and utterly
11:21 of the Amorites, who I that country.
Prov 8:31 always, rejoicing in his I world and delighting in
Is 13:20 It will never be I or dwelt in for
44:26 Jerusalem, 'She shall be I and of the cities
45:18 formed it to be I: "I am the LORD,
Jer 17:25 this city shall be I for ever.
46:26 Afterward Egypt shall be I as in the days
50:13 she shall not be I, but shall be an
50:39 more for ever, nor I for all generations.
Bar 4:35 time she will be I by demons.
Ezek 12:20 And the I cities shall be laid waste, and
26:19 cities that are not I, when I bring up
26:20 you will not be I or have a place
34:13 and in all the I places of the country.
35:9 perpetual desolation, and your cities shall not be I
36:10 the cities shall be I and the waste places
36:11 cause you to be I as in your former
36:33 the cities to be I, and the waste places
36:35 ruined cities are now I and fortified.'
38:12 places which are now I, and the people who
Joel 3:20 But Judah shall be I for ever, and Jerusalem
Zech 2:4 man, 'Jerusalem shall be I as villages without walls,
7:7 When Jerusalem was I and in prosperity, with her
7:7 and the lowland were I, were not these the
12:6 Jerusalem shall still be I in its place, in
14:11 And it shall be I, for there shall be
2Mac 3:1 the holy city was I in unbroken peace and
9:17 and would visit every I place to proclaim the
12:13 earthworks and walls, and I by all sorts of

INHABITS (2)

Is 42:11 the villages that Kedar I; let the inhabitants of
57:15 and lofty One who I eternity, whose name is

INHERIT (44)

Ex 32:13 descendants, and they shall I it for ever.'"
Lev 20:24 to you, 'You shall I their land, and I
25:46 sons after you, to I as a possession for
Num 26:55 of the tribes of their fathers they shall I
32:19 For we will not I with them on the
33:54 You shall I the land by lot according to
33:54 to the tribes of your fathers you shall I
34:13 land which you shall I by lot, which the
Deut 1:38 shall cause Israel to I it.
12:10 God gives you to I, and when he gives
16:20 you may live and I the land which the
Josh 1:6 cause this people to I the land which I
Judg 11:2 him, "You shall not I in our father's house;
1Sam 2:8 sit with princes and I a seat of honor.
2Kgs 2:9 pray you, let me I a double share of
2Chr 20:11 thy possession, which thou hast given us to I
Tob 4:12 and their posterity will I the land.
Job 13:26 me, and makest me I the iniquities of my
Ps 69:36 of his servants shall I it, and those who
Prov 3:35 The wise will I honor, but fools get disgrace.
11:29 troubles his household will I wind, and the fool
Sir 10:11 is dead he will I creeping things, and wild
19:3 Decay and worms will I him, and the reckless
37:26 among his people will I confidence, and his name
44:22 and cause them to I from sea to sea
Is 57:13 the land, and shall I my holy mountain.
65:9 mountains; my chosen shall I it, and my servants
Jer 12:14 my people Israel to I: "Behold, I will pluck
Zech 2:12 And the LORD will I Judah as his portion
Mt 5:5 meek, for they shall I the earth.
19:29 receive a hundredfold, and I eternal life.
25:34 blessed of my Father, I the kingdom prepared for
Mk 10:17 must I do to I eternal life?"
Lk 10:25 shall I do to I eternal life?"
18:18 shall I do to I eternal life?"
Rom 4:13 descendants, that they should I the world, did not
1Cor 6:9 the unrighteous will not I the kingdom of God?
6:10 revilers, nor robbers will I the kingdom of God.
15:50 flesh and blood cannot I the kingdom of God,
15:50 nor does the perishable I the imperishable.
Gal 4:30 the slave shall not I with the son of
5:21 such things shall not I the kingdom of God.
Heb 6:12 through faith and patience I the promises.
12:17 when he desired to I the blessing, he was

INHERITANCE (234)

Gen 31:14 there any portion or I left to us in
48:6 by the name of their brothers in their I
Ex 34:9 and our sin, and take us for thy I
Lev 27:16 which is his by I, then your valuation shall
27:22 of his possession by I,
27:24 whom the land belongs as a possession by I
Num 16:14 honey, nor given us I of fields and vineyards.
18:20 "You shall have no I in their land, neither

18:20 your portion and your I among the people of
18:21 in Israel for an I, in return for their
18:23 the people of Israel they shall have no I
18:24 the Levites for an I; therefore I have said
18:24 they shall have no I among the people of
18:26 from them for your I, then you shall present
26:53 shall be divided for I according to the number
26:54 shall give a large I, and to a small
26:54 shall give a small I; every tribe shall be
26:54 shall be given its I according to its numbers.
26:56 Their I shall be divided according to lot between
26:62 because there was no I given to them among
27:7 possession of an I among their father's brethren
27:7 brethren and cause the I of their father to
27:8 you shall cause his I to pass to his
27:9 you shall give his I to his brothers.
27:10 you shall give his I to his father's brothers.
27:11 you shall give his I to his kinsman that
32:18 the people of Israel have inherited each his I
32:19 and beyond; because our I has come to us
32:32 the possession of our I shall remain with us
33:54 shall give a large I, and to a small
33:54 shall give a small I; wherever the lot falls
34:2 to you for an I, the land of Canaan
34:14 houses have received their I, and also the half-tribe
34:15 half-tribe have received their I beyond the Jordan at
34:17 land to you for I: Eleazar the priest and
34:18 of every tribe, to divide the land for I
34:29 commanded to divide the I for the people of
35:2 the Levites, from the I of their possession, cities
35:8 in proportion to the I which it inherits, shall
36:2 give the land for I by lot to the
36:2 LORD to give the I of Zelophehad our brother
36:3 of Israel then their I will be taken from
36:3 be taken from the I of our fathers, and
36:3 and added to the I of the tribe to
36:3 be taken away from the lot of our I
36:4 Israel comes, then their I will be added to
36:4 be added to the I of the tribe to
36:4 they belong; and their I will be taken from
36:4 be taken from the I of the tribe of
36:7 The I of the people of Israel shall not
36:7 shall cleave to the I of the tribe of
36:8 daughter who possesses an I in any tribe of
36:8 Israel may possess the I of his fathers.
36:9 So no I shall be transferred from one tribe
36:9 people of Israel shall cleave to its own I
36:12 of Joseph, and their I remained in the tribe
Deut 4:21 the LORD your God gives you for an I
4:38 their land for an I, as at this day;
10:9 has no portion or I with his brothers; the
10:9 the LORD is his I, as the LORD your
12:9 rest and to the I which the LORD your
12:12 has no portion or I with you.
14:27 has no portion or I with you.
14:29 has no portion or I with you, and the
15:4 gives you for an I to possess),
18:1 have no portion or I with Israel; they shall
18:2 They shall have no I among their brethren; the
18:2 the LORD is their I, as he promised them.
19:10 gives you for an I, and so the guilt
19:14 "In the I which you will hold in the
20:16 gives you for an I, you shall save alive
21:16 his possessions as an I to his sons, he
21:23 the LORD your God gives you for an I
24:4 the LORD your God gives you for an I
25:19 gives you for an I to possess, you shall
26:1 gives you for an I, and have taken possession
29:8 gave it for an I to the Reubenites, the
32:8 to the nations their I, when he separated the
Josh 11:23 gave it for an I to Israel according to
13:6 to Israel for an I, as I have commanded
13:7 this land for an I to the nine tribes
13:8 the Gadites received their I, which Moses gave them,
13:14 alone Moses gave no I; the offerings by fire
13:14 of Israel are their I, as he said to
13:15 And Moses gave an I to the tribe of
13:23 This was the I of the Reubenites, according to
13:24 And Moses gave an I also to the tribe
13:28 This is the I of the Gadites according to
13:29 And Moses gave an I to the half-tribe of
13:33 Levi Moses gave no I; the LORD God of
13:33 of Israel is their I, as he said to
14:2 Their I was by lot, as the LORD had
14:3 Moses had given an I to the two and
14:3 Levites he gave no I among them.
14:9 trodden shall be an I for you and your
14:13 to Caleb the son of Jephunneh for an I
14:14 So Hebron became the I of Caleb the son
15:20 This is the I of the tribe of the
16:4 of Joseph, Manasseh and Ephraim, received their I
16:5 the boundary of their I on the east was
16:8 Such is the I of the tribe of the
16:9 the Ephraimites within the I of the Manassites, all
17:4 to give us an I along with our brethren."
17:4 he gave them an I among the brethren of
17:6 of Manasseh received an I along with his sons.
17:14 one portion as an I, although I am a
18:2 Israel seven tribes whose I had not yet been
18:7 Manasseh have received their I beyond the Jordan
18:20 This is the I of the tribe of Benjamin,
18:28 This is the I of the tribe of Benjamin
19:1 its families; and its I was in the midst
19:1 the midst of the I of the tribe of
19:2 it had for its I Beer-sheba, Sheba, Moladah,
19:8 This was the I of the tribe of Simeon
19:9 The I of the tribe of Simeon formed part
19:9 of Simeon obtained an I in the midst of
19:9 obtained an inheritance in the midst of their I
19:10 the territory of its I reached as far as
19:16 This is the I of the tribe of Zebulun,
19:23 This is the I of the tribe of Issachar,
19:31 This is the I of the tribe of Asher
19:39 This is the I of the tribe of Naphtali
19:41 territory of its I included Zorah, Eshtaol, Ir-shemesh,
19:48 This is the I of the tribe of Dan,
19:49 of Israel gave an I among them to Joshua
21:3 following cities and pasture lands out of their I
23:4 to you as an I for your tribes those
24:28 sent the people away, every man to his I
24:30 him in his own I at Timnath-serah, which is
24:32 money; it became an I of the descendants of
Judg 2:6 went each to his I to take possession of
2:9 the bounds of his I in Timnath-heres, in the
18:1 seeking for itself an I to dwell in; for
18:1 for until then no I among the tribes of
20:6 the country of the I of Israel; for they
21:17 "There must be an I for the survivors of
21:23 and returned to their I, and rebuilt the towns,
21:24 went out from there every man to his I
Ruth 4:5 restore the name of the dead to his I
4:6 it for myself, lest I impair my own I
4:10 the dead in his I, that the name of
2Sam 20:1 and we have no I in the son of
1Kgs 8:36 thou hast given to thy people as an I
12:16 We have no I in the son of Jesse.
21:3 should give you the I of my fathers."
21:4 not give you the I of my fathers." And
1Chr 16:18 land of Canaan, as your portion for an I
28:8 leave it for an I to your children after
2Chr 6:27 thou hast given to thy people as an I
10:16 We have no I in the son of Jesse.
Ezra 9:12 leave it for an I to your children for
Neh 11:20 the towns of Judah, every one in his I
Tob 6:11 her and to her I, for you are her
6:12 than any other man are entitled to the I
Jud 8:22 the desolation of our I --all this he will
9:12 father, God of the I of Israel, Lord of
13:5 time to help thy I, and to carry out
16:21 home to his own I, and Judith went to
Esth 10:12 And God remembered his people and vindicated his I
13:15 desire to destroy the I that has been thine
13:17 have mercy upon thy I; turn our mourning into
14:5 ancestors, for an everlasting I, and that thou didst
14:9 and to destroy thy I, to stop the mouths
Job 42:15 their father gave them I among their brothers.
Ps 78:71 shepherd of Jacob his people, of Israel his I
79:1 have come into thy I; they have defiled thy
105:11 land of Canaan as your portion for an I
Prov 13:22 good man leaves an I to his children's children,
17:2 and will share the I as one of the
20:21 An I gotten hastily in the beginning will in
28:10 pit; but the blameless will have a goodly I
Eccl 7:11 is good with an I, an advantage to those
Sir 9:6 give yourself to harlots lest you lose your I
22:21 that you may share with him in his I
23:12 be found in the I of Jacob!
24:8 in Israel receive your I
24:12 the portion of the Lord, who is their I
24:19 than honey, and my I sweeter than the honeycomb.
24:22 commanded us as an I for the congregations of
33:23 life, in the hour of death, distribute your I

36:11 and give them their I, as at the beginning.
41:6 The I of the children of sinners will perish,
42:3 and of dividing the I of friends;
44:12 their descendants, and their I to their children's
44:24 and gave him his I; he determined his portions,
45:22 people he has no I, and he has no
45:22 for the Lord himself is his portion and I
46:1 them, so that he might give Israel its I
46:8 bring them into their I, into a land flowing
46:9 obtained it for an I;
Jer 10:16 the tribe of his I; the LORD of hosts
16:18 and have filled my I with their abominations."
51:19 the tribe of his I; the LORD of hosts
Lam 5:2 Our I has been turned over to strangers, our
Ezek 35:15 you rejoiced over the I of the house of
36:12 you shall be their I, and you shall no
44:28 "They shall have no I; I am their inheritance:
44:28 inheritance; I am their I: and you shall give
46:16 sons out of his I, it shall belong to
46:16 to his sons, it is their property by I
46:17 gift out of his I to one of his
46:17 his sons may keep a gift from his I
46:18 take any of the I of the people, thrusting
46:18 give his sons their I out of his own
47:13 divide the land for I among the twelve tribes
47:14 this land shall fall to you as your I
47:22 allot it as an I for yourselves and for
47:22 shall be allotted an I among the tribes of
47:23 shall assign him his I, says the Lord GOD.
48:29 shall allot as an I among the tribes of
Mic 2:2 man and his house, a man and his I
7:14 the flock of thy I, who dwell alone in
7:18 passing over transgression for the remnant of his I
1Mac 2:56 the assembly, received an I in the land.
15:33 property, but only the I of our fathers, which
15:34 are firmly holding the I of our fathers.
2Mac 2:4 and had seen the I of God.
2:17 and has returned the I to all, and the
Mt 21:38 him and have his I
Mk 12:7 kill him, and the I will be ours.'
Lk 12:13 my brother divide the I with me."
20:14 kill him, that the I may be ours.'
Acts 7:5 he gave him no I in it, not even
13:19 their land as an I, for about four hundred
20:32 to give you the I among all those who
Gal 3:18 For if the I is by the law, it
Eph 1:14 the guarantee of our I until we acquire possession
1:18 riches of his glorious I in the saints,
5:5 an idolater), has any I in the kingdom of
Col 1:12 to share in the I of the saints in
3:24 you will receive the I as your reward; you
Heb 9:15 receive the promised eternal I, since a death has
11:8 to receive as an I; and he went out,
1Pet 1:4 dead, and to an I which is imperishable, undefiled,

INHERITANCES (6)

Josh 13:32 These are the I which Moses distributed in the
14:1 And these are the I which the people of
18:4 a view to their I, and then come to
19:49 of the land as I, the people of Israel
19:51 These are the I which Eleazar the priest and
1Mac 6:24 they have caught, and they have seized our I

INHERITED (9)

Lev 27:28 beast, or of his I field, shall be sold
Num 32:18 people of Israel have I each his inheritance.
Tob 14:13 He I their property and that of his father
Jud 4:12 the cities they had I to be destroyed, and
Prov 19:14 House and wealth are I from fathers, but a
Jer 16:19 say: "Our fathers have I nought but lies, worthless
1Mac 2:10 What nation has not I her palaces and has
2:57 because he was merciful, I the throne of the
1Pet 1:18 from the futile ways I from your fathers, not

INHERITORS

Is 65:9 Jacob, and from Judah I of my mountains; my

INHERITS

Num 35:8 the inheritance which it I, shall give of its

INHUMAN

2Tim 3:3 parents, ungrateful, unholy, I, implacable, slanderers,

INIQUITIES (52)

Lev 16:21 over him all the I of the people of
16:22 shall bear all their I upon him to a
26:39 also because of the I of their fathers they
Ezra 9:6 my God, for our I have risen higher than
9:7 guilt; and for our I we, our kings, and
9:13 us less than our I deserved and hast given
Neh 9:2 their sins and the I of their fathers.
Tob 13:5 afflict us for our I; and again he will
Job 13:23 How many are my I and my sins?
13:26 makest me inherit the I of my youth.
22:5 There is no end to your I
Ps 38:4 For my I have gone over my head; they
40:12 me without number; my I have overtaken me, till
51:9 from my sins, and blot out all my I
79:8 remember against us the I of our forefathers; let
90:8 Thou hast set our I before thee, our secret
103:10 our sins, nor requite us according to our I
107:17 and because of their I suffered affliction;
130:3 O LORD, shouldst mark I, Lord, who could stand?
130:8 And he will redeem Israel from all his I
Prov 5:22 The I of the wicked ensnare him, and he
Sir 17:16 Their I are not hidden from him, and all
Is 43:24 your sins, you have wearied me with your I
50:1 Behold, for your I you were sold, and for
53:5 was bruised for our I; upon him was the
53:11 be accounted righteous; and he shall bear their I
59:2 cannot hear; but your I have made a separation
59:12 and we know our I:
64:6 a leaf, and our I, like the wind, take
64:7 hast delivered us into the hand of our I
65:7 into their bosom their I and their fathers' iniquities
65:7 and their fathers' I together, says the LORD;
Jer 5:25 for the harvest.' Your I have turned these away,
11:10 turned back to the I of their forefathers, who
14:7 "Though our I testify against us, act, O LORD,
Lam 4:13 her prophets and the I of her priests, who
5:7 and are no more; and we bear their I
Bar 3:5 Remember not the I of our fathers, but in
3:8 punished for all the I of our fathers who
Ezek 24:23 pine away in your I and groan to one
28:18 the multitude of your I, in the unrighteousness of
36:31 loathe yourselves for your I and your abominable
36:33 you from all your I, I will cause the
43:10 plan, that they may be ashamed of their I
Dan 4:27 righteousness, and your I by showing mercy to
9:13 God, turning from our I and giving heed to
9:16 sins, and for the I of our fathers, Jerusalem
Amos 3:2 therefore I will punish you for all your I
Mic 7:19 he will tread our I under foot.
Rom 4:7 "Blessed are those whose I are forgiven, and whose
Heb 8:12 be merciful toward their I, and I will remember
Rev 18:5 high as heaven, and God has remembered her I

INIQUITOUS

Is 10:1 to those who decree I decrees, and the writers

INIQUITY (184)

Gen 15:16 fourth generation; for the I of the Amorites is
Ex 20:5 jealous God, visiting the I of the fathers upon
34:7 love for thousands, forgiving I and transgression and
34:7 the guilty, visiting the I of the fathers upon
34:9 people; and pardon our I and our sin, and
Lev 5:1 yet does not speak, he shall bear his I
5:17 yet he is guilty and shall bear his I
7:18 he who eats of it shall bear his I
10:17 you may bear the I of the congregation, to
17:16 or bathe his flesh, he shall bear his I
18:25 that I punished its I, and the land vomited
19:8 it shall bear his I, because he has profaned
20:17 uncovered his sister's nakedness, he shall bear his I
20:19 naked one's near kin; they shall bear their I
22:16 cause them to bear I and guilt, by eating
26:39 lands because of their I; and also because of
26:40 if they confess their I and the iniquity of
26:40 their iniquity and the I of their fathers in
26:41 make amends for their I;
26:43 make amends for their I, because they spurned my
Num 5:15 offering of remembrance, bringing I to
5:31 shall be free from I, but the woman shall
5:31 from iniquity, but the woman shall bear her I
14:18 in steadfast love, forgiving I and transgression, but he
14:18 the guilty, visiting the I of fathers upon children,
14:19 fourth generation.' Pardon the I of this people, I
14:34 you shall bear your I, forty years, and you
15:31 utterly cut off; his I shall be upon him."
18:1 with you shall bear I in connection with the
18:1 with you shall bear I in connection with your
18:23 they shall bear their I; it shall be a

30:15 heard of them, then he shall bear her I
Deut 5:9 jealous God, visiting the I of the fathers upon
32:4 of faithfulness and without I, just and right is
Josh 22:20 And he did not perish alone for his I
1Sam 3:13 for ever, for the I which he knew, because
3:14 of Eli that the I of Eli's house shall
15:23 and stubbornness is as I and idolatry.
2Sam 7:14 When he commits I, I will chasten him with
24:10 thee, take away the I of thy servant; for
1Chr 21:8 thee, take away the I of thy servant; for
Jud 5:17 the God who hates I is with them.
6:5 the day of your I, you shall not see
Job 4:8 seen, those who plow I and sow trouble reap
7:21 not pardon my transgression and take away my I
10:6 dost seek out my I and search for my
10:14 me, and dost not acquit me of my I
11:11 men; when he sees I, will he not consider
11:14 If I is in your hand, put it far
14:17 a bag, and thou wouldest cover over my I
15:5 For your I teaches your mouth, and you choose
15:16 a man who drinks I like water!
20:27 heavens will reveal his I, and the earth will
21:19 'God stores up their I for their sons.' Let
31:3 befall the unrighteous, and disaster the workers of I
31:11 that would be an I to be punished by
31:28 also would be an I to be punished by
31:33 men, by hiding my I in my bosom,
33:9 and there is no I in me.
34:32 if I have done I, I will do it
36:10 to instruction, and commands that they return from I
36:21 do not turn to I, for this you have
36:33 concerning him, who is jealous with anger against I
Ps 10:7 and oppression; under his tongue are mischief and I
32:2 the LORD imputes no I, and in whose spirit
32:5 did not hide my I; I said, "I will
36:2 own eyes that his I cannot be found out
38:18 I confess my I, I am sorry for my
49:5 of trouble, when the I of my persecutors surrounds
51:2 me thoroughly from my I, and cleanse me from
51:5 was brought forth in I, and in sin did
53:1 are corrupt, doing abominable I; there is none that
66:18 If I had cherished I in my heart, the
78:38 being compassionate, forgave their I, and did not
85:2 Thou didst forgive the I of thy people; thou
89:32 the rod and their I with scourges;
94:23 back on them their I and wipe them out
103:3 who forgives all your I, who heals all your
106:6 sinned; we have committed I, we have done
106:43 their purposes, and were brought low through their I
109:14 May the I of his fathers be remembered before
119:133 promise, and let no I get dominion over me.
141:4 with men who work I; and let me not
Prov 16:6 By loyalty and faithfulness I is atoned for, and
19:28 justice, and the mouth of the wicked devours I
Sir 7:6 be unable to remove I, lest you be partial
17:21 and turn away from I, and hate abominations
23:11 will be filled with I, and the scourge will
25:18 Any I is insignificant compared to a wife's iniquity;
25:18 compared to a wife's I; may a sinner's lot
27:10 prey; so does sin for the workers of I
41:18 or magistrate; and of I, before a congregation or
49:2 the people, and took away the abominations of I
Is 1:4 a people laden with I, offspring of evildoers, sons
1:13 I cannot endure I and solemn assembly.
5:18 to those who draw I with cords of falsehood,
13:11 the wicked for their I; I will put an
22:14 my ears: "Surely this I will not be forgiven
26:21 the earth for their I, and the earth will
30:13 on them; therefore this I shall be to you
31:2 and against the helpers of those who work I
32:6 and his mind plots I: to practice ungodliness, to
33:24 people who dwell there will be forgiven their I
40:2 is ended, that her I is pardoned, that she
53:6 laid on him the I of us all.
57:17 Because of the I of his covetousness I was
59:3 and your fingers with I; your lips have spoken
59:4 speak lies, they conceive mischief and bring forth I
59:6 works are works of I, and deeds of violence
59:7 thoughts are thoughts of I, desolation and destruction
64:9 LORD, and remember not I for ever.
Jer 9:5 speak lies; they commit I and are too weary
13:22 the greatness of your I that your skirts are
14:10 he will remember their I and punish their sins."
14:20 O LORD, and the I of our fathers, for
16:10 What is our I
16:17 me, nor is their I concealed from my eyes.
16:18 will doubly recompense their I and their sin, because
18:23 Forgive not their I, nor blot out their sin
25:12 the Chaldeans, for their I, says the LORD, making
31:34 I will forgive their I, and I will remember
36:3 I may forgive their I and their sin."
36:31 his servants for their I; I will bring upon
50:20 time, says the LORD, I shall be sought in
Lam 2:14 have not exposed your I to restore your fortunes,
4:22 The punishment of your I, O daughter of Zion,
4:22 no longer; but your I, O daughter of Edom,
Bar 3:7 our hearts all the I of our fathers who
Ezek 3:18 shall die in his I; but his blood I
3:19 shall die in his I; but you will have
3:20 his righteousness and commits I, and I lay a
7:13 and because of his I, none can maintain his
7:16 all of them moaning, every one over his I
7:19 For it was the stumbling block of their I
11:2 the men who devise I and who give wicked
14:3 stumbling block of their I before their faces; should
14:4 stumbling block of his I before his face, and
14:7 stumbling block of his I before his face, and
18:8 withholds his hand from I, executes true justice
18:17 withholds his hand from I, takes no interest or
18:17 die for his father's I; he shall surely live.
18:18 his people, behold, he shall die for his I
18:19 son suffer for the I of the father?' When
18:20 not suffer for the I of the father, nor
18:20 father suffer for the I of the son; the
18:24 his righteousness and commits I and does the same
18:26 his righteousness and commits I, he shall die for
18:26 for it; for the I which he has committed
18:30 all your transgressions, lest I be your ruin.
28:15 you were created, till I was found in you.
29:16 of Israel, recalling their I, when they turn to
33:6 taken away in his I, but his blood I
33:8 shall die in his I, but his blood I
33:9 shall die in his I, but you will have
33:13 his righteousness and commits I, none of his
33:13 remembered; but in the I that he has committed
33:15 of life, committing no I; he shall surely live,
33:18 his righteousness, and commits I, he shall die for
39:23 into captivity for their I, because they dealt so
44:12 a stumbling block of I to the house of
Dan 9:24 and to atone for I, to bring in everlasting
13:5 the Lord had said: I came forth from Babylon,
Hos 4:8 of my people; they are greedy for their I
8:13 he will remember their I, and punish their sins;
9:7 because of your great I and great hatred.
9:9 he will remember their I, he will punish their
10:10 them when they are chastised for their double I
10:13 You have plowed I, you have reaped injustice, you
12:11 If there is I in Gilead they shall surely
13:12 The I of Ephraim is bound up, his sin
14:1 God, for you have stumbled because of your I
14:2 him, "Take away all I; accept that which is
Mic 7:18 God like thee, pardoning I and passing over
Hab 2:12 town with blood, and founds a city on I
Zech 3:4 I have taken your I away from you, and
5:6 said, "This is their I in all the land."
Mal 2:6 peace and uprightness, and he turned many from I
Mt 23:27 but within you are full of hypocrisy and I
Lk 13:27 all you workers of I
Acts 8:23 gall of bitterness and in the bond of I
Rom 6:19 to greater and greater I, so now yield your
2Cor 6:14 For what partnership have righteousness and I
2Tim 2:19 names the name of the Lord depart from I
Tit 2:14 redeem us from all I and to purify for

INITIATE

Wis 8:4 For she is an I in the knowledge of

INITIATES

Wis 12:5 These I from the midst of a heathen cult,

INITIATIONS (2)

Wis 14:15 handed on to his dependents secret rites and I
14:23 kill children in their I, or celebrate secret mysteries,

INJECT

Sir 28:9 will disturb friends and I enmity among those who

INJURE (6)

Esth 12:6 and he sought to I Mordecai and his people
16:3 not only seek to I our subjects, but in
Ps 56:5 long they seek to I my cause; all their
Sir 13:12 will not hesitate to I or to imprison.

38:21 no good, and you I yourself.
1Mac 7:15 will not seek to I you or your friends."

INJURED (4)

Lev 21:19 man who has an I foot or an injured
21:19 injured foot or an I hand,
2Mac 12:22 that often they were I by their own men
Rom 14:15 your brother is being I by what you eat,

INJURES

Prov 8:36 he who misses me I himself; all who hate

INJURY (10)

Jud 7:25 done us a great I in not making peace
Prov 9:7 and he who reproves a wicked man incurs I
Wis 18:2 were doing them no I; and they begged their
Sir 10:6 your neighbor for any I, and do not attempt
31:30 a fool to his I, reducing his strength and
2Mac 3:39 and destroys those who come to do it I
9:4 upon the Jews the I done by those who
14:40 by arresting him he would do them an I
Acts 27:10 voyage will be with I and much loss, not
27:21 Crete and incurred this I and loss.

INJUSTICE (17)

Lev 19:15 "You shall do no I in judgment; you shall
Job 5:16 poor have hope, and I shuts her mouth.
Prov 13:23 much food, but it is swept away through I
16:8 a little with righteousness than great revenues with I
22:8 He who sows I will reap calamity, and the
Sir 7:3 sow the furrows of I, and you will not
10:7 and before men, and I is outrageous to both.
10:8 nation on account of I and insolence and wealth.
14:9 a portion, and mean I withers the soul.
20:27 and whoever pleases great men will atone for I
40:12 All bribery and I will be blotted out, but
Jer 22:13 his upper rooms by I; who makes his neighbor
Ezek 7:10 Your doom has come, I has blossomed, pride has
9:9 the city full of I; for they say, 'The
Hos 10:13 iniquity, you have reaped I, you have eaten the
1Mac 9:23 all the doers of I appeared.
Rom 9:14 Is there I on God's part?

INK (4)

Jer 36:18 I wrote them with I on the scroll."
2Cor 3:3 us, written not with I but with the Spirit
2Jn 1:12 not use paper and I, but I hope to
3Jn 1:13 write with pen and I

INLAID

Ezek 27:6 the coasts of Cyprus, I with ivory.

INMOST (2)

Wis 1:6 is witness of his I feelings, and a true
Rom 7:22 of God, in my I self,

INN (2)

Lk 2:7 there was no place for them in the I
10:34 brought him to an I, and took care of

INNER (73)

Ex 12:9 its legs and its I parts.
Lev 10:18 not brought into the I part of the sanctuary.
Num 25:8 of Israel into the I room, and pierced both
Judg 16:9 in wait in an I chamber.
16:12 wait were in an I chamber.
1Kgs 6:5 the nave and the I sanctuary; and he made
6:16 this within as an I sanctuary, as the most
6:17 in front of the I sanctuary, was forty cubits
6:19 The I sanctuary he prepared in the innermost part
6:20 The I sanctuary was twenty cubits long, twenty
6:21 in front of the I sanctuary, and overlaid it
6:22 that belonged to the I sanctuary he overlaid with
6:23 In the I sanctuary he made two cherubim of
6:29 open flowers, in the I and outer rooms.
6:30 with gold in the I and outer rooms.
6:31 the entrance to the I sanctuary he made doors
6:36 He built the I court with three courses of
7:12 beams; so had the I court of the house
7:49 the north, before the I sanctuary; the flowers, the
8:6 its place, in the I sanctuary of the house,
8:8 holy place before the I sanctuary; but they could
20:30 fled, and entered an I chamber in the city.
22:25 you go into an I chamber to hide yourself."
2Kgs 9:2 lead him to an I chamber.
10:25 and went into the I room of the house
1Chr 28:11 upper rooms, and its I chambers, and of the
2Chr 4:20 to burn before the I sanctuary, as prescribed;
4:22 the temple, for the I doors to the most
5:7 its place, in the I sanctuary of the house,
5:9 holy place before the I sanctuary; but they could
18:24 you go into an I chamber to hide yourself."
29:16 priests went into the I part of the house
Esth 4:11 the king inside the I court without being called,
5:1 and stood in the I court of the king's
Prov 18:8 go down into the I parts of the body.
26:22 go down into the I parts of the body.
Wis 17:4 For not even the I chamber that held them
17:13 from reason; and the I expectation of help, being
Sir 50:5 came out of the I sanctuary!
Ezek 8:3 the gateway of the I court that faces north,
8:16 brought me into the I court of the house
10:3 a cloud filled the I court.
40:7 the gate at the I end, one reed.
40:9 gate was at the I end.
40:15 the end of the I vestibule of the gate
40:19 the distance from the I front of the lower
40:19 outer front of the I court, a hundred cubits.
40:23 a gate to the I court; and he measured
40:27 the south of the I court; and he measured
40:28 brought me to the I court by the south
40:32 brought me to the I court on the east
40:44 from without into the I court, and behold, there
40:44 two chambers in the I court, one at the
41:3 he went into the I room and measured the
41:15 the temple and the I room and the outer
41:17 door, even to the I room, and on the
41:17 round about in the I room and the nave
42:1 me out into the I court, toward the north,
42:3 which belonged to the I court, and facing the
43:5 brought me into the I court; and behold, the
44:17 the gates of the I court, they shall wear
44:17 the gates of the I court, and within.
44:21 when he enters the I court.
44:27 holy place, into the I court, to minister in
45:19 the gate of the I court.
46:1 The gate of the I court that faces east
Jon 1:5 gone down into the I part of the ship
1Mac 9:54 the wall of the I court of the sanctuary.
Mt 24:26 he is in the I rooms,' do not believe
Acts 16:24 put them into the I prison and fastened their
2Cor 4:16 is wasting away, our I nature is being renewed
Eph 3:16 his Spirit in the I man,
Heb 6:19 that enters into the I shrine behind the curtain,

INNERMOST (7)

1Sam 24:3 were sitting in the I parts of the cave.
1Kgs 6:19 he prepared in the I part of the house,
6:27 the cherubim in the I part of the house;
7:50 the doors of the I part of the house,
Prov 20:27 LORD, searching all his I parts.
20:30 strokes make clean the I parts.
Amos 6:10 who is in the I parts of the house,

INNKEEPER

Lk 10:35 gave them to the I, saying, 'Take care of

INNOCENCE (5)

Gen 20:5 my heart and the I of my hands I
Ps 26:6 wash my hands in I, and go about thy
73:13 my heart clean and washed my hands in I
1Mac 2:37 all die in our I; heaven and earth testify
2:60 Daniel because of his I was delivered from the

INNOCENT (60)

Gen 20:4 wilt thou slay an I people?
Ex 23:7 do not slay the I and righteous, for I
Deut 19:10 to these three, lest I blood be shed in
19:13 purge the guilt of I blood from Israel, so
21:8 not the guilt of I blood in the midst
21:9 purge the guilt of I blood from your midst,
25:1 between them, acquitting the I and condemning the
27:25 bribe to slay an I person.' And all the
1Sam 19:5 will you sin against I blood by killing David
1Kgs 2:5 in war, and putting I blood upon the girdle
2Kgs 10:9 and said to all the people, "You are I
21:16 Manasseh shed very much I blood, till he had
24:4 and also for the I blood that he had
24:4 he filled Jerusalem with I blood, and the LORD
Tob 3:14 Lord, that I am I of any sin with
Esth 16:5 for the shedding of I blood, and have been
Job 4:7 now, who that was I ever perished?

9:15 Though I am I, I cannot answer him; I
9:20 Though I am I, my own mouth would condemn
9:23 death, he mocks at the calamity of the I
9:28 for I know thou wilt not hold me I
17:8 at this, and the I stirs himself up against
22:19 and are glad; the I laugh them to scorn,
22:30 He delivers the I man; you will be delivered
27:17 wear it, and the I will divide the silver.
34:5 has said, 'I am I, and God has taken
Ps 10:8 the villages; in hiding places he murders the I
15:5 and does not take a bribe against the I
19:13 shall be blameless, and I of great transgression.
94:21 righteous, and condemn the I to death.
106:38 demons; they poured out I blood, the blood of
Prov 1:11 us wantonly ambush the I;
6:17 and hands that shed I blood,
24:24 He who says to the wicked, "You are I
Wis 4:12 roving desire perverts the I mind.
Sir 26:20 will not be declared I of sin.
Is 5:23 bribe, and deprive the I of his right!
59:7 make haste to shed I blood; their thoughts are
Jer 2:35 you say, 'I am I; surely his anger has
7:6 the widow, or shed I blood in this place,
22:3 the widow, nor shed I blood in this place.
22:17 dishonest gain, for shedding I blood, and for
26:15 death, you will bring I blood upon yourselves and
Dan 13:46 loud voice, "I am I of the blood of
13:53 unjust judgments, condemning the I and letting the
13:53 put to death an I and righteous person.'
13:62 Thus I blood was saved that day.
Joel 3:19 because they have shed I blood in their land.
Jon 1:14 lay not on us I blood; for thou, O
1Mac 1:37 the sanctuary they shed I blood; they even defiled
2Mac 1:8 the gate and shed I blood.
8:4 lawless destruction of the I babies and the
Mt 10:16 wise as serpents and I as doves.
23:34 from the blood of I Abel to the blood
27:4 have sinned in betraying I blood." They said, "What
27:24 crowd, saying, "I am I of this righteous man's
Lk 23:46 praised God, and said, "Certainly this man was I
Acts 18:6 I am I
20:26 day that I am I of the blood of
Phil 2:15 may be blameless and I, children of God without

INNOCENTS

Jer 19:4 with the blood of I,

INNUMERABLE (5)

Jud 2:17 mules for transport, and I sheep and oxen and
Job 21:33 him, and those who go before him are I
Ps 104:25 which teems with things I, living things both small
Heb 11:12 heaven and as the I grains of sand by
12:22 heavenly Jerusalem, and to I angels in festal

INQUIRE (49)

Gen 25:22 So she went to I of the LORD.
Ex 18:15 come to me to I of God;
Lev 27:33 A man shall not I whether it is good
Num 27:21 the priest, who shall I for him by the
Deut 12:30 that you do not I about their gods, saying,
13:14 known, then you shall I and make search and
17:4 it; then you shall I diligently, and if it
19:18 days; the judges shall I diligently, and if the
Judg 18:5 they said to him, I of God, we pray
1Sam 9:9 a man went to I of God, he said,
17:56 And the king said, I whose son the stripling
28:7 go to her and I of her." And his
1Kgs 14:5 Jeroboam is coming to I of you concerning her
22:5 the king of Israel, I first for the word
22:7 prophet of the LORD of whom we may I
22:8 by whom we may I of the LORD, Micaiah
2Kgs 1:2 messengers, telling them, "Go, I of Baal-zebub, the
1:3 you are going to I of Baal-zebub, the god
1:6 you are sending to I of Baal-zebub, the god
1:16 have sent messengers to I of Baal-zebub, the god
1:16 God in Israel to I of his word?--therefore
3:11 through whom we may I of the LORD?" Then
8:8 man of God, and I of the LORD through
16:15 be for me to I by."
22:13 king's servant, saying, "Go, I of the LORD for
22:18 who sent you to I of the LORD, thus
1Chr 21:30 go before it to I of God, for he
2Chr 18:4 the king of Israel, I first for the word
18:6 prophet of the LORD of whom we may I
18:7 by whom we may I of the LORD, Micaiah
32:31 sent to him to I about the sign that
34:21 king's servant, saying, "Go, I of the LORD for
34:26 who sent you to I of the LORD, thus
Job 8:8 "For I, I pray you, of bygone ages, and
Ps 27:4 the LORD, and to I in his temple.
Wis 6:3 out your works and I into your plans.
Is 21:12 If you will I, inquire; come back again."
21:12 If you will inquire, I; come back again."
Jer 10:21 stupid, and do not I of the LORD; therefore
21:2 son of Ma-aseiah, saying, I of the LORD for
37:7 you to me to I of me, 'Behold, Pharaoh's
Ezek 14:7 to a prophet to I for himself of me,
20:1 of Israel came to I of the LORD, and
20:3 GOD, Is it to I of me that you
Hos 4:12 My people I of a thing of wood, and
Zeph 1:6 seek the LORD or I of him."
1Mac 3:48 of the law to I into those matters about
Acts 9:11 street called Straight, and I in the house of
23:20 they were going to I somewhat more closely about

INQUIRED (35)

Gen 43:27 And he I about their welfare, and said, "Is
Lev 10:16 Now Moses diligently I about the goat of the
Judg 1:1 the people of Israel I of the LORD, "Who
6:29 had made search and I, they said, "Gideon the
20:18 up to Bethel, and I of God, "Which of
20:23 the evening; and they I of the LORD, "Shall
20:27 the people of Israel I of the LORD (for
1Sam 10:22 So they I again of the LORD, "Did the
14:37 And Saul I of God, "Shall I go down
22:10 of Ahitub, and he I of the LORD for
22:13 a sword, and have I of God for him,
22:15 time that I have I of God for him?
23:2 Therefore David I of the LORD, "Shall I go
23:4 Then David I of the LORD again.
28:6 And when Saul I of the LORD, the LORD
30:8 And David I of the LORD, "Shall I pursue
2Sam 2:1 After this David I of the LORD, "Shall I
5:19 And David I of the LORD, "Shall I go
5:23 And when David I of the LORD, he said,
11:3 And David sent and I about the woman.
1Chr 14:10 And David I of God, "Shall I go up
14:14 And when David again I of God, God said
Esth 12:2 their conversation and I into their purposes, and
Ezek 14:3 I let myself be I of at all by
20:3 I will not be I of by you.
20:31 And shall I be I of by you, O
20:31 I will not be I of by you.
Dan 1:20 concerning which the king I of them, he found
2Mac 3:9 had come, and he I whether this really was
Mt 2:4 of the people, he I of them where the
Lk 18:36 multitude going by, he I what this meant.
Acts 4:7 in the midst, they I, "By what power or
21:33 He I who he was and what he had
1Pet 1:10 be yours searched and I about this salvation;
1:11 about this salvation; they I what person or time

INQUIRER

Ezek 14:10 the punishment of the I shall be alike--

INQUIRIES

Ezra 7:14 counselors to make I about Judah and Jerusalem

INQUIRING

Lk 1:62 signs to his father, I what he would have

INQUIRY (7)

Lev 19:20 given her freedom, an I shall be held.
Job 31:14 When he makes I, what shall I answer him?
Wis 1:9 For I will be made into the counsels of
6:8 But a strict I is in store for the
Sir 33:3 as dependable as an I by means of Urim.
41:4 years, there is no I about it in Hades.
Acts 10:17 by Cornelius, having made I for Simon's house, stood

INSATIABLE (5)

Sir 12:16 an opportunity his thirst for blood will be I
31:17 and do not be I, lest you give offense.
37:29 Do not have an I appetite for any luxury,
Ezek 16:28 Assyrians, because you were I; yea, you played the
2Pet 2:14 eyes full of adultery, I for sin.

INSCRIBE (2)

Is 30:8 on a tablet, and I it in a book,
1Mac 14:48 they gave orders to I this decree upon bronze

INSCRIBED (9)

Job 19:23 Oh that they were I in a book!
Sir 45:12 crown upon his turban, I like a signet with
Dan 5:24 the hand was sent, and this writing was I
5:25 the writing that was I: MENE, MENE, TEKEL, and
10:21 tell you what is I in the book of
Zech 14:20 day there shall be I on the bells of
Rev 19:12 he has a name I which no one knows
19:16 he has a name I, King of kings and
21:12 sons of Israel were I;

INSCRIPTION (8)

Ex 39:30 wrote upon it an I, like the engraving of
Zech 3:9 I will engrave its I, says the LORD of
Mt 22:20 them, "Whose likeness and I is this?"
Mk 12:16 them, "Whose likeness and I is this?" They said
15:26 And the I of the charge against him read,
Lk 20:24 Whose likeness and I has it?" They said, "Caesars."
23:37 There was also an I over him, "This is
Acts 17:23 an altar with this I, 'To an unknown god.'

INSCRUTABLE

Rom 11:33 his judgments and how I his ways!

INSECTS (4)

Lev 11:20 "All winged I that go upon all fours are
11:21 Yet among the winged I that go on all
11:23 But all other winged I which have four feet
Deut 14:19 And all winged I are unclean for you; they

INSECURELY

Wis 4:4 for a while, standing I they will be shaken

INSERTED

1Kgs 6:6 beams should not be I into the walls of

INSHORE

Acts 27:13 they weighed anchor and sailed along Crete, close I

INSIDE (32)

Gen 6:14 ark, and cover it I and out with pitch.
Ex 28:26 the breastpiece, on its I edge next to the
39:19 the breastpiece, on its I edge next to the
Lev 14:41 he shall cause the I of the house to
Josh 7:21 hidden in the earth I my tent, with the
Judg 7:16 empty jars, with torches I the jars.
2Sam 6:17 it in its place, I the tent which David
1Kgs 6:15 the house on the I with boards of cedar;
6:15 covered them on the I with wood; and he
6:21 And Solomon overlaid the I of the house with
2Kgs 16:18 which had been built I the palace, and the
1Chr 16:1 God, and set it I the tent which David
2Chr 3:4 overlaid it on the I with pure gold.
Esth 4:11 goes to the king I the inner court without
5:1 on his royal throne I the palace opposite the
Sir 19:12 so is a word I a fool.
Ezek 40:16 had windows round about I, and on the jambs
40:22 to it; and its vestibule was on the I
40:26 vestibule was on the I; and it had palm
40:41 tables were on the I, and four tables on
46:23 On the I, around each of the four courts
Dan 14:7 this is but clay I and brass outside, and
2Mac 1:15 with a few men I the wall of the
Mt 23:24 of the plate, but I they are full of
23:25 first cleanse the I of the cup and of
26:58 high priest, and going I he sat with the
Mk 15:16 soldiers led him away I the palace (that is,
Lk 11:39 of the dish, but I you are full of
11:40 the outside make the I also?
21:21 let those who are I the city depart, and
Acts 5:23 when we opened it we found no one I
1Cor 5:12 Is it not those I the church whom you

INSIGHT (15)

Ezra 8:16 who were men of I,
Job 34:35 his words are without I
Prov 1:2 instruction, understand words of I,
2:3 you cry out for I and raise your voice
3:5 heart, and do not rely on your own I
4:2 that you may gain I;
4:8 this: Get wisdom, and whatever you get, get I
7:4 and call I your intimate friend;
8:14 sound wisdom, I have I, I have strength.
9:6 and live, and walk in the way of I
9:10 and the knowledge of the Holy One is I
Wis 8:21 was a mark of I to know whose gift
Sir 6:37 he who will give I to your mind, and
Eph 1:9 in all wisdom and I the mystery of his
3:4 you can perceive my I into the mystery of

INSIGNIFICANT

Sir 25:18 Any iniquity is I compared to a wife's iniquity;

INSINCERELY

Gal 2:13 of the Jews acted I, so that even Barnabas

INSINCERITY (3)

Gal 2:13 that even Barnabas was carried away by their I
Jas 3:17 of mercy and good fruits, without uncertainty or I
1Pet 2:1 and all guile and I and envy and all

INSIST (2)

1Cor 13:5 Love does not I on its own way; it
Tit 3:8 I desire you to I on these things, so

INSISTED (3)

Jud 5:22 seacoast and from Moab I that he must be
Lk 22:57 an hour still another I, saying, "Certainly this man
Acts 12:15 But she I that it was so.

INSISTENTLY

1Mac 11:40 son of Alexander, and I urged him to hand

INSISTING

Col 2:18 one disqualify you, I on self-abasement and worship

INSOLENCE (13)

Esth 13:12 it was to in I or pride or for
Prov 13:10 By I the heedless make strife, but with those
Wis 12:17 and dost rebuke any I among those who know
Sir 10:6 and do not attempt anything by acts of I
10:8 account of injustice and I and wealth.
16:8 Lot, whom he loathed on account of their I
Is 16:6 his pride, and his I -- his boasts are
Jer 48:30 I know his I, says the LORD; his boasts
Bar 4:34 great population, and her I will be turned to
Dan 11:18 an end to his I; indeed he shall turn
11:18 he shall turn his I back upon him.
Hos 7:17 sword because of the I of their tongue.
2Mac 9:7 any way stop his I, but was even more

INSOLENT (13)

Ps 54:3 For I men have risen against me, ruthless men
75:5 high, or speak with I neck."
86:14 O God, I men have risen up against me;
119:21 Thou dost rebuke the I, accursed ones, who wander
Sir 8:11 up and leave an I fellow, lest he lie
32:18 an idea, and an I and proud man will
35:18 the multitude of the I, and breaks the scepters
Is 3:5 the youth will be I to the elder, and
14:4 oppressor has ceased, the I fury ceased!
33:19 see no more the I people, the people of
Jer 43:2 Kareah and all the I men said to Jeremiah,
2Mac 1:28 who oppress and are I with pride.
Rom 1:30 haters of God, I, haughty, boastful, inventors of

INSOLENTLY (5)

Neh 9:10 knewest that they acted I against our fathers; and
Job 16:10 they have struck me I upon the cheek, they
Ps 31:18 be dumb, which speak I against the righteous in
55:12 an adversary who deals I with me-- then
2Mac 12:14 of provisions, behaved most I toward Judas and his

INSPECT (2)

Job 5:24 safe, and you shall I your fold and miss
2Mac 5:18 the king sent to I the treasury.

INSPECTED (2)

Neh 2:13 Dung Gate, and I I the walls of Jerusalem
2:15 by the valley and I the wall; and I

INSPECTION (2)

2Mac 3:8 make a tour of I of the cities of
3:14 in to direct the I of these funds.

INSPECTORS

1Mac 1:51 And he appointed I over all the people and

INSPIRATION

2Mac 15:11 spears as with the I of brave words, and

INSPIRE (3)

Is 47:12 succeed, perhaps you may I terror.
Jer 49:16 The horror you I has deceived you, and the
Bar 6:4 on men's shoulders and I fear in the heathen.

INSPIRED (11)

Ex 35:34 And he has I him to teach, both him
Prov 16:10 I decisions are on the lips of a king;
Wis 15:11 who formed him and I him with an active
1Mac 4:35 observed the boldness which I those of Judas, and
Mt 22:43 it then that David, I by the Spirit, calls
Mk 12:36 David himself, I by the Holy Spirit, declared, 'The
Lk 2:27 And I by the Spirit he came into the
1Cor 12:11 All these are I by one and the same
1Thes 1:6 much affliction, with joy I by the Holy Spirit;
1Tim 1:18 pointed to you, that I by them you may
2Tim 3:16 All scripture is I by God and profitable for

INSPIRES (2)

1Cor 12:6 the same God who I them all in every
Col 1:29 energy which he mightily I within me.

INSTALLED (3)

Judg 17:5 ephod and teraphim, and I one of his sons,
17:12 And Micah I the Levite, and the young man
1Mac 12:38 he fortified it and I gates with bolts.

INSTANT (3)

Wis 18:12 them, since in one I their most valued children
Is 29:5 And in an I, suddenly,
30:13 comes suddenly, in an I;

INSTANTLY (4)

Mt 9:22 And I the woman was made well.
15:28 And her daughter was healed I
17:18 out of him, and the boy was cured I
Acts 22:29 him withdrew from him I; and the tribune also

INSTIGATED

Acts 6:11 Then they secretly I men, who said, "We have

INSTINCT (2)

2Pet 2:12 irrational animals, creatures of I, born to be caught
Jude 1:10 that they know by I as irrational animals do,

INSTITUTED

Rom 13:1 that exist have been I by God.

INSTITUTION

1Pet 2:13 sake to every human I, whether it be to

INSTRUCT (12)

1Sam 12:23 you; and I will I you in the good
2Chr 19:10 ordinances, then you shall I them, that they may
Neh 9:20 thy good Spirit to I them, and didst not
Ps 25:12 Him will he I in the way that he
32:8 [Selah] I will I you and teach you the
105:22 all his possessions, to I his princes at his
Sir 37:23 A wise man will I his own people, and
42:8 not be ashamed to I the stupid or foolish
Rom 15:14 knowledge, and able to I one another.
1Cor 2:16 Lord so as to I him?" But we have
14:19 mind, in order to I others, than ten thousand
2Tim 3:15 which are able to I you for salvation through

INSTRUCTED (21)

Gen 32:17 He I the foremost, "When Esau my brother meets
32:19 He likewise I the second and the third and
Ruth 2:15 rose to glean, Boaz I his young men, saying,
2Sam 11:19 the fighting; and he I the messenger, "When you
2Kgs 12:2 because Jehoiada the priest I him.
2Chr 26:5 days of Zechariah, who I him in the fear
Job 4:3 Behold, you have I many, and you have strengthened
Prov 21:11 a wise man is I, he gains knowledge.
Wis 6:11 words; long for them, and you will be I
6:25 Therefore be I by my words, and you will
Sir 40:29 is intelligent and well I guards against that.
42:8 you will be truly I, and will be approved
Is 28:26 For he is I aright; his God teaches him.
40:13 as his counselor has I him?
Jer 31:19 and after I was I, I smote upon my
38:27 as the king had I him.
2Mac 2:2 giving them the law I those who were being
Acts 7:22 And Moses was I in all the wisdom of
18:25 He had been I in the way of the
Rom 2:18 excellent, because you are I in the law,
Heb 8:5 the tent, he was I by God, saying, "See

INSTRUCTING (2)

Gen 32:4 the country of Edom, I them, "Thus you shall
Mt 11:1 when Jesus had finished I his twelve disciples, he

INSTRUCTION (59)

Ex 24:12 the commandment, which I have written for their I
Job 22:22 Receive I from his mouth, and lay up his
36:10 opens their ears to I, and commands that they
Prov 1:2 may know wisdom and I, understand words of
1:3 words of insight, receive I in wise dealing,
1:7 beginning of knowledge; fools despise wisdom and I
1:8 my son, your father's I, and reject not your
4:2 O sons, a father's I, and be attentive, that
4:14 Keep hold of I, do not let go; guard
8:10 Take my I instead of silver, and knowledge rather
8:33 Hear I and be wise, and do not neglect
9:9 Give I to a wise man, and he will
10:17 He who heeds I is on the path to
13:1 son hears his father's I, but a scoffer does
13:18 to him who ignores I, but he who heeds
15:5 fool despises his father's I, but he who heeds
15:32 He who ignores I despises himself, but he who
15:33 of the LORD is I in wisdom, and humility
19:20 to advice and accept I, that you may gain
19:27 my son, to hear I only to stray from
23:12 Apply your mind to I and your ear to
23:23 sell it; buy wisdom, I, and understanding.
24:32 saw and considered it; I looked and received I
Wis 3:11 whoever despises wisdom and I is miserable.
6:17 most sincere desire for I, and concern for instruction
6:17 instruction, and concern for I is love of her,
7:14 God, commended for the gifts that come from I
Sir 1:24 Lord is wisdom and I, and he delights in
6:18 your youth up choose I, and until you are
8:8 them you will gain I and learn how to
16:23 I will impart I by weight, and declare knowledge
23:7 Listen, my children, to I concerning speech; the one
24:25 It makes I shine forth like light, like the
24:30 I will again make I shine forth like the
24:32 for myself alone, but for all who seek I
33:4 heard; bind together your I, and make your answer.
33:17 for myself alone, but for all who seek I
39:8 He will reveal I in his teaching, and will
41:14 My children, observe I and be at peace; hidden
44:4 in their words of I;
50:27 I in understanding and knowledge I have written in
51:16 received her, and I found for myself much I
51:26 let your souls receive I; it is to be
51:28 Get I with a large sum of silver, and
Is 29:24 understanding, and those who murmur will accept I
30:9 will not hear the I of the LORD;
Jer 10:8 stupid and foolish; the I of idols is but
17:23 neck, that they might not hear and receive I
32:33 them persistently they have not listened to receive I
35:13 Will you not receive I and listen to my
Mal 2:6 True I was in his mouth, and no wrong
2:7 and men should seek I from his mouth, for
2:8 to stumble by your I; you have corrupted the
2:9 my ways but have shown partiality in your I
Rom 15:4 was written for our I, that by steadfastness and
1Cor 10:11 written down for our I, upon whom the end
Eph 6:4 in the discipline and I of the Lord.
Tit 1:8 be able to give I in sound doctrine and
Heb 6:2 faith toward God, with I about ablutions, the laying

INSTRUCTIONS (8)

Deut 17:11 you; according to the I which they give you,
Acts 15:24 we gave them no I,
23:31 soldiers, according to their I, took Paul and brought
1Cor 11:17 But in the following I I do not commend
Col 4:10 whom you have received I —if he comes to
1Thes 4:2 For you know what I we gave you through
1Tim 3:14 I am writing these I to you so that,
4:6 If you put these I before the brethren, you

INSTRUCTORS

Prov 5:13 my teachers or incline my ear to my I

INSTRUCTS (2)

Ps 16:7 night also my heart I me.
25:8 the LORD; therefore he I sinners in the way.

INSTRUMENT (5)

Num 35:16 him down with an I of iron, so that

Sir 43:2 forth, is a marvelous I, the work of the
43:8 in its phases, an I of the hosts on
Ezek 33:32 plays well on an I, for they hear what
Acts 9:15 he is a chosen I of mine to carry

INSTRUMENTS (21)

Gen 4:22 the forger of all I of bronze and iron.
1Sam 18:6 of joy, and with I of music.
1Chr 15:16 play loudly on musical I, on harps and lyres
16:42 for the music and I for sacred song.
23:5 the LORD with the I which I have made
2Chr 5:13 cymbals and other musical I, in praise to the
7:6 Levites also, with the I for music to the
23:13 singers with their musical I leading in the
29:26 Levites stood with the I of David, and the
29:27 trumpets, accompanied by the I of David king of
34:12 who were skilful with I of music,
Neh 12:36 Hanani, with the musical I of David the man
Ps 45:8 From ivory palaces stringed I make you glad;
Is 38:20 will sing to stringed I all the days of
Ezek 40:42 high, on which the I were to be laid
Amos 6:5 David invent for themselves I of music;
Hab 3:19 To the choirmaster: with stringed I
1Mac 13:51 and cymbals and stringed I, and with hymns and
Rom 6:13 members to sin as I of wickedness, but yield
6:13 members to God as I of righteousness.
1Cor 14:7 If even lifeless I, such as the flute or

INSUBORDINATE (2)

Tit 1:5 open to the charge of being profligate or I
1:9 For there are many I men, empty talkers and

INSULT (6)

Gen 39:14 us a Hebrew to I us; he came in
39:17 in to me to I me;
1Sam 25:39 who has avenged the I I received at the
Ps 69:9 insults of those who I thee have fallen on
Prov 12:16 at once, but the prudent man ignores an I
Wis 2:19 us test him with I and torture, that we

INSULTED

1Tim 1:13 blasphemed and persecuted and I him; but I received

INSULTING

Sir 23:15 man accustomed to use I words will never become

INSULTS (10)

Job 20:3 I hear censure which I me, and out of
Ps 69:9 consumed me, and the I of those who insult
69:20 I have broken my heart, so that I am
89:50 in my bosom the I of the peoples,
Prov 14:31 oppresses a poor man I his Maker, but he
17:5 who mocks the poor I his Maker; he who
Sir 22:22 precede the fire; so I precede bloodshed.
Lam 3:30 cheek to the smiter, and be filled with I
Mt 5:22 liable to judgment; whoever I his brother shall be
2Cor 12:10 content with weaknesses, I, hardships, persecutions,

INSURRECTION (3)

Mk 15:7 committed murder in the I, there was a man
Lk 23:18 into prison for an I started in the city,
23:24 thrown into prison for I and murder, whom they

INTACT

Tob 9:5 bags with their seals I and gave them to

INTEGRITY (26)

Gen 20:5 my brother.' In the I of my heart and
20:6 done this in the I of your heart, and
1Kgs 9:4 your father walked, with I of heart and uprightness,
Job 2:3 still holds fast his I, although you moved me
2:9 to him, "Do you still hold fast your I
4:6 your confidence, and the I of your ways your
27:5 not put away my I from me.
31:6 let God know my I
Ps 7:8 and according to the I that is in me.
25:21 May I and uprightness preserve me, for I wait
26:1 have walked in my I, and I have trusted
26:11 I walk in my I; redeem me, and be
41:12 me because of my I, and set me in
101:2 I will walk with I of heart within my
Prov 2:7 those who walk in I,
2:21 land, and men of I will remain in it;
10:9 He who walks in I walks securely, but he
11:3 The I of the upright guides them, but the
14:32 but the righteous finds refuge through his I
19:1 who walks in his I than a man who
20:7 who walks in his I – blessed are his
28:6 who walks in his I than a rich man
28:18 He who walks in I will be delivered, but
Sir 7:6 man, and thus put a blot on your I
2Mac 7:40 he died in his I, putting his whole trust
Tit 2:7 in your teaching show I, gravity,

INTELLIGENCE (8)

Ex 31:3 God, with ability and I, with knowledge and all
35:31 God, with ability, with I, with knowledge, and with
36:1 has put ability and I to know how to
Wis 15:18 by their lack of I;
Sir 19:21 God-fearing man who lacks I, than the highly
22:9 fool, for he lacks I; weep less bitterly for
2Mac 11:13 he was not without I, he pondered over the
Acts 13:7 Paulus, a man of I, who summoned Barnabas and

INTELLIGENT (17)

Prov 17:28 when he closes his lips, he is deemed I
18:15 An I mind acquires knowledge, and the ear of
Eccl 9:11 nor riches to the I, nor favor to the
Wis 7:22 a spirit that is I, holy, unique, manifold, subtle,
7:23 all spirits that are I and pure and most
Sir 3:27 The mind of the I man will ponder a
6:36 If you see an I man, visit him early;
7:21 your soul love an I servant; do not withhold
10:22 right to despise an I poor man, nor is
18:27 Every I man knows wisdom, and he praises the
19:2 Wine and women lead I men astray, and the
21:16 will be found in the speech of the I
22:15 mind settled on an I thought is like the
25:8 who lives with an I wife, and he who
26:19 want through poverty, and I men who are treated
36:19 of game, so an I mind detects false words.
40:29 a man who is I and well instructed guards

INTELLIGENTLY

Sir 14:20 man who meditates on wisdom and who reasons I

INTELLIGIBLE

1Cor 14:9 speech that is not I, how will any one

INTEND (17)

2Chr 28:10 And now you I to subjugate the people of
Neh 6:6 you and the Jews I to rebel; that is
Jud 9:5 the things thou didst I came to pass,
9:8 thy anger; for they I to defile thy sanctuary,
Esth 13:4 kingdom which we honorably I cannot be brought
Is 10:7 he does not so I, and his mind does
Jer 26:3 the evil which I I to do to them
36:3 the evil which I I to do to them,
1Mac 15:3 our fathers, and I I to lay claim to
15:4 have equipped warships, and I to make a landing
2Mac 7:2 said, "What do you I to ask and learn
Jn 7:35 "Where does this man I to go that we
7:35 Does he I to go to the Dispersion among
Acts 5:28 your teaching and you I to bring this man's
1Cor 16:5 through Macedonia, for I I to pass through,
2Cor 8:20 We I that no one should blame us about
2Pet 1:12 Therefore I I always to remind you of these

INTENDED (11)

Gen 31:20 tell him that he I to flee.
2Chr 11:22 his brothers, for he I to make him king.
32:2 Sennacherib had come and I to fight against
Neh 6:2 But they I to do me harm.
Jer 18:8 the evil that I I to do to it.
18:10 good which I had I to do to it.
1Mac 4:27 Israel as he had I, nor had they turned
2Mac 4:20 So this money was I by the sender for
11:2 He I to make the city a home for
Acts 25:4 and that he himself I to go there shortly.
Rom 1:13 that I have often I to come to you

INTENDING (10)

Sir 19:16 make a slip without I it.
Jer 41:17 Geruth Chimham near Bethlehem, I to go to Egypt
1Mac 11:63 with a large army, I to remove him from
2Mac 1:14 For under pretext of I to marry her, Antiochus
10:24 He came on, I to take Judea by storm.
12:7 were closed, he withdrew, I to come again and
Acts 12:4 soldiers to guard him, I after the Passover to
20:7 Paul talked with them, I to depart on the
20:13 set sail for Assos, I to take Paul aboard
20:13 so he had arranged, I himself to go by

INTENSE
2Mac 9:28 having endured the more I suffering, such as he

INTENSELY (3)
Wis 16:19 water it burned more I than fire, to destroy
Sir 17:21 and turn away from iniquity, and hate abominations I
Mk 9:3 his garments became glistening, I white, as no fuller

INTENSIFY
Wis 14:18 know the king to I their worship.

INTENSIFYING
2Mac 4:4 Coelesyria and Phoenicia, was I the malice of

INTENT (13)
Ex 32:12 Egyptians say, 'With evil I did he bring them
Num 35:11 kills any person without I may flee there.
35:15 kills any person without I may flee there.
Josh 20:3 kills any person without I or unwittingly may flee
20:9 killed a person without I could flee there, so
1Chr 12:38 to Hebron with full I to make David king
Prov 21:27 much more when he brings it with evil I
Wis 15:4 neither has the evil I of human art misled
Sir 38:28 sitting by the anvil, I upon his handiwork in
Bar 1:21 we each followed the I of his own wicked
1Mac 7:30 to him with treacherous I, and he was afraid
2Mac 4:14 priests were no longer I upon their service at
Acts 8:22 that, if possible, the I of your heart may

INTENTIONS (2)
2Mac 14:5 about the disposition and I of the Jews.
Heb 4:12 discerning the thoughts and I of the heart.

INTENTLY (7)
Tob 11:5 Now Anna sat looking I down the road for
Sir 9:5 Do not look I at a virgin, lest you
9:8 and do not look I at beauty belonging to
Mk 8:25 eyes; and he looked I and was restored, and
Acts 13:9 the Holy Spirit, looked I at him
14:9 speaking; and Paul, looking I at him and seeing
23:1 And Paul, looking I at the council, said, "Brethren,

INTENTS (2)
Jer 23:20 executed and accomplished the I of his mind.
30:24 executed and accomplished the I of his mind.

INTERCEDE (3)
1Sam 2:25 the LORD, who can I for him?" But they
Jer 7:16 them, and do not I with me, for I
27:18 them, then let them I with the LORD of

INTERCEDED
Tob 1:22 Ahikar I for me, and I returned to Nineveh.

INTERCEDES (3)
Rom 8:26 but the Spirit himself I for us with sighs
8:27 Spirit, because the Spirit I for the saints according
8:34 of God, who indeed I for us?

INTERCESSION (2)
Is 53:12 of many, and made I for the transgressors.
Heb 7:25 always lives to make I for them.

INTERCESSIONS
1Tim 2:1 urge that supplications, prayers, I, and thanksgivings

INTERCOURSE
2Mac 6:4 with harlots and had I with women within the

INTERDICT (7)
Dan 6:7 ordinance and enforce an I, that whoever makes
6:8 O king, establish the I and sign the document,
6:9 Therefore King Darius signed the document and I
6:12 the king, concerning the I, "O king!
6:12 you not sign an I, that any man who
6:13 O king, or the I you have signed, but
6:15 and Persians that no I or ordinance which the

INTEREST (22)
Ex 22:25 you shall not exact I from him.
Lev 25:36 Take no I from him or increase, but fear
25:37 him your money at I, nor give him your
Deut 23:19 shall not lend upon I to your brother, interest
23:19 brother, I on money, I on victuals, I on
23:19 victuals, interest on anything that is lent for I
23:20 you may lend upon I, but to your brother
23:20 shall not lend upon I; that the LORD your
Neh 5:7 them, "You are exacting I, each from his brother."
5:10 Let us leave off this I
Ps 15:5 out his money at I, and does not take
Prov 28:8 augments his wealth by I and increase gathers it
Sir 37:7 counsel, but some give counsel in their own I
37:8 first what is his I – for he will
Ezek 18:8 does not lend at I or take any increase,
18:13 commits abomination, lends at I, and takes increase;
18:17 from iniquity, takes no I or increase, observes my
22:12 shed blood; you take I and increase and make
Mt 25:27 should have received what was my own with I
Lk 19:23 have collected it with I

INTERESTS (5)
2Mac 14:8 genuinely concerned for the I of the king, and
1Cor 7:34 his wife, and his I are divided.
Phil 2:4 only to his own I, but also to the
2:4 but also to the I of others.
2:21 look after their own I, not those of Jesus

INTERIOR (2)
Ezek 42:15 had finished measuring the I of the temple area,
1Mac 4:48 the sanctuary and the I of the temple, and

INTERLACING
Jer 2:23 a restive young camel I her tracks,

INTERMARRY
Ezra 9:14 thy commandments again and I with the peoples

INTERMEDIARY (2)
Gal 3:19 and it was ordained by angels through an I
3:20 Now an I implies more than one; but God

INTERNAL
2Mac 9:5 relief and with sharp I tortures--

INTERPOSED (2)
Ps 106:30 Phinehas stood up and I, and the plague was
Heb 6:17 of his purpose, he I with an oath,

INTERPRET (13)
Gen 40:8 is no one to I them." And Joseph said
41:8 was none who could I it to Pharaoh.
41:15 no one who can I it; and I have
41:15 a dream you can I it."
Dan 5:12 knowledge, and understanding to I dreams,
Mt 16:3 You know how to I the appearance of the
16:3 sky, but you cannot I the signs of the
Lk 12:56 You know how to I the appearance of earth
12:56 not know how to I the present time?
1Cor 12:30 Do all I
14:13 a tongue should pray for the power to I
14:27 three, and each in turn; and let one I
14:28 is no one to I, let each of them

INTERPRETATION (39)
Gen 40:12 him, "This is its I: the three branches are
40:16 baker saw that the I was favorable, he said
40:18 answered, "This is its I: the three baskets are
41:12 to us, giving an I to each man according
Judg 7:15 the dream and its I, he worshiped; and he
Eccl 8:1 And who knows the I of a thing?
Dan 2:4 servants the dream, and we will show the I
2:5 the dream and its I, you shall be torn
2:6 the dream and its I, you shall receive from
2:6 Therefore show me the dream and its I
2:7 servants the dream, and we will show its I
2:9 shall know that you can show me its I
2:16 that he might show to the king the I
2:24 king, and I will show the king the I
2:25 who can make known to the king the I
2:26 the dream that I have seen and its I
2:30 in order that the I may be made known
2:36 dream; now we will tell the king its I
2:45 is certain, and its I sure."
4:6 known to me the I of the dream.
4:7 they could not make known to me its I
4:9 the dream which I saw; tell me its I
4:18 O Belteshazzar, declare the I, because all the wise
4:18 known to me the I, but you are able,
4:19 the dream or the I alarm you." Belteshazzar
4:19 hate you and its I for your enemies!
4:24 him'; this is the I, O king: It is
5:7 and shows me its I, shall be clothed with

5:8 writing or make known to the king the I
5:12 Daniel be called, and he will show the I
5:15 known to me its I; but they could not
5:15 could not show the I of the matter.
5:16 known to me its I, you shall be clothed
5:17 the king and make known to him the I
5:26 This is the I of the matter: MENE, God
7:16 known to me the I of the things.
1Cor 12:10 tongues, to another the I of tongues.
14:26 a lesson, a revelation, a tongue, or an I
2Pet 1:20 matter of one's own I,

INTERPRETATIONS (3)

Gen 40:8 to them, "Do not I belong to God?
Sir 47:17 parables, and for your I, the countries marveled at
Dan 5:16 that you can give I and solve problems.

INTERPRETED (4)

Gen 40:22 baker, as Joseph had I to them.
41:12 we told him, he I our dreams to us,
41:13 And as he I to us, so it came
Lk 24:27 all the prophets, he I to them in all

INTERPRETER

Gen 42:23 for there was an I between them.

INTERPRETING

1Cor 2:13 taught by the Spirit, I spiritual truths to those

INTERPRETS

1Cor 14:5 tongues, unless some one I, so that the church

INTERRUPT (2)

Sir 11:8 you have heard, nor I a speaker in the
32:3 knowledge, and do not I the music.

INTERVAL (2)

Lk 22:57 And after an I of about an hour still
Acts 5:7 After an I of about three hours his wife

INTERVENE

Is 59:16 was no one to I; then his own arm

INTERVENED

Wis 18:23 another in heaps, he I and held back the

INTERVENTION

2Mac 3:29 because of the divine I and deprived of any

INTERVIEW

2Mac 4:8 the king at an I three hundred and sixty

INTIMATE (5)

Job 19:19 All my I friends abhor me, and those whom
Prov 7:4 and call insight your I friend;
Dan 13:54 you see them being I with each other?" He
13:57 Israel, and they were I with you through fear;
13:58 you catch them being I with each other?" He

INTOLERABLE

2Mac 9:10 Because of his I stench no one was able

INTRICATE

Esth 16:13 our life, and with I craft and deceit asked

INTRICATELY

Ps 139:15 being made in secret, I wrought in the depths

INTRIGUE

Hos 7:7 their hearts burn with I; all night their anger

INTRIGUES

Sir 9:4 woman singer, lest you be caught in her I

INTRODUCED (5)

2Kgs 17:8 the customs which the kings of Israel had I
17:19 but walked in the customs which Israel had I
2Mac 4:11 ways of living and I new customs contrary to
Acts 24:2 excellent Felix, reforms are I on behalf of this
Heb 7:19 a better hope is I, through which we draw

INVADE (12)

2Kgs 13:20 of Moabites used to I the land in the
2Chr 20:10 wouldest not let Israel I when they came from
27:2 only he did not I the temple of the
Lam 1:10 has seen the nations I her sanctuary, those whom
Hab 3:16 come upon people who I us.
1Mac 4:35 and enlisted mercenaries, to I Judea again with an
12:25 them no opportunity to I his own country.
13:1 a large army to I the land of Judah
13:12 a large army to I the land of Judah,
13:20 this Trypho came to I the country and destroy
14:31 their enemies decided to I their country and lay
15:40 provoke the people and I Judea and take the

INVADED (8)

2Kgs 17:5 the king of Assyria I all the land and
2Chr 21:17 up against Judah, and I it, and carried away
28:17 the Edomites had again I and defeated Judah, and
32:1 of Assyria came and I Judah and encamped against
Jud 4:7 them Judea could be I, and it was easy
1Mac 1:17 So he I Egypt with a strong force, with
14:2 heard that Demetrius had I his territory, he sent
15:10 Antiochus set out and I the land of his

INVADING

2Mac 11:5 I Judea, he approached Bethzur, which was a

INVALIDS

Jn 5:3 lay a multitude of I, blind, lame, paralyzed.

INVASION (2)

2Mac 5:1 Antiochus made his second I of Egypt.
8:12 to Judas concerning Nicanor's I; and when he told

INVENT

Amos 6:5 harp, and like David I for themselves instruments of

INVENTED (2)

2Chr 26:15 Jerusalem he made engines, I by skilful men, to
Dan 13:43 that they have wickedly I against me!"

INVENTING

Neh 6:8 done, for you are I them out of your

INVENTION

Wis 14:12 of fornication, and the I of them was the

INVENTORS

Rom 1:30 God, insolent, haughty, boastful, I of evil, disobedient

INVEST (2)

Num 27:20 You shall I him with some of your authority,
1Cor 12:23 think less honorable we I with the greater honor,

INVESTED

Mt 25:27 you ought to have I my money with the

INVESTIGATE (4)

Wis 13:9 much that they could I the world, how did
Sir 3:20 difficult for you, nor I what is beyond your
11:7 find fault before you I; first consider, and then
Acts 25:20 a loss how to I these questions, I asked

INVESTIGATED (2)

Esth 2:23 When the affair was I and found to be
2Mac 1:34 the sacrifice, the king I the matter, and enclosed

INVESTIGATION (2)

Esth 16:7 hand on as from I of matters close at
Job 34:24 shatters the mighty without I, and sets others in

INVINCIBLE (3)

Jud 16:13 thou are great and glorious, wonderful in strength, I
Wis 5:19 take holiness as an I shield,
2Mac 11:13 that the Hebrews were I because the mighty God

INVIOLABILITY

2Mac 3:12 in the sanctity and I of the temple which

INVISIBLE (5)

Rom 1:20 of the world his I nature, namely, his eternal
Col 1:15 the image of the I God, the first-born of
1:16 on earth, visible and I, whether thrones or dominions
1Tim 1:17 King of ages, immortal, I, the only God, be
Heb 11:27 for he endured as seeing him who is I

INVITE (12)

1Sam 16:3 to the LORD.' And I Jesse to the sacrifice,
1Kgs 1:10 but he did not I Nathan the prophet or
Jud 12:10 only, and did not I any of his officers.
Job 1:4 they would send and I their three sisters to

Wis 1:12 Do not I death by the error of your
Sir 13:9 reserved; and he will I you the more often.
Lam 2:22 Thou didst I as to the day of an
Zech 3:10 one of you will I his neighbor under his
Mt 22:9 to the thoroughfares, and I to the marriage feast
Lk 14:12 a banquet, do not I your friends or your
14:12 neighbors, lest they also I you in return, and
14:13 you give a feast, I the poor, the maimed,

INVITED (35)

Num 25:2 These I the people to the sacrifices of their
Josh 24:9 and he sent and I Balaam the son of
Judg 14:15 Have you I us here to impoverish us?"
1Sam 9:13 bless the sacrifice; afterward those eat who are I
9:22 those who had been I, who were about thirty
16:5 and his sons, and I them to the sacrifice.
2Sam 11:13 And David I him, and he ate in his
13:23 near Ephraim, and Absalom I all the king's sons.
15:11 from Jerusalem who were I guests, and they went
1Kgs 1:9 beside En-rogel, and he I all his brothers, the
1:19 in abundance, and has I all the sons of
1:19 army; but Solomon your servant he has not I
1:25 in abundance, and has I all the king's sons,
1:26 Jehoiada, and your servant Solomon, he has not I
Tob 5:9 So Tobias I him in; he entered and they
Esth 5:12 tomorrow also I am I by her together with
2Mac 12:3 deed as this: they I the Jews who lived
14:5 purpose when he was I by Demetrius to a
Mt 22:3 call those who were I to the marriage feast;
22:4 'Tell those who are I, Behold, I have made
22:8 is ready, but those I were not worthy.
Lk 7:39 the Pharisee who had I him saw it, he
14:7 to those who were I, when he marked how
14:8 them, "When you are I by any one to
14:8 man than you be I by him;
14:9 him; and he who I you both will come
14:10 But when you are I, go and sit in
14:12 the man who had I him, "When you give
14:16 a great banquet, and I many;
14:17 those who had been I, 'Come; for all is
14:24 those men who were I shall taste my banquet.'"
Jn 2:2 there; Jesus also was I to the marriage, with
Acts 8:31 And he I Philip to come up and sit
28:14 found brethren, and were I to stay with them
Rev 19:9 are those who are I to the marriage supper

INVITES (4)

Ex 34:15 their gods and one I you, you eat of
Prov 18:6 strife, and his mouth I a flogging.
Sir 13:9 When a powerful man I you, be reserved; and
1Cor 10:27 one of the unbelievers I you to dinner and

INVITING

2Mac 8:11 cities on the seacoast, I them to buy Jewish

INVOCATION

2Mac 15:26 enemy in battle with I to God and prayers.

INVOKE (5)

2Sam 14:11 "Pray let the king I the LORD your God,
1Chr 16:4 of the LORD, to I, to thank, and to
Mt 26:74 Then he began to I a curse on himself
Mk 14:71 But he began to I a curse on himself
1Pet 1:17 And if you I as Father him who judges

INVOKED (4)

Ps 72:15 him continually, and blessings I for him all the
Jer 44:26 shall no more be I by the mouth of
Heb 11:20 By faith Isaac I future blessings on Jacob and
Jas 2:7 honorable name which was I over you?

INVOKING

Esth 15:2 Then, majestically adorned, after I the aid of the

INVOLVED (6)

Num 15:26 the whole population was I in the error.
Esth 16:5 blood, and have been I in irremediable calamities, by
Sir 12:14 a sinner and becomes I in his sins.
2Mac 2:24 the flood of numbers I and the difficulty there
5:18 happened that they were I in many sins, this
Heb 9:16 where a will is I, the death of the

INVOLVES

Sir 23:13 lewd vulgarity, for it I sinful speech.

INVULNERABLE (2)

Wis 7:22 mobile, clear, unpolluted, distinct, I, loving the good,
2Mac 8:36 therefore the Jews were I, because they followed the

INWARD (8)

2Sam 5:9 built the city round about from the Millo I
1Kgs 7:25 upon them, and all their hinder parts were I
2Chr 4:4 upon them, and all their hinder parts were I
Ps 51:6 desirest truth in the I being; therefore teach me
64:6 For the I mind and heart of a man
139:13 thou didst form my I parts, thou didst knit
Ezek 42:4 chambers was a passage I, ten cubits wide and
Mic 6:14 be hunger in your I parts; you shall put

INWARDLY (9)

Ps 62:4 with their mouths, but I they curse.
Prov 23:7 like one who is I reckoning.
Wis 8:17 I considered these things I, and thought upon them
Sir 19:23 down in mourning, but I he is full of
2Mac 5:11 So, raging I, he left Egypt and took the
Mt 7:15 in sheep's clothing but I are ravenous wolves.
Acts 10:17 Now while Peter was I perplexed as to what
Rom 2:29 Jew who is one I, and real circumcision is
8:23 of the Spirit, groan I as we wait for

INWARDS

Ezek 40:16 windows round about, narrowing I into their jambs in

IOB

Gen 46:13 of Issachar: Tola, Puvah, I, and Shimron.

IOTA

Mt 5:18 pass away, not an I, not a dot, will

IPHDEIAH

1Chr 8:25 Hananiah, Elam, Anthothijah, I, and Penuel were

IPHTAH

Josh 15:43 Libnah, Ether, Ashan, I, Ashnah, Nezib,

IPHTAHEL (2)

Josh 19:14 at the valley of I;
19:27 and the valley of I northward to Beth-emek and

IR

1Chr 7:12 were the sons of I, Hushim the sons of

IR-SHEMESH

Josh 19:41 inheritance included Zorah, Eshtaol, I,

IRA (6)

2Sam 20:26 Abiathar were priests; and I the Jairite was also
23:26 Harod, Helez the Paltite, I the son of Ikkesh
23:38 the son of Zeruiah, I the Ithrite, Gareb the
1Chr 11:28 Harod, Helez the Pelonite, I the son of Ikkesh
11:40 the son of Zeruiah, I the Ithrite, Gareb the
27:9 the sixth month, was I, the son of Ikkesh

IRAD (2)

Gen 4:18 To Enoch was born I; and Irad was the
4:18 was born Irad; and I was the father of

IRAM (2)

Gen 36:43 Teman, Mibzar, Magdiel, and I; these are the chiefs
1Chr 1:54 Teman, Mibzar, Magdiel, and I; these are the chiefs

IRI

1Chr 7:7 Uzzi, Uzziel, Jerimoth, and I, five, heads of fathers'

IRIJAH (2)

Jer 37:13 a sentry there named I the son of Shelemiah,
37:14 But I would not listen to him, and seized

IRKSOME

Phil 3:1 to you is not I to me, and is

IRNAHASH

1Chr 4:12 of Bethrapha, Paseah, and Tehinnah the father of I

IRON (106)

Gen 4:22 the forger of all instruments of bronze and I
Lev 26:19 make your heavens like I and your earth like
Num 31:22 silver, the bronze, the I, the tin, and the
35:16 with an instrument of I, so that he died,
Deut 3:11 was a bedstead of I; is it not in
4:20 forth out of the I furnace, out of Egypt,

I

8:9 land whose stones are I, and out of whose
27:5 shall lift up no I tool upon them.
28:23 brass, and the earth under you shall be I
28:48 put a yoke of I upon your neck, until
33:25 Your bars shall be I and bronze; and as
Josh 6:19 vessels of bronze and I, are sacred to the
6:24 of bronze and of I, they put into the
8:31 man has lifted an I tool"; and they offered
17:16 plain have chariots of I, both those in Beth-shean
17:18 they have chariots of I, and though they are
22:8 silver, gold, bronze, and I, and with much clothing;
Judg 1:19 of the plain, because they had chariots of I
4:3 nine hundred chariots of I, and oppressed the people
4:13 nine hundred chariots of I, and all the men
1Sam 17:7 six hundred shekels of I; and his shield-bearer went
2Sam 12:31 labor with saws and I picks and iron axes,
12:31 and iron picks and I axes, and made them
23:7 them arms himself with I and the shaft of
1Kgs 6:7 nor any tool of I was heard in the
8:51 the midst of the I furnace).
22:11 for himself horns of I, and said, "Thus says
2Kgs 6:6 there, and made the I float.
1Chr 20:3 labor with saws and I picks and axes; and
22:3 provided great stores of I for nails for the
22:14 silver, and bronze and I beyond weighing, for there
22:16 number, skilled in working gold, silver, bronze, and I
29:2 things of bronze, the I for the things of
29:2 for the things of I, and wood for the
29:7 of bronze, and a hundred thousand talents of I
2Chr 2:7 gold, silver, bronze, and I, and in purple, crimson,
2:14 in gold, silver, bronze, I, stone, and wood, and
18:10 for himself horns of I, and said, "Thus says
24:12 and also workers in I and bronze to repair
Job 19:24 Oh that with an I pen and lead they
20:24 will flee from an I weapon; a bronze arrow
28:2 I is taken out of the earth, and copper
40:18 tubes of bronze, his limbs like bars of I
41:27 He counts I as straw, and bronze as rotten
Ps 2:9 with a rod of I, and dash them in
105:18 in a collar of I;
107:16 bronze, and cuts in two the bars of I
149:8 nobles with fetters of I,
Prov 27:17 I sharpens iron, and one man sharpens another.
27:17 Iron sharpens I, and one man sharpens another.
Eccl 10:10 If the I is blunt, and one does not
Wis 13:15 in the wall, and fastens it there with I
17:16 prison not made of I;
Sir 13:2 pot associate with the I kettle?
22:13 and a piece of I are easier to bear
28:20 is a yoke of I, and its fetters are
38:28 upon his handiwork in I; the breath of the
39:26 water and fire and I and salt and wheat
48:17 the sheer rock with I and built pools for
Is 45:2 asunder the bars of I,
48:4 your neck is an I sinew and your forehead
60:17 gold, and instead of I I will bring silver;
60:17 silver; instead of wood, bronze, instead of stones, I
Jer 1:18 a fortified city, an I pillar, and bronze walls,
6:28 they are bronze and I, all of them act
11:4 of Egypt, from the I furnace, saying, Listen to
15:12 Can one break I, iron from the north, and
15:12 Can one break iron, I from the north, and
17:1 with a pen of I; with a point of
28:13 I will make in their place bars of I
28:14 all these nations an I yoke of servitude to
Ezek 4:3 And take an I plate, and place it as
4:3 place it as an I wall between you and
22:18 bronze and tin and I and lead in the
22:20 silver and bronze and I and lead and tin
27:12 of every kind; silver, I, tin, and lead they
27:19 for your wares; wrought I, cassia, and calamus were
Dan 2:33 bronze, its legs of I, its feet partly of
2:33 its feet partly of I and partly of clay.
2:34 on its feet of I and clay, and broke
2:35 in pieces; then the I, the clay, the bronze,
2:40 fourth kingdom, strong as I, because iron breaks to
2:40 strong as iron, because I breaks to pieces and
2:40 all things; and like I which crushes, it shall
2:41 clay and partly of I, it shall be a
2:41 of the firmness of I shall be in it,
2:41 just as you saw I mixed with the miry
2:42 the feet were partly I and partly clay, so
2:43 As you saw the I mixed with miry clay,
2:43 hold together, just as I does not mix with
2:45 broke in pieces the I, the bronze, the clay,
4:15 with a band of I and bronze, amid the
4:23 with a band of I and bronze, in the
5:4 gold and silver, bronze, I, wood, and stone.
5:23 and gold, of bronze, I, wood, and stone, which
7:7 and it had great I teeth; it devoured and
7:19 with its teeth of I and claws of bronze;
Amos 1:3 they have threshed Gilead with threshing sledges of I
Mic 4:13 will make your horn I and your hoofs bronze;
2Mac 11:9 men but the wildest beasts or walls of I
Acts 12:10 they came to the I gate leading into the
Rev 2:27 with a rod of I, as when earthen pots
9:9 they had scales like I breastplates, and the noise
12:5 with a rod of I, but her child was
18:12 of costly wood, bronze, I and marble,
19:15 with a rod of I; he will tread the

IRONS

Ps 107:10 in affliction and in I,

IRONSMITH

Is 44:12 The I fashions it and works it over the

IRPEEL

Josh 18:27 Mizpeh, Chephirah, Mozah, Rekem, I, Taralah,

IRRATIONAL (4)

Wis 11:15 astray to worship I serpents and worthless animals,
11:15 them a multitude of I creatures to punish them,
2Pet 2:12 But these, like I animals, creatures of instinct, born
Jude 1:10 know by instinct as I animals do, they are

IRRELIGION

Tit 2:12 training us to renounce I and worldly passions, and

IRRELIGIOUS

Heb 12:16 one be immoral or I like Esau, who sold

IRREMEDIABLE

Esth 16:5 have been involved in I calamities, by the persuasion

IRREPROACHABLE

Col 1:22 holy and blameless and I before him,

IRRESISTIBLE (2)

Wis 7:22 loving the good, keen, I,
2Mac 1:13 a force that seemed I, they were cut to

IRRESOLUTE

2Chr 13:7 Rehoboam was young and I and could not withstand

IRREVERENCE

2Mac 4:17 light thing to show I to the divine laws

IRREVOCABLE

Rom 11:29 the gifts and the call of God are I

IRRITABLE

1Cor 13:5 way; it is not I or resentful;

IRRITATE

1Sam 1:6 provoke her sorely, to I her, because the LORD

IRU

1Chr 4:15 the son of Jephunneh: I, Elah, and Naam; and

ISAAC (139)

Gen 17:19 a son, and you shall call his name I
17:21 establish my covenant with I, whom Sarah shall bear
21:3 was born to him, whom Sarah bore him, I
21:4 Abraham circumcised his son I when he was eight
21:5 old when his son I was born to him.
21:8 on the day that I was weaned.
21:9 had borne to Abraham, playing with her son I
21:10 woman shall not be heir with my son I
21:12 tells you, for through I shall your descendants be
22:2 son, your only son I, whom you love, and
22:3 him, and his son I; and he cut the
22:6 and laid it on I his son; and he
22:7 And I said to his father Abraham, "My father!"
22:9 in order, and bound I his son, and laid
24:4 kindred, and take a wife for my son I
24:14 one whom thou hast appointed for thy servant I
24:62 Now I had come from Beer-lahai-roi, and was
24:63 And I went out to meditate in the field
24:64 and when she saw I, she alighted from the
24:66 And the servant told I all the things that
24:67 Then I brought her into the tent, and took

24:67 So I was comforted after his mother's death.
25:5 Abraham gave all he had to I
25:6 away from his son I, eastward to the east
25:9 I and Ishmael his sons buried him in the
25:11 of Abraham God blessed I his son.
25:11 And I dwelt at Beer-lahai-roi.
25:19 are the descendants of I, Abraham's son: Abraham
25:19 was the father of I,
25:20 father of Isaac, and I was forty years old
25:21 And I prayed to the LORD for his wife,
25:26 I was sixty years old when she bore them.
25:28 I loved Esau, because he ate of his game;
26:1 And I went to Gerar, to Abimelech king of
26:6 So I dwelt in Gerar.
26:8 a window and saw I fondling Rebekah his wife.
26:9 So Abimelech called I, and said, "Behold, she is
26:9 I said to him, "Because I thought, 'Lest I
26:12 And I sowed in that land, and reaped in
26:16 And Abimelech said to I, "Go away from us;
26:17 So I departed from there, and encamped in the
26:18 And I dug again the wells of water which
26:19 But when I's servants dug in the valley and
26:20 quarreled with I's herdsmen, saying, "The water
26:25 And there I's servants dug a well.
26:27 I said to them, "Why have you come to
26:31 with one another; and I set them on their
26:32 That same day I's servants came and told him
26:35 made life bitter for I and Rebekah.
27:1 When I was old and his eyes were dim
27:5 Rebekah was listening when I spoke to his son
27:20 But I said to his son, "How is it
27:21 Then I said to Jacob, "Come near, that I
27:22 Jacob went near to I his father, who felt
27:26 Then his father I said to him, "Come near
27:30 As soon as I had finished blessing Jacob, when
27:30 from the presence of I his father, Esau his
27:32 His father I said to him, "Who are you?"
27:33 Then I trembled violently, and said, "Who was it
27:37 I answered Esau, "Behold, I have made him your
27:39 Then I his father answered him: "Behold, away from
27:46 Then Rebekah said to I, "I am weary of
28:1 Then I called Jacob and blessed him, and charged
28:5 Thus I sent Jacob away; and he went to
28:6 Now Esau saw that I had blessed Jacob and
28:8 women did not please I his father,
28:13 and the God of I; the land on which
31:18 to the land of Canaan to his father I
31:42 and the Fear of I, had not been on
31:53 Fear of his father I,
32:9 God of my father I, O LORD who didst
35:12 gave to Abraham and I I will give to
35:27 came to his father I at Mamre, or Kiriath-arba
35:27 Hebron), where Abraham and I had sojourned.
35:28 Now the days of I were a hundred and
35:29 And I breathed his last; and he died and
46:1 offered sacrifices to the God of his father I
48:15 my fathers Abraham and I walked, the God who
48:16 my fathers Abraham and I; and let them grow
49:31 wife; there they buried I and Rebekah his wife;
50:24 swore to Abraham, to I, and to Jacob."
Ex 2:24 covenant with Abraham, with I, and with Jacob.
3:6 Abraham, the God of I, and the God of
3:15 Abraham, the God of I, and the God of
3:16 God of Abraham, of I, and of Jacob, has
4:5 Abraham, the God of I, and the God of
6:3 appeared to Abraham, to I, and to Jacob, as
6:8 give to Abraham, to I, and to Jacob; I
32:13 Remember Abraham, I, and Israel, thy servants, to
33:1 I swore to Abraham, I, and Jacob, saying, 'To
Lev 26:42 remember my covenant with I and my covenant with
Num 32:11 give to Abraham, to I, and to Jacob, because
Deut 1:8 fathers, to Abraham, to I, and to Jacob, to
6:10 fathers, to Abraham, to I, and to Jacob, to
9:5 fathers, to Abraham, to I, and to Jacob.
9:27 Remember thy servants, Abraham, I, and Jacob; do
29:13 fathers, to Abraham, to I, and to Jacob.
30:20 fathers, to Abraham, to I, and to Jacob, to
34:4 swore to Abraham, to I, and to Jacob, 'I
Josh 24:3 I gave him I;
24:4 him Isaac; and to I I gave Jacob and
1Kgs 18:36 LORD, God of Abraham, I, and Israel, let it
2Kgs 13:23 his covenant with Abraham, I, and Jacob, and would
1Chr 1:28 The sons of Abraham: I and Ishmael.
1:34 Abraham was the father of I
1:34 The sons of I: Esau and Israel.
16:16 his sworn promise to I,
29:18 the God of Abraham, I, and Israel, our fathers,
2Chr 30:6 the God of Abraham, I, and Israel, that he
Tob 4:12 son, that Noah, Abraham, I, and Jacob, our fathers
Jud 8:26 and how he tested I, and what happened to
Ps 105:9 his sworn promise to I,
Sir 44:23 To I also he gave the same assurance for
Jer 33:26 the seed of Abraham, I, and Jacob.
Bar 2:34 to Abraham and to I and to Jacob, and
Dan 3:35 for the sake of I thy servant and Israel
Amos 7:9 the high places of I shall be made desolate,
7:16 against the house of I
2Mac 1:2 covenant with Abraham and I and Jacob, his faithful
Mt 1:2 was the father of I, and Isaac the father
1:2 father of Isaac, and I the father of Jacob,
8:11 at table with Abraham, I, and Jacob in the
22:32 and the God of I, and the God of
Mk 12:26 and the God of I, and the God of
Lk 3:34 Jacob, the son of I, the son of Abraham,
13:28 you see Abraham and I and Jacob and all
20:37 and the God of I and the God of
Acts 3:13 of Abraham and of I and of Jacob, the
7:8 became the father of I, and circumcised him on
7:8 the eighth day; and I became the father of
7:32 of Abraham and of I and of Jacob.' And
Rom 9:7 descendants; but "Through I shall your descendants
9:10 one man, our forefather I,
Gal 4:28 Now we, brethren, like I, are children of promise.
Heb 11:9 living in tents with I and Jacob, heirs with
11:17 was tested, offered up I, and he who had
11:18 it was said, "Through I shall your descendants be
11:20 By faith I invoked future blessings on Jacob and
Jas 2:21 he offered his son I upon the altar?

ISAIAH (56)

2Kgs 19:2 sackcloth, to the prophet I the son of Amoz.
19:5 King Hezekiah came to I,
19:6 Hezekiah came to Isaiah, I said to them, "Say
19:20 Then I the son of Amoz sent to Hezekiah,
20:1 And I the prophet the son of Amoz came
20:4 And before I had gone out of the middle
20:7 And I said, "Bring a cake of figs.
20:8 And Hezekiah said to I, "What shall be the
20:9 And I said, "This is the sign to you
20:11 And I the prophet cried to the LORD; and
20:14 Then I the prophet came to King Hezekiah, and
20:16 Then I said to Hezekiah, "Hear the word of
20:19 Then said Hezekiah to I, "The word of the
2Chr 26:22 from first to last, I the prophet the son
32:20 Hezekiah the king and I the prophet, the son
32:32 in the vision of I the prophet the son
Sir 48:20 heaven, and delivered them by the hand of I
48:22 David his father, which I the prophet commanded,
Is 1:1 The vision of I the son of Amoz,
2:1 The word which I the son of Amoz saw
7:3 the LORD said to I, "Go forth to meet
13:1 oracle concerning Babylon which I the son of Amoz
20:2 LORD had spoken by I the son of Amoz,
20:3 said, "As my servant I has walked naked and
37:2 sackcloth, to the prophet I the son of Amoz.
37:5 King Hezekiah came to I,
37:6 Hezekiah came to Isaiah, I said to them, "Say
37:21 Then I the son of Amoz sent to Hezekiah,
38:1 And I the prophet the son of Amoz came
38:4 the LORD came to I:
38:21 Now I had said, "Let them take a cake
39:3 Then I the prophet came to King Hezekiah, and
39:5 Then I said to Hezekiah, "Hear the word of
39:8 Then said Hezekiah to I, "The word of the
Mt 3:3 of by the prophet I when he said, "The
4:14 spoken by the prophet I might be fulfilled:
8:17 spoken by the prophet I, "He took our infirmities
12:17 spoken by the prophet I:
13:14 fulfilled the prophecy of I which says: 'You shall
15:7 Well did I prophesy of you, when he said:
Mk 1:2 it is written in I the prophet, "Behold, I
7:6 to them, "Well did I prophesy of you hypocrites,
Lk 3:4 of the words of I the prophet, "The voice
4:17 given to him the book of the prophet I
Jn 1:23 Lord,' as the prophet I said."
12:38 spoken by the prophet I might be fulfilled: "Lord,
12:39 For I again said,
12:41 I said this because he saw his glory and
Acts 8:28 in his chariot, he was reading the prophet I
8:30 and heard him reading I the prophet, and asked,
28:25 to your fathers through I the prophet:
Rom 9:27 And I cries out concerning Israel: "Though the

9:29 And as I predicted, "If the Lord of hosts
10:16 obeyed the gospel; for I says, "Lord, who has
10:20 Then I is so bold as to say, "I
15:12 praise him"; and further I says, "The root of

ISCAH

Gen 11:29 daughter of Haran the father of Milcah and I

ISCARIOT (11)

Mt 10:4 the Cananaean, and Judas I, who betrayed him.
26:14 who was called Judas I, went to the chief
Mk 3:19 the Cananaean, and Judas I, who betrayed him.
14:10 Then Judas I, who was one of the twelve,
Lk 6:16 of James, and Judas I, who became a traitor.
22:3 entered into Judas called I, who was of the
Jn 6:71 the son of Simon I, for he, one of
12:4 But Judas I, one of his disciples (he who
13:2 the heart of Judas I, Simon's son, to betray
13:26 gave it to Judas, the son of Simon I
14:22 Judas (not I said to him, "Lord, how is

ISH-BOSHETH (14)

2Sam 2:8 Saul's army, had taken I the son of Saul,
2:10 I, Saul's son, was forty years old when he
2:12 and the servants of I the son of Saul,
2:15 twelve for Benjamin and I the son of Saul,
3:7 daughter of Aiah; and I said to Abner, "Why
3:8 over the words of I, and said, "Am I
3:11 And I could not answer Abner another word, because
3:14 David sent messengers to I Saul's son, saying, "Give
3:15 And I sent, and took her from her husband
4:1 When I, Saul's son, heard that Abner had died
4:5 to the house of I, as he was taking
4:8 brought the head of I to David at Hebron.
4:8 is the head of I, the son of Saul,
4:12 took the head of I, and buried it in

ISHBAH

1Chr 4:17 bore Miriam, Shammai, and I, the father of

ISHBAK (2)

Gen 25:2 Zimran, Jokshan, Medan, Midian, I, and Shuah.
1Chr 1:32 Zimran, Jokshan, Medan, Midian, I, and Shuah.

ISHBI-BENOB

2Sam 21:16 And I, one of the descendants of the giants,

ISHHOD

1Chr 7:18 his sister Hammolecheth bore I, Abi-ezer, and

ISHI (5)

1Chr 2:31 The sons of Appa-im: I
2:31 The sons of I: Sheshan.
4:20 The sons of I: Zoheth and Ben-zoheth.
4:42 Uzziel, the sons of I;
5:24 fathers' houses: Epher, I, Eliel, Azriel, Jeremiah,

ISHMA

1Chr 4:3 sons of Etam: Jezreel, I, and Idbash; and the

ISHMAEL (48)

Gen 16:11 shall call his name I; because the LORD has
16:15 the name of his son, whom Hagar bore, I
16:16 old when Hagar bore I to Abram.
17:18 to God, "O that I might live in thy
17:20 As for I, I have heard you; behold, I
17:23 Then Abraham took I his son and all the
17:25 And I his son was thirteen years old when
17:26 Abraham and his son I were circumcised;
25:9 Isaac and I his sons buried him in the
25:12 the descendants of I, Abraham's son, whom Hagar
25:13 of the sons of I, named in the order
25:13 Nebaioth, the first-born of I; and Kedar, Adbeel,
25:16 are the sons of I and these are their
25:17 of the life of I, a hundred and thirty-seven
28:9 father, Esau went to I and took to wife,
28:9 Mahalath the daughter of I Abraham's son, the sister
36:3 the Hivite, and Basemath, I's daughter, the sister of
2Kgs 25:23 Gedaliah at Mizpah, namely, I the son of Nethaniah,
25:25 in the seventh month, I the son of Nethaniah,
1Chr 1:28 The sons of Abraham: Isaac and I
1:29 genealogies: the first-born of I, Nebaioth; and Kedar,
1:31 These are the sons of I
8:38 names: Azrikam, Bocheru, I, She-ariah, Obadiah, and
9:44 names: Azrikam, Bocheru, I, She-ariah, Obadiah, and
2Chr 19:11 Zebadiah the son of I, the governor of the
23:1 the son of Jeroham, I the son of Jehohanan,
Ezra 10:22 Pashhur: Eli-o-enai, Ma-aseiah, I, Nethanel,
Jer 40:8 to Gedaliah at Mizpah– I the son of Nethaniah,
40:14 the Ammonites has sent I the son of Nethaniah
40:15 me go and slay I the son of Nethaniah,
40:16 this thing, for you are speaking falsely of I
41:1 In the seventh month, I the son of Nethaniah,
41:2 together there at Mizpah, I the son of Nethaniah
41:3 I also slew all the Jews who were with
41:6 And I the son of Nethaniah came out from
41:7 came into the city, I the son of Nethaniah
41:8 them who said to I, "Do not kill us,
41:9 the cistern into which I cast all the bodies
41:9 Baasha king of Israel; I the son of Nethaniah
41:10 Then I took captive all the rest of the
41:10 I the son of Nethaniah took them captive and
41:11 all the evil which I the son of Nethaniah
41:12 went to fight against I the son of Nethaniah.
41:13 people who were with I saw Johanan the son
41:14 all the people whom I had carried away captive
41:15 But I the son of Nethaniah escaped from Johanan
41:16 of the people whom I the son of Nethaniah
41:18 afraid of them, because I the son of Nethaniah

ISHMAELITE (3)

2Sam 17:25 man named Ithra the I, who had married Abigal
1Chr 2:17 and the father of Amasa was Jether the I
27:30 camels was Obil the I; and over the she-asses

ISHMAELITES (7)

Gen 37:25 saw a caravan of I coming from Gilead, with
37:27 sell him to the I, and let not our
37:28 sold him to the I for twenty shekels of
39:1 bought him from the I who had brought him
Judg 8:24 earrings, because they were I
Jud 2:23 of Rassis and the I who lived along the
Ps 83:6 of Edom and the I, Moab and the Hagrites,

ISHMAIAH (2)

1Chr 12:4 Beracah, Jehu of Anathoth, I of Gibeon, a mighty
27:19 of Michael; for Zebulun, I the son of Obadiah;

ISHMERAI

1Chr 8:18 Zebadiah, Meshullam, Hizki, Heber, I, Izliah, and

ISHPAH

1Chr 8:16 Zebadiah, Arad, Eder, Michael, I, and Joha were sons

ISHPAN

1Chr 8:22 I, Eber, Eliel,

ISHVAH (2)

Gen 46:17 sons of Asher: Imnah, I, Ishvi, Beriah, with Serah
1Chr 7:30 sons of Asher: Imnah, I, Ishvi, Beriah, and their

ISHVI (4)

Gen 46:17 of Asher: Imnah, Ishvah, I, Beriah, with Serah their
Num 26:44 of the Imnites; of I, the family of the
1Sam 14:49 of Saul were Jonathan, I, and Malchishua; and the
1Chr 7:30 of Asher: Imnah, Ishvah, I, Beriah, and their sister

ISHVITES

Num 26:44 the family of the I; of Beriah, the family

ISLAND (10)

Acts 13:6 gone through the whole I as far as Paphos,
27:16 lee of a small I called Cauda, we managed
27:26 But we shall have to run on some I
28:1 then learned that the I was called Malta.
28:7 chief man of the I, named Publius, who received
28:9 the people on the I who had diseases also
28:11 had wintered in the I, a ship of Alexandria,
Rev 1:9 endurance, was on the I called Patmos on account
6:14 and every mountain and I was removed from its
16:20 And every I fled away, and no mountains were

ISLANDS (7)

Sir 43:23 great deep and planted I in it.
47:16 name reached to far-off I, and you were loved
Is 42:15 turn the rivers into I, and dry up the
1Mac 6:29 other kingdoms and from I of the seas.
8:11 The remaining kingdoms and I, as many as ever
11:38 had recruited from the I of the nations.
15:1 a letter from the I of the sea to

ISLES (5)

Ps 72:10 Tarshish and of the I render him tribute, may
Is 40:15 he takes up the I like fine dust.
Ezek 26:18 Now the I tremble on the day of your
26:18 your fall; yea, the I that are in the
1Mac 14:5 a way to the I of the sea.

ISMACHIAH

2Chr 31:13 Asahel, Jerimoth, Jozabad, Eliel, I, Mahath, and

ISOLATE

1Mac 12:36 city, in order to I it so that its

ISRAEL (2,724)

Gen 32:28 be called Jacob, but I, for you have striven
34:7 had wrought folly in I by lying with Jacob's
35:10 be called Jacob, but I shall be your name."
35:10 So his name was called I
35:21 I journeyed on, and pitched his tent beyond the
35:22 While I dwelt in that land Reuben went and
35:22 his father's concubine; and I heard of it.
37:3 Now I loved Joseph more than any other of
37:13 And I said to Joseph, "Are not your brothers
42:5 Thus the sons of I came to buy among
43:6 I said, "Why did you treat me so ill
43:8 And Judah said to I his father, "Send the
43:11 Then their father I said to them, "If it
45:21 The sons of I did so; and Joseph gave
45:28 father Jacob revived; and I said, "It is enough;
46:1 So I took his journey with all that he
46:2 And God spoke to I in visions of the
46:5 and the sons of I carried Jacob their father,
46:8 of the descendants of I, who came into Egypt,
46:29 went up to meet I his father in Goshen;
46:30 I said to Joseph, "Now let me die, since
47:27 Thus I dwelt in the land of Egypt, in
47:29 time drew near that I must die, he called
47:31 Then I bowed himself upon the head of his
48:2 come to you"; then I summoned his strength, and
48:8 When I saw Joseph's sons, he said, "Who are
48:10 Now the eyes of I were dim with age,
48:11 And I said to Joseph, "I had not thought
48:13 his right hand toward I's left hand, and Manasseh
48:13 his left hand toward I's right hand, and brought
48:14 And I stretched out his right hand and laid
48:20 day, saying, "By you I will pronounce blessings,
48:21 Then I said to Joseph, "Behold, I am about
49:2 Jacob, and hearken to I your father.
49:7 divide them in Jacob and scatter them in I
49:16 his people as one of the tribes of I
49:24 Shepherd, the Rock of I,
49:28 the twelve tribes of I; and this is what
50:2 So the physicians embalmed I;
50:25 of the sons of I, saying, "God will visit
Ex 1:1 of the sons of I who came to Egypt
1:6 But the descendants of I were fruitful and increased
1:8 "Behold, the people of I are too many and
1:11 Egyptians were in dread of the people of I
1:12 made the people of I serve with rigor,
2:23 And the people of I groaned under their bondage,
2:25 saw the people of I, and God knew their
3:9 of the people of I has come to me,
3:10 people, the sons of I, out of Egypt."
3:11 bring the sons of I out of Egypt?"
3:13 to the people of I and say to them,
3:14 to the people of I, 'I AM has sent
3:15 to the people of I, 'The LORD, the God
3:16 gather the elders of I together, and say to
3:18 and the elders of I shall go to the
4:22 'Thus says the LORD, I is my first-born son,
4:29 together all the elders of the people of I
4:31 visited the people of I and that he had
5:1 LORD, the God of I, 'Let my people go,
5:2 his voice and let I go?
5:2 I will not let I go."
5:14 of the people of I, whom Pharaoh's taskmasters had
5:15 of the people of I came and cried to
5:19 of the people of I saw that they were
6:5 of the people of I whom the Egyptians hold
6:6 to the people of I, 'I am the LORD,
6:9 to the people of I; but they did not
6:11 let the people of I go out of his
6:12 "Behold, the people of I have not listened to
6:13 to the people of I and to Pharaoh king
6:13 bring the people of I out of the land
6:14 Reuben, the first-born of I: Hanoch, Pallu, Hezron,
6:26 out the people of I from the land of
6:27 out the people of I from Egypt, this Moses
7:2 let the people of I go out of his
7:4 people the sons of I, out of the land
7:5 out the people of I from among them."
9:4 between the cattle of I and the cattle of
9:4 of all that belongs to the people of I
9:6 of the people of I not one died.
9:26 where the people of I were, there was no
9:35 let the people of I go; as the LORD
10:20 let the children of I go.
10:23 all the people of I had light where they
11:7 of the people of I, either man or beast,
11:7 makes a distinction between the Egyptians and I
11:10 let the people of I go out of his
12:3 all the congregation of I that on the tenth
12:6 of the congregation of I shall kill their lambs
12:15 day, that person shall be cut off from I
12:19 from the congregation of I, whether he is a
12:21 all the elders of I, and said to them,
12:27 of the people of I in Egypt, when he
12:28 Then the people of I went and did so;
12:31 and the people of I; and go, serve the
12:35 The people of I had also done as Moses
12:37 And the people of I journeyed from Rameses to
12:40 that the people of I dwelt in Egypt was
12:42 all the people of I throughout their generations.
12:47 All the congregation of I shall keep it.
12:50 all the people of I; as the LORD commanded
12:51 brought the people of I out of the land
13:2 among the people of I, both of man and
13:18 And the people of I went up out of
13:19 sworn the people of I, saying, "God will visit
14:2 "Tell the people of I to turn back and
14:3 of the people of I, 'They are entangled in
14:5 that we have let I go from serving us?"
14:8 pursued the people of I as they went forth
14:10 near, the people of I lifted up their eyes,
14:10 And the people of I cried out to the
14:15 Tell the people of I to go forward.
14:16 that the people of I may go on dry
14:19 before the host of I moved and went behind
14:20 the host of Egypt and the host of I
14:22 And the people of I went into the midst
14:25 us flee from before I; for the LORD fights
14:29 But the people of I walked on dry ground
14:30 Thus the LORD saved I that day from the
14:30 of the Egyptians; and I saw the Egyptians dead
14:31 And I saw the great work which the LORD
15:1 and the people of I sang this song to
15:19 but the people of I walked on dry ground
15:22 Then Moses led I onward from the Red Sea,
16:1 of the people of I came to the wilderness
16:2 of the people of I murmured against Moses and
16:6 all the people of I, "At evening you shall
16:9 of the people of I, 'Come near before the
16:10 of the people of I, they looked toward the
16:12 of the people of I; say to them, 'At
16:15 When the people of I saw it, they said
16:17 And the people of I did so; they gathered,
16:31 Now the house of I called its name manna;
16:35 And the people of I ate the manna forty
17:1 of the people of I moved on from the
17:5 of the elders of I; and take in your
17:6 so, in the sight of the elders of I
17:7 of the children of I, and because they put
17:8 Amalek and fought with I at Rephidim.
17:11 held up his hand, I prevailed; and whenever he
18:1 for Moses and for I his people, how the
18:1 the LORD had brought I out of Egypt.
18:8 to the Egyptians for I's sake, all the hardship
18:9 LORD had done to I, in that he had
18:12 all the elders of I to eat bread with
18:25 men out of all I, and made them heads
19:1 after the people of I had gone forth out
19:2 and there I encamped before the mountain.
19:3 tell the people of I:
19:6 which you shall speak to the children of I
20:22 to the people of I: 'You have seen for
24:1 of the elders of I, and worship afar off.
24:4 twelve pillars, according to the twelve tribes of I
24:5 of the people of I, who offered burnt offerings
24:9 of the elders of I went up,
24:10 saw the God of I; and there was under
24:11 of the people of I; they beheld God, and
24:17 mountain in the sight of the people of I

I

25:2 to the people of I, that they take for
25:22 give you in commandment for the people of I
27:20 command the people of I that they bring to
27:21 throughout their generations by the people of I
28:1 among the people of I, to serve me as
28:9 of the sons of I,
28:11 of the sons of I; you shall enclose them
28:12 for the sons of I; and Aaron shall bear
28:21 of the sons of I; they shall be like
28:29 of the sons of I in the breastpiece of
28:30 of the people of I upon his heart before
28:38 which the people of I hallow as their holy
29:28 from the people of I, for it is the
29:28 by the people of I from their peace offerings;
29:43 with the people of I, and it shall be
29:45 among the people of I, and will be their
30:12 of the people of I, then each shall give
30:16 from the people of I, and shall appoint it
30:16 bring the people of I to remembrance before the
30:31 to the people of I, 'This shall be my
31:13 to the people of I, 'You shall keep my
31:16 Therefore the people of I shall keep the sabbath,
31:17 and the people of I that in six days
32:4 are your gods, O I, who brought you up
32:8 are your gods, O I, who brought you up
32:13 Remember Abraham, Isaac, and I, thy servants, to
32:20 made the people of I drink it.
32:27 the LORD God of I, 'Put every man his
33:5 to the people of I, 'You are a stiff-necked
33:6 Therefore the people of I stripped themselves of
34:23 appear before the LORD God, the God of I
34:27 have made a covenant with you and with I
34:30 all the people of I saw Moses, behold, the
34:32 all the people of I came near, and he
34:34 told the people of I what he was commanded,
34:35 commanded, the people of I saw the face of
35:1 of the people of I, and said to them,
35:4 of the people of I, "This is the thing
35:20 of the people of I departed from the presence
35:29 women, the people of I, whose heart moved them
35:30 to the people of I, "See, the LORD has
36:3 which the people of I had brought for doing
39:6 according to the names of the sons of I
39:7 for the sons of I; as the LORD had
39:14 of the sons of I; they were like signets,
39:32 and the people of I had done according to
39:42 so the people of I had done all the

Lev 1:2 to the people of I, and say to them,
4:2 to the people of I, If any one sins
4:13 whole congregation of I commits a sin unwittingly
7:23 to the people of I, You shall eat no
7:29 to the people of I, He that offers the
7:34 from the people of I, out of the sacrifices
7:34 as a perpetual due from the people of I
7:36 by the people of I, on the day that
7:38 commanded the people of I to bring their offerings
9:1 and the elders of I;
9:3 to the people of I, 'Take a male goat
10:6 the whole house of I, may bewail the burning
10:11 teach the people of I all the statutes which
10:14 of the peace offerings of the people of I
11:2 to the people of I, These are the living
12:2 to the people of I, If a woman conceives,
15:2 to the people of I, When any man has
15:31 keep the people of I separate from their
16:5 of the people of I two male goats for
16:16 of the people of I, and because of their
16:17 his house and for all the assembly of I
16:19 it from the uncleannesses of the people of I
16:21 of the people of I, and all their transgressions,
16:34 for the people of I once in the year
17:2 all the people of I, This is the thing
17:3 of the house of I kills an ox or
17:5 that the people of I may bring their sacrifices
17:8 of the house of I, or of the strangers
17:10 of the house of I or of the strangers
17:12 to the people of I, No person among you
17:13 of the people of I, or of the strangers
17:14 to the people of I, You shall not eat
18:2 to the people of I, I am the LORD
19:2 of the people of I, You shall be holy;
20:2 to the people of I, Any man of the
20:2 of the people of I, or of the strangers
20:2 strangers that sojourn in I, who gives any of
21:24 his sons and to all the people of I
22:2 of the people of I, which they dedicate to
22:3 which the people of I dedicate to the LORD,
22:15 of the people of I, which they offer to
22:18 all the people of I, When any one of
22:18 of the house of I or of the sojourners
22:18 of the sojourners in I presents his offering, whether
22:32 among the people of I; I am the LORD
23:2 to the people of I, The appointed feasts of
23:10 to the people of I, When you come into
23:24 to the people of I, In the seventh month,
23:34 to the people of I, On the fifteenth day
23:42 that are native in I shall dwell in booths,
23:43 made the people of I dwell in booths when
23:44 to the people of I the appointed feasts of
24:2 "Command the people of I to bring you pure
24:8 of the people of I as a covenant for
24:10 among the people of I; and the Israelite woman's
24:10 and a man of I quarreled in the camp,
24:15 to the people of I, Whoever curses his God
24:23 to the people of I; and they brought him
24:23 Thus the people of I did as the LORD
25:2 to the people of I, When you come into
25:33 Levites are their possession among the people of I
25:46 brethren the people of I you shall not rule,
25:55 me the people of I are servants, they are
26:46 and the people of I on Mount Sinai by
27:2 to the people of I, When a man makes
27:34 for the people of I on Mount Sinai.

Num 1:2 of the people of I, by families, by fathers'
1:3 and upward, all in I who are able to
1:16 ancestral tribes, the heads of the clans of I
1:20 people of Reuben, I's first-born, their generations,
1:44 of the leaders of I, twelve men, each representing
1:45 of the people of I, by their fathers' houses,
1:45 forth to war in I –
1:49 among the people of I;
1:52 The people of I shall pitch their tents by
1:53 of the people of I; and the Levites shall
1:54 did the people of I; they did according to
2:2 Aaron, "The people of I shall encamp each by
2:32 are the people of I as numbered by their
2:33 among the people of I, as the LORD commanded
2:34 Thus did the people of I
3:8 for the people of I as they minister at
3:9 given to him from among the people of I
3:12 among the people of I instead of every first-born
3:12 that opens the womb among the people of I
3:13 all the first-born in I, both of man and
3:38 for the people of I; and any one else
3:40 of the people of I, from a month old
3:41 among the people of I, and the cattle of
3:41 firstlings among the cattle of the people of I
3:42 among the people of I, as the LORD commanded
3:45 among the people of I, and the cattle of
3:46 of the people of I, over and above the
3:50 of the people of I he took the money,
4:46 and the leaders of I numbered, by their families
5:2 "Command the people of I that they put out
5:4 And the people of I did so, and drove
5:4 so the people of I did.
5:6 to the people of I, When a man or
5:9 of the people of I, which they bring to
5:12 to the people of I, If any man's wife
6:2 to the people of I, When either a man
6:23 bless the people of I: you shall say to
6:27 upon the people of I, and I will bless
7:2 utensils, the leaders of I, heads of their fathers'
7:84 from the leaders of I: twelve silver plates, twelve
8:6 among the people of I, and cleanse them.
8:9 assemble the whole congregation of the people of I
8:10 LORD, the people of I shall lay their hands
8:11 from the people of I, that it may be
8:14 among the people of I, and the Levites shall
8:16 among the people of I; instead of all that
8:16 all the people of I, I have taken them
8:17 among the people of I are mine, both of
8:18 of all the first-born among the people of I
8:19 among the people of I, to do the service
8:19 for the people of I at the tent of
8:19 for the people of I, that there may be
8:19 among the people of I in case the people
8:19 case the people of I should come near the
8:20 of the people of I to the Levites; according
8:20 Levites, the people of I did to them.
9:2 "Let the people of I keep the passover at
9:4 told the people of I that they should keep
9:5 so the people of I did.

ISRAEL

9:7 at its appointed time among the people of I
9:10 to the people of I, If any man of
9:17 that the people of I set out; and in
9:17 there the people of I encamped.
9:18 LORD the people of I set out, and at
9:19 days, the people of I kept the charge of
9:22 there, the people of I remained in camp and
10:4 of the tribes of I, shall gather themselves to
10:12 and the people of I set out by stages
10:28 of the people of I according to their hosts,
10:29 good; for the LORD has promised good to I
10:36 O LORD, to the ten thousand thousands of I
11:4 and the people of I also wept again, and
11:16 of the elders of I, whom you know to
11:30 and the elders of I returned to the camp.
13:2 to the people of I; from each tribe of
13:3 men who were heads of the people of I
13:24 which the men of I cut down from there.
13:26 of the people of I in the wilderness of
13:32 to the people of I an evil report of
14:2 all the people of I murmured against Moses and
14:5 assembly of the congregation of the people of I
14:7 of the people of I, "The land, which we
14:10 tent of meeting to all the people of I
14:27 of the people of I, which they murmur against
14:39 all the people of I, and the people mourned
15:2 to the people of I, When you come into
15:18 to the people of I, When you come into
15:25 of the people of I, and they shall be
15:26 of the people of I shall be forgiven, and
15:29 among the people of I, and for the stranger
15:32 While the people of I were in the wilderness,
15:38 to the people of I, and bid them to
16:2 of the people of I, two hundred and fifty
16:9 that the God of I has separated you from
16:9 from the congregation of I, to bring you near
16:25 and the elders of I followed him.
16:34 And all I that were round about them fled
16:38 shall be a sign to the people of I
16:40 to the people of I, so that no one
16:41 of the people of I murmured against Moses and
17:2 to the people of I, and get from them
17:5 of the people of I, which they murmur against
17:6 to the people of I; and all their leaders
17:9 all the people of I; and they looked, and
17:12 And the people of I said to Moses, "Behold,
18:5 be wrath no more upon the people of I
18:6 among the people of I; they are a gift
18:8 of the people of I; I have given them
18:11 of the people of I; I have given them
18:14 Every devoted thing in I shall be yours.
18:19 which the people of I present to the LORD
18:20 portion and your inheritance among the people of I
18:21 given every tithe in I for an inheritance, in
18:22 henceforth the people of I shall not come near
18:23 among the people of I they shall have no
18:24 of the people of I, which they present as
18:24 shall have no inheritance among the people of I
18:26 from the people of I the tithe which I
18:28 from the people of I; and from it you
18:32 of the people of I, lest you die.'"
19:2 Tell the people of I to bring you a
19:9 of the people of I for the water for
19:10 to the people of I, and to the stranger
19:13 be cut off from I; because the water for
20:1 And the people of I, the whole congregation, came
20:12 of the people of I, therefore you shall not
20:13 where the people of I contended with the LORD,
20:14 "Thus says your brother I: You know all the
20:19 And the people of I said to him, "We
20:21 Edom refused to give I passage through his territory;
20:21 through his territory; so I turned away from him.
20:22 and the people of I, the whole congregation, came
20:24 to the people of I, because you rebelled against
20:29 all the house of I wept for Aaron thirty
21:1 the Negeb, heard that I was coming by the
21:1 Atharim, he fought against I, and took some of
21:2 And I vowed a vow to the LORD, and
21:3 to the voice of I, and gave over the
21:6 that many people of I died.
21:10 And the people of I set out, and encamped
21:17 Then I sang this song: "Spring up, O well!--
21:21 Then I sent messengers to Sihon king of the
21:23 Sihon would not allow I to pass through his
21:23 and went out against I to the wilderness, and
21:23 wilderness, and came to Jahaz, and fought against I
21:24 And I slew him with the edge of the
21:25 And I took all these cities, and Israel settled
21:25 all these cities, and I settled in all the
21:31 Thus I dwelt in the land of the Amorites.
22:1 Then the people of I set out, and encamped
22:2 Zippor saw all that I had done to the
22:3 was overcome with fear of the people of I
23:7 me, and come, denounce I
23:10 of Jacob, or number the fourth part of I
23:21 in Jacob; nor has he seen trouble in I
23:23 Jacob, no divination against I; now it shall be
23:23 said of Jacob and I, 'What has God wrought!'
24:1 the LORD to bless I, he did not go,
24:2 his eyes, and saw I encamping tribe by tribe.
24:5 are your tents, O Jacob, your encampments, O I
24:17 shall rise out of I; it shall crush the
24:18 shall be dispossessed, while I does valiantly.
25:1 While I dwelt in Shittim the people began to
25:3 So I yoked himself to Baal of Peor.
25:3 LORD was kindled against I;
25:4 anger of the LORD may turn away from I
25:5 to the judges of I, "Every one of you
25:6 of the people of I came and brought a
25:6 of the people of I, while they were weeping
25:8 after the man of I into the inner room,
25:8 them, the man of I and the woman, through
25:8 the plague was stayed from the people of I
25:11 from the people of I, in that he was
25:11 consume the people of I in my jealousy.
25:13 God, and made atonement for the people of I
25:14 the slain man of I, who was slain with
26:2 of the people of I, from twenty years old
26:2 fathers' houses, all in I who are able to
26:4 The people of I, who came forth out of
26:5 Reuben, the first-born of I; the sons of Reuben:
26:51 of the people of I, six hundred and one
26:62 among the people of I, because there was no
26:62 inheritance given to them among the people of I
26:63 numbered the people of I in the plains of
26:64 numbered the people of I in the wilderness of
27:8 to the people of I, 'If a man dies,
27:11 to the people of I a statute and ordinance,
27:12 which I have given to the people of I
27:20 of the people of I may obey.
27:21 all the people of I with him, the whole
28:2 "Command the people of I, and say to them,
29:40 told the people of I everything just as the
30:1 of the people of I, "This is what the
31:2 "Avenge the people of I on the Midianites;
31:4 of the tribes of I to the war."
31:5 of the thousands of I, a thousand from each
31:9 And the people of I took captive the women
31:12 of the people of I, at the camp on
31:16 caused the people of I, by the counsel of
31:30 from the people of I's half you shall take
31:42 From the people of I's half, which Moses separated
31:47 from the people of I's half Moses took one
31:54 for the people of I before the LORD.
32:4 before the congregation of I, is a land for
32:7 of the people of I from going over into
32:9 of the people of I from going into the
32:13 anger was kindled against I, and he made them
32:14 more the fierce anger of the LORD against I
32:17 before the people of I, until we have brought
32:18 until the people of I have inherited each his
32:22 the LORD and to I; and this land shall
32:28 houses of the tribes of the people of I
33:1 of the people of I, when they went forth
33:3 passover the people of I went out triumphantly in
33:5 So the people of I set out from Rameses,
33:38 after the people of I had come out of
33:40 heard of the coming of the people of I
33:51 to the people of I, When you pass over
34:2 "Command the people of I, and say to them,
34:13 commanded the people of I, saying, "This is the
34:29 for the people of I in the land of
35:2 "Command the people of I, that they give to
35:8 of the people of I, from the larger tribes
35:10 to the people of I, When you cross the
35:15 for the people of I, and for the stranger
35:34 dwell in the midst of the people of I
36:1 of the people of I;
36:2 to the people of I; and my lord was
36:3 of the people of I then their inheritance will
36:4 of the people of I comes, then their inheritance
36:5 commanded the people of I according to the word

I

36:7 of the people of I shall not be transferred
36:7 of the people of I shall cleave to the
36:8 of the people of I shall be wife to
36:8 of the people of I may possess the inheritance
36:9 of the people of I shall cleave to its
36:13 to the people of I in the plains of
Deut 1:1 Moses spoke to all I beyond the Jordan in
1:3 to the people of I according to all that
1:38 for he shall cause I to inherit it.
2:12 in their stead; as I did to the land
3:18 over armed before your brethren the people of I
4:1 "And now, O I, give heed to the statutes
4:44 before the children of I;
4:45 to the children of I when they came out
4:46 and the children of I defeated when they came
5:1 And Moses summoned all I, and said to them,
5:1 to them, "Hear, O I, the statutes and the
6:3 Hear therefore, O I, and be careful to do
6:4 "Hear, O I: The LORD our God is one
9:1 "Hear, O I; you are to pass over the
10:6 (The people of I journeyed from Be-eroth
10:12 give them.' "And now, I, what does the LORD
11:6 the midst of all I;
13:11 And all I shall hear, and fear, and never
17:4 has been done in I,
17:12 die; so you shall purge the evil from I
17:20 in his kingdom, he and his children, in I
18:1 portion or inheritance with I; they shall eat the
18:6 towns out of all I, where he lives–and
19:13 of innocent blood from I, so that it may
20:3 to them, 'Hear, O I, you draw near this
21:8 O LORD, thy people I, whom thou hast redeemed,
21:8 midst of thy people I; but let the guilt
21:21 your midst; and all I shall hear, and fear.
22:19 upon a virgin of I; and she shall be
22:21 has wrought folly in I by playing the harlot
22:22 woman; so you shall purge the evil from I
23:17 of the daughters of I, neither shall there be
23:17 be a cult prostitute of the sons of I
24:7 brethren, the people of I, and if he treats
25:6 his name may not be blotted out of I
25:7 his brother's name in I; he will not perform
25:10 shall be called in I, The house of him
26:15 and bless thy people I and the ground which
27:1 and the elders of I commanded the people, saying,
27:9 priests said to all I, "Keep silence and hear,
27:9 silence and hear, O I: this day you have
27:14 all the men of I with a loud voice:
29:1 with the people of I in the land of
29:2 And Moses summoned all I and said to them:
29:10 all the men of I,
29:21 all the tribes of I for calamity, in accordance
31:1 Moses continued to speak these words to all I
31:7 the sight of all I, "Be strong and of
31:9 the LORD, and to all the elders of I
31:11 of booths, when all I comes to appear before
31:11 this law before all I in their hearing.
31:19 to the people of I; put it in their
31:19 a witness for me against the people of I
31:22 day, and taught it to the people of I
31:23 bring the children of I into the land which
31:30 in the ears of all the assembly of I
32:45 these words to all I,
32:49 to the people of I for a possession;
32:51 of the people of I at the waters of
32:51 holy in the midst of the people of I
32:52 land which I give to the people of I
33:1 blessed the children of I before his death.
33:5 all the tribes of I together.
33:10 Jacob thy ordinances, and I thy law; they shall
33:21 of the people, with I he executed the commands
33:28 So I dwelt in safety, the fountain of Jacob
33:29 Happy are you, O I
34:8 And the people of I wept for Moses in
34:9 so the people of I obeyed him, and did
34:10 a prophet since in I like Moses, whom the
34:12 which Moses wrought in the sight of all I
Josh 1:2 am giving to them, to the people of I
2:2 "Behold, certain men of I have come here tonight
3:1 all the people of I; and they came to
3:7 the sight of all I, that they may know
3:9 to the people of I, "Come hither, and hear
3:12 from the tribes of I, from each tribe a
3:17 And while all I were passing over on dry
4:4 from the people of I, whom he had appointed,
4:5 of the people of I,
4:7 to the people of I a memorial for ever."
4:8 And the men of I did as Joshua commanded,
4:8 of the people of I, as the LORD told
4:12 before the people of I, as Moses had bidden
4:14 the sight of all I; and they stood in
4:21 to the people of I, "When your children ask
4:22 let your children know, I passed over this Jordan
5:1 for the people of I until they had crossed
5:1 spirit in them, because of the people of I
5:2 circumcise the people of I again the second time."
5:3 circumcised the people of I at Gibeath-haaraloth.
5:6 For the people of I walked forty years in
5:10 While the people of I were encamped in Gilgal
5:12 and the people of I had manna no more,
6:1 of the people of I; none went out, and
6:18 make the camp of I a thing for destruction,
6:23 kindred, and set them outside the camp of I
6:25 and she dwelt in I to this day, because
7:1 But the people of I broke faith in regard
7:1 of the LORD burned against the people of I
7:6 and the elders of I; and they put dust
7:8 can I say, when I has turned their backs
7:11 I has sinned; they have transgressed my covenant
7:12 Therefore the people of I cannot stand before their
7:13 the LORD, God of I, "There are devoted things
7:13 midst of you, O I; you cannot stand before
7:15 because he has done a shameful thing in I
7:16 the morning, and brought I near tribe by tribe,
7:19 the LORD God of I, and render praise to
7:20 the LORD God of I, and this is what
7:23 all the people of I; and they laid them
7:24 And Joshua and all I with him took Achan
7:25 And all I stoned him with stones; they burned
8:10 with the elders of I, before the people to
8:14 the Arabah to meet I in battle; but he
8:15 And Joshua and all I made a pretense of
8:17 not go out after I; they left the city
8:17 Israel; they left the city open, and pursued I
8:21 when Joshua and all I saw that the ambush
8:22 in the midst of I, some on this side,
8:22 on that side; and I smote them, until there
8:24 When I had finished slaughtering all the inhabitants
8:24 of the sword, all I returned to Ai, and
8:27 spoil of that city I took as their booty,
8:30 LORD, the God of I,
8:31 commanded the people of I, as it is written
8:32 of the people of I, he wrote upon the
8:33 And all I, sojourner as well as homeborn, with
8:33 first, that they should bless the people of I
8:35 all the assembly of I, and the women, and
9:2 together with one accord to fight Joshua and I
9:6 to the men of I, "We have come from
9:7 But the men of I said to the Hivites,
9:17 And the people of I set out and reached
9:18 But the people of I did not kill them,
9:18 to them by the LORD, the God of I
9:19 LORD, the God of I, and now we may
9:26 of the people of I; and they did not
10:1 had made peace with I and were among them,
10:4 peace with Joshua and with the people of I
10:10 into a panic before I, who slew them with
10:11 as they fled before I, while they were going
10:11 than the men of I killed with the sword.
10:12 to the men of I; and he said in
10:12 in the sight of I, "Sun, stand thou still
10:14 of a man; for the LORD fought for I
10:15 Joshua returned, and all I with him, to the
10:20 and the men of I had finished slaying them
10:21 his tongue against any of the people of I
10:24 all the men of I, and said to the
10:29 from Makkedah, and all I with him, to Libnah,
10:30 into the hand of I; and he smote it
10:31 from Libnah, and all I with him, to Lachish,
10:32 into the hand of I, and he took it
10:34 passed on with all I from Lachish to Eglon;
10:36 went up with all I from Eglon to Hebron;
10:38 Then Joshua, with all I, turned back to Debir
10:40 the LORD God of I commanded.
10:42 the LORD God of I fought for Israel.
10:42 because the LORD God of Israel fought for I
10:43 Joshua returned, and all I with him, to the
11:5 at the waters of Merom, to fight with I
11:6 of them, slain, to I; you shall hamstring their
11:8 into the hand of I, who smote them and
11:13 stood on mounds did I burn, except Hazor only;
11:14 cattle, the people of I took for their booty;

11:16 the hill country of I and its lowland
11:19 with the people of I, except the Hivites, the
11:20 they should come against I in battle, in order
11:21 the hill country of I; Joshua utterly destroyed them
11:22 of the people of I; only in Gaza, in
11:23 for an inheritance to I according to their tribal
12:1 whom the people of I defeated, and took possession
12:6 and the people of I defeated them; and Moses
12:7 and the people of I defeated on the west
12:7 to the tribes of I as a possession according
13:6 before the people of I; only allot the land
13:6 allot the land to I for an inheritance, as
13:13 Yet the people of I did not drive out
13:13 in the midst of I to this day.
13:14 the LORD God of I are their inheritance, as
13:22 soothsayer, the people of I killed with the sword
13:33 the LORD God of I is their inheritance, as
14:1 which the people of I received in the land
14:1 of the people of I distributed to them.
14:5 The people of I did as the LORD commanded
14:10 word to Moses, while I walked in the wilderness;
14:14 he wholly followed the LORD, the God of I
17:13 when the people of I grew strong, they put
18:1 of the people of I assembled at Shiloh, and
18:2 the people of I seven tribes whose inheritance
18:3 to the people of I, "How long will you
18:10 to the people of I, to each his portion.
19:49 inheritances, the people of I gave an inheritance
19:51 of the people of I distributed by lot at
20:2 to the people of I, 'Appoint the cities of
20:9 all the people of I, and for the stranger
21:1 of the people of I;
21:3 LORD the people of I gave to the Levites
21:8 lands the people of I gave by lot to
21:41 of the people of I were in all forty-eight
21:43 the LORD gave to I all the land which
21:45 to the house of I had failed; all came
22:9 from the people of I at Shiloh, which is
22:11 And the people of I heard say, "Behold, the
22:11 the side that belongs to the people of I
22:12 when the people of I heard of it, the
22:12 of the people of I gathered at Shiloh, to
22:13 Then the people of I sent to the Reubenites
22:14 the tribal families of I, every one of them
22:14 head of a family among the clans of I
22:16 against the God of I in turning away this
22:18 the whole congregation of I tomorrow.
22:20 and wrath fell upon all the congregation of I
22:21 of the families of I,
22:22 He knows; and let I itself know!
22:24 to do with the LORD, the God of I
22:30 of the families of I who were with him,
22:31 saved the people of I from the hand of
22:32 to the people of I, and brought back word
22:33 pleased the people of I; and the people of
22:33 and the people of I blessed God and spoke
23:1 had given rest to I from all their enemies
23:2 Joshua summoned all I, their elders and heads,
24:1 all the tribes of I to Shechem, and summoned
24:1 and the officers of I; and they presented themselves
24:2 LORD, the God of I, 'Your fathers lived of
24:9 arose and fought against I; and he sent and
24:23 your heart to the LORD, the God of I
24:31 And I served the LORD all the days of
24:31 all the work which the LORD did for I
24:32 which the people of I brought up from Egypt
Judg 1:1 Joshua the people of I inquired of the LORD,
1:28 When I grew strong, they put the Canaanites to
2:4 all the people of I, the people lifted up
2:6 people, the people of I went each to his
2:7 great work which the LORD had done for I
2:10 or the work which he had done for I
2:11 And the people of I did what was evil
2:14 LORD was kindled against I, and he gave them
2:20 LORD was kindled against I; and he said, "Because
2:22 them I may test I, whether they will take
3:1 LORD left, to test I by them, that is,
3:1 that is, all in I who had no experience
3:2 of the people of I might know war, that
3:4 for the testing of I, to know whether Israel
3:4 Israel, to know whether I would obey the
3:5 So the people of I dwelt among the Canaanites,
3:7 And the people of I did what was evil
3:8 LORD was kindled against I, and he sold them
3:8 and the people of I served Cushan-rishathaim eight
3:9 when the people of I cried to the LORD,
3:9 for the people of I, who delivered them, Othni-el
3:10 him, and he judged I; he went out to
3:12 And the people of I again did what was
3:12 king of Moab against I, because they had done
3:13 and went and defeated I; and they took possession
3:14 And the people of I served Eglon the king
3:15 when the people of I cried to the LORD,
3:15 The people of I sent tribute by him to
3:27 and the people of I went down with him
3:30 was subdued that day under the hand of I
3:31 Philistines with an oxgoad; and he too delivered I
4:1 And the people of I again did what was
4:3 Then the people of I cried to the LORD
4:3 oppressed the people of I cruelly for twenty years.
4:4 of Lappidoth, was judging I at that time.
4:5 and the people of I came up to her
4:6 LORD, the God of I, commands you, 'Go, gather
4:23 the king of Canaan before the people of I
4:24 of the people of I bore harder and harder
5:2 took the lead in I, that the people offered
5:3 make melody to the LORD, the God of I
5:5 yon Sinai before the LORD, the God of I
5:7 The peasantry ceased in I, they ceased until you
5:7 you arose, Deborah, arose as a mother in I
5:8 spear to be seen among forty thousand in I
5:9 commanders of I who offered themselves willingly
6:1 The people of I did what was evil in
6:2 of Midian prevailed over I; and because of Midian
6:2 Midian the people of I made for themselves the
6:4 leave no sustenance in I, and no sheep or
6:6 And I was brought very low because of Midian;
6:6 and the people of I cried for help to
6:7 When the people of I cried to the LORD
6:8 to the people of I; and he said to
6:8 LORD, the God of I: I led you up
6:14 of yours and deliver I from the hand of
6:15 to him, "Pray, Lord, how can I deliver I
6:36 "If thou wilt deliver I by my hand, as
6:37 that thou wilt deliver I by my hand, as
7:2 into their hand, lest I vaunt themselves against me,
7:8 all the rest of I every man to his
7:14 Joash, a man of I; into his hand God
7:15 to the camp of I, and said, "Arise; for
7:23 And the men of I were called out from
8:22 Then the men of I said to Gideon, "Rule
8:27 in Ophrah; and all I played the harlot after
8:28 before the people of I, and they lifted up
8:33 died, the people of I turned again and played
8:34 And the people of I did not remember the
8:35 all the good that he had done to I
9:22 Abimelech ruled over I three years.
9:55 when the men of I saw that Abimelech was
10:1 there arose to deliver I Tola the son of
10:2 And he judged I twenty-three years.
10:3 the Gileadite, who judged I twenty-two years.
10:6 And the people of I again did what was
10:7 LORD was kindled against I, and he sold them
10:8 oppressed the children of I that year.
10:8 all the people of I that were beyond the
10:9 of Ephraim; so that I was sorely distressed.
10:10 And the people of I cried to the LORD,
10:11 to the people of I, "Did I not deliver
10:15 And the people of I said to the LORD,
10:16 and he became indignant over the misery of I
10:17 and the people of I came together, and they
11:4 After a time the Ammonites made war against I
11:5 Ammonites made war against I, the elders of Gilead
11:13 of Jephthah, "Because I on coming from Egypt
11:15 him, "Thus says Jephthah: I did not take away
11:16 came up from Egypt, I went through the wilderness
11:17 I then sent messengers to the king of Edom,
11:17 So I remained at Kadesh.
11:19 I then sent messengers to Sihon king of the
11:19 king of Heshbon; and I said to him, 'Let
11:20 Sihon did not trust I to pass through his
11:20 together, and encamped at Jahaz, and fought with I
11:21 LORD, the God of I, gave Sihon and all
11:21 into the hand of I, and they defeated them;
11:21 they defeated them; so I took possession of all
11:23 LORD, the God of I, dispossessed the Amorites from
11:23 from before his people I; and are you to
11:25 he ever strive against I, or did he ever
11:26 While I dwelt in Heshbon and its villages, and
11:27 between the people of I and the people of
11:33 the Ammonites were subdued before the people of I
11:39 became a custom in I

11:40 that the daughters of I went year by year
12:7 Jephthah judged I six years.
12:8 After him Ibzan of Bethlehem judged I
12:9 And he judged I seven years.
12:11 Elon the Zebulunite judged I; and he judged Israel
12:11 Israel; and he judged I ten years.
12:13 Abdon the son of Hillel the Pirathonite judged I
12:14 asses; and he judged I eight years.
13:1 And the people of I again did what was
13:5 shall begin to deliver I from the hand of
14:4 At that time the Philistines had dominion over I
15:20 And he judged I in the days of the
16:31 He had judged I twenty years.
17:6 was no king in I; every man did what
18:1 In those days there was no king in I
18:1 among the tribes of I had fallen to them.
18:19 be priest to a tribe and family in I
18:29 who was born to I; but the name of
19:1 was no king in I, a certain Levite was
19:12 to the people of I; but we will pass
19:29 and sent her throughout all the territory of I
19:30 that the people of I came up out of
20:1 all the people of I came out, from Dan
20:2 all the tribes of I, presented themselves in the
20:3 that the people of I had gone up to
20:3 And the people of I said, "Tell us, how
20:6 of the inheritance of I; for they have committed
20:6 have committed abomination and wantonness in I
20:7 Behold, you people of I, all of you, give
20:10 all the tribes of I, and a hundred of
20:10 the wanton crime which they have committed in I
20:11 all the men of I gathered against the city,
20:12 And the tribes of I sent men through all
20:13 them to death, and put away evil from I
20:13 the voice of their brethren, the people of I
20:14 go out to battle against the people of I
20:17 And the men of I, apart from Benjamin, mustered
20:18 The people of I arose and went up to
20:19 Then the people of I rose in the morning,
20:20 And the men of I went out to battle
20:20 and the men of I drew up the battle
20:22 people, the men of I, took courage, and again
20:23 And the people of I went up and wept
20:24 So the people of I came near against the
20:25 of the people of I; all these were men
20:26 all the people of I, the whole army, went
20:27 And the people of I inquired of the LORD
20:29 So I set men in ambush round about Gibe-ah.
20:30 And the people of I went up against the
20:31 in the open country, about thirty men of I
20:32 But the men of I said, "Let us flee,
20:33 all the men of I rose up out of
20:33 and the men of I who were in ambush
20:34 men out of all I, and the battle was
20:35 LORD defeated Benjamin before I; and the men of
20:35 and the men of I destroyed twenty-five thousand one
20:36 The men of I gave ground to Benjamin, because
20:38 between the men of I and the men in
20:39 city the men of I should turn in battle.
20:39 about thirty men of I; they said, "Surely they
20:41 Then the men of I turned, and the men
20:42 before the men of I in the direction of
20:48 And the men of I turned back against the
21:1 Now the men of I had sworn at Mizpah,
21:3 LORD, the God of I, why has this come
21:3 come to pass in I, that there should be
21:3 there should be today one tribe lacking in I
21:5 And the people of I said, "Which of all
21:5 all the tribes of I did not come up
21:6 And the people of I had compassion for Benjamin
21:6 is cut off from I this day.
21:8 of the tribes of I that did not come
21:15 had made a breach in the tribes of I
21:17 that a tribe be not blotted out from I
21:18 For the people of I had sworn, "Cursed be
21:24 And the people of I departed from there at
21:25 was no king in I; every man did what
Ruth 2:12 LORD, the God of I, under whose wings you
4:7 in former times in I concerning redeeming and
4:7 and this was the manner of attesting in I
4:11 Leah, who together built up the house of I
4:14 kin; and may his name be renowned in I
1Sam 1:17 and the God of I grant your petition which
2:22 were doing to all I, and how they lay
2:28 all the tribes of I to be my priest,
2:28 my offerings by fire from the people of I
2:29 offering of my people I
2:30 LORD the God of I declares: 'I promised that
2:32 shall be bestowed upon I; and there shall not
3:11 do a thing in I, at which the two
3:20 And all I from Dan to Beer-sheba knew that
4:1 And the word of Samuel came to all I
4:1 Now I went out to battle against the Philistines;
4:2 up in line against I, and when the battle
4:2 when the battle spread, I was defeated by the
4:3 camp, the elders of I said, "Why has the
4:5 into the camp, all I gave a mighty shout,
4:10 the Philistines fought, and I was defeated, and they
4:10 for there fell of I thirty thousand foot soldiers.
4:17 tidings answered and said, I has fled before the
4:18 He had judged I forty years.
4:21 Ichabod, saying, "The glory has departed from I
4:22 glory has departed from I, for the ark of
5:7 of the God of I must not remain with
5:8 do with the ark of the God of I
5:8 of the God of I be brought around to
5:8 of the God of I there.
5:10 of the God of I to slay us and
5:11 of the God of I, and let it return
6:3 of the God of I, do not send it
6:5 to the God of I; perhaps he will lighten
7:2 all the house of I lamented after the LORD.
7:3 all the house of I, "If you are returning
7:4 So I put away the Baals and the Ashtaroth,
7:5 Samuel said, "Gather all I at Mizpah, and I
7:6 judged the people of I at Mizpah.
7:7 that the people of I had gathered at Mizpah,
7:7 the lords of the Philistines went up against I
7:7 when the people of I heard of it they
7:8 And the people of I said to Samuel, "Do
7:9 to the LORD for I, and the LORD answered
7:10 drew near to attack I; but the LORD thundered
7:10 them into confusion; and they were routed before I
7:11 And the men of I went out of Mizpah
7:13 and did not again enter the territory of I
7:14 Philistines had taken from I were restored to Israel,
7:14 Israel were restored to I, from Ekron to Gath;
7:14 Ekron to Gath; and I rescued their territory from
7:14 was peace also between I and the Amorites.
7:15 Samuel judged I all the days of his life.
7:16 Mizpah; and he judged I in all these places.
7:17 there, and there also he administered justice to I
8:1 became old, he made his sons judges over I
8:4 all the elders of I gathered together and came
8:22 to the men of I, "Go every man to
9:2 among the people of I more handsome than he;
9:9 (Formerly in I, when a man went to inquire
9:16 anoint him to be prince over my people I
9:20 for whom is all that is desirable in I
9:21 Benjaminite, from the least of the tribes of I
10:1 anointed you to be prince over his people I
10:18 to the people of I, "Thus says the LORD,
10:18 LORD, the God of I, 'I brought up Israel
10:18 Israel, 'I brought up I out of Egypt, and
10:20 all the tribes of I near, and the tribe
11:2 right eyes, and thus put disgrace upon all I
11:3 may send messengers through all the territory of I
11:7 all the territory of I by the hand of
11:8 Bezek, the men of I were three hundred thousand,
11:13 for today the LORD has wrought deliverance in I
11:15 all the men of I rejoiced greatly.
12:1 Samuel said to all I, "Behold, I have hearkened
13:1 and two years over I
13:2 three thousand men of I; two thousand were with
13:4 And all I heard it said that Saul had
13:4 Philistines, and also that I had become odious to
13:5 mustered to fight with I, thirty thousand chariots, and
13:6 When the men of I saw that they were
13:13 established your kingdom over I for ever.
13:19 all the land of I; for the Philistines said,
14:12 LORD has given them into the hand of I
14:18 went at that time with the people of I
14:22 all the men of I who had hid themselves
14:23 So the LORD delivered I that day; and the
14:24 And the men of I were distressed that day;
14:37 Wilt thou give them into the hand of I
14:39 LORD lives who saves I, though it be in
14:40 he said to all I, "You shall be on
14:41 "O LORD God of I, why hast thou not
14:41 O LORD, God of I, give Urim; but if
14:41 is in thy people I, give Thummim." And Jonathan
14:45 die, who has wrought this great victory in I

14:47 taken the kingship over I, he fought against all
14:48 the Amalekites, and delivered I out of the hands
15:1 king over his people I; now therefore hearken to
15:2 what Amalek did to I in opposing them on
15:6 all the people of I when they came up
15:17 you not the head of the tribes of I
15:17 The LORD anointed you king over I
15:26 LORD has rejected you from being king over I
15:28 torn the kingdom of I from you this day,
15:29 also the Glory of I will not lie or
15:30 my people and before I, and return with me,
15:35 repented that he had made Saul king over I
16:1 I have rejected him from being king over I
17:2 and the men of I were gathered, and encamped
17:3 the one side, and I stood on the mountain
17:8 to the ranks of I, "Why have you come
17:10 defy the ranks of I this day; give me
17:11 When Saul and all I heard these words of
17:19 all the men of I, were in the valley
17:21 And I and the Philistines drew up for battle,
17:24 All the men of I, when they saw the
17:25 And the men of I said, "Have you seen
17:25 come up to defy I; and the man who
17:25 daughter, and make his father's house free in I
17:26 this Philistine, and takes away the reproach from I
17:45 of the armies of I, whom you have defied.
17:46 is a God in I,
17:52 And the men of I and Judah rose with
18:6 all the cities of I, singing and dancing, to
18:16 But all I and Judah loved David; for he
18:18 my father's family in I, that I should be
18:28 David, and that all I loved him,
19:5 the LORD wrought a great victory for all I
20:12 LORD, the God of I, be witness!
23:10 LORD, the God of I, thy servant has surely
23:11 LORD, the God of I, I beseech thee, tell
23:17 shall be king over I, and I shall be
24:2 men out of all I, and went to seek
24:14 has the king of I come out?
24:20 that the kingdom of I shall be established in
25:1 Samuel died; and all I assembled and mourned for
25:30 appointed you prince over I,
25:32 LORD, the God of I, who sent you this
25:34 LORD the God of I lives, who has restrained
26:2 thousand chosen men of I, to seek David in
26:15 Who is like you in I
26:20 for the king of I has come out to
27:1 within the borders of I, and I shall escape
27:12 abhorred by his people I; therefore he shall be
28:1 gathered their forces for war, to fight against I
28:3 had died, and all I had mourned for him
28:4 and Saul gathered all I, and they encamped at
28:19 the LORD will give I also with you into
28:19 give the army of I also into the hand
29:3 of Saul, king of I, who has been with
30:25 and an ordinance for I to this day.
31:1 the Philistines fought against I; and the men of
31:1 and the men of I fled before the Philistines,
31:7 when the men of I who were on the
31:7 that the men of I had fled and that
2Sam 1:3 him, "I have escaped from the camp of I
1:12 for the house of I, because they had fallen
1:19 said: "Thy glory, O I, is slain upon thy
1:24 "Ye daughters of I, weep over Saul, who clothed
2:9 and Jezreel and Ephraim and Benjamin and all I
2:10 began to reign over I, and he reigned two
2:17 and the men of I were beaten before the
2:28 men stopped, and pursued I no more, nor did
3:10 throne of David over I and over Judah, from
3:12 to bring over all I to you."
3:17 with the elders of I, saying, "For some time
3:18 will save my people I from the hand of
3:19 at Hebron all that I and the whole house
3:21 and will gather all I to my lord the
3:37 the people and all I understood that day that
3:38 a great man has fallen this day in I
4:1 courage failed, and all I was dismayed.
5:1 all the tribes of I came to David at
5:2 out and brought in I; and the LORD said
5:2 shepherd of my people I, and you shall be
5:2 people Israel, and you shall be prince over I
5:3 all the elders of I came to the king
5:3 the LORD, and they anointed David king over I
5:5 he reigned over all I and Judah thirty-three years.
5:12 established him king over I, and that he had
5:12 his kingdom for the sake of his people I
5:17 been anointed king over I, all the Philistines went
6:1 the chosen men of I, thirty thousand.
6:5 all the house of I were making merry before
6:15 all the house of I brought up the ark
6:19 the whole multitude of I, both men and women,
6:20 "How the king of I honored himself today,
6:21 me as prince over I, the people of the
7:6 up the people of I from Egypt to this
7:7 all the people of I, did I speak a
7:7 of the judges of I, whom I commanded to
7:7 to shepherd my people I, saying, "Why have you
7:8 prince over my people I;
7:10 place for my people I, and will plant them,
7:11 judges over my people I; and I will give
7:23 is like thy people I, whom God went to
7:24 for thyself thy people I to be thy people
7:26 hosts is God over I and the house of
7:27 hosts, the God of I, hast made this revelation
8:15 David reigned over all I; and David administered
10:9 the picked men of I, and arrayed them against
10:15 had been defeated by I, they gathered themselves
10:17 David, he gathered all I together, and crossed the
10:18 the Syrians fled before I; and David slew of
10:19 had been defeated by I, they made peace with
10:19 they made peace with I, and became subject to
11:1 with him, and all I; and they ravaged the
11:11 David, "The ark and I and Judah dwell in
12:7 LORD, the God of I, 'I anointed you king
12:7 anointed you king over I, and I delivered you
12:8 you the house of I and of Judah; and
12:12 this thing before all I, and before the sun.'"
13:12 is not done in I; do not do this
13:13 be as one of the wanton fools in I
14:25 Now in all I there was no one so
15:2 is of such and such a tribe in I
15:6 did to all of I who came to the
15:6 Absalom stole the hearts of the men of I
15:10 all the tribes of I, saying, "As soon as
15:13 of the men of I have gone after Absalom."
16:3 'Today the house of I will give me back
16:15 people, the men of I, came to Jerusalem, and
16:18 all the men of I have chosen, his I
16:21 the house; and all I will hear that you
16:22 his father's concubines in the sight of all I
17:4 advice pleased Absalom and all the elders of I
17:10 with fear; for all I knows that your father
17:11 counsel is that all I be gathered to you,
17:13 a city, then all I will bring ropes to
17:14 all the men of I said, "The counsel of
17:15 and the elders of I; and thus and so
17:24 crossed the Jordan with all the men of I
17:26 And I and Absalom encamped in the land of
18:6 into the field against I; and the battle was
18:7 And the men of I were defeated there by
18:16 came back from pursuing I; for Joab restrained
18:17 of stones; and all I fled every one to
19:8 Now I had fled every man to his own
19:9 all the tribes of I, saying, "The king delivered
19:11 the word of all I has come to the
19:22 put to death in I this day?
19:22 know that I am this day king over I
19:40 half the people of I, brought the king on
19:41 all the men of I came to the king,
19:42 answered the men of I, "Because the king is
19:43 And the men of I answered the men of
19:43 fiercer than the words of the men of I
20:1 of Jesse; every man to his tents, O I
20:2 all the men of I withdrew from David, and
20:14 all the tribes of I to Abel of Beth-maacah;
20:19 peaceable and faithful in I; you seek to destroy
20:19 is a mother in I; why will you swallow
20:23 all the army of I; and Benaiah the son
21:2 of the people of I, but of the remnant
21:2 although the people of I had sworn to spare
21:2 for the people of I and Judah.
21:4 us to put any man to death in I
21:5 all the territory of I,
21:15 had war again with I, and David went down
21:17 to battle, lest you quench the lamp of I
21:21 And when he taunted I, Jonathan the son of
23:1 the sweet psalmist of I:
23:3 The God of I has spoken, the Rock of
23:3 spoken, the Rock of I has said to me:
23:9 and the men of I withdrew.
24:1 LORD was kindled against I, and he incited David
24:1 them, saying, "Go, number I and Judah."

24:2 all the tribes of I, from Dan to Beer-sheba,
24:4 of the king to number the people of I
24:9 to the king: in I there were eight hundred
24:15 sent a pestilence upon I from the morning until
24:25 the land, and the plague was averted from I
1Kgs 1:3 all the territory of I, and found Abishag the
1:20 the eyes of all I are upon you, to
1:30 LORD, the God of I, saying, 'Solomon your son
1:34 anoint him king over I; then blow the trumpet,
1:35 to be ruler over I and over Judah."
1:48 LORD, the God of I, who has granted one
2:4 on the throne of I
2:5 of the armies of I, Abner the son of
2:11 that David reigned over I was forty years; he
2:15 mine, and that all I fully expected me to
2:32 of the army of I, and Amasa the son
3:28 And all I heard of the judgment which the
4:1 was king over all I,
4:7 twelve officers over all I, who provided food for
4:20 Judah and I were as many as the sand
4:25 And Judah and I dwelt in safety, from Dan
5:13 labor out of all I; and the levy numbered
6:1 after the people of I came out of the
6:1 of Solomon's reign over I, in the month of
6:13 among the children of I, and will not forsake
6:13 of Israel, and will not forsake my people I
8:1 assembled the elders of I and all the heads
8:1 of the people of I, before King Solomon in
8:2 all the men of I assembled to King Solomon
8:3 all the elders of I came, and the priests
8:5 all the congregation of I, who had assembled before
8:9 with the people of I, when they came out
8:14 all the assembly of I, while all the assembly
8:14 all the assembly of I stood.
8:15 LORD, the God of I, who with his hand
8:16 I brought my people I out of Egypt, I
8:16 all the tribes of I in which to build
8:16 be over my people I
8:17 the name of the LORD, the God of I
8:20 on the throne of I, as the LORD promised,
8:20 the name of the LORD, the God of I
8:22 all the assembly of I, and spread forth his
8:23 "O LORD, God of I, there is no God
8:25 O LORD, God of I, keep with thy servant
8:25 upon the throne of I, if only your sons
8:26 therefore, O God of I, let thy word be
8:30 and of thy people I, when they pray toward
8:33 "When thy people I are defeated before the enemy
8:34 sin of thy people I, and bring them again
8:36 thy servants, thy people I, when thou dost teach
8:38 by all thy people I, each knowing the affliction
8:41 not of thy people I, comes from a far
8:43 as do thy people I, and that they may
8:52 supplication of thy people I, giving ear to them
8:55 all the assembly of I with a loud voice,
8:56 rest to his people I, according to all that
8:59 cause of his people I, as each day requires;
8:62 the king, and all I with him, offered sacrifice
8:63 all the people of I dedicated the house of
8:65 that time, and all I with him, a great
8:66 his servant and to I his people.
9:5 your royal throne over I for ever, as I
9:5 upon the throne of I
9:7 I will cut off I from the land which
9:7 of my sight; and I will become a proverb
9:20 of the people of I –
9:21 whom the people of I were unable to destroy
9:22 of the people of I Solomon made no slaves;
10:9 you and set you on the throne of I
10:9 Because the LORD loved I for ever, he has
11:2 to the people of I, "You shall not enter
11:9 LORD, the God of I, who had appeared to
11:16 (for Joab and all I remained there six months,
11:25 was an adversary of I all the days of
11:25 did; and he abhorred I, and reigned over Syria.
11:31 LORD, the God of I, 'Behold, I am about
11:32 all the tribes of I,
11:37 soul desires, and you shall be king over I
11:38 and I will give I to you.
11:42 in Jerusalem over all I was forty years.
12:1 to Shechem, for all I had come to Shechem
12:3 all the assembly of I came and said to
12:16 And when all I saw that the king did
12:16 To your tents, O I
12:16 So I departed to their tents.
12:17 over the people of I who dwelt in the
12:18 forced labor, and all I stoned him to death
12:19 So I has been in rebellion against the house
12:20 And when all I heard that Jeroboam had returned,
12:20 the assembly and made him king over all I
12:21 against the house of I, to restore the kingdom
12:24 or fight against your kinsmen the people of I
12:28 Behold your gods, O I, who brought you up
12:33 for the people of I, and went up to
14:7 LORD, the God of I: "Because I exalted you
14:7 leader over my people I,
14:10 bond and free in I, and will utterly consume
14:13 And all I shall mourn for him, and bury
14:13 LORD, the God of I, in the house of
14:14 himself a king over I, who shall cut off
14:15 the LORD will smite I, as a reed is
14:15 water, and root up I out of this good
14:16 And he will give I up because of the
14:16 and which he made I to sin."
14:18 And all I buried him and mourned for him,
14:19 Book of the Chronicles of the Kings of I
14:21 all the tribes of I, to put his name
14:24 the LORD drove out before the people of I
15:9 of Jeroboam king of I Asa began to reign
15:16 and Baasha king of I all their days.
15:17 Baasha king of I went up against Judah, and
15:19 with Baasha king of I, that he may withdraw
15:20 against the cities of I, and conquered Ijon, Dan,
15:25 began to reign over I in the second year
15:25 and he reigned over I two years.
15:26 sin which he made I to sin.
15:27 for Nadab and all I were laying siege to
15:30 and which he made I to sin, and because
15:30 which he provoked the LORD, the God of I
15:31 Book of the Chronicles of the Kings of I
15:32 and Baasha king of I all their days.
15:33 to reign over all I at Tirzah, and reigned
15:34 sin which he made I to sin.
16:2 leader over my people I, and you have walked
16:2 have made my people I to sin, provoking me
16:5 Book of the Chronicles of the Kings of I
16:8 began to reign over I in Tirzah, and reigned
16:13 and which they made I to sin, provoking the
16:13 the LORD God of I to anger with their
16:14 Book of the Chronicles of the Kings of I
16:16 the king"; therefore all I made Omri, the
16:16 the army, king over I that day in the
16:17 from Gibbethon, and all I with him, and they
16:19 which he committed, making I to sin.
16:20 Book of the Chronicles of the Kings of I
16:21 Then the people of I were divided into two
16:23 began to reign over I, and reigned for twelve
16:26 sins which he made I to sin, provoking the
16:26 LORD, the God of I, to anger by their
16:27 Book of the Chronicles of the Kings of I
16:29 began to reign over I, and Ahab the son
16:29 of Omri reigned over I in Samaria twenty-two years.
16:33 LORD, the God of I, to anger than all
16:33 all the kings of I who were before him.
17:1 LORD the God of I lives, before whom I
17:14 LORD the God of I, 'The jar of meal
18:17 to him, "Is it you, you troubler of I
18:18 "I have not troubled I; but you have, and
18:19 send and gather all I to me at Mount
18:20 all the people of I, and gathered the prophets
18:31 the LORD came, saying, I shall be your name";
18:36 of Abraham, Isaac, and I, let it be known
18:36 thou art God in I, and that I am
19:10 for the people of I have forsaken thy covenant,
19:14 for the people of I have forsaken thy covenant,
19:16 to be king over I; and Elisha the son
19:18 leave seven thousand in I, all the knees that
20:2 to Ahab king of I, and said to him,
20:4 And the king of I answered, "As you say,
20:7 Then the king of I called all the elders
20:11 And the king of I answered, "Tell him, 'Let
20:13 to Ahab king of I and said, "Thus says
20:15 all the people of I, seven thousand.
20:20 the Syrians fled and I pursued them, but Ben-hadad
20:21 And the king of I went out, and captured
20:22 to the king of I, and said to him,
20:26 and went up to Aphek, to fight against I
20:27 And the people of I were mustered, and were
20:27 them; the people of I encamped before them like
20:28 to the king of I, "Thus says the LORD,
20:29 and the people of I smote of the Syrians
20:31 of the house of I are merciful kings; let

20:31 to the king of I; perhaps he will spare
20:32 to the king of I and said, "Your servant
20:40 The king of I said to him, "So shall
20:41 and the king of I recognized him as one
20:43 And the king of I went to his house
21:7 wife said to him, "Do you now govern I
21:18 meet Ahab king of I, who is in Samaria;
21:21 bond or free, in I;
21:22 because you have made I to sin.
21:26 before the people of I
22:1 three years Syria and I continued without war.
22:2 of Judah came down to the king of I
22:3 And the king of I said to his servants,
22:4 to the king of I, "I am as you
22:5 to the king of I, "Inquire first for the
22:6 Then the king of I gathered the prophets together,
22:8 And the king of I said to Jehoshaphat, "There
22:9 Then the king of I summoned an officer and
22:10 Now the king of I and Jehoshaphat the king
22:17 said, "I saw all I scattered upon the mountains,
22:18 And the king of I said to Jehoshaphat, "Did
22:26 And the king of I said, "Seize Micaiah, and
22:29 So the king of I and Jehoshaphat the king
22:30 And the king of I said to Jehoshaphat, "I
22:30 And the king of I disguised himself and went
22:31 nor great, but only with the king of I
22:32 they said, "It is surely the king of I
22:33 not the king of I, they turned back from
22:34 struck the king of I between the scale armor
22:39 Book of the Chronicles of the Kings of I
22:41 in the fourth year of Ahab king of I
22:44 Jehoshaphat also made peace with the king of I
22:51 began to reign over I in Samaria in the
22:51 of Judah, and he reigned two years over I
22:52 of Nebat, who made I to sin.
22:53 LORD, the God of I, to anger in every
2Kgs 1:1 After the death of Ahab, Moab rebelled against I
1:3 is no God in I that you are going
1:6 is no God in I that you are sending
1:16 is no God in I to inquire of his
1:18 Book of the Chronicles of the Kings of I
2:12 the chariots of I and its horsemen!" And he
3:1 Ahab became king over I in Samaria, and he
3:3 Nebat, which he made I to sin; he did
3:4 to the king of I a hundred thousand lambs,
3:5 king of Moab rebelled against the king of I
3:6 of Samaria at that time and mustered all I
3:9 So the king of I went with the king
3:10 Then the king of I said, "Alas!
3:11 of the king of I's servants answered, "Elisha the
3:12 So the king of I and Jehoshaphat and the
3:13 to the king of I, "What have I to
3:13 But the king of I said to him, "No;
3:24 to the camp of I, the Israelites rose and
3:27 came great wrath upon I; and they withdrew from
5:2 from the land of I, and she waited on
5:4 so spoke the maiden from the land of I
5:5 will send a letter to the king of I
5:6 to the king of I, which read, "When this
5:7 when the king of I read the letter, he
5:8 that the king of I had rent his clothes,
5:8 may know that there is a prophet in I
5:12 of Damascus, better than all the waters of I
5:15 the earth but in I; so accept now a
6:8 Syria was warring against I, he took counsel with
6:9 to the king of I, "Beware that you do
6:10 And the king of I sent to the place
6:11 who of us is for the king of I
6:12 prophet who is in I, tells the king of
6:12 tells the king of I the words that you
6:21 When the king of I saw them he said
6:23 no more on raids into the land of I
6:26 as the king of I was passing by upon
7:6 "Behold, the king of I has hired against us
7:13 the whole multitude of I that have already perished;
8:12 to the people of I; you will set on
8:16 of Ahab, king of I, Jehoram the son of
8:18 of the kings of I, as the house of
8:25 of Ahab, king of I, Ahaziah the son of
8:26 she was a granddaughter of Omri king of I
9:3 anoint you king over I Then open the door
9:6 LORD the God of I, I anoint you king
9:6 king over the people of the LORD, over I
9:8 from Ahab every male, bond or free, in I
9:12 says the LORD, I anoint you king over I
9:14 (Now Joram with all I had been on guard
9:21 Then Joram king of I and Ahaziah king of
10:21 Jehu sent throughout all I; and all the worshipers
10:28 Thus Jehu wiped out Baal from I
10:29 Nebat, which he made I to sin, the golden
10:30 fourth generation shall sit on the throne of I
10:31 LORD the God of I with all his heart;
10:31 Jeroboam, which he made I to sin.
10:32 the LORD began to cut off parts of I
10:32 throughout the territory of I:
10:34 Book of the Chronicles of the Kings of I
10:36 Jehu reigned over I in Samaria was twenty-eight
13:1 began to reign over I in Samaria, and he
13:2 Nebat, which he made I to sin; he did
13:3 LORD was kindled against I, and he gave them
13:4 saw the oppression of I, how the king of
13:5 (Therefore the LORD gave I a savior, so that
13:5 and the people of I dwelt in their homes
13:6 Jeroboam, which he made I to sin, but walked
13:8 Book of the Chronicles of the Kings of I
13:10 began to reign over I in Samaria, and he
13:11 Nebat, which he made I to sin, but he
13:12 Book of the Chronicles of the Kings of I
13:13 was buried in Samaria with the kings of I
13:14 die, Joash king of I went down to him,
13:14 The chariots of I and its horsemen!"
13:16 to the king of I, "Draw the bow"; and
13:18 to the king of I, "Strike the ground with
13:22 king of Syria oppressed I all the days of
13:25 Joash defeated him and recovered the cities of I
14:1 of Joahaz, king of I, Amaziah the son of
14:8 of Jehu, king of I, saying, "Come, let us
14:9 And Jehoash king of I sent word to Amaziah
14:11 So Jehoash king of I went up, and he
14:12 Judah was defeated by I, and every man fled
14:13 And Jehoash king of I captured Amaziah king of
14:15 Book of the Chronicles of the Kings of I
14:16 with the kings of I; and Jeroboam his son
14:17 death of Jehoash son of Jehoahaz, king of I
14:23 of Joash, king of I, began to reign in
14:24 Nebat, which he made I to sin.
14:25 restored the border of I from the entrance of
14:25 LORD, the God of I, which he spoke by
14:26 that the affliction of I was very bitter, for
14:26 or free, and there was none to help I
14:27 out the name of I from under heaven, so
14:28 how he recovered for I Damascus and Hamath,
14:28 Book of the Chronicles of the Kings of I
14:29 fathers, the kings of I, and Zechariah his son
15:1 of Jeroboam king of I Azariah the son of
15:8 of Jeroboam reigned over I in Samaria six months.
15:9 Nebat, which he made I to sin.
15:11 Book of the Chronicles of the Kings of I
15:12 upon the throne of I to the fourth generation."
15:15 Book of the Chronicles of the Kings of I
15:17 began to reign over I, and he reigned ten
15:18 Nebat, which he made I to sin.
15:20 exacted the money from I, that is, from all
15:21 Book of the Chronicles of the Kings of I
15:23 began to reign over I in Samaria, and he
15:24 Nebat, which he made I to sin.
15:26 Book of the Chronicles of the Kings of I
15:27 began to reign over I in Samaria, and reigned
15:28 Nebat, which he made I to sin.
15:29 of Pekah king of I Tiglath-pileser king of Assyria
15:31 Book of the Chronicles of the Kings of I
15:32 of Remaliah, king of I, Jotham the son of
16:3 walked in the way of the kings of I
16:3 the LORD drove out before the people of I
16:5 of Remaliah, king of I, came up to wage
16:7 of the king of I, who are attacking me."
17:1 reign in Samaria over I, and he reigned nine
17:2 as the kings of I who were before him.
17:7 because the people of I had sinned against the
17:8 before the people of I, and in the customs
17:8 which the kings of I had introduced.
17:9 And the people of I did secretly against the
17:13 Yet the LORD warned I and Judah by every
17:18 was very angry with I, and removed them out
17:19 in the customs which I had introduced.
17:20 all the descendants of I, and afflicted them, and
17:21 When he had torn I from the house of
17:21 And Jeroboam drove I from following the LORD and
17:22 The people of I walked in all the sins
17:23 until the LORD removed I out of his sight,
17:23 So I was exiled from their own land to
17:24 of the people of I; and they took possession

17:34 commanded the children of Jacob, whom he named I
18:1 of Elah, king of I, Hezekiah the son of
18:4 days the people of I had burned incense to
18:5 LORD the God of I; so that there was
18:9 of Elah, king of I, Shalmaneser king of Assyria
18:10 of Hoshea king of I, Samaria was taken.
19:15 LORD the God of I, who art enthroned above
19:20 LORD, the God of I: Your prayer to me
19:22 Against the Holy One of I
21:2 the LORD drove out before the people of I
21:3 as Ahab king of I had done, and worshiped
21:7 all the tribes of I, I will put my
21:8 cause the feet of I to wander any more
21:9 whom the LORD destroyed before the people of I
21:12 LORD, the God of I, Behold, I am bringing
22:15 LORD, the God of I: 'Tell the man who
22:18 LORD, the God of I: Regarding the words which
23:13 Solomon the king of I had built for Ashtoreth
23:15 of Nebat, who made I to sin, that altar
23:19 Samaria, which kings of I had made, provoking the
23:22 the judges who judged I, or during all the
23:22 of the kings of I or of the kings
23:27 as I have removed I, and I will cast
24:13 which Solomon king of I had made, as the
1Chr 1:34 The sons of Isaac: Esau and I
2:1 are the sons of I: Reuben, Simeon, Levi, Judah,
2:7 Achar, the troubler of I, who transgressed in the
4:10 on the God of I, saying, "Oh that thou
5:1 Reuben the first-born of I (for he was the
5:1 Joseph the son of I, so that he is
5:3 Reuben, the first-born of I: Hanoch, Pallu, Hezron,
5:17 and in the days of Jeroboam king of I
5:26 So the God of I stirred up the spirit
6:38 of Levi, son of I;
6:49 to make atonement for I, according to all that
6:64 So the people of I gave the Levites the
7:29 dwelt the sons of Joseph the son of I
9:1 So all I was enrolled by genealogies; and these
9:1 written in the Book of the Kings of I
9:2 in their cities were I, the priests, the Levites,
10:1 the Philistines fought against I; and the men of
10:1 and the men of I fled before the Philistines,
10:7 all the men of I who were in the
11:1 Then all I gathered together to David at Hebron,
11:2 out and brought in I; and the LORD your
11:2 shepherd of my people I, and you shall be
11:2 and you shall be prince over my people I
11:3 all the elders of I came to the king
11:3 anointed David king over I, according to the word
11:4 And David and all I went to Jerusalem, that
11:10 kingdom, together with all I, to make him king,
11:10 according to the word of the LORD concerning I
12:32 times, to know what I ought to do, two
12:38 David king over all I; likewise all the rest
12:38 all the rest of I were of a single
12:40 oxen and sheep, for there was joy in I
13:2 all the assembly of I, "If it seems good
13:2 all the land of I, and with them to
13:5 So David assembled all I from the Shihor of
13:6 And David and all I went up to Baalah,
13:8 And David and all I were making merry before
14:2 established him king over I, and that his kingdom
14:2 highly exalted for the sake of his people I
14:8 anointed king over all I, all the Philistines went
15:3 And David assembled all I at Jerusalem, to bring
15:12 LORD, the God of I, to the place that
15:14 the ark of the LORD, the God of I
15:25 and the elders of I, and the commanders of
15:28 So all I brought up the ark of the
16:3 and distributed to all I, both men and women,
16:4 and to praise the LORD, the God of I
16:17 an everlasting covenant to I,
16:36 LORD, the God of I, from everlasting to everlasting!"
16:40 the law of the LORD which he commanded I
17:5 day I led up I to this day, but
17:6 have moved with all I, did I speak a
17:6 of the judges of I, whom I commanded to
17:7 prince over my people I;
17:9 place for my people I, and will plant them,
17:10 judges over my people I; and I will subdue
17:21 is like thy people I, whom God went to
17:22 didst make thy people I to be thy people
17:24 hosts, the God of I, is Israel's God,' and
17:24 God of Israel, is I's God,' and the house
18:14 David reigned over all I; and he administered justice
19:10 the picked men of I, and arrayed them against
19:16 had been defeated by I, they sent messengers and
19:17 David, he gathered all I together, and crossed the
19:18 the Syrians fled before I; and David slew of
19:19 had been defeated by I, they made peace with
20:7 And when he taunted I, Jonathan the son of
21:1 Satan stood up against I, and incited David to
21:1 up against Israel, and incited David to number I
21:2 the army, "Go, number I, from Beer-sheba to Dan,
21:3 Why should he bring guilt upon I
21:4 and went throughout all I, and came back to
21:5 In all I there were one million one hundred
21:7 was displeased with this thing, and he smote I
21:12 all the territory of I Now decide what answer
21:14 sent a pestilence upon I; and there fell seventy
21:14 Israel; and there fell seventy thousand men of I
22:1 and here the altar of burnt offering for I
22:2 in the land of I, and he set stonecutters
22:6 a house for the LORD, the God of I
22:9 peace and quiet to I in his days.
22:10 his royal throne in I for ever.'
22:12 gives you charge over I you may keep the
22:13 ordinances which the LORD commanded Moses for I
22:17 all the leaders of I to help Solomon his
23:1 days, he made Solomon his son king over I
23:2 all the leaders of I and the priests and
23:25 LORD, the God of I, has given peace to
24:19 the LORD God of I had commanded him.
26:29 to outside duties for I, as officers and judges.
26:30 had the oversight of I westward of the Jordan
27:1 of the people of I, the heads of fathers'
27:16 Over the tribes of I, for the Reubenites Eliezer
27:22 These were the leaders of the tribes of I
27:23 had promised to make I as many as the
27:24 yet wrath came upon I for this, and the
28:1 all the officials of I, the officials of the
28:4 the LORD God of I chose me from all
28:4 to be king over I for ever; for he
28:4 in me to make me king over all I
28:5 throne of the kingdom of the LORD over I
28:8 the sight of all I, the assembly of the
29:10 LORD, the God of I our father, for ever
29:18 of Abraham, Isaac, and I, our fathers, keep for
29:21 in abundance for all I;
29:23 he prospered, and all I obeyed him.
29:25 the sight of all I, and bestowed upon him
29:25 not been on any king before him in I
29:26 David the son of Jesse reigned over all I
29:27 that he reigned over I was forty years; he
29:30 upon him and upon I, and upon all the
2Chr 1:2 Solomon spoke to all I, to the commanders of
1:2 the leaders in all I, the heads of fathers'
1:13 And he reigned over I
2:4 LORD our God, as ordained for ever for I
2:12 the LORD God of I, who made heaven and
2:17 in the land of I, after the census of
5:2 assembled the elders of I and all the heads
5:2 of the people of I, in Jerusalem, to bring
5:3 all the men of I assembled before the king
5:4 all the elders of I came, and the Levites
5:6 all the congregation of I, who had assembled before
5:10 with the people of I, when they came out
6:3 all the assembly of I, while all the assembly
6:3 all the assembly of I stood.
6:4 LORD, the God of I, who with his hand
6:5 all the tribes of I in which to build
6:5 prince over my people I;
6:6 be over my people I
6:7 the name of the LORD, the God of I
6:10 on the throne of I, as the LORD promised,
6:10 the name of the LORD, the God of I
6:11 LORD which he made with the people of I
6:12 all the assembly of I, and spread forth his
6:13 all the assembly of I, and spread forth his
6:14 "O LORD, God of I, there is no God
6:16 O LORD, God of I, keep with thy servant
6:16 upon the throne of I, if only your sons
6:17 O LORD, God of I, let thy word be
6:21 and of thy people I, when they pray toward
6:24 "If thy people I are defeated before the enemy
6:25 sin of thy people I, and bring them again
6:27 thy servants, thy people I, when thou dost teach
6:29 by all thy people I, each knowing his own
6:32 not of thy people I, comes from a far
6:33 as do thy people I, and that they may
7:3 all the children of I saw the fire come
7:6 sounded trumpets; and all I stood.

7:8 seven days, and all I with him, a very
7:10 to Solomon and to I his people.
7:18 a man to rule I
8:2 settled the people of I in them.
8:7 who were not of I,
8:8 whom the people of I had not destroyed--these
8:9 of the people of I Solomon made no slaves
8:11 of David king of I, for the places to
9:8 Because your God loved I and would establish them
9:30 in Jerusalem over all I forty years.
10:1 to Shechem, for all I had come to Shechem
10:3 and Jeroboam and all I came and said to
10:16 And when all I saw that the king did
10:16 Each of you to your tents, O I
10:16 So all I departed to their tents.
10:17 over the people of I who dwelt in the
10:18 and the people of I stoned him to death
10:19 So I has been in rebellion against the house
11:1 warriors, to fight against I, to restore the kingdom
11:3 Judah, and to all I in Judah and Benjamin,
11:13 that were in all I resorted to him from
11:16 the LORD God of I came after them from
11:16 all the tribes of I to Jerusalem to sacrifice
12:1 the LORD, and all I with him.
12:6 Then the princes of I and the king humbled
12:13 all the tribes of I to put his name
13:4 and said, "Hear me, O Jeroboam and all I
13:5 the LORD God of I gave the kingship over
13:5 gave the kingship over I for ever to David
13:12 O sons of I, do not fight against the
13:15 defeated Jeroboam and all I before Abijah and
13:16 The men of I fled before Judah, and God
13:17 there fell slain of I five hundred thousand picked
13:18 Thus the men of I were subdued at that
15:3 For a long time I was without the true
15:4 LORD, the God of I, and sought him, he
15:9 deserted to him from I when they saw that
15:13 LORD, the God of I, should be put to
15:17 the high places were not taken out of I
16:1 Asa, Baasha king of I went up against Judah,
16:3 with Baasha king of I, that he may withdraw
16:4 against the cities of I, and they conquered Ijon,
16:11 the Book of the Kings of Judah and I
17:1 in his stead, and strengthened himself against I
17:4 commandments, and not according to the ways of I
18:3 Ahab king of I said to Jehoshaphat king of
18:4 to the king of I, "Inquire first for the
18:5 Then the king of I gathered the prophets together,
18:7 And the king of I said to Jehoshaphat, "There
18:8 Then the king of I summoned an officer and
18:9 Now the king of I and Jehoshaphat the king
18:16 said, "I saw all I scattered upon the mountains,
18:17 And the king of I said to Jehoshaphat, "Did
18:19 Ahab the king of I, that he may go
18:25 And the king of I said, "Seize Micaiah, and
18:28 So the king of I and Jehoshaphat the king
18:29 And the king of I said to Jehoshaphat, "I
18:29 And the king of I disguised himself; and they
18:30 nor great, but only with the king of I
18:31 Jehoshaphat, they said, "It is the king of I
18:32 not the king of I, they turned back from
18:33 struck the king of I between the scale armor
18:34 and the king of I propped himself up in
19:8 heads of families of I, to give judgment for
20:7 land before thy people I, and give it for
20:10 thou wouldest not let I invade when they came
20:19 LORD, the God of I, with a very loud
20:29 the LORD had fought against the enemies of I
20:34 recorded in the Book of the Kings of I
20:35 with Ahaziah king of I, who did wickedly.
21:4 sword, and also some of the princes of I
21:6 of the kings of I, as the house of
21:13 of the kings of I, and have led Judah
21:13 house of Ahab led I into unfaithfulness, and also
22:5 of Ahab king of I to make war against
23:2 of fathers' houses of I, and they came to
24:5 and gather from all I money to repair the
24:6 on the congregation of I for the tent of
24:9 of God laid upon I in the wilderness.
24:16 had done good in I, and toward God and
25:6 men of valor from I for a hundred talents
25:7 let the army of I go with you, for
25:7 LORD is not with I, with all these Ephraimites.
25:9 which I have given to the army of I
25:17 of Jehu, king of I, saying, "Come, let us
25:18 Joash the king of I sent word to Amaziah
25:21 So Joash king of I went up; and he
25:22 Judah was defeated by I, and every man fled
25:23 And Joash king of I captured Amaziah king of
25:25 of Joash the son of Jehoahaz, king of I
25:26 the Book of the Kings of Judah and I
27:7 of the Kings of I and Judah.
28:2 walked in the ways of the kings of I
28:3 the LORD drove out before the people of I
28:5 of the king of I, who defeated him with
28:8 The men of I took captive two hundred thousand
28:13 already great, and there is fierce wrath against I
28:19 of Ahaz king of I, for he had dealt
28:23 were the ruin of him, and of all I
28:26 the Book of the Kings of Judah and I
28:27 him into the tombs of the kings of I
29:7 in the holy place to the God of I
29:10 LORD, the God of I, that his fierce anger
29:24 on the altar, to make atonement for all I
29:24 the sin offering should be made for all I
29:27 accompanied by the instruments of David king of I
30:1 Hezekiah sent to all I and Judah, and wrote
30:1 the passover to the LORD the God of I
30:5 proclamation throughout all I, from Beer-sheba to
30:5 LORD the God of I, at Jerusalem; for they
30:6 couriers went throughout all I and Judah with letters
30:6 saying, "O people of I, return to the LORD,
30:6 of Abraham, Isaac, and I, that he may turn
30:21 And the people of I that were present at
30:25 that came out of I, and the sojourners who
30:25 of the land of I, and the sojourners who
30:26 of David king of I there had been nothing
31:1 this was finished, all I who were present went
31:1 all the people of I returned to their cities,
31:5 abroad, the people of I gave in abundance the
31:6 And the people of I and Judah who lived
31:8 heaps, they blessed the LORD and his people I
32:17 LORD the God of I and to speak against
32:32 the Book of the Kings of Judah and I
33:2 the LORD drove out before the people of I
33:7 all the tribes of I, I will put my
33:8 remove the foot of I from the land which
33:9 whom the LORD destroyed before the people of I
33:16 Judah to serve the LORD the God of I
33:18 LORD the God of I, behold, they are in
33:18 are in the Chronicles of the Kings of I
34:7 the incense altars throughout all the land of I
34:9 all the remnant of I and from all Judah
34:21 who are left in I and in Judah, concerning
34:23 LORD, the God of I: 'Tell the man who
34:26 LORD, the God of I: Regarding the words which
34:33 to the people of I, and made all who
34:33 all who were in I serve the LORD their
35:3 Levites who taught all I and who were holy
35:3 of David, king of I, built; you need no
35:3 serve the LORD your God and his people I
35:4 of David king of I and the directions of
35:17 And the people of I who were present kept
35:18 had been kept in I since the days of
35:18 of the kings of I had kept such a
35:18 and all Judah and I who were present, and
35:25 these an ordinance in I; behold, they are written
35:27 of the Kings of I and Judah.
36:8 of the Kings of I and Judah; and Jehoiachin
36:13 against turning to the LORD, the God of I
Ezra 1:3 LORD, the God of I -- he is the
2:2 of the people of I:
2:59 whether they belonged to I:
2:70 their towns, and all I in their towns.
3:1 and the sons of I were in the towns,
3:2 of the God of I, to offer burnt offerings
3:10 of David king of I;
3:11 for his steadfast love endures for ever toward I
4:1 LORD, the God of I,
4:3 of fathers' houses in I said to them, "You
4:3 LORD, the God of I, as King Cyrus the
5:1 of the God of I who was over them.
5:11 a great king of I built and finished.
6:14 of the God of I and by decree of
6:16 And the people of I, the priests and the
6:17 sin offering for all I twelve he-goats, according to
6:17 according to the number of the tribes of I
6:21 by the people of I who had returned from
6:21 land to worship the LORD, the God of I
6:22 of the house of God, the God of I
7:6 LORD the God of I had given; and the
7:7 of the people of I, and some of the

7:10 and to teach his statutes and ordinances in I
7:11 and his statutes for I:
7:13 of the people of I or their priests or
7:15 to the God of I, whose dwelling is in
7:28 gathered leading men from I to go up with
8:18 of Levi, son of I, namely Sherebiah with his
8:25 his lords and all I there present had offered;
8:29 of fathers' houses in I at Jerusalem, within the
8:35 to the God of I, twelve bulls for all
8:35 twelve bulls for all I, ninety-six rams, seventy-seven
9:1 said, "The people of I and the priests and
9:4 of the God of I, because of the faithlessness
9:15 LORD the God of I, thou art just, for
10:1 to him out of I; for the people wept
10:2 there is hope for I in spite of this.
10:5 and Levites and all I take oath that they
10:10 foreign women, and so increased the guilt of I
10:25 And of I: of the sons of Parosh: Ramiah,
Neh 1:6 for the people of I thy servants, confessing the
1:6 of the people of I, which we have sinned
2:10 to seek the welfare of the children of I
7:7 of the people of I:
7:61 whether they belonged to I:
7:73 temple servants, and all I, lived in their towns.
7:73 come, the children of I were in their towns.
8:1 of Moses which the LORD had given to I
8:14 that the people of I should dwell in booths
8:17 day the people of I had not done so.
9:1 month the people of I were assembled with fasting
10:33 to make atonement for I, and for all the
10:39 For the people of I and the sons of
11:3 property in their towns: I, the priests, the Levites,
11:20 And the rest of I, and of the priests
12:47 And all I in the days of Zerubbabel and
13:2 meet the children of I with bread and water,
13:3 law, they separated from I all those of foreign
13:18 bring more wrath upon I by profaning the sabbath."
13:26 not Solomon king of I sin on account of
13:26 him king over all I; nevertheless foreign women
Tob 1:4 in the land of I, while I was still
1:4 all the tribes of I, where all the tribes
1:6 is ordained for all I by an everlasting decree.
13:3 nations, O sons of I; for he has scattered
Jud 4:1 time the people of I living in Judea heard
4:8 the whole people of I, in session at Jerusalem,
4:9 And every man of I cried out to God
4:11 men and women of I, and their children, living
4:12 to the God of I not to give up
4:15 look with favor upon the whole house of I
5:1 that the people of I had prepared for war
6:2 against the people of I because their God will
6:10 and hand him over to the men of I
6:14 Then the men of I came down from their
6:17 had said so boastfully against the house of I
6:21 on the God of I for help.
7:19 The people of I cried out to the Lord
8:1 son of Salamiel, son of Sarasadai, son of I
8:6 and days of rejoicing of the house of I
8:33 the Lord will deliver I by my hand.
9:12 of the inheritance of I, Lord of heaven and
9:14 protects the people of I but thou alone!"
10:1 to the God of I, and had ended all
10:8 that the people of I may glory and Jerusalem
12:8 the Lord God of I to direct her way
13:7 me strength this day, O Lord God of I
13:11 show his power in I, and his strength against
13:14 from the house of I, but has destroyed our
14:4 within the borders of I shall pursue them and
14:5 despised the house of I and sent him to
14:10 that the God of I had done, he believed
14:10 joined the house of I, remaining so to this
15:3 Then the men of I, every one that was
15:4 all the frontiers of I, to tell what had
15:8 of the people of I who lived at Jerusalem,
15:8 Lord had done for I, and to see Judith
15:9 the great glory of I, you are the great
15:10 done great good to I, and God is well
15:12 all the women of I gathered to see her,
15:13 all the men of I followed, bearing their arms
16:1 this thanksgiving before all I, and all the people
16:8 her widow's mourning to exalt the oppressed in I
16:24 and the house of I mourned for her seven
16:25 among the people of I in the days of
Esth 10:9 my nation, this is I, who cried out to
10:13 generation to generation for ever among his people I
13:9 thee if it is thy will to save I

13:13 kiss the soles of his feet, to save I
13:18 And all I cried out mightily, for their death
14:3 the Lord God of I, and said: "O my
14:5 O Lord, didst take I out of all the
Ps 14:7 O that deliverance for I would come out of
14:7 people, Jacob shall rejoice, I shall be glad.
22:3 thou art holy, enthroned on the praises of I
22:23 in awe of him, all you sons of I
25:22 Redeem I, O God, out of all his troubles.
41:13 LORD, the God of I, from everlasting to everlasting!
50:7 I will speak, O I, I will testify against
53:6 O that deliverance for I would come from Zion!
53:6 Jacob will rejoice and I be glad.
59:5 Thou, LORD God of hosts, art God of I
68:8 at the presence of God, the God of I
68:26 you who are of I's fountain!"
68:34 whose majesty is over I, and his power is
68:35 sanctuary, the God of I, he gives power and
69:6 brought to dishonor through me, O God of I
71:22 thee with the lyre, O Holy One of I
72:18 LORD, the God of I, who alone does wondrous
76:1 God is known, his name is great in I
78:5 appointed a law in I, which he commanded our
78:21 his anger mounted against I;
78:31 them, and laid low the picked men of I
78:41 and again, and provoked the Holy One of I
78:55 settled the tribes of I in their tents.
78:59 was full of wrath, and he utterly rejected I
78:71 Jacob his people, of I his inheritance.
80:1 ear, O Shepherd of I, thou who leadest Joseph
81:4 is a statute for I, an ordinance of the
81:8 O I, if you would but listen to me!
81:11 listen to my voice; I would have none of
81:13 listen to me, that I would walk in my
83:4 let the name of I be remembered no more!"
89:18 LORD, our king to the Holy One of I
98:3 steadfast love and faithfulness to the house of I
103:7 to Moses, his acts to the people of I
105:10 as a statute, to I as an everlasting covenant,
105:23 Then I came to Egypt; Jacob sojourned in the
105:37 Then he led forth I with silver and gold,
106:48 LORD, the God of I, from everlasting to everlasting!
114:1 When I went forth from Egypt, the house of
114:2 Judah became his sanctuary, I his dominion.
115:9 O I, trust in the LORD!
115:12 bless the house of I; he will bless the
118:2 Let I say, "His steadfast love endures for ever."
121:4 Behold, he who keeps I will neither slumber nor
122:4 as was decreed for I, to give thanks to
124:1 on our side, let I now say—
125:5 Peace be in I
128:6 Peace be upon I
129:1 let I now say—
130:7 O I, hope in the LORD!
130:8 And he will redeem I from all his iniquities.
131:3 O I, hope in the LORD from this time
135:4 chosen Jacob for himself, I as his own possession.
135:12 as a heritage, a heritage to his people I
135:19 O house of I, bless the LORD!
136:11 for ever; and brought I out from among them,
136:14 for ever; and made I pass through the midst
136:22 ever; a heritage to I his servant, for his
147:2 builds up Jerusalem; he gathers the outcasts of I
147:19 word to Jacob, his statutes and ordinances to I
148:14 for the people of I who are near to
149:2 Let I be glad in his Maker, let the
Prov 1:1 of David, king of I:
Eccl 1:12 have been king over I in Jerusalem.
Song 3:7 the mighty men of I,
Sir 17:14 for every nation, but I is the Lord's own
24:8 in Jacob, and in I receive your inheritance.'
36:12 by thy name, upon I, whom thou hast likened
37:25 but the days of I are without number.
45:5 Jacob the covenant, and I his judgments.
45:11 of the tribes of I;
45:17 testimonies, and to enlighten I with his law.
45:23 goodness of his soul, and made atonement for I
46:1 that he might give I its inheritance.
46:10 all the sons of I might see that it
47:2 so David was selected from the sons of I
47:11 of kings and a throne of glory in I
47:18 called the God of I, you gathered gold like
47:23 of Nebat, who caused I to sin and gave
50:13 in their hands, before the whole congregation of I
50:20 of the sons of I, to pronounce the blessing
50:23 in our days in I, as in the days

Is	1:3	its master's crib; but I does not know, my
	1:4	the Holy One of I, they are utterly estranged.
	1:24	the Mighty One of I: "Ah, I will vent
	4:2	the pride and glory of the survivors of I
	5:7	is the house of I, and the men of
	5:19	the Holy One of I draw near, and let
	5:24	despised the word of the Holy One of I
	7:1	Remaliah the king of I came up to Jerusalem
	8:14	to both houses of I, a trap and a
	8:18	signs and portents in I from the LORD of
	9:8	it will light upon I;
	9:12	on the west devour I with open mouth.
	9:14	LORD cut off from I head and tail, palm
	10:17	The light of I will become a fire, and
	10:20	day the remnant of I and the survivors of
	10:20	the Holy One of I, in truth.
	10:22	For though your people I be as the sand
	11:12	assemble the outcasts of I, and gather the dispersed
	11:16	as there was for I when they came up
	12:6	in your midst is the Holy One of I
	14:1	and will again choose I, and will set them
	14:2	and the house of I will possess them in
	17:3	of the children of I, says the LORD of
	17:6	a fruit tree, says the LORD God of I
	17:7	the Holy One of I;
	17:9	of the children of I, and there will be
	19:24	In that day I will be the third with
	19:25	of my hands, and I my heritage."
	21:10	hosts, the God of I, I announce to you.
	21:17	LORD, the God of I, has spoken."
	24:15	the name of the LORD, the God of I
	27:6	Jacob shall take root, I shall blossom and put
	27:12	be gathered one by one, O people of I
	29:19	men shall exult in the Holy One of I
	29:23	will stand in awe of the God of I
	30:11	hear no more of the Holy One of I
	30:12	the Holy One of I, "Because you despise this
	30:15	the Holy One of I, "In returning and rest
	30:29	mountain of the LORD, to the Rock of I
	31:1	the Holy One of I or consult the LORD!
	31:6	whom you have deeply revolted, O people of I
	37:16	of hosts, God of I, who art enthroned above
	37:21	LORD, the God of I: Because you have prayed
	37:23	Against the Holy One of I
	40:27	Jacob, and speak, O I, "My way is hid
	41:8	But you, I, my servant, Jacob, whom I have
	41:14	Fear not, you worm Jacob, you men of I
	41:14	LORD; your Redeemer is the Holy One of I
	41:16	the Holy One of I you shall glory.
	41:17	I the God of I will not forsake them.
	41:20	the Holy One of I has created it.
	42:24	to the spoiler, and I to the robbers?
	43:1	who formed you, O I: "Fear not, for I
	43:3	the Holy One of I, your Savior.
	43:14	the Holy One of I: "For your sake I
	43:15	One, the Creator of I, your King."
	43:22	but you have been weary of me, O I
	43:28	to utter destruction and I to reviling.
	44:1	O Jacob my servant, I whom I have chosen!
	44:5	LORDs,' and surname himself by the name of I
	44:6	LORD, the King of I and his Redeemer, the
	44:21	things, O Jacob, and I, for you are my
	44:21	are my servant; O I, you will not be
	44:23	has redeemed Jacob, and will be glorified in I
	45:3	LORD, the God of I, who call you by
	45:4	my servant Jacob, and I my chosen, I call
	45:11	the Holy One of I, and his Maker: "Will
	45:15	thyself, O God of I, the Savior.
	45:17	But I is saved by the LORD with everlasting
	45:25	all the offspring of I shall triumph and glory."
	46:3	of the house of I, who have been borne
	46:13	salvation in Zion, for I my glory."
	47:4	his name—is the Holy One of I
	48:1	by the name of I, and who came forth
	48:1	confess the God of I, but not in truth
	48:2	on the God of I; the LORD of hosts
	48:12	me, O Jacob, and I, whom I called!
	48:17	the Holy One of I: "I am the LORD
	49:3	"You are my servant, I, in whom I will
	49:5	to him, and that I might be gathered to
	49:6	restore the preserved of I; I will give you
	49:7	LORD, the Redeemer of I and his Holy One,
	49:7	the Holy One of I, who has chosen you."
	52:12	and the God of I will be your rear
	54:5	the Holy One of I is your Redeemer, the
	55:5	the Holy One of I, for he has glorified
	56:8	gathers the outcasts of I, I will gather yet
	60:9	the Holy One of I, because he has glorified
	60:14	LORD, the Zion of the Holy One of I
	63:7	to the house of I which he has granted
	63:16	not know us and I does not acknowledge us;
Jer	2:3	I was holy to the LORD, the first fruits
	2:4	and all the families of the house of I
	2:14	"Is I a slave?
	2:26	so the house of I shall be shamed: they,
	2:31	been a wilderness to I, or a land of
	3:6	did, that faithless one, I, how she went up
	3:8	of that faithless one, I, I had sent her
	3:11	said to me, "Faithless I has shown herself less
	3:12	and say, 'Return, faithless I, says the LORD.
	3:18	join the house of I, and together they shall
	3:20	me, O house of I, says the LORD.'"
	3:21	weeping and pleading of I's sons, because they have
	3:23	the LORD our God is the salvation of I
	4:1	"If you return, O I, says the LORD, to
	5:11	For the house of I and the house of
	5:15	afar, O house of I, says the LORD.
	6:9	vine the remnant of I; like a grape-gatherer pass
	7:3	hosts, the God of I, Amend your ways and
	7:12	to it for the wickedness of my people I
	7:21	hosts, the God of I: "Add your burnt offerings
	9:15	hosts, the God of I: Behold, I will feed
	9:26	all the house of I is uncircumcised in heart."
	10:1	the LORD speaks to you, O house of I
	10:16	formed all things, and I is the tribe of
	11:3	LORD, the God of I: Cursed be the man
	11:10	them; the house of I and the house of
	11:17	which the house of I and the house of
	12:14	have given my people I to inherit: "Behold, I
	13:11	the whole house of I and the whole house
	13:12	LORD, the God of I, "Every jar shall be
	14:8	O thou hope of I, its savior in time
	16:9	hosts, the God of I: Behold, I will make
	16:14	up the people of I out of the land
	16:15	up the people of I out of the north
	17:13	LORD, the hope of I, all who forsake thee
	18:6	me: "O house of I, can I not do
	18:6	are you in my hand, O house of I
	18:13	The virgin I has done a very horrible thing.
	19:3	hosts, the God of I, Behold, I am bringing
	19:15	hosts, the God of I, Behold, I am bringing
	21:4	LORD, the God of I: Behold, I will turn
	23:2	LORD, the God of I, concerning the shepherds who
	23:6	will be saved, and I will dwell securely.
	23:7	up the people of I out of the land
	23:8	of the house of I out of the north
	23:13	and led my people I astray.
	24:5	LORD, the God of I: Like these good figs,
	25:15	LORD, the God of I, said to me: "Take
	25:27	hosts, the God of I: Drink, be drunk and
	27:4	hosts, the God of I: This is what you
	27:21	hosts, the God of I, concerning the vessels which
	28:2	hosts, the God of I: I have broken the
	28:14	hosts, the God of I: I have put upon
	29:4	hosts, the God of I, to all the exiles
	29:8	hosts, the God of I: Do not let your
	29:21	hosts, the God of I, concerning Ahab the son
	29:23	committed folly in I, they have committed adultery
	29:25	hosts, the God of I: You have sent letters
	30:2	LORD, the God of I: Write in a book
	30:3	fortunes of my people, I and Judah, says the
	30:4	the LORD spoke concerning I and Judah:
	30:10	nor be dismayed, O I; for lo, I will
	31:1	all the families of I, and they shall be
	31:2	in the wilderness; when I sought for rest,
	31:4	you, and you shall be built, O virgin I
	31:7	people, the remnant of I
	31:9	am a father to I, and Ephraim is my
	31:10	say, 'He who scattered I will gather him, and
	31:21	Return, O virgin I, return to these your cities.
	31:23	hosts, the God of I: "Once more they shall
	31:27	sow the house of I and the house of
	31:31	with the house of I and the house of
	31:33	with the house of I after those days, says
	31:36	shall the descendants of I cease from being a
	31:37	all the descendants of I for all that they
	32:14	hosts, the God of I: Take these deeds, both
	32:15	hosts, the God of I: Houses and fields and
	32:20	to this day in I and among all mankind,
	32:21	didst bring thy people I out of the land
	32:30	For the sons of I and the sons of
	32:30	youth; the sons of I have done nothing but

32:32 of the sons of I and the sons of
32:36 LORD, the God of I, concerning this city of
33:4 LORD, the God of I, concerning the houses of
33:7 and the fortunes of I, and rebuild them as
33:14 to the house of I and the house of
33:17 of the house of I,
34:2 LORD, the God of I: Go and speak to
34:13 LORD, the God of I: I made a covenant
35:13 hosts, the God of I: Go and say to
35:17 hosts, the God of I: Behold, I am bringing
35:18 hosts, the God of I: Because you have obeyed
35:19 hosts, the God of I: Jonadab the son of
36:2 spoken to you against I and Judah and all
37:7 the LORD, God of I: Thus shall you say
38:17 hosts, the God of I, If you will surrender
39:16 hosts, the God of I: Behold, I will fulfil
41:9 against Baasha king of I; Ishmael the son of
42:9 LORD, the God of I, to whom you sent
42:15 hosts, the God of I: If you set your
42:18 hosts, the God of I: As my anger and
43:10 hosts, the God of I: Behold, I will send
44:2 hosts, the God of I: You have seen all
44:7 hosts, the God of I: Why do you commit
44:11 hosts, the God of I: Behold, I will set
44:25 hosts, the God of I: You and your wives
45:2 LORD, the God of I, to you, O Baruch:
46:25 hosts, the God of I, said: "Behold, I am
46:27 nor be dismayed, O I; for lo, I will
48:1 hosts, the God of I: "Woe to Nebo, for
48:13 as the house of I was ashamed of Bethel,
48:27 Was not I a derision to you?
49:1 says the LORD: "Has I no sons?
49:2 burned with fire; then I shall dispossess those who
50:4 LORD, the people of I and the people of
50:17 I is a hunted sheep driven away by lions.
50:18 hosts, the God of I: Behold, I am bringing
50:19 I will restore I to his pasture, and he
50:20 shall be sought in I, and there shall be
50:29 proudly defied the LORD, the Holy One of I
50:33 hosts: The people of I are oppressed, and the
51:5 For I and Judah have not been forsaken by
51:5 full of guilt against the Holy One of I
51:19 formed all things, and I is the tribe of
51:33 hosts, the God of I: The daughter of Babylon
51:49 for the slain of I, as for Babylon have
Lam 2:1 earth the splendor of I; he has not remembered
2:3 all the might of I; he has withdrawn from
2:5 enemy, he has destroyed I; he has destroyed all
Bar 2:1 our judges who judged I, and against our kings
2:1 against the men of I and Judah.
2:11 O Lord God of I, who didst bring thy
2:15 Lord our God, for I and his descendants are
2:26 of the house of I and the house of
2:28 of the people of I, saying,
2:35 again remove my people I from the land which
3:1 Lord Almighty, God of I, the soul in anguish
3:4 Lord Almighty, God of I, hear now the prayer
3:4 of the dead of I and of the sons
3:9 commandments of life, O I; give ear, and learn
3:10 Why is it, O I, why is it that
3:24 O I, how great is the house of God!
3:36 his servant and to I whom he loved.
4:4 Happy are we, O I, for we know what
4:5 Take courage, my people, O memorial of I
5:7 level ground, so that I may walk safely in
5:8 fragrant tree have shaded I at God's command.
5:9 For God will lead I with joy, in the
Ezek 2:3 to the people of I, to a nation of
3:1 scroll, and go, speak to the house of I
3:4 to the house of I, and speak with my
3:5 to the house of I –
3:7 But the house of I will not listen to
3:7 all the house of I are of a hard
3:17 for the house of I; whenever you hear a
4:3 This is a sign for the house of I
4:4 of the house of I upon you; for the
4:5 you bear the punishment of the house of I
4:13 shall the people of I eat their bread unclean,
5:4 will come forth into all the house of I
6:2 toward the mountains of I, and prophesy against
6:3 say, You mountains of I, hear the word of
6:5 of the people of I before their idols; and
6:11 of the house of I; for they shall fall
7:2 to the land of I: An end!
8:4 of the God of I was there, like the
8:6 that the house of I are committing here, to
8:10 and all the idols of the house of I
8:11 of the house of I, with Ja-azaniah the son
8:12 of the house of I are doing in the
9:3 of the God of I had gone up from
9:8 all that remains of I in the outpouring of
9:9 of the house of I and Judah is exceedingly
10:19 of the God of I was over them.
10:20 underneath the God of I by the river Chebar;
11:5 think, O house of I; for I know the
11:10 at the border of I; and you shall know
11:11 at the border of I;
11:13 make a full end of the remnant of I
11:15 the whole house of I, all of them, are
11:17 you the land of I
11:22 of the God of I was over them.
12:6 made you a sign for the house of I
12:9 not the house of I, the rebellious house, said
12:10 all the house of I who are in it.'
12:19 in the land of I: They shall eat their
12:22 about the land of I, saying, 'The days grow
12:23 as a proverb in I But say to them,
12:24 vision or flattering divination within the house of I
12:27 of the house of I say, 'The vision that
13:2 against the prophets of I, prophesy and say to
13:4 prophets have been like foxes among ruins, O I
13:5 for the house of I, that it might stand
13:9 of the house of I, nor shall they enter
13:9 enter the land of I; and you shall know
13:16 prophets of I who prophesied concerning Jerusalem
14:1 of the elders of I to me; and sat
14:4 of the house of I who takes his idols
14:5 of the house of I, who are all estranged
14:6 to the house of I, Thus says the Lord
14:7 of the house of I, or of the strangers
14:7 strangers that sojourn in I, who separates himself
14:9 destroy him from the midst of my people I
14:11 that the house of I may go no more
17:2 to the house of I;
17:23 the mountain height of I will I plant it,
18:2 concerning the land of I, 'The fathers have eaten
18:3 shall no more be used by you in I
18:6 of the house of I, does not defile his
18:15 of the house of I, does not defile his
18:25 now, O house of I: Is my way not
18:29 Yet the house of I says, 'The way of
18:29 just.' O house of I, are my ways not
18:30 you, O house of I, every one according to
18:31 Why will you die, O house of I
19:1 for the princes of I,
19:9 no more be heard upon the mountains of I
20:1 of the elders of I came to inquire of
20:3 to the elders of I, and say to them,
20:5 day when I chose I, I swore to the
20:13 But the house of I rebelled against me in
20:27 to the house of I and say to them,
20:30 to the house of I, Thus says the Lord
20:31 be inquired of by you, O house of I
20:38 but they shall not enter the land of I
20:39 you, O house of I, thus says the Lord
20:40 the mountain height of I, says the Lord GOD,
20:40 all the house of I, all of them, shall
20:42 into the land of I, the country which I
20:44 doings, O house of I, says the Lord GOD."
21:2 against the land of I
21:3 to the land of I, Thus says the LORD:
21:12 all the princes of I; they are delivered over
21:25 wicked one, prince of I, whose day has come,
22:6 "Behold, the princes of I in you, every one
22:18 man, the house of I has become dross to
24:21 to the house of I, Thus says the Lord
25:3 over the land of I when it was made
25:6 against the land of I,
25:14 hand of my people I; and they shall do
27:17 and the land of I traded with you; they
28:24 for the house of I there shall be no
28:25 gather the house of I from the peoples among
29:6 to the house of I;
29:16 of the house of I, recalling their iniquity, when
29:21 to the house of I, and I will open
33:7 for the house of I; whenever you hear a
33:10 to the house of I, Thus have you said:
33:11 for why will you die, O house of I
33:20 just.' O house of I, I will judge each
33:24 in the land of I keep saying, 'Abraham was
33:28 and the mountains of I shall be so desolate
34:2 against the shepherds of I, prophesy, and say to

 ISRAEL

	34:2	GOD: Ho, shepherds of I who have been feeding
	34:13	on the mountains of I, by the fountains, and
	34:14	the mountain heights of I shall be their pasture;
	34:14	pasture they shall feed on the mountains of I
	34:30	they, the house of I, are my people, says
	35:5	over the people of I to the power of
	35:12	against the mountains of I, saying, 'They are laid
	35:15	of the house of I, because it was desolate,
	36:1	to the mountains of I, and say, O mountains
	36:1	say, O mountains of I, hear the word of
	36:4	therefore, O mountains of I, hear the word of
	36:6	concerning the land of I, and say to the
	36:8	you, O mountains of I, shall shoot forth your
	36:8	fruit to my people I; for they will soon
	36:10	the whole house of I, all of it; the
	36:12	you, even my people I; and they shall possess
	36:17	when the house of I dwelt in their own
	36:21	which the house of I caused to be profaned
	36:22	to the house of I, Thus says the Lord
	36:22	sake, O house of I, that I am about
	36:32	and confounded for your ways, O house of I
	36:37	let the house of I ask me to do
	37:11	man, these bones are the whole house of I
	37:12	will bring you home into the land of I
	37:16	and the children of I associated with him'; then
	37:16	all the house of I associated with him';
	37:19	and the tribes of I associated with him; and
	37:21	take the people of I from the nations among
	37:22	upon the mountains of I; and one king shall
	37:28	I the LORD sanctify I, when my sanctuary is
	38:8	upon the mountains of I, which had been a
	38:14	day when my people I are dwelling securely, you
	38:16	up against my people I, like a cloud covering
	38:17	servants the prophets of I, who in those days
	38:18	against the land of I, says the Lord GOD,
	38:19	in the land of I;
	39:2	against the mountains of I;
	39:4	upon the mountains of I, you and all your
	39:7	midst of my people I; and I will not
	39:7	I am the LORD, the Holy One in I
	39:9	in the cities of I will go forth and
	39:11	place for burial in I, the Valley of the
	39:12	months the house of I will be burying them,
	39:17	upon the mountains of I, and you shall eat
	39:22	The house of I shall know that I am
	39:23	that the house of I went into captivity for
	39:25	the whole house of I; and I will be
	39:29	upon the house of I, says the Lord GOD."
	40:2	into the land of I, and set me down
	40:4	all that you see to the house of I
	43:2	of the God of I came from the east;
	43:7	of the people of I for ever.
	43:7	And the house of I shall no more defile
	43:10	to the house of I the temple and its
	44:2	LORD, the God of I, has entered by it;
	44:6	to the house of I, Thus says the Lord
	44:6	GOD: O house of I, let there be an
	44:9	among the people of I, shall enter my sanctuary.
	44:10	after their idols when I went astray, shall bear
	44:12	to the house of I, therefore I have sworn
	44:15	when the people of I went astray from me,
	44:22	of the house of I, or a widow who
	44:28	them no possession in I; I am their possession.
	44:29	every devoted thing in I shall be theirs.
	45:6	it shall belong to the whole house of I
	45:8	It is to be his property in I
	45:8	let the house of I have the land according
	45:9	says the Lord GOD: Enough, O princes of I
	45:15	flock of two hundred, from the families of I
	45:16	shall give this offering to the prince in I
	45:17	of the house of I: he shall provide the
	45:17	offerings, to make atonement for the house of I
	47:13	land for inheritance among the twelve tribes of I
	47:18	and the land of I; to the eastern sea
	47:21	land among you according to the tribes of I
	47:22	as native-born sons of I; with you they shall
	47:22	be allotted an inheritance among the tribes of I
	48:11	when the people of I went astray, as the
	48:19	all the tribes of I, shall till it.
	48:29	among the tribes of I, and these are their
	48:31	the city being named after the tribes of I
Dan	1:3	of the people of I, both of the royal
	3:35	Isaac thy servant and I thy holy one,
	3:84	Bless the Lord, O I, sing praise to him
	9:7	Jerusalem, and to all I, those that are near
	9:11	All I has transgressed thy law and turned aside,
	9:20	sin of my people I, and presenting my supplication
	13:48	said, "Are you such fools, you sons of I
	13:48	condemned a daughter of I without examination and
	13:57	with the daughters of I, and they were intimate
Hos	1:1	of Jeroboam the son of Joash, king of I
	1:4	end to the kingdom of the house of I
	1:5	break the bow of I in the valley of
	1:6	on the house of I, to forgive them at
	1:10	of the people of I shall be like the
	1:11	and the people of I shall be gathered together,
	3:1	loves the people of I, though they turn to
	3:4	For the children of I shall dwell many days
	3:5	Afterward the children of I shall return and seek
	4:1	LORD, O people of I; for the LORD has
	4:15	play the harlot, O I, let not Judah become
	4:16	Like a stubborn heifer, I is stubborn; can the
	5:1	Give heed, O house of I
	5:3	I know Ephraim, and I is not hid from
	5:3	have played the harlot, I is defiled.
	5:5	The pride of I testifies to his face; Ephraim
	5:9	among the tribes of I I declare what is
	6:10	In the house of I I have seen a
	6:10	Ephraim's harlotry is there, I is defiled.
	7:2	when I would heal I, the corruption of Ephraim
	7:11	The pride of I witnesses against him; yet they
	8:2	cry, My God, we I know thee.
	8:3	I has spurned the good; the enemy shall pursue
	8:6	will it be till they are pure in I
	8:8	I is swallowed up; already they are among the
	8:14	For I has forgotten his Maker, and built palaces;
	9:1	Rejoice not, O I
	9:7	of recompense have come; I shall know it.
	9:10	Like grapes in the wilderness, I found I
	10:1	I is a luxuriant vine that yields its fruit.
	10:6	put to shame, and I shall be ashamed of
	10:8	Aven, the sin of I, shall be destroyed.
	10:9	you have sinned, O I; there they have continued.
	10:15	you, O house of I, because of your great
	10:15	storm the king of I shall be utterly cut
	11:1	When I was a child, I loved him, and
	11:8	How can I hand you over, O I
	11:12	and the house of I with deceit; but Judah
	12:12	land of Aram, there I did service for a
	12:13	prophet the LORD brought I up from Egypt, and
	13:1	he was exalted in I; but he incurred guilt
	13:9	will destroy you, O I; who can help you?
	14:1	Return, O I, to the LORD your God, for
	14:5	as the dew to I; he shall blossom as
Joel	2:27	in the midst of I, and that I, the
	3:2	and my heritage I, because they have scattered
	3:16	his people, a stronghold to the people of I
Amos	1:1	which he saw concerning I in the days of
	1:1	of Joash, king of I, two years before the
	2:6	"For three transgressions of I, and for four, I
	2:11	Is it not indeed so, O people of I
	3:1	you, O people of I, against the whole family
	3:12	shall the people of I who dwell in Samaria
	3:14	the day I punish I for his transgressions, I
	4:5	so you love to do, O people of I
	4:12	do to you, O I; because I will do
	4:12	to you, prepare to meet your God, O I
	5:1	lamentation, O house of I:
	5:2	rise, is the virgin I; forsaken on her land,
	5:3	shall have ten left to the house of I
	5:4	to the house of I: "Seek me and live;
	5:25	forty years in the wilderness, O house of I
	6:1	whom the house of I come!
	6:14	up against you a nation, O house of I
	7:8	midst of my people I; I will never again
	7:9	and the sanctuaries of I shall be laid waste,
	7:10	to Jeroboam king of I, saying, "Amos has conspired
	7:10	of the house of I; the land is not
	7:11	by the sword, and I must go into exile
	7:15	prophesy to my people I
	7:16	'Do not prophesy against I, and do not preach
	7:17	an unclean land, and I shall surely go into
	8:2	come upon my people I; I will never again
	9:7	like the Ethiopians to me, O people of I
	9:7	I not bring up I from the land of
	9:9	shake the house of I among all the nations
	9:14	fortunes of my people I, and they shall rebuild
Obad	1:20	of the people of I shall possess Phoenicia as
Mic	1:5	and for the sins of the house of I
	1:13	for in you were found the transgressions of I
	1:14	be a deceitful thing to the kings of I
	1:15	Mareshah; the glory of I shall come to Adullam.

2:12 gather the remnant of I; I will set them
3:1 of Jacob and rulers of the house of I
3:8 his transgression and to I his sin.
3:9 of the house of I, who abhor justice and
5:1 they strike upon the cheek the ruler of I
5:2 to be ruler in I, whose origin is from
5:3 his brethren shall return to the people of I
6:2 with his people, and he will contend with I
Nah 2:2 as the majesty of I, for plunderers have stripped
Zeph 2:9 hosts, the God of I, "Moab shall become like
3:13 who are left in I; they shall do no
3:14 Sing aloud, O daughter of Zion; shout, O I
3:15 The King of I, the LORD, is in your
Zech 1:19 which have scattered Judah, I, and Jerusalem."
8:13 Judah and house of I, so will I save
9:1 all the tribes of I;
11:14 annulling the brotherhood between Judah and I
12:1 of the LORD concerning I: Thus says the LORD,
Mal 1:1 of the LORD to I by Malachi.
1:5 "Great is the LORD, beyond the border of I
2:11 has been committed in I and in Jerusalem; for
2:16 LORD the God of I, and covering one's garment
4:4 that I commanded him at Horeb for all I
1Mac 1:11 men came forth from I, and misled many, saying,
1:20 He went up against I and came to Jerusalem
1:25 I mourned deeply in every community,
1:30 a severe blow, and destroyed many people of I
1:36 an evil adversary of I continually.
1:43 Many even from I gladly adopted his religion; they
1:53 the land; they drove I into hiding in every
1:58 kept using violence against I, against those found
1:62 But many in I stood firm and were resolved
1:64 And very great wrath came upon I
2:16 Many from I came to them; and Mattathias and
2:42 Hasideans, mighty warriors of I, every one who
2:46 boys that they found within the borders of I
2:55 he fulfilled the command, became a judge in I
2:70 And all I mourned for him with great lamentation.
3:2 his father helped him; they gladly fought for I
3:8 the land; thus he turned away wrath from I
3:10 a large force from Samaria to fight against I
3:15 him, to take vengeance on the sons of I
3:35 destroy the strength of I and the remnant of
3:41 get the sons of I for slaves.
3:46 opposite Jerusalem, because I formerly had a place
4:11 that there is one who redeems and saves I
4:25 Thus I had a great deliverance that day.
4:27 had not happened to I as he had intended,
4:30 thou, O Savior of I, who didst crush the
4:31 hand of thy people I, and let them be
4:59 all the assembly of I determined that every year
5:3 Akrabattene, because they kept lying in wait for I
5:60 of the people of I fell that day.
5:62 those men through whom deliverance was given to I
5:63 greatly honored in all I and among all the
6:18 the citadel kept hemming I in around the sanctuary.
7:5 and ungodly men of I; they were led by
7:9 him to take vengeance on the sons of I
7:13 among the sons of I to seek peace from
7:22 land of Judah and did great damage in I
7:23 among the sons of I; it was more than
7:26 who hated and detested I, and he commanded him
8:18 kingdom of the Greeks was completely enslaving I
9:20 And all I made great lamentation for him; they
9:21 "How is the mighty fallen, the savior of I
9:23 in all parts of I; all the doers of
9:27 was great distress in I, such as had not
9:51 And he placed garrisons in them to harass I
9:73 Thus the sword ceased from I
9:73 people, and he destroyed the ungodly out of I
10:46 Demetrius had done in I and how he had
10:61 pestilent men from I, lawless men, gathered together
11:23 of the elders of I and some of the
11:41 in the strongholds; for they kept fighting against I
12:52 great fear; and all I mourned deeply.
13:4 for the sake of I, and I alone am
13:26 All I bewailed him with great lamentation, and
13:41 Gentiles was removed from I,
13:51 great enemy had been crushed and removed from I
14:11 in the land, and I rejoiced with great joy.
14:26 have fought and repulsed I's enemies and established
16:2 fought the wars of I from our youth until
16:2 that we have delivered I many times.
2Mac 1:25 eternal, who dost rescue I from every evil, who
1:26 of all thy people I and preserve thy portion
9:5 Lord, the God of I, struck him an incurable

10:38 shows great kindness to I and gives them the
11:6 Lord to send a good angel to save I
Mt 2:6 come a ruler who will govern my people I
2:20 to the land of I, for those who sought
2:21 his mother, and went to the land of I
8:10 you, not even in I have I found such
9:33 saying, "Never was anything like this seen in I
10:6 to the lost sheep of the house of I
10:23 all the towns of I, before the Son of
15:24 to the lost sheep of the house of I
15:31 blind seeing; and they glorified the God of I
19:28 on twelve thrones, judging the twelve tribes of I
27:9 of the sons of I,
27:42 is the King of I; let him come down
Mk 12:29 first is, 'Hear, O I: The Lord our God,
15:31 Christ, the King of I, come down now from
Lk 1:16 of the sons of I to the Lord their
1:54 has helped his servant I, in remembrance of his
1:68 the Lord God of I, for he has visited
1:80 wilderness till the day of his manifestation to I
2:25 for the consolation of I, and the Holy Spirit
2:32 the Gentiles, and for glory to thy people I
2:34 rising of many in I, and for a sign
4:25 were many widows in I in the days of
4:27 were many lepers in I in the time of
7:9 you, not even in I have I found such
22:30 sit on thrones judging the twelve tribes of I
24:21 hoped that he was the one to redeem I
Jn 1:31 with water, that he might be revealed to I
1:49 You are the King of I
3:10 you a teacher of I, and yet you do
12:13 name of the Lord, even the King of I
Acts 1:6 you at this time restore the kingdom to I
2:22 be saved.' "Men of I, hear these words: Jesus
2:36 all the house of I therefore know assuredly that
3:12 the people, "Men of I, why do you wonder
4:10 all the people of I, that by the name
4:27 and the peoples of I,
5:21 all the senate of I, and sent to the
5:31 to give repentance to I and forgiveness of sins.
5:35 to them, "Men of I, take care what you
7:23 heart to visit his brethren, the sons of I
7:42 forty years in the wilderness, O house of I
9:15 and the sons of I;
10:36 which he sent to I, preaching good news of
13:16 hand said: "Men of I, and you that fear
13:17 God of this people I chose our fathers and
13:23 God has brought to I a Savior, Jesus, as
13:24 baptism of repentance to all the people of I
21:28 crying out, "Men of I, help!
28:20 of the hope of I that I am bound
Rom 9:6 who are descended from I belong to Israel,
9:6 from Israel belong to I,
9:27 Isaiah cries out concerning I: "Though the number of
9:27 of the sons of I be as the sand
9:31 faith; but that I who pursued the righteousness
10:19 Again I ask, did I not understand?
10:21 But of I he says, "All day long I
11:2 of Elijah, how he pleads with God against I
11:7 I failed to obtain what it sought.
11:11 so as to make I jealous.
11:25 come upon part of I, until the full number
11:26 in, and so all I will be saved; as
1Cor 10:18 Consider the people of I; are not those who
Gal 6:16 this rule, upon the I of God.
Eph 2:12 from the commonwealth of I, and strangers to the
Phil 3:5 of the people of I, of the tribe of
Heb 8:8 with the house of I and with the house
8:10 with the house of I after those days, says
Rev 2:14 before the sons of I, that they might eat
7:4 of the sons of I,
21:12 of the sons of I were inscribed;

ISRAELITE (5)

Lev 24:10 Now an I woman's son, whose father was an
24:10 of Israel; and the I woman's son and a
24:11 the camp, and the I woman's son blasphemed the
Jn 1:47 of him, "Behold, an I indeed, in whom is
Rom 11:1 I myself am an I, a descendant of Abraham,

ISRAELITES (35)

Gen 32:32 to this day the I do not eat the
36:31 of Edom, before any king reigned over the I
Ex 9:7 the cattle of the I was dead.
Judg 6:3 For whenever the I put in seed the Midianites
20:21 on that day twenty-two thousand men of the I

1Sam	2:14	Shiloh to all the I who came there.
	13:20	every one of the I went down to the
	14:21	to be with the I who were with Saul
	17:53	And the I came back from chasing the Philistines,
	29:1	at Aphek; and the I were encamped by the
2Kgs	3:24	camp of Israel, the I rose and attacked the
	17:6	and he carried the I away to Assyria, and
	18:11	of Assyria carried the I away to Assyria, and
1Chr	1:43	king reigned over the I: Bela the son of
Neh	9:2	And the I separated themselves from all foreigners,
Jud	4:8	So the I did as Joakim the high priest
	5:23	be afraid of the I; they are a people
	7:1	the hill country and make war on the I
	7:4	When the I saw their vast numbers they were
	7:6	full view of the I in Bethulia,
	7:10	For these people, the I, do not rely on
	7:17	the water supply and the springs of the I
	10:19	beauty, and admired the I, judging them by her,
	15:5	And when the I heard it, with one accord
	15:7	And the I, when they returned from the slaughter,
Is	66:20	LORD, just as the I bring their cereal offering
1Mac	5:9	gathered together against the I who lived in their
	5:45	gathered together all the I in Gilead, the small
	6:21	some of the ungodly I joined them.
Acts	7:37	who said to the I, 'God will raise up
Rom	9:4	They are I, and to them belong the sonship,
2Cor	3:7	such splendor that the I could not look at
	3:13	face so that the I might not see the
	11:22	Are they I
Heb	11:22	the exodus of the I and gave directions concerning

ISRAELTHEN

Judg	5:11	of his peasantry in I down to the gates

ISSACHAR (44)

Gen	30:18	to my husband"; so she called his name I
	35:23	first-born), Simeon, Levi, Judah, I, and Zebulun.
	46:13	The sons of I: Tola, Puvah, Iob, and Shimron.
	49:14	I is a strong ass, crouching between the sheepfolds;
Ex	1:3	Simeon, Levi, and Judah, I, Zebulun, and Benjamin,
Num	1:8	son of Amminadab; from I, Nethanel the son of
	1:28	Of the people of I, their generations, by their
	1:29	of the tribe of I was fifty-four thousand four
	2:5	be the tribe of I, the leader of the
	2:5	of the people of I being Nethanel the son
	7:18	Zuar, the leader of I, made an offering;
	10:15	of the men of I was Nethanel the son
	13:7	from the tribe of I, Igal the son of
	26:23	The sons of I according to their families: of
	26:25	are the families of I according to their number,
	34:26	of the sons of I a leader, Paltiel the
Deut	27:12	Simeon, Levi, Judah, I, Joseph, and Benjamin.
	33:18	your going out; and I, in your tents.
Josh	17:10	north Asher is reached, and on the east I
	17:11	Also in I and in Asher Manasseh had Beth-shean
	19:17	lot came out for I, for the tribe of
	19:17	for the tribe of I, according to its families.
	19:23	of the tribe of I, according to its families—
	21:6	of the tribe of I, from the tribe of
	21:28	of the tribe of I, Kishion with its pasture
Judg	5:15	staff; the princes of I came with Deborah, and
	5:15	came with Deborah, and I faithful to Barak; into
	10:1	Dodo, a man of I; and he lived at
1Kgs	4:17	son of Paruah, in I;
	15:27	of the house of I, conspired against him; and
1Chr	2:1	Reuben, Simeon, Levi, Judah, I, Zebulun,
	6:62	of the tribes of I, Asher, Naphtali, and Manasseh
	6:72	of the tribe of I: Kedesh with its pasture
	7:1	The sons of I: Tola, Puah, Jashub, and Shimron,
	7:5	all the families of I were in all eighty-seven
	12:32	Of I men who had understanding of the times,
	12:40	from as far as I and Zebulun and Naphtali,
	26:5	fifth, Ammiel the sixth, I the seventh, Pe-ullethai the
	27:18	of David's brothers; for I, Omri the son of
2Chr	30:18	them from Ephraim, Manasseh, I, and Zebulun, had
Ezek	48:25	side to the west, I, one portion.
	48:26	Adjoining the territory of I, from the east side
	48:33	Simeon, the gate of I, and the gate of
Rev	7:7	of the tribe of I,

ISSHIAH (6)

1Chr	7:3	Michael, Obadiah, Joel, and I, five, all of them
	12:6	Shephatiah the Haruphite; Elkanah, I, Azarel
	23:20	Micah the chief and I the second.
	24:21	the sons of Rehabiah, I the chief.
	24:25	The brother of Micah, I; of the sons of
	24:25	of the sons of I, Zechariah.

ISSHIJAH

Ezra	10:31	sons of Harim: Eliezer, I, Malchijah, Shemaiah,

ISSUE (10)

Deut	21:17	he is the first I of his strength; the
Ps	78:51	in Egypt, the first I of their strength in
	105:36	their land, the first I of all their strength.
Sir	27:28	Mockery and abuse I from the proud man, but
Is	22:24	house, the offspring and I, every small vessel, from
Ezek	23:20	of asses, and whose I was like that of
Dan	12:8	what shall be the I of these things?"
2Mac	4:28	summoned by the king on account of this I
	14:18	shrank from deciding the I by bloodshed.
Rev	4:5	From the throne I flashes of lightning, and voices

ISSUED (13)

Ezra	5:17	whether a decree was I by Cyrus the king
	6:3	king, Cyrus the king I a decree: Concerning the
Esth	3:14	document was to be I as a decree in
	3:15	and the decree was I in Susa the capital.
	4:8	of the written decree I in Susa for their
	8:13	written was to be I as a decree in
	8:14	and the decree was I in Susa the capital.
	9:14	done; a decree was I in Susa, and the
Dan	7:10	A stream of fire I and came forth from
1Mac	5:58	And they I orders to the men of the
2Mac	6:8	Ptolemy a decree was I to the neighboring Greek
Rev	1:16	stars, from his mouth I a sharp two-edged sword,
	9:17	and smoke and sulphur I from their mouths.

ISSUES (3)

1Tim	1:5	charge is love that I from a pure heart
Rev	19:15	From his mouth I a sharp sword with which
	19:21	horse, the sword that I from his mouth; and

ISSUING (3)

Ezek	47:1	and behold, water was I from below the threshold
Rev	9:18	and smoke and sulphur I from their mouths.
	16:13	And I saw, I from the mouth of the

ITALIAN

Acts	10:1	was known as the I Cohort,

ITALY (4)

Acts	18:2	Pontus, lately come from I with his wife Priscilla,
	27:1	we should sail for I, they delivered Paul and
	27:6	of Alexandria sailing for I, and put us on
Heb	13:24	Those who come from I send you greetings.

ITCH (13)

Lev	13:30	unclean; it is an I, a leprosy of the
	13:32	disease; and if the I has not spread, and
	13:32	yellow hair, and the I appears to be no
	13:33	shave himself, but the I he shall not shave;
	13:34	priest shall examine the I, and if the itch
	13:34	itch, and if the I has not spread in
	13:35	But if the I spreads in the skin after
	13:36	him, and if the I has spread in the
	13:37	in his eyes the I is checked, and black
	13:37	grown in it, the I is healed, he is
	14:54	leprous disease: for an I,
	22:22	a discharge or an I or scabs, you shall
Deut	28:27	the scurvy and the I, of which you cannot

ITCHING (5)

Lev	13:31	the priest examines the I disease, and it appears
	13:31	the person with the I disease for seven days,
	13:33	the person with the I disease for seven days
	21:20	his sight or an I disease or scabs or
2Tim	4:3	teaching, but having I ears they will accumulate

ITHAI

1Chr	11:31	of Baanah of Netophah, I the son of Ribai

ITHAMAR (21)

Ex	6:23	and she bore him Nadab, Abihu, Eleazar, and I
	28:1	and Aaron's sons, Nadab and Abihu, Eleazar and I
	38:21	under the direction of I the son of Aaron
Lev	10:6	and to Eleazar and I, his sons, "Do not
	10:12	and to Eleazar and I, his sons who were
	10:16	angry with Eleazar and I, the sons of Aaron
Num	3:2	and Abihu, Eleazar, and I;
	3:4	So Eleazar and I served as priests in the
	4:28	under the oversight of I the son of Aaron

I

4:33 under the hand of I the son of Aaron
7:8 under the direction of I the son of Aaron
26:60 to Aaron were born Nadab, Abihu, Eleazar and I
1Chr 6:3 The sons of Aaron: Nadab, Abihu, Eleazar, and I
24:1 The sons of Aaron: Nadab, Abihu, Eleazar, and I
24:2 children, so Eleazar and I became the priests.
24:3 of the sons of I, David organized them according
24:4 among the sons of I, they organized them under
24:4 of Eleazar, and eight of the sons of I
24:5 the sons of Eleazar and the sons of I
24:6 being chosen for Eleazar and one chosen for I
Ezra 8:2 Of the sons of I, Daniel.

ITHI-EL (3)
Neh 11:7 of Ma-aseiah, son of I, son of Jeshaiah.
Prov 30:1 The man says to I, to Ithi-el and Ucal:
30:1 says to Ithi-el, to I and Ucal:

ITHLAH
Josh 19:42 Eshtaol, Ir-shemesh, Sha-alabbin, Aijalon, I,

ITHMAH
1Chr 11:46 sons of Elna-am, and I the Moabite,

ITHNAN
Josh 15:23 Dimonah, Adadah, Kedesh, Hazor, I,

ITHRA
2Sam 17:25 of a man named I the Ishmaelite, who had

ITHRAN (3)
Gen 36:26 of Dishon: Hemdan, Eshban, I, and Cheran.
1Chr 1:41 of Dishon: Hamran, Eshban, I, and Cheran.
7:37 Bezer, Hod, Shamma, Shilshah, I, and Be-era.

ITHRE-AM
2Sam 3:5 Abital; and the sixth, I, of Eglah, David's wife.

ITHREAM
1Chr 3:3 by Abital; the sixth I, by his wife Eglah;

ITHRITE (4)
2Sam 23:38 of Zeruiah, Ira the I, Gareb the Ithrite,
23:38 the Ithrite, Gareb the I,
1Chr 11:40 of Zeruiah, Ira the I, Gareb the Ithrite,
11:40 the Ithrite, Gareb the I,

ITHRITES
1Chr 2:53 families of Kiriath-jearim: the I, the Puthites, the

ITINERANT
Acts 19:13 Then some of the I Jewish exorcists undertook to

ITSELF (66)
Gen 32:16 servants, every drove by I, and said to his
Ex 25:34 and on the lampstand I four cups made like
37:20 And on the lampstand I were four cups made
Lev 7:24 animal that dies of I, and the fat of
17:15 eats what dies of I or what is torn
22:8 That which dies of I or is torn by
25:5 What grows of I in your harvest you shall
25:11 reap what grows of I, nor gather the grapes
Num 23:9 alone, and not reckoning I among the nations!
23:24 a lion it lifts I; it does not lie
Deut 14:21 anything that dies of I; you may give it
Josh 22:22 knows; and let Israel I know!
Judg 18:1 Danites was seeking for I an inheritance to dwell
2Kgs 19:29 eat what grows of I, and in the second
Ezra 9:2 holy race has mixed I with the peoples of
Jud 8:6 sabbath and the sabbath I, the day before the
Esth 9:6 In Susa the capital I the Jews slew and
Job 6:16 dark with ice, and where the snow hides I
Prov 23:5 suddenly it takes to I wings, flying like an
Eccl 12:5 blossoms, the grasshopper drags I along and desire
Wis 2:11 what is weak proves I to be useless.
13:16 that it cannot help I, for it is only
16:24 hast made it, exerts I to punish the unrighteous,
Sir 13:2 against it, and will I be broken.
Is 10:15 Shall the axe vaunt I over him who hews
10:15 or the saw magnify I against him who wields
37:30 eat what grows of I, and in the second
60:20 nor your moon withdraw I; for the LORD will
Bar 6:15 but it cannot save I from war and robbers.
6:27 upright, it cannot move I; and if it is
6:27 over, it cannot straighten I; but gifts are placed
Ezek 4:14 eaten what died of I or was torn by
5:13 shall my anger spend I, and I will vent
17:14 humble and not lift I up, and that by
29:15 and never again exalt I above the nations; and
44:31 that has died of I or is torn.
Dan 8:11 It magnified I, even up to the Prince of
14:36 den, with the rushing sound of the wind I
Hos 10:6 Yea, the thing I shall be carried to Assyria,
Zech 12:12 mourn, each family by I; the family of the
12:12 house of David by I, and their wives by
12:12 house of Nathan by I, and their wives by
12:13 house of Levi by I, and their wives by
12:13 of the Shimeites by I, and their wives by
12:14 are left, each by I, and their wives by
2Mac 2:32 lengthen the preface while cutting short the history I
5:20 Therefore the place I shared in the misfortunes that
Mt 6:34 about tomorrow, for tomorrow will be anxious for I
12:25 "Every kingdom divided against I is laid waste, and
12:25 or house divided against I will stand;
Mk 3:24 kingdom is divided against I, that kingdom cannot
3:25 house is divided against I, that house will not
4:28 The earth produces of I, first the blade, then
Lk 11:17 "Every kingdom divided against I is laid waste, and
Jn 15:4 cannot bear fruit by I, unless it abides in
20:7 cloths but rolled up in a place by I
21:25 suppose that the world I could not contain the
Rom 8:21 hope; because the creation I will be set free
14:14 nothing is unclean in I; but it is unclean
1Cor 11:14 Does not nature I teach you that for a
2Cor 1:8 unbearably crushed that we despaired of life I
Eph 4:16 bodily growth and upbuilds I in love.
Heb 9:19 sprinkled both the book I and all the people,
9:24 one, but into heaven I, now to appear in
Jas 2:17 So faith by I, if it has no works,
3Jn 1:12 and from the truth I; I testify to him

ITTAI (8)
2Sam 15:19 the king said to I the Gittite, "Why do
15:21 But I answered the king, "As the LORD lives,
15:22 And David said to I, "Go then, pass on."
15:22 So I the Gittite passed on, with all his
18:2 under the command of I the Gittite.
18:5 Joab and Abishai and I, "Deal gently for my
18:12 you and Abishai and I, 'For my sake protect
23:29 of Baanah of Netophah, I the son of Ribai

ITURAEA
Lk 3:1 of the region of I and Trachonitis, and Lysani-as

IVORY (13)
1Kgs 10:18 also made a great I throne, and overlaid it
10:22 come bringing gold, silver, I, apes, and peacocks.
22:39 he did, and the I house which he built,
2Chr 9:17 also made a great I throne, and overlaid it
9:21 come bringing gold, silver, I, apes, and peacocks.
Ps 45:8 From I palaces stringed instruments make you glad;
Song 5:14 His body is I work, encrusted with sapphires.
7:4 neck is like an I tower.
Ezek 27:6 pines from the coasts of Cyprus, inlaid with I
27:15 brought you in payment I tusks and ebony.
Amos 3:15 and the houses of I shall perish, and the
6:4 lie upon beds of I, and stretch themselves upon
Rev 18:12 wood, all articles of I, all articles of costly

IVVAH (3)
2Kgs 18:34 Where are the gods of Sepharvaim, Hena, and I
19:13 the king of Hena, or the king of I
Is 37:13 the king of Hena, or the king of I

IVY
2Mac 6:7 in honor of Dionysus, wearing wreaths of I

IVY-WREATHED
2Mac 10:7 Therefore bearing I wands and beautiful branches

IYE-ABARIM (2)
Num 21:11 Oboth, and encamped at I, in the wilderness which
33:44 Oboth, and encamped at I, in the territory of

IYIM
Num 33:45 they set out from I, and encamped at Dibon-gad.

IZHAR (10)
Ex 6:18 sons of Kohath: Amram, I, Hebron, and Uzziel, the
6:21 The sons of I: Korah, Nepheg, and Zichri.
Num 3:19 by their families: Amram, I, Hebron, and Uzziel.
16:1 Korah the son of I, son of Kohath, son

1Chr	4:7	sons of Helah: Zereth, I, and Ethnan.
	6:2	sons of Kohath: Amram, I, Hebron, and Uzziel.
	6:18	sons of Kohath: Amram, I, Hebron, and Uzziel.
	6:38	of Korah, son of I, son of Kohath, son
	23:12	sons of Kohath: Amram, I, Hebron, and Uzziel, four.
	23:18	The sons of I: Shelomith the chief.

IZHARITES (4)

Num	3:27	the family of the I, and the family of
1Chr	24:22	Of the I, Shelomoth; of the sons of Shelomoth,
	26:23	Of the Amramites, the I, the Hebronites, and the
	26:29	Of the I, Chenaniah and his sons were appointed

IZLIAH

1Chr	8:18	Hizki, Heber, Ishmerai, I, and Jobab were the

IZRAHIAH (2)

1Chr	7:3	The sons of Uzzi: I
	7:3	And the sons of I: Michael, Obadiah, Joel, and

IZRAHITE

1Chr	27:8	month, was Shamhuth, the I; in his division were

IZRI

1Chr	25:11	twelve; the fourth to I, his sons and his

IZZIAH

Ezra	10:25	sons of Parosh: Ramiah, I, Malchijah, Mijamin,

J

JA-AKOBAH

1Chr	4:36	son of Asiel, Eli-o-enai, J, Jeshohaiah, Asaiah, Adi-el,

JA-ARESHIAH

1Chr	8:27	Shehariah, Athaliah, J, Elijah, and Zichri were

JA-AZANIAH (4)

2Kgs	25:23	Tanhumeth the Netophathite, and J the son of the
Jer	35:3	So I took J the son of Jeremiah, son
Ezek	8:11	house of Israel, with J the son of Shaphan
	11:1	I saw among them J the son of Azzur,

JA-AZIAH (2)

1Chr	24:26	The sons of J: Beno.
	24:27	sons of Merari: of J, Beno, Shoham, Zaccur, and

JA-AZIEL

1Chr	15:18	the second order, Zechariah, J, Shemiramoth, Jehiel,

JAAKAN

1Chr	1:42	The sons of Ezer: Bilhan, Zaavan, and J

JAALA

Neh	7:58	Perida, the sons of J, the sons of Darkon,

JAALAH

Ezra	2:56	Peruda, the sons of J, the sons of Darkon,

JAAR

Ps	132:6	Ephrathah, we found it in the fields of J

JAAREOREGIM

2Sam	21:19	Elhanan the son of J, the Bethlehemite, slew Goliath

JAASIEL (2)

1Chr	11:47	Eliel, and Obed, and J the Mezoba-ite.
	27:21	of Zechariah; for Benjamin, J the son of Abner;

JAASU

Ezra	10:37	Meremoth, Eliashib, Mattaniah, Mattenai, J

JABAL

Gen	4:20	Adah bore J; he was the father of those

JABBOK (7)

Gen	32:22	eleven children, and crossed the ford of the J
Num	21:24	the Arnon to the J, as far as to
Deut	2:37	banks of the river J and the cities of
	3:16	over as the river J, the boundary of the
Josh	12:2	far as the river J, the boundary of the
Judg	11:13	the Arnon to the J and to the Jordan;
	11:22	the Arnon to the J and from the wilderness

JABESH (12)

1Sam	11:1	all the men of J said to Nahash, "Make
	11:3	The elders of J said to him, "Give us
	11:5	told him the tidings of the men of J
	11:9	told the men of J, they were glad.
	11:10	Therefore the men of J said, "Tomorrow we will
	31:12	and they came to J and burnt them there.
	31:13	the tamarisk tree in J, and fasted seven days.
2Kgs	15:10	Shallum the son of J conspired against him, and
	15:13	Shallum the son of J began to reign in
	15:14	Shallum the son of J in Samaria and slew
1Chr	10:12	bodies of his sons, and brought them to J
	10:12	under the oak in J, and fasted seven days.

JABESH-GILEAD (12)

Judg	21:8	to the camp from J, to the assembly.
	21:9	of the inhabitants of J was there.
	21:10	smite the inhabitants of J with the edge of
	21:12	the inhabitants of J four hundred young virgins
	21:14	of the women of J; but they did not
1Sam	11:1	went up and besieged J; and all the men
	11:9	to the men of J: 'Tomorrow, by the time
	31:11	when the inhabitants of J heard what the Philistines
2Sam	2:4	was the men of J who buried Saul,"
	2:5	to the men of J, and said to them,
	21:12	from the men of J, who had stolen them
1Chr	10:11	But when all J heard all that the Philistines

JABEZ (4)

1Chr	2:55	scribes that dwelt at J: the Tirathites, the
	4:9	J was more honorable than his brothers; and his
	4:9	mother called his name J, saying, "Because I bore
	4:10	J called on the God of Israel, saying, "Oh

JABIN (9)

Josh	11:1	When J king of Hazor heard of this, he
Judg	4:2	into the hand of J king of Canaan, who
	4:7	Sisera, the general of J's army, to meet you
	4:17	there was peace between J the king of Hazor
	4:23	that day God subdued J the king of Canaan
	4:24	harder and harder on J the king of Canaan,
	4:24	Canaan, until they destroyed J king of Canaan.
1Sam	12:9	of the army of J king of Hazor, and
Ps	83:9	as to Sisera and J at the river Kishon,

JABNEEL (2)

Josh	15:11	and goes out to J; then the boundary comes
	19:33	Za-anannim, and Adami-nekeb, and J, as far as

JABNEH

2Chr	26:6	and the wall of J and the wall of

JACAN

1Chr	5:13	Michael, Meshullam, Sheba, Jorai, J, Zia, and Eber,

JACHIN (8)

Gen	46:10	Simeon: Jemuel, Jamin, Ohad, J, Zohar, and Shaul,
Ex	6:15	Simeon: Jemuel, Jamin, Ohad, J, Zohar, and Shaul,
Num	26:12	of the Jaminites; of J, the family of the
1Kgs	7:21	and called its name J; and he set up
1Chr	9:10	the priests: Jedaiah, Jehoiarib, J,
	24:17	Jehezkel, the twenty-first to J, the twenty-second to
2Chr	3:17	the south he called J, and that on the
Neh	11:10	the son of Joiarib, J,

JACHINITES

Num	26:12	the family of the J;

JACINTH (3)

Ex	28:19	the third row a J, an agate, and an
	39:12	the third row, a J, an agate, and an
Rev	21:20	tenth chrysoprase, the eleventh J, the twelfth

JACKAL

Neh	2:13	Valley Gate to the J's Well and to the

JACKALS (16)

Job	30:29	am a brother of J, and a companion of
Ps	44:19	in the place of J, and covered us with
	63:10	of the sword, they shall be prey for J
Is	13:22	in its towers, and J in the pleasant palaces;
	34:13	be the haunt of J, an abode for ostriches.
	35:7	water; the haunt of J shall become a swamp,
	43:20	will honor me, the J and the ostriches; for
Jer	9:11	ruins, a lair of J; and I will make
	10:22	cities of Judah a desolation, a lair of J

I

J

	14:6	pant for air like J; their eyes fail because
	49:33	become a haunt of J, an everlasting waste; no
	51:37	ruins, the haunt of J, a horror and a
Lam	4:3	Even the J give the breast and suckle their
	5:18	Zion which lies desolate; J prowl over it.
Mic	1:8	make lamentation like the J, and mourning like the
Mal	1:3	left his heritage to J of the desert."

JACOB (406)

Gen	25:26	of Esau's heel; so his name was called J
	25:27	of the field, while J was a quiet man,
	25:28	he ate of his game; but Rebekah loved J
	25:29	Once when J was boiling pottage, Esau came in
	25:30	And Esau said to J, "Let me eat some
	25:31	) J said, "First sell me your birthright."
	25:33	J said, "Swear to me first." So he swore
	25:33	swore to him, and sold his birthright to J
	25:34	Then J gave Esau bread and pottage of lentils,
	27:6	said to her son J, "I heard your father
	27:11	But J said to Rebekah his mother, "Behold, my
	27:15	and put them on J her younger son;
	27:17	had prepared, into the hand of her son J
	27:19	J said to his father, "I am Esau your
	27:21	Then Isaac said to J, "Come near, that I
	27:22	So J went near to Isaac his father, who
	27:22	said, "The voice is J's voice, but the hands
	27:30	Isaac had finished blessing J, when J had
	27:36	Esau said, "Is he not rightly named J
	27:41	Now Esau hated J because of the blessing with
	27:41	are approaching; then I will kill my brother J
	27:42	she sent and called J her younger son, and
	27:46	If J marries one of the Hittite women such
	28:1	Then Isaac called J and blessed him, and charged
	28:5	Thus Isaac sent J away; and he went to
	28:5	the brother of Rebekah, J's and Esau's mother.
	28:6	that Isaac had blessed J and sent him away
	28:7	and that J had obeyed his father and his
	28:10	J left Beer-sheba, and went toward Haran.
	28:16	Then J awoke from his sleep and said, "Surely
	28:18	So J rose early in the morning, and he
	28:20	Then J made a vow, saying, "If God will
	29:1	Then J went on his journey, and came to
	29:4	J said to them, "My brothers, where do you
	29:10	Now when J saw Rachel the daughter of Laban
	29:10	Laban his mother's brother, J went up and rolled
	29:11	Then J kissed Rachel, and wept aloud.
	29:12	And J told Rachel that he was her father's
	29:13	heard the tidings of J his sister's son, he
	29:13	J told Laban all these things,
	29:15	Then Laban said to J, "Because you are my
	29:18	J loved Rachel; and he said, "I will serve
	29:20	So J served seven years for Rachel, and they
	29:21	Then J said to Laban, "Give me my wife
	29:23	and brought her to J; and he went in
	29:25	it was Leah; and J said to Laban, "What
	29:28	J did so, and completed her week; then Laban
	29:30	be her maid.) So J went in to Rachel
	30:1	saw that she bore J no children, she envied
	30:1	and she said to J, "Give me children, or
	30:2	J's anger was kindled against Rachel, and he said,
	30:4	as a wife; and J went in to her.
	30:5	Bilhah conceived and bore J a son.
	30:7	conceived again and bore J a second son.
	30:9	and gave her to J as a wife.
	30:10	Leah's maid Zilpah bore J a son.
	30:12	Leah's maid Zilpah bore J a second son.
	30:16	When J came from the field in the evening,
	30:17	she conceived and bore J a fifth son.
	30:19	again, and she bore J a sixth son.
	30:25	Rachel had borne Joseph, J said to Laban, "Send
	30:29	J said to him, "You yourself know how I
	30:31	J said, "You shall not give me anything; if
	30:36	journey between himself and J; and Jacob fed the
	30:36	himself and Jacob; and J fed the rest of
	30:37	Then J took fresh rods of poplar and almond
	30:40	And J separated the lambs, and set the faces
	30:41	the flock were breeding J laid the rods in
	31:1	Now J heard that the sons of Laban were
	31:1	of Laban were saying, J has taken all that
	31:2	And J saw that Laban did not regard him
	31:3	the LORD said to J, "Return to the land
	31:4	So J sent and called Rachel and Leah into
	31:11	me in the dream, J and I said, 'Here
	31:17	So J arose, and set his sons and his
	31:20	And J outwitted Laban the Aramean, in that he
	31:22	the third day that J had fled,
	31:24	not a word to J, either good or bad."
	31:25	And Laban overtook J
	31:25	Now J had pitched his tent in the hill
	31:26	And Laban said to J, "What have you done,
	31:29	that you speak to J neither good nor bad.'
	31:31	J answered Laban, "Because I was afraid, for I
	31:32	Now J did not know that Rachel had stolen
	31:33	So Laban went into J's tent, and into Leah's
	31:36	Then J became angry, and upbraided Laban; Jacob
	31:36	angry, and upbraided Laban; J said to Laban, "What
	31:43	answered and said to J, "The daughters are my
	31:45	So J took a stone, and set it up
	31:46	And J said to his kinsmen, "Gather stones," and
	31:47	called it Jegar-sahadutha: but J called it Galeed.
	31:51	Then Laban said to J, "See this heap and
	31:53	So J swore by the Fear of his father
	31:54	his father Isaac, and J offered a sacrifice on
	32:1	J went on his way and the angels of
	32:2	met him; and when J saw them he said,
	32:3	And J sent messengers before him to Esau his
	32:4	Thus says your servant J, 'I have sojourned with
	32:6	the messengers returned to J, saying, "We came to
	32:7	Then J was greatly afraid and distressed; and he
	32:9	And J said, "O God of my father Abraham
	32:18	belong to your servant J; they are a present
	32:20	say, 'Moreover your servant J is behind us.'" For
	32:24	And J was left alone; and a man wrestled
	32:25	did not prevail against J, he touched the hollow
	32:25	of his thigh; and J's thigh was put out
	32:26	But J said, "I will not let you go,
	32:27	And he said, J
	32:28	no more be called J, but Israel, for you
	32:29	Then J asked him, "Tell me, I pray, your
	32:30	So J called the name of the place Peniel,
	32:32	touched the hollow of J's thigh on the sinew
	33:1	And J lifted up his eyes and looked, and
	33:5	J said, "The children whom God has graciously given
	33:8	J answered, "To find favor in the sight of
	33:10	J said, "No, I pray you, if I have
	33:13	But J said to him, "My lord knows that
	33:17	But J journeyed to Succoth, and built himself a
	33:18	And J came safely to the city of Shechem,
	34:1	she had borne to J, went out to visit
	34:3	Dinah the daughter of J; he loved the maiden
	34:5	Now J heard that he had defiled his daughter
	34:5	in the field, so J held his peace until
	34:6	Shechem went out to J to speak with him.
	34:7	The sons of J came in from the field
	34:7	Israel by lying with J's daughter, for such a
	34:13	The sons of J answered Shechem and his father
	34:19	he had delight in J's daughter.
	34:25	of the sons of J, Simeon and Levi, Dinah's
	34:27	And the sons of J came upon the slain,
	34:30	Then J said to Simeon and Levi, "You have
	35:1	God said to J, "Arise, go up to Bethel,
	35:2	So J said to his household and to all
	35:4	So they gave to J all the foreign gods
	35:4	in their ears; and J hid them under the
	35:5	that they did not pursue the sons of J
	35:6	And J came to Luz (that is, Bethel), which
	35:9	God appeared to J again, when he came from
	35:10	him, "Your name is J; no longer shall your
	35:10	your name be called J, but Israel shall be
	35:14	And J set up a pillar in the place
	35:15	So J called the name of the place where
	35:20	(that is, Bethlehem), and J set up a pillar
	35:22	Now the sons of J were twelve.
	35:23	sons of Leah: Reuben J's first-born), Simeon, Levi,
	35:26	were the sons of J who were born to
	35:27	And J came to his father Isaac at Mamre,
	35:29	his sons Esau and J buried him.
	36:6	went into a land away from his brother J
	37:1	J dwelt in the land of his father's sojournings,
	37:2	This is the history of the family of J
	37:34	Then J rent his garments, and put sackcloth upon
	42:1	When J learned that there was grain in Egypt,
	42:4	But J did not send Benjamin, Joseph's brother, with
	42:29	When they came to J their father in the
	42:36	And J their father said to them, "You have
	45:25	to the land of Canaan to their father J
	45:27	spirit of their father J revived;
	46:2	the night, and said, J, Jacob." And he said,
	46:2	in visions of the night, and said, "Jacob, J
	46:5	Then J set out from Beer-sheba; and the sons
	46:5	sons of Israel carried J their father, their little
	46:6	and came into Egypt, J and all his offspring

46:8 who came into Egypt, J and his sons.
46:8 Reuben, J's first-born,
46:15 whom she bore to J in Paddan-aram, together with
46:18 these she bore to J –sixteen persons).
46:19 The sons of Rachel, J's wife: Joseph and Benjamin.
46:22 who were born to J –fourteen persons in all).
46:25 these she bore to J –seven persons in all).
46:26 the persons belonging to J who came into Egypt,
46:26 offspring, not including J's sons' wives, were sixty-six
46:27 of the house of J, that came into Egypt,
47:7 Then Joseph brought in J his father, and set
47:7 him before Pharaoh, and J blessed Pharaoh.
47:8 And Pharaoh said to J, "How many are the
47:9 And J said to Pharaoh, "The days of the
47:10 And J blessed Pharaoh, and went out from the
47:28 And J lived in the land of Egypt seventeen
47:28 so the days of J, the years of his
48:2 it was told to J, "Your son Joseph has
48:3 And J said to Joseph, "God Almighty appeared to
49:1 Then J called his sons, and said, "Gather yourselves
49:2 hear, O sons of J, and hearken to Israel
49:7 will divide them in J and scatter them in
49:24 the Mighty One of J (by the name of
49:33 When J finished charging his sons, he drew up
50:24 he swore to Abraham, to Isaac, and to J
Ex 1:1 came to Egypt with J, each with his household:
1:4 All the offspring of J were seventy persons; Joseph
2:24 his covenant with Abraham, with Isaac, and with J
3:6 the God of Isaac, and the God of J
3:15 and the God of J, has sent me to
3:16 of Isaac, and of J, has appeared to me,
4:5 and the God of J, has appeared to you."
6:3 to Isaac, and to J, as God Almighty, but
6:8 to Isaac, and to J; I will give it
19:3 to the house of J, and tell the people
33:1 Abraham, Isaac, and J, saying, 'To your descendants
Lev 26:42 remember my covenant with J, and I will remember
Num 23:7 eastern mountains: 'Come, curse J for me, and come,
23:10 count the dust of J, or number the fourth
23:21 not beheld misfortune in J; nor has he seen
23:23 enchantment against J, no divination against Israel;
23:23 shall be said of J and Israel, 'What has
24:5 are your tents, O J, your encampments, O Israel!
24:17 come forth out of J, and a scepter shall
24:19 By J shall dominion be exercised, and the survivors
32:11 to Isaac, and to J, because they have not
Deut 1:8 to Isaac, and to J, to give to them
6:10 to Isaac, and to J, to give you, with
9:5 your fathers, to Abraham, to Isaac, and to J
9:27 servants, Abraham, Isaac, and J; do not regard the
29:13 your fathers, to Abraham, to Isaac, and to J
30:20 to Isaac, and to J, to give them."
32:9 portion is his people, J his allotted heritage.
33:4 law, as a possession for the assembly of J
33:10 They shall teach J thy ordinances, and Israel thy
33:28 safety, the fountain of J alone, in a land
34:4 to Isaac, and to J, 'I will give it
Josh 24:4 to Isaac I gave J and Esau.
24:4 Seir to possess, but J and his children went
24:32 portion of ground which J bought from the sons
1Sam 12:8 J went into Egypt and the Egyptians oppressed
2Sam 23:1 of the God of J, the sweet psalmist of
1Kgs 18:31 of the sons of J, to whom the word
2Kgs 13:23 with Abraham, Isaac, and J, and would not destroy
17:34 the children of J, whom he named Israel.
1Chr 16:13 his servant, sons of J, his chosen ones!
16:17 as a statute to J, as an everlasting covenant
Tob 4:12 Noah, Abraham, Isaac, and J, our fathers of old,
Jud 8:26 and what happened to J in Mesopotamia in Syria,
Ps 14:7 fortunes of his people, J shall rejoice, Israel shall
20:1 of the God of J protect you!
22:23 all you sons of J, glorify him, and stand
24:6 who seek the face of the God of J
44:4 King and my God, who ordainest victories for J
46:7 us; the God of J is our refuge.
46:11 us; the God of J is our refuge.
47:4 us, the pride of J whom he loves.
53:6 fortunes of his people, J will rejoice and Israel
59:13 that God rules over J to the ends of
75:9 I will sing praises to the God of J
76:6 rebuke, O God of J, both rider and horse
77:15 people, the sons of J and Joseph.
78:5 established a testimony in J, and appointed a law
78:21 fire was kindled against J, his anger mounted against
78:71 be the shepherd of J his people, of Israel
79:7 For they have devoured J, and laid waste his
81:1 strength; shout for joy to the God of J
81:4 for Israel, an ordinance of the God of J
84:8 hear my prayer; give ear, O God of J
85:1 thy land; thou didst restore the fortunes of J
87:2 Zion more than all the dwelling places of J
94:7 see; the God of J does not perceive."
99:4 thou hast executed justice and righteousness in J
105:6 his servant, sons of J, his chosen ones!
105:10 which he confirmed to J as a statute, to
105:23 Israel came to Egypt; J sojourned in the land
114:1 Egypt, the house of J from a people of
114:7 of the God of J,
132:2 the Mighty One of J,
132:5 a dwelling place for the Mighty One of J
135:4 the LORD has chosen J for himself, Israel as
146:5 is the God of J, whose hope is in
147:19 declares his word to J, his statutes and ordinances
Sir 23:12 it never be found in the inheritance of J
24:8 'Make your dwelling in J, and in Israel receive
24:22 us as an inheritance for the congregations of J
36:11 all the tribes of J, and give them their
44:24 upon the head of J; he acknowledged him with
45:5 and knowledge, to teach J the covenant, and Israel
45:17 and judgments, to teach J the testimonies, and to
46:14 the congregation, and the Lord watched over J
47:22 gave a remnant to J, and to David a
48:10 the son, and to restore the tribes of J
49:10 comforted the people of J and delivered them with
Is 2:3 of the God of J; that he may teach
2:5 O house of J, come, let us walk in
2:6 people, the house of J, because they are full
8:17 from the house of J, and I will hope
9:8 sent a word against J, and it will light
10:20 of the house of J will no more lean
10:21 return, the remnant of J, to the mighty God.
14:1 will have compassion on J and will again choose
14:1 them and will cleave to the house of J
17:4 day the glory of J will be brought low,
27:6 In days to come J shall take root, Israel
27:9 this the guilt of J will be expiated, and
29:22 concerning the house of J: "Jacob shall no more
29:22 the house of Jacob: J shall no more be
29:23 the Holy One of J, and will stand in
40:27 do you say, O J, and speak, O Israel,
41:8 you, Israel, my servant, J, whom I have chosen,
41:14 Fear not, you worm J, you men of Israel!
41:21 LORD; bring your proofs, says the King of J
42:24 Who gave up J to the spoiler, and Israel
43:1 who created you, O J, he who formed you,
43:22 call upon me, O J; but you have been
43:28 the sanctuary, I delivered J to utter destruction and
44:1 "But now hear, O J my servant, Israel whom
44:2 you: Fear not, O J my servant, Jeshurun whom
44:5 by the name of J, and another will write
44:21 Remember these things, O J, and Israel, for you
44:23 the LORD has redeemed J, and will be glorified
45:4 sake of my servant J, and Israel my chosen,
45:19 to the offspring of J, 'Seek me in chaos.'
46:3 me, O house of J, all the remnant of
48:1 this, O house of J, who are called by
48:12 "Hearken to me, O J, and Israel, whom I
48:20 earth; say, "The LORD has redeemed his servant J
49:5 his servant, to bring J back to him, and
49:6 up the tribes of J and to restore the
49:26 Savior, and your Redeemer, the Mighty One of J
58:1 to the house of J their sins.
58:14 with the heritage of J your father, for the
59:20 Redeemer, to those in J who turn from transgression,
60:16 Savior and your Redeemer, the Mighty One of J
65:9 bring forth descendants from J, and from Judah
Jer 2:4 LORD, O house of J, and all the families
5:20 in the house of J, proclaim it in Judah:
10:16 is the portion of J, for he is the
10:25 for they have devoured J; they have devoured him
30:7 time of distress for J; yet he shall be
30:10 "Then fear not, O J my servant, says the
30:10 J shall return and have quiet and ease, and
30:18 of the tents of J, and have compassion on
31:7 aloud with gladness for J, and raise shouts for
31:11 the LORD has ransomed J, and has redeemed him
33:26 reject the descendants of J and David my servant
33:26 rule over the seed of Abraham, Isaac, and J
46:27 "But fear not, O J my servant, nor be
46:27 J shall return and have quiet and ease, and
46:28 Fear not, O J my servant, says the LORD,
51:19 is the portion of J, for he is the

Lam 1:17 LORD has commanded against J that his neighbors
2:2 all the habitations of J; in his wrath he
2:3 a flaming fire in J, consuming all around.
Bar 2:34 to Isaac and to J, and they will rule
3:36 and gave her to J his servant and to
4:2 Turn, O J, and take her; walk toward the
Ezek 20:5 of the house of J, making myself known to
28:25 own land which I gave to my servant J
37:25 gave to my servant J; they and their children
39:25 restore the fortunes of J, and have mercy upon
Hos 10:11 yoke, Judah must plow, J must harrow for himself.
12:2 Judah, and will punish J according to his ways,
12:12 J fled to the land of Aram, there Israel
Amos 3:13 "Hear, and testify against the house of J
6:8 abhor the pride of J, and hate his strongholds;
7:2 How can J stand?
7:5 How can J stand?
8:7 by the pride of J: "Surely I will never
9:8 I will not utterly destroy the house of J
Obad 1:10 done to your brother J, shame shall cover you,
1:17 and the house of J shall possess their own
1:18 The house of J shall be a fire, and
Mic 1:5 for the transgression of J and for the sins
1:5 What is the transgression of J
2:7 Should this be said, O house of J
2:12 all of you, O J, I will gather the
3:1 Hear, you heads of J and rulers of the
3:8 might, to declare to J his transgression and to
3:9 of the house of J and rulers of the
4:2 of the God of J; that he may teach
5:7 Then the remnant of J shall be in the
5:8 And the remnant of J shall be among the
7:20 wilt show faithfulness to J and steadfast love to
Nah 2:2 restoring the majesty of J as the majesty of
Mal 1:2 "Is not Esau J's brother?" says the LORD.
1:2 "Yet I have loved J
2:12 from the tents of J, for the man who
3:6 you, O sons of J, are not consumed.
1Mac 1:28 all the house of J was clothed with shame.
3:7 kings, but he made J glad by his deeds,
3:45 Joy was taken from J; the flute and the
5:2 destroy the descendants of J who lived among them.
2Mac 1:2 Abraham and Isaac and J, his faithful servants.
Mt 1:2 Isaac the father of J, and Jacob the father
1:2 father of Jacob, and J the father of Judah
1:15 Matthan the father of J,
1:16 father of Jacob, and J the father of Joseph
8:11 with Abraham, Isaac, and J in the kingdom of
22:32 the God of Isaac, and the God of J
Mk 12:26 the God of Isaac, and the God of J
Lk 1:33 over the house of J for ever; and of
3:34 Judah, the son of J, the son of Isaac,
13:28 Abraham and Isaac and J and all the prophets
20:37 the God of Isaac and the God of J
Jn 4:5 near the field that J gave to his son
4:6 J's well was there, and so Jesus, wearied as
4:12 greater than our father J, who gave us the
Acts 3:13 of Isaac and of J, the God of our
7:8 became the father of J, and Jacob of the
7:8 father of Jacob, and J of the twelve patriarchs.
7:12 But when J heard that there was grain in
7:14 and called to him J his father and all
7:15 seventy-five souls; and J went down into Egypt.
7:32 of Isaac and of J And Moses trembled and
7:46 to find a habitation for the God of J
Rom 9:13 As it is written, J I loved, but Esau
11:26 will banish ungodliness from J;
Heb 11:9 tents with Isaac and J, heirs with him of
11:20 invoked future blessings on J and Esau.
11:21 By faith J, when dying, blessed each of the

JACOBS
Gen 30:42 so the feebler were Labans, and the stronger J

JADA (2)
1Chr 2:28 The sons of Onam: Shammai and J
2:32 The sons of J, Shammai's brother: Jether and

JADDAI
Ezra 10:43 Je-iel, Mattithiah, Zabad, Zebina, J, Joel, and

JADDU-A (3)
Neh 10:21 Meshullam, Hezir, Meshezabel, Zadok, J,
12:11 father of Jonathan, and Jonathan the father of J
12:22 Eliashib, Joiada, Johanan, and J, there were

JADON
Neh 3:7 Melatiah the Gibeonite and J the Meronothite, the

JAEL (6)
Judg 4:17 to the tent of J, the wife of Heber
4:18 And J came out to meet Sisera, and said
4:21 But J the wife of Heber took a tent
4:22 as Barak pursued Sisera, J went out to meet
5:6 in the days of J, caravans ceased and travelers
5:24 blessed of women be J, the wife of Heber

JAGUR
Josh 15:21 Edom, were Kabzeel, Eder, J,

JAHATH (8)
1Chr 4:2 was the father of J, and Jahath was the
4:2 father of Jahath, and J was the father of
6:20 Gershom: Libni his son, J his son, Zimmah his
6:43 of Shimei, son of J, son of Gershom, son
23:10 the sons of Shimei: J, Zina, and Jeush, and
23:11 J was the chief, and Zizah the second; but
24:22 the Izharites, Shelomoth; of the sons of Shelomoth,
2Chr 34:12 Over them were set J and Obadiah the Levites,

JAHAZ (7)
Num 21:23 wilderness, and came to J, and fought against Israel.
Deut 2:32 he and all his people, to battle at J
Josh 13:18 Bamoth-baal, and Beth-baal-meon, and J, and
21:36 with its pasture lands, J with its pasture lands,
Judg 11:20 together, and encamped at J, and fought with Israel.
Is 15:4 heard as far as J; therefore the armed men
Jer 48:34 out; as far as J they utter their voice,

JAHAZIEL (6)
1Chr 12:4 over the thirty; Jeremiah, J, Johanan, Jozabad of
16:6 cymbals, and Benaiah and J the priests were to
23:19 chief, Amariah the second, J the third, and
24:23 chief, Amariah the second, J the third, Jekameam
2Chr 20:14 the LORD came upon J the son of Zechariah,
Ezra 8:5 Shecaniah the son of J, and with him three

JAHDAI
1Chr 2:47 The sons of J: Regem, Jotham, Geshan, Pelet,

JAHDI-EL
1Chr 5:24 Azriel, Jeremiah, Hodaviah, and J, mighty warriors,

JAHDO
1Chr 5:14 of Jeshishai, son of J, son of Buz;

JAHLEEL (2)
Gen 46:14 Zebulun: Sered, Elon, and J
Num 26:26 of the Elonites; of J, the family of the

JAHLEELITES
Num 26:26 the Elonites; of Jahleel, the family of the J

JAHMAI
1Chr 7:2 Tola: Uzzi, Rephaiah, Jeri-el, J, Ibsam, and Shemuel,

JAHZAH (2)
1Chr 6:78 with its pasture lands, J with its pasture lands,
Jer 48:21 tableland, upon Holon, and J, and Mephaath,

JAHZEEL (2)
Gen 46:24 The sons of Naphtali: J, Guni, Jezer, and Shillem
Num 26:48 to their families: of J, the family of the

JAHZEELITES
Num 26:48 the family of the J; of Guni, the family

JAHZEIAH
Ezra 10:15 son of Asahel and J the son of Tikvah

JAHZERAH
1Chr 9:12 of Adi-el, son of J, son of Meshullam, son

JAHZI-EL
1Chr 7:13 The sons of Naphtali: J, Guni, Jezer, and Shallum,

JAILER (3)
Acts 16:23 into prison, charging the J to keep them safely.
16:27 When the J woke and saw that the prison
16:36 And the J reported the words to Paul, saying,

JAILERS
Mt 18:33 delivered him to the J, till he should pay

JAIR (10)
Num 32:41 And J the son of Manasseh went and took
Deut 3:14 J the Manassite took all the region of Argob,
Josh 13:30 all the towns of J, which are in Bashan,
Judg 10:3 After him arose J the Gileadite, who judged Israel
10:5 And J died, and was buried in Kamon.
1Kgs 4:13 had the villages of J the son of Manasseh,
1Chr 2:22 was the father of J, who had twenty-three cities
20:5 Elhanan the son of J slew Lahmi the brother
Esth 2:5 Mordecai, the son of J, son of Shimei, son
11:2 Mordecai the son of J, son of Shimei, son

JAIRITE
2Sam 20:26 priests; and Ira the J was also David's priest.

JAIRUS (2)
Mk 5:22 rulers of the synagogue, J by name; and seeing
Lk 8:41 came a man named J, who was a ruler

JAKEH
Prov 30:1 of Agur son of J of Massa.

JAKIM (2)
1Chr 8:19 J, Zichri, Zabdi,
24:12 Eliashib, the twelfth to J,

JALAM (4)
Gen 36:5 and Oholibamah bore Jeush, J, and Korah.
36:14 bore to Esau Jeush, J, and Korah.
36:18 wife: the chiefs Jeush, J, and Korah; these are
1Chr 1:35 Esau: Eliphaz, Reuel, Jeush, J, and Korah.

JALON
1Chr 4:17 The sons of Ezrah: Jether, Mered, Epher, and J

JAMBRES
2Tim 3:8 As Jannes and J opposed Moses, so these men

JAMBRI (2)
1Mac 9:36 But the sons of J from Medeba came out
9:37 brother, "The sons of J are celebrating a great

JAMBS (18)
Ezek 40:9 eight cubits; and its J, two cubits; and the
40:10 same size; and the J on either side were
40:16 narrowing inwards into their J in the side rooms,
40:16 inside, and on the J were palm trees.
40:21 either side, and its J and its vestibule were
40:24 and he measured its J and its vestibule; they
40:26 palm trees on its J, one on either side.
40:29 Its side rooms, its J, and its vestibule were
40:31 trees were on its J, and its stairway had
40:33 Its side rooms, its J, and its vestibule were
40:34 palm trees on its J, one on either side;
40:36 Its side rooms, its J, and its vestibule were
40:37 palm trees on its J, one on either side;
40:48 temple and measured the J of the vestibule, five
40:49 were pillars beside the J on either side.
41:1 nave, and measured the J; on each side six
41:1 side six cubits was the breadth of the J
41:3 room and measured the J of the entrance, two

JAMES (42)
Mt 4:21 saw two other brothers, J the son of Zebedee
10:2 and Andrew his brother; J the son of Zebedee,
10:3 Matthew the tax collector; J the son of Alphaeus,
13:55 are not his brethren J and Joseph and Simon
17:1 with him Peter and J and John his brother,
27:56 Mary the mother of J and Joseph, and the
Mk 1:19 little farther, he saw J the son of Zebedee
1:29 Simon and Andrew, with J and John.
3:17 whom he surnamed Peter; J the son of Zebedee
3:17 the brother of J, whom he surnamed Bo-anerges,
3:18 Matthew, and Thomas, and J the son of Alphaeus,
5:37 him except Peter and J and John the brother
5:37 Peter and James and John the brother of J
6:3 Mary and brother of J and Joses and Judas
9:2 with him Peter and J and John, and led
10:35 And J and John, the sons of Zebedee, came
10:41 to be indignant at J and John.
13:3 the temple, Peter and J and John and Andrew
14:33 with him Peter and J and John, and began
15:39 Mary the mother of J the younger and of
16:1 Mary the mother of J, and Salome, bought spices,
Lk 5:10 and so also were J and John, sons of
6:14 Andrew his brother, and J and John, and Philip,
6:15 Matthew, and Thomas, and J the son of Alphaeus,
6:16 Judas the son of J, and Judas Iscariot, who
8:51 Peter and John and J, and the father and
9:28 Peter and John and J, and went up on
9:54 And when his disciples J and John saw it,
24:10 Mary the mother of J and the other women
Acts 1:13 Peter and John and J and Andrew, Philip and
1:13 Bartholomew and Matthew, J the son of Alphaeus
1:13 Simon the Zealot and Judas the son of J
12:2 He killed J the brother of John with the
12:17 said, "Tell this to J and to the brethren."
15:13 After they finished speaking, J replied, "Brethren,
21:18 in with us to J; and all the elders
1Cor 15:7 Then he appeared to J, then to all the
Gal 1:19 the other apostles except J the Lord's brother.
2:9 was given to me, J and Cephas and John,
2:12 certain men came from J, he ate with the
Jas 1:1 J, a servant of God
Jude 1:1 Christ and brother of J, to those who are

JAMIN (6)
Gen 46:10 sons of Simeon: Jemuel, J, Ohad, Jachin, Zohar, and
Ex 6:15 sons of Simeon: Jemuel, J, Ohad, Jachin, Zohar, and
Num 26:12 of the Nemuelites; of J, the family of the
1Chr 2:27 first-born of Jerahmeel: Maaz, J, and Eker.
4:24 sons of Simeon: Nemuel, J, Jarib, Zerah, Shaul;
Neh 8:7 Also Jeshua, Bani, Sherebiah, J, Akkub, Shabbethai,

J

JAMINITES
Num 26:12 the family of the J; of Jachin, the family

JAMLECH
1Chr 4:34 Meshobab, J, Joshah the son of Amaziah,

JAMNIA (8)
Jud 2:28 Sur and Ocina and all who lived in J
1Mac 4:15 and to Azotus and J; and three thousand of
5:58 that were with them, and they marched against J
10:69 he assembled a large force and encamped against J
15:40 So Cendebeus came to J and began to provoke
2Mac 12:8 that the men in J meant in the same
12:9 attacked the people of J by night and set
12:40 of the idols of J, which the law forbids

JAN-OAH (3)
Josh 16:6 on the east to J,
16:7 it goes down from J to Ataroth and to
2Kgs 15:29 captured Ijon, Abel-beth-maacah, J, Kedesh, Hazor,

JANAI
1Chr 5:12 chief, Shapham the second, J, and Shaphat in

JANIM
Josh 15:53 Arab, Dumah, Eshan, J, Beth-tappuah, Aphekah,

JANNA-I
Lk 3:24 Melchi, the son of J, the son of Joseph,

JANNES
2Tim 3:8 As J and Jambres opposed Moses, so these men

JAPHETH (13)
Gen 5:32 Noah became the father of Shem, Ham, and J
6:10 And Noah had three sons, Shem, Ham, and J
7:13 Shem and Ham and J, and Noah's wife and
9:18 forth from the ark were Shem, Ham, and J
9:23 Then Shem and J took a garment, laid it
9:27 God enlarge J, and let him dwell in the
10:1 Noah, Shem, Ham, and J; sons were born to
10:2 The sons of J: Gomer, Magog, Madai, Javan, Tubal,
10:5 are the sons of J in their lands, each
10:21 the elder brother of J, children were born.
1Chr 1:4 Enoch, Thuselah, Lamech, Noah, Shem, Ham, and J
1:5 The sons of J: Gomer, Magog, Madai, Javan, Tubal,
Jud 2:25 the southern borders of J, fronting toward Arabia.

JAPHIA (5)
Josh 10:3 king of Jarmuth, to J king of Lachish, and
19:12 Daberath, then up to J;
2Sam 5:15 Solomon, Ibhar, Elishu-a, Nepheg, J,
1Chr 3:7 Elishama, Eliphelet, Nogah, Nepheg, J,
14:6 Elishu-a, Elpelet, Nogah, Nepheg, J,

JAPHLET (3)

1Chr 7:32 was the father of J, Shomer, Hotham, and their
7:33 The sons of J: Pasach, Bimhal, and Ashvath.
7:33 These are the sons of J

JAPHLETITES

Josh 16:3 the territory of the J, as far as the

JAR (25)

Gen 24:14 'Pray let down your J that I may drink,'
24:15 out with her water J upon her shoulder.
24:16 spring, and filled her J, and came up.
24:17 me a little water to drink from your J
24:18 quickly let down her J upon her hand, and
24:20 she quickly emptied her J into the trough and
24:43 little water from your J to drink,"
24:45 out with her water J on her shoulder; and
24:46 quickly let down her J from her shoulder, and
Ex 16:33 to Aaron, "Take a J, and put an omer
1Sam 26:11 his head, and the J of water, and let
26:12 the spear and the J of water from Saul's
26:16 spear is, and the J of water that was
1Kgs 14:3 some cakes, and a J of honey, and go
17:12 of meal in a J, and a little oil
17:14 God of Israel, 'The J of meal shall not
17:16 The J of meal was not spent, neither did
19:6 hot stones and a J of water.
2Kgs 4:2 the house, except a J of oil."
Sir 21:14 is like a broken J; it will hold no
Jer 13:12 God of Israel, "Every J shall be filled with
13:12 indeed know that every J will be filled with
Mk 14:13 a man carrying a J of water will meet
Lk 22:10 a man carrying a J of water will meet
Jn 4:28 woman left her water J, and went away into

JARAH (2)

1Chr 9:42 was the father of J, and Jarah of Alemeth,
9:42 father of Jarah, and J of Alemeth, Azmaveth, and

JARED (7)

Gen 5:15 lived sixty-five years, he became the father of J
5:16 after the birth of J eight hundred and thirty
5:18 When J had lived a hundred and sixty-two years
5:19 J lived after the birth of Enoch eight hundred
5:20 all the days of J were nine hundred and
1Chr 1:2 Seth, Enosh; Kenan, Mahalalel, J,
Lk 3:37 Enoch, the son of J, the son of Mahalale-el,

JARHA (2)

1Chr 2:34 Sheshan had an Egyptian slave, whose name was J
2:35 daughter in marriage to J his slave; and she

JARIB (3)

1Chr 4:24 of Simeon: Nemuel, Jamin, J, Zerah, Shaul;
Ezra 8:16 Ariel, Shemaiah, Elnathan, J, Elnathan, Nathan,
10:18 were found Ma-aseiah, Eliezer, J, and Gedaliah, of

JARMUTH (7)

Josh 10:3 to Piram king of J, to Japhia king of
10:5 Hebron, the king of J, the king of Lachish,
10:23 Hebron, the king of J, the king of Lachish,
12:11 one; the king of J, one; the king of
15:35 Zanoah, En-gannim, Tappuah, Enam, J, Adullam,
21:29 with its pasture lands, J with its pasture lands,
Neh 11:29 En-rimmon, in Zorah, in J,

JAROAH

1Chr 5:14 of Huri, son of J, son of Gilead, son

JARS (9)

Judg 7:8 So he took the J of the people from
7:16 of them and empty J, with torches inside the
7:16 them and empty jars, with torches inside the J
7:19 trumpets and smashed the J that were in their
7:20 trumpets and broke the J, holding in their left
1Kgs 18:33 he said, "Fill four J with water, and pour
Jer 48:12 vessels, and break his J in pieces.
Jn 2:6 Now six stone J were standing there, for the
2:7 to them, "Fill the J with water." And they

JASHAR (2)

Josh 10:13 Is this not written in the Book of J
2Sam 1:18 behold, it is written in the Book of J

JASHEN

2Sam 23:32 Sha-albon, the sons of J, Jonathan,

JASHOBE-AM (2)

1Chr 11:11 of David's mighty men: J, a Hachmonite, was chief
12:6 Isshiah, Azarel, Jo-ezer, and J, the Korahites;

JASHOBEAM

1Chr 27:2 division numbering twenty-four thousand: J the son

JASHUB (3)

Num 26:24 of the Punites; of J, the family of the
1Chr 7:1 of Issachar: Tola, Puah, J, and Shimron, four.
Ezra 10:29 were Meshullum, Malluch, Adaiah, J, Sheal, and

JASHUBITES

Num 26:24 the family of the J; of Shimron, the family

JASON (20)

1Mac 8:17 son of Accos, and J the son of Eleazar,
12:16 Antipater the son of J, and have sent them
14:22 Antipater the son of J, envoys of the Jews,
2Mac 1:7 in those years after J and his company revolted
2:23 been set forth by J of Cyrene in five
4:7 succeeded to the kingdom, J the brother of Onias
4:10 the king assented and J came to office, he
4:13 the surpassing wickedness of J, who was ungodly and
4:19 was present, the vile J sent envoys, chosen as
4:22 was welcomed magnificently by J and the city, and
4:23 period of three years J sent Menelaus, the brother
4:24 high-priesthood for himself, outbidding J by three
4:26 So J, who after supplanting his own brother was
5:5 that Antiochus was dead, J took no less than
5:6 But J kept relentlessly slaughtering his fellow,
Acts 17:5 attacked the house of J, seeking to bring them
17:6 find them, they dragged J and some of the
17:7 come here also, and J has received them; and
17:9 had taken security from J and the rest, they
Rom 16:21 so do Lucius and J and Sosipater, my kinsmen.

JASPER (7)

Ex 28:20 an onyx, and a J; they shall be set
39:13 an onyx, and a J; they were enclosed in
Ezek 28:13 covering, carnelian, topaz, and J, chrysolite, beryl,
Rev 4:3 sat there appeared like J and carnelian, and round
21:11 rare jewel, like a J, clear as crystal.
21:18 wall was built of J, while the city was
21:19 jewel; the first was J, the second sapphire, the

JATHAN

Tob 5:13 to know Ananias and J, the sons of the

JATHNI-EL

1Chr 26:2 second, Zebadiah the third, J the fourth,

JATTIR (4)

Josh 15:48 the hill country, Shamir, J, Socoh,
21:14 with its pasture lands, J with its pasture lands,
1Sam 30:27 of the Negeb, in J,
1Chr 6:57 with its pasture lands, J, Eshtemoa with its pasture

JAVAN (6)

Gen 10:2 Japheth: Gomer, Magog, Madai, J, Tubal, Meshech, .
10:4 The sons of J: Elishah, Tarshish, Kittim, and
1Chr 1:5 Japheth: Gomer, Magog, Madai, J, Tubal, Meshech,
1:7 The sons of J: Elishah, Tarshish, Kittim, and
Is 66:19 bow, to Tubal and J, to the coastlands afar
Ezek 27:13 J, Tubal, and Meshech traded with you; they

JAVELIN (8)

Josh 8:18 Joshua, "Stretch out the J that is in your
8:18 Joshua stretched out the J that was in his
8:26 he stretched out the J, until he had utterly
1Sam 17:6 his legs, and a J of bronze slung between
17:45 spear and with a J; but I come to
Job 39:23 rattle the quiver, the flashing spear and the J
41:26 avail; nor the spear, the dart, or the J
Ps 35:3 Draw the spear and J against my pursuers!

JAVELINS

Job 41:29 as stubble; he laughs at the rattle of J

JAW

Job 41:2 nose, or pierce his J with a hook?

JAWBONE (4)

Judg 15:15 he found a fresh J of an ass, and
15:16 Samson said, "With the J of an ass, heaps
15:16 upon heaps, with the J of an ass have

15:17 he threw away the J out of his hand;

JAWS (5)

Ps 22:15 tongue cleaves to my J; thou dost lay me
Is 30:28 to place on the J of the peoples a
Ezek 29:4 put hooks in your J, and make the fish
38:4 put hooks into your J, and I will bring
Hos 11:4 the yoke on their J, and I bent down

JAZER (15)

Num 21:24 to the Ammonites; for J was the boundary of
21:32 sent to spy out J; and they took its
32:1 saw the land of J and the land of
32:3 the congregation, "Ataroth, Dibon, J, Nimrah,
32:35 Dibon, Ataroth, Aroer, Atroth-shophan, J, Jogbehah,
Josh 13:25 Their territory was J, and all the cities of
21:39 with its pasture lands, J with its pasture lands--
2Sam 24:5 of the valley, toward Gad and on to J
1Chr 6:81 its pasture lands, and J with its pasture lands.
26:31 them were found at J in Gilead.)
Is 16:8 branches, which reached to J and strayed to the
16:9 with the weeping of J for the vine of
Jer 48:32 More than for J I weep for you, O
48:32 reached as far as J, upon your summer fruits
1Mac 5:8 He also took J and its villages; then he

JAZIZ

1Chr 27:30 Over the flocks was J the Hagrite.

JE-ATHERAI

1Chr 6:21 son, Zerah his son, J his son.

JE-IEL (12)

1Chr 5:7 was reckoned: the chief, J, and Zechariah,
8:29 J the father of Gibeon dwelt in Gibeon, and
9:35 the father of Gibeon, J, and the name of
11:44 the Ashterathite, Shama and J the sons of Hotham
15:18 Mikneiah, and the gatekeepers Obed-edom and J
15:21 Eliphelehu, Mikneiah, Obed-edom, J, and Azaziah
16:5 to him were Zechariah, J, Shemiramoth, Jehiel,
16:5 Eliab, Benaiah, Obed-edom, and J, who were to play
2Chr 20:14 of Benaiah, son of J, son of Mattaniah, a
26:11 the muster made by J the secretary and Ma-aseiah
35:9 brothers, and Hashabiah and J and Jozabad, the
Ezra 10:43 the sons of Nebo: J, Mattithiah, Zabad, Zebina,

JEALOUS (38)

Gen 37:11 And his brothers were J of him, but his
Ex 20:5 your God am a J God, visiting the iniquity
34:14 LORD, whose name is J, is a jealous God),
34:14 is Jealous, is a J God),
Num 5:14 him, and he is J of his wife who
5:14 him, and he is J of his wife, though
5:30 man and he is J of his wife; then
11:29 to him, "Are you J for my sake?
25:11 in that he was J with my jealousy among
25:13 priesthood, because he was J for his God, and
Deut 4:24 a devouring fire, a J God.
5:9 your God am a J God, visiting the iniquity
6:15 of you is a J God; lest the anger
Josh 24:19 God; he is a J God; he will not
1Kgs 19:10 "I have been very J for the LORD, the
19:14 "I have been very J for the LORD, the
Job 36:33 concerning him, who is J with anger against iniquity.
Ps 79:5 Will thy J wrath burn like fire?
106:16 in the camp were J of Moses and Aaron,
Wis 1:10 lawless deeds; because a J ear hears all things,
Sir 9:1 Do not be J of the wife of your
37:10 from those who are J of you.
Is 11:13 Ephraim shall not be J of Judah, and Judah
Ezek 36:6 I speak in my J wrath, because you have
39:25 and I will be J for my holy name.
Joel 2:18 Then the LORD became J for his land, and
Nah 1:2 The LORD is a J God and avenging, the
Zeph 1:18 the fire of his J wrath, all the earth
3:8 the fire of my J wrath all the earth
Zech 1:14 hosts: I am exceedingly J for Jerusalem and for
8:2 of hosts: I am J for Zion with great
8:2 jealousy, and I am J for her with great
Acts 7:9 "And the patriarchs, J of Joseph, sold him into
17:5 But the Jews were J, and taking some wicked
Rom 10:19 "I will make you J of those who are
11:11 to the Gentiles, so as to make Israel J
11:14 make my fellow Jews J, and thus save some
1Cor 13:4 kind; love is not J or boastful;

JEALOUSLY

Jas 4:5 scripture says, "He yearns J over the spirit which

JEALOUSY (41)

Num 5:14 if the spirit of J comes upon him, and
5:14 if the spirit of J comes upon him, and
5:15 a cereal offering of J, a cereal offering of
5:18 of remembrance, which is the cereal offering of J
5:25 the cereal offering of J out of the woman's
5:29 law in cases of J, when a wife, though
5:30 when the spirit of J comes upon a man
25:11 was jealous with my J among them, so that
25:11 not consume the people of Israel in my J
Deut 29:20 the LORD and his J would smoke against that
32:16 They stirred him to J with strange gods; with
32:21 have stirred me to J with what is no
32:21 will stir them to J with those who are
1Kgs 14:22 they provoked him to J with their sins which
Job 5:2 kills the fool, and J slays the simple.
Ps 78:58 they moved him to J with their graven images.
Prov 6:34 For J makes a man furious, and he will
27:4 anger is overwhelming; but who can stand before J
Song 8:6 is strong as death, J is cruel as the
Sir 30:24 J and anger shorten life, and anxiety brings on
Is 11:13 The J of Ephraim shall depart, and those who
Ezek 5:13 have spoken in my J, when I spend my
8:3 of the image of J, which provokes to jealousy.
8:3 of the image of jealousy, which provokes to J
8:5 gate, in the entrance, was this image of J
16:38 bring upon you the blood of wrath and J
16:42 on you, and my J shall depart from you;
36:5 speak in my hot J against the rest of
38:19 For in my J and in my blazing wrath
Zech 8:2 for Zion with great J, and I am jealous
1Mac 8:16 is no envy or J among them.
Acts 5:17 Sadducees, and filled with J
13:45 they were filled with J, and contradicted what was
Rom 13:13 and licentiousness, not in quarreling and J
1Cor 3:3 For while there is J and strife among you,
10:22 Shall we provoke the Lord to J
2Cor 11:2 I feel a divine J for you, for I
12:20 there may be quarreling, J, anger, selfishness,
Gal 5:20 idolatry, sorcery, enmity, strife, J, anger, selfishness,
Jas 3:14 if you have bitter J and selfish ambition in
3:16 For where J and selfish ambition exist, there will

JEARIM

Josh 15:10 northern shoulder of Mount J (that is, Chesalon), and

JEBERECHIAH

Is 8:2 Zechariah the son of J, to attest for me.

JEBUS (5)

Josh 18:28 Taralah, Zela, Ha-eleph, J (that is, Jerusalem),
Judg 19:10 departed, and arrived opposite J (that is, Jerusalem).
19:11 When they were near J, the day was far
1Chr 11:4 to Jerusalem, that is J, where the Jebusites were,
11:5 The inhabitants of J said to David, "You will

JEBUSITE (8)

Josh 15:8 southern shoulder of the J (that is, Jerusalem); and
2Sam 24:16 was by the threshing floor of Araunah the J
24:18 LORD on the threshing floor of Araunah the J
1Chr 21:15 standing by the threshing floor of Ornan the J
21:18 LORD on the threshing floor of Ornan the J
21:28 floor of Ornan the J, he made his sacrifices
2Chr 3:1 appointed, on the threshing floor of Ornan the J
Neh 9:8 Amorite, the Perizzite, the J, and the Girgashite; and

JEBUSITES (33)

Gen 10:16 and Heth, and the J, the Amorites, the Girgashites,
15:21 Amorites, the Canaanites, the Girgashites and the J
Ex 3:8 the Amorites, the Perizzites, the Hivites, and the J
3:17 the Hivites, and the J, a land flowing with
13:5 the Hivites, and the J, which he swore to
23:23 the Hivites, and the J, and I blot them
33:2 the Hittites, the Perizzites, the Hivites, and the J
34:11 the Hittites, the Perizzites, the Hivites, and the J
Num 13:29 Negeb; the Hittites, the J, and the Amorites dwell
Deut 7:1 the Hivites, and the J, seven nations greater and
20:17 the Hivites and the J, as the LORD your
Josh 3:10 Perizzites, the Girgashites, the Amorites, and the J
9:1 the Hivites, and the J, heard of this,
11:3 the Perizzites, and the J in the hill country,
12:8 the Hivites, and the J:
15:63 But the J, the inhabitants of Jerusalem, the people

15:63 drive out; so the J dwell with the people
18:16 the shoulder of the J, and downward to En-rogel;
24:11 the Hivites, and the J; and I gave them
Judg 1:21 not drive out the J who dwelt in Jerusalem;
1:21 in Jerusalem; so the J have dwelt with the
3:5 the Hivites, and the J;
19:11 this city of the J, and spend the night
2Sam 5:6 to Jerusalem against the J, the inhabitants of the
5:8 "Whoever would smite the J, let him get up
1Kgs 9:20 the Hivites, and the J, who were not of
1Chr 1:14 and Heth, and the J, the Amorites, the Girgashites,
11:4 is Jebus, where the J were, the inhabitants of
11:6 "Whoever shall smite the J first shall be chief
2Chr 8:7 the Hivites, and the J, who were not of
Ezra 9:1 the Perizzites, the J, the Ammonites, the Moabites,
Jud 5:16 the Perizzites and the J and the Shechemites and
Zech 9:7 in Judah, and Ekron shall be like the J

JECHONIAH (2)

Mt 1:11 Josiah the father of J and his brothers, at
1:12 the deportation to Babylon: J was the father of

JECOLIAH (2)

2Kgs 15:2 His mother's name was J of Jerusalem.
2Chr 26:3 His mother's name was J of Jerusalem.

JECONIAH (10)

1Chr 3:16 The descendants of Jehoiakim: J his son, Zedekiah
3:17 and the sons of J, the captive: Shealtiel his
Esth 2:6 captives carried away with J king of Judah, whom
11:4 brought from Jerusalem with J king of Judea.
Jer 24:1 into exile from Jerusalem J the son of Jehoiakim,
27:20 from Jerusalem to Babylon J the son of Jehoiakim,
28:4 back to this place J the son of Jehoiakim,
29:2 This was after King J, and the queen mother,
Bar 1:3 in the hearing of J the son of Jehoiakim,
1:9 carried away from Jerusalem J and the princes and

JEDAIAH (13)

1Chr 4:37 of Allon, son of J, son of Shimri, son
9:10 Of the priests: J, Jehoiarib, Jachin,
24:7 Jehoiarib, the second to J,
Ezra 2:36 priests: the sons of J, of the house of
Neh 3:10 Next to them J the son of Harumaph repaired
7:39 priests: the sons of J, namely the house of
11:10 Of the priests: J the son of Joiarib, Jachin,
12:6 Ma-adiah, Bilgah, Shemaiah, Joiarib, J,
12:7 Shemaiah, Joiarib, Jedaiah, Sallu, Amok, Hilkiah, J
12:19 of Joiarib, Mattenai; of J, Uzzi;
12:21 of Hilkiah, Hashabiah; of J, Nethanel.
Zech 6:10 exiles Heldai, Tobijah, and J, who have arrived from
6:14 reminder to Heldai, Tobijah, J, and Josiah the son

JEDIA-EL (6)

1Chr 7:6 Benjamin: Bela, Becher, and J, three.
7:10 The sons of J: Bilhan.
7:11 were the sons of J according to the heads
11:45 of Hotham the Aroerite, J the son of Shimri,
12:20 to him: Adnah, Jozabad, J, Michael, Jozabad, Elihu,
26:2 sons: Zechariah the first-born, J the second,

JEDIDAH

2Kgs 22:1 His mother's name was J the daughter of Adaiah

JEDIDIAH

2Sam 12:25 he called his name J, because of the LORD.

JEDUTHUN (14)

1Chr 9:16 of Galal, son of J, and Berechiah the son
16:38 Obed-edom, the son of J, and Hosah were to
16:41 them were Heman and J, and the rest of
16:42 Heman and J had trumpets and cymbals for the
16:42 The sons of J were appointed to the gate.
25:1 of Heman, and of J, who should prophesy with
25:3 Of J, the sons of Jeduthun: Gedaliah, Zeri, Jeshaiah,
25:3 Jeduthun, the sons of J: Gedaliah, Zeri, Jeshaiah,
25:3 direction of their father J, who prophesied with the
25:6 Asaph, J, and Heman were under the order of
2Chr 5:12 singers, Asaph, Heman, and J, their sons and
29:14 of the sons of J, Shemaiah and Uzziel.
35:15 Asaph, and Heman, and J the king's seer; and
Neh 11:17 son of Shammua, son of Galal, son of J

JEERED

2Kgs 2:23 of the city and J at him, saying, "Go

JEGAR-SAHADUTHA

Gen 31:47 Laban called it J: but Jacob called it Galeed.

JEHALLELEL (2)

1Chr 4:16 The sons of J: Ziph, Ziphah, Tiri-a, and Asarel.
2Chr 29:12 Azariah the son of J; and of the Gershonites,

JEHDEIAH (2)

1Chr 24:20 of Amram, Shuba-el; of the sons of Shuba-el, J
27:30 over the she-asses was J the Meronothite.

JEHEZKEL

1Chr 24:16 Pethahiah, the twentieth to J,

JEHIAH

1Chr 15:24 Obed-edom and J also were to be gatekeepers for

JEHIEL (13)

1Chr 15:18 order, Zechariah, Ja-aziel, Shemiramoth, J, Unni,
15:20 cymbals; Zechariah, Azi-el, Shemiramoth, J, Unni,
16:5 were Zechariah, Je-iel, Shemiramoth, J, Mattithiah,
3:8 The sons of Ladan: J the chief, and Zetham,
27:32 a scribe; he and J the son of Hachmoni
29:8 in the care of J the Gershonite.
2Chr 21:2 sons of Jehoshaphat: Azariah, J, Zechariah, Azariah,
31:13 brother as second; while J, Azaziah, Nahath, Asahel,
35:8 Hilkiah, Zechariah, and J, the chief officers of the
Ezra 8:9 Obadiah the son of J, and with him two
10:2 Shecaniah the son of J, of the sons of
10:21 Harim: Ma-aseiah, Elijah, Shemaiah, J, and Uzziah.
10:26 of Elam: Mattaniah, Zechariah, J, Abdi, Jeremoth,

JEHIELI (2)

1Chr 26:21 houses belonging to Ladan the Gershonite: J
26:22 The sons of J, Zetham and Joel his brother,

JEHIZKIAH

2Chr 28:12 the son of Meshillemoth, J the son of Shallum,

JEHO-ADDAN

2Chr 25:1 His mother's name was J of Jerusalem.

JEHO-ADDIN

2Kgs 14:2 His mother's name was J of Jerusalem.

JEHO-SHABE-ATH (2)

2Chr 22:11 But J, the daughter of the king, took Joash
22:11 Thus J, the daughter of King Jehoram and wife

JEHOADDAH (2)

1Chr 8:36 was the father of J; and Jehoaddah was the
8:36 father of Jehoaddah; and J was the father of

JEHOAHAZ (21)

2Kgs 10:35 And J his son reigned in his stead.
13:1 Ahaziah, king of Judah, J the son of Jehu
13:4 J besought the LORD, and the LORD hearkened
13:7 was not left to J an army of more
13:8 of the acts of J and all that he
13:9 So J slept with his fathers, and they buried
13:10 Jehoash the son of J began to reign over
13:22 of Syria oppressed Israel all the days of J
13:25 Jehoash the son of J took again from Ben-hadad
13:25 he had taken from J his father in war.
14:8 Jehoash the son of J, son of Jehu, king
14:17 of Jehoash son of J, king of Israel.
23:30 of the land took J the son of Josiah,
23:31 J was twenty-three years old when he began to
23:34 But he took J away; and he came to
2Chr 21:17 left to him except J, his youngest son.
25:17 Joash the son of J, son of Jehu, king
25:25 Joash the son of J, king of Israel.
36:1 of the land took J the son of Josiah
36:2 J was twenty-three years old when he began to
36:4 Jehoiakim; but Neco took J his brother and carried

JEHOASH (17)

2Kgs 11:21 J was seven years old when he began to
12:1 seventh year of Jehu J began to reign, and
12:2 And J did what was right in the eyes
12:4 J said to the priests, "All the money of
12:6 twenty-third year of King J the priests had made
12:7 Therefore King J summoned Jehoiada the priest and
12:18 go up against Jerusalem, J king of Judah took
13:10 Joash king of Judah J the son of Jehoahaz
13:25 Then J the son of Jehoahaz took again from

	14:8	Amaziah sent messengers to J the son of Jehoahaz,
	14:9	And J king of Israel sent word to Amaziah
	14:11	So J king of Israel went up, and he
	14:13	And J king of Israel captured Amaziah king of
	14:13	Judah, the son of J, son of Ahaziah, at
	14:15	of the acts of J which he did, and
	14:16	And J slept with his fathers, and was buried
	14:17	after the death of J son of Jehoahaz, king

JEHOHANAN (8)

1Chr	26:3	fourth, Elam the fifth, J the sixth, Eli-e-ho-enai the
2Chr	17:15	and next to him J the commander, with two
	23:1	Ishmael the son of J, Azariah the son of
Ezra	10:6	to the chamber of J the son of Eliashib,
	10:28	sons of Bebai were J, Hananiah, Zabbai, and Athlai.
Neh	6:18	Arah: and his son J had taken the daughter
	12:13	Ezra, Meshullam; of Amariah, J;
	12:42	Ma-aseiah, Shemaiah, Eleazar, Uzzi, J, Malchijah,

JEHOIACHIN (14)

2Kgs	24:6	with his fathers, and J his son reigned in
	24:8	J was eighteen years old when he became king,
	24:12	were besieging it; and J the king of Judah
	24:15	And he carried away J to Babylon; the king's
	24:17	of Babylon made Mattaniah, J's uncle, king in his
	25:27	of the exile of J king of Judah, in
	25:27	to reign, graciously freed J king of Judah from
	25:29	So J put off his prison garments.
2Chr	36:8	Israel and Judah; and J his son reigned in
	36:9	J was eight years old when he began to
Jer	52:31	of the captivity of J king of Judah, in
	52:31	up the head of J king of Judah and
	52:33	So J put off his prison garments.
Ezek	1:2	the exile of King J,

JEHOIADA (53)

2Sam	8:18	Benaiah the son of J was over the Cherethites
	20:23	Benaiah the son of J was in command of
	23:20	Benaiah the son of J was a valiant man
	23:22	Benaiah the son of J, and won a name
1Kgs	1:8	Benaiah the son of J, and Nathan the prophet,
	1:26	Benaiah the son of J, and your servant Solomon,
	1:32	Nathan the prophet, and Benaiah the son of J
	1:36	Benaiah the son of J answered the king, "Amen!
	1:38	Benaiah the son of J, and the Cherethites and
	1:44	Benaiah the son of J, and the Cherethites and
	2:25	Benaiah the son of J; and he struck him
	2:29	Benaiah the son of J, saying, "Go, strike him
	2:34	Benaiah the son of J went up, and struck
	2:35	Benaiah the son of J over the army in
	2:46	Benaiah the son of J; and he went out
	4:4	Benaiah the son of J was in command of
2Kgs	11:4	in the seventh year J sent and brought the
	11:9	according to all that J the priest commanded, and
	11:9	sabbath, and came to J the priest.
	11:15	Then J the priest commanded the captains who
	11:17	And J made a covenant between the LORD and
	12:2	all his days, because J the priest instructed him.
	12:7	Therefore King Jehoash summoned J the priest and
	12:9	Then J the priest took a chest, and bored
1Chr	11:22	Benaiah the son of J was a valiant man
	11:24	Benaiah the son of J, and won a name
	12:27	The prince J, of the house of Aaron, and
	18:17	Benaiah the son of J was over the Cherethites
	27:5	Benaiah, the son of J the priest, as chief;
	27:34	Ahithophel was succeeded by J the son of Benaiah,
2Chr	22:11	Jehoram and wife of J the priest, because she
	23:1	in the seventh year J took courage, and entered
	23:3	And J said to them, "Behold, the king's son!
	23:8	according to all that J the priest commanded.
	23:8	on the sabbath; for J the priest did not
	23:9	And J the priest delivered to the captains the
	23:11	proclaimed him king, and J and his sons anointed
	23:14	Then J the priest brought out the captains who
	23:16	And J made a covenant between himself and all
	23:18	And J posted watchmen for the house of the
	24:2	all the days of J the priest.
	24:3	J got for him two wives, and he had
	24:6	So the king summoned J the chief, and said
	24:12	And the king and J gave it to those
	24:14	before the king and J, and with it were
	24:14	of the LORD continually all the days of J
	24:15	But J grew old and full of days, and
	24:17	after the death of J the princes of Judah
	24:20	Zechariah the son of J the priest; and he
	24:22	remember the kindness which J, Zechariah's father,
	24:25	of the son of J the priest, and slew
Neh	13:28	of the sons of J, the son of Eliashib
Jer	29:26	you priest instead of J the priest, to have

JEHOIAKIM (38)

2Kgs	23:34	Josiah his father, and changed his name to J
	23:35	And J gave the silver and the gold to
	23:36	J was twenty-five years old when he began to
	24:1	Babylon came up, and J became his servant three
	24:5	of the deeds of J, and all that he
	24:6	So J slept with his fathers, and Jehoiachin his
	24:19	according to all that J had done.
1Chr	3:15	the first-born, the second J, the third Zedekiah, the
	3:16	The descendants of J: Jeconiah his son, Zedekiah his
2Chr	36:4	changed his name to J; but Neco took Jehoahaz
	36:5	J was twenty-five years old when he began to
	36:8	of the acts of J, and the abominations which
Jer	1:3	in the days of J the son of Josiah,
	22:18	says the LORD concerning J the son of Josiah,
	22:24	Coniah the son of J, king of Judah, were
	24:1	Jeconiah the son of J, king of Judah, together
	25:1	the fourth year of J the son of Josiah,
	26:1	of the reign of J the son of Josiah,
	26:21	And when King J, with all his warriors and
	26:22	Then King J sent to Egypt certain men, Elnathan
	26:23	brought him to King J, who slew him with
	27:20	Jeconiah the son of J, king of Judah, and
	28:4	Jeconiah the son of J, king of Judah, and
	35:1	in the days of J the son of Josiah,
	36:1	the fourth year of J the son of Josiah,
	36:9	the fifth year of J the son of Josiah,
	36:28	the first scroll, which J the king of Judah
	36:29	And concerning J king of Judah you shall say,
	36:30	says the LORD concerning J king of Judah, He
	36:32	of the scroll which J king of Judah had
	37:1	Judah, reigned instead of Coniah the son of J
	45:1	the fourth year of J the son of Josiah,
	46:2	the fourth year of J the son of Josiah,
	52:2	according to all that J had done.
Bar	1:3	Jeconiah the son of J, king of Judah, and
	1:7	it to Jerusalem to J the high priest, the
Dan	1:1	of the reign of J king of Judah, Nebuchadnezzar
	1:2	And the Lord gave J king of Judah into

JEHOIARIB (2)

1Chr	9:10	Of the priests: Jedaiah, J, Jachin,
	24:7	first lot fell to J, the second to Jedaiah,

JEHONADAB (3)

2Kgs	10:15	from there, he met J the son of Rechab
	10:15	And J answered, "It is." Jehu said, "If it
	10:23	house of Baal with J the son of Rechab;

JEHONATHAN (2)

2Chr	17:8	Zebadiah, Asahel, Shemiramoth, J, Adonijah,
Neh	12:18	Bilgah, Shammua; of Shemaiah, J;

JEHORAM (22)

1Kgs	22:50	David his father; and J his son reigned in
2Kgs	1:17	J, his brother, became king in his stead in
	1:17	the second year of J the son of Jehoshaphat,
	3:1	Jehoshaphat king of Judah, J the son of Ahab
	3:6	So King J marched out of Samaria at that
	3:8	J answered, "By the way of the wilderness of
	8:16	Ahab, king of Israel, J the son of Jehoshaphat,
	8:25	Ahaziah the son of J, king of Judah, began
	8:29	Ahaziah the son of J king of Judah went
	12:18	gifts that Jehoshaphat and J and Ahaziah, his fathers,
2Chr	17:8	and with these Levites, the priests Elishama and J
	21:1	city of David; and J his son reigned in
	21:3	gave the kingdom to J, because he was the
	21:4	When J had ascended the throne of his father
	21:5	J was thirty-two years old when he became king,
	21:9	Then J passed over with his commanders and all
	21:16	LORD stirred up against J the anger of the
	22:1	Ahaziah the son of J king of Judah reigned.
	22:5	counsel, and went with J the son of Ahab
	22:6	Ahaziah the son of J king of Judah went
	22:7	he went out with J to meet Jehu the
	22:11	the daughter of King J and wife of Jehoiada

JEHOSHAPHAT (85)

2Sam	8:16	over the army; and J the son of Ahilud
	20:24	the forced labor; and J the son of Ahilud
1Kgs	4:3	of Shisha were secretaries; J the son of Ahilud
	4:17	in Asher and Bealoth; J the son of Paruah,

15:24 David his father; and J his son reigned in
22:2 in the third year J the king of Judah
22:4 And he said to J, "Will you go with
22:4 And J said to the king of Israel, "I
22:5 And J said to the king of Israel, "Inquire
22:7 But J said, "Is there not here another prophet
22:8 of Israel said to J, "There is yet one
22:8 And J said, "Let not the king say so."
22:10 king of Israel and J the king of Judah
22:18 of Israel said to J, "Did I not tell
22:29 king of Israel and J the king of Judah
22:30 of Israel said to J, "I will disguise myself
22:32 of the chariots saw J, they said, "It is
22:32 fight against him; and J cried out.
22:41 J the son of Asa began to reign over
22:42 J was thirty-five years old when he began to
22:44 J also made peace with the king of Israel.
22:45 of the acts of J, and his might that
22:48 J made ships of Tarshish to go to Ophir
22:49 of Ahab said to J, "Let my servants go
22:49 but J was not willing.
22:50 And J slept with his fathers, and was buried
22:51 the seventeenth year of J king of Judah, and
2Kgs 1:17 Jehoram the son of J, king of Judah, because
3:1 the eighteenth year of J king of Judah, Jehoram
3:7 and sent word to J king of Judah, "The
3:11 And J said, "Is there no prophet of the
3:12 And J said, "The word of the LORD is
3:12 king of Israel and J and the king of
3:14 I have regard for J the king of Judah,
8:16 Jehoram the son of J, king of Judah, began
9:2 Jehu the son of J, son of Nimshi; and
9:14 Jehu the son of J the son of Nimshi
12:18 the votive gifts that J and Jehoram and Ahaziah,
1Chr 3:10 son, Asa his son, J his son,
18:15 over the army; and J the son of Ahilud
2Chr 17:1 J his son reigned in his stead, and strengthened
17:3 The LORD was with J, because he walked in
17:5 Judah brought tribute to J; and he had great
17:10 about Judah, and they made no war against J
17:11 of the Philistines brought J presents, and silver for
17:12 And J grew steadily greater.
18:1 Now J had great riches and honor; and he
18:3 of Israel said to J king of Judah, "Will
18:4 And J said to the king of Israel, "Inquire
18:6 But J said, "Is there not here another prophet
18:7 of Israel said to J, "There is yet one
18:7 And J said, "Let not the king say so."
18:9 king of Israel and J the king of Judah
18:17 of Israel said to J, "Did I not tell
18:28 king of Israel and J the king of Judah
18:29 of Israel said to J, "I will disguise myself
18:31 of the chariots saw J, they said, "It is
18:31 fight against him; and J cried out, and the
19:1 J the king of Judah returned in safety to
19:2 and said to King J, "Should you help the
19:4 J dwelt at Jerusalem; and he went out again
19:8 Moreover in Jerusalem J appointed certain Levites
20:1 the Me-unites, came against J for battle.
20:2 men came and told J, "A great multitude is
20:3 Then J feared, and set himself to seek the
20:5 And J stood in the assembly of Judah and
20:15 of Jerusalem, and King J: Thus says the LORD
20:18 Then J bowed his head with his face to
20:20 as they went out, J stood and said, "Hear
20:25 When J and his people came to take the
20:27 Judah and Jerusalem, and J at their head, returning
20:30 So the realm of J was quiet, for his
20:31 Thus J reigned over Judah.
20:34 of the acts of J, from first to last,
20:35 After this J king of Judah joined with Ahaziah
20:37 of Mareshah prophesied against J, saying, "Because
21:1 J slept with his fathers, and was buried with
21:2 brothers, the sons of J: Azariah, Jehiel, Zechariah,
21:2 were the sons of J king of Judah.
21:12 in the ways of J your father, or in
22:9 is the grandson of J, who sought the LORD
Joel 3:2 to the valley of J, and I will enter
3:12 to the valley of J; for there I will
Mt 1:8 Asa the father of J, and Jehoshaphat the father
1:8 father of Jehoshaphat, and J the father of Joram,

JEHOSHEBA

2Kgs 11:2 But J, the daughter of King Joram, sister of

JEHOZABAD (4)

2Kgs 12:21 son of Shimeath and J the son of Shomer,
1Chr 26:4 sons: Shemaiah the first-born, J the second, Joah the
2Chr 17:18 and next to him J with a hundred and
24:26 Shimeath the Ammonitess, and J the son of Shimrith

JEHOZADAK (8)

1Chr 6:14 of Seraiah, Seraiah of J;
6:15 Seraiah of Jehozadak; and J went into exile when
Hag 1:1 Joshua the son of J, the high priest,
1:12 Joshua the son of J, the high priest, with
1:14 Joshua the son of J, the high priest, and
2:2 Joshua the son of J, the high priest, and
2:4 O Joshua, son of J, the high priest; take
Zech 6:11 Joshua, the son of J, the high priest;

JEHU (61)

1Kgs 16:1 the LORD came to J the son of Hanani
16:7 came by the prophet J the son of Hanani
16:12 spoke against Baasha by J the prophet,
19:16 king over Syria; and J the son of Nimshi
19:17 sword of Hazael shall J slay; and him who
19:17 from the sword of J shall Elisha slay.
2Kgs 9:2 arrive, look there for J the son of Jehoshaphat,
9:5 And J said, "To which of us all?" And
9:11 When J came out to the servants of his
9:13 the trumpet, and proclaimed, J is king."
9:14 Thus J the son of Jehoshaphat the son of
9:15 king of Syria.) So J said, "If this is
9:16 Then J mounted his chariot, and went to Jezreel,
9:17 spied the company of J as he came, and
9:18 And J said, "What have you to do with
9:19 And J answered, "What have you to do with
9:20 like the driving of J the son of Nimshi;
9:21 and went to meet J, and met him at
9:22 And when Joram saw J, he said, "Is it
9:22 Joram saw Jehu, he said, "Is it peace, J
9:24 And J drew his bow with his full strength,
9:25 J said to Bidkar his aide, "Take him up,
9:27 And J pursued him, and said, "Shoot him also";
9:30 When J came to Jezreel, Jezebel heard of it;
9:31 And as J entered the gate, she said, "Is
10:1 So J wrote letters, and sent them to Samaria,
10:5 the guardians, sent to J, saying, "We are your
10:11 So J slew all that remained of the house
10:13 Beth-eked of the Shepherds, J met the kinsmen of
10:15 J said, "If it is, give me your hand."
10:15 And J took him up with him into the
10:18 Then J assembled all the people, and said to
10:18 Baal a little; but J will serve him much.
10:19 But J did it with cunning in order to
10:20 J ordered, "Sanctify a solemn assembly for Baal."
10:21 And J sent throughout all Israel; and all the
10:23 Then J went into the house of Baal with
10:24 Now J had stationed eighty men outside, and said,
10:25 offering the burnt offering, J said to the guard
10:28 Thus J wiped out Baal from Israel.
10:29 But J did not turn aside from the sins
10:30 the LORD said to J, "Because you have done
10:31 But J was not careful to walk in the
10:34 of the acts of J, and all that he
10:35 So J slept with his fathers, and they buried
10:36 The time that J reigned over Israel in Samaria
12:1 the seventh year of J Jehoash began to reign,
13:1 Jehoahaz the son of J began to reign over
14:8 of Jehoahaz, son of J, king of Israel, saying,
15:12 which he gave to J, "Your sons shall sit
1Chr 2:38 was the father of J, and Jehu of Azariah.
2:38 father of Jehu, and J of Azariah.
4:35 son of Amaziah, Joel, J the son of Joshibiah,
12:3 sons of Azmaveth; Beracah, J of Anathoth,
2Chr 19:2 But J the son of Hanani the seer went
20:34 in the chronicles of J the son of Hanani,
22:7 with Jehoram to meet J the son of Nimshi,
22:8 And when J was executing judgment upon the house
22:9 he was brought to J and put to death.
25:17 of Jehoahaz, son of J, king of Israel, saying,
Hos 1:4 punish the house of J for the blood of

JEHUBBAH

1Chr 7:34 Shemer his brother: Rohgah, J, and Aram.

JEHUCAL

Jer 37:3 King Zedekiah sent J the son of Shelemiah, and

JEHUD
Josh 19:45 Gibbethon, Baalath, J, Bene-berak, Gath-rimmon,

JEHUDI (4)
Jer 36:14 all the princes sent J the son of Nethaniah,
36:21 Then the king sent J to get the scroll,
36:21 Elishama the secretary; and J read it to the
36:23 As J read three or four columns, the king

JEHUEL
2Chr 29:14 the sons of Heman, J and Shimei; and of

JEKABZEEL
Neh 11:25 its villages, and in J and its villages,

JEKAMEAM (2)
1Chr 23:19 Jahaziel the third, and J the fourth.
24:23 second, Jahaziel the third, J the fourth.

JEKAMIAH (3)
1Chr 2:41 was the father of J, and Jekamiah of Elishama.
2:41 father of Jekamiah, and J of Elishama.
3:18 Malchiram, Pedaiah, Shenazzar, J, Hoshama, and

JEKUTHIEL
1Chr 4:18 father of Soco, and J the father of Zanoah.

JEMIMAH
Job 42:14 name of the first J; and the name of

JEMUEL (2)
Gen 46:10 The sons of Simeon: J, Jamin, Ohad, Jachin, Zohar,
Ex 6:15 The sons of Simeon: J, Jamin, Ohad, Jachin, Zohar,

JEOPARDED
Judg 5:18 is a people that J their lives to the

JEPHTHAH (30)
Judg 11:1 Now J the Gileadite was a mighty warrior, but
11:1 Gilead was the father of J
11:2 grew up, they thrust J out, and said to
11:3 Then J fled from his brothers, and dwelt in
11:3 worthless fellows collected round J, and went raiding
11:5 Gilead went to bring J from the land of
11:6 and they said to J, "Come and be our
11:7 But J said to the elders of Gilead, "Did
11:8 of Gilead said to J, "That is why we
11:9 J said to the elders of Gilead, "If you
11:10 of Gilead said to J, "The LORD will be
11:11 So J went with the elders of Gilead, and
11:11 leader over them; and J spoke all his words
11:12 Then J sent messengers to the king of the
11:13 answered the messengers of J, "Because Israel on
11:14 And J sent messengers again to the king of
11:15 to him, "Thus says J: Israel did not take
11:28 heed the message of J which he sent to
11:29 the LORD came upon J, and he passed through
11:30 And J made a vow to the LORD, and
11:32 So J crossed over to the Ammonites to fight
11:34 Then J came to his home at Mizpah; and
11:40 lament the daughter of J the Gileadite four days
12:1 Zaphon and said to J, "Why did you cross
12:2 And J said to them, "I and my people
12:4 Then J gathered all the men of Gilead and
12:7 J judged Israel six years.
12:7 Then J the Gileadite died, and was buried in
1Sam 12:11 Jerubbaal and Barak, and J, and Samuel, and
Heb 11:32 of Gideon, Barak, Samson, J, of David and Samuel

JEPHUNNEH (17)
Num 13:6 Caleb the son of J;
14:6 Caleb the son of J, who were among those
14:30 Caleb the son of J and Joshua the son
14:38 Caleb the son of J remained alive, of those
26:65 Caleb the son of J and Joshua the son
32:12 Caleb the son of J the Kenizzite and Joshua
34:19 the tribe of Judah, Caleb the son of J
Deut 1:36 Caleb the son of J; he shall see it,
Josh 14:6 Caleb the son of J the Kenizzite said to
14:13 Caleb the son of J for an inheritance.
14:14 Caleb the son of J the Kenizzite to this
15:13 Caleb the son of J a portion among the
21:12 Caleb the son of J as his possession.
1Chr 4:15 Caleb the son of J: Iru, Elah, and Naam;
6:56 villages they gave to Caleb the son of J
7:38 The sons of Jether: J, Pispa, and Ara.
Sir 46:7 Caleb the son of J: they withstood the congregation,

JERAH (2)
Gen 10:26 of Almodad, Sheleph, Hazarmaveth, J,
1Chr 1:20 of Almodad, Sheleph, Hazarmaveth, J,

JERAHMEEL (8)
1Chr 2:9 were born to him: J, Ram, and Chelubai.
2:25 The sons of J, the first-born of Hezron: Ram,
2:26 J also had another wife, whose name was Atarah;
2:27 Ram, the first-born of J: Maaz, Jamin, and Eker.
2:33 These were the descendants of J
2:42 Caleb the brother of J: Mareshah his first-born, who
24:29 Of Kish, the sons of Kish: J
Jer 36:26 And the king commanded J the king's son and

JERAHMEELITES (2)
1Sam 27:10 or "Against the Negeb of the J
30:29 the cities of the J, in the cities of

JERED
1Chr 4:18 his Jewish wife bore J the father of Gedor,

JEREMAI
Ezra 10:33 Mattenai, Mattattah, Zabad, Eliphelet, J, Manasseh,

JEREMIAH (156)
2Kgs 23:31 Hamutal the daughter of J of Libnah.
24:18 Hamutal the daughter of J of Libnah.
1Chr 5:24 Epher, Ishi, Eliel, Azriel, J, Hodaviah, and Jahdi-el,
12:4 leader over the thirty; J, Jahaziel, Johanan, Jozabad
12:10 Eliab third, Mishmannah fourth, J fifth,
12:13 Johanan eighth, Elzabad ninth, J tenth, Machbannai
2Chr 35:25 J also uttered a lament for Josiah; and all
36:12 not humble himself before J the prophet, who spoke
36:21 by the mouth of J, until the land had
36:22 by the mouth of J might be accomplished, the
Ezra 1:1 by the mouth of J might be accomplished, the
Neh 10:2 Hacaliah, Zedekiah, Seraiah, Azariah, J,
12:1 Shealtiel, and Jeshua: Seraiah, J, Ezra,
12:12 of Seraiah, Meraiah; of J, Hananiah;
12:34 Judah, Benjamin, Shemaiah, and J,
Sir 49:6 her streets desolate, according to the word of J
Jer 1:1 The words of J, the son of Hilkiah,
1:11 came to me, saying, J, what do you see?"
7:1 word that came to J from the LORD:
11:1 word that came to J from the LORD:
14:1 LORD which came to J concerning the drought:
18:1 word that came to J from the LORD:
18:18 us make plots against J, for the law shall
19:14 Then J came from Topheth, where the LORD had
20:1 of the LORD, heard J prophesying these things.
20:2 Then Pashhur beat J the prophet, and put him
20:3 when Pashhur released J from the stocks, J
21:1 word which came to J from the LORD, when
21:3 Then J said to them:
24:3 LORD said to me, "What do you see, J
25:1 word that came to J concerning all the people
25:2 king of Babylon), which J the prophet spoke to
25:13 in this book, which J prophesied against all the
26:7 all the people heard J speaking these words in
26:8 And when J had finished speaking all that the
26:9 the people gathered about J in the house of
26:12 Then J spoke to all the princes and all
26:20 against this land in words like those of J
26:24 of Shaphan was with J so that he was
27:1 this word came to J from the LORD.
28:5 Then the prophet J spoke to Hananiah the prophet
28:6 LORD; and the prophet J said, "Amen!
28:10 from the neck of J the prophet, and broke
28:11 But J the prophet went his way.
28:12 off the neck of J the prophet, the word
28:12 the LORD came to J:
28:15 And J the prophet said to the prophet Hananiah,
29:1 of the letter which J the prophet sent from
29:27 have you not rebuked J of Anathoth who is
29:29 in the hearing of J the prophet.
29:30 the LORD came to J:
30:1 word that came to J from the LORD:
32:1 word that came to J from the LORD in
32:2 was besieging Jerusalem, and J the prophet was shut
32:6 J said, "The word of the LORD came to
32:26 the LORD came to J:
33:1 the LORD came to J a second time, while
33:19 the LORD came to J:
33:23 the LORD came to J:

34:1 word which came to J from the LORD, when
34:6 Then J the prophet spoke all these words to
34:8 word which came to J from the LORD, after
34:12 the LORD came to J from the LORD:
35:1 word which came to J from the LORD in
35:3 Ja-azaniah the son of J, son of Habazziniah, and
35:12 the LORD came to J:
35:18 house of the Rechabites J said, "Thus says the
36:1 this word came to J from the LORD:
36:4 Then J called Baruch the son of Neriah, and
36:4 at the dictation of J all the words of
36:5 And J ordered Baruch, saying, "I am debarred from
36:8 Neriah did all that J the prophet ordered him
36:10 read the words of J from the scroll, in
36:19 and hide, you and J, and let no one
36:26 Baruch the secretary and J the prophet, but the
36:27 which Baruch wrote at J's dictation, the word of
36:27 the LORD came to J:
36:32 Then J took another scroll and gave it to
36:32 at the dictation of J all the words of
37:2 which he spoke through J the prophet.
37:3 son of Ma-aseiah, to J the prophet, saying, "Pray
37:4 Now J was still going in and out among
37:6 the LORD came to J the prophet:
37:12 of Pharaoh's army, J set out from Jerusalem
37:13 son of Hananiah, seized J the prophet, saying, "You
37:14 And J said, "It is false; I am not
37:14 to him, and seized J and brought him to
37:15 princes were enraged at J, and they beat him
37:16 When J had come to the dungeon cells, and
37:17 J said, "There is." Then he said, "You shall
37:18 J also said to King Zedekiah, "What wrong have
37:21 orders, and they committed J to the court of
37:21 So J remained in the court of the guard.
38:1 heard the words that J was saying to all
38:6 So they took J and cast him into the
38:6 of the guard, letting J down by ropes.
38:6 but only mire, and J sank in the mire.
38:7 that they had put J into the cistern--the
38:9 that they did to J the prophet by casting
38:10 from here, and lift J the prophet out of
38:11 he let down to J in the cistern by
38:12 the Ethiopian said to J, "Put the rags and
38:12 J did so.
38:13 Then they drew J up with ropes and lifted
38:13 And J remained in the court of the guard.
38:14 King Zedekiah sent for J the prophet and received
38:14 The king said to J, "I will ask you
38:15 J said to Zedekiah, "If I tell you, will
38:16 Zedekiah swore secretly to J, "As the LORD lives,
38:17 Then J said to Zedekiah, "Thus says the LORD,
38:19 King Zedekiah said to J, "I am afraid of
38:20 J said, "You shall not be given to them.
38:24 Then Zedekiah said to J, "Let no one know
38:27 the princes came to J and asked him, and
38:28 And J remained in the court of the guard
39:11 gave command concerning J through Nebuzaradan,
39:14 Babylon sent and took J from the court of
39:15 the LORD came to J while he was shut
40:1 word that came to J from the LORD after
40:2 of the guard took J and said to him,
40:6 Then J went to Gedaliah the son of Ahikam,
42:2 near and said to J the prophet, "Let our
42:4 J the prophet said to them, "I have heard
42:5 Then they said to J, "May the LORD be
42:7 days the word of the LORD came to J
43:1 When J finished speaking to all the people all
43:2 insolent men said to J, "You are telling a
43:6 son of Shaphan; also J the prophet and Baruch
43:8 the LORD came to J in Tahpanhes:
44:1 word that came to J concerning all the Jews
44:15 land of Egypt, answered J:
44:20 Then J said to all the people, men and
44:24 J said to all the people and all the
45:1 The word that J the prophet spoke to Baruch
45:1 at the dictation of J, in the fourth year
46:1 LORD which came to J the prophet concerning the
46:13 the LORD spoke to J the prophet about the
47:1 LORD that came to J the prophet concerning the
49:34 LORD that came to J the prophet concerning Elam,
50:1 of the Chaldeans, by J the prophet:
51:59 The word which J the prophet commanded Seraiah
51:60 J wrote in a book all the evil that
51:61 And J said to Seraiah: "When you come to
51:64 Thus far are the words of J
52:1 Hamutal the daughter of J of Libnah.

Bar 6:1 of a letter which J sent to those who
Dan 9:2 of the LORD to J the prophet, must pass
2Mac 2:1 in the records that J the prophet ordered those
2:5 And J came and found a cave, and he
2:7 When J learned of it, he rebuked them and
15:14 and the holy city, J, the prophet of God."
15:15 J stretched out his right hand and gave to
Mt 2:17 spoken by the prophet J:
16:14 say Elijah, and others J or one of the
27:9 spoken by the prophet J, saying, "And they took

JEREMOTH (8)

1Chr 7:8 Joash, Eliezer, Eli-o-enai, Omri, J, Abijah, Anathoth,
8:14 the inhabitants of Gath); and Ahio, Shashak, and J
23:23 Mushi: Mahli, Eder, and J, three.
25:22 to the fifteenth, to J, his sons and his
27:19 of Obadiah; for Naphtali, J the son of Azriel;
Ezra 10:26 Mattaniah, Zechariah, Jehiel, Abdi, J, and Elijah.
10:27 Zattu: Eli-o-enai, Eliashib, Mattaniah, J, Zabad, and
10:29 Meshullum, Malluch, Adaiah, Jashub, Sheal, and J

JERI-EL

1Chr 7:2 of Tola: Uzzi, Rephaiah, J, Jahmai, Ibsam, and

JERIAH (2)

1Chr 23:19 The sons of Hebron: J the chief, Amariah the
24:23 The sons of Hebron: J the chief, Amariah the

JERIBAI

1Chr 11:46 Eliel the Mahavite, and J, and Joshaviah, the sons

JERICHO (70)

Num 22:1 the plains of Moab beyond the Jordan at J
26:3 by the Jordan at J, saying,
26:63 the plains of Moab by the Jordan at J
31:12 the plains of Moab by the Jordan at J
33:48 by the Jordan at J;
33:50 by the Jordan at J,
34:15 the Jordan at J eastward, toward the sunrise."
35:1 by the Jordan at J,
36:13 the plains of Moab by the Jordan at J
Deut 32:49 land of Moab, opposite J; and view the land
34:1 to the top of Pisgah, which is opposite J
34:3 is, the valley of J the city of palm
Josh 2:1 as spies, saying, "Go, view the land, especially J
2:2 told the king of J, "Behold, certain men of
2:3 Then the king of J sent to Rahab, saying,
3:16 cut off; and the people passed over opposite J
4:13 the LORD for battle, to the plains of J
4:19 encamped in Gilgal on the east border of J
5:10 the month at evening in the plains of J
5:13 When Joshua was by J, he lifted up his
6:1 Now J was shut up from within and from
6:2 given into your hand J, with its king and
6:25 the messengers whom Joshua sent to spy out J
6:26 man that rises up and rebuilds this city, J
7:2 Joshua sent men from J to Ai, which is
8:2 as you did to J and its king; only
9:3 Joshua had done to J and to Ai,
10:1 he had done to J and its king, and
10:28 as he had done to the king of J
10:30 as he had done to the king of J
12:9 Jebusites): the king of J, one; the king of
13:32 plains of Moab, beyond the Jordan east of J
16:1 from the Jordan by J, east of the waters
16:1 of the waters of J, into the wilderness, going
16:1 wilderness, going up from J into the hill country
16:7 to Naarah, and touches J, ending at the Jordan.
18:12 the shoulder north of J, then up through the
18:21 to their families were J, Beth-hoglah, Emek-keziz,
20:8 the Jordan east of J, they appointed Bezer in
24:11 Jordan and came to J, and the men of
24:11 and the men of J fought against you, and
2Sam 10:5 king said, "Remain at J until your beards have
1Kgs 16:34 Hiel of Bethel built J; he laid its foundation
2Kgs 2:4 you; for the LORD has sent me to J
2:4 So they came to J
2:5 prophets who were at J drew near to Elisha,
2:15 prophets who were at J saw him over against
2:18 while he tarried at J, and he said to
25:5 in the plains of J; and all his army
1Chr 6:78 beyond the Jordan at J, on the east side
19:5 king said, "Remain at J until your beards have
2Chr 28:15 to their kinsfolk at J, the city of palm
Ezra 2:34 The sons of J, three hundred and forty-five.
Neh 3:2 him the men of J built.

	7:36	The sons of J, three hundred and forty-five.
Jud	4:4	Beth-horon and Belmain and J and to Choba and
Sir	24:14	like rose plants in J; like a beautiful olive
Jer	39:5	in the plains of J; and when they had
	52:8	in the plains of J; and all his army
1Mac	9:50	Judea: the fortress in J, and Emmaus, and
	16:11	over the plain of J, and he had much
	16:14	he went down to J with Mattathias and Judas
2Mac	12:15	engines of war overthrew J in the days of
Mt	20:29	they went out of J, a great crowd followed
Mk	10:46	And they came to J; and as he was
	10:46	as he was leaving J with his disciples and
Lk	10:30	down from Jerusalem to J, and he fell among
	18:35	he drew near to J, a blind man was
	19:1	He entered J and was passing through.
Heb	11:30	faith the walls of J fell down after they

JERIJAH

1Chr	26:31	Of the Hebronites, J was chief of the Hebronites

JERIMOTH (6)

1Chr	7:7	Bela: Ezbon, Uzzi, Uzziel, J, and Iri, five, heads
	12:5	Jozabad of Gederah, Eluzai, J, Bealiah, Shemariah,
	24:30	The sons of Mushi: Mahli, Eder, and J
	25:4	Uzziel, Shebuel, and J, Hananiah, Hanani, Eliathah,
2Chr	11:18	Mahalath the daughter of J the son of David,
	31:13	Jehiel, Azaziah, Nahath, Asahel, J, Jozabad, Eliel,

JERIOTH

1Chr	2:18	wife Azubah, and by J; and these were her

JEROBOAM (105)

1Kgs	11:26	J the son of Nebat, an Ephraimite of Zeredah,
	11:28	The man J was very able, and when Solomon
	11:29	at that time, when J went out of Jerusalem,
	11:31	And he said to J, "Take for yourself ten
	11:40	sought therefore to kill J; but Jeroboam arose, and
	11:40	to kill Jeroboam; but J arose, and fled into
	12:2	And when J the son of Nebat heard of
	12:2	from King Solomon), then J returned from Egypt.
	12:3	and called him; and J and all the assembly
	12:12	So J and all the people came to Rehoboam
	12:15	Ahijah the Shilonite to J the son of Nebat.
	12:20	all Israel heard that J had returned, they sent
	12:25	Then J built Shechem in the hill country of
	12:26	And J said in his heart, "Now the kingdom
	12:32	And J appointed a feast on the fifteenth day
	13:1	J was standing by the altar to burn incense.
	13:4	the altar at Bethel, J stretched out his hand
	13:33	After this thing J did not turn from his
	13:34	to the house of J, so as to cut
	14:1	Abijah the son of J fell sick.
	14:2	And J said to his wife, "Arise, and disguise
	14:2	are the wife of J, and go to Shiloh;
	14:4	J's wife did so; she arose, and went to
	14:5	"Behold, the wife of J is coming to inquire
	14:6	"Come in, wife of J; why do you pretend
	14:7	Go, tell J, 'Thus says the LORD, the God
	14:10	upon the house of J, and will cut off
	14:10	will cut off from J every male, both bond
	14:10	consume the house of J, as a man burns
	14:11	Any one belonging to J who dies in the
	14:13	for he only of J shall come to the
	14:13	the God of Israel, in the house of J
	14:14	off the house of J today.
	14:16	of the sins of J, which he sinned and
	14:17	Then J's wife arose, and departed, and came to
	14:19	of the acts of J, how he warred and
	14:20	And the time that J reigned was twenty-two years;
	14:30	war between Rehoboam and J continually.
	15:1	eighteenth year of King J the son of Nebat,
	15:6	war between Rehoboam and J all the days of
	15:7	And there was war between Abijam and J
	15:9	the twentieth year of J king of Israel Asa
	15:25	Nadab the son of J began to reign over
	15:29	all the house of J; he left to the
	15:29	to the house of J not one that breathed,
	15:30	for the sins of J which he sinned and
	15:34	in the way of J and in his sin
	16:2	in the way of J, and have made my
	16:3	like the house of J the son of Nebat.
	16:7	like the house of J, and also because he
	16:19	in the way of J, and for his sin
	16:26	all the way of J the son of Nebat,
	16:31	in the sins of J the son of Nebat,
	21:22	like the house of J the son of Nebat,
	22:52	in the way of J the son of Nebat,
2Kgs	3:3	to the sin of J the son of Nebat,
	9:9	like the house of J the son of Nebat,
	10:29	from the sins of J the son of Nebat,
	10:31	from the sins of J, which he made Israel
	13:2	followed the sins of J the son of Nebat,
	13:6	of the house of J, which he made Israel
	13:11	all the sins of J the son of Nebat,
	13:13	with his fathers, and J sat upon his throne;
	14:16	kings of Israel; and J his son reigned in
	14:23	Joash, king of Judah, J the son of Joash,
	14:24	all the sins of J the son of Nebat,
	14:27	by the hand of J the son of Joash.
	14:28	of the acts of J, and all that he
	14:29	And J slept with his fathers, the kings of
	15:1	the twenty-seventh year of J king of Israel Azariah
	15:8	Zechariah the son of J reigned over Israel in
	15:9	from the sins of J the son of Nebat,
	15:18	all the sins of J the son of Nebat,
	15:24	from the sins of J the son of Nebat,
	15:28	from the sins of J the son of Nebat,
	17:21	of David they made J the son of Nebat
	17:21	And J drove Israel from following the LORD and
	17:22	all the sins which J did; they did not
	23:15	high place erected by J the son of Nebat,
1Chr	5:17	in the days of J king of Israel.
2Chr	9:29	Iddo the seer concerning J the son of Nebat?
	10:2	And when J the son of Nebat heard of
	10:2	from King Solomon), then J returned from Egypt.
	10:3	and called him; and J and all Israel came
	10:12	So J and all the people came to Rehoboam
	10:15	Ahijah the Shilonite to J the son of Nebat.
	11:4	LORD, and returned and did not go against J
	11:14	Judah and Jerusalem, because J and his sons cast
	12:15	were continual wars between Rehoboam and J
	13:1	eighteenth year of King J Abijah began to reign
	13:2	Now there was war between Abijah and J
	13:3	thousand picked men; and J drew up his line
	13:4	said, "Hear me, O J and all Israel!
	13:6	Yet J the son of Nebat, a servant of
	13:8	the golden calves which J made you for gods.
	13:13	J had sent an ambush around to come on
	13:15	Judah shouted, God defeated J and all Israel before
	13:19	And Abijah pursued J, and took cities from him,
	13:20	J did not recover his power in the days
Sir	47:23	Also J the son of Nebat, who caused Israel
Hos	1:1	in the days of J the son of Joash,
Amos	1:1	in the days of J the son of Joash,
	7:9	against the house of J with the sword."
	7:10	of Bethel sent to J king of Israel, saying,
	7:11	thus Amos has said, J shall die by the

JEROHAM (10)

1Sam	1:1	Elkanah the son of J, son of Elihu, son
1Chr	6:27	son, Eliab his son, J his son, Elkanah his
	6:34	of Elkanah, son of J, son of Eliel, son
	8:27	Ja-areshiah, Elijah, and Zichri were the sons of J
	9:8	Ibneiah the son of J, Elah the son of
	9:12	Adaiah the son of J, son of Pashhur, son
	12:7	Zebadiah, the sons of J of Gedor.
	27:22	of Abner; for Dan, Azarel the son of J
2Chr	23:1	Azariah the son of J, Ishmael the son of
Neh	11:12	Adaiah the son of J, son of Pelaliah, son

JERUBBAAL (14)

Judg	6:32	day he was called J, that is to say,
	7:1	Then J (that is, Gideon) and all the people
	8:29	J the son of Joash went and dwelt in
	8:35	to the family of J (that is, Gideon) in
	9:1	Abimelech the son of J went to Shechem to
	9:2	of the sons of J rule over you, or
	9:5	brothers the sons of J, seventy men, upon one
	9:5	the youngest son of J was left, for he
	9:16	have dealt well with J and his house, and
	9:19	faith and honor with J and with his house
	9:24	the seventy sons of J might come and their
	9:28	not the son of J and Zebul his officer
	9:57	came the curse of Jotham the son of J
1Sam	12:11	And the LORD sent J and Barak, and Jephthah,

JERUBBESHETH

2Sam	11:21	Who killed Abimelech the son of J

JERUEL

2Chr	20:16	of the valley, east of the wilderness of J

JERUSALEM (940)

Josh 10:1 When Adoni-zedek king of J heard how Joshua had
10:3 So Adoni-zedek king of J sent to Hoham king
10:5 Amorites, the king of J, the king of Hebron,
10:23 cave, the king of J, the king of Hebron,
12:10 one; the king of J, one; the king of
15:8 the Jebusite (that is, J; and the boundary goes
15:63 Jebusites, the inhabitants of J, the people of Judah
15:63 people of Judah at J to this day.
18:28 Ha-eleph, Jebus (that is, J, Gibe-ah and
Judg 1:7 they brought him to J, and he died there.
1:8 of Judah fought against J, and took it, and
1:21 Jebusites who dwelt in J; so the Jebusites have
1:21 people of Benjamin in J to this day.
19:10 and departed, and arrived opposite Jebus (that is, J
1Sam 17:54 and brought it to J; but he put his
2Sam 5:5 six months; and at J he reigned over all
5:6 his men went to J against the Jebusites, the
5:13 concubines and wives from J, after he came from
5:14 born to him in J: Shammua, Shobab, Nathan,
8:7 the servants of Hadadezer, and brought them to J
9:13 So Mephibosheth dwelt in J; for he ate always
10:14 from fighting against the Ammonites, and came to J
11:1 But David remained at J
11:12 So Uriah remained in J that day, and the
12:31 Then David and all the people returned to J
14:23 and went to Geshur, and brought Absalom to J
14:28 two full years in J, without coming into the
15:8 bring me back to J, then I will offer
15:11 two hundred men from J who were invited guests,
15:14 were with him at J, "Arise, and let us
15:29 of God back to J; and they remained there.
15:37 into the city, just as Absalom was entering J
16:3 "Behold, he remains in J; for he said, 'Today
16:15 of Israel, came to J, and Ahithophel with him.
17:20 and could not find them, they returned to J
19:19 lord the king left J; let not the king
19:25 when he came from J to meet the king,
19:33 I will provide for you with me in J
19:34 I should go up with the king to J
20:2 followed their king steadfastly from the Jordan to J
20:3 to his house at J; and the king took
20:7 they went out from J to pursue Sheba the
20:22 And Joab returned to J to the king.
24:8 land, they came to J at the end of
24:16 forth his hand toward J to destroy it, the
1Kgs 2:11 seven years in Hebron, and thirty-three years in J
2:36 yourself a house in J, and dwell there, and
2:38 So Shimei dwelt in J many days.
2:41 Shimei had gone from J to Gath and returned,
3:1 house of the LORD and the wall around J
3:15 Then he came to J, and stood before the
8:1 before King Solomon in J, to bring up the
9:15 and the wall of J and Hazor and Megiddo
9:19 desired to build in J, in Lebanon, and in
10:2 She came to J with a very great retinue,
10:26 the chariot cities and with the king in J
10:27 silver as common in J as stone, and he
11:7 of the Ammonites, on the mountain east of J
11:13 for the sake of J which I have chosen."
11:29 Jeroboam went out of J, the prophet Ahijah the
11:32 for the sake of J, the city which I
11:36 lamp before me in J, the city where I
11:42 that Solomon reigned in J over all Israel was
12:18 haste to mount his chariot, to flee to J
12:21 When Rehoboam came to J, he assembled all the
12:27 of the LORD at J, then the heart of
12:28 have gone up to J long enough.
14:21 reigned seventeen years in J, the city which the
14:25 Egypt came up against J;
15:2 He reigned for three years in J
15:4 him a lamp in J, setting up his son
15:4 after him, and establishing J;
15:10 over Judah, and he reigned forty-one years in J
22:42 to reign, and he reigned twenty-five years in J
2Kgs 8:17 became king, and he reigned eight years in J
8:26 to reign, and he reigned one year in J
9:28 in a chariot to J, and buried him in
12:1 to reign, and he reigned forty years in J
12:17 to go up against J,
12:18 Then Hazael went away from J
14:2 to reign, and he reigned twenty-nine years in J
14:2 His mother's name was Jeho-addin of J
14:13 Beth-shemesh, and came to J, and broke down the
14:13 down the wall of J for four hundred cubits,
14:19 conspiracy against him in J, and he fled to
14:20 he was buried in J with his fathers in
15:2 to reign, and he reigned fifty-two years in J
15:2 His mother's name was Jecoliah of J
15:33 to reign, and he reigned sixteen years in J
16:2 to reign, and he reigned sixteen years in J
16:5 to wage war on J, and they besieged Ahaz
18:2 to reign, and he reigned twenty-nine years in J
18:17 great army from Lachish to King Hezekiah at J
18:17 And they went up and came to J
18:22 to Judah and to J, "You shall worship before
18:22 Jerusalem, "You shall worship before this altar in J
18:35 the LORD should deliver J out of my hand?"
19:10 you by promising that J will not be given
19:21 wags her head behind you--the daughter of J
19:31 upward; for out of J shall go forth a
21:1 to reign, and he reigned fifty-five years in J
21:4 LORD had said, "In J will I put my
21:7 this house, and in J, which I have chosen
21:12 I am bringing upon J and Judah such evil
21:13 I will stretch over J the measuring line of
21:13 and I will wipe J as one wipes a
21:16 till he had filled J from one end to
21:19 to reign, and he reigned two years in J
22:1 to reign, and he reigned thirty-one years in J
22:14 (now she dwelt in J in the Second Quarter);
23:1 elders of Judah and J were gathered to him.
23:2 all the inhabitants of J, and the priests and
23:4 he burned them outside J in the fields of
23:5 Judah and round about J; those also who burned
23:6 of the LORD, outside J, to the brook Kidron,
23:9 of the LORD in J, but they ate unleavened
23:13 that were east of J, to the south of
23:20 Then he returned to J
23:23 this passover was kept to the LORD in J
23:24 of Judah and in J, that he might establish
23:27 which I have chosen, J, and the house of
23:30 and brought him to J, and buried him in
23:31 to reign, and he reigned three months in J
23:33 might not reign in J, and laid upon the
23:36 to reign, and he reigned eleven years in J
24:4 shed; for he filled J with innocent blood, and
24:8 became king, and he reigned three months in J
24:8 name was Nehushta the daughter of Elnathan of J
24:10 Babylon came up to J, and the city was
24:14 He carried away all J, and all the princes,
24:15 took into captivity from J to Babylon.
24:18 became king, and he reigned eleven years in J
24:20 to the point in J and Judah that he
25:1 all his army against J, and laid siege to
25:8 servant of the king of Babylon, came to J
25:9 all the houses of J; every great house he
25:10 of the guard, broke down the walls around J
1Chr 3:4 And he reigned thirty-three years in J
3:5 born to him in J: Shimea, Shobab, Nathan and
6:10 priest in the house that Solomon built in J
6:15 LORD sent Judah and J into exile by the
6:32 of the LORD in J; and they performed their
8:28 These dwelt in J
8:32 opposite their kinsmen in J, with their kinsmen.
9:3 and Manasseh dwelt in J:
9:34 to their generations, leaders, who lived in J
9:38 opposite their kinsmen in J, with their kinsmen.
11:4 all Israel went to J, that is Jebus, where
14:3 took more wives in J, and David begot more
14:4 whom he had in J: Shammua, Shobab, Nathan,
15:3 assembled all Israel at J, to bring up the
18:7 the servants of Hadadezer, and brought them to J
19:15 Then Joab came to J
20:1 But David remained at J
20:3 Then David and all the people returned to J
21:4 went throughout all Israel, and came back to J
21:15 sent the angel to J to destroy it; but
21:16 his hand a drawn sword stretched out over J
23:25 and he dwells in J for ever.
28:1 David assembled at J all the officials of Israel,
29:27 seven years in Hebron, and thirty-three years in J
2Chr 1:4 tent for it in J
1:13 Gibeon, from before the tent of meeting, to J
1:14 the chariot cities and with the king in J
1:15 gold as common in J as stone, and he
2:7 me in Judah and J, whom David my father
2:16 so that you may take it up to J
3:1 of the LORD in J on Mount Moriah, where
5:2 people of Israel, in J, to bring up the
6:6 but I have chosen J that my name may
8:6 desired to build in J, in Lebanon, and in

9:1 Solomon she came to J to test him with
9:25 the chariot cities and with the king in J
9:27 silver as common in J as stone, and cedar
9:30 Solomon reigned in J over all Israel forty years.
10:18 haste to mount his chariot, to flee to J
11:1 When Rehoboam came to J, he assembled the house
11:5 Rehoboam dwelt in J, and he built cities for
11:14 came to Judah and J, because Jeroboam and his
11:16 tribes of Israel to J to sacrifice to the
12:2 Egypt came up against J
12:4 cities of Judah and came as far as J
12:5 who had gathered at J because of Shishak, and
12:7 be poured out upon J by the hand of
12:9 Egypt came up against J; he took away the
12:13 Rehoboam established himself in J and reigned.
12:13 reigned seventeen years in J, the city which the
13:2 He reigned for three years in J
14:15 Then they returned to J
15:10 They were gathered at J in the third month
17:13 He had soldiers, mighty men of valor, in J
19:1 Judah returned in safety to his house in J
19:4 Jehoshaphat dwelt at J; and he went out again
19:8 in J Jehoshaphat appointed certain Levites and
19:8 They had their seat at J
20:5 assembly of Judah and J, in the house of
20:15 Judah and inhabitants of J, and King Jehoshaphat:
20:17 behalf, O Judah and J Fear not, and be
20:18 and the inhabitants of J fell down before the
20:20 and said, "Hear me, Judah and inhabitants of J
20:27 man of Judah and J, and Jehoshaphat at their
20:27 their head, returning to J with joy, for the
20:28 They came to J, with harps and lyres and
20:31 to reign, and he reigned twenty-five years in J
21:5 became king, and he reigned eight years in J
21:11 led the inhabitants of J into unfaithfulness, and made
21:13 and the inhabitants of J into unfaithfulness, as the
21:20 reigned eight years in J; and he departed with
22:1 And the inhabitants of J made Ahaziah his youngest
22:2 to reign, and he reigned one year in J
23:2 fathers' houses of Israel, and they came to J
24:1 reigned forty years in J; his mother's name was
24:6 in from Judah and J the tax levied by
24:9 made throughout Judah and J, to bring in for
24:18 came upon Judah and J for this their guilt.
24:23 came to Judah and J, and destroyed all the
25:1 to reign, and he reigned twenty-nine years in J
25:1 His mother's name was Jeho-addan of J
25:23 and brought him to J, and broke down the
25:23 down the wall of J for four hundred cubits,
25:27 conspiracy against him in J, and he fled to
26:3 to reign, and he reigned fifty-two years in J
26:3 His mother's name was Jecoliah of J
26:9 Uzziah built towers in J at the Corner Gate
26:15 In J he made engines, invented by skilful men,
27:1 to reign, and he reigned sixteen years in J
27:8 to reign, and he reigned sixteen years in J
28:1 to reign, and he reigned sixteen years in J
28:10 people of Judah and J, male and female, as
28:24 he made himself altars in every corner of J
28:27 in the city, in J, for they did not
29:1 years old, and he reigned twenty-nine years in J
29:8 came on Judah and J, and he has made
30:1 of the LORD at J, to keep the passover
30:2 all the assembly in J had taken counsel to
30:3 the people assembled in J –
30:5 God of Israel, at J; for they had not
30:11 and of Zebulun humbled themselves and came to J
30:13 people came together in J to keep the feast
30:14 altars that were in J, and all the altars
30:21 that were present at J kept the feast of
30:26 was great joy in J, for since the time
30:26 Israel there had been nothing like this in J
31:4 people who lived in J to give the portion
32:2 intended to fight against J,
32:9 sent his servants to J to Hezekiah king of
32:9 Judah that were in J, saying,
32:10 are you relying, that you stand siege in J
32:12 and commanded Judah and J, "Before one altar you
32:18 to the people of J who were upon the
32:19 of the God of J as they spoke of
32:22 and the inhabitants of J from the hand of
32:23 to the LORD to J and precious things to
32:25 Therefore wrath came upon him and Judah and J
32:26 and the inhabitants of J, so that the wrath
32:33 and the inhabitants of J did him honor at
33:1 to reign, and he reigned fifty-five years in J
33:4 LORD had said, "In J shall my name be
33:7 this house, and in J, which I have chosen
33:9 and the inhabitants of J, so that they did
33:13 brought him again to J into his kingdom.
33:15 the LORD and in J, and he threw them
33:21 to reign, and he reigned two years in J
34:1 to reign, and he reigned thirty-one years in J
34:3 to purge Judah and J of the high places,
34:5 priests on their altars, and purged Judah and J
34:7 Then he returned to J
34:9 Judah and Benjamin and from the inhabitants of J
34:22 (now she dwelt in J in the Second Quarter)
34:29 gathered together all the elders of Judah and J
34:30 and the inhabitants of J and the priests and
34:32 who were present in J and in Benjamin stand
34:32 And the inhabitants of J did according to the
35:1 to the LORD in J; and they killed the
35:18 Israel who were present, and the inhabitants of J
35:24 in his second chariot and brought him to J
35:24 All Judah and J mourned for Josiah.
36:1 made him king in his father's stead in J
36:2 to reign; and he reigned three months in J
36:3 Egypt deposed him in J and laid upon the
36:4 king over Judah and J, and changed his name
36:5 to reign, and he reigned eleven years in J
36:9 he reigned three months and ten days in J
36:10 made his brother Zedekiah king over Judah and J
36:11 to reign, and he reigned eleven years in J
36:14 of the LORD which he had hallowed in J
36:19 down the wall of J, and burned all its
36:23 him a house at J, which is in Judah.
Ezra 1:2 him a house at J, which is in Judah.
1:3 him go up to J, which is in Judah,
1:3 God who is in J;
1:4 for the house of God which is in J
1:5 LORD which is in J;
1:7 had carried away from J and placed in the
1:11 the exiles were brought up from Babylonia to J
2:1 Babylonia; they returned to J and Judah, each to
2:68 LORD which is in J, made freewill offerings for
2:70 the people lived in J and its vicinity; and
3:1 towns, the people gathered as one man to J
3:8 house of God at J, in the second month,
3:8 who had come to J from the captivity.
4:6 an accusation against the inhabitants of Judah and J
4:8 wrote a letter against J to Artaxerxes the king
4:12 up from you to us have gone to J
4:20 kings have been over J, who ruled over the
4:23 to the Jews at J and by force and
4:24 God which is in J stopped; and it ceased
5:1 were in Judah and J, in the name of
5:2 God which is in J; and with them were
5:14 temple that was in J and brought into the
5:15 temple which is in J, and let the house
5:16 God which is in J; and from that time
5:17 the rebuilding of this house of God in J
6:3 house of God at J, let the house be
6:5 temple that is in J and brought to Babylon,
6:5 temple which is in J, each to its place;
6:9 as the priests at J require– let that
6:12 destroy this house of God which is in J
6:18 service of God at J, as it is written
7:7 went up also to J, in the seventh year
7:8 And he came to J in the fifth month,
7:9 month he came to J, for the good hand
7:13 offers to go to J, may go with you.
7:14 inquiries about Judah and J according to the law
7:15 whose dwelling is in J,
7:16 the house of their God which is in J
7:17 the house of your God which is in J
7:19 God, you shall deliver before the God of J
7:27 LORD which is in J,
8:29 houses in Israel at J, within the chambers of
8:30 to bring them to J, to the house of
8:31 month, to go to J; the hand of our
8:32 We came to J, and there we remained three
9:9 and to give us protection in Judea and J
10:7 made throughout Judah and J to all the returned
10:7 they should assemble at J,
10:9 and Benjamin assembled at J within the three days;
Neh 1:2 survived, who had escaped exile, and concerning J
1:3 shame; the wall of J is broken down, and
2:11 So I came to J and was there three
2:12 had put into my heart to do for J
2:13 inspected the walls of J which were broken down
2:17 we are in, how J lies in ruins with

2:17 build the wall of J, that we may no
2:20 have no portion or right or memorial in J
3:8 repaired; and they restored J as far as the
3:9 half the district of J, repaired.
3:12 half the district of J, repaired, he and his
4:7 of the walls of J was going forward and
4:8 come and fight against J and to cause confusion
4:22 pass the night within J, that they may be
6:7 proclaim concerning you in J, 'There is a king
7:2 the castle charge over J, for he was a
7:3 not the gates of J be opened until the
7:3 among the inhabitants of J, each to his station
7:6 exile; they returned to J and Judah, each to
8:15 their towns and in J, "Go out to the
11:1 the people lived in J; and the rest of
11:1 ten to live in J the holy city, while
11:2 the men who willingly offered to live in J
11:3 province who lived in J; but in the towns
11:4 And in J lived certain of the sons of
11:6 Perez who lived in J were four hundred and
11:22 of the Levites in J was Uzzi the son
12:27 of the wall of J they sought the Levites
12:27 to bring them to J to celebrate the dedication
12:28 from the circuit round J and from the villages
12:29 the singers had built for themselves villages around J
12:43 And the joy of J was heard afar off.
13:6 I was not in J, for in the thirty-second
13:7 king and came to J, and I then discovered
13:15 which they brought into J on the sabbath day;
13:16 sabbath to the people of Judah, and in J
13:19 at the gates of J before the sabbath, I
13:20 of wares lodged outside J once or twice.

Tob 1:4 of Naphtali my forefather deserted the house of J
1:6 alone went often to J for the feasts, as
1:7 Levi who ministered at J; a second tenth I
1:7 proceeds each year at J;
5:13 we went together to J to worship and offered
13:8 all men speak, and give him thanks in J
13:9 O J, the holy city, he will afflict you
13:16 For J will be built with sapphires and emeralds,
13:17 The streets of J will be paved with beryl
14:4 the good land, and J will be desolate.
14:5 captivity, and will rebuild J in splendor.

Jud 1:9 Jordan as far as J and Bethany and Chelous
4:2 were alarmed both for J and for the temple
4:6 priest, who was in J at the time, wrote
4:8 Israel, in session at J, had given order.
4:11 children, living at J, prostrated themselves before the
4:13 throughout Judea and in J before the sanctuary of
5:19 and have occupied J, where their sanctuary is,
9:1 house of God in J, Judith cried out to
10:8 Israel may glory and J may be exalted." And
11:13 of our God at J --although it is not
11:14 have sent men to J, because even the people
11:19 till you come to J; and I will set
13:4 work of my hands for the exaltation of J
15:5 Those in J and all the hill country also
15:8 Israel who lived at J, came to witness the
15:9 are the exaltation of J, you are the great
16:18 When they arrived at J they worshiped God.
16:20 people continued feasting in J before the sanctuary

Esth 2:6 been carried away from J among the captives
11:1 son of Ptolemy, one of the residents of J
11:4 Babylon had brought from J with Jeconiah king of

Ps 51:18 rebuild the walls of J,
68:29 of thy temple at J kings bear gifts to
79:1 temple; they have laid J in ruins.
79:3 like water round about J, and there was none
102:21 the LORD, and in J his praise,
116:19 house of the LORD, in your midst, O J
122:2 feet have been standing within your gates, O J
122:3 J, built as a city which is bound firmly
122:6 Pray for the peace of J
125:2 mountains are round about J, so the LORD is
128:5 see the prosperity of J all the days of
135:21 the LORD from Zion, he who dwells in J
137:5 I forget you, O J, let my right hand
137:6 I do not set J above my highest joy!
137:7 Edomites the day of J, how they said, "Rase
147:2 The LORD builds up J; he gathers the outcasts
147:12 Praise the LORD, O J

Eccl 1:1 the Preacher, the son of David, king in J
1:12 the Preacher have been king over Israel in J
1:16 all who were over J before me; and my
2:7 than any who had been before me in J
2:9 were before me in J; also my wisdom remained

J

Song 1:5 comely, O daughters of J, like the tents of
2:7 you, O daughters of J, by the gazelles or
3:5 you, O daughters of J, by the gazelles or
3:10 was lovingly wrought within by the daughters of J
5:8 you, O daughters of J, if you find my
5:16 and this is my friend, O daughters of J
6:4 my love, comely as J, terrible as an army
8:4 you, O daughters of J, that you stir not

Sir 24:11 resting place, and in J was my dominion.
36:13 city of thy sanctuary, J, the place of thy
50:27 son of Eleazar, of J, who out of his

Is 1:1 saw concerning Judah and J in the days of
2:1 the son of Amoz saw concerning Judah and J
2:3 law, and the word of the LORD from J
3:1 is taking away from J and from Judah stay
3:8 For J has stumbled, and Judah has fallen; because
4:3 Zion and remains in J will be called holy,
4:3 recorded for life in J,
4:4 cleansed the bloodstains of J from its midst by
5:3 now, O inhabitants of J and men of Judah,
5:14 and the nobility of J and her multitude go
7:1 Israel came up to J to wage war against
8:14 trap and a snare to the inhabitants of J
10:10 greater than those of J and Samaria,
10:11 I not do to J and her idols as
10:12 Mount Zion and on J he will punish the
10:32 of the daughter of Zion, the hill of J
22:10 counted the houses of J, and you broke down
22:21 to the inhabitants of J and to the house
24:23 Mount Zion and in J and before his elders
27:13 worship the LORD on the holy mountain at J
28:14 LORD, you scoffers, who rule this people in J
30:19 Zion who dwell at J; you shall weep no
31:5 of hosts will protect J; he will protect and
31:9 is in Zion, and whose furnace is in J
33:20 Your eyes will see J, a quiet habitation, an
36:2 to King Hezekiah at J, with a great army.
36:7 to Judah and to J, "You shall worship before
36:20 the LORD should deliver J out of my hand?"
37:10 you by promising that J will not be given
37:22 her head behind you-- the daughter of J
37:32 upward; for out of J shall go forth a
40:2 Speak tenderly to J, and cry to her that
40:9 voice with strength, O J, herald of good tidings,
41:27 and I give to J a herald of good
44:26 messengers; who says of J, 'She shall be inhabited,'
44:28 my purpose'; saying of J, 'She shall be built,'
51:17 yourself, stand up, O J, you who have drunk
52:1 your beautiful garments, O J, the holy city; for
52:2 dust, arise, O captive J; loose the bonds from
52:9 you waste places of J; for the LORD has
52:9 LORD has comforted his people, he has redeemed J
62:1 keep silent, and for J's sake I will not
62:6 Upon your walls, O J, I have set watchmen;
62:7 rest until he establishes J and makes it a
64:10 has become a wilderness, J a desolation.
65:18 for behold, I create J a rejoicing, and her
65:19 I will rejoice in J, and be glad in
66:10 "Rejoice with J, and be glad for her, all
66:13 will comfort you; you shall be comforted in J
66:20 to my holy mountain J, says the LORD, just

Jer 1:3 until the captivity of J in the fifth month.
1:15 of the gates of J, against all its walls
2:2 in the hearing of J, Thus says the LORD,
3:17 At that time J shall be called the throne
3:17 of the LORD in J, and they shall no
4:3 to the inhabitants of J: "Break up your fallow
4:4 Judah and inhabitants of J; lest my wrath go
4:5 Judah, and proclaim in J, and say, "Blow the
4:10 deceived this people and J, saying, 'It shall be
4:11 this people and to J, "A hot wind from
4:14 O J, wash your heart from wickedness, that you
4:16 is coming; announce to J, "Besiegers come from a
5:1 through the streets of J, look and take note!
6:1 O people of Benjamin, from the midst of J
6:6 her trees; cast up a siege mound against J
6:8 Be warned, O J, lest I be alienated from
7:17 cities of Judah and in the streets of J
7:34 from the streets of J the voice of mirth
8:1 of the inhabitants of J shall be brought out
9:11 I will make J a heap of ruins, a
11:2 the men of Judah and the inhabitants of J
11:6 in the streets of J: Hear the words of
11:9 the men of Judah and the inhabitants of J
11:12 and the inhabitants of J will go and cry
11:13 as the streets of J are the altars you

13:9 pride of Judah and the great pride of J
13:13 priests, the prophets, and all the inhabitants of J
13:27 Woe to you, O J
14:2 and the cry of J goes up.
14:16 in the streets of J, victims of famine and
15:4 son of Hezekiah, king of Judah, did in J
15:5 pity on you, O J, or who will bemoan
17:19 all the gates of J,
17:20 all the inhabitants of J, who enter by these
17:21 or bring it in by the gates of J
17:25 and the inhabitants of J; and this city shall
17:26 the places round about J, from the land of
17:27 by the gates of J on the sabbath day,
17:27 devour the palaces of J and shall not be
18:11 and the inhabitants of J: 'Thus says the LORD,
19:3 LORD, O kings of Judah and inhabitants of J
19:7 plans of Judah and J, and will cause their
19:13 The houses of J and the houses of the
22:19 dragged and cast forth beyond the gates of J
23:14 in the prophets of J I have seen a
23:15 from the prophets of J ungodliness has gone forth
24:1 taken into exile from J Jeconiah the son of
24:8 princes, the remnant of J who remain in this
25:2 all the inhabitants of J:
25:18 sent me drink it: J and the cities of
26:18 plowed as a field; J shall become a heap
27:3 who have come to J to Zedekiah king of
27:18 of Judah, and in J may not go to
27:20 took into exile from J to Babylon Jeconiah the
27:20 nobles of Judah and J –
27:21 of Judah, and in J:
29:1 the prophet sent from J to the elders of
29:1 taken into exile from J to Babylon.
29:2 princes of Judah and J, the craftsmen, and the
29:2 the craftsmen, and the smiths had departed from J
29:4 sent into exile from J to Babylon:
29:20 I sent away from J to Babylon:
29:25 people who are in J, and to Zephaniah the
32:2 of Babylon was besieging J, and Jeremiah the
32:32 the men of Judah and the inhabitants of J
32:44 in the places about J, and in the cities
33:10 and the streets of J that are desolate, without
33:13 Benjamin, the places about J, and in the cities
33:16 will be saved and J will dwell securely.
34:1 peoples were fighting against J and all of its
34:6 king of Judah, in J,
34:7 Babylon was fighting against J and against all the
34:8 all the people in J to make a proclamation
34:19 Judah, the princes of J, the eunuchs, the priests,
35:11 let us go to J for fear of the
35:11 of the Syrians.' So we are living in J
35:13 and the inhabitants of J, Will you not receive
35:17 all the inhabitants of J all the evil that
36:9 all the people in J and all the people
36:9 cities of Judah to J proclaimed a fast before
36:31 upon the inhabitants of J, and upon the men
37:5 Chaldeans who were besieging J heard news of
37:5 heard news of them, they withdrew from J
37:11 army had withdrawn from J at the approach of
37:12 Jeremiah set out from J to go to the
38:28 until the day that J was taken.
39:1 his army came against J and besieged it;
39:3 When J was taken, all the princes of the
39:8 the people, and broke down the walls of J
40:1 all the captives of J and Judah who were
42:18 on the inhabitants of J, so my wrath will
44:2 that I brought upon J and upon all the
44:6 in the streets of J; and they became a
44:9 land of Judah and in the streets of J
44:13 as I have punished J, with the sword, with
44:17 in the streets of J; for then we had
44:21 in the streets of J, you and your fathers,
51:35 let J say.
51:50 from afar, and let J come into your mind:
52:1 became king; and he reigned eleven years in J
52:3 such a pass in J and Judah that he
52:4 all his army against J, and they laid siege
52:12 who served the king of Babylon, entered J
52:13 all the houses of J; every great house he
52:14 guard, broke down all the walls round about J
52:29 away captive from J eight hundred and thirty-two
Lam 1:7 J remembers in the days of her affliction and
1:8 J sinned grievously, therefore she became filthy; all
1:17 should be his foes; J has become a filthy
2:10 sackcloth; the maidens of J have bowed their heads
2:13 you, to what compare you, O daughter of J
2:15 at the daughter of J; "Is this the city
4:12 foe or enemy could enter the gates of J
Bar 1:2 when the Chaldeans took J and burned it with
1:7 they sent it to J to Jehoiakim the high
1:7 the people who were present with him in J
1:9 had carried away from J Jeconiah and the princes
1:15 to the inhabitants of J,
2:2 he has done in J, in accordance with what
2:23 from the region about J the voice of mirth
4:8 up, and you grieved J, who reared you.
4:30 Take courage, O J, for he who named you
4:36 toward the east, O J, and see the joy
5:1 sorrow and affliction, O J, and put on for
5:5 Arise, O J, stand upon the height and look
Ezek 4:1 it a city, even J;
4:7 toward the siege of J, with your arm bared;
4:16 staff of bread in J; they shall eat bread
5:5 Lord GOD: This is J; I have set her
8:3 visions of God to J, to the entrance of
9:4 through the city, through J, and put a mark
9:8 Israel in the outpouring of thy wrath upon J
11:15 whom the inhabitants of J have said, 'They have
12:10 concerns the prince in J and all the house
12:19 concerning the inhabitants of J in the land of
13:16 Israel who prophesied concerning J and saw visions
14:21 when I send upon J my four sore acts
14:22 I have brought upon J, for all that I
15:6 so will I give up the inhabitants of J
16:2 man, make known to J her abominations,
16:3 the Lord GOD to J: Your origin and your
17:12 of Babylon came to J, and took her king
21:2 set your face toward J and preach against the
21:20 to Judah and to J the fortified.
21:22 comes the lot for J, to open the mouth
22:19 I will gather you into the midst of J
23:4 their names, Oholah is Samaria, and Oholibah is J
24:2 has laid siege to J this very day.
26:2 because Tyre said concerning J, 'Aha, the gate of
33:21 who had escaped from J came to me and
36:38 like the flock at J during her appointed feasts,
Dan 1:1 of Babylon came to J and besieged it.
3:28 upon us and upon J, the holy city of
5:2 of the temple in J be brought, that the
5:3 house of God in J; and the king and
6:10 upper chamber open toward J; and he got down
9:2 of the desolations of J, namely, seventy years.
9:7 to the inhabitants of J, and to all Israel,
9:12 the like of what has been done against J
9:16 away from thy city J, thy holy hill; because
9:16 iniquities of our fathers, J and thy people have
9:25 to restore and build J to the coming of
Joel 2:32 Mount Zion and in J there shall be those
3:1 fortunes of Judah and J,
3:6 people of Judah and J to the Greeks, removing
3:16 utters his voice from J, and the heavens and
3:17 And J shall be holy and strangers shall never
3:20 inhabited for ever, and J to all generations.
Amos 1:2 utters his voice from J; the pastures of the
2:5 Judah, and it shall devour the strongholds of J
Obad 1:11 and cast lots for J, you were like one
1:20 and the exiles of J who are in Sepharad
Mic 1:1 of Judah, which he saw concerning Samaria and J
1:5 Is it not J
1:9 reached to the gate of my people, to J
1:12 down from the LORD to the gate of J
3:10 Zion with blood and J with wrong.
3:12 plowed as a field; J shall become a heap
4:2 law, and the word of the LORD from J
4:8 shall come, the kingdom of the daughter of J
Zeph 1:4 all the inhabitants of J; and I will cut
1:12 time I will search J with lamps, and I
3:14 exult with all your heart, O daughter of J
3:16 shall be said to J: "Do not fear, O
Zech 1:12 have no mercy on J and the cities of
1:14 am exceedingly jealous for J and for Zion.
1:16 I have returned to J with compassion; my house
1:16 the measuring line shall be stretched out over J
1:17 LORD will again comfort Zion and again choose J
1:19 the horns which have scattered Judah, Israel, and J
2:2 to me, "To measure J, to see what is
2:4 to that young man, J shall be inhabited as
2:12 in the holy land, and will again choose J
3:2 LORD who has chosen J rebuke you!
7:7 When J was inhabited and in prosperity, with her
8:3 in the midst of J, and Jerusalem shall be
8:3 midst of Jerusalem, and J shall be called the

8:4 in the streets of J, each with staff in
8:8 in the midst of J; and they shall be
8:15 to do good to J and to the house
8:22 LORD of hosts in J, and to entreat the
9:9 Shout aloud, O daughter of J
9:10 the war horse from J; and the battle bow
12:2 am about to make J a cup of reeling
12:2 be against Judah also in the siege against J
12:3 day I will make J a heavy stone for
12:5 themselves, 'The inhabitants of J have strength
12:6 peoples round about, while J shall still be inhabited
12:6 shall still be inhabited in its place, in J
12:7 of the inhabitants of J may not be exalted
12:8 about the inhabitants of J so that the feeblest
12:9 to destroy all the nations that come against J
12:10 and the inhabitants of J a spirit of compassion
12:11 day the mourning in J will be as great
13:1 and the inhabitants of J to cleanse them from
14:2 all the nations against J to battle, and the
14:4 Olives which lies before J on the east; and
14:8 shall flow out from J, half of them to
14:10 a plain from Geba to Rimmon south of J
14:10 But J shall remain aloft upon its site from
14:11 be no more curse; J shall dwell in security.
14:12 that wage war against J: their flesh shall rot
14:14 of the other; even Judah will fight against J
14:16 that have come against J shall go up year
14:17 not go up to J to worship the King,
14:21 and every pot in J and Judah shall be
Mal 2:11 in Israel and in J; for Judah has profaned
3:4 offering of Judah and J will be pleasing to
1Mac 1:14 built a gymnasium in J, according to Gentile custom,
1:20 Israel and came to J with a strong force.
1:29 and he came to J with a large force.
1:35 collecting the spoils of J they stored them there,
1:38 them the residents of J fled; she became a
1:44 letters by messengers to J and the cities of
2:1 of Joarib, moved from J and settled in Modein.
2:6 committed in Judah and J,
2:18 that are left in J have done.
2:31 to the troops in J the city of David,
3:34 residents of Judea and J,
3:35 and the remnant of J; he was to banish
3:45 J was uninhabited like a wilderness; not one of
3:46 went to Mizpah, opposite J, because Israel formerly
6:7 upon the altar in J; and that they had
6:12 now I remember the evils I did in J
6:26 against the citadel in J to take it; they
6:48 army went up to J against them, and the
7:17 poured out round about J, and there was none
7:19 Then Bacchides departed from J and encamped in
7:27 So Nicanor came to J with a large force,
7:39 Nicanor went out from J and encamped in
7:47 and brought them and displayed them just outside J
8:22 tablets, and sent to J to remain with them
9:3 year they encamped against J;
9:50 Bacchides then returned to J and built strong cities
9:53 put them under guard in the citadel at J
10:7 Then Jonathan came to J and read the letter
10:10 And Jonathan dwelt in J and began to rebuild
10:31 And let J and her environs, her tithes and
10:32 of the citadel in J and give it to
10:39 to the sanctuary in J, to meet the necessary
10:43 at the temple in J, or in any of
10:45 rebuilding the walls of J and fortifying it round
10:66 And Jonathan returned to J in peace and gladness.
10:74 and set out from J, and Simon his brother
10:87 with him returned to J with much booty.
11:7 the river called Eleutherus; then he returned to J
11:20 attack the citadel in J, and he built many
11:34 who offer sacrifice in J, we have granted release
11:41 of the citadel from J, and the troops in
11:51 and they returned to J with much spoil.
11:62 their rulers as hostages and sent them to J
11:74 And Jonathan returned to J
12:25 he marched away from J and met them in
12:36 build the walls of J still higher, and to
13:2 he went up to J, and gathering the people
13:10 complete the walls of J, and he fortified it
13:39 has been collected in J shall be collected no
13:49 in the citadel at J were prevented from going
14:19 And these were read before the assembly in J
14:36 city of David in J, who had built themselves
14:37 built the walls of J higher.
15:7 I grant freedom to J and the sanctuary.
15:28 and the citadel in J; they are cities of
15:32 the king came to J, and when he saw
16:20 to take possession of J and the temple hill.
2Mac 1:1 The Jewish brethren in J and those in the
1:10 Those in J and those in Judea and the
3:6 that the treasury in J was full of untold
3:9 he had arrived at J and had been kindly
3:37 on another mission to J, he replied,
4:9 enrol the men of J as citizens of Antioch.
4:19 being Antiochian citizens from J, to carry three
4:21 Therefore upon arriving at Joppa he proceeded to J
5:22 afflict the people: at J, Philip, by birth a
5:25 this man arrived in J, he pretended to be
6:2 pollute the temple in J and call it the
8:31 and carried the rest of the spoils to J
8:36 of the people of J proclaimed that the Jews
9:4 there I will make J a cemetery of Jews."
10:15 who were banished from J, and endeavored to keep
11:5 about five leagues from J, and pressed it hard.
11:8 they were still near J, a horseman appeared at
12:9 light was seen in J, thirty miles distant.
12:29 to Scythopolis, which is seventy-five miles from J
12:31 they went up to J, as the feast of
12:43 and sent it to J to provide for a
14:23 Nicanor stayed on in J and did nothing out
14:37 of the elders of J, was denounced to Nicanor
15:30 Nicanor's head and arm and carry them to J
Mt 2:1 the East came to J, saying,
2:3 was troubled, and all J with him;
3:5 went out to him J and all Judea and
4:25 and the Decapolis and J and Judea and from
5:35 his footstool, or by J, for it is the
15:1 came to Jesus from J and said,
16:21 he must go to J and suffer many things
20:17 was going up to J, he took the twelve
20:18 are going up to J; and the Son of
21:1 they drew near to J and came to Bethphage,
21:10 And when he entered J, all the city was
23:36 "O J, Jerusalem, killing the prophets and stoning
23:36 "O Jerusalem, J, killing the prophets and stoning
Mk 1:5 all the people of J; and they were baptized
3:8 also from Judea and J and Idumea and from
3:22 who came down from J said, "He is possessed
7:1 who had come from J,
10:32 road, going up to J, and Jesus was walking
10:33 are going up to J; and the Son of
11:1 they drew near to J, to Bethphage and Bethany,
11:11 And he entered J, and went into the temple;
11:15 And they came to J
11:26 And they came again to J
15:40 other women who came up with him to J
Lk 2:22 brought him up to J to present him to
2:25 was a man in J, whose name was Simeon,
2:38 all who were looking for the redemption of J
2:41 his parents went to J every year at the
2:43 were returning, the boy Jesus stayed behind in J
2:45 him, they returned to J, seeking him.
4:9 he took him to J, and set him on
5:17 and Judea and from J; and the power of
6:17 from all Judea and J and the seacoast of
9:31 his departure, which he was to accomplish at J
9:51 up, he set his face to go to J
9:53 receive him, because his face was set toward J
10:30 was going down from J to Jericho, and he
13:4 offenders than all the others who dwelt in J
13:22 and villages, teaching, and journeying toward J
13:33 should perish away from J
13:34 from Jerusalem.' O J, Jerusalem, killing the prophets
13:34 from Jerusalem.' O Jerusalem, J, killing the prophets
17:11 On the way to J he was passing along
18:31 are going up to J, and everything that is
19:11 he was near to J, and because they supposed
19:28 this, he went on ahead, going up to J
21:20 "But when you see J surrounded by armies, then
21:24 among all nations; and J will be trodden down
23:7 who was himself in J at that time.
23:27 them said, "Daughters of J, do not weep for
24:13 about seven miles from J,
24:18 the only visitor to J who does not know
24:33 hour and returned to J; and they found the
24:47 in his name to all nations, beginning from J
24:52 him, and returned to J with great joy,
Jn 1:19 priests and Levites from J to ask him, "Who
2:13 was at hand, and Jesus went up to J
2:23 when he was in J at the Passover feast,
4:20 you say that in J is the place where
4:21 this mountain nor in J will you worship the

4:45 he had done in J at the feast, for
5:1 of the Jews, and Jesus went up to J
5:2 Now there is in J by the Sheep Gate
7:25 of the people of J therefore said, "Is not
10:22 of the Dedication at J;
11:18 Bethany was near J, about two miles off,
11:55 from the country to J before the Passover, to
12:12 the feast heard that Jesus was coming to J
Acts 1:4 not to depart from J, but to wait for
1:8 be my witnesses in J and in all Judea
1:12 Then they returned to J from the mount called
1:12 Olivet, which is near J, a sabbath day's journey
1:19 all the inhabitants of J, so that the field
2:5 there were dwelling in J Jews, devout men from
2:14 all who dwell in J, let this be known
4:5 were gathered together in J,
4:16 all the inhabitants of J, and we cannot deny
5:16 from the towns around J, bringing the sick and
5:28 here you have filled J with your teaching and
6:7 disciples multiplied greatly in J, and a great many
8:1 against the church in J; and they were all
8:14 when the apostles at J heard that Samaria had
8:25 Lord, they returned to J, preaching the gospel to
8:26 that goes down from J to Gaza." This is
8:27 treasure, had come to J to worship
9:2 or women, he might bring them bound to J
9:13 to thy saints at J;
9:21 who made havoc in J of those who called
9:26 he had come to J he attempted to join
9:28 out among them at J,
10:39 in the country of the Jews and in J
11:2 Peter went up to J, the circumcision party criticized
11:22 of the church in J, and they sent Barnabas
11:27 prophets came down from J to Antioch.
12:25 and Saul returned from J when they had fulfilled
13:13 them and returned to J;
13:27 those who live in J and their rulers, because
13:31 him from Galilee to J, who are now his
15:2 to go up to J to the apostles and
15:4 When they came to J, they were welcomed by
16:4 by the apostles and elders who were at J
19:21 Achaia and go to J, saying, "After I have
20:16 hastening to be at J, if possible, on the
20:22 I am going to J, bound in the Spirit,
21:4 they told Paul not to go on to J
21:11 shall the Jews at J bind the man who
21:12 there begged him not to go up to J
21:13 even to die at J for the name of
21:15 days we made ready and went up to J
21:17 we had come to J, the brethren received us
21:31 the cohort that all J was in confusion.
22:5 them in bonds to J to be punished.
22:17 I had returned to J and was praying in
22:18 get quickly out of J, because they will not
23:11 testified about me at J, so you must bear
24:10 up to worship at J;
25:1 he went up to J from Caesarea.
25:3 the man sent to J, planning an ambush to
25:7 had gone down from J stood about him, bringing
25:9 to go up to J, and there be tried
25:15 when I was at J, the chief priests and
25:20 wished to go to J and be tried there
25:24 petitioned me, both at J and here, shouting that
26:4 own nation and at J, is known by all
26:10 I did so in J; I not only shut
26:20 at Damascus, then at J and throughout all the
28:17 was delivered prisoner from J into the hands of
Rom 15:19 Spirit, so that from J and as far round
15:25 I am going to J with aid for the
15:26 among the saints at J;
15:31 that my service for J may be acceptable to
1Cor 16:3 accredit by letter to carry your gift to J
Gal 1:17 I go up to J to those who were
1:18 I went up to J to visit Cephas, and
2:1 went up again to J with Barnabas, taking Titus
4:25 corresponds to the present J, for she is in
4:26 But the J above is free, and she is
Heb 12:22 living God, the heavenly J, and to innumerable angels
Rev 3:12 my God, the new J which comes down from
21:2 the holy city, new J, coming down out of
21:10 me the holy city J coming down out of

JERUSHA
2Kgs 15:33 His mother's name was J the daughter of Zadok.

JERUSHAH
2Chr 27:1 His mother's name was J the daughter of Zadok.

JESHAIAH (7)
1Chr 3:21 of Hananiah: Pelatiah and J, his son Rephaiah, his
25:3 Gedaliah, Zeri, J, Shimei, Hashabiah, and Mattithiah,
25:15 twelve; the eighth to J, his sons and his
26:25 Rehabiah, and his son J, and his son Joram,
Ezra 8:7 the sons of Elam, J the son of Athaliah,
8:19 Hashabiah and with him J of the sons of
Neh 11:7 son of Ma-aseiah, son of Ithi-el, son of J

JESHANAH (2)
1Sam 7:12 up between Mizpah and J, and called its name
2Chr 13:19 with its villages and J with its villages and

JESHARELAH
1Chr 25:14 twelve; the seventh to J, his sons and his

JESHEBE-AB
1Chr 24:13 Huppah, the fourteenth to J,

JESHER
1Chr 2:18 these were her sons: J, Shobab, and Ardon.

JESHIMON (4)
1Sam 23:19 the hill of Hachilah, which is south of J
23:24 Maon, in the Arabah to the south of J
26:1 of Hachilah, which is on the east of J
26:3 is beside the road on the east of J

JESHISHAI
1Chr 5:14 of Michael, son of J, son of Jahdo, son

JESHOHAIAH
1Chr 4:36 of Asiel, Eli-o-enai, Ja-akobah, J, Asaiah, Adi-el,

JESHUA (31)
1Chr 24:11 Abijah, the ninth to J, the tenth to Shecaniah,
2Chr 31:15 Eden, Miniamin, J, Shemaiah, Amariah, and
Ezra 2:2 They came with Zerubbabel, J, Nehemiah, Seraiah,
2:6 namely the sons of J and Joab, two thousand
2:36 of the house of J, nine hundred and seventy-three.
2:40 Levites: the sons of J and Kadmi-el, of the
3:2 Then arose J the son of Jozadak, with his
3:8 son of Shealtiel and J the son of Jozadak
3:9 And J with his sons and his kinsmen, and
4:3 But Zerubbabel, J, and the rest of the heads
5:2 son of Shealtiel and J the son of Jozadak
8:33 Jozabad the son of J and No-adiah the son
10:18 of the sons of J the son of Jozadak
Neh 3:19 Ezer the son of J, ruler of Mizpah, repaired
7:7 They came with Zerubbabel, J, Nehemiah, Azariah,
7:11 namely the sons of J and Joab, two thousand
7:39 namely the house of J, nine hundred and
7:43 Levites: the sons of J, namely of Kadmi-el of
8:7 Also J, Bani, Sherebiah, Jamin, Akkub, Shabbethai,
8:17 from the days of J the son of Nun
9:4 of the Levites stood J, Bani, Kadmi-el, Shebaniah,
9:5 Then the Levites, J, Kadmi-el, Bani, Hashabneiah,
10:9 And the Levites: J the son of Azaniah, Binnui
11:26 its villages, and in J and in Moladah and
12:1 son of Shealtiel, and J: Seraiah, Jeremiah, Ezra,
12:7 and of their brethren in the days of J
12:8 And the Levites: J, Binnui, Kadmi-el, Sherebiah,
12:10 And J was the father of Joiakim, Joiakim the
12:24 Levites: Hashabiah, Sherebiah, and J the son of
12:26 Joiakim the son of J son of Jozadak, and
Sir 49:12 hand, and so was J the son of Jozadak;

JESHURUN (4)
Deut 32:15 "But J waxed fat, and kicked; you waxed fat,
33:5 LORD became king in J, when the heads of
33:26 none like God, O J, who rides through the
Is 44:2 O Jacob my servant, J whom I have chosen.

JESIMIEL
1Chr 4:36 Ja-akobah, Jeshohaiah, Asaiah, Adi-el, J, Benaiah,

JESSE (48)
Ruth 4:17 was the father of J, the father of David.
4:22 of Obed, Obed of J, and Jesse of David.
4:22 Obed of Jesse, and J of David.
1Sam 16:1 will send you to J the Bethlehemite, for I
16:3 the LORD.' And invite J to the sacrifice, and
16:5 And he consecrated J and his sons, and invited

16:8 Then J called Abinadab, and made him pass before
16:9 Then J made Shammah pass by.
16:10 And J made seven of his sons pass before
16:10 And Samuel said to J, "The LORD has not
16:11 And Samuel said to J, "Are all your sons
16:11 And Samuel said to J, "Send and fetch him;
16:18 seen a son of J the Bethlehemite, who is
16:19 Saul sent messengers to J, and said, "Send me
16:20 And J took an ass laden with bread, and
16:22 And Saul sent to J, saying, "Let David remain
17:12 Bethlehem in Judah, named J, who had eight sons.
17:13 three eldest sons of J had followed Saul to
17:17 And J said to David his son, "Take for
17:20 provisions, and went, as J had commanded him; and
17:58 son of your servant J the Bethlehemite."
20:27 not the son of J come to the meal,
20:30 chosen the son of J to your own shame,
20:31 as the son of J lives upon the earth,
22:7 will the son of J give every one of
22:8 with the son of J, none of you is
22:9 saw the son of J coming to Nob, to
22:13 and the son of J, in that you have
25:10 Who is the son of J
2Sam 20:1 in the son of J; every man to his
23:1 David, the son of J, the oracle of the
1Kgs 12:16 We have no inheritance in the son of J
1Chr 2:12 Salma of Boaz, Boaz of Obed, Obed of J
2:13 J was the father of Eliab his first-born, Abinadab
10:14 the kingdom over to David the son of J
12:18 O David; and with you, O son of J
29:26 David the son of J reigned over all Israel.
2Chr 10:16 We have no inheritance in the son of J
11:18 Eliab the son of J;
Ps 72:20 David, the son of J, are ended.
Sir 45:25 David, the son of J, of the tribe of
Is 11:1 from the stump of J, and a branch shall
11:10 day the root of J shall stand as an
Mt 1:5 Obed the father of J,
1:6 father of Jesse, and J the father of David
Lk 3:32 David, the son of J, the son of Obed,
Acts 13:22 David the son of J a man after my
Rom 15:12 says, "The root of J shall come, he who

JEST

Sir 8:4 Do not J with an ill-bred person, lest your

JESTING

Gen 19:14 But he seemed to his sons-in-law to be J

JESUS (930)

Sir 50:27 written in this book, J the son of Sirach,
Mt 1:1 of the genealogy of J Christ, the son of
1:16 of Mary, of whom J was born, who is
1:18 Now the birth of J Christ took place in
1:21 shall call his name J, for he will save
1:25 borne a son; and he called his name J
2:1 Now when J was born in Bethlehem of Judea
3:13 Then J came from Galilee to the Jordan to
3:15 But J answered him, "Let it be so now;
3:16 And when J was baptized, he went up immediately
4:1 Then J was led up by the Spirit into
4:7 J said to him, "Again it is written, 'You
4:10 Then J said to him, "Begone, Satan!
4:17 From that time J began to preach, saying, "Repent,
7:28 And when J finished these sayings, the crowds were
8:4 And J said to him, "See that you say
8:10 When J heard him, he marveled, and said to
8:13 And to the centurion J said, "Go; be it
8:14 And when J entered Peter's house, he saw his
8:18 Now when J saw great crowds around him, he
8:20 And J said to him, "Foxes have holes, and
8:22 But J said to him, "Follow me, and leave
8:34 came out to meet J; and when they saw
9:2 his bed; and when J saw their faith he
9:4 But J, knowing their thoughts, said, "Why do you
9:9 As J passed on from there, he saw a
9:10 and sat down with J and his disciples.
9:15 And J said to them, "Can the wedding guests
9:19 And J rose and followed him, with his disciples.
9:22 J turned, and seeing her he said, "Take heart,
9:23 And when J came to the ruler's house, and
9:27 And as J passed on from there, two blind
9:28 came to him; and J said to them, "Do
9:30 And J sternly charged them, "See that no one
9:35 And J went about all the cities and villages,
10:5 twelve J sent out, charging them, "Go nowhere
11:1 when J had finished instructing his twelve disciples,
11:4 And J answered them, "Go and tell John what
11:7 As they went away, J began to speak to
11:25 At that time J declared, "I thank thee, Father,
12:1 At that time J went through the grainfields on
12:15 J, aware of this, withdrew from there.
13:1 That same day J went out of the house
13:34 All this J said to the crowds in parables;
13:53 And when J had finished these parables, he went
13:57 But J said to them, "A prophet is not
14:1 about the fame of J;
14:12 and buried it; and they went and told J
14:13 Now when J heard this, he withdrew from there
14:16 J said, "They need not go away; you give
14:29 water and came to J;
14:31 J immediately reached out his hand and caught him,
15:1 and scribes came to J from Jerusalem and said,
15:21 And J went away from there and withdrew to
15:28 Then J answered her, "O woman, great is your
15:29 And J went on from there and passed along
15:32 Then J called his disciples to him and said,
15:34 And J said to them, "How many loaves have
16:6 J said to them, "Take heed and beware of
16:8 But J, aware of this, said, "O men of
16:13 Now when J came into the district of Caesarea
16:17 J answered him, "Blessed are you, Simon Bar-Jona!
16:21 From that time J began to show his disciples
16:24 Then J told his disciples, "If any man would
17:1 And after six days J took with him Peter
17:4 And Peter said to J, "Lord, it is well
17:7 But J came and touched them, saying, "Rise, and
17:8 saw no one but J only.
17:9 down the mountain, J commanded them, "Tell no
17:17 J answered, "O faithless and perverse generation,
17:18 And J rebuked him, and the demon came out
17:19 the disciples came to J privately and said, "Why
17:21 were gathering in Galilee, J said to them, "The
17:24 when he came home, J spoke to him first,
17:25 J said to him, "Then the sons are free.
18:1 the disciples came to J, saying, "Who is the
18:21 J said to him, "I do not say to
19:1 Now when J had finished these sayings, he went
19:14 rebuked the people; but J said, "Let the children
19:18 And J said, "You shall not kill, You shall
19:21 J said to him, "If you would be perfect,
19:23 And J said to his disciples, "Truly, I say
19:26 But J looked at them and said to them,
19:28 J said to them, "Truly, I say to you,
20:17 And as J was going up to Jerusalem, he
20:22 But J answered, "You do not know what you
20:25 But J called them to him and said, "You
20:30 when they heard that J was passing by, cried
20:32 And J stopped and called them, saying, "What do
20:34 And J in pity touched their eyes, and immediately
21:1 Mount of Olives, then J sent two disciples,
21:6 went and did as J had directed them;
21:11 "This is the prophet J from Nazareth of Galilee."
21:12 And J entered the temple of God and drove
21:16 And J said to them, "Yes; have you never
21:21 And J answered them, "Truly, I say to you,
21:24 J answered them, "I also will ask you a
21:27 So they answered J, "We do not know." And
21:31 J said to them, "Truly, I say to you,
21:42 J said to them, "Have you never read in
22:1 And again J spoke to them in parables, saying,
22:18 But J, aware of their malice, said, "Why put
22:20 And J said to them, "Whose likeness and inscription
22:29 But J answered them, "You are wrong, because you
22:41 Pharisees were gathered together, J asked them a
23:1 Then said J to the crowds and to his
24:1 J left the temple and was going away, when
24:4 And J answered them, "Take heed that no one
26:1 When J had finished all these sayings, he said
26:4 in order to arrest J by stealth and kill
26:6 Now when J was at Bethany in the house
26:10 But J, aware of this, said to them, "Why
26:17 the disciples came to J, saying, "Where will you
26:19 the disciples did as J had directed them, and
26:26 as they were eating, J took bread, and blessed,
26:31 Then J said to them, "You will all fall
26:34 J said to him, "Truly, I say to you,
26:36 Then J went with them to a place called
26:49 he came up to J at once and said,
26:50 J said to him, "Friend, why are you here?"
26:50 and laid hands on J and seized him.
26:51 those who were with J stretched out his hand

26:52 Then J said to him, "Put your sword back
26:55 At that hour J said to the crowds, "Have
26:57 those who had seized J led him to Caiaphas
26:59 sought false testimony against J that they might put
26:63 But J was silent.
26:64 J said to him, "You have said so.
26:69 "You also were with J the Galilean."
26:71 "This man was with J of Nazareth."
26:75 remembered the saying of J, "Before the cock crows,
27:1 people took counsel against J to put him to
27:11 Now J stood before the governor; and the governor
27:11 J said, "You have said so."
27:17 for you, Barabbas or J who is called Christ?"
27:20 the people to ask for Barabbas and destroy J
27:22 shall I do with J who is called Christ?"
27:26 Barabbas, and having scourged J, delivered him to
27:27 of the governor took J into the praetorium, and
27:37 which read, "This is J the King of the
27:46 about the ninth hour J cried with a loud
27:50 And J cried again with a loud voice and
27:54 him, keeping watch over J, saw the earthquake and
27:55 afar, who had followed J from Galilee, ministering to
27:57 named Joseph, who also was a disciple of J
27:58 to Pilate and asked for the body of J
28:5 know that you seek J who was crucified.
28:9 And behold, J met them and said, "Hail!" And
28:10 Then J said to them, "Do not be afraid;
28:16 the mountain to which J had directed them.
28:18 And J came and said to them, "All authority
Mk 1:1 of the gospel of J Christ, the Son of
1:9 In those days J came from Nazareth of Galilee
1:14 after John was arrested, J came into Galilee,
1:17 And J said to them, "Follow me and I
1:24 to do with us, J of Nazareth?
1:25 But J rebuked him, saying, "Be silent, and come
1:45 the news, so that J could no longer openly
2:5 And when J saw their faith, he said to
2:8 And immediately J, perceiving in his spirit that they
2:15 sinners were sitting with J and his disciples; for
2:17 And when J heard it, he said to them,
2:19 And J said to them, "Can the wedding guests
3:7 J withdrew with his disciples to the sea, and
5:6 And when he saw J from afar, he ran
5:7 to do with me, J, Son of the Most
5:9 And J asked him, "What is your name?" He
5:15 And they came to J, and saw the demoniac
5:17 they began to beg J to depart from their
5:20 the Decapolis how much J had done for him;
5:21 And when J had crossed again in the boat
5:27 heard the reports about J, and came up behind
5:30 And J, perceiving in himself that power had gone
5:36 ignoring what they said, J said to the ruler
6:4 And J said to them, "A prophet is not
6:14 heard of it; for J name had become known.
6:30 The apostles returned to J, and told him all
8:17 being aware of it, J said to them, "Why
8:27 And J went on with his disciples, to the
9:2 And after six days J took with him Peter
9:4 Elijah with Moses; and they were talking to J
9:5 And Peter said to J, "Master, it is well
9:8 one with them but J only.
9:21 And J asked his father, "How long has he
9:23 And J said to him, "If you can!
9:25 And when J saw that a crowd came running
9:27 But J took him by the hand and lifted
9:39 But J said, "Do not forbid him; for no
10:5 But J said to them, "For your hardness of
10:14 But when J saw it he was indignant, and
10:18 And J said to him, "Why do you call
10:21 And J looking upon him loved him, and said
10:23 And J looked around and said to his disciples,
10:24 But J said to them again, "Children, how hard
10:27 J looked at them and said, "With men it
10:29 J said, "Truly, I say to you, there is
10:32 up to Jerusalem, and J was walking ahead of
10:38 But J said to them, "You do not know
10:39 And J said to them, "The cup that I
10:42 And J called them to him and said to
10:47 heard that it was J of Nazareth, he began
10:47 cry out and say, J, Son of David, have
10:49 And J stopped and said, "Call him." And they
10:50 his mantle he sprang up and came to J
10:51 And J said to him, "What do you want
10:52 And J said to him, "Go your way; your
11:6 they told them what J had said; and they
11:7 brought the colt to J, and threw their garments
11:22 And J answered them, "Have faith in God.
11:28 J said to them, "I will ask you a
11:32 So they answered J, "We do not know." And
11:32 And J said to them, "Neither will I tell
12:17 J said to them, "Render to Caesar the things
12:24 J said to them, "Is not this why you
12:29 J answered, "The first is, 'Hear, O Israel: The
12:34 And when J saw that he answered wisely, he
12:35 And as J taught in the temple, he said,
13:2 And J said to him, "Do you see these
13:5 And J began to say to them, "Take heed
14:6 But J said, "Let her alone; why do you
14:18 were at table eating, J said, "Truly, I say
14:27 And J said to them, "You will all fall
14:30 And J said to him, "Truly, I say to
14:48 And J said to them, "Have you come out
14:53 And they led J to the high priest; and
14:55 council sought testimony against J to put him to
14:60 the midst, and asked J, "Have you no answer
14:62 And J said, "I am; and you will see
14:67 and said, "You also were with the Nazarene, J
14:72 And Peter remembered how J had said to him,
15:1 consultation; and they bound J and led him away
15:5 But J made no further answer, so that Pilate
15:15 Barabbas; and having scourged J, he delivered him
15:33 at the ninth hour J cried with a loud
15:36 And J uttered a loud cry, and breathed his
15:42 to Pilate, and asked for the body of J
16:6 be amazed; you seek J of Nazareth, who was
16:19 So then the Lord J, after he had spoken
Lk 1:31 a son, and you shall call his name J
2:21 circumcised, he was called J, the name given by
2:27 brought in the child J, to do for him
2:43 returning, the boy J stayed behind in Jerusalem.
2:52 And J increased in wisdom and in stature, and
3:21 were baptized, and when J also had been baptized
3:23 J, when he began his ministry, was about thirty
4:1 And J, full of the Holy Spirit, returned from
4:4 And J answered him, "It is written, 'Man shall
4:8 And J answered him, "It is written, 'You shall
4:12 And J answered him, "It is said, 'You shall
4:14 And J returned in the power of the Spirit
4:34 to do with us, J of Nazareth?
4:35 But J rebuked him, saying, "Be silent, and come
5:8 he fell down at J knees, saying, "Depart from
5:10 And J said to Simon, "Do not be afraid;
5:12 and when he saw J, he fell on his
5:18 and lay him before J;
5:19 bed through the tiles into the midst before J
5:22 J perceived their questionings, he answered them,
5:31 And J answered them, "Those who are well have
5:34 And J said to them, "Can you make wedding
6:3 And J answered, "Have you not read what David
6:9 And J said to them, "I ask you, is
6:11 with one another what they might do to J
7:3 When he heard of J, he sent to him
7:4 when they came to J, they besought him earnestly,
7:6 And J went with them.
7:9 When J heard this he marveled at him, and
7:40 And J answering said to him, "Simon, I have
8:28 When he saw J, he cried out and fell
8:28 to do with me, J, Son of the Most
8:30 demon into the desert.) J then asked him, "What
8:35 and they came to J, and found the man
8:35 at the feet of J, clothed and in his
8:39 whole city how much J had done for him.
8:40 Now when J returned, the crowd welcomed him, for
8:41 synagogue; and falling at J feet he besought him
8:45 And J said, "Who was it that touched me?"
8:46 But J said, "Some one touched me; for I
8:50 But J on hearing this answered him, "Do not
9:33 him, Peter said to J, "Master, it is well
9:36 the voice had spoken, J was found alone.
9:41 J answered, "O faithless and perverse generation,
9:42 But J rebuked the unclean spirit, and healed the
9:47 But when J perceived the thought of their hearts,
9:50 But J said to him, "Do not forbid him;
9:58 And J said to him, "Foxes have holes, and
9:62 J said to him, "No one who puts his
10:29 justify himself, said to J, "And who is my
10:30 J replied, "A man was going down from Jerusalem
10:37 And J said to him, "Go and do likewise."
13:12 And when J saw her, he called her and
13:14 the synagogue, indignant because J had healed on
14:3 And J spoke to the lawyers and Pharisees, saying,
17:13 their voices and said, J, Master, have mercy on

17:16 on his face at J feet, giving him thanks.
17:17 Then said J, "Were not ten cleansed?
18:16 But J called them to him, saying, "Let the
18:19 And J said to him, "Why do you call
18:22 And when J heard it, he said to him,
18:24 J looking at him said, "How hard it is
18:37 They told him, J of Nazareth is passing by."
18:38 And he cried, J, Son of David, have mercy
18:40 And J stopped, and commanded him to be brought
18:42 And J said to him, "Receive your sight; your
19:3 sought to see who J was, but could not,
19:5 And when J came to the place, he looked
19:9 And J said to him, "Today salvation has come
19:35 they brought it to J, and throwing their garments
19:35 the colt they set J upon it.
20:8 And J said to them, "Neither will I tell
20:34 And J said to them, "The sons of this
22:8 So J sent Peter and John, saying, "Go and
22:45 He drew near to J to kiss him;
22:46 to kiss him; but J said to him, "Judas,
22:49 But J said, "No more of this!" And he
22:50 Then J said to the chief priests and officers
22:61 men who were holding J mocked him and beat
23:8 When Herod saw J, he was very glad, for
23:19 more, desiring to release J;
23:24 they asked for; but J he delivered up to
23:25 on him the cross, to carry it behind J
23:27 But J turning to them said, "Daughters of Jerusalem,
23:33 And J said, "Father, forgive them; for they know
23:41 And he said, J, remember me when you come
23:45 Then J, crying with a loud voice, said, "Father,
23:51 to Pilate and asked for the body of J
24:15 talking and discussing together, J himself drew near
24:19 said to him, "Concerning J of Nazareth, who was
24:36 they were saying this, J himself stood among them,
Jn 1:17 and truth came through J Christ.
1:29 next day he saw J coming toward him, and
1:36 and he looked at J as he walked, and
1:37 disciples heard him say this, and they followed J
1:38 J turned, and saw them following, and said to
1:42 He brought him to J
1:42 J looked at him, and said, "So you are
1:43 The next day J decided to go to Galilee.
1:45 also the prophets wrote, J of Nazareth, the son
1:47 J saw Nathanael coming to him, and said of
1:48 J answered him, "Before Philip called you, when you
1:50 J answered him, "Because I said to you, I
2:1 and the mother of J was there;
2:2 of Jesus was there; J also was invited to
2:3 failed, the mother of J said to him, "They
2:4 And J said to her, "O woman, what have
2:7 J said to them, "Fill the jars with water."
2:11 first of his signs, J did at Cana in
2:13 was at hand, and J went up to Jerusalem.
2:19 J answered them, "Destroy this temple, and in three
2:22 and the word which J had spoken.
2:24 which he did; but J did not trust himself
3:2 This man came to J by night and said
3:3 J answered him, "Truly, truly, I say to you,
3:5 J answered, "Truly, truly, I say to you, unless
3:10 J answered him, "Are you a teacher of Israel,
3:22 After this J and his disciples went into the
4:1 Pharisees had heard that J was making and
4:2 disciples than John (although J himself did not
4:6 was there, and so J, wearied as he was
4:7 J said to her, "Give me a drink."
4:10 J answered her, "If you knew the gift of
4:13 J said to her, "Every one who drinks of
4:16 J said to her, "Go, call your husband, and
4:17 J said to her, "You are right in saying,
4:21 J said to her, "Woman, believe me, the hour
4:26 J said to her, "I who speak to you
4:34 J said to them, "My food is to do
4:44 For J himself testified that a prophet has no
4:47 When he heard that J had come from Judea
4:48 J therefore said to him, "Unless you see signs
4:50 J said to him, "Go; your son will live."
4:50 believed the word that J spoke to him and
4:53 was the hour when J had said to him,
4:54 the second sign that J did when he had
5:1 of the Jews, and J went up to Jerusalem.
5:5 When J saw him and knew that he had
5:7 J said to him, "Rise, take up your pallet,
5:12 who it was, for J had withdrawn, as there
5:13 Afterward, J found him in the temple, and said
5:14 Jews that it was J who had healed him.
5:15 why the Jews persecuted J, because he did this
5:16 But J answered them, "My Father is working still,
5:18 J said to them, "Truly, truly, I say to
6:1 After this J went to the other side of
6:3 J went up on the mountain, and there sat
6:5 was coming to him, J said to Philip, "How
6:10 J said, "Make the people sit down." Now there
6:11 J then took the loaves, and when he had
6:15 to make him king, J withdrew again to the
6:17 was now dark, and J had not yet come
6:19 four miles, they saw J walking on the sea
6:22 boat there, and that J had not entered the
6:24 the people saw that J was not there, nor
6:24 into the boats and went to Caperna-um, seeking J
6:26 J answered them, "Truly, truly, I say to you,
6:29 J answered them, "This is the work of God,
6:32 J then said to them, "Truly, truly, I say
6:35 J said to them, "I am the bread of
6:42 said, "Is not this J, the son of Joseph,
6:43 J answered them, "Do not murmur among
6:53 So J said to them, "Truly, truly, I say
6:61 But J, knowing in himself that his disciples
6:64 For J knew from the first who those were
6:67 J said to the twelve, "Do you also wish
6:70 J answered them, "Did I not choose you, the
7:1 After this J went about in Galilee; he would
7:6 J said to them, "My time has not yet
7:14 middle of the feast J went up into the
7:16 So J answered them, "My teaching is not mine,
7:21 J answered them, "I did one deed, and you
7:28 So J proclaimed, as he taught in the temple,
7:33 J then said, "I shall be with you a
7:37 feast, the great day, J stood up and proclaimed,
7:39 not been given, because J was not yet glorified.
8:1 But J went to the Mount of Olives.
8:6 J bent down and wrote with his finger on
8:9 with the eldest, and J was left alone with
8:10 J looked up and said to her, "Woman, where
8:11 And J said, "Neither do I condemn you; go,
8:12 Again J spoke to them, saying, "I am the
8:14 J answered, "Even if I do bear witness to
8:19 J answered, "You know neither me nor my Father;
8:25 J said to them, "Even what I have told
8:28 So J said, "When you have lifted up the
8:31 J then said to the Jews who had believed
8:34 J answered them, "Truly, truly, I say to you,
8:39 J said to them, "If you were Abraham's children,
8:42 J said to them, "If God were your Father,
8:49 J answered, "I have not a demon; but I
8:54 J answered, "If I glorify myself, my glory is
8:58 J said to them, "Truly, truly, I say to
8:59 throw at him; but J hid himself, and went
9:3 J answered, "It was not that this man sinned,
9:11 answered, "The man called J made clay and
9:14 a sabbath day when J made the clay and
9:35 J heard that they had cast him out, and
9:37 J said to him, "You have seen him, and
9:39 J said, "For judgment I came into this world,
9:41 J said to them, "If you were blind, you
10:6 This figure J used with them, but they did
10:7 So J again said to them, "Truly, truly, I
10:23 it was winter, and J was walking in the
10:25 J answered them, "I told you, and you do
10:32 J answered them, "I have shown you many good
10:34 J answered them, "Is it not written in your
11:4 But when J heard it he said, "This illness
11:5 Now J loved Martha and her sister and Lazarus.
11:9 J answered, "Are there not twelve hours in the
11:13 Now J had spoken of his death, but they
11:14 Then J told them plainly, "Lazarus is dead;
11:17 Now when J came, he found that Lazarus had
11:20 When Martha heard that J was coming, she went
11:21 Martha said to J, "Lord, if you had been
11:23 J said to her, "Your brother will rise again."
11:25 J said to her, "I am the resurrection and
11:30 Now J had not yet come to the village,
11:32 when she came where J was and saw him,
11:33 When J saw her weeping, and the Jews who
11:35 J wept.
11:38 Then J, deeply moved again, came to the tomb;
11:39 J said, "Take away the stone." Martha, the sister
11:40 J said to her, "Did I not tell you
11:41 And J lifted up his eyes and said, "Father,
11:44 J said to them, "Unbind him, and let him
11:46 and told them what J had done.
11:51 year he prophesied that J should die for the

11:54 J therefore no longer went about openly among the
11:56 They were looking for J and saying to one
12:1 days before the Passover, J came to Bethany, where
12:1 where Lazarus was, whom J had raised from the
12:3 anointed the feet of J and wiped his feet
12:7 J said, "Let her alone, let her keep it
12:9 only on account of J but also to see
12:11 the Jews were going away and believing in J
12:12 the feast heard that J was coming to Jerusalem.
12:14 And J found a young ass and sat upon
12:16 at first; but when J was glorified, then they
12:21 said to him, "Sir, we wish to see J
12:22 Andrew; Andrew went with Philip and they told J
12:23 And J answered them, "The hour has come for
12:30 J answered, "This voice has come for your sake,
12:35 J said to them, "The light is with you
12:36 When J had said this, he departed and hid
12:44 And J cried out and said, "He who believes
13:1 of the Passover, when J knew that his hour
13:3 son, to betray him, J, knowing that the Father
13:7 J answered him, "What I am doing you do
13:8 J answered him, "If I do not wash you,
13:10 J said to him, "He who has bathed does
13:21 When J had thus spoken, he was troubled in
13:23 of his disciples, whom J loved, was lying close
13:23 to the breast of J;
13:25 to the breast of J, he said to him,
13:26 J answered, "It is he to whom I shall
13:27 J said to him, "What you are going to
13:29 had the money box, J was telling him, "Buy
13:31 he had gone out, J said, "Now is the
13:36 J answered, "Where I am going you cannot follow
13:38 J answered, "Will you lay down your life for
14:6 J said to him, "I am the way, and
14:9 J said to him, "Have I been with you
14:23 J answered him, "If a man loves me, he
16:19 J knew that they wanted to ask him; so
16:31 J answered them, "Do you now believe?
17:1 When J had spoken these words, he lifted up
17:3 only true God, and J Christ whom thou hast
18:1 When J had spoken these words, he went forth
18:2 knew the place; for J often met there with
18:4 Then J, knowing all that was to befall him,
18:5 They answered him, J of Nazareth." Jesus said to
18:5 J said to them, "I am he." Judas, who
18:7 And they said, J of Nazareth."
18:8 J answered, "I told you that I am he;
18:11 J said to Peter, "Put your sword into its
18:12 of the Jews seized J and bound him.
18:15 Simon Peter followed J, and so did another disciple.
18:15 high priest along with J,
18:19 high priest then questioned J about his disciples and
18:20 J answered him, "I have spoken openly to the
18:22 officers standing by struck J with his hand, saying,
18:23 J answered him, "If I have spoken wrongly, bear
18:28 Then they led J from the house of Caiaphas
18:32 fulfill the word which J had spoken to show
18:33 praetorium again and called J, and said to him,
18:34 J answered, "Do you say this of your own
18:36 J answered, "My kingship is not of this world;
18:37 J answered, "You say that I am a king.
19:1 Then Pilate took J and scourged him.
19:5 So J came out, wearing the crown of thorns
19:9 again and said to J, "Where are you from?"
19:9 But J gave no answer.
19:11 J answered him, "You would have no power over
19:13 these words, he brought J out and sat down
19:17 So they took J, and he went out, bearing
19:18 on either side, and J between them.
19:19 the cross; it read, J of Nazareth, the King
19:20 for the place where J was crucified was near
19:23 the soldiers had crucified J they took his garments
19:25 by the cross of J were his mother, and
19:26 When J saw his mother, and the disciple whom
19:28 After this J, knowing that all was now finished,
19:30 When J had received the vinegar, he said, "It
19:33 when they came to J and saw that he
19:38 was a disciple of J, but secretly, for fear
19:38 away the body of J, and Pilate gave him
19:40 took the body of J, and bound it in
19:42 at hand, they laid J there.
20:2 disciple, the one whom J loved, and said to
20:12 where the body of J had lain, one at
20:14 turned round and saw J standing, but she did
20:14 but she did not know that it was J
20:15 J said to her, "Woman, why are you weeping?
20:16 J said to her, "Mary." She turned and said
20:17 J said to her, "Do not hold me, for
20:19 fear of the Jews, J came and stood among
20:21 J said to them again, "Peace be with you.
20:24 not with them when J came.
20:26 doors were shut, but J came and stood among
20:29 J said to him, "Have you believed because you
20:30 Now J did many other signs in the presence
20:31 you may believe that J is the Christ, the
21:1 After this J revealed himself again to the disciples
21:4 as day was breaking, J stood on the beach;
21:4 the disciples did not know that it was J
21:5 J said to them, "Children, have you any fish?"
21:7 That disciple whom J loved said to Peter, "It
21:10 J said to them, "Bring some of the fish
21:12 J said to them, "Come and have breakfast." Now
21:13 J came and took the bread and gave it
21:14 the third time that J was revealed to the
21:15 they had finished breakfast, J said to Simon Peter,
21:17 J said to him, "Feed my sheep.
21:20 them the disciple whom J loved, who had lain
21:21 him, he said to J, "Lord, what about this
21:22 J said to him, "If it is my will
21:23 not to die; yet J did not say to
21:25 many other things which J did; were every one
Acts 1:1 dealt with all that J began to do and
1:11 This J, who was taken up from you into
1:14 Mary the mother of J, and with his brothers.
1:16 Judas who was guide to those who arrested J
1:21 time that the Lord J went in and out
2:22 Israel, hear these words: J of Nazareth, a man
2:23 yourselves know-- this J, delivered up according to
2:32 This J God raised up, and of that we
2:36 Lord and Christ, this J whom you crucified."
2:38 in the name of J Christ for the forgiveness
3:6 in the name of J Christ of Nazareth, walk."
3:13 fathers, glorified his servant J, whom you delivered
3:16 faith which is through J has given the man
3:20 Christ appointed for you, J,
4:2 people and proclaiming in J the resurrection from
4:10 by the name of J Christ of Nazareth, whom
4:13 and they recognized that they had been with J
4:18 or teach at all in the name of J
4:27 against thy holy servant J, whom thou didst anoint,
4:30 performed through the name of thy holy servant J
4:33 resurrection of the Lord J, and great grace was
5:30 of our fathers raised J whom you killed by
5:40 in the name of J, and let them go.
5:42 cease teaching and preaching J as the Christ.
6:14 him say that this J of Nazareth will destroy
7:55 glory of God, and J standing at the right
7:59 Stephen, he prayed, "Lord J, receive my spirit."
8:12 and the name of J Christ, they were baptized,
8:16 been baptized in the name of the Lord J
8:35 scripture he told him the good news of J
9:5 he said, "I am J, whom you are persecuting;
9:17 "Brother Saul, the Lord J who appeared to you
9:20 synagogues immediately he proclaimed J, saying,
9:22 Damascus by proving that J was the Christ.
9:27 he had preached boldly in the name of J
9:34 said to him, "Aeneas, J Christ heals you; rise
10:36 news of peace by J Christ (he is Lord
10:38 preached: how God anointed J of Nazareth with the
10:48 in the name of J Christ.
11:17 believed in the Lord J Christ, who was I
11:20 spoke to the Greeks also, preaching the Lord J
13:23 to Israel a Savior, J, as he promised.
13:33 their children by raising J; as also it is
15:11 grace of the Lord J, just as they will."
15:26 sake of our Lord J Christ.
16:7 but the Spirit of J did not allow them;
16:18 in the name of J Christ to come out
16:31 "Believe in the Lord J, and you will be
17:3 dead, and saying, "This J, whom I proclaim to
17:7 of Caesar, saying that there is another king, J
17:18 divinities"--because he preached J and the.
18:5 testifying to the Jews that the Christ was J
18:25 accurately the things concerning J, though he knew
18:28 showing by the scriptures that the Christ was J
19:4 who was to come after him, that is, J
19:5 were baptized in the name of the Lord J
19:13 name of the Lord J over those who had
19:13 adjure you by the J whom Paul preaches."
19:15 evil spirit answered them, J I know, and Paul
19:17 name of the Lord J was extolled.
20:21 faith in our Lord J Christ.

20:24 received from the Lord J, to testify to the
20:35 words of the Lord J, how he said, 'It
21:13 at Jerusalem for the name of the Lord J
22:8 to me, 'I am J of Nazareth whom you
24:23 and heard him speak upon faith in Christ J
25:19 superstition and about one J, who was dead, but
26:9 opposing the name of J of Nazareth.
26:15 Lord said, 'I am J whom you are persecuting.
28:23 to convince them about J both from the law
28:30 teaching about the Lord J Christ quite openly and
Rom 1:1 Paul, a servant of J Christ, called to be
1:4 resurrection from the dead, J Christ our Lord,
1:6 called to belong to J Christ;
1:7 Father and the Lord J Christ.
1:8 thank my God through J Christ for all of
2:16 God judges the secrets of men by Christ J
3:22 God through faith in J Christ for all who
3:24 which is in Christ J,
3:26 that he justifies him who has faith in J
4:24 raised from the dead J our Lord,
5:1 God through our Lord J Christ.
5:11 God through our Lord J Christ, through whom we
5:15 of that one man J Christ abounded for many.
5:17 through the one man J Christ.
5:21 to eternal life through J Christ our Lord.
6:3 been baptized into Christ J were baptized into his
6:11 to sin and alive to God in Christ J
6:23 eternal life in Christ J our Lord.
7:25 be to God through J Christ our Lord!
8:1 no condemnation for those who are in Christ J
8:2 of life in Christ J has set me free
8:11 of him who raised J from the dead dwells
8:11 he who raised Christ J from the dead will
8:34 Is it Christ J, who died, yes, who was
8:39 of God in Christ J our Lord.
10:9 with your lips that J is Lord and believe
13:14 put on the Lord J Christ, and make no
14:14 persuaded in the Lord J that nothing is unclean
15:5 in accord with Christ J,
15:6 Father of our Lord J Christ.
15:16 a minister of Christ J to the Gentiles in
15:17 In Christ J, then, I have reason to be
15:30 brethren, by our Lord J Christ and by the
16:3 fellow workers in Christ J,
16:20 grace of our Lord J Christ be with you.
16:24 and the preaching of J Christ, according to the
16:26 glory for evermore through J Christ!
1Cor 1:1 an apostle of Christ J, and our brother Sosthenes,
1:2 those sanctified in Christ J, called to be saints
1:2 name of our Lord J Christ, both their Lord
1:3 Father and the Lord J Christ.
1:4 given you in Christ J,
1:7 revealing of our Lord J Christ;
1:8 day of our Lord J Christ.
1:9 fellowship of his Son, J Christ our Lord.
1:10 name of our Lord J Christ, that all of
1:30 your life in Christ J, whom God made our
2:2 nothing among you except J Christ and him crucified.
3:11 is laid, which is J Christ.
4:15 your father in Christ J through the gospel.
5:4 name of the Lord J on the man who
5:4 power of our Lord J,
5:5 be saved in the day of the Lord J
6:11 name of the Lord J Christ and in the
8:6 exist, and one Lord, J Christ, through whom are
9:1 Have I not seen J our Lord?
11:23 you, that the Lord J on the night when
12:3 of God ever says J be cursed!" and no
12:3 no one can say J is Lord" except by
15:31 I have in Christ J our Lord, I die
15:57 victory through our Lord J Christ.
16:23 grace of the Lord J be with you.
16:24 My love be with you all in Christ J
2Cor 1:1 an apostle of Christ J by the will of
1:2 Father and the Lord J Christ.
1:3 Father of our Lord J Christ, the Father of
1:14 of you, on the day of the Lord J
1:19 the Son of God, J Christ, whom we preached
4:5 is not ourselves, but J Christ as Lord, with
4:5 as your servants for J sake.
4:10 body the death of J, so that the life
4:10 that the life of J may also be manifested
4:11 up to death for J sake, so that the
4:11 that the life of J may be manifested in
4:14 who raised the Lord J will raise us also
4:14 raise us also with J and bring us with
8:9 grace of our Lord J Christ, that though he
11:4 comes and preaches another J than the one we
11:31 Father of the Lord J, he who is blessed
13:5 you not realize that J Christ is in you?--
13:14 grace of the Lord J Christ and the love
Gal 1:1 through man, but through J Christ and God the
1:3 Father and our Lord J Christ,
1:12 through a revelation of J Christ.
2:4 we have in Christ J, that they might bring
2:16 but through faith in J Christ, even we have
2:16 have believed in Christ J, in order to be
3:1 before whose eyes J Christ was publicly portrayed
3:14 that in Christ J the blessing of Abraham
3:22 promised to faith in J Christ might be given
3:26 custodian; for in Christ J you are all sons
3:28 female; for you are all one in Christ J
4:14 me as an angel of God, as Christ J
5:6 in Christ J neither circumcision nor uncircumcision is
5:24 who belong to Christ J have crucified the flesh
6:14 cross of our Lord J Christ, by which the
6:17 I bear on my body the marks of J
6:18 grace of our Lord J Christ be with your
Eph 1:1 an apostle of Christ J by the will of
1:1 also faithful in Christ J:
1:2 Father and the Lord J Christ.
1:3 Father of our Lord J Christ, who has blessed
1:5 be his sons through J Christ, according to the
1:15 faith in the Lord J and your love toward
1:17 God of our Lord J Christ, the Father of
2:6 heavenly places in Christ J,
2:7 his grace in kindness toward us in Christ J
2:10 workmanship, created in Christ J for good works,
2:13 But now in Christ J you who once were
2:20 apostles and prophets, Christ J himself being the
3:1 a prisoner for Christ J on behalf of you
3:6 the promise in Christ J through the gospel.
3:11 has realized in Christ J our Lord,
3:21 church and in Christ J to all generations, for
4:21 taught in him, as the truth is in J
5:20 name of our Lord J Christ to God the
6:23 Father and the Lord J Christ.
6:24 who love our Lord J Christ with love undying.
Phil 1:1 Timothy, servants of Christ J, To all the saints
1:1 the saints in Christ J who are at Philippi,
1:2 Father and the Lord J Christ.
1:6 at the day of J Christ.
1:8 for you all with the affection of Christ J
1:11 righteousness which come through J Christ, to the
1:19 of the Spirit of J Christ this will turn
1:26 to glory in Christ J, because of my coming
2:5 is yours in Christ J,
2:10 at the name of J every knee should bow,
2:11 every tongue confess that J Christ is Lord, to
2:19 hope in the Lord J to send Timothy to
2:21 interests, not those of J Christ.
3:3 and glory in Christ J, and put no confidence
3:8 worth of knowing Christ J my Lord.
3:12 my own, because Christ J has made me his
3:14 of the upward call of God in Christ J
3:20 a Savior, the Lord J Christ,
4:7 keep your hearts and your minds in Christ J
4:19 according to his riches in glory in Christ J
4:21 Greet every saint in Christ J
4:23 grace of the Lord J Christ be with your
Col 1:1 an apostle of Christ J by the will of
1:3 Father of our Lord J Christ, when we pray
1:4 your faith in Christ J and of the love
2:6 therefore you received Christ J the Lord, so live
3:17 name of the Lord J, giving thanks to God
4:11 you, receive him), and J who is called Justus.
4:12 a servant of Christ J, greets you, always
1Thes 1:1 Father and the Lord J Christ: Grace to you
1:3 hope in our Lord J Christ.
1:10 raised from the dead, J who delivers us from
2:14 of God in Christ J which are in Judea;
2:15 killed both the Lord J and the prophets, and
2:19 boasting before our Lord J at his coming?
3:11 himself, and our Lord J, direct our way to
3:13 coming of our Lord J with all his saints.
4:1 you in the Lord J, that as you learned
4:2 what instructions we gave you through the Lord J
4:14 since we believe that J died and rose again,
4:14 again, even so, through J, God will bring with
5:9 salvation through our Lord J Christ,
5:18 of God in Christ J for you.
5:23 coming of our Lord J Christ.

5:28 grace of our Lord J Christ be with you.
2Thes 1:1 father and the Lord J Christ:
1:2 Father and the Lord J Christ.
1:7 afflicted, when the Lord J is revealed from heaven
1:8 do not obey the gospel of our Lord J
1:12 name of our Lord J may be glorified in
1:12 God and the Lord J Christ.
2:1 coming of our Lord J Christ and our assembling
2:8 revealed, and the Lord J will slay him with
2:14 glory of our Lord J Christ.
2:16 Now may our Lord J Christ himself, and God
3:6 name of our Lord J Christ, that you keep
3:12 exhort in the Lord J Christ to do their
3:18 grace of our Lord J Christ be with you
1Tim 1:1 an apostle of Christ J by command of God
1:1 Savior and of Christ J our hope,
1:2 the Father and Christ J our Lord.
1:12 strength for this, Christ J our Lord, because he
1:14 the faith and love that are in Christ J
1:15 full acceptance, that Christ J came into the world
1:16 me, as the foremost, J Christ might display his
2:5 men, the man Christ J,
3:13 confidence in the faith which is in Christ J
4:6 good minister of Christ J, nourished on the words
5:21 God and of Christ J and of the elect
6:3 words of our Lord J Christ and the teaching
6:13 things, and of Christ J who in his testimony
6:14 appearing of our Lord J Christ;
2Tim 1:1 an apostle of Christ J by the will of
1:1 which is in Christ J,
1:2 the Father and Christ J our Lord.
1:9 gave us in Christ J ages ago,
1:10 of our Savior Christ J, who abolished death and
1:13 which are in Christ J;
2:1 that is in Christ J,
2:3 in suffering as a good soldier of Christ J
2:8 Remember J Christ, risen from the dead, descended
2:10 obtain salvation in Christ J with its eternal glory.
3:12 godly life in Christ J will be persecuted,
3:15 instruct you for salvation through faith in Christ J
4:1 God and of Christ J who is to judge
Tit 1:1 and an apostle of J Christ, to further the
1:3 the Father and Christ J our Savior.
2:13 great God and Savior J Christ,
3:6 upon us richly through J Christ our Savior,
Philem 1:1 a prisoner for Christ J, and Timothy our brother,
1:3 Father and the Lord J Christ.
1:5 have toward the Lord J and all the saints,
1:9 prisoner also for Christ J –
1:23 fellow prisoner in Christ J, sends greetings to you,
1:25 grace of the Lord J Christ be with your
Heb 2:9 But we see J, who for a little while
3:1 a heavenly call, consider J, the apostle and high
3:3 Yet J has been counted worthy of as much
4:14 passed through the heavens, J, the Son of God,
5:7 days of his flesh, J offered up prayers and
6:20 behind the curtain, where J has gone as a
7:22 This makes J the surety of a better covenant.
10:10 of the body of J Christ once for all.
10:19 by the blood of J,
12:2 before us, looking to J the pioneer and perfecter
12:24 made perfect, and to J, the mediator of a
13:8 J Christ is the same yesterday and today and
13:12 So J also suffered outside the gate in order
13:20 the dead our Lord J, the great shepherd of
13:21 in his sight, through J Christ; to whom be
Jas 1:1 and of the LORD J Christ, to the twelve
2:1 faith of our Lord J Christ, the Lord of
1Pet 1:1 Peter, an apostle of J Christ, to the Exiles
1:2 Spirit for obedience to J Christ and for sprinkling
1:3 Father of our Lord J Christ!
1:3 through the resurrection of J Christ from the dead,
1:7 at the revelation of J Christ.
1:13 at the revelation of J Christ.
2:5 acceptable to God through J Christ.
3:21 through the resurrection of J Christ,
4:11 may be glorified through J Christ.
2Pet 1:1 servant and apostle of J Christ, To those who
1:1 our God and Savior J Christ:
1:2 of God and of J our Lord.
1:8 knowledge of our Lord J Christ.
1:11 our Lord and Savior J Christ.
1:14 soon, as our Lord J Christ showed me.
1:16 coming of our Lord J Christ, but we were
2:20 our Lord and Savior J Christ, they are again
3:18 our Lord and Savior J Christ.
1Jn 1:3 and with his Son J Christ.
1:7 and the blood of J his Son cleanses us
2:1 advocate with the Father, J Christ the righteous;
2:22 he who denies that J is the Christ?
3:23 name of his Son J Christ and love one
4:2 spirit which confesses that J Christ has come in
4:3 which does not confess J is not of God.
4:15 Whoever confesses that J is the Son of God,
5:1 one who believes that J is the Christ is
5:5 he who believes that J is the Son of
5:6 by water and blood, J Christ, not with the
5:20 true, in his Son J Christ.
2Jn 1:3 the Father and from J Christ the Father's Son,
1:7 acknowledge the coming of J Christ in the flesh;
Jude 1:1 Jude, a servant of J Christ and brother of
1:1 Father and kept for J Christ:
1:4 only Master and Lord, J Christ.
1:17 apostles of our Lord J Christ;
1:21 mercy of our Lord J Christ unto eternal life.
1:25 God, our Savior through J Christ our Lord, be
Rev 1:1 THE revelation of J Christ, which God gave
1:2 to the testimony of J Christ, even to all
1:5 his throne, and from J Christ the faithful witness,
1:9 share with you in J the tribulation and the
1:9 the word of God and the testimony of J
12:17 the commandments of God and bear testimony to J
14:12 the commandments of God and the faith of J
17:6 saints and the blood of the martyrs of J
19:10 and your brethren who hold the testimony of J
19:10 For the testimony of J is the spirit of
20:4 for their testimony to J and for the word
22:16 "I J have sent my angel to you with
22:20 Come, Lord J
22:21 grace of the Lord J be with all the

JETHER (8)
Judg 8:20 And he said to J his first-born, "Rise, and
1Kgs 2:5 Amasa the son of J, whom he murdered, avenging
2:32 Amasa the son of J, commander of the army
1Chr 2:17 father of Amasa was J the Ishmaelite.
2:32 of Jada, Shammai's brother: J and Jonathan; and
2:32 Jether and Jonathan; and J died childless.
4:17 The sons of Ezrah: J, Mered, Epher, and Jalon.
7:38 The sons of J: Jephunneh, Pispa, and Ara.

JETHETH (2)
Gen 36:40 the chiefs Timna, Alvah, J,
1Chr 1:51 were: chiefs Timna, Aliah, J,

JETHRO (10)
Ex 3:1 flock of his father-in-law, J, the priest of Midian;
4:18 Moses went back to J his father-in-law and said
4:18 And J said to Moses, "Go in peace."
18:1 J, the priest of Midian, Moses' father-in-law, heard of
18:2 J, Moses' father-in-law, had taken Zipporah, Moses'
18:5 And J, Moses' father-in-law, came with his sons and
18:6 Moses, "Lo, your father-in-law J is coming to you
18:9 And J rejoiced for all the good which the
18:10 And J said, "Blessed be the LORD, who has
18:12 And J, Moses' father-in-law, offered a burnt offering

JETUR (3)
Gen 25:15 Massa, Hadad, Tema, J, Naphish, and Kedemah.
1Chr 1:31 Dumah, Massa, Hadad, Tema, J, Naphish, and
5:19 war upon the Hagrites, J, Naphish, and Nodab;

JEUEL (3)
1Chr 9:6 the sons of Zerah: J and their kinsmen, six
2Chr 29:13 of Eli-zaphan, Shimri and J; and of the sons
Ezra 8:13 their names being Eliphelet, J, and Shemaiah, and

JEUSH (9)
Gen 36:5 Reuel; and Oholibamah bore J, Jalam, and Korah.
36:14 she bore to Esau J, Jalam, and Korah.
36:18 Esau's wife: the chiefs J, Jalam, and Korah; these
1Chr 1:35 of Esau: Eliphaz, Reuel, J, Jalam, and Korah.
7:10 the sons of Bilhan: J, Benjamin, Ehud, Chenaanah,
8:39 brother: Ulam his first-born, J the second, and
23:10 Shimei: Jahath, Zina, and J, and Beriah.
23:11 Zizah the second; but J and Beriah had not
2Chr 11:19 she bore him sons, J, Shemariah, and Zaham.

JEUZ
1Chr 8:10 Jobab, Zibi-a, Mesha, Malcam, J, Sachia, and

J

JEW (37)

Esth 2:5 Now there was a J in Susa the capital
3:4 he had told them that he was a J
5:13 I see Mordecai the J sitting at the king's
6:10 so to Mordecai the J who sits at the
8:7 and to Mordecai the J, "Behold, I have given
9:29 Abihail, and Mordecai the J gave full written
9:31 seasons, as Mordecai the J and Queen Esther
10:3 For Mordecai the J was next in rank to
11:3 He was a J, dwelling in the city of
Jer 34:9 one should enslave a J, his brother.
Dan 14:28 king has become a J; he has destroyed Bel,
Zech 8:23 the robe of a J, saying, 'Let us go
1Mac 2:23 speaking these words, a J came forward in the
2Mac 6:6 so much as confess himself to be a J
9:17 also would become a J and would visit every
Jn 3:25 John's disciples and a J over purifying.
4:9 it that you, a J, ask a drink of
18:35 Pilate answered, "Am I a J
Acts 10:28 it is for a J to associate with or
18:2 And he found a J named Aquila, a native
18:24 Now a J named Apollos, a native of Alexandria,
19:34 that he was a J, for about two hours
21:39 replied, "I am a J, from Tarsus in Cilicia,
22:3 said: "I am a J, born at Tarsus in
Rom 1:16 has faith, to the J first and also to
2:9 who does evil, the J first and also the
2:10 who does good, the J first and also the
2:17 you call yourself a J and rely upon the
2:28 is not a real J who is one outwardly,
2:29 He is a J who is one inwardly, and
3:1 Then what advantage has the J
10:12 is no distinction between J and Greek; the same
1Cor 9:20 I became as a J, in order to win
Gal 2:14 "If you, though a J, live like a Gentile
2:14 and not like a J, how can you compel
3:28 There is neither J nor Greek, there is neither
Col 3:11 be Greek and J, circumcised and uncircumcised,

JEWEL (5)

Prov 20:15 but the lips of knowledge are a precious J
Song 4:9 your eyes, with one J of your necklace.
1Pet 3:4 heart with the imperishable J of a gentle and
Rev 21:11 like a most rare J, like a jasper, clear
21:19 were adorned with every J; the first was jasper,

JEWELER (2)

Ex 28:11 As a J engraves signets, so shall you engrave
Sir 45:11 the work of a J, for a reminder, in

JEWELRY (5)

Gen 24:53 the servant brought forth J of silver and of
Ex 3:22 sojourns in her house, J of silver and of
11:2 woman of her neighbor, J of silver and of
12:35 asked of the Egyptians J of silver and of
Hos 2:13 with her ring and J, and went after her

JEWELS (15)

Job 28:17 it be exchanged for J of fine gold.
Prov 3:15 is more precious than J, and nothing you desire
8:11 wisdom is better than J, and all that you
31:10 She is far more precious than J
Song 1:10 comely with ornaments, your neck with strings of J
5:14 His arms are rounded gold, set with J
7:1 rounded thighs are like J, the work of a
Is 61:10 and as a bride adorns herself with her J
Ezek 16:17 also took your fair J of my gold and
16:39 and take your fair J, and leave you naked
23:26 of your clothes and take away your fine J
Zech 9:16 people; for like the J of a crown they
Rev 17:4 bedecked with gold and J and pearls, holding in
18:12 cargo of gold, silver, J and pearls, fine linen,
18:16 bedecked with gold, with J, and with pearls!

JEWESS

Acts 24:23 Drusilla, who was a J; and he sent for

JEWISH (27)

1Chr 4:18 And his J wife bore Jered the father of
Neh 5:1 their wives against their J brethren.
5:8 have bought back our J brethren who have been
Esth 6:13 fall, is of the J people, you will not
1Mac 8:29 a treaty with the J people.
12:3 high priest and the J nation have sent us
12:6 the rest of the J people to their brethren
14:20 the rest of the J people, our brethren, greeting.
2Mac 1:1 The J brethren in Jerusalem and
1:1 of Judea, To their J brethren in Egypt, Greeting,
5:23 his malice toward the J citizens,
8:1 had continued in the J faith, and so they
8:11 inviting them to buy J slaves and promising to
9:19 content: "To his worthy J citizens, Antiochus their
Lk 23:49 named Joseph from the J town of Arimathea.
Jn 2:6 standing there, for the J rites of purification, each
19:42 So because of the J day of Preparation, as
Acts 10:22 of by the whole J nation, was directed by
12:11 from all that the J people were expecting."
13:6 magician, a J false prophet, named Bar-Jesus.
14:1 entered together into the J synagogue, and so spoke
16:1 the son of a J woman who was a
17:10 they went into the J synagogue.
19:13 of the itinerant J exorcists undertook to pronounce
19:14 Seven sons of a J high priest named Sceva
25:24 about whom the whole J people petitioned me, both
Tit 1:13 of giving heed to J myths or to commands

JEWS (344)

2Kgs 25:25 killed Gedaliah and the J and the Chaldeans who
Ezra 4:12 the king that the J who came up from
4:23 in haste to the J at Jerusalem and by
5:1 Iddo, prophesied to the J who were in Judah
5:5 the elders of the J, and they did not
6:7 the governor of the J and the elders of
6:7 the elders of the J rebuild this house of
6:8 these elders of the J for the rebuilding of
6:14 the elders of the J built and prospered, through
Neh 1:2 asked them concerning the J that survived, who had
2:16 not yet told the J, the priests, the nobles,
4:1 angry and greatly enraged, and he ridiculed the J
4:2 "What are these feeble J doing?
4:12 When the J who lived by them came they
5:17 hundred and fifty men, J and officials, besides those
6:6 that you and the J intend to rebel; that
13:23 also I saw the J who had married women
Esth 3:6 to destroy all the J, the people of Mordecai,
3:10 the son of Hammedatha, the enemy of the J
3:13 and to annihilate all J, young and old, women
4:3 great mourning among the J, with fasting and
4:7 the king's treasuries for the destruction of the J
4:13 will escape any more than all the other J
4:14 will rise for the J from another quarter, but
4:16 "Go, gather all the J to be found in
8:1 the house of Haman, the enemy of the J
8:3 the plot which he had devised against the J
8:5 wrote to destroy the J who are in all
8:7 gallows, because he would lay hands on the J
8:8 with regard to the J, in the name of
8:9 Mordecai commanded concerning the J to the
8:9 and also to the J in their script and
8:11 the king allowed the J who were in every
8:13 all peoples, and the J were to be ready
8:16 The J had light and gladness and joy and
8:17 and joy among the J, a feast and a
8:17 the country declared themselves J, for the fear of
8:17 the fear of the J had fallen upon them.
9:1 the enemies of the J hoped to get the
9:1 a day when the J should get the mastery
9:2 over their foes, the J gathered in their cities
9:3 officials also helped the J, for the fear of
9:5 So the J smote all their enemies with the
9:6 the capital itself the J slew and destroyed five
9:10 the enemy of the J; but they laid no
9:12 Susa the capital the J have slain five hundred
9:13 the king, let the J who are in Susa
9:15 The J who were in Susa gathered also on
9:16 Now the other J who were in the king's
9:18 But the J who were in Susa gathered on
9:19 Therefore the J of the villages, who live in
9:20 letters to all the J who were in all
9:22 days on which the J got relief from their
9:23 So the J undertook to do as they had
9:24 enemy of all the J, had plotted against the
9:24 had plotted against the J to destroy them, and
9:25 had devised against the J should come upon his
9:27 had befallen them, the J ordained and took it
9:28 into disuse among the J, nor should the
9:30 sent to all the J, to the hundred and
9:31 Esther enjoined upon the J, and as they had
10:3 was great among the J and popular with the
10:8 that gathered to destroy the name of the J
16:15 we find that the J, who were consigned to
16:19 place, and permit the J to live under their

Jer 32:12 presence of all the J who were sitting in
38:19 am afraid of the J who have deserted to
40:11 Likewise, when all the J who were in Moab
40:12 them, then all the J returned from all the
40:15 so that all the J who are gathered about
41:3 also slew all the J who were with Gedaliah
44:1 Jeremiah concerning all the J that dwelt in the
52:28 three thousand and twenty-three J;
52:30 away captive of the J seven hundred and forty-five
Dan 3:8 came forward and maliciously accused the J
3:12 There are certain J whom you have appointed over
13:4 his house; and the J used to come to
1Mac 4:2 the camp of the J and attack them suddenly.
4:20 flight, and that the J were burning the camp,
5:23 Then he took the J of Galilee and Arbatta,
5:30 stronghold, and attacking the J within.
6:6 and fled before the J; that the Jews had
6:6 the Jews; that the J had grown strong from
6:31 of war; but the J sallied out and burned
6:47 And when the J saw the royal might and
6:52 The J also made engines of war to match
6:60 he sent to the J an offer of peace,
6:61 On these conditions the J evacuated the stronghold.
7:45 The J pursued them a day's journey, from Adasa
7:47 Then the J seized the spoils and the plunder,
8:20 the people of the J have sent us to
8:23 the nation of the J at sea and on
8:25 the nation of the J shall act as their
8:27 the nation of the J, the Romans shall willingly
8:31 yoke heavy upon our friends and allies the J
10:23 a friendship with the J to strengthen himself.
10:25 the nation of the J, greeting.
10:29 and exempt all the J from payment of tribute
10:33 every one of the J taken as a captive
10:34 release for all the J who are in my
10:36 "Let J be enrolled in the king's forces to
11:30 the nation of the J, greeting.
11:33 the nation of the J, who are our friends
11:47 the king called the J to his aid, and
11:49 city saw that the J had gained control of
11:50 peace, and make the J stop fighting against us
11:51 So the J gained glory in the eyes of
12:21 the Spartans and the J that they are brethren
12:26 to fall upon the J by night.
13:36 and nation of the J, greeting.
13:42 high priest and commander and leader of the J
13:51 and seventy-first year, the J entered it with praise
14:22 Jason, envoys of the J, have come to us
14:33 stored, and he placed there a garrison of J
14:34 He settled J there, and provided in those cities
14:37 He settled J in it, and fortified it for
14:40 had heard that the J were addressed by the
14:41 "And the J and their priests decided that Simon
14:47 and ethnarch of the J and priests, and to
15:1 and ethnarch of the J, and to all the
15:2 the nation of the J, greeting.
15:17 The envoys of the J have come to us
15:17 the people of the J,
2Mac 1:7 and sixty-ninth year, we J wrote to you, in
1:10 king, and to the J in Egypt, Greeting, and
3:32 been perpetrated by the J with regard to Heliodorus,
4:11 royal concessions to the J, secured through John the
4:35 this reason not only J, but many also of
4:36 region of Cilicia, the J in the city appealed
4:41 But when the J became aware of Lysimachus'
5:25 day; then, finding the J not at work, he
6:1 senator to compel the J to forsake the laws
6:7 the king's birthday, the J were taken, under bitter
6:8 same policy toward the J and make them partake
8:10 by selling the captured J into slavery.
8:32 man, and one who had greatly troubled the J
8:34 merchants to buy the J,
8:36 Jerusalem proclaimed that the J had a Defender, and
8:36 and that therefore the J were invulnerable, because
9:4 of turning upon the J the injury done by
9:4 there I will make Jerusalem a cemetery of J
9:7 his rage against the J, and giving orders to
9:15 be free; and the J, whom he had not
9:18 and wrote to the J the following letter, in
10:8 whole nation of the J should observe these days
10:12 showing justice to the J because of the wrong
10:14 at every turn kept on warring against the J
10:15 strongholds, were harassing the J; they received
10:24 been defeated by the J before, gathered a
10:29 with golden bridles, and they were leading the J
11:2 and all his cavalry and came against the J
11:15 in behalf of the J which Maccabeus delivered to
11:16 letter written to the J by Lysias was to
11:16 the people of the J, greeting.
11:24 have heard that the J do not consent to
11:27 the senate of the J and to the other
11:27 and to the other J, greeting.
11:31 full permission for the J to enjoy their own
11:34 the people of the J, greeting.
12:1 the king, and the J went about their farming.
12:3 this: they invited the J who lived among them
12:3 ill will to the J;
12:8 to wipe out the J who were living among
12:17 to Charax, to the J who are called Toubiani.
12:28 But the J called upon the Sovereign who with
12:30 But when the J who dwelt there bore witness
12:34 a few of the J fell.
12:40 the law forbids the J to wear.
13:9 coming to show the J things far worse than
13:18 the daring of the J, tried strategy in attacking
13:19 strong fortress of the J, was turned back, attacked
13:21 the ranks of the J, gave secret information to
13:23 dismayed, called in the J, yielded and swore to
14:5 asked about the disposition and intentions of the J
14:6 answered: "Those of the J who are called Hasideans,
14:14 and calamities of the J would mean prosperity for
14:15 When the J heard of Nicanor's coming and the
14:37 his good will was called father of the J
14:39 he had for the J, sent more than five
15:2 And when the J who were compelled to follow
15:12 outstretched hands for the whole body of the J
Mt 2:2 he who has been born king of the J
27:11 asked him, "Are you the King of the J
27:29 they mocked him, saying, "Hail, King of the J
27:37 read, "This is Jesus the King of the J
28:15 been spread among the J to this day.
Mk 7:3 Pharisees, and all the J, do not eat unless
15:2 asked him, "Are you the King of the J
15:9 to release for you the King of the J
15:12 man whom you call the King of the J
15:18 began to salute him, "Hail, King of the J
15:26 charge against him read, "The King of the J
Lk 7:3 him elders of the J, asking him to come
23:3 asked him, "Are you the King of the J
23:36 the King of the J, save yourself!"
23:37 over him, "This is the King of the J
Jn 1:19 of John, when the J sent priests and Levites
2:13 The Passover of the J was at hand, and
2:18 The J then said to him, "What sign have
2:20 The J then said, "It has taken forty-six years
3:1 the Pharisees, named Nicodemus, a ruler of the J
4:9 For J have no dealings with Samaritans.
4:22 what we know, for salvation is from the J
5:1 a feast of the J, and Jesus went up
5:9 So the J said to the man who was
5:14 away and told the J that it was Jesus
5:15 this was why the J persecuted Jesus, because he
5:17 This was why the J sought all the more
6:4 the feast of the J, was at hand.
6:41 The J then murmured at him, because he said,
6:52 The J then disputed among themselves, saying, "How
7:1 in Judea, because the J sought to kill him.
7:2 Now the J feast of Tabernacles was at hand.
7:11 The J were looking for him at the feast,
7:13 for fear of the J no one spoke openly
7:15 The J marveled at it, saying, "How is it
7:35 The J said to one another, "Where does this
8:22 Then said the J, "Will he kill himself, since
8:31 then said to the J who had believed in
8:48 The J answered him, "Are we not right in
8:52 The J said to him, "Now we know that
8:57 The J then said to him, "You are not
9:18 The J did not believe that he had been
9:22 because they feared the J, for the Jews had
9:22 the Jews, for the J had already agreed that
10:19 a division among the J because of these words.
10:24 So the J gathered round him and said to
10:31 The J took up stones again to stone him.
10:33 The J answered him, "It is not for a
11:8 to him, "Rabbi, the J were but now seeking
11:19 and many of the J had come to Martha
11:31 When the J who were with her in the
11:33 her weeping, and the J who came with her
11:36 So the J said, "See how he loved him!"
11:45 Many of the J therefore, who had come with
11:54 about openly among the J, but went from there
11:55 the Passover of the J was at hand, and

12:9 great crowd of the J learned that he was
12:11 him many of the J were going away and
13:33 I said to the J so now I say
18:12 the officers of the J seized Jesus and bound
18:14 given counsel to the J that it was expedient
18:20 the temple, where all J come together; I have
18:31 The J said to him, "It is not lawful
18:33 to him, "Are you the King of the J
18:36 handed over to the J; but my kingship is
18:38 went out to the J again, and told them,
18:39 me release for you the King of the J
19:3 up to him, saying, "Hail, King of the J
19:7 The J answered him, "We have a law, and
19:12 release him, but the J cried out, "If you
19:14 He said to the J, "Behold your King!"
19:19 read, "Jesus of Nazareth, the King of the J
19:20 Many of the J read this title, for the
19:21 chief priests of the J then said to Pilate,
19:21 'The King of the J but, 'This man said,
19:21 'This man said, I am King of the J
19:31 a high day), the J asked Pilate that their
19:38 for fear of the J, asked Pilate that he
19:40 spices, as is the burial custom of the J
20:19 for fear of the J, Jesus came and stood
Acts 2:5 were dwelling in Jerusalem J, devout men from
2:10 visitors from Rome, both J and proselytes,
9:22 and confounded the J who lived in Damascus
9:23 days had passed, the J plotted to kill him,
10:39 the country of the J and in Jerusalem.
11:19 and Antioch, speaking the word to none except J
12:3 that it pleased the J, he proceeded to arrest
13:5 word of God in the synagogues of the J
13:43 synagogue broke up, many J and devout converts to
13:45 But when the J saw the multitudes, they were
13:50 But the J incited the devout women of high
14:1 company believed, both of J and of Greeks.
14:2 But the unbelieving J stirred up the Gentiles and
14:4 some sided with the J, and some with the
14:5 by both Gentiles and J, with their rulers, to
14:19 But J came there from Antioch and Iconium; and
16:3 him because of the J that were in those
16:20 said, "These men are J and they are disturbing
17:1 Thessalonica, where there was a synagogue of the J
17:5 But the J were jealous, and taking some wicked
17:11 Now these J were more noble than those in
17:13 But when the J of Thessalonica learned that the
17:17 the synagogue with the J and the devout persons,
18:2 had commanded all the J to leave Rome.
18:4 every sabbath, and persuaded J and Greeks.
18:5 preaching, testifying to the J that the Christ was
18:12 proconsul of Achaia, the J made a united attack
18:14 Gallio said to the J, "If it were a
18:14 bear with you, O J;
18:19 went into the synagogue and argued with the J
18:28 he powerfully confuted the J in public, showing by
19:10 of the Lord, both J and Greeks.
19:17 residents of Ephesus, both J and Greeks; and fear
19:33 prompted Alexander, whom the J had put forward.
20:3 against him by the J as he was about
20:19 the plots of the J;
20:21 house, testifying both to J and to Greeks of
21:11 Spirit, 'So shall the J at Jerusalem bind the
21:20 there are among the J of those who have
21:21 you teach all the J who are among the
21:27 were almost completed, the J from Asia, who had
22:12 of by all the J who lived there,
22:30 real reason why the J accused him, he unbound
23:12 it was day, the J made a plot and
23:20 And he said, "The J have agreed to ask
23:27 was seized by the J, and was about to
24:5 agitator among all the J throughout the world, and
24:8 The J also joined in the charge, affirming that
24:17 But some J from Asia--
24:26 desiring to do the J a favor, Felix left
25:2 principal men of the J informed him against Paul;
25:7 he had come, the J who had gone down
25:8 the law of the J, nor against the temple,
25:9 wishing to do the J a favor, said to
25:10 be tried; to the J I have done no
25:15 the elders of the J gave information about him,
26:2 the accusations of the J,
26:3 and controversies of the J; therefore I beg you
26:4 and at Jerusalem, is known by all the J
26:7 I am accused by J, O king!
26:21 For this reason the J seized me in the
28:17 local leaders of the J; and when they had
28:19 But when the J objected, I was compelled to
Rom 3:2 To begin with, the J are entrusted with the
3:9 Are we J any better off?
3:9 that all men, both J and Greeks, are under
3:29 God the God of J only?
9:24 called, not from the J only but also from
11:14 to make my fellow J jealous, and thus save
1Cor 1:22 For J demand signs and Greeks seek wisdom,
1:23 a stumbling block to J and folly to Gentiles,
1:24 who are called, both J and Greeks, Christ the
9:20 To the J I became as a Jew, in
9:20 in order to win J; to those under the
10:32 Give no offense to J or to Greeks or
12:13 baptized into one body-- J or Greeks, slaves or
2Cor 11:24 the hands of the J the forty lashes less
Gal 2:13 the rest of the J acted insincerely, so that
2:14 can you compel the Gentiles to live like J
2:15 We ourselves, who are J by birth and not
1Thes 2:14 they did from the J,
Rev 2:9 say that they are J and are not, but
3:9 say that they are J and are not, but

JEZANIAH

Jer 40:8 of Ephai the Netophathite, J the son of the

JEZEBEL (23)

1Kgs 16:31 he took for wife J the daughter of Ethbaal
18:4 LORD greatly; and when J cut off the prophets
18:13 what I did when J killed the prophets of
18:19 Asherah, who eat at J's table."
19:1 Ahab told J all that Elijah had done, and
19:2 Then J sent a messenger to Elijah, saying, "So
21:5 But J his wife came to him, and said
21:7 And J his wife said to him, "Do you
21:11 his city, did as J had sent word to
21:14 Then they sent to J, saying, "Naboth has been
21:15 As soon as J heard that Naboth had been
21:15 stoned and was dead, J said to Ahab, "Arise,
21:23 And of J the LORD also said, 'The dogs
21:23 'The dogs shall eat J within the bounds of
21:25 LORD like Ahab, whom J his wife incited.
2Kgs 9:7 I may avenge on J the blood of my
9:10 the dogs shall eat J in the territory of
9:22 sorceries of your mother J are so many?"
9:30 Jehu came to Jezreel, J heard of it; and
9:36 eat the flesh of J;
9:37 and the corpse of J shall be as dung
9:37 so that no one can say, This is J
Rev 2:20 you tolerate the woman J, who calls herself a

JEZER (3)

Gen 46:24 of Naphtali: Jahzeel, Guni, J, and Shillem
Num 26:49 of the Gunites; of J, the family of the
1Chr 7:13 of Naphtali: Jahzi-el, Guni, J, and Shallum, the

JEZERITES

Num 26:49 the family of the J; of Shillem, the family

JEZI-EL

1Chr 12:3 Shemaah of Gibe-ah; also J and Pelet the sons

JEZRAHIAH

Neh 12:42 the singers sang with J as their leader.

JEZREEL (39)

Josh 15:56 Maon, Carmel, Ziph, Juttah, J, Jokde-am, Zanoah,
17:16 its villages and those in the Valley of J
19:18 Its territory included J, Chesulloth, Shunem,
Judg 6:33 the Jordan they encamped in the Valley of J
1Sam 25:43 also took Ahino-am of J; and both of them
27:3 two wives, Ahino-am of J, and Abigail of Carmel,
29:1 were encamped by the fountain which is in J
29:11 But the Philistines went up to J
30:5 taken captive, Ahino-am of J, and Abigail the widow
2Sam 2:2 wives also, Ahino-am of J, and Abigail the widow
2:9 and the Ashurites and J and Ephraim and Benjamin
3:2 Amnon, of Ahino-am of J;
4:4 and Jonathan came from J; and his nurse took
1Kgs 4:12 is beside Zarethan below J, and from Beth-shean to
18:45 And Ahab rode and went to J
18:46 and ran before Ahab to the entrance of J
21:1 had a vineyard in J, beside the palace of
21:23 within the bounds of J
2Kgs 8:29 to be healed in J of the wounds which
8:29 son of Ahab in J, because he was sick.
9:10 in the territory of J, and none shall bury

9:15 to be healed in J of the wounds which
9:15 city to go and tell the news in J
9:16 chariot, and went to J, for Joram lay there.
9:17 on the tower in J, and he spied the
9:30 When Jehu came to J, Jezebel heard of it;
9:36 'In the territory of J the dogs shall eat
9:37 in the territory of J, so that no one
10:6 come to me at J tomorrow at this time."
10:7 in baskets, and sent them to him at J
10:11 house of Ahab in J, all his great men,
1Chr 4:3 the sons of Etam: J, Ishma, and Idbash; and
2Chr 22:6 to be healed in J of the wounds which
22:6 son of Ahab in J, because he was sick.
Hos 1:4 him, "Call his name J; for yet a little
1:4 for the blood of J, and I will put
1:5 the bow of Israel in the valley of J
1:11 land, for great shall be the day of J
2:22 and they shall answer J;

JEZREELITE (8)

1Kgs 21:1 Now Naboth the J had a vineyard in Jezreel,
21:4 of what Naboth the J had said to him;
21:6 spoke to Naboth the J, and said to him,
21:7 will give you the vineyard of Naboth the J
21:15 vineyard of Naboth the J, which he refused to
21:16 vineyard of Naboth the J, to take possession of
2Kgs 9:21 met him at the property of Naboth the J
9:25 belonging to Naboth the J; for remember, when you

JEZREELITESS

1Chr 3:1 Amnon, by Ahino-am the J; the second Daniel, by

JIDLAPH

Gen 22:22 Aram, Chesed, Hazo, Pildash, J, and Bethuel."

JO-ANAN

Lk 3:27 Joda, the son of J, the son of Rhesa,

JO-ANNA

Lk 24:10 was Mary Magdalene and J and Mary the mother

JO-EZER

1Chr 12:6 Haruphite; Elkanah, Isshiah, Azarel, J, and

JOAB (150)

1Sam 26:6 the Hittite, and to J's brother Abishai the son
2Sam 2:13 And J the son of Zeruiah, and the servants
2:14 And Abner said to J, "Let the young men
2:14 And J said, "Let them arise."
2:18 of Zeruiah were there, J, Abishai, and Asahel.
2:22 I lift up my face to your brother J
2:24 But J and Abishai pursued Abner; and as the
2:26 Then Abner called to J, "Shall the sword devour
2:27 And J said, "As God lives, if you had
2:28 So J blew the trumpet; and all the men
2:30 J returned from the pursuit of Abner; and when
2:32 And J and his men marched all night, and
3:22 of David arrived with J from a raid, bringing
3:23 When J and all the army that was with
3:23 came, it was told J, "Abner the son of
3:24 Then J went to the king and said, "What
3:26 When J came out from David's presence, he sent
3:27 Abner returned to Hebron, J took him aside into
3:29 upon the head of J, and upon all his
3:29 may the house of J never be without one
3:30 So J and Abishai his brother slew Abner, because
3:31 Then David said to J and to all the
8:16 And J the son of Zeruiah was over the
10:7 of it, he sent J and all the host
10:9 When J saw that the battle was set against
10:13 So J and the people who were with him
10:14 Then J returned from fighting against the
11:1 to battle, David sent J, and his servants with
11:6 David sent word to J, "Send me Uriah the
11:6 And J sent Uriah to David.
11:7 him, David asked how J was doing, and how
11:11 booths; and my lord J and the servants of
11:14 wrote a letter to J, and sent it by
11:16 And as J was besieging the city, he assigned
11:17 out and fought with J; and some of the
11:18 Then J sent and told David all the news
11:22 told David all that J had sent him to
11:25 shall you say to J, 'Do not let this
12:26 Now J fought against Rabbah of the Ammonites, and
12:27 And J sent messengers to David, and said, "I
14:1 Now J the son of Zeruiah perceived that the
14:2 And J sent to Tekoa, and fetched from there
14:3 So J put the words in her mouth.
14:19 "Is the hand of J with you in all
14:19 It was your servant J who bade me; it
14:20 of affairs your servant J did this.
14:21 the king said to J, "Behold now, I grant
14:22 And J fell on his face to the ground,
14:22 blessed the king; and J said, "Today your servant
14:23 So J arose and went to Geshur, and brought
14:29 Then Absalom sent for J, to send him to
14:29 to the king; but J would not come to
14:29 a second time, but J would not come.
14:30 to his servants, "See, J's field is next to
14:31 Then J arose and went to Absalom at his
14:32 Absalom answered J, "Behold, I sent word to you,
14:33 Then J went to the king, and told him;
17:25 had set Amasa over the army instead of J
17:25 Nahash, sister of Zeruiah, J's mother.
18:2 under the command of J, one third under the
18:2 the son of Zeruiah, J's brother, and one third
18:5 And the king ordered J and Abishai and Ittai,
18:10 saw it, and told J, "Behold, I saw Absalom
18:11 J said to the man who told him, "What,
18:12 the man said to J, "Even if I felt
18:14 J said, "I will not waste time like this
18:15 ten young men, J's armor-bearers, surrounded
18:16 Then J blew the trumpet, and the troops came
18:16 from pursuing Israel; for J restrained them.
18:20 And J said to him, "You are not to
18:21 Then J said to the Cushite, "Go, tell the
18:21 The Cushite bowed before J, and ran.
18:22 Zadok said again to J, "Come what may, let
18:22 And J said, "Why will you run, my son,
18:29 Ahima-az answered, "When J sent your servant, I
19:1 It was told J, "Behold, the king is weeping
19:5 Then J came into the house to the king,
19:13 commander of my army henceforth in place of J
20:7 went out after Abishai, J and the Cherethites and
20:8 Now J was wearing a soldier's garment, and over
20:9 And J said to Amasa, "Is it well with
20:9 And J took Amasa by the beard with his
20:10 sword which was in J's hand; so Joab struck
20:10 in Joab's hand; so J struck him with it
20:10 Then J and Abishai his brother pursued Sheba the
20:11 And one of J's men took his stand by
20:11 and said, "Whoever favors J, and whoever is for
20:11 and whoever is for David, let him follow J
20:13 people went on after J to pursue Sheba the
20:15 men who were with J came and besieged him
20:16 Tell J, 'Come here, that I may speak to
20:17 near her; and the woman said, "Are you J
20:20 J answered, "Far be it from me, far be
20:21 the woman said to J, "Behold, his head shall
20:22 son of Bichri, and threw it out to J
20:22 And J returned to Jerusalem to the king.
20:23 Now J was in command of all the army
23:18 Abishai, the brother of J, the son of Zeruiah,
23:24 Asahel the brother of J was one of the
23:37 Be-eroth, the armor-bearer of J the son of Zeruiah,
24:2 the king said to J and the commanders of
24:3 But J said to the king, "May the LORD
24:4 king's word prevailed against J and the commanders
24:4 So J and the commanders of the army went
24:9 And J gave the sum of the numbering of
1Kgs 1:7 He conferred with J the son of Zeruiah and
1:19 Abiathar the priest, and J the commander of the
1:25 all the king's sons, J the commander of the
1:41 And when J heard the sound of the trumpet,
2:5 you know also what J the son of Zeruiah
2:22 Abiathar the priest and J the son of Zeruiah."
2:28 the news came to J --for Joab had
2:28 to Joab --for J had supported Adonijah although
2:28 not supported Absalom-- J fled to the tent
2:29 was told King Solomon, J has fled to the
2:30 again, saying, "Thus said J, and thus he answered
2:31 for the blood which J shed without cause.
2:33 upon the head of J and upon the head
2:35 army in place of J, and the king put
11:15 was in Edom, and J the commander of the
11:16 male in Edom (for J and all Israel remained
11:21 his fathers and that J the commander of the
1Chr 2:16 sons of Zeruiah: Abishai, J, and Asahel, three.
4:14 was the father of J the father of Ge-harashim,
11:6 And J the son of Zeruiah went up first,
11:8 in complete circuit; and J repaired the rest of
11:20 Abishai, the brother of J, was chief of the

J

11:26 Asahel the brother of J, Elhanan the son of
11:39 Be-eroth, the armor-bearer of J the son of Zeruiah,
18:15 And J the son of Zeruiah was over the
19:8 of it, he sent J and all the army
19:10 When J saw that the battle was set against
19:14 So J and the people who were with him
19:15 likewise fled before Abishai, J's brother, and entered
19:15 Then J came to Jerusalem.
20:1 go forth to battle, J led out the army,
20:1 And J smote Rabbah, and overthrew it.
21:2 So David said to J and the commanders of
21:3 But J said, "May the LORD add to his
21:4 But the king's word prevailed against J
21:4 So J departed and went throughout all Israel, and
21:5 And J gave the sum of the numbering of
21:6 for the king's command was abhorrent to J
26:28 son of Ner, and J the son of Zeruiah
27:7 Asahel the brother of J was fourth, for the
27:24 J the son of Zeruiah began to number, but
27:34 J was commander of the king's army.
Ezra 2:6 sons of Jeshua and J, two thousand eight hundred
8:9 Of the sons of J, Obadiah the son of
Neh 7:11 sons of Jeshua and J, two thousand eight hundred

JOAH (11)

2Kgs 18:18 Shebnah the secretary, and J the son of Asaph,
18:26 Hilkiah, and Shebnah, and J, said to the Rabshakeh,
18:37 Shebna the secretary, and J the son of Asaph,
1Chr 6:21 son, Zimmah his son, J his son, Iddo his
26:4 first-born, Jehozabad the second, J the third, Sachar
2Chr 29:12 and of the Gershonites, J the son of Zimmah,
29:12 Eden the son of J;
34:8 of the city, and J the son of Joahaz,
Is 36:3 Shebna the secretary, and J the son of Asaph,
36:11 Then Eliakim, Shebna, and J said to the Rabshakeh,
36:22 Shebna the secretary, and J the son of Asaph,

JOAHAZ (2)

2Kgs 14:1 Joash the son of J, king of Israel, Amaziah
2Chr 34:8 Joah the son of J, the recorder, to repair

JOAKIM (10)

Jud 4:6 And J, the high priest, who was in Jerusalem
4:8 the Israelites did as J the high priest and
4:14 And J the high priest and all the priests
15:8 Then J the high priest, and the senate of
Dan 13:1 a man living in Babylon whose name was J
13:4 J was very rich, and had a spacious garden
13:6 men were frequently at J's house, and all who
13:28 house of her husband J, the two elders came,
13:29 daughter of Hilkiah, who is the wife of J
13:63 Susanna, and so did J her husband and all

JOANNA

Lk 8:3 had gone out, and J, the wife of Chuza,

JOARIB (2)

1Mac 2:1 of the sons of J, moved from Jerusalem and
14:29 of the sons of J, and his brothers, exposed

JOASH (50)

Judg 6:11 Ophrah, which belonged to J the Abiezrite, as his
6:29 "Gideon the son of J has done this thing."
6:30 the town said to J, "Bring out your son,
6:31 But J said to all who were arrayed against
7:14 Gideon the son of J, a man of Israel;
8:13 Gideon the son of J returned from the battle
8:29 Jerubbaal the son of J went and dwelt in
8:32 Gideon the son of J died in a good
8:32 in the tomb of J his father, at Ophrah
1Kgs 22:26 the city and to J the king's son;
2Kgs 11:2 sister of Ahaziah, took J the son of Ahaziah,
12:19 of the acts of J, and all that he
12:20 a conspiracy, and slew J in the house of
13:1 the twenty-third year of J the son of Ahaziah,
13:9 him in Samaria; and J his son reigned in
13:10 the thirty-seventh year of J king of Judah Jehoash
13:12 of the acts of J, and all that he
13:13 So J slept with his fathers, and Jeroboam sat
13:13 upon his throne; and J was buried in Samaria
13:14 he was to die, J king of Israel went
13:25 Three times J defeated him and recovered the cities
14:1 the second year of J the son of Joahaz,
14:1 Amaziah the son of J, king of Judah, began
14:3 in all things as J his father had done.
14:17 Amaziah the son of J, king of Judah, lived
14:23 Amaziah the son of J, king of Judah, Jeroboam
14:23 Jeroboam the son of J, king of Israel, began
14:27 by the hand of Jeroboam the son of J
1Chr 3:11 son, Ahaziah his son, J his son,
4:22 men of Cozeba, and J, and Saraph, who ruled
7:8 sons of Becher: Zemirah, J, Eliezer, Eli-o-enai, Omri,
12:3 chief was Ahiezer, then J, both sons of Shemaah
27:28 Gederite; and over the stores of oil was J
2Chr 18:25 the city and to J the king's son;
22:11 of the king, took J the son of Ahaziah,
24:1 J was seven years old when he began to
24:2 And J did what was right in the eyes
24:4 After this J decided to restore the house of
24:22 Thus J the king did not remember the kindness
24:23 the army of the Syrians came up against J
24:24 Thus they executed judgment on J
25:17 counsel and sent to J the son of Jehoahaz,
25:18 And J the king of Israel sent word to
25:21 So J king of Israel went up; and he
25:23 And J king of Israel captured Amaziah king of
25:23 Judah, the son of J, son of Ahaziah, at
25:25 Amaziah the son of J king of Judah lived
25:25 after the death of J the son of Jehoahaz,
Hos 1:1 Jeroboam the son of J, king of Israel.
Amos 1:1 Jeroboam the son of J, king of Israel, two

JOB (60)

Job 1:1 Uz, whose name was J; and that man was
1:5 had run their course, J would send and sanctify
1:5 of them all; for J said, "It may be
1:5 Thus J did continually.
1:8 you considered my servant J, that there is none
1:9 answered the LORD, "Does J fear God for nought?
1:14 came a messenger to J, and said, "The oxen
1:20 Then J arose, and rent his robe, and shaved
1:22 In all this J did not sin or charge
2:3 you considered my servant J, that there is none
2:7 the LORD, and afflicted J with loathsome sores from
2:10 In all this J did not sin with his
2:11 Now when J's three friends heard of all this
3:1 After this J opened his mouth and cursed the
3:2 And J said:
6:1 Then J answered:
9:1 Then J answered:
12:1 Then J answered:
16:1 Then J answered:
19:1 Then J answered:
21:1 Then J answered:
23:1 Then J answered:
26:1 Then J answered:
27:1 And J again took up his discourse, and said:
29:1 And J again took up his discourse, and said:
31:40 The words of J are ended.
32:1 men ceased to answer J, because he was righteous
32:2 He was angry at J because he justified himself
32:3 was angry also at J's three friends because they
32:3 although they had declared J to be in the
32:4 waited to speak to J because they were older
32:12 was none that confuted J, or that answered his
33:1 hear my speech, O J, and listen to all
33:31 Give heed, O J, listen to me; be silent,
34:5 For J has said, 'I am innocent, and God
34:7 What man is like J, who drinks up scoffing
34:35 hears me will say: J speaks without knowledge, his
34:36 without insight.' Would that J were tried to the
35:16 not greatly heed transgression, J opens his mouth in
37:14 "Hear this, O J; stop and consider the wondrous
38:1 Then the LORD answered J out of the whirlwind:
40:1 the LORD said to J:
40:3 Then J answered the LORD:
40:6 Then the LORD answered J out of the whirlwind:
42:1 Then J answered the LORD:
42:7 spoken these words to J, the LORD said to
42:7 right, as my servant J has.
42:8 go to my servant J, and offer up for
42:8 offering; and my servant J shall pray for you,
42:8 right, as my servant J has."
42:9 and the LORD accepted J's prayer.
42:10 restored the fortunes of J, when he had prayed
42:10 and the LORD gave J twice as much as
42:12 the latter days of J more than his beginning;
42:15 women so fair as J's daughters; and their father
42:16 And after this J lived a hundred and forty
42:17 And J died, an old man, and full of
Ezek 14:14 men, Noah, Daniel, and J, were in it, they
14:20 if Noah, Daniel, and J were in it, as

Jas 5:11 of the steadfastness of J, and you have seen

JOBAB (9)

Gen 10:29 Sheba, Ophir, Havilah, and J; all these were the
36:33 Bela died, and J the son of Zerah of
36:34 J died, and Husham of the land of the
Josh 11:1 this, he sent to J king of Madon, and
1Chr 1:23 Sheba, Ophir, Havilah, and J; all these were the
1:44 When Bela died, J the son of Zerah of
1:45 When J died, Husham of the land of the
8:9 by Hodesh his wife: J, Zibi-a, Mesha, Malcam,
8:18 Heber, Ishmerai, Izliah, and J were the sons of

JOCHEBED (2)

Ex 6:20 Amram took to wife J his father's sister and
Num 26:59 of Amram's wife was J the daughter of Levi,

JODA

Lk 3:26 Josech, the son of J,

JOED

Neh 11:7 of Meshullam, son of J, son of Pedaiah, son

JOEL (21)

1Sam 8:2 his first-born son was J, and the name of
1Chr 4:35 the son of Amaziah, J, Jehu the son of
5:4 The sons of J: Shemaiah his son, Gog his
5:8 of Shema, son of J, who dwelt in Aroer,
5:12 as far as Salecah: J the chief, Shapham the
6:28 The sons of Samuel: J his first-born, the second
6:33 singer the son of J, son of Samuel,
6:36 of Elkanah, son of J, son of Azariah, son
7:3 of Izrahiah: Michael, Obadiah, J, and Isshiah, five, all
11:38 the son of Ezbai, J the brother of Nathan,
15:7 the sons of Gershom, J the chief, with a
15:11 the Levites Uriel, Asaiah, J, Shemaiah, Eliel, and
15:17 Heman the son of J; and of his brethren
23:8 chief, and Zetham, and J, three.
26:22 of Jehieli, Zetham and J his brother, were in
27:20 the half-tribe of Manasseh, J the son of Pedaiah;
2Chr 29:12 son of Amasai, and J the son of Azariah,
Ezra 10:43 Mattithiah, Zabad, Zebina, Jaddai, J, and Benaiah.
Neh 11:9 J the son of Zichri was their overseer; and
Joel 1:1 LORD that came to J, the son of Pethuel:
Acts 2:16 spoken by the prophet J:

JOELAH

1Chr 12:7 Jashobe-am, the Korahites; and J and Zebadiah, the

JOGBEHAH (2)

Num 32:35 Ataroth, Aroer, Atroth-shophan, Jazer, J,
Judg 8:11 east of Nobah and J, and attacked the army;

JOGLI

Num 34:22 of Dan a leader, Bukki the son of J

JOHA (2)

1Chr 8:16 Eder, Michael, Ishpah, and J were sons of Beriah.
11:45 son of Shimri, and J his brother, the Tizite,

JOHANAN (26)

2Kgs 25:23 son of Nethaniah, and J the son of Kareah,
1Chr 3:15 The sons of Josiah: J the first-born, the second
3:24 Eliashib, Pelaiah, Akkub, J, Delaiah, and Anani,
6:9 of Azariah, Azariah of J,
6:10 Azariah of Johanan, and J of Azariah (it was
12:4 the thirty; Jeremiah, Jahaziel, J, Jozabad of,
12:12 Attai sixth, Eliel seventh, J eighth, Elzabad ninth,
2Chr 28:12 Azariah the son of J, Berechiah the son of
Ezra 8:12 the sons of Azgad, J the son of Hakkatan,
Neh 12:22 days of Eliashib, Joiada, J, and Jaddu-a, there were
12:23 until the days of J the son of Eliashib.
Jer 40:8 the son of Nethaniah, J the son of Kareah,
40:13 Now J the son of Kareah and all the
40:15 Then J the son of Kareah spoke secretly to
40:16 of Ahikam said to J the son of Kareah,
41:11 But when J the son of Kareah and all
41:13 were with Ishmael saw J the son of Kareah
41:14 back, and went to J the son of Kareah.
41:15 of Nethaniah escaped from J with eight men, and
41:16 Then J the son of Kareah and all the
41:16 children, and eunuchs, whom J brought back from
42:1 of the forces, and J the son of Kareah
42:8 Then he summoned J the son of Kareah and
43:2 son of Hoshaiah and J the son of Kareah
43:4 So J the son of Kareah and all the
43:5 But J the son of Kareah and all the

JOHN (152)

1Mac 2:1 Mattathias the son of J, son of Simeon, a
2:2 He had five sons, J surnamed Gaddi,
8:17 Eupolemus the son of J, son of Accos, and
9:36 came out and seized J and all that he
9:38 remembered the blood of J their brother, and went
13:53 And Simon saw that J his son had reached
16:1 J went up from Gazara and reported to Simon
16:2 older sons Judas and J, and said to them:
16:4 So J chose out of the country twenty thousand
16:9 Judas the brother of J was wounded, but John
16:9 John was wounded, but J pursued them until
16:10 fields of Azotus, and J burned it with fire,
16:19 to do away with J; he sent letters to
16:21 ahead and reported to J at Gazara that his
16:23 of the acts of J and his wars and
2Mac 4:11 the Jews, secured through J the father of
11:17 J and Absalom, who were sent by you, have
Mt 3:1 In those days came J the Baptist, preaching in
3:4 Now J wore a garment of camel's hair, and
3:13 to the Jordan to J, to be baptized by
3:14 J would have prevented him, saying, "I need to
4:12 when he heard that J had been arrested, he
4:21 son of Zebedee and J his brother, in the
9:14 Then the disciples of J came to him, saying,
10:2 son of Zebedee, and J his brother;
11:2 Now when J heard in prison about the deeds
11:4 them, "Go and tell J what you hear and
11:7 to the crowds concerning J: "What did you go
11:11 no one greater than J the Baptist; yet he
11:12 From the days of J the Baptist until now
11:13 the law prophesied until J;
11:18 did not mourn.' For J came neither eating nor
14:2 his servants, "This is J the Baptist, he has
14:3 For Herod had seized J and bound him and
14:4 brother Philip's wife; because J said to him, "It
14:8 me the head of J the Baptist here on
14:10 he sent and had J beheaded in the prison,
16:14 they said, "Some say J the Baptist, others say
17:1 Peter and James and J his brother, and led
17:13 speaking to them of J the Baptist.
21:25 The baptism of J, whence was it?
21:26 for all hold that J was a prophet."
21:32 For J came to you in the way of
Mk 1:4 J the baptizer appeared in the wilderness, preaching
1:6 Now J was clothed with camel's hair, and had
1:9 and was baptized by J in the Jordan.
1:14 Now after J was arrested, Jesus came into Galilee,
1:19 son of Zebedee and J his brother, who were
1:29 house of Simon and Andrew, with James and J
2:18 Now J's disciples and the Pharisees were fasting;
2:18 to him, "Why do J's disciples and the disciples
3:17 son of Zebedee and J the brother of James,
5:37 Peter and James and J the brother of James.
6:14 Some said, J the baptizer has been raised from
6:16 of it he said, J, whom I beheaded, has
6:17 had sent and seized J, and bound him in
6:18 For J said to Herod, "It is not lawful
6:20 not, for Herod feared J, knowing that he was
6:24 said, "The head of J the baptizer."
6:25 once the head of J the Baptist on a
8:28 And they told him, J the Baptist; and others
9:2 Peter and James and J, and led them up
9:38 J said to him, "Teacher, we saw a man
10:35 And James and J, the sons of Zebedee, came
10:41 they began to be indignant at James and J
11:29 Was the baptism of J from heaven or from
11:31 for all held that J was a real prophet.
13:3 Peter and James and J and Andrew asked him
14:33 Peter and James and J, and began to be
Lk 1:13 a son, and you shall call his name J
1:60 mother said, "Not so; he shall be called J
1:63 a writing tablet, and wrote, "His name is J
3:2 of God came to J the son of Zechariah
3:15 in their hearts concerning J, whether perhaps he
3:16 he were the Christ, J answered them all, "I
3:20 that he shut up J in prison.
5:10 also were James and J, sons of Zebedee, who
5:33 him, "The disciples of J fast often and offer
6:14 and James and J, and Philip, and Bartholomew,
7:18 The disciples of J told him of all these
7:19 And J, calling to him two of his disciples,
7:20 to him, they said, J the Baptist has sent
7:22 them, "Go and tell J what you have seen

J

7:24 When the messengers of J had gone, he began
7:24 to the crowds concerning J: "What did you go
7:28 none is greater than J; yet he who is
7:29 with the baptism of J;
7:33 did not weep.' For J the Baptist has come
8:51 him, except Peter and J and James, and the
9:7 said by some that J had been raised from
9:9 Herod said, J I beheaded; but who is this
9:19 And they answered, J the Baptist; but others say,
9:28 with him Peter and J and James, and went
9:49 J answered, "Master, we saw a man casting out
9:54 his disciples James and J saw it, they said,
11:1 us to pray, as J taught his disciples."
16:16 the prophets were until J; since then the good
20:4 Was the baptism of J from heaven or from
20:6 they are convinced that J was a prophet."
22:8 Jesus sent Peter and J, saying, "Go and prepare
Jn 1:6 a man sent from God, whose name was J
1:15 J bore witness to him, and cried, "This was
1:19 is the testimony of J, when the Jews sent
1:26 J answered them, "I baptize with water; but among
1:28 beyond the Jordan, where J was baptizing.
1:32 And J bore witness, "I saw the Spirit descend
1:35 The next day again J was standing with two
1:40 the two who heard J speak, and followed him,
1:42 said, "So you are Simon the son of J
3:23 J also was baptizing at Aenon near Salim, because
3:24 For J had not yet been put in prison.
3:25 a discussion arose between J's disciples and a Jew
3:26 And they came to J, and said to him,
3:27 J answered, "No one can receive anything except
4:1 baptizing more disciples than J
5:32 You sent to J, and he has borne witness
5:35 greater than that of J; for the works which
10:40 to the place where J at first baptized, and
10:41 him; and they said, J did no sign, but
10:41 sign, but everything that J said about this man
21:15 Peter, "Simon, son of J, do you love me
21:16 him, "Simon, son of J, do you love me?"
21:17 time, "Simon, son of J, do you love me?"
Acts 1:5 heard from me, for J baptized with water, but
1:13 were staying, Peter and J and James and Andrew,
1:22 from the baptism of J until the day when
3:1 Now Peter and J were going up to the
3:3 Seeing Peter and J about to go into the
3:4 gaze at him, with J, and said, "Look at
3:11 clung to Peter and J, all the people ran
4:6 priest and Caiaphas and J and Alexander, and all
4:13 boldness of Peter and J, and perceived that they
4:19 But Peter and J answered them, "Whether it is
8:14 to them Peter and J,
10:37 after the baptism which J preached:
11:16 Lord, how he said, J baptized with water, but
12:2 James the brother of J with the sword;
12:12 Mary, the mother of J whose other name was
12:25 mission, bringing with them J whose other name was
13:5 And they had J to assist them.
13:13 And J left them and returned to Jerusalem;
13:24 Before his coming J had preached a baptism of
13:25 And as J was finishing his course, he said,
15:36 to take with them J called Mark.
18:25 Jesus, though he knew only the baptism of J
19:3 They said, "Into J's baptism."
19:4 And Paul said, J baptized with the baptism of
Gal 2:9 James and Cephas and J, who were reputed to
Rev 1:1 angel to his servant J,
1:4 J to the seven churches that are in Asia:
1:9 I J, your brother, who share with you in
22:8 I J am he who heard and saw these

JOIADA (4)

Neh 3:6 And J the son of Paseah and Meshullam the
12:10 Eliashib the father of J,
12:11 the father of Joiada, J the father of Jonathan,
12:22 the days of Eliashib, J, Johanan, and Jaddu-a, there

JOIAKIM (4)

Neh 12:10 was the father of J, Joiakim the father of
12:10 the father of Joiakim, J the father of Eliashib,
12:12 in the days of J were priests, heads of
12:26 in the days of J the son of Jeshua

JOIARIB (5)

Ezra 8:16 leading men, and for J and Elnathan, who were
Neh 11:5 of Adaiah, son of J, son of Zechariah, son
11:10 Jedaiah the son of J, Jachin,
12:6 Mijamin, Ma-adiah, Bilgah, Shemaiah, J, Jedaiah,
12:19 of Shemaiah, Jehonathan; of J, Mattenai; of

JOIN (28)

Ex 1:9 war befall us, they J our enemies and fight
23:1 You shall not J hands with a wicked man,
Num 18:2 father, that they may J you, and minister to
18:4 They shall J you, and attend to the tent
Josh 23:12 you turn back, and J the remnant of these
1Sam 13:4 were called out to J Saul at Gilgal.
1Kgs 5:6 and my servants will J your servants, and I
Neh 10:29 knowledge and understanding, J with their brethren,
Jud 1:11 Assyrians, and refused to J him in the war;
12:11 in your care to J us and eat and
Job 16:4 my place; I could J words together against you,
Wis 5:20 sword, and creation will J with him to fight
Is 5:8 Woe to those who J house to house, who
14:1 land, and aliens will J them and will cleave
56:6 "And the foreigners who J themselves to the LORD,
Jer 3:18 house of Judah shall J the house of Israel,
50:5 saying, 'Come, let us J ourselves to the LORD
Ezek 37:17 associated with him'; and J them together into one
37:19 him; and I will J with it the stick
Dan 11:34 And many shall J themselves to them with flattery;
Zech 2:11 And many nations shall J themselves to the LORD
1Mac 13:14 he was about to J battle with him, so
2Mac 14:14 before Judas, flocked to J Nicanor, thinking that the
Acts 5:13 of the rest dared J them, but the people
8:29 Philip, "Go up and J this chariot."
9:26 Jerusalem he attempted to J the disciples; and they
Phil 3:17 Brethren, J in imitating me, and mark those who
1Pet 4:4 you do not now J them in the same

JOINED (61)

Gen 14:3 And all these J forces in the Valley of
14:8 went out, and they J battle in the Valley
29:34 my husband will be J to me, because I
49:6 my spirit, be not J to their company; for
Ex 26:24 be separate beneath, but J at the top, at
28:7 that it may be J together.
36:29 were separate beneath, but J at the top, at
39:4 for the ephod shoulder-pieces, J to it at its
Josh 11:5 And all these kings J their forces, and came
1Kgs 6:10 high, and it was J to the house with
20:29 day the battle was J; and the people of
2Kgs 23:3 and all the people J in the covenant.
2Chr 3:12 of five cubits, was J to the wing of
20:35 Jehoshaphat king of Judah J with Ahaziah king of
20:36 He J him in building ships to go to
20:37 saying, "Because you have J with Ahaziah, the LORD
35:22 mouth of God, but J battle in the plain
Ezra 6:21 every one who had J them and separated himself
Neh 4:6 all the wall was J together to half its
11:36 Levites in Judah were J to Benjamin.
Tob 1:5 All the tribes that J in apostasy used to
Jud 1:6 He was J by all the people of the
1:6 Many nations J the forces of the Chaldeans.
7:1 the allies who had J him, to break camp
14:10 and was circumcised, and J the house of Israel,
Esth 9:27 descendants and all who J them, that without fail
Job 41:17 They are J one to another; they clasp each
Ps 83:8 Tyre; Assyria also has J them; they are the
Eccl 9:4 But he who is J with all the living
Is 14:20 You will not be J with them in burial,
56:3 the foreigner who has J himself to the LORD
Hos 4:17 Ephraim is J to idols, let him alone.
1Mac 1:15 They J with the Gentiles and sold themselves to
1:52 who forsook the law, J them, and they did
2:43 to escape their troubles J them and reinforced them.
3:2 and all who had J his father helped him;
3:41 land of the Philistines J with them.
6:21 of the ungodly Israelites J them.
7:22 were troubling their people J him.
7:39 and the Syrian army J him.
11:69 from their places and J battle.
11:73 returned to him and J him in the pursuit
15:14 city, and the ships J battle from the sea;
2Mac 8:23 first division himself, he J battle with Nicanor.
10:28 breaking, the two armies J battle, the one having
12:34 When they J battle, it happened that a few
13:3 Menelaus also J them and with utter hypocrisy urged
13:12 When they had all J in the same petition
Mt 19:5 and mother and be J to his wife, and
19:6 What therefore God has J together, let not man
Mk 10:7 and mother and be J to his wife,
10:9 What therefore God has J together, let not man

20:28 J answered Saul, "David earnestly asked leave of me
20:30 anger was kindled against J, and he said to
20:32 Then J answered Saul his father, "Why should he
20:33 to smite him; so J knew that his father
20:34 And J rose from the table in fierce anger
20:35 In the morning J went out into the field
20:37 of the arrow which J had shot, Jonathan called
20:37 which Jonathan had shot, J called after the lad
20:38 And J called after the lad, "Hurry, make haste,
20:38 So J's lad gathered up the arrows, and came
20:39 lad knew nothing; only J and David knew the
20:40 And J gave his weapons to his lad, and
20:42 Then J said to David, "Go in peace, forasmuch
20:42 rose and departed; and J went into the city.
23:16 And J, Saul's son, rose, and went to David
23:18 remained at Horesh, and J went home.
31:2 and the Philistines slew J and Abinadab and
2Sam 1:4 Saul and his son J are also dead."
1:5 Saul and his son J are dead?"
1:12 for Saul and for J his son and for
1:17 lamentation over Saul and J his son,
1:22 mighty, the bow of J turned not back, and
1:23 "Saul and J, beloved and lovely!
1:25 J lies slain upon thy high places.
1:26 for you, my brother J; very pleasant have you
4:4 J, the son of Saul, had a son who
4:4 news about Saul and J came from Jezreel; and
9:1 show him kindness for J's sake?"
9:3 still a son of J; he is crippled in
9:6 Mephibosheth the son of J, son of Saul, came
9:7 sake of your father J, and I will restore
15:27 Ahima-az your son, and J the son of Abiathar.
15:36 Ahima-az, Zadok's son, and J, Abiathar's son; and by
17:17 Now J and Ahima-az were waiting at En-rogel; a
17:20 the house, they said, "Where are Ahima-az and J
21:7 son of Saul's son J, because of the oath
21:7 them, between David and J the son of Saul.
21:12 bones of his son J from the men of
21:13 bones of his son J; and they gathered the
21:14 Saul and his son J in the land of
21:21 when he taunted Israel, J the son of Shimei,
23:32 the sons of Jashen, J,
1Kgs 1:42 was still speaking, behold, J the son of Abiathar
1:43 J answered Adonijah, "No, for our lord King David
1Chr 2:32 Shammai's brother: Jether and J; and Jether died
2:33 The sons of J: Peleth and Zaza.
8:33 of Saul, Saul of J, Malchishua, Abinadab, and
8:34 and the son of J was Merib-baal; and Merib-baal
9:39 of Saul, Saul of J, Malchishua, Abinadab, and
9:40 and the son of J was Merib-baal; and Merib-baal
10:2 and the Philistines slew J and Abinadab and
11:34 Sha-albon, Hashem the Gizonite, J the son of Shagee
20:7 when he taunted Israel, J the son of Shimea,
27:25 in the towers, was J the son of Uzziah;
27:32 J, David's uncle, was a counselor, being a man
Ezra 8:6 Ebed the son of J, and with him fifty
10:15 Only J the son of Asahel and Jahzeiah the
Neh 12:11 Joiada the father of J, and Jonathan the father
12:11 father of Jonathan, and J the father of Jaddu-a.
12:14 Jehohanan; of Malluchi, J; of Shebaniah, Joseph;
12:35 Zechariah the son of J, son of Shemaiah, son
Jer 37:15 in the house of J the secretary, for it
37:20 to the house of J the secretary, lest I
38:26 to the house of J to die there.'"
1Mac 2:5 Eleazar called Avaran, and J called Apphus.
4:30 into the hands of J, the son of Saul,
5:17 in Galilee; I and J my brother will go
5:24 Judas Maccabeus and J his brother crossed the
5:55 Now while Judas and J were in Gilead and
9:19 Then J and Simon took Judas their brother and
9:28 assembled and said to J,
9:31 And J at that time accepted the leadership and
9:33 But J and Simon his brother and all who
9:35 And J sent his brother as leader of the
9:37 it was reported to J and Simon his brother,
9:44 And J said to those with him, "Let us
9:47 the battle began, and J stretched out his hand
9:48 Then J and the men with him leaped into
9:58 J and his men are living in quiet and
9:60 telling them to seize J and his men; but
9:61 And J's men seized about fifty of the men
9:62 Then J with his men, and Simon, withdrew to
9:65 But J left Simon his brother in the city,
9:70 When J learned of this, he sent ambassadors to
9:71 and he swore to J that he would not
9:73 And J dwelt in Michmash.
9:73 And J began to judge the people, and he
10:3 And Demetrius sent J a letter in peaceable words
10:7 Then J came to Jerusalem and read the letter
10:9 released the hostages to J, and he returned them
10:10 And J dwelt in Jerusalem and began to rebuild
10:15 Demetrius had sent to J, and men told him
10:15 of the battles that J and his brothers had
10:18 Alexander to his brother J, greeting.
10:21 So J put on the holy garments in the
10:46 When J and the people heard these words, they
10:59 the king wrote to J to come to meet
10:62 orders to take off J's garments and to clothe
10:66 And J returned to Jerusalem in peace and gladness.
10:69 the following message to J the high priest:
10:74 When J heard the words of Apollonius, his spirit
10:76 opened the gates, and J gained possession of Joppa.
10:78 J pursued him to Azotus, and the armies engaged
10:80 J learned that there was an ambush behind him,
10:81 men stood fast, as J commanded, and the enemy's
10:84 But J burned Azotus and the surrounding towns and
10:86 Then J departed from there and encamped against
10:87 And J and those with him returned to Jerusalem
10:88 these things, he honored J still more;
11:4 bodies of those whom J had burned in the
11:5 told the king what J had done, to throw
11:6 J met the king at Joppa with pomp, and
11:7 And J went with the king as far as
11:20 In those days J assembled the men of Judea
11:21 reported to him that J was besieging the citadel.
11:22 Ptolemais; and he wrote J not to continue the
11:23 When J heard this, he gave orders to continue
11:28 Then J asked the king to free Judea and
11:29 wrote a letter to J about all these things;
11:30 follows: "King Demetrius to J his brother and to
11:37 it be given to J and put up in
11:41 Now J sent to Demetrius the king the request
11:42 sent this message to J, "Not only will I
11:44 So J sent three thousand stalwart men to him
11:53 he became estranged from J and did not repay
11:53 repay the favors which J had done him, but
11:57 young Antiochus wrote to J, saying, "I confirm you
11:60 Then J set forth and traveled beyond the river
11:62 of Gaza pleaded with J, and he made peace
11:63 Then J heard that the officers of Demetrius had
11:67 J and his army encamped by the waters of
11:70 All the men with J fled; not one of
11:71 J rent his garments and put dust on his
11:74 And J returned to Jerusalem.
12:1 Now when J saw that the time was favorable
12:3 senate chamber and said, J the high priest and
12:5 of the letter which J wrote to the Spartans:
12:6 wrote to the Spartans: J the high priest, the
12:24 Now J heard that the commanders of Demetrius had
12:27 when the sun set, J commanded his men to
12:28 the enemy heard that J and his men were
12:29 But J and his men did not know it
12:30 Then J pursued them, but he did not overtake
12:31 So J turned aside against the Arabs who are
12:35 When J returned he convened the elders of the
12:40 He feared that J might not permit him to
12:41 J went out to meet him with forty thousand
12:44 Then he said to J, "Why have you wearied
12:46 J trusted him and did as he said; he
12:48 when J entered Ptolemais, the men of Ptolemais
12:49 Plain to destroy all J's soldiers.
12:50 But they realized that J had been seized and
12:52 and they mourned for J and his companions and
13:8 place of Judas and J your brother.
13:11 He sent J the son of Absalom to Joppa,
13:12 land of Judah, and J was with him under
13:14 up in place of J his brother, and that
13:15 for the money that J your brother owed the
13:19 Trypho broke his word and did not release J
13:23 approached Baskama, he killed J, and he was buried
13:25 took the bones of J his brother, and buried
14:16 away as Sparta, that J had died, and they
14:18 established with Judas and J his brothers.
14:30 J rallied the nation, and became their high priest,
2Mac 1:23 J led, and the rest responded, as did Nehemiah.
8:22 Simon and Joseph and J, each to command a

JOPPA (28)

Josh 19:46 and Rakkon with the territory over against J
2Chr 2:16 rafts by sea to J, so that you may
Ezra 3:7 to the sea, to J, according to the grant
Jon 1:3 He went down to J and found a ship

1Mac	10:75	He encamped before J, but the men of the
	10:75	its gates, for Apollonius had a garrison in J
	10:76	the gates, and Jonathan gained possession of J
	11:6	met the king at J with pomp, and they
	12:33	He turned aside to J and took it by
	13:11	son of Absalom to J, and with him a
	14:5	his honors he took J for a harbor, and
	14:34	He also fortified J, which is by the sea,
	15:28	"You hold control of J and Gazara and the
	15:35	As for J and Gazara, which you demand, they
2Mac	4:21	upon arriving at J he proceeded to Jerusalem.
	12:3	And some men of J did so ungodly a
	12:4	nothing, the men of J took them out to
	12:7	again and root out the whole community of J
Acts	9:36	Now there was at J a disciple named Tabitha,
	9:38	Since Lydda was near J, the disciples, hearing that
	9:42	became known throughout all J, and many believed
	9:43	And he stayed in J for many days with
	10:5	now send men to J, and bring one Simon
	10:8	related everything to them, he sent them to J
	10:23	of the brethren from J accompanied him.
	10:32	Send therefore to J and ask for Simon who
	11:5	in the city of J praying; and in a
	11:13	and saying, 'Send to J and bring Simon called

JORAH

Ezra	2:18	The sons of J, one hundred and twelve.

JORAI

1Chr	5:13	houses: Michael, Meshullam, Sheba, J, Jacan, Zia,

JORAM (31)

2Sam	8:10	Toi sent his son J to King David, to
	8:10	And J brought with him articles of silver, of
2Kgs	8:16	the fifth year of J the son of Ahab,
	8:21	Then J passed over to Zair with all his
	8:23	of the acts of J, and all that he
	8:24	So J slept with his fathers, and was buried
	8:25	the twelfth year of J the son of Ahab,
	8:28	He went with J the son of Ahab to
	8:28	at Ramoth-gilead, where the Syrians wounded J
	8:29	And King J returned to be healed in Jezreel
	8:29	went down to see J the son of Ahab
	9:14	Jehoshaphat the son of Nimshi conspired against J
	9:14	(Now J with all Israel had been on guard
	9:15	of Syria; but King J had returned to be
	9:16	went to Jezreel, for J lay there.
	9:16	king of Judah had come down to visit J
	9:17	And J said, "Take a horseman, and send to
	9:21	J said, "Make ready." And they made ready his
	9:21	Then J king of Israel and Ahaziah king of
	9:22	And when J saw Jehu, he said, "Is it
	9:23	Then J reined about and fled, saying to Ahaziah,
	9:24	full strength, and shot J between the shoulders, so
	9:29	the eleventh year of J the son of Ahab,
	11:2	the daughter of King J, sister of Ahaziah, took
1Chr	3:11	son, Jehoshaphat his son, J his son, Ahaziah his
	26:25	Jeshaiah, and his son J, and his son Zichri,
2Chr	22:5	And the Syrians wounded J,
	22:6	went down to see J the son of Ahab
	22:7	should come about through his going to visit J
Mt	1:8	Jehoshaphat the father of J, and Joram the father
	1:8	father of Joram, and J the father of Uzziah,

JORDAN (210)

Gen	13:10	and saw that the J valley was well watered
	13:11	for himself all the J valley, and Lot journeyed
	32:10	staff I crossed this J; and now I have
	50:10	which is beyond the J, they lamented there with
	50:11	place was named Abel-mizraim; it is beyond the J
Num	13:29	Canaanites dwell by the sea, and along the J
	22:1	of Moab beyond the J at Jericho.
	26:3	of Moab by the J at Jericho, saying,
	26:63	of Moab by the J at Jericho.
	31:12	of Moab by the J at Jericho.
	32:5	a possession; do not take us across the J
	32:19	other side of the J and beyond; because our
	32:19	this side of the J to the east."
	32:21	will pass over the J before the LORD, until
	32:29	with you over the J and the land shall
	32:32	our inheritance shall remain with us beyond the J
	33:48	of Moab by the J at Jericho;
	33:49	they encamped by the J from Beth-jeshimoth as far
	33:50	of Moab by the J at Jericho,
	33:51	you pass over the J into the land of
	34:12	go down to the J, and its end shall
	34:15	their inheritance beyond the J at Jericho eastward,
	35:1	of Moab by the J at Jericho,
	35:10	When you cross the J into the land of
	35:14	three cities beyond the J, and three cities in
	36:13	of Moab by the J at Jericho.
Deut	1:1	all Israel beyond the J in the wilderness, in
	1:5	Beyond the J, in the land of Moab, Moses
	2:29	I go over the J into the land which
	3:8	who were beyond the J, from the valley of
	3:17	Arabah also, with the J as the boundary, from
	3:20	gives them beyond the J; then you shall return
	3:25	good land beyond the J, that goodly hill country,
	3:27	eyes; for you shall not go over this J
	4:21	should not cross the J, and that I should
	4:22	not go over the J; but you shall go
	4:26	are going over the J to possess; you will
	4:41	the east beyond the J,
	4:46	of Egypt, beyond the J in the valley opposite
	4:47	the east beyond the J;
	4:49	east side of the J as far as the
	9:1	to pass over the J this day, to go
	11:30	they not beyond the J, west of the road,
	11:31	to pass over the J to go in to
	12:10	you go over the J, and live in the
	27:2	you pass over the J to the land which
	27:4	have passed over the J, you shall set up
	27:12	have passed over the J, these shall stand upon
	30:18	are going over the J to enter and possess.
	31:2	not go over this J
	31:13	are going over the J to possess."
	32:47	are going over the J to possess."
Josh	1:2	arise, go over this J, you and all this
	1:11	to pass over this J, to go in to
	1:14	gave you beyond the J; but all the men
	1:15	gave you beyond the J toward the sunrise."
	2:7	the way to the J as far as the
	2:10	that were beyond the J, to Sihon and Og,
	3:1	they came to the J, and lodged there before
	3:8	the waters of the J, you shall stand still
	3:8	the Jordan, you shall stand still in the J
	3:11	is to pass over before you into the J
	3:13	the waters of the J, the waters of the
	3:13	the waters of the J shall be stopped from
	3:14	to pass over the J with the priests bearing
	3:15	had come to the J, and the feet of
	3:15	of the water (the J overflows all its banks
	3:17	the midst of the J, until all the nation
	3:17	until all the nation finished passing over the J
	4:1	finished passing over the J, the LORD said to
	4:3	the midst of the J, from the very place
	4:5	the midst of the J, and take up each
	4:7	the waters of the J were cut off before
	4:7	it passed over the J, the waters of the
	4:7	the waters of the J were cut off.
	4:8	the midst of the J, according to the number
	4:9	the midst of the J, in the place where
	4:10	the midst of the J, until everything was finished
	4:16	the testimony to come up out of the J
	4:17	commanded the priests, "Come up out of the J
	4:18	the midst of the J, and the soles of
	4:18	the waters of the J returned to their place
	4:19	up out of the J on the tenth day
	4:20	took out of the J, Joshua set up in
	4:22	'Israel passed over this J on dry ground.'
	4:23	the waters of the J for you until you
	5:1	that were beyond the J to the west, and
	5:1	the waters of the J for the people of
	7:7	this people over the J at all, to give
	7:7	we had been content to dwell beyond the J
	9:1	who were beyond the J in the hill country
	9:10	who were beyond the J, Sihon the king of
	12:1	their land beyond the J toward the sunrising, from
	12:7	west side of the J, from Baal-gad in the
	13:8	gave them, beyond the J eastward, as Moses the
	13:23	of Reuben was the J as a boundary.
	13:27	of Heshbon, having the J as a boundary, to
	13:27	of the Sea of Chinnereth, eastward beyond the J
	13:32	of Moab, beyond the J east of Jericho.
	14:3	one-half tribes beyond the J; but to the Levites
	15:5	the Salt Sea, to the mouth of the J
	15:5	the mouth of the J;
	16:1	Joseph went from the J by Jericho, east of
	16:7	to Naarah, and touches Jericho, ending at the J
	17:5	other side of the J;
	18:7	inheritance beyond the J eastward, which Moses the
	18:12	boundary began at the J; then the boundary goes

J

18:19 south end of the J: this is the southern
18:20 The J forms its boundary on the eastern side.
19:22 boundary ends at the J --sixteen cities with their
19:33 it ended at the J;
19:34 west, and Judah on the east at the J
20:8 And beyond the J east of Jericho, they appointed
22:4 gave you on the other side of the J
22:7 their brethren in the land west of the J
22:10 the region about the J, that lies in the
22:10 an altar by the J, an altar of great
22:11 the region about the J, on the side that
22:25 LORD has made the J a boundary between us
23:4 cut off, from the J to the Great Sea
24:8 other side of the J; they fought with you,
24:11 you went over the J and came to Jericho,
Judg 3:28 the fords of the J against the Moabites, and
5:17 Gilead stayed beyond the J; and Dan, why did
6:33 together, and crossing the J they encamped in the
7:24 them, as far as Beth-barah, and also the J
7:24 waters as far as Beth-barah, and also the J
7:25 of Oreb and Zeeb to Gideon beyond the J
8:4 Gideon came to the J and passed over, he
10:8 that were beyond the J in the land of
10:9 the Ammonites crossed the J to fight also against
11:13 Jabbok and to the J; now therefore restore it
11:22 the Jabbok and from the wilderness to the J
12:5 the fords of the J against the Ephraimites.
12:6 and slew him at the fords of the J
1Sam 13:7 the fords of the J to the land of
31:7 and those beyond the J saw that the men
2Sam 2:29 Arabah; they crossed the J, and marching the whole
10:17 together, and crossed the J, and came to Helam.
16:14 arrived weary at the J; and there he refreshed
17:22 and they crossed the J; by daybreak not one
17:22 one was left who had not crossed the J
17:24 And Absalom crossed the J with all the men
19:15 came back to the J; and Judah came to
19:15 king and to bring the king over the J
19:17 rushed down to the J before the king,
19:18 about to cross the J,
19:31 the king to the J, to escort him over
19:31 to the Jordan, to escort him over the J
19:36 little way over the J with the king.
19:39 people went over the J, and the king went
19:41 his household over the J, and all David's men
20:2 king steadfastly from the J to Jerusalem.
24:5 They crossed the J, and began from Aroer, and
1Kgs 2:8 meet me at the J, I swore to him
7:46 the plain of the J the king cast them,
17:3 the brook Cherith, that is east of the J
17:5 the brook Cherith that is east of the J
2Kgs 2:6 for the LORD has sent me to the J
2:7 them, as they both were standing by the J
2:13 back and stood on the bank of the J
5:10 and wash in the J seven times, and your
5:14 seven times in the J, according to the word
6:2 us go to the J and each of us
6:4 they came to the J, they cut down trees.
7:15 as far as the J; and, lo, all the
10:33 of Israel: from the J eastward, all the land
1Chr 6:78 lands, and beyond the J at Jericho, on the
6:78 east side of the J, out of the tribe
12:15 men who crossed the J in the first month,
12:37 Manasseh from beyond the J, one hundred and
19:17 together, and crossed the J, and came to them,
26:30 Israel westward of the J for all the work
2Chr 4:17 the plain of the J the king cast them,
Jud 1:9 towns, and beyond the J as far as Jerusalem
5:15 and crossing over the J they took possession of
Job 40:23 he is confident though J rushes against his mouth.
Ps 42:6 from the land of J and of Hermon, from
114:3 sea looked and fled, J turned back.
114:5 O J, that you turn back?
Sir 24:24 Euphrates, and like the J at harvest time.
Is 9:1 the land beyond the J, Galilee of the nations.
Jer 12:5 will you do in the jungle of the J
49:19 the jungle of the J against a strong sheepfold,
50:44 the jungle of the J against a strong sheepfold,
Ezek 47:18 and Damascus; along the J between Gilead and the
Zech 11:3 the jungle of the J is laid waste!
1Mac 5:24 his brother crossed the J and went three days'
5:52 And they crossed the J into the large plain
9:34 and he with all his army crossed the J
9:42 brother, they returned to the marshes of the J
9:43 the sabbath day to the banks of the J
9:45 the water of the J is on this side
9:48 him leaped into the J and swam across to
9:48 did not cross the J to attack them.
Mt 3:5 the region about the J,
3:6 him in the river J, confessing their sins.
3:13 from Galilee to the J to John, to be
4:15 the sea, across the J, Galilee of the Gentiles--
4:25 and Jerusalem and Judea and from beyond the J
19:1 of Judea beyond the J;
Mk 1:5 him in the river J, confessing their sins.
1:9 Galilee and was baptized by John in the J
3:8 and from beyond the J and from about Tyre
10:1 Judea and beyond the J, and crowds gathered to
Lk 3:3 the region about the J, preaching a baptism of
4:1 Spirit, returned from the J, and was led by
Jn 1:28 in Bethany beyond the J, where John was baptizing.
3:26 with you beyond the J, to whom you bore
10:40 away again across the J to the place where

JORIM

Lk 3:29 Eliezer, the son of J, the son of Matthat,

JORKE-AM

1Chr 2:44 Raham, the father of J; and Rekem was the

JOSECH

Lk 3:26 Seme-in, the son of J, the son of Joda,

JOSEPH (259)

Gen 30:24 she called his name J, saying, "May the LORD
30:25 When Rachel had borne J, Jacob said to Laban,
33:2 children, and Rachel and J last of all.
33:7 bowed down; and last J and Rachel drew near,
35:24 The sons of Rachel: J and Benjamin.
37:2 J, being seventeen years old, was shepherding the
37:2 his father's wives; and J brought an ill report
37:3 Now Israel loved J more than any other of
37:5 Now J had a dream, and when he told
37:13 And Israel said to J, "Are not your brothers
37:17 So J went after his brothers, and found them
37:23 So when J came to his brothers, they stripped
37:28 by; and they drew J up and lifted him
37:28 silver; and they took J to Egypt.
37:29 pit and saw that J was not in the
37:31 Then they took J's robe, and killed a goat,
37:33 beast has devoured him; J is without doubt torn
39:1 Now J was taken down to Egypt, and Potiphar,
39:2 The LORD was with J, and he became a
39:4 So J found favor in his sight and attended
39:5 the Egyptian's house for J's sake; the blessing of
39:6 that he had in J's charge; and having him
39:6 Now J was handsome and good-looking.
39:7 cast her eyes upon J, and said, "Lie with
39:10 although she spoke to J day after day, he
39:20 And J's master took him and put him into
39:21 the LORD was with J and showed him steadfast
39:22 the prison committed to J's care all the prisoners
39:23 anything that was in J's care, because the LORD
40:3 in the prison where J was confined.
40:4 of the guard charged J with them, and he
40:6 When J came to them in the morning and
40:8 And J said to them, "Do not interpretations belong
40:9 told his dream to J, and said to him,
40:12 Then J said to him, "This is its interpretation:
40:16 favorable, he said to J, "I also had a
40:18 And J answered, "This is its interpretation: the three
40:22 the chief baker, as J had interpreted to them.
40:23 butler did not remember J, but forgot him.
41:14 Pharaoh sent and called J, and they brought him
41:15 And Pharaoh said to J, "I have had a
41:16 J answered Pharaoh, "It is not in me; God
41:17 Then Pharaoh said to J, "Behold, in my dream
41:25 Then J said to Pharaoh, "The dream of Pharaoh
41:39 So Pharaoh said to J, "Since God has shown
41:41 And Pharaoh said to J, "Behold, I have set
41:42 and put it on J's hand, and arrayed him
41:44 Moreover Pharaoh said to J, "I am Pharaoh, and
41:45 Pharaoh called J's name Zaphenath-paneah; and he
41:45 So J went out over the land of Egypt.
41:46 J was thirty years old when he entered the
41:46 And J went out from the presence of Pharaoh,
41:49 And J stored up grain in great abundance, like
41:50 year of famine came, J had two sons, whom
41:51 J called the name of the first-born Manasseh, "For,"
41:54 began to come, as J had said.
41:55 the Egyptians, "Go to J; what he says to
41:56 over all the land, J opened all the storehouses,

J

41:57 came to Egypt to J to buy grain, because
42:3 So ten of J's brothers went down to buy
42:4 did not send Benjamin, J's brother, with his brothers,
42:6 Now J was governor over the land; he it
42:6 And J's brothers came, and bowed themselves before
42:7 J saw his brothers, and knew them, but he
42:8 Thus J knew his brothers, but they did not
42:9 J remembered the dreams which he had dreamed
42:14 But J said to them, "It is as I
42:18 On the third day J said to them, "Do
42:23 did not know that J understood them, for there
42:25 And J gave orders to fill their bags with
42:36 me of my children: J is no more, and
43:15 and went down to Egypt, and stood before J
43:16 When J saw Benjamin with them, he said to
43:17 The man did as J bade him, and brought
43:17 brought the men to J's house.
43:18 they were brought to J's house, and they said,
43:19 to the steward of J's house, and spoke with
43:24 brought the men into J's house, and given them
43:25 ready the present for J's coming at noon, for
43:26 When J came home, they brought into the house
43:30 Then J made haste, for his heart yearned for
43:34 taken to them from J's table, but Benjamin's portion
44:2 And he did as J told him.
44:4 distance from the city, J said to his steward,
44:14 his brothers came to J's house, he was still
44:15 J said to them, "What deed is this that
45:1 Then J could not control himself before all those
45:1 stayed with him when J made himself known to
45:3 And J said to his brothers, "I am Joseph;
45:3 his brothers, "I am J; is my father still
45:4 So J said to his brothers, "Come near to
45:4 "I am your brother, J, whom you sold into
45:9 'Thus says your son J, God has made me
45:16 heard in Pharaoh's house, J's brothers have come," it
45:17 And Pharaoh said to J, "Say to your brothers,
45:21 Israel did so; and J gave them wagons, according
45:26 And they told him, J is still alive, and
45:27 all the words of J, which he had said
45:27 saw the wagons which J had sent to carry
45:28 said, "It is enough; J my son is still
46:4 you up again; and J's hand shall close your
46:19 of Rachel, Jacob's wife: J and Benjamin.
46:20 And to J in the land of Egypt were
46:27 and the sons of J, who were born to
46:28 Judah before him to J, to appear before him
46:29 Then J made ready his chariot and went up
46:30 Israel said to J, "Now let me die, since
46:31 J said to his brothers and to his father's
47:1 So J went in and told Pharaoh, "My father
47:5 Then Pharaoh said to J, "Your father and your
47:7 Then J brought in Jacob his father, and set
47:11 Then J settled his father and his brothers, and
47:12 And J provided his father, his brothers, and all
47:14 And J gathered up all the money that was
47:14 which they bought; and J brought the money into
47:15 the Egyptians came to J, and said, "Give us
47:16 And J answered, "Give your cattle, and I will
47:17 brought their cattle to J; and Joseph gave them
47:17 cattle to Joseph; and J gave them food in
47:20 So J bought all the land of Egypt for
47:23 Then J said to the people, "Behold, I have
47:26 So J made it a statute concerning the land
47:29 he called his son J and said to him,
48:1 After this J was told, "Behold, your father is
48:2 to Jacob, "Your son J has come to you";
48:3 And Jacob said to J, "God Almighty appeared to
48:8 When Israel saw J's sons, he said, "Who are
48:9 J said to his father, "They are my sons,
48:10 So J brought them near him; and he kissed
48:11 And Israel said to J, "I had not thought
48:12 Then J removed them from his knees, and he
48:13 And J took them both, Ephraim in his right
48:15 And he blessed J, and said, "The God before
48:17 When J saw that his father laid his right
48:18 And J said to his father, "Not so, my
48:21 Then Israel said to J, "Behold, I am about
49:22 J is a fruitful bough, a fruitful bough by
49:26 on the head of J, and on the brow
50:1 Then J fell on his father's face, and wept
50:2 And J commanded his servants the physicians to
50:4 for him were past, J spoke to the household
50:7 So J went up to bury his father; and
50:8 all the household of J, his brothers, and his
50:14 had buried his father, J returned to Egypt with
50:15 When J's brothers saw that their father was dead,
50:15 "It may be that J will hate us and
50:16 sent a message to J, saying, "Your father gave
50:17 he died, 'Say to J, Forgive, I pray you,
50:17 J wept when they spoke to him.
50:19 But J said to them, "Fear not, for am
50:22 So J dwelt in Egypt, he and his father's
50:22 his father's house; and J lived a hundred and
50:23 And J saw Ephraim's children of the third
50:23 Manasseh were born upon J's knees.
50:24 And J said to his brothers, "I am about
50:25 Then J took an oath of the sons of
50:26 So J died, being a hundred and ten years
Ex 1:4 Jacob were seventy persons; J was already in Egypt.
1:5 Then J died, and all his brothers, and all
1:7 new king over Egypt, who did not know J
13:19 took the bones of J with him; for Joseph
13:19 Joseph with him; for J had solemnly sworn the
Num 1:10 from the sons of J, from Ephraim, Elishama the
1:32 Of the people of J, namely, of the people
13:7 Igal the son of J;
13:11 from the tribe of J (that is from the
26:28 The sons of J according to their families: Manasseh
26:37 are the sons of J according to their families.
27:1 from the families of Manasseh the son of J
32:33 Manasseh the son of J, the kingdom of Sihon
34:23 Of the sons of J: of the tribe of
36:1 of the sons of J, came near and spoke
36:5 of the sons of J is right.
36:12 Manasseh the son of J, and their inheritance
Deut 27:12 Simeon, Levi, Judah, Issachar, J, and Benjamin.
33:13 And of J he said, "Blessed by the LORD
33:16 upon the head of J, and upon the crown
Josh 14:4 For the people of J were two tribes, Manasseh
16:1 of the descendants of J went from the Jordan
16:4 The people of J, Manasseh and Ephraim, received
17:1 of Manasseh, for he was the first-born of J
17:2 Manasseh the son of J, by their families.
17:14 And the tribe of J spoke to Joshua, saying,
17:16 The tribe of J said, "The hill country is
17:17 to the house of J, to Ephraim and Manasseh,
18:5 and the house of J in their territory on
18:11 the tribe of Judah and the tribe of J
24:32 The bones of J which the people of Israel
24:32 it became an inheritance of the descendants of J
Judg 1:22 The house of J also went up against Bethel;
1:23 And the house of J sent to spy out
1:35 of the house of J rested heavily upon them,
2Sam 19:20 all the house of J to come down to
1Kgs 11:28 all the forced labor of the house of J
1Chr 2:2 Issachar, Zebulun, Dan, J, Benjamin, Naphtali, Gad,
5:1 to the sons of J the son of Israel,
5:2 the birthright belonged to J,
7:29 dwelt the sons of J the son of Israel.
25:2 sons of Asaph: Zaccur, J, Nethaniah, and Asharelah,
25:9 fell for Asaph to J; the second to Gedaliah,
Ezra 10:42 Shelemiah, Shemariah, Shallum, Amariah, and J
Neh 12:14 Malluchi, Jonathan; of Shebaniah, J;
Jud 8:1 of Ox, son of J, son of Oziel, son
Ps 77:15 redeem thy people, the sons of Jacob and J
78:67 rejected the tent of J, he did not choose
80:1 Israel, thou who leadest J like a flock!
81:5 it a decree in J, when he went out
105:17 man ahead of them, J, who was sold as
Sir 49:15 And no man like J has been born, and
Ezek 37:16 write upon it, 'For J (the stick of Ephraim)
37:19 take the stick of J (which is in the
47:13 J shall have two portions.
48:32 gates, the gate of J, the gate of Benjamin,
Amos 5:6 in the house of J, and it devour, with
5:15 hosts, will be gracious to the remnant of J
6:6 but are not grieved over the ruin of J
Obad 1:18 and the house of J a flame, and the
Zech 10:6 Judah, and I will save the house of J
1Mac 2:53 J in the time of his distress kept the
5:18 But he left J, the son of Zechariah, and
5:56 in Galilee before Ptolemais, J, the son of Zechariah,
5:60 Then J and Azariah were routed, and were pursued
2Mac 8:22 brothers also, Simon and J and Jonathan, each to
10:19 Maccabeus left Simon and J, and also Zacchaeus
Mt 1:16 Jacob the father of J the husband of Mary,
1:18 had been betrothed to J, before they came together
1:19 Spirit; and her husband J, being a just man
1:20 in a dream, saying, J, son of David, do
1:24 When J woke from sleep, he did as the
2:13 the Lord appeared to J in a dream and

2:19 in a dream to J in Egypt, saying,
13:55 his brethren James and J and Simon and Judas?
27:56 mother of James and J, and the mother of
27:57 man from Arimathea, named J, who also was a
27:59 And J took the body, and wrapped it in
Mk 15:42 day before the sabbath, J of Arimathea, a respected
15:44 he was dead, he granted the body to J
Lk 1:27 man whose name was J, of the house of
2:4 And J also went up from Galilee, from the
2:16 and found Mary and J, and the babe lying
3:23 (as was supposed) of J, the son of Heli,
3:24 Janna-i, the son of J,
3:30 Judah, the son of J, the son of Jonam,
4:22 said, "Is not this J's son?"
23:49 was a man named J from the Jewish town
Jn 1:45 prophets wrote, Jesus of Nazareth, the son of J
4:5 the field that Jacob gave to his son J
6:42 Jesus, the son of J, whose father and mother
19:38 After this J of Arimathea, who was a disciple
Acts 1:23 they put forward two, J called Barsabbas, who was
4:36 Thus J who was surnamed by the apostles Barnabas
7:9 the patriarchs, jealous of J, sold him into Egypt;
7:13 at the second visit J made himself known to
7:13 to his brothers, and J's family became known to
7:14 And J sent and called to him Jacob his
7:18 over Egypt another king who had not known J
Heb 11:21 of the sons of J, bowing in worship over
11:22 By faith J, at the end of his life,
Rev 7:8 of the tribe of J, twelve thousand sealed out

JOSES (3)
Mk 6:3 brother of James and J and Judas and Simon,
15:39 the younger and of J, and Salome,
15:46 Mary the mother of J saw where he was

JOSHAH
1Chr 4:34 Meshobab, Jamlech, J the son of Amaziah,

JOSHAPHAT (2)
1Chr 11:43 son of Maacah, and J the Mithnite,
15:24 Shebaniah, J, Nethanel, Amasai, Zechariah, Benaiah,

JOSHAVIAH
1Chr 11:46 Mahavite, and Jeribai, and J, the sons of Elna-am,

JOSHBEKASHAH (2)
1Chr 25:4 Eliathah, Giddalti, and Romamti-ezer, J, Mallothi,
25:24 to the seventeenth, to J, his sons and his

JOSHEB-BASSHEBETH
2Sam 23:8 men whom David had: J a Tah-chemonite; he was

JOSHIBIAH
1Chr 4:35 Jehu the son of J, son of Seraiah, son

JOSHUA (225)
Ex 17:9 And Moses said to J, "Choose for us men,
17:10 So J did as Moses told him, and fought
17:13 And J mowed down Amalek and his people with
17:14 in the ears of J, that I will utterly
24:13 rose with his servant J, and Moses went up
32:17 When J heard the noise of the people as
33:11 the camp, his servant J the son of Nun,
Num 11:28 And J the son of Nun, the minister of
13:16 And Moses called Hoshea the son of Nun J
14:6 And J the son of Nun and Caleb the
14:30 son of Jephunneh and J the son of Nun.
14:38 But J the son of Nun and Caleb the
26:65 son of Jephunneh and J the son of Nun.
27:18 said to Moses, "Take J the son of Nun,
27:22 commanded him; he took J and caused him to
32:12 Jephunneh the Kenizzite and J the son of Nun,
32:28 the priest, and to J the son of Nun,
34:17 Eleazar the priest and J the son of Nun.
Deut 1:38 not go in there; J the son of Nun,
3:21 you.' And I commanded J at that time, 'Your
3:28 But charge J, and encourage and strengthen him; for
31:3 shall dispossess them; and J will go over at
31:7 Then Moses summoned J, and said to him in
31:14 you must die; call J, and present yourselves in
31:14 And Moses and J went and presented themselves in
31:23 And the LORD commissioned J the son of Nun
32:44 the people, he and J the son of Nun.
34:9 And J the son of Nun was full of
Josh 1:1 the LORD said to J the son of Nun,
1:10 Then J commanded the officers of the people,
1:12 the half-tribe of Manasseh J said,
1:16 And they answered J, "All that you have commanded
2:1 And J the son of Nun sent two men
2:23 over and came to J the son of Nun;
2:24 And they said to J, "Truly the LORD has
3:1 Early in the morning J rose and set out
3:5 And J said to the people, "Sanctify yourselves; for
3:6 And J said to the priests, "Take up the
3:7 the LORD said to J, "This day I will
3:9 And J said to the people of Israel, "Come
3:10 And J said, "Hereby you shall know that the
4:1 the LORD said to J,
4:4 Then J called the twelve men from the people
4:5 from each tribe; and J said to them, "Pass
4:8 of Israel did as J commanded, and took up
4:8 as the LORD told J; and they carried them
4:9 And J set up twelve stones in the midst
4:10 that the LORD commanded J to tell the people,
4:10 according to all that Moses had commanded J
4:14 day the LORD exalted J in the sight of
4:15 the LORD said to J,
4:17 J therefore commanded the priests, "Come up out of
4:20 out of the Jordan, J set up in Gilgal.
5:2 the LORD said to J, "Make flint knives and
5:3 So J made flint knives, and circumcised the people
5:4 is the reason why J circumcised them: all the
5:7 in their stead, that J circumcised; for they were
5:9 the LORD said to J, "This day I have
5:13 When J was by Jericho, he lifted up his
5:13 in his hand; and J went to him and
5:14 And J fell on his face to the earth,
5:15 LORD's army said to J, "Put off your shoes
5:15 And J did so.
6:2 the LORD said to J, "See, I have given
6:6 So J the son of Nun called the priests
6:8 And as J had commanded the people, the seven
6:10 But J commanded the people, "You shall not shout
6:12 Then J rose early in the morning, and the
6:16 had blown the trumpets, J said to the people,
6:22 And J said to the two men who had
6:25 who belonged to her, J saved alive; and she
6:25 hid the messengers whom J sent to spy out
6:26 J laid an oath upon them at that time,
6:27 the LORD was with J; and his fame was
7:2 J sent men from Jericho to Ai, which is
7:3 And they returned to J, and said to him,
7:6 Then J rent his clothes, and fell to the
7:7 And J said, "Alas, O Lord GOD, why hast
7:10 The LORD said to J, "Arise, why have you
7:16 So J rose early in the morning, and brought
7:19 Then J said to Achan, "My son, give glory
7:20 And Achan answered J, "Of a truth I have
7:22 So J sent messengers, and they ran to the
7:23 and brought them to J and all the people
7:24 And J and all Israel with him took Achan
7:25 And J said, "Why did you bring trouble on
8:1 the LORD said to J, "Do not fear or
8:3 So J arose, and all the fighting men, to
8:3 up to Ai; and J chose thirty thousand mighty
8:9 So J sent them forth; and they went to
8:9 west of Ai; but J spent that night among
8:10 And J arose early in the morning and mustered
8:13 But J spent that night in the valley.
8:15 And J and all Israel made a pretense of
8:16 and as they pursued J they were drawn away
8:18 the LORD said to J, "Stretch out the javelin
8:18 And J stretched out the javelin that was in
8:21 And when J and all Israel saw that the
8:23 Ai they took alive, and brought him to J
8:26 For J did not draw back his hand, with
8:27 the word of the LORD which he commanded J
8:28 So J burned Ai, and made it for ever
8:29 down of the sun J commanded, and they took
8:30 Then J built an altar in Mount Ebal to
8:35 that Moses commanded which J did not read before
9:2 one accord to fight J and Israel.
9:3 of Gibeon heard what J had done to Jericho
9:6 And they went to J in the camp at
9:8 They said to J, "We are your servants." And
9:8 And J said to them, "Who are you?
9:15 And J made peace with them, and made a
9:22 J summoned them, and he said to them, "Why
9:24 They answered J, "Because it was told to your
9:27 But J made them that day hewers of wood
10:1 of Jerusalem heard how J had taken Ai, and
10:4 has made peace with J and with the people

10:6 of Gibeon sent to J at the camp in
10:7 So J went up from Gilgal, he and all
10:8 the LORD said to J, "Do not fear them,
10:9 So J came upon them suddenly, having marched up
10:12 Then spoke J to the LORD in the day
10:15 Then J returned, and all Israel with him, to
10:17 And it was told J, "The five kings have
10:18 And J said, "Roll great stones against the mouth
10:20 When J and the men of Israel had finished
10:21 people returned safe to J in the camp at
10:22 Then J said, "Open the mouth of the cave,
10:24 those kings out to J, Joshua summoned all the
10:24 kings out to Joshua, J summoned all the men
10:25 And J said to them, "Do not be afraid
10:26 And afterward J smote them and put them to
10:27 down of the sun, J commanded, and they took
10:28 And J took Makkedah on that day, and smote
10:29 Then J passed on from Makkedah, and all Israel
10:31 And J passed on from Libnah, and all Israel
10:33 to help Lachish; and J smote him and his
10:34 And J passed on with all Israel from Lachish
10:36 Then J went up with all Israel from Eglon
10:38 Then J, with all Israel, turned back to Debir
10:40 So J defeated the whole land, the hill country
10:41 And J defeated them from Kadesh-barnea to Gaza,
10:42 And J took all these kings and their land
10:43 Then J returned, and all Israel with him, to
11:6 the LORD said to J, "Do not be afraid
11:7 So J came suddenly upon them with all his
11:9 And J did to them as the LORD bade
11:10 And J turned back at that time, and took
11:12 and all their kings, J took, and smote them
11:13 except Hazor only; that J burned.
11:15 servant, so Moses commanded J, and so Joshua did;
11:15 commanded Joshua, and so J did; he left nothing
11:16 So J took all that land, the hill country
11:18 J made war a long time with all those
11:21 And J came at that time, and wiped out
11:21 hill country of Israel; J utterly destroyed them with
11:23 So J took the whole land, according to all
11:23 spoken to Moses; and J gave it for an
12:7 of the land whom J and the people of
12:7 rises toward Seir (and J gave their land to
13:1 Now J was old and advanced in years; and
14:1 Eleazar the priest, and J the son of Nun,
14:6 of Judah came to J at Gilgal; and Caleb
14:13 Then J blessed him; and he gave Hebron to
15:13 of the LORD to J, he gave to Caleb
17:4 Eleazar the priest and J the son of Nun
17:14 of Joseph spoke to J, saying, "Why have you
17:15 And J said to them, "If you are a
17:17 Then J said to the house of Joseph, to
18:3 So J said to the people of Israel, "How
18:8 on their way; and J charged those who went
18:9 then they came to J in the camp at
18:10 camp at Shiloh, and J cast lots for them
18:10 the LORD; and there J apportioned the land to
19:49 inheritance among them to J the son of Nun.
19:51 Eleazar the priest and J the son of Nun
20:1 the LORD said to J,
21:1 the priest and to J the son of Nun
22:1 Then J summoned the Reubenites, and the Gadites,
22:6 So J blessed them, and sent them away; and
22:7 to the other half J had given a possession
22:7 And when J sent them away to their homes
23:1 enemies round about, and J was old and well
23:2 well advanced in years, J summoned all Israel, their
24:1 Then J gathered all the tribes of Israel to
24:2 And J said to all the people, "Thus says
24:19 But J said to the people, "You cannot serve
24:21 the people said to J, "Nay; but we will
24:22 Then J said to the people, "You are witnesses
24:24 the people said to J, "The LORD our God
24:25 So J made a covenant with the people that
24:26 And J wrote these words in the book of
24:27 And J said to all the people, "Behold, this
24:28 So J sent the people away, every man to
24:29 After these things J the son of Nun, the
24:31 all the days of J, and all the days
24:31 the elders who outlived J and had known all
Judg 1:1 After the death of J the people of Israel
2:6 When J dismissed the people, the people of Israel
2:7 all the days of J, and all the days
2:7 the elders who outlived J, who had seen all
2:8 And J the son of Nun, the servant of
2:21 of the nations that J left when he died,
2:23 did not give them into the power of J
1Sam 6:14 into the field of J of Beth-shemesh, and stopped
6:18 in the field of J of Beth-shemesh.
1Kgs 16:34 which he spoke by J the son of Nun.
2Kgs 23:8 of the gate of J the governor of the
1Chr 7:27 son, Nun his son, J his son.
Sir 46:1 J the son of Nun was mighty in war,
Hag 1:1 of Judah, and to J the son of Jehozadak,
1:12 son of Shealtiel, and J the son of Jehozadak,
1:14 and the spirit of J the son of Jehozadak,
2:2 of Judah, and to J the son of Jehozadak,
2:4 LORD; take courage, O J, son of Jehozadak, the
Zech 3:1 Then he showed me J the high priest standing
3:3 Now J was standing before the angel, clothed with
3:6 of the LORD enjoined J,
3:8 Hear now, O J the high priest, you and
3:9 I have set before J, upon a single stone
6:11 upon the head of J, the son of Jehozadak,
1Mac 2:55 J, because he fulfilled the command, became a judge
2Mac 12:15 in the days of J, rushed furiously upon the
Lk 3:29 Er, the son of J, the son of Eliezer,
Acts 7:45 brought it in with J when they dispossessed the
Heb 4:8 For if J had given them rest, God would

JOSIAH (59)

1Kgs 13:2 the house of David, J by name; and he
2Kgs 21:24 of the land made J his son king in
21:26 garden of Uzza; and J his son reigned in
22:1 J was eight years old when he began to
22:3 eighteenth year of King J, the king sent Shaphan
23:16 And as J turned, he saw the tombs there
23:19 the LORD to anger, J removed; he did to
23:23 eighteenth year of King J this passover was kept
23:24 Moreover J put away the mediums and the wizards
23:28 of the acts of J, and all that he
23:29 King J went to meet him; and Pharaoh Neco
23:30 Jehoahaz the son of J, and anointed him, and
23:34 Eliakim the son of J king in the place
23:34 in the place of J his father, and changed
1Chr 3:14 son, Amon his son, J his son.
3:15 The sons of J: Johanan the first-born, the second
2Chr 33:25 of the land made J his son king in
34:1 J was eight years old when he began to
34:33 And J took away all the abominations from all
35:1 J kept a passover to the LORD in Jerusalem;
35:7 Then J contributed to the lay people, as passover
35:16 the LORD, according to the command of King J
35:18 as was kept by J, and the priests and
35:19 of the reign of J this passover was kept.
35:20 After all this, when J had prepared the temple,
35:20 on the Euphrates and J went out against him.
35:22 Nevertheless J would not turn away from him, but
35:23 the archers shot King J; and the king said
35:24 All Judah and Jerusalem mourned for J
35:25 uttered a lament for J; and all the singing
35:25 women have spoken of J in their laments to
35:26 of the acts of J, and his good deeds
36:1 Jehoahaz the son of J and made him king
Sir 49:1 The memory of J is like a blending of
49:4 David and Hezekiah and J they all sinned greatly,
Jer 1:2 in the days of J the son of Amon,
1:3 Jehoiakim the son of J, king of Judah, and
1:3 Zedekiah, the son of J, king of Judah, until
3:6 the days of King J: "Have you seen what
22:11 Shallum the son of J, king of Judah, who
22:11 who reigned instead of J his father, and who
22:18 Jehoiakim the son of J, king of Judah: "They
25:1 Jehoiakim the son of J, king of Judah (that
25:3 the thirteenth year of J the son of Amon,
26:1 Jehoiakim the son of J, king of Judah, this
27:1 Zedekiah the son of J, king of Judah, this
35:1 Jehoiakim the son of J, king of Judah:
36:1 Jehoiakim the son of J, king of Judah, this
36:2 from the days of J until today.
36:9 Jehoiakim the son of J, king of Judah, in
37:1 Zedekiah the son of J, whom Nebuchadrezzar king
45:1 Jehoiakim the son of J, king of Judah:
46:2 Jehoiakim the son of J, king of Judah:
Bar 1:8 Zedekiah the son of J, king of Judah, had
Zeph 1:1 in the days of J the son of Amon,
Zech 6:10 to the house of J, the son of Zephaniah.
6:14 Heldai, Tobijah, Jedaiah, and J the son of Zephaniah.
Mt 1:10 Amos the father of J,
1:11 father of Josiah, and J the father of Jechoniah

JOSIPHIAH
Ezra 8:10 Shelomith the son of J, and with him a

JOSTLE
Joel 2:8 They do not J one another, each marches in

JOTBAH
2Kgs 21:19 name was Meshullemeth the daughter of Haruz of J

JOTBATHAH (3)
Num 33:33 they set out from Hor-haggidgad, and encamped at J
33:34 they set out from J, and encamped at Abronah.
Deut 10:7 and from Gudgodah to J, a land with brooks

JOTHAM (26)
Judg 9:5 upon one stone; but J the youngest son of
9:7 it was told to J, he went and stood
9:21 And J ran away and fled, and went to
9:57 came the curse of J the son of Jerubbaal.
2Kgs 15:5 And J the king's son was over the household,
15:7 city of David, and J his son reigned in
15:30 the twentieth year of J the son of Uzziah.
15:32 Remaliah, king of Israel, J the son of Uzziah,
15:36 of the acts of J, and all that he
15:38 J slept with his fathers, and was buried with
16:1 Ahaz the son of J, king of Judah, began
1Chr 2:47 sons of Jahdai: Regem, J, Geshan, Pelet, Ephah, and
3:12 son, Azariah his son, J his son,
5:17 in the days of J king of Judah, and
2Chr 26:21 And J his son was over the king's household,
26:23 And J his son reigned in his stead.
27:1 J was twenty-five years old when he began to
27:6 So J became mighty, because he ordered his ways
27:7 of the acts of J, and all his wars,
27:9 And J slept with his fathers, and they buried
Is 1:1 the days of Uzziah, J, Ahaz, and Hezekiah, kings
7:1 Ahaz the son of J, son of Uzziah, king
Hos 1:1 the days of Uzziah, J, Ahaz, and Hezekiah, kings
Mic 1:1 in the days of J, Ahaz, and Hezekiah, kings
Mt 1:9 Uzziah the father of J, and Jotham the father
1:9 father of Jotham, and J the father of Ahaz,

JOURNEY (74)
Gen 24:21 LORD had prospered his J or not.
29:1 Jacob went on his J, and came to the
30:36 distance of three days' J between himself and Jacob;
33:12 Esau said, "Let us J on our way, and
42:25 sack, and to give them provisions for the J
42:38 befall him on the J that you are to
45:21 of Pharaoh, and gave them provisions for the J
45:23 bread, and provision for his father on the J
46:1 So Israel took his J with all that he
Ex 3:18 go a three days' J into the wilderness, that
5:3 pray, a three days' J into the wilderness, and
8:27 must go three days' J into the wilderness and
Num 9:10 afar off on a J, he shall still keep
9:13 is not on a J, yet refrains from keeping
10:33 the LORD three days' J; and the ark of
10:33 before them three days' J, to seek out a
11:31 camp, about a day's J on this side and
11:31 side and a day's J on the other side,
33:8 went a three days' J in the wilderness of
Deut 1:2 It is eleven days' J from Horeb by the
1:7 turn and take your J, and go to the
1:40 for you, turn, and J into the wilderness in
2:24 'Rise up, take your J, and go over the
10:11 'Arise, go on your J at the head of
28:68 ships to Egypt, a J which I promised that
Josh 9:11 your hand for the J, and go to meet
9:12 our food for the J, on the day we
9:13 of ours are worn-out from the very long J
Judg 18:5 may know whether the J on which we are
18:6 The J on which you go is under the
19:9 the morning for your J, and go home."
1Sam 9:6 tell us about the J on which we have
21:5 it is a common J; how much more today
2Sam 11:10 to Uriah, "Have you not come from a J
1Kgs 18:27 he is on a J, or perhaps he is
19:4 himself went a day's J into the wilderness, and
19:7 and eat, else the J will be too great
Tob 5:16 "Get ready for the J, and good success to
5:16 So his son made the preparations for the J
5:21 go with him; his J will be successful, and
7:8 talked about on the J, and let the matter
9:5 So Raphael made the J and stayed over night
10:1 the days for the J had expired and they
11:1 he had made his J a success.
Prov 7:19 gone on a long J;
Wis 13:18 inexperienced; for a prosperous J, a thing that
18:3 for thy people's unknown J, and a harmless sun
19:5 experience an incredible J, but they themselves
Sir 21:16 a burden on a J, but delight will be
Jon 3:3 great city, three days' J in breadth.
3:4 to go into the city, going a day's J
1Mac 5:24 and went three days' J into the wilderness.
7:45 pursued them a day's J, from Adasa as far
8:19 Rome, a very long J; and they entered the
2Mac 3:8 set out on his J, ostensibly to make a
9:4 to drive without stopping until he completed the J
9:7 the Jews, and giving orders to hasten the J
Mt 10:10 no bag for your J, nor two tunics, nor
25:14 man going on a J called his servants and
Mk 6:8 take nothing for their J except a staff; no
10:17 setting out on his J, a man ran up
13:34 man going on a J, when he leaves home
Lk 2:44 they went a day's J, and they sought him
9:3 "Take nothing for your J, no staff, nor bag,
11:6 has arrived on a J, and I have nothing
15:13 had and took his J into a far country,
Jn 4:6 he was with his J, sat down beside the
Acts 1:12 Jerusalem, a sabbath day's J away;
10:9 they were on their J and coming near the
21:5 and went on our J; and they all, with
22:6 "As I made my J and drew near to
Rom 15:24 be sped on my J there by you, once
1Cor 16:6 speed me on my J, wherever I go.
3Jn 1:6 send them on their J as befits God's service.

JOURNEYED (25)
Gen 12:9 And Abram J on, still going toward the Negeb.
13:3 And he J on from the Negeb as far
13:11 Jordan valley, and Lot J east; thus they separated
20:1 From there Abraham J toward the territory of the
33:17 But Jacob J to Succoth, and built himself a
35:5 And as they J, a terror from God fell
35:16 Then they J from Bethel; and when they were
35:21 Israel J on, and pitched his tent beyond the
Ex 12:37 the people of Israel J from Rameses to Succoth,
Num 11:35 Kibroth-hattaavah the people J to Hazeroth; and
20:22 And they J from Kadesh, and the people of
Deut 2:1 "Then we turned, and J into the wilderness in
10:6 (The people of Israel J from Be-eroth Bene-jaakan
10:7 From there they J to Gudgodah, and from Gudgodah
Judg 11:18 Then they J through the wilderness, and went
17:8 place; and as he J, he came to the
1Chr 4:39 They J to the entrance of Gedor, to the
Wis 5:7 and destruction, and we J through trackless deserts,
11:2 They J through an uninhabited wilderness, and
Is 57:9 You J to Molech with oil and multiplied your
Lk 10:33 a Samaritan, as he J, came to where he
Acts 9:3 Now as he J he approached Damascus, and suddenly
22:5 the brethren, and I J to Damascus to take
26:12 "Thus I J to Damascus with the authority and
26:13 me and those who J with me.

JOURNEYING
Lk 13:22 and villages, teaching, and J toward Jerusalem.

JOURNEYS
2Cor 11:26 at sea; on frequent J, in danger from rivers,

JOY (196)
Judg 19:3 him, he came with J to meet him.
1Sam 18:6 timbrels, with songs of J, and with instruments of
1Kgs 1:40 and rejoicing with great J, so that the earth
1Chr 12:40 sheep, for there was J in Israel.
15:16 and lyres and cymbals, to raise sounds of J
16:27 before him; strength and J are in his place.
16:33 the wood sing for J before the LORD, for
2Chr 20:27 returning to Jerusalem with J, for the LORD had
30:26 So there was great J in Jerusalem, for since
Ezra 3:12 many shouted aloud for J;
6:16 the dedication of this house of God with J
6:22 bread seven days with J; for the LORD had
Neh 8:10 be grieved, for the J of the LORD is
12:43 them rejoice with great J; the women and children
12:43 And the J of Jerusalem was heard afar off.
Tob 7:18 and earth grant you J in place of this
13:10 tent may be raised for you again with J
Jud 4:12 desecrated to the malicious J of the Gentiles.
12:14 it will be a J to me until the
16:11 oppressed people shouted for J; my weak people

Esth	8:16	light and gladness and J and honor.
	8:17	there was gladness and J among the Jews, a
	10:13	with an assembly and J and gladness before God,
	14:18	servant has had no J since the day that
	16:21	day to be a J to his chosen people
Job	8:19	Behold, this is the J of his way; and
	20:5	is short, and the J of the godless but
	29:13	I caused the widow's heart to sing for J
	33:26	accepts him, he comes into his presence with J
	38:7	and all the sons of God shouted for J
Ps	4:7	Thou hast put more J in my heart than
	5:11	them ever sing for J; and do thou defend
	16:11	there is fulness of J, in thy right hand
	19:5	like a strong man runs its course with J
	20:5	May we shout for J over your victory, and
	21:6	him glad with the J of thy presence.
	27:6	sacrifices with shouts of J; I will sing and
	30:5	for the night, but J comes with the morning.
	32:11	righteous, and shout for J, all you upright in
	35:27	my vindication shout for J and be glad, and
	43:4	to God my exceeding J; and I will praise
	45:15	With J and gladness they are led along as
	47:1	Shout to God with loud songs of J
	48:2	in elevation, is the J of all the earth,
	51:8	Fill me with J and gladness; let the bones
	51:12	Restore to me the J of thy salvation, and
	63:7	the shadow of thy wings I sing for J
	65:8	the morning and the evening to shout for J
	65:12	hills gird themselves with J,
	65:13	with grain, they shout and sing together for J
	67:4	glad and sing for J, for thou dost judge
	68:3	exult before God; let them be jubilant with J
	71:23	lips will shout for J, when I sing praises
	81:1	our strength; shout for J to the God of
	84:2	and flesh sing for J to the living God.
	92:4	the works of thy hands I sing for J
	96:12	the wood sing for J
	97:11	for the righteous, and J for the upright in
	98:8	the hills sing for J together
	105:43	forth his people with J, his chosen ones with
	107:22	and tell of his deeds in songs of J
	119:111	yea, they are the J of my heart.
	126:2	tongue with shouts of J; then they said among
	126:5	who sow in tears reap with shouts of J
	126:6	home with shouts of J, bringing his sheaves with
	132:9	with righteousness, and let thy saints shout for J
	132:16	with salvation, and her saints will shout for J
	137:6	I do not set Jerusalem above my highest J
	149:5	let them sing for J on their couches.
Prov	12:20	devise evil, but those who plan good have J
	14:10	its own bitterness, and no stranger shares its J
	14:13	and the end of J is grief.
	15:21	Folly is a J to him who has no
	15:23	apt answer is a J to a man, and
	17:21	and the father of a fool has no J
	21:15	done, it is a J to the righteous, but
Eccl	2:26	wisdom and knowledge and J; but to the sinner
	5:20	keeps him occupied with J in his heart.
Wis	8:16	with her has no pain, but gladness and J
Sir	1:10	and gives gladness and J and long life.
	1:20	right moment, and then J will burst forth for
	2:9	good things, for everlasting J and mercy.
	4:12	who seek her early will be filled with J
	6:28	will be changed into J for you.
	30:16	is no gladness above J of heart.
Is	9:3	thou hast increased its J; they rejoice before thee
	9:3	before thee as with J at the harvest, as
	12:3	With J you will draw water from the wells
	12:6	Shout, and sing for J, O inhabitant of Zion,
	16:10	And J and gladness are taken away from the
	22:13	sackcloth; and behold, J and gladness, slaying oxen
	24:11	lack of wine; all J has reached its eventide;
	24:14	voices, they sing for J; over the majesty of
	26:19	dwellers in the dust, awake and sing for J
	29:19	meek shall obtain fresh J in the LORD, and
	32:14	dens for ever, a J of wild asses, a
	35:2	abundantly, and rejoice with J and singing.
	35:6	and the tongue of the dumb sing for J
	35:10	Zion with singing; everlasting J shall be upon their
	35:10	heads; they shall obtain J and gladness, and sorrow
	42:11	of Sela sing for J, let them shout from
	48:20	with a shout of J, proclaim it, send it
	49:13	Sing for J, O heavens, and exult, O earth;
	51:3	garden of the LORD; J and gladness will be
	51:11	Zion with singing; everlasting J shall be upon their
	51:11	heads; they shall obtain J and gladness, and sorrow
	52:8	together they sing for J; for eye to eye
	55:12	shall go out in J, and be led forth
	60:15	majestic for ever, a J from age to age.
	61:7	possess a double portion; yours shall be everlasting J
	65:18	create Jerusalem a rejoicing, and her people a J
	66:5	we may see your J; but it is they
	66:10	rejoice with her in J, all you who mourn
Jer	15:16	became to me a J and the delight of
	31:13	turn their mourning into J, I will comfort them,
	33:9	me a name of J, a praise and a
	48:33	Gladness and J have been taken away from the
	48:33	them with shouts of J; the shouting is not
	48:33	joy; the shouting is not the shout of J
	51:48	them, shall sing for J over Babylon; for the
Lam	2:15	perfection of beauty, the J of all the earth?"
	5:15	The J of our hearts has ceased; our dancing
Bar	4:11	With J I nurtured them, but I sent them
	4:22	to save you, and J has come to me
	4:23	back to me with J and gladness for ever.
	4:29	will bring you everlasting J with your salvation."
	4:36	Jerusalem, and see the J that is coming to
	5:9	will lead Israel with J, in the light of
Ezek	24:25	them their stronghold, their J and glory, the delight
	36:5	a possession with wholehearted J and utter
Joel	1:15	off before our eyes, J and gladness from the
Hab	3:18	the LORD, I will J in the God of
Zech	8:19	of Judah seasons of J and gladness, and cheerful
1Mac	3:45	J was taken from Jacob; the flute and the
	4:59	observed with gladness and J for eight days,
	5:54	Zion with gladness and J, and offered burnt
	14:11	in the land, and Israel rejoiced with great J
2Mac	3:30	disturbance, was filled with J and gladness, now that
	15:28	they were returning with J, they recognized Nicanor,
Mt	2:10	rejoiced exceedingly with great J;
	13:20	immediately receives it with J;
	13:44	up; then in his J he goes and sells
	25:21	much; enter into the J of your master.'
	25:23	much; enter into the J of your master.'
	28:8	with fear and great J, and ran to tell
Mk	4:16	immediately receive it with J;
Lk	1:14	And you will have J and gladness, and many
	1:44	ears, the babe in my womb leaped for J
	2:10	news of a great J which will come to
	6:23	day, and leap for J, for behold, your reward
	8:13	word, receive it with J; but these have no
	10:17	The seventy returned with J, saying, "Lord, even the
	15:7	there will be more J in heaven over one
	15:10	tell you, there is J before the angels of
	24:41	they still disbelieved for J, and wondered, he said
	24:52	to Jerusalem with great J,
Jn	3:29	bridegroom's voice; therefore this J of mine is now
	15:11	to you, that my J may be in you,
	15:11	you, and that your J may be full.
	16:20	be sorrowful, but your sorrow will turn into J
	16:21	remembers the anguish, for J that a child is
	16:22	one will take your J from you.
	16:24	will receive, that your J may be full.
	17:13	they may have my J fulfilled in themselves.
Acts	8:8	So there was much J in that city.
	12:14	Peter's voice, in her J she did not open
	13:52	disciples were filled with J and with the Holy
	15:3	and they gave great J to all the brethren.
Rom	14:17	righteousness and peace and J in the Holy Spirit;
	15:13	fill you with all J and peace in believing,
	15:32	come to you with J and be refreshed in
2Cor	1:24	with you for your J, for you stand firm
	2:3	of you, that my J would be the joy
	2:3	joy would be the J of you all.
	7:13	still more at the J of Titus, because his
	8:2	affliction, their abundance of J and their extreme
Gal	5:22	the Spirit is love, J, peace, patience, kindness,
Phil	1:4	making my prayer with J,
	1:25	for your progress and J in the faith,
	2:2	and sympathy, complete my J by being of the
	2:29	the Lord with all J; and honor such men,
	4:1	and long for, my J and crown, stand firm
Col	1:11	endurance and patience with J,
1Thes	1:6	in much affliction, with J inspired by the Holy
	2:19	is our hope or J or crown of boasting
	2:20	For you are our glory and J
	3:9	you, for all the J which we feel for
2Tim	1:4	see you, that I may be filled with J
Philem	1:7	I have derived much J and comfort from your
Heb	12:2	faith, who for the J that was set before
Jas	1:2	Count it all J, my brethren, when you meet
	4:9	to mourning and your J to dejection.

1Pet 1:8 in him and rejoice with unutterable and exalted J
1Jn 1:4 writing this that our J may be complete.
2Jn 1:12 face, so that our J may be complete.
3Jn 1:4 No greater J can I have than this, to

JOYFUL (22)

Deut 16:15 your hands, so that you will be altogether J
1Kgs 8:66 went to their homes J and glad of heart
2Chr 7:10 away to their homes, J and glad of heart
Ezra 3:13 the sound of the J shout from the sound
6:22 LORD had made them J, and had turned the
Tob 13:11 generations will give you J praise.
Jud 14:9 shout and made a J noise in their city.
Esth 5:9 went out that day J and glad of heart.
Job 3:7 be barren; let no J cry be heard in
Ps 63:5 mouth praises thee with J lips,
66:1 Make a J noise to God, all the earth;
68:3 let the righteous be J; let them exult before
95:1 let us make a J noise to the rock
95:2 let us make a J noise to him with
98:4 Make a J noise to the LORD, all the
98:6 the horn make a J noise before the King,
100:1 Make a J noise to the LORD, all the
Eccl 7:14 day of prosperity be J, and in the day
Is 32:13 joyous houses in the J city.
56:7 mountain, and make them J in my house of
Jer 49:25 city is forsaken, the J city!
Ezek 7:7 tumult, and not of J shouting upon the mountains.

JOYFULLY (4)

Is 64:5 Thou meetest him that J works righteousness, those
Lk 19:6 made haste and came down, and received him J
Heb 10:34 the prisoners, and you J accepted the plundering of
13:17 Let them do this J, and not sadly, for

JOYFULNESS

Deut 28:47 LORD your God with J and gladness of heart,

JOYOUS (3)

Ps 98:4 earth; break forth into J song and sing praises!
113:9 home, making her the J mother of children.
Is 32:13 yea, for all the J houses in the joyful

JOYOUSLY (2)

1Chr 29:17 here, offering freely and J to thee.
Ps 89:12 them; Tabor and Hermon J praise thy name.

JOZABAD (10)

1Chr 12:4 thirty; Jeremiah, Jahaziel, Johanan, J of Gederah,
12:20 deserted to him: Adnah, J, Jedia-el, Michael,
12:20 Jedia-el, Michael, J, Elihu, and Zillethai, chiefs
2Chr 31:13 Azaziah, Nahath, Asahel, Jerimoth, J, Eliel,
35:9 Hashabiah and Je-iel and J, the chiefs of the
Ezra 8:33 them were the Levites, J the son of Jeshua
10:22 Eli-o-enai, Ma-aseiah, Ishmael, Nethanel, J, and
10:23 Of the Levites: J, Shimei, Kelaiah (that is, Kelita),
Neh 8:7 Hodiah, Ma-aseiah, Kelita, Azariah, J, Hanan,
11:16 Bunni; and Shabbethai and J, of the chiefs of

JOZACAR

2Kgs 12:21 It was J the son of Shimeath and Jehozabad

JOZADAK (6)

Ezra 3:2 Jeshua the son of J, with his fellow priests,
3:8 Jeshua the son of J made a beginning, together
5:2 Jeshua the son of J arose and began to
10:18 Jeshua the son of J and his brethren.
Neh 12:26 of Jeshua son of J, and in the days
Sir 49:12 Jeshua the son of J; in their days they

JUBAL

Gen 4:21 His brother's name was J; he was the father

JUBILANT (2)

Ps 68:3 God; let them be J with joy!
Is 24:8 the noise of the J has ceased, the mirth

JUBILEE (21)

Lev 25:10 it shall be a J for you, when each
25:11 A J shall that fiftieth year be to you;
25:12 For it is a J; it shall be holy
25:13 "In this year of J each of you shall
25:15 of years after the J, you shall buy from
25:28 until the year of J; in the jubilee it
25:28 of jubilee; in the J it shall be released,
25:30 generations; it shall not be released in the J
25:31 redeemed, and they shall be released in the J
25:33 be released in the J; for the houses in
25:40 the year of the J;
25:50 until the year of J, and the price of
25:52 until the year of J, he shall make a
25:54 in the year of J, he and his children
27:17 from the year of J, it shall stand at
27:18 his field after the J, then the priest shall
27:18 until the year of J, and a deduction shall
27:21 is released in the J, shall be holy to
27:23 to the year of J, and the man shall
27:24 In the year of J the field shall return
Num 36:4 And when the J of the people of Israel

JUCAL

Jer 38:1 the son of Pashhur, J the son of Shelemiah,

JUDAH (883)

Gen 29:35 she called his name J; then she ceased bearing.
35:23 (Jacob's first-born), Simeon, Levi, J, Issachar, and
37:26 Then J said to his brothers, "What profit is
38:1 at that time that J went down from his
38:2 There J saw the daughter of a certain Canaanite
38:6 And J took a wife for Er his first-born,
38:7 But Er, J's first-born, was wicked in the sight
38:8 Then J said to Onan, "Go in to your
38:11 Then J said to Tamar his daughter-in-law, "Remain a
38:12 time the wife of J, Shua's daughter, died; and
38:12 daughter, died; and when J was comforted, he went
38:15 When J saw her, he thought her to be
38:20 When J sent the kid by his friend the
38:22 So he returned to J, and said, "I have
38:23 And J replied, "Let her keep the things as
38:24 About three months later J was told, "Tamar your
38:24 And J said, "Bring her out, and let her
38:26 Then J acknowledged them and said, "She is more
43:3 But J said to him, "The man solemnly warned
43:8 And J said to Israel his father, "Send the
44:14 When J and his brothers came to Joseph's house,
44:16 And J said, "What shall we say to my
44:18 Then J went up to him and said, "O
46:12 The sons of J: Er, Onan, Shelah, Perez, and
46:28 He sent J before him to Joseph, to appear
49:8 J, your brothers shall praise you; your hand shall
49:9 J is a lion's whelp; from the prey, my
49:10 shall not depart from J, nor the ruler's staff
Ex 1:2 Reuben, Simeon, Levi, and J,
31:2 of the tribe of J:
35:30 of the tribe of J;
38:22 of the tribe of J, made all that the
Num 1:7 son of Zurishaddai; from J, Nahshon the son of
1:26 Of the people of J, their generations, by their
1:27 of the tribe of J was seventy-four thousand six
2:3 of the camp of J by their companies, the
2:3 of the people of J being Nahshon the son
2:9 of the camp of J, by their companies, is
7:12 of the tribe of J;
10:14 of the men of J set out first by
13:6 from the tribe of J, Caleb the son of
26:19 The sons of J were Er and Onan; and
26:20 And the sons of J according to their families
26:22 are the families of J according to their number,
34:19 Of the tribe of J, Caleb the son of
Deut 27:12 the people: Simeon, Levi, J, Issachar, Joseph, and
33:7 this he said of J: "Hear, O LORD, the
33:7 LORD, the voice of J, and bring him in
34:2 all the land of J as far as the
Josh 7:1 of the tribe of J, took some of the
7:16 and the tribe of J was taken;
7:17 near the families of J, and the family of
7:18 of the tribe of J, was taken.
11:21 the hill country of J, and from all the
14:6 Then the people of J came to Joshua at
15:1 of the people of J according to their families
15:12 about the people of J according to their families.
15:13 among the people of J, Kiriath-arba, that is, Hebron
15:20 of the people of J according to their families.
15:21 of the people of J in the extreme South,
15:63 Jerusalem, the people of J could not drive out;
15:63 with the people of J at Jerusalem to this
18:5 it into seven portions, J continuing in his territory
18:11 between the tribe of J and the tribe of
18:14 Kiriath-jearim), a city belonging to the tribe of J
19:1 midst of the inheritance of the tribe of J
19:9 of the territory of J; because the portion of
19:9 of the tribe of J was too large for

JUDAH

19:34 on the west, and J on the east at
20:7 (that is, Hebron) in the hill country of J
21:4 from the tribes of J, Simeon, and Benjamin, thirteen
21:9 of the tribe of J and the tribe of
21:11 the hill country of J, along with the pasture
Judg 1:2 The LORD said, J shall go up; behold, I
1:3 And J said to Simeon his brother, "Come up
1:4 Then J went up and the LORD gave the
1:8 And the men of J fought against Jerusalem, and
1:9 afterward the men of J went down to fight
1:10 And J went against the Canaanites who dwelt in
1:16 with the people of J from the city of
1:16 into the wilderness of J, which lies in the
1:17 And J went with Simeon his brother, and they
1:18 J also took Gaza with its territory, and Ashkelon
1:19 the LORD was with J, and he took possession
10:9 to fight also against J and against Benjamin and
15:9 up and encamped in J, and made a raid
15:10 And the men of J said, "Why have you
15:11 three thousand men of J went down to the
17:7 man of Bethlehem in J, of the family of
17:7 of the family of J, who was a Levite;
17:8 town of Bethlehem in J, to live where he
17:9 Levite of Bethlehem in J, and I am going
18:12 and went up and encamped at Kiriath-jearim in J
19:1 took to himself a concubine from Bethlehem in J
19:2 house at Bethlehem in J, and was there some
19:18 passing from Bethlehem in J to the remote parts
19:18 went to Bethlehem in J; and I am going
20:18 And the LORD said, J shall go up first."
Ruth 1:1 man of Bethlehem in J went to sojourn in
1:2 Chilion; they were Ephrathites from Bethlehem in J
1:7 the way to return to the land of J
4:12 whom Tamar bore to J, because of the children
1Sam 11:8 and the men of J thirty thousand.
15:4 men on foot, and ten thousand men of J
17:1 which belongs to J, and encamped between Socoh
17:12 Ephrathite of Bethlehem in J, named Jesse, who had
17:52 men of Israel and J rose with a shout
18:16 But all Israel and J loved David; for he
22:5 stronghold; depart, and go into the land of J
23:3 are afraid here in J; how much more then
23:23 search him out among all the thousands of J
27:6 to the kings of J to this day.
27:10 David would say, "Against the Negeb of J
30:14 that which belongs to J and upon the Negeb
30:16 of the Philistines and from the land of J
30:26 friends, the elders of J, saying, "Here is a
2Sam 1:18 to the people of J; behold, it is written
2:1 go up into any of the cities of J
2:4 And the men of J came, and there they
2:4 they anointed David king over the house of J
2:7 and the house of J has anointed me king
2:10 But the house of J followed David.
2:11 over the house of J was seven years and
3:8 and said, "Am I a dog's head of J
3:10 over Israel and over J, from Dan to Beer-sheba."
5:5 Hebron he reigned over J seven years and six
5:5 over all Israel and J thirty-three years.
11:11 ark and Israel and J dwell in booths; and
12:8 of Israel and of J; and if this were
19:11 to the elders of J, 'Why should you be
19:14 all the men of J as one man; so
19:15 to the Jordan; and J came to Gilgal to
19:16 with the men of J to meet King David;
19:40 all the people of J, and also half the
19:41 brethren the men of J stolen you away, and
19:42 All the men of J answered the men of
19:43 answered the men of J, "We have ten shares
19:43 of the men of J were fiercer than the
20:2 but the men of J followed their king steadfastly
20:4 "Call the men of J together to me within
20:5 Amasa went to summon J; but he delayed beyond
21:2 his zeal for the people of Israel and J
24:1 David against them, saying, "Go, number Israel and J
24:7 to the Negeb of J at Beer-sheba.
24:9 and the men of J were five hundred thousand.
1Kgs 1:9 the royal officials of J,
1:35 him to be ruler over Israel and over J
2:32 son of Jether, commander of the army of J
4:19 there was one officer in the land of J
4:20 J and Israel were as many as the sand
4:25 And J and Israel dwelt in safety, from Dan
9:18 in the land of J,
12:17 of Israel who dwelt in the cities of J
12:20 but the tribe of J only.
12:21 all the house of J, and the tribe of
12:23 of Solomon, king of J, and to all the
12:23 all the house of J and Benjamin, and to
12:27 to Rehoboam king of J, and they will kill
12:27 kill me and return to Rehoboam king of J
12:32 feast that was in J, and he offered sacrifices
13:1 God came out of J by the word of
13:12 God who came from J had gone.
13:14 you the man of God who came from J
13:21 God who came from J, "Thus says the LORD,
14:21 Now Rehoboam the son of Solomon reigned in J
14:22 And J did what was evil in the sight
14:29 Book of the Chronicles of the Kings of J
15:1 son of Nebat, Abijam began to reign over J
15:7 Book of the Chronicles of the Kings of J
15:9 began to reign over J,
15:17 Israel went up against J, and built Ramah, that
15:17 out or come in to Asa king of J
15:22 a proclamation to all J, none was exempt, and
15:23 Book of the Chronicles of the Kings of J
15:25 of Asa king of J; and he reigned over
15:28 of Asa king of J, and reigned in his
15:33 of Asa king of J, Baasha the son of
16:8 of Asa king of J, Elah the son of
16:10 of Asa king of J, and reigned in his
16:15 of Asa king of J, Zimri reigned seven days
16:23 of Asa king of J, Omri began to reign
16:29 of Asa king of J, Ahab the son of
19:3 Beer-sheba, which belongs to J, and left his servant
22:2 Jehoshaphat the king of J came down to the
22:10 Jehoshaphat the king of J were sitting on their
22:29 Jehoshaphat the king of J went up to Ramoth-gilead.
22:41 began to reign over J in the fourth year
22:45 Book of the Chronicles of the Kings of J
22:51 of Jehoshaphat king of J, and he reigned two
2Kgs 1:17 of Jehoshaphat, king of J, because Ahaziah had no
3:1 of Jehoshaphat king of J, Jehoram the son of
3:7 to Jehoshaphat king of J, "The king of Moab
3:9 with the king of J and the king of
3:14 Jehoshaphat the king of J, I would neither look
8:16 of Jehoshaphat, king of J, began to reign.
8:19 LORD would not destroy J, for the sake of
8:20 from the rule of J, and set up a
8:22 from the rule of J to this day.
8:23 Book of the Chronicles of the Kings of J
8:25 of Jehoram, king of J, began to reign.
8:29 of Jehoram king of J went down to see
9:16 And Ahaziah king of J had come down to
9:21 and Ahaziah king of J set out, each in
9:27 Ahaziah the king of J saw this, he fled
9:29 son of Ahab, Ahaziah began to reign over J
10:13 of Ahaziah king of J, and he said, "Who
12:18 Jerusalem, Jehoash king of J took all the votive
12:18 fathers, the kings of J, had dedicated, and his
12:19 Book of the Chronicles of the Kings of J
13:1 of Ahaziah, king of J, Jehoahaz the son of
13:10 of Joash king of J Jehoash the son of
13:12 against Amaziah king of J, are they not written
14:1 of Joash, king of J, began to reign.
14:9 to Amaziah king of J, "A thistle on Lebanon
14:10 you fall, you and J with you?"
14:11 and Amaziah king of J faced one another in
14:11 in battle at Beth-shemesh, which belongs to J
14:12 And J was defeated by Israel, and every man
14:13 captured Amaziah king of J, the son of Jehoash,
14:15 with Amaziah king of J, are they not written
14:17 of Joash, king of J, lived fifteen years after
14:18 Book of the Chronicles of the Kings of J
14:21 all the people of J took Azariah, who was
14:22 and restored it to J, after the king slept
14:23 of Joash, king of J, Jeroboam the son of
14:28 which had belonged to J, are they not written
15:1 of Amaziah, king of J, began to reign.
15:6 Book of the Chronicles of the Kings of J
15:8 of Azariah king of J Zechariah the son of
15:13 of Uzziah king of J, and he reigned one
15:17 of Azariah king of J Menahem the son of
15:23 of Azariah king of J Pekahiah the son of
15:27 of Azariah king of J Pekah the son of
15:32 of Uzziah, king of J, began to reign.
15:36 Book of the Chronicles of the Kings of J
15:37 Syria and Pekah the son of Remaliah against J
16:1 of Jotham, king of J, began to reign.
16:6 drove the men of J from Elath; and the
16:19 Book of the Chronicles of the Kings of J
17:1 of Ahaz king of J Hoshea the son of

17:13 LORD warned Israel and J by every prophet and
17:18 but the tribe of J only.
17:19 J also did not keep the commandments of the
18:1 of Ahaz, king of J, began to reign.
18:5 all the kings of J after him, nor among
18:13 the fortified cities of J and took them.
18:14 And Hezekiah king of J sent to the king
18:14 of Hezekiah king of J three hundred talents of
18:16 which Hezekiah king of J had overlaid and gave
18:22 has removed, saying to J and to Jerusalem, "You
18:26 in the language of J within the hearing of
18:28 in the language of J: "Hear the word of
19:10 to Hezekiah king of J: 'Do not let your
19:30 of the house of J shall again take root
20:20 Book of the Chronicles of the Kings of J
21:11 "Because Manasseh king of J has committed these
21:11 him, and has made J also to sin with
21:12 bringing upon Jerusalem and J such evil that the
21:16 sin which he made J to sin so that
21:17 Book of the Chronicles of the Kings of J
21:25 Book of the Chronicles of the Kings of J
22:13 people, and for all J, concerning the words of
22:16 which the king of J has read.
22:18 to the king of J, who sent you to
23:1 all the elders of J and Jerusalem were gathered
23:2 all the men of J and all the inhabitants
23:5 whom the kings of J had ordained to burn
23:5 at the cities of J and round about Jerusalem;
23:8 of the cities of J, and defiled the high
23:11 that the kings of J had dedicated to the
23:12 which the kings of J had made, and the
23:17 God who came from J and predicted these things
23:22 of the kings of J;
23:24 in the land of J and in Jerusalem, that
23:26 anger was kindled against J, because of all the
23:27 said, "I will remove J also out of my
23:28 Book of the Chronicles of the Kings of J
24:2 and sent them against J to destroy it, according
24:3 Surely this came upon J at the command of
24:5 Book of the Chronicles of the Kings of J
24:12 Jehoiachin the king of J gave himself up to
24:20 point in Jerusalem and J that he cast them
25:21 So J was taken into exile out of its
25:22 in the land of J, whom Nebuchadnezzar king of
25:27 of Jehoiachin king of J, in the twelfth month,
25:27 freed Jehoiachin king of J from prison;
1Chr 2:1 Israel: Reuben, Simeon, Levi, J, Issachar, Zebulun,
2:3 The sons of J: Er, Onan, and Shelah; these
2:3 Now Er, J's first-born, was wicked in the sight
2:4 J had five sons in all.
2:10 father of Nahshon, prince of the sons of J
4:1 The sons of J: Perez, Hezron, Carmi, Hur, and
4:21 Shelah the son of J: Er the father of
4:27 all their family multiply like the men of J
4:41 of Hezekiah, king of J, and destroyed their tents
5:2 to the birthright; though J became strong among his
5:17 of Jotham king of J, and in the days
6:15 when the LORD sent J and Jerusalem into exile
6:55 in the land of J and its surrounding pasture
6:65 of the tribes of J, Simeon, and Benjamin these
9:1 And J was taken into exile in Babylon because
9:3 the people of J, Benjamin, Ephraim, and Manasseh
9:4 from the sons of Perez the son of J
12:16 men of Benjamin and J came to the stronghold
12:24 The men of J bearing shield and spear were
13:6 Kiriath-jearim which belongs to J, to bring up from
21:5 the sword, and in J four hundred and seventy
27:18 for Aaron, Zadok; for J, Elihu, one of David's
28:4 ever; for he chose J as leader, and in
28:4 in the house of J my father's house, and
2Chr 2:7 are with me in J and Jerusalem, whom David
9:11 like of them before in the land of J
10:17 of Israel who dwelt in the cities of J
11:1 assembled the house of J, and Benjamin, a hundred
11:3 of Solomon king of J, and to all Israel
11:3 to all Israel in J and Benjamin,
11:5 Jerusalem, and he built cities for defense in J
11:10 cities which are in J and in Benjamin.
11:12 So he held J and Benjamin.
11:14 holdings and came to J and Jerusalem, because
11:17 strengthened the kingdom of J, and for three years
11:23 all the districts of J and Benjamin, in all
12:4 the fortified cities of J and came as far
12:5 to the princes of J, who had gathered at
12:12 destruction; moreover, conditions were good in J
13:1 of King Jeroboam Abijah began to reign over J
13:13 were in front of J, and the ambush was
13:14 And when J looked, behold, the battle was before
13:15 Then the men of J raised the battle shout.
13:15 when the men of J shouted, God defeated Jeroboam
13:15 Jeroboam and all Israel before Abijah and J
13:16 of Israel fled before J, and God gave them
13:18 and the men of J prevailed, because they relied
14:4 the Asherim, and commanded J to seek the LORD,
14:5 all the cities of J the high places and
14:6 built fortified cities in J, for the land had
14:7 And he said to J, "Let us build these
14:8 three hundred thousand from J, armed with bucklers
14:12 before Asa and before J, and the Ethiopians fled.
14:13 The men of J carried away very much booty.
15:2 me, Asa, and all J and Benjamin: The LORD
15:8 all the land of J and Benjamin and from
15:9 And he gathered all J and Benjamin, and those
15:15 And all J rejoiced over the oath; for they
16:1 Israel went up against J, and built Ramah, that
16:1 out or come in to Asa king of J
16:6 King Asa took all J, and they carried away
16:7 to Asa king of J, and said to him,
16:11 of the Kings of J and Israel.
17:2 the fortified cities of J, and set garrisons in
17:2 in the land of J, and in the cities
17:5 his hand; and all J brought tribute to Jehoshaphat;
17:6 the high places and the Asherim out of J
17:7 in the cities of J;
17:9 And they taught in J, having the book of
17:9 all the cities of J and taught among the
17:10 that were round about J, and they made no
17:12 He built in J fortresses and store-cities,
17:13 he had great stores in the cities of J
17:14 by fathers' houses: Of J, the commanders of
17:19 had placed in the fortified cities throughout all J
18:3 to Jehoshaphat king of J, "Will you go with
18:9 Jehoshaphat the king of J were sitting on their
18:28 Jehoshaphat the king of J went up to Ramoth-gilead.
19:1 Jehoshaphat the king of J returned in safety to
19:5 the fortified cities of J, city by city,
19:11 of the house of J, in all the king's
20:3 the LORD, and proclaimed a fast throughout all J
20:4 And J assembled to seek help from the LORD;
20:4 all the cities of J they came to seek
20:5 in the assembly of J and Jerusalem, in the
20:13 all the men of J stood before the LORD,
20:15 he said, "Hearken, all J and inhabitants of
20:17 on your behalf, O J and Jerusalem.' Fear not,
20:18 the ground, and all J and the inhabitants of
20:20 and said, "Hear me, J and inhabitants of Jerusalem!
20:22 who had come against J, so that they were
20:24 When J came to the watchtower of the wilderness,
20:27 every man of J and Jerusalem, and Jehoshaphat
20:31 Thus Jehoshaphat reigned over J
20:35 this Jehoshaphat king of J joined with Ahaziah king
21:2 these were the sons of Jehoshaphat king of J
21:3 with fortified cities in J; but he gave the
21:8 from the rule of J, and set up a
21:10 from the rule of J to this day.
21:11 the hill country of J, and led the inhabitants
21:11 into unfaithfulness, and made J go astray.
21:12 of Asa king of J,
21:13 Israel, and have led J and the inhabitants of
21:17 they came up against J, and invaded it, and
22:1 of Jehoram king of J reigned.
22:6 of Jehoram king of J went down to see
22:8 met the princes of J and the sons of
22:10 destroyed all the royal family of house of J
23:2 they went about through J and gathered the Levites
23:2 all the cities of J, and the heads of
23:8 The Levites and all J did according to all
24:5 to the cities of J, and gather from all
24:6 to bring in from J and Jerusalem the tax
24:9 proclamation was made throughout J and
24:17 Jehoiada the princes of J came and did obeisance
24:18 And wrath came upon J and Jerusalem for this
24:23 They came to J and Jerusalem, and destroyed all
25:5 assembled the men of J, and set them by
25:5 of hundreds for all J and Benjamin.
25:10 became very angry with J, and returned home in
25:12 The men of J captured another ten thousand alive,
25:13 upon the cities of J, from Samaria to Beth-horon,
25:17 Then Amaziah king of J took counsel and sent
25:18 to Amaziah king of J, "A thistle on Lebanon
25:19 you fall, you and J with you?"
25:21 and Amaziah king of J faced one another in

25:21 in battle at Beth-shemesh, which belongs to J
25:22 And J was defeated by Israel, and every man
25:23 captured Amaziah king of J, the son of Joash,
25:25 of Joash king of J lived fifteen years after
25:26 of the Kings of J and Israel?
26:1 all the people of J took Uzziah, who was
26:2 and restored it to J, after the king slept
27:4 the hill country of J, and forts and towers
27:7 the Book of the Kings of Israel and J
28:6 and twenty thousand in J in one day, all
28:9 fathers, was angry with J, he gave them into
28:10 subjugate the people of J and Jerusalem, male and
28:17 again invaded and defeated J, and carried away
28:18 and the Negeb of J, and had taken Beth-shemesh,
28:19 For the LORD brought J low because of Ahaz
28:19 had dealt wantonly in J and had been faithless
28:25 In every city of J he made high places
28:26 of the Kings of J and Israel.
29:8 the LORD came on J and Jerusalem, and he
29:21 the kingdom and for the sanctuary and for J
30:1 to all Israel and J, and wrote letters also
30:6 throughout all Israel and J with letters from the
30:12 God was also upon J to give them one
30:24 For Hezekiah king of J gave the assembly a
30:25 The whole assembly of J, and the priests and
30:25 sojourners who dwelt in J, rejoiced.
31:1 to the cities of J and broke in pieces
31:1 the altars throughout all J and Benjamin, and in
31:6 people of Israel and J who lived in the
31:6 in the cities of J also brought in the
31:20 Hezekiah did throughout all J; and he did what
32:1 Assyria came and invaded J and encamped against
32:8 confidence from the words of Hezekiah king of J
32:9 to Hezekiah king of J and to all the
32:9 all the people of J that were in Jerusalem,
32:12 his altars and commanded J and Jerusalem, "Before
32:18 in the language of J to the people of
32:23 to Hezekiah king of J, so that he was
32:25 came upon him and J and Jerusalem.
32:32 of the Kings of J and Israel.
32:33 of David; and all J and the inhabitants of
33:9 Manasseh seduced J and the inhabitants of
33:14 the army in all the fortified cities in J
33:16 and he commanded J to serve the LORD
34:3 he began to purge J and Jerusalem of the
34:5 their altars, and purged J and Jerusalem.
34:9 Israel and from all J and Benjamin and from
34:11 which the kings of J had let go to
34:21 in Israel and in J, concerning the words of
34:24 book which was read before the king of J
34:26 to the king of J, who sent you to
34:29 all the elders of J and Jerusalem.
34:30 all the men of J and the inhabitants of
35:18 the Levites, and all J and Israel who were
35:21 we to do with each other, king of J
35:24 All J and Jerusalem mourned for Josiah.
35:27 the Book of the Kings of Israel and J
36:4 his brother king over J and Jerusalem, and changed
36:8 Kings of Israel and J; and Jehoiachin his son
36:10 brother Zedekiah king over J and Jerusalem.
36:23 him a house at Jerusalem, which is in J
Ezra 1:2 him a house at Jerusalem, which is in J
1:3 Jerusalem, which is in J, and rebuild the house
1:5 the fathers' houses of J and Benjamin, and the
1:8 counted them out to Shesh-bazzar the prince of J
2:1 returned to Jerusalem and J, each to his own
3:9 sons, the sons of J, together took the oversight
4:1 when the adversaries of J and Benjamin heard that
4:4 discouraged the people of J, and made them afraid
4:6 against the inhabitants of J and Jerusalem.
5:1 Jews who were in J and Jerusalem, in the
5:8 to the province of J, to the house of
7:14 to make inquiries about J and Jerusalem according
10:7 proclamation was made throughout J and Jerusalem
10:9 all the men of J and Benjamin assembled at
10:23 (that is, Kelita), Pethahiah, J, and Eliezer.
Neh 1:2 certain men out of J; and I asked them
2:5 you send me to J, to the city of
2:7 until I come to J;
4:10 But J said, "The strength of the burden-bearers is
4:16 all the house of J,
5:14 in the land of J, from the twentieth year
6:7 is a king in J And now it will
6:17 days the nobles of J sent many letters to
6:18 For many in J were bound by oath to
7:6 returned to Jerusalem and J, each to his town.
11:3 in the towns of J every one lived on
11:4 of the sons of J and of the sons
11:4 Of the sons of J: Athaiah the son of
11:9 was their overseer; and J the son of Hassenuah
11:20 all the towns of J, every one in his
11:24 Zerah the son of J, was at the king's
11:25 of the people of J lived in Kiriath-arba and
11:36 of the Levites in J were joined to Benjamin.
12:8 Jeshua, Binnui, Kadmi-el, Sherebiah, J, and
12:31 up the princes of J upon the wall, and
12:32 of the princes of J,
12:34 Azariah, Ezra, Meshullam, J, Benjamin, Shemaiah,
12:36 Milalai, Gilalai, Maai, Nethanel, J, and Hanani, with
12:44 of the towns; for J rejoiced over the priests
13:12 Then all J brought the tithe of the grain,
13:15 days I saw in J men treading wine presses
13:16 to the people of J, and in Jerusalem.
13:17 with the nobles of J and said to them,
13:24 speak the language of J, but the language of
Jud 14:7 said, "Blessed are you in every tent of J
Esth 2:6 with Jeconiah king of J, whom Nebuchadnezzar king
Ps 48:11 Let the daughters of J rejoice because of thy
60:7 Ephraim is my helmet; J is my scepter.
68:27 lead, the princes of J in their throng, the
69:35 rebuild the cities of J; and his servants shall
76:1 In J God is known, his name is great
78:68 chose the tribe of J, Mount Zion, which he
97:8 and the daughters of J rejoice, because of thy
108:8 Ephraim is my helmet; J my scepter.
114:2 of strange language, J became his sanctuary, Israel
Prov 25:1 of Hezekiah king of J copied.
Sir 45:25 of the tribe of J: the heritage of the
49:4 High; the kings of J came to an end;
Is 1:1 which he saw concerning J and Jerusalem in the
1:1 of Uzziah, Jotham, Ahaz, and Hezekiah, kings of J
2:1 of Amoz saw concerning J and Jerusalem.
3:1 from Jerusalem and from J stay and staff, the
3:8 Jerusalem has stumbled, and J has fallen; because
5:3 Jerusalem and men of J, judge, I pray you,
5:7 and the men of J are his pleasant planting;
7:1 of Uzziah, king of J, Rezin the king of
7:6 us go up against J and terrify it, and
7:17 that Ephraim departed from J -- the king of
8:8 will sweep on into J, it will overflow and
9:21 Ephraim Manasseh, and together they are against J
11:12 gather the dispersed of J from the four corners
11:13 and those who harass J shall be cut off;
11:13 not be jealous of J, and Judah shall not
11:13 jealous of Judah, and J shall not harass Ephraim.
19:17 And the land of J will become a terror
22:8 He has taken away the covering of J
22:21 inhabitants of Jerusalem and to the house of J
26:1 in the land of J: "We have a strong
36:1 the fortified cities of J and took them.
36:7 has removed, saying to J and to Jerusalem, "You
36:11 in the language of J within the hearing of
36:13 in the language of J: "Hear the words of
37:10 to Hezekiah king of J: 'Do not let your
37:31 of the house of J shall again take root
38:9 of Hezekiah king of J, after he had been
40:9 to the cities of J, "Behold your God!"
44:26 of the cities of J, 'They shall be built,
48:1 from the loins of J; who swear by the
65:9 from Jacob, and from J inheritors of my mountains;
Jer 1:2 of Amon, king of J, in the thirteenth year
1:3 of Josiah, king of J, and until the end
1:3 of Josiah, king of J, until the captivity of
1:15 round about, and against all the cities of J
1:18 against the kings of J, its princes, its priests,
2:28 many as your cities are your gods, O J
3:7 and her false sister J saw it.
3:8 yet her false sister J did not fear, but
3:10 this her false sister J did not return to
3:11 Israel has shown herself less guilty than false J
3:18 days the house of J shall join the house
4:3 to the men of J and to the inhabitants
4:4 hearts, O men of J and inhabitants of Jerusalem;
4:5 Declare in J, and proclaim in Jerusalem, and say,
4:16 distant land; they shout against the cities of J
5:11 and the house of J have been utterly faithless
5:20 Jacob, proclaim it in J:
7:2 all you men of J who enter these gates
7:17 in the cities of J and in the streets
7:30 "For the sons of J have done evil in
7:34 from the cities of J and from the streets
8:1 of the kings of J, the bones of its

9:11 the cities of J a desolation, without inhabitant."
9:26 yet uncircumcised– Egypt, J, Edom, the sons of
10:22 make the cities of J a desolation, a lair
11:2 to the men of J and the inhabitants of
11:6 in the cities of J, and in the streets
11:9 among the men of J and the inhabitants of
11:10 and the house of J have broken my covenant
11:12 Then the cities of J and the inhabitants of
11:13 as your cities, O J; and as many as
11:17 and the house of J have done, provoking me
12:14 up the house of J from among them.
13:9 spoil the pride of J and the great pride
13:11 the whole house of J cling to me, says
13:19 to open them; all J is taken into exile,
14:2 Jeremiah concerning the drought: J mourns and her
14:19 Hast thou utterly rejected J
15:4 of Hezekiah, king of J, did in Jerusalem.
17:1 "The sin of J is written with a pen
17:19 which the kings of J enter and by which
17:20 LORD, you kings of J, and all Judah, and
17:20 of Judah, and all J, and all the inhabitants
17:25 princes, the men of J and the inhabitants of
17:26 from the cities of J and the places round
18:11 to the men of J and the inhabitants of
19:3 LORD, O kings of J and inhabitants of Jerusalem.
19:4 nor the kings of J have known; and because
19:7 void the plans of J and Jerusalem, and will
19:13 of the kings of J –all the houses upon
20:4 I will give all J into the hand of
20:5 of the kings of J into the hand of
21:7 give Zedekiah king of J, and his servants, and
21:11 of the king of J say, 'Hear the word
22:1 of the king of J, and speak there this
22:2 LORD, O King of J, who sit on the
22:6 of the king of J: "You are as Gilead
22:11 of Josiah, king of J, who reigned instead of
22:18 of Josiah, king of J: "They shall not lament
22:24 of Jehoiakim, king of J, were the signet ring
22:30 the throne of David, and ruling again in J
23:6 In his days J will be saved, and Israel
24:1 of Jehoiakim, king of J, together with the princes
24:1 with the princes of J, the craftsmen, and the
24:5 good the exiles from J, whom I have sent
24:8 Zedekiah the king of J, his princes, the remnant
25:1 all the people of J, in the fourth year
25:1 of Josiah, king of J (that was the first
25:2 all the people of J and all the inhabitants
25:3 of Amon, king of J, to this day, the
25:18 and the cities of J, its kings and princes,
26:1 of Josiah, king of J, this word came from
26:2 all the cities of J which come to worship
26:10 When the princes of J heard these things, they
26:18 of Hezekiah king of J, and said to all
26:18 all the people of J: 'Thus says the LORD
26:19 Did Hezekiah king of J and all Judah put
26:19 of Judah and all J put him to death?
27:1 of Josiah, king of J, this word came to
27:3 have come to Jerusalem to Zedekiah king of J
27:12 To Zedekiah king of J I spoke in like
27:18 of the king of J, and in Jerusalem may
27:20 of Jehoiakim, king of J, and all the nobles
27:20 all the nobles of J and Jerusalem–
27:21 of the king of J, and in Jerusalem:
28:1 of Zedekiah king of J, in the fifth month
28:4 of Jehoiakim, king of J, and all the exiles
28:4 all the exiles from J who went to Babylon,
29:2 eunuchs, the princes of J and Jerusalem, the
29:3 whom Zedekiah king of J sent to Babylon to
29:22 all the exiles from J in Babylon: "The LORD
30:3 my people, Israel and J, says the LORD, and
30:4 spoke concerning Israel and J:
31:23 in the land of J and in its cities,
31:24 O holy hill!' And J and all its cities
31:27 and the house of J with the seed of
31:31 and the house of J,
32:1 of Zedekiah king of J, which was the eighteenth
32:2 was in the palace of the king of J
32:3 For Zedekiah king of J had imprisoned him, saying,
32:4 it; Zedekiah king of J shall not escape out
32:30 and the sons of J have done nothing but
32:32 and the sons of J which they did to
32:32 prophets, the men of J and the inhabitants of
32:35 this abomination, to cause J to sin.
32:44 in the cities of J, in the cities of
33:4 of the kings of J which were torn down
33:7 restore the fortunes of J and the fortunes of
33:10 in the cities of J and the streets of
33:13 in the cities of J, flocks shall again pass
33:14 the house of Israel and the house of J
33:16 In those days J will be saved and Jerusalem
34:2 to Zedekiah king of J and say to him,
34:4 word of the LORD, O Zedekiah king of J
34:6 to Zedekiah king of J, in Jerusalem,
34:7 all the cities of J that were left, Lachish
34:7 only fortified cities of J that remained.
34:19 the princes of J, the princes of Jerusalem,
34:21 And Zedekiah king of J, and his princes I
34:22 make the cities of J a desolation without inhabitant."
35:1 of Josiah, king of J:
35:13 to the men of J and the inhabitants of
35:17 I am bringing on J and all the inhabitants
36:1 of Josiah, king of J, this word came to
36:2 you against Israel and J and all the nations,
36:3 that the house of J will hear all the
36:6 all the men of J who come out of
36:9 of Josiah, king of J, in the ninth month,
36:9 from the cities of J to Jerusalem proclaimed a
36:28 Jehoiakim the king of J has burned.
36:29 concerning Jehoiakim king of J you shall say, 'Thus
36:30 concerning Jehoiakim king of J, He shall have none
36:31 upon the men of J, all the evil that
36:32 which Jehoiakim king of J had burned in the
37:1 in the land of J, reigned instead of Coniah
37:7 to the king of J who sent you to
38:22 of the king of J were being led out
39:1 of Zedekiah king of J, in the tenth month,
39:4 When Zedekiah king of J and all the soldiers
39:6 king of Babylon slew all the nobles of J
39:10 in the land of J some of the poor
40:1 captives of Jerusalem and J who were being exiled
40:5 of the cities of J, and dwell with him
40:11 left a remnant in J and had appointed Gedaliah
40:12 to the land of J, to Gedaliah at Mizpah;
40:15 and the remnant of J would perish?"
42:15 the word of the LORD, O remnant of J
42:19 you, O remnant of J, 'Do not go to
43:4 the LORD, to remain in the land of J
43:5 all the remnant of J who had returned to
43:5 in the land of J from all the nations
43:9 of the men of J,
44:2 upon Jerusalem and upon all the cities of J
44:6 in the cities of J and in the streets
44:7 from the midst of J, leaving you no remnant?
44:9 of the kings of J, the wickedness of their
44:9 in the land of J and in the streets
44:11 against you for evil, to cut off all J
44:12 take the remnant of J who have set their
44:14 of the remnant of J who have come to
44:14 to the land of J, to which they desire
44:17 in the cities of J and in the streets
44:21 in the cities of J and in the streets
44:24 LORD, all you of J who are in the
44:26 LORD, all you of J who dwell in the
44:26 of any man of J in all the land
44:27 all the men of J who are in the
44:28 to the land of J, few in number; and
44:28 all the remnant of J, who came to the
44:30 gave Zedekiah king of J into the hand of
45:1 of Josiah, king of J:
46:2 of Josiah, king of J:
49:34 beginning of the reign of Zedekiah king of J
50:4 and the people of J shall come together, weeping
50:20 none; and sin in J, and none shall be
50:33 and the people of J with them; all who
51:5 For Israel and J have not been forsaken by
51:59 with Zedekiah king of J to Babylon, in the
52:3 pass in Jerusalem and J that he cast them
52:10 all the princes of J at Riblah.
52:27 So J was carried captive out of its land.
52:31 of Jehoiachin king of J, in the twelfth month,
52:31 of Jehoiachin king of J and brought him out

Lam 1:3 J has gone into exile because of affliction and
1:15 in a wine press the virgin daughter of J
2:2 of the daughter of J; he has brought down
2:5 in the daughter of J mourning and lamentation.
5:11 ravished in Zion, virgins in the towns of J

Bar 1:3 of Jehoiakim, king of J, and in the hearing
1:8 to the land of J –the silver vessels which
1:8 of Josiah, king of J, had made,
1:15 to the men of J, to the inhabitants of
2:1 princes and against the men of Israel and J
2:23 from the cities of J and from the region

	2:26	the house of Israel and the house of J
Ezek	4:6	of the house of J; forty days I assign
	8:1	with the elders of J sitting before me, the
	8:17	for the house of J to commit the abominations
	9:9	house of Israel and J is exceedingly great; the
	21:20	the Ammonites and to J and to Jerusalem the
	25:3	over the house of J when it went into
	25:8	Behold, the house of J is like all the
	25:12	against the house of J and has grievously offended
	27:17	J and the land of Israel traded with you;
	37:16	write on it, 'For J, and the children of
	37:19	it the stick of J, and make them one
	48:7	side to the west, J, one portion.
	48:8	"Adjoining the territory of J, from the east side
	48:22	between the territory of J and the territory of
	48:31	Reuben, the gate of J, and the gate of
Dan	1:1	Jehoiakim king of J, Nebuchadnezzar king of
	1:2	gave Jehoiakim king of J into his hand, with
	1:6	Hananiah, Mishael, and Azariah of the tribe of J
	2:25	among the exiles from J a man who can
	5:13	of the exiles of J, whom the king my
	5:13	Judah, whom the king my father brought from J
	6:13	of the exiles from J, pays no heed to
	9:7	to the men of J, to the inhabitants of
	13:56	Canaan and not of J, beauty has deceived you
	13:57	but a daughter of J would not endure your
Hos	1:1	and Hezekiah, kings of J, and in the days
	1:7	on the house of J, and I will deliver
	1:11	And the people of J and the people of
	4:15	O Israel, let not J become guilty.
	5:5	stumble in his guilt; J also shall stumble with
	5:10	The princes of J have become like those who
	5:12	and like dry rot to the house of J
	5:13	saw his sickness, and J his wound, then Ephraim
	5:14	like a young lion to the house of J
	6:4	What shall I do with you, O J
	6:11	For you also, O J, a harvest is appointed.
	8:14	and built palaces; and J has multiplied fortified
	10:11	Ephraim to the yoke, J must plow, Jacob must
	11:12	Israel with deceit; but J is still known by
	12:2	has an indictment against J, and will punish Jacob
Joel	3:1	restore the fortunes of J and Jerusalem,
	3:6	sold the people of J and Jerusalem to the
	3:8	of the sons of J, and they will sell
	3:18	the stream beds of J shall flow with water;
	3:19	to the people of J, because they have shed
	3:20	But J shall be inhabited for ever, and Jerusalem
Amos	1:1	of Uzziah king of J and in the days
	2:4	"For three transgressions of J, and for four, I
	2:5	send a fire upon J, and it shall devour
	7:12	to the land of J, and eat bread there,
Obad	1:12	over the people of J in the day of
Mic	1:1	and Hezekiah, kings of J, which he saw concerning
	1:5	what is the sin of the house of J
	1:9	it has come to J, it has reached to
	5:2	among the clans of J, from you shall come
Nah	1:15	Keep your feasts, O J, fulfil your vows, for
Zeph	1:1	of Josiah the son of Amon, king of J
	1:4	out my hand against J, and against all the
	2:7	of the house of J, on which they shall
Hag	1:1	of Shealtiel, governor of J, and to Joshua the
	1:14	of Shealtiel, governor of J, and the spirit of
	2:2	of Shealtiel, governor of J, and to Joshua the
	2:21	to Zerubbabel, governor of J, saying, I am about
Zech	1:12	and the cities of J, against which thou hast
	1:19	horns which have scattered J, Israel, and Jerusalem."
	1:21	the horns which scattered J, so that no man
	1:21	against the land of J to scatter it."
	2:12	the LORD will inherit J as his portion in
	8:13	nations, O house of J and house of Israel,
	8:15	to the house of J; fear not.
	8:19	to the house of J seasons of joy and
	9:7	like a clan in J, and Ekron shall be
	9:13	For I have bent J as my bow; I
	10:3	flock, the house of J, and will make them
	10:6	strengthen the house of J, and I will save
	11:14	annulling the brotherhood between J and Israel.
	12:2	it will be against J also in the siege
	12:4	upon the house of J I will open my
	12:5	Then the clans of J shall say to themselves,
	12:6	make the clans of J like a blazing pot
	12:7	to the tents of J first, that the glory
	12:7	Jerusalem may not be exalted over that of J
	14:5	earthquake in the days of Uzziah king of J
	14:14	of the other; even J will fight against Jerusalem.
	14:21	pot in Jerusalem and J shall be sacred to
Mal	2:11	J has been faithless, and abomination has been
	2:11	and in Jerusalem; for J has profaned the sanctuary
	3:4	Then the offering of J and Jerusalem will be
1Mac	1:29	to the cities of J a chief collector of
	1:44	and the cities of J; he directed them to
	1:51	commanded the cities of J to offer sacrifice, city
	1:54	the surrounding cities of J,
	2:6	blasphemies being committed in J and Jerusalem,
	2:18	and the men of J and those that are
	3:8	through the cities of J; he destroyed the ungodly
	3:39	into the land of J and destroy it, as
	5:45	large company, to go to the land of J
	5:53	way till he came to the land of J
	5:68	the cities and returned to the land of J
	6:5	into the land of J had been routed;
	6:12	destroy the inhabitants of J without good reason.
	7:10	into the land of J; and he sent messengers
	7:22	of the land of J and did great damage
	7:50	So the land of J had rest for a
	9:1	into the land of J a second time, and
	9:57	and the land of J had rest for two
	9:72	from the land of J; then he turned and
	10:30	from the land of J or from the three
	10:33	from the land of J into any part of
	10:37	the king has commanded in the land of J
	12:4	the envoys safe conduct to the land of J
	12:46	troops, and they returned to the land of J
	12:52	reached the land of J safely, and they mourned
	13:1	invade the land of J and destroy it,
	13:12	invade the land of J, and Jonathan was with
Mt	1:2	Jacob the father of J and his brothers,
	1:3	and his brothers, and J the father of Perez
	2:6	in the land of J, are by no means
	2:6	among the rulers of J; for from you shall
Lk	1:39	to a city of J,
	3:30	Simeon, the son of J, the son of Joseph,
	3:33	Perez, the son of J,
Heb	7:14	Lord was descended from J, and in connection with
	8:8	with the house of J;
Rev	5:5	of the tribe of J, the Root of David,
	7:5	of the tribe of J, twelve thousand of the

JUDAISM (6)

2Mac	2:21	zealously on behalf of J, so that though few
	14:38	had been accused of J, and for Judaism he
	14:38	of Judaism, and for J he had with all
Acts	13:43	and devout converts to J followed Paul and
Gal	1:13	my former life in J, how I persecuted the
	1:14	and I advanced in J beyond many of my

JUDAS (165)

1Mac	2:4	Simon called Thassi, J called Maccabeus,
	2:66	J Maccabeus has been a mighty warrior from his
	3:1	Then J his son, who was called Maccabeus, took
	3:11	When J learned of it, he went out to
	3:12	seized their spoils; and J took the sword of
	3:13	Syrian army, heard that J had gathered a large
	3:14	will make war on J and his companions, who
	3:16	the ascent of Beth-horon, J went out to meet
	3:17	them, they said to J, "How can we, few
	3:18	J replied, "It is easy for many to be
	3:25	Then J and his brothers began to be feared,
	3:26	and the Gentiles talked of the battles of J
	3:42	Now J and his brothers saw that misfortunes had
	3:55	After this J appointed leaders of the people, in
	3:58	And J said, "Gird yourselves and be valiant.
	4:3	But J heard of it, and he and his
	4:5	entered the camp of J by night, he found
	4:6	At daybreak J appeared in the plain with three
	4:8	But J said to the men who were with
	4:13	Then the men with J blew their trumpets
	4:16	Then J and his force turned back from pursuing
	4:19	Just as J was finishing this speech, a detachment
	4:21	saw the army of J drawn up in the
	4:23	Then J returned to plunder the camp, and they
	4:29	encamped at Bethzur, and J met them with ten
	4:35	which inspired those of J, and how ready they
	4:36	Then said J and his brothers, "Behold, our enemies
	4:41	Then J detailed men to fight against those in
	4:59	Then J and his brothers and all the assembly
	5:3	But J made war on the sons of Esau
	5:10	Dathema, and sent to J and his brothers a
	5:16	When J and the people heard these messages, a
	5:17	Then J said to Simon his brother, "Choose your
	5:20	and eight thousand to J for Gilead.
	5:24	J Maccabeus and Jonathan his brother crossed the

5:28 Then J and his army quickly turned back by
5:31 So J saw that the battle had begun and
5:38 J sent men to spy out the camp, and
5:39 And J went to meet them.
5:40 Now as J and his army drew near to
5:42 When J approached the stream of water, he
5:44 they could stand before J no longer.
5:45 Then J gathered together all the Israelites in Gilead,
5:48 And J sent them this friendly message, "Let us
5:49 Then J ordered proclamation to be made to the
5:53 And J kept rallying the laggards and encouraging the
5:55 Now while J and Jonathan were in Gilead and
5:61 did not listen to J and his brothers.
5:63 The man J and his brothers were greatly honored
5:65 Then J and his brothers went forth and fought
5:68 But J turned aside to Azotus in the land
6:19 So J decided to destroy them, and assembled all
6:32 Then J marched away from the citadel and
6:42 But J and his army advanced to the battle,
7:6 accusation against the people: J and his brothers
7:7 all the ruin which J has brought upon us
7:10 he sent messengers to J and his brothers with
7:23 And J saw all the evil that Alcimus and
7:24 So J went out into all the surrounding parts
7:25 When Alcimus saw that J and those with him
7:27 and treacherously sent to J and his brothers this
7:29 So he came to J, and they greeted one
7:29 But the enemy were ready to seize J
7:30 It became known to J that Nicanor had come
7:31 went out to meet J in battle near Caphar-salama.
7:35 swore this oath, "Unless J and his army are
7:40 And J encamped in Adasa with three thousand men.
7:40 Then J prayed and said,
8:1 Now J heard of the fame of the Romans,
8:17 So J chose Eupolemus the son of John, son
8:20 and spoke as follows: J, who is also called
9:5 Now J was encamped in Elasa, and with him
9:7 When J saw that his army had slipped away
9:10 But J said, "Far be it from us to
9:12 and the men with J also blew their trumpets.
9:14 J saw that Bacchides and the strength of his
9:16 and followed close behind J and his men.
9:18 J also fell, and the rest fled.
9:19 Jonathan and Simon took J their brother and buried
9:22 of the acts of J, and his wars and
9:23 After the death of J, the lawless emerged in
9:26 for the friends of J, and brought them to
9:28 all the friends of J assembled and said to
9:29 death of your brother J there has been no
9:31 took the place of J his brother.
11:70 son of Absalom and J the son of Chalphi,
13:8 leader in place of J and Jonathan your brother.
14:18 they had established with J and Jonathan his
16:2 his two older sons J and John, and said
16:9 At that time J the brother of John was
16:14 Jericho with Mattathias and J his sons, in the
2Mac 1:10 and the senate and J, To Aristobulus, who is
2:14 In the same way J also collected all the
2:19 The story of J Maccabeus and his brothers, and
5:27 But J Maccabeus, with about nine others, got away
8:1 But J, who was also called Maccabeus, and his
8:12 Word came to J concerning Nicanor's invasion; and
12:5 When J heard of the cruelty visited on his
12:11 After a hard fight J and his men won
12:11 The defeated nomads besought J to grant them
12:12 J, thinking that they might really be useful in
12:14 behaved most insolently toward J and his men,
12:15 But J and his men, calling upon the great
12:21 of the approach of J, he sent off the
12:22 But when J first division appeared, terror and fear
12:23 And J pressed the pursuit with the utmost vigor,
12:26 Then J marched against Carnaim and the temple of
12:36 time and were weary, J called upon the Lord
12:38 Then J assembled his army and went to the
12:39 it had become necessary, J and his men went
12:42 And the noble J exhorted the people to keep
13:1 year word came to J and his men that
13:10 But when J heard of this, he ordered the
13:12 three days without ceasing, J exhorted them and
13:20 J sent in to the garrison whatever was necessary.
13:22 received theirs, withdrew, attacked J and his men,
14:1 later, word came to J and his men that
14:6 Hasideans, whose leader is J Maccabeus, are
14:10 For as long as J lives, it is impossible
14:11 who were hostile to J, quickly inflamed Demetrius
14:13 with orders to kill J and scatter his men,
14:14 who had fled before J, flocked to join Nicanor,
14:17 Simon, the brother of J, had encountered Nicanor,
14:18 of the valor of J and his men and
14:22 were set in place; J posted armed men in
14:24 And he kept J always in his presence; he
14:26 conspirator against the kingdom, J, to be his
14:33 you do not hand J over to me as
15:1 When Nicanor heard that J and his men were
15:6 monument of victory over J and his men.
15:15 hand and gave to J a golden sword, and
15:17 by the words of J, so noble and so
15:26 and battle songs; and J and his men met
Mt 10:4 Simon the Cananaean, and J Iscariot, who betrayed
13:55 his brethren James and Joseph and Simon and J
26:14 twelve, who was called J Iscariot, went to the
26:25 J, who betrayed him, said, "Is it I, Master?"
26:47 he was still speaking, J came, one of the
27:3 When J, his betrayer, saw that he was condemned,
Mk 3:19 Simon the Cananaean, and J Iscariot, who betrayed
6:3 James and Joses and J and Simon, and are
14:10 Then J Iscariot, who was one of the twelve,
14:43 he was still speaking, J came, one of the
Lk 6:16 called the Zealot, and J the son of James,
6:16 son of James, and J Iscariot, who became a
22:3 Then Satan entered into J called Iscariot, who was
22:45 and the man called J, one of the twelve,
22:46 Jesus said to him, J, would you betray the
Jn 6:71 He spoke of J the son of Simon Iscariot,
12:4 But J Iscariot, one of his disciples (he who
13:2 into the heart of J Iscariot, Simon's son, to
13:26 he gave it to J, the son of Simon
13:29 Some thought that, because J had the money box,
14:22 J (not Iscariot) said to him, "Lord, how is
18:2 Now J, who betrayed him, also knew the place;
18:3 So J, procuring a band of soldiers and some
18:5 J, who betrayed him, was standing with them.
Acts 1:13 Simon the Zealot and J the son of James.
1:16 mouth of David, concerning J who was guide to
1:25 and apostleship from which J turned aside, to go
5:37 After him J the Galilean arose in the days
9:11 in the house of J for a man of
15:22 They sent J called Barsabbas, and Silas, leading men
15:27 We have therefore sent J and Silas, who themselves
15:32 And J and Silas, who were themselves prophets,

JUDE

Jude 1:1 J, a servant of Jesus

JUDEA (98)

Ezra 9:9 give us protection in J and Jerusalem.
Tob 1:18 who came fleeing from J, I buried them secretly.
Jud 1:12 of Ammon, and all J, and every one in
3:9 the great ridge of J;
4:1 of Israel living in J heard of everything that
4:3 all the people of J were newly gathered together,
4:7 hills, since by them J could be invaded, and
4:13 fasted many days throughout J and in Jerusalem
8:21 we are captured all J will be captured and
11:19 through the middle of J, till you come to
Esth 11:4 had brought from Jerusalem with Jeconiah king of J
Dan 14:33 Now the prophet Habakkuk was in J
1Mac 3:34 for the residents of J and Jerusalem,
4:35 enlisted mercenaries, to invade J again with an even
5:8 Jazer and its villages; then he returned to J
5:18 of the forces, in J to guard it;
5:23 and led them to J with great rejoicing.
5:60 to the borders of J; as many as two
6:48 the king encamped in J and at Mount Zion.
6:53 who found safety in J from the Gentiles had
7:24 the surrounding parts of J, and took vengeance on
7:46 all the villages of J round about, and they
9:50 built strong cities in J: the fortress in Jericho,
9:60 all his allies in J, telling them to seize
9:63 forces, and sent orders to the men of J
10:38 have been added to J from the country of
10:38 be so annexed to J that they are considered
10:45 rebuilding the walls in J, also be paid from
11:20 assembled the men of J to attack the citadel
11:28 the king to free J and the three districts
11:34 both the territory of J and the three districts
11:34 them, were added to J from Samaria.
12:35 to build strongholds in J,
13:33 up the strongholds of J and walled them all
14:33 fortified the cities of J, and Bethzur on the
14:33 on the borders of J, where formerly the arms
15:30 outside the borders of J;

	15:39	him to encamp against J, and commanded him to
	15:40	the people and invade J and take the people
	15:41	along the highways of J, as the king had
	16:10	And he returned to J safely.
2Mac	1:1	in the land of J, To their Jewish brethren
	1:10	Jerusalem and those in J and the senate and
	5:11	it to mean that J was in revolt.
	8:9	nations, to wipe out the whole race of J
	10:24	on, intending to take J by storm.
	11:5	Invading J, he approached Bethzur, which was a
	13:1	a great army against J,
	13:13	king's army could enter J and get possession of
	14:12	appointed him governor of J, and sent him off
	14:14	And the Gentiles throughout J, who had fled before
	15:22	of Hezekiah king of J, and he slew fully
Mt	2:1	born in Bethlehem of J in the days of
	2:5	him, "In Bethlehem of J; for so it is
	2:22	that Archelaus reigned over J in place of his
	3:1	in the wilderness of J,
	3:5	him Jerusalem and all J and all the region
	4:25	Decapolis and Jerusalem and J and from beyond the
	19:1	entered the region of J beyond the Jordan;
	24:16	those who are in J flee to the mountains;
Mk	1:5	all the country of J, and all the people
	3:7	Galilee followed; also from J
	10:1	to the region of J and beyond the Jordan,
	13:14	those who are in J flee to the mountains;
Lk	1:5	of Herod, king of J, there was a priest
	1:65	the hill country of J;
	2:4	city of Nazareth, to J, to the city of
	3:1	Pilate being governor of J, and Herod being tetrarch
	4:44	And he was preaching in the synagogues of J
	5:17	village of Galilee and J and from Jerusalem; and
	6:17	of people from all J and Jerusalem and the
	7:17	through the whole of J and all the surrounding
	21:21	those who are in J flee to the mountains,
	23:5	people, teaching throughout all J, from Galilee even
Jn	3:22	into the land of J; there he remained with
	4:3	his disciples), he left J and departed again to
	4:47	Jesus had come from J to Galilee, he went
	4:54	he had come from J to Galilee.
	7:1	not go about in J, because the Jews sought
	7:3	here and go to J, that your disciples may
	11:7	"Let us go into J again."
Acts	1:8	Jerusalem and in all J and Samaria and to
	2:9	residents of Mesopotamia, J and Cappadocia, Pontus
	2:14	addressed them, "Men of J and all who dwell
	8:1	throughout the region of J and Samaria, except the
	9:31	the church throughout all J and Galilee and Samaria
	10:37	proclaimed throughout all J, beginning from Galilee
	11:1	brethren who were in J heard that the Gentiles
	11:29	brethren who lived in J;
	12:19	he went down from J to Caesarea, and remained
	15:1	men came down from J and were teaching the
	21:10	days, a prophet named Agabus came down from J
	26:20	all the country of J, and also to the
	28:21	received no letters from J about you, and none
Rom	15:31	from the unbelievers in J, and that my service
2Cor	1:16	have you send me on my way to J
Gal	1:22	churches of Christ in J;
1Thes	2:14	Jesus which are in J; for you suffered the

JUDGE (163)

Gen	16:5	May the LORD J between you and me!"
	18:25	Shall not the J of all the earth do
	19:9	came to sojourn, and he would play the J
	31:53	God of their father, J between us." So Jacob
	49:16	Dan shall J his people as one of the
Ex	2:14	a prince and a J over us?
	5:21	look upon you and J, because you have made
	18:13	morrow Moses sat to J the people, and the
	18:22	And let them J the people at all times;
Lev	19:15	in righteousness shall you J your neighbor.
Num	35:24	then the congregation shall J between the manslayer
Deut	1:16	between your brethren, and J righteously between a
	16:18	tribes; and they shall J the people with righteous
	17:9	priests, and to the J who is in office
	17:12	your God, or the J, that man shall die;
	25:2	to be beaten, the J shall cause him to
	32:27	lest their adversaries should J amiss, lest they should
Judg	2:18	LORD was with the J, and he saved them
	2:18	the days of the J; for the LORD was
	2:19	But whenever the J died, they turned back and
	11:27	me; the LORD, the J, decide this day between
1Sam	2:10	The LORD will J the ends of the earth;
	24:12	May the LORD J between me and you, may
	24:15	the LORD therefore be J, and give sentence between
2Sam	15:4	"Oh that I were J in the land!
1Kgs	8:32	heaven, and act, and J thy servants, condemning the
1Chr	16:33	for he comes to J the earth.
2Chr	6:23	heaven, and act, and J thy servants, requiting the
	19:6	you do, for you J not for man but
Ezra	7:25	and judges who may J all the people in
Jud	7:25	the elders, "God be J between you and us!
Job	22:13	Can he J through the deep darkness?
	23:7	I should be acquitted for ever by my J
Ps	7:8	LORD judges the peoples; J me, O LORD, according
	7:11	God is a righteous J, and a God who
	50:4	earth, that he may J his people:
	50:6	declare his righteousness, for God himself is J
	58:1	Do you J the sons of men uprightly?
	67:4	joy, for thou dost J the peoples with equity
	72:2	May he J thy people with righteousness, and thy
	75:2	I appoint I will J with equity.
	82:2	"How long will you J unjustly and show partiality
	82:8	Arise, O God, J the earth; for to thee
	94:2	Rise up, O J of the earth; render to
	96:10	be moved; he will J the peoples with equity."
	96:13	for he comes to J the earth.
	96:13	He will J the world with righteousness, and the
	98:9	for he comes to J the earth.
	98:9	He will J the world with righteousness, and the
	119:84	When wilt thou J those who persecute me?
Prov	31:9	Open your mouth, J righteously, maintain the rights
Eccl	3:17	my heart, God will J the righteous and the
Wis	9:7	people and to be J over thy sons and
	9:12	acceptable, and I shall J thy people justly, and
	12:18	sovereign in strength dost J with mildness, and with
	12:22	thy goodness when we J, and when we are
Sir	4:15	who obeys her will J the nations, and whoever
	7:6	seek to become a J, lest you be unable
	8:14	to law against a J, for the decision will
	10:23	The nobleman, and the J, and the ruler will
	11:9	with sinners when they J a case.
	31:15	J your neighbor's feelings by your own, and in
	35:12	the Lord is the J, and with him is
	38:33	not sit in the J's seat, nor do they
	41:18	a transgression, before a J or magistrate; and of
	45:26	in your heart to J his people in righteousness,
Is	2:4	He shall J between the nations, and shall decide
	3:2	and the soldier, the J and the prophet, the
	3:13	contend, he stands to J his people.
	5:3	and men of Judah, J, I pray you, between
	11:3	He shall not J by what his eyes see,
	11:4	with righteousness he shall J the poor, and decide
	33:22	the LORD is our J, the LORD is our
Jer	5:28	deeds of wickedness; they J not with justice the
Lam	3:59	to me, O LORD; J thou my cause.
Bar	6:54	They cannot J their own cause or deliver one
Ezek	7:3	upon you, and will J you according to your
	7:8	anger against you, and J you according to your
	7:27	own judgments I will J them; and they shall
	11:10	the sword; I will J you at the border
	11:11	of it; I will J you at the border
	16:38	And I will J you as women who break
	18:30	"Therefore I will J you, O house of Israel,
	20:4	Will you J them, son of man, will you
	20:4	of man, will you J them?
	21:30	your origin, I will J you.
	22:2	of man, will you J, will you judge the
	22:2	you judge, will you J the bloody city?
	23:24	them, and they shall J you according to their
	23:36	of man, will you J Oholah and Oholibah?
	24:14	your doings I will J you, says the Lord
	33:20	of Israel, I will J each of you according
	34:17	Lord GOD: Behold, I J between sheep and sheep,
	34:20	I, I myself will J between the fat sheep
	34:22	prey; and I will J between sheep and sheep.
	35:11	among you, when I J you.
	44:24	judges, and they shall J it according to my
Joel	3:12	I will sit to J all the nations round
Mic	4:3	He shall J between many peoples, and shall decide
	7:3	the prince and the J ask for a bribe,
1Mac	2:55	the command, became a J in Israel.
	7:42	against the sanctuary, and J him according to this
	9:73	And Jonathan began to J the people, and he
2Mac	12:6	upon God the righteous J, attacked the murderers of
	12:41	the Lord, the righteous J, who reveals the things
Mt	5:25	you over to the J, and the judge to
	5:25	the judge, and the J to the guard, and
	7:1	J not, that you be not judged.
Lk	6:37	J not, and you will not be judged; condemn

J

12:14 who made me a J or divider over you?"
12:57 why do you not J for yourselves what is
12:58 drag you to the J, and the judge hand
12:58 the judge, and the J hand you over to
18:2 city there was a J who neither feared God
18:6 "Hear what the unrighteous J says.
Jn 5:29 as I hear, I J; and my judgment is
7:24 Do not J by appearances, but judge with right
7:24 judge by appearances, but J with right judgment."
7:51 them, "Does our law J a man without first
8:15 You J according to the flesh, I judge no
8:15 to the flesh, I J no one.
8:16 even if I do J, my judgment is true,
8:16 not I alone that J, but I and he
8:26 you and much to J; but he who sent
8:50 who seeks it and he will be the J
12:47 them, I do not J him; for I did
12:47 did not come to J the world but to
12:48 my sayings has a J; the word that I
12:48 spoken will be his J on the last day.
18:31 "Take him yourselves and J him by your own
Acts 4:19 to God, you must J;
7:7 'But I will J the nation which they serve,'
7:27 a ruler and a J over us?
7:35 a ruler and a J God sent as both
10:42 by God to be J of the living and
13:46 it from you, and J yourselves unworthy of eternal
17:31 on which he will J the world in righteousness
18:15 refuse to be a J of these things."
23:3 Are you sitting to J me according to the
24:9 years you have been J over this nation, I
Rom 2:1 you are, when you J another; for in passing
2:1 yourself, because you, the J, are doing the very
2:3 man, that when you J those who do such
3:6 then how could God J the world?
14:22 has no reason to J himself for what he
1Cor 4:3 I do not even J myself.
5:12 those inside the church whom you are to J
6:2 that the saints will J the world?
6:3 that we are to J angels?
10:15 as to sensible men; J for yourselves what I
11:13 things are from God.) J for yourselves; is it
2Tim 4:1 Jesus who is to J the living and the
4:8 the Lord, the righteous J, will award to me
Heb 10:30 again, "The Lord will J his people."
12:23 heaven, and to a J who is God of
13:4 undefiled; for God will J the immoral and adulterous.
Jas 4:11 But if you J the law, you are not
4:11 not a doer of the law but a J
4:12 is one lawgiver and J, he who is able
4:12 are you that you J your neighbor?
5:9 be judged; behold, the J is standing at the
1Pet 4:5 who is ready to J the living and the
Rev 6:10 long before thou wilt J and avenge our blood

JUDGED (55)

Gen 30:6 Rachel said, "God has J me, and has also
Ex 18:26 And they J the people at all times; hard
Judg 3:10 upon him, and he J Israel; he went out
10:2 And he J Israel twenty-three years.
10:3 Jair the Gileadite, who J Israel twenty-two years.
12:7 Jephthah J Israel six years.
12:8 him Ibzan of Bethlehem J Israel.
12:9 And he J Israel seven years.
12:11 him Elon the Zebulunite J Israel; and he judged
12:11 judged Israel; and he J Israel ten years.
12:13 of Hillel the Pirathonite J Israel.
12:14 seventy asses; and he J Israel eight years.
15:20 And he J Israel in the days of the
16:31 He had J Israel twenty years.
1Sam 4:18 He had J Israel forty years.
7:6 And Samuel J the people of Israel at Mizpah.
7:15 Samuel J Israel all the days of his life.
7:16 and Mizpah; and he J Israel in all these
2Kgs 23:22 of the judges who J Israel, or during all
Ps 9:19 let the nations be J before thee!
Prov 27:21 and a man is J by his praise.
Wis 11:9 ungodly were tormented when J in wrath.
12:13 that thou hast not J unjustly;
12:21 what strictness thou hast J thy sons, to whose
12:22 and when we are J we may expect mercy.
15:18 than all others, when J by their lack of
Sir 46:14 of the Lord he J the congregation, and the
Jer 22:16 He J the cause of the poor and needy;
Bar 2:1 against our judges who J Israel, and against our
Ezek 16:38 and shed blood are J, and bring upon you
36:19 and their deeds I J them.
Mt 7:1 "Judge not, that you be not J
7:2 pronounce you will be J, and the measure you
Lk 6:37 you will not be J; condemn not, and you
7:43 to him, "You have J rightly."
Jn 16:11 judgment, because the ruler of this world is J
Acts 16:15 saying, "If you have J me to be faithful
Rom 2:12 the law will be J by the law.
3:4 in thy words, and prevail when thou art J
1Cor 2:15 is himself to be J by no one.
4:3 that I should be J by you or by
6:2 world is to be J by you, are you
11:31 But if we J ourselves truly, we should not
11:31 we judged ourselves truly, we should not be J
11:32 But when we are J by the Lord, we
1Tim 1:12 our Lord, because he J me faithful by appointing
Heb 4:1 any of you be J to have failed to
Jas 2:12 who are to be J under the law of
3:1 who teach shall be J with greater strictness.
5:9 you may not be J; behold, the Judge is
1Pet 4:6 the dead, that though J in the flesh like
Rev 11:18 the dead to be J, for rewarding thy servants,
19:2 and just; he has J the great harlot who
20:12 And the dead were J by what was written
20:13 them, and all were J by what they had

JUDGES (69)

Ex 21:22 shall pay as the J determine.
Num 25:5 Moses said to the J of Israel, "Every one
Deut 1:16 And I charged your J at that time, 'Hear
16:18 "You shall appoint J and officers in all your
17:9 the priests and the J who are in office
19:17 the priests and the J who are in office
19:18 in those days; the J shall inquire diligently, and
21:2 your elders and your J shall come forth, and
25:1 into court, and the J decide between them, acquitting
32:31 as our Rock, even our enemies themselves being J
Josh 8:33 and officers and their J, stood on opposite sides
23:2 elders and heads, their J and officers, and said
24:1 elders, the heads, the J, and the officers of
Judg 2:16 the LORD raised up J, who saved them out
2:17 not listen to their J; for they played the
2:18 the LORD raised up J for them, the LORD
Ruth 1:1 the days when the J ruled there was a
1Sam 8:1 he made his sons J over Israel.
8:2 second, Abijah; they were J in Beer-sheba.
2Sam 7:7 with any of the J of Israel, whom I
7:11 time that I appointed J over my people Israel;
2Kgs 23:22 the days of the J who judged Israel, or
1Chr 17:6 with any of the J of Israel, whom I
17:10 time that I appointed J over my people Israel;
23:4 shall be officers and J,
26:29 to outside duties for Israel, as officers and J
2Chr 1:2 of hundreds, to the J, and to all the
19:5 He appointed J in the land in all the
19:6 and said to the J, "Consider what you do,
Ezra 4:9 of their associates, the J, the governors, the officials,
7:25 hand, appoint magistrates and J who may judge all
10:14 them the elders and J of every city, till
Job 9:24 the faces of its J -- if it is
12:17 counselors away stripped, and J he makes fools.
21:22 knowledge, seeing that he J those that are on
31:11 be punished by the J;
31:28 be punished by the J, for I should have
36:31 For by these he J peoples; he gives food
Ps 7:8 The LORD J the peoples; judge me, O LORD,
9:8 for judgment; and he J the world with righteousness,
9:8 world with righteousness, he J the peoples with
58:11 is a God who J on earth."
Prov 29:14 If a king J the poor with equity his
Wis 6:1 and understand; learn, O J of the ends of
Sir 16:12 also his reproof; he J a man according to
35:19 their devices; till he J the case of his
46:11 The J also, with their respective names, those whose
Is 1:26 I will restore your J as at the first,
16:5 of David one who J and seeks justice and
Bar 2:1 us, and against our J who judged Israel, and
Ezek 44:24 they shall act as J, and they shall judge
Dan 13:5 two elders from the people were appointed as J
13:5 from elders who were J, who were supposed to
13:41 of the people and J; and they condemned her
Zeph 3:3 are roaring lions; her J are evening wolves that
Mt 12:27 Therefore they shall be your J
Lk 11:19 Therefore they shall be your J
Jn 5:21 The Father J no one, but has given all
Acts 13:20 that he gave them J until Samuel the prophet.
Rom 2:16 to my gospel, God J the secrets of men

1Cor	2:15	The spiritual man J all things, but is himself
	4:4	is the Lord who J me.
	5:13	God J those outside.
Jas	2:4	among yourselves, and become J with evil thoughts?
	4:11	against a brother or J his brother, speaks evil
	4:11	against the law and J the law.
1Pet	1:17	as Father him who J each one impartially according
	2:23	trusted to him who J justly.
Rev	18:8	the Lord God who J her."
	19:11	and in righteousness he J and makes war.

JUDGEST

Jer	11:20	LORD of hosts, who J righteously, who triest the

JUDGING (9)

Judg	4:4	wife of Lappidoth, was J Israel at that time.
Jud	10:19	and admired the Israelites, J them by her, and
Esth	16:9	our methods and always J what comes before our
Prov	24:23	Partiality in J is not good.
Wis	12:10	But J them little by little thou gavest them
Sir	4:9	not be fainthearted in J a case.
Mt	19:28	sit on twelve thrones, J the twelve tribes of
Lk	22:30	and sit on thrones J the twelve tribes of
1Cor	5:12	I to do with J outsiders?

JUDGMENT (208)

Gen	15:14	but I will bring J on the nation which
Ex	6:6	with great acts of J,
	7:4	the land of Egypt by great acts of J
	28:15	make a breastpiece of J, in skilled work; like
	28:29	in the breastpiece of J upon his heart, when
	28:30	in the breastpiece of J you shall put the
	28:30	Aaron shall bear the J of the people of
Lev	19:15	do no injustice in J; you shall not be
	19:35	do no wrong in J, in measures of length
Num	27:21	for him by the J of the Urim before
	35:12	die until he stands before the congregation for J
Deut	1:17	not be partial in J; you shall hear the
	1:17	of man, for the J is Gods; and the
	16:18	and they shall judge the people with righteous J
	32:41	hand takes hold on J, I will take vengeance
Josh	20:6	before the congregation for J, until the death of
Judg	4:5	people of Israel came up to her for J
2Sam	15:2	before the king for J, Absalom would call to
	15:6	to the king for J; so Absalom stole the
1Kgs	3:28	Israel heard of the J which the king had
	7:7	he was to pronounce J, even the Hall of
	7:7	even the Hall of J; it was finished with
	20:40	him, "So shall your J be; you yourself have
2Chr	19:6	the LORD; he is with you in giving J
	19:8	of Israel, to give J for the LORD and
	20:9	upon us, the sword, J, or pestilence, or famine,
	20:12	wilt thou not execute J upon them?
	22:8	when Jehu was executing J upon the house of
	24:24	Thus they executed J on Joash.
Ezra	7:26	of the king, let J be strictly executed upon
Tob	3:2	render true and righteous J for ever.
Jud	9:6	in advance, and thy J is with foreknowledge.
	16:17	in the day of J; fire and worms he
Esth	1:13	versed in law and J,
	13:3	among us in sound J, and is distinguished for
Job	11:10	imprisons, and calls to J, who can hinder him?
	14:3	and bring him into J with thee?
	19:29	sword, that you may know there is a J
	22:4	you, and enters into J with you?
	24:1	are not times of J kept by the Almighty,
	34:23	for any man to go before God in J
	36:17	are full of the J on the wicked; judgment
	36:17	judgment on the wicked; J and justice seize you.
Ps	1:5	not stand in the J, nor sinners in the
	7:6	awake, O my God; thou hast appointed a J
	9:4	thou hast sat on the throne giving righteous J
	9:7	established his throne for J;
	9:16	known, he has executed J; the wicked are snared
	51:4	justified in thy sentence and blameless in thy J
	75:7	is God who executes J, putting down one and
	76:8	heavens thou didst utter J; the earth feared and
	76:9	God arose to establish J to save all the
	82:1	the gods he holds J:
	110:6	He will execute J among the nations, filling them
	119:66	Teach me good J and knowledge, for I believe
	122:5	There thrones for J were set, the thrones of
	143:2	Enter not into J with thy servant; for no
	149:9	execute on them the J written!
Prov	16:10	a king; his mouth does not sin in J
	18:1	seeks pretexts to break out against all sound J
	20:8	on the throne of J winnows all evil with
Eccl	11:9	all these things God will bring you into J
	12:14	bring every deed into J, with every secret thing,
Wis	6:5	and swiftly, because severe J falls on those in
	7:15	that I speak with J and have thought worthy
	8:11	be found keen in J, and in the sight
	9:3	and righteousness, and pronounce J in uprightness of
	9:5	with little understanding of J and laws;
	12:12	Or will resist thy J
	12:25	thou didst send thy J to mock them.
	12:26	will experience the deserved J of God.
	16:18	being pursued by the J of God;
Sir	3:23	For their hasty J has led many astray, and
	6:23	son, and accept my J; do not reject my
	18:19	Before J, examine yourself, and in the hour of
	21:5	of God, and his J comes speedily.
	25:4	an attractive thing is J in gray-haired men, and
	32:18	A man of J will not overlook an idea,
	35:17	and does justice for the righteous, and executes J
	38:33	the sentence of J; they cannot expound discipline
	38:33	cannot expound discipline or J, and they are not
	42:2	covenant, and of rendering J to acquit the ungodly;
	43:13	driving snow and speeds the lightnings of his J
	45:10	with the oracle of J, Urim and Thummim;
Is	3:14	The LORD enters into J with the elders and
	4:4	by a spirit of J and by a spirit
	28:6	him who sits in J, and strength to those
	28:7	they err in vision, they stumble in giving J
	32:4	rash will have good J, and the tongue of
	34:5	behold, it descends for J upon Edom, upon the
	41:1	them speak; let us together draw near for J
	53:8	By oppression and J he was taken away; and
	54:17	confute every tongue that rises against you in J
	66:16	will the LORD execute J, and by his sword,
Jer	2:35	will bring you to J for saying, 'I have
	4:12	I who speak in J upon them."
	25:31	he is entering into J with all flesh, and
	48:21	J has come upon the tableland, upon Holon, and
	48:47	Thus far is the J on Moab.
	51:9	own country; for her J has reached up to
	51:52	when I will execute J upon her images, and
Ezek	14:21	four sore acts of J, sword, famine, evil beasts,
	16:52	for you have made J favorable to your sisters;
	17:20	Babylon and enter into J with him there for
	20:35	I will enter into J with you face to
	20:36	As I entered into J with your fathers in
	20:36	I will enter into J with you, says the
	23:10	byword among women, when J had been executed
	23:24	I will commit the J to them, and they
	23:45	righteous men shall pass J on them with the
	30:14	will execute acts of J upon Thebes.
	30:19	will execute acts of J upon Egypt.
	38:22	I will enter into J with him; and I
	39:21	nations shall see my J which I have executed,
Dan	3:31	done to us, thou hast done in true J
	7:10	the court sat in J, and the books were
	7:22	of Days came, and J was given for the
	7:26	court shall sit in J, and his dominion shall
	13:49	Return to the place of J
Hos	5:1	For the J pertains to you; for you have
	5:11	is oppressed, crushed in J, because he was
	6:5	my mouth, and my J goes forth as the
	10:4	they make covenants; so J springs up like poisonous
Joel	3:2	I will enter into J with them there, on
Amos	7:4	was calling for a J by fire, and it
Mic	3:11	Its heads give J for a bribe, its priests
	7:9	my cause and executes J for me.
Hab	1:12	ordained them as a J; and thou, O Rock,
Mal	3:5	near to you for J; I will be a
2Mac	1:17	God, who has brought J upon those who have
	2:29	adornment, such in my J is the case with
	7:35	not yet escaped the J of the almighty, all-seeing
	7:36	but you, by the J of God, will receive
	8:11	talent, not expecting the J from the Almighty that
	9:4	But the J of heaven rode with him!
	9:18	way abate, for the J of God had justly
	11:37	some men, so that we may have your J
Mt	5:21	shall be liable to J
	5:22	shall be liable to J; whoever insults his brother
	7:2	For with the J you pronounce you will be
	10:15	on the day of J for the land of
	11:22	on the day of J for Tyre and Sidon
	11:24	on the day of J for the land of
	12:36	on the day of J men will render account
	12:41	will arise at the J with this generation and
	12:42	will arise at the J with this generation and

26:66 What is your J
27:19 was sitting on the J seat, his wife sent
Lk 10:14 more tolerable in the J for Tyre and Sidon
11:31 will arise at the J with the men of
11:32 will arise at the J with this generation and
Jn 3:19 And this is the J, that the light has
5:21 but has given all J to the Son,
5:23 does not come into J, but has passed from
5:26 him authority to execute J, because he is the
5:28 who have done evil, to the resurrection of J
5:29 I judge; and my J is just, because I
7:24 not judge by appearances, but judge with right J
8:16 I do judge, my J is true, for it
9:39 Jesus said, "For J I came into this world,
12:31 Now is the J of this world, now shall
16:8 sin and righteousness and J:
16:11 me no more; concerning J, because the ruler of
19:13 sat down on the J seat at a place
Acts 15:19 of old.' Therefore my J is that we should
21:25 a letter with our J that they should abstain
24:24 and self-control and future J, Felix was alarmed and
Rom 2:1 another; for in passing J upon him you condemn
2:2 We know that the J of God rightly falls
2:3 you will escape the J of God?
2:5 wrath when God's righteous J will be revealed.
5:16 the J following one trespass brought condemnation,
12:3 to think with sober J, each according to the
13:2 has appointed, and those who resist will incur J
14:3 him who abstains pass J on him who eats;
14:4 are you to pass J on the servant of
14:10 Why do you pass J on your brother?
14:10 all stand before the J seat of God;
14:13 us no more pass J on one another, but
1Cor 1:10 united in the same mind and the same J
4:5 Therefore do not pronounce J before the time,
5:3 I have already pronounced J
7:40 But in my J she is happier if she
11:29 body eats and drinks J upon himself.
2Cor 5:10 all appear before the J seat of Christ, so
Gal 5:10 you will bear his J, whoever he is.
Col 2:16 let no one pass J on you in questions
2Thes 1:5 evidence of the righteous J of God, that you
1Tim 5:24 are conspicuous, pointing to J, but the sins of
Heb 6:2 hands, the resurrection of the dead, and eternal J
9:27 and after that comes J,
10:27 a fearful prospect of J, and a fury of
Jas 2:13 For J is without mercy to one who has
2:13 has shown no mercy; yet mercy triumphs over J
1Pet 4:17 time has come for J to begin with the
2Pet 2:4 be kept until the J;
2:9 until the day of J,
2:11 not pronounce a reviling J upon them before the
3:7 until the day of J and destruction of ungodly
1Jn 4:17 for the day of J, because as he is
Jude 1:6 nether gloom until the J of the great day;
1:9 to pronounce a reviling J upon him, but said,
1:15 holy myriads, to execute J on all, and to
Rev 14:7 the hour of his J has come; and worship
17:1 will show you the J of the great harlot
18:10 one hour has thy J come."
18:20 for God has given J for you against her!"
20:4 were those to whom J was committed.

JUDGMENTS (49)

Ex 12:12 Egypt I will execute J: I am the LORD.
Num 33:4 them; upon their gods also the LORD executed J
1Chr 16:12 wonders he wrought, the J he uttered,
16:14 LORD our God; his J are in all the
Tob 3:5 And now thy many J are true in exacting
Ps 10:5 at all times; thy J are on high, out
36:6 mountains of God, thy J are like the great
48:11 the daughters of Judah rejoice because of thy J
97:8 rejoice, because of thy J, O God.
105:5 his miracles, and the J he uttered,
105:7 LORD our God; his J are in all the
119:75 O LORD, that thy J are right, and that
119:120 of thee, and I am afraid of thy J
119:137 art thou, O LORD, and right are thy J
Wis 17:1 Great are thy J and hard to describe; therefore
Sir 17:10 them an eternal covenant, and showed them his J
18:13 his discipline and who are eager for his J
20:3 a man who executes J by violence.
32:16 Lord will form true J, and like a light
45:5 to teach Jacob the covenant, and Israel his J
45:17 authority and statutes and J, to teach Jacob the
48:7 rebuke at Sinai and J of vengeance at Horeb;
Is 26:8 the path of thy J, O LORD, we wait
26:9 For when thy J are in the earth, the
58:2 ask of me righteous J, they delight to draw
Jer 1:16 I will utter my J against them, for all
Ezek 5:8 and I will execute J in the midst of
5:10 and I will execute J on you, and any
5:15 you, when I execute J on you in anger
7:27 according to their own J I will judge them;
11:9 of foreigners, and execute J upon you.
16:41 your houses and execute J upon you in the
23:24 and they shall judge you according to their J
25:11 and I will execute J upon Moab.
28:22 LORD when I execute J in her, and manifest
28:26 securely, when I execute J upon all their neighbors
44:24 and they shall judge it according to my J
Dan 3:27 right, and all thy J are truth.
3:28 Thou hast executed true J in all that thou
13:9 from looking to Heaven or remembering righteous J
13:53 past, pronouncing unjust J, condemning the innocent
Zeph 3:15 has taken away the J against you, he has
Zech 7:9 of hosts, Render true J, show kindness and mercy
8:16 render in your gates J that are true and
Rom 11:33 How unsearchable are his J and how inscrutable his
Rev 15:4 worship thee, for thy J have been revealed."
16:5 thou in these thy J, thou who art and
16:7 God the Almighty, true and just are thy J
19:2 our God, for his J are true and just;

JUDICIOUS

Prov 16:23 wise makes his speech J, and adds persuasiveness to

JUDITH (34)

Gen 26:34 he took to wife J the daughter of Be-eri
Jud 8:1 At that time J heard about these things: she
8:4 J had lived at home as a widow for
8:9 When J heard the wicked words spoken by the
8:32 J said to them, "Listen to me.
9:1 Then J fell upon her face, and put ashes
9:1 of God in Jerusalem, J cried out to the
10:1 When J had ceased crying out to the God
10:10 they had done this, J went out, she and
10:23 And when J came into the presence of Holofernes
11:5 J replied to him, "Accept the words of your
12:2 But J said, "I cannot eat it, lest it
12:4 J replied, "As your soul lives, my lord, your
12:14 And J said, "Who am I, to refuse my
12:16 Then J came in and lay down, and Holofernes'
12:18 J said, "I will drink now, my lord, because
13:2 So J was left alone in the tent,
13:3 Now J had told her maid to stand outside
13:4 Then J, standing beside his bed, said in her
13:11 J called out from afar to the watchmen at
14:1 Then J said to them, "Listen to me, my
14:7 up he fell at J's feet, and knelt before
14:8 Then J described to him in the presence of
14:14 for he supposed that he was sleeping with J
14:17 to the tent where J had stayed, and when
15:8 Israel, and to see J and to greet her.
15:11 They gave J the tent of Holofernes and all
16:1 Then J began this thanksgiving before all Israel, and
16:2 And J said, Begin a song to my God
16:7 set upon him; but J the daughter of Merari
16:19 J also dedicated to God all the vessels of
16:20 for three months, and J remained with them.
16:21 his own inheritance, and J went to Bethulia, and
16:25 in the days of J, or for a long

JUICE (3)

Num 6:3 shall not drink any J of grapes or eat
Song 8:2 wine to drink, the J of my pomegranates.
1Mac 6:34 showed the elephants the J of grapes and mulberries,

JULIA

Rom 16:15 Greet Philologus, J, Nereus and his sister, and

JULIUS (2)

Acts 27:1 to a centurion of the Augustan Cohort, named J
27:3 in at Sidon; and J treated Paul kindly, and

JUNGLE (4)

Jer 12:5 you do in the J of the Jordan?
49:19 coming up from the J of the Jordan against
50:44 coming up from the J of the Jordan against
Zech 11:3 the lions, for the J of the Jordan is

JUNIAS

Rom	16:7	Greet Andronicus and J, my kinsmen and my fellow

JURISDICTION (3)

Neh	3:7	who were under the J of the governor of
Lk	20:20	to the authority and J of the governor.
	23:7	he belonged to Herod's J, he sent him over

JUSHAB-HESED

1Chr	3:20	Ohel, Berechiah, Hasadiah, and J, five.

JUST (172)

Gen	26:29	do us no harm, J as we have not
Lev	4:10	away with the kidneys J as these are taken
	19:36	You shall have J balances, just weights, a just
	19:36	shall have just balances, J weights, a just ephah,
	19:36	balances, just weights, a J ephah, and a just
	19:36	just ephah, and a J hin: I am the
Num	22:33	aside from me, surely J now I would have
	29:40	people of Israel everything J as the LORD had
Deut	1:30	himself fight for you, J as he did for
	1:41	go up and fight, J as the LORD our
	12:22	J as the gazelle or the hart is eaten,
	18:16	you shall heed– J as you desired of
	25:15	A full and J weight you shall have, a
	25:15	have, a full and J measure you shall have;
	32:4	faithfulness and without iniquity, J and right is he.
	33:21	the commands and J decrees of the LORD."
Josh	1:17	J as we obeyed Moses in all things, so
	21:44	rest on every side J as he had sworn
	23:15	But J as all the good things which the
Judg	7:19	watch, when they had J set the watch; and
Ruth	3:6	threshing floor and did J as her mother-in-law had
1Sam	9:12	is; behold, he is J ahead of you.
	9:12	haste; he has come J now to the city,
2Sam	3:22	J then the servants of David arrived with Joab
	15:37	came into the city, J as Absalom was entering
2Kgs	5:22	to say, 'There have J now come to me
1Chr	24:31	brother alike, cast lots, J as their brethren the
	26:12	chief men, had duties, J as their brethren did,
Ezra	9:15	of Israel, thou art J, for we are left
Neh	9:33	Yet thou hast been J in all that has
Tob	14:5	all generations for ever, J as the prophets said
	14:9	and be merciful and J, so that it may
Jud	2:1	on the whole region, J as he said.
	2:13	to carry them out J as I have ordered
	10:16	heart, but tell him J what you have said,
Esth	2:20	for Esth obeyed Mordecai J as when she was
	6:4	Now Haman had J entered the outer court of
Job	9:2	can a man be J before God?
	12:4	he answered me, a J and blameless man, am
	27:17	it up, but the J will wear it, and
	31:6	be weighed in a J balance, and let God
	35:2	Elihu said: "Do you think this to be J
Ps	9:4	thou hast maintained my J cause; thou hast sat
	17:1	Hear a J cause, O LORD; attend to my
	111:7	hands are faithful and J; all his precepts are
	119:121	have done what is J and right; do not
	145:17	The LORD is J in all his ways, and
Prov	8:15	rulers decree what is J;
	11:1	the LORD, but a J weight is his delight.
	12:5	of the righteous are J; the counsels of the
	16:11	A J balance and scales are the LORDs; all
	21:7	away, because they refuse to do what is J
Eccl	2:16	the wise man dies J like the fool!
	5:16	is a grievous evil: J as he came, so
Wis	14:30	But J penalties will overtake them on two counts:
	14:31	men swear, but the J penalty for those who
	19:17	loss of sight– J as were those at
Sir	18:6	has finished, he is J beginning, and when he
	24:26	J as the first man did not know her
	39:23	will incur his wrath, J as he turns fresh
	39:24	his ways are straight, J as they are obstacles
	39:25	created for good people, J as evil things for
	39:27	good to the godly, J as they turn into
Is	66:20	Jerusalem, says the LORD, J as the Israelites bring
Jer	3:4	Have you not J now called to me, 'My
	10:24	O LORD, but in J measure; not in thy
	30:11	will chasten you in J measure, and I will
	32:42	thus says the LORD: J as I have brought
	46:28	will chasten you in J measure, and I will
Bar	4:28	For J as you purposed to go astray from
	4:33	For J as she rejoiced at your fall and
	6:17	For J as one's dish is useless when it
	6:18	And J as the gates are shut on every
	6:20	They are J like a beam of the temple,
	6:27	are placed before them J as before the dead.
	6:73	Better therefore is a J man who has no
Ezek	18:25	the Lord is not J Hear now, O house
	18:25	O house of Israel: Is my way not J
	18:25	Is it not your ways that are not J
	18:29	the Lord is not J O house of Israel,
	18:29	O house of Israel, are my ways not J
	18:29	Is it not your ways that are not J
	33:17	the Lord is not J; when it is their
	33:17	it is their own way that is not J
	33:20	the Lord is not J O house of Israel,
	45:10	"You shall have J balances, a just ephah, and
	45:10	have just balances, a J ephah, and a just
	45:10	just ephah, and a J bath.
Dan	2:41	shall be in it, J as you saw iron
	2:43	will not hold together, J as iron does not
	2:45	shall stand for ever; J as you saw that
	3:27	For thou art J in all that thou hast
	4:37	and his ways are J; and those who walk
1Mac	4:19	J as Judas was finishing this speech, a detachment
	7:12	Bacchides to ask for J terms.
	7:47	them and displayed them J outside Jerusalem.
	10:37	by their own laws, J as the king has
2Mac	1:24	awe-inspiring and strong and J and merciful, who
	1:25	bountiful, who alone art J and almighty and eternal,
	2:10	J as Moses prayed to the Lord, and fire
	2:27	and loss of sleep, J as it is not
	3:28	this man who had J entered the aforesaid treasury
	5:18	as he came forward, J as Heliodorus was, whom
	7:36	of God, will receive J punishment for your arrogance.
	9:8	Thus he who had J been thinking that he
	10:28	J as dawn was breaking, the two armies joined
	11:14	to settle everything on J terms, promising that he
	11:31	own food and laws, J as formerly, and none
	13:8	And this was eminently J; because he had committed
	13:11	the people who had J begun to revive fall
	13:17	This happened, J as day was dawning, because the
	15:39	For J as it is harmful to drink wine
Mt	1:19	husband Joseph, being a J man and unwilling to
	5:45	sends rain on the J and on the unjust.
	9:18	saying, "My daughter has J died; but come and
	13:40	J as the weeds are gathered and burned with
Mk	4:36	them in the boat, J as he was.
Lk	1:2	been accomplished among us, J as they were
	1:17	the wisdom of the J, to make ready for
	14:14	will be repaid at the resurrection of the J
	15:7	sheep which was lost.' J so, I tell you,
	15:10	which I had lost.' J so, I tell you,
	24:24	tomb, and found it J as the women had
Jn	4:27	J then his disciples came.
	5:29	and my judgment is J, because I seek not
	15:10	abide in my love, J as I have kept
	21:4	J as day was breaking, Jesus stood on the
	21:10	fish that you have J caught."
Acts	10:47	received the Holy Spirit J as we have?"
	11:15	Spirit fell on them J as on us at
	15:8	them the Holy Spirit J as he did to
	15:11	of the Lord Jesus, J as they will."
	22:14	will, to see the J One and to hear
	24:14	resurrection of both the J and the unjust.
Rom	3:8	Their condemnation is J
	6:19	For J as you once yielded your members to
	7:12	commandment is holy and J and good.
	8:4	in order that the J requirement of the law
	11:30	J as you were once disobedient to God but
1Cor	9:18	J this: that in my preaching I may make
	10:33	the church of God, J as I try to
	12:12	For J as the body is one and has
	15:49	J as we have borne the image of the
	16:7	to see you now J in passing; I hope
2Cor	7:14	put to shame; but J as everything we said
Gal	2:7	gospel to the uncircumcised, J as Peter had been
Eph	4:4	body and one Spirit, J as you were called
Phil	2:23	therefore to send him J as soon as I
	4:8	is honorable, whatever is J, whatever is pure,
Col	2:7	established in the faith, J as you were taught,
1Thes	2:4	made with guile; but J as we have been
	3:4	were to suffer affliction; J as it has come
	4:1	and to please God, J as you are doing,
	5:11	build one another up, J as you are doing.
2Thes	1:6	indeed God deems it J to repay with affliction
1Tim	1:9	laid down for the J but for the lawless
Heb	2:2	or disobedience received a J retribution,
	3:2	him who appointed him, J as Moses also was
	4:2	news came to us J as to them; but
	5:4	is called by God, J as Aaron was.

9:27 And J as it is appointed for men to
12:23 to the spirits of J men made perfect,
2Pet 2:1 arose among the people, J as there will be
1Jn 1:9 he is faithful and J, and will forgive our
2:27 and is no lie, J as it has taught
3:23 and love one another, J as he has commanded
2Jn 1:4 children following the truth, J as we have been
Jude 1:7 of the great day; J as Sodom and Gomorrah
Rev 15:3 J and true are thy ways, O King of
16:5 angel of water say, J art thou in these
16:7 the Almighty, true and J are thy judgments!"
19:2 judgments are true and J; he has judged the

JUSTICE (142)

Gen 18:19 by doing righteousness and J; so that the LORD
Ex 23:2 so as to pervert J;
23:6 shall not pervert the J due to your poor
Deut 10:18 He executes J for the fatherless and the widow,
16:19 You shall not pervert J; you shall not show
16:20 J, and only justice, you shall follow, that you
16:20 Justice, and only J, you shall follow, that you
24:17 shall not pervert the J due to the sojourner
27:19 he who perverts the J due to the sojourner,
32:4 work is perfect; for all his ways are J
1Sam 7:17 there also he administered J to Israel.
8:3 aside after gain; they took bribes and perverted J
2Sam 8:15 Israel; and David administered J and equity to all
15:4 come to me, and I would give him J
1Kgs 3:28 wisdom of God was in him, to render J
10:9 that you may execute J and righteousness."
1Chr 18:14 Israel; and he administered J and equity to all
2Chr 9:8 that you may execute J and righteousness."
19:7 is no perversion of J with the LORD our
Esth 16:4 will escape the evil-hating J of God, who always
Job 8:3 Does God pervert J
9:19 is a matter of J, who can summon him?
19:7 answered; I call aloud, but there is no J
29:14 it clothed me; my J was like a robe
34:12 do wickedly, and the Almighty will not pervert J
34:17 Shall one who hates J govern?
36:17 the wicked; judgment and J seize you.
37:23 great in power and J, and abundant righteousness he
Ps 10:18 thy ear to do J to the fatherless and
33:5 He loves righteousness and J; the earth is full
37:28 For the LORD loves J; he will not forsake
37:30 the righteous utters wisdom, and his tongue speaks J
72:1 Give the king thy J, O God, and thy
72:2 thy people with righteousness, and thy poor with J
82:3 [Selah] Give J to the weak and the fatherless;
89:14 Righteousness and J are the foundation of thy
94:15 abandon his heritage; for J will return to the
97:2 about him; righteousness and J are the foundation of
99:4 Mighty King, lover of J, thou hast established equity;
99:4 equity; thou hast executed J and righteousness in
101:1 of loyalty and of J; to thee, O LORD,
103:6 LORD works vindication and J for all who are
106:3 are they who observe J, who do righteousness at
112:5 generously and lends, who conducts his affairs with J
119:149 O LORD, in thy J preserve my life.
119:156 O LORD; give me life according to thy J
140:12 the afflicted, and executes J for the needy.
146:7 for ever; who executes J for the oppressed; who
Prov 1:3 in wise dealing, righteousness, J, and equity;
2:8 guarding the paths of J and preserving the way
2:9 will understand righteousness and J and equity, every
8:20 in the paths of J,
17:23 from the bosom to pervert the ways of J
18:5 man, or to deprive a righteous man of J
19:28 worthless witness mocks at J, and the mouth of
21:3 To do righteousness and J is more acceptable to
21:15 When J is done, it is a joy to
28:5 men do not understand J, but those who seek
29:4 By J a king gives stability to the land,
29:26 ruler, but from the LORD a man gets J
Eccl 3:16 in the place of J, even there was wickedness,
5:8 the poor oppressed and J and right violently taken
Wis 1:8 will escape notice, and J, when it punishes, will
5:18 breastplate, and wear impartial J as a helmet;
8:7 teaches self-control and prudence, J and courage;
11:20 breath when pursued by J and scattered by the
Sir 16:20 Who will announce his acts of J
27:8 If you pursue J, you will attain it and
35:17 visits him, and does J for the righteous, and
Is 1:17 to do good; seek J, correct oppression; defend the
1:21 become a harlot, she that was full of J
1:27 shall be redeemed by J, and those in her
5:7 and he looked for J, but behold, bloodshed; for
5:16 hosts is exalted in J, and the Holy God
9:7 to uphold it with J and with righteousness from
10:2 aside the needy from J and to rob the
16:3 "Give counsel, grant J; make your shade like night
16:5 who judges and seeks J and is swift to
28:6 and a spirit of J to him who sits
28:17 And I will make J the line, and righteousness
30:18 is a God of J; blessed are all those
32:1 reign in righteousness, and princes will rule in J
32:16 Then J will dwell in the wilderness, and
33:5 will fill Zion with J and righteousness;
40:14 him the path of J, and taught him knowledge,
42:1 he will bring forth J to the nations.
42:3 will not quench; he will faithfully bring forth J
42:4 till he has established J in the earth; and
51:4 from me, and my J for a light to
56:1 says the LORD: "Keep J, and do righteousness, for
59:8 and there is no J in their paths; they
59:9 Therefore J is far from us, and righteousness does
59:11 doves; we look for J, but there is none;
59:14 J is turned back, and righteousness stands afar off;
59:15 and it displeased him that there was no J
61:8 I the LORD love J, I hate robbery and
Jer 4:2 lives,' in truth, in J, and in uprightness, then
5:1 man, one who does J and seeks truth; that
5:28 they judge not with J the cause of the
7:5 if you truly execute J one with another,
9:24 who practice steadfast love, J, and righteousness in
21:12 says the LORD: "Execute J in the morning, and
22:3 says the LORD: Do J and righteousness, and deliver
22:15 and drink and do J and righteousness?
23:5 wisely, and shall execute J and righteousness in the
33:15 and he shall execute J and righteousness in the
Bar 2:17 not ascribe glory or J to the Lord,
Ezek 18:8 from iniquity, executes true J between man and man,
34:16 will watch over; I will feed them in J
45:9 oppression, and execute J and righteousness; cease
Dan 3:28 for in truth and J thou hast brought all
Hos 2:19 in righteousness and in J, in steadfast love, and
12:6 fast to love and J, and wait continually for
Amos 5:7 O you who turn J to wormwood, and cast
5:15 love good, and establish J in the gate; it
5:24 But let J roll down like waters, and righteousness
6:12 But you have turned J into poison and the
Mic 3:1 for you to know J –
3:8 the LORD, and with J and might, to declare
3:9 of Israel, who abhor J and pervert all equity,
6:8 you but to do J, and to love kindness,
Hab 1:4 law is slacked and J never goes forth.
1:4 surround the righteous, so J goes forth perverted.
1:7 terrible are they; their J and dignity proceed from
Zeph 3:5 he shows forth his J, each dawn he does
Mal 2:17 Or by asking, "Where is the God of J
1Mac 2:29 were seeking righteousness and J went down to the
6:22 you fail to do J and to avenge our
7:18 is no truth or J in them, for they
14:35 and because of the J and loyalty which he
2Mac 4:34 with no regard for J, he immediately put him
8:13 and distrustful of God's J ran off and got
10:12 the lead in showing J to the Jews because
Mt 12:18 and he shall proclaim J to the Gentiles.
12:20 wick, till he brings J to victory;
23:22 matters of the law, J and mercy and faith;
Lk 11:42 every herb, and neglect J and the love of
Acts 8:33 In his humiliation J was denied him.
24:24 as he argued about J and self-control and future
28:4 escaped from the sea, J has not allowed him
Rom 3:5 serves to show the J of God, what shall
Heb 11:33 faith conquered kingdoms, enforced J, received

JUSTICES (2)

Dan 3:2 counselors, the treasurers, the J, the magistrates,
3:3 the treasurers, the J, the magistrates, and all

JUSTIFICATION (3)

Rom 4:25 death for our trespasses and raised for our J
5:16 but the free gift following many trespasses brings J
Gal 2:21 of God; for if J were through the law,

JUSTIFIED (35)

Job 32:2 at Job because he J himself rather than God;
40:8 Will you condemn me that you may be J
Ps 51:4 so that thou art J in thy sentence and
Sir 1:19 Unrighteous anger cannot be J, for a man's anger
23:11 he will not be J, for his house will

31:5 gold will not be J, and he who pursues
Mt 11:19 sinners!' Yet wisdom is J by her deeds."
12:37 words you will be J, and by your words
Lk 7:29 and the tax collectors J God, having been baptized
7:35 sinners!' Yet wisdom is J by all her children."
18:14 down to his house J rather than the other;
Rom 2:13 the doers of the law who will be J
3:4 "That thou mayest be J in thy words, and
3:20 human being will be J in his sight by
3:24 of God, they are J by his grace as
3:28 that a man is J by faith apart from
4:2 For if Abraham was J by works, he has
5:1 Therefore, since we are J by faith, we have
5:9 therefore, we are now J by his blood, much
8:30 he called he also J; and those whom he
8:30 and those whom he J he also glorified.
10:4 that every one who has faith may be J
10:10 heart and so is J, and he confesses with
1Cor 6:11 were sanctified, you were J in the name of
Gal 2:16 a man is not J by works of the
2:16 in order to be J by faith in Christ,
2:16 works of the law shall no one be J
2:17 our endeavor to be J in Christ, we ourselves
3:11 that no man is J before God by the
3:24 that we might be J by faith.
5:4 you who would be J by the law; you
Tit 3:7 that we might be J by his grace and
Jas 2:21 not Abraham our father J by works, when he
2:24 that a man is J by works and not
2:25 also Rahab the harlot J by works when she

JUSTIFIES (4)

Prov 17:15 He who J the wicked and he who condemns
Rom 3:26 righteous and that he J him who has faith
4:5 but trusts him who J the ungodly, his faith
8:33 It is God who J;

JUSTIFY (9)

Job 33:32 for I desire to J you.
Sir 10:28 Who will J the man that sins against himself?
13:21 unseemly words, and they J him.
Is 43:9 bring their witnesses to J them, and let them
Lk 10:29 But he, desiring to J himself, said to Jesus,
16:15 "You are those who J yourselves before men, but
Acts 19:40 we can give to J this commotion."
Rom 3:30 one; and he will J the circumcised on the
Gal 3:8 foreseeing that God would J the Gentiles by faith,

JUSTLY (10)

2Sam 23:3 me: When one rules J over men, ruling in
Wis 9:12 shall judge thy people J, and shall be worthy
19:13 of thunder, for they J suffered because of their
Is 59:4 No one enters suit J, no one goes to
2Mac 7:38 the Almighty which has J fallen on our whole
9:6 and that very J, for he had tortured
9:18 judgment of God had J come upon him, he
Lk 23:40 And we indeed J; for we are receiving the
Col 4:1 Masters, treat your slaves J and fairly, knowing that
1Pet 2:23 threaten; but he trusted to him who judges J

JUSTUS (3)

Acts 1:23 Barsabbas, who was surnamed J, and Matthias.
18:7 a man named Titius J, a worshiper of God;
Col 4:11 you, receive him), and Jesus who is called J

JUTTAH (2)

Josh 15:55 Maon, Carmel, Ziph, J,
21:16 with its pasture lands, J with its pasture lands,

K

KAB

2Kgs 6:25 fourth part of a K of dove's dung for

KABZEEL (3)

Josh 15:21 boundary of Edom, were K, Eder, Jagur,
2Sam 23:20 a valiant man of K, a doer of great
1Chr 11:22 a valiant man of K, a doer of great

KADESH (19)

Gen 14:7 to Enmishpat (that is, K, and subdued all the
16:14 Beer-lahai-roi; it lies between K and Bered.
20:1 Negeb, and dwelt between K and Shur; and he
Num 13:26 wilderness of Paran, at K; they brought back word
20:1 the people stayed in K; and Miriam died there,
20:14 Moses sent messengers from K to the king of
20:16 here we are in K, a city on the
20:22 And they journeyed from K, and the people of
27:14 waters of Meribah of K in the wilderness of
33:36 encamped in the wilderness of Zin (that is, K
33:37 they set out from K, and encamped at Mount
Deut 1:46 So you remained at K many days, the days
Judg 11:16 wilderness to the Red Sea and came to K
11:17 So Israel remained at K
2Sam 24:6 to Gilead, and to K in the land of
Jud 1:9 Bethany and Chelous and K and the river of
Ps 29:8 the wilderness, the LORD shakes the wilderness of K
1Mac 11:63 Demetrius had come to K in Galilee with a
11:73 pursuit as far as K, to their camp, and

KADESH-BARNEA (11)

Num 32:8 I sent them from K to see the land.
34:4 shall be south of K; then it shall go
Deut 1:2 Horeb by the way of Mount Seir to K
1:19 our God commanded us; and we came to K
2:14 time from our leaving K until we crossed the
9:23 LORD sent you from K, saying, 'Go up and
Josh 10:41 Joshua defeated them from K to Gaza, and all
14:6 man of God in K concerning you and me.
14:7 LORD sent me from K to spy out the
15:3 goes up south of K, along by Hezron, up
Jud 5:14 way of Sinai and K, and drove out all

KADMI-EL (8)

Ezra 2:40 sons of Jeshua and K, of the sons of
3:9 and his kinsmen, and K and his sons, the
Neh 7:43 of Jeshua, namely of K of the sons of
9:4 Levites stood Jeshua, Bani, K, Shebaniah, Bunni,
9:5 Then the Levites, Jeshua, K, Bani, Hashabneiah,
10:9 the sons of Henadad, K;
12:8 the Levites: Jeshua, Binnui, K, Sherebiah, Judah, and
12:24 Jeshua the son of K, with their brethren over

KADMONITES

Gen 15:19 Kenites, the Kenizzites, the K,

KAIN (2)

Num 24:22 in the rock; nevertheless K shall be wasted.
Josh 15:57 Jezreel, Jokde-am, Zanoah, K, Gibe-ah, and Timnah:

KAIWAN

Amos 5:26 Sakkuth your king, and K your star-god, your images,

KALLAI

Neh 12:20 Jedaiah, Uzzi; of Sallai, K; of Amok, Eber;

KAMON

Judg 10:5 And Jair died, and was buried in K

KANAH (3)

Josh 16:8 westward to the brook K, and ends at the
17:9 Then the boundary went down to the brook K
19:28 Cabul, Ebron, Rehob, Hammon, K, as far as Sidon

KAREAH (14)

2Kgs 25:23 Johanan the son of K, and Seraiah the son
Jer 40:8 Johanan the son of K, Seraiah the son of
40:13 Johanan the son of K and all the leaders
40:15 Johanan the son of K spoke secretly to Gedaliah
40:16 Johanan the son of K, "You shall not do
41:11 Johanan the son of K and all the leaders
41:13 Johanan the son of K and all the leaders
41:14 back, and went to Johanan the son of K
41:16 Johanan the son of K and all the leaders
42:1 Johanan the son of K and Azariah the son
42:8 Johanan the son of K and all the commanders
43:2 Johanan the son of K and all the insolent
43:4 Johanan the son of K and all the commanders
43:5 Johanan the son of K and all the commanders

KARKA

Josh 15:3 Addar, turns about to K,

KARKOR

Judg 8:10 and Zalmunna were in K with their army, about

KARNAIM

Amos 6:13 our own strength taken K for ourselves?"

KARTAH

Josh 21:34 with its pasture lands, K with its pasture lands,

KARTAN

Josh 21:32 its pasture lands, and K with its pasture lands—

KATTATH

Josh 19:15 valley of Iphtahel; and K, Nahalal, Shimron, Idalah,

KEDAR (12)

Gen 25:13 first-born of Ishmael; and K, Adbeel, Mibsam,
1Chr 1:29 of Ishmael, Nebaioth; and K, Adbeel, Mibsam,
Ps 120:5 Meshech, that I dwell among the tents of K
Song 1:5 like the tents of K, like the curtains of
Is 21:16 all the glory of K will come to an
21:17 of the sons of K will be few; for
42:11 voice, the villages that K inhabits; let the inhabitants
60:7 All the flocks of K shall be gathered to
Jer 2:10 see, or send to K and examine with care;
49:28 Concerning K and the kingdoms of Hazor which
49:28 Thus says the LORD: "Rise up, advance against K
Ezek 27:21 all the princes of K were your favored dealers

KEDEMAH (2)

Gen 25:15 Massa, Hadad, Tema, Jetur, Naphish, and K
1Chr 1:31 Dumah, Massa, Hadad, Tema, Jetur, Naphish, and K

KEDEMOTH (4)

Deut 2:26 from the wilderness of K to Sihon the king
Josh 13:18 Beth-baal-meon, and Jahaz, and K, and Mephaath,
21:37 with its pasture lands, K with its pasture lands,
1Chr 6:79 with its pasture lands, K with its pasture lands,

KEDESH (13)

Josh 12:22 one; the king of K, one; the king of
15:23 Kinah, Dimonah, Adadah, K, Hazor, Ithnan,
19:37 Adamah, Ramah, Hazor, K, Edre-i, En-hazor,
20:7 So they set apart K in Galilee in the
21:32 the tribe of Naphtali, K in Galilee with its
Judg 4:6 son of Abino-am from K in Naphtali, and said
4:9 Then Deborah arose, and went with Barak to K
4:10 Zebulun and Naphtali to K; and ten thousand men
4:11 as the oak in Za-anannim, which is near K
2Kgs 15:29 captured Ijon, Abel-beth-maacah, Jan-oah, K, Hazor,
1Chr 6:72 the tribe of Issachar: K with its pasture lands,
6:76 the tribe of Naphtali: K in Galilee with its
Tob 1:2 to the south of K Naphtali in Galilee above

KEDRON (3)

1Mac 15:39 him to build up K and fortify its gates,
15:41 He built up K and stationed there horsemen and
16:9 them until Cendebeus reached K, which he had built.

KEEL

Wis 5:10 nor track of its K in the waves;

KEEN (2)

Wis 7:22 invulnerable, loving the good, K, irresistible,
8:11 I shall be found K in judgment, and in

KEEP (412)

Gen 2:15 to till it and K it.
6:19 into the ark, to K them alive with you;
6:20 in to you, to K them alive.
7:3 male and female, to K their kind alive upon
17:9 for you, you shall K my covenant, you and
17:10 covenant, which you shall K, between me and you
18:19 household after him to K the way of the
28:15 with you and will K you wherever you go,
28:20 with me, and will K me in this way
30:31 feed your flock and K it:
33:9 have enough, my brother; K what you have for
38:23 Judah replied, "Let her K the things as her
41:35 cities, and let them K it.
45:7 on earth, and to K alive for you many
Ex 12:6 goats; and you shall K it until the fourteenth
12:14 day, and you shall K it as a feast
12:25 has promised, you shall K this service.
12:47 congregation of Israel shall K it.
12:48 with you and would K the passover to the
12:48 may come near and K it; he shall be
13:5 and honey, you shall K this service in this
13:10 You shall therefore K this ordinance at its appointed
15:26 to his commandments and K all his statutes, I
16:28 do you refuse to K my commandments and my
19:5 obey my voice and K my covenant, you shall
20:6 who love me and K my commandments.
20:8 the sabbath day, to K it holy.
22:7 money or goods to K, and it is stolen
22:10 or any beast to K, and it dies or
23:7 K far from a false charge, and do not
23:14 the year you shall K a feast to me.
23:15 You shall K the feast of unleavened bread; as
23:16 You shall K the feast of harvest, of the
23:16 You shall K the feast of ingathering at the
31:13 of Israel, 'You shall K my sabbaths, for this
31:14 You shall K the sabbath, because it is holy
31:16 people of Israel shall K the sabbath, observing the
34:18 he feast of unleavened bread you shall K
Lev 15:31 "Thus you shall K the people of Israel separate
18:4 do my ordinances and K my statutes and walk
18:5 You shall therefore K my statutes and my
18:26 But you shall K my statutes and my ordinances
18:30 So K my charge never to practice any of
19:3 father, and you shall K my sabbaths: I am
19:19 "You shall K my statutes.
19:30 You shall K my sabbaths and reverence my
20:8 K my statutes, and do them; I am the
20:22 "You shall therefore K all my statutes and all
22:2 and his sons to K away from the holy
22:9 LORD.' They shall therefore K my charge, lest they
22:31 "So you shall K my commandments and do them:
23:32 to evening shall you K your sabbath."
23:39 the land, you shall K the feast of the
23:41 You shall K it as a feast to the
23:41 your generations; you shall K it in the seventh
24:3 of meeting, Aaron shall K it in order from
24:4 He shall K the lamps in order upon the
25:2 you, the land shall K a sabbath to the
25:18 do my statutes, and K my ordinances and perform
26:2 You shall K my sabbaths and reverence my
Num 1:53 and the Levites shall K charge of the tabernacle
6:24 LORD bless you and K you:
8:26 tent of meeting, to K the charge, and they
9:2 the people of Israel K the passover at its
9:3 the evening, you shall K it at its appointed
9:3 its ordinances you shall K it."
9:4 Israel that they should K the passover.
9:6 that they could not K the passover on that
9:10 journey, he shall still K the passover to the
9:11 the evening they shall K it; they shall eat
9:12 the passover they shall K it.
9:14 among you, and will K the passover to the
29:12 work, and you shall K a feast to the
31:18 by lying with him, K alive for yourselves.
Deut 4:2 it; that you may K the commandments of the
4:6 K them and do them; for that will be
4:9 "Only take heed, and K your soul diligently, lest
4:40 Therefore you shall K his statutes and his
5:10 who love me and K my commandments.
5:12 the sabbath day, to K it holy, as the
5:15 God commanded you to K the sabbath day.
5:29 fear me and to K all my commandments, that
6:17 shall diligently K the commandments of the LORD
7:9 who love him and K his commandments, to a
7:12 to these ordinances, and K and do them, the
7:12 LORD your God will K with you the covenant
7:12 to your fathers to K;
8:2 heart, whether you would K his commandments, or
8:6 So you shall K the commandments of the LORD
10:13 your soul, and to K the commandments and statutes
11:1 LORD your God, and K his charge, his statutes,
11:8 "You shall therefore K all the commandment which I
13:4 and fear him, and K his commandments and obey
16:1 month of Abib, and K the passover to the
16:10 Then you shall K the feast of weeks to
16:13 "You shall K the feast of booths seven days,
16:15 seven days you shall K the feast to the
19:9 you are careful to K all this commandment, which
23:9 camp, then you shall K yourself from every evil
26:17 in his ways, and K his statutes and his
26:18 that you are to K all his commandments,
27:1 the people, saying, K all the commandment which
27:9 said to all Israel, K silence and hear, O
28:9 to you, if you K the commandments of the
28:45 LORD your God, to K his commandments and his
30:8 of the LORD, and K all his commandments which
30:10 LORD your God, to K his commandments and his
Josh 6:18 But you, K yourselves from the things devoted to
22:3 have been careful to K the charge of the
22:5 his ways, and to K his commandments, and to
23:6 be very steadfast to K and do all that

Judg 18:19 they said to him, K quiet, put your hand
Ruth 2:8 leave this one, but K close to my maidens.
2:21 to me, 'You shall K close by my servants,
1Sam 17:34 "Your servant used to K sheep for his father;
2Sam 3:8 This day I K showing loyalty to the house
14:14 devises means not to K his banished one an
15:16 left ten concubines to K the house.
16:21 he has left to K the house; and all
18:18 have no son to K my name in remembrance";
22:44 the peoples; thou didst K me as the head
1Kgs 2:3 yourself a man, and K the charge of the
6:12 obey my ordinances and K all my commandments
8:25 LORD, God of Israel, K with thy servant David
8:58 his ways, and to K his commandments, his statutes,
9:6 children, and do not K my commandments and my
11:10 but he did not K what the LORD commanded.
20:39 to me, and said, K this man; if by
22:3 to us, and we K quiet and do not
2Kgs 17:13 your evil ways and K my commandments and my
17:19 Judah also did not K the commandments of the
23:3 the LORD and to K his commandments and his
23:21 commanded all the people, K the passover to the
1Chr 4:10 and that thou wouldst K me from harm so
10:13 that he did not K the command of the
22:12 over Israel you may K the law of the
23:32 Thus they shall K charge of the tent of
29:18 and Israel, our fathers, K for ever such purposes
29:19 whole heart he may K thy commandments, thy
2Chr 6:16 LORD, God of Israel, K with thy servant David
13:11 every evening; for we K the charge of the
14:4 their fathers, and to K the law and the
23:6 all the people shall K the charge of the
30:1 LORD at Jerusalem, to K the passover to the
30:2 had taken counsel to K the passover in the
30:3 for they could not K it in its time
30:5 people should come and K the passover to the
30:13 together in Jerusalem to K the feast of unleavened
30:23 assembly agreed together to K the feast for another
34:31 the LORD and to K his commandments and his
35:16 prepared that day, to K the passover and to
Ezra 6:6 province Beyond the River, K away;
8:29 Guard them and K them until you weigh them
Neh 1:5 who love him and K his commandments;
1:9 return to me and K my commandments and do
5:2 we may eat and K alive."
13:22 guard the gates, to K the sabbath day holy.
Tob 3:5 because we did not K thy commandments.
3:15 for whom I should K myself as wife.
14:9 But K the law and the commandments, and be
Jud 7:12 in your camp, and K all the men in
7:13 and camp there to K watch that not a
11:10 what he said, but K it in your mind,
Esth 3:8 and they do not K the king's laws, so
4:14 For if you K silence at such a time
9:21 them that they should K the fourteenth day of
9:27 without fail they would K these two days according
Job 4:2 Yet who can K from speaking?
13:5 Oh that you would K silent, and it would
14:16 steps, thou wouldest not K watch over my sin;
22:15 of heaven.' Will you K to the old way
30:10 They abhor me, they K aloof from me; they
36:6 He does not K the wicked alive, but gives
36:19 your cry avail to K you from distress, or
41:12 "I will not K silence concerning his limbs, or
Ps 16:8 I K the LORD always before me; because he
17:8 K me as the apple of the eye; hide
19:13 K back thy servant also from presumptuous sins; let
22:9 the womb; thou didst K me safe upon my
22:29 and he who cannot K himself alive.
25:10 faithfulness, for those who K his covenant and his
32:9 else it will not K with you.
33:19 soul from death, and K them alive in famine.
34:13 K your tongue from evil, and your lips from
37:34 for the LORD, and K to his way, and
50:3 comes, he does not K silence, before him is
50:18 of his; and you K company with adulterers.
55:19 of old; because they K no law, and do
66:7 for ever, whose eyes K watch on the nations—
74:11 hand, why dost thou K thy right hand in
75:3 it is I who K steady its pillars.
78:7 works of God, but K his commandments;
78:10 They did not K God's covenant, but refused to
78:42 They did not K in mind his power, or
83:1 O God, do not K silence; do not hold
89:28 steadfast love I will K for him for ever,
89:31 statutes and do not K my commandments,
103:9 chide, nor will he K his anger for ever.
103:18 children, to those who K his covenant and remember
105:45 end that they should K his statutes, and observe
119:2 Blessed are those who K his testimonies, who seek
119:9 can a young man K his way pure?
119:33 statutes; and I will K it to the end.
119:34 understanding, that I may K thy law and observe
119:44 I will K thy law continually, for ever and
119:55 night, O LORD, and K thy law.
119:57 portion; I promise to K thy words.
119:60 do not delay to K thy commandments.
119:63 thee, of those who K thy precepts.
119:67 astray; but now I K thy word.
119:69 my whole heart I K thy precepts;
119:88 life, that I may K the testimonies of thy
119:100 the aged, for I K thy precepts.
119:101 way, in order to K thy word.
119:115 evildoers, that I may K the commandments of my
119:133 K steady my steps according to thy promise, and
119:134 oppression, that I may K thy precepts.
119:136 because men do not K thy law.
119:145 I will K thy statutes.
119:158 because they do not K thy commands.
119:168 I K thy precepts and testimonies, for all my
121:7 The LORD will K you from all evil; he
121:7 all evil; he will K your life.
121:8 The LORD will K your going out and your
132:12 If your sons K my covenant and my testimonies
141:3 my mouth, O LORD, K watch over the door
141:9 K me from the trap which they have laid
Prov 2:20 of good men and K to the paths of
3:1 but let your heart K my commandments;
3:21 My son, K sound wisdom and discretion; let them
3:26 your confidence and will K your foot from being
4:5 hold fast my words; K my commandments, and live;
4:7 her, and she will K you, love her, and
4:14 K hold of instruction, do not let go; guard
4:22 escape from your sight; K them within your heart.
4:24 K your heart with all vigilance; for from it
5:2 understanding; that you may K discretion, and your
5:8 K your way far from her, and do not
6:20 My son, K your father's commandment, and forsake
7:1 My son, K my words and treasure up my
7:2 my commandments with you; K my commandments
7:2 my commandments and live, K my teachings as the
8:32 happy are those who K my ways.
20:3 for a man to K aloof from strife; but
22:5 who guards himself will K far from them.
22:12 eyes of the LORD K watch over knowledge, but
22:18 be pleasant if you K them within you, if
28:4 wicked, but those who K the law strive against
Eccl 2:10 desired I did not K from them; I kept
3:6 lose; a time to K, and a time to
3:7 sew; a time to K silence, and a time
8:2 K the king's command, and because of your sacred
12:13 Fear God, and K his commandments; for this is
Wis 1:11 of useless murmuring, and K your tongue from
6:4 not rule rightly, nor K the law, nor walk
13:7 among his works they K searching, and they trust
14:24 customs, they no longer K either their lives or
Sir 1:23 If you desire wisdom, K the commandments, and the
1:26 in men's sight, and K watch over your lips.
2:15 who love him will K his ways.
4:1 living, and do not K needy eyes waiting.
6:13 K yourself far from your enemies, and be on
6:18 are old you will K finding wisdom.
6:26 all your soul, and K her ways with all
7:22 are profitable to you, K them.
8:17 not be able to K a secret.
9:13 K far from a man who has the power
11:19 in the Lord and K at your toil; for
13:12 he who does not K words to himself; he
13:13 K words to yourself and be very watchful, for
15:15 you will, you can K the commandments, and to
17:17 Lord, and he will K a person's kindness like
22:25 lips, that it may K me from falling, so
26:10 K strict watch over a headstrong daughter, lest, when
26:20 A merchant can hardly K from wrongdoing, and a
27:17 Love your friend and K faith with him; but
27:22 and no one can K him from them.
29:3 Confirm your word and K faith with him, and
35:3 To K from wickedness is pleasing to the Lord,
38:34 But they K stable the fabric of the world,
42:11 K strict watch over a headstrong daughter, lest she
Is 7:21 day a man will K alive a young cow
10:1 and the writers who K writing oppression,

26:3 Thou dost K him in perfect peace, whose mind
33:23 in its place, or K the sail spread out.
45:20 their wooden idols, and K on praying to a
56:1 Thus says the LORD: K justice, and do righteousness,
56:4 "To the eunuchs who K my sabbaths, who choose
62:1 sake I will not K silent, and for Jerusalem's
64:12 Wilt thou K silent, and afflict us sorely?
65:5 their vessels; who say, K to yourself, do not
65:6 me: "I will not K silent, but I will
Jer 2:25 K your feet from going unshod and your throat
4:19 beating wildly; I cannot K silent; for I hear
8:7 turtledove, swallow, and crane K the time of their
15:6 says the LORD, you K going backward; so I
17:22 do any work, but K the sabbath day holy,
17:24 the sabbath day, but K the sabbath day holy
17:27 listen to me, to K the sabbath day holy,
31:10 gather him, and will K him as a shepherd
31:16 Thus says the LORD: K your voice from weeping,
34:18 covenant and did not K the terms of the
42:4 tell you; I will K nothing back from you."
49:11 fatherless children, I will K them alive; and let
Lam 4:22 is accomplished, he will K you in exile no
Bar 6:35 them and does not K it, they will not
Ezek 11:20 in my statutes and K my ordinances and obey
13:18 to my people, and K other souls alive for
33:24 the land of Israel K saying, 'Abraham was only
38:7 "Be ready and K ready, you and all the
44:8 have set foreigners to K my charge in my
44:14 will appoint them to K charge of the temple,
44:16 me, and they shall K my charge.
44:24 They shall K my laws and my statutes in
44:24 feasts, and they shall K my sabbaths holy.
46:17 only his sons may K a gift from his
Dan 9:4 who love him and K his commandments,
Amos 5:13 who is prudent will K silent in such a
Nah 1:15 K your feasts, O Judah, fulfil your vows, for
Hab 1:17 Is he then to K on emptying his net,
2:20 let all the earth K silence before him.
Zech 3:7 in my ways and K my charge, then you
11:12 wages; but if not, K them." And they weighed
14:16 of hosts, and to K the feast of booths.
14:18 not go up to K the feast of booths.
14:19 not go up to K the feast of booths.
1Mac 4:60 towers round about, to K the Gentiles from coming
8:26 decided; and they shall K their obligations without
8:28 decided; and they shall K these obligations and do
10:20 take our side and K friendship with us."
10:27 now continue still to K faith with us, and
12:27 be alert and to K their arms at hand
2Mac 1:9 now see that you K the feast of booths
2:16 Will you therefore please K the days?
3:15 deposits, that he should K them safe for those
3:22 Lord that he would K what had been entrusted
6:6 A man could neither K the sabbath, nor observe
7:17 K on, and see how his mighty power will
9:25 to my kingdom K watching for opportunities and
10:15 Jerusalem, and endeavored to K up the war.
12:42 exhorted the people to K themselves free from sin,
14:36 Lord of all holiness, K undefiled for ever this
15:8 the Gentiles, but to K in mind the former
Mt 19:17 you would enter life, K the commandments."
26:18 at hand; I will K the passover at your
28:14 will satisfy him and K you out of trouble."
Mk 7:9 God, in order to K your tradition!
Lk 11:28 word of God and K it!"
Jn 8:55 know him and I K his word.
9:16 for he does not K the sabbath." But others
10:24 "How long will you K us in suspense?
12:7 her alone, let her K it for the day
12:25 in this world will K it for eternal life.
12:47 sayings and does not K them, I do not
14:15 love me, you will K my commandments.
14:23 loves me, he will K my word, and my
14:24 love me does not K my words; and the
15:10 If you K my commandments, you will abide in
15:20 my word, they will K yours also.
16:1 this to you to K you from falling away.
17:11 Holy Father, K them in thy name, which thou
17:15 but that thou shouldst K them from the evil
Acts 5:3 Holy Spirit and to K back part of the
5:38 case I tell you, K away from these men
7:53 angels and did not K it."
15:5 to charge them to K the law of Moses."
15:29 If you K yourselves from these, you will do
16:23 charging the jailer to K them safely.
Rom 2:27 are physically uncircumcised but K the law will
14:22 faith that you have, K between yourself and God;
1Cor 7:37 in his heart, to K her as his betrothed,
14:28 let each of them K silence in church and
14:34 saints, the women should K silence in the churches.
2Cor 2:11 presence of Christ, to K Satan from gaining the
4:4 of the unbelievers, to K them from seeing the
10:13 beyond limit, but will K to the limits God
12:7 And to K me from being too elated by
12:7 to harass me, to K me from being too
Gal 5:3 he is bound to K the whole law.
6:13 circumcision do not themselves K the law, but they
Eph 6:18 To that end K alert with all perseverance, making
Phil 4:7 passes all understanding, will K your hearts and your
1Thes 5:6 do, but let us K awake and be sober.
2Thes 3:6 Jesus Christ, that you K away from any brother
1Tim 2:12 men; she is to K silent.
5:21 I charge you to K these rules without favor,
5:22 in another man's sins; K yourself pure.
6:14 I charge you to K the commandment unstained and
Philem 1:13 have been glad to K him with me, in
Heb 10:39 who have faith and K their souls.
13:5 K your life free from love of money, and
Jas 1:26 their affliction, and to K oneself unstained from the
1Pet 3:10 good days, let him K his tongue from evil
3:16 gentleness and reverence; and K your conscience
4:7 is at hand; therefore K sane and sober for
2Pet 1:8 yours and abound, they K you from being ineffective
2:9 from trial, and to K the unrighteous under
1Jn 2:3 know him, if we K his commandments.
3:22 we ask, because we K his commandments and do
3:24 All who K his commandments abide in him, and
5:3 of God, that we K his commandments.
5:21 Little children, K yourselves from idols.
Jude 1:6 angels that did not K their own position but
1:21 in the Holy Spirit; K yourselves in the love
1:24 who is able to K you from falling and
Rev 1:3 who hear, and who K what is written therein;
3:3 you received and heard; K that, and repent.
3:10 patient endurance, I will K you from the hour
3:18 clothe you and to K the shame of your
12:17 offspring, on those who K the commandments of God
14:12 the saints, those who K the commandments of God
22:9 and with those who K the words of this

KEEPER (19)

Gen 4:2 Now Abel was a K of sheep, and Cain
4:9 "I do not know; am I my brother's K
39:21 the sight of the K of the prison.
39:22 And the K of the prison committed to Joseph's
39:23 doer of it; the K of the prison paid
1Sam 17:20 the sheep with a K, and took the provisions,
17:22 in charge of the K of the baggage, and
2Kgs 22:14 Tikvah, son of Harhas, K of the wardrobe (now
2Chr 31:14 of Imnah the Levite, K of the east gate,
34:22 Tokhath, son of Hasrah, K of the wardrobe (now
Neh 2:8 letter to Asaph, the K of the king's forest,
3:29 son of Shecaniah, the K of the East Gate,
Tob 1:22 Now Ahikar was cupbearer, K of the signet, and
Ps 121:5 The LORD is your K; the LORD is your
Song 1:6 me, they made me K of the vineyards; but,
Sir 37:12 know to be a K of the commandments, whose
Is 27:3 the LORD, am its K; every moment I water
Jer 35:4 the son of Shallum, K of the threshold.
Acts 19:35 the Ephesians is temple K of the great Artemis,

KEEPERS (13)

Gen 46:32 for they have been K of cattle; and they
46:34 'Your servants have been K of cattle from our
2Kgs 22:4 the LORD, which the K of the threshold have
23:4 second order, and the K of the threshold, to
25:18 priest, and the three K of the threshold;
1Chr 9:19 work of the service, K of the thresholds of
9:19 camp of the LORD, K of the entrance.
2Chr 34:9 which the Levites, the K of the threshold, had
Eccl 12:3 the day when the K of the house tremble,
Song 8:11 out the vineyard to K; each one was to
8:12 the thousand, and the K of the fruit two
Jer 4:17 Like K of a field are they against her
52:24 priest, and the three K of the threshold;

KEEPEST (2)

Neh 9:32 and terrible God, who K covenant and steadfast love,
Dan 9:4 and terrible God, who K covenant and steadfast love

KEEPING (48)

Ex 3:1 Now Moses was K the flock of his father-in-law,

34:7 steadfast love and faithfulness, K steadfast love for
Num 9:13 journey, yet refrains from K the passover, that person
Deut 6:2 your son's son, by K all his statutes and
7:8 loves you, and is K the oath which he
8:11 your God, by not K his commandments and his
13:18 the LORD your God, K all his commandments which
17:19 LORD his God, by K all the words of
27:10 the LORD your God, K his commandments and his
30:16 his ways, and by K his commandments and his
1Sam 16:11 but behold, he is K the sheep." And Samuel
25:16 we were with them K the sheep.
1Kgs 2:3 in his ways and K his statutes, his commandments,
3:14 walk in my ways, K my statutes and my
8:23 or on earth beneath, K covenant and showing
8:61 in his statutes and K his commandments, as at
9:4 have commanded you, and K my statutes and my
11:33 in my sight and K my statutes and my
11:38 in my eyes by K my statutes and my
1Chr 28:7 he continues resolute in K my commandments and
2Chr 6:14 heaven or on earth, K covenant and showing
7:17 have commanded you and K my statutes and my
31:18 they were faithful in K themselves holy.
Jud 8:26 Syria, while he was K the sheep of Laban,
Ps 19:11 thy servant warned; in K them there is great
42:4 of thanksgiving, a multitude K festival.
119:5 may be steadfast in K thy statutes!
Prov 15:3 are in every place, K watch on the evil
Wis 6:18 of her is the K of her laws, and
Sir 20:4 is one who by K silent is found wise,
32:23 for this is the K of the commandments.
42:3 acquit the ungodly; of K accounts with a partner
Ezek 13:19 should not die and K alive persons who should
17:14 up, and that by K his covenant it might
Mal 3:14 the good of our K his charge or of
1Mac 10:54 and to her in K with your position."
2Mac 8:17 but to fight nobly, K before their eyes the
14:6 is Judas Maccabeus, are K up war and stirring
15:3 who had commanded the K of the sabbath day.
Mt 27:54 who were with him, K watch over Jesus, saw
Lk 2:8 out in the field, K watch over their flock
17:7 a servant plowing or K sheep, say to him
Acts 10:30 this hour, I was K the ninth hour of
22:20 by and approving, and K the garments of those
1Cor 7:19 nor uncircumcision, but K the commandments of God
1Tim 3:4 his own household well, K his children submissive
Heb 13:17 them; for they are K watch over your souls,
Rev 16:15 he who is awake, K his garments that he

KEEPS (54)

Ex 21:18 does not die but K his bed,
Deut 7:9 the faithful God who K covenant and steadfast love
Neh 1:5 and terrible God who K covenant and steadfast love
Tob 4:10 delivers from death and K you from entering the
Job 33:18 pride from man; he K back his soul from
Ps 34:20 He K all his bones; not one of them
41:2 LORD protects him and K him alive; he is
119:129 wonderful; therefore my soul K them.
119:167 My soul K thy testimonies; I love them exceedingly.
121:3 be moved, he who K you will not slumber.
121:4 Behold, he who K Israel will neither slumber nor
146:6 is in them; who K faith for ever;
Prov 11:5 righteousness of the blameless K his way straight,
11:13 is trustworthy in spirit K a thing hidden.
17:28 Even a fool who K silent is considered wise;
19:8 loves himself; he who K understanding will prosper.
19:16 He who K the commandment keeps his life; he
19:16 who keeps the commandment K his life; he who
21:23 He who K his mouth and his tongue keeps
21:23 mouth and his tongue K himself out of trouble.
24:12 Does not he who K watch over your soul
28:7 He who K the law is a wise son,
29:3 glad, but one who K company with harlots squanders
29:18 blessed is he who K the law.
Eccl 5:20 his life because God K him occupied with joy
Sir 20:1 is a man who K silent but is wise.
20:5 There is one who K silent because he has
20:5 no answer, while another K silent because he knows
21:11 Whoever K the law controls his thoughts, and
29:1 him with his hand K the commandments.
35:1 He who K the law makes many offerings; he
37:14 a man's soul sometimes K him better informed than
42:9 A daughter K her father secretly wakeful, and worry
Is 26:2 the righteous nation which K faith may enter in.
56:2 holds it fast, who K the sabbath, not profaning
56:2 not profaning it, and K his hand from doing
56:6 servants, every one who K the sabbath, and does
Jer 5:24 the spring rain, and K for us the weeks
6:7 As a well K its water fresh, so she
6:7 water fresh, so she K fresh her wickedness; violence
31:10 him as a shepherd K his flock.'
48:10 cursed is he who K back his sword from
Ezek 18:21 he has committed and K all my statutes and
Nah 1:2 on his adversaries and K wrath for his enemies.
Jn 7:19 Yet none of you K the law.
8:51 you, if any one K my word, he will
8:52 say, 'If any one K my word, he will
14:21 has my commandments and K them, he it is
Rom 2:26 man who is uncircumcised K the precepts of the
Jas 2:10 For whoever K the whole law but fails in
1Jn 2:5 in him; but whoever K his word, in him
5:18 was born of God K him, and the evil
Rev 2:26 who conquers and who K my works until the
22:7 Blessed is he who K the words of the

KEHELATHAH (2)

Num 33:22 they set out from Rissah, and encamped at K
33:23 they set out from K, and encamped at Mount

KEILAH (18)

Josh 15:44 Iphtah, Ashnah, Nezib, K, Achzib, and Mareshah:
1Sam 23:1 Philistines are fighting against K, and are robbing
23:2 David, "Go and attack the Philistines and save K
23:3 if we go to K against the armies of
23:4 "Arise, go down to K; for I will give
23:5 his men went to K, and fought with the
23:5 So David delivered the inhabitants of K
23:6 fled to David to K, he came down with
23:7 was told Saul that David had come to K
23:8 to go down to K, to besiege David and
23:10 seeks to come to K, to destroy the city
23:11 Will the men of K surrender me into his
23:12 "Will the men of K surrender me and my
23:13 arose and departed from K, and they went wherever
23:13 David had escaped from K, he gave up the
1Chr 4:19 were the fathers of K the Garmite and Eshtemoa
Neh 3:17 half the district of K, repaired for his district.
3:18 half the district of K;

KELAIAH

Ezra 10:23 the Levites: Jozabad, Shimei, K (that is, Kelita),

KELITA (3)

Ezra 10:23 Shimei, Kelaiah (that is, K, Pethahiah, Judah, and
Neh 8:7 Akkub, Shabbethai, Hodiah, Ma-aseiah, K, Azariah,
10:10 their brethren, Shebaniah, Hodiah, K, Pelaiah,

KEMUEL (3)

Gen 22:21 first-born, Buz his brother, K the father of Aram,
Num 34:24 of Ephraim a leader, K the son of Shiphtan.
1Chr 27:17 Hashabiah the son of K; for Aaron, Zadok;

KENAN (6)

Gen 5:9 lived ninety years, he became the father of K
5:10 after the birth of K eight hundred and fifteen
5:12 When K had lived seventy years, he became the
5:13 K lived after the birth of Mahalalel eight hundred
5:14 all the days of K were nine hundred and
1Chr 1:2 Adam, Seth, Enosh; K, Mahalalel, Jared,

KENATH (2)

Num 32:42 Nobah went and took K and its villages, and
1Chr 2:23 took from them Havvoth-jair, K and its villages, sixty

KENAZ (11)

Gen 36:11 of Eliphaz were Teman, Omar, Zepho, Gatam, and K
36:15 chiefs Teman, Omar, Zepho, K,
36:42 Oholibamah, Elah, Pinon, K, Teman, Mibzar,
Josh 15:17 Othni-el the son of K, the brother of Caleb,
Judg 1:13 Othni-el the son of K, Caleb's younger brother, took
3:9 Othni-el the son of K, Caleb's younger brother.
3:11 Othni-el the son of K died.
1Chr 1:36 Teman, Omar, Zephi, Gatam, K, Timna, and Amalek.
1:53 Oholibamah, Elah, Pinon, K, Teman, Mibzar,
4:13 The sons of K: Othni-el and Seraiah; and the
4:15 Elah, and Naam; and the sons of Elah: K

KENITE (6)

Num 24:21 he looked on the K, and took up his
Judg 1:16 the descendants of the K, Moses' father-in-law, went
4:11 Now Heber the K had separated from the Kenites,
4:17 wife of Heber the K; for there was peace
4:17 of Hazor and the house of Heber the K

K

5:24 wife of Heber the K, of tent-dwelling women most

KENITES (7)

Gen 15:19 the land of the K, the Kenizzites, the Kadmonites,
Judg 4:11 had separated from the K, the descendants of Hobab
1Sam 15:6 Saul said to the K, "Go, depart, go down
15:6 So the K departed from among the Amalekites.
27:10 or, "Against the Negeb of the K
30:29 the cities of the K,
1Chr 2:55 These are the K who came from Hammath, the

KENIZZITE (3)

Num 32:12 son of Jephunneh the K and Joshua the son
Josh 14:6 son of Jephunneh the K said to him, "You
14:14 son of Jephunneh the K to this day, because

KENIZZITES

Gen 15:19 of the Kenites, the K, the Kadmonites,

KEPT (216)

Gen 20:6 it was I who K you from sinning against
26:5 obeyed my voice and K my charge, my
29:9 father's sheep; for she K them.
37:11 him, but his father K the saying in mind.
39:9 am; nor has he K back anything from me
50:20 many people should be K alive, as they are
Ex 12:42 a night of watching K to the LORD by
16:23 lay by to be K till the morning.'"
16:32 omer of it be K throughout your generations, that
16:33 the LORD, to be K throughout your generations."
16:34 Aaron placed it before the testimony, to be K
21:29 warned but has not K it in, and it
21:36 its owner has not K it in, he shall
36:3 They still K bringing him freewill offerings every
Lev 6:9 the altar shall be K burning on it.
6:12 the altar shall be K burning on it, it
6:13 Fire shall be K burning upon the altar continually;
24:2 a light may be K burning continually.
26:10 eat old store long K, and you shall clear
Num 9:5 And they K the passover in the first month,
9:7 man; why are we K from offering the LORD's
9:19 the people of Israel K the charge of the
9:23 they set out; they K the charge of the
17:10 the testimony, to be K as a sign for
18:8 given you whatever is K of the offerings made
19:9 and they shall be K for the congregation of
Deut 32:10 cared for him, he K him as the apple
33:9 observed thy word, and K thy covenant.
Josh 5:10 encamped in Gilgal they K the passover on the
14:10 behold, the LORD has K me alive, as he
22:2 to them, "You have K all that Moses the
Judg 5:6 caravans ceased and travelers K to the byways.
16:2 They K quiet all night, saying, "Let us wait
Ruth 2:23 So she K close to the maidens of Boaz,
1Sam 9:24 said, "See, what was K is set before you.
9:24 Eat; because it was K for you until the
13:13 foolishly; you have not K the commandment of the
13:14 because you have not K what the LORD commanded
21:4 the young men have K themselves from women."
21:5 truth women have been K from us as always
25:33 be you, who have K me this day from
25:39 of Nabal, and has K back his servant from
26:15 then have you not K watch over your lord
26:16 because you have not K watch over your lord,
2Sam 13:34 the young man who K the watch lifted up
15:12 the people with Absalom K increasing.
22:22 For I have K the ways of the LORD,
22:24 before him, and I K myself from guilt.
1Kgs 2:43 then have you not K your oath to the
3:6 thee; and thou hast K for him this great
8:24 their heart; who hast K with thy servant David
11:11 and you have not K my covenant and my
11:34 whom I chose, who K my commandments and my
13:21 LORD, and have not K the commandment which the
14:8 my servant David, who K my commandments, and
14:27 of the guard, who K the door of the
2Kgs 18:6 from following him, but K the commandments which
23:22 such passover had been K since the days of
23:23 Josiah this passover was K to the LORD in
1Chr 4:33 their settlements, and they K a genealogical record.
12:22 day to day men K coming to David to
12:29 the majority had hitherto K their allegiance to the
2Chr 6:15 their heart; who hast K with thy servant David
7:9 assembly; for they had K the dedication of the
12:10 of the guard, who K the door of the
30:5 for they had not K it in great numbers
30:21 were present at Jerusalem K the feast of unleavened
30:23 seven days; so they K it for another seven
34:21 our fathers have not K the word of the
35:1 Josiah K a passover to the LORD in Jerusalem;
35:17 Israel who were present K the passover at that
35:18 like it had been K in Israel since the
35:18 kings of Israel had K such a passover as
35:18 a passover as was K by Josiah, and the
35:19 of the reign of Josiah this passover was K
36:16 dwelling place; but they K mocking the messengers
36:21 it lay desolate it K sabbath, to fulfil seventy
Ezra 3:4 And they K the feast of booths, as it
6:19 month the returned exiles K the passover.
6:22 And they K the feast of unleavened bread seven
Neh 1:7 thee, and have not K the commandments, the
4:23 off our clothes; each K his weapon in his
8:18 They K the feast seven days; and on the
9:34 our fathers have not K thy law or heeded
11:19 and their brethren, who K watch at the gates,
Tob 1:11 the Gentiles; but I K myself from eating it,
Jud 6:12 and all the slingers K them from coming up
12:1 his silver dishes were K, and ordered them to
Esth 9:28 should be remembered and K throughout every
12:1 of the king who K watch in the courtyard.
Job 21:32 the grave, watch is K over his tomb.
23:11 his steps; I have K his way and have
24:1 not times of judgment K by the Almighty, and
29:21 me, and waited, and K silence for my counsel.
31:34 me, so that I K silence, and did not
Ps 18:21 For I have K the ways of the LORD,
18:23 before him, and I K myself from guilt.
56:8 Thou hast K count of my tossings; put thou
66:9 be heard, who has K us among the living,
73:13 in vain have I K my heart clean and
99:7 pillar of cloud; they K his testimonies, and the
116:10 I K my faith, even when I said, "I
119:4 thy precepts to be K diligently.
119:22 contempt, for I have K thy testimonies.
119:56 me, that I have K thy precepts.
Eccl 2:10 keep from them; I K my heart from no
5:13 the sun: riches were K by their owner to
Song 1:6 vineyards; but, my own vineyard I have not K
Wis 4:17 and for what he K him safe.
10:5 blameless before God, and K him strong in the
10:12 from his enemies, and K him safe from those
14:16 strong with time, was K as a law, and
17:16 down, and thus was K shut up in a
18:4 darkness, those who had K thy sons imprisoned,
19:6 thy children might be K unharmed.
Sir 3:1 that you may be K in safety.
8:18 that is to be K secret, for you do
20:2 his fault will be K from loss.
44:21 him in glory; he K the law of the
Is 30:29 a holy feast is K; and gladness of heart,
42:6 by the hand and K you; I have given
42:14 my peace, I have K still and restrained myself;
49:8 helped you; I have K you and given you
Jer 5:25 and your sins have K good from you.
16:11 me and have not K my law,
35:14 no wine, has been K; and they drink none
35:16 son of Rechab have K the command which their
35:18 Jonadab your father, and K all his precepts, and
Bar 2:9 And the Lord has K the calamities ready, and
Ezek 5:7 in my statutes or K my ordinances, but have
44:8 And you have not K charge of my holy
44:15 sons of Zadok, who K the charge of my
48:11 sons of Zadok, who K my charge, who did
Dan 5:19 whom he would he K alive; whom he would
7:28 color changed; but I K the matter in my
9:14 Therefore the LORD has K ready the calamity and
Hos 11:2 went from me; they K sacrificing to the Baals,
13:12 up, his sin is K in store.
Amos 1:11 tore perpetually, and he K his wrath for ever.
2:4 LORD, and have not K his statutes, but their
Mic 6:16 For you have K the statutes of Omri, and
Mal 2:9 as you have not K my ways but have
3:7 statutes and have not K them.
1Mac 1:58 They K using violence against Israel, against those
2:53 time of his distress K the commandment, and
5:3 at Akrabattene, because they K lying in wait for
5:53 And Judas K rallying the laggards and encouraging
6:18 men in the citadel K hemming Israel in around
7:45 and as they followed K sounding the battle call
8:12 on them they have K friendship.
10:26 Since you have K your agreement with us and
11:5 him; but the king K silent.

11:8 the sea, and he K devising evil designs against
11:25 men of his nation K making complaints against him,
11:41 the strongholds; for they K fighting against Israel.
12:40 on him, so he K seeking to seize and
12:47 He K with himself three thousand men, two thousand
12:50 encouraged one another and K marching in close
13:20 Simon and his army K marching along opposite him
13:21 men in the citadel K sending envoys to Trypho
15:25 shut Trypho up and K him from going out
2Mac 2:12 Likewise Solomon also K the eight days.
3:19 the maidens who were K indoors ran together to
4:28 captain of the citadel K requesting payment, for the
5:6 Jason K relentlessly slaughtering his fellow citizens,
5:27 to the wilderness, and K himself and his companions
6:11 together, because their piety K them from defending
8:27 of their spoils, they K the sabbath, giving great
10:14 and at every turn K on warring against the
10:30 armor and weapons, they K him from being
12:38 the custom, and they K the sabbath there.
14:4 During that day he K quiet.
14:24 And he K Judas always in his presence; he
15:34 is he who has K his own place undefiled."
Mt 27:36 they sat down and K watch over him there.
Mk 6:20 and holy man, and K him safe.
9:10 So they K the matter to themselves, questioning
Lk 2:19 But Mary K all these things, pondering them in
2:51 them; and his mother K all these things in
4:42 him, and would have K him from leaving them;
8:29 seized him; he was K under guard, and bound
9:36 And they K silence and told no one in
18:3 in that city who K coming to him and
19:20 your pound, which I K laid away in a
24:16 But their eyes were K from recognizing him.
Jn 2:10 wine; but you have K the good wine until
11:37 the blind man have K this man from dying?"
15:10 just as I have K my Father's commandments and
15:20 persecute you; if they K my word, they will
17:6 me, and they have K thy word
17:12 was with them, I K them in thy name,
18:16 to the maid who K the door, and brought
18:17 The maid who K the door said to Peter,
Acts 5:2 his wife's knowledge he K back some of the
7:19 they might not be K alive.
12:5 So Peter was K in prison; but earnest prayer
15:12 And all the assembly K silence; and they listened
24:22 that he should be K in custody but should
25:4 that Paul was being K at Caesarea, and that
25:21 had appealed to be K in custody for the
27:43 wishing to save Paul, K them from carrying out
Rom 11:4 "I have K for myself seven thousand men who
16:24 the mystery which was K secret for long ages
Gal 3:23 confined under the law, K under restraint until faith
1Thes 5:23 soul and body be K sound and blameless at
2Tim 4:7 the race, I have K the faith.
Heb 11:28 By faith he K the Passover and sprinkled the
Jas 5:4 your fields, which you K back by fraud, cry
1Pet 1:4 undefiled, and unfading, K in heaven for you,
2Pet 2:4 nether gloom to be K until the judgment;
3:7 up for fire, being K until the day of
Jude 1:1 God the Father and K for Jesus Christ:
1:6 proper dwelling have been K by him in eternal
Rev 3:8 and yet you have K my word and have
3:10 Because you have K my word of patient endurance,
8:12 of the day was K from shining, and likewise

KEREN-HAPPUCH

Job 42:14 second Keziah; and the name of the third K

KERIOTH (2)

Jer 48:24 Beth-gamul, and Beth-meon, and K, and Bozrah, and
Amos 2:2 devour the strongholds of K, and Moab shall die

KERIOTH-HEZRON

Josh 15:25 Ziph, Telem, Bealoth, Hazor-hadattah, K (that is,

KERNEL

1Cor 15:37 be, but a bare K, perhaps of wheat or

KEROS (2)

Ezra 2:44 Tabbaoth, the sons of K, the sons of Siaha,
Neh 7:47 Tabbaoth, the sons of K, the sons of Sia,

KETTLE (3)

1Sam 2:14 into the pan, or K, or caldron, or pot;
Sir 13:2 can the clay pot associate with the iron K
Mic 3:3 like meat in a K, like flesh in a

KETURAH (4)

Gen 25:1 Abraham took another wife, whose name was K
25:4 All these were the children of K
1Chr 1:32 The sons of K, Abraham's concubine: she bore
1:33 All these were the descendants of K

KEY (7)

Judg 3:25 chamber, they took the K and opened them; and
Is 22:22 on his shoulder the K of the house of
2Mac 14:22 men in readiness at K places to prevent sudden
Lk 11:52 have taken away the K of knowledge; you did
Rev 3:7 one, who has the K of David, who opens
9:1 he was given the K of the shaft of
20:1 in his hand the K of the bottomless pit

KEYS (2)

Mt 16:19 will give you the K of the kingdom of
Rev 1:18 and I have the K of Death and Hades.

KEZIAH

Job 42:14 name of the second K; and the name of

KIBROTH-HATTAAVAH (5)

Num 11:34 that place was called K, because there they buried
11:35 From K the people journeyed to Hazeroth; and they
33:16 from the wilderness of Sinai, and encamped at K
33:17 they set out from K, and encamped at Hazeroth.
Deut 9:22 at Massah, and at K, you provoked the LORD

KIBZA-IM

Josh 21:22 with its pasture lands, K with its pasture lands,

KICK

Acts 26:14 It hurts you to K against the goads.'

KICKED

Deut 32:15 Jeshurun waxed fat, and K; you waxed fat, you

KID (16)

Gen 38:17 will send you a K from the flock." And
38:20 When Judah sent the K by his friend the
38:23 see, I sent this K, and you could not
Ex 23:19 shall not boil a K in its mother's milk.
34:26 shall not boil a K in its mother's milk."
Deut 14:21 shall not boil a K in its mother's milk.
Judg 6:19 house and prepared a K, and unleavened cakes from
13:15 you, and prepare a K for you."
13:19 So Manoah took the K with the cereal offering,
14:6 as one tears a K; and he had nothing
15:1 his wife with a K; and he said, "I
1Sam 16:20 of wine and a K, and sent them by
Tob 2:12 also gave her a K;
2:13 said to her, "Where did you get the K
Is 11:6 lie down with the K, and the calf and
Lk 15:29 never gave me a K, that I might make

KIDNAPERS

1Tim 1:10 manslayers, immoral persons, sodomites, K, liars,

KIDNEYS (18)

Ex 29:13 liver, and the two K with the fat that
29:22 liver, and the two K with the fat that
Lev 3:4 entrails, and the two K with the fat that
3:4 liver which he shall take away with the K
3:10 entrails, and the two K with the fat that
3:10 liver which he shall take away with the K
3:15 entrails, and the two K with the fat that
3:15 liver which he shall take away with the K
4:9 entrails, and the two K with the fat that
4:9 take away with the K
7:4 the entrails, the two K with the fat that
7:4 take away with the K;
8:16 liver, and the two K with their fat, and
8:25 liver, and the two K with their fat, and
9:10 the fat and the K and the appendage of
9:19 the entrails, and the K, and the appendage of
Job 16:13 He slashes open my K, and does not spare;
Is 34:6 the fat of the K of rams.

KIDRON (12)

2Sam 15:23 king crossed the brook K, and all the people
1Kgs 2:37 and cross the brook K, know for certain that
15:13 her image and burned it at the brook K
2Kgs 23:4 the fields of the K, and carried their ashes
23:6 Jerusalem, to the brook K, and burned it at
23:6 it at the brook K, and beat it to

K

23:12 cast the dust of them into the brook K
2Chr 15:16 crushed it, and burned it at the brook K
29:16 it and carried it out to the brook K
30:14 and threw into the K valley.
Jer 31:40 far as the brook K, to the corner of
Jn 18:1 his disciples across the K valley, where there was

KIDS (9)
Gen 27:9 fetch me two good K, that I may prepare
27:16 the skins of the K she put upon his
Num 15:11 for each of the male lambs or the K
1Sam 10:3 there, one carrying three K, another carrying three
2Chr 35:7 were present, lambs and K from the flock to
35:8 six hundred lambs and K and three hundred bulls.
35:9 five thousand lambs and K and five hundred bulls.
Song 1:8 flock, and pasture your K beside the shepherds' tents.
Is 5:17 their pasture, fatlings and K shall feed among the

KILL (174)
Gen 4:15 came upon him should K him.
12:12 wife'; then they will K me, but they will
20:11 place, and they will K me because of my
26:7 of the place should K me for the sake
27:41 approaching; then I will K my brother Jacob."
27:42 himself by planning to K you.
37:18 conspired against him to K him.
37:20 Come now, let us K him and throw him
Ex 1:15 a son, you shall K him; but if it
2:14 Do you mean to K me as you killed
2:15 it, he sought to K Moses.
4:24 him and sought to K him.
5:21 in their hand to K us."
12:6 congregation of Israel shall K their lambs in the
12:21 to your families, and K the passover lamb.
16:3 into this wilderness to K this whole assembly with
17:3 out of Egypt, to K us and our children
20:13 "You shall not K
21:14 willfully attacks another to K him treacherously, you
22:24 burn, and I will K you with the sword,
29:11 bull, and you shall K the bull before the
29:20 ram, and you shall K the ram, and take
Lev 1:5 Then he shall K the bull before the LORD;
1:11 blemish; and he shall K it on the north
3:2 of his offering and K it at the door
3:13 upon its head, and K it before the tent
4:4 of the bull, and K the bull before the
4:24 of the goat, and K it in the place
4:24 the place where they K the burnt offering before
4:29 the sin offering, and K the sin offering in
4:33 the sin offering, and K it for a sin
4:33 the place where they K the burnt offering.
7:2 the place where they K the burnt offering they
7:2 burnt offering they shall K the guilt offering, and
14:5 shall command them to K one of the birds
14:13 LORD; and he shall K the lamb in the
14:13 the place where they K the sin offering and
14:19 And afterward he shall K the burnt offering;
14:25 And he shall K the lamb of the guilt
14:50 and hyssop, and shall K one of the birds
16:11 his house; he shall K the bull as a
16:15 "Then he shall K the goat of the sin
20:15 death; and you shall K the beast.
20:16 with it, you shall K the woman and the
22:28 ewe, you shall not K both her and her
Num 11:15 deal thus with me, K me at once, if
14:15 Now if thou dost K this people as one
16:13 milk and honey, to K us in the wilderness,
22:29 for then I would K you."
31:17 Now therefore, K every male among the little ones,
31:17 the little ones, and K every woman who has
Deut 5:17 "'You shall not K
12:21 you, then you may K any of your herd
13:9 him; but you shall K him; your hand shall
32:39 god beside me; I K and I make alive;
Josh 9:18 of Israel did not K them, because the leaders
9:26 and they did not K them.
Judg 9:54 "Draw your sword and K me, lest men say
13:23 LORD had meant to K us, he would not
15:13 hands; we will not K you." So they bound
16:2 morning; then we will K him."
20:5 night; they meant to K me, and they ravished
20:31 began to smite and K some of the people,
20:39 begun to smite and K about thirty men of
1Sam 15:3 not spare them, but K both man and woman,
16:2 hears it, he will K me." And the LORD
17:9 fight with me and K me, then we will
17:9 prevail against him and K him, then you shall
19:1 servants, that they should K David.
19:2 my father seeks to K you; therefore take heed
19:11 him, that he might K him in the morning.
19:15 bed, that I may K him."
19:17 go; why should I K you?"
22:17 about him, "Turn and K the priests of the
24:10 and some bade me K you, but I spared
24:11 robe, and did not K you, you may know
24:18 that you did not K me when the LORD
30:15 that you will not K me, or deliver me
2Sam 13:28 you, 'Strike Amnon,' then K him.
14:7 brother, that we may K him for the life
14:32 in me, let him K me.'"
21:16 new sword, thought to K David.
1Kgs 11:40 Solomon sought therefore to K Jeroboam; but
12:27 Judah, and they will K me and return to
18:9 hand of Ahab, to K me?
18:12 find you, he will K me, although I your
18:14 here'"; and he will K me."
20:36 me, a lion shall K you." And as soon
2Kgs 5:7 "Am I God, to K and to make alive,
7:4 live, and if they K us we shall but
2Chr 30:17 the Levites had to K the passover lamb for
35:6 And K the passover lamb, and sanctify yourselves,
Neh 4:11 midst of them and K them and stop the
6:10 they are coming to K you, at night they
6:10 they are coming to K you."
Jud 1:12 Syria, that he would K them by the sword,
11:12 they have planned to K their cattle and have
16:5 up my territory, and K my young men with
Job 20:16 of a viper will K him.
24:14 dark, that he may K the poor and needy;
Eccl 3:3 planted; a time to K, and a time to
Wis 11:19 sight of them could K by fright.
14:23 For whether they K children in their initiations, or
14:24 they either treacherously K one another, or grieve
18:5 they had resolved to K the babes of thy
Sir 9:13 has the power to K, and you will not
47:4 youth did he not K a giant, and take
Is 14:30 safety; but I will K your root with famine,
Jer 20:17 because he did not K me in the womb;
41:8 to Ishmael, "Do not K us, for we have
41:8 refrained and did not K them with their companions.
43:3 Chaldeans, that they may K us or take us
Dan 14:29 or else we will K you and your household."
1Mac 5:2 So they began to K and destroy among the
9:32 this, he tried to K him.
11:10 he has tried to K me."
11:45 and they wanted to K the king.
12:40 seeking to seize and K him, and he marched
15:40 the people captive and K them.
16:21 has sent men to K you also."
2Mac 4:34 aside, urged him to K Onias.
14:13 off with orders to K Judas and scatter his
Mt 5:21 old, 'You shall not K; and whoever kills shall
10:28 not fear those who K the body but cannot
10:28 the body but cannot K the soul; rather fear
17:22 men, and they will K him, and he will
19:18 said, "You shall not K, You shall not commit
21:38 heir; come, let us K him and have his
23:33 of whom you will K and crucify, and some
26:4 Jesus by stealth and K him.
Mk 3:4 to do harm, to save life or to K
6:19 him, and wanted to K him.
9:31 men, and they will K him; and when he
10:19 commandments: 'Do not K, Do not commit adultery,
10:34 and scourge him, and K him; and after three
12:7 heir; come, let us K him, and the inheritance
14:1 him by stealth, and K him;
Lk 11:49 of whom they will K and persecute,'
12:4 not fear those who K the body, and after
13:31 for Herod wants to K you."
15:23 the fatted calf and K it, and let us
18:20 commit adultery, Do not K, Do not steal, Do
18:33 will scourge him and K him, and on the
20:14 the heir; let us K him, that the inheritance
Jn 5:17 all the more to K him, because he not
7:1 the Jews sought to K him.
7:19 do you seek to K me?"
7:20 Who is seeking to K you?"
7:25 not this the man whom they seek to K
8:22 the Jews, "Will he K himself, since he says,
8:37 yet you seek to K me, because my word
8:40 now you seek to K me, a man who
10:10 only to steal and K and destroy; I came

Acts 5:33 enraged and wanted to K them.
7:28 Do you want to K me as you killed
9:23 the Jews plotted to K him,
9:24 day and night, to K him;
9:29 they were seeking to K him.
10:13 to him, "Rise, Peter; K and eat."
11:7 to me, 'Rise, Peter; K and eat.'
16:27 and was about to K himself, supposing that the
21:31 they were trying to K him, word came to
23:15 we are ready to K him before he comes
25:3 planning an ambush to K him on the way.
26:21 temple and tried to K me.
27:42 soldiers' plan was to K the prisoners, lest any
Rom 13:9 adultery, You shall not K, You shall not steal,
Jas 2:11 said also, "Do not K
2:11 commit adultery but do K, you have become a
4:2 You desire and do not have; so you K
Rev 6:8 of the earth, to K with sword and with
9:5 months, but not to K them, and their torture
9:15 and the year, to K a third of mankind.
11:7 and conquer them and K them,

KILLED (170)

Gen 4:8 his brother Abel, and K him.
34:25 the city unawares, and K all the males.
37:31 took Joseph's robe, and K a goat, and dipped
Ex 2:12 seeing no one he K the Egyptian and hid
2:14 kill me as you K the Egyptian?" Then Moses
Lev 4:15 the bull shall be K before the LORD.
6:25 the burnt offering is K shall the sin offering
6:25 the sin offering be K before the LORD; it
8:15 And Moses K it, and took the blood, and
8:19 And Moses K it, and threw the blood upon
8:23 And Moses K it, and took some of its
9:8 to the altar, and K the calf of the
9:12 And he K the burnt offering; and Aaron's sons
9:15 for the people, and K it, and offered it
9:18 He K the ox also and the ram, the
14:6 the bird that was K over the running water;
14:51 the bird that was K and in the running
Num 16:41 Aaron, saying, "You have K the people of the
31:19 whoever of you has K any person, and whoever
Deut 21:1 is not known who K him,
Josh 7:5 the men of Ai K about thirty-six men of
10:11 the men of Israel K with the sword.
13:22 the people of Israel K with the sword among
20:5 his hand; because he K his neighbor unwittingly,
20:9 that any one who K a person without intent
Judg 3:29 And they K at that time about ten thousand
3:31 son of Anath, who K six hundred of the
7:25 Oreb and Zeeb; they K Oreb at the rock
7:25 Oreb, and Zeeb they K at the wine press
9:45 took the city, and K the people that were
9:54 of me, 'A woman K him.'" And his young
14:19 down to Ashkelon and K thirty men of the
1Sam 14:13 Jonathan, and his armor-bearer K them after him;
17:35 and smote him and K him.
17:36 Your servant has K both lions and bears; and
17:50 struck the Philistine, and K him; there was no
17:51 of its sheath, and K him, and cut off
18:27 with his men, and K two hundred of the
19:11 save your life tonight, tomorrow you will be K
21:9 the Philistine, whom you K in the valley of
22:18 the priests, and he K on that day eighty-five
22:21 David that Saul had K the priests of the
25:11 meat that I have K for my shearers, and
28:24 house, and she quickly K it, and she took
30:2 small and great; they K no one, but carried
2Sam 3:30 Abner, because he had K their brother Asahel in
4:12 young men, and they K them, and cut off
11:21 Who K Abimelech the son of Jerubbesheth?
13:32 suppose that they have K all the young men
14:6 struck the other and K him.
18:15 and struck him, and K him.
21:12 the day the Philistines K Saul on Gilboa;
21:17 attacked the Philistine and K him.
1Kgs 2:34 struck him down and K him; and he was
13:24 on the road and K him.
15:28 So Baasha K him in the third year of
15:29 he was king, he K all the house of
16:10 struck him down and K him, in the twenty-seventh
16:11 on his throne, he K all the house of
16:16 conspired, and he has K the king"; therefore all
18:13 I did when Jezebel K the prophets of the
18:40 the brook Kishon, and K them there.
20:20 And each K his man; the Syrians fled and
20:21 horses and chariots, and K the Syrians with a
20:36 lion met him and K him.
21:19 LORD, "Have you K, and also taken possession?"'
2Kgs 14:5 in his hand he K his servants who had
14:7 He K ten thousand Edomites in the Valley of
15:10 down at Ibleam, and K him, and reigned in
16:9 to Kir, and he K Rezin.
17:25 lions among them, which K some of them.
21:23 conspired against him, and K the king in his
25:25 men, and attacked and K Gedaliah and the Jews
1Chr 19:18 thousand foot soldiers, and K also Shophach the
2Chr 18:2 And Ahab K an abundance of sheep and oxen
21:13 and also you have K your brothers, of your
22:8 attended Ahaziah, and he K them.
24:22 had shown him, but K his son.
25:3 in his hand he K his servants who had
25:13 Samaria to Beth-horon, and K three thousand people
29:22 So they K the bulls, and the priests received
29:22 the altar; and they K the rams and their
29:22 the altar; and they K the lambs and their
29:24 them, and the priests K them and made a
30:15 And they K the passover lamb on the fourteenth
33:24 conspired against him and K him in his house.
35:1 in Jerusalem; and they K the passover lamb on
35:11 And they K the passover lamb, and the priests
Ezra 6:20 So they K the passover lamb for all the
Neh 9:26 behind their back and K thy prophets, who had
Tob 1:21 two of Sennacherib's sons K him, and they fled
7:8 very warmly; and they K a ram from the
Jud 2:25 territory of Cilicia, and K every one who resisted
Prov 1:32 For the simple are K by their turning away,
Wis 16:9 For they were K by the bites of locusts
Jer 41:2 with the sword, and K him, whom the king
1Mac 2:9 Her babes have been K in her streets, her
2:24 anger; he ran and K him upon the altar.
2:25 the same time he K the king's officer who
3:11 and he defeated and K him.
5:13 of Tob have been K; the enemy have captured
5:28 took the city, and K every male by the
5:35 took it; and he K every male in it,
6:45 to reach it; he K men right and left,
6:46 it from beneath, and K it; but it fell
7:4 So the army K them, and Demetrius took his
7:16 sixty of them and K them in one day,
7:19 of the people, and K them and threw them
9:2 they took it and K many people.
9:61 in this treachery, and K them.
9:69 the country, and he K many of them.
11:18 in the strongholds were K by the inhabitants of
11:47 the city; and they K on that day as
12:48 entered with him they K with the sword.
13:23 he approached Baskama, he K Jonathan, and he was
13:31 young king Antiochus; he K him
16:16 banquet hall, and they K him and his two
16:22 to destroy him and K them, for he had
2Mac 4:42 many of them, and K some, and put them
4:42 temple robber himself they K close by the treasury.
5:26 his armed men and K great numbers of people.
8:30 Timothy and Bacchides they K more than twenty
8:32 They K the commander of Timothy's forces, a most
10:37 They K Timothy, who was hidden in a cistern,
12:28 into their hands, and K as many as twenty-five
Mt 2:16 and he sent and K all the male children
16:21 and scribes, and be K, and on the third
21:35 servants and beat one, K another, and stoned another.
21:39 of the vineyard, and K him.
22:4 my fat calves are K, and everything is ready;
22:6 treated them shamefully, and K them.
Mk 8:31 the scribes, and be K, and after three days
9:31 and when he is K, after three days he
12:5 another, and him they K; and so with many
12:5 many others, some they beat and some they K
12:8 they took him and K him, and cast him
Lk 9:22 and scribes, and be K, and on the third
11:47 the tombs of the prophets whom your fathers K
11:48 your fathers; for they K them, and you build
12:5 who, after he has K, has power to cast
13:4 in Siloam fell and K them, do you think
15:27 and your father has K the fatted calf, because
15:30 living with harlots, you K for him the fatted
20:15 of the vineyard and K him.
Acts 2:23 God, you crucified and K by the hands of
3:15 granted to you, and K the Author of life,
5:30 raised Jesus whom you K by hanging him on
7:28 kill me as you K the Egyptian yesterday?'
7:52 And they K those who announced beforehand the

K

12:2 He K James the brother of John with the
13:28 death, yet they asked Pilate to have him K
22:20 garments of those who K him.'
23:12 drink till they had K Paul.
23:14 food till we have K Paul.
23:21 drink till they have K him; and now they
23:27 was about to be K by them, when I
Rom 7:11 me and by it K me.
8:36 sake we are being K all the day long;
11:3 "Lord, they have K thy prophets, they have
2Cor 6:9 punished, and yet not K;
1Thes 2:15 from the Jews, who K both the Lord Jesus
Heb 11:37 in two, they were K with the sword; they
Jas 5:6 have condemned, you have K the righteous man; he
2Pet 2:12 to be caught and K, reviling in matters of
Rev 2:13 faithful one, who was K among you, where Satan
6:11 who were to be K as they themselves had
9:18 third of mankind was K, by the fire and
9:20 mankind, who were not K by these plagues, did
11:5 harm them, thus he is doomed to be K
11:13 seven thousand people were K in the earthquake,

KILLING (12)

Lev 3:8 of his offering and K it before the tent
Judg 9:56 against his father in K his seventy brothers;
1Sam 19:5 against innocent blood by K David without cause?"
2Kgs 17:26 and behold, they are K them, because they do
Is 22:13 gladness, slaying oxen and K sheep, eating flesh and
Hos 4:2 swearing, lying, K, stealing, and committing adultery;
1Mac 2:37 us that you are K us unjustly."
9:40 the ambush and began K them.
2Mac 5:13 Then there was K of young and old, destruction
10:17 those whom they encountered, K no fewer than
Mt 23:36 "O Jerusalem, Jerusalem, K the prophets and
Lk 13:34 Jerusalem.' O Jerusalem, Jerusalem, K the prophets

KILLS (26)

Ex 21:29 it in, and it K a man or a
22:1 or a sheep, and K it or sells it,
Lev 17:3 the house of Israel K an ox or a
17:3 in the camp, or K it outside the camp,
24:17 He who K a man shall be put to
24:18 He who K a beast shall make it good,
24:21 He who K a beast shall make it good;
24:21 good; and he who K a man shall be
Num 35:11 that the manslayer who K any person without intent
35:15 that any one who K any person without intent
35:30 If any one K a person, the murderer shall
Deut 4:42 might flee there, who K his neighbor unintentionally,
19:4 If any one K his neighbor unintentionally without
Josh 20:3 that the manslayer who K any person without intent
1Sam 2:6 The LORD K and brings to life; he brings
17:25 and the man who K him, the king will
17:26 for the man who K this Philistine, and takes
17:27 to the man who K him."
Job 5:2 Surely vexation K the fool, and jealousy slays the
Prov 21:25 desire of the sluggard K him for his hands
Wis 16:14 man in his wickedness K another, but he cannot
Sir 34:20 Like one who K a son before his father's
Is 66:3 is like him who K a man; he who
Mt 5:21 not kill; and whoever K shall be liable to
Jn 16:2 is coming when whoever K you will think he
2Cor 3:6 for the written code K, but the Spirit gives

KILN (4)

Ex 9:8 of ashes from the K, and let Moses throw
9:10 took ashes from the K, and stood before Pharaoh,
19:18 the smoke of a K, and the whole mountain
Sir 27:5 The K tests the potter's vessels; so the test

KIN (18)

Lev 18:6 any one near of K to him to uncover
20:19 make naked one's near K; they shall bear their
21:2 for his nearest of K, his mother, his father,
25:25 then his next of K shall come and redeem
Ruth 2:20 a relative of ours, one of our nearest K
3:9 over your maidservant, for you are next of K
3:13 of the next of K for you, well; let
3:13 of the next of K for you, then, as
3:13 of the next of K for you.
4:1 behold, the next of K, of whom Boaz had
4:3 to the next of K, "Naomi, who has come
4:6 Then the next of K said, "I cannot redeem
4:8 when the next of K said to Boaz, "Buy
4:14 day without next of K; and may his name
2Sam 19:42 king is near of K to us.
Jud 16:24 who were next of K to her husband Manasseh,
Sir 23:16 with his near of K will never cease until
Mk 6:4 and among his own K, and in his own

KINAH

Josh 15:22 were Kabzeel, Eder, Jagur, K, Dimonah, Adadah,

KIND (73)

Gen 1:11 each according to its K, upon the earth." And
1:12 which is their seed, each according to its K
1:21 kinds, and every winged bird according to its K
1:25 that creeps upon the ground according to its K
6:20 ground according to its K, two of every sort
7:3 female, to keep their K alive upon the face
7:14 beast according to its K, and all the cattle
7:14 earth according to its K, and every bird according
7:14 bird according to its K, every bird of every
Ex 22:9 clothing, or for any K of lost thing, of
Lev 11:14 falcon according to its K,
11:15 raven according to its K,
11:16 hawk according to its K,
11:19 heron according to its K, the hoopoe, and the
11:22 locust according to its K, the bald locust according
11:22 locust according to its K, the cricket according to
11:22 cricket according to its K, and the grasshopper
11:22 its kind, and the grasshopper according to its K
11:29 lizard according to its K,
19:19 breed with a different K; you shall not sow
Deut 14:14 every raven after its K;
17:8 requiring decision between one K of homicide and
17:8 homicide and another, one K of legal right and
17:8 and another, or one K of assault and another,
27:21 who lies with any K of beast.' And all
1Kgs 9:13 Therefore he said, "What K of cities are these
2Kgs 1:7 said to them, "What K of man was he
1Chr 28:21 has skill for any K of service; also the
2Chr 10:7 "If you will be K to this people and
34:13 did work in every K of service; and some
Ps 107:18 affliction; they loathed any K of food, and they
145:17 all his ways, and K in all his doings.
Prov 11:17 A man who is K benefits himself, but a
14:21 is he who is K to the poor.
14:31 but he who is K to the needy honors
19:17 He who is K to the poor lends to
28:8 for him who is K to the poor.
Wis 12:19 righteous man must be K, and thou hast filled
15:1 thou, our God, art K and true, patient, and
19:11 saw also a new K of birds, when desire
19:21 the crystalline, easily melted K of heavenly food.
Sir 27:9 Birds flock with their K; so truth returns to
41:16 good to retain every K of shame, and not
Ezek 27:12 great wealth of every K; silver, iron, tin, and
27:18 great wealth of every K; wine of Helbon, and
38:21 I will summon every K of terror against Gog,
Dan 3:5 harp, bagpipe, and every K of music, you are
3:7 harp, bagpipe, and every K of music, all the
3:10 harp, bagpipe, and every K of music, shall fall
3:15 harp, bagpipe, and every K of music, to fall
6:23 the den, and no K of hurt was found
Hag 2:12 or oil, or any K of food, does it
1Mac 6:11 For I was K and beloved in my power.'
2Mac 1:24 art King and art K,
12:30 shown them and their K treatment of them in
Mt 13:47 gathered fish of every K;
Mk 9:29 said to them, "This K cannot be driven out
Lk 6:35 High; for he is K to the ungrateful and
Acts 10:33 and you have been K enough to come.
1Cor 5:1 you, and of a K that is not found
7:7 God, one of one K and one of another.
13:4 Love is patient and K; love is not jealous
15:35 With what K of body do they come?"
15:38 chosen, and to each K of seed its own
15:39 but there is one K for men, another for
Eph 4:19 greedy to practice every K of uncleanness.
4:32 all malice, and be K to one another, tenderhearted,
Phil 4:14 Yet it was K of you to share my
1Thes 1:5 You know what K of men we proved to
Tit 2:5 be sensible, chaste, domestic, K, and submissive to
Jas 1:17 we should be a K of first fruits of
3:7 For every K of beast and bird, of reptile
1Pet 2:18 not only to the K and gentle but also

KINDLE (16)

Ex 35:3 to death; you shall K no fire in all
Sir 8:10 Do not K the coals of a sinner, lest
28:8 given to anger will K strife,

	32:16	a light they will K righteous deeds.
	51:4	which I did not K,
Is	50:11	Behold, all you who K a fire, who set
Jer	7:18	gather wood, the fathers K fire, and the women
	17:27	day, then I will K a fire in its
	21:14	the LORD; I will K a fire in her
	43:12	He shall K a fire in the temples of
	49:27	And I will K a fire in the wall
	50:32	up, and I will K a fire in his
Ezek	20:47	GOD, Behold, I will K a fire in you,
	24:10	Heap on the logs, K the fire, boil well
Amos	1:14	So I will K a fire in the wall
Mal	1:10	that you might not K fire upon my altar

KINDLED (64)

Gen	30:2	Jacob's anger was K against Rachel, and he said,
	39:19	his anger was K
Ex	4:14	of the LORD was K against Moses and he
	22:6	is consumed, he that K the fire shall make
Lev	10:6	may bewail the burning which the LORD has K
Num	11:1	it, his anger was K, and the fire of
	11:33	of the LORD was K against the people, and
	12:9	of the LORD was K against them, and he
	22:22	But God's anger was K because he went; and
	22:27	and Balaam's anger was K, and he struck the
	24:10	And Balak's anger was K against Balaam, and he
	25:3	of the LORD was K against Israel;
	32:10	the LORD's anger was K on that day, and
	32:13	the LORD's anger was K against Israel, and he
Deut	6:15	LORD your God be K against you, and he
	7:4	the LORD would be K against you, and he
	11:17	of the LORD be K against you, and he
	29:27	of the LORD was K against this land, bringing
	31:17	my anger will be K against them in that
	32:22	For a fire is K by my anger, and
Josh	23:16	the LORD will be K against you, and you
Judg	2:14	of the LORD was K against Israel, and he
	2:20	of the LORD was K against Israel; and he
	3:8	of the LORD was K against Israel, and he
	9:30	Gaal the son of Ebed, his anger was K
	10:7	of the LORD was K against Israel, and he
1Sam	11:6	heard these words, and his anger was greatly K
	17:28	and Eliab's anger was K against David, and he
	20:30	Then Saul's anger was K against Jonathan, and he
2Sam	6:7	of the LORD was K against Uzzah; and God
	12:5	David's anger was greatly K against the man; and
	24:1	of the LORD was K against Israel, and he
2Kgs	13:3	of the LORD was K against Israel, and he
	22:13	the LORD that is K against us, because our
	22:17	my wrath will be K against this place, and
	23:26	which his anger was K against Judah, because of
1Chr	13:10	of the LORD was K against Uzzah; and he
Jud	7:5	and when they had K fires on their towers
	13:13	admitted them, and they K a fire for light,
Job	19:11	He has K his wrath against me, and counts
	42:7	Temanite: "My wrath is K against you and against
Ps	2:12	in the way; for his wrath is quickly K
	78:21	wrath; a fire was K against Jacob, his anger
	106:40	of the LORD was K against his people, and
	124:3	when their anger was K against us;
Wis	2:2	reason is a spark K by the beating of
Sir	9:8	by it passion is K like a fire.
	16:6	a fire will be K, and in a disobedient
	16:6	kindled, and in a disobedient nation wrath was K
	40:30	sweet, but in his stomach a fire is K
Is	5:25	of the LORD was K against his people, and
	10:16	a burning will be K, like the burning of
	50:11	fire, and by the brands which you have K
Jer	15:14	anger a fire is K which shall burn for
	17:4	anger a fire is K which shall burn for
	44:6	were poured forth and K in the cities of
Lam	4:11	hot anger; and he K a fire in Zion,
Ezek	20:48	I the LORD have K it; it shall not
1Mac	12:28	at heart; so they K fires in their camp
2Mac	10:36	to the towers; they K fires and burned the
Lk	12:49	the earth; and would that it were already K
	22:53	and when they had K a fire in the
Acts	28:2	unusual kindness, for they K a fire and welcomed
2Pet	3:12	the heavens will be K and dissolved, and the

KINDLES (6)

Job	41:21	His breath K coals, and a flame comes forth
Sir	28:11	A hasty quarrel K fire, and urgent strife sheds
Is	9:18	briers and thorns; it K the thickets of the
	30:33	a stream of brimstone, K it.
	44:15	and warms himself, he K a fire and bakes
	64:2	as when fire K brushwood and the fire

KINDLINESS

Esth	16:10	quite devoid of our K, having become our guest,

KINDLING

Prov	26:21	a quarrelsome man for K strife.

KINDLY (18)

Josh	2:12	as I have dealt K with you, you also
	2:12	you also will deal K with my father's house,
	2:14	then we will deal K and faithfully with you
Judg	1:24	and we will deal K with you."
	19:3	after her, to speak K to her and bring
Ruth	1:8	May the LORD deal K with you, as you
	2:13	comforted me and spoken K to your maidservant,
1Sam	20:8	Therefore deal K with your servant, for you have
2Sam	19:7	go out and speak K to your servants; for
2Kgs	25:28	prison; and he spoke K to him, and gave
Wis	1:6	For wisdom is a K spirit and will not
Sir	13:6	will speak to you K and say, "What do
Jer	52:32	prison; and he spoke K to him, and gave
2Mac	3:9	Jerusalem and had been K welcomed by the high
	6:22	death, and be treated K on account of his
Acts	27:3	and Julius treated Paul K, and gave him leave
1Thes	3:6	you always remember us K and long to see
2Tim	2:24	not be quarrelsome but K to every one, an

KINDNESS (55)

Gen	19:19	have shown me great K in saving my life;
	20:13	her, 'This is the K you must do me:
	40:14	and do me the K, I pray you, to
Judg	8:35	they did not show K to the family of
Ruth	2:20	by the LORD, whose K has not forsaken the
	3:10	have made this last K greater than the first,
1Sam	15:6	them; for you showed K to all the people
2Sam	9:1	I may show him K for Jonathan's sake?"
	9:3	I may show the K of God to him?"
	9:7	I will show you K for the sake of
2Chr	24:22	did not remember the K which Jehoiada, Zechariah's
Esth	13:2	acting reasonably and with K, I have determined to
	16:2	by the too great K of their benefactors, the
Job	6:14	"He who withholds K from a friend forsakes the
Ps	109:12	be none to extend K to him, nor any
	109:16	not remember to show K, but pursued the poor
	141:5	or rebuke me in K, but let the oil
Prov	21:21	who pursues righteousness and K will find life and
	31:26	and the teaching of K is on her tongue.
Wis	16:2	punishment thou didst show K to thy people, and
	16:11	forgetfulness and become unresponsive to thy K
	16:24	the unrighteous, and in K relaxes on behalf of
Sir	3:14	For K to a father will not be forgotten,
	7:33	living, and withhold not K from the dead.
	12:1	If you do a K, know to whom you
	17:17	will keep a person's K like the apple of
	19:22	are people who distort K to gain a verdict.
	29:15	not forget all the K of your surety, for
	30:6	one to repay the K of his friends.
	35:2	He who returns a K offers fine flour, and
	36:23	If K and humility mark her speech, her husband
	37:11	a merciless man about K, with an idler about
	40:17	K is like a garden of blessings, and almsgiving
Bar	2:27	God, in all thy K and in all thy
Hos	4:1	is no faithfulness or K, and no knowledge of
Mic	6:8	justice, and to love K, and to walk humbly
Zech	7:9	Render true judgments, show K and mercy each to
2Mac	2:22	the Lord with great K became gracious to them–
	6:13	punish them immediately, is a sign of great K
	9:27	policy and will treat you with moderation and K
	10:38	Lord who shows great K to Israel and gives
	14:9	nation with the gracious K which you show to
Acts	24:4	beg you in your K to hear us briefly.
	28:2	natives showed us unusual K, for they kindled a
Rom	2:4	the riches of his K and forbearance and patience?
	2:4	not know that God's K is meant to lead
	11:22	Note then the K and the severity of God:
	11:22	have fallen, but God's K to you, provided you
	11:22	you continue in his K; otherwise you too will
2Cor	6:6	by purity, knowledge, forbearance, K, the Holy Spirit,
Gal	5:22	love, joy, peace, patience, K, goodness, faithfulness,
Eph	2:7	of his grace in K toward us in Christ
Col	3:12	holy and beloved, compassion, K, lowliness,
Tit	3:4	the goodness and loving K of God our Savior
1Pet	2:3	you have tasted the K of the Lord.

KINDRED (22)

Gen 12:1 your country and your K and your father's house
24:4 country and to my K, and take a wife
24:38 house and to my K, and take a wife
24:40 my son from my K and from my father's
24:41 you come to my K; and if they will
25:17 was gathered to his K
31:3 fathers and to your K, and I will be
32:9 country and to your K, and I will do
43:7 about ourselves and our K, saying, 'Is your father
Num 10:30 depart to my own land and to my K
Josh 6:23 they brought all her K, and set them outside
Jud 16:24 her husband Manasseh, and to her own nearest K
Esth 2:10 known her people or K, for Mordecai had charged
2:20 not made known her K or her people, as
8:6 I endure to see the destruction of my K
Wis 7:3 and fell upon the K earth, and my first
Dan 13:30 with her parents, her children, and all her K
13:63 husband and all her K, because nothing shameful
2Mac 5:6 the cost of one's K is the greatest misfortune,
Lk 1:61 her, "None of your K is called by this
Acts 7:3 land and from your K and go into the
7:14 father and all his K, seventy-five souls;

KINDS (51)

Gen 1:12 according to their own K, and trees bearing fruit
1:21 swarm, according to their K, and every winged bird
1:24 creatures according to their K: cattle and creeping
1:24 and beasts of the earth according to their K
1:25 earth according to their K and the cattle according
1:25 cattle according to their K, and everything that
6:20 birds according to their K, and of the animals
6:20 animals according to their K, of every creeping thing
7:14 cattle according to their K, and every creeping thing
Ex 1:13 brick, and in all K of work in the
Lev 19:19 your field with two K of seed; nor shall
19:19 cloth made of two K of stuff.
19:23 land and plant all K of trees for food,
Deut 14:13 the kite, after their K;
14:15 the hawk, after their K;
14:18 the heron, after their K; the hoopoe and the
22:9 your vineyard with two K of seed, lest the
25:13 in your bag two K of weights, a large
25:14 in your house two K of measures, a large
2Kgs 8:9 present with him, all K of goods of Damascus,
1Chr 22:15 masons, carpenters, and all K of craftsmen without
2Chr 16:14 been filled with various K of spices prepared by
32:27 shields, and for all K of costly vessels;
32:28 and stalls for all K of cattle, and sheepfolds.
Neh 13:15 grapes, figs, and all K of burdens, which they
13:16 in fish and all K of wares and sold
13:20 and sellers of all K of wares lodged outside
Esth 1:7 goblets, goblets of different K, and the royal wine
Ps 45:13 the people with all K of wealth.
Eccl 2:5 planted in them all K of fruit trees.
Sir 16:28 good things; with all K of living beings he
25:2 My soul hates three K of men, and I
36:19 the palate tastes the K of game, so an
43:25 and marvelous works, all K of living things, and
50:9 gold adorned with all K of precious stones;
Jer 15:3 appoint over them four K of destroyers, says the
Ezek 8:10 round about, were all K of creeping things, and
17:23 it will dwell all K of beasts; in the
27:22 the best of all K of spices, and all
39:20 mighty men and all K of warriors,' says the
44:30 first fruits of all K, and every offering of
44:30 every offering of all K from all your offerings,
47:10 be of very many K, like the fish of
47:12 there will grow all K of trees for food.
Mt 5:11 you and utter all K of evil against you
Acts 10:12 In it were all K of animals and reptiles
Rom 7:8 wrought in me all K of covetousness.
1Cor 12:10 spirits, to another various K of tongues, to another
12:28 administrators, speakers in various K of tongues.
Rev 18:12 silk and scarlet, all K of scented wood, all
22:2 life with its twelve K of fruit, yielding its

KING (2,926)

Gen 14:1 the days of Amraphel K of Shinar, Arioch king
14:1 king of Shinar, Arioch K of Ellasar, Ched-or-laomer
14:1 king of Ellasar, Ched-or-laomer K of Elam, and Tidal
14:1 of Elam, and Tidal K of Goiim,
14:2 made war with Bera K of Sodom, Birsha king
14:2 king of Sodom, Birsha K of Gomorrah, Shinab king
14:2 king of Gomorrah, Shinab K of Admah, Shemeber
14:2 king of Admah, Shemeber K of Zeboiim, and the
14:2 of Zeboiim, and the K of Bela (that is,
14:8 Then the K of Sodom, the king of Gomorrah,
14:8 king of Sodom, the K of Gomorrah, the king
14:8 king of Gomorrah, the K of Admah, the king
14:8 king of Admah, the K of Zeboiim, and the
14:8 of Zeboiim, and the K of Bela (that is,
14:9 of Siddim with Ched-or-laomer K of Elam, Tidal king
14:9 king of Elam, Tidal K of Goiim, Amraphel king
14:9 king of Goiim, Amraphel K of Shinar, and Arioch
14:9 of Shinar, and Arioch K of Ellasar, four kings
14:17 were with him, the K of Sodom went out
14:17 Shaveh (that is, the K's Valley).
14:18 And Melchizedek K of Salem brought out bread and
14:21 And the K of Sodom said to Abram, "Give
14:22 Abram said to the K of Sodom, "I have
20:2 And Abimelech K of Gerar sent and took Sarah.
26:1 to Gerar, to Abimelech K of the Philistines.
26:8 a long time, Abimelech K of the Philistines looked
36:31 of Edom, before any K reigned over the Israelites.
39:20 the place where the K's prisoners were confined, and
40:1 the butler of the K of Egypt and his
40:1 offended their lord the K of Egypt.
40:5 the baker of the K of Egypt, who were
41:46 the service of Pharaoh K of Egypt.
Ex 1:7 there arose a new K over Egypt, who did
1:14 Then the K of Egypt said to the Hebrew
1:16 not do as the K of Egypt commanded them,
1:17 So the K of Egypt called the midwives, and
2:23 those many days the K of Egypt died.
3:18 shall go to the K of Egypt and say
3:19 I know that the K of Egypt will not
5:4 But the K of Egypt said to them, "Moses
6:11 "Go in, tell Pharaoh K of Egypt to let
6:13 Israel and to Pharaoh K of Egypt to bring
6:27 who spoke to Pharaoh K of Egypt about bringing
6:29 the LORD; tell Pharaoh K of Egypt all that
14:5 When the K of Egypt was told that the
14:8 the heart of Pharaoh K of Egypt and he
Num 20:14 from Kadesh to the K of Edom, "Thus says
20:17 will go along the K's Highway, we will not
21:1 When the Canaanite, the K of Arad, who dwelt
21:21 sent messengers to Sihon K of the Amorites, saying,
21:22 will go by the K's Highway, until we have
21:26 city of Sihon the K of the Amorites, who
21:26 fought against the former K of Moab and taken
21:29 captives, to an Amorite K, Sihon.
21:33 Bashan; and Og the K of Bashan came out
21:34 you did to Sihon K of the Amorites, who
22:4 of Zippor, who was K of Moab at that
22:10 the son of Zippor, K of Moab, has sent
23:7 has brought me, the K of Moab from the
23:21 the shout of a K is among them.
24:7 in many waters, his K shall be higher than
32:33 the kingdom of Sihon K of the Amorites and
32:33 the kingdom of Og K of Bashan, the land
33:40 And the Canaanite, the K of Arad, who dwelt
Deut 1:4 had defeated Sihon the K of the Amorites, who
1:4 Heshbon, and Og the K of Bashan, who lived
2:24 hand Sihon the Amorite, K of Heshbon, and his
2:26 Kedemoth to Sihon the K of Heshbon, with words
2:30 us.' But Sihon the K of Heshbon would not
3:1 Bashan; and Og the K of Bashan came out
3:2 did to Sihon the K of the Amorites, who
3:3 hand Og also, the K of Bashan, and all
3:6 did to Sihon the K of Heshbon, destroying every
3:11 (For only Og the K of Bashan was left
4:46 land of Sihon the K of the Amorites, who
4:47 land of Og the K of Bashan, the two
7:8 the hand of Pharaoh K of Egypt.
11:3 Egypt to Pharaoh the K of Egypt and to
17:14 'I will set a K over me, like all
17:15 may indeed set as K over you him whom
17:15 you shall set as K over you; you may
28:36 bring you, and your K whom you set over
29:7 this place, Sihon the K of Heshbon and Og
29:7 Heshbon and Og the K of Bashan came out
33:5 Thus the LORD became K in Jeshurun, when the
Josh 2:2 it was told the K of Jericho, "Behold, certain
2:3 Then the K of Jericho sent to Rahab, saying,
6:2 hand Jericho, with its K and mighty men of
8:1 into your hand the K of Ai, and his
8:2 to Ai and its K as you did to
8:2 to Jericho and its K; only its spoil and
8:14 And when the K of Ai saw this he
8:23 But the K of Ai they took alive, and
8:29 And he hanged the K of Ai on a

9:10 the Jordan, Sihon the K of Heshbon, and Og
9:10 of Heshbon, and Og K of Bashan, who dwelt
10:1 Adoni-zedek K of Jerusalem heard how Joshua had
10:1 to Ai and its K as he had done
10:1 to Jericho and its K, and how the inhabitants
10:3 So Adoni-zedek K of Jerusalem sent to Hoham king
10:3 Jerusalem sent to Hoham K of Hebron, to Piram
10:3 of Hebron, to Piram K of Jarmuth, to Japhia
10:3 of Jarmuth, to Japhia K of Lachish, and to
10:3 Lachish, and to Debir K of Eglon, saying,
10:5 of the Amorites, the K of Jerusalem, the king
10:5 king of Jerusalem, the K of Hebron, the king
10:5 king of Hebron, the K of Jarmuth, the king
10:5 king of Jarmuth, the K of Lachish, and the
10:5 of Lachish, and the K of Eglon, gathered their
10:23 from the cave, the K of Jerusalem, the king
10:23 king of Jerusalem, the K of Hebron, the king
10:23 king of Hebron, the K of Jarmuth, the king
10:23 king of Jarmuth, the K of Lachish, and the
10:23 of Lachish, and the K of Eglon.
10:28 smote it and its K with the edge of
10:28 he did to the K of Makkedah as he
10:28 had done to the K of Jericho.
10:30 it also and its K into the hand of
10:30 he did to its K as he had done
10:30 had done to the K of Jericho.
10:33 Then Horam K of Gezer came up to help
10:37 the sword, and its K and its towns, and
10:39 took it with its K and all its towns;
10:39 to Libnah and its K, so he did to
10:39 so he did to Debir and to its K
11:1 When Jabin K of Hazor heard of this, he
11:1 he sent to Jobab K of Madon, and to
11:1 Madon, and to the K of Shimron, and to
11:1 Shimron, and to the K of Achshaph,
11:10 Hazor, and smote its K with the sword; for
12:2 the Arabah eastward: Sihon K of the Amorites who
12:4 of Pisgah; and Og K of Bashan, one of
12:5 the boundary of Sihon K of Heshbon.
12:9 and the Jebusites): the K of Jericho, one; the
12:9 of Jericho, one; the K of Ai, which is
12:10 beside Bethel, one; the K of Jerusalem, one; the
12:10 of Jerusalem, one; the K of Hebron, one;
12:11 of Hebron, one; the K of Jarmuth, one; the
12:11 of Jarmuth, one; the K of Lachish, one;
12:12 of Lachish, one; the K of Eglon, one; the
12:12 of Eglon, one; the K of Gezer, one;
12:13 of Gezer, one; the K of Debir, one; the
12:13 of Debir, one; the K of Geder, one;
12:14 of Geder, one; the K of Hormah, one; the
12:14 of Hormah, one; the K of Arad, one;
12:15 of Arad, one; the K of Libnah, one; the
12:15 of Libnah, one; the K of Adullam, one;
12:16 of Adullam, one; the K of Makkedah, one; the
12:16 of Makkedah, one; the K of Bethel, one;
12:17 of Bethel, one; the K of Tappuah, one; the
12:17 of Tappuah, one; the K of Hepher, one;
12:18 of Hepher, one; the K of Aphek, one; the
12:18 of Aphek, one; the K of Lasharon, one;
12:19 of Lasharon, one; the K of Madon, one; the
12:19 of Madon, one; the K of Hazor, one;
12:20 of Hazor, one; the K of Shimron-meron, one; the
12:20 of Shimron-meron, one; the K of Achshaph, one;
12:21 of Achshaph, one; the K of Taanach, one; the
12:21 of Taanach, one; the K of Megiddo, one;
12:22 of Megiddo, one; the K of Kedesh, one; the
12:22 of Kedesh, one; the K of Jokne-am in Carmel,
12:23 in Carmel, one; the K of Dor in Naphath-dor,
12:23 in Naphath-dor, one; the K of Goiim in Galilee,
12:24 in Galilee, one; the K of Tirzah, one: in
13:10 the cities of Sihon K of the Amorites, who
13:21 the kingdom of Sihon K of the Amorites, who
13:27 the kingdom of Sihon K of Heshbon, having the
13:30 whole kingdom of Og K of Bashan, and all
24:9 the son of Zippor, K of Moab, arose and
Judg 3:8 the hand of Cushan-rishathaim K of Mesopotamia;
3:10 LORD gave Cushan-rishathaim K of Mesopotamia
3:12 LORD strengthened Eglon the K of Moab against
3:14 Israel served Eglon the K of Moab eighteen years.
3:15 him to Eglon the K of Moab.
3:17 the tribute to Eglon K of Moab.
3:19 "I have a secret message for you, O K
4:2 the hand of Jabin K of Canaan, who reigned
4:17 peace between Jabin the K of Hazor and the
4:23 God subdued Jabin the K of Canaan before the
4:24 harder on Jabin the K of Canaan, until they
4:24 until they destroyed Jabin K of Canaan.
8:18 of them; they resembled the sons of a K
9:6 went and made Abimelech K, by the oak of
9:8 forth to anoint a K over them; and they
9:15 you are anointing me K over you, then come
9:16 when you made Abimelech K, and if you have
9:18 son of his maidservant, K over the citizens of
11:12 sent messengers to the K of the Ammonites and
11:13 And the K of the Ammonites answered the
11:14 messengers again to the K of the Ammonites
11:17 sent messengers to the K of Edom, saying, 'Let
11:17 your land'; but the K of Edom would not
11:17 sent also to the K of Moab, but he
11:19 sent messengers to Sihon K of the Amorites, king
11:19 king of the Amorites, K of Heshbon; and Israel
11:25 the son of Zippor, K of Moab?
11:28 But the K of the Ammonites did not heed
17:6 days there was no K in Israel; every man
18:1 days there was no K in Israel.
19:1 when there was no K in Israel, a certain
21:25 days there was no K in Israel; every man
1Sam 2:10 give strength to his K, and exalt the power
8:5 appoint for us a K to govern us like
8:6 said, "Give us a K to govern us." And
8:7 rejected me from being K over them.
8:9 the ways of the K who shall reign over
8:10 who were asking a K from him.
8:11 the ways of the K who will reign over
8:18 out because of your K, whom you have chosen
8:19 we will have a K over us,
8:20 nations, and that our K may govern us and
8:22 "Hearken to their voice, and make them a K
10:19 but set a K over us.' Now therefore present
10:24 And all the people shouted, "Long live the K
11:15 there they made Saul K before the LORD in
12:1 and have made a K over you.
12:2 And now, behold, the K walks before you; and
12:9 the army of Jabin K of Hazor, and into
12:9 the hand of the K of Moab; and they
12:12 saw that Nahash the K of the Ammonites came
12:12 me, 'No, but a K shall reign over us,'
12:12 us,' when the LORD your God was your K
12:13 And now behold the K whom you have chosen,
12:13 LORD has set a K over you.
12:14 both you and the K who reigns over you
12:15 the LORD will be against you and your K
12:17 of the LORD, in asking for yourselves a K
12:19 sins this evil, to ask for ourselves a K
12:25 shall be swept away, both you and your K
15:1 me to anoint you K over his people Israel;
15:8 he took Agag the K of the Amalekites alive,
15:11 I have made Saul K; for he has turned
15:17 The LORD anointed you K over Israel.
15:20 have brought Agag the K of Amalek, and I
15:23 LORD, he has also rejected you from being K
15:26 rejected you from being K over Israel."
15:32 to me Agag the K of the Amalekites." And
15:35 he had made Saul K over Israel.
16:1 rejected him from being K over Israel?
16:1 provided for myself a K among his sons."
17:25 who kills him, the K will enrich with great
17:55 your soul lives, O K, I cannot tell."
17:56 And the K said, "Inquire whose son the stripling
18:6 and dancing, to meet K Saul, with timbrels, with
18:18 Israel, that I should be son-in-law to the K
18:22 and say, 'Behold, the K has delight in you,
18:22 now then become the K's son-in-law.'"
18:23 thing to become the K's son-in-law, seeing that I
18:25 say to David, 'The K desires no marriage present
18:25 be avenged of the K's enemies.'" Now Saul thought
18:26 well to be the K's son-in-law.
18:27 full number to the K, that he might become
18:27 he might become the K's son-in-law.
19:4 him, "Let not the K sin against his servant
20:5 at table with the K; but let me go,
20:24 new moon came, the K sat down to eat
20:25 The K sat upon his seat, as at other
20:29 not come to the K's table."
21:2 Ahimelech the priest, "The K has charged me with
21:8 with me, because the K's business required haste."
21:10 went to Achish the K of Gath.
21:11 not this David the K of the land?
21:12 afraid of Achish the K of Gath.
22:3 he said to the K of Moab, "Pray let
22:4 left them with the K of Moab, and they
22:11 Then the K sent to summon Ahimelech the priest,

22:11 Nob; and all of them came to the K
22:14 Then Ahimelech answered the K, "And who among
22:14 David, who is the K's son-in-law, and captain over
22:15 Let not the K impute anything to his servant
22:16 And the K said, "You shall surely die, Ahimelech,
22:17 And the K said to the guard who stood
22:17 the servants of the K would not put forth
22:18 Then the K said to Doeg, "You turn and
23:17 you; you shall be K over Israel, and I
23:20 Now come down, O K, according to all your
23:20 surrender him into the K's hand."
24:8 cave, and called after Saul, "My lord the K
24:14 After whom has the K of Israel come out?
24:20 you shall surely be K, and that the kingdom
25:36 in his house, like the feast of a K
26:14 answered, "Who are you that calls to the K
26:15 you not kept watch over your lord the K
26:15 in to destroy the K your lord.
26:16 now see where the K's spear is, and the
26:17 said, "It is my voice, my lord, O K
26:19 let my lord the K hear the words of
26:20 the LORD; for the K of Israel has come
26:22 David made answer, "Here is the spear, O K
27:2 the son of Maoch, K of Gath.
28:13 The K said to her, "Have no fear; what
29:3 the servant of Saul, K of Israel, who has
29:8 fight against the enemies of my lord the K
2Sam 2:4 there they anointed David K over the house of
2:7 Judah has anointed me K over them."
2:9 and he made him K over Gilead and the
2:11 time that David was K in Hebron over the
3:3 the daughter of Talmai K of Geshur;
3:17 been seeking David as K over you.
3:21 to my lord the K, that they may make
3:23 Ner came to the K, and he has let
3:24 Joab went to the K and said, "What have
3:31 And K David followed the bier.
3:32 at Hebron; and the K lifted up his voice
3:33 And the K lamented for Abner, saying, "Should
3:36 as everything that the K did pleased all the
3:37 had not been the K's will to slay Abner
3:38 And the K said to his servants, "Do you
3:39 day weak, though anointed K; these men the sons
4:8 they said to the K, "Here is the head
4:8 avenged my lord the K this day on Saul
5:2 past, when Saul was K over us, it was
5:3 Israel came to the K at Hebron; and King
5:3 king at Hebron; and K David made a covenant
5:3 and they anointed David K over Israel.
5:6 And the K and his men went to Jerusalem
5:11 And Hiram K of Tyre sent messengers to David,
5:12 LORD had established him K over Israel, and that
5:17 David had been anointed K over Israel, all the
6:12 And it was told K David, "The LORD has
6:16 the window, and saw K David leaping and dancing
6:20 and said, "How the K of Israel honored himself
7:1 Now when the K dwelt in his house, and
7:2 enemies round about, the K said to Nathan the
7:3 Nathan said to the K, "Go, do all that
7:18 Then K David went in and sat before the
8:3 the son of Rehob, K of Zobah, as he
8:5 came to help Hadadezer K of Zobah, David slew
8:8 Berothai, cities of Hadadezer, K David took very
8:9 When Toi K of Hamath heard that David had
8:10 his son Joram to K David, to greet him,
8:11 of bronze; these also K David dedicated to the
8:12 the son of Rehob, K of Zobah.
9:2 to David; and the K said to him, "Are
9:3 And the K said, "Is there not still some
9:3 Ziba said to the K, "There is still a
9:4 The K said to him, "Where is he?" And
9:4 Ziba said to the K, "He is in the
9:5 Then K David sent and brought him from the
9:9 Then the K called Ziba, Saul's servant, and said
9:11 Ziba said to the K, "According to all that
9:11 that my lord the K commands his servant, so
9:11 like one of the K's sons.
9:13 ate always at the K's table.
10:1 After this the K of the Ammonites died, and
10:5 And the K said, "Remain at Jericho until your
10:6 foot soldiers, and the K of Maacah with a
11:2 the roof of the K's house, that he saw
11:8 went out of the K's house, and there followed
11:8 and there followed him a present from the K
11:9 the door of the K's house with all the
11:19 the fighting to the K,
11:20 king, then, if the K's anger rises, and if
11:24 wall; some of the K's servants are dead; and
12:7 Israel, 'I anointed you K over Israel, and I
12:30 the crown of their K from his head; the
13:4 "O son of the K, why are you so
13:6 ill; and when the K came to see him,
13:6 Amnon said to the K, "Pray let my sister
13:13 you, speak to the K; for he will not
13:18 virgin daughters of the K clad of old.
13:21 When K David heard of all these things, he
13:23 Absalom invited all the K's sons.
13:24 Absalom came to the K, and said, "Behold, your
13:24 sheepshearers; pray let the K and his servants go
13:25 But the K said to Absalom, "No, my son,
13:26 And the K said to him, "Why should he
13:27 Amnon and all the K's sons go with him.
13:29 Then all the K's sons arose, and each mounted
13:30 has slain all the K's sons, and not one
13:31 Then the K arose, and rent his garments, and
13:32 the young men the K's sons, for Amnon alone
13:33 not my lord the K so take it to
13:33 suppose that all the K's sons are dead; for
13:35 Jonadab said to the K, "Behold, the king's sons
13:35 the king, "Behold, the K's sons have come; as
13:36 finished speaking, behold, the K's sons came, and
13:36 and wept; and the K also and all his
13:37 the son of Ammihud, K of Geshur.
13:39 the spirit of the K longed to go forth
14:1 Zeruiah perceived that the K's heart went out to
14:3 and go to the K, and speak thus to
14:4 Tekoa came to the K, she fell on her
14:4 ground, and did obeisance, and said, "Help, O K
14:5 And the K said to her, "What is your
14:8 Then the K said to the woman, "Go to
14:9 Tekoa said to the K, "On me be the
14:9 guilt, my lord the K, and on my father's
14:9 father's house; let the K and his throne be
14:10 The K said, "If any one says anything to
14:11 said, "Pray let the K invoke the LORD your
14:12 handmaid speak a word to my lord the K
14:13 giving this decision the K convicts himself, inasmuch
14:13 himself, inasmuch as the K does not bring his
14:15 to my lord the K because the people have
14:15 will speak to the K; it may be that
14:15 may be that the K will perform the request
14:16 For the K will hear, and deliver his servant
14:17 of my lord the K will set me at
14:17 for my lord the K is like the angel
14:18 Then the K answered the woman, "Do not hide
14:18 "Let my lord the K speak."
14:19 The K said, "Is the hand of Joab with
14:19 live, my lord the K, one cannot turn to
14:19 that my lord the K has said.
14:21 Then the K said to Joab, "Behold now, I
14:22 obeisance, and blessed the K; and Joab said, "Today
14:22 sight, my lord the K, in that the king
14:22 king, in that the K has granted the request
14:24 And the K said, "Let him dwell apart in
14:24 not come into the K's presence.
14:26 hundred shekels by the K's weight.
14:28 without coming into the K's presence.
14:29 send him to the K; but Joab would not
14:32 send you to the K, to ask, "Why have
14:32 the presence of the K; and if there is
14:33 Joab went to the K, and told him; and
14:33 he came to the K, and bowed himself on
14:33 the ground before the K; and the king kissed
14:33 the king; and the K kissed Absalom.
15:2 to come before the K for judgment, Absalom would
15:3 man deputed by the K to hear you."
15:6 who came to the K for judgment; so Absalom
15:7 Absalom said to the K, "Pray let me go
15:9 The K said to him, "Go in peace." So
15:10 then say, 'Absalom is K at Hebron!'"
15:15 And the K's servants said to the king, "Behold,
15:15 servants said to the K, "Behold, your servants are
15:15 whatever my lord the K decides."
15:16 So the K went forth, and all his household
15:16 And the K left ten concubines to keep the
15:17 And the K went forth, and all the people
15:18 followed him from Gath, passed on before the K
15:19 Then the K said to Ittai the Gittite, "Why
15:19 and stay with the K; for you are a
15:21 But Ittai answered the K, "As the LORD lives,
15:21 as my lord the K lives, wherever my lord
15:21 wherever my lord the K shall be, whether for

15:23 passed by, and the K crossed the brook Kidron,
15:25 Then the K said to Zadok, "Carry the ark
15:27 The K also said to Zadok the priest, "Look,
15:34 be your servant, O K; as I have been
15:35 you hear from the K's house, tell it to
16:2 And the K said to Ziba, "Why have you
16:2 asses are for the K's household to ride on,
16:3 And the K said, "And where is your master's
16:3 Ziba said to the K, "Behold, he remains in
16:4 Then the K said to Ziba, "Behold, all that
16:4 find favor in your sight, my lord the K
16:5 When K David came to Bahurim, there came out
16:6 all the servants of K David; and all the
16:9 Zeruiah said to the K, "Why should this dead
16:9 should this dead dog curse my lord the K
16:10 But the K said, "What have I to do
16:14 And the K, and all the people who were
16:16 Absalom, Hushai said to Absalom, "Long live the K
16:16 Long live the K
17:2 will strike down the K only,
17:16 pass over; lest the K and all the people
17:17 would go and tell K David; for they must
17:21 and went and told K David.
18:2 And the K said to the men, "I myself
18:4 The K said to them, "Whatever seems best to
18:4 So the K stood at the side of the
18:5 And the K ordered Joab and Abishai and Ittai,
18:5 people heard when the K gave orders to all
18:12 my hand against the K's son; for in our
18:12 in our hearing the K commanded you and Abishai
18:13 nothing hidden from the K, then you yourself would
18:18 which is in the K's Valley, for he said,
18:19 carry tidings to the K that the LORD has
18:20 no tidings, because the K's son is dead."
18:21 Cushite, "Go, tell the K what you have seen."
18:25 And the watchman called out and told the K
18:25 And the K said, "If he is alone, there
18:26 The K said, "He also brings tidings."
18:27 And the K said, "He is a good man,
18:28 cried out to the K, "All is well." And
18:28 he bowed before the K with his face to
18:28 who raised their hand against my lord the K
18:29 And the K said, "Is it well with the
18:30 And the K said, "Turn aside, and stand here."
18:31 Cushite said, "Good tidings for my lord the K
18:32 The K said to the Cushite, "Is it well
18:32 of my lord the K, and all who rise
18:33 And the K was deeply moved, and went up
19:1 told Joab, "Behold, the K is weeping and mourning
19:2 heard that day, "The K is grieving for his
19:4 The K covered his face, and the king cried
19:4 his face, and the K cried with a loud
19:5 the house to the K, and said, "You have
19:8 Then the K arose, and took his seat in
19:8 all told, "Behold, the K is sitting in the
19:8 gate"; and all the people came before the K
19:9 of Israel, saying, "The K delivered us from the
19:10 nothing about bringing the K back?"
19:11 And K David sent this message to Zadok and
19:11 last to bring the K back to his house,
19:11 word of all Israel has come to the K
19:12 to bring back the K
19:14 sent word to the K, "Return, both you and
19:15 So the K came back to the Jordan; and
19:15 Gilgal to meet the K and to bring the
19:15 and to bring the K over the Jordan.
19:16 of Judah to meet K David;
19:17 the Jordan before the K,
19:18 to bring over the K's household, and to do
19:18 fell down before the K, as he was about
19:19 and said to the K, "Let not my lord
19:19 day my lord the K left Jerusalem; let not
19:19 Jerusalem; let not the K bear it in mind.
19:20 to come down to meet my lord the K
19:22 I am this day K over Israel?"
19:23 And the K said to Shimei, "You shall not
19:23 And the K gave him his oath.
19:24 down to meet the K; he had neither dressed
19:24 from the day the K departed until the day
19:25 Jerusalem to meet the K, the king said to
19:25 meet the king, the K said to him, "Why
19:26 answered, "My lord, O K, my servant deceived me;
19:26 and go with the K For your servant is
19:27 has slandered your servant to my lord the K
19:27 But my lord the K is like the angel
19:28 before my lord the K; but you set your
19:28 right have I, then, to cry to the K
19:29 And the K said to him, "Why speak any
19:30 Mephibosheth said to the K, "Oh, let him take
19:30 since my lord the K has come safely home."
19:31 went on with the K to the Jordan, to
19:32 he had provided the K with food while he
19:33 And the K said to Barzillai, "Come over with
19:34 Barzillai said to the K, "How many years have
19:34 go up with the K to Jerusalem?
19:35 be an added burden to my lord the K
19:36 a little way over the Jordan with the K
19:36 Why should the K recompense me with such a
19:37 with my lord the K; and do for him
19:38 And the K answered, "Chimham shall go over with
19:39 the Jordan, and the K went over; and the
19:39 went over; and the K kissed Barzillai and blessed
19:40 The K went on to Gilgal, and Chimham went
19:40 of Israel, brought the K on his way.
19:41 Israel came to the K, and said to the
19:41 and said to the K, "Why have our brethren
19:41 away, and brought the K and his household over
19:42 of Israel, "Because the K is near of kin
19:42 at all at the K's expense?
19:43 ten shares in the K, and in David also
19:43 the first to speak of bringing back our K
20:2 Judah followed their K steadfastly from the Jordan
20:3 at Jerusalem; and the K took the ten concubines
20:4 Then the K said to Amasa, "Call the men
20:21 up his hand against K David; give up him
20:22 And Joab returned to Jerusalem to the K
21:2 So the K called the Gibeonites.
21:5 They said to the K, "The man who consumed
21:6 And the K said, "I will give them."
21:7 But the K spared Mephibosheth, the son of Saul's
21:8 The K took the two sons of Rizpah the
21:14 did all that the K commanded.
22:51 he gives to his K, and shows steadfast love
24:2 So the K said to Joab and the commanders
24:3 Joab said to the K, "May the LORD your
24:3 of my lord the K still see it; but
24:3 does my lord the K delight in this thing?"
24:4 But the K's word prevailed against Joab and the
24:4 the presence of the K to number the people
24:9 the people to the K: in Israel there were
24:20 down, he saw the K and his servants coming
24:20 did obeisance to the K with his face to
24:21 has my lord the K come to his servant?"
24:22 "Let my lord the K take and offer up
24:23 All this, O K, Araunah gives to the king."
24:23 All this, O king, Araunah gives to the K
24:23 Araunah said to the K, "The LORD your God
24:24 But the K said to Araunah, "No, but I
1Kgs 1:1 Now K David was old and
1:2 for my lord the K, and let her wait
1:2 her wait upon the K, and be his nurse;
1:2 that my lord the K may be warm."
1:3 Abishag the Shunammite, and brought her to the K
1:4 and she became the K's nurse and ministered to
1:4 to him; but the K knew her not.
1:5 saying, "I will be K; and he prepared for
1:9 all his brothers, the K's sons, and all the
1:11 of Haggith has become K and David our lord
1:13 in at once to K David, and say to
1:13 not, my lord the K, swear to your maidservant,
1:13 Why then is Adonijah K
1:14 still speaking with the K, I also will come
1:15 Bathsheba went to the K into his chamber (now
1:15 his chamber (now the K was very old, and
1:15 Abishag the Shunammite was ministering to the K
1:16 did obeisance to the K, and the king said,
1:16 the king, and the K said, "What do you
1:18 now, behold, Adonijah is K, although you, my lord
1:18 you, my lord the K, do not know it.
1:19 the sons of the K, Abiathar the priest, and
1:20 now, my lord the K, the eyes of all
1:20 of my lord the K after him.
1:21 when my lord the K sleeps with his fathers,
1:22 still speaking with the K, Nathan the prophet came
1:23 And they told the K, "Here is Nathan the
1:23 came in before the K, he bowed before the
1:23 he bowed before the K, with his face to
1:24 said, "My lord the K, have you said, 'Adonijah
1:25 has invited all the K's sons, Joab the commander
1:25 and saying, 'Long live K Adonijah!'
1:27 by my lord the K and you have not
1:27 of my lord the K after him?"

1:28 Then K David answered, "Call Bathsheba to me." So
1:28 she came into the K's presence, and stood before
1:28 into the king's presence, and stood before the K
1:29 And the K swore, saying, "As the LORD lives,
1:31 did obeisance to the K, and said, "May my
1:31 said, "May my lord K David live for ever!"
1:32 K David said, "Call to me Zadok the priest,
1:32 So they came before the K
1:33 And the K said to them, "Take with you
1:34 prophet there anoint him K over Israel; then blow
1:34 and say, 'Long live K Solomon!'
1:35 for he shall be K in my stead; and
1:36 of Jehoiada answered the K, "Amen!
1:36 of my lord the K, say so.
1:37 with my lord the K, even so may he
1:37 throne of my lord K David."
1:38 Solomon to ride on K David's mule, and brought
1:39 people said, "Long live K Solomon!"
1:43 "No, for our lord K David has made Solomon
1:43 David has made Solomon K;
1:44 Solomon king; and the K has sent with him
1:44 to ride on the K's mule;
1:45 prophet have anointed him K at Gihon; and they
1:47 Moreover the K's servants came to congratulate our
1:47 to congratulate our lord K David, saying, 'Your God
1:47 your throne.' And the K bowed himself upon the
1:48 And the K also said, 'Blessed be the LORD,
1:51 Solomon, "Behold, Adonijah fears K Solomon; for, lo,
1:51 the altar, saying, 'Let K Solomon swear to me
1:53 So K Solomon sent, and they brought him down
1:53 and did obeisance to K Solomon; and Solomon said
2:17 he said, "Pray ask K Solomon—he will not
2:18 well; I will speak for you to the K
2:19 So Bathsheba went to K Solomon, to speak to
2:19 And the K rose to meet her, and bowed
2:19 seat brought for the K's mother; and she sat
2:20 And the K said to her, "Make your request,
2:22 K Solomon answered his mother, "And why do you
2:23 Then K Solomon swore by the LORD, saying, "God
2:25 So K Solomon sent Benaiah the son of Jehoiada;
2:26 Abiathar the priest the K said, "Go to Anathoth,
2:29 when it was told K Solomon, "Joab has fled
2:30 said to him, "The K commands, 'Come forth.'" But
2:30 Then Benaiah brought the K word again, saying,
2:31 The K replied to him, "Do as he has
2:35 The K put Benaiah the son of Jehoiada over
2:35 of Joab, and the K put Zadok the priest
2:36 Then the K sent and summoned Shimei, and said
2:38 Shimei said to the K, "What you say is
2:38 as my lord the K has said, so will
2:39 Achish, son of Maacah, K of Gath.
2:42 Gath and returned, the K sent and summoned
2:44 The K also said to Shimei, "You know in
2:45 But K Solomon shall be blessed, and the throne
2:46 Then the K commanded Benaiah the son of
3:1 marriage alliance with Pharaoh K of Egypt; he took
3:4 And the K went to Gibeon to sacrifice there,
3:7 hast made thy servant K in place of David
3:13 so that no other K shall compare with you,
3:16 harlots came to the K, and stood before him.
3:22 Thus they spoke before the K
3:23 Then the K said, "The one says, 'This is
3:24 And the K said, "Bring me a sword." So
3:24 So a sword was brought before the K
3:25 And the K said, "Divide the living child in
3:26 alive said to the K, because her heart yearned
3:27 Then the K answered and said, "Give the living
3:28 the judgment which the K had rendered; and they
3:28 in awe of the K, because they perceived that
4:1 K Solomon was king over all Israel,
4:1 King Solomon was K over all Israel,
4:5 Nathan was priest and K's friend;
4:7 provided food for the K and his household; each
4:19 the country of Sihon K of the Amorites and
4:19 Amorites and of Og K of Bashan.
4:27 officers supplied provisions for K Solomon, and for
4:27 all who came to K Solomon's table, each one
5:1 Now Hiram K of Tyre sent his servants to
5:1 they had anointed him K in place of his
5:13 K Solomon raised a levy of forced labor out
5:17 At the K's command, they quarried out great, costly
6:2 The house which K Solomon built for the LORD
7:13 And K Solomon sent and brought Hiram from Tyre.
7:14 He came to K Solomon, and did all his
7:40 that he did for K Solomon on the house
7:45 Hiram made for K Solomon, were of burnished
7:46 of the Jordan the K cast them, in the
7:51 all the work that K Solomon did on the
8:1 people of Israel, before K Solomon in Jerusalem, to
8:2 of Israel assembled to K Solomon at the feast
8:5 And K Solomon and all the congregation of Israel,
8:14 Then the K faced about, and blessed all the
8:62 Then the K, and all Israel with him, offered
8:63 So the K and all the people of Israel
8:64 The same day the K consecrated the middle of
8:66 and they blessed the K, and went to their
9:1 the LORD and the K's house and all that
9:10 the LORD and the K's house,
9:11 king's house, and Hiram K of Tyre had supplied
9:11 much as he desired, K Solomon gave to Hiram
9:14 had sent to the K one hundred and twenty
9:15 the forced labor which K Solomon levied to build
9:16 Megiddo and Gezer (Pharaoh K of Egypt had gone
9:26 K Solomon built a fleet of ships at Ezion-geber,
9:28 they brought it to K Solomon.
10:3 nothing hidden from the K which he could not
10:6 she said to the K, "The report was true
10:9 he has made you K, that you may execute
10:10 Then she gave the K a hundred and twenty
10:10 of Sheba gave to K Solomon.
10:12 And the K made of the almug wood supports
10:12 LORD, and for the K's house, lyres also and
10:13 And K Solomon gave to the queen of Sheba
10:13 by the bounty of K Solomon.
10:16 K Solomon made two hundred large shields of
10:17 each shield; and the K put them in the
10:18 The K also made a great ivory throne, and
10:21 All K Solomon's drinking vessels were of gold, and
10:22 For the K had a fleet of ships of
10:23 Thus K Solomon excelled all the kings of the
10:26 cities and with the K in Jerusalem.
10:27 And the K made silver as common in Jerusalem
10:28 and Kue, and the K's traders received them from
10:29 and so through the K's traders they were exported
11:1 Now K Solomon loved many foreign women: the
11:18 to Egypt, to Pharaoh K of Egypt, who gave
11:23 from his master Hadadezer K of Zobah.
11:24 there, and made him K in Damascus.
11:26 widow, also lifted up his hand against the K
11:27 why he lifted up his hand against the K
11:37 and you shall be K over Israel.
11:40 into Egypt, to Shishak K of Egypt, and was
12:1 Israel had come to Shechem to make him K
12:2 he had fled from K Solomon), then Jeroboam
12:6 Then K Rehoboam took counsel with the old men,
12:12 third day, as the K said, "Come to me
12:13 And the K answered the people harshly, and
12:15 So the K did not hearken to the people;
12:16 Israel saw that the K did not hearken to
12:16 the people answered the K, "What portion have we
12:18 Then K Rehoboam sent Adoram, who was
12:18 And K Rehoboam made haste to mount his chariot,
12:20 assembly and made him K over all Israel.
12:23 the son of Solomon, K of Judah, and to
12:27 their lord, to Rehoboam K of Judah, and they
12:27 and return to Rehoboam K of Judah."
12:28 So the K took counsel, and made two calves
13:4 And when the K heard the saying of the
13:6 And the K said to the man of God,
13:6 the LORD; and the K's hand was restored to
13:7 And the K said to the man of God,
13:8 God said to the K, "If you give me
13:11 had spoken to the K, they told to their
14:2 that I should be K over this people.
14:14 up for himself a K over Israel, who shall
14:25 the fifth year of K Rehoboam, Shishak king of
14:25 of King Rehoboam, Shishak K of Egypt came up
14:26 the treasures of the K's house; he took away
14:27 Solomon had made; and K Rehoboam made in their
14:27 the door of the K's house.
14:28 as often as the K went into the house
15:1 the eighteenth year of K Jeroboam the son of
15:9 twentieth year of Jeroboam K of Israel Asa began
15:16 between Asa and Baasha K of Israel all their
15:17 Baasha K of Israel went up against Judah, and
15:17 come in to Asa K of Judah.
15:18 the treasures of the K's house, and gave them
15:18 of his servants; and K Asa sent them to
15:18 the son of Hezi-on, K of Syria, who dwelt
15:19 your league with Baasha K of Israel, that he
15:20 And Ben-hadad hearkened to K Asa, and sent the
15:22 Then K Asa made a proclamation to all Judah,

15:22 building; and with them K Asa built Geba of
15:25 second year of Asa K of Judah; and he
15:28 third year of Asa K of Judah, and reigned
15:29 soon as he was K, he killed all the
15:32 between Asa and Baasha K of Israel all their
15:33 third year of Asa K of Judah, Baasha the
16:8 twenty-sixth year of Asa K of Judah, Elah the
16:10 twenty-seventh year of Asa K of Judah, and reigned
16:15 twenty-seventh year of Asa K of Judah, Zimri
16:16 he has killed the K; therefore all Israel made
16:16 commander of the army, K over Israel that day
16:18 the citadel of the K's house, and burned the
16:18 house, and burned the K's house over him with
16:21 Ginath, to make him K, and half followed Omri.
16:22 of Ginath; so Tibni died, and Omri became K
16:23 thirty-first year of Asa K of Judah, Omri began
16:29 thirty-eighth year of Asa K of Judah, Ahab the
16:31 the daughter of Ethbaal K of the Sidonians, and
19:15 anoint Hazael to be K over Syria;
19:16 shall anoint to be K over Israel; and Elisha
20:1 Ben-hadad the K of Syria gathered all his army
20:2 the city to Ahab K of Israel, and said
20:4 And the K of Israel answered, "As you say,
20:4 say, my lord, O K, I am yours, and
20:7 Then the K of Israel called all the elders
20:9 "Tell my lord the K, 'All that you first
20:11 And the K of Israel answered, "Tell him, 'Let
20:13 came near to Ahab K of Israel and said,
20:20 pursued them, but Ben-hadad K of Syria escaped on
20:21 And the K of Israel went out, and captured
20:22 came near to the K of Israel, and said
20:22 in the spring the K of Syria will come
20:23 the servants of the K of Syria said to
20:28 and said to the K of Israel, "Thus says
20:31 go out to the K of Israel; perhaps he
20:32 and went to the K of Israel and said,
20:38 and waited for the K by the way, disguising
20:39 And as the K passed, he cried to the
20:39 he cried to the K and said, "Your servant
20:40 The K of Israel said to him, "So shall
20:41 his eyes; and the K of Israel recognized him
20:43 And the K of Israel went to his house
21:1 the palace of Ahab K of Samaria.
21:10 cursed God and the K Then take him out,
21:13 the people, saying, "Naboth cursed God and the K
21:18 down to meet Ahab K of Israel, who is
22:2 third year Jehoshaphat the K of Judah came down
22:2 came down to the K of Israel.
22:3 And the K of Israel said to his servants,
22:3 the hand of the K of Syria?"
22:4 Jehoshaphat said to the K of Israel, "I am
22:5 Jehoshaphat said to the K of Israel, "Inquire first
22:6 Then the K of Israel gathered the prophets together,
22:6 will give it into the hand of the K
22:8 And the K of Israel said to Jehoshaphat, "There
22:8 said, "Let not the K say so."
22:9 Then the K of Israel summoned an officer and
22:10 Now the K of Israel and Jehoshaphat the king
22:10 Israel and Jehoshaphat the K of Judah were sitting
22:12 will give it into the hand of the K
22:13 are favorable to the K; let your word be
22:15 had come to the K, the king said to
22:15 to the king, the K said to him, "Micaiah,
22:15 will give it into the hand of the K
22:16 But the K said to him, "How many times
22:18 And the K of Israel said to Jehoshaphat, "Did
22:26 And the K of Israel said, "Seize Micaiah, and
22:26 and to Joash the K's son;
22:27 say, 'Thus says the K, "Put this fellow in
22:29 So the K of Israel and Jehoshaphat the king
22:29 Israel and Jehoshaphat the K of Judah went up
22:30 And the K of Israel said to Jehoshaphat, "I
22:30 And the K of Israel disguised himself and went
22:31 Now the K of Syria had commanded the thirty-two
22:31 but only with the K of Israel."
22:32 "It is surely the K of Israel." So they
22:33 it was not the K of Israel, they turned
22:34 venture, and struck the K of Israel between the
22:35 that day, and the K was propped up in
22:37 So the K died, and was brought to Samaria;
22:37 and they buried the K in Samaria.
22:41 fourth year of Ahab K of Israel.
22:44 made peace with the K of Israel.
22:47 There was no K in Edom; a deputy was
22:47 was no king in Edom; a deputy was K
22:51 seventeenth year of Jehoshaphat K of Judah, and he

2Kgs 1:3 the messengers of the K of Samaria, and say
1:5 messengers returned to the K, and he said to
1:6 'Go back to the K who sent you, and
1:9 Then the K sent to him a captain of
1:9 man of God, the K says, 'Come down.'"
1:11 Again the K sent to him another captain of
1:11 God, this is the K's order, 'Come down quickly!'"
1:13 Again the K sent the captain of a third
1:15 with him to the K,
1:17 Jehoram, his brother, became K in his stead in
1:17 the son of Jehoshaphat, K of Judah, because Ahaziah
3:1 eighteenth year of Jehoshaphat K of Judah, Jehoram
3:1 son of Ahab became K over Israel in Samaria,
3:4 Now Mesha K of Moab was a sheep breeder;
3:4 deliver annually to the K of Israel a hundred
3:5 when Ahab died, the K of Moab rebelled against
3:5 Moab rebelled against the K of Israel.
3:6 So K Jehoram marched out of Samaria at that
3:7 sent word to Jehoshaphat K of Judah, "The king
3:7 king of Judah, "The K of Moab has rebelled
3:9 So the K of Israel went with the king
3:9 Israel went with the K of Judah and the
3:9 of Judah and the K of Edom.
3:10 Then the K of Israel said, "Alas!
3:11 Then one of the K of Israel's servants answered,
3:12 So the K of Israel and Jehoshaphat and the
3:12 and Jehoshaphat and the K of Edom went down
3:13 Elisha said to the K of Israel, "What have
3:13 But the K of Israel said to him, "No;
3:14 regard for Jehoshaphat the K of Judah, I would
3:26 When the K of Moab saw that the battle
3:26 break through, opposite the K of Edom; but they
4:13 your behalf to the K or to the commander
5:1 the army of the K of Syria, was a
5:5 And the K of Syria said, "Go now, and
5:5 a letter to the K of Israel." So he
5:6 the letter to the K of Israel, which read,
5:7 And when the K of Israel read the letter,
5:8 God heard that the K of Israel had rent
5:8 he sent to the K, saying, "Why have you
6:8 Once when the K of Syria was warring against
6:9 sent word to the K of Israel, "Beware that
6:10 And the K of Israel sent to the place
6:11 the mind of the K of Syria was greatly
6:11 us is for the K of Israel?"
6:12 "None, my lord, O K; but Elisha, the prophet
6:12 in Israel, tells the K of Israel the words
6:21 When the K of Israel saw them he said
6:24 Afterward Ben-hadad K of Syria mustered his entire
6:26 Now as the K of Israel was passing by
6:26 out to him, saying, "Help, my lord, O K
6:28 And the K asked her, "What is your trouble?"
6:30 When the K heard the words of the woman
6:32 Now the K had dispatched a man from his
6:33 speaking with them, the K came down to him
7:2 on whose hand the K leaned said to the
7:6 one another, "Behold, the K of Israel has hired
7:9 go and tell the K's household."
7:11 was told within the K's household.
7:12 And the K rose in the night, and said
7:14 mounted men, and the K sent them after the
7:15 And the messengers returned, and told the K
7:17 Now the K had appointed the captain on whose
7:17 had said when the K came down to him.
7:18 had said to the K, "Two measures of barley
8:3 to appeal to the K for her house and
8:4 Now the K was talking with Gehazi the servant
8:5 he was telling the K how Elisha had restored
8:5 life appealed to the K for her house and
8:5 said, "My lord, O K, here is the woman,
8:6 And when the K asked the woman, she told
8:6 So the K appointed an official for her, saying,
8:7 Ben-hadad the K of Syria was sick; and when
8:8 the K said to Hazael, "Take a present with
8:9 said, "Your son Ben-hadad K of Syria has sent
8:13 you are to be K over Syria."
8:15 And Hazael became K in his stead.
8:16 the son of Ahab, K of Israel, Jehoram the
8:16 the son of Jehoshaphat, K of Judah, began to
8:17 old when he became K, and he reigned eight
8:20 and set up a K of their own.
8:25 the son of Ahab, K of Israel, Ahaziah the
8:25 the son of Jehoram, K of Judah, began to
8:26 a granddaughter of Omri K of Israel.
8:28 war against Hazael K of Syria at Ramoth-gilead,
8:29 And K Joram returned to be healed in Jezreel

K

8:29 he fought against Hazael K of Syria.
8:29 the son of Jehoram K of Judah went down
9:3 LORD, I anoint you K over Israel.' Then open
9:6 Israel, I anoint you K over the people of
9:12 LORD, I anoint you K over Israel.'"
9:13 they blew the trumpet, and proclaimed, "Jehu is K
9:14 at Ramoth-gilead against Hazael K of Syria;
9:15 king of Syria; but K Joram had returned to
9:15 he fought with Hazael K of Syria.) So Jehu
9:16 And Ahaziah K of Judah had come down to
9:18 said, "Thus says the K, 'Is it peace?" And
9:19 and said, "Thus the K has said, 'Is it
9:21 Then Joram K of Israel and Ahaziah king of
9:21 of Israel and Ahaziah K of Judah set out,
9:27 When Ahaziah the K of Judah saw this, he
9:34 for she is a K's daughter."
10:5 not make any one K; do whatever is good
10:6 Now the K's sons, seventy persons, were with the
10:7 them, they took the K's sons, and slew them,
10:8 the heads of the K's sons," he said, "Lay
10:13 the kinsmen of Ahaziah K of Judah, and he
11:2 Jehosheba, the daughter of K Joram, sister of
11:2 away from among the K's sons who were about
11:4 he showed them the K's son.
11:5 sabbath and guard the K's house
11:8 LORD, shall surround the K, each with his weapons
11:8 Be with the K when he goes out and
11:10 shields that had been K Davids, which were in
11:12 he brought out the K's son, and put the
11:12 and they proclaimed him K, and anointed him; and
11:12 clapped their hands, and said, "Long live the K
11:14 looked, there was the K standing by the pillar,
11:14 the trumpeters beside the K, and all the people
11:16 horses' entrance to the K's house, and there she
11:17 the LORD and the K and people, that they
11:17 and also between the K and the people.
11:19 and they brought the K down from the house
11:19 the guards to the K's house.
11:20 the sword at the K's house.
12:6 the twenty-third year of K Jehoash the priests had
12:7 Therefore K Jehoash summoned Jehoiada the priest
12:10 in the chest, the K's secretary and the high
12:17 At that time Hazael K of Syria went up
12:18 up against Jerusalem, Jehoash K of Judah took all
12:18 LORD and of the K's house, and sent these
12:18 sent these to Hazael K of Syria.
13:1 the son of Ahaziah, K of Judah, Jehoahaz the
13:3 the hand of Hazael K of Syria and into
13:4 of Israel, how the K of Syria oppressed them.
13:7 thousand footmen; for the K of Syria had destroyed
13:10 thirty-seventh year of Joash K of Judah Jehoash the
13:12 he fought against Amaziah K of Judah, are they
13:14 was to die, Joash K of Israel went down
13:16 he said to the K of Israel, "Draw the
13:16 his hands upon the K's hands.
13:18 he said to the K of Israel, "Strike the
13:22 Now Hazael K of Syria oppressed Israel all the
13:24 When Hazael K of Syria died, Ben-hadad his son
13:24 Ben-hadad his son became K in his stead.
14:1 the son of Joahaz, K of Israel, Amaziah the
14:1 the son of Joash, K of Judah, began to
14:5 who had slain the K his father.
14:8 Jehoahaz, son of Jehu, K of Israel, saying, "Come,
14:9 And Jehoash K of Israel sent word to Amaziah
14:9 sent word to Amaziah K of Judah, "A thistle
14:11 So Jehoash K of Israel went up, and he
14:11 and he and Amaziah K of Judah faced one
14:13 And Jehoash K of Israel captured Amaziah king of
14:13 of Israel captured Amaziah K of Judah, the son
14:14 the treasuries of the K's house, also hostages, and
14:15 he fought with Amaziah K of Judah, are they
14:17 the son of Joash, K of Judah, lived fifteen
14:17 Jehoash son of Jehoahaz, K of Israel.
14:21 old, and made him K instead of his father
14:22 to Judah, after the K slept with his fathers.
14:23 the son of Joash, K of Judah, Jeroboam the
14:23 the son of Joash, K of Israel, began to
15:1 twenty-seventh year of Jeroboam K of Israel Azariah
15:1 the son of Amaziah, K of Judah, began to
15:5 the LORD smote the K, so that he was
15:5 And Jotham the K's son was over the household,
15:8 thirty-eighth year of Azariah K of Judah Zechariah
15:13 thirty-ninth year of Uzziah K of Judah, and he
15:17 thirty-ninth year of Azariah K of Judah Menahem
15:19 Pul the K of Assyria came against the land;
15:20 to give to the K of Assyria.
15:20 So the K of Assyria turned back, and did
15:23 fiftieth year of Azariah K of Judah Pekahiah the
15:25 the citadel of the K's house; he slew him,
15:27 fifty-second year of Azariah K of Judah Pekah the
15:29 the days of Pekah K of Israel Tiglath-pileser king
15:29 king of Israel Tiglath-pileser K of Assyria came and
15:32 the son of Remaliah, K of Israel, Jotham the
15:32 the son of Uzziah, K of Judah, began to
15:37 to send Rezin the K of Syria and Pekah
16:1 the son of Jotham, K of Judah, began to
16:5 Then Rezin K of Syria and Pekah the son
16:5 the son of Remaliah, K of Israel, came up
16:6 At that time the K of Edom recovered Elath
16:7 messengers to Tiglath-pileser K of Assyria, saying, "I
16:7 the hand of the K of Syria and from
16:7 the hand of the K of Israel, who are
16:8 the treasures of the K's house, and sent a
16:8 a present to the K of Assyria.
16:9 And the K of Assyria hearkened to him; the
16:9 hearkened to him; the K of Assyria marched up
16:10 K Ahaz went to Damascus to meet Tiglath-pileser
16:10 Damascus to meet Tiglath-pileser K of Assyria, he
16:10 And K Ahaz sent to Uriah the priest a
16:11 accordance with all that K Ahaz had sent from
16:11 priest made it, before K Ahaz arrived from
16:12 And when the K came from Damascus, the king
16:12 came from Damascus, the K viewed the altar.
16:12 Then the K drew near to the altar, and
16:15 K Ahaz commanded Uriah the priest, saying, "Upon
16:15 cereal offering, and the K's burnt offering, and his
16:16 did all this, as K Ahaz commanded.
16:17 And K Ahaz cut off the frames of the
16:18 outer entrance for the K he removed from the
16:18 LORD, because of the K of Assyria.
17:1 twelfth year of Ahaz K of Judah Hoshea the
17:3 him came up Shalmaneser K of Assyria; and Hoshea
17:4 But the K of Assyria found treachery in Hoshea;
17:4 sent messengers to So, K of Egypt, and offered
17:4 no tribute to the K of Assyria, as he
17:4 by year; therefore the K of Assyria shut him
17:5 Then the K of Assyria invaded all the land
17:6 year of Hoshea the K of Assyria captured Samaria,
17:7 the hand of Pharaoh K of Egypt, and had
17:21 David they made Jeroboam the son of Nebat K
17:24 And the K of Assyria brought people from Babylon,
17:26 So the K of Assyria was told, "The nations
17:27 Then the K of Assyria commanded, "Send there one
18:1 Hoshea son of Elah, K of Israel, Hezekiah the
18:1 the son of Ahaz, K of Judah, began to
18:7 He rebelled against the K of Assyria, and would
18:9 the fourth year of K Hezekiah, which was the
18:9 Hoshea son of Elah, K of Israel, Shalmaneser king
18:9 king of Israel, Shalmaneser K of Assyria came up
18:10 ninth year of Hoshea K of Israel, Samaria was
18:11 The K of Assyria carried the Israelites away to
18:13 the fourteenth year of K Hezekiah Sennacherib king
18:13 of King Hezekiah Sennacherib K of Assyria came up
18:14 And Hezekiah K of Judah sent to the king
18:14 Judah sent to the K of Assyria at Lachish,
18:14 And the K of Assyria required of Hezekiah king
18:14 Assyria required of Hezekiah K of Judah three
18:15 the treasuries of the K's house.
18:16 the doorposts which Hezekiah K of Judah had
18:16 gave it to the K of Assyria.
18:17 And the K of Assyria sent the Tartan, the
18:17 army from Lachish to K Hezekiah at Jerusalem.
18:18 they called for the K, there came out to
18:19 'Thus says the great K, the king of Assyria:
18:19 the great king, the K of Assyria: On what
18:21 Such is Pharaoh K of Egypt to all who
18:23 with my master the K of Assyria: I will
18:28 word of the great K, the king of Assyria!
18:28 the great king, the K of Assyria!
18:29 Thus says the K: 'Do not let Hezekiah deceive
18:30 the hand of the K of Assyria.'
18:31 for thus says the K of Assyria: 'Make your
18:33 the hand of the K of Assyria?
18:36 a word, for the K's command was, "Do not
19:1 When K Hezekiah heard it, he rent his clothes,
19:4 whom his master the K of Assyria has sent
19:5 When the servants of K Hezekiah came to Isaiah,
19:6 the servants of the K of Assyria have reviled
19:8 returned, and found the K of Assyria fighting against
19:8 he heard that the K had left Lachish.
19:9 And when the K heard concerning Tirhakah king of
19:9 heard concerning Tirhakah K of Ethiopia, "Behold,

19:10 you speak to Hezekiah K of Judah: 'Do not
19:10 the hand of the K of Assyria.
19:13 Where is the K of Hamath, the king of
19:13 king of Hamath, the K of Arpad, the king
19:13 king of Arpad, the K of the city of
19:13 city of Sepharvaim, the K of Hena, or the
19:13 of Hena, or the K of Ivvah?"
19:20 to me about Sennacherib K of Assyria I have
19:32 the LORD concerning the K of Assyria, He shall
19:36 Then Sennacherib K of Assyria departed, and went
20:6 the hand of the K of Assyria, and I
20:12 the son of Baladan, K of Babylon, sent envoys
20:14 the prophet came to K Hezekiah, and said to
20:18 the palace of the K of Babylon."
21:3 an Asherah, as Ahab K of Israel had done,
21:11 the prophets, "Because Manasseh K of Judah has
21:23 him, and killed the K in his house.
21:24 who had conspired against K Amon, and the people
21:24 made Josiah his son K in his stead.
22:3 the eighteenth year of K Josiah, the king sent
22:3 of King Josiah, the K sent Shaphan the son
22:9 secretary came to the K, and reported to the
22:9 and reported to the K, "Your servants have emptied
22:10 the secretary told the K, "Hilkiah the priest has
22:10 And Shaphan read it before the K
22:11 And when the K heard the words of the
22:12 And the K commanded Hilkiah the priest, and
22:12 secretary, and Asaiah the K's servant, saying,
22:16 the book which the K of Judah has read.
22:18 But as to the K of Judah, who sent
22:20 And they brought back word to the K
23:1 Then the K sent, and all the elders of
23:2 And the K went up to the house of
23:3 And the K stood by the pillar and made
23:4 And the K commanded Hilkiah, the high priest, and
23:13 And the K defiled the high places that were
23:13 corruption, which Solomon the K of Israel had built
23:21 And the K commanded all the people, "Keep the
23:23 the eighteenth year of K Josiah this passover was
23:25 him there was no K like him, who turned
23:29 his days Pharaoh Neco K of Egypt went up
23:29 went up to the K of Assyria to the
23:29 K Josiah went to meet him; and Pharaoh Neco
23:30 him, and made him K in his father's stead.
23:34 the son of Josiah K in the place of
24:1 In his days Nebuchadnezzar K of Babylon came up,
24:7 And the K of Egypt did not come again
24:7 his land, for the K of Babylon had taken
24:7 that belonged to the K of Egypt from the
24:8 old when he became K, and he reigned three
24:10 the servants of Nebuchadnezzar K of Babylon came
24:11 And Nebuchadnezzar K of Babylon came to the city,
24:12 it; and Jehoiachin the K of Judah gave himself
24:12 himself up to the K of Babylon, himself, and
24:12 The K of Babylon took him prisoner in the
24:13 the treasures of the K's house, and cut in
24:13 the LORD, which Solomon K of Israel had made,
24:15 Jehoiachin to Babylon; the K's mother, the king's
24:15 the king's mother, the K's wives, his officials, and
24:16 And the K of Babylon brought captive to Babylon
24:17 And the K of Babylon made Mattaniah, Jehoiachin's
24:17 made Mattaniah, Jehoiachin's uncle, K in his stead,
24:18 old when he became K, and he reigned eleven
24:20 Zedekiah rebelled against the K of Babylon.
25:1 of the month, Nebuchadnezzar K of Babylon came
25:2 the eleventh year of K Zedekiah.
25:4 in the city; the K with all the men
25:4 two walls, by the K's garden, though the Chaldeans
25:5 the Chaldeans pursued the K, and overtook him in
25:6 Then they captured the K, and brought him up
25:6 him up to the K of Babylon at Riblah,
25:8 year of K Nebuchadnezzar, K of Babylon--
25:8 a servant of the K of Babylon, came to
25:9 the LORD, and the K's house and all the
25:11 had deserted to the K of Babylon, together with
25:19 five men of the K's council who were found
25:20 brought them to the K of Babylon at Riblah.
25:21 And the K of Babylon smote them, and put
25:22 of Judah, whom Nebuchadnezzar K of Babylon had
25:23 men heard that the K of Babylon had appointed
25:24 land, and serve the K of Babylon, and it
25:27 the exile of Jehoiachin K of Judah, in the
25:27 of the month, Evil-merodach K of Babylon, in the
25:27 reign, graciously freed Jehoiachin K of Judah from
25:29 dined regularly at the K's table;
25:30 given him by the K, every day a portion,

1Chr 1:43 of Edom before any K reigned over the Israelites:
3:2 the daughter of Talmai, K of Geshur; the fourth
4:23 dwelt there with the K for his work.
4:41 the days of Hezekiah, K of Judah, and destroyed
5:6 his son, whom Tilgath-pilneser K of Assyria carried
5:17 the days of Jotham K of Judah, and in
5:17 the days of Jeroboam K of Israel.
5:26 the spirit of Pul K of Assyria, the spirit
5:26 the spirit of Tilgath-pilneser K of Assyria, and he
9:18 stationed hitherto in the K's gate on the east
11:2 even when Saul was K, it was you that
11:3 Israel came to the K at Hebron; and David
11:3 and they anointed David K over Israel, according to
11:10 Israel, to make him K, according to the word
12:31 were expressly named to come and make David K
12:38 intent to make David K over all Israel; likewise
12:38 were of a single mind to make David K
14:1 And Hiram K of Tyre sent messengers to David,
14:2 LORD had established him K over Israel, and that
14:8 David had been anointed K over all Israel, all
15:29 the window, and saw K David dancing and making
17:16 Then K David went in and sat before the
18:3 David also defeated Hadadezer K of Zobah, toward
18:5 came to help Hadadezer K of Zobah, David slew
18:9 When Tou K of Hamath heard that David had
18:9 whole army of Hadadezer, K of Zobah,
18:10 his son Hadoram to K David, to greet him,
18:11 of bronze; these also K David dedicated to the
18:17 the chief officials in the service of the K
19:1 after this Nahash the K of the Ammonites died,
19:5 And the K said, "Remain at Jericho until your
19:7 thousand chariots and the K of Maacah with his
20:2 the crown of their K from his head; he
21:3 not, my lord the K, all of them my
21:4 But the K's word prevailed against Joab.
21:6 the numbering, for the K's command was abhorrent
21:23 let my lord the K do what seems good
21:24 But K David said to Ornan, "No, but I
23:1 made Solomon his son K over Israel.
24:6 the presence of the K, and the princes, and
24:31 in the presence of K David, Zadok, Ahimelech, and
25:2 Asaph, who prophesied under the direction of the K
25:5 sons of Heman the K's seer, according to the
25:6 and Heman were under the order of the K
26:26 gifts which David the K, and the heads of
26:30 the LORD and for the service of the K
26:32 at Jazer in Gilead.) K David appointed him and
26:32 to God and for the affairs of the K
27:1 officers who served the K in all matters concerning
27:24 in the chronicles of K David.
27:25 Over the K's treasuries was Azmaveth the son of
27:31 these were stewards of K David's property.
27:32 of Hachmoni attended the K's sons.
27:33 Ahithophel was the K's counselor, and Hushai the
27:33 the Archite was the K's friend.
27:34 was commander of the K's army.
28:1 divisions that served the K, the commanders of
28:1 and cattle of the K and his sons, together
28:2 Then K David rose to his feet and said:
28:4 father's house to be K over Israel for ever;
28:4 me to make me K over all Israel.
29:1 And David the K said to all the assembly,
29:6 the officers over the K's work.
29:9 the LORD; David the K also rejoiced greatly.
29:20 worshiped the LORD, and did obeisance to the K
29:22 the son of David K the second time, and
29:23 of the LORD as K instead of David his
29:24 all the sons of K David, pledged their allegiance
29:24 pledged their allegiance to K Solomon.
29:25 not been on any K before him in Israel.
29:29 Now the acts of K David, from first to
2Chr 1:8 and hast made me K in his stead.
1:9 thou hast made me K over a people as
1:11 I have made you K,
1:14 cities and with the K in Jerusalem.
1:15 And the K made silver and gold as common
1:16 and Kue, and the K's traders received them from
2:3 word to Huram the K of Tyre: "As you
2:11 Then Huram the K of Tyre answered in a
2:11 he has made you K over them."
2:12 earth, who has given K David a wise son,
4:11 that he did for K Solomon on the house
4:16 of burnished bronze for K Solomon for the house
4:17 of the Jordan the K cast them, in the
5:3 Israel assembled before the K at the feast which
5:6 And K Solomon and all the congregation of Israel,

6:3 Then the K faced about, and blessed all the
7:4 Then the K and all the people offered sacrifice
7:5 K Solomon offered as a sacrifice twenty-two
7:5 So the K and all the people dedicated the
7:6 to the LORD which K David had made for
7:11 the LORD and the K's house; all that Solomon
8:10 the chief officers of K Solomon, two hundred and
8:11 the house of David K of Israel, for the
8:15 aside from what the K had commanded the priests
8:18 and brought it to K Solomon.
9:5 she said to the K, "The report was true
9:8 on his throne as K for the LORD your
9:8 he has made you K over them, that you
9:9 Then she gave the K a hundred and twenty
9:9 of Sheba gave to K Solomon.
9:11 And the K made of the algum wood steps
9:11 LORD and for the K's house, lyres also and
9:12 And K Solomon gave to the queen of Sheba
9:12 asked besides what she had brought to the K
9:15 K Solomon made two hundred large shields of
9:16 each shield; and the K put them in the
9:17 The K also made a great ivory throne, and
9:20 All K Solomon's drinking vessels were of gold, and
9:21 For the K's ships went to Tarshish with the
9:22 Thus K Solomon excelled all the kings of the
9:25 cities and with the K in Jerusalem.
9:27 And the K made silver as common in Jerusalem
10:1 Israel had come to Shechem to make him K
10:2 he had fled from K Solomon), then Jeroboam
10:6 Then K Rehoboam took counsel with the old men,
10:12 third day, as the K said, "Come to me
10:13 And the K answered them harshly, and forsaking the
10:14 of the old men, K Rehoboam spoke to them
10:15 So the K did not hearken to the people;
10:16 Israel saw that the K did not hearken to
10:16 the people answered the K, "What portion have we
10:18 Then K Rehoboam sent Hadoram, who was
10:18 And K Rehoboam made haste to mount his chariot,
11:3 the son of Solomon K of Judah, and to
11:22 his brothers, for he intended to make him K
12:2 the fifth year of K Rehoboam, because they had
12:2 to the LORD, Shishak K of Egypt came up
12:6 of Israel and the K humbled themselves and said,
12:9 So Shishak K of Egypt came up against Jerusalem;
12:9 the treasures of the K's house; he took away
12:10 Solomon had made; and K Rehoboam made in their
12:10 the door of the K's house.
12:11 as often as the K went into the house
12:13 So K Rehoboam established himself in Jerusalem
13:1 the eighteenth year of K Jeroboam Abijah began to
15:16 Even Maacah, his mother, K Asa removed from being
16:1 reign of Asa, Baasha K of Israel went up
16:1 come in to Asa K of Judah.
16:2 the LORD and the K's house, and sent them
16:2 sent them to Ben-hadad K of Syria, who dwelt
16:3 your league with Baasha K of Israel, that he
16:4 And Ben-hadad hearkened to K Asa, and sent the
16:6 Then K Asa took all Judah, and they carried
16:7 seer came to Asa K of Judah, and said
16:7 you relied on the K of Syria, and did
16:7 the army of the K of Syria has escaped
17:19 the service of the K, besides those whom the
17:19 besides those whom the K had placed in the
18:3 Ahab K of Israel said to Jehoshaphat king of
18:3 Israel said to Jehoshaphat K of Judah, "Will you
18:4 Jehoshaphat said to the K of Israel, "Inquire first
18:5 Then the K of Israel gathered the prophets together,
18:5 will give it into the hand of the K
18:7 And the K of Israel said to Jehoshaphat, "There
18:7 said, "Let not the K say so."
18:8 Then the K of Israel summoned an officer and
18:9 Now the K of Israel and Jehoshaphat the king
18:9 Israel and Jehoshaphat the K of Judah were sitting
18:11 will give it into the hand of the K
18:12 are favorable to the K; let your word be
18:14 had come to the K, the king said to
18:14 to the king, the K said to him, "Micaiah,
18:15 But the K said to him, "How many times
18:17 And the K of Israel said to Jehoshaphat, "Did
18:19 will entice Ahab the K of Israel, that he
18:25 And the K of Israel said, "Seize Micaiah, and
18:25 and to Joash the K's son;
18:26 say, 'Thus says the K, Put this fellow in
18:28 So the K of Israel and Jehoshaphat the king
18:28 Israel and Jehoshaphat the K of Judah went up
18:29 And the K of Israel said to Jehoshaphat, "I
18:29 And the K of Israel disguised himself; and they
18:30 Now the K of Syria had commanded the captains
18:30 but only with the K of Israel."
18:31 said, "It is the K of Israel." So they
18:32 it was not the K of Israel, they turned
18:33 venture, and struck the K of Israel between the
18:34 that day, and the K of Israel propped himself
19:1 Jehoshaphat the K of Judah returned in safety to
19:2 him, and said to K Jehoshaphat, "Should you help
19:11 Judah, in all the K's matters; and the Levites
20:15 inhabitants of Jerusalem, and K Jehoshaphat: Thus
20:35 After this Jehoshaphat K of Judah joined with
20:35 Judah joined with Ahaziah K of Israel, who did
21:2 the sons of Jehoshaphat K of Judah.
21:5 old when he became K, and he reigned eight
21:8 and set up a K of their own.
21:12 the ways of Asa K of Judah,
21:17 that belonged to the K's house, and also his
22:1 Ahaziah his youngest son K in his stead; for
22:1 the son of Jehoram K of Judah reigned.
22:5 the son of Ahab K of Israel to make
22:5 war against Hazael K of Syria at Ramoth-gilead.
22:6 he fought against Hazael K of Syria.
22:6 the son of Jehoram K of Judah went down
22:11 the daughter of the K, took Joash the son
22:11 away from among the K's sons who were about
22:11 Jeho-shabe-ath, the daughter of K Jehoram and wife
23:3 a covenant with the K in the house of
23:3 to them, "Behold, the K's son!
23:5 shall be at the K's house and one third
23:7 Levites shall surround the K, each with his weapons
23:7 Be with the K when he comes in, and
23:9 shields that had been K Davids, which were in
23:10 a guard for the K, every man with his
23:11 he brought out the K's son, and put the
23:11 and they proclaimed him K, and Jehoiada and his
23:11 anointed him, and they said, "Long live the K
23:12 running and praising the K, she went into the
23:13 looked, there was the K standing by his pillar
23:13 the trumpeters beside the K, and all the people
23:15 horse gate of the K's house, and they slew
23:16 the people and the K that they should be
23:20 and they brought the K down from the house
23:20 upper gate to the K's house.
23:20 And they set the K upon the royal throne.
24:6 So the K summoned Jehoiada the chief, and said
24:8 So the K commanded, and they made a chest,
24:11 was brought to the K's officers by the Levites,
24:11 money in it, the K's secretary and the officer
24:12 And the K and Jehoiada gave it to those
24:14 the money before the K and Jehoiada, and with
24:17 did obeisance to the K; then the king hearkened
24:17 the king; then the K hearkened to them.
24:21 by command of the K they stoned him with
24:22 Thus Joash the K did not remember the kindness
24:23 their spoil to the K of Damascus.
25:3 who had slain the K his father.
25:7 him and said, "O K, do not let the
25:16 he was speaking the K said to him, "Have
25:17 Then Amaziah K of Judah took counsel and sent
25:17 Jehoahaz, son of Jehu, K of Israel, saying, "Come,
25:18 And Joash the K of Israel sent word to
25:18 sent word to Amaziah K of Judah, "A thistle
25:21 So Joash K of Israel went up; and he
25:21 and he and Amaziah K of Judah faced one
25:23 And Joash K of Israel captured Amaziah king of
25:23 of Israel captured Amaziah K of Judah, the son
25:24 the treasuries of the K's house, and hostages, and
25:25 the son of Joash K of Judah lived fifteen
25:25 the son of Jehoahaz, K of Israel.
26:1 old, and made him K instead of his father
26:2 to Judah, after the K slept with his fathers.
26:11 Hananiah, one of the K's commanders.
26:13 power, to help the K against the enemy.
26:18 valor; and they withstood K Uzziah, and said to
26:21 And K Uzziah was a leper to the day
26:21 son was over the K's household, governing the people
27:5 He fought with the K of the Ammonites and
28:5 the hand of the K of Syria, who defeated
28:5 the hand of the K of Israel, who defeated
28:7 Ephraim, slew Ma-aseiah the K's son and Azrikam
28:7 and Elkanah the next in authority to the K
28:16 At that time K Ahaz sent to the king
28:16 Ahaz sent to the K of Assyria for help.
28:19 low because of Ahaz K of Israel, for he
28:20 So Tilgath-pilneser K of Assyria came against him,

28:21 the house of the K and of the princes,
28:21 gave tribute to the K of Assyria; but it
28:22 the LORD--this same K Ahaz.
29:15 went in as the K had commanded, by the
29:18 in to Hezekiah the K and said, "We have
29:19 All the utensils which K Ahaz discarded in his
29:20 Then Hezekiah the K rose early and gathered the
29:23 were brought to the K and the assembly, and
29:24 For the K commanded that the burnt offering and
29:25 and of Gad the K's seer and of Nathan
29:27 the instruments of David K of Israel.
29:29 offering was finished, the K and all who were
29:30 And Hezekiah the K and the princes commanded the
30:2 For the K and his princes and all the
30:4 seemed right to the K and all the assembly.
30:6 with letters from the K and his princes, as
30:6 his princes, as the K had commanded, saying, "O
30:12 to do what the K and the princes commanded
30:24 For Hezekiah K of Judah gave the assembly a
30:26 the son of David K of Israel there had
31:3 The contribution of the K from his own possessions
31:13 appointment of Hezekiah the K and Azariah the
32:1 acts of faithfulness Sennacherib K of Assyria came
32:7 or dismayed before the K of Assyria and all
32:8 the words of Hezekiah K of Judah.
32:9 this Sennacherib K of Assyria, who was besieging
32:9 to Jerusalem to Hezekiah K of Judah and to
32:10 saying, "Thus says Sennacherib K of Assyria, 'On
32:11 the hand of the K of Assyria"?
32:20 Then Hezekiah the K and Isaiah the prophet, the
32:21 the camp of the K of Assyria.
32:22 the hand of Sennacherib K of Assyria and from
32:23 precious things to Hezekiah K of Judah, so that
33:11 the army of the K of Assyria, who took
33:25 who had conspired against K Amon; and the people
33:25 made Josiah his son K in his stead.
34:16 the book to the K, and further reported to
34:16 further reported to the K, "All that was committed
34:18 the secretary told the K, "Hilkiah the priest has
34:18 And Shaphan read it before the K
34:19 When the K heard the words of the law
34:20 And the K commanded Hilkiah, Ahikam the son of
34:20 secretary, and Asaiah the K's servant, saying,
34:22 and those whom the K had sent went to
34:24 was read before the K of Judah.
34:26 But to the K of Judah, who sent you
34:28 And they brought back word to the K
34:29 Then the K sent and gathered together all the
34:30 And the K went up to the house of
34:31 And the K stood in his place and made
35:3 the son of David, K of Israel, built; you
35:4 the directions of David K of Israel and the
35:7 these were from the K's possessions.
35:10 divisions according to the K's command.
35:15 and Jeduthun the K's seer; and the gatekeepers
35:16 to the command of K Josiah.
35:20 prepared the temple, Neco K of Egypt went up
35:21 do with each other, K of Judah?
35:23 And the archers shot K Josiah; and the king
35:23 King Josiah; and the K said to his servants,
36:1 Josiah and made him K in his father's stead
36:3 Then the K of Egypt deposed him in Jerusalem
36:4 And the K of Egypt made Eliakim his brother
36:4 Eliakim his brother K over Judah and Jerusalem,
36:6 him came up Nebuchadnezzar K of Babylon, and
36:10 spring of the year K Nebuchadnezzar sent and
36:10 his brother Zedekiah K over Judah and Jerusalem.
36:13 also rebelled against K Nebuchadnezzar, who had
36:17 up against them the K of the Chaldeans, who
36:18 the treasures of the K and of his princes,
36:22 first year of Cyrus K of Persia, that the
36:22 the spirit of Cyrus K of Persia so that
36:23 writing: "Thus says Cyrus K of Persia, 'The LORD,
Ezra 1:1 first year of Cyrus K of Persia, that the
1:1 the spirit of Cyrus K of Persia so that
1:2 writing: "Thus says Cyrus K of Persia: The LORD,
1:7 Cyrus the K also brought out the vessels of
1:8 Cyrus K of Persia brought these out in charge
2:1 exiles whom Nebuchadnezzar the K of Babylon had
3:7 they had from Cyrus K of Persia.
3:10 the directions of David K of Israel;
4:2 the days of Esarhaddon K of Assyria who brought
4:3 God of Israel, as K Cyrus the king of
4:3 as King Cyrus the K of Persia has commanded
4:5 the days of Cyrus K of Persia, even until
4:5 the reign of Darius K of Persia.
4:7 associates wrote to Artaxerxes K of Persia; the
4:8 Jerusalem to Artaxerxes the K as follows--
4:11 "To Artaxerxes the K: Your servants, the men
4:12 it known to the K that the Jews who
4:13 it known to the K that, if this city
4:14 us to witness the K's dishonor, therefore we send
4:14 send and inform the K,
4:16 make known to the K that, if this city
4:17 The K sent an answer: "To Rehum the commander
4:22 should damage grow to the hurt of the K
4:23 when the copy of K Artaxerxes' letter was read
4:24 the reign of Darius K of Persia.
5:6 sent to Darius the K;
5:7 follows: "To Darius the K, all peace.
5:8 it known to the K that we went to
5:11 ago, which a great K of Israel built and
5:12 the hand of Nebuchadnezzar K of Babylon, the
5:13 first year of Cyrus K of Babylon, Cyrus the
5:13 of Babylon, Cyrus the K made a decree that
5:14 Babylon, these Cyrus the K took out of the
5:17 seem good to the K, let search be made
5:17 issued by Cyrus the K for the rebuilding of
5:17 And let the K send us his pleasure in
6:1 Then Darius the K made a decree, and search
6:3 year of Cyrus the K, Cyrus the king issued
6:3 the king, Cyrus the K issued a decree: Concerning
6:10 the life of the K and his sons.
6:12 dwell there overthrow any K or people that shall
6:13 sent by Darius the K, Tattenai, the governor of
6:13 diligence what Darius the K had ordered.
6:14 and Darius and Artaxerxes K of Persia;
6:15 sixth year of the reign of Darius the K
6:22 the heart of the K of Assyria to them,
7:1 the reign of Artaxerxes K of Persia, Ezra the
7:6 had given; and the K granted him all that
7:7 year of Artaxerxes the K, some of the people
7:8 seventh year of the K;
7:11 of the letter which K Artaxerxes gave to Ezra
7:12 statutes for Israel: "Artaxerxes, K of kings, to Ezra
7:14 are sent by the K and his seven counselors
7:15 and gold which the K and his counselors have
7:20 it out of the K's treasury.
7:21 "And I, Artaxerxes the K, make a decree to
7:23 the realm of the K and his sons.
7:26 the law of the K, let judgment be strictly
7:27 the heart of the K, to beautify the house
7:28 steadfast love before the K and his counselors, and
7:28 and before all the K's mighty officers.
8:1 reign of Artaxerxes the K:
8:22 ashamed to ask the K for a band of
8:22 we had told the K, "The hand of our
8:25 our God which the K and his counselors and
8:36 They also delivered the K's commissions to the king's
8:36 king's commissions to the K's satraps and to the
Neh 1:11 Now I was cupbearer to the K
2:1 the twentieth year of K Artaxerxes, when wine was
2:1 up the wine and gave it to the K
2:2 And the K said to me, "Why is your
2:3 I said to the K, "Let the king live
2:3 the king, "Let the K live for ever!
2:4 Then the K said to me, "For what do
2:5 I said to the K, "If it pleases the
2:5 "If it pleases the K, and if your servant
2:6 And the K said to me (the queen sitting
2:6 So it pleased the K to send me; and
2:7 I said to the K, "If it pleases the
2:7 "If it pleases the K, let letters be given
2:8 the keeper of the K's forest, that he may
2:8 And the K granted me what I asked, for
2:9 and gave them the K's letters.
2:9 Now the K had sent with me officers of
2:14 Gate and to the K's Pool; but there was
2:18 the words which the K had spoken to me.
2:19 Are you rebelling against the K
3:15 of Shelah of the K's garden, as far as
3:25 upper house of the K at the court of
5:4 borrowed money for the K's tax upon our fields
5:14 year of Artaxerxes the K, twelve years, neither I
6:6 wish to become their K, according to this report.
6:7 Jerusalem, 'There is a K in Judah.' And now
6:7 be reported to the K according to these words.
7:6 exiles whom Nebuchadnezzar the K of Babylon had
9:22 the land of Sihon K of Heshbon and the
9:22 the land of Og K of Bashan.
11:23 a command from the K concerning them, and a
11:24 Judah, was at the K's hand in all matters

K

13:6 thirty-second year of Artaxerxes K of Babylon I went
13:6 Artaxerxes king of Babylon I went to the K
13:6 asked leave of the K
13:26 Did not Solomon K of Israel sin on account
13:26 nations there was no K like him, and he
13:26 and God made him K over all Israel; nevertheless
Tob 1:2 the days of Shalmaneser, K of the Assyrians, was
1:18 And if Sennacherib the K put to death any
1:18 were sought by the K, they were not found.
1:19 went and informed the K about me, that I
12:7 the secret of a K, but gloriously to reveal
12:11 the secret of a K, but gloriously to reveal
13:6 righteousness, and exalt the K of the ages.
13:7 my soul exalts the K of heaven, and will
13:10 Lord, and praise the K of the ages, that
13:11 hands, gifts for the K of heaven.
13:15 Let my soul praise God the great K
Jud 1:2 he is the K who built walls about
1:5 in those days that K Nebuchadnezzar made war
1:5 Nebuchadnezzar made war against K Arphaxad in
1:7 Then Nebuchadnezzar K of the Assyrians sent to all
1:11 the orders of Nebuchadnezzar K of the Assyrians,
1:13 led his forces against K Arphaxad, and defeated him
2:1 the palace of Nebuchadnezzar K of the Assyrians
2:4 forth his plan, Nebuchadnezzar K of the Assyrians
2:5 "Thus says the Great K, the lord of the
2:19 to go ahead of K Nebuchadnezzar and to cover
3:2 of Nebuchadnezzar, the Great K, lie prostrate before
4:1 general of Nebuchadnezzar the K of the Assyrians,
5:3 rules over them as K, leading their army?
5:11 So the K of Egypt became hostile to them;
6:3 deliver them--we the K's servants will destroy them
6:4 So says K Nebuchadnezzar, the lord of the whole
9:12 Creator of the waters, K of all thy creation,
11:1 to serve Nebuchadnezzar, the K of all the earth.
11:4 servants of my lord K Nebuchadnezzar."
11:7 Nebuchadnezzar the K of the whole earth lives, and
11:23 in the house of K Nebuchadnezzar and be renowned
14:18 upon the house of K Nebuchadnezzar!
Esth 1:2 in those days when K Ahasuerus sat on his
1:5 days were completed, the K gave for all the
1:5 the garden of the K's palace.
1:7 was lavished according to the bounty of the K
1:8 was compelled; for the K had given orders to
1:9 palace which belonged to K Ahasuerus.
1:10 the heart of the K was merry with wine,
1:10 seven eunuchs who served K Ahasuerus as
1:11 Queen Vashti before the K with her royal crown,
1:12 to come at the K's command conveyed by the
1:12 At this the K was enraged, and his anger
1:13 Then the K said to the wise men who
1:13 for this was the K's procedure toward all who
1:14 Media, who saw the K's face, and sat first
1:15 performed the command of K Ahasuerus conveyed
1:16 in presence of the K and the princes, "Not
1:16 "Not only to the K has Queen Vashti done
1:16 all the provinces of K Ahasuerus.
1:17 they will say, K Ahasuerus commanded Queen Vashti
1:18 it to all the K's princes, and there will
1:19 If it please the K, let a royal order
1:19 come no more before K Ahasuerus; and let the
1:19 Ahasuerus; and let the K give her royal position
1:20 decree made by the K is proclaimed throughout all
1:21 This advice pleased the K and the princes, and
1:21 the princes, and the K did as Memucan proposed;
2:1 when the anger of K Ahasuerus had abated, he
2:2 Then the K's servants who attended him said, "Let
2:2 beautiful young virgins be sought out for the K
2:3 And let the K appoint officers in all the
2:3 custody of Hegai the K's eunuch who is in
2:4 maiden who pleases the K be queen instead of
2:4 This pleased the K, and he did so.
2:6 with Jeconiah K of Judah, whom Nebuchadnezzar
2:6 of Judah, whom Nebuchadnezzar K of Babylon had
2:8 So when the K's order and his edict were
2:8 was taken into the K's palace and put in
2:9 chosen maids from the K's palace, and advanced her
2:12 to go in to K Ahasuerus, after being twelve
2:13 went in to the K in this way she
2:13 the harem to the K's palace.
2:14 custody of Sha-ashgaz the K's eunuch who was in
2:14 go in to the K again, unless the king
2:14 king again, unless the K delighted in her and
2:15 go in to the K, she asked for nothing
2:15 except what Hegai the K's eunuch, who had charge
2:16 Esther was taken to K Ahasuerus into his royal
2:17 of his reign, the K loved Esther more than
2:18 Then the K gave a great banquet to all
2:19 was sitting at the K's gate.
2:21 was sitting at the K's gate, Bigthan and Teresh,
2:21 Teresh, two of the K's eunuchs, who guarded the
2:21 to lay hands on K Ahasuerus.
2:22 and Esther told the K in the name of
2:23 of the Chronicles in the presence of the K
3:1 things K Ahasuerus promoted Haman the Agagite,
3:2 And all the K's servants who were at the
3:2 who were at the K's gate bowed down and
3:2 to Haman; for the K had so commanded concerning
3:3 Then the K's servants who were at the king's
3:3 who were at the K's gate said to Mordecai,
3:3 do you transgress the K's command?"
3:7 the twelfth year of K Ahasuerus, they cast Pur,
3:8 Then Haman said to K Ahasuerus, "There is a
3:8 do not keep the K's laws, so that it
3:8 is not for the K's profit to tolerate them.
3:9 If it please the K, let it be decreed
3:9 have charge of the K's business, that they may
3:9 put it into the K's treasuries."
3:10 So the K took his signet ring from his
3:11 And the K said to Haman, "The money is
3:12 Then the K's secretaries were summoned on the
3:12 was written to the K's satraps and to the
3:12 in the name of K Ahasuerus and sealed with
3:12 and sealed with the K's ring.
3:13 couriers to all the K's provinces, to destroy, to
3:15 by order of the K, and the decree was
3:15 And the K and Haman sat down to drink;
4:2 the entrance of the K's gate, for no one
4:2 one might enter the K's gate clothed with sackcloth.
4:3 province, wherever the K's command and his decree
4:5 Hathach, one of the K's eunuchs, who had been
4:6 in front of the K's gate,
4:7 to pay into the K's treasuries for the destruction
4:8 to go to the K to make supplication to
4:8 is next to the K, spoke against us for
4:8 and speak to the K concerning us and deliver
4:11 Mordecai, saying, "All the K's servants and the
4:11 the people of the K's provinces know that if
4:11 woman goes to the K inside the inner court
4:11 one to whom the K holds out the golden
4:11 come in to the K these thirty days."
4:13 not that in the K's palace you will escape
4:16 will go to the K, though it is against
5:1 inner court of the K's palace, opposite the king's
5:1 king's palace, opposite the K's hall.
5:1 The K was sitting on his royal throne inside
5:2 palace; and when the K saw Queen Esther standing
5:3 And the K said to her, "What is it,
5:4 "If it please the K, let the king and
5:4 the king, let the K and Haman come this
5:4 a dinner that I have prepared for the K
5:5 Then said the K, "Bring Haman quickly, that we
5:5 So the K and Haman came to the dinner
5:6 were drinking wine, the K said to Esther, "What
5:8 the sight of the K, and if it please
5:8 if it please the K to grant my petition
5:8 my request, let the K and Haman come tomorrow
5:8 will do as the K has said."
5:9 saw Mordecai in the K's gate, that he neither
5:11 promotions with which the K had honored him, and
5:11 above the princes and the servants of the K
5:12 one come with the K to the banquet she
5:12 I am invited by her together with the K
5:13 Jew sitting at the K's gate."
5:14 the morning tell the K to have Mordecai hanged
5:14 go merrily with the K to the dinner." This
6:1 On that night the K could not sleep; and
6:1 the chronicles, and they were read before the K
6:2 Teresh, two of the K's eunuchs, who guarded the
6:2 to lay hands upon K Ahasuerus.
6:3 And the K said, "What honor or dignity has
6:3 The K's servants who attended him said, "Nothing
6:4 And the K said, "Who is in the court?"
6:4 outer court of the K's palace to speak to
6:4 to speak to the K about having Mordecai hanged
6:5 So the K's servants told him, "Haman is there,
6:5 And the K said, "Let him come in."
6:6 came in, and the K said to him, "What
6:6 the man whom the K delights to honor?" And
6:6 himself, "Whom would the K delight to honor more
6:7 Haman said to the K, "For the man whom
6:7 the man whom the K delights to honor,

6:8 be brought, which the K has worn, and the
6:8 the horse which the K has ridden, and on
6:9 to one of the K's most noble princes; let
6:9 the man whom the K delights to honor, and
6:9 the man whom the K delights to honor.'"
6:10 Then the K said to Haman, "Make haste, take
6:10 who sits at the K's gate.
6:11 the man whom the K delights to honor."
6:12 Mordecai returned to the K's gate.
6:14 talking with him, the K's eunuchs arrived and
7:1 So the K and Haman went in to feast
7:2 were drinking wine, the K again said to Esther,
7:3 in your sight, O K, and if it please
7:3 if it please the K, let my life be
7:4 to be compared with the loss to the K
7:5 Then K Ahasuerus said to Queen Esther, "Who is
7:6 in terror before the K and the queen.
7:7 And the K rose from the feast in wrath
7:7 that evil was determined against him by the K
7:8 And the K returned from the palace garden to
7:8 Esther was; and the K said, "Will he even
7:8 the mouth of the K, they covered Haman's face.
7:9 in attendance on the K, "Moreover, the gallows
7:9 whose word saved the K, is standing in Haman's
7:10 And the K said, "Hang him on that." So
7:10 the anger of the K abated.
8:1 On that day K Ahasuerus gave to Queen Esther
8:1 Mordecai came before the K, for Esther had told
8:2 to her; and the K took off his signet
8:3 spoke again to the K; she fell at his
8:4 And the K held out the golden scepter to
8:5 Esther, and Esther rose and stood before the K
8:5 "If it please the K, and if I have
8:5 seem right before the K, and I be pleasing
8:5 who are in all the provinces of the K
8:7 Then K Ahasuerus said to Queen Esther and to
8:8 the name of the K, and seal it with
8:8 seal it with the K's ring; for an edict
8:8 the name of the K and sealed with the
8:8 and sealed with the K's ring cannot be revoked."
8:9 The K's secretaries were summoned at that time, in
8:10 in the name of K Ahasuerus and sealed with
8:10 and sealed with the K's ring, and letters were
8:10 were used in the K's service, bred from the
8:11 By these the K allowed the Jews who were
8:12 all the provinces of K Ahasuerus, on the thirteenth
8:14 were used in the K's service, rode out in
8:14 haste, urged by the K's command; and the decree
8:15 the presence of the K in royal robes of
8:17 every city, wherever the K's command and his edict
9:1 the same, when the K's command and edict were
9:2 all the provinces of K Ahasuerus to lay hands
9:4 was great in the K's house, and his fame
9:11 in Susa the capital was reported to the K
9:12 And the K said to Queen Esther, "In Susa
9:12 the rest of the K's provinces!
9:13 "If it please the K, let the Jews who
9:14 So the K commanded this to be done; a
9:16 who were in the K's provinces also gathered to
9:20 all the provinces of K Ahasuerus, both near and
9:25 Esther came before the K, he gave orders in
10:1 K Ahasuerus laid tribute on the land and on
10:2 Mordecai, to which the K advanced him, are they
10:3 next in rank to K Ahasuerus, and he was
10:6 is Esther, whom the K married and made queen.
11:3 great man, serving in the court of the K
11:4 captives whom Nebuchadnezzar K of Babylon had
11:4 from Jerusalem with Jeconiah K of Judea.
12:1 two eunuchs of the K who kept watch in
12:2 hands upon Artaxerxes the K; and he informed the
12:2 and he informed the K concerning them.
12:3 Then the K examined the two eunuchs, and when
12:4 led to execution, The K made a permanent record
12:5 And the K ordered Mordecai to serve in the
12:6 great honor with the K, and he sought to
12:6 people because of the two eunuchs of the K
13:1 the letter: "The Great K, Artaxerxes, to the rulers
13:9 said: "O Lord, Lord, K who rulest over all
13:15 O Lord God and K, God of Abraham, spare
14:3 thou only art our K; help me, who am
14:10 idols, and to magnify for ever a mortal K
14:12 give me courage, O K of the gods and
14:17 have not honored the K's feast or drunk the
15:6 through all the doors, she stood before the K
15:8 the spirit of the K to gentleness, and in
15:16 And the K was agitated, and all his servants
16:1 this letter: "The Great K, Artaxerxes, to the rulers

Job 15:24 against him, like a K prepared for battle.
18:14 is brought to the K of terrors.
29:25 I dwelt like a K among his troops, like
34:18 who says to a K, 'Worthless one,' and to
41:34 is high; he is K over all the sons

Ps 2:6 "I have set my K on Zion, my holy
5:2 of my cry, my K and my God, for
10:16 The LORD is K for ever and ever; the
18:50 he gives to his K, and shows steadfast love
20:9 Give victory to the K, O LORD; answer us
21:1 In thy strength the K rejoices, O LORD; and
21:7 For the K trusts in the LORD; and through
24:7 that the K of glory may come in.
24:8 Who is the K of glory?
24:9 that the K of glory may come in.
24:10 Who is this K of glory?
24:10 hosts, he is the K of glory!
29:10 LORD sits enthroned as K for ever.
33:16 A K is not saved by his great army;
44:4 Thou art my K and my God, who ordainest
45:1 my verses to the K; my tongue is like
45:5 the heart of the K's enemies; the peoples fall
45:11 father's house; and the K will desire your beauty.
45:14 is led to the K, with her virgin companions,
45:15 along as they enter the palace of the K
47:2 is terrible, a great K over all the earth.
47:6 Sing praises to our K, sing praises!
47:7 For God is the K of all the earth;
48:2 the far north, the city of the great K
61:6 the life of the K; may his years endure
63:11 But the K shall rejoice in God; all who
68:24 of my God, my K, into the sanctuary--
72:1 Give the K thy justice, O God, and thy
74:12 Yet God my K is from of old, working
84:3 LORD of hosts, my K and my God.
89:18 to the LORD, our K to the Holy One
95:3 God, and a great K above all gods.
98:6 joyful noise before the K, the LORD!
99:4 Mighty K, lover of justice, thou hast established
105:20 The K sent and released him, the ruler of
135:11 slew mighty kings, Sihon, K of the Amorites, and
135:11 the Amorites, and Og, K of Bashan, and all
136:19 endures for ever; Sihon, K of the Amorites, for
136:20 for ever; and Og, K of Bashan, for his
145:1 thee, my God and K, and bless thy name
149:2 let the sons of Zion rejoice in their K

Prov 1:1 Solomon, son of David, K of Israel:
14:28 the glory of a K, but without people a
14:35 deals wisely has the K's favor, but his wrath
16:10 the lips of a K; his mouth does not
16:13 the delight of a K, and he loves him
16:14 A K's wrath is a messenger of death, and
16:15 the light of a K's face there is life,
19:12 A K's wrath is like the growling of a
20:2 dread wrath of a K is like the growling
20:8 A K who sits on the throne of judgment
20:26 A wise K winnows the wicked, and drives the
20:28 and faithfulness preserve the K, and his throne is
21:1 The K's heart is a stream of water in
22:11 gracious, will have the K as his friend.
24:21 the LORD and the K, and do not disobey
25:1 the men of Hezekiah K of Judah copied.
25:5 the presence of the K, and his throne will
25:6 yourself forward in the K's presence or stand in
29:4 By justice a K gives stability to the land,
29:14 If a K judges the poor with equity his
30:22 slave when he becomes K, and a fool when
30:27 the locusts have no K, yet all of them
30:31 the he-goat, and a K striding before his people.
31:1 The words of Lemuel, K of Massa, which his

Eccl 1:1 the son of David, K in Jerusalem.
1:12 the Preacher have been K over Israel in Jerusalem.
2:12 can the man do who comes after the K
4:13 an old and foolish K, who will no longer
5:9 But in all, a K is an advantage to
8:2 Keep the K's command, and because of your sacred
8:4 the word of the K is supreme, and who
9:14 it; and a great K came against it and
10:16 O land, when your K is a child, and
10:17 O land, when your K is the son of
10:20 do not curse the K, nor in your bedchamber

Song 1:4 The K has brought me into his chambers.
1:12 While the K was on his couch, my nard
3:9 K Solomon made himself a palanquin from the wood
3:11 of Zion, and behold K Solomon, with the crown

7:5 are like purple; a K is held captive in
Wis 6:24 world, and a sensible K is the stability of
7:5 For no K has had a different beginning of
9:7 chosen me to be K of thy people and
11:10 ungodly as a stern K does in condemnation.
12:14 unjustly; nor can any K or monarch confront thee
14:17 visible image of the K whom they honored, so
14:18 did not know the K to intensify their worship.
18:11 same loss as the K;
Sir 7:4 office, nor the seat of honor from the K
7:5 the Lord, nor display your wisdom before the K
10:3 An undisciplined K will ruin his people, but a
10:10 baffles the physician; the K of today will die
38:2 and he will receive a gift from the K
45:25 the heritage of the K is from son to
46:20 and revealed to the K his death, and lifted
48:23 backward, and he lengthened the life of the K
50:15 the Most High, the K of all.
51:1 thee, O Lord and K, and will praise thee
51:6 the slander of an unrighteous tongue to the K
Is 6:1 In the year that K Uzziah died I saw
6:5 eyes have seen the K, the LORD of hosts!"
7:1 Jotham, son of Uzziah, K of Judah, Rezin the
7:1 of Judah, Rezin the K of Syria and Pekah
7:1 son of Remaliah the K of Israel came up
7:6 son of Tabeel as K in the midst of
7:17 from Judah-- the K of Assyria."
7:20 River-- with the K of Assyria-- the
8:4 carried away before the K of Assyria."
8:7 mighty and many, the K of Assyria and all
8:21 and will curse their K and their God, and
10:12 arrogant boasting of the K of Assyria and his
14:4 this taunt against the K of Babylon: "How the
14:28 In the year that K Ahaz died came this
19:4 master; and a fierce K will rule over them,
20:1 sent by Sargon the K of Assyria, came to
20:4 Ethiopia, so shall the K of Assyria lead away
20:6 be delivered from the K of Assyria!
23:15 for seventy years, like the days of one K
30:33 prepared; yea, for the K it is made ready,
32:1 Behold, a K will reign in righteousness, and princes
33:17 eyes will see the K in his beauty; they
33:22 the LORD is our K; he will save us.
36:1 the fourteenth year of K Hezekiah, Sennacherib king
36:1 of King Hezekiah, Sennacherib K of Assyria came up
36:2 And the K of Assyria sent the Rabshakeh from
36:2 from Lachish to K Hezekiah at Jerusalem, with
36:4 'Thus says the great K, the king of Assyria:
36:4 the great king, the K of Assyria: On what
36:6 Such is Pharaoh K of Egypt to all who
36:8 with my master the K of Assyria: I will
36:13 words of the great K, the king of Assyria!
36:13 the great king, the K of Assyria!
36:14 Thus says the K: 'Do not let Hezekiah deceive
36:15 the hand of the K of Assyria."
36:16 for thus says the K of Assyria: Make your
36:18 the hand of the K of Assyria?
36:21 a word, for the K's command was, "Do not
37:1 When K Hezekiah heard it, he rent his clothes,
37:4 whom his master the K of Assyria has sent
37:5 When the servants of K Hezekiah came to Isaiah,
37:6 the servants of the K of Assyria have reviled
37:8 returned, and found the K of Assyria fighting against
37:8 had heard that the K had left Lachish.
37:9 the K heard concerning Tirhakah king of Ethiopia,
37:9 king heard concerning Tirhakah K of Ethiopia, "He
37:10 you speak to Hezekiah K of Judah: 'Do not
37:10 the hand of the K of Assyria.
37:13 Where is the K of Hamath, the king of
37:13 king of Hamath, the K of Arpad, the king
37:13 king of Arpad, the K of the city of
37:13 city of Sepharvaim, the K of Hena, or the
37:13 of Hena, or the K of Ivvah?'"
37:21 to me concerning Sennacherib K of Assyria,
37:33 the LORD concerning the K of Assyria: He shall
37:37 Then Sennacherib K of Assyria departed, and went
38:6 the hand of the K of Assyria, and defend
38:9 A writing of Hezekiah K of Judah, after he
39:1 the son of Baladan, K of Babylon, sent envoys
39:3 the prophet came to K Hezekiah, and said to
39:7 the palace of the K of Babylon."
41:21 your proofs, says the K of Jacob.
43:15 your Holy One, the Creator of Israel, your K
44:6 says the LORD, the K of Israel and his
Jer 1:2 the son of Amon, K of Judah, in the
1:3 the son of Josiah, K of Judah, and until

1:3 the son of Josiah, K of Judah, until the
3:6 in the days of K Josiah: "Have you seen
4:9 courage shall fail both K and princes; the priests
8:19 Is her K not in her?" "Why have they
10:7 not fear thee, O K of the nations?
10:10 he is the living God and the everlasting K
13:18 Say to the K and the queen mother: "Take
15:4 the son of Hezekiah, K of Judah, did in
20:4 the hand of the K of Babylon; he shall
21:1 from the LORD, when K Zedekiah sent to him
21:2 for us, for Nebuchadrezzar K of Babylon is making
21:4 are fighting against the K of Babylon and against
21:7 I will give Zedekiah K of Judah, and his
21:7 the hand of Nebuchadrezzar K of Babylon and into
21:10 the hand of the K of Babylon, and he
21:11 the house of the K of Judah say, 'Hear
22:1 the house of the K of Judah, and speak
22:2 of the LORD, O K of Judah, who sit
22:6 the house of the K of Judah: "'You are
22:11 the son of Josiah, K of Judah, who reigned
22:15 think you are a K because you compete in
22:18 the son of Josiah, K of Judah: "They shall
22:24 the son of Jehoiakim, K of Judah, were the
22:25 the hand of Nebuchadrezzar K of Babylon and into
23:5 he shall reign as K and deal wisely, and
24:1 After Nebuchadrezzar K of Babylon had taken into
24:1 the son of Jehoiakim, K of Judah, together with
24:8 I treat Zedekiah the K of Judah, his princes,
25:1 the son of Josiah, K of Judah (that was
25:1 first year of Nebuchadrezzar K of Babylon),
25:3 the son of Amon, K of Judah, to this
25:9 and for Nebuchadrezzar the K of Babylon, my
25:11 nations shall serve the K of Babylon seventy years.
25:12 I will punish the K of Babylon and that
25:19 at this day; Pharaoh K of Egypt, his servants,
25:26 And after them the K of Babylon shall drink.
26:1 the son of Josiah, K of Judah, this word
26:10 came up from the K's house to the house
26:18 the days of Hezekiah K of Judah, and said
26:19 wooded height.' Did Hezekiah K of Judah and all
26:21 And when K Jehoiakim, with all his warriors and
26:21 heard his words, the K sought to put him
26:22 Then K Jehoiakim sent to Egypt certain men,
26:23 and brought him to K Jehoiakim, who slew him
27:1 the son of Josiah, K of Judah, this word
27:3 Send word to the K of Edom, the king
27:3 king of Edom, the K of Moab, the king
27:3 king of Moab, the K of the sons of
27:3 sons of Ammon, the K of Tyre, and the
27:3 of Tyre, and the K of Sidon by the
27:3 to Jerusalem to Zedekiah K of Judah.
27:6 hand of Nebuchadnezzar, the K of Babylon, my
27:8 not serve this Nebuchadnezzar K of Babylon, and put
27:8 the yoke of the K of Babylon, I will
27:9 shall not serve the K of Babylon.'
27:11 the yoke of the K of Babylon and serve
27:12 To Zedekiah K of Judah I spoke in like
27:12 the yoke of the K of Babylon, and serve
27:13 will not serve the K of Babylon?
27:14 shall not serve the K of Babylon,' for it
27:17 to them; serve the K of Babylon and live.
27:18 the house of the K of Judah, and in
27:20 this city, which Nebuchadnezzar K of Babylon did not
27:20 the son of Jehoiakim, K of Judah, and all
27:21 the house of the K of Judah, and in
28:1 the reign of Zedekiah K of Judah, in the
28:2 the yoke of the K of Babylon.
28:3 LORD's house, which Nebuchadnezzar K of Babylon
28:4 the son of Jehoiakim, K of Judah, and all
28:4 the yoke of the K of Babylon."
28:11 the yoke of Nebuchadnezzar K of Babylon from the
28:14 of servitude to Nebuchadnezzar K of Babylon, and
29:2 This was after K Jeconiah, and the queen mother,
29:3 of Hilkiah, whom Zedekiah K of Judah sent to
29:3 to Babylon to Nebuchadnezzar K of Babylon.
29:16 the LORD concerning the K who sits on the
29:21 the hand of Nebuchadrezzar K of Babylon, and he
29:22 and Ahab, whom the K of Babylon roasted in
30:9 God and David their K, whom I will raise
32:1 tenth year of Zedekiah K of Judah, which was
32:2 the army of the K of Babylon was besieging
32:2 the palace of the K of Judah.
32:3 For Zedekiah K of Judah had imprisoned him,
32:3 the hand of the K of Babylon, and he
32:4 shall take it; Zedekiah K of Judah shall not
32:4 the hand of the K of Babylon, and shall

32:28 the hand of Nebuchadrezzar K of Babylon, and he
32:36 the hand of the K of Babylon by sword,
34:1 the LORD, when Nebuchadrezzar K of Babylon and
34:2 and speak to Zedekiah K of Judah and say
34:2 the hand of the K of Babylon, and he
34:3 you shall see the K of Babylon eye to
34:4 the LORD, O Zedekiah K of Judah!
34:6 these words to Zedekiah K of Judah, in Jerusalem,
34:7 the army of the K of Babylon was fighting
34:8 from the LORD, after K Zedekiah had made a
34:21 And Zedekiah K of Judah, and his princes I
34:21 the army of the K of Babylon which has
35:1 the son of Josiah, K of Judah:
35:11 But when Nebuchadrezzar K of Babylon came up
36:1 the son of Josiah, K of Judah, this word
36:9 the son of Josiah, K of Judah, in the
36:12 went down to the K's house, into the secretary's
36:16 "We must report all these words to the K
36:20 the court to the K, having put the scroll
36:20 and they reported all the words to the K
36:21 Then the K sent Jehudi to get the scroll,
36:21 read it to the K and all the princes
36:21 and all the princes who stood beside the K
36:22 ninth month, and the K was sitting in the
36:23 or four columns, the K would cut them off
36:24 Yet neither the K, nor any of his servants
36:25 and Gemariah urged the K not to burn the
36:26 And the K commanded Jerahmeel the king's son and
36:26 king commanded Jerahmeel the K's son and Seraiah
36:27 Now, after the K had burned the scroll with
36:28 scroll, which Jehoiakim the K of Judah has burned.
36:29 And concerning Jehoiakim K of Judah you shall say,
36:29 in it that the K of Babylon will certainly
36:30 the LORD concerning Jehoiakim K of Judah, He
36:32 the scroll which Jehoiakim K of Judah had burned
37:1 Josiah, whom Nebuchadrezzar K of Babylon made
37:1 king of Babylon made K in the land of
37:3 K Zedekiah sent Jehucal the son of Shelemiah, and
37:7 you say to the K of Judah who sent
37:17 remained there many days, K Zedekiah sent for him,
37:17 The K questioned him secretly in his house, and
37:17 the hand of the K of Babylon."
37:18 Jeremiah also said to K Zedekiah, "What wrong
37:19 to you, saying, 'The K of Babylon will not
37:20 O my lord the K: let my humble plea
37:21 So K Zedekiah gave orders, and they committed
38:3 the army of the K of Babylon and be
38:4 princes said to the K, "Let this man be
38:5 K Zedekiah said, "Behold, he is in your hands;
38:5 your hands; for the K can do nothing against
38:6 cistern of Malchiah, the K's son, which was in
38:7 who was in the K's house, heard that they
38:7 into the cistern--the K was sitting in the
38:8 Ebed-melech went from the K's house and said to
38:8 and said to the K,
38:9 king, "My lord the K, these men have done
38:10 Then the K commanded Ebed-melech, the Ethiopian,
38:11 the house of the K, to a wardrobe of
38:14 K Zedekiah sent for Jeremiah the prophet and
38:14 The K said to Jeremiah, "I will ask you
38:16 Then K Zedekiah swore secretly to Jeremiah, "As
38:17 the princes of the K of Babylon, then your
38:18 the princes of the K of Babylon, then this
38:19 K Zedekiah said to Jeremiah, "I am afraid of
38:22 the house of the K of Judah were being
38:22 the princes of the K of Babylon and were
38:23 be seized by the K of Babylon; and this
38:25 you said to the K and what the king
38:25 king and what the K said to you; hide
38:26 humble plea to the K that he would not
38:27 answered them as the K had instructed him.
39:1 ninth year of Zedekiah K of Judah, in the
39:1 the tenth month, Nebuchadrezzar K of Babylon and
39:3 the princes of the K of Babylon came and
39:3 the officers of the K of Babylon.
39:4 When Zedekiah K of Judah and all the soldiers
39:4 by way of the K's garden through the gate
39:5 him up to Nebuchadrezzar K of Babylon, at Riblah,
39:6 The K of Babylon slew the sons of Zedekiah
39:6 his eyes; and the K of Babylon slew all
39:8 The Chaldeans burned the K's house and the house
39:11 Nebuchadrezzar K of Babylon gave command
39:13 chief officers of the K of Babylon
40:5 of Shaphan, whom the K of Babylon appointed
40:7 men heard that the K of Babylon had appointed
40:9 land, and serve the K of Babylon, and it
40:11 lands heard that the K of Babylon had left
40:14 know that Baalis the K of the Ammonites has
41:1 chief officers of the K, came with ten men
41:2 killed him, whom the K of Babylon had appointed
41:9 the large cistern which K Asa had made for
41:9 for defense against Baasha K of Israel; Ishmael the
41:10 were in Mizpah, the K's daughters and all the
41:18 of Ahikam, whom the K of Babylon had made
42:11 Do not fear the K of Babylon, of whom
43:10 and take Nebuchadrezzar the K of Babylon, my
44:30 will give Pharaoh Hophra K of Egypt into the
44:30 as I gave Zedekiah K of Judah into the
44:30 the hand of Nebuchadrezzar K of Babylon, who was
45:1 the son of Josiah, K of Judah:
46:2 army of Pharaoh Neco, K of Egypt, which was
46:2 and which Nebuchadrezzar K of Babylon defeated in
46:2 the son of Josiah, K of Judah:
46:13 the coming of Nebuchadrezzar K of Babylon to
46:17 the name of Pharaoh, K of Egypt, 'Noisy one
46:18 I live, says the K, whose name is the
46:26 the hand of Nebuchadrezzar K of Babylon and his
48:15 to slaughter, says the K, whose name is the
49:28 Hazor which Nebuchadrezzar K of Babylon smote.
49:30 For Nebuchadrezzar K of Babylon has made a plan
49:34 the reign of Zedekiah K of Judah.
49:38 Elam, and destroy their K and princes, says the
50:17 First the K of Assyria devoured him, and now
50:17 at last Nebuchadrezzar K of Babylon has gnawed
50:18 bringing punishment on the K of Babylon and his
50:18 as I punished the K of Assyria.
50:43 "The K of Babylon heard the report of them,
51:31 another, to tell the K of Babylon that his
51:34 "Nebuchadrezzar the K of Babylon has devoured
51:57 not wake, says the K, whose name is the
51:59 he went with Zedekiah K of Judah to Babylon,
52:1 old when he became K; and he reigned eleven
52:3 Zedekiah rebelled against the K of Babylon.
52:4 of the month, Nebuchadrezzar K of Babylon came
52:5 the eleventh year of K Zedekiah.
52:7 two walls, by the K's garden, while the Chaldeans
52:8 the Chaldeans pursued the K, and overtook Zedekiah
52:9 Then they captured the K, and brought him up
52:9 him up to the K of Babylon at Riblah
52:10 The K of Babylon slew the sons of Zedekiah
52:11 in fetters, and the K of Babylon took him
52:12 nineteenth year of K Nebuchadrezzar, king of
52:12 year of King Nebuchadrezzar, K of Babylon--
52:12 bodyguard who served the K of Babylon, entered
52:13 the LORD, and the K's house and all the
52:15 had deserted to the K of Babylon, together with
52:20 stands, which Solomon the K had made for the
52:25 seven men of the K's council, who were found
52:26 brought them to the K of Babylon at Riblah.
52:27 And the K of Babylon smote them, and put
52:31 the captivity of Jehoiachin K of Judah, in the
52:31 of the month, Evil-merodach K of Babylon, in the
52:31 year that he became K, lifted up the head
52:31 the head of Jehoiachin K of Judah and brought
52:33 dined regularly at the K's table;
52:34 given him by the K until the day of
Lam 2:6 fierce indignation has spurned K and priest.
2:9 broken her bars; her K and princes are among
Bar 1:3 the son of Jehoiakim, K of Judah, and in
1:8 the son of Josiah, K of Judah, had made,
1:9 had made, after Nebuchadnezzar K of Babylon had
1:11 the life of Nebuchadnezzar K of Babylon, and for
1:12 the protection of Nebuchadnezzar K of Babylon, and
2:21 shoulders and serve the K of Babylon, and you
2:22 will not serve the K of Babylon,
2:24 voice, to serve the K of Babylon; and thou
6:1 as captives by the K of the Babylonians, to
6:2 as captives by Nebuchadnezzar, K of the
6:18 who has offended a K, as though he were
6:34 cannot set up a K or depose one.
6:53 cannot set up a K over a country or
6:56 no resistance to a K or any enemies.
6:59 better to be a K who shows his courage,
Ezek 1:2 of the exile of K Jehoiachin),
7:27 The K mourns, the prince is wrapped in despair,
17:12 Tell them, Behold, the K of Babylon came to
17:12 Jerusalem, and took her K and her princes and
17:16 the place where the K dwells who made him
17:16 dwells who made him K, whose oath he despised,
19:9 brought him to the K of Babylon; they brought
20:33 out, I will be K over you.
21:19 the sword of the K of Babylon to come;

21:21 For the K of Babylon stands at the parting
24:2 The K of Babylon has laid siege to Jerusalem
26:7 from the north Nebuchadrezzar K of Babylon, king
26:7 Nebuchadrezzar king of Babylon, K of kings, with
28:12 a lamentation over the K of Tyre, and say
29:2 your face against Pharaoh K of Egypt, and prophesy
29:3 am against you, Pharaoh K of Egypt, the great
29:18 "Son of man, Nebuchadrezzar K of Babylon made
29:19 of Egypt to Nebuchadrezzar K of Babylon; and he
30:10 the hand of Nebuchadrezzar K of Babylon.
30:21 the arm of Pharaoh K of Egypt; and lo,
30:22 I am against Pharaoh K of Egypt, and will
30:24 the arms of the K of Babylon, and put
30:25 the arms of the K of Babylon, but the
30:25 the hand of the K of Babylon, he shall
31:2 man, say to Pharaoh K of Egypt and to
32:2 a lamentation over Pharaoh K of Egypt, and say
32:11 The sword of the K of Babylon shall come
37:22 of Israel; and one K shall be king over
37:22 one king shall be K over them all; and
37:24 servant David shall be K over them; and they
Dan 1:1 the reign of Jehoiakim K of Judah, Nebuchadnezzar
1:1 king of Judah, Nebuchadnezzar K of Babylon came
1:2 the Lord gave Jehoiakim K of Judah into his
1:3 Then the K commanded Ashpenaz, his chief eunuch,
1:4 to serve in the K's palace, and to teach
1:5 The K assigned them a daily portion of the
1:5 rich food which the K ate, and of the
1:5 that time they were to stand before the K
1:8 defile himself with the K's rich food, or with
1:10 lest my lord the K, who appointed your food
1:10 So you would endanger my head with the K
1:13 youths who eat the K's rich food be observed
1:15 youths who ate the K's rich food.
1:18 the time, when the K had commanded that they
1:19 And the K spoke with them, and among them
1:19 and Azariah; therefore they stood before the K
1:20 understanding concerning which the K inquired of
1:21 the first year of K Cyrus.
2:2 Then the K commanded that the magicians, the
2:2 summoned, to tell the K his dreams.
2:2 So they came in and stood before the K
2:3 And the K said to them, "I had a
2:4 Chaldeans said to the K, "O king, live for
2:4 to the king, "O K, live for ever!
2:5 The K answered the Chaldeans, "The word from me
2:7 second time, "Let the K tell his servants the
2:8 The K answered, "I know with certainty that you
2:10 The Chaldeans answered the K, "There is not a
2:10 who can meet the K's demand; for no great
2:10 no great and powerful K has asked such a
2:11 The thing that the K asks is difficult, and
2:11 show it to the K except the gods, whose
2:12 Because of this the K was angry and very
2:14 the captain of the K's guard, who had gone
2:15 said to Arioch, the K's captain, "Why is the
2:15 the decree of the K so severe?" Then Arioch
2:16 in and besought the K to appoint him a
2:16 might show to the K the interpretation.
2:23 known to us the K's matter."
2:24 to Arioch, whom the K had appointed to destroy
2:24 me in before the K, and I will show
2:24 I will show the K the interpretation."
2:25 in Daniel before the K in haste, and said
2:25 make known to the K the interpretation."
2:26 The K said to Daniel, whose name was Belteshazzar,
2:27 Daniel answered the K, "No wise men, enchanters,
2:27 can show to the K the mystery which the
2:27 the mystery which the K has asked,
2:28 has made known to K Nebuchadnezzar what will be
2:29 these: To you, O K, as you lay in
2:30 made known to the K, and that you may
2:31 "You saw, O K, and behold, a great image.
2:36 we will tell the K its interpretation.
2:37 You, O K, the king of kings, to whom
2:37 You, O king, the K of kings, to whom
2:45 made known to the K what shall be hereafter.
2:46 Then K Nebuchadnezzar fell upon his face, and did
2:47 The K said to Daniel, "Truly, your God is
2:48 Then the K gave Daniel high honors and many
2:49 made request of the K, and he appointed Shadrach,
2:49 Daniel remained at the K's court.
3:1 K Nebuchadnezzar made an image of gold, whose
3:2 Then K Nebuchadnezzar sent to assemble the
3:2 of the image which K Nebuchadnezzar had set up.
3:3 of the image that K Nebuchadnezzar had set up;
3:5 the golden image that K Nebuchadnezzar has set up;
3:7 the golden image which K Nebuchadnezzar had set
3:9 They said to K Nebuchadnezzar, "O king, live for
3:9 to King Nebuchadnezzar, "O K, live for ever!
3:10 You, O K, have made a decree, that every
3:12 These men, O K, pay no heed to you;
3:13 Then they brought these men before the K
3:16 Abednego answered the K, "O Nebuchadnezzar, we
3:17 will deliver us out of your hand, O K
3:18 known to you, O K, that we will not
3:22 Because the K's order was strict and the furnace
3:32 and to an unjust K, the most wicked in
3:46 Now the K's servants who threw them in did
3:92 Then K Nebuchadnezzar was astonished and rose up
3:92 They answered the K, "True, O king."
3:92 They answered the king, "True, O K
3:95 governors, and the K's counselors gathered together
3:96 set at nought the K's command, and yielded up
3:98 Then the K promoted Shadrach, Meshach, and
4:1 K Nebuchadnezzar to all peoples, nations, and
4:18 men.' This dream I, K Nebuchadnezzar, saw.
4:19 The K said, "Belteshazzar, let not the dream or
4:22 it is you, O K, who have grown and
4:23 And whereas the K saw a watcher, a holy
4:24 is the interpretation, O K: It is a decree
4:24 upon my lord the K,
4:27 Therefore, O K, let my counsel be acceptable to
4:28 All this came upon K Nebuchadnezzar.
4:30 of Babylon, and the K said, "Is not this
4:31 were still in the K's mouth, there fell a
4:31 voice from heaven, "O K Nebuchadnezzar, to you it
4:37 extol and honor the K of heaven; for all
5:1 K Belshazzar made a great feast for a thousand
5:2 be brought, that the K and his lords, his
5:3 in Jerusalem; and the K and his lords, his
5:5 the wall of the K's palace, opposite the lampstand;
5:5 the lampstand; and the K saw the hand as
5:6 Then the K's color changed, and his thoughts
5:7 The K cried aloud to bring in the enchanters,
5:7 The K said to the wise men of Babylon,
5:8 Then all the K's wise men came in, but
5:8 make known to the K the interpretation.
5:9 Then K Belshazzar was greatly alarmed, and his
5:10 the words of the K and his lords, came
5:10 the queen said, "O K, live for ever!
5:11 found in him, and K Nebuchadnezzar, your father,
5:12 this Daniel, whom the K named Belteshazzar.
5:13 Then Daniel was brought in before the K
5:13 The K said to Daniel, "You are that Daniel,
5:13 of Judah, whom the K my father brought from
5:17 Daniel answered before the K, "Let your gifts be
5:17 the writing to the K and make known to
5:18 O K, the Most High God gave Nebuchadnezzar your
5:30 night Belshazzar the Chaldean K was slain.
6:2 account, so that the K might suffer no loss.
6:3 in him; and the K planned to set him
6:6 by agreement to the K and said to him,
6:6 said to him, "O K Darius, live for ever!
6:7 are agreed that the K should establish an ordinance
6:7 except to you, O K, shall be cast into
6:8 Now, O K, establish the interdict and sign the
6:9 Therefore K Darius signed the document and
6:12 and said before the K, concerning the interdict, "O
6:12 said before the king, concerning the interdict, "O K
6:12 except to you, O K, shall be cast into
6:12 The K answered, "The thing stands fast, according to
6:13 they answered before the K, "That Daniel, who is
6:13 heed to you, O K, or the interdict you
6:14 Then the K, when he heard these words, was
6:15 by agreement to the K, and said to the
6:15 and said to the K, "Know, O king, that
6:15 the king, "Know, O K, that it is a
6:15 ordinance which the K establishes can be changed."
6:16 Then the K commanded, and Daniel was brought and
6:16 The K said to Daniel, "May your God, whom
6:17 the den, and the K sealed it with his
6:18 Then the K went to his palace, and spent
6:19 break of day, the K arose and went in
6:21 Daniel said to the K, "O king, live for
6:21 to the king, "O K, live for ever!
6:22 also before you, O K, I have done no
6:23 Then the K was exceedingly glad, and commanded
6:24 And the K commanded, and those men who had
6:25 Then K Darius wrote to all the peoples, nations,
7:1 first year of Belshazzar K of Babylon, Daniel had
8:1 of the reign of K Belshazzar a vision appeared

8:21 the he-goat is the K of Greece; and the
8:21 great horn between his eyes is the first K
8:23 their full measure, a K of bold countenance, one
8:27 and went about the K's business; but I was
9:1 a Mede, who became K over the realm of
10:1 third year of Cyrus K of Persia a word
11:3 Then a mighty K shall arise, who shall rule
11:5 "Then the K of the south shall be strong,
11:6 the daughter of the K of the south shall
11:6 shall come to the K of the north to
11:7 the fortress of the K of the north, and
11:8 refrain from attacking the K of the north.
11:9 the realm of the K of the south but
11:11 Then the K of the south, moved with anger,
11:11 and fight with the K of the north; and
11:13 For the K of the north shall again raise
11:14 shall rise against the K of the south; and
11:15 Then the K of the north shall come and
11:25 his courage against the K of the south with
11:25 great army; and the K of the south shall
11:36 "And the K shall do according to his will;
11:40 of the end the K of the south shall
11:40 attack him; but the K of the north shall
14:1 When K Astyages was laid with his fathers, Cyrus
14:2 a companion of the K, and was the most
14:4 The K revered it and went every day to
14:5 And the K said to him, "Why do you
14:6 The K said to him, "Do you not think
14:7 not be deceived, O K; for this is but
14:8 Then the K was angry, and he called his
14:9 Daniel said to the K, "Let it be done
14:10 And the K went with Daniel into the temple
14:11 outside; you yourself, O K, shall set forth the
14:14 had gone out, the K set forth the food
14:14 the presence of the K alone.
14:14 sealed it with the K's signet, and departed.
14:16 in the morning the K rose and came, and
14:17 And the K said, "Are the seals unbroken, Daniel?"
14:17 He answered, "They are unbroken, O K
14:18 doors were opened, the K looked at the table,
14:19 laughed, and restrained the K from going in, and
14:20 The K said, "I see the footsteps of men
14:21 Then the K was enraged, and he seized the
14:22 Therefore the K put them to death, and gave
14:24 And the K said to Daniel, "You cannot deny
14:26 But if you, O K, will give me permission,
14:26 The K said, "I give you permission."
14:28 and conspired against the K, saying, "The king has
14:28 the king, saying, "The K has become a Jew;
14:29 Going to the K, they said, "Hand Daniel over
14:30 The K saw that they were pressing him hard,
14:40 the seventh day the K came to mourn for
14:41 And the K shouted with a loud voice, "Thou
Hos 1:1 the son of Joash, K of Israel.
3:4 dwell many days without K or prince, without
3:5 God, and David their K; and they shall come
5:1 Hearken, O house of the K
5:13 went to Assyria, and sent to the great K
7:4 wickedness they make the K glad, and the princes
7:6 the day of our K the princes became sick
8:10 little while from anointing K and princes.
10:3 say: "We have no K, for we fear not
10:3 the LORD, and a K, what could he do
10:6 carried to Assyria, as tribute to the great K
10:7 Samaria's K shall perish, like a chip on the
10:15 In the storm the K of Israel shall be
11:5 Assyria shall be their K, because they have refused
13:10 Where now is your K, to save you; where
13:10 said, "Give me a K and princes"?
Amos 1:1 the days of Uzziah K of Judah and in
1:1 the son of Joash, K of Israel, two years
1:15 the whirlwind; and their K shall go into exile,
2:1 the bones of the K of Edom.
5:26 take up Sakkuth your K, and Kaiwan your star-god,
7:1 latter growth after the K's mowings.
7:10 Bethel sent to Jeroboam K of Israel, saying, "Amos
7:13 for it is the K's sanctuary, and it is
Jon 3:6 Then tidings reached the K of Nineveh, and he
3:7 the decree of the K and his nobles: Let
Mic 2:13 Their K will pass on before them, the LORD
4:9 Is there no K in you?
6:5 people, remember what Balak K of Moab devised,
Nah 3:18 shepherds are asleep, O K of Assyria; your nobles
Zeph 1:1 the son of Amon, K of Judah.
1:8 the officials and the K's sons and all who
3:15 The K of Israel, the LORD, is in your
Hag 1:1 year of Darius the K, in the sixth month,
2:1 year of Darius the K, in the seventh month,
Zech 7:1 the fourth year of K Darius, the word of
9:5 The K shall perish from Gaza; Ashkelon shall be
9:9 Lo, your K comes to you; triumphant and victorious
11:6 the hand of his K; and they shall crush
14:5 the days of Uzziah K of Judah.
14:9 the LORD will become K over all the earth;
14:10 of Hananel to the K's wine presses.
14:16 year to worship the K, the LORD of hosts,
14:17 Jerusalem to worship the K, the LORD of hosts,
Mal 1:14 I am a great K, says the LORD of
1Mac 1:1 Kittim, had defeated Darius, K of the Persians and
1:1 Persians and the Medes, he succeeded him as K
1:1 (He had previously become K of Greece.)
1:10 son of Antiochus the K; he had been a
1:13 some of the people eagerly went to the K
1:16 he determined to become K of the land of
1:18 He engaged Ptolemy K of Egypt in battle, and
1:29 Two years later the K sent to the cities
1:41 Then the K wrote to his whole kingdom that
1:43 All the Gentiles accepted the command of the K
1:44 And the K sent letters by messengers to Jerusalem
1:50 the command of the K shall die."
1:57 the decree of the K condemned him to death.
2:15 the K's officers who were enforcing the apostasy
2:17 Then the K's officers spoke to Mattathias as follows:
2:18 and do what the K commands, as all the
2:18 the friends of the K, and you and your
2:19 the rule of the K obey him, and have
2:22 will not obey the K's words by turning aside
2:23 Modein, according to the K's command.
2:25 time he killed the K's officer who was forcing
2:31 was reported to the K's officers, and to the
2:31 who had rejected the K's command had gone down
2:33 and do what the K commands, and you will
2:34 we do what the K commands and so profane
3:14 companions, who scorn the K's command."
3:26 His fame reached the K, and the Gentiles talked
3:27 When K Antiochus heard these reports, he was
3:32 in charge of the K's affairs from the river
3:37 Then the K took the remaining half of his
3:38 the friends of the K,
3:39 destroy it, as the K had commanded.
3:42 also learned what the K had commanded to do
4:3 out to attack the K's force in Emmaus
4:27 turned out as the K had commanded him.
6:1 K Antiochus was going through the upper provinces
6:2 of Philip, the Macedonian K who first reigned over
6:8 When the K heard this news, he was astounded
6:15 his son and bring him up to be K
6:16 Thus Antiochus the K died there in the one
6:17 Lysias learned that the K was dead, he set
6:17 set up Antiochus the K's son to reign.
6:22 They went to the K and said, "How long
6:28 The K was enraged when he heard this.
6:32 at Beth-zechariah, opposite the camp of the K
6:33 in the morning the K rose and took his
6:40 a part of the K's army was spread out
6:42 hundred men of the K's army fell.
6:43 he supposed that the K was upon it.
6:48 The soldiers of the K's army went up to
6:48 against them, and the K encamped in Judea and
6:50 So the K took Bethzur and stationed a guard
6:55 heard that Philip, whom K Antiochus while still living
6:55 his son to be K,
6:56 had gone with the K, and that he was
6:57 and said to the K, to the commanders of
6:60 The speech pleased the K and the commanders, and
6:61 So the K and the commanders gave them their
6:62 But when the K entered Mount Zion and saw
7:6 they brought to the K this accusation against the
7:7 the land of the K, and let him punish
7:8 So the K chose Bacchides, one of the king's
7:8 Bacchides, one of the K's friends, governor of the
7:8 in the kingdom and was faithful to the K
7:20 help him; then Bacchides went back to the K
7:25 he returned to the K and brought wicked charges
7:26 Then the K sent Nicanor, one of his honored
7:33 burnt offering that was being offered for the K
7:41 messengers from the K spoke blasphemy, thy angel
8:5 Philip, and Perseus K of the Macedonians, and the
8:6 defeated Antiochus the Great, K of Asia, who went
8:8 took from him and gave to Eumenes the K
8:31 concerning the wrongs which K Demetrius is doing
9:57 he returned to the K, and the land of

10:2 When Demetrius the K heard of it, he assembled
10:8 they heard that the K had given him authority
10:15 Now Alexander the K heard of all the promises
10:18 in the following words: K Alexander to his brother
10:20 to be called the K's friend" (and he sent
10:25 in the following words: K Demetrius to the nation
10:36 be enrolled in the K's forces to the number
10:36 is due to all the forces of the K
10:37 great strongholds of the K, and let some of
10:37 laws, just as the K has commanded in the
10:40 yearly out of the K's revenues from appropriate
10:43 owes money to the K or has any debt,
10:44 sanctuary be paid from the revenues of the K
10:45 also be paid from the revenues of the K
10:48 Now Alexander the K assembled large forces and
10:51 sent ambassadors to Ptolemy K of Egypt with the
10:55 Ptolemy the K replied and said, "Happy was the
10:58 Alexander the K met him, and Ptolemy gave him
10:59 Then Alexander the K wrote to Jonathan to come
10:61 accuse him; but the K paid no attention to
10:62 The K gave orders to take off Jonathan's garments
10:63 The K also seated him at his side; and
10:65 Thus the K honored him and enrolled him among
10:68 When Alexander the K heard of it, he was
10:88 When Alexander the K heard of these things, he
11:1 Then the K of Egypt gathered great forces, like
11:2 him, for Alexander the K had commanded them to
11:5 They also told the K what Jonathan had done,
11:5 on him; but the K kept silent.
11:6 Jonathan met the K at Joppa with pomp, and
11:7 Jonathan went with the K as far as the
11:8 So K Ptolemy gained control of the coastal cities
11:9 envoys to Demetrius the K, saying, "Come, let us
11:14 Now Alexander the K was in Cilicia at that
11:16 find protection there, and K Ptolemy was exalted.
11:18 But K Ptolemy died three days later, and his
11:19 So Demetrius became K in the one hundred and
11:21 nation went to the K and reported to him
11:24 he went to the K at Ptolemais, taking silver
11:26 complaints against him, the K treated him as his
11:28 Then Jonathan asked the K to free Judea and
11:29 The K consented, and wrote a letter to Jonathan
11:30 contents were as follows: K Demetrius to Jonathan
11:32 K Demetrius to Lasthenes his father, greeting.
11:34 royal taxes which the K formerly received from them
11:38 Now when Demetrius the K saw that the land
11:40 to him, to become K in place of his
11:41 sent to Demetrius the K the request that he
11:44 they came to the K, the king rejoiced at
11:44 to the king, the K rejoiced at their arrival.
11:45 twenty thousand, and they wanted to kill the K
11:46 But the K fled into the palace.
11:47 So the K called the Jews to his aid,
11:48 spoil on that day, and they saved the K
11:49 cried out to the K with this entreaty,
11:51 the eyes of the K and of all the
11:52 So Demetrius the K sat on the throne of
11:57 make you one of the friends of the K
12:7 from Arius, who was K among you, stating that
12:20 sent to Onias: "Arius, K of the Spartans, to
12:39 Trypho attempted to become K in Asia and put
12:39 and to raise his hand against Antiochus the K
13:31 treacherously with the young K Antiochus; he killed
13:32 killed him and became K in his place, putting
13:34 them to Demetrius the K with a request to
13:35 Demetrius the K sent him a favorable reply to
13:36 a letter as follows, K Demetrius to Simon, the
14:1 seventy-second year Demetrius the K assembled his
14:2 When Arsaces the K of Persia and Media heard
14:38 view of these things K Demetrius confirmed him in
14:39 him one of the K's friends and paid him
15:1 son of Demetrius the K, sent a letter from
15:2 contents were as follows: K Antiochus to Simon the
15:16 of the Romans, to K Ptolemy, greeting.
15:22 thing to Demetrius the K and to Attalus and
15:25 Antiochus the K besieged Dor anew, continually
15:32 the friend of the K came to Jerusalem, and
15:32 the words of the K,
15:36 in wrath to the K and reported to him
15:36 And the K was greatly angered.
15:38 the K made Cendebeus commander-in-chief of the
15:39 the people; but the K pursued Trypho.
15:41 of Judea, as the K had ordered him.
16:18 sent it to the K, asking him to send
2Mac 1:10 teacher of Ptolemy the K, and to the Jews
1:11 him greatly for taking our side against the K
1:20 been commissioned by the K of Persia, sent the
1:24 merciful, who alone art K and art kind,
1:33 was reported to the K of the Persians that,
1:34 of the sacrifice, the K investigated the matter, and
1:35 those persons whom the K favored he exchanged
3:3 that even Seleucus, the K of Asia, defrayed from
3:6 them to fall under the control of the K
3:7 When Apollonius met the K, he told him of
3:7 The K chose Heliodorus, who was in charge of
3:8 to carry out the K's purpose.
3:13 Heliodorus, because of the K's commands which he
3:13 be confiscated for the K's treasury.
3:32 priest, fearing that the K might get the notion
3:35 he marched off with his forces to the K
3:37 When the K asked Heliodorus what sort of person
4:5 betook himself to the K, not accusing his fellow
4:6 saw that without the K's attention public affairs
4:8 by corruption, promising the K at an interview three
4:10 When the K assented and Jason came to office,
4:18 at Tyre and the K was present,
4:21 coronation of Philometor as K, Antiochus learned
4:23 the money to the K and to complete the
4:24 when presented to the K, extolled him with an
4:25 After receiving the K's orders he returned,
4:27 regularly any of the money promised to the K
4:28 were summoned by the K on account of this
4:30 present to Antiochis, the K's concubine.
4:31 So the K went hastily to settle the trouble,
4:36 When the K returned from the region of Cilicia,
4:44 When the K came to Tyre, three men sent
4:45 Ptolemy son of Dorymenes to win over the K
4:46 Ptolemy, taking the K aside into a colonnade
4:46 for refreshment, induced the K to change his mind.
5:11 had happened reached the K, he took it to
5:18 was, whom Seleucus the K sent to inspect the
6:1 long after this, the K sent an Athenian senator
6:7 monthly celebration of the K's birthday, the Jews
6:21 been commanded by the K,
7:1 being compelled by the K, under torture with whips
7:3 The K fell into a rage, and gave orders
7:5 was utterly helpless, the K ordered them to take
7:9 present life, but the K of the universe will
7:12 As a result the K himself and those with
7:16 he looked at the K, and said, "Because you
7:25 him at all, the K called the mother to
7:30 will not obey the K's command, but I obey
7:39 The K fell into a rage, and handled him
8:8 for aid to the K's government.
8:9 Patroclus, one of the K's chief friends, and sent
8:10 make up for the K the tribute due to
9:19 Jewish citizens, Antiochus their K and general sends
9:25 son Antiochus to be K, whom I have often
10:13 before Eupator by the K's friends.
11:1 after this, Lysias, the K's guardian and kinsman, who
11:14 he would persuade the K, constraining him to be
11:15 For the K granted every request in behalf of
11:18 I have informed the K of everything that needed
11:22 The K's letter ran thus: "King Antiochus to his
11:22 king's letter ran thus: K Antiochus to his brother
11:27 To the nation the K's letter was as follows:
11:27 letter was as follows: K Antiochus to the senate
11:35 the kinsman of the K has granted you, we
11:36 be referred to the K, as soon as you
12:1 Lysias returned to the K, and the Jews went
13:4 But the K of kings aroused the anger of
13:9 The K with barbarous arrogance was coming to
13:13 of God before the K's army could enter Judea
13:15 men, he attacked the K's pavilion at night and
13:18 The K, having had a taste of the daring
13:22 The K negotiated a second time with the people
13:26 This is how the K's attack and withdrawal turned
14:4 altar, and went to K Demetrius in about the
14:8 the interests of the K, and second because I
14:9 you are acquainted, O K, with the details of
14:11 the rest of the K's friends, who were hostile
14:27 The K became excited and, provoked by the false
14:29 possible to oppose the K, he watched for an
15:5 arms and finish the K's business." Nevertheless, he
15:22 the time of Hezekiah K of Judea, and he
Mt 1:6 Jesse, and Jesse the father of David the K
2:1 days of Herod the K, behold, wise men from
2:2 who has been born K of the Jews?
2:3 When Herod the K heard this, he was troubled,
2:9 they had heard the K they went their way;
5:35 for it is the city of the great K
14:9 And the K was sorry; but because of his

	18:22	be compared to a K who wished to settle
	21:5	of Zion, Behold, your K is coming to you,
	22:2	be compared to a K who gave a marriage
	22:7	The K was angry, and he sent his troops
	22:11	"But when the K came in to look at
	22:13	Then the K said to the attendants, 'Bind him
	25:34	Then the K will say to those at his
	25:40	visit thee?' And the K will answer them, 'Truly,
	27:11	him, "Are you the K of the Jews?" Jesus
	27:29	mocked him, saying, "Hail, K of the Jews!"
	27:37	"This is Jesus the K of the Jews."
	27:42	He is the K of Israel; let him come
Mk	6:14	K Herod heard of it; for Jesus' name had
	6:22	his guests; and the K said to the girl,
	6:25	with haste to the K, and asked, saying, "I
	6:26	And the K was exceedingly sorry; but because of
	6:27	And immediately the K sent a soldier of the
	15:2	him, "Are you the K of the Jews?" And
	15:9	release for you the K of the Jews?"
	15:12	whom you call the K of the Jews?"
	15:18	to salute him, "Hail, K of the Jews!"
	15:26	against him read, "The K of the Jews."
	15:31	Let the Christ, the K of Israel, come down
Lk	1:5	the days of Herod, K of Judea, there was
	14:31	to finish.' Or what K, going to encounter another
	14:31	going to encounter another K in war, will not
	19:38	saying, "Blessed is the K who comes in the
	23:2	and saying that he himself is Christ a K
	23:3	him, "Are you the K of the Jews?" And
	23:36	"If you are the K of the Jews, save
	23:37	him, "This is the K of the Jews."
Jn	1:49	You are the K of Israel!"
	6:15	force to make him K, Jesus withdrew again to
	12:13	the Lord, even the K of Israel!"
	12:15	of Zion; behold, your K is coming, sitting on
	18:33	him, "Are you the K of the Jews?"
	18:37	Pilate said to him, "So you are a K
	18:37	Jesus answered, "You say that I am a K
	18:39	release for you the K of the Jews?"
	19:3	to him, saying, "Hail, K of the Jews!" and
	19:12	who makes himself a K sets himself against Caesar."
	19:14	He said to the Jews, "Behold your K
	19:15	Pilate said to them, "Shall I crucify your K
	19:15	answered, "We have no K but Caesar."
	19:19	"Jesus of Nazareth, the K of the Jews."
	19:21	"Do not write, 'The K of the Jews,' but,
	19:21	man said, I am K of the Jews.'"
Acts	7:10	and wisdom before Pharaoh, K of Egypt, who made
	7:18	arose over Egypt another K who had not known
	12:1	that time Herod the K laid violent hands upon
	12:20	persuaded Blastus, the K's chamberlain, they asked
	12:20	country depended on the K's country for food.
	13:21	they asked for a K; and God gave them
	13:22	David to be their K; of whom he testified
	17:7	that there is another K, Jesus."
	25:13	had passed, Agrippa the K and Bernice arrived at
	25:14	Paul's case before the K, saying, "There is a
	25:24	And Festus said, K Agrippa and all who are
	25:26	and, especially before you, K Agrippa, that, after we
	26:2	it is before you, K Agrippa, I am to
	26:7	this hope I am accused by Jews, O K
	26:13	At midday, O K, I saw on the way
	26:19	in me.' "Wherefore, O K Agrippa, I was not
	26:26	For the K knows about these things, and to
	26:27	K Agrippa, do you believe the prophets?
	26:30	Then the K rose, and the governor and Bernice
2Cor	11:32	Damascus, the governor under K Aretas guarded the
1Tim	1:17	To the K of ages, immortal, invisible, the only
	6:15	and only Sovereign, the K of kings and Lord
Heb	7:1	For this Melchizedek, K of Salem, priest of the
	7:2	translation of his name, K of righteousness, and then
	7:2	then he is also K of Salem, that is,
	7:2	of Salem, that is, K of peace.
	11:23	not afraid of the K's edict.
	11:27	the anger of the K; for he endured as
Rev	9:11	They have as K over them the angel of
	15:3	are thy ways, O K of the ages!
	17:14	Lord of lords and K of kings, and those
	19:16	has a name inscribed, K of kings and Lord

KINGDOM (375)

Gen	10:10	The beginning of his K was Babel, Erech, and
	20:9	on me and my K a great sin?
Ex	19:6	be to me a K of priests and a
Num	24:7	than Agag, and his K shall be exalted.
	32:33	son of Joseph, the K of Sihon king of
	32:33	the Amorites and the K of Og king of
Deut	3:4	region of Argob, the K of Og in Bashan.
	3:10	Edre-i, cities of the K of Og in Bashan.
	3:13	and all Bashan, the K of Og, that is,
	17:18	the throne of his K, he shall write for
	17:20	continue long in his K, he and his children,
Josh	13:12	to Salecah; all the K of Og in Bashan,
	13:21	tableland, and all the K of Sihon king of
	13:27	the rest of the K of Sihon king of
	13:30	all Bashan, the whole K of Og king of
	13:31	the cities of the K of Og in Bashan;
1Sam	10:16	the matter of the K, of which Samuel had
	11:14	us go to Gilgal and there renew the K
	13:13	would have established your K over Israel for ever.
	13:14	But now your K shall not continue; the LORD
	15:28	LORD has torn the K of Israel from you
	18:8	and what more can he have but the K
	20:31	neither you nor your K shall be established.
	24:20	king, and that the K of Israel shall be
	28:17	LORD has torn the K out of your hand,
2Sam	3:10	him, to transfer the K from the house of
	3:28	said, "I and my K are for ever guiltless
	5:12	he had exalted his K for the sake of
	7:12	from your body, and I will establish his K
	7:13	the throne of his K for ever.
	7:16	your house and your K shall be made sure
	16:3	give me back the K of my father.'"
	16:8	LORD has given the K into the hand of
1Kgs	2:12	his father; and his K was firmly established.
	2:15	"You know that the K was mine, and that
	2:15	to reign; however the K has turned about and
	2:22	Ask for him the K also; for he is
	2:46	So the K was established in the hand of
	10:20	like of it was never made in any K
	11:11	will surely tear the K from you and will
	11:13	tear away all the K; but I will give
	11:31	about to tear the K from the hand of
	11:34	not take the whole K out of his hand;
	11:35	I will take the K out of his son's
	12:21	Israel, to restore the K to Rehoboam the son
	12:26	his heart, "Now the K will turn back to
	14:8	Israel, and tore the K away from the house
	18:10	is no nation or K whither my lord has
	18:10	an oath of the K or nation, that they
1Chr	10:14	him, and turned the K over to David the
	11:10	strong support in his K, together with all Israel,
	12:23	Hebron, to turn the K of Saul over to
	14:2	Israel, and that his K was highly exalted for
	16:20	to nation, from one K to another people,
	17:11	your own sons, and I will establish his K
	17:14	house and in my K for ever and his
	28:5	the throne of the K of the LORD over
	28:7	I will establish his K for ever if he
	29:11	thine; thine is the K, O LORD, and thou
2Chr	1:1	established himself in his K, and the LORD his
	9:19	like of it was never made in any K
	11:1	Israel, to restore the K to Rehoboam.
	11:17	They strengthened the K of Judah, and for three
	13:8	think to withstand the K of the LORD in
	14:5	And the K had rest under him.
	17:5	the LORD established the K in his hand; and
	21:3	but he gave the K to Jehoram, because he
	22:9	Ahaziah had no one able to rule the K
	29:21	sin offering for the K and for the sanctuary
	32:15	of any nation or K has been able to
	33:13	and brought him again to Jerusalem into his K
	36:20	the establishment of the K of Persia,
	36:22	proclamation throughout all his K and also put it
Ezra	1:1	proclamation throughout all his K and also put it
	7:13	or Levites in my K, who freely offers to
Neh	9:35	serve thee in their K, and in thy great
Tob	1:21	the accounts of his K and over the entire
	13:1	who lives for ever, and blessed is his K
Jud	1:12	by his throne and K that he would surely
	2:12	the power of my K, what I have spoken
	11:8	man in the whole K, thoroughly informed and
Esth	1:14	sat first in the K—:
	1:20	proclaimed throughout all his K, vast as it is,
	2:3	the provinces of his K to gather all the
	3:6	Mordecai, throughout the whole K of Ahasuerus.
	3:8	the provinces of your K; their laws are different
	4:14	not come to the K for such a time
	5:3	given you, even to the half of my K
	5:6	the half of my K, it shall be fulfilled."
	7:2	the half of my K, it shall be fulfilled."
	9:30	twenty-seven provinces of the K of Ahasuerus, in

13:2 order to make my K peaceable and open to
13:3 second place in the K,
13:4 the unifying of the K which we honorably intend
13:5 can so that our K may not attain stability.
16:8 care to render our K quiet and peaceable for
16:12 deprive us of our K and our life,
16:13 blameless partner of our K, together with their
16:14 and would transfer the K of the Persians to
16:16 who has directed the K both for us an
Ps 103:19 the heavens, and his K rules over all.
105:13 to nation, from one K to another people,
145:11 the glory of thy K, and tell of thy
145:12 mighty deeds, and the glorious splendor of thy K
145:13 Thy K is an everlasting kingdom, and thy dominion
145:13 kingdom is an everlasting K, and thy dominion
Eccl 4:14 or in his own K had been born poor.
Wis 6:4 as servants of his K you did not rule
6:20 so the desire for wisdom leads to a K
10:10 she showed him the K of God, and gave
10:14 the scepter of a K and authority over his
Sir 46:13 the Lord, established the K and anointed rulers over
47:21 divided and a disobedient K arose out of Ephraim.
Is 9:7 David, and over his K, to establish it, and
17:3 from Ephraim, and the K from Damascus; and the
19:2 neighbor, city against city, K against kingdom;
19:2 against city, kingdom against K;
34:12 shall name it No K There, and all its
60:12 For the nation and K that will not serve
Jer 18:7 a nation or a K, that I will pluck
18:9 a nation or a K that I will build
27:8 if any nation or K will not serve this
Lam 2:2 ground in dishonor the K and its rulers.
Ezek 17:14 taken away, that the K might be humble and
29:14 origin; and there they shall be a lowly K
Dan 1:20 magicians and enchanters that were in all his K
2:37 heaven has given the K, the power, and the
2:39 you shall arise another K inferior to you, and
2:39 and yet a third K of bronze, which shall
2:40 shall be a fourth K, strong as iron, because
2:41 shall be a divided K; but some of the
2:42 partly clay, so the K shall be partly strong
2:44 will set up a K which shall never be
3:56 the throne of thy K and to be extolled
4:3 His K is an everlasting kingdom, and his dominion
4:3 kingdom is an everlasting K, and his dominion is
4:17 Most High rules the K of men, and gives
4:18 wise men of my K are not able to
4:25 Most High rules the K of men, and gives
4:26 of the tree, your K shall be sure for
4:31 it is spoken: The K has departed from you,
4:32 Most High rules the K of men and gives
4:34 dominion, and his K endures from generation to
4:36 the glory of my K, my majesty and splendor
4:36 was established in my K, and still more greatness
5:7 and shall be the third ruler in the K
5:11 There is in your K a man in whom
5:16 and shall be the third ruler in the K
5:21 High God rules the K of men, and sets
5:26 the days of your K and brought it to
5:28 found wanting; PERES, your K is divided and given
5:29 he should be the third ruler in the K
5:31 the Mede received the K, being about sixty-two
6:1 to set over the K a hundred and twenty
6:1 be throughout the whole K;
6:3 king planned to set him over the whole K
6:4 with regard to the K; but they could find
6:7 the presidents of the K, the prefects and the
6:26 enduring for ever; his K shall never be destroyed,
7:14 dominion and glory and K, that all peoples, nations,
7:14 pass away, and his K one that shall not
7:18 High shall receive the K, and possess the kingdom
7:18 kingdom, and possess the K for ever, for ever
7:22 the time came when the saints received the K
7:23 shall be a fourth K on earth, which shall
7:24 horns, out of this K ten kings shall arise,
7:27 And the K and the dominion and the greatness
7:27 the Most High; their K shall be an everlasting
7:27 shall be an everlasting K, and all dominions shall
10:13 The prince of the K of Persia withstood me
10:13 the prince of the K of Persia
11:2 up all against the K of Greece.
11:4 he has arisen, his K shall be broken and
11:4 he ruled; for his K shall be plucked up
11:17 strength of his whole K, and he shall bring
11:17 women to destroy the K; but it shall not
11:20 the glory of the K; but within a few
11:21 warning and obtain the K by flatteries.
14:1 with his fathers, Cyrus the Persian received his K
Hos 1:4 an end to the K of the house of
Amos 7:13 sanctuary, and it is a temple of the K
9:8 are upon the sinful K, and I will destroy
Obad 1:21 Mount Esau; and the K shall be the LORDs.
Mic 4:8 dominion shall come, the K of the daughter of
1Mac 1:6 youth, and divided his K among them while he
1:10 thirty-seventh year of the K of the Greeks.
1:16 Antiochus saw that his K was established, he
1:41 wrote to his whole K that all should be
1:51 In such words he wrote to his whole K
2:57 the throne of the K for ever.
3:14 name for myself and win honor in the K
3:27 the forces of his K, a very strong army.
6:14 friends, and made him ruler over all his K
6:57 the affairs of the K press urgently upon us.
7:4 took his seat upon the throne of his K
7:8 great man in the K and was faithful to
8:18 they saw that the K of the Greeks was
10:33 any part of my K, I set free without
10:34 for all the Jews who are in my K
10:37 be put in positions of trust in the K
10:43 and receive back all his property in my K
10:52 have returned to my K and have taken my
10:53 the throne of his K --
10:55 took your seat on the throne of their K
11:1 get possession of Alexander's K by trickery and add
11:1 by trickery and add it to his own K
11:9 wife, and you shall reign over your father's K
11:11 threw blame on Alexander because he coveted his K
11:51 the people in his K, and they returned to
11:52 the throne of his K, and the land was
15:3 gained control of the K of our fathers, and
15:3 lay claim to the K so that I may
15:4 many cities in my K,
15:9 gain control of our K, we will bestow great
15:28 citadel in Jerusalem; they are cities of my K
15:29 have taken possession of many places in my K
2Mac 1:7 holy land and the K
4:7 Epiphanes succeeded to the K, Jason the brother of
9:25 the neighbors to my K keep watching for
10:11 he succeeded to the K, appointed one Lysias to
11:23 the subjects of the K be undisturbed in caring
14:6 will not let the K attain tranquillity.
14:26 that conspirator against the K, Judas, to be his
Mt 3:2 Judea, "Repent, for the K of heaven is at
4:17 saying, "Repent, for the K of heaven is at
4:23 the gospel of the K and healing every disease
5:3 for theirs is the K of heaven.
5:10 for theirs is the K of heaven.
5:19 called least in the K of heaven; but he
5:19 called great in the K of heaven.
5:20 will never enter the K of heaven.
6:10 Thy K come.
6:33 But seek first his K and his righteousness, and
7:21 Lord,' shall enter the K of heaven, but he
8:11 and Jacob in the K of heaven,
8:12 the sons of the K will be thrown into
9:35 the gospel of the K, and healing every disease
10:7 you go, saying, 'The K of heaven is at
11:11 is least in the K of heaven is greater
11:12 Baptist until now the K of heaven has suffered
12:25 said to them, "Every K divided against itself is
12:26 how then will his K stand?
12:28 out demons, then the K of God has come
13:11 the secrets of the K of heaven, but to
13:19 the word of the K and does not understand
13:24 before them, saying, "The K of heaven may be
13:31 before them, saying, "The K of heaven is like
13:33 "The K of heaven is like leaven which a
13:38 the sons of the K; the weeds are the
13:41 gather out of his K all causes of sin
13:43 the sun in the K of their Father.
13:44 "The K of heaven is like treasure hidden in
13:45 "Again, the K of heaven is like a merchant
13:47 "Again, the K of heaven is like a net
13:52 been trained for the K of heaven is like
16:19 the keys of the K of heaven, and whatever
16:28 see the Son of man coming in his K
18:1 the greatest in the K of heaven?"
18:3 will never enter the K of heaven.
18:4 the greatest in the K of heaven.
18:22 "Therefore the K of heaven may be compared to
19:12 the sake of the K of heaven.
19:14 to such belongs the K of heaven."

19:23 man to enter the K of heaven.
19:24 man to enter the K of God."
20:1 "For the K of heaven is like a householder
20:21 hand and one at your left, in your K
21:31 harlots go into the K of God before you.
21:43 I tell you, the K of God will be
22:2 in parables, saying, "The K of heaven may be
23:13 because you shut the K of heaven against men;
24:7 rise against nation, and K against kingdom, and there
24:7 nation, and kingdom against K, and there will be
24:14 this gospel of the K will be preached throughout
25:1 "Then the K of heaven shall be compared to
25:34 my Father, inherit the K prepared for you from
26:29 drink it new with you in my Father's K
Mk 1:15 is fulfilled, and the K of God is at
3:24 If a K is divided against itself, that kingdom
3:24 divided against itself, that K cannot stand.
4:11 the secret of the K of God, but for
4:26 And he said, "The K of God is as
4:30 can we compare the K of God, or what
6:23 I will give you, even half of my K
9:1 they see that the K of God has come
9:45 you to enter the K of God with one
10:14 to such belongs the K of God.
10:15 does not receive the K of God like a
10:23 riches to enter the K of God!"
10:24 riches to enter the K of God!
10:25 man to enter the K of God."
11:10 Blessed is the K of our father David that
12:34 not far from the K of God." And after
13:8 rise against nation, and K against kingdom; there
13:8 nation, and kingdom against K; there will be
14:25 it new in the K of God."
15:42 himself looking for the K of God, took courage
Lk 1:33 ever; and of his K there will be no
4:43 good news of the K of God to the
6:20 for yours is the K of God.
7:28 is least in the K of God is greater
8:1 good news of the K of God.
8:10 the secrets of the K of God; but for
9:2 out to preach the K of God and to
9:11 to them of the K of God, and cured
9:27 before they see the K of God."
9:60 go and proclaim the K of God."
9:62 is fit for the K of God."
10:9 say to them, 'The K of God has come
10:11 know this, that the K of God has come
11:2 Thy K come.
11:17 said to them, "Every K divided against itself is
11:18 himself, how will his K stand?
11:20 out demons, then the K of God has come
12:31 Instead, seek his K, and these things shall be
12:32 your Father's good pleasure to give you the K
13:18 therefore, "What is the K of God like?
13:20 shall I compare the K of God?
13:28 the prophets in the K of God and you
13:29 at table in the K of God.
14:15 eat bread in the K of God!"
16:16 good news of the K of God is preached,
17:20 the Pharisees when the K of God was coming,
17:20 he answered them, "The K of God is not
17:21 'There!' for behold, the K of God is in
18:16 to such belongs the K of God.
18:17 does not receive the K of God like a
18:24 riches to enter the K of God!
18:25 man to enter the K of God."
18:29 the sake of the K of God,
19:11 they supposed that the K of God was to
21:10 rise against nation, and K against kingdom;
21:10 nation, and kingdom against K;
21:31 you know that the K of God is near.
22:16 is fulfilled in the K of God."
22:18 the vine until the K of God comes."
22:29 assigned to me, a K,
22:30 my table in my K, and sit on thrones
23:41 "Jesus, remember me when you come into your K
23:50 was looking for the K of God.
Jn 3:3 he cannot see the K of God."
3:5 he cannot enter the K of God.
Acts 1:3 and speaking of the K of God.
1:6 this time restore the K to Israel?"
8:12 good news about the K of God and the
14:22 we must enter the K of God.
19:8 and pleading about the K of God;
20:25 have gone preaching the K will see my face
28:23 evening, testifying to the K of God and trying
28:30 to him, preaching the K of God and teaching
Rom 14:17 For the K of God is not food and
1Cor 4:20 For the K of God does not consist in
6:9 will not inherit the K of God?
6:10 robbers will inherit the K of God.
15:24 when he delivers the K to God the Father
15:50 blood cannot inherit the K of God, nor does
Gal 5:21 shall not inherit the K of God.
Eph 5:5 any inheritance in the K of Christ and of
Col 1:13 transferred us to the K of his beloved Son,
4:11 fellow workers for the K of God, and they
1Thes 2:12 you into his own K and glory.
2Thes 1:5 made worthy of the K of God, for which
2Tim 4:1 his appearing and his K:
4:18 every evil and save me for his heavenly K
Heb 1:8 the righteous scepter is the scepter of thy K
12:28 grateful for receiving a K that cannot be shaken,
Jas 2:5 and heirs of the K which he has promised
2Pet 1:11 entrance into the eternal K of our Lord and
Rev 1:6 and made us a K, priests to his God
1:9 the tribulation and the K and the patient endurance,
5:10 hast made them a K and priests to our
11:15 in heaven, saying, "The K of the world has
11:15 world has become the K of our Lord and
12:10 the power and the K of our God and
16:10 the beast, and its K was in darkness; men

KINGDOMS (61)

Deut 3:21 do to all the K into which you are
28:25 horror to all the K of the earth.
Josh 11:10 Hazor formerly was the head of all those K
1Sam 10:18 hand of all the K that were oppressing you.'
1Kgs 4:21 ruled over all the K from the Euphrates to
2Kgs 19:15 alone, of all the K of the earth; thou
19:19 hand, that all the K of the earth may
1Chr 29:30 and upon all the K of the countries.
2Chr 12:8 the service of the K of the countries."
17:10 fell upon all the K of the lands that
20:6 rule over all the K of the nations?
20:29 came on all the K of the countries when
36:23 given me all the K of the earth, and
Ezra 1:2 given me all the K of the earth, and
Neh 9:22 thou didst give them K and peoples, and didst
Ps 46:6 The nations rage, the K totter; he utters his
68:32 Sing to God, O K of the earth; sing
79:6 thee, and on the K that do not call
102:22 gather together, and K, to worship the LORD.
135:11 Bashan, and all the K of Canaan,
Sir 44:3 who ruled in their K, and were men renowned
Is 10:10 has reached to the K of the idols whose
13:4 Hark, an uproar of K, of nations gathering together!
13:19 Babylon, the glory of K, the splendor and pride
14:16 earth tremble, who shook K,
23:11 he has shaken the K; the LORD has given
23:17 harlot with all the K of the world upon
37:16 alone, of all the K of the earth; thou
37:20 hand, that all the K of the earth may
47:5 shall no more be called the mistress of K
Jer 1:10 over nations and over K, to pluck up and
1:15 the tribes of the K of the north, says
10:7 and in all their K there is none like
15:4 horror to all the K of the earth because
24:9 horror to all the K of the earth, to
25:26 another, and all the K of the world which
28:8 and pestilence against many countries and great K
29:18 horror to all the K of the earth, to
34:1 army and all the K of the earth under
34:17 horror to all the K of the earth.
49:28 Concerning Kedar and the K of Hazor which
51:20 with you I destroy K;
51:27 summon against her the K, Ararat, Minni, and
Bar 2:4 subjection to all the K around us, to be
Ezek 29:15 most lowly of the K, and never again exalt
37:22 two nations, and no longer divided into two K
Dan 2:44 in pieces all these K and bring them to
7:23 different from all the K, and it shall devour
7:27 the greatness of the K under the whole heaven
8:22 four others arose, four K shall arise from his
Amos 6:2 Are they better than these K
Nah 3:5 on your nakedness and K on your shame.
Zeph 3:8 gather nations, to assemble K, to pour out upon
Hag 2:22 overthrow the throne of K; I am about to
2:22 the strength of the K of the nations, and
1Mac 1:16 of Egypt, that he might reign over both K
6:29 to him from other K and from islands of
8:11 The remaining K and islands, as many as ever

Mt 4:8 showed him all the K of the world and
Lk 4:5 showed him all the K of the world in
Heb 11:33 through faith conquered K, enforced justice, received

KINGLY (3)

Dan 5:20 was deposed from his K throne, and his glory
Lk 19:12 country to receive a K power and then return.
19:15 having received the K power, he commanded these

KINGS (365)

Gen 14:2 king of Goiim, these K made war with Bera
14:5 year Ched-or-laomer and the K who were with him
14:9 king of Ellasar, four K against five.
14:10 pits; and as the K of Sodom and Gomorrah
14:17 of Ched-or-laomer and the K who were with him,
17:6 nations of you, and K shall come forth from
17:16 a mother of nations; K of peoples shall come
35:11 come from you, and K shall spring from you.
36:31 These are the K who reigned in the land
Num 31:8 They slew the K of Midian with the rest
31:8 and Reba, the five K of Midian; and they
Deut 3:8 hand of the two K of the Amorites who
3:21 done to these two K; so will the LORD
4:47 of Bashan, the two K of the Amorites, who
7:24 he will give their K into your hand, and
31:4 Sihon and Og, the K of the Amorites, and
Josh 2:10 did to the two K of the Amorites that
5:1 When all the K of the Amorites that were
5:1 west, and all the K of the Canaanites that
9:1 When all the K who were beyond the Jordan
9:10 did to the two K of the Amorites who
10:5 Then the five K of the Amorites, the king
10:6 us; for all the K of the Amorites that
10:16 These five K fled, and hid themselves in the
10:17 told Joshua, "The five K have been found, hidden
10:22 and bring those five K out to me from
10:23 and brought those five K out to him from
10:24 when they brought those K out to Joshua, Joshua
10:24 put your feet upon the necks of these K
10:40 slopes, and all their K; he left none remaining,
10:42 Joshua took all these K and their land at
11:2 Achshaph, and to the K who were in the
11:5 And all these K joined their forces, and came
11:12 the cities of those K, and all their kings,
11:12 kings, and all their K, Joshua took, and smote
11:17 he took all their K, and smote them, and
11:18 made war a long time with all those K
12:1 Now these are the K of the land, whom
12:7 And these are the K of the land whom
12:24 the king of Tirzah, one: in all, thirty-one K
24:12 before you, the two K of the Amorites; it
Judg 1:7 And Adoni-bezek said, "Seventy K with their thumbs
5:3 "Hear, O K; give ear, O princes; to the
5:19 "The K came, they fought; then fought the kings
5:19 fought; then fought the K of Canaan, at Taanach,
8:5 Zebah and Zalmunna, the K of Midian."
8:12 and took the two K of Midian, Zebah and
8:26 garments worn by the K of Midian, and besides
1Sam 14:47 against Edom, against the K of Zobah, and against
27:6 has belonged to the K of Judah to this
2Sam 10:19 And when all the K who were servants of
11:1 year, the time when K go forth to battle,
1Kgs 4:24 Gaza, over all the K west of the Euphrates;
4:34 and from all the K of the earth, who
10:15 and from all the K of Arabia and from
10:23 Solomon excelled all the K of the earth in
10:29 exported to all the K of the Hittites and
10:29 the Hittites and the K of Syria.
14:19 the Chronicles of the K of Israel.
14:29 the Chronicles of the K of Judah?
15:7 the Chronicles of the K of Judah?
15:23 the Chronicles of the K of Judah?
15:31 the Chronicles of the K of Israel?
16:5 the Chronicles of the K of Israel?
16:14 the Chronicles of the K of Israel?
16:20 the Chronicles of the K of Israel?
16:27 the Chronicles of the K of Israel?
16:33 anger than all the K of Israel who were
20:1 his army together; thirty-two K were with him, and
20:12 was drinking with the K in the booths, he
20:16 he and the thirty-two K who helped him.
20:24 do this: remove the K, each from his post,
20:31 have heard that the K of the house of
20:31 of Israel are merciful K; let us put sackcloth
22:39 the Chronicles of the K of Israel?
22:45 the Chronicles of the K of Judah?
2Kgs 1:18 the Chronicles of the K of Israel?
3:10 has called these three K to give them into
3:13 has called these three K to give them into
3:21 Moabites heard that the K had come up to
3:23 "This is blood; the K have surely fought together,
7:6 hired against us the K of the Hittites and
7:6 the Hittites and the K of Egypt to come
8:18 the way of the K of Israel, as the
8:23 the Chronicles of the K of Judah?
10:4 said, "Behold, the two K could not stand before
10:34 the Chronicles of the K of Israel?
11:19 took his seat on the throne of the K
12:18 Ahaziah, his fathers, the K of Judah, had dedicated,
12:19 the Chronicles of the K of Judah?
13:8 the Chronicles of the K of Israel?
13:12 the Chronicles of the K of Israel?
13:13 in Samaria with the K of Israel.
14:15 the Chronicles of the K of Israel?
14:16 in Samaria with the K of Israel; and Jeroboam
14:18 the Chronicles of the K of Judah?
14:28 the Chronicles of the K of Israel?
14:29 with his fathers, the K of Israel, and Zechariah
15:6 the Chronicles of the K of Judah?
15:11 the Chronicles of the K of Israel.
15:15 the Chronicles of the K of Israel.
15:21 the Chronicles of the K of Israel?
15:26 the Chronicles of the K of Israel.
15:31 the Chronicles of the K of Israel.
15:36 the Chronicles of the K of Judah?
16:3 the way of the K of Israel.
16:19 the Chronicles of the K of Judah?
17:2 yet not as the K of Israel who were
17:8 the customs which the K of Israel had introduced.
18:5 him among all the K of Judah after him,
19:11 have heard what the K of Assyria have done
19:17 truth, O LORD, the K of Assyria have laid
20:20 the Chronicles of the K of Judah?
21:17 the Chronicles of the K of Judah?
21:25 the Chronicles of the K of Judah?
23:5 idolatrous priests whom the K of Judah had ordained
23:11 the horses that the K of Judah had dedicated
23:12 of Ahaz, which the K of Judah had made,
23:19 cities of Samaria, which K of Israel had made,
23:22 the days of the K of Israel or of
23:22 Israel or of the K of Judah;
23:28 the Chronicles of the K of Judah?
24:5 the Chronicles of the K of Judah?
25:28 the seats of the K who were with him
1Chr 1:43 These are the K who reigned in the land
9:1 the Book of the K of Israel.
16:21 oppress them; he rebuked K on their account,
19:9 the city, and the K who had come were
20:1 year, the time when K go forth to battle,
2Chr 1:12 as none of the K had who were before
1:17 exported to all the K of the Hittites and
1:17 the Hittites and the K of Syria.
9:14 brought; and all the K of Arabia and the
9:22 Solomon excelled all the K of the earth in
9:23 And all the K of the earth sought the
9:26 ruled over all the K from the Euphrates to
16:11 the Book of the K of Judah and Israel.
20:34 the Book of the K of Israel.
21:6 the way of the K of Israel, as the
21:13 the way of the K of Israel, and have
21:20 David, but not in the tombs of the K
24:16 of David among the K, because he had done
24:25 not bury him in the tombs of the K
24:27 in the Commentary on the Book of the K
25:26 the Book of the K of Judah and Israel?
26:23 which belonged to the K, for they said, "He
27:7 the Book of the K of Israel and Judah.
28:2 the ways of the K of Israel.
28:23 the gods of the K of Syria helped them,
28:26 the Book of the K of Judah and Israel.
28:27 the tombs of the K of Israel.
30:6 the hand of the K of Assyria.
32:4 saying, "Why should the K of Assyria come and
32:32 the Book of the K of Judah and Israel.
33:18 the Chronicles of the K of Israel.
34:11 the buildings which the K of Judah had let
35:18 prophet; none of the K of Israel had kept
35:27 the Book of the K of Israel and Judah.
36:8 the Book of the K of Israel and Judah;
Ezra 4:15 rebellious city, hurtful to K and provinces, and that
4:19 old has risen against K, and that rebellion and
4:20 And mighty K have been over Jerusalem, who ruled

KINGS

	7:12	Israel: "Artaxerxes, king of K, to Ezra the priest,
	9:7	our iniquities we, our K, and our priests have
	9:7	the hand of the K of the lands, to
	9:9	steadfast love before the K of Persia, to grant
Neh	9:24	their hands, with their K and the peoples of
	9:32	upon us, upon our K, our princes, our priests,
	9:32	the time of the K of Assyria until this
	9:34	have acted wickedly; our K, our princes, our priests,
	9:37	yield goes to the K whom thou hast set
Esth	10:2	the Chronicles of the K of Media and Persia?
	13:4	the ordinances of the K, so that the unifying
Job	3:14	been at rest, with K and counselors of the
	12:18	looses the bonds of K, and binds a waistcloth
	36:7	the righteous, but with K upon the throne he
Ps	2:2	The K of the earth set themselves, and the
	2:10	Now therefore, O K, be wise; be warned, O
	45:9	you glad; daughters of K are among your ladies
	48:4	For lo, the K assembled, they came on together.
	68:12	bore the tidings: "The K of the armies, they
	68:14	When the Almighty scattered K there, snow fell on
	68:29	thy temple at Jerusalem K bear gifts to thee.
	72:10	May the K of Tarshish and of the isles
	72:10	him tribute, may the K of Sheba and Seba
	72:11	May all K fall down before him, all nations
	76:12	is terrible to the K of the earth.
	89:27	the highest of the K of the earth.
	102:15	LORD, and all the K of the earth thy
	105:14	oppress them; he rebuked K on their account,
	105:30	with frogs, even in the chambers of their K
	110:5	hand; he will shatter K on the day of
	119:46	of thy testimonies before K, and shall not be
	135:10	nations and slew mighty K,
	136:17	him who smote great K, for his steadfast love
	136:18	ever; and slew famous K, for his steadfast love
	138:4	All the K of the earth shall praise thee,
	144:10	who givest victory to K, who rescuest David thy
	148:11	K of the earth and all peoples, princes and
	149:8	peoples, to bind their K with chains and their
Prov	8:15	By me K reign, and rulers decree what is
	16:12	is an abomination to K to do evil, for
	22:29	he will stand before K; he will not stand
	25:2	but the glory of K is to search things
	25:3	so the mind of K is unsearchable.
	30:28	yet it is in K palaces.
	31:3	to women, your ways to those who destroy K
	31:4	It is not for K, O Lemuel, it is
	31:4	it is not for K to drink wine, or
Eccl	2:8	and the treasure of K and provinces; I got
Wis	6:1	Listen therefore, O K, and understand; learn, O
	10:16	Lord, and withstood dread K with wonders and signs.
Sir	8:2	ruined many, and has perverted the minds of K
	11:5	Many K have had to sit on the ground,
	45:3	the Lord glorified him in the presence of K
	47:11	him the covenant of K and a throne of
	48:6	Most High; who brought K down to destruction, and
	48:8	at Horeb; who anointed K to inflict retribution, and
	49:4	the Most High; the K of Judah came to
Is	1:1	Jotham, Ahaz, and Hezekiah, K of Judah.
	7:16	land before whose two K you are in dread
	10:8	for he says: "Are not my commanders all K
	14:9	thrones all who were K of the nations.
	14:18	go home?' All the K of the nations lie
	19:11	son of the wise, a son of ancient K
	24:21	in heaven, and the K of the earth, on
	37:11	have heard what the K of Assyria have done
	37:18	truth, O LORD, the K of Assyria have laid
	41:2	so that he tramples K under foot; he makes
	45:1	ungird the loins of K, to open doors before
	49:7	the servant of rulers: K shall see and arise;
	49:23	K shall be your foster fathers, and their queens
	52:15	he startle many nations; K shall shut their mouths
	60:3	to your light, and K to the brightness of
	60:10	your walls, and their K shall minister to you;
	60:11	the nations, with their K led in procession.
	60:16	suck the breast of K; and you shall know
	62:2	vindication, and all the K your glory; and you
Jer	1:18	whole land, against the K of Judah, its princes,
	2:26	be shamed: they, their K, their princes, their priests,
	8:1	the bones of the K of Judah, the bones
	13:13	of this land: the K who sit on David's
	17:19	Gate, by which the K of Judah enter and
	17:20	of the LORD, you K of Judah, and all
	17:25	gates of this city K who sit on the
	19:3	of the LORD, O K of Judah and inhabitants
	19:4	their fathers nor the K of Judah have known;
	19:13	the houses of the K of Judah—all the
	20:5	the treasures of the K of Judah into the
	22:4	gates of this house K who sit on the
	25:14	many nations and great K shall make slaves even
	25:18	cities of Judah, its K and princes, to make
	25:20	among them; all the K of the land of
	25:20	Uz and all the K of the land of
	25:22	of Ammon; all the K of Tyre, all the
	25:22	of Tyre, all the K of Sidon, and the
	25:22	of Sidon, and the K of the coastland across
	25:24	their hair; all the K of Arabia and all
	25:24	Arabia and all the K of the mixed tribes
	25:25	the desert; all the K of Zimri, all the
	25:25	of Zimri, all the K of Elam, and all
	25:25	Elam, and all the K of Media;
	25:26	of Media; all the K of the north, far
	27:7	many nations and great K shall make him their
	32:32	me to anger—their K and their princes, their
	33:4	the houses of the K of Judah which were
	34:5	your fathers, the former K who were before you,
	44:9	the wickedness of the K of Judah, the wickedness
	44:17	and our fathers, our K and our princes, in
	44:21	and your fathers, your K and your princes, and
	46:25	her gods and her K, upon Pharaoh and those
	50:41	mighty nation and many K are stirring from the
	51:11	the spirit of the K of the Medes, because
	51:28	war against her, the K of the Medes, with
	52:32	the seats of the K who were with him
Lam	4:12	The K of the earth did not believe, or
Bar	1:16	Jerusalem, and to our K and our princes and
	2:1	Israel, and against our K and against our princes
	2:19	our fathers or our K that we bring before
	2:24	the bones of our K and the bones of
	6:51	all the nations and K that they are not
	6:66	neither curse nor bless K;
Ezek	26:7	of Babylon, king of K, with horses and chariots,
	27:33	merchandise you enriched the K of the earth.
	27:35	at you; and their K are horribly afraid, their
	28:17	I exposed you before K, to feast their eyes
	32:10	at you, and their K shall shudder because of
	32:29	"Edom is there, her K and all her princes,
	43:7	neither they, nor their K, by their harlotry, and
	43:7	dead bodies of their K,
	43:9	dead bodies of their K far from me, and
Dan	2:21	and seasons; he removes K and sets up kings;
	2:21	kings and sets up K; he gives wisdom to
	2:37	king, the king of K, to whom the God
	2:44	the days of those K the God of heaven
	2:47	gods and Lord of K, and a revealer of
	7:17	great beasts are four K who shall arise out
	7:24	of this kingdom ten K shall arise, and another
	7:24	the former ones, and shall put down three K
	8:20	horns, these are the K of Media and Persia.
	9:6	thy name to our K, our princes, and our
	9:8	of face, to our K, to our princes, and
	11:2	Behold, three more K shall arise in Persia; and
	11:27	as for the two K, their minds shall be
Hos	1:1	Jotham, Ahaz, and Hezekiah, K of Judah, and in
	7:8	All their K have fallen; and none of them
	8:4	They made K, but not through me.
	13:11	I have given you K in my anger, and
Mic	1:1	Jotham, Ahaz, and Hezekiah, K of Judah, which he
	1:14	deceitful thing to the K of Israel.
Hab	1:10	At K they scoff, and of rulers they make
1Mac	1:2	put to death the K of the earth.
	2:48	of the Gentiles and K, and they never let
	3:7	He embittered many K, but he made Jacob glad
	3:30	he used to give more lavishly than preceding K
	8:4	They also subdued the K who came against them
	8:12	They have subdued K far and near, and as
	8:13	help and to make K, they make kings, and
	8:13	make kings, they make K, and those whom they
	10:49	The two K met in battle, and the army
	10:58	with great pomp, as K do.
	10:60	and met the two K; he gave them and
	10:89	the custom to give to the kinsmen of K
	12:13	have encircled us; the K round about us have
	13:36	priest and friend of K, and to the elders
	14:13	fight them, and the K were crushed in those
	15:5	tax remissions that the K before me have granted
	15:15	with letters to the K and countries, in which
	15:19	to write to the K and countries that they
2Mac	2:13	the books about the K and prophets, and the
	2:13	David, and letters of K about votive offerings.
	3:2	came about that the K themselves honored the place
	5:16	votive offerings which other K had made to enhance
	13:4	But the King of K aroused the anger of

Mt 10:18 dragged before governors and K for my sake, to
11:8 soft raiment are in K houses.
17:24 From whom do K of the earth take toll
Mk 13:9 stand before governors and K for my sake, to
Lk 7:25 in luxury are in K courts.
10:24 that many prophets and K desired to see what
21:12 will be brought before K and governors for my
22:25 said to them, "The K of the Gentiles exercise
Acts 4:26 The K of the earth set themselves in array,
9:15 before the Gentiles and K and the sons of
1Cor 4:8 Without us you have become K
1Tim 2:2 for all men, for K and all who are
6:15 Sovereign, the King of K and Lord of lords,
Heb 7:1 the slaughter of the K and blessed him;
Rev 1:5 and the ruler of K on earth.
6:15 Then the K of the earth and the great
10:11 about many peoples and nations and tongues and K
16:12 the way for the K from the east.
16:14 go abroad to the K of the whole world,
17:2 waters, with whom the K of the earth have
17:10 they are also seven K, five of whom have
17:12 you saw are ten K who have not yet
17:12 to receive authority as K for one hour, together
17:14 lords and King of K, and those with him
17:18 has dominion over the K of the earth."
18:3 impure passion, and the K of the earth have
18:9 And the K of the earth, who committed fornication
19:16 name inscribed, King of K and Lord of lords.
19:18 eat the flesh of K, the flesh of captains,
19:19 the beast and the K of the earth with
21:24 nations walk; and the K of the earth shall

KINGSHIP (8)

1Sam 10:25 and duties of the K; and he wrote them
14:47 Saul had taken the K over Israel, he fought
2Chr 13:5 of Israel gave the K over Israel for ever
Dan 5:18 Nebuchadnezzar your father K and greatness and
2Mac 2:17 to all, and the K and priesthood and consecration,
Jn 18:36 Jesus answered, "My K is not of this world;
18:36 this world; if my K were of this world,
18:36 the Jews; but my K is not from the

KINSFOLK (7)

1Sam 18:18 and who are my K, my father's family in
2Chr 28:8 thousand of their K, women, sons, and daughters;
28:11 the captives from your K whom you have taken,
28:15 brought them to their K at Jericho, the city
Job 19:14 My K and my close friends have failed me;
Lk 1:58 And her neighbors and K heard that the Lord
2:44 sought him among their K and acquaintances;

KINSHIP (2)

Wis 8:17 my mind, that in K with wisdom there is
2Mac 5:9 in hope of finding protection because of their K

KINSMAN (24)

Gen 14:14 Abram heard that his K had been taken captive,
14:16 also brought back his K Lot with his goods,
24:48 daughter of my master's K for his son.
29:12 he was her father's K, and that he was
29:15 "Because you are my K, should you therefore serve
Lev 25:49 him, or a near K belonging to his family
Num 5:8 the man has no K to whom restitution may
27:11 his inheritance to his K that is next to
Judg 9:18 because he is your K –
Ruth 2:1 Now Naomi had a K of her husbands, a
3:2 is not Boaz our K, with whose maidens you
3:12 I am a near K, yet there is a
3:12 yet there is a K nearer than I.
4:3 which belonged to our K Elimelech.
Tob 3:15 his heir, no near K or kinsman's son for
3:15 no near kinsman or K's son for whom I
6:11 her inheritance, for you are her only eligible K
Sir 41:21 the appeal of a K; of taking away some
Amos 6:10 And when a man's K, he who burns him,
1Mac 11:31 you to Lasthenes our K we have written to
2Mac 11:1 the king's guardian and K, who was in charge
11:35 to what Lysias the K of the king has
Jn 18:26 the high priest, a K of the man whose
Rom 16:11 Greet my K Herodion.

KINSMEN (62)

Gen 13:8 your herdsmen and my herdsmen; for we are K
16:12 and he shall dwell over against all his K
24:27 the way to the house of my master's K
31:23 fled, he took his K with him and pursued
31:25 and Laban with his K encamped in the hill
31:32 the presence of our K point out what I
31:37 it here before my K and your kinsmen, that
31:37 my kinsmen and your K, that they may decide
31:46 Jacob said to his K, "Gather stones," and they
31:54 mountain and called his K to eat bread; and
Ex 4:18 I pray, to my K in Egypt and see
Judg 5:14 you, Benjamin, with your K; from Machir marched
9:1 Shechem to his mother's K and said to them
9:3 And his mother's K spoke all these words on
9:26 into Shechem with his K; and the men of
9:31 of Ebed and his K have come to Shechem,
9:41 out Gaal and his K, so that they could
14:3 the daughters of your K, or among all our
2Sam 19:12 You are my K, you are my bone and
1Kgs 12:24 or fight against your K the people of Israel.
16:11 single male of his K or his friends.
2Kgs 10:13 Shepherds, Jehu met the K of Ahaziah king of
10:13 answered, "We are the K of Ahaziah, and we
1Chr 5:7 And his K by their families, when the genealogy
5:13 their K according to their fathers' houses: Michael,
7:5 Their K belonging to all the families of Issachar
8:32 also dwelt opposite their K in Jerusalem, with their
8:32 opposite their kinsmen in Jerusalem, with their K
9:6 Zerah: Jeuel and their K, six hundred and ninety.
9:9 of Ibnijah; and their K according to their
9:13 of Immer; besides their K, heads of their fathers'
9:17 Talmon, Ahiman, and their K (Shallum being the
9:19 of Korah, and his K of his fathers' house,
9:25 and south; and their K who were in their
9:32 Also some of their K of the Kohathites had
9:38 also dwelt opposite their K in Jerusalem, with their
9:38 opposite their kinsmen in Jerusalem, with their K
12:2 or the left hand; they were Benjaminites, Saul's K
12:29 Of the Benjaminites, the K of Saul, three thousand,
12:32 chiefs, and all their K under their command.
23:22 but only daughters; their K, the sons of Kish,
2Chr 5:12 Jeduthun, their sons and K, arrayed in fine linen,
Ezra 3:2 of Shealtiel with his K, and they built the
3:9 his sons and his K, and Kadmi-el and his
3:9 of Henadad and the Levites, their sons and K
8:18 with his sons and K, eighteen;
8:19 of Merari, with his K and their sons, twenty;
8:24 and ten of their K with them.
Neh 12:36 of Asaph; and his K, Shemaiah, Azarel, Milalai,
Ps 38:11 my plague, and my K stand afar off.
Jer 7:15 cast out all your K, all the offspring of
29:16 in this city, your K who did not go
51:35 me and to my K be upon Babylon," let
1Mac 10:89 to give to the K of kings.
2Mac 8:1 villages and summoned their K and enlisted those
12:39 to lie with their K in the sepulchres of
Lk 14:12 your brothers or your K or rich neighbors, lest
21:16 parents and brothers and K and friends, and some
Acts 10:24 had called together his K and close friends.
Rom 9:3 of my brethren, my K by race.
16:7 Andronicus and Junias, my K and my fellow
16:21 so do Lucius and Jason and Sosipater, my K

KINSWOMAN (3)

Lev 18:12 your father's sister; she is your father's near K
18:13 mother's sister, for she is your mother's near K
Lk 1:36 And behold, your K Elizabeth in her old age

KINSWOMEN

Lev 18:17 they are your near K; it is wickedness.

KIR (5)

2Kgs 16:9 its people captive to K, and he killed Rezin.
Is 15:1 Moab is undone; because K is laid waste in
22:6 chariots and horsemen, and K uncovered the shield.
Amos 1:5 people of Syria shall go into exile to K
9:7 the Philistines from Caphtor and the Syrians from K

KIR-HARESETH (2)

2Kgs 3:25 stones were left in K, and the slingers surrounded
Is 16:7 Mourn, utterly stricken, for the raisin-cakes of K

KIR-HERES (3)

Is 16:11 a lyre for Moab, and my heart for K
Jer 48:31 for the men of K I mourn.
48:36 for the men of K; therefore the riches they

KIRIATH-ARBA (9)

Gen 23:2 And Sarah died at K (that is, Hebron) in
35:27 Isaac at Mamre, or K (that is, Hebron), where

Josh 14:15 of Hebron formerly was K; this Arba was the
15:13 the people of Judah, K, that is, Hebron (Arba
15:54 Beth-tappuah, Aphekah, Humtah, K (that is,
20:7 country of Ephraim, and K (that is, Hebron) in
21:11 They gave them K (Arba being the father of
Judg 1:10 of Hebron was formerly K; and they defeated
Neh 11:25 of Judah lived in K and its villages, and

KIRIATH-BAAL (2)

Josh 15:60 K (that is, Kiriath-jearim), and Rabbah: two cities
18:14 and it ends at K (that is, Kiriath-jearim), a

KIRIATH-HUZOTH

Num 22:39 Balaam went with Balak, and they came to K

KIRIATH-JEARIM (19)

Josh 9:17 their cities were Gibeon, Chephirah, Be-eroth, and K
15:9 to Baalah (that is, K;
15:60 Kiriath-baal (that is, K, and Rabbah: two cities with
18:14 at Kiriath-baal (that is, K, a city belonging to
18:15 at the outskirts of K; and the boundary goes
18:28 is, Jerusalem), Gibe-ah and K--fourteen cities with
Judg 18:12 up and encamped at K in Judah.
18:12 to this day; behold, it is west of K
1Sam 6:21 to the inhabitants of K, saying, "The Philistines have
7:1 And the men of K came and took up
7:2 ark was lodged at K, a long time passed,
1Chr 2:50 Shobal the father of K,
2:52 Shobal the father of K had other sons: Haroeh,
2:53 And the families of K: the Ithrites, the Puthites,
13:5 Hamath, to bring the ark of God from K
13:6 Baalah, that is, to K which belongs to Judah,
2Chr 1:4 ark of God from K to the place that
Neh 7:29 The men of K, Chephirah, and Be-eroth, seven
Jer 26:20 the LORD, Uriah the son of Shemaiah from K

KIRIATH-SANNAH

Josh 15:49 Shamir, Jattir, Socoh, Dannah, K (that is, Debir),

KIRIATH-SEPHER (4)

Josh 15:15 Debir; now the name of Debir formerly was K
15:16 Caleb said, "Whoever smites K, and takes it, to
Judg 1:11 The name of Debir was formerly K
1:12 said, "He who attacks K and takes it, I

KIRIATHAIM (6)

Num 32:37 Reuben built Heshbon, Elealeh, K,
Josh 13:19 and Mephaath, and K, and Sibmah, and Zereth-sha
1Chr 6:76 its pasture lands, and K with its pasture lands.
Jer 48:1 K is put to shame, it is taken; the
48:23 Beth-diblathaim, and K, and Beth-gamul, and
Ezek 25:9 of the country, Beth-jeshimoth, Baal-meon, and K

KIRIATHARIM

Ezra 2:25 The sons of K, Chephirah, and Be-eroth, seven

KISH (23)

1Sam 9:1 Benjamin whose name was K, the son of Abiel,
9:3 Now the asses of K, Saul's father, were lost.
9:3 So K said to Saul his son, "Take one
10:11 another, "What has come over the son of K
10:21 Saul the son of K was taken by lot.
14:51 of Ner, Saul's uncle; K was the father of
2Sam 21:14 in the tomb of K his father; and they
1Chr 8:30 son: Abdon, then Zur, K, Baal, Nadab,
8:33 was the father of K, Kish of Saul, Saul
8:33 the father of Kish, K of Saul, Saul of
9:36 son Abdon, then Zur, K, Baal, Ner, Nadab,
9:39 was the father of K, Kish of Saul, Saul
9:39 the father of Kish, K of Saul, Saul of
12:1 Saul the son of K; and they were among
23:21 The sons of Mahli: Eleazar and K
23:22 kinsmen, the sons of K, married them.
24:29 Of K, the sons of Kish: Jerahmeel.
24:29 Kish, the sons of K: Jerahmeel.
26:28 Saul the son of K, and Abner the son
2Chr 29:12 the sons of Merari, K the son of Abdi,
Esth 2:5 of Shimei, son of K, a Benjaminite,
11:2 of Shimei, son of K, of the tribe of
Acts 13:21 Saul the son of K, a man of the

KISHI

1Chr 6:44 Ethan the son of K, son of Abdi, son

KISHION (2)

Josh 19:20 Haphara-im, Shion, Anaharath, Rabbith, K, Ebez,
21:28 the tribe of Issachar, K with its pasture lands,

KISHON (6)

Judg 4:7 you by the river K with his chariots and
4:13 with him, from Harosheth-ha-goiim to the river K
5:21 The torrent K swept them away, the onrushing
5:21 them away, the onrushing torrent, the torrent K
1Kgs 18:40 down to the brook K, and killed them there.
Ps 83:9 Jabin at the river K,

KISS (23)

Gen 27:26 him, "Come near and K me, my son."
31:28 not permit me to K my sons and my
2Sam 15:5 hold of him, and K him.
20:9 his right hand to K him.
1Kgs 19:20 and said, "Let me K my father and my
Esth 13:13 have been willing to K the soles of his
Ps 2:12 with fear, with trembling K his feet, lest he
85:10 righteousness and peace will K each other.
Song 1:2 O that you would K me with the kisses
8:1 you outside, I would K you, and none would
Sir 29:5 A man will K another's hands until he gets
Hos 13:2 Men K calves!
Mt 26:48 "The one I shall K is the man; seize
Mk 14:44 "The one I shall K is the man; seize
Lk 7:45 You gave me no K, but from the time
7:45 has not ceased to K my feet.
22:45 near to Jesus to K him;
22:46 you betray the Son of man with a K
Rom 16:16 Greet one another with a holy K
1Cor 16:20 Greet one another with a holy K
2Cor 13:12 Greet one another with a holy K
1Thes 5:26 Greet all the brethren with a holy K
1Pet 5:14 one another with the K of love.

KISSED (25)

Gen 27:27 he came near and K him; and he smelled
29:11 Then Jacob K Rachel, and wept aloud.
29:13 and embraced him and K him, and brought him
31:55 morning Laban arose, and K his grandchildren and
33:4 on his neck and K him, and they wept.
45:15 And he K all his brothers and wept upon
48:10 near him; and he K them and embraced them.
50:1 wept over him, and K him.
Ex 4:27 mountain of God and K him.
18:7 and did obeisance and K him; and they asked
Ruth 1:9 Then she K them, and they lifted up their
1:14 wept again; and Orpah K her mother-in-law, but Ruth
1Sam 10:1 on his head, and K him and said, "Has
20:41 three times; and they K one another, and wept
2Sam 14:33 king; and the king K Absalom.
19:39 over; and the king K Barzillai and blessed him,
1Kgs 19:18 mouth that has not K him."
Tob 7:6 Raguel sprang up and K him and wept.
10:12 And he K her.
Job 31:27 and my mouth has K my hand;
Mt 26:49 And he K him.
Mk 14:45 And he K him.
Lk 7:38 of her head, and K his feet, and anointed
15:20 and embraced him and K him.
Acts 20:37 and embraced Paul and K him,

KISSES (5)

Prov 7:13 She seizes him and K him, and with impudent
24:26 gives a right answer K the lips.
27:6 friend; profuse are the K of an enemy.
Song 1:2 kiss me with the K of your mouth!
7:9 like apples, and your K like the best wine

KITCHENS

Ezek 46:24 me, "These are the K where those who minister

KITE (2)

Lev 11:14 vulture, the osprey, the K, the falcon according to
Deut 14:13 osprey, the buzzard, the K, after their kinds;

KITES

Is 34:15 yea, there shall the K be gathered, each one

KITRON

Judg 1:30 out the inhabitants of K, or the inhabitants of

KITTIM (5)

Gen 10:4 of Javan: Elishah, Tarshish, K, and Dodanim.
Num 24:24 ships shall come from K and shall afflict Asshur
1Chr 1:7 of Javan: Elishah, Tarshish, K, and Rodanim.

Dan 11:30 For ships of K shall come against him, and
1Mac 1:1 from the land of K, had defeated Darius, king

KNAVE (2)

Is 32:5 called noble, nor the K said to be honorable.
32:7 The knaveries of the K are evil; he devises

KNAVERIES

Is 32:7 The K of the knave are evil; he devises

KNEAD (2)

Gen 18:6 measures of fine meal, K it, and make cakes."
Jer 7:18 fire, and the women K dough, to make cakes

KNEADED (2)

1Sam 28:24 she took flour, and K it and baked unleavened
2Sam 13:8 she took dough, and K it, and made cakes

KNEADING (3)

Ex 8:3 your ovens and your K bowls;
12:34 it was leavened, their K bowls being bound up
Hos 7:5 the fire, from the K of the dough until

KNEADING-TROUGH (2)

Deut 28:5 Blessed shall be your basket and your K
28:17 Cursed shall be your basket and your K

KNEADS

Wis 15:7 For when a potter K the soft earth and

KNEE (5)

Gen 41:43 chariot; and they cried before him, "Bow the K
Is 45:23 return: 'To me every K shall bow, every tongue
Rom 11:4 have not bowed the K to Baal."
14:11 says the Lord, every K shall bow to me,
Phil 2:10 name of Jesus every K should bow, in heaven

KNEE-DEEP

Ezek 47:4 led me through the water; and it was K

KNEEL (2)

Gen 24:11 he made the camels K down outside the city
Ps 95:6 bow down, let us K before the LORD, our

KNEELING (5)

Mt 17:14 up to him and K before him said,
20:20 with her sons, and K before him she asked
27:29 And K before him they mocked him, saying, "Hail,
Mk 1:40 him beseeching him, and K said to him, "If
Acts 21:5 outside the city; and K down on the beach

KNEELS

Judg 7:5 likewise every one that K down to drink."

KNEES (26)

Gen 30:3 may bear upon my K, and even I may
48:12 removed them from his K, and he bowed himself
50:23 the son of Manasseh were born upon Joseph's K
Deut 28:35 smite you on the K and on the legs
Judg 16:19 him sleep upon her K; and she called a
1Kgs 18:42 the earth, and put his face between his K
19:18 in Israel, all the K that have not bowed
2Kgs 1:13 and fell on his K before Elijah, and entreated
2Chr 6:13 he knelt upon his K in the presence of
Ezra 9:5 and fell upon my K and spread out my
Job 3:12 Why did the K receive me?
4:4 stumbling, and you have made firm the feeble K
Ps 109:24 My K are weak through fasting; my body has
Sir 25:22 Drooping hands and weak K are caused by the
Is 35:3 the weak hands, and make firm the feeble K
66:12 carried upon her hip, and dandled upon her K
Ezek 7:17 are feeble, and all K weak as water.
21:7 will faint and all K will be weak as
Dan 5:6 gave way, and his K knocked together.
6:10 got down upon his K three times a day
10:10 and set me trembling on my hands and K
Nah 2:10 Hearts faint and K tremble, anguish is on all
Mt 18:25 servant fell on his K, imploring him, 'Lord, have
Lk 5:8 fell down at Jesus' K, saying, "Depart from me,
Eph 3:14 reason I bow my K before the Father,
Heb 12:12 and strengthen your weak K,

KNELT (13)

Judg 7:6 rest of the people K down to drink water.
1Kgs 8:54 LORD, where he had K with hands outstretched
2Chr 6:13 Then he K upon his knees in the presence
Jud 14:7 at Judith's feet, and K before her, and said,
Mt 8:2 came to him and K before him, saying, "Lord,
9:18 ruler came in and K before him, saying, "My
15:25 But she came and K before him, saying, "Lord,
Mk 10:17 man ran up and K before him, and asked
15:19 upon him, and they K down in homage to
Lk 22:41 a stone's throw, and K down and prayed,
Acts 7:60 And he K down and cried with a loud
9:40 them all outside and K down and prayed; then
20:36 had spoken thus, he K down and prayed with

KNEW (95)

Gen 3:7 were opened, and they K that they were naked;
4:1 Now Adam K Eve his wife, and she conceived
4:17 Cain K his wife, and she conceived and bore
4:25 And Adam K his wife again, and she bore
8:11 olive leaf; so Noah K that the waters had
9:24 from his wine and K what his youngest son
38:9 But Onan K that the offspring would not be
42:7 saw his brothers, and K them, but he treated
42:8 Thus Joseph K his brothers, but they did not
Ex 2:25 of Israel, and God K their condition.
Deut 7:15 of Egypt, which you K, will he inflict upon
9:24 the day that I K you.
34:10 Moses, whom the LORD K face to face,
Judg 13:21 Then Manoah K that he was the angel of
19:25 to them; and they K her, and abused her
1Sam 1:19 And Elkanah K Hannah his wife, and the LORD
3:13 the iniquity which he K, because his sons were
3:20 from Dan to Beer-sheba K that Samuel was
10:11 And when all who K him before saw how
18:28 when Saul saw and K that the LORD was
20:9 If I K that it was determined by my
20:33 smite him; so Jonathan K that his father was
20:39 But the lad K nothing; only Jonathan and David
20:39 only Jonathan and David K the matter.
22:17 with David, and they K that he fled, and
22:22 said to Abiathar, "I K on that day, when
23:9 David K that Saul was plotting evil against him;
26:12 man saw it, or K it, nor did any
28:14 And Saul K that it was Samuel, and he
2Sam 11:16 the place where he K there were valiant men.
15:11 in their simplicity, and K nothing.
1Kgs 1:4 him; but the king K her not.
2Chr 33:13 Then Manasseh K that the LORD was God.
Esth 1:13 the wise men who K the times— for
Job 20:20 "Because his greed K no rest, he will not
23:3 Oh, that I K where I might find him,
Ps 35:15 me; cripples whom I K not slandered me without
Wis 19:1 pitiless anger, for God K in advance even their
Is 48:7 should say, 'Behold, I K them.'
48:8 For I K that you would deal very treacherously,
55:5 not, and nations that K you not shall run
Jer 1:5 in the womb I K you, and before you
11:18 to me and I K; then thou didst show
32:8 for yourself.' Then I K that this was the
41:4 Gedaliah, before any one K of it,
44:3 other gods that they K not, neither they, nor
44:15 all the men who K that their wives had
Ezek 10:20 river Chebar; and I K that they were cherubim.
Dan 5:21 of heaven, until he K that the Most High
5:22 your heart, though you K all this,
6:10 When Daniel K that the document had been signed,
Hos 13:5 It was I who K you in the wilderness,
Jon 1:10 For the men K that he was fleeing from
4:2 to Tarshish; for I K that thou art a
Zech 11:11 who were watching me, K that it was the
1Mac 13:17 Simon K that they were speaking deceitfully to him,
15:12 the sea; for he K that troubles had converged
2Mac 15:21 works wonders; for he K that it is not
Mt 1:25 took his wife, but K her not until she
7:23 to them, 'I never K you; depart from me,
25:24 forward, saying, 'Master, I K you to be a
25:26 You K that I reap where I have not
27:18 For he K that it was out of envy
Mk 1:34 to speak, because they K him.
6:33 saw them going, and K them, and they ran
Lk 4:41 to speak, because they K that he was the
6:8 But he K their thoughts, and he said to
12:47 And that servant who K his master's will, but
19:22 You K that I was a severe man, taking
19:42 that even today you K the things that make
Jn 1:10 him, yet the world K him not.
2:9 had drawn the water K, the steward of the
2:25 to them, because he K all men and needed
2:25 man; for he himself K what was in man.

4:1 Now when the Lord K that the Pharisees had
4:10 answered her, "If you K the gift of God,
4:53 The father K that was the hour when Jesus
5:5 Jesus saw him and K that he had been
6:6 him, for he himself K what he would do.
6:64 For Jesus K from the first who those were
8:19 my Father; if you K me, you would know
11:42 I K that thou hearest me always, but I
11:57 that if any one K where he was, he
13:1 the Passover, when Jesus K that his hour had
13:11 For he K who was to betray him; that
13:28 one at the table K why he said this
16:19 Jesus K that they wanted to ask him; so
18:2 who betrayed him, also K the place; for Jesus
21:12 They K it was the Lord.
Acts 9:30 And when the brethren K it, they brought him
16:3 places, for they all K that his father was
18:25 concerning Jesus, though he K only the baptism of
Rom 1:21 excuse; for although they K God they did not
2Cor 5:21 to be sin who K no sin, so that
Heb 10:34 your property, since you K that you yourselves had

KNEWEST

Neh 9:10 his land, for thou K that they acted insolently

KNIFE (4)

Gen 22:6 took in his hand the fire and the K
22:10 hand, and took the K to slay his son.
Judg 19:29 house, he took a K, and laying hold of
Prov 23:2 you; and put a K to your throat if

KNIT (8)

1Sam 18:1 soul of Jonathan was K to the soul of
1Chr 12:17 my heart will be K to you; but if
Job 10:11 skin and flesh, and K me together with bones
40:17 of his thighs are K together.
Ps 139:13 inward parts, thou didst K me together in my
Eph 4:16 whole body, joined and K together by every joint
Col 2:2 encouraged as they are K together in love, to
2:19 whole body, nourished and K together through its

KNIVES (3)

Josh 5:2 to Joshua, "Make flint K and circumcise the people
5:3 So Joshua made flint K, and circumcised the people
Prov 30:14 swords, whose teeth are K, to devour the poor

KNOCK (4)

Mt 7:7 and you will find; K, and it will be
Lk 11:9 and you will find; K, and it will be
13:25 stand outside and to K at the door, saying,
Rev 3:20 at the door and K; if any one hears

KNOCKED (3)

Jud 14:14 Bagoas went in and K at the door of
Dan 5:6 way, and his knees K together.
Acts 12:13 And when he K at the door of the

KNOCKING (2)

Song 5:2 my beloved is K
Acts 12:16 But Peter continued K; and when they opened, they

KNOCKS (4)

Ex 21:27 If he K out the tooth of his slave,
Mt 7:8 and to him who K it will be opened.
Lk 11:10 and to him who K it will be opened.
12:36 to him at once when he comes and K

KNOTS

Wis 13:13 crooked and full of K, he takes and carves

KNOW (1,005)

Gen 4:9 said, "I do not K; am I my brother's
12:11 Sarai his wife, "I K that you are a
15:8 how am I to K that I shall possess
15:13 LORD said to Abram, K of a surety that
18:21 come to me; and if not, I will K
19:5 us, that we may K them."
19:33 father; he did not K when she lay down
19:35 and he did not K when she lay down
20:6 the dream, "Yes, I K that you have done
20:7 do not restore her, K that you shall surely
21:26 said, "I do not K who has done this
22:12 him; for now I K that you fear God,
24:14 By this I shall K that thou hast shown
27:2 old; I do not K the day of my
27:21 you, my son, to K whether you are really
28:16 and I did not K it."
29:5 to them, "Do you K Laban the son of
29:5 They said, "We K him."
30:26 me go; for you K the service which I
30:29 to him, "You yourself K how I have served
31:6 You K that I have served your father with
31:32 Now Jacob did not K that Rachel had stolen
38:16 for he did not K that she was his
42:8 but they did not K him.
42:23 They did not K that Joseph understood them, for
42:33 'By this I shall K that you are honest
42:34 me; then I shall K that you are not
43:7 we in any way K that he would say,
43:22 We do not K who put our money in
44:15 Do you not K that such a man as
44:27 said to us, 'You K that my wife bore
46:30 seen your face and K that you are still
47:6 Goshen; and if you K any able men among
48:19 refused, and said, "I K, my son, I know;
48:19 know, my son, I K; he also shall become
Ex 1:7 Egypt, who did not K Joseph.
2:4 at a distance, to K what would be done
3:7 of their taskmasters; I K their sufferings,
3:19 LORD our God.' I K that the king of
4:14 I K that he can speak well; and behold,
5:2 I do not K the LORD, and moreover I
6:7 God; and you shall K that I am the
7:5 And the Egyptians shall K that I am the
7:17 "By this you shall K that I am the
8:10 say, that you may K that there is no
8:22 there; that you may K that I am the
9:14 people, that you may K that there is none
9:29 hail, that you may K that the earth is
9:30 and your servants, I K that you do not
10:2 them; that you may K that I am the
10:26 and we do not K with what we must
11:7 growl; that you may K that the LORD makes
14:4 and the Egyptians shall K that I am the
14:18 And the Egyptians shall K that I am the
16:6 "At evening you shall K that it was the
16:12 bread; then you shall K that I am the
16:15 For they did not K what it was.
18:11 Now I K that the LORD is greater than
18:16 and I make them K the statutes of God
18:20 decisions, and make them K the way in which
23:9 oppress a stranger; you K the heart of a
29:46 And they shall K that I am the LORD
31:13 generations, that you may K that I, the LORD,
32:1 Egypt, we do not K what has become of
32:22 lord burn hot; you K the people, that they
32:23 Egypt, we do not K what has become of
33:5 you, that I may K what to do with
33:12 hast not let me K whom thou wilt send
33:12 thou hast said, 'I K you by name, and
33:13 ways, that I may K thee and find favor
33:17 my sight, and I K you by name."
34:29 mountain, Moses did not K that the skin of
36:1 ability and intelligence to K how to do any
Lev 5:1 seen or come to K the matter, yet does
5:3 when he comes to K it he shall be
5:4 when he comes to K it he shall in
5:17 though he does not K it, yet he is
23:43 that your generations may K that I made the
Num 10:31 pray you, for you K how we are to
11:16 of Israel, whom you K to be the elders
14:31 in, and they shall K the land which you
14:34 years, and you shall K my displeasure.'
16:28 said, "Hereby you shall K that the LORD has
16:30 Sheol, then you shall K that these men have
20:14 your brother Israel: You K all the adversity that
22:6 the land; for I K that he whom you
22:19 also, that I may K what more the LORD
22:34 for I did not K that thou didst stand
24:14 I will let you K what this people will
Deut 3:19 and your cattle (I K that you have many
4:35 shown, that you might K that the LORD is
4:39 as at this day; K therefore this day, and
7:9 K therefore that the LORD your God is God,
8:2 you, testing you to K what was in your
8:3 which you did not K, nor did your fathers
8:3 nor did your fathers K; that he might make
8:3 he might make you K that man does not
8:5 K then in your heart that, as a man
8:16 your fathers did not K, that he might humble
9:2 the Anakim, whom you K, and of whom you
9:3 the sons of Anak?' K therefore this day that

K

9:6 K therefore, that the LORD your God is not
13:3 is testing you, to K whether you love the
18:21 heart, 'How may we K the word which the
20:20 the trees which you K are not trees for
22:2 if you do not K him, you shall bring
29:6 drink; that you may K that I am the
29:16 "You K how we dwelt in the land of
31:21 their descendants); for I K the purposes which they
31:27 For I K how rebellious and stubborn you are;
31:29 For I K that after my death you will
Josh 2:4 but I did not K where they came from;
2:5 went I do not K; pursue them quickly, for
2:9 to the men, "I K that the LORD has
3:4 it, that you may K the way you shall
3:7 Israel, that they may K that, as I was
3:10 said, "Hereby you shall K that the living God
4:22 shall let your children K, 'Israel passed over this
4:24 of the earth may K that the hand of
8:14 but he did not K that there was an
14:6 said to him, "You K what the LORD said
22:22 He knows; and let Israel itself K
22:31 the Manassites, "Today we K that the LORD is
23:13 women and they yours, K assuredly that the LORD
23:14 the earth, and you K in your hearts and
Judg 2:10 them, who did not K the LORD or the
3:2 people of Israel might K war, that he might
3:4 testing of Israel, to K whether Israel would obey
6:37 ground, then I shall K that thou wilt deliver
13:16 (For Manoah did not K that he was the
14:4 and mother did not K that it was from
15:11 Samson, "Do you not K that the Philistines are
16:20 And he did not K that the LORD had
17:13 Micah said, "Now I K that the LORD will
18:5 thee, that we may K whether the journey on
18:14 their brethren, "Do you K that in these houses
19:22 house, that we may K him."
20:34 the Benjaminites did not K that disaster was close
Ruth 2:11 that you did not K before.
3:11 all my fellow townsmen K that you are a
4:4 me, that I may K, for there is no
1Sam 3:7 Samuel did not yet K the LORD, and the
6:9 not, then we shall K that it is not
12:17 rain; and you shall K and see that your
14:3 the people did not K that Jonathan had gone.
14:38 of the people; and K and see how this
17:28 I K your presumption, and the evil of your
17:46 all the earth may K that there is a
17:47 all this assembly may K that the LORD saves
20:3 thinks, 'Let not Jonathan K this, lest he be
20:7 he is angry, then K that evil is determined
20:30 woman, do I not K that you have chosen
21:2 me, 'Let no one K anything of the matter
22:3 with you, till I K what God will do
23:22 make yet more sure; K and see the place
24:11 kill you, you may K and see that there
24:20 And now, behold, I K that you shall surely
25:11 from I do not K where?"
25:17 Now therefore K this and consider what you should
28:2 "Very well, you shall K what your servant can
28:9 to him, "Surely you K what Saul has done,
29:9 answer to David, "I K that you are as
2Sam 1:5 him, "How do you K that Saul and his
2:26 Do you not K that the end will be
3:25 You K that Abner the son of Ner came
3:25 deceive you, and to K your going out and
3:25 coming in, and to K all that you are
3:26 but David did not K about it.
3:38 servants, "Do you not K that a prince and
7:21 to make thy servant K it.
11:20 Did you not K that they would shoot from
14:20 angel of God to K all things that are
15:20 seeing I go I K not where?
17:8 Hushai said moreover, "You K that your father and
18:29 but I do not K what it was."
19:22 For do I not K that I am this
24:2 people, that I may K the number of the
1Kgs 1:11 our lord does not K it?
1:18 the king, do not K it.
2:5 of Israel.' "Moreover you K also what Joab the
2:9 wise man; you will K what you ought to
2:15 He said, "You K that the kingdom was mine,
2:37 cross the brook Kidron, K for certain that you
2:42 solemnly admonish you, saying, K for certain that on
2:44 said to Shimei, "You K in your own heart
3:7 child; I do not K how to go out
5:3 word to Hiram, "You K that David my father
5:6 you set; for you K that there is no
8:43 of the earth may K thy name and fear
8:43 and that they may K that this house which
8:60 of the earth may K that the LORD is
17:24 to Elijah, "Now I K that you are a
18:12 carry you whither I K not; and so, when
18:37 that this people may K that thou, O LORD,
20:13 day; and you shall K that I am the
20:28 hand, and you shall K that I am the
22:3 his servants, "Do you K that Ramoth-gilead belongs
2Kgs 2:3 to him, "Do you K that today the LORD
2:3 he said, "Yes, I K it; hold your peace."
2:5 to him, "Do you K that today the LORD
2:5 he answered, "Yes, I K it; hold your peace."
4:1 is dead; and you K that your servant feared
5:6 this letter reaches you, K that I have sent
5:8 me, that he may K that there is a
5:15 he said, "Behold, I K that there is no
7:12 They K that we are hungry; therefore they have
8:12 He answered, "Because I K the evil that you
9:11 said to them, "You K the fellow and his
10:10 K then that there shall fall to the earth
17:26 of Samaria do not K the law of the
17:26 because they do not K the law of the
19:19 of the earth may K that thou, O LORD,
19:27 "But I K your sitting down and your going
1Chr 12:32 of the times, to K what Israel ought to
21:2 report, that I may K their number."
28:9 you, Solomon my son, K the God of your
29:17 I K, my God, that thou triest the heart,
2Chr 2:8 from Lebanon, for I K that your servants know
2:8 know that your servants K how to cut timber
6:33 of the earth may K thy name and fear
6:33 and that they may K that this house which
12:8 him, that they may K my service and the
13:5 Ought you not to K that the LORD God
20:12 We do not K what to do, but our
25:16 stopped, but said, "I K that God has determined
32:13 Do you not K what I and my fathers
32:31 try him and to K all that was in
Ezra 7:25 River, all such as K the laws of your
7:25 those who do not K them, you shall teach.
Neh 2:16 the officials did not K where I had gone
4:11 said, "They will not K or see till we
Tob 2:10 I did not K that there were sparrows on
2:14 You seem to K everything!"
3:8 her, "Do you not K that you strangle your
5:2 when I do not K the man?"
5:5 but Tobias did not K it.
5:11 "I should like to K, my brother, your people
5:13 For I used to K Ananias and Jathan, the
6:12 For I K that Raguel, according to the law
7:4 to them, "Do you K our brother Tobit?" And
11:7 Raphael said, "I K, Tobias, that your father will
Jud 5:8 they had come to K; hence they drove them
8:13 but you will never K anything!
8:20 But we K no other god but him, and
9:7 bow and sling, and K not that thou art
9:14 and every tribe to K and understand that thou
Esth 4:11 of the king's provinces K that if any man
16:4 boasts of those who K nothing of goodness they
Job 5:24 You shall K that your tent is safe, and
5:25 You shall K also that your descendants shall be
5:27 Hear, and K it for your good."
7:10 nor does his place K him any more.
8:9 but of yesterday, and K nothing, for our days
9:2 Job answered: "Truly I K that it is so:
9:5 removes mountains, and they K it not, when he
9:28 my suffering, for I K thou wilt not hold
10:2 condemn me; let me K why thou dost contend
10:13 in thy heart; I K that this was thy
11:6 K then that God exacts of you less than
11:8 Deeper than Sheol—what can you K
12:3 Who does not K such things as these?
12:9 all these does not K that the hand of
13:2 What you K, I also know; I am not
13:2 you know, I also K; I am not inferior
13:18 prepared my case; I K that I shall be
13:23 Make me K my transgression and my sin.
14:21 and he does not K it; they are brought
15:9 What do you K that we do not know?
15:9 What do you know that we do not K
19:6 an argument against me, K then that God has
19:25 For I K that my Redeemer lives, and at
19:29 sword, that you may K there is a judgment."
20:4 Do you not K this from of old, since

KNOW

21:19 themselves, that they may K it.
21:27 "Behold, I K your thoughts, and your schemes to
22:13 Therefore you say, 'What does God K
24:1 why do those who K him never see his
24:16 up; they do not K the light.
28:13 Man does not K the way to it, and
29:16 the cause of him whom I did not K
30:23 Yea, I K that thou wilt bring me to
31:6 balance, and let God K my integrity!)
32:22 For I do not K how to flatter, else
33:3 and what my lips K they speak sincerely.
34:2 to me, you who K;
34:33 choose, and not I; therefore declare what you K
36:26 is great, and we K him not; the number
37:7 that all men may K his work.
37:15 Do you K how God lays his command upon
37:16 Do you K the balancings of the clouds, the
38:5 Who determined its measurements--surely you K
38:12 caused the dawn to K its place,
38:18 Declare, if you K all this.
38:21 You K, for you were born then, and the
38:33 Do you K the ordinances of the heavens?
39:1 "Do you K when the mountain goats bring forth?
39:2 fulfil, and do you K the time when they
42:2 answered the LORD: "I K that thou canst do
42:3 too wonderful for me, which I did not K
Ps 4:3 [Selah] But K that the LORD has set apart
9:10 And those who K thy name put their trust
9:20 Let the nations K that they are but men!
20:6 Now I K that the LORD will help his
25:4 Make me to K thy ways, O LORD; teach
35:11 of things that I K not.
36:10 love to those who K thee, and thy salvation
39:4 tongue: "LORD, let me K my end, and what
39:4 my days; let me K how fleeting my life
39:13 me, that I may K gladness, before I depart
41:11 By this I K that thou art pleased with
46:10 "Be still, and K that I am God.
50:11 I K all the birds of the air, and
51:3 For I K my transgressions, and my sin is
56:9 This I K, that God is for me.
59:13 more, that men may K that God rules over
73:11 And they say, "How can God K
78:6 the next generation might K them, the children yet
79:6 nations that do not K thee, and on the
83:18 Let them K that thou alone, whose name is
87:4 [Selah] Among those who K me I mention Rahab
89:15 are the people who K the festal shout, who
92:6 The dull man cannot K, the stupid cannot understand
100:3 K that the LORD is God!
101:4 from me; I will K nothing of evil.
109:27 Let them K that this is thy hand; thou,
119:75 I K, O LORD, that thy judgments are right,
119:79 me, that they may K thy testimonies.
119:125 understanding, that I may K thy testimonies!
135:5 For I K that the LORD is great, and
139:23 me, O God, and K my heart!
139:23 Try me and K my thoughts!
140:12 I K that the LORD maintains the cause of
147:20 nation; they do not K his ordinances.
Prov 1:2 Israel: That men may K wisdom and instruction,
4:20 darkness; they do not K over what they stumble.
5:6 and she does not K it.
7:23 snare; he does not K that it will cost
9:18 But he does not K that the dead are
10:32 lips of the righteous K what is acceptable, but
24:12 "Behold, we did not K this," does not he
24:12 watch over your soul K it, and will he
24:14 K that wisdom is such to your soul; if
27:1 for you do not K what a day may
27:23 K well the condition of your flocks, and give
28:22 wealth, and does not K that want will come
30:4 Surely you K
Eccl 1:17 applied my mind to K wisdom and to know
1:17 know wisdom and to K madness and folly.
3:12 I K that there is nothing better for them
3:14 I K that whatever God does endures for ever;
5:1 for they do not K that they are doing
7:25 turned my mind to K and to search out
7:25 of things, and to K the wickedness of folly
8:5 a wise man will K the time and way.
8:7 For he does not K what is to be,
8:12 his life, yet I K that it will be
8:16 applied my mind to K wisdom, and to see
8:17 wise man claims to K, he cannot find it
9:1 it is love or hate man does not K
9:5 For the living K that they will die, but
9:5 die, but the dead K nothing, and they have
9:12 For man does not K his time.
10:15 that he does not K the way to the
11:2 to eight, for you K not what evil may
11:5 As you do not K how the spirit comes
11:5 so you do not K the work of God
11:6 for you do not K which will prosper, this
11:9 But K that for all these things God will
Song 1:8 If you do not K, O fairest among women,
Wis 2:22 and they did not K the secret purposes of
7:12 but I did not K that she was their
7:17 of what exists, to K the structure of the
8:21 mark of insight to K whose gift she was--
12:17 insolence among those who K it.
12:27 God him whom they had before refused to K
13:1 that are seen to K him who exists, nor
13:3 be gods, let them K how much better than
13:9 had the power to K so much that they
14:18 those who did not K the king to intensify
15:2 not sin, because we K that we are accounted
15:3 For to K thee is complete righteousness, and to
15:3 complete righteousness, and to K thy power is the
15:11 because he failed to K the one who formed
16:16 the ungodly, refusing to K thee, were scourged by
16:18 seeing this they might K that they were being
16:22 so that they might K that the crops of
Sir 8:18 for you do not K what he will divulge
9:11 for you do not K what his end will
9:13 K that you are walking in the midst of
9:14 you can, aim to K your neighbors, and consult
11:17 he does not K how much time will pass
12:1 you do a kindness, K to whom you do
12:11 mirror, and you will K that it was not
24:26 first man did not K her perfectly, the last
27:27 and he will not K where it came from.
36:5 us; and let them K thee, as we have
36:17 on the earth will K that thou art the
37:12 godly man whom you K to be a keeper
46:6 that the nations might K his armament, that he
Is 1:3 but Israel does not K, my people does not
5:19 come, that we may K it!"
9:9 all the people will K, Ephraim and the inhabitants
19:21 and the Egyptians will K the LORD in that
37:20 of the earth may K that thou alone art
37:28 'I K your sitting down and your going out
41:20 men may see and K, may consider and understand
41:22 them, that we may K their outcome; or declare
41:23 hereafter, that we may K that you are gods;
41:26 beginning, that we might K, and beforetime, that we
42:16 a way that they K not, in paths that
43:10 chosen, that you may K and believe me and
44:8 is no Rock; I K not any."
44:9 witnesses neither see nor K, that they may be
44:18 They K not, nor do they discern; for he
45:3 places, that you may K that it is I,
45:4 though you do not K me.
45:5 though you do not K me,
45:6 me, that men may K, from the rising of
47:8 as a widow or K the loss of children":
47:11 suddenly, of which you K nothing.
48:4 Because I K that you are obstinate, and your
49:23 Then you will K that I am the LORD;
49:26 Then all flesh shall K that I am the
50:4 taught, that I may K how to sustain with
50:7 a flint, and I K that I shall not
51:7 to me, you who K righteousness, the people in
52:6 Therefore my people shall K my name; therefore in
52:6 that day they shall K that it is I
55:5 call nations that you K not, and nations that
58:2 daily, and delight to K my ways, as if
59:8 way of peace they K not, and there is
59:12 with us, and we K our iniquities:
60:16 kings; and you shall K that I, the LORD,
63:16 though Abraham does not K us and Israel does
66:18 "For I K their works and their thoughts, and
Jer 1:6 Behold, I do not K how to speak, for
2:8 the law did not K me; the rulers transgressed
2:19 K and see that it is evil and bitter
2:23 way in the valley; K what you have done--
4:22 people are foolish, they K me not; they are
4:22 to do good they K not."
5:4 for they do not K the way of the
5:5 to them; for they K the way of the
5:15 language you do not K, nor can you understand
5:28 They K no bounds in deeds of wickedness; they

6:15 ashamed; they did not K how to blush.
6:18 hear, O nations, and K, O congregation, what will
6:27 people, that you may K and assay their ways.
8:7 coming; but my people K not the ordinance of
8:12 ashamed; they did not K how to blush.
9:3 and they do not K me, says the LORD.
9:6 deceit, they refuse to K me, says the LORD.
10:23 I K, O LORD, that the way of man
10:25 upon the nations that K thee not, and upon
11:19 I did not K it was against me they
13:12 'Do we not indeed K that every jar will
15:14 which you do not K, for in my anger
15:15 take me not away; K that for thy sake
16:21 I will make them K, this once I will
16:21 I will make them K my power and my
16:21 might, and they shall K that my name is
17:4 which you do not K, for in my anger
22:16 Is not this to K me?
22:28 cast into a land which they do not K
24:7 them a heart to K that I am the
26:15 Only K for certain that if you put me
29:11 For I K the plans I have for you,
31:34 each his brother, saying, K the LORD,' for they
31:34 for they shall all K me, from the least
36:19 and let no one K where you are."
38:24 Jeremiah, "Let no one K of these words and
40:14 to him, "Do you K that Baalis the king
40:15 and no one will K it.
42:19 not go to Egypt.' K for a certainty that
42:22 Now therefore K for a certainty that you shall
44:28 Egypt to live, shall K whose word will stand,
44:29 order that you may K that my words will
48:17 him, and all who K his name; say, 'How
48:30 I K his insolence, says the LORD; his boasts
50:24 and you did not K it; you were found
Bar 2:15 all the earth may K that thou art the
2:30 For I K that they will not obey me,
2:31 themselves, and they will K that I am the
4:4 O Israel, for we K what is pleasing to
6:23 From this you will K that they are not
6:29 Since you K by these things that they are
6:52 then can fail to K that they are not
6:65 Since you K then that they are not gods,
6:72 upon them you will K that they are not
Ezek 2:5 rebellious house) they will K that there has been
5:13 myself; and they shall K that I, the LORD,
6:7 you, and you shall K that I am the
6:10 And they shall K that I am the LORD;
6:13 And you shall K that I am the LORD,
6:14 Then they will K that I am the LORD."
7:4 Then you will K that I am the LORD.
7:9 Then you will K that I am the LORD,
7:27 them; and they shall K that I am the
11:5 of Israel; for I K the things that come
11:10 Israel; and you shall K that I am the
11:12 Israel; and you shall K that I am the
12:15 And they shall K that I am the LORD,
12:16 they go, and may K that I am the
12:20 desolation; and you shall K that I am the
13:9 Israel; and you shall K that I am the
13:14 it; and you shall K that I am the
13:21 prey; and you shall K that I am the
13:23 Then you will K that I am the LORD."
14:8 people; and you shall K that I am the
14:23 doings; and you shall K that I have not
15:7 them; and you will K that I am the
16:62 you, and you shall K that I am the
17:12 house, Do you not K what these things mean?
17:21 wind; and you shall K that I, the LORD,
17:24 of the field shall K that I the LORD
20:4 Then let them K the abominations of their fathers,
20:12 them, that they might K that I the LORD
20:20 you, that you may K that I the LORD
20:26 it that they might K that I am the
20:38 Then you will K that I am the LORD.
20:42 And you shall K that I am the LORD,
20:44 And you shall K that I am the LORD,
21:5 and all flesh shall K that I the LORD
22:16 nations; and you shall K that I am the
22:22 it; and you shall K that I the LORD
23:49 idolatry; and you shall K that I am the
24:24 comes, then you will K that I am the
24:27 them; and they will K that I am the
25:5 Then you will K that I am the LORD.
25:7 Then you will K that I am the LORD.
25:11 Then they will K that I am the LORD.
25:14 wrath; and they shall K my vengeance, says the
25:17 Then they will K that I am the LORD,
26:6 Then they will K that I am the LORD.
28:19 All who K you among the peoples are appalled
28:22 And they shall K that I am the LORD
28:23 Then they will K that I am the LORD.
28:24 Then they will K that I am the Lord
28:26 Then they will K that I am the LORD
29:6 inhabitants of Egypt shall K that I am the
29:9 Then they will K that I am the LORD.
29:16 Then they will K that I am the Lord
29:21 Then they will K that I am the LORD."
30:8 Then they will K that I am the LORD,
30:19 Then they will K that I am the LORD."
30:25 fall; and they shall K that I am the
30:26 Then they will K that I am the LORD."
32:15 it, then they will K that I am the
33:29 Then they will K that I am the LORD,
33:33 will!--then they will K that a prophet has
34:27 land; and they shall K that I am the
34:30 And they shall K that I, the LORD their
35:4 desolation; and you shall K that I am the
35:9 Then you will K that I am the LORD.
35:12 And you shall K that I, the LORD, have
35:15 Then they will K that I am the LORD.
36:11 Then you will K that I am the LORD.
36:23 and the nations will K that I am the
36:36 round about you shall K that I, the LORD,
36:38 Then they will K that I am the LORD."
37:6 live; and you shall K that I am the
37:13 And you shall K that I am the LORD,
37:14 land; then you shall K that I, the LORD,
37:28 Then the nations will K that I the LORD
38:16 that the nations may K me, when through you,
38:23 Then they will K that I am the LORD.
39:6 coastlands; and they shall K that I am the
39:7 and the nations shall K that I am the
39:22 house of Israel shall K that I am the
39:23 And the nations shall K that the house of
39:28 Then they shall K that I am the LORD
Dan 2:3 spirit is troubled to K the dream."
2:8 The king answered, "I K with certainty that you
2:9 dream, and I shall K that you can show
2:30 and that you may K the thoughts of your
3:45 Let them K that thou art the Lord, the
4:9 the magicians, because I K that the spirit of
4:17 that the living may K that the Most High
4:25 over you, till you K that the Most High
4:26 the time that you K that Heaven rules.
5:23 see or hear or K, but the God in
6:15 said to the king, K, O king, that it
7:19 "Then I desired to K the truth concerning the
9:25 K therefore and understand that from the going forth
10:20 he said, "Do you K why I have come
11:32 but the people who K their God shall stand
11:38 his fathers did not K he shall honor with
14:35 seen Babylon, and I K nothing about the den."
Hos 2:8 And she did not K that it was I
2:20 faithfulness; and you shall K the LORD.
5:3 I K Ephraim, and Israel is not hid from
5:4 within them, and they K not the LORD.
6:3 Let us K, let us press on to know
6:3 us press on to K the LORD; his going
8:2 My God, we Israel K thee.
9:7 have come; Israel shall K it.
11:3 but they did not K that I healed them.
13:4 land of Egypt; you K no God but me,
14:9 is discerning, let him K them; for the ways
Joel 2:27 You shall K that I am in the midst
3:17 "So you shall K that I am the LORD
Amos 3:10 "They do not K how to do right," says
5:12 For I K how many are your transgressions, and
Jon 1:7 lots, that we may K on whose account this
1:12 for you; for I K it is because of
4:11 persons who do not K their right hand from
Mic 3:1 not for you to K justice?--
4:12 But they do not K the thoughts of the
6:5 Gilgal, that you may K the saving acts of
Zech 2:9 Then you will K that the LORD of hosts
2:11 you, and you shall K that the LORD of
4:5 me, "Do you not K what these are?" I
4:9 Then you will K that the LORD of hosts
4:13 me, "Do you not K what these are?" I
6:15 LORD; and you shall K that the LORD of
Mal 2:4 So shall you K that I have sent this
1Mac 2:65 "Now behold, I K that Simeon your brother is

K

4:11 all the Gentiles will K that there is one
4:33 and let all who K thy name praise thee
6:13 I K that it is because of this that
11:31 so that you may K what it says.
12:29 his men did not K it until morning, for
13:3 to them, "You yourselves K what great things I
13:3 and the sanctuary; you K also the wars and
2Mac 1:27 and let the Gentiles K that thou art our
7:22 them, "I do not K how you came into
9:24 troubled, for they would K to whom the government
11:26 so that they may K our policy and be
14:32 that they did not K where the man was
Mt 6:3 let your left hand K what your right hand
7:11 then, who are evil, K how to give good
7:16 You will K them by their fruits.
7:20 Thus you will K them by their fruits.
9:6 But that you may K that the Son of
13:11 has been given to K the secrets of the
15:12 to him, "Do you K that the Pharisees were
16:3 red and threatening.' You K how to interpret the
17:12 and they did not K him, but did to
20:22 answered, "You do not K what you are asking.
20:25 him and said, "You K that the rulers of
21:27 So they answered Jesus, "We do not K
22:16 Herodi-ans, saying, "Teacher, we K that you are true,
22:29 are wrong, because you K neither the scriptures nor
24:32 forth its leaves, you K that summer is near.
24:33 all these things, you K that he is near,
24:39 and they did not K until the flood came
24:42 for you do not K on what day your
24:43 But K this, that if the householder had known
24:50 hour he does not K,
25:12 you, I do not K you.'
25:13 Watch therefore, for you K neither the day nor
26:2 to his disciples, "You K that after two days
26:70 saying, "I do not K what you mean."
26:72 oath, "I do not K the man."
26:74 swear, "I do not K the man." And immediately
28:5 be afraid; for I K that you seek Jesus
Mk 1:24 I K who you are, the Holy One of
2:10 But that you may K that the Son of
5:43 that no one should K this, and told them
7:23 not have any one K it; yet he could
9:6 For he did not K what to say, for
9:30 not have any one K it;
10:19 You K the commandments: 'Do not kill, Do not
10:38 them, "You do not K what you are asking.
10:42 said to them, "You K that those who are
11:32 So they answered Jesus, "We do not K
12:14 to him, "Teacher, we K that you are true,
12:24 are wrong, that you K neither the scriptures nor
13:28 forth its leaves, you K that summer is near.
13:29 things taking place, you K that he is near,
13:33 for you do not K when the time will
13:35 for you do not K when the master of
14:40 and they did not K what to answer him.
14:68 it, saying, "I neither K nor understand what you
14:71 swear, "I do not K this man of whom
Lk 1:4 Theophilus, that you may K the truth concerning the
1:18 angel, "How shall I K this?
2:43 His parents did not K it,
2:49 Did you not K that I must be in
4:34 I K who you are, the Holy One of
5:24 But that you may K that the Son of
8:10 has been given to K the secrets of the
10:11 off against you; nevertheless K this, that the kingdom
11:13 then, who are evil, K how to give good
12:39 But K this, that if the householder had known
12:46 hour he does not K, and will punish him,
12:48 he who did not K, and did what deserved
12:56 You K how to interpret the appearance of earth
12:56 why do you not K how to interpret the
13:25 you, 'I do not K where you come from.'
13:27 you, I do not K where you come from;
18:20 You K the commandments: 'Do not commit adultery,
19:15 him, that he might K what they had gained
19:44 because you did not K the time of your
20:7 that they did not K whence it was.
20:21 asked him, "Teacher, we K that you speak and
21:20 surrounded by armies, then K that its desolation has
21:30 see for yourselves and K that the summer is
21:31 things taking place, you K that the kingdom of
22:34 times deny that you K me."
22:55 "Woman, I do not K him."
22:58 "Man, I do not K what you are saying."
23:33 forgive them; for they K not what they do."
24:18 Jerusalem who does not K the things that have
Jn 1:26 whom you do not K,
1:31 I myself did not K him; but for this
1:33 I myself did not K him; but he who
1:48 him, "How do you K me?" Jesus answered him,
2:9 wine, and did not K where it came from
3:2 to him, "Rabbi, we K that you are a
3:8 but you do not K whence it comes or
3:11 speak of what we K, and bear witness to
4:22 what you do not K; we worship what we
4:22 we worship what we K, for salvation is from
4:25 said to him, "I K that Messiah is coming
4:32 food to eat of which you do not K
4:42 for ourselves, and we K that this is indeed
5:12 been healed did not K who it was, for
5:31 to me, and I K that the testimony which
5:41 But I K that you have not the love
6:42 son of Joseph, whose father and mother we K
6:69 and have come to K, that you are the
7:17 his will, he shall K whether the teaching is
7:26 that the authorities really K that this is the
7:27 Yet we K where this man comes from; and
7:27 appears, no one will K where he comes from."
7:28 in the temple, "You K me, and you know
7:28 know me, and you K where I come from?
7:28 me is true, and him you do not K
7:29 I K him, for I come from him, and
7:49 crowd, who do not K the law, are accursed."
8:14 is true, for I K whence I have come
8:14 but you do not K whence I come or
8:19 Jesus answered, "You K neither me nor my Father;
8:19 knew me, you would K my Father also."
8:28 man, then you will K that I am he,
8:32 disciples, and you will K the truth, and the
8:37 I K that you are descendants of Abraham; yet
8:52 to him, "Now we K that you have a
8:55 not known him; I K him.
8:55 said, I do not K him, I should be
8:55 you; but I do K him and I keep
9:12 He said, "I do not K
9:20 His parents answered, "We K that this is our
9:21 sees we do not K, nor do we know
9:21 know, nor do we K who opened his eyes.
9:24 God the praise; we K that this man is
9:25 sinner, I do not K; one thing I know,
9:25 know; one thing I K, that though I was
9:29 We K that God has spoken to Moses, but
9:29 man, we do not K where he comes from."
9:30 You do not K where he comes from, and
9:31 We K that God does not listen to sinners,
10:4 follow him, for they K his voice.
10:5 for they do not K the voice of strangers."
10:14 the good shepherd; I K my own and my
10:14 own and my own K me,
10:15 knows me and I K the Father; and I
10:27 my voice, and I K them, and they follow
10:38 works, that you may K and understand that the
11:22 And even now I K that whatever you ask
11:24 said to him, "I K that he will rise
11:49 said to them, "You K nothing at all;
11:57 he should let them K, so that they might
12:35 the darkness does not K where he goes.
12:50 And I K that his commandment is eternal life.
13:7 doing you do not K now, but afterward you
13:12 to them, "Do you K what I have done
13:17 If you K these things, blessed are you if
13:18 of you all; I K whom I have chosen;
13:35 this all men will K that you are my
14:4 And you K the way where I am going."
14:5 "Lord, we do not K where you are going;
14:5 going; how can we K the way?"
14:7 Father also; henceforth you K him and have seen
14:9 yet you do not K me, Philip?
14:17 nor knows him; you K him, for he dwells
14:20 that day you will K that I am in
14:31 that the world may K that I love the
15:15 the servant does not K what his master is
15:18 the world hates you, K that it has hated
15:21 because they do not K him who sent me.
16:18 We do not K what he means."
16:30 Now we K that you know all things, and
16:30 we know that you K all things, and need
17:3 eternal life, that they K thee the only true
17:7 thy word Now they K that everything that thou
17:8 have received them and K in truth that I
17:23 that the world may K that thou hast sent

17:25 known thee; and these K that thou hast sent
18:21 said to them; they K what I said."
19:4 you, that you may K that I find no
19:10 Do you not K that I have power to
20:2 and we do not K where they have laid
20:9 yet they did not K the scripture, that he
20:13 and I do not K where they have laid
20:14 but she did not K that it was Jesus.
21:4 the disciples did not K that it was Jesus.
21:15 him, "Yes, Lord; you K that I love you."
21:16 him, "Yes, Lord; you K that I love you."
21:17 to him, "Lord, you K everything; you know that
21:17 you know everything; you K that I love you."
21:24 these things; and we K that his testimony is
Acts 1:7 not for you to K times or seasons which
2:22 midst, as you yourselves K --
2:36 house of Israel therefore K assuredly that God has
3:16 whom you see and K; and the faith which
3:17 "And now, brethren, I K that you acted in
7:40 Egypt, we do not K what has become of
10:28 to them, "You yourselves K how unlawful it is
10:36 You K the word which he sent to Israel,
12:9 him; he did not K that what was done
15:7 to them, "Brethren, you K that in the early
17:19 Are-opagus, saying, "May we K what this new
17:20 ears; we wish to K therefore what these things
19:15 answered them, "Jesus I K, and Paul I know;
19:15 know, and Paul I K; but who are you?"
19:25 and said, "Men, you K that from this business
19:32 of them did not K why they had come
19:35 there who does not K that the city of
20:18 to them: "You yourselves K how I lived among
20:25 And now, behold, I K that all you among
20:29 I K that after my departure fierce wolves will
20:34 You yourselves K that these hands ministered to my
21:24 Thus all will K that there is nothing in
21:37 he said, "Do you K Greek?
22:14 fathers appointed you to K his will, to see
22:19 'Lord, they themselves K that in every synagogue
22:30 the morrow, desiring to K the real reason why
23:5 said, "I did not K, brethren, that he was
23:28 And desiring to K the charge on which they
25:10 no wrong, as you K very well.
26:27 I K that you believe."
28:22 to this sect we K that everywhere it is
Rom 1:13 I want you to K, brethren, that I have
1:32 Though they K God's decree that those who do
2:2 We K that the judgment of God rightly falls
2:4 Do you not K that God's kindness is meant
2:18 relation to God and K his will and approve
3:17 and the way of peace they do not K
3:19 Now we K that whatever the law says it
6:3 Do you not K that all of us who
6:6 We K that our old self was crucified with
6:9 For we K that Christ being raised from the
6:16 Do you not K that if you yield yourselves
7:1 Do you not K, brethren--for I am speaking
7:1 speaking to those who K the law--that the
7:14 We K that the law is spiritual; but I
7:18 For I K that nothing good dwells within me,
8:22 We K that the whole creation has been groaning
8:26 for we do not K how to pray as
8:28 We K that in everything God works for good
11:2 Do you not K what the scripture says of
13:11 Besides this you K what hour it is, how
14:14 I K and am persuaded in the Lord Jesus
15:29 to Spain; and I K that when I come
1Cor 1:16 that, I do not K whether I baptized any
1:21 the world did not K God through wisdom, it
2:2 For I decided to K nothing among you except
3:16 Do you not K that you are God's temple
5:6 Do you not K that a little leaven leavens
6:2 Do you not K that the saints will judge
6:3 Do you not K that we are to judge
6:9 Do you not K that the unrighteous will not
6:15 Do you not K that your bodies are members
6:16 Do you not K that he who joins himself
6:19 Do you not K that your body is a
7:16 Wife, how do you K whether you will save
7:16 Husband, how do you K whether you will save
8:1 offered to idols: we K that "all of us
8:2 he does not yet K as he ought to
8:2 does not yet know as he ought to K
8:4 offered to idols, we K that "an idol has
9:13 Do you not K that those who are employed
9:24 Do you not K that in a race all
10:1 I want you to K, brethren, that our fathers
12:2 You K that when you were heathen, you were
13:12 Now I K in part; then I shall understand
14:7 how will any one K what is played?
14:9 how will any one K what is said?
14:11 if I do not K the meaning of the
14:16 when he does not K what you are saying?
14:35 anything they desire to K, let them ask their
16:15 Now, brethren, you K that the household of
2Cor 1:7 is unshaken; for we K that as you share
2:4 but to let you K the abundant love that
2:9 might test you and K whether you are obedient
5:1 For we K that if the earthly tent we
5:6 of good courage; we K that while we are
8:1 We want you to K, brethren, about the grace
8:9 For you K the grace of our Lord Jesus
9:2 the saints, for I K your readiness, of which
12:2 I K a man in Christ who fourteen years
12:2 body I do not K, God knows.
12:3 And I K that this man was caught up
12:3 body I do not K, God knows--
Gal 1:11 I would have you K, brethren, that the gospel
2:16 Gentile sinners, yet who K that a man is
4:8 when you did not K God, you were in
4:9 you have come to K God, or rather to
4:13 me no wrong; you K it was because of
Eph 1:18 enlightened, that you may K what is the hope
3:19 and depth, and to K the love of Christ
6:21 that you also may K how I am and
6:22 purpose, that you may K how we are, and
Phil 1:12 I want you to K, brethren, that what has
1:19 For I K that through your prayers and the
1:25 Convinced of this, I K that I shall remain
2:22 But Timothy's worth you K, how as a son
3:10 faith; that I may K him and the power
4:5 Let all men K your forbearance.
4:12 I K how to be abased, and I know
4:12 be abased, and I K how to abound; in
4:15 And you Philippians yourselves K that in the
Col 2:1 I want you to K how greatly I strive
4:6 so that you may K how you ought to
4:8 purpose, that you may K how we are and
1Thes 1:4 For we K, brethren beloved by God, that he
1:5 You K what kind of men we proved to
2:1 For you yourselves K, brethren, that our visit to
2:2 at Philippi, as you K, we had courage in
2:5 of flattery, as you K, or a cloak for
2:11 you believers; for you K how, like a father
3:3 You yourselves K that this is to be our
3:4 it has come to pass, and as you K
3:5 sent that I might K your faith, for fear
4:2 For you K what instructions we gave you through
4:4 each one of you K how to take a
4:5 heathen who do not K God;
5:2 For you yourselves K well that the day of
2Thes 1:8 those who do not K God and upon those
2:6 And you K what is restraining him now so
3:7 For you yourselves K how you ought to imitate
1Tim 1:8 Now we K that the law is good, if
3:5 a man does not K how to manage his
3:15 am delayed, you may K how one ought to
4:3 those who believe and K the truth.
2Tim 1:12 not ashamed, for I K whom I have believed,
1:18 Day--and you well K all the service he
2:23 stupid, senseless controversies; you K that they breed
2:25 repent and come to K the truth,
Tit 1:15 They profess to K God, but they deny him
Heb 8:11 one his brother, saying, K the Lord,' for all
8:11 Lord,' for all shall K me, from the least
10:30 For we K him who said, "Vengeance is mine,
12:17 For you K that afterward, when he desired to
Jas 1:3 various trials, for you K that the testing of
1:18 K this, my beloved brethren.
3:1 my brethren, for you K that we who teach
4:4 Do you not K that friendship with the world
4:14 whereas you do not K about tomorrow.
5:20 him back, let him K that whoever brings back
1Pet 1:18 You K that you were ransomed from the futile
2Pet 1:12 these things, though you K them and are established
1:14 of reminder, since I K that the putting off
1Jn 2:3 be sure that we K him, if we keep
2:4 He who says "I K him" but disobeys his
2:11 darkness, and does not K where he is going,
2:13 you, fathers, because you K him who is from
2:13 you, children, because you K the Father.
2:14 you, fathers, because you K him who is from

2:18 have come; therefore we K that it is the
2:20 anointed by the Holy One, and you all K
2:21 because you do not K the truth, but because
2:21 truth, but because you K it, and know that
2:21 you know it, and K that no lie is
2:29 If you K that he is righteous, you may
3:1 the world does not K us is that it
3:1 that it did not K him.
3:2 shall be, but we K that when he appears
3:5 You K that he appeared to take away sins,
3:14 We K that we have passed out of death
3:15 a murderer, and you K that no murderer has
3:16 By this we K love, that he laid down
3:19 By this we shall K that we are of
3:24 And by this we K that he abides in
4:2 By this you K the Spirit of God: every
4:6 By this we K the spirit of truth and
4:8 not love does not K God; for God is
4:13 By this we K that we abide in him
4:16 So we K and believe the love God has
5:2 By this we K that we love the children
5:13 God, that you may K that you have eternal
5:15 And if we K that he hears us in
5:15 whatever we ask, we K that we have obtained
5:18 We K that any one born of God does
5:19 We K that we are of God, and the
5:20 And we K that the Son of God has
5:20 given us understanding, to K him who is true;
2Jn 1:1 but also all who K the truth,
3Jn 1:2 be in health; I K that it is well
1:12 him too, and you K my testimony is true.
Jude 1:10 those things that they K by instinct as irrational
Rev 2:2 "I K your works, your toil and your patient
2:3 to be false; I K you are enduring patiently
2:9 "I K your tribulation and your poverty (but you
2:13 "I K where you dwell, where Satan's throne is;
2:19 "I K your works, your love and faith and
2:23 all the churches shall K that I am he
3:1 "I K your works; you have the name of
3:3 and you will not K at what hour I
3:8 "I K your works.
3:8 able to shut; I K that you have but
3:15 "I K your works: you are neither cold nor
7:14 I said to him, "Sir, you K

KNOWEST (27)

2Sam 7:20 For thou K thy servant, O Lord GOD!
1Kgs 8:39 each whose heart thou K, according to all his
8:39 (for thou, thou only, K the hearts of all
1Chr 17:18 For thou K thy servant.
2Chr 6:30 each whose heart thou K, according to all his
6:30 (for thou, thou only, K the hearts of the
Tob 3:14 Thou K, O Lord, that I am innocent of
Esth 13:12 Thou K all things; thou knowest, O Lord, that
13:12 knowest all things; thou K, O Lord, that it
14:15 all things; and thou K that I hate the
14:16 Thou K my necessity _ that I abhor the
Job 10:7 my sin, although thou K that I am not
Ps 40:9 my lips, as thou K, O LORD.
69:5 O God, thou K my folly; the wrongs I
69:19 Thou K my reproach, and my shame and my
139:2 Thou K when I sit down and when I
139:4 lo, O LORD, thou K it altogether.
139:14 Thou K me right well;
142:3 spirit is faint, thou K my way!
Jer 12:3 But thou, O LORD, K me; thou seest me,
15:15 O LORD, thou K; remember me and visit me,
17:16 day of disaster, thou K; that which came out
18:23 Yet, thou, O LORD, K all their plotting to
Ezek 37:3 And I answered, "O Lord GOD, thou K
Dan 13:43 come to be, thou K that these men have
1Mac 3:52 to destroy us; thou K what they plot against
Acts 1:24 and said, "Lord, who K the hearts of all

KNOWING (44)

Gen 3:5 will be like God, K good and evil."
3:22 like one of us, K good and evil; and
1Kgs 8:38 thy people Israel, each K the affliction of his
2Kgs 4:39 pot of pottage, not K what they were.
2Chr 6:29 thy people Israel, each K his own affliction, and
Tob 8:12 him without any one K about it."
Job 34:25 Thus, K their works, he overturns them in the
Wis 8:9 to live with me, K that she would give
15:2 sin we are thine, K thy power; but we
18:19 might not perish without K why they suffered.
Mt 9:4 But Jesus, K their thoughts, said, "Why do you
12:25 K their thoughts, he said to them, "Every kingdom
Mk 5:33 But the woman, K what had been done to
6:20 for Herod feared John, K that he was a
12:15 But K their hypocrisy, he said to them, "Why
Lk 8:53 they laughed at him, K that she was dead.
9:33 one for Elijah"—not K what he said.
11:17 But he, K their thoughts, said to them, "Every
11:44 walk over them without K it."
Jn 6:61 But Jesus, K in himself that his disciples murmured
13:3 to betray him, Jesus, K that the Father had
18:4 Then Jesus, K all that was to befall him,
19:28 After this Jesus, K that all was now finished,
Acts 2:30 therefore a prophet, and K that God had sworn
5:7 wife came in, not K what had happened.
20:22 in the Spirit, not K what shall befall me
Rom 5:3 our sufferings, K that suffering produces endurance,
1Cor 15:58 work of the Lord, K that in the Lord
2Cor 4:14 and so we speak, K that he who raised
5:11 Therefore, K the fear of the Lord, we persuade
Eph 6:8 and not to men, K that whatever good any
6:9 them, and forbear threatening, K that he who is
Phil 1:16 it out of love, K that I am put
3:8 the surpassing worth of K Christ Jesus my Lord.
Col 3:24 Lord and not men, K that from the Lord
4:1 slaves justly and fairly, K that you also have
2Tim 3:14 and have firmly believed, K from whom you learned
Tit 3:11 to do with him, K that such a person
Philem 1:21 I write to you, K that you will do
Heb 11:8 he went out, not K where he was to
1Pet 5:9 firm in your faith, K that the same experience
2Pet 2:21 of righteousness than after K it to turn back
3:17 You therefore, beloved, K this beforehand, beware
Rev 3:17 I need nothing; not K that you are wretched,

KNOWLEDGE (186)

Gen 2:9 the tree of the K of good and evil.
2:17 the tree of the K of good and evil
Ex 31:3 ability and intelligence, with K and all craftsmanship,
35:31 with intelligence, with K, and with all craftsmanship,
Num 15:24 done unwittingly without the K of the congregation,
24:16 God, and knows the K of the Most High,
Deut 1:39 this day have no K of good or evil,
1Sam 2:3 is a God of K, and by him actions
1Kgs 2:32 head, because, without the K of my father David,
2Chr 1:10 me now wisdom and K to go out and
1:11 have asked wisdom and K for yourself that you
1:12 you king, wisdom and K are granted to you.
Neh 10:28 daughters, all who have K and understanding,
Esth 2:22 this came to the K of Mordecai, and he
14:15 Thou hast K of all things; and thou knowest
Job 15:2 man answer with windy K, and fill himself with
21:14 do not desire the K of thy ways.
21:22 Will any teach God K, seeing that he judges
26:3 who has no wisdom, and plentifully declared sound K
34:35 say: 'Job speaks without K, his words are without
35:16 mouth in empty talk, he multiplies words without K
36:3 I will fetch my K from afar, and ascribe
36:4 who is perfect in K is with you.
36:12 they perish by the sword, and die without K
37:16 who is perfect in K,
38:2 is this that darkens counsel by words without K
42:3 that hides counsel without K Therefore I have
Ps 14:4 Have they no K, all the evildoers who eat
19:2 pours forth speech, and night to night declares K
71:15 the day, for their number is past my K
73:11 Is there K in the Most High?"
82:5 They have neither K nor understanding, they walk
94:10 He who teaches men K,
119:66 me good judgment and K, for I believe in
139:6 Such K is too wonderful for me; it is
Prov 1:4 given to the simple, K and discretion to the
1:7 is the beginning of K; fools despise wisdom and
1:22 scoffers delight in their scoffing and fools hate K
1:29 Because they hated K and did not choose the
2:5 LORD and find the K of God.
2:6 from his mouth come K and understanding;
2:10 into your heart, and K will be pleasant to
3:20 the heavens; by his K the deeps broke forth,
5:2 may keep discretion, and your lips may guard K
8:9 who understands and right to those who find K
8:10 instead of silver, and K rather than choice gold;
8:12 prudence, and I find K and discretion.
9:10 of wisdom, and the K of the Holy One
10:14 Wise men lay up K, but the babbling of
11:9 his neighbor, but by K the righteous are delivered.
12:1 Whoever loves discipline loves K, but he who hates

K

12:23 prudent man conceals his K, but fools proclaim their
13:16 prudent man acts with K, but a fool flaunts
14:6 wisdom in vain, but K is easy for a
14:7 for there you do not meet words of K
14:18 acquire folly, but the prudent are crowned with K
15:2 of the wise dispenses K, but the mouths of
15:7 of the wise spread K; not so the minds
15:14 who has understanding seeks K, but the mouths of
17:27 restrains his words has K, and he who has
18:15 An intelligent mind acquires K, and the ear of
18:15 knowledge, and the ear of the wise seeks K
19:2 man to be without K, and he who makes
19:25 a man of understanding, and he will gain K
19:27 instruction only to stray from the words of K
20:15 but the lips of K are a precious jewel.
21:11 when a wise man is instructed, he gains K
22:12 LORD keep watch over K, but he overthrows the
22:17 your mind to my K;
22:20 sayings of admonition and K,
23:12 to instruction and your ear to words of K
24:4 it is established; by K the rooms are filled
24:5 and a man of K than he who has
28:2 men of understanding and K its stability will long
29:7 poor; a wicked man does not understand such K
30:3 wisdom, nor have I K of the Holy One.
Eccl 1:16 mind has had great experience of wisdom and K
1:18 and he who increases K increases sorrow.
2:21 toiled with wisdom and K and skill must leave
2:26 God gives wisdom and K and joy; but to
7:12 and the advantage of K is that wisdom preserves
9:10 work or thought or K or wisdom in Sheol,
12:9 also taught the people K, weighing and studying and
Wis 2:13 He professes to have K of God, and calls
6:22 of creation, and make K of her clear, and
7:17 who gave me unerring K of what exists, to
8:4 an initiate in the K of God, and an
10:10 God, and gave him K of angels; she prospered
14:22 to err about the K of God, but they
18:6 might rejoice in sure K of the oaths in
Sir 1:17 he rained down K and discerning comprehension,
6:33 listen you will gain K, and if you incline
10:29 is honored for his K, while a rich man
16:22 my son, and acquire K, and pay close attention
16:23 by weight, and declare K accurately.
17:6 He filled them with K and understanding, and
17:9 He bestowed K upon them, and allotted to them
19:19 But the K of wickedness is not wisdom, nor
21:13 The K of a wise man will increase like
21:14 like a broken jar; it will hold no K
21:18 a fool; and the K of the ignorant is
32:3 should, but with accurate K, and do not interrupt
33:11 the fulness of his K the Lord distinguished them
39:7 direct his counsel and K aright, and meditate on
45:5 law of life and K, to teach Jacob the
50:27 Instruction in understanding and K I have written in
Is 5:13 exile for want of K; their honored men are
11:2 might, the spirit of K and the fear of
11:9 be full of the K of the LORD as
28:9 "Whom will he teach K, and to whom will
33:6 of salvation, wisdom, and K; the fear of the
40:14 justice, and taught him K, and showed him the
44:19 considers, nor is there K or discernment to say,
44:25 back, and makes their K foolish;
45:20 They have no K who carry about their wooden
47:10 your wisdom and your K led you astray, and
53:11 be satisfied; by his K shall the righteous one,
56:10 they are all without K; they are all dumb
58:3 and thou takest no K of it?' Behold, in
Jer 3:15 will feed you with K and understanding.
10:14 is stupid and without K; every goldsmith is put
14:18 their trade through the land, and have no K
51:17 is stupid and without K; every goldsmith is put
Bar 3:20 learned the way to K, nor understood her paths,
3:27 them the way to K;
3:36 the whole way to K, and gave her to
Dan 1:4 all wisdom, endowed with K, understanding learning,
2:21 to the wise and K to those who have
5:12 because an excellent spirit, K, and understanding to
12:4 to and fro, and K shall increase."
Hos 4:1 or kindness, and no K of God in the
4:6 destroyed for lack of K; because you have rejected
4:6 because you have rejected K, I reject you from
6:6 and not sacrifice, the K of God, rather than
8:4 They set up princes, but without my K
Hab 2:14 be filled with the K of the glory of
Mal 2:7 a priest should guard K, and men should seek
2Mac 6:30 Lord in his holy K that, though I might
Lk 1:77 his ways, to give K of salvation to his
11:52 away the key of K; you did not enter
Acts 5:2 and with his wife's K he kept back some
24:21 having a rather accurate K of the Way, put
Rom 2:20 law the embodiment of K and truth–
3:20 through the law comes K of sin.
11:33 riches and wisdom and K of God!
15:14 goodness, filled with all K, and able to instruct
1Cor 1:5 all speech and all K –
8:1 idols: we know that "all of us possess K
8:1 K
8:7 However, not all possess this K
8:10 you, a man of K, at table in an
8:11 And so by your K this weak man is
12:8 another the utterance of K according to the same
13:2 all mysteries and all K, and if I have
13:8 will cease; as for K, it will pass away.
13:9 For our K is imperfect and our prophecy is
14:6 you some revelation or K or prophecy or teaching?
15:34 For some have no K of God.
2Cor 2:14 the fragrance of the K of him everywhere.
4:6 the light of the K of the glory of
6:6 hunger; by purity, K, forbearance, kindness, the Holy
8:7 faith, in utterance, in K, in all earnestness, and
10:5 proud obstacle to the K of God, and take
11:6 I am not in K; in every way we
Eph 1:17 of revelation in the K of him,
3:19 of Christ which surpasses K, that you may be
4:13 faith and of the K of the Son of
Phil 1:9 more and more, with K and all discernment,
Col 1:9 be filled with the K of his will in
1:10 and increasing in the K of God.
2:2 assured understanding and the K of God's mystery, of
2:3 are hid all the treasures of wisdom and K
3:10 is being renewed in K after the image of
1Tim 2:4 to come to the K of the truth.
6:20 what is falsely called K,
2Tim 3:7 never arrive at a K of the truth.
Tit 1:1 God's elect and their K of the truth which
Philem 1:6 faith may promote the K of all the good
Heb 10:26 deliberately after receiving the K of the truth, there
2Pet 1:2 to you in the K of God and of
1:3 and godliness, through the K of him who called
1:5 virtue, and virtue with K,
1:6 knowledge, and K with self-control, and self-control
1:8 or unfruitful in the K of our Lord Jesus
2:20 the world through the K of our Lord and
3:18 in the grace and K of our Lord and

KNOWN (245)

Gen 19:8 daughters who have not K man; let me bring
24:16 look upon, a virgin, whom no man had K
41:21 no one would have K that they had eaten
45:1 when Joseph made himself K to his brothers.
Ex 2:14 was afraid, and thought, "Surely the thing is K
6:3 did not make myself K to them.
21:36 Or if it is K that the ox has
33:16 how shall it be K that I have found
Lev 4:14 they have committed becomes K, the assembly shall
4:23 has committed is made K to him, he shall
4:28 has committed is made K to him he shall
Num 12:6 the LORD make myself K to him in a
31:17 every woman who has K man by lying with
31:18 girls who have not K man by lying with
31:35 women who had not K man by lying with
Deut 2:11 Anakim they are also K as Rephaim, but the
2:20 possession.' (That also is K as a land of
4:9 your life; make them K to your children and
11:2 children who have not K or seen it), consider
11:28 go after other gods which you have not K
13:2 which you have not K, 'and let us serve
13:6 nor your fathers have K,
13:13 which you have not K,
21:1 and it is not K who killed him,
28:33 which you have not K shall eat up the
28:36 nor your fathers have K; and there you shall
28:64 stone, which neither you nor your fathers have K
29:26 whom they had not K and whom he had
31:13 children, who have not K it, may hear and
32:17 gods they had never K, to new gods that
Josh 24:31 outlived Joshua and had K all the work which
Judg 3:2 least as had not K it before.
11:39 She had never K a man.
16:9 So the secret of his strength was not K
21:12 virgins who had not K man by lying with

Ruth 3:3 do not make yourself K to the man until
3:14 "Let it not be K that the woman came
1Sam 6:3 and it will be K to you why his
9:27 that I may make K to you the word
22:15 for your servant has K nothing of all this,
2Sam 17:19 it; and nothing was K of it.
22:44 whom I had not K served me.
1Kgs 14:2 that it be not K that you are the
18:36 Israel, let it be K this day that thou
1Chr 16:8 on his name, make K his deeds among the
17:19 this greatness, in making K all these great things.
Ezra 4:12 And now be it K to the king that
4:13 Now be it K to the king that, if
4:16 We make K to the king that, if this
5:8 Be it K to the king that we went
Neh 4:15 heard that it was K to us and that
9:14 and thou didst make K to them thy holy
Tob 13:4 Make his greatness K there, and exalt him in
Esth 1:17 queen will be made K to all women, causing
2:10 Esther had not made K her people or kindred,
2:10 Mordecai had charged her not to make it K
2:20 Esther had not made K her kindred or her
3:6 as they had made K to him the people
14:12 O Lord; make thyself K in this time of
Job 42:11 and all who had K him before, and ate
Ps 9:16 LORD has made himself K, he has executed
18:43 whom I had not K served me.
25:14 him, and he makes K to them his covenant.
38:9 all my longing is K to thee, my sighing
67:2 thy way may be K upon earth, thy saving
69:19 my foes are all K to thee.
76:1 In Judah God is K, his name is great
78:3 we have heard and K, that our fathers have
79:10 of thy servants be K among the nations before
81:5 voice I had not K:
88:12 Are thy wonders K in the darkness, or thy
98:2 The LORD has made K his victory, he has
103:7 He made K his ways to Moses, his acts
105:1 on his name, make K his deeds among the
106:8 that he might make K his mighty power.
119:152 Long have I K from thy testimonies that thou
139:1 hast searched me and K me!
145:12 thy power, to make K to the sons of
Prov 1:23 will make my words K to you.
12:16 of a fool is K at once, but the
14:33 but it is not K in the heart of
20:11 a child makes himself K by his acts, whether
22:19 I have made them K to you today, even
31:23 Her husband is K in the gates, when he
Eccl 6:5 seen the sun or K anything; yet it finds
6:10 named, and it is K what man is, and
Wis 2:1 no one has been K to return from Hades.
4:1 immortality, because it is K both by God and
5:7 the way of the Lord we have not K
6:13 hastens to make herself K to those who desire
16:28 sun, to make it K that one must rise
18:6 That night was made K beforehand to our fathers,
18:18 down half dead, made K why they were dying;
Sir 4:24 For wisdom is K through speech, and education
6:27 and she will become K to you; and when
11:26 a man will be K through his children.
12:8 friend will not be K in prosperity, nor will
16:15 I shall not be K, for what is my
19:26 A man is K by his appearance, and a
19:26 a sensible man is K by his face, when
21:7 mighty in speech is K from afar; but the
23:20 was created, it was K to him; so it
26:6 a tongue-lashing makes it K to all.
26:9 eyes, and she is K by her eyelids.
36:5 thee, as we have K that there is not
38:5 tree in order that his power might be K
42:18 all that may be K, and he looks into
46:15 his words he became K as a trustworthy seer.
Is 12:4 upon his name; make K his deeds among the
12:5 gloriously; let this be K in all the earth.
19:12 tell you and make K what the LORD of
19:21 LORD will make himself K to the Egyptians; and
38:19 day; the father makes K to the children thy
40:21 Have you not K
40:28 Have you not K
42:16 that they have not K I will guide them.
48:3 and I made them K; then suddenly I did
48:6 new things, hidden things which you have not K
48:8 heard, you have never K, from of old your
61:9 Their descendants shall be K among the nations, and
64:2 to make thy name K to thy adversaries, and
66:14 and it shall be K that the hand of
Jer 7:9 that you have not K,
9:16 nor their fathers have K; and I will send
11:18 The LORD made it K to me and I
16:13 nor your fathers have K, and there you shall
19:4 kings of Judah have K; and because they have
28:9 then it will be K that the LORD has
33:3 great and hidden things which you have not K
Bar 6:50 it will afterward be K that they are false.
Ezek 16:2 "Son of man, make K to Jerusalem her
20:5 of Jacob, making myself K to them in the
20:9 sight I made myself K to them in bringing
32:9 nations, into the countries which you have not K
35:11 I will make myself K among you, when I
36:32 GOD; let that be K to you.
38:23 holiness and make myself K in the eyes of
39:7 name I will make K in the midst of
43:11 whole form; and make K to them all its
Dan 2:5 you do not make K to me the dream
2:9 not make the dream K to me, there is
2:15 Arioch made the matter K to Daniel.
2:17 and made the matter K to Hananiah, Mishael, and
2:23 and hast now made K to me what we
2:23 for thou hast made K to us the king's
2:25 man who can make K to the king the
2:26 you able to make K to me the dream
2:28 and he has made K to King Nebuchadnezzar what
2:29 who reveals mysteries made K to you what is
2:30 interpretation may be made K to the king, and
2:45 great God has made K to the king what
3:18 if not, be it K to you, O king,
4:6 that they might make K to me the interpretation
4:7 they could not make K to me its interpretation.
4:18 not able to make K to me the interpretation,
5:8 the writing or make K to the king the
5:15 this writing and make K to me its interpretation;
5:16 the writing and make K to me its interpretation,
5:17 the king and make K to him the interpretation.
7:16 told me, and made K to me the interpretation
8:19 "Behold, I will make K to you what shall
Hos 11:12 but Judah is still K by God, and is
Amos 3:2 "You only have I K of all the families
Hab 3:2 the years make it K; in wrath remember mercy.
Zech 7:14 among all the nations which they had not K
14:7 continuous day (it is K to the LORD), not
1Mac 6:3 because his plan became K to the men of
7:3 when this act became K to him, he said,
7:30 It became K to Judas that Nicanor had come
8:10 them, but this became K to them, and they
9:60 unable to do it, because their plan became K
2Mac 1:33 When this matter became K, and it was reported
Mt 10:26 be revealed, or hidden that will not be K
12:7 And if you had K what this means, 'I
12:16 all, and ordered them not to make him K
12:33 for the tree is K by its fruit.
24:43 if the householder had K in what part of
Mk 3:12 he strictly ordered them not to make him K
6:14 heard of it; for Jesus' name had become K
Lk 2:15 the Lord has made K to us."
2:17 saw it they made K the saying which had
6:44 for each tree is K by its own fruit.
7:39 prophet, he would have K who and what sort
8:17 that shall not be K and come to light.
12:2 be revealed, or hidden that will not be K
12:39 if the householder had K at what hour the
24:35 and how he was K to them in the
Jn 1:18 bosom of the Father, he has made him K
7:4 he seeks to be K openly.
8:55 But you have not K him; I know him.
14:7 If you had K me, you would have known
14:7 me, you would have K my Father also; henceforth
15:15 Father I have made K to you.
16:3 because they have not K the Father, nor me.
17:25 the world has not K thee, but I have
17:25 thee, but I have K thee; and these know
17:26 I made K to them thy name, and I
17:26 I will make it K, that the love with
18:15 As this disciple was K to the high priest,
18:16 other disciple, who was K to the high priest,
Acts 1:19 And it became K to all the inhabitants of
2:14 Jerusalem, let this be K to you, and give
2:28 Thou hast made K to me the ways of
4:10 been healed, be it K to you all, and
7:13 visit Joseph made himself K to his brothers, and
7:13 and Joseph's family became K to Pharaoh.
7:18 king who had not K Joseph.

9:24 but their plot became K to Saul.
9:42 And it became K throughout all Joppa, and many
10:1 centurion of what was K as the Italian Cohort,
13:38 Let it be K to you therefore, brethren, that
15:18 has made these things K from of old.'
19:17 And this became K to all residents of Ephesus,
26:4 and at Jerusalem, is K by all the Jews.
26:5 They have K for a long time, if they
28:28 them.' Let it be K to you then that
Rom 1:19 For what can be K about God is plain
7:7 I should not have K sin.
7:7 I should not have K what it is to
9:22 wrath and to make K his power, has endured
9:23 in order to make K the riches of his
11:34 "For who has K the mind of the Lord,
16:19 while your obedience is K to all, so that
16:25 prophetic writings is made K to all nations, according
1Cor 2:16 "For who has K the mind of the Lord
8:3 loves God, one is K by him.
2Cor 3:2 your hearts, to be K and read by all
5:11 what we are is K to God, and I
5:11 I hope it is K also to your conscience.
Gal 1:22 I was still not K by sight to the
4:9 or rather to be K by God, how can
Eph 1:9 For he has made K to us in all
3:3 the mystery was made K to me by revelation,
3:5 which was not made K to the sons of
3:10 might now be made K to the principalities and
Phil 1:13 it has become K throughout the whole praetorian
4:6 your requests be made K to God.
Col 1:8 behalf and has made K to us your love
1:25 word of God fully K,
1:27 God chose to make K how great among the
Heb 3:10 hearts; they have not K my ways.'
2Pet 1:16 myths when we made K to you the power
2:21 them never to have K the way of righteousness
1Jn 3:6 either seen him or K him.
Rev 1:1 and he made it K by sending his angel

KNOWS (112)

Gen 3:5 For God K that when you eat of it
33:13 to him, "My lord K that the children are
Num 24:16 words of God, and K the knowledge of the
Deut 2:7 of your hands; he K your going through this
34:6 Beth-peor; but no man K the place of his
Josh 22:22 He K; and let Israel itself know!
1Sam 20:3 David replied, "Your father K well that I have
23:17 Saul my father also K this."
2Sam 12:22 for I said, 'Who K whether the LORD will
14:22 said, "Today your servant K that I have found
17:10 fear; for all Israel K that your father is
19:20 For your servant K that I have sinned; therefore,
1Kgs 5:6 one among us who K how to cut timber
Tob 13:6 right before him; who K if he will accept
Esth 4:14 And who K whether you have not come to
Job 11:11 For he K worthless men; when he sees iniquity,
15:23 'Where is it?' He K that a day of
18:21 place of him who K not God."
23:10 But he K the way that I take; when
28:7 no bird of prey K, and the falcon's eye
28:23 to it, and he K its place.
Ps 1:6 righteous; for the LORD K the way of the
37:18 The LORD K the days of the blameless, and
39:6 man heaps up, and K not who will gather!
44:21 For he K the secrets of the heart.
74:9 none among us who K how long.
91:14 protect him, because he K my name.
94:11 men knowledge, the LORD, K the thoughts of man,
103:14 For he K our frame; he remembers that we
103:16 gone, and its place K it no more.
104:19 the seasons; the sun K its time for setting.
138:6 but the haughty he K from afar.
Prov 9:13 she is wanton and K no shame.
14:10 The heart K its own bitterness, and no stranger
24:22 rise suddenly, and who K the ruin that will
29:7 A righteous man K the rights of the poor;
Eccl 2:19 after me; and who K whether he will be
3:21 Who K whether the spirit of man goes upward
6:8 poor man have who K how to conduct himself
6:12 For who K what is good for man while
7:22 cursing you; your heart K that many times you
8:1 And who K the interpretation of a thing?
10:14 words, though no man K what is to be,
Wis 1:7 holds all things together K what is said;
5:12 so that no one K its pathway.
8:8 for wide experience, she K the things of old,
9:9 thee is wisdom, who K thy works and was
9:11 For she K and understands all things, and she
13:16 not fall, because he K that it cannot help
15:13 more than all others, K that he sins when
Sir 1:5 Her clever devices--who K them?
15:19 fear him, and he K every deed of man.
18:27 Every intelligent man K wisdom, and he praises the
20:5 keeps silent because he K when to speak.
32:8 be as one who K and yet holds his
34:9 An educated man K many things, and one with
34:10 He that is inexperienced K few things, but he
42:18 For the Most High K all that may be
Is 1:3 The ox K its owner, and the ass its
7:15 and honey when he K how to refuse the
7:16 For before the child K how to refuse the
8:4 for before the child K how to cry 'My
29:15 Who K us?"
59:8 who goes in them K peace.
Jer 8:7 stork in the heavens K her times; and the
9:24 that he understands and K me, that I am
29:23 am the one who K, and I am witness,
Bar 3:31 No one K the way to her, or is
3:32 But he who K all things knows her, he
3:32 who knows all things K her, he found her
Dan 2:22 and mysterious things; he K what is in the
Hos 7:10 his strength, and he K it not; gray hairs
7:10 upon him, and he K it not.
Joel 2:14 Who K whether he will not turn and repent,
Jon 3:9 Who K, God may yet repent and turn from
Nah 1:7 day of trouble; he K those who take refuge
3:17 fly away; no one K where they are.
Zeph 3:5 fail; but the unjust K no shame.
Mt 6:8 them, for your Father K what you need before
6:32 and your heavenly Father K that you need them
9:30 "See that no one K it."
11:27 Father; and no one K the Son except the
11:27 Father, and no one K the Father except the
24:36 and hour no one K, not even the angels
Mk 4:27 sprout and grow, he K not how.
13:32 that hour no one K, not even the angels
Lk 10:22 Father; and no one K who the Son is
12:30 things; and your Father K that you need them.
16:15 before men, but God K your hearts; for what
Jn 10:15 me, as the Father K me and I know
14:17 neither sees him nor K him; you know him,
19:35 is true, and he K that he tells the
Acts 15:8 And God who K the heart bore witness to
26:26 For the king K about these things, and to
Rom 8:27 the hearts of men K what is the mind
1Cor 2:11 For what person K a man's thoughts except the
3:20 and again, "The Lord K that the thoughts of
8:2 one imagines that he K something, he does not
2Cor 11:11 God K I do!
11:31 is blessed for ever, K that I do not
12:2 of the body I do not know, God K
12:3 do not know, God K –
1Tim 6:4 up with conceit, he K nothing; he has a
2Tim 2:19 this seal: "The Lord K those who are his,"
Jas 4:17 Whoever K what is right to do and fails
2Pet 2:9 deeds), then the Lord K how to rescue the
1Jn 3:20 our hearts, and he K everything.
4:6 Whoever K God listens to us, and he who
4:7 born of God and K God.
Rev 2:17 stone which no one K except him who receives
12:12 great wrath, because he K that his time is
19:12 inscribed which no one K but himself.

KOA

Ezek 23:23 Pekod and Shoa and K, and all the Assyrians

KOHATH (26)

Gen 46:11 sons of Levi: Gershon, K, and Merari.
Ex 6:16 to their generations: Gershon, K, and Merari, the
6:18 The sons of K: Amram, Izhar, Hebron, and Uzziel,
6:18 of the life of K being a hundred and
Num 3:17 their names: Gershon and K and Merari.
3:19 And the sons of K by their families: Amram,
3:27 Of K were the family of the Amramites, and
3:29 of the sons of K were to encamp on
4:2 of the sons of K from among the sons
4:4 of the sons of K in the tent of
4:15 that the sons of K shall come to carry
4:15 which the sons of K are to carry.
7:9 to the sons of K he gave none, because
16:1 of Izhar, son of K, son of Levi, and
26:57 of the Gershonites; of K, the family of the

	26:58	And K was the father of Amram.
1Chr	6:1	sons of Levi: Gershom, K, and Merari.
	6:2	The sons of K: Amram, Izhar, Hebron, and Uzziel.
	6:16	sons of Levi: Gershom, K, and Merari.
	6:18	The sons of K: Amram, Izhar, Hebron, and Uzziel.
	6:22	The sons of K: Amminadab his son, Korah his
	6:38	of Izhar, son of K, son of Levi, son
	6:66	of the sons of K had cities of their
	15:5	of the sons of K, Uriel the chief, with
	23:6	sons of Levi: Gershom, K, and Merari.
	23:12	The sons of K: Amram, Izhar, Hebron, and Uzziel,

KOHATHITE

Josh	21:20	Kohathites belonging to the K families of the Levites,

KOHATHITES (20)

Num	3:27	the Uzzielites; these are the families of the K
	3:30	the fathers' house of the families of the K
	4:18	the families of the K be destroyed from among
	4:34	the sons of the K, by their families and
	4:37	the families of the K, all who served in
	10:21	Then the K set out, carrying the holy things,
	26:57	the family of the K; of Merari, the family
Josh	21:4	lot came out for the families of the K
	21:5	the rest of the K received by lot from
	21:10	the families of the K who belonged to the
	21:20	the rest of the K belonging to the Kohathite
	21:26	the rest of the K were ten in all
1Chr	6:33	the sons of the K: Heman the singer the
	6:54	of the families of K, for theirs was the
	6:61	the rest of the K were given by lot
	6:70	for the rest of the families of the K
	9:32	their kinsmen of the K had charge of the
2Chr	20:19	the Levites, of the K and the Korahites, stood
	29:12	the sons of the K; and of the sons
	34:12	the sons of the K, to have oversight.

KOLA

Jud	15:4	Bebai and Choba and K, and to all the

KOLAIAH (2)

Neh	11:7	of Pedaiah, son of K, son of Ma-aseiah, son
Jer	29:21	Ahab the son of K and Zedekiah the son

KONA

Jud	4:4	of Samaria, and to K and Beth-horon and Belmain

KORAH (28)

Gen	36:5	Reuel; and Oholibamah bore Jeush, Jalam, and K
	36:14	wife: she bore to Esau Jeush, Jalam, and K
	36:16	Omar, Zepho, Kenaz, K, Gatam, and Amalek; these
	36:18	chiefs Jeush, Jalam, and K; these are the chiefs
Ex	6:21	The sons of Izhar: K, Nepheg, and Zichri.
	6:24	The sons of K: Assir, Elkanah, and Abiasaph; these
Num	16:1	Now K the son of Izhar, son of Kohath,
	16:5	and he said to K and all his company,
	16:6	Do this: take censers, K and all his company;
	16:8	And Moses said to K, "Hear now, you sons
	16:16	And Moses said to K, "Be present, you and
	16:19	Then K assembled all the congregation against them
	16:24	about the dwelling of K, Dathan, and Abiram."
	16:27	about the dwelling of K, Dathan, and Abiram; and
	16:32	men that belonged to K and all their goods.
	16:40	lest he become as K and as his company--
	16:49	besides those who died in the affair of K
	26:9	in the company of K, when they contended against
	26:10	them up together with K, when that company died,
	26:11	Notwithstanding, the sons of K did not die.
	27:3	in the company of K, but died for his
1Chr	1:35	sons of Esau: Eliphaz, Reuel, Jeush, Jalam, and K
	2:43	The sons of Hebron: K, Tappuah, Rekem, and Shema.
	6:22	Kohath: Amminadab his son, K his son, Assir his
	6:37	of Ebiasaph, son of K,
	9:19	of Ebiasaph, son of K, and his kinsmen of
Sir	45:18	and the company of K, in wrath and anger.
Jude	1:11	error, and perish in K's rebellion.

KORAHITE

1Chr	9:31	first-born of Shallum the K, was in charge of

KORAHITES (7)

Ex	6:24	and Abiasaph; these are the families of the K
Num	26:58	family of the Mushites, the family of the K
1Chr	9:19	his fathers' house, the K, were in charge of
	12:6	Jo-ezer, and Jashobe-am, the K;
	26:1	the gatekeepers: of the K, Meshelemiah the son of
	26:19	the gatekeepers among the K and the sons of
2Chr	20:19	the Kohathites and the K, stood up to praise

KORE (3)

1Chr	9:19	Shallum the son of K, son of Ebiasaph, son
	26:1	Meshelemiah the son of K, of the sons of
2Chr	31:14	And K the son of Imnah the Levite, keeper

KOZ

1Chr	4:8	K was the father of Anub, Zobebah, and the

KUE (4)

1Kgs	10:28	was from Egypt and K, and the king's traders
	10:28	traders received them from K at a price.
2Chr	1:16	was from Egypt and K, and the king's traders
	1:16	traders received them from K for a price.

KUSHAIAH

1Chr	15:17	Ethan the son of K;

L

LA-ODICEA (6)

Col	2:1	and for those at L, and for all who
	4:13	and for those in L and in Hi-erapolis.
	4:15	to the brethren at L, and to Nympha and
	4:16	see that you read also the letter from L
Rev	1:11	and to Sardis and to Philadelphia and to L
	3:14	of the church in L write: 'The words of

LA-ODICEANS

Col	4:16	the church of the L; and see that you

LAADAH

1Chr	4:21	the father of Lecah, L the father of Mareshah,

LABAN (58)

Gen	24:29	brother whose name was L; and Laban ran out
	24:29	name was Laban; and L ran out to the
	24:32	into the house; and L ungirded the camels, and
	24:50	Then L and Bethuel answered, "The thing comes
	25:20	Paddan-aram, the sister of L the Aramean.
	27:43	voice; arise, flee to L my brother in Haran,
	28:2	of the daughters of L your mother's brother.
	28:5	went to Paddan-aram to L, the son of Bethuel
	29:5	them, "Do you know L the son of Nahor?"
	29:10	Rachel the daughter of L his mother's brother, and
	29:10	and the sheep of L his mother's brother, Jacob
	29:10	watered the flock of L his mother's brother.
	29:13	When L heard the tidings of Jacob his sister's
	29:13	Jacob told L all these things,
	29:14	all these things, and L said to him, "Surely
	29:15	Then L said to Jacob, "Because you are my
	29:16	Now L had two daughters; the name of the
	29:19	L said, "It is better that I give her
	29:21	Then Jacob said to L, "Give me my wife
	29:22	So L gathered together all the men of the
	29:24	L gave his maid Zilpah to his daughter Leah
	29:25	and Jacob said to L, "What is this you
	29:26	L said, "It is not so done in our
	29:28	completed her week; then L gave him his daughter
	29:29	L gave his maid Bilhah to his daughter Rachel
	29:30	than Leah, and served L for another seven years.
	30:25	Joseph, Jacob said to L, "Send me away, that
	30:27	But L said to him, "If you will allow
	30:34	L said, "Good!
	30:35	But that day L removed the he-goats that were
	30:36	fed the rest of L's flock.
	30:40	in the flock of L; and he put his
	30:40	not put them with L's flock.
	31:1	that the sons of L were saying, "Jacob has
	31:2	And Jacob saw that L did not regard him
	31:12	have seen all that L is doing to you.
	31:19	L had gone to shear his sheep, and Rachel
	31:20	And Jacob outwitted L the Aramean, in that he
	31:22	When it was told L on the third day
	31:24	But God came to L the Aramean in a
	31:25	And L overtook Jacob.
	31:25	the hill country, and L with his kinsmen encamped
	31:26	And L said to Jacob, "What have you done,
	31:31	Jacob answered L, "Because I was afraid, for I
	31:33	So L went into Jacob's tent, and into Leah's
	31:34	L felt all about the tent, but did not
	31:36	angry, and upbraided L; Jacob said to Laban,

K
L

31:36 Laban; Jacob said to L, "What is my offense?
31:43 Then L answered and said to Jacob, "The daughters
31:47 L called it Jegar-sahadutha: but Jacob called it
31:48 L said, "This heap is a witness between you
31:51 Then L said to Jacob, "See this heap and
31:55 Early in the morning L arose, and kissed his
32:4 'I have sojourned with L, and stayed until now;
46:18 sons of Zilpah, whom L gave to Leah his
46:25 sons of Bilhah, whom L gave to Rachel his
Deut 1:1 between Paran and Tophel, L, Hazeroth, and
Jud 8:26 keeping the sheep of L, his mother's brother.

LABANS
Gen 30:42 so the feebler were L, and the stronger Jacobs.

LABOR (71)
Gen 31:42 my affliction and the L of my hands, and
35:16 from Ephrath, Rachel travailed, and she had hard L
35:17 was in her hard L, the midwife said to
38:28 when she was in L, one put out a
49:15 to bear, and became a slave at forced L
Ex 5:9 men that they may L at it and pay
20:9 Six days you shall L, and do all your
23:16 first fruits of your L, of what you sow
23:16 in from the field the fruit of your L
Deut 5:13 Six days you shall L, and do all your
20:11 it shall do forced L for you and shall
Josh 16:10 day but have become slaves to do forced L
17:13 the Canaanites to forced L, and did not utterly
Judg 1:28 the Canaanites to forced L, but did not utterly
1:30 dwelt among them, and became subject to forced L
1:33 became subject to forced L for them.
1:35 upon them, and they became subject to forced L
2Sam 12:31 and set them to L with saws and iron
20:24 charge of the forced L; and Jehoshaphat the son
1Kgs 4:6 of Abda was in charge of the forced L
5:13 a levy of forced L out of all Israel;
9:15 account of the forced L which King Solomon levied
11:28 over all the forced L of the house of
12:18 taskmaster over the forced L, and all Israel stoned
1Chr 20:3 and set them to L with saws and iron
2Chr 10:18 taskmaster over the forced L, and the people of
Neh 4:22 by night and may L by day."
5:13 house and from his L who does not perform
Job 9:29 why then do I L in vain?
39:11 great, and will you leave to him your L
39:16 not hers; though her L be in vain, yet
Ps 78:46 the fruit of their L to the locust.
104:23 work and to his L until the evening.
107:12 bowed down with hard L; they fell down, with
127:1 those who build it L in vain.
128:2 the fruit of the L of your hands; you
Prov 12:24 while the slothful will be put to forced L
21:25 sluggard kills him for his hands refuse to L
Wis 9:16 hand we find with L; but who has traced
Sir 7:15 Do not hate toilsome L, or farm work, which
19:11 like a woman in L with a child.
40:1 Much L was created for every man, and a
Is 22:4 bitter tears; do not L to comfort me for
31:8 his young men shall be put to forced L
55:2 not bread, and your L for that which does
65:23 They shall not L in vain, or bear children
66:7 "Before she was in L she gave birth; before
66:8 as Zion was in L she brought forth her
Jer 30:6 hands on his loins like a woman in L
51:58 The peoples L for nought, and the nations weary
Ezek 23:29 the fruit of your L, and leave you naked
29:18 Babylon made his army L hard against Tyre; every
29:18 to pay for the L that he had performed
Jon 4:10 which you did not L, nor did you make
Hab 2:13 of hosts that peoples L only for fire, and
Mt 11:28 to me, all who L and are heavy laden,
Jn 4:38 which you did not L; others have labored, and
4:38 have labored, and you have entered into their L
6:27 Do not L for the food which perishes, but
1Cor 3:8 each shall receive his wages according to his L
4:12 and homeless, and we L, working with our own
15:58 in the Lord your L is not in vain.
Eph 4:28 but rather let him L, doing honest work with
Phil 1:22 flesh, that means fruitful L for me.
2:16 run in vain or L in vain.
1Thes 1:3 work of faith and L of love and steadfastness
2:9 For you remember our L and toil, brethren; we
3:5 you and that our L would be in vain.
5:12 to respect those who L among you and are
2Thes 3:8 but with toil and L we worked night and
1Tim 5:17 honor, especially those who L in preaching and

LABORED (17)
Josh 24:13 which you had not L, and cities which you
2Chr 24:13 engaged in the work L, and the repairing went
Neh 4:17 each with one hand L on the work and
4:21 So we L at the work, and half of
Sir 24:32 that I have not L for myself alone, but
33:17 that I have not L for myself alone, but
51:27 eyes that I have L little and found myself
Is 47:12 with which you have L from your youth; perhaps
47:15 with whom you have L, who have trafficked with
49:4 I said, "I have L in vain, I have
62:8 for which you have L;
Jer 3:24 for which our fathers L, their flocks and their
Ezek 29:20 recompense for which he L, because they worked for
Dan 6:14 deliver Daniel; and he L till the sun went
Jn 4:38 not labor; others have L, and you have entered
Gal 4:11 am afraid I have L over you in vain.
Phil 4:3 women, for they have L side by side with

LABORER (7)
Jud 4:10 resident alien and hired L and purchased slave–they
Eccl 5:12 the sleep of a L, whether he eats little
Sir 7:20 faithfully, or a hired L who devotes himself to
Mt 10:10 a staff; for the L deserves his food.
Lk 10:7 they provide, for the L deserves his wages; do
1Cor 16:16 such men and to every fellow worker and L
1Tim 5:18 and, "The L deserves his wages."

LABORERS (8)
Mt 9:37 is plentiful, but the L are few;
9:38 harvest to send out L into his harvest."
20:1 the morning to hire L for his vineyard.
20:2 After agreeing with the L for a denarius a
20:8 his steward, 'Call the L and pay them their
Lk 10:2 is plentiful, but the L are few; pray therefore
10:2 harvest to send out L into his harvest.
Jas 5:4 the wages of the L who mowed your fields,

LABORIOUS (12)
Lev 23:7 you shall do no L work.
23:8 you shall do no L work."
23:21 you shall do no L work: it is a
23:25 You shall do no L work; and you shall
23:35 you shall do no L work.
23:36 you shall do no L work.
Num 28:18 you shall do no L work,
28:25 you shall do no L work.
28:26 you shall do no L work,
29:1 you shall do no L work.
29:12 you shall do no L work, and you shall
29:35 you shall do no L work,

LABORIOUSLY
Wis 15:7 the soft earth and L molds each vessel for

LABORS (20)
Deut 28:33 and of all your L; and you shall be
Prov 5:10 your strength, and your L go to the house
Eccl 2:20 the toil of my L under the sun,
Wis 3:11 hope is vain, their L are unprofitable, and their
3:15 the fruit of good L is renowned, and the
5:1 him, and those who make light of his L
8:7 one loves righteousness, her L are virtues; for she
8:18 delight, and in the L of her hands, unfailing
10:10 prospered him in his L, and increased the fruit
10:17 the reward of their L; she guided them along
Sir 14:15 the fruit of your L to another, and what
16:25 weary, and they do not cease from their L
38:27 and master workman who L by night as well
Bar 3:18 and are anxious, whose L are beyond measure?
Hag 1:11 upon men and cattle, and upon all their L
2Cor 6:5 beatings, imprisonments, tumults, L, watching,
10:15 limit, in other men's L; but our hope is
11:23 madman–with far greater L, far more
Heb 4:10 also ceases from his L as God did from
Rev 14:13 may rest from their L, for their deeds follow

LACE (4)
Ex 28:28 the ephod with a L of blue, that it
28:37 the turban by a L of blue; it shall
39:21 the ephod with a L of blue, so that
39:31 tied to it a L of blue, to fasten

L

LACEDAEMONIANS
2Mac 5:9 to go to the L in hope of finding

LACHISH (24)
Josh 10:3 to Japhia king of L, and to Debir king
10:5 Jarmuth, the king of L, and the king of
10:23 Jarmuth, the king of L, and the king of
10:31 Israel with him, to L, and laid siege to
10:32 and the LORD gave L into the hand of
10:33 came up to help L; and Joshua smote him
10:34 with all Israel from L to Eglon; and they
10:35 destroyed that day, as he had done to L
12:11 one; the king of L, one;
15:39 Dilean, Mizpeh, Joktheel, L, Bozkath, Eglon,
2Kgs 14:19 against him in Jerusalem, and he fled to L
14:19 sent after him to L, and slew him there.
18:14 king of Assyria at L, saying, "I have done
18:17 a great army from L to King Hezekiah at
19:8 for he heard that the king had left L
2Chr 11:9 Gath, Mareshah, Ziph, Adoraim, L, Azekah,
25:27 against him in Jerusalem, and he fled to L
25:27 sent after him to L, and slew him there.
32:9 Assyria, who was besieging L with all his forces,
Neh 11:30 Adullam, and their villages, L and its fields, and
Is 36:2 sent the Rabshakeh from L to King Hezekiah at
37:8 he had heard that the king had left L
Jer 34:7 Judah that were left, L and Azekah; for these
Mic 1:13 chariots, inhabitants of L; you were the beginning

LACK (36)
Gen 18:28 the whole city for L of five?" And he
Ex 16:18 gathered little had no L; each gathered according to
Deut 8:9 in which you will L nothing, a land whose
Judg 18:10 where there is no L of anything that is
19:19 servants; there is no L of anything."
1Sam 21:15 Do I L madmen, that you have brought this
Jud 8:9 they were faint for L of water, and when
Job 4:11 strong lion perishes for L of prey, and the
31:19 any one perish for L of clothing, or a
38:41 and wander about for L of food?
Ps 34:10 who seek the LORD L no good thing.
Prov 5:23 He dies for L of discipline, and because of
10:21 but fools die for L of sense.
26:20 For L of wood the fire goes out; and
31:11 he will have no L of gain.
Wis 11:17 formless matter, did not L the means to send
15:18 when judged by their L of intelligence;
Sir 19:25 And if by L of strength he is prevented
23:10 under torture will not L bruises, so also the
Is 24:11 in the streets for L of wine; all joy
50:2 their fish stink for L of water, and die
Jer 33:17 LORD: David shall never L a man to sit
33:18 Levitical priests shall never L a man in my
35:19 of Rechab shall never L a man to stand
Ezek 4:17 this that they may L bread and water, and
Hos 4:6 people are destroyed for L of knowledge; because
Amos 4:6 all your cities, and L of bread in all
1Mac 2:61 trust in him will L strength.
Mt 19:20 these I have observed; what do I still L
Mk 10:21 said to him, "You L one thing; go, sell
Lk 18:22 he said to him, "One thing you still L
22:35 sandals, did you L anything?" They said, "Nothing."
1Cor 7:5 Satan tempt you through L of self-control.
2Cor 8:15 over, and he who gathered little had no L
Tit 3:13 way; see that they L nothing.
Jas 2:15 is ill-clad and in L of daily food,

LACKED (5)
Deut 2:7 with you; you have L nothing.'
1Kgs 11:22 him, "What have you L with me that you
Neh 9:21 the wilderness, and they L nothing; their clothes did
Wis 19:4 which their torments still L,
Jer 44:18 to her, we have L everything and have been

LACKING (18)
Gen 18:28 Suppose five of the fifty righteous are L
Lev 2:13 with your God be L from your cereal offering;
Judg 18:7 Sidonians, quiet and unsuspecting, L nothing that is
21:3 be today one tribe L in Israel?"
1Kgs 4:27 one in his month; they let nothing be L
Prov 10:19 many, transgression is not L, but he who restrains
Eccl 1:15 straight, and what is L cannot be numbered.
9:8 let not oil be L on your head.
Sir 3:13 even if he is L in understanding, show forbearance;
14:10 bread, and it is L at his table.
37:21 Lord, since he is L in all wisdom.
47:23 ample in folly and L in understanding, Rehoboam,
51:24 you say you are L in these things, and
Is 59:15 Truth is L, and he who departs from evil
1Cor 1:7 that you are not L in any spiritual gift,
Col 1:24 I complete what is L in Christ's afflictions for
1Thes 3:10 and supply what is L in your faith?
Jas 1:4 be perfect and complete, L in nothing.

LACKS (18)
2Sam 3:29 the sword, or who L bread!"
Prov 10:13 back of him who L sense.
11:12 who belittles his neighbor L sense, but a man
12:9 the great man but L bread.
28:16 A ruler who L understanding is a cruel oppressor;
Eccl 6:2 honor, so that he L nothing of all that
10:3 on the road, he L sense, and he says
Song 7:2 rounded bowl that never L mixed wine.
Wis 14:4 even if a man L skill, he may put
Sir 10:26 goes about boasting, but L bread.
11:12 and needs help, who L strength and abounds in
19:20 a fool who merely L wisdom.
19:21 the God-fearing man who L intelligence, than the
22:9 the dead, for he L the light; and weep
22:9 the fool, for he L intelligence; weep less bitterly
25:2 adulterous old man who L good sense.
Jas 1:5 If any of you L wisdom, let him ask
2Pet 1:9 For whoever L these things is blind and shortsighted

LAD (38)
Gen 21:12 displeased because of the L and because of your
21:17 the voice of the L; and the angel of
21:17 the voice of the L where he is.
21:18 Arise, lift up the L, and hold him fast
21:19 water, and gave the L a drink.
21:20 God was with the L, and he grew up;
22:5 ass; I and the L will go yonder and
22:12 your hand on the L or do anything to
37:2 brothers; he was a L with the sons of
37:30 brothers, and said, "The L is gone; and I,
42:22 not tell you not to sin against the L
43:8 his father, "Send the L with me, and we
44:22 to my lord, 'The L cannot leave his father,
44:30 my father, and the L is not with us,
44:30 bound up in the L's life,
44:31 he sees that the L is not with us,
44:32 became surety for the L to my father, saying,
44:33 remain instead of the L as a slave to
44:33 lord; and let the L go back with his
44:34 my father if the L is not with me?
Judg 16:26 Samson said to the L who held him by
1Sam 20:21 I will send the L, saying, 'Go, find the
20:21 I say to the L, 'Look, the arrows are
20:35 appointment with David, and with him a little L
20:36 he said to his L, "Run and find the
20:36 As the L ran, he shot an arrow beyond
20:37 And when the L came to the place of
20:37 Jonathan called after the L and said, "Is not
20:38 Jonathan called after the L, "Hurry, make haste, stay
20:38 So Jonathan's L gathered up the arrows, and came
20:39 But the L knew nothing; only Jonathan and David
20:40 his weapons to his L, and said to him,
20:41 as soon as the L had gone, David rose
2Sam 17:18 But a L saw them, and told Absalom; so
Tob 10:4 said to him, "The L has perished; his long
Dan 13:45 spirit of a young L named Daniel;
Jn 6:9 him, "There is a L here who has five
Acts 20:12 And they took the L away alive, and were

LADAN (7)
1Chr 7:26 son, Tahan his son, L his son, Ammihud his
23:7 sons of Gershom were L and Shimei.
23:8 The sons of L: Jehiel the chief, and Zetham,
23:9 were the heads of the fathers' houses of L
26:21 The sons of L, the sons of the Gershonites
26:21 the Gershonites belonging to L, the heads of the
26:21 fathers' houses belonging to L the Gershonite:

LADDER (2)
Gen 28:12 that there was a L set up on the
1Mac 11:59 made governor from the L of Tyre to the

LADDERS
1Mac 5:30 not be counted, carrying L and engines of war

LADEN (5)
1Sam 16:20 Jesse took an ass L with bread, and a

Neh 4:17 who carried burdens were L in such a way
Is 1:4 sinful nation, a people L with iniquity, offspring of
Ezek 27:25 were filled and heavily L in the heart of
Mt 11:28 labor and are heavy L, and I will give

LADIES (3)

Judg 5:29 his chariots?' Her wisest L make answer, nay, she
Esth 1:18 This very day the L of Persia and Media
Ps 45:9 kings are among your L of honor; at your

LADS

Gen 48:16 all evil, bless the L; and in them let

LADY (2)

2Jn 1:1 elder to the elect L and her children, whom
1:5 now I beg you, L, not as though I

LAEL

Num 3:24 Eliasaph, the son of L as head of the

LAGGARDS

1Mac 5:53 Judas kept rallying the L and encouraging the people

LAGGED

Deut 25:18 your rear all who L behind you; and he

LAHAD

1Chr 4:2 and Jahath was the father of Ahumai and L

LAHMAM

Josh 15:40 Lachish, Bozkath, Eglon, Cabbon, L, Chitlish,

LAHMI

1Chr 20:5 son of Jair slew L the brother of Goliath

LAID (263)

L

Gen 9:23 Japheth took a garment, L it upon both their
15:10 them in two, and L each half over against
22:6 the burnt offering, and L it on Isaac his
22:9 an altar there, and L the wood in order,
22:9 Isaac his son, and L him on the altar,
30:41 flock were breeding Jacob L the rods in the
39:16 Then she L up his garment by her until
48:14 his right hand and L it upon the head
48:17 saw that his father L his right hand upon
Ex 5:9 Let heavier work be L upon the men that
16:24 So they L it by till the morning, as
21:30 If a ransom is L on him, then he
21:30 his life whatever is L upon him.
Lev 8:14 Aaron and his sons L their hands upon the
8:18 Aaron and his sons L their hands on the
8:22 Aaron and his sons L their hands on the
10:1 fire in it, and L incense on it, and
Num 16:18 fire in them and L incense upon them, and
21:30 as Dibon, and we L waste until fire spread
27:23 whole congregation, and he L his hands upon him,
Deut 26:6 and afflicted us, and L upon us hard bondage.
32:34 "Is not this L up in store with me,
34:9 wisdom, for Moses had L his hands upon him;
Josh 2:6 flax which she had L in order on the
2:19 if a hand is L upon any one who
4:8 where they lodged, and L them down there.
6:26 Joshua L an oath upon them at that time,
7:23 of Israel; and they L them down before the
10:31 him, to Lachish, and L siege to it, and
10:34 to Eglon; and they L siege to it, and
Judg 6:26 stronghold here, with stones L in due order; then
9:24 and their blood be L upon Abimelech their brother,
9:34 up by night, and L wait against Shechem in
9:43 into three companies, and L wait in the fields;
9:48 took it up and L it on his shoulder.
Ruth 3:15 measures of barley, and L it upon her; then
4:16 took the child and L him in her bosom,
1Sam 10:25 in a book and L it up before the
14:24 that day; for Saul L an oath on the
15:27 to go away, Saul L hold upon the skirt
19:13 took an image and L it on the bed
25:18 cakes of figs, and L them on asses.
2Sam 13:19 she wore; and she L her hand on her
22:16 of the world were L bare, at the rebuke
1Kgs 1:51 for, lo, he has L hold of the horns
3:20 your maidservant slept, and L it in her bosom,
3:20 in her bosom, and L her dead son in
6:37 of the LORD was L, in the month of
9:9 land of Egypt, and L hold on other gods,
11:30 Then Ahijah L hold of the new garment that
12:11 now, whereas my father L upon you a heavy
13:29 man of God and L it upon the ass,
13:30 And he L the body in his own grave;
16:34 Bethel built Jericho; he L its foundation at the
17:19 where he lodged, and L him upon his own
18:33 bull in pieces and L it on the wood.
2Kgs 4:21 she went up and L him on the bed
4:31 went on ahead and L the staff upon the
5:23 two festal garments, and L them upon two of
11:16 So they L hands on her; and she went
13:16 And Elisha L his hands upon the king's hands.
19:17 kings of Assyria have L waste the nations and
23:33 reign in Jerusalem, and L upon the land a
25:1 army against Jerusalem, and L siege to it; and
2Chr 7:22 land of Egypt, and L hold on other gods,
8:16 of the LORD was L until it was finished.
10:11 now, whereas my father L upon you a heavy
16:14 They L him on a bier which had been
23:15 So they L hands on her; and she went
24:9 the servant of God L upon Israel in the
29:23 the assembly, and they L their hands upon them,
31:6 LORD their God, and L them in heaps.
36:3 him in Jerusalem and L upon the land a
Ezra 3:6 the temple of the LORD was not yet L
3:10 And when the builders L the foundation of the
3:11 foundation of the house of the LORD was L
3:12 of this house being L, though many shouted aloud
4:15 why this city was L waste.
5:8 stones, and timber is L in the walls; this
5:16 this Shesh-bazzar came and L the foundations of the
Neh 3:3 the Fish Gate; they L its beams and set
3:6 the Old Gate; they L its beams and set
5:15 who were before me L heavy burdens upon the
Esth 9:10 the Jews; but they L no hand on the
9:15 in Susa; but they L no hands on the
9:16 hated them; but they L no hands on the
9:31 and as they had L down for themselves and
10:1 King Ahasuerus L tribute on the land and on
Job 6:2 and all my calamity L in the balances!
14:10 man dies, and is L low; man breathes his
15:20 the years that are L up for the ruthless.
16:15 my skin, and have L my strength in the
20:26 Utter darkness is L up for his treasures; a
29:9 refrained from talking, and L their hand on their
34:13 the earth and who L on him the whole
38:4 were you when I L the foundation of the
38:6 bases sunk, or who L its cornerstone,
41:9 is disappointed; he is L low even at the
Ps 18:15 of the world were L bare, at thy rebuke,
31:19 goodness, which thou hast L up for those who
78:31 strongest of them, and L low the picked men
79:1 holy temple; they have L Jerusalem in ruins.
79:7 have devoured Jacob, and L waste his habitation.
89:40 his walls; thou hast L his strongholds in ruins.
104:3 a tent, who hast L the beams of thy
116:3 the pangs of Sheol L hold on me; I
119:11 I have L up thy word in my heart,
119:110 The wicked have L a snare for me, but
141:9 trap which they have L for me, and from
Prov 7:26 a victim has she L low; yea, all her
13:22 the sinner's wealth is L up for the righteous.
Eccl 9:1 But all this I L to heart, examining it
Song 7:13 old, which I have L up for you, O
Sir 21:4 the proud will be L waste.
47:19 But you L your loins beside women, and through
50:2 He L the foundations for the high double walls,
Is 14:8 saying, 'Since you were L low, no hewer comes
14:12 the ground, you who L the nations low!
15:1 Because Ar is L waste in a night Moab
15:1 undone; because Kir is L waste in a night
15:7 and what they have L up they carry away
23:1 Tarshish, for Tyre is L waste, without house or
23:14 for your stronghold is L waste.
24:3 earth shall be utterly L waste and utterly despoiled;
32:19 city will be utterly L low.
37:18 kings of Assyria have L waste all the nations
44:28 and of the temple, 'Your foundation shall be L
48:13 My hand L the foundation of the earth, and
49:17 destroyers, and those who L you waste go forth
51:13 out the heavens and L the foundations of the
53:6 and the LORD has L on him the iniquity
60:12 nations shall be utterly L waste.
Jer 4:20 the whole land is L waste.
4:26 all its cities were L in ruins before the
9:10 wilderness, because they are L waste so that no
9:12 the land ruined and L waste like a wilderness,

	10:25	consumed him, and have L waste his habitation.
	18:22	to take me, and L snares for my feet.
	26:8	and all the people L hold of him, saying,
	48:1	Nebo, for it is L waste!
	48:20	Arnon, that Moab is L waste.
	49:3	Heshbon, for Ai is L waste!
	52:4	against Jerusalem, and they L siege to it and
Lam	2:5	destroyed all its palaces, L in ruins its strongholds;
	2:6	that of a garden, L in ruins the place
	3:28	silence when he has L it on him;
	4:6	moment, no hand being L on it.
Bar	3:20	understood her paths, nor L hold of her.
Ezek	11:7	slain whom you have L in the midst of
	12:20	inhabited cities shall be L waste, and the land
	13:14	its foundation will be L bare; when it falls,
	16:36	Because your shame was L bare and your nakedness
	19:7	ravaged their strongholds, and L waste their cities;
	21:29	for you--to be L on the necks of
	24:2	king of Babylon has L siege to Jerusalem this
	26:2	now that she is L waste,'
	26:19	make you a city L waste, like the cities
	29:12	among cities that are L waste.
	30:7	of cities that are L waste.
	32:19	Go down, and be L with the uncircumcised.'
	32:27	war, whose swords were L under their heads, and
	32:29	all their might are L with those who are
	32:32	therefore he shall be L among the uncircumcised,
	35:12	Israel, saying, 'They are L desolate, they are given
	39:21	hand which I have L on them.
	40:42	instruments were to be L with which the burnt
	40:43	the flesh of the offering was to be L
Dan	2:5	your houses shall be L in ruins.
	3:97	limb, and their houses L in ruins; for there
	6:17	stone was brought and L upon the mouth of
	13:34	of the people, and L their hands upon her
	14:1	When King Astyages was L with his fathers, Cyrus
Joel	1:7	It has L waste my vines, and splintered my
	1:10	The fields are L waste, the ground mourns; because
Amos	4:9	blight and mildew; I L waste your gardens and
	7:9	of Israel shall be L waste, and I will
Mic	5:1	a wall; siege is L against us; with a
Nah	1:5	melt; the earth is L waste before him, the
Zeph	1:13	plundered, and their houses L waste.
	2:14	cedar work will be L bare.
	3:6	in ruins; I have L waste their streets so
Hag	2:18	the LORD's temple was L, consider:
Zech	4:9	hands of Zerubbabel have L the foundation of this
	8:9	LORD of hosts was L, that the temple might
	10:11	of Assyria shall be L low, and the scepter
	11:3	of the Jordan is L waste!
Mal	1:3	hated Esau; I have L waste his hill country
1Mac	2:12	our glory have been L waste; the Gentiles have
2Mac	1:21	wood and what was L upon it.
	12:45	splendid reward that is L up for those who
	14:7	Therefore I have L aside my ancestral glory –
	15:27	in their hearts, they L low no less than
Mt	3:10	now the axe is L to the root of
	12:25	divided against itself is L waste, and no city
	19:15	And he L his hands on them and went
	26:50	they came up and L hands on Jesus and
	27:60	clean linen shroud, and L it in his own
Mk	6:5	there, except that he L his hands upon a
	6:29	took his body, and L it in a tomb.
	6:56	cities, or country, they L the sick in the
	8:23	on his eyes and L his hands upon him,
	8:25	Then again he L his hands upon his eyes;
	14:46	And they L hands on him and seized him.
	15:45	the linen shroud, and L him in a tomb
	15:46	the mother of Joses saw where he was L
	16:6	the place where they L him.
Lk	1:66	all who heard them L them up in their
	2:7	in swaddling cloths, and L him in a manger,
	3:9	now the axe is L to the root of
	4:40	to him; and he L his hands on every
	6:48	who dug deep, and L the foundation upon rock;
	11:17	divided against itself is L waste, and a divided
	12:19	you have ample goods L up for many years;
	13:13	And he L his hands upon her, and immediately
	14:29	Otherwise, when he has L a foundation, and is
	19:20	pound, which I kept L away in a napkin;
	23:25	from the country, and L on him the cross,
	23:52	a linen shroud, and L him in a rock-hewn
	23:52	tomb, where no one had ever yet been L
	23:54	how his body was L;
Jn	7:30	him; but no one L hands on him, because
	7:44	him, but no one L hands on him.
	11:34	said, "Where have you L him?" They said to
	13:4	God, rose from supper, L aside his garments, and
	19:41	new tomb where no one had ever been L
	19:42	close at hand, they L Jesus there.
	20:2	know where they have L him."
	20:13	know where they have L him."
	20:15	me where you have L him, and I will
Acts	3:2	being carried, whom they L daily at that gate
	4:35	what was sold and L it at the apostles'
	4:37	brought the money and L it at the apostles'
	5:2	only a part and L it at the apostles'
	5:15	into the streets, and L them on beds and
	6:6	and they prayed and L their hands upon them.
	7:16	back to Shechem and L in the tomb that
	7:58	him; and the witnesses L down their garments at
	8:17	Then they L their hands on them and they
	9:37	had washed her, they L her in an upper
	12:1	time Herod the king L violent hands upon some
	13:3	fasting and praying they L their hands on them
	13:29	from the tree, and L him in a tomb.
	13:36	fell asleep, and was L with his fathers, and
	19:6	And when Paul had L his hands upon them,
	21:27	all the crowd, and L hands on him,
	24:1	They L before the governor their case against Paul;
	24:13	our fathers, believing everything L down by the law
	25:14	there many days, Festus L Paul's case before the
	25:16	defense concerning the charge L against him.
1Cor	3:10	skilled master builder I L a foundation, and another
	3:11	than that which is L, which is Jesus Christ.
	9:16	For necessity is L upon me.
Gal	2:2	by revelation; and I L before them (but privately
Col	1:5	because of the hope L up for you in
1Tim	1:9	the law is not L down for the just
	4:14	the council of elders L their hands upon you.
2Tim	4:8	Henceforth there is L up for me the crown
Heb	4:13	all are open and L bare to the eyes
Jas	5:3	You have L up treasure for the last days.
1Jn	3:16	know love, that he L down his life for
Rev	1:17	But he L his right hand upon me, saying,
	18:17	this wealth has been L waste." And all shipmasters
	18:19	hour she has been L waste.

LAIN (12)

Gen	26:10	people might easily have L with your wife, and
Num	5:19	'If no man has L with you, and if
	5:20	than your husband has L with you,
Judg	21:11	every woman that has L with a male you
Job	3:13	then I should have L down and been quiet;
	31:9	woman, and I have L in wait at my
Jer	3:2	have you not been L with?
Bar	6:43	the passers-by and is L with, she derides the
Ezek	23:8	her youth men had L with her and handled
Jon	1:5	the ship and had L down, and was fast
Jn	20:12	body of Jesus had L, one at the head
	21:20	Jesus loved, who had L close to his breast

LAIR (3)

Jer	9:11	heap of ruins, a L of jackals; and I
	10:22	Judah a desolation, a L of jackals.
Zeph	2:15	she has become, a L for wild beasts!

LAIRS

Job	37:8	beasts go into their L, and remain in their

LAISH (6)

Judg	18:7	departed, and came to L, and saw the people
	18:14	out the country of L said to their brethren,
	18:27	the Danites came to L, to a people quiet
	18:29	of the city was L at the first.
1Sam	25:44	Palti the son of L, who was of Gallim.
2Sam	3:15	her from her husband Paltiel the son of L

LAISHAH

Is	10:30	Hearken, O L

LAKE (14)

Deut	33:23	the LORD, possess the L and the south."
Job	14:11	waters fail from a L, and a river wastes
2Mac	12:16	so that the adjoining L, a quarter of a
Lk	5:1	was standing by the L of Gennesaret.
	5:2	two boats by the L; but the fishermen had
	8:22	go across to the other side of the L
	8:23	came down on the L, and they were filling
	8:33	steep bank into the L and were drowned.
Rev	19:20	thrown alive into the L of fire that burns
	20:10	was thrown into the L of fire and sulphur

L

	20:14	were thrown into the L of fire.
	20:14	the second death, the L of fire;
	20:15	was thrown into the L of fire.
	21:8	shall be in the L that burns with fire

LAKKUM

Josh	19:33	Jabneel, as far as L; and it ended at

LAMA (2)

Mt	27:46	loud voice, "Eli, Eli, L sabach-thani?" that is, "My
Mk	15:33	"Elo-i, Elo-i, L sabach-thani?" which means, "My

LAMB (113)

Gen	22:7	but where is the L for a burnt offering?"
	22:8	will provide himself the L for a burnt offering,
	30:32	sheep and every black L, and the spotted and
	30:35	on it, and every L that was black, and
Ex	12:3	take every man a L according to their fathers'
	12:3	their fathers' houses, a L for a household;
	12:4	too small for a L, then a man and
	12:4	eat you shall make your count for the L
	12:5	Your L shall be without blemish, a male a
	12:21	according to your families, and kill the passover L
	13:13	shall redeem with a L, or if you will
	29:39	One L you shall offer in the morning, and
	29:39	morning, and the other L you shall offer in
	29:40	and with the first L a tenth measure of
	29:41	And the other L you shall offer in the
	34:20	shall redeem with a L, or if you will
Lev	3:7	If he offers a L for his offering, then
	4:32	"If he brings a L as his offering for
	4:35	the fat of the L is removed from the
	5:6	from the flock, a L or a goat, for
	5:7	he cannot afford a L, then he shall bring,
	9:3	a calf and a L, both a year old
	12:6	tent of meeting a L a year old for
	12:8	she cannot afford a L, then she shall take
	14:10	blemish, and one ewe L a year old without
	14:13	he shall kill the L in the place where
	14:21	shall take one male L for a guilt offering
	14:24	priest shall take the L of the guilt offering,
	14:25	he shall kill the L of the guilt offering;
	17:3	an ox or a L or a goat in
	22:23	A bull or a L which has a part
	23:12	shall offer a male L a year old without
Num	6:12	and bring a male L a year old for
	6:14	the LORD, one male L a year old without
	6:14	offering, and one ewe L a year old without
	7:15	one ram, one male L a year old, for
	7:21	one ram, one male L a year old, for
	7:27	one ram, one male L a year old, for
	7:33	one ram, one male L a year old, for
	7:39	one ram, one male L a year old, for
	7:45	one ram, one male L a year old, for
	7:51	one ram, one male L a year old, for
	7:57	one ram, one male L a year old, for
	7:63	one ram, one male L a year old, for
	7:69	one ram, one male L a year old, for
	7:75	one ram, one male L a year old, for
	7:81	one ram, one male L a year old, for
	15:5	burnt offering, or for the sacrifice, for each L
	28:4	The one L you shall offer in the morning,
	28:4	morning, and the other L you shall offer in
	28:7	a hin for each L; in the holy place
	28:8	The other L you shall offer in the evening;
	28:13	cereal offering for every L; for a burnt offering
	28:14	a hin for a L; this is the burnt
1Sam	7:9	Samuel took a sucking L and offered it as
	17:34	bear, and took a L from the flock,
2Sam	12:3	but one little ewe L, which he had bought.
	12:4	took the poor man's L, and prepared it for
	12:6	he shall restore the L fourfold, because he did
2Chr	30:15	they killed the passover L on the fourteenth day
	30:17	to kill the passover L for every one who
	35:1	they killed the passover L on the fourteenth day
	35:6	And kill the passover L, and sanctify yourselves, and
	35:11	they killed the passover L, and the priests sprinkled
	35:13	they roasted the passover L with fire according to
Ezra	6:20	they killed the passover L for all the returned
Sir	13:16	What fellowship has a wolf with a L
	46:16	side, and he offered in sacrifice a sucking L
Is	11:6	shall dwell with the L, and the leopard shall
	53:7	his mouth; like a L that is led to
	65:25	The wolf and the L shall feed together, the
	66:3	he who sacrifices a L, like him who breaks
Jer	11:19	was like a gentle L led to the slaughter.
Ezek	46:13	"He shall provide a L a year old without
	46:15	Thus the L and the meal offering and the
Hos	4:16	feed them like a L in a broad pasture?
Mk	14:12	they sacrificed the passover L, his disciples said to
Lk	22:7	on which the passover L had to be sacrificed.
Jn	1:29	and said, "Behold, the L of God, who takes
	1:36	and said, "Behold, the L of God!"
Acts	8:32	the slaughter or a L before its shearer is
1Cor	5:7	For Christ, our paschal L, has been sacrificed.
1Pet	1:19	like that of a L without blemish or spot.
Rev	5:6	elders, I saw a L standing, as though it
	5:8	fell down before the L, each holding a harp,
	5:12	voice, "Worthy is the L who was slain, to
	5:13	throne and to the L be blessing and honor
	6:1	I saw when the L opened one of the
	6:16	the wrath of the L;
	7:9	throne and before the L, clothed in white robes,
	7:10	who sits upon the throne, and to the L
	7:14	made them white in the blood of the L
	7:17	For the L in the midst of the throne
	8:1	When the L opened the seventh seal, there was
	12:11	the blood of the L and by the word
	13:8	of life of the L that was slain.
	13:11	two horns like a L and it spoke like
	14:1	Mount Zion stood the L, and with him a
	14:4	these who follow the L wherever he goes; these
	14:4	for God and the L,
	14:10	holy angels and in the presence of the L
	15:3	the song of the L, saying, "Great and wonderful
	17:14	make war on the L, and the Lamb will
	17:14	the Lamb, and the L will conquer them, for
	19:7	the marriage of the L has come, and his
	19:9	are invited to the marriage supper of the L
	21:9	show you the Bride, the wife of the L
	21:14	twelve names of the twelve apostles of the L
	21:22	is the Lord God the Almighty and the L
	21:23	is its light, and its lamp is the L
	21:27	are written in the L's book of life.
	22:1	God and of the L
	22:3	God and of the L shall be in it,

LAMBS (90)

Gen	21:28	Abraham set seven ewe L of the flock apart.
	21:29	of these seven ewe L which you have set
	21:30	said, "These seven ewe L you will take from
	30:33	and black among the L, if found with me,
	30:40	And Jacob separated the L, and set the faces
Ex	12:6	Israel shall kill their L in the evening.
	12:21	said to them, "Select L for yourselves according to
	29:38	upon the altar: two L a year old day
Lev	14:10	shall take two male L without blemish, and one
	14:12	one of the male L, and offer it for
	23:18	with the bread seven L a year old without
	23:19	offering, and two male L a year old as
	23:20	LORD, with the two L; they shall be holy
Num	7:17	goats, and five male L a year old.
	7:23	goats, and five male L a year old.
	7:29	goats, and five male L a year old.
	7:35	goats, and five male L a year old.
	7:41	goats, and five male L a year old.
	7:47	goats, and five male L a year old.
	7:53	goats, and five male L a year old.
	7:59	goats, and five male L a year old.
	7:65	goats, and five male L a year old.
	7:71	goats, and five male L a year old.
	7:77	goats, and five male L a year old.
	7:83	goats, and five male L a year old.
	7:87	twelve rams, twelve male L a year old, with
	7:88	goats sixty, the male L a year old sixty.
	15:11	each of the male L or the kids.
	28:3	the LORD: two male L a year old without
	28:9	sabbath day two male L a year old without
	28:11	one ram, seven male L a year old without
	28:19	ram, and seven male L a year old; see
	28:21	each of the seven L;
	28:27	one ram, seven male L a year old;
	28:29	each of the seven L;
	29:2	one ram, seven male L a year old without
	29:4	each of the seven L;
	29:8	one ram, seven male L a year old; they
	29:10	each of the seven L:
	29:13	two rams, fourteen male L a year old; they
	29:15	each of the fourteen L;
	29:17	two rams, fourteen male L a year old without
	29:18	rams, and for the L, by number, according to
	29:20	two rams, fourteen male L a year old without

29:21 rams, and for the L, by number, according to
29:23 two rams, fourteen male L a year old without
29:24 rams, and for the L, by number, according to
29:26 two rams, fourteen male L a year old without
29:27 rams, and for the L, by number, according to
29:29 two rams, fourteen male L a year old without
29:30 rams, and for the L, by number, according to
29:32 two rams, fourteen male L a year old without
29:33 rams, and for the L, by number, according to
29:36 one ram, seven male L a year old without
29:37 ram, and for the L, by number, according to
Deut 32:14 flock, with fat of L and rams, herds of
1Sam 15:9 the fatlings, and the L, and all that was
2Kgs 3:4 Israel a hundred thousand L, and the wool of
1Chr 29:21 rams, and a thousand L, with their drink offerings,
2Chr 29:21 bulls, seven rams, seven L, and seven he-goats for
29:22 and they killed the L and their blood was
29:32 rams, and two hundred L; all these were for
35:7 all that were present, L and kids from the
35:8 two thousand six hundred L and kids and three
35:9 passover offerings five thousand L and kids and five
Ezra 6:17 hundred rams, four hundred L, and as a sin
7:17 buy bulls, rams, and L, with their cereal offerings
8:35 Israel, ninety-six rams, seventy-seven L, and as a sin
Ps 114:4 The mountains skipped like rams, the hills like L
114:6 O hills, like L
Prov 27:26 mountains is gathered, the L will provide your
Wis 19:9 horses, and leaped like L, praising thee, O Lord,
Sir 47:3 with bears as with L of the flock.
Is 1:11 of bulls, or of L, or of he-goats.
5:17 Then shall the L graze as in their pasture,
16:1 They have sent L to the ruler of the
34:6 with the blood of L and goats, with the
40:11 he will gather the L in his arms, he
Jer 51:40 bring them down like L to the slaughter, like
Ezek 27:21 your favored dealers in L, rams, and goats; in
39:18 earth—of rams, of L, and of goats, of
46:4 day shall be six L without blemish and a
46:5 cereal offering with the L shall be as much
46:6 without blemish, and six L and a ram, which
46:7 ram, and with the L as much as he
46:11 ephah, and with the L as much as one
Dan 3:39 of thousands of fat L;
Amos 6:4 their couches, and eat L from the flock, and
Lk 10:3 send you out as L in the midst of
Jn 21:15 He said to him, "Feed my L

LAME (31)

Lev 21:18 a man blind or L, or one who has
Deut 15:21 blemish, if it is L or blind, or has
2Sam 4:4 fled in her haste, he fell, and became L
5:6 the blind and the L will ward you off"—
5:8 shaft to attack the L and the blind, who
5:8 "The blind and the L shall not come into
9:13 Now he was L in both his feet.
19:26 go with the king.' For your servant is L
Job 29:15 eyes to the blind, and feet to the L
Prov 26:7 Like a L man's legs, which hang useless, is
Is 33:23 be divided; even the L will take the prey.
35:6 unstopped; then shall the L man leap like a
Jer 31:8 the blind and the L, the woman with child
Mic 4:6 I will assemble the L and gather those who
4:7 have afflicted; and the L I will make the
Zeph 3:19 I will save the L and gather the outcast,
Mal 1:8 offer those that are L or sick, is that
1:13 by violence or is L or sick, and this
Mt 11:5 their sight and the L walk, lepers are cleansed
15:30 bringing with them the L, the maimed, the blind,
15:31 the maimed whole, the L walking, and the blind
18:8 enter life maimed or L than with two hands
21:14 the blind and the L came to him in
Mk 9:44 you to enter life L than with two feet
Lk 7:22 receive their sight, the L walk, lepers are cleansed,
14:13 poor, the maimed, the L, the blind,
14:21 maimed and blind and L
Jn 5:3 multitude of invalids, blind, L, paralyzed.
Acts 3:2 And a man L from birth was being carried,
8:7 who were paralyzed or L were healed.
Heb 12:13 so that what is L may not be put

LAMECH (12)

Gen 4:18 of Me-thusha-el, and Me-thusha-el the father of L
4:19 And L took two wives; the name of the
4:23 L said to his wives: "Adah and Zillah, hear
4:23 voice; you wives of L, hearken to what I
4:24 is avenged sevenfold, truly L seventy-sevenfold."
5:25 and eighty-seven years, he became the father of L
5:26 after the birth of L seven hundred and eighty-two
5:28 When L had lived a hundred and eighty-two years,
5:30 L lived after the birth of Noah five hundred
5:31 all the days of L were seven hundred and
1Chr 1:3 Mahalalel, Jared, Enoch, Thuselah, L,
Lk 3:36 Noah, the son of L,

LAMENT (22)

Judg 11:40 year by year to L the daughter of Jephthah
2Chr 35:25 Jeremiah also uttered a L for Josiah; and all
Wis 18:10 back, and their piteous L for their children was
Sir 38:16 as one who is suffering grievously begin the L
Is 3:26 And her gates shall L and mourn; ravaged, she
19:8 fishermen will mourn and L, all who cast hook
Jer 4:8 gird you with sackcloth, L and wail; for the
9:20 to your daughters a L, and each to her
14:2 gates languish; her people L on the ground, and
16:5 mourning, or go to L, or bemoan them; for
16:6 and no one shall L for them or cut
22:18 Judah: "They shall not L for him, saying, 'Ah
22:18 sister!' They shall not L for him, saying, 'Ah
34:5 spices for you and L for you, saying, "Alas,
49:3 Gird yourselves with sackcloth, L, and run to and
Lam 2:8 rampart and wall to L, they languish together.
Ezek 27:32 lamentation for you, and L over you: 'Who was
Joel 1:8 L like a virgin girded with sackcloth for the
1:12 Gird on sackcloth and L, O priests, wail, O
Mic 1:8 For this I will L and wail; I will
1Mac 1:27 bridegroom took up the L; she who sat in
Jn 16:20 you will weep and L, but the world will

LAMENTATION (35)

Gen 50:10 very great and sorrowful L; and he made a
2Sam 1:17 David lamented with this L over Saul and Jonathan
11:26 was dead, she made L for her husband.
Tob 2:6 turned into mourning, and all your festivities into L
Jud 7:30 Then great and general L arose throughout the
Job 27:15 the pestilence buries, and their widows make no L
Ps 78:64 by the sword, and their widows made no L
Is 29:2 shall be moaning and L, and she shall be
Jer 6:26 only son, most bitter L; for suddenly the destroyer
7:29 it away; raise a L on the bare heights,
9:10 the mountains, and a L for the pastures of
31:15 is heard in Ramah, L and bitter weeping.
48:38 there is nothing but L; for I have broken
Lam 2:5 multiplied in the daughter of Judah mourning and L
Ezek 2:10 on it words of L and mourning and woe.
19:1 you, take up a L for the princes of
19:14 This is a L, and has become a lamentation.
19:14 This is a lamentation, and has become a L
26:17 they will raise a L over you, and say
27:2 of man, raise a L over Tyre,
27:32 wailing they raise a L for you, and lament
28:12 of man, raise a L over the king of
32:2 of man, raise a L over Pharaoh king of
32:16 This is a L which shall be chanted; the
Amos 5:1 up over you in L, O house of Israel:
5:16 who are skilled in L,
8:10 all your songs into L; I will bring sackcloth
Mic 1:8 naked; I will make L like the jackals, and
2:4 and wail with bitter L, and say, "We are
1Mac 2:70 And all Israel mourned for him with great L
4:39 and mourned with great L, and sprinkled themselves
9:20 all Israel made great L for him; they mourned
13:26 bewailed him with great L, and mourned for him
Mt 2:18 Ramah, wailing and loud L, Rachel weeping for her
Acts 8:2 Stephen, and made great L over him.

LAMENTATIONS (2)

Is 43:14 shouting of the Chaldeans will be turned to L
2Mac 11:6 all the people, with L and tears, besought the

LAMENTED (8)

Gen 50:10 beyond the Jordan, they L there with a very
1Sam 7:2 the house of Israel L after the LORD.
2Sam 1:17 And David L with this lamentation over Saul and
3:33 And the king L for Abner, saying, "Should Abner
Sir 51:19 to the heavens, and L my ignorance of her.
Jer 16:4 They shall not be L, nor shall they be
25:33 They shall not be L, or gathered, or buried;
Lk 23:26 women who bewailed and L him.

LAMENTING (4)

Esth 4:3 fasting and weeping and L, and most of them
9:31 descendants, with regard to their fasts and their L

Wis 19:3 at mourning, and were L at the graves of
Nah 2:7 carried off, her maidens L, moaning like doves, and

LAMENTS (3)

2Chr 35:25 of Josiah in their L to this day.
35:25 in Israel; behold, they are written in the L
Ps 35:14 about as one who L his mother, bowed down

LAMP (38)

Ex 27:20 the light, that a L may be set up
Lev 24:2 beaten olives for the L, that a light may
1Sam 3:3 his own place; the L of God had not
2Sam 21:17 lest you quench the L of Israel."
22:29 Yea, thou art my L, O LORD, and my
1Kgs 11:36 may always have a L before me in Jerusalem,
15:4 God gave him a L in Jerusalem, setting up
2Kgs 4:10 a chair, and a L, so that whenever he
8:19 promised to give a L to him and to
2Chr 21:7 promised to give a L to him and to
Job 18:6 his tent, and his L above him is put
21:17 is it that the L of the wicked is
29:3 over me; when his L shone upon my head,
Ps 18:28 thou dost light my L; the LORD my God
119:105 Thy word is a L to my feet and
132:17 I have prepared a L for my anointed.
Prov 6:23 the commandment is a L and the teaching a
13:9 righteous rejoices, but the L of the wicked will
20:20 or his mother, his L will be put out
20:27 of man is the L of the LORD, searching
21:4 a proud heart, the L of the wicked, are
24:20 has no future; the L of the wicked will
31:18 Her L does not go out at night.
Sir 26:17 Like the shining L on the holy lampstand, so
Jer 25:10 of the millstones and the light of the L
Mt 5:15 do men light a L and put it under
6:22 "The eye is the L of the body.
Mk 4:21 to them, "Is a L brought in to be
Lk 8:16 one after lighting a L covers it with a
11:33 one after lighting a L puts it in a
11:34 Your eye is the L of your body; when
11:36 bright, as when a L with its rays gives
15:8 does not light a L and sweep the house
Jn 5:34 a burning and shining L, and you were willing
2Pet 1:19 this as to a L shining in a dark
Rev 18:23 the light of a L shall shine in thee
21:23 its light, and its L is the Lamb.
22:5 need no light of L or sun, for the

LAMPS (36)

Ex 25:6 wood, oil for the L, spices for the anointing
25:37 shall make the seven L for it; and the
25:37 for it; and the L shall be set up
30:7 when he dresses the L he shall burn it,
30:8 Aaron sets up the L in the evening, he
35:14 its utensils and its L, and the oil for
37:23 he made its seven L and its snuffers and
39:37 pure gold and its L with the lamps set
39:37 its lamps with the L set and all its
Lev 24:4 He shall keep the L in order upon the
Num 4:9 the light, with its L, its snuffers, its trays,
8:2 you set up the L, the seven lamps shall
8:2 the lamps, the seven L shall give light in
8:3 he set up its L to give light in
1Kgs 7:49 sanctuary; the flowers, the L, and the tongs, of
1Chr 28:15 golden lampstands and their L, the weight of gold
28:15 each lampstand and its L, the weight of silver
28:15 a lampstand and its L, according to the use
2Chr 4:20 the lampstands and their L of pure gold to
4:21 prescribed; the flowers, the L, and the tongs, of
13:11 golden lampstand that its L may burn every evening;
29:7 and put out the L, and have not burned
Jud 10:22 the tent, with silver L carried before him.
Bar 6:19 They light L, even more than they light for
Zeph 1:12 will search Jerusalem with L, and I will punish
Zech 4:2 of it, and seven L on it, with seven
4:2 on each of the L which are on the
1Mac 4:50 altar and lighted the L on the lampstand, and
2Mac 1:8 and we lighted the L and we set out
10:3 burned incense and lighted L and set out the
Mt 25:1 maidens who took their L and went to meet
25:3 the foolish took their L, they took no oil
25:4 the wise took flasks of oil with their L
25:7 Then all those maidens rose and trimmed their L
25:8 your oil, for our L are going out.'
Lk 12:35 be girded and your L burning,

LAMPSTAND (38)

Ex 25:31 you shall make a L of pure gold.
25:31 the shaft of the L shall be made of
25:32 three branches of the L out of one side
25:32 three branches of the L out of the other
25:33 going out of the L;
25:34 lampstand; and on the L itself four cups made
25:35 of the six branches going out from the L
26:35 the veil, and the L on the south side
30:27 its utensils, and the L and its utensils, and
31:8 utensils, and the pure L with all its utensils,
35:14 of the Presence; the L also for the light,
37:17 He also made the L of pure gold.
37:17 the shaft of the L were made of hammered
37:18 three branches of the L out of one side
37:18 three branches of the L out of the other
37:19 for the six branches going out of the L
37:20 And on the L itself were four cups made
39:37 of the Presence; the L of pure gold and
Lev 24:4 in order upon the L of pure gold before
Num 3:31 ark, the table, the L, the altars, the vessels
4:9 blue, and cover the L for the light, with
8:2 lamps shall give light in front of the L
8:3 in front of the L, as the LORD commanded
8:4 the workmanship of the L, hammered work of gold;
8:4 LORD had shown Moses, so he made the L
1Chr 28:15 of gold for each L and its lamps, the
28:15 of silver for a L and its lamps, according
28:15 the use of each L in the service,
2Chr 13:11 care for the golden L that its lamps may
Sir 26:17 lamp on the holy L, so is a beautiful
Dan 5:5 king's palace, opposite the L; and the king saw
Zech 4:2 see, and behold, a L all of gold, with
4:11 on the right and the left of the L
1Mac 1:21 the golden altar, the L for the light, and
4:49 vessels, and brought the L, the altar of incense,
4:50 the lamps on the L, and these gave light
Heb 9:2 in which were the L and the table and
Rev 2:5 you and remove your L from its place, unless

LAMPSTANDS (11)

1Kgs 7:49 of the Presence, the L of pure gold, five
1Chr 28:15 weight of the golden L and their lamps, the
2Chr 4:7 he made ten golden L as prescribed, and set
4:20 of the Presence, the L and their lamps of
Jer 52:19 the pots, and the L, and the dishes for
Rev 1:12 I saw seven golden L,
1:13 the midst of the L one like a son
1:20 and the seven golden L, the seven stars are
1:20 churches and the seven L are the seven churches.
2:1 right hand, who walks among the seven golden L
11:4 trees and the two L which stand before the

LANCES (2)

1Kgs 18:28 custom with swords and L, until the blood gushed
2Mac 5:2 companies fully armed with L and drawn swords--

LAND (1,927)

Gen 1:9 and let the dry L appear." And it was
1:10 God called the dry L Earth, and the waters
2:11 flows around the whole L of Havilah, where there
2:12 the gold of that L is good; bdellium and
2:13 flows around the whole L of Cush.
4:16 and dwelt in the L of Nod, east of
7:22 everything on the dry L in whose nostrils was
10:10 of them in the L of Shinar.
10:11 From that L he went into Assyria, and built
11:2 a plain in the L of Shinar and settled
11:28 father Terah in the L of his birth, in
11:31 to go into the L of Canaan; but when
12:1 father's house to the L that I will show
12:5 to go to the L of Canaan.
12:5 had come to the L of Canaan,
12:6 Abram passed through the L to the place at
12:6 At that time the Canaanites were in the L
12:7 said, "To your descendants I will give this L
12:10 Now there was a famine in the L
12:10 there, for the famine was severe in the L
13:6 tents, so that the L could not support both
13:7 the Canaanites and the Perizzites dwelt in the L
13:9 Is not the whole L before you?
13:10 the LORD, like the L of Egypt, in the
13:12 Abram dwelt in the L of Canaan, while Lot
13:15 westward; for all the L which you see I
13:17 the breadth of the L, for I will give
15:7 to give you this L to possess."

15:13 be sojourners in a L that is not theirs,
15:18 descendants I give this L, from the river of
15:19 the river Euphrates, the L of the Kenites, the
16:3 ten years in the L of Canaan, Sarai, Abram's
17:8 descendants after you, the L of your sojournings, all
17:8 your sojournings, all the L of Canaan, for an
19:28 and toward all the L of the valley, and
19:28 the smoke of the L went up like the
20:15 Abimelech said, "Behold, my L is before you; dwell
21:21 for him from the L of Egypt.
21:23 me and with the L where you have sojourned."
21:32 and returned to the L of the Philistines.
21:34 many days in the L of the Philistines.
22:2 and go to the L of Moriah, and offer
23:2 is, Hebron) in the L of Canaan; and Abraham
23:7 bowed to the Hittites, the people of the L
23:12 Abraham bowed down before the people of the L
23:13 the people of the L, "But if you will,
23:15 me; a piece of L worth four hundred shekels
23:19 is, Hebron) in the L of Canaan.
24:5 follow me to this L; must I then take
24:5 son back to the L from which you came?"
24:7 house and from the L of my birth, and
24:7 I will give this L he will send his
24:37 the Canaanites, in whose L I dwell;
26:1 a famine in the L, besides the former famine
26:2 Egypt; dwell in the L of which I shall
26:3 Sojourn in this L, and I will be with
26:12 Isaac sowed in that L, and reaped in the
26:22 us, and we shall be fruitful in the L
27:46 the women of the L, what good will my
28:4 take possession of the L of your sojournings which
28:13 God of Isaac; the L on which you lie
28:15 you back to this L; for I will not
29:1 and came to the L of the people of
31:3 Jacob, "Return to the L of your fathers and
31:13 go forth from this L, and return to the
31:13 and return to the L of your birth.'"
31:18 to go to the L of Canaan to his
32:3 his brother in the L of Seir, the country
33:18 which is in the L of Canaan, on his
33:19 money the piece of L on which he had
34:1 the women of the L;
34:2 the prince of the L, saw her, he seized
34:10 with us; and the L shall be open to
34:21 them dwell in the L and trade in it,
34:21 it, for behold, the L is large enough for
34:30 the inhabitants of the L, the Canaanites and the
35:6 which is in the L of Canaan, he and
35:12 The L which I gave to Abraham and Isaac
35:12 I will give the L to your descendants after
35:22 Israel dwelt in that L Reuben went and lay
36:5 to him in the L of Canaan.
36:6 had acquired in the L of Canaan; and he
36:6 he went into a L away from his brother
36:7 to dwell together; the L of their sojournings could
36:16 of Eliphaz in the L of Edom; they are
36:17 of Reuel in the L of Edom; they are
36:20 the inhabitants of the L: Lotan, Shobal, Zibeon,
36:21 of Seir in the L of Edom.
36:30 their clans in the L of Seir.
36:31 who reigned in the L of Edom, before any
36:34 and Husham of the L of the Temanites reigned
36:43 dwelling places in the L of their possession.
37:1 Jacob dwelt in the L of his father's sojournings,
37:1 father's sojournings, in the L of Canaan.
40:15 stolen out of the L of the Hebrews; and
41:19 seen in all the L of Egypt.
41:29 plenty throughout all the L of Egypt,
41:30 be forgotten in the L of Egypt; the famine
41:30 famine will consume the L,
41:31 be unknown in the L by reason of that
41:33 set him over the L of Egypt.
41:34 appoint overseers over the L, and take the fifth
41:34 the produce of the L of Egypt during the
41:36 a reserve for the L against the seven years
41:36 are to befall the L of Egypt, so that
41:36 Egypt, so that the L may not perish through
41:41 you over all the L of Egypt."
41:43 him over all the L of Egypt.
41:44 foot in all the L of Egypt."
41:45 went out over the L of Egypt.
41:46 went through all the L of Egypt.
41:48 was plenty in the L of Egypt, and stored
41:52 me fruitful in the L of my affliction."
41:53 that prevailed in the L of Egypt came to
41:54 but in all the L of Egypt there was
41:55 When all the L of Egypt was famished, the
41:56 spread over all the L, Joseph opened all the
41:56 was severe in the L of Egypt.
42:5 famine was in the L of Canaan.
42:6 was governor over the L; he it was who
42:6 who sold to all the people of the L
42:7 They said, "From the L of Canaan, to buy
42:9 have come to see the weakness of the L
42:12 the weakness of the L that you have come
42:13 one man in the L of Canaan; and behold,
42:29 their father in the L of Canaan, they told
42:30 the lord of the L, spoke roughly to us,
42:30 and took us to be spies of the L
42:32 our father in the L of Canaan.'
42:33 the lord of the L, said to us, 'By
42:34 your brother, and you shall trade in the L
43:1 Now the famine was severe in the L
43:11 choice fruits of the L in your bags, and
44:8 to you from the L of Canaan; how then
45:6 has been in the L these two years; and
45:8 ruler over all the L of Egypt.
45:10 shall dwell in the L of Goshen, and you
45:17 go back to the L of Canaan;
45:18 the best of the L of Egypt, and you
45:18 the fat of the L
45:19 take wagons from the L of Egypt for your
45:20 best of all the L of Egypt is yours.'"
45:25 and came to the L of Canaan to their
45:26 ruler over all the L of Egypt." And his
46:6 had gained in the L of Canaan, and came
46:12 Onan died in the L of Canaan); and the
46:20 to Joseph in the L of Egypt were born
46:28 they came into the L of Goshen.
46:31 who were in the L of Canaan, have come
46:34 may dwell in the L of Goshen; for every
47:1 have come from the L of Canaan; they are
47:1 are now in the L of Goshen."
47:4 to sojourn in the L; for there is no
47:4 is severe in the L of Canaan; and now,
47:4 servants dwell in the L of Goshen."
47:6 The L of Egypt is before you; settle your
47:6 the best of the L; let them dwell in
47:6 them dwell in the L of Goshen; and if
47:11 a possession in the L of Egypt, in the
47:11 the best of the L, in the land of
47:11 the land, in the L of Rameses, as Pharaoh
47:13 food in all the L; for the famine was
47:13 severe, so that the L of Egypt and the
47:13 of Egypt and the L of Canaan languished by
47:14 was found in the L of Egypt and in
47:14 Egypt and in the L of Canaan, for the
47:15 all spent in the L of Egypt and in
47:15 Egypt and in the L of Canaan, all the
47:19 die before your eyes, both we and our L
47:19 Buy us and our L for food, and we
47:19 and we with our L will be slaves to
47:19 die, and that the L may not be desolate."
47:20 Joseph bought all the L of Egypt for Pharaoh;
47:20 The L became Pharaohs;
47:22 Only the L of the priests he did not
47:22 gave them; therefore they did not sell their L
47:23 bought you and your L for Pharaoh.
47:23 seed for you, and you shall sow the L
47:26 a statute concerning the L of Egypt, and it
47:26 have the fifth; the L of the priests alone
47:27 Israel dwelt in the L of Egypt, in the
47:27 of Egypt, in the L of Goshen; and they
47:28 Jacob lived in the L of Egypt seventeen years;
48:3 at Luz in the L of Canaan and blessed
48:4 and will give this L to your descendants after
48:5 to you in the L of Egypt before I
48:7 sorrow died in the L of Canaan on the
48:21 you again to the L of your fathers.
49:15 good, and that the L was pleasant; so he
49:30 of Mamre, in the L of Canaan, which Abraham
50:5 for myself in the L of Canaan, there shall
50:7 the elders of the L of Egypt,
50:8 were left in the L of Goshen.
50:11 the inhabitants of the L, the Canaanites, saw the
50:13 carried him to the L of Canaan, and buried
50:24 up out of this L to the land which
50:24 this land to the L which he swore to

Ex 1:6 strong; so that the L was filled with them.
1:9 and fight against us and escape from the L
2:15 and stayed in the L of Midian; and he

2:22 "I have been a sojourner in a foreign L
3:8 up out of that L to a good and
3:8 a good and broad L, a land flowing with
3:8 and broad land, a L flowing with milk and
3:17 of Egypt, to the L of the Canaanites, the
3:17 and the Jebusites, a L flowing with milk and
4:20 went back to the L of Egypt; and in
5:5 the people of the L are now many and
5:12 abroad throughout all the L of Egypt, to gather
6:1 hand he will drive them out of his L
6:4 to give them the L of Canaan, the land
6:4 land of Canaan, the L in which they dwelt
6:8 bring you into the L which I swore to
6:11 the people of Israel go out of his L
6:13 Israel out of the L of Egypt.
6:26 of Israel from the L of Egypt by their
6:28 to Moses in the L of Egypt,
7:2 the people of Israel go out of his L
7:3 and wonders in the L of Egypt,
7:4 Israel, out of the L of Egypt by great
7:19 blood throughout all the L of Egypt, both in
7:21 blood throughout all the L of Egypt.
8:5 to come upon the L of Egypt!'"
8:6 up and covered the L of Egypt.
8:7 brought frogs upon the L of Egypt.
8:14 in heaps, and the L stank.
8:16 gnats throughout all the L of Egypt.'"
8:17 gnats throughout all the L of Egypt.
8:22 will set apart the L of Goshen, where my
8:24 and in all the L of Egypt the land
8:24 land of Egypt the L was ruined by reason
8:25 said, "Go, sacrifice to your God within the L
9:5 the LORD will do this thing in the L
9:9 dust over all the L of Egypt, and become
9:9 beast throughout all the L of Egypt."
9:22 hail in all the L of Egypt, upon man
9:22 the field, throughout the L of Egypt."
9:23 rained hail upon the L of Egypt;
9:24 been in all the L of Egypt since it
9:25 field throughout all the L of Egypt, both man
9:26 Only in the L of Goshen, where the people
10:5 the face of the L, so that no one
10:5 one can see the L; and they shall eat
10:12 your hand over the L of Egypt for the
10:12 may come upon the L of Egypt, and eat
10:12 every plant in the L, all that the hail
10:13 his rod over the L of Egypt, and the
10:13 east wind upon the L all that day and
10:14 up over all the L of Egypt, and settled
10:15 face of the whole L, so that the land
10:15 land, so that the L was darkened, and they
10:15 the plants in the L and all the fruit
10:15 field, through all the L of Egypt.
10:21 be darkness over the L of Egypt, a darkness
10:22 darkness in all the L of Egypt three days;
11:3 very great in the L of Egypt, in the
11:5 the first-born in the L of Egypt shall die,
11:6 cry throughout all the L of Egypt, such as
11:9 be multiplied in the L of Egypt."
11:10 the people of Israel go out of his L
12:1 and Aaron in the L of Egypt,
12:12 will pass through the L of Egypt that night,
12:12 the first-born in the L of Egypt, both man
12:13 when I smite the L of Egypt.
12:17 hosts out of the L of Egypt: therefore you
12:19 is a sojourner or a native of the L
12:25 you come to the L which the LORD will
12:29 the first-born in the L of Egypt, from the
12:33 them out of the L in haste; for they
12:41 went out from the L of Egypt.
12:42 them out of the L of Egypt; so this
12:48 he shall be as a native of the L
12:51 Israel out of the L of Egypt by their
13:5 brings you into the L of the Canaanites, the
13:5 to give you, a L flowing with milk and
13:11 brings you into the L of the Canaanites, as
13:15 the first-born in the L of Egypt, both the
13:17 by way of the L of the Philistines, although
13:18 up out of the L of Egypt equipped for
14:3 are entangled in the L; the wilderness has shut
14:21 made the sea dry L, and the waters were
16:1 had departed from the L of Egypt.
16:3 the LORD in the L of Egypt, when we
16:6 you out of the L of Egypt,
16:32 you out of the L of Egypt.'"
16:35 came to a habitable L; they ate the manna,
16:35 the border of the L of Canaan.
18:3 sojourner in a foreign L,
19:1 forth out of the L of Egypt, on that
20:2 you out of the L of Egypt, out of
20:12 be long in the L which the LORD your
22:21 were strangers in the L of Egypt.
23:9 were strangers in the L of Egypt.
23:10 you shall sow your L and gather in its
23:26 be barren in your L; I will fulfil the
23:29 one year, lest the L become desolate and the
23:30 you, until you are increased and possess the L
23:31 the inhabitants of the L into your hand, and
23:33 not dwell in your L, lest they make you
29:46 forth out of the L of Egypt that I
32:1 up out of the L of Egypt, we do
32:4 up out of the L of Egypt!"
32:7 up out of the L of Egypt, have corrupted
32:8 up out of the L of Egypt!'"
32:11 forth out of the L of Egypt with great
32:13 heaven, and all this L that I have promised
32:23 up out of the L of Egypt, we do
33:1 up out of the L of Egypt, to the
33:1 of Egypt, to the L of which I swore
33:3 Go up to a L flowing with milk and
34:12 the inhabitants of the L whither you go, lest
34:15 the inhabitants of the L, and when they play
34:24 any man desire your L, when you go up
Lev 11:30 kind, the gecko, the L crocodile, the lizard, the
11:45 up out of the L of Egypt, to be
14:34 you come into the L of Canaan, which I
14:34 a house in the L of your possession,
16:22 him to a solitary L; and he shall let
18:3 they do in the L of Egypt, where you
18:3 they do in the L of Canaan, to which
18:25 defiled themselves; and the L became defiled, so that
18:25 its iniquity, and the L vomited out its inhabitants.
18:27 the men of the L did, who were before
18:27 you, so that the L became defiled);
18:28 became defiled); lest the L vomit you out, when
19:9 the harvest of your L, you shall not reap
19:23 you come into the L and plant all kinds
19:29 a harlot, lest the L fall into harlotry and
19:29 into harlotry and the L become full of wickedness.
19:33 with you in your L, you shall not do
19:34 were strangers in the L of Egypt: I am
19:36 you out of the L of Egypt.
20:2 the people of the L shall stone him with
20:4 the people of the L do at all hide
20:22 do them; that the L where I am bringing
20:24 'You shall inherit their L, and I will give
20:24 you to possess, a L flowing with milk and
22:24 or sacrifice within your L;
22:33 you out of the L of Egypt to be
23:10 you come into the L which I give you
23:22 the harvest of your L, you shall not reap
23:39 the produce of the L, you shall keep the
23:43 them out of the L of Egypt: I am
25:2 you come into the L which I give you,
25:2 I give you, the L shall keep a sabbath
25:4 solemn rest for the L, a sabbath to the
25:5 be a year of solemn rest for the L
25:6 The sabbath of the L shall provide food for
25:7 that are in your L all its yield shall
25:9 shall send abroad the trumpet throughout all your L
25:10 proclaim liberty throughout the L to all its
25:18 will dwell in the L securely.
25:19 The L will yield its fruit, and you will
25:23 The L shall not be sold in perpetuity, for
25:23 in perpetuity, for the L is mine; for you
25:24 possess, you shall grant a redemption of the L
25:34 the fields of common L belonging to their cities
25:38 forth out of the L of Egypt to give
25:38 to give you the L of Canaan, and to
25:42 forth out of the L of Egypt; they shall
25:45 been born in your L; and they may be
25:55 forth out of the L of Egypt: I am
26:1 figured stone in your L, to bow down to
26:4 their season, and the L shall yield its increase,
26:5 and dwell in your L securely.
26:6 give peace in the L, and you shall lie
26:6 evil beasts from the L, and the sword shall
26:6 and the sword shall not go through your L
26:13 forth out of the L of Egypt, that you
26:20 in vain, for your L shall not yield its
26:20 the trees of the L shall not yield their
26:32 I will devastate the L, so that your enemies

26:33 after you; and your L shall be a desolation,
26:34 "Then the L shall enjoy its sabbaths as long
26:34 are in your enemies' L; then the land shall
26:34 enemies' land; then the L shall rest, and enjoy
26:38 the nations, and the L of your enemies shall
26:41 brought them into the L of their enemies; if
26:42 covenant with Abraham, and I will remember the L
26:43 But the L shall be left by them, and
26:44 they are in the L of their enemies, I
26:45 forth out of the L of Egypt in the
27:16 LORD part of the L which is his by
27:24 bought, to whom the L belongs as a possession
27:30 the tithe of the L, whether of the seed
27:30 the seed of the L or of the fruit
Num 1:1 come out of the L of Egypt, saying,
3:13 the first-born in the L of Egypt, I consecrated
8:17 the first-born in the L of Egypt I consecrated
9:1 come out of the L of Egypt, saying,
10:9 to war in your L against the adversary who
10:30 depart to my own L and to my kindred."
11:12 sucking child, to the L which thou didst swear
13:2 to spy out the L of Canaan, which I
13:16 men whom Moses sent to spy out the L
13:17 to spy out the L of Canaan, and said
13:18 and see what the L is, and whether the
13:19 many, and whether the L that they dwell in
13:20 strongholds, and whether the L is rich or poor,
13:20 and bring some of the fruit of the L
13:21 and spied out the L from the wilderness of
13:25 forty days they returned from spying out the L
13:26 congregation, and showed them the fruit of the L
13:27 "We came to the L to which you sent
13:28 who dwell in the L are strong, and the
13:29 Amalekites dwell in the L of the Negeb; the
13:32 evil report of the L which they had spied
13:32 spied out, saying, "The L, through which we have
13:32 it out, is a L that devours its inhabitants;
14:2 had died in the L of Egypt!
14:3 bring us into this L, to fall by the
14:6 had spied out the L, rent their clothes,
14:7 people of Israel, "The L, which we passed through
14:7 to spy it out, is an exceedingly good L
14:8 bring us into this L and give it to
14:8 it to us, a L which flows with milk
14:9 the people of the L, for they are bread
14:14 and they will tell the inhabitants of this L
14:16 this people into the L which he swore to
14:23 voice, shall see the L which I swore to
14:24 will bring into the L into which he went,
14:30 shall come into the L where I swore that
14:31 they shall know the L which you have despised.
14:34 you spied out the L, forty days, for every
14:36 to spy out the L, and who returned and
14:36 evil report against the L,
14:37 evil report of the L, died by plague before
14:38 those men who went to spy out the L
15:2 you come into the L you are to inhabit,
15:18 you come into the L to which I bring
15:19 the food of the L, you shall present an
15:41 you out of the L of Egypt, to be
16:13 up out of a L flowing with milk and
16:14 brought us into a L flowing with milk and
18:13 that is in their L, which they bring to
18:20 no inheritance in their L, neither shall you have
20:12 this assembly into the L which I have given
20:17 Now let us pass through your L
20:23 the border of the L of Edom,
20:24 shall not enter the L which I have given
21:4 to go around the L of Edom; and the
21:22 me pass through your L; we will not turn
21:24 took possession of his L from the Arnon to
21:26 and taken all his L out of his hand,
21:31 Israel dwelt in the L of the Amorites.
21:34 his people, and his L; and you shall do
21:35 survivor left to him; and they possessed his L
22:5 the River, in the L of Amaw to call
22:6 drive them from the L; for I know that
22:13 "Go to your own L; for the LORD has
26:4 forth out of the L of Egypt, were:
26:19 Onan died in the L of Canaan.
26:53 Moses: "To these the L shall be divided for
26:55 But the L shall be divided by lot; according
27:12 Abarim, and see the L which I have given
32:1 and they saw the L of Jazer and the
32:1 of Jazer and the L of Gilead, and behold,
32:4 Nebo, and Beon, the L which the LORD smote
32:4 of Israel, is a L for cattle; and your
32:5 your sight, let this L be given to your
32:7 going over into the L which the LORD has
32:8 I sent them from Kadesh-barnea to see the L
32:9 Eshcol, and saw the L, they discouraged the heart
32:9 from going into the L which the LORD had
32:11 upward, shall see the L which I swore to
32:17 fortified cities because of the inhabitants of the L
32:22 before him and the L is subdued before the
32:22 to Israel; and this L shall be your possession
32:29 the Jordan and the L shall be subdued before
32:29 shall give them the L of Gilead for a
32:30 among you in the L of Canaan."
32:32 the LORD into the L of Canaan, and the
32:33 king of Bashan, the L and its cities with
32:33 the cities of the L throughout the country.
33:1 forth out of the L of Egypt by their
33:37 the edge of the L of Edom.
33:38 come out of the L of Egypt, on the
33:40 the Negeb in the L of Canaan, heard of
33:51 the Jordan into the L of Canaan,
33:52 the inhabitants of the L from before you, and
33:53 take possession of the L and settle in it,
33:53 I have given the L to you to possess
33:54 You shall inherit the L by lot according to
33:55 the inhabitants of the L from before you, then
33:55 trouble you in the L where you dwell.
34:2 When you enter the L of Canaan (this is
34:2 Canaan (this is the L that shall fall to
34:2 for an inheritance, the L of Canaan in its
34:12 This shall be your L with its boundaries all
34:13 saying, "This is the L which you shall inherit
34:17 who shall divide the L to you for inheritance:
34:18 tribe, to divide the L for inheritance.
34:29 of Israel in the L of Canaan."
35:5 to them as pasture L for their cities.
35:10 the Jordan into the L of Canaan,
35:14 three cities in the L of Canaan, to be
35:28 may return to the L of his possession.
35:32 to dwell in the L before the death of
35:33 not thus pollute the L in which you live;
35:33 for blood pollutes the L, and no expiation can
35:33 be made for the L, for the blood that
35:34 shall not defile the L in which you live,
36:2 lord to give the L for inheritance by lot
Deut 1:5 the Jordan, in the L of Moab, Moses undertook
1:7 by the seacoast, the L of the Canaanites, and
1:8 I have set the L before you; go in
1:8 take possession of the L which the LORD swore
1:21 God has set the L before you; go up,
1:22 they may explore the L for us, and bring
1:25 the fruit of the L and brought it down
1:25 'It is a good L which the LORD our
1:27 forth out of the L of Egypt, to give
1:35 shall see the good L which I swore to
1:36 I will give the L upon which he has
2:5 you any of their L, no, not so much
2:9 you any of their L for a possession, because
2:12 Israel did to the L of their possession, which
2:19 you any of the L of the sons of
2:20 is known as a L of Rephaim; Rephaim formerly
2:24 of Heshbon, and his L; begin to take possession,
2:27 me pass through your L; I will go only
2:29 the Jordan into the L which the LORD our
2:31 give Sihon and his L over to you; begin
2:31 you may occupy his L
2:37 Only to the L of the sons of Ammon
3:2 his people and his L into your hand; and
3:8 So we took the L at that time out
3:12 took possession of this L at that time, I
3:13 Bashan is called the L of Rephaim.
3:18 has given you this L to possess; all your
3:20 they also occupy the L which the LORD your
3:25 and see the good L beyond the Jordan, that
3:28 in possession of the L which you shall see.'
4:1 take possession of the L which the LORD, the
4:5 do them in the L which you are entering
4:14 do them in the L which you are going
4:21 not enter the good L which the LORD your
4:22 must die in this L, I must not go
4:22 go over and take possession of that good L
4:25 grown old in the L, if you act corruptly
4:26 utterly perish from the L which you are going
4:38 to give you their L for an inheritance, as
4:40 your days in the L which the LORD your
4:46 opposite Beth-peor, in the L of Sihon the king

4:47 took possession of his L and the land of
4:47 his land and the L of Og the king
5:6 you out of the L of Egypt, out of
5:15 a servant in the L of Egypt, and the
5:16 with you, in the L which the LORD your
5:31 do them in the L which I give them
5:33 live long in the L which you shall possess.
6:1 do them in the L to which you are
6:3 promised you, in a L flowing with milk and
6:10 brings you into the L which he swore to
6:12 you out of the L of Egypt, out of
6:18 possession of the good L which the LORD swore
6:23 and give us the L which he swore to
7:1 brings you into the L which you are entering
7:13 your flock, in the L which he swore to
8:1 in and possess the L which the LORD swore
8:7 you into a good L, a land of brooks
8:7 a good land, a L of brooks of water,
8:8 valleys and hills, a L of wheat and barley,
8:8 trees and pomegranates, a L of olive trees and
8:9 trees and honey, a L in which you will
8:9 will lack nothing, a L whose stones are iron,
8:10 God for the good L he has given you.
8:14 you out of the L of Egypt, out of
9:4 in to possess this L; whereas it is because
9:5 in to possess their L; but because of the
9:6 giving you this good L to possess because of
9:7 came out of the L of Egypt, until you
9:23 take possession of the L which I have given
9:28 their sin, lest the L from which thou didst
9:28 bring them into the L which he promised them,
10:7 Gudgodah to Jotbathah, a L with brooks of water.
10:11 in and possess the L, which I swore to
10:19 were sojourners in the L of Egypt.
11:3 and to all his L;
11:8 take possession of the L which you are going
11:9 live long in the L which the LORD swore
11:9 to their descendants, a L flowing with milk and
11:10 For the L which you are entering to take
11:10 is not like the L of Egypt, from which
11:11 of vegetables; but the L which you are going
11:11 to possess is a L of hills and valleys,
11:12 rain from heaven, a L which the LORD your
11:14 the rain for your L in its season, the
11:17 no rain, and the L yield no fruit, and
11:17 quickly off the good L which the LORD gives
11:21 be multiplied in the L which the LORD swore
11:25 you upon all the L that you shall tread,
11:29 brings you into the L which you are entering
11:30 the sun, in the L of the Canaanites who
11:31 take possession of the L which the LORD your
12:1 to do in the L which the LORD, the
12:10 and live in the L which the LORD your
12:19 Levite as long as you live in your L
12:29 and dwell in their L,
13:5 you out of the L of Egypt and redeemed
13:10 you out of the L of Egypt, out of
15:4 bless you in the L which the LORD your
15:7 your towns within your L which the LORD your
15:11 cease out of the L; therefore I command you,
15:11 the needy and to the poor, in the L
15:15 a slave in the L of Egypt, and the
16:3 came out of the L of Egypt in hurried
16:3 came out of the L of Egypt.
16:20 live and inherit the L which the LORD your
17:14 you come to the L which the LORD your
18:9 you come into the L which the LORD your
19:1 off the nations whose L the LORD your God
19:2 for you in the L which the LORD your
19:3 the area of the L which the LORD your
19:8 gives you all the L which he promised to
19:10 be shed in your L which the LORD your
19:14 will hold in the L that the LORD your
20:1 up out of the L of Egypt.
21:1 "If in the L which the LORD your God
21:23 shall not defile your L which the LORD your
23:7 Egyptian, because you were a sojourner in his L
23:20 you undertake in the L which you are entering
24:4 bring guilt upon the L which the LORD your
24:14 who are in your L within your towns;
24:22 a slave in the L of Egypt; therefore I
25:15 be prolonged in the L which the LORD your
25:19 round about, in the L which the LORD your
26:1 you come into the L which the LORD your
26:2 you harvest from your L that the LORD your
26:3 have come into the L which the LORD swore
26:9 and gave us this L, a land flowing with
26:9 us this land, a L flowing with milk and
26:15 to our fathers, a L flowing with milk and
27:2 the Jordan to the L which the LORD your
27:3 over to enter the L which the LORD your
27:3 God gives you, a L flowing with milk and
28:8 bless you in the L which the LORD your
28:11 your ground, within the L which the LORD swore
28:12 the rain of your L in its season and
28:21 consumed you off the L which you are entering
28:24 the rain of your L powder and dust; from
28:52 down throughout all your L; and they shall besiege
28:52 towns throughout all your L, which the LORD your
28:63 be plucked off the L which you are entering
29:1 of Israel in the L of Moab, besides the
29:2 your eyes in the L of Egypt, to Pharaoh
29:2 and to all his L,
29:8 them; we took their L, and gave it for
29:16 we dwelt in the L of Egypt, and how
29:22 comes from a far L, would say, when they
29:22 the afflictions of that L and the sicknesses with
29:23 sick-- the whole L brimstone and salt, and
29:24 'Why has the LORD done thus to this L
29:25 them out of the L of Egypt,
29:27 was kindled against this L, bringing upon it all
29:28 uprooted them from their L in anger and fury
29:28 cast them into another L, as at this day.'
30:5 bring you into the L which your fathers possessed,
30:16 bless you in the L which you are entering
30:18 live long in the L which you are going
30:20 may dwell in the L which the LORD swore
31:4 Amorites, and to their L, when he destroyed them.
31:7 this people into the L which the LORD has
31:13 you live in the L which you are going
31:16 strange gods of the L, where they go to
31:20 brought them into the L flowing with milk and
31:21 brought them into the L that I swore to
31:23 of Israel into the L which I swore to
32:10 him in a desert L, and in the howling
32:43 makes expiation for the L of his people."
32:47 live long in the L which you are going
32:49 which is in the L of Moab, opposite Jericho;
32:49 Jericho; and view the L of Canaan, which I
32:52 you shall see the L before you; but you
32:52 go there, into the L which I give to
33:13 the LORD be his L, with the choicest gifts
33:21 the best of the L for himself, for there
33:28 Jacob alone, in a L of grain and wine;
34:1 showed him all the L, Gilead as far as
34:2 Dan, all Naphtali, the L of Ephraim and Manasseh,
34:2 and Manasseh, all the L of Judah as far
34:4 him, "This is the L of which I swore
34:5 died there in the L of Moab, according to
34:6 the valley in the L of Moab opposite Beth-peor;
34:11 to do in the L of Egypt, to Pharaoh
34:11 and to all his L,

Josh 1:2 this people, into the L which I am giving
1:4 river Euphrates, all the L of the Hittites to
1:6 people to inherit the L which I swore to
1:11 take possession of the L which the LORD your
1:13 will give you this L
1:14 shall remain in the L which Moses gave you
1:15 take possession of the L which the LORD your
1:15 shall return to the L of your possession, and
1:15 shall possess it, the L which Moses the servant
2:1 saying, "Go, view the L, especially Jericho." And they
2:2 have come here tonight to search out the L
2:3 they have come to search out all the L
2:9 has given you the L, and that the fear
2:9 the inhabitants of the L melt away before you.
2:14 with you when the LORD gives us the L
2:18 we come into the L, you shall bind this
2:24 has given all the L into our hands; and
2:24 the inhabitants of the L are fainthearted because of
5:6 let them see the L which the LORD had
5:6 to give us, a L flowing with milk and
5:11 the produce of the L, unleavened cakes and parched
5:12 the produce of the L; and the people of
5:12 the fruit of the L of Canaan that year.
6:22 had spied out the L, "Go into the harlot's
6:27 Joshua; and his fame was in all the L
7:2 to them, "Go up and spy out the L
7:9 the inhabitants of the L will hear of it,
8:1 his city, and his L;
9:24 give you all the L, and to destroy all
9:24 the inhabitants of the L from before you; so

L

10:40 Joshua defeated the whole L, the hill country and
10:42 these kings and their L at one time, because
11:3 under Hermon in the L of Mizpah.
11:16 Joshua took all that L, the hill country and
11:16 Negeb and all the L of Goshen and the
11:22 Anakim left in the L of the people of
11:23 Joshua took the whole L, according to all that
11:23 And the L had rest from war.
12:1 the kings of the L, whom the people of
12:1 took possession of their L beyond the Jordan toward
12:6 the LORD gave their L for a possession to
12:7 the kings of the L whom Joshua and the
12:7 (and Joshua gave their L to the tribes of
12:8 in the Negeb, the L of the Hittites, the
13:1 remains yet very much L to be possessed.
13:2 This is the L that yet remains: all the
13:4 the south, all the L of the Canaanites, and
13:5 the Amorites, and the L of the Gebalites, and
13:6 Israel; only allot the L to Israel for an
13:7 Now therefore divide this L for an inheritance to
13:21 the princes of Sihon, who dwelt in the L
13:25 Gilead, and half the L of the Ammonites, to
14:1 Israel received in the L of Canaan, which Eleazar
14:4 the Levites in the L, but only cities to
14:5 as the LORD commanded Moses; they allotted the L
14:7 to spy out the L; and I brought him
14:9 day, saying, 'Surely the L on which your foot
14:15 And the L had rest from war.
15:19 set me in the L of the Negeb, give
17:5 ten portions, besides the L of Gilead and Bashan,
17:6 The L of Gilead was allotted to the rest
17:8 The L of Tappuah belonged to Manasseh, but the
17:10 at the sea; the L to the south being
17:12 but the Canaanites persisted in dwelling in that L
17:15 for yourselves in the L of the Perizzites and
18:1 of meeting there; the L lay subdued before them.
18:3 take possession of the L, which the LORD, the
18:4 up and down the L, writing a description of
18:6 you shall describe the L in seven divisions and
18:8 the description of the L, saying, "Go up and
18:8 a description of the L, and come again to
18:9 and down in the L and set down in
18:10 there Joshua apportioned the L to the people of
19:49 several territories of the L as inheritances, the
19:51 So they finished dividing the L
21:2 at Shiloh in the L of Canaan, "The LORD
21:43 to Israel all the L which he swore to
22:4 your home in the L where your possession lies,
22:7 their brethren in the L west of the Jordan.
22:9 which is in the L of Canaan, to go
22:9 to go to the L of Gilead, their own
22:9 of Gilead, their own L of which they had
22:10 that lies in the L of Canaan, the Reubenites
22:11 the frontier of the L of Canaan, in the
22:13 of Manasseh, in the L of Gilead, Phinehas the
22:15 of Manasseh, in the L of Gilead, and they
22:19 But now, if your L is unclean, pass over
22:19 over into the LORD's L where the LORD's
22:32 the Gadites in the L of Gilead to the
22:32 of Gilead to the L of Canaan, to the
22:33 them, to destroy the L where the Reubenites and
23:5 you shall possess their L, as the LORD your
23:13 from off this good L which the LORD your
23:15 from off this good L which the LORD your
23:16 from off the good L which he has given
24:3 him through all the L of Canaan, and made
24:8 brought you to the L of the Amorites, who
24:8 took possession of their L, and I destroyed them
24:13 I gave you a L on which you had
24:15 the Amorites in whose L you dwell; but as
24:17 fathers up from the L of Egypt, out of
24:18 who lived in the L; therefore we also will
Judg 1:2 I have given the L into his hand."
1:15 set me in the L of the Negeb, give
1:26 man went to the L of the Hittites and
1:27 but the Canaanites persisted in dwelling in that L
1:32 the inhabitants of the L; for they did not
1:33 the inhabitants of the L; nevertheless the inhabitants
2:1 brought you into the L which I swore to
2:2 the inhabitants of this L; you shall break down
2:6 to his inheritance to take possession of the L
2:12 them out of the L of Egypt; they went
3:11 So the L had rest forty years.
3:30 And the L had rest for eighty years.
5:31 And the L had rest for forty years.
6:4 the produce of the L, as far as the
6:5 that they wasted the L as they came in.
6:9 and gave you their L;
6:10 the Amorites, in whose L you dwell.' But you
8:28 And the L had rest forty years in the
9:37 the center of the L, and one company is
10:4 which are in the L of Gilead.
10:8 the Jordan in the L of the Amorites, which
11:3 and dwelt in the L of Tob; and worthless
11:5 bring Jephthah from the L of Tob;
11:12 have come to me to fight against my L
11:13 Egypt took away my L, from the Arnon to
11:15 not take away the L of Moab or the
11:15 of Moab or the L of the Ammonites,
11:17 we pray, through your L; but the king of
11:18 and went around the L of Edom and the
11:18 of Edom and the L of Moab, and arrived
11:18 east side of the L of Moab, and camped
11:19 we pray, through your L to our country.'
11:21 possession of all the L of the Amorites, who
12:12 at Aijalon in the L of Zebulun.
12:15 at Pirathon in the L of Ephraim, in the
18:2 to spy out the L and to explore it;
18:2 they said to them, "Go and explore the L
18:9 we have seen the L, and behold, it is
18:9 to go, and enter in and possess the L
18:10 The L is broad; yea, God has given it
18:17 to spy out the L went up, and entered
18:30 until the day of the captivity of the L
19:30 up out of the L of Egypt until this
20:1 to Beer-sheba, including the L of Gilead, and the
21:12 which is in the L of Canaan.
21:21 and go to the L of Benjamin.
Ruth 1:1 a famine in the L, and a certain man
1:7 to return to the L of Judah.
2:11 mother and your native L and came to a
4:3 selling the parcel of L which belonged to our
1Sam 6:5 mice that ravage the L, and give glory to
6:5 from off you and your gods and your L
6:9 way to its own L, to Beth-shemesh, then it
9:4 and passed through the L of Shalishah, but they
9:4 they passed through the L of Shaalim, but they
9:4 they passed through the L of Benjamin, but did
9:5 they came to the L of Zuph, Saul said
9:16 a man from the L of Benjamin, and you
12:6 up out of the L of Egypt.
13:3 trumpet throughout all the L, saying, "Let the
13:7 the Jordan to the L of Gad and Gilead.
13:17 toward Ophrah, to the L of Shual,
13:19 found throughout all the L of Israel; for the
14:14 half a furrow's length in an acre of L
14:29 father has troubled the L; see how my eyes
21:11 "Is not this David the king of the L
22:5 and go into the L of Judah." So David
23:23 he is in the L, I will search him
23:27 the Philistines have made a raid upon the L
27:1 should escape to the L of the Philistines; then
27:8 the inhabitants of the L from of old, as
27:8 as Shur, to the L of Egypt.
27:9 And David smote the L, and left neither man
28:3 the mediums and the wizards out of the L
28:9 off the mediums and the wizards from the L
29:11 to return to the L of the Philistines.
30:16 abroad over all the L, eating and drinking and
30:16 had taken from the L of the Philistines and
30:16 Philistines and from the L of Judah.
31:9 sent messengers throughout the L of the Philistines,
2Sam 3:12 "To whom does the L belong?
5:6 the inhabitants of the L, who said to David,
9:7 to you all the L of Saul your father;
9:10 servants shall till the L for him, and shall
10:2 servants came into the L of the Ammonites.
15:4 moreover, "Oh that I were judge in the L
17:26 Absalom encamped in the L of Gilead.
19:9 fled out of the L from Absalom.
19:29 have decided: you and Ziba shall divide the L
21:14 son Jonathan in the L of Benjamin in Zela,
21:14 And after that God heeded supplications for the L
24:6 to Kadesh in the L of the Hittites; and
24:8 gone through all the L, they came to Jerusalem
24:13 years of famine come to you in your L
24:13 shall there be three days' pestilence in your L
24:25 heeded supplications for the L, and the plague was
1Kgs 4:10 Socoh and all the L of Hepher);
4:19 of Uri, in the L of Gilead, the country
4:19 one officer in the L of Judah.
4:21 the Euphrates to the L of the Philistines and

6:1 came out of the L of Egypt, in the
8:9 came out of the L of Egypt.
8:21 them out of the L of Egypt."
8:34 them again to the L which thou gavest to
8:36 grant rain upon thy L, which thou hast given
8:37 is famine in the L, if there is pestilence
8:40 they live in the L which thou gavest to
8:46 away captive to the L of the enemy, far-off
8:47 to heart in the L to which they have
8:47 to thee in the L of their captors, saying,
8:48 their heart in the L of their enemies, who
8:48 to thee toward their L, which thou gavest to
9:7 off Israel from the L which I have given
9:8 done thus to this L and to this house?'
9:9 fathers out of the L of Egypt, and laid
9:11 twenty cities in the L of Galilee.
9:13 they are called the L of Cabul to this
9:18 the wilderness, in the L of Judah,
9:19 and in all the L of his dominion.
9:21 after them in the L, whom the people of
9:26 Red Sea, in the L of Edom.
10:6 heard in my own L of your affairs and
10:13 back to her own L, with her servants.
10:15 of Arabia and from the governors of the L
11:18 him an allowance of food, and gave him L
12:28 up out of the L of Egypt."
14:15 out of this good L which he gave to
14:24 there were also male cult prostitutes in the L
15:12 prostitutes out of the L, and removed all the
15:20 Chinneroth, with all the L of Naphtali.
17:7 up, because there was no rain in the L
18:5 Obadiah, "Go through the L to all the springs
18:6 So they divided the L between them to pass
20:7 the elders of the L, and said, "Mark, now,
22:46 of his father Asa, he exterminated from the L
2Kgs 2:19 is bad, and the L is unfruitful."
3:19 every good piece of L with stones."
3:25 every good piece of L every man threw a
3:27 withdrew from him and returned to their own L
4:38 Gilgal when there was a famine in the L
5:2 little maid from the L of Israel, and she
5:4 the maiden from the L of Israel."
6:23 on raids into the L of Israel.
8:1 will come upon the L for seven years."
8:2 and sojourned in the L of the Philistines seven
8:3 woman returned from the L of the Philistines, she
8:3 to the king for her house and her L
8:5 to the king for her house and her L
8:6 that she left the L until now."
10:33 Jordan eastward, all the L of Gilead, the Gadites,
11:3 of the LORD, while Athaliah reigned over the L
11:14 the people of the L rejoicing and blowing trumpets.
11:18 the people of the L went to the house
11:19 the people of the L; and they brought the
11:20 the people of the L rejoiced; and the city
13:20 used to invade the L in the spring of
15:5 over the household, governing the people of the L
15:19 Assyria came against the L; and Menahem gave Pul
15:20 back, and did not stay there in the L
15:29 and Galilee, all the L of Naphtali; and he
16:15 the people of the L, and their cereal offering,
17:5 Assyria invaded all the L and came to Samaria,
17:7 up out of the L of Egypt from under
17:23 exiled from their own L to Assyria until this
17:26 the god of the L; therefore he has sent
17:26 know the law of the god of the L
17:27 them the law of the god of the L
17:36 you out of the L of Egypt with great
18:25 Go up against this L, and destroy it.'"
18:32 you away to a L like your own land,
18:32 land like your own L, a land of grain
18:32 your own land, a L of grain and wine,
18:32 grain and wine, a L of bread and vineyards,
18:32 bread and vineyards, a L of olive trees and
18:33 nations ever delivered his L out of the hand
19:7 return to his own L; and I will cause
19:7 to fall by the sword in his own L
19:37 and escaped into the L of Ararat.
21:8 more out of the L which I gave to
21:24 the people of the L slew all those who
21:24 the people of the L made Josiah his son
23:24 were seen in the L of Judah and in
23:30 the people of the L took Jehoahaz the son
23:33 at Riblah in the L of Hamath, that he
23:33 and laid upon the L a tribute of a
23:35 but he taxed the L to give the money
23:35 the people of the L, from every one according
24:7 again out of his L, for the king of
24:14 none remained, except the poorest people of the L
24:15 chief men of the L, he took into captivity
25:3 was no food for the people of the L
25:12 the poorest of the L to be vinedressers and
25:19 the people of the L; and sixty men of
25:19 the people of the L who were found in
25:21 at Riblah in the L of Hamath.
25:21 Judah was taken into exile out of its L
25:22 remained in the L of Judah, whom Nebuchadnezzar
25:24 officials; dwell in the L, and serve the king
1Chr 1:43 who reigned in the L of Edom before any
1:45 died, Husham of the L of the Temanites reigned
2:22 twenty-three cities in the L of Gilead.
4:40 good pasture, and the L was very broad, quiet,
5:9 had multiplied in the L of Gilead.
5:11 against them in the L of Bashan as far
5:23 Manasseh dwelt in the L; they were very numerous
5:25 the peoples of the L, whom God had destroyed
6:55 gave Hebron in the L of Judah and its
7:21 were born in the L slew, because they came
10:9 sent messengers throughout the L of the Philistines,
11:4 where the Jebusites were, the inhabitants of the L
13:2 remain in all the L of Israel, and with
16:18 I will give the L of Canaan, as your
19:2 to Hanun in the L of the Ammonites, to
19:3 and to overthrow and to spy out the L
21:12 LORD, pestilence upon the L, and the angel of
22:2 who were in the L of Israel, and he
22:18 the inhabitants of the L into my hand; and
22:18 my hand; and the L is subdued before the
28:8 may possess this good L, and leave it for
2Chr 2:17 who were in the L of Israel, after the
6:5 people out of the L of Egypt, I chose
6:25 them again to the L which thou gavest to
6:27 grant rain upon thy L, which thou hast given
6:28 is famine in the L, if there is pestilence
6:31 they live in the L which thou gavest to
6:36 away captive to a L far or near;
6:37 to heart in the L to which they have
6:37 to thee in the L of their captivity, saying,
6:38 their heart in the L of their captivity, to
6:38 and pray toward their L, which thou gavest to
7:13 locust to devour the L, or send pestilence among
7:14 and will forgive their sin and heal their L
7:20 you up from the L which I have given
7:21 done thus to this L and to this house?"
7:22 them out of the L of Egypt, and laid
8:6 and in all the L of his dominion.
8:8 after them in the L, whom the people of
8:17 the sea, in the L of Edom.
9:5 heard in my own L of your affairs and
9:11 them before in the L of Judah.
9:12 back to her own L, with her servants.
9:14 the governors of the L brought gold and silver
9:26 the Euphrates to the L of the Philistines, and
14:1 In his days the L had rest for ten
14:6 in Judah, for the L had rest.
14:7 gates and bars; the L is still ours, because
15:8 idols from all the L of Judah and Benjamin
17:2 set garrisons in the L of Judah, and in
19:3 Asherahs out of the L, and have set your
19:5 appointed judges in the L in all the fortified
20:7 the inhabitants of this L before thy people Israel,
20:10 they came from the L of Egypt, and whom
22:12 house of God, while Athaliah reigned over the L
23:13 the people of the L rejoicing and blowing trumpets,
23:20 the people of the L; and they brought the
23:21 the people of the L rejoiced; and the city
26:21 the king's household, governing the people of the L
30:9 compassion with their captors, and return to this L
30:25 came out of the L of Israel, and the
31:19 the fields of common L belonging to their cities,
32:4 that flowed through the L, saying, "Why should the
32:21 returned with shame of face to his own L
32:31 been done in the L, God left him to
33:8 of Israel from the L which I appointed for
33:25 the people of the L slew all those who
33:25 the people of the L made Josiah his son
34:7 altars throughout all the L of Israel.
34:8 he had purged the L and the house, he
36:1 The people of the L took Jehoahaz the son
36:3 and laid upon the L a tribute of a
36:21 of Jeremiah, until the L had enjoyed its sabbaths.
Ezra 4:4 the people of the L discouraged the people of

6:21 the peoples of the L to worship the LORD,
9:11 the prophets, saying, 'The L which you are entering,
9:11 of it, is a L unclean with the pollutions
9:12 the good of the L, and leave it for
10:2 the peoples of the L, but even now there
10:11 the peoples of the L and from the foreign
Neh 4:4 be plundered in a L where they are captives.
5:14 their governor in the L of Judah, from the
5:16 wall, and acquired no L; and all my servants
9:8 to his descendants the L of the Canaanite, the
9:10 the people of his L, for thou knewest that
9:11 the sea on dry L; and thou didst cast
9:15 in to possess the L which thou hadst sworn
9:22 took possession of the L of Sihon king of
9:22 of Heshbon and the L of Og king of
9:23 bring them into the L which thou hadst told
9:24 in and possessed the L, and thou didst subdue
9:24 the inhabitants of the L, the Canaanites, and didst
9:24 the peoples of the L, that they might do
9:25 cities and a rich L, and took possession of
9:35 the large and rich L which thou didst set
9:36 this day; in the L that thou gavest to
10:30 the peoples of the L or take their daughters
10:31 the peoples of the L bring in wares or
Tob 1:3 with me into the L of the Assyrians, to
1:4 own country, in the L of Israel, while I
3:15 my father in the L of my captivity.
4:12 their children, and their posterity will inherit the L
6:3 the fish and threw it up on the L
13:6 him thanks in the L of my captivity, and
14:4 earth from the good L, and Jerusalem will be
14:5 them back into their L; and they will rebuild
Jud 1:9 Raamses and the whole L of Goshen,
1:12 the inhabitants of the L of Moab, and the
3:3 buildings, and all our L, and all our wheat
3:8 the gods of the L, so that all nations
5:9 and go to the L of Canaan.
5:12 he afflicted the whole L of Egypt with incurable
5:15 they lived in the L of the Amorites, and
7:4 face of the whole L; neither the high mountains
7:18 whole face of the L, and their tents and
8:22 the captivity of the L and the desolation of
Esth 10:1 laid tribute on the L and on the coastlands
13:16 thyself out of the L of Egypt.
Job 1:1 a man in the L of Uz, whose name
1:10 hands, and his possessions have increased in the L
10:21 not return, to the L of gloom and deep
10:22 and deep darkness, the L of gloom and chaos,
12:15 if he sends them out, they overwhelm the L
15:19 to whom alone the L was given, and no
22:8 with power possessed the L, and the favored man
24:18 is cursed in the L; no treader turns toward
28:13 not found in the L of the living.
30:8 brood, they have been whipped out of the L
31:38 "If my L has cried out against me, and
37:13 correction, or for his L, or for love, he
38:26 bring rain on a L where no man is,
38:27 the waste and desolate L, and to make the
39:6 home, and the salt L for his dwelling place?
42:15 And in all the L there were no women
Ps 10:16 and ever; the nations shall perish from his L
16:3 the saints in the L, they are the noble,
25:13 in prosperity, and his children shall possess the L
27:13 the LORD in the L of the living!
35:20 are quiet in the L they conceive words of
37:3 will dwell in the L, and enjoy security.
37:9 who wait for the LORD shall possess the L
37:11 meek shall possess the L, and delight themselves in
37:22 LORD shall possess the L, but those cursed by
37:29 righteous shall possess the L, and dwell upon it
37:34 you to possess the L; you will look on
41:2 called blessed in the L; thou dost not give
42:6 remember thee from the L of Jordan and of
44:3 did they win the L, nor did their own
52:5 uproot you from the L of the living.
60:2 Thou hast made the L to quake, thou hast
63:1 a dry and weary L where no water is.
66:6 the sea into dry L; men passed through the
68:6 prosperity; but the rebellious dwell in a parched L
72:16 of grain in the L; on the tops of
74:8 all the meeting places of God in the L
74:20 dark places of the L are full of the
78:12 wrought marvels in the L of Egypt, in the
78:54 them to his holy L, to the mountain which
80:9 it; it took deep root and filled the L
81:5 went out over the L of Egypt.
81:10 up out of the L of Egypt.
85:1 wast favorable to thy L; thou didst restore the
85:9 fear him, that glory may dwell in our L
85:12 is good, and our L will yield its increase.
88:12 saving help in the L of forgetfulness?
94:17 have dwelt in the L of silence.
95:5 made it; for his hands formed the dry L
101:6 the faithful in the L, that they may dwell
101:8 the wicked in the L, cutting off all the
105:11 I will give the L of Canaan as your
105:16 a famine on the L, and broke every staff
105:23 Jacob sojourned in the L of Ham.
105:27 and miracles in the L of Ham.
105:28 darkness, and made the L dark; they rebelled against
105:30 Their L swarmed with frogs, even in the chambers
105:32 for rain, and lightning that flashed through their L
105:35 the vegetation in their L, and ate up the
105:36 the first-born in their L, the first issue of
106:22 wondrous works in the L of Ham, and terrible
106:24 they despised the pleasant L, having no faith in
106:38 of Canaan; and the L was polluted with blood.
107:34 thirsty ground, a fruitful L into a salty waste,
107:35 of water, a parched L into springs of water.
112:2 be mighty in the L; the generation of the
116:9 the LORD in the L of the living.
125:3 not rest upon the L allotted to the righteous,
135:12 Canaan, and gave their L as a heritage, a
136:21 ever; and gave their L as a heritage, for
137:4 we sing the LORD's song in a foreign L
140:11 be established in the L; let evil hunt down
141:7 and shatters on the L, so shall their bones
142:5 my portion in the L of the living.
143:6 my soul thirsts for thee like a parched L
Prov 2:21 upright will inhabit the L, and men of integrity
2:22 cut off from the L, and the treacherous will
10:30 but the wicked will not dwell in the L
12:11 He who tills his L will have plenty of
21:19 live in a desert L than with a contentious
28:2 When a L transgresses it has many rulers; but
28:19 He who tills his L will have plenty of
29:4 gives stability to the L, but one who exacts
31:23 when he sits among the elders of the L
Eccl 5:9 an advantage to a L with cultivated fields.
10:16 Woe to you, O L, when your king is
10:17 Happy are you, O L, when your king is
Song 2:12 voice of the turtledove is heard in our L
Wis 12:3 old in thy holy L
12:7 our fathers, that the L most precious of all
14:5 billows on a raft they come safely to L
16:19 fire, to destroy the crops of the unrighteous L
18:15 the midst of the L that was doomed, a
19:7 the camp, and dry L emerging where water had
19:19 For L animals were transformed into water
19:19 and creatures that swim moved over to the L
Sir 37:3 formed to cover the L with deceit?
39:22 blessing covers the dry L like a river, and
43:3 noon it parches the L; and who can withstand
45:22 But in the L of the people he has
46:8 their inheritance, into a L flowing with milk and
47:24 many, so as to remove them from their L
48:15 away captive from their L and were scattered over
Is 1:7 presence aliens devour your L; it is desolate, as
1:19 the good of the L;
2:7 Their L is filled with silver and gold, and
2:7 to their treasures; their L is filled with horses,
2:8 Their L is filled with idols; they bow down
4:2 the fruit of the L shall be the pride
5:8 to dwell alone in the midst of the L
5:30 one look to the L, behold, darkness and distress;
6:11 without men, and the L is utterly desolate,
6:12 places are many in the midst of the L
7:16 choose the good, the L before whose two kings
7:18 which is in the L of Assyria.
7:22 is left in the L will eat curds and
7:24 there, for all the L will be briers and
8:8 the breadth of your L, O Immanu-el."
8:21 pass through the L, greatly distressed and hungry;
9:1 brought into contempt the L of Zebulun and the
9:1 of Zebulun and the L of Naphtali, but in
9:1 of the sea, the L beyond the Jordan, Galilee
9:2 who dwelt in a L of deep darkness, on
9:19 LORD of hosts the L is burned, and the
10:18 and of his fruitful L the LORD will destroy,
11:16 came up from the L of Egypt.
13:5 come from a distant L, from the end of
13:14 and every man will flee to his own L

L

14:1 them in their own L, and aliens will join
14:2 them in the LORD's L as male and female
14:20 you have destroyed your L, you have slain your
14:25 the Assyrian in my L, and upon my mountains
15:8 has gone round the L of Moab; the wailing
15:9 Moab who escape, for the remnant of the L
16:1 the ruler of the L, from Sela, by way
16:4 has vanished from the L,
18:1 Ah, L of whirring wings which is beyond the
18:2 mighty and conquering, whose L the rivers divide.
18:7 mighty and conquering, whose L the rivers divide, to
19:10 the pillars of the L will be crushed, and
19:17 And the L of Judah will become a terror
19:18 five cities in the L of Egypt which speak
19:19 the midst of the L of Egypt, and a
19:20 of hosts in the L of Egypt; when they
21:1 it comes from the desert, from a terrible L
21:14 O inhabitants of the L of Tema.
22:18 ball into a wide L; there you shall die,
23:1 From the L of Cyprus it is revealed to
23:10 Overflow your L like the Nile, O daughter of
23:13 Behold the L of the Chaldeans!
26:1 be sung in the L of Judah: "We have
26:10 learn righteousness; in the L of uprightness he deals
26:15 thou hast enlarged all the borders of the L
26:19 light, and on the L of the shades thou
27:13 were lost in the L of Assyria and those
27:13 driven out to the L of Egypt will come
28:22 the Lord GOD of hosts upon the whole L
30:6 Through a L of trouble and anguish, from where
32:2 shade of a great rock in a weary L
33:9 The L mourns and languishes; Lebanon is
33:17 they will behold a L that stretches afar.
34:6 great slaughter in the L of Edom.
34:7 Their L shall be soaked with blood, and their
34:9 soil into brimstone; her L shall become burning
35:1 wilderness and the dry L shall be glad, the
36:10 come up against this L to destroy it?
36:10 Go up against this L, and destroy it.'"
36:17 you away to a L like your own land,
36:17 land like your own L, a land of grain
36:17 your own land, a L of grain and wine,
36:17 grain and wine, a L of bread and vineyards.
36:18 the nations delivered his L out of the hand
37:7 return to his own L; and I will make
37:7 him fall by the sword in his own L
37:38 and escaped into the L of Ararat.
38:11 the LORD in the L of the living; I
41:18 water, and the dry L springs of water.
44:3 water on the thirsty L, and streams on the
45:19 in secret, in a L of darkness; I did
49:8 people, to establish the L, to apportion the desolate
49:12 and these from the L of Syene."
49:19 places and your devastated L -- surely now you
53:8 off out of the L of the living, stricken
57:13 me shall possess the L, and shall inherit my
60:18 be heard in your L, devastation or destruction within
60:21 they shall possess the L for ever, the shoot
61:7 lot; therefore in your L you shall possess a
62:4 termed Forsaken, and your L shall no more be
62:4 in her, and your L Married; for the LORD
62:4 in you, and your L shall be married.
65:16 blesses himself in the L shall bless himself by
65:16 an oath in the L shall swear by the
66:8 Shall a L be born in one day?
Jer 1:1 in Anathoth in the L of Benjamin,
1:14 break forth upon all the inhabitants of the L
1:18 walls, against the whole L, against the kings of
1:18 princes, its priests, and the people of the L
2:2 the wilderness, in a L not sown.
2:6 us up from the L of Egypt, who led
2:6 the wilderness, in a L of deserts and pits,
2:6 and pits, in a L of drought and deep
2:6 deep darkness, in a L that none passes through,
2:7 you into a plentiful L to enjoy its fruits
2:7 in you defiled my L, and made my heritage
2:15 They have made his L a waste; his cities
2:31 to Israel, or a L of thick darkness?
3:1 Would not that L be greatly polluted?
3:2 You have polluted the L with your vile harlotry.
3:9 she polluted the L, committing adultery with stone
3:16 and increased in the L, in those days, says
3:18 shall come from the L of the north to
3:18 the north to the L that I gave your
3:19 give you a pleasant L, a heritage most beauteous
4:5 the trumpet through the L; cry aloud and say,
4:7 place to make your L a waste; your cities
4:16 come from a distant L; they shout against the
4:20 on disaster, the whole L is laid waste.
4:26 and lo, the fruitful L was a desert, and
4:27 the LORD, "The whole L shall be a desolation;
5:19 foreign gods in your L, so you shall serve
5:19 serve strangers in a L that is not yours.'"
5:30 has happened in the L:
6:8 lest I make you a desolation, an uninhabited L
6:12 out my hand against the inhabitants of the L
6:20 from Sheba, or sweet cane from a distant L
7:7 this place, in the L that I gave of
7:22 them out of the L of Egypt, I did
7:25 came out of the L of Egypt to this
7:34 the bride; for the L shall become a waste.
8:16 their stallions the whole L quakes.
8:16 come and devour the L and all that fills
8:19 and breadth of the L: "Is the LORD not
9:3 grown strong in the L; for they proceed from
9:12 Why is the L ruined and laid waste like
9:19 we have left the L, because they have cast
10:18 the inhabitants of the L at this time, and
11:4 them out of the L of Egypt, from the
11:5 to give them a L flowing with milk and
11:7 up out of the L of Egypt, warning them
11:19 him off from the L of the living, that
12:4 How long will the L mourn, and the grass
12:5 if in a safe L you fall down, how
12:11 The whole L is made desolate, but no man
12:12 one end of the L to the other; no
12:14 them up from their L, and I will pluck
12:15 each to his heritage and each to his L
13:13 the inhabitants of this L: the kings who sit
14:4 no rain on the L, the farmers are ashamed,
14:8 a stranger in the L, like a wayfarer who
14:15 not come on this L: By sword and famine
14:18 their trade through the L, and have no knowledge.'"
15:7 the gates of the L; I have bereaved them,
15:10 man of strife and contention to the whole L
15:14 your enemies in a L which you do not
16:3 begot them in this L:
16:6 shall die in this L; they shall not be
16:13 you out of this L into a land which
16:13 this land into a L which neither you nor
16:14 Israel out of the L of Egypt,'
16:15 back to their own L which I gave to
16:18 they have polluted my L with the carcasses of
17:4 your enemies in a L which you do not
17:6 places of the wilderness, in an uninhabited salt L
17:26 about Jerusalem, from the L of Benjamin, from the
18:16 the highway, making their L a horror, a thing
22:10 shall return no more to see his native L
22:12 shall never see this L again."
22:27 But to the L to which they will long
22:28 and cast into a L which they do not
22:29 O L, land, land, hear the word of the
22:29 O land, L, land, hear the word of the
22:29 O land, land, L, hear the word of the
23:5 and shall execute justice and righteousness in the L
23:7 Israel out of the L of Egypt,'
23:8 them.' Then they shall dwell in their own L
23:10 For the L is full of adulterers; because of
23:10 of the curse the L mourns, and the pastures
23:15 Jerusalem ungodliness has gone forth into all the L
24:5 this place to the L of the Chaldeans.
24:6 and I will bring them back to this L
24:8 who remain in this L, and those who dwell
24:8 who dwell in the L of Egypt.
24:10 utterly destroyed from the L which I gave to
25:5 and dwell upon the L which the LORD has
25:9 bring them against this L and its inhabitants, and
25:11 This whole L shall become a ruin and a
25:12 and that nation, the L of the Chaldeans, for
25:12 the LORD, making the L an everlasting waste.
25:13 will bring upon that L all the words which
25:20 the kings of the L of Uz and all
25:20 the kings of the L of the Philistines (Ashkelon,
25:38 his covert, for their L has become a waste
26:17 the elders of the L arose and spoke to
26:20 city and against this L in words like those
27:7 time of his own L comes; then many nations
27:10 removed far from your L, and I will drive
27:11 leave on its own L, to till it and
30:3 them back to the L which I gave to
30:10 your offspring from the L of their captivity.
31:16 come back from the L of the enemy.

 LAND

31:23 these words in the L of Judah and in
31:32 them out of the L of Egypt, my covenant
32:8 at Anathoth in the L of Benjamin, for the
32:15 be bought in this L
32:20 and wonders in the L of Egypt, and to
32:21 Israel out of the L of Egypt with signs
32:22 thou gavest them this L, which thou didst swear
32:22 to give them, a L flowing with milk and
32:41 plant them in this L in faithfulness, with all
32:43 be bought in this L of which you are
32:44 and witnessed, in the L of Benjamin, in the
33:11 the fortunes of the L as at first, says
33:13 the Negeb, in the L of Benjamin, the places
33:15 he shall execute justice and righteousness in the L
34:13 them out of the L of Egypt, out of
34:19 the people of the L who passed between the
35:7 many days in the L where you sojourn.'
35:11 came up against the L, we said, 'Come, and
35:15 shall dwell in the L which I gave to
36:29 come and destroy this L, and will cut off
37:1 made king in the L of Judah, reigned instead
37:2 the people of the L listened to the words
37:7 about to return to Egypt, to its own L
37:12 to go to the L of Benjamin to receive
37:19 will not come against you and against this L
39:5 at Riblah, in the L of Hamath; and he
39:10 guard, left in the L of Judah some of
40:4 See, the whole L is before you; go wherever
40:6 among the people who were left in the L
40:7 Ahikam governor in the L, and had committed to
40:7 the poorest of the L who had not been
40:9 Dwell in the L, and serve the king of
40:12 and came to the L of Judah, to Gedaliah
41:2 king of Babylon had appointed governor in the L
41:18 king of Babylon had made governor over the L
42:10 will remain in this L, then I will build
42:12 you and let you remain in your own L
42:13 not remain in this L disobeying the voice of
42:14 will go to the L of Egypt, where we
42:16 you there in the L of Egypt; and the
43:4 to remain in the L of Judah.
43:5 to live in the L of Judah from all
43:7 they came into the L of Egypt, for they
43:11 come and smite the L of Egypt, giving to
43:12 he shall clean the L of Egypt, as a
43:13 which is in the L of Egypt; and the
44:1 that dwelt in the L of Egypt, at Migdol,
44:1 Memphis, and in the L of Pathros,
44:8 other gods in the L of Egypt where you
44:9 they committed in the L of Judah and in
44:12 to come to the L of Egypt to live,
44:12 be consumed; in the L of Egypt they shall
44:13 who dwell in the L of Egypt, as I
44:14 to live in the L of Egypt shall escape
44:14 or return to the L of Judah, to which
44:15 in Pathros in the L of Egypt, answered Jeremiah:
44:21 the people of the L, did not the LORD
44:22 you committed; therefore your L has become a
44:24 who are in the L of Egypt,
44:26 who dwell in the L of Egypt: Behold, I
44:26 Judah in all the L of Egypt, saying, 'As
44:27 who are in the L of Egypt shall be
44:28 shall return from the L of Egypt to the
44:28 of Egypt to the L of Judah, few in
44:28 who came to the L of Egypt to live,
45:4 I am plucking up--that is, the whole L
46:13 Babylon to smite the L of Egypt:
46:16 people and to the L of our birth, because
46:27 your offspring from the L of their captivity.
47:2 they shall overflow the L and all that fills
47:2 every inhabitant of the L shall wail.
48:24 the cities of the L of Moab, far and
48:33 away from the fruitful L of Moab; I have
50:1 Babylon, concerning the L of the Chaldeans, by
50:3 which shall make her L a desolation, and none
50:8 go out of the L of the Chaldeans, and
50:16 and every one shall flee to his own L
50:18 of Babylon and his L, as I punished the
50:21 "Go up against the L of Merathaim, and against
50:22 battle is in the L, and great destruction!
50:25 to do in the L of the Chaldeans.
50:28 and escape from the L of Babylon, to declare
50:38 For it is a L of images, and they
50:45 has formed against the L of the Chaldeans: Surely
51:2 they shall empty her L, when they come against
51:4 down slain in the L of the Chaldeans, and
51:5 of hosts; but the L of the Chaldeans is
51:28 and deputies, and every L under their dominion.
51:29 The L trembles and writhes in pain, for the
51:29 stand, to make the L of Babylon a desolation,
51:43 become a horror, a L of drought and a
51:43 and a desert, a L in which no one
51:46 report heard in the L, when a report comes
51:46 violence is in the L, and ruler is against
51:47 of Babylon; her whole L shall be put to
51:52 and through all her L the wounded shall groan.
51:54 great destruction from the L of the Chaldeans!
52:6 was no food for the people of the L
52:9 at Riblah in the L of Hamath, and he
52:16 the poorest of the L to be vinedressers and
52:25 the people of the L; and sixty men of
52:25 the people of the L, who were found in
52:27 at Riblah in the L of Hamath.
52:27 So Judah was carried captive out of its L
Lam 4:21 Edom, dweller in the L of Uz; but to
Bar 1:8 return them to the L of Judah--the silver
1:9 the people of the L, and brought them to
1:19 fathers out of the L of Egypt until today,
1:20 fathers out of the L of Egypt to give
1:20 give to us a L flowing with milk and
2:11 people out of the L of Egypt with a
2:21 will remain in the L which I gave to
2:23 bride, and the whole L will be a desolation
2:30 But in the L of their exile they will
2:32 praise me in the L of their exile, and
2:34 them again into the L which I swore to
2:35 people Israel from the L which I have given
3:10 you are in the L of your enemies, that
6:61 seen; and the wind likewise blows in every L
6:72 be consumed, and be a reproach in the L
Ezek 1:3 of Buzi, in the L of the Chaldeans by
6:14 them, and make the L desolate and waste,
7:2 Lord GOD to the L of Israel: An end!
7:2 has come upon the four corners of the L
7:7 O inhabitant of the L; the time has come,
7:23 "Because the L is full of bloody crimes and
7:27 the people of the L are palsied by terror.
8:12 not see us, the LORD has forsaken the L
8:17 they should fill the L with violence, and provoke
9:9 is exceedingly great; the L is full of blood,
9:9 LORD has forsaken the L, and the LORD does
11:15 LORD; to us this L is given for a
11:17 will give you the L of Israel.'
12:6 may not see the L; for I have made
12:12 may not see the L with his eyes.
12:13 to Babylon in the L of the Chaldeans, yet
12:19 the people of the L, Thus says the Lord
12:19 of Jerusalem in the L of Israel: They shall
12:19 in dismay, because their L will be stripped of
12:20 laid waste, and the L shall become a desolation;
12:22 you have about the L of Israel, saying, 'The
13:9 shall they enter the L of Israel; and you
14:13 of man, when a L sins against me by
14:15 to pass through the L, and they ravage it,
14:16 be delivered, but the L would be desolate.
14:17 a sword upon that L, and say, Let a
14:17 sword go through the L; and I cut off
14:19 a pestilence into that L, and pour out my
15:8 I will make the L desolate, because they have
16:3 birth are of the L of the Canaanites; your
16:29 also with the trading L of Chaldea; and even
17:4 carried it to a L of trade, and set
17:5 the seed of the L and planted it in
17:13 chief men of the L he had taken away,
18:2 this proverb concerning the L of Israel, 'The fathers
19:4 with hooks to the L of Egypt.
19:7 their cities; and the L was appalled and all
19:13 in the wilderness, in a dry and thirsty L
20:5 to them in the L of Egypt, I swore
20:6 them out of the L of Egypt into a
20:6 of Egypt into a L that I had searched
20:6 out for them, a L flowing with milk and
20:8 the midst of the L of Egypt.
20:9 them out of the L of Egypt.
20:10 them out of the L of Egypt and brought
20:15 bring them into the L which I had given
20:15 had given them, a L flowing with milk and
20:28 brought them into the L which I swore to
20:36 the wilderness of the L of Egypt, so I
20:38 them out of the L where they sojourn, but
20:38 shall not enter the L of Israel.
20:40 serve me in the L; there I will accept

20:42 bring you into the L of Israel, the country
20:46 prophesy against the forest L in the Negeb;
21:2 sanctuaries; prophesy against the L of Israel
21:3 and say to the L of Israel, Thus says
21:19 of them shall come forth from the same L
21:30 were created, in the L of your origin, I
21:32 the midst of the L; you shall be no
22:24 her, You are a L that is not cleansed,
22:29 The people of the L have practiced extortion and
22:30 before me for the L, that I should not
23:15 of Babylonians whose native L was Chaldea.
23:19 the harlot in the L of Egypt
23:27 harlotry brought from the L of Egypt; so that
23:48 to lewdness in the L, that all women may
25:3 profaned, and over the L of Israel when it
25:6 within you against the L of Israel,
26:20 a place in the L of the living.
27:17 Judah and the L of Israel traded with you;
28:25 dwell in their own L which I gave to
29:9 and beast; and the L of Egypt shall be
29:10 I will make the L of Egypt an utter
29:12 I will make the L of Egypt a desolation
29:14 them back to the L of Pathros, the land
29:14 land of Pathros, the L of their origin; and
29:19 I will give the L of Egypt to Nebuchadrezzar
29:20 have given him the L of Egypt as his
30:5 the people of the L that is in league,
30:11 in to destroy the L; and they shall draw
30:11 Egypt, and fill the L with the slain.
30:12 and will sell the L into the hand of
30:12 bring desolation upon the L and everything in it,
30:13 a prince in the L of Egypt; so I
30:13 put fear in the L of Egypt.
30:25 it out against the L of Egypt;
31:12 the watercourses of the L; and all the peoples
32:6 I will drench the L even to the mountains
32:8 put darkness upon your L, says the Lord GOD.
32:15 When I make the L of Egypt desolate and
32:15 desolate and when the L is stripped of all
32:23 spread terror in the L of the living.
32:24 spread terror in the L of the living, and
32:25 was spread in the L of the living, and
32:26 spread terror in the L of the living.
32:27 men was in the L of the living.
32:32 spread terror in the L of the living; therefore
33:2 the sword upon a L, and the people of
33:2 the people of the L take a man from
33:3 sword coming upon the L and blows the trumpet
33:24 waste places in the L of Israel keep saying,
33:24 got possession of the L; but we are many;
33:24 we are many; the L is surely given us
33:25 and shed blood; shall you then possess the L
33:26 his neighbor's wife; shall you then possess the L
33:28 I will make the L a desolation and a
33:29 I have made the L a desolation and a
34:13 them into their own L; and I will feed
34:14 down in good grazing L, and on fat pasture
34:25 wild beasts from the L, so that they may
34:27 be secure in their L; and they shall know
34:28 the beasts of the L devour them; they shall
34:29 with hunger in the L, and no longer suffer
36:5 Edom, who gave my L to themselves as a
36:6 Therefore prophesy concerning the L of Israel, and
36:17 dwelt in their own L, they defiled it by
36:18 had shed in the L, for the idols with
36:20 go out of his L
36:24 the countries, and bring you into your own L
36:28 shall dwell in the L which I gave to
36:34 And the L that was desolate shall be tilled,
36:35 they will say, 'This L that was desolate has
37:12 you home into the L of Israel.
37:14 you in your own L; then you shall know
37:21 them to their own L;
37:22 one nation in the L, upon the mountains of
37:25 shall dwell in the L where your fathers dwelt
38:2 toward Gog, of the L of Magog, the chief
38:8 will go against the L that is restored from
38:8 restored from war, the L where people were
38:9 a cloud covering the L you and all your
38:11 go up against the L of unwalled villages; I
38:16 my people Israel, like a cloud covering the L
38:16 bring you against my L, that the nations may
38:18 shall come against the L of Israel, says the
38:19 great shaking in the L of Israel;
39:12 be burying them, in order to cleanse the L
39:13 the people of the L will bury them; and
39:14 to pass through the L continually and bury those
39:14 the face of the L, so as to cleanse
39:15 these pass through the L and any one sees
39:16 is there also.) Thus shall they cleanse the L
39:26 dwell securely in their L with none to make
39:28 nations, and then gathered them into their own L
40:2 of God into the L of Israel, and set
45:1 "When you allot the L as a possession, you
45:1 a portion of the L as a holy district,
45:4 holy portion of the L; it shall be for
45:7 prince shall belong the L on both sides of
45:7 the western to the eastern boundary of the L
45:8 of Israel have the L according to their tribes.
45:16 the people of the L shall give this offering
45:22 the people of the L a young bull for
46:3 The people of the L shall worship at the
46:9 the people of the L come before the LORD
47:13 you shall divide the L for inheritance among the
47:14 your fathers, and this L shall fall to you
47:15 the boundary of the L: On the north side,
47:18 between Gilead and the L of Israel; to the
47:21 you shall divide this L among you according to
48:12 holy portion of the L, a most holy place,
48:14 choice portion of the L, for it is holy
48:17 city shall have open L: on the north two
48:29 This is the L which you shall allot as
Dan 1:2 brought them to the L of Shinar, to the
8:9 south, toward the east, and toward the glorious L
9:6 fathers, and to all the people of the L
9:15 people out of the L of Egypt with a
11:9 the south but shall return into his own L
11:16 stand in the glorious L, and all of it
11:19 fortresses of his own L; but he shall stumble
11:28 shall return to his L with great substance, but
11:28 work his will, and return to his own L
11:39 and shall divide the L for a price.
11:41 He shall come into the glorious L
11:42 the countries, and the L of Egypt shall not
Hos 1:2 of harlotry, for the L commits great harlotry by
1:11 go up from the L, for great shall be
2:3 her like a parched L, and slay her with
2:15 came out of the L of Egypt.
2:18 and war from the L; and I will make
2:23 I will sow him for myself in the L
4:1 has a controversy with the inhabitants of the L
4:1 of God in the L;
4:3 Therefore the L mourns, and all who dwell in
7:17 their derision in the L of Egypt.
9:3 not remain in the L of the LORD; but
11:5 shall return to the L of Egypt, and Assyria
11:11 like doves from the L of Assyria; and I
12:9 your God from the L of Egypt; I will
12:12 (Jacob fled to the L of Aram, there Israel
13:4 your God from the L of Egypt; you know
13:5 the wilderness, in the L of drought;
Joel 1:2 aged men, give ear, all inhabitants of the L
1:6 come up against my L, powerful and without
1:13 the inhabitants of the L to the house of
2:1 the inhabitants of the L tremble, for the day
2:3 The L is like the garden of Eden before
2:18 became jealous for his L, and had pity on
2:20 a parched and desolate L, his front into the
2:21 "Fear not, O L; be glad and rejoice, for
3:2 have divided up my L,
3:19 because they have shed innocent blood in their L
Amos 2:10 up out of the L of Egypt, and led
2:10 wilderness, to possess the L of the Amorite.
3:1 up out of the L of Egypt:
3:9 the strongholds in the L of Egypt, and say,
3:11 adversary shall surround the L, and bring down your
5:2 Israel; forsaken on her L, with none to raise
7:2 the grass of the L, I said, "O Lord
7:4 the great deep and was eating up the L
7:10 house of Israel; the L is not able to
7:11 Israel must go into exile away from his L
7:12 flee away to the L of Judah, and eat
7:17 the sword, and your L shall be parceled out
7:17 die in an unclean L, and Israel shall surely
7:17 shall surely go into exile away from its L
8:4 the poor of the L to an end,
8:8 Shall not the L tremble on this account, and
8:11 a famine on the L; not a famine of
9:7 up Israel from the L of Egypt, and the
9:15 plant them upon their L, and they shall never
9:15 up out of the L which I have given
Obad 1:19 of the Shephelah the L of the Philistines; they

1:19 they shall possess the L of Ephraim and the
1:19 of Ephraim and the L of Samaria and Benjamin
Jon 1:9 heaven, who made the sea and the dry L
1:13 the ship back to L, but they could not,
2:6 went down to the L whose bars closed upon
2:10 and it vomited out Jonah upon the dry L
Mic 5:5 Assyrian comes into our L and treads upon our
5:6 they shall rule the L of Assyria with the
5:6 the sword, and the L of Nimrod with the
5:6 he comes into our L and treads within our
5:11 the cities of your L and throw down all
6:4 you up from the L of Egypt, and redeemed
7:14 midst of a garden L; let them feed in
7:15 came out of the L of Egypt I will
Nah 3:13 The gates of your L are wide open to
Hab 3:7 the curtains of the L of Midian did tremble.
Zeph 2:3 you humble of the L, who do his commands;
2:5 against you, O Canaan, L of the Philistines; and
2:9 Ammonites like Gomorrah, a L possessed by nettles
Hag 1:11 a drought upon the L and the hills, upon
2:4 you people of the L, says the LORD; work,
2:6 sea and the dry L;
Zech 1:21 their horns against the L of Judah to scatter
2:6 Flee from the L of the north, says the
2:12 portion in the holy L, and will again choose
3:9 the guilt of this L in a single day.
5:3 face of the whole L; for every one who
5:6 said, "This is their iniquity in all the L
5:11 to me, "To the L of Shinar, to build
7:5 the people of the L and the priests, When
7:14 Thus the L they left was desolate, so that
7:14 fro, and the pleasant L was made desolate."
9:1 LORD is against the L of Hadrach and will
9:16 of a crown they shall shine on his L
10:10 them home from the L of Egypt, and gather
10:10 bring them to the L of Gilead and to
11:6 the inhabitants of this L, says the LORD.
11:16 raising up in the L a shepherd who does
12:12 The L shall mourn, each family by itself; the
13:2 the idols from the L, so that they shall
13:2 will remove from the L the prophets and the
13:5 the soil; for the L has been my possession
13:8 In the whole L, says the LORD, two thirds
14:10 The whole L shall be turned into a plain
Mal 3:12 you will be a L of delight, says the
4:6 come and smite the L with a curse."
1Mac 1:1 who came from the L of Kittim, had defeated
1:16 become king of the L of Egypt, that he
1:19 fortified cities in the L of Egypt, and he
1:19 and he plundered the L of Egypt.
1:24 Taking them all, he departed to his own L
1:28 Even the L shook for its inhabitants, and all
1:44 customs strange to the L,
1:52 did evil in the L;
2:56 in the assembly, received an inheritance in the L
3:8 ungodly out of the L; thus he turned away
3:24 rest fled into the L of the Philistines.
3:29 had caused in the L by abolishing the laws
3:36 aliens in all their territory, and distribute their L
3:39 to go into the L of Judah and destroy
3:41 from Syria and the L of the Philistines joined
4:22 all fled into the L of the Philistines.
5:13 who were in the L of Tob have been
5:45 to go to the L of Judah.
5:48 us pass through your L to get to our
5:48 pass through your land to get to our L
5:53 he came to the L of Judah.
5:65 of Esau in the L to the south.
5:66 to go into the L of the Philistines, and
5:68 to Azotus in the L of the Philistines; he
5:68 and returned to the L of Judah.
6:5 had gone into the L of Judah had been
6:13 am perishing of deep grief in a strange L
6:49 since it was a sabbatical year for the L
7:6 friends, and have driven us out of our L
7:7 us and upon the L of the king, and
7:10 large force into the L of Judah; and he
7:22 gained control of the L of Judah and did
7:50 So the L of Judah had rest for a
8:3 had done in the L of Spain to get
8:10 plundered them, conquered the L, tore down their
8:16 to control all their L; they all heed the
8:23 at sea and on L for ever, and may
8:32 rights and fight you on sea and on L
9:1 and Alcimus into the L of Judah a second
9:53 leading men of the L as hostages and put
9:57 the king, and the L of Judah had rest
9:69 Then he decided to depart to his own L
9:72 formerly taken from the L of Judah; then he
9:72 departed to his own L, and came no more
10:13 left his place and departed to his own L
10:30 collect them from the L of Judah or from
10:33 a captive from the L of Judah into any
10:37 has commanded in the L of Judah.
10:39 Ptolemais and the L adjoining it I have given
10:55 you returned to the L of your fathers and
10:67 from Crete to the L of his fathers.
10:72 were twice put to flight in their own L
11:34 the crops of the L and the fruit of
11:38 king saw that the L was quiet before him
11:52 his kingdom, and the L was quiet before him.
12:4 safe conduct to the L of Judah.
12:46 they returned to the L of Judah.
12:52 they all reached the L of Judah safely, and
13:1 army to invade the L of Judah and destroy
13:12 army to invade the L of Judah, and Jonathan
13:22 and went into the L of Gilead.
13:24 Trypho turned back and departed to his own L
13:32 Asia; and he brought great calamity upon the L
14:4 The L had rest all the days of Simon.
14:8 They tilled their L in peace; the ground gave
14:11 established peace in the L, and Israel rejoiced with
14:13 was left in the L to fight them, and
15:10 out and invaded the L of his fathers.
15:14 the city hard from L and sea, and permitted
15:29 great damage in the L, and you have taken
15:33 have neither taken foreign L nor seized foreign
15:35 people and to our L; for them we will
2Mac 1:1 and those in the L of Judea, To their
1:7 revolted from the holy L and the kingdom
2:21 they seized the whole L and pursued the barbarian
4:26 a fugitive into the L of Ammon.
5:21 could sail on the L and walk on the
9:28 pitiable fate, among the mountains in a strange L
Mt 2:6 O Bethlehem, in the L of Judah, are by
2:20 and go to the L of Israel, for those
2:21 and went to the L of Israel.
4:15 might be fulfilled: "The L of Zebulun and the
4:15 of Zebulun and the L of Naphtali, toward the
10:15 of judgment for the L of Sodom and Gomorrah
11:24 of judgment for the L of Sodom than for
14:24 furlongs distant from the L, beaten by the waves;
14:34 over, they came to L at Gennesaret.
23:14 you traverse sea and L to make a single
27:45 darkness over all the L until the ninth hour.
Mk 4:1 whole crowd was beside the sea on the L
6:47 the sea, and he was alone on the L
6:53 over, they came to L at Gennesaret, and moored
15:32 darkness over the whole L until the ninth hour.
Lk 4:25 famine over all the L;
4:26 to Zarephath, in the L of Sidon, to a
5:3 him to put out a little from the L
5:11 brought their boats to L, they left everything and
8:27 he stepped out on L, there met him a
12:16 a parable, saying, "The L of a rich man
14:35 fit neither for the L nor for the dunghill;
23:43 darkness over the whole L until the ninth hour,
Jn 3:22 disciples went into the L of Judea; there he
6:21 boat was at the L to which they were
21:8 not far from the L, but about a hundred
21:9 they got out on L, they saw a charcoal
Acts 5:3 keep back part of the proceeds of the L
5:8 whether you sold the L for so much." And
7:3 him, 'Depart from your L and from your kindred
7:3 and go into the L which I will show
7:4 he departed from the L of the Chaldeans, and
7:4 from there into this L in which you are
7:6 be aliens in a L belonging to others, who
7:29 an exile in the L of Midian, where he
7:40 us out from the L of Egypt, we do
13:17 their stay in the L of Egypt, and with
13:19 seven nations in the L of Canaan, he gave
13:19 he gave them their L as an inheritance, for
20:13 he had arranged, intending himself to go by L
27:14 struck down from the L;
27:27 the sailors suspected that they were nearing L
27:39 did not recognize the L, but they noticed a
27:43 and make for the L,
27:44 And so it was that all escaped to L
Heb 6:7 For L which has drunk the rain that often
8:9 them out of the L of Egypt; for they
11:9 he sojourned in the L of promise, as in

L

11:9 as in a foreign L, living in tents with
11:15 been thinking of that L from which they had
11:29 as if on dry L; but the Egyptians, when
Jude 1:5 people out of the L of Egypt, afterward destroyed
Rev 10:2 left foot on the L,
10:5 standing on sea and L lifted up his right
10:8 is standing on the sea and on the L

LANDED (3)

1Mac 10:1 the son of Antiochus, L and occupied Ptolemais.
Acts 18:22 When he had L at Caesarea, he went up
21:3 sailed to Syria, and L at Tyre; for there

LANDING

1Mac 15:4 intend to make a L in the country so

LANDINGS

Judg 5:17 coast of the sea, settling down by his L

LANDMARK (5)

Deut 19:14 not remove your neighbor's L, which the men of
27:17 who removes his neighbor's L And all the people
Prov 22:28 Remove not the ancient L which your fathers have
23:10 not remove an ancient L or enter the fields
Hos 5:10 those who remove the L; upon them I will

LANDMARKS

Job 24:2 Men remove L; they seize flocks and pasture them.

LANDS (161)

Gen 10:5 of Japheth in their L, each with his own
10:20 families, their languages, their L, and their nations.
10:31 families, their languages, their L, and their nations.
26:3 will give all these L, and I will fulfil
26:4 your descendants all these L; and by your
41:54 was famine in all L; but in all the
47:18 of my lord but our bodies and our L
Lev 26:36 their hearts in the L of their enemies; the
26:39 away in your enemies' L because of their iniquity;
Num 35:2 to the Levites pasture L round about the cities.
35:3 in, and their pasture L shall be for their
35:4 The pasture L of the cities, which you shall
35:7 the Levites shall be forty-eight, with their pasture L
Josh 14:4 in, with their pasture L for their cattle and
21:2 along with their pasture L for our cattle."
21:3 following cities and pasture L out of their
21:8 cities and their pasture L the people of Israel
21:11 along with the pasture L round about it.
21:13 slayer, with its pasture L, Libnah with its pasture
21:13 Libnah with its pasture L,
21:14 Jattir with its pasture L, Eshtemoa with its pasture
21:14 Eshtemoa with its pasture L,
21:15 Holon with its pasture L, Debir with its pasture
21:15 Debir with its pasture L,
21:16 Ain with its pasture L, Juttah with its pasture
21:16 Juttah with its pasture L, Beth-shemesh with its
21:16 Beth-shemesh with its pasture L --nine cities out of
21:17 Gibeon with its pasture L, Geba with its pasture
21:17 Geba with its pasture L,
21:18 Anathoth with its pasture L, and Almon with its
21:18 Almon with its pasture L --four cities.
21:19 were in all thirteen cities with their pasture L
21:21 slayer, with its pasture L in the hill country
21:21 Gezer with its pasture L,
21:22 Kibza-im with its pasture L, Beth-horon with its
21:22 Beth-horon with its pasture L --four cities;
21:23 Elteke with its pasture L, Gibbethon with its pasture
21:23 Gibbethon with its pasture L,
21:24 Aijalon with its pasture L, Gath-rimmon with its
21:24 Gath-rimmon with its pasture L --four cities;
21:25 Taanach with its pasture L, and Gath-rimmon with
21:25 Gath-rimmon with its pasture L --two cities.
21:26 Kohathites were ten in all with their pasture L
21:27 Bashan with its pasture L, the city of refuge
21:27 Beeshterah with its pasture L --two cities;
21:28 Kishion with its pasture L, Daberath with its pasture
21:28 Daberath with its pasture L,
21:29 Jarmuth with its pasture L, En-gannim with its
21:29 En-gannim with its pasture L --four cities;
21:30 Mishal with its pasture L, Abdon with its pasture
21:30 Abdon with its pasture L,
21:31 Helkath with its pasture L, and Rehob with its
21:31 Rehob with its pasture L --four cities;
21:32 Galilee with its pasture L, the city of refuge
21:32 Hammoth-dor with its pasture L, and Kartan with its
21:32 Kartan with its pasture L --three cities.
21:33 were in all thirteen cities with their pasture L
21:34 Jokne-am with its pasture L, Kartah with its pasture
21:34 Kartah with its pasture L,
21:35 Dimnah with its pasture L, Nahalal with its pasture
21:35 Nahalal with its pasture L --four cities;
21:36 Bezer with its pasture L, Jahaz with its pasture
21:36 Jahaz with its pasture L,
21:37 Kedemoth with its pasture L, and Mephaath with its
21:37 Mephaath with its pasture L --four cities;
21:38 Gilead with its pasture L, the city of refuge
21:38 Mahanaim with its pasture L,
21:39 Heshbon with its pasture L, Jazer with its pasture
21:39 Jazer with its pasture L --four cities in all.
21:41 were in all forty-eight cities with their pasture L
21:42 had each its pasture L round about it; so
2Kgs 19:11 have done to all L, destroying them utterly.
19:17 the nations and their L,
1Chr 5:16 in all the pasture L of Sharon to their
6:55 and its surrounding pasture L,
6:57 Libnah with its pasture L, Jattir, Eshtemoa with its
6:57 Eshtemoa with its pasture L,
6:58 Hilen with its pasture L, Debir with its pasture
6:58 Debir with its pasture L,
6:59 Ashan with its pasture L, and Beth-shemesh with its
6:59 Beth-shemesh with its pasture L;
6:60 Geba with its pasture L, Alemeth with its pasture
6:60 Alemeth with its pasture L, and Anathoth with its
6:60 its pasture lands, and Anathoth with its pasture L
6:64 gave the Levites the cities with their pasture L
6:67 Shechem with its pasture L in the hill country
6:67 Gezer with its pasture L,
6:68 Jokmeam with its pasture L, Beth-horon with its
6:68 Beth-horon with its pasture L,
6:69 Aijalon with its pasture L, Gath-rimmon with its
6:69 Gath-rimmon with its pasture L,
6:70 Aner with its pasture L, and Bile-am with its
6:70 Bile-am with its pasture L, for the rest of
6:71 Bashan with its pasture L and Ashtaroth with its
6:71 Ashtaroth with its pasture L;
6:72 Kedesh with its pasture L, Daberath with its pasture
6:72 Daberath with its pasture L,
6:73 Ramoth with its pasture L, and Anem with its
6:73 Anem with its pasture L;
6:74 Mashal with its pasture L, Abdon with its pasture
6:74 Abdon with its pasture L,
6:75 Hukok with its pasture L, and Rehob with its
6:75 Rehob with its pasture L;
6:76 Galilee with its pasture L, Hammon with its pasture
6:76 Hammon with its pasture L, and Kiriathaim with its
6:76 its pasture lands, and Kiriathaim with its pasture L
6:77 Rimmono with its pasture L, Tabor with its pasture
6:77 Tabor with its pasture L,
6:78 steppe with its pasture L, Jahzah with its pasture
6:78 Jahzah with its pasture L,
6:79 Kedemoth with its pasture L, and Mephaath with its
6:79 Mephaath with its pasture L;
6:80 Gilead with its pasture L, Mahanaim with its pasture
6:80 Mahanaim with its pasture L,
6:81 Heshbon with its pasture L, and Jazer with its
6:81 its pasture lands, and Jazer with its pasture L
13:2 cities that have pasture L, that they may come
14:17 went out into all L, and the LORD brought
22:5 and glory throughout all L; I will therefore make
2Chr 9:28 imported for Solomon from Egypt and from all L
11:14 Levites left their common L and their holdings and
13:9 priests for yourselves like the peoples of other L
15:5 disturbances afflicted all the inhabitants of the L
17:10 the kingdoms of the L that were round about
26:10 and in the fertile L, for he loved the
32:13 have done to all the peoples of other L
32:13 the nations of those L at all able to
32:13 able to deliver their L out of my hand?
32:17 the nations of the L who have not delivered
Ezra 3:3 the peoples of the L, and they offered burnt
9:1 the peoples of the L with their abominations, from
9:2 has mixed itself with the peoples of the L
9:7 the kings of the L, to the sword, to
9:11 the peoples of the L, with their abominations which
Neh 9:30 into the hand of the peoples of the L
10:28 the peoples of the L to the law of
Jud 2:27 cities and ravaged their L and put to death
Ps 49:11 generations, though they named L their own.
100:1 a joyful noise to the LORD, all the L
105:44 he gave them the L of the nations; and
106:27 among the nations, scattering them over the L
107:3 gathered in from the L, from the east and

Sir 10:16 Lord has overthrown the L of the nations, and
39:4 will travel through the L of foreign nations, for
Is 37:11 have done to all L, destroying them utterly.
37:18 the nations and their L,
Jer 27:6 have given all these L into the hand of
40:11 Edom and in other L heard that the king
Ezek 20:6 milk and honey, the most glorious of all L
20:15 most glorious of all L,
30:23 the nations, and disperse them throughout the L
39:27 them from their enemies' L, and through them have
Dan 9:7 away, in all the L to which thou hast
Zeph 2:11 its place, all the L of the nations.
1Mac 6:25 also against all the L on their borders.
Mt 19:29 mother or children or L, for my name's sake,
Mk 10:29 father or children or L, for my sake and
10:30 mothers and children and L, with persecutions, and
Acts 4:34 as were possessors of L or houses sold them,
28:7 of that place were L belonging to the chief
2Cor 10:16 preach the gospel in L beyond you, without boasting

LANES (2)

Tob 13:18 of Ophir; all her L will cry 'Hallelujah!' and
Lk 14:21 to the streets and L of the city, and

LANGUAGE (40)

Gen 10:5 each with his own L, by their families, in
11:1 whole earth had one L and few words.
11:6 they have all one L; and this is only
11:7 and there confuse their L, that they may not
11:9 the LORD confused the L of all the earth;
Deut 28:49 flies, a nation whose L you do not understand,
2Kgs 18:26 servants in the Aramaic L, for we understand it;
18:26 to us in the L of Judah within the
18:28 loud voice in the L of Judah: "Hear the
2Chr 32:18 loud voice in the L of Judah to the
Neh 13:24 their children spoke the L of Ashdod, and they
13:24 could not speak the L of Judah, but the
13:24 of Judah, but the L of each people.
Esth 1:22 people in its own L, that every man be
1:22 speak according to the L of his people.
3:12 people in its own L; it was written in
8:9 people in its own L, and also to the
8:9 to the Jews in their script and their L
Ps 114:1 a people of strange L,
Is 19:18 Egypt which speak the L of Canaan and swear
36:11 to us in the L of Judah within the
36:13 loud voice in the L of Judah: "Hear the
Jer 5:15 nation, a nation whose L you do not know,
Bar 4:15 nation, of a strange L, who had no respect
Ezek 3:5 speech and a hard L, but to the house
3:6 speech and a hard L, whose words you cannot
Dan 1:4 them the letters and L of the Chaldeans.
3:97 Any people, nation, or L that speaks anything against
2Mac 7:8 He replied in the L of his fathers, and
7:21 of them in the L of their fathers.
12:37 In the L of their fathers he raised the
15:29 Sovereign Lord in the L of their fathers.
15:36 Adar in the Syrian L – the day
Acts 1:19 was called in their L Akeldama, that is, Field
2:6 each one heard them speaking in his own L
2:8 hear, each of us in his own native L
21:40 them in the Hebrew L, saying:
22:2 them in the Hebrew L, they were the more
26:14 me in the Hebrew L, 'Saul, Saul, why do
1Cor 14:11 the meaning of the L, I shall be a

LANGUAGES (9)

Gen 10:20 by their families, their L, their lands, and their
10:31 by their families, their L, their lands, and their
Dan 3:4 O peoples, nations, and L,
3:7 the peoples, nations, and L fell down and worshiped
4:1 all peoples, nations, and L, that dwell in all
5:19 all peoples, nations, and L trembled and feared
6:25 the peoples, nations, and L that dwell in all
7:14 all peoples, nations, and L should serve him; his
1Cor 14:10 are doubtless many different L in the world, and

LANGUISH (7)

Is 16:8 the fields of Heshbon L, and the vine of
19:8 Nile; and they will L who spread nets upon
24:4 and withers; the heavens L together with the earth.
Jer 14:2 mourns and her gates L; her people lament on
31:12 garden, and they shall L no more.
Lam 2:8 wall to lament, they L together.
Hos 4:3 who dwell in it L, and also the beasts

LANGUISHED (3)

Gen 47:13 the land of Canaan L by reason of the
Ps 68:9 thy heritage as it L;
Jer 15:9 who bore seven has L; she has swooned away;

LANGUISHES (6)

Ps 119:81 My soul L for thy salvation; I hope in
Is 24:4 and withers, the world L and withers; the heavens
24:7 wine mourns, the vine L, all the merry-hearted sigh.
33:9 The land mourns and L; Lebanon is confounded and
Joel 1:10 grain is destroyed, the wine fails, the oil L
1:11 The vine withers, the fig tree L

LANGUISHING (3)

Deut 28:65 failing eyes, and a L soul;
Ps 6:2 LORD, for I am L; O LORD, heal me,
Jer 31:25 weary soul, and every L soul I will replenish."

LANTERNS

Jn 18:3 Pharisees, went there with L and torches and

LAP (5)

2Kgs 4:20 child sat on her L till noon, and then
4:39 gathered from it his L full of wild gourds,
Neh 5:13 also shook out my L and said, "So may
Prov 16:33 is cast into the L, but the decision is
Lk 6:38 together, running over, will be put into your L

LAPPED (2)

Judg 7:6 number of those that L, putting their hands to
7:7 three hundred men that L I will deliver you,

LAPPIDOTH

Judg 4:4 prophetess, the wife of L, was judging Israel at

LAPS (2)

Judg 7:5 Gideon, "Every one that L the water with his
7:5 tongue, as a dog L, you shall set by

LAPSE

2Mac 10:3 offered sacrifices, after a L of two years, and

LARGE (77)

Gen 29:2 the well's mouth was L,
30:43 exceedingly rich, and had L flocks, maidservants and
34:21 behold, the land is L enough for them; let
Num 13:28 are fortified and very L; and besides, we saw
26:54 To a L tribe you shall give a large
26:54 you shall give a L inheritance, and to a
33:54 your families; to a L tribe you shall give
33:54 you shall give a L inheritance, and to a
Deut 25:13 kinds of weights, a L and a small.
25:14 kinds of measures, a L and a small.
27:2 you shall set up L stones, and plaster them
Josh 19:9 of Judah was too L for them, the tribe
1Kgs 10:16 Solomon made two hundred L shields of beaten
2Chr 9:15 Solomon made two hundred L shields of beaten
23:9 the spears and the L and small shields that
26:10 cisterns, for he had L herds, both in the
Neh 7:4 city was wide and L, but the people within
9:35 them, and in the L and rich land which
13:5 prepared for Tobiah a L chamber where they had
Tob 7:8 the flock and set L servings of food before
Jud 5:3 How L is their army, and in what does
Sir 51:28 Get instruction with a L sum of silver, and
Is 5:9 houses shall be desolate, L and beautiful houses,
8:1 to me, "Take a L tablet and write upon
30:23 cattle will graze in L pastures;
Jer 41:9 had slain was the L cistern which King Asa
43:9 "Take in your hands L stones, and hide them
Ezek 17:15 him horses and a L army.
23:32 which is deep and L; you shall be laughed
31:5 forest; its boughs grew L and its branches long,
1Mac 1:17 cavalry and with a L fleet.
1:29 to Jerusalem with a L force.
3:10 together Gentiles and a L force from Samaria to
3:13 Judas had gathered a L company, including a body
3:31 regions and raise a L fund.
5:26 cities were strong and L –
5:30 up, and behold, a L company, that could not
5:38 it is a very L force.
5:45 and goods, a very L company, to go to
5:46 This was a L and very strong city on
5:52 the Jordan into the L plain before Beth-shan.
6:41 the army was very L and strong.
7:10 and came with a L force into the land

L

7:11 had come with a L force.
7:27 to Jerusalem with a L force, and treacherously sent
8:6 chariots and a very L army.
9:37 from Nadabath with a L escort."
9:43 he came with a L force on the sabbath
9:60 to come with a L force, and secretly sent
10:2 he assembled a very L army and marched out
10:48 Alexander the king assembled L forces and
10:69 and he assembled a L force and encamped against
10:77 thousand cavalry and a L army, and went to
10:77 for he had a L troop of cavalry and
11:63 in Galilee with a L army, intending to remove
12:42 had come with a L army, he was afraid
13:1 Trypho had assembled a L army to invade the
13:12 from Ptolemais with a L army to invade the
14:24 to Rome with a L gold shield weighing a
16:5 plain, and behold, a L force of infantry and
2Mac 1:31 should be poured upon L stones.
Mt 19:2 beyond the Jordan; and L crowds followed him, and
26:9 been sold for a L sum, and given to
Mk 4:1 And a very L crowd gathered about him, so
4:32 shrubs, and puts forth L branches, so that the
12:41 rich people put in L sums.
14:15 will show you a L upper room furnished and
16:4 stone was rolled back; --it was very L
Lk 5:29 and there was a L company of tax collectors
7:12 a widow; and a L crowd from the city
8:32 Now a L herd of swine was feeding there
22:12 will show you a L upper room furnished; there
Jn 21:11 net ashore, full of L fish, a hundred and
Acts 11:24 And a L company was added to the Lord.
11:26 church, and taught a L company of people; and
22:28 this citizenship for a L sum." Paul said, "But
Gal 6:11 See with what L letters I am writing to

LARGENESS

1Kgs 4:29 understanding beyond measure, and L of mind like

L

LARGER (7)

Num 26:56 to lot between the L and the smaller."
35:8 of Israel, from the L tribes you shall take
Deut 20:1 chariots and an army L than your own, you
Ezek 43:14 smaller ledge to the L ledge, four cubits, with
1Mac 4:35 again with an even L army.
12:24 had returned, with a L force than before, to
Lk 12:18 my barns, and build L ones; and there I

LASEA

Acts 27:8 Fair Havens, near which was the city of L

LASHA

Gen 10:19 Sodom, Gomorrah, Admah, and Zeboiim, as far as L

LASHARON

Josh 12:18 one; the king of L, one;

LASHED

Wis 5:11 found; the light air, L by the beat of

LASHES

2Cor 11:24 the Jews the forty L less one.

LAST (116)

Gen 2:23 man said, "This at L is bone of my
19:4 the people to the L man, surrounded the house;
19:34 younger, "Behold, I lay L night with my father;
25:8 Abraham breathed his L and died in a good
25:17 years; he breathed his L and died, and was
31:29 father spoke to me L night, saying, 'Take heed
31:42 hands, and rebuked you L night."
33:2 and Rachel and Joseph L of all.
33:7 and bowed down; and L Joseph and Rachel drew
35:29 And Isaac breathed his L; and he died and
49:33 bed, and breathed his L, and was gathered to
Lev 26:5 And your threshing shall L to the time of
26:5 and the vintage shall L to the time for
Num 2:31 They shall set out L, standard by standard."
14:33 your faithlessness, until the L of your dead bodies
Deut 28:54 bosom, and to the L of the children who
Josh 8:24 them to the very L had fallen by the
Ruth 3:10 you have made this L kindness greater than the
2Sam 15:17 they halted at the L house.
19:11 should you be the L to bring the king
19:12 should you be the L to bring back the
23:1 Now these are the L words of David: The
1Chr 23:27 for by the L words of David these
29:29 David, from first to L, are written in the
2Chr 9:29 Solomon, from first to L, are they not written
12:15 Rehoboam, from first to L, are they not written
16:11 Asa, from first to L, are written in the
20:34 Jehoshaphat, from first to L, are written in the
25:26 Amaziah, from first to L, are they not written
26:22 Uzziah, from first to L, Isaiah the prophet the
28:26 ways, from first to L, behold, they are written
35:27 his acts, first and L, behold, they are written
Neh 8:18 first day to the L day, he read from
Jud 7:28 and children draw their L breath.
Job 11:20 them, and their hope is to breathe their L
14:10 low; man breathes his L, and where is he?
19:25 Redeemer lives, and at L he will stand upon
Ps 68:25 in front, the minstrels L, between them maidens
81:15 and their fate would L for ever.
Prov 23:32 At the L it bites like a serpent, and
27:24 for riches do not L for ever; and does
Wis 2:16 unclean; he calls the L end of the righteous
Sir 6:28 For at L you will find the rest she
12:12 of honor, and at L you will realize the
24:26 know her perfectly, the L one has not fathomed
32:11 do not be the L; go home quickly and
33:16 I was the L on watch; I was like
48:24 might he saw the L things, and comforted those
51:14 and I will search for her to the L
Is 41:4 first, and with the L; I am He.
44:6 and I am the L; besides me there is
48:12 I am the first, and I am the L
Jer 32:14 vessel, that they may L for a long time.
50:12 she shall be the L of the nations, a
50:17 him, and now at L Nebuchadrezzar king of Babylon
Dan 4:8 At L Daniel came in before me--he who
8:3 the other, and the higher one came up L
Amos 4:2 with hooks, even the L of you with fishhooks.
1Mac 6:53 Gentiles had consumed the L of the stores.
2Mac 3:31 lying quite at his L breath.
5:5 forced back and at L the city was being
7:9 he was at his L breath, he said, "You
7:41 L of all, the mother died, after her sons.
Mt 5:26 you have paid the L penny.
12:45 dwell there; and the L state of that man
19:30 are first will be L, and the last first.
19:30 be last, and the L first.
20:8 wages, beginning with the L, up to the first.'
20:12 householder, saying, 'These L worked only one hour,
20:14 to give to this L as I give to
20:16 my generosity?' So the L will be first, and
20:16 the last will be first, and the first L
26:60 At L two came forward
27:64 the dead,' and the L fraud will be worse
Mk 9:35 first, he must be L of all and servant
10:31 are first will be L, and the last first."
10:31 be last, and the L first."
12:22 L of all the woman also died.
15:36 Jesus uttered a loud cry, and breathed his L
15:38 he thus breathed his L, he said, "Truly this
Lk 11:26 dwell there; and the L state of that man
12:59 have paid the very L copper."
13:30 And behold, some are L who will be first,
13:30 first, and some are first who will be L
23:45 And having said this he breathed his L
Jn 6:39 it up at the L day.
6:40 him up at the L day."
6:44 him up at the L day.
6:54 him up at the L day.
7:37 On the L day of the feast, the great
11:24 the resurrection at the L day."
12:48 his judge on the L day.
Acts 2:17 Joel: 'And in the L days it shall be,
27:20 being saved was at L abandoned.
Rom 1:10 I may now at L succeed in coming to
1Cor 4:9 exhibited us apostles as L of all, like men
15:8 L of all, as to one untimely born, he
15:26 The L enemy to be destroyed is death.
15:45 a living being"; the L Adam became a life-giving
15:52 an eye, at the L trumpet.
2Cor 9:2 has been ready since L year; and your zeal
1Thes 2:16 But God's wrath has come upon them at L
2Tim 3:1 this, that in the L days there will come
Heb 1:2 prophets, but in these L days he has spoken
Jas 5:3 up treasure for the L days.
1Pet 1:5 be revealed in the L time.
2Pet 2:20 and overpowered, the L state has become worse
3:3 will come in the L days with scoffing, following
1Jn 2:18 Children, it is the L hour; and as you

2:18 that it is the L hour.
Jude 1:18 to you, "In the L time there will be
Rev 1:17 the first and the L,
2:8 the first and the L, who died and came
15:1 plagues, which are the L, for with them the
21:9 full of the seven L plagues, and spoke to
22:13 the first and the L, the beginning and the

LASTED (3)
Judg 14:17 days that their feast L; and on the seventh
Tob 8:19 feast for them which L fourteen days.
Jud 13:1 because the banquet had L long.

LASTHENES (2)
1Mac 11:31 wrote concerning you to L our kinsman we have
11:32 'King Demetrius to L his father, greeting.

LASTING (8)
Deut 28:59 severe and L, and sicknesses grievous and L
Esth 1:5 and small, a banquet L for seven days, in
13:2 of my subjects in L tranquillity and, in order
Sir 11:15 he approves will have L success.
11:31 he give you a L blemish.
49:13 of Nehemiah also is L; he raised for us
Heb 13:14 here we have no L city, but we seek

LASTS (2)
Sir 22:10 Mourning for the dead L seven days, but for
22:10 an ungodly man it L all his life.

LATCH
Song 5:4 his hand to the L, and my heart was

LATE (12)
Ex 9:32 ruined, for they are L in coming up.)
Deut 32:17 had come in of L, whom your fathers had
2Sam 11:2 It happened, L one afternoon, when David arose
Ps 127:2 up early and go L to rest, eating the
Is 5:11 strong drink, who tarry L into the evening till
1Mac 10:80 from early morning till L afternoon.
2Mac 8:25 were obliged to return because the hour was L
Mk 6:35 And when it grew L, his disciples came to
6:35 the hour is now L;
11:11 as it was already L, he went out to
Jas 5:7 the early and the L rain.
Jude 1:12 winds; fruitless trees in L autumn, twice dead,

LATELY
Acts 18:2 a native of Pontus, L come from Italy with

LATER (21)
Gen 30:33 will answer for me L, when you come to
38:24 About three months L Judah was told, "Tamar your
Deut 11:14 early rain and the L rain, that you may
1Sam 25:38 And about ten days L the LORD smote Nabal;
Ezra 8:13 Adonikam, those who came L, their names being
Eccl 1:11 be any remembrance of L things yet to happen
4:16 Yet those who come L will not rejoice in
Sir 27:23 admires your words; but L he will twist his
1Mac 1:29 Two years L the king sent to the cities
11:18 Ptolemy died three days L, and his troops in
2Mac 4:17 a fact which L events will make clear.
14:1 Three years L, word came to Judas and his
Lk 15:13 Not many days L, the younger son gathered all
22:56 And a little L some one else saw him
Jn 20:26 Eight days L, his disciples were again in the
1Tim 4:1 expressly says that in L times some will depart
5:24 to judgment, but the sins of others appear L
Heb 3:5 were to be spoken L,
4:8 God would not speak L of another day.
7:28 the oath, which came L than the law, appoints
12:11 painful rather than pleasant; L it yields the peaceful

LATIN
Jn 19:20 written in Hebrew, in L, and in Greek.

LATRINE
2Kgs 10:27 and made it a L to this day.

LATTER (33)
Ex 4:8 they may believe the L sign.
Num 24:14 your people in the L days."
Deut 4:30 upon you in the L days, you will return
24:3 man's wife, and the L husband dislikes her and
24:3 house, or if the L husband dies, who took
32:29 they would discern their L end!
Job 8:7 beginning was small, your L days will be very
42:12 the LORD blessed the L days of Job more
Wis 19:16 the aliens; but the L, after receiving them with
Is 2:2 to pass in the L days that the mountain
9:1 Naphtali, but in the L time he will make
Jer 12:4 will not see our L end."
23:20 In the L days you will understand it clearly.
30:24 In the L days you will understand this.
48:47 of Moab in the L days, says the LORD."
49:39 "But in the L days I will restore the
Ezek 38:8 be mustered; in the L years you will go
38:16 In the L days I will bring you against
Dan 2:28 will be in the L days.
8:19 shall be at the L end of the indignation;
8:23 And at the L end of their rule, when
10:14 your people in the L days.
11:9 Then the L shall come into the realm of
Hos 3:5 his goodness in the L days.
Joel 2:23 the early and the L rain, as before.
Amos 7:1 shooting up of the L growth; and lo, it
7:1 lo, it was the L growth after the king's
Mic 4:1 to pass in the L days that the mountain
Hag 2:9 The L splendor of this house shall be greater
1Mac 11:34 Lydda and Rathamin; the L, with all the region
2Mac 14:31 When the L became aware that he had been
Phil 1:16 The L do it out of love, knowing that
Rev 2:19 endurance, and that your L works exceed the first.

LATTICE (4)
Judg 5:28 Sisera gazed through the L: 'Why is his chariot
2Kgs 1:2 Ahaziah fell through the L in his upper chamber
Prov 7:6 looked out through my L,
Song 2:9 gazing in at the windows, looking through the L

LAUD
Ps 145:4 One generation shall L thy works to another, and

LAUGH (17)
Gen 18:13 Abraham, "Why did Sarah L, and say, 'Shall I
18:15 saying, "I did not L; for she was afraid.
18:15 He said, "No, but you did L
21:6 one who hears will L over me."
Jud 12:12 embrace her she will L at us."
Job 5:22 and famine you shall L, and shall not fear
22:19 are glad; the innocent L them to scorn,
Ps 52:6 and fear, and shall L at him, saying,
59:8 thou, O LORD, dost L at them; thou dost
80:6 neighbors; and our enemies L among themselves.
Prov 1:26 reproof, I also will L at your calamity; I
Eccl 3:4 and a time to L; a time to mourn,
Wis 4:18 but the Lord will L them to scorn.
Sir 30:10 Do not L with him, lest you have sorrow
Hab 1:10 They L at every fortress, for they heap up
Lk 6:21 are you that weep now, for you shall L
6:25 "Woe to you that L now, for you shall

LAUGHED (11)
Gen 17:17 on his face and L, and said to himself,
18:12 So Sarah L to herself, saying, "After I have
38:23 own, lest we be L at; you see, I
2Chr 30:10 as Zebulun; but they L them to scorn, and
Tob 2:8 And my neighbors L at me and said, "He
Ezek 23:32 large; you shall be L at and held in
Dan 14:7 Then Daniel L, and said, "Do not be deceived,
14:19 Then Daniel L, and restrained the king from going
Mt 9:24 And they L at him.
Mk 5:40 And they L at him.
Lk 8:53 And they L at him, knowing that she was

LAUGHINGSTOCK (9)
Job 12:4 I am a L to my friends; I, who
12:4 me, a just and blameless man, am a L
Ps 44:14 among the nations, a L among the peoples.
Sir 6:4 and make him the L of his enemies.
18:30 will make you the L of your enemies.
42:11 she make you a L to your enemies, a
Jer 20:7 I have become a L all the day; every
Lam 3:14 I have become the L of all peoples, the
1Mac 10:70 I have become a L and reproach because of

LAUGHS (8)
Job 39:18 herself to flee, she L at the horse and
39:22 He L at fear, and is not dismayed; he
41:29 counted as stubble; he L at the rattle of
Ps 2:4 sits in the heavens L; the LORD has them
37:13 him; but the LORD L at the wicked, for

L

Prov 29:9 fool only rages and L, and there is no
31:25 her clothing, and she L at the time to
Sir 21:20 his voice when he L, but a clever man

LAUGHTER (11)
Gen 21:6 said, "God has made L for me; every one
Job 8:21 fill your mouth with L, and your lips with
Ps 126:2 mouth was filled with L, and our tongue with
Prov 14:13 Even in L the heart is sad, and the
Eccl 2:2 I said of L, "It is mad," and of
7:3 Sorrow is better than L, for by sadness of
7:6 pot, so is the L of the fools; this
10:19 Bread is made for L, and wine gladdens life,
Sir 19:27 man's attire and open-mouthed L, and a man's
27:13 is offensive, and their L is wantonly sinful.
Jas 4:9 Let your L be turned to mourning and your

LAUNCHED
2Mac 4:40 three thousand men and L an unjust attack, under

LAVER (12)
Ex 30:18 shall also make a L of bronze, with its
30:28 its utensils and the L and its base;
31:9 its utensils, and the L and its base,
35:16 all its utensils, the L and its base;
38:8 And he made the L of bronze and its
39:39 all its utensils; the L and its base;
Lev 8:11 its utensils, and the L and its base, to
1Kgs 7:30 at the four corners were supports for a L
7:38 lavers of bronze; each L held forty baths, each
7:38 held forty baths, each L measured four cubits, and
7:38 and there was a L for each of the
2Kgs 16:17 stands, and removed the L from them, and he

LAVERS (4)
1Kgs 7:38 And he made ten L of bronze; each laver
7:43 stands, and the ten L upon the stands;
2Chr 4:6 He also made ten L in which to wash,
4:14 stands also, and the L upon the stands,

LAVISH
Is 46:6 Those who L gold from the purse, and weigh

LAVISHED (4)
Esth 1:7 the royal wine was L according to the bounty
Ezek 16:15 of your renown, and L your harlotries on any
Hos 2:8 the oil, and who L upon her silver and
Eph 1:8 his grace which he L upon us.

LAVISHLY
1Mac 3:30 used to give more L than preceding kings.

LAW (498)
Ex 12:49 There shall be one L for the native and
13:9 your eyes, that the L of the LORD may
16:4 will walk in my L or not.
24:12 of stone, with the L and the commandment, which
Lev 6:9 saying, This is the L of the burnt offering.
6:14 "And this is the L of the cereal offering.
6:25 sons, This is the L of the sin offering.
7:1 "This is the L of the guilt offering.
7:7 offering, there is one L for them; the priest
7:11 "And this is the L of the sacrifice of
7:37 This is the L of the burnt offering, of
11:46 This is the L pertaining to beast and bird
12:7 This is the L for her who bears a
13:59 This is the L for a leprous disease in
14:2 "This shall be the L of the leper for
14:32 This is the L for him in whom is
14:54 This is the L for any leprous disease: for
14:57 This is the L for leprosy.
15:3 And this is the L of his uncleanness for
15:32 This is the L for him who has a
24:22 You shall have one L for the sojourner and
Num 5:29 "This is the L in cases of jealousy, when
5:30 the priest shall execute upon her all this L
6:13 "And this is the L for the Nazirite, when
6:21 "This is the L for the Nazirite who takes
6:21 do according to the L for his separation as
15:16 One L and one ordinance shall be for you
15:29 You shall have one L for him who does
19:2 the statute of the L which the LORD has
19:14 "This is the L when a man dies in
31:21 the statute of the L which the LORD has
Deut 1:5 undertook to explain this L, saying,
4:8 righteous as all this L which I set before
4:44 This is the L which Moses set before the
17:18 a copy of this L, from that which is
17:19 the words of this L and these statutes, and
27:3 the words of this L, when you pass over
27:8 the words of this L very plainly."
27:26 the words of this L by doing them.' And
28:58 the words of this L which are written in
28:61 the book of this L, the LORD will bring
29:21 the covenant written in this book of the L
29:29 we may do all the words of this L
30:10 this book of the L, if you turn to
31:9 And Moses wrote this L, and gave it to
31:11 you shall read this L before all Israel in
31:12 the words of this L,
31:24 the words of this L in a book, to
31:26 this book of the L, and put it by
32:46 careful to do all the words of this L
33:4 Moses commanded us a L, as a possession for
33:10 ordinances, and Israel thy L; they shall put incense
Josh 1:7 according to all the L which Moses my servant
1:8 This book of the L shall not depart out
8:31 the book of the L of Moses, "an altar
8:32 a copy of the L of Moses, which he
8:34 the words of the L, the blessing and the
8:34 that is written in the book of the L
22:5 the commandment and the L which Moses the
23:6 the book of the L of Moses, turning aside
24:26 the book of the L of God; and he
1Kgs 2:3 is written in the L of Moses, that you
2Kgs 10:31 to walk in the L of the LORD the
14:6 the book of the L of Moses, where the
17:13 accordance with all the L which I commanded your
17:26 do not know the L of the god of
17:26 do not know the L of the god of
17:27 and teach them the L of the god of
17:34 the ordinances or the L or the commandment which
17:37 the ordinances and the L and the commandment
21:8 according to all the L that my servant Moses
22:8 the book of the L in the house of
22:11 the book of the L, he rent his clothes.
23:24 the words of the L which were written in
23:25 according to all the L of Moses; nor did
1Chr 16:40 is written in the L of the LORD which
22:12 you may keep the L of the LORD your
2Chr 6:16 to walk in my L as you have walked
12:1 strong, he forsook the L of the LORD, and
14:4 and to keep the L and the commandment.
15:3 teaching priest, and without L;
17:9 the book of the L of the LORD with
19:10 cities, concerning bloodshed, L or commandment,
23:18 is written in the L of Moses, with rejoicing
25:4 is written in the L, in the book of
30:16 posts according to the L of Moses the man
31:3 is written in the L of the LORD.
31:4 give themselves to the L of the LORD.
31:21 in accordance with the L and the commandments,
33:8 commanded them, all the L, the statutes, and the
34:14 the book of the L of the LORD given
34:15 the book of the L in the house of
34:19 the words of the L he rent his clothes.
35:26 is written in the L of the LORD,
Ezra 3:2 is written in the L of Moses the man
7:6 scribe skilled in the L of Moses which the
7:10 heart to study the L of the LORD, and
7:12 the scribe of the L of the God of
7:14 Jerusalem according to the L of your God, which
7:21 the scribe of the L of the God of
7:26 will not obey the L of your God and
7:26 your God and the L of the king, let
10:3 and let it be done according to the L
Neh 8:1 the book of the L of Moses which the
8:2 the priest brought the L before the assembly, both
8:3 people were attentive to the book of the L
8:7 people to understand the L, while the people
8:8 the book, from the L of God, clearly; and
8:9 wept when they heard the words of the L
8:13 in order to study the words of the L
8:14 it written in the L that the LORD had
8:18 the book of the L of God.
9:3 the book of the L of the LORD their
9:14 and statutes and a L by Moses thy servant.
9:26 thee and cast thy L behind their back and
9:29 in order to turn them back to thy L
9:34 have not kept thy L or heeded thy commandments
10:28 the lands to the L of God, their wives,
10:29 to walk in God's L which was given by

	10:34	our God, as it is written in the L
	10:36	is written in the L, and the firstlings of
	12:44	portions required by the L for the priests and
	13:3	the people heard the L, they separated from Israel
Tob	6:12	Raguel, according to the L of Moses, cannot give
	7:12	"Take her right now, in accordance with the L
	7:13	her according to the L of Moses, and take
	14:9	But keep the L and the commandments, and be
Esth	1:8	was according to the L, no one was compelled;
	1:13	who were versed in L and judgment,
	1:15	: "According to the L, what is to be
	4:11	there is but one L; all alike are to
	4:16	it is against the L; and if I perish,
	15:10	not die, for our L applies only to the
Ps	1:2	delight is in the L of the LORD, and
	1:2	LORD, and on his L he meditates day and
	19:7	The L of the LORD is perfect, reviving the
	37:31	The L of his God is in his heart;
	40:8	O my God; thy L is within my heart."
	55:19	because they keep no L, and do not fear
	78:5	Jacob, and appointed a L in Israel, which he
	78:10	covenant, but refused to walk according to his L
	89:30	his children forsake my L and do not walk
	94:12	teach out of thy L
	119:1	who walk in the L of the LORD!
	119:18	I may behold wondrous things out of thy L
	119:29	far from me; and graciously teach me thy L
	119:34	I may keep thy L and observe it with
	119:44	I will keep thy L continually, for ever and
	119:51	but I do not turn away from thy L
	119:53	me because of the wicked, who forsake thy L
	119:55	in the night, O LORD, and keep thy L
	119:61	wicked ensnare me, I do not forget thy L
	119:70	gross like fat, but I delight in thy L
	119:72	The L of thy mouth is better to me
	119:77	may live; for thy L is my delight.
	119:85	me, men who do not conform to thy L
	119:92	If thy L had not been my delight, I
	119:97	Oh, how I love thy L
	119:109	hand continually, but I do not forget thy L
	119:113	I hate double-minded men, but I love thy L
	119:126	to act, for thy L has been broken.
	119:136	of tears, because men do not keep thy L
	119:142	for ever, and thy L is true.
	119:150	with evil purpose; they are far from thy L
	119:153	deliver me, for I do not forget thy L
	119:163	hate and abhor falsehood, but I love thy L
	119:165	those who love thy L; nothing can make them
	119:174	O LORD, and thy L is my delight.
Prov	28:4	Those who forsake the L praise the wicked, but
	28:4	those who keep the L strive against them.
	28:7	He who keeps the L is a wise son,
	28:9	ear from hearing the L, even his prayer is
	29:18	restraint, but blessed is he who keeps the L
Wis	2:11	our might be our L of right, for what
	2:12	for sins against the L, and accuses us of
	6:4	rightly, nor keep the L, nor walk according to
	14:16	was kept as a L, and at the command
	16:6	remind them of thy L's command.
	18:4	imperishable light of the L was to be given
	18:9	agreed to the divine L, that the saints would
Sir	2:16	who love him will be filled with the L
	8:14	Do not go to L against a judge, for
	9:15	discussion be about the L of the Most High.
	15:1	who holds to the L will obtain wisdom.
	17:9	allotted to them the L of life.
	19:17	him; and let the L of the Most High
	19:18	all wisdom there is the fulfilment of the L
	19:21	than the highly prudent man who transgresses the L
	21:11	Whoever keeps the L controls his thoughts, and
	23:23	she has disobeyed the L of the Most High;
	24:22	Most High God, the L which Moses commanded us
	32:15	He who seeks the L will be filled with
	32:24	He who believes the L gives heed to the
	33:2	will not hate the L, but he who is
	33:3	will trust in the L; for him the law
	33:3	law; for him the L is as dependable as
	34:8	Without such deceptions the L will be fulfilled, and
	35:1	He who keeps the L makes many offerings; he
	39:1	the study of the L of the Most High
	39:8	will glory in the L of the Lord's covenant.
	41:8	who have forsaken the L of the Most High
	42:2	to sin: of the L of the Most High
	44:21	glory; he kept the L of the Most High,
	45:5	face to face, the L of life and knowledge,
	45:17	the testimonies, and to enlighten Israel with his L
	46:14	By the L of the Lord he judged the
	49:4	for they forsook the L of the Most High;
Is	2:3	shall go forth the L, and the word of
	5:24	they have rejected the L of the LORD of
	42:4	the earth; and the coastlands wait for his L
	42:21	sake, to magnify his L and make it glorious.
	42:24	not walk, and whose L they would not obey?
	51:4	my nation; for a L will go forth from
	51:7	whose heart is my L; fear not the reproach
	59:4	no one goes to L honestly; they rely on
Jer	2:8	Those who handle the L did not know me;
	5:4	of the LORD, the L of their God.
	5:5	of the LORD, the L of their God." But
	6:19	and as for my L, they have rejected it.
	8:8	are wise, and the L of the LORD is
	9:13	they have forsaken my L which I set before
	16:11	have not kept my L,
	18:18	against Jeremiah, for the L shall not perish from
	26:4	to walk in my L which I have set
	31:33	I will put my L within them, and I
	32:23	or walk in thy L; they did nothing of
	44:10	nor walked in my L and my statutes which
	44:23	or walk in his L and in his statutes
Lam	2:9	among the nations; the L is no more, and
Bar	2:2	is written in the L of Moses,
	2:28	him to write thy L in the presence of
	4:1	of God, and the L that endures for ever.
	4:12	turned away from the L of God.
Ezek	7:26	the prophet, but the L perishes from the priest,
	22:26	done violence to my L and have profaned my
	43:12	This is the L of the temple: the whole
	43:12	Behold, this is the L of the temple.
Dan	6:5	in connection with the L of his God."
	6:8	changed, according to the L of the Medes and
	6:12	fast, according to the L of the Medes and
	6:15	that it is a L of the Medes and
	7:25	the times and the L; and they shall be
	9:11	Israel has transgressed thy L and turned aside,
	9:11	are written in the L of Moses the servant
	9:13	is written in the L of Moses, all this
	13:3	daughter according to the L of Moses.
	13:6	who had suits at L came to them.
	13:62	in accordance with the L of Moses, they put
Hos	4:6	you have forgotten the L of your God, I
	8:1	have broken my covenant, and transgressed my L
Amos	2:4	they have rejected the L of the LORD, and
Mic	4:2	shall go forth the L, and the word of
Hab	1:4	So the L is slacked and justice never goes
Zeph	3:4	what is sacred, they do violence to the L
Zech	7:12	they should hear the L and the words which
Mal	4:4	"Remember the L of my servant Moses, the statutes
1Mac	1:49	they should forget the L and change all the
	1:52	one who forsook the L, joined them, and they
	1:56	The books of the L which they found they
	1:57	one adhered to the L, the decree of the
	2:21	us to desert the L and the ordinances.
	2:26	with zeal for the L, as Phinehas did against
	2:27	is zealous for the L and supports the covenant
	2:42	every one who offered himself willingly for the L
	2:48	They rescued the L out of the hands of
	2:50	show zeal for the L, and give your lives
	2:58	great zeal for the L was taken up into
	2:64	grow strong in the L, for by it you
	2:67	all who observe the L, and avenge the wrong
	2:68	and heed what the L commands."
	3:48	the book of the L to inquire into those
	3:56	should return to his home, according to the L
	4:42	priests devoted to the L,
	4:47	unhewn stones, as the L directs, and built a
	4:53	offered sacrifice, as the L directs, on the new
	10:14	who had forsaken the L and the commandments, for
	13:48	and settled in it men who observed the L
	14:14	he sought out the L, and did away with
	14:29	their sanctuary and the L might be perserved; and
	15:21	that he may punish them according to their L
2Mac	1:4	your heart to his L and his commandments, and
	2:2	after giving them the L instructed those who were
	2:3	exhorted them that the L should not depart from
	2:18	and consecration, as he promised through the L
	3:15	who had given the L about deposits, that he
	4:11	living and introduced new customs contrary to the L
	6:23	to the holy God-given L, he declared himself quickly,
	7:30	the command of the L that was given to
	10:26	their adversaries, as the L declares.
	12:40	of Jamnia, which the L forbids the Jews to
	13:10	being deprived of the L and their country and

15:9 Encouraging them from the L and the prophets, and
Mt 5:17 come to abolish the L and the prophets; I
5:18 will pass from the L until all is accomplished.
7:12 for this is the L and the prophets.
11:13 the prophets and the L prophesied until John;
12:5 not read in the L how on the sabbath
22:36 "Teacher, which is the great commandment in the L
22:40 commandments depend all the L and the prophets."
23:22 weightier matters of the L, justice and mercy and
Lk 2:22 purification according to the L of Moses, they
2:23 is written in the L of the Lord, "Every
2:24 is said in the L of the Lord, "a
2:27 the custom of the L,
2:39 everything according to the L of the Lord, they
5:17 and teachers of the L sitting by, who had
10:26 said to him, "What is written in the L
16:16 "The L and the prophets were until John; since
16:17 one dot of the L to become void.
24:44 about me in the L of Moses and the
Jn 1:17 For the L was given through Moses; grace and
1:45 whom Moses in the L and also the prophets
7:19 Did not Moses give you the L
7:19 Yet none of you keeps the L
7:23 circumcision, so that the L of Moses may not
7:49 do not know the L, are accursed."
7:51 to them, "Does our L judge a man without
8:5 Now in the L Moses commanded us to stone
8:17 In your L it is written that the testimony
10:34 not written in your L, 'I said, you are
12:34 have heard from the L that the Christ remains
15:25 is written in their L, 'They hated me without
18:31 him yourselves and judge him by your own L
19:7 him, "We have a L, and by that law
19:7 law, and by that L he ought to die,
Acts 5:34 a teacher of the L, held in honor by
6:13 holy place and the L;
7:53 you who received the L as delivered by angels
13:15 the reading of the L and the prophets, the
13:39 be freed by the L of Moses.
15:5 them to keep the L of Moses."
18:13 persuading men to worship God contrary to the L
18:15 names and your own L, see to it yourselves;
21:20 all zealous for the L,
21:24 that you yourself live in observance of the L
21:28 the people and the L and this place; moreover
22:3 strict manner of the L of our fathers, being
22:12 man according to the L, well spoken of by
23:3 me according to the L, and yet contrary to
23:3 yet contrary to the L you order me to
23:29 about questions of their L, but charged with nothing
24:13 laid down by the L or written in the
25:8 defense, "Neither against the L of the Jews, nor
28:23 Jesus both from the L of Moses and from
Rom 2:12 have sinned without the L will also perish without
2:12 also perish without the L, and all who have
2:12 have sinned under the L will be judged by
2:12 under the law will be judged by the L
2:13 the hearers of the L who are righteous before
2:13 the doers of the L who will be justified.
2:14 who have not the L do by nature what
2:14 by nature what the L requires, they are a
2:14 requires, they are a L to themselves, even though
2:14 themselves, even though they do not have the L
2:15 show that what the L requires is written on
2:17 and rely upon the L and boast of your
2:18 are instructed in the L,
2:20 children, having in the L the embodiment of
2:23 who boast in the L, do you dishonor God
2:23 law, do you dishonor God by breaking the L
2:25 if you obey the L; but if you break
2:25 if you break the L, your circumcision becomes
2:26 the precepts of the L, will not his uncircumcision
2:27 uncircumcised but keep the L will condemn you who
2:27 the written code and circumcision but break the L
3:19 know that whatever the L says it speaks to
3:19 who are under the L, so that every mouth
3:20 by works of the L, since through the law
3:20 law, since through the L comes knowledge of sin.
3:21 been manifested apart from L, although the law and
3:21 from law, although the L and the prophets bear
3:28 is justified by faith apart from works of L
3:31 we then overthrow the L by this faith?
3:31 On the contrary, we uphold the L
4:13 come through the L but through the righteousness
4:14 the adherents of the L who are to be
4:15 For the L brings wrath, but where there is
4:15 where there is no L there is no transgression.
4:16 the adherents of the L but also to those
5:13 the world before the L was given, but sin
5:13 sin is not counted where there is no L
5:20 L came in, to increase the trespass; but where
6:14 you are not under L but under grace.
6:15 we are not under L but under grace?
7:1 those who know the L --that the law is
7:1 the law--that the L is binding on a
7:2 woman is bound by L to her husband as
7:2 is discharged from the L concerning the husband.
7:3 is free from that L, and if she marries
7:4 have died to the L through the body of
7:5 passions, aroused by the L, were at work in
7:6 are discharged from the L, dead to that which
7:7 That the L is sin?
7:7 not been for the L, I should not have
7:7 to covet if the L had not said, "You
7:8 Apart from the L sin lies dead.
7:9 alive apart from the L, but when the commandment
7:12 So the L is holy, and the commandment is
7:14 We know that the L is spiritual; but I
7:16 I agree that the L is good.
7:21 it to be a L that when I want
7:22 I delight in the L of God, in my
7:23 in my members another L at war with the
7:23 at war with the L of my mind and
7:23 me captive to the L of sin which dwells
7:25 of myself serve the L of God with my
7:25 flesh I serve the L of sin.
8:2 For the L of the Spirit of life in
8:2 me free from the L of sin and death.
8:3 has done what the L, weakened by the flesh,
8:4 just requirement of the L might be fulfilled in
8:7 not submit to God's L, indeed it cannot;
9:4 the giving of the L, the worship, and the
9:31 which is based on L did not succeed in
9:31 on law did not succeed in fulfilling that L
10:4 the end of the L, that every one who
10:5 is based on the L shall live by it.
13:8 he who loves his neighbor has fulfilled the L
13:10 neighbor; therefore love is the fulfilling of the L
1Cor 6:1 he dare go to L before the unrighteous instead
6:6 but brother goes to L against brother, and that
9:8 Does not the L say the same?
9:9 is written in the L of Moses, "You shall
9:20 to those under the L I became as one
9:20 as one under the L --though not being myself
9:20 being myself under the L --that I might win
9:20 law--that I might win those under the L
9:21 To those outside the L I became as one
9:21 as one outside the L --not being without law
9:21 law--not being without L toward God but under
9:21 God but under the L of Christ--that I
9:21 Christ--that I might win those outside the L
14:21 In the L it is written, "By men of
14:34 subordinate, as even the L says.
15:56 sin, and the power of sin is the L
Gal 2:16 by works of the L but through faith in
2:16 by works of the L, because by works of
2:16 by works of the L shall no one be
2:19 For I through the L died to the law,
2:19 law died to the L, that I might live
2:21 justification were through the L, then Christ died to
3:2 by works of the L, or by hearing with
3:5 by works of the L, or by hearing with
3:10 on works of the L are under a curse;
3:10 the book of the L, and do them."
3:11 before God by the L; for "He who through
3:12 shall live"; but the L does not rest on
3:13 the curse of the L, having become a curse
3:17 what I mean: the L, which came four hundred
3:18 inheritance is by the L, it is no longer
3:19 Why then the L
3:21 Is the L then against the promises of God?
3:21 not; for if a L had been given which
3:21 alive, then righteousness would indeed be by the L
3:23 were confined under the L, kept under restraint until
3:24 So that the L was our custodian until Christ
4:4 woman, born under the L,
4:5 who were under the L, so that we might
4:21 desire to be under L, do you not hear
4:21 be under law, do you not hear the L
5:3 that he is bound to keep the whole L
5:4 be justified by the L; you have fallen away
5:14 For the whole L is fulfilled in one word,

5:18 by the Spirit you are not under the L
5:23 gentleness, self-control; against such there is no L
6:2 and so fulfil the L of Christ.
6:13 not themselves keep the L, but they desire to
Eph 2:15 in his flesh the L of commandments and ordinances,
Phil 3:5 Hebrews; as to the L a Pharisee,
3:6 to righteousness under the L blameless.
3:9 my own, based on L, but that which is
1Tim 1:7 be teachers of the L, without understanding either
1:8 we know that the L is good, if any
1:9 understanding this, that the L is not laid down
Tit 3:9 and quarrels over the L, for they are unprofitable
Heb 7:5 a commandment in the L to take tithes from
7:11 the people received the L, what further need would
7:12 a change in the L as well.
7:19 and uselessness (for the L made nothing perfect); on
7:28 Indeed, the L appoints men in their weakness as
7:28 came later than the L, appoints a Son who
8:4 are priests who offer gifts according to the L
9:19 every commandment of the L had been declared by
9:22 Indeed, under the L almost everything is purified
10:1 For since the L has but a shadow of
10:8 offered according to the L,
10:28 who has violated the L of Moses dies without
Jas 1:24 looks into the perfect L, the law of liberty,
1:24 the perfect law, the L of liberty, and perseveres,
2:8 really fulfil the royal L, according to the scripture,
2:9 are convicted by the L as transgressors.
2:10 whoever keeps the whole L but fails in one
2:11 kill, you have become a transgressor of the L
2:12 be judged under the L of liberty.
4:11 speaks evil against the L and judges the law.
4:11 speaks evil against the law and judges the L
4:11 if you judge the L, you are not a
4:11 a doer of the L but a judge.

LAWBREAKER

2Mac 13:7 about that Menelaus the L died, without even burial

LAWFUL (37)

Ezra 7:24 it shall not be L to impose tribute, custom,
Jud 11:13 although it is not L for any of the
Ezek 18:5 and does what is L and right–
18:19 has done what is L and right, and has
18:21 and does what is L and right, he shall
18:27 and does what is L and right, he shall
33:14 and does what is L and right,
33:16 has done what is L and right, he shall
33:19 and does what is L and right, he shall
2Mac 4:11 and he destroyed the L ways of living and
Mt 12:2 doing what is not L to do on the
12:4 which it was not L for him to eat
12:10 asked him, "Is it L to heal on the
12:12 So it is L to do good on the
14:4 him, "It is not L for you to have
19:3 by asking, "Is it L to divorce one's wife
22:17 Is it L to pay taxes to Caesar, or
27:6 said, "It is not L to put them into
Mk 2:24 doing what is not L on the sabbath?"
2:26 which it is not L for any but the
3:4 to them, "Is it L on the sabbath to
6:18 Herod, "It is not L for you to have
10:2 him asked, "Is it L for a man to
12:14 Is it L to pay taxes to Caesar, or
Lk 6:2 doing what is not L to do on the
6:4 which it is not L for any but the
6:9 ask you, is it L on the sabbath to
14:3 Pharisees, saying, "Is it L to heal on the
20:22 Is it L for us to give tribute to
Jn 5:9 sabbath, it is not L for you to carry
18:31 him, "It is not L for us to put
Acts 16:21 which it is not L for us Romans to
22:25 standing by, "Is it L for you to scourge
1Cor 6:12 "All things are L for me," but not all
6:12 "All things are L for me," but I will
10:23 "All things are L
10:23 "All things are L

LAWFULLY

1Tim 1:8 any one uses it L,

LAWGIVER

Jas 4:12 There is one L and judge, he who is

LAWLESS (30)

Wis 1:9 convict him of his L deeds;
3:14 hands have done no L deed, and who has
4:20 reckoned up, and their L deeds will convict them
15:17 what he makes with L hands is dead, for
17:2 For when L men supposed that they held the
Sir 16:4 through a tribe of L men it will be
34:18 the gifts of the L are not acceptable.
Dan 3:32 into the hands of L enemies, most hateful rebels,
1Mac 1:11 In those days L men came forth from Israel,
1:34 there a sinful people, L men.
2:44 in their anger and L men in their wrath;
3:5 out and pursued the L; he burned those who
3:6 L men shrank back for fear of him; all
7:5 to him all the L and ungodly men of
9:23 death of Judas, the L emerged in all parts
9:58 Then all the L plotted and said, "See!
9:69 greatly enraged at the L men who had counseled
10:61 pestilent men from Israel, L men, gathered together
11:21 But certain L men who hated their nation went
11:25 Although certain L men of his nation kept making
14:14 did away with every L and wicked man.
2Mac 8:4 to remember also the L destruction of the innocent
8:17 before their eyes the L outrage which the Gentiles
Acts 2:23 by the hands of L men.
2Thes 2:8 And then the L one will be revealed, and
2:9 The coming of the L one by the activity
1Tim 1:9 just but for the L and disobedient, for the
1Pet 4:3 drunkenness, revels, carousing, and L idolatry.
2Pet 2:8 after day with their L deeds),
3:17 with the error of L men and lose your

LAWLESSLY

Dan 3:29 we have sinfully and L departed from thee, and

LAWLESSNESS (10)

Prov 11:30 tree of life, but L takes away lives.
Wis 5:7 of the paths of L and destruction, and we
5:23 L will lay waste the whole earth, and evil-doing
Sir 21:3 All L is like a two-edged sword; there is
1Mac 3:20 in great pride and L to destroy us and
2Thes 2:3 and the man of L is revealed, the son
2:7 For the mystery of L is already at work;
Heb 1:9 loved righteousness and hated L; therefore God, thy
1Jn 3:4 sin is guilty of L; sin is lawlessness.
3:4 commits sin is guilty of lawlessness; sin is L

LAWS (51)

Gen 26:5 charge, my commandments, my statutes, and my L
Ex 16:28 you refuse to keep my commandments and my L
Lev 26:46 statutes and ordinances and L which the LORD
Ezra 7:25 such as know the L of your God; and
Neh 9:13 right ordinances and true L, good statutes and
Jud 11:12 that God by his L has forbidden them to
Esth 1:19 be written among the L of the Persians and
3:8 of your kingdom; their L are different from those
3:8 not keep the king's L, so that it is
13:4 hostile people, who have L contrary to those of
13:5 manner of life and L, and is ill-disposed to
16:15 governed by most righteous L
16:19 permit the Jews to live under their own L
Ps 105:45 they should keep his statutes, and observe his L
Wis 6:18 the keeping of her L, and giving heed to
6:18 giving heed to her L is assurance of immortality,
9:5 understanding of judgment and L;
Is 24:5 they have transgressed the L, violated the statutes,
Ezek 43:11 ordinances and all its L; and write it down
43:11 and perform all its L and all its ordinances.
44:5 LORD and all its L; and mark well those
44:24 They shall keep my L and my statutes in
Dan 9:10 God by following his L, which he set before
Hos 8:12 write for him my L by ten thousands, they
1Mac 3:21 but we fight for our lives and our L
3:29 land by abolishing the L that had existed from
6:59 them live by their L as they did before;
6:59 on account of their L which we abolished that
10:37 live by their own L, just as the king
13:3 have done for the L and the sanctuary; you
2Mac 2:22 city and restored the L that were about to
3:1 unbroken peace and the L were very well observed
4:2 his fellow countrymen, and a zealot for the L
4:17 irreverence to the divine L – a fact
5:8 a rebel against the L, and abhorred as the
5:15 traitor both to the L and to his country.
6:1 Jews to forsake the L of their fathers and
6:1 to live by the L of God,
6:5 abominable offerings which were forbidden by the L
6:28 willingly and nobly for the revered and holy L

L

7:2 rather than transgress the L of our fathers."
7:9 of life, because we have died for his L
7:11 and because of his L I disdain them, and
7:23 now forget yourselves for the sake of his L
7:37 and life for the L of our fathers, appealing
8:21 to die for their L and their country; then
8:36 because they followed the L ordained by him.
11:31 their own food and L, just as formerly, and
13:14 the death for the L, temple, city, country, and
Heb 8:10 I will put my L into their minds, and
10:16 I will put my L on their hearts, and

LAWSUITS (2)

Sir 29:19 into suretyship and pursues gain will fall into L
1Cor 6:7 To have L at all with one another is

LAWYER (3)

Mt 22:35 one of them, a L, asked him a question,
Lk 10:25 And behold, a L stood up to put him
Tit 3:13 to speed Zenas the L and Apollos on their

LAWYERS (5)

Lk 7:30 the Pharisees and the L rejected the purpose of
11:45 One of the L answered him, "Teacher, in saying
11:46 said, "Woe to you L also!
11:52 Woe to you L!
14:3 Jesus spoke to the L and Pharisees, saying, "Is

LAY (255)

Gen 9:21 and became drunk, and L uncovered in his tent.
19:4 But before they L down, the men of the
19:33 first-born went in, and L with her father; he
19:33 not know when she L down or when she
19:34 the younger, "Behold, I L last night with my
19:35 the younger arose, and L with him; and he
19:35 not know when she L down or when she
22:12 He said, "Do not L your hand on the
28:11 under his head and L down in that place
30:16 So he L with her that night.
30:42 flock he did not L them there; so the
34:2 he seized her and L with her and humbled
35:22 land Reuben went and L with Bilhah his father's
37:22 in the wilderness, but L no hand upon him"—
41:35 that are coming, and L up grain under the
Ex 5:8 made heretofore you shall L upon them, you shall
7:4 you; then I will L my hand upon Egypt
7:23 and he did not L even this to heart.
16:13 in the morning dew L round about the camp.
16:23 that is left over L by to be kept
21:22 the woman's husband shall L upon him; and he
24:11 And he did not L his hand on the
29:10 and his sons shall L their hands upon the
29:15 and his sons shall L their hands upon the
29:19 and his sons shall L their hands upon the
Lev 1:4 the LORD; he shall L his hand upon the
1:7 on the altar, and L wood in order upon
1:8 sons the priests shall L the pieces, the head,
1:12 and the priest shall L them in order upon
2:15 oil upon it, and L frankincense on it; it
3:2 And he shall L his hand upon the head
3:13 before the LORD, and L his hand upon its
4:4 before the LORD, and L his hand on the
4:15 of the congregation shall L their hands upon the
4:24 without blemish, and shall L his hand upon the
4:29 And he shall L his hand on the head
4:33 female without blemish, and L his hand upon the
6:12 morning, and he shall L the burnt offering in
16:21 goat; and Aaron shall L both his hands upon
24:14 all who heard him L their hands upon his
26:31 And I will L your cities waste, and will
Num 8:10 people of Israel shall L their hands upon the
8:12 Then the Levites shall L their hands upon the
11:11 sight, that thou dost L the burden of all
16:46 off the altar, and L incense on it, and
22:27 of the LORD, she L down under Balaam; and
24:9 He couched, he L down like a lion, and
27:18 is the spirit, and L your hand upon him;
Deut 4:39 therefore this day, and L it to your heart,
7:15 you, but he will L them upon all who
9:18 Then I L prostrate before the LORD as before,
9:25 "So I L prostrate before the LORD for these
11:18 "You shall therefore L up these words of mine
11:25 LORD your God will L the fear of you
14:28 the same year, and L it up within your
22:22 die, the man who L with the woman, and
22:25 only the man who L with her shall die.
22:29 then the man who L with her shall give
32:46 he said to them, L to heart all the
Josh 2:8 Before they L down, she came up to them
4:3 over with you, and L them down in the
6:26 his first-born shall he L its foundation, and at
8:2 as booty for yourselves; L an ambush against the
8:9 place of ambush, and L between Bethel and Ai,
18:1 meeting there; the land L subdued before them.
Judg 3:25 opened them; and there L their lord dead on
4:22 her tent; and there L Sisera dead, with the
5:27 sank, he fell, he L still at her feet;
7:12 people of the East L along the valley like
7:13 so that the tent L flat."
16:2 surrounded the place and L in wait for him
16:3 But Samson L till midnight, and at midnight he
Ruth 3:7 uncovered his feet, and L down.
3:8 and behold, a woman L at his feet!
3:14 So she L at his feet until the morning,
1Sam 2:22 Israel, and how they L with the women who
3:5 So he went and L down.
3:9 So Samuel went and L down in his place.
3:15 Samuel L until morning; then he opened the doors
9:25 the roof, and he L down to sleep.
15:5 city of Amalek, and L in wait in the
19:24 prophesied before Samuel, and L naked all that day
26:5 the place where Saul L, with Abner the son
26:7 by night; and there L Saul sleeping within the
26:7 Abner and the army L around him.
2Sam 4:7 the house, as he L on his bed in
11:4 to him, and he L with her.
12:16 and went in and L all night upon the
12:24 in to her, and L with her; and she
13:6 So Amnon L down, and pretended to be ill;
13:14 he forced her, and L with her.
13:31 rent his garments, and L on the earth; and
20:12 And Amasa L wallowing in his blood in the
1Kgs 3:19 the night, because she L on it.
5:17 stones in order to L the foundation of the
8:47 near; yet if they L it to heart in
13:4 from the altar, saying, L hold of him." And
13:31 of God is buried; L my bones beside his
18:23 it in pieces and L it on the wood,
18:23 the other bull and L it on the wood,
19:5 And he L down and slept under a broom
19:6 ate and drank, and L down again.
20:6 of your servants, and L hands on whatever pleases
21:4 And he L down on his bed, and turned
21:27 flesh, and fasted and L in sackcloth, and went
2Kgs 1:2 chamber in Samaria, and L sick; so he sent
4:29 do not reply; and L my staff upon the
4:34 he went up and L upon the child, putting
9:16 to Jezreel, for Joram L there.
10:8 he said, L them in two heaps at the
20:7 let them take and L it on the boil,
1Chr 9:27 God; for upon them L the duty of watching,
2Chr 6:37 near; yet if they L it to heart in
35:5 of your brethren the L people, and let there
35:7 Josiah contributed to the L people, as passover
35:12 fathers' houses of the L people, to offer to
35:13 quickly to all the L people.
36:21 the days that it L desolate it kept sabbath,
Neh 10:32 We also L upon ourselves the obligation to charge
13:21 so again I will L hands on you." From
Tob 6:16 ashes of incense and L upon them some of
12:13 order to go and L out the dead, your
Jud 10:2 rose from where she L prostrate and called her
12:16 Judith came in and L down, and Holofernes' heart
13:15 canopy beneath which he L in his drunken stupor.
Esth 2:21 angry and sought to L hands on King Ahasuerus.
3:6 But he disdained to L hands on Mordecai alone.
4:3 and most of them L in sackcloth and ashes.
6:2 who had sought to L hands upon King Ahasuerus.
8:7 gallows, because he would L hands on the Jews.
9:2 of King Ahasuerus to L hands on such as
12:2 they were preparing to L hands upon Artaxerxes the
Job 9:33 between us, who might L his hand upon us
17:3 L down a pledge for me with thyself; who
21:5 and be appalled, and L your hand upon your
22:22 from his mouth, and L up his words in
22:24 your tents, if you L gold in the dust,
23:4 I would L my case before him and fill
40:4 I L my hand on my mouth.
41:8 L hands on him; think of the battle; you
Ps 7:5 to the ground, and L my soul in the
22:15 my jaws; thou dost L me in the dust
38:12 who seek my life L their snares, those who

	50:21	I rebuke you, and L the charge before you.
	66:11	the net; thou didst L affliction on our loins;
	76:6	both rider and horse L stunned.
	83:3	They L crafty plans against thy people; they consult
	84:3	herself, where she may L her young, at thy
	102:25	Of old thou didst L the foundation of the
Prov	3:18	life to those who L hold of her; those
	10:14	Wise men L up knowledge, but the babbling of
Eccl	2:3	wisdom--and how to L hold on folly, till
	7:2	and the living will L it to heart.
Song	7:8	the palm tree and L hold of its branches.
Wis	5:23	Lawlessness will L waste the whole earth, and
	10:12	safe from those who L in wait for him;
	17:2	their power they themselves L as captives of
	17:7	of their magic art L humbled, and their boasted
Sir	21:4	Terror and violence will L waste riches; thus the
	29:11	L up your treasure according to the commandments
	38:16	L out his body with the honor due him,
Is	3:17	and the LORD will L bare their secret parts.
	13:11	of the arrogant, and L low the haughtiness of
	21:2	Go up, O Elam, L siege, O Media; all
	24:1	Behold, the LORD will L waste the earth and
	25:11	but the LORD will L low his pride together
	25:12	he will bring down, L low, and cast to
	27:5	Or let them L hold of my protection, let
	29:21	be an offender, and L a snare for him
	34:15	the owl nest and L and hatch and gather
	42:15	I will L waste mountains and hills, and dry
	47:7	that you did not L these things to heart
	54:11	stones in antimony, and L your foundations with
Jer	6:21	LORD: 'Behold, I will L before this people stumbling
	6:23	They L hold on bow and spear, they are
	50:42	They L hold of bow and spear; they are
Lam	2:8	The LORD determined to L in ruins the wall
	4:19	on the mountains, they L in wait for us
Ezek	3:20	commits iniquity, and I L a stumbling block before
	4:1	take a brick and L it before you, and
	4:4	side, and I will L the punishment of the
	6:5	And I will L the dead bodies of the
	14:5	idols, that I may L hold of the hearts
	25:9	nations, therefore I will L open the flank of
	25:14	And I will L my vengeance upon Edom by
	25:17	the LORD, when I L my vengeance upon them."
	35:4	I will L your cities waste, and you shall
	36:29	make it abundant and L no famine upon you.
	37:6	And I will L sinews upon you, and will
	44:19	have been ministering, and L them in the holy
Dan	2:28	your head as you L in bed are these:
	2:29	O king, as you L in bed came thoughts
	4:5	me afraid; as I L in bed the fancies
	4:10	my head as I L in bed were these:
	4:13	my head as I L in bed, and behold,
	7:1	his head as he L in his bed.
	8:27	Daniel, was overcome and L sick for some days;
	13:37	came to her and L with her.
Hos	2:12	And I will L waste her vines and her
Amos	2:8	name is profaned; they L themselves down beside
Jon	1:14	this man's life, and L not on us innocent
Mic	1:7	her idols I will L waste; for from the
	7:16	their might; they shall L their hands on their
Zech	14:13	so that each will L hold on the hand
Mal	2:2	if you will not L it to heart to
	2:2	because you do not L it to heart.
1Mac	6:9	He L there for many days, because deep grief
	14:31	invade their country and L hands on their sanctuary,
	15:3	and I intend to L claim to the kingdom
	16:5	them; and a stream L between them.
2Mac	3:29	While he L prostrate, speechless because of the
	15:18	for brethren and relatives, L upon them less heavily;
Mt	6:19	"Do not L up for yourselves treasures on earth,
	6:20	in and steal, but L up for yourselves treasures
	8:20	man has nowhere to L his head."
	9:18	died; but come and L your hand on her,
	12:11	the sabbath, will not L hold of it and
	19:13	him that he might L his hands on them
	23:4	hard to bear, and L them on men's shoulders;
	28:6	Come, see the place where he L
Mk	1:30	Now Simon's mother-in-law L sick with a fever, and
	2:4	let down the pallet on which the paralytic L
	5:23	Come and L your hands on her, so that
	7:31	they besought him to L his hand upon him.
	16:18	hurt them; they will L their hands on the
Lk	5:18	bring him in and L him before Jesus;
	5:25	that on which he L, and went home, glorifying
	9:58	man has nowhere to L his head."
	16:20	And at his gate L a poor man named
	19:21	what you did not L down, and reap what
	19:22	what I did not L down and reaping what
	20:19	chief priests tried to L hands on him at
	21:12	all this they will L their hands on you
	22:51	temple, you did not L hands on me.
Jn	5:3	In these L a multitude of invalids, blind, lame,
	10:15	the Father; and I L down my life for
	10:17	loves me, because I L down my life, that
	10:18	from me, but I L it down of my
	10:18	I have power to L it down, and I
	11:38	cave, and a stone L upon it.
	13:37	I will L down my life for you."
	13:38	Jesus answered, "Will you L down your life for
	15:13	this, that a man L down his life for
Acts	8:19	one on whom I L my hands may receive
	9:12	Ananias come in and L his hands on him
	15:28	and to us to L upon you no greater
	27:20	and no small tempest L on us, all hope
	28:8	the father of Publius L sick with fever and
1Cor	3:11	foundation can any one L than that which is
	6:4	cases, why do you L them before those who
	7:35	own benefit, not to L any restraint upon you,
2Cor	12:14	children ought not to L up for their parents,
Heb	12:1	witnesses, let us also L aside every weight, and
1Jn	3:16	and we ought to L down our lives for
Rev	2:24	say, I do not L upon you any other

LAYEST

Ps	139:5	behind and before, and L thy hand upon me.

LAYING (23)

Lev	3:8	it before the LORD, L his hand upon the
Judg	6:37	said, behold, I am L a fleece of wool
	19:29	took a knife, and L hold of his concubine
1Sam	28:9	Why then are you L a snare for my
1Kgs	15:27	and all Israel were L siege to Gibbethon.
Tob	4:9	So you will be L up a good treasure
Ps	64:5	purpose; they talk of L snares secretly, thinking,
Is	28:16	GOD, "Behold, I am L in Zion for a
	51:16	out the heavens and L the foundations of the
Jer	51:55	For the LORD is L Babylon waste, and stilling
Ezek	42:14	the outer court without L there the garments in
Hab	3:13	head of the wicked, L him bare from thigh
Mk	10:16	arms and blessed them, L his hands upon them.
Acts	8:18	was given through the L on of the apostles'
	9:17	And L his hands on him he said, "Brother
	27:30	sea, under pretense of L out anchors from the
Rom	9:33	written, "Behold, I am L in Zion a stone
1Tim	5:22	be hasty in the L on of hands, nor
	6:19	liberal and generous, thus L up for themselves a
2Tim	1:6	within you through the L on of my hands;
Heb	6:1	on to maturity, not L again a foundation of
	6:2	instruction about ablutions, the L on of hands, the
1Pet	2:6	scripture: "Behold, I am L in Zion a stone,

LAYS (14)

Job	8:15	does not stand; he L hold of it, but
	18:9	the heel, a snare L hold of him.
	37:15	you know how God L his command upon them,
Prov	29:25	The fear of man L a snare, but he
Sir	3:4	is like one who L up treasure.
	50:28	things, and he who L them to heart will
Is	26:5	He L it low, lays it low to the
	26:5	He lays it low, L it low to the
	30:32	punishment which the LORD L upon them will be
	57:1	perishes, and no one L it to heart; devout
Jer	12:11	desolate, but no man L it to heart.
Lk	12:21	So is he who L up treasure for himself,
	15:5	has found it, he L it on his shoulders,
Jn	10:11	The good shepherd L down his life for the

LAZARUS (16)

Lk	16:20	a poor man named L, full of sores,
	16:23	saw Abraham far-off and L in his bosom.
	16:24	upon me, and send L to dip the end
	16:25	your good things, and L in like manner evil
Jn	11:1	certain man was ill, L of Bethany, the village
	11:2	her hair, whose brother L was ill.
	11:5	Now Jesus loved Martha and her sister and L
	11:11	to them, "Our friend L has fallen asleep, but
	11:14	Jesus told them plainly, L is dead;
	11:17	came, he found that L had already been in
	11:43	with a loud voice, L, come out."
	12:1	came to Bethany, where L was, whom Jesus had
	12:2	supper; Martha served, and L was one of those
	12:9	but also to see L, whom he had raised

L

12:10 priests planned to put L also to death,
12:17 him when he called L out of the tomb

LAZY (2)

Sir 37:11 his work, with a L servant about a big
Tit 1:11 always liars, evil beasts, L gluttons."

LE-UMMIM

Gen 25:3 The sons of Dedan were Asshurim, Letushim, and L

LEAD (88)

Gen 33:14 servant, and I will L on slowly, according to
Ex 13:17 go, God did not L them by way of
13:21 pillar of cloud to L them along the way,
15:10 them; they sank as L in the mighty waters.
32:34 But now go, L the people to the place
Num 27:17 before them, who shall L them out and bring
31:22 the tin, and the L,
Deut 28:37 where the LORD will L you away.
29:19 my heart.' This would L to the sweeping away
32:12 the LORD alone did L him, and there was
Judg 4:9 are going will not L to your glory, for
5:2 the leaders took the L in Israel, that the
5:12 Arise, Barak, L away your captives, O son of
1Sam 30:22 that each man may L away his wife and
2Kgs 9:2 among his fellows, and L him to an inner
1Chr 15:21 and Azaziah were to L with lyres according to
Neh 9:12 of cloud thou didst L them in the day,
Jud 2:9 overflow; and I will L them away captive to
11:19 Then I will L you through the middle of
11:19 it; and you will L them like sheep that
Job 19:24 an iron pen and L they were graven in
38:32 Can you L forth the Mazzaroth in their season,
Ps 5:8 L me, O LORD, in thy righteousness because of
25:5 L me in thy truth, and teach me, for
27:11 way, O LORD; and L me on a level
31:3 for thy name's sake L me and guide me,
43:3 thy truth; let them L me, let them bring
60:9 Who will L me to Edom?
61:2 L thou me to the rock that is higher
68:27 of them, in the L, the princes of Judah
77:20 Thou didst L thy people like a flock by
108:10 Who will L me to Edom?
110:3 on the day you L your host upon the
119:35 L me in the path of thy commandments, for
125:5 ways the LORD will L away with evildoers!
139:10 there thy hand shall L me, and thy right
139:24 way in me, and L me in the way
143:10 Let thy good spirit L me on a level
Prov 6:22 you walk, they will L you; when you lie
21:5 plans of the diligent L surely to abundance, but
Eccl 5:6 Let not your mouth L you into sin, and
Song 8:2 I would L you and bring you into the
Wis 16:13 and death; thou dost L men down to the
Sir 19:2 Wine and women L intelligent men astray, and the
22:12 What is heavier than L
40:28 My son, do not L the life of a
42:1 do not let partiality L you to sin:
47:18 gathered gold like tin and amassed silver like L
Is 9:16 tail; for those who L this people lead them
9:16 who lead this people L them astray, and those
11:6 a little child shall L them.
20:4 the king of Assyria L away the Egyptians captives
40:11 his bosom, and gently L those that are with
42:16 And I will L the blind in a way
49:10 pity on them will L them, and by springs
57:18 heal him; I will L him and requite him
63:14 So thou didst L thy people, to make for
Jer 6:29 bellows blow fiercely, the L is consumed by the
23:32 who tell them and L my people astray by
31:9 with consolations I will L them back, I will
Bar 5:9 For God will L Israel with joy, in the
Ezek 14:22 it any survivors to L out sons and daughters,
22:18 tin and iron and L in the furnace, have
22:20 bronze and iron and L and tin into a
27:12 silver, iron, tin, and L they exchanged for your
39:2 of the north, and L you against the mountains
Hos 9:13 a prey; Ephraim must L forth his sons to
Mic 3:5 concerning the prophets who L my people astray,
2Mac 10:12 called Macron, took the L in showing justice to
Mt 6:13 forgiven our debtors; And L us not into temptation,
24:5 Christ,' and they will L many astray.
24:11 prophets will arise and L many astray.
24:24 wonders, so as to L astray, if possible, even
Mk 13:6 he!' and they will L many astray.
13:22 signs and wonders, to L astray, if possible, the
14:44 man; seize him and L him away under guard."
Lk 6:39 "Can a blind man L a blind man?
11:4 indebted to us; and L us not into temptation."
13:15 from the manger, and L it away to water
Acts 13:11 about seeking people to L him by the hand.
Rom 2:4 kindness is meant to L you to repentance?
1Cor 7:17 Only, let every one L the life which the
Eph 4:1 Lord, beg you to L a life worthy of
Col 1:10 wisdom and understanding, to L a life worthy of
1Thes 2:12 and charged you to L a life worthy of
1Tim 2:2 positions, that we may L a quiet and peaceable
2Tim 2:16 chatter, for it will L people into more and
Heb 8:9 by the hand to L them out of the

LEADEN (2)

Zech 5:7 And behold, the L cover was lifted, and there
5:8 and thrust down the L weight upon its mouth.

LEADER (77)

Num 2:3 by their companies, the L of the people of
2:5 tribe of Issachar, the L of the people of
2:7 tribe of Zebulun, the L of the people of
2:10 by their companies, the L of the people of
2:12 tribe of Simeon, the L of the people of
2:14 tribe of Gad, the L of the people of
2:18 by their companies, the L of the people of
2:20 tribe of Manasseh, the L of the people of
2:22 tribe of Benjamin, the L of the people of
2:25 by their companies, the L of the people of
2:27 tribe of Asher, the L of the people of
2:29 tribe of Naphtali, the L of the people of
7:11 offer their offerings, one L each day, for the
7:18 son of Zuar, the L of Issachar, made an
7:24 son of Helon, the L of the men of
7:30 son of Shedeur, the L of the men of
7:36 son of Zurishaddai, the L of the men of
7:42 son of Deuel, the L of the men of
7:48 son of Ammihud, the L of the men of
7:54 son of Pedahzur, the L of the men of
7:60 son of Gideoni, the L of the men of
7:66 son of Ammishaddai, the L of the men of
7:72 son of Ochran, the L of the men of
7:78 son of Enan, the L of the men of
13:2 man, every one a L among them."
17:6 rods, one for each L, according to their fathers'
34:18 You shall take one L of every tribe, to
34:22 sons of Dan a L, Bukki the son of
34:23 sons of Manasseh a L, Hanniel the son of
34:24 sons of Ephraim a L, Kemuel the son of
34:25 sons of Zebulun a L, Eli-zaphan the son of
34:26 sons of Issachar a L, Paltiel the son of
34:27 sons of Asher a L, Ahihud the son of
34:28 sons of Naphtali a L, Pedahel the son of
Judg 11:6 "Come and be our L, that we may fight
11:11 made him head and L over them; and Jephthah
1Kgs 11:24 about him and became L of a marauding band,
14:7 people, and made you L over my people Israel,
16:2 dust and made you L over my people Israel,
1Chr 11:42 Shiza the Reubenite, a L of the Reubenites, and
12:4 the thirty and a L over the thirty; Jeremiah,
13:1 of thousands and of hundreds, with every L
15:22 Chenaniah, L of the Levites in music, should direct
15:27 singers, and Chenaniah the L of the music of
28:4 he chose Judah as L, and in the house
Neh 9:17 neck and appointed a L to return to their
11:17 Asaph, who was the L to begin the thanksgiving
12:42 And the singers sang with Jezrahiah as their L
Jud 5:5 Then Achior, the L of all the Ammonites, said
13:18 the head of the L of our enemies.
Sir 9:17 craftsmen; so a people's L is proved wise by
10:20 Among brothers their L is worthy of honor, and
45:24 that he should be L of the sanctuary and
50:1 The L of his brethren and the pride of
Is 3:6 you shall be our L, and this heap of
3:7 shall not make me L of the people."
55:4 to the peoples, a L and commander for the
Dan 3:38 prince, or prophet, or L, no burnt offering, or
1Mac 2:17 follows: "You are a L, honored and great in
5:6 band and many people with Timothy as their L
5:18 Zechariah, and Azariah, a L of the people, with
9:30 as our ruler and L, to fight our battle."
9:35 sent his brother as L of the multitude and
12:53 said, "They have no L or helper.
13:8 voice, "You are our L in place of Judas
13:42 priest and commander and L of the Jews."
14:35 they made him their L and high priest, because

14:41 Simon should be their L and high priest for
2Mac 1:13 For when the L reached Persia with a force
1:16 and struck down the L and his men, and
10:28 other made rage their L in the fight.
12:36 himself their ally and L in the battle.
14:6 are called Hasideans, whose L is Judas Maccabeus,
14:16 the command of the L, they set out from
14:20 fully considered, and the L had informed the people,
Lk 22:26 the youngest, and the L as one who serves.
Acts 5:31 his right hand as L and Savior, to give

LEADERS (68)

Ex 15:15 of Edom dismayed; the L of Moab, trembling seizes
16:22 and when all the L of the congregation came
34:31 Aaron and all the L of the congregation returned
35:27 And the L brought onyx stones and stones to
Num 1:16 the congregation, the L of their ancestral tribes,
1:44 the help of the L of Israel, twelve men,
3:32 be chief over the L of the Levites, and
4:34 and Aaron and the L of the congregation numbered
4:46 and Aaron and the L of Israel numbered, by
7:2 all its utensils, the L of Israel, heads of
7:2 their fathers' houses, the L of the tribes, who
7:3 every two of the L, and for each one
7:10 And the L offered offerings for the dedication of
7:10 was anointed; and the L offered their offering before
7:84 was anointed, from the L of Israel: twelve silver
10:4 only one, then the L, the heads of the
16:2 two hundred and fifty L of the congregation, chosen
17:2 house, from all their L according to their fathers'
17:6 Israel; and all their L gave him rods, one
27:2 priest, and before the L and all the congregation,
31:13 priest, and all the L of the congregation, went
32:2 priest and to the L of the congregation,
36:1 Moses and before the L, the heads of the
Josh 9:15 them live; and the L of the congregation swore
9:18 kill them, because the L of the congregation had
9:18 Then all the congregation murmured against the L
9:19 But all the L said to all the congregation,
9:21 And the L said to them, "Let them live."
9:21 the congregation, as the L had said of them.
13:21 Moses defeated with the L of Midian, Evi and
17:4 of Nun and the L, and said, "The LORD
Judg 5:2 that day: "That the L took the lead in
10:18 And the people, the L of Gilead, said one
1Sam 14:38 "Come hither, all you L of the people; and
1Kgs 8:1 of the tribes, the L of the fathers' houses
1Chr 4:42 Seir, having as their L Pelatiah, Neariah, Rephaiah,
9:34 to their generations, L, who lived in Jerusalem.
22:17 also commanded all the L of Israel to help
23:2 David assembled all the L of Israel and the
27:22 These were the L of the tribes of Israel.
29:6 as did also the L of the tribes, the
29:24 All the L and the mighty men, and also
2Chr 1:2 and to all the L in all Israel, the
5:2 of the tribes, the L of the fathers' houses
Neh 4:16 of mail; and the L stood behind all the
11:1 Now the L of the people lived in Jerusalem;
Jud 6:17 presence of the Assyrian L, and all that Holofernes
7:8 Esau and all the L of the Moabites and
14:19 When the L of the Assyrian army heard this,
Sir 33:18 the people, and you L of the congregation, hearken.
44:4 , and proclaiming prophecies; L of the people in
46:18 he wiped out the L of the people of
Is 3:12 O my people, your L mislead you, and confuse
14:9 you, all who were L of the earth; it
Jer 40:13 Kareah and all the L of the forces in
41:11 Kareah and all the L of the forces with
41:13 Kareah and all the L of the forces with
41:16 Kareah and all the L of the forces with
Zech 10:3 I will punish the L; for the LORD of
1Mac 3:55 After this Judas appointed L of the people, in
9:61 the country who were L in this treachery, and
10:37 Let their officers and L be of their own
2Mac 10:21 Maccabeus, he gathered the L of the people, and
14:21 And the L set a day on which to
Acts 28:17 called together the local L of the Jews; and
Heb 13:7 Remember your L, those who spoke to you the
13:17 Obey your L and submit to them; for they
13:24 Greet all your L and all the saints.

LEADERSHIP (5)

Num 33:1 their hosts under the L of Moses and Aaron.
Sir 32:2 account and receive a wreath for your excellent L
1Mac 9:31 that time accepted the L and took the place
2Mac 4:40 unjust attack, under the L of a certain Auranus,
Heb 3:16 left Egypt under the L of Moses?

LEADEST

Ps 80:1 of Israel, thou who L Joseph like a flock!

LEADING (26)

2Chr 23:13 with their musical instruments L in the celebration.
36:14 All the L priests and the people likewise were
Ezra 7:28 me, and I gathered L men from Israel to
8:16 Nathan, Zechariah, and Meshullam, L men, and for
8:17 them to Iddo, the L man at the place
8:24 apart twelve of the L priests: Sherebiah, Hashabiah,
10:5 arose and made the L priests and Levites and
Jud 5:3 over them as king, L their army?
15:13 people in the dance, L all the women, while
Ps 68:18 ascend the high mount, L captives in thy train,
Ezek 40:26 there were seven steps L up to it, and
1Mac 5:11 fled, and Timothy is L their forces.
9:53 the sons of the L men of the land
2Mac 8:23 watchword, "God's help"; then, L the first division
10:1 his followers, the Lord L them on, recovered the
10:29 bridles, and they were L the Jews.
13:15 He stabbed the L elephant and its rider.
Mk 6:21 and officers and the L men of Galilee.
Lk 22:45 of the twelve, was L them.
Jn 7:12 said, "No, he is L the people astray."
Acts 12:10 to the iron gate L into the city.
13:50 high standing and the L men of the city,
15:22 called Barsabbas, and Silas, L men among the
16:12 Philippi, which is the L city of the district
17:4 a few of the L women.
Heb 3:12 an evil, unbelieving heart, L you to fall away

LEADS (32)

Tob 13:2 he shows mercy; he L down to Hades, and
Job 12:17 He L counselors away stripped, and judges he makes
12:19 He L priests away stripped, and overthrows the
12:23 he enlarges nations, and L them away.
Ps 23:2 He L me beside still waters;
23:3 He L me in paths of righteousness for his
25:9 He L the humble in what is right, and
68:6 to dwell in; he L out the prisoners to
Prov 10:16 wage of the righteous L to life, the gain
12:26 way of the wicked L them astray.
12:28 the way of error L to death.
15:24 The wise man's path L upward to life, that
16:29 entices his neighbor and L him in a way
19:23 fear of the LORD L to life; and he
Wis 6:20 the desire for wisdom L to a kingdom.
7:12 them all, because wisdom L them; but I did
Sir 27:15 strife of the proud L to bloodshed, and their
37:30 brings sickness, and gluttony L to nausea.
Is 30:28 peoples a bridle that L astray.
48:17 you to profit, who L you in the way
1Mac 9:2 by the road which L to Gilgal and encamped
Mt 7:13 way is easy, that L to destruction, and those
7:14 way is hard, that L to life, and those
15:14 if a blind man L a blind man, both
24:4 heed that no one L you astray.
Mk 13:5 heed that no one L you astray.
Jn 10:3 sheep by name and L them out.
Rom 5:18 man's act of righteousness L to acquittal and life
6:16 either of sin, which L to death, or of
6:16 or of obedience, which L to righteousness?
2Cor 2:14 who in Christ always L us in triumph, and
7:10 produces a repentance that L to salvation and brings

LEAF (10)

Gen 8:11 a freshly plucked olive L; so Noah knew that
Ex 39:3 And gold L was hammered out and cut into
Lev 26:36 sound of a driven L shall put them to
Job 13:25 thou frighten a driven L and pursue dry chaff?
Ps 1:3 its season, and its L does not wither.
Prov 11:28 but the righteous will flourish like a green L
Is 1:30 like an oak whose L withers, and like a
64:6 all fade like a L, and our iniquities, like
Mk 11:13 a fig tree in L, he went to see
Lk 21:30 they come out in L, you see for yourselves

LEAFY (5)

Lev 23:40 trees, and boughs of L trees, and willows of
Neh 8:15 myrtle, palm, and other L trees to make booths,
Ezek 6:13 tree, and under every L oak, wherever they offered
20:28 high hill or any L tree, there they offered
Mk 11:8 road, and others spread L branches which they had

LEAGUE (9)

1Sam 22:8 my son makes a L with the son of
1Kgs 15:19 "Let there be a L between me and you,
15:19 gold; go, break your L with Baasha king of
2Chr 16:3 "Let there be a L between me and you,
16:3 gold; go, break your L with Baasha king of
Job 5:23 you shall be in L with the stones of
Is 7:2 told, "Syria is in L with Ephraim," his heart
30:1 and who make a L, but not of my
Ezek 30:5 land that is in L, shall fall with them

LEAGUES

2Mac 11:5 fortified place about five L from Jerusalem, and

LEAH (34)

Gen 29:16 of the older was L, and the name of
29:17 L's eyes were weak, but Rachel was beautiful and
29:23 he took his daughter L and brought her to
29:24 Zilpah to his daughter L to be her maid.)
29:25 morning, behold, it was L; and Jacob said to
29:30 loved Rachel more than L, and served Laban for
29:31 the LORD saw that L was hated, he opened
29:32 And L conceived and bore a son, and she
30:9 When L saw that she had ceased bearing children,
30:10 Then L's maid Zilpah bore Jacob a son.
30:11 And L said, "Good fortune!" so she called his
30:12 L's maid Zilpah bore Jacob a second son.
30:13 And L said, "Happy am I!
30:14 the field, and brought them to his mother L
30:14 Then Rachel said to L, "Give me, I pray,
30:16 field in the evening, L went out to meet
30:17 And God hearkened to L, and she conceived and
30:18 L said, "God has given me my hire because
30:19 And L conceived again, and she bore Jacob a
30:20 Then L said, "God has endowed me with a
31:4 and called Rachel and L into the field where
31:14 Then Rachel and L answered him, "Is there any
31:33 Jacob's tent, and into L's tent, and into the
31:33 he went out of L's tent, and entered Rachels.
33:1 divided the children among L and Rachel and the
33:2 children in front, then L with her children, and
33:7 children, and bowed down; L likewise and her
34:1 Dinah the daughter of L, whom she had borne
35:23 The sons of L: Reuben (Jacob's first-born), Simeon,
35:26 The sons of Zilpah, L's maid: Gad and Asher.
46:15 are the sons of L, whom she bore to
46:18 whom Laban gave to L his daughter; and these
49:31 and there I buried L –
Ruth 4:11 house, like Rachel and L, who together built up

LEAKS

Eccl 10:18 roof sinks in, and through indolence the house L

LEAN (8)

Gen 41:27 The seven L and gaunt cows that came up
Judg 16:26 rests, that I may L against them."
Sir 15:4 He will L on her and will not fall,
Is 10:20 Jacob will no more L upon him that smote
10:20 smote them, but will L upon the LORD, the
17:4 and the fat of his flesh will grow L
Ezek 34:20 fat sheep and the L sheep.
Mic 3:11 for money; yet they L upon the LORD and

LEANED (6)

Judg 16:29 house rested, and he L his weight upon them,
2Kgs 7:2 whose hand the king L said to the man
7:17 on whose hand he L to have charge of
Ps 71:6 Upon thee I have L from my birth; thou
Ezek 29:7 shoulders; and when they L upon you, you broke,
Amos 5:19 into the house and L with his hand against

LEANING (6)

2Sam 1:6 and there was Saul L upon his spear; and
2Kgs 5:18 Rimmon to worship there, L on my arm, and
Esth 15:3 two maids with her, L daintily on one,
Ps 62:3 of you, like a L wall, a tottering fence?
Song 8:5 up from the wilderness, L upon her beloved?
2Mac 7:27 But, L close to him, she spoke in their

LEANNESS

Job 16:8 against me; and my L has risen up against

LEANS (4)

Num 21:15 seat of Ar, and L to the border of
2Kgs 18:21 of any man who L on it.
Job 8:15 He L against his house, but it does not
Is 36:6 of any man who L on it.

LEAP (13)

Gen 31:12 all the goats that L upon the flock are
Lev 11:21 feet, with which to L on the earth.
2Sam 22:30 my God I can L over a wall.
Job 39:20 Do you make him L like the locust?
41:19 torches; sparks of fire L forth.
Ps 18:29 my God I can L over a wall.
Wis 5:21 true aim, and will L to the target as
Is 33:4 caterpillar gathers; as locusts L, men leap upon it.
33:4 as locusts leap, men L upon it.
35:6 shall the lame man L like a hart, and
Joel 2:5 rumbling of chariots, they L on the tops of
2:9 They L upon the city, they run upon the
Lk 6:23 in that day, and L for joy, for behold,

LEAPED (9)

Gen 31:10 that the he-goats which L upon the flock were
Tob 6:2 A fish L up from the river and would
Wis 18:15 gone, thy all-powerful word L from heaven, from the
19:9 ranged like horses, and L like lambs, praising thee,
1Mac 9:48 the men with him L into the Jordan and
13:44 in the siege engine L out into the city,
Lk 1:41 of Mary, the babe L in her womb; and
1:44 babe in my womb L for joy.
Acts 19:16 the evil spirit was L on them, mastered all

LEAPING (6)

2Sam 6:16 and saw King David L and dancing before the
Song 2:8 Behold, he comes, L upon the mountains, bounding
Wis 17:19 the unseen running of L animals, or the sound
Mal 4:2 You shall go forth L like calves from the
Acts 3:8 And L up he stood and walked and entered
3:8 with them, walking and L and praising God.

LEAPS (3)

Deut 33:22 a lion's whelp, that L forth from Bashan."
Job 37:1 my heart trembles, and L out of its place.
Zeph 1:9 punish every one who L over the threshold, and

LEARN (63)

Gen 24:21 her in silence to L whether the LORD had
Deut 4:10 so that they may L to fear me all
5:1 day, and you shall L them and be careful
14:23 flock; that you may L to fear the LORD
17:19 life, that he may L to fear the LORD
18:9 you, you shall not L to follow the abominable
31:12 they may hear and L to fear the LORD
31:13 it, may hear and L to fear the LORD
Ruth 3:18 my daughter, until you L how the matter turns
1Sam 19:3 you; and if I L anything I will tell
Ezra 4:15 of the records and L that this city is
Tob 5:8 so that I may L to what tribe he
5:13 because I tried to L your tribe and family.
Esth 2:11 of the harem, to L how Esther was and
4:5 go to Mordecai to L what this was and
Job 23:5 I would L what he would answer me, and
Ps 119:7 upright heart, when I L thy righteous ordinances.
119:71 afflicted, that I might L thy statutes.
119:73 understanding that I may L thy commandments.
141:6 them, then they shall L that the word of
Prov 8:5 O simple ones, L prudence; O foolish men, pay
19:25 and the simple will L prudence; reprove a man
22:25 wrathful man, lest you L his ways and entangle
Wis 6:1 O kings, and understand; L, O judges of the
6:9 directed, that you may L wisdom and not transgress.
9:10 and that I may L what is pleasing to
9:13 For what man can L the counsel of God?
10:12 so that he might L that godliness is more
11:16 them, that they might L that one is punished
16:26 love, O Lord, might L that it is not
Sir 8:8 will gain instruction and L how to serve great
8:9 will gain understanding and L how to give an
18:18 Before you speak, L, and before you fall ill,
37:8 of a counselor, and L first what is his
Is 1:17 cease to do evil, L to do good; seek
2:4 nation, neither shall they L war any more.
26:9 inhabitants of the world L righteousness.
26:10 wicked, he does not L righteousness; in the land
Jer 10:2 Thus says the LORD: L not the way of
12:16 if they will diligently L the ways of my
Bar 3:9 Israel; give ear, and L wisdom!
3:14 L where there is wisdom, where there is strength,
Mic 4:3 nation, neither shall they L war any more;
1Mac 7:42 today; let the rest L that Nicanor has spoken

L

	10:72	Ask and L who I am and who the
2Mac	7:2	intend to ask and L from us?
Mt	9:13	Go and L what this means, 'I desire mercy,
	11:29	yoke upon you, and L from me; for I
	24:32	"From the fig tree L its lesson: as soon
Mk	13:28	"From the fig tree L its lesson: as soon
Acts	21:34	as he could not L the facts because of
	24:7	will be able to L from him about everything
1Cor	4:6	brethren, that you may L by us not to
	14:31	so that all may L and all be encouraged;
Eph	4:20	You did not so L Christ!--
	5:10	true), and try to L what is pleasing to
1Tim	1:20	Satan that they may L not to blaspheme.
	2:11	Let a woman L in silence with all submissiveness.
	5:4	grandchildren, let them first L their religious duty to
	5:13	Besides that, they L to be idlers, gadding about
Tit	3:14	And let our people L to apply themselves to
Rev	3:9	before your feet, and L that I have loved
	14:3	No one could L that song except the hundred

LEARNED (56)

Gen	30:27	say so, I have L by divination that the
	42:1	When Jacob L that there was grain in Egypt,
1Sam	4:6	And when they L that the ark of the
	26:4	sent out spies, and L of a certainty that
Ezra	7:11	the priest, the scribe, L in matters of the
Tob	1:19	When I L that I was being searched for,
Jud	11:16	when I, your servant, L all this, I fled
Esth	4:1	When Mordecai L all that had been done, Mordecai
	12:2	into their purposes, and L that they were preparing
Ps	106:35	with the nations and L to do as they
Prov	30:3	I have not L wisdom, nor have I knowledge
Wis	7:13	I L without guile and I impart without grudging;
	7:21	virtues of roots; I L both what is secret
	9:17	Who has L thy counsel, unless thou hast given
	11:9	disciplined in mercy, they L how the ungodly were
Sir	8:9	aged, for they themselves L from their fathers;
Is	29:13	a commandment of men L by rote;
Bar	3:20	but they have not L the way to knowledge,
	3:23	for understanding, have not L the way to wisdom,
Ezek	19:3	young lion, and he L to catch prey; he
	19:6	young lion, and he L to catch prey; he
Dan	4:32	you, until you have L that the Most High
1Mac	2:39	Mattathias and his friends L of it, they mourned
	3:11	When Judas L of it, he went out to
	3:42	They also L what the king had commanded to
	6:17	And when Lysias L that the king was dead,
	7:31	When Nicanor L that his plan had been disclosed,
	9:32	When Bacchides L of this, he tried to kill
	9:63	When Bacchides L of this, he assembled all his
	9:70	When Jonathan L of this, he sent ambassadors to
	10:80	Jonathan L that there was an ambush behind him,
	12:22	now that we have L this, please write us
	13:14	Trypho L that Simon had risen up in place
2Mac	2:7	When Jeremiah L of it, he rebuked them and
	4:21	Philometor as king, Antiochus L that Philometor had
	12:21	When Timothy L of the approach of Judas, he
Mk	15:44	And when he L from the centurion that he
Lk	7:37	a sinner, when she L that he was at
	9:11	When the crowds L it, they followed him; and
	23:7	And when he L that he belonged to Herod's
Jn	6:45	who has heard and L from the Father comes
	12:9	crowd of the Jews L that he was there,
Acts	14:6	to stone them, they L of it and fled
	17:13	the Jews of Thessalonica L that the word of
	23:27	and rescued him, having L that he was a
	23:34	When he L that he was from Cilicia
	28:1	had escaped, we then L that the island was
Phil	4:9	What you have L and received and heard and
	4:11	want; for I have L, in whatever state I
	4:12	all circumstances I have L the secret of facing
Col	1:7	in truth, as you L it from Epaphras our
1Thes	4:1	Jesus, that as you L from us how you
2Tim	3:14	in what you have L and have firmly believed,
	3:14	knowing from whom you L it
Heb	5:8	was a Son, he L obedience through what he
Rev	2:24	teaching, who have not L what some call the

LEARNING (10)

Prov	1:5	hear and increase in L, and the man of
	9:9	a righteous man and he will increase in L
Sir	44:4	and in understanding of L for the people, wise
Dan	1:4	endowed with knowledge, understanding L, and
	1:17	youths, God gave them L and skill in all
	13:48	without examination and without L the facts?
2Mac	12:8	But L that the men in Jamnia meant in

Jn	7:15	that this man has L, when he has never
	7:51	him a hearing and L what he does?"
Acts	26:24	are mad; your great L is turning you mad."

LEASH

Job	41:5	you put him on L for your maidens?

LEAST (37)

Gen	24:55	us a while, at L ten days; after that
	32:10	not worthy of the L of all the steadfast
Ex	5:11	your work will not be lessened in the L
Num	11:32	quails; he who gathered L gathered ten homers; and
Judg	3:2	war to such at L as had not known
	6:15	and I am the L in my family."
1Sam	9:21	a Benjaminite, from the L of the tribes of
2Kgs	18:24	single captain among the L of my master's servants,
Ps	68:27	There is Benjamin, the L of them, in the
Wis	16:3	food, might lose the L remnant of appetite because
Sir	23:21	city, and where he L suspects it, he will
Is	36:9	single captain among the L of my master's servants,
	60:22	The L one shall become a clan, and the
Jer	6:13	"For from the L to the greatest of them,
	8:10	conquerors, because from the L to the greatest every
	31:34	know me, from the L of them to the
	42:1	the people from the L to the greatest, came
	42:8	the people from the L to the greatest,
	44:12	be consumed; from the L to the greatest, they
Jon	3:5	of them to the L of them.
2Mac	8:35	regarded as of the L account, took off his
Mt	2:6	are by no means L among the rulers of
	5:19	relaxes one of the L of these commandments and
	5:19	so, shall be called L in the kingdom of
	11:11	yet he who is L in the kingdom of
	25:40	to one of the L of these my brethren,
	25:45	to one of the L of these, you did
Lk	7:28	yet he who is L in the kingdom of
	9:48	for he who is L among you all is
Acts	5:15	Peter came by at L his shadow might fall
	8:10	to him, from the L to the greatest, saying,
1Cor	6:4	before those who are L esteemed by the church?
	9:2	not an apostle, at L I am to you;
	15:9	For I am the L of the apostles, unfit
2Cor	11:5	am not in the L inferior to these superlative
Eph	3:8	I am the very L of all the saints,
Heb	8:11	know me, from the L of them to the

LEATHER (4)

2Kgs	1:8	with a girdle of L about his loins." And
Ezek	16:10	and shod you with L, I swathed you in
Mt	3:4	camel's hair, and a L girdle around his waist;
Mk	1:6	hair, and had a L girdle around his waist,

LEAVE (149)

Gen	28:15	for I will not L you until I have
	33:15	Esau said, "Let me L with you some of
	42:33	you are honest men: L one of your brothers
	44:22	lord, 'The lad cannot L his father, for if
	44:22	for if he should L his father, his father
Ex	16:19	them, "Let no man L any of it till
	23:11	eat; and what they L the wild beasts may
Lev	7:15	offering; he shall not L any of it until
	16:23	holy place, and shall L them there;
	19:10	your vineyard; you shall L them for the poor
	22:30	same day, you shall L none of it until
	23:22	your harvest; you shall L them for the poor
Num	9:12	They shall L none of it until the morning,
	10:31	he said, "Do not L us, I pray you,
Deut	13:5	bondage, to make you L the way in which
	28:51	who also shall not L you grain, wine, or
Josh	11:14	and they did not L any that breathed.
Judg	6:4	neighborhood of Gaza, and L no sustenance in Israel,
	9:9	to them, 'Shall I L my fatness, by which
	9:11	to them, 'Shall I L my sweetness and my
	9:13	to them, 'Shall I L my wine which cheers
	16:17	then my strength will L me, and I shall
Ruth	1:16	"Entreat me not to L you or to return
	2:8	in another field or L this one, but keep
	2:16	bundles for her, and L it for her to
1Sam	10:9	turned his back to L Samuel, God gave him
	14:36	light; let us not L a man of them."
	20:6	say, 'David earnestly asked L of me to run
	20:28	Saul, "David earnestly asked L of me to go
	25:22	if by morning I L so much as one
2Sam	14:7	which is left, and L to my husband neither
1Kgs	8:57	fathers; may he not L us or forsake us;
	16:11	Baasha; he did not L him a single male

L

19:18 Yet I will L seven thousand in Israel, all
2Kgs 2:2 live, I will not L you." So they went
2:4 live, I will not L you." So they came
2:6 live, I will not L you." So the two
4:30 live, I will not L you." So he arose
1Chr 28:8 this good land, and L it for an inheritance
Ezra 9:8 LORD our God, to L us a remnant, and
9:12 of the land, and L it for an inheritance
Neh 5:10 Let us L off this interest.
6:3 work stop while I L it and come down
13:6 some time I asked L of the king
Tob 8:20 that he should not L until the fourteen days
9:3 that I should not L;
12:13 hesitate to rise and L your dinner in order
14:8 "So now, my son, L Nineveh, because what the
Jud 2:5 whole earth: When you L my presence, take with
5:9 God commanded them to L the place where they
Esth 6:10 L out nothing that you have mentioned."
13:7 violence to Hades, and L our government completely
Job 39:11 great, and will you L to him your labor?
Ps 17:14 than enough; may they L something over to their
49:10 alike must perish and L their wealth to others.
119:121 and right; do not L me to my oppressors.
141:8 thee I seek refuge; L me not defenseless!
Prov 9:6 L simpleness, and live, and walk in the way
14:7 L the presence of a fool, for there you
Eccl 2:18 seeing that I must L it to the man
2:21 knowledge and skill must L all to be enjoyed
10:4 against you, do not L your place, for deference
Wis 2:9 revelry, everywhere let us L signs of enjoyment,
8:13 have immortality, and L an everlasting remembrance
10:14 prison she did not L him, until she brought
12:11 one that thou didst L them unpunished for their
Sir 8:11 not get up and L an insolent fellow, lest
14:15 Will you not L the fruit of your labors
23:11 the scourge will not L his house; if he
23:26 She will L her memory for a curse, and
24:31 teaching like prophecy, and L it to all future
27:12 for a chance to L, but among thoughtful people
32:11 L in good time and do not be the
33:25 you will find rest; L his hands idle, and
38:12 him; let him not L you, for there is
39:11 lives long, he will L a name greater than
Is 10:3 and where will you L your wealth?
30:11 smooth things, prophesy illusions, L the way, turn
32:6 concerning the LORD, to L the craving of the
65:15 You shall L your name to my chosen for
Jer 9:2 place, that I might L my people and go
14:9 called by thy name; L us not."
17:11 his days they will L him, and at his
18:14 the snow of Lebanon L the crags of Sirion?
27:11 serve him, I will L on its own land,
30:11 will by no means L you unpunished.
46:28 will by no means L you unpunished."
48:28 L the cities, and dwell in the rock, O
49:9 you, would they not L gleanings?
49:11 L your fatherless children, I will keep them alive;
50:20 pardon those whom I L as a remnant.
Ezek 6:8 "Yet I will L some of you alive.
16:39 your fair jewels, and L you naked and bare.
23:29 of your labor, and L you naked and bare,
31:12 cut it down and L it.
31:12 from its shadow and L it.
39:28 I will L none of them remaining among the
Dan 4:15 But L the stump of its roots in the
4:23 and destroy it, but L the stump of its
4:26 it was commanded to L the stump of the
Hos 12:14 so his LORD will L his bloodguilt upon him,
Joel 2:14 turn and repent, and L a blessing behind him,
2:16 Let the bridegroom L his room, and the bride
Obad 1:5 you, would they not L gleanings?
Zeph 3:3 are evening wolves that L nothing till the morning.
3:12 For I will L in the midst of you
Mal 4:1 so that it will L them neither root nor
1Mac 1:48 unclean animals, and to L their sons uncircumcised.
9:10 for our brethren, and L no cause to question
15:14 permitted no one to L or enter it.
2Mac 6:28 my old age and L to the young a
Mt 5:24 has something against you, L your gift there before
8:22 him, "Follow me, and L the dead to bury
8:34 they begged him to L their neighborhood.
10:14 your feet as you L that house or town.
18:11 astray, does he not L the ninety-nine on the
19:5 reason a man shall L his father and mother
Mk 5:13 So he gave them L
6:10 stay there until you L the place.
6:11 hear you, when you L, shake off the dust
6:46 after he had taken L of them, he went
7:8 precepts of men.' You L the commandment of God,
10:7 reason a man shall L his father and mother
Lk 8:32 So he gave them L
9:5 receive you, when you L that town shake off
9:39 him, and will hardly L him.
9:60 he said to him, L the dead to bury
15:4 of them, does not L the ninety-nine in the
19:44 and they will not L one stone upon another
Jn 7:3 brothers said to him, L here and go to
14:18 "I will not L you desolate; I will come
14:27 Peace I L with you; my peace I give
16:32 his home, and will L me alone; yet I
19:38 the body of Jesus, and Pilate gave him L
Acts 7:46 of God and asked L to find a habitation
14:17 yet he did not L himself without witness, for
16:39 and asked them to L the city.
18:2 all the Jews to L Rome.
18:18 longer, and then took L of the brethren and
18:21 declined; but on taking L of them he said,
20:1 having exhorted them took L of them and departed
21:40 he had given him L, Paul, standing on the
27:3 kindly, and gave him L to go to his
Rom 12:19 never avenge yourselves, but L it to the wrath
2Cor 2:13 So I took L of them and went on
12:8 this, that it should L me;
Eph 5:31 reason a man shall L his father and mother
Heb 6:1 Therefore let us L the elementary doctrine of Christ
Rev 11:2 court outside the temple; L that out, for it

LEAVEN (22)

Ex 12:15 you shall put away L out of your houses,
12:19 For seven days no L shall be found in
13:7 with you, and no L shall be seen with
34:25 of my sacrifice with L; neither shall the sacrifice
Lev 2:11 shall be made with L; for you shall burn
2:11 you shall burn no L nor any honey as
6:17 It shall not be baked with L
23:17 shall be baked with L, as first fruits to
Deut 16:4 No L shall be seen with you in all
Mt 13:33 of heaven is like L which a woman took
16:6 and beware of the L of the Pharisees and
16:11 Beware of the L of the Pharisees and Sadducees."
16:12 to beware of the L of bread, but of
Mk 8:15 heed, beware of the L of the Pharisees and
8:15 the Pharisees and the L of Herod."
Lk 12:1 first, "Beware of the L of the Pharisees, which
13:21 It is like L which a woman took and
1Cor 5:6 know that a little L leavens the whole lump?
5:7 Cleanse out the old L that you may be
5:8 not with the old L, the leaven of malice
5:8 the old leaven, the L of malice and evil,
Gal 5:9 A little L leavens the whole lump.

LEAVENED (14)

Ex 12:15 one eats what is L, from the first day
12:19 one eats what is L, that person shall be
12:20 You shall eat nothing L; in all your dwellings
12:34 dough before it was L, their kneading bowls being
12:39 for it was not L, because they were thrust
13:3 from this place; no L bread shall be eaten.
13:7 for seven days; no L bread shall be seen
23:18 of my sacrifice with L bread, or let the
Lev 7:13 offering with cakes of L bread.
Deut 16:3 You shall eat no L bread with it; seven
Hos 7:5 the kneading of the dough until it is L
Amos 4:5 of that which is L, and proclaim freewill offerings,
Mt 13:33 three measures of flour, till it was all L
Lk 13:21 three measures of flour, till it was all L

LEAVENS (2)

1Cor 5:6 that a little leaven L the whole lump?
Gal 5:9 A little leaven L the whole lump.

LEAVES (39)

Gen 2:24 Therefore a man L his father and his mother
3:7 and they sewed fig L together and made themselves
Ex 21:33 "When a man L a pit open, or when
1Kgs 6:34 cypress wood; the two L of the one door
6:34 folding, and the two L of the other door
Job 16:6 how much of it L me?
30:4 pick mallow and the L of bushes, and to
39:14 For she L her eggs to the earth, and
41:32 Behind him he L a shining wake; one would
Prov 13:22 A good man L an inheritance to his children's

28:3 a beating rain that L no food.
Sir 6:3 You will devour your L and destroy your fruit,
11:17 will pass until he L them to others and
14:18 Like flourishing L on a spreading tree which sheds
23:22 with a woman who L her husband and provides
33:31 ill-treat him, and he L and runs away, which
Is 33:9 desert; and Bashan and Carmel shake off their L
34:4 host shall fall, as L fall from the vine,
34:4 from the vine, like L falling from the fig
Jer 3:20 as a faithless wife L her husband, so have
8:13 fig tree; even the L are withered, and what
17:8 heat comes, for its L remain green, and is
Ezek 17:9 all its fresh sprouting L wither?
41:24 The doors had two L apiece, two swinging leaves
41:24 leaves apiece, two swinging L for each door.
47:12 Their L will not wither nor their fruit fail,
47:12 for food, and their L for healing."
Dan 4:12 Its L were fair and its fruit abundant, and
4:14 branches, strip off its L and scatter its fruit;
4:21 the whole earth; whose L were fair and its
Mt 21:19 nothing on it but L only.
24:32 and puts forth its L, you know that summer
Mk 11:13 he found nothing but L, for it was not
12:19 man's brother dies and L a wife, but leaves
12:19 leaves a wife, but L no child, the man
13:28 and puts forth its L, you know that summer
13:34 a journey, when he L home and puts his
Jn 10:12 the wolf coming and L the sheep and flees;
Rev 22:2 each month; and the L of the tree were

LEAVING (21)

Ex 23:5 you shall refrain from L him with it, you
Deut 2:14 the time from our L Kadesh-barnea until we crossed
2Kgs 7:7 horses, and their asses, L the camp as it
2Chr 24:25 had departed from him, L him severely wounded, his
Ps 19:5 forth like a bridegroom L his chamber, and like
Jer 44:7 the midst of Judah, L you no remnant?
2Mac 2:28 endure the uncomfortable toil, L the responsibility
4:31 to settle the trouble, L Andronicus, a man of
6:31 this way he died, L in his death an
Mt 4:13 withdrew into Galilee; and L Nazareth he went and
21:17 And L them, he went out of the city
26:44 So, L them again, he went away and prayed
Mk 4:36 And L the crowd, they took him with them
10:46 and as he was L Jericho with his disciples
12:21 took her, and died, L no children; and the
Lk 4:42 have kept him from L them;
10:30 beat him, and departed, L him half dead.
Jn 16:28 world; again, I am L the world and going
Acts 21:3 in sight of Cyprus, L it on the left
23:32 returned to the barracks, L the horsemen to go
1Pet 2:21 also suffered for you, L you an example, that

LEBANA

Neh 7:48 Padon, the sons of L, the sons of Hagaba,

LEBANAH

Ezra 2:45 Padon, the sons of L, the sons of Hagabah,

LEBANON (75)

Deut 1:7 of the Canaanites, and L, as far as the
3:25 goodly hill country, and L
11:24 from the wilderness and L and from the River,
Josh 1:4 the wilderness and this L as far as the
9:1 the Great Sea toward L, the Hittites, the Amorites,
11:17 in the valley of L below Mount Hermon.
12:7 in the valley of L to Mount Halak, that
13:5 the Gebalites, and all L, toward the sunrising, from
13:6 the hill country from L to Misrephoth-maim, even all
Judg 3:3 who dwelt on Mount L, from Mount Baal-hermon as
9:15 devour the cedars of L
1Kgs 4:33 cedar that is in L to the hyssop that
5:6 command that cedars of L be cut for me;
5:9 to the sea from L; and I will make
5:14 he sent them to L, ten thousand a month
5:14 be a month in L and two months at
7:2 of the Forest of L; its length was a
9:19 build in Jerusalem, in L, and in all the
10:17 them in the House of the Forest of L
10:21 of the Forest of L were of pure gold;
2Kgs 14:9 Judah, "A thistle on L sent to a cedar
14:9 to a cedar on L, saying, 'Give your daughter
14:9 a wild beast of L passed by and trampled
19:23 the far recesses of L; I felled its tallest
2Chr 2:8 and algum timber from L, for I know that
2:8 your servants know how to cut timber in L
2:16 timber you need from L, and bring it to
8:6 build in Jerusalem, in L, and in all the
9:16 them in the House of the Forest of L
9:20 of the Forest of L were of pure gold;
25:18 Judah, "A thistle on L sent to a cedar
25:18 to a cedar on L, saying, 'Give your daughter
25:18 a wild beast of L passed by and trampled
Ezra 3:7 bring cedar trees from L to the sea, to
Jud 1:7 Cilicia and Damascus and L and Antilebanon and all
Ps 29:5 the cedars, the LORD breaks the cedars of L
29:6 He makes L to skip like a calf, and
37:35 man overbearing, and towering like a cedar of L
72:16 its fruit be like L; and may men blossom
92:12 palm tree, and grow like a cedar in L
104:16 abundantly, the cedars of L which he planted.
Song 3:9 made himself a palanquin from the wood of L
4:8 Come with me from L, my bride; come with
4:8 from Lebanon, my bride; come with me from L
4:11 of your garments is like the scent of L
4:15 well of living water, and flowing streams from L
5:15 His appearance is like L, choice as the cedars.
7:4 like a tower of L, overlooking Damascus.
Sir 24:13 like a cedar in L, and like a cypress
50:8 a green shoot on L on a summer day;
50:12 a young cedar on L; and they surrounded him
Is 2:13 all the cedars of L, lofty and lifted up;
10:34 with an axe, and L with its majestic trees
14:8 you, the cedars of L, saying, 'Since you were
29:17 very little while until L shall be turned into
33:9 land mourns and languishes; L is confounded and
35:2 The glory of L shall be given to it,
37:24 the far recesses of L; I felled its tallest
40:16 L would not suffice for fuel, nor are its
60:13 The glory of L shall come to you, the
Jer 18:14 Does the snow of L leave the crags of
22:6 as the summit of L, yet surely I will
22:20 "Go up to L, and cry out, and lift
22:23 O inhabitant of L, nested among the cedars, how
Ezek 17:3 many colors, came to L and took the top
27:5 took a cedar from L to make a mast
31:3 to a cedar in L, with fair branches and
31:15 stopped; I will clothe L in gloom for it,
31:16 choice and best of L, all that drink water,
Hos 14:6 be like the olive, and his fragrance like L
14:7 their fragrance shall be like the wine of L
Nah 1:4 wither, the bloom of L fades.
Hab 2:17 The violence done to L will overwhelm you; the
Zech 10:10 of Gilead and to L, till there is no
11:1 Open your doors, O L, that the fire may

LEBAOTH

Josh 15:32 Ziklag, Madmannah, Sansannah, L, Shilhim, Ain,

LEBONAH

Judg 21:19 up from Bethel to Shechem, and south of L

LECAH

1Chr 4:21 Er the father of L, Laadah the father of

LED (140)

Gen 14:14 been taken captive, he L forth his trained men,
24:27 me, the LORD has L me in the way
24:48 master Abraham, who had L me by the right
48:15 the God who has L me all my life
Ex 3:1 of Midian; and he L his flock to the
13:18 But God L the people round by the way
15:13 "Thou hast L in thy steadfast love the people
15:22 Then Moses L Israel onward from the Red Sea,
Deut 8:2 LORD your God has L you these forty years
8:15 house of bondage, who L you through the great
29:5 I have L you forty years in the wilderness;
Josh 24:3 beyond the River and L him through all the
Judg 6:8 God of Israel: I L you up from Egypt,
2Sam 5:2 it was you that L out and brought in
2Kgs 6:19 And he L them to Samaria.
1Chr 11:2 it was you that L out and brought in
17:5 since the day I L up Israel to this
20:1 forth to battle, Joab L out the army, and
2Chr 21:11 country of Judah, and L the inhabitants of Jerusalem
21:13 of Israel, and have L Judah and the inhabitants
21:13 the house of Ahab L Israel into unfaithfulness, and
25:11 Amaziah took courage, and L out his people, and
Neh 9:19 pillar of cloud which L them in the way
Tob 12:3 For he has L me back to you safely,
Jud 1:13 the seventeenth year he L his forces against King
5:14 before them, and he L them by the way

L

5:18 many battles and were L away captive to a
6:11 slaves took him and L him out of the
7:6 the second day Holofernes L out all his cavalry
10:20 servants came out and L her into the tent.
Esth 12:3 they confessed they were L to execution,
Ps 42:4 with the throng, and L them in procession to
45:14 many-colored robes she is L to the king, with
45:15 and gladness they are L along as they enter
78:14 In the daytime he L them with a cloud,
78:26 by his power he L out the south wind;
78:52 Then he L forth his people like sheep, and
78:53 He L them in safety, so that they were
105:37 Then he L forth Israel with silver and gold,
105:43 So he L forth his people with joy, his
106:9 became dry; and he L them through the deep
107:7 from their distress; he L them by a straight
136:16 ever; to him who L his people through the
Prov 4:12 of wisdom; I have L you in the paths
20:1 brawler; and whoever is L astray by it is
Wis 2:21 reasoned, but they were L astray, for their
10:18 the Red Sea, and L them through deep waters;
11:15 and wicked thoughts, which L them astray to
19:11 of birds, when desire L them to ask for
Sir 3:23 their hasty judgment has L many astray, and wrong
13:8 care not to be L astray, and not to
15:12 "It was he who L me astray"; for he
31:5 pursues money will be L astray by it.
45:5 hear his voice, and L him into the thick
49:2 He was L aright in converting the people, and
Is 9:16 and those who are L by them are swallowed
19:13 of her tribes have L Egypt astray.
44:20 a deluded mind has L him astray, and he
47:10 wisdom and your knowledge L you astray, and you
48:21 thirsted not when he L them through the deserts;
53:7 a lamb that is L to the slaughter, and
55:12 in joy, and be L forth in peace; the
60:11 nations, with their kings L in procession.
63:13 everlasting name, who L them through the depths?
Jer 2:6 land of Egypt, who L us in the wilderness,
2:17 your God, when he L you in the way?
11:19 like a gentle lamb L to the slaughter.
23:8 who brought up and L the descendants of the
23:13 prophesied by Baal and L my people Israel astray.
38:22 of Judah were being L out to the princes
38:23 your sons shall be L out to the Chaldeans,
50:6 sheep; their shepherds have L them astray, turning
Lam 3:11 lion in hiding; he L me off my way
Bar 4:16 They L away the widow's beloved sons, and bereaved
5:6 from you on foot, L away by their enemies;
6:43 one of them is L off by one of
Ezek 20:10 So I L them out of the land of
37:2 And he L me round among them; and behold,
40:22 east; and seven steps L up to it; and
40:24 And he L me toward the south, and behold,
40:49 cubits; and ten steps L up to it; and
41:7 the temple a stairway L upward, and thus one
42:1 Then he L me out into the inner court,
42:15 the temple area, he L me out by the
46:21 the outer court, and L me to the four
47:2 the north gate, and L me round on the
47:3 thousand cubits, and then L me through the water;
47:4 measured a thousand, and L me through the water;
47:4 measured a thousand, and L me through the water;
47:6 Then he L me back along the bank of
Dan 13:45 as she was being L away to be put
Hos 4:12 spirit of harlotry has L them astray, and they
11:4 I L them with cords of compassion, with the
Amos 2:4 but their lies have L them astray, after which
2:10 land of Egypt, and L you forty years in
1Mac 5:23 all they possessed, and L them to Judea with
7:5 of Israel; they were L by Alcimus, who wanted
2Mac 1:19 our fathers were being L captive to Persia, the
1:23 Jonathan L, and the rest responded, as did
2:2 Lord, nor to be L astray in their thoughts
4:38 off his garments, and L him about the whole
6:25 longer, they should be L astray because of me,
Mt 4:1 Then Jesus was L up by the Spirit into
17:1 John his brother, and L them up a high
26:57 who had seized Jesus L him to Caiaphas the
27:2 they bound him and L him away and delivered
27:31 clothes on him, and L him away to crucify
Mk 8:23 by the hand, and L him out of the
9:2 James and John, and L them up a high
14:53 And they L Jesus to the high priest; and
15:1 they bound Jesus and L him away and delivered
15:16 And the soldiers L him away inside the palace
15:20 And they L him out to crucify him.
Lk 4:1 the Jordan, and was L by the Spirit
4:29 of the city, and L him to the brow
21:8 that you are not L astray; for many will
21:24 the sword, and be L captive among all nations;
22:52 they seized him and L him away, bringing him
22:64 and scribes; and they L him away to their
23:25 And as they L him away, they seized one
23:31 who were criminals, were L away to be put
24:50 Then he L them out as far as Bethany,
Jn 7:47 answered them, "Are you L astray, you also?
18:13 First they L him to Annas; for he was
18:28 Then they L Jesus from the house of Caiaphas
Acts 7:36 He L them out, having performed wonders and signs
7:40 for this Moses who L us out from the
8:32 this: "As a sheep L to the slaughter or
9:8 see nothing; so they L him by the hand
13:17 with uplifted arm he L them out of it.
21:38 up a revolt and L the four thousand men
22:11 that light, I was L by the hand by
Rom 5:18 as one man's trespass L to condemnation for all
8:14 For all who are L by the Spirit of
1Cor 12:2 were heathen, you were L astray to dumb idols,
2Cor 11:3 your thoughts will be L astray from a sincere
Gal 5:18 But if you are L by the Spirit you
Eph 4:8 ascended on high he L a host of captives,
Tit 3:3 were once foolish, disobedient, L astray, slaves to
Heb 13:9 Do not be L away by diverse and strange

LEDGE (8)

Ex 27:5 set it under the L of the altar so
38:4 of bronze, under its L, extending halfway down.
Ezek 43:14 ground to the lower L, two cubits, with a
43:14 and from the smaller L to the larger ledge,
43:14 ledge to the larger L, four cubits, with a
43:17 The L also shall be square, fourteen cubits long
43:20 four corners of the L, and upon the rim
45:19 four corners of the L of the altar, and

LEE (3)

Acts 27:4 we sailed under the L of Cyprus, because the
27:7 we sailed under the L of Crete off Salmone.
27:16 And running under the L of a small island

LEECH

Prov 30:15 The L has two daughters; "Give, give," they cry.

LEEKS

Num 11:5 cucumbers, the melons, the L, the onions, and the

LEES (4)

Is 25:6 of wine on the L, of fat things full
25:6 of wine on the L well refined.
Jer 48:11 has settled on his L; he has not been
Zeph 1:12 are thickening upon their L, those who say in

LEFT (441)

Gen 7:23 Only Noah was L, and those that were with
11:8 the earth, and they L off building the city.
13:9 If you take the L hand, then I will
13:9 right hand, then I will go to the L
24:49 turn to the right hand or to the L
28:10 Jacob L Beer-sheba, and went toward Haran.
31:14 any portion or inheritance L to us in our
32:8 the company which is L will escape."
32:24 And Jacob was L alone; and a man wrestled
39:6 So he L all that he had in Joseph's
39:12 But he L his garment in her hand, and
39:13 saw that he had L his garment in her
39:15 voice and cried, he L his garment with me,
39:18 voice and cried, he L his garment with me,
42:38 his brother is dead, and he only is L
44:20 and he alone is L of his mother's children;
44:28 me two sons; one L me, and I said,
47:18 lords; there is nothing L in the sight of
48:13 right hand toward Israel's L hand, and Manasseh in
48:13 and Manasseh in his L hand toward Israel's right
48:14 the younger, and his L hand upon the head
50:8 and their herds were L in the land of
Ex 2:20 Why have you L the man?
8:9 your houses and be L only in the Nile."
8:11 people; they shall be L only in the Nile."
9:21 word of the LORD L his slaves and his
10:5 shall eat what is L to you after the
10:12 in the land, all that the hail has L
10:15 which the hail had L; not a green thing

LEFT

10:19 a single locust was L in all the country
10:26 a hoof shall be L behind, for we must
14:22 them on their right hand and on their L
14:29 them on their right hand and on their L
16:20 listen to Moses; some L part of it till
16:23 and all that is L over lay by to
34:25 of the passover be L until the morning.
Lev 2:3 And what is L of the cereal offering shall
2:10 And what is L of the cereal offering shall
10:12 his sons who were L, "Take the cereal offering
10:16 of Aaron who were L, saying,
14:15 palm of his own L hand,
14:16 that is in his L hand, and sprinkle some
14:26 palm of his own L hand;
14:27 that is in his L hand seven times before
19:6 the morrow; and anything L over until the third
26:36 of you that are L, I will send faintness
26:39 of you that are L shall pine away in
26:43 the land shall be L by them, and enjoy
Num 20:17 hand or to the L, until we have passed
21:35 was not one survivor L to him; and they
22:26 turn either to the right or to the L
25:7 it, he rose and L the congregation, and took
26:65 There was not L a man of them, except
Deut 2:27 aside neither to the right nor to the L
2:34 women, and children; we L none remaining;
3:3 until no survivor was L to him.
3:11 king of Bashan was L of the remnant of
4:27 and you will be L few in number among
5:32 aside to the right hand or to the L
7:20 until those who are L and hide themselves from
17:11 either to the right hand or to the L
17:20 hand or to the L; so that he may
28:14 hand or to the L, to go after other
28:55 because he has nothing L him, in the siege
28:62 multitude, you shall be L few in number; because
Josh 1:7 hand or to the L, that you may have
2:11 there was no courage L in any man, because
8:17 was not a man L in Ai or Bethel,
8:17 out after Israel; they L the city open, and
8:22 them, until there was L none that survived or
10:28 person in it, he L none remaining; and he
10:30 person in it; he L none remaining in it;
10:33 his people, until he L none remaining.
10:37 person in it; he L none remaining, as he
10:39 person in it; he L none remaining; as he
10:40 all their kings; he L none remaining, but utterly
11:8 smote them, until they L none remaining.
11:11 them; there was none L that breathed, and he
11:15 so Joshua did; he L nothing undone of all
11:22 none of the Anakim L in the land of
13:12 Edre-i (he alone was L of the remnant of
23:6 hand nor to the L,
23:7 mixed with these nations L here among you, or
23:12 remnant of these nations L here among you, and
Judg 2:21 the nations that Joshua L when he died,
2:23 So the LORD L those nations, not driving them
3:1 nations which the LORD L, to test Israel by
3:21 Ehud reached with his L hand, took the sword
4:16 edge of the sword; not a man was L
7:20 jars, holding in their L hands the torches, and
8:10 men, all who were L of all the army
9:5 son of Jerubbaal was L, for he hid himself.
16:19 him, and his strength L him.
16:20 that the LORD had L him.
16:29 the one and his L hand on the other.
18:24 priest, and go away, and what have I L
21:7 for those who are L, since we have sworn
21:16 for those who are L, since the women are
Ruth 1:3 died, and she was L with her two sons.
2:11 me, and how you L your father and mother
2:14 and she had some L over.
2:18 what food she had L over after being satisfied.
4:14 LORD, who has not L you this day without
1Sam 2:36 every one who is L in your house shall
5:4 trunk of Dagon was L to him.
6:12 right nor to the L, and the lords of
11:11 two of them were L together.
17:20 in the morning, and L the sheep with a
17:22 And David L the things in charge of the
17:28 with whom have you L those few sheep in
22:4 And he L them with the king of Moab,
24:7 Saul rose up and L the cave, and went
25:34 there had not been L to Nabal so much
27:9 smote the land, and L neither man nor woman
30:9 those stayed who were L behind.
30:13 Amalekite; and my master L me behind because I
30:21 and who had been L at the brook Besor;
2Sam 2:19 hand nor to the L from following Abner.
2:21 hand or to your L, and seize one of
5:21 And the Philistines L their idols there, and David
8:4 the chariot horses, but L enough for a hundred
9:1 there still any one L of the house of
13:30 king's sons, and not one of them is L
14:7 my coal which is L, and leave to my
14:19 hand or to the L from anything that my
15:16 And the king L ten concubines to keep the
16:6 were on his right hand and on his L
16:21 concubines, whom he has L to keep the house;
17:12 the men with him not one will be L
17:22 daybreak not one was L who had not crossed
18:9 oak, and he was L hanging between heaven and
19:19 my lord the king L Jerusalem; let not the
20:3 concubines whom he had L to care for the
1Kgs 7:47 And Solomon L all the vessels unweighed, because
9:20 the people who were L of the Amorites, the
9:21 their descendants who were L after them in the
15:18 the gold that were L in the treasures of
15:29 house of Jeroboam; he L to the house of
17:17 there was no breath L in him.
18:22 even I only, am L a prophet of the
19:3 belongs to Judah, and L his servant there.
19:10 even I only, am L; and they seek my
19:14 even I only, am L; and they seek my
19:20 And he L the oxen, and ran after Elijah,
20:30 fell upon twenty-seven thousand men that were L
22:19 hand and on his L;
2Kgs 3:25 only its stones were L in Kir-hareseth, and the
4:43 the LORD, 'They shall eat and have some L
4:44 ate, and had some L, according to the word
7:13 that those who are L here will fare like
8:6 the day that she L the land until now."
10:11 his priests, until he L him none remaining.
10:21 was not a man L who did not come.
13:7 For there was not L to Jehoahaz an army
14:26 for there was none L, bond or free, and
17:18 his sight; none was L but the tribe of
19:4 up your prayer for the remnant that is L
19:8 that the king had L Lachish.
20:17 Babylon; nothing shall be L, says the LORD.
22:2 aside to the right hand or to the L
23:8 which were on one's L at the gate of
25:11 the people who were L in the city and
25:12 captain of the guard L some of the poorest
25:22 king of Babylon had L, he appointed Gedaliah the
1Chr 6:44 On the L hand were their brethren the sons
12:2 the right or the L hand; they were Benjaminites,
14:12 And they L their gods there, and David gave
16:37 So David L Asaph and his brethren there before
16:39 And he L Zadok the priest and his brethren
18:4 the chariot horses, but L enough for a hundred
2Chr 8:7 the people who were L of the Hittites, the
8:8 their descendants who were L after them in the
11:14 For the Levites L their common lands and their
18:18 hand and on his L;
21:17 that no son was L to him except Jehoahaz,
28:14 So the armed men L the captives and the
31:10 enough and have plenty L; for the LORD has
31:10 people, so that we have this great store L
32:31 in the land, God L him to himself, in
34:2 turn aside to the right or to the L
34:21 for those who are L in Israel and in
Ezra 9:15 just, for we are L a remnant that has
Neh 6:1 there was no breach L in it (although up
8:4 and Meshullam on his L hand.
12:38 thanks went to the L, and I followed them
Tob 1:8 me, for I was L an orphan by my
1:14 Rages in Media I L ten talents of silver
1:19 put to death, I L home in fear.
1:20 confiscated and nothing was L to me except my
4:1 money which he had L in trust with Gabael
4:20 of silver which I L in trust with Gabael
10:7 by which they had L; she ate nothing in
11:2 brother, of how you L your father?
Jud 2:14 So Holofernes L the presence of his master, and
5:8 For they had L the ways of their ancestors,
6:13 they bound Achior and L him lying at the
7:23 there was no strength L in them any longer.
8:7 her husband Manasseh had L her gold and silver,
10:19 them had better be L alive, for if we
13:2 So Judith was L alone in the tent,
13:4 small or great, was L in the bedchamber.

14:8 from the day she L until the moment of
Esth 7:8 As the words L the mouth of the king,
Job 20:21 There was nothing L after he had eaten; therefore
20:26 devour him; what is L in his tent will
21:34 There is nothing L of your answers but falsehood."
22:20 off, and what they L the fire has consumed.'
23:9 perceive him; on the L hand I seek him,
Ps 106:11 covered their adversaries; not one of them was L
Prov 3:16 right hand; in her L hand are riches and
4:28 right or to the L; turn your foot away
25:28 city broken into and L without walls.
29:15 wisdom, but a child L to himself brings shame
31:8 of all who are L desolate.
Eccl 10:2 the right, but a fool's heart toward the L
Song 2:6 O that his L hand were under my head,
8:3 O that his L hand were under my head,
Wis 4:19 foundations; they will be L utterly dry and barren,
10:8 the good, but also L for mankind a reminder
14:6 guided by thy hand L to the world the
Sir 6:3 fruit, and will be L like a withered tree.
15:11 of the Lord I L the right way"; for
15:14 the beginning, and he L him in the power
30:4 dead, for he has L behind him one like
30:6 not grieved; he has L behind him an avenger
39:32 thought this out and L it in writing:
44:9 of them who have L a name, so that
44:18 therefore a remnant was L to the earth when
47:23 with his fathers, and L behind him one of
48:15 earth; the people were L very few in number,
Is 1:8 daughter of Zion is L like a booth in
1:9 of hosts had not L us a few survivors,
4:3 And he who is L in Zion and remains
7:22 every one that is L in the land will
9:20 they devour on the L, but are not satisfied;
11:11 the remnant which is L of his people, from
11:16 the remnant which is L of his people, as
17:6 Gleanings will be L in it, as when an
18:6 all of them be L to the birds of
24:6 the earth are scorched, and few men are L
24:12 Desolation is L in the city, the gates are
30:17 flee, till you are L like a flagstaff on
30:21 the right or when you turn to the L
37:4 up your prayer for the remnant that is L
37:8 that the king had L Lachish.
39:6 Babylon; nothing shall be L, says the LORD.
49:21 Behold, I was L alone; whence then have these
54:3 right and to the L, and your descendants will
Jer 9:19 shamed, because we have L the land, because they
11:23 by famine; and none of them shall be L
25:38 a lion he has L his covert, for their
27:18 the vessels which are L in the house of
27:19 the vessels which are L in this city,
27:21 the vessels which are L in the house of
34:7 of Judah that were L, Lachish and Azekah; for
38:4 the soldiers who are L in this city, and
38:9 there is no bread L in the city."
38:22 Behold, all the women L in the house of
38:27 So they L off speaking with him, for the
39:9 the people who were L in the city, those
39:10 captain of the guard, L in the land of
40:6 the people who were L in the land.
40:11 king of Babylon had L a remnant in Judah
41:10 people who were L at Mizpah, whom Nebuzaradan,
42:2 remnant (for we are L but a few of
43:6 of the guard had L with Gedaliah the son
44:18 But since we L off burning incense to the
50:26 utterly; let nothing be L of her.
52:15 the people who were L in the city and
52:16 captain of the guard L some of the poorest
Lam 1:13 me back; he has L me stunned, faint all
Bar 2:13 us, for we are L, few in number, among
4:12 of many; I was L desolate because of the
4:19 for I have been L desolate.
6:47 They have L only lies and reproach for those
Ezek 1:10 an ox on the L side, and the four
4:4 "Then lie upon your L side, and I will
6:12 and he that is L and is preserved shall
9:8 smiting, and I was L alone, I fell upon
14:22 if there should be L in it any survivors
21:16 sharply to right and L where your edge is
24:21 your daughters whom you L behind shall fall by
36:36 the nations that are L round about you shall
39:3 your bow from your L hand, and will make
41:9 the platform which was L free was five cubits.
41:11 the platform that was L free, one door toward
41:11 the part that was L free was five cubits

47:11 they are to be L for salt.
Dan 2:1 troubled, and his sleep L him.
2:44 shall its sovereignty be L to another people.
10:8 So I was L alone and saw this great
10:8 and no strength was L in me; my radiant
10:13 help me, so I L him there with the
10:17 and no breath is L in me."
12:7 right hand and his L hand toward heaven; and
Hos 4:12 astray, and they have L their God to play
9:12 children, I will bereave them till none is L
Joel 1:4 What the cutting locust L, the swarming locust has
1:4 What the swarming locust L, the hopping locust has
1:4 what the hopping locust L, the destroying locust has
Amos 5:3 shall have a hundred L, and that which went
5:3 hundred shall have ten L to the house of
9:1 people; and what are L of them I will
Jon 4:11 right hand from their L, and also much cattle?"
Zeph 2:5 I will destroy you till no inhabitant is L
3:13 LORD, those who are L in Israel; they shall
Hag 2:3 and say, 'Who is L among you that saw
Zech 4:3 of the bowl and the other on its L
4:11 the right and the L of the lampstand?"
7:14 Thus the land they L was desolate, so that
11:9 let those that are L devour the flesh of
12:6 right and to the L all the peoples round
12:14 the families that are L, each by itself, and
13:8 one third shall be L alive.
Mal 1:3 his hill country and L his heritage to jackals
1Mac 2:18 and those that are L in Jerusalem have done.
2:22 religion to the right hand or to the L
2:28 to the hills and L all that they had
3:32 He L Lysias, a distinguished man of royal lineage,
5:18 But he L Joseph, the son of Zechariah, and
5:46 right or to the L; they had to go
6:2 , breastplates, and weapons L there by Alexander,
6:36 it, and they never L it.
6:45 killed men right and L, and they parted before
6:54 Few men were L in the sanctuary, because famine
7:20 of the country and L with him a force
7:46 the sword; not even one of them was L
9:6 no more than eight hundred of them were L
9:8 to those who were L, "Let us rise and
9:16 When those on the L wing saw that the
9:65 But Jonathan L Simon his brother in the city,
10:13 had built fled; each L his place and departed
10:79 Now Apollonius had secretly L a thousand cavalry
11:64 to meet them, but L his brother Simon in
11:70 one of them was L except Mattathias the son
12:47 thousand of whom he L in Galilee, while a
13:4 the sake of Israel, and I alone am L
14:13 No one was L in the land to fight
2Mac 1:31 the liquid that was L should be poured upon
4:29 Menelaus L his own brother Lysimachus as deputy in
4:29 the high-priesthood, while Sostratus L Crates, the
5:11 So, raging inwardly, he L Egypt and took the
5:22 And he L governors to afflict the people: at
9:24 they would know to whom the government was L
10:19 withstand a siege, Maccabeus L Simon and Joseph,
12:18 one place he had L a very strong garrison.
12:19 those whom Timothy had L in the stronghold, more
13:23 Philip, who had been L in charge of the
13:24 received Maccabeus, L Hegemonides as governor
Mt 4:11 Then the devil L him, and behold, angels came
4:20 Immediately they L their nets and followed him.
4:22 Immediately they L the boat and their father, and
6:3 do not let your L hand know what your
8:15 hand, and the fever L her, and she rose
13:36 Then he L the crowds and went into the
14:20 of the broken pieces L over.
15:37 of the broken pieces L over.
16:4 So he L them and departed.
19:27 reply, "Lo, we have L everything and followed you.
19:29 every one who has L houses or brothers or
20:21 and one at your L, in your kingdom."
20:23 hand and at my L is not mine to
22:22 they marveled; and they L him and went away.
22:25 and having no children L his wife to his
24:1 Jesus L the temple and was going away, when
24:2 there will not be L here one stone upon
24:40 the field; one is taken and one is L
24:41 the mill; one is taken and one is L
25:33 his right hand, but the goats at the L
25:41 to those at his L hand, 'Depart from me,
27:38 one on the right and one on the L
Mk 1:18 And immediately they L their nets and followed him.
1:20 called them; and they L their father Zebedee in

1:29 And immediately he L the synagogue, and entered
1:31 up, and the fever L her; and she served
1:42 And immediately the leprosy L him, and he was
7:16 entered the house, and L the people, his disciples
7:28 way; the demon has L your daughter."
8:8 up the broken pieces L over, seven baskets full.
8:13 And he L them, and getting into the boat
10:1 And he L there and went to the region
10:28 him, "Lo, we have L everything and followed you."
10:29 no one who has L house or brothers or
10:37 and one at your L, in your glory."
10:40 hand or at my L is not mine to
12:12 against them; so they L him and went away.
12:20 and when he died L no children;
12:22 likewise; and the seven L no children.
13:2 There will not be L here one stone upon
14:52 seized him, but he L the linen cloth and
15:27 one on his right and one on his L
Lk 4:38 And he arose and L the synagogue, and entered
4:39 the fever, and it L her; and immediately she
5:11 boats to land, they L everything and followed him.
5:13 And immediately the leprosy L him.
5:28 And he L everything, and rose and followed him.
9:17 took up what was L over, twelve baskets of
10:40 that my sister has L me to serve alone?
12:39 and would not have L his house to be
17:34 bed; one will be taken and the other L
17:35 together; one will be taken and the other L
18:28 said, "Lo, we have L our homes and followed
18:29 no man who has L house or wife or
20:31 and likewise all seven L no children and died.
21:6 there shall not be L here one stone upon
23:32 one on the right and one on the L
Jn 4:3 only his disciples), he L Judea and departed again
4:28 So the woman L her water jar, and went
4:52 seventh hour the fever L him."
6:12 "Gather up the fragments L over, that nothing may
6:13 the five barley loaves, L by those who had
8:9 eldest, and Jesus was L alone with the woman
8:29 me; he has not L me alone, for I
Acts 5:41 Then they L the presence of the council, rejoicing
12:10 and immediately the angel L him.
13:13 And John L them and returned to Jerusalem;
18:1 After this he L Athens and went to Corinth.
18:7 And he L there and went to the house
18:19 to Ephesus, and he L them there; but he
19:12 the sick, and diseases L them and the evil
21:3 leaving it on the L we sailed to Syria,
24:26 Jews a favor, Felix L Paul in prison.
25:14 "There is a man L prisoner by Felix;
27:40 off the anchors and L them in the sea,
Rom 9:29 of hosts had not L us children, we would
11:3 and I alone am L, and they seek my
2Cor 6:7 hand and for the L;
Phil 4:15 the gospel, when I L Macedonia, no church entered
1Thes 3:1 were willing to be L behind at Athens alone,
4:15 are alive, who are L until the coming of
4:17 are alive, who are L, shall be caught up
1Tim 5:5 real widow, and is L all alone, has set
2Tim 4:13 the cloak that I L with Carpus at Troas,
4:20 at Corinth; Trophimus I L ill at Miletus.
Tit 1:4 This is why I L you in Crete, that
Heb 2:8 subjection to him, he L nothing outside his control.
3:16 not all those who L Egypt under the leadership
11:27 By faith he L Egypt, not being afraid of
12:8 If you are L without discipline, in which all
Jude 1:6 their own position but L their proper dwelling have
Rev 10:2 the sea, and his L foot on the land,

LEFT-HANDED (2)

Judg 3:15 Gera, the Benjaminite, a L man.
20:16 picked men who were L; every one could sling

LEG

1Sam 9:24 cook took up the L and the upper portion

LEGAL (3)

Deut 17:8 another, one kind of L right and another, or
Col 2:14 against us with its L demands; this he set
Heb 7:16 not according to a L requirement concerning bodily

LEGION (3)

Mk 5:9 replied, "My name is L; for we are many."
5:15 who had had the L; and they were afraid.
Lk 8:30 And he said, L; for many demons had entered

LEGIONS

Mt 26:53 me more than twelve L of angels?

LEGS (24)

Ex 12:9 its head with its L and its inner parts.
25:26 rings to the four corners at its four L
29:17 its entrails and its L, and put them with
37:13 rings to the four corners at its four L
Lev 1:9 its entrails and its L he shall wash with
1:13 the entrails and the L he shall wash with
4:11 with its head, its L, its entrails, and its
8:21 the entrails and the L were washed with water,
9:14 the entrails and the L, and burned them with
11:21 eat those which have L above their feet, with
Deut 28:35 knees and on the L with grievous boils of
1Sam 17:6 of bronze upon his L, and a javelin of
Ps 147:10 his pleasure in the L of a man;
Prov 26:7 Like a lame man's L, which hang useless, is
Song 5:15 His L are alabaster columns, set upon bases of
Is 47:2 your robe, uncover your L, pass through the rivers.
Ezek 1:7 Their L were straight, and the soles of their
Dan 2:33 thighs of bronze, its L of iron, its feet
10:6 torches, his arms and L like the gleam of
Amos 3:12 of the lion two L, or a piece of
Jn 19:31 asked Pilate that their L might be broken, and
19:32 came and broke the L of the first, and
19:33 was already dead, they did not break his L
Rev 10:1 the sun, and his L like pillars of fire.

LEHABIM (2)

Gen 10:13 father of Ludim, Anamim, L, Naph-tuhim,
1Chr 1:11 father of Ludim, Anamim, L, Naph-tuhim,

LEHEM

1Chr 4:22 Moab and returned to L (now the records are

LEHI (5)

Judg 15:9 encamped in Judah, and made a raid on L
15:14 When he came to L, the Philistines came shouting
15:19 place that is at L, and there came water
15:19 En-hakkore; it is at L to this day.
2Sam 23:11 Philistines gathered together at L, where there was

LEISURE (4)

Esth 14:16 it on the days when I am at L
Wis 13:13 with care in his L, and shapes it with
Sir 38:24 on the opportunity of L; and he who has
Mk 6:31 and they had no L even to eat.

LEMUEL (2)

Prov 31:1 The words of L, king of Massa, which his
31:4 not for kings, O L, it is not for

LEND (21)

Ex 22:25 "If you L money to any of my people
Lev 25:37 You shall not L him your money at interest,
Deut 15:6 you, and you shall L to many nations, but
15:8 hand to him, and L him sufficient for his
23:19 "You shall not L upon interest to your brother,
23:20 a foreigner you may L upon interest, but to
23:20 brother you shall not L upon interest; that the
28:12 hands; and you shall L to many nations, but
28:44 He shall L to you, and you shall not
28:44 and you shall not L to him; he shall
Jud 11:22 before the people, to L strength to our hands
Sir 8:12 Do not L to a man who is stronger
8:12 but if you do L anything, be as one
29:1 that shows mercy will L to his neighbor, and
29:2 L to your neighbor in the time of his
29:7 many have refused to L; they have been afraid
Ezek 18:8 a garment, does not L at interest or take
Lk 6:34 And if you L to those from whom you
6:34 Even sinners L to sinners, to receive as much
6:35 and do good, and L, expecting nothing in return;
11:5 say to him, 'Friend, L me three loaves;

LENDER (3)

Prov 22:7 and the borrower is the slave of the L
Sir 29:6 If the L exert pressure, he will hardly get
Is 24:2 seller; as with the L, so with the borrower;

LENDING (2)

Neh 5:10 and my servants are L them money and grain.
Ps 37:26 ever giving liberally and L, and his children become

L

LENDS (4)
Ps 112:5 who deals generously and L, who conducts his affairs
Prov 19:17 kind to the poor L to the LORD, and
Sir 20:14 a herald; today he L and tomorrow he asks
Ezek 18:13 the idols, commits abomination, L at interest, and

LENGTH (77)
Gen 6:15 to make it: the L of the ark three
13:17 Arise, walk through the L and the breadth of
Ex 25:10 half shall be its L, a cubit and a
25:17 half shall be its L, and a cubit and
25:23 cubits shall be its L, a cubit its breadth,
26:2 The L of each curtain shall be twenty-eight cubits,
26:8 The L of each curtain shall be thirty cubits,
26:13 what remains in the L of the curtains of
26:16 cubits shall be the L of a frame, and
27:11 And likewise for its L on the north side
27:18 The L of the court shall be a hundred
28:16 double, a span its L and a span its
30:2 cubit shall be its L, and a cubit its
36:9 The L of each curtain was twenty-eight cubits, and
36:15 The L of each curtain was thirty cubits, and
36:21 Ten cubits was the L of a frame, and
37:1 a half was its L, a cubit and a
37:6 a half was its L, and a cubit and
37:10 two cubits was its L, a cubit its breadth,
37:25 of acacia wood; its L was a cubit, and
38:1 five cubits was its L, and five cubits its
39:9 double, a span its L and a span its
Lev 19:35 judgment, in measures of L or weight or quantity.
Deut 3:11 Nine cubits was its L, and four cubits its
30:20 life to you and L of days, that you
Judg 3:16 edges, a cubit in L; and he girded it
1Sam 14:14 were half a furrow's L in an acre of
28:20 fell at once full L upon the ground, filled
1Kgs 6:24 Five cubits was the L of one wing of
6:24 and five cubits the L of the other wing
7:2 Forest of Lebanon; its L was a hundred cubits,
7:6 Hall of Pillars; its L was fifty cubits, and
2Chr 3:3 house of God: the L, in cubits of the
3:8 most holy place; its L, corresponding to the breadth
Jud 7:3 as Balbaim and in L from Bethulia to Cyamon,
Job 12:12 aged, and understanding in L of days.
Ps 21:4 gavest it to him, L of days for ever
Prov 3:2 keep my commandments; for L of days and years
Wis 4:8 is not honored for L of time, nor measured
8:12 I speak at greater L they will put their
Sir 30:22 of a man is L of days.
Is 57:10 were wearied with the L of your way, but
Jer 8:19 my people from the L and breadth of the
Bar 3:14 discern where there is L of days, and life,
Ezek 31:7 its greatness, in the L of its branches; for
40:5 temple area, and the L of the measuring reed
40:5 and a handbreadth in L; so he measured the
40:18 gates, corresponding to the L of the gates; this
40:20 He measured its L and its breadth.
40:21 the first gate; its L was fifty cubits, and
40:25 of the others; its L was fifty cubits, and
40:29 in its vestibule; its L was fifty cubits, and
40:33 in its vestibule; its L was fifty cubits, and
40:36 windows round about; its L was fifty cubits, and
40:49 The L of the vestibule was twenty cubits, and
41:2 and he measured the L of the nave forty
41:4 And he measured the L of the room, twenty
41:12 round about, and its L ninety cubits.
41:15 Then he measured the L of the building facing
42:2 The L of the building which was on the
42:11 north, of the same L and breadth, with the
45:7 the east, corresponding in L to one of the
48:8 in breadth, and in L equal to one of
48:9 twenty-five thousand cubits in L, and twenty
48:10 and twenty-five thousand in L on the southern side,
48:13 twenty-five thousand cubits in L and ten thousand in
48:13 The whole L shall be twenty-five thousand cubits and
48:15 and twenty-five thousand in L, shall be for ordinary
48:18 The remainder of the L alongside the holy portion
Zech 2:2 what is its breadth and what is its L
5:2 a flying scroll; its L is twenty cubits, and
Lk 23:9 questioned him at some L; but he made no
Acts 7:5 not even a foot's L, but promised to give
Eph 3:18 is the breadth and L and height and depth,
Phil 4:10 greatly that now at L you have revived your
Rev 21:16 city lies foursquare, its L the same as its
21:16 twelve thousand stadia; its L and breadth and height

LENGTHEN (5)
1Kgs 3:14 walked, then I will L your days."
2Kgs 20:10 for the shadow to L ten steps; rather let
Is 54:2 out; hold not back, L your cords and strengthen
Jer 6:4 the day declines, for the shadows of evening L
2Mac 2:32 it is foolish to L the preface while cutting

LENGTHENED
Sir 48:23 went backward, and he L the life of the

LENGTHENING
Dan 4:27 may perhaps be a L of your tranquillity."

LENT (7)
Deut 15:2 release what he has L to his neighbor; he
23:19 on anything that is L for interest.
1Sam 1:28 Therefore I have L him to the LORD; as
1:28 he lives, he is L to the LORD." And
2:20 the loan which she L to the LORD"; so
Wis 15:8 the soul that was L him.
Jer 15:10 I have not L, nor have I borrowed, yet

LENTILS (4)
Gen 25:34 bread and pottage of L, and he ate and
2Sam 17:28 parched grain, beans and L,
23:11 of ground full of L; and the men fled
Ezek 4:9 and barley, beans and L, millet and spelt, and

LEOPARD (7)
Sir 28:23 a lion; like a L it will mangle them.
Is 11:6 the lamb, and the L shall lie down with
Jer 5:6 A L is watching against their cities, every one
13:23 his skin or the L his spots?
Dan 7:6 lo, another, like a L, with four wings of
Hos 13:7 a lion, like a L I will lurk beside
Rev 13:2 saw was like a L, its feet were like

LEOPARDS (2)
Song 4:8 the dens of lions, from the mountains of L
Hab 1:8 horses are swifter than L, more fierce than the

LEPER (16)
Lev 13:45 "The L who has the disease shall wear torn
14:2 the law of the L for the day of
14:3 is healed in the L,
22:4 Aaron who is a L or suffers a discharge
Num 5:2 of the camp every L, and every one having
2Kgs 5:1 mighty man of valor, but he was a L
5:11 his hand over the place, and cure the L
5:27 from his presence a L, as white as snow.
15:5 that he was a L to the day of
2Chr 26:21 King Uzziah was a L to the day of
26:21 death, and being a L dwelt in a separate
26:23 the kings, for they said, "He is a L
Mt 8:2 him; and behold, a L came to him and
26:6 house of Simon the L,
Mk 1:40 And a L came to him beseeching him, and
14:3 house of Simon the L, as he sat at

LEPERS (7)
2Kgs 7:3 four men who were L at the entrance to
7:8 And when these L came to the edge of
Mt 10:8 raise the dead, cleanse L, cast out demons.
11:5 and the lame walk, L are cleansed and the
Lk 4:27 And there were many L in Israel in the
7:22 sight, the lame walk, L are cleansed, and the
17:12 was met by ten L, who stood at a

LEPROSY (28)
Lev 13:8 the priest shall pronounce him unclean; it is L
13:9 man is afflicted with L, he shall be brought
13:11 it is a chronic L in the skin of
13:12 And if the L breaks out in the skin,
13:12 skin, so that the L covers all the skin
13:13 examination, and if the L has covered all his
13:15 unclean; raw flesh is unclean, for it is L
13:20 is the disease of L, it has broken out
13:25 skin, then it is L; it has broken out
13:30 is an itch, a L of the head or
13:42 diseased spot, it is L breaking out on his
13:43 like the appearance of L in the skin of
13:51 disease is a malignant L; it is unclean.
13:52 it is a malignant L; it shall be burned
14:7 to be cleansed of L; then he shall pronounce
14:44 it is a malignant L in the house; it
14:55 for an itch, for L in a garment or

	14:57	This is the law for L
Deut	24:8	in an attack of L, to be very careful
2Kgs	5:3	He would cure him of his L
	5:6	servant, that you may cure him of his L
	5:7	to me to cure a man of his L
	5:27	Therefore the L of Naaman shall cleave to you,
2Chr	26:19	angry with the priests L broke out on his
Mt	8:3	And immediately his L was cleansed.
Mk	1:42	And immediately the L left him, and he was
Lk	5:12	a man full of L; and when he saw
	5:13	And immediately the L left him.

LEPROUS (18)

Ex	4:6	behold, his hand was L, as white as snow.
Lev	13:2	it turns into a L disease on the skin
	13:3	body, it is a L disease; when the priest
	13:25	unclean; it is a L disease.
	13:27	unclean; it is a L disease.
	13:44	body, he is a L man, he is unclean;
	13:47	"When there is a L disease in a garment,
	13:49	skin, it is a L disease and shall be
	13:55	the fire, whether the L spot is on the
	13:59	the law for a L disease in a garment
	14:3	Then, if the L disease is healed in the
	14:32	in whom is a L disease, who cannot afford
	14:34	and I put a L disease in a house
	14:54	the law for any L disease: for an itch,
Num	12:10	tent, behold, Miriam was L, as white as snow.
	12:10	turned towards Miriam, and behold, she was L
2Sam	3:29	discharge, or who is L, or who holds a
2Chr	26:20	and behold, he was L in his forehead!

LESHEM (2)

Josh	19:47	up and fought against L, and after capturing it
	19:47	settled in it, calling L, Dan, after the name

LESS (35)

Ex	16:17	Israel did so; they gathered, some more, some L
	30:15	poor shall not give L, than the half-shekel, when
Num	22:18	my God, to do L or more.
1Kgs	8:27	contain thee; how much L this house which I
2Chr	6:18	contain thee; how much L this house which I
	32:15	How much L will your God deliver you out
Ezra	9:13	God, hast punished us L than our iniquities deserved
Job	11:6	God exacts of you L than your guilt deserves.
	15:16	his sight; how much L one who is abominable
	25:6	his sight; how much L man, who is a
	35:14	How much L when you say that you do
Ps	8:5	hast made him little L than God, and dost
Prov	17:7	to a fool; still L is false speech to
	19:10	live in luxury, much L for a slave to
Wis	15:10	his life is of L worth than clay,
Sir	22:9	he lacks intelligence; weep L bitterly for the dead,
Is	40:17	accounted by him as L than nothing and emptiness.
Jer	3:11	Israel has shown herself L guilty than false Judah.
Ezek	15:5	for nothing; how much L, when the fire has
2Mac	4:40	in years and no L advanced in folly.
	5:5	dead, Jason took no L than a thousand men
	10:18	When no L than nine thousand took refuge in
	12:4	and drowned them, not L than two hundred.
	12:10	against Timothy, not L than five thousand Arabs
	15:18	relatives, lay upon them L heavily; their greatest and
	15:27	they laid low no L than thirty-five thousand men,
1Cor	12:15	not make it any L a part of the
	12:16	not make it any L a part of the
	12:23	body which we think L honorable we invest with
2Cor	11:24	Jews the forty lashes L one.
	12:13	in what were you L favored than the rest
	12:15	the more, am I to be loved the L
Phil	2:28	that I may be L anxious.
1Tim	5:9	if she is not L than sixty years of
Heb	12:25	them on earth, much L shall we escape if

LESSEN (4)

Ex	5:8	shall by no means L it; for they are
	5:19	shall by no means L your daily number of
Sir	17:20	in his presence and L your offenses.
	28:8	strife, and you will L sins; for a man

LESSENED (2)

Ex	5:11	work will not be L in the least.'"
Sir	19:6	and for one who hates gossip evil is L

LESSER (2)

Gen	1:16	the day, and the L light to rule the
1Chr	12:14	of the army, the L over a hundred and

LESSON (4)

Sir	9:1	teach her an evil L to your own hurt.
Mt	24:32	fig tree learn its L: as soon as its
Mk	13:28	fig tree learn its L: as soon as its
1Cor	14:26	has a hymn, a L, a revelation, a tongue,

LEST (268)

Gen	3:3	shall you touch it, L you die.'"
	3:22	and evil; and now, L he put forth his
	4:15	a mark on Cain, L any who came upon
	11:4	a name for ourselves, L we be scattered abroad
	14:23	anything that is yours, L you should say, 'I
	19:15	daughters who are here, L you be consumed in
	19:17	flee to the hills, L you be consumed."
	19:19	flee to the hills, L the disaster overtake me,
	26:7	thinking, L the men of the place should kill
	26:9	him, "Because I thought, L I die because of
	32:11	for I fear him, L he come and slay
	38:9	semen on the ground, L he should give offspring
	38:23	things as her own, L we be laughed at;
	45:11	of famine to come; L you and your household,
Ex	1:9	deal shrewdly with them, L they multiply, and, if
	5:3	the LORD our God, L he fall upon us
	13:17	near; for God said, L the people repent when
	19:21	and warn the people, L they break through to
	19:22	the LORD consecrate themselves, L the LORD break
	19:24	up to the LORD, L he break out against
	20:19	God speak to us, L we die."
	23:29	you in one year, L the land become desolate
	23:33	dwell in your land, L they make you sin
	28:35	when he comes out, L he die.
	28:43	in the holy place; L they bring guilt upon
	30:20	shall wash with water, L they die.
	30:21	hands and their feet, L they die: it shall
	33:3	go up among you, L I consume you in
	34:12	Take heed to yourself, L you make a covenant
	34:12	land whither you go, L it become a snare
	34:15	is a jealous God), L you make a covenant
Lev	8:35	the LORD has charged, L you die; for so
	10:6	not rend your clothes, L you die, and lest
	10:6	lest you die, and L wrath come upon all
	10:7	the tent of meeting, L you die; for the
	10:9	the tent of meeting, L you die; it shall
	11:43	defile yourselves with them, L you become unclean.
	14:36	to examine the disease, L all that is in
	15:31	separate from their uncleanness, L they die in their
	16:2	is upon the ark, L he die; for I
	16:13	is upon the testimony, L he die;
	18:28	the land became defiled); L the land vomit you
	19:17	reason with your neighbor, L you bear sin because
	19:29	making her a harlot, L the land fall into
	22:9	therefore keep my charge, L they bear sin for
Num	4:15	touch the holy things, L they die.
	4:20	even for a moment, L they die."
	14:42	Do not go up L you be struck down
	16:26	touch nothing of theirs, L you be swept away
	16:34	cry; for they said, L the earth swallow us
	16:40	incense before the LORD, L he become as Korah
	17:10	their murmurings against me, L they die."
	18:3	or to the altar, L they, and you, die.
	18:22	the tent of meeting, L they bear sin and
	18:32	the people of Israel, L you die.'"
	20:18	shall not pass through, L I come out with
Deut	1:42	the midst of you; L you be defeated before
	4:9	keep your soul diligently, L you forget the things
	4:9	eyes have seen, and L they depart from your
	4:16	of the fire, beware L you act corruptly by
	4:19	And beware L you lift up your eyes to
	4:23	Take heed to yourselves, L you forget the covenant
	6:12	full, then take heed L you forget the LORD,
	6:15	is a jealous God; L the anger of the
	7:22	of them at once, L the wild beasts grow
	7:25	take it for yourselves, L you be ensnared by
	8:11	"Take heed L you forget the LORD your God,
	8:12	command you this day: L, when you have eaten
	8:17	Beware L you say in your heart, 'My power
	9:28	wickedness, or their sin, L the land from which
	11:16	Take heed L your heart be deceived, and you
	15:9	Take heed L there be a base thought in
	17:17	multiply wives for himself, L his heart turn away;
	18:16	great fire any more, L I die.'
	19:6	and save his life; L the avenger of blood
	19:10	cities to these three, L innocent blood be shed
	20:5	back to his house, L he die in the
	20:6	back to his house, L he die in the
	20:7	back to his house, L he die in the

	20:8	back to his house, L the heart of his
	22:9	two kinds of seed, L the whole yield be
	24:15	his heart upon it); L he cry against you
	25:3	him, but not more; L, if one should go
	29:18	Beware L there be among you a man or
	29:18	gods of those nations; L there be among you
	32:27	provocation by the enemy, L their adversaries should
	32:27	adversaries should judge amiss, L they should say,
Josh	2:16	"Go into the hills, L the pursuers meet you;
	6:18	things devoted to destruction, L when you have
	9:20	and let them live, L wrath be upon us,
	22:27	sacrifices and peace offerings; L your children say to
	24:27	a witness against you, L you deal falsely with
Judg	7:2	Midianites into their hand, L Israel vaunt themselves
	9:54	sword and kill me, L men say of me,
	14:15	what the riddle is, L we burn you and
	18:25	be heard among us, L angry fellows fall upon
Ruth	2:22	out with his maidens, L in another field you
	4:6	redeem it for myself, L I impair my own
1Sam	4:9	like men, O Philistines, L you become slaves to
	9:5	let us go back, L my father cease to
	13:19	for the Philistines said, L the Hebrews make
	15:6	from among the Amalekites, L I destroy you with
	20:3	not Jonathan know this, L he be grieved.' But
	27:11	tidings to Gath, thinking, L they should tell about
	29:4	with us to battle, L in the battle he
	31:4	me through with it, L these uncircumcised come and
2Sam	1:20	the streets of Ashkelon; L the daughters of the
	1:20	of the Philistines rejoice, L the daughters of the
	12:28	city, and take it; L I take the city,
	13:25	us not all go, L we be burdensome to
	15:14	Absalom; go in haste, L he overtake us quickly,
	17:16	all means pass over; L the king and all
	20:6	servants and pursue him, L he get himself fortified
	21:17	with us to battle, L you quench the lamp
1Kgs	18:44	chariot and go down, L the rain stop you.'"
1Chr	10:4	me through with it, L these uncircumcised come and
2Chr	35:21	who is with me, L he destroy you."
Ezra	7:23	the God of heaven, L his wrath be against
Jud	7:9	lord hear a word, L his army be defeated.
	12:2	"I cannot eat it, L it be an offense;
Job	32:13	Beware L you say, 'We have found wisdom; God
	36:18	Beware L wrath entice you into scoffing; and let
Ps	2:12	trembling kiss his feet, L he be angry, and
	7:2	pursuers, and deliver me, L like a lion they
	13:3	God; lighten my eyes, L I sleep the sleep
	13:4	the sleep of death; L my enemy say, "I
	13:4	have prevailed over him"; L my foes rejoice because
	28:1	not deaf to me, L, if thou be silent
	50:22	you who forget God, L I rend, and there
	59:11	Slay them not, L my people forget; make them
	91:12	will bear you up, L you dash your foot
	125:3	allotted to the righteous, L the righteous put forth
	143:7	thy face from me, L I be like those
Prov	5:9	door of her house; L you give your honor
	5:10	years to the merciless; L strangers take their fill
	20:13	Love not sleep, L you come to poverty; open
	22:25	with a wrathful man, L you learn his ways
	24:18	glad when he stumbles; L the LORD see it,
	25:10	not disclose another's secret; L he who hears you
	25:16	only enough for you, L you be sated with
	25:17	in your neighbor's house, L he become weary of
	26:4	according to his folly, L you be like him
	26:5	according to his folly, L he be wise in
	30:6	add to his words, L he rebuke you, and
	30:9	is needful for me, L I be full, and
	30:9	or L I be poor, and steal, and profane
	30:10	servant to his master, L he curse you, and
	31:5	to desire strong drink; L they drink and forget
Eccl	7:21	things that men say, L you hear your servant
Wis	4:11	He was caught up L evil change his understanding
	16:11	then were quickly delivered, L they should fall into
Sir	1:27	Do not exalt yourself L you fall, and thus
	2:7	and turn not aside, L you fall.
	6:2	through your soul's counsel, L your soul be torn
	7:6	to become a judge, L you be unable to
	7:6	unable to remove iniquity, L you be partial to
	8:1	with a powerful man, L you fall into his
	8:2	with a rich man, L his resources outweigh yours;
	8:4	with an ill-bred person, L your ancestors be
	8:10	coals of a sinner, L you be burned in
	8:11	leave an insolent fellow, L he lie in ambush
	8:15	with a foolhardy fellow, L he be burdensome to
	8:19	thoughts to every one, L you drive away your
	9:3	meet a loose woman, L you fall into her
	9:4	with a woman singer, L you be caught in
	9:5	intently at a virgin, L you stumble and incur
	9:6	give yourself to harlots L you lose your inheritance.
	9:9	with her at wine; L your heart turn aside
	9:13	him, make no misstep, L he rob you of
	11:31	for he devises evil, L he give you a
	12:5	give it to him, L by means of it
	12:12	him next to you, L he overthrow you and
	12:12	sit at your right, L he try to take
	13:10	Do not push forward, L you be repulsed; and
	13:10	remain at a distance, L you be forgotten.
	18:31	revel in great luxury, L you become impoverished by
	23:14	sit among great men; L you be forgetful in
	26:10	over a headstrong daughter, L, when she finds liberty,
	28:26	Beware L you err with your tongue, lest you
	28:26	err with your tongue, L you fall before him
	29:20	take heed to yourself L you fall.
	30:10	not laugh with him, L you have sorrow with
	30:12	while he is young, L he become stubborn and
	31:16	do not chew greedily, L you be hated.
	31:17	do not be insatiable, L you give offense.
	33:19	your property to another, L you change your mind
	37:8	thought for himself— L he cast the lot
	42:9	when she is young, L she do not marry,
	42:9	marry, or if married, L she be hated;
	42:10	hated; while a virgin, L she be defiled or
	42:10	or having a husband, L she prove unfaithful, or,
	42:10	unfaithful, or, though married, L she be barren.
	42:11	over a headstrong daughter, L she make you a
Is	6:10	and shut their eyes; L they see with their
	14:21	guilt of their fathers, L they rise and possess
	27:3	L any one harm it, I guard it night
	28:22	therefore do not scoff, L your bonds be made
	33:15	who shakes his hands, L they hold a bribe,
	36:18	Beware L Hezekiah mislead you by saying, "The
	48:5	announced them to you, L you should say, 'My
	48:7	never heard of them, L you should say, 'Behold,
Jer	1:17	be dismayed by them, L I dismay you before
	4:4	and inhabitants of Jerusalem; L my wrath go forth
	6:8	Be warned, O Jerusalem, L I be alienated from
	6:8	be alienated from you; L I make you a
	10:24	not in thy anger, L thou bring me to
	21:12	who has been robbed, L my wrath go forth
	37:20	of Jonathan the secretary, L I die there."
	38:19	deserted to the Chaldeans, L I be handed over
Bar	6:27	are made to stand, L they fall to the
Ezek	18:30	from all your transgressions, L iniquity be your ruin.
	44:19	put on other garments, L they communicate holiness
Dan	1:10	to Daniel, "I fear L my lord the king,
Hos	2:3	from between her breasts; L I strip her naked
Amos	5:6	the LORD and live, L he break out like
Zech	7:12	their hearts like adamant L they should hear the
Mal	4:6	children to their fathers, L I come and smite
1Mac	4:45	to tear it down, L it bring reproach upon
	13:17	money and the sons, L he arouse great hostility
2Mac	6:24	he said, L many of the young should suppose
Mt	4:6	will bear you up, L you strike your foot
	5:25	with him to court, L your accuser hand you
	7:6	your pearls before swine, L they trample them under
	13:15	eyes they have closed, L they should perceive with
	13:29	But he said, 'No; L in gathering the weeds
	15:32	send them away hungry, L they faint on the
	26:5	"Not during the feast, L there be a tumult
	27:64	until the third day, L his disciples go and
Mk	3:9	because of the crowd, L they should crush him;
	4:12	hear but not understand; L they should turn again,
	13:36	in the morning— L he come suddenly and
	14:2	"Not during the feast, L there be a tumult
Lk	4:11	will bear you up, L you strike your foot
	11:35	Therefore be careful L the light in you be
	12:58	him on the way, L he drag you to
	14:8	a place of honor, L a more eminent man
	14:12	kinsmen or rich neighbors, L they also invite you
	16:28	he may warn them, L they also come into
	21:34	take heed to yourselves L your hearts be weighed
Jn	3:20	come to the light, L his deeds should be
	12:35	you have the light, L the darkness overtake you;
	12:40	and hardened their heart, L they should see with
	12:42	did not confess it, L they should be put
Acts	13:40	Beware, therefore, L there come upon you what is
	27:42	to kill the prisoners, L any should swim away
	28:27	eyes they have closed; L they should perceive with
Rom	11:25	L you be wise in your own conceits, I
	15:20	has already been named, L I build on another
1Cor	1:15	except Crispus and Gaius; L any one should say
	1:17	not with eloquent wisdom, L the cross of Christ
	7:5	then come together again, L Satan tempt you

	8:9	Only take care L this liberty of yours somehow
	8:13	will never eat meat, L I cause my brother
	9:27	body and subdue it, L after preaching to others
	10:12	he stands take heed L he fall.
	11:34	him eat at home-- L you come together to
2Cor	9:4	said you would be; L if some Macedonians come
Gal	2:2	preach among the Gentiles, L somehow I should be
	6:1	Look to yourself, L you too be tempted.
Eph	2:9	not because of works, L any man should boast.
Phil	2:27	but on me also, L I should have sorrow
Col	3:21	provoke your children, L they become discouraged.
Heb	2:1	what we have heard, L we drift away from
	3:12	Take care, brethren, L there be in any of
	4:1	remains, let us fear L any of you be
2Pet	3:17	knowing this beforehand, beware L you be carried
Rev	18:4	of her, my people, L you take part in
	18:4	part in her sins, L you share in her

LET (1,712)

Gen	1:3	And God said, L there be light"; and there
	1:6	And God said, L there be a firmament in
	1:6	of the waters, and L it separate the waters
	1:9	And God said, L the waters under the heavens
	1:9	into one place, and L the dry land appear."
	1:11	And God said, L the earth put forth vegetation,
	1:14	And God said, L there be lights in the
	1:14	from the night; and L them be for signs
	1:15	days and years, and L them be lights in
	1:20	And God said, L the waters bring forth swarms
	1:20	of living creatures, and L birds fly above the
	1:22	in the seas, and L birds multiply on the
	1:24	And God said, L the earth bring forth living
	1:26	Then God said, L us make man in our
	1:26	after our likeness; and L them have dominion over
	4:8	to Abel his brother, L us go out to
	9:26	God be Shem; and L Canaan be his slave.
	9:27	God enlarge Japheth, and L him dwell in the
	9:27	tents of Shem; and L Canaan be his slave."
	11:3	to one another, "Come, L us make bricks, and
	11:4	Then they said, "Come, L us build ourselves a
	11:4	in the heavens, and L us make a name
	11:7	Come, L us go down, and there confuse their
	12:12	me, but they will L you live.
	13:8	Abram said to Lot, L there be no strife
	14:24	who went with me; L Aner, Eshcol, and Mamre
	18:4	L a little water be brought, and wash your
	18:30	Then he said, "Oh L not the Lord be
	18:32	Then he said, "Oh L not the Lord be
	19:8	have not known man; L me bring them out
	19:20	L me escape there--is it not a little
	19:32	Come, L us make our father drink wine, and
	19:34	night with my father; L us make him drink
	20:6	therefore I did not L you touch her.
	21:16	bowshot; for she said, L me not look upon
	23:9	For the full price L him give it to
	24:14	L the maiden to whom I shall say, 'Pray
	24:14	I shall say, 'Pray L down your jar that
	24:14	will water your camels-- L her be the one
	24:18	lord"; and she quickly L down her jar upon
	24:43	the spring of water; L the young woman who
	24:44	L her be the woman whom the LORD has
	24:45	said to her, 'Pray L me drink.'
	24:46	me drink.' She quickly L down her jar from
	24:51	her and go, and L her be the wife
	24:55	and her mother said, L the maiden remain with
	24:56	has prospered my way; L me go that I
	25:30	Esau said to Jacob, L me eat some of
	26:28	you; so we say, L there be an oath
	26:28	you and us, and L us make a covenant
	27:29	L peoples serve you, and nations bow down to
	27:31	said to his father, L my father arise, and
	30:26	have served you, and L me go; for you
	30:32	flock and keep it: L me pass through all
	30:34	L it be as you have said."
	31:35	said to her father, L not my lord be
	31:44	Come now, L us make a covenant, you and
	31:44	you and I; and L it be a witness
	32:26	Then he said, L me go, for the day
	32:26	said, "I will not L you go, unless you
	33:12	Then Esau said, L us journey on our way,
	33:14	L my lord pass on before his servant, and
	33:15	So Esau said, L me leave with you some
	33:15	L me find favor in the sight of my
	34:11	and to her brothers, L me find favor in
	34:21	are friendly with us; L them dwell in the
	34:21	large enough for them; L us take their daughters
	34:21	daughters in marriage, and L us give them our
	34:23	Only L us agree with them, and they will
	35:3	change your garments; then L us arise and go
	37:17	I heard them say, L us go to Dothan.'"
	37:20	Come now, L us kill him and throw him
	37:21	of their hands, saying, L us not take his
	37:27	Come, L us sell him to the Ishmaelites, and
	37:27	to the Ishmaelites, and L not our hand be
	38:16	side, and said, "Come, L me come in to
	38:23	And Judah replied, L her keep the things as
	38:24	"Bring her out, and L her be burned."
	41:33	Now therefore L Pharaoh select a man discreet and
	41:34	L Pharaoh proceed to appoint overseers over the
	41:35	And L them gather all the food of these
	41:35	in the cities, and L them keep it.
	42:16	one of you, and L him bring your brother,
	42:19	you are honest men, L one of your brothers
	42:19	in your prison, and L the rest go and
	43:9	him before you, then L me bear the blame
	43:31	controlling himself he said, L food be served."
	44:9	servants it be found, L him die, and we
	44:10	He said, L it be as you say: he
	44:18	said, "O my lord, L your servant, I pray
	44:18	my lord's ears, and L not your anger burn
	44:33	my life.' Now therefore, L your servant, I pray
	44:33	to my lord; and L the lad go back
	46:30	said to Joseph, "Now L me die, since I
	47:4	now, we pray you, L your servants dwell in
	47:6	best of the land; L them dwell in the
	47:30	me in Egypt, but L me lie with my
	48:11	and lo, God has L me see your children
	48:16	lads; and in them L my name be perpetuated,
	48:16	Abraham and Isaac; and L them grow into a
	49:21	Naphtali is a hind L loose, that bears comely
	50:5	bury me.' Now therefore L me go up, I
Ex	1:9	Come, L us deal shrewdly with them, lest they
	1:16	Egypt commanded them, but L the male children
	1:17	you done this, and L the male children live?"
	1:21	Nile, but you shall L every daughter live."
	3:18	now, we pray you, L us go a three
	3:19	of Egypt will not L you go unless compelled
	3:20	after that he will L you go.
	4:18	and said to him, L me go back, I
	4:21	that he will not L the people go.
	4:23	I say to you, L my son go that
	4:23	if you refuse to L him go, behold, I
	4:26	So he L him alone.
	5:1	the God of Israel, L my people go, that
	5:2	heed his voice and L Israel go?
	5:2	moreover I will not L Israel go."
	5:3	has met with us; L us go, we pray,
	5:7	make bricks, as heretofore; L them go and gather
	5:8	idle; therefore they cry, L us go and offer
	5:9	sacrifice to our God.' L heavier work be laid
	5:17	idle; therefore you say, L us go and sacrifice
	6:11	king of Egypt to L the people of Israel
	7:2	shall tell Pharaoh to L the people of Israel
	7:14	hardened, he refuses to L the people go.
	7:16	me to you, saying, L my people go, that
	8:1	'Thus says the LORD, L my people go, that
	8:2	if you refuse to L them go, behold, I
	8:8	people; and I will L the people go to
	8:20	'Thus says the LORD, L my people go, that
	8:21	if you will not L my people go, behold,
	8:28	Pharaoh said, "I will L you go, to sacrifice
	8:29	his people, tomorrow; only L not Pharaoh deal
	8:32	also, and did not L the people go.
	9:1	God of the Hebrews, L my people go, that
	9:2	if you refuse to L them go and still
	9:7	and he did not L the people go.
	9:8	from the kiln, and L Moses throw them toward
	9:13	God of the Hebrews, L my people go, that
	9:16	this purpose have I L you live, to show
	9:17	people, and will not L them go.
	9:28	and hail; I will L you go, and you
	9:35	and he did not L the people of Israel
	10:3	L my people go, that they may serve me.
	10:4	if you refuse to L my people go, behold,
	10:7	L the men go, that they may serve the
	10:10	you, if ever I L you and your little
	10:20	and he did not L the children of Israel
	10:24	go with you; only L your flocks and your
	10:25	said, "You must also L us have sacrifices and
	10:27	and he would not L them go.
	11:1	Egypt; afterwards he will L you go hence; when
	11:10	and he did not L the people of Israel

12:10 And you shall L none of it remain until
12:36 Egyptians, so that they L them have what they
12:48 passover to the LORD, L all his males be
13:15 Pharaoh stubbornly refused to L us go, the LORD
13:17 When Pharaoh L the people go, God did not
14:5 done, that we have L Israel go from serving
14:12 to you in Egypt, L us alone and let
14:12 'Let us alone and L us serve the Egyptians?
14:25 and the Egyptians said, L us flee from before
16:19 Moses said to them, L no man leave any
16:29 you in his place, L no man go out
16:32 the LORD has commanded: L an omer of it
18:22 And L them judge the people at all times;
18:27 Then Moses L his father-in-law depart, and he went
19:10 today and tomorrow, and L them wash their
19:22 And also L the priests who come near to
19:24 you; but do not L the priests and the
20:19 we will hear; but L not God speak to
21:8 himself, then he shall L her be redeemed; he
21:13 for him, but God L him fall into his
21:26 destroys it, he shall L the slave go free
21:27 or female, he shall L the slave go free
22:13 is torn by beasts, L him bring it as
23:11 seventh year you shall L it rest and lie
23:13 of other gods, nor L such be heard out
23:18 with leavened bread, or L the fat of my
24:14 whoever has a cause, L him go to them."
25:8 And L them make me a sanctuary, that I
32:10 stiff-necked people; now therefore L me alone, that
32:22 And Aaron said, L not the anger of my
32:24 I said to them, L any who have gold
32:25 loose (for Aaron had L them break loose, to
33:12 but thou hast not L me know whom thou
34:3 up with you, and L no man be seen
34:3 throughout all the mountain; L no flocks or herds
34:9 thy sight, O Lord, L the Lord, I pray
35:5 of a generous heart, L him bring the LORD's
35:10 "And L every able man among you come and
36:6 proclaimed throughout the camp, L neither man nor
Lev 2:13 salt; you shall not L the salt of the
4:3 on the people, then L him offer for the
10:6 his sons, "Do not L the hair of your
13:45 wear torn clothes and L the hair of his
14:7 him clean, and shall L the living bird go
14:53 stuff; and he shall L the living bird go
16:22 land; and he shall L the goat go in
19:19 You shall not L your cattle breed with a
21:10 the garments, shall not L the hair of his
24:14 him who cursed; and L all who heard him
24:14 upon his head, and L all the congregation stone
25:27 means to redeem it, L him reckon the years
26:22 And I will L loose the wild beasts among
Num 4:18 to Moses and Aaron, L not the tribe of
5:21 lain with you, then' L the priest make the
6:5 be holy; he shall L the locks of hair
8:7 expiation upon them, and L them go with a
8:8 Then L them take a young bull and its
9:2 land of Egypt, saying, L the people of Israel
10:35 "Arise, O LORD, and L thy enemies be scattered;
10:35 enemies be scattered; and L them that hate thee
11:16 tent of meeting, and L them take their stand
11:31 from the sea, and L them fall beside the
12:12 L her not be as one dead, of whom
12:14 L her be shut up outside the camp seven
13:30 before Moses, and said, L us go up at
14:4 said to one another, L us choose a captain,
14:17 now, I pray thee, L the power of the
16:17 and Aaron, tomorrow; and L every one of you
16:38 of their lives; so L them be made into
20:17 Now L us pass through your land.
20:19 will pay for it; L me only pass through
21:22 of the Amorites, saying, L me pass through your
21:27 say, "Come to Heshbon, L it be built, let
21:27 let it be built, L the city of Sihon
22:13 LORD has refused to L me go with you."
22:16 the son of Zippor: L nothing hinder you from
22:33 have slain you and L her live."
23:10 L me die the death of the righteous, and
23:10 of the righteous, and L my end be like
24:14 people; come, I will L you know what this
27:16 said to the LORD, L the LORD, the God
31:15 to them, "Have you L all the women live?
32:5 favor in your sight, L this land be given
33:55 of them whom you L remain shall be as
36:6 the daughters of Zelophehad, L them marry whom
Deut 1:22 near me, and said, L us send men before
2:27 words of peace, saying, L me pass through your
2:28 I may drink; only L me pass through on
2:30 of Heshbon would not L us pass by him;
3:25 L me go over, I pray, and see the
3:26 LORD said to me, L it suffice you; speak
4:10 me, that I may L them hear my words,
4:36 Out of heaven he L you hear his voice,
4:36 and on earth he L you see his great
8:3 he humbled you and L you hunger and fed
9:14 is a stubborn people; L me alone, that I
13:2 and if he says, L us go after other
13:2 have not known, 'and L us serve them,'
13:6 entices you secretly, saying, L us go and serve
13:13 of the city, saying, L us go and serve
15:12 seventh year you shall L him go free from
15:13 And when you L him go free from you,
15:13 you, you shall not L him go empty-handed;
15:18 to you, when you L him go free from
18:16 assembly, when you said, L me not hear again
20:3 battle against your enemies: L not your heart faint;
20:5 L him go back to his house, lest he
20:6 L him go back to his house, lest he
20:7 L him go back to his house, lest he
20:8 L him go back to his house, lest the
21:8 thy people Israel; but L the guilt of blood
21:14 in her, you shall L her go where she
22:7 the young; you shall L the mother go, but
32:1 I will speak; and L the earth hear the
32:38 L them rise up and help you, let them
32:38 up and help you, L them be your protection!
33:6 L Reuben live, and not die, nor let his
33:6 and not die, nor L his men be few."
33:16 L these come upon the head of Joseph, and
33:24 above sons be Asher; L him be the favorite
33:24 of his brothers, and L him dip his foot
34:4 your descendants.' I have L you see it with
Josh 2:15 Then she L them down by a rope through
2:18 window through which you L us down; and you
4:22 mean?' then you shall L your children know, 'Israel
5:6 that he would not L them see the land
6:6 of the covenant, and L seven priests bear seven
6:7 around the city, and L the armed men pass
6:10 shall not shout or L your voice be heard,
7:3 and said to him, L not all the people
7:3 people go up, but L about two or three
9:15 covenant with them, to L them live; and the
9:20 do to them, and L them live, lest wrath
9:21 leaders said to them, L them live." So they
10:4 and help me, and L us smite Gibeon; for
10:19 their rear, do not L them enter their cities;
22:22 He knows; and L Israel itself know!
22:26 Therefore we said, L us now build an altar,
Judg 1:25 the sword, but they L the man and all
6:31 he is a god, L him contend for himself,
6:32 that is to say, L Baal contend against him,"
6:39 Gideon said to God, L not thy anger burn
6:39 anger burn against me, L me speak but this
6:39 but this once; pray, L me make trial only
6:39 with the fleece; pray, L it be dry only
6:39 on all the ground L there be dew."
7:3 is fearful and trembling, L him return home."' And
7:7 into your hand; and L all the others go
8:24 Gideon said to them, L me make a request
9:15 shade; but if not, L fire come out of
9:19 rejoice in Abimelech, and L him also rejoice in
9:20 you; but if not, L fire come out from
9:20 Shechem, and Beth-millo; and L fire come out from
10:14 whom you have chosen; L them deliver you in
11:17 king of Edom, saying, L us pass, we pray,
11:19 Israel said to him, L us pass, we pray,
11:37 said to her father, L this thing be done
11:37 be done for me; L me alone two months,
12:5 fugitives of Ephraim said, L me go over," the
13:8 LORD, I pray thee, L the man of God
13:13 said to the woman L her beware.
13:14 from the vine, neither L her drink wine or
13:14 that I commanded her L her observe."
13:15 of the LORD, "Pray, L us detain you, and
14:12 Samson said to them, L me now put a
15:5 to the torches, he L the foxes go into
16:2 quiet all night, saying, L us wait till the
16:26 him by the hand, L me feel the pillars
16:30 And Samson said, L me die with the Philistines."
18:9 They said, "Arise, and L us go up against
18:25 to him, "Do not L your voice be heard
19:6 spend the night, and L your heart be merry."

19:9 close; lodge here and L your heart be merry;
19:11 his master, "Come now, L us turn aside to
19:13 his servant, "Come and L us draw near to
19:24 daughter and his concubine; L me bring them out
19:25 began to break, they L her go.
19:28 to her, "Get up, L us be going." But
20:32 men of Israel said, L us flee, and draw
Ruth 2:2 Moabitess said to Naomi, L me go to the
2:7 She said, 'Pray, L me glean and gather among
2:9 L your eyes be upon the field which they
2:15 his young men, saying, L her glean even among
3:13 kin for you, well; L him do it; but
3:14 another; and he said, L it not be known
1Sam 1:18 And she said, L your maidservant find favor in
2:3 more so very proudly, L not arrogance come from
2:16 man said to him, L them burn the fat
3:18 "It is the LORD; L him do what seems
3:19 was with him and L none of his words
4:3 L us bring the ark of the covenant of
5:8 They answered, L the ark of the God of
5:11 God of Israel, and L it return to its
6:6 them, did not they L the people go, and
6:8 send it off, and L it go its way.
9:5 was with him, "Come, L us go back, lest
9:6 L us go there; perhaps he can tell us
9:9 God, he said, "Come, L us go to the
9:10 servant, "Well said; come, L us go." So they
9:19 the morning I will L you go and will
11:14 to the people, "Come, L us go to Gilgal
13:3 all the land, saying, L the Hebrews hear."
14:1 bore his armor, "Come, L us go over to
14:6 bore his armor, "Come, L us go over to
14:34 and say to them, L every man bring his
14:36 Then Saul said, L us go down after the
14:36 until the morning light; L us not leave a
14:36 But the priest said, L us draw near hither
16:16 L our lord now command your servants, who are
16:22 sent to Jesse, saying, L David remain in my
17:8 man for yourselves, and L him come down to
17:32 David said to Saul, L no man's heart fail
18:2 day, and would not L him return to his
18:17 For Saul thought, L not my hand be upon
18:17 be upon him, but L the hand of the
18:21 Saul thought, L me give her to him, that
19:4 and said to him, L not the king sin
19:12 So Michal L David down through the window; and
19:17 deceived me thus, and L my enemy go, so
19:17 "He said to me, L me go; why should
20:3 eyes; and he thinks, L not Jonathan know this,
20:5 with the king; but L me go, that I
20:11 said to David, "Come, L us go out into
20:16 face of the earth, L not the name of
20:29 to Bethlehem; he said, L me go; for our
20:29 favor in your eyes, L me get away, and
21:2 and said to me, L no one know anything
21:13 of the gate, and L his spittle run down
22:3 king of Moab, "Pray L my father and my
22:15 L not the king impute anything to his servant
24:19 his enemy, will he L him go away safe?
25:8 Therefore L my young men find favor in your
25:24 be the guilt; pray L your handmaid speak in
25:25 L not my lord regard this ill-natured fellow, Nabal;
25:26 own hand, now then L your enemies and those
25:27 And now L this present which your servant has
26:8 this day; now therefore L me pin him to
26:11 jar of water, and L us go."
26:19 Now therefore L my lord the king hear the
26:20 other gods.' Now therefore, L not my blood fall
26:22 L one of the young men come over and
27:5 favor in your eyes, L a place be given
28:22 hearken to your handmaid; L me set a morsel
2Sam 1:21 "Ye mountains of Gilboa, L there be no dew
2:7 Now therefore L your hands be strong, and be
2:14 Abner said to Joab, L the young men arise
2:14 And Joab said, L them arise."
3:23 king, and he has L him go, and he
5:8 would smite the Jebusites, L him get up the
10:12 of good courage, and L us play the man
11:12 and tomorrow I will L you depart." So Uriah
11:25 to Joab, 'Do not L this matter trouble you,
13:5 you, say to him, L my sister Tamar come
13:6 to the king, "Pray L my sister Tamar come
13:24 servant has sheepshearers; pray L the king and his
13:25 Absalom, "No, my son, L us not all go,
13:26 said, "If not, pray L my brother Amnon go
13:27 pressed him until he L Amnon and all the
13:32 Shimeah, David's brother, said, L not my lord suppose
13:33 Now therefore L not my lord the king so
14:9 on my father's house; L the king and his
14:11 Then she said, "Pray L the king invoke the
14:12 the woman said, "Pray L your handmaid speak a
14:18 And the woman said, L my lord the king
14:24 And the king said, L him dwell apart in
14:32 Now therefore L me go into the presence of
14:32 is guilt in me, L him kill me.'"
15:7 to the king, "Pray L me go and pay
15:14 at Jerusalem, "Arise, and L us flee; or else
15:25 bring me back and L me see both it
15:26 behold, here I am, L him do to me
16:4 said, "I do obeisance; L me ever find favor
16:9 L me go over and take off his head."
16:11 L him alone, and let him curse; for the
16:11 Let him alone, and L him curse; for the
17:1 Ahithophel said to Absalom, L me choose twelve
17:5 the Archite also, and L us hear what he
18:19 the son of Zadok, L me run, and carry
18:22 Joab, "Come what may, L me also run after
19:19 said to the king, L not my lord hold
19:19 the king left Jerusalem; L not the king bear
19:30 to the king, "Oh, L him take it all,
19:37 Pray L your servant return, that I may die
19:37 is your servant Chimham; L him go over with
20:11 whoever is for David, L him follow Joab."
20:18 say in old time, L them but ask counsel
21:6 the territory of Israel, L seven of his sons
24:14 am in great distress; L us fall into the
24:14 mercy is great; but L me not fall into
24:17 L thy hand, I pray thee, be against me
24:22 Araunah said to David, L my lord the king
1Kgs 1:2 servants said to him, L a young maiden be
1:2 lord the king, and L her wait upon the
1:2 and be his nurse; L her lie in your
1:12 Now therefore come, L me give you counsel, that
1:34 down to Gihon; and L Zadok the priest and
1:51 of the altar, saying, L King Solomon swear to
2:6 wisdom, but do not L his gray head go
2:7 Barzillai the Gileadite, and L them be among those
2:21 She said, L Abishag the Shunammite be given to
4:27 in his month; they L nothing be lacking.
8:26 O God of Israel, L thy word be confirmed,
8:52 L thy eyes be open to the supplication of
8:59 L these words of mine, wherewith I have made
8:61 L your heart therefore be wholly true to the
11:21 Hadad said to Pharaoh, L me depart, that I
11:22 said to him, "Only L me go."
15:19 dwelt in Damascus, saying, L there be a league
17:21 "O LORD my God, L this child's soul come
18:23 L two bulls be given to us; and let
18:23 given to us; and L them choose one bull
18:36 Abraham, Isaac, and Israel, L it be known this
18:40 the prophets of Baal; L not one of them
19:20 after Elijah, and said, L me kiss my father
20:11 Israel answered, "Tell him, L not him that girds
20:23 stronger than we; but L us fight against them
20:31 Israel are merciful kings; L us put sackcloth on
20:32 servant Ben-hadad says, 'Pray, L me live.'" And he
20:34 Ahab said, "I will L you go on these
20:34 covenant with him and L him go.
20:42 LORD, 'Because you have L go out of your
21:7 and eat bread, and L your heart be cheerful;
21:10 fellows opposite him, and L them bring a charge
22:8 And Jehoshaphat said, L not the king say so."
22:13 favorable to the king; L your word be like
22:17 'These have no master; L each return to his
22:49 Ahab said to Jehoshaphat, L my servants go with
2Kgs 1:10 a man of God, L fire come down from
1:12 a man of God, L fire come down from
1:13 God, I pray you, L my life, and the
1:14 their fifties; but now L my life be precious
2:9 said, "I pray you, L me inherit a double
2:16 fifty strong men; pray, L them go, and seek
4:10 L us make a small roof chamber with walls,
4:27 man of God said, L her alone, for she
5:8 L him come now to me, that he may
5:17 not, I pray you, L there be given to
6:2 L us go to the Jordan and each of
6:2 there a log, and L us make a place
7:4 If we say, L us enter the city,' the
7:4 So now come, L us go over to the
7:9 us; now therefore come, L us go and tell
7:13 of his servants said, L some men take five
7:13 that have already perished; L us send and see."

9:15 is your mind, then L no one slip out
9:17 to meet them, and L him say, 'Is it
10:19 and all his priests; L none be missing, for
10:25 in and slay them; L not a man escape."
11:15 For the priest said, L her not be slain
12:5 house of the LORD, L the priests take, each
12:5 from his acquaintance; and L them repair the house
14:8 of Israel, saying, "Come, L us look one another
17:27 carried away thence; and L him go and dwell
18:29 the king: 'Do not L Hezekiah deceive you, for
18:30 Do not L Hezekiah make you to rely on
19:10 of Judah: 'Do not L your God on whom
20:7 And L them take and lay it on the
20:10 lengthen ten steps; rather L the shadow go back
22:5 from the people; and L it be given into
22:5 of the LORD; and L them give it to
23:18 And he said, L him be; let no man
23:18 said, "Let him be; L no man move his
23:18 So they L his bones alone, with the bones
1Chr 13:2 the LORD our God, L us send abroad to
13:3 Then L us bring again the ark of our
16:10 in his holy name; L the hearts of those
16:31 L the heavens be glad, and let the earth
16:31 heavens be glad, and L the earth rejoice, and
16:31 the earth rejoice, and L them say among the
16:32 L the sea roar, and all that fills it,
16:32 all that fills it, L the field exult, and
17:23 And now, O LORD, L the word which thou
19:13 of good courage, and L us play the man
21:13 am in great distress; L me fall into the
21:13 is very great; but L me not fall into
21:17 L thy hand, I pray thee, O LORD my
21:17 my father's house; but L not the plague be
21:23 David, "Take it; and L my lord the king
2Chr 1:9 O LORD God, L thy promise to David my
2:15 my lord has spoken, L him send to his
6:17 LORD, God of Israel, L thy word be confirmed,
6:40 Now, O my God, L thy eyes be open
6:41 L thy priests, O LORD God, be clothed with
6:41 clothed with salvation, and L thy saints rejoice in
14:7 he said to Judah, L us build these cities,
14:11 thou art our God; L not man prevail against
15:7 Do not L your hands be weak, for your
16:3 dwelt in Damascus, saying, L there be a league
16:5 stopped building Ramah, and L his work cease.
18:7 And Jehoshaphat said, L not the king say so."
18:12 favorable to the king; L your word be like
18:16 'These have no master; L each return to his
19:7 Now then, L the fear of the LORD be
20:10 whom thou wouldest not L Israel invade when they
23:3 L him reign, as the LORD spoke concerning the
23:6 L no one enter the house of the LORD
25:7 "O king, do not L the army of Israel
25:17 of Israel, saying, "Come, L us look one another
32:15 Now therefore do not L Hezekiah deceive you or
34:11 kings of Judah had L go to ruin.
35:5 the lay people, and L there be for each
36:23 L him go up.'"
Ezra 1:3 be with him, and L him go up to
1:4 is in Jerusalem; and L each survivor, in whatever
4:2 and said to them, L us build with you;
5:15 is in Jerusalem, and L the house of God
5:17 good to the king, L search be made in
5:17 And L the king send us his pleasure in
6:3 of God at Jerusalem, L the house be rebuilt,
6:4 one course of timber; L the cost be paid
6:5 And also L the gold and silver vessels of
6:7 the River, keep away; L the work on this
6:7 house of God alone; L the governor of the
6:9 at Jerusalem require-- L that be given to
6:12 Darius make a decree; L it be done with
7:23 the God of heaven, L it be done in
7:26 law of the king, L judgment be strictly executed
10:3 Therefore L us make a covenant with our God
10:3 of our God; and L it be done according
10:14 L our officials stand for the whole assembly; let
10:14 for the whole assembly; L all in our cities
Neh 1:6 and keep his commandments; L thy ear be attentive,
1:11 O Lord, L thy ear be attentive to the
2:3 said to the king, L the king live for
2:7 it pleases the king, L letters be given me
2:7 River, that they may L me pass through until
2:17 Come, L us build the wall of Jerusalem, that
2:18 And they said, L us rise up and build."
4:5 cover their guilt, and L not their sin be
4:22 people at that time, L every man and his
5:2 daughters, we are many; L us get grain, that
5:10 L us leave off this interest.
6:2 me, saying, "Come and L us meet together in
6:7 So now come, and L us take counsel together."
6:10 shut up, he said, L us meet together in
6:10 within the temple, and L us close the doors
7:3 I said to them, L not the gates of
7:3 are still standing guard L them shut and bar
9:32 covenant and steadfast love, L not all the hardship
Tob 4:7 uprightly, and do not L your eye begrudge the
4:15 wine to excess or L drunkenness go with you
4:16 charity, and do not L your eye begrudge the
4:19 commands, and do not L them be blotted out
4:20 And now L me explain to you about the
7:8 on the journey, and L the matter be settled."
7:10 But L me explain the true situation to you.
8:4 "Sister, get up, and L us pray that the
8:5 L the heavens and all thy creatures bless thee.
8:6 man should be alone; L us make a helper
8:12 if he is not, L us bury him without
8:15 L thy saints and all thy creatures bless thee;
8:15 thy creatures bless thee; L all thy angels and
10:5 my child, that I L you go, you who
10:12 L me hear a good report of you.
11:3 L us run ahead of your wife and prepare
13:8 L all men speak, and give him thanks in
13:15 L my soul praise God the great King.
Jud 5:5 Ammonites, said to him, L my lord now hear
5:21 in their nation, then L my lord pass them
5:24 Therefore L us go up, Lord Holofernes, and they
7:9 to him and said, L our lord hear a
7:12 forces with you; only L your servants take possession
7:29 L him not do this day the things which
7:31 L us hold out for five more days; by
8:17 wait for his deliverance, L us call upon him
8:24 "Now therefore, brethren, L us set an example to
8:25 In spite of everything L us give thanks to
10:19 alive, for if we L them go they will
11:5 of your servant, and L your maidservant speak in
12:6 to Holofernes and said, L my lord now command
12:12 a disgrace if we L such a woman go
14:2 and the sun rises, L every valiant man take
14:5 Ammonite to me, and L him see and recognize
16:14 L all thy creatures serve thee, for thou didst
Esth 1:19 it please the king, L a royal order go
1:19 forth from him, and L it be written among
1:19 before King Ahasuerus; and L the king give her
2:2 who attended him said, L beautiful young virgins be
2:3 And L the king appoint officers in all the
2:3 charge of the women; L their ointments be given
2:4 And L the maiden who pleases the king be
3:9 it please the king, L it be decreed that
5:4 it please the king, L the king and Haman
5:8 and fulfil my request, L the king and Haman
5:12 added, "Even Queen Esther L no one come with
5:14 friends said to him, L a gallows fifty cubits
6:5 And the king said, L him come in."
6:8 king delights to honor, L royal robes be brought,
6:9 crown is set; and L the robes and the
6:9 king's most noble princes; L him array the man
6:9 delights to honor, and L him conduct the man
7:3 it please the king, L my life be given
8:5 pleasing in his eyes, L an order be written
9:13 it please the king, L the Jews who are
9:13 And L the ten sons of Haman be hanged
14:11 being; and do not L them mock at our
Job 3:3 And Job said: L the day perish wherein
3:4 'A man-child is conceived.' L that day be darkness!
3:5 L gloom and deep darkness claim it.
3:5 L clouds dwell upon it; let the blackness of
3:5 clouds dwell upon it; L the blackness of the
3:6 That night-- L thick darkness seize it!
3:6 L it not rejoice among the days of the
3:6 days of the year, L it not come into
3:7 Yea, L that night be barren; let no joyful
3:7 that night be barren; L no joyful cry be
3:8 L those curse it who curse the day, who
3:9 L the stars of its dawn be dark; let
3:9 its dawn be dark; L it hope for light,
6:9 me, that he would L loose his hand and
6:29 Turn, I pray, L no wrong be done.
7:16 L me alone, for my days are a breath.
7:19 away from me, nor L me alone till I
9:18 cause; he will not L me get my breath,
9:34 L him take his rod away from me, and
9:34 away from me, and L not dread of him

LET

10:2 Do not condemn me; L me know why thou
10:20 L me alone, that I may find a little
11:14 it far away, and L not wickedness dwell in
13:13 L me have silence, and I will speak, and
13:13 I will speak, and L come on me what
13:17 to my words, and L my declaration be in
13:21 far from me, and L not dread of thee
13:22 I will answer; or L me speak, and do
15:13 spirit against God, and L such words go out
15:31 L him not trust in emptiness, deceiving himself; for
16:18 not my blood, and L my cry find no
17:4 therefore thou wilt not L them triumph.
20:13 he is loath to L it go, and holds
21:2 to my words, and L this be your consolation.
21:19 iniquity for their sons.' L him recompense it to
21:20 L their own eyes see their destruction, and let
21:20 see their destruction, and L them drink of the
27:6 righteousness, and will not L it go; my heart
27:7 L my enemy be as the wicked, and let
27:7 as the wicked, and L him that rises up
31:6 has hastened to deceit; L me be weighed in
31:6 a just balance, and L God know my integrity!)
31:8 to my hands; then L me sow, and another
31:8 and another eat; and L what grows for me
31:10 my neighbor's door; then L my wife grind for
31:10 grind for another, and L others bow down upon
31:22 in the gate; then L my shoulder blade fall
31:22 from my shoulder, and L my arm be broken
31:30 him (I have not L my mouth sin by
31:35 L the Almighty answer me!) Oh, that I had
31:40 death of its owners; L thorns grow instead of
32:7 I said, L days speak, and many years teach
32:10 say, 'Listen to me; L me also declare my
33:25 have found a ransom; L his flesh become fresh
33:25 become fresh with youth; L him return to the
34:4 L us choose what is right; let us determine
34:4 choose what is right; L us determine among
36:18 you into scoffing; and L not the greatness of
39:5 "Who has L the wild ass go free?
40:2 who argues with God, L him answer it."
40:19 the works of God; L him who made him
Ps 2:3 and his anointed, saying, L us burst their bonds
5:10 their guilt, O God; L them fall by their
5:11 But L all who take refuge in thee rejoice,
5:11 refuge in thee rejoice, L them ever sing for
7:5 my enemy without cause, L the enemy pursue me
7:5 and overtake me, and L him trample my life
7:7 L the assembly of the peoples be gathered about
7:9 O L the evil of the wicked come to
9:19 L not man prevail; let the nations be judged
9:19 Let not man prevail; L the nations be judged
9:20 L the nations know that they are but men!
10:2 hotly pursue the poor; L them be caught in
16:10 up to Sheol, or L thy godly one see
17:2 From thee L my vindication come!
17:2 L thy eyes see the right!
19:13 also from presumptuous sins; L them not have
19:14 L the words of my mouth and the meditation
22:8 cause to the LORD; L him deliver him, let
22:8 let him deliver him, L him rescue him, for
25:2 in thee I trust, L me not be put
25:2 be put to shame; L not my enemies exult
25:3 Yea, L none that wait for thee be put
25:3 be put to shame; L them be ashamed who
25:20 life, and deliver me; L me not be put
27:14 LORD; be strong, and L your heart take courage;
30:1 up, and hast not L my foes rejoice over
31:1 do I seek refuge; L me never be put
31:16 L thy face shine on thy servant; save me
31:17 L me not be put to shame, O LORD,
31:17 I call on thee; L the wicked be put
31:17 be put to shame, L them go dumbfounded to
31:18 L the lying lips be dumb, which speak insolently
31:24 Be strong, and L your heart take courage, all
32:6 [Selah] Therefore L every one who is godly offer
33:8 L all the earth fear the LORD, let all
33:8 earth fear the LORD, L all the inhabitants of
33:22 L thy steadfast love, O LORD, be upon us,
34:2 boast in the LORD; L the afflicted hear and
34:3 LORD with me, and L us exalt his name
35:4 L them be put to shame and dishonor who
35:4 L them be turned back and confounded who devise
35:5 L them be like chaff before the wind, with
35:6 L their way be dark and slippery, with the
35:8 L ruin come upon them unawares!
35:8 And L the net which they hid ensnare them;
35:8 they hid ensnare them; L them fall therein to
35:19 L not those rejoice over me who are wrongfully
35:19 wrongfully my foes, and L not those wink the
35:24 to thy righteousness; and L them not rejoice over
35:25 L them not say to themselves, "Aha, we have
35:25 L them not say, "We have swallowed him up."
35:26 L them be put to shame and confusion altogether
35:26 L them be clothed with shame and dishonor who
35:27 L those who desire my vindication shout for joy
36:11 L not the foot of arrogance come upon me,
37:33 to his power, or L him be condemned when
38:16 For I pray, "Only L them not rejoice over
39:4 with my tongue: "LORD, L me know my end,
39:4 measure of my days; L me know how fleeting
40:11 thy mercy from me, L thy steadfast love and
40:14 L them be put to shame and confusion altogether
40:14 snatch away my life; L them be turned back
40:15 L them be appalled because of their shame who
43:3 light and thy truth; L them lead me, let
43:3 let them lead me, L them bring me to
45:4 to defend the right; L your right hand teach
48:11 is filled with victory; L Mount Zion be glad!
48:11 L the daughters of Judah rejoice because of thy
51:8 with joy and gladness; L the bones which thou
55:15 L death come upon them; let them go down
55:15 death come upon them; L them go down to
55:15 down to Sheol alive; L them go away in
57:5 L thy glory be over all the earth!
57:11 L thy glory be over all the earth!
58:7 L them vanish like water that runs away; like
58:7 runs away; like grass L them be trodden down
58:8 L them be like the snail which dissolves into
59:10 me; my God will L me look in triumph
59:12 words of their lips, L them be trapped in
61:4 L me dwell in thy tent for ever!
64:10 L the righteous rejoice in the LORD, and take
64:10 L all the upright in heart glory!
66:7 on the nations-- L not the rebellious exalt
66:8 our God, O peoples, L the sound of his
66:9 living, and has not L our feet slip.
66:12 our loins; thou didst L men ride over our
67:3 L the peoples praise thee, O God; let all
67:3 praise thee, O God; L all the peoples praise
67:4 L the nations be glad and sing for joy,
67:5 [Selah] L the peoples praise thee, O God; let
67:5 praise thee, O God; L all the peoples praise
67:7 God has blessed us; L all the ends of
68:1 L God arise, let his enemies be scattered; let
68:1 Let God arise, L his enemies be scattered; let
68:1 his enemies be scattered; L those who hate him
68:2 wax melts before fire, L the wicked perish before
68:3 But L the righteous be joyful; let them exult
68:3 the righteous be joyful; L them exult before God;
68:3 them exult before God; L them be jubilant with
68:31 L bronze be brought from Egypt; let Ethiopia hasten
68:31 be brought from Egypt; L Ethiopia hasten to stretch
69:6 L not those who hope in thee be put
69:6 Lord GOD of hosts; L not those who seek
69:14 sinking in the mire; L me be delivered from
69:15 L not the flood sweep over me, or the
69:22 L their own table before them become a snare;
69:22 them become a snare; L their sacrificial feasts be
69:23 L their eyes be darkened, so that they cannot
69:24 indignation upon them, and L thy burning anger
69:25 camp be a desolation, L no one dwell in
69:28 L them be blotted out of the book of
69:28 book of the living; L them not be enrolled
69:29 afflicted and in pain; L thy salvation, O God,
69:32 L the oppressed see it and be glad; you
69:32 you who seek God, L your hearts revive.
69:34 L heaven and earth praise him, the seas and
70:2 L them be put to shame and confusion who
70:2 L them be turned back and brought to dishonor
70:3 L them be appalled because of their shame who
71:1 do I take refuge; L me never be put
72:3 L the mountains bear prosperity for the people, and
74:21 L not the downtrodden be put to shame; let
74:21 be put to shame; L the poor and needy
76:11 God, and perform them; L all around him bring
78:13 divided the sea and L them pass through it,
78:28 of the seas; he L them fall in the
78:49 He L loose on them his fierce anger, wrath,
79:8 iniquities of our forefathers; L thy compassion come
79:10 L the avenging of the outpoured blood of thy
79:11 L the groans of the prisoners come before thee;
80:3 Restore us, O God; L thy face shine, that

80:7 O God of hosts; L thy face shine, that
80:17 But L thy hand be upon the man of
80:19 L thy face shine, that we may be saved!
83:4 They say, "Come, L us wipe them out as
83:4 out as a nation; L the name of Israel
83:12 and Zalmunna, who said, L us take possession for
83:17 L them be put to shame and dismayed for
83:17 and dismayed for ever; L them perish in disgrace.
83:18 L them know that thou alone, whose name is
85:8 L me hear what God the LORD will speak,
88:2 L my prayer come before thee, incline thy ear
89:5 [Selah] L the heavens praise thy wonders, O LORD,
90:16 L thy work be manifest to thy servants, and
90:17 L the favor of the Lord our God be
95:1 O come, L us sing to the LORD; let
95:1 sing to the LORD; L us make a joyful
95:2 L us come into his presence with thanksgiving; let
95:2 his presence with thanksgiving; L us make a joyful
95:6 O come, L us worship and bow down, let
95:6 worship and bow down, L us kneel before the
96:11 L the heavens be glad, and let the earth
96:11 heavens be glad, and L the earth rejoice; let
96:11 let the earth rejoice; L the sea roar, and
96:12 all that fills it; L the field exult, and
97:1 The LORD reigns; L the earth rejoice; let the
97:1 let the earth rejoice; L the many coastlands be
98:7 L the sea roar, and all that fills it;
98:8 L the floods clap their hands; let the hills
98:8 floods clap their hands; L the hills sing for
99:1 The LORD reigns; L the peoples tremble!
99:1 enthroned upon the cherubim; L the earth quake!
99:3 L them praise thy great and terrible name!
102:1 my prayer, O LORD; L my cry come to
102:18 L this be recorded for a generation to come,
104:35 L sinners be consumed from the earth, and let
104:35 from the earth, and L the wicked be no
105:3 in his holy name; L the hearts of those
106:48 And L all the people say, "Amen!" Praise the
107:2 L the redeemed of the LORD say so, whom
107:8 L them thank the LORD for his steadfast love,
107:15 L them thank the LORD for his steadfast love,
107:21 L them thank the LORD for his steadfast love,
107:22 And L them offer sacrifices of thanksgiving, and tell
107:31 L them thank the LORD for his steadfast love,
107:32 L them extol him in the congregation of the
107:38 and he does not L their cattle decrease.
107:43 Whoever is wise, L him give heed to these
107:43 heed to these things; L men consider the steadfast
108:5 L thy glory be over all the earth!
109:6 wicked man against him; L an accuser bring him
109:7 When he is tried, L him come forth guilty;
109:7 him come forth guilty; L his prayer be counted
109:12 L there be none to extend kindness to him,
109:14 before the LORD, and L not the sin of
109:15 L them be before the LORD continually; and may
109:17 He loved to curse; L curses come on him!
109:27 L them know that this is thy hand; thou,
109:28 L them curse, but do thou bless!
109:28 L my assailants be put to shame; may thy
118:2 L Israel say, "His steadfast love endures for ever."
118:3 L the house of Aaron say, "His steadfast love
118:4 L those who fear the LORD say, "His steadfast
118:24 the LORD has made; L us rejoice and be
119:10 heart I seek thee; L me not wander from
119:31 thy testimonies, O LORD; L me not be put
119:41 L thy steadfast love come to me, O LORD,
119:76 L thy steadfast love be ready to comfort me
119:77 L thy mercy come to me, that I may
119:78 L the godless be put to shame, because they
119:79 L those who fear thee turn to me, that
119:116 I may live, and L me not be put
119:122 thy servant for good; L not the godless oppress
119:133 to thy promise, and L no iniquity get dominion
119:169 L my cry come before thee, O LORD; give
119:170 L my supplication come before thee; deliver me
119:173 L thy hand be ready to help me, for
119:175 L me live, that I may praise thee, and
119:175 may praise thee, and L thy ordinances help me.
121:3 He will not L your foot be moved, he
122:1 they said to me, L us go to the
124:1 was on our side, L Israel now say–
129:1 L Israel now say–
129:6 L them be like the grass on the housetops,
130:2 L thy ears be attentive to the voice of
132:7 L us go to his dwelling place; let us
132:7 to his dwelling place; L us worship at his
132:9 L thy priests be clothed with righteousness, and let
132:9 clothed with righteousness, and L thy saints shout for
137:5 forget you, O Jerusalem, L my right hand wither!
137:6 L my tongue cleave to the roof of my
139:11 If I say, L only darkness cover me, and
140:9 lift up their head, L the mischief of their
140:10 L burning coals fall upon them!
140:10 L them be cast into pits, no more to
140:11 L not the slanderer be established in the land;
140:11 established in the land; L evil hunt down the
141:2 L my prayer be counted as incense before thee,
141:4 who work iniquity; and L me not eat of
141:5 L a good man strike or rebuke me in
141:5 me in kindness, but L the oil of the
141:10 L the wicked together fall into their own nets,
143:8 L me hear in the morning of thy steadfast
143:10 L thy good spirit lead me on a level
145:21 of the LORD, and L all flesh bless his
148:5 L them praise the name of the LORD!
148:13 L them praise the name of the LORD, for
149:2 L Israel be glad in his Maker, let the
149:2 glad in his Maker, L the sons of Zion
149:3 L them praise his name with dancing, making
149:5 L the faithful exult in glory; let them sing
149:5 faithful exult in glory; L them sing for joy
149:6 L the high praises of God be in their
150:6 L everything that breathes praise the LORD!
Prov 1:11 say, "Come with us, L us lie in wait
1:11 in wait for blood, L us wantonly ambush the
1:12 the innocent; like Sheol L us swallow them alive
3:1 forget my teaching, but L your heart keep my
3:3 L not loyalty and faithfulness forsake you; bind them
3:21 sound wisdom and discretion; L them not escape
4:5 and said to me, L your heart hold fast
4:14 of instruction, do not L go; guard her, for
4:22 L them not escape from your sight; keep them
4:26 L your eyes look directly forward, and your gaze
5:17 L them be for yourself alone, and not for
5:18 L your fountain be blessed, and rejoice in the
5:19 L her affection fill you at all times with
6:25 heart, and do not L her capture you with
7:18 Come, L us take our fill of love till
7:18 of love till morning; L us delight ourselves with
7:25 L not your heart turn aside to her ways,
9:4 town, "Whoever is simple, L him turn in here!"
9:16 way, "Whoever is simple, L him turn in here!"
10:3 The LORD does not L the righteous go hungry,
17:12 L a man meet a she-bear robbed of her
23:17 L not your heart envy sinners, but continue in
23:25 L your father and mother be glad, let her
23:25 and mother be glad, L her who bore you
23:26 me your heart, and L your eyes observe my
24:17 your enemy falls, and L not your heart be
25:17 L your foot be seldom in your neighbor's house,
27:2 L another praise you, and not your own mouth;
28:17 the blood of another, L him be a fugitive
28:17 a fugitive until death; L no one help him.
31:7 those in bitter distress; L them drink and forget
31:31 of her hands, and L her works praise her
Eccl 5:2 with your mouth, nor L your heart be hasty
5:2 you upon earth; therefore L your words be few.
5:6 L not your mouth lead you into sin, and
5:12 the rich will not L him sleep.
9:8 L your garments be always white; let not oil
9:8 garments be always white; L not oil be lacking
11:8 man lives many years, L him rejoice in them
11:8 in them all; but L him remember that the
11:9 in your youth, and L your heart cheer you
Song 1:4 Draw me after you, L us make haste.
2:14 covert of the cliff, L me see your face,
2:14 me see your face, L me hear your voice,
3:4 him, and would not L him go until I
4:16 Blow upon my garden, L its fragrance be wafted
4:16 L my beloved come to his garden, and eat
7:11 Come, my beloved, L us go forth into the
7:12 lodge in the villages; L us go out early
8:11 vineyard at Baal-hamon; he L out the vineyard to
8:13 listening for your voice; L me hear it.
Wis 2:6 "Come, therefore, L us enjoy the good things that
2:7 L us take our fill of costly wine and
2:7 wine and perfumes, and L no flower of spring
2:8 L us crown ourselves with rosebuds before they.
2:9 L none of us fail to share in our
2:9 in our revelry, everywhere L us leave signs of
2:10 L us oppress the righteous poor man; let us
2:10 the righteous poor man; L us not spare the

2:11 But L our might be our law of right,
2:12 L us lie in wait for the righteous man,
2:17 L us see if his words are true, and
2:17 words are true, and L us test what will
2:19 L us test him with insult and torture, that
2:20 L us condemn him to a shameful death, for,
13:3 them to be gods, L them know how much
13:4 their power and working, L them perceive from
Sir 2:18 L us fall into the hands of the Lord,
4:31 L not your hand be extended to receive, but
5:10 in your understanding, and L your speech be.
6:6 L those that are at peace with you be
6:6 you be many, but L your advisers be one
6:27 of her, do not L her go.
6:35 narrative, and do not L wise proverbs escape you.
6:36 man, visit him early; L your foot wear out
7:21 L your soul love an intelligent servant; do not
9:15 L your conversation be with men of understanding,
9:15 men of understanding, and L all your discussion be
9:16 L righteous men be your dinner companions, and let
9:16 your dinner companions, and L your glorying be in
14:14 of a happy day; L not your share of
18:21 L nothing hinder you from paying a vow promptly,
19:10 L it die with you.
19:17 you threaten him; and L the law of the
23:1 to their counsel, and L me not fall because
23:6 L neither gluttony nor lust overcome me, and do
27:19 hand, so you have L your neighbor go, and
29:10 friend, and do not L it rust under a
29:26 have anything at hand, L me have it to
31:10 L it be for him a ground for boasting.
33:20 in you, do not L any one take your
33:30 you have a servant, L him be as yourself,
36:3 against foreign nations and L them see thy might.
36:5 magnified before us; and L them know thee, as
36:8 the appointed time, and L people recount thy mighty
36:9 L him who survives be consumed in the fiery
36:16 wait for thee, and L thy prophets be found
38:12 the Lord created him; L him not leave you,
38:16 My son, L your tears fall for the dead,
38:17 L your weeping be bitter and your wailing fervent;
38:23 dead is at rest, L his remembrance cease, and
42:1 ashamed, and do not L partiality lead you to
42:7 Whatever you deal out, L it be by number
44:1 L us now praise famous men, and our fathers
50:24 And L him deliver us in our days!
51:26 under the yoke, and L your souls receive instruction;
Is 1:18 "Come now, L us reason together, says the LORD:
2:3 come, and say: "Come, L us go up to
2:5 house of Jacob, come, L us walk in the
4:1 our own clothes, only L us be called by
5:1 L me sing for my beloved a love song
5:19 cart ropes, who say: L him make haste, let
5:19 "Let him make haste, L him speed his work
5:19 we may see it; L the purpose of the
5:19 Israel draw near, and L it come, that we
7:4 fear, and do not L your heart be faint
7:6 evil against you, saying, L us go up against
7:6 and terrify it, and L us conquer it for
7:11 the LORD your God; L it be deep as
7:25 place where cattle are L loose and where sheep
8:13 shall regard as holy; L him be your fear,
8:13 be your fear, and L him be your dread.
12:5 he has done gloriously; L this be known in
14:17 cities, who did not L his prisoners go home?'
16:4 betray not the fugitive; L the outcasts of Moab
16:7 Therefore L Moab wail, let every one wail for
16:7 Therefore let Moab wail, L every one wail for
19:12 L them tell you and make known what the
21:6 "Go, set a watchman, L him announce what he
21:7 asses, riders on camels, L him listen diligently, very
22:4 "Look away from me, L me weep bitter tears;
22:13 L us eat and drink, for tomorrow we die."
25:9 have waited for him; L us be glad and
26:11 L them see thy zeal for thy people, and
26:11 L the fire for thy adversaries consume them.
26:19 the shades thou wilt L it fall.
27:5 Or L them lay hold of my protection, let
27:5 hold of my protection, L them make peace with
27:5 make peace with me, L them make peace with
29:1 Add year to year; L the feasts run their
30:11 aside from the path, L us hear no more
32:20 beside all waters, who L the feet of the
34:1 L the earth listen, and all that fills it;
36:14 the king: 'Do not L Hezekiah deceive you, for
36:15 Do not L Hezekiah make you rely on the
37:10 of Judah: 'Do not L your God on whom
38:21 Now Isaiah had said, L them take a cake
41:1 in silence, O coastlands; L the peoples renew their
41:1 peoples renew their strength; L them approach, then
41:1 let them approach, then L them speak; let us
41:1 then let them speak; L us together draw near
41:22 L them bring them, and tell us what is
42:10 L the sea roar and all that fills it,
42:11 L the desert and its cities lift up their
42:11 villages that Kedar inhabits; L the inhabitants of
42:11 Sela sing for joy, L them shout from the
42:12 L them give glory to the LORD, and declare
43:9 L all the nations gather together, and let the
43:9 nations gather together, and L the peoples assemble.
43:9 L them bring their witnesses to justify them, and
43:9 to justify them, and L them hear and say,
43:26 Put me in remembrance, L us argue together; set
44:7 L him proclaim it, let him declare and set
44:7 Let him proclaim it, L him declare and set
44:7 L them tell us what is yet to be.
44:11 craftsmen are but men; L them all assemble, let
44:11 let them all assemble, L them stand forth, they
45:8 heavens, from above, and L the skies rain down
45:8 skies rain down righteousness; L the earth open, that
45:8 may sprout forth, and L it cause righteousness to
45:21 and present your case; L them take counsel
47:13 with your many counsels; L them stand forth and
50:8 L us stand up together.
50:8 L him come near to me.
54:2 of your tent, and L the curtains of your
55:7 while he is near; L the wicked forsake his
55:7 unrighteous man his thoughts; L him return to the
56:3 L not the foreigner who has joined himself to
56:3 from his people"; and L not the eunuch say,
56:12 they say, L us get wine, let us fill
56:12 "let us get wine, L us fill ourselves with
57:13 When you cry out, L your collection of idols
58:6 of the yoke, to L the oppressed go free,
66:5 name's sake have said, L the LORD be glorified,
Jer 2:28 L them arise, if they can save you, in
3:25 L us lie down in our shame, and let
3:25 in our shame, and L our dishonor cover us;
4:5 and say, 'Assemble, and L us go into the
5:24 say in their hearts, L us fear the LORD
6:4 against her; up, and L us attack at noon!"
6:5 "Up, and L us attack by night, and destroy
7:3 doings, and I will L you dwell in this
7:7 hurt, then I will L you dwell in this
8:14 Gather together, L us go into the fortified cities
9:4 L every one beware of his neighbor, and put
9:18 skilful women to come; L them make haste and
9:20 of the LORD, and L your ear receive the
9:23 Thus says the LORD: L not the wise man
9:23 glory in his wisdom, L not the mighty man
9:23 glory in his might, L not the rich man
9:24 in his riches; but L him who glories glory
11:19 they devised schemes, saying, L us destroy the tree
11:19 tree with its fruit, L us cut him off
11:20 heart and the mind, L me see thy vengeance
14:17 to them this word: L my eyes run down
14:17 night and day, and L them not cease, for
15:1 of my sight, and L them go!
15:11 So L it be, O LORD, if I have
17:15 L it come!"
17:18 L those be put to shame who persecute me,
17:18 who persecute me, but L me not be put
17:18 be put to shame; L them be dismayed, but
17:18 them be dismayed, but L me not be dismayed;
18:2 and there I will L you hear my words."
18:18 Then they said, "Come, L us make plots against
18:18 Come, L us smite him with the tongue, and
18:18 with the tongue, and L us not heed any
18:21 power of the sword, L their wives become childless
18:23 L them be overthrown before thee; deal with them
20:10 L us denounce him!" say all my familiar friends,
20:12 heart and the mind, L me see thy vengeance
20:14 my mother bore me, L it not be blessed!
20:16 L that man be like the cities which the
20:16 LORD overthrew without pity; L him hear a cry
23:28 L the prophet who has a dream tell the
23:28 tell the dream, but L him who has my
27:18 is with them, then L them intercede with the
29:8 of Israel: Do not L your prophets and your
31:6 of Ephraim: 'Arise, and L us go up to
35:11 we said, 'Come, and L us go to Jerusalem
36:19 you and Jeremiah, and L no one know where

L

37:20 my lord the king: L my humble plea come
38:4 said to the king, L this man be put
38:11 worn-out clothes, which he L down to Jeremiah in
38:24 Zedekiah said to Jeremiah, L no one know of
40:1 of the guard had L him go from Ramah,
40:5 and a present, and L him go.
40:15 to Gedaliah at Mizpah, L me go and slay
42:2 to Jeremiah the prophet, L our supplication come
42:12 mercy on you and L you remain in your
46:9 L the warriors go forth: men of Ethiopia and
46:16 to another, 'Arise, and L us go back to
48:2 evil against her: 'Come, L us cut her off
49:11 keep them alive; and L your widows trust in
50:5 toward it, saying, 'Come, L us join ourselves to
50:26 and destroy her utterly; L nothing be left of
50:27 Slay all her bulls, L them go down to
50:29 Encamp round about her; L no one escape.
50:33 fast, they refuse to L them go.
51:3 L not the archer bend his bow, and let
51:3 bend his bow, and L him not stand up
51:6 the midst of Babylon, L every man save his
51:9 Forsake her, and L us go each to his
51:10 forth our vindication; come, L us declare in Zion
51:35 L the inhabitant of Zion say.
51:35 L Jerusalem say.
51:45 L every man save his life from the fierce
51:46 L not your heart faint, and be not fearful
51:50 LORD from afar, and L Jerusalem come into your
Lam 1:21 thou hast announced, and L them be as I
1:22 L all their evil-doing come before thee; and deal
2:18 L tears stream down like a torrent day and
3:28 L him sit alone in silence when he has
3:29 laid it on him; L him put his mouth
3:30 may yet be hope; L him give his cheek
3:40 L us test and examine our ways, and return
3:41 L us lift up our hearts and hands to
Bar 2:13 L thy anger turn away from us, for we
4:12 L no one rejoice over me, a widow and
4:14 L the neighbors of Zion come; remember the
6:5 the foreigners or to L fear for these gods
Ezek 1:24 they stood still, they L down their wings.
1:25 they stood still, they L down their wings.
3:27 he that will hear, L him hear; and he
3:27 will refuse to hear, L him refuse; for they
4:3 face toward it, and L it be in a
4:15 me, "See, I will L you have cow's dung
7:3 you, and I will L loose my anger upon
7:12 L not the buyer rejoice, nor the seller mourn,
12:16 But I will L a few of them escape
13:20 arms; and I will L the souls that you
14:3 their faces; should I L myself be inquired of
14:17 that land, and say, L a sword go through
20:4 Then L them know the abominations of their fathers,
20:32 never happen—the thought, L us be like the
20:37 rod, and I will L you go in by
21:14 clap your hands and L the sword come down
24:10 out the broth, and L the bones be burned
36:12 Yea, I will L men walk upon you, even
36:15 and I will not L you hear any more
36:32 says the Lord GOD; L that be known to
36:37 This also I will L the house of Israel
39:7 and I will not L my holy name be
43:9 Now L them put away their idolatry and the
44:6 O house of Israel, L there be an end
44:20 shave their heads or L their locks grow long;
45:8 people; but they shall L the house of Israel
Dan 1:12 servants for ten days; L us be given vegetables
1:13 Then L our appearance and the appearance of the
2:7 answered a second time, L the king tell his
3:43 L all who do harm to thy servants be
3:44 be put to shame; L them be disgraced and
3:44 power and dominion, and L their strength be broken.
3:45 L them know that thou art the Lord, the
3:75 L the earth bless the Lord; let it sing
3:75 earth bless the Lord; L it sing praise to
4:14 and scatter its fruit; L the beasts flee from
4:15 L him be wet with the dew of heaven;
4:15 the dew of heaven; L his lot be with
4:16 grass of the earth; L his mind be changed
4:16 from a mans, and L a beast's mind be
4:16 given to him; and L seven times pass over
4:19 The king said, "Belteshazzar, L not the dream or
4:23 of the field; and L him be wet with
4:23 dew of heaven; and L his lot be with
4:27 Therefore, O king, L my counsel be acceptable to
5:10 L not your thoughts alarm you or your color
5:12 Now L Daniel be called, and he will show
5:17 answered before the king, L your gifts be for
9:16 all thy righteous acts, L thy anger and thy
10:19 was strengthened and said, L my lord speak, for
13:13 said to each other, L us go home, for
14:9 said to the king, L it be done as
Hos 4:4 Yet L no one contend, and let none accuse,
4:4 no one contend, and L none accuse, for with
4:15 the harlot, O Israel, L not Judah become guilty.
4:17 is joined to idols, L him alone.
6:1 seek me, saying, "Come, L us return to the
6:3 L us know, let us press on to know
6:3 Let us know, L us press on to know
14:9 Whoever is wise, L him understand these things;
14:9 things; whoever is discerning, L him know them; for
Joel 1:3 children of it, and L your children tell their
2:1 L all the inhabitants of the land tremble, for
2:16 L the bridegroom leave his room, and the bride
2:17 vestibule and the altar L the priests, the ministers
3:9 L all the men of war draw near, let
3:9 of war draw near, L them come up.
3:10 pruning hooks into spears; L the weak say, "I
3:12 L the nations bestir themselves, and come up to
Amos 5:24 But L justice roll down like waters, and
Obad 1:1 L us rise against her for battle!"
Jon 1:7 to one another, "Come, L us cast lots, that
1:14 beseech thee, O LORD, L us not perish for
3:7 king and his nobles: L neither man nor beast,
3:7 nor flock, taste anything; L them not feed, or
3:8 or drink water, but L man and beast be
3:8 covered with sackcloth, and L them cry mightily to
3:8 mightily to God; yea, L every one turn from
Mic 1:2 is in it; and L the Lord GOD be
4:2 come, and say: "Come, L us go up to
4:11 assembled against you, saying, L her be profaned,
4:11 her be profaned, and L our eyes gaze upon
6:1 before the mountains, and L the hills hear your
7:14 of a garden land; L them feed in Bashan
Nah 3:5 face; and I will L nations look on your
Hab 2:20 in his holy temple; L all the earth keep
Zeph 3:16 not fear, O Zion; L not your hands grow
Zech 3:5 And I said, L them put a clean turban
7:10 or the poor; and L none of you devise
8:9 the LORD of hosts: L your hands be strong,
8:13 Fear not, but L your hands be strong."
8:21 go to another, saying, L us go at once
8:23 of a Jew, saying, L us go with you,
11:9 What is to die, L it die; what is
11:9 is to be destroyed, L it be destroyed; and
11:9 it be destroyed; and L those that are left
11:17 L his arm be wholly withered, his right eye
Mal 2:15 heed to yourselves, and L none be faithless to
1Mac 1:11 and misled many, saying, L us go and make
2:27 a loud voice, saying: L every one who is
2:37 places, for they said, L us all die in
2:41 this decision that day: L us fight against every
2:41 on the sabbath day; L us not all die
2:48 kings, and they never L the sinner gain the
3:43 said to one another, L us repair the destruction
4:10 And now L us cry to Heaven, to see
4:31 thy people Israel, and L them be ashamed of
4:32 boldness of their strength; L them tremble in their
4:33 who love thee, and L all who know thy
4:36 our enemies are crushed; L us go up to
5:48 them this friendly message, L us pass through your
5:57 So they said, L us also make a name
5:57 a name for ourselves; L us go and make
6:58 Now then L us come to terms with these
6:59 nation, and agree to L them live by their
7:3 he said, "Do not L me see their faces!"
7:7 man whom you trust; L him go and see
7:7 of the king, and L him punish them and
7:28 brothers this peaceable message, L there be no
7:38 on his army, and L them fall by the
7:38 remember their blasphemies, and L them live no
7:42 army before us today; L the rest learn that
9:8 those who were left, L us rise and go
9:9 L us rather save our own lives now, and
9:9 own lives now, and L us come back with
9:10 our time has come, L us die bravely for
9:44 to those with him, L us rise up now
9:58 So now L us bring Bacchides back, and he
10:4 him; for he said, L us act first to
10:31 And L Jerusalem and her environs, her tithes and
10:33 free without payment; and L all officials cancel also
10:34 a feast — L them all be days

 LET

	10:36	L Jews be enrolled in the king's forces to
	10:36	thirty thousand men, and L the maintenance be
	10:37	L some of them be stationed in the great
	10:37	of the king, and L some of them be
	10:37	L their officers and leaders be of their own
	10:37	their own number, and L them live by their
	10:38	the country of Samaria, L them be so annexed
	10:43	or has any debt, L him be released and
	10:44	L the cost of rebuilding and restoring the structures
	10:45	And L the cost of rebuilding the walls of
	10:54	kingdom-- now therefore L us establish friendship
	10:63	about any matter, and L no one annoy him
	10:71	to meet us, and L us match strength with
	11:9	the king, saying, "Come, L us make a covenant
	11:37	copy of this, and L it be given to
	12:53	Now therefore L us make war on them and
	13:38	you remain valid, and L the strongholds that you
	13:40	enrolled in our bodyguard, L them be enrolled, and
	13:40	them be enrolled, and L there be peace between
2Mac	1:27	rejected and despised, and L the Gentiles know that
	2:32	At this point therefore L us begin our narrative,
	6:13	In fact, not to L the impious alone for
	6:17	L what we have said serve as a reminder;
	7:42	L this be enough, then, about the eating of
	10:20	receiving seventy thousand drachmas L some of
	10:36	open the gates and L in the rest of
	12:2	of Cyprus, would not L them live quietly and
	12:24	he besought them to L him go in safety,
	12:25	restore them unharmed, they L him go, for the
	13:11	temple, and not to L the people who had
	14:6	sedition, and will not L the kingdom attain
	15:36	public vote never to L this day go unobserved,
Mt	3:15	But Jesus answered him, L it be so now;
	5:16	L your light so shine before men, that they
	5:31	'Whoever divorces his wife, L him give her a
	5:37	L what you say be simply 'Yes' or 'No';
	5:40	and take your coat, L him have your cloak
	6:3	give alms, do not L your left hand know
	6:34	L the day's own trouble be sufficient for the
	7:4	say to your brother, L me take the speck
	8:21	said to him, "Lord, L me first go and
	10:13	the house is worthy, L your peace come upon
	10:13	it is not worthy, L your peace return to
	11:15	has ears to hear, L him hear.
	13:9	He who has ears, L him hear."
	13:30	L both grow together until the harvest; and at
	13:43	He who has ears, L him hear.
	15:4	of father or mother, L him surely die.'
	15:14	L them alone; they are blind guides.
	16:24	would come after me, L him deny himself and
	18:16	even to the church, L him be to you
	19:6	God has joined together, L not man put asunder."
	19:12	able to receive this, L him receive it."
	19:14	people; but Jesus said, L the children come to
	20:33	said to him, "Lord, L our eyes be opened."
	21:33	built a tower, and L it out to tenants,
	21:38	is the heir; come, L us kill him and
	21:41	a miserable death, and L out the vineyard to
	24:15	in the holy place L the reader understand),
	24:16	the reader understand), then L those who are in
	24:17	flee to the mountains; L him who is on
	24:18	in his house; and L him who is in
	24:43	and would not have L his house be broken
	26:39	if it be possible, L this cup pass from
	26:46	Rise, L us be going; see, my betrayer is
	27:22	They all said, L him be crucified."
	27:23	shouted all the more, L him be crucified."
	27:42	the King of Israel; L him come down now
	27:43	He trusts in God; L God deliver him now,
	27:49	the others said, "Wait, L us see whether Elijah
Mk	1:38	he said to them, L us go on to
	2:4	made an opening, they L down the pallet on
	4:9	has ears to hear, L him hear."
	4:23	has ears to hear, L him hear."
	4:35	he said to them, L us go across to
	5:12	us to the swine, L us enter them."
	7:10	of father or mother, L him surely die';
	7:26	he said to her, L the children first be
	8:34	would come after me, L him deny himself and
	9:5	that we are here; L us make three booths,
	10:9	God has joined together, L not man put asunder."
	10:14	and said to them, L the children come to
	10:51	said to him, "Master, L me receive my sight."
	11:6	had said; and they L them go.
	12:1	built a tower, and L it out to tenants,
	12:7	is the heir; come, L us kill him, and
	12:15	me a coin, and L me look at it."
	13:14	ought not to be L the reader understand), then
	13:14	the reader understand), then L those who are in
	13:15	flee to the mountains; L him who is on
	13:16	take anything away; and L him who is in
	14:6	But Jesus said, L her alone; why do you
	14:42	Rise, L us be going; see, my betrayer is
	14:49	But L the scriptures be fulfilled."
	15:31	L the Christ, the King of Israel, come down
	15:35	to drink, saying, "Wait, L us see whether Elijah
Lk	1:38	handmaid of the Lord; L it be to me
	2:15	said to one another, L us go over to
	3:11	who has two coats, L him share with him
	3:11	he who has food, L him do likewise."
	5:4	into the deep and L down your nets for
	5:5	your word I will L down the nets."
	5:19	on the roof and L him down with his
	6:42	to your brother, 'Brother, L me take out the
	7:7	say the word, and L my servant be healed.
	8:8	has ears to hear, L him hear."
	8:22	he said to them, L us go across to
	8:32	they begged him to L them enter these.
	9:23	would come after me, L him deny himself and
	9:33	that we are here; L us make three booths,
	9:44	said to his disciples, L these words sink into
	9:59	But he said, "Lord, L me first go and
	9:61	follow you, Lord; but L me first say farewell
	12:35	L your loins be girded and your lamps burning,
	13:8	And he answered him, L it alone, sir, this
	14:4	and healed him, and L him go.
	14:35	has ears to hear, L him hear."
	15:23	and kill it, and L us eat and make
	16:29	Moses and the prophets; L them hear them.'
	17:31	On that day, L him who is on the
	17:31	them away; and likewise L him who is in
	18:16	them to him, saying, L the children come to
	18:41	He said, "Lord, L me receive my sight."
	20:9	planted a vineyard, and L it out to tenants,
	20:14	'This is the heir; L us kill him, that
	21:21	Then L those who are in Judea flee to
	21:21	to the mountains, and L those who are inside
	21:21	the city depart, and L not those who are
	22:26	so with you; rather L the greatest among you
	22:36	to them, "But now, L him who has a
	22:36	And L him who has no sword sell his
	23:34	saying, "He saved others; L him save himself, if
Jn	1:22	L us have an answer for those who sent
	7:37	"If any one thirst, L him come to me
	8:7	and said to them, L him who is without
	11:7	said to the disciples, L us go into Judea
	11:15	But L us go to him."
	11:16	to his fellow disciples, L us also go, that
	11:44	them, "Unbind him, and L him go."
	11:48	If we L him go on thus, every one
	11:57	he was, he should L them know, so that
	12:7	Jesus said, L her alone, let her keep it
	12:7	said, "Let her alone, L her keep it for
	14:1	L not your hearts be troubled; believe in God,
	14:27	L not your hearts be troubled, neither let them
	14:27	hearts be troubled, neither L them be afraid.
	14:31	Rise, L us go hence.
	18:8	if you seek me, L these men go."
	19:24	said to one another, L us not tear it,
Acts	1:20	the book of Psalms, L his habitation become
	1:20	habitation become desolate, and L there be no one
	1:20	it'; and 'His office L another take.'
	2:14	who dwell in Jerusalem, L this be known to
	2:27	soul to Hades, nor L thy Holy One see
	2:36	stool for thy feet.' L all the house of
	4:17	further among the people, L us warn them to
	4:21	further threatened them, they L them go, finding no
	5:38	from these men and L them alone; for if
	5:40	name of Jesus, and L them go.
	9:25	him by night and L him down over the
	10:11	like a great sheet, L down by four corners
	11:5	like a great sheet, L down from heaven by
	13:35	psalm, 'Thou wilt not L thy Holy One see
	13:38	L it be known to you therefore, brethren, that
	15:35	said to Barnabas, "Come, L us return and visit
	16:35	sent the police, saying, L those men go."
	16:36	magistrates have sent to L you go; now therefore
	16:37	L them come themselves and take us out."
	17:9	and the rest, they L them go.
	19:30	the disciples would not L him;
	19:38	and there are proconsuls; L them bring charges
	21:39	city; I beg you, L me speak to the

L

24:19 Or else L these men themselves say what
25:5 said he, L the men of authority among you
25:5 wrong about the man, L them accuse him."
27:29 on the rocks, they L out four anchors from
27:32 of the boat, and L it go.
28:28 me to heal them.' L it be known to
Rom 3:4 L God be true though every man be false,
6:12 L not sin therefore reign in your mortal bodies,
11:9 And David says, L their table become a snare
11:10 a retribution for them; L their eyes be darkened
12:6 grace given to us, L us use them: if
12:9 L love be genuine; hate what is evil, hold
13:1 L every person be subject to the governing
13:12 L us then cast off the works of darkness
13:13 the armor of light; L us conduct ourselves
14:3 L not him who eats despise him who abstains,
14:3 him who abstains, and L not him who abstains
14:5 L every one be fully convinced in his own
14:13 Then L us no more pass judgment on one
14:15 Do not L what you eat cause the ruin
14:16 So do not L your good be spoken of
14:19 L us then pursue what makes for peace and
15:2 not to please ourselves; L each of us please
15:11 Lord, all Gentiles, and L all the peoples praise
1Cor 1:31 as it is written, L him who boasts, boast
3:10 L each man take care how he builds upon
3:18 L no one deceive himself.
3:18 wise in this age, L him become a fool
3:21 So L no one boast of men.
5:2 L him who has done this be removed from
5:8 L us, therefore, celebrate the festival, not with the
7:11 (but if she does, L her remain single or
7:15 partner desires to separate, L it be so; in
7:17 Only, L every one lead the life which the
7:18 L him not seek to remove the marks of
7:18 L him not seek circumcision.
7:24 each was called, there L him remain with God.
7:29 short; from now on, L those who have wives
7:36 it has to be, L him do as he
7:36 do as he wishes: L them marry--it is
10:12 Therefore L any one who thinks that he stands
10:13 and he will not L you be tempted beyond
10:24 L no one seek his own good, but the
11:6 be shorn or shaven, L her wear a veil.
11:28 L a man examine himself, and so eat of
11:34 any one is hungry, L him eat at home--
14:26 L all things be done for edification.
14:27 speak in a tongue, L there be only two
14:27 each in turn; and L one interpret.
14:28 no one to interpret, L each of them keep
14:29 L two or three prophets speak, and let the
14:29 three prophets speak, and L the others weigh what
14:30 to another sitting by, L the first be silent.
14:35 they desire to know, L them ask their husbands
15:32 dead are not raised, L us eat and drink,
16:11 So L no one despise him.
16:14 L all that you do be done in love.
16:22 love for the Lord, L him be accursed.
2Cor 2:4 you pain but to L you know the abundant
4:6 the God who said, L light shine out of
7:1 have these promises, beloved, L us cleanse ourselves
10:7 that he is Christs, L him remind himself that
10:11 L such people understand that what we say by
10:17 L him who boasts, boast of the Lord."
11:16 I repeat, L no one think me foolish; but
11:33 me, but I was L down in a basket
Gal 1:8 we preached to you, L him be accursed.
1:9 that which you received, L him be accursed.
3:2 L me ask you only this: Did you receive
5:25 live by the Spirit, L us also walk by
5:26 L us have no self-conceit, no provoking of one
6:4 But L each one test his own work, and
6:6 L him who is taught the word share all
6:9 And L us not grow weary in well-doing, for
6:10 as we have opportunity, L us do good to
6:17 Henceforth L no man trouble me; for I bear
Eph 4:25 putting away falsehood, L every one speak the
4:26 not sin; do not L the sun go down
4:28 L the thief no longer steal, but rather let
4:28 longer steal, but rather L him labor, doing honest
4:29 L no evil talk come out of your mouths,
4:31 L all bitterness and wrath and anger and clamor
5:4 L there be no filthiness, nor silly talk, nor
5:4 not fitting; but instead L there be thanksgiving.
5:6 L no one deceive you with empty words, for
5:24 subject to Christ, so L wives also be subject
5:33 and the church; however, L each one of you
5:33 wife as himself, and L the wife see that
Phil 1:27 Only L your manner of life be worthy of
2:4 L each of you look not only to his
3:15 L those of us who are mature be thus
3:16 Only L us hold true to what we have
4:5 L all men know your forbearance.
4:6 supplication with thanksgiving L your requests be
Col 2:16 Therefore L no one pass judgment on you in
2:18 L no one disqualify you, insisting on self-abasement
3:15 And L the peace of Christ rule in your
3:16 L the word of Christ dwell in you richly,
4:6 L your speech always be gracious, seasoned with
1Thes 5:6 So then L us not sleep, as others do,
5:6 as others do, but L us keep awake and
5:8 belong to the day, L us be sober, and
2Thes 2:3 L no one deceive you in any way; for
3:10 one will not work, L him not eat.
1Tim 2:11 L a woman learn in silence with all submissiveness.
3:10 And L them also be tested first; then if
3:10 themselves blameless L them serve as deacons.
3:12 L deacons be the husband of one wife, and
3:12 of one wife, and L them manage their children
4:12 L no one despise your youth, but set the
5:4 has children or grandchildren, L them first learn
5:9 L a widow be enrolled if she is not
5:16 relatives who are widows, L her assist them; let
5:16 let her assist them; L the church not be
5:17 L the elders who rule well be considered worthy
6:1 L all who are under the yoke of slavery
2Tim 2:19 and, L every one who names the name of
Tit 2:15 L no one disregard you.
3:14 And L our people learn to apply themselves to
Heb 1:6 the world, he says, L all God's angels worship
4:1 entering his rest remains, L us fear lest any
4:11 L us therefore strive to enter that rest, that
4:14 the Son of God, L us hold fast our
4:16 L us then with confidence draw near to the
6:1 L us leave the elementary doctrine of Christ
10:22 the house of God, L us draw near with
10:23 L us hold fast the confession of our hope
10:24 promised is faithful; and L us consider how to
12:1 a cloud of witnesses, L us also lay aside
12:1 clings so closely, and L us run with perseverance
12:28 Therefore L us be grateful for receiving a kingdom
12:28 be shaken, and thus L us offer to God
13:1 L brotherly love continue.
13:4 L marriage be held in honor among all, and
13:4 honor among all, and L the marriage bed be
13:13 Therefore L us go forth to him outside the
13:15 Through him then L us continually offer up a
13:17 L them do this joyfully, and not sadly, for
Jas 1:4 And L steadfastness have its full effect, that you
1:5 of you lacks wisdom, L him ask God, who
1:6 But L him ask in faith, with no doubting,
1:8 L the lowly brother boast in his exaltation,
1:12 L no one say when he is tempted, "I
1:18 L every man be quick to hear, slow to
3:1 L not many of you become teachers, my brethren,
3:13 By his good life L him show his works
4:9 L your laughter be turned to mourning and your
5:12 any other oath, but L your yes be yes
5:13 L him pray.
5:13 L him sing praise.
5:14 L him call for the elders of the church,
5:14 of the church, and L them pray over him,
5:20 one brings him back, L him know that whoever
1Pet 3:3 L not yours be the outward adorning with braiding
3:4 of fine clothing, but L it be the hidden
3:6 you do right and L nothing terrify you.
3:10 and see good days, L him keep his tongue
3:11 lips from speaking guile; L him turn away from
3:11 evil and do right; L him seek peace and
4:3 L the time that is past suffice for doing
4:15 But L none of you suffer as a murderer,
4:16 suffers as a Christian, L him not be ashamed,
4:16 but under that name L him glorify God.
4:19 Therefore L those who suffer according to God's will
1Jn 2:24 L what you heard from the beginning abide in
3:7 Little children, L no one deceive you.
3:18 Little children, L us not love in word or
4:7 Beloved, L us love one another; for love is
Rev 2:7 who has an ear, L him hear what the
2:11 who has an ear, L him hear what the
2:17 who has an ear, L him hear what the
2:29 who has an ear, L him hear what the

3:6 who has an ear, L him hear what the
3:13 who has an ear, L him hear what the
3:22 who has an ear, L him hear what the
11:9 bodies and refuse to L them be placed in
13:9 one has an ear, L him hear:
13:18 This calls for wisdom: L him who has understanding
19:7 L us rejoice and exult and give him the
22:11 L the evildoer still do evil, and the filthy
22:17 And L him who hears say, "Come." And let
22:17 And L him who is thirsty come, let him
22:17 who is thirsty come, L him who desires take

LETHECH

Hos 3:2 a homer and a L of barley.

LETS (8)

Ex 11:1 go hence; when he L you go, he will
22:5 be grazed over, or L his beast loose and
Lev 16:26 And he who L the goat go to Azazel
Job 37:3 the whole heaven he L it go, and his
39:14 to the earth, and L them be warmed on
Ps 107:36 And there he L the hungry dwell, and they
Is 44:14 or an oak and L it grow strong among
Jer 46:17 Egypt, 'Noisy one who L the hour go by.'

LETTER (77)

2Sam 11:14 morning David wrote a L to Joab, and sent
11:15 In the L he wrote, "Set Uriah in the
2Kgs 5:5 I will send a L to the king of
5:6 And he brought the L to the king of
5:6 which read, "When this L reaches you, know that
5:7 of Israel read the L, he rent his clothes
10:2 as soon as this L comes to you, seeing
10:6 to them a second L, saying, "If you are
10:7 And when the L came to them, they took
19:14 Hezekiah received the L from the hand of the
2Chr 2:11 Tyre answered in a L which he sent to
21:12 And a L came to him from Elijah the
Ezra 4:7 king of Persia; the L was written in Aramaic
4:8 scribe wrote a L against Jerusalem to Artaxerxes
4:11 a copy of the L that they sent--
4:18 And now the L which you sent to us
4:23 copy of King Artaxerxes' L was read before Rehum
5:5 answer be returned by L concerning it.
5:6 The copy of the L which Tattenai the governor
7:11 a copy of the L which King Artaxerxes gave
Neh 2:8 to Judah; and a L to Asaph, the keeper
6:5 me with an open L in his hand.
Esth 9:26 was written in this L, and of what they
9:29 authority, confirming this second L about Purim.
11:1 to Egypt the preceding L of Purim, which they
13:1 a copy of the L: "The Great King, Artaxerxes,
16:1 a copy of this L: "The Great King, Artaxerxes,
16:19 a copy of this L publicly in every place,
Is 37:14 Hezekiah received the L from the hand of the
Jer 29:1 the words of the L which Jeremiah the prophet
29:3 The L was sent by the hand of Elasah
29:29 the priest read this L in the hearing of
Bar 6:1 A copy of a L which Jeremiah sent to
1Mac 5:10 and his brothers a L which said, "The Gentiles
5:14 While the L was still being read, behold, other
8:22 a copy of the L which they wrote in
10:3 Demetrius sent Jonathan a L in peaceable words to
10:7 Jerusalem and read the L in the hearing of
10:17 And he wrote a L and sent it to
11:29 consented, and wrote a L to Jonathan about all
11:31 This copy of the L which we wrote concerning
12:5 a copy of the L which Jonathan wrote to
12:7 in time past a L was sent to Onias
12:8 honor, and received the L, which contained a clear
12:10 since you sent your L to us.
12:17 deliver to you this L from us concerning the
12:19 a copy of the L which they sent to
13:35 and wrote him a L as follows,
14:20 a copy of the L which the Spartans sent:
15:1 the king, sent a L from the islands of
2Mac 9:18 the Jews the following L, in the form of
11:16 The L written to the Jews by Lysias was
11:22 The king's L ran thus: "King Antiochus to his
11:27 the nation the king's L was as follows: "King
11:34 also sent them a L, which read thus: "Quintus
Acts 15:23 brethren, with the following L: "The brethren, both
15:30 the congregation together, they delivered the L
21:25 we have sent a L with our judgment that
23:25 And he wrote a L to this effect:
23:33 Caesarea and delivered the L to the governor, they
23:34 On reading the L, he asked to what province
Rom 16:22 the writer of this L, greet you in the
1Cor 5:9 to you in my L not to associate with
16:3 whom you accredit by L to carry your gift
2Cor 3:2 You yourselves are our L of recommendation,
3:3 that you are a L from Christ delivered by
7:8 you sorry with my L, I do not regret
7:8 I see that that L grieved you, though only
10:11 what we say by L when absent, we do
Col 4:16 And when this L has been read among you,
4:16 you read also the L from La-odicea.
1Thes 5:27 the Lord that this L be read to all
2Thes 2:2 by word, or by L purporting to be from
2:15 us, either by word of mouth or by L
3:14 we say in this L, note that man, and
3:17 the mark in every L of mine; it is
2Pet 3:1 is now the second L that I have written

LETTERS (43)

1Kgs 21:8 So she wrote L in Ahab's name and sealed
21:8 and she sent the L to the elders and
21:9 she wrote in the L, "Proclaim a fast, and
21:11 was written in the L which she had sent
2Kgs 10:1 So Jehu wrote L, and sent them to Samaria,
20:12 Babylon, sent envoys with L and a present to
2Chr 30:1 and Judah, and wrote L also to Ephraim and
30:6 Israel and Judah with L from the king and
32:17 And he wrote L to cast contempt on the
Neh 2:7 pleases the king, let L be given me to
2:9 Beyond the River, and gave them the king's L
6:17 of Judah sent many L to Tobiah, and Tobiah's
6:17 to Tobiah, and Tobiah's L came to them.
6:19 And Tobiah sent L to make me afraid.
Esth 1:22 Memucan proposed; he sent L to all the royal
3:13 L were sent by couriers to all the king's
8:5 written to revoke the L devised by Haman the
8:10 the king's ring, and L were sent by mounted
9:20 these things, and sent L to all the Jews
9:30 L were sent to all the Jews, to the
13:6 to you in the L of Haman, who is
16:17 put in execution the L sent by Haman the
Sir 45:11 a reminder, in engraved L, according to the number
Is 39:1 Babylon, sent envoys with L and a present to
Jer 29:25 Israel: You have sent L in your name to
Dan 1:4 to teach them the L and language of the
1:17 and skill in all L and wisdom; and Daniel
1Mac 1:44 And the king sent L by messengers to Jerusalem
9:60 force, and secretly sent L to all his allies
12:2 He also sent L to the same effect to
12:4 the Romans gave them L to the people in
15:15 arrived from Rome, with L to the kings and
16:19 with John; he sent L to the captains asking
2Mac 2:13 writings of David, and L of kings about votive
Acts 9:2 and asked him for L to the synagogues at
22:5 From them I received L to the brethren, and
28:21 "We have received no L from Judea about you,
2Cor 3:1 need, as some do, L of recommendation to you,
3:7 of death, carved in L on stone, came with
10:9 would not seem to be frightening you with L
10:10 For they say, "His L are weighty and strong,
Gal 6:11 See with what large L I am writing to
2Pet 3:16 of this as he does in all his L

LETTEST

Lk 2:29 and said, "Lord, now L thou thy servant depart

LETTING (5)

Ex 8:29 falsely again by not L the people go to
2Chr 25:13 Amaziah sent back, not L them go with him
Prov 17:14 of strife is like L out water; so quit
Jer 38:6 court of the guard, L Jeremiah down by ropes.
Dan 13:53 condemning the innocent and L the guilty go free,

LETUSHIM

Gen 25:3 of Dedan were Asshurim, L, and Le-ummim.

LEVEL (12)

Ps 26:12 My foot stands on L ground; in the great
27:11 lead me on a L path because of my
143:10 lead me on a L path!
Prov 15:19 the upright is a L highway.
Is 26:7 of the righteous is L; thou dost make smooth
40:4 uneven ground shall become L, and the rough places
42:16 the rough places into L ground.
45:2 go before you and L the mountains, I will
Bar 5:7 filled up, to make L ground, so that Israel

L

2Mac 9:14 he was hastening to L to the ground and
14:33 a prisoner, I will L this precinct of God
Lk 6:17 and stood on a L place, with a great

LEVELED (3)

Is 28:25 When he has L its surface, does he not
Jer 51:58 of Babylon shall be L to the ground and
2Mac 8:3 and about to be L to the ground, and

LEVI (71)

Gen 29:34 him three sons"; therefore his name was called L
34:25 of Jacob, Simeon and L, Dinah's brothers, took their
34:30 said to Simeon and L, "You have brought trouble
35:23 Reuben (Jacob's first-born), Simeon, L, Judah,
46:11 The sons of L: Gershon, Kohath, and Merari.
49:5 Simeon and L are brothers; weapons of violence are
Ex 1:2 his household: Reuben, Simeon, L, and Judah,
2:1 from the house of L went and took to
2:1 went and took to wife a daughter of L
6:16 of the sons of L according to their generations:
6:16 of the life of L being a hundred and
32:26 all the sons of L gathered themselves together to
32:28 And the sons of L did according to the
Num 1:49 "Only the tribe of L you shall not number,
3:6 "Bring the tribe of L near, and set them
3:15 "Number the sons of L, by fathers' houses and
3:17 were the sons of L by their names: Gershon
4:2 among the sons of L, by their families and
16:1 of Kohath, son of L, and Dathan and Abiram
16:7 You have gone too far, sons of L
16:8 now, you sons of L:
16:10 brethren the sons of L with you?
17:3 and write Aaron's name upon the rod of L
17:8 for the house of L had sprouted and put
18:2 also, the tribe of L, the tribe of your
26:58 are the families of L: the family of the
26:59 Jochebed the daughter of L, who was born to
26:59 who was born to L in Egypt; and she
Deut 10:8 apart the tribe of L to carry the ark
10:9 Therefore L has no portion or inheritance with his
18:1 all the tribe of L, shall have no portion
21:5 priests the sons of L shall come forward, for
27:12 bless the people: Simeon, L, Judah, Issachar, Joseph,
31:9 priests the sons of L, who carried the ark
33:8 And of L he said, "Give to Levi thy
33:8 he said, "Give to L thy Thummim, and thy
Josh 13:14 To the tribe of L alone Moses gave no
13:33 to the tribe of L Moses gave no inheritance;
1Chr 2:1 of Israel: Reuben, Simeon, L, Judah, Issachar,
6:1 The sons of L: Gershom, Kohath, and Merari.
6:16 The sons of L: Gershom, Kohath, and Merari.
6:38 of Kohath, son of L, son of Israel;
6:43 son of Jahath, son of Gershom, son of L
6:47 of Merari, son of L;
21:6 he did not include L and Benjamin in the
23:6 to the sons of L: Gershom, Kohath, and Merari.
23:14 of God were named among the tribe of L
23:24 were the sons of L by their fathers' houses,
24:20 of the sons of L: of the sons of
27:17 son of Maacah; for L, Hashabiah the son of
Ezra 8:15 I found there none of the sons of L
8:18 Mahli the son of L, son of Israel, namely
Neh 10:39 and the sons of L shall bring the contribution
12:23 The sons of L, heads of fathers' houses, were
Tob 1:7 to the sons of L who ministered at Jerusalem;
Ps 135:20 O house of L, bless the LORD!
Sir 45:6 holy man like him, of the tribe of L
Ezek 40:46 among the sons of L may come near to
48:31 and the gate of L, the gates of the
Zech 12:13 of the house of L by itself, and their
Mal 2:4 that my covenant with L may hold, says the
2:8 corrupted the covenant of L, says the LORD of
3:3 purify the sons of L and refine them like
Mk 2:14 passed on, he saw L the son of Alphaeus
Lk 3:24 Matthat, the son of L, the son of Melchi,
3:29 Matthat, the son of L,
5:27 a tax collector, named L, sitting at the tax
5:29 And L made him a great feast in his
Heb 7:5 And those descendants of L who receive the priestly
7:9 might even say that L himself, who receives tithes,
Rev 7:7 of the tribe of L, twelve thousand of the

LEVIATHAN (6)

Job 3:8 the day, who are skilled to rouse up L
41:1 "Can you draw out L with a fishhook, or
Ps 74:14 crush the heads of L, thou didst give him
104:26 go the ships, and L which thou didst form
Is 27:1 strong sword will punish L the fleeing serpent,
27:1 Leviathan the fleeing serpent, L the twisting serpent,

LEVIED (2)

1Kgs 9:15 labor which King Solomon L to build the house
2Chr 24:6 and Jerusalem the tax L by Moses, the servant

LEVIES

1Mac 10:29 salt tax and crown L,

LEVITE (29)

Ex 4:14 said, "Is there not Aaron, your brother, the L
Deut 12:12 your maidservants, and the L that is within your
12:18 your maidservant, and the L who is within your
12:19 do not forsake the L as long as you
14:27 shall not forsake the L who is within your
14:29 your towns; and the L, because he has no
16:11 and your maidservant, the L who is within your
16:14 and your maidservant, the L, the sojourner, the
18:6 "And if a L comes from any of your
26:11 house, you, and the L, and the sojourner who
26:12 giving it to the L, the sojourner, the fatherless,
26:13 given it to the L, the sojourner, the fatherless,
Judg 17:7 Judah, who was a L; and he sojourned there.
17:9 him, "I am a L of Bethlehem in Judah,
17:11 And the L was content to dwell with the
17:12 And Micah installed the L, and the young man
17:13 because I have a L as priest."
18:3 voice of the young L; and they turned aside
18:15 house of the young L, at the home of
19:1 in Israel, a certain L was sojourning in the
20:4 And the L, the husband of the woman who
1Chr 24:6 son of Nethanel, a L, recorded them in the
2Chr 20:14 son of Mattaniah, a L of the sons of
31:12 them was Conaniah the L, with Shimei his brother
31:14 son of Imnah the L, keeper of the east
Ezra 10:15 Meshullum and Shabbethai the L supported them.
Esth 11:1 a priest and a L, and Ptolemy his son
Lk 10:32 So likewise a L, when he came to the
Acts 4:36 Son of encouragement), a L, a native of Cyprus,

LEVITES (253)

Ex 6:19 the families of the L according to their generations.
6:25 fathers' houses of the L by their families.
38:21 the work of the L under the direction of
Lev 25:32 the cities of the L, the houses in the
25:32 of their possession, the L may redeem at any
25:33 if one of the L does not exercise his
25:33 the cities of the L are their possession among
Num 1:47 But the L were not numbered by their ancestral
1:50 Israel; but appoint the L over the tabernacle of
1:51 to set out, the L shall take it down;
1:51 to be pitched, the L shall set it up.
1:53 own standard; but the L shall encamp around the
1:53 of Israel; and the L shall keep charge of
2:17 the camp of the L in the midst of
2:33 But the L were not numbered among the people
3:9 you shall give the L to Aaron and his
3:12 I have taken the L from among the people
3:12 The L shall be mine,
3:20 the families of the L, by their fathers' houses.
3:32 the leaders of the L, and to have oversight
3:39 were numbered of the L, whom Moses and Aaron
3:41 you shall take the L for me—I am
3:41 the cattle of the L instead of all the
3:45 to Moses, "Take the L instead of all the
3:45 the cattle of the L instead of their cattle;
3:45 their cattle; and the L shall be mine: I
3:46 number of the male L,
3:49 those redeemed by the L;
4:18 destroyed from among the L;
4:46 were numbered of the L, whom Moses and Aaron
7:5 give them to the L, to each man according
7:6 and the oxen, and gave them to the L
8:6 to Moses, "Take the L from among the people
8:9 you shall present the L before the tent of
8:10 When you present the L before the LORD, the
8:10 their hands upon the L,
8:11 Aaron shall offer the L before the LORD as
8:12 Then the L shall lay their hands upon the
8:12 to the LORD, to make atonement for the L
8:13 you shall cause the L to attend Aaron and
8:14 you shall separate the L from among the people
8:14 of Israel, and the L shall be mine.
8:15 And after that the L shall go in to

 LEVITES

8:18 I have taken the L instead of all the
8:19 I have given the L as a gift to
8:20 of Israel to the L; according to all that
8:20 commanded Moses concerning the L, the people of
8:21 And the L purified themselves from sin, and washed
8:22 And after that the L went in to do
8:22 commanded Moses concerning the L, so they did to
8:24 what pertains to the L: from twenty-five years old
8:26 you do to the L in assigning their duties."
18:6 taken your brethren the L from among the people
18:21 "To the L I have given every tithe in
18:23 But the L shall do the service of the
18:24 have given to the L for an inheritance; therefore
18:26 shall say to the L, 'When you take from
18:30 be reckoned to the L as produce of the
26:57 These are the L as numbered according to their
31:30 give them to the L who have charge of
31:47 gave them to the L who had charge of
35:2 they give to the L, from the inheritance of
35:2 shall give to the L pasture lands round about
35:4 shall give to the L, shall reach from the
35:6 you give to the L shall be the six
35:7 you give to the L shall be forty-eight, with
35:8 inherits, shall give of its cities to the L
Deut 27:14 And the L shall declare to all the men
31:25 end, Moses commanded the L who carried the ark
Josh 14:3 Jordan; but to the L he gave no inheritance
14:4 was given to the L in the land, but
18:7 The L have no portion among you, for the
21:1 fathers' houses of the L came to Eleazar the
21:3 Israel gave to the L the following cities and
21:4 So those L who were descendants of Aaron the
21:8 by lot to the L, as the LORD had
21:10 who belonged to the L; since the lot fell
21:20 Kohathite families of the L, the cities allotted to
21:27 the families of the L, were given out of
21:34 the rest of the L, the Merarite families, were
21:40 the families of the L, those allotted to them
21:41 The cities of the L in the midst of
1Sam 6:15 And the L took down the ark of the
2Sam 15:24 also, with all the L, bearing the ark of
1Kgs 8:4 the priests and the L brought them up.
12:31 all the people, who were not of the L
1Chr 6:19 the families of the L according to their fathers.
6:48 and their brethren the L were appointed for all
6:64 of Israel gave the L the cities with their
9:2 Israel, the priests, the L, and the temple servants.
9:14 Of the L: Shemaiah the son of Hasshub, son
9:18 were the gatekeepers of the camp of the L
9:26 chief gatekeepers, who were L, were in charge of
9:31 Mattithiah, one of the L, the first-born of Shallum
9:33 fathers' houses of the L, dwelling in the chambers
9:34 fathers' houses of the L, according to their
12:26 Of the L four thousand six hundred.
13:2 to the priests and L in the cities that
15:2 "No one but the L may carry the ark
15:4 of Aaron and the L:
15:11 and Abiathar, and the L Uriel, Asaiah, Joel,
15:12 fathers' houses of the L; sanctify yourselves, you and
15:14 the priests and the L sanctified themselves to bring
15:15 And the L carried the ark of God upon
15:16 the chiefs of the L to appoint their brethren
15:17 So the L appointed Heman the son of Joel;
15:22 Chenaniah, leader of the L in music, should direct
15:26 because God helped the L who were carrying the
15:27 also were all the L who were carrying the
16:4 appointed certain of the L as ministers before the
23:2 leaders of Israel and the priests and the L
23:3 The L, thirty years old and upward, were numbered,
23:26 And so the L no longer need to carry
23:27 the number of the L from twenty years old
24:6 priests and of the L; one father's house being
24:30 the sons of the L according to their fathers'
24:31 fathers' houses of the priests and of the L
26:20 And of the L, Ahijah had charge of the
28:13 priests and of the L, and all the work
28:21 the priests and the L for all the service
2Chr 5:4 Israel came, and the L took up the ark.
5:5 the priests and the L brought them up.
7:6 at their posts; the L also, with the instruments
8:14 their service, and the L for their offices of
8:15 commanded the priests and L concerning any matter
11:13 the priests and the L that were in all
11:14 For the L left their common lands and their
13:9 of Aaron, and the L, and made priests for
13:10 sons of Aaron, and L for their service.
17:8 and with them the L, Shemaiah, Nethaniah,
17:8 Tobadonijah; and with these L, the priests Elishama
19:8 Jerusalem Jehoshaphat appointed certain L and
19:11 king's matters; and the L will serve you as
20:19 And the L, of the Kohathites and the Korahites,
23:2 Judah and gathered the L from all the cities
23:4 of you priests and L who come off duty
23:6 the priests and ministering L; they may enter, for
23:7 The L shall surround the king, each with his
23:8 The L and all Judah did according to all
23:18 Levitical priests and the L whom David had
24:5 the priests and the L, and said to them,
24:5 But the L did not hasten it.
24:6 you not required the L to bring in from
24:11 king's officers by the L, when they saw that
29:4 the priests and the L, and assembled them in
29:5 the east, and said to them, "Hear me, L
29:12 Then the L arose, Mahath the son of Amasai,
29:16 the LORD; and the L took it and carried
29:25 And he stationed the L in the house of
29:26 The L stood with the instruments of David, and
29:30 the princes commanded the L to sing praises to
29:34 themselves their brethren the L helped them, until
29:34 was finished—for the L were more upright in
30:15 the priests and the L were put to shame,
30:16 which they received from the hand of the L
30:17 sanctified themselves; therefore the L had to kill the
30:21 great gladness; and the L and the priests praised
30:22 encouragingly to all the L who showed good skill
30:25 the priests and the L, and the whole assembly
30:27 the priests and the L arose and blessed the
31:2 priests and of the L, division by division, each
31:2 the priests and the L, for burnt offerings and
31:4 the priests and the L, that they might give
31:9 the priests and the L about the heaps.
31:17 houses; that of the L from twenty years old
31:19 every one among the L who was enrolled.
34:9 of God, which the L, the keepers of the
34:12 Jahath and Obadiah the L, of the sons of
34:12 The L, all who were skilful with instruments of
34:13 and some of the L were scribes, and officials,
34:30 the priests and the L, all the people both
35:3 he said to the L who taught all Israel
35:5 a part of a father's house of the L
35:8 the people, to the priests, and to the L
35:9 the chiefs of the L, gave to the Levites
35:9 Levites, gave to the L for the passover offerings
35:10 their place, and the L in their divisions according
35:11 from them while the L flayed the victims.
35:14 until night; so the L prepared for themselves and
35:15 for their brethren the L prepared for them.
35:18 the priests and the L, and all Judah and
Ezra 1:5 the priests and the L, every one whose spirit
2:40 The L: the sons of Jeshua and Kadmi-el, of
2:70 The priests, the L, and some of the people
3:8 the priests and the L and all who had
3:8 They appointed the L, from twenty years old and
3:9 of Henadad and the L, their sons and kinsmen.
3:10 with trumpets, and the L, the sons of Asaph,
3:12 of the priests and L and heads of fathers'
6:16 the priests and the L, and the rest of
6:18 their divisions and the L in their courses, for
6:20 the priests and the L had purified themselves
7:7 of the priests and L, the singers and gatekeepers,
7:13 or their priests or L in my kingdom, who
7:24 of the priests, the L, the singers, the doorkeepers,
8:20 his officials had set apart to attend the L.
8:29 chief priests and the L and the heads of
8:30 the priests and the L took over the weight
8:33 with them were the L, Jozabad the son of
9:1 the priests and the L have not separated themselves
10:5 the leading priests and L and all Israel take
10:23 Of the L: Jozabad, Shimei, Kelaiah (that is, Kelita),
Neh 3:17 After him the L repaired: Rehum the son of
7:1 the singers, and the L had been appointed,
7:43 The L: the sons of Jeshua, namely of Kadmi-el
7:73 So the priests, the L, the gatekeepers, the singers,
8:7 Jozabad, Hanan, Pelaiah, the L, helped the people to
8:9 and scribe, and the L who taught the people
8:11 So the L stilled all the people, saying, "Be
8:13 the priests and the L, came together to Ezra
9:4 the stairs of the L stood Jeshua, Bani, Kadmi-el,
9:5 Then the L, Jeshua, Kadmi-el, Bani, Hashabneiah, ,
9:38 and our princes, our L, and our priests set
10:9 And the L: Jeshua the son of Azaniah, Binnui
10:28 people, the priests, the L, the gatekeepers, the

10:34 lots, the priests, the L, and the people, for
10:37 to bring to the L the tithes from our
10:37 for it is the L who collect the tithes
10:38 shall be with the L when the Levites receive
10:38 the Levites when the L receive the tithes; and
10:38 the tithes; and the L shall bring up the
11:3 Israel, the priests, the L, the temple servants, and
11:15 And of the L: Shemaiah the son of Hasshub,
11:16 the chiefs of the L, who were over the
11:18 All the L in the holy city were two
11:20 the priests and the L, were in all the
11:22 The overseer of the L in Jerusalem was Uzzi
11:36 certain divisions of the L in Judah were joined
12:1 the priests and the L who came up with
12:8 And the L: Jeshua, Binnui, Kadmi-el, Sherebiah,
12:22 As for the L, in the days of Eliashib,
12:24 the chiefs of the L: Hashabiah, Sherebiah, and
12:27 Jerusalem they sought the L in all their places,
12:30 the priests and the L purified themselves; and they
12:44 priests and for the L according to the fields
12:44 the priests and the L who ministered.
12:47 which was for the L; and the Levites set
12:47 the Levites; and the L set apart that which
13:5 by commandment to the L, singers, and gatekeepers,
13:10 the portions of the L had not been given
13:10 them; so that the L and the singers, who
13:13 and Pedaiah of the L, and as their assistant
13:22 And I commanded the L that they should purify
13:29 and the covenant of the priesthood and the L
13:30 of the priests and L, each in his work;
Is 66:21 for priests and for L, says the LORD.
Ezek 44:10 But the L who went far from me, going
45:5 shall be for the L who minister at the
48:11 went astray, as the L did.
48:12 most holy place, adjoining the territory of the L
48:13 of the priests, the L shall have an allotment
48:22 the property of the L and the property of
Jn 1:19 Jews sent priests and L from Jerusalem to ask

L

LEVITICAL (15)

Deut 17:9 and coming to the L priests, and to the
17:18 the charge of the L priests;
18:1 "The L priests, that is, all the tribe of
24:8 to all that the L priests shall direct you;
27:9 And Moses and the L priests said to all
Josh 3:3 being carried by the L priests, then you shall
8:33 the ark before the L priests who carried the
2Chr 5:12 divisions; and all the L singers, Asaph, Heman, and
23:18 the direction of the L priests and the Levites
Jer 33:18 of Israel, and the L priests shall never lack
33:21 my covenant with the L priests my ministers.
33:22 my servant, and the L priests who minister to
Ezek 43:19 shall give to the L priests of the family
44:15 "But the L priests, the sons of Zadok, who
Heb 7:11 been attainable through the L priesthood (for under

LEVITY

Eph 5:4 nor silly talk, nor L, which are not fitting;

LEVY (7)

Num 31:28 And L for the LORD a tribute from the
1Kgs 5:13 King Solomon raised a L of forced labor out
5:13 all Israel; and the L numbered thirty thousand men.
5:14 at home; Adoniram was in charge of the L
9:21 Solomon made a forced L of slaves, and so
2Chr 8:8 Solomon made a forced L and so they are
2Mac 11:3 for Greeks, and to L tribute on the temple

LEWD (3)

Sir 23:13 accustom your mouth to L vulgarity, for it involves
Jer 13:27 adulteries and neighings, your L harlotries, on the
Ezek 16:27 were ashamed of your L behavior.

LEWDLY

Ezek 22:11 wife; another L defiles his daughter-in-law;

LEWDNESS (13)

Ezek 16:43 "Have you not committed L in addition to all
16:58 the penalty of your L and your abominations, says
22:9 the mountains; men commit L in your midst.
23:21 you longed for the L of your youth, when
23:27 an end to your L and your harlotry brought
23:29 Your L and your harlotry
23:35 the consequences of your L and harlotry."
23:44 in to Oholah and to Oholibah to commit L
23:48 put an end to L in the land, that
23:48 warning and not commit L as you have done.
23:49 And your L shall be requited upon you, and
24:13 Its rust is your filthy L
Hos 2:10 I will uncover her L in the sight of

LIABLE (5)

1Mac 14:45 of them shall be L to punishment."
Mt 5:21 whoever kills shall be L to judgment.'
5:22 his brother shall be L to judgment; whoever insults
5:22 his brother shall be L to the council, and
5:22 'You fool!' shall be L to the hell of

LIAR (15)

Job 24:25 will prove me a L, and show that there
34:6 I am counted a L; my wound is incurable,
Prov 17:4 wicked lips; and a L gives heed to a
19:22 and a poor man is better than a L
30:6 he rebuke you, and you be found a L
Sir 20:24 preferable to a habitual L, but the lot of
20:25 The disposition of a L brings disgrace, and his
25:2 man who is a L, and an adulterous old
Jn 8:44 for he is a L and the father of
8:55 I should be a L like you; but I
1Jn 1:10 we make him a L, and his word is
2:4 his commandments is a L, and the truth is
2:22 Who is the L but he who denies that
4:20 brother, he is a L; for he who does
5:10 has made him a L, because he has not

LIARS (7)

Ps 63:11 for the mouths of L will be stopped.
Sir 15:8 men of pride, and L will never think of
Is 44:25 frustrates the omens of L, and makes fools of
1Tim 1:10 immoral persons, sodomites, kidnapers, L, perjurers,
4:2 through the pretensions of L whose consciences are
Tit 1:11 said, "Cretans are always L, evil beasts, lazy"
Rev 21:8 sorcerers, idolaters, and all L, their lot shall be

LIBATION (6)

Ex 29:40 fourth of a hin of wine for a L
29:41 cereal offering and its L, as in the morning,
30:9 you shall pour no L thereon.
Sir 50:15 cup and poured a L of the blood of
Jer 52:19 the dishes for incense, and the bowls for L
Phil 2:17 be poured as a L upon the sacrificial offering

LIBATIONS (11)

Ex 25:29 with which to pour L; of pure gold you
37:16 its bowls and flagons with which to pour L
2Chr 29:35 and there were the L for the burnt offerings.
Esth 14:17 king's feast or drunk the wine of the L
Ps 16:4 multiply their sorrows; their L of blood I will
Jer 44:17 heaven and pour out L to her, as we
44:18 heaven and pouring out L to her, we have
44:19 heaven and poured out L to her, was it
44:19 image and poured out L to her?"
44:25 and to pour out L to her.' Then confirm
Hos 9:4 They shall not pour L of wine to the

LIBERAL (4)

Prov 11:25 A L man will be enriched, and one who
Sir 31:23 the one who is L with food, and their
2Cor 8:20 blame us about this L gift which we are
1Tim 6:18 rich in good deeds, L and generous,

LIBERALITY (3)

Esth 2:18 to the provinces, and gave gifts with royal L
Rom 12:8 he who contributes, in L; he who gives aid,
2Cor 8:2 in a wealth of L on their part.

LIBERALLY (3)

Deut 15:14 you shall furnish him L out of your flock,
Ps 37:26 He is ever giving L and lending, and his
Acts 10:2 his household, gave alms L to the people, and

LIBERTY (18)

Lev 25:10 fiftieth year, and proclaim L throughout the land to
Ps 119:45 I shall walk at L, for I have sought
Sir 26:10 lest, when she finds L, she use it to
33:25 leave his hands idle, and he will seek L
Is 61:1 the brokenhearted, to proclaim L to the captives, and
Jer 34:8 make a proclamation of L to them,
34:15 my eyes by proclaiming L, each to his neighbor,
34:17 obeyed me by proclaiming L, every one to his
34:17 I proclaim to you L to the sword, to
Ezek 46:17 to the year of L; then it shall revert

Lk	4:18	blind, to set at L those who are oppressed,
Acts	24:22	but should have some L, and that none of
	28:18	to set me at L, because there was no
Rom	8:21	and obtain the glorious L of the children of
1Cor	8:9	take care lest this L of yours somehow become
	10:29	For why should my L be determined by another
Jas	1:24	law, the law of L, and perseveres, being no
	2:12	are to be judged under the law of L

LIBNAH (18)

Num	33:20	they set out from Rimmon-perez, and encamped at L
	33:21	they set out from L, and encamped at Rissah.
Josh	10:29	Israel with him, to L, and fought against Libnah;
	10:29	Libnah, and fought against L;
	10:31	Joshua passed on from L, and all Israel with
	10:32	person in it, as he had done to L
	10:39	to Hebron and to L and its king, so
	12:15	one; the king of L, one; the king of
	15:42	L, Ether, Ashan,
	21:13	with its pasture lands, L with its pasture lands,
2Kgs	8:22	Then L revolted at the same time.
	19:8	of Assyria fighting against L; for he heard that
	23:31	name was Hamutal the daughter of Jeremiah of L
	24:18	name was Hamutal the daughter of Jeremiah of L
1Chr	6:57	cities of refuge: Hebron, L with its pasture lands,
2Chr	21:10	At that time L also revolted from his rule,
Is	37:8	of Assyria fighting against L; for he had heard
Jer	52:1	name was Hamutal the daughter of Jeremiah of L

LIBNI (5)

Ex	6:17	The sons of Gershon: L and Shimei, by their
Num	3:18	Gershon by their families: L and Shimei.
1Chr	6:17	the sons of Gershom: L and Shimei.
	6:20	Of Gershom: L his son, Jahath his son, Zimmah
	6:29	sons of Merari: Mahli, L his son, Shimei his

LIBNITES (2)

Num	3:21	the family of the L and the family of
	26:58	the family of the L, the family of the

LIBRARY

2Mac	2:13	that he founded a L and collected the books

LIBYA (2)

Ezek	30:5	and all Arabia, and L, and the people of
Acts	2:10	and the parts of L belonging to Cyrene, and

LIBYANS (4)

2Chr	12:3	with him from Egypt-- L, Sukki-im, and Ethiopians.
	16:8	the Ethiopians and the L a huge army with
Dan	11:43	of Egypt; and the L and the Ethiopians shall
Nah	3:9	limit; Put and the L were her helpers.

LICENTIOUS

2Pet	2:18	folly, they entice with L passions of the flesh

LICENTIOUSNESS (9)

Mk	7:21	coveting, wickedness, deceit, L, envy, slander, pride,
Rom	13:13	not in debauchery and L, not in quarreling and
2Cor	12:21	the impurity, immorality, and L which they have
Gal	5:19	are plain: fornication, impurity, L,
Eph	4:19	given themselves up to L, greedy to practice every
1Pet	4:3	to do, living in L, passions, drunkenness, revels,
2Pet	2:2	many will follow their L, and because of them
	2:7	greatly distressed by the L of the wicked
Jude	1:4	of our God into L and deny our only

LICK (6)

Num	22:4	"This horde will now L up all that is
1Kgs	21:19	of Naboth shall dogs L your own blood."'"
Jud	7:4	"These men will now L up the face of
Ps	72:9	him, and his enemies L the dust!
Is	49:23	down to you, and L the dust of your
Mic	7:17	be deaf; they shall L the dust like a

LICKED (4)

1Kgs	18:38	and the dust, and L up the water that
	21:19	the place where dogs L up the blood of
	22:38	Samaria, and the dogs L up his blood, and
Lk	16:21	the dogs came and L his sores.

LICKS

Num	22:4	us, as the ox L up the grass of

LID

2Kgs	12:9	a hole in the L of it, and set

LIE (161)

Gen	19:32	wine, and we will L with him, that we
	19:34	you go in and L with him, that we
	28:13	land on which you L I will give to
	30:15	said, "Then he may L with you tonight for
	38:26	And he did not L with her again.
	39:7	upon Joseph, and said, L with me."
	39:10	listen to her, to L with her or to
	39:12	by his garment, saying, L with me." But he
	39:14	in to me to L with me, and I
	47:30	Egypt, but let me L with my fathers; carry
Ex	21:13	if he did not L in wait for him,
	23:11	let it rest and L fallow, that the poor
	25:27	frame the rings shall L, as holders for the
	28:28	blue, that it may L upon the skilfully woven
	39:21	so that it should L upon the skilfully woven
Lev	18:20	And you shall not L carnally with your neighbor's
	18:22	You shall not L with a male as with
	18:23	And you shall not L with any beast and
	18:23	to a beast to L with it: it is
	19:11	nor deal falsely, nor L to one another.
	26:6	land, and you shall L down, and none shall
Num	23:19	man, that he should L, or a son of
	23:24	itself; it does not L down till it devours
Deut	6:7	way, and when you L down, and when you
	11:19	way, and when you L down, and when you
	25:2	shall cause him to L down and be beaten
	28:30	and another man shall L with her; you shall
Josh	8:4	them, "Behold, you shall L in ambush against the
Judg	9:32	are with you, and L in wait in the
	21:20	Benjaminites, saying, "Go and L in wait in the
Ruth	3:4	uncover his feet and L down; and he will
	3:7	merry, he went to L down at the end
	3:13	L down until the morning."
1Sam	3:5	"I did not call; L down again." So he
	3:6	not call, my son; L down again."
	3:9	said to Samuel, "Go, L down; and if he
	15:29	of Israel will not L or repent; for he
	22:8	servant against me, to L in wait, as at
	22:13	risen against me, to L in wait, as at
2Sam	7:12	are fulfilled and you L down with your fathers,
	8:2	a line, making them L down on the ground;
	11:11	to drink, and to L with my wife?
	11:13	he went out to L on his couch with
	12:3	from his cup, and L in his bosom, and
	12:11	neighbor, and he shall L with your wives in
	13:5	Jonadab said to him, L down on your bed,
	13:11	said to her, "Come, L with me, my sister."
1Kgs	1:2	his nurse; let her L in your bosom, that
2Kgs	4:16	of God; do not L to your maidservant."
Jud	3:2	Nebuchadnezzar, the Great King, L prostrate before
	3:3	sheepfolds with their tents, L before you; do with
Job	6:28	for I will not L to your face.
	7:4	When I L down I say, 'When shall I
	7:21	For now I shall L in the earth; thou
	11:19	You will L down, and none will make you
	20:11	vigor, but it will L down with him in
	21:26	They L down alike in the dust, and the
	24:7	They L all night naked, without clothing, and have
	38:40	in their dens, or L in wait in their
Ps	3:5	[Selah] I L down and sleep; I wake again,
	4:8	peace I will both L down and sleep; for
	23:2	want; he makes me L down in green pastures.
	36:12	There the evildoers L prostrate, they are thrust
	57:4	I L in the midst of lions that greedily
	59:3	For, lo, they L in wait for my life;
	88:5	like the slain that L in the grave, like
	89:35	holiness; I will not L to David.
	102:7	the waste places; I L awake, I am like
	104:22	get them away and L down in their dens.
	119:95	The wicked L in wait to destroy me; but
Prov	1:11	with us, let us L in wait for blood,
	1:18	bird; but these men L in wait for their
	3:24	be afraid; when you L down, your sleep will
	6:9	How long will you L there, O sluggard?
	6:22	lead you; when you L down, they will watch
	12:6	words of the wicked L in wait for blood,
	14:5	faithful witness does not L, but a false witness
	15:11	Sheol and Abaddon L open before the LORD, how
	24:15	L not in wait as a wicked man against
Eccl	4:11	Again, if two L together, they are warm; but
	11:3	place where the tree falls, there it will L
Song	1:7	where you make it L down at noon; for
Wis	2:12	"Let us L in wait for the righteous man,
Sir	5:14	slanderer, and do not L in ambush with your
	7:12	Do not devise a L against your brother, nor

L

7:13 Refuse to utter any L, for the habit of
8:11 insolent fellow, lest he L in ambush against your
14:22 like a hunter, and L in wait on her
20:23 A L is an ugly blot on a man;
41:17 mother; and of a L, before a prince or
43:32 things greater than these L hidden, for we have
46:12 revive from where they L, and may the name
49:10 revive from where they L, for they comforted the
Is 6:11 he said: "Until cities L waste without inhabitant, and
11:6 and the leopard shall L down with the kid,
11:7 feed; their young shall L down together; and the
13:20 will make their flocks L down there.
13:21 But wild beasts will L down there, and its
14:18 kings of the nations L in glory, each in
14:30 feed, and the needy L down in safety; but
17:2 for flocks, which will L down, and none will
33:8 The highways L waste, the wayfaring man ceases.
34:10 to generation it shall L waste; none shall pass
43:17 army and warrior; they L down, they cannot rise,
44:20 "Is there not a L in my right hand?"
50:11 my hand: you shall L down in torment.
51:20 sons have fainted, they L at the head of
65:10 place for herds to L down, for my people
Jer 3:25 Let us L down in our shame, and let
8:8 of the scribes has made it into a L
27:10 For it is a L which they are prophesying
27:14 for it is a L which they are prophesying
27:16 for it is a L which they are prophesying
28:15 you have made this people trust in a L
29:9 for it is a L which they are prophesying
29:21 who are prophesying a L to you in my
29:31 you trust in a L,
43:2 men said to Jeremiah, "You are telling a L
Lam 2:21 dust of the streets L the young and the
4:1 The holy stones L scattered at the head of
4:5 brought up in purple L on ash heaps.
Ezek 4:4 "Then L upon your left side, and I will
4:4 the days that you L upon it, you shall
4:6 completed these, you shall L down a second time,
4:9 of days that you L upon your side, three
6:13 LORD, when their slain L among their idols round
13:6 falsehood and divined a L; they say, 'Says the
31:12 and its boughs will L broken in all the
31:18 nether world; you shall L among the uncircumcised,
32:20 and with her shall L all her multitudes.
32:21 have come down, they L still, the uncircumcised,
32:27 And they do not L with the fallen mighty
32:28 shall be broken and L among the uncircumcised,
32:29 by the sword; they L with the uncircumcised, with
32:30 by their might; they L uncircumcised with those who
34:14 pasture; there they shall L down in good grazing
34:15 I will make them L down, says the Lord
48:22 of the prince shall L between the territory of
Dan 13:20 give your consent, and L with us.
Hos 2:18 I will make you L down in safety.
6:9 As robbers L in wait for a man, so
Amos 6:4 "Woe to those who L upon beds of ivory,
Mic 7:2 among men; they all L in wait for blood,
Hab 2:3 it hastens to the end—it will not L
Zeph 2:7 of Ashkelon they shall L down at evening.
2:14 Herds shall L down in the midst of her,
3:13 they shall pasture and L down, and none shall
2Mac 5:10 cast out many to L unburied had no one
12:39 bring them back to L with their kinsmen in
Acts 5:3 filled your heart to L to the Holy Spirit
23:21 forty of their men L in ambush for him,
Rom 1:25 about God for a L and worshiped and served
2Cor 11:31 blessed for ever, knows that I do not L
Gal 1:20 God, I do not L
Col 3:9 Do not L to one another, seeing that you
1Jn 1:6 walk in darkness, we L and do not live
2:21 and know that no L is of the truth.
2:27 true, and is no L, just as it has
Rev 3:9 and are not, but L --behold, I will make
11:8 their dead bodies will L in the street of
14:5 in their mouth no L was found, for they

LIED (8)

Lev 6:3 what was lost and L about it, swearing falsely—
Josh 7:11 they have stolen, and L, and put them among
1Kgs 13:18 But he L to him.
Ps 78:36 with their mouths; they L to him with their
Is 57:11 fear, so that you L, and did not remember
Dan 13:55 You have L against your own head, for the
13:59 You also have L against your own head, for
Acts 5:4 You have not L to men but to God."

LIES (139)

Gen 16:14 was called Beer-lahai-roi; it L between Kadesh and
Ex 22:16 is not betrothed, and L with her, he shall
22:19 "Whoever L with a beast shall be put to
Lev 14:47 evening; and he who L down in the house
15:4 who has the discharge L shall be unclean; and
15:18 If a man L with a woman and has
15:20 everything upon which she L during her impurity
15:24 And if any man L with her, and her
15:24 bed on which he L shall be unclean.
15:26 bed on which she L, all the days of
15:33 for the man who L with a woman who
19:20 "If a man L carnally with a woman who
20:11 The man who L with his father's wife has
20:12 If a man L with his daughter-in-law, both of
20:13 If a man L with a male as with
20:15 If a man L with a beast, he shall
20:16 approaches any beast and L with it, you shall
20:18 If a man L with a woman having her
20:20 If a man L with his uncle's wife, he
26:34 as long as it L desolate, while you are
26:35 As long as it L desolate it shall have
26:43 its sabbaths while it L desolate without them; and
Num 5:13 him, if a man L with her carnally, and
14:33 of your dead bodies L in the wilderness.
Deut 19:11 hates his neighbor, and L in wait for him,
22:23 in the city and L with her,
22:25 man seizes her and L with her, then only
22:28 and seizes her and L with her, and they
27:20 "'Cursed be he who L with his father's wife,
27:21 "'Cursed be he who L with any kind of
27:22 "'Cursed be he who L with his sister, whether
27:23 "'Cursed be he who L with his mother-in-law.' And
Josh 15:8 of the mountain that L over against the valley
18:13 the mountain that L south of Lower Beth-horon.
18:14 from the mountain that L to the south, opposite
22:4 land where your possession L, which Moses the
22:10 about the Jordan, that L in the land of
Judg 1:16 wilderness of Judah, which L in the Negeb near
16:5 wherein his great strength L, and by what means
16:6 wherein your great strength L, and how you might
16:10 me, and told me L; please tell me how
16:13 me, and told me L; tell me how you
16:15 have not told me wherein your great strength L
Ruth 3:4 But when he L down, observe the place where
3:4 the place where he L; then, go and uncover
2Sam 1:25 "Jonathan L slain upon thy high places.
2:24 hill of Ammah, which L before Giah on the
Neh 2:3 of my fathers' sepulchres, L waste, and its gates
2:17 are in, how Jerusalem L in ruins with its
Job 13:4 you, you whitewash with L; worthless physicians are
14:12 dries up, so man L down and rises not
40:21 the lotus plants he L, in the covert of
Ps 4:2 will you love vain words, and seek after L
5:6 destroyest those who speak L; the LORD abhors
7:14 and is pregnant with mischief, and brings forth L
12:2 Every one utters L to his neighbor; with flattering
41:8 he will not rise again from where he L
58:3 the womb, they err from their birth, speaking L
59:12 For the cursing and L which they utter,
69:4 would destroy me, those who attack me with L
88:7 Thy wrath L heavy upon me, and thou dost
101:7 no man who utters L shall continue in my
119:69 godless besmear me with L, but with my whole
144:8 aliens, whose mouths speak L, and whose right hand
144:11 aliens, whose mouths speak L, and whose right hand
Prov 6:19 witness who breathes out L, and a man who
7:12 at every corner she L in wait.
14:5 not lie, but a false witness breathes out L
14:25 but one who utters L is a betrayer.
19:5 and he who utters L will not escape.
19:9 and he who utters L will perish.
23:28 She L in wait like a robber and increases
23:34 be like one who L down in the midst
23:34 sea, like one who L on the top of
Eccl 6:1 the sun, and it L heavy upon men:
8:6 way, although man's trouble L heavy upon him.
Song 1:13 bag of myrrh, that L between my breasts.
Wis 14:28 in exultation, or prophesy L, or live unrighteously, or
Sir 11:29 your weakness; for he L in wait, turning good
11:30 coals, and a sinner L in wait to shed
27:10 A lion L in wait for prey; so does
27:28 proud man, but vengeance L in wait for him
28:26 fall before him who L in wait.
38:13 a time when success L in the hands of
51:2 of a slanderous tongue, from lips that utter L

Is 1:7 Your country L desolate, your cities are burned with
9:15 the prophet who teaches L is the tail;
24:5 The earth L polluted under its inhabitants; for they
24:20 a hut; its transgression L heavy upon it, and
27:10 calf grazes, there he L down, and strips its
28:15 for we have made L our refuge, and in
28:17 away the refuge of L, and waters will overwhelm
59:3 lips have spoken L, your tongue mutters wickedness.
59:4 empty pleas, they speak L, they conceive mischief
Jer 9:5 their tongue to speak L; they commit iniquity and
13:25 because you have forgotten me and trusted in L
14:14 "The prophets are prophesying L in my name; I
16:19 have inherited nought but L, worthless things in
23:14 adultery and walk in L; they strengthen the hands
23:25 have said who prophesy L in my name, saying,
23:26 long shall there be L in the heart of
23:26 the prophets who prophesy L, and who prophesy the
23:32 people astray by their L and their recklessness, when
Lam 5:18 for Mount Zion which L desolate; jackals prowl over
Bar 6:47 They have left only L and reproach for those
Ezek 13:8 uttered delusions and seen L, therefore behold, I am
13:19 not live, by your L to my people, who
13:19 your lies to my people, who listen to L
21:29 visions, while they divine L for you--to be
22:28 false visions and divining L for them, saying, 'Thus
29:3 the great dragon that L in the midst of
47:16 Zedad, Berothah, Sibraim (which L on the border
Dan 11:27 mischief; they shall speak L at the same table,
14:12 will, who is telling L about us."
Hos 7:14 them, but they speak L against me.
10:13 reaped injustice, you have eaten the fruit of L
11:12 has encompassed me with L, and the house of
Amos 2:4 his statutes, but their L have led them astray,
Mic 2:11 and utter wind and L, saying, "I will preach
6:12 violence; your inhabitants speak L, and their tongue
7:5 mouth from her who L in your bosom;
Nah 3:1 city, all full of L and booty--no end
Hab 2:18 shaped it, a metal image, a teacher of L
Zeph 3:13 wrong and utter no L, nor shall there be
Hag 1:4 houses, while this house L in ruins?
1:9 of my house that L in ruins, while you
Zech 10:2 and the diviners see L; the dreamers tell false
13:3 live, for you speak L in the name of
14:4 Mount of Olives which L before Jerusalem on the
Jn 8:44 When he L, he speaks according to his own
8:44 he is a liar and the father of L
Rom 7:8 from the law sin L dead.
7:21 to do right, evil L close at hand.
2Cor 3:15 is read a veil L over their minds;
Phil 3:13 I do, forgetting what L behind and straining forward
3:13 straining forward to what L ahead,
Tit 1:2 which God, who never L, promised ages ago
Rev 9:10 men for five months L in their tails.
21:16 The city L foursquare, its length the same as

LIFE (694)

Gen 1:30 has the breath of L, I have given every
2:7 nostrils the breath of L; and man became a
2:9 food, the tree of L also in the midst
3:14 you shall eat all the days of your L
3:17 the days of your L;
3:22 of the tree of L, and eat, and live
3:24 to guard the way to the tree of L
6:17 is the breath of L from under heaven; everything
7:11 hundredth year of Noah's L, in the second month,
7:15 flesh in which there was the breath of L
7:22 was the breath of L died.
9:4 eat flesh with its L, that is, its blood.
9:5 I will require the L of man.
12:13 you, and that my L may be spared on
19:17 said, "Flee for your L; do not look back
19:19 kindness in saving my L; but I cannot flee
19:20 little one?--and my L will be saved!"
23:1 the years of the L of Sarah.
25:7 the years of Abraham's L, a hundred and seventy-five
25:17 the years of the L of Ishmael, a hundred
26:35 Hittite; and they made L bitter for Isaac and
27:46 am weary of my L because of the Hittite
27:46 what good will my L be to me?"
32:30 face, and yet my L is preserved."
37:21 their hands, saying, "Let us not take his L
42:15 be tested: by the L of Pharaoh, you shall
42:16 or else, by the L of Pharaoh, surely you
44:30 us, then, as his L is bound up in
44:30 up in the lad's L,
44:32 my father all my L
45:5 for God sent me before you to preserve L
47:8 are the days of the years of your L
47:9 the years of my L, and they have not
47:9 the years of the L of my fathers in
47:28 the years of his L, were a hundred and
48:15 led me all my L long to this day,
Ex 4:19 who were seeking your L are dead."
6:16 the years of the L of Levi being a
6:18 the years of the L of Kohath being a
6:20 the years of the L of Amram being one
21:6 an awl; and he shall serve him for L
21:23 then you shall give L for life,
21:23 shall give life for L,
21:30 the redemption of his L whatever is laid upon
Lev 17:11 For the L of the flesh is in the
17:11 blood that makes atonement, by reason of the L
17:14 "For the L of every creature is the blood
17:14 any creature, for the L of every creature is
19:16 stand forth against the L of your neighbor: I
24:18 shall make it good, L for life.
24:18 a beast shall make it good, life for L
26:16 the eyes and cause L to pine away.
Num 22:30 have ridden all your L long to this day?
35:31 no ransom for the L of a murderer, who
Deut 4:9 the days of your L; make them known to
4:42 he might save his L:
6:2 the days of your L; and that your days
12:23 the blood is the L, and you shall not
12:23 shall not eat the L with the flesh.
16:3 the days of your L you may remember the
17:19 the days of his L, that he may learn
19:4 manslayer, who by fleeing there may save his L
19:5 cities and save his L;
19:21 pity; it shall be L for life, eye for
19:21 shall be life for L, eye for eye, tooth
24:6 would be taking a L in pledge.
28:66 a languishing soul; your L shall hang in doubt
28:66 in dread, and have no assurance of your L
30:15 before you this day L and good, death and
30:19 have set before you L and death, blessing and
30:19 and curse; therefore choose L, that you and your
30:20 him; for that means L to you and length
32:47 but it is your L, and thereby you shall
Josh 1:5 the days of your L; as I was with
2:14 said to her, "Our L for yours!
4:14 awe of Moses, all the days of his L
Judg 9:17 you, and risked his L, and rescued you from
12:3 me, I took my L in my hand, and
13:12 the boy's manner of L, and what is he
16:30 than those whom he had slain during his L
18:25 and you lose your L with the lives of
Ruth 4:15 you a restorer of L and a nourisher of
1Sam 1:11 the days of his L, and no razor shall
2:6 kills and brings to L; he brings down to
7:15 Samuel judged Israel all the days of his L
19:5 for he took his L in his hand and
19:11 do not save your L tonight, tomorrow you will
20:1 sin before your father, that he seeks my L
22:23 he that seeks my L seeks your life; with
22:23 my life seeks your L; with me you shall
23:15 because Saul had come out to seek his L
24:11 though you hunt my L to take it.
25:29 and to seek your L, the life of my
25:29 seek your life, the L of my lord shall
26:20 out to seek my L, like one who hunts
26:21 you harm, because my L was precious in your
26:24 Behold, as your L was precious this day in
26:24 sight, so may my L be precious in the
28:2 well, I will make you my bodyguard for L
28:9 a snare for my L to bring about my
28:21 I have taken my L in my hand, and
2Sam 1:9 me, and yet my L still lingers.'
1:23 In L and in death they were not divided;
4:8 enemy, who sought your L; the LORD has avenged
4:9 who has redeemed my L out of every adversity,
14:7 kill him for the L of his brother whom
14:14 not take away the L of him who devises
15:21 for death or for L, there also will your
16:11 own son seeks my L; how much more now
17:3 You seek the L of only one man, and
18:13 dealt treacherously against his L (and there is
19:5 this day saved your L, and the lives of
1Kgs 1:12 may save your own L and the life of
1:12 own life and the L of your son Solomon.
2:23 if this word does not cost Adonijah his L
3:11 asked for yourself long L or riches or the

L

3:11 or riches or the L of your enemies, but
4:21 and served Solomon all the days of his L
11:34 the days of his L, for the sake of
15:5 the days of his L, except in the matter
15:6 Rehoboam and Jeroboam all the days of his L
19:2 do not make your L as the life of
19:2 your life as the L of one of them
19:3 and went for his L, and came to Beer-sheba,
19:4 LORD, take away my L; for I am no
19:10 and they seek my L, to take it away."
19:14 and they seek my L, to take it away."
20:31 king of Israel; perhaps he will spare your L
20:39 he be missing, your L shall be for his
20:39 shall be for his L, or else you shall
20:42 to destruction, therefore your L shall go for his
20:42 shall go for his L, and your people for
2Kgs 1:13 pray you, let my L, and the life of
1:13 my life, and the L of these fifty servants
1:14 but now let my L be precious in your
4:31 but there was no sound or sign of L
8:1 he had restored to L, "Arise, and depart with
8:5 restored the dead to L, behold, the woman whose
8:5 he had restored to L appealed to the king
8:5 here is her son whom Elisha restored to L
10:24 into your hands to escape shall forfeit his L
20:6 And I will add fifteen years to your L
25:29 every day of his L he dined regularly at
2Chr 1:11 wealth, honor, or the L of those who hate
1:11 not even asked long L, but have asked wisdom
Ezra 6:10 and pray for the L of the king and
Tob 1:3 the days of my L, and I performed many
3:15 thee to take my L, command that respect be
4:3 the days of your L; do what is pleasing
4:5 the days of your L, and do not walk
5:19 For the L that is given to us by
12:9 will have fulness of L;
14:3 grown old and am about to depart this L
Jud 8:29 the beginning of your L all the people have
10:15 "You have saved your L by hurrying down to
12:18 my lord, because my L means more to me
13:20 not spare your own L when our nation was
16:22 the days of her L after Manasseh her husband
Esth 7:3 the king, let my L be given me at
7:7 stayed to beg his L from Queen Esther, for
13:5 a strange manner of L and laws, and is
16:12 our kingdom and our L,
Job 2:4 a man has he will give for his L
2:6 he is in your power; only spare his L
3:20 is in misery, and L to the bitter in
7:7 "Remember that my L is a breath; my eye
7:16 I loathe my L; I would not live for
9:21 blameless; I regard not myself; I loathe my L
10:1 "I loathe my L; I will give free utterance
10:12 Thou hast granted me L and steadfast love; and
10:20 the days of my L few?
11:17 And your L will be brighter than the noonday;
12:10 his hand is the L of every living thing
13:14 teeth, and put my L in my hand.
24:22 Yet God prolongs the L of the mighty by
24:22 power; they rise up when they despair of L
27:8 cuts him off, when God takes away his L
31:30 by asking for his L with a curse);
33:4 and the breath of the Almighty gives me L
33:18 from the Pit, his L from perishing by the
33:20 bones; so that his L loathes bread, and his
33:22 the Pit, and his L to those who bring
33:28 the Pit, and my L shall see the light.'
33:30 Pit, that he may see the light of L
36:14 in youth, and their L ends in shame.
Ps 6:4 O LORD, save my L; deliver me for the
7:5 let him trample my L to the ground, and
16:11 me the path of L; in thy presence there
17:13 Deliver my L from the wicked by thy sword,
17:14 men whose portion in L is of the world.
21:4 He asked L of thee; thou gavest it to
22:20 from the sword, my L from the power of
23:6 the days of my L; and I shall dwell
25:20 Oh guard my L, and deliver me; let me
26:9 with sinners, nor my L with bloodthirsty men,
27:1 the stronghold of my L; of whom shall I
27:4 the days of my L, to behold the beauty
30:3 Sheol, restored me to L from among those gone
31:10 For my L is spent with sorrow, and my
31:13 against me, as they plot to take my L
34:12 is there who desires L, and covets many days,
34:22 The LORD redeems the L of his servants; none
35:4 to shame and dishonor who seek after my L
35:7 without cause they dug a pit for my L
35:17 from their ravages, my L from the lions!
36:9 is the fountain of L; in thy light do
38:12 Those who seek my L lay their snares, those
39:4 know how fleeting my L is!
40:14 to snatch away my L; let them be turned
42:8 me, a prayer to the God of my L
49:7 the price of his L,
49:8 the ransom of his L is costly, and can
54:3 ruthless men seek my L; they do not set
54:4 helper; the Lord is the upholder of my L
56:6 have waited for my L,
56:13 may walk before God in the light of L
59:3 in wait for my L; fierce men band themselves
61:6 Prolong the L of the king; may his years
63:3 love is better than L, my lips will praise
63:9 seek to destroy my L shall go down into
64:1 my complaint; preserve my L from dread of the
70:2 put to shame and confusion who seek my L
71:10 who watch for my L consult together,
72:14 violence he redeems their L; and precious is their
74:19 do not forget the L of thy poor for
80:18 from thee; give us L, and we will call
86:2 Preserve my L, for I am godly; save thy
86:14 ruthless men seek my L, and they do not
88:3 of troubles, and my L draws near to Sheol.
89:47 what the measure of L is, for what vanity
90:10 The years of our L are threescore and ten,
91:16 With long L I will satisfy him, and show
94:21 band together against the L of the righteous, and
103:4 diseases, who redeems your L from the Pit, who
109:20 LORD, of those who speak evil against my L
116:4 LORD: "O LORD, I beseech thee, save my L
119:37 vanities; and give me L in thy ways.
119:40 for thy precepts; in thy righteousness give me L
119:50 in my affliction that thy promise gives me L
119:88 steadfast love spare my L, that I may keep
119:93 precepts; for by them thou hast given me L
119:107 sorely afflicted; give me L, O LORD, according to
119:109 I hold my L in my hand continually, but
119:149 love; O LORD, in thy justice preserve my L
119:154 redeem me; give me L according to thy promise!
119:156 O LORD; give me L according to thy justice.
119:159 Preserve my L according to thy steadfast love.
121:7 you from all evil; he will keep your L
128:5 prosperity of Jerusalem all the days of your L
133:3 has commanded the blessing, L for evermore.
138:7 thou dost preserve my L; thou dost stretch out
143:3 he has crushed my L to the ground; he
143:11 For thy name's sake, O LORD, preserve my L
Prov 1:19 it takes away the L of its possessors.
2:19 back nor do they regain the paths of L
3:2 days and years of L and abundant welfare will
3:16 Long L is in her right hand; in her
3:18 is a tree of L to those who lay
3:22 and they will be L for your soul and
4:11 the years of your L may be many.
4:14 let go; guard her, for she is your L
4:23 For they are L to him who finds them,
4:24 vigilance; for from it flow the springs of L
5:6 to the path of L; her ways wander, and
5:11 the end of your L you groan, when your
6:23 are the way of L,
6:26 bread, but an adulteress stalks a man's very L
7:23 not know that it will cost him his L
8:35 who finds me finds L and obtains favor from
9:11 multiplied, and years will be added to your L
10:11 is a fountain of L, but the mouth of
10:16 the righteous leads to L, the gain of the
10:17 on the path to L, but he who rejects
10:27 of the LORD prolongs L, but the years of
11:30 is a tree of L, but lawlessness takes away
12:10 has regard for the L of his beast, but
12:28 path of righteousness is L, but the way of
13:3 his mouth preserves his L; he who opens wide
13:8 ransom of a man's L is his wealth, but
13:12 but a desire fulfilled is a tree of L
13:14 is a fountain of L, that one may avoid
14:27 is a fountain of L, that one may avoid
14:30 A tranquil mind gives L to the flesh, but
15:4 is a tree of L, but perverseness in it
15:24 path leads upward to L, that he may avoid
16:15 king's face there is L, and his favor is
16:17 evil; he who guards his way preserves his L
16:22 is a fountain of L to him who has

16:31 of glory; it is gained in a righteous L
18:21 Death and L are in the power of the
19:16 the commandment keeps his L; he who despises the
19:23 the LORD leads to L; and he who has
20:2 he who provokes him to anger forfeits his L
21:21 and kindness will find L and honor.
22:4 of the LORD is riches and honor and L
22:23 cause and despoil of L those who despoil them.
23:14 you will save his L from Sheol.
29:10 who is blameless, and the wicked seek his L
29:24 thief hates his own L; he hears the curse,
31:12 and not harm, all the days of her L
Eccl 2:3 under heaven during the few days of their L
2:17 So I hated L, because what is done under
5:18 few days of his L which God has given
5:20 the days of his L because God keeps him
6:3 he does not enjoy L's good things, and also
6:12 days of his vain L, which he passes like
7:12 that wisdom preserves the L of him who has
7:15 In my vain L I have seen everything; there
7:15 man who prolongs his L in his evil-doing.
8:12 times and prolongs his L, yet I know that
8:15 through the days of L which God gives him
9:9 Enjoy L with the wife whom you love, all
9:9 days of your vain L which he has given
9:9 is your portion in L and in your toil
10:19 laughter, and wine gladdens L, and money answers
11:10 and the dawn of L are vanity.
Wis 1:12 the error of your L, nor bring on destruction
2:1 and sorrowful is our L, and there is no
2:4 remember our works; our L will pass away like
2:15 because his manner of L is unlike that of
2:17 the end of his L;
4:9 men, and a blameless L is ripe old age.
5:4 We thought that his L was madness and that
7:6 mankind one entrance into L, and a common
8:5 a desirable possession in L, what is richer than
8:7 and courage; nothing in L is more profitable for
8:16 has no bitterness, and L with her has no
12:23 who in folly of L lived unrighteously thou didst
13:11 useful vessel that serves L's needs,
13:18 that is weak; for L he prays to a
14:12 was the corruption of L,
15:9 die or that his L is brief, but he
15:10 than dirt, and his L is of less worth
15:12 an idle game, and L a festival held for
15:17 worships, since he has L, but they never have.
16:13 thou hast power over L and death; thou dost
Sir 1:10 heart, and gives gladness and joy and long L
1:18 root of wisdom, and her branches are long L
2:3 may be honored at the end of your L
3:6 father will have long L, and whoever obeys the
4:12 Whoever loves her loves L, and those who seek
6:16 is an elixir of L; and those who fear
7:36 the end of your L, and then you will
9:13 no misstep, lest he rob you of your L
10:9 for even in L his bowels decay.
10:28 will honor the man that dishonors his own L
11:14 Good things and bad, L and death, poverty and
11:25 close of a man's L his deeds will be
15:17 Before a man are L and death, and whichever
17:9 them, and allotted to them the law of L
20:21 man may lose his L through shame, or lose
22:9 attained rest; but the L of the fool is
22:10 or an ungodly man it lasts all his L
23:1 and Ruler of my L, do not abandon me
23:4 and God of my L, do not give me
25:2 greatly offended at their L: a beggar who is
28:6 the end of your L, and cease from enmity,
29:15 he has given his L for you.
29:21 The essentials for L are water and bread and
29:22 Better is the L of a poor man under
29:24 It is a miserable L to go from house
30:17 better than a miserable L, and eternal rest than
30:22 of heart is the L of man, and the
30:24 Jealousy and anger shorten L, and anxiety brings on
31:27 Wine is like L to men, if you drink
31:27 What is L to a man who is without
33:14 opposite of evil, and L the opposite of death;
33:23 the days of your L, in the hour of
34:17 eyes; he grants healing, L, and blessing.
34:21 the needy is the L of the poor; whoever
37:18 appear, good and evil, L and death; and it
37:25 The L of a man is numbered by days,
37:31 who is careful to avoid it prolongs his L
38:14 and in healing, for the sake of preserving L
38:19 sorrow continues, and the L of the poor man
38:20 sorrow; drive it away, remembering the end of L
39:26 the needs of man's L are water and fire
40:18 L is sweet for the self-reliant and the worker,
40:28 do not lead the L of a beggar; it
40:29 of another, his existence cannot be considered as L
41:3 and the end of L; this is the decree
41:4 Whether L is for ten or a hundred or
41:13 days of a good L are numbered, but a
45:5 face, the law of L and knowledge, to teach
48:14 As in his L he did wonders, so in
48:23 and he lengthened the L of the king.
50:1 Onias, who in his L repaired the house, and
51:3 those who sought my L, from the many afflictions
51:6 to death, and my L was very near to
Is 4:3 has been recorded for L in Jerusalem,
38:5 behold, I will add fifteen years to your L
38:12 have rolled up my L; he cuts me off
38:16 all these is the L of my spirit.
38:17 hast held back my L from the pit of
38:20 the days of our L, at the house of
43:4 return for you, peoples in exchange for your L
57:10 hopeless"; you found new L for your strength, and
57:16 spirit, and I have made the breath of L
Jer 4:10 you'; whereas the sword has reached their very L
4:30 Your lovers despise you; they seek your L
8:3 shall be preferred to L by all the remnant
11:21 Anathoth, who seek your L, and say, "Do not
18:20 Yet they have dug a pit for my L
19:7 by the hand of those who seek their L
19:9 those who seek their L afflict them.'
20:13 he has delivered the L of the needy from
21:8 you the way of L and the way of
21:9 and shall have his L as a prize of
22:25 those who seek your L, into the hand of
31:12 and the herd; their L shall be like a
38:2 he shall have his L as a prize of
38:16 the hand of these men who seek your L
38:17 of Babylon, then your L shall be spared, and
38:20 with you, and your L shall be spared.
39:18 you shall have your L as a prize of
40:14 Ishmael the son of Nethaniah to take your L
40:15 should he take your L, so that all the
44:30 those who seek his L, as I gave Zedekiah
44:30 Babylon, who was his enemy and sought his L
45:5 will give you your L as a prize of
46:26 those who seek their L, into the hand of
49:37 those who seek their L; I will bring evil
51:6 midst of Babylon, let every man save his L
51:13 the thread of your L is cut.
51:45 every man save his L from the fierce anger
52:33 every day of his L he dined regularly at
Lam 2:12 the city, as their L is poured out on
3:58 my cause, O Lord, thou hast redeemed my L
Bar 1:11 and pray for the L of Nebuchadnezzar king of
1:11 Babylon, and for the L of Belshazzar his son,
3:9 Hear the commandments of L, O Israel; give ear,
3:14 length of days, and L, where there is light
Ezek 3:18 order to save his L, that wicked man shall
3:19 his iniquity; but you will have saved your L
3:21 took warning; and you will have saved your L
7:13 because of his iniquity, none can maintain his L
13:22 way to save his L;
18:27 is lawful and right, he shall save his L
20:25 they could not have L;
32:10 one for his own L, on the day of
33:5 had taken warning, he would have saved his L
33:9 his iniquity, but you will have saved your L
33:15 in the statutes of L, committing no iniquity; he
Dan 12:2 awake, some to everlasting L, and some to shame
Amos 2:14 the mighty save his L;
2:15 the horse save his L;
Jon 1:14 perish for this man's L, and lay not on
2:6 didst bring up my L from the Pit, O
4:3 O LORD, take my L from me, I beseech
Hab 2:10 cutting off many peoples; you have forfeited your L
Mal 2:5 was a covenant of L and peace, and I
2:15 made and sustained for us the spirit of L
1Mac 3:12 used it in battle the rest of his L
6:44 So he gave his L to save his people
13:5 me to spare my L in any time of
2Mac 3:31 High and to grant L to one who was
3:33 his sake the Lord has granted you your L
3:35 the Savior of his L, and having bidden Onias
4:10 his countrymen over to the Greek way of L
6:19 with honor rather than L with pollution, went up

1Thes	2:12	you to lead a L worthy of God, who
1Tim	1:16	who were to believe in him for eternal L
	2:2	a quiet and peaceable L, godly and respectful in
	4:8	promise for the present L and also for the
	4:8	and also for the L to come.
	6:12	hold of the eternal L to which you were
	6:13	of God who gives L to all things, and
	6:19	take hold of the L which is life indeed.
	6:19	the life which is L indeed.
2Tim	1:1	the promise of the L which is in Christ
	1:10	abolished death and brought L and immortality to
	3:10	conduct, my aim in L, my faith, my patience,
	3:12	to live a godly L in Christ Jesus will
Tit	1:2	in hope of eternal L which God, who never
	3:7	grace and become heirs in hope of eternal L
Heb	7:3	days nor end of L, but resembling the Son
	7:16	descent but by the power of an indestructible L
	11:22	the end of his L, made mention of the
	11:35	that they might rise again to a better L
	13:5	Keep your L free from love of money, and
	13:7	the outcome of their L, and imitate their faith.
Jas	1:11	receive the crown of L which God has promised
	3:13	By his good L let him show his works
	4:14	What is your L
1Pet	3:7	of the grace of L, in order that your
	3:10	"He that would love L and see good days,
2Pet	1:3	things that pertain to L and godliness, through the
1Jn	1:1	concerning the word of L –
	1:2	of life– the L was made manifest, and
	1:2	to you the eternal L which was with the
	2:16	and the pride of L, is not of the
	2:25	this is what he has promised us, eternal L
	3:14	out of death into L, because we love the
	3:15	no murderer has eternal L abiding in him.
	3:16	he laid down his L for us; and we
	5:11	God gave us eternal L, and this life is
	5:11	eternal life, and this L is in his Son.
	5:12	has the Son has L; he who has not
	5:12	has not the Son of God has not L
	5:13	that you may know that you have eternal L
	5:16	God will give him L for those whose sin
	5:20	This is the true God and eternal L
3Jn	1:3	the truth of your L, as indeed you do
Jude	1:21	mercy of our Lord Jesus Christ unto eternal L
Rev	2:7	of the tree of L, which is in the
	2:8	and the last, who died and came to L
	2:10	and I will give you the crown of L
	3:5	of the book of L; I will confess his
	11:11	days a breath of L from God entered them,
	13:8	in the book of L of the Lamb that
	17:8	in the book of L from the foundation of
	20:4	They came to L, and reigned with Christ a
	20:5	did not come to L until the thousand years
	20:12	book was opened, which is the book of L
	20:15	in the book of L, he was thrown into
	21:6	of the water of L without payment.
	21:27	who are written in the Lamb's book of L
	22:1	of the water of L, bright as crystal, flowing
	22:2	river, the tree of L with its twelve kinds
	22:14	to the tree of L and that they may
	22:17	take the water of L without price.
	22:19	in the tree of L and in the holy

LIFE-GIVING

1Cor	15:45	last Adam became a L spirit.

LIFEBLOOD (5)

Gen	9:5	For your L I will surely require a reckoning;
1Chr	11:19	Shall I drink the L of these men?
Is	63:3	in my wrath; their L is sprinkled upon my
	63:6	I poured out their L on the earth."
Jer	2:34	skirts is found the L of guiltless poor; you

LIFELESS (4)

Wis	13:17	ashamed to address a L thing.
	14:29	because they trust in L idols they swear wicked
	15:5	that they desire the L form of a dead
1Cor	14:7	If even L instruments, such as the flute or

LIFELIKE

Sir	38:27	heart on painting a L image, and he is

LIFELONG

Heb	2:15	death were subject to L bondage.

LIFETIME (5)

Num	3:4	as priests in the L of Aaron their father.
2Sam	18:18	Now Absalom in his L had taken and set
Ps	30:5	a moment, and his favor is for a L
	39:5	few handbreadths, and my L is as nothing in
Lk	16:25	that you in your L received your good things,

LIFT (99)

Gen	13:14	had separated from him, L up your eyes, and
	21:18	Arise, L up the lad, and hold him fast
	31:12	am!' And he said, L up your eyes and
	40:13	three days Pharaoh will L up your head and
	40:19	three days Pharaoh will L up your head–from
	41:44	consent no man shall L up hand or foot
Ex	14:16	L up your rod, and stretch out your hand
	23:5	shall help him to L it up.
Num	6:26	to you: The LORD L up his countenance upon
Deut	3:27	top of Pisgah, and L up your eyes westward
	4:19	And beware lest you L up your eyes to
	22:4	shall help him to L them up again.
	27:5	of stones; you shall L up no iron tool
	32:40	For I L up my hand to heaven, and
2Sam	2:22	How then could I L up my face to
2Kgs	19:4	God has heard; therefore L up your prayer for
Ezra	9:6	ashamed and blush to L my face to thee,
Job	10:15	am righteous, I cannot L up my head, for
	10:16	And if I L myself up, thou dost hunt
	11:15	Surely then you will L up your face without
	22:26	in the Almighty, and L up your face to
	38:34	"Can you L up your voice to the clouds,
Ps	4:6	L up the light of thy countenance upon us,
	7:6	LORD, in thy anger, L thyself up against the
	10:12	O LORD; O God, L up thy hand; forget
	24:4	heart, who does not L up his soul to
	24:7	[Selah] L up your heads, O gates!
	24:9	L up your heads, O gates!
	25:1	thee, O LORD, I L up my soul.
	28:2	for help, as I L up my hands toward
	63:4	I live; I will L up my hands and
	68:4	praises to his name; L up a song to
	75:4	the wicked, "Do not L up your horn;
	75:5	your horn; do not L up your horn on
	86:4	O Lord, do I L up my soul.
	93:3	their voice, the floods L up their roaring.
	110:7	way; therefore he will L up his head.
	116:13	I will L up the cup of salvation and
	121:1	I L up my eyes to the hills.
	123:1	To thee I L up my eyes, O thou
	134:2	L up your hands to the holy place, and
	139:20	maliciously defy thee, who L themselves up against
	140:9	Those who surround me L up their head, let
	143:8	for to thee I L up my soul.
Prov	30:13	lofty are their eyes, how high their eyelids L
Eccl	4:10	they fall, one will L up his fellow; but
	4:10	has not another to L him up.
Sir	11:1	a humble man will L up his head, and
	13:2	Do not L a weight beyond your strength, nor
	36:3	L up thy hand against foreign nations and let
	40:26	Riches and strength L up the heart, but the
Is	2:4	hooks; nation shall not L up sword against nation,
	10:15	if a staff should L him who is not
	10:24	with the rod and L up their staff against
	10:26	sea, and he will L it as he did
	24:14	They L up their voices, they sing for joy;
	33:10	LORD, "now I will L myself up; now I
	37:4	God has heard; therefore L up your prayer for
	40:9	herald of good tidings; L up your voice with
	40:9	herald of good tidings, L it up, fear not;
	40:26	L up your eyes on high and see: who
	42:2	will not cry or L up his voice, or
	42:11	desert and its cities L up their voice, the
	46:7	They L it upon their shoulders, they carry it,
	49:18	L up your eyes round about and see; they
	49:22	GOD: "Behold, I will L up my hand to
	51:6	L up your eyes to the heavens, and look
	52:8	Hark, your watchmen L up their voice, together they
	58:1	"Cry aloud, spare not, L up your voice like
	60:4	L up your eyes round about, and see; they
	62:10	clear it of stones, L up an ensign over
Jer	3:2	L up your eyes to the bare heights, and
	7:16	for this people, or L up cry or prayer
	11:14	for this people, or L up a cry or
	13:20	L up your eyes and see those who come
	13:26	I myself will L up your skirts over your
	22:20	and cry out, and L up your voice in
	23:39	behold, I will surely L you up and cast

38:10 you from here, and L Jeremiah the prophet out
Lam 2:19 L your hands to him for the lives of
3:41 Let us L up our hearts and hands to
Ezek 8:5 me, "Son of man, L up your eyes now
12:6 their sight you shall L the baggage upon your
12:12 is among them shall L his baggage upon his
17:14 be humble and not L itself up, and that
18:6 upon the mountains or L up his eyes to
18:15 upon the mountains or L up his eyes to
21:22 with a cry, to L up the voice with
23:27 that you shall not L up your eyes to
33:25 with the blood, and L up your eyes to
Dan 11:14 your own people shall L themselves up in order
Mic 4:3 hooks; nation shall not L up sword against nation,
Nah 3:5 of hosts, and will L up your skirts over
Zech 5:5 and said to me, L your eyes, and see
12:3 the peoples; all who L it shall grievously hurt
Mt 12:11 hold of it and L it out?
Lk 18:13 far-off, would not even L up his eyes to
Jn 4:35 I tell you, L up your eyes, and see
Heb 12:12 Therefore L your drooping hands and strengthen

LIFTED (127)

Gen 13:10 And Lot L up his eyes, and saw that
18:2 He L up his eyes and looked, and behold,
21:16 against him, the child L up his voice and
22:4 the third day Abraham L up his eyes and
22:13 And Abraham L up his eyes and looked, and
24:63 the evening; and he L up his eyes and
24:64 And Rebekah L up her eyes, and when she
27:38 And Esau L up his voice and wept.
31:10 of the flock I L up my eyes, and
33:1 And Jacob L up his eyes and looked, and
37:28 drew Joseph up and L him out of the
39:15 he heard that I L up my voice and
39:18 as soon as I L up my voice and
40:20 all his servants, and L up the head of
43:29 And he L up his eyes, and saw his
Ex 7:20 of his servants, he L up the rod and
10:19 strong west wind, which L the locusts and drove
14:10 the people of Israel L up their eyes, and
Lev 9:22 Then Aaron L up his hands toward the people
Num 20:11 And Moses L up his hand and struck the
24:2 And Balaam L up his eyes, and saw Israel
Deut 8:14 then your heart be L up, and you forget
17:20 heart may not be L up above his brethren,
Josh 4:18 the priests' feet were L up on dry ground,
5:13 was by Jericho, he L up his eyes and
8:31 which no man has L an iron tool"; and
Judg 2:4 of Israel, the people L up their voices and
8:28 of Israel, and they L up their heads no
19:17 And he L up his eyes, and saw the
21:2 before God, and they L up their voices and
Ruth 1:9 kissed them, and they L up their voices and
1:14 Then they L up their voices and wept again;
1Sam 6:13 valley; and when they L up their eyes and
24:16 And Saul L up his voice and wept.
2Sam 3:32 Hebron; and the king L up his voice and
13:34 who kept the watch L up his eyes, and
13:36 king's sons came, and L up their voice and
18:24 wall, and when he L up his eyes and
20:21 son of Bichri, has L up his hand against
1Kgs 11:26 Zeruah, a widow, also L up his hand against
11:27 the reason why he L up his hand against
2Kgs 4:20 And when he had L him, and brought him
9:32 And he L up his face to the window,
14:10 and your heart has L you up.
19:22 your voice and haughtily L your eyes?
1Chr 21:16 And David L his eyes and saw the angel
2Chr 25:19 and your heart has L you up in boastfulness.
Jud 11:2 I would never have L my spear against them;
16:11 the enemy trembled; they L up their voices, and
Job 5:11 those who mourn are L to safety.
Ps 24:7 and be L up, O ancient doors!
24:9 and be L up, O ancient doors!
27:6 my head shall be L up above my enemies
41:9 of my bread, has L his heel against me.
93:3 The floods have L up, O LORD, the floods
93:3 LORD, the floods have L up their voice, the
107:25 the stormy wind, which L up the waves of
131:1 my heart is not L up, my eyes are
Sir 46:2 he was when he L his hands and stretched
46:20 king his death, and L up his voice out
47:4 the people, when he L his hand with a
48:18 sent the Rabshakeh; he L up his hand against
50:20 Simon came down, and L up his hands over
Is 2:12 against all that is L up and high;
2:13 of Lebanon, lofty and L up; and against all
6:1 a throne, high and L up; and his train
26:11 LORD, thy hand is L up, but they see
37:23 your voice and haughtily L your eyes?
40:4 Every valley shall be L up, and every mountain
52:13 shall be exalted and L up, and shall be
63:9 he redeemed them; he L them up and carried
Jer 12:8 the forest, she has L up her voice against
13:22 that your skirts are L up, and you suffer
38:13 up with ropes and L him out of the
51:9 heaven and has been L up even to the
52:31 that he became king, L up the head of
Ezek 3:12 Then the Spirit L me up, and as the
3:14 The Spirit L me up and took me away,
8:3 head; and the Spirit L me up between earth
8:5 So I L up my eyes toward the north,
10:16 and when the cherubim L up their wings to
10:19 And the cherubim L up their wings and mounted
11:1 The Spirit L me up, and brought me to
11:22 Then the cherubim L up their wings, with the
11:24 And the Spirit L me up and brought me
43:5 facing east, the Spirit L me up, and brought
Dan 4:34 the days I, Nebuchadnezzar, L my eyes to heaven,
5:20 when his heart was L up and his spirit
5:23 this, but you have L up yourself against the
7:4 off, and it was L up from the ground
10:5 is, the Tigris, I L up my eyes and
14:36 of his head, and L him by his hair
Hos 13:6 and their heart was L up; therefore they forgot
Mic 5:9 Your hand shall be L up over your adversaries,
Hab 3:10 forth its voice, it L its hands on high.
Zech 1:18 And I L my eyes and saw, and behold,
1:21 of the nations who L up their horns against
2:1 And I L my eyes and saw, and behold,
5:1 Again I L my eyes and saw, and behold,
5:7 the leaden cover was L, and there was a
5:9 Then I L my eyes and saw, and behold,
5:9 a stork, and they L up the ephah between
6:1 And again I L my eyes and saw, and
1Mac 1:3 and his heart was L up.
16:13 His heart was L up; he determined to get
Mt 17:8 And when they L up their eyes, they saw
Mk 1:31 by the hand and L her up, and the
9:27 by the hand and L him up, and he
Lk 6:20 And he L up his eyes on his disciples,
16:23 being in torment, he L up his eyes, and
17:13 at a distance and L up their voices and
Jn 3:14 And as Moses L up the serpent in the
3:14 Son of man be L up,
8:28 said, "When you have L up the Son of
11:41 And Jesus L up his eyes and said, "Father,
12:32 I, when I am L up from the earth,
12:34 of man must be L up?
13:18 ate my bread has L his heel against me.'
17:1 spoken these words, he L up his eyes to
Acts 1:9 looking on, he was L up, and a cloud
2:14 standing with the eleven, L up his voice and
4:24 they heard it, they L their voices together to
9:41 her his hand and L her up.
10:26 But Peter L him up, saying, "Stand up; I
14:11 Paul had done, they L up their voices, saying
22:22 to him; then they L up their voices and
Rev 10:5 on sea and land L up his right hand

LIFTER

Ps 3:3 my glory, and the L of my head.

LIFTEST (2)

Job 30:22 Thou L me up on the wind, thou makest
Ps 9:13 me, O thou who L me up from the

LIFTING (9)

Neh 8:6 L up their hands; and they bowed their heads
Esth 15:7 L his face, flushed with splendor, he looked at
Ps 75:6 from the wilderness comes L up;
75:7 putting down one and L up another.
141:2 before thee, and the L up of my hands
Is 33:3 peoples flee, at the L up of thyself nations
Lk 24:50 far as Bethany, and L up his hands he
Jn 6:5 L up his eyes, then, and seeing that a
1Tim 2:8 the men should pray, L holy hands without anger

LIFTS (11)

Num 23:24 as a lion it L itself; it does not
1Sam 2:8 from the dust; he L the needy from the

Job 27:21 The east wind L him up and he is
Ps 113:7 from the dust, and L the needy from the
146:8 The LORD L up those who are bowed down;
147:6 The LORD L up the downtrodden, he casts the
Sir 11:12 for his good; he L him out of his
34:17 He L up the soul and gives light to
38:3 skill of the physician L up his head, and
Is 10:15 should wield him who L it, or as if
Ezek 18:12 not restore the pledge, L up his eyes to

LIGAMENTS

Col 2:19 through its joints and L, grows with a growth

LIGHT (287)

Gen 1:3 said, "Let there be L; and there was light.
1:3 said, "Let there be light"; and there was L
1:4 God saw that the L was good; and God
1:4 and God separated the L from the darkness.
1:5 God called the L Day, and the darkness he
1:15 the heavens to give L upon the earth." And
1:16 great lights, the greater L to rule the day,
1:16 day, and the lesser L to rule the night;
1:17 the heavens to give L upon the earth,
1:18 and to separate the L from the darkness.
44:3 as the morning was L, the men were sent
Ex 10:23 people of Israel had L where they dwelt.
13:21 fire to give them L, that they might travel
25:37 so as to give L upon the space in
27:20 olive oil for the L, that a lamp may
35:8 wood, oil for the L, spices for the anointing
35:14 lampstand also for the L, with its utensils and
35:14 the oil for the L;
35:28 and oil for the L, and for the anointing
39:37 the oil for the L;
Lev 24:2 the lamp, that a L may be kept burning
Num 4:9 the lampstand for the L, with its lamps, its
4:16 the oil for the L, the fragrant incense, the
8:2 seven lamps shall give L in front of the
8:3 its lamps to give L in front of the
Judg 16:2 us wait till the L of the morning; then
19:26 house where her master was, till it was L
1Sam 14:36 them until the morning L; let us not leave
25:36 told him nothing at all until the morning L
29:10 morning, and depart as soon as you have L
2Sam 17:12 found, and we shall L upon him as the
23:4 them like the morning L, like the sun shining
1Kgs 16:31 it had been a L thing for him to
2Kgs 3:18 beasts.' This is a L thing in the sight
7:9 wait until the morning L, punishment will overtake
Neh 9:12 in the night to L for them the way
Tob 10:5 you who are the L of my eyes?"
14:10 he brought him from L into darkness, and with
Jud 13:13 kindled a fire for L, and gathered around them.
Esth 8:16 The Jews had L and gladness and joy and
10:6 river, and there was L and the sun and
11:11 river, with abundant water; L came, and the sun
Job 3:4 not seek it, nor L shine upon it.
3:9 let it hope for L, but have none, nor
3:16 untimely birth, as infants that never see the L
3:20 "Why is L given to him that is in
3:23 Why is L given to a man whose way
10:22 gloom and chaos, where L is as darkness."
12:22 out of darkness, and brings deep darkness to L
12:25 in the dark without L; and he makes them
17:12 night into day; 'The L they say, 'is near
18:5 "Yea, the L of the wicked is put out,
18:6 The L is dark in his tent, and his
18:18 He is thrust from L into darkness, and driven
22:11 terror overwhelms you; your L is darkened, so that
22:28 established for you, and L will shine on your
24:13 who rebel against the L, who are not acquainted
24:16 shut themselves up; they do not know the L
25:3 Upon whom does his L not arise?
26:10 at the boundary between L and darkness.
28:11 thing that is hid he brings forth to L
29:3 head, and by his L I walked through darkness;
29:24 no confidence; and the L of my countenance they
30:26 when I waited for L, darkness came.
33:28 life shall see the L
33:30 he may see the L of life.
37:21 cannot look on the L when it is bright
38:15 From the wicked their L is withheld, and their
38:19 to the dwelling of L, and where is the
38:24 the place where the L is distributed, or where
41:18 His sneezings flash forth L, and his eyes are
Ps 4:6 Lift up the L of thy countenance upon us,
18:28 Yea, thou dost L my lamp; the LORD my
27:1 The LORD is my L and my salvation; whom
36:9 of life; in thy L do we see light.
36:9 of life; in thy light do we see L
37:6 your vindication as the L, and your right as
38:10 fails me; and the L of my eyes--it
43:3 Oh send out thy L and thy truth; let
44:3 thy arm, and the L of thy countenance; for
49:19 his fathers, who will never more see the L
56:13 before God in the L of life.
78:14 cloud, and all the night with a fiery L
89:15 O LORD, in the L of thy countenance,
90:8 secret sins in the L of thy countenance.
97:11 L dawns for the righteous, and joy for the
104:2 who coverest thyself with L as with a garment,
105:39 and fire to give L by night.
112:4 L rises in the darkness for the upright; the
118:27 LORD is God, and he has given us L
119:105 my feet and a L to my path.
119:130 of thy words gives L; it imparts understanding to
139:11 cover me, and the L about me be night,"
139:12 for darkness is as L with thee.
Prov 4:19 righteous is like the L of dawn, which shines
6:23 and the teaching a L, and the reproofs of
13:9 The L of the righteous rejoices, but the lamp
15:30 The L of the eyes rejoices the heart, and
16:15 In the L of a king's face there is
23:5 When your eyes L upon it, it is gone;
29:13 together; the LORD gives L to the eyes of
Eccl 2:13 wisdom excels folly as L excels darkness.
11:7 L is sweet, and it is pleasant for the
12:2 the sun and the L and the moon and
Wis 5:1 and those who make L of his labors.
5:6 of truth, and the L of righteousness did not
5:11 passage is found; the L air, lashed by the
5:14 wind, and like a L hoarfrost driven away by
7:10 have her rather than L, because her radiance never
7:26 a reflection of eternal L, a spotless mirror of
7:29 Compared with the L she is found to be
12:26 heeded the warning of L rebukes will experience the
16:28 the dawning of the L;
17:5 was able to give L, nor did the brilliant
17:20 was illumined with brilliant L, and was engaged in
18:1 for thy holy ones there was very great L
18:4 to be deprived of L and imprisoned in darkness,
18:4 through whom the imperishable L of the law was
Sir 17:26 Yet its L fails.
22:9 for he lacks the L; and weep for the
24:25 instruction shine forth like L, like the Gihon at
32:16 judgments, and like a L they will kindle righteous
34:17 the soul and gives L to the eyes; he
42:16 on everything with its L, and the work of
43:7 for feast days, a L that wanes when it
50:29 all things, for the L of the Lord is
Is 2:5 us walk in the L of the LORD.
5:20 who put darkness for L and light for darkness,
5:20 darkness for light and L for darkness, who put
5:30 and distress; and the L is darkened by its
9:2 have seen a great L; those who dwelt in
9:2 darkness, on them has L shined.
9:8 Jacob, and it will L upon Israel;
10:17 The L of Israel will become a fire, and
13:10 will not give their L; the sun will be
13:10 rising and the moon will not shed its L
26:19 is a dew of L, and on the land
30:26 Moreover the L of the moon will be as
30:26 will be as the L of the sun, and
30:26 the sun, and the L of the sun will
30:26 be sevenfold, as the L of seven days, in
42:6 to the people, a L to the nations,
42:16 darkness before them into L, the rough places into
45:7 I form L and create darkness, I make weal
49:6 says: "It is too L a thing that you
49:6 give you as a L to the nations, that
50:10 darkness and has no L, yet trusts in the
50:11 Walk by the L of your fire, and by
51:4 my justice for a L to the peoples.
58:8 Then shall your L break forth like the dawn,
58:10 afflicted, then shall your L rise in the darkness
59:9 us; we look for L, and behold, darkness, and
60:1 Arise, shine; for your L has come, and the
60:3 shall come to your L, and kings to the
60:19 be no more your L by day, nor for
60:19 shall the moon give L to you by night;
60:19 will be your everlasting L, and your God will
60:20 will be your everlasting L, and your days of

Jer 3:9 Because harlotry was so L to her, she polluted
4:23 and to the heavens, and they had no L
13:16 while you look for L he turns it into
25:10 the millstones and the L of the lamp.
31:35 gives the sun for L by day and the
31:35 and the stars for L by night, who stirs
Lam 3:2 into darkness without any L;
Bar 1:12 and he will give L to our eyes, and
3:14 life, where there is L for the eyes, and
3:20 men have seen the L of day, and have
3:33 who sends forth the L, and it goes, called
4:2 take her; walk toward the shining of her L
5:9 with joy, in the L of his glory, with
6:19 They L lamps, even more than they light for
6:19 even more than they L for themselves, though their
6:22 Bats, swallows, and birds L on their bodies and
6:67 the sun or give L like the moon.
Ezek 32:7 cloud, and the moon shall not give its L
Dan 2:22 the darkness, and the L dwells with him.
3:71 Bless the Lord, L and darkness, sing praise to
5:11 days of your father L and understanding and wisdom,
5:14 in you, and that L and understanding and excellent
Hos 6:5 mouth, and my judgment goes forth as the L
Amos 5:18 is darkness, and not L;
5:20 LORD darkness, and not L, and gloom with no
Mic 7:8 LORD will be a L to me.
7:9 me forth to the L; I shall behold his
Hab 3:4 brightness was like the L, rays flashed from his
3:11 their habitation at the L of thine arrows as
Zech 14:7 night, for at evening time there shall be L
1Mac 1:21 the lampstand for the L, and all its utensils.
4:50 lampstand, and these gave L in the temple.
2Mac 1:32 up; but when the L from the altar shone
2:26 abbreviating, it is no L matter but calls for
4:17 For it is no L thing to show irreverence
12:9 the glow of the L was seen in Jerusalem,
Mt 4:16 have seen a great L, and for those who
4:16 and shadow of death L has dawned."
5:14 "You are the L of the world.
5:15 Nor do men L a lamp and put it
5:15 stand, and it gives L to all in the
5:16 Let your L so shine before men, that they
6:22 will be full of L;
6:23 If then the L in you is darkness, how
10:27 dark, utter in the L; and what you hear
11:30 my yoke is easy, and my burden is L
17:2 the sun, and his garments became white as L
22:5 feast.' But they made L of it and went
24:29 will not give its L, and the stars will
Mk 4:22 nor is anything secret, except to come to L
13:24 will not give its L,
Lk 1:79 on high to give L to those who sit
2:32 of all peoples, a L for revelation to the
8:16 stand, that those who enter may see the L
8:17 that shall not be known and come to L
11:33 stand, that those who enter may see the L
11:34 body is full of L; but when it is
11:35 be careful lest the L in you be darkness.
11:36 body is full of L, having no part dark,
11:36 when a lamp with its rays gives you L
12:3 be heard in the L, and what you have
12:48 beating, shall receive a L beating.
15:8 one coin, does not L a lamp and sweep
16:8 with their own generation than the sons of L
22:54 he sat in the L and gazing at him,
23:44 hour, while the sun's L failed; and the curtain
Jn 1:4 the life was the L of men.
1:5 The L shines in the darkness, and the darkness
1:7 bear witness to the L, that all might believe
1:8 He was not the L, but came to bear
1:8 light, but came to bear witness to the L
1:9 The true L that enlightens every man was coming
3:19 the judgment, that the L has come into the
3:19 loved darkness rather than L, because their deeds
3:20 does evil hates the L, and does not come
3:20 not come to the L, lest his deeds should
3:21 true comes to the L, that it may be
5:34 willing to rejoice for a while in his L
8:12 saying, "I am the L of the world; he
8:12 but will have the L of life."
9:5 world, I am the L of the world."
11:9 because he sees the L of this world.
11:10 he stumbles, because the L is not in him."
12:35 said to them, "The L is with you for
12:35 while you have the L, lest the darkness overtake
12:36 While you have the L, believe in the light,
12:36 light, believe in the L, that you may become
12:36 the light, that you may become sons of L
12:46 I have come as L into the world, that
Acts 9:3 Damascus, and suddenly a L from heaven flashed
12:7 Lord appeared, and a L shone in the cell;
13:47 you to be a L for the Gentiles, that
22:6 about noon a great L from heaven suddenly shone
22:9 with me saw the L but did not hear
22:11 the brightness of that L, I was led by
26:13 on the way a L from heaven, brighter than
26:18 turn from darkness to L and from the power
26:23 dead, he would proclaim L both to the people
Rom 2:19 to the blind, a L to those who are
13:12 on the armor of L;
1Cor 4:5 who will bring to L the things now hidden
2Cor 4:4 them from seeing the L of the gospel of
4:6 God who said, "Let L shine out of darkness,"
4:6 hearts to give the L of the knowledge of
6:14 Or what fellowship has L with darkness?
11:14 even Satan disguises himself as an angel of L
Eph 5:8 but now you are L in the Lord; walk
5:8 walk as children of L
5:9 (for the fruit of L is found in all
5:13 is exposed by the L it becomes visible, for
5:13 visible, for anything that becomes visible is L
5:14 from the dead, and Christ shall give you L
Col 1:12 share in the inheritance of the saints in L
1Thes 5:5 are all sons of L and sons of the
1Tim 6:16 and dwells in unapproachable L, whom no man has
2Tim 1:10 life and immortality to L through the gospel.
1Pet 2:9 called you out of darkness into his marvelous L
1Jn 1:5 you, that God is L and in him is
1:7 we walk in the L, as he is in
1:7 he is in the L, we have fellowship with
2:8 away and the true L is already shining.
2:9 he is in the L and hates his brother
2:10 brother abides in the L, and in it there
Rev 8:12 a third of their L was darkened; a third
18:23 no more; and the L of a lamp shall
21:23 of God is its L, and its lamp is
21:24 By its L shall the nations walk; and the
22:5 more; they need no L of lamp or sun,
22:5 God will be their L, and they shall reign

LIGHTED (5)

Neh 9:19 fire by night which L for them the way
Ps 77:18 the whirlwind; thy lightnings L up the world; the
1Mac 4:50 on the altar and L the lamps on the
2Mac 1:8 cereal offering, and we L the lamps and we
10:3 they burned incense and L lamps and set out

LIGHTEN (10)

1Sam 6:5 Israel; perhaps he will L his hand from off
1Kgs 12:4 Now therefore L the hard service of your father
12:9 have said to me, L the yoke that your
12:10 heavy, but do you L it for us'; thus
2Chr 10:4 Now therefore L the hard service of your father
10:9 have said to me, L the yoke that your
10:10 heavy, but do you L it for us'; thus
Ps 13:3 O LORD my God; L my eyes, lest I
97:4 His lightnings L the world; the earth sees and
Jon 1:5 into the sea, to L it for them.

LIGHTENED

Acts 27:38 had eaten enough, they L the ship, throwing out

LIGHTENS (2)

2Sam 22:29 LORD, and my God L my darkness.
Ps 18:28 the LORD my God L my darkness.

LIGHTER

Ps 62:9 up; they are together L than a breath.

LIGHTING (2)

Lk 8:16 "No one after L a lamp covers it with
11:33 "No one after L a lamp puts it in

LIGHTLY (5)

1Sam 2:30 despise me shall be L esteemed.
Jer 2:36 have not sinned.' How L you gad about, changing
6:14 wound of my people L, saying, 'Peace, peace,' when
8:11 wound of my people L, saying, 'Peace, peace,' when
Heb 12:5 son, do not regard L the discipline of the

LIGHTMINDED

Sir 19:4 others too quickly is L, and one who sins

LIGHTNING (28)

2Sam 22:15 arrows, and scattered them; L, and routed them.
Job 28:26 a way for the L of the thunder;
36:30 Behold, he scatters his L about him, and covers
36:32 his hands with the L, and commands it to
37:3 it go, and his L to the corners of
37:11 thick cloud with moisture; the clouds scatter his L
37:15 them, and causes the L of his cloud to
Ps 105:32 hail for rain, and L that flashed through their
144:6 Flash forth the L and scatter them, send out
Wis 5:21 Shafts of L will fly with true aim, and
Sir 32:10 L speeds before the thunder, and approval precedes a
Bar 6:61 So also the L, when it flashes, is widely
Ezek 1:13 bright, and out of the fire went forth L
1:14 darted to and fro, like a flash of L
21:10 sharpened for slaughter, polished to flash like L
21:15 it is made like L, it is polished for
21:28 and to flash like L --
Dan 10:6 like the appearance of L, his eyes like flaming
Nah 2:4 squares; they gleam like torches, they dart like L
Zech 9:14 arrow go forth like L; the Lord GOD will
Mt 24:27 For as the L comes from the east and
28:3 His appearance was like L, and his raiment white
Lk 10:18 saw Satan fall like L from heaven.
17:24 For as the L flashes and lights up the
Rev 4:5 throne issue flashes of L, and voices and peals
8:5 thunder, voices, flashes of L, and an earthquake.
11:19 there were flashes of L, voices, peals of thunder,
16:18 there were flashes of L, voices, peals of thunder,

LIGHTNINGS (12)

Ex 19:16 there were thunders and L, and a thick cloud
20:18 the thunderings and the L and the sound of
Job 37:4 does not restrain the L when his voice is
38:35 Can you send forth L, that they may go
Ps 18:14 them; he flashed forth L, and routed them.
77:18 in the whirlwind; thy L lighted up the world;
97:4 His L lighten the world; the earth sees and
135:7 the earth, who makes L for the rain and
Sir 43:13 snow and speeds the L of his judgment.
Jer 10:13 He makes L for the rain, and he brings
51:16 He makes L for the rain, and he brings
Dan 3:74 Bless the Lord, L and clouds, sing praise to

LIGHTS (10)

Gen 1:14 said, "Let there be L in the firmament of
1:15 and let them be L in the firmament of
1:16 made the two great L, the greater light to
Ps 136:7 who made the great L, for his steadfast love
Ezek 32:8 All the bright L of heaven will I make
Lk 17:24 the lightning flashes and L up the sky from
Acts 16:29 And he called for L and rushed in, and
20:8 There were many L in the upper chamber where
Phil 2:15 whom you shine as L in the world,
Jas 1:16 from the Father of L with whom there is

LIKELY

Wis 9:14 and our designs are L to fail,

LIKEN (5)

Wis 7:9 Neither did I L to her any priceless gem,
Is 40:18 whom then will you L God, or what likeness
46:5 "To whom will you L me and make me
Lam 2:13 What can I L to you, that I may
Ezek 31:3 Behold, I will L you to a cedar in

LIKENED (2)

Sir 25:11 to whom shall be L the one who holds
36:12 Israel, whom thou hast L to a first-born son.

LIKENESS (35)

Gen 1:26 our image, after our L; and let them have
5:1 made him in the L of God.
5:3 son in his own L, after his image, and
Ex 20:4 graven image, or any L of anything that is
Deut 4:16 of any figure, the L of male or female,
4:17 male or female, the L of any beast that
4:17 on the earth, the L of any winged bird
4:18 in the air, the L of anything that creeps
4:18 on the ground, the L of any fish that
5:8 graven image, or any L of anything that is
Wis 14:19 ruler, skilfully forced the L to take more beautiful
Sir 34:3 this against that, the L of a face confronting
Is 40:18 liken God, or what L compare with him?
Ezek 1:5 of it came the L of four living creatures.
1:10 As for the L of their faces, each had
1:16 four had the same L, their construction being as
1:22 creatures there was the L of a firmament, shining
1:26 heads there was the L of a throne, in
1:26 and seated above the L of a throne was
1:26 a throne was a L as it were of
1:28 the appearance of the L of the glory of
10:10 four had the same L, as if a wheel
10:22 And as for the L of their faces, they
Dan 10:16 behold, one in the L of the sons of
Mt 22:20 said to them, "Whose L and inscription is this?"
Mk 12:16 said to them, "Whose L and inscription is this?"
Lk 20:24 Whose L and inscription has it?" They said,
Acts 14:11 to us in the L of men!"
Rom 8:3 own Son in the L of sinful flesh and
2Cor 3:18 being changed into his L from one degree of
4:4 Christ, who is the L of God.
Eph 4:24 nature, created after the L of God in true
Phil 2:7 being born in the L of men.
Heb 7:15 priest arises in the L of Melchizedek,
Jas 3:9 are made in the L of God.

LIKENESSES (2)

Wis 13:10 fashioned with skill, and L of animals, or a
Ezek 41:17 the nave were carved L

LIKES

3Jn 1:9 church; but Diotrephes, who L to put himself first,

LIKEWISE (73)

Gen 32:19 He L instructed the second and the third and
32:23 across the stream, and L everything that he had.
33:7 and bowed down; Leah L and her children drew
Ex 22:30 You shall do L with your oxen and with
23:11 You shall do L with your vineyard, and with
26:4 the first set; and L you shall make loops
27:11 And L for its length on the north side
36:11 of the first set; L he made them on
Deut 12:30 I also may do L
15:17 And to your bondwoman you shall do L
Judg 1:3 the Canaanites; and I L will go with you
7:5 shall set by himself; L every one that kneels
7:17 at me, and do L; when I come to
1Sam 14:22 L, when all the men of Israel who had
2Sam 10:14 the Syrians fled, they L fled before Abishai, and
1Kgs 7:18 he made pomegranates; in two rows round about
8:41 L when a foreigner, who is not of thy
2Kgs 17:41 graven images; their children L, and their children's
1Chr 12:38 king over all Israel; L all the rest of
19:15 the Syrians fled, they L fled before Abishai, Joab's
23:30 praising the LORD, and L at evening,
2Chr 1:17 a hundred and fifty; L through them these were
6:32 L when a foreigner, who is not of thy
32:29 He L provided cities for himself, and flocks and
36:14 priests and the people L were exceedingly unfaithful,
Neh 5:18 six choice sheep; fowls L were prepared for me,
10:34 We have L cast lots, the priests, the Levites,
Tob 12:12 the dead, I was L present with you.
Sir 13:18 the prey of lions; L the poor are pastures
13:19 to a proud man; L a poor man is
24:11 In the beloved city L he gave me a
33:15 the Most High; they L are in pairs, one
40:14 will be made glad; L transgressors will utterly fail.
49:7 afflict and destroy, and L to build and to
Jer 40:11 L, when all the Jews who were in Moab
Bar 6:28 use the money; and L their wives preserve some
6:35 L they are not able to give either wealth
6:61 seen; and the wind L blows in every land.
Ezek 18:14 and does not do L,
40:16 the side rooms, and L the vestibule had windows
2Mac 2:12 L Solomon also kept the eight days.
15:13 Then L a man appeared, distinguished by his gray
Mk 12:21 children; and the third L;
Lk 3:11 and he who has food, let him do L
10:32 So L a Levite, when he came to the
10:37 And Jesus said to him, "Go and do L
13:3 repent you will all L perish.
13:5 repent you will all L perish."
17:28 L as it was in the days of Lot--
17:31 take them away; and L let him who is
20:31 third took her, and L all seven left no
22:20 And L the cup after supper, saying, "This cup
22:36 purse take it, and L a bag.
Jn 5:18 for whatever he does, that the Son does L
Rom 1:27 unnatural, and the men L gave up natural relations
4:12 reckoned to them, and L the father of the
7:4 L, my brethren, you have died to the law

L

8:26 L the Spirit helps us in our weakness; for
1Cor 7:3 her conjugal rights, and L the wife to her
7:4 but the husband does; L the husband does not
7:22 L he who was free when called is a
Phil 2:18 L you also should be glad and rejoice with
1Tim 3:8 Deacons L must be serious, not double-tongued, not
3:11 The women L must be serious, no slanderers, but
Tit 2:3 Bid the older women L to be reverent in
2:6 L urge the younger men to control themselves.
Heb 2:14 and blood, he himself L partook of the same
1Pet 3:1 L you wives, be submissive to your husbands, so
3:7 L you husbands, live considerately with your wives,
5:5 L you that are younger be subject to the
5:13 at Babylon, who is L chosen, sends you greetings;
Jude 1:7 the surrounding cities, which L acted immorally and
Rev 8:12 kept from shining, and L a third of the

LIKHI
1Chr 7:19 Shemida were Ahian, Shechem, L, and Aniam.

LIKING (2)
Wis 16:21 took it, was changed to suit every one's L
Sir 32:17 and will find a decision according to his L

LIKINGS
2Tim 4:3 to suit their own L,

LILIES (9)
Song 2:16 am his, he pastures his flock among the L
4:5 twins of a gazelle, that feed among the L
5:13 His lips are L, distilling liquid myrrh.
6:2 his flock in the gardens, and to gather L
6:3 is mine; he pastures his flock among the L
7:2 belly is a heap of wheat, encircled with L
Sir 50:8 the first fruits, like L by a spring of
Mt 6:28 Consider the L of the field, how they grow;
Lk 12:27 Consider the L, how they grow; they neither toil

L

LILY (6)
1Kgs 7:26 the flower of a L; it held two thousand
2Chr 4:5 the flower of a L; it held over three
Song 2:1 rose of Sharon, a L of the valleys.
2:2 As a L among brambles, so is my love
Sir 39:14 like frankincense, and put forth blossoms like a L
Hos 14:5 shall blossom as the L, he shall strike root

LILY-WORK (2)
1Kgs 7:19 the vestibule were of L, four cubits.
7:22 And upon the tops of the pillars was L

LIMB (10)
Lev 21:18 mutilated face or a L too long,
Judg 19:29 concubine he divided her, L by limb, into twelve
19:29 divided her, limb by L, into twelve pieces, and
Dan 2:5 you shall be torn L from limb, and your
2:5 be torn limb from L, and your houses shall
3:97 Abednego shall be torn L from limb, and their
3:97 be torn limb from L, and their houses laid
2Mac 7:7 have your body punished L by limb?"
7:7 rather than have your body punished limb by L
9:7 as to torture every L of his body.

LIMBS (4)
Job 18:13 is consumed, the first-born of death consumes his L
40:18 tubes of bronze, his L like bars of iron.
41:12 keep silence concerning his L, or his mighty strength,
Dan 5:6 thoughts alarmed him; his L gave way, and his

LIME (2)
Is 33:12 as if burned to L, like thorns cut down,
Amos 2:1 because he burned to L the bones of the

LIMIT (8)
Job 11:7 you find out the L of the Almighty?
15:8 And do you L wisdom to yourself?
Ps 119:96 I have seen a L to all perfection, but
Prov 8:29 to the sea its L, so that the waters
Sir 39:18 done, and none can L his saving power.
Nah 3:9 too, and that without L; Put and the Libyans
2Cor 10:13 will not boast beyond L, but will keep to
10:15 do not boast beyond L, in other men's labors;

LIMITATIONS
Rom 6:19 speaking in human terms, because of your natural L

LIMITED
Sir 17:2 men few days, a L time, but granted them

LIMITS (2)
1Chr 5:16 all the pasture lands of Sharon to their L
2Cor 10:13 will keep to the L God has apportioned us,

LIMPED
1Kgs 18:26 And they L about the altar which they had

LIMPING (2)
Gen 32:31 as he passed Penuel, L because of his thigh.
1Kgs 18:21 long will you go L with two different opinions?

LINE (44)
Lev 22:4 None of the L of Aaron who is a
Num 34:7 shall mark out your L to Mount Hor;
Judg 20:20 drew up the battle L against them at Gibe-ah.
20:22 again formed the battle L in the same place
1Sam 4:2 Philistines drew up in L against Israel, and when
4:12 ran from the battle L, and came to Shiloh
17:2 and drew up in L of battle against the
17:20 forth to the battle L, shouting the war cry.
17:48 quickly toward the battle L to meet the Philistine.
2Sam 8:2 measured them with a L, making them lie down
8:2 death, and one full L to be spared.
1Kgs 7:15 one pillar, and a L of twelve cubits measured
7:23 cubits high, and a L of thirty cubits measured
2Kgs 21:13 over Jerusalem the measuring L of Samaria, and the
2Chr 4:2 cubits high, and a L of thirty cubits measured
13:3 Jeroboam drew up his L of battle against him
Job 38:5 Or who stretched the L upon it?
Ps 89:29 I will establish his L for ever and his
89:36 His L shall endure for ever, his throne as
Is 28:10 precept, precept upon precept, L upon line, line upon
28:10 upon precept, line upon L, line upon line, here
28:10 precept, line upon line, L upon line, here a
28:10 upon line, line upon L, here a little, there
28:13 precept, precept upon precept, L upon line, line upon
28:13 upon precept, line upon L, line upon line, here
28:13 precept, line upon line, L upon line, here a
28:13 upon line, line upon L, here a little, there
28:17 make justice the L, and righteousness the plummet;
34:11 He shall stretch the L of confusion over it,
34:17 to them with the L; they shall possess it
44:13 The carpenter stretches a L, he marks it out
Jer 31:39 And the measuring L shall go out farther, straight
Lam 2:8 it off by the L; he restrained not his
Ezek 40:3 like bronze, with a L of flax and a
47:3 on eastward with a L in his hand, the
Amos 7:7 built with a plumb L, with a plumb line
7:7 line, with a plumb L in his hand.
7:8 And I said, "A plumb L
7:8 am setting a plumb L in the midst of
7:17 be parceled out by L; you yourself shall die
Mic 2:5 none to cast the L by lot in the
Zech 1:16 hosts, and the measuring L shall be stretched out
2:1 man with a measuring L in his hand!
1Mac 7:14 "A priest of the L of Aaron has come

LINEAGE (3)
Tob 5:13 relative of mine, of a good and noble L
1Mac 3:32 distinguished man of royal L, in charge of the
Lk 2:4 of the house and L of David,

LINED (4)
1Kgs 6:15 He L the walls of the house on the
2Chr 3:5 The nave he L with cypress, and covered it
3:7 So he L the house with gold--its beams,
1Mac 16:6 he and his army L up against them.

LINEN (105)
Gen 41:42 in garments of fine L, and put a gold
Ex 25:4 stuff and fine twined L, goats' hair,
26:1 curtains of fine twined L and blue and purple
26:31 stuff and fine twined L; in skilled work shall
26:36 and fine twined L, embroidered with needlework.
27:9 hangings of fine twined L a hundred cubits long
27:16 and fine twined L, embroidered with needlework; it
27:18 hangings of fine twined L and bases of bronze.
28:5 and purple and scarlet stuff, and fine twined L
28:6 and of fine twined L, skilfully worked.
28:8 and purple and scarlet stuff, and fine twined L
28:15 stuff, and fine twined L shall you make it.
28:39 checker work of fine L, and you shall make
28:39 a turban of fine L, and you shall make

28:42 shall make for them L breeches to cover their
35:6 stuff and fine twined L; goats' hair,
35:23 scarlet stuff or fine L or goats' hair or
35:25 stuff and fine twined L;
35:35 stuff and fine twined L, or by a weaver--
36:8 made of fine twined L and blue and purple
36:35 stuff and fine twined L; with cherubim skilfully
36:37 and fine twined L, embroidered with needlework;
38:9 were of fine twined L, a hundred cubits;
38:16 round about the court were of fine twined L
38:18 stuff and fine twined L; it was twenty cubits
38:23 and purple and scarlet stuff and fine twined L
39:2 and purple and scarlet stuff, and fine twined L
39:3 into the fine twined L, in skilled design.
39:5 stuff, and fine twined L; as the LORD had
39:8 and purple and scarlet stuff, and fine twined L
39:24 and purple and scarlet stuff and fine twined L
39:27 coats, woven of fine L, for Aaron and his
39:28 the turban of fine L, and the caps of
39:28 the caps of fine L, and the linen breeches
39:28 fine linen, and the L breeches of fine twined
39:28 breeches of fine twined L,
39:29 girdle of fine twined L and of blue and
Lev 6:10 shall put on his L garment, and put his
6:10 garment, and put his L breeches upon his body,
13:47 a woolen or a L garment,
13:48 warp or woof of L or wool, or in
13:52 or woof, woolen or L, or anything of skin,
13:59 garment of wool or L, either in warp or
16:4 put on the holy L coat, and shall have
16:4 and shall have the L breeches on his body,
16:4 be girded with the L girdle, and wear the
16:4 girdle, and wear the L turban; these are the
16:23 shall put off the L garments which he put
16:32 atonement, wearing the holy L garments;
Deut 22:11 mingled stuff, wool and L together.
Judg 14:12 will give you thirty L garments and thirty festal
14:13 shall give me thirty L garments and thirty festal
1Sam 2:18 boy girded with a L ephod.
22:18 persons who wore the L ephod.
2Sam 6:14 was girded with a L ephod.
1Chr 4:21 of the house of L workers at Beth-ashbea;
15:27 a robe of fine L, as also were all
15:27 and David wore a L ephod.
2Chr 2:14 crimson fabrics and fine L, and to do all
3:14 crimson fabrics and fine L, and worked cherubim on
5:12 kinsmen, arrayed in fine L, with cymbals, harps, and
Jud 16:8 and put on a L gown to deceive him.
Esth 1:6 with cords of fine L and purple to silver
8:15 a mantle of fine L and purple, while the
Prov 7:16 colored spreads of Egyptian L;
31:22 her clothing is fine L and purple.
31:24 She makes L garments and sells them; she delivers
Sir 45:8 symbols of authority, the L breeches, the long robe,
Is 3:23 garments of gauze, the L garments, the turbans, and
Jer 13:1 "Go and buy a L waistcloth, and put it
Bar 6:72 By the purple and L that rot upon them
Ezek 9:2 a man clothed in L, with a writing case
9:3 the man clothed in L, who had the writing
9:11 the man clothed in L, with the writing case
10:2 the man clothed in L, "Go in among the
10:6 the man clothed in L, "Take fire from between
10:7 the man clothed in L, who took it and
16:10 swathed you in fine L and covered you with
16:13 raiment was of fine L, and silk, and embroidered
27:7 Of fine embroidered L from Egypt was your sail,
27:16 purple, embroidered work, fine L, coral, and agate.
44:17 court, they shall wear L garments; they shall have
44:18 They shall have L turbans upon their heads, and
44:18 upon their heads, and L breeches upon their loins;
Dan 10:5 a man clothed in L, whose loins were girded
12:6 the man clothed in L, who was above the
12:7 The man clothed in L, who was above the
Mt 27:59 it in a clean L shroud,
Mk 14:51 with nothing but a L cloth about his body;
14:52 but he left the L cloth and ran away
15:45 And he bought a L shroud, and taking him
15:45 wrapped him in the L shroud, and laid him
Lk 16:19 in purple and fine L and who feasted sumptuously
23:52 wrapped it in a L shroud, and laid him
24:12 in, he saw the L clothes by themselves; and
Jn 19:40 and bound it in L cloths with the spices,
20:5 in, he saw the L cloths lying there, but
20:6 tomb; he saw the L cloths lying,
20:7 not lying with the L cloths but rolled up
Rev 15:6 robed in pure bright L, and their breasts girded
18:12 jewels and pearls, fine L, purple, silk and scarlet,
18:16 was clothed in fine L, in purple and scarlet,
19:8 be clothed with fine L, bright and pure"—
19:8 for the fine L is the righteous deeds
19:14 heaven, arrayed in fine L, white and pure, followed

LINES (3)

2Sam 8:2 on the ground; two L he measured to be
2Chr 14:10 they drew up their L of battle in the
Ps 16:6 The L have fallen for me in pleasant places;

LINGER

Sir 32:11 the last; go home quickly and do not L

LINGERED

Gen 19:16 But he L; so the men seized him and

LINGERS

2Sam 1:9 yet my life still L

LINTEL (4)

Ex 12:7 two doorposts and the L of the houses in
12:22 basin, and touch the L and the two doorposts
12:23 the blood on the L and on the two
1Kgs 6:31 doors of olivewood; the L and the doorposts formed

LINUS

2Tim 4:21 as do Pudens and L and Claudia and all

LION (104)

Gen 49:9 Judah is a L's whelp; from the prey, my
49:9 he couched as a L, and as a lioness;
Num 23:24 up and as a L it lifts itself; it
24:9 lay down like a L, and like a lioness;
Deut 33:20 Gad couches like a L, he tears the arm,
33:22 said, "Dan is a L's whelp, that leaps forth
Judg 14:5 And behold, a young L roared against him;
14:6 and he tore the L asunder as one tears
14:8 the carcass of the L, and behold, there was
14:8 the body of the L, and honey.
14:9 taken the honey from the carcass of the L
14:18 What is stronger than a L
1Sam 17:34 when there came a L, or a bear, and
17:37 the paw of the L and from the paw
2Sam 17:10 the heart of a L, will utterly melt with
23:20 down and slew a L in a pit on
1Kgs 13:24 he went away a L met him on the
13:24 stood beside it; the L also stood beside the
13:25 the road, and the L standing by the body.
13:26 given him to the L, which has torn him
13:28 the ass and the L standing beside the body.
13:28 The L had not eaten the body or torn
20:36 gone from me, a L shall kill you." And
20:36 departed from him, a L met him and killed
1Chr 11:22 down and slew a L in a pit on
Esth 14:13 my mouth before the L, and turn his heart
Job 4:10 The roar of the L, the voice of the
4:10 voice of the fierce L, the teeth of the
4:11 The strong L perishes for lack of prey, and
10:16 hunt me like a L, and again work wonders
28:8 not trodden it; the L has not passed over
38:39 the prey for the L, or satisfy the appetite
Ps 7:2 me, lest like a L they rend me, dragging
10:9 in secret like a L in his covert; he
17:12 They are like a L eager to tear, as
17:12 tear, as a young L lurking in ambush.
22:13 mouths at me, like a ravening and roaring L
22:21 the mouth of the L, my afflicted soul from
91:13 will tread on the L and the adder, the
91:13 the adder, the young L and the serpent you
Prov 19:12 the growling of a L, but his favor is
20:2 the growling of a L; he who provokes him
22:13 says, "There is a L outside!
26:13 says, "There is a L in the road!
26:13 There is a L in the streets!"
28:1 pursues, but the righteous are bold as a L
28:15 Like a roaring L or a charging bear is
30:30 in their stride: the L, which is mightiest among
Eccl 9:4 a living dog is better than a dead L
Sir 4:30 not be like a L in your home, nor
21:2 Its teeth are L's teeth, and destroy the souls
25:15 rather dwell with a L and a dragon than
27:10 A L lies in wait for prey; so does
27:28 vengeance lies in wait for him like a L
28:23 against them like a L; like a leopard it
Is 5:29 roaring is like a L, like young lions they

11:6 the calf and the L and the fatling together,
11:7 down together; and the L shall eat straw like
15:9 Dibon even more, a L for those of Moab
30:6 the lioness and the L, the viper and the
31:4 to me, As a L or a young lion
31:4 lion or a young L growls over his prey,
35:9 No L shall be there, nor shall any ravenous
38:13 until morning; like a L he breaks all my
65:25 shall feed together, the L shall eat straw like
Jer 2:30 own sword devoured your prophets like a ravening L
4:7 A L has gone up from his thicket, a
5:6 Therefore a L from the forest shall slay them,
12:8 to me like a L in the forest, she
25:38 Like a L he has left his covert, for
49:19 Behold, like a L coming up from the jungle
50:44 "Behold, like a L coming up from the jungle
Lam 3:10 in wait, like a L in hiding;
Ezek 1:10 the face of a L on the right side,
10:14 the face of a L, and the fourth the
19:3 he became a young L, and he learned to
19:5 of her whelps and made him a young L
19:6 he became a young L, and he learned to
22:25 are like a roaring L tearing the prey; they
32:2 "You consider yourself a L among the nations, but
41:19 face of a young L toward the palm tree
Dan 7:4 first was like a L and had eagles' wings.
Hos 5:14 will be like a L to Ephraim, and like
5:14 and like a young L to the house of
11:10 will roar like a L; yea, he will roar,
13:7 to them like a L, like a leopard I
13:8 devour them like a L, as a wild beast
Amos 3:4 Does a L roar in the forest, when he
3:4 Does a young L cry out from his den,
3:8 The L has roared; who will not fear?
3:12 the mouth of the L two legs, or a
5:19 man fled from a L, and a bear met
Mic 5:8 many peoples, like a L among the beasts of
5:8 forest, like a young L among the flocks of
Nah 2:11 young lions, where the L brought his prey, where
2:12 The L tore enough for his whelps and strangled
1Mac 3:4 He was like a L in his deeds, like
3:4 his deeds, like a L's cub roaring for prey.
2Tim 4:17 was rescued from the L's mouth.
1Pet 5:8 around like a roaring L, seeking some one to
Rev 4:7 living creature like a L, the second living creature
5:5 "Weep not; lo, the L of the tribe of
10:3 loud voice, like a L roaring; when he called
13:2 mouth was like a L's mouth.

LIONESS (7)

Gen 49:9 lion, and as a L; who dares rouse him
Num 23:24 As a L it rises up and as a
24:9 lion, and like a L; who will rouse him
Job 4:11 the whelps of the L are scattered.
Is 30:6 from where come the L and the lion, the
Ezek 19:2 and say: What a L was your mother among
Joel 1:6 teeth, and it has the fangs of a L

LIONESSES

Nah 2:12 strangled prey for his L; he filled his caves

LIONS (54)

1Sam 17:36 servant has killed both L and bears; and this
2Sam 1:23 were swifter than eagles, they were stronger than L
1Kgs 7:29 in the frames were L, oxen, and cherubim.
7:29 above and below the L and oxen, there were
7:36 panels, he carved cherubim, L, and palm trees,
10:19 arm rests and two L standing beside the arm
10:20 arm rests, while twelve L stood there, one on
2Kgs 17:25 therefore the LORD sent L among them, which
17:26 therefore he has sent L among them, and behold,
1Chr 12:8 like the faces of L, and who were swift
2Chr 9:18 arm rests and two L standing beside the arm
9:19 arm rests, while twelve L stood there, one on
Job 4:10 teeth of the young L, are broken.
38:39 appetite of the young L,
Ps 34:10 The young L suffer want and hunger; but those
35:17 me from their ravages, my life from the L
57:4 in the midst of L that greedily devour the
58:6 fangs of the young L, O LORD!
104:21 The young L roar for their prey, seeking their
Song 4:8 from the dens of L, from the mountains of
Wis 11:17 of bears, or bold L,
Sir 13:18 are the prey of L; likewise the poor are
47:3 He played with L as with young goats, and
Is 5:29 a lion, like young L they roar; they growl
Jer 2:15 The L have roared against him, they have roared
50:17 "Israel is a hunted sheep driven away by L
51:38 shall roar together like L; they shall growl like
51:38 they shall growl like L whelps.
Ezek 19:2 say: What a lioness was your mother among L
19:2 the midst of young L, rearing her whelps.
19:6 He prowled among the L; he became a young
Dan 6:7 king, shall be cast into the den of L
6:12 king, shall be cast into the den of L
6:16 was brought and cast into the den of L
6:19 and went in haste to the den of L
6:20 continually, been able to deliver you from the L
6:22 angel and shut the L mouths, and they have
6:24 into the den of L – they, their children, and
6:24 of the den the L overpowered them and broke
6:27 has saved Daniel from the power of the L
14:31 threw Daniel into the L den, and he was
14:32 There were seven L in the den, and every
14:34 to Daniel, in the L den."
Joel 1:6 number; its teeth are L teeth, and it has
Nah 2:11 Where is the L den, the cave of the
2:11 cave of the young L, where the lion brought
2:13 shall devour your young L; I will cut off
Zeph 3:3 within her are roaring L; her judges are evening
Zech 11:3 the roar of the L, for the jungle of
1Mac 2:60 innocence was delivered from the mouth of the L
2Mac 11:11 They hurled themselves like L against the enemy,
Heb 11:33 stopped the mouths of L,
Rev 9:8 and their teeth like L teeth;
9:17 the horses were like L heads, and fire and

LIP

Lev 13:45 shall cover his upper L and cry, 'Unclean, unclean.'

LIPS (138)

Ex 6:12 to me, who am a man of uncircumcised L
6:30 I am of uncircumcised L; how then shall Pharaoh
Lev 5:4 one utters with his L a rash oath to
Num 30:6 thoughtless utterance of her L by which she has
30:8 thoughtless utterance of her L, by which she bound
30:12 proceeds out of her L concerning her vows, or
Deut 23:23 what has passed your L, for you have voluntarily
1Sam 1:13 her heart; only her L moved, and her voice
Jud 2:2 fully, with his own L, all the wickedness of
9:10 the deceit of my L strike down the slave
15:13 and wearing garlands and with songs on their L
Job 2:10 all this Job did not sin with his L
8:21 with laughter, and your L with shouting.
11:5 speak, and open his L to you,
13:6 reasoning, and listen to the pleadings of my L
15:6 not I; your own L testify against you.
16:5 the solace of my L would assuage your pain.
23:12 the commandment of his L; I have treasured in
27:4 in my nostrils; my L will not speak falsehood,
32:20 I must open my L and answer.
33:3 heart, and what my L know they speak sincerely.
Ps 12:2 his neighbor; with flattering L and a double heart
12:3 cut off all flattering L, the tongue that makes
12:4 we will prevail, our L are with us; who
16:4 pour out or take their names upon my L
17:1 to my prayer from L free of deceit!
17:4 the word of thy L I have avoided the
21:2 and hast not withheld the request of his L
31:18 Let the lying L be dumb, which speak insolently
34:13 from evil, and your L from speaking deceit.
40:9 have not restrained my L, as thou knowest, O
45:2 is poured upon your L; therefore God has blessed
50:16 my statutes, or take my covenant on your L
51:15 Lord, open thou my L, and my mouth shall
59:7 and snarling with their L – for "Who," they
59:12 the words of their L, let them be trapped
63:3 better than life, my L will praise thee.
63:5 praises thee with joyful L,
66:14 vows, that which my L uttered and my mouth
71:23 My L will shout for joy, when I sing
89:34 alter the word that went forth from my L
119:13 With my L I declare all the ordinances of
119:171 My L will pour forth praise that thou dost
120:2 O LORD, from lying L, from a deceitful tongue."
140:3 serpents, and under their L is the poison of
140:9 the mischief of their L overwhelm them!
141:3 LORD, keep watch over the door of my L
Prov 5:2 keep discretion, and your L may guard knowledge.
5:3 For the L of a loose woman drip honey,
6:2 the utterance of your L, caught in the words
8:6 things, and from my L will come what is

L

8:7 utter truth; wickedness is an abomination to my L
10:13 On the L of him who has understanding wisdom
10:18 conceals hatred has lying L, and he who utters
10:19 he who restrains his L is prudent.
10:21 The L of the righteous feed many, but fools
10:32 The L of the righteous know what is acceptable,
12:13 the transgression of his L, but the righteous escapes
12:19 Truthful L endure for ever, but a lying tongue
12:22 Lying L are an abomination to the LORD, but
13:3 who opens wide his L comes to ruin.
14:3 his back, but the L of the wise will
15:7 The L of the wise spread knowledge; not so
16:10 decisions are on the L of a king; his
16:13 Righteous L are the delight of a king, and
16:23 his speech judicious, and adds persuasiveness to his L
16:30 he who compresses his L brings evil to pass.
17:4 evildoer listens to wicked L; and a liar gives
17:28 when he closes his L, he is deemed intelligent.
18:6 A fool's L bring strife, and his mouth invites
18:7 his ruin, and his L are a snare to
18:20 he is satisfied by the yield of his L
20:15 costly stones; but the L of knowledge are a
22:18 if all of them are ready on your L
23:16 will rejoice when your L speak what is right.
24:2 devise violence, and their L talk of mischief.
24:26 He who gives a right answer kisses the L
24:28 without cause, and do not deceive with your L
26:23 earthen vessel are smooth L with an evil heart.
26:24 hates, dissembles with his L and harbors deceit in
27:2 own mouth; a stranger, and not your own L
Eccl 10:12 him favor, but the L of a fool consume
Song 4:3 Your L are like a scarlet thread, and your
4:11 Your L distil nectar, my bride; honey and milk
5:13 His L are lilies, distilling liquid myrrh.
7:9 down smoothly, gliding over L and teeth.
Sir 1:21 right moment, and the L of many will tell
1:26 in men's sight, and keep watch over your L
12:16 speak sweetly with his L, but in his mind
14:1 not blunder with his L and need not suffer
15:9 not fitting on the L of a sinner, for
20:18 is continually on the L of the ignorant.
20:19 proverb from a fool's L will be rejected, for
20:23 is continually on the L of the ignorant.
21:5 man goes from his L to the ears of
21:25 The L of strangers will speak of these things,
22:25 of prudence upon my L, that it may keep
23:8 is overtaken through his L, the reviler and the
34:8 fulfilled, and wisdom is made perfect in truthful L
37:22 of his understanding may be trustworthy on his L
39:15 with songs on your L, and with lyres; and
50:20 the Lord with his L, and to glory in
51:2 a slanderous tongue, from L that utter lies.
Is 6:5 a man of unclean L, and I dwell in
6:5 a people of unclean L; for my eyes have
6:7 this has touched your L; your guilt is taken
11:4 the breath of his L he shall slay the
28:11 by men of strange L and with an alien
29:13 honor me with their L, while their hearts are
30:27 thick rising smoke; his L are full of indignation,
57:18 creating for his mourners the fruit of the L
59:3 fingers with iniquity; your L have spoken lies, your
Jer 7:28 has perished; it is cut off from their L
17:16 came out of my L was before thy face.
Lam 3:62 The L and thoughts of my assailants are against
Ezek 24:17 do not cover your L, nor eat the bread
24:22 shall not cover your L, nor eat the bread
29:21 I will open your L among them.
33:31 it; for with their L they show much love,
Dan 10:16 of men touched my L; then I opened my
Hos 8:1 the trumpet to your L, for a vulture is
14:2 and we will render the fruit of our L
Mic 3:7 shall all cover their L, for there is no
Hab 3:16 my body trembles, my L quiver at the sound;
Zech 4:2 on it, with seven L on each of the
Mal 2:6 mouth, and no wrong was found on his L
2:7 For the L of a priest should guard knowledge,
Mt 15:8 honors me with their L, but their heart is
Mk 7:6 honors me with their L, but their heart is
Lk 22:69 We have heard it ourselves from his own L
Rom 3:13 "The venom of asps is under their L
10:8 near you, on your L and in your heart
10:9 you confess with your L that Jesus is Lord
10:10 he confesses with his L and so is saved.
1Cor 14:21 tongues and by the L of foreigners will I
Heb 13:15 is, the fruit of L that acknowledge his name.
1Pet 2:22 no sin; no guile was found on his L
3:10 from evil and his L from speaking guile;

LIQUID (7)

Ex 30:23 the finest spices: of L myrrh five hundred shekels,
Song 5:5 myrrh, my fingers with L myrrh, upon the handles
5:13 lips are lilies, distilling L myrrh.
2Mac 1:20 found fire but thick L, he ordered them to
1:21 priests to sprinkle the L on the wood and
1:31 Nehemiah ordered that the L that was left should
1:33 hidden the fire, the L had appeared with which

LIST (2)

1Chr 25:1 The L of those who did the work and
27:1 This is the L of the people of Israel,

LISTEN (164)

Gen 23:15 answered Abraham, "My lord, L to me; a piece
34:17 if you will not L to us and be
39:10 day, he would not L to her, to lie
42:21 and we would not L; therefore is this distress
42:22 But you would not L
Ex 4:1 not believe me or L to my voice, for
6:9 but they did not L to Moses, because of
6:12 how then shall Pharaoh L to me, who am
6:30 how then shall Pharaoh L to me?"
7:4 Egypt, Pharaoh will not L to you; then I
7:13 and he would not L to them; as the
7:22 and he would not L to them; as the
8:15 heart, and would not L to them; as the
8:19 and he would not L to them; as the
9:12 and he did not L to them; as the
11:9 Moses, "Pharaoh will not L to you; that my
16:20 But they did not L to Moses; some left
18:19 L now to my voice; I will give you
Deut 13:3 them,' you shall not L to the words of
13:8 yield to him or L to him, nor shall
Josh 24:10 but I would not L to Balaam; therefore he
Judg 2:17 yet they did not L to their judges; for
9:7 and said to them, L to me, you men
9:7 Shechem, that God may L to you.
11:17 land'; but the king of Edom would not L
19:25 the men would not L to him.
20:13 the Benjaminites would not L to the voice of
Ruth 2:8 said to Ruth, "Now, L, my daughter, do not
1Sam 2:25 But they would not L to the voice of
8:19 the people refused to L to the voice of
24:9 Saul, "Why do you L to the words of
30:24 Who would L to you in this matter?
2Sam 12:18 and he did not L to us; how then
13:14 But he would not L to her; and being
13:16 But he would not L to her.
19:35 Can I still L to the voice of singing
20:17 she said to him, L to the words of
2Kgs 14:11 But Amaziah would not L
17:14 But they would not L, but were stubborn, as
17:40 However they would not L, but they did according
18:31 of Assyria.' Do not L to Hezekiah; for thus
18:32 And do not L to Hezekiah when he misleads
21:9 But they did not L, and Manasseh seduced them
2Chr 25:20 But Amaziah would not L; for it was of
35:22 He did not L to the words of Neco
Neh 13:27 Shall we then L to you and do all
Tob 6:12 Now L to my plan.
6:15 Now L to me, brother, for she will become
Jud 8:11 she said to them, L to me, rulers of
8:32 Judith said to them, L to me.
14:1 Judith said to them, L to me, my brethren,
Esth 3:4 and he would not L to them, they told
Job 13:6 now my reasoning, and L to the pleadings of
13:17 L carefully to my words, and let my declaration
21:2 Then Job answered: L carefully to my words,
32:10 Therefore I say, L to me; let me also
33:1 speech, O Job, and L to all my words.
33:31 Give heed, O Job, L to me; be silent,
33:33 If not, L to me; be silent, and I
34:16 have understanding, hear this; L to what I say.
Ps 34:11 Come, O sons, L to me, I will teach
61:1 my cry, O God, L to my prayer;
81:8 if you would but L to me!
81:11 my people did not L to my voice; Israel
81:13 that my people would L to me, that Israel
Prov 1:24 and you refused to L, have stretched out my
5:7 And now, O sons, L to me, and do
5:13 I did not L to the voice of my
7:24 And now, O sons, L to me, and be
8:32 And now, my sons, L to me: happy are

13:1 a scoffer does not L to rebuke.
19:20 L to advice and accept instruction, that you may
Eccl 5:1 to draw near to L is better than to
Wis 6:1 L therefore, O kings, and understand; learn, O judges
Sir 3:1 L to me your father, O children; and act
6:23 L, my son, and accept my judgment; do not
6:33 If you love to L you will gain knowledge,
6:35 Be ready to L to every narrative, and do
14:23 her windows will also L at her doors;
16:22 L to me, my son, and acquire knowledge, and
21:24 for a man to L at a door, and
23:7 L, my children, to instruction concerning speech; the
31:22 L to me, my son, and do not disregard
34:24 another curses, to whose voice will the Lord L
34:26 same things, who will L to his prayer?
35:13 man; and he will L to the prayer of
39:13 L to me, O you holy sons, and bud
Is 1:15 prayers, I will not L; your hands are full
21:7 on camels, let him L diligently, very diligently."
34:1 Let the earth L, and all that fills it;
36:16 Do not L to Hezekiah; for thus says the
41:1 L to me in silence, O coastlands; let the
42:23 this, will attend and L for the time to
49:1 L to me, O coastlands, and hearken, you peoples
51:4 L to me, my people, and give ear to
65:12 spoke, you did not L, but you did what
66:4 spoke they did not L; but they did what
Jer 6:10 are closed, they cannot L; behold, the word of
7:13 persistently you did not L, and when I called
7:26 yet they did not L to me, or incline
7:27 but they will not L to you.
11:4 the iron furnace, saying, L to my voice, and
11:11 me, I will not L to them.
11:14 for I will not L when they call to
12:17 any nation will not L, then I will utterly
13:11 praise, and a glory, but they would not L
13:17 if you will not L, my soul will weep
16:12 evil will, refusing to L to me;
17:23 Yet they did not L or incline their ear,
17:24 "But if you L to me, says the LORD,
17:27 if you do not L to me, to keep
22:21 said, 'I will not L This has been your
23:16 of hosts: "Do not L to the words of
26:3 may be they will L, and every one turn
26:4 If you will not L to me, to walk
27:9 So do not L to your prophets, your diviners,
27:14 Do not L to the words of the prophets
27:16 the LORD: Do not L to the words of
27:17 Do not L to them; serve the king of
28:15 to the prophet Hananiah, L, Hananiah, the LORD has
29:8 you, and do not L to the dreams which
29:19 but you would not L, says the LORD.--
34:14 your fathers did not L to me or incline
35:13 not receive instruction and L to my words?
35:15 incline your ear or L to me.
36:25 scroll, he would not L to them.
37:14 But Irijah would not L to him, and seized
38:15 counsel, you will not L to me."
44:5 But they did not L or incline their ear,
44:16 LORD, we will not L to you.
Ezek 3:6 to such, they would L to you.
3:7 of Israel will not L to you; for they
3:7 are not willing to L to me; because all
13:19 to my people, who L to lies.
20:8 me and would not L to me; they did
20:39 if you will not L to me; but my
Amos 5:23 the melody of your harps I will not L
Mal 2:2 If you will not L, if you will not
1Mac 2:65 wise in counsel; always L to him; he shall
5:61 deed, they did not L to Judas and his
2Mac 7:25 young man would not L to him at all,
Mt 10:14 not receive you or L to your words, shake
17:5 I am well pleased; L to him."
18:15 if he does not L, take one or two
18:16 If he refuses to L to them, tell it
18:16 if he refuses to L even to the church,
Mk 4:3 and in his teaching he said to them: L
9:7 is my beloved Son; L to him."
Lk 9:35 my Son, my Chosen; L to him!"
Jn 6:60 hard saying; who can L to it?"
9:27 have told you already, and you would not L
9:31 that God does not L to sinners, but if
10:20 he is mad; why L to him?"
Acts 3:22 You shall L to him in whatever he tells
3:23 soul that does not L to that prophet shall
4:19 sight of God to L to you rather than
13:16 "Men of Israel, and you that fear God, L
15:13 speaking, James replied, "Brethren, L to me.
26:3 I beg you to L to me patiently.
28:28 has been sent to the Gentiles; they will L
1Cor 14:21 then they will not L to me, says the
2Tim 3:7 various impulses, who will L to anybody and can
Jas 2:5 L, my beloved brethren.
1Jn 4:6 of God does not L to us.

LISTENED (27)

Gen 3:17 said, "Because you have L to the voice of
Ex 6:12 of Israel have not L to me; how then
Judg 13:9 And God L to the voice of Manoah, and
2Kgs 18:12 LORD commanded; they neither L nor obeyed.
2Chr 25:16 this and have not L to my counsel."
Ezra 8:23 for this, and he L to our entreaty.
Job 15:8 Have you L in the council of God?
29:21 in my hand.' "Men L to me, and waited,
32:11 for your words, I L for your wise sayings,
Ps 66:18 in my heart, the Lord would not have L
66:19 But truly God has L; he has given heed
Jer 8:6 have given heed and L, but they have not
23:18 who has given heed to his word and L
25:3 spoken persistently to you, but you have not L
25:4 You have neither L nor inclined your ears to
25:7 Yet you have not L to me, says the
32:33 persistently they have not L to receive instruction.
35:14 but you have not L to me.
35:17 and they have not L, I have called to
37:2 people of the land L to the words of
Dan 9:6 ordinances; we have not L to thy servants the
Lk 10:39 the Lord's feet and L to his teaching.
Acts 14:9 He L to Paul speaking; and Paul, looking intently
15:12 kept silence; and they L to Barnabas and Paul
22:22 to this word they L to him; then they
27:21 "Men, you should have L to me, and should
2Cor 6:2 acceptable time I have L to you, and helped

LISTENERS

Sir 25:9 good sense, and he who speaks to attentive L

LISTENING (10)

Gen 18:10 And Sarah was L at the tent door behind
27:5 Now Rebekah was L when Isaac spoke to his
2Sam 20:17 And he answered, "I am L
Job 9:16 believe that he was L to my voice.
Prov 25:12 wise reprover to a L ear.
Song 8:13 gardens, my companions are L for your voice; let
Jer 18:10 in my sight, not L to my voice, then
Lk 2:46 sitting among the teachers, L to them and asking
Acts 16:25 and the prisoners were L to them,
2Tim 4:4 will turn away from L to the truth and

LISTENS (10)

Prov 1:33 them; but he who L to me will dwell
8:34 is the man who L to me, watching daily
12:15 but a wise man L to advice.
17:4 An evildoer L to wicked lips; and a liar
29:12 If a ruler L to falsehood, all his officials
Zeph 3:2 She L to no voice, she accepts no correction.
Mt 18:14 If he L to you, you have gained your
Jn 9:31 does his will, God L to him.
1Jn 4:5 world, and the world L to them.
4:6 Whoever knows God L to us, and he who

LITERAL

Rom 2:29 a matter of the heart, spiritual and not L

LITTER (2)

Song 3:7 Behold, it is the L of Solomon!
2Mac 9:8 and carried in a L, making the power of

LITTERED

2Kgs 7:15 all the way was L with garments and equipment

LITTERS

Is 66:20 in chariots, and in L, and upon mules, and

LITTLE (245)

Gen 18:4 Let a L water be brought, and wash your
19:20 and it is a L one.
19:20 is it not a L one?--and my life
24:17 "Pray give me a L water to drink from
24:43 "Pray give me a L water from your jar
30:30 For you had L before I came, and it
34:29 their wealth, all their L ones and their wives,

LITTLE

43:2 again, buy us a L food."
43:8 you and also our L ones.
43:11 man a present, a L balm and a little
43:11 little balm and a L honey, gum, myrrh, pistachio
44:25 again, buy us a L food,'
45:19 of Egypt for your L ones and for your
46:5 Jacob their father, their L ones, and their wives,
47:24 as food for your L ones."
50:21 for you and your L ones." Thus he reassured
Ex 10:10 let you and your L ones go!
16:18 and he that gathered L had no lack; each
23:30 L by little I will drive them out from
23:30 Little by L I will drive them out from
Num 14:3 Our wives and our L ones will become a
14:31 But your L ones, who you said would become
16:27 their sons, and their L ones.
31:9 of Midian and their L ones; and they took
31:17 every male among the L ones, and kill every
32:16 and cities for our L ones,
32:17 their place; and our L ones shall live in
32:24 Build cities for your L ones, and folds for
32:26 Our L ones, our wives, our flocks, and all
Deut 1:39 Moreover your L ones, who you said would become
3:19 But your wives, your L ones, and your cattle
7:22 these nations before you L by little; you may
7:22 before you little by L; you may not make
14:16 after their kinds; the L owl and the great
20:14 the women and the L ones, the cattle, and
28:38 field, and shall gather L in; for the locust
29:11 men of Israel, your L ones, your wives, and
31:12 people, men, women, and L ones, and the sojourner
Josh 1:14 land.' Your wives, your L ones, and your cattle
8:35 the women, and the L ones, and the sojourners
Judg 4:19 "Pray, give me a L water to drink; for
18:21 and departed, putting the L ones and the cattle
21:10 the women and the L ones.
1Sam 2:19 make for him a L robe and take it
14:29 because I tasted a L of this honey.
14:43 him, "I tasted a L honey with the tip
15:17 said, "Though you are L in your own eyes,
18:23 seem to you a L thing to become the
20:35 and with him a L lad.
22:15 has known nothing of all this, much or L
2Sam 12:3 had nothing but one L ewe lamb, which he
12:8 if this were too L, I would add to
15:22 men and all the L ones who were with
16:1 David had passed a L beyond the summit, Ziba
19:36 servant will go a L way over the Jordan
1Kgs 3:7 I am but a L child; I do not
11:17 Hadad being yet a L child.
12:10 say to them, 'My L finger is thicker than
17:10 said, "Bring me a L water in a vessel,
17:12 a jar, and a L oil in a cruse;
17:13 first make me a L cake of it and
18:44 he said, "Behold, a L cloud like a man's
18:45 And in a L while the heavens grew black
20:27 before them like two L flocks of goats, but
2Kgs 5:2 had carried off a L maid from the land
5:14 the flesh of a L child, and he was
8:12 dash in pieces their L ones, and rip up
10:18 "Ahab served Baal a L; but Jehu will serve
1Chr 16:19 in number, and of L account, and sojourners in
2Chr 10:10 say to them, 'My L finger is thicker than
20:13 the LORD, with their L ones, their wives, and
31:18 enrolled with all their L children, their wives, their
Ezra 9:8 and grant us a L reviving in our bondage.
Neh 9:32 all the hardship seem L to thee that has
Tob 4:8 give according to the L you have.
12:8 A L with righteousness is better than much with
Jud 16:16 thee is a very L thing, but he who
Job 10:20 I may find a L comfort
21:11 They send forth their L ones like a flock,
24:24 They are exalted a L while, and then are
36:2 "Bear with me a L, and I will show
Ps 8:5 thou hast made him L less than God, and
37:10 Yet a L while, and the wicked will be
37:16 Better is a L that the righteous has than
105:12 few in number, of L account, and sojourners in
137:9 be who takes your L ones and dashes them
Prov 6:10 A L sleep, a little slumber, a little folding
6:10 A little sleep, a L slumber, a little folding
6:10 a little slumber, a L folding of the hands
10:20 the wicked is of L worth.
13:11 but he who gathers L by little will increase
13:11 who gathers little by L will increase it.
15:16 Better is a L with the fear of the
16:8 Better is a L with righteousness than great revenues
24:33 A L sleep, a little slumber, a little folding
24:33 A little sleep, a L slumber, a little folding
24:33 a little slumber, a L folding of the hands
Eccl 5:12 laborer, whether he eats L or much; but the
9:14 There was a L city with few men in
10:1 evil odor; so a L folly outweighs wisdom and
Song 2:15 us the foxes, the L foxes, that spoil the
8:8 We have a L sister, and she has no
Wis 3:5 Having been disciplined a L, they will receive great
7:9 gold is but a L sand in her sight,
9:5 and short-lived, with L understanding of judgment
12:2 Therefore thou dost correct L by little those who
12:2 dost correct little by L those who trespass, and
12:8 army, to destroy them L by little,
12:8 destroy them little by L,
12:10 But judging them L by little thou gavest them
12:10 judging them little by L thou gavest them a
13:6 Yet these men are L to be blamed, for
15:8 before and after a L while goes to the
16:6 were troubled for a L while as a warning,
Sir 6:19 you will toil a L while, and soon you
19:1 small things will fail L by little.
19:1 who despises small things will fail little by L
20:11 buys much for a L, but pays for it
20:14 He gives L and upbraids much, he opens his
29:23 Be content with L or much.
31:19 How ample a L is for a well-disciplined man!
38:24 and he who has L business may become wise.
40:6 He gets L or no rest, and afterward in
42:4 of acquiring much or L;
51:16 inclined my ear a L and received her, and
51:27 that I have labored L and found myself much
Is 7:13 Is it too L for you to weary men,
10:25 For in a very L while my indignation will
11:6 fatling together, and a L child shall lead them.
26:20 hide yourselves for a L while until the wrath
28:10 upon line, here a L, there a little."
28:10 line upon line, here a little, there a L
28:13 upon line, here a L, there a little; that
28:13 a little, there a L; that they may go,
29:17 not yet a very L while until Lebanon shall
32:10 In L more than a year you will shudder,
63:18 possessed thy sanctuary a L while; our adversaries
Jer 49:20 of Teman: Even the L ones of the flock
50:45 the Chaldeans: Surely the L ones of their flock
51:33 is trodden; yet a L while and the time
Ezek 9:6 young men and maidens, L children and women, but
16:47 abominations; within a very L time you were more
Dan 7:8 them another horn, a L one, before which three
8:9 them came forth a L horn, which grew exceedingly
11:34 they shall receive a L help.
Hos 1:4 Jezreel; for yet a L while, and I will
8:10 shall cease for a L while from anointing king
13:16 by the sword, their L ones shall be dashed
Amos 6:11 into fragments, and the L house into bits.
Mic 5:2 Bethlehem Ephrathah, who are L to be among the
Nah 3:10 went into captivity; her L ones were dashed in
Hag 1:6 sown much, and harvested L; you eat, but you
1:9 lo, it came to L; and when you brought
2:6 Once again, in a L while, I will shake
Zech 1:15 was angry but a L they furthered the disaster.
13:7 my hand against the L ones.
1Mac 16:15 them treacherously in the L stronghold called Dok,
2Mac 3:14 There was no L distress throughout the whole city.
3:30 the temple, which a L while before was full
5:17 was angered for a L while because of the
6:29 And those who a L before had acted toward
7:33 is angry for a L while, to rebuke and
8:8 man was gaining ground L by little, and that
8:8 gaining ground little by L, and that he was
8:33 had fled into one L house; so these received
9:10 the man who a L while before had thought
15:19 city were in no L distress, being anxious over
Mt 6:30 you, O men of L faith?
8:26 afraid, O men of L faith?" Then he rose
10:42 to one of these L ones even a cup
14:31 him, "O man of L faith, why did you
16:8 said, "O men of L faith, why do you
17:20 them, "Because of your L faith.
18:6 causes one of these L ones who believe in
18:10 despise one of these L ones; for I tell
18:13 that one of these L ones should perish.
25:21 been faithful over a L, I will set you
25:23 been faithful over a L, I will set you
26:39 And going a L farther he fell on his

26:73 After a L while the bystanders came up and
Mk 1:19 And going on a L farther, he saw James
5:23 besought him, saying, "My L daughter is at the
5:41 "Talitha cumi"; which means, L girl, I say to
7:24 a woman, whose L daughter was possessed by
9:42 causes one of these L ones who believe in
14:35 And going a L farther, he fell on the
14:70 And after a L while again the bystanders said
Lk 5:3 to put out a L from the land.
7:47 he who is forgiven L, loves little."
7:47 much; but he who is forgiven little, loves L
12:28 you, O men of L faith!
12:32 "Fear not, L flock, for it is your Father's
16:10 faithful in a very L is faithful also in
16:10 dishonest in a very L is dishonest also in
17:2 cause one of these L ones to sin.
19:17 faithful in a very L, you shall have authority
22:56 And a L later some one else saw him
Jn 6:7 bread for each of them to get a L
7:33 be with you a L longer, and then I
12:35 with you for a L longer.
13:33 L children, yet a little while I am with
13:33 Little children, yet a L while I am with
14:19 Yet a L while, and the world will see
16:16 "A L while, and you will see me no
16:16 no more; again a L while, and you will
16:17 says to us, 'A L while, and you will
16:17 me, and again a L while, and you will
16:18 he mean by 'a L while?
16:19 meant by saying, 'A L while, and you will
16:19 me, and again a L while, and you will
Acts 14:28 And they remained no L time with the disciples.
19:23 time there arose no L stir concerning the Way.
19:24 of Artemis, brought no L business to the craftsmen.
20:12 and were not a L comforted.
27:28 found twenty fathoms; a L farther on they sounded
Rom 15:24 once I have enjoyed your company for a L
1Cor 5:6 not know that a L leaven leavens the whole
2Cor 8:15 and he who gathered L had no lack."
10:8 if I boast a L too much of our
11:1 with me in a L foolishness.
11:16 fool, so that I too may boast a L
Gal 4:19 My L children, with whom I am again in
5:9 A L leaven leavens the whole lump.
1Tim 5:23 water, but use a L wine for the sake
Heb 2:7 make him for a L while lower than the
2:9 Jesus, who for a L while was made lower
10:37 "For yet a L while, and the coming one
Jas 3:5 the tongue is a L member and boasts of
4:14 that appears for a L time and then vanishes.
1Pet 1:6 though now for a L while you may have
5:10 you have suffered a L while, the God of
1Jn 2:1 My L children, I am writing this to you
2:12 am writing to you, L children, because your sins
2:28 And now, L children, abide in him, so that
3:7 L children, let no one deceive you.
3:18 L children, let us not love in word or
4:4 L children, you are of God, and have overcome
5:21 L children, keep yourselves from idols.
Rev 3:8 that you have but L power, and yet you
6:11 told to rest a L longer, until the number
10:2 He had a L scroll open in his hand.
10:9 to give me the L scroll; and he said
10:10 And I took the L scroll from the hand
17:10 must remain only a L while.
20:3 be loosed for a L while.

LIVE (398)

Gen 3:22 life, and eat, and L for ever"–
12:12 will kill me, but they will let you L
17:18 "O that Ishmael might L in thy sight!"
20:7 he will pray for you, and you shall L
25:22 said, "If it is thus, why do I L
27:40 your sword you shall L, and you shall serve
31:32 with whom you find your gods shall not L
42:2 there, that we may L, and not die."
42:18 this and you will L, for I fear God:
43:8 go, that we may L and not die, both
47:19 seed, that we may L, and not die, and
Ex 1:15 but if it is a daughter, she shall L
1:16 Egypt commanded them, but let the male children L
1:17 you done this, and let the male children L
1:21 the Nile, but you shall let every daughter L
9:16 have I let you L, to show you my
19:13 man, he shall not L When the trumpet sounds
21:35 they shall sell the L ox and divide the
22:18 "You shall not permit a sorceress to L
33:20 face; for man shall not see me and L
Lev 16:20 he shall present the L goat;
16:21 the head of the L goat, and confess over
18:5 which a man shall L: I am the LORD.
25:35 a sojourner he shall L with you.
25:36 that your brother may L beside you.
Num 4:19 them, that they may L and not die when
14:21 but truly, as I L, and as all the
14:28 to them, 'As I L says the LORD, 'what
21:8 who is bitten, when he sees it, shall L
21:9 he would look at the bronze serpent and L
22:33 I would have slain you and let her L
24:23 said, "Alas, who shall L when God does this?
31:15 to them, "Have you let all the women L
32:17 our little ones shall L in the fortified cities
35:25 fled, and he shall L in it until the
35:33 land in which you L; for blood pollutes the
35:34 land in which you L, in the midst of
Deut 2:4 sons of Esau, who L in Seir; and they
2:8 sons of Esau who L in Seir, away from
2:22 sons of Esau, who L in Seir, when he
2:29 sons of Esau who L in Seir and the
2:29 and the Moabites who L in Ar did for
4:1 them; that you may L, and go in and
4:10 the days that they L upon the earth, and
4:26 possess; you will not L long upon it, but
4:33 the fire, as you have heard, and still L
5:24 seen God speak with man and man still L
5:33 you, that you may L, and that it may
5:33 and that you may L long in the land
8:1 do, that you may L and multiply, and go
8:3 that man does not L by bread alone, but
8:12 built goodly houses and L in them,
11:9 and that you may L long in the land
11:30 of the Canaanites who L in the Arabah, over
11:31 you possess it and L in it,
12:1 the days that you L upon the earth.
12:10 over the Jordan, and L in the land which
12:10 about, so that you L in safety,
12:19 as long as you L in your land.
16:20 follow, that you may L and inherit the land
22:7 and that you may L long.
26:1 possession of it, and L in it,
30:6 and with all your soul, that you may L
30:16 ordinances, then you shall L and multiply, and the
30:18 perish; you shall not L long in the land
30:19 and your descendants may L,
31:13 as long as you L in the land which
31:21 witness (for it will L unforgotten in the mouths
32:40 and swear, As I L for ever,
32:47 and thereby you shall L long in the land
33:6 "Let Reuben L, and not die, nor let his
Josh 6:17 in her house shall L, because she hid the
9:7 the Hivites, "Perhaps you L among us; then how
9:15 them, to let them L; and the leaders of
9:20 them, and let them L, lest wrath be upon
9:21 And the leaders said to them, "Let them L
Judg 9:41 that they could not L on at Shechem.
17:8 Bethlehem in Judah, to L where he could find
1Sam 1:26 As you L, my lord, I am the woman
10:24 the people shouted, "Long L the king!"
25:28 be found in you so long as you L
2Sam 1:10 that he could not L after he had fallen;
11:11 As you L, and as your soul lives, I
12:22 that the child may L
14:19 "As surely as you L, my lord the king,
16:16 said to Absalom, "Long L the king!
16:16 Long L the king!"
19:34 have I still to L, that I should go
1Kgs 1:25 him, and saying, 'Long L King Adonijah!'
1:31 my lord King David L for ever!"
1:34 trumpet, and say, 'Long L King Solomon!'
1:39 the people said, "Long L King Solomon!"
8:40 the days that they L in the land which
20:32 said, "Your servant Ben-hadad says, 'Pray, let me L
20:32 And he said, "Does he still L
2Kgs 2:2 and as you yourself L, I will not leave
2:4 and as you yourself L, I will not leave
2:6 and as you yourself L, I will not leave
4:7 and your sons can L on the rest."
4:30 and as you yourself L, I will not leave
7:4 our lives we shall L, and if they kill
10:19 offer to Baal; whoever is missing shall not L
11:12 hands, and said, "Long L the king!"
18:32 honey, that you may L, and not die.

2Chr	6:31	the days that they L in the land which
	8:11	"My wife shall not L in the house of
	19:10	from your brethren who L in their cities, concerning
	23:11	and they said, "Long L the king."
Ezra	4:17	of their associates who L in Samaria and in
Neh	2:3	king, "Let the king L for ever!
	4:12	the places where they L they will come up
	6:11	as I could go into the temple and L
	9:29	which a man shall L, and turned a stubborn
	11:1	out of ten to L in Jerusalem the holy
	11:2	who willingly offered to L in Jerusalem.
Tob	3:6	to die than to L, because I have heard
	3:15	Why should I L
	4:5	L uprightly all the days of your life, and
	4:7	possessions to all who L uprightly, and do not
	5:3	as long as I L; and go and get
	6:16	chamber, you shall take L ashes of incense and
	8:2	and he took the L ashes of incense and
	14:10	And do not L in Nineveh any longer.
Jud	2:12	For as I L, and by the power of
	5:4	alone, of all who L in the west, refused
	7:10	the mountains where they L, for it is not
	7:14	be strewn about in the streets where they L
	11:2	if your people who L in the hill country
	11:4	Have courage; you will L, tonight and from now
	11:7	of the air will L by your power under
	11:23	God, and you shall L in the house of
	14:4	you and all who L within the borders of
Esth	4:11	holds out the golden scepter that he may L
	9:19	of the villages, who L in the open towns,
	13:17	feasting, that we may L and sing praise to
	16:19	permit the Jews to L under their own laws.
Job	7:16	life; I would not L for ever.
	14:14	man die, shall he L again?
	18:19	people, and no survivor where he used to L
	21:7	Why do the wicked L, reach old age, and
	28:4	away from where men L; they are forgotten by
Ps	22:26	May your hearts L for ever!
	49:9	he should continue to L on for ever, and
	55:23	and treachery shall not L out half their days.
	63:4	as long as I L; I will lift up
	72:5	May he L while the sun endures, and as
	72:15	Long may he L, may gold of Sheba be
	89:48	What man can L and never see death?
	103:5	as long as you L so that your youth
	104:33	as long as I L; I will sing praise
	107:36	establish a city to L in;
	116:2	will call on him as long as I L
	118:17	die, but I shall L, and recount the deeds
	119:17	servant, that I may L and observe thy word.
	119:77	me, that I may L; for thy law is
	119:116	promise, that I may L, and let me not
	119:144	for ever; give me understanding that I may L
	119:175	Let me L, that I may praise thee, and
	146:2	as long as I L; I will sing praises
Prov	4:5	keep my commandments, and L;
	7:2	keep my commandments and L, keep my teachings
	9:6	Leave simpleness, and L, and walk in the way
	11:19	steadfast in righteousness will L, but he who pursues
	15:27	his household, but he who hates bribes will L
	19:10	for a fool to L in luxury, much less
	21:9	It is better to L in a corner of
	21:19	It is better to L in a desert land
	25:24	It is better to L in a corner of
Eccl	3:12	as long as they L;
	6:6	Even though he should L a thousand years twice
	9:3	their hearts while they L, and after that they
Wis	3:17	Even if they L long they will be held
	5:15	But the righteous L for ever, and their reward
	8:9	to take her to L with me, knowing that
	13:7	For as they L among his works they keep
	14:22	of God, but they L in great strife due
	14:28	or prophesy lies, or L unrighteously, or readily
Sir	9:12	not be held guiltless as long as they L
	13:5	own something, he will L with you; he will
	14:4	others; and others will L in luxury on his
	25:1	and a husband who L in harmony.
	33:19	as long as you L; and do not give
	34:13	fear the Lord will L, for their hope is
	37:26	and his name will L for ever.
	37:27	your soul while you L; see what is bad
	38:32	can neither sojourn nor L there.
	39:9	and his name will L through all generations.
	41:19	and of theft, in the place where you L
	42:23	All these things L and remain for ever for
	46:12	who have been honored L again in their sons!
	48:11	adorned in love; for we also shall surely L
	50:26	no nation: Those who L on Mount Seir, and
	51:18	For I resolved to L according to wisdom, and
Is	26:14	dead, they will not L; they are shades, they
	26:19	Thy dead shall L, their bodies shall rise.
	38:16	by these things men L, and in all these
	38:16	Oh, restore me to health and make me L
	49:18	As I L, says the LORD, you shall put
	55:3	that your soul may L; and I will make
Jer	21:9	are besieging you shall L and shall have his
	22:24	"As I L, says the LORD, though Coniah the
	27:12	Babylon, and serve him and his people, and L
	27:17	to them; serve the king of Babylon and L
	29:5	Babylon: Build houses and L in them; plant gardens
	29:28	long; build houses and L in them, and plant
	35:7	vineyard; but you shall L in tents all your
	35:7	days, that you may L many days in the
	38:2	to the Chaldeans shall L; he shall have his
	38:2	his life as a prize of war, and L
	38:17	with fire, and you and your house shall L
	42:15	Egypt and go to L there,
	42:17	go to Egypt to L there shall die by
	42:22	the place where you desire to go to L
	43:2	go to Egypt to L there';
	43:5	who had returned to L in the land of
	44:8	you have come to L, that you may be
	44:12	land of Egypt to L, and they shall all
	44:14	who have come to L in the land of
	44:28	land of Egypt to L, shall know whose word
	46:18	go by.' "As I L, says the King, whose
	49:16	your heart, you who L in the clefts of
Lam	4:20	his shadow we shall L among the nations."
Bar	1:12	eyes, and we shall L under the protection of
	4:1	hold her fast will L, and those who forsake
	6:46	them will certainly not L very long themselves; how
Ezek	3:21	sin, he shall surely L, because he took warning;
	5:11	Wherefore, as I L, says the Lord GOD, surely,
	7:13	return to what he has sold, while they L
	13:19	persons who should not L, by your lies to
	14:16	in it, as I L, says the Lord GOD,
	14:18	in it, as I L, says the Lord GOD,
	14:20	in it, as I L, says the Lord GOD,
	16:6	you in your blood, L,
	16:48	As I L, says the Lord GOD, your sister
	17:16	As I L, says the Lord GOD, surely in
	17:19	Lord GOD: As I L, surely my oath which
	18:3	As I L, says the Lord GOD, this proverb
	18:9	righteous, he shall surely L, says the Lord GOD.
	18:13	at interest, and takes increase; shall he then L
	18:13	He shall not L
	18:17	die for his father's iniquity; he shall surely L
	18:19	to observe all my statutes, he shall surely L
	18:21	right, he shall surely L; he shall not die.
	18:22	the righteousness which he has done he shall L
	18:23	that he should turn from his way and L
	18:24	things that the wicked man does, shall he L
	18:28	committed, he shall surely L, he shall not die.
	18:32	one, says the Lord GOD; so turn, and L
	20:3	As I L, says the Lord GOD, I will
	20:11	my ordinances, by whose observance man shall L
	20:13	whose observance man shall L; and my sabbaths
	20:21	observance man shall L; they profaned my sabbaths.
	20:31	As I L, says the Lord GOD, I will
	20:33	and stone.' "As I L, says the Lord GOD,
	33:10	how then can we L
	33:11	to them, As I L, says the Lord GOD,
	33:11	from his way and L; turn back, turn back
	33:12	not be able to L by his righteousness when
	33:13	that he shall surely L, yet if he trusts
	33:15	iniquity; he shall surely L, he shall not die.
	33:16	what is lawful and right, he shall surely L
	33:19	and right, he shall L by it.
	33:27	Lord GOD: As I L, surely those who are
	34:8	the LORD: As I L, says the Lord GOD,
	35:6	punishment; therefore, as I L, says the Lord GOD,
	35:11	therefore, as I L, says the Lord GOD,
	37:3	to me, "Son of man, can these bones L
	37:5	cause breath to enter you, and you shall L
	37:6	you, and you shall L; and you shall know
	37:9	and breathe upon these slain, that they may L
	37:14	you, and you shall L, and I will place
	45:5	possession for cities to L in.
	47:9	creature which swarms will L, and there will be
	47:9	fresh; so everything will L where the river goes.
Dan	2:4	the king, "O king, L for ever!
	3:9	King Nebuchadnezzar, "O king, L for ever!

	5:10	queen said, "O king, L for ever!
	6:6	him, "O King Darius, L for ever!
	6:21	the king, "O king, L for ever!
Hos	6:2	up, that we may L before him.
Amos	5:4	Israel: "Seek me and L;
	5:6	Seek the LORD and L, lest he break out
	5:14	evil, that you may L; and so the LORD,
Obad	1:3	deceived you, you who L in the clefts of
Jon	4:3	is better for me to die than to L
	4:8	is better for me to die than to L
Hab	2:4	but the righteous shall L by his faith.
Zeph	2:9	Therefore, as I L
Zech	1:5	the prophets, do they L for ever?
	10:9	their children they shall L and return.
	13:3	him, 'You shall not L, for you speak lies
1Mac	2:13	Why should we L any longer?"
	2:19	all the nations that L under the rule of
	2:20	and my brothers will L by the covenant of
	2:33	do what the king commands, and you will L
	4:35	they were either to L or to die nobly,
	6:23	serve your father, to L by what he said
	6:59	agree to let them L by their laws as
	7:38	blasphemies, and let them L no longer."
	10:37	number, and let them L by their own laws,
2Mac	5:27	do; they continued to L on what grew wild,
	6:1	fathers and cease to L by the laws of
	6:26	men, yet whether I L or die I shall
	11:25	them and that they L according to the customs
	12:2	would not let them L quietly and in peace.
	12:4	because they wished to L peaceably and suspected
Mt	4:4	written, 'Man shall not L by bread alone, but
	9:18	lay your hand on her, and she will L
Mk	5:23	so that she may be made well, and L
	7:5	do your disciples not L according to the tradition
Lk	4:4	written, 'Man shall not L by bread alone.'"
	7:25	are gorgeously appareled and L in luxury are in
	10:28	have answered right; do this, and you will L
	20:38	the living; for all L to him."
Jn	4:50	Jesus said to him, "Go; your son will L
	4:53	him, "Your son will L; and he himself believed,
	5:24	Son of God, and those who hear will L
	6:51	this bread, he will L for ever; and the
	6:57	sent me, and I L because of the Father,
	6:57	who eats me will L because of me.
	6:58	eats this bread will L for ever."
	11:25	die, yet shall he L,
	14:19	see me; because I L, you will live also.
	14:19	I live, you will L also.
Acts	1:20	be no one to L in it'; and 'His
	13:27	For those who L in Jerusalem and their rulers,
	17:24	and earth, does not L in shrines made by
	17:26	nation of men to L on all the face
	17:28	for 'In him we L and move and have
	21:24	but that you yourself L in observance of the
	22:22	For he ought not to L
	25:24	he ought not to L any longer.
	28:4	the sea, justice has not allowed him to L
Rom	1:17	written, "He who through faith is righteous shall L
	6:2	died to sin still L in it?
	6:8	that we shall also L with him.
	8:5	For those who L according to the flesh set
	8:5	flesh, but those who L according to the Spirit
	8:12	to the flesh, to L according to the flesh--
	8:13	for if you L according to the flesh
	8:13	death the deeds of the body you will L
	10:5	on the law shall L by it.
	12:16	L in harmony with one another; do not be
	12:18	it depends upon you, L peaceably with all.
	14:8	If we L, we live to the Lord, and
	14:8	If we live, we L to the Lord, and
	14:8	so then, whether we L or whether we die,
	14:11	is written, "As I L, says the Lord, every
	15:5	encouragement grant you to L in such harmony with
1Cor	7:12	and she consents to L with him, he should
	7:13	and he consents to L with her, she should
	7:29	those who have wives L as though they had
2Cor	4:11	For while we L we are always being given
	5:1	the earthly tent we L in is destroyed, we
	5:15	all, that those who L might live no longer
	5:15	those who live might L no longer for themselves
	6:9	dying, and behold we L; as punished, and yet
	6:16	God said, "I will L in them and move
	7:3	die together and to L together.
	10:3	For though we L in the world we are
	13:4	with you we shall L with him by the
	13:11	agree with one another, L in peace, and the
Gal	2:14	you, though a Jew, L like a Gentile and
	2:14	compel the Gentiles to L like Jews?"
	2:19	law, that I might L to God.
	2:20	no longer I who L, but Christ who lives
	2:20	the life I now L in the flesh I
	2:20	in the flesh I L by faith in the
	3:11	faith is righteous shall L;
	3:12	who does them shall L by them."
	5:25	If we L by the Spirit, let us also
Eph	1:12	destined and appointed to L for the praise of
	4:17	you must no longer L as the Gentiles do,
	6:3	and that you may L long on the earth."
Phil	1:21	For to me to L is Christ, and to
	3:17	mark those who so L as you have an
	3:18	you even with tears, L as enemies of the
Col	2:6	Jesus the Lord, so L in him,
	2:20	universe, why do you L as if you still
1Thes	3:8	faith; for now we L, if you stand fast
	4:1	how you ought to L and to please God,
	4:11	more, to aspire to L quietly, to mind your
	5:10	or sleep we might L with him.
2Tim	2:11	him, we shall also L with him;
	3:12	all who desire to L a godly life in
Tit	2:12	worldly passions, and to L sober, upright, and godly
Heb	10:38	my righteous one shall L by faith, and if
	12:9	be subject to the Father of spirits and L
Jas	4:15	Lord wills, we shall L and we shall do
1Pet	2:16	L as free men, yet without using your freedom
	2:16	pretext for evil; but L as servants of God.
	2:24	die to sin and L to righteousness.
	3:7	you husbands, L considerately with your wives,
	4:2	sin, so as to L for the rest of
	4:6	like men, they might L in the spirit like
2Pet	2:18	escaped from those who L in error.
1Jn	1:6	lie and do not L according to the truth;
	4:9	so that we might L through him.

LIVED (136)

Gen	5:3	When Adam had L a hundred and thirty years,
	5:5	the days that Adam L were nine hundred and
	5:6	When Seth had L a hundred and five years,
	5:7	Seth L after the birth of Enosh eight hundred
	5:9	When Enosh had L ninety years, he became the
	5:10	Enosh L after the birth of Kenan eight hundred
	5:12	When Kenan had L seventy years, he became the
	5:13	Kenan L after the birth of Mahalalel eight hundred
	5:15	When Mahalalel had L sixty-five years, he became
	5:16	Mahalalel L after the birth of Jared eight hundred
	5:18	When Jared had L a hundred and sixty-two years
	5:19	Jared L after the birth of Enoch eight hundred
	5:21	When Enoch had L sixty-five years, he became the
	5:25	When Methuselah had L a hundred and eighty-seven
	5:26	Methuselah L after the birth of Lamech seven
	5:28	When Lamech had L a hundred and eighty-two
	5:30	Lamech L after the birth of Noah five hundred
	9:28	After the flood Noah L three hundred and fifty
	10:30	territory in which they L extended from Mesha in
	11:11	the flood; and Shem L after the birth of
	11:12	When Arpachshad had L thirty-five years, he became
	11:13	of Shelah; and Arpachshad L after the birth of
	11:14	When Shelah had L thirty years, he became the
	11:15	of Eber; and Shelah L after the birth of
	11:16	When Eber had L thirty-four years, he became the
	11:17	of Peleg; and Eber L after the birth of
	11:18	When Peleg had L thirty years, he became the
	11:19	of Reu; and Peleg L after the birth of
	11:20	When Reu had L thirty-two years, he became the
	11:21	of Serug; and Reu L after the birth of
	11:22	When Serug had L thirty years, he became the
	11:23	of Nahor; and Serug L after the birth of
	11:24	When Nahor had L twenty-nine years, he became
	11:25	of Terah; and Nahor L after the birth of
	11:26	When Terah had L seventy years, he became the
	21:20	he grew up; he L in the wilderness, and
	21:21	He L in the wilderness of Paran; and his
	23:1	Sarah L a hundred and twenty-seven years; these
	47:22	allowance from Pharaoh, and L on the allowance
	47:28	And Jacob L in the land of Egypt seventeen
	50:22	father's house; and Joseph L a hundred and ten
Deut	1:4	of the Amorites, who L in Heshbon, and Og
	1:4	king of Bashan, who L in Ashtaroth and in
	1:44	Then the Amorites who L in that hill country
	2:10	possession.' (The Emim formerly L there, a people
	2:12	The Horites also L in Seir formerly, but the
	2:20	Rephaim formerly L there, but the Ammonites
	2:23	for the Avvim, who L in villages as far

4:46 of the Amorites, who L at Heshbon, whom Moses
4:47 of the Amorites, who L to the east beyond
5:26 of fire, as we have, and has still L
Josh 8:35 and the sojourners who L among them.
24:2 of Israel, 'Your fathers L of old beyond the
24:7 to Egypt; and you L in the wilderness a
24:8 of the Amorites, who L on the other side
24:18 peoples, the Amorites who L in the land; therefore
Judg 10:1 of Issachar; and he L at Shamir in the
Ruth 1:4 They L there about ten years;
2:23 wheat harvests; and she L with her mother-in-law.
2Kgs 4:8 where a wealthy woman L, who urged him to
14:17 Joash, king of Judah, L fifteen years after the
25:30 every day a portion, as long as he L
1Chr 9:34 their generations, leaders, who L in Jerusalem.
2Chr 11:13 resorted to him from all places where they L
25:25 Joash king of Judah L fifteen years after the
31:4 commanded the people who L in Jerusalem to give
31:6 Israel and Judah who L in the cities of
Ezra 2:70 some of the people L in Jerusalem and its
2:70 and the temple servants L in their towns, and
Neh 4:12 When the Jews who L by them came they
7:73 servants, and all Israel, L in their towns.
11:1 leaders of the people L in Jerusalem; and the
11:3 of the province who L in Jerusalem; but in
11:3 of Judah every one L on his property in
11:4 And in Jerusalem L certain of the sons of
11:6 sons of Perez who L in Jerusalem were four
11:21 But the temple servants L on Ophel; and Ziha
11:25 the people of Judah L in Kiriath-arba and its
11:31 people of Benjamin also L from Geba onward, at
13:16 of Tyre also, who L in the city, brought
Jud 1:6 and all those who L along the Euphrates and
1:7 sent to all who L in Persia and to
1:7 and to all who L in the west, those
1:7 the west, those who L in Cilicia and Damascus
1:7 Antilebanon and all who L along the seacoast,
1:10 Memphis, and all who L in Egypt as far
1:11 But all who L in the whole region disregarded
2:23 and the Ishmaelites who L along the desert, south
2:28 all the people who L along the seacoast, at
2:28 Tyre, and those who L in Sur and Ocina
2:28 Ocina and all who L in Jamnia.
2:28 Those who L in Azotus and Ascalon feared him
5:7 At one time they L in Mesopotamia, because they
5:8 fled to Mesopotamia, and L there for a long
5:10 down to Egypt and L there as long as
5:15 So they L in the land of the Amorites,
5:16 all the Gergesites, and L there a long time.
8:4 Judith had L at home as a widow for
10:2 the house where she L on sabbaths and on
15:8 people of Israel who L at Jerusalem, came to
Job 15:28 his loins, and has L in desolate cities, in
42:16 And after this Job L a hundred and forty
Wis 12:23 in folly of life L unrighteously thou didst torment
14:17 their presence, since they L at a distance, they
Sir 44:10 though they had not L; they have become as
Jer 35:10 seed; but we have L in tents, and have
52:34 day of his death as long as he L
Bar 3:37 appeared upon earth and L among men.
Ezek 16:46 sister is Samaria, who L with her daughters to
16:46 your younger sister, who L to the south of
37:10 into them, and they L, and stood upon their
1Mac 5:2 descendants of Jacob who L among them.
5:9 against the Israelites who L in their territory, and
9:71 try to harm him as long as he L
2Mac 12:3 invited the Jews who L among them to embark,
Mt 23:29 saying, 'If we had L in the days of
Mk 5:3 an unclean spirit, who L among the tombs; and
Lk 2:36 a great age, having L with her husband seven
8:27 no clothes, and he L not in a house
Acts 7:2 in Mesopotamia, before he L in Haran,
7:4 of the Chaldeans, and L in Haran.
9:22 confounded the Jews who L in Damascus by proving
9:32 to the saints that L at Lydda.
11:29 to the brethren who L in Judea;
17:21 and the foreigners who L there spent their time
20:18 yourselves know how I L among you all the
22:12 all the Jews who L there,
23:1 said, "Brethren, I have L before God in all
26:5 our religion I have L as a Pharisee.
28:29 And he L there two whole years at his
Rom 14:9 end Christ died and L again, that he might
Eph 2:3 these we all once L in the passions of
Col 3:7 once walked, when you L in them.
Jas 5:5 You have L on the earth in luxury and
2Pet 2:8 and heard as he L among them, he was
Rev 13:14 the sword and yet L;

LIVELIHOOD

Sir 31:4 man toils as his L diminishes, and when he

LIVER (17)

Ex 29:13 the appendage of the L, and the two kidneys
29:22 the appendage of the L, and the two kidneys
Lev 3:4 the appendage of the L which he shall take
3:10 the appendage of the L which he shall take
3:15 the appendage of the L which he shall take
4:9 the appendage of the L which he shall take
7:4 the appendage of the L which he shall take
8:16 the appendage of the L, and the two kidneys
8:25 the appendage of the L, and the two kidneys
9:10 the appendage of the L from the sin offering
9:19 the appendage of the L;
Tob 6:4 take the heart and L and gall and put
6:6 what use is the L and heart and gall
6:7 for the heart and L, if a demon or
6:16 of the heart and L of the fish so
8:2 put the heart and L of the fish upon
Ezek 21:21 he consults the teraphim, he looks at the L

LIVES (161)

Gen 9:3 Every moving thing that L shall be food for
47:25 "You have saved our L; may it please my
Ex 1:13 rigor, and made their L bitter with hard service,
Lev 25:6 and the sojourner who L with you;
Num 16:38 the cost of their L; so let them be
Deut 8:3 alone, but that man L by everything that proceeds
18:6 all Israel, where he L –and he may come
21:19 the place where he L,
Josh 2:13 them, and deliver our L from death."
9:24 feared greatly for our L because of you, and
Judg 5:18 people that jeoparded their L to the death; Naphtali
8:19 mother; as the LORD L, if you had saved
18:25 your life with the L of your household."
Ruth 3:13 then, as the LORD L, I will do the
1Sam 1:28 as long as he L, he is lent to
14:39 For as the LORD L who saves Israel, though
14:45 As the LORD L, there shall not one hair
17:55 said, "As your soul L, O king, I cannot
19:6 swore, "As the LORD L, he shall not be
20:3 truly, as the LORD L and as your soul
20:3 and as your soul L, there is but a
20:21 for, as the LORD L, it is safe for
20:31 the son of Jesse L upon the earth, neither
25:26 lord, as the LORD L, and as your soul
25:26 and as your soul L, seeing the LORD has
25:29 your God; and the L of your enemies he
25:34 the God of Israel L, who has restrained me
26:10 said, "As the LORD L, the LORD will smite
26:16 As the LORD L, you deserve to die, because
28:10 LORD, "As the LORD L, no punishment shall come
29:6 him, "As the LORD L, you have been honest,
2Sam 2:27 Joab said, "As God L, if you had not
4:9 Be-erothite, "As the LORD L, who has redeemed my
11:11 and as your soul L, I will not do
12:5 Nathan, "As the LORD L, the man who has
14:11 said, "As the LORD L, not one hair of
15:21 king, "As the LORD L, and as my lord
15:21 my lord the king L, wherever my lord the
19:5 your life, and the L of your sons and
19:5 your daughters, and the L of your wives and
22:47 "The LORD L; and blessed be my rock, and
23:17 men who went at the risk of their L
1Kgs 1:29 saying, "As the LORD L, who has redeemed my
2:24 therefore as the LORD L, who has established me,
17:1 the God of Israel L, before whom I stand,
17:12 the LORD your God L, I have nothing baked,
17:23 his mother; and Elijah said, "See, your son L
18:10 the LORD your God L, there is no nation
18:15 the LORD of hosts L, before whom I stand,
22:14 said, "As the LORD L, what the LORD says
2Kgs 2:2 said, "As the LORD L, and as you yourself
2:4 said, "As the LORD L, and as you yourself
2:6 said, "As the LORD L, and as you yourself
3:14 the LORD of hosts L, whom I serve, were
4:30 said, "As the LORD L, and as you yourself
5:16 said, "As the LORD L, whom I serve, I
5:20 As the LORD L, I will run after him,
7:4 if they spare our L we shall live, and
7:7 camp as it was, and fled for their L
1Chr 11:19 the risk of their L they brought it." Therefore

2Chr 18:13 said, "As the LORD L, what my God says,
Tob 6:14 die and bring the L of my father and
8:17 Lord; and bring their L to fulfilment in health
12:10 commit sin are the enemies of their own L
13:1 "Blessed is God who L for ever, and blessed
Jud 5:3 people is this that L in the hill country?
7:28 be slaves, but our L will be spared, and
8:24 our brethren, for their L depend upon us, and
11:7 of the whole earth L, and as his power
12:4 replied, "As your soul L, my lord, your servant
13:16 As the Lord L, who has protected me in
Esth 8:11 gather and defend their L, to destroy, to slay,
9:16 gathered to defend their L, and got relief from
13:2 determined to settle the L of my subjects in
Job 8:17 about the stoneheap; he L among the rocks.
19:25 know that my Redeemer L, and at last he
27:2 and said: "As God L, who has taken away
Ps 18:46 The LORD L; and blessed be my rock, and
49:18 Though, while he L, he counts himself happy, and
72:13 needy, and saves the L of the needy.
78:50 death, but gave their L over to the plague.
97:10 evil; he preserves the L of his saints; he
Prov 1:18 blood, they set an ambush for their own L
11:30 a tree of life, but lawlessness takes away L
14:25 A truthful witness saves L, but one who utters
Eccl 6:3 a hundred children, and L many years, so that
6:12 for man while he L the few days of
11:8 For if a man L many years, let him
Wis 7:28 as the man who L with wisdom.
12:6 parents who murder helpless L, thou didst will to
14:5 therefore men trust their L even to the smallest
14:24 longer keep either their L or their marriages pure,
Sir 3:12 as long as he L;
18:1 He who L for ever created the whole universe;
25:7 children; a man who L to see the downfall
25:8 happy is he who L with an intelligent wife,
39:11 his praise; if he L long, he will leave
41:1 you to one who L at peace among his
44:15 peace, and their name L to all generations.
Is 65:20 it an infant that L but a few days,
Jer 4:2 swear, 'As the LORD L in truth, in justice,
5:2 Though they say, "As the LORD L'
12:16 name, 'As the LORD L even as they taught
16:14 said, 'As the LORD L who brought up the
16:15 but 'As the LORD L who brought up the
17:21 the sake of your L, and do not bear
21:7 into the hand of those who seek their L
23:7 say, 'As the LORD L who brought up the
23:8 but 'As the LORD L who brought up and
34:20 into the hand of those who seek their L
34:21 those who seek their L, into the hand of
38:16 Jeremiah, "As the LORD L, who made our souls,
42:20 have gone astray at the cost of your L
44:26 'As the Lord GOD L
Lam 2:19 to him for the L of your children, who
5:9 the peril of our L, because of the sword
Bar 6:7 is with you, and he is watching your L
Ezek 14:14 deliver but their own L by their righteousness, says
14:20 deliver but their own L by their righteousness.
17:17 and siege walls built to cut off many L
22:25 have devoured human L; they have taken treasure
22:27 prey, shedding blood, destroying L to get dishonest
Dan 4:34 and honored him who L for ever; for his
7:12 taken away, but their L were prolonged for a
12:7 swear by him who L for ever that it
Hos 4:15 to Beth-aven, and swear not, "As the LORD L
Amos 8:14 say, 'As thy god L, O Dan,' and, 'As
8:14 the way of Beer-sheba L they shall fall, and
Hab 1:16 for by them he L in luxury, and his
1Mac 2:40 the Gentiles for our L and for our ordinances,
2:50 law, and give your L for the covenant of
3:21 we fight for our L and our laws.
9:9 rather save our own L now, and let us
9:44 and fight for our L, for today things are
12:51 would fight for their L, they turned back.
2Mac 11:7 others to risk their L with him to aid
14:10 as long as Judas L, it is impossible for
Lk 21:19 By your endurance you will gain your L
Jn 11:26 he live, and whoever L and believes in me
Acts 15:26 who have risked their L for the sake of
27:10 cargo and the ship, but also of our L
Rom 6:10 but the life he L he lives to God.
6:10 life he lives he L to God.
7:2 as long as he L; but if her husband
7:3 an adulteress if she L with another man while
14:7 None of us L to himself, and none of
1Cor 7:39 bound to her husband as long as he L
2Cor 13:4 crucified in weakness, but L by the power of
Gal 2:20 live, but Christ who L in me; and the
1Tim 5:6 who is self-indulgent is dead even while she L
Tit 2:12 sober, upright, and godly L in this world,
Heb 5:13 for every one who L on milk is unskilled
7:8 one of whom it is testified that he L
7:25 him, since he always L to make intercession for
2Pet 3:11 you to be in L of holiness and godliness,
1Jn 3:16 to lay down our L for the brethren.
Rev 4:9 on the throne, who L for ever and ever,
4:10 and worship him who L for ever and ever;
10:6 swore by him who L for ever and ever,
12:11 they loved not their L even unto death.
15:7 wrath of God who L for ever and ever;

LIVESTOCK (3)

Gen 31:18 his cattle, all his L which he had gained,
Num 35:3 cattle and for their L and for all their
1Chr 5:21 They carried off their L: fifty thousand of their

LIVING (237)

Gen 1:20 bring forth swarms of L creatures, and let birds
1:21 sea monsters and every L creature that moves, with
1:24 the earth bring forth L creatures according to their
1:28 air and over every L thing that moves upon
2:7 and man became a L being.
2:19 the man called every L creature, that was its
3:20 Eve, because she was the mother of all L
6:19 And of every L thing of all flesh, you
7:4 forty nights; and every L thing that I have
7:23 He blotted out every L thing that was upon
8:17 forth with you every L thing that is with
8:21 ever again destroy every L creature as I have
9:10 you, and with every L creature that is with
9:12 and you and every L creature that is with
9:15 and you and every L creature of all flesh;
9:16 between God and every L creature of all flesh
14:13 the Hebrew, who was L by the oaks of
25:6 while he was still L he sent them away
Lev 11:2 Israel, These are the L things which you may
11:10 waters and of the L creatures that are in
11:46 and bird and every L creature that moves through
11:47 clean and between the L creature that may be
11:47 be eaten and the L creature that may not
14:4 to be cleansed two L clean birds and cedarwood
14:6 He shall take the L bird with the cedarwood
14:6 dip them and the L bird in the blood
14:7 and shall let the L bird go into the
14:51 stuff, along with the L bird, and dip them
14:52 water, and with the L bird, and with the
14:53 he shall let the L bird go out of
Num 16:48 the dead and the L; and the plague was
Deut 5:26 the voice of the L God speaking out of
11:6 their tents, and every L thing that followed them,
Josh 3:10 shall know that the L God is among you,
Judg 17:10 year, and a suit of apparel, and your L
Ruth 2:20 has not forsaken the L or the dead!" Naomi
1Sam 17:26 the armies of the L God?"
17:36 the armies of the L God."
25:29 the bundle of the L in the care of
2Sam 20:3 day of their death, L as if in widowhood.
1Kgs 3:22 woman said, "No, the L child is mine, and
3:22 is yours, and the L child is mine." Thus
3:23 my son is the L one.'"
3:25 king said, "Divide the L child in two, and
3:26 lord, give her the L child, and by no
3:27 and said, "Give the L child to the first
2Kgs 19:4 sent to mock the L God, and will rebuke
19:16 sent to mock the L God.
Neh 3:26 and the temple servants L on Ophel repaired to
Tob 12:6 presence of all the L for what he has
13:4 presence of all the L; because he is our
Jud 4:1 the people of Israel L in Judea heard of
4:11 Israel, and their children, L at Jerusalem, prostrated
5:9 place where they were L and go to the
10:3 used to wear while her husband Manasseh was L
11:7 you to direct every L soul, not only do
11:14 because even the people L there have been doing
Esth 16:16 High, the most mighty L God, who has directed
Job 12:10 the life of every L thing and the breath
28:13 is not found in the land of the L
28:21 the eyes of all L, and concealed from the
30:23 death, and to the house appointed for all L
Ps 27:13 of the LORD in the land of the L
42:2 for God, for the L God.

	52:5	will uproot you from the land of the L
	66:9	kept us among the L, and has not let
	69:28	the book of the L; let them not be
	84:2	for joy to the L God.
	104:25	teems with things innumerable, L things both small
	116:9	before the LORD in the land of the L
	142:5	refuge, my portion in the land of the L
	143:2	servant; for no man L is righteous before thee.
	145:16	the desire of every L thing.
Eccl	4:2	more fortunate than the L who are still alive;
	4:15	I saw all the L who move about under
	6:8	who knows how to conduct himself before the L
	7:2	all men, and the L will lay it to
	9:4	joined with all the L has hope, for a
	9:4	has hope, for a L dog is better than
	9:5	For the L know that they will die, but
Song	4:15	fountain, a well of L water, and flowing streams
Wis	1:13	does not delight in the death of the L
	4:10	by him, and while L among sinners he was
	4:16	the ungodly who are L, and youth that is
	8:3	her noble birth by L with God, and the
	11:26	they are thine, O Lord who lovest the L
	15:11	breathed into him a L spirit.
	18:12	For the L were not sufficient even to bury
	18:23	wrath, and cut off its way to the L
Sir	4:1	the poor of his L, and do not keep
	7:33	graciously to all the L, and withhold not kindness
	13:15	his neighbor; all L beings associate by species,
	14:17	All L beings become old like a garment, for
	16:28	with all kinds of L beings he covered its
	17:4	of them in all L beings, and granted them
	18:12	Lord is for all L beings.
	34:22	take away a neighbor's L is to murder him;
	43:25	works, all kinds of L things, and huge creatures
	44:7	men furnished with resources, L peaceably in their
	45:16	out of all the L to offer sacrifice to
	49:16	and Adam above every L being in the creation.
Is	8:19	they consult the dead on behalf of the L
	37:4	sent to mock the L God, and will rebuke
	37:17	sent to mock the L God.
	38:11	the land of the L; I shall look upon
	38:19	The L, the living, he thanks thee, as I
	38:19	The living, the L, he thanks thee, as I
	53:8	the land of the L, stricken for the transgression
Jer	2:13	me, the fountain of L waters, and hewed out
	10:10	God; he is the L God and the everlasting
	11:19	the land of the L, that his name be
	17:13	LORD, the fountain of L water.
	23:36	the words of the L God, the LORD of
	29:32	not have any one L among this people to
	35:11	Syrians.' So we are L in Jerusalem."
Lam	3:39	Why should a L man complain, a man, about
Ezek	1:5	the likeness of four L creatures.
	1:13	the midst of the L creatures there was something
	1:13	and fro among the L creatures; and the fire
	1:14	And the L creatures darted to and fro, like
	1:15	I looked at the L creatures, I saw a
	1:15	the earth beside the L creatures, one for each
	1:19	And when the L creatures went, the wheels went
	1:19	them; and when the L creatures rose from the
	1:20	the spirit of the L creatures was in the
	1:21	the spirit of the L creatures was in the
	1:22	the heads of the L creatures there was the
	3:13	the wings of the L creatures as they touched
	10:15	These were the L creatures that I saw by
	10:17	the spirit of the L creatures was in them.
	10:20	These were the L creatures that I saw underneath
	26:20	have a place in the land of the L
	32:23	who spread terror in the land of the L
	32:24	the land of the L, and they bear their
	32:25	the land of the L, and they bear their
	32:26	they spread terror in the land of the L
	32:27	mighty men was in the land of the L
	32:32	the land of the L; therefore he shall be
	47:9	the river goes every L creature which swarms will
Dan	2:30	more than all the L has this mystery been
	4:17	the end that the L may know that the
	6:20	Daniel, servant of the L God, has your God,
	6:26	for he is the L God, enduring for ever;
	13:1	There was a man L in Babylon whose name
	14:5	man-made idols, but the L God, who created heaven
	14:6	that Bel is a L God?
	14:24	that this is a L god; so worship him."
	14:25	for he is the L God.
Hos	1:10	them, "Sons of the L God."
Zech	14:8	On that day L waters shall flow out from

1Mac	6:55	King Antiochus while still L had appointed to bring
	9:58	and his men are L in quiet and confidence.
2Mac	4:11	the lawful ways of L and introduced new customs
	4:16	those whose ways of L they admired and wished
	6:25	for the sake of L a brief moment longer,
	7:33	And if our L Lord is angry for a
	9:9	while he was still L in anguish and pain,
	11:24	their own way of L and ask that their
	12:8	the Jews who were L among them,
	15:4	declared, "It is the L Lord himself, the Sovereign
Mt	16:16	the Son of the L God."
	22:32	not God of the dead, but of the L
	26:63	adjure you by the L God, tell us if
Mk	12:27	dead, but of the L; you are quite wrong."
	12:44	has put in everything she had, her whole L
Lk	8:43	had spent all her L upon physicians, and could
	15:12	And he divided his L between them.
	15:13	and there he squandered his property in loose L
	15:30	who has devoured your L with harlots, you killed
	20:38	dead, but of the L; for all live to
	21:4	put in all the L that she had."
	24:5	do you seek the L among the dead?
Jn	4:10	would have given you L water."
	4:11	do you get that L water?
	4:51	him and told him that his son was L
	6:51	I am the L bread which came down from
	6:57	As the L Father sent me, and I live
	7:38	shall flow rivers of L water.'"
Acts	7:4	which you are now L;
	7:38	fathers; and he received L oracles to give to
	10:42	be judge of the L and the dead.
	14:15	vain things to a L God who made the
Rom	7:5	While we were L in the flesh, our sinful
	9:26	called 'sons of the L God.'"
	12:1	your bodies as a L sacrifice, holy and acceptable
	14:9	Lord both of the dead and of the L
1Cor	5:1	for a man is L with his father's wife.
	9:6	no right to refrain from working for a L
	9:14	gospel should get their L by the gospel.
	15:45	man Adam became a L being"; the last Adam
2Cor	3:3	the Spirit of the L God, not on tablets
	6:16	the temple of the L God; as God said,
1Thes	1:9	idols, to serve a L and true God,
2Thes	3:6	any brother who is L in idleness and not
	3:11	some of you are L in idleness, mere busybodies,
	3:12	work in quietness and to earn their own L
1Tim	3:15	the church of the L God, the pillar and
	4:10	hope set on the L God, who is the
2Tim	4:1	is to judge the L and the dead, and
Heb	3:12	fall away from the L God.
	4:12	word of God is L and active, sharper than
	9:14	works to serve the L God.
	10:20	by the new and L way which he opened
	10:31	the hands of the L God.
	11:9	in a foreign land, L in tents with Isaac
	12:22	the city of the L God, the heavenly Jerusalem,
1Pet	1:3	born anew to a L hope through the resurrection
	1:23	of imperishable, through the L and abiding word of
	2:4	to him, to that L stone, rejected by men
	2:5	and precious; and like L stones be yourselves built
	4:3	Gentiles like to do, L in licentiousness, passions,
	4:5	ready to judge the L and the dead.
Rev	1:18	the last, and the L one; I died, and
	4:6	the throne, are four L creatures, full of eyes
	4:7	and behind: the first L creature like a lion,
	4:7	a lion, the second L creature like an ox,
	4:7	an ox, the third L creature with the face
	4:7	man, and the fourth L creature like a flying
	4:8	And the four L creatures, each of them with
	4:9	And whenever the L creatures give glory and honor
	5:6	throne and the four L creatures and among the
	5:8	the scroll, the four L creatures and the twenty-four
	5:11	the throne and the L creatures and the elders
	5:14	And the four L creatures said, "Amen!" and the
	6:1	one of the four L creatures say, as with
	6:3	I heard the second L creature say, "Come!"
	6:5	I heard the third L creature say, "Come!" And
	6:6	midst of the four L creatures saying, "A quart
	6:7	voice of the fourth L creature say, "Come!"
	7:2	the seal of the L God, and he called
	7:11	elders and the four L creatures, and they fell
	7:17	them to springs of L water; and God will
	8:9	a third of the L creatures in the sea
	14:3	and before the four L creatures and before the
	15:7	one of the four L creatures gave the seven
	16:3	dead man, and every L thing died that was

19:4 elders and the four L creatures fell down and

LIZARD (4)

Lev 11:29 the mouse, the great L according to its kind,
11:30 the land crocodile, the L, the sand lizard, and
11:30 the lizard, the sand L, and the chameleon.
Prov 30:28 march in rank; the L you can take in

LO (123)

Gen 8:11 in the evening, and L, in her mouth a
15:12 fell on Abram; and L, a dread and great
19:28 valley, and beheld, and L, the smoke of the
29:2 in the field, and L, three flocks of sheep
37:7 in the field, and L, my sheaf arose and
39:8 to his master's wife, L, having me my master
48:11 see your face; and L, God has let me
Ex 2:6 saw the child; and L, the babe was crying.
3:2 and he looked, and L, the bush was burning,
18:6 when one told Moses, L, your father-in-law Jethro is
19:9 LORD said to Moses, L, I am coming to
Num 22:38 Balaam said to Balak, L, I have come to
23:6 returned to him, and L, he and all the
23:9 hills I behold him; L, a people dwelling alone,
23:17 came to him, and, L, he was standing beside
Deut 22:17 he spurns her; and L, he has made shameful
Josh 14:10 the wilderness; and now, L, I am this day
Judg 7:13 dreamed a dream; and L, a cake of barley
13:5 eat nothing unclean, for L, you shall conceive and
1Sam 21:14 Achish to his servants, L, you see the man
24:10 L, this day your eyes have seen how the
25:36 came to Nabal; and, L, he was holding a
2Sam 1:6 upon his spear; and L, the chariots and the
15:24 Abiathar came up, and L, Zadok came also, with
24:17 the people, and said, L, I have sinned, and
1Kgs 1:51 fears King Solomon; for, L, he has laid hold
2Kgs 1:14 L, fire came down from heaven, and consumed the
6:20 and they saw; and L, they were in the
7:15 as the Jordan; and, L, all the way was
13:21 man was being buried, L, a marauding band was
2Chr 29:9 For L, our fathers have fallen by the sword
Jud 9:6 presented themselves and said, L, we are here'; for
Job 5:27 L, this we have searched out; it is true.
9:11 L, he passes by me, and I see him
13:1 L, my eye has seen all this, my ear
26:14 L, these are but the outskirts of his ways;
Ps 11:2 to the mountains; for L, the wicked bend the
37:36 I passed by, and, L, he was no more;
40:7 Then I said, L, I come; in the roll
40:9 in the great congregation; L, I have not restrained
48:4 For L, the kings assembled, they came on together.
59:3 For, L, they lie in wait for my life;
68:33 heavens, the ancient heavens; L, he sends forth his
73:27 For L, those who are far from thee shall
83:2 For L, thy enemies are in tumult; those who
92:9 For, L, thy enemies, O LORD, for, lo, thy
92:9 enemies, O LORD, for, L, thy enemies shall perish;
127:3 L, sons are a heritage from the LORD, the
128:4 L, thus shall the man be blessed who fears
132:6 L, we heard of it in Ephrathah, we found
139:4 is on my tongue, L, O LORD, thou knowest
Prov 7:10 And L, a woman meets him, dressed as a
24:31 man without sense; and L, it was all overgrown
Song 2:11 and come away; for L, the winter is past,
Sir 24:29 my garden plot"; and L, my canal became a
Is 5:26 of the earth; and L, swiftly, speedily it comes!
25:9 said on that day, L, this is our God;
38:17 L, it was for my welfare that I had
49:12 L, these shall come from afar, and lo, these
49:12 come from afar, and L, these from the north
Jer 1:15 For, L, I am calling all the tribes of
4:23 on the earth, and L, it was waste and
4:24 on the mountains, and L, they were quaking, and
4:25 I looked, and L, there was no man, and
4:26 I looked, and L, the fruitful land was a
8:9 be dismayed and taken; L, they have rejected the
30:10 dismayed, O Israel; for L, I will save you
46:27 dismayed, O Israel; for L, I will save you
50:12 L, she shall be the last of the nations,
Ezek 2:9 out to me, and, L, a written scroll was
3:23 into the plain; and, L, the glory of the
8:2 Then I beheld, and, L, a form that had
8:8 dug in the wall, L, there was a door.
8:17 L, they put the branch to their nose.
9:2 And L, six men came from the direction of
9:11 And L, the man clothed in linen, with the
15:4 L, it is given to the fire for fuel;
23:39 And L, this is what they did in my
23:40 messenger was sent, and L, they came.
30:9 of Egypt's doom; for, L, it comes!
30:21 king of Egypt; and L, it has not been
33:32 And, L, you are to them like one who
37:2 upon the valley; and L, they were very dry.
Dan 7:6 this I looked, and L, another, like a leopard,
10:20 am through with him, L, the prince of Greece
Amos 4:13 For L, he who forms the mountains, and creates
7:1 the latter growth; and L, it was the latter
9:9 "For L, I will command, and shake the house
Hab 1:6 For L, I am rousing the Chaldeans, that bitter
Hag 1:9 looked for much, and, L, it came to little;
Zech 2:10 daughter of Zion; for L, I come and I
9:4 But L, the Lord will strip her of her
9:9 L, your king comes to you; triumphant and victorious
11:6 L, I will cause men to fall each into
11:16 For L, I am raising up in the land
12:2 of man within him: L, I am about to
Mt 2:9 went their way; and L, the star which they
3:17 alighting on him; and L, a voice from heaven,
17:5 was still speaking, when L, a bright cloud
19:27 Peter said in reply, L, we have left everything
24:23 one says to you, L, here is the Christ!'
24:25 L, I have told you beforehand.
24:26 they say to you, L, he is in the
24:26 out; if they say, L, he is in the
28:7 L, I have told you."
28:20 have commanded you; and L, I am with you
Mk 10:28 to say to him, L, we have left everything
Lk 13:7 said to the vinedresser, L, these three years I
15:29 he answered his father, L, these many years I
17:21 nor will they say, L, here it is!' or
17:23 will say to you, L, there!' or 'Lo, here!'
17:23 you, 'Lo, there!' or L, here!' Do not go,
18:28 And Peter said, L, we have left our homes
Acts 27:24 stand before Caesar; and L, God has granted you
1Cor 15:51 L! I tell you a mystery. We shall
Heb 10:7 Then I said, L, I have come to do
10:9 law), then he added, L, I have come to
Rev 4:1 this I looked, and L, in heaven an open
4:2 in the Spirit, and L, a throne stood in
5:5 to me, "Weep not; L, the Lion of the
14:1 Then I looked, and L, on Mount Zion stood
14:14 Then I looked, and L, a white cloud, and
16:15 L, I am coming like a thief!

LO-DEBAR (4)

2Sam 9:4 house of Machir the son of Ammiel, at L
9:5 house of Machir the son of Ammiel, at L
17:27 son of Ammiel from L, and Barzillai the Gileadite
Amos 6:13 you who rejoice in L, who say, "Have we

LOAD (3)

Gen 45:17 your brothers, 'Do this: L your beasts and go
Lk 11:46 for you L men with burdens hard to bear,
Gal 6:5 each man will have to bear his own L

LOADED (6)

Gen 42:26 Then they L their asses with their grain, and
44:13 clothes, and every man L his ass, and they
45:23 as follows: ten asses L with the good things
45:23 Egypt, and ten she-asses L with grain, bread, and
Jud 15:11 she took them and L her mule and hitched
Is 46:1 things you carry are L as burdens on weary

LOADING

Neh 13:15 heaps of grain and L them on asses; and

LOADS (4)

2Kgs 8:9 all kinds of goods of Damascus, forty camel L
Job 37:11 He L the thick cloud with moisture; the clouds
Lam 5:13 and boys stagger under L of wood.
Hab 2:6 for how long?--and L himself with pledges!"

LOAF (6)

Ex 29:23 of ordination), and one L of bread, and one
1Sam 2:36 of silver or a L of bread, and shall
1Chr 16:3 women, to each a L of bread, a portion
Prov 6:26 be hired for a L of bread, but an
Jer 37:21 the guard; and a L of bread was given
Mk 8:14 they had only one L with them in the

LOAN (5)

Deut 24:10 make your neighbor a L of any sort, you
24:11 whom you make the L shall bring the pledge

1Sam 2:20 this woman for the L which she lent to
Sir 29:4 Many persons regard a L as a windfall, and
29:5 until he gets a L, and will lower his

LOATH

Job 20:13 tongue, though he is L to let it go,

LOATHE (10)

Ex 7:18 and the Egyptians will L to drink water from
Num 21:5 no water, and we L this worthless food."
Job 7:16 I L my life; I would not live for
9:21 regard not myself; I L my life.
10:1 "I L my life; I will give free utterance
Ps 139:21 And do I not L them that rise up
Sir 11:2 his good looks, nor L a man because of
Jer 14:19 Does thy soul L Zion?
Ezek 20:43 yourselves; and you shall L yourselves for all the
36:31 good; and you will L yourselves for your iniquities

LOATHED (8)

Ps 95:10 For forty years I L that generation and said,
107:18 iniquities suffered affliction; they L any kind of food,
Sir 16:8 of Lot, whom he L on account of their
20:7 many words will be L, and whoever usurps the
Is 14:19 your sepulchre, like a L untimely birth, clothed with
Ezek 16:37 and all those you L; I will gather them
16:45 of your mother, who L her husband and her
16:45 of your sisters, who L their husbands and their

LOATHES (2)

Job 33:20 so that his life L bread, and his appetite
Prov 27:7 He who is sated L honey, but to one

LOATHING

Wis 11:24 that exist, and hast L for none of the

LOATHSOME (6)

Num 11:20 your nostrils and becomes L to you, because you
Job 2:7 and afflicted Job with L sores from the sole
6:7 as food that is L to me.
19:17 repulsive to my wife, L to the sons of
Ezek 6:9 and they will be L in their own sight
8:10 of creeping things, and L beasts, and all the

LOAVES (34)

Lev 23:17 from your dwellings two L of bread to be
Judg 8:5 of Succoth, "Pray, give L of bread to the
1Sam 10:3 kids, another carrying three L of bread, and another
10:4 and give you two L of bread, which you
17:17 grain, and these ten L, and carry them quickly
21:3 Give me five L of bread, or whatever is
25:18 and took two hundred L, and two skins of
2Sam 16:1 saddled, bearing two hundred L of bread, a hundred
1Kgs 14:3 Take with you ten L, some cakes, and a
2Kgs 4:42 the first fruits, twenty L of barley, and fresh
2Mac 1:8 lighted the lamps and we set out the L
Mt 4:3 these stones to become L of bread."
14:17 "We have only five L here and two fish."
14:19 and taking the five L and the two fish
14:19 broke and gave the L to the disciples, and
15:34 to them, "How many L have you?" They said,
15:36 he took the seven L and the fish, and
16:9 not remember the five L of the five thousand,
16:10 Or the seven L of the four thousand, and
Mk 6:38 to them, "How many L have you?
6:41 And taking the five L and the two fish
6:41 blessed, and broke the L, and gave them to
6:44 those who ate the L were five thousand men.
6:52 not understand about the L, but their hearts were
8:5 asked them, "How many L have you?" They said,
8:6 he took the seven L, and having given thanks
8:19 I broke the five L for the five thousand,
Lk 9:13 no more than five L and two fish—unless
9:16 And taking the five L and the two fish
11:5 'Friend, lend me three L;
Jn 6:9 who has five barley L and two fish; but
6:11 Jesus then took the L, and when he had
6:13 from the five barley L, left by those who
6:26 but because you ate your fill of the L

LOCAL (2)

Bar 6:14 Like a L ruler the god holds a scepter,
Acts 28:17 he called together the L leaders of the Jews;

LOCK (3)

Sir 28:24 your property with thorns, L up your silver and
42:6 there are many hands, L things up.
Ezek 8:3 took me by a L of my head; and

LOCKED (5)

Judg 3:23 chamber upon him, and L them.
3:24 the roof chamber were L, they thought, "He is
Song 4:12 A garden L is my sister, my bride, a
4:12 my bride, a garden L, a fountain sealed.
Acts 5:23 found the prison securely L and the sentries standing

LOCKS (9)

Num 6:5 he shall let the L of hair of his
Judg 16:13 you weave the seven L of my head with
16:14 Delilah took the seven L of his head and
16:19 shave off the seven L of his head.
Song 5:2 wet with dew, my L with the drops of
5:11 the finest gold; his L are wavy, black as
7:5 Carmel, and your flowing L are like purple; a
Bar 6:18 secure with doors and L and bars, in order
Ezek 44:20 heads or let their L grow long; they shall

LOCUST (22)

Ex 10:19 Sea; not a single L was left in all
Lev 11:22 you may eat: the L according to its kind,
11:22 its kind, the bald L according to its kind,
Deut 28:38 little in; for the L shall consume it.
28:42 of your ground the L shall possess.
1Kgs 8:37 blight or mildew or L or caterpillar; if their
2Chr 6:28 blight or mildew or L or caterpillar; if their
7:13 rain, or command the L to devour the land,
Job 39:20 Do you make him leap like the L
Ps 78:46 and the fruit of their labor to the L
109:23 at evening; I am shaken off like a L
Joel 1:4 What the cutting L left, the swarming locust has
1:4 locust left, the swarming L has eaten.
1:4 What the swarming L left, the hopping locust has
1:4 locust left, the hopping L has eaten, and what
1:4 and what the hopping L left, the destroying locust
1:4 locust left, the destroying L has eaten.
2:25 years which the swarming L has eaten, the hopper,
Amos 4:9 your olive trees the L devoured; yet you did
Nah 3:15 It will devour you like the L
3:15 yourselves like the L, multiply like the grasshopper!
3:16 The L spreads its wings and flies away.

LOCUSTS (24)

Ex 10:4 tomorrow I will bring L into your country,
10:12 of Egypt for the L, that they may come
10:13 was morning the east wind had brought the L
10:14 And the L came up over all the land
10:14 a dense swarm of L as had never been
10:19 wind, which lifted the L and drove them into
Judg 6:5 their tents, coming like L for number; both they
7:12 along the valley like L for multitude; and their
Jud 2:20 like a swarm of L, like the dust of
Ps 105:34 He spoke, and the L came, and young locusts
105:34 locusts came, and young L without number;
Prov 30:27 in the rocks; the L have no king, yet
Wis 16:9 by the bites of L and flies, and no
Sir 43:17 its descent is like L alighting.
Is 33:4 the caterpillar gathers; as L leap, men leap upon
Jer 46:23 are more numerous than L; they are without number.
51:14 men, as many as L, and they shall raise
51:27 marshal against her, bring up horses like bristling L
Amos 7:1 behold, he was forming L in the beginning of
Nah 3:17 scribes like clouds of L settling on the fences
Mt 3:4 and his food was L and wild honey.
Mk 1:6 his waist, and ate L and wild honey.
Rev 9:3 from the smoke came L on the earth, and
9:7 In appearance the L were like horses arrayed for

LOD (4)

1Chr 8:12 who built Ono and L with its towns,
Ezra 2:33 The sons of L, Hadid, and Ono, seven hundred
Neh 7:37 The sons of L, Hadid, and Ono, seven hundred
11:35 Hadid, Zeboim, Neballat, L, and Ono, the valley

LODGE (21)

Gen 24:23 house for us to L in?"
24:25 enough, and room to L in."
Num 22:8 he said to them, L here this night, and
Josh 4:3 the place where you L tonight.'"
Judg 19:9 draws to its close; L here and let your
Ruth 1:16 go, and where you L I will lodge; your
1:16 you lodge I will L; your people shall be
2Sam 17:16 tell David, 'Do not L tonight at the fords

L

Neh 13:21 them, "Why do you L before the wall?
Ps 55:7 wander afar, I would L in the wilderness, [Selah]
Song 7:11 into the fields, and L in the villages;
Sir 14:25 near her, and will L in an excellent lodging
24:7 place; I sought in whose territory I might L
51:23 who are untaught, and L in my school.
Is 1:8 a vineyard, like a L in a cucumber field,
10:29 pass, at Geba they L for the night; Ramah
21:13 in Arabia you will L, O caravans of Dedanites.
Jer 4:14 shall your evil thoughts L within you?
Zeph 2:14 and the hedgehog shall L in her capitals; the
Lk 9:12 country round about, to L and get provisions; for
Acts 21:16 Cyprus, an early disciple, with whom we should L

LODGED (18)

Gen 32:13 So he L there that night, and took from
32:21 him; and he himself L that night in the
Josh 2:1 name was Rahab, and L there.
3:1 to the Jordan, and L there before they passed
4:8 the place where they L, and laid them down
Judg 18:2 house of Micah, and L there.
19:4 ate and drank, and L there.
19:7 urged him, till he L there again.
1Sam 7:2 that the ark was L at Kiriath-jearim, a long
1Kgs 17:19 upper chamber, where he L, and laid him upon
19:9 to a cave, and L there; and behold, the
1Chr 9:27 And they L round about the house of God;
Neh 13:20 all kinds of wares L outside Jerusalem once or
Job 31:32 (the sojourner has not L in the street; I
Is 1:21 Righteousness L in her, but now murderers.
2Mac 3:17 at him the pain L in his heart.
Mt 21:17 city to Bethany and L there.
Lk 21:37 he went out and L on the mount called

LODGES (2)

Eccl 7:9 to anger, for anger L in the bosom of
Sir 36:26 has no home, and L wherever night finds him?

LODGING (11)

Gen 42:27 ass provender at the L place, he saw his
43:21 we came to the L place we opened our
Ex 4:24 At a L place on the way the LORD
Sir 14:25 lodge in an excellent L place;
29:28 has feeling: scolding about L and the reproach of
Jer 9:2 the desert a wayfarers' L place, that I might
1Mac 3:45 citadel; it was a L place for the Gentiles.
Acts 10:6 called Peter; he is L with Simon, a tanner,
10:18 was called Peter was L there.
10:32 called Peter; he is L in the house of
28:23 to him at his L in great numbers.

LOFTILY

Ps 73:8 and speak with malice; L they threaten oppression.

LOFTINESS

Jer 48:29 very proud--of his L, his pride, and his

LOFTY (20)

Job 22:12 the highest stars, how L they are!
Ps 104:13 From thy L abode thou waterest the mountains; the
Prov 30:13 There are those--how L are their eyes, how
Is 2:12 that is proud and L, against all that is
2:13 the cedars of Lebanon, L and lifted up; and
2:14 and against all the L hills;
10:33 hewn down, and the L will be brought low.
26:5 of the height, the L city.
30:25 And upon every L mountain and every high hill
57:7 Upon a high and L mountain you have set
57:15 says the high and L One who inhabits eternity,
Ezek 16:24 and made yourself a L place in every square;
16:25 street you built your L place and prostituted your
16:31 street, and making your L place in every square.
16:39 and break down your L places; they shall strip
17:22 a sprig from the L top of the cedar,
17:22 upon a high and L mountain;
31:14 waters may grow to L height or set their
Zeph 1:16 cities and against the L battlements.
1Cor 2:1 testimony of God in L words or wisdom.

LOG (13)

Lev 14:10 with oil, and one L of oil.
14:12 offering, along with the L of oil, and wave
14:15 take some of the L of oil, and pour
14:21 cereal offering, and a L of oil;
14:24 guilt offering, and the L of oil, and the
2Kgs 6:2 us get there a L, and let us make
6:5 one was felling a L, his axe head fell
Mt 7:3 do not notice the L that is in your
7:4 when there is the L in your own eye?
7:5 hypocrite, first take the L out of your own
Lk 6:41 do not notice the L that is in your
6:42 do not see the L that is in your
6:42 hypocrite, first take the L out of your own

LOGS (3)

Eccl 10:9 and he who splits L is endangered by them.
Ezek 24:5 the flock, pile the L under it; boil its
24:10 Heap on the L, kindle the fire, boil well

LOINS (62)

Gen 37:34 put sackcloth upon his L, and mourned for his
Ex 12:11 shall eat it: your L girded, your sandals on
28:42 naked flesh; from the L to the thighs they
Lev 3:4 on them at the L, and the appendage of
3:10 on them at the L, and the appendage of
3:15 on them at the L, and the appendage of
4:9 on them at the L, and the appendage of
7:4 on them at the L, and the appendage of
Deut 33:11 his hands; crush the L of his adversaries, of
2Sam 20:8 sheath fastened upon his L, and as he went
1Kgs 2:5 the girdle about my L, and upon the sandals
12:10 'My little finger is thicker than my father's L
18:46 he girded up his L and ran before Ahab
20:31 put sackcloth on our L and ropes upon our
20:32 girded sackcloth on their L, and put ropes on
2Kgs 1:8 haircloth, with a girdle of leather about his L
4:29 Gehazi, "Gird up your L, and take my staff
9:1 him, "Gird up your L, and take this flask
2Chr 10:10 'My little finger is thicker than my father's L
Jud 4:14 the Lord, with their L girded with sackcloth, offered
8:5 girded sackcloth about her L and wore the garments
Job 12:18 of kings, and binds a waistcloth on their L
15:27 gathered fat upon his L,
31:20 without covering; if his L have not blessed me,
38:3 Gird up your L like a man, I will
40:7 whirlwind: "Gird up your L like a man; I
40:16 his strength in his L, and his power in
Ps 38:7 For my L are filled with burning, and there
66:11 lay affliction on our L;
69:23 see; and make their L tremble continually.
Prov 31:17 She girds her L with strength and makes her
Sir 35:18 till he crushes the L of the unmerciful and
47:19 But you laid your L beside women, and through
Is 11:5 his waist, and faithfulness the girdle of his L
20:2 the sackcloth from your L and take off your
21:3 Therefore my L are filled with anguish; pangs have
32:11 yourselves bare, and gird sackcloth upon your L
45:1 him and ungird the L of kings, to open
48:1 came forth from the L of Judah; who swear
Jer 1:17 you, gird up your L; arise, and say to
13:1 put it on your L, and do not dip
13:2 of the LORD, and put it on my L
13:4 which is upon your L, and arise, go to
13:11 waistcloth clings to the L of a man, so
30:6 his hands on his L like a woman in
48:37 gashes, and on the L is sackcloth.
Ezek 1:27 the appearance of his L I saw as it
1:27 the appearance of his L I saw as it
8:2 appeared to be his L it was fire, and
8:2 fire, and above his L it was like the
23:15 with belts on their L, with flowing turbans on
29:7 and made all their L to shake;
44:18 linen breeches upon their L; they shall not gird
47:4 the water; and it was up to the L
Dan 10:5 clothed in linen, whose L were girded with gold
Amos 8:10 bring sackcloth upon all L, and baldness on every
Nah 2:1 the road; gird your L; collect all your strength.
2:10 anguish is on all L, all faces grow pale!
2Mac 10:25 heads and girded their L with sackcloth, in
Lk 12:35 "Let your L be girded and your lamps burning,
Eph 6:14 therefore, having girded your L with truth, and
Heb 7:10 was still in the L of his ancestor when

LOIS

2Tim 1:5 first in your grandmother L and your mother Eunice

LONELY (12)

Ps 25:16 me; for I am L and afflicted.
102:7 I am like a L bird on the housetop.
Lam 1:1 How L sits the city that
Bar 4:16 sons, and bereaved the L woman of her daughters.
Mt 14:13 a boat to a L place apart.

14:15 said, "This is a L place, and the day
Mk 1:35 went out to a L place, and there he
6:31 by yourselves to a L place, and rest a
6:32 the boat to a L place by themselves.
6:35 said, "This is a L place, and the hour
Lk 4:42 and went into a L place.
9:12 are here in a L place."

LONG (332)

Gen 26:8 had been there a L time, Abimelech king of
37:3 he made him a L robe with sleeves.
37:23 of his robe, the L robe with sleeves that
37:32 and they sent the L robe with sleeves and
48:15 me all my life L to this day,
Ex 10:3 of the Hebrews, 'How L will you refuse to
10:7 said to him, "How L shall this man be
16:28 said to Moses, "How L do you refuse to
19:13 the trumpet sounds a L blast, they shall come
20:12 your days may be L in the land which
27:1 acacia wood, five cubits L and five cubits broad;
27:9 linen a hundred cubits L for one side;
27:11 hangings a hundred cubits L, their pillars twenty and
27:16 a screen twenty cubits L, of blue and purple
38:18 it was twenty cubits L and five cubits high
Lev 13:46 shall remain unclean as L as he has the
21:18 or a limb too L,
22:23 has a part too L or too short you
26:10 shall eat old store L kept, and you shall
26:34 enjoy its sabbaths as L as it lies desolate,
26:35 As L as it lies desolate it shall have
Num 6:5 the locks of hair of his head grow L
9:18 LORD they encamped; as L as the cloud rested
14:11 said to Moses, "How L will this people despise
14:11 And how L will they not believe in me,
14:27 and to Aaron, "How L shall this wicked congregation
20:15 dwelt in Egypt a L time; and the Egyptians
22:30 ridden all your life L to this day?
24:22 How L shall Asshur take you away captive?"
Deut 1:6 Horeb, 'You have stayed L enough at this mountain;
2:3 about this mountain country L enough; turn
4:26 you will not live L upon it, but will
5:33 that you may live L in the land which
11:9 that you may live L in the land which
11:21 to give them, as L as the heavens are
12:19 forsake the Levite as L as you live in
14:24 the way is too L for you, so that
17:20 that he may continue L in his kingdom, he
19:6 because the way is L, and wound him mortally,
20:19 a city for a L time, making war against
22:7 well with you, and that you may live L
30:18 you shall not live L in the land which
31:13 LORD your God, as L as you live in
32:47 thereby you shall live L in the land which
33:12 him all the day L, and makes his dwelling
Josh 6:5 when they make a L blast with the ram's
9:13 worn-out from the very L journey."
11:18 Joshua made war a L time with all those
18:3 people of Israel, "How L will you be slack
23:1 A L time afterward, when the LORD had given
24:7 in the wilderness a L time.
Judg 5:28 is his chariot so L in coming?
18:31 which he made, as L as the house of
1Sam 1:14 said to her, "How L will you be drunken?
1:28 to the LORD; as L as he lives, he
7:2 lodged at Kiriath-jearim, a L time passed, some
10:24 all the people shouted, L live the king!"
16:1 said to Samuel, "How L will you grieve over
20:31 For as L as the son of Jesse lives
25:15 in the fields, as L as we went with
25:28 found in you so L as you live.
2Sam 2:26 How L will it be before you bid your
3:1 There was a L war between the house of
13:18 she was wearing a L robe with sleeves; for
13:19 head, and rent the L robe which she wore;
16:16 Hushai said to Absalom, L live the king!
16:16 L live the king!"
1Kgs 1:25 before him, and saying, L live King Adonijah!'
1:34 the trumpet, and say, L live King Solomon!'
1:39 all the people said, L live King Solomon!"
3:11 not asked for yourself L life or riches or
6:2 LORD was sixty cubits L, twenty cubits wide, and
6:3 house was twenty cubits L, equal to the width
6:17 front of the inner sanctuary, was forty cubits L
6:20 sanctuary was twenty cubits L, twenty cubits wide,
7:27 stand was four cubits L, four cubits wide, and
8:8 the poles were so L that the ends of
12:28 gone up to Jerusalem L enough.
18:21 people, and said, "How L will you go limping
2Kgs 9:22 can there be, so L as the harlotries and
11:12 their hands, and said, L live the king!"
19:25 that I determined it L ago?
25:30 day a portion, as L as he lived.
2Chr 1:11 have not even asked L life, but have asked
3:4 house was twenty cubits L, equal to the width
4:1 of bronze, twenty cubits L, and twenty cubits wide,
5:9 the poles were so L that the ends of
6:13 bronze platform five cubits L, five cubits wide, and
15:3 For a L time Israel was without the true
23:11 him, and they said, L live the king."
26:5 of God; and as L as he sought the
Neh 2:6 sitting beside him), "How L will you be gone,
Tob 5:3 pay him wages as L as I live; and
9:4 and if I delay L he will be greatly
10:4 lad has perished; his L delay proves it." Then
Jud 1:2 thick and six cubits L; he made the walls
5:8 lived there for a L time.
5:10 and lived there as L as they had food;
5:16 and lived there a L time.
5:17 As L as they did not sin against their
13:1 all were weary because the banquet had lasted L
16:25 Judith, or for a L time after her death.
Esth 5:13 me no good, so L as I see Mordecai
13:7 that those who have L been and are now
Job 3:21 bitter in soul, who L for death, but it
7:4 But the night is L, and I am full
7:19 How L wilt thou not look away from me,
8:2 the Shuhite answered: "How L will you say these
14:15 answer thee; thou wouldest L for the work of
18:2 the Shuhite answered: "How L will you hunt for
19:2 Then Job answered: "How L will you torment me,
27:3 my soul bitter; as L as my breath is
36:20 Do not L for the night, when peoples are
Ps 4:2 O men, how L shall my honor suffer shame?
4:2 How L will you love vain words, and seek
6:3 But thou, O LORD—how L
13:1 How L, O LORD?
13:1 How L wilt thou hide thy face from me?
13:2 How L must I bear pain in my soul,
13:2 How L shall my enemy be exalted over me?
25:5 salvation; for thee I wait all the day L
32:3 body wasted away through my groaning all day L
35:17 How L, O LORD, wilt thou look on?
35:28 righteousness and of thy praise all the day L
38:12 of ruin, and meditate treachery all the day L
39:1 bridle my mouth, so L as the wicked are
44:15 All day L my disgrace is before me, and
44:22 slain all the day L, and accounted as sheep
56:1 upon me; all day L foemen oppress me;
56:2 upon me all day L, for many fight against
56:5 All day L they seek to injure my cause;
62:3 How L will you set upon a man to
63:4 will bless thee as L as I live; I
71:24 help all the day L, for they have been
72:5 sun endures, and as L as the moon, throughout
72:15 L may he live, may gold of Sheba be
72:17 his fame continue as L as the sun!
73:14 For all the day L I have been stricken,
74:9 there is none among us who knows how L
74:10 How L, O God, is the foe to scoff?
77:5 I remember the years L ago.
79:5 How L, O LORD?
80:4 God of hosts, how L wilt thou be angry
82:2 he holds judgment: "How L will you judge unjustly
88:17 a flood all day L; they close in upon
89:36 ever, his throne as L as the sun before
89:46 [Selah] How L, O LORD?
89:46 How L will thy wrath burn like fire?
90:13 How L
91:16 With L life I will satisfy him, and show
94:3 O LORD, how L shall the wicked, how long
94:3 shall the wicked, how L shall the wicked exult?
103:5 you with good as L as you live so
104:33 to the LORD as L as I live; I
116:2 call on him as L as I live.
119:40 Behold, I L for thy precepts; in thy righteousness
119:84 How L must thy servant endure?
119:131 I pant, because I L for thy commandments.
119:152 L have I known from thy testimonies that thou
119:174 I L for thy salvation, O LORD, and thy
120:6 Too L have I had my dwelling among those
123:4 Too L our soul has been sated with the
129:3 my back; they made L their furrows."

143:3 in darkness like those L dead.
146:2 praise the LORD as L as I live; I
Prov 1:22 gates she speaks: "How L, O simple ones, will
1:22 How L will scoffers delight in their scoffing and
3:16 L life is in her right hand; in her
6:9 How L will you lie there, O sluggard?
7:19 has gone on a L journey;
21:26 All day L the wicked covets, but the righteous
23:30 Those who tarry L over wine, those who go
28:2 knowledge its stability will L continue.
Eccl 2:16 all will have been L forgotten.
3:12 and enjoy themselves as L as they live;
Wis 3:17 Even if they live L they will be held
4:2 imitate it, and they L for it when it
4:13 short time, he fulfilled L years;
6:11 desire on my words; L for them, and you
11:14 mockingly rejected him who L before had been cast
17:2 darkness and prisoners of L night, shut in under
18:20 the wrath did not L continue.
18:24 For upon his L robe the whole world was
Sir 1:10 gladness and joy and L life.
1:18 and her branches are L life.
3:6 his father will have L life, and whoever obeys
3:12 not grieve him as L as he lives;
9:12 be held guiltless as L as they live.
10:10 A L illness baffles the physician; the king of
33:19 power over yourself, as L as you live; and
39:11 praise; if he lives L, he will leave a
45:8 the linen breeches, the L robe, and the ephod.
46:4 one day become as L as two?
Is 6:11 Then I said, "How L, O Lord?" And he
22:11 him who planned it L ago.
30:33 a burning place has L been prepared; yea, for
37:26 that I determined it L ago?
42:14 For a L time I have held my peace,
45:21 Who told this L ago?
48:7 are created now, not L ago; before today you
51:9 old, the generations of L ago.
57:11 peace, even for a L time, and so you
64:5 we have been a L time, and shall we
65:22 and my chosen shall L enjoy the work of
Jer 2:20 "For L ago you broke your yoke and burst
4:14 How L shall your evil thoughts lodge within you?
4:21 How L must I see the standard, and hear
12:4 How L will the land mourn, and the grass
13:27 How L will it be before you are made
20:8 for me a reproach and derision all day L
22:27 to which they will L to return, there they
23:26 I have dreamed!' How L shall there be lies
29:28 "Your exile will be L; build houses and live
31:22 How L will you waver, O faithless daughter?
32:14 may last for a L time.
47:5 of the Anakim, how L will you gash yourselves?
47:6 How L till you are quiet?
52:34 of his death as L as he lived.
Lam 1:13 has left me stunned, faint all the day L
2:17 threat; as he ordained L ago, he has demolished
3:3 his hand again and again the whole day L
3:6 like the dead of L ago.
3:14 peoples, the burden of their songs all day L
3:62 my assailants are against me all the day L
5:20 why dost thou so L forsake us?
Bar 4:35 days, and for a L time she will be
6:3 many years, for a L time, up to seven
6:46 certainly not live very L themselves; how then can
Ezek 4:5 of their punishment; so L shall you bear the
12:22 saying, 'The days grow L, and every vision comes
17:3 with great wings and L pinions, rich in plumage
31:5 large and its branches L, from abundant water in
40:5 man's hand was six L cubits, each being a
40:7 side rooms, one reed L, and one reed broad;
40:30 round about, twenty-five cubits L and five cubits
40:42 cubit and a half L, and a cubit and
40:43 And hooks, a handbreadth L, were fastened round
40:47 court, a hundred cubits L, and a hundred cubits
41:8 full reed of six L cubits.
41:13 temple, a hundred cubits L; and the yard and
41:13 walls, a hundred cubits L;
41:22 cubits high, two cubits L, and two cubits broad;
42:4 and a hundred cubits L, and their doors were
42:7 the outer court, opposite the chambers, fifty cubits L
42:8 court were fifty cubits L, while those opposite the
42:8 those opposite the temple were a hundred cubits L
42:20 it, five hundred cubits L and five hundred cubits
43:16 be square, twelve cubits L by twelve broad.
43:17 be square, fourteen cubits L by fourteen broad, with
44:20 let their locks grow L; they shall only trim
45:1 twenty-five thousand cubits L and twenty thousand
45:3 section twenty-five thousand cubits L and ten
45:5 twenty-five thousand cubits L and ten thousand
45:6 and twenty-five thousand cubits L; it shall belong to
46:22 small courts, forty cubits L and thirty broad; the
Dan 4:33 his hair grew as L as eagles' feathers, and
8:13 that spoke, "For how L is the vision concerning
12:6 of the stream, "How L shall it be till
Hos 8:5 How L will it be till they are pure
12:1 east wind all day L; they multiply falsehood and
Hab 1:2 O LORD, how L shall I cry for help,
2:6 his own—for how L —and loads himself with
Zech 1:12 LORD of hosts, how L wilt thou have no
1Mac 6:22 king and said, "How L will you fail to
8:19 to Rome, a very L journey; and they entered
9:71 to harm him as L as he lived.
2Mac 6:1 Not L after this, the king sent an Athenian
6:13 the impious alone for L, but to punish them
6:21 aside, because of their L acquaintance with him, and
10:6 booths, remembering how not L before, during the
12:36 been fighting for a L time and were weary,
14:10 For as L as Judas lives, it is impossible
Mt 9:15 wedding guests mourn as L as the bridegroom is
11:21 they would have repented L ago in sackcloth and
17:17 and perverse generation, how L am I to be
17:17 How L am I to bear with you?
23:5 broad and their fringes L,
25:19 Now after a L time the master of those
Mk 2:19 As L as they have the bridegroom with them,
8:3 them have come a L way."
9:19 "O faithless generation, how L am I to be
9:19 How L am I to bear with you?
9:21 asked his father, "How L has he had this?"
12:38 to go about in L robes, and to have
12:40 for a pretense make L prayers.
Lk 8:27 had demons; for a L time he had worn
9:41 and perverse generation, how L am I to be
10:13 they would have repented L ago, sitting in sackcloth
18:7 Will he delay L over them?
20:9 another country for a L while.
20:46 to go about in L robes, and love salutations
20:47 for a pretense make L prayers.
23:8 glad, for he had L desired to see him,
Jn 5:5 been lying there a L time, he said to
9:5 As L as I am in the world, I
10:24 said to him, "How L will you keep us
14:9 been with you so L, and yet you do
Acts 8:11 him, because for a L time he had amazed
14:3 they remained for a L time, speaking boldly for
20:11 conversed with them a L while, until daybreak, and
26:5 have known for a L time, if they are
26:29 said, "Whether short or L, I would to God
27:21 As they had been L without food, Paul then
28:6 they had waited a L time and saw no
Rom 1:11 For I L to see you, that I may
7:2 to her husband as L as he lives; but
8:36 killed all the day L; we are regarded as
10:21 he says, "All day L I have held out
16:24 was kept secret for L ages
1Cor 7:39 to her husband as L as he lives.
11:14 a man to wear L hair is degrading to
11:15 if a woman has L hair, it is her
2Cor 5:2 indeed we groan, and L to put on our
9:14 all others; while they L for you and pray
Gal 4:1 that the heir, as L as he is a
Eph 6:3 that you may live L on the earth."
Phil 4:1 whom I love and L for, my joy and
1Thes 3:6 remember us kindly and L to see us, as
3:6 see us, as we L to see you—
2Tim 1:4 remember your tears, I L night and day to
Heb 3:13 another every day, as L as it is called
4:7 saying through David so L afterward, in the words
9:8 not yet opened as L as the outer tent
9:17 not in force as L as the one who
1Pet 1:12 things into which angels L to look.
2:2 Like newborn babes, L for the pure spiritual milk,
2Pet 1:13 think it right, as L as I am in
3:5 of God heavens existed L ago, and an earth
Jude 1:4 gained by some who L ago were designated for
Rev 1:13 man, clothed with a L robe and with a
6:10 holy and true, how L before thou wilt judge
9:6 find it; they will L to die, and death

LONG-HAIRED

Deut 32:42 the captives, from the L heads of the enemy.'

LONGED (8)

Gen 31:30 gone away because you L greatly for your father's
2Sam 13:39 spirit of the king L to go forth to
Is 21:4 me; the twilight I L for has been turned
Lam 2:16 is the day we L for; now we have
Ezek 23:21 Thus you L for the lewdness of your youth,
Mt 13:17 prophets and righteous men L to see what you
Rom 15:23 and since I have L for many years to
Rev 18:14 for which thy soul L has gone from thee,

LONGER (125)

Gen 4:12 ground, it shall no L yield to you its
17:5 No L shall your name be Abram, but your
35:10 name is Jacob; no L shall your name be
Ex 2:3 could hide him no L she took for him
5:7 foremen, "You shall no L give the people straw
9:28 let you go, and you shall stay no L
9:33 and the rain no L poured upon the earth.
Num 9:22 a month, or a L time, that the cloud
Deut 10:16 heart, and be no L stubborn.
31:2 day; I am no L able to go out
32:5 him, they are no L his children because of
Josh 5:1 and there was no L any spirit in them,
Judg 2:14 that they could no L withstand their enemies.
1Sam 1:18 her countenance was no L sad.
27:1 of seeking me any L within the borders of
2Kgs 6:33 Why should I wait for the LORD any L
1Chr 23:26 so the Levites no L need to carry the
2Chr 35:3 built; you need no L carry it upon your
Neh 2:17 that we may no L suffer disgrace."
Tob 1:15 that I could no L go into Media.
2:8 said, "He is no L afraid that he will
14:10 And do not live in Nineveh any L
Jud 7:23 there was no strength left in them any L
8:31 and we will no L be faint."
10:10 and they could no L see her.
Job 11:9 Its measure is L than the earth, and broader
24:20 their name is no L remembered; so wickedness is
Ps 12:1 for there is no L any that is godly;
74:9 signs; there is no L any prophet, and there
Eccl 4:13 king, who will no L take advice,
Wis 14:24 strange customs, they no L keep either their lives
Sir 41:12 will remain for you L than a thousand great
Is 7:8 that it will no L be a people.)
Jer 16:14 when it shall no L be said, 'As the
23:7 when men shall no L say, 'As the LORD
31:29 days they shall no L say: 'The fathers have
31:34 And no L shall each man teach his neighbor
33:24 that they are no L a nation in their
44:22 The LORD could no L bear your evil-doings and
48:42 destroyed and be no L a people, because he
51:44 The nations shall no L flow to him; the
Lam 4:15 the nations, "They shall stay with us no L
4:22 you in exile no L; but your iniquity, O
Ezek 12:25 It will no L be delayed, but in your
12:28 will be delayed any L, but the word which
24:27 speak and be no L dumb.
30:13 Memphis; there shall no L be a prince in
33:22 and I was no L dumb.
34:10 feeding the sheep; no L shall the shepherds feed
34:22 flock, they shall no L be a prey; and
34:29 the land, and no L suffer the reproach of
36:12 and you shall no L bereave them of children.
36:14 therefore you shall no L devour men and no
36:14 devour men and no L bereave your nation of
36:15 and you shall no L bear the disgrace of
36:15 the peoples and no L cause your nation to
37:22 they shall be no L two nations, and no
37:22 two nations, and no L divided into two kingdoms.
Hos 2:16 'My husband,' and no L will you call me,
Zeph 3:11 and you shall no L be haughty in my
Zech 11:6 For I will no L have pity on the
14:21 And there shall no L be a trader in
Mal 2:13 groaning because he no L regards the offering or
1Mac 2:11 been taken away; no L free, she has become
2:13 Why should we live any L
5:44 was conquered; they could stand before Judas no L
7:38 remember their blasphemies, and let them live no L
9:55 that he could no L say a word or
13:39 been collected in Jerusalem shall be collected no L
2Mac 4:14 the priests were no L intent upon their service
6:25 living a brief moment L, they should be led
9:13 Lord, who would no L have mercy on him,
Mt 5:13 It is no L good for anything except to
19:6 So they are no L two but one.
Mk 1:45 that Jesus could no L openly enter a town,
2:2 that there was no L room for them, not
7:12 then you no L permit him to do
9:8 looking around they no L saw any one with
10:8 So they are no L two but one.
Lk 15:19 you; I am no L worthy to be called
15:21 you; I am no L worthy to be called
16:2 for you can no L be steward.'
20:40 For they no L dared to ask him any
Jn 4:42 woman, "It is no L because of your words
6:66 drew back and no L went about with him.
7:33 with you a little L, and then I go
11:6 he stayed two days L in the place where
11:54 Jesus therefore no L went about openly among the
12:35 "The light is with you for a little L
14:30 I will no L talk much with you, for
15:15 No L do I call you servants, for the
16:21 the child, she no L remembers the anguish, for
16:25 when I shall no L speak to you in
Acts 18:18 Paul stayed many days L, and then took leave
18:20 to stay for a L period, he declined;
20:9 as Paul talked still L; and being overcome by
25:24 shouting that he ought not to live any L
Rom 6:6 and we might no L be enslaved to sin.
6:9 die again; death no L has dominion over him.
7:17 then it is no L I that do it,
7:20 want, it is no L I that do it,
11:6 grace, it is no L on the basis of
11:6 otherwise grace would no L be grace.
14:15 eat, you are no L walking in love.
15:23 now, since I no L have any room for
2Cor 5:15 live might live no L for themselves but for
5:16 point of view, we regard him thus no L
Gal 2:20 Christ; it is no L I who live, but
3:18 law, it is no L by promise; but God
3:25 come, we are no L under a custodian;
4:7 God you are no L a slave but a
Eph 2:19 then you are no L strangers and sojourners, but
4:14 that we may no L be children, tossed to
4:17 that you must no L live as the Gentiles
4:28 Let the thief no L steal, but rather let
1Thes 3:1 could bear it no L, we were willing to
3:5 could bear it no L, I sent that I
1Tim 5:23 No L drink only water, but use a little
Philem 1:16 back for ever, no L as a slave but
Heb 10:2 cleansed, they would no L have any consciousness of
10:18 these, there is no L any offering for sin.
10:26 the truth, there no L remains a sacrifice for
1Pet 4:2 in the flesh no L by human passions but
Rev 6:11 to rest a little L, until the number of
12:8 and there was no L any place for them

LONGING (7)

Deut 28:32 on and fail with L for them all the
Ps 38:9 Lord, all my L is known to thee, my
119:20 soul is consumed with L for thy ordinances at
Rom 8:19 creation waits with eager L for the revealing of
2Cor 7:7 told us of your L, your mourning, your zeal
7:11 what alarm, what L, what zeal, what punishment!
Phil 2:26 for he has been L for you all, and

LONGINGLY (2)

2Sam 23:15 And David said L, "O that some one would
1Chr 11:17 And David said L, "O that some one would

LONGS (7)

Gen 34:8 of my son Shechem L for your daughter; I
Job 7:2 Like a slave who L for the shadow, and
Ps 12:5 place him in the safety for which he L
42:1 As a hart L for flowing streams, so longs
42:1 for flowing streams, so L my soul for thee,
84:2 My soul L, yea, faints for the courts of
Wis 8:8 And if any one L for wide experience, she

LOOK (212)

Gen 9:16 the clouds, I will L upon it and remember
13:14 up your eyes, and L from the place where
15:5 him outside and said, L toward heaven, and number
19:17 your life; do not L back or stop anywhere
21:16 said, "Let me not L upon the death of
24:16 was very fair to L upon, a virgin, whom
26:7 she was fair to L upon.
30:33 when you come to L into my wages with
42:1 sons, "Why do you L at one another?"
Ex 3:6 he was afraid to L at God.
5:21 to them, "The LORD L upon you and judge,
10:10 L, you have some evil purpose in mind.

L

Lev 14:39 the seventh day, and L; and if the disease
14:44 priest shall go and L; and if the disease
Num 4:20 not go in to L upon the holy things
11:6 but this manna to L at."
15:39 you a tassel to L upon and remember all
21:9 any man, he would L at the bronze serpent
24:1 at other times, to L for omens, but set
Deut 26:15 L down from thy holy habitation, from heaven, and
28:32 people, while your eyes L on and fail with
Judg 7:17 he said to them, L at me, and do
9:36 he said to Zebul, L, men are coming down
9:37 spoke again and said, L, men are coming down
1Sam 1:11 if thou wilt indeed L on the affliction of
2:29 Why then L with greedy eye at my sacrifices
2:32 in distress you will L with envious eye on
9:3 and arise, go and L for the asses."
14:11 and the Philistines said, L, Hebrews are coming out
16:7 to Samuel, "Do not L on his appearance or
20:21 say to the lad, L, the arrows are on
20:22 say to the youth, L, the arrows are beyond
2Sam 9:8 servant, that you should L upon a dead dog
15:27 to Zadok the priest, L, go back to the
16:12 that the LORD will L upon my affliction, and
1Kgs 12:16 L now to your own house, David." So Israel
18:43 servant, "Go up now, L toward the sea." And
2Kgs 3:14 Judah, I would neither L at you, nor see
4:25 to Gehazi his servant, L, yonder is the Shunammite;
6:32 L, when the messenger comes, shut the door, and
9:2 And when you arrive, L there for Jehu the
14:8 saying, "Come, let us L one another in the
2Chr 10:16 L now to your own house, David." So all
25:17 saying, "Come, let us L one another in the
Tob 3:3 Remember me and L favorably upon me; do not
5:4 So he went to L for a man; and
Jud 4:15 all their might to L with favor upon the
6:9 be taken, do not L downcast!
6:19 of our people, and L this day upon the
13:4 God of all might, L in this hour upon
14:18 For L, here is Holofernes lying on the ground,
Esth 1:17 women, causing them to L with contempt upon their
Job 6:19 The caravans of Tema L, the travelers of Sheba
6:28 now, be pleased to L at me; for I
7:19 long wilt thou not L away from me, nor
10:15 filled with disgrace and L upon my affliction.
14:6 that he cannot pass, L away from him, and
17:13 the darkness.' If I L for Sheol as my
20:17 He will not L upon the rivers, the streams
21:5 L at me, and be appalled, and lay your
31:1 how then could I L upon a virgin?
35:5 L at the heavens, and see; and behold the
37:21 "And now men cannot L on the light when
40:11 of your anger, and L on every one that
40:12 L on every one that is proud, and bring
Ps 8:3 When I L at thy heavens, the work of
34:5 L to him, and be radiant; so your faces
35:17 O LORD, wilt thou L on?
37:10 no more; though you L well at his place,
37:34 the land; you will L on the destruction of
39:13 L away from me, that I may know gladness,
59:10 God will let me L in triumph on my
68:16 Why L you with envy, O many-peaked mountain, at
80:14 L down from heaven, and see; have regard for
84:9 our shield, O God; L upon the face of
85:11 ground, and righteousness will L down from the sky.
91:8 You will only L with your eyes and see
101:6 I will L with favor on the faithful in
104:27 These all L to thee, to give them their
118:7 help me; I shall L in triumph on those
119:153 L on my affliction and deliver me, for I
119:158 I L at the faithless with disgust, because they
123:2 the eyes of servants L to the hand of
123:2 mistress, so our eyes L to the LORD our
142:4 I L to the right and watch, but there
145:15 The eyes of all L to thee, and thou
Prov 4:26 Let your eyes L directly forward, and your gaze
23:31 Do not L at wine when it is red,
29:16 but the righteous will L upon their downfall.
Eccl 12:3 few, and those that L through the windows are
Song 6:11 the nut orchard, to L at the blossoms of
6:13 return, that we may L upon you.
6:13 Why should you L upon the Shulammite, as upon
Wis 17:10 trembling fear, refusing to L even at the air,
Sir 7:22 L after them; if they are profitable to you,
9:5 Do not L intently at a virgin, lest you
9:7 Do not L around in the streets of a
9:8 woman, and do not L intently at beauty belonging
11:12 eyes of the Lord L upon him for his
14:16 in Hades one cannot L for luxury.
20:21 shame, or lose it because of his foolish L
23:19 than the sun; they L upon all the ways
33:15 L upon all the works of the Most High;
33:21 than that you should L to the hand of
34:15 To whom does he L
36:1 God of all, and L upon us,
42:12 Do not L upon any one for beauty, and
43:11 L upon the rainbow, and praise him who made
Is 5:30 And if one L to the land, behold, darkness
8:22 upward; and they will L to the earth, but
13:8 They will L aghast at one another; their faces
17:7 and their eyes will L to the Holy One
17:8 and they will not L to what their own
18:3 when a signal is raised on the mountains, L
18:4 me: "I will quietly L from my dwelling like
22:4 Therefore I said: L away from me, let me
22:11 But you did not L to him who did
31:1 strong, but do not L to the Holy One
33:20 L upon Zion, the city of our appointed feasts!
38:11 the living; I shall L upon man no more
41:28 But when I L there is no one; among
42:18 Hear, you deaf; and L, you blind, that you
51:1 who seek the LORD; L to the rock from
51:2 L to Abraham your father and to Sarah who
51:6 to the heavens, and L at the earth beneath;
53:2 comeliness that we should L at him, and no
59:9 not overtake us; we L for light, and behold,
59:11 moan like doves; we L for justice, but there
63:15 L down from heaven and see, from thy holy
66:2 to whom I will L, he that is humble
66:24 shall go forth and L on the dead bodies
Jer 2:23 L at your way in the valley; know what
3:12 I will not L on you in anger, for
5:1 the streets of Jerusalem, L and take note!
5:3 do not thy eyes L for truth?
6:16 by the roads, and L, and ask for the
13:16 mountains, and while you L for light he turns
20:4 their enemies while you L on.
39:12 guard, saying, "Take him, L after him well and
40:4 come, and I will L after you well; but
46:5 fled in haste; they L not back—terror on
47:3 their wheels, the fathers L not back to their
Lam 1:11 L, O LORD, and behold, for I am despised."
1:12 L and see if there is any sorrow like
2:20 L, O LORD, and see!
Bar 2:16 O Lord, L down from thy holy habitation, and
4:36 L toward the east, O Jerusalem, and see the
5:5 upon the height and L toward the east, and
Ezek 4:17 bread and water, and L at one another in
40:4 me, "Son of man, L with your eyes, and
Dan 13:20 to her, and said: L, the garden doors are
14:19 going in, and said, L at the floor, and
Hos 14:8 I who answer and L after you.
Amos 5:22 beasts I will not L upon.
Jon 2:4 how shall I again L upon thy holy temple?'
Mic 7:7 for me, I will L to the LORD, I
Nah 3:5 I will let nations L on your nakedness and
3:7 And all who L on you will shrink from
Hab 1:3 me see wrongs and L upon trouble?
1:5 L among the nations, and see; wonder and be
1:13 evil and canst not L on wrong, why dost
1:13 wrong, why dost thou L on faithless men, and
2:1 on the tower, and L forth to see what
Zech 12:10 so that, when they L on him whom they
1Mac 9:45 For L
2Mac 1:27 slaves among the Gentiles, L upon those who are
7:28 you, my child, to L at the heaven and
8:2 besought the Lord to L upon the people who
11:29 to return home and L after your own affairs.
15:8 heaven, and now to L for the victory which
Mt 6:16 you fast, do not L dismal, like the hypocrites,
6:26 L at the birds of the air: they neither
11:3 come, or shall we L for another?"
12:2 they said to him, L, your disciples are doing
22:11 king came in to L at the guests, he
Mk 2:24 Pharisees said to him, L, why are they doing
8:24 see men; but they L like trees, walking."
11:21 And Peter remembered and said to him, "Master, L
12:15 coin, and let me L at it."
13:1 disciples said to him, L, Teacher, what wonderful
13:21 one says to you, L, here is the Christ!'
13:21 is the Christ!' or L, there he is!' do
Lk 7:19 come, or shall we L for another?"
7:20 come, or shall we L for another?"

9:38 I beg you to L upon my son, for
21:28 begin to take place, L up and raise your
21:29 told them a parable: L at the fig tree,
22:38 And they said, L, Lord, here are two swords."
Jn 12:19 you can do nothing; L, the world has gone
19:37 scripture says, "They shall L on him whom they
20:5 first; and stooping to L in, he saw the
20:11 wept she stooped to L into the tomb;
Acts 3:4 with John, and said, L at us."
4:29 And now, Lord, L upon their threats, and grant
7:31 he drew near to L, the voice of the
7:32 And Moses trembled and did not dare to L
11:25 went to Tarsus to L for Saul;
2Cor 3:7 the Israelites could not L at Moses' face because
4:18 all comparison, because we L not to the things
10:7 L at what is before your eyes.
Gal 6:1 L to yourself, lest you too be tempted.
Eph 5:15 L carefully then how you walk, not as unwise
Phil 2:4 Let each of you L not only to his
2:21 They all L after their own interests, not those
3:2 L out for the dogs, look out for the
3:2 out for the dogs, L out for the evil-workers,
3:2 out for the evil-workers, L out for those who
2Thes 3:15 Do not L on him as an enemy, but
Jas 3:4 L at the ships also; though they are so
1Pet 1:12 from heaven, things into which angels long to L
2Jn 1:8 L to yourselves, that you may not lose what
Rev 5:3 the scroll or to L into it,

LOOKED (154)

Gen 8:13 of the ark, and L, and behold, the face
16:4 she had conceived, she L with contempt on her
16:5 she had conceived, she L on me with contempt.
18:2 up his eyes and L, and behold, three men
18:16 from there, and they L toward Sodom; and Abraham
19:26 Lot's wife behind him L back, and she became
19:28 the LORD; and he L down toward Sodom and
22:13 up his eyes and L, and behold, behind him
24:63 up his eyes and L, and behold, there were
26:8 king of the Philistines L out of a window
29:2 As he L, he saw a well in the
29:32 "Because the LORD has L upon my affliction; surely
33:1 up his eyes and L, and behold, Esau was
43:33 youth; and the men L at one another in
Ex 2:11 to his people and L on their burdens; and
2:12 He L this way and that, and seeing no
3:2 a bush; and he L, and lo, the bush
14:24 fire and of cloud L down upon the host
16:10 people of Israel, they L toward the wilderness, and
33:8 his tent door, and L after Moses, until he
Num 17:9 of Israel; and they L, and each man took
24:20 Then he L on Amalek, and took up his
24:21 And he L on the Kenite, and took up
Deut 9:16 And I L, and behold, you had sinned against
Josh 5:13 up his eyes and L, and behold, a man
8:20 the men of Ai L back, behold, the smoke
Judg 9:43 the fields; and he L and saw the men
13:20 Manoah and his wife L on; and they fell
16:27 men and women, who L on while Samson made
20:40 of smoke, the Benjaminites L behind them; and
1Sam 6:19 of Beth-shemesh, because they L into the ark of
14:16 in Gibe-ah of Benjamin L; and behold, the multitude
16:6 When they came, he L on Eliab and thought,
17:42 And when the Philistine L, and saw David, he
24:8 And when Saul L behind him, David bowed with
2Sam 1:7 And when he L behind him, he saw me,
2:20 Then Abner L behind him and said, "Is it
6:16 the daughter of Saul L out of the window,
13:34 up his eyes, and L, and behold, many people
18:24 up his eyes and L, he saw a man
22:42 They L, but there was none to save; they
24:20 And when Araunah L down, he saw the king
1Kgs 3:21 dead; but when I L at it closely in
18:43 he went up and L, and said, "There is
19:6 And he L, and behold, there was at his
2Kgs 6:30 wall--and the people L, and behold, he had
9:30 adorned her head, and L out of the window.
9:32 Two or three eunuchs L out at him.
11:14 people; and when she L, there was the king
1Chr 15:29 the daughter of Saul L out of the window,
21:21 came to Ornan, Ornan L and saw David and
2Chr 13:14 And when Judah L, behold, the battle was before
20:24 of the wilderness, they L toward the multitude; and
23:13 people; and when she L, there was the king
26:20 and all the priests, L at him, and behold,
Neh 4:14 And I L, and arose, and said to the
Jud 1:11 afraid of him, but L upon him as only
4:13 heard their prayers and L upon their affliction; for
Esth 15:5 perfect beauty, and she L happy, as if beloved,
15:7 flushed with splendor, he L at her in fierce
Job 30:26 But when I L for good, evil came; and
31:26 much; if I have L at the sun when
36:25 All men have L on it; man beholds it
Ps 54:7 and my eye has L in triumph on my
63:2 So I have L upon thee in the sanctuary,
69:20 I L for pity, but there was none; and
102:19 the LORD: that he L down from his holy
102:19 from heaven the LORD L at the earth,
114:3 The sea L and fled, Jordan turned back.
Prov 7:6 my house I have L out through my lattice,
24:32 and considered it; I L and received instruction.
Sir 16:27 After this the Lord L upon the earth, and
51:7 to help me; I L for the assistance of
Is 5:2 in it; and he L for it to yield
5:4 When I L for it to yield grapes, why
5:7 pleasant planting; and he L for justice, but behold,
22:8 In that day you L to the weapons of
57:8 their bed, you have L on nakedness.
63:5 I L, but there was no one to help;
64:3 terrible things which we L not for, thou camest
Jer 4:23 I L on the earth, and lo, it was
4:24 I L on the mountains, and lo, they were
4:25 I L, and lo, there was no man, and
4:26 I L, and lo, the fruitful land was a
8:15 We L for peace, but no good came, for
14:19 We L for peace, but no good came; for
31:26 Thereupon I awoke and L, and my sleep was
Ezek 1:4 As I L, behold, a stormy wind came out
1:13 there was something that L like burning coals of
1:15 Now as I L at the living creatures, I
2:9 And when I L, behold, a hand was stretched
8:7 court; and when I L, behold, there was a
10:1 Then I L, and behold, on the firmament that
10:9 And I L, and behold, there were four wheels
16:8 by you again and L upon you, behold, you
37:8 And as I L, there were sinews on them,
44:4 the temple; and I L, and behold, the glory
Dan 2:34 As you L, a stone was cut out by
7:4 Then as I L its wings were plucked off,
7:6 flesh.' After this I L, and lo, another, like
7:9 As I L, thrones were placed and one that
7:11 I L then because of the sound of the
7:11 And as I L, the beast was slain, and
7:21 As I L, this horn made war with the
10:5 up my eyes and L, and behold, a man
12:5 Then I Daniel L, and behold, two others stood,
13:35 And she, weeping, L up toward heaven, for her
14:18 were opened, the king L at the table, and
14:40 to the den he L in, and there sat
Hab 3:6 measured the earth; he L and shook the nations;
Hag 1:9 You have L for much, and, lo, it came
1Mac 4:5 one there, so he L for them in the
4:12 When the foreigners L up and saw them coming
5:30 At dawn they L up, and behold, a large
9:39 raised their eyes and L, and saw a tumultuous
2Mac 3:17 showed to those who L at him the pain
7:4 brothers and the mother L on.
7:16 But he L at the king, and said, "Because
Mt 14:19 the two fish he L up to heaven, and
19:26 But Jesus L at them and said to them,
Mk 3:5 And he L around at them with anger, grieved
5:32 And he L around to see who had done
6:41 the two fish he L up to heaven, and
8:24 And he L up and said, "I see men;
8:25 his eyes; and he L intently and was restored,
10:23 And Jesus L around and said to his disciples,
10:27 Jesus L at them and said, "With men it
11:11 and when he had L round at everything, as
14:67 Peter warming himself, she L at him, and said,
Lk 1:25 the days when he L on me, to take
6:10 And he L around on them all, and said
9:16 the two fish he L up to heaven, and
19:5 to the place, he L up and said to
20:17 But he L at them and said, "What then
21:1 He L up and saw the rich putting their
22:59 the Lord turned and L at Peter.
Jn 1:36 his disciples; and he L at Jesus as he
1:42 Jesus L at him, and said, "So you are
8:10 Jesus L up and said to her, "Woman, where
13:22 The disciples L at one another, uncertain of whom
Acts 13:9 with the Holy Spirit, L intently at him
Heb 11:10 For he L forward to the city which has

L

11:26 of Egypt, for he L to the reward.
1Jn 1:1 eyes, which we have L upon and touched with
Rev 4:1 After this I L, and lo, in heaven an
4:3 was a rainbow that L like an emerald.
5:11 Then I L, and I heard around the throne
6:12 the sixth seal, I L, and behold, there was
7:9 After this I L, and behold, a great multitude
8:13 Then I L, and I heard an eagle crying
9:7 their heads were what L like crowns of gold;
14:1 Then I L, and lo, on Mount Zion stood
14:14 Then I L, and lo, a white cloud, and
15:5 After this I L, and the temple of the

LOOKEST

Dan 3:55 sittest upon cherubim and L upon the deeps, and

LOOKING (40)

Gen 37:25 down to eat; and L up they saw a
Tob 5:11 he answered, "Are you L for a tribe and
11:5 Now Anna sat L intently down the road for
Ps 119:37 Turn my eyes from L at vanities; and give
Song 2:9 in at the windows, L through the lattice.
Sir 41:20 who greet you; of L at a woman who
Is 33:15 shuts his eyes from L upon evil,
38:14 eyes are weary with L upward.
Ezek 23:15 heads, all of them L like officers, a picture
Dan 13:9 away their eyes from L to Heaven or remembering
2Mac 12:45 But if he was L to the splendid reward
15:20 When all were now L forward to the coming
15:34 And they all, L to heaven, blessed the Lord
Mt 27:55 also many women there, L on from afar, who
Mk 3:34 And L around on those who sat about him,
7:33 touched his tongue; and L up to heaven, he
9:8 And suddenly L around they no longer saw any
10:21 And Jesus L upon him loved him, and said
15:39 There were also women L on from afar, among
15:42 who was also himself L for the kingdom of
16:4 And L up, they saw that the stone was
Lk 2:25 was righteous and devout, L for the consolation of
2:38 to all who were L for the redemption of
2:48 and I have been L for you anxiously."
18:24 Jesus L at him said, "How hard it is
23:50 deed, and he was L for the kingdom of
24:12 the tomb; stooping and L in, he saw the
24:17 And they stood still, L sad.
Jn 7:11 The Jews were L for him at the feast,
11:56 They were L for Jesus and saying to one
Acts 1:9 this, as they were L on, he was lifted
1:11 why do you stand L into heaven?
10:19 "Behold, three men are L for you.
10:21 the one you are L for; what is the
11:6 L at it closely I observed animals and beasts
14:9 Paul speaking; and Paul, L intently at him and
23:1 And Paul, L intently at the council, said, "Brethren,
27:12 a harbor of Crete, L northeast and southeast, and
Heb 12:2 is set before us, L to Jesus the pioneer
Jude 1:12 carouse together, L after themselves; waterless

LOOKS (31)

Num 21:20 top of Pisgah which L down upon the desert.
1Sam 13:18 toward the border that L down upon the valley
16:7 as man sees; man L on the outward appearance,
16:7 appearance, but the LORD L on the heart."
Job 7:2 like a hireling who L for his wages,
28:24 For he L to the ends of the earth,
Ps 14:2 The LORD L down from heaven upon the children
33:13 The LORD L down from heaven, he sees all
33:14 he sits enthroned he L forth on all the
53:2 God L down from heaven upon the sons of
101:5 The man of haughty L and arrogant heart I
104:32 in his works, who L on the earth and
113:6 seated on high, who L far down upon the
Prov 14:15 everything, but the prudent L where he is going.
25:23 brings forth rain; and a backbiting tongue, angry L
31:27 She L well to the ways of her household,
Song 6:10 "Who is this that L forth like the dawn,
Sir 11:2 man for his good L, nor loathe a man
16:17 with trembling when he L upon them.
37:10 consult the one who L at you suspiciously; hide
40:29 When a man L to the table of another,
42:16 The sun L down on everything with its light,
42:18 be known, and he L into the signs of
Is 2:11 The haughty L of man shall be brought low,
Lam 3:50 the LORD from heaven L down and sees;
Ezek 2:6 be dismayed at their L, for they are a
3:9 be dismayed at their L, for they are a

21:21 consults the teraphim, he L at the liver.
Mt 5:28 that every one who L at a woman lustfully
Lk 9:62 to the plow and L back is fit for
Jas 1:24 But he who L into the perfect law, the

LOOM (2)

Judg 16:14 away the pin, the L, and the web.
Is 38:12 me off from the L; from day to night

LOOMS

Jer 6:1 on Beth-haccherem; for evil L out of the north,

LOOPS (14)

Ex 26:4 And you shall make L of blue on the
26:4 likewise you shall make L on the edge of
26:5 Fifty L you shall make on the one curtain,
26:5 one curtain, and fifty L you shall make on
26:5 the second set; the L shall be opposite one
26:10 you shall make fifty L on the edge of
26:10 one set, and fifty L on the edge of
26:11 the clasps into the L, and couple the tent
36:11 And he made L of blue on the edge
36:12 set; he made fifty L on the one curtain,
36:12 and he made fifty L on the edge of
36:12 the second set; the L were opposite one another.
36:17 And he made fifty L on the edge of
36:17 one set, and fifty L on the edge of

LOOSE (34)

Gen 27:40 but when you break L you shall break his
49:21 is a hind let L, that bears comely fawns.
Ex 22:5 or lets his beast L and it feeds in
28:28 breastpiece shall not come L from the ephod.
32:25 the people had broken L (for Aaron had let
32:25 had let them break L, to their shame among
39:21 breastpiece should not come L from the ephod; as
Lev 10:6 of your heads hang L, and do not rend
13:45 of his head hang L, and he shall cover
21:10 of his head hang L, nor rend his clothes;
26:22 And I will let L the wild beasts among
Job 6:9 that he would let L his hand and cut
38:31 of the Pleiades, or L the cords of Orion?
Ps 78:49 He let L on them his fierce anger, wrath,
Prov 2:16 be saved from the L woman, from the adventuress
5:3 the lips of a L woman drip honey, and
5:20 my son, with a L woman and embrace the
7:5 preserve you from the L woman, from the
22:14 The mouth of a L woman is a deep
Sir 9:3 go to meet a L woman, lest you fall
22:14 will not be torn L by an earthquake; so
Is 5:27 not a waistcloth is L, not a sandal-thong broken;
7:25 where cattle are let L and where sheep tread.
20:2 Amoz, saying, "Go, and L the sackcloth from your
33:23 Your tackle hangs L; it cannot hold the mast
52:2 arise, O captive Jerusalem; L the bonds from your
58:6 that I choose: to L the bonds of wickedness,
Ezek 5:16 spoken-- when I L against you my deadly
5:16 destruction, which I will L to destroy you, and
7:3 and I will let L my anger upon you,
Dan 3:93 I see four men L, walking in the midst
Mt 16:19 heaven, and whatever you L on earth shall be
18:17 heaven, and whatever you L on earth shall be
Lk 15:13 squandered his property in L living.

LOOSED (12)

Jud 9:2 the strangers who had L the girdle of a
Job 30:11 Because God has L my cord and humbled me,
39:5 Who has L the bonds of the swift ass,
Ps 30:11 into dancing; thou hast L my sackcloth and girded
116:16 Thou hast L my bonds.
Mt 16:19 on earth shall be L in heaven."
18:17 on earth shall be L in heaven.
Lk 1:64 opened and his tongue L, and he spoke, blessing
13:16 for eighteen years, be L from this bond on
Acts 2:24 raised him up, having L the pangs of death,
Rev 20:3 that he must be L for a little while.
20:7 ended, Satan will be L from his prison

LOOSEN

Jer 17:4 You shall L your hand from your heritage which

LOOSENING

Acts 27:40 at the same time L the ropes that tied

LOOSES (2)

Job 12:18 He L the bonds of kings, and binds a

12:21 contempt on princes, and L the belt of the

LOOTED

Obad 1:13 you should not have L his goods in the

LOP

Is 10:33 LORD of hosts will L the boughs with terrifying

LORD (8,408)

Gen 2:4 the day that the L God made the earth
2:5 sprung up–for the L God had not caused
2:7 ground-- then the L God formed man of
2:8 And the L God planted a garden in Eden,
2:9 of the ground the L God made to grow
2:15 The L God took the man and put him
2:16 And the L God commanded the man, saying, "You
2:18 Then the L God said, "It is not good
2:19 of the ground the L God formed every beast
2:21 So the L God caused a deep sleep to
2:22 the rib which the L God had taken from
3:1 wild creature that the L God had made.
3:8 the sound of the L God walking in the
3:8 the presence of the L God among the trees
3:9 But the L God called to the man, and
3:13 Then the L God said to the woman, "What
3:14 The L God said to the serpent, "Because you
3:21 And the L God made for Adam and for
3:22 Then the L God said, "Behold, the man has
3:23 ever"-- therefore the L God sent him forth
4:1 gotten a man with the help of the L
4:3 Cain brought to the L an offering of the
4:4 And the L had regard for Abel and his
4:6 The L said to Cain, "Why are you angry,
4:9 Then the L said to Cain, "Where is Abel
4:10 And the L said, "What have you done?
4:13 Cain said to the L, "My punishment is greater
4:15 Then the L said to him, "Not so!
4:15 And the L put a mark on Cain, lest
4:16 the presence of the L, and dwelt in the
4:26 began to call upon the name of the L
5:29 the ground which the L has cursed this one
6:3 Then the L said, "My spirit shall not abide
6:5 The L saw that the wickedness of man was
6:6 And the L was sorry that he had made
6:7 So the L said, "I will blot out man
6:8 Noah found favor in the eyes of the L
7:1 Then the L said to Noah, "Go into the
7:5 did all that the L had commanded him.
7:16 commanded him; and the L shut him in.
8:20 an altar to the L, and took of every
8:21 And when the L smelled the pleasing odor, the
8:21 the pleasing odor, the L said in his heart,
9:26 said, "Blessed by the L my God be Shem;
10:9 mighty hunter before the L; therefore it is said,
10:9 said, "Like Nimrod a mighty hunter before the L
11:5 And the L came down to see the city
11:6 And the L said, "Behold, they are one people,
11:8 So the L scattered them abroad from there over
11:9 Babel, because there the L confused the language of
11:9 and from there the L scattered them abroad over
12:1 Now the L said to Abram, "Go from your
12:4 Abram went, as the L had told him; and
12:7 Then the L appeared to Abram, and said, "To
12:7 an altar to the L, who had appeared to
12:8 an altar to the L and called on the
12:8 LORD and called on the name of the L
12:17 But the L afflicted Pharaoh and his house with
13:4 there Abram called on the name of the L
13:10 the garden of the L, like the land of
13:10 was before the L destroyed Sodom and Gomorrah.
13:13 of Sodom were wicked, great sinners against the L
13:14 The L said to Abram, after Lot had separated
13:18 and there he built an altar to the L
14:22 have sworn to the L God Most High, maker
15:1 the word of the L came to Abram in
15:2 But Abram said, "O L GOD, what wilt thou
15:4 the word of the L came to him, "This
15:6 And he believed the L; and he reckoned it
15:7 him, "I am the L who brought you from
15:8 But he said, "O L GOD, how am I
15:13 Then the L said to Abram, "Know of a
15:18 On that day the L made a covenant with
16:2 Abram, "Behold now, the L has prevented me from
16:5 May the L judge between you and me!"
16:7 The angel of the L found her by a
16:9 The angel of the L said to her, "Return
16:10 The angel of the L also said to her,
16:11 the angel of the L said to her, "Behold,
16:11 name Ishmael; because the L has given heed to
16:13 the name of the L who spoke to her,
17:1 ninety-nine years old the L appeared to Abram, and
18:1 And the L appeared to him by the oaks
18:3 earth, and said, "My L, if I have found
18:10 The L said, "I will surely return to you
18:13 The L said to Abraham, "Why did Sarah laugh,
18:14 am old?' Is anything too hard for the L
18:17 The L said, "Shall I hide from Abraham what
18:19 the way of the L by doing righteousness and
18:19 justice; so that the L may bring to Abraham
18:20 Then the L said, "Because the outcry against Sodom
18:22 toward Sodom; but Abraham still stood before the L
18:26 And the L said, "If I find at Sodom
18:27 to speak to the L, I who am but
18:30 "Oh let not the L be angry, and I
18:31 have taken upon myself to speak to the L
18:32 "Oh let not the L be angry, and I
18:33 And the L went his way, when he had
19:13 become great before the L, and the LORD has
19:13 the LORD, and the L has sent us to
19:14 this place; for the L is about to destroy
19:16 by the hand, the L being merciful to him,
19:24 Then the L rained on Sodom and Gomorrah
19:24 and fire from the L out of heaven;
19:27 had stood before the L;
20:4 her; so he said, L, wilt thou slay an
20:18 For the L had closed all the wombs of
21:1 The L visited Sarah as he had said, and
21:1 had said, and the L did to Sarah as
21:33 the name of the L, the Everlasting God.
22:11 the angel of the L called to him from
22:14 of that place The L will provide; as it
22:14 the mount of the L it shall be provided."
22:15 the angel of the L called to Abraham a
22:16 have sworn, says the L, because you have done
23:6 Abraham, "Hear us, my L; you are a mighty
23:11 his city, "No, my L, hear me; I give
23:15 Ephron answered Abraham, "My L, listen to me; a
24:1 in years; and the L had blessed Abraham in
24:3 you swear by the L, the God of heaven
24:7 The L, the God of heaven, who took me
24:12 And he said, "O L, God of my master
24:18 She said, "Drink, my L; and she quickly let
24:21 to learn whether the L had prospered his journey
24:26 head and worshiped the L,
24:27 said, "Blessed be the L, the God of my
24:27 As for me, the L has led me in
24:31 O blessed of the L; why do you stand
24:35 The L has greatly blessed my master, and he
24:40 said to me, 'The L, before whom I walk,
24:42 spring, and said, 'O L, the God of my
24:44 the woman whom the L has appointed for my
24:48 head and worshiped the L, and blessed the LORD,
24:48 LORD, and blessed the L, the God of my
24:50 thing comes from the L; we cannot speak to
24:51 master's son, as the L has spoken."
24:52 he bowed himself to the earth before the L
24:56 delay me, since the L has prospered my way;
25:21 Isaac prayed to the L for his wife, because
25:21 was barren; and the L granted his prayer, and
25:22 So she went to inquire of the L
25:23 And the L said to her, "Two nations are
26:2 And the L appeared to him, and said, "Do
26:12 The L blessed him,
26:22 saying, "For now the L has made room for
26:24 And the L appeared to him the same night
26:25 the name of the L, and pitched his tent
26:28 see plainly that the L is with you; so
26:29 You are now the blessed of the L
27:7 bless you before the L before I die.'
27:20 He answered, "Because the L your God granted me
27:27 a field which the L has blessed!
27:29 Be L over your brothers, and may your mother's
27:37 have made him your L, and all his brothers
28:13 And behold, the L stood above it and said,
28:13 said, "I am the L, the God of Abraham
28:16 and said, "Surely the L is in this place;
28:21 in peace, then the L shall be my God,
29:31 When the L saw that Leah was hated, he
29:32 she said, "Because the L has looked upon my
29:33 and said, "Because the L has heard that I
29:35 I will praise the L; therefore she called his
30:24 Joseph, saying, "May the L add to me another

L

30:27 by divination that the L has blessed me because
30:30 increased abundantly; and the L has blessed you
31:3 Then the L said to Jacob, "Return to the
31:35 father, "Let not my L be angry that I
31:49 for he said, "The L watch between you and
32:4 shall say to my L Esau: Thus says your
32:5 sent to tell my L, in order that I
32:9 my father Isaac, O L who didst say to
32:18 present sent to my L Esau; and moreover he
33:8 "To find favor in the sight of my L
33:13 said to him, "My L knows that the children
33:14 Let my L pass on before his servant, and
33:14 I come to my L in Seir."
33:15 me find favor in the sight of my L
38:7 the sight of the L; and the LORD slew
38:7 the LORD; and the L slew him.
38:10 the sight of the L, and he slew him
39:2 The L was with Joseph, and he became a
39:3 master saw that the L was with him, and
39:3 him, and that the L caused all that he
39:5 that he had the L blessed the Egyptian's house
39:5 the blessing of the L was upon all that
39:21 But the L was with Joseph and showed him
39:23 Joseph's care, because the L was with him; and
39:23 whatever he did, the L made it prosper.
40:1 his baker offended their L the king of Egypt.
42:10 to him, "No, my L, but to buy food
42:30 saying, "The man, the L of the land, spoke
42:33 Then the man, the L of the land, said
43:20 and said, "Oh, my L, we came down the
44:5 from this that my L drinks, and by this
44:7 him, "Why does my L speak such words as
44:8 or gold from your L's house?
44:9 also will be my L's slaves."
44:16 Judah said, "What shall we say to my L
44:16 behold, we are my L's slaves, both we and
44:18 and said, "O my L, let your servant, I
44:18 a word in my L's ears, and let not
44:19 My L asked his servants, saying, 'Have you a
44:20 we said to my L, 'We have a father,
44:22 We said to my L, 'The lad cannot leave
44:24 father we told him the words of my L
44:33 a slave to my L; and let the lad
45:8 father to Pharaoh, and L of all his house
45:9 God has made me L of all Egypt; come
47:18 not hide from my L that our money is
47:18 the sight of my L but our bodies and
47:25 may it please my L, we will be slaves
49:18 I wait for thy salvation, O L
Ex 3:2 the angel of the L appeared to him in
3:4 When the L saw that he turned aside to
3:7 Then the L said, "I have seen the affliction
3:15 people of Israel, 'The L, the God of your
3:16 say to them, 'The L, the God of your
3:18 say to him, 'The L, the God of the
3:18 may sacrifice to the L our God.'
4:1 they will say, 'The L did not appear to
4:2 The L said to him, "What is that in
4:4 But the L said to Moses, "Put out your
4:5 may believe that the L, the God of their
4:6 Again, the L said to him, "Put your hand
4:10 Moses said to the L, "Oh, my Lord, I
4:10 the LORD, "Oh, my L, I am not eloquent,
4:11 Then the L said to him, "Who has made
4:11 Is it not I, the L
4:13 he said, "Oh, my L, send, I pray, some
4:14 the anger of the L was kindled against Moses
4:19 And the L said to Moses in Midian, "Go
4:21 And the L said to Moses, "When you go
4:22 Pharaoh, 'Thus says the L, Israel is my first-born
4:24 on the way the L met him and sought
4:27 The L said to Aaron, "Go into the wilderness
4:28 the words of the L with which he had
4:30 the words which the L had spoken to Moses,
4:31 they heard that the L had visited the people
5:1 said, "Thus says the L, the God of Israel,
5:2 said, "Who is the L, that I should heed
5:2 do not know the L, and moreover I will
5:3 and sacrifice to the L our God, lest he
5:17 and sacrifice to the L
5:21 said to them, "The L look upon you and
5:22 turned again to the L and said, "O LORD,
5:22 LORD and said, "O L, why hast thou done
6:1 But the L said to Moses, "Now you shall
6:2 And God said to Moses, "I am the L
6:3 by my name the L I did not make
6:6 Israel, 'I am the L, and I will bring
6:7 that I am the L your God, who has
6:8 I am the L
6:10 And the L said to Moses,
6:12 Moses said to the L, "Behold, the people of
6:13 But the L spoke to Moses and Aaron, and
6:26 Moses to whom the L said: "Bring out the
6:28 the day when the L spoke to Moses in
6:29 land of Egypt, the L said to Moses, "I
6:29 Moses, "I am the L; tell Pharaoh king of
6:30 Moses said to the L, "Behold, I am of
7:1 And the L said to Moses, "See, I make
7:5 that I am the L, when I stretch forth
7:6 they did as the L commanded them.
7:8 And the L said to Moses and Aaron,
7:10 and did as the L commanded; Aaron cast down
7:13 to them; as the L had said.
7:14 Then the L said to Moses, "Pharaoh's heart is
7:16 say to him, 'The L, the God of the
7:17 Thus says the L, "By this you shall know
7:17 that I am the L: behold, I will strike
7:19 And the L said to Moses, "Say to Aaron,
7:20 Aaron did as the L commanded; in the sight
7:22 to them; as the L had said.
7:25 days passed after the L had struck the Nile.
8:1 Then the L said to Moses, "Go in to
8:1 him, 'Thus says the L, "Let my people go,
8:5 And the L said to Moses, "Say to Aaron,
8:8 and said, "Entreat the L to take away the
8:8 let the people go to sacrifice to the L
8:10 no one like the L our God.
8:12 Moses cried to the L concerning the frogs, as
8:13 And the L did according to the word of
8:15 to them; as the L had said.
8:16 Then the L said to Moses, "Say to Aaron,
8:19 to them; as the L had said.
8:20 Then the L said to Moses, "Rise up early
8:20 him, 'Thus says the L, "Let my people go,
8:22 that I am the L in the midst of
8:24 And the L did so; there came great swarms
8:26 shall sacrifice to the L our God offerings abominable
8:27 and sacrifice to the L our God as he
8:28 to sacrifice to the L your God in the
8:29 will pray to the L that the swarms of
8:29 letting the people go to sacrifice to the L
8:30 went out from Pharaoh and prayed to the L
8:31 And the L did as Moses asked, and removed
9:1 Then the L said to Moses, "Go in to
9:1 him, 'Thus says the L, the God of the
9:3 the hand of the L will fall with a
9:4 But the L will make a distinction between the
9:5 And the L set a time, saying, "Tomorrow the
9:5 time, saying, "Tomorrow the L will do this thing
9:6 on the morrow the L did this thing; all
9:8 And the L said to Moses and Aaron, "Take
9:12 But the L hardened the heart of Pharaoh, and
9:12 to them; as the L had spoken to Moses.
9:13 Then the L said to Moses, "Rise up early
9:13 him, 'Thus says the L, the God of the
9:20 the word of the L among the servants of
9:21 the word of the L left his slaves and
9:22 And the L said to Moses, "Stretch forth your
9:23 toward heaven; and the L sent thunder and hail,
9:23 And the L rained hail upon the land of
9:27 sinned this time; the L is in the right,
9:28 Entreat the L; for there has been enough of
9:29 my hands to the L; the thunder will cease,
9:30 not yet fear the L God."
9:33 his hands to the L; and the thunder and
9:35 Israel go; as the L had spoken through Moses.
10:1 Then the L said to Moses, "Go in to
10:2 that you may know that I am the L
10:3 him, "Thus says the L, the God of the
10:7 they may serve the L their God; do you
10:8 them, "Go, serve the L your God; but who
10:9 for we must hold a feast to the L
10:10 said to them, "The L be with you, if
10:11 you, and serve the L, for that is what
10:12 Then the L said to Moses, "Stretch out your
10:13 of Egypt, and the L brought an east wind
10:16 have sinned against the L your God, and against
10:17 once, and entreat the L your God only to
10:18 he went out from Pharaoh, and entreated the L
10:19 And the L turned a very strong west wind,
10:20 But the L hardened Pharaoh's heart, and he did
10:21 Then the L said to Moses, "Stretch out your

10:24 said, "Go, serve the L; your children also may
10:25 may sacrifice to the L our God.
10:26 them to serve the L our God, and we
10:26 we must serve the L until we arrive there."
10:27 But the L hardened Pharaoh's heart, and he would
11:1 The L said to Moses, "Yet one plague more
11:3 And the L gave the people favor in the
11:4 said, "Thus says the L: About midnight I will
11:7 may know that the L makes a distinction between
11:9 Then the L said to Moses, "Pharaoh will not
11:10 before Pharaoh; and the L hardened Pharaoh's
12:1 The L said to Moses and Aaron in the
12:11 It is the L's passover.
12:12 Egypt I will execute judgments: I am the L
12:14 a feast to the L; throughout your generations you
12:23 For the L will pass through to slay the
12:23 the two doorposts, the L will pass over the
12:25 the land which the L will give you, as
12:27 the sacrifice of the L's passover, for he passed
12:28 did so; as the L had commanded Moses and
12:29 At midnight the L smote all the first-born in
12:31 and go, serve the L, as you have said.
12:36 and clothing; and the L had given the people
12:41 the hosts of the L went out from the
12:42 of watching by the L, to bring them out
12:42 watching kept to the L by all the people
12:43 And the L said to Moses and Aaron, "This
12:48 the passover to the L, let all his males
12:50 of Israel; as the L commanded Moses and Aaron,
12:51 that very day the L brought the people of
13:1 The L said to Moses,
13:3 strength of hand the L brought you out from
13:5 And when the L brings you into the land
13:6 day there shall be a feast to the L
13:8 because of what the L did for me when
13:9 the law of the L may be in your
13:9 a strong hand the L has brought you out
13:11 "And when the L brings you into the land
13:12 set apart to the L all that first opens
13:14 strength of hand the L brought us out of
13:15 let us go, the L slew all the first-born
13:15 I sacrifice to the L all the males that
13:16 a strong hand the L brought us out of
13:21 And the L went before them by day in
14:1 Then the L said to Moses,
14:4 the Egyptians shall know that I am the L
14:8 And the L hardened the heart of Pharaoh king
14:10 cried out to the L;
14:13 the salvation of the L, which he will work
14:14 The L will fight for you, and you have
14:15 The L said to Moses, "Why do you cry
14:18 that I am the L, when I have gotten
14:21 the sea; and the L drove the sea back
14:24 the morning watch the L in the pillar of
14:25 before Israel; for the L fights for them against
14:26 Then the L said to Moses, "Stretch out your
14:27 into it, and the L routed the Egyptians in
14:30 Thus the L saved Israel that day from the
14:31 great work which the L did against the Egyptians,
14:31 the people feared the L; and they believed in
14:31 they believed in the L and in his servant
15:1 this song to the L, saying, "I will sing
15:1 will sing to the L, for he has triumphed
15:2 The L is my strength and my song, and
15:3 The L is a man of war; the LORD
15:3 man of war; the L is his name.
15:6 Thy right hand, O L, glorious in power, thy
15:6 thy right hand, O L, shatters the enemy.
15:11 is like thee, O L, among the gods?
15:16 till thy people, O L, pass by, till the
15:17 mountain, the place, O L, which thou hast made
15:17 abode, the sanctuary, O L, which thy hands have
15:18 The L will reign for ever and ever."
15:19 into the sea, the L brought back the waters
15:21 them: "Sing to the L, for he has triumphed
15:25 he cried to the L; and the LORD showed
15:25 the LORD; and the L showed him a tree,
15:25 There the L made for them a statute and
15:26 the voice of the L your God, and do
15:26 for I am the L, your healer."
16:3 the hand of the L in the land of
16:4 Then the L said to Moses, "Behold, I will
16:6 that it was the L who brought you out
16:7 the glory of the L, because he has heard
16:7 because he has heard your murmurings against the L
16:8 Moses said, "When the L gives you in the
16:8 the full, because the L has heard your murmurings
16:8 murmurings are not against us but against the L
16:9 'Come near before the L, for he has heard
16:10 the glory of the L appeared in the cloud.
16:11 And the L said to Moses,
16:12 that I am the L your God.'"
16:15 the bread which the L has given you to
16:16 This is what the L has commanded: 'Gather of
16:23 "This is what the L has commanded: 'Tomorrow is
16:23 holy sabbath to the L; bake what you will
16:25 a sabbath to the L; today you will not
16:28 And the L said to Moses, "How long do
16:29 The L has given you the sabbath, therefore on
16:32 "This is what the L has commanded: 'Let an
16:33 place it before the L, to be kept throughout
16:34 As the L commanded Moses, so Aaron placed it
17:1 commandment of the L, and camped at Rephidim;
17:2 do you put the L to the proof?"
17:4 Moses cried to the L, "What shall I do
17:5 And the L said to Moses, "Pass on before
17:7 because they put the L to the proof by
17:7 by saying, "Is the L among us or not?"
17:14 And the L said to Moses, "Write this as
17:15 name of it, The L is my banner,
17:16 saying, "A hand upon the banner of the L
17:16 The L will have war with Amalek from generation
18:1 his people, how the L had brought Israel out
18:8 father-in-law all that the L had done to Pharaoh
18:8 way, and how the L had delivered them.
18:9 the good which the L had done to Israel,
18:10 said, "Blessed be the L, who has delivered you
18:11 I know that the L is greater than all
19:3 to God, and the L called to him out
19:7 these words which the L had commanded him.
19:8 said, "All that the L has spoken we will
19:8 reported the words of the people to the L
19:9 And the L said to Moses, "Lo, I am
19:9 told the words of the people to the L
19:10 And the L said to Moses, "Go to the
19:11 the third day the L will come down upon
19:18 in smoke, because the L descended upon it in
19:20 And the L came down upon Mount Sinai, to
19:20 the mountain; and the L called Moses to the
19:21 And the L said to Moses, "Go down and
19:21 break through to the L to gaze and many
19:22 come near to the L consecrate themselves, lest the
19:22 consecrate themselves, lest the L break out upon
19:23 Moses said to the L, "The people cannot come
19:24 And the L said to him, "Go down, and
19:24 come up to the L, lest he break out
20:2 saying, "I am the L your God, who brought
20:5 them; for I the L your God am a
20:7 the name of the L your God in vain;
20:7 in vain; for the L will not hold him
20:10 a sabbath to the L your God; in it
20:11 in six days the L made heaven and earth,
20:11 seventh day; therefore the L blessed the sabbath day
20:12 the land which the L your God gives you.
20:22 And the L said to Moses, "Thus you shall
22:11 an oath by the L shall be between them
22:20 god, save to the L only, shall be utterly
23:17 males appear before the L GOD.
23:19 the house of the L your God.
23:25 You shall serve the L your God, and I
24:1 "Come up to the L, you and Aaron, Nadab,
24:2 come near to the L; but the others shall
24:3 the words of the L and all the ordinances;
24:3 the words which the L has spoken we will
24:4 And Moses wrote all the words of the L
24:5 and sacrificed peace offerings of oxen to the L
24:7 said, "All that the L has spoken we will
24:8 the covenant which the L has made with you
24:12 The L said to Moses, "Come up to me
24:16 The glory of the L settled on Mount Sinai,
24:17 the glory of the L was like a devouring
25:1 The L said to Moses,
27:21 tend it from evening to morning before the L
28:12 their names before the L upon his two shoulders
28:29 bring them to continual remembrance before the L
28:30 goes in before the L; thus Aaron shall bear
28:30 his heart before the L continually.
28:35 holy place before the L, and when he comes
28:36 signet, 'Holy to the L
28:38 forehead, that they may be accepted before the L
29:11 the bull before the L, at the door of
29:18 burnt offering to the L; it is a pleasing

L

7:29 peace offerings to the L shall bring his offering
7:29 his offering to the L; from the sacrifice of
7:30 by fire to the L; he shall bring the
7:30 be waved as a wave offering before the L
7:35 by fire to the L, consecrated to them on
7:35 as priests of the L;
7:36 of the LORD; the L commanded this to be
7:38 offerings, which the L commanded Moses on Mount
7:38 their offerings to the L, in the wilderness of
8:1 The L said to Moses,
8:4 Moses did as the L commanded him; and the
8:5 the thing which the L has commanded to be
8:9 holy crown, as the L commanded Moses.
8:13 on them, as the L commanded Moses.
8:17 the camp, as the L commanded Moses.
8:21 by fire to the L, as the LORD commanded
8:21 the LORD, as the L commanded Moses.
8:26 which was before the L he took one unleavened
8:27 waved them as a wave offering before the L
8:28 pleasing odor, an offering by fire to the L
8:29 wave offering before the L; it was Moses' portion
8:29 of ordination, as the L commanded Moses.
8:34 been done today, the L has commanded to be
8:35 days, performing what the L has charged, lest you
8:36 the things which the L commanded by Moses.
9:2 both without blemish, and offer them before the L
9:4 to sacrifice before the L, and a cereal offering
9:4 oil; for today the L will appear to you.'"
9:5 the congregation drew near and stood before the L
9:6 the thing which the L commanded you to do;
9:6 the glory of the L will appear to you."
9:7 for them; as the L has commanded."
9:10 the altar, as the L commanded Moses.
9:21 wave offering before the L; as Moses commanded.
9:23 the glory of the L appeared to all the
9:24 forth from before the L and consumed the burnt
10:1 unholy fire before the L, such as he had
10:2 the presence of the L and devoured them, and
10:2 and devoured them, and they died before the L
10:3 "This is what the L has said, 'I will
10:6 the burning which the L has kindled.
10:7 anointing oil of the L is upon you." And
10:8 And the L spoke to Aaron, saying,
10:11 the statutes which the L has spoken to them
10:12 by fire to the L, and eat it unleavened
10:13 by fire to the L; for so I am
10:15 wave offering before the L, and it shall be
10:15 for ever; as the L has commanded."
10:17 to make atonement for them before the L
10:19 burnt offering before the L; and yet such things
10:19 have been acceptable in the sight of the L
11:1 And the L said to Moses and Aaron,
11:44 For I am the L your God; consecrate yourselves
11:45 For I am the L who brought you up
12:1 The L said to Moses,
12:7 offer it before the L, and make atonement for
13:1 The L said to Moses and Aaron,
14:1 The L said to Moses,
14:11 these things before the L, at the door of
14:12 wave offering before the L;
14:16 oil with his finger seven times before the L
14:18 priest shall make atonement for him before the L
14:23 of meeting, before the L;
14:24 wave them for a wave offering before the L
14:27 seven times before the L;
14:29 cleansed, to make atonement for him before the L
14:31 make atonement before the L for him who is
14:33 The L said to Moses and Aaron,
15:1 The L said to Moses and Aaron,
15:14 and come before the L to the door of
15:15 for him before the L for his discharge.
15:30 for her before the L for her unclean discharge.
16:1 The L spoke to Moses, after the death of
16:1 drew near before the L and died;
16:2 and died; and the L said to Moses, "Tell
16:7 set them before the L at the door of
16:8 one lot for the L and the other lot
16:9 lot fell for the L, and offer it as
16:10 presented alive before the L to make atonement
16:12 the altar before the L, and two handfuls of
16:13 the fire before the L, that the cloud of
16:18 which is before the L and make atonement for
16:30 your sins you shall be clean before the L
16:34 Moses did as the L commanded him.
17:1 And the L said to Moses,
17:2 the thing which the L has commanded.
17:4 a gift to the L before the tabernacle of
17:4 the tabernacle of the L, bloodguilt shall be imputed
17:5 bring them to the L, to the priest at
17:5 peace offerings to the L;
17:6 the altar of the L at the door of
17:6 the fat for a pleasing odor to the L
17:9 sacrifice it to the L; that man shall be
18:1 And the L said to Moses,
18:2 Israel, I am the L your God.
18:4 I am the L your God.
18:5 which a man shall live: I am the L
18:6 I am the L
18:21 the name of your God: I am the L
18:30 them: I am the L your God."
19:1 And the L said to Moses,
19:2 holy; for I the L your God am holy.
19:3 sabbaths: I am the L your God.
19:4 gods: I am the L your God.
19:5 peace offerings to the L, you shall offer it
19:8 holy thing of the L; and that person shall
19:10 sojourner: I am the L your God.
19:12 the name of your God: I am the L
19:14 you shall fear your God: I am the L
19:16 the life of your neighbor: I am the L
19:18 love your neighbor as yourself: I am the L
19:21 for himself to the L, to the door of
19:22 guilt offering before the L for his sin which
19:24 be holy, an offering of praise to the L
19:25 you: I am the L your God.
19:28 tattoo any marks upon you: I am the L
19:30 sabbaths and reverence my sanctuary: I am the L
19:31 them: I am the L your God.
19:32 you shall fear your God: I am the L
19:34 Egypt: I am the L your God.
19:36 hin: I am the L your God, who brought
19:37 my ordinances, and do them: I am the L
20:1 The L said to Moses,
20:7 for I am the L your God.
20:8 them; I am the L who sanctify you.
20:24 honey.' I am the L your God, who have
20:26 me; for I the L am holy, and have
21:1 And the L said to Moses, "Speak to the
21:6 by fire to the L, the bread of their
21:8 you; for I the L, who sanctify you, am
21:12 his God is upon him: I am the L
21:15 for I am the L who sanctify him."
21:16 And the L said to Moses,
21:21 near to offer the L's offerings by fire; since
21:23 for I am the L who sanctify them."
22:1 And the L said to Moses,
22:2 not profane my holy name; I am the L
22:3 Israel dedicate to the L, while he has an
22:3 cut off from my presence: I am the L
22:8 it: I am the L
22:9 it: I am the L who sanctify them.
22:15 they offer to the L,
22:16 for I am the L who sanctify them."
22:17 And the L said to Moses,
22:18 is offered to the L as a burnt offering,
22:21 peace offerings to the L, to fulfil a vow
22:22 not offer to the L or make of them
22:22 offering by fire upon the altar to the L
22:24 not offer to the L or sacrifice within your
22:26 And the L said to Moses,
22:27 acceptable as an offering by fire to the L
22:29 of thanksgiving to the L, you shall sacrifice it
22:30 none of it until morning: I am the L
22:31 my commandments and do them: I am the L
22:32 Israel; I am the L who sanctify you,
22:33 Egypt to be your God: I am the L
23:1 The L said to Moses,
23:2 appointed feasts of the L which you shall proclaim
23:3 a sabbath to the L in all your dwellings.
23:4 appointed feasts of the L, the holy convocations,
23:5 the evening, is the L's passover.
23:6 unleavened bread to the L; seven days you shall
23:8 by fire to the L seven days; on the
23:9 And the L said to Moses,
23:11 the sheaf before the L, that you may find
23:12 without blemish as a burnt offering to the L
23:13 by fire to the L, a pleasing odor; and
23:16 a cereal offering of new grain to the L
23:17 baked with leaven, as first fruits to the L
23:18 burnt offering to the L, with their cereal offering
23:18 offering by fire, a pleasing odor to the L
23:20 wave offering before the L, with the two lambs;

23:20 be holy to the L for the priest.
23:22 stranger: I am the L your God."
23:23 And the L said to Moses,
23:25 shall present an offering by fire to the L
23:26 And the L said to Moses,
23:27 and present an offering by fire to the L
23:28 for you before the L your God.
23:33 And the L said to Moses,
23:34 days is the feast of booths to the L
23:36 by fire to the L; on the eighth day
23:36 by fire to the L; it is a solemn
23:37 appointed feasts of the L, which you shall proclaim
23:37 for presenting to the L offerings by fire, burnt
23:38 the sabbaths of the L, and besides your gifts,
23:38 your freewill offerings, which you give to the L
23:39 the feast of the L seven days; on the
23:40 shall rejoice before the L your God seven days.
23:41 a feast to the L seven days in the
23:43 Egypt: I am the L your God."
23:44 people of Israel the appointed feasts of the L
24:1 The L said to Moses,
24:3 to morning before the L continually; it shall be
24:4 pure gold before the L continually.
24:7 portion to be offered by fire to the L
24:8 in order before the L continually on behalf of
24:9 by fire to the L, a perpetual due."
24:12 the will of the L should be declared to
24:13 And the L said to Moses,
24:16 the name of the L shall be put to
24:22 for I am the L your God."
24:23 Israel did as the L commanded Moses.
25:1 The L said to Moses on Mount Sinai,
25:2 the land shall keep a sabbath to the L
25:4 a sabbath to the L; you shall not sow
25:17 for I am the L your God.
25:38 I am the L your God, who brought you
25:55 Egypt: I am the L your God.
26:1 for I am the L your God.
26:2 sabbaths and reverence my sanctuary: I am the L
26:13 I am the L your God, who brought you
26:44 for I am the L their God;
26:45 I might be their God: I am the L
26:46 and laws which the L made between him and
27:1 The L said to Moses,
27:2 of persons to the L at your valuation,
27:9 an offering to the L, all of such that
27:9 man gives to the L is holy.
27:11 an offering to the L, then the man shall
27:14 be holy to the L, the priest shall value
27:16 man dedicates to the L part of the land
27:21 be holy to the L, as a field that
27:22 he dedicates to the L a field which he
27:23 that day as a holy thing to the L
27:26 firstling belongs to the L, no man may dedicate;
27:28 man devotes to the L, of anything that he
27:28 every devoted thing is most holy to the L
27:30 is the LORDs; it is holy to the L
27:32 the herdsman's staff, shall be holy to the L
27:34 commandments which the L commanded Moses for
Num 1:1 The L spoke to Moses in
1:19 by head, as the L commanded Moses.
1:48 For the L said to Moses,
1:54 to all that the L commanded Moses.
2:1 The L said to Moses and Aaron,
2:33 of Israel, as the L commanded Moses.
2:34 to all that the L commanded Moses, so they
3:1 the time when the L spoke with Moses on
3:4 Abihu died before the L when they offered unholy
3:4 unholy fire before the L in the wilderness of
3:5 And the L said to Moses,
3:11 And the L said to Moses,
3:13 beast; they shall be mine: I am the L
3:14 And the L said to Moses in the wilderness
3:16 the word of the L, as he was commanded.
3:39 the commandment of the L, by families, all the
3:40 And the L said to Moses, "Number all the
3:41 me--I am the L --instead of all the
3:42 of Israel, as the L commanded him.
3:44 And the L said to Moses,
3:45 the Levites shall be mine: I am the L
3:51 the word of the L, as the LORD commanded
3:51 the LORD, as the L commanded Moses.
4:1 The L said to Moses and Aaron,
4:17 The L said to Moses and Aaron,
4:21 The L said to Moses,
4:37 the commandment of the L by Moses.
4:41 numbered according to the commandment of the L
4:45 the commandment of the L by Moses.
4:49 the commandment of the L through Moses they
4:49 by him, as the L commanded Moses.
5:1 The L said to Moses,
5:4 the camp; as the L said to Moses, so
5:5 And the L said to Moses,
5:6 breaking faith with the L, and that person is
5:8 shall go to the L for the priest, in
5:11 And the L said to Moses,
5:16 set her before the L;
5:18 the woman before the L, and unbind the hair
5:21 to the woman) 'the L make you an execration
5:21 your people, when the L makes your thigh fall
5:25 cereal offering before the L and bring it to
5:30 the woman before the L, and the priest shall
6:1 And the L said to Moses,
6:2 separate himself to the L,
6:5 separates himself to the L, he shall be holy;
6:6 separates himself to the L he shall not go
6:8 of his separation he is holy to the L
6:12 separate himself to the L for the days of
6:14 his gift to the L, one male lamb a
6:16 present them before the L and offer his sin
6:17 peace offering to the L, with the basket of
6:20 wave offering before the L; they are a holy
6:21 His offering to the L shall be according to
6:22 The L said to Moses,
6:24 say to them, The L bless you and keep
6:25 and keep you: The L make his face to
6:26 gracious to you: The L lift up his countenance
7:3 their offerings before the L, six covered wagons and
7:4 Then the L said to Moses,
7:11 And the L said to Moses, "They shall offer
7:89 to speak with the L, he heard the voice
8:1 Now the L said to Moses,
8:3 the lampstand, as the L commanded Moses.
8:4 the pattern which the L had shown Moses, so
8:5 And the L said to Moses,
8:10 the Levites before the L, the people of Israel
8:11 the Levites before the L as a wave offering
8:11 be theirs to do the service of the L
8:12 burnt offering to the L, to make atonement for
8:13 offer them as a wave offering to the L
8:20 to all that the L commanded Moses concerning the
8:21 wave offering before the L, and Aaron made
8:22 his sons; as the L had commanded Moses concerning
8:23 And the L said to Moses,
9:1 And the L spoke to Moses in the wilderness
9:5 to all that the L commanded Moses, so the
9:7 kept from offering the L's offering at its appointed
9:8 may hear what the L will command concerning you."
9:9 The L said to Moses,
9:10 he shall still keep the passover to the L
9:13 did not offer the L's offering at its appointed
9:14 the passover to the L, according to the statute
9:18 the command of the L the people of Israel
9:18 the command of the L they encamped; as long
9:19 the charge of the L, and did not set
9:20 the command of the L they remained in camp;
9:20 the command of the L they set out.
9:23 the command of the L they encamped, and at
9:23 the command of the L they set out; they
9:23 the charge of the L, at the command of
9:23 the command of the L by Moses.
10:1 The L said to Moses,
10:9 be remembered before the L your God, and you
10:10 God: I am the L your God."
10:13 the command of the L by Moses.
10:29 place of which the L said, 'I will give
10:29 you good; for the L has promised good to
10:32 us, whatever good the L will do to us,
10:33 the mount of the L three days' journey; and
10:33 the covenant of the L went before them three
10:34 the cloud of the L was over them by
10:35 Moses said, "Arise, O L, and let thy enemies
10:36 he said, "Return, O L, to the ten thousand
11:1 the hearing of the L about their misfortunes; and
11:1 misfortunes; and when the L heard it, his anger
11:1 the fire of the L burned among them, and
11:2 Moses prayed to the L, and the fire abated.
11:3 the fire of the L burned among them.
11:10 the anger of the L blazed hotly, and Moses
11:11 Moses said to the L, "Why hast thou dealt
11:16 And the L said to Moses, "Gather for me
11:18 the hearing of the L, saying, "Who will give

11:18 Therefore the L will give you meat, and you
11:20 you have rejected the L who is among you,
11:23 And the L said to Moses, "Is the LORD's
11:23 to Moses, "Is the L's hand shortened?
11:24 the words of the L; and he gathered seventy
11:25 Then the L came down in the cloud and
11:28 chosen men, said, "My L Moses, forbid them."
11:29 Would that all the L's people were prophets, that
11:29 were prophets, that the L would put his spirit
11:31 a wind from the L, and it brought quails
11:33 the anger of the L was kindled against the
11:33 the people, and the L smote the people with
12:2 they said, "Has the L indeed spoken only through
12:2 And the L heard it.
12:4 And suddenly the L said to Moses and to
12:5 And the L came down in a pillar of
12:6 among you, I the L make myself known to
12:8 speech; and he beholds the form of the L
12:9 the anger of the L was kindled against them,
12:11 to Moses, "Oh, my L, do not punish us
12:13 Moses cried to the L, "Heal her, O God,
12:14 But the L said to Moses, "If her father
13:1 The L said to Moses,
13:3 the command of the L, all of them men
14:3 Why does the L bring us into this land,
14:8 If the L delights in us, he will bring
14:9 not rebel against the L; and do not fear
14:9 from them, and the L is with us; do
14:10 the glory of the L appeared at the tent
14:11 And the L said to Moses, "How long will
14:13 Moses said to the L, "Then the Egyptians will
14:14 heard that thou, O L, art in the midst
14:14 people; for thou, O L, art seen face to
14:16 will say, 'Because the L was not able to
14:17 the power of the L be great as thou
14:18 hast promised, saying, 'The L is slow to anger,
14:20 Then the L said, "I have pardoned, according to
14:21 the glory of the L,
14:26 And the L said to Moses and to Aaron,
14:28 I live,' says the L, 'what you have said
14:35 my displeasure.' I, the L, have spoken; surely this
14:37 of the land, died by plague before the L
14:40 the place which the L has promised; for we
14:41 the command of the L, for that will not
14:42 your enemies, for the L is not among you.
14:43 back from following the L, the LORD will not
14:43 following the LORD, the L will not be with
14:44 the covenant of the L, nor Moses, departed out
15:1 The L said to Moses,
15:3 you offer to the L from the herd or
15:3 pleasing odor to the L,
15:4 shall offer to the L a cereal offering of
15:7 hin of wine, a pleasing odor to the L
15:8 peace offerings to the L,
15:10 offering by fire, a pleasing odor to the L
15:13 offering by fire, a pleasing odor to the L
15:14 pleasing odor to the L, he shall do as
15:15 are, so shall the sojourner be before the L
15:17 The L said to Moses,
15:19 land, you shall present an offering to the L
15:21 shall give to the L an offering throughout your
15:22 commandments which the L has spoken to Moses,
15:23 Moses, all that the L has commanded you by
15:23 the day that the L gave commandment, and onward
15:24 pleasing odor to the L, with its cereal offering
15:25 by fire to the L, and their sin offering
15:25 sin offering before the L, for their error.
15:28 make atonement before the L for the person who
15:30 a sojourner, reviles the L, and that person shall
15:31 the word of the L, and has broken his
15:35 And the L said to Moses, "The man shall
15:36 with stones, as the L commanded Moses.
15:37 The L said to Moses,
15:39 the commandments of the L, to do them, not
15:41 I am the L your God, who brought you
15:41 God: I am the L your God."
16:3 of them, and the L is among them; why
16:3 you exalt yourselves above the assembly of the L
16:5 "In the morning the L will show who is
16:7 upon them before the L tomorrow, and the man
16:7 the man whom the L chooses shall be the
16:9 the tabernacle of the L, and to stand before
16:11 it is against the L that you and all
16:15 and said to the L, "Do not respect their
16:16 your company, before the L, you and they, and
16:17 you bring before the L his censer, two hundred
16:19 the glory of the L appeared to all the
16:20 And the L said to Moses and to Aaron,
16:23 And the L said to Moses,
16:28 shall know that the L has sent me to
16:29 all men, then the L has not sent me.
16:30 But if the L creates something new, and the
16:30 shall know that these men have despised the L
16:35 came forth from the L, and consumed the two
16:36 Then the L said to Moses,
16:38 offered them before the L; therefore they are holy.
16:40 burn incense before the L, lest he become as
16:40 his company--as the L said to Eleazar through
16:41 saying, "You have killed the people of the L
16:42 the glory of the L appeared.
16:44 of meeting, and the L said to Moses,
16:46 gone forth from the L, the plague has begun."
17:1 The L said to Moses,
17:7 the rods before the L in the tent of
17:9 rods from before the L to all the people
17:10 And the L said to Moses, "Put back the
17:11 did Moses; as the L commanded him, so he
17:13 the tabernacle of the L, shall die.
18:1 So the L said to Aaron, "You and your
18:6 you, given to the L, to do the service
18:8 Then the L said to Aaron, "And behold, I
18:12 they give to the L, I give to you.
18:13 they bring to the L, shall be yours; every
18:15 they offer to the L, shall be yours; nevertheless
18:17 pleasing odor to the L;
18:19 Israel present to the L I give to you,
18:19 for ever before the L for you and for
18:20 And the L said to Aaron, "You shall have
18:24 an offering to the L, I have given to
18:25 And the L said to Moses,
18:26 from it to the L, a tithe of the
18:28 an offering to the L from all your tithes,
18:28 you shall give the L's offering to Aaron the
18:29 offering due to the L, from all the best
19:1 Now the L said to Moses and to Aaron,
19:2 the law which the L has commanded: Tell the
19:13 the tabernacle of the L, and that person shall
19:20 the sanctuary of the L; because the water for
20:3 had died when our brethren died before the L
20:4 the assembly of the L into this wilderness, that
20:6 the glory of the L appeared to them,
20:7 to them, and the L said to Moses,
20:9 rod from before the L, as he commanded him.
20:12 And the L said to Moses and Aaron, "Because
20:13 Israel contended with the L, and he showed himself
20:16 we cried to the L, he heard our voice,
20:23 And the L said to Moses and Aaron at
20:27 Moses did as the L commanded; and they went
21:2 a vow to the L, and said, "If thou
21:3 And the L hearkened to the voice of Israel,
21:6 Then the L sent fiery serpents among the people,
21:7 have spoken against the L and against you; pray
21:7 you; pray to the L, that he take away
21:8 And the L said to Moses, "Make a fiery
21:14 the Wars of the L, "Waheb in Suphah, and
21:16 well of which the L said to Moses, "Gather
21:34 But the L said to Moses, "Do not fear
22:8 to you, as the L speaks to me"; so
22:13 own land; for the L has refused to let
22:18 the command of the L my God, to do
22:19 know what more the L will say to me."
22:22 the angel of the L took his stand in
22:23 the angel of the L standing in the road,
22:24 the angel of the L stood in a narrow
22:25 the angel of the L, she pushed against the
22:26 the angel of the L went ahead, and stood
22:27 the angel of the L, she lay down under
22:28 Then the L opened the mouth of the ass,
22:31 Then the L opened the eyes of Balaam, and
22:31 the angel of the L standing in the way,
22:32 the angel of the L said to him, "Why
22:34 the angel of the L, "I have sinned, for
22:35 the angel of the L said to Balaam, "Go
23:3 will go; perhaps the L will come to meet
23:5 And the L put a word in Balaam's mouth,
23:8 I denounce whom the L has not denounced?
23:12 to speak what the L puts in my mouth?"
23:15 while I meet the L yonder."
23:16 And the L met Balaam, and put a word
23:17 him, "What has the L spoken?"
23:21 The L their God is with them, and the
23:26 you, 'All that the L says, that I must

24:1 that it pleased the L to bless Israel, he
24:6 like aloes that the L has planted, like cedar
24:11 honor you,' but the L has held you back
24:13 the word of the L, to do either good
24:13 own will; what the L speaks, that will I
25:3 the anger of the L was kindled against Israel;
25:4 against Israel; and the L said to Moses, "Take
25:4 the sun before the L, that the fierce anger
25:4 fierce anger of the L may turn away from
25:10 And the L said to Moses,
25:16 And the L said to Moses,
26:1 After the plague the L said to Moses and
26:4 as the L commanded Moses.
26:9 they contended against the L,
26:52 The L said to Moses:
26:61 died when they offered unholy fire before the L
26:65 For the L had said of them, "They shall
27:3 themselves together against the L in the company of
27:5 Moses brought their case before the L
27:6 And the L said to Moses,
27:11 and ordinance, as the L commanded Moses.'"
27:12 The L said to Moses, "Go up into this
27:15 Moses said to the L,
27:16 the LORD, "Let the L, the God of the
27:17 the congregation of the L may not be as
27:18 And the L said to Moses, "Take Joshua the
27:21 the Urim before the L; at his word they
27:22 Moses did as the L commanded him; he took
27:23 commissioned him as the L directed through Moses.
28:1 The L said to Moses,
28:3 shall offer to the L: two male lambs a
28:6 pleasing odor, an offering by fire to the L
28:7 a drink offering of strong drink to the L
28:8 offering by fire, a pleasing odor to the L
28:11 burnt offering to the L: two young bulls, one
28:13 pleasing odor, an offering by fire to the L
28:15 sin offering to the L; it shall be offered
28:16 first month is the L's passover.
28:19 burnt offering to the L: two young bulls, one
28:24 pleasing odor to the L; it shall be offered
28:26 new grain to the L at your feast of
28:27 pleasing odor to the L; two young bulls, one
29:2 pleasing odor to the L: one young bull, one
29:6 pleasing odor, an offering by fire to the L
29:8 burnt offering to the L, a pleasing odor: one
29:12 a feast to the L seven days;
29:13 pleasing odor to the L, thirteen young bulls, two
29:36 pleasing odor to the L: one bull, one ram,
29:39 shall offer to the L at your appointed feasts,
29:40 everything just as the L had commanded Moses.
30:1 "This is what the L has commanded.
30:2 a vow to the L, or swears an oath
30:3 a vow to the L, and binds herself by
30:5 shall stand; and the L will forgive her, because
30:8 bound herself; and the L will forgive her.
30:12 them void, and the L will forgive her.
30:16 the statutes which the L commanded Moses, as
31:1 The L said to Moses,
31:3 Midian, to execute the L's vengeance on Midian.
31:7 Midian, as the L commanded Moses, and slew
31:16 act treacherously against the L in the matter of
31:16 the plague came among the congregation of the L
31:21 the law which the L has commanded Moses:
31:25 The L said to Moses,
31:28 And levy for the L a tribute from the
31:29 Eleazar the priest as an offering to the L
31:30 who have charge of the tabernacle of the L
31:31 priest did as the L commanded Moses.
31:37 hundred sheep, and the L's tribute of sheep was
31:38 thousand, of which the L's tribute was seventy-two.
31:39 hundred, of which the L's tribute was sixty-one.
31:40 thousand, of which the L's tribute was thirty-two.
31:41 the offering for the L, to Eleazar the priest,
31:41 the priest, as the L commanded Moses.
31:47 the tabernacle of the L; as the LORD commanded
31:47 the LORD; as the L commanded Moses.
31:50 we have brought the L's offering, what each man
31:50 beads, to make atonement for ourselves before the L
31:52 they offered to the L, from the commanders of
31:54 memorial for the people of Israel before the L
32:4 the land which the L smote before the congregation
32:7 the land which the L has given them?
32:9 the land which the L had given them.
32:10 And the L's anger was kindled on that day,
32:12 have wholly followed the L
32:13 the LORD.' And the L's anger was kindled against
32:13 the sight of the L was consumed.
32:14 fierce anger of the L against Israel!
32:20 to go before the L for the war,
32:21 the Jordan before the L, until he has driven
32:22 is subdued before the L; then after that you
32:22 of obligation to the L and to Israel; and
32:22 this land shall be your possession before the L
32:23 have sinned against the L; and be sure your
32:25 will do as my L commands.
32:27 for war, before the L to battle, as my
32:27 to battle, as my L orders."
32:29 to battle before the L, will pass with you
32:31 Reuben answered, "As the L has said to your
32:32 over armed before the L into the land of
33:2 by command of the L; and these are their
33:4 their first-born, whom the L had struck down among
33:4 their gods also the L executed judgments.
33:38 the command of the L, and died there, in
33:50 And the L said to Moses in the plains
34:1 The L said to Moses,
34:13 by lot, which the L has commanded to give
34:16 The L said to Moses,
34:29 the men whom the L commanded to divide the
35:1 The L said to Moses in the plains of
35:9 And the L said to Moses,
35:34 dwell; for I the L dwell in the midst
36:2 Israel; they said, "The L commanded my lord to
36:2 "The LORD commanded my L to give the land
36:2 of Israel; and my L was commanded by the
36:2 was commanded by the L to give the inheritance
36:5 the word of the L, saying, "The tribe of
36:6 is what the L commands concerning the daughters
36:10 Zelophehad did as the L commanded Moses;
36:13 the ordinances which the L commanded by Moses to
Deut 1:3 to all that the L had given him in
1:6 this law, saying, "The L our God said to
1:8 the land which the L swore to your fathers,
1:10 to bear you; the L your God has multiplied
1:11 May the L, the God of your fathers, make
1:19 the Amorites, as the L our God commanded us;
1:20 the Amorites, which the L our God gives us.
1:21 Behold, the L your God has set the land
1:21 take possession, as the L, the God of your
1:25 good land which the L our God gives us.'
1:26 the command of the L your God;
1:27 and said, 'Because the L hated us he has
1:30 The L your God who goes before you will
1:31 have seen how the L your God bore you,
1:32 did not believe the L your God,
1:34 "And the L heard your words, and was angered,
1:36 has wholly followed the L
1:37 followed the LORD!' The L was angry with me
1:41 have sinned against the L; we will go up
1:41 fight, just as the L our God commanded us.'
1:42 And the L said to me, 'Say to them,
1:43 the command of the L, and were presumptuous and
1:45 and wept before the L; but the LORD did
1:45 the LORD; but the L did not hearken to
2:1 Red Sea, as the L told me; and for
2:2 Then the L said to me,
2:7 For the L your God has blessed you in
2:7 these forty years the L your God has been
2:9 And the L said to me, 'Do not harass
2:12 their possession, which the L gave to them.)
2:14 the camp, as the L had sworn to them.
2:15 the hand of the L was against them, to
2:17 among the people, the L said to me,
2:21 the Anakim; but the L destroyed them before them;
2:29 the land which the L our God gives to
2:30 by him; for the L your God hardened his
2:31 And the L said to me, 'Behold, I have
2:33 And the L our God gave him over to
2:36 high for us; the L our God gave all
2:37 country, and wherever the L our God forbade us.
3:2 But the L said to me, 'Do not fear
3:3 at Heshbon.' So the L our God gave into
3:18 that time, saying, 'The L your God has given
3:20 given you, until the L gives rest to your
3:20 the land which the L your God gives them
3:21 seen all that the L your God has done
3:21 kings; so will the L do to all the
3:22 for it is the L your God who fights
3:23 "And I besought the L at that time, saying,
3:24 that time, saying, 'O L GOD, thou hast only
3:26 and Lebanon.' But the L was angry with me
3:26 to me; and the L said to me, 'Let

4:1	the land which the L, the God of your
4:2	the commandments of the L your God which I
4:3	have seen what the L did at Baal-peor; for
4:3	at Baal-peor; for the L your God destroyed from
4:4	held fast to the L your God are all
4:5	and ordinances, as the L my God commanded me,
4:7	to it as the L our God is to
4:10	you stood before the L your God at Horeb,
4:10	God at Horeb, the L said to me, 'Gather
4:12	Then the L spoke to you out of the
4:14	And the L commanded me at that time to
4:15	the day that the L spoke to you at
4:19	them, things which the L your God has allotted
4:20	But the L has taken you, and brought you
4:21	Furthermore the L was angry with me on your
4:21	good land which the L your God gives you
4:23	the covenant of the L your God, which he
4:23	of anything which the L your God has forbidden
4:24	For the L your God is a devouring fire,
4:25	the sight of the L your God, so as
4:27	And the L will scatter you among the peoples,
4:27	the nations where the L will drive you.
4:29	you will seek the L your God, and you
4:30	will return to the L your God and obey
4:31	his voice, for the L your God is a
4:34	to all that the L your God did for
4:35	might know that the L is God; there is
4:39	your heart, that the L is God in heaven
4:40	the land which the L your God gives you
5:2	The L our God made a covenant with us
5:3	our fathers did the L make this covenant, but
5:4	The L spoke with you face to face at
5:5	I stood between the L and you at that
5:5	the word of the L; for you were afraid
5:6	said: "'I am the L your God, who brought
5:9	them; for I the L your God am a
5:11	the name of the L your God in vain:
5:11	in vain: for the L will not hold him
5:12	it holy, as the L your God commanded you.
5:14	a sabbath to the L your God; in it
5:15	of Egypt, and the L your God brought you
5:15	outstretched arm; therefore the L your God
5:16	your mother, as the L your God commanded you;
5:16	the land which the L your God gives you.
5:22	neighbors.' "These words the L spoke to all your
5:24	you said, 'Behold, the L our God has shown
5:25	the voice of the L our God any more,
5:27	hear all that the L our God will say;
5:27	us all that the L our God will speak
5:28	do it.' "And the L heard your words, when
5:28	to me; and the L said to me, 'I
5:32	do therefore as the L your God has commanded
5:33	the way which the L your God has commanded
6:1	the ordinances which the L your God commanded
6:2	you may fear the L your God, you and
6:3	multiply greatly, as the L, the God of your
6:4	"Hear, O Israel: The L our God is one
6:4	our God is one L;
6:5	you shall love the L your God with all
6:10	"And when the L your God brings you into
6:12	lest you forget the L, who brought you out
6:13	You shall fear the L your God; you shall
6:15	about you; for the L your God in the
6:15	the anger of the L your God be kindled
6:16	shall not put the L your God to the
6:17	the commandments of the L your God, and his
6:18	the sight of the L, that it may go
6:18	good land which the L swore to give to
6:19	before you, as the L has promised.
6:20	the ordinances which the L our God has commanded
6:21	in Egypt; and the L brought us out of
6:22	mighty hand; and the L showed signs and wonders,
6:24	And the L commanded us to do all these
6:24	statutes, to fear the L our God, for our
6:25	this commandment before the L our God, as he
7:1	commanded us.' "When the L your God brings you
7:2	yourselves, and when the L your God gives them
7:4	the anger of the L would be kindled against
7:6	people holy to the L your God; the LORD
7:6	LORD your God; the L your God has chosen
7:7	other people that the L set his love upon
7:8	it is because the L loves you, and is
7:8	your fathers, that the L has brought you out
7:9	Know therefore that the L your God is God,
7:12	and do them, the L your God will keep
7:15	And the L will take away from you all
7:16	the peoples that the L your God will give
7:18	shall remember what the L your God did to
7:19	arm, by which the L your God brought you
7:19	out; so will the L your God do to
7:20	Moreover the L your God will send hornets among
7:21	of them; for the L your God is in
7:22	The L your God will clear away these nations
7:23	But the L your God will give them over
7:25	an abomination to the L your God.
8:1	the land which the L swore to give to
8:2	the way which the L your God has led
8:3	that proceeds out of the mouth of the L
8:5	disciplines his son, the L your God disciplines you.
8:6	the commandments of the L your God, by walking
8:7	For the L your God is bringing you into
8:10	you shall bless the L your God for the
8:11	lest you forget the L your God, by not
8:14	and you forget the L your God, who brought
8:18	You shall remember the L your God, for it
8:19	if you forget the L your God and go
8:20	the nations that the L makes to perish before
8:20	the voice of the L your God.
9:3	devouring fire is the L your God; he will
9:3	perish quickly, as the L has promised you.
9:4	your heart, after the L your God has thrust
9:4	my righteousness that the L has brought me in
9:4	these nations that the L is driving them out
9:5	of these nations the L your God is driving
9:5	the word which the L swore to your fathers,
9:6	"Know therefore, that the L your God is not
9:7	how you provoked the L your God to wrath
9:7	this place, you have been rebellious against the L
9:8	Horeb you provoked the L to wrath, and the
9:8	to wrath, and the L was so angry with
9:9	the covenant which the L made with you, I
9:10	And the L gave me the two tables of
9:10	the words which the L had spoken with you
9:11	and forty nights the L gave me the two
9:12	Then the L said to me, 'Arise, go down
9:13	molten image.' "Furthermore the L said to me, 'I
9:16	had sinned against the L your God; you had
9:16	the way which the L had commanded you.
9:18	lay prostrate before the L as before, forty days
9:18	the sight of the L, to provoke him to
9:19	hot displeasure which the L bore against you, so
9:19	But the L hearkened to me that time also.
9:20	And the L was so angry with Aaron that
9:22	Kibroth-hattaavah, you provoked the L to wrath.
9:23	And when the L sent you from Kadesh-barnea,
9:23	the commandment of the L your God, and did
9:24	been rebellious against the L from the day that
9:25	lay prostrate before the L for these forty days
9:25	forty nights, because the L had said he would
9:26	I prayed to the L, 'O Lord GOD, destroy
9:26	to the LORD, 'O L GOD, destroy not thy
9:28	us say, "Because the L was not able to
10:1	"At that time the L said to me, 'Hew
10:4	ten commandments which the L had spoken to you
10:4	the assembly; and the L gave them to me.
10:5	they are, as the L commanded me.
10:8	At that time the L set apart the tribe
10:8	the covenant of the L, to stand before the
10:8	to stand before the L to minister to him
10:9	with his brothers; the L is his inheritance, as
10:9	his inheritance, as the L your God said to
10:10	forty nights, and the L hearkened to me that
10:10	that time also; the L was unwilling to destroy
10:11	And the L said to me, 'Arise, go on
10:12	Israel, what does the L your God require of
10:12	but to fear the L your God, to walk
10:12	him, to serve the L your God with all
10:13	and statutes of the L, which I command you
10:14	Behold, to the L your God belong heaven and
10:15	in it; yet the L set his heart in
10:17	For the L your God is God of gods
10:17	God of gods and L of lords, the great,
10:20	You shall fear the L your God; you shall
10:22	persons; and now the L your God has made
11:1	shall therefore love the L your God, and keep
11:2	the discipline of the L your God, his greatness,
11:4	you, and how the L has destroyed them to
11:7	great work of the L which he did.
11:9	the land which the L swore to your fathers
11:12	a land which the L your God cares for;
11:12	the eyes of the L your God are always
11:13	day, to love the L your God, and to

11:17 the anger of the L be kindled against you,
11:17 good land which the L gives you.
11:21 the land which the L swore to your fathers
11:22 to do, loving the L your God, walking in
11:23 to him, then the L will drive out all
11:25 stand against you; the L your God will lay
11:27 the commandments of the L your God, which I
11:28 the commandments of the L your God, but turn
11:29 And when the L your God brings you into
11:31 the land which the L your God gives you;
12:1 the land which the L, the God of your
12:4 do so to the L your God.
12:5 the place which the L your God will choose
12:7 shall eat before the L your God, and you
12:7 undertake, in which the L your God has blessed
12:9 the inheritance which the L your God gives you.
12:10 the land which the L your God gives you
12:11 the place which the L your God will choose,
12:11 your votive offerings which you vow to the L
12:12 shall rejoice before the L your God, you and
12:14 the place which the L will choose in one
12:15 the blessing of the L your God which he
12:18 eat them before the L your God in the
12:18 the place which the L your God will choose,
12:18 shall rejoice before the L your God in all
12:20 "When the L your God enlarges your territory, as
12:21 the place which the L your God will choose
12:21 your flock, which the L has given you, as
12:25 what is right in the sight of the L
12:26 the place which the L will choose,
12:27 the altar of the L your God; the blood
12:27 the altar of the L your God, but the
12:28 the sight of the L your God.
12:29 "When the L your God cuts off before you
12:31 do so to the L your God; for every
12:31 abominable thing which the L hates they have done
13:3 of dreams; for the L your God is testing
13:3 whether you love the L your God with all
13:4 shall walk after the L your God and fear
13:5 taught rebellion against the L your God, who brought
13:5 way in which the L your God commanded you
13:10 you away from the L your God, who brought
13:12 your cities, which the L your God gives you
13:16 burnt offering to the L your God; it shall
13:17 your hand; that the L may turn from the
13:18 the voice of the L your God, keeping all
13:18 the sight of the L your God.
14:1 the sons of the L your God; you shall
14:2 people holy to the L your God, and the
14:2 your God, and the L has chosen you to
14:21 people holy to the L your God.
14:23 And before the L your God, in the place
14:23 learn to fear the L your God always.
14:24 the tithe, when the L your God blesses you,
14:24 from you, which the L your God chooses, to
14:25 the place which the L your God chooses,
14:26 eat there before the L your God and rejoice,
14:29 be filled; that the L your God may bless
15:2 his brother, because the L's release has been
15:4 among you (for the L will bless you in
15:4 the land which the L your God gives you
15:5 the voice of the L your God, being careful
15:6 For the L your God will bless you, as
15:7 your land which the L your God gives you,
15:9 he cry to the L against you, and it
15:10 because for this the L your God will bless
15:14 wine press; as the L your God has blessed
15:15 of Egypt, and the L your God redeemed you;
15:18 So the L your God will bless you in
15:19 shall consecrate to the L your God; you shall
15:20 your household, before the L your God year by
15:20 the place which the L will choose.
15:21 sacrifice it to the L your God.
16:1 the passover to the L your God; for in
16:1 month of Abib the L your God brought you
16:2 passover sacrifice to the L your God, from the
16:2 the place which the L will choose, to make
16:5 your towns which the L your God gives you;
16:6 the place which the L your God will choose,
16:7 the place which the L your God will choose;
16:8 solemn assembly to the L your God; you shall
16:10 of weeks to the L your God with the
16:10 shall give as the L your God blesses you;
16:11 shall rejoice before the L your God, you and
16:11 the place which the L your God will choose,
16:15 the feast to the L your God at the
16:15 the place which the L will choose; because the
16:15 will choose; because the L your God will bless
16:16 shall appear before the L your God at the
16:16 not appear before the L empty-handed;
16:17 the blessing of the L your God which he
16:18 your towns which the L your God gives you,
16:20 the land which the L your God gives you.
16:21 the altar of the L your God which you
16:22 a pillar, which the L your God hates.
17:1 not sacrifice to the L your God an ox
17:1 an abomination to the L your God.
17:2 your towns which the L your God gives you,
17:2 the sight of the L your God, in transgressing
17:8 the place which the L your God will choose,
17:10 that place which the L will choose; and you
17:12 minister there before the L your God, or the
17:14 the land which the L your God gives you,
17:15 you him whom the L your God will choose.
17:16 multiply horses, since the L has said to you,
17:19 learn to fear the L his God, by keeping
18:1 by fire to the L, and his rightful dues.
18:2 among their brethren; the L is their inheritance, as
18:5 For the L your God has chosen him out
18:5 the name of the L, him and his sons
18:6 the place which the L will choose,
18:7 the name of the L his God, like all
18:7 Levites who stand to minister there before the L
18:9 the land which the L your God gives you,
18:12 an abomination to the L; and because of these
18:12 these abominable practices the L your God is driving
18:13 be blameless before the L your God.
18:14 as for you, the L your God has not
18:15 "The L your God will raise up for you
18:16 you desired of the L your God at Horeb
18:16 the voice of the L my God, or see
18:17 I die.' And the L said to me, 'They
18:21 the word which the L has not spoken?–
18:22 the name of the L, if the word does
18:22 a word which the L has not spoken; the
19:1 "When the L your God cuts off the nations
19:1 nations whose land the L your God gives you,
19:2 the land which the L your God gives you
19:3 the land which the L your God gives you
19:8 And if the L your God enlarges your border,
19:9 day, by loving the L your God and by
19:10 your land which the L your God gives you
19:14 the land that the L your God gives you
19:17 shall appear before the L, before the priests and
20:1 of them; for the L your God is with
20:4 of them; for the L your God is he
20:13 it; and when the L your God gives it
20:14 your enemies, which the L your God has given
20:16 these peoples that the L your God gives you
20:17 the Jebusites, as the L your God has commanded;
20:18 to sin against the L your God.
21:1 the land which the L your God gives you
21:5 come forward, for the L your God has chosen
21:5 the name of the L, and by their word
21:8 Forgive, O L, thy people Israel, whom thou hast
21:9 what is right in the sight of the L
21:10 your enemies, and the L your God gives them
21:23 your land which the L your God gives you
22:5 an abomination to the L your God.
23:1 off shall not enter the assembly of the L
23:2 the assembly of the L; even to the tenth
23:2 his descendants shall enter the assembly of the L
23:3 the assembly of the L; even to the tenth
23:3 the assembly of the L for ever;
23:5 Nevertheless the L your God would not hearken to
23:5 to Balaam; but the L your God turned the
23:5 for you, because the L your God loved you.
23:8 to them may enter the assembly of the L
23:14 Because the L your God walks in the midst
23:18 the house of the L your God in payment
23:18 an abomination to the L your God.
23:20 upon interest; that the L your God may bless
23:21 a vow to the L your God, you shall
23:21 pay it; for the L your God will surely
23:23 voluntarily vowed to the L your God what you
24:4 an abomination before the L, and you shall not
24:4 the land which the L your God gives you
24:9 Remember what the L your God did to Miriam
24:13 to you before the L your God.
24:15 against you to the L, and it be sin
24:18 in Egypt and the L your God redeemed you
24:19 the widow; that the L your God may bless

25:15 the land which the L your God gives you.
25:16 an abomination to the L your God.
25:19 Therefore when the L your God has given you
25:19 the land which the L your God gives you
26:1 the land which the L your God gives you
26:2 your land that the L your God gives you,
26:2 the place which the L your God will choose,
26:3 this day to the L your God that I
26:3 the land which the L swore to our fathers
26:4 the altar of the L your God.
26:5 make response before the L your God, 'A wandering
26:7 we cried to the L the God of our
26:7 our fathers, and the L heard our voice, and
26:8 our oppression; and the L brought us out of
26:10 ground, which thou, O L, hast given me.' And
26:10 it down before the L your God, and worship
26:10 and worship before the L your God;
26:11 the good which the L your God has given
26:13 shall say before the L your God, 'I have
26:14 the voice of the L my God, I have
26:16 honey.' "This day the L your God commands you
26:17 this day concerning the L that he is your
26:18 his voice; and the L has declared this day
26:19 people holy to the L your God, as he
27:2 the land which the L your God gives you,
27:3 the land which the L your God gives you,
27:3 and honey, as the L, the God of your
27:5 an altar to the L your God, an altar
27:6 an altar to the L your God of unhewn
27:6 on it to the L your God;
27:7 shall rejoice before the L your God.
27:9 the people of the L your God.
27:10 the voice of the L your God, keeping his
27:15 an abomination to the L, a thing made by
28:1 the voice of the L your God, being careful
28:1 you this day, the L your God will set
28:2 the voice of the L your God.
28:7 "The L will cause your enemies who rise against
28:8 The L will command the blessing upon you in
28:8 the land which the L your God gives you.
28:9 The L will establish you as a people holy
28:9 the commandments of the L your God, and walk
28:10 the name of the L; and they shall be
28:11 And the L will make you abound in prosperity,
28:11 the land which the L swore to your fathers
28:12 The L will open to you his good treasury
28:13 And the L will make you the head, and
28:13 the commandments of the L your God, which I
28:15 the voice of the L your God or be
28:20 "The L will send upon you curses, confusion, and
28:21 The L will make the pestilence cleave to you
28:22 The L will smite you with consumption, and with
28:24 The L will make the rain of your land
28:25 "The L will cause you to be defeated before
28:27 The L will smite you with the boils of
28:28 The L will smite you with madness and blindness
28:35 The L will smite you on the knees and
28:36 "The L will bring you, and your king whom
28:37 the peoples where the L will lead you away.
28:45 the voice of the L your God, to keep
28:47 did not serve the L your God with joyfulness
28:48 your enemies whom the L will send against you,
28:49 The L will bring a nation against you from
28:52 your land, which the L your God has given
28:53 and daughters, whom the L your God has given
28:58 and awful name, the L your God,
28:59 your God, then the L will bring on you
28:61 of this law, the L will bring upon you,
28:62 the voice of the L your God.
28:63 And as the L took delight in doing you
28:63 multiplying you, so the L will take delight in
28:64 And the L will scatter you among all peoples,
28:65 your foot; but the L will give you there
28:68 And the L will bring you back in ships
29:1 the covenant which the L commanded Moses to
29:2 seen all that the L did before your eyes
29:4 to this day the L has not given you
29:6 that I am the L your God.
29:10 of you before the L your God; the heads
29:12 sworn covenant of the L your God, which the
29:12 your God, which the L your God makes with
29:15 this day before the L our God.
29:18 this day from the L our God to go
29:20 The L would not pardon him, but rather the
29:20 the anger of the L and his jealousy would
29:20 upon him, and the L would blot out his
29:21 And the L would single him out from all
29:22 sicknesses with which the L has made it sick--
29:23 and Zeboiim, which the L overthrew in his anger
29:24 say, 'Why has the L done thus to this
29:25 the covenant of the L, the God of their
29:27 the anger of the L was kindled against this
29:28 this book; and the L uprooted them from their
29:29 things belong to the L our God; but the
30:1 the nations where the L your God has driven
30:2 and return to the L your God, you and
30:3 your soul; then the L your God will restore
30:3 the peoples where the L your God has scattered
30:4 heaven, from there the L your God will gather
30:5 fetch you; and the L your God will bring
30:6 And the L your God will circumcise your heart
30:6 you will love the L your God with all
30:7 And the L your God will put all these
30:8 the voice of the L, and keep all his
30:9 The L your God will make you abundantly
30:9 your ground; for the L will again take delight
30:10 the voice of the L your God, to keep
30:10 you turn to the L your God with all
30:16 the commandments of the L your God which I
30:16 day, by loving the L your God, by walking
30:16 and multiply, and the L your God will bless
30:20 may live, loving the L your God, obeying his
30:20 the land which the L swore to your fathers,
31:2 The L has said to me, 'You shall not
31:3 over this Jordan.' The L your God himself will
31:3 your head, as the L has spoken.
31:4 And the L will do to them as he
31:5 And the L will give them over to you,
31:6 for it is the L your God who goes
31:7 the land which the L has sworn to their
31:8 It is the L who goes before you; he
31:9 the covenant of the L, and to all the
31:11 to appear before the L your God at the
31:12 learn to fear the L your God, and be
31:13 learn to fear the L your God, as long
31:14 And the L said to Moses, "Behold, the days
31:15 And the L appeared in the tent in a
31:16 And the L said to Moses, "Behold, you are
31:23 And the L commissioned Joshua the son of Nun
31:25 the covenant of the L,
31:26 the covenant of the L your God, that it
31:27 been rebellious against the L; how much more after
31:29 the sight of the L, provoking him to anger
32:3 For I will proclaim the name of the L
32:6 you thus requite the L, you foolish and senseless
32:9 For the L's portion is his people, Jacob his
32:12 on its pinions, the L alone did lead him,
32:19 "The L saw it, and spurned them, because of
32:27 hand is triumphant, the L has not wrought all
32:30 sold them, and the L had given them up?
32:36 For the L will vindicate his people and have
32:48 And the L said to Moses that very day,
33:2 He said, "The L came from Sinai, and dawned
33:5 Thus the L became king in Jeshurun, when the
33:7 of Judah: "Hear, O L, the voice of Judah,
33:11 Bless, O L, his substance, and accept the work
33:12 "The beloved of the L, he dwells in safety
33:13 said, "Blessed by the L be his land, with
33:21 executed the commands and just decrees of the L
33:23 the blessing of the L, possess the lake and
33:29 people saved by the L, the shield of your
34:1 And the L showed him all the land, Gilead
34:4 And the L said to him, "This is the
34:5 the servant of the L died there in the
34:5 the word of the L,
34:9 and did as the L had commanded Moses.
34:10 like Moses, whom the L knew face to face,
34:11 the wonders which the L sent him to do
Josh 1:1 the servant of the L, the LORD said to
1:1 of the LORD, the L said to Joshua the
1:9 be dismayed; for the L your God is with
1:11 the land which the L your God gives you
1:13 the servant of the L commanded you, saying, 'The
1:13 commanded you, saying, 'The L your God is providing
1:15 help them, until the L gives rest to your
1:15 the land which the L your God is giving
1:15 the servant of the L gave you beyond the
1:17 you; only may the L your God be with
2:9 "I know that the L has given you the
2:10 have heard how the L dried up the water
2:11 of you; for the L your God is he
2:12 to me by the L that as I have

L

2:14 with you when the L gives us the land."
2:24 to Joshua, "Truly the L has given all the
3:3 the covenant of the L your God being carried
3:5 yourselves; for tomorrow the L will do wonders
3:7 And the L said to Joshua, "This day I
3:9 the words of the L your God."
3:11 the covenant of the L of all the earth
3:13 the ark of the L, the Lord of all
3:13 of the LORD, the L of all the earth,
3:17 the covenant of the L stood on dry ground
4:1 over the Jordan, the L said to Joshua,
4:5 the ark of the L your God into the
4:7 the covenant of the L; when it passed over
4:8 of Israel, as the L told Joshua; and they
4:10 was finished that the L commanded Joshua to tell
4:11 the ark of the L and the priests passed
4:13 passed over before the L for battle, to the
4:14 On that day the L exalted Joshua in the
4:15 And the L said to Joshua,
4:18 the covenant of the L came up from the
4:23 dry ground.' For the L your God dried up
4:23 passed over, as the L your God did to
4:24 the hand of the L is mighty; that you
4:24 you may fear the L your God for ever."
5:1 sea, heard that the L had dried up the
5:2 At that time the L said to Joshua, "Make
5:6 the voice of the L; to them the LORD
5:6 LORD; to them the L swore that he would
5:6 the land which the L had sworn to their
5:9 And the L said to Joshua, "This day I
5:14 the army of the L I have now come."
5:14 him, "What does my L bid his servant?"
5:15 the commander of the L's army said to Joshua,
6:2 And the L said to Joshua, "See, I have
6:6 of rams' horns before the ark of the L
6:7 men pass on before the ark of the L
6:8 rams' horns before the L went forward, blowing the
6:8 the covenant of the L following them.
6:11 the ark of the L to compass the city,
6:12 the priests took up the ark of the L
6:13 the ark of the L passed on, blowing the
6:13 the ark of the L, while the trumpets blew
6:16 people, "Shout; for the L has given you the
6:17 be devoted to the L for destruction; only Rahab
6:19 are sacred to the L; they shall go into
6:19 they shall go into the treasury of the L
6:24 into the treasury of the house of the L
6:26 saying, "Cursed before the L be the man that
6:27 So the L was with Joshua; and his fame
7:1 the anger of the L burned against the people
7:6 the ark of the L until the evening, he
7:7 Joshua said, "Alas, O L GOD, why hast thou
7:8 O L, what can I say, when Israel has
7:10 The L said to Joshua, "Arise, why have you
7:13 for thus says the L, God of Israel, "There
7:14 the tribe which the L takes shall come near
7:14 the family which the L takes shall come near
7:14 the household which the L takes shall come near
7:15 the covenant of the L, and because he has
7:19 give glory to the L God of Israel, and
7:20 have sinned against the L God of Israel, and
7:23 Israel; and they laid them down before the L
7:25 The L brings trouble on you today." And all
7:26 this day; then the L turned from his burning
8:1 And the L said to Joshua, "Do not fear
8:7 the city; for the L your God will give
8:8 fire, doing as the L has bidden; see, I
8:18 Then the L said to Joshua, "Stretch out the
8:27 the word of the L which he commanded Joshua.
8:30 Mount Ebal to the L, the God of Israel,
8:31 the servant of the L had commanded the people
8:31 burnt offerings to the L, and sacrificed peace
8:33 the covenant of the L, half of them in
8:33 the servant of the L had commanded at the
9:9 the name of the L your God; for we
9:14 provisions, and did not ask direction from the L
9:18 to them by the L, the God of Israel.
9:19 to them by the L, the God of Israel,
9:24 a certainty that the L your God had commanded
9:27 the altar of the L, to continue to this
10:8 And the L said to Joshua, "Do not fear
10:10 And the L threw them into a panic before
10:11 ascent of Beth-horon, the L threw down great stones
10:12 spoke Joshua to the L in the day when
10:12 the day when the L gave the Amorites over
10:14 or since, when the L hearkened to the voice
10:14 a man; for the L fought for Israel.
10:19 their cities; for the L your God has given
10:25 courage; for thus the L will do to all
10:30 against Libnah; and the L gave it also and
10:32 assaulted it: and the L gave Lachish into the
10:40 that breathed, as the L God of Israel commanded.
10:42 one time, because the L God of Israel fought
11:6 And the L said to Joshua, "Do not be
11:8 And the L gave them into the hand of
11:9 to them as the L bade him; he hamstrung
11:12 the servant of the L had commanded.
11:15 As the L had commanded Moses his servant, so
11:15 of all that the L had commanded Moses.
11:20 For it was the L's doing to harden their
11:20 be exterminated, as the L commanded Moses.
11:23 to all that the L had spoken to Moses;
12:6 the servant of the L, and the people of
12:6 the servant of the L gave their land for
13:1 in years; and the L said to him, "You
13:8 the servant of the L gave them:
13:14 by fire to the L God of Israel are
13:33 gave no inheritance; the L God of Israel is
14:2 by lot, as the L had commanded Moses for
14:5 Israel did as the L commanded Moses; they allotted
14:6 "You know what the L said to Moses the
14:7 the servant of the L sent me from Kadesh-barnea
14:8 I wholly followed the L my God.
14:9 have wholly followed the L my God.'
14:10 And now, behold, the L has kept me alive,
14:10 the time that the L spoke this word to
14:12 country of which the L spoke on that day;
14:12 may be that the L will be with me,
14:12 them out as the L said."
14:14 he wholly followed the L, the God of Israel.
15:13 the commandment of the L to Joshua, he gave
17:4 leaders, and said, "The L commanded Moses to give
17:4 the commandment of the L he gave them an
17:14 people, since hitherto the L has blessed me?"
18:3 the land, which the L, the God of your
18:6 you here before the L our God.
18:7 the priesthood of the L is their heritage; and
18:7 the servant of the L gave them."
18:8 you here before the L in Shiloh."
18:10 in Shiloh before the L; and there Joshua apportioned
19:50 By command of the L they gave him the
19:51 at Shiloh before the L, at the door of
20:1 Then the L said to Joshua,
21:2 land of Canaan, "The L commanded through Moses
21:3 by command of the L the people of Israel
21:8 Levites, as the L had commanded through Moses.
21:43 Thus the L gave to Israel all the land
21:44 And the L gave them rest on every side
21:44 withstood them, for the L had given all their
21:45 good promises which the L had made to the
22:2 the servant of the L commanded you, and have
22:3 the charge of the L your God.
22:4 And now the L your God has given rest
22:4 the servant of the L gave you on the
22:5 the servant of the L commanded you, to love
22:5 you, to love the L your God, and to
22:9 by command of the L through Moses.
22:16 whole congregation of the L, 'What is this treachery
22:16 day from following the L, by building yourselves an
22:16 an altar this day in rebellion against the L
22:17 the congregation of the L,
22:18 must turn away this day from following the L
22:18 you rebel against the L today he will be
22:19 pass over into the L's land where the LORD's
22:19 LORD's land where the L's tabernacle stands, and
22:19 not rebel against the L, or make us as
22:19 the altar of the L our God.
22:22 families of Israel, "The Mighty One, God, the L
22:22 The Mighty One, God, the L
22:22 of faith toward the L, spare us not today
22:23 away from following the L; or if we did
22:23 on it, may the L himself take vengeance.
22:24 to do with the L, the God of Israel?
22:25 For the L has made the Jordan a boundary
22:25 no portion in the L So your children might
22:25 might make our children cease to worship the L
22:27 the service of the L in his presence with
22:27 no portion in the L
22:28 the altar of the L, which our fathers made,
22:29 should rebel against the L, and turn away this
22:29 day from following the L by building an altar
22:29 the altar of the L our God that stands

22:31 we know that the L is in the midst
22:31 this treachery against the L; now you have saved
22:31 people of Israel from the hand of the L
22:34 between us that the L is God."
23:1 time afterward, when the L had given rest to
23:3 seen all that the L your God has done
23:3 for it is the L your God who has
23:5 The L your God will push them back before
23:5 their land, as the L your God promised you.
23:8 but cleave to the L your God as you
23:9 For the L has driven out before you great
23:10 since it is the L your God who fights
23:11 therefore, to love the L your God.
23:13 know assuredly that the L your God will not
23:13 good land which the L your God has given
23:14 good things which the L your God promised
23:15 good things which the L your God promised
23:15 for you, so the L will bring upon you
23:15 good land which the L your God has given
23:16 the covenant of the L your God, which he
23:16 the anger of the L will be kindled against
24:2 people, "Thus says the L, the God of Israel,
24:7 they cried to the L, he put darkness between
24:14 "Now therefore fear the L, and serve him in
24:14 the River, and in Egypt, and serve the L
24:15 unwilling to serve the L, choose this day whom
24:15 me and my house, we will serve the L
24:16 we should forsake the L, to serve other gods;
24:17 for it is the L our God who brought
24:18 we passed; and the L drove out before us
24:18 also will serve the L, for he is our
24:19 "You cannot serve the L; for he is a
24:20 If you forsake the L and serve foreign gods,
24:21 to Joshua, "Nay; but we will serve the L
24:22 you have chosen the L, to serve him." And
24:23 your heart to the L, the God of Israel."
24:24 said to Joshua, "The L our God we will
24:26 under the oak in the sanctuary of the L
24:27 the words of the L which he spoke to
24:29 the servant of the L, died, being a hundred
24:31 And Israel served the L all the days of
24:31 the work which the L did for Israel.
Judg 1:1 Israel inquired of the L, "Who shall go up
1:2 The L said, "Judah shall go up; behold, I
1:4 went up and the L gave the Canaanites and
1:19 And the L was with Judah, and he took
1:22 against Bethel; and the L was with them.
2:1 the angel of the L went up from Gilgal
2:4 the angel of the L spoke these words to
2:5 place Bochim; and they sacrificed there to the L
2:7 the people served the L all the days of
2:7 great work which the L had done for Israel.
2:8 the servant of the L, died at the age
2:10 did not know the L or the work which
2:11 the sight of the L and served the Baals;
2:12 and they forsook the L, the God of their
2:12 and they provoked the L to anger.
2:13 They forsook the L, and served the Baals and
2:14 the anger of the L was kindled against Israel,
2:15 the hand of the L was against them for
2:15 for evil, as the L had warned, and as
2:15 warned, and as the L had sworn to them;
2:16 Then the L raised up judges, who saved them
2:17 the commandments of the L, and they did not
2:18 Whenever the L raised up judges for them, the
2:18 judges for them, the L was with the judge,
2:18 the judge; for the L was moved to pity
2:20 the anger of the L was kindled against Israel;
2:22 the way of the L as their fathers did,
2:23 So the L left those nations, not driving them
3:1 the nations which the L left, to test Israel
3:4 the commandments of the L, which he commanded
3:7 the sight of the L, forgetting the LORD their
3:7 the LORD, forgetting the L their God, and serving
3:8 the anger of the L was kindled against Israel,
3:9 Israel cried to the L, the LORD raised up
3:9 to the LORD, the L raised up a deliverer
3:10 The Spirit of the L came upon him, and
3:10 to war, and the L gave Cushan-rishathaim king of
3:12 the sight of the L; and the LORD strengthened
3:12 the LORD; and the L strengthened Eglon the king
3:12 what was evil in the sight of the L
3:15 Israel cried to the L, the LORD raised up
3:15 to the LORD, the L raised up for them
3:25 and there lay their L dead on the floor.
3:28 after me; for the L has given your enemies
4:1 the sight of the L, after Ehud died.
4:2 And the L sold them into the hand of
4:3 Israel cried to the L for help; for he
4:6 said to him, "The L, the God of Israel,
4:9 your glory, for the L will sell Sisera into
4:14 day in which the L has given Sisera into
4:14 Does not the L go out before you?" So
4:15 And the L routed Sisera and all his chariots
4:18 him, "Turn aside, my L, turn aside to me;
5:2 the people offered themselves willingly, bless the L
5:3 O princes; to the L I will sing, I
5:3 make melody to the L, the God of Israel.
5:4 L, when thou didst go forth from Seir, when
5:5 mountains quaked before the L, yon Sinai before the
5:5 yon Sinai before the L, the God of Israel.
5:9 Bless the L
5:11 the triumphs of the L, the triumphs of his
5:11 to the gates marched the people of the L
5:13 the people of the L marched down for him
5:23 the angel of the L, curse bitterly its inhabitants,
5:23 the help of the L, to the help of
5:23 the help of the L against the mighty.
5:31 as spoil?' "So perish all thine enemies, O L
6:1 the sight of the L; and the LORD gave
6:1 the LORD; and the L gave them into the
6:6 people of Israel cried for help to the L
6:7 Israel cried to the L on account of the
6:8 of the Midianites, the L sent a prophet to
6:8 them, "Thus says the L, the God of Israel:
6:10 you, 'I am the L your God; you shall
6:11 the angel of the L came and sat under
6:12 the angel of the L appeared to him and
6:12 said to him, "The L is with you, you
6:13 "Pray, sir, if the L is with us, why
6:13 saying, 'Did not the L bring us up from
6:13 Egypt?' But now the L has cast us off,
6:14 And the L turned to him and said, "Go
6:15 said to him, "Pray, L, how can I deliver
6:16 And the L said to him, "But I will
6:21 the angel of the L reached out the tip
6:21 the angel of the L vanished from his sight.
6:22 the angel of the L; and Gideon said, "Alas,
6:22 Gideon said, "Alas, O L GOD!
6:22 the angel of the L face to face."
6:23 But the L said to him, "Peace be to
6:24 altar there to the L, and called it, The
6:24 and called it, The L is peace.
6:25 That night the L said to him, "Take your
6:26 an altar to the L your God on the
6:27 and did as the L had told him; but
6:34 the Spirit of the L took possession of Gideon;
7:2 The L said to Gideon, "The people with you
7:4 And the L said to Gideon, "The people are
7:5 the water; and the L said to Gideon, "Every
7:7 And the L said to Gideon, "With the three
7:9 That same night the L said to him, "Arise,
7:15 said, "Arise; for the L has given the host
7:18 and shout, 'For the L and for Gideon.'"
7:20 "A sword for the L and for Gideon!"
7:22 three hundred trumpets, the L set every man's sword
8:7 "Well then, when the L has given Zebah and
8:19 my mother; as the L lives, if you had
8:23 rule over you; the L will rule over you."
8:34 did not remember the L their God, who had
10:6 the sight of the L, and served the Baals
10:6 and they forsook the L, and did not serve
10:7 the anger of the L was kindled against Israel,
10:10 Israel cried to the L, saying, "We have sinned
10:11 And the L said to the people of Israel,
10:15 Israel said to the L, "We have sinned; do
10:16 them and served the L; and he became indignant
11:9 the Ammonites, and the L gives them over to
11:10 said to Jephthah, "The L will be witness between
11:11 his words before the L at Mizpah.
11:21 And the L, the God of Israel, gave Sihon
11:23 So then the L, the God of Israel, dispossessed
11:24 And all that the L our God has dispossessed
11:27 war on me; the L, the Judge, decide this
11:29 the Spirit of the L came upon Jephthah, and
11:30 a vow to the L, and said, "If thou
11:32 against them; and the L gave them into his
11:35 my mouth to the L, and I cannot take
11:36 your mouth to the L, do to me according
11:36 mouth, now that the L has avenged you on
12:3 the Ammonites, and the L gave them into my
13:1 the sight of the L; and the LORD gave

L

13:1 the LORD; and the L gave them into the
13:3 the angel of the L appeared to the woman
13:8 Then Manoah entreated the L, and said, "O, LORD,
13:8 LORD, and said, "O, L, I pray thee, let
13:13 the angel of the L said to Manoah, "Of
13:15 the angel of the L, "Pray, let us detain
13:16 the angel of the L said to Manoah, "If
13:16 a burnt offering, then offer it to the L
13:16 the angel of the L
13:17 the angel of the L, "What is your name,
13:18 the angel of the L said to him, "Why
13:19 the rock to the L, to him who works
13:20 the angel of the L ascended in the flame
13:21 The angel of the L appeared no more to
13:21 knew that he was the angel of the L
13:23 to him, "If the L had meant to kill
13:24 boy grew, and the L blessed him.
13:25 the Spirit of the L began to stir him
14:4 it was from the L; for he was seeking
14:6 the Spirit of the L came mightily upon him,
14:19 the Spirit of the L came mightily upon him,
15:14 the Spirit of the L came mightily upon him,
15:18 he called on the L and said, "Thou hast
16:20 not know that the L had left him.
16:28 Samson called to the L and said, "O Lord
16:28 LORD and said, "O L GOD, remember me, I
17:2 mother said, "Blessed be my son by the L
17:3 the silver to the L from my hand for
17:13 I know that the L will prosper me, because
18:6 you go is under the eye of the L
20:1 one man to the L at Mizpah.
20:18 And the L said, "Judah shall go up first."
20:23 and wept before the L until the evening; and
20:23 they inquired of the L, "Shall we again draw
20:23 And the L said, "Go up against them."
20:26 sat there before the L, and fasted that day
20:26 burnt offerings and peace offerings before the L
20:27 Israel inquired of the L (for the ark of
20:28 And the L said, "Go up; for tomorrow I
20:35 And the L defeated Benjamin before Israel; and the
21:3 And they said, "O L, the God of Israel,
21:5 not come up in the assembly to the L
21:5 come up to the L to Mizpah, saying, "He
21:7 have sworn by the L that we will not
21:8 come up to the L to Mizpah?" And behold,
21:15 on Benjamin because the L had made a breach
21:19 yearly feast of the L at Shiloh, which is
Ruth 1:6 of Moab that the L had visited his people
1:8 May the L deal kindly with you, as you
1:9 The L grant that you may find a home,
1:13 the hand of the L has gone forth against
1:17 May the L do so to me and more
1:21 away full, and the L has brought me back
1:21 me Naomi, when the L has afflicted me and
2:4 to the reapers, "The L be with you!" And
2:4 And they answered, "The L bless you."
2:12 The L recompense you for what you have done,
2:12 given you by the L, the God of Israel,
2:13 gracious to me, my L, for you have comforted
2:20 be he by the L, whose kindness has not
3:10 be blessed by the L, my daughter; you have
3:13 you, then, as the L lives, I will do
4:11 May the L make the woman, who is coming
4:12 the children that the L will give you by
4:13 to her, and the L gave her conception, and
4:14 Naomi, "Blessed be the L, who has not left
1Sam 1:3 to sacrifice to the L of hosts at Shiloh,
1:3 Eli, Hophni and Phinehas, were priests of the L
1:5 one portion, because the L had closed her womb.
1:6 irritate her, because the L had closed her womb.
1:7 the house of the L, she used to provoke
1:9 beside the doorpost of the temple of the L
1:10 and prayed to the L, and wept bitterly.
1:11 vow and said, "O L of hosts, if thou
1:11 give him to the L all the days of
1:12 praying before the L, Eli observed her mouth.
1:15 Hannah answered, "No, my L, I am a woman
1:15 have been pouring out my soul before the L
1:19 and worshiped before the L; then they went back
1:19 his wife, and the L remembered her;
1:20 she said, "I have asked him of the L
1:21 to offer to the L the yearly sacrifice, and
1:22 the presence of the L, and abide there for
1:23 him; only, may the L establish his word." So
1:24 the house of the L at Shiloh; and the
1:26 And she said, "Oh, my L
1:26 As you live, my L, I am the woman
1:26 standing here in your presence, praying to the L
1:27 I prayed; and the L has granted me my
1:28 lent him to the L; as long as he
1:28 as he lives, he is lent to the L
1:28 And they worshiped the L there.
2:1 heart exults in the L; my strength is exalted
2:1 the LORD; my strength is exalted in the L
2:2 none holy like the L, there is none besides
2:3 your mouth; for the L is a God of
2:6 The L kills and brings to life; he brings
2:7 The L makes poor and makes rich; he brings
2:10 The adversaries of the L shall be broken to
2:10 The L will judge the ends of the earth;
2:11 boy ministered to the L, in the presence of
2:12 worthless men; they had no regard for the L
2:17 the sight of the L; for the men treated
2:17 the offering of the L with contempt.
2:18 was ministering before the L, a boy girded with
2:20 wife, and say, "The L give you children by
2:20 she lent to the L; so then they would
2:21 And the L visited Hannah, and she conceived and
2:21 boy Samuel grew in the presence of the L
2:24 the people of the L spreading abroad.
2:25 man sins against the L, who can intercede for
2:25 the will of the L to slay them.
2:26 in favor with the L and with men.
2:27 to him, "Thus the L has said, 'I revealed
2:30 people Israel?' Therefore the L the God of Israel
2:30 ever'; but now the L declares: 'Far be it
3:1 was ministering to the L under Eli.
3:1 the word of the L was rare in those
3:3 the temple of the L, where the ark of
3:4 Then the L called, "Samuel!
3:6 And the L called again, "Samuel!" And Samuel
3:7 not yet know the L, and the word of
3:7 the word of the L had not yet been
3:8 And the L called Samuel again the third time.
3:8 Eli perceived that the L was calling the boy.
3:9 you shall say, 'Speak, L, for thy servant hears.'"
3:10 And the L came and stood forth, calling as
3:11 Then the L said to Samuel, "Behold, I am
3:15 opened the doors of the house of the L
3:18 said, "It is the L; let him do what
3:19 Samuel grew, and the L was with him and
3:20 Samuel was established as a prophet of the L
3:21 And the L appeared again at Shiloh, for the
3:21 at Shiloh, for the L revealed himself to Samuel
3:21 Samuel at Shiloh by the word of the L
4:3 said, "Why has the L put us to rout
4:3 the covenant of the L here from Shiloh, that
4:4 the covenant of the L of hosts, who is
4:5 the covenant of the L came into the camp,
4:6 the ark of the L had come to the
5:3 on the ground before the ark of the L
5:4 the ark of the L, and the head of
5:6 The hand of the L was heavy upon the
5:9 the hand of the L was against the city,
6:1 The ark of the L was in the country
6:2 shall we do with the ark of the L
6:8 the ark of the L and place it on
6:11 the ark of the L on the cart, and
6:14 the cows as a burnt offering to the L
6:15 the ark of the L and the box that
6:15 and sacrificed sacrifices on that day to the L
6:17 guilt offering to the L: one for Ashdod, one
6:18 the ark of the L, is a witness to
6:19 the ark of the L; he slew seventy men
6:19 people mourned because the L had made a great
6:20 to stand before the L, this holy God?
6:21 "The Philistines have returned the ark of the L
7:1 the ark of the L, and brought it to
7:1 to have charge of the ark of the L
7:2 all the house of Israel lamented after the L
7:3 are returning to the L with all your heart,
7:3 your heart to the L, and serve him only,
7:4 and they served the L only.
7:5 will pray to the L for you."
7:6 it out before the L, and fasted on that
7:6 and said there, "We have sinned against the L
7:8 to cry to the L our God for us,
7:9 burnt offering to the L; and Samuel cried to
7:9 Samuel cried to the L for Israel, and the
7:9 for Israel, and the L answered him.
7:10 attack Israel; but the L thundered with a mighty
7:12 he said, "Hitherto the L has helped us."

7:13 the hand of the L was against the Philistines
7:17 And he built there an altar to the L
8:6 And Samuel prayed to the L
8:7 And the L said to Samuel, "Hearken to the
8:10 the words of the L to the people who
8:18 for yourselves; but the L will not answer you
8:21 he repeated them in the ears of the L
8:22 And the L said to Samuel, "Hearken to their
9:15 before Saul came, the L had revealed to Samuel:
9:17 Samuel saw Saul, the L told him, "Here is
10:1 said, "Has not the L anointed you to be
10:1 the people of the L and you will save
10:1 to you that the L has anointed you to
10:6 the spirit of the L will come mightily upon
10:17 people together to the L at Mizpah;
10:18 Israel, "Thus says the L, the God of Israel,
10:19 present yourselves before the L by your tribes and
10:22 inquired again of the L, "Did the man come
10:22 and the L said, "Behold, he has hidden himself
10:24 see him whom the L has chosen?
10:25 a book and laid it up before the L
11:7 the dread of the L fell upon the people,
11:13 day, for today the L has wrought deliverance in
11:15 Saul king before the L in Gilgal.
11:15 peace offerings before the L, and there Saul and
12:3 against me before the L and before his anointed.
12:5 said to them, "The L is witness against you,
12:6 to the people, "The L is witness, who appointed
12:7 with you before the L concerning all the saving
12:7 saving deeds of the L which he performed for
12:8 fathers cried to the L and the LORD sent
12:8 the LORD and the L sent Moses and Aaron,
12:9 But they forgot the L their God; and he
12:10 they cried to the L, and said, 'We have
12:10 we have forsaken the L, and have served the
12:11 serve thee.' And the L sent Jerubbaal and Barak,
12:12 over us,' when the L your God was your
12:13 have asked; behold, the L has set a king
12:14 you will fear the L and serve him and
12:14 the commandment of the L, and if both you
12:14 you will follow the L your God, it will
12:15 the voice of the L, but rebel against the
12:15 the commandment of the L, then the hand of
12:15 the hand of the L will be against you
12:16 great thing, which the L will do before your
12:17 will call upon the L, that he may send
12:17 the sight of the L, in asking for yourselves
12:18 Samuel called upon the L, and the LORD sent
12:18 the LORD, and the L sent thunder and rain
12:18 people greatly feared the L and Samuel.
12:19 your servants to the L your God, that we
12:20 aside from following the L, but serve the LORD
12:20 LORD, but serve the L with all your heart;
12:22 For the L will not cast away his people,
12:22 it has pleased the L to make you a
12:23 should sin against the L by ceasing to pray
12:24 Only fear the L, and serve him faithfully with
13:12 the favor of the L; so I forced myself,
13:13 the commandment of the L your God, which he
13:13 you; for now the L would have established your
13:14 shall not continue; the L has sought out a
13:14 own heart; and the L has appointed him to
13:14 not kept what the L commanded you."
14:3 the priest of the L in Shiloh, wearing an
14:6 may be that the L will work for us;
14:6 nothing can hinder the L from saving by many
14:10 go up; for the L has given them into
14:12 after me; for the L has given them into
14:23 So the L delivered Israel that day; and the
14:33 are sinning against the L, by eating with the
14:34 not sin against the L by eating with the
14:35 an altar to the L; it was the first
14:35 the first altar that he built to the L
14:39 For as the L lives who saves Israel, though
14:41 Therefore Saul said, "O L God of Israel, why
14:41 Jonathan my son, O L, God of Israel, give
14:45 As the L lives, there shall not one hair
15:1 said to Saul, "The L sent me to anoint
15:1 now therefore hearken to the words of the L
15:2 Thus says the L of hosts, 'I will punish
15:10 The word of the L came to Samuel:
15:11 he cried to the L all night.
15:13 be you to the L; I have performed the
15:13 LORD; I have performed the commandment of the L
15:15 to sacrifice to the L your God; and the
15:16 tell you what the L said to me this
15:17 The L anointed you king over Israel.
15:18 And the L sent you on a mission, and
15:19 did you not obey the voice of the L
15:19 what was evil in the sight of the L
15:20 the voice of the L, I have gone on
15:20 mission on which the L sent me, I have
15:21 to sacrifice to the L your God in Gilgal."
15:22 Samuel said, "Has the L as great delight in
15:22 sacrifices, as in obeying the voice of the L
15:23 the word of the L, he has also rejected
15:24 the commandment of the L and your words, because
15:25 return with me, that I may worship the L
15:26 the word of the L, and the LORD has
15:26 the LORD, and the L has rejected you from
15:28 said to him, "The L has torn the kingdom
15:30 I may worship the L your God."
15:31 turned back after Saul; and Saul worshiped the L
15:33 in pieces before the L in Gilgal.
15:35 And the L repented that he had made Saul
16:1 The L said to Samuel, "How long will you
16:2 And the L said, "Take a heifer with you,
16:2 to sacrifice to the L
16:4 Samuel did what the L commanded, and came to
16:5 to sacrifice to the L; consecrate yourselves, and
16:6 and thought, "Surely the L's anointed is before him."
16:7 But the L said to Samuel, "Do not look
16:7 rejected him; for the L sees not as man
16:7 outward appearance, but the L looks on the heart."
16:8 said, "Neither has the L chosen this one."
16:9 said, "Neither has the L chosen this one."
16:10 said to Jesse, "The L has not chosen these."
16:12 And the L said, "Arise, anoint him; for this
16:13 the Spirit of the L came mightily upon David
16:14 the Spirit of the L departed from Saul, and
16:14 evil spirit from the L tormented him.
16:16 Let our L now command your servants, who are
16:18 good presence; and the L is with him."
17:37 And David said, "The L who delivered me from
17:37 David, "Go, and the L be with you!"
17:45 the name of the L of hosts, the God
17:46 This day the L will deliver you into my
17:47 may know that the L saves not with sword
17:47 the battle is the L's and he will give
18:12 of David, because the L was with him but
18:14 his undertakings; for the L was with him.
18:17 me and fight the L's battles." For Saul thought,
18:28 and knew that the L was with David, and
19:5 the Philistine, and the L wrought a great victory
19:6 Saul swore, "As the L lives, he shall not
19:9 evil spirit from the L came upon Saul, as
20:3 But truly, as the L lives and as your
20:12 said to David, "The L, the God of Israel,
20:13 do you harm, the L do so to Jonathan,
20:13 May the L be with you, as he has
20:14 loyal love of the L, that I may not
20:15 When the L cuts off every one of the
20:16 And may the L take vengeance on David's enemies."
20:21 come, for, as the L lives, it is safe
20:22 then go; for the L has sent you away.
20:23 have spoken, behold, the L is between you and
20:42 the name of the L, saying, 'The LORD shall
20:42 the LORD, saying, 'The L shall be between me
21:6 removed from before the L, to be replaced by
21:7 day, detained before the L; his name was Doeg
22:10 he inquired of the L for him, and gave
22:12 And he answered, "Here I am, my L
22:17 the priests of the L; because their hand also
22:17 hand to fall upon the priests of the L
22:21 that Saul had killed the priests of the L
23:2 David inquired of the L, "Shall I go and
23:2 And the L said to David, "Go and attack
23:4 David inquired of the L again.
23:4 And the L answered him, "Arise, go down to
23:10 Then said David, "O L, the God of Israel,
23:11 O L, the God of Israel, I beseech thee,
23:11 And the L said, "He will come down."
23:12 And the L said, "They will surrender you."
23:18 a covenant before the L; David remained at Horesh,
23:21 be blessed by the L; for you have had
24:4 day of which the L said to you, 'Behold,
24:6 to his men, "The L forbid that I should
24:6 this thing to my L, the LORD's anointed, to
24:6 to my lord, the L's anointed, to put forth
24:6 seeing he is the L's anointed."
24:8 called after Saul, "My L the king!" And when
24:10 have seen how the L gave you today into

24:10 my hand against my L; for he is the
24:10 for he is the L's anointed.'
24:12 May the L judge between me and you, may
24:12 and you, may the L avenge me upon you;
24:15 May the L therefore be judge, and give sentence
24:18 kill me when the L put me into your
24:19 So may the L reward you with good for
24:21 me therefore by the L that you will not
25:24 "Upon me alone, my L, be the guilt; pray
25:25 Let not my L regard this ill-natured fellow, Nabal;
25:25 young men of my L, whom you sent.
25:26 Now then, my L, as the LORD lives, and
25:26 my lord, as the L lives, and as your
25:26 soul lives, seeing the L has restrained you from
25:26 do evil to my L be as Nabal.
25:27 has brought to my L be given to the
25:27 given to the young men who follow my L
25:28 your handmaid; for the L will certainly make my
25:28 will certainly make my L a sure house, because
25:28 sure house, because my L is fighting the battles
25:28 the battles of the L; and evil shall not
25:29 the life of my L shall be bound in
25:29 the care of the L your God; and the
25:30 And when the L has done to my lord
25:30 has done to my L according to all the
25:31 prince over Israel, my L shall have no cause
25:31 cause or for my L taking vengeance himself.
25:31 And when the L has dealt well with my
25:31 well with my L, then remember your handmaid."
25:32 Abigail, "Blessed be the L, the God of Israel,
25:34 as surely as the L the God of Israel
25:38 ten days later the L smote Nabal; and he
25:39 said, "Blessed be the L who has avenged the
25:39 servant from evil; the L has returned the evil-doing
25:41 wash the feet of the servants of my L
26:9 his hand against the L's anointed, and be guiltless?"
26:10 David said, "As the L lives, the LORD will
26:10 the LORD lives, the L will smite him; or
26:11 The L forbid that I should put forth my
26:11 my hand against the L's anointed; but take now
26:12 deep sleep from the L had fallen upon them.
26:15 kept watch over your L the king?
26:15 people came in to destroy the king your L
26:16 As the L lives, you deserve to die, because
26:16 kept watch over your L, the LORD's anointed.
26:16 over your lord, the L's anointed.
26:17 is my voice, my L, O king."
26:18 said, "Why does my L pursue after his servant?
26:19 Now therefore let my L the king hear the
26:19 If it is the L who has stirred you
26:19 be cursed before the L, for they have driven
26:19 the heritage of the L, saying, 'Go, serve other
26:20 the presence of the L; for the king of
26:23 The L rewards every man for his righteousness and
26:23 his faithfulness; for the L gave you into my
26:23 my hand against the L's anointed.
26:24 the sight of the L, and may he deliver
28:6 Saul inquired of the L, the LORD did not
28:6 of the LORD, the L did not answer him,
28:10 to her by the L, "As the LORD lives,
28:10 the LORD, "As the L lives, no punishment shall
28:16 ask me, since the L has turned from you
28:17 The L has done to you as he spoke
28:17 by me; for the L has torn the kingdom
28:18 the voice of the L, and did not carry
28:18 against Amalek, therefore the L has done this thing
28:19 Moreover the L will give Israel also with you
28:19 be with me; the L will give the army
29:4 how could this fellow reconcile himself to his L
29:6 to him, "As the L lives, you have been
29:8 the enemies of my L the king?"
29:10 the servants of your L who came with you;
30:6 strengthened himself in the L his God.
30:8 David inquired of the L, "Shall I pursue after
30:23 brothers, with what the L has given us; he
30:26 the enemies of the L;
2Sam 1:10 and I have brought them here to my L
1:12 the people of the L and for the house
1:14 hand to destroy the L's anointed?"
1:16 'I have slain the L's anointed.'"
2:1 David inquired of the L, "Shall I go up
2:1 And the L said to him, "Go up." David
2:5 be blessed by the L, because you showed this
2:5 loyalty to Saul your L, and buried him!
2:6 Now may the L show steadfast love and faithfulness
2:7 valiant; for Saul your L is dead, and the

L

3:9 for David what the L has sworn to him,
3:18 it about; for the L has promised David, saying,
3:21 all Israel to my L the king, that they
3:28 ever guiltless before the L for the blood of
3:39 The L requite the evildoer according to his
4:8 sought your life; the L has avenged my lord
4:8 LORD has avenged my L the king this day
4:9 the Be-erothite, "As the L lives, who has redeemed
5:2 in Israel; and the L said to you, 'You
5:3 at Hebron before the L, and they anointed David
5:10 and greater, for the L, the God of hosts,
5:12 David perceived that the L had established him king
5:19 David inquired of the L, "Shall I go up
5:19 And the L said to David, "Go up; for
5:20 and he said, "The L has broken through my
5:23 David inquired of the L, he said, "You shall
5:24 yourself; for then the L has gone out before
5:25 David did as the L commanded him, and smote
6:2 the name of the L of hosts who sits
6:5 making merry before the L with all their might,
6:7 the anger of the L was kindled against Uzzah;
6:8 was angry because the L had broken forth upon
6:9 was afraid of the L that day; and he
6:9 the ark of the L come to me?"
6:10 the ark of the L into the city of
6:11 the ark of the L remained in the house
6:11 three months; and the L blessed Obed-edom and all
6:12 told King David, "The L has blessed the household
6:13 the ark of the L had gone six paces,
6:14 David danced before the L with all his might;
6:15 the ark of the L with shouting, and with
6:16 the ark of the L came into the city
6:16 and dancing before the L; and she despised him
6:17 the ark of the L, and set it in
6:17 burnt offerings and peace offerings before the L
6:18 the name of the L of hosts,
6:21 "It was before the L, who chose me above
6:21 the people of the L --and I will make
6:21 LORD--and I will make merry before the L
7:1 his house, and the L had given him rest
7:3 your heart; for the L is with you."
7:4 the word of the L came to Nathan,
7:5 David, 'Thus says the L: Would you build me
7:8 David, 'Thus says the L of hosts, I took
7:11 Moreover the L declares to you that the LORD
7:11 to you that the L will make you a
7:18 and sat before the L, and said, "Who am
7:18 "Who am I, O L GOD, and what is
7:19 in thy eyes, O L GOD; thou hast spoken
7:19 me future generations, O L GOD!
7:20 knowest thy servant, O L GOD!
7:22 thou art great, O L God; for there is
7:24 ever; and thou, O L, didst become their God.
7:25 And now, O L God, confirm for ever the
7:26 for ever, saying, 'The L of hosts is God
7:27 For thou, O L of hosts, the God of
7:28 And now, O L GOD, thou art God, and
7:29 thee; for thou, O L GOD, hast spoken, and
8:6 And the L gave victory to David wherever he
8:11 David dedicated to the L, together with the silver
8:14 And the L gave victory to David wherever he
9:11 to all that my L the king commands his
10:3 said to Hanun their L, "Do you think, because
10:12 God; and may the L do what seems good
11:9 the servants of his L, and did not go
11:11 in booths; and my L Joab and the servants
11:11 the servants of my L are camping in the
11:13 the servants of his L, but he did not
11:27 the thing that David had done displeased the L
12:1 And the L sent Nathan to David.
12:5 to Nathan, "As the L lives, the man who
12:7 Thus says the L, the God of Israel, 'I
12:9 the word of the L, to do what is
12:11 wife.' Thus says the L, 'Behold, I will raise
12:13 said to Nathan, "I have sinned against the L
12:13 said to David, "The L also has put away
12:14 have utterly scorned the L, the child that is
12:15 And the L struck the child that Uriah's wife
12:20 the house of the L, and worshiped; he then
12:22 'Who knows whether the L will be gracious to
12:24 And the L loved him,
12:25 he called his name Jedidiah, because of the L
13:32 said, "Let not my L suppose that they have
13:33 therefore let not my L the king so take
14:9 be the guilt, my L the king, and on
14:11 the king invoke the L your God, that the

14:11 He said, "As the L lives, not one hair
14:12 a word to my L the king." He said,
14:15 say this to my L the king because the
14:17 'The word of my L the king will set
14:17 at rest'; for my L the king is like
14:17 The L your God be with you!"
14:18 woman said, "Let my L the king speak."
14:19 as you live, my L the king, one cannot
14:19 from anything that my L the king has said.
14:20 But my L has wisdom like the wisdom of
14:22 in your sight, my L the king, in that
15:7 have vowed to the L, in Hebron.
15:8 Aram, saying, 'If the L will indeed bring me
15:8 Jerusalem, then I will offer worship to the L
15:15 to do whatever my L the king decides."
15:20 you; and may the L show steadfast love and
15:21 the king, "As the L lives, and as my
15:21 lives, and as my L the king lives, wherever
15:21 king lives, wherever my L the king shall be,
15:25 the eyes of the L, he will bring me
15:31 And David said, "O L, I pray thee, turn
16:4 in your sight, my L the king."
16:8 The L has avenged upon you all the blood
16:8 have reigned; and the L has given the kingdom
16:9 dead dog curse my L the king?
16:10 is cursing because the L has said to him,
16:11 him curse; for the L has bidden him.
16:12 may be that the L will look upon my
16:12 affliction, and that the L will repay me with
16:18 "No; for whom the L and this people and
17:14 For the L had ordained to defeat the good
17:14 Ahithophel, so that the L might bring evil upon
18:19 the king that the L has delivered him from
18:28 said, "Blessed be the L your God, who has
18:28 their hand against my L the king."
18:31 "Good tidings for my L the king!
18:31 For the L has delivered you this day from
18:32 the enemies of my L the king, and all
19:7 I swear by the L, if you do not
19:19 king, "Let not my L hold me guilty or
19:19 on the day my L the king left Jerusalem;
19:20 down to meet my L the king."
19:21 because he cursed the L's anointed?"
19:26 He answered, "My L, O king, my servant deceived
19:27 your servant to my L the king.
19:27 But my L the king is like the angel
19:28 to death before my L the king; but you
19:30 it all, since my L the king has come
19:35 added burden to my L the king?
19:37 go over with my L the king; and do
20:6 than Absalom; take your L's servants and pursue him,
20:19 will you swallow up the heritage of the L
21:1 year; and David sought the face of the L
21:1 And the L said, "There is bloodguilt on Saul
21:3 that you may bless the heritage of the L
21:6 them up before the L at Gibeon on the
21:6 LORD at Gibeon on the mountain of the L
21:7 the oath of the L which was between them,
21:9 the mountain before the L, and the seven of
22:1 David spoke to the L the words of this
22:1 the day when the L delivered him from the
22:2 He said, "The L is my rock, and my
22:4 I call upon the L, who is worthy to
22:7 I called upon the L; to my God I
22:14 The L thundered from heaven, and the Most High
22:16 the rebuke of the L, at the blast of
22:19 my calamity; but the L was my stay.
22:21 "The L rewarded me according to my righteousness;
22:22 the ways of the L, and have not wickedly
22:25 Therefore the L has recompensed me according to
22:29 art my lamp, O L, and my God lightens
22:31 the promise of the L proves true; he is
22:32 "For who is God, but the L
22:42 they cried to the L, but he did not
22:47 "The L lives; and blessed be my rock, and
22:50 will extol thee, O L, among the nations, and
23:2 "The Spirit of the L speaks by me, his
23:10 the sword; and the L wrought a great victory
23:12 the Philistines; and the L wrought a great victory.
23:16 it out to the L,
23:17 it from me, O L, that I should do
24:1 the anger of the L was kindled against Israel,
24:3 the king, "May the L your God add to
24:3 the eyes of my L the king still see
24:3 but why does my L the king delight in
24:10 David said to the L, "I have sinned greatly
24:10 But now, O L, I pray thee, take away
24:11 the word of the L came to the prophet
24:12 David, 'Thus says the L, Three things I offer
24:14 the hand of the L, for his mercy is
24:15 So the L sent a pestilence upon Israel from
24:16 to destroy it, the L repented of the evil,
24:16 the angel of the L was by the threshing
24:17 David spoke to the L when he saw the
24:18 an altar to the L on the threshing floor
24:19 Gad's word, as the L commanded.
24:21 said, "Why has my L the king come to
24:21 an altar to the L, that the plague may
24:22 to David, "Let my L the king take and
24:23 to the king, "The L your God accept you."
24:24 burnt offerings to the L my God which cost
24:25 an altar to the L, and offered burnt offerings
24:25 So the L heeded supplications for the land, and
1Kgs 1:2 be sought for my L the king, and let
1:2 your bosom, that my L the king may be
1:11 king and David our L does not know it?
1:13 'Did you not, my L the king, swear to
1:17 said to him, "My L, you swore to your
1:17 maidservant by the L your God, saying, 'Solomon
1:18 king, although you, my L the king, do not
1:20 And now, my L the king, the eyes of
1:20 the throne of my L the king after him.
1:21 to pass, when my L the king sleeps with
1:24 And Nathan said, "My L the king, have you
1:27 brought about by my L the king and you
1:27 the throne of my L the king after him?"
1:29 swore, saying, "As the L lives, who has redeemed
1:30 to you by the L, the God of Israel,
1:31 and said, "May my L King David live for
1:33 the servants of your L, and cause Solomon my
1:36 May the L, the God of my lord the
1:36 the God of my L the king, say so.
1:37 As the L has been with my lord the
1:37 has been with my L the king, even so
1:37 the throne of my L King David."
1:43 Adonijah, "No, for our L King David has made
1:47 came to congratulate our L King David, saying, 'Your
1:48 said, 'Blessed be the L, the God of Israel,
2:3 the charge of the L your God, walking in
2:4 you turn; that the L may establish his word
2:8 to him by the L, saying, 'I will not
2:15 my brothers, for it was his from the L
2:23 Solomon swore by the L, saying, "God do so
2:24 Now therefore as the L lives, who has established
2:26 the ark of the L GOD before David my
2:27 being priest to the L, thus fulfilling the word
2:27 the word of the L which he had spoken
2:28 the tent of the L and caught hold of
2:29 the tent of the L, and behold, he is
2:30 the tent of the L, and said to him,
2:32 The L will bring back his bloody deeds upon
2:33 be peace from the L for evermore."
2:38 is good; as my L the king has said,
2:42 you swear by the L, and solemnly admonish you,
2:43 your oath to the L and the commandment with
2:44 my father; so the L will bring back your
2:45 be established before the L for ever."
3:1 the house of the L and the wall around
3:2 yet been built for the name of the L
3:3 Solomon loved the L, walking in the statutes of
3:5 At Gibeon the L appeared to Solomon in a
3:7 And now, O L my God, thou hast made
3:10 It pleased the L that Solomon had asked this.
3:15 the covenant of the L, and offered up burnt
3:17 woman said, "Oh, my L, this woman and I
3:26 her son, "Oh, my L, give her the living
5:3 the name of the L his God because of
5:3 surrounded him, until the L put them under the
5:4 But now the L my God has given me
5:5 the name of the L my God, as the
5:5 my God, as the L said to David my
5:7 said, "Blessed be the L this day, who has
5:12 And the L gave Solomon wisdom, as he promised
6:1 he began to build the house of the L
6:2 Solomon built for the L was sixty cubits long,
6:11 the word of the L came to Solomon,
6:19 there the ark of the covenant of the L
6:37 the house of the L was laid, in the
7:9 the house of the L to the great court.
7:12 the house of the L, and the vestibule of
7:40 the house of the L:
7:45 the house of the L, which Hiram made for

L

7:48 the house of the L: the golden altar, the
7:51 the house of the L was finished.
7:51 in the treasuries of the house of the L
8:1 the covenant of the L out of the city
8:4 the ark of the L, the tent of meeting,
8:6 the covenant of the L to its place, in
8:9 at Horeb, where the L made a covenant with
8:10 the house of the L,
8:11 the glory of the L filled the house of
8:11 of the LORD filled the house of the L
8:12 Then Solomon said, "The L has set the sun
8:15 said, "Blessed be the L, the God of Israel,
8:17 the name of the L, the God of Israel.
8:18 But the L said to David my father, 'Whereas
8:20 my name.' Now the L has fulfilled his promise
8:20 of Israel, as the L promised, and I have
8:20 the name of the L, the God of Israel.
8:21 the covenant of the L which he made with
8:22 the altar of the L in the presence of
8:23 heaven; and said, "O L, God of Israel, there
8:25 Now therefore, O L, God of Israel, keep with
8:28 to his supplication, O L my God, hearkening to
8:44 they pray to the L toward the city which
8:53 out of Egypt, O L GOD."
8:54 and supplication to the L, he arose from before
8:54 the altar of the L, where he had knelt
8:56 saying, "Blessed be the L who has given rest
8:57 The L our God be with us, as he
8:59 made supplication before the L, be near to the
8:59 be near to the L our God day and
8:60 may know that the L is God; there is
8:61 wholly true to the L our God, walking in
8:62 all Israel with him, offered sacrifice before the L
8:63 peace offerings to the L twenty-two thousand oxen
8:63 people of Israel dedicated the house of the L
8:64 the house of the L; for there he offered
8:64 that was before the L was too small to
8:65 of Egypt, before the L our God, seven days.
8:66 the goodness that the L had shown to David
9:1 the house of the L and the king's house
9:2 desired to build, the L appeared to Solomon a
9:3 And the L said to him, "I have heard
9:8 say, 'Why has the L done thus to this
9:9 'Because they forsook the L their God who brought
9:9 served them; therefore the L has brought all this
9:10 the house of the L and the king's house,
9:15 the house of the L and his own house
9:25 he built to the L, burning incense before the
9:25 built to the LORD, burning incense before the L
10:1 the name of the L, she came to test
10:5 the house of the L, there was no more
10:9 Blessed be the L your God, who has delighted
10:9 Because the L loved Israel for ever, he has
10:12 the house of the L, and for the king's
11:2 nations concerning which the L had said to the
11:4 wholly true to the L his God, as was
11:6 the sight of the L, and did not wholly
11:6 not wholly follow the L, as David his father
11:9 And the L was angry with Solomon, because his
11:9 turned away from the L, the God of Israel,
11:10 not keep what the L commanded.
11:11 Therefore the L said to Solomon, "Since this has
11:14 And the L raised up an adversary against Solomon,
11:31 for thus says the L, the God of Israel,
12:15 brought about by the L that he might fulfil
12:15 his word, which the L spoke by Ahijah the
12:24 people, 'Thus says the L, You shall not go
12:24 the word of the L, and went home again,
12:24 home again, according to the word of the L
12:27 the house of the L at Jerusalem, then the
12:27 turn again to their L, to Rehoboam king of
13:1 the word of the L to Bethel.
13:2 the word of the L, and said, "O altar,
13:2 altar, thus says the L: 'Behold, a son shall
13:3 the sign that the L has spoken: 'Behold, the
13:5 God had given by the word of the L
13:6 the favor of the L your God, and pray
13:6 of God entreated the L; and the king's hand
13:9 the word of the L, saying, 'You shall neither
13:17 the word of the L, 'You shall neither eat
13:18 the word of the L, saying, 'Bring him back
13:20 the word of the L came to the prophet
13:21 Judah, "Thus says the L, 'Because you have
13:21 the word of the L, and have not kept
13:21 commandment which the L your God commanded
13:26 the word of the L; therefore the LORD has
13:26 the LORD; therefore the L has given him to
13:26 the word which the L spoke to him."
13:32 the word of the L against the altar in
14:5 And the L said to Ahijah, "Behold, the wife
14:7 Jeroboam, 'Thus says the L, the God of Israel:
14:11 shall eat; for the L has spoken it.'"
14:13 something pleasing to the L, the God of Israel,
14:14 Moreover the L will raise up for himself a
14:15 And henceforth the L will smite Israel, as a
14:15 their Asherim, provoking the L to anger.
14:18 the word of the L, which he spoke by
14:21 the city which the L had chosen out of
14:22 the sight of the L, and they provoked him
14:24 the nations which the L drove out before the
14:26 the house of the L and the treasures of
14:28 the house of the L, the guard bore them
15:3 wholly true to the L his God, as the
15:4 for David's sake the L his God gave him
15:5 the eyes of the L, and did not turn
15:11 the eyes of the L, as David his father
15:14 wholly true to the L all his days.
15:15 the house of the L the votive gifts of
15:18 the house of the L and the treasures of
15:26 the sight of the L, and walked in the
15:29 the word of the L which he spoke by
15:30 which he provoked the L, the God of Israel.
15:34 the sight of the L, and walked in the
16:1 the word of the L came to Jehu the
16:7 the word of the L came by the prophet
16:7 the sight of the L, provoking him to anger
16:12 the word of the L, which he spoke against
16:13 to sin, provoking the L God of Israel to
16:19 the sight of the L, walking in the way
16:25 the sight of the L, and did more evil
16:26 to sin, provoking the L, the God of Israel,
16:30 the sight of the L more than all that
16:33 more to provoke the L, the God of Israel,
16:34 the word of the L, which he spoke by
17:1 to Ahab, "As the L the God of Israel
17:2 the word of the L came to him,
17:5 the word of the L; he went and dwelt
17:8 the word of the L came to him,
17:12 she said, "As the L your God lives, I
17:14 For thus says the L the God of Israel,
17:14 the day that the L sends rain upon the
17:16 the word of the L which he spoke by
17:20 he cried to the L, "O LORD my God,
17:20 to the LORD, "O L my God, hast thou
17:21 and cried to the L, "O LORD my God,
17:21 to the LORD, "O L my God, let this
17:22 And the L hearkened to the voice of Elijah;
17:24 the word of the L in your mouth is
18:1 the word of the L came to Elijah, in
18:3 (Now Obadiah revered the L greatly;
18:4 the prophets of the L, Obadiah took a hundred
18:7 "Is it you, my L Elijah?"
18:8 Go, tell your L, 'Behold, Elijah is here.'"
18:10 As the L your God lives, there is no
18:10 or kingdom whither my L has not sent to
18:11 say, 'Go, tell your L, "Behold, Elijah is here."'
18:12 the Spirit of the L will carry you whither
18:12 servant have revered the L from my youth.
18:13 not been told my L what I did when
18:13 the prophets of the L, how I hid a
18:13 hundred men of the L's prophets by fifties in
18:14 say, 'Go, tell your L, "Behold, Elijah is here"';
18:15 Elijah said, "As the L of hosts lives, before
18:18 the commandments of the L and followed the Baals.
18:21 If the L is God, follow him; but if
18:22 a prophet of the L; but Baal's prophets are
18:24 the name of the L; and the God who
18:30 the altar of the L that had been thrown
18:31 the word of the L came, saying, "Israel shall
18:32 built an altar in the name of the L
18:36 near and said, "O L, God of Abraham, Isaac,
18:37 Answer me, O L, answer me, that this people
18:37 know that thou, O L, art God, and that
18:38 the fire of the L fell, and consumed the
18:39 and they said, "The L, he is God; the
18:39 he is God; the L, he is God."
18:46 the hand of the L was on Elijah; and
19:4 is enough; now, O L, take away my life;
19:7 the angel of the L came again a second
19:9 the word of the L came to him, and
19:10 very jealous for the L, the God of hosts;
19:11 forth, and stand upon the mount before the L

19:11 And behold, the L passed by, and a great
19:11 the rocks before the L, but the LORD was
19:11 the LORD, but the L was not in the
19:11 an earthquake, but the L was not in the
19:12 a fire, but the L was not in the
19:14 very jealous for the L, the God of hosts;
19:15 And the L said to him, "Go, return on
20:4 "As you say, my L, O king, I am
20:9 of Ben-hadad, "Tell my L the king, 'All that
20:13 said, "Thus says the L, Have you seen all
20:13 and you shall know that I am the L
20:14 said, "Thus says the L, By the servants of
20:28 Israel, "Thus says the L, 'Because the Syrians have
20:28 Syrians have said, "The L is a god of
20:28 and you shall know that I am the L
20:35 the command of the L, "Strike me, I pray."
20:36 the voice of the L, behold, as soon as
20:42 him, "Thus says the L, 'Because you have let
21:3 said to Ahab, "The L forbid that I should
21:17 the word of the L came to Elijah the
21:19 him, 'Thus says the L, "Have you killed, and
21:19 him, 'Thus says the L: "In the place where
21:20 what is evil in the sight of the L
21:23 And of Jezebel the L also said, 'The dogs
21:25 the sight of the L like Ahab, whom Jezebel
21:26 had done, whom the L cast out before the
21:28 the word of the L came to Elijah the
22:5 Israel, "Inquire first for the word of the L
22:6 "Go up; for the L will give it into
22:7 another prophet of the L of whom we may
22:8 may inquire of the L, Micaiah the son of
22:11 said, "Thus says the L, 'With these you shall
22:12 Ramoth-gilead and triumph; the L will give it into
22:14 Micaiah said, "As the L lives, what the LORD
22:14 LORD lives, what the L says to me, that
22:15 up and triumph; the L will give it into
22:16 but the truth in the name of the L
22:17 no shepherd; and the L said, 'These have no
22:19 the word of the L: I saw the LORD
22:19 LORD: I saw the L sitting on his throne,
22:20 his left; and the L said, 'Who will entice
22:21 and stood before the L, saying, 'I will entice
22:22 entice him.' And the L said to him, 'By
22:23 Now therefore behold, the L has put a lying
22:23 these your prophets; the L has spoken evil
22:24 the Spirit of the L go from me to
22:28 return in peace, the L has not spoken by
22:38 the word of the L which he had spoken.
22:43 the sight of the L; yet the high places
22:52 the sight of the L, and walked in the
22:53 him, and provoked the L, the God of Israel,
2Kgs 1:3 the angel of the L said to Elijah the
1:4 therefore thus says the L, 'You shall not come
1:6 him, Thus says the L, Is it because there
1:15 the angel of the L said to Elijah, "Go
1:16 him, "Thus says the L, 'Because you have sent
1:17 the word of the L which Elijah had spoken.
2:1 Now when the L was about to take Elijah
2:2 pray you; for the L has sent me as
2:2 Elisha said, "As the L lives, and as you
2:3 know that today the L will take away your
2:4 pray you; for the L has sent me to
2:4 he said, "As the L lives, and as you
2:5 know that today the L will take away your
2:6 pray you; for the L has sent me to
2:6 he said, "As the L lives, and as you
2:14 saying, "Where is the L, the God of Elijah?"
2:16 the Spirit of the L has caught him up
2:19 is pleasant, as my L sees; but the water
2:21 said, "Thus says the L, I have made this
2:24 he cursed them in the name of the L
3:2 the sight of the L, though not like his
3:10 The L has called these three kings to give
3:11 no prophet of the L here, through whom we
3:11 here, through whom we may inquire of the L
3:12 "The word of the L is with him." So
3:13 "No; it is the L who has called these
3:14 Elisha said, "As the L of hosts lives, whom
3:15 the power of the L came upon him.
3:16 said, "Thus says the L, 'I will make this
3:17 For thus says the L, 'You shall not see
3:18 the sight of the L; he will also give
4:1 your servant feared the L, but the creditor has
4:16 she said, "No, my L, O man of God;
4:27 bitter distress; and the L has hidden it from
4:28 "Did I ask my L for a son?
4:30 child said, "As the L lives, and as you
4:33 the two of them, and prayed to the L
4:43 for thus says the L, 'They shall eat and
4:44 some left, according to the word of the L
5:1 because by him the L had given victory to
5:3 mistress, "Would that my L were with the prophet
5:4 in and told his L, "Thus and so spoke
5:11 the name of the L his God, and wave
5:16 he said, "As the L lives, whom I serve,
5:17 offering or sacrifice to any god but the L
5:18 this matter may the L pardon your servant: when
5:18 house of Rimmon, the L pardon your servant in
5:20 As the L lives, I will run after him,
6:12 servants said, "None, my L, O king; but Elisha,
6:17 prayed, and said, "O L, I pray thee, open
6:17 So the L opened the eyes of the young
6:18 Elisha prayed to the L, and said, "Strike this
6:20 Samaria, Elisha said, "O L, open the eyes of
6:20 So the L opened their eyes, and they saw;
6:26 him, saying, "Help, my L, O king!"
6:27 he said, "If the L will not help you,
6:33 him and said, "This trouble is from the L
6:33 I wait for the L any longer?"
7:1 the word of the L: thus says the LORD,
7:1 LORD: thus says the L, Tomorrow about this time
7:2 of God, "If the L himself should make windows
7:6 For the L had made the army of the
7:16 a shekel, according to the word of the L
7:19 of God, "If the L himself should make windows
8:1 you can; for the L has called for a
8:5 And Gehazi said, "My L, O king, here is
8:8 and inquire of the L through him, saying, 'Shall
8:10 certainly recover'; but the L has shown me that
8:12 "Why does my L weep?" He answered, "Because
8:13 Elisha answered, "The L has shown me that you
8:18 what was evil in the sight of the L
8:19 Yet the L would not destroy Judah, for the
8:27 the sight of the L, as the house of
9:3 say, 'Thus says the L, I anoint you king
9:6 him, "Thus says the L the God of Israel,
9:6 the people of the L, over Israel.
9:7 the blood of all the servants of the L
9:12 saying, 'Thus says the L, I anoint you king
9:25 his father, how the L uttered this oracle against
9:26 his sons--says the L --I will requite you
9:26 ground, in accordance with the word of the L
9:36 the word of the L, which he spoke by
10:10 the word of the L, which the LORD spoke
10:10 the LORD, which the L spoke concerning the house
10:10 of Ahab; for the L has done what he
10:16 with me, and see my zeal for the L
10:17 the word of the L which he spoke to
10:23 no servant of the L here among you, but
10:30 And the L said to Jehu, "Because you have
10:31 the law of the L the God of Israel
10:32 In those days the L began to cut off
11:3 the house of the L, while Athaliah reigned over
11:4 the house of the L; and he made a
11:4 the house of the L, and he showed them
11:7 the house of the L,
11:10 the house of the L;
11:13 the house of the L to the people;
11:15 not be slain in the house of the L
11:17 a covenant between the L and the king and
11:17 they should be the L's people; and also between
11:18 priest posted watchmen over the house of the L
11:19 the house of the L, marching through the gate
12:2 the eyes of the L all his days, because
12:4 the house of the L, the money for which
12:4 the house of the L,
12:9 the house of the L; and the priests who
12:9 that was brought into the house of the L
12:10 that was found in the house of the L
12:11 the house of the L; and they paid it
12:11 the house of the L,
12:12 the house of the L, and for any outlay
12:13 the house of the L basins of silver, snuffers,
12:13 the house of the L,
12:14 the house of the L with it.
12:16 the house of the L; it belonged to the
12:18 the house of the L and of the king's
13:2 the sight of the L, and followed the sins
13:3 the anger of the L was kindled against Israel,
13:4 Jehoahaz besought the L, and the LORD hearkened
13:4 the LORD, and the L hearkened to him; for
13:5 (Therefore the L gave Israel a savior, so that

L

13:11 the sight of the L; he did not depart
13:17 And he said, "The L's arrow of victory, the
13:23 But the L was gracious to them and had
14:3 the eyes of the L, yet not like David
14:6 Moses, where the L commanded, "The fathers shall
14:14 the house of the L and in the treasuries
14:24 the sight of the L; he did not depart
14:25 the word of the L, the God of Israel,
14:26 For the L saw that the affliction of Israel
14:27 But the L had not said that he would
15:3 the eyes of the L, according to all that
15:5 And the L smote the king, so that he
15:9 the sight of the L, as his fathers had
15:12 the promise of the L which he gave to
15:18 the sight of the L; he did not depart
15:24 the sight of the L; he did not turn
15:28 the sight of the L; he did not depart
15:34 the eyes of the L, according to all that
15:35 the upper gate of the house of the L
15:37 In those days the L began to send Rezin
16:2 the eyes of the L his God, as his
16:3 the nations whom the L drove out before the
16:8 the house of the L and in the treasures
16:14 which was before the L he removed from the
16:14 the house of the L, and put it on
16:18 the house of the L, because of the king
17:2 the sight of the L, yet not as the
17:7 had sinned against the L their God, who had
17:8 the nations whom the L drove out before the
17:9 did secretly against the L their God things that
17:11 nations did whom the L carried away before them.
17:11 wicked things, provoking the L to anger,
17:12 idols, of which the L had said to them,
17:13 Yet the L warned Israel and Judah by every
17:14 not believe in the L their God.
17:15 them, concerning whom the L had commanded them
17:16 the commandments of the L their God, and made
17:17 the sight of the L, provoking him to anger.
17:18 Therefore the L was very angry with Israel, and
17:19 the commandments of the L their God, but walked
17:20 And the L rejected all the descendants of Israel,
17:21 Israel from following the L and made them commit
17:23 from them, until the L removed Israel out of
17:25 did not fear the L; therefore the LORD sent
17:25 the LORD; therefore the L sent lions among them,
17:28 and taught them how they should fear the L
17:32 They also feared the L, and appointed from among
17:33 So they feared the L but also served their
17:34 do not fear the L, and they do not
17:34 commandment which the L commanded the children
17:35 The L made a covenant with them, and commanded
17:36 you shall fear the L, who brought you out
17:39 you shall fear the L your God, and he
17:41 these nations feared the L, and also served their
18:3 the eyes of the L, according to all that
18:5 He trusted in the L the God of Israel;
18:6 held fast to the L; he did not depart
18:6 the commandments which the L commanded Moses.
18:7 And the L was with him; wherever he went
18:12 the voice of the L their God but transgressed
18:12 servant of the L commanded; they neither listened
18:15 the house of the L, and in the treasuries
18:16 the temple of the L, and from the doorposts
18:22 "We rely on the L our God," is it
18:25 is it without the L that I have come
18:25 The L said to me, Go up against this
18:30 to rely on the L by saying, The LORD
18:30 LORD by saying, The L will surely deliver us,
18:32 you by saying, The L will deliver us.
18:35 my hand, that the L should deliver Jerusalem out
19:1 sackcloth, and went into the house of the L
19:4 may be that the L your God heard all
19:4 the words which the L your God has heard;
19:6 master, 'Thus says the L: Do not be afraid
19:14 the house of the L, and spread it before
19:14 of the LORD, and spread it before the L
19:15 Hezekiah prayed before the L, and said: "O LORD
19:15 LORD, and said: "O L the God of Israel,
19:16 Incline thy ear, O L, and hear; open thy
19:16 open thy eyes, O L, and see; and hear
19:17 Of a truth, O L, the kings of Assyria
19:19 So now, O L our God, save us, I
19:19 know that thou, O L, art God alone."
19:20 saying, "Thus says the L, the God of Israel:
19:21 the word that the L has spoken concerning him:
19:23 you have mocked the L, and you have said,
19:31 The zeal of the L will do this.
19:32 "Therefore thus says the L concerning the king of
19:33 shall not come into this city, says the L
19:35 the angel of the L went forth, and slew
20:1 him, "Thus says the L, 'Set your house in
20:2 and prayed to the L, saying,
20:3 saying, "Remember now, O L, I beseech thee, how
20:4 the word of the L came to him:
20:5 people, Thus says the L, the God of David
20:5 shall go up to the house of the L
20:8 the sign that the L will heal me, and
20:8 the house of the L on the third day?"
20:9 to you from the L, that the LORD will
20:9 the LORD, that the L will do the thing
20:11 prophet cried to the L; and he brought the
20:16 the word of the L:
20:17 to Babylon; nothing shall be left, says the L
20:19 "The word of the L which you have spoken
21:2 the sight of the L, according to the abominable
21:2 the nations whom the L drove out before the
21:4 the house of the L, of which the LORD
21:4 LORD, of which the L had said, "In Jerusalem
21:5 the two courts of the house of the L
21:6 the sight of the L, provoking him to anger.
21:7 house of which the L said to David and
21:9 had done whom the L destroyed before the people
21:10 And the L said by his servants the prophets,
21:12 therefore thus says the L, the God of Israel,
21:16 what was evil in the sight of the L
21:20 the sight of the L, as Manasseh his father
21:22 them; he forsook the L, the God of his
21:22 did not walk in the way of the L
22:2 the eyes of the L, and walked in all
22:3 the house of the L, saying,
22:4 the house of the L, which the keepers of
22:5 the house of the L; and let them give
22:5 the house of the L, repairing the house,
22:8 of the law in the house of the L
22:9 have the oversight of the house of the L
22:13 "Go, inquire of the L for me, and for
22:13 the wrath of the L that is kindled against
22:15 them, "Thus says the L, the God of Israel:
22:16 me, Thus says the L, Behold, I will bring
22:18 to inquire of the L, thus shall you say
22:18 him, Thus says the L, the God of Israel:
22:19 humbled yourself before the L, when you heard how
22:19 me, I also have heard you, says the L
23:2 the house of the L, and with him all
23:2 had been found in the house of the L
23:3 a covenant before the L, to walk after the
23:3 to walk after the L and to keep his
23:4 the temple of the L all the vessels made
23:6 the house of the L, outside Jerusalem, to the
23:7 the house of the L, where the women wove
23:9 the altar of the L in Jerusalem, but they
23:11 the house of the L, by the chamber of
23:12 the house of the L, he pulled down and
23:16 the word of the L which the man of
23:19 had made, provoking the L to anger, Josiah removed;
23:21 the passover to the L your God, as it
23:23 was kept to the L in Jerusalem.
23:24 the priest found in the house of the L
23:25 who turned to the L with all his heart
23:26 Still the L did not turn from the fierceness
23:27 And the L said, "I will remove Judah also
23:32 the sight of the L, according to all that
23:37 the sight of the L, according to all that
24:2 And the L sent against him bands of the
24:2 the word of the L which he spoke by
24:3 the command of the L, to remove them out
24:4 innocent blood, and the L would not pardon.
24:9 the sight of the L, according to all that
24:13 the house of the L, and the treasures of
24:13 the temple of the L, which Solomon king of
24:13 had made, as the L had foretold.
24:19 the sight of the L, according to all that
24:20 the anger of the L it came to the
25:9 the house of the L, and the king's house
25:13 the house of the L, and the stands and
25:13 the house of the L, the Chaldeans broke in
25:16 the house of the L, the bronze of all
1Chr 2:3 the sight of the L, and he slew him.
6:15 into exile when the L sent Judah and Jerusalem
6:31 the house of the L, after the ark rested
6:32 the house of the L in Jerusalem; and they
9:19 the camp of the L, keepers of the entrance.

9:20 in time past; the L was with him.
9:23 the house of the L, that is, the house
10:13 was unfaithful to the L in that he did
10:13 the command of the L, and also consulted a
10:14 guidance, and did not seek guidance from the L
10:14 Therefore the L slew him, and turned the kingdom
11:2 in Israel; and the L your God said to
11:3 at Hebron before the L, and they anointed David
11:3 the word of the L by Samuel.
11:9 and greater, for the L of hosts was with
11:10 the word of the L concerning Israel.
11:14 the Philistines; and the L saved them by a
11:18 it out to the L,
12:23 to him, according to the word of the L
13:2 the will of the L our God, let us
13:6 the name of the L who sits enthroned above
13:10 the anger of the L was kindled against Uzzah;
13:11 was angry because the L had broken forth upon
13:14 three months; and the L blessed the household of
14:2 David perceived that the L had established him king
14:10 And the L said to him, "Go up, and
14:17 all lands, and the L brought the fear of
15:2 of God, for the L chose them to carry
15:2 the ark of the L and to minister to
15:3 the ark of the L to its place, which
15:12 the ark of the L, the God of Israel,
15:13 the first time, the L our God broke forth
15:14 the ark of the L, the God of Israel.
15:15 had commanded according to the word of the L
15:25 the covenant of the L from the house of
15:26 the covenant of the L, they sacrificed seven bulls
15:28 the covenant of the L with shouting, to the
15:29 the covenant of the L came to the city
16:2 the name of the L,
16:4 the ark of the L, to invoke, to thank,
16:4 and to praise the L, the God of Israel.
16:7 be sung to the L by Asaph and his
16:8 give thanks to the L, call on his name,
16:10 those who seek the L rejoice!
16:11 Seek the L and his strength, seek his presence
16:14 He is the L our God; his judgments are
16:23 Sing to the L, all the earth!
16:25 For great is the L, and greatly to be
16:26 are idols; but the L made the heavens.
16:28 Ascribe to the L, O families of the peoples,
16:28 peoples, ascribe to the L glory and strength!
16:29 Ascribe to the L the glory due his name;
16:29 Worship the L in holy array;
16:31 among the nations, "The L reigns!"
16:33 for joy before the L, for he comes to
16:34 give thanks to the L, for he is good;
16:36 Blessed be the L, the God of Israel, from
16:36 and praised the L
16:37 the covenant of the L to minister continually before
16:39 the tabernacle of the L in the high place
16:40 burnt offerings to the L upon the altar of
16:40 the law of the L which he commanded Israel.
16:41 give thanks to the L, for his steadfast love
17:1 the covenant of the L is under a tent."
17:3 the word of the L came to Nathan,
17:4 David, 'Thus says the L: You shall not build
17:7 David, 'Thus says the L of hosts, I took
17:10 to you that the L will build you a
17:16 and sat before the L, and said, "Who am
17:16 "Who am I, O L God, and what is
17:17 me future generations, O L God!
17:19 thy servant's sake, O L, and according to thy
17:20 none like thee, O L, and there is no
17:22 ever; and thou, O L, didst become their God.
17:23 And now, O L, let the word which thou
17:24 for ever, saying, 'The L of hosts, the God
17:26 And now, O L, thou art God, and thou
17:27 for what thou, O L, hast blessed is blessed
18:6 And the L gave victory to David wherever he
18:11 David dedicated to the L, together with the silver
18:13 And the L gave victory to David wherever he
19:13 God; and may the L do what seems good
21:3 Joab said, "May the L add to his people
21:3 Are they not, my L the king, all of
21:3 all of them my L's servants?
21:3 Why then should my L require this?
21:9 And the L spoke to Gad, David's seer, saying,
21:10 David, 'Thus says the L, Three things I offer
21:11 him, "Thus says the L, 'Take which you will:
21:12 the sword of the L, pestilence upon the land,
21:12 the angel of the L destroying throughout all the
21:13 the hand of the L, for his mercy is
21:14 So the L sent a pestilence upon Israel; and
21:15 to destroy it, the L saw, and he repented
21:15 the angel of the L was standing by the
21:16 the angel of the L standing between earth and
21:17 I pray thee, O L my God, be against
21:18 the angel of the L commanded Gad to say
21:18 an altar to the L on the threshing floor
21:19 he had spoken in the name of the L
21:22 an altar to the L --give it to me
21:23 it; and let my L the king do what
21:24 not take for the L what is yours, nor
21:26 an altar to the L and presented burnt offerings
21:26 and called upon the L, and he answered him
21:27 Then the L commanded the angel; and he put
21:28 David saw that the L had answered him at
21:29 the tabernacle of the L, which Moses had made
21:30 of the sword of the angel of the L
22:1 the house of the L God and here the
22:5 be built for the L must be exceedingly magnificent,
22:6 a house for the L, the God of Israel.
22:7 the name of the L my God.
22:8 the word of the L came to me, saying,
22:11 Now, my son, the L be with you, so
22:11 the house of the L your God, as he
22:12 may the L grant you discretion and understanding,
22:12 the law of the L your God.
22:13 ordinances which the L commanded Moses for
22:14 the house of the L a hundred thousand talents
22:16 The L be with you!"
22:18 saying, "Is not the L your God with you?
22:18 is subdued before the L and his people.
22:19 heart to seek the L your God.
22:19 the sanctuary of the L God, so that the
22:19 the covenant of the L and the holy vessels
22:19 a house built for the name of the L
23:4 the house of the L, six thousand shall be
23:5 offer praises to the L with the instruments which
23:13 burn incense before the L, and minister to him
23:24 for the service of the house of the L
23:25 For David said, "The L, the God of Israel,
23:28 the house of the L, having the care of
23:30 thanking and praising the L, and likewise at evening,
23:31 are offered to the L on sabbaths, new moons,
23:31 number required of them, continually before the L
23:32 for the service of the house of the L
24:19 the house of the L according to the procedure
24:19 their father, as the L God of Israel had
25:3 the lyre in thanksgiving and praise to the L
25:6 the house of the L with cymbals, harps, and
25:7 in singing to the L, all who were skilful,
26:12 the house of the L;
26:22 of the treasuries of the house of the L
26:27 for the maintenance of the house of the L
26:30 the work of the L and for the service
27:23 of age, for the L had promised to make
28:2 the covenant of the L, and for the footstool
28:4 shed blood.' Yet the L God of Israel chose
28:5 my sons (for the L has given me many
28:5 the kingdom of the L over Israel.
28:8 the assembly of the L, and in the hearing
28:8 the commandments of the L your God; that you
28:9 willing mind; for the L searches all hearts, and
28:10 heed now, for the L has chosen you to
28:12 the house of the L, all the surrounding chambers,
28:13 the house of the L; for all the vessels
28:13 the house of the L,
28:18 covered the ark of the covenant of the L
28:19 the hand of the L concerning it, all the
28:20 not dismayed; for the L God, even my God,
28:20 the house of the L is finished.
29:1 man but for the L God.
29:5 offer willingly, consecrating himself today to the L
29:8 the house of the L, in the care of
29:9 offered freely to the L; David the king also
29:10 Therefore David blessed the L in the presence of
29:10 "Blessed art thou, O L, the God of Israel
29:11 Thine, O L, is the greatness, and the power,
29:11 is the kingdom, O L, and thou art exalted
29:16 O L our God, all this abundance that we
29:18 O L, the God of Abraham, Isaac, and Israel,
29:20 the assembly, "Bless the L your God." And all
29:20 the assembly blessed the L, the God of their
29:20 heads, and worshiped the L, and did obeisance to
29:21 performed sacrifices to the L, and on the next
29:21 burnt offerings to the L, a thousand bulls, a

29:22 and drank before the L on that day with
29:22 as prince for the L, and Zadok as priest.
29:23 the throne of the L as king instead of
29:25 And the L gave Solomon great repute in the
2Chr 1:1 his kingdom, and the L his God was with
1:3 the servant of the L had made in the
1:5 made, was there before the tabernacle of the L
1:5 And Solomon and the assembly sought the L
1:6 bronze altar before the L, which was at the
1:9 O L God, let thy promise to David my
2:1 the name of the L, and a royal palace
2:4 the name of the L my God and dedicate
2:4 appointed feasts of the L our God, as ordained
2:11 to Solomon, "Because the L loves his people he
2:12 said, "Blessed be the L God of Israel, who
2:12 a temple for the L, and a royal palace
2:14 the craftsmen of my L, David your father.
2:15 wine, of which my L has spoken, let him
3:1 the house of the L in Jerusalem on Mount
3:1 Mount Moriah, where the L had appeared to David
4:16 for King Solomon for the house of the L
5:1 the house of the L was finished.
5:2 the covenant of the L out of the city
5:7 the covenant of the L to its place, in
5:10 at Horeb, where the L made a covenant with
5:13 and thanksgiving to the L, and when the song
5:13 in praise to the L, "For he is good,
5:13 the house of the L, was filled with a
5:14 the glory of the L filled the house of
6:1 Then Solomon said, "The L has said that he
6:4 said, "Blessed be the L, the God of Israel,
6:7 the name of the L, the God of Israel.
6:8 But the L said to David my father, 'Whereas
6:10 my name.' Now the L has fulfilled his promise
6:10 of Israel, as the L promised, and I have
6:10 the name of the L, the God of Israel.
6:11 the covenant of the L which he made with
6:12 the altar of the L in the presence of
6:14 heaven; and said, "O L, God of Israel, there
6:16 Now therefore, O L, God of Israel, keep with
6:17 me.' Now therefore, O L, God of Israel, let
6:19 to his supplication, O L my God, hearkening to
6:41 "And now arise, O L God, and go to
6:41 Let thy priests, O L God, be clothed with
6:42 O L God, do not turn away the face
7:1 the glory of the L filled the temple.
7:2 the house of the L, because the glory of
7:2 the glory of the L filled the LORD's house.
7:2 the LORD filled the L's house.
7:3 the glory of the L upon the temple, they
7:3 gave thanks to the L, saying, "For he is
7:4 and all the people offered sacrifice before the L
7:6 for music to the L which King David had
7:6 giving thanks to the L—for his steadfast love
7:7 the house of the L; for there he offered
7:10 the goodness that the L had shown to David
7:11 the house of the L and the king's house;
7:11 the house of the L and in his own
7:12 Then the L appeared to Solomon in the night
7:21 say, 'Why has the L done thus to this
7:22 'Because they forsook the L the God of their
8:1 the house of the L and his own house,
8:11 the ark of the L has come are holy."
8:12 burnt offerings to the L upon the altar of
8:12 the altar of the L which he had built
8:16 the house of the L was laid until it
8:16 the house of the L was completed.
9:4 the house of the L, there was no more
9:8 Blessed be the L your God, who has delighted
9:8 as king for the L your God!
9:11 the house of the L and for the king's
10:15 by God that the L might fulfil his word,
11:2 the word of the L came to Shemaiah the
11:4 Benjamin, 'Thus says the L, You shall not go
11:4 the word of the L, and returned and did
11:14 as priests of the L,
11:16 hearts to seek the L God of Israel came
11:16 to sacrifice to the L, the God of their
12:1 the law of the L, and all Israel with
12:2 been unfaithful to the L, Shishak king of Egypt
12:5 them, "Thus says the L, 'You abandoned me, so
12:6 themselves and said, "The L is righteous."
12:7 When the L saw that they humbled themselves, the
12:7 the word of the L came to Shemaiah: "They
12:9 the house of the L and the treasures of
12:11 the house of the L, the guard came and
12:12 the wrath of the L turned from him, so
12:13 the city which the L had chosen out of
12:14 did not set his heart to seek the L
13:5 to know that the L God of Israel gave
13:6 and rebelled against his L;
13:8 the kingdom of the L in the hand of
13:9 the priests of the L, the sons of Aaron,
13:10 as for us, the L is our God, and
13:10 priests ministering to the L who are sons of
13:11 They offer to the L every morning and every
13:11 the charge of the L our God, but you
13:12 not fight against the L, the God of your
13:14 they cried to the L, and the priests blew
13:18 they relied upon the L, the God of their
13:20 of Abijah; and the L smote him, and he
14:2 the eyes of the L his God.
14:4 Judah to seek the L, the God of their
14:6 those years, for the L gave him peace.
14:7 we have sought the L our God; we have
14:11 Asa cried to the L his God, "O LORD,
14:11 LORD his God, "O L, there is none like
14:11 Help us, O L our God, for we rely
14:11 O L, thou art our God; let not man
14:12 So the L defeated the Ethiopians before Asa and
14:13 were broken before the L and his army.
14:14 the fear of the L was upon them.
15:2 Judah and Benjamin: The L is with you, while
15:4 they turned to the L, the God of Israel,
15:8 the altar of the L that was in front
15:8 of the vestibule of the house of the L
15:9 they saw that the L his God was with
15:11 They sacrificed to the L on that day, from
15:12 covenant to seek the L, the God of their
15:13 would not seek the L, the God of Israel,
15:14 took oath to the L with a loud voice,
15:15 by them, and the L gave them rest round
16:2 the house of the L and the king's house,
16:7 not rely on the L your God, the army
16:8 you relied on the L, he gave them into
16:9 the eyes of the L run to and fro
16:12 did not seek the L, but sought help from
17:3 The L was with Jehoshaphat, because he walked in
17:5 Therefore the L established the kingdom in his hand;
17:6 the ways of the L; and furthermore he took
17:9 the law of the L with them; they went
17:10 the fear of the L fell upon all the
17:16 the service of the L, with two hundred thousand
18:4 Israel, "Inquire first for the word of the L
18:6 another prophet of the L of whom we may
18:7 may inquire of the L, Micaiah the son of
18:10 said, "Thus says the L, 'With these you shall
18:11 Ramoth-gilead and triumph; the L will give it into
18:13 Micaiah said, "As the L lives, what my God
18:15 but the truth in the name of the L
18:16 no shepherd; and the L said, 'These have no
18:18 the word of the L: I saw the LORD
18:18 LORD: I saw the L sitting on his throne,
18:19 his left; and the L said, 'Who will entice
18:20 and stood before the L, saying, 'I will entice
18:20 entice him.' And the L said to him, 'By
18:22 Now therefore behold, the L has put a lying
18:22 these your prophets; the L has spoken evil
18:23 the Spirit of the L go from me to
18:27 return in peace, the L has not spoken by
18:31 cried out, and the L helped him.
19:2 the wicked and love those who hate the L
19:2 wrath has gone out against you from the L
19:4 them back to the L, the God of their
19:6 man but for the L; he is with you
19:7 the fear of the L be upon you; take
19:7 of justice with the L our God, or partiality,
19:8 give judgment for the L and to decide disputed
19:9 the fear of the L, in faithfulness, and with
19:10 incur guilt before the L and wrath may not
19:11 all matters of the L; and Zebadiah the son
19:11 courageously, and may the L be with the upright!"
20:3 himself to seek the L, and proclaimed a fast
20:4 seek help from the L; from all the cities
20:4 cities of Judah they came to seek the L
20:5 the house of the L, before the new court,
20:6 court, and said, "O L, God of our fathers,
20:13 Judah stood before the L, with their little ones,
20:14 the Spirit of the L came upon Jahaziel the
20:15 Jehoshaphat: Thus says the L to you, 'Fear not,
20:17 the victory of the L on your behalf, O
20:17 against them, and the L will be with you."

L

20:18 Jerusalem fell down before the L, worshiping the L
20:19 up to praise the L, the God of Israel,
20:20 Believe in the L your God, and you will
20:21 to sing to the L and praise him in
20:21 "Give thanks to the L, for his steadfast love
20:22 sing and praise, the L set an ambush against
20:26 there they blessed the L; therefore the name of
20:27 with joy, for the L had made them rejoice
20:28 lyres and trumpets, to the house of the L
20:29 they heard that the L had fought against the
20:32 what was right in the sight of the L
20:37 joined with Ahaziah, the L will destroy what you
21:6 what was evil in the sight of the L
21:7 Yet the L would not destroy the house of
21:10 he had forsaken the L, the God of his
21:12 saying, "Thus says the L, the God of David
21:14 than yourself; behold, the L will bring a great
21:16 And the L stirred up against Jehoram the anger
21:18 after all this the L smote him in his
22:4 the sight of the L, as the house of
22:7 of Nimshi, whom the L had anointed to destroy
22:9 Jehoshaphat, who sought the L with all his heart."
23:3 him reign, as the L spoke concerning the sons
23:5 in the courts of the house of the L
23:6 the house of the L except the priests and
23:6 the people shall keep the charge of the L
23:12 the house of the L to the people;
23:14 not slay her in the house of the L
23:16 they should be the L's people.
23:18 the house of the L under the direction of
23:18 the house of the L, to offer burnt offerings
23:18 burnt offerings to the L, as it is written
23:19 the house of the L so that no one
23:20 the house of the L, marching through the upper
24:2 the eyes of the L all the days of
24:4 Joash decided to restore the house of the L
24:6 the servant of the L, on the congregation of
24:7 the house of the L for the Baals.
24:8 outside the gate of the house of the L
24:9 bring in for the L the tax that Moses
24:12 the house of the L, and they hired masons
24:12 the house of the L, and also workers in
24:12 and bronze to repair the house of the L
24:14 the house of the L, both for the service
24:14 the house of the L continually all the days
24:18 the house of the L, the God of their
24:19 them back to the L; these testified against them,
24:20 the commandments of the L, so that you cannot
24:20 you have forsaken the L, he has forsaken you.'"
24:21 in the court of the house of the L
24:22 he said, "May the L see and avenge!"
24:24 with few men, the L delivered into their hand
24:24 they had forsaken the L, the God of their
25:2 the eyes of the L, yet not with a
25:4 of Moses, where the L commanded, "The fathers
25:7 with you, for the L is not with Israel,
25:9 of God answered, "The L is able to give
25:15 Therefore the L was angry with Amaziah and sent
25:27 turned away from the L they made a conspiracy
26:4 the eyes of the L, according to all that
26:5 as he sought the L, God made him prosper.
26:16 was false to the L his God, and entered
26:16 the temple of the L to burn incense on
26:17 eighty priests of the L who were men of
26:18 burn incense to the L, but for the priests
26:18 no honor from the L God."
26:19 the house of the L, by the altar of
26:20 go out, because the L had smitten him.
26:21 he was excluded from the house of the L
27:2 the eyes of the L according to all that
27:2 he did not invade the temple of the L
27:3 the house of the L, and did much building
27:6 his ways before the L his God.
28:1 the eyes of the L, like his father David,
28:3 the nations whom the L drove out before the
28:5 Therefore the L his God gave him into the
28:6 they had forsaken the L, the God of their
28:9 a prophet of the L was there, whose name
28:9 them, "Behold, because the L, the God of your
28:10 your own against the L your God?
28:11 fierce wrath of the L is upon you."
28:13 us guilt against the L in addition to our
28:19 For the L brought Judah low because of Ahaz
28:19 in Judah and had been faithless to the L
28:21 the house of the L and the house of
28:22 more faithless to the L–this same King Ahaz.
28:24 the house of the L; and he made himself
28:25 provoking to anger the L, the God of his
29:2 the eyes of the L, according to all that
29:3 the house of the L, and repaired them.
29:5 the house of the L, the God of your
29:6 the sight of the L our God; they have
29:6 the habitation of the L, and turned their backs.
29:8 the wrath of the L came on Judah and
29:10 a covenant with the L, the God of Israel,
29:11 be negligent, for the L has chosen you to
29:15 the words of the L, to cleanse the house
29:15 the LORD, to cleanse the house of the L
29:16 the house of the L to cleanse it, and
29:16 the temple of the L into the court of
29:16 the house of the L; and the Levites took
29:17 the vestibule of the L; then for eight days
29:17 the house of the L, and on the sixteenth
29:18 the house of the L, the altar of burnt
29:19 behold, they are before the altar of the L
29:20 and went up to the house of the L
29:21 to offer them on the altar of the L
29:25 the house of the L with cymbals, harps, and
29:25 commandment was from the L through his prophets.
29:27 the song to the L began also, and the
29:30 sing praises to the L with the words of
29:31 consecrated yourselves to the L; come near, bring
29:31 and thank offerings to the house of the L
29:32 these were for a burnt offering to the L
29:35 the house of the L was restored.
30:1 the house of the L at Jerusalem, to keep
30:1 the passover to the L the God of Israel.
30:5 the passover to the L the God of Israel,
30:6 Israel, return to the L, the God of Abraham,
30:7 were faithless to the L God of their fathers,
30:8 yield yourselves to the L, and come to his
30:8 ever, and serve the L your God, that his
30:9 you return to the L, your brethren and your
30:9 For the L your God is gracious and merciful,
30:12 the princes commanded by the word of the L
30:15 brought burnt offerings into the house of the L
30:17 not clean, to make it holy to the L
30:18 them, saying, "The good L pardon every one
30:19 to seek God, the L the God of his
30:20 And the L heard Hezekiah, and healed the people.
30:21 the priests praised the L day by day, singing
30:21 day, singing with all their might to the L
30:22 showed good skill in the service of the L
30:22 giving thanks to the L the God of their
31:2 the camp of the L and to give thanks
31:3 it is written in the law of the L
31:4 might give themselves to the law of the L
31:6 been consecrated to the L their God, and laid
31:8 heaps, they blessed the L and his people Israel.
31:10 the house of the L we have eaten and
31:10 plenty left; for the L has blessed his people,
31:11 the house of the L; and they prepared them.
31:14 contribution reserved for the L and the most holy
31:16 the house of the L as the duty of
31:20 and faithful before the L his God.
32:8 with us is the L our God, to help
32:11 he tells you, "The L our God will deliver
32:16 still more against the L GOD and against his
32:17 cast contempt on the L the God of Israel
32:21 And the L sent an angel, who cut off
32:22 So the L saved Hezekiah and the inhabitants of
32:23 brought gifts to the L to Jerusalem and precious
32:24 he prayed to the L; and he answered him
32:26 the wrath of the L did not come upon
33:2 the sight of the L, according to the abominable
33:2 the nations whom the L drove out before the
33:4 the house of the L, of which the LORD
33:4 LORD, of which the L had said, "In Jerusalem
33:5 the two courts of the house of the L
33:6 the sight of the L, provoking him to anger.
33:9 the nations whom the L destroyed before the people
33:10 The L spoke to Manasseh and to his people,
33:11 Therefore the L brought upon them the commanders
33:12 the favor of the L his God and humbled
33:13 Manasseh knew that the L was God.
33:15 the house of the L, and all the altars
33:15 the house of the L and in Jerusalem, and
33:16 the altar of the L and offered upon it
33:16 Judah to serve the L the God of Israel.
33:17 but only to the L their God.
33:18 the name of the L the God of Israel,
33:22 the sight of the L, as Manasseh his father

	33:23	humble himself before the L, as Manasseh his father
	34:2	the eyes of the L, and walked in the
	34:8	the house of the L his God.
	34:10	the house of the L; and the workmen who
	34:10	the house of the L gave it for repairing
	34:14	the house of the L, Hilkiah the priest found
	34:14	the law of the L given through Moses.
	34:15	the house of the L; and Hilkiah gave the
	34:17	the house of the L and have delivered it
	34:21	"Go, inquire of the L for me and for
	34:21	the wrath of the L that is poured out
	34:21	the word of the L, to do according to
	34:23	them, "Thus says the L, the God of Israel:
	34:24	me, Thus says the L, Behold, I will bring
	34:26	to inquire of the L, thus shall you say
	34:26	him, Thus says the L, the God of Israel:
	34:27	me, I also have heard you, says the L
	34:30	the house of the L, with all the men
	34:30	had been found in the house of the L
	34:31	a covenant before the L, to walk after the
	34:31	to walk after the L and to keep his
	34:33	in Israel serve the L their God.
	34:33	away from following the L the God of their
	35:1	a passover to the L in Jerusalem; and they
	35:2	in the service of the house of the L
	35:3	were holy to the L, "Put the holy ark
	35:3	Now serve the L your God and his people
	35:6	the word of the L by Moses."
	35:12	to offer to the L, as it is written
	35:16	the service of the L was prepared that day,
	35:16	the altar of the L, according to the command
	35:26	the law of the L,
	36:5	the sight of the L his God.
	36:7	the house of the L to Babylon and put
	36:9	what was evil in the sight of the L
	36:10	the house of the L, and made his brother
	36:12	the sight of the L his God.
	36:12	prophet, who spoke from the mouth of the L
	36:13	against turning to the L, the God of Israel.
	36:14	the house of the L which he had hallowed
	36:15	The L, the God of their fathers, sent persistently
	36:16	the wrath of the L rose against his people,
	36:18	the house of the L, and the treasures of
	36:21	the word of the L by the mouth of
	36:22	the word of the L by the mouth of
	36:22	might be accomplished, the L stirred up the spirit
	36:23	king of Persia, 'The L, the God of heaven,
	36:23	his people, may the L his God be with
Ezra	1:1	the word of the L by the mouth of
	1:1	might be accomplished, the L stirred up the spirit
	1:2	king of Persia: The L, the God of heaven,
	1:3	the house of the L, the God of Israel–
	1:5	the house of the L which is in Jerusalem;
	1:7	the house of the L which Nebuchadnezzar had
	2:68	the house of the L which is in Jerusalem,
	3:3	upon it to the L, burnt offerings morning and
	3:5	appointed feasts of the L, and the offerings of
	3:5	one who made a freewill offering to the L
	3:6	they began to offer burnt offerings to the L
	3:6	the temple of the L was not yet laid.
	3:8	of the work of the house of the L
	3:10	the temple of the L, the priests in their
	3:10	cymbals, to praise the L, according to the directions
	3:11	giving thanks to the L, "For he is good,
	3:11	when they praised the L, because the foundation of
	3:11	the house of the L was laid.
	4:1	a temple to the L, the God of Israel,
	4:3	will build to the L, the God of Israel,
	6:21	land to worship the L, the God of Israel.
	6:22	with joy; for the L had made them joyful,
	7:6	of Moses which the L the God of Israel
	7:6	the hand of the L his God was upon
	7:10	the law of the L, and to do it,
	7:11	the commandments of the L and his statutes for
	7:27	Blessed be the L, the God of our fathers,
	7:27	the house of the L which is in Jerusalem,
	7:28	the hand of the L my God was upon
	8:28	are holy to the L, and the vessels are
	8:28	freewill offering to the L, the God of your
	8:29	within the chambers of the house of the L
	8:35	all this was a burnt offering to the L
	9:5	my hands to the L my God,
	9:8	been shown by the L our God, to leave
	9:15	O L the God of Israel, thou art just,
	10:3	the counsel of my L and of those who
	10:11	make confession to the L the God of your
Neh	1:5	And I said, "O L God of heaven, the
	1:11	O L, let thy ear be attentive to the
	3:5	put their necks to the work of their L
	4:14	Remember the L, who is great and terrible, and
	5:13	and praised the L
	8:1	of Moses which the L had given to Israel.
	8:6	And Ezra blessed the L, the great God; and
	8:6	heads and worshiped the L with their faces to
	8:9	is holy to the L your God; do not
	8:10	is holy to our L; and do not be
	8:10	the joy of the L is your strength."
	8:14	the law that the L had commanded by Moses
	9:3	the law of the L their God for a
	9:3	confession and worshiped the L their God.
	9:4	loud voice to the L their God.
	9:5	up and bless the L your God from everlasting
	9:6	said: "Thou art the L, thou alone; thou hast
	9:7	Thou art the L, the God who didst choose
	10:29	the commandments of the L our Lord and his
	10:29	of the LORD our L and his ordinances and
	10:34	the altar of the L our God, as it
	10:35	the house of the L;
Tob	2:2	is mindful of the L, and I will wait
	3:2	"Righteous art thou, O L; all thy deeds and
	3:11	"Blessed art thou, O L my God, and blessed
	3:12	And now, O L, I have turned my eyes
	3:14	Thou knowest, O L, that I am innocent of
	4:5	"Remember the L our God all your days, my
	4:19	Bless the L God on every occasion; ask him
	4:19	has understanding; but the L himself gives all good
	5:19	to us by the L is enough for us."
	7:18	brave, my child; the L of heaven and earth
	8:4	us pray that the L may have mercy upon
	8:7	himself.' And now, O L, I am not taking
	8:17	Show them mercy, O L; and bring their lives
	10:12	said to Tobias, "The L of heaven bring you
	10:12	daughter Sarah, that I may rejoice before the L
	12:22	the angel of the L had appeared to them.
	13:4	because he is our L and God, he is
	13:6	Praise the L of righteousness, and exalt the King
	13:10	thanks worthily to the L, and praise the King
	13:11	the name of the L God, bearing gifts in
	13:13	and will praise the L of the righteous.
	14:2	continued to fear the L God and to praise
	14:6	turn to fear the L God in truth, and
	14:7	Gentiles will praise the L, and his people will
	14:7	to God, and the L will exalt his people.
	14:7	all who love the L God in truth and
Jud	2:5	the Great King, the L of the whole earth:
	2:15	by divisions as his L had ordered him to
	4:2	the temple of the L their God.
	4:11	heads and spread out their sackcloth before the L
	4:13	So the L heard their prayers and looked upon
	4:13	the sanctuary of the L Almighty.
	4:14	who stood before the L and ministered to the
	4:14	and ministered to the L, with their loins girded
	4:15	cried out to the L with all their might
	5:5	to him, "Let my L now hear a word
	5:20	therefore, my master and L, if there is any
	5:21	nation, then let my L pass them by; for
	5:21	them by; for their L will defend them, and
	5:24	let us go up, L Holofernes, and they will
	6:4	says King Nebuchadnezzar, the L of the whole earth.
	6:19	him, and said, "O L God of heaven, behold
	7:9	and said, "Let our L hear a word, lest
	7:11	Therefore, my L, do not fight against them in
	7:19	cried out to the L their God, for their
	7:29	and our God, the L of our fathers, who
	7:30	cried out to the L God with a loud
	7:31	by that time the L our God will restore
	8:11	our enemies unless the L turns and helps us
	8:13	You are putting the L Almighty to the test–
	8:14	do not provoke the L our God to anger.
	8:16	the purposes of the L our God; for God
	8:23	into favor, but the L our God will turn
	8:25	give thanks to the L our God, who is
	8:27	upon us; but the L scourges those who draw
	8:31	devout woman, and the L will send us rain
	8:33	to our enemies, the L will deliver Israel by
	8:35	peace, and may the L God go before you,
	9:1	cried out to the L with a loud voice,
	9:2	voice, and said, "O L God of my father
	9:7	that thou art the L who crushest wars; the
	9:7	who crushest wars; the L is thy name.
	9:12	the inheritance of Israel, L of heaven and earth,
	10:15	by hurrying down to the presence of our L

LORD

11:4 the servants of my L King Nebuchadnezzar."
11:5 nothing false to my L this night.
11:6 through you, and my L will not fail to
11:10 Therefore, my L and master, do not disregard what
11:11 in order that my L may not be defeated
11:17 and night; therefore, my L, I will remain with
11:22 bring destruction upon those who have slighted my L
12:4 your soul lives, my L, your servant will not
12:4 with me before the L carries out by my
12:6 and said, "Let my L now command that your
12:8 spring she prayed the L God of Israel to
12:13 please come to my L and be honored in
12:14 Judith said, "Who am I, to refuse my L
12:18 will drink now, my L, because my life means
13:4 in her heart, "O L God of all might,
13:7 strength this day, O L God of Israel!"
13:15 The L has struck him down by the hand
13:16 As the L lives, who has protected me in
13:18 and blessed be the L God, who created the
14:13 affairs, "Wake up our L, for the slaves have
15:8 good things which the L had done for Israel,
15:10 May the Almighty L bless you for ever!" And
16:2 tambourines, sing to my L with cymbals.
16:3 For God is the L who crushes wars; for
16:6 But the L Almighty has foiled them by the
16:12 fugitives, they perished before the army of my L
16:13 a new song: O L, thou are great and
16:16 he who fears the L shall be great for
16:17 The L Almighty will take vengeance on them in
16:19 she gave as a votive offering to the L
Esth 1:22 that every man be L in his own house
4:8 Beseech the L and speak to the king concerning
10:9 The L has saved his people; the Lord has
10:9 saved his people; the L has delivered us from
13:8 Mordecai prayed to the L, calling to remembrance
13:8 calling to remembrance all the works of the L
13:9 He said: "O L, Lord, King who rulest over
13:9 He said: "O Lord, L, King who rulest over
13:11 heaven, and thou art L of all, and there
13:11 one who can resist thee, who art the L
13:12 things; thou knowest, O L, that it was to
13:14 thee, who art my L; and I will not
13:15 And now, O L God and King, God of
13:17 to thy name, O L; do not destroy the
14:1 anxiety, fled to the L;
14:3 she prayed to the L God of Israel, and
14:3 and said: "O my L, thou only art our
14:5 family that thou, O L, didst take Israel out
14:7 Thou art righteous, O L
14:11 O L, do not surrender thy scepter to what
14:12 Remember, O L; make thyself known in this time
14:14 alone and have no helper but thee, O L
14:18 except in thee, O L God of Abraham.
15:13 "I saw you, my L, like an angel of
15:14 you are wonderful, my L, and your countenance is
Job 1:6 present themselves before the L, and Satan also
1:7 The L said to Satan, "Whence have you come?"
1:7 Satan answered the L, "From going to and fro
1:8 And the L said to Satan, "Have you considered
1:9 Then Satan answered the L, "Does Job fear God
1:12 And the L said to Satan, "Behold, all that
1:12 Satan went forth from the presence of the L
1:21 shall I return; the L gave, and the LORD
1:21 LORD gave, and the L has taken away; blessed
1:21 taken away; blessed be the name of the L
2:1 present themselves before the L, and Satan also
2:1 came among them to present himself before the L
2:2 And the L said to Satan, "Whence have you
2:2 Satan answered the L, "From going to and fro
2:3 And the L said to Satan, "Have you considered
2:4 Then Satan answered the L, "Skin for skin!
2:6 And the L said to Satan, "Behold, he is
2:7 the presence of the L, and afflicted Job with
12:9 the hand of the L has done this?
28:28 the fear of the L, that is wisdom; and
38:1 Then the L answered Job out of the whirlwind:
40:1 And the L said to Job:
40:3 Then Job answered the L:
40:6 Then the L answered Job out of the whirlwind:
42:1 Then Job answered the L:
42:7 After the L had spoken these words to Job,
42:7 words to Job, the L said to Eliphaz the
42:9 and did what the L had told them; and
42:9 told them; and the L accepted Job's prayer.
42:10 And the L restored the fortunes of Job, when
42:10 his friends; and the L gave Job twice as
42:11 the evil that the L had brought upon him;
42:12 And the L blessed the latter days of Job
Ps 1:2 the law of the L, and on his law
1:6 the righteous; for the L knows the way of
2:2 counsel together, against the L and his anointed,
2:4 the heavens laughs; the L has them in derision.
2:7 the decree of the L: He said to me,
2:11 Serve the L with fear, with trembling
3:1 O L, how many are my foes!
3:3 [Selah] But thou, O L, art a shield about
3:4 cry aloud to the L, and he answers me
3:5 wake again, for the L sustains me.
3:7 Arise, O L
3:8 Deliverance belongs to the L; thy blessing be upon
4:3 But know that the L has set apart the
4:3 godly for himself; the L hears when I call
4:5 right sacrifices, and put your trust in the L
4:6 the light of thy countenance upon us, O L
4:8 for thou alone, O L, makest me dwell in
5:1 to my words, O L; give heed to my
5:3 O L, in the morning thou dost hear my
5:6 who speak lies; the L abhors bloodthirsty and
5:8 Lead me, O L, in thy righteousness because of
5:12 bless the righteous, O L; thou dost cover him
6:1 O L, rebuke me not in thy anger, nor
6:2 gracious to me, O L, for I am languishing;
6:2 I am languishing; O L, heal me, for my
6:3 But thou, O L --how long?
6:4 Turn, O L, save my life; deliver me for
6:8 of evil; for the L has heard the sound
6:9 The L has heard my supplication; the LORD accepts
6:9 heard my supplication; the L accepts my prayer.
7:1 O L my God, in thee do I take
7:3 O L my God, if I have done this,
7:6 [Selah] Arise, O L, in thy anger, lift thyself
7:8 The L judges the peoples; judge me, O LORD,
7:8 judge me, O L, according to my righteousness
7:17 will give to the L the thanks due to
7:17 the name of the L, the Most High.
8:1 O L, our Lord, how majestic is thy name
8:1 O LORD, our L, how majestic is thy name
8:9 O L, our Lord, how majestic is thy name
8:9 O LORD, our L, how majestic is thy name
9:1 give thanks to the L with my whole heart;
9:7 But the L sits enthroned for ever, he has
9:9 The L is a stronghold for the oppressed, a
9:10 thee, for thou, O L, hast not forsaken those
9:11 Sing praises to the L, who dwells in Zion!
9:13 Be gracious to me, O L
9:16 The L has made himself known, he has executed
9:19 Arise, O L
9:20 Put them in fear, O L
10:1 [Selah] Why dost thou stand afar off, O L
10:3 man greedy for gain curses and renounces the L
10:12 Arise, O L; O God, lift up thy hand;
10:16 The L is king for ever and ever; the
10:17 O L, thou wilt hear the desire of the
11:1 In the L I take refuge; how can you
11:4 The L is in his holy temple, the LORD's
11:4 his holy temple, the L's throne is in heaven;
11:5 The L tests the righteous and the wicked, and
11:7 For the L is righteous, he loves righteous deeds;
12:1 Help, L; for there is no longer any that
12:3 May the L cut off all flattering lips, the
12:5 says the L; "I will place him in the
12:6 The promises of the L are promises that are
12:7 Do thou, O L, protect us, guard us ever
13:1 How long, O L
13:3 and answer me, O L my God; lighten my
13:6 will sing to the L, because he has dealt
14:2 The L looks down from heaven upon the children
14:4 eat bread, and do not call upon the L
14:6 the poor, but the L is his refuge.
14:7 When the L restores the fortunes of his people,
15:1 O L, who shall sojourn in thy tent?
15:4 those who fear the L; who swears to his
16:2 I say to the L, "Thou art my Lord;
16:2 LORD, "Thou art my L; I have no good
16:5 The L is my chosen portion and my cup;
16:7 I bless the L who gives me counsel; in
16:8 I keep the L always before me; because he
17:1 a just cause, O L; attend to my cry!
17:13 Arise, O L
17:14 by thy hand, O L, from men whose portion
18:1 I love thee, O L, my strength.
18:2 The L is my rock, and my fortress, and

18:3 I call upon the L, who is worthy to
18:6 I called upon the L; to my God I
18:13 The L also thundered in the heavens, and the
18:15 at thy rebuke, O L, at the blast of
18:18 my calamity; but the L was my stay.
18:20 The L rewarded me according to my righteousness;
18:21 the ways of the L, and have not wickedly
18:24 Therefore the L has recompensed me according to
18:28 light my lamp; the L my God lightens my
18:30 the promise of the L proves true; he is
18:31 For who is God, but the L
18:41 they cried to the L, but he did not
18:46 The L lives; and blessed be my rock, and
18:49 will extol thee, O L, among the nations, and
19:7 The law of the L is perfect, reviving the
19:7 the testimony of the L is sure, making wise
19:8 the precepts of the L are right, rejoicing the
19:8 the commandment of the L is pure, enlightening the
19:9 the fear of the L is clean, enduring for
19:9 the ordinances of the L are true, and righteous
19:14 in thy sight, O L, my rock and my
20:1 The L answer you in the day of trouble!
20:5 May the L fulfil all your petitions!
20:6 I know that the L will help his anointed;
20:7 the name of the L our God.
20:9 to the king, O L; answer us when we
21:1 the king rejoices, O L; and in thy help
21:7 king trusts in the L; and through the steadfast
21:9 The L will swallow them up in his wrath;
21:13 Be exalted, O L, in thy strength!
22:8 his cause to the L; let him deliver him,
22:19 But thou, O L, be not far-off!
22:23 You who fear the L, praise him!
22:26 satisfied; those who seek him shall praise the L
22:27 and turn to the L; and all the families
22:28 dominion belongs to the L, and he rules over
22:30 shall tell of the L to the coming generation,
23:1 The L is my shepherd, I shall not want;
23:6 the house of the L for ever.
24:1 The earth is the L's and the fulness thereof,
24:3 Who shall ascend the hill of the L
24:5 receive blessing from the L, and vindication from the
24:8 The L, strong and mighty, the LORD, mighty in
24:8 strong and mighty, the L, mighty in battle!
24:10 The L of hosts, he is the King of
25:1 [Selah] To thee, O L, I lift up my
25:4 know thy ways, O L; teach me thy paths.
25:6 of thy mercy, O L, and of thy steadfast
25:7 love remember me, for thy goodness' sake, O L
25:8 and upright is the L; therefore he instructs sinners
25:10 the paths of the L are steadfast love and
25:11 thy name's sake, O L, pardon my guilt, for
25:12 Who is the man that fears the L
25:14 The friendship of the L is for those who
25:15 are ever toward the L, for he will pluck
26:1 Vindicate me, O L, for I have walked in
26:1 have trusted in the L without wavering.
26:2 Prove me, O L, and try me; test my
26:6 about thy altar, O L,
26:8 O L, I love the habitation of thy house,
26:12 in the great congregation I will bless the L
27:1 The L is my light and my salvation; whom
27:1 The L is the stronghold of my life; of
27:4 I asked of the L, that will I seek
27:4 the house of the L all the days of
27:4 the beauty of the L, and to inquire in
27:6 I will sing and make melody to the L
27:7 Hear, O L, when I cry aloud, be gracious
27:8 to thee, "Thy face, L, do I seek."
27:10 forsaken me, but the L will take me up.
27:11 me thy way, O L; and lead me on
27:13 the goodness of the L in the land of
27:14 Wait for the L; be strong, and let your
27:14 your heart take courage; yea, wait for the L
28:1 To thee, O L, I call; my rock, be
28:5 the works of the L, or the work of
28:6 Blessed be the L
28:7 The L is my strength and my shield; in
28:8 The L is the strength of his people, he
29:1 Ascribe to the L, O heavenly beings, ascribe to
29:1 beings, ascribe to the L glory and strength.
29:2 Ascribe to the L the glory of his name;
29:2 his name; worship the L in holy array.
29:3 The voice of the L is upon the waters;
29:3 of glory thunders, the L, upon many waters.
29:4 The voice of the L is powerful, the voice
29:4 the voice of the L is full of majesty.
29:5 The voice of the L breaks the cedars, the
29:5 breaks the cedars, the L breaks the cedars of
29:7 The voice of the L flashes forth flames of
29:8 The voice of the L shakes the wilderness, the
29:8 shakes the wilderness, the L shakes the wilderness
29:9 The voice of the L makes the oaks to
29:10 The L sits enthroned over the flood; the LORD
29:10 over the flood; the L sits enthroned as king
29:11 May the L give strength to his people!
29:11 May the L bless his people with peace!
30:1 will extol thee, O L, for thou hast drawn
30:2 O L my God, I cried to thee for
30:3 O L, thou hast brought up my soul from
30:4 Sing praises to the L, O you his saints,
30:7 By thy favor, O L, thou hadst established me
30:8 To thee, O L, I cried; and to the
30:8 cried; and to the L I made supplication:
30:10 Hear, O L, and be gracious to me!
30:10 O L, be thou my helper!"
30:12 O L my God, I will give thanks to
31:1 In thee, O L, do I seek refuge; let
31:5 hast redeemed me, O L, faithful God.
31:6 to vain idols; but I trust in the L
31:9 gracious to me, O L, for I am in
31:14 trust in thee, O L, I say, "Thou art
31:17 put to shame, O L, for I call on
31:21 Blessed be the L, for he has wondrously shown
31:23 Love the L, all you his saints!
31:23 The L preserves the faithful, but abundantly requites
31:24 take courage, all you who wait for the L
32:2 man to whom the L imputes no iniquity, and
32:5 my transgressions to the L; then thou didst forgive
32:10 steadfast love surrounds him who trusts in the L
32:11 Be glad in the L, and rejoice, O righteous,
33:1 Rejoice in the L, O you righteous!
33:2 Praise the L with the lyre, make melody to
33:4 the word of the L is upright; and all
33:5 is full of the steadfast love of the L
33:6 the word of the L the heavens were made,
33:8 the earth fear the L, let all the inhabitants
33:10 The L brings the counsel of the nations to
33:11 The counsel of the L stands for ever, the
33:12 whose God is the L, the people whom he
33:13 The L looks down from heaven, he sees all
33:18 the eye of the L is on those who
33:20 soul waits for the L; he is our help
33:22 thy steadfast love, O L, be upon us, even
34:1 I will bless the L at all times; his
34:2 its boast in the L; let the afflicted hear
34:3 O magnify the L with me, and let us
34:4 I sought the L, and he answered me, and
34:6 man cried, and the L heard him, and saved
34:7 The angel of the L encamps around those who
34:8 and see that the L is good!
34:9 O fear the L, you his saints, for those
34:10 those who seek the L lack no good thing.
34:11 I will teach you the fear of the L
34:15 The eyes of the L are toward the righteous,
34:16 The face of the L is against evildoers, to
34:17 cry for help, the L hears, and delivers them
34:18 The L is near to the brokenhearted, and saves
34:19 the righteous; but the L delivers him out of
34:22 The L redeems the life of his servants; none
35:1 Contend, O L, with those who contend with me;
35:5 the angel of the L driving them on!
35:6 the angel of the L pursuing them!
35:9 shall rejoice in the L, exulting in his deliverance.
35:10 bones shall say, "O L, who is like thee,
35:17 How long, O L, wilt thou look on?
35:22 Thou hast seen, O L; be not silent!
35:22 O L, be not far from me!
35:23 right, for my cause, my God and my L
35:24 Vindicate me, O L, my God, according to thy
35:27 evermore, "Great is the L, who delights in the
36:5 Thy steadfast love, O L, extends to the heavens,
36:6 great deep; man and beast thou savest, O L
37:3 Trust in the L, and do good; so you
37:4 Take delight in the L, and he will give
37:5 your way to the L; trust in him, and
37:7 Be still before the L, and wait patiently for
37:9 who wait for the L shall possess the land.
37:13 at him; but the L laughs at the wicked,
37:17 be broken; but the L upholds the righteous.
37:18 The L knows the days of the blameless, and
37:20 the enemies of the L are like the glory

37:22 those blessed by the L shall possess the land,
37:23 man are from the L, and he establishes him
37:24 cast headlong, for the L is the stay of
37:28 For the L loves justice; he will not forsake
37:33 The L will not abandon him to his power,
37:34 Wait for the L, and keep to his way,
37:39 righteous is from the L; he is their refuge
37:40 The L helps them and delivers them; he delivers
38:1 O L, rebuke me not in thy anger, nor
38:9 L, all my longing is known to thee, my
38:15 But for thee, O L, do I wait; it
38:15 it is thou, O L my God, who wilt
38:21 Do not forsake me, O L
38:22 to help me, O L, my salvation!
39:4 spoke with my tongue: L, let me know my
39:7 "And now, L, for what do I wait?
39:12 "Hear my prayer, O L, and give ear to
40:1 waited patiently for the L; he inclined to me
40:3 and fear, and put their trust in the L
40:4 man who makes the L his trust, who does
40:5 Thou hast multiplied, O L my God, thy wondrous
40:9 not restrained my lips, as thou knowest, O L
40:11 Do not thou, O L, withhold thy mercy from
40:13 Be pleased, O L, to deliver me!
40:13 O L, make haste to help me!
40:16 love thy salvation say continually, "Great is the L
40:17 and needy; but the L takes thought for me.
41:1 The L delivers him in the day of trouble;
41:2 day of trouble; the L protects him and keeps
41:3 The L sustains him on his sickbed; in his
41:4 me, I said, "O L, be gracious to me;
41:10 But do thou, O L, be gracious to me,
41:13 Blessed be the L, the God of Israel, from
42:8 By day the L commands his steadfast love; and
44:23 Why sleepest thou, O L
45:11 Since he is your L, bow to him;
46:7 The L of hosts is with us; the God
46:8 the works of the L, how he has wrought
46:11 The L of hosts is with us; the God
47:2 For the L, the Most High, is terrible, a
47:5 with a shout, the L with the sound of
48:1 Great is the L and greatly to be praised
48:8 the city of the L of hosts, in the
50:1 Mighty One, God the L, speaks and summons the
51:15 O L, open thou my lips, and my mouth
54:4 is my helper; the L is the upholder of
54:6 to thy name, O L, for it is good.
55:9 Destroy their plans, O L, confuse their tongues; for
55:16 upon God; and the L will save me.
55:22 your burden on the L, and he will sustain
56:10 I praise, in the L, whose word I praise,
57:9 thanks to thee, O L, among the peoples; I
58:6 out the fangs of the young lions, O L
59:3 sin of mine, O L,
59:5 Thou, L God of hosts, art God of Israel.
59:8 But thou, O L, dost laugh at them; thou
59:11 bring them down, O L, our shield!
62:12 that to thee, O L, belongs steadfast love.
64:10 righteous rejoice in the L, and take refuge in
66:18 in my heart, the L would not have listened.
68:4 his name is the L, exult before him!
68:11 The L gives the command; great is the host
68:16 abode, yea, where the L will dwell for ever?
68:17 thousands upon thousands, the L came from Sinai
68:18 the rebellious, that the L God may dwell there.
68:19 Blessed be the L, who daily bears us up;
68:20 and to GOD, the L, belongs escape from death.
68:22 The L said, "I will bring them back from
68:26 the great congregation, the L, O you who are
68:32 sing praises to the L, [Selah]
69:6 shame through me, O L GOD of hosts; let
69:13 for me, my prayer is to thee, O L
69:16 Answer me, O L, for thy steadfast love is
69:31 This will please the L more than an ox
69:33 For the L hears the needy, and does not
70:1 O L, make haste to help me!
70:5 and my deliverer; O L, do not tarry!
71:1 In thee, O L, do I take refuge; let
71:5 For thou, O L, art my hope, my trust,
71:5 hope, my trust, O L, from my youth.
71:16 mighty deeds of the L GOD I will come,
72:18 Blessed be the L, the God of Israel, who
73:28 I have made the L GOD my refuge, that
74:18 Remember this, O L, how the enemy scoffs, and
75:8 the hand of the L there is a cup,
76:11 your vows to the L your God, and perform
77:2 trouble I seek the L; in the night my
77:7 my spirit: "Will the L spurn for ever, and
77:11 the deeds of the L; yea, I will remember
78:4 glorious deeds of the L, and his might, and
78:21 Therefore, when the L heard, he was full of
78:65 Then the L awoke as from sleep, like a
79:5 How long, O L
79:12 taunts with which they have taunted thee, O L
80:4 O L God of hosts, how long wilt thou
80:19 Restore us, O L God of hosts!
81:10 I am the L your God, who brought you
81:15 Those who hate the L would cringe toward him,
83:16 shame, that they may seek thy name, O L
83:18 whose name is the L, art the Most High
84:1 thy dwelling place, O L of hosts!
84:2 the courts of the L; my heart and flesh
84:3 at thy altars, O L of hosts, my King
84:8 O L God of hosts, hear my prayer; give
84:11 For the L God is a sun and shield;
84:11 good thing does the L withhold from those who
84:12 O L of hosts, blessed is the man who
85:1 L, thou wast favorable to thy land; thou didst
85:7 thy steadfast love, O L, and grant us thy
85:8 hear what God the L will speak, for he
85:12 Yea, the L will give what is good, and
86:1 Incline thy ear, O L, and answer me, for
86:3 gracious to me, O L, for to thee do
86:4 for to thee, O L, do I lift up
86:5 For thou, O L, art good and forgiving, abounding
86:6 Give ear, O L, to my prayer; hearken to
86:8 among the gods, O L, nor are there any
86:9 down before thee, O L, and shall glorify thy
86:11 me thy way, O L, that I may walk
86:12 thanks to thee, O L my God, with my
86:15 But thou, O L, art a God merciful and
86:17 to shame because thou, L, hast helped me and
87:2 city he founded; the L loves the gates of
87:6 The L records as he registers the peoples, "This
88:1 O L, my God, I call for help by
88:9 call upon thee, O L; I spread out my
88:13 But I, O L, cry to thee; in the
88:14 O L, why dost thou cast me off?
89:1 thy steadfast love, O L, for ever; with my
89:5 praise thy wonders, O L, thy faithfulness in the
89:6 in the skies can be compared to the L
89:6 beings is like the L,
89:8 O L God of hosts, who is mighty as
89:8 as thou art, O L, with thy faithfulness round
89:15 shout, who walk, O L, in the light of
89:18 shield belongs to the L, our king to the
89:46 [Selah] How long, O L
89:47 Remember, O L, what the measure of life is,
89:49 [Selah] L, where is thy steadfast love of old,
89:50 Remember, O L, how thy servant is scorned; how
89:51 thy enemies taunt, O L, with which they mock
89:52 Blessed be the L for ever!
90:1 L, thou hast been our dwelling place in all
90:13 Return, O L
90:17 the favor of the L our God be upon
91:2 will say to the L, "My refuge and my
91:9 you have made the L your refuge, the Most
92:1 give thanks to the L, to sing praises to
92:4 For thou, O L, hast made me glad by
92:5 How great are thy works, O L
92:8 ever, but thou, O L, art on high for
92:9 lo, thy enemies, O L, for, lo, thy enemies
92:13 the house of the L, they flourish in the
92:15 to show that the L is upright; he is
93:1 The L reigns; he is robed in majesty; the
93:1 robed in majesty; the L is robed, he is
93:3 have lifted up, O L, the floods have lifted
93:4 of the sea, the L on high is mighty!
93:5 befits thy house, O L, for evermore.
94:1 O L, thou God of vengeance, thou God of
94:3 O L, how long shall the wicked, how long
94:5 crush thy people, O L, and afflict thy heritage.
94:7 and they say, "The L does not see; the
94:11 teaches men knowledge, the L, knows the thoughts
94:12 thou dost chasten, O L, and whom thou dost
94:14 For the L will not forsake his people; he
94:17 If the L had not been my help, my
94:18 thy steadfast love, O L, held me up.
94:22 But the L has become my stronghold, and my
94:23 for their wickedness; the L our God will wipe
95:1 us sing to the L; let us make a
95:3 For the L is a great God, and a

95:6 us kneel before the L, our Maker!
96:1 O sing to the L a new song; sing
96:1 song; sing to the L, all the earth!
96:2 Sing to the L, bless his name; tell of
96:4 For great is the L, and greatly to be
96:5 are idols; but the L made the heavens.
96:7 Ascribe to the L, O families of the peoples,
96:7 peoples, ascribe to the L glory and strength!
96:8 Ascribe to the L the glory due his name;
96:9 Worship the L in holy array; tremble before him,
96:10 among the nations, "The L reigns!
96:13 for joy before the L, for he comes, for
97:1 The L reigns; let the earth rejoice; let the
97:5 like wax before the L, before the Lord of
97:5 the LORD, before the L of all the earth.
97:9 For thou, O L, art most high over all
97:10 The L loves those who hate evil; he preserves
97:12 Rejoice in the L, O you righteous, and give
98:1 O sing to the L a new song, for
98:2 The L has made known his victory, he has
98:4 joyful noise to the L, all the earth; break
98:5 Sing praises to the L with the lyre, with
98:6 make a joyful noise before the King, the L
98:9 joy together before the L, for he comes to
99:1 The L reigns; let the peoples tremble!
99:2 The L is great in Zion; he is exalted
99:5 Extol the L our God; worship at his footstool!
99:6 They cried to the L, and he answered them.
99:8 O L our God, thou didst answer them; thou
99:9 Extol the L our God, and worship at his
99:9 holy mountain; for the L our God is holy!
100:1 joyful noise to the L, all the lands!
100:2 Serve the L with gladness!
100:3 Know that the L is God!
100:5 For the L is good; his steadfast love endures
101:1 justice; to thee, O L, I will sing.
101:8 all the evildoers from the city of the L
102:1 Hear my prayer, O L; let my cry come
102:12 But thou, O L, art enthroned for ever; thy
102:15 the name of the L, and all the kings
102:16 For the L will build up Zion, he will
102:18 unborn may praise the L:
102:19 height, from heaven the L looked at the earth,
102:21 the name of the L, and in Jerusalem his
102:22 gather together, and kingdoms, to worship the L
103:1 Bless the L, O my soul; and all that
103:2 Bless the L, O my soul, and forget not
103:6 The L works vindication and justice for all who
103:8 The L is merciful and gracious, slow to anger
103:13 his children, so the L pities those who fear
103:17 steadfast love of the L is from everlasting to
103:19 The L has established his throne in the heavens,
103:20 Bless the L, O you his angels, you mighty
103:21 Bless the L, all his hosts, his ministers that
103:22 Bless the L, all his works, in all places
103:22 Bless the L, O my soul!
104:1 Bless the L, O my soul!
104:1 O L my God, thou art very great!
104:16 The trees of the L are watered abundantly, the
104:24 O L, how manifold are thy works!
104:31 the glory of the L endure for ever, may
104:31 for ever, may the L rejoice in his works,
104:33 will sing to the L as long as I
104:34 pleasing to him, for I rejoice in the L
104:35 Bless the L, O my soul!
104:35 Praise the L
105:1 give thanks to the L, call on his name,
105:3 those who seek the L rejoice!
105:4 Seek the L and his strength, seek his presence
105:7 He is the L our God; his judgments are
105:19 the word of the L tested him.
105:21 free; he made him L of his house, and
105:24 And the L made his people very fruitful, and
105:45 Praise the L
106:1 Praise the L
106:1 give thanks to the L, for he is good;
106:2 mighty doings of the L, or show forth all
106:4 Remember me, O L, when thou showest favor to
106:16 holy one of the L,
106:25 and did not obey the voice of the L
106:29 dead; they provoked the L to anger with their
106:34 the peoples, as the L commanded them,
106:40 the anger of the L was kindled against his
106:47 Save us, O L our God, and gather us
106:48 Blessed be the L, the God of Israel, from
106:48 Praise the L
107:1 give thanks to the L, for he is good;
107:2 the redeemed of the L say so, whom he
107:6 they cried to the L in their trouble, and
107:8 Let them thank the L for his steadfast love,
107:13 they cried to the L in their trouble, and
107:15 Let them thank the L for his steadfast love,
107:19 they cried to the L in their trouble, and
107:21 Let them thank the L for his steadfast love,
107:24 the deeds of the L, his wondrous works in
107:28 they cried to the L in their trouble, and
107:31 Let them thank the L for his steadfast love,
107:43 let men consider the steadfast love of the L
108:3 thanks to thee, O L, among the peoples, I
109:14 be remembered before the L, and let not the
109:15 them be before the L continually; and may his
109:20 my accusers from the L, of those who speak
109:21 thou, O GOD my L, deal on my behalf
109:26 Help me, O L my God!
109:27 thy hand; thou, O L, hast done it!
109:30 great thanks to the L; I will praise him
110:1 The L says to my lord: "Sit at my
110:1 LORD says to my L: "Sit at my right
110:2 The L sends forth from Zion your mighty scepter.
110:4 The L has sworn and will not change his
110:5 The L is at your right hand; he will
111:1 Prasie the L
111:1 give thanks to the L with my whole heart,
111:2 the works of the L, studied by all who
111:4 to be remembered; the L is gracious and merciful.
111:10 The fear of the L is the beginning of
112:1 Praise the L
112:1 man who fears the L, who greatly delights in
112:4 for the upright; the L is gracious, merciful, and
112:7 tidings; his heart is firm, trusting in the L
113:1 Praise the L
113:1 O servants of the L, praise the name of
113:1 of the LORD, praise the name of the L
113:2 the name of the L from this time forth
113:3 the name of the L is to be praised!
113:4 The L is high above all nations, and his
113:5 Who is like the L our God, who is
113:9 Praise the L
114:7 the presence of the L, at the presence of
115:1 Not to us, O L, not to us, but
115:9 O Israel, trust in the L
115:10 house of Aaron, put your trust in the L
115:11 You who fear the L, trust in the LORD!
115:11 You who fear the LORD, trust in the L
115:12 The L has been mindful of us; he will
115:13 those who fear the L, both small and great.
115:14 May the L give you increase, you and your
115:15 be blessed by the L, who made heaven and
115:16 The heavens are the L's heavens, but the earth
115:17 do not praise the L, nor do any that
115:18 we will bless the L from this time forth
115:18 Praise the L
116:1 I love the L, because he has heard my
116:4 the name of the L: "O LORD, I beseech
116:4 of the LORD: "O L, I beseech thee, save
116:5 Gracious is the L, and righteous; our God is
116:6 The L preserves the simple; when I was brought
116:7 your rest; for the L has dealt bountifully with
116:9 I walk before the L in the land of
116:12 I render to the L for all his bounty
116:13 the name of the L,
116:14 my vows to the L in the presence of
116:15 the sight of the L is the death of
116:16 O L, I am thy servant; I am thy
116:17 thanksgiving and call on the name of the L
116:18 my vows to the L in the presence of
116:19 the house of the L, in your midst, O
116:19 Praise the L
117:1 Praise the L, all nations!
117:2 the faithfulness of the L endures for ever.
117:2 Praise the L
118:1 give thanks to the L, for he is good;
118:4 those who fear the L say, "His steadfast love
118:5 I called on the L; the LORD answered me
118:5 on the LORD; the L answered me and set
118:6 With the L on my side I do not
118:7 The L is on my side to help me;
118:8 take refuge in the L than to put confidence
118:9 take refuge in the L than to put confidence
118:10 the name of the L I cut them off!
118:11 the name of the L I cut them off!
118:12 the name of the L I cut them off!

118:13 was falling, but the L helped me.
118:14 The L is my strength and my song; he
118:15 right hand of the L does valiantly,
118:16 right hand of the L is exalted, the right
118:16 right hand of the L does valiantly!"
118:17 shall live, and recount the deeds of the L
118:18 The L has chastened me sorely, but he has
118:19 enter through them and give thanks to the L
118:20 the gate of the L; the righteous shall enter
118:23 This is the L's doing; it is marvelous in
118:24 the day which the L has made; let us
118:25 Save us, we beseech thee, O L
118:25 O L, we beseech thee, give us success!
118:26 he who enters in the name of the L
118:26 We bless you from the house of the L
118:27 The L is God, and he has given us
118:29 give thanks to the L, for he is good;
119:1 blameless, who walk in the law of the L
119:12 Blessed be thou, O L; teach me thy statutes!
119:31 to thy testimonies, O L; let me not be
119:33 Teach me, O L, the way of thy statutes;
119:41 come to me, O L, thy salvation according to
119:52 ordinances from of old, I take comfort, O L
119:55 in the night, O L, and keep thy law.
119:57 The L is my portion; I promise to keep
119:64 The earth, O L, is full of thy steadfast
119:65 with thy servant, O L, according to thy word.
119:75 I know, O L, that thy judgments are right,
119:89 For ever, O L, thy word is firmly fixed
119:107 give me life, O L, according to thy word!
119:108 offerings of praise, O L, and teach me thy
119:126 is time for the L to act, for thy
119:137 Righteous art thou, O L, and right are thy
119:145 my whole heart I cry; answer me, O L
119:149 thy steadfast love; O L, in thy justice preserve
119:151 thou art near, O L, and all thy commandments
119:156 is thy mercy, O L; give me life according
119:166 for thy salvation, O L, and I do thy
119:169 come before thee, O L; give me understanding
119:174 for thy salvation, O L, and thy law is
120:1 I cry to the L, that he may answer
120:2 me: "Deliver me, O L, from lying lips, from
121:2 help comes from the L, who made heaven and
121:5 The L is your keeper; the LORD is your
121:5 is your keeper; the L is your shade on
121:7 The L will keep you from all evil; he
121:8 The L will keep your going out and your
122:1 "Let us go to the house of the L
122:4 the tribes of the L, as was decreed for
122:4 to give thanks to the name of the L
122:9 the house of the L our God, I will
123:2 eyes look to the L our God, till he
123:3 mercy upon us, O L, have mercy upon us,
124:1 had not been the L who was on our
124:2 had not been the L who was on our
124:6 Blessed be the L, who has not given us
124:8 the name of the L, who made heaven and
125:1 who trust in the L are like Mount Zion,
125:2 about Jerusalem, so the L is round about his
125:4 Do good, O L, to those who are good,
125:5 their crooked ways the L will lead away with
126:1 When the L restored the fortunes of Zion, we
126:2 among the nations, "The L has done great things
126:3 The L has done great things for us; we
126:4 Restore our fortunes, O L, like the watercourses in
127:1 Unless the L builds the house, those who build
127:1 Unless the L watches over the city, the watchman
127:3 a heritage from the L, the fruit of the
128:1 one who fears the L, who walks in his
128:4 shall the man be blessed who fears the L
128:5 The L bless you from Zion!
129:4 The L is righteous; he has cut the cords
129:8 "The blessing of the L be upon you!
129:8 We bless you in the name of the L
130:1 of the depths I cry to thee, O L
130:2 L, hear my voice!
130:3 If thou, O L, shouldst mark iniquities, Lord, who
130:3 LORD, shouldst mark iniquities, L, who could stand?
130:5 I wait for the L, my soul waits, and
130:6 soul waits for the L more than watchmen for
130:7 O Israel, hope in the L
130:7 For with the L there is steadfast love, and
131:1 O L, my heart is not lifted up, my
131:3 Israel, hope in the L from this time forth
132:1 Remember, O L, in David's favor, all the hardships
132:2 he swore to the L and vowed to the
132:5 a place for the L, a dwelling place for
132:8 Arise, O L, and go to thy resting place,
132:11 The L swore to David a sure oath from
132:13 For the L has chosen Zion; he has desired
133:3 For there the L has commanded the blessing, life
134:1 Come, bless the L, all you servants of the
134:1 you servants of the L, who stand by night
134:1 stand by night in the house of the L
134:2 hands to the holy place, and bless the L
134:3 May the L bless you from Zion, he who
135:1 Praise the L
135:1 the name of the L, give praise, O servants
135:1 O servants of the L,
135:2 the house of the L, in the courts of
135:3 Praise the L, for the LORD is good; sing
135:3 the LORD, for the L is good; sing to
135:4 For the L has chosen Jacob for himself, Israel
135:5 I know that the L is great, and that
135:5 great, and that our L is above all gods.
135:6 Whatever the L pleases he does, in heaven and
135:13 Thy name, O L, endures for ever, thy renown,
135:13 ever, thy renown, O L, throughout all ages.
135:14 For the L will vindicate his people, and have
135:19 O house of Israel, bless the L
135:19 O house of Aaron, bless the L
135:20 O house of Levi, bless the L
135:20 You that fear the L, bless the LORD!
135:20 You that fear the LORD, bless the L
135:21 Blessed be the L from Zion, he who dwells
135:21 Praise the L
136:1 give thanks to the L, for he is good,
136:3 give thanks to the L of lords, for his
137:4 shall we sing the L's song in a foreign
137:7 Remember, O L, against the Edomites the day of
138:1 give thee thanks, O L, with my whole heart;
138:4 shall praise thee, O L, for they have heard
138:5 the ways of the L, for great is the
138:5 LORD, for great is the glory of the L
138:6 For though the L is high, he regards the
138:8 The L will fulfil his purpose for me; thy
138:8 thy steadfast love, O L, endures for ever.
139:1 O L, thou hast searched me and known me!
139:4 my tongue, lo, O L, thou knowest it altogether.
139:21 I not hate them that hate thee, O L
140:1 Deliver me, O L, from evil men; preserve me
140:4 [Selah] Guard me, O L, from the hands of
140:6 I say to the L, Thou art my God;
140:6 ear to the voice of my supplications, O L
140:7 O L, my Lord, my strong deliverer, thou hast
140:7 O LORD, my L, my strong deliverer, thou hast
140:8 Grant not, O L, the desires of the wicked;
140:12 I know that the L maintains the cause of
141:1 call upon thee, O L; make haste to me!
141:3 over my mouth, O L, keep watch over the
141:6 the word of the L is true.
141:8 are toward thee, O L God; in thee I
142:1 my voice to the L, with my voice I
142:1 make supplication to the L,
142:5 cry to thee, O L; I say, Thou art
143:1 Hear my prayer, O L; give ear to my
143:7 [Selah] Make haste to answer me, O L
143:9 Deliver me, O L, from my enemies!
143:11 thy name's sake, O L, preserve my life!
144:1 Blessed be the L, my rock, who trains my
144:3 O L, what is man that thou dost regard
144:5 Bow thy heavens, O L, and come down!
144:15 Happy the people whose God is the L
145:3 Great is the L, and greatly to be praised,
145:8 The L is gracious and merciful, slow to anger
145:9 The L is good to all, and his compassion
145:10 thanks to thee, O L, and all thy saints
145:13 The L is faithful in all his words, and
145:14 The L upholds all who are falling, and raises
145:17 The L is just in all his ways, and
145:18 The L is near to all who call upon
145:20 The L preserves all who love him; but all
145:21 the praise of the L, and let all flesh
146:1 Praise the L
146:1 Praise the L, O my soul!
146:2 I will praise the L as long as I
146:5 hope is in the L his God,
146:7 The L sets the prisoners free;
146:8 the prisoners free; the L opens the eyes of
146:8 The L lifts up those who are bowed down;
146:8 are bowed down; the L loves the righteous.
146:9 The L watches over the sojourners, he upholds the

L

146:10 The L will reign for ever, thy God, O
146:10 Praise the L
147:1 Praise the L
147:2 The L builds up Jerusalem; he gathers the outcasts
147:5 Great is our L, and abundant in power; his
147:6 The L lifts up the downtrodden, he casts the
147:7 Sing to the L with thanksgiving; make melody to
147:11 a man; but the L takes pleasure in those
147:12 Praise the L, O Jerusalem!
147:20 Praise the L
148:1 Praise the L
148:1 Praise the L from the heavens, praise him in
148:5 Let them praise the name of the L
148:7 Praise the L from the earth, you sea monsters
148:13 the name of the L, for his name alone
148:14 Praise the L
149:1 Praise the L
149:1 Sing to the L a new song, his praise
149:4 For the L takes pleasure in his people; he
149:9 Praise the L
150:1 Praise the L
150:6 Let everything that breathes praise the L
150:6 Praise the L

Prov 1:7 The fear of the L is the beginning of
1:29 the fear of the L,
2:5 the fear of the L and find the knowledge
2:6 For the L gives wisdom; from his mouth come
3:5 Trust in the L with all your heart, and
3:7 own eyes; fear the L, and turn away from
3:9 Honor the L with your substance and with the
3:11 do not despise the L's discipline or be weary
3:12 his reproof, for the L reproves him whom he
3:19 The L by wisdom founded the earth; by
3:26 it comes; for the L will be your confidence
3:32 an abomination to the L, but the upright are
3:33 The L's curse is on the house of the
5:21 the eyes of the L, and he watches all
6:16 six things which the L hates, seven which are
8:13 The fear of tQhe L is hatred of evil.
8:22 The L created me at the beginning of his
8:35 obtains favor from the L;
9:10 The fear of the L is the beginning of
10:3 The L does not let the righteous go hungry,
10:22 The blessing of the L makes rich, and he
10:27 The fear of the L prolongs life, but the
10:29 The L is a stronghold to him whose way
11:1 an abomination to the L, but a just weight
11:20 an abomination to the L, but those of blameless
12:2 obtains favor from the L, but a man of
12:22 an abomination to the L, but those who act
14:2 in uprightness fears the L, but he who is
14:26 the fear of the L one has strong confidence,
14:27 The fear of the L is a fountain of
15:3 The eyes of the L are in every place,
15:8 an abomination to the L, but the prayer of
15:9 an abomination to the L, but he loves him
15:11 lie open before the L, how much more the
15:16 the fear of the L than great treasure and
15:25 The L tears down the house of the proud,
15:26 an abomination to the L, the words of the
15:29 The L is far from the wicked, but he
15:33 The fear of the L is instruction in wisdom,
16:1 the answer of the tongue is from the L
16:2 own eyes, but the L weighs the spirit.
16:3 your work to the L, and your plans will
16:4 The L has made everything for its purpose, even
16:5 an abomination to the L; be assured, he will
16:6 the fear of the L a man avoids evil.
16:7 man's ways please the L, he makes even his
16:9 his way, but the L directs his steps.
16:20 and happy is he who trusts in the L
16:33 lap, but the decision is wholly from the L
17:3 for gold, and the L tries hearts.
17:15 righteous are both alike an abomination to the L
18:10 The name of the L is a strong tower;
18:22 a good thing, and obtains favor from the L
19:3 way to ruin, his heart rages against the L
19:14 fathers, but a prudent wife is from the L
19:17 poor lends to the L, and he will repay
19:21 the purpose of the L that will be established.
19:23 The fear of the L leads to life; and
20:10 measures are both alike an abomination to the L
20:12 the seeing eye, the L has made them both.
20:22 evil"; wait for the L, and he will help
20:23 an abomination to the L, and false scales are
20:24 are ordered by the L; how then can man
20:27 the lamp of the L, searching all his innermost
21:1 the hand of the L; he turns it wherever
21:2 own eyes, but the L weighs the heart.
21:3 more acceptable to the L than sacrifice.
21:30 no understanding, no counsel, can avail against the L
21:31 of battle, but the victory belongs to the L
22:2 poor meet together; the L is the maker of
22:4 and fear of the L is riches and honor
22:12 The eyes of the L keep watch over knowledge,
22:14 he with whom the L is angry will fall
22:19 may be in the L, I have made them
22:23 the gate; for the L will plead their cause
23:17 the fear of the L all the day.
24:18 he stumbles; lest the L see it, and be
24:21 My son, fear the L and the king, and
25:22 his head, and the L will reward you.
28:5 those who seek the L understand it completely.
28:14 man who fears the L always; but he who
28:25 who trusts in the L will be enriched.
29:13 oppressor meet together; the L gives light to the
29:25 who trusts in the L is safe.
29:26 ruler, but from the L a man gets justice.
30:9 and deny thee, and say, "Who is the L
31:30 woman who fears the L is to be praised.

Wis 1:1 earth, think of the L with uprightness, and seek
1:7 the Spirit of the L has filled the world,
1:9 will come to the L, to convict him of
2:13 God, and calls himself a child of the L
3:8 over peoples, and the L will reign over them
3:10 and rebelled against the L;
3:14 wicked things against the L; for special favor will
3:14 of great delight in the temple of the L
4:14 was pleasing to the L, therefore he took him
4:17 not understand what the L purposed for him, and
4:18 for him, but the L will laugh them to
5:7 the way of the L we have not known.
5:15 reward is with the L; the Most High takes
5:16 the hand of the L, because with his right
5:17 The L will take his zeal as his whole
6:3 given you from the L, and your sovereignty from
6:7 For the L of all will not stand in
8:3 with God, and the L of all loves her.
8:21 I appealed to the L and besought him, and
9:1 of my fathers and L of mercy, who hast
9:13 can discern what the L wills?
10:16 a servant of the L, and withstood dread kings
10:20 they sang hymns, O L, to thy holy name,
11:13 perceived it was the L's doing.
11:26 they are thine, O L who lovest the living.
12:2 wickedness and put their trust in thee, O L
13:3 than these is their L, for the author of
13:9 to find sooner the L of these things?
16:12 was thy word, O L, which heals all men.
16:26 thou didst love, O L, might learn that it
19:9 lambs, praising thee, O L, who didst deliver them.
19:22 For in everything, O L, thou hast exalted and

Sir 1:1 wisdom comes from the L and is with him
1:7 The L himself created wisdom; he saw her and
1:9 The fear of the L is glory and exultation,
1:10 The fear of the L delights the heart, and
1:11 him who fears the L it will go well
1:12 To fear the L is the beginning of wisdom
1:14 To fear the L is wisdom's full measure; she
1:16 The fear of the L is the crown of
1:18 To fear the L is the root of wisdom,
1:23 the commandments, and the L will supply it for
1:24 the fear of the L is wisdom and instruction,
1:25 the fear of the L; do not approach him
1:27 The L will reveal your secrets and cast you
1:27 the fear of the L, and your heart was
2:1 to serve the L, prepare yourself for temptation.
2:7 You who fear the L, wait for his mercy;
2:8 You who fear the L, trust in him, and
2:9 you who fear the L, hope for good things,
2:10 ever trusted in the L and was put to
2:10 the fear of the L and was forsaken?
2:11 For the L is compassionate and merciful; he forgives
2:14 you do when the L punishes you?
2:15 Those who fear the L will not disobey his
2:16 Those who fear the L will seek his approval,
2:17 Those who fear the L will prepare their hearts,
2:18 the hands of the L, but not into the
3:2 For the L honored the father above the children,
3:6 and whoever obeys the L will refresh his mother;
3:16 whoever angers his mother is cursed by the L
3:18 will find favor in the sight of the L

3:19 the might of the L; he is glorified by
4:13 obtain glory, and the L will bless the place
4:14 the Holy One; the L loves those who love
4:28 the truth and the L God will fight for
5:3 for the L will surely punish you.
5:4 for the L is slow to anger.
5:7 to turn to the L, nor postpone it from
5:7 the wrath of the L will go forth, and
6:16 those who fear the L will find him.
6:17 Whoever fears the L directs his friendship aright, for
6:37 the statutes of the L, and meditate at all
7:4 not seek from the L the highest office, nor
7:5 righteousness before the L, nor display your wisdom
7:29 your soul fear the L, and honor his priests.
7:31 Fear the L and honor the priest, and give
9:16 your glorying be in the fear of the L
10:4 the hands of the L, and over it he
10:5 the hands of the L, and he confers his
10:7 is hateful before the L and before men, and
10:12 to depart from the L; his heart has forsaken
10:13 the L brought upon them extraordinary afflictions,
10:14 The L has cast down the thrones of rulers,
10:15 The L has plucked up the roots of the
10:16 The L has overthrown the lands of the nations,
10:19 Those who fear the L
10:20 those who fear the L are worthy of honor
10:21 their glory is the fear of the L
10:23 is greater than the man who fears the L
11:4 the works of the L are wonderful, and his
11:12 the eyes of the L look upon him for
11:14 and death, poverty and wealth, come from the L
11:15 The gift of the L endures for those who
11:19 but trust in the L and keep at your
11:19 the sight of the L to enrich a poor
11:20 The blessing of the L is the reward of
11:24 the sight of the L to reward a man
14:11 your means, and present worthy offerings to the L
15:1 man who fears the L will do this, and
15:9 for it has not been sent from the L
15:10 in wisdom, and the L will prosper it.
15:11 say, "Because of the L I left the right
15:13 The L hates all abominations, and they are not
15:18 the wisdom of the L; he is mighty in
16:2 the fear of the L is in them.
16:11 wrath are with the L; he is mighty to
16:15 be hidden from the L, and who from on
16:24 The works of the L have existed from the
16:27 After this the L looked upon the earth, and
17:1 The L created man out of earth, and turned
17:14 but Israel is the L's own portion.
17:16 him, and all their sins are before the L
17:17 a signet with the L, and he will keep
17:20 Turn to the L and forsake your sins; pray
17:23 and well sings the L's praises.
17:24 the mercy of the L, and his forgiveness for
18:2 the whole universe; the L alone will be declared
18:5 it possible to trace the wonders of the L
18:10 Therefore the L is patient with them and pours
18:12 the compassion of the L is for all living
18:22 not be like a man who tempts the L
18:25 change, and all things move swiftly before the L
19:18 the fear of the L, and in all wisdom
21:6 he that fears the L will repent in his
21:11 is the fulfilment of the fear of the L
23:1 O L, Father and Ruler of my life, do
23:4 O L, Father and God of my life, do
23:19 the eyes of the L are ten thousand times
23:27 the fear of the L, and nothing sweeter than
23:27 sweeter than to heed the commandments of the L
24:12 the portion of the L, who is their inheritance.
25:1 the sight of the L and of men; agreement
25:6 and their boast is the fear of the L
25:10 no one superior to him who fears the L
25:11 The fear of the L surpasses everything; to whom
26:3 the blessings of the man who fears the L
26:14 a gift of the L, and there is nothing
26:16 the heights of the L, so is the beauty
26:19 to sin– the L will prepare him for
27:3 the fear of the L, his house will be
27:24 to him; even the L will hate him.
28:1 suffer vengeance from the L, and he will firmly
28:3 another, and yet seek for healing from the L
28:23 Those who forsake the L will fall into its
30:19 is afflicted by the L;
32:14 He who fears the L will accept his discipline,
32:16 Those who fear the L will form true judgments,
32:24 he who trusts the L will not suffer loss.
33:1 man who fears the L, but in trial he
33:8 By the L's decision they were distinguished, and he
33:11 knowledge the L distinguished them and appointed
33:16 the blessing of the L I excelled, and like
34:13 those who fear the L will live, for their
34:14 He who fears the L will not be timid,
34:15 the soul of the man who fears the L
34:16 The eyes of the L are upon those who
34:24 whose voice will the L listen?
35:3 is pleasing to the L, and to forsake unrighteousness
35:4 not appear before the L empty-handed,
35:8 Glorify the L generously, and do not stint the
35:11 For the L is the one who repays, and
35:12 unrighteous sacrifice; for the L is the judge, and
35:16 is pleasing to the L will be accepted, and
35:17 until it reaches the L; he will not desist
35:18 And the L will not delay, neither will he
36:1 mercy upon us, O L, the God of all,
36:5 that there is not God but thee, O L
36:12 Have mercy, O L, upon the people called by
36:17 Hearken, O L, to the prayer of thy servants,
36:17 that thou art the L, the God of the
37:21 given him by the L, since he is lacking
38:1 of him, for the L created him;
38:4 The L created medicines from the earth, and a
38:9 but pray to the L, and he will heal
38:12 his place, for the L created him; let him
38:14 will pray to the L that he should grant
39:5 early to seek the L who made him, and
39:6 If the great L is willing, he will be
39:6 give thanks to the L in prayer.
39:8 the law of the L's covenant.
39:14 of praise; bless the L for all his works;
39:16 the works of the L, for they are very
39:33 The works of the L are all good, and
39:35 and voice, and bless the name of the L
40:26 the fear of the L is better than both.
40:26 the fear of the L, and with it there
40:27 The fear of the L is like a garden
41:3 the decree from the L for all flesh,
42:15 the works of the L, and will declare what
42:15 the words of the L his works are done.
42:16 the work of the L is full of his
42:17 The L has not enabled his holy ones to
42:17 marvelous works, which the L the Almighty has
43:5 Great is the L who made it; and at
43:9 a gleaming array in the heights of the L
43:29 Terrible is the L and very great, and marvelous
43:30 When you praise the L, exalt him as much
43:33 For the L has made all things, and to
44:2 The L apportioned to them great glory, his majesty
44:17 Enoch pleased the L, and was taken up; he
44:22 Therefore the L assured him by an oath that
45:1 From his descendants the L brought forth a man
45:3 signs to cease; the L glorified him in the
45:15 to minister to the L and serve as priest
45:16 offer sacrifice to the L, incense and a pleasing
45:19 The L saw it and was not pleased, and
45:21 the sacrifices to the L, which he gave to
45:22 the people; for the L himself is his portion
45:23 the fear of the L, and stood fast, when
45:26 May the L grant you wisdom in your heart
46:3 For he waged the wars of the L
46:6 side, and the great L answered him with hailstones
46:6 the sight of the L; for he wholly followed
46:9 And the L gave Caleb strength, which remained with
46:10 see that it is good to follow the L
46:11 turn away from the L – may their memory
46:13 Samuel, beloved by his L, a prophet of the
46:13 a prophet of the L, established the kingdom and
46:14 the law of the L he judged the congregation,
46:14 the congregation, and the L watched over Jacob.
46:16 He called upon the L, the Mighty One, when
46:17 Then the L thundered from heaven, and made his
46:19 to witness before the L and his anointed: "I
47:5 he appealed to the L, the Most High, and
47:6 the blessings of the L, when the glorious diadem
47:11 The L took away his sins, and exalted his
47:18 the name of the L God, who is called
47:22 But the L will never give up his mercy,
48:3 the word of the L he shut up the
48:20 they called upon the L who is merciful, spreading
48:21 The L smote the camp of the Assyrians, and
48:22 was pleasing to the L, and he held strongly
49:3 his heart upon the L; in the days of

L

49:12 temple holy to the L, prepared for everlasting glory.
50:13 their splendor with the L's offering in their hands,
50:17 faces to worship their L, the Almighty, God Most
50:19 the people besought the L Most High in prayer
50:19 of worship of the L was ended; so they
50:20 the blessing of the L with his lips, and
50:29 the light of the L is his path.
51:1 thanks to thee, O L and King, and will
51:8 remembered thy mercy, O L, and thy work from
51:10 I appealed to the L, the Father of my
51:10 the Father of my L, not to forsake me
51:12 and I will bless the name of the L
51:22 The L gave me a tongue as my reward,
Is 1:2 O earth; for the L has spoken: "Sons have
1:4 They have forsaken the L, they have despised the
1:9 If the L of hosts had not left us
1:10 the word of the L, you rulers of Sodom!
1:11 says the L; I have had enough of burnt
1:18 reason together, says the L: though your sins are
1:20 the mouth of the L has spoken."
1:24 Therefore the L says, the LORD of hosts, the
1:24 the Lord says, the L of hosts, the Mighty
1:28 those who forsake the L shall be consumed.
2:2 the house of the L shall be established as
2:3 the mountain of the L, to the house of
2:3 the word of the L from Jerusalem.
2:5 let us walk in the light of the L
2:10 the terror of the L, and from the glory
2:11 be humbled; and the L alone will be exalted
2:12 For the L of hosts has a day against
2:17 brought low; and the L alone will be exalted
2:19 the terror of the L, and from the glory
2:21 the terror of the L, and from the glory
3:1 For, behold, the L, the LORD of hosts, is
3:1 behold, the Lord, the L of hosts, is taking
3:8 deeds are against the L, defying his glorious
3:13 The L has taken his place to contend, he
3:14 The L enters into judgment with the elders and
3:15 says the L GOD of hosts.
3:16 The L said: Because the daughters of Zion are
3:17 with their feet; the L will smite with a
3:17 of Zion, and the L will lay bare their
3:18 In that day the L will take away the
4:2 the branch of the L shall be beautiful and
4:4 in Jerusalem, when the L shall have washed away
4:5 Then the L will create over the whole site
5:7 the vineyard of the L of hosts is the
5:9 The L of hosts has sworn in my hearing:
5:12 the deeds of the L, or see the work
5:16 But the L of hosts is exalted in justice,
5:24 the law of the L of hosts, and have
5:25 the anger of the L was kindled against his
6:1 died I saw the L sitting upon a throne,
6:3 holy, holy is the L of hosts; the whole
6:5 seen the King, the L of hosts!"
6:8 the voice of the L saying, "Whom shall I
6:11 Then I said, "How long, O L
6:12 utterly desolate, and the L removes men far away,
7:3 And the L said to Isaiah, "Go forth to
7:7 thus says the L GOD: It shall not stand,
7:10 Again the L spoke to Ahaz,
7:11 a sign of the L your God; let it
7:12 will not put the L to the test."
7:14 Therefore the L himself will give you a sign.
7:17 The L will bring upon you and upon your
7:18 In that day the L will whistle for the
7:20 In that day the L will shave with a
8:1 Then the L said to me, "Take a large
8:3 Then the L said to me, "Call his name
8:5 The L spoke to me again:
8:7 Remaliah; therefore, behold, the L is bringing up
8:11 For the L spoke thus to me with his
8:13 But the L of hosts, him you shall regard
8:17 will wait for the L, who is hiding his
8:18 the children whom the L has given me are
8:18 in Israel from the L of hosts, who dwells
9:7 The zeal of the L of hosts will do
9:8 The L has sent a word against Jacob, and
9:11 So the L raises adversaries against them, and stirs
9:13 them, nor seek the L of hosts.
9:14 So the L cut off from Israel head and
9:17 Therefore the L does not rejoice over their young
9:19 the wrath of the L of hosts the land
10:12 When the L has finished all his work on
10:16 Therefore the L, the LORD of hosts, will send
10:16 Therefore the Lord, the L of hosts, will send
10:18 his fruitful land the L will destroy, both soul
10:20 will lean upon the L, the Holy One of
10:23 For the L, the LORD of hosts, will make
10:23 For the Lord, the L of hosts, will make
10:24 Therefore thus says the L, the LORD of hosts:
10:24 says the Lord, the L of hosts: "O my
10:26 And the L of hosts will wield against them
10:33 Behold, the L, the LORD of hosts will lop
10:33 Behold, the Lord, the L of hosts will lop
11:2 the Spirit of the L shall rest upon him,
11:2 spirit of knowledge and the fear of the L
11:3 delight shall be in the fear of the L
11:9 the knowledge of the L as the waters cover
11:11 In that day the L will extend his hand
11:15 And the L will utterly destroy the tongue of
12:1 thanks to thee, O L, for though thou wast
12:2 be afraid; for the L GOD is my strength
12:4 "Give thanks to the L, call upon his name;
12:5 "Sing praises to the L, for he has done
13:4 The L of hosts is mustering a host for
13:5 of the heavens, the L and the weapons of
13:6 the day of the L is near; as destruction
13:9 the day of the L comes, cruel, with wrath
13:13 the wrath of the L of hosts in the
14:1 The L will have compassion on Jacob and will
14:2 possess them in the L's land as male and
14:3 When the L has given you rest from your
14:5 The L has broken the staff of the wicked,
14:22 says the L of hosts, "and will cut off
14:22 and remnant, offspring and posterity, says the L
14:23 of destruction, says the L of hosts."
14:24 The L of hosts has sworn: "As I have
14:27 For the L of hosts has purposed, and who
14:32 "The L has founded Zion, and in her the
16:13 the word which the L spoke concerning Moab in
16:14 But now the L says, "In three years, like
17:3 of Israel, says the L of hosts.
17:6 fruit tree, says the L God of Israel.
18:4 For thus the L said to me: "I will
18:7 be brought to the L of hosts from a
18:7 the name of the L of hosts.
19:1 Behold, the L is riding on a swift cloud
19:4 over them, says the L, the LORD of hosts.
19:4 says the Lord, the L of hosts.
19:12 make known what the L of hosts has purposed
19:14 The L has mingled within her a spirit of
19:16 the hand which the L of hosts shakes over
19:17 the purpose which the L of hosts has purposed
19:18 swear allegiance to the L of hosts.
19:19 an altar to the L in the midst of
19:19 a pillar to the L at its border.
19:20 a witness to the L of hosts in the
19:20 they cry to the L because of oppressors he
19:21 And the L will make himself known to the
19:21 Egyptians will know the L in that day and
19:21 make vows to the L and perform them.
19:22 And the L will smite Egypt, smiting and healing,
19:22 will return to the L, and he will heed
19:25 the earth, whom the L of hosts has blessed,
20:2 at that time the L had spoken by Isaiah
20:3 and barefoot-- the L said, "As my servant
21:6 For thus the L said to me: "Go, set
21:8 watchtower I stand, O L, continually by day, and
21:10 have heard from the L of hosts, the God
21:16 For thus the L said to me, "Within a
21:17 be few; for the L, the God of Israel,
22:5 For the L GOD of hosts has a day
22:12 In that day the L GOD of hosts called
22:14 The L of hosts has revealed himself in my
22:14 says the L GOD of hosts.
22:15 Thus says the L GOD of hosts, "Come, go
22:17 Behold, the L will hurl you away violently, O
22:25 that day, says the L of hosts, the peg
22:25 cut off, for the L has spoken."
23:9 The L of hosts has purposed it, to defile
23:11 shaken the kingdoms; the L has given command
23:17 of seventy years, the L will visit Tyre, and
23:18 be dedicated to the L; it will not be
23:18 fine clothing for those who dwell before the L
24:1 Behold, the L will lay waste the earth and
24:3 utterly despoiled; for the L has spoken this word.
24:14 the majesty of the L they shout from the
24:15 give glory to the L; in the coastlands of
24:15 the name of the L, the God of Israel.
24:21 On that day the L will punish the host
24:23 sun ashamed; for the L of hosts will reign

45:25 In the L all the offspring of Israel shall
47:4 Our Redeemer– the L of hosts is his
48:1 the name of the L, and confess the God
48:2 God of Israel; the L of hosts is his
48:14 The L loves him; he shall perform his purpose
48:16 And now the L GOD has sent me and
48:17 Thus says the L, your Redeemer, the Holy One
48:17 Israel: "I am the L your God, who teaches
48:20 the earth; say, "The L has redeemed his servant
48:22 says the L, "for the wicked."
49:1 The L called me from the womb, from the
49:4 right is with the L, and my recompense with
49:5 And now the L says, who formed me from
49:5 the eyes of the L, and my God has
49:7 Thus says the L, the Redeemer of Israel and
49:7 themselves; because of the L, who is faithful, the
49:8 Thus says the L: "In a time of favor
49:13 For the L has comforted his people, and will
49:14 But Zion said, "The L has forsaken me, my
49:14 has forsaken me, my L has forgotten me."
49:18 I live, says the L, you shall put them
49:22 Thus says the L GOD: "Behold, I will lift
49:23 that I am the L; those who wait for
49:25 Surely, thus says the L: "Even the captives of
49:26 that I am the L your Savior, and your
50:1 Thus says the L: "Where is your mother's bill
50:4 The L GOD has given me the tongue of
50:5 The L GOD has opened my ear, and I
50:7 For the L GOD helps me; therefore I have
50:9 Behold, the L GOD helps me; who will declare
50:10 among you fears the L and obeys the voice
50:10 the name of the L and relies upon his
51:1 you who seek the L; look to the rock
51:3 For the L will comfort Zion; he will comfort
51:3 the garden of the L; joy and gladness will
51:9 O arm of the L; awake, as in days
51:11 the ransomed of the L shall return, and come
51:13 and have forgotten the L, your Maker, who stretched
51:15 For I am the L your God, who stirs
51:15 waves roar– the L of hosts is his
51:17 the hand of the L the cup of his
51:20 the wrath of the L, the rebuke of your
51:22 wine: Thus says your L, the LORD, your God
51:22 says your Lord, the L, your God who pleads
52:3 For thus says the L: "You were sold for
52:4 For thus says the L GOD: My people went
52:5 I here, says the L, seeing that my people
52:5 rulers wail, says the L, and continually all the
52:8 the return of the L to Zion.
52:9 of Jerusalem; for the L has comforted his people,
52:10 The L has bared his holy arm before the
52:11 yourselves, you who bear the vessels of the L
52:12 in flight, for the L will go before you,
53:1 the arm of the L been revealed?
53:6 own way; and the L has laid on him
53:10 the will of the L to bruise him; he
53:10 the will of the L shall prosper in his
54:1 children of her that is married, says the L
54:5 is your husband, the L of hosts is his
54:6 For the L has called you like a wife
54:8 on you, says the L, your Redeemer.
54:10 be removed, says the L, who has compassion on
54:13 be taught by the L, and great shall be
54:17 the servants of the L and their vindication from
54:17 LORD and their vindication from me, says the L
55:5 you, because of the L your God, and of
55:6 "Seek the L while he may be found, call
55:7 him return to the L, that he may have
55:8 neither are your ways my ways, says the L
55:13 shall be to the L for a memorial, for
56:1 Thus says the L: "Keep justice, and do righteousness,
56:3 joined himself to the L say, "The LORD will
56:3 the LORD say, "The L will surely separate me
56:4 For thus says the L: "To the eunuchs who
56:6 join themselves to the L, to minister to him,
56:6 the name of the L, and to be his
56:8 Thus says the L GOD, who gathers the outcasts
57:19 the near, says the L; and I will heal
58:5 a fast, and a day acceptable to the L
58:8 the glory of the L shall be your rear
58:9 shall call, and the L will answer; you shall
58:11 And the L will guide you continually, and satisfy
58:13 holy day of the L honorable; if you honor
58:14 take delight in the L, and I will make
58:14 the mouth of the L has spoken."
59:1 Behold, the L's hand is not shortened, that it
59:13 transgressing, and denying the L, and turning away
59:15 The L saw it, and it displeased him that
59:19 the name of the L from the west, and
59:19 the wind of the L drives.
59:20 in Jacob who turn from transgression, says the L
59:21 with them, says the L: my spirit which is
59:21 children's children, says the L, from this time forth
60:1 the glory of the L has risen upon you.
60:2 the peoples; but the L will arise upon you,
60:6 frankincense, and shall proclaim the praise of the L
60:9 the name of the L your God, and for
60:14 the City of the L, the Zion of the
60:16 know that I, the L, am your Savior and
60:19 by night; but the L will be your everlasting
60:20 withdraw itself; for the L will be your everlasting
60:22 nation; I am the L; in its time I
61:1 The Spirit of the L GOD is upon me,
61:1 upon me, because the L has anointed me to
61:2 the year of the L's favor, and the day
61:3 the planting of the L, that he may be
61:6 the priests of the L, men shall speak of
61:8 For I the L love justice, I hate robbery
61:9 a people whom the L has blessed.
61:10 greatly rejoice in the L, my soul shall exult
61:11 spring up, so the L GOD will cause righteousness
62:2 the mouth of the L will give.
62:3 the hand of the L, and a royal diadem
62:4 land Married; for the L delights in you, and
62:6 You who put the L in remembrance, take no
62:8 The L has sworn by his right hand and
62:9 it and praise the L, and those who gather
62:11 Behold, the L has proclaimed to the end of
62:12 The redeemed of the L; and you shall be
63:7 steadfast love of the L, the praises of the
63:7 the praises of the L, according to all that
63:7 to all that the L has granted us, and
63:14 the Spirit of the L gave them rest.
63:16 acknowledge us; thou, O L, art our Father, our
63:17 O L, why dost thou make us err from
64:8 Yet, O L, thou art our Father; we are
64:9 exceedingly angry, O L, and remember not iniquity
64:12 Wilt thou restrain thyself at these things, O L
65:7 iniquities together, says the L; because they burned
65:8 Thus says the L: "As the wine is found
65:11 you who forsake the L, who forget my holy
65:13 thus says the L GOD: "Behold, my servants
65:15 a curse, and the L GOD will slay you;
65:23 the blessed of the L, and their children with
65:25 destroy in all my holy mountain, says the L
66:1 Thus says the L: "Heaven is my throne and
66:2 so all these things are mine, says the L
66:5 the word of the L, you who tremble at
66:5 have said, 'Let the L be glorified, that we
66:6 The voice of the L, rendering recompense to his
66:9 says the L; shall I, who cause to bring
66:12 For thus says the L: "Behold, I will extend
66:14 the hand of the L is with his servants,
66:15 "For behold, the L will come in fire, and
66:16 by fire will the L execute judgment, and by
66:16 those slain by the L shall be many.
66:17 shall come to an end together, says the L
66:20 an offering to the L, upon horses, and in
66:20 mountain Jerusalem, says the L, just as the Israelites
66:20 a clean vessel to the house of the L
66:21 take for priests and for Levites, says the L
66:22 before me, says the L; so shall your descendants
66:23 shall come to worship before me, says the L
Jer 1:2 the word of the L came in the days
1:4 the word of the L came to me saying,
1:6 Then I said, "Ah, L GOD!
1:7 But the L said to me, "Do not say,
1:8 am with you to deliver you, says the L
1:9 Then the L put forth his hand and touched
1:9 my mouth; and the L said to me, "Behold,
1:11 the word of the L came to me, saying,
1:12 Then the L said to me, "You have seen
1:13 The word of the L came to me a
1:14 Then the L said to me, "Out of the
1:15 the north, says the L; and they shall come
1:19 with you, says the L, to deliver you."
2:1 The word of the L came to me, saying,
2:2 Jerusalem, Thus says the L, I remember the devotion
2:3 was holy to the L, the first fruits of
2:3 became guilty; evil came upon them, says the L
2:4 the word of the L, O house of Jacob,
2:5 Thus says the L: "What wrong did your fathers

2:6 say, 'Where is the L who brought us up
2:8 say, 'Where is the L Those who handle the
2:9 with you, says the L, and with your children's
2:12 utterly desolate, says the L,
2:17 yourself by forsaking the L your God, when he
2:19 you to forsake the L your God; the fear
2:19 in you, says the L GOD of hosts.
2:22 before me, says the L GOD.
2:29 You have all rebelled against me, says the L
2:31 you, O generation, heed the word of the L
2:37 your head, for the L has rejected those in
3:1 says the L
3:6 The L said to me in the days of
3:10 her whole heart, but in pretense, says the L
3:11 And the L said to me, "Faithless Israel has
3:12 north, and say, 'Return, faithless Israel, says the L
3:12 am merciful, says the L; I will not be
3:13 you rebelled against the L your God and scattered
3:13 you have not obeyed my voice, says the L
3:14 faithless children, says the L; for I am your
3:16 those days, says the L, they shall no more
3:16 say, "The ark of the covenant of the L
3:17 the throne of the L, and all nations shall
3:17 the presence of the L in Jerusalem, and they
3:20 to me, O house of Israel, says the L
3:21 they have forgotten the L their God.
3:22 for thou art the L our God.
3:23 Truly in the L our God is the salvation
3:25 have sinned against the L our God, we and
3:25 the voice of the L our God."
4:1 O Israel, says the L, to me you should
4:2 you swear, 'As the L lives,' in truth, in
4:3 For thus says the L to the men of
4:4 Circumcise yourselves to the L, remove the foreskin
4:8 fierce anger of the L has not turned back
4:9 that day, says the L, courage shall fail both
4:10 Then I said, "Ah, L GOD, surely thou hast
4:17 because she has rebelled against me, says the L
4:26 in ruins before the L, before his fierce anger.
4:27 For thus says the L, "The whole land shall
5:2 they say, "As the L lives," yet they swear
5:3 O L, do not thy eyes look for truth?
5:4 the way of the L, the law of their
5:5 the way of the L, the law of their
5:9 says the L; and shall I not avenge myself
5:11 have been utterly faithless to me, says the L
5:12 spoken falsely of the L, and have said, 'He
5:14 Therefore thus says the L, the God of hosts:
5:15 from afar, O house of Israel, says the L
5:18 those days, says the L, I will not make
5:19 say, 'Why has the L our God done all
5:22 says the L; Do you not tremble before me?
5:24 'Let us fear the L our God, who gives
5:29 says the L, and shall I not avenge myself
6:6 For thus says the L of hosts: "Hew down
6:9 Thus says the L of hosts: "Glean thoroughly as
6:10 the word of the L is to them an
6:11 the wrath of the L; I am weary of
6:12 says the L
6:15 says the L
6:16 Thus says the L: "Stand by the roads, and
6:21 Therefore thus says the L: 'Behold, I will lay
6:22 Thus says the L: "Behold, a people is coming
6:30 are called, for the L has rejected them."
7:1 to Jeremiah from the L:
7:2 the gate of the L's house, and proclaim there
7:2 the word of the L, all you men of
7:2 Judah who enter these gates to worship the L
7:3 Thus says the L of hosts, the God of
7:4 the temple of the L, the temple of the
7:4 the temple of the L, the temple of the
7:4 the temple of the L
7:11 Behold, I myself have seen it, says the L
7:13 these things, says the L, and when I spoke
7:19 says the L
7:20 Therefore thus says the L GOD: Behold, my anger
7:21 Thus says the L of hosts, the God of
7:28 the voice of the L their God, and did
7:29 bare heights, for the L has rejected and forsaken
7:30 my sight, says the L; they have set their
7:32 are coming, says the L, when it will no
8:1 that time, says the L, the bones of the
8:3 driven them, says the L of hosts.
8:4 them, Thus says the L: When men fall, do
8:7 my people know not the ordinance of the L
8:8 the law of the L is with us?

8:9 the word of the L, and what wisdom is
8:12 punish them, they shall be overthrown, says the L
8:13 gather them, says the L, there are no grapes
8:14 perish there; for the L our God has doomed
8:14 to drink, because we have sinned against the L
8:17 says the L
8:19 the land: "Is the L not in Zion?
9:3 and they do not know me, says the L
9:6 deceit, they refuse to know me, says the L
9:7 Therefore thus says the L of hosts: "Behold, I
9:9 says the L; and shall I not avenge myself
9:12 the mouth of the L spoken, that he may
9:13 And the L says: "Because they have forsaken my
9:15 Therefore thus says the L of hosts, the God
9:17 Thus says the L of hosts: "Consider, and call
9:20 the word of the L, and let your ear
9:22 Speak, "Thus says the L: 'The dead bodies of
9:23 Thus says the L: "Let not the wise man
9:24 that I am the L who practice steadfast love,
9:24 for in these things I delight, says the L
9:25 are coming, says the L, when I will punish
10:1 the word which the L speaks to you, O
10:2 Thus says the L: "Learn not the way of
10:6 none like thee, O L; thou art great, and
10:10 But the L is the true God; he is
10:16 of his inheritance; the L of hosts is his
10:18 For thus says the L: "Behold, I am slinging
10:21 not inquire of the L; therefore they have not
10:23 I know, O L, that the way of man
10:24 Correct me, O L, but in just measure; not
11:1 to Jeremiah from the L:
11:3 them, Thus says the L, the God of Israel:
11:5 Then I answered, "So be it, L
11:6 And the L said to me, "Proclaim all these
11:9 Again the L said to me, "There is revolt
11:11 Therefore, thus says the L, Behold, I am bringing
11:16 The L once called you, 'A green olive tree,
11:17 The L of hosts, who planted you, has pronounced
11:18 The L made it known to me and I
11:20 But, O L of hosts, who judgest righteously, who
11:21 Therefore thus says the L concerning the men of
11:21 the name of the L, or you will die
11:22 therefore thus says the L of hosts: "Behold, I
12:1 Righteous art thou, O L, when I complain to
12:3 But thou, O L, knowest me; thou seest me,
12:12 the sword of the L devours from one end
12:13 harvests because of the fierce anger of the L
12:14 Thus says the L concerning all my evil neighbors
12:16 my name, 'As the L lives,' even as they
12:17 pluck it up and destroy it, says the L
13:1 Thus said the L to me, "Go and buy
13:2 the word of the L, and put it on
13:3 the word of the L came to me a
13:5 the Euphrates, as the L commanded me.
13:6 after many days the L said to me, "Arise,
13:8 the word of the L came to me:
13:9 me: "Thus says the L: Even so will I
13:11 to me, says the L, that they might be
13:12 word: 'Thus says the L, the God of Israel,
13:13 them, 'Thus says the L: Behold, I will fill
13:14 against another, fathers and sons together, says the L
13:15 not proud, for the L has spoken.
13:16 Give glory to the L your God before he
13:17 with tears, because the L's flock has been taken
13:25 to you, says the L, because you have forgotten
14:1 The word of the L which came to Jeremiah
14:7 against us, act, O L, for thy name's sake;
14:9 Yet thou, O L, art in the midst of
14:10 Thus says the L concerning this people: "They have
14:10 their feet; therefore the L does not accept them,
14:11 The L said to me: "Do not pray for
14:13 Then I said: "Ah, L GOD, behold, the prophets
14:14 And the L said to me: "The prophets are
14:15 Therefore thus says the L concerning the prophets
14:20 acknowledge our wickedness, O L, and the iniquity of
14:22 thou not he, O L our God?
15:1 Then the L said to me, "Though Moses and
15:2 them, 'Thus says the L: "Those who are for
15:3 of destroyers, says the L: the sword to slay,
15:6 rejected me, says the L, you keep going backward;
15:9 to the sword before their enemies, says the L
15:11 let it be, O L, if I have not
15:15 O L, thou knowest; remember me and visit me,
15:16 by thy name, O L, God of hosts.
15:19 Therefore thus says the L: "If you return, I
15:20 to save you and deliver you, says the L

16:1 The word of the L came to me:
16:3 For thus says the L concerning the sons and
16:5 "For thus says the L: Do not enter the
16:5 this people, says the L, my steadfast love and
16:9 For thus says the L of hosts, the God
16:10 you, 'Why has the L pronounced all this great
16:10 have committed against the L our God?'
16:11 forsaken me, says the L, and have gone after
16:14 are coming, says the L, when it shall no
16:14 be said, 'As the L lives who brought up
16:15 Egypt,' but 'As the L lives who brought up
16:16 many fishers, says the L, and they shall catch
16:19 O L, my strength and my stronghold, my refuge
16:21 they shall know that my name is the L
17:5 Thus says the L: "Cursed is the man who
17:5 his arm, whose heart turns away from the L
17:7 who trusts in the L, whose trust is the
17:7 trusts in the LORD, whose trust is the L
17:10 "I the L search the mind and try the
17:13 O L, the hope of Israel, all who forsake
17:13 they have forsaken the L, the fountain of living
17:14 Heal me, O L, and I shall be healed;
17:15 to me, "Where is the word of the L
17:19 Thus said the L to me: "Go and stand
17:20 the word of the L, you kings of Judah,
17:21 Thus says the L: Take heed for the sake
17:24 to me, says the L, and bring in no
17:26 bringing thank offerings to the house of the L
18:1 to Jeremiah from the L:
18:5 the word of the L came to me:
18:6 says the L
18:11 Jerusalem: 'Thus says the L, Behold, I am shaping
18:13 "Therefore thus says the L: Ask among the nations,
18:19 heed to me, O L, and hearken to my
18:23 Yet, thou, O L, knowest all their plotting to
19:1 Thus said the L, "Go, buy a potter's earthen
19:3 the word of the L, O kings of Judah
19:3 Thus says the L of hosts, the God of
19:6 are coming, says the L, when this place shall
19:11 them, 'Thus says the L of hosts: So will
19:12 this place, says the L, and to its inhabitants,
19:14 from Topheth, where the L had sent him to
19:14 the court of the L's house, and said to
19:15 people: "Thus says the L of hosts, the God
20:1 the house of the L, heard Jeremiah prophesying
20:2 upper Benjamin Gate of the house of the L
20:3 said to him, "The L does not call your
20:4 For thus says the L: Behold, I will make
20:7 O L, thou hast deceived me, and I was
20:8 the word of the L has become for me
20:11 But the L is with me as a dread
20:12 O L of hosts, who triest the righteous, who
20:13 Sing to the L; praise the LORD!
20:13 Sing to the LORD; praise the L
20:16 the cities which the L overthrew without pity; let
21:1 to Jeremiah from the L, when King Zedekiah sent
21:2 saying, "Inquire of the L for us, for Nebuchadrezzar
21:2 against us; perhaps the L will deal with us
21:4 Zedekiah, 'Thus says the L, the God of Israel:
21:7 Afterward, says the L, I will give Zedekiah king
21:8 say: 'Thus says the L: Behold, I set before
21:10 for good, says the L: it shall be given
21:11 the word of the L,
21:12 Thus says the L: "'Execute justice in the morning,
21:13 the plain, says the L; you who say, 'Who
21:14 your doings, says the L; I will kindle a
22:1 Thus says the L: "Go down to the house
22:2 the word of the L, O King of Judah,
22:3 Thus says the L: Do justice and righteousness, and
22:5 by myself, says the L, that this house shall
22:6 For thus says the L concerning the house of
22:8 neighbor, "Why has the L dealt thus with this
22:9 the covenant of the L their God, and worshiped
22:11 For thus says the L concerning Shallum the son
22:16 says the L
22:18 thus says the L concerning Jehoiakim the son
22:18 for him, saying, 'Ah L or 'Ah his majesty!'
22:24 I live, says the L, though Coniah the son
22:29 land, land, land, hear the word of the L
22:30 Thus says the L: "Write this man down as
23:1 says the L
23:2 Therefore thus says the L, the God of Israel,
23:2 attend to you for your evil-doings, says the L
23:4 dismayed, neither shall any be missing, says the L
23:5 are coming, says the L, when I will raise
23:6 will be called: 'The L is our righteousness.'
23:7 are coming, says the L, when men shall no
23:7 longer say, 'As the L lives who brought up
23:8 Egypt,' but 'As the L lives who brought up
23:9 wine, because of the L and because of his
23:11 house I have found their wickedness, says the L
23:12 in the year of their punishment, says the L
23:15 Therefore thus says the L of hosts concerning the
23:16 Thus says the L of hosts: "Do not listen
23:16 own minds, not from the mouth of the L
23:17 the word of the L, 'It shall be well
23:18 the council of the L to perceive and to
23:19 Behold, the storm of the L
23:20 The anger of the L will not turn back
23:23 at hand, says the L, and not a God
23:24 says the L
23:24 says the L
23:28 says the L
23:29 like fire, says the L, and like a hammer
23:30 the prophets, says the L, who steal my words
23:31 the prophets, says the L, who use their tongues
23:31 and say, 'Says the L
23:32 lying dreams, says the L, and who tell them
23:32 not profit this people at all, says the L
23:33 the burden of the L you shall say to
23:33 you off, says the L
23:34 'The burden of the L I will punish that
23:35 brother, 'What has the L answered?' or 'What has
23:35 or 'What has the L spoken?'
23:36 'the burden of the L you shall mention no
23:36 the living God, the L of hosts, our God.
23:37 prophet, 'What has the L answered you?' or 'What
23:37 or 'What has the L spoken?'
23:38 'The burden of the L thus says the LORD,
23:38 LORD,' thus says the L, 'Because you have said
23:38 have said these words, "The burden of the L
23:38 "You shall not say, 'The burden of the L
24:1 them to Babylon, the L showed me this vision:
24:1 of figs placed before the temple of the L
24:3 And the L said to me, "What do you
24:4 the word of the L came to me:
24:5 me: "Thus says the L, the God of Israel:
24:7 that I am the L; and they shall be
24:8 "But thus says the L: Like the bad figs
25:3 the word of the L has come to me,
25:4 to hear, although the L persistently sent to you
25:5 the land which the L has given to you
25:7 to me, says the L, that you might provoke
25:8 "Therefore thus says the L of hosts: Because you
25:9 the north, says the L, and for Nebuchadrezzar the
25:12 their iniquity, says the L, making the land an
25:15 Thus the L, the God of Israel, said to
25:17 the cup from the L's hand, and made all
25:17 nations to whom the L sent me drink it:
25:27 them, 'Thus says the L of hosts, the God
25:28 them, 'Thus says the L of hosts: You must
25:29 the earth, says the L of hosts.'
25:30 say to them: 'The L will roar from on
25:31 the earth, for the L has an indictment against
25:31 the sword, says the L
25:32 LORD.' "Thus says the L of hosts: Behold, evil
25:33 those slain by the L on that day shall
25:36 For the L is despoiling their pasture,
25:37 devastated, because of the fierce anger of the L
26:1 word came from the L,
26:2 LORD, "Thus says the L: Stand in the court
26:2 the court of the L's house, and speak to
26:2 the house of the L all the words that
26:4 them, 'Thus says the L: If you will not
26:7 speaking these words in the house of the L
26:8 speaking all that the L had commanded him to
26:9 the name of the L, saying, 'This house shall
26:9 gathered about Jeremiah in the house of the L
26:10 the house of the L and took their seat
26:10 the New Gate of the house of the L
26:12 the people, saying, "The L sent me to prophesy
26:13 the voice of the L your God, and the
26:13 your God, and the L will repent of the
26:15 for in truth the L sent me to you
26:16 the name of the L our God."
26:18 Judah: 'Thus says the L of hosts, Zion shall
26:19 he not fear the L and entreat the favor
26:19 the favor of the L, and did not the
26:19 and did not the L repent of the evil
26:20 the name of the L, Uriah the son of
27:1 Judah, this word came to Jeremiah from the L
27:2 Thus the L said to me: "Make yourself thongs

27:4 masters: 'Thus says the L of hosts, the God
27:8 with pestilence, says the L, until I have consumed
27:11 to till it and dwell there, says the L
27:13 by pestilence, as the L has spoken concerning any
27:15 sent them, says the L, but they are prophesying
27:16 saying, "Thus says the L: Do not listen to
27:16 the vessels of the L's house will now shortly
27:18 the word of the L is with them, then
27:18 them intercede with the L of hosts, that the
27:18 the house of the L, in the house of
27:19 For thus says the L of hosts concerning the
27:21 thus says the L of hosts, the God
27:21 the house of the L, in the house of
27:22 when I give attention to them, says the L
28:1 the house of the L, in the presence of
28:2 saying, "Thus says the L of hosts, the God
28:3 vessels of the L's house, which Nebuchadnezzar king
28:4 to Babylon, says the L, for I will break
28:5 the house of the L;
28:6 May the L do so; may the LORD make
28:6 do so; may the L make the words which
28:6 the house of the L, and all the exiles.
28:9 be known that the L has truly sent the
28:11 saying, "Thus says the L: Even so will I
28:12 the word of the L came to Jeremiah:
28:13 Hananiah, 'Thus says the L: You have broken wooden
28:14 For thus says the L of hosts, the God
28:15 Hananiah, "Listen, Hananiah, the L has not sent you,
28:16 Therefore thus says the L: 'Behold, I will remove
28:16 die, because you have uttered rebellion against the L
29:4 said: "Thus says the L of hosts, the God
29:7 and pray to the L on its behalf, for
29:8 For thus says the L of hosts, the God
29:9 name; I did not send them, says the L
29:10 "For thus says the L: When seventy years are
29:11 for you, says the L, plans for welfare and
29:14 by you, says the L, and I will restore
29:14 driven you, says the L, and I will bring
29:15 you have said, 'The L has raised up prophets
29:16 Thus says the L concerning the king who
29:17 exile: 'Thus says the L of hosts, Behold, I
29:19 my words, says the L, which I persistently sent
29:19 not listen, says the L --
29:20 the word of the L, all you exiles whom
29:21 Babylon: 'Thus says the L of hosts, the God
29:22 Judah in Babylon: "The L make you like Zedekiah
29:23 who knows, and I am witness, says the L
29:25 say: "Thus says the L of hosts, the God
29:26 the priests, saying, 'The L has made you priest
29:26 the house of the L over every madman who
29:30 the word of the L came to Jeremiah:
29:31 'Thus says the L concerning Shemaiah of Nehelam:
29:32 therefore thus says the L: Behold, I will punish
29:32 my people, says the L, for he has talked
29:32 LORD, for he has talked rebellion against the L
30:1 to Jeremiah from the L:
30:2 LORD: "Thus says the L, the God of Israel:
30:3 are coming, says the L, when I will restore
30:3 and Judah, says the L, and I will bring
30:4 the words which the L spoke concerning Israel and
30:5 Judah: "Thus says the L: We have heard a
30:8 that day, says the L of hosts, that I
30:9 they shall serve the L their God and David
30:10 my servant, says the L, nor be dismayed, O
30:11 save you, says the L; I will make a
30:12 "For thus says the L: Your hurt is incurable,
30:17 will heal, says the L, because they have called
30:18 cares!' "Thus says the L: Behold, I will restore
30:21 says the L
30:23 Behold the storm of the L
30:24 fierce anger of the L will not turn back
31:1 that time, says the L, I will be the
31:2 Thus says the L: "The people who survived the
31:3 sought for rest, the L appeared to him from
31:6 to Zion, to the L our God.'"
31:7 For thus says the L: "Sing aloud with gladness
31:7 praise, and say, 'The L has saved his people,
31:10 the word of the L, O nations, and declare
31:11 his flock.' For the L has ransomed Jacob, and
31:12 the goodness of the L, over the grain, the
31:14 shall be satisfied with my goodness, says the L
31:15 Thus says the L: "A voice is heard in
31:16 Thus says the L: "Keep your voice from weeping,
31:16 be rewarded, says the L, and they shall come
31:17 your future, says the L, and your children shall
31:18 for thou art the L my God.
31:20 will surely have mercy on him, says the L
31:22 For the L has created a new thing on
31:23 Thus says the L of hosts, the God of
31:23 restore their fortunes: 'The L bless you, O habitation
31:27 are coming, says the L, when I will sow
31:28 them to build and to plant, says the L
31:31 are coming, says the L, when I will make
31:32 broke, though I was their husband, says the L
31:33 those days, says the L: I will put my
31:34 brother, saying, 'Know the L for they shall all
31:34 the greatest, says the L; for I will forgive
31:35 Thus says the L, who gives the sun for
31:35 its waves roar--the L of hosts is his
31:36 before me, says the L, then shall the descendants
31:37 Thus says the L: "If the heavens above can
31:37 for all that they have done, says the L
31:38 are coming, says the L, when the city shall
31:38 be rebuilt for the L from the tower of
31:40 toward the east, shall be sacred to the L
32:1 to Jeremiah from the L in the tenth year
32:3 say, 'Thus says the L: Behold, I am giving
32:5 visit him, says the L; though you fight against
32:6 "The word of the L came to me:
32:8 the word of the L, and said to me,
32:8 knew that this was the word of the L
32:14 saying, 'Thus says the L of hosts, the God
32:15 For thus says the L of hosts, the God
32:16 I prayed to the L, saying:
32:17 the LORD, saying: 'Ah L GOD!
32:18 whose name is the L of hosts,
32:25 Yet thou, O L GOD, hast said to me,
32:26 The word of the L came to Jeremiah:
32:27 "Behold, I am the L, the God of all
32:28 Therefore, thus says the L: Behold, I am giving
32:30 by the work of their hands, says the L
32:36 therefore thus says the L, the God of Israel,
32:42 "For thus says the L: Just as I have
32:44 for I will restore their fortunes, says the L
33:1 The word of the L came to Jeremiah a
33:2 guard: "Thus says the L who made the earth,
33:2 made the earth, the L who formed it to
33:2 to establish it--the L is his name:
33:4 For thus says the L, the God of Israel,
33:10 "Thus says the L: In this place of which
33:11 the house of the L: 'Give thanks to the
33:11 'Give thanks to the L of hosts, for the
33:11 of hosts, for the L is good, for his
33:11 of the land as at first, says the L
33:12 "Thus says the L of hosts: In this place
33:13 of the one who counts them, says the L
33:14 are coming, says the L, when I will fulfil
33:16 will be called: 'The L is our righteousness.'
33:17 "For thus says the L: David shall never lack
33:19 The word of the L came to Jeremiah:
33:20 Jeremiah: "Thus says the L: If you can break
33:23 The word of the L came to Jeremiah:
33:24 people are saying, 'The L has rejected the two
33:25 Thus says the L: If I have not established
34:1 to Jeremiah from the L, when Nebuchadrezzar king
34:2 cities: "Thus says the L, the God of Israel:
34:2 him, 'Thus says the L: Behold, I am giving
34:4 the word of the L, O Zedekiah king of
34:4 Thus says the L concerning you: 'You shall not
34:5 for you, saying, "Alas, L For I have spoken
34:5 For I have spoken the word, says the L
34:8 to Jeremiah from the L, after King Zedekiah had
34:12 The word of the L came to Jeremiah from
34:12 to Jeremiah from the L:
34:13 LORD: "Thus says the L, the God of Israel:
34:17 Therefore, thus says the L: You have not obeyed
34:17 sword, to pestilence, and to famine, says the L
34:22 will command, says the L, and will bring them
35:1 to Jeremiah from the L in the days of
35:2 the house of the L, into one of the
35:4 the house of the L into the chamber of
35:12 the word of the L came to Jeremiah:
35:13 Jeremiah: "Thus says the L of hosts, the God
35:13 says the L
35:17 Therefore, thus says the L, the God of hosts,
35:18 said, "Thus says the L of hosts, the God
35:19 therefore thus says the L of hosts, the God
36:1 to Jeremiah from the L:
36:4 the words of the L which he had spoken
36:5 the house of the L;
36:6 the people in the L's house you shall read
36:6 the words of the L from the scroll which

36:7 will come before the L, and that every one
36:7 and wrath that the L has pronounced against this
36:8 the words of the L in the LORD's house.
36:8 the LORD in the L's house.
36:9 Judah to Jerusalem proclaimed a fast before the L
36:10 the house of the L, in the chamber of
36:10 New Gate of the L's house.
36:11 the words of the L from the scroll,
36:26 the prophet, but the L hid them.
36:27 the word of the L came to Jeremiah:
36:29 say, 'Thus says the L, You have burned this
36:30 Therefore thus says the L concerning Jehoiakim king
37:2 the words of the L which he spoke through
37:3 for us to the L our God."
37:6 the word of the L came to Jeremiah the
37:7 prophet: "Thus says the L, God of Israel: Thus
37:9 Thus says the L, Do not deceive yourselves, saying,
37:17 and said, "Is there any word from the L
37:20 pray you, O my L the king: let my
38:2 people, "Thus says the L, He who stays in
38:3 Thus says the L, This city shall surely be
38:9 to the king, "My L the king, these men
38:14 the third entrance of the temple of the L
38:16 to Jeremiah, "As the L lives, who made our
38:17 Zedekiah, "Thus says the L, the God of hosts,
38:20 the voice of the L in what I say
38:21 the vision which the L has shown to me:
39:15 The word of the L came to Jeremiah while
39:16 Ethiopian, 'Thus says the L of hosts, the God
39:17 that day, says the L, and you shall not
39:18 have put your trust in me, says the L
40:1 Jeremiah from the L after Nebuzaradan the captain
40:2 said to him, "The L your God pronounced this
40:3 against this place; the L has brought it about,
40:3 you sinned against the L, and did not obey
41:5 incense to present at the temple of the L
42:2 and pray to the L your God for us,
42:3 see us), that the L your God may show
42:4 will pray to the L your God according to
42:4 request, and whatever the L answers you I will
42:5 to Jeremiah, "May the L be a true and
42:5 word with which the L your God sends you
42:6 the voice of the L our God to whom
42:6 the voice of the L our God."
42:7 the word of the L came to Jeremiah.
42:9 them, "Thus says the L, the God of Israel,
42:11 fear him, says the L, for I am with
42:13 the voice of the L your God
42:15 the word of the L, O remnant of Judah.
42:15 Thus says the L of hosts, the God of
42:18 "For thus says the L of hosts, the God
42:19 The L has said to you, O remnant of
42:20 sent me to the L your God, saying, 'Pray
42:20 for us to the L our God, and whatever
42:20 God, and whatever the L our God says declare
42:21 the voice of the L your God in anything
43:1 these words of the L their God, with which
43:1 God, with which the L their God had sent
43:2 The L our God did not send you to
43:4 the voice of the L, to remain in the
43:7 they did not obey the voice of the L
43:8 the word of the L came to Jeremiah in
43:10 them, 'Thus says the L of hosts, the God
44:2 Pathros, "Thus says the L of hosts, the God
44:7 now thus says the L God of hosts, the
44:11 "Therefore thus says the L of hosts, the God
44:16 the name of the L, we will not listen
44:21 land, did not the L remember it?
44:22 The L could no longer bear your evil-doings and
44:23 you sinned against the L and did not obey
44:23 the voice of the L or walk in his
44:24 the word of the L, all you of Judah
44:25 Egypt, Thus says the L of hosts, the God
44:26 the word of the L, all you of Judah
44:26 great name, says the L, that my name shall
44:26 Egypt, saying, 'As the L GOD lives.'
44:29 to you, says the L, that I will punish
44:30 evil: Thus says the L, Behold, I will give
45:2 Judah: "Thus says the L, the God of Israel,
45:3 for the L has added sorrow to my pain;
45:4 him, Thus says the L: Behold, what I have
45:5 all flesh, says the L; but I will give
46:1 The word of the L which came to Jeremiah
46:5 says the L
46:10 the day of the L GOD of hosts, a
46:10 For the L GOD of hosts holds a sacrifice
46:13 The word which the L spoke to Jeremiah the
46:15 Because the L thrust him down.
46:18 whose name is the L of hosts, like Tabor
46:23 her forest, says the L, though it is impenetrable,
46:25 The L of hosts, the God of Israel, said:
46:26 as in the days of old, says the L
46:28 my servant, says the L, for I am with
47:1 The word of the L that came to Jeremiah
47:2 "Thus says the L: Behold, waters are rising out
47:4 For the L is destroying the Philistines, the remnant
47:6 Ah, sword of the L
47:7 be quiet, when the L has given it a
48:1 Thus says the L of hosts, the God of
48:8 be destroyed, as the L has spoken.
48:10 the work of the L with slackness; and cursed
48:12 are coming, says the L, when I shall send
48:15 whose name is the L of hosts.
48:25 off, and his arm is broken, says the L
48:26 magnified himself against the L; so that Moab shall
48:30 his insolence, says the L; his boasts are false,
48:35 in Moab, says the L, him who offers sacrifice
48:38 vessel for which no one cares, says the L
48:40 For thus says the L: "Behold, one shall fly
48:42 a people, because he magnified himself against the L
48:43 says the L
48:44 in the year of their punishment, says the L
48:47 of Moab in the latter days, says the L
49:1 Thus says the L: "Has Israel no sons?
49:2 are coming, says the L, when I will cause
49:2 dispossess those who dispossessed him, says the L
49:5 upon you, says the L GOD of hosts, from
49:6 restore the fortunes of the Ammonites, says the L
49:7 Thus says the L of hosts: "Is wisdom no
49:12 For thus says the L: "If those who did
49:13 by myself, says the L, that Bozrah shall become
49:14 heard tidings from the L, and a messenger has
49:16 will bring you down from there, says the L
49:18 were overthrown, says the L, no man shall dwell
49:20 the plan which the L has made against Edom
49:26 that day, says the L of hosts.
49:28 Thus says the L: "Rise up, advance against Kedar!
49:30 says the L
49:31 dwells securely, says the L, that has no gates
49:32 calamity from every side of them, says the L
49:34 The word of the L that came to Jeremiah
49:35 Thus says the L of hosts: "Behold, I will
49:37 evil upon them, my fierce anger, says the L
49:38 and destroy their king and princes, says the L
49:39 will restore the fortunes of Elam, says the L
50:1 The word which the L spoke concerning Babylon,
50:4 that time, says the L, the people of Israel
50:4 they shall seek the L their God.
50:5 join ourselves to the L in an everlasting covenant
50:7 have sinned against the L, their true habitation, the
50:7 their true habitation, the L, the hope of their
50:10 who plunder her shall be sated, says the L
50:13 the wrath of the L she shall not be
50:14 no arrows, for she has sinned against the L
50:15 the vengeance of the L: take vengeance on her,
50:18 Therefore, thus says the L of hosts, the God
50:20 that time, says the L, iniquity shall be sought
50:21 after them, says the L, and do all that
50:24 found and caught, because you strove against the L
50:25 The L has opened his armory, and brought out
50:25 his wrath, for the L GOD of hosts has
50:28 the vengeance of the L our God, vengeance for
50:29 has proudly defied the L, the Holy One of
50:30 shall be destroyed on that day, says the L
50:31 proud one, says the L GOD of hosts; for
50:33 "Thus says the L of hosts: The people of
50:34 Redeemer is strong; the L of hosts is his
50:35 the Chaldeans, says the L, and upon the inhabitants
50:40 neighbor cities, says the L, so no man shall
50:45 the plan which the L has made against Babylon,
51:1 Thus says the L: "Behold, I will stir up
51:5 by their God, the L of hosts; but the
51:6 the time of the L's vengeance, the requital he
51:7 golden cup in the L's hand, making all the
51:10 The L has brought forth our vindication; come, let
51:10 the work of the L our God.
51:11 The L has stirred up the spirit of the
51:11 the vengeance of the L, the vengeance for his
51:12 the ambushes; for the L has both planned and
51:14 The L of hosts has sworn by himself: Surely
51:19 of his inheritance; the L of hosts is his
51:24 that they have done in Zion, says the L

51:25 destroying mountain, says the L, which destroys the
51:26 you shall be a perpetual waste, says the L
51:29 in pain, for the L's purposes against Babylon stand,
51:33 For thus says the L of hosts, the God
51:36 Therefore thus says the L: "Behold, I will plead
51:39 a perpetual sleep and not wake, says the L
51:45 his life from the fierce anger of the L
51:48 against them out of the north, says the L
51:50 Remember the L from afar, and let Jerusalem come
51:51 holy places of the L's house.'
51:52 are coming, says the L, when I will execute
51:53 would come from me upon her, says the L
51:55 For the L is laying Babylon waste, and stilling
51:56 in pieces; for the L is a God of
51:57 whose name is the L of hosts.
51:58 "Thus says the L of hosts: The broad wall
51:62 words, and say, 'O L, thou hast said concerning
52:2 the sight of the L, according to all that
52:3 the anger of the L things came to such
52:13 the house of the L, and the king's house
52:17 the house of the L, and the stands and
52:17 the house of the L, the Chaldeans broke in
52:20 the house of the L, the bronze of all
Lam 1:5 enemies prosper, because the L has made her suffer
1:9 "O L, behold my affliction, for the enemy has
1:11 "Look, O L, and behold, for I am despised."
1:12 upon me, which the L inflicted on the day
1:14 strength to fail; the L gave me into the
1:15 "The L flouted all my mighty men in the
1:15 my young men; the L has trodden as in
1:17 to comfort her; the L has commanded against Jacob
1:18 "The L is in the right, for I have
1:20 "Behold, O L, for I am in distress, my
2:1 How the L in his anger has set the
2:2 The L has destroyed without mercy all the
2:5 The L has become like an enemy, he has
2:6 his appointed feasts; the L has brought to an
2:7 The L has scorned his altar, disowned his sanctuary;
2:7 the house of the L as on the day
2:8 The L determined to lay in ruins the wall
2:9 and her prophets obtain no vision from the L
2:17 The L has done what he purposed, has carried
2:18 Cry aloud to the L
2:19 heart like water before the presence of the L
2:20 Look, O L, and see!
2:20 prophet be slain in the sanctuary of the L
2:22 the anger of the L none escaped or survived;
3:18 is my glory, and my expectation from the L
3:22 steadfast love of the L never ceases, his mercies
3:24 "The L is my portion," says my soul, "therefore
3:25 The L is good to those who wait for
3:26 should wait quietly for the salvation of the L
3:31 For the L will not cast off for ever,
3:36 in his cause, the L does not approve.
3:37 to pass, unless the L has ordained it?
3:40 and examine our ways, and return to the L
3:50 without respite, until the L from heaven looks down
3:55 on thy name, O L, from the depths of
3:58 up my cause, O L, thou hast redeemed my
3:59 done to me, O L; judge thou my cause.
3:61 heard their taunts, O L, all their devices against
3:64 wilt requite them, O L, according to the work
3:66 and destroy them from under thy heavens, O L
4:11 The L gave full vent to his wrath, he
4:16 The L himself has scattered them, he will regard
4:20 of our nostrils, the L's anointed, was taken in
5:1 Remember, O L, what has befallen us; behold, and
5:19 But thou, O L, dost reign for ever; thy
5:21 us to thyself, O L, that we may be
Bar 1:5 and prayed before the L;
1:8 the house of the L, which had been carried
1:10 the altar of the L our God;
1:12 And the L will give us strength, and he
1:13 for us to the L our God, for we
1:13 have sinned against the L our God, and to
1:13 the anger of the L and his wrath have
1:14 the house of the L on the days of
1:15 'Righteousness belongs to the L our God, but
1:17 have sinned before the L,
1:18 the voice of the L our God, to walk
1:18 the statutes of the L which he set before
1:19 the day when the L brought our fathers out
1:19 been disobedient to the L our God, and we
1:20 the curse which the L declared through Moses his
1:21 the voice of the L our God in all
1:21 the sight of the L our God.
2:1 "So the L confirmed his word, which he spoke
2:4 surrounding peoples, where the L has scattered
2:5 we sinned against the L our God, in not
2:6 "Righteousness belongs to the L our God, but
2:7 calamities with which the L threatened us have
2:8 the favor of the L by turning away, each
2:9 And the L has kept the calamities ready, and
2:9 calamities ready, and the L has brought them upon
2:9 upon us, for the L is righteous in all
2:10 the statutes of the L which he set before
2:11 "And now, O L God of Israel, who didst
2:12 have done wrong, O L our God, against all
2:14 Hear, O L, our prayer and our supplication, and
2:15 that thou art the L our God, for Israel
2:16 O L, look down from thy holy habitation, and
2:16 Incline thy ear, O L, and hear;
2:17 open thy eyes, O L, and see; for the
2:17 or justice to the L,
2:18 will ascribe to thee glory and righteousness, O L
2:19 prayer for mercy, O L our God.
2:21 saying: "Thus says the L: Bend your shoulders and
2:22 the voice of the L and will not serve
2:27 dealt with us, O L our God, in all
2:31 that I am the L their God.
2:33 ways of their fathers, who sinned before the L
3:1 "O L Almighty, God of Israel, the soul in
3:2 Hear, O L, and have mercy, for we have
3:4 O L Almighty, God of Israel, hear now the
3:4 the voice of the L their God, so that
3:6 For thou art the L our God, and thee,
3:6 God, and thee, O L, will we praise.
3:8 fathers who forsook the L our God.'"
6:6 "It is thou, O L, whom we must worship."
Ezek 1:3 the word of the L came to Ezekiel the
1:3 the hand of the L was upon him there.
1:28 of the likeness of the glory of the L
2:4 them, 'Thus says the L GOD.'
3:11 them, 'Thus says the L GOD'; whether they hear
3:12 the glory of the L arose from its place,
3:14 the hand of the L being strong upon me;
3:16 the word of the L came to me:
3:22 the hand of the L was there upon me;
3:23 the glory of the L stood there, like the
3:27 them, 'Thus says the L GOD'; he that will
4:13 And the L said, "Thus shall the people of
4:14 Then I said, "Ah L GOD!
5:5 Thus says the L GOD: This is Jerusalem; I
5:7 Therefore thus says the L GOD: Because you are
5:8 therefore thus says the L GOD: Behold, I, even
5:11 I live, says the L GOD, surely, because you
5:13 know that I, the L, have spoken in my
5:15 furious chastisements--I, the L, have spoken--
5:17 I, the L, have spoken."
6:1 The word of the L came to me:
6:3 the word of the L GOD!
6:3 Thus says the L GOD to the mountains and
6:7 and you shall know that I am the L
6:10 that I am the L; I have not said
6:11 Thus says the L GOD: "Clap your hands, and
6:13 that I am the L, when their slain lie
6:14 Then they will know that I am the L
7:1 The word of the L came to me:
7:2 man, thus says the L GOD to the land
7:4 Then you will know that I am the L
7:5 "Thus says the L GOD: Disaster after disaster!
7:9 that I am the L, who smite.
7:19 the wrath of the L; they cannot satisfy their
7:27 and they shall know that I am the L
8:1 the hand of the L GOD fell there upon
8:12 For they say, 'The L does not see us,
8:12 not see us, the L has forsaken the land.'"
8:14 the house of the L; and behold, there sat
8:16 the house of the L; and behold, at the
8:16 the temple of the L, between the porch and
8:16 the temple of the L, and their faces toward
9:4 And the L said to him, "Go through the
9:8 face, and cried, "Ah L GOD!
9:9 for they say, 'The L has forsaken the land,
9:9 the land, and the L does not see.'
10:4 the glory of the L went up from the
10:4 of the brightness of the glory of the L
10:18 the glory of the L went forth from the
10:19 the house of the L; and the glory of
11:1 the house of the L, which faces east.
11:5 the Spirit of the L fell upon me, and
11:5 "Say, Thus says the L: So you think, O

LORD

11:7 Therefore thus says the L GOD: Your slain whom
11:8 upon you, says the L GOD.
11:10 and you shall know that I am the L
11:12 that I am the L; for you have not
11:13 voice, and said, "Ah L GOD!
11:14 the word of the L came to me:
11:15 gone far from the L; to us this land
11:16 say, 'Thus says the L GOD: Though I removed
11:17 say, 'Thus says the L GOD: I will gather
11:21 own heads, says the L GOD."
11:23 the glory of the L went up from the
11:25 the things that the L had showed me.
12:1 The word of the L came to me:
12:8 the word of the L came to me:
12:10 them, 'Thus says the L GOD: This oracle concerns
12:15 that I am the L, when I disperse them
12:16 go, and may know that I am the L
12:17 the word of the L came to me:
12:19 land, Thus says the L GOD concerning the inhabitants
12:20 and you shall know that I am the L
12:21 the word of the L came to me:
12:23 therefore, 'Thus says the L GOD: I will put
12:25 But I the L will speak the word which
12:25 perform it, says the L GOD."
12:26 the word of the L came to me:
12:28 them, Thus says the L GOD: None of my
12:28 be performed, says the L GOD."
13:1 The word of the L came to me:
13:2 the word of the L
13:3 LORD!' Thus says the L GOD, Woe to the
13:5 stand in battle in the day of the L
13:6 they say, 'Says the L when the LORD has
13:6 the LORD,' when the L has not sent them,
13:7 have said, 'Says the L although I have not
13:8 Therefore thus says the L God: "Because you have
13:8 against you, says the L GOD.
13:9 that I am the L GOD.
13:13 Therefore thus says the L GOD: I will make
13:14 and you shall know that I am the L
13:16 no peace, says the L GOD.
13:18 say, Thus says the L GOD: Woe to the
13:20 "Wherefore thus says the L GOD: Behold, I am
13:21 and you shall know that I am the L
13:23 Then you will know that I am the L
14:2 the word of the L came to me:
14:4 them, Thus says the L GOD: Any man of
14:4 the prophet, I the L will answer him myself
14:6 Israel, Thus says the L GOD: Repent and turn
14:7 of me, I the L will answer him myself;
14:8 and you shall know that I am the L
14:9 a word, I, the L, have deceived that prophet,
14:11 their God, says the L GOD."
14:12 the word of the L came to me:
14:14 their righteousness, says the L GOD.
14:16 I live, says the L GOD, they would deliver
14:18 I live, says the L GOD, they would deliver
14:20 I live, says the L GOD, they would deliver
14:21 "For thus says the L GOD: How much more
14:23 in it, says the L GOD."
15:1 the word of the L came to me:
15:6 Therefore thus says the L GOD: Like the wood
15:7 that I am the L, when I set my
15:8 acted faithlessly, says the L GOD."
16:1 the word of the L came to me:
16:3 say, Thus says the L GOD to Jerusalem: Your
16:8 with you, says the L GOD, and you became
16:14 upon you, says the L GOD.
16:19 pleasing odor, says the L GOD.
16:23 says the L GOD),
16:30 your heart, says the L GOD, seeing you did
16:35 the word of the L:
16:36 LORD: Thus says the L GOD, Because your shame
16:43 your head, says the L GOD.
16:48 I live, says the L GOD, your sister Sodom
16:58 of your lewdness and your abominations, says the L
16:59 "Yea, thus says the L GOD: I will deal
16:62 that I am the L,
16:63 have done, says the L GOD."
17:1 The word of the L came to me:
17:3 say, Thus says the L GOD: A great eagle
17:9 Say, Thus says the L GOD: Will it thrive?
17:11 the word of the L came to me:
17:16 I live, says the L GOD, surely in the
17:19 Therefore thus says the L GOD: As I live,
17:21 know that I, the L, have spoken."
17:22 Thus says the L GOD: "I myself will take
17:24 know that I the L bring low the high
17:24 I the L have spoken, and I will do
18:1 The word of the L came to me again:
18:3 I live, says the L GOD, this proverb shall
18:9 surely live, says the L GOD.
18:23 the wicked, says the L GOD, and not rather
18:25 'The way of the L is not just.' Hear
18:29 'The way of the L is not just.' O
18:30 his ways, says the L GOD.
18:32 any one, says the L GOD; so turn, and
20:1 to inquire of the L, and sat before me.
20:2 the word of the L came to me:
20:3 them, Thus says the L GOD, Is it to
20:3 I live, says the L GOD, I will not
20:5 them, Thus says the L GOD: On the day
20:5 saying, I am the L your God.
20:7 Egypt; I am the L your God.
20:12 know that I the L sanctify them.
20:19 I the L am your God; walk in my
20:20 know that I the L am your God.
20:26 that they might know that I am the L
20:27 them, Thus says the L GOD: In this again
20:30 Israel, Thus says the L GOD: Will you defile
20:31 I live, says the L GOD, I will not
20:33 I live, says the L GOD, surely with a
20:36 with you, says the L GOD.
20:38 Then you will know that I am the L
20:39 Israel, thus says the L GOD: Go serve every
20:40 of Israel, says the L GOD, there all the
20:42 that I am the L, when I bring you
20:44 that I am the L, when I deal with
20:44 of Israel, says the L GOD."
20:45 the word of the L came to me:
20:47 the word of the L: Thus says the Lord
20:47 LORD: Thus says the L GOD, Behold, I will
20:48 see that I the L have kindled it; it
20:49 Then I said, "Ah L GOD!
21:1 The word of the L came to me:
21:3 Israel, Thus says the L: Behold, I am against
21:5 know that I the L have drawn my sword
21:7 says the L GOD.
21:8 the word of the L came to me:
21:9 say, Thus says the L, Say: A sword, a
21:13 says the L GOD.
21:17 my fury; I the L have spoken."
21:18 The word of the L came to me again:
21:24 "Therefore thus says the L GOD: Because you have
21:26 punishment, thus says the L GOD: Remove the
21:28 say, Thus says the L GOD concerning the Ammonites,
21:32 remembered; for I the L have spoken."
22:1 the word of the L came to me, saying,
22:3 say, Thus says the L GOD: A city that
22:12 forgotten me, says the L GOD.
22:14 I the L have spoken, and I will do
22:16 and you shall know that I am the L
22:17 the word of the L came to me:
22:19 Therefore thus says the L GOD: Because you have
22:22 know that I the L have poured out my
22:23 the word of the L came to me:
22:28 saying, 'Thus says the L GOD,' when the LORD
22:28 Lord GOD,' when the L has not spoken.
22:31 their heads, says the L GOD."
23:1 The word of the L came to me:
23:22 Oholibah, thus says the L GOD: "Behold, I will
23:28 For thus says the L GOD: Behold, I will
23:32 Thus says the L GOD: "You shall drink your
23:34 have spoken, says the L GOD.
23:35 Therefore thus says the L GOD: Because you have
23:36 The L said to me: "Son of man, will
23:46 For thus says the L GOD: "Bring up a
23:49 that I am the L GOD."
24:1 the word of the L came to me:
24:3 them, Thus says the L GOD: Set on the
24:6 "Therefore thus says the L GOD: Woe to the
24:9 Therefore thus says the L GOD: Woe to the
24:14 I the L have spoken; it shall come to
24:14 judge you, says the L GOD."
24:15 the word of the L came to me:
24:20 "The word of the L came to me:
24:21 Israel, Thus says the L GOD: Behold, I will
24:24 that I am the L GOD.'
24:27 and they will know that I am the L
25:1 The word of the L came to me:
25:3 the word of the L GOD: Thus says the
25:3 GOD: Thus says the L GOD, Because you said,
25:5 Then you will know that I am the L

25:6 For thus says the L GOD: Because you have
25:7 Then you will know that I am the L
25:8 "Thus says the L GOD: Because Moab said, Behold,
25:11 Then they will know that I am the L
25:12 "Thus says the L GOD: Because Edom acted
25:13 therefore thus says the L GOD, I will stretch
25:14 my vengeance, says the L GOD.
25:15 "Thus says the L GOD: Because the Philistines acted
25:16 therefore thus says the L GOD, Behold, I will
25:17 that I am the L, when I lay my
26:1 the word of the L came to me:
26:3 therefore thus says the L GOD: Behold, I am
26:5 have spoken, says the L GOD; and she shall
26:6 Then they will know that I am the L
26:7 "For thus says the L GOD: Behold, I will
26:14 rebuilt; for I the L have spoken, says the
26:14 have spoken, says the L GOD.
26:15 "Thus says the L GOD to Tyre: Will not
26:19 "For thus says the L GOD: When I make
26:21 found again, says the L GOD."
27:1 The word of the L came to me:
27:3 coastlands, thus says the L GOD: "O Tyre, you
28:1 The word of the L came to me:
28:2 Tyre, Thus says the L GOD: "Because your heart
28:6 therefore thus says the L GOD: "Because you
28:10 have spoken, says the L GOD."
28:11 the word of the L came to me:
28:12 him, Thus says the L GOD: "You were the
28:20 The word of the L came to me:
28:22 say, Thus says the L GOD: "Behold, I am
28:22 that I am the L when I execute judgments
28:23 Then they will know that I am the L
28:24 that I am the L GOD.
28:25 "Thus says the L GOD: When I gather the
28:26 that I am the L their God."
29:1 the word of the L came to me:
29:3 say, Thus says the L GOD: "Behold, I am
29:6 of Egypt shall know that I am the L
29:8 therefore thus says the L GOD: Behold, I will
29:9 Then they will know that I am the L
29:13 "For thus says the L GOD: At the end
29:16 that I am the L GOD."
29:17 the word of the L came to me:
29:19 Therefore thus says the L GOD: Behold, I will
29:20 for me, says the L GOD.
29:21 Then they will know that I am the L
30:1 The word of the L came to me:
30:2 say, Thus says the L GOD: "Wail, 'Alas for
30:3 the day of the L is near; it will
30:6 "Thus says the L: Those who support Egypt shall
30:6 the sword, says the L GOD.
30:8 that I am the L, when I have set
30:10 "Thus says the L GOD: I will put an
30:12 of foreigners; I, the L, have spoken.
30:13 "Thus says the L GOD: I will destroy the
30:19 Then they will know that I am the L
30:20 the word of the L came to me:
30:22 Therefore thus says the L GOD: Behold, I am
30:25 and they shall know that I am the L
30:26 Then they will know that I am the L
31:1 the word of the L came to me:
31:10 "Therefore thus says the L GOD: Because it towered
31:15 "Thus says the L GOD: When it goes down
31:18 his multitude, says the L GOD."
32:1 the word of the L came to me:
32:3 Thus says the L GOD: I will throw my
32:8 your land, says the L GOD.
32:11 For thus says the L GOD: The sword of
32:14 like oil, says the L GOD.
32:15 then they will know that I am the L
32:16 chant it, says the L GOD."
32:17 the word of the L came to me:
32:31 the sword, says the L GOD.
32:32 his multitude, says the L GOD."
33:1 The word of the L came to me:
33:11 I live, says the L GOD, I have no
33:17 'The way of the L is not just'; when
33:20 'The way of the L is not just.' O
33:22 the hand of the L had been upon me
33:23 The word of the L came to me:
33:25 them, Thus says the L GOD: You eat flesh
33:27 them, Thus says the L GOD: As I live,
33:29 that I am the L, when I have made
33:30 comes forth from the L
34:1 The word of the L came to me:
34:2 shepherds, Thus says the L GOD: Ho, shepherds of
34:7 the word of the L:
34:8 I live, says the L GOD, because my sheep
34:9 the word of the L:
34:10 LORD: Thus says the L GOD, Behold, I am
34:11 "For thus says the L GOD: Behold, I, I
34:15 lie down, says the L GOD.
34:17 flock, thus says the L GOD: Behold, I judge
34:20 "Therefore, thus says the L GOD to them: Behold,
34:24 And I, the L, will be their God, and
34:24 among them; I, the L, have spoken.
34:27 that I am the L, when I break the
34:30 know that I, the L their God, am with
34:30 my people, says the L GOD.
34:31 your God, says the L GOD."
35:1 The word of the L came to me:
35:3 it, Thus says the L GOD: Behold, I am
35:4 and you shall know that I am the L
35:6 I live, says the L GOD, I will prepare
35:9 Then you will know that I am the L
35:10 of them,--although the L was there--
35:11 I live, says the L GOD, I will deal
35:12 know that I, the L, have heard all the
35:14 Thus says the L GOD: For the rejoicing of
35:15 Then they will know that I am the L
36:1 mountains of Israel, hear the word of the L
36:2 Thus says the L GOD: Because the enemy said
36:3 say, Thus says the L GOD: Because, yea, because
36:4 the word of the L GOD: Thus says the
36:4 GOD: Thus says the L GOD to the mountains
36:5 therefore thus says the L GOD: I speak in
36:6 valleys, Thus says the L GOD: Behold, I speak
36:7 therefore thus says the L GOD: I swear that
36:11 Then you will know that I am the L
36:13 Thus says the L GOD: Because men say to
36:14 of children, says the L GOD;
36:15 to stumble, says the L GOD."
36:16 The word of the L came to me:
36:20 the people of the L, and yet they had
36:22 Israel, Thus says the L GOD: It is not
36:23 that I am the L, says the Lord GOD,
36:23 the LORD, says the L GOD, when through you
36:32 will act, says the L GOD; let that be
36:33 "Thus says the L GOD: On the day that
36:36 know that I, the L, have rebuilt the ruined
36:36 was desolate; I, the L, have spoken, and I
36:37 "Thus says the L GOD: This also I will
36:38 Then they will know that I am the L
37:1 The hand of the L was upon me, and
37:1 the Spirit of the L, and set me down
37:3 And I answered, "O L GOD, thou knowest."
37:4 O dry bones, hear the word of the L
37:5 Thus says the L GOD to these bones: Behold,
37:6 and you shall know that I am the L
37:9 breath, Thus says the L GOD: Come from the
37:12 them, Thus says the L GOD: Behold, I will
37:13 that I am the L, when I open your
37:14 know that I, the L, have spoken, and I
37:14 spoken, and I have done it, says the L
37:15 The word of the L came to me:
37:19 them, Thus says the L GOD: Behold, I am
37:21 them, Thus says the L GOD: Behold, I will
37:28 know that I the L sanctify Israel, when my
38:1 The word of the L came to me:
38:3 say, Thus says the L GOD: Behold, I am
38:10 "Thus says the L GOD: On that day thoughts
38:14 Gog, Thus says the L GOD: On that day
38:17 "Thus says the L GOD: Are you he of
38:18 of Israel, says the L GOD, my wrath will
38:21 against Gog, says the L GOD; every man's sword
38:23 Then they will know that I am the L
39:1 say, Thus says the L GOD: Behold, I am
39:5 have spoken, says the L GOD.
39:6 and they shall know that I am the L
39:7 that I am the L, the Holy One in
39:8 brought about, says the L GOD.
39:10 plundered them, says the L GOD.
39:13 my glory, says the L GOD.
39:17 man, thus says the L GOD: Speak to the
39:20 of warriors,' says the L GOD.
39:22 that I am the L their God, from that
39:25 "Therefore thus says the L GOD: Now I will
39:28 that I am the L their God because I
39:29 of Israel, says the L GOD."
40:1 the hand of the L was upon me,
40:46 come near to the L to minister to him.
41:22 "This is the table which is before the L

L

42:13 priests who approach the L shall eat the most
43:4 the glory of the L entered the temple by
43:5 the glory of the L filled the temple.
43:18 man, thus says the L GOD: These are the
43:19 to me, says the L GOD, a bull for
43:24 present them before the L, and the priests shall
43:24 them up as a burnt offering to the L
43:27 accept you, says the L GOD."
44:2 by it; for the L, the God of Israel,
44:3 eat bread before the L; he shall enter by
44:4 the glory of the L filled the temple of
44:4 the temple of the L; and I fell upon
44:5 And the L said to me, "Son of man,
44:5 the temple of the L and all its laws;
44:6 Israel, Thus says the L GOD: O house of
44:9 "Therefore thus says the L GOD: No foreigner,
44:12 concerning them, says the L GOD, that they shall
44:15 the blood, says the L GOD;
44:27 sin offering, says the L GOD.
45:1 set apart for the L a portion of the
45:4 sanctuary and approach the L to minister to him;
45:9 "Thus says the L GOD: Enough, O princes of
45:9 my people, says the L GOD.
45:15 for them, says the L GOD.
45:18 "Thus says the L GOD: In the first month,
45:23 burnt offering to the L seven young bulls and
46:1 "Thus says the L GOD: The gate of the
46:3 that gate before the L on the sabbaths and
46:4 prince offers to the L on the sabbath day
46:9 land come before the L at the appointed feasts,
46:12 freewill offering to the L, the gate facing east
46:13 burnt offering to the L daily; morning by morning
46:14 cereal offering to the L; this is the ordinance
46:16 "Thus says the L GOD: If the prince makes
47:13 Thus says the L GOD: "These are the boundaries
47:23 his inheritance, says the L GOD.
48:9 set apart for the L shall be twenty-five thousand
48:10 the sanctuary of the L in the midst of
48:14 the land, for it is holy to the L
48:29 several portions, says the L GOD.
48:35 henceforth shall be, The L is there."

L

Dan 1:2 And the L gave Jehoiakim king of Judah into
1:10 "I fear lest my L the king, who appointed
2:47 God of gods and L of kings, and a
3:24 flames, singing hymns to God and blessing the L
3:26 "Blessed art thou, O L, God of our fathers,
3:37 For we, O L, have become fewer than any
3:43 works, and give glory to thy name, O L
3:45 that thou art the L, the only God, glorious
3:49 the angel of the L came down into the
3:52 "Blessed art thou, O L, God of our fathers,
3:58 "Bless the L, all works of the Lord, sing
3:58 all works of the L, sing praise to him
3:59 Bless the L, you heavens, sing praise to him
3:60 Bless the L, you angels of the Lord, sing
3:60 you angels of the L, sing praise to him
3:61 Bless the L, all waters above the heaven, sing
3:62 Bless the L, all powers, sing praise to him
3:63 Bless the L, sun and moon, sing praise to
3:64 Bless the L, stars of heaven, sing praise to
3:65 Bless the L, all rain and dew, sing praise
3:66 Bless the L, all winds, sing praise to him
3:67 Bless the L, fire and heat, sing praise to
3:68 Bless the L, winter cold and summer heat, sing
3:69 Bless the L, dews and snows, sing praise to
3:70 Bless the L, nights and days, sing praise to
3:71 Bless the L, light and darkness, sing praise to
3:72 Bless the L, ice and cold, sing praise to
3:73 Bless the L, frosts and snows, sing praise to
3:74 Bless the L, lightnings and clouds, sing praise to
3:75 the earth bless the L; let it sing praise
3:76 Bless the L, mountains and hills, sing praise to
3:77 Bless the L, all things that grow on the
3:78 Bless the L, you springs, sing praise to him
3:79 Bless the L, seas and rivers, sing praise to
3:80 Bless the L, you whales and all creatures that
3:81 Bless the L, all birds of the air, sing
3:82 Bless the L, all beasts and cattle, sing praise
3:83 Bless the L, you sons of men, sing praise
3:84 Bless the L, O Israel, sing praise to him
3:85 Bless the L, you priests of the Lord, sing
3:85 you priests of the L, sing praise to him
3:86 Bless the L, you servants of the Lord, sing
3:86 you servants of the L, sing praise to him
3:87 Bless the L, spirits and souls of the righteous,
3:88 Bless the L, you who are holy and humble

3:89 Bless the L, Hananiah, Azariah, and Mishael, sing
3:90 Give thanks to the L, for he is good,
3:91 all who worship the L, the God of gods,
4:19 Belteshazzar answered, "My L, may the dream be
4:24 has come upon my L the king,
5:23 up yourself against the L of heaven; and the
9:2 the word of the L to Jeremiah the prophet,
9:3 my face to the L God, seeking him by
9:4 I prayed to the L my God and made
9:4 made confession, saying, "O L, the great and terrible
9:7 To thee, O L, belongs righteousness, but to us
9:8 To us, O L, belongs confusion of face, to
9:9 To the L our God belong mercy and forgiveness;
9:10 the voice of the L our God by following
9:13 the favor of the L our God, turning from
9:14 Therefore the L has kept ready the calamity and
9:14 upon us; for the L our God is righteous
9:15 And now, O L our God, who didst bring
9:16 O L, according to all thy righteous acts, let
9:17 thy own sake, O L, cause thy face to
9:19 O L, hear; O LORD, forgive; O LORD, give
9:19 O LORD, hear; O L, forgive; O LORD, give
9:19 O LORD, forgive; O L, give heed and act;
9:20 my supplication before the L my God for the
10:16 before me, "O my L, by reason of the
10:17 How can my L's servant talk with my lord?
10:17 How can my lord's servant talk with my L
10:19 and said, "Let my L speak, for you have
12:8 I said, "O my L, what shall be the
13:2 very beautiful woman and one who feared the L
13:5 Concerning them the L had said: "Iniquity came
13:23 than to sin in the sight of the L
13:35 toward heaven, for her heart trusted in the L
13:44 The L heard her cry.
13:53 go free, though the L said, 'Do not put
14:25 "I will worship the L my God, for he
14:34 the angel of the L said to Habakkuk, "Take
14:36 the angel of the L took him by the
14:41 "Thou art great, O L God of Daniel, and
Hos 1:1 The word of the L that came to Hosea
1:2 When the L first spoke through Hosea, the LORD
1:2 spoke through Hosea, the L said to Hosea, "Go,
1:2 the land commits great harlotry by forsaking the L
1:4 And the L said to him, "Call his name
1:6 And the L said to him, "Call her name
1:7 deliver them by the L their God; I will
1:9 And the L said, "Call his name Not my
2:13 after her lovers, and forgot me, says the L
2:16 that day, says the L, you will call me,
2:20 me in faithfulness; and you shall know the L
2:21 that day, says the L, I will answer the
3:1 And the L said to me, "Go again, love
3:1 adulteress; even as the L loves the people of
3:5 return and seek the L their God, and David
3:5 in fear to the L and to his goodness
4:1 the word of the L, O people of Israel;
4:1 of Israel; for the L has a controversy with
4:10 they have forsaken the L to cherish harlotry.
4:15 swear not, "As the L lives."
4:16 is stubborn; can the L now feed them like
5:4 is within them, and they know not the L
5:6 go to seek the L, but they will not
5:7 dealt faithlessly with the L; for they have borne
6:1 us return to the L; for he has torn,
6:3 on to know the L; his going forth is
7:11 not return to the L their God, nor seek
8:1 the house of the L, because they have broken
8:13 eat it; but the L has no delight in
9:3 the land of the L; but Ephraim shall return
9:4 of wine to the L; and they shall not
9:4 shall not come to the house of the L
9:5 on the day of the feast of the L
9:14 Give them, O L—what wilt thou give?
10:2 The L will break down their altars, and destroy
10:3 we fear not the L, and a king, what
10:12 time to seek the L, that he may come
11:10 shall go after the L, he will roar like
11:11 will return them to their homes, says the L
12:2 The L has an indictment against Judah, and will
12:5 him—the L the God of hosts,
12:5 God of hosts, the L is his name:
12:9 I am the L your God from the land
12:13 By a prophet the L brought Israel up from
12:14 bitter provocation; so his L will leave his bloodguilt
13:4 I am the L your God from the land
13:15 the wind of the L, shall come, rising from

	14:1	O Israel, to the L your God, for you
	14:2	and return to the L; say to him, "Take
	14:9	the ways of the L are right, and the
Joel	1:1	The word of the L that came to Joel,
	1:9	are cut off from the house of the L
	1:9	The priests mourn, the ministers of the L
	1:13	the house of the L your God; and cry
	1:13	the LORD your God; and cry to the L
	1:14	the day of the L is near, and as
	1:18	Unto thee, O L, I cry.
	2:1	the day of the L is coming, it is
	2:11	The L utters his voice before his army, for
	2:11	the day of the L is great and very
	2:12	says the L, "return to me with all your
	2:13	Return to the L, your God, for he is
	2:14	drink offering for the L, your God?
	2:17	the ministers of the L, weep and say, "Spare
	2:17	"Spare thy people, O L, and make not thy
	2:18	Then the L became jealous for his land, and
	2:19	The L answered and said to his people, "Behold,
	2:21	and rejoice, for the L has done great things!
	2:23	and rejoice in the L, your God; for he
	2:26	the name of the L your God, who has
	2:27	and that I, the L, am your God and
	2:31	terrible day of the L comes.
	2:32	the name of the L shall be delivered; for
	2:32	who escape, as the L has said, and among
	2:32	be those whom the L calls.
	3:8	nation far-off; for the L has spoken."
	3:11	Bring down thy warriors, O L
	3:14	the day of the L is near in the
	3:16	And the L roars from Zion, and utters his
	3:16	But the L is a refuge to his people,
	3:17	that I am the L your God, who dwell
	3:18	the house of the L and water the valley
	3:21	the guilty, for the L dwells in Zion."
Amos	1:2	And he said: "The L roars from Zion, and
	1:3	says the L: "For three transgressions of Damascus,
	1:5	says the L
	1:6	Thus says the L: "For three transgressions of Gaza,
	1:8	says the L GOD.
	1:9	Thus says the L: "For three transgressions of Tyre,
	1:11	Thus says the L: "For three transgressions of Edom,
	1:13	Thus says the L: "For three transgressions of the
	1:15	says the L
	2:1	Thus says the L: "For three transgressions of Moab,
	2:3	says the L
	2:4	Thus says the L: "For three transgressions of Judah,
	2:4	the law of the L, and have not kept
	2:6	Thus says the L: "For three transgressions of Israel,
	2:11	says the L
	2:16	says the L
	3:1	this word that the L has spoken against you,
	3:6	a city, unless the L has done it?
	3:7	Surely the L GOD does nothing, without revealing his
	3:8	The L GOD has spoken; who can but prophesy?"
	3:10	says the L, "those who store up violence and
	3:11	Therefore thus says the L GOD: "An adversary shall
	3:12	Thus says the L: "As the shepherd rescues from
	3:13	says the L GOD, the God of hosts,
	3:15	says the L
	4:2	we may drink!' The L GOD has sworn by
	4:3	says the L
	4:5	says the L GOD.
	4:6	says the L
	4:8	says the L
	4:9	says the L
	4:10	says the L
	4:11	says the L
	4:13	of the earth–the L, the God of hosts,
	5:3	For thus says the L GOD: "The city that
	5:4	For thus says the L to the house of
	5:6	Seek the L and live, lest he break out
	5:8	of the earth, the L is his name,
	5:14	live; and so the L, the God of hosts,
	5:15	may be that the L, the God of hosts,
	5:16	Therefore thus says the L, the God of hosts,
	5:16	God of hosts, the L: "In all the squares
	5:17	says the L
	5:18	to you who desire the day of the L
	5:18	Why would you have the day of the L
	5:20	the day of the L darkness, and not light,
	5:27	says the L, whose name is the God of
	6:8	The L GOD has sworn by himself (says the
	6:8	by himself (says the L, the God of hosts):
	6:10	We must not mention the name of the L
	6:11	For behold, the L commands, and the great house
	6:14	says the L, the God of hosts; "and they
	7:1	Thus the L GOD showed me: behold, he was
	7:2	land, I said, "O L GOD, forgive, I beseech
	7:3	The L repented concerning this; "It shall not be,"
	7:3	said the L
	7:4	Thus the L GOD showed me: behold, the Lord
	7:4	showed me: behold, the L GOD was calling for
	7:5	Then I said, "O L GOD, cease, I beseech
	7:6	The L repented concerning this; "This also shall not
	7:6	said the L GOD.
	7:7	showed me: behold, the L was standing beside a
	7:8	And the L said to me, "Amos, what do
	7:8	Then the L said, "Behold, I am setting a
	7:15	sycamore trees, and the L took me from following
	7:15	the flock, and the L said to me, 'Go,
	7:16	Israel.' "Now therefore hear the word of the L
	7:17	Therefore thus says the L: 'Your wife shall be
	8:1	Thus the L GOD showed me: behold, a basket
	8:2	Then the L said to me, "The end has
	8:3	says the L GOD; "the dead bodies shall be
	8:7	The L has sworn by the pride of Jacob:
	8:9	says the L GOD, "I will make the sun
	8:11	says the L GOD, "when I will send a
	8:11	water, but of hearing the words of the L
	8:12	the word of the L, but they shall not
	9:1	I saw the L standing beside the altar, and
	9:5	The L, GOD of hosts, he who touches the
	9:6	the earth– the L is his name.
	9:7	says the L
	9:8	the eyes of the L GOD are upon the
	9:8	says the L
	9:12	says the L who does this.
	9:13	says the L, "when the plowman shall overtake the
	9:15	says the L your God.
Obad	1:1	Thus says the L GOD concerning Edom: We have
	1:1	heard tidings from the L, and a messenger has
	1:4	thence I will bring you down, says the L
	1:8	that day, says the L, destroy the wise men
	1:15	the day of the L is near upon all
	1:18	of Esau; for the L has spoken.
Jon	1:1	the word of the L came to Jonah the
	1:3	flee to Tarshish from the presence of the L
	1:3	to Tarshish, away from the presence of the L
	1:4	But the L hurled a great wind upon the
	1:9	and I fear the L, the God of heaven,
	1:10	the presence of the L, because he had told
	1:14	they cried to the L, "We beseech thee, O
	1:14	"We beseech thee, O L, let us not perish
	1:14	blood; for thou, O L, hast done as it
	1:16	the men feared the L exceedingly, and they offered
	1:16	a sacrifice to the L and made vows.
	1:17	And the L appointed a great fish to swallow
	2:1	Jonah prayed to the L his God from the
	2:2	"I called to the L, out of my distress,
	2:6	from the Pit, O L my God.
	2:7	me, I remembered the L; and my prayer came
	2:9	Deliverance belongs to the L
	2:10	And the L spoke to the fish, and it
	3:1	the word of the L came to Jonah the
	3:3	to Nineveh, according to the word of the L
	4:2	he prayed to the L and said, "I pray
	4:2	said, "I pray thee, L, is not this what
	4:3	Therefore now, O L, take my life from me,
	4:4	And the L said, "Do you do well to
	4:6	And the L God appointed a plant, and made
	4:10	And the L said, "You pity the plant, for
Mic	1:1	The word of the L that came to Micah
	1:2	it; and let the L GOD be a witness
	1:2	witness against you, the L from his holy temple.
	1:3	For behold, the L is coming forth out of
	1:12	come down from the L to the gate of
	2:3	thus says the L: Behold, against this family
	2:5	line by lot in the assembly of the L
	2:7	the Spirit of the L impatient?
	2:13	on before them, the L at their head.
	3:4	will cry to the L, but he will not
	3:5	Thus says the L concerning the prophets who lead
	3:8	the Spirit of the L, and with justice and
	3:11	they lean upon the L and say, "Is not
	3:11	say, "Is not the L in the midst of
	4:1	the house of the L shall be established as
	4:2	the mountain of the L, to the house of
	4:2	the word of the L from Jerusalem.
	4:4	the mouth of the L of hosts has spoken.
	4:5	the name of the L our God for ever

L

4:6 that day, says the L, I will assemble the
4:7 strong nation; and the L will reign over them
4:10 be rescued, there the L will redeem you from
4:12 the thoughts of the L, they do not understand
4:13 their gain to the L, their wealth to the
4:13 their wealth to the L of the whole earth.
5:4 the strength of the L, in the majesty of
5:4 the name of the L his God.
5:7 like dew from the L, like showers upon the
5:10 that day, says the L, I will cut off
6:1 Hear what the L says: Arise, plead your case
6:2 the controversy of the L, and you enduring
6:2 the earth; for the L has a controversy with
6:5 you may know the saving acts of the L
6:6 I come before the L, and bow myself before
6:7 Will the L be pleased with thousands of rams,
6:8 and what does the L require of you but
6:9 The voice of the L cries to the city--
7:7 will look to the L, I will wait for
7:8 sit in darkness, the L will be a light
7:9 the indignation of the L because I have sinned
7:10 me, "Where is the L your God?" My eyes
7:17 in dread to the L our God, and they
Nah 1:2 The L is a jealous God and avenging, the
1:2 God and avenging, the L is avenging and wrathful;
1:2 avenging and wrathful; the L takes vengeance on his
1:3 The L is slow to anger and of great
1:3 great might, and the L will by no means
1:7 The L is good, a stronghold in the day
1:9 What do you plot against the L
1:11 plotted evil against the L, and counseled villainy?
1:12 Thus says the L, "Though they be strong and
1:14 The L has given commandment about you: "No more
2:2 (For the L is restoring the majesty of Jacob
2:13 against you, says the L of hosts, and I
3:5 against you, says the L of hosts, and will
Hab 1:2 O L, how long shall I cry for help,
1:12 not from everlasting, O L my God, my Holy
1:12 O L, thou hast ordained them as a judgment;
2:2 And the L answered me: "Write the vision; make
2:13 it not from the L of hosts that peoples
2:14 the glory of the L, as the waters cover
2:16 The cup in the L's right hand will come
2:20 But the L is in his holy temple; let
3:2 O L, I have heard the report of thee,
3:2 and thy work, O L, do I fear.
3:8 Was thy wrath against the rivers, O L
3:18 will rejoice in the L, I will joy in
3:19 GOD, the L, is my strength; he makes my
Zeph 1:1 The word of the L which came to Zephaniah
1:2 says the L
1:3 says the L
1:5 and swear to the L and yet swear by
1:6 back from following the L, who do not seek
1:6 do not seek the L or inquire of him."
1:7 Be silent before the L GOD!
1:7 the day of the L is at hand; the
1:7 is at hand; the L has prepared a sacrifice
1:8 the day of the L's sacrifice--"I will punish
1:10 says the L, "a cry will be heard from
1:12 in their hearts, 'The L will not do good,
1:14 great day of the L is near, near and
1:14 the day of the L is bitter, the mighty
1:17 have sinned against the L; their blood shall be
1:18 on the day of the wrath of the L
2:2 fierce anger of the L, before there comes upon
2:2 you the day of the wrath of the L
2:3 Seek the L, all you humble of the land,
2:3 on the day of the wrath of the L
2:5 The word of the L is against you, O
2:7 For the L their God will be mindful of
2:9 says the L of hosts, the God of Israel,
2:10 the people of the L of hosts.
2:11 The L will be terrible against them; yea, he
3:2 not trust in the L, she does not draw
3:5 The L within her is righteous, he does no
3:8 says the L, "for the day when I arise
3:9 the name of the L and serve him with
3:12 the name of the L,
3:15 The L has taken away the judgments against you,
3:15 King of Israel, the L, is in your midst;
3:17 The L, your God, is in your midst, a
Hag 1:1 the word of the L came by Haggai the
1:2 priest, "Thus says the L of hosts: This people
1:2 yet come to rebuild the house of the L
1:3 the word of the L came by Haggai the
1:5 therefore thus says the L of hosts: Consider how
1:7 "Thus says the L of hosts: Consider how you
1:8 I may appear in my glory, says the L
1:9 says the L of hosts.
1:12 the voice of the L their God, and the
1:12 the prophet, as the L their God had sent
1:12 sent him; and the people feared before the L
1:13 the messenger of the L, spoke to the people
1:13 the people with the L's message, "I am with
1:13 LORD's message, "I am with you, says the L
1:14 And the L stirred up the spirit of Zerubbabel
1:14 the house of the L of hosts, their God,
2:1 the word of the L came by Haggai the
2:4 O Zerubbabel, says the L; take courage, O Joshua,
2:4 the land, says the L; work, for I am
2:4 with you, says the L of hosts,
2:6 For thus says the L of hosts: Once again,
2:7 with splendor, says the L of hosts.
2:8 is mine, says the L of hosts.
2:9 the former, says the L of hosts; and in
2:9 give prosperity, says the L of hosts.'"
2:10 the word of the L came by Haggai the
2:11 prophet, "Thus says the L of hosts: Ask the
2:14 before me, says the L; and so with every
2:15 the temple of the L,
2:17 you did not return to me, says the L
2:18 the foundation of the L's temple was laid, consider:
2:20 The word of the L came a second time
2:23 that day, says the L of hosts, I will
2:23 of Shealtiel, says the L, and make you like
2:23 chosen you, says the L of hosts."
Zech 1:1 the word of the L came to Zechariah the
1:2 the prophet, saying, "The L was very angry with
1:3 them, Thus says the L of hosts: Return to
1:3 to me, says the L of hosts, and I
1:3 to you, says the L of hosts.
1:4 out, 'Thus says the L of hosts, Return from
1:4 did not hear or heed me, says the L
1:6 and said, As the L of hosts purposed to
1:7 the word of the L came to Zechariah the
1:9 'What are these, my L The angel who talked
1:10 are they whom the L has sent to patrol
1:11 the angel of the L who was standing among
1:12 the angel of the L said, 'O LORD of
1:12 the LORD said, 'O L of hosts, how long
1:13 seventy years?' And the L answered gracious and
1:14 out, Thus says the L of hosts: I am
1:16 Therefore, thus says the L, I have returned to
1:16 in it, says the L of hosts, and the
1:17 again, Thus says the L of hosts: My cities
1:17 with prosperity, and the L will again comfort Zion
1:20 Then the L showed me four smiths.
2:5 round about, says the L, and I will be
2:6 the north, says the L; for I have spread
2:6 the four winds of the heavens, says the L
2:8 For thus said the L of hosts, after his
2:9 will know that the L of hosts has sent
2:10 dwell in the midst of you, says the L
2:11 join themselves to the L in that day, and
2:11 shall know that the L of hosts has sent
2:12 And the L will inherit Judah as his portion
2:13 all flesh, before the L; for he has roused
3:1 the angel of the L, and Satan standing at
3:2 And the L said to Satan, "The LORD rebuke
3:2 said to Satan, "The L rebuke you, O Satan!
3:2 The L who has chosen Jerusalem rebuke you!
3:5 the angel of the L was standing by.
3:6 the angel of the L enjoined Joshua,
3:7 Joshua, "Thus says the L of hosts: If you
3:9 its inscription, says the L of hosts, and I
3:10 that day, says the L of hosts, every one
4:4 who talked with me, "What are these, my L
4:5 I said, "No, my L
4:6 the word of the L to Zerubbabel: Not by
4:6 my Spirit, says the L of hosts.
4:8 the word of the L came to me, saying,
4:9 will know that the L of hosts has sent
4:10 the eyes of the L, which range through the
4:13 I said, "No, my L
4:14 who stand by the L of the whole earth."
5:4 it forth, says the L of hosts, and it
6:4 who talked with me, "What are these, my L
6:5 presenting themselves before the L of all the earth.
6:9 the word of the L came to me:
6:12 him, 'Thus says the L of hosts, "Behold, the
6:12 and he shall build the temple of the L

6:13 the temple of the L, and shall bear royal
6:14 the temple of the L as a reminder to
6:15 the temple of the L; and you shall know
6:15 shall know that the L of hosts has sent
6:15 the voice of the L your God."
7:1 the word of the L came to Zechariah in
7:2 the favor of the L,
7:3 the house of the L of hosts and the
7:4 the word of the L of hosts came to
7:7 the words which the L proclaimed by the former
7:8 the word of the L came to Zechariah, saying,
7:9 saying, "Thus says the L of hosts, Render true
7:12 the words which the L of hosts had sent
7:12 wrath came from the L of hosts.
7:13 says the L of hosts,
8:1 the word of the L of hosts came to
8:2 saying, "Thus says the L of hosts: I am
8:3 Thus says the L: I will return to Zion,
8:3 the mountain of the L of hosts, the holy
8:4 Thus says the L of hosts: Old men and
8:6 Thus says the L of hosts: If it is
8:6 my sight, says the L of hosts?
8:7 Thus says the L of hosts: Behold, I will
8:9 Thus says the L of hosts: "Let your hands
8:9 the house of the L of hosts was laid,
8:11 former days, says the L of hosts.
8:14 For thus says the L of hosts: "As I
8:14 not relent, says the L of hosts,
8:17 for all these things I hate, says the L
8:18 the word of the L of hosts came to
8:19 saying, "Thus says the L of hosts: The fast
8:20 "Thus says the L of hosts: Peoples shall yet
8:21 the favor of the L, and to seek the
8:21 and to seek the L of hosts; I am
8:22 come to seek the L of hosts in Jerusalem,
8:22 Jerusalem, and to entreat the favor of the L
8:23 Thus says the L of hosts: In those days
9:1 The word of the L is against the land
9:1 For to the L belong the cities of Aram,
9:4 But lo, the L will strip her of her
9:14 Then the L will appear over them, and his
9:14 forth like lightning; the L GOD will sound the
9:15 The L of hosts will protect them, and they
9:16 On that day the L their God will save
10:1 Ask rain from the L in the season of
10:1 spring rain, from the L who makes the storm
10:3 the leaders; for the L of hosts cares for
10:5 shall fight because the L is with them, and
10:6 for I am the L their God and I
10:7 and rejoice, their hearts shall exult in the L
10:12 them strong in the L and they shall glory
10:12 says the L
11:4 Thus said the L my God: "Become shepherd of
11:5 say, 'Blessed be the L, I have become rich';
11:6 on the inhabitants of this land, says the L
11:11 knew that it was the word of the L
11:13 Then the L said to me, "Cast it into
11:13 into the treasury in the house of the L
11:15 Then the L said to me, "Take once more
12:1 The word of the L concerning Israel: Thus says
12:1 Israel: Thus says the L, who stretched out the
12:4 that day, says the L, I will strike every
12:5 have strength through the L of hosts, their God.'
12:7 "And the L will give victory to the tents
12:8 On that day the L will put a shield
12:8 the angel of the L, at their head.
13:2 that day, says the L of hosts, I will
13:3 the name of the L; and his father and
13:7 says the L of hosts.
13:8 whole land, says the L, two thirds shall be
13:9 they will say, 'The L is my God.'"
14:1 a day of the L is coming, when the
14:3 Then the L will go forth and fight against
14:5 Then the L your God will come, and all
14:7 is known to the L, not day and not
14:9 And the L will become king over all the
14:9 on that day the L will be one and
14:12 plague with which the L will smite all the
14:13 great panic from the L shall fall on them,
14:16 worship the King, the L of hosts, and to
14:17 worship the King, the L of hosts, there will
14:18 plague with which the L afflicts the nations that
14:20 the bells of the horses, "Holy to the L
14:20 the house of the L shall be as the
14:21 be sacred to the L of hosts, so that
14:21 the house of the L of hosts on that

Mal 1:1 the word of the L to Israel by Malachi.
1:2 says the L
1:2 says the L
1:4 the L of hosts says, "They may build, but
1:4 people with whom the L is angry for ever."
1:5 say, "Great is the L, beyond the border of
1:6 says the L of hosts to you, O priests,
1:7 By thinking that the L's table may be despised.
1:8 says the L of hosts.
1:9 says the L of hosts.
1:10 in you, says the L of hosts, and I
1:11 the nations, says the L of hosts.
1:12 you say that the L's table is polluted, and
1:13 at me, says the L of hosts.
1:13 says the L
1:14 yet sacrifices to the L what is blemished; for
1:14 great King, says the L of hosts, and my
2:2 my name, says the L of hosts, then I
2:4 may hold, says the L of hosts.
2:7 the messenger of the L of hosts.
2:8 of Levi, says the L of hosts,
2:11 the sanctuary of the L, which he loves, and
2:12 May the L cut off from the tents of
2:12 an offering to the L of hosts!
2:13 You cover the L's altar with tears, with weeping
2:14 Because the L was witness to the covenant between
2:16 hate divorce, says the L the God of Israel,
2:16 with violence, says the L of hosts.
2:17 You have wearied the L with your words.
2:17 the sight of the L, and he delights in
3:1 before me, and the L whom you seek will
3:1 is coming, says the L of hosts.
3:3 silver, till they present right offerings to the L
3:4 be pleasing to the L as in the days
3:5 fear me, says the L of hosts.
3:6 "For I the L do not change; therefore you,
3:7 to you, says the L of hosts.
3:10 the test, says the L of hosts, if I
3:11 to bear, says the L of hosts.
3:12 of delight, says the L of hosts.
3:13 words have been stout against me, says the L
3:14 in mourning before the L of hosts?
3:16 those who feared the L spoke with one another;
3:16 with one another; the L heeded and heard them,
3:16 those who feared the L and thought on his
3:17 be mine, says the L of hosts, my special
4:1 them up, says the L of hosts, so that
4:3 I act, says the L of hosts.
4:5 terrible day of the L comes.
1Mac 2:53 the commandment, and became L of Egypt.
2Mac 1:8 We besought the L and we were heard, and
1:24 to this effect: "O L, Lord God, Creator of
1:24 this effect: "O Lord, L God, Creator of all
2:2 the commandments of the L, nor to be led
2:8 And then the L will disclose these things, and
2:8 the glory of the L and the cloud will
2:10 Moses prayed to the L, and fire came down
2:22 be abolished, while the L with great kindness
3:22 calling upon the Almighty L that he would keep
3:30 recovery, they praised the L who had acted
3:30 now that the Almighty L had appeared.
3:33 for his sake the L has granted you your
3:35 offered sacrifice to the L and made very great
4:38 The L thus repaid him with the punishment he
5:17 not perceive that the L was angered for a
5:19 But the L did not choose the nation for
5:20 glory when the great L became reconciled.
6:14 the other nations the L waits patiently to punish
6:30 is clear to the L in his holy knowledge
7:6 die nobly, saying, "The L God is watching over
7:20 good courage because of her hope in the L
7:33 And if our living L is angry for a
7:40 his integrity, putting his whole trust in the L
8:2 They besought the L to look upon the people
8:5 the wrath of the L had turned to mercy.
8:14 same time besought the L to rescue those who
8:27 and thanks to the L, who had preserved them
8:29 and besought the merciful L to be wholly reconciled
8:35 the help of the L by opponents whom he
9:5 But the all-seeing L, the God of Israel, struck
9:13 a vow to the L, who would no longer
10:1 and his followers, the L leading them on, recovered
10:4 prostrate and besought the L that they might never
10:28 their reliance upon the L, while the other made
10:38 thanksgivings they blessed the L who shows great
11:6 and tears, besought the L to send a good

11:10 heavenly ally, for the L had mercy on them.
12:36 Judas called upon the L to show himself their
12:41 the ways of the L, the righteous Judge, who
13:10 to call upon the L day and night, now
13:12 had besought the merciful L with weeping and
13:17 was dawning, because the L's help protected him.
14:35 in these words: "O L of all, who hast
14:36 now, O holy One, L of all holiness, keep
14:46 crowd, calling upon the L of life and spirit
15:4 "It is the living L himself, the Sovereign in
15:7 confidence that he would get help from the L
15:21 and called upon the L who works wonders; for
15:21 arms, but as the L decides, that he gains
15:22 in these words: "O L, thou didst send thy
15:29 they blessed the Sovereign L in the language of
15:34 to heaven, blessed the L who had manifested himself,
15:35 to every one of the help of the L
Mt 1:20 an angel of the L appeared to him in
1:22 to fulfil what the L had spoken by the
1:24 the angel of the L commanded him; he took
2:13 an angel of the L appeared to Joseph in
2:15 to fulfil what the L had spoken by the
2:19 an angel of the L appeared in a dream
3:3 the way of the L, make his paths straight."
4:7 shall not tempt the L your God.'"
4:10 'You shall worship the L your God and him
5:33 shall perform to the L what you have sworn.'
7:21 who says to me, L, Lord,' shall enter the
7:21 says to me, 'Lord, L shall enter the kingdom
7:22 will say to me, L, Lord, did we not
7:22 say to me, 'Lord, L, did we not prophesy
8:2 knelt before him, saying, L, if you will, you
8:6 beseeching him and saying, L, my servant is lying
8:8 the centurion answered him, L, I am not worthy
8:21 disciples said to him, L, let me first go
8:25 woke him, saying, "Save, L; we are perishing."
9:28 They said to him, "Yes, L
9:38 few; pray therefore the L of the harvest to
11:25 "I thank thee, Father, L of heaven and earth,
12:8 Son of man is L of the sabbath."
14:28 And Peter answered him, L, if it is you,
14:30 sink he cried out, L, save me."
15:22 mercy on me, O L, Son of David; my
15:25 knelt before him, saying, L, help me."
15:27 She said, "Yes, L, yet even the dogs eat
16:22 and began to rebuke him, saying, "God forbid, L
17:4 Peter said to Jesus, L, it is well that
17:15 kneeling before him said, L, have mercy on my
18:20 and said to him, L, how often shall my
18:24 could not pay, his L ordered him to be
18:25 his knees, imploring him, L, have patience with me,
18:26 pity for him the L of that servant released
18:30 and reported to their L all that had taken
18:31 Then his L summoned him and said to him,
18:33 And in anger his L delivered him to the
20:25 rulers of the Gentiles L it over them, and
20:31 cried out the more, L, have mercy on us,
20:33 They said to him, L, let our eyes be
21:3 you shall say, 'The L has need of them,'
21:9 he who comes in the name of the L
21:42 corner; this was the L's doing, and it is
22:37 "You shall love the L your God with all
22:43 the Spirit, calls him L, saying,
22:44 him Lord, saying, 'The L said to my Lord,
22:44 Lord said to my L, Sit at my right
22:45 David thus calls him L, how is he his
23:38 he who comes in the name of the L
24:42 on what day your L is coming.
25:11 maidens came also, saying, L, lord, open to us.'
25:11 came also, saying, 'Lord, L, open to us.'
25:37 righteous will answer him, L, when did we see
25:44 they also will answer, L, when did we see
26:22 to him one after another, "Is it I, L
27:10 potter's field, as the L directed me."
28:2 an angel of the L descended from heaven and
Mk 1:3 the way of the L, make his paths straight–
2:28 Son of man is L even of the sabbath."
5:19 them how much the L has done for you,
7:27 she answered him, "Yes, L; yet even the dogs
10:42 rule over the Gentiles L it over them, and
11:3 doing this?' say, 'The L has need of it
11:9 he who comes in the name of the L
12:11 corner; this was the L's doing, and it is
12:29 'Hear, O Israel: The L our God, the Lord
12:29 Lord our God, the L is one;
12:30 you shall love the L your God with all
12:36 Holy Spirit, declared, 'The L said to my Lord,
12:36 Lord said to my L, Sit at my right
12:37 David himself calls him L; so how is he
13:20 And if the L had not shortened the days,
16:19 So then the L Jesus, after he had spoken
16:20 preached everywhere, while the L worked with them
Lk 1:6 and ordinances of the L blameless.
1:9 the temple of the L and burn incense.
1:11 an angel of the L standing on the right
1:15 be great before the L, and he shall drink
1:16 of Israel to the L their God,
1:17 make ready for the L a people prepared."
1:25 herself, saying, "Thus the L has done to me
1:28 full of grace, the L is with you!"
1:32 Most High; and the L God will give to
1:38 the handmaid of the L; let it be to
1:43 the mother of my L should come to me?
1:45 of what was spoken to her from the L
1:46 "My soul magnifies the L,
1:58 kinsfolk heard that the L had shown great mercy
1:66 the hand of the L was with him.
1:68 saying, "Blessed be the L God of Israel, for
1:76 will go before the L to prepare his ways,
2:9 an angel of the L appeared to them, and
2:9 the glory of the L shone around them, and
2:11 of David a Savior, who is Christ the L
2:15 has happened, which the L has made known to
2:22 present him to the L
2:23 the law of the L, "Every male that opens
2:23 called holy to the L
2:24 the law of the L, "a pair of turtledoves,
2:26 he had seen the L's Christ.
2:29 blessed God and said, L, now lettest thou thy
2:39 the law of the L, they returned into Galilee,
3:4 the way of the L, make his paths straight.
4:8 'You shall worship the L your God, and him
4:12 shall not tempt the L your God.'"
4:18 "The Spirit of the L is upon me, because
4:19 oppressed, to proclaim the acceptable year of the L
5:8 me, for I am a sinful man, O L
5:12 face and besought him, L, if you will, you
5:17 the power of the L was with him to
6:5 Son of man is L of the sabbath."
6:46 do you call me L, Lord,' and not do
6:46 you call me 'Lord, L and not do what
7:6 him, saying to him, L, do not trouble yourself,
7:13 And when the L saw her, he had compassion
7:19 sent them to the L, saying, "Are you he
9:54 saw it, they said, L, do you want us
9:59 But he said, L, let me first go and
9:61 "I will follow you, L; but let me first
10:1 After this the L appointed seventy others, and sent
10:2 few; pray therefore the L of the harvest to
10:17 returned with joy, saying, L, even the demons are
10:21 "I thank thee, Father, L of heaven and earth,
10:27 "You shall love the L your God with all
10:39 who sat at the L's feet and listened to
10:40 to him and said, L, do you not care
10:41 But the L answered her, "Martha, Martha, you are
11:1 disciples said to him, L, teach us to pray,
11:39 And the L said to him, "Now you Pharisees
12:41 Peter said, L, are you telling this parable for
12:42 And the L said, "Who then is the faithful
13:15 Then the L answered him, "You hypocrites!
13:23 one said to him, L, will those who are
13:25 at the door, saying, L, open to us.' He
13:35 he who comes in the name of the L
17:5 apostles said to the L, "Increase our faith!"
17:6 And the L said, "If you had faith as
17:36 And they said to him, "Where, L
18:6 And the L said, "Hear what the unrighteous judge
18:41 He said, L, let me receive my sight."
19:8 and said to the L, "Behold, Lord, the half
19:8 to the Lord, "Behold, L, the half of my
19:16 came before him, saying, L, your pound has made
19:18 the second came, saying, L, your pound has made
19:20 Then another came, saying, L, here is your pound,
19:25 they said to him, L, he has ten pounds!')
19:31 shall say this, 'The L has need of it.'"
19:34 And they said, "The L has need of it."
19:38 King who comes in the name of the L
20:37 where he calls the L the God of Abraham
20:42 Book of Psalms, 'The L said to my Lord,
20:42 Lord said to my L, Sit at my right
20:44 David thus calls him L; so how is he
22:33 he said to him, L, I am ready to

22:38 And they said, "Look, L, here are two swords."
22:47 would follow, they said, L, shall we strike with
22:59 And the L turned and looked at Peter.
22:59 the word of the L, how he had said
24:34 them, who said, "The L has risen indeed, and
Jn 1:23 the way of the L as the prophet Isaiah
4:1 Now when the L knew that the Pharisees had
6:23 the bread after the L had given thanks.
6:34 They said to him, L, give us this bread
6:68 Simon Peter answered him, L, to whom shall we
8:11 She said, "No one, L
9:38 He said, L, I believe"; and he worshipped him.
11:2 Mary who anointed the L with ointment and wiped
11:3 sent to him, saying, L, he whom you love
11:12 disciples said to him, L, if he has fallen
11:21 Martha said to Jesus, L, if you had been
11:27 said to him, "Yes, L; I believe that you
11:32 feet, saying to him, L, if you had been
11:34 They said to him, L, come and see."
11:39 man, said to him, L, by this time there
12:13 the name of the L, even the King of
12:38 Isaiah might be fulfilled: L, who has believed our
12:38 the arm of the L been revealed?"
13:6 Peter said to him, L, do you wash my
13:9 Peter said to him, L, not my feet only
13:13 call me Teacher and L; and you are right,
13:14 If I then, your L and Teacher, have washed
13:25 he said to him, L, who is it?"
13:36 Peter said to him, L, where are you going?"
13:37 Peter said to him, L, why cannot I follow
14:5 Thomas said to him, L, we do not know
14:8 Philip said to him, L, show us the Father,
14:22 Iscariot) said to him, L, how is it that
20:2 "They have taken the L out of the tomb,
20:13 have taken away my L, and I do not
20:18 "I have seen the L; and she told them
20:20 the disciples were glad when they saw the L
20:25 other disciples told him, "We have seen the L
20:28 Thomas answered him, "My L and my God!"
21:7 Jesus loved said to Peter, "It is the L
21:7 that it was the L, he put on his
21:12 They knew it was the L
21:15 said to him, "Yes, L; you know that I
21:16 said to him, "Yes, L; you know that I
21:17 he said to him, L, you know everything; you
21:20 supper and had said, L, who is it that
21:21 he said to Jesus, L, what about this man?"
Acts 1:6 together, they asked him, L, will you at this
1:21 the time that the L Jesus went in and
1:24 they prayed and said, L, who knowest the hearts
2:20 the day of the L comes, the great and
2:21 the name of the L shall be saved.'
2:25 him, 'I saw the L always before me, for
2:34 he himself says, 'The L said to my Lord,
2:34 Lord said to my L, Sit at my right
2:36 has made him both L and Christ, this Jesus
2:39 every one whom the L our God calls to
2:47 And the L added to their number day by
3:19 the presence of the L,
3:22 Moses said, 'The L God will raise up for
4:24 God and said, "Sovereign L, who didst make the
4:26 together, against the L and against his Anointed--
4:29 And now, L, look upon their threats, and grant
4:33 the resurrection of the L Jesus, and great grace
5:9 agreed together to tempt the Spirit of the L
5:14 were added to the L, multitudes both of men
5:19 an angel of the L opened the prison doors
7:31 the voice of the L came,
7:33 And the L said to him, 'Take off the
7:49 for me, says the L, or what is the
7:59 stoning Stephen, he prayed, L Jesus, receive my
7:60 with a loud voice, L, do not hold this
8:16 the name of the L Jesus.
8:22 and pray to the L that, if possible, the
8:24 for me to the L, that nothing of what
8:25 the word of the L, they returned to Jerusalem,
8:26 an angel of the L said to Philip, "Rise
8:38 the Spirit of the L caught up Philip; and
9:1 the disciples of the L, went to the high
9:5 And he said, "Who are you, L
9:10 The L said to him in a vision, "Ananias."
9:10 And he said, "Here I am, L
9:11 And the L said to him, "Rise and go
9:13 But Ananias answered, L, I have heard from many
9:15 But the L said to him, "Go, for he
9:17 said, "Brother Saul, the L Jesus who appeared to
9:27 he had seen the L, who spoke to him,
9:29 Jerusalem, preaching boldly in the name of the L
9:31 the fear of the L and in the comfort
9:35 Sharon saw him, and they turned to the L
9:42 throughout all Joppa, and many believed in the L
10:4 him in terror, and said, "What is it, L
10:14 But Peter said, "No, L; for I have never
10:33 all that you have been commanded by the L
10:36 Jesus Christ (he is L of all),
11:8 But I said, 'No, L; for nothing common or
11:16 the word of the L, how he said, 'John
11:17 we believed in the L Jesus Christ, who was
11:20 Greeks also, preaching the L Jesus.
11:21 the hand of the L was with them, and
11:21 a great number that believed turned to the L
11:23 remain faithful to the L with steadfast purpose;
11:24 And a large company was added to the L
12:7 an angel of the L appeared, and a light
12:11 am sure that the L has sent his angel
12:17 to them how the L had brought him out
12:23 an angel of the L smote him, because he
13:2 they were worshiping the L and fasting, the Holy
13:10 stop making crooked the straight paths of the L
13:11 the hand of the L is upon you, and
13:12 he was astonished at the teaching of the L
13:47 For so the L has commanded us, saying, 'I
13:49 the word of the L spread throughout all the
14:3 speaking boldly for the L, who bore witness to
14:23 committed them to the L in whom they believed.
15:11 the grace of the L Jesus, just as they
15:17 men may seek the L, and all the Gentiles
15:18 my name, says the L, who has made these
15:26 the sake of our L Jesus Christ.
15:34 the word of the L, with many others also.
15:35 the word of the L, and see how they
15:39 by the brethren to the grace of the L
16:14 The L opened her heart to give heed to
16:15 be faithful to the L, come to my house
16:31 said, "Believe in the L Jesus, and you will
16:32 the word of the L to him and to
17:24 everything in it, being L of heaven and earth,
18:8 synagogue, believed in the L, together with all his
18:9 And the L said to Paul one night in
18:25 the way of the L; and being fervent in
19:5 the name of the L Jesus.
19:10 the word of the L, both Jews and Greeks.
19:13 the name of the L Jesus over those who
19:17 the name of the L Jesus was extolled.
19:20 the word of the L grew and prevailed mightily.
20:19 in Asia, serving the L with all humility and
20:21 of faith in our L Jesus Christ.
20:24 I received from the L Jesus, to testify to
20:28 the church of the L which he obtained with
20:35 the words of the L Jesus, how he said,
21:13 the name of the L Jesus."
21:14 "The will of the L be done."
22:8 answered, 'Who are you, L And he said to
22:10 'What shall I do, L And the Lord said
22:10 do, Lord?' And the L said to me, 'Rise,
22:19 me.' And I said, L, they themselves know that
23:11 The following night the L stood by him and
25:26 to write to my L about him.
26:15 said, 'Who are you, L And the Lord said,
26:15 you, Lord?' And the L said, 'I am Jesus
28:30 and teaching about the L Jesus Christ quite openly
Rom 1:4 dead, Jesus Christ our L,
1:7 our Father and the L Jesus Christ.
4:8 man against whom the L will not reckon his
4:24 the dead Jesus our L,
5:1 with God through our L Jesus Christ.
5:11 in God through our L Jesus Christ, through whom
5:21 to eternal life through Jesus Christ our L
6:23 God is eternal life in Christ Jesus our L
7:25 Thanks be to God through Jesus Christ our L
8:39 the love of God in Christ Jesus our L
9:28 be saved; for the L will execute his sentence
9:29 Isaiah predicted, "If the L of hosts had not
10:9 lips that Jesus is L and believe in your
10:12 and Greek; the same L is Lord of all
10:12 the same Lord is L of all and bestows
10:13 the name of the L will be saved."
10:16 gospel; for Isaiah says, L, who has believed what
11:3 L, they have killed thy prophets, they have
11:34 the mind of the L, or who has been
12:11 zeal, be aglow with the Spirit, serve the L
12:19 "Vengeance is mine, I will repay, says the L

L

13:14 But put on the L Jesus Christ, and make
14:6 the day, observes it in honor of the L
14:6 in honor of the L, since he gives thanks
14:6 in honor of the L and gives thanks to
14:8 we live to the L, and if we die,
14:8 we die to the L; so then, whether we
14:9 that he might be L both of the dead
14:11 I live, says the L, every knee shall bow
14:14 am persuaded in the L Jesus that nothing is
15:6 and Father of our L Jesus Christ.
15:11 and again, "Praise the L, all Gentiles, and let
15:30 you, brethren, by our L Jesus Christ and by
16:2 receive her in the L as befits the saints,
16:8 Greet Ampliatus, my beloved in the L
16:11 Greet those in the L who belong to the
16:12 those workers in the L, Tryphaena and Tryphosa.
16:12 beloved Persis, who has worked hard in the L
16:13 Rufus, eminent in the L, also his mother and
16:18 do not serve our L Christ, but their own
16:20 The grace of our L Jesus Christ be with
16:22 writer of this letter, greet you in the L
1Cor 1:2 the name of our L Jesus Christ, both their
1:2 Jesus Christ, both their L and ours:
1:3 our Father and the L Jesus Christ.
1:7 the revealing of our L Jesus Christ;
1:8 the day of our L Jesus Christ.
1:9 the fellowship of his Son, Jesus Christ our L
1:10 the name of our L Jesus Christ, that all
1:31 written, "Let him who boasts, boast of the L
2:8 not have crucified the L of glory.
2:16 the mind of the L so as to instruct
3:5 you believed, as the L assigned to each.
3:20 and again, "The L knows that the thoughts of
4:4 It is the L who judges me.
4:5 the time, before the L comes, who will bring
4:17 faithful child in the L, to remind you of
4:19 you soon, if the L wills, and I will
5:4 the name of the L Jesus on the man
5:4 the power of our L Jesus,
5:5 the day of the L Jesus.
6:11 the name of the L Jesus Christ and in
6:13 immorality, but for the L, and the Lord for
6:13 the Lord, and the L for the body.
6:14 And God raised the L and will also raise
6:17 is united to the L becomes one spirit with
7:10 not I but the L, that the wife should
7:12 I say, not the L, that if any brother
7:17 the life which the L has assigned to him,
7:22 was called in the L as a slave is
7:22 as a slave is a freedman of the L
7:25 no command of the L, but I give my
7:25 one who by the L's mercy is trustworthy.
7:32 the affairs of the L, how to please the
7:32 how to please the L;
7:34 the affairs of the L, how to be holy
7:35 and to secure your undivided devotion to the L
7:39 married to whom she wishes, only in the L
8:6 we exist, and one L, Jesus Christ, through whom
9:1 Have I not seen Jesus our L
9:1 Are not you my workmanship in the L
9:2 are the seal of my apostleship in the L
9:5 the brothers of the L and Cephas?
9:14 the same way, the L commanded that those who
10:9 must not put the L to the test, as
10:21 the cup of the L and the cup of
10:21 the table of the L and the table of
10:22 Shall we provoke the L to jealousy?
11:11 (Nevertheless, in the L woman is not independent of
11:20 it is not the L's supper that you eat.
11:23 I received from the L what I also delivered
11:23 to you, that the L Jesus on the night
11:26 cup, you proclaim the L's death until he comes.
11:27 the cup of the L in an unworthy manner
11:27 of profaning the body and blood of the L
11:32 are judged by the L, we are chastened so
12:3 and no one can say "Jesus is L
12:5 service, but the same L;
14:21 they will not listen to me, says the L
14:37 writing to you is a command of the L
15:31 in Christ Jesus our L, I die every day!
15:57 the victory through our L Jesus Christ.
15:58 the work of the L, knowing that in the
15:58 knowing that in the L your labor is not
16:7 with you, if the L permits.
16:10 the work of the L, as I am.
16:19 their house, send you hearty greetings in the L
16:22 no love for the L, let him be accursed.
16:22 Our L, come!
16:23 The grace of the L Jesus be with you.
2Cor 1:2 our Father and the L Jesus Christ.
1:3 and Father of our L Jesus Christ, the Father
1:14 the day of the L Jesus.
1:24 Not that we L it over your faith; we
2:12 for me in the L;
3:16 man turns to the L the veil is removed.
3:17 Now the L is the Spirit, and where the
3:17 the Spirit of the L is, there is freedom.
3:18 the glory of the L, are being changed into
3:18 this comes from the L who is the Spirit.
4:5 but Jesus Christ as L, with ourselves as your
4:14 he who raised the L Jesus will raise us
5:6 are away from the L,
5:8 from the body and at home with the L
5:11 the fear of the L, we persuade men; but
6:17 from them, says the L, and touch nothing unclean;
6:18 and daughters, says the L Almighty."
8:5 gave themselves to the L and to us by
8:9 the grace of our L Jesus Christ, that though
8:19 the glory of the L and to show our
8:21 not only in the L's sight but also in
10:8 our authority, which the L gave for building you
10:17 "Let him who boasts, boast of the L
10:18 the man whom the L commends.
11:17 say not with the L's authority but as a
11:31 and Father of the L Jesus, he who is
12:1 go on to visions and revelations of the L
12:8 times I besought the L about this, that it
13:10 the authority which the L has given me for
13:14 The grace of the L Jesus Christ and the
Gal 1:3 the Father and our L Jesus Christ,
1:19 apostles except James the L's brother.
5:10 have confidence in the L that you will take
6:14 the cross of our L Jesus Christ, by which
6:18 The grace of our L Jesus Christ be with
Eph 1:2 our Father and the L Jesus Christ.
1:3 and Father of our L Jesus Christ, who has
1:15 your faith in the L Jesus and your love
1:17 the God of our L Jesus Christ, the Father
2:21 holy temple in the L;
3:11 in Christ Jesus our L,
4:1 a prisoner for the L, beg you to lead
4:5 to your call, one L, one faith, one baptism,
4:17 and testify in the L, that you must no
5:8 are light in the L; walk as children of
5:10 try to learn what is pleasing to the L
5:17 the will of the L is.
5:19 making melody to the L with all your heart,
5:20 the name of our L Jesus Christ to God
5:22 be subject to your husbands, as to the L
6:1 your parents in the L, for this is right.
6:4 up in the discipline and instruction of the L
6:7 will as to the L and not to men,
6:8 same again from the L, whether he is a
6:10 be strong in the L and in the strength
6:21 faithful minister in the L will tell you everything.
6:23 the Father and the L Jesus Christ.
6:24 all who love our L Jesus Christ with love
Phil 1:2 our Father and the L Jesus Christ.
1:14 confident in the L because of my imprisonment,
2:11 that Jesus Christ is L, to the glory of
2:19 I hope in the L Jesus to send Timothy
2:24 I trust in the L that shortly I myself
2:29 receive him in the L with all joy; and
3:1 Finally, my brethren, rejoice in the L
3:8 the surpassing worth of knowing Christ Jesus my L
3:20 await a Savior, the L Jesus Christ,
4:1 firm thus in the L, my beloved.
4:2 and I entreat Syntyche to agree in the L
4:4 Rejoice in the L always; again I will say,
4:5 The L is at hand.
4:10 I rejoice in the L greatly that now at
4:23 The grace of the L Jesus Christ be with
Col 1:3 the Father of our L Jesus Christ, when we
1:10 life worthy of the L, fully pleasing to him,
2:6 received Christ Jesus the L, so live in him,
3:13 each other; as the L has forgiven you, so
3:17 the name of the L Jesus, giving thanks to
3:18 to your husbands, as is fitting in the L
3:20 your parents in everything, for this pleases the L
3:22 but in singleness of heart, fearing the L
3:23 heartily, as serving the L and not men,
3:24 knowing that from the L you will receive the

3:24 you are serving the L Christ.
4:7 and faithful minister and fellow servant in the L
4:17 the ministry which you have received in the L
1Thes 1:1 the Father and the L Jesus Christ: Grace to
1:3 of hope in our L Jesus Christ.
1:6 us and of the L, for you received the
1:8 the word of the L sounded forth from you
2:15 who killed both the L Jesus and the prophets,
2:19 of boasting before our L Jesus at his coming?
3:8 we live, if you stand fast in the L
3:11 Father himself, and our L Jesus, direct our way
3:12 you; and may the L make you increase and
3:13 the coming of our L Jesus with all his
4:1 exhort you in the L Jesus, that as you
4:2 gave you through the L Jesus.
4:6 this matter, because the L is an avenger in
4:15 the word of the L, that we who are
4:15 the coming of the L, shall not precede those
4:16 For the L himself will descend from heaven with
4:17 clouds to meet the L in the air; and
4:17 and so we shall always be with the L
5:2 the day of the L will come like a
5:9 obtain salvation through our L Jesus Christ,
5:12 over you in the L and admonish you,
5:23 the coming of our L Jesus Christ.
5:27 adjure you by the L that this letter be
5:28 The grace of our L Jesus Christ be with
2Thes 1:1 our father and the L Jesus Christ:
1:2 the Father and the L Jesus Christ.
1:7 are afflicted, when the L Jesus is revealed from
1:8 the gospel of our L Jesus.
1:9 the presence of the L and from the glory
1:12 the name of our L Jesus may be glorified
1:12 our God and the L Jesus Christ.
2:1 the coming of our L Jesus Christ and our
2:2 the day of the L has come.
2:8 be revealed, and the L Jesus will slay him
2:13 brethren beloved by the L, because God chose you
2:14 the glory of our L Jesus Christ.
2:16 Now may our L Jesus Christ himself, and God
3:1 the word of the L may speed on and
3:3 But the L is faithful; he will strengthen you
3:4 have confidence in the L about you, that you
3:5 May the L direct your hearts to the love
3:6 the name of our L Jesus Christ, that you
3:12 and exhort in the L Jesus Christ to do
3:16 Now may the L of peace himself give you
3:16 The L be with you all.
3:18 The grace of our L Jesus Christ be with
1Tim 1:2 from God the Father and Christ Jesus our L
1:12 this, Christ Jesus our L, because he judged me
1:14 the grace of our L overflowed for me with
6:3 sound words of our L Jesus Christ and the
6:14 the appearing of our L Jesus Christ;
6:15 King of kings and L of lords,
2Tim 1:2 from God the Father and Christ Jesus our L
1:8 of testifying to our L, nor of me his
1:16 May the L grant mercy to the household of
1:18 me-- may the L grant him to find
1:18 find mercy from the L on that Day--and
2:7 I say, for the L will grant you understanding
2:14 charge them before the L to avoid disputing about
2:19 bearing this seal: "The L knows those who are
2:19 the name of the L depart from iniquity."
2:22 who call upon the L from a pure heart.
2:24 And the L's servant must not be quarrelsome but
3:11 from them all the L rescued me.
4:8 of righteousness, which the L, the righteous judge,
4:14 me great harm; the L will requite him for
4:17 But the L stood by me and gave me
4:18 The L will rescue me from every evil and
4:22 The L be with your spirit.
Philem 1:3 our Father and the L Jesus Christ.
1:5 you have toward the L Jesus and all the
1:16 you, both in the flesh and in the L
1:20 I want some benefit from you in the L
1:25 The grace of the L Jesus Christ be with
Heb 1:10 And, "Thou, L, didst found the earth in the
2:3 at first by the L, and it was attested
7:14 is evident that our L was descended from Judah,
7:21 with an oath, "The L has sworn and will
8:2 set up not by man but by the L
8:8 will come, says the L, when I will establish
8:9 I paid no heed to them, says the L
8:10 those days, says the L: I will put my
8:11 brother, saying, 'Know the L for all shall know
10:16 those days, says the L: I will put my
10:30 And again, "The L will judge his people."
12:5 the discipline of the L, nor lose courage when
12:6 For the L disciplines him whom he loves, and
12:14 holiness without which no one will see the L
13:6 can confidently say, "The L is my helper, I
13:20 from the dead our L Jesus, the great shepherd
Jas 1:1 God and of the L Jesus Christ, to the
1:7 all his ways, will receive anything from the L
2:1 the faith of our L Jesus Christ, the Lord
2:1 Lord Jesus Christ, the L of glory.
3:9 it we bless the L and Father, and with
4:10 Humble yourselves before the L and he will exalt
4:15 to say, "If the L wills, we shall live
5:4 the ears of the L of hosts.
5:7 patient, therefore, brethren, until the coming of the L
5:8 the coming of the L is at hand.
5:10 prophets who spoke in the name of the L
5:11 the purpose of the L, how the Lord is
5:11 the Lord, how the L is compassionate and merciful.
5:14 the name of the L;
5:15 sick man, and the L will raise him up;
1Pet 1:3 and Father of our L Jesus Christ!
1:25 the word of the L abides for ever." That
2:3 for you have tasted the kindness of the L
2:13 Be subject for the L's sake to every human
3:6 husbands, as Sarah obeyed Abraham, calling him L
3:12 the eyes of the L are upon the righteous,
3:12 the face of the L is against those that
3:15 troubled, but in your hearts reverence Christ as L
2Pet 1:2 the knowledge of God and of Jesus our L
1:8 the knowledge of our L Jesus Christ.
1:11 eternal kingdom of our L and Savior Jesus Christ.
1:14 be soon, as our L Jesus Christ showed me.
1:16 and coming of our L Jesus Christ, but we
2:9 lawless deeds), then the L knows how to rescue
2:11 a reviling judgment upon them before the L
2:20 the knowledge of our L and Savior Jesus Christ,
3:2 the commandment of the L and Savior through your
3:8 beloved, that with the L one day is as
3:9 The L is not slow about his promise as
3:10 the day of the L will come like a
3:15 the forbearance of our L as salvation.
3:18 and knowledge of our L and Savior Jesus Christ.
Jude 1:4 our only Master and L, Jesus Christ.
1:9 him, but said, "The L rebuke you."
1:14 prophesied, saying, "Behold, the L came with his
1:17 the apostles of our L Jesus Christ;
1:21 the mercy of our L Jesus Christ unto eternal
1:25 Jesus Christ our L, be glory, majesty, dominion,
Rev 1:8 says the L God, who is and who was
1:10 the Spirit on the L's day, and I heard
4:8 holy, holy, is the L God Almighty, who was
4:11 "Worthy art thou, our L and God, to receive
6:10 loud voice, "O Sovereign L, holy and true, how
11:4 which stand before the L of the earth.
11:8 and Egypt, where their L was crucified.
11:15 the kingdom of our L and of his Christ,
11:17 give thanks to thee, L God Almighty, who art
14:13 who die in the L henceforth." "Blessed indeed," says
15:3 are thy deeds, O L God the Almighty!
15:4 shall not fear and glorify thy name, O L
16:7 the altar cry, "Yea, L God the Almighty, true
17:14 them, for he is L of lords and King
18:8 for mighty is the L God who judges her."
19:6 For the L our God the Almighty reigns.
19:16 King of kings and L of lords.
21:22 its temple is the L God the Almighty and
22:5 or sun, for the L God will be their
22:6 And the L, the God of the spirits of
22:20 Come, L Jesus!
22:21 The grace of the L Jesus be with all

LORDED (2)

Neh 5:15 Even their servants L it over the people.
2Mac 5:23 besides these Menelaus, who L it over his fellow

LORDLY (2)

Judg 5:25 him curds in a L bowl.
Zech 11:13 --the L price at which I was paid

LORDS (58)

Gen 19:2 earth, and said, "My L, turn aside, I pray
19:18 them, "Oh, no, my L;
47:18 of cattle are my L; there is nothing left
Ex 9:29 you may know that the earth is the L

13:12 your cattle that are males shall be the L
Lev 3:16 All fat is the L
27:26 dedicate; whether ox or sheep, it is the L
27:30 the trees, is the L; it is holy to
Num 21:28 Ar of Moab, the L of the heights of
Deut 10:17 gods and Lord of L, the great, the mighty,
Judg 3:3 the nations: the five L of the Philistines, and
11:31 Ammonites, shall be the L, and I will offer
16:5 And the L of the Philistines came to her
16:8 Then the L of the Philistines brought her seven
16:18 sent and called the L of the Philistines, saying,
16:18 Then the L of the Philistines came up to
16:23 Now the L of the Philistines gathered to offer
16:27 and women; all the L of the Philistines were
16:30 house fell upon the L and upon all the
1Sam 2:8 the earth are the L, and on them he
5:8 gathered together all the L of the Philistines, and
5:11 gathered together all the L of the Philistines, and
6:4 the number of the L of the Philistines; for
6:4 was upon all of you and upon your L
6:12 the left, and the L of the Philistines went
6:16 And when the five L of the Philistines saw
6:18 belonging to the five L, both fortified cities and
7:7 gathered at Mizpah, the L of the Philistines went
29:2 As the L of the Philistines were passing on
29:6 Nevertheless the L do not approve of you.
29:7 may not displease the L of the Philistines."
Ezra 8:25 his counselors and his L and all Israel there
Ps 136:3 to the Lord of L, for his steadfast love
Prov 16:11 and scales are the L; all the weights in
Eccl 8:9 the sun, while man L it over man to
Is 16:8 vine of Sibmah; the L of the nations have
26:13 LORD our God, other L besides thee have ruled
44:5 say, 'I am the L another will call himself
44:5 on his hand, 'The L and surname himself by
Jer 5:10 away her branches, for they are not the L
25:34 roll in ashes, you L of the flock, for
25:35 nor escape for the L of the flock.
25:36 the wail of the L of the flock!
Dan 4:36 My counselors and my L sought me, and I
5:1 a thousand of his L, and drank wine in
5:2 the king and his L, his wives, and his
5:3 the king and his L, his wives, and his
5:9 color changed; and his L were perplexed.
5:10 the king and his L, came into the banqueting
5:23 and you and your L, your wives, and your
6:17 the signet of his L, that nothing might be
Obad 1:21 Mount Esau; and the kingdom shall be the L
Rom 14:8 live or whether we die, we are the L
1Cor 8:5 and many L –
10:26 "the earth is the L, and everything in it."
1Tim 6:15 kings and Lord of L,
Rev 17:14 he is Lord of L and King of kings,
19:16 name inscribed, King of kings and Lord of L

LORDSHIP

Lk 22:25 of the Gentiles exercise L over them; and those

LOSE (29)

Judg 18:25 upon you, and you L your life with the
1Kgs 18:5 mules alive, and not L some of the animals."
Eccl 3:6 and a time to L; a time to keep,
Wis 16:3 they desired food, might L the least remnant of
Sir 9:6 to harlots lest you L your inheritance.
19:7 conversation, and you will L nothing at all.
20:21 A man may L his life through shame, or
20:21 life through shame, or L it because of his
29:10 L your silver for the sake of a brother
Zeph 3:7 correction; she will not L sight of all that
2Mac 9:11 spirit, he began to L much of his arrogance
Mt 5:29 is better that you L one of your members
5:30 is better that you L one of your members
10:39 finds his life will L it, and he who
10:42 you, he shall not L his reward."
16:25 save his life will L it, and whoever loses
Mk 8:35 save his life will L it; and whoever loses
9:41 will by no means L his reward.
Lk 9:24 save his life will L it; and whoever loses
17:33 gain his life will L it, but whoever loses
18:1 to pray and not L heart.
Jn 6:39 me, that I should L nothing of all that
2Cor 4:1 God, we do not L heart.
4:16 So we do not L heart.
Gal 6:9 if we do not L heart.
Eph 3:13 ask you not to L heart over what I
Heb 12:5 of the Lord, nor L courage when you are
2Pet 3:17 of lawless men and L your own stability.
2Jn 1:8 that you may not L what you have worked

LOSES (9)

Deut 22:3 your brothers, which he L and you find; you
Mt 10:39 it, and he who L his life for my
16:25 lose it, and whoever L his life for my
Mk 8:35 lose it; and whoever L his life for my
Lk 9:24 lose it; and whoever L his life for my
9:25 the whole world and L or forfeits himself?
15:8 silver coins, if she L one coin, does not
17:33 lose it, but whoever L his life will preserve
Jn 12:25 who loves his life L it, and he who

LOSING

Jud 10:13 the hill country without L one of his men,

LOSS (26)

Gen 31:39 you; I bore the L of it myself; of
Ex 21:19 shall pay for the L of his time, and
Judg 3:25 were utterly at a L; but when he still
Tob 4:13 in shiftlessness there is L and great want, because
Esth 7:4 be compared with the L to the king."
Wis 18:11 man suffered the same L as the king;
19:17 were stricken also with L of sight– just
Sir 18:6 when he stops, he will be at a L
20:2 who confesses his fault will be kept from L
20:8 adversity, and a windfall may result in a L
22:3 and the birth of a daughter is a L
32:24 he who trusts the Lord will not suffer L
40:26 There is no L in the fear of the
Is 47:8 widow or know the L of children":
47:9 in one day; the L of children and widowhood
Dan 6:2 account, so that the king might suffer no L
2Mac 2:26 calls for sweat and L of sleep,
Acts 25:20 Being at a L how to investigate these questions,
27:10 with injury and much L, not only of the
27:21 sail from Crete and incurred this injury and L
27:22 there will be no L of life among you,
1Cor 3:15 up, he will suffer L, though he himself will
2Cor 7:9 that you suffered no L through us.
Phil 3:7 had, I counted as L for the sake of
3:8 I count everything as L because of the surpassing
3:8 I have suffered the L of all things, and

LOSSES

Sir 20:10 There are L because of glory, and there are

LOST (50)

Ex 22:9 for any kind of L thing, of which one
Lev 6:3 has found what was L and lied about it,
6:4 to him, or the L thing which he found,
Deut 22:3 shall do with any L thing of your brothers,
Josh 19:47 of the Danites was L to them, the Danites
1Sam 9:3 Now the asses of Kish, Saul's father, were L
9:20 your asses that were L three days ago, do
2Sam 22:46 Foreigners L heart, and came trembling out of their
1Kgs 20:25 army that you have L, horse for horse, and
Tob 7:7 heard that Tobit had L his sight, he was
14:2 years old when he L his sight, and after
Jud 7:23 Their children L heart, and the women
Job 11:20 of escape will be L to them, and their
Ps 18:45 Foreigners L heart, and came trembling out of their
119:176 gone astray like a L sheep; seek thy servant,
Prov 5:23 and because of his great folly he is L
Eccl 5:14 and those riches were L in a bad venture;
9:5 more reward; but the memory of them is L
Sir 2:14 to you who have L your endurance!
8:12 as one who has L it.
29:10 let it rust under a stone and be L
29:14 a man who has L his sense of shame
41:2 is contrary, and has L his patience!
Is 6:5 For I am L; for I am a man
27:13 and those who were L in the land of
Jer 50:6 "My people have been L sheep; their shepherds have
Lam 3:54 'I said, I am L
Ezek 19:5 that her hope was L, she took another of
34:4 not brought back, the L you have not sought,
34:16 I will seek the L, and I will bring
37:11 and our hope is L; we are clean cut
2Mac 2:14 books that had been L on account of the
Mt 5:13 but if salt has L its taste, how shall
10:6 go rather to the L sheep of the house
15:24 sent only to the L sheep of the house
Mk 2:22 and the wine is L, and so are the
9:48 if the salt has L its saltness, how will

Lk 14:34 but if salt has L its taste, how shall
15:4 sheep, if he has L one of them, does
15:4 the one which is L, until he finds it?
15:6 my sheep which was L
15:9 coin which I had L
15:24 alive again; he was L, and is found.' And
15:32 is alive; he was L, and is found.'"
19:10 man came to seek and to save the L
Jn 6:12 the fragments left over, that nothing may be L
17:12 none of them is L but the son of
18:9 thou gavest me I L not one."
Acts 27:9 much time had been L, and the voyage was
Rev 18:14 and thy splendor are L to thee, never to

LOT (114)

Gen 11:27 and Haran; and Haran was the father of L
11:31 Abram his son and L the son of Haran,
12:4 had told him; and L went with him.
12:5 Sarai his wife, and L his brother's son, and
13:1 that he had, and L with him, into the
13:5 And L, who went with Abram, also had flocks
13:7 and the herdsmen of L's cattle.
13:8 Then Abram said to L, "Let there be no
13:10 And L lifted up his eyes, and saw that
13:11 So L chose for himself all the Jordan valley,
13:11 the Jordan valley, and L journeyed east; thus they
13:12 land of Canaan, while L dwelt among the cities
13:14 said to Abram, after L had separated from him,
14:12 way; they also took L, the son of Abram's
14:16 brought back his kinsman L with his goods, and
19:1 in the evening; and L was sitting in the
19:1 When L saw them, he rose to meet them,
19:5 and they called to L, "Where are the men
19:6 L went out of the door to the men,
19:9 hard against the man L, and drew near to
19:10 their hands and brought L into the house to
19:12 the men said to L, "Have you any one
19:14 So L went out and said to his sons-in-law,
19:15 dawned, the angels urged L, saying, "Arise, take your
19:18 And L said to them, "Oh, no, my lords;
19:23 on the earth when L came to Zoar.
19:26 But L's wife behind him looked back, and she
19:29 remembered Abraham, and sent L out of the midst
19:29 the cities in which L dwelt.
19:30 Now L went up out of Zoar, and dwelt
19:36 both the daughters of L were with child by
Lev 16:8 the two goats, one L for the LORD and
16:8 LORD and the other L for Azazel.
16:9 goat on which the L fell for the LORD,
16:10 goat on which the L fell for Azazel shall
Num 26:55 shall be divided by L; according to the names
26:56 be divided according to L between the larger and
33:54 inherit the land by L according to your families;
33:54 small inheritance; wherever the L falls to any man,
34:13 you shall inherit by L, which the LORD has
36:2 land for inheritance by L to the people of
36:3 taken away from the L of our inheritance.
Deut 2:9 to the sons of L for a possession.'
2:19 to the sons of L for a possession.'
Josh 14:2 Their inheritance was by L, as the LORD had
15:1 The L for the tribe of the people of
17:14 given me but one L and one portion as
17:17 shall not have one L only,
18:11 The L of the tribe of Benjamin according to
19:1 The second L came out for Simeon, for the
19:10 The third L came up for the tribe of
19:17 The fourth L came out for Issachar, for the
19:24 The fifth L came out for the tribe of
19:32 The sixth L came out for the tribe of
19:40 The seventh L came out for the tribe of
19:51 of Israel distributed by L at Shiloh before the
21:4 The L came out for the families of the
21:4 the priest received by L from the tribes of
21:5 the Kohathites received by L from the families of
21:6 The Gersonites received by L from the families of
21:8 of Israel gave by L to the Levites, as
21:10 the Levites; since the L fell to them first.
Judg 20:9 up against it by L,
1Sam 10:20 and the tribe of Benjamin was taken by L
10:21 Matrites was taken by L; finally he brought the
10:21 Saul the son of Kish was taken by L
14:42 Saul said, "Cast the L between me and my
1Chr 6:54 for theirs was the L,
6:61 Kohathites were given by L out of the family
6:65 also gave them by L out of the tribes
24:5 They organized them by L, all alike, for there
24:7 The first L fell to Jehoiarib, the second to
25:9 The first L fell for Asaph to Joseph; the
26:14 The L for the east fell to Shelemiah.
26:14 shrewd counselor, and his L came out for the
Esth 3:7 Pur, that is the L, before Haman day after
9:24 Pur, that is the L, to crush and destroy
Ps 16:5 chosen portion and my cup; thou holdest my L
83:8 are the strong arm of the children of L
Prov 1:14 spoil; throw in your L among us, we will
16:33 The L is cast into the lap, but the
18:18 The L puts an end to disputes and decides
Eccl 3:22 for that is his L; who can bring him
5:18 God has given him, for this is his L
5:19 and to accept his L and find enjoyment in
Wis 2:9 because this is our portion, and this our L
5:5 And why is his L among the saints?
8:19 soul fell to my L;
Sir 14:15 you acquired by toil to be divided by L
16:8 spare the neighbors of L, whom he loathed on
20:24 habitual liar, but the L of both is ruin.
25:18 iniquity; may a sinner's L befall her!
37:8 lest he cast the L against you
41:9 and when you die, a curse is your L
Is 17:14 despoil us, and the L of those who plunder
34:17 He has cast the L for them, his hand
57:6 they, they, are your L; to them you have
61:7 shall rejoice in your L; therefore in your land
Jer 13:25 This is your L, the portion I have measured
Ezek 21:22 right hand comes the L for Jerusalem, to open
Dan 4:15 of heaven; let his L be with the beasts
4:23 heaven; and let his L be with the beasts
Jon 1:7 cast lots, and the L fell upon Jonah.
Mic 2:5 cast the line by L in the assembly of
Zeph 2:10 This shall be their L in return for their
Lk 1:9 fell to him by L to enter the temple
17:28 in the days of L —they ate, they drank,
17:29 on the day when L went out from Sodom
17:32 Remember L's wife.
Acts 1:26 for them, and the L fell on Matthias; and
8:21 have neither part nor L in this matter, for
1Thes 3:3 yourselves know that this is to be our L
2Pet 2:7 if he rescued righteous L, greatly distressed by the
Rev 21:8 and all liars, their L shall be in the

LOTAN (7)

Gen 36:20 inhabitants of the land: L, Shobal, Zibeon, Anah,
36:22 The sons of L were Hori and Heman; and
36:22 Hori and Heman; and L's sister was Timna.
36:29 the Horites: the chiefs L, Shobal, Zibeon, Anah,
1Chr 1:38 The sons of Seir: L, Shobal, Zibeon, Anah, Dishon,
1:39 The sons of L: Hori and Homam; and Lotan's
1:39 Hori and Homam; and L's sister was Timna.

LOTS (25)

Lev 16:8 and Aaron shall cast L upon the two goats,
Josh 18:6 and I will cast L for you here before
18:8 and I will cast L for you here before
18:10 Shiloh, and Joshua cast L for them in Shiloh
1Chr 24:31 younger brother alike, cast L, just as their brethren
25:8 And they cast L for their duties, small and
26:13 LORD; and they cast L by fathers' houses, small
26:14 They cast L also for his son Zechariah, a
Neh 10:34 We have likewise cast L, the priests, the Levites,
11:1 of the people cast L to bring one out
Esth 10:10 purpose he made two L, one for the people
10:11 And these two L came to the hour and
Job 6:27 You would even cast L over the fatherless, and
Ps 22:18 among them, and for my raiment they cast L
Joel 3:3 land, and have cast L for my people, and
Obad 1:11 his gates and cast L for Jerusalem, you were
Jon 1:7 "Come, let us cast L, that we may know
1:7 So they cast L, and the lot fell upon
Nah 3:10 for her honored men L were cast, and all
Mt 27:35 among them by casting L;
Mk 15:24 garments among them, casting L for them, to decide
Lk 23:33 And they cast L to divide his garments.
Jn 19:24 tear it, but cast L for it to see
19:24 among them, and for my clothing they cast L
Acts 1:26 And they cast L for them, and the lot

LOTUS (2)

Job 40:21 Under the L plants he lies, in the covert
40:22 For his shade the L trees cover him; the

LOUD (95)

Gen 39:14 cried out with a L voice;

Ex 19:16 mountain, and a very L trumpet blast, so that
Lev 25:9 shall send abroad the L trumpet on the tenth
Num 14:1 the congregation raised a L cry; and the people
Deut 5:22 thick darkness, with a L voice; and he added
27:14 of Israel with a L voice:
Judg 5:22 "Then L beat the horses' hoofs with the galloping,
1Sam 28:12 cried out with a L voice; and the woman
2Sam 19:4 king cried with a L voice, "O my son
1Kgs 8:55 of Israel with a L voice, saying,
2Kgs 18:28 called out in a L voice in the language
1Chr 15:28 and cymbals, and made L music on harps and
2Chr 15:14 the LORD with a L voice, and with shouting,
20:19 Israel, with a very L voice.
32:18 shouted it with a L voice in the language
Ezra 3:12 house, wept with a L voice when they saw
10:12 assembly answered with a L voice, "It is so;
Neh 9:4 they cried with a L voice to the LORD
Jud 7:24 cried out with a L voice, and said before
7:30 Lord God with a L voice.
9:1 the Lord with a L voice, and said,
13:14 to them with a L voice, "Praise God, O
14:16 cried out with a L voice and wept and
14:19 greatly dismayed, and their L cries and shouts arose
Esth 4:1 city, wailing with a L and bitter cry;
Ps 33:3 on the strings, with L shouts.
47:1 Shout to God with L songs of joy!
102:5 Because of my L groaning my bones cleave to
150:5 cymbals; praise him with L clashing cymbals!
Prov 7:11 She is L and wayward, her feet do not
27:14 his neighbor with a L voice, rising early in
Sir 40:13 and crash like a L clap of thunder in
Is 36:13 called out in a L voice in the language
Ezek 8:18 my ears with a L voice, I will not
9:1 my ears with a L voice, saying, "Draw near,
11:13 and cried with a L voice, and said, "Ah
Dan 13:24 cried out with a L voice, and the two
13:42 cried out with a L voice, and said, "O
13:46 he cried with a L voice, "I am innocent
14:18 and shouted in a L voice, "You are great,
14:41 king shouted with a L voice, "Thou art great,
Zeph 1:10 the Second Quarter, a L crash from the hills.
3:17 exult over you with L singing
1Mac 2:19 and said in a L voice: "Even if all
2:27 the city with a L voice, saying: "Let every
3:54 trumpets and gave a L shout.
5:31 Heaven with trumpets and L shouts,
13:8 they answered in a L voice, "You are our
13:45 cried out with a L voice, asking Simon to
Mt 2:18 Ramah, wailing and L lamentation, Rachel weeping
24:31 his angels with a L trumpet call, and they
27:46 Jesus cried with a L voice, "Eli, Eli, lama
27:50 cried again with a L voice and yielded up
Mk 1:26 and crying with a L voice, came out of
5:7 crying out with a L voice, he said, "What
15:33 Jesus cried with a L voice, "Elo-i, Elo-i, lama
15:36 And Jesus uttered a L cry, and breathed his
Lk 1:42 she exclaimed with a L cry, "Blessed are you
4:33 cried out with a L voice,
8:28 and said with a L voice, "What have you
17:15 praising God with a L voice;
19:37 praise God with a L voice for all the
23:22 were urgent, demanding with L cries that he should
23:45 Jesus, crying with a L voice, said, "Father, into
Jn 11:43 he cried with a L voice, "Lazarus, come out."
Acts 7:57 cried out with a L voice and stopped their
7:60 and cried with a L voice, "Lord, do not
8:7 possessed, crying with a L voice; and many who
14:10 well, said in a L voice, "Stand upright on
16:28 Paul cried with a L voice, "Do not harm
26:24 Festus said with a L voice, "Paul, you are
Heb 5:7 prayers and supplications, with L cries and tears, to
2Pet 2:18 For, uttering L boasts of folly, they entice with
3:10 pass away with a L noise, and the elements
Rev 1:10 heard behind me a L voice like a trumpet
5:2 angel proclaiming with a L voice, "Who is worthy
5:12 thousands, saying with a L voice, "Worthy is the
6:10 cried out with a L voice, "O Sovereign Lord,
7:2 he called with a L voice to the four
7:10 crying out with a L voice, "Salvation belongs to
8:13 eagle crying with a L voice, as it flew
10:3 called out with a L voice, like a lion
11:12 Then they heard a L voice from heaven saying
11:15 trumpet, and there were L voices in heaven, saying,
12:10 And I heard a L voice in heaven, saying,
14:2 like the sound of L thunder; the voice I
14:7 he said with a L voice, "Fear God and
14:9 them, saying with a L voice, "If any one
14:15 temple, calling with a L voice to him who
14:18 he called with a L voice to him who
16:1 Then I heard a L voice from the temple
16:17 the air, and a L voice came out of
19:1 seemed to be the L voice of a great
19:17 sun, and with a L voice he called to
21:3 and I heard a L voice from the throne

LOUD-MOUTHED

Jude 1:16 following their own passions, L boasters, flattering

LOUDER (2)

Ex 19:19 of the trumpet grew L and louder, Moses spoke,
19:19 trumpet grew louder and L, Moses spoke, and God

LOUDLY (5)

1Chr 15:16 singers who should play L on musical instruments, on
Jud 16:1 and all the people L sang this song of
Jer 2:15 lions have roared against him, they have roared L
Dan 13:60 all the assembly shouted L and blessed God, who
Mk 5:38 saw a tumult, and people weeping and wailing L

LOVE (569)

Gen 22:2 son Isaac, whom you L, and go to the
24:12 thee, and show steadfast L to my master Abraham.
24:14 thou hast shown steadfast L to my master."
24:27 not forsaken his steadfast L and his faithfulness
27:4 food, such as I L, and bring it to
29:20 days because of the L he had for her.
29:32 now my husband will L me."
32:10 of all the steadfast L and all the faithfulness
39:21 and showed him steadfast L, and gave him favor
Ex 15:13 led in thy steadfast L the people whom thou
20:6 me, but showing steadfast L to thousands of those
20:6 thousands of those who L me and keep my
21:5 slave plainly says, 'I L my master, my wife,
34:6 and abounding in steadfast L and faithfulness,
34:7 and faithfulness, keeping steadfast L for thousands,
Lev 19:18 people, but you shall L your neighbor as yourself:
19:34 you, and you shall L him as yourself; for
Num 14:18 and abounding in steadfast L, forgiving iniquity and
14:19 greatness of thy steadfast L, and according as thou
Deut 5:10 me, but showing steadfast L to thousands of those
5:10 thousands of those who L me and keep my
6:5 LORD; and you shall L the LORD your God
7:7 the LORD set his L upon you and chose
7:9 keeps covenant and steadfast L with those who love
7:9 love with those who L him and keep his
7:12 covenant and the steadfast L which he swore to
7:13 to keep; he will L you, bless you, and
10:12 all his ways, to L him, to serve the
10:15 set his heart in L upon your fathers and
10:19 L the sojourner therefore; for you were sojourners in
11:1 "You shall therefore L the LORD your God, and
11:13 you this day, to L the LORD your God,
13:3 to know whether you L the LORD your God
30:6 so that you will L the LORD your God
Josh 22:5 LORD commanded you, to L the LORD your God,
23:11 to yourselves, therefore, to L the LORD your God.
Judg 14:16 me, you do not L me; you have put
16:15 can you say, 'I L you,' when your heart
1Sam 18:22 and all his servants L you; now then become
20:14 show me the loyal L of the LORD, that
20:17 swear again by his L for him; for he
2Sam 1:26 been to me; your L to me was wonderful,
1:26 was wonderful, passing the L of women.
2:6 the LORD show steadfast L and faithfulness to you!
7:15 not take my steadfast L from him, as I
13:4 said to him, "I L Tamar, my brother Absalom's
13:15 was greater than the L with which he had
15:20 the LORD show steadfast L and faithfulness to you."
19:6 your concubines, because you L those who hate you
19:6 and hate those who L you.
22:51 king, and shows steadfast L to his anointed, to
1Kgs 3:6 shown great and steadfast L to thy servant David
3:6 this great and steadfast L, and hast given him
8:23 covenant and showing steadfast L to thy servants
11:2 after their gods"; Solomon clung to these in L
1Chr 16:34 good; for his steadfast L endures for ever!
16:41 LORD, for his steadfast L endures for ever.
17:13 not take my steadfast L from him, as I
2Chr 1:8 shown great and steadfast L to David my father,
5:13 good, for his steadfast L endures for ever," the
6:14 covenant and showing steadfast L to thy servants
6:42 Remember thy steadfast L for David thy servant."

7:3 good, for his steadfast L endures for ever."
7:6 LORD--for his steadfast L endures for ever--
19:2 help the wicked and L those who hate the
20:21 LORD, for his steadfast L endures for ever."
Ezra 3:11 good, for his steadfast L endures for ever toward
7:28 to me his steadfast L before the king and
9:9 to us his steadfast L before the kings of
Neh 1:5 keeps covenant and steadfast L with those who love
1:5 love with those who L him and keep his
9:17 and abounding in steadfast L, and didst not forsake
9:32 keepest covenant and steadfast L, let not all the
13:22 me according to the greatness of thy steadfast L
Tob 4:13 So now, my son, L your brethren, and in
6:14 a demon is in L with her, and he
6:17 things, he fell in L with her and yearned
13:10 who are captives, and L those within you who
13:12 will be all who L you.
13:14 blessed are those who L you!
14:7 And all who L the Lord God in truth
Esth 13:12 pride or for any L of glory that I
Job 10:12 me life and steadfast L; and thy care has
37:13 his land, or for L, he causes it to
39:13 but are they the pinions and plumage of L
Ps 4:2 How long will you L vain words, and seek
5:7 abundance of thy steadfast L will enter thy house,
5:11 them, that those who L thy name may exult
6:4 deliver me for the sake of thy steadfast L
13:5 trusted in thy steadfast L; my heart shall rejoice
17:7 Wondrously show thy steadfast L, O savior of those
18:1 I L thee, O LORD, my strength.
18:50 king, and shows steadfast L to his anointed, to
21:7 and through the steadfast L of the Most High
25:6 and of thy steadfast L, for they have been
25:7 according to thy steadfast L remember me, for thy
25:10 the LORD are steadfast L and faithfulness, for those
26:3 For thy steadfast L is before my eyes, and
26:8 O LORD, I L the habitation of thy house,
31:7 glad for thy steadfast L, because thou hast seen
31:16 on thy servant; save me in thy steadfast L
31:21 wondrously shown his steadfast L to me when I
31:23 L the LORD, all you his saints!
32:10 the wicked; but steadfast L surrounds him who trusts
33:5 full of the steadfast L of the LORD.
33:18 hope in his steadfast L,
33:22 Let thy steadfast L, O LORD, be upon us,
36:5 Thy steadfast L, O LORD, extends to the heavens,
36:7 precious is thy steadfast L, O God!
36:10 O continue thy steadfast L to those who know
40:10 not concealed thy steadfast L and thy faithfulness
40:11 me, let thy steadfast L and thy faithfulness ever
40:16 thee; may those who L thy salvation say continually,
42:8 LORD commands his steadfast L; and at night his
44:26 Deliver us for the sake of thy steadfast L
45:7 scepter of equity; you L righteousness and hate
48:9 thought on thy steadfast L, O God, in the
51:1 according to thy steadfast L; according to thy
52:3 You L evil more than good, and lying more
52:4 [Selah] You L all words that devour, O deceitful
52:8 trust in the steadfast L of God for ever
57:3 send forth his steadfast L and his faithfulness!
57:10 For thy steadfast L is great to the heavens,
59:10 God in his steadfast L will meet me; my
59:16 aloud of thy steadfast L in the morning.
59:17 my fortress, the God who shows me steadfast L
61:7 before God; bid steadfast L and faithfulness watch
62:12 and that to thee, O Lord, belongs steadfast L
63:3 Because thy steadfast L is better than life, my
66:20 or removed his steadfast L from me!
69:13 abundance of thy steadfast L answer me.
69:16 LORD, for thy steadfast L is good; according to
69:36 it, and those who L his name shall dwell
70:4 May those who L thy salvation say evermore, "God
77:8 Has his steadfast L for ever ceased?
85:7 Show us thy steadfast L, O LORD, and grant
85:10 Steadfast L and faithfulness will meet; righteousness
86:5 forgiving, abounding in steadfast L to all who call
86:13 great is thy steadfast L toward me; thou hast
86:15 and abounding in steadfast L and faithfulness.
88:11 [Selah] Is thy steadfast L declared in the grave,
89:1 sing of thy steadfast L, O LORD, for ever;
89:2 For thy steadfast L was established for ever, thy
89:14 of thy throne; steadfast L and faithfulness go before
89:24 faithfulness and my steadfast L shall be with him,
89:28 My steadfast L I will keep for him for
89:33 from him my steadfast L, or be false to
89:49 where is thy steadfast L of old, which by
90:14 morning with thy steadfast L, that we may rejoice
91:14 cleaves to me in L, I will deliver him;
92:2 to declare thy steadfast L in the morning, and
94:18 thy steadfast L, O LORD, held me up.
98:3 has remembered his steadfast L and faithfulness to
100:5 is good; his steadfast L endures for ever, and
103:4 crowns you with steadfast L and mercy,
103:8 gracious, slow to anger and abounding in steadfast L
103:11 great is his steadfast L toward those who fear
103:17 But the steadfast L of the LORD is from
106:1 good; for his steadfast L endures for ever!
106:7 abundance of thy steadfast L, but rebelled against
106:45 according to the abundance of his steadfast L
107:1 good; for his steadfast L endures for ever!
107:8 LORD for his steadfast L, for his wonderful works
107:15 LORD for his steadfast L, for his wonderful works
107:21 LORD for his steadfast L, for his wonderful works
107:31 LORD for his steadfast L, for his wonderful works
107:43 men consider the steadfast L of the LORD.
108:4 For thy steadfast L is great above the heavens,
109:4 In return for my L they accuse me, even
109:5 me evil for good, and hatred for my L
109:21 sake; because thy steadfast L is good, deliver me!
109:26 Save me according to thy steadfast L
115:1 sake of thy steadfast L and thy faithfulness!
116:1 I L the LORD, because he has heard my
117:2 great is his steadfast L toward us; and the
118:1 is good; his steadfast L endures for ever!
118:2 Israel say, "His steadfast L endures for ever."
118:3 Aaron say, "His steadfast L endures for ever."
118:4 LORD say, "His steadfast L endures for ever."
118:29 good; for his steadfast L endures for ever!
119:41 Let thy steadfast L come to me, O LORD,
119:47 find my delight in thy commandments, which I L
119:48 thy commandments, which I L, and I will meditate
119:64 full of thy steadfast L; teach me thy statutes!
119:76 Let thy steadfast L be ready to comfort me
119:88 In thy steadfast L spare my life, that I
119:97 Oh, how I L thy law!
119:113 double-minded men, but I L thy law.
119:119 as dross; therefore I L thy testimonies.
119:124 according to thy steadfast L, and teach me thy
119:127 Therefore I L thy commandments above gold, above
119:132 wont toward those who L thy name.
119:149 voice in thy steadfast L; O LORD, in thy
119:159 Consider how I L thy precepts!
119:159 Preserve my life according to thy steadfast L
119:163 abhor falsehood, but I L thy law.
119:165 peace have those who L thy law; nothing can
119:167 keeps thy testimonies; I L them exceedingly.
122:6 "May they prosper who L you!
130:7 LORD there is steadfast L, and with him is
136:1 good, for his steadfast L endures for ever.
136:2 gods, for his steadfast L endures for ever.
136:3 lords, for his steadfast L endures for ever;
136:4 wonders, for his steadfast L endures for ever;
136:5 heavens, for his steadfast L endures for ever;
136:6 waters, for his steadfast L endures for ever;
136:7 lights, for his steadfast L endures for ever;
136:8 day, for his steadfast L endures for ever;
136:9 night, for his steadfast L endures for ever;
136:10 Egypt, for his steadfast L endures for ever;
136:11 them, for his steadfast L endures for ever;
136:12 arm, for his steadfast L endures for ever;
136:13 sunder, for his steadfast L endures for ever;
136:14 it, for his steadfast L endures for ever;
136:15 Sea, for his steadfast L endures for ever;
136:16 wilderness, for his steadfast L endures for ever;
136:17 kings, for his steadfast L endures for ever;
136:18 kings, for his steadfast L endures for ever;
136:19 Amorites, for his steadfast L endures for ever;
136:20 Bashan, for his steadfast L endures for ever;
136:21 heritage, for his steadfast L endures for ever;
136:22 servant, for his steadfast L endures for ever.
136:23 estate, for his steadfast L endures for ever;
136:24 foes, for his steadfast L endures for ever;
136:25 flesh, for his steadfast L endures for ever.
136:26 heaven, for his steadfast L endures for ever.
138:2 name for thy steadfast L and thy faithfulness; for
138:8 for me; thy steadfast L, O LORD, endures for
143:8 morning of thy steadfast L, for in thee I
143:12 And in thy steadfast L cut off my enemies,
145:8 merciful, slow to anger and abounding in steadfast L
145:20 LORD preserves all who L him; but all the
147:11 him, in those who hope in his steadfast L
Prov 1:22 simple ones, will you L being simple?

3:24 L Your Neighbor
4:7 she will keep you, L her, and she will
5:19 times with delight, be infatuated always with her L
7:18 take our fill of L till morning; let us
7:18 love till morning; let us delight ourselves with L
8:17 I L those who love me, and those who
8:17 I love those who L me, and those who
8:21 with wealth those who L me, and filling their
8:36 all who hate me L death."
9:8 man, and he will L you.
10:12 stirs up strife, but L covers all offenses.
15:17 dinner of herbs where L is than a fatted
17:9 forgives an offense seeks L, but he who repeats
18:21 tongue, and those who L it will eat its
20:13 L not sleep, lest you come to poverty; open
27:5 Better is open rebuke than hidden L
Eccl 3:8 speak; a time to L, and a time to
9:1 God; whether it is L or hate man does
9:6 Their L and their hate and their envy have
9:9 the wife whom you L, all the days of
Song 1:2 For your L is better than wine,
1:3 out; therefore the maidens L you.
1:4 we will extol your L more than wine; rightly
1:4 wine; rightly do they L you.
1:9 I compare you, my L, to a mare of
1:15 you are beautiful, my L; behold, you are beautiful;
2:2 brambles, so is my L among maidens.
2:4 banqueting house, and his banner over me was L
2:5 me with apples; for I am sick with L
2:7 not up nor awaken L until it please.
2:10 to me: "Arise, my L, my fair one, and
2:13 Arise, my L, my fair one, and come away.
3:5 not up nor awaken L until it please.
4:1 you are beautiful, my L, behold, you are beautiful!
4:7 are all fair, my L; there is no flaw
4:10 How sweet is your L, my sister, my bride!
4:10 much better is your L than wine, and the
5:2 me, my sister, my L, my dove, my perfect
5:8 that you tell him I am sick with L
6:4 beautiful as Tirzah, my L, comely as Jerusalem,
7:12 There I will give you my L
8:4 not up nor awaken L until it please.
8:6 upon your arm; for L is strong as death,
8:7 Many waters cannot quench L, neither can floods
8:7 a man offered for L all the wealth of
Wis 1:1 L righteousness, you rulers of
3:9 abide with him in L, because grace and mercy
6:12 discerned by those who L her, and is found
6:17 concern for instruction is L of her,
6:18 love of her, and L of her is the
16:26 sons, whom thou didst L, O Lord, might learn
Sir 1:8 her to those who L him.
2:15 words, and those who L him will keep his
2:16 approval, and those who L him will be filled
4:10 High, and he will L you more than does
4:14 Lord loves those who L her.
6:33 If you L to listen you will gain knowledge,
7:21 Let your soul L an intelligent servant; do not
7:30 With all your might L your Maker, and do
27:17 L your friend and keep faith with him; but
34:16 are upon those who L him, a mighty protection
40:20 the heart, but the L of wisdom is better
48:11 have been adorned in L; for we also shall
Is 5:1 for my beloved a L song concerning his vineyard:
16:5 be established in steadfast L and on it will
43:4 and honored, and I L you, I give men
54:8 you, but with everlasting L I will have compassion
54:10 removed, but my steadfast L shall not depart from
55:3 covenant, my steadfast, sure L for David.
56:6 minister to him, to L the name of the
61:8 For I the LORD L justice, I hate robbery
63:7 will recount the steadfast L of the LORD, the
63:7 mercy, according to the abundance of his steadfast L
63:9 saved them; in his L and in his pity
66:10 her, all you who L her; rejoice with her
Jer 2:2 of your youth, your L as a bride, how
5:31 their direction; my people L to have it so,
9:24 LORD who practice steadfast L, justice, and
16:5 the LORD, my steadfast L and mercy.
31:3 you with an everlasting L; therefore I have continued
32:18 thee, who showest steadfast L to thousands, but dost
33:11 good, for his steadfast L endures for ever!' For
Lam 3:22 have hope: The steadfast L of the LORD never
3:32 abundance of his steadfast L;
Ezek 16:8 at the age for L; and I spread my
23:17 into the bed of L, and they defiled her
33:31 lips they show much L, but their heart is
33:32 like one who sings L songs with a beautiful
Dan 9:4 keepest covenant and steadfast L with those who L
13:20 and we are in L with you; so give
14:38 not forsaken those who L thee."
Hos 2:19 in justice, in steadfast L, and in mercy.
3:1 to me, "Go again, L a woman who is
3:1 to other gods and L cakes of raisins."
4:18 themselves to harlotry; they L shame more than
6:4 Your L is like a morning cloud, like the
6:6 For I desire steadfast L and not sacrifice, the
8:13 They L sacrifice; they sacrifice flesh and eat it;
9:15 I will L them no more; all their princes
10:12 the fruit of steadfast L; break up your fallow
11:4 with the bands of L, and I became to
12:6 return, hold fast to L and justice, and wait
14:4 their faithlessness; I will L them freely, for my
Joel 2:13 and abounding in steadfast L, and repents of evil.
Amos 4:5 them; for so you L to do, O people
5:15 Hate evil, and L good, and establish justice in
Jon 4:2 and abounding in steadfast L, and repentest of evil.
Mic 3:2 hate the good and L the evil, who tear
6:8 do justice, and to L kindness, and to walk
7:18 anger for ever because he delights in steadfast L
7:20 to Jacob and steadfast L to Abraham, as thou
Zeph 3:17 renew you in his L; he will exult over
Zech 8:17 against one another, and L no false oath, for
8:19 and cheerful feasts; therefore L truth and peace.
1Mac 4:33 sword of those who L thee, and let all
2Mac 6:20 even for the natural L of life.
Mt 5:43 was said, 'You shall L your neighbor and hate
5:44 I say to you, L your enemies and pray
5:46 For if you L those who love you, what
5:46 you love those who L you, what reward have
6:5 the hypocrites; for they L to stand and pray
6:24 hate the one and L the other, or he
19:19 mother, and, You shall L your neighbor as yourself."
22:37 to him, "You shall L the Lord your God
22:39 like it, You shall L your neighbor as yourself.
23:6 fringes long, and they L the place of honor
24:12 is multiplied, most men's L will grow cold.
Mk 12:30 one; and you shall L the Lord your God
12:31 is this, 'You shall L your neighbor as yourself.'
12:33 but he; and to L him with all the
12:33 the strength, and to L one's neighbor as oneself,
Lk 6:27 to you that hear, L your enemies, do good
6:32 "If you L those who love you, what credit
6:32 you love those who L you, what credit is
6:32 For even sinners L those who love them.
6:32 sinners love those who L them.
6:35 But L your enemies, and do good, and lend,
7:42 which of them will L him more?"
10:27 he answered, "You shall L the Lord your God
11:42 neglect justice and the L of God; these you
11:43 for you L the best seat in the synagogues
16:13 hate the one and L the other, or he
20:46 in long robes, and L salutations in the market
Jn 5:41 you have not the L of God within you.
8:42 your Father, you would L me, for I proceeded
11:3 "Lord, he whom you L is ill."
13:34 to you, that you L one another; even as
13:34 you, that you also L one another.
13:35 disciples, if you have L for one another."
14:15 "If you L me, you will keep my commandments.
14:21 Father, and I will L him and manifest myself
14:23 and my Father will L him, and we will
14:24 He who does not L me does not keep
14:31 may know that I L the Father.
15:9 so have I loved you; abide in my L
15:10 will abide in my L, just as I have
15:10 kept my Father's commandments and abide in his L
15:12 my commandment, that you L one another as I
15:13 Greater L has no man than this, that a
15:17 I command you, to L one another.
15:19 world, the world would L its own; but because
17:24 given me in thy L for me before the
17:26 it known, that the L with which thou hast
21:15 of John, do you L me more than these?"
21:15 you know that I L you." He said to
21:16 of John, do you L me?" He said to
21:16 you know that I L you." He said to
21:17 of John, do you L me?" Peter was grieved
21:17 third time, "Do you L me?" And he said
21:17 you know that I L you." Jesus said to
Rom 5:5 disappoint us, because God's L has been poured into
5:8 But God shows his L for us in that

8:28 good with those who L him, who are called
8:35 separate us from the L of Christ?
8:39 separate us from the L of God in Christ
12:9 Let L be genuine; hate what is evil, hold
12:10 to what is good; L one another with brotherly
13:8 one anything, except to L one another; for he
13:9 sentence, "You shall L your neighbor as yourself."
13:10 L does no wrong to a neighbor; therefore love
13:10 to a neighbor; therefore L is the fulfilling of
14:15 you eat, you are no longer walking in L
15:30 Christ and by the L of the Spirit, to
1Cor 2:9 prepared for those who L him,"
4:21 a rod, or with L in a spirit of
8:1 puffs up, but L builds up.
13:1 angels, but have not L, I am a noisy
13:2 mountains, but have not L, I am nothing.
13:3 burned, but have not L, I gain nothing.
13:4 L is patient and kind; love is not jealous
13:4 is patient and kind; L is not jealous or
13:5 L does not insist on its own way; it
13:7 L bears all things, believes all things, hopes all
13:8 L never ends; as for prophecies, they will pass
13:13 So faith, hope, L abide, these three; but the
13:13 these three; but the greatest of these is L
14:1 Make L your aim, and earnestly desire the spiritual
16:14 Let all that you do be done in L
16:22 any one has no L for the Lord, let
16:24 My L be with you all in Christ Jesus.
2Cor 2:4 you know the abundant L that I have for
2:8 you to reaffirm your L for him.
5:14 For the L of Christ controls us, because we
6:6 the Holy Spirit, genuine L,
8:7 earnestness, and in your L for us--see that
8:8 of others that your L also is genuine.
8:24 the churches, of your L and of our boasting
11:11 Because I do not L you?
12:15 If I L you the more, am I to
13:11 and the God of L and peace will be
13:14 Jesus Christ and the L of God and the
Gal 5:6 is of any avail, but faith working through L
5:13 the flesh, but through L be servants of one
5:14 one word, "You shall L your neighbor as yourself."
5:22 of the Spirit is L, joy, peace, patience, kindness,
Eph 1:5 He destined us in L to be his sons
1:15 Lord Jesus and your L toward all the saints,
2:4 out of the great L with which he loved
3:17 rooted and grounded in L,
3:19 and to know the L of Christ which surpasses
4:2 forbearing one another in L,
4:15 speaking the truth in L, we are to grow
4:16 makes bodily growth and upbuilds itself in L
5:2 And walk in L, as Christ loved us and
5:25 Husbands, L your wives, as Christ loved the church
5:28 Even so husbands should L their wives as their
5:33 each one of you L his wife as himself,
6:23 to the brethren, and L with faith, from God
6:24 be with all who L our Lord Jesus Christ
6:24 Lord Jesus Christ with L undying.
Phil 1:9 my prayer that your L may abound more and
1:16 do it out of L, knowing that I am
2:1 Christ, any incentive of L, any participation in the
2:2 mind, having the same L, being in full accord
4:1 my brethren, whom I L and long for, my
Col 1:4 Jesus and of the L which you have for
1:8 known to us your L in the Spirit.
2:2 are knit together in L, to have all the
3:14 all these put on L, which binds everything together
3:19 Husbands, L your wives, and do not be harsh
1Thes 1:3 faith and labor of L and steadfastness of hope
3:6 of your faith and L and reported that you
3:12 increase and abound in L to one another and
4:9 But concerning L of the brethren you have no
4:9 taught by God to L one another;
4:10 and indeed you do L all the brethren throughout
5:8 breastplate of faith and L, and for a helmet
5:13 them very highly in L because of their work.
2Thes 1:3 growing abundantly, and the L of every one of
2:10 because they refused to L the truth and so
3:5 your hearts to the L of God and to
1Tim 1:5 of our charge is L that issues from a
1:14 with the faith and L that are in Christ
2:15 continues in faith and L and holiness, with modesty.
4:12 speech and conduct, in L, in faith, in purity.
6:10 For the L of money is the root of
6:11 at righteousness, godliness, faith, L, steadfastness,
2Tim 1:7 spirit of power and L and self-control.
1:13 in the faith and L which are in Christ
2:22 aim at righteousness, faith, L, and peace, along with
3:10 faith, my patience, my L, my steadfastness,
4:10 For Demas, in L with this present world, has
Tit 2:2 sound in faith, in L, and in steadfastness.
2:4 the young women to L their husbands and children,
3:15 Greet those who L us in the faith.
Philem 1:5 I hear of your L and of the faith
1:7 and comfort from your L, my brother, because the
1:9 is required, yet for L's sake I prefer to
Heb 6:10 your work and the L which you showed for
10:24 up one another to L and good works,
13:1 Let brotherly L continue.
13:5 your life free from L of money, and be
Jas 1:11 promised to those who L him.
2:5 promised to those who L him?
2:8 the scripture, "You shall L your neighbor as yourself,"
1Pet 1:8 having seen him you L him; though you do
1:22 truth for a sincere L of the brethren, love
1:22 love of the brethren, L one another earnestly from
2:17 L the brotherhood.
3:8 unity of spirit, sympathy, L of the brethren, a
3:10 For "He that would L life and see good
4:8 all hold unfailing your L for one another, since
4:8 for one another, since L covers a multitude of
5:14 Greet one another with the kiss of L
2Pet 1:7 brotherly affection, and brotherly affection with L
1Jn 2:5 word, in him truly L for God is perfected.
2:15 Do not L the world or the things in
2:15 one loves the world, L for the Father is
3:1 See what L the Father has given us, that
3:10 he who does not L his brother.
3:11 beginning, that we should L one another,
3:14 into life, because we L the brethren.
3:14 He who does not L abides in death.
3:16 By this we know L, that he laid down
3:17 him, how does God's L abide in him?
3:18 children, let us not L in word or speech
3:23 Son Jesus Christ and L one another, just as
4:7 Beloved, let us L one another; for love is
4:7 love one another; for L is of God, and
4:8 He who does not L does not know God;
4:8 love does not know God; for God is L
4:9 In this the L of God was made manifest
4:10 In this is L, not that we loved God
4:11 we also ought to L one another.
4:12 seen God; if we L one another, God abides
4:12 in us and his L is perfected in us.
4:16 know and believe the L God has for us.
4:16 God is L, and he who abides in love
4:16 he who abides in L abides in God, and
4:17 In this is L perfected with us, that we
4:18 is no fear in L, but perfect love casts
4:18 in love, but perfect L casts out fear.
4:18 and he who fears is not perfected in L
4:19 We L, because he first loved us.
4:20 any one says, "I L God," and hates his
4:20 he who does not L his brother whom he
4:20 he has seen, cannot L God whom he has
4:21 who loves God should L his brother also.
5:2 we know that we L the children of God,
5:2 of God, when we L God and obey his
5:3 For this is the L of God, that we
2Jn 1:1 her children, whom I L in the truth, and
1:3 Jesus Christ the Father's Son, in truth and L
1:5 the beginning, that we L one another.
1:6 And this is L, that we follow his commandments;
1:6 have heard from the beginning, that you follow L
3Jn 1:1 beloved Gaius, whom I L in the truth.
1:6 have testified to your L before the church.
Jude 1:2 May mercy, peace, and L be multiplied to you.
1:12 are blemishes on your L feasts, as they boldly
1:21 keep yourselves in the L of God; wait for
Rev 2:4 you have abandoned the L you had at first.
2:19 know your works, your L and faith and service
3:19 Those whom I L, I reprove and chasten; so

LOVED (105)

Gen 24:67 his wife; and he L her.
25:28 Isaac L Esau, because he ate of his game;
25:28 his game; but Rebekah L Jacob.
27:14 mother prepared savory food, such as his father L
29:18 Jacob L Rachel; and he said, "I will serve
29:30 Rachel also, and he L Rachel more than Leah,
34:3 daughter of Jacob; he L the maiden and spoke
37:3 Now Israel L Joseph more than any other of

L

37:4 saw that their father L him more than all
Deut 4:37 And because he L your fathers and chose their
21:15 two wives, the one L and the other disliked,
21:15 him children, both the L and the disliked, and
21:16 the son of the L as the first-born in
23:5 the LORD your God L you.
33:3 Yea, he L his people; all those consecrated to
Judg 16:4 After this he L a woman in the valley
1Sam 1:5 daughters; and, although he L Hannah, he would give
16:21 And Saul L him greatly, and he became his
18:1 of David, and Jonathan L him as his own
18:3 with David, because he L him as his own
18:16 all Israel and Judah L David; for he went
18:20 Now Saul's daughter Michal L David; and they told
18:28 and that all Israel L him,
20:17 for him; for he L him as he loved
20:17 loved him as he L his own soul.
2Sam 12:24 And the LORD L him,
13:1 time Amnon, David's son, L her.
13:15 with which he had L her.
1Kgs 3:3 Solomon L the LORD, walking in the statutes of
5:1 father; for Hiram always L David.
10:9 Because the LORD L Israel for ever, he has
11:1 King Solomon L many foreign women: the daughter
2Chr 9:8 Because your God L Israel and would establish them
11:21 Rehoboam L Maacah the daughter of Absalom
26:10 fertile lands, for he L the soil.
Esth 2:17 his reign, the king L Esther more than all
14:2 every part that she L to adorn she covered
Job 19:19 and those whom I L have turned against me.
Ps 109:17 He L to curse; let curses come on him!
Song 7:6 pleasant you are, O L one, delectable maiden!
Wis 4:10 pleased God and was L by him, and while
7:10 I L her more than health and beauty, and
8:2 I L her and sought her from my youth,
Sir 3:17 then you will be L by those whom God
7:35 man, because for such deeds you will be L
15:13 and they are not L by those who fear
47:8 his heart, and he L his Maker.
47:16 islands, and you were L for your peace.
47:22 posterity of him who L him; so he gave
Is 57:8 with them, you have L their bed, you have
Jer 2:25 hopeless, for I have L strangers, and after them
8:2 heaven, which they have L and served, which they
14:10 this people: "They have L to wander thus, they
31:3 I have L you with an everlasting love; therefore
Bar 3:36 Jacob his servant and to Israel whom he L
Ezek 16:37 pleasure, all those you L and all those you
Hos 9:1 You have L a harlot's hire upon all threshing
9:10 Baal, and became detestable like the thing they L
10:11 a trained heifer that L to thresh, and I
11:1 was a child, I L him, and out of
Mal 1:2 "I have L you," says the LORD.
1:2 say, "How hast thou L us?" "Is not Esau
1:2 "Yet I have L Jacob
2Mac 14:37 as a man who L his fellow citizens and
Mk 10:21 Jesus looking upon him L him, and said to
Lk 7:47 are forgiven, for she L much; but he who
Jn 3:16 For God so L the world that he gave
3:19 the world, and men L darkness rather than light,
11:5 Now Jesus L Martha and her sister and Lazarus.
11:36 said, "See how he L him!"
12:43 the synagogue: for they L the praise of men
13:1 to the Father, having L his own who were
13:1 in the world, he L them to the end.
13:23 his disciples, whom Jesus L, was lying close to
13:34 even as I have L you, that you also
14:21 loves me will be L by my Father, and
14:28 to you.' If you L me, you would have
15:9 As the Father has L me, so have I
15:9 me, so have I L you; abide in my
15:12 another as I have L you.
16:27 you, because you have L me and have believed
17:23 sent me and hast L them even as thou
17:23 even as thou hast L me.
17:26 with which thou hast L me may be in
19:26 the disciple whom he L standing near, he said
20:2 the one whom Jesus L, and said to them,
21:7 That disciple whom Jesus L said to Peter, "It
21:20 the disciple whom Jesus L, who had lain close
Rom 8:37 conquerors through him who L us.
9:13 is written, "Jacob I L, but Esau I hated."
2Cor 12:15 am I to be L the less?
Gal 2:20 Son of God, who L me and gave himself
Eph 2:4 love with which he L us,
5:2 in love, as Christ L us and gave himself
5:25 your wives, as Christ L the church and gave
2Thes 2:16 God our Father, who L us and gave us
2Tim 4:8 to all who have L his appearing.
Heb 1:9 Thou hast L righteousness and hated lawlessness;
2Pet 2:15 son of Beor, who L gain from wrongdoing,
1Jn 4:10 love, not that we L God but that he
4:10 God but that he L us and sent his
4:11 Beloved, if God so L us, we also ought
4:19 love, because he first L us.
Rev 3:9 learn that I have L you.
12:11 their testimony, for they L not their lives even

LOVELINESS

Sir 24:17 a vine I caused L to bud, and my

LOVELY (9)

Gen 29:17 eyes were weak, but Rachel was beautiful and L
2Sam 1:23 "Saul and Jonathan, beloved and L
Jud 8:7 and had a very L face; and her husband
Esth 2:7 maiden was beautiful and L, and when her father
Ps 84:1 How L is thy dwelling place, O LORD of
Prov 5:19 of your youth, a L hind, a graceful doe.
Song 1:16 Behold, you are beautiful, my beloved, truly L
4:3 like a scarlet thread, and your mouth is L
Phil 4:8 is pure, whatever is L, whatever is gracious, if

LOVER (5)

Ps 88:18 Thou hast caused L and friend to shun me;
99:4 Mighty King, L of justice, thou hast established
Is 47:8 therefore hear this, you L of pleasures, who sit
1Tim 3:3 not quarrelsome, and no L of money.
Tit 1:7 gain, but hospitable, a L of goodness, master of

LOVERS (29)

Song 5:1 Eat, O friends, and drink: drink deeply, O L
Wis 15:6 L of evil things and fit for such objects
Jer 2:33 "How well you direct your course to seek L
3:1 the harlot with many L; and would you return
3:2 you have sat awaiting L like an Arab in
4:30 Your L despise you; they seek your life.
22:20 Abarim, for all your L are destroyed.
22:22 your shepherds, and your L shall go into captivity;
30:14 All your L have forgotten you; they care nothing
Lam 1:2 cheeks; among all her L she has none to
1:19 "I called to my L but they deceived me;
Ezek 16:33 gifts to all your L, bribing them to come
16:36 your harlotries with your L, and because of all
16:37 will gather all your L, with whom you took
16:39 the hand of your L, and they shall throw
23:5 she doted on her L the Assyrians,
23:9 the hands of her L, into the hands of
23:22 rouse against you your L from whom you turned
Hos 2:5 will go after my L, who give me my
2:7 She shall pursue her L, but not overtake them;
2:10 the sight of her L, and no one shall
2:12 my hire, which my L have given me.' I
2:13 and went after her L, and forgot me, says
8:9 a wild ass wandering alone; Ephraim has hired L
Lk 16:14 The Pharisees, who were L of money, heard all
2Tim 3:2 For men will be L of self, lovers of
3:2 be lovers of self, L of money, proud, arrogant,
3:4 reckless, swollen with conceit, L of pleasure rather
3:4 of pleasure rather than L of God,

LOVES (81)

Gen 27:9 father, such as he L;
44:20 children; and his father L him.'
Deut 7:8 is because the LORD L you, and is keeping
10:18 and the widow, and L the sojourner, giving him
15:16 from you,' because he L you and your household,
Ruth 4:15 for your daughter-in-law who L you, who is more
2Chr 2:11 Solomon, "Because the LORD L his people he has
Ps 11:5 soul hates him that L violence.
11:7 LORD is righteous, he L righteous deeds; the upright
33:5 He L righteousness and justice; the earth is full
37:28 For the LORD L justice; he will not forsake
47:4 for us, the pride of Jacob whom he L
78:68 the tribe of Judah, Mount Zion, which he L
87:2 he founded; the LORD L the gates of Zion
97:10 The LORD L those who hate evil; he preserves
119:140 tried, and thy servant L it.
146:8 bowed down; the LORD L the righteous.
Prov 3:12 reproves him whom he L, as a father the
12:1 Whoever L discipline L knowledge, but he who hates
13:24 son, but he who L him is diligent to
15:9 the LORD, but he L him who pursues righteousness.

16:13 a king, and he L him who speaks what
17:17 A friend L at all times, and a brother
17:19 He who L transgression loves strife; he who makes
17:19 He who loves transgression L strife; he who makes
19:8 He who gets wisdom L himself; he who keeps
21:17 He who L pleasure will be a poor man;
21:17 poor man; he who L wine and oil will
22:11 He who L purity of heart, and whose speech
29:3 He who L wisdom makes his father glad, but
Eccl 5:10 He who L money will not be satisfied with
5:10 money; nor he who L wealth, with gain: this
Song 1:7 you whom my soul L, where you pasture your
3:1 him whom my soul L; I sought him, but
3:2 squares; I will seek him whom my soul L
3:3 Have you seen him whom my soul L
3:4 them, when I found him whom my soul L
Wis 7:28 and prophets; for God L nothing so much as
8:3 the Lord of all L her.
8:7 And if any one L righteousness, her labors are
Sir 3:24 the end, and whoever L danger will perish by
4:12 Whoever L her loves life, and those who seek
4:12 Whoever loves her L life, and those who seek
4:14 Holy One; the Lord L those who love her.
13:14 Every creature L its like, and every person his
30:1 He who L his son will whip him often,
31:5 He who L gold will not be justified, and
Is 1:23 Every one L a bribe and runs after gifts.
48:14 The LORD L him; he shall perform his purpose
Bar 6:9 for a girl who L ornaments;
Hos 3:1 even as the LORD L the people of Israel,
12:7 are false balances, he L to oppress.
Mal 2:11 the LORD, which he L, and has married the
2Mac 15:14 is a man who L the brethren and prays
Mt 10:37 He who L father or mother more than me
10:37 me; and he who L son or daughter more
Lk 7:5 for him, for he L our nation, and he
7:47 who is forgiven little, L little."
Jn 3:35 the Spirit; the Father L the Son, and has
5:19 For the Father L the Son, and shows him
10:17 this reason the Father L me, because I lay
12:25 He who L his life loses it, and he
14:21 he it is who L me; and he who
14:21 me; and he who L me will be loved
14:23 him, "If a man L me, he will keep
16:27 for the Father himself L you, because you have
Rom 13:8 another; for he who L his neighbor has fulfilled
1Cor 8:3 But if one L God, one is known by
2Cor 9:7 under compulsion, for God L a cheerful giver.
Eph 5:28 He who L his wife loves himself.
5:28 who loves his wife L himself.
Heb 12:6 disciplines him whom he L, and chastises every son
1Jn 2:10 He who L his brother abides in the light,
2:15 If any one L the world, love for the
4:7 God, and he who L is born of God
4:21 him, that he who L God should love his
5:1 and every one who L the parent loves the
5:1 who loves the parent L the child.
Rev 1:5 To him who L us and has freed us
22:15 and every one who L and practices falsehood.

LOVESICK

Ezek 16:30 "How L is your heart, says the Lord GOD,

LOVEST (2)

Wis 11:24 For thou L all things that exist, and hast
11:26 thine, O Lord who L the living.

LOVING (7)

Deut 11:22 command you to do, L the LORD your God,
19:9 you this day, by L the LORD your God
30:16 you this day, by L the LORD your God,
30:20 your descendants may live, L the LORD your God,
Wis 7:22 clear, unpolluted, distinct, invulnerable, L the good,
Is 56:10 bark; dreaming, lying down, L to slumber.
Tit 3:4 when the goodness and L kindness of God our

LOVINGLY

Song 3:10 of purple; it was L wrought within by the

LOW (61)

Judg 6:6 Israel was brought very L because of Midian; and
11:35 have brought me very L, and you have become
1Sam 2:7 makes rich; he brings L, he also exalts.
2Chr 28:19 the LORD brought Judah L because of Ahaz king
Jud 13:20 our nation was brought L, but have avenged our
Esth 1:20 will give honor to their husbands, high and L
Job 6:5 grass, or the ox L over his fodder?
14:10 dies, and is laid L; man breathes his last,
14:21 it; they are brought L, and he perceives it
40:12 proud, and bring him L; and tread down the
41:9 disappointed; he is laid L even at the sight
Ps 49:2 of the world, both L and high, rich and
62:9 [Selah] Men of L estate are but a breath,
78:31 of them, and laid L the picked men of
79:8 to meet us, for we are brought very L
106:43 purposes, and were brought L through their iniquity.
107:39 diminished and brought L through oppression,
116:6 when I was brought L, he saved me.
136:23 remembered us in our L estate, for his steadfast
142:6 to my cry; for I am brought very L
Prov 7:26 victim has she laid L; yea, all her slain
29:23 pride will bring him L, but he who is
Eccl 10:6 rich sit in a L place.
12:4 of the grinding is L, and one rises up
12:4 of song are brought L;
Sir 4:7 congregation; bow your head L to a great man.
6:12 if you are brought L he will turn against
11:12 him out of his L estate
33:12 he cursed and brought L, and he turned them
Is 2:9 and men are brought L -- forgive them not!
2:11 man shall be brought L, and the pride of
2:17 men shall be brought L; and the LORD alone
5:15 and men are brought L, and the eyes of
10:33 hewn down, and the lofty will be brought L
13:11 the arrogant, and lay L the haughtiness of the
14:8 'Since you were laid L, no hewer comes up
14:12 to the ground, you who laid the nations L
17:4 Jacob will be brought L, and the fat of
25:11 the LORD will lay L his pride together with
25:12 will bring down, lay L, and cast to the
26:5 For he has brought L the inhabitants of the
26:5 He lays it L, lays it low to the
26:5 it low, lays it L to the ground, casts
29:4 you shall speak, from L in the dust your
32:19 down, and the city will be utterly laid L
40:4 and hill be made L; the uneven ground shall
60:14 you shall come bending L to you; and all
Bar 2:5 They were brought L and not raised up, because
5:7 everlasting hills be made L and the valleys filled
Ezek 17:6 sprouted and became a L spreading vine, and its
17:24 I the LORD bring L the high tree, and
17:24 and make high the L tree, dry up the
21:26 exalt that which is L, and abase that which
Dan 3:37 nation, and are brought L this day in all
Hab 3:6 were scattered, the everlasting hills sank L
Zech 10:11 Assyria shall be laid L, and the scepter of
2Mac 15:27 their hearts, they laid L no less than thirty-five
Lk 1:48 he has regarded the L estate of his handmaiden.
1:52 and exalted those of L degree;
3:5 hill shall be brought L, and the crooked shall
1Cor 1:28 God chose what is L and despised in the

LOWER (24)

Gen 6:16 side; make it with L, second, and third decks.
Ex 28:27 in front to the L part of the two
39:20 in front to the L part of the two
Deut 28:43 you shall come down L and lower.
28:43 higher; and you shall come down lower and L
Josh 13:27 a boundary, to the L end of the Sea
15:19 upper springs and the L springs.
16:3 as the territory of L Beth-horon, then to Gezer,
18:13 that lies south of L Beth-horon.
Judg 1:15 upper springs and the L springs.
1Kgs 9:17 Solomon rebuilt Gezer) and L Beth-horon
1Chr 7:24 Sheerah, who built both L and Upper Beth-horon,
2Chr 8:5 built Upper Beth-horon and L Beth-horon, fortified
Prov 25:7 than to be put L in the presence of
Sir 29:5 a loan, and will L his voice in speaking
Is 22:9 the waters of the L pool,
Ezek 40:18 gates; this was the L pavement.
40:19 inner front of the L gate to the outer
42:5 them than from the L and middle chambers in
42:6 ground more than the L and the middle ones.
43:14 the ground to the L ledge, two cubits, with
Eph 4:9 also descended into the L parts of the earth?
Heb 2:7 for a little while L than the angels, thou
2:9 little while was made L than the angels, crowned

LOWERED (4)

Gen 44:11 Then every man quickly L his sack to the
Ex 17:11 prevailed; and whenever he L his hand, Amalek
Acts 27:17 on the Syrtis, they L the gear, and so

L

27:30 the ship, and had L the boat into the

LOWERING

Acts 9:25 down over the wall, L him in a basket.

LOWEST (7)

1Kgs 6:6 The L story was five cubits broad, the middle
6:8 The entrance for the L story was on the
Neh 4:13 So in the L parts of the space behind
Ps 55:23 them down into the L pit; men of blood
Ezek 41:7 went up from the L story to the top
Lk 14:9 shame to take the L place.
14:10 and sit in the L place, so that when

LOWING (3)

1Sam 6:12 Beth-shemesh along one highway, L as they went;
15:14 my ears, and the L of the oxen which
Jer 9:10 passes through, and the L of cattle is not

LOWLAND (10)

Deut 1:7 country and in the L, and in the Negeb,
Josh 9:1 country and in the L all along the coast
10:40 the Negeb and the L and the slopes, and
11:2 Chinneroth, and in the L, and in Naphoth-dor on
11:16 of Goshen and the L and the Arabah and
11:16 of Israel and its L
12:8 hill country, in the L, in the Arabah, in
15:33 And in the L, Eshtaol, Zorah, Ashnah,
Judg 1:9 hill country, in the Negeb, and in the L
Zech 7:7 the South and the L were inhabited, were not

LOWLIEST (2)

Wis 6:6 For the L man may be pardoned in mercy,
Dan 4:17 sets over it the L of men.'

LOWLINESS (3)

Esth 4:8 the days of your L, when you were cared
Eph 4:2 been called, with all L and meekness, with patience,
Col 3:12 beloved, compassion, kindness, L, meekness, and

LOWLY (16)

Jud 9:11 art God of the L, helper of the oppressed,
Esth 11:11 sun rose, and the L were exalted and consumed
Job 5:11 high those who are L, and those who mourn
22:29 God abases the proud, but he saves the L
Ps 138:6 high, he regards the L; but the haughty he
Prov 16:19 to be of a L spirit with the poor
29:23 but he who is L in spirit will obtain
Sir 10:14 and has seated the L in their place.
Jer 13:18 queen mother: "Take a L seat, for your beautiful
Ezek 29:14 they shall be a L kingdom.
29:15 shall be the most L of the kingdoms, and
Zeph 3:12 the midst of you a people humble and L
Mt 11:29 I am gentle and L in heart, and you
Rom 12:16 but associate with the L; never be conceited.
Phil 3:21 who will change our L body to be like
Jas 1:8 Let the L brother boast in his exaltation,

LOYAL (10)

1Sam 20:14 alive, show me the L love of the LORD,
2Sam 22:26 "With the L thou dost show thyself loyal; with
22:26 thou dost show thyself L; with the blameless man
Esth 16:1 to those who are L to our government, greeting.
16:23 for us and the L Persians, but that for
Ps 18:25 With the L thou dost show thyself loyal; with
18:25 thou dost show thyself L; with the blameless man
Sir 26:2 A L wife rejoices her husband, and he will
46:7 Moses he did a L deed, he and Caleb
3Jn 1:5 Beloved, it is a L thing you do when

LOYALLY (8)

Gen 21:23 as I have dealt L with you, you will
24:49 if you will deal L and truly with my
47:29 and promise to deal L and truly with me.
2Sam 10:2 said, "I will deal L with Hanun the son
10:2 as his father dealt L with me." So David
1Kgs 2:7 But deal L with the sons of Barzillai the
1Chr 19:2 said, "I will deal L with Hanun the son
19:2 for his father dealt L with me." So David

LOYALTY (14)

1Sam 20:15 not cut off your L from my house for
2Sam 2:5 because you showed this L to Saul your lord,
3:8 day I keep showing L to the house of
16:17 Hushai, "Is this your L to your friend?
1Kgs 2:7 table; for with such L they met me when

Ps 101:1 I will sing of L and of justice; to
Prov 3:3 Let not L and faithfulness forsake you; bind them
14:22 who devise good meet L and faithfulness.
16:6 By L and faithfulness iniquity is atoned for, and
19:22 in a man is L, and a poor man
20:6 man proclaims his own L, but a faithful man
20:28 L and faithfulness preserve the king, and his throne
Jon 2:8 pay regard to vain idols forsake their true L
1Mac 14:35 of the justice and L which he had maintained

LUCIUS (3)

1Mac 15:16 the following was written: L, consul of the Romans,
Acts 13:1 who was called Niger, L of Cyrene, Mana-en a
Rom 16:21 greets you; so do L and Jason and Sosipater,

LUCK

Sir 8:19 every one, lest you drive away your good L

LUD (7)

Gen 10:22 Shem: Elam, Asshur, Arpachshad, L, and Aram.
1Chr 1:17 Shem: Elam, Asshur, Arpachshad, L, Aram, Uz, Hul,
Jud 2:23 and ravaged Put and L, and plundered all the
Is 66:19 to Tarshish, Put, and L, who draw the bow,
Jer 46:9 the shield, men of L, skilled in handling the
Ezek 27:10 "Persia and L and Put were in your army
30:5 Ethiopia, and Put, and L, and all Arabia, and

LUDIM (2)

Gen 10:13 became the father of L, Anamim, Lehabim,
1Chr 1:11 was the father of L, Anamim, Lehabim, Naph-tuhim,

LUHITH (2)

Is 15:5 at the ascent of L they go up weeping;
Jer 48:5 at the ascent of L they go up weeping;

LUKE (3)

Col 4:14 L the beloved physician and Demas greet you.
2Tim 4:11 L alone is with me.
Philem 1:24 Mark, Aristarchus, Demas, and L, my fellow workers.

LUKEWARM

Rev 3:16 So, because you are L, and neither cold nor

LUMINARIES (2)

Ps 74:16 thou hast established the L and the sun.
Wis 13:2 turbulent water, of the L of heaven were the

LUMP (5)

Rom 9:21 out of the same L one vessel for beauty
11:16 so is the whole L; and if the root
1Cor 5:6 know that a little leaven leavens the whole L
5:7 may be a new L, as you really are
Gal 5:9 A little leaven leavens the whole L

LURED

Jas 1:13 tempted when he is L and enticed by his

LURK (3)

Ps 56:6 band themselves together, they L, they watch my
Jer 5:26 among my people; they L like fowlers lying in
Hos 13:7 a leopard I will L beside the way.

LURKING (2)

1Sam 23:23 note of all the L places where he hides,
Ps 17:12 as a young lion L in ambush.

LURKS (2)

Ps 10:9 for the hapless, he L in secret like a
10:9 in his covert; he L that he may seize

LUST (16)

Tob 8:7 of mine because of L, but with sincerity.
Ps 68:30 under foot those who L after tribute; scatter the
Prov 11:6 but the treacherous are taken captive by their L
Sir 23:6 Let neither gluttony nor L overcome me, and do
Is 57:5 you who burn with L among the oaks, under
Jer 2:24 Who can restrain her L
Ezek 23:8 and poured out their L upon her.
23:17 defiled her with their L; and after she was
Dan 13:14 the other for the reason, they confessed their L
13:56 has deceived you and L has perverted your heart.
1Thes 4:5 in the passion of L like heathen who do
2Pet 2:10 who indulge in the L of defiling passion and
1Jn 2:16 in the world, the L of the flesh and
2:16 the flesh and the L of the eyes and
2:17 passes away, and the L of it; but he

Jude 1:7 and indulged in unnatural L, serve as an example

LUSTER

Ps 132:18 but upon himself his crown will shed its L

LUSTFUL (3)

Sir 26:9 harlotry shows in her L eyes, and she is
Ezek 16:26 with the Egyptians, your L neighbors, multiplying
Dan 13:11 ashamed to disclose their L desire to possess her.

LUSTFULLY

Mt 5:28 looks at a woman L has already committed adultery

LUSTS (2)

Rom 1:24 them up in the L of their hearts to
Eph 4:22 is corrupt through deceitful L,

LUSTY

Jer 5:8 They were well-fed L stallions, each neighing for his

LUTE (2)

Ps 92:3 the music of the L and the harp, to
150:3 sound; praise him with L and harp!

LUTES

1Mac 4:54 songs and harps and L and cymbals.

LUXURIANT

Hos 10:1 Israel is a L vine that yields its fruit.

LUXURIOUS

Wis 19:11 them to ask for L food;

LUXURY (9)

Prov 19:10 fool to live in L, much less for a
Sir 11:25 hour makes one forget L, and at the close
14:4 others will live in L on his goods.
14:16 yourself, because in Hades one cannot look for L
18:31 not revel in great L, lest you become impoverished
37:29 insatiable appetite for any L, and do not give
Hab 1:16 them he lives in L, and his food is
Lk 7:25 appareled and live in L are in kings' courts.
Jas 5:5 on the earth in L and in pleasure; you

LUZ (8)

Gen 28:19 of the city was L at the first.
35:6 And Jacob came to L (that is, Bethel), which
48:3 appeared to me at L in the land of
Josh 16:2 going from Bethel to L, it passes along to
18:13 in the direction of L, to the shoulder of
18:13 to the shoulder of L (the same is Bethel),
Judg 1:23 the city was formerly L
1:26 and called its name L; that is its name

LYCAONIA

Acts 14:6 and Derbe, cities of L, and to the surrounding

LYCAONIAN

Acts 14:11 their voices, saying in L, "The gods have come

LYCIA (2)

1Mac 15:23 to Pamphylia, and to L, and to Halicarnassus, and
Acts 27:5 Cilicia and Pamphylia, we came to Myra in L

LYDDA (4)

1Mac 11:34 districts of Aphairema and L and Rathamin; the
Acts 9:32 down also to the saints that lived at L
9:35 all the residents of L and Sharon saw him,
9:38 Since L was near Joppa, the disciples, hearing that

LYDIA (3)

1Mac 8:8 provinces, the country of India and Media and L
Acts 16:14 was a woman named L, from the city of
16:40 the prison, and visited L; and when they had

LYE (3)

Job 9:30 cleanse my hands with L,
Is 1:25 your dross as with L and remove all your
Jer 2:22 you wash yourself with L and use much soap,

LYING (80)

Gen 29:2 three flocks of sheep L beside it; for out
34:7 folly in Israel by L with Jacob's daughter, for
Ex 5:9 pay no regard to L words."
23:5 one who hates you L under its burden, you
Num 21:20 Bamoth to the valley L in the region of
31:17 has known man by L with him.
31:18 not known man by L with him, keep alive
31:35 not known man by L with him.
35:20 or hurled at him, L in wait, so that
35:22 anything on him without L in wait,
Deut 21:1 one is found slain, L in the open country,
22:22 a man is found L with the wife of
Judg 4:21 ground, as he was L fast asleep from weariness.
16:9 Now she had men L in wait in an
16:12 And the men L in wait were in an
19:27 there was his concubine L at the door of
21:12 not known man by L with him; and they
1Sam 3:2 could not see, was L down in his own
3:3 out, and Samuel was L down within the temple
5:4 both his hands were L cut off upon the
26:5 his army; Saul was L within the encampment, while
2Sam 13:8 house, where he was L down.
1Kgs 22:22 and will be a L spirit in the mouth
22:23 LORD has put a L spirit in the mouth
2Kgs 4:32 he saw the child L dead on his bed.
2Chr 18:21 and will be a L spirit in the mouth
18:22 LORD has put a L spirit in the mouth
20:24 they were dead bodies L on the ground; none
Jud 6:13 Achior and left him L at the foot of
14:18 look, here is Holofernes L on the ground, and
Ps 31:18 Let the L lips be dumb, which speak insolently
52:3 more than good, and L more than speaking the
109:2 speaking against me with L tongues.
120:2 me, O LORD, from L lips, from a deceitful
139:3 my path and my L down, and art acquainted
Prov 6:17 him: haughty eyes, a L tongue, and hands that
10:18 who conceals hatred has L lips, and he who
12:19 for ever, but a L tongue is but for
12:22 L lips are an abomination to the LORD, but
21:6 of treasures by a L tongue is a fleeting
26:28 A L tongue hates its victims, and a flattering
30:8 from me falsehood and L; give me neither poverty
Wis 1:11 without result, and a L mouth destroys the soul.
Sir 7:13 for the habit of L serves no good.
51:5 an unclean tongue and L words—
Is 30:9 are a rebellious people, L sons, sons who will
32:7 ruin the poor with L words, even when the
56:10 cannot bark; dreaming, L down, loving to slumber.
59:13 uttering from the heart L words.
Jer 5:26 they lurk like fowlers L in wait.
14:14 prophesying to you a L vision, worthless divination,
23:32 those who prophesy L dreams, says the LORD,
29:23 spoken in my name L words which I did
Lam 3:10 me like a bear L in wait, like a
Ezek 13:7 vision, and uttered a L divination, whenever you have
13:9 visions and who give L divinations; they shall not
Dan 2:9 have agreed to speak L and corrupt words before
Hos 4:2 land; there is swearing, L, killing, stealing, and
1Mac 5:3 Akrabattene, because they kept L in wait for Israel.
11:4 destroyed, and the corpses L about, and the charred
2Mac 3:31 to one who was L quite at his last
4:41 the ashes that were L about, and threw them
13:12 weeping and fasting and L prostrate for three days
15:28 joy, they recognized Nicanor, L dead, in full armor.
Mt 8:6 "Lord, my servant is L paralyzed at home, in
8:14 he saw his mother-in-law L sick with a fever;
9:2 to him a paralytic, L on his bed; and
Mk 7:29 and found the child L in bed, and the
Lk 2:12 in swaddling cloths and L in a manger."
2:16 Joseph, and the babe L in a manger.
11:54 speak of many things, L in wait for him,
Jn 5:5 that he had been L there a long time,
13:23 whom Jesus loved, was L close to the breast
13:25 So L thus, close to the breast of Jesus,
20:5 saw the linen cloths L there, but he did
20:6 saw the linen cloths L,
20:7 on his head, not L with the linen cloths
21:9 fire there, with fish L on it, and bread.
Rom 9:1 Christ, I am not L; my conscience bears me
1Tim 2:7 truth, I am not L, a teacher of the

LYRE (29)

Gen 4:21 those who play the L and pipe.
31:27 away with mirth and songs, with tambourine and L
1Sam 10:5 tambourine, flute, and L before them, prophesying.
16:16 skilful in playing the L; and when the evil
16:23 Saul, David took the L and played it with
18:10 David was playing the L, as he did day
19:9 in his hand; and David was playing the L
1Chr 25:3 who prophesied with the L in thanksgiving and
Job 21:12 the tambourine and the L, and rejoice to the

L

30:31 My L is turned to mourning, and my pipe
Ps 33:2 the LORD with the L, make melody to him
43:4 praise thee with the L, O God, my God.
49:4 solve my riddle to the music of the L
57:8 Awake, O harp and L
71:22 to thee with the L, O Holy One of
81:2 the timbrel, the sweet L with the harp.
92:3 and the harp, to the melody of the L
98:5 the LORD with the L, with the lyre and
98:5 the lyre, with the L and the sound of
108:2 Awake, O harp and L
147:7 thanksgiving; make melody to our God upon the L
149:3 dancing, making melody to him with timbrel and L
Is 5:12 They have L and harp, timbrel and flute and
16:11 soul moans like a L for Moab, and my
24:8 the mirth of the L is stilled.
Dan 3:5 of the horn, pipe, L, trigon, harp, bagpipe, and
3:7 of the horn, pipe, L, trigon, harp, bagpipe, and
3:10 of the horn, pipe, L, trigon, harp, bagpipe, and
3:15 of the horn, pipe, L, trigon, harp, bagpipe, and

LYRES (18)
2Sam 6:5 might, with songs and L and harps and tambourines
1Kgs 10:12 for the king's house, L also and harps for
1Chr 13:8 might, with song and L and harps and tambourines
15:16 instruments, on harps and L and cymbals, to raise
15:21 were to lead with L according to the Sheminith.
15:28 cymbals, and made loud music on harps and L
16:5 to play harps and L; Asaph was to sound
25:1 who should prophesy with L, with harps, and with
25:6 with cymbals, harps, and L for the service of
2Chr 5:12 with cymbals, harps, and L, stood east of the
9:11 for the king's house, L also and harps for
20:28 Jerusalem, with harps and L and trumpets, to the
29:25 with cymbals, harps, and L, according to the
Neh 12:27 and with singing, with cymbals, harps, and L
Ps 137:2 On the willows there we hung up our L
Sir 39:15 your lips, and with L; and this you shall
Is 30:32 sound of timbrels and L; battling with brandished
Ezek 26:13 the sound of your L shall be heard no

LYSANI-AS
Lk 3:1 Ituraea and Trachonitis, and L tetrarch of Abilene,

LYSIAS (31)
1Mac 3:32 He left L, a distinguished man of royal lineage,
3:33 L was also to take care of Antiochus his
3:34 he turned over to L half of his troops
3:35 of Judea and Jerusalem, L was to send a
3:38 L chose Ptolemy the son of Dorymenes, and Nicanor
4:26 went and reported to L all that had happened.
4:34 of the army of L five thousand men; they
4:35 And when L saw the rout of his troops
6:6 had been routed; that L had gone first with
6:17 And when L learned that the king was dead,
6:17 L had brought him up as a boy, and
6:55 Then L heard that Philip, whom King Antiochus
7:2 army seized Antiochus and L to bring them to
2Mac 10:11 the kingdom, appointed one L to have charge of
11:1 Very soon after this, L, the king's guardian and
11:6 men got word that L was besieging the strongholds,
11:12 and wounded, and L himself escaped by disgraceful
11:15 agreed to all that L urged.
11:15 which Maccabeus delivered to L in writing.
11:16 to the Jews by L was to this effect:
11:16 was to this effect: L to the people of
11:22 Antiochus to his brother L, greeting.
11:35 With regard to what L the kinsman of the
12:1 agreement had been reached, L returned to the king,
12:27 a fortified city where L dwelt with multitudes of
13:2 Judea, and with him L, his guardian, who had
13:4 the scoundrel; and when L informed him that this
13:26 L took the public platform, made the best possible
14:2 having made away with Antiochus and his guardian L
Acts 23:26 to this effect: "Claudius L to his Excellency the
24:21 them off, saying, "When L the tribune comes down,

LYSIMACHUS (7)
Esth 11:1 had been translated by L the son of Ptolemy,
2Mac 4:29 left his own brother L as deputy in the
4:39 in the city by L with the connivance of
4:39 the populace gathered against L, because many of
4:40 and filled with anger, L armed about three thousand
4:41 Jews became aware of L attack, some picked up
4:41 in wild confusion at L and his men.

LYSTRA (6)
Acts 14:6 it and fled to L and Derbe, cities of
14:8 Now at L there was a man sitting, who
14:21 disciples, they returned to L and to Iconium and
16:1 And he came also to Derbe and to L
16:2 by the brethren at L and Iconium.
2Tim 3:11 at Iconium, and at L, what persecutions I endured;

M

MA-ACATHITE (3)
2Kgs 25:23 the Netophathite, and Ja-azaniah the son of the M
1Chr 4:19 fathers of Keilah the Garmite and Eshtemoa the M
Jer 40:8 the son of the M, they and their men.

MA-ACATHITES (4)
Deut 3:14 the Geshurites and the M, and called the villages
Josh 12:5 the Geshurites and the M, and over half of
13:11 of the Geshurites and M, and all Mount Hermon,
13:13 the Geshurites or the M; but Geshur and Maacath

MA-ADAI
Ezra 10:34 the sons of Bani: M, Amram, Uel,

MA-ADIAH
Neh 12:5 Iddo, Ginnethoi, Abijah, Mijamin, M, Bilgah,

MA-ASEIAH (23)
1Chr 15:18 Jehiel, Unni, Eliab, Benaiah, M, Mattithiah,
15:20 Jehiel, Unni, Eliab, M, and Benaiah were to
2Chr 23:1 the son of Obed, M the son of Adaiah,
26:11 Je-iel the secretary and M the officer, under the
28:7 man of Ephraim, slew M the king's son and
34:8 son of Azaliah, and M the governor of the
Ezra 10:18 foreign women were found M, Eliezer, Jarib, and
10:21 the sons of Harim: M, Elijah, Shemaiah, Jehiel, and
10:22 sons of Pashhur: Eli-o-enai, M, Ishmael, Nethanel,
10:30 Pahath-moab: Adna, Chelal, Benaiah, M, Mattaniah,
Neh 3:23 Azariah the son of M, son of Ananiah repaired
8:4 Anaiah, Uriah, Hilkiah, and M on his right hand;
8:7 Hodiah, M, Kelita, Azariah, Jozabad, Hanan
10:25 Pilha, Shobek, Rehum, Hashabnah, M,
11:5 sons of Perez; and M the son of Baruch,
11:7 of Kolaiah, son of M, son of Ithi-el, son
12:41 priests Eliakim, M, Miniamin, Micaiah, Eli-o-enai,
12:42 Hananiah, with trumpets; and M, Shemaiah, Eleazar,
Jer 21:1 priest, the son of M, saying,
29:21 Zedekiah the son of M, who are prophesying a
29:25 Zephaniah the son of M the priest, and to
35:4 above the chamber of M the son of Shallum,
37:3 priest, the son of M, to Jeremiah the prophet,

MA-AZIAH (2)
1Chr 24:18 the twenty-third to Delaiah, the twenty-fourth to M
Neh 10:8 Abijah, Mijamin, M, Bilgai, Shemaiah; these are

MAACAH (22)
Gen 22:24 was Reumah, bore Tebah, Gaham, Tahash, and M
2Sam 3:3 Absalom the son of M the daughter of Talmai
10:6 and the king of M with a thousand men,
10:8 men of Tob and M, were by themselves in
23:34 son of Ahasbai of M, Eliam the son of
1Kgs 2:39 to Achish, son of M, king of Gath.
15:2 His mother's name was M the daughter of
15:10 mother's name was M the daughter of Abishalom.
15:13 He also removed M his mother from being queen
1Chr 2:48 M, Caleb's concubine, bore Sheber and Tirhanah.
3:2 Absalom, whose mother was M, the daughter of
7:15 The name of his sister was M
7:16 And M the wife of Machir bore a son,
8:29 Gibeon, and the name of his wife was M
9:35 of his wife was M,
11:43 Hanan the son of M, and Joshaphat the Mithnite,
19:7 and the king of M with his army, who
27:16 Shephatiah the son of M;
2Chr 11:20 After her he took M the daughter of Absalom,
11:21 Rehoboam loved M the daughter of Absalom above
11:22 Abijah the son of M as chief prince among
15:16 Even M, his mother, King Asa removed from being

MAACATH
Josh 13:13 Ma-acathites; but Geshur and M dwell in the midst

MAAI
Neh 12:36 Azarel, Milalai, Gilalai, M, Nethanel, Judah, and

MAARATH
Josh 15:59 Bethzur, Gedor, M, Beth-anoth, and Eltekon: six

MAASAI
1Chr 9:12 son of Malchijah, and M the son of Adi-el,

MAATH
Lk 3:26 Naggai, the son of M, the son of Mattathias,

MAAZ
1Chr 2:27 the first-born of Jerahmeel: M, Jamin, and Eker.

MACCABEUS (31)
1Mac 2:4 called Thassi, Judas called M,
2:66 Judas M has been a mighty warrior from his
3:1 son, who was called M, took command in his
5:24 Judas M and Jonathan his brother crossed the
5:34 realized that it was M, they fled before him,
8:20 who is also called M, and his brothers and
2Mac 2:19 The story of Judas M and his brothers, and
5:27 But Judas M, with about nine others, got away
8:1 who was also called M, and his companions secretly
8:5 As soon as M got his army organized, the
8:16 But M gathered his men together, to the number
10:1 Now M and his followers, the Lord leading them
10:16 But M and his men, after making solemn
10:19 to withstand a siege, M left Simon and Joseph,
10:21 had happened came to M, he gathered the leaders
10:25 As he drew near, M and his men sprinkled
10:30 Surrounding M and protecting him with their own
10:33 Then M and his men were glad, and they
10:35 in the army of M, fired with anger because
11:6 When M and his men got word that Lysias
11:7 M himself was the first to take up arms,
11:15 M, having regard for the common good, agreed to
11:15 of the Jews which M delivered to Lysias in
12:19 who were captains under M, marched out and
12:20 But M arranged his army in divisions, set men
13:24 He received M, left Hegemonides as governor from
14:6 whose leader is Judas M, are keeping up war
14:27 commanding him to send M to Antioch as a
14:30 But M, noticing that Nicanor was more austere in
15:7 But M did not cease to trust with all
15:21 deployed on the flanks, M, perceiving the hosts that

MACEDONIA (24)
Acts 16:9 night: a man of M was standing beseeching him
16:9 saying, "Come over to M and help us."
16:10 to go on into M, concluding that God had
16:12 of the district of M, and a Roman colony.
18:5 and Timothy arrived from M, Paul was occupied with
19:21 Spirit to pass through M and Achaia and go
19:22 And having sent into M two of his helpers,
20:1 them took leave of them and departed for M
20:3 sail for Syria, he determined to return through M
Rom 15:26 For M and Achaia have been pleased to make
1Cor 16:5 you after passing through M, for I intend to
16:5 intend to pass through M,
2Cor 1:16 on my way to M, and to come back
1:16 back to you from M and have you send
2:13 took leave of them and went on to M
7:5 when we came into M, our bodies had no
8:1 in the churches of M,
9:2 to the people of M, saying that Achaia has
11:9 were supplied by the brethren who came from M
Phil 4:15 gospel, when I left M, no church entered into
1Thes 1:7 all the believers in M and in Achaia.
1:8 forth from you in M and Achaia, but your
4:10 indeed you do love all the brethren throughout M
1Tim 1:3 I was going to M, remain at Ephesus that

MACEDONIAN (4)
Esth 16:10 son of Hammedatha, a M (really an alien to
1Mac 1:1 son of Philip, the M, who came from the
6:2 son of Philip, the M king who first reigned
Acts 27:2 accompanied by Aristarchus, a M from Thessalonica.

MACEDONIANS (6)
Esth 16:14 transfer the kingdom of the Persians to the M
1Mac 8:5 Perseus king of the M, and the others who
2Mac 8:20 thousand M; and when the M were hard-pressed, the
Acts 19:29 and Aristarchus, M who were Paul's companions
2Cor 9:4 be; lest if some M come with me and

MACH-PELAH (6)
Gen 23:9 me the cave of M, which he owns; it
23:17 field of Ephron in M, which was to the
23:19 of the field of M east of Mamre (that
25:9 in the cave of M, in the field of
49:30 in the field at M, to the east of
50:13 of the field at M, to the east of

MACHBANNAI
1Chr 12:13 Elzabad ninth, Jeremiah tenth, M eleventh.

MACHBENAH
1Chr 2:49 Sheva the father of M and the father of

MACHI
Num 13:15 the tribe of Gad, Geuel the son of M

MACHINES (3)
1Mac 6:51 throw fire and stones, M to shoot arrows, and
9:64 many days and made M of war.
9:67 set fire to the M of war.

MACHIR (21)
Gen 50:23 the children also of M the son of Manasseh
Num 26:29 sons of Manasseh: of M, the family of the
26:29 of the Machirites; and M was the father of
27:1 of Gilead, son of M, son of Manasseh, from
32:39 And the sons of M the son of Manasseh
32:40 Moses gave Gilead to M the son of Manasseh,
36:1 Gilead the son of M, son of Manasseh, of
Deut 3:15 to this day.) To M I gave Gilead,
Josh 13:31 to the people of M the son of Manasseh
17:1 To M the first-born of Manasseh, the father of
17:3 of Gilead, son of M, son of Manasseh, had
Judg 5:14 with your kinsmen; from M marched down the
2Sam 9:4 in the house of M the son of Ammiel,
9:5 from the house of M the son of Ammiel,
17:27 of the Ammonites, and M the son of Ammiel
1Chr 2:21 to the daughter of M the father of Gilead,
2:23 these were descendants of M, the father of Gilead.
7:14 concubine bore; she bore M the father of Gilead.
7:15 And M took a wife for Huppim and for
7:16 Maacah the wife of M bore a son, and
7:17 Gilead the son of M, son of Manasseh.

MACHIRITES (2)
Num 26:29 the family of the M; and Machir was the
Josh 13:31 the half of the M according to their families.

MACHNADEBAI
Ezra 10:40 Shelemiah, Nathan, Adaiah, M, Shashai, Sharai,

MACRON
2Mac 10:12 Ptolemy, who was called M, took the lead in

MAD (15)
Deut 28:34 you shall be driven M by the sight which
1Sam 21:13 them, and feigned himself M in their hands, and
21:14 see the man is M; why then have you
2Kgs 9:11 Why did this M fellow come to you?" And
Eccl 2:2 I said of laughter, "It is M
Jer 50:38 images, and they are M over idols.
51:7 drank of her wine, therefore the nations went M
Hos 9:7 of the spirit is M, because of your great
2Mac 14:5 opportunity that furthered his M purpose when he
Jn 10:20 demon, and he is M; why listen to him?"
Acts 12:15 They said to her, "You are M
26:24 voice, "Paul, you are M; your great learning is
26:24 are mad; your great learning is turning you M
26:25 said, "I am not M, most excellent Festus, but
1Cor 14:23 enter, will they not say that you are M

MADAI (2)
Gen 10:2 Japheth: Gomer, Magog, M, Javan, Tubal, Meshech,
1Chr 1:5 of Japheth: Gomer, Magog, M, Javan, Tubal,

MADE (1,431)
Gen 1:7 And God M the firmament and separated the waters
1:16 And God M the two great lights, the greater
1:16 rule the night; he M the stars also.
1:25 And God M the beasts of the earth according
1:31 everything that he had M, and behold, it was
2:4 that the LORD God M the earth and the
2:9 ground the LORD God M to grow every tree
2:22 from the man he M into a woman and
3:1 other wild creature that the LORD God had M

M

3:7 fig leaves together and M themselves aprons.
3:21 And the LORD God M for Adam and for
5:1 God created man, he M him in the likeness
6:6 sorry that he had M man on the earth,
6:7 sorry that I have M them."
7:4 thing that I have M I will blot out
8:1 And God M a wind blow over the earth,
8:6 ark which he had M,
9:6 be shed; for God M man in his own
13:4 place where he had M an altar at the
14:2 of Goiim, these kings M war with Bera king
14:23 should say, 'I have M Abram rich.'
15:18 that day the LORD M a covenant with Abram,
17:5 Abraham; for I have M you the father of
19:3 his house; and he M them a feast, and
19:33 So they M their father drink wine that night;
19:35 So they M their father drink wine that night
21:6 Sarah said, "God has M laughter for me; every
21:8 was weaned; and Abraham M a great feast on
21:27 and the two men M a covenant.
21:32 So they M a covenant at Beer-sheba.
23:17 its whole area, was M over
23:20 is in it were M over to Abraham as
24:11 And he M the camels kneel down outside the
24:37 My master M me swear, saying, 'You shall not
26:22 now the LORD has M room for us, and
26:30 So he M them a feast, and they ate
26:35 the Hittite; and they M life bitter for Isaac
27:37 Esau, "Behold, I have M him your lord, and
28:20 Then Jacob M a vow, saying, "If God will
29:22 of the place, and M a feast.
31:13 anointed a pillar and M a vow to me.
31:46 they took stones, and M a heap; and they
33:17 himself a house, and M booths for his cattle;
34:29 houses, they captured and M their prey.
37:3 old age; and he M him a long robe
38:29 a breach you have M for yourself!" Therefore his
39:4 attended him, and he M him overseer of his
39:5 the time that he M him overseer in his
39:23 he did, the LORD M it prosper.
40:20 was Pharaoh's birthday, he M a feast for all
41:43 his neck; and he M him to ride in
41:51 he said, "God has M me forget all my
41:52 Ephraim, "For God has M me fruitful in the
43:25 their asses provender, they M ready the present for
43:28 bowed their heads and M obeisance.
43:30 Then Joseph M haste, for his heart yearned for
45:1 with him when Joseph M himself known to his
45:8 God; and he has M me a father to
45:9 son Joseph, God has M me lord of all
46:29 Then Joseph M ready his chariot and went up
47:21 for the people, he M slaves of them from
47:26 So Joseph M it a statute concerning the land
49:24 unmoved, his arms were M agile by the hands
50:5 Pharaoh, saying, My father M me swear, saying, 'I
50:6 your father, as he M you swear."
50:10 sorrowful lamentation; and he M a mourning for his
Ex 1:12 So they M the people of Israel serve with
1:13 serve with rigor, and M their lives bitter with
1:13 all their work they M them serve with rigor.
2:3 for him a basket M of bulrushes, and daubed
2:14 He answered, "Who M you a prince and a
4:11 to him, "Who has M man's mouth?
5:8 of bricks which they M heretofore you shall lay
5:21 judge, because you have M us offensive in the
9:20 the servants of Pharaoh M his slaves and his
10:2 son how I have M sport of the Egyptians
14:6 So he M ready his chariot and took his
14:21 wind all night, and M the sea dry land,
15:17 LORD, which thou hast M for thy abode, the
15:25 There the LORD M for them a statute and
16:31 it was like wafers M with honey.
18:25 of all Israel, and M them heads over the
20:11 six days the LORD M heaven and earth, the
24:8 which the LORD has M with you in accordance
25:31 the lampstand shall be M of hammered work; its
25:33 of it; three cups M like almonds, each with
25:33 branch, and three cups M like almonds, each with
25:34 lampstand itself four cups M like almonds, with their
25:39 gold shall it be M, with all these utensils.
26:31 work shall it be M, with cherubim;
27:8 you on the mountain, so shall it be M
29:33 with which atonement was M, to ordain and
31:17 six days the LORD M heaven and earth, and
31:18 Moses, when he had M an end of speaking
32:4 a graving tool, and M a molten calf; and
32:5 it; and Aaron M proclamation and said, "Tomorrow
32:8 them; they have M for themselves a molten
32:20 calf which they had M, and burnt it with
32:20 upon the water, and M the people of Israel
32:31 great sin; they have M for themselves gods of
32:35 the people, because they M the calf which Aaron
32:35 people, because they made the calf which Aaron M
34:8 And Moses M haste to bow his head toward
34:27 these words I have M a covenant with you
36:8 men among the workmen M the tabernacle with ten
36:8 ten curtains; they were M of fine twined linen
36:11 And he M loops of blue on the edge
36:11 first set; likewise he M them on the edge
36:12 the second set; he M fifty loops on the
36:12 one curtain, and he M fifty loops on the
36:13 And he M fifty clasps of gold, and coupled
36:14 He also M curtains of goats' hair for a
36:14 over the tabernacle; he M eleven curtains.
36:17 And he M fifty loops on the edge of
36:18 And he M fifty clasps of bronze to couple
36:19 And he M for the tent a covering of
36:20 Then he M the upright frames for the tabernacle
36:23 for the tabernacle he M thus: twenty frames for
36:24 south side; and he M forty bases of silver
36:25 the north side, he M twenty frames
36:27 the tabernacle westward he M six frames.
36:28 And he M two frames for corners of the
36:29 the first ring; he M two of them thus,
36:31 And he M bars of acacia wood, five for
36:33 And he M the middle bar to pass through
36:34 frames with gold, and M their rings of gold
36:35 And he M the veil of blue and purple
36:35 cherubim skilfully worked he M it.
36:36 And for it he M four pillars of acacia,
36:37 He also M a screen for the door of
37:1 Bezalel M the ark of acacia wood; two cubits
37:2 within and without, and M a molding of gold
37:4 And he M poles of acacia wood, and overlaid
37:6 And he M a mercy seat of pure gold;
37:7 And he M two cherubim of hammered gold; on
37:7 the mercy seat he M them,
37:8 the mercy seat he M the cherubim on its
37:10 He also M the table of acacia wood; two
37:11 with pure gold, and M a molding of gold
37:12 And he M around it a frame a handbreadth
37:12 a handbreadth wide, and M a molding of gold
37:15 He M the poles of acacia wood to carry
37:16 And he M the vessels of pure gold which
37:17 He also M the lampstand of pure gold.
37:17 of the lampstand were M of hammered work; its
37:19 of it; three cups M like almonds, each with
37:19 branch, and three cups M like almonds, each with
37:20 itself were four cups M like almonds, with their
37:23 And he M its seven lamps and its snuffers
37:24 He M it and all its utensils of a
37:25 He M the altar of incense of acacia wood;
37:26 its horns; and he M a molding of gold
37:27 round about it, and M two rings of gold
37:28 And he M the poles of acacia wood, and
37:29 He M the holy anointing oil also, and the
38:1 He M the altar of burnt offering also of
38:2 He M horns for it on its four corners;
38:3 And he M all the utensils of the altar,
38:3 all its utensils he M of bronze.
38:4 And he M for the altar a grating, a
38:6 for the poles; he M the poles of acacia
38:7 it with them; he M it hollow, with boards.
38:8 And he M the laver of bronze and its
38:9 And he M the court; for the south side
38:22 the tribe of Judah, M all that the LORD
38:28 and seventy-five shekels he M hooks for the pillars,
38:28 overlaid their capitals and M fillets for them.
38:30 shekels; with it he M the bases for the
39:1 and scarlet stuff they M finely wrought garments, for
39:1 the holy place; they M the holy garments for
39:2 And he M the ephod of gold, blue and
39:4 They M for the ephod shoulder-pieces, joined to it
39:8 He M the breastpiece, in skilled work, like the
39:9 square; the breastpiece was M double, a span its
39:15 And they M on the breastpiece twisted chains like
39:16 pure gold; and they M two settings of gold
39:19 Then they M two rings of gold, and put
39:20 And they M two rings of gold, and attached
39:22 He also M the robe of the ephod woven
39:24 of the robe they M pomegranates of blue and
39:25 They also M bells of pure gold, and put

MADE

39:27 They also M the coats, woven of fine linen,
39:30 And they M the plate of the holy crown
Lev 2:7 pan, it shall be M of fine flour with
2:8 cereal offering that is M of these things to
2:11 the LORD shall be M with leaven; for you
4:23 he has committed is M known to him, he
4:28 he has committed is M known to him he
6:21 It shall be M with oil on a griddle;
7:25 offering by fire is M to the LORD shall
7:35 sons from the offerings M by fire to the
13:48 skin or in anything M of skin,
13:49 skin or in anything M of skin, it is
16:17 comes out and has M atonement for himself and
16:20 "And when he has M an end of atoning
16:30 day shall atonement be M for you, to cleanse
16:34 that atonement may be M for the people of
19:19 a garment of cloth M of two kinds of
20:18 her nakedness, he has M naked her fountain, and
22:5 which he may be M unclean or a man
23:17 bread to be waved, M of two tenths of
23:43 may know that I M the people of Israel
25:30 walled city shall be M sure in perpetuity to
26:13 of your yoke and M you walk erect.
26:46 laws which the LORD M between him and the
27:18 a deduction shall be M from your valuation.
Num 5:8 whom restitution may be M for the wrong, the
5:8 with which atonement is M for him.
5:27 And when he has M her drink the water,
6:3 shall drink no vinegar M from wine or strong
7:18 the leader of Issachar, M an offering;
8:4 shown Moses, so he M the lampstand.
8:21 the LORD, and Aaron M atonement for them to
11:8 it in pots, and M cakes of it; and
14:36 and who returned and M all the congregation to
15:34 it had not been M plain what should be
16:38 so let them be M into hammered plates as
16:47 on the incense, and M atonement for the people.
18:8 kept of the offerings M to me, all the
20:5 And why have you M us come up out
21:9 So Moses M a bronze serpent, and set it
21:29 He has M his sons fugitives, and his daughters
22:29 ass, "Because you have M sport of me.
25:13 for his God, and M atonement for the people
30:12 stand: her husband has M them void, and the
32:13 against Israel, and he M them wander in the
35:33 no expiation can be M for the land, for
Deut 1:28 Our brethren have M our hearts melt, saying, "The
2:30 hardened his spirit and M his heart obstinate, that
4:23 your God, which he M with you, and make
5:2 The LORD our God M a covenant with us
9:9 covenant which the LORD M with you, I remained
9:12 them; they have M themselves a molten image.'
9:16 your God; you had M yourselves a molten calf;
9:21 calf which you had M, and burned it with
10:3 the ark.' So I M an ark of acacia
10:5 ark which I had M; and there they are,
10:22 LORD your God has M you as the stars
11:4 their chariots; how he M the water of the
20:9 when the officers have M an end of speaking
22:17 and lo, he has M shameful charges against her,
26:19 nations that he has M, in praise and in
27:15 the LORD, a thing M by the hands of
29:1 covenant which he had M with them at Horeb.
29:22 which the LORD has M it sick--
29:25 their fathers, which he M with them when he
31:16 covenant which I have M with them.
32:6 who created you, who M you and established you?
32:13 He M him ride on the high places of
32:13 the field; and he M him suck honey out
32:15 he forsook God who M him, and scoffed at
Josh 2:17 yours which you have M us swear.
2:20 oath which you have M us swear."
2:22 for the pursuers had M search all along the
5:3 So Joshua M flint knives, and circumcised the people
8:14 men of the city, M haste and went out
8:15 Joshua and all Israel M a pretense of being
8:19 took it; and they M haste to set the
8:28 Joshua burned Ai, and M it for ever a
9:4 cunning, and went and M ready provisions, and took
9:15 And Joshua M peace with them, and made a
9:15 peace with them, and M a covenant with them,
9:16 days after they had M a covenant with them,
9:27 But Joshua M them that day hewers of wood
10:1 inhabitants of Gibeon had M peace with Israel and
10:4 Gibeon; for it has M peace with Joshua and
10:5 encamped against Gibeon, and M war against it.

11:18 Joshua M war a long time with all those
11:19 not a city that M peace with the people
14:8 went up with me M the heart of the
17:1 Then allotment was M to the tribe of Manasseh,
17:2 And allotments were M to the rest of the
21:45 which the LORD had M to the house of
22:25 For the LORD has M the Jordan a boundary
22:28 LORD, which our fathers M, not for burnt offerings,
24:3 land of Canaan, and M his offspring many.
24:7 and the Egyptians, and M the sea come upon
24:25 So Joshua M a covenant with the people that
24:25 people that day, and M statutes and ordinances for
Judg 3:16 And Ehud M for himself a sword with two
6:2 the people of Israel M for themselves the dens
6:29 And after they had M search and inquired, they
8:27 And Gideon M an ephod of it and put
8:33 after the Baals, and M Baal-berith their god.
9:6 and they went and M Abimelech king, by the
9:16 and honor when you M Abimelech king, and if
9:18 one stone, and have M Abimelech, the son of
9:57 brothers; and God also M all the wickedness of
11:4 a time the Ammonites M war against Israel.
11:5 And when the Ammonites M war against Israel, the
11:11 Gilead, and the people M him head and leader
11:30 And Jephthah M a vow to the LORD, and
11:39 her according to his vow which he had M
14:10 the woman, and Samson M a feast there; for
15:9 encamped in Judah, and M a raid on Lehi.
16:14 And she M them tight with the pin, and
16:19 She M him sleep upon her knees; and she
16:25 the prison, and he M sport before them.
16:25 They M him stand between the pillars;
16:27 looked on while Samson M sport.
17:4 to the silversmith, who M it into a graven
17:5 a shrine, and he M an ephod and teraphim,
18:24 my gods which I M, and the priest, and
18:27 taking what Micah had M, and the priest who
18:31 graven image which he M, as long as the
19:4 father-in-law, the girl's father, M him stay, and he
20:37 the men in ambush M haste and rushed upon
20:38 was that when they M a great cloud of
21:15 because the LORD had M a breach in the
Ruth 3:10 my daughter; you have M this last kindness greater
1Sam 1:17 petition which you have M to him."
1:27 my petition which I M to him.
6:6 After he had M sport of them, did not
6:19 because the LORD had M a great slaughter among
8:1 Samuel became old, he M his sons judges over
11:15 Gilgal, and there they M Saul king before the
12:1 to me, and have M a king over you.
12:8 out of Egypt, and M them dwell in this
14:14 Jonathan and his armor-bearer M, was of about
15:11 repent that I have M Saul king; for he
15:33 "As your sword has M women childless, so shall
15:35 repented that he had M Saul king over Israel.
16:8 Jesse called Abinadab, and M him pass before
16:9 Then Jesse M Shammah pass by.
16:10 And Jesse M seven of his sons pass before
18:3 Then Jonathan M a covenant with David, because he
18:7 one another as they M merry, "Saul has slain
18:13 from his presence, and M him a commander of
19:8 with the Philistines, and M a great slaughter among
20:17 And Jonathan M David swear again by his love
21:2 charged you.' I have M an appointment with the
21:13 in their hands, and M marks on the doors
23:5 away their cattle, and M a great slaughter among
23:18 the two of them M a covenant before the
23:27 for the Philistines have M a raid upon the
25:18 Then Abigail M haste, and took two hundred loaves,
25:23 Abigail saw David, she M haste, and alighted from
25:34 you, unless you had M haste and come to
25:42 And Abigail M haste and rose and mounted on
26:22 And David M answer, "Here is the spear, O
27:8 men went up, and M raids upon the Geshurites,
27:10 "Against whom have you M a raid today?" David
27:12 David, thinking, "He has M himself utterly abhorred
29:9 And Achish M answer to David, "I know that
30:1 day, the Amalekites had M a raid upon the
30:14 We had M a raid upon the Negeb of
30:25 that day forward he M it a statute and
2Sam 2:9 to Mahanaim; and he M him king over Gilead
3:20 David at Hebron, David M a feast for Abner
5:3 Hebron; and King David M a covenant with them
7:16 your kingdom shall be M sure for ever before
7:27 God of Israel, hast M this revelation to thy
10:19 defeated by Israel, they M peace with Israel, and

11:13 drank, so that he M him drunk; and in
11:26 husband was dead, she M lamentation for her
12:31 and iron axes, and M them toil at the
13:2 so tormented that he M himself ill because of
13:8 and kneaded it, and M cakes in his sight,
13:10 the cakes she had M, and brought them into
14:15 because the people have M me afraid; and your
16:21 hear that you have M yourself odious to your
19:6 For you have M it clear today that commanders
19:16 the Benjaminite, from Bahurim, M haste to come
22:12 He M darkness around him his canopy, thick clouds,
22:33 strong refuge, and has M my way safe.
22:34 He M my feet like hinds' feet, and set
22:36 salvation, and thy help M me great.
23:5 For he has M with me an everlasting covenant,
1Kgs 1:43 lord King David has M Solomon king;
2:24 father, and who has M me a house, as
3:1 Solomon M a marriage alliance with Pharaoh king
3:7 my God, thou hast M thy servant king in
3:15 and peace offerings, and M a feast for all
5:12 the two of them M a treaty.
6:4 And he M for the house windows with recessed
6:5 inner sanctuary; and he M side chambers all around.
6:6 of the house he M offsets on the wall
6:9 finished it; and he M the ceiling of the
6:20 He also M an altar of cedar.
6:23 inner sanctuary he M two cherubim of olivewood,
6:31 the inner sanctuary he M doors of olivewood; the
6:33 So also he M for the entrance to the
7:6 And he M the Hall of Pillars; its length
7:7 And he M the Hall of the Throne where
7:8 Solomon also M a house like this hall for
7:9 All these were M of costly stones, hewn according
7:16 He also M two capitals of molten bronze, to
7:17 Then he M two nets of checker work with
7:18 Likewise he M pomegranates; in two rows round
7:23 Then he M the molten sea; it was round,
7:26 and its brim was M like the brim of
7:27 He also M the ten stands of bronze; each
7:31 as a pedestal is M, a cubit and a
7:33 The wheels were M like a chariot wheel; their
7:37 After this manner he M the ten stands; all
7:38 And he M ten lavers of bronze; each laver
7:40 Hiram also M the pots, the shovels, and the
7:45 the LORD, which Hiram M for King Solomon, were
7:48 So Solomon M all the vessels that were in
8:7 so that the cherubim M a covering above the
8:9 Horeb, where the LORD M a covenant with the
8:20 his promise which he M; for I have risen
8:21 the LORD which he M with our fathers, when
8:31 his neighbor and is M to take an oath,
8:38 prayer, whatever supplication is M by any man or
8:59 wherewith I have M supplication before the LORD,
9:3 supplication, which you have M before me; I have
9:21 destroy utterly--these Solomon M a forced levy of
9:22 people of Israel Solomon M no slaves; they were
10:9 for ever, he has M you king, that you
10:12 And the king M of the almug wood supports
10:16 King Solomon M two hundred large shields of
10:17 And he M three hundred shields of beaten gold;
10:18 The king also M a great ivory throne, and
10:20 of it was never M in any kingdom.
10:27 And the king M silver as common in Jerusalem
10:27 as stone, and he M cedar as plentiful as
11:24 and dwelt there, and M him king in Damascus.
12:4 to Rehoboam, "Your father M our yoke heavy.
12:10 to you, 'Your father M our yoke heavy, but
12:14 men, saying, "My father M your yoke heavy, but
12:18 And King Rehoboam M haste to mount his chariot,
12:20 to the assembly and M him king over all
12:28 king took counsel, and M two calves of gold.
12:31 He also M houses on high places, and appointed
12:32 Bethel, sacrificing to the calves that he had M
12:32 priests of the high places that he had M
12:33 altar which he had M in Bethel on the
13:33 his evil way, but M priests for the high
14:7 among the people, and M you leader over my
14:9 and have gone and M for yourself other gods,
14:15 Euphrates, because they have M their Asherim,
14:16 sinned and which he M Israel to sin."
14:26 gold which Solomon had M;
14:27 made; and King Rehoboam M in their stead shields
15:12 removed all the idols that his fathers had M
15:13 had an abominable image M for Asherah; and Asa
15:22 Then King Asa M a proclamation to all Judah,
15:26 his sin which he M Israel to sin.
15:30 sinned and which he M Israel to sin, and
15:34 his sin which he M Israel to sin.
16:2 of the dust and M you leader over my
16:2 of Jeroboam, and have M my people Israel to
16:13 sinned, and which they M Israel to sin, provoking
16:16 king"; therefore all Israel M Omri, the commander
16:20 the conspiracy which he M, are they not written
16:26 the sins which he M Israel to sin, provoking
16:33 And Ahab M an Asherah.
18:26 they limped about the altar which they had M
18:32 And he M a trench about the altar, as
20:34 So he M a covenant with him and let
20:41 Then he M haste to take the bandage away
21:22 and because you have M Israel to sin.
22:11 the son of Chenaanah M for himself horns of
22:44 Jehoshaphat also M peace with the king of Israel.
22:48 Jehoshaphat M ships of Tarshish to go to Ophir
22:52 son of Nebat, who M Israel to sin.
2Kgs 2:21 the LORD, I have M this water wholesome;
3:2 the pillar of Baal which his father had M
3:3 of Nebat, which he M Israel to sin; he
3:9 And when they had M a circuitous march of
6:6 it in there, and M the iron float.
7:6 For the Lord had M the army of the
9:21 And they M ready his chariot.
10:25 soon as he had M an end of offering
10:27 house of Baal, and M it a latrine to
10:29 of Nebat, which he M Israel to sin, the
10:31 of Jeroboam, which he M Israel to sin.
11:4 the LORD; and he M a covenant with them
11:17 And Jehoiada M a covenant between the LORD and
12:6 Jehoash the priests had M no repairs on the
12:13 But there were not M for the house of
12:20 His servants arose and M a conspiracy, and slew
13:2 of Nebat, which he M Israel to sin; he
13:6 of Jeroboam, which he M Israel to sin, but
13:7 had destroyed them and M them like the dust
13:11 of Nebat, which he M Israel to sin, but
13:17 Aphek until you have M an end of them."
13:19 Syria until you had M an end of it,
14:19 And they M a conspiracy against him in Jerusalem,
14:21 sixteen years old, and M him king instead of
14:24 of Nebat, which he M Israel to sin.
15:9 of Nebat, which he M Israel to sin.
15:15 the conspiracy which he M, behold, they are written
15:18 of Nebat, which he M Israel to sin.
15:24 of Nebat, which he M Israel to sin.
15:28 of Nebat, which he M Israel to sin.
15:30 the son of Elah M a conspiracy against Pekah
16:11 so Uriah the priest M it, before King Ahaz
17:15 his covenant that he M with their fathers, and
17:16 LORD their God, and M for themselves molten
17:16 two calves; and they M an Asherah, and worshiped
17:21 house of David they M Jeroboam the son of
17:21 following the LORD and M them commit great sin.
17:29 But every nation still M gods of its own,
17:29 which the Samaritans had M, every nation in the
17:30 the men of Babylon M Succoth-benoth, the men of
17:30 the men of Cuth M Nergal, the men of
17:30 the men of Hamath M Ashima,
17:31 Ashima, and the Avvites M Nibhaz and Tartak; and
17:35 The LORD M a covenant with them, and
17:38 covenant that I have M with you.
18:4 serpent that Moses had M, for until those days
19:15 the earth; thou hast M heaven and earth.
20:20 might, and how he M the pool and the
21:3 altars for Baal, and M an Asherah, as Ahab
21:7 Asherah that he had M he set in the
21:11 before him, and has M Judah also to sin
21:16 the sin which he M Judah to sin so
21:24 people of the land M Josiah his son king
23:3 by the pillar and M a covenant before the
23:4 LORD all the vessels M for Baal, for Asherah,
23:12 kings of Judah had M, and the altars which
23:12 altars which Manasseh had M in the two courts
23:15 son of Nebat, who M Israel to sin, that
23:19 kings of Israel had M, provoking the LORD to
23:30 and anointed him, and M him king in his
23:34 And Pharaoh Neco M Eliakim the son of Josiah
24:13 king of Israel had M, as the LORD had
24:17 the king of Babylon M Mattaniah, Jehoiachin's uncle,
25:4 Then a breach was M in the city; the
25:16 stands, which Solomon had M for the house of
1Chr 5:10 days of Saul they M war on the Hagrites,
5:19 They M war upon the Hagrites, Jetur, Naphish, and
6:49 Aaron and his sons M offerings upon the altar

	11:3	at Hebron; and David M a covenant with them
	12:18	David received them, and M them officers of his
	12:39	for their brethren had M preparation for them.
	14:9	Philistines had come and M a raid in the
	14:13	the Philistines yet again M a raid in the
	15:28	trumpets, and cymbals, and M loud music on harps
	16:16	the covenant which he M with Abraham, his sworn
	16:26	idols; but the LORD M the heavens.
	18:8	bronze; with it Solomon M the bronze sea and
	19:6	saw that they had M themselves odious to David,
	19:19	defeated by Israel, they M peace with David, and
	21:28	Ornan the Jebusite, he M his sacrifices there.
	21:29	LORD, which Moses had M in the wilderness, and
	23:1	full of days, he M Solomon his son king
	23:5	instruments which I have M for praise."
	26:10	the first-born, his father M him chief),
	26:31	David's reign search was M and men of great
	28:2	our God; and I M preparations for building.
	28:18	the altar of incense M of refined gold, and
	28:19	All this he M clear by the writing from
	29:6	heads of fathers' houses M their freewill offerings, as
	29:19	for which I have M provision."
	29:22	And they M Solomon the son of David king
2Chr	1:1	was with him and M him exceedingly great.
	1:3	of the LORD had M in the wilderness, was
	1:5	son of Hur, had M, was there before the
	1:8	my father, and hast M me king in his
	1:9	fulfilled, for thou hast M me king over a
	1:11	over whom I have M you king,
	1:15	And the king M silver and gold as common
	1:15	as stone, and he M cedar as plentiful as
	2:11	his people he has M you king over them."
	2:12	God of Israel, who M heaven and earth, who
	3:5	with fine gold, and M palms and chains on
	3:8	And he M the most holy place; its length,
	3:10	most holy place he M two cherubim of wood
	3:14	And he M the veil of blue and purple
	3:15	of the house he M two pillars thirty-five cubits
	3:16	He M chains like a necklace and put them
	3:16	the pillars; and he M a hundred pomegranates, and
	4:1	He M an altar of bronze, twenty cubits long,
	4:2	Then he M the molten sea; it was round,
	4:5	and its brim was M like the brim of
	4:6	He also M ten lavers in which to wash,
	4:7	And he M ten golden lampstands as prescribed, and
	4:8	He also M ten tables, and placed them in
	4:8	And he M a hundred basins of gold.
	4:9	He M the court of the priests, and the
	4:11	Huram also M the pots, the shovels, and the
	4:14	He M the stands also, and the lavers upon
	4:16	for these Huram-abi M of burnished bronze for
	4:18	Solomon M all these things in great quantities, so
	4:19	So Solomon M all the things that were in
	5:8	so that the cherubim M a covering above the
	5:10	Horeb, where the LORD M a covenant with the
	6:10	his promise which he M; for I have risen
	6:11	the LORD which he M with the people of
	6:13	Solomon had M a bronze platform five cubits long,
	6:22	his neighbor and is M to take an oath,
	6:29	prayer, whatever supplication is M by any man or
	7:6	which King David had M for giving thanks to
	7:7	bronze altar Solomon had M could not hold the
	7:15	the prayer that is M in this place.
	8:8	not destroyed--these Solomon M a forced levy and
	8:9	people of Israel Solomon M no slaves for his
	9:8	for ever, he has M you king over them,
	9:11	And the king M of the algum wood steps
	9:15	King Solomon M two hundred large shields of
	9:16	And he M three hundred shields of beaten gold;
	9:17	The king also M a great ivory throne, and
	9:19	of it was never M in any kingdom.
	9:27	And the king M silver as common in Jerusalem
	10:4	to Rehoboam, "Your father M our yoke heavy.
	10:10	to you, 'Your father M our yoke heavy, but
	10:14	men, saying, "My father M your yoke heavy, but
	10:18	And King Rehoboam M haste to mount his chariot,
	11:11	He M the fortresses strong, and put commanders in
	11:12	all the cities, and M them very strong.
	11:15	satyrs, and for the calves which he had M
	11:17	for three years they M Rehoboam the son of
	12:9	gold which Solomon had M;
	12:10	made; and King Rehoboam M in their stead shields
	13:8	golden calves which Jeroboam M you for gods.
	13:9	and the Levites, and M priests for yourselves like
	15:16	mother because she had M an abominable image for
	16:14	perfumer's art; and they M a very great fire
	17:10	Judah, and they M no war against Jehoshaphat.
	18:1	and honor; and he M a marriage alliance with
	18:10	the son of Chenaanah M for himself horns of
	20:23	and when they had M an end of the
	20:27	for the LORD had M them rejoice over their
	20:37	Ahaziah, the LORD will destroy what you have M
	21:7	covenant which he had M with David, and since
	21:11	Moreover he M high places in the hill country
	21:11	Jerusalem into unfaithfulness, and M Judah go
	21:19	His people M no fire in his honor, like
	21:19	honor, like the fires M for his fathers.
	22:1	the inhabitants of Jerusalem M Ahaziah his youngest
	23:3	And all the assembly M a covenant with the
	23:16	And Jehoiada M a covenant between himself and all
	24:8	king commanded, and they M a chest, and set
	24:9	proclamation was M throughout Judah and
	24:14	and with it were M utensils for the house
	25:16	to him, "Have we M you a royal counselor?
	25:27	from the LORD they M a conspiracy against him
	26:1	sixteen years old, and M him king instead of
	26:5	sought the LORD, God M him prosper.
	26:6	He went out and M war against the Philistines,
	26:11	numbers in the muster M by Je-iel the secretary
	26:15	In Jerusalem he M engines, invented by skilful men,
	28:2	He even M molten images for the Baals;
	28:18	And the Philistines had M raids on the cities
	28:24	the LORD; and he M himself altars in every
	28:25	city of Judah he M high places to burn
	29:8	Jerusalem, and he has M them an object of
	29:19	was faithless, we have M ready and sanctified; and
	29:24	priests killed them and M a sin offering with
	29:24	sin offering should be M for all Israel.
	30:7	fathers, so that he M them a desolation, as
	32:5	He also M weapons and shields in abundance.
	32:27	and honor; and he M for himself treasuries for
	33:3	to the Baals, and M Asherahs, and worshiped all
	33:7	idol which he had M he set in the
	33:22	Manasseh his father had M, and served them.
	33:25	people of the land M Josiah his son king
	34:4	molten images, and he M dust of them and
	34:31	in his place and M a covenant before the
	34:32	Then he M all who were present in Jerusalem
	34:33	people of Israel, and M all who were in
	35:25	They M these an ordinance in Israel; behold, they
	36:1	son of Josiah and M him king in his
	36:4	the king of Egypt M Eliakim his brother king
	36:10	of the LORD, and M his brother Zedekiah king
	36:13	Nebuchadnezzar, who had M him swear by God;
	36:22	Persia so that he M a proclamation throughout all
Ezra	1:1	Persia so that he M a proclamation throughout all
	2:68	which is in Jerusalem, M freewill offerings for the
	3:5	of every one who M a freewill offering to
	3:8	the son of Jozadak M a beginning, together with
	4:4	people of Judah, and M them afraid to build,
	4:15	that search may be M in the book of
	4:19	And I M a decree, and search has been
	4:19	and search has been M, and it has been
	4:19	and sedition have been M in it.
	4:21	that these men be M to cease, and that
	4:21	until a decree is M by me.
	4:23	by force and power M them cease.
	5:13	Babylon, Cyrus the king M a decree that this
	5:14	Shesh-bazzar, whom he had M governor;
	5:17	king, let search be M in the royal archives
	6:1	Then Darius the king M a decree, and search
	6:1	decree, and search was M in Babylonia, in the
	6:11	his house shall be M a dunghill.
	6:22	for the LORD had M them joyful, and had
	10:1	While Ezra prayed and M confession, weeping and
	10:5	Then Ezra arose and M the leading priests and
	10:7	And a proclamation was M throughout Judah and
Neh	8:4	pulpit which they had M for the purpose; and
	8:16	and brought them and M booths for themselves, each
	8:17	returned from the captivity M booths and dwelt in
	9:3	fourth of it they M confession and worshiped the
	9:6	thou alone; thou hast M heaven, the heaven of
	9:18	Even when they had M for themselves a molten
	9:27	of their enemies, who M them suffer; and in
	12:43	rejoiced, for God had M them rejoice with great
	13:25	their hair; and I M them take oath in
	13:26	his God, and God M him king over all
	13:26	nevertheless foreign women M even him to sin.
Tob	4:16	the gift when you M it.
	4:19	your ways may be M straight and that all
	5:16	So his son M the preparations for the journey.
	8:2	fish upon them and M a smoke.

8:16 thou, because thou hast M me glad.
9:5 So Raphael M the journey and stayed over night
11:1 God because he had M his journey a success.
13:14 and they will be M glad for ever.
Jud 1:2 six cubits long; he M the walls seventy cubits
1:4 the foundations; and he M its gates, which were
1:5 King Nebuchadnezzar M war against King Arphaxad
5:11 and humbled them and M slaves of them.
6:1 When the disturbance M by the men outside the
8:14 search out God, who M all these things, and
8:18 ours which worshiped gods M with hands, as was
8:30 we have promised, and M us take an oath
10:4 all her ornaments, and M herself very beautiful, to
10:23 she prostrated herself and M obeisance to him, and
14:9 a great shout and M a joyful noise in
16:14 thee, for thou didst speak, and they were M
Esth 1:17 the queen will be M known to all women,
1:20 So when the decree M by the king is
2:10 Esther had not M known her people or kindred,
2:17 on her head and M her queen instead of
2:20 Now Esther had not M known her kindred or
3:6 So, as they had M known to him the
5:14 fifty cubits high be M, and in the morning
5:14 counsel pleased Haman, and he had the gallows M
6:11 he arrayed Mordecai and M him ride through the
9:17 day they rested and M that a day of
10:6 the king married and M queen.
10:10 For this purpose he M two lots, one for
12:4 to execution, The king M a permanent record of
13:10 For thou hast M heaven and earth and every
16:5 of authority have been M in part responsible for
16:21 over all things, has M this day to be
16:24 It shall be M not only impassable for men,
Job 1:17 formed three companies, and M a raid upon the
2:11 They M an appointment together to come to condole
4:4 stumbling, and you have M firm the feeble knees.
4:14 me, and trembling, which M all my bones shake.
7:20 Why hast thou M me thy mark?
9:9 of the sea; who M the Bear and Orion,
10:8 Thy hands fashioned and M me; and now thou
10:9 Remember that thou hast M me of clay; and
16:7 me out; he has M desolate all my company.
17:6 "He has M me a byword of the peoples,
23:16 God has M my heart faint; the Almighty has
26:13 wind the heavens were M fair; his hand pierced
27:2 the Almighty, who has M my soul bitter;
28:18 No mention shall be M of coral or of
28:26 by measure; when he M a decree for the
29:17 of the unrighteous, and M him drop his prey
31:1 "I have M a covenant with my eyes; how
31:15 Did not he who M me in the womb
31:24 "If I have M gold my trust, or called
33:4 spirit of God has M me, and the breath
38:9 the womb; when I M clouds its garment, and
39:17 fear; because God has M her forget wisdom, and
40:15 "Behold, Behemoth, which I M as I made you;
40:15 I made as I M you; he eats grass
40:19 God; let him who M him bring near his
41:15 His back is M of rows of shields, shut
Ps 7:15 and falls into the hole which he has M
8:5 Yet thou hast M him little less than God,
9:15 the pit which they M; in the net which
9:16 The LORD has M himself known, he has executed
18:11 He M darkness his covering around him, his canopy
18:32 me with strength, and M my way safe.
18:33 He M my feet like hinds' feet, and set
18:35 me, and thy help M me great.
30:8 to the LORD I M supplication:
33:6 LORD the heavens were M, and all their host
39:5 Behold, thou hast M my days a few handbreadths,
44:10 Thou hast M us turn back from the foe;
44:11 Thou hast M us like sheep for slaughter, and
44:13 Thou hast M us the taunt of our neighbors,
44:14 Thou hast M us a byword among the nations,
50:5 my faithful ones, who M a covenant with me
60:2 Thou hast M the land to quake, thou hast
60:3 Thou hast M thy people suffer hard things; thou
60:3 wine to drink that M us reel.
69:11 When I M sackcloth my clothing, I became a
71:20 Thou who hast M me see many sore troubles
72:15 May prayer be M for him continually, and blessings
73:28 near God; I have M the Lord GOD my
74:17 the earth; thou hast M summer and winter.
78:13 pass through it, and M the waters stand like
78:16 He M streams come out of the rock, and
78:33 So he M their days vanish like a breath,
78:50 He M a path for his anger; he did
78:64 sword, and their widows M no lamentation.
80:17 man whom thou hast M strong for thyself!
81:5 He M it a decree in Joseph, when he
86:9 the nations thou hast M shall come and bow
88:8 shun me; thou hast M me a thing of
89:3 hast said, "I have M a covenant with my
89:42 his foes; thou hast M all his enemies rejoice.
89:43 and thou hast not M him stand in battle.
91:9 Because you have M the LORD your refuge, the
92:4 thou, O LORD, hast M me glad by thy
95:5 is his, for he M it; for his hands
96:5 idols; but the LORD M the heavens.
98:2 The LORD has M known his victory, he has
100:3 It is he that M us, and we are
103:7 He M known his ways to Moses, his acts
104:19 Thou hast M the moon to mark the seasons;
104:24 In wisdom hast thou M them all; the earth
105:9 the covenant which he M with Abraham, his sworn
105:21 set him free; he M him lord of his
105:24 And the LORD M his people very fruitful, and
105:24 people very fruitful, and M them stronger than their
105:28 He sent darkness, and M the land dark; they
106:19 They M a calf in Horeb and worshiped a
106:33 their account; for they M his spirit bitter, and
107:29 from their distress; he M the storm be still,
115:15 by the LORD, who M heaven and earth!
118:24 which the LORD has M; let us rejoice and
119:49 in which thou hast M me hope.
119:73 Thy hands have M and fashioned me; give me
119:87 They have almost M an end of me on
121:2 from the LORD, who M heaven and earth.
124:8 of the LORD, who M heaven and earth.
129:3 upon my back; they M long their furrows."
134:3 from Zion, he who M heaven and earth!
136:5 him who by understanding M the heavens, for his
136:7 ever; to him who M the great lights, for
136:14 endures for ever; and M Israel pass through the
139:15 when I was being M in secret, intricately wrought
143:3 the ground; he has M me sit in darkness
145:9 his compassion is over all that he has M
146:6 LORD his God, who M heaven and earth, the
Prov 4:17 sleep unless they have M some one stumble.
8:26 forth; before he had M the earth with its
8:28 the deep, when he M firm the skies above,
16:4 The LORD has M everything for its purpose, even
20:9 can say, "I have M my heart clean; I
20:12 eye, the LORD has M them both.
21:31 The horse is M ready for the day of
22:19 the LORD, I have M them known to you
Eccl 1:15 is crooked cannot be M straight, and what is
2:4 I M great works; I built houses and planted
2:5 vineyards for myself; I M myself gardens and parks,
2:6 I M myself pools from which to water the
3:11 busy with He has M everything beautiful in its
3:14 from it; God has M it so, in order
7:3 countenance the heart is M glad.
7:13 straight what he has M crooked?
7:14 adversity consider; God has M the one as well
7:29 I found, that God M man upright, but they
10:19 Bread is M for laughter, and wine gladdens life,
Song 1:6 angry with me, they M me keeper of the
3:9 King Solomon M himself a palanquin from the wood
3:10 He M its posts of silver, its back of
Wis 1:9 For inquiry will be M into the counsels of
1:16 pined away, and they M a covenant with him,
2:23 man for incorruption, and M him in the image
5:4 held in derision and M a byword of reproach—
6:7 greatness; because he himself M both small and
6:10 For they will be M holy who observe holy
9:1 of mercy, who hast M all things by thy
9:2 the creatures thou hast M,
10:11 stood by him and M him rich.
10:21 of the dumb, and M the tongues of babes
11:24 things which thou hast M, for thou wouldst not
11:24 thou wouldst not have M anything if thou hadst
14:8 But the idol M with hands is accursed, and
14:8 so is he who M it; because he did
14:15 at an untimely bereavement, M an image of his
14:17 appearance far away, and M a visible image of
15:8 this man who was M of earth a short
15:16 For a man M them, and one whose spirit
16:24 serving thee who hast M it, exerts itself to
17:16 in a prison not M of iron;
18:6 That night was M known beforehand to our fathers,
18:18 hurled down half dead, M known why they were

Sir 19:4 to this end, and M them forget what had
19:14 to them, but these M slaves of guests who
Sir 1:13 She M among men an eternal foundation, and
14:19 and the man who M it will pass away
16:4 men it will be M desolate.
16:24 creation, and when he M them, he determined their
17:3 like his own, and M them in his own
17:5 He M for them tongue and eyes; he gave
24:5 Alone I have M the circuit of the vault
25:8 he who has not M a slip with his
29:6 and he has needlessly M him his enemy; he
32:13 things bless him who M you and satisfies you
33:9 some of them he M ordinary days.
33:12 some of them he M holy and brought near
33:13 hand of him who M them, to give them
34:4 thing what will be M clean?
34:8 fulfilled, and wisdom is M perfect in truthful lips.
38:5 Was not water M sweet with a tree in
39:5 seek the Lord who M him, and will make
39:31 his commands, and be M ready on earth for
40:14 generous man will be M glad; likewise transgressors
42:24 other, and he has M nothing incomplete.
43:5 is the Lord who M it; and at his
43:6 He M the moon also, to serve in its
43:11 and praise him who M it, exceedingly beautiful in
43:33 For the Lord has M all things, and to
44:19 Everlasting covenants were M with him that all flesh
44:24 and the covenant he M to rest upon the
45:2 He M him equal in glory to the holy
45:2 the holy ones, and M him great in the
45:5 He M him hear his voice, and led him
45:7 He M an everlasting covenant with him, and gave
45:23 of his soul, and M atonement for Israel.
46:17 thundered from heaven, and M his voice heard with
48:2 by his zeal he M them few in number.
48:18 hand against Zion and M great boasts in his
49:6 of the sanctuary, and M her streets desolate,
50:11 the holy altar, he M the court of the
50:16 of hammered work, they M a great noise to
50:17 all the people together M haste and fell to
51:17 I M progress therein; to him who gives wisdom
Is 2:8 their hands, to what their own fingers have M
2:20 of gold, which they M for themselves to worship,
5:8 room, and you are M to dwell alone in
14:3 with which you were M to serve,
14:16 this the man who M the earth tremble, who
14:17 who shook kingdoms, who M the world like a
17:8 their own fingers have M, either the Asherim or
19:14 confusion; and they have M Egypt stagger in all
22:11 You M a reservoir between the two walls for
23:13 razed her palaces, they M her a ruin.
25:2 For thou hast M the city a heap, the
27:11 discernment; therefore he who M them will not have
28:15 have said, "We have M a covenant with death,
28:15 us; for we have M lies our refuge, and
28:22 lest your bonds be M strong; for I have
29:16 clay; that the thing M should say of its
30:33 the king it is M ready, its pyre made
30:33 made ready, its pyre M deep and wide, with
31:7 your hands have sinfully M for you.
33:1 and when you have M an end of dealing
34:7 blood, and their soil M rich with fat.
37:16 the earth; thou hast M heaven and earth.
40:4 mountain and hill be M low; the uneven ground
43:7 created for my glory, whom I formed and M
44:2 says the LORD who M you, who formed you
44:24 am the LORD, who M all things, who stretched
45:12 I M the earth, and created man upon it;
45:18 formed the earth and M it (he established it;
46:4 I have M, and I will bear; I will
47:6 on the aged you M your yoke exceedingly heavy.
48:3 my mouth and I M them known; then suddenly
48:21 through the deserts; he M water flow for them
49:2 He M my mouth like a sharp sword, in
49:2 he hid me; he M me a polished arrow,
51:2 I blessed him and M him many.
51:12 of man who is M like grass,
51:23 over'; and you have M your back like the
53:5 was the chastisement that M us whole, and with
53:9 And they M his grave with the wicked and
53:12 sin of many, and M intercession for the transgressors.
55:4 Behold, I M him a witness to the peoples,
57:8 to it, you have M it wide; and you
57:8 wide; and you have M a bargain for yourself
57:16 spirit, and I have M the breath of life.
59:2 but your iniquities have M a separation between you
59:8 their paths; they have M their roads crooked, no
63:6 in my anger, I M them drunk in my
66:2 things my hand has M, and so all these
Jer 2:7 defiled my land, and M my heritage an abomination.
2:15 They have M his land a waste; his cities
2:28 your gods that you M for yourself?
3:16 it shall not be M again.
5:3 They have M their faces harder than rock; they
6:27 "I have M you an assayer and tester among
7:12 in Shiloh, where I M my name dwell at
8:8 of the scribes has M it into a lie.
10:12 It is he who M the earth by his
11:10 my covenant which I M with their fathers.
11:18 The LORD M it known to me and I
12:10 my portion, they have M my pleasant portion a
12:11 They have M it a desolation; desolate, it mourns
12:11 The whole land is M desolate, but no man
13:11 a man, so I M the whole house of
13:27 be before you are M clean?"
15:8 I have M their widows more in number than
15:8 at noonday; I have M anguish and terror fall
25:17 the LORD's hand, and M all the nations to
27:5 my outstretched arm have M the earth, with the
28:15 you, and you have M this people trust in
29:26 saying, 'The LORD has M you priest instead of
29:31 send him, and has M you trust in a
31:32 the covenant which I M with their fathers when
32:17 is thou who hast M the heavens and the
32:20 all mankind, and hast M thee a name, as
32:23 Therefore thou hast M all this evil come upon
33:2 says the LORD who M the earth, the LORD
33:14 fulfil the promise I M to the house of
34:8 after King Zedekiah had M a covenant with all
34:13 God of Israel: I M a covenant with your
34:15 his neighbor, and you M a covenant before me
34:18 the covenant which they M before me, I will
37:1 Nebuchadrezzar king of Babylon M king in the land
37:15 for it had been M a prison.
38:16 the LORD lives, who M our souls, I will
38:26 say to them, 'I M a humble plea to
39:2 month, a breach was M in the city.
41:9 which King Asa had M for defense against Baasha
41:18 king of Babylon had M governor over the land.
44:19 husbands' approval that we M cakes for her bearing
44:25 vows that we have M, to burn incense to
48:33 of Moab; I have M the wine cease from
49:20 which the LORD has M against Edom and the
49:30 king of Babylon has M a plan against you,
50:45 which the LORD has M against Babylon, and the
51:15 "It is he who M the earth by his
51:34 crushed me; he has M me an empty vessel,
52:7 Then a breach was M in the city; and
52:20 Solomon the king had M for the house of
Lam 1:5 because the LORD has M her suffer for the
1:13 into my bones he M it descend; he spread
2:17 without pity; he has M the enemy rejoice over
3:4 He has M my flesh and my skin waste
3:6 and tribulation; he has M me dwell in darkness
3:9 hewn stones, he has M my paths crooked.
3:11 to pieces; he has M me desolate;
3:16 He has M my teeth grind on gravel, and
3:16 grind on gravel, and M me cower in ashes;
3:45 Thou hast M us offscouring and refuse among the
Bar 1:8 king of Judah, had M,
2:11 outstretched arm, and hast M thee a name, as
2:26 thy name thou hast M as it is today,
3:34 gladness for him who M them.
4:7 you provoked him who M you, by sacrificing to
5:7 the everlasting hills be M low and the valleys
6:4 you will see gods M of silver and gold
6:27 them these gods are M to stand, lest they
6:39 These things that are M of wood and overlaid
6:45 They are M by carpenters and goldsmiths; they can
6:46 the things that are M by them be gods?
6:50 Since they are M of wood and overlaid with
6:57 Gods M of wood and overlaid with silver and
Ezek 3:8 Behold, I have M your face hard against their
3:9 than flint have I M your forehead; fear them
3:17 of man, I have M you a watchman for
7:14 blown the trumpet and M all ready; but none
7:20 for vainglory, and they M their abominable images
12:6 land; for I have M you a sign for
14:15 it, and it be M desolate, so that no
16:16 of your garments, and M for yourself gaily decked
16:17 had given you, and M for yourself images of
16:24 a vaulted chamber, and M yourself a lofty place

M

16:51 than they, and have M your sisters appear righteous
16:52 also, for you have M judgment favorable to your
16:52 disgrace, for you have M your sisters appear
17:13 the seed royal and M a covenant with him,
17:16 the king dwells who M him king, whose oath
19:5 of her whelps and M him a young lion.
20:9 in whose sight I M myself known to them
21:15 it is M like lightning, it is polished for
21:24 GOD: Because you have M your guilt to be
22:4 idols which you have M; and you have brought
22:4 Therefore I have M you a reproach to the
22:13 gain which you have M, and at the blood
22:25 precious things; they have M many widows in the
22:26 holy things; they have M no distinction between the
25:3 Israel when it was M desolate, and over the
26:15 groan, when slaughter is M in the midst of
27:4 the seas; your builders M perfect your beauty.
27:5 They M all your planks of fir trees from
27:6 oaks of Bashan they M your oars; they made
27:6 made your oars; they M your deck of pines
27:11 walls round about; they M perfect your beauty.
27:24 bound with cords and M secure; in these they
29:3 is my own; I M it.'
29:7 you, you broke, and M all their loins to
29:9 is mine, and I M it,'
29:18 Nebuchadrezzar king of Babylon M his army labor
29:18 Tyre; every head was M bald and every shoulder
31:4 nourished it, the deep M it grow tall, making
31:6 birds of the air M their nests in its
31:9 I M it beautiful in the mass of its
32:25 They have M her a bed among the slain
33:7 of man, I have M a watchman for the
33:29 LORD, when I have M the land a desolation
36:3 Because, yea, because they M you desolate, and
46:23 of masonry, with hearths M at the bottom of
Dan 2:15 Then Arioch M the matter known to Daniel.
2:17 to his house and M the matter known to
2:23 strength, and hast now M known to me what
2:23 thee, for thou hast M known to us the
2:28 mysteries, and he has M known to King
2:29 he who reveals mysteries M known to you what
2:30 the interpretation may be M known to the king,
2:45 A great God has M known to the king
2:48 many great gifts, and M him ruler over the
2:49 Daniel M request of the king, and he appointed
3:1 King Nebuchadnezzar M an image of gold, whose
3:10 You, O king, have M a decree, that every
3:15 image which I have M, well and good; but
3:50 of the furnace, and M the midst of the
4:5 had a dream which M me afraid; as I
4:6 Therefore I M a decree that all the wise
4:25 field; you shall be M to eat grass like
4:32 and you shall be M to eat grass like
5:1 King Belshazzar M a great feast for a thousand
5:11 King Nebuchadnezzar, your father, M him chief of
5:21 and his mind was M like that of a
5:29 neck, and proclamation was M concerning him, that
7:4 from the ground and M to stand upon two
7:16 he told me, and M known to me the
7:21 I looked, this horn M war with the saints,
9:4 LORD my God and M confession, saying, "O Lord,
9:15 mighty hand, and hast M thee a name, as
11:23 that an alliance is M with him he shall
14:13 the table they had M a hidden entrance, through
14:27 boiled them together and M cakes, which he fed
Hos 5:2 And they have M deep the pit of Shittim;
8:4 They M kings, but not through me.
8:4 silver and gold they M idols for their own
8:6 A workman M it; it is not God.
13:2 molten images, idols skilfully M of their silver, all
Joel 1:7 down; their branches are M white.
Amos 2:12 "But you M the Nazirites drink wine, and
3:3 together, unless they have M an appointment?
4:10 your horses; and I M the stench of your
5:8 He who M the Pleiades and Orion, and turns
5:26 your images, which you M for yourselves;
7:9 of Isaac shall be M desolate, and the sanctuaries
Jon 1:9 God of heaven, who M the sea and the
1:16 to the LORD and M vows.
3:7 he M proclamation and published through Nineveh,
4:2 That is why I M haste to flee to
4:5 of the city, and M a booth for himself
4:6 appointed a plant, and M it come up over
Mic 3:4 time, because they have M their deeds evil.
Zeph 2:8 taunted my people and M boasts against their
3:6 their cities have been M desolate, without a man,
Hag 2:5 the promise that I M you when you came
Zech 7:12 They M their hearts like adamant lest they should
7:14 the pleasant land was M desolate."
9:13 my bow; I have M Ephraim its arrow.
11:10 covenant which I had M with all the peoples.
Mal 2:15 not the one God M and sustained for us
1Mac 2:41 So they M this decision that day: "Let us
3:7 many kings, but he M Jacob glad by his
4:49 They M new holy vessels, and brought the
5:3 But Judas M war on the sons of Esau
5:14 came from Galilee and M a similar report;
5:49 ordered proclamation to be M to the army that
6:14 of his friends, and M him ruler over all
6:33 Beth-zechariah, and his troops M ready for battle
6:41 who heard the noise M by their multitude, by
6:49 He M peace with the men of Bethzur, and
6:52 The Jews also M engines of war to match
7:9 ungodly Alcimus, whom he M high priest; and he
8:1 well-disposed toward all who M an alliance with
8:31 follows, 'Why have you M your yoke heavy upon
9:20 And all Israel M great lamentation for him; they
9:26 vengeance on them and M sport of them.
9:64 for many days and M machines of war.
10:65 his chief friends, and M him general and governor
11:27 had formerly had, and M him to be regarded
11:51 down their arms and M peace.
11:59 Simon his brother he M governor from the Ladder
11:62 with Jonathan, and he M peace with them, and
13:27 and his brothers; he M it high that it
13:38 grants that we have M to you remain valid,
13:43 He M a siege engine, brought it up to
13:53 reached manhood, so he M him commander of all
14:15 He M the sanctuary glorious, and added to the
14:27 So they M a record on bronze tablets and
14:35 his nation, and they M him their leader and
14:39 the high-priesthood, and he M him one of the
15:27 agreements he formerly had M with Simon, and
15:38 the king M Cendebeus commander-in-chief of the
16:13 the country, and M treacherous plans against Simon
2Mac 1:34 enclosed the place and M it sacred.
2:9 It was also M clear that being possessed of
3:4 Benjamin, who had been M captain of the temple,
3:9 disclosure that had been M and stated why he
3:20 to heaven, they all M entreaty.
3:35 to the Lord and M very great vows to
5:1 About this time Antiochus M his second invasion of
5:3 up, attacks and counterattacks M on this side and
5:5 thousand men and suddenly M an assault upon the
5:16 which other kings had M to enhance the glory
8:15 sake of the covenants M with their fathers, and
8:21 with good courage and M them ready to die
8:29 done this, they M common supplication and besought
8:35 his splendid uniform and M his way alone like
9:13 Then the abominable fellow M a vow to the
9:23 the occasions when he M expeditions into the upper
10:3 purified the sanctuary, and M another altar of
10:28 Lord, while the other M rage their leader in
12:27 before the walls and M a vigorous defense; and
12:45 Therefore he M atonement for the dead, that they
13:26 took the public platform, M the best possible
14:2 of the country, having M away with Antiochus and
14:26 covenant that had been M and went to Demetrius.
15:1 region of Samaria, he M plans to attack them
15:9 they had won, he M them the more eager.
Mt 9:16 from the garment, and a worse tear is M
9:21 garment, I shall be M well."
9:22 daughter; your faith has M you well." And instantly
9:22 instantly the woman was M well.
14:22 Then he M the disciples get into the boat
14:36 as touched it were M well.
15:6 your tradition, you have M void the word of
18:24 all that he had, and payment to be M
19:4 read that he who M them from the beginning
19:4 them from the beginning M them male and female,
19:12 eunuchs who have been M eunuchs by men, and
19:12 are eunuchs who have M themselves eunuchs for the
20:12 hour, and you have M them equal to us
22:4 invited, Behold, I have M ready my dinner, my
22:5 marriage feast.' But they M light of it and
23:16 the temple that has M the gold sacred?
25:16 with them; and he M five talents more.
25:17 had the two talents M two talents more.
25:20 talents; here I have M five talents more.'
25:22 talents; here I have M two talents more.'
27:12 priests and elders, he M no answer.
27:64 the sepulchre to be M secure until the third

27:66 So they went and M the sepulchre secure by
Mk 1:42 him, and he was M clean.
2:4 and when they had M an opening, they let
2:21 from the old, and a worse tear is M
2:23 grainfields; and as they M their way his disciples
2:27 them, "The sabbath was M for man, not man
4:22 hid, except to be M manifest; nor is anything
5:23 that she may be M well, and live."
5:28 garments, I shall be M well."
5:34 "Daughter, your faith has M you well; go in
6:45 Immediately he M his disciples get into the boat
6:56 as touched it were M well.
10:6 beginning of creation, 'God M them male and
10:52 way; your faith has M you well." And immediately
11:17 But you have M it a den of robbers."
14:58 this temple that is M with hands, and in
14:58 will build another, not M with hands.'"
14:61 he was silent and M no answer.
15:5 But Jesus M no further answer, so that Pilate
Lk 1:22 the temple; and he M signs to them and
1:62 And they M signs to his father, inquiring what
2:15 which the Lord has M known to us."
2:17 they saw it they M known the saying which
3:5 the crooked shall be M straight, and the rough
3:5 rough ways shall be M smooth;
5:29 And Levi M him a great feast in his
8:17 that shall not be M manifest, nor anything secret
8:48 "Daughter, your faith has M you well; go in
9:15 they did so, and M them all sit down.
11:40 Did not he who M the outside make the
12:14 to him, "Man, who M me a judge or
13:13 and immediately she was M straight, and she praised
13:19 birds of the air M nests in its branches."
17:19 way; your faith has M you well."
18:42 sight; your faith has M you well."
19:6 So he M haste and came down, and received
19:16 'Lord, your pound has M ten pounds more.'
19:18 'Lord, your pound has M five pounds.'
19:46 prayer'; but you have M it a den of
23:9 some length; but he M no answer.
Jn 1:3 God; all things were M through him, and without
1:3 him was not anything M that was made.
1:3 without him was not anything made that was M
1:10 and the world was M through him, yet the
1:18 the Father, he has M him known.
4:46 Galilee, where he had M the water wine.
7:23 on the sabbath I M a man's whole body
8:33 say, 'You will be M free'?"
9:3 of God might be M manifest in him.
9:6 on the ground and M clay of the spittle
9:11 "The man called Jesus M clay and anointed my
9:14 sabbath day when Jesus M the clay and opened
12:2 There they M him a supper; Martha served, and
15:3 You are already M clean by the word which
15:15 my Father I have M known to you.
17:5 I had with thee before the world was M
17:26 I M known to them thy name, and I
18:18 servants and officers had M a charcoal fire, because
19:7 die, because he has M himself the Son of
19:23 took his garments and M four parts, one for
Acts 2:28 Thou hast M known to me the ways of
2:36 assuredly that God has M him both Lord and
3:7 feet and ankles were M strong.
3:12 or piety we had M him walk?
3:16 in his name, has M this man strong whom
4:35 feet; and distribution was M to each as any
7:10 king of Egypt, who M him governor over Egypt
7:13 the second visit Joseph M himself known to his
7:27 him aside, saying, 'Who M you a ruler and
7:35 they refused, saying, 'Who M you a ruler and
7:41 of him.' And they M a calf in those
7:43 the figures which you M to worship; and I
7:48 not dwell in houses M with hands; as the
8:2 men buried Stephen, and M great lamentation over
9:21 this the man who M havoc in Jerusalem of
9:39 other garments which Dorcas M while she was with
10:17 sent by Cornelius, having M inquiry for Simon's
10:40 the third day and M him manifest;
12:5 prayer for him was M to God by the
12:21 upon the throne, and M an oration to them.
13:17 chose our fathers and M the people great during
14:5 When an attempt was M by both Gentiles and
14:9 had faith to be M well,
14:15 a living God who M the heaven and the
14:21 that city and had M many disciples, they returned
15:7 the early days God M choice among you, that
15:9 to us; and he M no distinction between us
15:18 the Lord, who has M these things known from
16:11 therefore from Troas, we M a direct voyage to
17:24 The God who M the world and everything in
17:24 not live in shrines M by man,
17:26 And he M from one every nation of men
18:12 of Achaia, the Jews M a united attack upon
19:24 Demetrius, a silversmith, who M silver shrines of
19:26 people, saying that gods M with hands are not
20:3 when a plot was M against him by the
20:28 the Holy Spirit has M you overseers, to care
21:15 After these days we M ready and went up
22:6 "As I M my journey and drew near to
23:12 was day, the Jews M a plot and bound
23:13 more than forty who M this conspiracy.
25:17 came together here, I M no delay, but on
26:1 out his hand and M his defense:
26:6 hope in the promise M by God to our
26:24 And as he thus M his defense, Festus said
27:40 to the wind they M for the beach.
28:13 And from there we M a circuit and arrived
28:25 after Paul had M one statement: "The Holy
Rom 1:20 clearly perceived in the things that have been M
4:17 is written, "I have M you the father of
4:20 No distrust M him waver concerning the promise of
5:19 man's disobedience many were M sinners, so by one
5:19 obedience many will be M righteous.
9:20 molder, "Why have you M me thus?"
9:22 the vessels of wrath M for destruction,
9:29 like Sodom and been M like Gomorrah."
16:25 the prophetic writings is M known to all nations,
1Cor 1:20 Has not God M foolish the wisdom of the
1:30 Christ Jesus, whom God M our wisdom, our
9:12 Nevertheless, we have not M use of this right,
9:15 But I have M no use of any of
9:19 all men, I have M myself a slave to
11:8 (For man was not M from woman, but woman
11:12 for as woman was M from man, so man
12:13 free--and all were M to drink of one
14:30 If a revelation is M to another sitting by,
15:22 Christ shall all be M alive.
16:2 contributions need not be M when I come.
16:17 Achaicus, because they have M up for your absence;
2Cor 2:1 For I M up my mind not to make
2:3 those who should have M me rejoice, for I
3:6 from God, who has M us competent to be
5:1 God, a house not M with hands, eternal in
5:21 For our sake he M him to be sin
7:8 For even if I M you sorry with my
8:6 as he had already M a beginning, he should
9:7 do as he has M up his mind, not
11:6 every way we have M this plain to you
11:29 Who is M to fall, and I am not
12:9 for my power is M perfect in weakness." I
Gal 3:16 Now the promises were M to Abraham and to
3:19 the promise had been M; and it was ordained
4:18 always good to be M much of, and not
Eph 1:9 For he has M known to us in all
1:20 from the dead and M him sit at his
1:22 his feet and has M him the head over
2:1 And you he M alive, when you were dead
2:5 dead through our trespasses, M us alive together
2:6 up with him, and M us sit with him
2:11 the circumcision, which is M in the flesh by
2:14 our peace, who has M us both one, and
3:3 how the mystery was M known to me by
3:5 Christ, which was not M known to the sons
3:7 this gospel I was M a minister according to
3:10 God might now be M known to the principalities
Phil 1:14 the brethren have been M confident in the Lord
3:12 because Christ Jesus has M me his own.
3:13 consider that I have M it my own; but
4:6 let your requests be M known to God.
Col 1:8 our behalf and has M known to us your
1:26 and generations but now M manifest to his saints.
2:11 circumcised with a circumcision M without hands, by
2:13 of your flesh, God M alive together with him,
2:15 principalities and powers and M a public example of
1Thes 2:3 uncleanness, nor is it M with guile;
2:6 though we might have M demands as apostles of
2Thes 1:5 that you may be M worthy of the kingdom
1Tim 1:19 certain persons have M shipwreck of their faith,
2:1 intercessions, and thanksgivings be M for all men,
6:12 were called when you M the good confession in
6:13 testimony before Pontius Pilate M the good
6:15 and this will be M manifest at the proper

M

Heb 1:3 When he had M purification for sins, he sat
2:9 a little while was M lower than the angels,
2:17 he had to be M like his brethren in
5:5 exalt himself to be M a high priest, but
5:9 he suffered; and being M perfect he became the
6:13 For when God M a promise to Abraham, since
7:19 uselessness (for the law M nothing perfect); on the
7:28 Son who has been M perfect for ever.
8:9 the covenant that I M with their fathers on
9:6 preparations having thus been M, the priests go
9:11 more perfect tent (not M with hands, that is,
9:16 of the one who M it must be established.
9:17 as the one who M it is alive.
9:24 not into a sanctuary M with hands, a copy
10:13 his enemies should be M a stool for his
11:3 what is seen was M out of things which
11:22 end of his life, M mention of the exodus
11:40 they should not be M perfect.
12:19 a voice whose words M the hearers entreat that
12:23 spirits of just men M perfect,
12:27 of what has been M, in order that what
Jas 2:4 have you not M distinctions among yourselves, and
3:9 curse men, who are M in the likeness of
4:5 spirit which he has M to dwell in us"?
1Pet 1:20 the world but was M manifest at the end
3:18 in the flesh but M alive in the spirit;
2Pet 1:16 devised myths when we M known to you the
1:19 have the prophetic word M more sure.
2:6 them to extinction and M them an example to
1Jn 1:2 the life was M manifest, and we saw
1:2 the Father and was M manifest to us--
4:9 love of God was M manifest among us, that
5:10 not believe God has M him a liar, because
5:15 have obtained the requests M of him.
Rev 1:1 take place; and he M it known by sending
1:6 by his blood and M us a kingdom, priests
5:10 and nation, and hast M them a kingdom and
7:14 washed their robes and M them white in the
8:6 had the seven trumpets M ready to blow them.
8:11 water, because it was M bitter.
10:10 it my stomach was M bitter.
14:7 and worship him who M heaven and earth, the
14:8 the great, she who M all nations drink the
18:1 and the earth was M bright with his splendor.
19:7 and his Bride has M herself ready;
21:21 each of the gates M of a single pearl,

MADEST (2)

Tob 3:4 captivity, and death; thou M us a byword of
8:6 Thou M Adam and gavest him Eve his wife

MADMAN (4)

1Sam 21:15 fellow to play the M in my presence?
Prov 26:18 Like a M who throws firebrands, arrows, and death,
Jer 29:26 the LORD over every M who prophesies, to put
2Cor 11:23 am talking like a M --with far greater labors,

MADMANNAH (2)

Josh 15:31 Eltolad, Chesil, Hormah, Ziklag, M, Sansannah,
1Chr 2:49 Shaaph the father of M, Sheva the father of

MADMEN (3)

1Sam 21:15 Do I lack M, that you have brought this
Wis 5:20 will join with him to fight against the M
Jer 48:2 nation!' You also, O M, shall be brought to

MADMENAH

Is 10:31 M is in flight, the inhabitants of Gebim flee

MADNESS (11)

Deut 28:28 will smite you with M and blindness and confusion
Eccl 1:17 wisdom and to know M and folly.
2:12 to consider wisdom and M and folly; for what
7:25 wickedness of folly and the foolishness which is M
9:3 full of evil, and M is in their hearts
10:13 and the end of his talk is wicked M
Wis 5:4 that his life was M and that his end
Sir 22:11 and you will never be wearied by his M
Zech 12:4 every horse with panic, and its rider with M
2Mac 6:29 he had uttered were in their opinion sheer M
2Pet 2:16 with human voice and restrained the prophet's M

MADON (2)

Josh 11:1 to Jobab king of M, and to the king
12:19 one; the king of M, one; the king of

MAGADAN

Mt 15:39 the boat and went to the region of M

MAGBISH

Ezra 2:30 The sons of M, one hundred and fifty-six.

MAGDALENE (12)

Mt 27:56 among whom were Mary M, and Mary the mother
27:61 Mary M and the other Mary were there, sitting
28:1 of the week, Mary M and the other Mary
Mk 15:39 among whom were Mary M, and Mary the mother
15:46 Mary M and Mary the mother of Joses saw
16:1 sabbath was past, Mary M, and Mary the mother
16:9 appeared first to Mary M, from whom he had
Lk 8:2 infirmities: Mary, called M, from whom seven
24:10 Now it was Mary M and Jo-anna and Mary
Jn 19:25 sister, Mary the wife of Clopas, and Mary M
20:1 of the week Mary M came to the tomb
20:18 Mary M went and said to the disciples, "I

MAGDIEL (2)

Gen 36:43 Kenaz, Teman, Mibzar, M, and Iram; these are
1Chr 1:54 Kenaz, Teman, Mibzar, M, and Iram; these are

MAGGOT

Job 25:6 man, who is a M, and the son of

MAGGOTS

Is 14:11 sound of your harps; M are the bed beneath

MAGIC (8)

Prov 17:8 bribe is like a M stone in the eyes
Wis 17:7 The delusions of their M art lay humbled, and
18:13 everything because of their M arts, yet, when their
Ezek 13:18 the women who sew M bands upon all wrists,
13:20 I am against your M bands with which you
Acts 8:9 who had previously practiced M in the city and
8:11 long time he had amazed them with his M
19:19 of those who practiced M arts brought their books

MAGICIAN (4)

Is 3:3 counselor and the skilful M and the expert in
Dan 2:10 a thing of any M or enchanter or Chaldean.
Acts 13:6 came upon a certain M, a Jewish false prophet,
13:8 But Elymas the M (for that is the meaning

MAGICIANS (15)

Gen 41:8 called for all the M of Egypt and all
41:24 told it to the M, but there was no
Ex 7:11 and they also, the M of Egypt, did the
7:22 But the M of Egypt did the same by
8:7 But the M did the same by their secret
8:18 The M tried by their secret arts to bring
8:19 And the M said to Pharaoh, "This is the
9:11 And the M could not stand before Moses because
9:11 boils were upon the M and upon all the
Dan 1:20 better than all the M and enchanters that were
2:2 king commanded that the M, the enchanters, the
2:27 "No wise men, enchanters, M, or astrologers can
4:7 Then the M, the enchanters, the Chaldeans, and the
4:9 Belteshazzar, chief of the M, because I know that
5:11 chief of the M, enchanters, Chaldeans, and

MAGISTRATE (4)

Sir 10:1 A wise M will educate his people, and the
10:2 Like the M of the people, so are his
41:18 before a judge or M; and of iniquity, before
Lk 12:58 your accuser before the M, make an effort to

MAGISTRATES (9)

Ezra 7:25 in your hand, appoint M and judges who may
Jud 6:14 placed him before the M of their city,
Dan 3:2 treasurers, the justices, the M, and all the officials
3:3 treasurers, the justices, the M, and all the officials
Acts 16:20 brought them to the M they said, "These men
16:22 attacking them; and the M tore the garments off
16:35 it was day, the M sent the police, saying,
16:36 to Paul, saying, "The M have sent to let
16:38 these words to the M, and they were afraid

MAGNIFICENCE (2)

1Mac 15:32 plate, and his great M, he was amazed.
Acts 19:27 be deposed from her M, she whom all Asia

MAGNIFICENT (3)

1Chr 22:5 LORD must be exceedingly M, of fame and glory

Tob	14:11	Tobias gave him a M funeral.
	14:13	his father-in-law and mother-in-law M funerals.

MAGNIFICENTLY (3)

2Mac	3:25	appeared to them a M caparisoned horse, with a
	4:22	He was welcomed M by Jason and the city,
	4:49	of the crime, provided M for their funeral.

MAGNIFIED (9)

2Sam	7:26	thy name will be M for ever, saying, 'The
1Chr	17:24	will be established and M for ever, saying, 'The
Sir	36:4	in them be thou M before us;
Jer	48:26	him drunk, because he M himself against the LORD;
	48:42	a people, because he M himself against the LORD.
Ezek	35:13	to devour.' And you M yourselves against me with
Dan	8:4	as he pleased and M himself.
	8:8	Then the he-goat M himself exceedingly; but when
	8:11	It M itself, even up to the Prince of

MAGNIFIES

Lk	1:46	Mary said, "My soul M the Lord,

MAGNIFY (13)

Esth	14:10	vain idols, and to M for ever a mortal
Job	19:5	If indeed you M yourselves against me, and make
Ps	34:3	O M the LORD with me, and let us
	35:26	shame and dishonor who M themselves against me!
	69:30	a song; I will M him with thanksgiving.
Sir	49:11	How shall we M Zerubbabel?
Is	10:15	it, or the saw M itself against him who
	42:21	his righteousness' sake, to M his law and make
Dan	8:25	own mind he shall M himself.
	11:36	shall exalt himself and M himself above every god,
	11:37	god, for he shall M himself above all.
	11:39	acknowledge him he shall M with honor.
Rom	11:13	to the Gentiles, I M my ministry

MAGOG (5)

Gen	10:2	sons of Japheth: Gomer, M, Madai, Javan, Tubal,
1Chr	1:5	Japheth: Gomer, M, Madai, Javan, Tubal, Meshech,
Ezek	38:2	of the land of M, the chief prince of
	39:6	will send fire on M and on those who
Rev	20:8	that is, Gog and M, to gather them for

MAGPIASH

Neh	10:20	Hariph, Anathoth, Nebai, M, Meshullam, Hezir,

MAHALAB

Josh	19:29	ends at the sea; M, Achzib,

MAHALALE-EL

Lk	3:37	Jared, the son of M, the son of Ca-inan,

MAHALALEL (7)

Gen	5:12	lived seventy years, he became the father of M
	5:13	after the birth of M eight hundred and forty
	5:15	When M had lived sixty-five years, he became the
	5:16	M lived after the birth of Jared eight hundred
	5:17	all the days of M were eight hundred and
1Chr	1:2	Adam, Seth, Enosh; Kenan, M, Jared,
Neh	11:4	of Shephatiah, son of M, of the sons of

MAHALATH (2)

Gen	28:9	the wives he had, M the daughter of Ishmael
2Chr	11:18	Rehoboam took as wife M the daughter of Jerimoth

MAHANAIM (13)

Gen	32:2	So he called the name of that place M
Josh	13:26	and Betonim, and from M to the territory of
	13:30	Their region extended from M, through all Bashan,
	21:38	refuge for the slayer, M with its pasture lands,
2Sam	2:8	brought him over to M;
	2:12	Saul, went out from M to Gibeon.
	2:29	and marching the whole forenoon they came to M
	17:24	Then David came to M
	17:27	When David came to M, Shobi the son of
	19:32	while he stayed at M; for he was a
1Kgs	2:8	when I went to M; but when he came
	4:14	son of Iddo, in M;
1Chr	6:80	with its pasture lands, M with its pasture lands,

MAHANEH-DAN (2)

Judg	13:25	to stir him in M, between Zorah and Eshtaol.
	18:12	that place is called M to this day; behold,

MAHARAI (3)

2Sam	23:28	Hushathite, Zalmon the Ahohite, M of Netophah,
1Chr	11:30	Hushathite, Ilai the Ahohite, M of Netophah, Heled
	27:13	the tenth month, was M of Netophah, of the

MAHATH (3)

1Chr	6:35	of Elkanah, son of M, son of Amasai,
2Chr	29:12	Then the Levites arose, M the son of Amasai,
	31:13	Eliel, Ismachiah, M, and Benaiah were overseers

MAHAVITE

1Chr	11:46	the Tizite, Eliel the M, and Jeribai, and Joshaviah,

MAHAZI-OTH (2)

1Chr	25:4	Eliathah, Giddalti, and Romamti-ezer, Joshbekasha
	25:30	to the twenty-third, to M, his sons and his

MAHER-SHALAL-HASH-BAZ (2)

Is	8:1	write upon it in common characters, 'Belonging to M
	8:3	me, "Call his name M;

MAHLAH (5)

Num	26:33	daughters of Zelophehad were M, Noah, Hoglah,
	27:1	of his daughters were: M, Noah, Hoglah, Milcah, and
	36:11	LORD commanded Moses; for M, Tirzah, Hoglah,
Josh	17:3	names of his daughters: M, Noah, Hoglah, Milcah,
1Chr	7:18	sister Hammolecheth bore Ishhod, Abi-ezer, and M

MAHLI (12)

Ex	6:19	The sons of Merari: M and Mushi.
Num	3:20	Merari by their families: M and Mushi.
1Chr	6:19	The sons of Merari: M and Mushi.
	6:29	The sons of Merari: M, Libni his son, Shimei
	6:47	of Shemer, son of M, son of Mushi, son
	23:21	The sons of Merari: M and Mushi.
	23:21	The sons of M: Eleazar and Kish.
	23:23	The sons of Mushi: M, Eder, and Jeremoth, three.
	24:26	The sons of Merari: M and Mushi.
	24:28	Of M: Eleazar, who had no sons.
	24:30	The sons of Mushi: M, Eder, and Jerimoth.
Ezra	8:18	of the sons of M the son of Levi,

MAHLITES (2)

Num	3:33	the family of the M and the family of
	26:58	the family of the M, the family of the

MAHLON (4)

Ruth	1:2	his two sons were M and Chilion; they were
	1:5	ten years; and both M and Chilion died, so
	4:9	and all that belonged to Chilion and to M
	4:10	Moabitess, the widow of M, I have bought to

MAHOL

1Kgs	4:31	Darda, the sons of M; and his fame was

MAHSEIAH (3)

Jer	32:12	of Neriah son of M, in the presence of
	51:59	of Neriah, son of M, when he went with
Bar	1:1	of Neraiah, son of M, son of Zedekiah, son

MAID (45)

Gen	16:1	She had an Egyptian M whose name was Hagar;
	16:2	go in to my M; it may be that
	16:3	Hagar the Egyptian, her M, and gave her to
	16:5	I gave my M to your embrace, and when
	16:6	to Sarai, "Behold, your M is in your power;
	16:8	And he said, "Hagar, M of Sarai, where have
	25:12	Hagar the Egyptian, Sarah's M, bore to Abraham.
	29:24	(Laban gave his M Zilpah to his daughter Leah
	29:24	Leah to be her M
	29:29	(Laban gave his M Bilhah to his daughter Rachel
	29:29	Rachel to be her M
	30:3	said, "Here is my M Bilhah; go in to
	30:4	she gave him her M Bilhah as a wife;
	30:7	Rachel's M Bilhah conceived again and bore Jacob a
	30:9	children, she took her M Zilpah and gave her
	30:10	Then Leah's M Zilpah bore Jacob a son.
	30:12	Leah's M Zilpah bore Jacob a second son.
	30:18	because I gave my M to my husband"; so
	35:25	sons of Bilhah, Rachel's M: Dan and Naphtali.
	35:26	sons of Zilpah, Leah's M: Gad and Asher.
Ex	2:5	reeds and sent her M to fetch it.
2Kgs	5:2	carried off a little M from the land of
Tob	8:13	So the M opened the door and went in,
Jud	8:10	days, she sent her M, who was in charge
	8:33	go out with my M; and within the days

M

10:2 prostrate and called her M and went down into
10:5 And she gave her M a bottle of wine
10:10 out, she and her M with her; and the
10:17 accompany her and her M, and they brought them
12:15 woman's finery, and her M went and spread on
12:19 before him what her M had prepared.
13:3 Judith had told her M to stand outside the
13:9 Holofernes' head to her M,
16:23 She set her M free.
Esth 15:7 the head of the M who went before her.
Ps 123:2 the eyes of a M to the hand of
Prov 30:23 a husband, and a M when she succeeds her
Is 24:2 master; as with the M, so with her mistress;
Mt 26:69 And a M came up to him, and said,
26:71 to the porch, another M saw him, and she
Mk 14:69 And the M saw him, and began again to
Lk 22:54 Then a M, seeing him as he sat in
Jn 18:16 and spoke to the M who kept the door,
18:17 The M who kept the door said to Peter,
Acts 12:13 of the gateway, a M named Rhoda came to

MAIDEN (28)

Gen 24:14 Let the M to whom I shall say, 'Pray
24:16 The M was very fair to look upon, a
24:28 Then the M ran and told her mother's household
24:55 mother said, "Let the M remain with us a
24:57 "We will call the M, and ask her."
34:3 Jacob; he loved the M and spoke tenderly to
34:4 saying, "Get me this M for my wife."
34:12 only give me the M to be my wife."
Judg 5:30 dividing the spoil?--A M or two for every
Ruth 2:5 of the reapers, "Whose M is this?"
2:6 "It is the Moabite M, who came back with
1Kgs 1:2 him, "Let a young M be sought for my
1:3 sought for a beautiful M throughout all the territory
1:4 The M was very beautiful; and she became the
2Kgs 5:4 and so spoke the M from the land of
Esth 2:4 And let the M who pleases the king be
2:7 father nor mother; the M was beautiful and lovely,
2:9 And the M pleased him and won his favor;
2:12 turn came for each M to go in to
2:13 women-- when the M went in to the
Prov 30:19 and the way of a man with a M
Song 7:1 graceful are your feet in sandals, O queenly M
7:6 and pleasant you are, O loved one, delectable M
Sir 20:3 desire to violate a M is a man who
30:20 eunuch who embraces a M and groans.
Jer 2:32 Can a M forget her ornaments, or a bride
51:22 young man and the M;
Amos 2:7 in to the same M, so that my holy

MAIDENHOOD

Ezek 16:7 and arrived at full M; your breasts were formed,

MAIDENS (32)

Ex 2:5 the river, and her M walked beside the river;
Ruth 2:8 leave this one, but keep close to my M
2:22 go out with his M, lest in another field
2:23 kept close to the M of Boaz, gleaning until
3:2 our kinsman, with whose M you were?
1Sam 9:11 city, they met young M coming out to draw
25:42 ass, and her five M attended her; she went
Esth 2:8 proclaimed, and when many M were gathered in
Job 41:5 will you put him on leash for your M
Ps 68:25 minstrels last, between them M playing timbrels:
78:63 young men, and their M had no marriage song.
148:12 Young men and M together, old men and children!
Prov 27:27 food of your household and maintenance for your M
31:15 food for her household and tasks for her M
Song 1:3 poured out; therefore the M love you.
2:2 lily among brambles, so is my love among M
6:8 and eighty concubines, and M without number.
6:9 The M saw her and called her happy; the
Jer 31:13 Then shall the M rejoice in the dance, and
Lam 1:4 her priests groan; her M have been dragged away,
1:18 behold my suffering; my M and my young men
2:10 put on sackcloth; the M of Jerusalem have bowed
2:21 and the old; my M and my young men
3:51 fate of all the M of my city.
Ezek 9:6 young men and M, little children and women,
Nah 2:7 is carried off, her M lamenting, moaning like doves,
Zech 9:17 the young men flourish, and new wine the M
1Mac 1:26 rulers and elders groaned, M and young men became
2Mac 3:19 Some of the M who were kept indoors ran
Mt 25:1 be compared to ten M who took their lamps
25:7 him.' Then all those M rose and trimmed their
25:11 Afterward the other M came also, saying, 'Lord, lord,

MAIDS (23)

Gen 24:61 Then Rebekah and her M arose, and rode upon
32:22 two wives, his two M, and his eleven children,
33:1 children among Leah and Rachel and the two M
33:2 And he put the M with their children in
33:6 Then the M drew near, they and their children,
2Sam 6:20 eyes of his servants' M, as one of the
6:22 eyes; but by the M of whom you have
Tob 3:7 reproached by her father's M,
3:8 So the M said to her, "Do you not
8:12 "Send one of the M to see whether he
Esth 2:9 and with seven chosen M from the king's palace,
2:9 advanced her and her M to the best place
4:4 When Esther's M and her eunuchs came and told
4:16 I and my M will also fast as you
15:2 she took her two M with her,
Prov 9:3 has sent out her M to call from the
Dan 13:15 before with only two M, and wished to bathe
13:17 She said to her M, "Bring me oil and
13:19 When the M had gone out, the two elders
13:21 why you sent your M away."
13:36 came in with two M, shut the garden doors,
13:36 maids, shut the garden doors, and dismissed the M
Mk 14:66 courtyard, one of the M of the high priest

MAIDSERVANT (32)

Ex 11:5 the first-born of the M who is behind the
20:10 your manservant, or your M, or your cattle, or
20:17 his manservant, or his M, or his ox, or
Deut 5:14 your manservant, or your M, or your ox, or
5:14 your manservant and your M may rest as well
5:21 his manservant, or his M, his ox, or his
12:18 your manservant and your M, and the Levite who
16:11 your manservant and your M, the Levite who is
16:14 your manservant and your M, the Levite, the
Judg 9:18 the son of his M, king over the citizens
19:19 for me and your M and the young man
Ruth 2:13 spoken kindly to your M, though I am not
3:9 "I am Ruth, your M; spread your skirt over
3:9 your skirt over your M, for you are next
1Sam 1:11 the affliction of thy M, and remember me, and
1:11 and not forget thy M, but wilt give to
1:11 wilt give to thy M a son, then I
1:16 Do not regard your M as a base woman,
1:18 she said, "Let your M find favor in your
2Sam 17:17 waiting at En-rogel; a M used to go and
20:17 to him, "Listen to the words of your M
1Kgs 1:13 king, swear to your M, saying, "Solomon your son
1:17 you swore to your M by the LORD your
3:20 beside me, while your M slept, and laid it
2Kgs 4:2 And she said, "Your M has nothing in the
4:16 man of God; do not lie to your M
Jud 11:5 servant, and let your M speak in your presence,
11:6 the words of your M, God will accomplish something
12:13 and said, "This beautiful M will please come to
Job 31:13 my manservant or my M, when they brought a
Wis 9:5 the son of thy M, a man who is
Sir 41:22 of meddling with his M -- and do not

MAIDSERVANTS (16)

Gen 12:16 oxen, he-asses, menservants, M, she-asses, and
24:35 and gold, menservants and M, camels and asses.
30:43 and had large flocks, M and menservants, and
31:33 tent of the two M, but he did not
32:5 asses, flocks, menservants, and M; and I have sent
Deut 12:12 your menservants and your M, and the Levite that
Ruth 2:13 maidservant, though I am not one of your M
1Sam 8:16 take your menservants and M, and the best of
2Kgs 5:26 vineyards, sheep and oxen, menservants and M
Ezra 2:65 besides their menservants and M, of whom there
Neh 7:67 besides their menservants and M, of whom there
Jud 16:12 The sons of M have pierced them through; they
Job 19:15 have forgotten me; my M count me as a
Joel 2:29 upon the menservants and M in those days, I
Lk 12:45 the menservants and the M, and to eat and
Acts 2:18 my menservants and my M in those days I

MAIL (8)

1Sam 17:5 with a coat of M, and the weight of
17:38 head, and clothed him with a coat of M
2Chr 26:14 spears, helmets, coats of M, bows, and stones for
Neh 4:16 bows, and coats of M; and the leaders stood
Job 41:13 Who can penetrate his double coat of M
Jer 46:4 polish your spears, put on your coats of M

51:3 him not stand up in his coat of M
1Mac 6:35 armed with coats of M, and with brass helmets

MAIMED (7)

Zech 11:16 wandering, or heal the M, or nourish the sound,
Mt 15:30 them the lame, the M, the blind, the dumb,
15:31 the dumb speaking, the M whole, the lame walking,
18:8 you to enter life M or lame than with
Mk 9:43 you to enter life M than with two hands
Lk 14:13 invite the poor, the M, the lame, the blind,
14:21 in the poor and M and blind and lame.'

MAIN (4)

Josh 8:13 stationed the forces, the M encampment which was
Dan 11:41 and Moab and the M part of the Ammonites.
1Mac 11:46 the city seized the M streets of the city
2Mac 12:35 dragging him off by M strength, wishing to take

MAINLAND (3)

Ezek 26:6 her daughters on the M shall be slain by
26:8 your daughters on the M; he will set up
26:17 inhabitants, who imposed your terror on all the M

MAINSTAY

Jer 49:35 bow of Elam, the M of their might;

MAINTAIN (17)

Lev 25:35 becomes poor, and cannot M himself with you, you
25:35 with you, you shall M him; as a stranger
1Kgs 8:45 and their supplication, and M their cause.
8:49 and their supplication, and M their cause
8:59 night, and may he M the cause of his
2Chr 6:35 and their supplication, and M their cause.
6:39 their supplications, and M their cause and forgive
Job 16:21 God, that he would M the right of a
Ps 82:3 weak and the fatherless; M the right of the
Prov 31:9 your mouth, judge righteously, M the rights of the
Ezek 7:13 his iniquity, none can M his life.
2Mac 9:26 to you and to M your present good will,
10:12 them, and attempted to M peaceful relations with
11:19 If you will M your good will toward the
1Cor 11:2 me in everything and M the traditions even as
Eph 4:3 in love, eager to M the unity of the
1Pet 2:12 M good conduct among the Gentiles, so that in

MAINTAINED (5)

Jud 8:7 and fields; and she M this estate.
Ps 9:4 For thou hast M my just cause; thou hast
1Mac 14:35 loyalty which he had M toward his nation.
2Mac 10:14 of the region, he M a force of mercenaries,
15:30 citizens, the man who M his youthful good will

MAINTAINS (3)

Ps 140:12 know that the LORD M the cause of the
Prov 15:25 of the proud, but M the widow's boundaries.
Sir 28:5 he himself, being flesh, M wrath, who will make

MAINTENANCE (3)

1Chr 26:27 dedicated gifts for the M of the house of
Prov 27:27 of your household and M for your maidens.
1Mac 10:36 men, and let the M be given them that

MAJESTIC (13)

Ex 15:11 Who is like thee, M in holiness, terrible in
Job 37:4 he thunders with his M voice and he does
39:20 His M snorting is terrible.
Ps 8:1 LORD, our Lord, how M is thy name in
8:9 LORD, our Lord, how M is thy name in
76:4 Glorious art thou, more M than the everlasting
Sir 18:4 Who can measure his M power?
Is 10:34 and Lebanon with its M trees will fall.
30:30 LORD will cause his M voice to be heard
60:15 I will make you M for ever, a joy
Ezek 32:18 and the daughters of M nations, to the nether
2Mac 3:34 to all men the M power of God." Having
2Pet 1:17 to him by the M Glory, "This is my

MAJESTICALLY

Esth 15:2 Then, M adorned, after invoking the aid of the

MAJESTY (54)

Ex 15:7 greatness of thy M thou overthrowest thy
Deut 33:17 His firstling bull has M, and his horns are
33:26 help, and in his M through the skies.
1Chr 16:27 Honor and M are before him; strength and joy
29:11 the victory, and the M; for all that is
29:25 upon him such royal M as had not been
Tob 13:6 show his power and M to a nation of
13:7 King of heaven, and will rejoice in his M
Esth 1:4 and pomp of his M for many days, a
15:6 full array of his M, all covered with gold
Job 13:11 Will not his M terrify you, and the dread
31:23 God, and I could not have faced his M
37:22 golden splendor; God is clothed with terrible M
40:10 "Deck yourself with M and dignity; clothe yourself
Ps 21:5 thy help; splendor and M thou dost bestow upon
29:4 the voice of the LORD is full of M
45:3 thigh, O mighty one, in your glory and M
45:4 In your M ride forth victoriously for the cause
68:34 power to God, whose M is over Israel, and
93:1 he is robed in M; the LORD is robed,
96:6 Honor and M are before him; strength and beauty
104:1 clothed with honor and M,
111:3 Full of honor and M is his work, and
145:5 glorious splendor of thy M, and on thy wondrous
Wis 18:24 of stones, and thy M on the diadem upon
Sir 2:18 men; for as his M is, so also is
17:7 to show them the M of his works.
17:11 eyes saw his glorious M, and their ears heard
39:15 all his works; ascribe M to his name and
43:15 In his M he amasses the clouds, and the
44:2 them great glory, his M from the beginning.
Is 2:10 the LORD, and from the glory of his M
2:19 the glory of his M, when he rises to
2:21 the glory of his M, when he rises to
24:14 for joy; over the M of the LORD they
26:10 does not see the M of the LORD.
33:21 there the LORD in M will be for us
35:2 given to it, the M of Carmel and Sharon.
35:2 of the LORD, the M of our God.
Jer 22:18 lord!' or 'Ah his M
Lam 1:6 the daughter of Zion has departed all her M
Dan 4:30 royal residence and for the glory of my M
4:36 of my kingdom, my M and splendor returned to
5:18 greatness and glory and M;
11:21 person to whom royal M has not been given;
Mic 5:4 the LORD, in the M of the name of
Nah 2:2 LORD is restoring the M of Jacob as the
2:2 of Jacob as the M of Israel, for plunderers
2Mac 15:13 dignity, and of marvelous M and authority.
Lk 9:43 were astonished at the M of God.
Heb 1:3 right hand of the M on high,
8:1 the throne of the M in heaven,
2Pet 1:16 Jesus Christ, but we were eyewitnesses of his M
Jude 1:25 our Lord, be glory, M, dominion, and authority,

MAJORITY (3)

1Chr 12:29 thousand, of whom the M had hitherto kept their
Acts 27:12 to winter in, the M advised to put to
2Cor 2:6 this punishment by the M is enough;

MAKAZ

1Kgs 4:9 of Ephraim; Ben-deker, in M, Sha-albim,

MAKE (1,189)

Gen 1:26 God said, "Let us M man in our image,
2:18 be alone; I will M him a helper fit
3:6 to be desired to M one wise, she took
6:13 "I have determined to M an end of all
6:14 M yourself an ark of gopher wood; make rooms
6:14 ark of gopher wood; M rooms in the ark,
6:15 how you are to M it: the length of
6:16 M a roof for the ark, and finish it
6:16 ark in its side; M it with lower, second,
9:12 the covenant which I M between me and you
11:3 another, "Come, let us M bricks, and burn them
11:4 heavens, and let us M a name for ourselves,
12:2 And I will M of you a great nation,
12:2 will bless you, and M your name great, so
13:16 I will M your descendants as the dust of
17:2 And I will M my covenant between me and
17:6 I will M you exceedingly fruitful; and I will
17:6 fruitful; and I will M nations of you, and
17:20 will bless him and M him fruitful and multiply
17:20 princes, and I will M him a great nation.
18:6 to Sarah, and said, M ready quickly three measures
18:6 meal, knead it, and M cakes."
19:22 M haste, escape there; for I can do nothing
19:32 Come, let us M our father drink wine, and
19:34 my father; let us M him drink wine tonight
21:13 And I will M a nation of the son
21:18 hand; for I will M him a great nation."

M

24:3 thigh, and I will M you swear by the
26:28 us, and let us M a covenant with you,
28:3 Almighty bless you and M you fruitful and multiply
31:44 Come now, let us M a covenant, you and
32:12 do you good, and M your descendants as the
34:9 M marriages with us; give your daughters to us,
35:1 and dwell there; and M there an altar to
35:3 Bethel, that I may M there an altar to
40:14 I pray you, to M mention of me to
42:38 that you are to M, you would bring down
43:16 slaughter an animal and M ready, for the men
43:18 fall upon us, to M slaves of us and
45:1 him; and he cried, M every one go out
45:9 M haste and go up to my father and
45:13 M haste and bring my father down here."
46:3 for I will there M of you a great
48:4 me, 'Behold, I will M you fruitful, and multiply
48:4 you, and I will M of you a company
48:20 pronounce blessings, saying, 'God M you as Ephraim
Ex 5:5 now many and you M them rest from their
5:7 the people straw to M bricks, as heretofore; let
5:16 they say to us, M bricks!' And behold, your
6:3 LORD I did not M myself known to them.
7:1 to Moses, "See, I M you as God to
8:28 M entreaty for me."
9:4 But the LORD will M a distinction between the
12:4 can eat you shall M your count for the
18:16 his neighbor, and I M them know the statutes
18:20 and the decisions, and M them know the way
20:4 "You shall not M for yourself a graven image,
20:23 You shall not M gods of silver to be
20:23 me, nor shall you M for yourselves gods of
20:24 of earth you shall M for me and sacrifice
20:25 And if you M me an altar of stone,
21:34 of the pit shall M it good; he shall
22:1 He shall M restitution; if he has nothing, then
22:5 man's field, he shall M restitution from the best
22:6 kindled the fire shall M full restitution.
22:11 and he shall not M restitution.
22:12 from him, he shall M restitution to its owner.
22:13 evidence; he shall not M restitution for what has
22:14 with it, he shall M full restitution.
22:15 it, he shall not M restitution; if it was
22:16 present for her, and M her his wife.
23:13 said to you; and M no mention of the
23:27 come, and I will M all your enemies turn
23:32 You shall M no covenant with them or with
23:33 your land, lest they M you sin against me;
25:8 And let them M me a sanctuary, that I
25:9 furniture, so you shall M it.
25:10 "They shall M an ark of acacia wood; two
25:11 it, and you shall M upon it a molding
25:13 You shall M poles of acacia wood, and overlay
25:17 Then you shall M a mercy seat of pure
25:18 And you shall M two cherubim of gold; of
25:18 hammered work shall you M them, on the two
25:19 M one cherub on the one end, and one
25:19 mercy seat shall you M the cherubim on its
25:23 "And you shall M a table of acacia wood;
25:24 with pure gold, and M a molding of gold
25:25 And you shall M around it a frame a
25:26 And you shall M for it four rings of
25:28 You shall M the poles of acacia wood, and
25:29 And you shall M its plates and dishes for
25:29 pure gold you shall M them.
25:31 "And you shall M a lampstand of pure gold.
25:37 And you shall M the seven lamps for it;
25:40 And see that you M them after the pattern
26:1 "Moreover you shall M the tabernacle with ten
26:1 skilfully worked shall you M them.
26:4 And you shall M loops of blue on the
26:4 and likewise you shall M loops on the edge
26:5 Fifty loops you shall M on the one curtain,
26:5 fifty loops you shall M on the edge of
26:6 And you shall M fifty clasps of gold, and
26:7 "You shall also M curtains of goats' hair for
26:7 tent over the tabernacle; eleven curtains shall you M
26:10 And you shall M fifty loops on the edge
26:11 "And you shall M fifty clasps of bronze, and
26:14 And you shall M for the tent a covering
26:15 "And you shall M upright frames for the tabernacle
26:18 You shall M the frames for the tabernacle: twenty
26:19 of silver you shall M under the twenty frames,
26:22 tabernacle westward you shall M six frames.
26:23 And you shall M two frames for corners of
26:26 "And you shall M bars of acacia wood, five
26:29 with gold, and shall M their rings of gold
26:31 "And you shall M a veil of blue and
26:36 "And you shall M a screen for the door
26:37 And you shall M for the screen five pillars
27:1 "You shall M the altar of acacia wood, five
27:2 And you shall M horns for it on its
27:3 You shall M pots for it to receive its
27:3 its utensils you shall M of bronze.
27:4 You shall also M for it a grating, a
27:4 the net you shall M four bronze rings at
27:6 And you shall M poles for the altar, poles
27:8 You shall M it hollow, with boards; as it
27:9 "You shall M the court of the tabernacle.
28:2 And you shall M holy garments for Aaron your
28:3 mind, that they M Aaron's garments to consecrate
28:4 garments which they shall M: a breastpiece, an
28:4 a girdle; they shall M holy garments for Aaron
28:6 And they shall M the ephod of gold, of
28:13 And you shall M settings of gold filigree,
28:15 "And you shall M a breastpiece of judgment, in
28:15 the ephod you shall M it; of gold, blue
28:15 twined linen shall you M it.
28:22 And you shall M for the breastpiece twisted chains
28:23 gold; and you shall M for the breastpiece two
28:26 And you shall M two rings of gold, and
28:27 And you shall M two rings of gold, and
28:31 "And you shall M the robe of the ephod
28:33 its skirts you shall M pomegranates of blue and
28:36 "And you shall M a plate of pure gold,
28:39 linen, and you shall M a turban of fine
28:39 linen, and you shall M a girdle embroidered with
28:40 Aaron's sons you shall M coats and girdles and
28:40 and caps; you shall M them for glory and
28:42 And you shall M for them linen breeches to
29:2 You shall M them of fine wheat flour.
29:36 the altar, when you M atonement for it, and
29:37 Seven days you shall M atonement for the altar,
30:1 "You shall M an altar to burn incense upon;
30:1 acacia wood shall you M it.
30:3 horns; and you shall M for it a molding
30:4 golden rings shall you M for it; under its
30:4 of it shall you M them, and they shall
30:5 You shall M the poles of acacia wood, and
30:10 Aaron shall M atonement upon its horns once a
30:10 of atonement he shall M atonement for it once
30:15 the LORD's offering to M atonement for yourselves.
30:16 LORD, so as to M atonement for yourselves."
30:18 Moses, "You shall also M a laver of bronze,
30:25 hin; and you shall M of these a sacred
30:32 men, and you shall M no other like it
30:35 an equal part), and M an incense blended as
30:37 incense which you shall M according to its
30:37 composition, you shall not M for yourselves; it shall
31:6 ability, that they may M all that I have
32:1 said to him, "Up, M us gods, who shall
32:10 of you I will M a great nation."
32:23 they said to me, M us gods, who shall
32:30 LORD; perhaps I can M atonement for your sin."
33:19 he said, "I will M all my goodness pass
34:10 he said, "Behold, I M a covenant.
34:12 to yourself, lest you M a covenant with the
34:15 jealous God), lest you M a covenant with the
34:16 after their gods and M your sons play the
34:17 "You shall M for yourself no molten gods.
35:10 among you come and M all that the LORD
35:24 Every one who could M an offering of silver
Lev 1:4 accepted for him to M atonement for him.
4:20 and the priest shall M atonement for them, and
4:26 so the priest shall M atonement for him for
4:31 and the priest shall M atonement for him, and
4:35 and the priest shall M atonement for him for
5:6 and the priest shall M atonement for him for
5:10 and the priest shall M atonement for him for
5:13 Thus the priest shall M atonement for him for
5:16 He shall also M restitution for what he has
5:16 and the priest shall M atonement for him with
5:18 and the priest shall M atonement for him for
6:7 and the priest shall M atonement for him before
6:30 tent of meeting to M atonement in the holy
8:15 and consecrated it, to M atonement for it.
8:34 to be done to M atonement for you.
9:7 your burnt offering, and M atonement for yourself
9:7 of the people, and M atonement for them; as
10:17 of the congregation, to M atonement for them before
11:43 You shall not M yourselves abominable with any
11:47 upon the earth, to M a distinction between the

12:7 before the LORD, and M atonement for her; then
12:8 and the priest shall M atonement for her, and
13:8 and the priest shall M an examination, and if
13:10 and the priest shall M an examination, and if
13:13 then the priest shall M an examination, and if
13:20 and the priest shall M an examination, and if
13:39 spots, the priest shall M an examination, and if
14:3 and the priest shall M an examination.
14:18 Then the priest shall M atonement for him before
14:19 the sin offering, to M atonement for him who
14:20 Thus the priest shall M atonement for him, and
14:21 to be waved, to M atonement for him, and
14:29 to be cleansed, to M atonement for him before
14:31 and the priest shall M atonement before the LORD
14:53 field; so he shall M atonement for the house,
15:15 and the priest shall M atonement for him before
15:30 and the priest shall M atonement for her before
16:6 for himself, and shall M atonement for himself and
16:10 before the LORD to M atonement over it, that
16:11 for himself, and shall M atonement for himself and
16:16 seat; thus he shall M atonement for the holy
16:17 when he enters to M atonement in the holy
16:18 before the LORD and M atonement for it, and
16:24 of the people, and M atonement for himself and
16:27 was brought in to M atonement in the holy
16:32 father's place shall M atonement, wearing the holy
16:33 garments; he shall M atonement for the sanctuary,
16:33 sanctuary, and he shall M atonement for the tent
16:33 altar, and he shall M atonement for the priests
17:11 upon the altar to M atonement for your souls;
19:4 turn to idols or M for yourselves molten gods:
19:22 And the priest shall M atonement for him with
19:28 You shall not M any cuttings in your flesh
20:19 for that is to M naked one's near kin;
20:25 shall therefore M a distinction between the clean
20:25 clean; you shall not M yourselves abominable by
21:5 They shall not M tonsures upon their heads, nor
21:5 of their beards, nor M any cuttings in their
22:22 to the LORD or M of them an offering
23:21 And you shall M proclamation on the same day;
23:28 day of atonement, to M atonement for you before
24:18 kills a beast shall M it good, life for
24:21 kills a beast shall M it good; and he
25:39 you, you shall not M him serve as a
25:46 for ever; you may M slaves of them, but
25:52 of jubilee, he shall M a reckoning with him;
26:1 "You shall M for yourselves no idols and erect
26:6 down, and none shall M you afraid; and I
26:9 regard for you and M you fruitful and multiply
26:10 out the old to M way for the new.
26:11 And I will M my abode among you, and
26:19 power, and I will M your heavens like iron
26:22 destroy your cattle, and M you few in number,
26:31 cities waste, and will M your sanctuaries desolate,
26:41 is humbled and they M amends for their iniquity;
26:43 them; and they shall M amends for their iniquity,
27:25 sanctuary: twenty gerahs shall M a shekel.
Num 5:7 committed; and he shall M full restitution for his
5:19 Then the priest shall M her take an oath,
5:21 then' (let the priest M the woman take the
5:21 the woman) 'the LORD M you an execration and
5:22 into your bowels and M your body swell and
5:24 bitterness; and he shall M the woman drink the
5:26 altar, and afterward shall M the woman drink the
6:7 they die, shall he M himself unclean; because his
6:11 a burnt offering, and M atonement for him, because
6:25 keep you: The LORD M his face to shine
8:12 to the LORD, to M atonement for the Levites.
8:19 of meeting, and to M atonement for the people
10:2 LORD said to Moses, M two silver trumpets; of
10:2 hammered work you shall M them; and you shall
12:6 you, I the LORD M myself known to him
14:12 them, and I will M of you a nation
14:30 swore that I would M you dwell, except Caleb
15:3 your appointed feasts, to M a pleasing odor to
15:25 And the priest shall M atonement for all the
15:28 And the priest shall M atonement before the LORD
15:28 he sins unwittingly, to M atonement for him; and
15:38 and bid them to M tassels on the corners
16:13 that you must also M yourself a prince over
16:46 to the congregation, and M atonement for them; for
17:5 sprout; thus I will M to cease from me
17:10 rebels, that you may M an end of their
21:8 LORD said to Moses, M a fiery serpent, and
28:22 a sin offering, to M atonement for you.
28:30 one male goat, to M atonement for you.
29:5 a sin offering, to M atonement for you;
30:8 disapproval, then he shall M void her vow which
30:13 or her husband may M void.
31:50 earrings, and beads, to M atonement for ourselves
Deut 1:11 God of your fathers, M you a thousand times
4:9 days of your life; M them known to your
4:23 made with you, and M a graven image in
5:3 fathers did the LORD M this covenant, but with
5:8 "You shall not M for yourself a graven image,
7:2 destroy them; you shall M no covenant with them,
7:3 You shall not M marriages with them, giving your
7:22 little; you may not M an end of them
7:24 hand, and you shall M their name perish from
8:3 know; that he might M you know that man
9:3 drive them out, and M them perish quickly, as
9:14 heaven; and I will M of you a nation
10:1 on the mountain, and M an ark of wood.
12:5 put his name and M his habitation there; thither
12:11 God will choose, to M his name dwell there,
13:5 house of bondage, to M you leave the way
13:14 you shall inquire and M search and ask diligently;
14:1 not cut yourselves or M any baldness on your
14:23 he will choose, to M his name dwell there,
16:2 LORD will choose, to M his name dwell there.
16:6 God will choose, to M his name dwell in
16:11 God will choose, to M his name dwell there.
16:13 seven days, when you M your ingathering from your
16:21 of the LORD your God which you shall M
22:8 new house, you shall M a parapet for your
22:12 "You shall M yourself tassels on the four corners
23:21 "When you M a vow to the LORD your
24:10 "When you M your neighbor a loan of any
24:11 man to whom you M the loan shall bring
26:2 God will choose, to M his name to dwell
26:5 "And you shall M response before the LORD your
28:11 And the LORD will M you abound in prosperity,
28:13 And the LORD will M you the head, and
28:21 The LORD will M the pestilence cleave to you
28:24 The LORD will M the rain of your land
28:68 that you should never M again; and there you
29:1 LORD commanded Moses to M with the people of
29:14 you only that I M this sworn covenant,
30:5 it; and he will M you more prosperous and
30:9 LORD your God will M you abundantly prosperous in
32:26 them afar, I will M the remembrance of them
32:39 I kill and I M alive; I wound and
32:42 I will M my arrows drunk with blood, and
Josh 1:8 for then you shall M your way prosperous, and
5:2 LORD said to Joshua, M flint knives and circumcise
6:5 And when they M a long blast with the
6:18 the devoted things and M the camp of Israel
7:3 attack Ai; do not M the whole people toil
9:6 far country; so now M a covenant with us."
9:7 then how can we M a covenant with you?"
9:11 your servants; come now, M a covenant with us."'
22:12 gathered at Shiloh, to M war against them.
22:19 against the LORD, or M us as rebels by
22:25 So your children might M our children cease to
23:7 here among you, or M mention of the names
23:12 here among you, and M marriages with them, so
Judg 2:2 you, and you shall M no covenant with the
5:3 will sing, I will M melody to the LORD,
5:29 chariots?' Her wisest ladies M answer, nay, she gives
6:39 once; pray, let me M trial only this once
8:24 to them, "Let me M a request of you;
9:48 have seen me do, M haste to do, as
13:16 food; but if you M ready a burnt offering,
16:13 with the web and M it tight with the
16:25 Samson, that he may M sport for us." So
17:3 for my son, to M a graven image and
Ruth 3:3 floor; but do not M yourself known to the
4:11 May the LORD M the woman, who is coming
1Sam 2:8 the ash heap, to M them sit with princes
2:19 his mother used to M for him a little
6:5 So you must M images of your tumors and
8:12 his harvest, and to M his implements of war
8:22 to their voice, and M them a king." Samuel
9:12 M haste; he has come just now to the
9:27 while, that I may M known to you the
11:1 Jabesh said to Nahash, M a treaty with us,
11:2 this condition I will M a treaty with you,
12:22 pleased the LORD to M you a people for
13:19 "Lest the Hebrews M themselves swords or spears";
17:25 him his daughter, and M his father's house free
18:25 Now Saul thought to M David fall by the
20:38 after the lad, "Hurry, M haste, stay not." So

M

22:7 and vineyards, will he M you all commanders of
23:22 Go, M yet more sure; know and see the
23:27 came to Saul, saying, M haste and come; for
25:28 the LORD will certainly M my lord a sure
25:39 and wooed Abigail, to M her his wife.
28:2 "Very well, I will M you my bodyguard for
31:4 thrust me through, and M sport of me." But
2Sam 3:12 M your covenant with me, and behold, my hand
3:13 said, "Good; I will M a covenant with you;
3:21 king, that they may M a covenant with you,
6:21 LORD--and I will M merry before the LORD.
6:22 I will M myself yet more contemptible than this,
7:9 you; and I will M for you a great
7:11 that the LORD will M you a house.
7:21 all this greatness, to M thy servant know it.
13:6 sister Tamar come and M a couple of cakes
15:20 and shall I today M you wander about with
21:3 And how shall I M expiation, that you may
22:40 the battle; thou didst M my assailants sink under
22:41 Thou didst M my enemies turn their backs to
1Kgs 1:37 be with Solomon, and M his throne greater than
1:47 David, saying, 'Your God M the name of Solomon
1:47 famous than yours, and M his throne greater than
2:16 have one request to M of you; do not
2:20 one small request to M of you; do not
2:20 king said to her, M your request, my mother;
2:42 him, "Did I not M you swear by the
4:7 each man had to M provision for one month
5:9 Lebanon; and I will M it into rafts to
8:33 name, and pray and M supplication to thee in
8:47 captive, and repent, and M supplication to thee in
11:34 hand; but I will M him ruler all the
12:1 come to Shechem to M him king.
16:3 house, and I will M your house like the
16:21 son of Ginath, to M him king, and half
17:13 have said; but first M me a little cake
17:13 to me, and afterward M for yourself and your
19:2 if I do not M your life as the
21:22 Israel; and I will M your house like the
2Kgs 3:16 the LORD, 'I will M this dry stream-bed full
4:10 Let us M a small roof chamber with walls,
5:7 to kill and to M alive, that this man
6:2 log, and let us M a place for us
7:2 the LORD himself should M windows in heaven,
7:19 the LORD himself should M windows in heaven,
8:28 son of Ahab to M war against Hazael king
9:9 And I will M the house of Ahab like
9:21 Joram said, M ready." And they made ready his
10:5 We will not M any one king; do whatever
18:23 Come now, M a wager with my master the
18:30 Do not let Hezekiah M you to rely on
18:31 the king of Assyria: M your peace with me
1Chr 6:49 holy place, and to M atonement for Israel, according
10:4 these uncircumcised come and M sport of me." But
11:10 with all Israel, to M him king, according to
12:31 named to come and M David king.
12:38 with full intent to M David king over all
12:38 a single mind to M David king.
16:8 call on his name, M known his deeds among
17:8 you; and I will M for you a name,
17:22 And thou didst M thy people Israel to be
22:5 lands; I will therefore M preparation for it." So
27:23 LORD had promised to M Israel as many as
28:4 pleasure in me to M me king over all
29:12 hand it is to M great and to give
2Chr 2:18 hundred as overseers to M the people work.
5:13 trumpeters and singers to M themselves heard in
6:24 name, and pray and M supplication to thee in
6:37 captive, and repent, and M supplication to thee in
7:20 my sight, and will M it a proverb and
10:1 come to Shechem to M him king.
11:22 for he intended to M him king.
12:12 so as not to M a complete destruction; moreover,
22:5 king of Israel to M war against Hazael king
26:13 five hundred, who could M war with mighty power,
29:10 in my heart to M a covenant with the
29:24 on the altar, to M atonement for all Israel.
30:5 So they decreed to M a proclamation throughout all
30:17 was not clean, to M it holy to the
32:25 But Hezekiah did not M return according to the
35:21 has commanded me to M haste.
Ezra 4:16 We M known to the king that, if this
4:21 Therefore M a decree that these men be made
6:8 Moreover I M a decree regarding what you shall
6:11 Also I M a decree that if any one
6:12 I Darius M a decree; let it be done
7:13 And now I M a decree that any one
7:14 his seven counselors to M inquiries about Judah and
7:21 I, Artaxerxes the king, M a decree to all
10:3 Therefore let us M a covenant with our God
10:11 Now then M confession to the LORD the God
Neh 1:9 I have chosen, to M my name dwell there.'
2:4 "For what do you M request?" So I prayed
2:8 give me timber to M beams for the gates
2:20 God of heaven will M us prosper, and we
6:14 prophets who wanted to M me afraid.
6:19 Tobiah sent letters to M me afraid.
8:12 send portions and to M great rejoicing, because they
8:15 other leafy trees to M booths, as it is
9:8 before thee, and didst M with him the covenant
9:14 commandments, and thou didst M known to them thy
9:31 mercies thou didst not M an end of them
9:38 of all this we M a firm covenant and
10:33 the sin offerings to M atonement for Israel, and
Tob 4:7 the gift when you M it.
4:8 you have many possessions, M your gift from them
6:7 to any one, you M a smoke from these
6:16 fish so as to M a smoke.
7:11 nothing here until you M a binding agreement with
7:16 said to her, "Sister, M up the other room,
8:6 be alone; let us M a helper for him
13:4 M his greatness known there, and exalt him in
Jud 6:2 tell us not to M war against the people
7:1 the hill country and M war on the Israelites.
9:13 M my deceitful words to be their wound and
Esth 2:10 charged her not to M it known.
4:8 to the king to M supplication to him and
6:10 king said to Haman, M haste, take the robes
9:2 And no one could M a stand against them,
9:22 holiday; that they should M them days of feasting
13:2 and, in order to M my kingdom peaceable and
14:11 plan against themselves, and M an example of the
14:12 Remember, O Lord; M thyself known in this time
Job 6:22 Have I said, M me a gift?
6:24 I will be silent; M me understand how I
7:17 man, that thou dost M so much of him,
8:5 will seek God and M supplication to the Almighty,
11:19 down, and none will M you afraid; many will
13:23 M me know my transgression and my sin.
17:12 They M night into day; 'The light,' they say,
19:5 yourselves against me, and M my humiliation an
22:3 to him if you M your ways blameless?
22:27 You will M your prayer to him, and he
24:11 of the wicked they M oil; they tread the
27:15 buries, and their widows M no lamentation.
30:1 "But now they M sport of me, men who
31:15 me in the womb M him?
34:11 his ways he will M it befall him.
34:33 Will he then M requital to suit you, because
38:27 desolate land, and to M the ground put forth
39:20 Do you M him leap like the locust?
41:3 Will he M many supplications to you?
41:4 Will he M a covenant with you to take
41:28 The arrow cannot M him flee; for him slingstones
Ps 2:8 me, and I will M the nations your heritage,
5:8 because of my enemies; M thy way straight before
5:10 M them bear their guilt, O God; let them
18:39 the battle; thou didst M my assailants sink under
18:40 Thou didst M my enemies turn their backs to
18:43 the peoples; thou didst M me the head of
21:6 Yea, thou dost M him most blessed for ever;
21:6 for ever; thou dost M him glad with the
21:9 You will M them as a blazing oven when
22:7 mock at me, they M mouths at me, they
25:4 M me to know thy ways, O LORD; teach
27:6 I will sing and M melody to the LORD.
33:2 LORD with the lyre, M melody to him with
38:22 M haste to help me, O Lord, my salvation!
39:8 M me not the scorn of the fool!
40:13 O LORD, M haste to help me!
45:8 ivory palaces stringed instruments M you glad;
45:16 your sons; you will M them princes in all
46:4 a river whose streams M glad the city of
52:7 man who would not M God his refuge, but
57:7 I will sing and M melody!
59:4 mine, they run and M ready.
59:11 lest my people forget; M them totter by thy
66:1 M a joyful noise to God, all the earth;
66:15 of rams; I will M an offering of bulls
67:1 and bless us and M his face to shine
69:12 gate, and the drunkards M songs about me.
69:17 I am in distress, M haste to answer me.

M

69:23 they cannot see; and M their loins tremble
70:1 O LORD, M haste to help me!
71:12 me; O my God, M haste to help me!
73:18 slippery places; thou dost M them fall to ruin.
76:11 M your vows to the LORD your God, and
80:6 Thou dost M us the scorn of our neighbors;
83:5 accord; against thee they M a covenant--
83:11 M their nobles like Oreb and Zeeb, all their
83:13 O my God, M them like whirling dust, like
84:6 valley of Baca they M it a place of
85:13 go before him, and M his footsteps a way.
89:27 salvation.' And I will M him the first-born, the
90:15 M us glad as many days as thou hast
95:1 the LORD; let us M a joyful noise to
95:2 with thanksgiving; let us M a joyful noise to
97:7 put to shame, who M their boast in worthless
98:4 M a joyful noise to the LORD, all the
98:6 sound of the horn M a joyful noise before
100:1 M a joyful noise to the LORD, all the
104:15 of man, oil to M his face shine, and
105:1 call on his name, M known his deeds among
106:8 sake, that he might M known his mighty power.
106:26 them that he would M them fall in the
108:1 I will sing and M melody!
109:4 me, even as I M prayer for them.
110:1 right hand, till I M your enemies your footstool."
113:8 the ash heap, to M them sit with princes,
115:7 and they do not M a sound in their
115:8 Those who M them are like them; so are
119:27 M me understand the way of thy precepts, and
119:135 M thy face shine upon thy servant, and teach
119:165 thy law; nothing can M them stumble.
132:17 There I will M a horn to sprout for
135:18 them be those who M them!-- yea, every
139:8 If I M my bed in Sheol, thou art
140:3 They M their tongue sharp as a serpents, and
141:1 upon thee, O LORD; M haste to me!
142:1 with my voice I M supplication to the LORD,
143:7 [Selah] M haste to answer me, O LORD!
145:12 of thy power, to M known to the sons
147:7 the LORD with thanksgiving; M melody to our God
Prov 1:16 to evil, and they M haste to shed blood.
1:23 to you; I will M my words known to
3:6 him, and he will M straight your paths.
6:18 wicked plans, feet that M haste to run to
13:10 By insolence the heedless M strife, but with those
15:23 To M an apt answer is a joy to
20:30 cleanse away evil; strokes M clean the innermost
22:24 M no friendship with a man given to anger,
27:9 Oil and perfume M the heart glad, but the
27:11 wise, my son, and M my heart glad, that
30:26 not mighty, yet they M their homes in the
Eccl 2:1 "Come now, I will M a test of pleasure;
7:13 of God; who can M straight what he has
7:16 overmuch, and do not M yourself overwise; why
10:1 Dead flies M the perfumer's ointment give off an
10:4 place, for deference will M amends for great
Song 1:4 after you, let us M haste.
1:7 your flock, where you M it lie down at
1:11 We will M you ornaments of gold, studded with
8:14 M haste, my beloved, and be like a gazelle
Wis 1:13 because God did not M death, and he does
2:6 things that exist, and M use of the creation
2:19 gentle he is, and M trial of his forbearance.
5:1 him, and those who M light of his labors.
6:13 She hastens to M herself known to those who
6:22 beginning of creation, and M knowledge of her clear,
9:9 present when thou didst M the world, and who
12:12 for the destruction of nations which thou didst M
13:11 then with pleasing workmanship M a useful vessel
15:6 are those who either M or desire or worship
16:28 of the sun, to M it known that one
Sir 2:6 he will help you; M your ways straight, and
4:7 M yourself beloved in the congregation; bow your
6:4 who has it, and M him the laughingstock of
6:11 In prosperity he will M himself your equal, and
7:9 gifts, and when I M an offering to the
7:23 Discipline them, and M them obedient from their
9:13 if you approach him, M no misstep, lest he
10:25 Do not M a display of your wisdom when
16:14 He will M room for every act of mercy;
18:30 base desire, it will M you the laughingstock of
19:10 It will not M you burst!
19:16 A person may M a slip without intending it.
20:22 man may for shame M promises to a friend,
20:22 a friend, and needlessly M him an enemy.
22:17 pricks an eye will M tears fall, and one
24:8 And he said, M your dwelling in Jacob, and
24:30 I will again M instruction shine forth like the
24:30 dawn, and I will M it shine afar;
25:22 wife who does not M her husband happy.
27:14 end, and their quarrels M a man stop his
28:5 maintains wrath, who will M expiation for his sins?
28:25 your silver and gold, M balances and scales for
28:25 for your words, and M a door and a
29:8 circumstances, and do not M him wait for your
30:3 teaches his son will M his enemies envious, and
31:27 has been created to M men glad.
32:1 If they M you master of the feast, do
33:4 together your instruction, and M your answer.
33:28 he does not obey, M his fetters heavy.
36:6 and work further wonders; M thy hand and thy
39:5 made him, and will M supplication before the Most
39:5 mouth in prayer and M supplication for his sins.
40:21 flute and the harp M pleasant melody, but a
40:25 Gold and silver M the foot stand sure, but
42:7 number and weight, and M a record of all
42:11 headstrong daughter, lest she M you a laughingstock
43:6 in its season to M the times and to
45:9 as he walked, to M their ringing heard in
45:16 a memorial portion, to M atonement for the people.
47:9 before the altar, to M sweet melody with their
Is 1:15 you; even though you M many prayers, I will
1:16 Wash yourselves; M yourselves clean; remove the
3:4 And I will M boys their princes, and babes
3:7 mantle; you shall not M me leader of the
5:6 I will M it a waste; it shall not
5:19 who say: "Let him M haste, let him speed
6:10 but do not perceive.' M the heart of this
9:1 latter time he will M glorious the way of
10:2 and that they may M the fatherless their prey!
10:23 LORD of hosts, will M a full end, as
12:4 call upon his name; M known his deeds among
13:9 and fierce anger, to M the earth a desolation
13:12 I will M men more rare than fine gold,
13:13 Therefore I will M the heavens tremble, and the
13:20 there, no shepherds will M their flocks lie down
14:14 the clouds, I will M myself like the Most
14:23 And I will M it a possession of the
16:3 "Give counsel, grant justice; M your shade like night
17:2 down, and none will M them afraid.
17:11 alien god, though you M them grow on the
17:11 you plant them, and M them blossom in the
19:12 them tell you and M known what the LORD
19:21 And the LORD will M himself known to the
19:21 offering, and they will M vows to the LORD
23:16 M sweet melody, sing many songs, that you may
24:1 waste the earth and M it desolate, and he
25:6 LORD of hosts will M for all peoples a
26:7 is level; thou dost M smooth the path of
27:5 my protection, let them M peace with me, let
27:5 with me, let them M peace with me."
27:11 broken; women come and M a fire of them.
28:17 haste.' And I will M justice the line, and
29:16 maker, "He did not M me"; or the thing
29:21 who by a word M a man out to
30:1 not mine; and who M a league, but not
32:11 complacent ones; strip, and M yourselves bare, and
35:3 the weak hands, and M firm the feeble knees.
36:8 Come now, M a wager with my master the
36:15 Do not let Hezekiah M you rely on the
36:16 the king of Assyria: M your peace with me
37:7 land; and I will M him fall by the
37:26 pass, that you should M fortified cities crash into
38:8 promised: Behold, I will M the shadow cast by
38:16 me to health and M me live!
40:3 way of the LORD, M straight in the desert
41:15 Behold, I will M of you a threshing sledge,
41:15 them, and you shall M the hills like chaff;
41:18 the valleys; I will M the wilderness a pool
42:2 up his voice, or M it heard in the
42:21 magnify his law and M it glorious.
43:19 I will M a way in the wilderness and
44:9 All who M idols are nothing, and the things
44:19 eaten; and shall I M the residue of it
45:7 and create darkness, I M weal and create woe,
45:13 righteousness, and I will M straight all his ways;
45:14 They will M supplication to you, saying: 'God is
46:5 you liken me and M me equal, and compare
48:6 this time forth I M you hear new things,
49:11 And I will M all my mountains a way,
49:20 too narrow for me; M room for me to

49:26 I will M your oppressors eat their own flesh,
50:2 up the sea, I M the rivers a desert;
50:3 heavens with blackness, and M sackcloth their
51:3 waste places, and will M her wilderness like Eden,
51:10 great deep; that didst M the depths of the
53:11 righteous one, my servant, M many to be accounted
54:12 I will M your pinnacles of agate, your gates
55:3 live; and I will M with you an everlasting
56:7 my holy mountain, and M them joyful in my
58:4 this day will not M your voice to be
58:11 with good things, and M your bones strong; and
58:14 LORD, and I will M you ride upon the
59:6 men will not cover themselves with what they M
59:7 to evil, and they M haste to shed innocent
60:13 sanctuary; and I will M the place of my
60:15 passing through, I will M you majestic for ever,
60:17 I will M your overseers peace and your taskmasters
61:8 recompense, and I will M an everlasting covenant
63:12 waters before them to M for himself an everlasting
63:14 lead thy people, to M for thyself a glorious
63:17 LORD, why dost thou M us err from thy
64:2 to boil– to M thy name known to
66:22 earth which I will M shall remain before me,
Jer 1:18 And I, behold, I M you this day a
4:7 from his place to M your land a waste;
4:27 yet I will not M a full end.
5:10 vine-rows and destroy, but M not a full end;
5:18 LORD, I will not M a full end of
5:28 of the fatherless, to M it prosper, and they
6:8 from you; lest I M you a desolation, an
6:26 and roll in ashes; M mourning as for an
7:18 women knead dough, to M cakes for the queen
7:34 And I will M to cease from the cities
9:11 I will M Jerusalem a heap of ruins, a
9:11 jackals; and I will M the cities of Judah
9:18 to come; let them M haste and raise a
10:11 gods who did not M the heavens and the
10:22 the north country to M the cities of Judah
15:4 And I will M them a horror to all
15:14 I will M you serve your enemies in a
15:20 And I will M you to this people a
16:6 or cut himself or M himself bald for them.
16:9 Israel: Behold, I will M to cease from this
16:20 Can man M for himself gods?
16:21 "Therefore, behold, I will M them know, this once
16:21 this once I will M them know my power
17:4 you, and I will M you serve your enemies
18:18 said, "Come, let us M plots against Jeremiah, for
19:7 this place I will M void the plans of
19:8 And I will M this city a horror, a
19:9 And I will M them eat the flesh of
20:4 LORD: Behold, I will M you a terror to
21:2 wonderful deeds, and will M him withdraw from us."
22:6 yet surely I will M you a desert, an
23:27 heart, who think to M my people forget my
24:9 I will M them a horror to all the
25:9 utterly destroy them, and M them a horror, a
25:14 and great kings shall M slaves even of them;
25:15 wine of wrath, and M all the nations to
25:18 kings and princes, to M them a desolation and
26:6 heeded, then I will M this house like Shiloh,
26:6 Shiloh, and I will M this city a curse
27:2 LORD said to me: M yourself thongs and yoke-bars,
27:7 and great kings shall M him their slave.
28:6 so; may the LORD M the words which you
28:13 bars, but I will M in their place bars
29:17 pestilence, and I will M them like vile figs
29:18 and pestilence, and will M them a horror to
29:22 in Babylon: "The LORD M you like Zedekiah and
30:8 strangers shall no more M servants of them.
30:10 ease, and none shall M him afraid.
30:11 the LORD; I will M a full end of
30:11 you I will not M a full end.
30:16 on you I will M a prey.
30:19 voices of those who M merry.
30:19 be few; I will M them honored, and they
30:21 their midst; I will M him draw near, and
31:9 them back, I will M them walk by brooks
31:21 up waymarks for yourself, M yourself guideposts;
31:31 LORD, when I will M a new covenant with
31:33 covenant which I will M with the house of
32:37 place, and I will M them dwell in safety.
32:40 I will M with them an everlasting covenant, that
33:4 were torn down to M a defense against the
33:18 cereal offerings, and to M sacrifices for ever."
34:8 people in Jerusalem to M a proclamation of liberty
34:17 I will M you a horror to all the
34:18 before me, I will M like the calf which
34:22 I will M the cities of Judah a desolation
46:27 ease, and none shall M him afraid.
46:28 I will M a full end of all the
46:28 you I will not M a full end.
48:26 M him drunk, because he magnified himself against
49:15 For behold, I will M you small among the
49:16 Though you M your nest as high as the
49:19 sheepfold, I will suddenly M them run away from
50:3 against her, which shall M her land a desolation,
50:44 sheepfold, I will suddenly M them run away from
51:12 the walls of Babylon; M the watch strong; set
51:25 from the crags, and M you a burnt mountain.
51:29 against Babylon stand, to M the land of Babylon
51:36 up her sea and M her fountain dry;
51:39 them a feast and M them drunk, till they
51:57 I will M drunk her princes and her wise
Bar 1:14 are sending you, to M your confession in the
2:23 of Babylon, I will M to cease from the
2:35 I will M an everlasting covenant with them to
5:7 valleys filled up, to M level ground, so that
6:9 People take gold and M crowns for the heads
6:18 death, so the priests M their temples secure with
6:46 The men that M them will certainly not live
Ezek 3:26 people; and I will M your tongue cleave to
4:9 a single vessel, and M bread of them.
5:14 Moreover I will M you a desolation and an
6:14 hand against them, and M the land desolate and
7:20 it; therefore I will M it an unclean thing
7:23 and profane it, and M a desolation.
11:13 wilt thou M a full end of the remnant
13:13 Lord GOD: I will M a stormy wind break
13:18 upon all wrists, and M veils for the heads
14:8 that man, I will M him a sign and
15:3 taken from it to M anything?
15:8 And I will M the land desolate, because they
16:2 me: "Son of man, M known to Jerusalem her
16:41 many women; I will M you stop playing the
17:24 the high tree, and M high the low tree,
17:24 the green tree, and M the dry tree flourish.
20:13 in the wilderness, to M a full end of
20:17 not destroy them or M a full end of
20:37 I will M you pass under the rod, and
21:10 Or do we M mirth?
21:19 And M a signpost, make it at the head
21:19 And make a signpost, M it at the head
21:27 ruin, ruin I will M it; there shall not
22:12 interest and increase and M gain of your neighbors
23:46 host against them, and M them an object of
24:9 I also will M the pile great.
24:17 Sigh, but not aloud; M no mourning for the
25:4 encampments among you and M their dwellings in
25:5 I will M Rabbah a pasture for camels and
25:7 the peoples and will M you perish out of
25:13 beast; and I will M it desolate; from Teman
26:4 soil from her, and M her a bare rock.
26:12 They will M a spoil of your riches and
26:14 I will M you a bare rock; you shall
26:19 Lord GOD: When I M you a city laid
26:20 old, and I will M you to dwell in
27:5 cedar from Lebanon to M a mast for you.
27:31 wallow in ashes; they M themselves bald for you,
29:4 in your jaws, and M the fish of your
29:10 streams, and I will M the land of Egypt
29:12 And I will M the land of Egypt a
29:15 nations; and I will M them so small that
30:14 I will M Pathros a desolation, and will set
30:22 broken; and I will M the sword fall from
31:15 to Sheol I will M the deep mourn for
31:16 I will M the nations quake at the sound
32:7 cover the heavens, and M their stars dark; I
32:8 of heaven will I M dark over you, and
32:10 I will M many peoples appalled at you, and
32:14 Then I will M their waters clear, and cause
32:15 When I M the land of Egypt desolate and
33:2 from among them, and M him their watchman;
33:28 And I will M the land a desolation and
34:15 sheep, and I will M them lie down, says
34:25 "I will M with them a covenant of peace
34:26 And I will M them and the places round
34:28 securely, and none shall M them afraid.
35:3 you, and I will M you a desolation and
35:7 I will M Mount Seir a waste and a
35:9 I will M you a perpetual desolation, and your
35:11 them; and I will M myself known among you,

35:14 whole earth I will M you desolate.
36:29 summon the grain and M it abundant and lay
36:30 I will M the fruit of the tree and
37:19 stick of Judah, and M them one stick, that
37:22 land; and I will M them one nation in
37:26 I will M a covenant of peace with them;
38:23 and my holiness and M myself known in the
39:3 left hand, and will M your arrows drop out
39:7 holy name I will M known in the midst
39:9 will go forth and M fires of the weapons
39:9 spears, and they will M fires of them for
39:10 forests, for they will M their fires of the
39:14 seven months they will M their search.
39:26 land with none to M them afraid,
42:20 hundred cubits broad, to M a separation between the
43:11 its whole form; and M known to them all
43:20 cleanse the altar and M atonement for it.
43:26 Seven days shall they M atonement for the altar
45:13 offering which you shall M: one sixth of an
45:15 and peace offerings, to M atonement for them, says
45:17 and peace offerings, to M atonement for the house
45:20 ignorance; so you shall M atonement for the temple.
45:25 the feast, he shall M the same provision for
Dan 2:5 if you do not M known to me the
2:9 if you do not M the dream known to
2:25 a man who can M known to the king
2:26 "Are you able to M known to me the
3:36 thou didst promise to M their descendants as many
3:38 incense, no place to M an offering before thee
3:97 Therefore I M a decree: Any people, nation, or
4:6 me, that they might M known to me the
4:7 but they could not M known to me its
4:18 are not able to M known to me the
5:8 read the writing or M known to the king
5:15 read this writing and M known to me its
5:16 read the writing and M known to me its
5:17 to the king and M known to him the
6:26 I M a decree, that in all my royal
8:16 and it called, "Gabriel, M this man understand the
8:19 said, "Behold, I will M known to you what
8:25 his cunning he shall M deceit prosper under his
9:27 And he shall M a strong covenant with many
10:14 Persia and came to M you understand what is
11:6 some years they shall M an alliance, and the
11:6 of the north to M peace; but she shall
11:33 who are wise shall M many understand, though they
11:35 cleanse them and to M them white, until the
11:39 He shall M them rulers over many and shall
12:10 shall purify themselves, and M themselves white, and
Hos 2:3 strip her naked and M her as in the
2:3 she was born, and M her like a wilderness,
2:12 given me.' I will M them a forest, and
2:15 her her vineyards, and M the Valley of Achor
2:18 And I will M for you a covenant on
2:18 land; and I will M you lie down in
4:13 of the mountains, and M offerings upon the hills,
7:4 By their wickedness they M the king glad, and
10:4 empty oaths they M covenants; so judgment springs
11:8 How can I M you like Admah!
12:1 falsehood and violence; they M a bargain with
12:9 Egypt; I will again M you dwell in tents,
13:2 more and more, and M for themselves molten
Joel 2:17 people, O LORD, and M not thy heritage a
2:19 I will no more M you a reproach among
Amos 8:5 sale, that we may M the ephah small and
8:9 Lord GOD, "I will M the sun go down
8:10 every head; I will M it like the mourning
9:14 wine, and they shall M gardens and eat their
Obad 1:2 Behold, I will M you small among the nations,
Jon 4:10 labor, nor did you M it grow, which came
Mic 1:6 Therefore I will M Samaria a heap in the
1:8 and naked; I will M lamentation like the jackals,
1:16 M yourselves bald and cut off your hair, for
1:16 children of your delight; M yourselves as bald as
4:4 tree, and none shall M them afraid; for the
4:7 the lame I will M the remnant; and those
4:13 Zion, for I will M your horn iron and
6:16 counsels; that I may M you a desolation, and
Nah 1:8 overflowing flood he will M a full end of
1:9 He will M a full end; he will not
1:14 I will M your grave, for you are vile."
3:6 you with contempt, and M you a gazingstock.
Hab 1:3 Why dost thou M me see wrongs and look
1:10 and of rulers they M sport.
2:2 me: "Write the vision; M it plain upon tablets,
2:7 those awake who will M you tremble?
3:2 midst of the years M it known; in wrath
Zeph 1:18 sudden end he will M of all the inhabitants
2:13 Assyria; and he will M Nineveh a desolation, a
3:7 they were eager to M all their deeds corrupt."
3:13 down, and none shall M them afraid."
Hag 2:23 says the LORD, and M you like a signet
Zech 6:11 silver and gold, and M a crown, and set
8:16 that are true and M for peace,
9:6 Ashdod; and I will M an end of the
9:17 Grain shall M the young men flourish, and new
10:3 of Judah, and will M them like his proud
10:12 I will M them strong in the LORD and
12:2 I am about to M Jerusalem a cup of
12:3 that day I will M Jerusalem a heavy stone
12:6 that day I will M the clans of Judah
Mal 2:9 hosts, and so I M you despised and abased
1Mac 1:11 "Let us go and M a covenant with the
1:48 were to M themselves abominable by everything
2:15 city of Modein to M them offer sacrifice.
3:14 he said, "I will M a name for myself
3:14 I will M war on Judas and his companions,
5:42 man to encamp, but M them all enter the
5:57 said, "Let us also M a name for ourselves;
5:57 let us go and M war on the Gentiles
6:58 with these men, and M peace with them and
8:13 to help and to M kings, they make kings,
8:13 to make kings, they M kings, and those whom
8:29 these terms the Romans M a treaty with the
8:30 deletion that they may M shall be valid.
9:70 ambassadors to him to M peace with him and
10:4 us act first to M peace with him before
10:16 Come now, we will M him our friend and
10:54 your son-in-law, and will M gifts to you and
11:9 saying, "Come, let us M a covenant with each
11:37 therefore take care to M a copy of this,
11:50 "Grant us peace, and M the Jews stop fighting
11:57 the four districts and M you one of the
12:40 do so, but might M war on him, so
12:53 Now therefore let us M war on them and
13:37 we are ready to M a general peace with
13:45 voice, asking Simon to M peace with them;
13:50 cried to Simon to M peace with them, and
14:1 so that he could M war against Trypho.
14:12 there was none to M them afraid.
15:4 warships, and intend to M a landing in the
15:19 seek their harm or M war against them and
15:19 and their country, or M alliance with those who
15:39 its gates, and to M war on the people;
15:41 might go out and M raids along the highways
2Mac 1:26 preserve thy portion and M it holy.
2:25 wish to read, to M it easy for those
3:8 his journey, ostensibly to M a tour of inspection
3:18 houses in crowds to M a general supplication
4:17 which later events will M clear.
6:8 toward the Jews and M them partake of the
7:24 oaths that he would M him rich and enviable
7:28 that God did not M them out of things
7:37 afflictions and plagues to M you confess that he
8:10 Nicanor determined to M up for the king the
9:4 get there I will M Jerusalem a cemetery of
9:14 the ground and to M a cemetery, he was
9:15 to pick, he would M, all of them, equal
11:2 He intended to M the city a home for
11:36 so that we may M proposals appropriate for you.
11:37 Therefore M haste and send some men, so that
12:12 many ways, agreed to M peace with them; and
Mt 3:3 way of the Lord, M his paths straight."
4:19 me, and I will M you fishers of men."
5:25 M friends quickly with your accuser, while you are
5:36 head, for you cannot M one hair white or
8:2 you will, you can M me clean."
12:16 ordered them not to M him known.
12:33 "Either M the tree good, and its fruit good;
12:33 its fruit good; or M the tree bad, and
13:32 the air come and M nests in its branches."
17:4 you wish, I will M three booths here, one
21:13 of prayer'; but you M it a den of
23:5 by men; for they M their phylacteries broad and
23:14 sea and land to M a single proselyte, and
23:14 becomes a proselyte, you M him twice as much
26:62 up and said, "Have you no answer to M
27:65 guard of soldiers; go, M it as secure as
28:19 Go therefore and M disciples of all nations, baptizing
Mk 1:3 way of the Lord, M his paths straight—"
1:17 me and I will M you become fishers of
1:40 you will, you can M me clean."

3:12 ordered them not to M him known.
4:32 of the air can M nests in its shade."
5:39 them, "Why do you M a tumult and weep?
9:5 are here; let us M three booths, one for
12:40 and for a pretense M long prayers.
12:42 two copper coins, which M a penny.
14:60 and asked Jesus, "Have you no answer to M
15:4 again asked him, "Have you no answer to M
Lk 1:17 of the just, to M ready for the Lord
3:4 way of the Lord, M his paths straight.
5:12 you will, you can M me clean."
5:14 to the priest, and M an offering for your
5:34 to them, "Can you M wedding guests fast while
9:14 said to his disciples, M them sit down in
9:33 are here; let us M three booths, one for
9:52 of the Samaritans, to M ready for him;
11:40 who made the outside M the inside also?
12:47 will, but did not M ready or act according
12:58 accuser before the magistrate, M an effort to settle
14:18 all alike began to M excuses.
15:23 let us eat and M merry;
15:24 And they began to M merry.
15:29 kid, that I might M merry with my friends.
15:32 It was fitting to M merry and be glad,
16:9 And I tell you, M friends for yourselves by
19:5 said to him, "Zacchaeus, M haste and come down;
19:42 knew the things that M for peace!
20:43 right hand, till I M thy enemies a stool
20:47 and for a pretense M long prayers.
22:12 upper room furnished; there M ready."
Jn 1:23 crying in the wilderness, M straight the way of
2:16 away; you shall not M my Father's house a
6:10 Jesus said, M the people sit down." Now there
6:15 him by force to M him king, Jesus withdrew
8:32 and the truth will M you free."
10:33 you, being a man, M yourself God."
14:23 come to him and M our home with him.
17:26 name, and I will M it known, that the
Acts 2:28 of life; thou wilt M me full of gladness
2:35 right hand, till I M thy enemies a stool
4:24 "Sovereign Lord, who didst M the heaven and the
7:40 Egypt, saying to Aaron, M for us gods to
7:44 Moses directed him to M it, according to the
7:50 Did not my hand M all these things?'
9:34 heals you; rise and M your bed." And immediately
15:10 therefore why do you M trial of God by
19:33 his hand, wishing to M a defense to the
22:1 defense which I now M before you."
22:18 him saying to me, M haste and get quickly
24:9 this nation, I cheerfully M my defense.
24:18 before you and to M an accusation, if they
25:16 and had opportunity to M his defense concerning the
26:2 Agrippa, I am to M my defense today against
26:11 synagogues and tried to M them blaspheme; and in
26:28 time you think to M me a Christian!"
27:43 themselves overboard first and M for the land,
Rom 4:11 The purpose was to M him the father of
6:12 your mortal bodies, to M you obey their passions.
9:21 over the clay, to M out of the same
9:22 his wrath and to M known his power, has
9:23 destruction, in order to M known the riches of
9:33 a stone that will M men stumble, a rock
9:33 a rock that will M them fall; and he
10:19 Moses says, "I will M you jealous of those
10:19 foolish nation I will M you angry."
11:11 Gentiles, so as to M Israel jealous.
11:14 ministry in order to M my fellow Jews jealous,
13:14 Lord Jesus Christ, and M no provision for the
14:4 Master is able to M him stand.
14:20 for any one to M others fall by what
15:26 have been pleased to M some contribution for the
1Cor 4:14 not write this to M you ashamed, but to
6:15 members of Christ and M them members of a
9:18 my preaching I may M the gospel free of
12:15 that would not M it any less a part
12:16 that would not M it any less a part
14:1 M love your aim, and earnestly desire the spiritual
2Cor 1:9 but that was to M us rely not on
1:17 Do I M my plans like a worldly man,
2:1 my mind not to M you another painful visit.
2:2 who is there to M me glad but the
5:9 home or away, we M it our aim to
7:1 body and spirit, and M holiness perfect in the
Gal 3:17 God, so as to M the promise void.
3:21 been given which could M alive, then righteousness
4:17 They M much of you, but for no good
4:17 out, that you may M much of them.
6:12 those who want to M a good showing in
Eph 3:9 of Christ, and to M all men see what
Phil 3:12 I press on to M it my own, because
Col 1:25 me for you, to M the word of God
1:27 them God chose to M known how great among
4:4 prison, that I may M it clear, as I
1Thes 3:12 and may the Lord M you increase and abound
2Thes 1:11 that our God may M you worthy of his
2:11 a strong delusion, to M them believe what is
1Tim 1:7 things about which they M assertions.
5:4 their own family and M some return to their
2Tim 3:6 them are those who M their way into households
Heb 1:13 right hand, till I M thy enemies a stool
2:7 Thou didst M him for a little while lower
2:10 sons to glory, should M the pioneer of their
2:17 service of God, to M expiation for the sins
7:25 he always lives to M intercession for them.
8:5 saying, "See that you M everything according to the
8:10 covenant that I will M with the house of
10:1 offered year after year, M perfect those who draw
10:16 covenant that I will M with them after those
11:14 people who speak thus M it clear that they
12:13 your weak knees, and M straight paths for your
Jas 3:2 For we all M many mistakes, and if any
3:18 peace by those who M peace.
1Pet 2:8 "A stone that will M men stumble, a rock
2:8 a rock that will M them fall"; for they
3:15 Always be prepared to M a defense to any
2Pet 1:5 For this very reason M every effort to supplement
1Jn 1:10 have not sinned, we M him a liar, and
Rev 3:9 Behold, I will M those of the synagogue of
3:9 lie--behold, I will M them come and bow
3:12 who conquers, I will M him a pillar in
11:7 the bottomless pit will M war upon them and
11:10 rejoice over them and M merry and exchange
12:17 and went off to M war on the rest
13:7 it was allowed to M war on the saints
13:14 on earth, bidding them M an image for the
16:19 remembered great Babylon, to M her drain the cup
17:14 the beast; they will M war on the Lamb,
17:16 the harlot; they will M her desolate and naked,
19:19 their armies gathered to M war against him who
21:5 throne said, "Behold, I M all things new." Also

MAKED (2)

1Mac 5:26 in Alema and Chaspho, M and Carnaim" –
5:36 on and took Chaspho, M, and Bosor, and the

MAKER (26)

Gen 14:19 by God Most High, M of heaven and earth;
14:22 LORD God Most High, M of heaven and earth,
Job 4:17 Can a man be pure before his M
32:22 flatter, else would my M soon put an end
35:10 'Where is God my M, who gives songs in
36:3 from afar, and ascribe righteousness to my M
Ps 95:6 down, let us kneel before the LORD, our M
149:2 be glad in his M, let the sons of
Prov 14:31 poor man insults his M, but he who is
17:5 the poor insults his M; he who is glad
22:2 the LORD is the M of them all.
Sir 7:30 your might love your M, and do not forsake
10:12 from the Lord; his heart has forsaken his M
38:15 who sins before his M, may he fall into
39:28 their strength and calm the anger of their M
47:8 with all his heart, and he loved his M
Is 17:7 men will regard their M, and their eyes will
29:16 should say of its M, "He did not make
45:9 who strives with his M, an earthen vessel with
45:11 of Israel, and his M: "Will you question me
51:13 forgotten the LORD, your M, who stretched out the
54:5 For your M is your husband, the LORD of
Ezek 20:49 'Is he not a M of allegories?'"
Hos 8:14 Israel has forgotten his M, and built palaces; and
Hab 2:18 an idol when its M has shaped it, a
Heb 11:10 foundations, whose builder and M is God.

MAKERS

Is 45:16 shame and confounded, the M of idols go in

MAKES (161)

Ex 4:11 Who M him dumb, or deaf, or seeing, or
11:7 know that the LORD M a distinction between the
25:2 every man whose heart M him willing you shall
30:38 Whoever M any like it to use as perfume
Lev 7:7 them; the priest who M atonement with it shall

14:48 the priest comes and M an examination, and the
17:11 is the blood that M atonement, by reason of
27:2 Israel, When a man M a special vow of
27:10 good; and if he M any exchange of beast
Num 5:21 people, when the LORD M your thigh fall away
6:2 man or a woman M a special vow, the
30:12 But if her husband M them null and void
30:15 But if he M them null and void after
Deut 8:20 nations that the LORD M to perish before you,
20:12 But if it M no peace with you, but
20:12 peace with you, but M war against you, then
20:20 against the city that M war with you, until
27:15 be the man who M a graven or molten
29:12 the LORD your God M with you this day;
32:43 on his adversaries, and M expiation for the land
33:12 the day long, and M his dwelling between his
1Sam 2:7 The LORD M poor and makes rich; he brings
2:7 LORD makes poor and M rich; he brings low,
22:8 me when my son M a league with the
2Sam 23:4 morning, like rain that M grass to sprout from
Job 12:17 stripped, and judges he M fools.
12:23 He M nations great, and he destroys them: he
12:24 of the earth, and M them wander in a
12:25 without light; and he M them stagger like a
25:2 are with God; he M peace in his high
27:18 spider's web, like a booth which a watchman M
31:14 When he M inquiry, what shall I answer him?
32:8 of the Almighty, that M him understand.
35:11 of the earth, and M us wiser than the
39:27 eagle mounts up and M his nest on high?
39:28 rock he dwells and M his home in the
40:17 He M his tail stiff like a cedar; the
41:31 He M the deep boil like a pot; he
41:31 like a pot; he M the sea like a
Ps 7:15 He M a pit, digging it out, and falls
12:3 lips, the tongue that M great boasts,
23:2 shall not want; he M me lie down in
25:14 fear him, and he M known to them his
29:6 He M Lebanon to skip like a calf, and
29:9 voice of the LORD M the oaks to whirl,
34:2 My soul M its boast in the LORD; let
40:4 is the man who M the LORD his trust,
46:9 He M wars cease to the end of the
107:40 contempt upon princes and M them wander in
107:41 out of affliction, and M their families like flocks.
119:98 Thy commandment M me wiser than my enemies,
135:7 He it is who M the clouds rise at
135:7 of the earth, who M lightnings for the rain
147:8 for the earth, he M grass grow upon the
147:14 He M peace in your borders; he fills you
147:18 and melts them; he M his wind blow, and
Prov 6:34 For jealousy M a man furious, and he will
10:1 A wise son M a glad father, but a
10:4 hand of the diligent M rich.
10:10 he who boldly reproves M peace.
10:22 blessing of the LORD M rich, and he adds
12:25 but a good word M him glad.
13:12 Hope deferred M the heart sick, but a desire
14:30 the flesh, but passion M the bones rot.
15:13 A glad heart M a cheerful countenance, but by
15:20 A wise son M a glad father, but a
15:27 greedy for unjust gain M trouble for his household,
16:7 please the LORD, he M even his enemies to
16:23 mind of the wise M his speech judicious, and
17:19 loves strife; he who M his door high seeks
18:16 A man's gift M room for him and brings
19:2 knowledge, and he who M haste with his feet
19:11 Good sense M a man slow to anger, and
20:11 Even a child M himself known by his acts,
29:3 He who loves wisdom M his father glad, but
31:17 loins with strength and M her arms strong.
31:22 She M herself coverings; her clothing is fine linen
31:24 She M linen garments and sells them; she delivers
Eccl 7:7 Surely oppression M the wise man foolish, and a
8:1 A man's wisdom M his face shine, and the
11:5 work of God who M everything.
Wis 7:27 into holy souls and M them friends of God,
13:14 of a man, or M it like some worthless
13:15 with paint; then he M for it a niche
15:13 he sins when he M from earthy matter fragile
15:17 mortal, and what he M with lawless hands is
Sir 11:25 misery of an hour M one forget luxury, and
18:17 of a grudging man M the eyes dim.
20:12 The wise man M himself beloved through his words,
22:17 who pricks the heart M it show feeling.
24:24 It M them full of understanding, like the Euphrates,
24:25 It M instruction shine forth like light, like the
26:6 rival, and a tongue-lashing M it known to all.
27:14 men given to swearing M one's hair stand on
35:1 who keeps the law M many offerings; he who
35:19 of his people and M them rejoice in his
38:8 away pain; the pharmacist M of them a compound.
38:30 with his arm and M it pliable with his
Is 27:9 his sin: when he M all the stones of
38:19 this day; the father M known to the children
40:23 princes to nought, and M the rulers of the
41:2 kings under foot; he M them like dust with
43:16 says the LORD, who M a way in the
44:15 bakes bread; also he M a god and worships
44:15 and worships it, he M it a graven image
44:17 rest of it he M into a god, his
44:25 omens of liars, and M fools of diviners; who
44:25 wise men back, and M their knowledge foolish;
46:6 a goldsmith, and he M it into a god;
53:10 to grief; when he M himself an offering for
59:15 who departs from evil M himself a prey.
62:7 he establishes Jerusalem and M it a praise in
66:3 swine's blood; he who M a memorial offering of
Jer 10:13 the heavens, and he M the mist rise from
10:13 He M lightnings for the rain, and he brings
13:16 it into gloom and M it deep darkness.
17:5 trusts in man and M flesh his arm, whose
22:13 rooms by injustice; who M his neighbor serve him
46:22 "She M a sound like a serpent gliding away;
51:16 the heavens, and he M the mist rise from
51:16 He M lightnings for the rain, and he brings
Bar 6:35 or money; if one M a vow to them
Ezek 22:3 may come, and that M idols to defile herself!
46:16 GOD: If the prince M a gift to any
46:17 But if he M a gift out of his
Dan 6:7 an interdict, that whoever M petition to any god
6:12 that any man who M petition to any god
6:13 you have signed, but M his petition three times
8:13 offering, the transgression that M desolate, and the
9:27 shall come one who M desolate, until the decreed
11:31 up the abomination that M desolate.
12:11 and the abomination that M desolate is set up,
Amos 4:13 is his thought; who M the morning darkness, and
5:9 is his name, who M destruction flash forth against
Nah 1:4 rebukes the sea and M it dry, he dries
Hab 2:15 Woe to him who M his neighbors drink of
2:15 of his wrath, and M them drunk, to gaze
2:18 own creation when he M dumb idols!
3:19 is my strength; he M my feet like hinds'
3:19 like hinds' feet, he M me tread upon my
Zech 10:1 from the LORD who M the storm clouds, who
1Mac 8:26 to the enemy who M war they shall not
10:4 with him before he M peace with Alexander against
Mt 5:32 the ground of unchastity, M her an adulteress; and
5:45 in heaven; for he M his sun rise on
23:18 or the altar that M the gift sacred?
Mk 7:36 things well; he even M the deaf hear and
Jn 8:36 So if the Son M you free, you will
19:12 friend; every one who M himself a king sets
Rom 14:19 us then pursue what M for peace and for
14:21 or do anything that M your brother stumble.
2Cor 11:20 it if a man M slaves of you, or
Gal 2:6 something (what they were M no difference to me;
Eph 4:16 is working properly, M bodily growth and upbuilds
Col 2:8 it that no one M a prey of you
Heb 1:7 angels he says, "Who M his angels winds, and
7:22 This M Jesus the surety of a better covenant.
Jas 3:2 and if any one M no mistakes in what
4:4 friend of the world M himself an enemy of
Rev 13:12 in its presence, and M the earth and its
19:11 righteousness he judges and M war.

MAKEST (9)

Job 13:26 things against me, and M me inherit the iniquities
30:22 on the wind, thou M me ride on it,
Ps 4:8 thou alone, O LORD, M me dwell in safety.
65:8 at thy signs; thou M the outgoings of the
104:3 on the waters, who M the clouds thy chariot,
104:4 of the wind, who M the winds thy messengers,
104:10 Thou M springs gush forth in the valleys; they
104:20 Thou M darkness, and it is night, when all
Hab 1:14 For thou M men like the fish of the

MAKHELOTH (2)

Num 33:25 they set out from Haradah, and encamped at M
33:26 they set out from M, and encamped at Tahath.

MAKING (89)

Gen 34:30 trouble on me by M me odious to the
Ex 5:14 all your task of M bricks today, as hitherto?"
Lev 19:29 profane your daughter by M her a harlot, lest
Deut 4:16 you act corruptly by M a graven image for
4:25 you act corruptly by M a graven image in
20:19 for a long time, M war against it in
Josh 22:33 spoke no more of M war against them, to
Judg 11:27 do me wrong by M war on me; the
19:22 As they were M their hearts merry, behold, the
1Sam 23:26 mountain; and David was M haste to get away
2Sam 3:6 of David, Abner was M himself strong in the
6:5 house of Israel were M merry before the LORD
7:23 to be his people, M himself a name, and
8:2 them with a line, M them lie down on
1Kgs 7:14 understanding, and skill, for M any work in bronze.
16:19 sin which he committed, M Israel to sin.
2Kgs 12:12 and quarried stone for M repairs on the house
1Chr 9:31 was in charge of M the flat cakes.
13:8 and all Israel were M merry before God with
15:29 King David dancing and M merry; and she despised
17:19 all this greatness, in M known all these great
17:21 to be his people, M for thyself a name
2Chr 25:14 gods, and worshiped them, M offerings to them.
Jud 5:11 and set them to M bricks, and humbled them
5:23 strength or power for M war.
7:25 great injury in not M peace with the Assyrians.
Esth 9:18 on the fifteenth day, M that a day of
Ps 7:13 his deadly weapons, M his arrows fiery shafts.
19:7 the LORD is sure, M wise the simple;
40:2 feet upon a rock, M my steps secure.
113:9 barren woman a home, M her the joyous mother
149:3 his name with dancing, M melody to him with
Prov 2:2 my commandments with you, M your ear attentive to
20:25 to reflect only after M his vows.
Eccl 12:12 Of M many books there is no end, and
Wis 14:12 For the idea of M idols was the beginning
15:7 those for contrary uses, M all in like manner;
Sir 1:16 the crown of wisdom, M peace and perfect health
18:22 Before M a vow, prepare yourself; and do not
31:31 not afflict him by M demands of him.
38:27 each is diligent in M a great variety; he
41:22 do not upbraid after M a gift;
43:2 sun, when it appears, M proclamation as it goes
Is 45:9 to him who fashions it, 'What are you M
55:10 but water the earth, M it bring forth and
57:4 Of whom are you M sport?
Jer 5:14 word, behold, I am M my words in your
18:4 the vessel he was M of clay was spoiled
18:16 bypaths, not the highway, M their land a horror,
19:12 and to its inhabitants, M this city like Topheth.
20:15 M him very glad.
21:2 king of Babylon is M war against us; perhaps
25:12 iniquity, says the LORD, M the land an everlasting
51:7 in the LORD's hand, M all the earth drunken;
Ezek 16:31 of every street, and M your lofty place in
20:5 the house of Jacob, M myself known to them
20:26 their very gifts in M them offer by fire
24:6 piece after piece, without M any choice.
31:4 made it grow tall, M its rivers flow round
Dan 2:38 birds of the air, M you rule over them
6:11 and found Daniel M petition and supplication before
Mic 6:13 begun to smite you, M you desolate because of
1Mac 11:25 of his nation kept M complaints against him,
15:25 forces against it and M engines of war; and
2Mac 3:33 the high priest was M the offering of atonement,
6:23 But M a high resolve, worthy of his years
9:8 carried in a litter, M the power of God
10:16 his men, after M solemn supplication and beseeching
Mt 9:23 players, and the crowd M a tumult,
Mk 6:48 saw that they were M headway painfully, for the
7:13 father or mother, thus M void the word of
Jn 2:15 And M a whip of cords, he drove them
4:1 heard that Jesus was M and baptizing more disciples
5:17 called God his Father, M himself equal with God.
Acts 11:12 to go with them, M no distinction.
13:10 will you not stop M crooked the straight paths
Rom 7:23 of my mind and M me captive to the
15:20 gospel of Christ, thus M it my ambition to
1Cor 9:18 free of charge, not M full use of my
2Cor 5:20 ambassadors for Christ, God M his appeal through
6:10 rejoicing; as poor, yet M many rich; as having
Eph 2:15 of the two, so M peace,
5:16 men but as wise, M the most of the
5:19 spiritual songs, singing and M melody to the Lord
6:18 alert with all perseverance, M supplication for all the
Phil 1:4 mine for you all M my prayer with joy,
Col 1:20 earth or in heaven, M peace by the blood
4:5 yourselves wisely toward outsiders, M the most of
Rev 13:13 works great signs, even M fire come down from

MAKKEDAH (9)

Josh 10:10 and smote them as far as Azekah and M
10:16 fled, and hid themselves in the cave at M
10:17 have been found, hidden in the cave at M
10:21 in the camp at M; not a man moved
10:28 And Joshua took M on that day, and smote
10:28 to the king of M as he had done
10:29 Joshua passed on from M, and all Israel with
12:16 one; the king of M, one; the king of
15:41 Beth-dagon, Naamah, and M: sixteen cities with

MALACHI

Mal 1:1 the word of the LORD to Israel by M

MALCAM

1Chr 8:9 wife: Jobab, Zibi-a, Mesha, M,

MALCHI-EL (3)

Gen 46:17 of Beriah: Heber and M
Num 26:45 of the Heberites; of M, the family of the
1Chr 7:31 of Beriah: Heber and M, who was the father

MALCHI-ELITES

Num 26:45 the Heberites; of Malchi-el, the family of the M

MALCHIAH (3)

Jer 21:1 Pashhur the son of M and Zephaniah the priest,
38:1 Pashhur the son of M heard the words that
38:6 into the cistern of M, the king's son, which

MALCHIJAH (12)

1Chr 6:40 of Ba-aseiah, son of M,
9:12 of Pashhur, son of M, and Maasai the son
24:9 Se-orim, the fifth to M, the sixth to Mijamin,
Ezra 10:25 of Parosh: Ramiah, Izziah, M, Mijamin, Eleazar,
10:31 of Harim: Eliezer, Isshijah, M, Shemaiah, Shime-on,
Neh 3:11 M the son of Harim and Hasshub the son
3:14 M the son of Rechab, ruler of the district
3:31 After him M, one of the goldsmiths, repaired as
8:4 hand; and Pedaiah, Mishael, M, Hashum,
10:3 Azariah, Jeremiah, Pashhur, Amariah, M,
11:12 of Pashhur, son of M,
12:42 Shemaiah, Eleazar, Uzzi, Jehohanan, M, Elam, and

MALCHIRAM

1Chr 3:18 captive: Shealtiel his son, M, Pedaiah, Shenazzar,

MALCHISHUA (5)

1Sam 14:49 were Jonathan, Ishvi, and M; and the names of
31:2 Jonathan and Abinadab and M, the sons of Saul.
1Chr 8:33 Saul, Saul of Jonathan, M, Abinadab, and Eshbaal;
9:39 Saul, Saul of Jonathan, M, Abinadab, and Eshbaal;
10:2 Jonathan and Abinadab and M, the sons of Saul.

MALCHUS

Jn 18:10 The slave's name was M

MALCONTENTS

Jude 1:16 are grumblers, M, following their own passions-

MALE (188)

Gen 1:27 God he created him; M and female he created
5:2 M and female he created them, and he blessed
6:19 you; they shall be M and female.
7:2 all clean animals, the M and his mate; and
7:2 are not clean, the M and his mate;
7:3 of the air also, M and female, to keep
7:9 ground, two and two, M and female, went into
7:16 And they that entered, M and female of all
17:10 descendants after you: Every M among you shall be
17:12 shall be circumcised; every M throughout you,
17:14 Any uncircumcised M who is not circumcised in the
17:23 with his money, every M among the men of
20:14 sheep and oxen, and M and female slaves, and
34:15 we are and every M of you be circumcised.
34:22 one people: that every M among us be circumcised
34:24 son Shechem; and every M was circumcised, all who
Ex 1:16 them, but let the M children live.
1:17 this, and let the M children live?"
12:5 be without blemish, a M a year old; you
21:7 go out as the M slaves do.

21:20 man strikes his slave, M or female, with a
21:26 eye of his slave, M or female, and destroys
21:27 tooth of his slave, M or female, he shall
21:32 ox gores a slave, M or female, the owner
34:19 is mine, all your M cattle, the firstlings of
Lev 1:3 he shall offer a M without blemish; he shall
1:10 he shall offer a M without blemish;
3:1 animal from the herd, M or female, he shall
3:6 animal from the flock, M or female, he shall
4:23 offering a goat, a M without blemish,
6:18 Every M among the children of Aaron may eat
6:29 Every M among the priests may eat of it;
7:6 Every M among the priests may eat of it;
9:3 of Israel, 'Take a M goat for a sin
12:2 conceives, and bears a M child, then she shall
12:7 bears a child, either M or female.
14:10 he shall take two M lambs without blemish, and
14:12 take one of the M lambs, and offer it
14:21 he shall take one M lamb for a guilt
15:33 is, for any one, M or female, who has
16:5 people of Israel two M goats for a sin
18:22 not lie with a M as with a woman;
20:13 man lies with a M as with a woman,
22:19 you shall offer a M without blemish, of the
23:12 you shall offer a M lamb a year old
23:19 you shall offer one M goat for a sin
23:19 sin offering, and two M lambs a year old
25:6 yourself and for your M and female slaves and
25:44 As for your M and female slaves whom you
25:44 have: you may buy M and female slaves from
27:3 your valuation of a M from twenty years old
27:5 shall be for a M twenty shekels, and for
27:6 shall be for a M five shekels of silver,
27:7 your valuation for a M shall be fifteen shekels,
Num 1:2 number of names, every M, head by head;
1:20 head by head, every M from twenty years old
1:22 head by head, every M from twenty years old
3:15 and by families; every M from a month old
3:46 the number of the M Levites,
5:3 shall put out both M and female, putting them
6:12 separation, and bring a M lamb a year old
6:14 to the LORD, one M lamb a year old
7:15 bull, one ram, one M lamb a year old,
7:16 a burnt offering; one M goat for a sin
7:17 oxen, five rams, five M goats, and five male
7:17 male goats, and five M lambs a year old.
7:21 bull, one ram, one M lamb a year old,
7:22 a burnt offering; one M goat for a sin
7:23 oxen, five rams, five M goats, and five male
7:23 male goats, and five M lambs a year old.
7:27 bull, one ram, one M lamb a year old,
7:28 a burnt offering; one M goat for a sin
7:29 oxen, five rams, five M goats, and five male
7:29 male goats, and five M lambs a year old.
7:33 bull, one ram, one M lamb a year old,
7:34 a burnt offering; one M goat for a sin
7:35 oxen, five rams, five M goats, and five male
7:35 male goats, and five M lambs a year old.
7:39 bull, one ram, one M lamb a year old,
7:40 a burnt offering; one M goat for a sin
7:41 oxen, five rams, five M goats, and five male
7:41 male goats, and five M lambs a year old.
7:45 bull, one ram, one M lamb a year old,
7:46 a burnt offering; one M goat for a sin
7:47 oxen, five rams, five M goats, and five male
7:47 male goats, and five M lambs a year old.
7:51 bull, one ram, one M lamb a year old,
7:52 a burnt offering; one M goat for a sin
7:53 oxen, five rams, five M goats, and five male
7:53 male goats, and five M lambs a year old.
7:57 bull, one ram, one M lamb a year old,
7:58 a burnt offering; one M goat for a sin
7:59 oxen, five rams, five M goats, and five male
7:59 male goats, and five M lambs a year old.
7:63 bull, one ram, one M lamb a year old,
7:64 a burnt offering; one M goat for a sin
7:65 oxen, five rams, five M goats, and five male
7:65 male goats, and five M lambs a year old.
7:69 bull, one ram, one M lamb a year old,
7:70 a burnt offering; one M goat for a sin
7:71 oxen, five rams, five M goats, and five male
7:71 male goats, and five M lambs a year old.
7:75 bull, one ram, one M lamb a year old,
7:76 a burnt offering; one M goat for a sin
7:77 oxen, five rams, five M goats, and five male
7:77 male goats, and five M lambs a year old.
7:81 bull, one ram, one M lamb a year old,
7:82 a burnt offering; one M goat for a sin
7:83 oxen, five rams, five M goats, and five male
7:83 male goats, and five M lambs a year old.
7:87 bulls, twelve rams, twelve M lambs a year old,
7:87 cereal offering; and twelve M goats for a sin
7:88 the rams sixty, the M goats sixty, the male
7:88 male goats sixty, the M lambs a year old
15:11 for each of the M lambs or the kids.
15:24 the ordinance, and one M goat for a sin
18:10 eat of it; every M may eat of it;
26:62 were twenty-three thousand, every M from a month
28:3 to the LORD: two M lambs a year old
28:9 the sabbath day two M lambs a year old
28:11 bulls, one ram, seven M lambs a year old
28:15 Also one M goat for a sin offering to
28:19 one ram, and seven M lambs a year old;
28:22 seven lambs; also one M goat for a sin
28:27 bulls, one ram, seven M lambs a year old;
28:30 seven lambs; with one M goat, to make atonement
29:2 bull, one ram, seven M lambs a year old
29:5 seven lambs; with one M goat for a sin
29:8 bull, one ram, seven M lambs a year old;
29:11 seven lambs: also one M goat for a sin
29:13 bulls, two rams, fourteen M lambs a year old;
29:16 fourteen lambs; also one M goat for a sin
29:17 bulls, two rams, fourteen M lambs a year old
29:19 the ordinance; also one M goat for a sin
29:20 bulls, two rams, fourteen M lambs a year old
29:22 the ordinance; also one M goat for a sin
29:23 bulls, two rams, fourteen M lambs a year old
29:25 the ordinance; also one M goat for a sin
29:26 bulls, two rams, fourteen M lambs a year old
29:28 the ordinance; also one M goat for a sin
29:29 bulls, two rams, fourteen M lambs a year old
29:31 the ordinance; also one M goat for a sin
29:32 bulls, two rams, fourteen M lambs a year old
29:34 the ordinance; also one M goat for a sin
29:36 bull, one ram, seven M lambs a year old
29:38 the ordinance; also one M goat for a sin
31:7 as the LORD commanded Moses, and slew every M
31:17 Now therefore, kill every M among the little ones,
Deut 4:16 figure, the likeness of M or female,
7:14 there shall not be M or female barren among
23:1 are crushed or whose M member is cut off
28:68 to your enemies as M and female slaves, but
Josh 17:2 these were the M descendants of Manasseh the
Judg 21:11 you shall do; every M and every woman that
21:11 has lain with a M you shall utterly destroy."
1Sam 25:22 so much as one M of all who belong
25:34 been left to Nabal so much as one M
1Kgs 11:15 slain, he slew every M in Edom
11:16 had cut off every M in Edom);
14:10 off from Jeroboam every M, both bond and free
14:24 and there were also M cult prostitutes in the
15:12 He put away the M cult prostitutes out of
16:11 leave him a single M of his kinsmen or
21:21 off from Ahab every M, bond or free, in
22:46 the remnant of the M cult prostitutes who remained
2Kgs 9:8 off from Ahab every M, bond or free, in
23:7 the houses of the M cult prostitutes which were
2Chr 28:10 of Judah and Jerusalem, M and female, as your
31:19 distribute portions to every M among the priests and
Ezra 2:65 they had two hundred M and female singers.
Neh 7:67 hundred and forty-five singers, M and female.
Eccl 2:7 I bought M and female slaves, and had slaves
Is 14:2 the LORD's land as M and female slaves; they
Jer 34:9 free his Hebrew slaves, M and female, so that
34:10 set free his slave, M or female, so that
34:11 and took back the M and female slaves they
34:16 you took back his M and female slaves, whom
Mal 1:14 cheat who has a M in his flock, and
1Mac 5:28 city, and killed every M by the edge of
5:35 and he killed every M in it, plundered it,
5:51 He destroyed every M by the edge of the
Mt 2:16 and killed all the M children in Bethlehem and
19:4 the beginning made them M and female,
Mk 10:6 creation, 'God made them M and female.'
Lk 2:23 of the Lord, "Every M that opens the womb
Gal 3:28 free, there is neither M nor female; for you
Rev 12:5 she brought forth a M child, one who is
12:13 who had borne the M child.

MALES (17)

Gen 34:25 upon the city unawares, and killed all the M
Ex 12:48 LORD, let all his M be circumcised, then he

M

13:12 your cattle that are M shall be the LORDs.
13:15 the LORD all the M that first open the
23:17 year shall all your M appear before the Lord
34:23 year shall all your M appear before the LORD
Num 3:22 number of all the M from a month old
3:28 number of all the M, from a month old
3:34 number of all the M from a month old
3:39 by families, all the M from a month old
3:40 "Number all the first-born M of the people of
3:43 And all the first-born M, according to the number
Deut 15:19 "All the firstling M that are born of your
16:16 a year all your M shall appear before the
20:13 shall put all its M to the sword,
Josh 5:4 circumcised them: all the M of the people who
2Chr 31:16 those enrolled by genealogy, M from three years old

MALICE (13)
Ps 41:5 say of me in M: "When will he die,
73:8 scoff and speak with M; loftily they threaten
Ezek 25:6 rejoiced with all the M within you against the
25:15 and took vengeance with M of heart to destroy
2Mac 4:4 Phoenicia, was intensifying the M of Simon.
5:23 In his M toward the Jewish citizens,
Mt 22:18 Jesus, aware of their M, said, "Why put me
Rom 1:29 all manner of wickedness, evil, covetousness, M
1Cor 5:8 leaven, the leaven of M and evil, but with
Eph 4:31 from you, with all M,
Col 3:8 all away: anger, wrath, M, slander, and foul talk
Tit 3:3 passing our days in M and envy, hated by
1Pet 2:1 So put away all M and all guile and

MALICIOUS (4)
Ex 23:1 man, to be a M witness.
Deut 19:16 If a M witness rises against any man to
Jud 4:12 and desecrated to the M joy of the Gentiles.
Ps 35:11 M witnesses rise up; they ask me of things

MALICIOUSLY (2)
Ps 139:20 from me, men who M defy thee, who lift
Dan 3:8 Chaldeans came forward and M accused the Jews.

MALIGN
Mt 10:25 much more will they M those of his household.

MALIGNANT (3)
Lev 13:51 the disease is a M leprosy; it is unclean.
13:52 for it is a M leprosy; it shall be
14:44 house, it is a M leprosy in the house;

MALIGNITY
Rom 1:29 envy, murder, strife, deceit, M, they are gossips,

MALLET
Judg 5:26 hand to the workmen's M; she struck Sisera a

MALLOTHI (2)
1Chr 25:4 and Romamti-ezer, Joshbekashah, M, Hothir,
25:26 to the nineteenth, to M, his sons and his

MALLOW (2)
Job 24:24 and fade like the M; they are cut off
30:4 desolate ground; they pick M and the leaves of

MALLUCH (6)
1Chr 6:44 of Abdi, son of M,
Ezra 10:29 of Bani were Meshullum, M, Adaiah, Jashub, Sheal,
10:32 Shemaiah, Shime-on, Benjamin, M, and Shemariah.
Neh 10:4 Amariah, Malchijah, Hattush, Shebaniah, M,
10:27 Ahiah, Hanan, Anan, M, Harim, Baanah.
12:2 Seraiah, Jeremiah, Ezra, Amariah, M, Hattush,

MALLUCHI
Neh 12:14 of Amariah, Jehohanan; of M, Jonathan; of

MALLUS
2Mac 4:30 of Tarsus and of M revolted because their cities

MALTA
Acts 28:1 we then learned that the island was called M

MALTREATED (2)
2Mac 7:13 too had died, they M and tortured the fourth
7:15 forward the fifth and M him.

MAMMON (4)
Mt 6:24 You cannot serve God and M
Lk 16:9 by means of unrighteous M, so that when it
16:11 faithful in the unrighteous M, who will entrust to
16:13 You cannot serve God and M

MAMRE (10)
Gen 13:18 by the oaks of M, which are at Hebron;
14:13 by the oaks of M the Amorite, brother of
14:24 let Aner, Eshcol, and M take their share."
18:1 by the oaks of M, as he sat at
23:17 to the east of M, the field with the
23:19 of Mach-pelah east of M (that is, Hebron) in
25:9 the Hittite, east of M,
35:27 his father Isaac at M, or Kiriath-arba (that is,
49:30 to the east of M, in the land of
50:13 to the east of M, which Abraham bought with

MAN (2,792)
Gen 1:26 said, "Let us make M in our image, after
1:27 So God created M in his own image, in
2:5 and there was no M to till the ground;
2:7 the LORD God formed M of dust from the
2:7 breath of life; and M became a living being.
2:8 there he put the M whom he had formed.
2:15 LORD God took the M and put him in
2:16 LORD God commanded the M, saying, "You may
2:18 not good that the M should be alone; I
2:19 brought them to the M to see what he
2:19 and whatever the M called every living creature,
2:20 The M gave names to all cattle, and to
2:20 field; but for the M there was not found
2:21 to fall upon the M, and while he slept
2:22 had taken from the M he made into a
2:22 into a woman and brought her to the M
2:23 Then the M said, "This at last is bone
2:23 called Woman, because she was taken out of M
2:24 Therefore a M leaves his father and his mother
2:25 And the M and his wife were both naked,
3:8 the day, and the M and his wife hid
3:9 God called to the M, and said to him,
3:12 The M said, "The woman whom thou gavest to
3:20 The M called his wife's name Eve, because she
3:22 God said, "Behold, the M has become like one
3:24 He drove out the M; and at the east
4:1 "I have gotten a M with the help of
4:23 I have slain a M for wounding me, a
4:23 wounding me, a young M for striking me.
5:1 When God created M, he made him in the
5:2 them and named them M when they were created.
6:3 shall not abide in M for ever, for he
6:5 that the wickedness of M was great in the
6:6 that he had made M on the earth, and
6:7 "I will blot out M whom I have created
6:7 face of the ground, M and beast and creeping
6:9 Noah was a righteous M, blameless in his
7:21 the earth, and every M;
7:23 face of the ground, M and animals and creeping
8:21 the ground because of M, for the imagination of
8:21 for the imagination of M's heart is evil from
9:5 require it and of M; of every man's brother
9:5 of man; of every M's brother I will require
9:5 man's brother I will require the life of M
9:6 sheds the blood of M, by man shall his
9:6 blood of man, by M shall his blood be
9:6 shed; for God made M in his own image.
10:8 the first on earth to be a mighty M
15:4 came to him, "This M shall not be your
16:12 wild ass of a M, his hand against every
16:12 his hand against every M and every man's hand
16:12 every man and every M's hand against him; and
17:17 be born to a M who is a hundred
19:4 people to the last M, surrounded the house;
19:8 who have not known M; let me bring them
19:9 pressed hard against the M Lot, and drew near
19:31 there is not a M on earth to come
20:3 you are a dead M, because of the woman
20:3 for she is a M's wife."
20:7 Now then restore the M's wife; for he is
24:16 a virgin, whom no M had known.
24:21 The M gazed at her in silence to learn
24:22 had done drinking, the M took a gold ring
24:26 The M bowed his head and worshiped the LORD,
24:29 ran out to the M, to the spring.
24:30 his sister, "Thus the M spoke to me," he
24:30 he went to the M; and behold, he was
24:32 So the M came into the house; and Laban
24:58 said to her, "Will you go with this M

24:61 camels and followed the M; thus the servant took
24:65 servant, "Who is the M yonder, walking in the
25:8 old age, an old M and full of years,
25:27 a skilful hunter, a M of the field, while
25:27 Jacob was a quiet M, dwelling in tents.
26:11 saying, "Whoever touches this M or his wife shall
26:13 blessed him, and the M became rich, and gained
27:11 Esau is a hairy M, and I am a
27:11 a hairy man, and I am a smooth M
29:19 her to any other M; stay with me."
30:43 Thus the M grew exceedingly rich, and had large
31:50 my daughters, although no M is with us, remember,
32:24 left alone; and a M wrestled with him until
32:25 When the M saw that he did not prevail
34:19 And the young M did not delay to do
37:15 And a M found him wandering in the fields;
37:15 the fields; and the M asked him, "What are
37:17 And the M said, "They have gone away, for
38:25 her father-in-law, "By the M to whom these belong,
39:2 he became a successful M; and he was in
41:12 an interpretation to each M according to his dream.
41:33 let Pharaoh select a M discreet and wise, and
41:38 we find such a M as this, in whom
41:44 without your consent no M shall lift up hand
42:11 all sons of one M, we are honest men,
42:13 the sons of one M in the land of
42:25 and to replace every M's money in his sack,
42:30 befallen them, saying, "The M, the lord of the
42:33 of Canaan.' Then the M, the lord of the
42:35 their sacks, behold, every M's bundle of money was
43:3 said to him, "The M solemnly warned us, saying,
43:5 go down, for the M said to us, 'You
43:6 as to tell the M that you had another
43:7 They replied, "The M questioned us carefully about
43:11 carry down to the M a present, a little
43:13 go again to the M;
43:14 you mercy before the M, that he may send
43:17 The M did as Joseph bade him, and brought
43:21 and there was every M's money in the mouth
43:24 And when the M had brought the men into
43:27 father well, the old M of whom you spoke?
44:1 carry, and put each M's money in the mouth
44:11 Then every M quickly lowered his sack to the
44:11 the ground, and every M opened his sack.
44:13 their clothes, and every M loaded his ass, and
44:15 know that such a M as I can indeed
44:17 Only the M in whose hand the cup was
44:20 a father, an old M, and a young brother,
44:26 we cannot see the M's face unless our youngest
Ex 2:1 Now a M from the house of Levi went
2:13 he said to the M that did the wrong,
2:20 Why have you left the M
2:21 to dwell with the M, and he gave Moses
4:11 him, "Who has made M's mouth?
6:12 me, who am a M of uncircumcised lips?"
7:12 For every M cast down his rod, and they
8:17 there came gnats on M and beast; all the
8:18 there were gnats on M and beast.
9:9 out in sores on M and beast throughout all
9:10 out in sores on M and beast.
9:19 come down upon every M and beast that is
9:22 land of Egypt, upon M and beast and every
9:25 land of Egypt, both M and beast; and the
10:7 "How long shall this M be a snare to
11:2 that they ask, every M of his neighbor and
11:3 Moreover, the M Moses was very great in the
11:7 people of Israel, either M or beast, not a
12:3 they shall take every M a lamb according to
12:4 a lamb, then a M and his neighbor next
12:12 land of Egypt, both M and beast; and on
13:2 of Israel, both of M and of beast, is
13:13 Every first-born of M among your sons you shall
13:15 both the first-born of M and the first-born of
15:3 The LORD is a M of war; the LORD
16:16 'Gather of it, every M of you, as much
16:19 to them, "Let no M leave any of it
16:29 two days; remain every M of you in his
16:29 his place, let no M go out of his
18:16 I decide between a M and his neighbor, and
19:13 shot; whether beast or M, he shall not live.'
21:7 "When a M sells his daughter as a slave,
21:12 "Whoever strikes a M so that he dies shall
21:14 But if a M willfully attacks another to kill
21:16 "Whoever steals a M, whether he sells him or
21:18 his fist and the M does not die but
21:19 bed, then if the M rises again and walks
21:20 "When a M strikes his slave, male or female,
21:26 "When a M strikes the eye of his slave,
21:28 an ox gores a M or a woman to
21:29 and it kills a M or a woman, the
21:31 If it gores a M's son or daughter, he
21:33 "When a M leaves a pit open, or when
21:33 open, or when a M digs a pit and
21:35 "When one M's ox hurts anothers, so that it
22:1 "If a M steals an ox or a sheep,
22:5 "When a M causes a field or vineyard to
22:5 it feeds in another M's field, he shall make
22:7 "If a M delivers to his neighbor money or
22:7 stolen out of the M's house, then, if the
22:10 "If a M delivers to his neighbor an ass
22:14 "If a M borrows anything of his neighbor, and
22:16 "If a M seduces a virgin who is not
23:1 hands with a wicked M, to be a malicious
23:3 partial to a poor M in his suit.
25:2 an offering; from every M whose heart makes him
32:1 for this Moses, the M who brought us up
32:23 for this Moses, the M who brought us up
32:27 of Israel, 'Put every M his sword on his
32:27 camp, and slay every M his brother, and every
32:27 his brother, and every M his companion, and every
32:27 his companion, and every M his neighbor.'"
33:4 they mourned; and no M put on his ornaments.
33:8 rose up, and every M stood at his tent
33:10 up and worship, every M at his tent door.
33:11 to face, as a M speaks to his friend.
33:11 of Nun, a young M, did not depart from
33:20 see my face; for M shall not see me
34:3 No M shall come up with you, and let
34:3 you, and let no M be seen throughout all
34:24 borders; neither shall any M desire your land, when
35:10 "And let every able M among you come and
35:22 of gold objects, every M dedicating an offering of
35:23 And every M with whom was found blue or
35:24 LORD's offering; and every M with whom was found
36:1 Oholiab and every able M in whom the LORD
36:2 Oholiab and every able M in whose mind the
36:6 the camp, "Let neither M nor woman do anything
Lev 1:2 to them, When any M of you brings an
3:1 "If a M's offering is a sacrifice of peace
5:5 When a M is guilty in any of these,
7:8 priest who offers any M's burnt offering shall have
7:21 whether the uncleanness of M or an unclean beast
13:2 and Aaron, "When a M has on the skin
13:9 "When a M is afflicted with leprosy, he shall
13:29 "When a M or woman has a disease on
13:38 "When a M or a woman has spots on
13:40 "If a M's hair has fallen from his head,
13:41 And if a M's hair has fallen from his
13:44 he is a leprous M, he is unclean; the
14:11 him shall set the M who is to be
15:2 of Israel, When any M has a discharge from
15:16 "And if a M has an emission of semen,
15:18 If a M lies with a woman and has
15:24 And if any M lies with her, and her
15:33 discharge, and for the M who lies with a
16:17 There shall be no M in the tent of
16:21 the hand of a M who is in readiness.
17:3 If any M of the house of Israel kills
17:4 be imputed to that M; he has shed blood;
17:4 shed blood; and that M shall be cut off
17:8 say to them, Any M of the house of
17:9 to the LORD; that M shall be cut off
17:10 "If any M of the house of Israel or
17:13 Any M also of the people of Israel, or
18:5 by doing which a M shall live: I am
19:20 "If a M lies carnally with a woman who
19:20 slave, betrothed to another M and not yet ransomed
19:32 face of an old M, and you shall fear
20:2 people of Israel, Any M of the people of
20:3 my face against that M, and will cut him
20:4 their eyes from that M, when he gives one
20:5 my face against that M and against his family,
20:10 "If a M commits adultery with the wife of
20:11 The M who lies with his father's wife has
20:12 If a M lies with his daughter-in-law, both of
20:13 If a M lies with a male as with
20:14 If a M takes a wife and her mother
20:15 If a M lies with a beast, he shall
20:17 "If a M takes his sister, a daughter of
20:18 If a M lies with a woman having her
20:20 If a M lies with his uncle's wife, he
20:21 If a M takes his brother's wife, it is

20:27 "A M or a woman who is a medium
21:18 shall draw near, a M blind or lame, or
21:19 too long, or a M who has an injured
21:20 a dwarf, or a M with a defect in
21:21 or crushed testicles; no M of the descendants of
22:4 the dead or a M who has had an
22:5 made unclean or a M from whom he may
22:14 And if a M eats of a holy thing
24:10 woman's son and a M of Israel quarreled in
24:17 He who kills a M shall be put to
24:19 When a M causes a disfigurement in his neighbor,
24:20 he has disfigured a M, he shall be disfigured.
24:21 he who kills a M shall be put to
25:26 If a M has no one to redeem it,
25:27 the overpayment to the M to whom he sold
25:29 "If a M sells a dwelling house in a
27:2 of Israel, When a M makes a special vow
27:8 And if a M is too poor to pay
27:9 of such that any M gives to the LORD
27:11 the LORD, then the M shall bring the animal
27:14 "When a M dedicates his house to be holy
27:16 "If a M dedicates to the LORD part of
27:20 the field to another M, it shall not be
27:23 of jubilee, and the M shall give the amount
27:26 to the LORD, no M may dedicate; whether ox
27:28 devoted thing that a M devotes to the LORD,
27:28 he has, whether of M or beast, or of
27:31 If a M wishes to redeem any of his
27:33 A M shall not inquire whether it is good
Num 1:4 be with you a M from each tribe, each
1:4 from each tribe, each M being the head of
1:26 old and upward, every M able to go forth
1:28 old and upward, every M able to go forth
1:30 old and upward, every M able to go forth
1:32 old and upward, every M able to go forth
1:34 old and upward, every M able to go forth
1:36 old and upward, every M able to go forth
1:38 old and upward, every M able to go forth
1:40 old and upward, every M able to go forth
1:42 old and upward, every M able to go forth
1:45 old and upward, every M able to go forth
1:52 by their companies, every M by his own camp
1:52 own camp and every M by his own standard;
3:13 in Israel, both of M and of beast; they
5:6 of Israel, When a M or woman commits any
5:8 But if the M has no kinsman to whom
5:10 be his; and every M's holy things shall be
5:10 be his; whatever any M gives to the priest
5:12 of Israel, If any M's wife goes astray and
5:13 against him, if a M lies with her carnally,
5:15 defiled herself; then the M shall bring his wife
5:19 oath, saying, 'If no M has lain with you,
5:20 defiled yourself, and some M other than your
5:30 jealousy comes upon a M and he is jealous
5:31 The M shall be free from iniquity, but the
6:2 Israel, When either a M or a woman makes
6:9 "And if any M dies very suddenly beside him,
7:5 the Levites, to each M according to his service."
8:17 are mine, both of M and of beast; on
9:6 dead body of a M, so that they could
9:7 dead body of a M; why are we kept
9:10 of Israel, If any M of you or of
9:13 But the M who is clean and is not
9:13 its appointed time; that M shall bear his sin.
11:10 throughout their families, every M at the door of
11:27 And a young M ran and told Moses, "Eldad
12:3 Now the M Moses was very meek, more than
13:2 shall you send a M, every one a leader
14:15 this people as one M, then the nations who
15:32 wilderness, they found a M gathering sticks on the
15:35 said to Moses, "The M shall be put to
16:7 LORD tomorrow, and the M whom the LORD
16:18 So every M took his censer, and they put
16:22 all flesh, shall one M sin, and wilt thou
17:2 Write each M's name upon his rod,
17:5 the rod of the M whom I choose shall
17:9 they looked, and each M took his rod.
18:15 of all flesh, whether M or beast, which they
18:15 nevertheless the first-born of M you shall redeem,
19:9 And a M who is clean shall gather up
19:13 the body of any M who has died, and
19:14 the law when a M dies in a tent:
19:16 a bone of a M, or a grave, shall
19:20 "But the M who is unclean and does not
21:9 a serpent bit any M, he would look at
23:19 Zippor: God is not M, that he should lie,
23:19 or a son of M, that he should repent.
24:3 the oracle of the M whose eye is opened,
24:15 the oracle of the M whose eye is opened,
25:8 and went after the M of Israel into the
25:8 both of them, the M of Israel and the
25:14 name of the slain M of Israel, who was
26:64 there was not a M of those numbered by
26:65 was not left a M of them, except Caleb
27:8 of Israel, 'If a M dies, and has no
27:16 all flesh, appoint a M over the congregation,
27:18 son of Nun, a M in whom is the
30:2 When a M vows a vow to the LORD,
30:16 Moses, as between a M and his wife, and
31:11 the booty, both of M and of beast.
31:17 woman who has known M by lying with him.
31:18 who have not known M by lying with him,
31:26 was taken, both of M and of beast, you
31:35 who had not known M by lying with him.
31:49 there is not a M missing from us.
31:50 LORD's offering, what each M found, articles of gold,
31:53 had taken booty, every M for himself.)
32:21 war, and every armed M of you will pass
32:27 will pass over, every M who is armed for
32:29 sons of Reuben, every M who is armed to
33:54 lot falls to any M, that shall be his;
35:17 hand, by which a M may die, and he
35:18 hand, by which a M may die, and he
35:23 stone, by which a M may die, and without
35:28 For the M must remain in his city of
Deut 1:16 judge righteously between a M and his brother or
1:17 of the face of M, for the judgment is
1:23 men of you, one M for each tribe;
1:31 bore you, as a M bears his son, in
1:41 commanded us.' And every M of you girded on
3:20 you shall return every M to his possession which
4:32 day that God created M upon the earth, and
5:24 seen God speak with M and man still live.
5:24 speak with man and M still live.
7:24 under heaven; not a M shall be able to
8:3 make you know that M does not live by
8:3 bread alone, but that M lives by everything that
8:5 heart that, as a M disciplines his son, the
11:25 No M shall be able to stand against you;
12:8 here this day, every M doing whatever is right
15:7 among you a poor M, one of your brethren,
15:12 your brother, a Hebrew M, or a Hebrew woman,
16:17 the LORD empty-handed; every M shall give as he
17:2 God gives you, a M or woman who does
17:5 to your gates that M or woman who has
17:5 you shall stone that M or woman to death
17:12 The M who acts presumptuously, by not obeying the
17:12 or the judge, that M shall die; so you
19:5 as when a M goes into the forest
19:6 him mortally, though the M did not deserve to
19:11 "But if any M hates his neighbor, and lies
19:11 he dies, and the M flees into one of
19:15 not prevail against a M for any crime or
19:16 witness rises against any M to accuse him of
20:5 the people, saying, 'What M is there that has
20:5 the battle and another M dedicate it.
20:6 And what M is there that has planted a
20:6 the battle and another M enjoy its fruit.
20:7 And what M is there that has betrothed a
20:7 the battle and another M take her.'
20:8 people, and say, What M is there that is
21:3 nearest to the slain M shall take a heifer
21:6 nearest to the slain M shall wash their hands
21:15 "If a M has two wives, the one loved
21:18 "If a M has a stubborn and rebellious son,
21:22 "And if a M has committed a crime punishable
21:23 day, for a hanged M is accursed by God;
22:5 that pertains to a M, nor shall a man
22:5 man, nor shall a M put on a woman's
22:13 "If any M takes a wife, and goes in
22:16 my daughter to this M to wife, and he
22:18 city shall take the M and whip him;
22:22 "If a M is found lying with the wife
22:22 the wife of another M, both of them shall
22:22 them shall die, the M who lay with the
22:23 betrothed virgin, and a M meets her in the
22:24 the city, and the M because he violated his
22:25 the open country a M meets a young woman
22:25 is betrothed, and the M seizes her and lies
22:25 her, then only the M who lay with her
22:26 like that of a M attacking and murdering his
22:28 "If a M meets a virgin who is not

22:29 are found, then the M who lay with her
22:30 "A M shall not take his father's wife, nor
23:10 is among you any M who is not clean
24:1 "When a M takes a wife and marries her,
24:2 goes and becomes another M's wife,
24:5 "When a M is newly married, he shall not
24:6 "No M shall take a mill or an upper
24:7 "If a M is found stealing one of his
24:11 stand outside, and the M to whom you make
24:12 he is a poor M, you shall not sleep
24:16 for the fathers; every M shall be put to
25:2 then if the guilty M deserves to be beaten,
25:7 And if the M does not wish to take
25:9 be done to the M who does not build
27:15 voice: "'Cursed be the M who makes a graven
27:18 who misleads a blind M on the road.' And
28:30 a wife, and another M shall lie with her;
28:54 The M who is the most tender and delicately
28:68 female slaves, but no M will buy you."
29:18 be among you a M or woman or family
29:20 would smoke against that M, and the curses written
32:25 terror, destroying both young M and virgin, the
32:25 sucking child with the M of gray hairs.
33:1 with which Moses the M of God blessed the
34:6 opposite Beth-peor; but no M knows the place of
Josh 1:5 No M shall be able to stand before you
2:11 courage left in any M, because of you; for
3:12 the tribes of Israel, from each tribe a M
4:2 from each tribe a M,
4:4 he had appointed, a M from each tribe;
5:13 looked, and behold, a M stood before him with
6:5 shall go up every M straight before him."
6:20 into the city, every M straight before him, and
6:26 the LORD be the M that rises up and
7:14 takes shall come near M by man.
7:14 the LORD takes shall come near man by M
7:17 family of the Zerahites M by man, and Zabdi
7:17 the Zerahites man by M, and Zabdi was taken;
7:18 brought near his household M by man, and Achan
7:18 his household man by M, and Achan the son
8:17 There was not a M left in Ai or
8:31 stones, upon which no M has lifted an iron
10:8 there shall not a M of them stand before
10:14 the voice of a M; for the LORD fought
10:21 at Makkedah; not a M moved his tongue against
11:14 their booty; but every M they smote with the
14:6 said to Moses the M of God in Kadesh-barnea
14:15 Arba was the greatest M among the Anakim.
17:1 because he was a M of war.
23:9 as for you, no M has been able to
23:10 One M of you puts to flight a thousand,
24:28 the people away, every M to his inheritance.
Judg 1:24 the spies saw a M coming out of the
1:25 but they let the M and all his family
1:26 And the M went to the land of the
3:15 the son of Gera, the Benjaminite, a left-handed M
3:17 Now Eglon was a very fat M
3:28 and allowed not a M to pass over.
3:29 able-bodied men; not a M escaped.
4:16 the sword; not a M was left.
4:20 tent, and if any M comes and asks you,
4:22 will show you the M whom you are seeking."
5:30 or two for every M; spoil of dyed stuffs
6:12 with you, you mighty M of valor."
6:16 and you shall smite the Midianites as one M
7:4 say to you, 'This M shall go with you,'
7:4 say to you, 'This M shall not go with
7:7 the others go every M to his home."
7:8 rest of Israel every M to his tent, but
7:13 Gideon came, behold, a M was telling a dream
7:14 son of Joash, a M of Israel; into his
7:21 They stood every M in his place round about
7:22 the LORD set every M's sword against his fellow
8:14 he caught a young M of Succoth, and questioned
8:21 us; for as the M is, so is his
8:24 you; give me every M of you the earrings
8:25 a garment, and every M cast in it the
9:54 hastily to the young M his armor-bearer, and said
9:54 And his young M thrust him through, and he
9:55 dead, they departed every M to his home.
10:1 son of Dodo, a M of Issachar; and he
10:18 another, "Who is the M that will begin to
11:39 She had never known a M
13:2 there was a certain M of Zorah, of the
13:6 told her husband, "A M of God came to
13:8 pray thee, let the M of God whom thou
13:10 her husband, "Behold, the M who came to me
13:11 and came to the M and said to him,
13:11 him, "Are you the M who spoke to this
14:20 to his companion, who had been his best M
16:7 shall become weak, and be like any other M
16:11 shall become weak, and be like any other M
16:13 shall become weak, and be like any other M
16:17 shall become weak, and be like any other M
16:19 and she called a M, and had him shave
17:1 There was a M of the hill country of
17:5 And the M Micah had a shrine, and he
17:6 king in Israel; every M did what was right
17:7 there was a young M of Bethlehem in Judah,
17:8 And the M departed from the town of Bethlehem
17:11 to dwell with the M; and the young man
17:11 man; and the young M became to him like
17:12 Levite, and the young M became his priest, and
18:19 the house of one M, or to be priest
19:6 father said to the M, "Be pleased to spend
19:7 And when the M rose up to go, his
19:9 And when the M and his concubine and his
19:10 But the M would not spend the night; he
19:15 the city; for no M took them into his
19:16 And behold, an old M was coming from his
19:16 field at evening; the M was from the hill
19:17 city; and the old M said, "Where are you
19:19 maidservant and the young M with your servants;
19:20 And the old M said, "Peace be to you;
19:22 said to the old M, the master of the
19:22 house, "Bring out the M who came into your
19:23 And the M, the master of the house, went
19:23 wickedly; seeing that this M has come into my
19:24 you; but against this M do not do so
19:25 So the M seized his concubine, and put her
19:26 the door of the M's house where her master
19:28 the ass; and the M rose up and went
20:1 congregation assembled as one M to the LORD at
20:8 people arose as one M, saying, "We will not
20:11 Israel gathered against the city, united as one M
21:12 who had not known M by lying with him;
21:21 vineyards and seize each M his wife from the
21:22 not take for each M of them his wife
21:24 at that time, every M to his tribe and
21:24 out from there every M to his inheritance.
21:25 king in Israel; every M did what was right
Ruth 1:1 land, and a certain M of Bethlehem in Judah
1:2 The name of the M was Elimelech and the
2:1 of her husbands, a M of wealth, of the
2:19 Blessed be the M who took notice of you."
2:19 worked, and said, "The M's name with whom I
2:20 said to her, "The M is a relative of
3:3 yourself known to the M until he has finished
3:8 At midnight the M was startled, and turned over,
3:16 her all that the M had done for her,
3:18 turns out, for the M will not rest, but
1Sam 1:1 There was a certain M of Ramathaim-zophim of the
1:3 Now this M used to go up year by
1:21 And the M Elkanah and all his house went
2:9 by might shall a M prevail.
2:13 was that when any M offered sacrifice, the priest's
2:15 and say to the M who was sacrificing, "Give
2:16 And if the M said to him, "Let them
2:25 If a M sins against a man, God will
2:25 man sins against a M, God will mediate for
2:25 him; but if a M sins against the LORD,
2:27 And there came a M of God to Eli,
2:31 not be an old M in your house.
2:32 not be an old M in your house for
2:33 The M of you whom I shall not cut
4:10 and they fled, every M to his home; and
4:12 A M of Benjamin ran from the battle line,
4:13 And when the M came into the city and
4:14 Then the M hastened and came and told Eli.
4:16 And the M said to Eli, "I am he
4:18 he was an old M, and heavy.
8:22 of Israel, "Go every M to his city."
9:1 There was a M of Benjamin whose name was
9:1 Aphiah, a Benjaminite, a M of wealth;
9:2 son whose name was Saul, a handsome young M
9:2 There was not a M among the people of
9:6 "Behold, there is a M of God in this
9:6 and he is a M that is held in
9:7 if we go, what can we bring the M
9:7 to bring to the M of God.
9:8 give it to the M of God, to tell
9:9 in Israel, when a M went to inquire of

9:10 the city where the M of God was.
9:16 send to you a M from the land of
9:17 him, "Here is the M of whom I spoke
10:6 prophesy with them and be turned into another M
10:12 And a M of the place answered, "And who
10:21 of the Matrites near M by man, and Saul
10:21 Matrites near man by M, and Saul the son
10:22 the LORD, "Did the M come hither?" and the
10:27 said, "How can this M save us?" And they
11:7 the people, and they came out as one M
11:13 Saul said, "Not a M shall be put to
12:4 taken anything from any M's hand."
13:2 he sent home, every M to his tent.
13:14 has sought out a M after his own heart;
14:1 said to the young M who bore his armor,
14:6 said to the young M who bore his armor,
14:20 battle; and behold, every M's sword was against his
14:24 saying, "Cursed be the M who eats food until
14:26 was dropping, but no M put his hand to
14:28 saying, 'Cursed be the M who eats food this
14:34 to them, 'Let every M bring his ox or
14:36 us not leave a M of them." And they
14:39 there was not a M among all the people
14:52 Saul saw any strong M, or any valiant man,
14:52 man, or any valiant M, he attached him to
15:3 them, but kill both M and woman, infant and
15:29 he is not a M, that he should repent."
16:7 LORD sees not as M sees; man looks on
16:7 not as man sees; M looks on the outward
16:16 to seek out a M who is skilful in
16:17 "Provide for me a M who can play well,
16:18 skilful in playing, a M of valor, a man
16:18 man of valor, a M of war, prudent in
16:18 in speech, and a M of good presence; and
17:8 Choose a M for yourselves, and let him come
17:10 day; give me a M, that we may fight
17:12 days of Saul the M was already old and
17:24 when they saw the M, fled from him, and
17:25 "Have you seen this M who has come up?
17:25 defy Israel; and the M who kills him, the
17:26 be done for the M who kills this Philistine,
17:27 be done to the M who kills him."
17:32 to Saul, "Let no M's heart fail because of
17:33 he has been a M of war from his
17:58 said to him, "Whose son are you, young M
18:23 I am a poor M and of no repute?"
21:7 Now a certain M of the servants of Saul
21:14 "Lo, you see the M is mad; why then
24:19 For if a M finds his enemy, will he
25:2 And there was a M in Maon, whose business
25:2 The M was very rich; he had three thousand
25:3 the name of the M was Nabal, and the
25:3 beautiful, but the M was churlish and ill-behaved;
25:13 to his men, "Every M gird on his sword!"
25:13 And every M of them girded on his sword;
26:12 No M saw it, or knew it, nor did
26:15 David said to Abner, "Are you not a M
26:23 The LORD rewards every M for his righteousness
27:3 and his men, every M with his household, and
27:9 land, and left neither M nor woman alive, but
27:11 And David saved neither M nor woman alive, to
28:14 she said, "An old M is coming up; and
29:4 to him, "Send the M back, that he may
30:13 "I am a young M of Egypt, servant to
30:17 day; and not a M of them escaped, except
30:22 recovered, except that each M may lead away his
2Sam 1:2 third day, behold, a M came from Saul's camp,
1:5 said to the young M who told him, "How
1:6 And the young M who told him said, "By
1:13 said to the young M who told him, "Where
3:38 prince and a great M has fallen this day
4:2 sons of Rimmon a M of Benjamin from Be-eroth
4:11 have slain a righteous M in his own house
10:12 let us play the M for our people, and
12:2 The rich M had very many flocks and herds;
12:3 herds; but the poor M had nothing but one
12:4 traveler to the rich M, and he was unwilling
12:4 he took the poor M's lamb, and prepared it
12:4 prepared it for the M who had come to
12:5 greatly kindled against the M; and he said to
12:5 the LORD lives, the M who has done this
12:7 Nathan said to David, "You are the M
13:3 David's brother; and Jonadab was a very crafty M
13:17 He called the young M who served him and
13:34 And the young M who kept the watch lifted
14:7 say, 'Give up the M who struck his brother,
14:16 the hand of the M who would destroy me
14:21 bring back the young M Absalom."
15:2 gate; and when any M had a suit to
15:3 but there is no M deputed by the king
15:4 Then every M with a suit or cause might
15:5 And whenever a M came near to do obeisance
16:5 there came out a M of the family of
16:7 cursed, "Begone, begone, you M of blood, you
16:8 for you are a M of blood."
17:3 life of only one M, and all the people
17:10 Then even the valiant M, whose heart is like
17:10 father is a mighty M, and that those who
17:18 the house of a M at Bahurim, who had
17:25 the son of a M named Ithra the Ishmaelite,
18:5 sake with the young M Absalom." And all the
18:10 And a certain M saw it, and told Joab,
18:11 Joab said to the M who told him, "What,
18:12 But the M said to Joab, "Even if I
18:12 sake protect the young M Absalom.'
18:24 looked, he saw a M running alone.
18:26 the watchman saw another M running; and the
18:26 and said, "See, another M running alone!" The king
18:27 "He is a good M, and comes with good
18:29 with the young M Absalom?" Ahima-az answered,
18:32 well with the young M Absalom?" And the Cushite
18:32 against you for evil, be like that young M
19:7 not go, not a M will stay with you
19:8 Israel had fled every M to his own home.
19:14 of Judah as one M; so that they sent
19:32 was a very aged M, eighty years old; and
19:32 at Mahanaim; for he was a very wealthy M
20:1 son of Jesse; every M to his tents, O
20:12 stopped; and when the M saw that all the
20:21 But a M of the hill country of Ephraim,
20:22 from the city, every M to his home.
21:4 us to put any M to death in Israel."
21:5 to the king, "The M who consumed us and
21:20 where there was a M of great stature, who
22:26 loyal; with the blameless M thou dost show thyself
23:1 the oracle of the M who was raised on
23:7 the hand; but the M who touches them arms
23:20 Jehoiada was a valiant M of Kabzeel, a doer
23:21 And he slew an Egyptian, a handsome M
24:14 let me not fall into the hand of M
1Kgs 1:6 also a very handsome M; and he was born
1:42 you are a worthy M and bring good news."
1:52 to be a worthy M, not one of his
2:2 and show yourself a M,
2:4 not fail you a M on the throne of
2:9 you are a wise M; you will know what
4:7 and his household; each M had to make provision
4:25 even to Beer-sheba, every M under his vine and
7:14 his father was a M of Tyre, a worker
8:25 never fail you a M before me to sit
8:31 "If a M sins against his neighbor and is
8:38 is made by any M or by all thy
8:46 for there is no M who does not sin—
9:5 not fail you a M upon the throne of
11:28 The M Jeroboam was very able, and when Solomon
11:28 saw that the young M was industrious he gave
12:22 came to Shemaiah the M of God:
12:24 Return every M to his home, for this thing
13:1 And behold, a M of God came out of
13:2 And the M cried against the altar by the
13:4 the saying of the M of God, which he
13:5 the sign which the M of God had given
13:6 king said to the M of God, "Entreat now
13:6 And the M of God entreated the LORD; and
13:7 king said to the M of God, "Come home
13:8 And the M of God said to the king,
13:11 him all that the M of God had done
13:12 the way which the M of God who came
13:14 he went after the M of God, and found
13:14 him, "Are you the M of God who came
13:21 he cried to the M of God who came
13:26 said, "It is the M of God, who disobeyed
13:29 the body of the M of God and laid
13:31 grave in which the M of God is buried;
14:10 of Jeroboam, as a M burns up dung until
17:18 you against me, O M of God?
17:24 that you are a M of God, and that
18:44 little cloud like a M's hand is rising out
20:7 and see how this M is seeking trouble; for
20:20 And each killed his M; the Syrians fled and
20:28 And a M of God came near and said
20:35 And a certain M of the sons of the

20:35 But the M refused to strike him.
20:37 Then he found another M, and said, "Strike me,
20:37 And the M struck him, smiting and wounding him.
20:39 turned and brought a M to me, and said,
20:39 and said, 'Keep this M; if by any means
20:42 of your hand the M whom I had devoted
22:8 "There is yet one M by whom we may
22:34 But a certain M drew his bow at a
22:36 through the army, "Every M to his city, and
22:36 his city, and every M to his country!"
2Kgs 1:6 him, "There came a M to meet us, and
1:7 them, "What kind of M was he who came
1:9 said to him, "O M of God, the king
1:10 "If I am a M of God, let fire
1:11 said to him, "O M of God, this is
1:12 "If I am a M of God, let fire
1:13 and entreated him, "O M of God, I pray
3:25 piece of land every M threw a stone, until
4:7 came and told the M of God, and he
4:9 this is a holy M of God, who is
4:16 "No, my lord, O M of God; do not
4:21 the bed of the M of God, and shut
4:22 quickly go to the M of God, and come
4:25 and came to the M of God at Mount
4:25 When the M of God saw her coming, he
4:27 the mountain to the M of God, she caught
4:27 But the M of God said, "Let her alone,
4:40 they cried out, "O M of God, there is
4:42 A M came from Baal-shalishah, bringing the man of
4:42 from Baal-shalishah, bringing the M of God bread of
5:1 Syria, was a great M with his master and
5:1 He was a mighty M of valor, but he
5:7 make alive, that this M sends word to me
5:7 me to cure a M of his leprosy?
5:8 But when Elisha the M of God heard that
5:14 the word of the M of God; and his
5:15 he returned to the M of God, he and
5:20 servant of Elisha the M of God, said, "See,
5:26 in spirit when the M turned from his chariot
6:6 Then the M of God said, "Where did it
6:9 But the M of God sent word to the
6:10 place of which the M of God told him.
6:15 the servant of the M of God rose early
6:17 eyes of the young M, and he saw; and
6:19 bring you to the M whom you seek." And
6:32 king had dispatched a M from his presence; but
7:2 leaned said to the M of God, "If the
7:17 he died, as the M of God had said
7:18 For when the M of God had said to
7:19 captain had answered the M of God, "If the
8:2 the word of the M of God; she went
8:4 the servant of the M of God, saying, "Tell
8:7 was told him, "The M of God has come
8:8 go to meet the M of God, and inquire
8:11 And the M of God wept.
9:4 the young M, the prophet, went to Ramoth-gilead.
9:6 house; and the young M poured the oil on
9:13 Then in haste every M of them took his
9:18 So a M on horseback went to meet him,
10:21 there was not a M left who did not
10:24 outside, and said, "The M who allows any of
10:25 them; let not a M escape." So when they
11:11 the guards stood, every M with his weapons in
12:4 money for which each M is assessed—the money
12:4 the money which a M's heart prompts him to
13:19 Then the M of God was angry with him,
13:21 And as a M was being buried, lo, a
13:21 was seen and the M was cast into the
13:21 as soon as the M touched the bones of
14:6 the fathers; but every M shall die for his
14:12 by Israel, and every M fled to his home.
15:20 of silver from every M, to give to the
18:21 the hand of any M who leans on it.
22:15 of Israel: 'Tell the M who sent you to
23:16 the LORD which the M of God proclaimed, who
23:17 the tomb of the M of God who came
23:18 him be; let no M move his bones." So
1Chr 11:22 Jehoiada was a valiant M of Kabzeel, a doer
11:23 slew an Egyptian, a M of great stature, five
12:4 of Gibeon, a mighty M among the thirty and
12:28 Zadok, a young M mighty in valor, and twenty-two
19:13 let us play the M for our people, and
20:6 where there was a M of great stature, who
21:13 let me not fall into the hand of M
22:9 he shall be a M of peace.
23:14 sons of Moses the M of God were named
27:6 who was a mighty M of the thirty and
27:32 a counselor, being a M of understanding and a
28:21 will be every willing M who has skill for
29:1 will not be for M but for the LORD
2Chr 2:7 now send me a M skilled to work in
2:13 a skilled M, endued with understanding, Huram-abi,
2:14 his father was a M of Tyre.
6:5 and I chose no M as prince over my
6:16 never fail you a M before me to sit
6:18 God dwell indeed with M on the earth?
6:22 "If a M sins against his neighbor and is
6:29 is made by any M or by all thy
6:36 for there is no M who does not sin—
7:18 not fail you a M to rule Israel.'
8:14 for so David the M of God had commanded.
11:2 came to Shemaiah the M of God:
11:4 Return every M to his home, for this thing
14:11 our God; let not M prevail against thee."
15:13 whether young or old, M or woman.
17:17 Benjamin: Eliada, a mighty M of valor, with two
18:7 "There is yet one M by whom we may
18:33 But a certain M drew his bow at a
19:6 you judge not for M but for the LORD;
20:27 they returned, every M of Judah and Jerusalem,
23:10 for the king, every M with his weapon in
25:4 the fathers; but every M shall die for his
25:7 But a M of God came to him and
25:9 Amaziah said to the M of God, "But what
25:9 The M of God answered, "The LORD is able
25:22 by Israel, and every M fled to his home.
28:7 And Zichri, a mighty M of Ephraim, slew Ma-aseiah
30:16 law of Moses the M of God; the priests
31:1 to their cities, every M to his possession.
34:23 of Israel: 'Tell the M who sent you to
36:17 no compassion on young M or virgin, old man
36:17 man or virgin, old M or aged; he gave
Ezra 3:1 people gathered as one M to Jerusalem.
3:2 law of Moses the M of God.
8:17 to Iddo, the leading M at the place Casiphia,
8:18 they brought us a M of discretion, of the
Neh 1:11 grant him mercy in the sight of this M
4:18 The M who sounded the trumpet was beside me.
4:22 that time, "Let every M and his servant pass
5:13 God shake out every M from his house and
6:11 said, "Should such a M as I flee?
6:11 And what M such as I could go into
7:2 more faithful and God-fearing M than many.
8:1 people gathered as one M into the square before
9:29 observance of which a M shall live, and turned
12:24 commandment of David the M of God, watch
12:36 instruments of David the M of God; and Ezra
Tob 1:4 was still a young M, the whole tribe of
1:9 When I became a M I married Anna, a
2:2 and bring whatever poor M of our brethren you
3:14 of any sin with M,
4:7 away from any poor M, and the face of
4:14 the wages of any M who works for you,
4:18 advice from every wise M, and do not despise
5:2 the money when I do not know the M
5:3 to him, "Find a M to go with you
5:4 to look for a M; and he found Raphael,
5:8 he is a reliable M to go with you."
5:11 family or for a M whom you will pay
5:16 him, "Go with this M; God who dwells in
5:16 departed, and the young M's dog was with them.
6:2 Then the young M went down to wash himself.
6:2 have swallowed the young M;
6:3 So the young M seized the fish and threw
6:5 So the young M did as the angel told
6:6 Then the young M said to the angel, "Brother
6:7 from these before the M or woman, and that
6:8 anoint with it a M who has white films
6:10 said to the young M, "Brother, today we shall
6:12 give her to another M without incurring the penalty
6:12 rather than any other M are entitled to the
6:13 Then the young M said to the angel, "Brother
7:2 much the young M resembles my cousin Tobit!"
7:7 and exclaimed, "Son of that good and noble M
8:6 not good that the M should be alone; let
11:6 and so is the M who went with him!"
12:1 the wages of the M who went with you;
12:4 The old M said, "He deserves it."
Jud 1:11 him as only one M, and they sent back
2:18 of food for every M, and a huge amount
4:9 And every M of Israel cried out to God
6:3 the king's servants will destroy them as one M

7:5 Then each M took up his weapons, and when
7:11 array, and not a M of your army will
7:13 watch that not a M gets out of the
8:14 find out what a M is thinking; how do
8:16 God is not like M, to be threatened, nor
10:19 Surely not a M of them had better be
11:8 are the one good M in the whole kingdom,
14:2 rises, let every valiant M take his weapons and
14:5 see and recognize the M who despised the house
14:11 the wall, and every M took his weapons, and
Esth 1:8 to do as every M desired.
1:22 own language, that every M be lord in his
4:11 know that if any M or woman goes to
6:6 be done to the M whom the king delights
6:7 the king, "For the M whom the king delights
6:9 let him array the M whom the king delights
6:9 let him conduct the M on horseback through the
6:9 be done to the M whom the king delights
6:11 be done to the M whom the king delights
9:4 the provinces; for the M Mordecai grew more and
11:3 of Susa, a great M, serving in the court
13:14 set the glory of M above the glory of
14:11 an example of the M who began this against
14:13 heart to hate the M who is fighting against
16:15 annihilation by this thrice-accursed M, are not
16:18 of Hammedatha, because the M himself who did
Job 1:1 There was a M in the land of
1:1 was Job; and that M was blameless and upright,
1:3 servants; so that this M was the greatest of
1:8 a blameless and upright M, who fears God and
2:3 a blameless and upright M, who fears God and
2:4 All that a M has he will give for
3:23 light given to a M whose way is hid,
4:17 a voice: 'Can mortal M be righteous before God?
4:17 Can a M be pure before his Maker?
5:7 from the ground; but M is born to trouble
5:17 "Behold, happy is the M whom God reproves;
6:26 speech of a despairing M is wind?
7:1 "Has not M a hard service upon earth, and
7:17 What is M, that thou dost make so much
8:13 hope of the godless M shall perish.
8:20 not reject a blameless M, nor take the hand
9:2 But how can a M be just before God?
9:32 he is not a M, as I am, that
10:4 Dost thou see as M sees?
10:5 as the days of M, or thy years as
10:5 or thy years as M's years,
11:2 go unanswered, and a M full of talk be
11:12 But a stupid M will get understanding, when a
11:12 when a wild ass's colt is born a M
12:4 a just and blameless M, am a laughingstock.
12:14 if he shuts a M in, none can open.
12:25 and he makes them stagger like a drunken M
13:9 can you deceive him, as one deceives a M
13:16 salvation, that a godless M shall not come before
13:28 M wastes away like a rotten thing, like a
14:1 M that is born of a woman is of
14:10 But M dies, and is laid low; man breathes
14:10 and is laid low; M breathes his last, and
14:12 and dries up, so M lies down and rises
14:14 If a M die, shall he live again?
14:19 the earth; so thou destroyest the hope of M
15:2 "Should a wise M answer with windy knowledge,
15:7 "Are you the first M that was born?
15:14 What is M, that he can be clean?
15:16 abominable and corrupt, a M who drinks iniquity like
15:20 The wicked M writhes in pain all his days,
15:28 in houses which no M should inhabit, which were
16:21 the right of a M with God, like that
16:21 like that of a M with his neighbor.
17:10 not find a wise M among you.
20:4 from of old, since M was placed upon earth,
20:29 This is the wicked M's portion from God, the
21:4 As for me, is my complaint against M
21:30 testimony that the wicked M is spared in the
22:2 Temanite answered: "Can a M be profitable to God?
22:8 The M with power possessed the land, and the
22:8 land, and the favored M dwelt in it.
22:30 He delivers the innocent M; you will be delivered
23:7 There an upright M could reason with him, and
24:6 and they glean the vineyard of the wicked M
25:4 How then can M be righteous before God?
25:6 sight; how much less M, who is a maggot,
25:6 and the son of M, who is a worm!"
27:13 portion of a wicked M with God, and the
28:9 M puts his hand to the flinty rock, and
28:13 M does not know the way to it, and
28:28 And he said to M, 'Behold, the fear of
31:19 clothing, or a poor M without covering;
32:8 the spirit in a M, the breath of the
32:13 may vanquish him, not M
32:21 to any person or use flattery toward any M
33:12 God is greater than M
33:14 and in two, though M does not perceive it.
33:17 that he may turn M aside from his deed,
33:17 cut off pride from M;
33:19 M is also chastened with pain upon his bed,
33:23 thousand, to declare to M what is right for
33:26 his youthful vigor'; then M prays to God, and
33:29 three times, with a M,
34:7 am without transgression.' What M is like Job, who
34:9 said, 'It profits a M nothing that he should
34:11 the work of a M he will requite him,
34:15 would perish together, and M would return to dust.
34:18 and to nobles, 'Wicked M;
34:21 the ways of a M, and he sees all
34:23 a time for any M to go before God
34:29 a nation or a M –
34:30 that a godless M should not reign, that
34:34 me, and the wise M who hears me will
35:8 Your wickedness concerns a M like yourself, and
35:8 like yourself, and your righteousness a son of M
36:25 have looked on it; M beholds it from afar.
36:28 down, and drop upon M abundantly.
37:7 the hand of every M, that all men may
37:20 Did a M ever wish that he would be
38:3 your loins like a M, I will question you,
38:26 a land where no M is, on the desert
38:26 which there is no M;
40:7 your loins like a M; I will question you,
41:9 the hope of a M is disappointed; he is
42:17 Job died, an old M, and full of days.
Ps 1:1 Blessed is the M who walks not in
7:12 If a M does not repent, God will whet
7:14 Behold, the wicked M conceives evil, and is pregnant
8:4 hast established; what is M that thou art mindful
8:4 and the son of M that thou dost care
9:19 Let not M prevail; let the nations be judged
10:3 his heart, and the M greedy for gain curses
10:18 the oppressed, so that M who is of the
18:25 loyal; with the blameless M thou dost show thyself
19:5 and like a strong M runs its course with
22:6 a worm, and no M; scorned by men, and
25:12 Who is the M that fears the LORD?
32:2 Blessed is the M to whom the LORD imputes
34:6 This poor M cried, and the LORD heard him,
34:8 Happy is the M who takes refuge in him!
34:12 What M is there who desires life, and covets
36:6 like the great deep; M and beast thou savest,
37:7 his way, over the M who carries out evil
37:23 The steps of a M are from the LORD,
37:35 have seen a wicked M overbearing, and towering
37:37 Mark the blameless M, and behold the upright, for
37:37 is posterity for the M of peace.
38:13 am like a deaf M, I do not hear,
38:13 hear, like a dumb M who does not open
38:14 I am like a M who does not hear,
39:5 Surely every M stands as a mere breath!
39:6 [Selah] Surely M goes about as a shadow!
39:6 are they in turmoil; M heaps up, and knows
39:11 When thou dost chasten M with rebukes for sin,
39:11 to him; surely every M is a mere breath!
40:4 Blessed is the M who makes the LORD his
49:7 Truly no M can ransom himself, or give to
49:12 M cannot abide in his pomp, he is like
49:18 happy, and though a M gets praise when he
49:20 M cannot abide in his pomp, he is like
52:1 you boast, O mighty M, of mischief done against
52:7 him, saying, "See the M who would not make
56:11 What can M do to me?
60:11 the foe, for vain is the help of M
62:3 you set upon a M to shatter him, all
62:12 thou dost requite a M according to his work.
64:6 and heart of a M are deep!
71:4 from the grasp of the unjust and cruel M
78:25 M ate of the bread of the angels; he
78:65 sleep, like a strong M shouting because of wine.
80:17 hand be upon the M of thy right hand,
80:17 hand, the son of M whom thou hast made
84:12 hosts, blessed is the M who trusts in thee!
88:4 Pit; I am a M who has no strength,
89:48 What M can live and never see death?

90:3 Thou turnest M back to the dust, and sayest,
92:6 The dull M cannot know, the stupid cannot
94:11 knows the thoughts of M, that they are but
94:12 Blessed is the M whom thou dost chasten, O
101:5 The M of haughty looks and arrogant heart I
101:7 No M who practices deceit shall dwell in my
101:7 in my house; no M who utters lies shall
103:15 As for M, his days are like grass; he
104:14 cattle, and plants for M to cultivate, that he
104:15 gladden the heart of M, oil to make his
104:15 and bread to strengthen M's heart.
104:23 M goes forth to his work and to his
105:17 he had sent a M ahead of them, Joseph,
108:12 the foe, for vain is the help of M
109:6 Appoint a wicked M against him; let an accuser
112:1 Blessed is the M who fears the LORD, who
112:5 is well with the M who deals generously and
112:10 The wicked M sees it and is angry; he
112:10 desire of the wicked M comes to nought.
118:6 What can M do to me?
118:8 in the LORD than to put confidence in M
119:9 How can a young M keep his way pure?
119:134 Redeem me from M's oppression, that I may keep
127:5 Happy is the M who has his quiver full
128:4 Lo, thus shall the M be blessed who fears
135:8 of Egypt, both of M and of beast;
140:11 hunt down the violent M speedily!
141:5 Let a good M strike or rebuke me in
142:4 remains to me, no M cares for me.
143:2 thy servant; for no M living is righteous before
144:3 O LORD, what is M that thou dost regard
144:3 or the son of M that thou dost think
144:4 M is like a breath, his days are like
146:3 in a son of M, in whom there is
147:10 the legs of a M;
Prov 1:5 youth– the wise M also may hear and
1:5 in learning, and the M of understanding acquire skill,
3:4 good repute in the sight of God and M
3:13 Value Happy is the M who finds wisdom, and
3:13 finds wisdom, and the M who gets understanding,
3:30 not contend with a M for no reason, when
3:31 Do not envy a M of violence and do
3:32 ways; for the perverse M is an abomination to
5:21 For a M's ways are before the eyes of
6:11 like a vagabond, and want like an armed M
6:12 worthless person, a wicked M, goes about with
6:19 out lies, and a M who sows discord among
6:26 an adulteress stalks a M's very life.
6:27 Can a M carry fire in his bosom and
6:34 For jealousy makes a M furious, and he will
7:7 the youths, a young M without sense,
8:34 Happy is the M who listens to me, watching
9:7 who reproves a wicked M incurs injury.
9:8 you; reprove a wise M, and he will love
9:9 instruction to a wise M, and he will be
9:9 wiser; teach a righteous M and he will increase
10:15 A rich M's wealth is his strong city; the
10:23 is pleasure to a M of understanding.
11:9 his mouth the godless M would destroy his neighbor,
11:12 lacks sense, but a M of understanding remains silent.
11:17 A M who is kind benefits himself, but a
11:17 himself, but a cruel M hurts himself.
11:18 A wicked M earns deceptive wages, but one who
11:21 Be assured, an evil M will not go unpunished,
11:24 One M gives freely, yet grows all the richer;
11:25 A liberal M will be enriched, and one who
12:2 A good M obtains favor from the LORD, but
12:2 the LORD, but a M of evil devices he
12:3 A M is not established by wickedness, but the
12:8 A M is commended according to his good sense,
12:9 Better is a M of humble standing who works
12:9 who plays the great M but lacks bread.
12:10 A righteous M has regard for the life of
12:13 An evil M is ensnared by the transgression of
12:14 of his words a M is satisfied with good,
12:14 the work of a M's hand comes back to
12:15 eyes, but a wise M listens to advice.
12:16 once, but the prudent M ignores an insult.
12:23 A prudent M conceals his knowledge, but fools
12:25 Anxiety in a M's heart weighs him down, but
12:26 A righteous M turns away from evil, but the
12:27 A slothful M will not catch his prey, but
12:27 prey, but the diligent M will get precious wealth.
13:2 his mouth a good M eats good, but the
13:5 A righteous M hates falsehood, but a wicked man
13:5 falsehood, but a wicked M acts shamefully and
13:7 One M pretends to be rich, yet has nothing;
13:8 The ransom of a M's life is his wealth,
13:8 wealth, but a poor M has no means of
13:16 In everything a prudent M acts with knowledge, but
13:22 A good M leaves an inheritance to his children's
14:6 is easy for a M of understanding.
14:8 wisdom of a prudent M is to discern his
14:12 seems right to a M, but its end is
14:14 A perverse M will be filled with the fruit
14:14 ways, and a good M with the fruit of
14:16 A wise M is cautious and turns away from
14:17 A M of quick temper acts foolishly, but a
14:17 acts foolishly, but a M of discretion is patient.
14:31 who oppresses a poor M insults his Maker, but
14:33 the mind of a M of understanding, but it
15:18 A hot-tempered M stirs up strife, but he who
15:20 father, but a foolish M despises his mother.
15:21 no sense, but a M of understanding walks aright.
15:23 a joy to a M, and a word in
15:24 The wise M's path leads upward to life, that
16:1 the mind belong to M, but the answer of
16:2 the ways of a M are pure in his
16:6 of the LORD a M avoids evil.
16:7 When a M's ways please the LORD, he makes
16:9 A M's mind plans his way, but the LORD
16:14 death, and a wise M will appease it.
16:21 heart is called a M of discernment, and pleasant
16:25 seems right to a M, but its end is
16:27 A worthless M plots evil, and his speech is
16:28 A perverse M spreads strife, and a whisperer
16:29 A M of violence entices his neighbor and leads
17:10 goes deeper into a M of understanding than a
17:11 An evil M seeks only rebellion, and a cruel
17:12 Let a M meet a she-bear robbed of her
17:13 If a M returns evil for good, evil will
17:18 A M without sense gives a pledge, and becomes
17:20 A M of crooked mind does not prosper, and
17:23 A wicked M accepts a bribe from the bosom
17:24 A M of understanding sets his face toward wisdom,
17:26 fine on a righteous M is not good; to
17:27 cool spirit is a M of understanding.
18:4 The words of a M's mouth are deep waters;
18:5 partial to a wicked M, or to deprive a
18:5 to deprive a righteous M of justice.
18:10 strong tower; the righteous M runs into it and
18:11 A rich M's wealth is his strong city, and
18:12 destruction a M's heart is haughty, but humility
18:14 A M's spirit will endure sickness; but a broken
18:16 A M's gift makes room for him and brings
18:20 of his mouth a M is satisfied; he is
19:1 Better is a poor M who walks in his
19:1 his integrity than a M who is perverse in
19:2 not good for a M to be without knowledge,
19:3 When a M's folly brings his way to ruin,
19:4 friends, but a poor M is deserted by his
19:6 favor of a generous M, and every one is
19:6 a friend to a M who gives gifts.
19:7 All a poor M's brothers hate him; how much
19:11 Good sense makes a M slow to anger, and
19:19 A M of great wrath will pay the penalty;
19:21 the mind of a M, but it is the
19:22 is desired in a M is loyalty, and a
19:22 loyalty, and a poor M is better than a
19:25 learn prudence; reprove a M of understanding, and
20:3 an honor for a M to keep aloof from
20:5 The purpose in a M's mind is like deep
20:5 deep water, but a M of understanding will draw
20:6 Many a M proclaims his own loyalty, but a
20:6 loyalty, but a faithful M who can find?
20:7 A righteous M who walks in his integrity–
20:16 Take a M's garment when he has given surety
20:17 is sweet to a M, but afterward his mouth
20:24 A M's steps are ordered by the LORD; how
20:24 LORD; how then can M understand his way?
20:25 a snare for a M to say rashly, "It
20:27 The spirit of M is the lamp of the
21:2 Every way of a M is right in his
21:11 wise; when a wise M is instructed, he gains
21:16 A M who wanders from the way of understanding
21:17 will be a poor M; he who loves wine
21:20 remains in a wise M's dwelling, but a foolish
21:20 dwelling, but a foolish M devours it.
21:22 A wise M scales the city of the mighty
21:24 of the proud, haughty M who acts with arrogant
21:28 the word of a M who hears will endure.
21:29 A wicked M puts on a bold face, but

21:29 face, but an upright M considers his ways.
22:3 A prudent M sees danger and hides himself; but
22:24 no friendship with a M given to anger, nor
22:24 go with a wrathful M,
22:29 Do you see a M skillful in his work?
23:2 if you are a M given to appetite.
23:6 the bread of a M who is stingy; do
23:21 drowsiness will clothe a M with rags.
24:5 A wise M is mightier than a strong man,
24:5 mightier than a strong M, and a man of
24:5 strong man, and a M of knowledge than he
24:12 will he not requite M according to his work?
24:15 wait as a wicked M against the dwelling of
24:16 home; for a righteous M falls seven times, and
24:20 wicked; for the evil M has no future; the
24:29 I will pay the M back for what he
24:30 the vineyard of a M without sense;
24:34 like a robber, and want like an armed M
25:14 without rain is a M who boasts of a
25:18 A M who bears false witness against his neighbor
25:19 Trust in a faithless M in time of trouble
25:26 fountain is a righteous M who gives way before
25:28 A M without self-control is like a city broken
26:7 Like a lame M's legs, which hang useless, is
26:12 Do you see a M who is wise in
26:19 and death, is the M who deceives his neighbor
26:21 so is a quarrelsome M for kindling strife.
27:8 its nest, is a M who strays from his
27:12 A prudent M sees danger and hides himself; but
27:13 Take a M's garment when he has given surety
27:17 sharpens iron, and one M sharpens another.
27:19 so the mind of M reflects the man.
27:19 face, so the mind of man reflects the M
27:20 satisfied, and never satisfied are the eyes of M
27:21 for gold, and a M is judged by his
28:3 A poor M who oppresses the poor is a
28:6 Better is a poor M who walks in his
28:6 integrity than a rich M who is perverse in
28:11 A rich M is wise in his own eyes,
28:11 eyes, but a poor M who has understanding will
28:14 Blessed is the M who fears the LORD always;
28:17 If a M is burdened with the blood of
28:20 A faithful M will abound with blessings, but he
28:21 piece of bread a M will do wrong.
28:22 A miserly M hastens after wealth, and does not
28:23 He who rebukes a M will afterward find more
28:24 the companion of a M who destroys.
28:25 A greedy M stirs up strife, but he who
29:5 A M who flatters his neighbor spreads a net
29:6 An evil M is ensnared in his transgression, but
29:6 transgression, but a righteous M sings and rejoices.
29:7 A righteous M knows the rights of the poor;
29:7 the poor; a wicked M does not understand such
29:9 If a wise M has an argument with a
29:11 anger, but a wise M quietly holds it back.
29:13 The poor M and the oppressor meet together; the
29:20 Do you see a M who is hasty in
29:22 A M of wrath stirs up strife, and a
29:22 up strife, and a M given to anger causes
29:23 A M's pride will bring him low, but he
29:25 The fear of M lays a snare, but he
29:26 from the LORD a M gets justice.
29:27 An unjust M is an abomination to the righteous,
30:1 The M says to Ithi-el, to Ithi-el and Ucal:
30:2 Surely I am too stupid to be a M
30:2 I have not the understanding of a M
30:19 the way of a M with a maiden.
Eccl 1:3 What does M gain by all the toil at
1:8 full of weariness; a M cannot utter it; the
2:8 women, and many concubines, M's delight.
2:12 for what can the M do who comes after
2:14 The wise M has his eyes in his head,
2:16 For of the wise M as of the fool
2:16 How the wise M dies just like the fool!
2:18 leave it to the M who will come after
2:19 will be a wise M or a fool?
2:21 sun, because sometimes a M who has toiled with
2:21 be enjoyed by a M who did not toil
2:22 What has a M from all the toil and
2:24 nothing better for a M than that he should
2:26 For to the M who pleases him God gives
3:11 has put eternity into M's mind, yet so that
3:13 is God's gift to M that every one should
3:19 the same breath, and M has no advantage over
3:21 whether the spirit of M goes upward and the
3:22 better than that a M should enjoy his work,
4:4 work come from a M's envy of his neighbor.
4:12 And though a M might prevail against one who
5:19 Every M also to whom God has given wealth
6:2 heavy upon men: a M to whom God gives
6:3 If a M begets a hundred children, and lives
6:7 All the toil of M is for his mouth,
6:8 advantage has the wise M over the fool?
6:8 what does the poor M have who knows how
6:10 it is known what M is, and that he
6:11 vanity, and what is M the better?
6:12 what is good for M while he lives the
6:12 For who can tell M what will be after
7:5 is better for a M to hear the rebuke
7:7 oppression makes the wise M foolish, and a bribe
7:14 the other, so that M may not find out
7:15 there is a righteous M who perishes in his
7:15 there is a wicked M who prolongs his life
7:19 strength to the wise M more than ten rulers
7:20 is not a righteous M on earth who does
7:28 One M among a thousand I found, but a
7:29 found, that God made M upright, but they have
8:1 Who is like the wise M
8:1 A M's wisdom makes his face shine, and the
8:5 mind of a wise M will know the time
8:6 time and way, although M's trouble lies heavy upon
8:8 No M has power to retain the spirit, or
8:9 under the sun, while M lords it over man
8:9 man lords it over M to his hurt.
8:15 I commend enjoyment, for M has no good thing
8:17 work of God, that M cannot find out the
8:17 However much M may toil in seeking, he will
8:17 even though a wise M claims to know, he
9:1 is love or hate M does not know.
9:2 As is the good M, so is the sinner;
9:12 For M does not know his time.
9:15 it a poor wise M, and he by his
9:15 Yet no one remembered that poor M
9:16 might, though the poor M's wisdom is despised, and
10:2 A wise M's heart inclines him toward the right,
10:12 words of a wise M's mouth win him favor,
10:14 multiplies words, though no M knows what is to
11:8 For if a M lives many years, let him
11:9 Rejoice, O young M, in your youth, and let
12:5 and desire fails; because M goes to his eternal
12:13 commandments; for this is the whole duty of M
Song 8:7 If a M offered for love all the wealth
Wis 1:9 counsels of an ungodly M, and a report of
2:1 no remedy when a M comes to his end,
2:10 oppress the righteous poor M; let us not spare
2:12 wait for the righteous M, because he is inconvenient
2:18 for if the righteous M is God's son, he
2:23 souls; for God created M for incorruption, and made
3:10 disregarded the righteous M and rebelled against
4:7 But the righteous M, though he die early, will
4:16 The righteous M who had died will condemn the
4:16 condemn the prolonged old age of the unrighteous M
4:17 end of the wise M, and will not understand
5:1 the righteous M will stand with great confidence
5:4 say, "This is the M whom we once held
5:14 hope of the ungodly M is like chaff carried
6:6 For the lowliest M may be pardoned in mercy,
7:2 the seed of a M and the pleasure of
7:28 so much as the M who lives with wisdom.
9:2 thy wisdom hast formed M, to have dominion over
9:5 of thy maidservant, a M who is weak and
9:13 For what M can learn the counsel of God?
10:3 But when an unrighteous M departed from her in
10:4 it, steering the righteous M by a paltry piece
10:5 recognized the righteous M and preserved him
10:6 Wisdom rescued a righteous M when the ungodly
10:10 When a righteous M fled from his brother's wrath,
10:13 When a righteous M was sold, wisdom did not
12:19 people that the righteous M must be kind, and
13:13 the image of a M,
14:4 that even if a M lacks skill, he may
14:9 God are the ungodly M and his ungodliness,
14:20 whom shortly before they had honored as a M
15:8 same clay-- this M who was made of
15:13 For this M, more than all others, knows that
15:16 For a M made them, and one whose spirit
15:16 formed them; for no M can form a god
16:14 A M in his wickedness kills another, but he
16:26 of crops that feeds M, but that thy word
16:29 hope of an ungrateful M will melt like wintry
18:11 master, and the common M suffered the same loss
18:21 For a blameless M was quick to act as

27:18 For as a M destroys his enemy, so you
27:27 If a M does evil, it will roll back
27:28 issue from the proud M, but vengeance lies in
27:30 abominations, and the sinful M will possess them.
28:3 Does a M harbor anger against another, and yet
28:4 no mercy toward a M like himself, and yet
28:8 lessen sins; for a M given to anger will
28:9 strife, and a sinful M will disturb friends and
28:10 the strength of the M will be his anger,
28:19 Happy is the M who is protected from it,
29:5 A M will kiss another's hands until he gets
29:8 be patient with a M in humble circumstances, and
29:9 Help a poor M for the commandment's sake, and
29:14 A good M will be surety for his neighbor,
29:14 his neighbor, but a M who has lost his
29:22 life of a poor M under the shelter of
29:22 sumptuous food in another M's house.
29:28 to bear for a M who has feeling: scolding
30:14 off is a poor M who is well and
30:14 constitution than a rich M who is severely afflicted
30:22 is the life of M, and the rejoicing of
30:22 the rejoicing of a M is length of days.
30:25 A M of cheerful and good heart will give
31:3 The rich M toils as his wealth accumulates, and
31:4 The poor M toils as his livelihood diminishes, and
31:8 Blessed is the rich M who is found blameless,
31:12 you seated at the table of a great M
31:19 How ample a little is for a well-disciplined M
31:27 is life to a M who is without wine?
32:7 Speak, young M, if there is need of you,
32:10 the thunder, and approval precedes a modest M
32:17 A sinful M will shun reproof, and will find
32:18 A M of judgment will not overlook an idea,
32:18 an insolent and proud M will not cower in
33:1 evil will befall the M who fears the Lord,
33:2 A wise M will not hate the law, but
33:3 A M of understanding will trust in the law;
34:1 A M of no understanding has vain and false
34:9 An educated M knows many things, and one with
34:15 the soul of the M who fears the Lord!
34:20 father's eyes is the M who offers a sacrifice
34:21 of it is a M of blood.
34:25 If a M washes after touching a dead body,
34:26 So if a M fasts for his sins, and
35:6 offering of a righteous M anoints the altar, and
35:7 sacrifice of a righteous M is acceptable, and the
35:13 case of a poor M; and he will listen
35:19 till he repays the M according to his deeds,
36:20 cause grief, but a M of experience will pay
36:21 woman will accept any M, but one daughter is
36:25 is no wife, a M will wander about and
36:26 who will trust a M that has no home,
37:11 selling, with a grudging M about gratitude or with
37:11 or with a merciless M about kindness, with an
37:11 work or with a M hired for a year
37:12 constantly with a godly M whom you know to
37:14 For a M's soul sometimes keeps him better informed
37:19 A M may be shrewd and the teacher of
37:20 A M skilled in words may be hated; he
37:22 A M may be wise to his own advantage,
37:23 A wise M will instruct his own people, and
37:24 A wise M will have praise heaped upon him,
37:25 The life of a M is numbered by days,
38:4 earth, and a sensible M will not despise them.
38:19 life of the poor M weighs down his heart.
39:26 all the needs of M's life are water and
40:1 was created for every M, and a heavy yoke
40:3 of death, from the M who sits on a
40:4 and ashes, from the M who wears purple and
40:8 With all flesh, both M and beast, and upon
40:14 A generous M will be made glad; likewise
40:19 a city establish a M's name, but a blameless
40:27 blessing, and covers a M better than any glory.
40:29 When a M looks to the table of another,
40:29 pollutes himself with another M's food, but a man
40:29 man's food, but a M who is intelligent and
41:1 his possessions, to a M without distractions, who is
41:15 Better is the M who hides his folly than
41:15 his folly than the M who hides his wisdom.
41:21 of gazing at another M's wife;
41:23 proper shame, and will find favor with every M
42:8 foolish or the aged M who quarrels with the
42:14 the wickedness of a M than a woman who
43:4 A M tending a furnace works in burning heat,
45:1 Lord brought forth a M of mercy, who found
45:1 beloved by God and M, Moses, whose memory is

45:6 of Moses, a holy M like him, of the
46:19 And no M accused him.
47:5 hand to slay a M mighty in war, to
49:15 And no M like Joseph has been born, and
Is 2:9 So M is humbled, and men are brought low—
2:11 The haughty looks of M shall be brought low,
2:17 And the haughtiness of M shall be humbled, and
2:22 Turn away from M in whose nostrils is breath,
3:2 of water; the mighty M and the soldier, the
3:3 of fifty and the M of rank, the counselor
3:5 oppress one another, every M his fellow and every
3:5 his fellow and every M his neighbor; the youth
3:6 When a M takes hold of his brother in
4:1 take hold of one M in that day, saying,
5:15 M is bowed down, and men are brought low,
6:5 for I am a M of unclean lips, and
7:21 In that day a M will keep alive a
9:15 the elder and honored M is the head, and
9:19 for the fire; no M spares his brother.
10:18 as when a sick M wastes away.
13:7 be feeble, and every M's heart will melt,
13:14 to gather them, every M will turn to his
13:14 own people, and every M will flee to his
14:16 you: 'Is this the M who made the earth
19:2 they will fight, every M against his brother and
19:2 his brother and every M against his neighbor, city
19:14 doings as a drunken M staggers in his vomit.
22:17 will hurl you away violently, O you strong M
24:20 staggers like a drunken M, it sways like a
28:4 the summer: when a M sees it, he eats
29:8 As when a hungry M dreams he is eating
29:8 as when a thirsty M dreams he is drinking
29:21 a word make a M out to be an
31:8 a sword, not of M; and a sword, not
31:8 a sword, not of M, shall devour him; and
33:8 lie waste, the wayfaring M ceases.
33:8 witnesses are despised, there is no regard for M
35:6 then shall the lame M leap like a hart,
36:6 the hand of any M who leans on it.
38:11 I shall look upon M no more among the
42:13 forth like a mighty M, like a man of
42:13 mighty man, like a M of war he stirs
44:13 the figure of a M, with the beauty of
44:13 the beauty of a M, to dwell in a
44:15 becomes fuel for a M; he takes a part
45:12 the earth, and created M upon it; it was
46:11 from the east, the M of my counsel from
47:3 will take vengeance, and I will spare no M
50:2 Why, when I came, was there no M
51:12 you are afraid of M who dies, of the
51:12 of the son of M who is made like
53:3 rejected by men; a M of sorrows, and acquainted
53:9 and with a rich M in his death, although
55:7 way, and the unrighteous M his thoughts; let him
56:2 Blessed is the M who does this, and the
56:2 and the son of M who holds it fast,
57:1 The righteous M perishes, and no one lays it
57:1 For the righteous M is taken away from calamity,
58:5 a day for a M to humble himself?
59:16 that there was no M, and wondered that there
62:5 For as a young M marries a virgin, so
65:20 days, or an old M who does not fill
66:2 But this is the M to whom I will
66:3 him who kills a M; he who sacrifices a
Jer 2:6 passes through, where no M dwells?'
3:1 "If a M divorces his wife and she goes
3:1 him and becomes another M's wife, will he return
4:25 lo, there was no M, and all the birds
4:29 are forsaken, and no M dwells in them.
5:1 you can find a M, one who does justice
6:23 in array as a M for battle, against you,
7:20 on this place, upon M and beast, upon the
8:6 not spoken aright; no M repents of his wickedness,
9:12 Who is the M so wise that he can
9:23 "Let not the wise M glory in his wisdom,
9:23 let not the mighty M glory in his might,
9:23 let not the rich M glory in his riches;
10:14 Every M is stupid and without knowledge; every
10:23 that the way of M is not in himself,
10:23 it is not in M who walks to direct
11:3 Israel: Cursed be the M who does not heed
12:11 made desolate, but no M lays it to heart.
13:11 the loins of a M, so I made the
14:9 thou be like a M confused, like a mighty
14:9 confused, like a mighty M who cannot save?
15:10 you bore me, a M of strife and contention

M

16:20 Can M make for himself gods?
17:5 LORD: "Cursed is the M who trusts in man
17:5 man who trusts in M and makes flesh his
17:7 "Blessed is the M who trusts in the LORD,
17:10 to give to every M according to his ways,
20:15 Cursed be the M who brought the news to
20:16 Let that M be like the cities which the
21:6 of this city, both M and beast; they shall
22:8 this city, and every M will say to his
22:28 Is this M Coniah a despised, broken pot, a
22:30 the LORD: "Write this M down as childless, a
22:30 down as childless, a M who shall not succeed
23:9 am like a drunken M, like a man overcome
23:9 drunken man, like a M overcome by wine, because
23:24 Can a M hide himself in secret places so
23:34 I will punish that M and his household.
23:36 the burden is every M's own word, and you
26:11 all the people, "This M deserves the sentence of
26:16 and the prophets, "This M does not deserve the
26:20 There was another M who prophesied in the name
30:6 and see, can a M bear a child?
30:6 do I see every M with his hands on
31:22 thing on the earth: a woman protects a M
31:27 with the seed of M and the seed of
31:30 his own sin; each M who eats sour grapes,
31:34 no longer shall each M teach his neighbor and
32:19 of men, rewarding every M according to his ways
32:43 is a desolation, without M or beast; it is
33:10 is a waste without M or beast,' in the
33:10 that are desolate, without M or inhabitant or beast,
33:12 which is waste, without M or beast, and in
33:17 shall never lack a M to sit on the
33:18 shall never lack a M in my presence to
35:4 son of Igdaliah, the M of God, which was
35:19 shall never lack a M to stand before me."
36:29 cut off from it M and beast?"
37:10 only wounded men, every M in his tent, they
38:4 the king, "Let this M be put to death,
38:4 For this M is not seeking the welfare of
44:7 cut off from you M and woman, infant and
44:26 the mouth of any M of Judah in all
49:5 be driven out, every M straight before him, with
49:18 says the LORD, no M shall dwell there, no
49:18 shall dwell there, no M shall sojourn in her.
49:33 an everlasting waste; no M shall dwell there, no
49:33 shall dwell there, no M shall sojourn in her."
50:3 dwell in it; both M and beast shall flee
50:40 the LORD, so no M shall dwell there, and
50:40 and no son of M shall sojourn in her.
50:42 horses, arrayed as a M for battle against you,
51:6 of Babylon, let every M save his life!
51:17 Every M is stupid and without knowledge; every
51:22 I break in pieces M and woman; with you
51:22 in pieces the old M and the youth; with
51:22 in pieces the young M and the maiden;
51:43 which no son of M passes.
51:45 Let every M save his life from the fierce
51:62 dwell in it, neither M nor beast, and it
Lam 3:1 I am the M who has seen affliction under
3:27 is good for a M that he bear the
3:35 the right of a M in the presence of
3:36 High, to subvert a M in his cause, the
3:39 Why should a living M complain, a man, about
3:39 living man complain, a M, about the punishment of
Bar 4:15 respect for an old M, and had no pity
6:18 every side upon a M who has offended a
6:32 funeral feast for a M who has died.
6:36 They cannot save a M from death or rescue
6:37 sight to a blind M; they cannot rescue a
6:37 they cannot rescue a M who is in distress.
6:41 they see a dumb M, who cannot speak, they
6:41 pray Bel that the M may speak, as though
6:73 therefore is a just M who has no idols,
Ezek 1:10 the face of a M in front; the four
2:1 to me, "Son of M, stand upon your feet,
2:3 to me, "Son of M, I send you to
2:6 And you, son of M, be not afraid of
2:8 "But you, son of M, hear what I say
3:1 to me, "Son of M, eat what is offered
3:3 to me, "Son of M, eat this scroll that
3:4 to me, "Son of M, go, get you to
3:10 to me, "Son of M, all my words that
3:17 to me: "Son of M, I have made you
3:18 his life, that wicked M shall die in his
3:20 Again, if a righteous M turns from his righteousness
3:21 you warn the righteous M not to sin, and
3:25 you, O son of M, behold, cords will be
4:1 you, O son of M, take a brick and
4:16 to me, "Son of M, behold, I will break
5:1 you, O son of M, take a sharp sword;
6:2 to me: "Son of M, set your face toward
7:2 you, O son of M, thus says the Lord
8:2 the appearance of a M; below what appeared to
8:5 to me, "Son of M, lift up your eyes
8:6 to me, "Son of M, do you see what
8:8 to me, "Son of M, dig in the wall";
8:12 to me, "Son of M, have you seen what
8:12 in the dark, every M in his room of
8:15 me, "Have you seen this, O son of M
8:17 me, "Have you seen this, O son of M
9:2 which faces north, every M with his weapon for
9:2 with them was a M clothed in linen, with
9:3 he called to the M clothed in linen, who
9:11 And lo, the M clothed in linen, with the
10:2 he said to the M clothed in linen, "Go
10:3 the house, when the M went in; and a
10:6 when he commanded the M clothed in linen, "Take
10:7 the hands of the M clothed in linen, who
10:14 the face of a M, and the third the
11:2 to me, "Son of M, these are the men
11:4 prophesy against them, prophesy, O son of M
11:15 to me: "Son of M, your brethren, even your
12:2 to me: "Son of M, you dwell in the
12:3 Therefore, son of M, prepare for yourself an exile's
12:9 to me: "Son of M, has not the house
12:18 to me: "Son of M, eat your bread with
12:22 to me: "Son of M, what is this proverb
12:27 to me: "Son of M, behold, they of the
13:2 to me: "Son of M, prophesy against the prophets
13:17 "And you, son of M, set your face against
14:3 to me: "Son of M, these men have taken
14:4 the Lord GOD: Any M of the house of
14:8 my face against that M, I will make him
14:13 to me: "Son of M, when a land sins
14:13 cut off from it M and beast,
14:15 desolate, so that no M may pass through because
14:17 cut off from it M and beast;
14:19 cut off from it M and beast;
14:21 cut off from it M and beast!
15:2 to me: "Son of M, how does the wood
16:2 to me: "Son of M, make known to Jerusalem
17:2 to me: "Son of M, propound a riddle, and
17:15 Can a M escape who does such things?
18:5 "If a M is righteous and does what is
18:8 executes true justice between M and man,
18:8 justice between man and M,
18:14 "But if this M begets a son who sees
18:21 "But if a wicked M turns away from all
18:24 But when a righteous M turns away from his
18:24 things that the wicked M does, shall he live?
18:26 a righteous M turns away from his righteousness
18:27 Again, when a wicked M turns away from the
20:3 to me: "Son of M, speak to the elders
20:4 judge them, son of M, will you judge them?
20:8 they did not every M cast away the detestable
20:11 ordinances, by whose observance M shall live.
20:13 ordinances, by whose observance M shall live; and
20:21 by whose observance M shall live; they profaned
20:27 "Therefore, son of M, speak to the house of
20:46 to me: "Son of M, set your face toward
21:2 to me: "Son of M, set your face toward
21:6 Sigh therefore, son of M; sigh with breaking heart
21:9 to me: "Son of M, prophesy and say, Thus
21:12 and wail, son of M, for it is against
21:14 "Prophesy therefore, son of M; clap your hands and
21:19 me again: "Son of M, mark two ways for
21:28 "And you, son of M, prophesy, and say, Thus
22:2 "And you, son of M, will you judge, will
22:18 to me: "Son of M, the house of Israel
22:24 to me: "Son of M, say to her, You
22:30 I sought for a M among them who should
23:2 to me: "Son of M, there were two women,
23:36 to me: "Son of M, will you judge Oholah
24:2 to me: "Son of M, write down the name
24:16 to me: "Son of M, behold, I am about
24:25 "And you, son of M, on the day when
25:2 to me: "Son of M, set your face toward
25:13 cut off from it M and beast; and I
26:2 to me: "Son of M, because Tyre said concerning
27:2 "Now you, son of M, raise a lamentation over
28:2 to me: "Son of M, say to the prince
28:2 you are but a M, and no god, though

M

28:9 you are but a M, and no god, in
28:12 to me: "Son of M, raise a lamentation over
28:21 to me: "Son of M, set your face toward
29:2 to me: "Son of M, set your face against
29:8 cut off from you M and beast;
29:11 No foot of M shall pass through it, and
29:18 to me: "Son of M, Nebuchadrezzar king of Babylon
30:2 to me: "Son of M, prophesy, and say, Thus
30:21 to me: "Son of M, I have broken the
30:24 before him like a M mortally wounded.
31:2 to me: "Son of M, say to Pharaoh king
32:2 to me: "Son of M, raise a lamentation over
32:13 and no foot of M shall trouble them any
32:18 to me: "Son of M, wail over the multitude
33:2 to me: "Son of M, speak to your people
33:2 the land take a M from among them, and
33:6 one of them; that M is taken away in
33:7 "So you, son of M, I have made a
33:8 the wicked, O wicked M, you shall surely die,
33:8 his way, that wicked M shall die in his
33:10 "And you, son of M, say to the house
33:12 And you, son of M, say to your people,
33:21 of the month, a M who had escaped from
33:22 by the time the M came to me in
33:24 to me: "Son of M, the inhabitants of these
33:24 'Abraham was only one M, yet he got possession
33:30 for you, son of M, your people who talk
34:2 to me: "Son of M, prophesy against the shepherds
35:2 to me: "Son of M, set your face against
36:1 "And you, son of M, prophesy to the mountains
36:11 will multiply upon you M and beast; and they
36:17 to me: "Son of M, when the house of
37:3 to me, "Son of M, can these bones live?"
37:9 breath, prophesy, son of M, and say to the
37:11 to me, "Son of M, these bones are the
37:16 to me: "Son of M, take a stick and
38:2 to me: "Son of M, set your face toward
38:14 spoil?' "Therefore, son of M, prophesy, and say to
38:21 the Lord GOD; every M's sword will be against
39:1 "And you, son of M, prophesy against Gog, and
39:15 any one sees a M's bone, then he shall
39:17 for you, son of M, thus says the Lord
40:3 behold, there was a M, whose appearance was like
40:4 And the M said to me, "Son of man,
40:4 to me, "Son of M, look with your eyes,
40:5 measuring reed in the M's hand was six long
41:19 the face of a M toward the palm tree
43:6 While the M was standing beside me, I heard
43:7 to me, "Son of M, this is the place
43:10 "And you, son of M, describe to the house
43:18 to me, "Son of M, thus says the Lord
44:5 to me, "Son of M, mark well, see with
47:3 in his hand, the M measured a thousand cubits,
47:6 to me, "Son of M, have you seen this?"
Dan 2:10 "There is not a M on earth who can
2:25 exiles from Judah a M who can make known
3:10 a decree, that every M who hears the sound
5:5 the fingers of a M's hand appeared and wrote
5:11 in your kingdom a M in whom is the
6:7 to any god or M for thirty days, except
6:12 an interdict, that any M who makes petition to
6:12 to any god or M within thirty days except
7:4 two feet like a M; and the mind of
7:4 the mind of a M was given to it.
7:8 the eyes of a M, and a mouth speaking
7:13 like a son of M, and he came to
8:15 before me one having the appearance of a M
8:16 And I heard a M's voice between the banks
8:16 called, "Gabriel, make this M understand the vision."
8:17 "Understand, O son of M, that the vision is
9:21 speaking in prayer, the M Gabriel, whom I had
10:5 looked, and behold, a M clothed in linen, whose
10:11 to me, "O Daniel, M greatly beloved, give heed
10:18 the appearance of a M touched me and strengthened
10:19 And he said, "O M greatly beloved, fear not,
12:6 I said to the M clothed in linen, who
12:7 The M clothed in linen, who was above the
13:1 There was a M living in Babylon whose name
13:21 you that a young M was with you, and
13:37 Then a young M, who had been hidden, came
13:39 could not hold the M, for he was too
13:40 her who the young M was, but she would
Hos 3:3 or belong to another M; so will I also
6:9 in wait for a M, so the priests are
9:7 is a fool, the M of the spirit is
11:9 am God and not M, the Holy One in
Amos 2:7 of the afflicted; a M and his father go
4:13 wind, and declares to M what is his thought;
5:19 light; as if a M fled from a lion,
6:10 And when a M's kinsman, he who burns him,
Obad 1:9 Teman, so that every M from Mount Esau will
Jon 1:14 not perish for this M's life, and lay not
3:7 his nobles: Let neither M nor beast, herd nor
3:8 drink water, but let M and beast be covered
Mic 2:2 away; they oppress a M and his house, a
2:2 and his house, a M and his inheritance.
2:11 If a M should go about and utter wind
4:4 they shall sit every M under his vine and
6:8 has showed you, O M, what is good; and
6:11 Shall I acquit the M with wicked scales and
7:2 The godly M has perished from the earth, and
7:3 bribe, and the great M utters the evil desire
7:6 against her mother-in-law; a M's enemies are the
Nah 2:1 M the ramparts; watch the road; gird your loins;
Hab 1:13 wicked swallows up the M more righteous than he?
2:5 is treacherous; the arrogant M shall not abide.
Zeph 1:3 "I will sweep away M and beast; I will
1:14 is bitter, the mighty M cries aloud there.
3:6 made desolate, without a M, without an inhabitant.
Zech 1:8 night, and behold, a M riding upon a red
1:10 they are.' So the M who was standing among
1:21 Judah, so that no M raised his head; and
2:1 saw, and behold, a M with a measuring line
2:4 say to that young M, 'Jerusalem shall be inhabited
4:1 waked me, like a M that is wakened out
6:12 of hosts, "Behold, the M whose name is the
8:10 was no wage for M or any wage for
8:10 for I set every M against his fellow.
12:1 formed the spirit of M within him:
13:7 my shepherd, against the M who stands next to
Mal 2:12 of Jacob, for the M who does this, any
3:8 shall we return?' Will M rob God?
3:17 spare them as a M spares his son who
1Mac 2:8 has become like a M without honor;
2:41 us fight against every M who comes to attack
3:32 left Lysias, a distinguished M of royal lineage, in
4:30 Saul, and of the M who carried his armor.
5:42 this command, "Permit no M to encamp, but make
5:63 The M Judas and his brothers were greatly honored
7:7 Now then send a M whom you trust; let
7:8 he was a great M in the kingdom and
7:38 Take vengeance on this M and on his army,
8:16 They trust one M each year to rule over
8:16 all heed the one M, and there is no
10:16 So he said, "Shall we find another such M
11:38 all his troops, each M to his own place,
14:12 Each M sat under his vine and his fig
14:14 and did away with every lawless and wicked M
2Mac 3:4 But a M named Simon, of the tribe of
3:11 son of Tobias, a M of very prominent position,
3:17 had come over the M, which plainly showed to
3:28 carried him away, this M who had just entered
3:32 offered sacrifice for the M's recovery.
4:2 the government the M who was the benefactor
4:26 was supplanted by another M, was driven as a
4:31 trouble, leaving Andronicus, a M of high rank, to
4:35 and displeased at the unjust murder of the M
4:40 a certain Auranus, a M advanced in years and
5:18 in many sins, this M would have been scourged
5:22 more barbarous than the M who appointed him;
5:25 When this M arrived in Jerusalem, he pretended to
6:6 A M could neither keep the sabbath, nor observe
6:18 in high position, a M now advanced in age
6:21 unlawful sacrifice took the M aside, because of their
7:12 astonished at the young M's spirit, for he regarded
7:21 woman's reasoning with a M's courage, and said to
7:23 shaped the beginning of M and devised the origin
7:25 Since the young M would not listen to him
7:30 still speaking, the young M said, "What are you
8:8 Philip saw that the M was gaining ground little
8:9 a general and a M of experience in military
8:32 forces, a most unholy M, and one who had
9:9 And so the ungodly M's body swarmed with worms,
9:10 able to carry the M who a little while
10:10 son of that ungodly M, and will give a
10:11 This M, when he succeeded to the kingdom,
12:35 and was a strong M, caught hold of Gorgias,
12:35 to take the accursed M alive, when one of
12:43 took up a collection, M by man, to the
12:43 a collection, man by M, to the amount of
13:4 informed him that this M was to blame for
13:6 push to destruction any M guilty of sacrilege or

M

13:21 But Rhodocus, a M from the ranks of the
14:24 his presence; he was warmly attached to the M
14:27 accusations of that depraved M, wrote to Nicanor,
14:28 their agreement when the M had done no wrong.
14:31 cleverly outwitted by the M, he went to the
14:31 them to hand the M over.
14:32 not know where the M was whom he sought,
14:37 to Nicanor as a M who loved his fellow
15:12 a noble and good M, of modest bearing and
15:13 Then likewise a M appeared, distinguished by his
15:14 saying, "This is a M who loves the brethren
15:30 And the M who was ever in body and
15:30 his fellow citizens, the M who maintained his
15:32 head and that profane M's arm, which had been
Mt 1:19 Joseph, being a just M and unwilling to put
4:4 answered, "It is written, M shall not live by
7:9 Or what M of you, if his son asks
7:24 be like a wise M who built his house
7:26 be like a foolish M who built his house
8:9 For I am a M under authority, with soldiers
8:20 but the Son of M has nowhere to lay
8:27 saying, "What sort of M is this, that even
9:3 said to themselves, "This M is blaspheming."
9:6 that the Son of M has authority on earth
9:9 there, he saw a M called Matthew sitting at
9:33 cast out, the dumb M spoke; and the crowds
10:23 before the Son of M comes.
10:35 come to set a M against his father, and
10:36 her mother-in-law; and a M's foes will be those
10:41 who receives a righteous M because he is a
10:41 he is a righteous M shall receive a righteous
10:41 shall receive a righteous M's reward.
11:8 To see a M clothed in soft raiment?
11:19 demon'; the Son of M came eating and drinking,
12:8 For the Son of M is lord of the
12:10 behold, there was a M with a withered hand.
12:11 said to them, "What M of you, if he
12:12 more value is a M than a sheep!
12:13 he said to the M, "Stretch out your hand."
12:13 And the M stretched it out, and it was
12:22 so that the dumb M spoke and saw.
12:24 of demons, that this M casts out demons."
12:29 one enter a strong M's house and plunder his
12:29 his goods, unless he first binds the strong M
12:32 against the Son of M will be forgiven; but
12:35 The good M out of his good treasure brings
12:35 good, and the evil M out of his evil
12:40 will the Son of M be three days and
12:43 gone out of a M, he passes through waterless
12:45 last state of that M becomes worse than the
12:47 he replied to the M who told him, "Who
13:24 be compared to a M who sowed good seed
13:31 mustard seed which a M took and sowed in
13:37 is the Son of M;
13:41 The Son of M will send his angels, and
13:44 a field, which a M found and covered up;
13:54 said, "Where did this M get this wisdom and
13:56 Where then did this M get all this?"
14:31 saying to him, "O M of little faith, why
15:11 the mouth defiles a M, but what comes out
15:11 comes out of the mouth, this defiles a M
15:14 And if a blind M leads a blind man,
15:14 man leads a blind M, both will fall into
15:18 proceeds from the heart, and this defiles a M
15:20 are what defile a M; but to eat with
15:20 eat with unwashed hands does not defile a M
16:13 that the Son of M is?"
16:24 his disciples, "If any M would come after me,
16:26 will it profit a M, if he gains the
16:26 Or what shall a M give in return for
16:27 For the Son of M is to come with
16:27 he will repay every M for what he has
16:28 see the Son of M coming in his kingdom."
17:9 until the Son of M is raised from the
17:12 also the Son of M will suffer at their
17:14 to the crowd, a M came up to him
17:21 them, "The Son of M is to be delivered
18:7 but woe to the M by whom the temptation
18:11 If a M has a hundred sheep, and one
19:5 'For this reason a M shall leave his father
19:6 joined together, let not M put asunder."
19:10 the case of a M with his wife, it
19:20 The young M said to him, "All these I
19:22 When the young M heard this he went away
19:23 hard for a rich M to enter the kingdom
19:24 than for a rich M to enter the kingdom
19:28 when the Son of M shall sit on his
20:18 and the Son of M will be delivered to
20:28 as the Son of M came not to be
21:28 A M had two sons; and he went to
22:11 he saw there a M who had no wedding
22:16 and care for no M; for you do not
22:24 Moses said, 'If a M dies, having no children,
23:9 And call no M your father on earth, for
24:27 will be the coming of the Son of M
24:30 of the Son of M in heaven, and then
24:30 see the Son of M coming on the clouds
24:37 will be the coming of the Son of M
24:39 will be the coming of the Son of M
24:44 for the Son of M is coming at an
25:14 be as when a M going on a journey
25:24 to be a hard M, reaping where you did
25:31 "When the Son of M comes in his glory,
26:2 and the Son of M will be delivered up
26:24 The Son of M goes as it is written
26:24 but woe to that M by whom the Son
26:24 whom the Son of M is betrayed!
26:24 been better for that M if he had not
26:45 and the Son of M is betrayed into the
26:48 shall kiss is the M; seize him."
26:64 see the Son of M seated at the right
26:71 to the bystanders, "This M was with Jesus of
26:72 with an oath, "I do not know the M
26:74 and to swear, "I do not know the M
27:19 do with that righteous M, for I have suffered
27:24 innocent of this righteous M's blood; see to it
27:32 they came upon a M of Cyrene, Simon by
27:32 Simon by name; this M they compelled to carry
27:47 hearing it said, "This M is calling Elijah."
27:57 came a rich M from Arimathea, named Joseph,
Mk 1:23 in their synagogue a M with an unclean spirit;
2:7 hearts, "Why does this M speak thus?
2:10 that the Son of M has authority on earth
2:27 sabbath was made for M, not man for the
2:27 made for man, not M for the sabbath;
2:28 so the Son of M is lord even of
3:1 the synagogue, and a M was there who had
3:3 he said to the M who had the withered
3:5 and said to the M, "Stretch out your hand."
3:27 can enter a strong M's house and plunder his
3:27 first binds the strong M; then indeed he may
4:23 If any M has ears to hear, let him
4:26 is as if a M should scatter seed upon
5:2 of the tombs a M with an unclean spirit,
5:8 "Come out of the M, you unclean spirit!"
5:15 his right mind, the M who had had the
5:18 into the boat, the M who had been possessed
6:2 saying, "Where did this M get all this?
6:20 a righteous and holy M, and kept him safe.
7:11 you say, 'If a M tells his father or
7:15 is nothing outside a M which by going into
7:15 come out of a M are what defile him."
7:17 whatever goes into a M from outside cannot defile
7:19 comes out of a M is what defiles a
7:19 out of a man is what defiles a M
7:20 of the heart of M, come evil thoughts, fornication,
7:22 things come from within, and they defile a M
7:31 brought to him a M who was deaf and
8:22 to him a blind M, and begged him to
8:23 he took the blind M by the hand, and
8:31 that the Son of M must suffer many things,
8:34 to them, "If any M would come after me,
8:36 does it profit a M, to gain the whole
8:37 For what can a M give in return for
8:38 will the Son of M also be ashamed, when
9:9 until the Son of M should have risen from
9:12 of the Son of M, that he should suffer
9:31 them, "The Son of M will be delivered into
9:38 "Teacher, we saw a M casting out demons in
10:2 it lawful for a M to divorce his wife?"
10:4 said, "Moses allowed a M to write a certificate
10:7 'For this reason a M shall leave his father
10:9 joined together, let not M put asunder."
10:17 on his journey, a M ran up and knelt
10:25 than for a rich M to enter the kingdom
10:33 and the Son of M will be delivered to
10:45 For the Son of M also came not to
10:49 they called the blind M, saying to him, "Take
10:51 And the blind M said to him, "Master, let
12:1 "A M planted a vineyard, and set a hedge
12:14 and care for no M; for you do not
12:19 us that if a M's brother dies and leaves

12:19 leaves no child, the M must take the wife,
13:26 see the Son of M coming in clouds with
13:34 It is like a M going on a journey,
14:13 the city, and a M carrying a jar of
14:21 For the Son of M goes as it is
14:21 but woe to that M by whom the Son
14:21 whom the Son of M is betrayed!
14:21 been better for that M if he had not
14:41 come; the Son of M is betrayed into the
14:44 shall kiss is the M; seize him and lead
14:51 And a young M followed him, with nothing but
14:62 see the Son of M seated at the right
14:69 to the bystanders, "This M is one of them."
14:71 do not know this M of whom you speak."
15:7 insurrection, there was a M called Barabbas.
15:12 I do with the M whom you call the
15:38 he said, "Truly this M was the Son of
16:5 they saw a young M sitting on the right
Lk 1:18 I am an old M, and my wife is
1:27 virgin betrothed to a M whose name was Joseph,
2:25 Now there was a M in Jerusalem, whose name
2:25 was Simeon, and this M was righteous and devout,
2:52 in stature, and in favor with God and M
4:4 him, "It is written, M shall not live by
4:33 synagogue there was a M who had the spirit
5:8 I am a sinful M, O Lord."
5:12 cities, there came a M full of leprosy; and
5:18 on a bed a M who was paralyzed, and
5:20 their faith he said, M, your sins are forgiven
5:24 that the Son of M has authority on earth
5:24 he said to the M who was paralyzed–"I
6:5 them, "The Son of M is lord of the
6:6 synagogue and taught, a M was there whose right
6:8 he said to the M who had the withered
6:22 as evil, on account of the Son of M
6:39 parable: "Can a blind M lead a blind man?
6:39 parable: "Can a blind man lead a blind M
6:45 The good M out of the good treasure of
6:45 good, and the evil M out of his evil
6:48 he is like a M building a house, who
6:49 them is like a M who built a house
7:8 For I am a M set under authority, with
7:12 the city, behold, a M who had died was
7:14 And he said, "Young M, I say to you,
7:15 And the dead M sat up, and began to
7:25 A M clothed in soft clothing?
7:34 demon.' The Son of M has come eating and
7:39 to himself, "If this M were a prophet, he
8:27 there met him a M from the city who
8:29 the unclean spirit to come out of the M
8:33 came out of the M and entered the swine,
8:35 Jesus, and found the M from whom the demons
8:38 The M from whom the demons had gone begged
8:41 And there came a M named Jairus, who was
8:49 was still speaking, a M from the ruler's house
9:22 saying, "The Son of M must suffer many things,
9:23 to all, "If any M would come after me,
9:25 does it profit a M if he gains the
9:26 will the Son of M be ashamed when he
9:38 And behold, a M from the crowd cried, "Teacher,
9:44 for the Son of M is to be delivered
9:49 "Master, we saw a M casting out demons in
9:57 along the road, a M said to him, "I
9:58 but the Son of M has nowhere to lay
10:30 Jesus replied, "A M was going down from Jerusalem
10:36 proved neighbor to the M who fell among the
11:14 gone out, the dumb M spoke, and the people
11:21 When a strong M, fully armed, guards his own
11:24 gone out of a M, he passes through waterless
11:26 last state of that M becomes worse than the
11:30 will the Son of M be to this generation.
12:8 men, the Son of M also will acknowledge before
12:10 against the Son of M will be forgiven; but
12:14 he said to him, M, who made me a
12:15 all covetousness; for a M's life does not consist
12:16 land of a rich M brought forth plentifully;
12:40 for the Son of M is coming at an
13:6 told this parable: "A M had a fig tree
13:19 mustard seed which a M took and sowed in
14:2 behold, there was a M before him who had
14:8 lest a more eminent M than you be invited
14:9 'Give place to this M and then you will
14:12 said also to the M who had invited him,
14:16 said to him, "A M once gave a great
14:30 mock him, saying, 'This M began to build, and
15:2 scribes murmured, saying, "This M receives sinners
15:4 them this parable: "What M of you, having a
15:11 said, "There was a M who had two sons;
16:1 "There was a rich M who had a steward,
16:1 to him that this M was wasting his goods.
16:19 "There was a rich M, who was clothed in
16:20 gate lay a poor M named Lazarus, full of
16:21 fell from the rich M's table; moreover the dogs
16:22 The poor M died and was carried by the
16:22 The rich M also died and was buried;
17:22 of the Son of M, and you will not
17:24 will the Son of M be in his day.
17:26 be in the days of the Son of M
17:30 when the Son of M is revealed.
18:2 feared God nor regarded M;
18:4 fear God nor regard M,
18:8 when the Son of M comes, will he find
18:14 I tell you, this M went down to his
18:25 than for a rich M to enter the kingdom
18:29 you, there is no M who has left house
18:31 of the Son of M by the prophets will
18:35 to Jericho, a blind M was sitting by the
19:2 And there was a M named Zacchaeus; he was
19:7 the guest of a M who is a sinner."
19:10 For the Son of M came to seek and
19:14 do not want this M to reign over us.'
19:21 you are a severe M; you take up what
19:22 I was a severe M, taking up what I
20:9 people this parable: "A M planted a vineyard, and
20:28 us that if a M's brother dies, having a
20:28 but no children, the M must take the wife
21:27 see the Son of M coming in a cloud
21:36 place, and to stand before the Son of M
22:10 entered the city, a M carrying a jar of
22:22 For the Son of M goes as it has
22:22 but woe to that M by whom he is
22:45 a crowd, and the M called Judas, one of
22:46 betray the Son of M with a kiss?"
22:54 at him, said, "This M also was with him."
22:56 But Peter said, M, I am not."
22:57 insisted, saying, "Certainly this M also was with him;
22:58 But Peter said, M, I do not know what
22:67 on the Son of M shall be seated at
23:2 saying, "We found this M perverting our nation, and
23:4 the multitudes, "I find no crime in this M
23:6 he asked whether the M was a Galilean.
23:14 "You brought me this M as one who was
23:14 did not find this M guilty of any of
23:17 together, "Away with this M, and release to us
23:18 us Barabbas"– a M who had been thrown
23:24 He released the M who had been thrown into
23:40 our deeds; but this M has done nothing wrong."
23:46 and said, "Certainly this M was innocent!"
23:49 Now there was a M named Joseph from the
23:49 a good and righteous M,
23:51 This M went to Pilate and asked for the
24:7 that the Son of M must be delivered into
Jn 1:6 There was a M sent from God, whose name
1:9 light that enlightens every M was coming into the
1:13 of the will of M, but of God.
1:30 'After me comes a M who ranks before me,
1:51 God ascending and descending upon the Son of M
2:10 said to him, "Every M serves the good wine
2:25 to bear witness of M; for he himself knew
2:25 man; for he himself knew what was in M
3:1 Now there was a M of the Pharisees, named
3:2 This M came to Jesus by night and said
3:4 him, "How can a M be born when he
3:13 he who descended from heaven, the Son of M
3:14 must the Son of M be lifted up,
4:29 people, "Come, see a M who told me all
4:50 The M believed the word that Jesus spoke to
5:4 One M was there, who had been ill for
5:6 The sick M answered him, "Sir, I have no
5:6 "Sir, I have no M to put me into
5:8 And at once the M was healed, and he
5:9 Jews said to the M who was cured, "It
5:10 he answered them, "The M who healed me said
5:11 him, "Who is the M who said to you,
5:12 Now the M who had been healed did not
5:14 The M went away and told the Jews that
5:26 execute judgment, because he is the Son of M
5:33 I receive is from M; but I say this
6:27 which the Son of M will give to you;
6:50 from heaven, that a M may eat of it
6:52 saying, "How can this M give us his flesh
6:53 of the Son of M and drink his blood,

6:62 see the Son of M ascending where he was
7:4 For no M works in secret if he seeks
7:12 While some said, "He is a good M
7:15 is it that this M has learning, when he
7:17 sent me; if any M's will is to do
7:22 and you circumcise a M upon the sabbath.
7:23 on the sabbath a M receives circumcision, so that
7:23 sabbath I made a M's whole body well?
7:25 "Is not this the M whom they seek to
7:27 we know where this M comes from; and when
7:31 more signs than this M has done?"
7:35 another, "Where does this M intend to go that
7:46 The officers answered, "No M ever spoke like this
7:46 officers answered, "No man ever spoke like this M
7:51 our law judge a M without first giving him
8:28 up the Son of M, then you will know
8:40 to kill me, a M who has told you
9:1 by, he saw a M blind from his birth.
9:2 "Rabbi, who sinned, this M or his parents, that
9:3 was not that this M sinned, or his parents,
9:6 spittle and anointed the M's eyes with the clay,
9:8 "Is not this the M who used to sit
9:9 He said, "I am the M
9:11 He answered, "The M called Jesus made clay and
9:13 to the Pharisees the M who had formerly been
9:16 the Pharisees said, "This M is not from God,
9:16 said, "How can a M who is a sinner
9:17 said to the blind M, "What do you say
9:18 the parents of the M who had received his
9:24 time they called the M who had been blind,
9:24 we know that this M is a sinner."
9:29 but as for this M, we do not know
9:30 The M answered, "Why, this is a marvel!
9:32 the eyes of a M born blind.
9:33 If this M were not from God, he could
9:35 said, "Do you believe in the Son of M
10:1 by another way, that M is a thief and
10:33 because you, being a M, make yourself God."
10:41 John said about this M was true."
11:1 Now a certain M was ill, Lazarus of Bethany,
11:37 eyes of the blind M have kept this man
11:37 man have kept this M from dying?"
11:39 sister of the dead M, said to him, "Lord,
11:44 The dead M came out, his hands and feet
11:47 For this M performs many signs.
11:50 for you that one M should die for the
12:23 for the Son of M to be glorified.
12:34 that the Son of M must be lifted up?
12:34 Who is this Son of M
13:31 is the Son of M glorified, and in him
14:23 answered him, "If a M loves me, he will
15:6 If a M does not abide in me, he
15:13 Greater love has no M than this, that a
15:13 than this, that a M lay down his life
16:32 will be scattered, every M to his home, and
18:14 was expedient that one M should die for the
18:17 also one of this M's disciples?" He said, "I
18:26 a kinsman of the M whose ear Peter had
18:29 said, "What accusation do you bring against this M
18:30 answered him, "If this M were not an evildoer,
18:31 us to put any M to death."
18:39 I should release one M for you at the
18:40 again, "Not this M, but Barabbas!" Now Barabbas
19:5 Pilate said to them, "Behold the M
19:12 "If you release this M, you are not Caesar's
19:21 the Jews,' but, 'This M said, I am King
21:21 he said to Jesus, "Lord, what about this M
Acts 1:18 (Now this M bought a field with the reward
2:22 Jesus of Nazareth, a M attested to you by
3:2 And a M lame from birth was being carried,
3:16 name, has made this M strong whom you see
3:16 Jesus has given the M this perfect health in
4:9 by what means this M has been healed,
4:10 dead, by him this M is standing before you
4:14 But seeing the M that had been healed standing
4:22 For the M on whom this sign of healing
5:1 But a M named Ananias with his wife Sapphira
5:28 intend to bring this M's blood upon us."
6:5 they chose Stephen, a M full of faith and
6:13 witnesses who said, "This M never ceases to speak
7:24 he defended the oppressed M and avenged him by
7:27 each other?' But the M who was wronging his
7:56 and the Son of M standing at the right
7:58 feet of a young M named Saul.
8:9 But there was a M named Simon who had
8:10 the greatest, saying, "This M is that power of
9:11 of Judas for a M of Tarsus named Saul;
9:12 he has seen a M named Ananias come in
9:13 from many about this M, how much evil he
9:21 "Is not this the M who made havoc in
9:33 There he found a M named Aeneas, who had
10:1 Caesarea there was a M named Cornelius, a
10:2 Italian Cohort, a devout M who feared God with
10:22 an upright and God-fearing M, who is well spoken
10:26 up, saying, "Stand up; I too am a M
10:28 should not call any M common or unclean.
10:30 house; and behold, a M stood before me in
11:12 and we entered the M's house.
11:24 he was a good M, full of the Holy
12:22 "The voice of a god, and not of M
13:7 proconsul, Sergius Paulus, a M of intelligence, who
13:21 son of Kish, a M of the tribe of
13:22 son of Jesse a M after my heart, who
13:23 my will.' Of this M's posterity God has brought
13:38 brethren, that through this M forgiveness of sins is
14:8 Lystra there was a M sitting, who could not
16:9 in the night: a M of Macedonia was standing
17:24 in shrines made by M,
17:29 a representation by the art and imagination of M
17:31 in righteousness by a M whom he has appointed,
18:7 the house of a M named Titius Justus, a
18:10 with you, and no M shall attack you to
18:13 the tribunal, saying, "This M is persuading men to
18:24 He was an eloquent M, well versed in the
19:16 And the M in whom the evil spirit was
19:24 For a M named Demetrius, a silversmith, who made
19:35 "Men of Ephesus, what M is there who does
20:9 And a young M named Eutychus was sitting in
21:11 at Jerusalem bind the M who owns this girdle
21:28 This is the M who is teaching men everywhere
22:12 one Ananias, a devout M according to the law,
22:25 you to scourge a M who is a Roman
22:26 For this M is a Roman citizen."
23:9 and contended, "We find nothing wrong in this M
23:17 said, "Take this young M to the tribune; for
23:18 to bring this young M to you, as he
23:22 tribune dismissed the young M, charging him, "Tell
23:27 This M was seized by the Jews, and was
23:30 a plot against the M, I sent him to
24:5 we have found this M a pestilent fellow, an
25:3 favor to have the M sent to Jerusalem, planning
25:5 anything wrong about the M, let them accuse him."
25:14 saying, "There is a M left prisoner by Felix;
25:17 tribunal and ordered the M to be brought in.
25:22 like to hear the M myself." "Tomorrow," said he,
25:24 us, you see this M about whom the whole
26:31 to one another, "This M is doing nothing to
26:32 said to Festus, "This M could have been set
28:4 another, "No doubt this M is a murderer.
28:7 belonging to the chief M of the island, named
Rom 1:23 for images resembling mortal M or birds or animals
2:1 have no excuse, O M, whoever you are, when
2:3 Do you suppose, O M, that when you judge
2:6 will render to every M according to his works:
2:26 So, if a M who is uncircumcised keeps the
3:4 be true though every M be false, as it
3:28 we hold that a M is justified by faith
4:6 a blessing upon the M to whom God reckons
4:8 covered; blessed is the M against whom the Lord
5:7 die for a righteous M —though perhaps for a
5:7 perhaps for a good M one will dare even
5:12 the world through one M and death through sin,
5:15 many died through one M's trespass, much more
5:15 grace of that one M Jesus Christ abounded for
5:16 effect of that one M's sin.
5:17 If, because of one M's trespass, death reigned
5:17 reigned through that one M, much more will those
5:17 life through the one M Jesus Christ.
5:18 Then as one M's trespass led to condemnation for
5:18 all men, so one M's act of righteousness leads
5:19 For as by one M's disobedience many were made
5:19 sinners, so by one M's obedience many will be
7:3 she lives with another M while her husband is
7:3 if she marries another M she is not an
7:24 Wretched M that I am!
9:10 conceived children by one M, our forefather Isaac,
9:16 it depends not upon M's will or exertion, but
9:20 who are you, a M, to answer back to
10:5 Moses writes that the M who practices the
10:10 For M believes with his heart and so is
14:1 As for the M who is weak in faith,
14:2 anything, while the weak M eats only vegetables.

M

14:5 One M esteems one day as better than another,
14:5 than another, while another M esteems all days alike.
15:20 I build on another M's foundation,
1Cor 1:20 Where is the wise M
2:9 nor the heart of M conceived, what God has
2:11 what person knows a M's thoughts except the spirit
2:11 the spirit of the M which is in him?
2:14 The unspiritual M does not receive the gifts of
2:15 The spiritual M judges all things, but is himself
3:10 a foundation, and another M is building upon it.
3:10 Let each M take care how he builds upon
3:13 hay, straw— each M's work will become manifest;
3:14 the work which any M has built on the
3:15 If any M's work is burned up, he will
4:5 every M will receive his commendation from God.
5:1 among pagans; for a M is living with his
5:4 Lord Jesus on the M who has done such
5:5 are to deliver this M to Satan for the
6:5 that there is no M among you wise enough
6:18 other sin which a M commits is outside the
6:18 body; but the immoral M sins against his own
7:1 is well for a M not to touch a
7:2 temptation to immorality, each M should have his
7:32 The unmarried M is anxious about the affairs of
7:33 Lord; but the married M is anxious about worldly
8:10 one sees you, a M of knowledge, at table
8:11 knowledge this weak M is destroyed, the brother
10:13 has overtaken you that is not common to M
10:28 of consideration for the M who informed you, and
10:29 be determined by another M's scruples?
11:3 the head of every M is Christ, the head
11:4 Any M who prays or prophesies with his head
11:7 For a M ought not to cover his head,
11:7 of God; but woman is the glory of M
11:8 (For M was not made from woman, but woman
11:8 was not made from woman, but woman from M
11:9 Neither was M created for woman, but woman for
11:9 woman, but woman for M
11:11 is not independent of M nor man of woman;
11:11 independent of man nor M of woman;
11:12 woman was made from M, so man is now
11:12 made from man, so M is now born of
11:14 you that for a M to wear long hair
11:28 Let a M examine himself, and so eat of
13:11 when I became a M, I gave up childish
14:17 enough, but the other M is not edified.
15:21 For as by a M came death, by a
15:21 came death, by a M has come also the
15:36 You foolish M
15:45 is written, "The first M Adam became a living
15:47 The first M was from the earth, a man
15:47 from the earth, a M of dust; the second
15:47 of dust; the second M is from heaven.
15:48 As was the M of dust, so are those
15:48 and as is the M of heaven, so are
15:49 the image of the M of dust, we shall
15:49 the image of the M of heaven.
2Cor 1:17 plans like a worldly M, ready to say Yes
3:16 minds; but when a M turns to the Lord
4:2 commend ourselves to every M's conscience in the
5:12 pride themselves on a M's position and not on
8:12 according to what a M has, not according to
10:18 it is not the M who commends himself that
10:18 is accepted, but the M whom the Lord commends.
11:20 bear it if a M makes slaves of you,
12:2 I know a M in Christ who fourteen years
12:3 I know that this M was caught up into
12:4 cannot be told, which M may not utter.
12:5 On behalf of this M I will boast, but
Gal 1:1 from men nor through M, but through Jesus Christ
1:11 by me is not M's gospel.
1:12 not receive it from M, nor was I taught
2:16 who know that a M is not justified by
3:11 is evident that no M is justified before God
3:15 one annuls even a M's will, or adds to
5:3 testify again to every M who receives circumcision
6:1 Brethren, if a M is overtaken in any trespass,
6:5 For each M will have to bear his own
6:7 mocked, for whatever a M sows, that he will
6:17 Henceforth let no M trouble me; for I bear
Eph 2:9 of works, lest any M should boast.
2:15 in himself one new M in place of the
3:16 Spirit in the inner M,
5:5 no fornicator or impure M, or one who is
5:29 For no M ever hates his own flesh, but
5:31 "For this reason a M shall leave his father

Phil 3:4 If any other M thinks he has reason for
Col 1:28 we proclaim, warning every M and teaching every
1:28 man and teaching every M in all wisdom, that
1:28 we may present every M mature in Christ.
3:11 barbarian, Scythian, slave, free M, but Christ is all,
1Thes 4:6 know God; that no M transgress, and wrong his
4:8 disregards this, disregards not M but God, who gives
2Thes 2:3 comes first, and the M of lawlessness is revealed,
3:14 this letter, note that M, and have nothing to
1Tim 2:5 God and men, the M Christ Jesus,
3:5 way; for if a M does not know how
5:1 not rebuke an older M but exhort him as
5:22 participate in another M's sins; keep yourself pure.
6:11 But as for you, M of God, shun all
6:16 unapproachable light, whom no M has ever seen or
2Tim 3:17 in righteousness, that the M of God may be
Tit 1:5 directed you, if any M is blameless, the husband
3:10 As for a M who is factious, after admonishing
Heb 2:6 testified somewhere, "What is M that thou art
2:6 or the son of M, that thou carest for
7:6 But this M who has not their genealogy received
8:2 set up not by M but by the Lord.
10:28 A M who has violated the law of Moses
10:29 be deserved by the M who has spurned the
11:12 Therefore from one M, and him as good as
13:6 be afraid; what can M do to me?"
Jas 1:7 suppose that a double-minded M, unstable in all his
1:10 So will the rich M fade away in the
1:11 Blessed is the M who endures trial, for when
1:18 Let every M be quick to hear, slow to
1:19 for the anger of M does not work the
1:22 he is like a M who observes his natural
1:25 deceives his heart, this M's religion is vain.
2:2 For if a M with gold rings and in
2:2 assembly, and a poor M in shabby clothing also
2:3 say to the poor M, "Stand there," or, "Sit
2:6 But you have dishonored the poor M
2:14 my brethren, if a M says he has faith
2:20 be shown, you shallow M, that faith apart from
2:24 You see that a M is justified by works
3:2 he is a perfect M, able to bridle the
5:6 have killed the righteous M; he does not resist
5:15 will save the sick M, and the Lord will
5:16 prayer of a righteous M has great power in
5:17 Elijah was a M of like nature with ourselves
1Pet 4:18 And "If the righteous M is scarcely saved, where
2Pet 1:21 by the impulse of M, but men moved by
2:8 by what that righteous M saw and heard as
2:19 for whatever overcomes a M, to that he is
1Jn 4:12 No M has ever seen God; if we love
Rev 1:13 like a son of M, clothed with a long
4:7 the face of a M, and the fourth living
7:9 great multitude which no M could number, from
9:5 torture of a scorpion, when it stings a M
14:14 like a son of M, with a golden crown
16:3 blood of a dead M, and every living thing
21:17 forty-four cubits by a M's measure, that is, an

MAN-CHILD

Job 3:3 night which said, 'A M is conceived.'

MAN-MADE

Dan 14:5 I do not revere M idols, but the living

MANA-EN

Acts 13:1 Niger, Lucius of Cyrene, M a member of the

MANACLES

Sir 21:19 his feet, and like M on his right hand.

MANAGE (3)

1Tim 3:4 He must M his own household well, keeping his
3:5 not know how to M his own household, how
3:12 wife, and let them M their children and their

MANAGED

Acts 27:16 island called Cauda, we M with difficulty to secure

MANAHATH (3)

Gen 36:23 sons of Shobal: Alvan, M, Ebal, Shepho, and Onam.
1Chr 1:40 sons of Shobal: Alian, M, Ebal, Shephi, and Onam.
8:6 carried into exile to M:

MANAHATHITES

1Chr 2:54 and half of the M, the Zorites.

MANASSEH (147)

Gen 41:51 name of the first-born M, "For," he said, "God
46:20 of Egypt were born M and Ephraim, whom Asenath,
48:1 him his two sons, M and Ephraim.
48:5 are mine; Ephraim and M shall be mine, as
48:13 Israel's left hand, and M in his left hand
48:14 upon the head of M, crossing his hands, for
48:14 crossing his hands, for M was the first-born.
48:17 from Ephraim's head to M's head.
48:20 as Ephraim and as M; and thus he put
48:20 as Manasseh"; and thus he put Ephraim before M
50:23 Machir the son of M were born upon Joseph's
Num 1:10 of Ammihud, and from M, Gamaliel the son of
1:34 Of the people of M, their generations, by their
1:35 of the tribe of M was thirty-two thousand two
2:20 be the tribe of M, the leader of the
2:20 of the people of M being Gamaliel the son
7:54 of the men of M:
10:23 of the men of M was Gamaliel the son
13:11 from the tribe of M, Gaddi the son of
26:28 according to their families: M and Ephraim.
26:29 The sons of M: of Machir, the family of
26:34 are the families of M; and their number was
27:1 of Machir, son of M, from the families of
27:1 from the families of M the son of Joseph.
32:33 to the half-tribe of M the son of Joseph,
32:39 Machir the son of M went to Gilead and
32:40 Machir the son of M, and he settled in
32:41 Jair the son of M went and took their
34:14 also the half-tribe of M;
34:23 of the sons of M a leader, Hanniel the
36:1 of Machir, son of M, of the fathers' houses
36:12 of the sons of M the son of Joseph,
Deut 3:13 of Argob, I gave to the half-tribe of M
33:17 of Ephraim, and such are the thousands of M
34:2 land of Ephraim and M, all the land of
Josh 1:12 and the half-tribe of M Joshua said,
4:12 and the half-tribe of M passed over armed before
12:6 Reubenites and the Gadites and the half-tribe of M
13:7 the nine tribes and half the tribe of M
13:8 of the tribe of M the Reubenites and the
13:29 to the half-tribe of M; it was allotted to
13:31 Machir the son of M for the half of
14:4 Joseph were two tribes, M and Ephraim; and no
16:4 The people of Joseph, M and Ephraim, received
17:1 to the tribe of M, for he was the
17:1 Machir the first-born of M, the father of Gilead,
17:2 of the tribe of M, by their families, Abi-ezer,
17:2 the male descendants of M the son of Joseph,
17:3 of Machir, son of M, had no sons, but
17:5 Thus there fell to M ten portions, besides the
17:6 because the daughters of M received an inheritance
17:7 territory of M reached from Asher to Mich-methath,
17:8 of Tappuah belonged to M, but the town of
17:8 on the boundary of M belonged to the sons
17:9 among the cities of M, belong to Ephraim.
17:9 Then the boundary of M goes on the north
17:11 Issachar and in Asher M had Beth-shean and its
17:12 Yet the sons of M could not take possession
17:17 Joseph, to Ephraim and M, "You are a numerous
18:7 half the tribe of M have received their inheritance
20:8 and Golan in Bashan, from the tribe of M
21:5 and the half-tribe of M, ten cities.
21:6 from the half-tribe of M in Bashan, thirteen cities.
21:25 of the half-tribe of M, Taanach with its pasture
21:27 of the half-tribe of M, Golan in Bashan with
22:1 and the half-tribe of M,
22:7 of the tribe of M Moses had given a
22:9 and the half-tribe of M returned home, parting from
22:10 and the half-tribe of M built there an altar
22:11 and the half-tribe of M have built an altar
22:13 and the half-tribe of M, in the land of
22:15 and the half-tribe of M, in the land of
22:21 and the half-tribe of M said in answer to
Judg 1:27 M did not drive out the inhabitants of Beth-shean
6:15 is the weakest in M, and I am the
6:35 sent messengers throughout all M; and they too
7:23 Asher and from all M, and they pursued after
11:29 passed through Gilead and M, and passed on to
12:4 you Gileadites, in the midst of Ephraim and M
1Kgs 4:13 Jair the son of M, which are in Gilead,
2Kgs 20:21 with his fathers; and M his son reigned in
21:1 M was twelve years old when he began to
21:9 did not listen, and M seduced them to do
21:11 servants the prophets, "Because M king of Judah has
21:16 Moreover M shed very much innocent blood, till he
21:17 of the acts of M, and all that he
21:18 And M slept with his fathers, and was buried
21:20 of the LORD, as M his father had done.
23:12 and the altars which M had made in the
23:26 the provocations with which M had provoked him.
24:3 for the sins of M, according to all that
1Chr 3:13 son, Hezekiah his son, M his son,
5:18 and the half-tribe of M had valiant men, who
5:23 of the half-tribe of M dwelt in the land;
5:26 and the half-tribe of M, and brought them to
6:61 half-tribe, the half of M, ten cities.
6:62 Issachar, Asher, Naphtali, and M in Bashan.
6:70 of the half-tribe of M, Aner with its pasture
6:71 of the half-tribe of M: Golan in Bashan with
7:14 The sons of M: Asriel, whom his Aramean concubine
7:17 of Gilead the son of Machir, son of M
9:3 Benjamin, Ephraim, and M dwelt in Jerusalem:
12:19 of the men of M deserted to David when
12:20 Ziklag these men of M deserted to him: Adnah,
12:20 Elihu, and Zillethai, chiefs of thousands in M
12:31 Of the half-tribe of M eighteen thousand, who were
12:37 and the half-tribe of M from beyond the Jordan,
27:20 for the half-tribe of M, Joel the son of
27:21 for the half-tribe of M in Gilead, Iddo the
2Chr 15:9 and those from Ephraim, M, and Simeon who were
30:1 also to Ephraim and M, that they should come
30:10 country of Ephraim and M, and as far as
30:11 men of Asher, of M, and of Zebulun humbled
30:18 of them from Ephraim, M, Issachar, and Zebulun,
31:1 and in Ephraim and M, until they had destroyed
32:33 And M his son reigned in his stead.
33:1 M was twelve years old when he began to
33:9 M seduced Judah and the inhabitants of Jerusalem,
33:10 The LORD spoke to M and to his people,
33:11 of Assyria, who took M with hooks and bound
33:13 Then M knew that the LORD was God.
33:18 of the acts of M, and his prayer to
33:20 So M slept with his fathers, and they buried
33:22 of the LORD, as M his father had done.
33:22 all the images that M his father had made,
33:23 before the LORD, as M his father had humbled
34:6 in the cities of M, Ephraim, and Simeon, and
34:9 threshold, had collected from M and Ephraim and
Ezra 10:30 Benaiah, Ma-aseiah, Mattaniah, Bezalel, Binnui,
10:33 Mattattah, Zabad, Eliphelet, Jeremai, M, and
Jud 8:2 Her husband M, who belonged to her tribe and
8:7 face; and her husband M had left her gold
10:3 wear while her husband M was living.
16:22 of her life after M her husband died and
16:23 cave of her husband M,
16:24 kin to her husband M, and to her own
Ps 60:7 Gilead is mine; M is mine; Ephraim is my
80:2 shine forth before Ephraim and Benjamin and M
108:8 Gilead is mine; M is mine; Ephraim is my
Is 9:21 devours his neighbor's flesh, M Ephraim, and
9:21 Manasseh Ephraim, and Ephraim M, and together
Jer 15:4 earth because of what M the son of Hezekiah,
Ezek 48:4 side to the west, M, one portion.
48:5 Adjoining the territory of M, from the east side
Mt 1:10 Hezekiah the father of M, and Manasseh the father
1:10 father of Manasseh, and M the father of Amos,
Rev 7:6 of the tribe of M,

MANASSEHS

Josh 17:10 to the north being M, with the sea forming

MANASSITE

Deut 3:14 Jair the M took all the region of Argob,

MANASSITES (10)

Deut 4:43 the Gadites, and Golan in Bashan for the M
29:8 Reubenites, the Gadites, and the half-tribe of the M
Josh 13:29 the half-tribe of the M according to their families.
16:9 the inheritance of the M, all those towns with
17:6 Gilead was allotted to the rest of the M
22:30 the Gadites and the M spoke, it pleased them
22:31 the Gadites and the M, "Today we know that
2Kgs 10:33 the Reubenites, and the M, from Aroer, which is
1Chr 7:29 the borders of the M, Beth-shean and its towns,
26:32 the half-tribe of the M for everything pertaining to

MANDRAKES (6)

Gen 30:14 Reuben went and found M in the field, and
30:14 "Give me, I pray, some of your son's M
30:15 take away my son's M also?" Rachel said, "Then
30:15 may lie with you tonight for your son's M

30:16 for I have hired you with my son's M
Song 7:13 The M give forth fragrance, and over our doors

MANFULLY (3)
1Mac 6:31 out and burned these with fire, and fought M
2Mac 6:27 Therefore, by M giving up my life now, I
14:43 on the wall, and M threw himself down into

MANGER (4)
Lk 2:7 laid him in a M, because there was no
2:12 wrapped in swaddling cloths and lying in a M
2:16 and Joseph, and the babe lying in a M
13:15 his ass from the M, and lead it away

MANGLE
Sir 28:23 a leopard it will M them.

MANHOOD (3)
Hos 12:3 heel, and in his M he strove with God.
1Mac 13:53 his son had reached M, so he made him
Eph 4:13 of God, to mature M, to the measure of

MANIFEST (27)
Ps 90:16 Let thy work be M to thy servants, and
Wis 7:21 secret and what is M,
Sir 6:22 name, and is not M to many.
Is 24:23 his elders he will M his glory.
Bar 6:51 It will be M to all the nations and
Ezek 20:41 scattered; and I will M my holiness among you
28:22 Sidon, and I will M my glory in the
28:22 judgments in her, and M my holiness in her;
28:25 they are scattered, and M my holiness in them
1Mac 11:12 from Alexander, and their enmity became M
15:9 your glory will become M in all the earth."
2Mac 9:8 the power of God M to all.
Mk 4:22 except to be made M; nor is anything secret,
Lk 8:17 shall not be made M, nor anything secret that
Jn 9:3 God might be made M in him.
14:21 will love him and M myself to him."
14:22 it that you will M yourself to us, and
Acts 2:20 comes, the great and M day.
4:16 performed through them is M to all the inhabitants
10:40 day and made him M;
1Cor 3:13 man's work will become M; for the Day will
Col 1:26 generations but now made M to his saints.
1Tim 6:15 this will be made M at the proper time
1Pet 1:20 world but was made M at the end of
1Jn 1:2 the life was made M, and we saw it,
1:2 Father and was made M to us--
4:9 of God was made M among us, that God

MANIFESTATION (5)
2Mac 3:24 caused so great a M that all who had
12:22 the enemy at the M to them of him
15:27 men, and were greatly gladdened by God's M
Lk 1:80 the day of his M to Israel.
1Cor 12:7 each is given the M of the Spirit for

MANIFESTATIONS
1Cor 14:12 you are eager for M of the Spirit, strive

MANIFESTED (12)
Ps 77:14 workest wonders, who hast M thy might among the
Wis 16:21 thy sustenance M thy sweetness toward thy children;
2Mac 15:34 the Lord who had M himself, saying, "Blessed is
Jn 2:11 Cana in Galilee, and M his glory; and his
17:6 "I have M thy name to the men whom
Rom 3:21 of God has been M apart from law, although
2Cor 4:10 Jesus may also be M in our bodies.
4:11 of Jesus may be M in our mortal flesh.
1Tim 3:16 our religion: He was M in the flesh, vindicated
2Tim 1:10 ago, and now has M through the appearing of
Tit 1:3 at the proper time M in his word through
1Pet 5:4 the chief Shepherd is M you will obtain the

MANIFESTING
2Mac 14:15 his own heritage by M himself.

MANIFESTS
Wis 1:2 to the test, and M himself to those who

MANIFOLD (5)
Job 11:6 For he is M in understanding.
Ps 104:24 O LORD, how M are thy works!
Wis 7:22 is intelligent, holy, unique, M, subtle, mobile, clear,
Lk 18:30 who will not receive M more in this time,
Eph 3:10 through the church the M wisdom of God might

MANIUS
2Mac 11:34 "Quintus Memmius and Titus M, envoys of the

MANKIND (17)
Tob 8:6 them the race of M has sprung.
Job 12:10 every living thing and the breath of all M
Wis 7:6 there is for all M one entrance into life,
10:8 but also left for M a reminder of their
14:21 a hidden trap for M, because men, in bondage
Sir 45:4 and meekness; he chose him out of all M
Is 13:12 than fine gold, and M than the gold of
Jer 32:20 Israel and among all M, and hast made thee
Bar 6:26 men's shoulders, revealing to M their worthlessness.
Zeph 1:3 I will cut off M from the face of
2Mac 7:28 Thus also M comes into being.
Eph 2:3 nature children of wrath, like the rest of M
Rev 9:4 but only those of M who have not the
9:15 and the year, to kill a third of M
9:18 plagues a third of M was killed, by the
9:20 The rest of M, who were not killed by
14:4 have been redeemed from M as first fruits for

MANLINESS
2Mac 15:17 arousing valor and awaking M in the souls of

MANNA (17)
Ex 16:31 Israel called its name M; it was like coriander
16:33 put an omer of M in it, and place
16:35 of Israel ate the M forty years, till they
16:35 land; they ate the M, till they came to
Num 11:6 at all but this M to look at."
11:7 Now the M was like coriander seed, and its
11:9 in the night, the M fell with it.
Deut 8:3 and fed you with M, which you did not
8:16 in the wilderness with M which your fathers did
Josh 5:12 And the M ceased on the morrow, when they
5:12 people of Israel had M no more, but ate
Neh 9:20 didst not withhold thy M from their mouth, and
Ps 78:24 rained down upon them M to eat, and gave
Jn 6:31 Our fathers ate the M in the wilderness; as
6:49 Your fathers ate the M in the wilderness, and
Heb 9:4 golden urn holding the M, and Aaron's rod that
Rev 2:17 some of the hidden M, and I will give

MANNER (33)
Gen 18:11 with Sarah after the M of women.
19:31 to us after the M of all the earth.
Ex 12:11 In this M you shall eat it: your loins
Deut 15:2 And this is the M of the release: every
Josh 6:15 city in the same M seven times: it was
Judg 13:12 to be the boy's M of life, and what
18:7 in security, after the M of the Sidonians, quiet
Ruth 4:7 and this was the M of attesting in Israel.
1Kgs 7:37 After this M he made the ten stands; all
2Kgs 17:33 own gods, after the M of the nations from
17:34 this day they do according to the former M
17:40 listen, but they did according to their former M
Neh 6:4 way and I answered them in the same M
Esth 13:5 perversely following a strange M of life and laws,
Ps 144:13 be full, providing all M of store; may our
Wis 2:15 to us, because his M of life is unlike
15:7 making all in like M; but which shall be
Sir 19:27 laughter, and a man's M of walking, show what
Jer 27:12 I spoke in like M: "Bring your necks under
Ezek 20:30 defile yourselves after the M of your fathers and
Amos 4:10 a pestilence after the M of Egypt; I slew
2Mac 10:6 with rejoicing, in the M of the feast of
14:46 This was the M of his death.
15:12 modest bearing and gentle M, one who spoke
Mk 4:16 And these in like M are the ones sown
Lk 16:25 and Lazarus in like M evil things; but now
Acts 22:3 according to the strict M of the law of
26:4 "My M of life from my youth, spent from
Rom 1:29 filled with all M of wickedness, evil, covetousness,
1Cor 11:27 Lord in an unworthy M will be guilty of
Eph 4:22 belongs to your former M of life and is
Phil 1:27 Only let your M of life be worthy of
Jude 1:8 Yet in like M these men in their dreamings

MANNERS
Sir 31:17 the sake of good M, and do not be

MANOAH (17)
Judg 13:2 Danites, whose name was M; and his wife was

13:8 Then M entreated the LORD, and said, "O, LORD,
13:9 to the voice of M, and the angel of
13:9 in the field; but M her husband was not
13:11 And M arose and went after his wife, and
13:12 And M said, "Now when your words come true,
13:13 the LORD said to M, "Of all that I
13:15 M said to the angel of the LORD, "Pray,
13:16 the LORD said to M, "If you detain me,
13:16 (For M did not know that he was the
13:17 of the LORD.) And M said to the angel
13:19 So M took the kid with the cereal offering,
13:20 of the altar while M and his wife looked
13:21 appeared no more to M and to his wife.
13:21 Then M knew that he was the angel of
13:22 And M said to his wife, "We shall surely
16:31 in the tomb of M his father.

MANS
Dan 4:16 be changed from a M, and let a beast's

MANSERVANT (9)
Ex 20:10 or your daughter, your M, or your maidservant, or
20:17 neighbor's wife, or his M, or his maidservant, or
Deut 5:14 your daughter, or your M, or your maidservant, or
5:14 your gates, that your M and your maidservant may
5:21 his field, or his M, or his maidservant, his
12:18 and your daughter, your M and your maidservant,
16:11 and your daughter, your M and your maidservant, the
16:14 and your daughter, your M and your maidservant, the
Job 31:13 the cause of my M or my maidservant, when

MANSLAYER (13)
Num 35:6 you shall permit the M to flee, and in
35:11 for you, that the M who kills any person
35:12 the avenger, that the M may not die until
35:24 shall judge between the M and the avenger of
35:25 congregation shall rescue the M from the hand of
35:26 But if the M shall at any time go
35:27 of blood slays the M, he shall not be
35:28 the high priest the M may return to the
Deut 4:42 the Jordan, that the M might flee there, who
19:3 possession, so that any M can flee to them.
19:4 the provision for the M, who by fleeing there
19:6 hot anger pursue the M and overtake him, because
Josh 20:3 through Moses, that the M who kills any person

MANSLAYERS
1Tim 1:9 murderers of mothers, for M,

MANTELET
Nah 2:5 to the wall, the M is set up.

MANTLE (26)
Gen 25:25 body like a hairy M; so they called his
Ex 22:27 covering, it is his M for his body; in
Josh 7:21 the spoil a beautiful M from Shinar, and two
7:24 the silver and the M and the bar of
Ruth 3:15 he said, "Bring the M you are wearing and
1Kgs 19:13 his face in his M and went out and
19:19 him and cast his M upon him.
2Kgs 2:8 Then Elijah took his M, and rolled it up,
2:13 he took up the M of Elijah that had
2:14 Then he took the M of Elijah that had
Ezra 9:3 my garments and my M, and pulled hair from
9:5 my garments and my M rent, and fell upon
Esth 8:15 golden crown and a M of fine linen and
Ps 109:29 wrapped in their own shame as in a M
Song 5:7 they took away my M, those watchmen of the
Is 3:6 saying: "You have a M; you shall be our
3:7 is neither bread nor M; you shall not make
59:17 clothing, and wrapped himself in fury as a M
61:3 instead of mourning, the M of praise instead of
Zech 13:4 put on a hairy M in order to deceive,
Mt 24:18 the field not turn back to take his M
Mk 10:50 And throwing off his M he sprang up and
13:16 the field not turn back to take his M
Lk 22:36 no sword sell his M and buy one.
Acts 12:8 to him, "Wrap your M around you and follow
Heb 1:12 a garment, like a M thou wilt roll them

MANTLES (4)
Ex 12:34 bound up in their M on their shoulders.
Is 3:22 the festal robes, the M, the cloaks, and the
Dan 3:21 were bound in their M, their tunics, their hats,
3:95 was not singed, their M were not harmed, and

MANURE
Lk 13:8 till I dig about it and put on M

MANY (684)
Gen 9:10 earth with you, as M as came out of
21:34 And Abraham sojourned M days in the land of
37:34 mourned for his son M days.
45:7 keep alive for you M survivors.
47:8 said to Jacob, "How M are the days of
50:3 for it, for so M are required for embalming.
50:20 bring it about that M people should be kept
Ex 1:8 of Israel are too M and too mighty for
2:23 the course of those M days the king of
5:5 the land are now M and you make them
12:38 with them, and very M cattle, both flocks and
19:21 LORD to gaze and M of them perish.
Lev 11:42 fours, or whatever has M feet, all the swarming
15:25 discharge of blood for M days, not at the
25:16 If the years are M you shall increase the
25:51 If there are still M years, according to them
26:21 upon you, sevenfold as M as your sins.
Num 9:19 continued over the tabernacle M days, the people of
13:18 they are few or M,
20:20 out against them with M men, and with a
21:6 the people, so that M people of Israel died.
22:3 people, because they were M; Moab was overcome
24:7 seed shall be in M waters, his king shall
35:8 tribes you shall take M, and from the smaller
Deut 1:11 a thousand times as M as you are, and
1:46 you remained at Kadesh M days, the days that
2:1 told me; and for M days we went about
2:10 a people great and M, and tall as the
2:21 a people great and M, and tall as the
3:5 and bars, besides very M unwalled villages.
3:19 know that you have M cattle) shall remain in
7:1 it, and clears away M nations before you, the
15:6 you shall lend to M nations, but you shall
15:6 you shall rule over M nations, but they shall
23:24 fill of grapes, as M as you wish, but
28:12 you shall lend to M nations, but you shall
31:17 will be devoured; and M evils and troubles will
31:21 And when M evils and troubles have come upon
32:7 consider the years of M generations; ask your father,
Josh 11:4 the seashore, with very M horses and chariots.
22:3 forsaken your brethren these M days, down to this
22:8 wealth, and with very M cattle, with silver, gold,
24:3 the land of Canaan, and made his offspring M
Judg 7:2 with you are too M for me to give
7:4 people are still too M; take them down to
8:30 offspring, for he had M wives.
9:40 fled before him; and M fell wounded, up to
16:24 country, who has slain M of us."
1Sam 2:5 but she who has M children is forlorn.
14:6 LORD from saving by M or by few."
25:10 There are M servants nowadays who are breaking
26:25 You will do M things and will succeed in
2Sam 1:4 from the battle, and M of the people also
12:2 rich man had very M flocks and herds;
13:34 and looked, and behold, M people were coming from
14:2 who has been mourning M days for the dead;
19:34 to the king, "How M years have I still
22:17 drew me out of M waters.
24:3 a hundred times as M as they are, while
1Kgs 2:38 Shimei dwelt in Jerusalem M days.
4:20 and Israel were as M as the sand by
7:47 because there were so M of them; the weight
8:5 the ark, sacrificing so M sheep and oxen that
11:1 King Solomon loved M foreign women: the daughter
17:15 her household ate for M days.
18:1 After M days the word of the LORD came
18:25 first, for you are M; and call on the
22:16 said to him, "How M times shall I adjure
2Kgs 9:22 the sorceries of your mother Jezebel are so M
19:23 have said, 'With my M chariots I have gone
1Chr 4:27 his brothers had not M children, nor did all
5:22 For M fell slain, because the war was of
7:4 thousand, for they had M wives and sons.
7:22 Ephraim their father mourned M days, and his
8:40 warriors, bowmen, having M sons and grandsons,
21:3 a hundred times as M as they are!
23:11 and Beriah had not M sons, therefore they became
23:17 sons, but the sons of Rehabiah were very M
27:23 to make Israel as M as the stars of
28:5 LORD has given me M sons) he has chosen
2Chr 1:9 over a people as M as the dust of
5:6 the ark, sacrificing so M sheep and oxen that

16:8 army with exceedingly M chariots and horsemen?
18:15 said to him, "How M times shall I adjure
24:27 sons, and of the M oracles against him, and
26:10 wilderness, and hewed out M cisterns, for he had
30:13 And M people came together in Jerusalem to keep
30:17 For there were M in the assembly who had
30:18 multitude of the people, M of them from Ephraim,
32:4 A great M people were gathered, and they stopped
32:23 And M brought gifts to the LORD to Jerusalem
Ezra 3:12 But M of the priests and Levites and heads
3:12 house being laid, though M shouted aloud for joy;
5:11 house that was built M years ago, which a
10:13 But the people are M, and it is a
Neh 5:2 our daughters, we are M; let us get grain,
6:17 nobles of Judah sent M letters to Tobiah, and
6:18 For M in Judah were bound by oath to
7:2 was a more faithful and God-fearing man than M
9:28 hear from heaven, and M times thou didst deliver
9:30 M years thou didst bear with them, and didst
13:26 Among the M nations there was no king like
Tob 1:3 life, and I performed M acts of charity to
1:16 of Shalmaneser I performed M acts of charity to
1:18 his anger he put M to death.
3:5 And now thy M judgments are true in exacting
4:4 son, that she faced M dangers for you while
4:8 If you have M possessions, make your gift from
13:11 M nations will come from afar to the name
Jud 1:6 M nations joined the forces of the Chaldeans.
4:13 for the people fasted M days throughout Judea and
5:9 and silver and very M cattle.
5:18 were utterly defeated in M battles and were led
8:11 helps us within so M days.
11:16 the whole world, as M as shall hear about
16:22 M desired to marry her, but she remained a
Esth 1:4 of his majesty for M days, a hundred and
2:8 proclaimed, and when M maidens were gathered in
8:17 And M from the peoples of the country declared
13:2 "Having become ruler of M nations and master of
16:2 the more proud do M men become.
16:5 And often M of those who are set in
Job 1:3 hundred she-asses, and very M servants; so that this
4:3 Behold, you have instructed M, and you have
5:25 your descendants shall be M, and your offspring as
11:19 will make you afraid; M will entreat your favor.
13:23 How M are my iniquities and my sins?
16:2 answered: "I have heard M such things; miserable
23:14 appoints for me; and M such things are in
32:7 'Let days speak, and M years teach wisdom.'
41:3 Will he make M supplications to you?
Ps 3:1 O LORD, how M are my foes!
3:1 M are rising against me;
3:2 are rising against me; M are saying of me,
4:6 There are M who say, "O that we might
5:10 because of their M transgressions cast them out,
18:16 drew me out of M waters.
22:12 M bulls encompass me, strong bulls of Bashan
25:19 Consider how M are my foes, and with what
29:3 thunders, the LORD, upon M waters.
31:13 hear the whispering of M – terror on every
32:10 M are the pangs of the wicked; but steadfast
34:12 desires life, and covets M days, that he may
34:19 M are the afflictions of the righteous; but the
37:16 than the abundance of M wicked.
38:19 cause are mighty, and M are those who hate
40:3 M will see and fear, and put their trust
55:18 that I wage, for M are arrayed against me.
56:2 all day long, for M fight against me proudly.
71:7 as a portent to M; but thou art my
71:20 hast made me see M sore troubles wilt revive
90:15 Make us glad as M days as thou hast
90:15 afflicted us, and as M years as we have
93:4 than the thunders of M waters, mightier than the
94:19 of my heart are M, thy consolations cheer my
97:1 earth rejoice; let the M coastlands be glad!
106:43 M times he delivered them, but they were rebellious
119:157 M are my persecutors and my adversaries, but I
135:10 his servants; who smote M nations and slew mighty
144:7 deliver me from the M waters, from the hand
Prov 4:11 that the years of your life may be M
7:26 into her paths; for M a victim has she
10:19 When words are M, transgression is not lacking, but
10:21 of the righteous feed M, but fools die for
14:20 but the rich has M friends.
15:22 go wrong, but with M advisers they succeed.
19:4 Wealth brings M new friends, but a poor man
19:6 M seek the favor of a generous man, and
19:21 M are the plans in the mind of a
20:6 M a man proclaims his own loyalty, but a
28:2 land transgresses it has M rulers; but with men
28:27 his eyes will get M a curse.
29:26 M seek the favor of a ruler, but from
31:29 and he praises her: M women have done excellently,
Eccl 2:8 men and women, and M concubines, man's delight.
5:3 a fool's voice with M words.
5:7 increase, empty words grow M: but do you fear
6:3 hundred children, and lives M years, so that the
6:3 of his years are M, but he does not
7:22 your heart knows that M times you have yourself
7:29 they have sought out M devices.
10:6 folly is set in M high places, and the
11:1 will find it after M days.
11:8 if a man lives M years, let him rejoice
11:8 remember that the days of darkness will be M
12:12 Of making M books there is no end, and
Song 8:7 M waters cannot quench love, neither can floods
Wis 6:2 multitudes, and boast of M nations.
18:12 death, had corpses too M to count.
Sir 1:21 and the lips of M will tell of his
3:23 hasty judgment has led M astray, and wrong opinion
6:6 peace with you be M, but let your advisers
6:22 like her name, and is not manifest to M
8:2 for gold has ruined M, and has perverted the
9:8 beauty belonging to another; M have been misled by
11:5 M kings have had to sit on the ground,
11:6 M rulers have been greatly disgraced, and illustrious
11:10 not busy yourself with M matters; if you multiply
11:13 his head, so that M are amazed at him.
11:27 into your home, for M are the wiles of
11:30 spark of fire come M burning coals, and a
13:21 slips, his helpers are M; he speaks unseemly words,
16:5 M such things my eye has seen, and my
16:15 Among so M people I shall not be known,
20:7 Whoever uses too M words will be loathed, and
20:13 nothing, for he has M eyes instead of one.
20:16 How M will ridicule him, and how often!
23:11 A man who swears M oaths will be filled
27:1 M have committed sin for a trifle, and whoever
27:24 I have hated M things, but none to be
28:13 for he has destroyed M who were at peace.
28:14 Slander has shaken M, and scattered them from
28:18 M have fallen by the edge of the sword,
28:18 sword, but not so M as have fallen because
29:4 M persons regard a loan as a windfall, and
29:7 of such wickedness, therefore, M have refused to
29:18 Being surety has ruined M men who were
30:23 for sorrow has destroyed M, and there is no
31:6 M have come to ruin because of gold, and
31:18 you are seated among M persons, do not reach
31:25 be valiant over wine, for wine has destroyed M
34:7 For dreams have deceived M, and those who put
34:9 An educated man knows M things, and one with
34:11 I have seen M things in my travels, and
35:1 keeps the law makes M offerings; he who heeds
37:19 and the teacher of M, and yet be unprofitable
37:31 M have died of gluttony, but he who is
39:9 M will praise his understanding, and it will never
40:15 will not put forth M branches; they are unhealthy
42:6 and where there are M hands, lock things up.
43:32 M things greater than these lie hidden, for we
45:9 with pomegranates, with very M golden bells round
47:24 Their sins became exceedingly M, so as to remove
51:3 my life, from the M afflictions that I endured,
Is 1:15 even though you make M prayers, I will not
2:3 flow to it, and M peoples shall come, and
2:4 and shall decide for M peoples; and they shall
5:9 in my hearing: "Surely M houses shall be desolate,
6:12 the forsaken places are M in the midst of
8:7 the River, mighty and M, the king of Assyria
8:15 And M shall stumble thereon; they shall fall and
17:12 Ah, the thunder of M peoples, they thunder like
17:13 like the roaring of M waters, but he will
22:9 city of David were M, and you collected the
23:3 sea and were on M waters; your revenue was
23:16 Make sweet melody, sing M songs, that you may
24:22 a prison, and after M days they will be
31:1 chariots because they are M and in horsemen
37:24 have said, With my M chariots I have gone
42:20 He sees M things, but does not observe them;
47:9 in spite of your M sorceries and the great
47:12 your enchantments and your M sorceries, with which
47:13 are wearied with your M counsels; let them stand
51:2 him, and I blessed him and made him M

52:14 As M were astonished at him– his appearance
52:15 so shall he startle M nations; kings shall shut
53:11 one, my servant, make M to be accounted righteous;
53:12 bore the sin of M, and made intercession for
58:12 up the foundations of M generations; you shall be
61:4 cities, the devastations of M generations.
66:16 and those slain by the LORD shall be M
Jer 2:28 of trouble; for as M as your cities are
3:1 played the harlot with M lovers; and would you
5:6 because their transgressions are M, their apostasies
11:13 gods have become as M as your cities, O
11:13 O Judah; and as M as the streets of
12:10 M shepherds have destroyed my vineyard, they have
13:6 And after M days the LORD said to me,
14:7 for our backslidings are M, we have sinned against
16:16 I am sending for M fishers, says the LORD,
16:16 I will send for M hunters, and they shall
20:10 For I hear M whispering.
22:8 "And M nations will pass by this city, and
25:14 For M nations and great kings shall make slaves
27:7 own land comes; then M nations and great kings
28:8 famine, and pestilence against M countries and great
35:7 that you may live M days in the land
36:32 in the fire; and M similar words were added
37:16 cells, and remained there M days,
42:2 but a few of M, as your eyes see
46:11 vain you have used M medicines; there is no
50:41 a mighty nation and M kings are stirring from
51:13 you who dwell by M waters, rich in treasures,
51:14 you with men, as M as locusts, and they
51:55 Their waves roar like M waters, the noise of
Lam 1:22 for my groans are M and my heart is
Bar 1:12 we shall serve them M days and find favor
4:12 widow and bereaved of M; I was left desolate
4:35 from the Everlasting for M days, and for a
6:3 will remain there for M years, for a long
Ezek 1:24 like the sound of M waters, like the thunder
3:6 Israel– not to M peoples of foreign speech
12:27 he sees is for M days hence, and he
16:41 in the sight of M women; I will make
17:3 rich in plumage of M colors, came to Lebanon
17:9 a strong arm or M people to pull it
17:17 built to cut off M lives.
21:15 hearts may melt, and M fall at all their
22:25 things; they have made M widows in the midst
26:3 and will bring up M nations against you, as
26:7 and a host of M soldiers.
26:10 horses will be so M that their dust will
27:3 of the peoples on M coastlands, thus says the
27:15 Rhodes traded with you; M coastlands were your
27:33 the seas, you satisfied M peoples; with your abundant
31:15 restrain its rivers, and M waters shall be stopped;
32:3 with a host of M peoples; and I will
32:9 trouble the hearts of M peoples, when I carry
32:10 I will make M peoples appalled at you, and
32:13 its beasts from beside M waters; and no foot
33:24 land; but we are M; the land is surely
37:2 behold, there were very M upon the valley; and
38:6 with all his hordes– M peoples are with you.
38:8 After M days you will be mustered; in the
38:8 people were gathered from M nations upon the
38:9 all your hordes, and M peoples with you.
38:15 the north, you and M peoples with you, all
38:22 his hordes and the M peoples that are with
38:23 in the eyes of M nations.
39:27 in the sight of M nations.
43:2 like the sound of M waters; and the earth
47:7 of the river very M trees on the one
47:9 there will be very M fish; for this water
47:10 will be of very M kinds, like the fish
Dan 2:48 Daniel high honors and M great gifts, and made
3:36 make their descendants as M as the stars of
8:25 warning he shall destroy M; and he shall even
8:26 for it pertains to M days hence."
9:27 a strong covenant with M for one week; and
11:14 "In those times M shall rise against the king
11:18 coastlands, and shall take M of them; but a
11:26 be swept away, and M shall fall down slain.
11:33 are wise shall make M understand, though they shall
11:34 And M shall join themselves to them with flattery;
11:39 make them rulers over M and shall divide the
11:40 and horsemen, and with M ships; and he shall
11:44 with great fury to exterminate and utterly destroy M
12:2 And M of those who sleep in the dust
12:3 and those who turn M to righteousness, like the
12:4 M shall run to and fro, and knowledge shall

12:10 M shall purify themselves, and make themselves
Hos 3:3 dwell as mine for M days; you shall not
3:4 of Israel shall dwell M days without king or
Amos 5:12 For I know how M are your transgressions, and
8:3 dead bodies shall be M; in every place they
Mic 4:2 flow to it, and M nations shall come, and
4:3 He shall judge between M peoples, and shall decide
4:11 Now M nations are assembled against you, saying,
4:13 shall beat in pieces M peoples, and shall devote
5:7 in the midst of M peoples like dew from
5:8 in the midst of M peoples, like a lion
Nah 1:12 they be strong and M, they will be cut
Hab 2:8 Because you have plundered M nations, all the
2:10 house by cutting off M peoples; you have forfeited
Zech 2:11 And M nations shall join themselves to the LORD
7:3 have done for so M years?"
8:20 even the inhabitants of M cities;
8:22 hosts; I am going.' M peoples and strong nations
10:8 they shall be as M as of old.
Mal 2:6 uprightness, and he turned M from iniquity.
2:8 way; you have caused M to stumble by your
1Mac 1:2 of Greece.) He fought M battles, conquered
1:3 the earth, and plundered M nations.
1:9 sons after them for M years; and they caused
1:9 years; and they caused M evils on the earth.
1:11 from Israel, and misled M, saying, "Let us go
1:11 we separated from them M evils have come upon
1:18 fled before him, and M were wounded and fell.
1:30 severe blow, and destroyed M people of Israel.
1:43 M even from Israel gladly adopted his religion; they
1:52 M of the people, every one who forsook the
1:62 But M in Israel stood firm and were resolved
2:16 M from Israel came to them; and Mattathias and
2:18 silver and gold and M gifts."
2:29 Then M who were seeking righteousness and justice
2:32 M pursued them, and overtook them; they encamped
3:7 He embittered M kings, but he made Jacob glad
3:11 M were wounded and fell, and the rest fled.
3:18 "It is easy for M to be hemmed in
3:18 difference between saving by M or by few.
5:6 a strong band and M people with Timothy as
5:7 He engaged in M battles with them and they
5:12 from their hands, for M of us have fallen,
5:21 to Galilee and fought M battles against the Gentiles,
5:22 of Ptolemais, and as M as three thousand of
5:26 their brethren in Gilead: M of them have been
5:34 As M as eight thousand of them fell that
5:60 borders of Judea; as M as two thousand of
6:9 He lay there for M days, because deep grief
6:24 put to death as M of us as they
6:31 against Bethzur, and for M days they fought and
6:51 before the sanctuary for M days.
6:52 theirs, and fought for M days.
7:19 he sent and seized M of the men who
8:10 M of them were wounded and fell, and the
8:11 kingdoms and islands, as M as ever opposed them,
8:12 and near, and as M as have heard of
9:2 took it and killed M people.
9:6 were greatly frightened, and M slipped away from
9:17 battle became desperate, and M on both sides were
9:20 for him; they mourned M days and said,
9:22 have not been recorded, for they were very M
9:39 tambourines and musicians and M weapons.
9:40 M were wounded and fell, and the rest fled
9:64 fought against it for M days and made machines
9:69 country, and he killed M of them.
10:28 We will grant you M immunities and give you
10:60 silver and gold and M gifts, and found favor
11:1 by the seashore, and M ships; and he tried
11:20 Jerusalem, and he built M engines of war to
11:27 high-priesthood and in as M other honors as he
11:40 and he stayed there M days.
11:47 on that day as M as a hundred thousand
11:65 fought against it for M days and hemmed it
11:74 As M as three thousand of the foreigners fell
12:13 But as for ourselves, M afflictions and many wars
12:13 many afflictions and M wars have encircled us;
13:26 and mourned for him M days.
13:49 were very hungry, and M of them perished from
15:4 those who have devastated M cities in my kingdom,
15:29 have taken possession of M places in my kingdom.
16:2 we have delivered Israel M times.
16:8 put to flight, and M of them were wounded
2Mac 1:20 But after M years had passed, when it pleased
1:35 king favored he exchanged M excellent gifts.
2:27 secure the gratitude of M we will gladly endure

3:26 scourged him continuously, inflicting M blows on him.
4:35 not only Jews, but M also of other nations,
4:39 When M acts of sacrilege had been committed in
4:39 gathered against Lysimachus, because M of the gold
4:42 a result, they wounded M of them, and killed
5:9 he who had driven M from their own country
5:10 who had cast out M to lie unburied had
5:14 hand-to-hand fighting; and as M were sold into
5:18 they were involved in M sins, this man would
6:24 he said, "lest M of the young should suppose
9:6 bowels of others with M and strange inflictions.
9:16 back, all of them, M times over; and the
12:12 really be useful in M ways, agreed to make
12:23 sword, and destroyed as M as thirty thousand men.
12:25 And when with M words he had confirmed his
12:28 hands, and killed as M as twenty-five thousand of
13:8 because he had committed M sins against the altar
13:15 night and slew as M as two thousand men
Mt 3:7 But when he saw M of the Pharisees and
6:7 be heard for their M words.
7:13 destruction, and those who enter by it are M
7:22 On that day M will say to me, 'Lord,
7:22 your name, and do M mighty works in your
8:11 I tell you, M will come from east and
8:16 they brought to him M who were possessed with
8:30 Now a herd of M swine was feeding at
9:10 in the house, behold, M tax collectors and sinners
10:31 of more value than M sparrows.
12:15 And M followed him, and he healed them all,
13:3 And he told them M things in parables, saying:
13:17 I say to you, M prophets and righteous men
13:58 he did not do M mighty works there, because
14:24 by this time was M furlongs distant from the
14:36 his garment; and as M as touched it were
15:30 blind, the dumb, and M others, and they put
15:34 said to them, "How M loaves have you?" They
16:9 five thousand, and how M baskets you gathered?
16:10 four thousand, and how M baskets you gathered?
16:21 to Jerusalem and suffer M things from the elders
18:20 As M as seven times?"
19:30 But M that are first will be last, and
20:28 to give his life as a ransom for M
22:9 the marriage feast as M as you find.'
22:14 gnash their teeth.' For M are called, but few
24:5 For M will come in my name, saying, 'I
24:5 and they will lead M astray.
24:10 And then M will fall away, and betray one
24:11 And M false prophets will arise and lead many
24:11 will arise and lead M astray.
26:28 is poured out for M for the forgiveness of
26:60 they found none, though M false witnesses came
27:13 you not hear how M things they testify against
27:52 also were opened, and M bodies of the saints
27:53 went into the holy city and appeared to M
27:55 There were also M women there, looking on from
Mk 1:34 And he healed M who were sick with various
1:34 diseases, and cast out M demons; and he would
2:2 And M were gathered together, so that there was
2:15 table in his house, M tax collectors and sinners
2:15 disciples; for there were M who followed him.
3:10 for he had healed M, so that all who
4:2 And he taught them M things in parables, and
4:33 With M such parables he spoke the word to
5:9 replied, "My name is Legion; for we are M
5:26 had suffered much under M physicians, and had
6:2 in the synagogue; and M who heard him were
6:13 And they cast out M demons, and anointed with
6:13 and anointed with oil M that were sick and
6:31 For M were coming and going, and they had
6:33 Now M saw them going, and knew them, and
6:34 began to teach them M things.
6:38 said to them, "How M loaves have you?
6:56 his garment; and as M as touched it were
7:4 themselves; and there are M other traditions which
7:13 And M such things you do."
8:5 he asked them, "How M loaves have you?" They
8:19 the five thousand, how M baskets full of broken
8:20 the four thousand, how M baskets full of broken
8:31 of man must suffer M things, and be rejected
9:12 that he should suffer M things and be treated
10:31 But M that are first will be last, and
10:45 to give his life as a ransom for M
10:48 And M rebuked him, telling him to be silent;
11:8 And M spread their garments on the road, and
12:5 killed; and so with M others, some they beat
12:41 M rich people put in large sums.
13:6 M will come in my name, saying, 'I am
13:6 and they will lead M astray.
14:24 of the covenant, which is poured out for M
14:56 For M bore false witness against him, and their
15:3 priests accused him of M things.
15:4 See how M charges they bring against you."
15:40 to him; and also M other women who came
Lk 1:1 Inasmuch as M have undertaken to compile
1:14 joy and gladness, and M will rejoice at his
1:16 And he will turn M of the sons of
2:34 fall and rising of M in Israel, and for
2:35 that thoughts out of M hearts may be revealed."
3:18 So, with M other exhortations, he preached good
4:25 tell you, there were M widows in Israel in
4:27 And there were M lepers in Israel in the
4:41 also came out of M, crying, "You are the
7:21 that hour he cured M of diseases and plagues
7:21 evil spirits, and on M that were blind he
7:47 her sins, which are M, are forgiven, for she
8:3 steward, and Susanna, and M others, who provided
8:29 (For M a time it had seized him; he
8:30 he said, "Legion"; for M demons had entered him.
9:22 of man must suffer M things, and be rejected
10:24 I tell you that M prophets and kings desired
10:41 anxious and troubled about M things;
11:53 him to speak of M things,
12:1 the meantime, when so M thousands of the multitude
12:7 of more value than M sparrows.
12:19 goods laid up for M years; take your ease,
13:24 the narrow door; for M, I tell you, will
14:16 great banquet, and invited M;
15:13 Not M days later, the younger son gathered all
15:17 himself he said, 'How M of my father's hired
15:29 his father, 'Lo, these M years I have served
17:25 first he must suffer M things and be rejected
21:8 not led astray; for M will come in my
22:63 And they spoke M other words against him, reviling
Jn 2:23 at the Passover feast, M believed in his name
4:39 M Samaritans from that city believed in him because
4:41 And M more believed because of his word.
6:9 two fish; but what are they among so M
6:60 M of his disciples, when they heard it, said,
6:66 After this M of his disciples drew back and
7:31 Yet M of the people believed in him; they
8:30 As he spoke thus, M believed in him.
10:20 M of them said, "He has a demon, and
10:32 "I have shown you M good works from the
10:41 And M came to him; and they said, "John
10:42 And M believed in him there.
11:19 two miles off, and M of the Jews had
11:45 M of the Jews therefore, who had come with
11:47 For this man performs M signs.
11:55 was at hand, and M went up from the
12:11 on account of him M of the Jews were
12:37 he had done so M signs before them, yet
12:42 Nevertheless M even of the authorities believed in
14:2 my Father's house are M rooms; if it were
16:12 "I have yet M things to say to you,
19:20 M of the Jews read this title, for the
20:30 Now Jesus did M other signs in the presence
21:11 although there were so M, the net was not
21:25 But there are also M other things which Jesus
Acts 1:3 after his passion by M proofs, appearing to them
1:5 with water, but before M days you shall be
2:40 And he testified with M other words and exhorted
2:43 upon every soul; and M wonders and signs were
4:4 But M of those who heard the word believed;
4:34 among them, for as M as were possessors of
5:12 Now M signs and wonders were done among the
6:7 Jerusalem, and a great M of the priests were
8:7 spirits came out of M who were possessed, crying
8:7 a loud voice; and M who were paralyzed or
8:25 the gospel to M villages of the Samaritans.
9:13 I have heard from M about this man, how
9:23 When M days had passed, the Jews plotted to
9:42 throughout all Joppa, and M believed in the Lord.
9:43 stayed in Joppa for M days with one Simon,
10:27 went in and found M persons gathered;
12:12 name was Mark, where M were gathered together
13:31 the dead; and for M days he appeared to
13:43 the synagogue broke up, M Jews and devout
13:48 of God; and as M as were ordained to
14:21 city and had made M disciples, they returned to
14:22 and saying that through M tribulations we must nter
15:32 exhorted the brethren with M words and
15:34 of the Lord, with M others also.

16:18 this she did for M days.
16:23 when they had inflicted M blows upon them, they
17:4 as did a great M of the devout Greeks
17:12 M of them therefore believed, with not a few
18:8 all his household; and M of the Corinthians hearing
18:10 you; for I have M people in this city."
18:18 After this Paul stayed M days longer, and then
19:18 M also of those who were now believers came,
20:8 There were M lights in the upper chamber where
21:20 "You see, brother, how M thousands there are among
24:9 replied: "Realizing that for M years you have been
25:7 him, bringing against him M serious charges which
25:14 as they stayed there M days, Festus laid Paul's
26:9 I ought to do M things in opposing the
26:10 not only shut up M of the saints in
27:20 nor stars appeared for M a day, and no
28:10 They presented M gifts to us; and when we
Rom 4:17 you the father of M nations" —in the
4:18 become the father of M nations; as he had
5:15 For if M died through one man's trespass, much
5:15 of that one man Jesus Christ abounded for M
5:16 free gift following M trespasses brings justification.
5:19 by one man's disobedience M were made sinners, so
5:19 by one man's obedience M will be made righteous.
8:29 be the first-born among M brethren.
12:4 one body we have M members, and all the
12:5 function, so we, though M, are one body in
15:23 I have longed for M years to come to
16:2 been a helper of M and of myself as
1Cor 1:26 your call, brethren; not M of you were wise
1:26 to worldly standards, not M were powerful, not many
1:26 many were powerful, not M were of noble birth;
4:15 you do not have M fathers.
8:5 as indeed there are M "gods" and many "lords"—
8:5 and M "lords"—
10:17 bread, we who are M are one body, for
10:33 advantage, but that of M, that they may be
11:30 That is why M of you are weak and
12:12 is one and has M members, and all the
12:12 of the body, though M, are one body, so
12:14 does not consist of one member but of M
12:20 it is, there are M parts, yet one body.
14:10 are doubtless M different languages in the world,
16:9 me, and there are M adversaries.
2Cor 1:11 by prayer, so that M will give thanks on
1:11 us in answer to M prayers.
2:4 of heart and with M tears, not to cause
2:17 are not, like so M, peddlers of God's word;
6:10 as poor, yet making M rich; as having nothing,
8:22 and found earnest in M matters, but who is
9:12 but also overflows in M thanksgivings to God.
11:18 this boastful confidence; since M boast of worldly
11:27 toil and hardship, through M a sleepless night, in
12:21 have to mourn over M of those who sinned
Gal 1:14 advanced in Judaism beyond M of my own age
3:4 Did you experience so M things in vain?—if
3:16 referring to M; but, referring to one, "And to
3:27 For as M of you as were baptized into
4:27 the desolate one are M more than the children
Phil 3:18 For M, of whom I have often told you
1Tim 6:9 into a snare, into M senseless and hurtful desires
6:10 pierced their hearts with M pangs.
6:12 in the presence of M witnesses.
2Tim 2:2 from me before M witnesses entrust to faithful
Tit 1:9 For there are M insubordinate men, empty talkers
Heb 1:1 In M and various ways God
2:10 things exist, in bringing M sons to glory, should
7:23 The former priests were M in number, because they
9:28 bear the sins of M, will appear a second
11:12 were born descendants as M as the stars of
12:15 and by it the M become defiled;
Jas 3:1 Let not M of you become teachers, my brethren,
3:2 For we all make M mistakes, and if any
2Pet 2:2 And M will follow their licentiousness, and because
1Jn 2:18 is coming, so now M antichrists have come; therefore
4:1 are of God; for M false prophets have gone
2Jn 1:7 For M deceivers have gone out into the world,
Rev 1:15 like the sound of M waters;
5:11 elders the voice of M angels, numbering myriads of
8:11 waters became wormwood, and M men died of the
9:9 like the noise of M chariots with horses rushing
10:11 must again prophesy about M peoples and nations
14:2 like the sound of M waters and like the
17:1 who is seated upon M waters,
19:6 like the sound of M waters and like the
19:12 on his head are M diadems; and he has

MANY-COLORED

Ps 45:14 with gold-woven robes; in M robes she is led

MANY-PEAKED (2)

Ps 68:15 mountain of Bashan; O M mountain, mountain of
68:16 you with envy, O M mountain, at the mount

MAOCH

1Sam 27:2 Achish the son of M, king of Gath.

MAON (7)

Josh 15:55 M, Carmel, Ziph, Juttah,
1Sam 23:24 in the wilderness of M, in the Arabah to
23:25 the rock which is in the wilderness of M
23:25 he pursued after David in the wilderness of M
25:2 was a man in M, whose business was in
1Chr 2:45 The son of Shammai: M; and Maon was the
2:45 of Shammai: Maon; and M was the father of

MAONITES

Judg 10:12 the Amalekites, and the M, oppressed you; and you

MAR

Lev 19:27 on your temples or M the edges of your

MARA

Ruth 1:20 me Naomi, call me M, for the Almighty has

MARAH (5)

Ex 15:23 When they came to M, they could not drink
15:23 drink the water of M because it was bitter;
15:23 because it was bitter; therefore it was named M
Num 33:8 in the wilderness of Etham, and encamped at M
33:9 they set out from M, and came to Elim;

MARAUDER

Jer 18:22 when thou bringest the M suddenly upon them!

MARAUDING (2)

1Kgs 11:24 became leader of a M band, after the slaughter
2Kgs 13:21 being buried, lo, a M band was seen and

MARBLE (4)

1Chr 29:2 colored stones, all sorts of precious stones, and M
Esth 1:6 to silver rings and M pillars, and also couches
1:6 pavement of porphyry, M, mother-of-pearl and
Rev 18:12 wood, bronze, iron and M,

MARCH (23)

Num 2:9 They shall set out first on the M
2:24 They shall set out third on the M
10:28 was the order of M of the people of
12:15 set out on the M till Miriam was brought
Josh 6:3 You shall M around the city, all the men
6:4 seventh day you shall M around the city seven
6:7 the people, "Go forward; M around the city, and
Judg 5:4 Seir, when thou didst M from the region of
5:21 M on, my soul, with might!
1Sam 29:6 right that you should M out and in with
2Kgs 3:8 Then he said, "By which way shall we M
3:9 had made a circuitous M of seven days, there
Jud 1:4 that his armies could M out in force and
Ps 68:7 when thou didst M through the wilderness, [Selah]
Prov 30:27 yet all of them M in rank;
Jer 46:22 away; for her enemies M in force, and come
Joel 2:7 They M each on his way, they do not
Hab 1:6 and hasty nation, who M through the breadth of
Zech 9:8 so that none shall M to and fro; no
9:14 sound the trumpet, and M forth in the whirlwinds
1Mac 6:33 army by a forced M along the road to
2Mac 12:10 from there, on their M against Timothy, not less
13:13 elders, he determined to M out and decide the

MARCHED (39)

Josh 6:14 the second day they M around the city once,
6:15 dawn of day, and M around the city in
6:15 that day that they M around the city seven
10:9 upon them suddenly, having M up all night from
Judg 2:15 Whenever they M out, the hand of the LORD
5:11 down to the gates M the people of the
5:13 Then down M the remnant of the noble; the
5:13 people of the LORD M down for him against
5:14 kinsmen; from Machir M down the commanders,
2Sam 2:32 Joab and his men M all night, and the
18:4 while all the army M out by hundreds and
2Kgs 3:6 So King Jehoram M out of Samaria at that

M

16:9 the king of Assyria M up against Damascus, and
Jud 2:21 They M for three days from Nineveh to the
1Mac 3:57 Then the army M out and encamped to the
5:36 From there he M on and took Chaspho, Maked,
5:58 with them, and they M against Jamnia.
5:66 Then he M off to go into the land
6:32 Then Judas M away from the citadel and encamped
7:10 So they M away and came with a large
9:4 against Jerusalem; then they M off and went to
9:11 the army of Bacchides M out from the camp
10:2 very large army and M out to meet him
11:15 Ptolemy M out and met him with a strong
11:67 in the morning they M to the plain of
12:25 So he M away from Jerusalem and met them
12:32 went to Damascus, and M through all that region.
12:33 also went forth and M through the country as
12:40 kill him, and he M forth and came to
13:22 He M off and went into the land of
14:1 assembled his forces and M into Media to secure
16:4 horsemen, and they M against Cendebeus and
16:5 morning they arose and M into the plain, and
2Mac 3:35 bidden Onias farewell, he M off with his forces
4:22 Then he M into Phoenicia.
12:19 captains under Maccabeus, M out and destroyed
12:26 Then Judas M against Carnaim and the temple of
12:27 destruction of these, he M also against Ephron, a
Rev 20:9 And they M up over the broad earth and

MARCHES (2)
Wis 4:2 throughout all time it M crowned in triumph, victor
Joel 2:8 jostle one another, each M in his path; they

MARCHING (10)
Ex 14:10 behold, the Egyptians were M after them; and they
2Sam 2:29 crossed the Jordan, and M the whole forenoon they
5:24 hear the sound of M in the tops of
2Kgs 11:19 house of the LORD, M through the gate of
1Chr 14:15 hear the sound of M in the tops of
2Chr 23:20 house of the LORD, M through the upper gate
Is 63:1 glorious in his apparel, M in the greatness of
1Mac 6:41 their multitude, by the M of the multitude and
12:50 one another and kept M in close formation, ready
13:20 and his army kept M along opposite him to

MARE
Song 1:9 my love, to a M of Pharaoh's chariots.

MAREAL
Josh 19:11 westward, and on to M, and touches Dabbesheth,

MARESHAH (9)
Josh 15:44 Nezib, Keilah, Achzib, and M: nine cities with their
1Chr 2:42 the brother of Jerahmeel: M his first-born, who was
2:42 The sons of M: Hebron.
4:21 Laadah the father of M, and the families of
2Chr 11:8 Bethzur, Soco, Adullam, Gath, M, Ziph,
14:9 three hundred chariots, and came as far as M
14:10 of battle in the valley of Zephathah at M
20:37 son of Do-davahu of M prophesied against
Mic 1:15 upon you, inhabitants of M; the glory of Israel

MARINERS (4)
Ezek 27:9 the sea with their M were in you, to
27:27 wares, your merchandise, your M and your pilots,
27:29 The M and all the pilots of the sea
Jon 1:5 Then the M were afraid, and each cried to

MARISA (2)
1Mac 5:66 the land of the Philistines, and passed through M
2Mac 12:35 off his arm; so Gorgias escaped and reached M

MARITAL
Ex 21:10 her clothing, or her M rights.

MARK (46)
Gen 4:15 the LORD put a M on Cain, lest any
38:25 And she said, M, I pray you, whose these
Ex 13:16 shall be as a M on your hand or
Num 34:7 Great Sea you shall M out your line to
34:8 Mount Hor you shall M it out to the
34:10 "You shall M out your eastern boundary from
1Sam 20:20 of it, as though I shot at a M
2Sam 13:28 Absalom commanded his servants, M when Amnon's
1Kgs 20:7 the land, and said, M, now, and see how
Job 7:20 Why hast thou made me thy M
10:14 I sin, thou dost M me, and dost not
36:32 the lightning, and commands it to strike the M
Ps 37:37 M the blameless man, and behold the upright, for
50:22 M this, then, you who forget God, lest I
104:19 made the moon to M the seasons; the sun
130:3 thou, O LORD, shouldst M iniquities, Lord, who could
Wis 8:21 and it was a M of insight to know
Sir 13:25 The M of a happy heart is a cheerful
36:23 If kindness and humility M her speech, her husband
Lam 3:12 set me as a M for his arrow.
Ezek 9:4 Jerusalem, and put a M upon the foreheads of
9:6 but touch no one upon whom is the M
21:19 again: "Son of man, M two ways for the
21:20 way to a city; M a way for the
44:5 me, "Son of man, M well, see with your
44:5 all its laws; and M well those who may
1Mac 8:14 worn purple as a M of pride,
2Mac 2:6 him came up to M the way, but could
Jn 20:25 my finger in the M of the nails, and
Acts 12:12 other name was M, where many were gathered
12:25 bringing with them John whose other name was M
15:36 Barnabas wanted to take with them John called M
15:38 each other; Barnabas took M with him and sailed
Phil 3:17 in imitating me, and M those who so live
Col 4:10 prisoner greets you, and M the cousin of Barnabas
2Thes 3:17 This is the M in every letter of mine;
1Tim 6:21 some have missed the M as regards the faith.
2Tim 4:11 Get M and bring him with you; for he
Philem 1:24 you, and so do M, Aristarchus, Demas, and Luke,
1Pet 5:13 sends you greetings; and so does my son M
Rev 13:17 unless he has the M, that is, the name
14:9 image, and receives a M on his forehead or
14:11 and whoever receives the M of its name."
16:2 men who bore the M of the beast and
19:20 who had received the M of the beast and
20:4 had not received its M on their foreheads or

MARKED (5)
Prov 8:29 his command, when he M out the foundations of
Is 40:12 of his hand and M off the heavens with
Lam 2:8 daughter of Zion; he M it off by the
Lk 14:7 were invited, when he M how they chose the
Rev 13:16 and slave, to be M on the right hand

MARKET (16)
Tob 2:3 and thrown into the M place."
Ps 55:11 not depart from its M place.
Prov 7:12 street, now in the M, and at every corner
2Mac 3:4 administration of the city M;
Mt 11:16 children sitting in the M places and calling to
20:3 standing idle in the M place;
23:7 and salutations in the M places, and being called
Mk 6:56 the sick in the M places, and besought him
7:4 they come from the M place, they do not
12:38 have salutations in the M places
Lk 7:32 children sitting in the M place and calling to
11:43 and salutations in the M places.
20:46 love salutations in the M places and the best
Acts 16:19 dragged them into the M place before the rulers;
17:17 persons, and in the M place every day with
1Cor 10:25 sold in the meat M without raising any question

MARKETS (3)
Jud 1:14 its towers, plundered its M, and turned its beauty
Prov 1:20 the street; in the M she raises her voice;
Ezek 27:15 were your own special M, they brought you in

MARKS (7)
Lev 19:28 dead or tattoo any M upon you: I am
1Sam 21:13 their hands, and made M on the doors of
Is 44:13 stretches a line, he M it out with a
44:13 it with planes, and M it with a compass;
1Mac 1:15 and removed the M of circumcision, and abandoned
1Cor 7:18 seek to remove the M of circumcision.
Gal 6:17 on my body the M of Jesus.

MAROTH
Mic 1:12 For the inhabitants of M wait anxiously for good,

MARRED
Is 52:14 his appearance was so M, beyond human semblance

MARRIAGE (53)
Gen 34:8 I pray you, give her to him in M
34:12 ever so much as M present and gift, and
34:21 take their daughters in M, and let us give
38:14 she had not been given to him in M

M

41:45 he gave him in M Asenath, the daughter of
Ex 22:16 he shall give the M present for her, and
22:17 money equivalent to the M present for virgins.
Judg 12:9 daughters he gave in M outside his clan, and
21:1 give his daughter in M to Benjamin."
1Sam 18:25 'The king desires no M present except a hundred
1Kgs 3:1 Solomon made a M alliance with Pharaoh king of
7:8 for Pharaoh's daughter whom he had taken in M
11:2 shall not enter into M with them, neither shall
11:19 he gave him in M the sister of his
1Chr 2:35 gave his daughter in M to Jarha his slave;
2Chr 18:1 and he made a M alliance with Ahab.
Tob 3:17 daughter of Raguel in M to Tobias the son
6:10 given to you in M,
6:12 we return from Rages we will celebrate the M
6:15 night she will be given to you in M
11:19 Nadab came, and Tobias' M was celebrated for seven
Ps 78:63 their maidens had no M song.
Wis 7:2 seed of a man and the pleasure of M
13:17 about possessions and his M and children, he is
14:26 sex perversion, disorder in M, adultery, and
Sir 7:25 Give a daughter in M; you will have finished
23:18 man who breaks his M vows says to himself,
Jer 29:6 give your daughters in M, that they may bear
Dan 2:43 with one another in M, but they will not
1Mac 10:58 Cleopatra his daughter in M, and celebrated her
11:9 will give you in M my daughter who was
Mt 22:2 king who gave a M feast for his son,
22:3 were invited to the M feast; but they would
22:4 ready; come to the M feast.'
22:9 and invite to the M feast as many as
22:30 nor are given in M, but are like angels
24:38 marrying and giving in M, until the day when
25:10 with him to the M feast; and the door
Mk 12:25 nor are given in M, but are like angels
Lk 12:36 come home from the M feast, so that they
14:8 any one to a M feast, do not sit
17:27 they were given in M, until the day when
20:34 and are given in M;
20:35 nor are given in M,
Jn 2:1 day there was a M at Cana in Galilee,
2:2 was invited to the M, with his disciples.
1Cor 7:27 Do not seek M
7:38 he who refrains from M will do better.
1Tim 4:3 are seared, who forbid M and enjoin abstinence from
Heb 13:4 Let M be held in honor among all, and
13:4 all, and let the M bed be undefiled; for
Rev 19:7 the glory, for the M of the Lamb has
19:9 are invited to the M supper of the Lamb."

MARRIAGES (4)

Gen 34:9 Make M with us; give your daughters to us,
Deut 7:3 You shall not make M with them, giving your
Josh 23:12 among you, and make M with them, so that
Wis 14:24 their lives or their M pure, but they either

MARRIED (41)

Gen 38:2 name was Shua; he M her and went in
Ex 21:3 if he comes in M, then his wife shall
Lev 22:12 a priest's daughter is M to an outsider she
Num 12:1 woman whom he had M, for he had married
12:1 married, for he had M a Cushite woman;
30:6 And if she is M to a husband, while
36:3 But if they are M to any of the
36:11 daughters of Zelophehad, were M to sons of their
36:12 They were M into the families of the sons
Deut 24:5 a man is newly M, he shall not go
25:5 dead shall not be M outside the family to
2Sam 17:25 the Ishmaelite, who had M Abigal the daughter of
1Chr 2:19 When Azubah died, Caleb M Ephrath, who bore him
2:21 of Gilead, whom he M when he was sixty
4:17 of Pharaoh, whom Mered M; and she conceived and
23:22 the sons of Kish, M them.
Ezra 10:2 our God and have M foreign women from the
10:10 "You have trespassed and M foreign women, and so
10:17 the men who had M foreign women.
10:18 the priests who had M foreign women were found
10:44 All these had M foreign women, and they put
Neh 13:23 the Jews who had M women of Ashdod, Ammon,
Tob 1:9 became a man I M Anna, a member of
Esth 10:6 Esther, whom the king M and made queen.
Sir 42:9 not marry, or if M, lest she be hated;
42:10 prove unfaithful, or, though M, lest she be barren.
Is 54:1 of her that is M, says the LORD.
62:4 her, and your land M; for the LORD delights
62:4 delights in you, and your land shall be M
Mal 2:11 he loves, and has M the daughter of a
2Mac 14:25 have children; so he M, settled down, and shared
Mt 22:25 among us; the first M, and died, and having
Mk 6:17 wife; because he had M her.
Lk 14:20 another said, 'I have M a wife, and therefore
17:27 ate, they drank, they M, they were given in
Rom 7:2 Thus a M woman is bound by law to
1Cor 7:10 To the M I give charge, not I but
7:33 the Lord; but the M man is anxious about
7:34 and spirit; but the M woman is anxious about
7:39 is free to be M to whom she wishes,
Gal 4:27 more than the children of her that is M

MARRIES (13)

Gen 27:46 If Jacob M one of the Hittite women such
Deut 24:1 takes a wife and M her, if then she
Is 62:5 as a young man M a virgin, so shall
Mt 5:32 an adulteress; and whoever M a divorced woman
19:9 for unchastity, and M another, commits adultery; and
19:9 adultery; and he who M a divorced woman, commits
Mk 10:11 divorces his wife and M another, commits adultery
10:12 her husband and M another, she commits adultery."
Lk 16:18 divorces his wife and M another commits adultery,
16:18 adultery, and he who M a woman divorced from
Rom 7:3 law, and if she M another man she is
1Cor 7:28 and if a girl M she does not sin.
7:38 So that he who M his betrothed does well;

MARROW (4)

Job 21:24 of fat and the M of his bones moist.
Ps 63:5 is feasted as with M and fat, and my
Is 25:6 fat things full of M, of wine on the
Heb 4:12 spirit, of joints and M, and discerning the thoughts

MARRY (29)

Gen 19:14 sons-in-law, who were to M his daughters, "Up, get
28:1 him, "You shall not M one of the Canaanite
28:6 him, "You shall not M one of the Canaanite
Lev 21:7 They shall not M a harlot or a woman
21:7 defiled; neither shall they M a woman divorced from
21:14 these he shall not M; but he shall take
Num 36:6 of Zelophehad, 'Let them M whom they think best;
36:6 best; only, they shall M within the family of
Josh 23:12 them, so that you M their women and they
Tob 4:12 fathers and do not M a foreign woman, who
Jud 16:22 Many desired to M her, but she remained a
Sir 42:9 lest she do not M, or if married, lest
Is 62:5 so shall your sons M you, and as the
Ezek 44:22 They shall not M a widow, or a divorced
2Mac 1:14 pretext of intending to M her, Antiochus came to
14:25 he urged him to M and have children; so
Mt 19:10 with his wife, it is not expedient to M
22:24 children, his brother must M the widow, and raise
22:30 the resurrection they neither M nor are given in
Mk 12:25 the dead, they neither M nor are given in
Lk 20:34 sons of this age M and are given in
20:35 from the dead neither M nor are given in
1Cor 7:9 if they cannot exercise self-control, they should M
7:9 it is better to M than to be aflame
7:28 But if you M, you do not sin, and
7:28 Yet those who M will have worldly troubles, and
7:36 he wishes: let them M --it is no sin.
1Tim 5:11 Christ they desire to M,
5:14 would have younger widows M, bear children, rule

MARRYING (3)

Ruth 1:13 Would you therefore refrain from M
Neh 13:27 against our God by M foreign women?"
Mt 24:38 were eating and drinking, M and giving in marriage,

MARSENA

Esth 1:14 Admatha, Tarshish, Meres, M, and Memucan, the

MARSH (3)

Job 8:11 "Can papyrus grow where there is no M
40:21 the covert of the reeds and in the M
1Mac 9:45 and on that, with M and thicket; there is

MARSHAL (2)

Judg 5:14 those who bear the M's staff;
Jer 51:27 and Ashkenaz; appoint a M against her, bring up

MARSHALED

Jud 2:16 a great army is M for a campaign.

MARSHALS

Sir 17:27 He M the host of the height of heaven;

MARSHES (2)

Ezek 47:11 But its swamps and M will not become fresh;
1Mac 9:42 they returned to the M of the Jordan.

MARTHA (13)

Lk 10:38 and a woman named M received him into her
10:40 But M was distracted with much serving; and she
10:41 the Lord answered her, M, Martha, you are anxious
10:41 Lord answered her, "Martha, M, you are anxious and
Jn 11:1 Bethany, the village of Mary and her sister M
11:5 Now Jesus loved M and her sister and Lazarus.
11:19 Jews had come to M and Mary to console
11:20 When M heard that Jesus was coming, she went
11:21 M said to Jesus, "Lord, if you had been
11:24 M said to him, "I know that he will
11:30 in the place where M had met him.
11:39 M, the sister of the dead man, said to
12:2 made him a supper; M served, and Lazarus was

MARTYRS

Rev 17:6 the blood of the M of Jesus.

MARVEL (8)

Sir 43:24 its dangers, and we M at what we hear.
Jn 3:7 Do not M that I said to you, 'You
5:19 these will he show him, that you may M
5:27 Do not M at this; for the hour is
7:21 deed, and you all M at it.
9:30 The man answered, "Why, this is a M
Rev 17:7 But the angel said to me, "Why M
17:8 of the world, will M to behold the beast,

MARVELED (22)

Jud 10:19 And they M at her beauty, and admired the
10:23 his servants, they all M at the beauty of
11:20 his servants, and they M at her wisdom and
Wis 11:14 of the events they M at him, for their
Sir 47:17 your interpretations, the countries M at you.
2Mac 1:22 a great fire blazed up, so that all M
Mt 8:10 Jesus heard him, he M, and said to those
8:27 And the men M, saying, "What sort of man
9:33 spoke; and the crowds M, saying, "Never was
21:20 disciples saw it they M, saying, "How did the
22:22 they heard it, they M; and they left him
Mk 5:20 Jesus had done for him; and all men M
6:6 And he M because of their unbelief.
Lk 1:63 And they all M
2:33 father and his mother M at what was said
7:9 Jesus heard this he M at him, and turned
8:25 were afraid, and they M, saying to one another,
11:14 out, the dumb man spoke, and the people M
Jn 4:27 They M that he was talking with a woman,
7:15 The Jews M at it, saying, "How is it
2Thes 1:10 saints, and to be M at in all who
Rev 17:6 I saw her I M greatly.

MARVELING (2)

Lk 9:43 while they were all M at everything he did,
20:26 what he said; but M at his answer they

MARVELOUS (27)

1Chr 16:24 among the nations, his M works among all the
Jud 11:8 kingdom, thoroughly informed and M in military
Job 5:9 things and unsearchable, M things without number:
9:10 things beyond understanding, and M things without
Ps 96:3 among the nations, his M works among all the
98:1 for he has done M things!
118:23 LORD's doing; it is M in our eyes.
131:1 too great and too M for me.
Wis 10:17 guided them along a M way, and became a
19:8 nation, after gazing on M wonders.
Sir 38:6 be glorified in his M works.
39:20 them, and nothing is M to him.
42:17 to recount all his M works, which the Lord
43:2 goes forth, is a M instrument, the work of
43:25 it are strange and M works, all kinds of
43:29 and very great, and M is his power.
48:14 did wonders, so in death his deeds were M
Is 29:14 I will again do M things with this people,
29:14 this people, wonderful and M; and the wisdom of
Dan 3:43 in accordance with thy M works, and give glory
Mic 7:15 I will show them M things.
Zech 8:6 hosts: If it is M in the sight of
8:6 should it also be M in my sight, says
2Mac 15:13 and dignity, and of M majesty and authority.
Mt 21:42 doing, and it is M in our eyes?
Mk 12:11 doing, and it is M in our eyes'?"
1Pet 2:9 of darkness into his M light.

MARVELOUSLY (4)

2Chr 26:15 far, for he was M helped, till he was
Jud 10:14 was in their eyes M beautiful—they said to
Sir 43:8 for the moon, increasing M in its phases, an
2Mac 3:30 Lord who had acted M for his own place.

MARVELS (3)

Ex 34:10 people I will do M, such as have not
Ps 78:12 their fathers he wrought M in the land of
Sir 43:18 The eye M at the beauty of its whiteness,

MARY (54)

Mt 1:16 Joseph the husband of M, of whom Jesus was
1:18 When his mother M had been betrothed to Joseph,
1:20 not fear to take M your wife, for that
2:11 saw the child with M his mother, and they
13:55 Is not his mother called M
27:56 him; among whom were M Magdalene, and Mary
27:56 were Mary Magdalene, and M the mother of James
27:61 M Magdalene and the other Mary were there,
27:61 Magdalene and the other M were there, sitting
28:1 day of the week, M Magdalene and the other
28:1 Magdalene and the other M went to see the
Mk 6:3 carpenter, the son of M and brother of James
15:39 afar, among whom were M Magdalene, and Mary
15:39 were Mary Magdalene, and M the mother of James
15:46 M Magdalene and Mary the mother of Joses saw
15:46 Mary Magdalene and M the mother of Joses saw
16:1 the sabbath was past, M Magdalene, and Mary the
16:1 past, Mary Magdalene, and M the mother of James,
16:9 he appeared first to M Magdalene, from whom he
Lk 1:27 house of David; and the virgin's name was M
1:30 "Do not be afraid, M, for you have found
1:34 And M said to the angel, "How shall this
1:38 And M said, "Behold, I am the handmaid of
1:39 In those days M arose and went with haste
1:41 heard the greeting of M, the babe leaped in
1:46 And M said, "My soul magnifies the Lord,
1:56 And M remained with her about three months, and
2:5 to be enrolled with M, his betrothed, who was
2:16 with haste, and found M and Joseph, and the
2:19 But M kept all these things, pondering them in
2:34 them and said to M his mother, "Behold, this
8:2 evil spirits and infirmities: M, called Magdalene,
10:39 had a sister called M, who sat at the
10:42 M has chosen the good portion, which shall not
24:10 Now it was M Magdalene and Jo-anna and Mary
24:10 Magdalene and Jo-anna and M the mother of James
Jn 11:1 Bethany, the village of M and her sister Martha.
11:2 It was M who anointed the Lord with ointment
11:19 come to Martha and M to console them concerning
11:20 and met him, while M sat in the house.
11:28 and called her sister M, saying quietly, "The Teacher
11:31 house, consoling her, saw M rise quickly and go
11:32 Then M, when she came where Jesus was and
11:45 who had come with M and had seen what
12:3 M took a pound of costly ointment of pure
19:25 and his mother's sister, M the wife of Clopas,
19:25 wife of Clopas, and M Magdalene.
20:1 day of the week M Magdalene came to the
20:11 But M stood weeping outside the tomb, and as
20:16 Jesus said to her, M
20:18 M Magdalene went and said to the disciples, "I
Acts 1:14 with the women and M the mother of Jesus,
12:12 to the house of M, the mother of John
Rom 16:6 Greet M, who has worked hard among you.

MASH

Gen 10:23 The sons of Aram: Uz, Hul, Gether, and M

MASHAL

1Chr 6:74 the tribe of Asher: M with its pasture lands,

MASONRY

Ezek 46:23 was a row of M, with hearths made at

MASONS (7)

2Sam 5:11 trees, also carpenters and M who built David a
2Kgs 12:12 LORD, and to the M and the stonecutters, as
22:6 builders, and to the M, as well as for

1Chr 14:1 and cedar trees, also M and carpenters to build
22:15 workmen: stonecutters, M, carpenters, and all kinds
2Chr 24:12 LORD, and they hired M and carpenters to restore
Ezra 3:7 gave money to the M and the carpenters, and

MASREKAH (2)

Gen 36:36 died, and Samlah of M reigned in his stead.
1Chr 1:47 Hadad died, Samlah of M reigned in his stead.

MASS (5)

Job 16:10 upon the cheek, they M themselves together against
38:38 dust runs into a M and the clods cleave
Ezek 19:11 its height with the M of its branches.
31:9 it beautiful in the M of its branches, and
2Mac 2:24 history because of the M of material,

MASSA (4)

Gen 25:14 Adbeel, Mibsam, Mishma, Dumah, M,
1Chr 1:30 Adbeel, Mibsam, Mishma, Dumah, M, Hadad, Tema,
Prov 30:1 The words of Agur son of Jakeh of M
31:1 of Lemuel, king of M, which his mother taught

MASSACRED

2Mac 12:6 burned the boats, and M those who had taken

MASSAH (5)

Ex 17:7 name of the place M and Meribah, because of
Deut 6:16 to the test, as you tested him at M
9:22 Taberah also, and at M, and at Kibroth-hattaavah,
33:8 thou didst test at M, with whom thou didst
Ps 95:8 on the day at M in the wilderness,

MASSING

2Mac 5:3 that, brandishing of shields, M of spears, hurling of

MAST (3)

Prov 23:34 one who lies on the top of a M
Is 33:23 it cannot hold the M firm in its place,
Ezek 27:5 Lebanon to make a M for you.

MASTER (182)

Gen 4:7 you, but you must M it."
24:9 thigh of Abraham his M, and swore to him
24:10 took ten of his M's camels and departed, taking
24:10 choice gifts from his M; and he arose, and
24:12 LORD, God of my M Abraham, grant me success
24:12 steadfast love to my M Abraham.
24:14 that thou hast shown steadfast love to my M
24:27 the God of my M Abraham, who has not
24:27 his steadfast love and his faithfulness toward my M
24:27 the house of my M's kinsmen."
24:35 has greatly blessed my M, and he has become
24:36 And Sarah my M's wife bore a son to
24:36 a son to my M when she was old;
24:37 My M made me swear, saying, 'You shall not
24:39 I said to my M, 'Perhaps the woman will
24:42 the God of my M Abraham, if now thou
24:44 has appointed for my M's son.'
24:48 the God of my M Abraham, who had led
24:48 the daughter of my M's kinsman for his son.
24:49 and truly with my M, tell me; and if
24:51 the wife of your M's son, as the LORD
24:54 morning, he said, "Send me back to my M
24:56 me go that I may go to my M
24:65 The servant said, "It is my M
39:2 the house of his M the Egyptian,
39:3 the Egyptian, and his M saw that the LORD
39:7 after a time his M's wife cast her eyes
39:8 and said to his M's wife, "Lo, having me
39:8 "Lo, having me my M has no concern about
39:16 by her until his M came home,
39:19 When his M heard the words which his wife
39:20 And Joseph's M took him and put him into
40:7 in custody in his M's house, "Why are your
Ex 21:4 If his M gives him a wife and she
21:4 children shall be her M's and he shall go
21:5 says, 'I love my M, my wife, and my
21:6 out free,' then his M shall bring him to
21:6 the doorpost; and his M shall bore his ear
21:8 does not please her M, who has designated her
21:32 shall give to their M thirty shekels of silver,
Deut 23:15 give up to his M a slave who has
23:15 has escaped from his M to you;
Judg 19:11 servant said to his M, "Come now, let us
19:12 And his M said to him, "We will not
19:22 the old man, the M of the house, "Bring
19:23 And the man, the M of the house, went
19:26 man's house where her M was, till it was
19:27 And her M rose up in the morning, and
1Sam 20:38 gathered up the arrows, and came to his M
25:14 wilderness to salute our M; and he railed at
25:17 is determined against our M and against all his
30:13 an Amalekite; and my M left me behind because
30:15 the hands of my M, and I will take
2Sam 9:9 have given to your M's son.
9:10 the produce, that your M's son may have bread
9:10 eat; but Mephibosheth your M's son shall always eat
12:8 I gave you your M's house, and your master's
12:8 master's house, and your M's wives into your bosom,
16:3 "And where is your M's son?" Ziba said to
1Kgs 11:23 had fled from his M Hadadezer king of Zobah.
22:17 said, 'These have no M; let each return to
2Kgs 2:3 will take away your M from over you?" And
2:5 will take away your M from over you?" And
2:16 go, and seek your M; it may be that
5:1 great man with his M and in high favor,
5:18 your servant: when my M goes into the house
5:20 God, said, "See, my M has spared this Naaman
5:22 My M has sent me to say, 'There have
5:25 and stood before his M, and Elisha said to
6:5 the water; and he cried out, "Alas, my M
6:15 And the servant said, "Alas, my M
6:22 may eat and drink and go to their M
6:23 sent them away, and they went to their M
6:32 the sound of his M's feet behind him?"
8:14 and came to his M, who said to him,
9:7 house of Ahab your M, that I may avenge
9:11 the servants of his M, they said to him,
9:31 "Is it peace, you Zimri, murderer of your M
10:2 to you, seeing your M's sons are with you,
10:3 and fittest of your M's sons and set him
10:3 and fight for your M's house."
10:6 the heads of your M's sons, and come to
10:9 who conspired against my M, and slew him; but
18:23 a wager with my M the king of Assyria:
18:24 the least of my M's servants, when you rely
18:27 to them, "Has my M sent me to speak
18:27 these words to your M and to you, and
19:4 the Rabshakeh, whom his M the king of Assyria
19:6 them, "Say to your M, 'Thus says the LORD:
1Chr 12:19 will desert to his M Saul.")
2Chr 18:16 said, 'These have no M; let each return to
Jud 2:14 the presence of his M, and called together all
5:20 Now therefore, my M and lord, if there is
6:13 foot of the hill, and returned to their M
11:10 Therefore, my lord and M, do not disregard what
13:1 the attendants from his M's presence; and they went
Esth 13:2 of many nations and M of the whole world,
14:12 of the gods and M of all dominion!
Job 3:19 there, and the slave is free from his M
Ps 12:4 our lips are with us; who is our M
123:2 the hand of their M, as the eyes of
Prov 8:30 beside him, like a M workman; and I was
27:18 he who guards his M will be honored.
30:10 a servant to his M, lest he curse you,
Eccl 2:19 Yet he will be M of all for which
Song 7:1 the work of a M hand.
Wis 18:11 same penalty as the M, and the common man
Sir 28:22 It will not be M over the godly, and
32:1 If they make you M of the feast, do
38:27 is every craftsman and M workman who labors by
Is 1:3 and the ass its M's crib; but Israel does
19:4 hand of a hard M; and a fierce king
22:18 you shame of your M's house.
24:2 slave, so with his M; as with the maid,
36:8 a wager with my M the king of Assyria:
36:9 the least of my M's servants, when you rely
36:12 Rabshakeh said, "Has my M sent me to speak
36:12 these words to your M and to you, and
37:4 the Rabshakeh, whom his M the king of Assyria
37:6 them, "Say to your M, 'Thus says the LORD:
Jer 3:14 for I am your M; I will take you,
Zeph 1:9 those who fill their M's house with violence and
Mal 1:6 son honors his father, and a servant his M
1:6 if I am a M, where is my fear?
2Mac 2:29 For as the M builder of a new house
Mt 10:24 a servant above his M;
10:25 like his teacher, and the servant like his M
10:25 they have called the M of the house Be-elzebul,
23:10 for you have one M, the Christ.
24:45 wise servant, whom his M has set over his
24:46 that servant whom his M when he comes will

	24:48	says to himself, 'My M is delayed,'
	24:50	with the drunken, the M of that servant will
	25:18	ground and hid his M's money.
	25:19	a long time the M of those servants came
	25:20	five talents more, saying, M, you delivered to me
	25:21	five talents more.' His M said to him, 'Well
	25:21	the joy of your M
	25:22	talents came forward, saying, M, you delivered to me
	25:23	two talents more.' His M said to him, 'Well
	25:23	the joy of your M
	25:24	talent came forward, saying, M, I knew you to
	25:26	is yours.' But his M answered him, 'You wicked
	26:25	Judas, who betrayed him, said, "Is it I, M
	26:49	up to Jesus at once and said, "Hail, M
Mk	9:5	Peter said to Jesus, M, it is well that
	10:51	man said to him, M, let me receive my
	11:21	and said to him, M, look!
	13:35	not know when the M of the house will
	14:45	went up to him at once, and said, M
Lk	5:5	And Simon answered, M, we toiled all night and
	8:24	and woke him, saying, M, Master, we are perishing!"
	8:24	woke him, saying, "Master, M, we are perishing!"
	8:45	denied it, Peter said, M, the multitudes surround you
	9:33	Peter said to Jesus, M, it is well that
	9:49	John answered, M, we saw a man casting out
	12:36	are waiting for their M to come home from
	12:37	those servants whom the M finds awake when he
	12:42	wise steward, whom his M will set over his
	12:43	that servant whom his M when he comes will
	12:45	says to himself, 'My M is delayed in coming,'
	12:46	and get drunk, the M of that servant will
	12:47	servant who knew his M's will, but did not
	14:21	the servant came and reported this to his M
	14:23	is room.' And the M said to the servant,
	16:3	I do, since my M is taking the stewardship
	16:5	stewardship.' So, summoning his M's debtors one by
	16:5	do you owe my M
	16:8	eighty.' The M commended the dishonest steward
	17:13	voices and said, "Jesus, M, have mercy on us."
Jn	13:16	not greater than his M; nor is he who
	15:15	not know what his M is doing; but I
	15:20	not greater than his M If they persecuted me,
Rom	14:4	is before his own M that he stands or
	14:4	be upheld, for the M is able to make
1Cor	3:10	me, like a skilled M builder I laid a
Eph	6:9	who is both their M and yours is in
Col	4:1	you also have a M in heaven.
2Tim	2:21	and useful to the M of the house, ready
Tit	1:7	a lover of goodness, M of himself, upright, holy,
2Pet	2:1	heresies, even denying the M who bought them,
Jude	1:4	and deny our only M and Lord, Jesus Christ.

MASTERED

Acts	19:16	was leaped on them, M all of them, and

MASTERS (18)

1Sam	25:10	nowadays who are breaking away from their M
Prov	25:13	send him, he refreshes the spirit of his M
Wis	10:14	scepter of a kingdom and authority over his M
Sir	3:7	mother; he will serve his parents as his M
Jer	27:4	this charge for their M: 'Thus says the LORD
	27:4	shall say to your M:
Mt	6:24	one can serve two M; for either he will
	15:27	that fall from their M table."
	23:10	Neither be called M, for you have one master,
Lk	16:13	servant can serve two M; for either he will
Eph	6:5	who are your earthly M, with fear and trembling,
	6:9	M, do the same to them, and forbear threatening,
Col	3:22	who are your earthly M, not with eye-service, as
	4:1	M, treat your slaves justly and fairly, knowing that
1Tim	6:1	of slavery regard their M as worthy of all
	6:2	who have believing M must not be disrespectful
Tit	2:9	be submissive to their M and to give satisfaction
1Pet	2:18	be submissive to your M with all respect, not

MASTERY (3)

Esth	9:1	hoped to get the M over them, but which
	9:1	Jews should get the M over their foes,
Sir	9:2	so that she gains M over your strength.

MASTIC

Dan	13:54	He answered, "Under a M tree."

MATCH (3)

1Mac	6:52	engines of war to M theirs, and fought for
	10:71	us, and let us M strength with each other
Lk	5:36	the new will not M the old.

MATCHED

2Cor	8:11	desiring it may be M by your completing it

MATE (4)

Gen	7:2	the male and his M; and a pair of
	7:2	the male and his M;
Is	34:15	the kites be gathered, each one with her M
	34:16	shall be missing; none shall be without her M

MATERIAL (4)

Prov	25:4	and the smith has M for a vessel;
2Mac	2:24	of the mass of M,
Rom	15:27	service to them in M blessings.
1Cor	9:11	if we reap your M benefits?

MATERIALS (6)

Ex	28:8	the same workmanship and M, of gold, blue and
	39:5	was of the same M and workmanship, of gold,
1Chr	22:5	So David provided M in great quantity before his
2Mac	1:21	And when the M for the sacrifices were presented,
	1:31	And when the M of the sacrifice were consumed,
	1:33	associates had burned the M of the sacrifice,

MATING

Gen	31:10	In the M season of the flock I lifted

MATRED (2)

Gen	36:39	Mehetabel, the daughter of M, daughter of
1Chr	1:50	the daughter of M, the daughter of Mezahab.

MATRITES (2)

1Sam	10:21	the family of the M was taken by lot;
	10:21	the family of the M near man by man,

MATTAN (3)

2Kgs	11:18	pieces, and they slew M the priest of Baal
2Chr	23:17	pieces, and they slew M the priest of Baal
Jer	38:1	Shephatiah the son of M, Gedaliah the son of

MATTANAH (2)

Num	21:18	they went on to M,
	21:19	to Mattanah, and from M to Nahaliel, and from

MATTANIAH (16)

2Kgs	24:17	king of Babylon made M, Jehoiachin's uncle, king in
1Chr	9:15	Bakbakkar, Heresh, Galal, and M the son of Mica,
	25:4	sons of Heman: Bukkiah, M, Uzziel, Shebuel, and
	25:16	twelve; the ninth to M, his sons and his
2Chr	20:14	of Je-iel, son of M, a Levite of the
	29:13	of Asaph, Zechariah and M;
Ezra	10:26	the sons of Elam: M, Zechariah, Jehiel, Abdi,
	10:27	Eli-o-enai, Eliashib, M, Jeremoth, Zabad, and Aziza.
	10:30	Adna, Chelal, Benaiah, Ma-aseiah, M, Bezalel,
	10:37	Vaniah, Meremoth, Eliashib, M, Mattenai, Jaasu.
Neh	11:17	house of God; and M the son of Mica,
	11:22	of Hashabiah, son of M, son of Mica, of
	12:8	Kadmi-el, Sherebiah, Judah, and M, who with his
	12:25	M, Bakbukiah, Obadiah, Meshullam, Talmon, and
	12:35	of Shemaiah, son of M, son of Micaiah, son
	13:13	of Zaccur, son of M, for they were counted

MATTATHA

Lk	3:31	Menna, the son of M, the son of Nathan,

MATTATHIAS (16)

1Mac	2:1	In those days M the son of John, son
	2:14	And M and his sons rent their clothes, put
	2:16	came to them; and M and his sons were
	2:17	king's officers spoke to M as follows: "You are
	2:19	But M answered and said in a loud voice:
	2:24	When M saw it, be burned with zeal and
	2:27	Then M cried out in the city with a
	2:39	When M and his friends learned of it, they
	2:45	And M and his friends went about and tore
	2:49	days drew near for M to die, and he
	11:70	them was left except M the son of Absalom
	14:29	Simon the son of M, a priest of the
	16:14	down to Jericho with M and Judas his sons,
2Mac	14:19	Posidonius and Theodotus and M to give and receive
Lk	3:25	Joseph, the son of M, the son of Amos,
	3:26	Maath, the son of M, the son of Seme-in,

MATTATTAH

Ezra	10:33	sons of Hashum: Mattenai, M, Zabad, Eliphelet,

MATTENAI (3)
Ezra 10:33 the sons of Hashum: M, Mattattah, Zabad, Eliphelet,
10:37 Vaniah, Meremoth, Eliashib, Mattaniah, M, Jaasu.
Neh 12:19 Shemaiah, Jehonathan; of Joiarib, M; of Jedaiah,

MATTER (92)
Gen 24:9 his master, and swore to him concerning this M
30:15 "Is it a small M that you have taken
Ex 18:22 all times; every great M they shall bring to
18:22 you, but any small M they shall decide themselves;
18:26 Moses, but any small M they decided themselves.
Lev 5:1 come to know the M, yet does not speak,
6:2 his neighbor in a M of deposit or security,
Num 25:18 beguiled you in the M of Peor, and in
25:18 Peor, and in the M of Cozbi, the daughter
31:16 the LORD in the M of Peor, and so
Deut 3:26 you; speak no more to me of this M
Josh 22:20 break faith in the M of the devoted things,
Ruth 3:18 you learn how the M turns out, for the
3:18 but will settle the M today."
1Sam 10:16 But about the M of the kingdom, of which
11:4 Saul, they reported the M in the ears of
20:19 hid yourself when the M was in hand, and
20:23 And as for the M of which you and
20:39 knew nothing; only Jonathan and David knew the M
21:2 charged me with a M, and said to me,
21:2 know anything of the M about which I send
30:24 Who would listen to you in this M
2Sam 11:25 'Do not let this M trouble you, for the
19:42 Why then are you angry over this M
20:18 counsel at Abel'; and so they settled a M
21:4 "It is not a M of silver or gold
1Kgs 5:8 you desire in the M of cedar and cypress
15:5 life, except in the M of Uriah the Hittite.
2Kgs 5:18 In this M may the LORD pardon your servant:
5:18 Rimmon, the LORD pardon your servant in this M
1Chr 2:7 who transgressed in the M of the devoted thing;
2Chr 8:15 and Levites concerning any M and concerning the
24:5 to year; and see that you hasten the M
32:31 And so in the M of the envoys of
Ezra 4:22 be slack in this M; why should damage grow
5:17 the king send us his pleasure in this M
10:9 trembling because of this M and because of the
10:13 two; for we have greatly transgressed in this M
10:14 our God over this M be averted from us."
10:16 down to examine the M;
Tob 7:8 journey, and let the M be settled."
Esth 9:26 had faced in this M, and of what had
Job 9:19 If it is a M of justice, who can
19:28 'The root of the M is found in him';
22:28 will decide on a M, and it will be
Prov 17:9 he who repeats a M alienates a friend.
Eccl 3:1 a time for every M under heaven:
3:17 a time for every M, and for every work.
5:8 be amazed at the M; for the high official
8:3 not delay when the M is unpleasant, for he
8:6 For every M has its time and way, although
10:20 your voice, or some winged creature tell the M
12:13 The end of the M; all has been heard.
Wis 11:17 world out of formless M, did not lack the
15:13 he makes from earthy M fragile vessels and graven
Sir 11:9 not argue about a M which does not concern
15:15 act faithfully is a M of your own choice.
31:15 own, and in every M be thoughtful.
37:11 to these in any M of counsel.
Ezek 16:20 harlotries so small a M
Dan 1:14 to them in this M, and tested them for
1:20 And in every M of wisdom and understanding
2:15 Then Arioch made the M known to Daniel.
2:17 house and made the M known to Hananiah, Mishael,
2:23 thou hast made known to us the king's M
3:16 have no need to answer you in this M
5:15 they could not show the interpretation of the M
5:26 interpretation of the M: MENE, God has numbered
7:1 the dream, and told the sum of the M
7:28 obey them.' "Here is the end of the M
7:28 but I kept the M in my mind."
1Mac 10:35 them or annoy any of them about any M
10:63 against him about any M, and let no one
2Mac 1:33 When this M became known, and it was reported
1:34 the king investigated the M, and enclosed the place
2:26 it is no light M but calls for sweat
13:13 out and decide the M by the help of
14:9 the details of this M, deign to take thought
15:17 and to decide the M, by fighting hand-to-hand with
Mk 9:10 So they kept the M to themselves, questioning what
10:10 house the disciples asked him again about this M
Acts 8:21 nor lot in this M, for your heart is
15:6 the elders were gathered together to consider this M
18:14 "If it were a M of wrongdoing or vicious
18:15 since it is a M of questions about words
28:23 And he expounded the M to them from morning
Rom 2:29 real circumcision is a M of the heart, spiritual
2Cor 7:11 point you have proved yourselves guiltless in the M
8:10 And in this M I give my advice: it
8:14 but that as a M of equality your abundance
1Thes 4:6 his brother in this M, because the Lord is
2Pet 1:20 of scripture is a M of one's own interpretation,

MATTERS (21)
1Chr 27:1 the king in all M concerning the divisions that
2Chr 19:11 over you in all M of the LORD; and
19:11 in all the king's M; and the Levites will
Ezra 7:11 the scribe, learned in M of the commandments of
Neh 11:24 king's hand in all M concerning the people.
Esth 10:5 I had concerning these M, and none of them
16:7 as from investigation of M close at hand.
Sir 3:22 beyond your tasks, for M too great for human
5:15 In great and small M do not act amiss,
11:10 busy yourself with many M; if you multiply activities
1Mac 3:48 to inquire into those M about which the Gentiles
2Mac 2:30 ground and to discuss M from every side and
11:17 have asked about the M indicated therein.
11:20 And concerning these M and their details, I have
11:36 But as to the M which he decided are
15:37 This, then, is how M turned out with Nicanor.
Mt 23:22 have neglected the weightier M of the law, justice
1Cor 6:3 How much more, M pertaining to this life!
7:1 Now concerning the M about which you wrote.
2Cor 8:22 found earnest in many M, but who is now
2Pet 2:12 and killed, reviling in M of which they are

MATTHAN (2)
Mt 1:15 Eleazar the father of M, and Matthan the father
1:15 father of Matthan, and M the father of Jacob,

MATTHAT (2)
Lk 3:24 Heli, the son of M, the son of Levi,
3:29 Jorim, the son of M, the son of Levi,

MATTHEW (5)
Mt 9:9 saw a man called M sitting at the tax
10:3 Thomas and M the tax collector; James
Mk 3:18 Philip, and Bartholomew, and M, and Thomas, and
Lk 6:15 Philip, and Bartholomew, and M, and Thomas, and
Acts 1:13 and Thomas, Bartholomew and M, James the son of

MATTHIAS (2)
Acts 1:23 called Barsabbas, who was surnamed Justus, and M
1:26 the lot fell on M; and he was enrolled

MATTITHIAH (8)
1Chr 9:31 of the spices, and M, one of the Levites,
15:18 Benaiah, Ma-aseiah, M, Eliphelehu, and Mikneiah,
15:21 Alamoth; but M, Eliphelehu, Mikneiah, Obed-edom,
16:5 Zechariah, Je-iel, Shemiramoth, Jehiel, M, Eliab,
25:3 Jeshaiah, Shimei, Hashabiah, and M, six, under the
25:21 twelve; to the fourteenth, M, his sons and his
Ezra 10:43 sons of Nebo: Je-iel, M, Zabad, Zebina, Jaddai, Joel,
Neh 8:4 beside him stood M, Shema, Anaiah, Uriah, Hilkiah,

MATTOCK
1Sam 13:20 sharpen his plowshare, his M, his axe, or his

MATTOCKS
1Sam 13:21 plowshares and for the M, and a third of

MATURE (9)
1Mac 16:3 by His mercy are M in years.
Lk 8:14 pleasures of life, and their fruit does not M
1Cor 2:6 Yet among the M we do impart wisdom, although
14:20 be babes in evil, but in thinking be M
Eph 4:13 Son of God, to M manhood, to the measure
Phil 3:15 of us who are M be thus minded; and
Col 1:28 may present every man M in Christ.
4:12 that you may stand M and fully assured in
Heb 5:14 food is for the M, for those who have

MATURITY (3)
Wis 3:16 will not come to M, and the offspring of
4:5 before they come to M, and their fruit will
Heb 6:1 and go on to M, not laying again a

MAXIMS (2)
Job 13:12 Your M are proverbs of ashes, your defenses are
Sir 8:8 busy yourself with their M; because from them you

MAYEST (5)
1Kgs 8:29 be there,' that thou M hearken to the prayer
2Chr 6:20 thy name, that thou M hearken to the prayer
Ps 10:14 and vexation, that thou M take it into thy
130:4 with thee, that thou M be feared.
Rom 3:4 is written, "That thou M be justified in thy

MAZZAROTH
Job 38:32 you lead forth the M in their season, or

ME-HUJA-EL (2)
Gen 4:18 was the father of M, and Me-huja-el the father
4:18 of Me-huja-el, and M the father of Me-thusha-el,

ME-JARKON
Josh 19:46 Jehud, Bene-berak, Gath-rimmon, and M and

ME-THUSHA-EL (2)
Gen 4:18 Me-huja-el the father of M, and Me-thusha-el the
4:18 father of Me-thusha-el, and M the father of Lamech.

ME-UNIM (3)
1Chr 4:41 their tents and the M who were found there,
Ezra 2:50 Asnah, the sons of M, the sons of Nephisim,
Neh 7:52 Besai, the sons of M, the sons of Nephushesim,

ME-UNITES (2)
2Chr 20:1 them some of the M, came against Jehoshaphat for
26:7 Arabs that dwelt in Gurbaal, and against the M

MEADOWS (2)
Ps 65:13 with joy, the M clothe themselves with flocks,
Zeph 2:6 seacoast, shall be pastures, M for shepherds and

MEAL (24)
Gen 18:6 three measures of fine M, knead it, and make
Num 5:15 an ephah of barley M; he shall pour no
15:20 first of your coarse M you shall present a
15:21 first of your coarse M you shall give to
1Sam 20:27 Jesse come to the M, either yesterday or today?"
2Sam 17:28 earthen vessels, wheat, barley, M, parched grain,
1Kgs 4:22 and sixty cors of M,
17:12 only a handful of M in a jar, and
17:14 Israel, 'The jar of M shall not be spent,
17:16 The jar of M was not spent, neither did
2Kgs 4:41 He said, "Then bring M
7:1 a measure of fine M shall be sold for
7:16 a measure of fine M was sold for a
7:18 a measure of fine M for a shekel, about
1Chr 12:40 oxen, abundant provisions of M, cakes of figs, clusters
Neh 10:37 first of our coarse M, and our contributions, the
Sir 31:21 the middle of the M, and you will have
Is 47:2 the millstones and grind M, put off your veil,
Ezek 44:30 first of your coarse M, that a blessing may
46:15 the lamb and the M offering and the oil
Hos 8:7 it shall yield no M; if it were to
2Mac 6:21 flesh of the sacrificial M which had been
1Cor 11:21 ahead with his own M, and one is hungry
Heb 12:16 Esau, who sold his birthright for a single M

MEALS (3)
Sir 25:17 Her husband takes his M among the neighbors, and
41:19 of selfish behavior at M, of surliness in receiving
Bar 6:30 Women serve M for gods of silver and gold

MEALTIME (2)
Ruth 2:14 And at M Boaz said to her, "Come here,
Dan 13:13 other, "Let us go home, for it is M

MEAN (40)
Gen 33:8 said, "What do you M by all this company
Ex 2:14 Do you M to kill me as you killed
12:26 you, 'What do you M by this service?'
13:14 you, 'What does this M you shall say to
Josh 4:6 'What do those stones M to you?'
4:21 'What do these stones M
1Sam 4:6 great shouting in the camp of the Hebrews M
1Kgs 1:41 said, "What does this uproar in the city M
Esth 16:23 and hereafter it may M salvation for us and
Sir 14:5 If a man is M to himself, to whom
14:9 with a portion, and M injustice withers the soul.
Is 3:15 What do you M by crushing my people, by
22:1 What do you M that you have gone up,
Jer 4:30 one, what do you M that you dress in
Ezek 17:12 house, Do you not know what these things M
18:2 again: "What do you M by repeating this proverb
24:19 us what these things M for us, that you
37:18 show us what you M by these?'
Jon 1:6 him, "What do you M, you sleeper?
2Mac 5:11 he took it to M that Judea was in
14:7 glory – I M the high-priesthood –
14:14 of the Jews would M prosperity for themselves.
Mt 26:70 all, saying, "I do not know what you M
Mk 14:68 saying, "I neither know nor understand what you M
Jn 7:36 What does he M by saying, 'You will seek
16:18 said, "What does he M by 'a little while?
Acts 2:12 perplexed, saying to one another, "What does this M
10:17 he had seen might M, behold, the men that
17:20 we wish to know therefore what these things M
21:39 a citizen of no M city; I beg you,
Rom 11:12 Gentiles, how much more will their full inclusion M
11:15 what will their acceptance M but life from the
1Cor 1:12 What I M is that each one of you
7:29 I M, brethren, the appointed time has grown very
10:29 conscience' sake– I M his conscience, not yours–
15:29 Otherwise, what do people M by being baptized on
2Cor 8:13 I do not M that others should be eased
Gal 3:17 This is what I M: the law, which came
4:1 I M that the heir, as long as he
Eph 4:9 what does it M but that he had also

MEANER
Sir 14:6 No one is M than the man who is

MEANING (8)
Gen 21:29 Abraham, "What is the M of these seven ewe
40:5 own dream, and each dream with its own M
41:11 I, each having a dream with its own M
Deut 6:20 come, 'What is the M of the testimonies and
Acts 13:8 (for that is the M of his name) withstood
1Cor 5:10 men; not at all M the immoral of this
14:10 and none is without M;
14:11 do not know the M of the language, I

MEANINGS
Sir 39:3 seek out the hidden M of proverbs and be

MEANS (77)
Gen 41:32 doubling of Pharaoh's dream M that the thing is
Ex 5:8 you shall by no M lessen it; for they
5:19 "You shall by no M lessen your daily number
34:7 who will by no M clear the guilty, visiting
Lev 25:26 prosperous and finds sufficient M to redeem it,
25:28 he has not sufficient M to get it back
25:54 not redeemed by these M, then he shall be
Num 14:18 he will by no M clear the guilty, visiting
Deut 29:24 What M the heat of this great anger?'
30:20 to him; for that M life to you and
Judg 16:5 lies, and by what M we may overpower him,
1Sam 6:3 empty, but by all M return him a guilt
2Sam 14:14 of him who devises M not to keep his
17:16 wilderness, but by all M pass over; lest the
1Kgs 3:26 child, and by no M slay it." But the
3:27 woman, and by no M slay it; she is
20:39 man; if by any M he be missing, your
22:22 to him, 'By what M And he said, 'I
2Chr 18:20 to him, 'By what M
Jud 12:18 lord, because my life M more to me today
Prov 13:8 poor man has no M of redemption.
Wis 11:17 did not lack the M to send upon them
12:27 gods, being punished by M of them, they saw
15:12 get money however one can, even by base M
18:8 For by the same M by which thou didst
Sir 8:13 give surety beyond your M, but if you give
12:5 to him, lest by M of it he subdue
14:11 according to your M, and present worthy offerings
33:3 as an inquiry by M of Urim.
Jer 30:11 I will by no M leave you unpunished.
46:28 I will by no M leave you unpunished."
Nah 1:3 LORD will by no M clear the guilty.
1Mac 14:10 furnished them with the M of defense, till his
2Mac 1:36 which M purification, but by most people it is
Mt 1:23 (which M, God with us).
2:6 Judah, are by no M least among the rulers
9:13 and learn what this M, 'I desire mercy, and
12:7 had known what this M, 'I desire mercy, and
13:38 and the good seed M the sons of the
27:33 place called Golgotha (which M the place of a

Mk 5:41 her, "Talitha cumi"; which M, "Little girl, I say
9:41 Christ, will by no M lose his reward.
15:22 place called Golgotha (which M the place of a
15:33 which M, "My God, my God, why hast thou
Lk 8:3 others, who provided for them out of their M
16:9 friends for yourselves by M of unrighteous mammon,
Jn 1:38 (which M Teacher), "where are you staying?"
1:41 (which M Christ).
1:42 (which M Peter).
9:7 (which M Sent).
11:4 may be glorified by M of it."
16:18 We do not know what he M
20:16 (which M Teacher).
Acts 4:9 a cripple, by what M this man has been
4:36 Barnabas (which M, Son of encouragement),
9:36 disciple named Tabitha, which M Dorcas.
Rom 3:4 By no M
3:6 (I speak in a human way.) By no M
3:31 By no M
6:2 By no M
6:15 By no M
7:7 By no M
7:13 By no M
9:8 This M that it is not the children of
9:14 By no M
11:1 By no M
11:11 By no M
11:12 Now if their trespass M riches for the world,
11:12 and if their failure M riches for the Gentiles,
11:15 For if their rejection M the reconciliation of the
1Cor 9:22 I might by all M save some.
2Cor 8:3 gave according to their M, as I can testify,
8:3 testify, and beyond their M, of their own free
Phil 1:22 in the flesh, that M fruitful labor for me.
1Tim 6:5 that godliness is a M of gain.
2Pet 3:5 of water and by M of water,
Rev 9:19 with heads, and by M of them they wound.

MEANT (16)

Gen 50:20 As for you, you M evil against me; but
50:20 against me; but God M it for good, to
Deut 19:19 him as he had M to do to his
Judg 13:23 "If the LORD had M to kill us, he
20:5 me by night; they M to kill me, and
2Mac 12:8 the men in Jamnia M in the same way
Mk 6:48 He M to pass by them,
9:10 questioning what the rising from the dead M
Lk 8:9 him what this parable M,
15:26 one of the servants and asked what this M
18:36 a multitude going by, he inquired what this M
Jn 11:13 they thought that he M taking rest in sleep.
16:19 asking yourselves, what I M by saying, 'A little
Rom 2:4 that God's kindness is M to lead you to
1Cor 6:13 "Food is M for the stomach and the stomach
6:13 The body is not M for immorality, but for

MEANTIME

Lk 12:1 In the M, when so many thousands of the

MEANWHILE (3)

Gen 37:36 M the Midianites had sold him in Egypt to
2Chr 20:13 M all the men of Judah stood before the
Jn 4:31 M the disciples besought him, saying, "Rabbi, eat."

MEARAH

Josh 13:4 of the Canaanites, and M which belongs to the

MEASURE (70)

Gen 41:49 until he ceased to M it, for it could
Ex 26:2 four cubits; all the curtains shall have one M
26:8 cubits; the eleven curtains shall have the same M
29:40 first lamb a tenth M of fine flour mingled
36:9 four cubits; all the curtains had the same M
36:15 four cubits; the eleven curtains had the same M
Num 35:5 And you shall M, outside the city, for the
Deut 21:2 forth, and they shall M the distance to the
25:15 a full and just M you shall have; that
1Kgs 4:29 wisdom and understanding beyond M, and largeness
6:25 cherubim had the same M and the same form.
7:9 stones, hewn according to M, sawed with saws, back
7:37 alike, of the same M and the same form.
2Kgs 7:1 about this time a M of fine meal shall
7:16 So a M of fine meal was sold for
7:18 a shekel, and a M of fine meal for
Job 11:9 Its M is longer than the earth, and broader
28:25 out the waters by M;
Ps 39:4 and what is the M of my days; let
80:5 and given them tears to drink in full M
89:47 O Lord, what the M of life is, for
147:5 abundant in power; his understanding is beyond M
Wis 11:20 arranged all things by M and number and weight.
Sir 1:14 Lord is wisdom's full M; she satisfies men with
6:15 and no scales can M his excellence.
18:4 Who can M his majestic power?
Is 5:14 opened its mouth beyond M, and the nobility of
27:8 M by measure, by exile thou didst contend with
27:8 Measure by M, by exile thou didst contend with
40:12 the earth in a M and weighed the mountains
47:9 upon you in full M, in spite of your
56:12 tomorrow will be like this day, great beyond M
65:7 the hills, I will M into their bosom payment
Jer 10:24 LORD, but in just M; not in thy anger,
30:11 chasten you in just M, and I will by
46:28 chasten you in just M, and I will by
Bar 3:18 silver, and are anxious, whose labors are beyond M
Ezek 4:11 you shall drink by M, the sixth part of
4:16 shall drink water by M and in dismay.
45:3 holy district you shall M off a section twenty-five
45:11 be of the same M, the bath containing one
45:11 a homer; the homer shall be the standard M
48:30 five hundred cubits by M,
48:33 five hundred cubits by M, three gates, the gate
Dan 8:23 have reached their full M, a king of bold
Mic 6:10 wicked, and the scant M that is accursed?
Zech 2:2 said to me, "To M Jerusalem, to see what
2Mac 6:14 have reached the full M of their sins; but
Mt 7:2 be judged, and the M you give will be
7:2 give will be the M you get.
23:31 Fill up, then, the M of your fathers.
Mk 4:24 what you hear; the M you give will be
4:24 give will be the M you get, and still
7:36 they were astonished beyond M, saying, "He has
Lk 6:38 given to you; good M, pressed down, shaken together,
6:38 For the M you give will be the measure
6:38 give will be the M you get back."
Jn 3:34 it is not by M that he gives the
Rom 7:13 the commandment might become sinful beyond M
12:3 each according to the M of faith which God
2Cor 2:5 me, but in some M --not to put it
10:12 But when they M themselves by one another, and
Eph 4:7 us according to the M of Christ's gift.
4:13 mature manhood, to the M of the stature of
1Thes 2:16 to fill up the M of their sins.
Rev 11:1 was told: "Rise and M the temple of God
11:2 there, but do not M the court outside the
18:7 give her a like M of torment and mourning.
21:15 rod of gold to M the city and its
21:17 cubits by a man's M, that is, an angels.

MEASURED (54)

Gen 41:49 to measure it, for it could not be M
Ex 16:18 But when they M it with an omer, he
Ruth 3:15 held it, and he M out six measures of
2Sam 8:2 he defeated Moab, and M them with a line,
8:2 ground; two lines he M to be put to
1Kgs 6:25 The other cherub also M ten cubits; both cherubim
7:15 line of twelve cubits M its circumference; it was
7:23 line of thirty cubits M its circumference.
7:38 forty baths, each laver M four cubits, and there
2Chr 4:2 line of thirty cubits M its circumference.
Jud 7:21 day, because it was M out to them to
Wis 4:8 length of time, nor M by number of years;
Is 40:12 Who has M the waters in the hollow of
Jer 13:25 the portion I have M out to you, says
31:37 heavens above can be M, and the foundations of
33:22 the sea cannot be M, so I will multiply
Ezek 40:5 in length; so he M the thickness of the
40:6 up its steps, and M the threshold of the
40:8 Then he M the vestibule of the gateway, eight
40:11 Then he M the breadth of the opening of
40:13 Then he M the gate from the back of
40:14 He M also the vestibule, twenty cubits; and round
40:19 Then he M the distance from the inner front
40:20 He M its length and its breadth.
40:23 inner court; and he M from gate to gate,
40:24 the south; and he M its jambs and its
40:27 inner court; and he M from gate to gate
40:28 south gate, and he M the south gate; it
40:32 east side, and he M the gate; it was
40:35 north gate, and he M it; it had the
40:47 And he M the court, a hundred cubits long,
40:48 of the temple and M the jambs of the

41:1 to the nave, and M the jambs; on each
41:2 either side; and he M the length of the
41:3 the inner room and M the jambs of the
41:4 And he M the length of the room, twenty
41:5 Then he M the wall of the temple, six
41:8 of the side chambers M a full reed of
41:13 Then he M the temple, a hundred cubits long;
41:15 Then he M the length of the building facing
42:15 which faced east, and M the temple area round
42:16 He M the east side with the measuring reed,
42:17 Then he turned and M the north side, five
42:18 Then he turned and M the south side, five
42:19 the west side and M, five hundred cubits by
42:20 He M it on the four sides.
47:3 his hand, the man M a thousand cubits, and
47:4 Again he M a thousand, and led me through
47:4 Again he M a thousand, and led me through
47:5 Again he M a thousand, and it was a
Hos 1:10 which can be neither M nor numbered; and in
Hab 3:6 He stood and M the earth; he looked and
Rev 21:16 its breadth; and he M the city with his
21:17 He also M its wall, a hundred and forty-four

MEASUREMENT

1Kgs 7:11 stones, hewn according to M, and cedar.

MEASUREMENTS (2)

2Chr 3:3 These are Solomon's M for building the house of
Job 38:5 Who determined its M --surely you know!

MEASURES (20)

Gen 18:6 "Make ready quickly three M of fine meal, knead
Lev 19:35 wrong in judgment, in M of length or weight
Deut 25:14 house two kinds of M, a large and a
Ruth 3:15 he measured out six M of barley, and laid
3:17 her, saying, "These six M of barley he gave
1Sam 25:18 ready dressed, and five M of parched grain, and
1Kgs 18:32 as would contain two M of seed.
2Kgs 7:1 a shekel, and two M of barley for a
7:16 a shekel, and two M of barley for a
7:18 to the king, "Two M of barley shall be
1Chr 23:29 with oil, and all M of quantity or size.
Prov 20:10 Diverse weights and diverse M are both alike an
Hag 2:16 a heap of twenty M, there were but ten;
2:16 winevat to draw fifty M, there were but twenty.
2Mac 4:21 government, and he took M for his own security.
Mt 13:33 and hid in three M of flour, till it
Lk 13:21 and hid in three M of flour, till it
16:6 He said, 'A hundred M of oil.' And he
16:7 He said, 'A hundred M of wheat.' He said
Acts 27:17 it up, they took M to undergird the ship;

MEASURING (15)

2Kgs 21:13 stretch over Jerusalem the M line of Samaria, and
Jer 31:39 And the M line shall go out farther, straight
Ezek 40:3 of flax and a M reed in his hand;
40:5 the length of the M reed in the man's
42:15 when he had finished M the interior of the
42:16 east side with the M reed, five hundred cubits
42:16 hundred cubits by the M reed.
42:17 hundred cubits by the M reed.
42:18 hundred cubits by the M reed.
42:19 hundred cubits by the M reed.
48:10 have an allotment M twenty-five thousand cubits on
Zech 1:16 of hosts, and the M line shall be stretched
2:1 a man with a M line in his hand!
Rev 11:1 I was given a M rod like a staff,
21:15 to me had a M rod of gold to

MEAT (29)

Num 11:4 "O that we had M to eat!
11:13 am I to get M to give to all
11:13 and say, 'Give us M, that we may eat.'
11:18 and you shall eat M; for you have wept
11:18 "Who will give us M to eat?
11:18 LORD will give you M, and you shall eat.
11:21 'I will give them M, that they may eat
11:33 While the M was yet between their teeth, before
Judg 6:19 ephah of flour; the M he put in a
6:20 to him, "Take the M and the unleavened cakes,
6:21 hand, and touched the M and the unleavened cakes;
1Sam 2:13 would come, while the M was boiling, with a
2:15 who was sacrificing, "Give M for the priest to
2:15 will not accept boiled M from you, but raw."
25:11 my water and my M that I have killed
2Sam 6:19 bread, a portion of M, and a cake of
1Kgs 17:6 brought him bread and M in the morning, and
17:6 morning, and bread and M in the evening; and
1Chr 16:3 bread, a portion of M, and a cake of
Job 31:31 been filled with his M
Ps 78:20 give bread, or provide M for his people?"
Prov 23:20 among gluttonous eaters of M;
Is 44:16 eats flesh, he roasts M and is satisfied; also
Dan 10:3 ate no delicacies, no M or wine entered my
Mic 3:3 chop them up like M in a kettle, like
2Mac 6:21 urged him to bring M of his own providing,
Rom 14:21 right not to eat M or drink wine or
1Cor 8:13 I will never eat M, lest I cause my
10:25 is sold in the M market without raising any

MEBUNNAI

2Sam 23:27 Tekoa, Abi-ezer, of Anathoth, M the Hushathite,

MECHERATHITE

1Chr 11:36 of Ur, Hepher the M, Ahijah the Pelonite,

MECONAH

Neh 11:28 villages, in Ziklag, in M and its villages,

MEDAD (2)

Num 11:26 and the other named M, and the spirit rested
11:27 told Moses, "Eldad and M are prophesying in the

MEDAN (2)

Gen 25:2 bore him Zimran, Jokshan, M, Midian, Ishbak, and
1Chr 1:32 she bore Zimran, Jokshan, M, Midian, Ishbak, and

MEDDLE

Sir 3:22 Do not M in what is beyond your tasks,

MEDDLES

Prov 26:17 He who M in a quarrel not his own

MEDDLING

Sir 41:22 another man's wife; of M with his maidservant--

MEDE (3)

Dan 5:31 And Darius the M received the kingdom, being about
9:1 Ahasuerus, by birth a M, who became king over
11:1 year of Darius the M, I stood up to

MEDEBA (6)

Num 21:30 and we laid waste until fire spread to M
Josh 13:9 all the tableland of M as far as Dibon;
13:16 all the tableland by M;
1Chr 19:7 with his army, who came and encamped before M
Is 15:2 over Nebo and over M Moab wails.
1Mac 9:36 sons of Jambri from M came out and seized

MEDES (14)

2Kgs 17:6 of Gozan, and in the cities of the M
18:11 the cities of the M,
Jud 1:1 who ruled over the M in Ecbatana--
16:10 at her boldness, the M were daunted at her
Esth 1:19 the Persians and the M so that it may
Is 13:17 am stirring up the M against them, who have
Jer 51:11 the kings of the M, because his purpose concerning
51:28 the kings of the M, with their governors and
Dan 5:28 and given to the M and Persians."
6:8 the law of the M and the Persians, which
6:12 the law of the M and Persians, which cannot
6:15 a law of the M and Persians that no
1Mac 1:1 the Persians and the M, he succeeded him as
Acts 2:9 Parthians and M and Elamites and residents of

MEDIA (24)

Ezra 6:2 in the province of M, a scroll was found
Tob 1:14 used to go into M, and once at Rages
1:14 once at Rages in M I left ten talents
1:15 so that I could no longer go into M
3:7 day, at Ecbatana in M, it also happened that
4:1 Gabael at Rages in M, and he said to
4:20 Gabael the son of Gabrias at Rages in M
5:5 "Can you go with me to Rages in M
9:2 Gabael at Rages in M and get the money
11:15 great things that had happened to him in M
14:4 Go to M, my son, for I fully believe
14:4 But in M there will be peace for a
14:14 died in Ecbatana of M at the age of
Esth 1:3 chiefs of Persia and M and the nobles and
1:14 princes of Persia and M, who saw the king's
1:18 ladies of Persia and M who have heard of

M

	18:16	So Obadiah went to M Ahab, and told him;
	18:16	and Ahab went to M Elijah.
	21:18	"Arise, go down to M Ahab king of Israel,
2Kgs	1:3	"Arise, go up to M the messengers of the
	1:6	came a man to M us, and said to
	1:7	he who came to M you and told you
	2:15	And they came to M him, and bowed to
	4:26	run at once to M her, and say to
	4:29	If you M any one, do not salute him;
	4:31	Therefore he returned to M him, and told him,
	5:21	from the chariot to M him, and said, "Is
	5:26	from his chariot to M you?
	8:8	you and go to M the man of God,
	8:9	So Hazael went to M him, and took a
	9:17	horseman, and send to M them, and let him
	9:18	on horseback went to M him, and said, "Thus
	9:21	chariot, and went to M Jehu, and met him
	10:15	of Rechab coming to M him; and he greeted
	16:10	went to Damascus to M Tiglath-pileser king of
	23:29	King Josiah went to M him; and Pharaoh Neco
1Chr	12:17	David went out to M them and said to
	19:5	men, he sent to M them, for the men
2Chr	14:10	Asa went out to M him, and they drew
	15:2	he went out to M Asa, and said to
	19:2	seer went out to M him, and said to
	22:7	out with Jehoram to M Jehu the son of
	28:9	he went out to M the army that came
Neh	6:2	"Come and let us M together in one of
	6:10	he said, "Let us M together in the house
	13:2	for they did not M the children of Israel
Tob	11:9	Then Anna ran to M them, and embraced her
	11:16	Tobit went out to M his daughter-in-law at the
Jud	5:4	to come out and M me?"
Job	5:14	They M with darkness in the daytime, and grope
	30:27	of affliction come to M me.
	39:21	he goes out to M the weapons.
Ps	10:6	generations I shall not M adversity."
	21:3	[Selah] For thou dost M him with goodly blessings;
	59:10	his steadfast love will M me; my God will
	79:8	compassion come speedily to M us, for we are
	85:10	love and faithfulness will M; righteousness and
Prov	7:15	have come out to M you, to seek you
	14:7	there you do not M words of knowledge.
	14:22	Those who devise good M loyalty and faithfulness.
	17:12	Let a man M a she-bear robbed of her
	22:2	rich and the poor M together; the LORD is
	29:13	man and the oppressor M together; the LORD gives
Eccl	8:5	obeys a command will M no harm, and the
Wis	19:5	but they themselves might M a strange death.
Sir	9:3	Do not go to M a loose woman, lest
	15:2	She will come to M him like a mother,
	19:26	his face, when you M him.
	36:9	who harm thy people M destruction.
Is	7:3	Isaiah, "Go forth to M Ahaz, you and Shear-jashub
	14:9	is stirred up to M you when you come,
	21:14	the thirsty bring water, M the fugitive with bread,
	34:14	And wild beasts shall M with hyenas, the satyr
Jer	18:21	May their men M death by pestilence, their youths
	41:6	out from Mizpah to M them, weeping as he
	51:31	One runner runs to M another, and one messenger
	51:31	and one messenger to M another, to tell the
Dan	2:10	on earth who can M the king's demand; for
Amos	4:12	to you, prepare to M your God, O Israel!"
	9:10	shall not overtake or M us.'
Zech	2:3	angel came forward to M him,
1Mac	3:11	he went out to M him, and he defeated
	3:16	Judas went out to M him with a small
	3:17	the army coming to M them, they said to
	5:39	And Judas went to M them.
	5:59	of the city to M them in battle.
	7:30	him and would not M him again.
	7:31	he went out to M Judas in battle near
	9:39	and his brothers to M them with tambourines and
	10:2	and marched out to M him in battle.
	10:39	sanctuary in Jerusalem, to M the necessary expenses
	10:56	as you wrote, but M me at Ptolemais, so
	10:59	Jonathan to come to M him.
	10:71	to the plain to M us, and let us
	10:86	city came out to M him with great pomp.
	11:2	him and went to M him, for Alexander the
	11:2	had commanded them to M him, since he was
	11:22	the siege, but to M him for a conference
	11:64	He went to M them, but left his brother
	12:41	Jonathan went out to M him with forty thousand
	16:5	horsemen was coming to M them; and a stream
2Mac	14:21	day on which to M by themselves.
Mt	8:34	city came out to M Jesus; and when they
	25:1	lamps and went to M the bridegroom.
	25:6	Come out to M him.'
Mk	14:13	jar of water will M you; follow him,
Lk	14:31	with ten thousand to M him who comes against
	22:10	jar of water will M you; follow him into
Jn	12:13	and went out to M him, crying, "Hosanna!
	12:18	the crowd went to M him was that they
Acts	22:30	all the council to M, and he brought Paul
	28:15	and Three Taverns to M us.
1Cor	11:20	When you M together, it is not the Lord's
2Cor	13:5	indeed you fail to M the test!
1Thes	4:17	in the clouds to M the Lord in the
2Thes	2:1	and our assembling to M him, we beg you,
Heb	4:2	because it did not M with faith in the
	10:25	works, not neglecting to M together, as is the
Jas	1:2	my brethren, when you M various trials,

MEETEST

Is	64:5	Thou M him that joyfully works righteousness, those

MEETING (138)

Ex	27:21	In the tent of M, outside the veil which
	28:43	into the tent of M, or when they come
	29:4	of the tent of M, and wash them with
	29:10	shall bring the bull before the tent of M
	29:11	of the tent of M,
	29:30	into the tent of M to minister in the
	29:32	basket, at the door of the tent of M
	29:42	of the tent of M before the LORD, where
	29:44	consecrate the tent of M and the altar; Aaron
	30:16	of the tent of M; that it may bring
	30:18	between the tent of M and the altar, and
	30:20	into the tent of M, or when they come
	30:26	it the tent of M and the ark of
	30:36	in the tent of M where I shall meet
	31:7	you: the tent of M, and the ark of
	33:7	camp; and he called it the tent of M
	33:7	to the tent of M, which was outside the
	35:21	for the tent of M, and for all its
	38:8	ministered at the door of the tent of M
	38:30	of the tent of M, the bronze altar and
	39:32	of the tent of M was finished; and the
	39:40	for the tent of M;
Lev	1:1	from the tent of M, saying,
	1:3	of the tent of M, that he may be
	1:5	is at the door of the tent of M
	3:2	of the tent of M; and Aaron's sons the
	3:8	before the tent of M; and Aaron's sons shall
	3:13	before the tent of M; and the sons of
	4:4	of the tent of M before the LORD, and
	4:5	to the tent of M;
	4:7	in the tent of M, and the rest of
	4:7	is at the door of the tent of M
	4:14	before the tent of M;
	4:16	to the tent of M,
	4:18	in the tent of M before the LORD; and
	4:18	is at the door of the tent of M
	6:16	of the tent of M they shall eat it.
	6:26	eaten, in the court of the tent of M
	6:30	into the tent of M to make atonement in
	8:3	congregation at the door of the tent of M
	8:4	assembled at the door of the tent of M
	8:31	of the tent of M, and there eat it
	8:33	of the tent of M for seven days, until
	8:35	of the tent of M you shall remain day
	9:5	before the tent of M; and all the congregation
	9:23	into the tent of M; and when they came
	10:7	of the tent of M, lest you die; for
	10:9	into the tent of M, lest you die; it
	12:6	of the tent of M a lamb a year
	14:11	LORD, at the door of the tent of M
	14:23	of the tent of M, before the LORD;
	15:14	of the tent of M, and give them to
	15:29	priest, to the door of the tent of M
	16:7	of the tent of M;
	16:16	for the tent of M, which abides with them
	16:17	in the tent of M when he enters to
	16:20	and the tent of M and the altar, he
	16:23	into the tent of M, and shall put off
	16:33	for the tent of M and for the altar,
	17:4	of the tent of M, to offer it as
	17:5	of the tent of M, and slay them as
	17:6	of the tent of M, and burn the fat
	17:9	of the tent of M, to sacrifice it to
	19:21	of the tent of M, a ram for a

24:3 in the tent of M, Aaron shall keep it
Num 1:1 in the tent of M, on the first day
2:2 facing the tent of M on every side.
2:17 "Then the tent of M shall set out, with
3:7 before the tent of M, as they minister at
3:8 of the tent of M, and attend to the
3:25 in the tent of M was to be the
3:25 of the tent of M,
3:38 before the tent of M toward the sunrise, were
4:3 to do the work in the tent of M
4:4 in the tent of M: the most holy things.
4:15 of the tent of M which the sons of
4:23 to do the work in the tent of M
4:25 and the tent of M with its covering, and
4:25 of the tent of M,
4:28 in the tent of M, and their work is
4:30 to do the work of the tent of M
4:31 in the tent of M: the frames of the
4:33 in the tent of M, under the hand of
4:35 in the tent of M;
4:37 in the tent of M, whom Moses and Aaron
4:39 in the tent of M –
4:41 in the tent of M, whom Moses and Aaron
4:43 in the tent of M –
4:47 in the tent of M,
6:10 of the tent of M,
6:13 of the tent of M,
6:18 of the tent of M, and shall take the
7:5 of the tent of M, and give them to
7:89 into the tent of M to speak with the
8:9 before the tent of M, and assemble the whole
8:15 at the tent of M, when you have cleansed
8:19 at the tent of M, and to make atonement
8:22 in the tent of M in attendance upon Aaron
8:24 of the tent of M;
8:26 in the tent of M, to keep the charge,
10:3 you at the entrance of the tent of M
11:16 to the tent of M, and let them take
12:4 "Come out, you three, to the tent of M
14:10 at the tent of M to all the people
16:18 of the tent of M with Moses and Aaron.
16:19 them at the entrance of the tent of M
16:42 toward the tent of M; and behold, the cloud
16:43 of the tent of M,
16:50 of the tent of M, when the plague was
17:4 in the tent of M before the testimony, where
18:4 to the tent of M, for all the service
18:6 to do the service of the tent of M
18:21 they serve, their service in the tent of M
18:22 near the tent of M, lest they bear sin
18:23 of the tent of M, and they shall bear
18:31 return for your service in the tent of M
19:4 of the tent of M seven times.
20:6 of the tent of M, and fell on their
25:6 weeping at the door of the tent of M
27:2 of the tent of M, saying,
31:54 into the tent of M, as a memorial for
Deut 31:14 in the tent of M, that I may commission
31:14 went and presented themselves in the tent of M
Josh 18:1 up the tent of M there; the land lay
19:51 LORD, at the door of the tent of M
1Sam 2:22 served at the entrance to the tent of M
1Kgs 8:4 LORD, the tent of M, and all the holy
1Chr 6:32 of the tent of M, until Solomon had built
9:21 gatekeeper at the entrance of the tent of M
23:32 of the tent of M and the sanctuary, and
2Chr 1:3 for the tent of M of God, which Moses
1:6 at the tent of M, and offered a thousand
1:13 before the tent of M, to Jerusalem.
5:5 ark, the tent of M, and all the holy
Ps 74:8 they burned all the M places of God in
2Mac 14:5 by Demetrius to a M of the council and
14:30 with him and was M him more rudely than
Acts 13:43 And when the M of the synagogue broke up,

MEETS (10)
Gen 32:17 "When Esau my brother M you, and asks you,
Num 35:19 to death; when he M him, he shall put
35:21 to death, when he M him.
Deut 22:23 virgin, and a man M her in the city
22:25 open country a man M a young woman who
22:28 "If a man M a virgin who is not
Prov 7:10 And lo, a woman M him, dressed as a
Wis 6:16 in their paths, and M them in every thought.
Sir 40:23 or a companion never M one amiss, but a
Is 41:2 the east whom victory M at every step?

MEGIDDO (12)
Josh 12:21 one; the king of M, one;
17:11 and the inhabitants of M and its villages; the
Judg 1:27 or the inhabitants of M and its villages; but
5:19 by the waters of M; they got no spoils
1Kgs 4:12 of Ahilud, in Taanach, M, and all Beth-shean which
9:15 Jerusalem and Hazor and M and Gezer
2Kgs 9:27 And he fled to M, and died there.
23:29 Neco slew him at M, when he saw him.
23:30 in a chariot from M, and brought him to
1Chr 7:29 Taanach and its towns, M and its towns, Dor
2Chr 35:22 God, but joined battle in the plain of M
Zech 12:11 the mourning for Hadadrimmon in the plain of M

MEHETABEL (3)
Gen 36:39 his wife's name was M, the daughter of Matred,
1Chr 1:50 and his wife's name M the daughter of Matred,
Neh 6:10 of Delaiah, son of M, who was shut up,

MEHIDA (2)
Ezra 2:52 Bazluth, the sons of M, the sons of Harsha,
Neh 7:54 Bazlith, the sons of M, the sons of Harsha,

MEHIR
1Chr 4:11 was the father of M, who was the father

MEHOLATHITE (2)
1Sam 18:19 given to Adriel the M for a wife.
2Sam 21:8 son of Barzillai the M;

MEHUMAN
Esth 1:10 with wine, he commanded M, Biztha, Harbona,

MELATIAH
Neh 3:7 next to them repaired M the Gibeonite and Jadon

MELCHI (2)
Lk 3:24 Levi, the son of M, the son of Janna-i,
3:28 Neri, the son of M, the son of Addi,

MELCHIEL
Jud 6:15 son of Gothoniel, and Charmis the son of M

MELCHIZEDEK (10)
Gen 14:18 And M king of Salem brought out bread and
Ps 110:4 a priest for ever after the order of M
Heb 5:6 a priest for ever, after the order of M
5:10 God a high priest after the order of M
6:20 high priest for ever after the order of M
7:1 For this M, king of Salem, priest of the
7:10 of his ancestor when M met him.
7:11 after the order of M, rather than one named
7:15 in the likeness of M,
7:17 a priest for ever, after the order of M

MELE-A
Lk 3:31 Eliakim, the son of M, the son of Menna,

MELECH (2)
1Chr 8:35 sons of Micah: Pithon, M, Tarea, and Ahaz.
9:41 sons of Micah: Pithon, M, Tahre-a, and Ahaz;

MELODIOUS
Wis 17:18 whistling wind, or a M sound of birds in

MELODY (16)
Judg 5:3 sing, I will make M to the LORD, the
Ps 27:6 will sing and make M to the LORD.
33:2 with the lyre, make M to him with the
57:7 I will sing and make M
92:3 the harp, to the M of the lyre.
98:5 lyre, with the lyre and the sound of M
108:1 I will sing and make M
147:7 LORD with thanksgiving; make M to our God upon
149:3 name with dancing, making M to him with timbrel
Sir 32:6 of gold is the M of music with good
40:21 the harp make pleasant M, but a pleasant voice
47:9 altar, to make sweet M with their voices.
50:18 him with their voices in sweet and full-toned M
Is 23:16 Make sweet M, sing many songs, that you may
Amos 5:23 your songs; to the M of your harps I
Eph 5:19 songs, singing and making M to the Lord with

MELONS
Num 11:5 nothing, the cucumbers, the M, the leeks, the onions,

MELT (23)

Deut 1:28 have made our hearts M, saying, "The people are
20:8 heart of his fellows M as his heart.'
Josh 2:9 inhabitants of the land M away before you.
14:8 heart of the people M; yet I wholly followed
2Sam 17:10 a lion, will utterly M with fear; for all
Jud 16:15 presence the rocks shall M like wax, but to
Ps 97:5 The mountains M like wax before the LORD, before
Wis 16:29 an ungrateful man will M like wintry frost, and
19:21 them, nor did they M the crystalline, easily melted
Sir 3:15 weather, your sins will M away.
Is 8:6 that flow gently, and M in fear before Rezin
13:7 every man's heart will M,
14:31 gate; cry, O city; M in fear, O Philistia,
19:1 of the Egyptians will M within them.
Jer 49:23 heard evil tidings; they M in fear, they are
Ezek 21:7 comes, every heart will M and all hands will
21:15 that their hearts may M, and many fall at
22:20 it in order to M it; so I will
22:20 put you in and M you.
Mic 1:4 And the mountains will M under him and the
Nah 1:5 before him, the hills M; the earth is laid
1Mac 4:32 Fill them with cowardice; M the boldness of their
2Pet 3:12 and the elements will M with fire!

MELTED (15)

Ex 15:15 inhabitants of Canaan have M away.
16:21 eat; but when the sun grew hot, it M
Josh 2:11 heard it, our hearts M, and there was no
5:1 crossed over, their heart M, and there was no
7:5 hearts of the people M, and became as water.
Judg 15:14 fire, and his bonds M off his hands.
Ps 22:14 like wax, it is M within my breast;
107:26 the depths; their courage M away in their evil
Wis 16:27 destroyed by fire was M when simply warmed by
19:21 melt the crystalline, easily M kind of heavenly food.
Bar 6:20 say their hearts have M, when worms from the
Ezek 22:21 and you shall be M in the midst of
22:22 As silver is M in a furnace, so you
22:22 so you shall be M in the midst of
24:11 its filthiness may be M in it, its rust

MELTING

Wis 16:22 ice withstood fire without M, so that they might

MELTS (8)

Ps 46:6 kingdoms totter; he utters his voice, the earth M
68:2 them away; as wax M before fire, let the
112:10 gnashes his teeth and M away; the desire of
119:28 My soul M away for sorrow; strengthen me
147:18 forth his word, and M them; he makes his
Sir 38:28 breath of the fire M his flesh, and he
Is 15:3 every one wails and M in tears.
Amos 9:5 the earth and it M, and all who dwell

MEMBER (11)

Lev 25:47 you, or to a M of the stranger's family,
Deut 23:1 crushed or whose male M is cut off shall
Tob 1:9 I married Anna, a M of our family, and
Mk 15:42 of Arimathea, a respected M of the council, who
Lk 23:49 He was a M of the council, a good
Acts 13:1 of Cyrene, Mana-en a M of the court of
Rom 11:1 descendant of Abraham, a M of the tribe of
1Cor 12:14 not consist of one M but of many.
12:26 If one M suffers, all suffer together; if one
12:26 suffer together; if one M is honored, all rejoice
Jas 3:5 tongue is a little M and boasts of great

MEMBERS (30)

Gen 36:6 daughters, and all the M of his household, his
1Chr 5:23 The M of the half-tribe of Manasseh dwelt in
Job 17:7 grief, and all my M are like a shadow.
Ezek 23:20 her paramours there, whose M were like those of
Mt 5:29 lose one of your M than that your whole
5:30 lose one of your M than that your whole
Rom 6:13 Do not yield your M to sin as instruments
6:13 to life, and your M to God as instruments
6:19 you once yielded your M to impurity and to
6:19 now yield your M to righteousness for sanctification.
7:5 at work in our M to bear fruit for
7:23 I see in my M another law at war
7:23 the law of sin which dwells in my M
12:4 body we have many M, and all the members
12:4 members, and all the M do not have the
12:5 in Christ, and individually M one of another.
1Cor 6:5 enough to decide between M of the brotherhood,
6:15 that your bodies are M of Christ?
6:15 I therefore take the M of Christ and make
6:15 Christ and make them M of a prostitute?
12:12 one and has many M, and all the members
12:12 members, and all the M of the body, though
12:25 body, but that the M may have the same
12:27 of Christ and individually M of it.
Eph 2:19 with the saints and M of the household of
3:6 Gentiles are fellow heirs, M of the same body,
4:25 neighbor, for we are M one of another.
5:30 church, because we are M of his body.
Jas 3:6 unrighteous world among our M, staining the whole
4:1 your passions that are at war in your M

MEMMIUS

2Mac 11:34 read thus: "Quintus M and Titus Manius, envoys

MEMOIRS

2Mac 2:13 records and in the M of Nehemiah, and also

MEMORABLE

Esth 6:1 bring the book of M deeds, the chronicles, and

MEMORIAL (25)

Ex 12:14 be for you a M day, and you shall
13:9 hand and as a M between your eyes, that
17:14 "Write this as a M in a book and
Lev 2:2 burn this as its M portion upon the altar,
2:9 the cereal offering its M portion and burn this
2:16 shall burn as its M portion part of the
5:12 of it as its M portion and burn this
6:15 burn this as its M portion on the altar,
23:24 of solemn rest, a M proclaimed with blast of
24:7 the bread as a M portion to be offered
Num 5:26 cereal offering, as its M portion, and burn it
31:54 of meeting, as a M for the people of
Josh 4:7 people of Israel a M for ever."
Neh 2:20 portion or right or M in Jerusalem."
Sir 38:11 sweet-smelling sacrifice, and a M portion of fine
44:10 some who have no M, who have perished as
45:16 pleasing odor as a M portion, to make atonement
Is 26:8 wait for thee; thy M name is the desire
55:13 the LORD for a M, for an everlasting sign
66:3 he who makes a M offering of frankincense, like
Bar 4:5 courage, my people, O M of Israel!
1Mac 8:22 them there as a M of peace and alliance:
13:29 armor for a permanent M, and beside the suits
2Mac 6:31 of nobility and a M of courage, not only
Acts 10:4 have ascended as a M before God.

MEMORIZE

2Mac 2:25 who are inclined to M, and to profit all

MEMORY (22)

Job 18:17 His M perishes from the earth, and he has
Ps 9:6 rooted out; the very M of them has perished.
109:15 continually; and may his M be cut off from
Prov 10:7 The M of the righteous is a blessing, but
Eccl 9:5 more reward; but the M of them is lost.
Wis 4:1 virtue, for in the M of virtue is immortality,
4:19 suffer anguish, and the M of them will perish.
11:12 a groaning at the M of what had occurred.
Sir 10:17 and has extinguished the M of them from the
23:26 She will leave her M for a curse, and
35:7 is acceptable, and the M of it will not
39:9 be blotted out; his M will not disappear, and
45:1 and man, Moses, whose M is blessed.
46:11 Lord-- may their M be blessed!
49:1 The M of Josiah is like a blending of
49:13 The M of Nehemiah also is lasting; he raised
1Mac 3:7 his deeds, and his M is blessed for ever.
3:35 was to banish the M of them from the
12:53 and blot out the M of them from among
2Mac 7:20 was especially admirable and worthy of honorable M
Mt 26:13 will be told in M of her."
Mk 14:9 will be told in M of her."

MEMPHIS (8)

Jud 1:10 even beyond Tanis and M, and all who lived
Is 19:13 and the princes of M are deluded; those who
Jer 2:16 Moreover, the men of M and Tahpanhes have broken
44:1 Migdol, at Tahpanhes, at M, and in the land
46:14 in Migdol; proclaim in M and Tahpanhes; Say, 'Stand
46:19 For M shall become a waste, a ruin, without
Ezek 30:13 to the images, in M; there shall no longer
Hos 9:6 Egypt shall gather them, M shall bury them.

MEMUCAN (3)

Esth 1:14 Tarshish, Meres, Marsena, and M, the seven princes
1:16 Then M said in presence of the king and
1:21 the king did as M proposed;

MEN (2,184)

Gen 4:26 At that time M began to call upon the
6:1 When M began to multiply on the face of
6:2 that the daughters of M were fair; and they
6:4 to the daughters of M, and they bore children
6:4 These were the mighty M that were of old,
6:4 were of old, the M of renown.
11:2 And as M migrated from the east, they found
11:5 which the sons of M had built.
12:20 And Pharaoh gave M orders concerning him; and
13:13 Now the M of Sodom were wicked, great sinners
14:14 led forth his trained M, born in his house,
14:24 but what the young M have eaten, and the
14:24 the share of the M who went with me;
17:23 every male among the M of Abraham's house, and
17:27 circumcised; and all the M of his house, those
18:2 looked, and behold, three M stood in front of
18:16 Then the M set out from there, and they
18:22 So the M turned from there, and went toward
19:4 they lay down, the M of the city, the
19:4 of the city, the M of Sodom, both young
19:5 Lot, "Where are the M who came to you
19:6 the door to the M, shut the door after
19:8 do nothing to these M, for they have come
19:10 But the M put forth their hands and brought
19:11 struck with blindness the M who were at the
19:12 Then the M said to Lot, "Have you any
19:16 he lingered; so the M seized him and his
20:8 these things; and the M were very much afraid.
21:27 Abimelech, and the two M made a covenant.
22:3 two of his young M with him, and his
22:5 said to his young M, "Stay here with the
22:19 returned to his young M, and they arose and
24:13 the daughters of the M of the city are
24:32 the feet of the M who were with him.
24:54 And he and the M who were with him
24:59 and her nurse, and Abraham's servant and his M
26:7 When the M of the place asked him about
26:7 thinking, "lest the M of the place should kill
29:22 gathered together all the M of the place, and
32:6 you, and four hundred M with him."
32:28 with God and with M, and have prevailed."
33:1 coming, and four hundred M with him.
33:15 you some of the M who are with me."
34:7 of it; and the M were indignant and very
34:20 and spoke to the M of their city, saying,
34:21 their city, saying, "These M are friendly with us;
34:22 this condition will the M agree to dwell with
38:21 And he asked the M of the place, "Where
38:22 her; and also the M of the place said,
39:11 and none of the M of the house was
39:14 she called to the M of her household and
41:8 and all its wise M; and Pharaoh told them
42:11 man, we are honest M, your servants are not
42:19 if you are honest M, let one of your
42:31 him, 'We are honest M, we are not spies;
42:33 that you are honest M: leave one of your
42:34 not spies but honest M, and I will deliver
43:15 So the M took the present, and they took
43:16 his house, "Bring the M into the house, and
43:16 make ready, for the M are to dine with
43:17 him, and brought the M to Joseph's house.
43:18 And the M were afraid because they were brought
43:24 man had brought the M into Joseph's house, and
43:33 his youth; and the M looked at one another
44:1 his house, "Fill the M's sacks with food, as
44:3 morning was light, the M were sent awy with
44:4 "Up, follow after the M; and when you overtake
46:32 to me; and the M are shepherds, for they
47:2 brothers he took five M and presented them to
47:6 you know any able M among them, put them
49:6 their anger they slay M, and in their wantonness

Ex 4:19 Egypt; for all the M who were seeking your
5:9 be laid upon the M that they may labor
7:11 Pharaoh summoned the wise M and the sorcerers;
10:7 Let the M go, that they may serve the
10:11 Go, the M among you, and serve the LORD,
12:33 haste; for they said, "We are all dead M
12:37 six hundred thousand M on foot, besides women
17:9 Joshua, "Choose for us M, and go out, fight
18:21 Moreover choose able M from all the people, such
18:21 such as fear God, M who are trustworthy and
18:21 bribe; and place such M over the people as
18:25 Moses chose able M out of all Israel, and
21:18 "When M quarrel and one strikes the other with
21:22 "When M strive together, and hurt a woman with
22:31 "You shall be M consecrated to me; therefore you
24:5 And he sent young M of the people of
24:11 hand on the chief M of the people of
30:32 the bodies of ordinary M, and you shall make
31:6 given to all able M ability, that they may
32:28 of the people that day about three thousand M
35:22 So they came, both M and women; all who
35:29 All the M and women, the people of Israel,
36:4 that all the able M who were doing every
36:8 And all the able M among the workmen made
38:26 hundred and three thousand, five hundred and fifty M

Lev 5:4 of rash oath that M swear, and it is
6:3 all the things which M do and sin therein,
18:27 of these abominations the M of the land did,
27:9 an animal such as M offer as an offering
27:29 utterly destroyed from among M, shall be ransomed;

Num 1:5 the names of the M who shall attend you.
1:17 and Aaron took these M who have been named,
1:44 leaders of Israel, twelve M, each representing his
5:6 of the sins that M commit by breaking faith
7:24 the leader of the M of Zebulun:
7:30 the leader of the M of Reuben:
7:36 the leader of the M of Simeon:
7:42 the leader of the M of Gad:
7:48 the leader of the M of Ephraim:
7:54 the leader of the M of Manasseh:
7:60 the leader of the M of Benjamin:
7:66 the leader of the M of Dan:
7:72 the leader of the M of Asher:
7:78 the leader of the M of Naphtali:
9:6 And there were certain M who were unclean
9:7 that day; and those M said to him, "We
10:14 the camp of the M of Judah set out
10:15 the tribe of the M of Issachar was Nethanel
10:16 the tribe of the M of Zebulun was Eliab
10:19 the tribe of the M of Simeon was Shelumi-el
10:20 the tribe of the M of Gad was Eliasaph
10:22 the camp of the M of Ephraim set out
10:23 the tribe of the M of Manasseh was Gamaliel
10:24 the tribe of the M of Benjamin was Abidan
10:25 the camp of the M of Dan, acting as
10:26 the tribe of the M of Asher was Pagiel
10:27 the tribe of the M of Naphtali was Ahira
11:16 "Gather for me seventy M of the elders of
11:24 and he gathered seventy M of the elders of
11:26 Now two M remained in the camp, one named
11:28 one of his chosen M, said, "My lord Moses,
12:3 meek, more than all M that were on the
13:2 said to Moses, "Send M to spy out the
13:3 LORD, all of them M who were heads of
13:16 the names of the M whom Moses sent to
13:24 the cluster which the M of Israel cut down
13:31 Then the M who had gone up with him
13:32 saw in it are M of great stature.
14:22 LORD, none of the M who have seen my
14:36 And the M whom Moses sent to spy out
14:37 against the land, the M who brought up an
14:38 remained alive, of those M who went to spy
16:2 sons of Reuben, took M; and they rose up
16:2 from the assembly, well-known M;
16:14 Will you put out the eyes of these M
16:26 tents of these wicked M, and touch nothing of
16:29 If these M die the common death of all
16:29 common death of all M, or if they are
16:29 the fate of all M, then the LORD has
16:30 shall know that these M have despised the LORD."
16:32 households and all the M that belonged to Korah
16:35 two hundred and fifty M offering the incense.
16:38 the censers of these M who have sinned at
20:20 against them with many M, and with a strong
21:23 He gathered all his M together, and went out
22:9 said, "Who are these M with you?"
22:20 to him, "If the M have come to call
22:35 Balaam, "Go with the M; but only the word
25:5 of you slay his M who have yoked themselves
26:10 two hundred and fifty M; and they became a
31:3 to the people, "Arm M from among you for
31:21 priest said to the M of war who had
31:28 a tribute from the M of war who went
31:32 the spoil that the M of war took was:
31:42 from that of the M who had gone to

18:2 Danites sent five able M from the whole number
18:7 Then the five M departed, and came to Laish,
18:11 And six hundred M of the tribe of Dan,
18:14 Then the five M who had gone to spy
18:16 Now the six hundred M of the Danites, armed
18:17 gate; and the five M who had gone to
18:17 with the six hundred M armed with weapons of
18:22 home of Micah, the M who were in the
19:6 So the two M sat and ate and drank
19:16 sojourning in Gibe-ah; the M of the place were
19:22 hearts merry, behold, the M of the city, base
19:25 But the M would not listen to him.
20:2 God, four hundred thousand M on foot that drew
20:5 And the M of Gibe-ah rose against me, and
20:10 we will take ten M of a hundred throughout
20:11 So all the M of Israel gathered against the
20:12 tribes of Israel sent M through all the tribe
20:13 therefore give up the M, the base fellows in
20:15 that day twenty-six thousand M that drew the sword,
20:15 of Gibe-ah, who mustered seven hundred picked M
20:16 were seven hundred picked M who were left-handed;
20:17 And the M of Israel, apart from Benjamin, mustered
20:17 mustered four hundred thousand M that drew sword;
20:17 sword; all these were M of war.
20:20 And the M of Israel went out to battle
20:20 against Benjamin; and the M of Israel drew up
20:21 that day twenty-two thousand M of the Israelites.
20:22 But the people, the M of Israel, took courage,
20:25 the ground eighteen thousand M of the people of
20:25 Israel; all these were M who drew the sword.
20:29 So Israel set M in ambush round about Gibe-ah.
20:31 open country, about thirty M of Israel.
20:32 But the M of Israel said, "Let us flee,
20:33 And all the M of Israel rose up out
20:33 at Baal-tamar; and the M of Israel who were
20:34 Gibe-ah ten thousand picked M out of all Israel,
20:35 Israel; and the M of Israel destroyed twenty-five
20:35 twenty-five thousand one hundred M of Benjamin
20:35 day; all these were M who drew the sword.
20:36 The M of Israel gave ground to Benjamin, because
20:36 they trusted to the M in ambush whom they
20:37 And the M in ambush made haste and rushed
20:37 rushed upon Gibe-ah; the M in ambush moved out
20:38 appointed signal between the M of Israel and the
20:38 of Israel and the M in ambush was that
20:39 of the city the M of Israel should turn
20:39 and kill about thirty M of Israel; they said,
20:41 Then the M of Israel turned, and the men
20:41 Israel turned, and the M of Benjamin were,
20:42 their backs before the M of Israel in the
20:44 Eighteen thousand M of Benjamin fell, all of them
20:44 fell, all of them M of valor.
20:45 of Rimmon; five thousand M of them were cut
20:45 Gidom, and two thousand M of them were slain.
20:46 Benjamin were twenty-five thousand M that drew
20:46 sword, all of them M of valor.
20:47 But six hundred M turned and fled toward the
20:48 And the M of Israel turned back against the
20:48 edge of the sword, M and beasts and all
21:1 Now the M of Israel had sworn at Mizpah,
21:10 of their bravest M, and commanded them, "Go
Ruth 2:9 not charged the young M not to molest you?
2:9 drink what the young M have drawn."
2:15 Boaz instructed his young M, saying, "Let her glean
3:10 not gone after young M, whether poor or rich.
4:2 And he took ten M of the elders of
1Sam 2:12 of Eli were worthless M; they had no regard
2:17 sin of the young M was very great in
2:17 the LORD; for the M treated the offering of
2:26 and in favor with the LORD and with M
2:33 your house shall die by the sword of M
4:2 slew about four thousand M on the field of
4:9 and acquit yourselves like M, O Philistines, lest you
4:9 you; acquit yourselves like M and fight."
5:7 And when the M of Ashdod saw how things
5:9 and he afflicted the M of the city, both
5:12 very heavy there; the M who did not die
6:10 The M did so, and took two milch cows
6:15 great stone; and the M of Beth-shemesh offered
6:19 slew some of the M of Beth-shemesh, because they
6:19 LORD; he slew seventy M of them, and the
6:20 Then the M of Beth-shemesh said, "Who is able
7:1 And the M of Kiriath-jearim came and took up
7:11 And the M of Israel went out of Mizpah
8:22 then said to the M of Israel, "Go every
10:2 you will meet two M by Rachel's tomb in
10:3 oak of Tabor; three M going up to God
10:26 and with him went M of valor whose hearts
11:1 Jabesh-gilead; and all the M of Jabesh said to
11:5 the tidings of the M of Jabesh.
11:8 them at Bezek, the M of Israel were three
11:8 hundred thousand, and the M of Judah thirty.
11:9 you say to the M of Jabesh-gilead: 'Tomorrow, by
11:9 came and told the M of Jabesh, they were
11:10 Therefore the M of Jabesh said, "Tomorrow we will
11:12 over us?' Bring the M, that we may put
11:15 Saul and all the M of Israel rejoiced greatly.
13:2 Saul chose three thousand M of Israel; two thousand
13:6 When the M of Israel saw that they were
13:15 who were present with him, about six hundred M
14:2 were about six hundred M,
14:8 cross over to the M, and we will show
14:12 And the M of the garrison hailed Jonathan and
14:14 was of about twenty M within as it were
14:22 Likewise, when all the M of Israel who had
14:24 And the M of Israel were distressed that day;
15:4 Telaim, two hundred thousand M on foot, and ten
15:4 foot, and ten thousand M of Judah.
16:18 One of the young M answered, "Behold, I have
17:2 And Saul and the M of Israel were gathered,
17:19 they, and all the M of Israel, were in
17:24 All the M of Israel, when they saw the
17:25 And the M of Israel said, "Have you seen
17:26 David said to the M who stood by him,
17:28 he spoke to the M; and Eliab's anger was
17:52 And the M of Israel and Judah rose with
18:5 set him over the M of war.
18:27 went, along with his M, and killed two hundred
21:2 appointment with the young M for such and such
21:4 if only the young M have kept themselves from
21:5 vessels of the young M are holy, even when
22:2 And there were with him about four hundred M
22:6 was discovered, and the M who were with him.
22:19 to the sword; both M and women, children and
23:3 But David's M said to him, "Behold, we are
23:5 And David and his M went to Keilah, and
23:8 down to Keilah, to besiege David and his M
23:11 Will the M of Keilah surrender me into his
23:12 said David, "Will the M of Keilah surrender me
23:12 surrender me and my M into the hand of
23:13 Then David and his M, who were about six
23:24 Now David and his M were in the wilderness
23:25 And Saul and his M went to seek him.
23:26 and David and his M on the other side
23:26 as Saul and his M were closing in upon
23:26 upon David and his M to capture them,
24:2 took three thousand chosen M out of all Israel,
24:2 seek David and his M in front of the
24:3 Now David and his M were sitting in the
24:4 And the M of David said to him, "Here
24:6 He said to his M, "The LORD forbid that
24:7 So David persuaded his M with these words, and
24:9 to the words of M who say, 'Behold, David
24:22 but David and his M went up to the
25:5 David sent ten young M; and David said to
25:5 said to the young M, "Go up to Carmel,
25:8 Ask your young M, and they will tell you.
25:8 Therefore let my young M find favor in your
25:9 When David's young M came, they said all this
25:11 and give it to M who come from I
25:12 So David's young M turned away, and came back
25:13 David said to his M, "Every man gird on
25:13 and about four hundred M went up after David,
25:14 one of the young M told Abigail, Nabal's wife,
25:15 Yet the M were very good to us, and
25:19 said to her young M, "Go on before me;
25:20 behold, David and his M came down toward her;
25:25 not see the young M of my lord, whom
25:27 given to the young M who follow my lord.
25:29 If M rise up to pursue you and to
26:2 with three thousand chosen M of Israel, to seek
26:19 but if it is M, may they be cursed
26:22 one of the young M come over and fetch
27:2 and the six hundred M who were with him,
27:3 Gath, he and his M, every man with his
27:8 Now David and his M went up, and made
28:1 that you and your M are to go out
28:8 went, he and two M with him; and they
29:2 and David and his M were passing on in
29:4 the heads of the M here?
29:11 set out with his M early in the morning,
30:1 when David and his M came to Ziklag on

30:3 when David and his M came to the city,
30:9 and the six hundred M who were with him,
30:10 he and four hundred M; two hundred stayed behind,
30:17 except four hundred young M, who mounted camels
30:21 to the two hundred M, who had been too
30:22 base fellows among the M who had gone with
30:31 where David and his M had roamed.
31:1 against Israel; and the M of Israel fled before
31:6 armor-bearer, and all his M, on the same day
31:7 And when the M of Israel who were on
31:7 Jordan saw that the M of Israel had fled
31:12 Saul, all the valiant M arose, and went all
2Sam 1:11 so did all the M who were with him;
1:15 one of the young M and said, "Go, fall
2:3 David brought up his M who were with him,
2:4 And the M of Judah came, and there they
2:4 David, "It was the M of Jabesh-gilead who buried
2:5 sent messengers to the M of Jabesh-gilead, and said
2:14 Joab, "Let the young M arise and play before
2:17 and Abner and the M of Israel were beaten
2:21 one of the young M, and take his spoil."
2:27 not spoken, surely the M would have given up
2:28 trumpet; and all the M stopped, and pursued Israel
2:29 And Abner and his M went all that night
2:30 of David's servants nineteen M besides Asahel.
2:31 of Benjamin three hundred and sixty of Abner's M
2:32 And Joab and his M marched all night, and
3:20 Abner came with twenty M to David at Hebron,
3:20 for Abner and the M who were with him.
3:39 though anointed king; these M the sons of Zeruiah
4:2 Saul's son had two M who were captains of
4:11 much more, when wicked M have slain a righteous
4:12 David commanded his young M, and they killed
5:6 the king and his M went to Jerusalem against
5:21 and David and his M carried them away.
6:1 gathered all the chosen M of Israel, thirty thousand.
6:19 multitude of Israel, both M and women, to each
7:10 no more; and violent M shall afflict them no
7:14 with the rod of M, with the stripes of
7:14 of the sons of M;
8:5 David slew twenty-two thousand M of the Syrians.
10:5 meet them, for the M were greatly ashamed.
10:6 Maacah with a thousand M, and the men of
10:6 thousand men, and the M of Tob, twelve thousand
10:6 men, and the men of Tob, twelve thousand M
10:7 Joab and all the host of the mighty M
10:8 of Rehob, and the M of Tob and Maacah,
10:9 some of the picked M of Israel, and arrayed
10:10 the rest of his M he put in the
10:18 of the Syrians the M of seven hundred chariots,
11:16 the place where he knew there were valiant M
11:17 And the M of the city came out and
11:23 said to David, "The M gained an advantage over
12:1 him, "There were two M in a certain city,
13:32 killed all the young M the king's sons, for
15:1 and horses, and fifty M to run before him.
15:6 the hearts of the M of Israel.
15:11 Absalom went two hundred M from Jerusalem who
15:13 "The hearts of the M of Israel have gone
15:22 on, with all his M and all the little
16:2 fruit for the young M to eat, and the
16:6 and all the mighty M were on his right
16:13 So David and his M went on the road,
16:15 all the people, the M of Israel, came to
16:18 people and all the M of Israel have chosen,
17:1 me choose twelve thousand M, and I will set
17:8 your father and his M are mighty men, and
17:8 his men are mighty M, and that they are
17:10 that those who are with him are valiant M
17:12 him and all the M with him not one
17:14 Absalom and all the M of Israel said, "The
17:21 they had gone, the M came up out of
17:24 Jordan with all the M of Israel.
18:1 Then David mustered the M who were with him,
18:2 king said to the M, "I myself will also
18:3 But the M said, "You shall not go out.
18:7 And the M of Israel were defeated there by
18:7 there was great on that day, twenty thousand M
18:15 young M, Joab's armor-bearers, surrounded Absalom
18:28 has delivered up the M who raised their hand
19:14 heart of all the M of Judah as one
19:16 come down with the M of Judah to meet
19:17 him were a thousand M from Benjamin.
19:28 father's house were but M doomed to death before
19:35 the voice of singing M and singing women?
19:41 Then all the M of Israel came to the
19:41 have our brethren the M of Judah stolen you
19:41 Jordan, and all David's M with him?"
19:42 All the M of Judah answered the men of
19:42 of Judah answered the M of Israel, "Because the
19:43 And the M of Israel answered the men of
19:43 of Israel answered the M of Judah, "We have
19:43 the words of the M of Judah were fiercer
19:43 the words of the M of Israel.
20:2 So all the M of Israel withdrew from David,
20:2 of Bichri; but the M of Judah followed their
20:4 to Amasa, "Call the M of Judah together to
20:7 and all the mighty M; they went out from
20:11 And one of Joab's M took his stand by
20:15 And all the M who were with Joab came
21:12 son Jonathan from the M of Jabesh-gilead, who had
21:17 Then David's M adjured him, "You shall no more
22:49 didst deliver me from M of violence.
23:3 one rules justly over M, ruling in the fear
23:6 But godless M are all like thorns that are
23:8 the mighty M whom David had: Josheb-basshebeth
23:9 among the three mighty M was Eleazar the son
23:9 for battle, and the M of Israel withdrew.
23:10 that day; and the M returned after him only
23:11 of lentils; and the M fled from the Philistines.
23:13 of the thirty chief M went down, and came
23:16 Then the three mighty M broke through the camp
23:17 the blood of the M who went at the
23:17 These things did the three mighty M
23:18 spear against three hundred M and slew them, and
23:22 and won a name beside the three mighty M
24:9 hundred thousand valiant M who drew the sword,
24:9 the sword, and the M of Judah were five
24:15 people from Dan to Beer-sheba seventy thousand M
1Kgs 1:5 and horsemen, and fifty M to run before him.
1:8 Rei, and David's mighty M were not with Adonijah.
1:10 Benaiah or the mighty M or Solomon his brother.
2:32 with the sword two M more righteous and better
4:31 wiser than all other M, wiser than Ethan the
4:34 And M came from all peoples to hear the
5:13 all Israel; and the levy numbered thirty thousand M
5:18 Hiram's builders and the M of Gebal did the
8:2 And all the M of Israel assembled to King
8:39 all the children of M;
11:18 to Paran, and took M with them from Paran
11:24 And he gathered M about him and became leader
12:6 counsel with the old M, who had stood before
12:8 counsel which the old M gave him, and took
12:8 counsel with the young M who had grown up
12:10 And the young M who had grown up with
12:13 counsel which the old M had given him,
12:14 counsel of the young M, saying, "My father made
13:2 incense upon you, and M's bones shall be burned
13:25 And behold, M passed by, and saw the body
18:13 I hid a hundred M of the LORD's prophets
18:22 but Baal's prophets are four hundred and fifty M
20:12 he said to his M, "Take your positions." And
20:17 they reported to him, M are coming out from
20:30 fell upon twenty-seven thousand M that were left.
20:33 Now the M were watching for an omen, and
21:11 And the M of his city, the elders and
22:6 together, about four hundred M, and said to them,
2Kgs 1:9 a captain of fifty M with his fifty.
1:11 another captain of fifty M with his fifty.
1:14 former captains of fifty M with their fifties; but
2:7 Fifty M of the sons of the prophets also
2:16 your servants fifty strong M; pray, let them go,
2:17 They sent therefore fifty M; and for three days
2:19 Now the M of the city said to Elisha,
4:40 poured out for the M to eat.
4:41 "Pour out for the M, that they may eat."
4:42 said, "Give to the M, that they may eat."
4:43 am I to set this before a hundred M
4:43 "Give them to the M, that they may eat,
5:22 of Ephraim two young M of the sons of
5:24 and he sent the M away, and they departed.
6:20 the eyes of these M, that they may see."
7:3 Now there were four M who were lepers at
7:13 servants said, "Let some M take five of the
7:14 they took two mounted M, and the king sent
8:12 will slay their young M with the sword, and
10:6 were with the great M of the city, who
10:11 Jezreel, all his great M, and his familiar friends,
10:24 Jehu had stationed eighty M outside, and said, "The
11:9 and each brought his M who were to go
12:15 an accounting from the M into whose hand they
15:20 from all the wealthy M, fifty shekels of silver

15:25 against him with fifty M of the Gileadites, and
16:6 Edom, and drove the M of Judah from Elath;
17:30 they dwelt; the M of Babylon made Succoth-benoth,
17:30 Babylon made Succoth-benoth, the M of Cuth made
17:30 Cuth made Nergal, the M of Hamath made Ashima,
18:27 and not to the M sitting on the wall,
19:18 but the work of M's hands, wood and stone;
19:35 the Assyrians; and when M arose early in the
20:14 him, "What did these M say?
23:2 with him all the M of Judah and all
23:14 and filled their places with the bones of M
23:17 And the M of the city told him, "It
23:20 burned the bones of M upon them.
24:14 and all the mighty M of valor, ten thousand
24:15 officials, and the chief M of the land, he
24:16 to Babylon all the M of valor, seven thousand,
25:4 king with all the M of war fled by
25:19 in command of the M of war, and five
25:19 of war, and five M of the king's council
25:19 the land; and sixty M of the people of
25:23 open country and their M heard that the king
25:23 they came with their M to Gedaliah at Mizpah,
25:24 to them and their M, saying, "Do not be
25:25 family, came with ten M, and attacked and killed
1Chr 4:12 These are the M of Recah.
4:22 and Jokim, and the M of Cozeba, and Joash,
4:27 family multiply like the M of Judah.
4:42 of them, five hundred M of the Simeonites, went
5:18 of Manasseh had valiant M, who carried shield and
5:21 and a hundred thousand M alive.
5:24 Jahdi-el, mighty warriors, famous M, heads of their
6:31 These are the M whom David put in charge
6:33 These are the M who served and their sons.
7:3 all of them chief M;
7:21 and Ele-ad, whom the M of Gath who were
7:40 All of these were M of Asher, heads of
7:40 for service in war, was twenty-six thousand M
8:28 houses, according to their generations, chief M
8:40 sons of Ulam were M who were mighty warriors,
9:13 and sixty, very able M for the work of
10:1 against Israel; and the M of Israel fled before
10:7 And when all the M of Israel who were
10:12 Saul, all the valiant M arose, and took away
11:10 chiefs of David's mighty M, who gave him strong
11:11 account of David's mighty M: Jashobe-am,
11:12 among the three mighty M was Eleazar the son
11:13 of barley, and the M fled from the Philistines.
11:15 of the thirty chief M went down to the
11:18 Then the three mighty M broke through the camp
11:19 Shall I drink the lifeblood of these M
11:19 These things did the three mighty M
11:20 spear against three hundred M and slew them, and
11:24 and won a name beside the three mighty M
11:26 The mighty M of the armies were Asahel the
12:1 Now these are the M who came to David
12:1 were among the mighty M who helped him in
12:15 These are the M who crossed the Jordan in
12:16 And some of the M of Benjamin and Judah
12:19 Some of the M of Manasseh deserted to David
12:20 went to Ziklag these M of Manasseh deserted to
12:21 they were all mighty M of valor, and were
12:22 from day to day M kept coming to David
12:24 The M of Judah bearing shield and spear were
12:25 Of the Simeonites, mighty M of valor for war,
12:30 thousand eight hundred, mighty M of valor, famous
12:30 men of valor, famous M in their fathers' houses.
12:32 Of Issachar M who had understanding of the times,
12:34 were thirty-seven thousand M armed with shield and
12:35 thousand six hundred M equipped for battle.
12:37 hundred and twenty thousand M armed with all the
12:38 All these, M of war, arrayed in battle order,
16:3 to all Israel, both M and women, to each
17:9 no more; and violent M shall waste them no
18:5 David slew twenty-two thousand M of the Syrians.
19:5 was told concerning the M, he sent to meet
19:5 meet them, for the M were greatly ashamed.
19:8 Joab and all the army of the mighty M
19:10 some of the picked M of Israel, and arrayed
19:11 the rest of his M he put in the
19:18 of the Syrians the M of seven thousand chariots,
21:5 million one hundred thousand M who drew the
21:14 there fell seventy thousand M of Israel.
23:3 numbered, and the total was thirty-eight thousand M
24:4 Since more chief M were found among the sons
26:6 houses, for they were M of great ability.
26:7 whose brethren were able M, Elihu and Semachiah.
26:8 sons and brethren, able M qualified for the service;
26:9 sons and brethren, able M, eighteen.
26:12 corresponding to their chief M, had duties, just as
26:30 one thousand seven hundred M of ability, had the
26:31 search was made and M of great ability among
26:32 two thousand seven hundred M of ability, heads of
28:1 palace officials, the mighty M, and all the seasoned
29:24 leaders and the mighty M, and also all the
2Chr 2:2 Solomon assigned seventy thousand M to bear
5:3 And all the M of Israel assembled before the
6:30 of the children of M;
10:6 counsel with the old M, who had stood before
10:8 counsel which the old M gave him, and took
10:8 counsel with the young M who had grown up
10:10 And the young M who had grown up with
10:13 counsel of the old M,
10:14 counsel of the young M, saying, "My father made
13:3 an army of valiant M of war, four hundred
13:3 four hundred thousand picked M; and Jeroboam
13:15 Then the M of Judah raised the battle shout.
13:15 And when the M of Judah shouted, God defeated
13:16 The M of Israel fled before Judah, and God
13:17 fell slain of Israel five hundred thousand picked M
13:18 Thus the M of Israel were subdued at that
13:18 that time, and the M of Judah prevailed, because
14:8 and eighty thousand M from Benjamin, that carried
14:8 all these were mighty M of valor.
14:9 army of a million M and three hundred chariots,
14:13 The M of Judah carried away very much booty.
17:13 He had soldiers, mighty M of valor, in Jerusalem.
17:14 three hundred thousand mighty M of valor,
17:16 two hundred thousand mighty M of valor.
17:17 with two hundred thousand M armed with bow and
18:5 prophets together, four hundred M, and said to them,
20:2 Some M came and told Jehoshaphat, "A great
20:10 And now behold, the M of Ammon and Moab
20:13 Meanwhile all the M of Judah stood before the
20:22 an ambush against the M of Ammon, Moab, and
20:23 For the M of Ammon and Moab rose against
22:1 for the band of M that came with the
23:8 They each brought his M, who were to go
24:24 had come with few M, the LORD delivered into
25:5 Then Amaziah assembled the M of Judah, and set
25:5 three hundred thousand picked M, fit for war, able
25:6 a hundred thousand mighty M of valor from Israel
25:11 and smote ten thousand M of Seir.
25:12 The M of Judah captured another ten thousand alive,
25:13 But the M of the army whom Amaziah sent
25:14 the gods of the M of Seir, and set
26:12 fathers' houses of mighty M of valor was two
26:15 engines, invented by skilful M, to be on the
26:17 the LORD who were M of valor;
28:6 day, all of them M of valor, because they
28:8 The M of Israel took captive two hundred thousand
28:12 chiefs also of the M of Ephraim, Azariah the
28:14 So the armed M left the captives and the
28:15 And the M who have been mentioned by name
30:11 Only a few M of Asher, of Manasseh, and
31:19 their cities, there were M in the several cities
32:3 officers and his mighty M to stop the water
32:19 are the work of M's hands.
34:12 And the M did the work faithfully.
34:30 LORD, with all the M of Judah and the
35:25 and all the singing M and singing women have
36:17 who slew their young M with the sword in
Ezra 1:4 be assisted by the M of his place with
2:2 The number of the M of the people of
2:22 The M of Netophah, fifty-six.
2:23 The M of Anathoth, one hundred and twenty-eight.
2:27 The M of Michmas, one hundred and twenty-two.
2:28 The M of Bethel and Ai, two hundred and
3:12 of fathers' houses, old M who had seen the
4:9 the Persians, the M of Erech, the Babylonians,
4:9 Erech, the Babylonians, the M of Susa, that is,
4:11 king: Your servants, the M of the province Beyond
4:21 a decree that these M be made to cease,
5:4 the names of the M who are building this
5:10 the names of the M at their head.
6:8 be paid to these M in full and without
7:28 and I gathered leading M from Israel to go
8:3 with whom were registered one hundred and fifty M
8:4 son of Zerahiah, and with him two hundred M
8:5 son of Jahaziel, and with him three hundred M
8:6 the son of Jonathan, and with him fifty M
8:7 the son of Athaliah, and with him seventy M
8:8 the son of Michael, and with him eighty M

8:9 Jehiel, and with him two hundred and eighteen M
8:10 Josiphiah, and with him a hundred and sixty M
8:11 the son of Bebai, and with him twenty-eight M
8:12 Hakkatan, and with him a hundred and ten M
8:13 Jeuel, and Shemaiah, and with them sixty M
8:14 Bigvai, Uthai and Zaccur, and with them seventy M
8:16 Zechariah, and Meshullam, leading M, and for
8:16 and Elnathan, who were M of insight,
9:2 the officials and chief M has been foremost."
10:1 great assembly of M, women, and children, gathered
10:9 Then all the M of Judah and Benjamin assembled
10:16 Ezra the priest selected M, heads of fathers' houses,
10:17 end of all the M who had married foreign
Neh 1:2 brethren, came with certain M out of Judah; and
2:12 I and a few M with me; and I
3:2 next to him the M of Jericho built.
3:7 Jadon the Meronothite, the M of Gibeon and of
3:16 pool, and to the house of the mighty M
3:22 him the priests, the M of the Plain, repaired.
4:23 my servants nor the M of the guard who
5:5 help it, for other M have our fields and
5:17 a hundred and fifty M, Jews and officials, besides
7:7 The number of the M of the people of
7:26 The M of Bethlehem and Netophah, a hundred and
7:27 The M of Anathoth, a hundred and twenty-eight.
7:28 The M of Beth-azmaveth, forty-two.
7:29 M of Kiriath-jearim, Chephirah, and Be-eroth, seven
7:30 The M of Ramah and Geba, six hundred and
7:31 The M of Michmas, a hundred and twenty-two.
7:32 The M of Bethel and Ai, a hundred and
7:33 The M of the other Nebo, fifty-two.
8:2 before the assembly, both M and women and all
8:3 the presence of the M and the women and
11:2 people blessed all the M who willingly offered to
11:6 were four hundred and sixty-eight valiant M
11:14 and their brethren, mighty M of valor, a hundred
12:44 On that day M were appointed over the chambers
13:15 I saw in Judah M treading wine presses on
13:16 M of Tyre also, who lived in the city,
Tob 1:19 Then one of the M of Nineveh went and
13:8 Let all M speak, and give him thanks in
Jud 2:5 take with you M confident in their strength,
2:27 death all their young M with the edge of
3:5 The M came to Holofernes and told him all
3:6 cities and took picked M from them as his
4:7 wide enough for two M at the most.
4:11 And all the M and women of Israel, and
5:22 saying this, all the M standing around the tent
5:22 officers and all the M from the seacoast and
6:1 disturbance made by the M outside the council died
6:10 him over to the M of Israel.
6:12 When the M of the city saw them, they
6:14 Then the M of Israel came down from their
6:16 and all their young M and their women ran
7:2 day; their force of M of war was one
7:4 to his neighbor, "These M will now lick up
7:12 and keep all the M in your forces with
7:18 sent some of their M toward the south and
7:23 the women and young M fainted from thirst and
7:24 the people, the young M, the women, and the
8:3 he stood overseeing the M who were binding sheaves
8:7 gold and silver, and M and women slaves, and
8:12 the place of God among the sons of M
9:11 nor thy might upon M of strength; for thou
10:4 the eyes of all M who might see her.
10:9 they ordered the young M to open the gate
10:10 with her; and the M of the city watched
10:13 losing one of his M, captured or slain."
10:14 When the M heard her words, and observed her
10:17 their number a hundred M to accompany her and
11:7 soul, not only do M serve him because of
11:9 his words, for the M of Bethulia spared him
11:14 They have sent M to Jerusalem, because even the
13:12 When the M of her city heard her voice,
13:19 from the hearts of M, as they remember the
14:6 of one of the M at the gathering of
15:1 When the M in the tents heard it, they
15:3 Then the M of Israel, every one that was
15:4 And Uzziah sent M to Betomasthaim and Bebai and
15:13 women, while all the M of Israel followed, bearing
16:5 and kill my young M with the sword, and
16:7 hands of the young M, nor did the sons
Esth 1:13 said to the wise M who knew the times—
1:14 law and judgment, the M next to him being
2:23 to be so, the M were both hanged on
6:13 Then his wise M and his wife Zeresh said

7:4 sold merely as slaves, M and women, I would
9:6 and destroyed five hundred M,
9:12 have slain five hundred M and also the ten
9:15 they slew three hundred M in Susa; but they
13:2 the peace which all M desire.
13:5 in opposition to all M, perversely following a strange
16:2 more proud do many M become.
16:4 away thankfulness from among M, but, carried away
16:6 public affairs, when these M by the false trickery
16:8 and peaceable for all M,
16:24 not only impassable for M, but also most hateful
Job 4:13 deep sleep falls on M,
7:20 do I do to thee, thou watcher of M
11:3 Should your babble silence M, and when you mock,
11:11 For he knows worthless M; when he sees iniquity,
15:18 will declare (what wise M have told, and their
16:10 M have gaped at me with their mouth, they
17:6 am one before whom M spit.
17:8 Upright M are appalled at this, and the innocent
21:33 sweet to him; all M follow after him, and
22:15 old way which wicked M have trod?
24:2 M remove landmarks; they seize flocks and pasture
28:3 M put an end to darkness, and search out
28:4 valley away from where M live; they are forgotten
28:4 they hang afar from M, they swing to and
29:8 the square, the young M saw me and withdrew,
29:21 new in my hand.' M listened to me, and
30:1 make sport of me, M who are younger than
30:2 strength of their hands, M whose vigor is gone?
30:5 driven out from among M; they shout after them
31:31 a curse); if the M of my tent have
31:33 concealed my transgressions from M, by hiding my
32:1 So these three M ceased to answer Job, because
32:5 mouth of these three M, he became angry.
33:15 deep sleep falls upon M, while they slumber on
33:16 opens the ears of M, and terrifies them with
33:26 He recounts to M his salvation,
33:27 and he sings before M, and says: 'I sinned,
34:2 my words, you wise M, and give ear to
34:8 in company with evildoers and walks with wicked M
34:10 "Therefore, hear me, you M of understanding, far be
34:26 in the sight of M,
34:34 M of understanding will say to me, and the
34:36 to the end, because he answers like wicked M
35:12 not answer, because of the pride of evil M
36:24 his work, of which M have sung.
36:25 All M have looked on it; man beholds it
37:7 every man, that all M may know his work.
37:21 "And now M cannot look on the light when
37:24 Therefore M fear him; he does not regard any
Ps 4:2 O M, how long shall my honor suffer shame?
5:6 lies; the LORD abhors bloodthirsty and deceitful M
9:20 Let the nations know that they are but M
11:4 eyes behold, his eyelids test, the children of M
12:1 faithful have vanished from among the sons of M
12:8 as vileness is exalted among the sons of M
14:2 upon the children of M, to see if there
17:4 to the works of M, by the word of
17:14 by thy sword, from M by thy hand, O
17:14 hand, O LORD, from M whose portion in life
18:48 didst deliver me from M of violence.
21:10 and their children from among the sons of M
22:6 no man; scorned by M, and despised by the
22:30 Posterity shall serve him; M shall tell of the
26:4 not sit with false M, nor do I consort
26:9 my life with bloodthirsty M,
26:10 life with bloodthirsty men, M in whose hands are
31:19 thee, in the sight of the sons of M
31:20 from the plots of M; thou holdest them safe
33:13 all the sons of M;
36:7 The children of M take refuge in the shadow
42:3 day and night, while M say to me continually,
43:1 from deceitful and unjust M deliver me!
45:2 of the sons of M; grace is poured upon
49:6 my persecutors surrounds me, M who trust in their
53:2 upon the sons of M to see if there
54:3 For insolent M have risen against me, ruthless men
54:3 risen against me, ruthless M seek my life; they
55:23 into the lowest pit; M of blood and treachery
56:1 me, O God, for M trample upon me; all
57:4 devour the sons of M; their teeth are spears
58:1 judge the sons of M uprightly?
58:11 M will say, "Surely there is a reward for
59:2 who work evil, and save me from bloodthirsty M
59:3 for my life; fierce M band themselves against me.
59:13 are no more, that M may know that God

M

	17:27	of heaven; but all M are dust and ashes.
	19:2	and women lead intelligent M astray, and the man
	20:10	glory, and there are M who have raised their
	20:26	himself, and a sensible man will please great M
	20:27	and whoever pleases great M will atone for injustice.
	21:2	are lion's teeth, and destroy the souls of M
	21:26	the mouth of wise M is in their mind.
	23:14	you sit among great M; lest you be forgetful
	23:16	Two sorts of M multiply sins, and a third
	23:19	to the eyes of M, and he does not
	23:19	all the ways of M, and perceive even the
	24:23	It fills M with wisdom, like the Pishon, and
	25:1	Lord and of M; agreement between brothers,
	25:2	hates three kinds of M, and I am greatly
	25:4	is judgment in gray-haired M, and for the aged
	25:5	aged, and understanding and counsel in honorable M
	26:19	through poverty, and intelligent M who are treated
	27:7	him reason, for this is the test of M
	27:14	The talk of M given to swearing makes one's
	28:14	strong cities, and overturned the houses of great M
	29:18	surety has ruined many M who were prosperous, and
	29:18	sea; it has driven M of power into exile,
	31:23	M will praise the one who is liberal with
	31:27	is like life to M, if you drink it
	31:27	been created to make M glad.
	33:10	All M are from the ground, and Adam was
	33:13	he pleases– so M are in the hand
	35:19	and the works of M according to their devices;
	36:23	her speech, her husband is not like other M
	38:3	the presence of great M he is admired.
	38:6	he gave skill to M that he might be
	38:32	cannot be established, and M can neither sojourn nor
	39:2	discourse of notable M and penetrate the subtleties
	39:4	will serve among great M and appear before rulers;
	39:4	he tests the good and the evil among M
	41:8	Woe to you, ungodly M, who have forsaken the
	41:11	The mourning of M is about their bodies, but
	42:8	truly instructed, and will be approved before all M
	42:18	and the hearts of M, and considers their crafty
	44:1	us now praise famous M, and our fathers in
	44:3	their kingdoms, and were M renowned for their
	44:6	verses in writing; rich M furnished with resources,
	44:9	a name, so that M declare their praise.
	44:11	But these were M of mercy, whose righteous deeds
	44:24	The blessing of all M and the covenant he
	45:18	and Abiram and their M and the company of
	46:19	eternal sleep, Samuel called M to witness before the
	48:6	to destruction, and famous M from their beds;
	49:3	the days of wicked M he strengthened godliness.
	49:16	Seth were honored among M, and Adam above every
	51:7	for the assistance of M, and there was none.
Is	2:9	man is humbled, and M are brought low–
	2:11	and the pride of M shall be humbled; and
	2:17	and the pride of M shall be brought low;
	2:19	And M shall enter the caves of the rocks
	2:20	In that day M will cast forth their idols
	3:25	Your M shall fall by the sword and your
	3:25	sword and your mighty M in battle.
	5:3	inhabitants of Jerusalem and M of Judah, judge, I
	5:7	of Israel, and the M of Judah are his
	5:13	of knowledge; their honored M are dying of hunger,
	5:15	is bowed down, and M are brought low, and
	5:22	drinking wine, and valiant M in mixing strong drink,
	6:11	inhabitant, and houses without M, and the land is
	6:12	and the LORD removes M far away, and the
	7:13	for you to weary M, that you weary my
	7:24	With bow and arrows M will come there, for
	9:3	at the harvest, as M rejoice when they divide
	9:17	rejoice over their young M, and has no compassion
	10:14	the peoples; and as M gather eggs that have
	11:15	into seven channels that M may cross dryshod.
	13:3	have summoned my mighty M to execute my anger,
	13:12	I will make M more rare than fine gold,
	13:18	will slaughter the young M; they will have no
	15:4	Jahaz; therefore the armed M of Moab cry aloud;
	17:7	In that day M will regard their Maker, and
	19:12	Where then are your wise M
	21:17	archers of the mighty M of the sons of
	23:4	have neither reared young M nor brought up virgins."
	24:6	are scorched, and few M are left.
	28:11	Nay, but by M of strange lips and with
	29:11	When M give it to one who can read,
	29:13	is a commandment of M learned by rote;
	29:14	wisdom of their wise M shall perish, and the
	29:14	discernment of their discerning M shall be hid."
	29:19	and the poor among M shall exult in the
	31:3	The Egyptians are M, and not God; and their
	31:8	sword, and his young M shall be put to
	33:4	gathers; as locusts leap, M leap upon it.
	36:12	and not to the M sitting on the wall,
	37:19	but the work of M's hands, wood and stone;
	37:36	the Assyrians; and when M arose early in the
	38:16	Lord, by these things M live, and in all
	39:3	him, "What did these M say?
	40:30	be weary, and young M shall fall exhausted;
	41:14	you worm Jacob, you M of Israel!
	41:20	the pine together; that M may see and know,
	43:4	love you, I give M in return for you,
	44:11	the craftsmen are but M; let them all assemble,
	44:25	diviners; who turns wise M back, and makes their
	45:6	not know me, that M may know, from the
	45:14	Ethiopia, and the Sabeans, M of stature, shall come
	51:7	not the reproach of M, and be not dismayed
	52:14	of the sons of M –
	53:3	despised and rejected by M; a man of sorrows,
	53:3	as one from whom M hide their faces he
	57:1	it to heart; devout M are taken away, while
	59:6	not serve as clothing; M will not cover themselves
	59:10	those in full vigor we are like dead M
	60:11	not be shut; that M may bring to you
	61:6	priests of the LORD, M shall speak of you
	66:24	dead bodies of the M that have rebelled against
Jer	2:16	Moreover, the M of Memphis and Tahpanhes have
	4:3	the LORD to the M of Judah and to
	4:4	of your hearts, O M of Judah and inhabitants
	5:16	like an open tomb, they are all mighty M
	5:26	For wicked M are found among my people; they
	5:26	They set a trap; they catch M
	6:11	the gatherings of young M, also; both husband and
	7:2	the LORD, all you M of Judah who enter
	8:4	says the LORD: When M fall, do they not
	8:9	The wise M shall be put to shame, they
	9:2	they are all adulterers, a company of treacherous M
	9:21	streets and the young M from the squares.
	9:22	'The dead bodies of M shall fall like dung
	10:4	M deck it with silver and gold; they fasten
	10:9	purple; they are all the work of skilled M
	11:2	and speak to the M of Judah and the
	11:9	is revolt among the M of Judah and the
	11:21	the LORD concerning the M of Anathoth, who seek
	11:22	punish them; the young M shall die by the
	11:23	bring evil upon the M of Anathoth, the year
	12:4	are swept away, because M said, "He will not
	12:5	you have raced with M on foot, and they
	15:8	the mothers of young M a destroyer at noonday;
	17:25	and their princes, the M of Judah and the
	18:11	therefore, say to the M of Judah and the
	18:21	May their M meet death by pestilence, their youths
	19:10	the sight of the M who go with you,
	19:11	M shall bury in Topheth because there will be
	23:7	says the LORD, when M shall no longer say,
	26:22	sent to Egypt certain M, Elnathan the son of
	27:5	the earth, with the M and animals that are
	31:13	dance, and the young M and the old shall
	32:19	all the ways of M, rewarding every man according
	32:32	and their prophets, the M of Judah and the
	33:5	the dead bodies of M whom I shall smite
	34:5	were before you, so M shall burn spices for
	34:18	And the M who transgressed my covenant and did
	35:13	and say to the M of Judah and the
	36:6	hearing of all the M of Judah who come
	36:31	Jerusalem, and upon the M of Judah, all the
	37:10	of them only wounded M, every man in his
	38:9	lord the king, these M have done evil in
	38:10	the Ethiopian, "Take three M with you from here,
	38:11	So Ebed-melech took the M with him and went
	38:16	the hand of these M who seek your life."
	39:17	the hand of the M of whom you are
	40:7	open country and their M heard that the king
	40:7	had committed to him M, women, and children, those
	40:8	the son of the Ma-acathite, they and their M
	40:9	to them and their M, saying, "Do not be
	41:1	king, came with ten M to Gedaliah the son
	41:2	Nethaniah and the ten M with him rose up
	41:5	knew of it, eighty M arrived from Shechem and
	41:7	of Nethaniah and the M with him slew them,
	41:8	But there were ten M among them who said
	41:9	the bodies of the M whom he had slain
	41:12	they took all their M and went to fight
	41:15	from Johanan with eight M, and went to the
	42:17	All the M who set their faces to go
	43:2	and all the insolent M said to Jeremiah, "You

M

Amos 2:11 some of your young M for Nazirites.
4:10 I slew your young M with the sword; I
6:1 of Samaria, the notable M of the first of
6:9 And if ten M remain in one house, they
8:13 virgins and the young M shall faint for thirst.
Obad 1:8 LORD, destroy the wise M out of Edom, and
1:9 And your mighty M shall be dismayed, O Teman,
Jon 1:10 Then the M were exceedingly afraid, and said to
1:10 For the M knew that he was fleeing from
1:13 Nevertheless the M rowed hard to bring the ship
1:16 Then the M feared the LORD exceedingly, and they
Mic 2:12 flock in its pasture, a noisy multitude of M
5:5 and eight princes of M;
5:7 which tarry not for M nor wait for the
5:7 for men nor wait for the sons of M
6:12 Your rich M are full of violence; your inhabitants
7:2 is none upright among M; they all lie in
7:6 man's enemies are the M of his own house.
Nah 2:3 shield of his mighty M is red, his soldiers
3:10 street; for her honored M lots were cast, and
3:10 and all her great M were bound in chains.
Hab 1:11 and go on, guilty M, whose own might is
1:13 thou look on faithless M, and art silent when
1:14 For thou makest M like the fish of the
2:8 for the blood of M and violence to the
2:17 for the blood of M and violence to the
Zeph 1:12 I will punish the M who are thickening upon
1:17 will bring distress on M, so that they shall
3:4 prophets are wanton, faithless M; her priests profane
Hag 1:11 ground brings forth, upon M and cattle, and upon
Zech 2:4 of the multitude of M and cattle in it.
3:8 you, for they are M of good omen: behold,
7:2 and Regem-melech and their M, to entreat the favor
8:4 LORD of hosts: Old M and old women shall
8:23 In those days ten M from the nations of
9:17 shall make the young M flourish, and new wine
10:1 storm clouds, who gives M showers of rain, to
10:5 shall be like mighty M in battle, trampling the
11:6 Lo, I will cause M to fall each into
Mal 2:7 guard knowledge, and M should seek instruction
1Mac 1:11 In those days lawless M came forth from Israel,
1:26 maidens and young M became faint, the beauty
1:34 And they stationed there a sinful people, lawless M
2:18 the Gentiles and the M of Judah and those
2:31 city of David, that M who had rejected the
2:44 their anger and lawless M in their wrath; the
2:47 hunted down the arrogant M, and the work
3:6 Lawless M shrank back for fear of him; all
3:13 a body of faithful M who stayed with him
3:15 strong army of ungodly M went up with him
3:38 Nicanor and Gorgias, mighty M among the friends of
4:2 M from the citadel were his guides.
4:3 he and his mighty M moved out to attack
4:5 because he said, "These M are fleeing from us."
4:6 plain with three thousand M, but they did not
4:7 about it; and these M were trained in war.
4:8 Judas said to the M who were with him,
4:13 Then the M with Judas blew their trumpets
4:29 Bethzur, and Judas met them with ten thousand M
4:34 of Lysias five thousand M; they fell in action.
4:41 Then Judas detailed M to fight against those in
5:13 destroyed about a thousand M there."
5:15 had gathered together M of Ptolemais and Tyre
5:17 his brother, "Choose your M and go and rescue
5:20 Then three thousand M were assigned to Simon to
5:27 and destroy all these M in one day."
5:32 he said to the M of his forces, "Fight
5:38 Judas sent M to spy out the camp, and
5:47 But the M of the city shut them out
5:50 So the M of the forces encamped, and he
5:58 issued orders to the M of the forces that
5:59 And Gorgias and his M came out of the
5:62 the family of those M through whom deliverance
5:64 M gathered to them and praised them.
6:3 became known to the M of the city
6:18 Now the M in the citadel kept hemming Israel
6:35 they stationed a thousand M armed with coats of
6:37 each were four armed M who fought from there,
6:42 battle, and six hundred M of the king's army
6:45 reach it; he killed M right and left, and
6:49 made peace with the M of Bethzur, and they
6:54 Few M were left in the sanctuary, because famine
6:57 forces, and to the M, "We daily grow weaker,
6:58 to terms with these M, and make peace with
7:1 sailed with a few M to a city by
7:5 the lawless and ungodly M of Israel; they were
7:19 seized many of the M who had deserted to
7:24 took vengeance on the M who had deserted, and
7:28 come with a few M to see you face
7:32 About five hundred M of the army of Nicanor
7:40 Judas encamped in Adasa with three thousand M
7:46 And M came out of all the villages of
8:2 M told him of their wars and of the
9:5 Elasa, and with him were three thousand picked M
9:12 the trumpets; and the M with Judas also blew
9:14 then all the stouthearted M went with him,
9:16 turned and followed close behind Judas and his M
9:48 Then Jonathan and the M with him leaped into
9:49 one thousand of Bacchides' M fell that day.
9:53 sons of the leading M of the land as
9:58 Jonathan and his M are living in quiet and
9:60 seize Jonathan and his M; but they were unable
9:61 And Jonathan's M seized about fifty of the men
9:61 about fifty of the M of the country who
9:62 Then Jonathan with his M, and Simon, withdrew to
9:63 sent orders to the M of Judea.
9:65 country; and he went with only a few M
9:67 and Simon and his M sallied out from the
9:69 enraged at the lawless M who had counseled him
10:7 people and of the M in the citadel.
10:9 But the M in the citadel released the hostages
10:15 sent to Jonathan, and M told him of the
10:32 may station in it M of his own choice
10:36 of thirty thousand M, and let the maintenance
10:61 A group of pestilent M from Israel, lawless men,
10:61 from Israel, lawless M, gathered together against
10:72 M will tell you that you cannot stand before
10:74 He chose ten thousand M and set out from
10:75 before Joppa, but the M of the city closed
10:76 against it, and the M of the city became
10:80 shot arrows at his M from early morning till
10:81 But his M stood fast, as Jonathan commanded, and
10:85 with those burned alive, came to eight thousand M
10:86 against Askalon, and the M of the city came
11:20 days Jonathan assembled the M of Judea to attack
11:21 But certain lawless M who hated their nation went
11:25 Although certain lawless M of his nation kept
11:43 well to send me M who will help me,
11:44 sent three thousand stalwart M to him at Antioch,
11:45 Then the M of the city assembled within the
11:46 Then the M of the city seized the main
11:47 that day as many as a hundred thousand M
11:49 When the M of the city saw that the
11:61 to Gaza, but the M of Gaza shut him
11:69 Then the M in ambush emerged from their places
11:70 All the M with Jonathan fled; not one of
11:73 When his M who were fleeing saw this, they
12:1 for him, he chose M and sent them to
12:27 set, Jonathan commanded his M to be alert and
12:28 that Jonathan and his M were prepared for battle,
12:29 But Jonathan and his M did not know it
12:34 the stronghold to the M whom Demetrius had sent.
12:41 forty thousand picked fighting M, and he came to
12:45 for yourself a few M to stay with you,
12:47 with himself three thousand M, two thousand of
12:48 Jonathan entered Ptolemais, the M of Ptolemais
12:50 perished along with his M, and they encouraged one
12:53 blot out the memory of them from among M
13:21 Now the M in the citadel kept sending envoys
13:34 Simon also chose M and sent them to Demetrius
13:44 The M in the siege engine leaped out into
13:45 The M in the city, with their wives and
13:48 and settled in it M who observed the law.
13:49 The M in the citadel at Jerusalem were prevented
13:52 and he and his M dwelt there.
14:9 Old M sat in the streets; they all talked
14:23 people to receive these M with honor and to
14:32 money; he armed the M of his nation's forces
14:36 as were also the M in the city of
14:42 the sanctuary and appoint M over its tasks and
15:3 Whereas certain pestilent M have gained control of
15:21 Therefore if any pestilent M have fled to you
15:26 Antiochus two thousand picked M, to fight for him,
16:6 first; and when his M saw him, they crossed
16:15 great banquet, and hid M there.
16:16 drunk, Ptolemy and his M rose up, took their
16:19 He sent other M to Gazara to do away
16:20 and he sent other M to take possession of
16:21 that "he has sent M to kill you also."
16:22 and he seized the M who came to destroy
2Mac 1:15 come with a few M inside the wall of
1:16 the leader and his M, and dismembered them and

3:26 Two young M also appeared to him, remarkably
3:27 came over him, his M took him up and
3:33 atonement, the same young M appeared again to
3:34 heaven, report to all M the majestic power of
3:36 bore testimony to all M of the deeds of
4:9 and to enrol the M of Jerusalem as citizens
4:12 noblest of the young M to wear the Greek
4:40 armed about three thousand M and launched an
4:41 them in wild confusion at Lysimachus and his M
4:44 came to Tyre, three M sent by the senate
4:47 to death those unfortunate M, who would have been
5:4 Therefore all M prayed that the apparition might
5:5 less than a thousand M and suddenly made an
5:8 city, pursued by all M, hated as a rebel
5:24 slay all the grown M and to sell the
5:25 work, he ordered his M to parade under arms.
5:26 city with his armed M and killed great numbers
6:20 out the flesh, as M ought to go who
6:26 avoid the punishment of M, yet whether I live
7:14 at the hands of M and to cherish the
7:16 you have authority among M, mortal though you are,
7:34 most defiled of all M, do not be elated
8:1 faith, and so they gathered about six thousand M
8:2 been profaned by ungodly M,
8:16 But Maccabeus gathered his M together, to the
8:22 division, putting fifteen hundred M under each.
9:2 and Antiochus and his M were defeated, with the
10:16 But Maccabeus and his M, after making solemn
10:19 also Zacchaeus and his M, a force sufficient to
10:20 But the M with Simon, who were money-hungry,
10:21 people, and accused these M of having sold their
10:22 Then he slew these M who had turned traitor,
10:25 near, Maccabeus and his M sprinkled dust upon their
10:29 heaven five resplendent M on horses with golden
10:33 Then Maccabeus and his M were glad, and they
10:34 The M within, relying on the strength of the
10:35 fifth day, twenty young M in the army of
11:2 gathered about eighty thousand M and all his cavalry
11:6 When Maccabeus and his M got word that Lysias
11:9 to assail not only M but the wildest beasts
11:20 I have ordered these M and my representatives to
11:37 haste and send some M, so that we may
12:3 And some M of Joppa did so ungodly a
12:4 and suspected nothing, the M of Joppa took them
12:5 gave orders to his M
12:8 But learning that the M in Jamnia meant in
12:11 fight Judas and his M won the victory, by
12:14 toward Judas and his M, railing at them and
12:15 But Judas and his M, calling upon the great
12:19 left in the stronghold, more than ten thousand M
12:20 army in divisions, set M in command of the
12:22 injured by their own M and pierced by the
12:23 sword, and destroyed as many as thirty thousand M
12:24 the hands of Dositheus and Sosipater and their M
12:27 Stalwart young M took their stand before the walls
12:35 one of Bacenor's M, who was on horseback
12:36 As Esdris and his M had been fighting for
12:37 he charged against Gorgias' M when they were not
12:39 necessary, Judas and his M went to take up
12:40 this was why these M had fallen.
13:1 to Judas and his M that Antiochus Eupator was
13:14 world and exhorting his M to fight nobly to
13:15 He gave his M the watchword, "God's victory," and
13:15 of the bravest young M, he attacked the king's
13:15 many as two thousand M in the camp.
13:22 attacked Judas and his M, was defeated
14:1 to Judas and his M that Demetrius, the son
14:13 Judas and scatter his M, and to set up
14:18 of Judas and his M and their courage in
14:22 place; Judas posted armed M in readiness at key
14:30 a few of his M, and went into hiding
15:1 that Judas and his M were in the region
15:6 public monument of victory over Judas and his M
15:8 And he exhorted his M not to fear the
15:25 Nicanor and his M advanced with trumpets and
15:26 and Judas and his M met the enemy in
15:27 thirty-five thousand M, and were greatly gladdened
Mt 2:1 the king, behold, wise M from the East came
2:7 Herod summoned the wise M secretly and
2:16 tricked by the wise M, was in a furious
2:16 time which he had ascertained from the wise M
4:19 me, and I will make you fishers of M
5:11 "Blessed are you when M revile you and persecute
5:12 in heaven, for so M persecuted the prophets who
5:13 be thrown out and trodden under foot by M
5:15 Nor do M light a lamp and put it
5:16 light so shine before M, that they may see
5:19 these commandments and teaches M so, shall be
5:21 was said to the M of old, 'You shall
5:33 was said to the M of old, 'You shall
6:1 practicing your piety before M in order to be
6:2 the streets, that they may be praised by M
6:5 street corners, that they may be seen by M
6:14 For if you forgive M their trespasses, your heavenly
6:15 you do not forgive M their trespasses, neither will
6:16 faces that their fasting may be seen by M
6:18 not be seen by M but by your Father
6:30 more clothe you, O M of little faith?
7:12 whatever you wish that M would do to you,
8:12 the outer darkness; there M will weep and gnash
8:26 are you afraid, O M of little faith?" Then
8:27 And the M marveled, saying, "What sort of man
9:8 glorified God, who had given such authority to M
9:27 from there, two blind M followed him, crying aloud,
9:28 the house, the blind M came to him; and
10:17 Beware of M; for they will deliver you up
10:32 acknowledges me before M, I also will acknowledge
10:33 whoever denies me before M, I also will deny
11:12 has suffered violence, and M of violence take it
12:31 blasphemy will be forgiven M, but the blasphemy
12:36 the day of judgment M will render account for
12:41 The M of Nineveh will arise at the judgment
13:17 many prophets and righteous M longed to see what
13:25 his field; but while M were sleeping, his enemy
13:42 furnace of fire; there M will weep and gnash
13:48 when it was full, M drew it ashore and
13:50 furnace of fire; there M will weep and gnash
14:21 about five thousand M, besides women and children.
14:35 And when the M of that place recognized him,
15:9 worship me, teaching as doctrines the precepts of M
15:38 ate were four thousand M, besides women and
16:8 of this, said, "O M of little faith, why
16:13 his disciples, "Who do M say that the Son
16:23 not on the side of God, but of M
17:21 into the hands of M,
19:11 to them, "Not all M can receive this saying,
19:12 been made eunuchs by M, and there are eunuchs
19:26 said to them, "With M this is impossible, but
20:25 them, and their great M exercise authority over
20:30 And behold, two blind M sitting by the roadside,
21:25 From heaven or from M
21:26 if we say, 'From M we are afraid of
22:13 the outer darkness; there M will weep and gnash
22:16 for you do not regard the position of M
23:4 and lay them on M's shoulders; but they themselves
23:5 to be seen by M; for they make their
23:7 the market places, and being called rabbi by M
23:13 kingdom of heaven against M; for you neither enter
23:18 he is bound by his oath.' You blind M
23:26 are full of dead M's bones and all uncleanness.
23:27 outwardly appear righteous to M, but within you are
23:33 you prophets and wise M and scribes, some of
24:12 wickedness is multiplied, most M's love will grow
24:40 Then two M will be in the field; one
24:51 with the hypocrites; there M will weep and gnash
25:30 the outer darkness; there M will weep and gnash
26:62 is it that these M testify against you?"
28:4 him the guards trembled and became like dead M
Mk 1:17 and I will make you become fishers of M
2:3 bringing to him a paralytic carried by four M
3:28 forgiven the sons of M, and whatever blasphemies
5:20 for him; and all M marveled.
6:12 out and preached that M should repent.
6:21 officers and the leading M of Galilee.
6:44 those who ate the loaves were five thousand M
7:7 doctrines the precepts of M
7:8 of God, and hold fast the tradition of M
8:4 can one feed these M with bread here in
8:24 and said, "I see M; but they look like
8:27 his disciples, "Who do M say that I am?"
8:33 not on the side of God, but of M
9:31 into the hands of M, and they will kill
10:27 them and said, "With M it is impossible, but
10:42 them, and their great M exercise authority over
11:29 the baptism of John from heaven or from M
11:31 shall we say, 'From M —they were afraid of
12:14 regard the position of M, but truly teach the
14:60 is it that these M testify against you?"
Lk 1:25 on me, to take away my reproach among M
2:14 on earth peace among M with whom he is
3:15 in expectation, and all M questioned in their hearts
5:10 not be afraid; henceforth you will be catching M

M

5:18 And behold, M were bringing on a bed a
6:22 "Blessed are you when M hate you, and when
6:26 to you, when all M speak well of you,
6:31 as you wish that M would do to you,
7:20 And when the M had come to him, they
7:31 shall I compare the M of this generation, and
9:14 For there were about five thousand M
9:30 And behold, two M talked with him, Moses and
9:32 glory and the two M who stood with him.
9:33 And as the M were parting from him, Peter
9:44 is to be delivered into the hands of M
11:30 a sign to the M of Nineveh, so will
11:31 the judgment with the M of this generation and
11:32 The M of Nineveh will arise at the judgment
11:44 are not seen, and M walk over them without
11:46 for you load M with burdens hard to bear,
12:8 who acknowledges me before M, the Son of man
12:9 who denies me before M will be denied before
12:28 he clothe you, O M of little faith!
12:36 burning, and be like M who are waiting for
12:48 of him to whom M commit much they will
13:29 And M will come from east and west, and
14:24 you, none of those M who were invited shall
14:35 nor for the dunghill; M throw it away.
16:15 who justify yourselves before M, but God knows your
16:15 what is exalted among M is an abomination in
18:10 and despised others: "Two M went up into the
18:11 am not like other M, extortioners, unjust, adulterers,
18:27 "What is impossible with M is possible with God."
19:47 scribes and the principal M of the people sought
20:4 the baptism of John from heaven or from M
20:6 if we say, 'From M all the people will
21:26 sea and the waves, M fainting with fear and
22:61 Now the M who were holding Jesus mocked him
24:4 about this, behold, two M stood by them in
24:5 to the ground, the M said to them, "Why
24:7 the hands of sinful M, and be crucified, and
24:25 to them, "O foolish M, and slow of heart
Jn 1:4 life, and the life was the light of M
2:10 wine first; and when M have drunk freely, then
2:25 because he knew all M and needed no one
3:19 into the world, and M loved darkness rather than
4:20 is the place where M ought to worship."
5:40 I do not receive glory from M
6:10 the place; so the M sat down, in number
8:17 the testimony of two M is true;
12:32 earth, will draw all M to myself."
12:43 loved the praise of M more than the praise
13:35 By this all M will know that you are
17:6 thy name to the M whom thou gavest me
18:8 seek me, let these M go."
Acts 1:10 he went, behold, two M stood by them in
1:11 white robes, and said, M of Galilee, why do
1:21 So one of the M who have accompanied us
1:22 us--one of these M must become with us
1:24 the hearts of all M, show which one of
2:5 in Jerusalem Jews, devout M from every nation
2:14 voice and addressed them, M of Judea and all
2:15 For these M are not drunk, as you suppose,
2:17 prophesy, and your young M shall see visions, and
2:17 visions, and your old M shall dream dreams;
2:22 Lord shall be saved.' M of Israel, hear these
2:23 crucified and killed by the hands of lawless M
3:12 he addressed the people, M of Israel, why do
4:4 the number of the M came to about five
4:12 under heaven given among M by which we must
4:13 they were uneducated, common M, they wondered;
4:16 another, saying, "What shall we do with these M
4:21 the people; for all M praised God for what
5:4 have not lied to M but to God."
5:6 The young M rose and wrapped him up and
5:10 When the young M came in they found her
5:14 Lord, multitudes both of M and women,
5:25 and told them, "The M whom you put in
5:29 answered, "We must obey God rather than M
5:34 up and ordered the M to be put outside
5:35 he said to them, M of Israel, take care
5:35 Israel, take care what you do with these M
5:36 and a number of M, about four hundred, joined
5:38 keep away from these M and let them alone;
5:38 this undertaking is of M, it will fail;
6:3 from among you seven M of good repute, full
6:11 Then they secretly instigated M, who said, "We have
7:26 have reconciled them, saying, M, you are brethren,
8:2 Devout M buried Stephen, and made great
8:3 house, he dragged off M and women and committed
8:12 they were baptized, both M and women.
9:2 belonging to the Way, M or women, he might
9:7 The M who were traveling with him stood
9:38 was there, sent two M to him entreating him,
10:5 And now send M to Joppa, and bring one
10:17 might mean, behold, the M that were sent by
10:19 to him, "Behold, three M are looking for you.
10:21 went down to the M and said, "I am
11:3 you go to uncircumcised M and eat with them?"
11:11 that very moment three M arrived at the house
11:20 were some of them, M of Cyprus and Cyrene,
13:16 with his hand said: M of Israel, and you
13:50 standing and the leading M of the city, and
14:11 come down to us in the likeness of M
14:15 among the multitude, crying, M, why are you doing
14:15 We also are M, of like nature with you,
15:1 But some M came down from Judea and were
15:17 that the rest of M may seek the Lord,
15:22 whole church, to choose M from among them and
15:22 Barsabbas, and Silas, leading M among the brethren,
15:25 one accord, to choose M and send them to
15:26 beloved Barnabas and Paul, M who have risked their
16:17 and us, crying, "These M are servants of the
16:20 magistrates they said, "These M are Jews and they
16:30 them out and said, M, what must I do
16:35 police, saying, "Let those M go."
16:37 beaten us publicly, uncondemned, M who are Roman
17:6 city authorities, crying, "These M who have turned
17:12 Greek women of high standing as well as M
17:22 of the Are-opagus, said: M of Athens, I perceive
17:25 himself gives to all M life and breath and
17:26 one every nation of M to live on all
17:30 now he commands all M everywhere to repent,
17:31 given assurance to all M by raising him from
17:34 But some M joined him and believed, among them
18:13 "This man is persuading M to worship God contrary
19:25 like occupation, and said, M, you know that from
19:35 the crowd, he said, M of Ephesus, what man
19:37 you have brought these M here who are neither
20:30 own selves will arise M speaking perverse things, to
21:23 We have four M who are under a vow;
21:24 a vow; take these M and purify yourself along
21:26 Then Paul took the M, and the next day
21:28 on him, crying out, M of Israel, help!
21:28 man who is teaching M everywhere against the
21:38 led the four thousand M of the Assassins out
22:4 delivering to prison both M and women,
22:15 for him to all M of what you have
23:21 than forty of their M lie in ambush for
24:15 have a clear conscience toward God and toward M
24:19 Or else let these M themselves say what wrongdoing
25:2 priests and the principal M of the Jews informed
25:5 said he, "let the M of authority among you
25:23 tribunes and the prominent M of the city.
27:21 among them and said, M, you should have listened
27:25 you.' So take heart, M, for I have faith
27:31 the soldiers, "Unless these M stay in the ship,
Rom 1:18 ungodliness and wickedness of M who by their
1:27 for unnatural, and the M likewise gave up natural
1:27 passion for one another, M committing shameless
1:27 committing shameless acts with M and receiving in
2:16 judges the secrets of M by Christ Jesus.
2:29 praise is not from M but from God.
3:9 already charged that all M, both Jews and Greeks,
5:12 death spread to all M because all men sinned--
5:12 all men because all M sinned--
5:18 to condemnation for all M, so one man's act
5:18 righteousness leads to acquittal and life for all M
6:13 yourselves to God as M who have been brought
8:27 searches the hearts of M knows what is the
9:33 stone that will make M stumble, a rock that
10:14 But how are M to call upon him in
10:15 And how can M preach unless they are sent?
11:4 for myself seven thousand M who have not bowed
11:32 God has consigned all M to disobedience, that he
14:18 Christ is acceptable to God and approved by M
16:7 fellow prisoners; they are M of note among the
1Cor 1:25 God is wiser than M, and the weakness of
1:25 and the weakness of God is stronger than M
2:5 in the wisdom of M but in the power
3:1 address you as spiritual M, but as men of
3:1 spiritual men, but as M of the flesh, as
3:3 not of the flesh, and behaving like ordinary M
3:4 are you not merely M
3:21 So let no one boast of M
4:9 last of all, like M sentenced to death; because

M

4:9 spectacle to the world, to angels and to M
5:9 to associate with immoral M;
7:23 with a price; do not become slaves of M
9:19 am free from all M, I have made myself
9:22 all things to all M, that I might by
10:15 speak as to sensible M; judge for yourselves what
10:33 try to please all M in everything I do,
13:1 in the tongues of M and of angels, but
14:2 tongue speaks not to M but to God; for
14:3 who prophesies speaks to M for their upbuilding and
14:21 it is written, "By M of strange tongues and
15:19 we are of all M most to be pitied.
15:39 is one kind for M, another for animals, another
16:16 be subject to such M and to every fellow
16:18 Give recognition to such M
2Cor 2:17 God's word; but as M of sincerity, as commissioned
3:2 and read by all M;
5:11 the Lord, we persuade M; but what we are
8:21 Lord's sight but also in the sight of M
8:24 and of our boasting about you to these M
10:15 beyond limit, in other M's labors; but our hope
11:13 For such M are false apostles, deceitful workmen,
Gal 1:1 an apostle--not from M nor through man, but
1:10 seeking the favor of M, or of God?
1:10 Or am I trying to please M
1:10 I were still pleasing M, I should not be
2:12 For before certain M came from James, he ate
3:7 see that it is M of faith who are
3:9 then, those who are M of faith are blessed
6:10 do good to all M, and especially to those
Eph 3:5 to the sons of M in other generations as
3:9 and to make all M see what is the
4:8 host of captives, and he gave gifts to M
4:14 by the cunning of M, by their craftiness in
5:15 walk, not as unwise M but as wise,
6:7 Lord and not to M,
Phil 2:7 a servant, being born in the likeness of M
2:29 joy; and honor such M,
4:5 Let all M know your forbearance.
Col 3:23 the Lord and not M,
4:11 These are the only M of the circumcision among
1Thes 1:5 know what kind of M we proved to be
2:4 speak, not to please M, but to please God
2:6 we seek glory from M, whether from you or
2:13 as the word of M but as what it
2:15 God and oppose all M
3:12 another and to all M, as we do to
2Thes 3:2 from wicked and evil M; for not all have
1Tim 2:1 be made for all M,
2:4 Savior, who desires all M to be saved and
2:5 mediator between God and M, the man Christ Jesus,
2:8 in every place the M should pray, lifting holy
2:12 to have authority over M; she is to keep
4:10 the Savior of all M, especially of those who
5:1 a father; treat younger M like brothers,
5:24 The sins of some M are conspicuous, pointing to
6:5 suspicions, and wrangling among M who are
6:9 hurtful desires that plunge M into ruin and
2Tim 2:2 witnesses entrust to faithful M who will be able
3:2 For M will be lovers of self, lovers of
3:8 opposed Moses, so these M also oppose the truth,
3:8 also oppose the truth, M of corrupt mind and
3:9 to all, as was that of those two M
3:13 be persecuted, while evil M and impostors will go
Tit 1:9 many insubordinate M, empty talkers and deceivers,
1:13 or to commands of M who reject the truth.
2:2 Bid the older M be temperate, serious, sensible,
2:6 Likewise urge the younger M to control themselves.
2:11 the salvation of all M,
3:2 gentle, and to show perfect courtesy toward all M
3:3 and envy, hated by M and hating one another;
3:8 good deeds; these are excellent and profitable to M
Heb 5:1 priest chosen from among M is appointed to act
5:1 act on behalf of M in relation to God,
6:16 M indeed swear by a greater than themselves, and
7:8 are received by mortal M; there, by one of
7:28 Indeed, the law appoints M in their weakness as
9:27 it is appointed for M to die once, and
11:2 For by it the M of old received divine
11:19 was able to raise M even from the dead;
12:14 for peace with all M, and for the holiness
12:23 the spirits of just M made perfect,
13:17 over your souls, as M who will have to
Jas 1:5 who gives to all M generously and without
3:9 with it we curse M, who are made in
4:8 purify your hearts, you M of double mind.
1Pet 2:4 living stone, rejected by M but in God's sight
2:8 stone that will make M stumble, a rock that
2:15 should put to silence the ignorance of foolish M
2:16 Live as free M, yet without using your freedom
2:17 Honor all M
4:6 in the flesh like M, they might live in
2Pet 1:21 impulse of man, but M moved by the Holy
2:18 passions of the flesh M who have barely escaped
3:7 the day of judgment and destruction of ungodly M
3:17 the error of lawless M and lose your own
1Jn 2:13 writing to you, young M, because you have overcome
2:14 write to you, young M, because you are strong,
5:9 receive the testimony of M, the testimony of God
2Jn 1:7 out into the world, M who will not acknowledge
3Jn 1:8 ought to support such M, that we may be
Jude 1:8 in like manner these M in their dreamings defile
1:10 But these M revile whatever they do not understand,
Rev 2:2 you cannot bear evil M but have tested those
5:9 thy blood didst ransom M for God from every
6:4 the earth, so that M should slay one another;
6:15 earth and the great M and the generals and
8:11 became wormwood, and many M died of the water,
9:6 And in those days M will seek death and
9:10 their power of hurting M for five months lies
11:9 days and a half M from the peoples and
13:4 M worshiped the dragon, for he had given his
13:13 in the sight of M;
16:2 sores came upon the M who bore the mark
16:6 For M have shed the blood of saints and
16:8 was allowed to scorch M with fire;
16:9 scorch men with fire; M were scorched by the
16:10 kingdom was in darkness; M gnawed their tongues in
16:18 had never been since M were on the earth,
16:21 M from heaven, till M cursed God for the
18:17 all shipmasters and seafaring M, sailors and all
18:23 merchants were the great M of the earth, and
19:18 the flesh of mighty M, the flesh of horses
19:18 the flesh of all M, both free and slave,
21:3 saying, "Behold, the dwelling of God is with M

MEN-PLEASERS (2)

Eph 6:6 way of eye-service, as M, but as servants of
Col 3:22 not with eye-service, as M, but in singleness of

MENAHEM (8)

2Kgs 15:14 Then M the son of Gadi came up from
15:16 At that time M sacked Tappuah and all who
15:17 Azariah king of Judah M the son of Gadi
15:19 against the land; and M gave Pul a thousand
15:20 M exacted the money from Israel, that is, from
15:21 of the deeds of M, and all that he
15:22 And M slept with his fathers, and Pekahiah his
15:23 Pekahiah the son of M began to reign over

MEND (2)

Jn 4:52 when he began to M, and they said to
2Cor 13:11 M your ways, heed my appeal, agree with one

MENDED (2)

Josh 9:4 worn-out and torn and M,
Jer 19:11 potter's vessel, so that it can never be M

MENDING (2)

Mt 4:21 with Zebedee their father, M their nets, and he
Mk 1:19 were in their boat M the nets.

MENE (3)

Dan 5:25 was inscribed: M, M, TEKEL, and PARSIN.
5:26 interpretation of the matter: M, God has numbered

MENELAUS (17)

2Mac 4:23 three years Jason sent M, the brother of the
4:27 And M held the office, but he did not
4:29 M left his own brother Lysimachus as deputy in
4:32 But M, thinking he had obtained a suitable
4:34 M, taking Andronicus aside, urged him to kill
4:39 with the connivance of M, and when report of
4:43 Charges were brought against M about this incident.
4:45 But M, already as good as beaten, promised a
4:47 M, the cause of all the evil, he acquitted
4:50 But M, because of the cupidity of those in
5:5 city was being taken, M took refuge in the
5:15 the world, guided by M, who had become a
5:23 Andronicus; and besides these M, who lorded it over
11:29 M has informed us that you wish to return
11:32 I have also sent M to encourage you.

13:3 M also joined them and with utter hypocrisy urged
13:7 it came about that M the lawbreaker died, without

MENESTHEUS (2)
2Mac 4:4 Apollonius, the son of M and governor of Coelesyria
4:21 Apollonius the son of M was sent to Egypt

MENIAL
Rom 9:21 beauty and another for M use?

MENNA
Lk 3:31 Mele-a, the son of M, the son of Mattatha,

MENSERVANTS (12)
Gen 12:16 sheep, oxen, he-asses, M, maidservants, she-asses,
24:35 herds, silver and gold, M and maidservants, camels
30:43 large flocks, maidservants and M, and camels and
32:5 have oxen, asses, flocks, M, and maidservants; and I
Deut 12:12 and your daughters, your M and your maidservants,
1Sam 8:16 He will take your M and maidservants, and the
2Kgs 5:26 vineyards, sheep and oxen, M and maidservants?
Ezra 2:65 and sixty, besides their M and maidservants, of
Neh 7:67 and sixty, besides their M and maidservants, of
Joel 2:29 Even upon the M and maidservants in those days,
Lk 12:45 begins to beat the M and the maidservants, and
Acts 2:18 yea, and on my M and my maidservants in

MENSTRUAL
Lev 18:19 she is in her M uncleanness.

MENSTRUATION (3)
Lev 12:2 the time of her M, she shall be unclean.
12:5 weeks, as in her M; and she shall continue
Bar 6:29 touched by women in M or at childbirth.

MENSTRUOUS
Esth 14:16 abhor it like a M rag, and I do

MENTION (10)
Gen 40:14 pray you, to make M of me to Pharaoh,
Ex 23:13 you; and make no M of the names of
Josh 23:7 among you, or make M of the names of
Job 28:18 No M shall be made of coral or of
Ps 87:4 who know me I M Rahab and Babylon; behold,
Jer 20:9 say, "I will not M him, or speak any
23:36 the LORD' you shall M no more, for the
Amos 6:10 We must not M the name of the LORD."
Rom 1:9 that without ceasing I M you always in my
Heb 11:22 of his life, made M of the exodus of

MENTIONED (12)
Josh 21:9 gave the following cities M by name,
1Sam 4:18 When he M the ark of God, Eli fell
1Chr 4:38 of Shemaiah-- these M by name were princes
6:65 these cities which are M by name.
2Chr 28:15 men who have been M by name rose and
Ezra 8:20 These were all M by name.
Esth 6:10 Leave out nothing that you have M
Is 19:17 to whom it is M will fear because of
Hos 2:17 and they shall be M by name no more.
2Mac 4:1 The previously M Simon, who had informed about
4:23 brother of the previously M Simon, to carry the
14:8 those whom I have M our whole nation is

MENTIONING
1Thes 1:2 for you all, constantly M you in our prayers.

MENUHOTH
1Chr 2:52 Kiriath-jearim had other sons: Haroeh, half of the M

MEONOTHAI (2)
1Chr 4:13 Seraiah; and the sons of Othni-el: Hathath and M
4:14 M was the father of Ophrah; and Seraiah was

MEPHAATH (4)
Josh 13:18 Jahaz, and Kedemoth, and M,
21:37 its pasture lands, and M with its pasture lands--
1Chr 6:79 its pasture lands, and M with its pasture lands;
Jer 48:21 Holon, and Jahzah, and M,

MEPHIBOSHETH (15)
2Sam 4:4 And his name was M
9:6 And M the son of Jonathan, son of Saul,
9:6 And David said, M
9:10 bread to eat; but M your master's son shall
9:11 So M ate at David's table, like one of
9:12 And M had a young son, whose name was
9:12 in Ziba's house became M's servants.
9:13 So M dwelt in Jerusalem; for he ate always
16:1 Ziba the servant of M met him, with a
16:4 all that belonged to M is now yours." And
19:24 And M the son of Saul came down to
19:25 him, "Why did you not go with me, M
19:30 And M said to the king, "Oh, let him
21:7 But the king spared M, the son of Saul's
21:8 to Saul, Armoni and M; and the five sons

MERAB (4)
1Sam 14:49 of the first-born was M, and the name of
18:17 is my elder daughter M; I will give her
18:19 at the time when M, Saul's daughter, should have
2Sam 21:8 the five sons of M the daughter of Saul,

MERAIAH
Neh 12:12 fathers' houses: of Seraiah, M; of Jeremiah,

MERAIOTH (7)
1Chr 6:6 of Zerahiah, Zerahiah of M,
6:7 Zerahiah, Zerahiah of Meraioth, M of Amariah,
6:52 son, Zerahiah his son, M his son, Amariah his
9:11 of Zadok, son of M, son of Ahitub, the
Ezra 7:3 of Azariah, son of M,
Neh 11:11 of Zadok, son of M, son of Ahitub, ruler
12:15 of Harim, Adna; of M, Helkai;

MERARI (36)
Gen 46:11 The sons of Levi: Gershon, Kohath, and M
Ex 6:16 generations: Gershon, Kohath, and M, the years of
6:19 The sons of M: Mahli and Mushi.
Num 3:17 Levi by their names: Gershon and Kohath and M
3:20 And the sons of M by their families: Mahli
3:33 Of M were the family of the Mahlites and
3:33 of the Mushites: these are the families of M
3:35 of the families of M was Zuriel the son
3:36 of the sons of M was to be the
4:29 for the sons of M, you shall number them
4:33 of the sons of M, the whole of their
4:42 of the sons of M, by their families and
4:45 of the sons of M, whom Moses and Aaron
7:8 to the sons of M, according to their service,
10:17 and the sons of M, who carried the tabernacle,
26:57 of the Kohathites; of M, the family of the
1Chr 6:1 The sons of Levi: Gershom, Kohath, and M
6:16 The sons of Levi: Gershom, Kohath, and M
6:19 The sons of M: Mahli and Mushi.
6:29 The sons of M: Mahli, Libni his son, Shimei
6:44 brethren the sons of M: Ethan the son of
6:47 of Mushi, son of M, son of Levi;
9:14 of the sons of M;
15:6 of the sons of M, Asaiah the chief, with
15:17 of the sons of M, their brethren, Ethan the
23:6 to the sons of Levi: Gershom, Kohath, and M
23:21 The sons of M: Mahli and Mushi.
24:26 The sons of M: Mahli and Mushi.
24:27 The sons of M: of Ja-aziah, Beno, Shoham, Zaccur,
26:10 of the sons of M, had sons: Shimri the
26:19 gatekeepers among the Korahites and the sons of M
2Chr 29:12 of the sons of M, Kish the son of
34:12 of the sons of M, and Zechariah and Meshullam,
Ezra 8:19 of the sons of M, with his kinsmen and
Jud 8:1 was the daughter of M the son of Ox,
16:7 Judith the daughter of M undid him with the

MERARITE (2)
Josh 21:34 of the Levites, the M families, were given out
21:40 cities of the several M families, that is, the

MERARITES (4)
Num 26:57 the Kohathites; of Merari, the family of the M
Josh 21:7 The M according to their families received from the
1Chr 6:63 To the M according to their families were allotted
6:77 the rest of the M were allotted out of

MERATHAIM
Jer 50:21 against the land of M, and against the inhabitants

MERCENARIES (3)
1Mac 4:35 to Antioch and enlisted M, to invade Judea again
2Mac 10:14 maintained a force of M, and at every turn
10:24 a tremendous force of M and collected the cavalry

MERCENARY (2)

1Mac 6:29 And M forces came to him from other kingdoms
15:3 recruited a host of M troops and have equipped

MERCHANDISE (13)

Prov 31:18 She perceives that her M is profitable.
Is 23:18 Her M and her hire will be dedicated to
23:18 or hoarded, but her M will supply abundant food
45:14 of Egypt and the M of Ethiopia, and the
Ezek 26:12 a prey of your M; they will break down
27:13 of men and vessels of bronze for your M
27:17 they exchanged for your M wheat, olives and early
27:19 iron, cassia, and calamus were bartered for your M
27:25 ships of Tarshish traveled for you with your M
27:27 riches, your wares, your M, your mariners and your
27:27 caulkers, your dealers in M, and all your men
27:33 your abundant wealth and M you enriched the kings
27:34 of the waters; your M and all your crew

MERCHANT (8)

Prov 31:14 the ships of the M, she brings her food
31:24 and sells them; she delivers girdles to the M
Song 3:6 frankincense, with all the fragrant powders of the M
Sir 26:20 A M can hardly keep from wrongdoing, and a
37:11 about war, with a M about barter or with
Is 23:3 Nile; you were the M of the nations.
Ezek 27:3 entrance to the sea, M of the peoples on
Mt 13:45 heaven is like a M in search of fine

MERCHANTS (20)

Gen 23:16 silver, according to the weights current among the M
1Kgs 10:15 the traffic of the M, and from all the
2Chr 9:14 which the traders and M brought; and all the
Neh 3:31 servants and of the M, opposite the Muster Gate,
3:32 the goldsmiths and the M repaired.
13:20 Then the M and sellers of all kinds of
Job 41:6 Will they divide him up among the M
Sir 42:5 profit from dealing with M, and of much discipline
Is 23:2 of the coast, O M of Sidon; your messengers
23:8 bestower of crowns, whose M were princes, whose
Bar 3:23 on the earth, the M of Merran and Teman,
Ezek 17:4 trade, and set it in a city of M
27:36 The M among the peoples hiss at you; you
38:13 and Dedan and the M of Tarshish and all
Nah 3:16 You increased your M more than the stars of
2Mac 8:34 had brought the thousand M to buy the Jews,
Rev 18:3 with her, and the M of the earth have
18:11 And the M of the earth weep and mourn
18:15 The M of these wares, who gained wealth from
18:23 no more; for thy M were the great men

MERCIES (8)

Neh 9:19 thou in thy great M didst not forsake them
9:27 according to thy great M thou didst give them
9:28 times thou didst deliver them according to thy M
9:31 Nevertheless in thy great M thou didst not make
Sir 18:4 And who can fully recount his M
Lam 3:22 LORD never ceases, his M never come to an
Rom 12:1 therefore, brethren, by the M of God, to present
2Cor 1:3 Christ, the Father of M and God of all

MERCIFUL (38)

Gen 19:16 hand, the LORD being M to him, and they
Ex 34:6 the LORD, a God M and gracious, slow to
Deut 4:31 your God is a M God; he will not
1Kgs 20:31 house of Israel are M kings; let us put
2Chr 30:9 God is gracious and M, and will not turn
Neh 9:17 to forgive, gracious and M, slow to anger and
9:31 art a gracious and M God.
Tob 6:17 cry out to the M God, and he will
7:12 The M God will guide you both for the
11:17 that God had been M to him.
14:9 the commandments, and be M and just, so that
Ps 57:1 Be M to me, O God, be merciful to
57:1 me, O God, be M to me, for in
86:15 Lord, art a God M and gracious, slow to
103:8 The LORD is M and gracious, slow to anger
111:4 to be remembered; the LORD is gracious and M
112:4 the LORD is gracious, M, and righteous.
116:5 is the LORD, and righteous; our God is M
145:8 LORD is gracious and M, slow to anger and
Wis 11:23 But thou art M to all, for thou canst
Sir 2:11 Lord is compassionate and M; he forgives sins and
48:20 the Lord who is M, spreading forth their hands
50:19 before him who is M, till the order of
Jer 3:12 anger, for I am M, says the LORD; I
Joel 2:13 he is gracious and M, slow to anger, and
Jon 4:2 a gracious God and M, slow to anger, and
1Mac 2:57 David, because he was M, inherited the throne of
2Mac 1:24 strong and just and M, who alone art King
8:29 supplication and besought the M Lord to be wholly
11:9 all together praised the M God, and were
13:12 and had besought the M Lord with weeping and
Mt 5:7 "Blessed are the M, for they shall obtain mercy.
Lk 6:36 Be M, even as your Father is merciful.
6:36 Be merciful, even as your Father is M
18:13 breast, saying, 'God, be M to me a sinner!'
Heb 2:17 he might become a M and faithful high priest
8:12 For I will be M toward their iniquities, and
Jas 5:11 the Lord, how the Lord is compassionate and M

MERCILESS (4)

Prov 5:9 your years to the M;
Wis 12:5 and unholy rites, their M slaughter of children, and
Sir 37:11 gratitude or with a M man about kindness, with
Jer 30:14 the punishment of a M foe, because your guilt

MERCILESSLY

Hab 1:17 emptying his net, and M slaying nations for ever?

MERCY (212)

Gen 43:14 God Almighty grant you M before the man, that
Ex 25:17 you shall make a M seat of pure gold;
25:18 two ends of the M seat.
25:19 one piece with the M seat shall you make
25:20 wings above, overshadowing the M seat with their
25:20 to another; toward the M seat shall the faces
25:21 you shall put the M seat on the top
25:22 and from above the M seat, from between the
26:34 You shall put the M seat upon the ark
30:6 the testimony, before the M seat that is over
31:7 the testimony, and the M seat that is thereon,
33:19 gracious, and will show M on whom I will
33:19 will show mercy on whom I will show M
35:12 with its poles, the M seat, and the veil
37:6 And he made a M seat of pure gold;
37:7 two ends of the M seat he made them,
37:8 one piece with the M seat he made the
37:9 wings above, overshadowing the M seat with their
37:9 to another; toward the M seat were the faces
39:35 its poles and the M seat;
Lev 16:2 the veil, before the M seat which is upon
16:2 the cloud upon the M seat.
16:13 incense may cover the M seat which is upon
16:14 the front of the M seat, and before the
16:14 seat, and before the M seat he shall sprinkle
16:15 sprinkling it upon the M seat and before the
16:15 seat and before the M seat;
Num 7:89 him from above the M seat that was upon
Deut 7:2 them, and show no M to them.
13:17 anger, and show you M, and have compassion on
Josh 11:20 and should receive no M but be exterminated, as
2Sam 24:14 the LORD, for his M is great; but let
1Chr 21:13 the LORD, for his M is very great; but
28:11 the room for the M seat;
Neh 1:11 today, and grant him M in the sight of
Tob 3:2 all thy ways are M and truth, and thou
6:17 save you and have M on you.
8:4 the Lord may have M upon us."
8:7 that I may find M and may grow old
8:16 thou hast treated us according to thy great M
8:17 Show them M, O Lord; and bring their lives
8:17 lives to fulfilment in health and happiness and M
11:15 but thou hast had M upon me; here I
13:2 afflicts, and he shows M; he leads down to
13:5 again he will show M, and will gather us
13:6 accept you and have M on you?
13:9 again he will show M to the sons of
14:5 God will again have M on them, and bring
14:7 righteousness will rejoice, showing M to our
Jud 7:31 restore to us his M, for he will not
13:14 has not withdrawn his M from the house of
16:15 who fear thee thou wilt continue to show M
Esth 13:6 enemies, without pity or M, on the fourteenth day
13:17 my prayer, and have M upon thy inheritance; turn
Job 9:15 I must appeal for M to my accuser.
Ps 23:6 Surely goodness and M shall follow me all the
25:6 Be mindful of thy M, O LORD, and of
40:11 O LORD, withhold thy M from me, let thy
51:1 Have M on me, O God, according to thy
51:1 according to thy abundant M blot out my
69:16 according to thy abundant M, turn to me.

18:25 these he feared; for M to test the wrath
Sir 19:20 is a fool who M lacks wisdom.
Rom 4:12 circumcised who are not M circumcised but also
1Cor 3:4 are you not M men?

MEREMOTH (6)
Ezra 8:33 into the hands of M the priest, son of
10:36 Benaiah, Bedeiah, Cheluhi, Vaniah, M, Eliashib,
Neh 3:4 And next to them M the son of Uriah,
3:21 After him M the son of Uriah, son of
10:5 Hattush, Shebaniah, Malluch, Harim, M, Obadiah,
12:3 Malluch, Hattush, Shecaniah, Rehum, M,

MERES
Esth 1:14 Carshena, Shethar, Admatha, Tarshish, M, Marsena,

MERI-BATH-ADESH
Deut 32:51 at the waters of M, in the wilderness of

MERIB-BAAL (4)
1Chr 8:34 son of Jonathan was M; and Merib-baal was the
8:34 Jonathan was Merib-baal; and M was the father of
9:40 son of Jonathan was M; and Merib-baal was the
9:40 Jonathan was Merib-baal; and M was the father of

MERIBAH (8)
Ex 17:7 the place Massah and M, because of the faultfinding
Num 20:13 are the waters of M, where the people of
20:24 rebelled against my command at the waters of M
27:14 are the waters of M of Kadesh in the
Deut 33:8 at the waters of M;
Ps 81:7 thunder; I tested you at the waters of M
95:8 your hearts, as at M, as on the day
106:32 at the waters of M, and it went ill

MERIBATH-KADESH (2)
Ezek 47:19 as the waters of M, thence along the Brook
48:28 to the waters of M, thence along the Brook

MERIT
Sir 38:17 mourning according to his M, for one day, or

MERODACH
Jer 50:2 is put to shame, M is dismayed.

MERODACH-BALADAN (2)
2Kgs 20:12 At that time M the son of Baladan, king
Is 39:1 At that time M the son of Baladan, king

MEROM (2)
Josh 11:5 at the waters of M, to fight with Israel.
11:7 by the waters of M, and fell upon them.

MERONOTHITE (2)
1Chr 27:30 and over the she-asses was Jehdeiah the M
Neh 3:7 Gibeonite and Jadon the M, the men of Gibeon

MEROZ
Judg 5:23 "Curse M, says the angel of the LORD, curse

MERRAN
Bar 3:23 the merchants of M and Teman, the story-tellers

MERRILY
Esth 5:14 upon it; then go M with the king to

MERRY (28)
Gen 43:34 they drank and were M with him.
Judg 16:25 when their hearts were M, they said, "Call Samson,
19:6 spend the night, and let your heart be M
19:9 let your heart be M; and tomorrow you shall
19:22 were making their hearts M, behold, the men of
Ruth 3:7 and his heart was M, he went to lie
1Sam 18:7 another as they made M, "Saul has slain his
25:36 And Nabal's heart was M within him, for he
2Sam 6:5 of Israel were making M before the LORD with
6:21 and I will make M before the LORD.
13:28 when Amnon's heart is M with wine, and when
1Chr 13:8 all Israel were making M before God with all
15:29 David dancing and making M; and she despised him
Tob 7:9 "Eat, drink, and be M;
7:11 But for the present be M
Jud 12:13 drink wine and be M with us, and become
12:17 "Drink now, and be M with us!"
Esth 1:10 of the king was M with wine, he commanded
Eccl 9:7 your wine with a M heart; for God has
Sir 32:2 that you may be M on their account and
Jer 30:19 thanksgiving, and the voices of those who make M
31:13 the young men and the old shall be M
Lk 12:19 ease, eat, drink, be M
15:23 us eat and make M;
15:24 and is found.' And they began to make M
15:29 that I might make M with my friends.
15:32 was fitting to make M and be glad, for
Rev 11:10 over them and make M and exchange presents,

MERRY-HEARTED
Is 24:7 vine languishes, all the M sigh.

MERRYMAKERS (2)
Jer 15:17 in the company of M, nor did I rejoice;
31:4 shall go forth in the dance of the M

MERRYMAKING
Sir 31:31 despise him in his M; speak no word of

MESALOTH
1Mac 9:2 Gilgal and encamped against M in Arbela, and they

MESHA (3)
Gen 10:30 they lived extended from M in the direction of
2Kgs 3:4 Now M king of Moab was a sheep breeder;
1Chr 8:9 his wife: Jobab, Zibi-a, M, Malcam,

MESHACH (15)
Dan 1:7 Shadrach, Mishael he called M, and Azariah he
2:49 and he appointed Shadrach, M, and Abednego over
3:12 province of Babylon: Shadrach, M, and Abednego.
3:13 rage commanded that Shadrach, M, and Abednego
3:14 it true, O Shadrach, M, and Abednego, that you
3:16 Shadrach, M, and Abednego answered the king, "O
3:19 was changed against Shadrach, M, and Abednego.
3:20 army to bind Shadrach, M, and Abednego, and to
3:22 who took up Shadrach, M, and Abednego.
3:23 three men, Shadrach, M, and Abednego, fell bound
3:94 furnace and said, "Shadrach, M, and Abednego,
3:94 Then Shadrach, M, and Abednego came out from the
3:96 the God of Shadrach, M, and Abednego, who has
3:97 the God of Shadrach, M, and Abednego shall be
3:98 the king promoted Shadrach, M, and Abednego in

MESHECH (9)
Gen 10:2 Magog, Madai, Javan, Tubal, M, and Tiras.
1Chr 1:5 Magog, Madai, Javan, Tubal, M, and Tiras.
1:17 Asshur, Arpachshad, Lud, Aram, Uz, Hul, Gether, and
M
Ps 120:5 that I sojourn in M, that I dwell among
Ezek 27:13 Javan, Tubal, and M traded with you; they exchanged
32:26 M and Tubal are there, and all their multitude,
38:2 the chief prince of M and Tubal, and prophesy
38:3 Gog, chief prince of M and Tubal;
39:1 Gog, chief prince of M and Tubal;

MESHELEMIAH (4)
1Chr 9:21 Zechariah the son of M was gatekeeper at the
26:1 gatekeepers: of the Korahites, M the son of Kore,
26:2 And M had sons: Zechariah the first-born, Jedia-el
26:9 And M had sons and brethren, able men, eighteen.

MESHEZABEL (3)
Neh 3:4 of Berechiah, son of M repaired.
10:21 Magpiash, Meshullam, Hezir, M, Zadok, Jaddu-a,
11:24 Pethahiah the son of M, of the sons of

MESHILLEMITH
1Chr 9:12 of Meshullam, son of M, son of Immer;

MESHILLEMOTH (2)
2Chr 28:12 Berechiah the son of M, Jehizkiah the son of
Neh 11:13 of Ahzai, son of M, son of Immer,

MESHOBAB
1Chr 4:34 M, Jamlech, Joshah the son of Amaziah,

MESHULLAM (23)
2Kgs 22:3 of Azaliah, son of M, the secretary, to the
1Chr 3:19 the sons of Zerubbabel: M and Hananiah, and
5:13 their fathers' houses: Michael, M, Sheba, Jorai, ,
8:17 Zebadiah, M, Hizki, Heber,
9:7 Sallu the son of M, son of Hodaviah, son
9:8 son of Michri, and M the son of Shephatiah,
9:11 of Hilkiah, son of M, son of Zadok, son

9:12 of Jahzerah, son of M, son of Meshillemith, son
2Chr 34:12 Merari, and Zechariah and M, of the sons of
Ezra 8:16 Elnathan, Nathan, Zechariah, and M, leading men,
Neh 3:4 And next to them M the son of Berechiah,
3:6 son of Paseah and M the son of Besodeiah
3:30 After him M the son of Berechiah repaired opposite
6:18 taken the daughter of M the son of Berechiah
8:4 Hash-baddanah, Zechariah, and M on his left hand.
10:7 Daniel, Ginnethon, Baruch, M, Abijah, Mijamin,
10:20 Hariph, Anathoth, Nebai, Magpiash, M, Hezir,
11:7 Sallu the son of M, son of Joed, son
11:11 of Hilkiah, son of M, son of Zadok, son
12:13 Jeremiah, Hananiah; of Ezra, M; of Amariah,
12:16 Iddo, Zechariah; of Ginnethon, M;
12:25 Obadiah, M, Talmon, and Akkub were gate
12:33 Judah, and Azariah, Ezra, M,

MESHULLEMETH

2Kgs 21:19 His mother's name was M the daughter of Haruz

MESHULLUM (2)

Ezra 10:15 Tikvah opposed this, and M and Shabbethai the
10:29 sons of Bani were M, Malluch, Adaiah, Jashub,

MESOPOTAMIA (11)

Gen 24:10 arose, and went to M, to the city of
Deut 23:4 Beor from Pethor of M, to curse you.
Judg 3:8 of Cushan-rishathaim king of M; and the people of
3:10 gave Cushan-rishathaim king of M into his hand; and
1Chr 19:6 chariots and horsemen from M, from Aram-maacah,
Jud 2:24 Euphrates and passed through M and destroyed all
5:7 time they lived in M, because they would not
5:8 and they fled to M, and lived there for
8:26 happened to Jacob in M in Syria, while he
Acts 2:9 Elamites and residents of M, Judea and Cappadocia,
7:2 when he was in M, before he lived in

MESSAGE (34)

Gen 50:16 So they sent a M to Joseph, saying, "Your
Num 22:7 they came to Balaam, and gave him Balak's M
Judg 3:19 "I have a secret M for you, O king."
3:20 said, "I have a M from God for you."
11:28 did not heed the M of Jephthah which he
2Sam 12:25 him, and sent a M by Nathan the prophet;
19:11 King David sent this M to Zadok and Abiathar
1Kgs 5:8 "I have heard the M which you have sent
20:12 When Ben-hadad heard this M as he was drinking
Esth 4:10 and gave him a M for Mordecai, saying,
Prov 26:6 He who sends a M by the hand of
Is 28:9 knowledge, and to whom will he explain the M
28:19 it will be sheer terror to understand the M
Bar 6:1 to give them the M which God had commanded
Jon 3:2 proclaim to it the M that I tell you."
Hag 1:13 people with the LORD's M, "I am with you,
1Mac 5:48 sent them this friendly M, "Let us pass through
7:27 his brothers this peaceable M,
10:25 So he sent a M to them in the
10:51 Egypt with the following M:
10:69 he sent the following M to Jonathan the high
11:42 And Demetrius sent this M to Jonathan, "Not only
2Mac 14:28 When this M came to Nicanor, he was troubled
Mk 16:20 them and confirmed the M by the signs that
Acts 11:14 declare to you a M by which you will
13:26 has been sent the M of this salvation.
1Cor 2:4 my speech and my M were not in plausible
2Cor 5:19 entrusting to us the M of reconciliation.
2Tim 4:15 of him yourself, for he strongly opposed our M
4:17 strength to proclaim the M fully, that all the
Heb 2:2 For if the M declared by angels was valid
4:2 to them; but the M which they heard did
1Jn 1:5 This is the M we have heard from him
3:11 For this is the M which you have heard

MESSAGES (2)

1Mac 5:16 the people heard these M, a great assembly was
Heb 12:19 entreat that no further M be spoken to them.

MESSENGER (35)

1Sam 23:27 capture them, when a M came to Saul, saying,
2Sam 11:19 and he instructed the M, "When you have finished
11:22 So the M went, and came and told David
11:23 The M said to David, "The men gained an
11:25 David said to the M, "Thus shall you say
15:13 And a M came to David, saying, "The hearts
1Kgs 19:2 Then Jezebel sent a M to Elijah, saying, "So
22:13 And the M who went to summon Micaiah said
2Kgs 5:10 And Elisha sent a M to him, saying, "Go
6:32 presence; but before the M arrived Elisha said to
6:32 Look, when the M comes, shut the door, and
9:18 watchman reported, saying, "The M reached them,
10:8 When the M came and told him, "They have
2Chr 18:12 And the M who went to summon Micaiah said
Job 1:14 and there came a M to Job, and said,
Prov 13:17 A bad M plunges men into trouble, but a
16:14 king's wrath is a M of death, and a
17:11 rebellion, and a cruel M will be sent against
25:13 harvest is a faithful M to those who send
Eccl 5:6 not say before the M that it was a
Sir 43:26 Because of him his M finds the way, and
Is 42:19 or deaf as my M whom I send?
Jer 49:14 the LORD, and a M has been sent among
51:31 meet another, and one M to meet another, to
Ezek 23:40 far, to whom a M was sent, and lo,
Obad 1:1 the LORD, and a M has been sent among
Hag 1:13 Then Haggai, the M of the LORD, spoke to
Mal 2:7 for he is the M of the LORD of
3:1 "Behold, I send my M to prepare the way
3:1 to his temple; the M of the covenant in
Mt 11:10 'Behold, I send my M before thy face, who
Mk 1:2 "Behold, I send my M before thy face, who
Lk 7:27 'Behold, I send my M before thy face, who
2Cor 12:7 in the flesh, a M of Satan, to harass
Phil 2:25 fellow soldier, and your M and minister to my

MESSENGERS (88)

Gen 32:3 And Jacob sent M before him to Esau his
32:6 And the M returned to Jacob, saying, "We came
Num 20:14 Moses sent M from Kadesh to the king of
21:21 Then Israel sent M to Sihon king of the
22:5 at that time, sent M to Balaam the son
24:12 I not tell your M whom you sent to
Deut 2:26 you.' "So I sent M from the wilderness of
Josh 6:17 because she hid the M that we sent.
6:25 because she hid the M whom Joshua sent to
7:22 So Joshua sent M, and they ran to the
Judg 6:35 And he sent M throughout all Manasseh; and they
6:35 And he sent M to Asher, Zebulun, and Naphtali;
7:24 And Gideon sent M throughout all the hill country
9:31 And he sent M to Abimelech at Arumah, saying,
11:12 Then Jephthah sent M to the king of the
11:13 Ammonites answered the M of Jephthah, "Because
11:14 And Jephthah sent M again to the king of
11:17 Israel then sent M to the king of Edom,
11:19 Israel then sent M to Sihon king of the
1Sam 6:21 So they sent M to the inhabitants of Kiriath-jearim,
11:3 that we may send M through all the territory
11:4 When the M came to Gibe-ah of Saul, they
11:7 by the hand of M, saying, "Whoever does not
11:9 they said to the M who had come, "Thus
11:9 When the M came and told the men of
16:19 Therefore Saul sent M to Jesse, and said, "Send
19:11 That night Saul sent M to David's house to
19:14 And when Saul sent M to take David, she
19:15 Then Saul sent the M to see David, saying,
19:16 And when the M came in, behold, the image
19:20 Then Saul sent M to take David; and when
19:20 God came upon the M of Saul, and they
19:21 Saul, he sent other M, and they also prophesied.
19:21 And Saul sent M again the third time, and
25:14 wife, "Behold, David sent M out of the wilderness
25:42 she went after the M of David, and became
31:9 his armor, and sent M throughout the land of
2Sam 2:5 David sent M to the men of Jabesh-gilead, and
3:12 And Abner sent M to David at Hebron, saying,
3:14 Then David sent M to Ish-bosheth Saul's son, saying,
3:26 David's presence, he sent M after Abner, and they
5:11 king of Tyre sent M to David, and cedar
11:4 So David sent M, and took her; and she
12:27 And Joab sent M to David, and said, "I
15:10 But Absalom sent secret M throughout all the tribes
1Kgs 20:2 And he sent M into the city to Ahab
20:5 The M came again, and said, "Thus says Ben-hadad:
20:9 he said to the M of Ben-hadad, "Tell my
20:9 And the M departed and brought him word again.
2Kgs 1:2 sick; so he sent M, telling them, "Go, inquire
1:3 up to meet the M of the king of
1:5 The M returned to the king, and he said
1:16 'Because you have sent M to inquire of Baal-zebub,
7:15 And the M returned, and told the king.
14:8 Then Amaziah sent M to Jehoash the son of
16:7 So Ahaz sent M to Tiglath-pileser king of Assyria,
17:4 for he had sent M to So, king of

19:9 he sent M again to Hezekiah, saying,
19:14 the hand of the M, and read it; and
19:23 By your M you have mocked the LORD, and
1Chr 10:9 his armor, and sent M throughout the land of
14:1 king of Tyre sent M to David, and cedar
19:2 So David sent M to console him concerning his
19:16 by Israel, they sent M and brought out the
2Chr 36:15 to them by his M, because he had compassion
36:16 they kept mocking the M of God, despising his
Neh 6:3 And I sent M to them, saying, "I am
Tob 10:8 and I will send M to your father, and
Jud 1:11 they sent back his M empty-handed and shamefaced.
3:1 So they sent M to sue for peace, and
Ps 104:4 makest the winds thy M, fire and flame thy
Is 14:32 will one answer the M of the nation?
18:2 Go, you swift M, to a nation, tall and
23:2 merchants of Sidon; your M passed over the sea
37:9 heard it, he sent M to Hezekiah, saying,
37:14 the hand of the M, and read it; and
44:26 the counsel of his M; who says of Jerusalem,
Ezek 23:16 upon them, and sent M to them in Chaldea.
30:9 "On that day swift M shall go forth from
Nah 2:13 the voice of your M shall no more be
1Mac 1:44 king sent letters by M to Jerusalem and the
5:14 read, behold, other M, with their garments rent,
7:10 Judah; and he sent M to Judas and his
7:41 and said, "When the M from the king spoke
Lk 7:24 When the M of John had gone, he began
9:52 And he sent M ahead of him, who went
2Cor 8:23 our brethren, they are M of the churches, the
Jas 2:25 when she received the M and sent them out

MESSIAH (2)

Jn 1:41 and said to him, "We have found the M
4:25 him, "I know that M is coming (he who

MET (71)

Gen 32:1 the angels of God M him;
33:8 you mean by all this company which I M
Ex 3:18 of the Hebrews, has M with us; and now,
4:24 the way the LORD M him and sought to
4:27 So he went, and M him at the mountain
5:3 of the Hebrews has M with us; let us
5:20 They M Moses and Aaron, who were waiting for
Num 23:4 And God M Balaam; and Balaam said to him,
23:16 And the LORD M Balaam, and put a word
1Sam 9:11 to the city, they M young maidens coming out
10:10 a band of prophets M him; and the spirit
25:20 toward her; and she M them.
2Sam 2:13 David, went out and M them at the pool
16:1 the servant of Mephibosheth M him, with a couple
1Kgs 2:7 with such loyalty they M me when I fled
13:24 went away a lion M him on the road
18:7 way, behold, Elijah M him; and Obadiah recognized
20:36 from him, a lion M him and killed him.
2Kgs 9:21 to meet Jehu, and M him at the property
10:13 of the Shepherds, Jehu M the kinsmen of Ahaziah
10:15 departed from there, he M Jehonadab the son of
2Chr 22:8 house of Ahab, he M the princes of Judah
Tob 7:1 house of Raguel, Sarah M them and greeted them.
Jud 10:11 and an Assyrian patrol M her
15:9 And when they M her they all blessed her
Song 8:1 If I M you outside, I would kiss you,
Sir 31:6 and their destruction has M them face to face.
Jer 41:6 As he M them, he said to them, "Come
Dan 13:14 But turning back, they M again; and when each
Hos 12:4 He M God at Bethel, and there God spoke
Amos 5:19 lion, and a bear M him; or went into
1Mac 4:29 at Bethzur, and Judas M them with ten thousand
5:25 encountered the Nabateans, who M them peaceably
7:43 So the armies M in battle on the thirteenth
10:49 The two kings M in battle, and the army
10:53 of our country; I M him in battle, and
10:58 Alexander the king M him, and Ptolemy gave him
10:60 pomp to Ptolemais and M the two kings; he
10:74 and Simon his brother M him to help him.
11:6 Jonathan M the king at Joppa with pomp, and
11:15 Ptolemy marched out and M him with a strong
11:60 people of the city M him and paid him
11:68 army of the foreigners M him in the plain;
11:68 mountains, but they themselves M him face to face.
12:25 away from Jerusalem and M them in the region
2Mac 3:7 When Apollonius M the king, he told him of
5:8 Finally he M a miserable end.
5:12 relentlessly every one they M and to slay those
8:14 Nicanor before he ever M them,
10:35 with savage fury cut down every one they M
13:8 ashes were holy, he M his death in ashes.
15:26 Judas and his men M the enemy in battle
Mt 8:28 the Gadarenes, two demoniacs M him, coming out of
28:9 And behold, Jesus M them and said, "Hail!" And
Mk 5:2 of the boat, there M him out of the
Lk 8:27 out on land, there M him a man from
9:37 mountain, a great crowd M him.
17:12 a village, he was M by ten lepers, who
Jn 4:51 going down, his servants M him and told him
11:20 coming, she went and M him, while Mary sat
11:30 place where Martha had M him.
18:2 place; for Jesus often M there with his disciples.
Acts 10:25 When Peter entered, Cornelius M him and fell down
11:26 a whole year they M with the church, and
16:16 of prayer, we were M by a slave girl
17:18 Epicurean and Stoic philosophers M him.
20:14 And when he M us at Assos, we took
25:16 one before the accused M the accusers face to
2Cor 13:7 may appear to have M the test, but that
Heb 7:1 the Most High God, M Abraham returning from the
7:10 his ancestor when Melchizedek M him.

METAL

Hab 2:18 has shaped it, a M image, a teacher of

METED

Job 28:25 wind its weight, and M out the waters by

METHEG-AMMAH

2Sam 8:1 them, and David took M out of the hand

METHOD

2Mac 13:4 to death by the M which is the custom

METHODS

Esth 16:9 men, by changing our M and always judging what

METHUSELAH (6)

Gen 5:21 lived sixty-five years, he became the father of M
5:22 after the birth of M three hundred years, and
5:25 When M had lived a hundred and eighty-seven years,
5:26 M lived after the birth of Lamech seven hundred
5:27 all the days of M were nine hundred and
Lk 3:37 Lamech, the son of M, the son of Enoch,

MEZAHAB (2)

Gen 36:39 Mehetabel, the daughter of Matred, daughter of M
1Chr 1:50 the daughter of Matred, the daughter of M

MEZOBA-ITE

1Chr 11:47 the Moabite, Eliel, and Obed, and Jaasiel the M

MIBHAR

1Chr 11:38 the brother of Nathan, M the son of Hagri,

MIBSAM (3)

Gen 25:13 Ishmael; and Kedar, Adbeel, M,
1Chr 1:29 Nebaioth; and Kedar, Adbeel, M,
4:25 Shallum was his son, M his son, Mishma his

MIBZAR (2)

Gen 36:42 Elah, Pinon, Kenaz, Teman, M,
1Chr 1:53 Elah, Pinon, Kenaz, Teman, M,

MICA (5)

2Sam 9:12 Mephibosheth had a young son, whose name was M
1Chr 9:15 Mattaniah the son of M, son of Zichri, son
Neh 10:11 Hodiah, Kelita, Pelaiah, Hanan, M, Rehob,
11:17 Mattaniah the son of M, son of Zabdi, son
11:22 of Mattaniah, son of M, of the sons of

MICAH (34)

Judg 17:1 the hill country of Ephraim, whose name was M
17:4 image; and it was in the house of M
17:5 And the man M had a shrine, and he
17:8 hill country of Ephraim to the house of M
17:9 And M said to him, "From where do you
17:10 And M said to him, "Stay with me, and
17:12 And M installed the Levite, and the young man
17:12 his priest, and was in the house of M
17:13 Then M said, "Now I know that the LORD
18:2 to the house of M, and lodged there.
18:3 by the house of M, they recognized the voice
18:4 "Thus and thus has M dealt with me: he
18:13 of Ephraim, and came to the house of M

M

18:15 at the home of M, and asked him of
18:18 when these went into M's house and took the
18:22 from the home of M, the men who were
18:22 in the houses near M's house were called out,
18:23 round and said to M, "What ails you that
18:26 their way; and when M saw that they were
18:27 And taking what M had made, and the priest
18:31 So they set up M's graven image which he
1Chr 5:5 son, Shimei his son, M his son, Re-aiah his
8:34 was Merib-baal; and Merib-baal was the father of M
8:35 The sons of M: Pithon, Melech, Tarea, and Ahaz.
9:40 was Merib-baal; and Merib-baal was the father of M
9:41 The sons of M: Pithon, Melech, Tahre-a, and Ahaz;
23:20 The sons of Uzziel: M the chief and Isshiah
24:24 The sons of Uzziel, M; of the sons of
24:24 of the sons of M, Shamir.
24:25 The brother of M, Isshiah; of the sons of
2Chr 34:20 Abdon the son of M, Shaphan the secretary, and
Jud 6:15 Uzziah the son of M, of the tribe of
Jer 26:18 people, saying, M of Moresheth prophesied in
Mic 1:1 LORD that came to M of Moresheth in the

MICAIAH (27)
1Kgs 22:8 inquire of the LORD, M the son of Imlah;
22:9 and said, "Bring quickly M the son of Imlah."
22:13 who went to summon M said to him, "Behold,
22:14 But M said, "As the LORD lives, what the
22:15 king said to him, M, shall we go to
22:19 And M said, "Therefore hear the word of the
22:24 came near and struck M on the cheek, and
22:25 And M said, "Behold, you shall see on that
22:26 of Israel said, "Seize M, and take him back
22:28 And M said, "If you return in peace, the
2Kgs 22:12 Achbor the son of M, and Shaphan the secretary,
2Chr 13:2 His mother's name was M the daughter of Uriel
17:7 Obadiah, Zechariah, Nethanel, and M, to teach in the
18:7 inquire of the LORD, M the son of Imlah;
18:8 and said, "Bring quickly M the son of Imlah."
18:12 who went to summon M said to him, "Behold,
18:13 But M said, "As the LORD lives, what my
18:14 king said to him, M, shall we go to
18:18 And M said, "Therefore hear the word of the
18:23 came near and struck M on the cheek, and
18:24 And M said, "Behold, you shall see on that
18:25 of Israel said, "Seize M, and take him back
18:27 And M said, "If you return in peace, the
Neh 12:35 of Mattaniah, son of M, son of Zaccur, son
12:41 priests Eliakim, Ma-aseiah, Miniamin, M, Eli-o-enai,
Jer 36:11 When M the son of Gemariah, son of Shaphan,
36:13 And M told them all the words that he

MICE (5)
1Sam 6:4 tumors and five golden M, according to the number
6:5 and images of your M that ravage the land,
6:11 box with the golden M and the images of
6:18 Ekron; also the golden M, according to the number
Is 66:17 and the abomination and M, shall come to an

MICH-METHATH (2)
Josh 16:6 on the north is M; then on the east
17:7 reached from Asher to M, which is east of

MICHAEL (15)
Num 13:13 Sethur the son of M;
1Chr 5:13 to their fathers' houses: M, Meshullam, Sheba, Jorai,
5:14 of Gilead, son of M, son of Jeshishai, son
6:40 of Shimea, son of M, son of Ba-aseiah, son
7:3 the sons of Izrahiah: M, Obadiah, Joel, and Isshiah,
8:16 Zebadiah, Arad, Eder, M, Ishpah, and Joha were
12:20 Adnah, Jozabad, Jedia-el, M, Jozabad, Elihu, and
27:18 Omri the son of M;
2Chr 21:2 Azariah, Jehiel, Zechariah, Azariah, M, and
Ezra 8:8 Zebadiah the son of M, and with him eighty
Dan 10:13 me twenty-one days; but M, one of the chief
10:21 side against these except M, your prince.
12:1 that time shall arise M, the great prince who
Jude 1:9 when the archangel M, contending with the devil,
Rev 12:7 war arose in heaven, M and his angels fighting

MICHAL (16)
1Sam 14:49 name of the younger M;
18:20 Now Saul's daughter M loved David; and they told
18:27 gave him his daughter M for a wife.
19:11 But M, David's wife, told him, "If you do
19:12 So M let David down through the window; and
19:13 M took an image and laid it on the
19:17 Saul said to M, "Why have you deceived me
19:17 And M answered Saul, "He said to me, 'Let
25:44 Saul had given M his daughter, David's wife, to
2Sam 3:13 unless you first bring M, Saul's daughter, when you
3:14 "Give me my wife M, whom I betrothed at
6:16 the city of David, M the daughter of Saul
6:20 But M the daughter of Saul came out to
6:21 And David said to M, "It was before the
6:23 And M the daughter of Saul had no child
1Chr 15:29 the city of David, M the daughter of Saul

MICHMAS (2)
Ezra 2:27 The men of M, one hundred and twenty-two.
Neh 7:31 The men of M, a hundred and twenty-two.

MICHMASH (10)
1Sam 13:2 were with Saul in M and the hill country
13:5 up and encamped in M, to the east of
13:11 Philistines had mustered at M,
13:16 of Benjamin; but the Philistines encamped in M
13:23 the Philistines went out to the pass of M
14:5 north in front of M, and the other on
14:31 Philistines that day from M to Aijalon.
Neh 11:31 from Geba onward, at M, Aija, Bethel and its
Is 10:28 passed through Migron, at M he stores his baggage;
1Mac 9:73 And Jonathan dwelt in M

MICHRI
1Chr 9:8 of Uzzi, son of M, and Meshullam the son

MID-COURSE
Ps 102:23 broken my strength in M; he has shortened my

MIDDAY (3)
1Kgs 18:29 And as M passed, they raved on until the
Neh 8:3 from early morning until M, in the presence of
Acts 26:13 At M, O king, I saw on the way

MIDDIN
Josh 15:61 In the wilderness, Beth-arabah, M, Secacah,

MIDDLE (34)
Ex 26:28 The M bar, halfway up the frames, shall pass
36:33 And he made the M bar to pass through
Num 35:5 city being in the M; this shall belong to
Deut 3:16 the Arnon, with the M of the valley as
Josh 12:2 Arnon, and from the M of the valley as
13:9 that is in the M of the valley, and
13:16 that is in the M of the valley, and
Judg 7:19 the beginning of the M watch, when they had
16:29 Samson grasped the two M pillars upon which the
2Sam 10:4 their garments in the M, at their hips, and
24:5 that is in the M of the valley, toward
1Kgs 6:6 five cubits broad, the M one was six cubits
6:8 by stairs to the M story, and from the
6:8 story, and from the M story to the third.
6:27 each other in the M of the house.
8:64 the king consecrated the M of the court that
2Kgs 20:4 gone out of the M court, the word of
1Chr 19:4 their garments in the M, at their hips, and
2Chr 7:7 And Solomon consecrated the M of the court that
Jud 11:19 lead you through the M of Judea, till you
Wis 7:18 beginning and end and M of times, the alternations
Sir 31:21 get up in the M of the meal, and
Jer 39:3 sat in the M gate: Nergal-sharezer, Samgar-nebo,
Ezek 15:4 of it, and the M of it is charred,
41:7 top story through the M story.
42:5 from the lower and M chambers in the building.
42:6 the lower and the M ones.
1Mac 10:63 with him into the M of the city and
2Mac 14:44 he fell in the M of the empty space.
Lk 22:53 a fire in the M of the courtyard and
Jn 7:14 About the M of the feast Jesus went up
Acts 1:18 burst open in the M and all his bowels
17:22 Paul, standing in the M of the Are-opagus, said:
Rev 22:2 the Lamb through the M of the street of

MIDHEAVEN (3)
Rev 8:13 as it flew in M, "Woe, woe, woe to
14:6 another angel flying in M, with an eternal gospel
19:17 birds that fly in M, "Come, gather for the

MIDIAN (51)
Gen 25:2 him Zimran, Jokshan, Medan, M, Ishbak, and Shuah.
25:4 The sons of M were Ephah, Epher, Hanoch, Abida,
36:35 of Bedad, who defeated M in the country of

Ex 2:15 in the land of M; and he sat down
2:16 Now the priest of M had seven daughters; and
3:1 Jethro, the priest of M; and he led his
4:19 said to Moses in M, "Go back to Egypt;
18:1 Jethro, the priest of M, Moses' father-in-law, heard
Num 22:4 to the elders of M, "This horde will now
22:7 and the elders of M departed with the fees
25:15 of the people of a fathers' house in M
25:18 of the prince of M, their sister, who was
31:3 they may go against M, to execute the LORD's
31:3 Midian, to execute the LORD's vengeance on M
31:7 warred against M, as the LORD commanded Moses,
31:8 slew the kings of M with the rest of
31:8 the five kings of M; and they also slew
31:9 captive the women of M and their little ones;
Josh 13:21 with the leaders of M, Evi and Rekem and
Judg 6:1 into the hand of M seven years.
6:2 And the hand of M prevailed over Israel; and
6:2 Israel; and because of M the people of Israel
6:6 very low because of M; and the people of
6:13 off, and given us into the hand of M
6:14 from the hand of M; do not I send
7:1 and the camp of M was north of them,
7:8 and the camp of M was below him in
7:13 into the camp of M, and came to the
7:14 hand God has given M and all the host."
7:15 given the host of M into your hand."
7:23 and from all Manasseh, and they pursued after M
7:25 the two princes of M, Oreb and Zeeb; they
7:25 Zeeb, as they pursued M; and they brought the
8:1 call us when you went to fight with M
8:3 hands the princes of M, Oreb and Zeeb; what
8:5 pursuing after Zebah and Zalmunna, the kings of M
8:12 the two kings of M, Zebah and Zalmunna, and
8:22 have delivered us out of the hand of M
8:26 by the kings of M, and besides the collars
8:28 So M was subdued before the people of Israel,
9:17 from the hand of M;
1Kgs 11:18 They set out from M and came to Paran,
1Chr 1:32 bore Zimran, Jokshan, Medan, M, Ishbak, and
1:33 The sons of M: Ephah, Epher, Hanoch, Abida, and
1:46 of Bedad, who defeated M in the country of
Ps 83:9 as thou didst to M, as to Sisera and
Is 9:4 thou hast broken as on the day of M
10:26 as when he smote M at the rock of
60:6 the young camels of M and Ephah; all those
Hab 3:7 of the land of M did tremble.
Acts 7:29 in the land of M, where he became the

MIDIANITE (5)

Gen 37:28 Then M traders passed by; and they drew Joseph
Num 10:29 son of Reuel the M, Moses' father-in-law, "We are
25:6 came and brought a M woman to his family,
25:14 was slain with the M woman, was Zimri the
25:15 the name of the M woman who was slain

MIDIANITES (13)

Gen 37:36 Meanwhile the M had sold him in Egypt to
Num 25:17 to Moses, "Harass the M, and smite them;
31:2 of Israel on the M; afterward you shall be
Judg 6:3 put in seed the M and the Amalekites and
6:7 on account of the M,
6:11 the wine press, to hide it from the M
6:16 you shall smite the M as one man."
6:33 Then all the M and the Amalekites and the
7:2 me to give the M into their hand, lest
7:7 you, and give the M into your hand; and
7:12 And the M and the Amalekites and all the
7:24 "Come down against the M and seize the waters
Jud 2:26 He surrounded all the M, and burned their tents

MIDNIGHT (15)

Ex 11:4 says the LORD: About M I will go forth
12:29 At M the LORD smote all the first-born in
Judg 16:3 But Samson lay till M, and at midnight he
16:3 till midnight, and at M he arose and took
Ruth 3:8 At M the man was startled, and turned over,
1Kgs 3:20 And she arose at M, and took my son
Jud 12:5 her into the tent, and she slept until M
Job 34:20 moment they die; at M the people are shaken
Ps 119:62 At M I rise to praise thee, because of
Mt 25:6 But at M there was a cry, 'Behold, the
Mk 13:35 the evening, or at M, or at cockcrow, or
Lk 11:5 go to him at M and say to him,
Acts 16:25 But about M Paul and Silas were praying and
20:7 the morrow; and he prolonged his speech until M
27:27 sea of Adria, about M the sailors suspected that

MIDST (286)

Gen 1:6 a firmament in the M of the waters, and
2:9 life also in the M of the garden, and
3:3 which is in the M of the garden, neither
19:29 Lot out of the M of the overthrow, when
48:16 a multitude in the M of the earth."
Ex 3:2 fire out of the M of a bush; and
8:22 the LORD in the M of the earth.
9:24 flashing continually in the M of the hail, very
11:4 go forth in the M of Egypt;
14:22 Israel went into the M of the sea on
14:23 after them into the M of the sea, all
14:27 the Egyptians in the M of the sea.
15:19 dry ground in the M of the sea.
23:25 sickness away from the M of you.
24:16 Moses out of the M of the cloud.
25:8 a sanctuary, that I may dwell in their M
34:9 thee, go in the M of us, although it
34:12 a snare in the M of you.
Lev 15:31 by defiling my tabernacle that is in their M
16:16 with them in the M of their uncleannesses.
Num 2:17 the Levites in the M of the camps; as
5:3 their camp, in the M of which I dwell."
14:14 LORD, art in the M of this people; for
16:33 they perished from the M of the assembly.
16:45 "Get away from the M of this congregation, that
16:47 and ran into the M of the assembly; and
19:6 cast them into the M of the burning of
19:20 cut off from the M of the assembly, since
33:8 and passed through the M of the sea into
35:34 you live, in the M of which I dwell;
35:34 LORD dwell in the M of the people of
Deut 1:42 am not in the M of you; lest you
4:12 you out of the M of the fire; you
4:15 Horeb out of the M of the fire,
4:33 speaking out of the M of the fire, as
4:34 for himself from the M of another nation, by
4:36 words out of the M of the fire.
5:4 mountain, out of the M of the fire,
5:22 mountain out of the M of the fire, the
5:23 voice out of the M of the darkness, while
5:24 voice out of the M of the fire; we
5:26 speaking out of the M of fire, as we
6:15 your God in the M of you is a
7:21 God is in the M of you, a great
9:10 mountain out of the M of the fire on
10:4 mountain out of the M of the fire on
11:6 followed them, in the M of all Israel;
13:5 the evil from the M of you.
13:16 its spoil into the M of its open square,
17:7 the evil from the M of you.
19:19 the evil from the M of you.
21:8 innocent blood in the M of thy people Israel;
21:9 innocent blood from your M, when you do what
21:21 the evil from your M; and all Israel shall
22:21 the evil from the M of you.
22:24 the evil from the M of you.
23:14 God walks in the M of your camp, to
23:16 with you, in your M, in the place which
24:7 the evil from the M of you.
29:16 we came through the M of the nations through
32:51 with me in the M of the people of
32:51 as holy in the M of the people of
Josh 3:17 dry ground in the M of the Jordan, until
4:3 here out of the M of the Jordan, from
4:5 your God into the M of the Jordan, and
4:8 stones out of the M of the Jordan, according
4:9 twelve stones in the M of the Jordan, in
4:10 ark stood in the M of the Jordan, until
4:18 came up from the M of the Jordan, and
7:13 devoted things in the M of you, O Israel;
8:22 they were in the M of Israel, some on
10:13 sun stayed in the M of heaven, and did
13:13 Maacath dwell in the M of Israel to this
16:10 have dwelt in the M of Ephraim to this
19:1 inheritance was in the M of the inheritance of
19:9 an inheritance in the M of their inheritance.
21:41 the Levites in the M of the possession of
22:31 LORD is in the M of us, because you
24:5 I did in the M of it; and afterwards
Judg 12:4 you Gileadites, in the M of Ephraim and Manasseh."
18:20 and went in the M of the people.
20:42 destroyed them in the M of them.
1Sam 11:11 they came into the M of the camp in

M

	16:13	anointed him in the M of his brothers; and
2Sam	1:25	mighty fallen in the M of the battle!
	3:27	him aside into the M of the gate to
	23:12	his stand in the M of the plot, and
1Kgs	3:8	servant is in the M of thy people whom
	8:51	of Egypt, from the M of the iron furnace).
	20:39	went out into the M of the battle; and
2Kgs	6:20	they were in the M of Samaria.
1Chr	11:14	his stand in the M of the plot, and
2Chr	20:14	of Asaph, in the M of the assembly.
Neh	4:11	we come into the M of them and kill
	9:11	they went through the M of the sea on
Jud	6:16	set Achior in the M of all their people,
	11:19	your throne in the M of it; and you
	14:19	shouts arose in the M of the camp.
	16:3	his camp, in the M of the people.
Esth	4:1	went out into the M of the city, wailing
Ps	22:22	my brethren; in the M of the congregation I
	46:5	God is in the M of her, she shall
	48:9	O God, in the M of thy temple.
	55:11	ruin is in its M; oppression and fraud do
	57:4	I lie in the M of lions that greedily
	74:4	have roared in the M of thy holy place;
	74:12	working salvation in the M of the earth.
	78:28	them fall in the M of their camp, all
	82:1	divine council; in the M of the gods he
	102:24	not hence in the M of my days, thou
	109:30	praise him in the M of the throng.
	110:2	Rule in the M of your foes!
	116:19	the LORD, in your M, O Jerusalem.
	135:9	beast; who in thy M, O Egypt, sent signs
	136:14	Israel pass through the M of it, for his
	138:7	I walk in the M of trouble, thou dost
Prov	23:34	lies down in the M of the sea, like
Wis	4:14	him quickly from the M of wickedness.
	12:5	These initiates from the M of a heathen cult,
	16:19	time even in the M of water it burned
	18:15	royal throne, into the M of the land that
Sir	1:27	you down in the M of the congregation, because
	9:13	are walking in the M of snares, and that
	11:8	a speaker in the M of his words.
	14:27	will dwell in the M of her glory.
	15:5	his mouth in the M of the assembly.
	24:1	will glory in the M of her people.
	42:12	not sit in the M of women;
	48:17	brought water into the M of it; he tunneled
	51:4	side and from the M of fire which I
Is	4:4	of Jerusalem from its M by a spirit of
	5:2	a watchtower in the M of it, and hewed
	5:8	dwell alone in the M of the land.
	5:25	as refuse in the M of the streets.
	6:5	I dwell in the M of a people of
	6:12	are many in the M of the land.
	7:6	as king in the M of it,"
	10:23	as decreed, in the M of all the earth.
	12:6	for great in your M is the Holy One
	19:19	the LORD in the M of the land of
	19:24	a blessing in the M of the earth,
	24:13	shall be in the M of the earth among
	25:11	his hands in the M of it as a
	29:23	my hands, in his M, they will sanctify my
	41:18	and fountains in the M of the valleys; I
	52:11	go out from the M of her, purify yourselves,
	58:9	take away from the M of you the yoke,
	61:9	their offspring in the M of the peoples; all
	63:11	who put in the M of them his holy
	66:17	following one in the M, eating swine's flesh and
Jer	6:1	of Benjamin, from the M of Jerusalem!
	12:16	built up in the M of my people.
	14:9	LORD, art in the M of us, and we
	17:11	by right; in the M of his days they
	21:4	them together into the M of this city.
	30:21	come forth from their M; I will make him
	44:7	and child, from the M of Judah, leaving you
	46:21	hired soldiers in her M are like fatted calves;
	50:8	fathers.' "Flee from the M of Babylon, and go
	50:37	foreign troops in her M, that they may become
	51:6	"Flee from the M of Babylon, let every man
	51:45	"Go out of the M of her, my people!
	51:47	shall fall in the M of her.
	51:63	cast it into the M of the Euphrates,
	52:25	were found in the M of the city.
Lam	1:3	overtaken her in the M of her distress.
	1:15	mighty men in the M of me; he summoned
	4:13	who shed in the M of her the blood
Ezek	1:4	continually, and in the M of the fire, as
	1:5	And from the M of it came the likeness
	1:13	In the M of the living creatures there was
	5:2	the fire in the M of the city, when
	5:8	execute judgments in the M of you in the
	5:10	their sons in the M of you, and sons
	5:12	with famine in the M of you; a third
	6:7	shall fall in the M of you, and you
	7:4	your ways, while your abominations are in your M
	7:9	your ways, while your abominations are in your M
	11:7	have laid in the M of it, they are
	11:7	forth out of the M of it.
	11:9	forth out of the M of it, and give
	11:11	the flesh in the M of it; I will
	11:23	went up from the M of the city, and
	12:2	you dwell in the M of a rebellious house,
	13:14	shall perish in the M of it; and you
	14:8	him off from the M of my people; and
	14:9	destroy him from the M of my people Israel.
	16:53	own fortunes in the M of them,
	19:2	She couched in the M of young lions, rearing
	20:8	against them in the M of the land of
	21:32	shall be in the M of the land; you
	22:3	sheds blood in the M of her, that her
	22:7	suffers extortion in your M; the fatherless and the
	22:9	the mountains; men commit lewdness in your M
	22:13	has been in the M of you.
	22:19	gather you into the M of Jerusalem.
	22:21	be melted in the M of it.
	22:22	be melted in the M of it; and you
	22:25	Her princes in the M of her are like
	22:25	many widows in the M of her.
	22:27	Her princes in the M of her are like
	24:7	is still in the M of her; she put
	25:4	their dwellings in your M; they shall eat your
	26:5	shall be in the M of the sea a
	26:12	will cast into the M of the waters.
	26:15	is made in the M of you?
	27:27	that is in your M, sink into the heart
	27:32	like Tyre in the M of the sea?
	28:14	of God; in the M of the stones of
	28:16	you out from the M of the stones of
	28:18	forth fire from the M of you; it consumed
	28:22	my glory in the M of you.
	28:23	shall fall in the M of her, by the
	29:3	that lies in the M of his streams, that
	29:4	up out of the M of your streams, with
	29:12	a desolation in the M of desolated countries; and
	30:7	be desolated in the M of desolated countries and
	30:7	shall be in the M of cities that are
	32:21	helpers, out of the M of Sheol: 'They have
	37:1	me down in the M of the valley; it
	37:26	my sanctuary in the M of them for evermore.
	37:28	sanctuary is in the M of them for evermore."
	39:7	make known in the M of my people Israel;
	43:7	will dwell in the M of the people of
	43:9	will dwell in their M for ever.
	48:8	the sanctuary in the M of it.
	48:10	the LORD in the M of it.
	48:15	In the M of it shall be the city;
	48:21	the temple in its M,
	48:22	shall be in the M of that which belongs
Dan	3:24	walked about in the M of the flames, singing
	3:25	this prayer; in the M of the fire he
	3:50	furnace, and made the M of the furnace like
	3:89	delivered us from the M of the burning fiery
	3:89	fiery furnace; from the M of the fire he
	3:93	loose, walking in the M of the fire, and
	4:10	a tree in the M of the earth; and
	13:34	stood up in the M of the people, and
	13:48	his stand in the M of them, he said,
Hos	11:9	Holy One in your M, and I will not
Joel	2:27	I am in the M of Israel, and that
Amos	2:3	the ruler from its M, and will slay all
	3:9	tumults within her, and the oppressions in her M
	5:17	will pass through the M of you," says the
	6:4	and calves from the M of the stall;
	7:8	plumb line in the M of my people Israel;
	7:10	against you in the M of the house of
Mic	3:11	the LORD in the M of us?
	5:7	shall be in the M of many peoples like
	5:8	the nations, in the M of many peoples, like
	7:14	a forest in the M of a garden land;
Nah	3:13	Behold, your troops are women in your M
Hab	3:2	In the M of the years renew it; in
	3:2	renew it; in the M of the years make
Zeph	2:14	lie down in the M of her, all the

M

	11:10	the chiefs of David's M men, who gave him
	11:11	an account of David's M men: Jashobe-am,
	11:12	him among the three M men was Eleazar the
	11:18	Then the three M men broke through the camp
	11:19	things did the three M men.
	11:24	name beside the three M men.
	11:26	The M men of the armies were Asahel the
	12:1	they were among the M men who helped him
	12:4	Ishmaiah of Gibeon, a M man among the thirty
	12:8	in the wilderness M and experienced warriors,
	12:21	for they were all M men of valor, and
	12:25	Of the Simeonites, M men of valor for war,
	12:28	Zadok, a young man M in valor, and twenty-two
	12:30	twenty thousand eight hundred, M men of valor,
	19:8	the army of the M men.
	27:6	Benaiah who was a M man of the thirty
	28:1	the palace officials, the M men, and all the
	29:24	the leaders and the M men, and also all
2Chr	6:32	great name, and thy M hand, and thy outstretched
	13:3	eight hundred thousand picked M warriors.
	13:21	But Abijah grew M
	14:8	bows; all these were M men of valor.
	14:11	to help, between the M and the weak.
	17:13	He had soldiers, M men of valor, in Jerusalem.
	17:14	with three hundred thousand M men of valor,
	17:16	with two hundred thousand M men of valor.
	17:17	Of Benjamin: Eliada, a M man of valor, with
	25:6	also a hundred thousand M men of valor from
	26:12	of fathers' houses of M men of valor was
	26:13	could make war with M power, to help the
	27:6	So Jotham became M, because he ordered his ways
	28:7	And Zichri, a M man of Ephraim, slew Ma-aseiah
	32:3	his officers and his M men to stop the
	32:21	cut off all the M warriors and commanders and
Ezra	4:20	And M kings have been over Jerusalem, who ruled
	7:28	before all the king's M officers.
Neh	3:16	the house of the M men.
	9:11	as a stone into M waters.
	9:32	God, the great and M and terrible God, who
	11:14	Immer, and their brethren, M men of valor, a
Jud	16:7	For their M one did not fall by the
Esth	16:16	Most High, the most M living God, who has
Job	5:15	mouth, the needy from the hand of the M
	9:4	wise in heart, and M in strength --who
	12:19	leads priests away stripped, and overthrows the M
	21:7	old age, and grow M in power?
	24:22	the life of the M by his power; they
	34:17	who is righteous and M,
	34:20	pass away, and the M are taken away by
	34:24	He shatters the M without investigation, and sets
	35:9	for help because of the arm of the M
	36:5	"Behold, God is M, and does not despise any;
	36:5	despise any; he is M in strength of understanding.
	41:12	his limbs, or his M strength, or his goodly
	41:25	raises himself up the M are afraid; at the
Ps	18:17	for they were too M for me.
	20:6	his holy heaven with M victories by his right
	24:8	The LORD, strong and M, the LORD, mighty in
	24:8	and mighty, the LORD, M in battle!
	35:18	great congregation; in the M throng I will praise
	38:19	foes without cause are M, and many are those
	45:3	upon your thigh, O M one, in your glory
	50:1	The M One, God the LORD, speaks and summons
	50:3	round about him a M tempest.
	52:1	do you boast, O M man, of mischief done
	62:7	and my honor; my M rock, my refuge is
	68:15	O M mountain, mountain of Bashan; O many-peaked
	68:17	With M chariotry, twice ten thousand, thousands
	68:33	forth his voice, his M voice.
	69:4	hate me without cause; M are those who would
	71:16	With the M deeds of the Lord GOD I
	77:12	and muse on thy M deeds.
	80:10	with its shade, the M cedars with its branches;
	89:8	of hosts, who is M as thou art, O
	89:10	thy enemies with thy M arm.
	89:13	Thou hast a M arm; strong is thy hand,
	89:19	upon one who is M, I have exalted one
	93:4	of the sea, the LORD on high is M
	99:4	M King, lover of justice, thou hast established equity;
	103:20	you his angels, you M ones who do his
	106:2	Who can utter the M doings of the LORD,
	106:8	might make known his M power.
	110:2	forth from Zion your M scepter.
	112:2	His descendants will be M in the land; the
	132:2	and vowed to the M One of Jacob,
	132:5	dwelling place for the M One of Jacob."
	135:10	many nations and slew M kings,
	145:4	and shall declare thy M acts.
	145:12	sons of men thy M deeds, and the glorious
	150:1	praise him in his M firmament!
	150:2	Praise him for his M deeds; praise him according
Prov	7:26	her slain are a M host.
	16:32	is better than the M, and he who rules
	21:22	the city of the M and brings down the
	30:26	are a people not M, yet they make their
Song	3:7	About it are sixty M men of the mighty
	3:7	mighty men of the M men of Israel,
Wis	5:23	relentlessly overwhelm them; a M wind will rise
	6:6	pardoned in mercy, but M men will be mightily
	6:8	a strict inquiry is in store for the M
	18:5	all together by a M flood.
Sir	15:18	the Lord; he is M in power and sees
	16:11	the Lord; he is M to forgive, and he
	18:3	can search out his M deeds?
	21:7	He who is M in speech is known from
	29:13	affliction; more than a M shield and more than
	34:16	who love him, a M protection and strong support,
	36:8	let people recount thy M deeds.
	46:1	son of Nun was M in war, and was
	46:5	the Most High, the M One, when enemies pressed
	46:6	him with hailstones of M power.
	46:6	he wholly followed the M One.
	46:16	upon the Lord, the M One, when his enemies
	46:17	voice heard with a M sound;
	47:5	to slay a man M in war, to exalt
Is	1:24	LORD of hosts, the M One of Israel: "Ah,
	3:2	stay of water; the M man and the soldier,
	3:25	the sword and your M men in battle.
	8:7	waters of the River, M and many, the king
	9:6	"Wonderful Counselor, M God, Everlasting Father,
	10:21	of Jacob, to the M God.
	13:3	ones, have summoned my M men to execute my
	17:12	like the roaring of M waters!
	18:2	and far, a nation M and conquering, whose land
	18:7	and far, a nation M and conquering, whose land
	21:17	the archers of the M men of the sons
	28:2	has one who is M and strong; like a
	28:2	like a storm of M, overflowing waters, he will
	34:7	young steers with the M bulls.
	42:13	goes forth like a M man, like a man
	42:13	aloud, he shows himself M against his foes.
	43:16	a path in the M waters,
	49:24	be taken from the M, or the captives of
	49:25	the captives of the M shall be taken, and
	49:26	and your Redeemer, the M One of Jacob."
	56:11	The dogs have a M appetite; they never have
	60:16	and your Redeemer, the M One of Jacob.
	60:22	the smallest one a M nation; I am the
	62:8	hand and by his M arm: "I will not
	63:1	is I, announcing vindication, M to save."
Jer	5:16	tomb, they are all M men.
	9:23	wisdom, let not the M man glory in his
	14:9	man confused, like a M man who cannot save?
	32:18	them, O great and M God whose name is
	32:19	great in counsel and M in deed; whose eyes
	48:14	'We are heroes and M men of war?
	48:17	name; say, 'How the M scepter is broken, the
	50:41	from the north; a M nation and many kings
	51:55	waste, and stilling her M voice.
Lam	1:15	LORD flouted all my M men in the midst
Bar	1:4	the hearing of the M men and the princes,
	1:9	the prisoners and the M men and the people
	2:11	of Egypt with a M hand and with signs
Ezek	17:17	Pharaoh with his M army and great company will
	20:33	GOD, surely with a M hand and an outstretched
	20:34	are scattered, with a M hand and an outstretched
	26:11	the sword; and your M pillars will fall to
	26:17	city renowned, that was M on the sea, you
	31:11	the hand of a M one of the nations;
	32:12	by the swords of M ones, all of them
	32:21	The M chiefs shall speak of them, with their
	32:27	lie with the fallen M men of old who
	32:27	the terror of the M men was in the
	38:15	a great host, a M army;
	39:18	the flesh of the M, and drink the blood
	39:20	horses and riders, with M men and all kinds
Dan	2:31	This image, M and of exceeding brightness, stood
	3:20	And he ordered certain M men of his army
	4:3	are his signs, how M his wonders!
	4:30	have built by my M power as a royal
	8:6	at him in his M wrath.
	8:24	he does, and destroy M men and the people

M

9:15 of Egypt with a M hand, and hast made
11:3 Then a M king shall arise, who shall rule
11:25 an exceedingly great and M army; but he shall
Joel 3:9 war, stir up the M men.
Amos 2:14 strength, nor shall the M save his life;
2:16 of heart among the M shall flee away naked
Obad 1:9 And your M men shall be dismayed, O Teman,
Jon 1:4 and there was a M tempest on the sea,
Nah 2:3 The shield of his M men is red, his
Hab 3:15 horses, the surging of M waters.
Zeph 1:14 LORD is bitter, the M man cries aloud there.
Zech 10:5 they shall be like M men in battle, trampling
10:7 shall become like a M warrior, and their hearts
1Mac 2:42 a company of Hasideans, M warriors of Israel, every
2:66 Maccabeus has been a M warrior from his youth;
3:38 and Nicanor and Gorgias, M men among the friends
4:3 and he and his M men moved out to
4:30 the attack of the M warrior by the hand
9:21 said, "How is the M fallen, the savior of
10:19 that you are a M warrior and worthy to
2Mac 7:17 and see how his M power will torture you
11:13 were invincible because the M God fought on their
Mt 7:22 name, and do many M works in your name?'
11:20 where most of his M works had been done,
11:21 for if the M works done in you had
11:23 For if the M works done in you had
13:54 this wisdom and these M works?
13:58 did not do many M works there, because of
Mk 6:2 What M works are wrought by his hands!
6:5 he could do no M work there, except that
9:39 one who does a M work in my name
Lk 1:49 for he who is M has done great things
1:52 has put down the M from their thrones, and
10:13 for if the M works done in you had
19:37 voice for all the M works that they had
24:19 who was a prophet M in deed and word
Acts 2:2 the rush of a M wind, and it filled
2:11 our own tongues the M works of God."
2:22 you by God with M works and wonders and
7:22 Egyptians, and he was M in his words and
2Cor 12:12 signs and wonders and M works.
2Thes 1:7 from heaven with his M angels in flaming fire,
Heb 11:34 out of weakness, became M in war, put foreign
1Pet 5:6 yourselves therefore under the M hand of God, that
Rev 10:1 Then I saw another M angel coming down from
18:2 called out with a M voice, "Fallen, fallen is
18:8 burned with fire; for M is the Lord God
18:10 thou great city, thou M city, Babylon!
18:21 Then a M angel took up a stone like
19:6 the sound of M thunderpeals, crying, "Hallelujah!
19:18 captains, the flesh of M men, the flesh of

MIGRATED
Gen 11:2 And as men M from the east, they found

MIGRON (2)
1Sam 14:2 tree which is at M; the people who were
Is 10:28 he has passed through M, at Michmash he stores

MIJAMIN (4)
1Chr 24:9 Malchijah, the sixth to M,
Ezra 10:25 Ramiah, Izziah, Malchijah, M, Eleazar, Hashabiah,
Neh 10:7 Ginnethon, Baruch, Meshullam, Abijah, M,
12:5 Iddo, Ginnethoi, Abijah, M, Ma-adiah, Bilgah,

MIKLOTH (3)
1Chr 8:32 Gedor, Ahio, Zecher, and M (he was the father
9:37 Gedor, Ahio, Zechariah and M;
9:38 Zechariah and Mikloth; and M was the father of

MIKNEIAH (2)
1Chr 15:18 Ma-aseiah, Mattithiah, Eliphelehu, and M, and the
15:21 but Mattithiah, Eliphelehu, M, Obed-edom, Je-iel,

MILALAI
Neh 12:36 kinsmen, Shemaiah, Azarel, M, Gilalai, Maai,

MILCAH (11)
Gen 11:29 name of Nahor's wife, M, the daughter of Haran
11:29 Haran the father of M and Iscah.
22:20 told Abraham, "Behold, M also has borne children
22:23 These eight M bore to Nahor, Abraham's brother.
24:15 Bethuel the son of M, the wife of Nahor,
24:24 Bethuel the son of M, whom she bore to
24:47 Bethuel, Nahor's son, whom M bore to him.' So
Num 26:33 were Mahlah, Noah, Hoglah, M, and Tirzah.
27:1 were: Mahlah, Noah, Hoglah, M, and Tirzah.
36:11 Mahlah, Tirzah, Hoglah, M, and Noah, the daughters
Josh 17:3 daughters: Mahlah, Noah, Hoglah, M, and Tirzah.

MILCH (3)
Gen 32:15 and twenty rams, thirty M camels and their colts,
1Sam 6:7 new cart and two M cows upon which there
6:10 so, and took two M cows and yoked them

MILCOM (6)
1Kgs 11:5 the Sidonians, and after M the abomination of the
11:33 god of Moab, and M the god of the
2Kgs 23:13 of Moab, and for M the abomination of the
Jer 49:1 Why then has M dispossessed Gad, and his people
49:3 For M shall go into exile, with his priests
Zeph 1:5 and yet swear by M;

MILDEW (5)
Deut 28:22 with blasting, and with M; they shall pursue you
1Kgs 8:37 pestilence or blight or M or locust or caterpillar;
2Chr 6:28 pestilence or blight or M or locust or caterpillar;
Amos 4:9 you with blight and M; I laid waste your
Hag 2:17 toil with blight and M and hail; yet you

MILDNESS
Wis 12:18 dost judge with M, and with great forbearance

MILE (3)
2Mac 12:10 gone more than a M from there, on their
12:16 a quarter of a M wide, appeared to be
Mt 5:41 you to go one M, go with him two

MILES (7)
2Mac 12:9 seen in Jerusalem, thirty M distant.
12:17 they had gone ninety-five M from there, they came
12:29 Scythopolis, which is seventy-five M from Jerusalem.
Mt 5:41 to go one mile, go with him two M
Lk 24:13 named Emmaus, about seven M from Jerusalem,
Jn 6:19 about three or four M, they saw Jesus walking
11:18 near Jerusalem, about two M off,

MILETUS (3)
Acts 20:15 and the day after that we came to M
20:17 And from M he sent to Ephesus and called
2Tim 4:20 remained at Corinth; Trophimus I left ill at M

MILITARY (4)
Jud 11:8 informed and marvelous in M strategy.
1Mac 15:26 and gold and much M equipment.
2Mac 8:9 man of experience in M service.
Acts 25:23 audience hall with the M tribunes and the prominent

MILK (50)
Gen 18:8 he took curds, and M, and the calf which
49:12 red with wine, and his teeth white with M
Ex 3:8 a land flowing with M and honey, to the
3:17 a land flowing with M and honey."'
13:5 a land flowing with M and honey, you shall
23:19 shall not boil a kid in its mother's M
33:3 a land flowing with M and honey; but I
34:26 shall not boil a kid in its mother's M
Lev 20:24 a land flowing with M and honey.' I am
Num 13:27 us; it flows with M and honey, and this
14:8 land which flows with M and honey.
16:13 a land flowing with M and honey, to kill
16:14 a land flowing with M and honey, nor given
Deut 6:3 a land flowing with M and honey.
11:9 a land flowing with M and honey.
14:21 shall not boil a kid in its mother's M
26:9 a land flowing with M and honey.
26:15 a land flowing with M and honey.'
27:3 a land flowing with M and honey, as the
31:20 the land flowing with M and honey, which I
32:14 from the herd, and M from the flock, with
Josh 5:6 a land flowing with M and honey.
Judg 4:19 opened a skin of M and gave him a
5:25 and she gave him M, she brought him curds
Job 10:10 pour me out like M and curdle me like
29:6 steps were washed with M, and the rock poured
Prov 27:27 will be enough goats' M for your food, for
30:33 For pressing M produces curds, pressing the nose
Song 4:11 my bride; honey and M are under your tongue;
5:1 my honey, I drink my wine with my M
5:12 of water, bathed in M, fitly set.
Sir 39:26 and wheat flour and M and honey, the blood
46:8 a land flowing with M and honey.

M

Is 7:22 of the abundance of M which they give, he
28:9 are weaned from the M, those taken from the
55:1 Come, buy wine and M without money and without
60:16 You shall suck the M of nations, you shall
Jer 11:5 a land flowing with M and honey, as at
32:22 a land flowing with M and honey;
Lam 4:7 than snow, whiter than M; their bodies were more
Bar 1:20 a land flowing with M and honey.
Ezek 20:6 a land flowing with M and honey, the most
20:15 a land flowing with M and honey, the most
25:4 eat your fruit, and they shall drink your M
Joel 3:18 hills shall flow with M, and all the stream
1Cor 3:2 I fed you with M, not solid food; for
9:7 tends a flock without getting some of the M
Heb 5:12 You need M, not solid food;
5:13 one who lives on M is unskilled in the
1Pet 2:2 for the pure spiritual M, that by it you

MILL (5)
Ex 11:5 who is behind the M; and all the first-born
Deut 24:6 man shall take a M or an upper millstone
Judg 16:21 he ground at the M in the prison.
Lam 5:13 to grind at the M; and boys stagger under
Mt 24:41 be grinding at the M; one is taken and

MILLET
Ezek 4:9 barley, beans and lentils, M and spelt, and put

MILLION (3)
1Chr 21:5 Israel there were one M one hundred thousand men
22:14 talents of gold, a M talents of silver, and
2Chr 14:9 an army of a M men and three hundred

MILLO (7)
2Sam 5:9 round about from the M inward.
1Kgs 9:15 own house and the M and the wall of
9:24 had built for her; then he built the M
11:27 Solomon built the M, and closed up the breach
2Kgs 12:20 in the house of M, on the way that
1Chr 11:8 round about from the M in complete circuit; and
2Chr 32:5 and he strengthened the M in the city of

MILLS
Num 11:8 and ground it in M or beat it in

MILLSTONE (9)
Deut 24:6 mill or an upper M in pledge; for he
Judg 9:53 woman threw an upper M upon Abimelech's head,
2Sam 11:21 woman cast an upper M upon him from the
Job 41:24 hard as a stone, hard as the nether M
Mt 18:6 to have a great M fastened round his neck
Mk 9:42 him if a great M were hung round his
Lk 17:2 for him if a M were hung round his
Rev 18:21 stone like a great M and threw it into
18:22 the sound of the M shall be heard in

MILLSTONES (2)
Is 47:2 Take the M and grind meal, put off your
Jer 25:10 the grinding of the M and the light of

MINA
Ezek 45:12 ten shekels, and your M shall be fifty shekels.

MINAS (6)
1Kgs 10:17 of beaten gold; three M of gold went into
Ezra 2:69 of gold, five thousand M of silver, and one
Neh 7:71 two thousand two hundred M of silver.
7:72 of gold, two thousand M of silver, and sixty-seven
1Mac 14:24 shield weighing a thousand M, to confirm the
15:18 have brought a gold shield weighing a thousand M

MINCING
Is 3:16 wantonly with their eyes, M along as they go,

MIND (209)
Gen 37:11 him, but his father kept the saying in M
Ex 10:10 Look, you have some evil purpose in M
14:5 people had fled, the M of Pharaoh and his
28:3 endowed with an able M, that they make Aaron's
36:2 able man in whose M the LORD had put
Deut 5:29 they had such a M as this always, to
28:28 blindness and confusion of M;
29:4 not given you a M to understand, or eyes
30:1 you call them to M among all the nations
Judg 16:17 told her all his M, and said to her,
16:18 told her all his M, she sent and called
16:18 once, for he has told me all his M
1Sam 2:35 heart and in my M; and I will build
9:19 will tell you all that is on your M
9:20 do not set your M on them, for they
14:7 "Do all that your M inclines to; behold, I
14:7 you, as is your M so is mine."
2Sam 19:19 Jerusalem; let not the king bear it in M
1Kgs 3:9 servant therefore an understanding M to govern thy
3:12 a wise and discerning M, so that none like
4:29 measure, and largeness of M like the sand on
8:48 repent with all their M and with all their
10:2 she told him all that was on her M
10:24 his wisdom, which God had put into his M
11:11 this has been your M and you have not
2Kgs 6:11 And the M of the king of Syria was
9:15 "If this is your M, then let no one
1Chr 12:38 were of a single M to make David king.
22:19 Now set your M and heart to seek the
28:9 and with a willing M; for the LORD searches
28:12 that he had in M for the courts of
2Chr 6:38 repent with all their M and with all their
9:1 she told him all that was on her M
9:23 his wisdom, which God had put into his M
Neh 4:6 the people had a M to work.
6:8 you are inventing them out of your own M
7:5 put it into my M to assemble the nobles
Tob 4:19 not let them be blotted out of your M
Jud 8:14 and find out his M or comprehend his thought?
11:10 keep it in your M, for it is true:
16:9 her beauty captivated his M, and the sword severed
Esth 11:12 had it on his M and sought all day
Job 7:17 thou dost set thy M upon him,
23:14 me; and many such things are in his M
Ps 26:2 and try me; test my heart and my M
31:12 have passed out of M like one who is
64:6 For the inward M and heart of a man
77:11 I will call to M the deeds of the
78:42 did not keep in M his power, or the
110:4 will not change his M, "You are a priest
Prov 10:20 is choice silver; the M of the wicked is
11:20 Men of perverse M are an abomination to the
12:8 but one of perverse M is despised.
14:30 A tranquil M gives life to the flesh, but
14:33 Wisdom abides in the M of a man of
15:14 The M of him who has understanding seeks
15:28 The M of the righteous ponders how to answer,
16:1 The plans of the M belong to man, but
16:9 A man's M plans his way, but the LORD
16:23 The M of the wise makes his speech judicious,
17:16 hand to buy wisdom, when he has no M
17:20 A man of crooked M does not prosper, and
18:15 An intelligent M acquires knowledge, and the ear of
19:21 the plans in the M of a man, but
20:5 purpose in a man's M is like deep water,
22:17 wise, and apply your M to my knowledge;
23:12 Apply your M to instruction and your ear to
23:19 wise, and direct your M in the way.
23:33 strange things, and your M utter perverse things.
25:3 for depth, so the M of kings is unsearchable.
27:19 to face, so the M of man reflects the
28:26 trusts in his own M is a fool; but
Eccl 1:13 And I applied my M to seek and to
1:16 before me; and my M has had great experience
1:17 And I applied my M to know wisdom and
2:3 I searched with my M how to cheer my
2:3 body with wine—my M still guiding me with
2:23 in the night his M does not rest.
3:11 put eternity into man's M, yet so that he
7:7 wise man foolish, and a bribe corrupts the M
7:25 I turned my M to know and to search
7:28 the sum, which my M has sought repeatedly, but
8:5 no harm, and the M of a wise man
8:9 observed while applying my M to all that is
8:16 When I applied my M to know wisdom, and
11:10 Remove vexation from your M, and put away pain
Wis 4:12 is good, and roving desire perverts the innocent M
8:17 upon them in my M, that in kinship with
9:15 soul, and this earthy tent burdens the thoughtful M
Sir 1:25 Lord; do not approach him with a divided M
3:24 A stubborn M will be afflicted at the end,
3:25 A stubborn M will be burdened by troubles, and
3:27 The M of the intelligent man will ponder a
4:3 troubles of an angry M, nor delay your gift
6:37 give insight to your M, and your desire for
11:28 cage, so is the M of a proud man,
12:16 lips, but in his M he will plan to

14:21 who reflects in his M on her ways will
16:18 And no M will reflect on this.
17:5 them ears and a M for thinking.
21:14 The M of a fool is like a broken
21:26 The M of fools is in their mouth, but
21:26 the mouth of wise men is in their M
22:14 an earthquake; so the M firmly fixed on a
22:15 A M settled on an intelligent thought is like
23:2 thoughts, and the discipline of wisdom over my M
25:22 A dejected M, a gloomy face, and a wounded
27:6 a thought discloses the cultivation of a man's M
32:12 what you have in M, but do not sin
33:19 lest you change your M and must ask for
34:5 woman in travail the M has fancies.
34:6 do not give your M to them.
36:19 game, so an intelligent M detects false words.
36:20 A perverse M will cause grief, but a man
40:5 his bed, his sleep at night confuses his M
40:6 the visions of his M like one who has
42:15 will now call to M the works of the
43:18 its whiteness, and the M is amazed at its
Is 10:7 so intend, and his M does not so think;
10:7 it is in his M to destroy, and to
21:4 My M reels, horror has appalled me; the twilight
26:3 in perfect peace, whose M is stayed on thee,
32:4 The M of the rash will have good judgment,
32:6 speaks folly, and his M plots iniquity: to practice
33:18 Your M will muse on the terror: "Where is
44:20 on ashes; a deluded M has led him astray,
46:8 consider, recall it to M, you transgressors,
65:17 things shall not be remembered or come into M
Jer 3:16 shall not come to M, or be remembered, or
7:31 not command, nor did it come into my M
11:20 the heart and the M, let me see thy
12:3 me, and triest my M toward thee.
17:10 the LORD search the M and try the heart,
19:5 it come into my M;
20:12 the heart and the M, let me see thy
23:20 has executed and accomplished the intents of his M
30:24 has executed and accomplished the intents of his M
32:35 it enter into my M, that they should do
44:21 Did it not come into his M
51:50 Jerusalem come into your M:
Lam 3:21 this I call to M, and therefore I have
Ezek 11:5 I know the things that come into your M
20:32 "What is in your M shall never happen--the
38:10 will come into your M, and you will devise
40:4 ears, and set your M upon all that I
Dan 2:30 that you may know the thoughts of your M
4:16 the earth; let his M be changed from a
4:16 and let a beast's M be given to him;
5:21 among men, and his M was made like that
6:14 distressed, and set his M to deliver Daniel; and
7:4 a man; and the M of a man was
7:28 changed; but I kept the matter in my M
8:25 and in his own M he shall magnify himself.
10:12 that you set your M to understand and humbled
1Mac 3:31 was greatly perplexed in M, and determined to go
2Mac 4:46 for refreshment, induced the king to change his M
5:21 the sea, because his M was elated.
14:20 they were of one M, they agreed to the
15:8 but to keep in M the former times when
Mt 22:37 with all your soul, and with all your M
Mk 5:15 and in his right M, the man who had
12:30 and with all your M, and with all your
Lk 1:29 and considered in her M what sort of greeting
8:35 and in his right M; and they were afraid.
10:27 and with all your M; and your neighbor as
12:29 you are to drink, nor be of anxious M
Rom 1:28 up to a base M and to improper conduct.
7:23 the law of my M and making me captive
7:25 of God with my M, but with my flesh
8:6 To set the M on the flesh is death,
8:6 but to set the M on the Spirit is
8:7 For the M that is set on the flesh
8:27 knows what is the M of the Spirit, because
11:34 who has known the M of the Lord, or
12:2 the renewal of your M, that you may prove
14:5 every one be fully convinced in his own M
1Cor 1:10 united in the same M and the same judgment.
2:16 who has known the M of the Lord so
2:16 But we have the M of Christ.
7:21 Never M
14:14 spirit prays but my M is unfruitful.
14:15 will pray with the M also; I will sing
14:15 will sing with the M also.
14:19 five words with my M, in order to instruct
15:34 Come to your right M, and sin no more.
2Cor 2:1 I made up my M not to make you
2:13 the Lord; but my M could not rest because
5:13 are in our right M, it is for you.
7:13 of Titus, because his M has been set at
9:7 has made up his M, not reluctantly or under
Eph 2:3 desires of body and M, and so we were
Phil 1:27 one spirit, with one M striving side by side
2:2 being of the same M, having the same love,
2:2 love, being in full accord and of one M
2:5 Have this M among yourselves, which is yours in
Col 1:21 estranged and hostile in M, doing evil deeds,
2:18 reason by his sensuous M,
1Thes 4:11 to live quietly, to M your own affairs, and
2Thes 2:2 be quickly shaken in M or excited, either by
1Tim 6:5 who are depraved in M and bereft of the
2Tim 3:8 truth, men of corrupt M and counterfeit faith;
Heb 7:21 will not change his M, 'Thou art a priest
Jas 4:8 and purify your hearts, you men of double M
1Pet 3:8 the brethren, a tender heart and a humble M
2Pet 3:1 have aroused your sincere M by way of reminder;
Rev 2:23 am he who searches M and heart, and I
17:9 This calls for a M with wisdom: the seven
17:13 These are of one M and give over their
17:17 by being of one M and giving over their

MINDED (2)

Phil 3:15 are mature be thus M; and if in anything
3:15 anything you are otherwise M, God will reveal that

MINDFUL (13)

1Chr 16:15 He is M of his covenant for ever, of
Neh 9:17 obey, and were not M of the wonders which
Tob 2:2 may find who is M of the Lord, and
Ps 8:4 man that thou art M of him, and the
9:12 who avenges blood is M of them; he does
25:6 Be M of thy mercy, O LORD, and of
105:8 He is M of his covenant for ever, of
111:5 him; he is ever M of his covenant.
115:12 The LORD has been M of us; he will
Sir 4:25 the truth, but be M of your ignorance.
Zeph 2:7 their God will be M of them and restore
Heb 2:6 man that thou art M of him, or the
1Pet 2:19 one is approved if, M of God, he endures

MINDS (34)

Job 17:4 thou hast closed their M to understanding, therefore
Ps 7:9 thou who triest the M and hearts, thou righteous
Prov 15:7 knowledge; not so the M of fools.
24:2 with them; for their M devise violence, and their
Wis 19:2 they would change their M and pursue them.
Sir 8:2 and has perverted the M of kings.
21:17 and they will ponder his words in their M
Is 44:18 cannot see, and their M, so that they cannot
Jer 14:14 worthless divination, and the deceit of their own M
23:16 visions of their own M, not from the mouth
Ezek 13:2 out of their own M: 'Hear the word of
13:17 out of their own M; prophesy against them
Dan 11:27 the two kings, their M shall be bent on
13:9 And they perverted their M and turned away their
Lk 21:14 it therefore in your M, not to meditate beforehand
24:45 he opened their M to understand the scriptures,
Acts 14:2 Gentiles and poisoned their M against the brethren.
15:24 with words, unsettling your M, although we gave
28:6 him, they changed their M and said that he
Rom 1:21 thinking and their senseless M were darkened.
8:5 the flesh set their M on the things of
8:5 the Spirit set their M on the things of
2Cor 3:14 But their M were hardened; for to this day,
3:15 veil lies over their M;
4:4 world has blinded the M of the unbelievers, to
Eph 4:17 the futility of their M;
4:23 the spirit of your M,
Phil 3:19 in their shame, with M set on earthly things.
4:7 your hearts and your M in Christ Jesus.
Col 3:2 Set your M on things that are above, not
Tit 1:14 is pure; their very M and consciences are corrupted.
Heb 8:10 my laws into their M, and write them on
10:16 on their hearts, and write them on their M
1Pet 1:13 Therefore gird up your M, be sober, set your

MINES

1Mac 8:3 the silver and gold M there,

MINGLE (2)
Ps 102:9 ashes like bread, and M tears with my drink,
Rev 8:3 given much incense to M with the prayers of

MINGLED (8)
Ex 29:40 measure of fine flour M with a fourth of
Deut 22:11 shall not wear a M stuff, wool and linen
Ps 106:35 commanded them, but they M with the nations and
Is 19:14 The LORD has M within her a spirit of
Mt 27:34 him wine to drink, M with gall; but when
Mk 15:23 they offered him wine M with myrrh; but he
Lk 13:1 whose blood Pilate had M with their sacrifices.
Rev 15:2 a sea of glass M with fire, and those

MINGLING
2Mac 14:38 when there was no M with the Gentiles, he

MINIAMIN (3)
2Chr 31:15 Eden, M, Jeshua, Shemaiah, Amariah, and
Neh 12:17 of Abijah, Zichri; of M, of Moadiah, Piltai;
12:41 the priests Eliakim, Ma-aseiah, M, Micaiah,

MINISTER (60)
Ex 28:43 near the altar to M in the holy place;
29:30 tent of meeting to M in the holy place.
30:20 near the altar to M, to burn an offering
Num 3:3 whom he ordained to M in the priest's office.
3:6 priest, that they may M to him.
3:7 of meeting, as they M at the tabernacle;
3:8 of Israel as they M at the tabernacle.
3:31 with which the priests M, and the screen; all
8:26 serve no more, but M to their brethren in
11:28 son of Nun, the M of Moses, one of
16:9 before the congregation to M to them;
18:2 may join you, and M to you while you
Deut 10:8 before the LORD to M to him and to
17:12 priest who stands to M there before the LORD
18:5 tribes, to stand and M in the name of
18:7 choose, then he may M in the name of
18:7 Levites who stand to M there before the LORD.
21:5 has chosen them to M to him and to
Josh 1:1 son of Nun, Moses' M,
1Kgs 8:11 could not stand to M because of the cloud;
1Chr 15:2 the LORD and to M to him for ever."
16:37 of the LORD to M continually before the ark
23:13 before the LORD, and M to him and pronounce
2Chr 5:14 could not stand to M because of the cloud;
29:11 in his presence, to M to him, and to
31:2 and peace offerings, to M in the gates of
Neh 10:36 to the priests who M in the house of
10:39 and the priests that M, and the gatekeepers and
Jud 11:13 for the priests who M in the presence of
Ps 101:6 that is blameless shall M to me.
Sir 4:14 who serve her will M to the Holy One;
45:15 days of heaven, to M to the Lord and
Is 56:6 to the LORD, to M to him, to love
60:7 rams of Nebaioth shall M to you; they shall
60:10 and their kings shall M to you; for in
Jer 33:22 the Levitical priests who M to me."
Ezek 40:46 to the LORD to M to him.
42:14 garments in which they M, for these are holy;
43:19 near to me to M to me, says the
44:15 near to me to M to me; and they
44:16 approach my table, to M to me, and they
44:17 on them, while they M at the gates of
44:27 the inner court, to M in the holy place,
45:4 for the priests, who M in the sanctuary and
45:4 approach the LORD to M to him; and it
45:5 for the Levites who M at the temple, as
46:24 kitchens where those who M at the temple shall
1Mac 10:42 to the priests who M there.
Mt 25:44 prison, and did not M to thee?'
Acts 8:27 Ethiopian, a eunuch, a M of the Candace, queen
Rom 15:16 God to be a M of Christ Jesus to
Eph 3:7 I was made a M according to the gift
6:21 beloved brother and faithful M in the Lord will
Phil 2:25 and your messenger and M to my need,
Col 1:7 He is a faithful M of Christ on our
1:23 heaven, and of which I, Paul, became a M
1:25 which I became a M according to the divine
4:7 beloved brother and faithful M and fellow servant in
1Tim 4:6 will be a good M of Christ Jesus, nourished
Heb 8:2 Majesty in heaven, a M in the sanctuary and

MINISTERED (16)
Ex 38:8 the ministering women who M at the door of
Deut 10:6 and his son Eleazar M as priest in his
Judg 20:28 Eleazar, son of Aaron, M before it in those
1Sam 2:11 And the boy M to the LORD, in the
1Kgs 1:4 the king's nurse and M to him; but the
19:21 went after Elijah, and M to him.
1Chr 6:32 They M with song before the tabernacle of the
Neh 12:44 rejoiced over the priests and the Levites who M
Tob 1:7 sons of Levi who M at Jerusalem; a second
Jud 4:14 before the Lord and M to the Lord, with
Sir 24:10 the holy tabernacle I M before him, and so
Ezek 44:12 Because they M to them before their idols and
Mt 4:11 behold, angels came and M to him.
Mk 1:13 beasts; and the angels M to him.
15:40 Galilee, followed him, and M to him; and also
Acts 20:34 know that these hands M to my necessities, and

MINISTERING (15)
Ex 35:19 finely wrought garments for M in the holy place,
38:8 the mirrors of the M women who ministered at
39:1 finely wrought garments, for M in the holy place;
39:26 of the robe for M; as the LORD had
39:41 finely worked garments for M in the holy place,
1Sam 2:18 Samuel was M before the LORD, a boy girded
3:1 the boy Samuel was M to the LORD under
1Kgs 1:15 Abishag the Shunammite was M to the king).
1Chr 26:12 as their brethren did, M in the house of
2Chr 13:10 We have priests M to the LORD who are
23:6 except the priests and M Levites; they may enter,
Wis 16:21 children; and the bread, M to the desire of
Ezek 44:19 which they have been M, and lay them in
Mt 27:55 followed Jesus from Galilee, M to him;
Heb 1:14 Are they not all M spirits sent forth to

MINISTERS (17)
Ex 28:35 upon Aaron when he M, and its sound shall
1Chr 16:4 of the Levites as M before the ark of
2Chr 29:11 and to be his M and burn incense to
Ezra 8:17 namely, to send us M for the house of
Ps 103:21 all his hosts, his M that do his will!
104:4 the winds thy messengers, fire and flame thy M
Sir 7:30 love your Maker, and do not forsake his M
Is 61:6 of you as the M of our God; you
Jer 33:21 and my covenant with the Levitical priests my M
Ezek 44:11 They shall be M in my sanctuary, having oversight
Joel 1:9 The priests mourn, the M of the LORD.
1:12 O priests, wail, O M of the altar.
1:12 night in sackcloth, O M of my God!
2:17 let the priests, the M of the LORD, weep
Lk 1:2 beginning were eyewitnesses and M of the word,
Rom 13:6 for the authorities are M of God, attending to
2Cor 3:6 us competent to be M of a new covenant,

MINISTRY (17)
2Chr 7:6 offered praises by their M; opposite them the priests
8:14 offices of praise and M before the priests as
Wis 18:21 the shield of his M, prayer and propitiation by
Lk 3:23 when he began his M, was about thirty years
Acts 1:17 us, and was allotted his share in this M
1:25 the place in this M and apostleship from which
6:4 prayer and to the M of the word."
20:24 my course and the M which I received from
21:19 God had done among the Gentiles through his M
Rom 11:13 Gentiles, I magnify my M
2Cor 4:1 Therefore, having this M by the mercy of God,
5:18 and gave us the M of reconciliation;
6:3 be found with our M,
Eph 4:12 for the work of M, for building up the
Col 4:17 that you fulfil the M which you have received
2Tim 4:5 do the work of an evangelist, fulfil your M
Heb 8:6 Christ has obtained a M which is as much

MINNI
Jer 51:27 her the kingdoms, Ararat, M, and Ashkenaz; appoint

MINNITH
Judg 11:33 to the neighborhood of M, twenty cities, and as

MINSTREL (2)
2Kgs 3:15 But now bring me a M
3:15 And when the M played, the power of the

MINSTRELS (2)
Ps 68:25 singers in front, the M last, between them maidens
Rev 18:22 sound of harpers and M, of flute players and

MINT (3)

1Mac	15:6	I permit you to M your own coinage as
Mt	23:22	for you tithe M and dill and cummin, and
Lk	11:42	for you tithe M and rue and every herb,

MIRACLE

Ex	7:9	yourselves by working a M then you shall say

MIRACLES (12)

Ex	4:21	before Pharaoh all the M which I have put
Ps	78:11	had done, and the M that he had shown
	78:43	in Egypt, and his M in the fields of
	105:5	he has done, his M, and the judgments he
	105:27	signs among them, and M in the land of
Acts	8:13	seeing signs and great M performed, he was amazed.
	19:11	And God did extraordinary M by the hands of
1Cor	12:10	another the working of M, to another prophecy, to
	12:28	teachers, then workers of M, then healers, helpers,
	12:29	Do all work M
Gal	3:5	to you and works M among you do so
Heb	2:4	and wonders and various M and by gifts of

MIRE (13)

2Sam	22:43	them down like the M of the streets.
Job	30:19	cast me into the M, and I have become
	41:30	spreads himself like a threshing sledge on the M
Ps	18:42	them out like the M of the streets.
	69:2	I sink in deep M, where there is no
	69:14	from sinking in the M; let me be delivered
Is	10:6	them down like the M of the streets.
	57:20	its waters toss up M and dirt.
Jer	38:6	the cistern, but only M, and Jeremiah sank in
	38:6	but only mire, and Jeremiah sank in the M
	38:22	are sunk in the M, they turn away from
Mic	7:10	trodden down like the M of the streets.
2Pet	2:22	sow is washed only to wallow in the M

MIRIAM (15)

Ex	15:20	Then M, the prophetess, the sister of Aaron, took
	15:21	And M sang to them: "Sing to the LORD,
Num	12:1	M and Aaron spoke against Moses because of the
	12:4	and to Aaron and M, "Come out, you three,
	12:5	and called Aaron and M; and they both came
	12:10	over the tent, behold, M was leprous, as white
	12:10	And Aaron turned towards M, and behold, she was
	12:15	So M was shut up outside the camp seven
	12:15	on the march till M was brought in again.
	20:1	stayed in Kadesh; and M died there, and was
	26:59	Aaron and Moses and M their sister.
Deut	24:9	your God did to M on the way as
1Chr	4:17	she conceived and bore M, Shammai, and Ishbah,
	6:3	The children of Amram: Aaron, Moses, and M
Mic	6:4	and I sent before you Moses, Aaron, and M

MIRMAH

1Chr	8:10	Jobab, Zibi-a, Mesha, Malcam, Jeuz, Sachia, and M

MIRROR (5)

Job	37:18	spread out the skies, hard as a molten M
Wis	7:26	eternal light, a spotless M of the working of
Sir	12:11	who has polished a M, and you will know
1Cor	13:12	we see in a M dimly, but then face
Jas	1:22	natural face in a M;

MIRRORS

Ex	38:8	of bronze, from the M of the ministering women

MIRTH (12)

Gen	31:27	sent you away with M and songs, with tambourine
Ps	137:3	songs, and our tormentors, M, saying, "Sing us one
Eccl	7:4	heart of fools is in the house of M
Is	24:8	The M of the timbrels is stilled, the noise
	24:8	jubilant has ceased, the M of the lyre is
Jer	7:34	Jerusalem the voice of M and the voice of
	16:9	days, the voice of M and the voice of
	25:10	them the voice of M and the voice of
	33:11	again the voice of M and the voice of
Bar	2:23	Jerusalem the voice of M and the voice of
Ezek	21:10	Or do we make M
Hos	2:11	end to all her M, her feasts, her new

MIRY (3)

Ps	40:2	pit, out of the M bog, and set my
Dan	2:41	iron mixed with the M clay.
	2:43	the iron mixed with M clay, so they will

MISCARRIAGE (2)

Ex	21:22	that there is a M, and yet no harm
2Kgs	2:21	henceforth neither death nor M shall come from it."

MISCARRIED

Gen	31:38	your she-goats have not M, and I have not

MISCARRYING

Hos	9:14	Give them a M womb and dry breasts.

MISCHANCE

Ps	144:14	with young, suffering no M or failure in bearing;

MISCHIEF (18)

Judg	15:3	regard to the Philistines, when I do them M
1Kgs	11:25	days of Solomon, doing M as Hadad did; and
Job	15:35	They conceive M and bring forth evil and their
Ps	7:14	and is pregnant with M, and brings forth lies.
	7:16	His M returns upon his own head, and on
	10:7	under his tongue are M and iniquity.
	21:11	you, if they devise M, they will not succeed.
	28:3	with their neighbors, while M is in their hearts.
	36:3	of his mouth are M and deceit; he has
	36:4	He plots M while on his bed; he sets
	41:6	while his heart gathers M; when he goes out,
	52:1	O mighty man, of M done against the godly?
	55:10	on its walls; and M and trouble are within
	94:20	with thee, who frame M by statute?
	140:9	their head, let the M of their lips overwhelm
Prov	24:2	minds devise violence, and their lips talk of M
Is	59:4	speak lies, they conceive M and bring forth iniquity.
Dan	11:27	shall be bent on M; they shall speak lies

MISCHIEF-MAKER (2)

Prov	24:8	plans to do evil will be called a M
1Pet	4:15	a wrongdoer, or a M;

MISCHIEVOUS

Prov	17:4	gives heed to a M tongue.

MISDEEDS

Heb	10:17	their sins and their M no more."

MISERABLE (8)

Job	16:2	heard many such things; M comforters are you all.
Wis	3:11	for whoever despises wisdom and instruction is M
	13:10	But M, with their hopes set on dead things,
	15:14	most foolish, and more M than an infant, are
Sir	29:24	It is a M life to go from house
	30:17	is better than a M life, and eternal rest
2Mac	5:8	Finally he met a M end.
Mt	21:41	those wretches to a M death, and let out

MISERIES

Jas	5:1	and howl for the M that are coming upon

MISERLY

Prov	28:22	A M man hastens after wealth, and does not

MISERY (11)

Judg	10:16	became indignant over the M of Israel.
Job	3:20	him that is in M, and life to the
	7:3	emptiness, and nights of M are apportioned to me.
	11:16	You will forget your M; you will remember it
	20:22	all the force of M will come upon him.
Ps	31:10	fails because of my M, and my bones waste
Prov	31:7	poverty, and remember their M no more.
Sir	11:25	The M of an hour makes one forget luxury,
Bar	2:25	They perished in great M, by famine and sword
2Mac	6:9	could see, therefore, the M that had come upon
Rom	3:16	paths are ruin and M,

MISFORTUNE (11)

Num	23:21	He has not beheld M in Jacob; nor has
1Kgs	5:4	on every side; there is neither adversary nor M
Job	12:5	there is contempt for M; it is ready for
Prov	13:21	M pursues sinners, but prosperity rewards the
Wis	14:21	men, in bondage to M or to royal authority,
Obad	1:12	the day of his M; you should not have
2Mac	4:1	and had been the real cause of the M
	5:6	kindred is the greatest M, but imagining that he
	12:30	them in times of M,
	14:8	our whole nation is now in no small M
Acts	28:6	time and saw no M come to him, they

MITHNITE
1Chr 11:43 Maacah, and Joshaphat the M,

MITHREDATH (2)
Ezra 1:8 out in charge of M the treasurer, who counted
4:7 of Artaxerxes, Bishlam and M and Tabeel and the

MITYLENE
Acts 20:14 we took him on board and came to M

MIX (5)
Sir 18:14 My son, do not M reproach with your good
Dan 2:43 clay, so they will M with one another in
2:43 as iron does not M with clay.
14:11 forth the food and M and place the wine,
Rev 18:6 double for her deeds; M a double draught for

MIXED (56)
Ex 12:38 A M multitude also went up with them, and
29:2 unleavened bread, unleavened cakes M with oil, and
Lev 2:4 cakes of fine flour M with oil, or unleavened
2:5 of fine flour unleavened, M with oil;
6:21 shall bring it well M, in baked pieces like
7:10 And every cereal offering, M with oil or dry,
7:12 thank offering unleavened cakes M with oil,
7:12 of fine flour well M with oil.
9:4 and a cereal offering M with oil; for today
14:10 ephah of fine flour M with oil, and one
14:21 ephah of fine flour M with oil for a
23:13 ephah of fine flour M with oil, to be
Num 6:15 cakes of fine flour M with oil, and unleavened
7:13 full of fine flour M with oil for a
7:19 full of fine flour M with oil for a
7:25 full of fine flour M with oil for a
7:31 full of fine flour M with oil for a
7:37 full of fine flour M with oil for a
7:43 full of fine flour M with oil for a
7:49 full of fine flour M with oil for a
7:55 full of fine flour M with oil for a
7:61 full of fine flour M with oil for a
7:67 full of fine flour M with oil for a
7:73 full of fine flour M with oil for a
7:79 full of fine flour M with oil for a
8:8 offering of fine flour M with oil, and you
15:4 ephah of fine flour, M with a fourth of
15:6 ephah of fine flour, M with a third of
15:9 ephah of fine flour, M with half a hin
28:5 for a cereal offering, M with a fourth of
28:9 for a cereal offering, M with oil, and its
28:12 for a cereal offering, M with oil, for each
28:12 for a cereal offering, M with oil, for the
28:13 tenth of fine flour M with oil as a
28:20 offering of fine flour M with oil; three tenths
28:28 offering of fine flour M with oil, three tenths
29:3 offering of fine flour M with oil, three tenths
29:9 offering of fine flour M with oil, three tenths
29:14 offering of fine flour M with oil, three tenths
Josh 23:7 you may not be M with these nations left
1Chr 23:29 baked offering, the offering M with oil, and all
Ezra 9:2 the holy race has M itself with the peoples
Jud 2:20 with them went a M crowd like a swarm
Ps 75:8 with foaming wine, well M; and he will pour
Prov 9:2 her beasts, she has M her wine, she has
9:5 bread and drink of the wine I have M
23:30 who go to try M wine.
Song 7:2 bowl that never lacks M wine.
Is 1:22 become dross, your wine M with water.
65:11 and fill cups of M wine for Destiny;
Jer 25:24 the kings of the M tribes that dwell in
Dan 2:41 as you saw iron M with the miry clay.
2:43 you saw the iron M with miry clay, so
2Mac 15:39 water alone, while wine M with water is sweet
Rev 8:7 followed hail and fire, M with blood, which fell
18:6 double draught for her in the cup she M

MIXES
Hos 7:9 Ephraim M himself with the peoples; Ephraim is a

MIXING (2)
1Chr 9:30 the priests, prepared the M of the spices,
Is 5:22 and valiant men in M strong drink,

MIXTURE
Jn 19:39 night, came bringing a M of myrrh and aloes,

MIZAR
Ps 42:6 land of Jordan and of Hermon, from Mount M

MIZPAH (44)
Gen 31:49 Galeed, and the pillar M, for he said, "The
Josh 11:3 the Hivites under Hermon in the land of M
Judg 10:17 of Israel came together, and they encamped at M
11:11 spoke all his words before the LORD at M
11:29 and passed on to M of Gilead, and from
11:29 of Gilead, and from M of Gilead he passed
11:34 to his home at M; and behold, his daughter
20:1 assembled as one man to the LORD at M
20:3 had gone up to M And the people of
21:1 Israel had sworn at M, "No one of us
21:5 to the LORD to M, saying, "He shall be
21:8 did not come up to the LORD to M
1Sam 7:5 "Gather all Israel at M, and I will pray
7:6 So they gathered at M, and drew water and
7:6 And Samuel judged the people of Israel at M
7:7 Israel had gathered at M, the lords of the
7:11 Israel went out of M and pursued the Philistines,
7:12 set it up between M and Jeshanah, and called
7:16 to Bethel, Gilgal, and M; and he judged Israel
10:17 to the LORD at M;
1Kgs 15:22 them King Asa built Geba of Benjamin and M
2Kgs 25:23 men to Gedaliah at M, namely, Ishmael the son
25:25 and the Chaldeans who were with him at M
2Chr 16:6 building, and with them he built Geba and M
Neh 3:7 of Gibeon and of M, who were under the
3:15 of the district of M, repaired the Fountain Gate;
3:19 of Jeshua, ruler of M, repaired another section
Jer 40:6 son of Ahikam, at M, and dwelt with him
40:8 went to Gedaliah at M --Ishmael the son of
40:10 I will dwell at M, to stand for you
40:12 Judah, to Gedaliah at M; and they gathered wine
40:13 came to Gedaliah at M
40:15 secretly to Gedaliah at M, "Let me go and
41:1 men to Gedaliah the son of Ahikam, at M
41:1 bread together there at M,
41:3 were with Gedaliah at M, and the Chaldean soldiers
41:6 Nethaniah came out from M to meet them, weeping
41:10 people who were in M, the king's daughters and
41:10 who were left at M, whom Nebuzaradan, the captain
41:14 carried away captive from M turned about and came
41:16 carried away captive from M after he had slain
Hos 5:1 been a snare at M, and a net spread
1Mac 3:46 and went to M, opposite Jerusalem, because Israel
3:46 Israel formerly had a place of prayer in M

MIZPEH (4)
Josh 11:8 as the valley of M; and they smote them,
15:38 Zenan, Hadashah, Migdal-gad, Dilean, M, Joktheel,
18:26 Gibeon, Ramah, Be-eroth, M, Chephirah, Mozah,
1Sam 22:3 went from there to M of Moab; and he

MIZZAH (3)
Gen 36:13 the sons of Reuel: Nahath, Zerah, Shammah, and M
36:17 Zerah, Shammah, and M; these are the chiefs
1Chr 1:37 The sons of Reuel: Nahath, Zerah, Shammah, and M

MNASON
Acts 21:16 to the house of M of Cyprus, an early

MOAB (171)
Gen 19:37 and called his name M; he is the father
36:35 in the country of M, reigned in his stead,
Ex 15:15 dismayed; the leaders of M, trembling seizes them;
Num 21:11 wilderness which is opposite M, toward the sunrise.
21:13 is the boundary of M, between Moab and the
21:13 boundary of Moab, between M and the Amorites.
21:15 of Ar, and leans to the border of M
21:20 in the region of M by the top of
21:26 the former king of M and taken all his
21:28 It devoured Ar of M, the lords of the
21:29 Woe to you, O M
22:1 in the plains of M beyond the Jordan at
22:3 And M was in great dread of the people,
22:3 because they were many; M was overcome with fear
22:4 And M said to the elders of Midian, "This
22:4 who was king of M at that time,
22:7 So the elders of M and the elders of
22:8 so the princes of M stayed with Balaam.
22:10 of Zippor, king of M, has sent to me,
22:14 So the princes of M rose and went to
22:21 his ass, and went with the princes of M
22:36 at the city of M, on the boundary formed

23:6 all the princes of M were standing beside his
23:7 me, the king of M from the eastern mountains:
23:17 and the princes of M with him.
24:17 crush the forehead of M, and break down all
25:1 to play the harlot with the daughters of M
26:3 in the plains of M by the Jordan at
26:63 in the plains of M by the Jordan at
31:12 on the plains of M by the Jordan at
33:44 and encamped at Iye-abarim, in the territory of M
33:48 in the plains of M by the Jordan at
33:49 as far as Abel-shittim in the plains of M
33:50 in the plains of M by the Jordan at
35:1 in the plains of M by the Jordan at
36:13 in the plains of M by the Jordan at
Deut 1:5 in the land of M, Moses undertook to explain
2:8 went in the direction of the wilderness of M
2:9 me, 'Do not harass M or contend with them
2:18 over the boundary of M at Ar;
29:1 in the land of M, besides the covenant which
32:49 in the land of M, opposite Jericho; and view
34:1 from the plains of M to Mount Nebo, to
34:5 in the land of M, according to the word
34:6 in the land of M opposite Beth-peor; but no
34:8 in the plains of M thirty days; then the
Josh 13:32 in the plains of M, beyond the Jordan east
24:9 of Zippor, king of M, arose and fought against
Judg 3:12 Eglon the king of M against Israel, because they
3:14 Eglon the king of M eighteen years.
3:15 tribute by him to Eglon the king of M
3:17 he presented the tribute to Eglon king of M
3:30 So M was subdued that day under the hand
10:6 Sidon, the gods of M, the gods of the
11:15 away the land of M or the land of
11:17 to the king of M, but he would not
11:18 and the land of M, and arrived on the
11:18 of the land of M, and camped on the
11:18 enter the territory of M, for the Arnon was
11:18 Moab, for the Arnon was the boundary of M
11:25 than Balak the son of Zippor, king of M
Ruth 1:1 in the country of M, he and his wife
1:2 into the country of M and remained there.
1:6 from the country of M, for she had heard
1:6 in the country of M that the LORD had
1:22 with her, who returned from the country of M
2:6 came back with Naomi from the country of M
4:3 from the country of M, is selling the parcel
1Sam 12:9 of the king of M; and they fought against
14:47 on every side, against M, against the Ammonites,
22:3 there to Mizpeh of M; and he said to
22:3 to the king of M, "Pray let my father
22:4 with the king of M, and they stayed with
2Sam 8:2 And he defeated M, and measured them with a
8:12 subdued, from Edom, M, the Ammonites, the
23:20 of great deeds; he smote two ariels of M
1Kgs 11:7 Chemosh the abomination of M, and for Molech the
11:33 Chemosh the god of M, and Milcom the god
2Kgs 1:1 the death of Ahab, M rebelled against Israel.
3:4 Now Mesha king of M was a sheep breeder;
3:5 died, the king of M rebelled against the king
3:7 Judah, "The king of M has rebelled against me;
3:7 will you go with me to battle against M
3:10 kings to give them into the hand of M
3:13 kings to give them into the hand of M
3:23 Now then, M, to the spoil!"
3:26 When the king of M saw that the battle
23:13 Chemosh the abomination of M, and for Milcom the
1Chr 1:46 in the country of M, reigned in his stead;
4:22 Saraph, who ruled in M and returned to Lehem
8:8 in the country of M after he had sent
11:22 of great deeds; he smote two ariels of M
18:2 And he defeated M, and the Moabites became
18:11 from Edom, M, the Ammonites, the Philistines,
2Chr 20:10 men of Ammon and M and Mount Seir, whom
20:22 the men of Ammon, M, and Mount Seir, who
20:23 men of Ammon and M rose against the inhabitants
Neh 13:23 of Ashdod, Ammon, and M;
Jud 1:12 of the land of M, and the people of
5:2 all the princes of M and the commanders of
5:22 the seacoast and from M insisted that he must
Ps 60:8 M is my washbasin; upon Edom I cast my
83:6 Edom and the Ishmaelites, M and the Hagrites,
108:9 M is my washbasin; upon Edom I cast my
Is 11:14 hand against Edom and M, and the Ammonites shall
15:1 An oracle concerning M
15:1 waste in a night M is undone; because Kir
15:1 waste in a night M is undone.
15:2 Nebo and over Medeba M wails.
15:4 the armed men of M cry aloud; his soul
15:5 heart cries out for M; his fugitives flee to
15:8 round the land of M; the wailing reaches to
15:9 lion for those of M who escape, for the
16:2 are the daughters of M at the fords of
16:4 let the outcasts of M sojourn among you; be
16:6 of the pride of M, how proud he was;
16:7 Therefore let M wail, let every one wail for
16:7 let Moab wail, let every one wail for M
16:11 like a lyre for M, and my heart for
16:12 And when M presents himself, when he wearies
16:13 the LORD spoke concerning M in the past.
16:14 hireling, the glory of M will be brought into
25:10 on this mountain, and M shall be trodden down
Jer 9:26 the sons of Ammon, M, and all who dwell
25:21 remnant of Ashdod); Edom, M, and the sons of
27:3 Edom, the king of M, the king of the
40:11 Jews who were in M and among the Ammonites
48:1 Concerning M
48:2 down; the renown of M is no more.
48:4 'Desolation and great destruction!' M is destroyed; a
48:9 "Give wings to M, for she would fly away;
48:11 M has been at ease from his youth and
48:13 Then M shall be ashamed of Chemosh, as the
48:15 The destroyer of M and his cities has come
48:16 The calamity of M is near at hand and
48:18 For the destroyer of M has come up against
48:20 say, 'What has happened?' M is put to shame,
48:20 by the Arnon, that M is laid waste.
48:24 of the land of M, far and near.
48:25 The horn of M is cut off, and his
48:26 the LORD; so that M shall wallow in his
48:28 and dwell in the rock, O inhabitants of M
48:29 of the pride of M --he is very proud--
48:31 Therefore I wail for M; I cry out for
48:31 cry out for all M; for the men of
48:33 the fruitful land of M; I have made the
48:35 to an end in M, says the LORD, him
48:36 my heart moans for M like a flute, and
48:38 all the housetops of M and in the squares
48:38 for I have broken M like a vessel for
48:39 How M has turned his back in shame!
48:39 So M has become a derision and a horror
48:40 spread his wings against M;
48:41 of the warriors of M shall be in that
48:42 woman in her pangs; M shall be destroyed and
48:43 and snare are before you, O inhabitant of M
48:44 bring these things upon M in the year of
48:45 destroyed the forehead of M, the crown of the
48:46 Woe to you, O M
48:47 restore the fortunes of M in the latter days,
48:47 Thus far is the judgment on M
Ezek 25:8 the Lord GOD: Because M said, Behold, the house
25:9 open the flank of M from the cities on
25:11 the nations, and I will execute judgments upon M
Dan 11:41 his hand: Edom and M and the main part
Amos 2:1 "For three transgressions of M, and for four, I
2:2 send a fire upon M, and it shall devour
2:2 strongholds of Kerioth, and M shall die amid uproar,
Mic 6:5 what Balak king of M devised, and what Balaam
Zeph 2:8 heard the taunts of M and the revilings of
2:9 the God of Israel, M shall become like Sodom,

MOABITE (6)

Deut 23:3 "No Ammonite or M shall enter the assembly of
Ruth 1:4 These took M wives; the name of the one
2:6 answered, "It is the M maiden, who came back
1Kgs 11:1 daughter of Pharaoh, and M, Ammonite, Edomite,
1Chr 11:46 Elna-am, and Ithmah the M,
Neh 13:1 that no Ammonite or M should ever enter the

MOABITES (19)

Gen 19:37 the father of the M to this day.
Deut 2:11 as Rephaim, but the M call them Emim.
2:29 in Seir and the M who live in Ar
Judg 3:28 given your enemies the M into your hand." So
3:28 the Jordan against the M, and allowed not a
3:29 ten thousand of the M, all strong, able-bodied men;
2Sam 8:2 And the M became servants to David and brought
2Kgs 3:18 will also give the M into your hand,
3:21 When all the M heard that the kings had
3:22 upon the water, the M saw the water opposite
3:24 rose and attacked the M, till they fled before
3:24 went forward, slaughtering the M as they went.
13:20 Now bands of M used to invade the land

24:2 and bands of the M, and bands of the
1Chr 18:2 defeated Moab, and the M became servants to David
2Chr 20:1 After this the M and Ammonites, and with them
Ezra 9:1 Jebusites, the Ammonites, the M, the Egyptians, and
Jud 6:1 Achior and all the M in the presence of
7:8 the leaders of the M and the commanders of

MOABITESS (6)
Ruth 1:22 returned, and Ruth the M her daughter-in-law with
2:2 And Ruth the M said to Naomi, "Let me
2:21 And Ruth the M said, "Besides, he said to
4:5 also buying Ruth the M, the widow of the
4:10 Also Ruth the M, the widow of Mahlon, I
2Chr 24:26 and Jehozabad the son of Shimrith the M

MOADIAH
Neh 12:17 Zichri; of Miniamin, of M, Piltai;

MOAN (5)
Ps 55:17 utter my complaint and M, and he will hear
77:3 of God, and I M; I meditate, and my
Is 38:14 crane I clamor, I M like a dove.
59:11 growl like bears, we M and moan like doves;
59:11 bears, we moan and M like doves; we look

MOANING (4)
Ps 6:6 am weary with my M; every night I flood
Is 29:2 and there shall be M and lamentation, and she
Ezek 7:16 valleys, all of them M, every one over his
Nah 2:7 her maidens lamenting, M like doves, and beating

MOANS (3)
Is 16:11 Therefore my soul M like a lyre for Moab,
Jer 48:36 Therefore my heart M for Moab like a flute,
48:36 flute, and my heart M like a flute for

MOAT
Dan 9:25 again with squares and M, but in a troubled

MOB (2)
Sir 26:5 the gathering of a M, and false accusation--all
Acts 21:36 the crowd; for the M of the people followed,

MOBILE (2)
Wis 7:22 holy, unique, manifold, subtle, M, clear, unpolluted,
7:24 For wisdom is more M than any motion; because

MOCHMUR
Jud 7:18 Acraba, which is near Chusi beside the brook M

MOCK (14)
2Kgs 19:4 Assyria has sent to M the living God, and
19:16 he has sent to M the living God.
Esth 14:11 do not let them M at our downfall; but
Job 11:3 men, and when you M, shall no one shame
21:3 after I have spoken, M on.
Ps 22:7 All who see me M at me, they make
89:51 LORD, with which they M the footsteps of thy
Prov 1:26 your calamity; I will M when panic strikes you,
Wis 12:25 send thy judgment to M them.
Is 37:4 Assyria has sent to M the living God, and
37:17 he has sent to M the living God.
Ezek 22:5 far from you will M you, you infamous one,
Mk 10:34 Gentiles; and they will M him, and spit upon
Lk 14:29 see it begin to M him,

MOCKED (24)
Judg 16:10 Samson, "Behold, you have M me, and told me
16:13 "Until now you have M me, and told me
16:15 You have M me these three times, and you
1Kgs 18:27 And at noon Elijah M them, saying, "Cry aloud,
2Kgs 19:22 "Whom have you M and reviled?
19:23 your messengers you have M the LORD, and you
2Chr 30:10 them to scorn, and M them.
Ps 35:16 without ceasing; they impiously M more and more,
79:4 taunt to our neighbors, M and derided by those
Is 37:23 'Whom have you M and reviled?
37:24 your servants you have M the Lord, and you
1Mac 7:34 But he M them and derided them and defiled
Mt 20:19 the Gentiles to be M and scourged and crucified,
27:29 kneeling before him they M him, saying, "Hail, King
27:31 And when they had M him, they stripped him
27:41 the scribes and elders, M him, saying,
Mk 15:20 And when they had M him, they stripped him
15:30 also the chief priests M him to one another
Lk 18:32 Gentiles, and will be M and shamefully treated and
22:61 who were holding Jesus M him and beat him;
23:11 him with contempt and M him; then, arraying him
23:35 The soldiers also M him, coming up and offering
Acts 17:32 of the dead, some M; but others said, "We
Gal 6:7 deceived; God is not M, for whatever a man

MOCKER
Prov 20:1 Wine is a M, strong drink a brawler; and

MOCKERS (2)
Job 17:2 Surely there are M about me, and my eye
Hos 7:6 of wine; he stretched out his hand with M

MOCKERY
Sir 27:28 M and abuse issue from the proud man, but

MOCKING (7)
Gen 27:12 shall seem to be M him, and bring a
2Chr 36:16 place; but they kept M the messengers of God,
Sir 33:6 stallion is like a M friend; he neighs under
Lam 1:7 foe gloated over her, M at her downfall.
Ezek 22:4 the nations, and a M to all the countries.
Acts 2:13 But others M said, "They are filled with new
Heb 11:36 Others suffered M and scourging, and even chains

MOCKINGLY
Wis 11:14 For though they had M rejected him who long

MOCKS (5)
Job 9:23 brings sudden death, he M at the calamity of
Prov 17:5 He who M the poor insults his Maker; he
19:28 A worthless witness M at justice, and the mouth
30:17 The eye that M a father and scorns to
Jer 20:7 the day; every one M me.

MODEIN (9)
1Mac 2:1 of Joarib, moved from Jerusalem and settled in M
2:15 to the city of M to make them offer
2:23 upon the altar in M, according to the king's
2:70 buried in the tomb of his fathers at M
9:19 of their fathers at M,
13:25 and buried him in M, the city of his
13:30 which he built in M; it remains to this
16:4 against Cendebeus and camped for the night in M
2Mac 13:14 and commonwealth, he pitched his camp near M

MODEL (2)
2Kgs 16:10 Uriah the priest a M of the altar, and
Tit 2:7 in all respects a M of good deeds, and

MODERATE
Sir 31:20 Healthy sleep depends on M eating; he rises early,

MODERATION (3)
Sir 31:27 life to men, if you drink it in M
2Mac 4:37 wept because of the M and good conduct of
9:27 will treat you with M and kindness."

MODEST (3)
Sir 26:15 A M wife adds charm to charm, and no
32:10 and approval precedes a M man.
2Mac 15:12 and good man, of M bearing and gentle manner,

MODESTLY
1Tim 2:9 women should adorn themselves M and sensibly in

MODESTY (2)
1Cor 12:23 are treated with greater M,
1Tim 2:15 continues in faith and love and holiness, with M

MOIST (3)
Deut 29:19 the sweeping away of M and dry alike.
Job 21:24 of fat and the marrow of his bones M
Dan 3:50 the furnace like a M whistling wind, so that

MOISTEN
Ezek 46:14 hin of oil to M the flour, as a

MOISTURE (2)
Job 37:11 the thick cloud with M; the clouds scatter his
Lk 8:6 up, it withered away, because it had no M

MOLADAH (4)
Josh 15:26 is, Hazor), Amam, Shema, M,
19:2 its inheritance Beer-sheba, Sheba, M,
1Chr 4:28 They dwelt in Beer-sheba, M, Hazar-shual,

M

Neh 11:26 in Jeshua and in M and Beth-pelet,

MOLD

Nah 3:14 tread the mortar, take hold of the brick M

MOLDED (2)

Wis 7:1 a mother I was M into flesh,
Rom 9:20 Will what is M say to its molder, "Why

MOLDER

Rom 9:20 molded say to its M, "Why have you made

MOLDING (10)

Ex 25:11 make upon it a M of gold round about.
25:24 gold, and make a M of gold around it.
25:25 handbreadth wide, and a M of gold around the
30:3 make for it a M of gold round about.
30:4 for it; under its M on two opposite sides
37:2 without, and made a M of gold around it.
37:11 gold, and made a M of gold around it.
37:12 wide, and made a M of gold around the
37:26 and he made a M of gold round about
37:27 on it under its M, on two opposite sides

MOLDS (2)

Wis 15:7 soft earth and laboriously M each vessel for our
15:9 his glory that he M counterfeit gods.

MOLDY (2)

Josh 9:5 clothes; and all their provisions were dry and M
9:12 it is dry and M;

MOLECH (9)

Lev 18:21 them by fire to M, and so profane the
20:2 of his children to M shall be put to
20:3 of his children to M, defiling my sanctuary and
20:4 of his children to M, and do not put
20:5 who follow him in playing the harlot after M
1Kgs 11:7 of Moab, and for M the abomination of the
2Kgs 23:10 son or his daughter as an offering to M
Is 57:9 You journeyed to M with oil and multiplied your
Jer 32:35 sons and daughters to M, though I did not

M

MOLES

Is 2:20 to worship, to the M and to the bats,

MOLEST (2)

Ruth 2:9 young men not to M you?
Acts 14:5 with their rulers, to M them and to stone

MOLESTED (2)

Ruth 2:22 his maidens, lest in another field you be M
2Mac 11:31 of them shall be M in any way for

MOLID

1Chr 2:29 was Abihail, and she bore him Ahban and M

MOLOCH

Acts 7:43 up the tent of M, and the star of

MOLTEN (31)

Ex 32:4 tool, and made a M calf; and they said,
32:8 made for themselves a M calf, and have worshiped
34:17 make for yourself no M gods.
Lev 19:4 or make for yourselves M gods: I am the
Num 33:52 and destroy all their M images, and demolish all
Deut 9:12 have made themselves a M image.'
9:16 had made yourselves a M calf; you had turned
27:15 makes a graven or M image, an abomination to
Judg 17:3 graven image and a M image; now therefore I
17:4 graven image and a M image; and it was
18:14 graven image, and a M image?
18:17 the teraphim, and the M image, while the priest
18:18 the teraphim, and the M image, the priest said
1Kgs 7:16 made two capitals of M bronze, to set upon
7:23 Then he made the M sea; it was round,
14:9 yourself other gods, and M images, provoking me to
2Kgs 17:16 and made for themselves M images of two calves;
2Chr 4:2 Then he made the M sea; it was round,
28:2 He even made M images for the Baals;
34:3 the graven and the M images.
34:4 the graven and the M images, and he made
Neh 9:18 made for themselves a M calf and said, 'This
Job 37:18 skies, hard as a M mirror?
Ps 106:19 Horeb and worshiped a M image.
Is 30:22 images and your gold-plated M images.
41:29 works are nothing; their M images are empty wind.
42:17 images, who say to M images, "You are our
48:5 graven image and my M image commanded them.'
Dan 11:8 their gods with their M images and with their
Hos 13:2 and make for themselves M images, idols skilfully
Nah 1:14 graven image and the M image.

MOMENT (44)

Ex 33:5 if for a single M I should go up
Num 4:20 things even for a M, lest they die."
16:21 congregation, that I may consume them in a M
16:45 congregation, that I may consume them in a M
Ruth 2:7 morning until now, without resting even for a M
Ezra 9:8 now for a brief M favor has been shown
Tob 3:17 At that very M Tobit returned and entered his
Jud 13:9 the posts; after a M she went out, and
14:8 she left until the M of her speaking to
Esth 10:11 to the hour and M and day of decision
Job 7:18 visit him every morning, and test him every M
20:5 the joy of the godless but for a M
34:20 In a M they die; at midnight the people
Ps 6:10 back, and be put to shame in a M
30:5 is but for a M, and his favor is
73:19 are destroyed in a M, swept away utterly by
Prov 6:15 him suddenly; in a M he will be broken
12:19 but a lying tongue is but for a M
Sir 1:20 endure until the right M, and then joy will
1:21 words until the right M, and the lips of
3:29 the future; at the M of his falling he
18:23 death, and of the M of vengeance when he
20:6 silent until the right M, but a braggart and
20:6 a braggart and fool goes beyond the right M
40:7 the battle-front; at the M of his rescue he
Is 27:3 am its keeper; every M I water it.
47:9 to you in a M, in one day; the
54:7 For a brief M I forsook you, but with
54:8 overflowing wrath for a M I hid my face
66:8 Shall a nation be brought forth in one M?
Jer 4:20 my tents are destroyed, my curtains in a M
Lam 4:6 was overthrown in a M, no hand being laid
Ezek 26:16 ground and tremble every M, and be appalled at
32:10 they shall tremble every M, every one for his
Dan 4:19 was dismayed for a M, and his thoughts alarmed
2Mac 6:25 of living a brief M longer, they should be
9:11 God, for he was tortured with pain every M
Mt 8:13 And the servant was healed at that very M
26:16 And from that M he sought an opportunity to
Lk 4:5 the world in a M of time,
Acts 11:11 At that very M three men arrived at the
1Cor 15:52 be changed, in a M, in the twinkling of
Gal 2:5 submission even for a M, that the truth of
Heb 12:11 For the M all discipline seems painful rather than

MOMENTARY

2Cor 4:17 For this slight M affliction is preparing for us

MONARCH

Wis 12:14 can any king or M confront thee about those

MONARCHS (5)

Wis 6:9 To you then, O M, my words are directed,
6:21 thrones and scepters, O M over the peoples, honor
8:15 subject to me; dread M will be afraid of
14:16 the command of M graven images were worshiped.
14:17 men could not honor M in their presence, since

MONEY (184)

Gen 17:12 or bought with your M from any foreigner who
17:13 is bought with your M, shall be circumcised.
17:23 or bought with his M, every male among the
17:27 and those bought with M from a foreigner, were
31:15 been using up the M given for us.
33:19 a hundred pieces of M the piece of land
42:25 to replace every man's M in his sack, and
42:27 place, he saw his M in the mouth of
42:28 to his brothers, "My M has been put back;
42:35 every man's bundle of M was in his sack;
42:35 saw their bundles of M, they were dismayed.
43:12 Take double the M with you; carry back with
43:12 back with you the M that was returned in
43:15 they took double the M with them, and Benjamin;
43:18 is because of the M, which was replaced in
43:21 there was every man's M in the mouth of
43:21 of his sack, our M in full weight; so
43:22 we have brought other M down in our hand
43:22 know who put our M in our sacks."

43:23 in your sacks for you; I received your M
44:1 and put each man's M in the mouth of
44:2 the youngest, with his M for the grain." And
44:8 Behold, the M which we found in the mouth
47:14 gathered up all the M that was found in
47:14 and Joseph brought the M into Pharaoh's house.
47:15 And when the M was all spent in the
47:15 For our M is gone."
47:16 your cattle, if your M is gone."
47:18 my lord that our M is all spent; and
Ex 12:44 that is bought for M may eat of it
21:11 shall go out for nothing, without payment of M
21:21 to be punished; for the slave is his M
21:34 good; he shall give M to its owner, and
22:7 delivers to his neighbor M or goods to keep,
22:17 him, he shall pay M equivalent to the marriage
22:25 "If you lend M to any of my people
30:16 shall take the atonement M from the people of
Lev 22:11 as his property for M, the slave may eat
25:37 not lend him your M at interest, nor give
25:52 he shall refund the M for his redemption.
27:15 of the valuation in M to it, and it
27:19 of the valuation in M to it, and it
Num 3:48 them, and give the M by which the excess
3:49 Moses took the redemption M from those who were
3:50 Israel he took the M, one thousand three hundred
3:51 Moses gave the redemption M to Aaron and his
Deut 2:6 food from them for M, that you may eat;
2:6 water of them for M, that you may drink.
2:28 sell me food for M, that I may eat,
2:28 give me water for M, that I may drink;
14:25 shall turn it into M, and bind up the
14:25 and bind up the M in your hand, and
14:26 chooses, and spend the M for whatever you desire,
21:14 not sell her for M, you shall not treat
23:19 your brother, interest on M, interest on victuals,
Josh 24:32 a hundred pieces of M; it became an inheritance
Judg 16:18 her, and brought the M in their hands.
17:4 when he restored the M to his mother, his
1Kgs 21:2 you, I will give you its value in M
21:6 me your vineyard for M; or else, if it
21:15 to give you for M; for Naboth is not
2Kgs 5:26 a time to accept M and garments, olive orchards
12:4 the priests, "All the M of the holy things
12:4 of the LORD, the M for which each man
12:4 man is assessed--the M from the assessment of
12:4 of persons--and the M which a man's heart
12:7 therefore take no more M from your acquaintances,
12:8 should take no more M from the people, and
12:9 in it all the M that was brought into
12:10 that there was much M in the chest, the
12:10 up in bags the M that was found in
12:11 they would give the M that was weighed out
12:13 of silver, from the M that was brought into
12:15 hand they delivered the M to pay out to
12:16 The M from the guilt offerings and the money
12:16 guilt offerings and the M from the sin offerings
15:20 Menahem exacted the M from Israel, that is, from
22:4 the amount of the M which has been brought
22:7 from them for the M which is delivered into
22:9 have emptied out the M that was found in
23:35 land to give the M according to the command
2Chr 24:5 gather from all Israel M to repair the house
24:11 that there was much M in it, the king's
24:11 after day, and collected M in abundance.
24:14 the rest of the M before the king and
34:9 priest and delivered the M that had been brought
34:14 were bringing out the M that had been brought
34:17 have emptied out the M that was found in
Ezra 3:7 So they gave M to the masons and the
7:17 With this M, then, you shall with all diligence
Neh 5:4 said, "We have borrowed M for the king's tax
5:10 servants are lending them M and grain.
5:11 and the hundredth of M, grain, wine, and oil
Tob 2:11 my wife Anna earned M at women's work.
4:1 day Tobit remembered the M which he had left
4:2 to him about the M before I die?"
5:2 can I obtain the M when I do not
5:3 as I live; and go and get the M
5:18 Do not add M to money, but consider it
5:18 not add money to M, but consider it as
9:2 Media and get the M for me; and bring
9:5 Gabael brought out the M bags with their seals
10:2 there is no one to give him the M
10:10 half of his property in slaves, cattle, and M
12:3 wife, he obtained the M for me, and he

Esth 3:11 said to Haman, "The M is given to you,
4:7 the exact sum of M that Haman had promised
Job 42:11 him a piece of M and a ring of
Ps 15:5 not put out his M at interest, and does
Prov 7:20 took a bag of M with him; at full
Eccl 5:10 He who loves M will not be satisfied with
5:10 not be satisfied with M; nor he who loves
7:12 like the protection of M; and the advantage of
10:19 wine gladdens life, and M answers everything.
Wis 15:12 says one must get M however one can, even
Sir 7:18 exchange a friend for M, or a real brother
18:32 by feasting with borrowed M, when you have nothing
21:8 house with other people's M is like one who
29:5 speaking of his neighbor's M; but at the time
29:6 robbed him of his M, and he has needlessly
31:5 and he who pursues M will be led astray
51:25 and said, Get these things for yourselves without M
Is 43:24 me sweet cane with M, or satisfied me with
52:3 for nothing, and you shall be redeemed without M
55:1 he who has no M, come, buy and eat!
55:1 wine and milk without M and without price.
55:2 do you spend your M for that which is
Jer 32:9 and weighed out the M to him, seventeen shekels
32:10 witnesses, and weighed the M on scales.
32:25 "Buy the field for M and get witnesses"--though
32:44 shall be bought for M, and deeds shall be
Bar 1:6 Lord; and they collected M, each giving what he
1:10 "Herewith we send you M; so buy with the
1:10 so buy with the M burnt offerings and sin
6:28 gods and use the M; and likewise their wives
6:35 give either wealth or M; if one makes a
Mic 3:11 its prophets divine for M; yet they lean upon
1Mac 3:29 he saw that the M in the treasury was
8:26 or supply grain, arms, M, or ships, as Rome
8:28 given no grain, arms, M, or ships, as Rome
10:43 precincts, because he owes M to the king or
13:15 "It is for the M that Jonathan your brother
13:17 sent to get the M and the sons, lest
13:18 not send him the M and the sons, he
14:32 sums of his own M; he armed the men
15:6 your own coinage as M for your country,
15:30 seized and the tribute M of the places which
15:31 caused and the tribute M of the cities, five
2Mac 3:6 of untold sums of M, so that the amount
3:7 told him of the M about which he had
3:7 commands to effect the removal of the aforesaid M
3:11 orphans, and also some M of Hyrcanus, son of
3:13 had, said that this M must in any case
4:1 had informed about the M against his own country,
4:19 Those who carried the M, however, thought best not
4:20 So this M was intended by the sender for
4:23 Simon, to carry the M to the king and
4:27 regularly any of the M promised to the king.
8:25 They captured the M of those who had come
10:21 sold their brethren for M by setting their enemies
Mt 22:19 Show me the M for the tax." And they
25:18 dug in the ground and hid his master's M
25:27 to have invested my M with the bankers, and
27:6 them into the treasury, since they are blood M
28:12 gave a sum of M to the soldiers
28:15 So they took the M and did as they
Mk 6:8 bread, no bag, no M in their belts;
12:41 watched the multitude putting M into the treasury.
14:11 they were glad, and promised to give him M
Lk 9:3 bag, nor bread, nor M; and do not have
16:14 who were lovers of M, heard all this, and
19:15 he had given the M, to be called to
19:23 you not put my M into the bank, and
22:5 they were glad, and engaged to give him M
Jn 12:6 as he had the M box he used to
13:29 because Judas had the M box, Jesus was telling
Acts 4:37 him, and brought the M and laid it at
8:18 hands, he offered them M,
8:20 you could obtain the gift of God with M
24:25 time he hoped that M would be given him
1Tim 3:3 but gentle, not quarrelsome, and no lover of M
6:10 For the love of M is the root of
2Tim 3:2 lovers of M, proud, arrogant, abusive, disobedient
Heb 13:5 free from love of M, and be content with

MONEY-CHANGERS (4)

Mt 21:12 the tables of the M and the seats of
Mk 11:15 the tables of the M and the seats of
Jn 2:14 and pigeons, and the M at their business.
2:15 the coins of the M and overturned their tables.

M

MONEY-HUNGRY
2Mac 10:20 with Simon, who were M, were bribed by some

MONEY-MAKING
Wis 13:19 take a step; for M and work and success

MONEY-VALUE
Lev 27:18 priest shall compute the M for it according to

MONEYLENDER
Sir 29:28 scolding about lodging and the reproach of the M

MONGREL
Zech 9:6 shall be uninhabited; a M people shall dwell in

MONSTER (2)
Job 7:12 sea, or a sea M, that thou settest a
Jer 51:34 swallowed me like a M; he has filled his

MONSTERS (2)
Gen 1:21 created the great sea M and every living creature
Ps 148:7 the earth, you sea M and all deeps,

MONSTROUS
Wis 17:15 now were driven by M specters, and now were

MONTH (268)
Gen 7:11 life, in the second M, on the seventeenth day
7:11 seventeenth day of the M, on that day all
8:4 and in the seventh M, on the seventeenth day
8:4 seventeenth day of the M, the ark came to
8:5 abate until the tenth M; in the tenth month,
8:5 month; in the tenth M, on the first day
8:5 first day of the M, the tops of the
8:13 year, in the first M, the first day of
8:13 first day of the M, the waters were dried
8:14 In the second M, on the twenty-seventh day of
8:14 twenty-seventh day of the M, the earth was dry.
29:14 And he stayed with him a M
Ex 12:2 land of Egypt, "This M shall be for you
12:2 shall be the first M of the year for
12:3 tenth day of this M they shall take every
12:6 fourteenth day of this M, when the whole assembly
12:18 In the first M, on the fourteenth day of
12:18 fourteenth day of the M at evening, you shall
12:18 twenty-first day of the M at evening.
13:4 go forth, in the M of Abib.
13:5 honey, you shall keep this service in this M
16:1 day of the second M after they had departed
23:15 appointed time in the M of Abib, for in
34:18 time appointed in the M Abib; for in the
34:18 Abib; for in the M Abib you came out
Lev 16:29 that in the seventh M, on the tenth day
16:29 tenth day of the M, you shall afflict yourselves,
23:5 In the first M, on the fourteenth day of
23:5 fourteenth day of the M in the evening, is
23:6 day of the same M is the feast of
23:24 Israel, In the seventh M, on the first day
23:24 first day of the M, you shall observe a
23:27 day of this seventh M is the day of
23:32 ninth day of the M beginning at evening, from
23:34 day of this seventh M and for seven days
23:39 day of the seventh M, when you have gathered
23:41 generations; you shall keep it in the seventh M
25:9 day of the seventh M; on the day of
27:6 person is from a M old up to five
Num 1:1 day of the second M, in the second year
1:18 day of the second M, they assembled the whole
3:15 every male from a M old and upward you
3:22 the males from a M old and upward was
3:28 the males, from a M old and upward, there
3:34 the males from a M old and upward was
3:39 the males from a M old and upward, were
3:40 of Israel, from a M old and upward, taking
3:43 of names, from a M old and upward as
9:1 Sinai, in the first M of the second year
9:3 fourteenth day of this M, in the evening, you
9:5 passover in the first M, on the fourteenth day
9:5 fourteenth day of the M, in the evening, in
9:11 In the second M on the fourteenth day in
9:22 two days, or a M, or a longer time,
10:11 year, in the second M, on the twentieth day
10:11 twentieth day of the M, the cloud was taken
11:20 days, but a whole M, until it comes out
11:21 may eat a whole M
18:16 redemption price (at a M old you shall redeem
20:1 Zin in the first M, and the people stayed
26:62 every male from a M old and upward; for
28:14 burnt offering of each M throughout the months of
28:16 day of the first M is the LORD's passover.
28:17 fifteenth day of this M is a feast; seven
29:1 day of the seventh M you shall have a
29:7 day of this seventh M you shall have a
29:12 day of the seventh M you shall have a
33:3 Rameses in the first M, on the fifteenth day
33:3 day of the first M; on the day after
33:38 Egypt, on the first day of the fifth M
Deut 1:3 day of the eleventh M, Moses spoke to the
16:1 "Observe the M of Abib, and keep the passover
16:1 God; for in the M of Abib the LORD
21:13 her mother a full M; after that you may
Josh 4:19 day of the first M, and they encamped in
5:10 fourteenth day of the M at evening in the
1Sam 20:34 second day of the M, for he was grieved
1Kgs 4:7 make provision for one M in the year.
4:27 each one in his M; they let nothing be
5:14 Lebanon, ten thousand a M in relays; they would
5:14 they would be a M in Lebanon and two
6:1 over Israel, in the M of Ziv, which is
6:1 which is the second M, he began to build
6:37 was laid, in the M of Ziv.
6:38 eleventh year, in the M of Bul, which is
6:38 which is the eighth M, the house was finished
8:2 the feast in the M Ethanim, which is the
8:2 in the month Ethanim, which is the seventh M
12:32 day of the eighth M like the feast that
12:33 day in the eighth M, in the month which
12:33 eighth month, in the M which he had devised
2Kgs 15:13 and he reigned one M in Samaria.
25:1 reign, in the tenth M, on the tenth day
25:1 tenth day of the M, Nebuchadnezzar king of Babylon
25:3 day of the fourth M the famine was so
25:8 In the fifth M, on the seventh day of
25:8 seventh day of the M --which was the nineteenth
25:25 But in the seventh M, Ishmael the son of
25:27 Judah, in the twelfth M, on the twenty-seventh day
25:27 twenty-seventh day of the M, Evil-merodach king of
1Chr 12:15 Jordan in the first M, when it was overflowing
27:1 that came and went, M after month throughout the
27:1 and went, month after M throughout the year, each
27:2 division in the first M; in his division were
27:3 the commanders of the army for the first M
27:4 division of the second M; in his division were
27:5 commander, for the third M, was Benaiah, the son
27:7 fourth, for the fourth M, and his son Zebadiah
27:8 commander, for the fifth M, was Shamhuth, the
27:9 Sixth, for the sixth M, was Ira, the son
27:10 Seventh, for the seventh M, was Helez the Pelonite,
27:11 Eighth, for the eighth M, was Sibbecai the
27:12 Ninth, for the ninth M, was Abi-ezer of Anathoth,
27:13 Tenth, for the tenth M, was Maharai of Netophah,
27:14 Eleventh, for the eleventh M, was Benaiah of
27:15 Twelfth, for the twelfth M, was Heldai the
2Chr 3:2 build in the second M of the fourth year
5:3 at the feast which is in the seventh M
7:10 day of the seventh M he sent the people
15:10 Jerusalem in the third M of the fifteenth year
29:3 reign, in the first M, he opened the doors
29:17 day of the first M, and on the eighth
29:17 eighth day of the M they came to the
29:17 day of the first M they finished.
30:2 passover in the second M --
30:13 bread in the second M, a very great assembly.
30:15 lamb on the fourteenth day of the second M
31:7 In the third M they began to pile up
31:7 the heaps, and finished them in the seventh M
35:1 lamb on the fourteenth day of the first M
Ezra 3:1 When the seventh M came, and the sons of
3:6 day of the seventh M they began to offer
3:8 Jerusalem, in the second M, Zerubbabel the son of
6:15 third day of the M of Adar, in the
6:19 day of the first M the returned exiles kept
7:8 Jerusalem in the fifth M, which was in the
7:9 day of the first M he began to go
7:9 day of the fifth M he came to Jerusalem,
8:31 day of the first M, to go to Jerusalem;
10:9 it was the ninth M, on the twentieth day
10:9 ninth month, on the twentieth day of the M
10:16 day of the tenth M they sat down to
10:17 day of the first M they had come to
Neh 1:1 it happened in the M of Chislev, in the
2:1 In the M of Nisan, in the twentieth year

6:15 twenty-fifth day of the M Elul, in fifty-two days.
7:73 And when the seventh M had come, the children
8:2 understanding, on the first day of the seventh M
8:14 feast of the seventh M,
9:1 twenty-fourth day of this M the people of Israel
Jud 2:1 day of the first M, there was talk in
3:10 remained for a whole M in order to assemble
Esth 2:16 palace in the tenth M, which is the month
2:16 month, which is the M of Tebeth, in the
3:7 In the first M, which is the month of
3:7 month, which is the M of Nisan, in the
3:7 and they cast it M after month till the
3:7 cast it month after M till the twelfth month,
3:7 month till the twelfth M, which is the month
3:7 month, which is the M of Adar.
3:12 day of the first M, and an edict, according
3:13 day of the twelfth M, which is the month
3:13 month, which is the M of Adar, and to
8:9 time, in the third M, which is the month
8:9 month, which is the M of Sivan, on the
8:12 day of the twelfth M, which is the month
8:12 month, which is the M of Adar.
9:1 Now in the twelfth M, which is the month
9:1 month, which is the M of Adar, on the
9:15 fourteenth day of the M of Adar and they
9:17 thirteenth day of the M of Adar, and on
9:19 fourteenth day of the M of Adar as a
9:21 fourteenth day of the M Adar and also the
9:22 enemies, and as the M that had been turned
10:13 these days in the M of Adar, on the
10:13 and fifteenth of that M, with an assembly and
13:6 day of the twelfth M, Adar, of this present
16:20 day of the twelfth M, Adar, on that very
Sir 43:8 The M is named for the moon, increasing
Jer 1:3 until the captivity of Jerusalem in the fifth M
2:24 weary themselves; in her M they will find her.
28:1 Judah, in the fifth M of the fourth year,
28:17 year, in the seventh M, the prophet Hananiah died.
36:9 Judah, in the ninth M, all the people in
36:22 It was the ninth M, and the king was
39:1 Judah, in the tenth M, Nebuchadrezzar king of
39:2 Zedekiah, in the fourth M, on the ninth day
39:2 ninth day of the M, a breach was made
41:1 In the seventh M, Ishmael the son of Nethaniah,
52:4 reign, in the tenth M, on the tenth day
52:4 tenth day of the M, Nebuchadrezzar king of Babylon
52:6 day of the fourth M the famine was so
52:12 In the fifth M, on the tenth day of
52:12 tenth day of the M --which was the nineteenth
52:31 Judah, in the twelfth M, on the twenty-fifth day
52:31 twenty-fifth day of the M, Evil-merodach king of,
Bar 1:2 seventh day of the M, at the time when
Ezek 1:1 year, in the fourth M, on the fifth day
1:1 day of the in M, as I was among
1:2 fifth day of the M (it was the fifth
8:1 year, in the sixth M, on the fifth day
8:1 fifth day of the M, as I sat in
20:1 year, in the fifth M, on the tenth day
20:1 tenth day of the M, certain of the elders
24:1 year, in the tenth M, on the tenth day
24:1 tenth day of the M, the word of the
26:1 first day of the M, the word of the
29:1 year, in the tenth M, on the twelfth day
29:1 twelfth day of the M, the word of the
29:17 year, in the first M, on the first day
29:17 first day of the M, the word of the
30:20 year, in the first M, on the seventh day
30:20 seventh day of the M, the word of the
31:1 year, in the third M, on the first day
31:1 first day of the M, the word of the
32:1 year, in the twelfth M, on the first day
32:1 first day of the M, the word of the
32:17 year, in the first M, on the fifteenth day
32:17 fifteenth day of the M, the word of the
33:21 exile, in the tenth M, on the fifth day
33:21 fifth day of the M, a man who had
40:1 tenth day of the M, in the fourteenth year
45:18 GOD: In the first M, on the first day
45:18 first day of the M, you shall take a
45:20 seventh day of the M for any one who
45:21 "In the first M, on the fourteenth day of
45:21 fourteenth day of the M, you shall celebrate the
45:25 In the seventh M, on the fifteenth day of
45:25 fifteenth day of the M and for the seven
47:12 bear fresh fruit every M, because the water for
Dan 10:4 day of the first M, as I was standing
Hag 1:1 king, in the sixth M, on the first day
1:1 first day of the M, the word of the
1:15 twenty-fourth day of the M, in the sixth month.
1:15 twenty-fourth day of the month, in the sixth M
2:1 king, in the seventh M, on the twenty-first day
2:1 twenty-first day of the M, the word of the
2:10 day of the ninth M, in the second year
2:18 onward, from the twenty-fourth day of the ninth M
2:20 twenty-fourth day of the M,
Zech 1:1 In the eighth M, in the second year
1:7 day of the eleventh M which is the month
1:7 month which is the M of Shebat, in the
7:1 day of the ninth M, which is Chislev.
7:3 fast in the fifth M, as I have done
7:5 mourned in the fifth M and in the seventh,
8:19 fast of the fourth M, and the fast of
11:8 In one M I destroyed the three shepherds.
1Mac 1:58 Israel, against those found M after month in the
1:58 those found month after M in the cities.
1:59 twenty-fifth day of the M they offered sacrifice on
4:52 day of the ninth M, which is the month
4:52 month, which is the M of Chislev, in the
4:59 twenty-fifth day of the M of Chislev.
7:43 thirteenth day of the M of Adar.
9:3 In the first M of the one hundred and
9:54 year, in the second M, Alcimus gave orders to
10:21 garments in the seventh M of the one hundred
13:51 day of the second M, in the one hundred
16:14 year, in the eleventh M, which is the month
16:14 month, which is the M of Shebat.
2Mac 1:9 of booths in the M of Chislev, in the
10:5 day of the same M, which was Chislev.
15:36 day of the twelfth M -- which is
Lk 1:26 In the sixth M the angel Gabriel was sent
1:36 this is the sixth M with her who was
Rev 9:15 hour, the day, the M, and the year, to
22:2 yielding its fruit each M; and the leaves of

MONTHLY

2Mac 6:7 On the M celebration of the king's birthday, the

MONTHS (62)

Gen 38:24 About three M later Judah was told, "Tamar your
Ex 2:2 was a goodly child, she hid him three M
12:2 you the beginning of M; it shall be the
Num 10:10 the beginnings of your M, you shall blow the
28:11 the beginnings of your M you shall offer a
28:14 each month throughout the M of the year.
Deut 33:14 rich yield of the M,
Judg 11:37 let me alone two M, that I may go
11:38 her away for two M; and she departed, she
11:39 the end of two M, she returned to her
19:2 Bethlehem in Judah, and was there some four M
20:47 and abode at the rock of Rimmon four M
1Sam 6:1 was in the country of the Philistines seven M
27:7 of the Philistines was a year and four M
2Sam 2:11 house of Judah was seven years and six M
5:5 seven years and six M; and at Jerusalem he
6:11 Obed-edom the Gittite three M; and the LORD
24:8 the end of nine M and twenty days.
24:13 will you flee three M before your foes while
1Kgs 5:14 in Lebanon and two M at home; Adoniram was
11:16 Israel remained there six M, until he had cut
2Kgs 15:8 of Jeroboam reigned over Israel in Samaria six M
23:31 and he reigned three M in Jerusalem.
24:8 and he reigned three M in Jerusalem.
1Chr 3:4 where he reigned for seven years and six M
13:14 in his house three M; and the LORD blessed
21:12 of famine; or three M of devastation by your
2Chr 36:2 and he reigned three M in Jerusalem.
36:9 and he reigned three M and ten days in
Jud 8:4 as a widow for three years and four M
16:20 the sanctuary for three M, and Judith remained with
Esth 2:12 Ahasuerus, after being twelve M under the
2:12 of their beautifying, six M with oil of myrrh
2:12 of myrrh and six M with spices and ointments
Job 3:6 it not come into the number of the M
7:3 so I am allotted M of emptiness, and nights
14:5 the number of his M is with thee, and
21:21 the number of their M is cut off?
29:2 were as in the M of old, as in
39:2 Can you number the M that they fulfil, and
Wis 7:2 the period of ten M, compacted with blood, from
Ezek 39:12 For seven M the house of Israel will be
39:14 the end of seven M they will make their
Dan 4:29 the end of twelve M he was walking on

M

7:10 on the gallows which he had prepared for M
8:1 And M came before the king, for Esther had
8:2 had taken from Haman, and gave it to M
8:2 And Esther set M over the house of Haman.
8:7 Queen Esther and to M the Jew, "Behold, I
8:9 to all that M commanded concerning the Jews
8:15 Then M went out from the presence of the
9:3 for the fear of M had fallen upon them.
9:4 For M was great in the king's house, and
9:4 provinces; for the man M grew more and more
9:20 And M recorded these things, and sent letters to
9:23 had begun, and as M had written to them.
9:29 daughter of Abihail, and M the Jew gave full
9:31 their appointed seasons, as M the Jew and Queen
10:2 the high honor of M, to which the king
10:3 For M the Jew was next in rank to
10:4 And M said, "These things have come from God.
11:2 first day of Nisan, M the son of Jair,
11:12 M saw in his dream what God had determined
12:1 Now M took his rest in the courtyard with
12:4 of these things, and M wrote an account of
12:5 And the king ordered M to serve in the
12:6 he sought to injure M and his people because
13:8 Then M prayed to the Lord, calling to remembrance
16:13 asked for destruction of M, our savior and perpetual
2Mac 15:36 the day before M's day.

MORE (665)
Gen 3:1 Now the serpent was M subtle than any other
8:12 and she did not return to him any M
26:13 became rich, and gained M and more until he
26:13 and gained more and M until he became very
29:30 and he loved Rachel M than Leah, and served
32:28 "Your name shall no M be called Jacob, but
37:3 Now Israel loved Joseph M than any other of
37:4 their father loved him M than all his brothers,
37:5 to his brothers they only hated him the M
37:8 they hated him yet M for his dreams and
38:26 and said, "She is M righteous than I, inasmuch
42:13 day with our father, and one is no M
42:32 father; one is no M, and the youngest is
42:36 children: Joseph is no M, and Simeon is no
42:36 and Simeon is no M, and now you would
44:23 see my face no M
Ex 1:11 But the M they were oppressed, the more they
1:11 they were oppressed, the M they multiplied and the
1:11 they multiplied and the M they spread abroad.
9:29 there will be no M hail, that you may
11:1 Moses, "Yet one plague M I will bring upon
16:17 so; they gathered, some M, some less.
30:15 rich shall not give M, and the poor shall
36:5 "The people bring much M than enough for doing
36:6 nor woman do anything M for the offering for
36:7 was sufficient to do all the work, and M
Lev 13:5 him up seven days M;
13:33 disease for seven days M;
13:54 it up seven days M;
17:7 So they shall no M slay their sacrifices for
19:25 that they may yield M richly for you: I
26:21 me, I will bring M plagues upon you, sevenfold
27:20 not be redeemed any M;
Num 8:25 service and serve no M,
11:25 But they did so no M
12:3 Moses was very meek, M than all men that
18:5 there be wrath no M upon the people of
20:19 let me only pass through on foot, nothing M
22:15 again Balak sent princes, M in number and more
22:15 more in number and M honorable than they.
22:18 the LORD my God, to do less or M
22:19 I may know what M the LORD will say
32:14 men, to increase still M the fierce anger of
Deut 3:26 suffice you; speak no M to me of this
5:22 with a loud voice; and he added no M
5:25 LORD our God any M, we shall die.
7:7 not because you were M in number than any
18:16 this great fire any M, lest I die.'
25:3 given him, but not M; lest, if one should
25:3 to beat him with M stripes than these, your
30:5 he will make you M prosperous and numerous than
31:27 the LORD; how much M after my death!
Josh 5:12 Israel had manna no M, but ate of the
7:12 be with you no M, unless you destroy the
10:11 they died; there were M who died because of
22:33 God and spoke no M of making war against
Judg 8:28 Israel, and they lifted up their heads no M
10:13 other gods; therefore I will deliver you no M
13:21 the LORD appeared no M to Manoah and to
16:30 at his death were M than those whom he
Ruth 1:17 so to me and M also if even death
1:18 determined to go with her, she said no M
4:15 loves you, who is M to you than seven
1Sam 1:8 Am I not M to you than ten sons?"
2:3 Talk no M so very proudly, let not arrogance
3:17 so to you and M also, if you hide
9:2 the people of Israel M handsome than he; from
14:19 of the Philistines increased M and more; and Saul
14:19 Philistines increased more and M; and Saul said to
14:44 so to me and M also; you shall surely
18:8 ascribed thousands; and what M can he have but
18:29 him, Saul was still M afraid of David.
18:30 came out David had M success than all the
20:13 so to Jonathan, and M also, if I do
21:5 journey; how much M today will their vessels
23:3 in Judah; how much M then if we go
23:22 Go, make yet M sure; know and see the
24:17 to David, "You are M righteous than I; for
25:22 so to David and M also, if by morning
26:21 for I will no M do you harm, because
27:4 fled to Gath, he sought for him no M
28:15 and answers me no M, either by prophets or
30:4 until they had no M strength to weep.
2Sam 2:28 and pursued Israel no M, nor did they fight
2:28 Israel no more, nor did they fight any M
3:9 so to Abner, and M also, if I do
3:35 so to me and M also, if I taste
4:11 How much M, when wicked men have slain a
5:13 David took M concubines and wives from Jerusalem,
5:13 came from Hebron; and M sons and daughters were
6:22 will make myself yet M contemptible than this, and
7:10 and be disturbed no M; and violent men shall
7:10 shall afflict them no M, as formerly,
7:20 And what M can David say to thee?
10:19 the Syrians feared to help the Ammonites any M
12:8 little, I would add to you as much M
14:11 of blood slay no M, and my son be
16:11 my life; how much M now may this Benjaminite!
18:8 and the forest devoured M people that day than
19:13 so to me, and M also, if you are
19:29 him, "Why speak any M of your affairs?
19:43 David also we have M than you.
20:6 Bichri will do us M harm than Absalom; take
21:17 him, "You shall no M go out with us
1Kgs 1:47 the name of Solomon M famous than yours, and
2:23 so to me and M also if this word
2:32 the sword two men M righteous and better than
10:5 LORD, there was no M spirit in her.
14:22 sins which they committed, M than all that their
16:25 the LORD, and did M evil than all who
16:30 sight of the LORD M than all that were
16:33 Ahab did M to provoke the LORD, the God
19:2 do to me, and M also, if I do
20:10 so to me, and M also, if the dust
2Kgs 2:12 And he saw him no M
6:10 he saved himself there M than once or twice.
6:16 are with us are M than those who are
6:23 the Syrians came no M on raids into the
6:31 so to me, and M also, if the head
9:35 her, they found no M of her than the
12:7 take no M money from your acquaintances,
12:8 they should take no M money from the people,
13:7 Jehoahaz an army of M than fifty horsemen and
21:8 Israel to wander any M out of the land
21:9 seduced them to do M evil than the nations
21:11 and has done things M wicked than all that
1Chr 4:9 Jabez was M honorable than his brothers; and his
14:3 And David took M wives in Jerusalem, and David
14:3 Jerusalem, and David begot M sons and daughters.
17:9 and be disturbed no M; and violent men shall
17:9 shall waste them no M, as formerly,
17:18 And what M can David say to thee for
19:19 were not willing to help the Ammonites any M
24:4 Since M chief men were found among the sons
2Chr 9:4 LORD, there was no M spirit in her.
15:19 And there was no M war until the thirty-fifth
20:25 took for themselves until they could carry no M
25:9 to give you much M than this."
28:22 distress he became yet M faithless to the LORD--
29:34 for the Levites were M upright in heart than
32:16 his servants said still M against the Lord GOD
33:8 and I will no M remove the foot of
33:9 so that they did M evil than the nations
33:23 this Amon incurred guilt M and more.

	33:23	himself, but this Amon incurred guilt more and M
Neh	7:2	for he was a M faithful and God-fearing man
	13:18	Yet you bring M wrath upon Israel by profaning
Tob	3:13	the earth and that I hear reproach no M
	3:15	upon me, and that I hear reproach no M
	12:1	with you; and he must also be given M
	12:21	they stood up; but they saw him no M
Jud	7:31	hold out for five M days; by that time
	12:3	where can we get M like it for you?
	12:18	because my life means M to me today than
	12:20	quantity of wine, much M than he had ever
	16:23	She became M and more famous, and grew old
	16:23	She became more and M famous, and grew old
Esth	1:19	is to come no M before King Ahasuerus; and
	2:17	the king loved Esther M than all the women,
	2:17	favor in his sight M than all the virgins,
	4:13	you will escape any M than all the other
	6:6	king delight to honor M than me?"
	9:4	the man Mordecai grew M and more powerful.
	9:4	Mordecai grew more and M powerful.
	16:2	"The M often they are honored by the too
	16:2	of their benefactors, the M proud do many men
	16:7	so much from the M ancient records which we
	16:9	before our eyes with M equitable consideration.
Job	3:21	and dig for it M than for hid treasures;
	4:19	with error; how much M those who dwell in
	7:8	will behold me no M; while thy eyes are
	7:10	up; he returns no M to his house, nor
	7:10	house, nor does his place know him any M
	8:22	the tent of the wicked will be no M
	14:12	the heavens are no M he will not awake,
	20:9	will see him no M, nor will his place
	20:9	will his place any M behold him.
	27:19	will do so no M; he opens his eyes,
	32:15	discomfited, they answer no M; they have not a
	32:16	speak, because they stand there, and answer no M
	34:19	nor regards the rich M than the poor, for
	34:31	will not offend any M;
	34:32	have done iniquity, I will do it no M
	35:11	night, who teaches us M than the beasts of
	42:12	latter days of Job M than his beginning; and
Ps	4:7	Thou hast put M joy in my heart than
	10:18	is of the earth may strike terror no M
	17:14	may their children have M than enough; may they
	19:10	M to be desired are they than gold, even
	28:5	break them down and build them up no M
	35:16	they impiously mocked M and more, gnashing at
	35:16	impiously mocked more and M, gnashing at me with
	37:10	wicked will be no M; though you look well
	37:36	lo, he was no M; though I sought him,
	39:13	know gladness, before I depart and be no M
	40:5	them, they would be M than can be numbered.
	40:12	cannot see; they are M than the hairs of
	49:19	fathers, who will never M see the light.
	52:3	You love evil M than good, and lying more
	52:3	than good, and lying M than speaking the truth.
	59:13	till they are no M, that men may know
	69:4	M in number than the hairs of my head
	69:26	him whom thou hast wounded, they afflict still M
	69:31	will please the LORD M than an ox or
	71:14	will praise thee yet M and more.
	71:14	continually, and will praise thee yet more and M
	72:7	and peace abound, till the moon be no M
	76:4	[Selah] Glorious art thou, M majestic than the
	78:17	Yet they sinned still M against him, rebelling against
	83:4	let the name of Israel be remembered no M
	87:2	the gates of Zion M than all the dwelling
	88:5	thou dost remember no M, for they are cut
	103:16	is gone, and its place knows it no M
	104:35	the earth, and let the wicked be no M
	119:99	I have M understanding than all my teachers, for
	119:100	I understand M than the aged, for I keep
	120:3	And what M shall be done to you, you
	123:3	for we have had M than enough of contempt.
	130:6	waits for the LORD M than watchmen for the
	130:6	watchmen for the morning, M than watchmen for
	139:18	count them, they are M than the sand.
	140:10	cast into pits, no M to rise!
Prov	3:15	She is M precious than jewels, and nothing you
	10:25	the wicked is no M, but the righteous is
	11:31	on earth, how much M the wicked and the
	12:7	overthrown and are no M, but the house of
	15:11	the LORD, how much M the hearts of men!
	19:7	hate him; how much M do his friends go
	21:3	and justice is M acceptable to the LORD
	21:27	an abomination; how much M when he brings it
	26:12	There is M hope for a fool than for
	28:23	man will afterward find M favor than he who
	29:20	There is M hope for a fool than for
	31:7	their poverty, and remember their misery no M
	31:10	She is far M precious than jewels.
Eccl	2:7	of herds and flocks, M than any who had
	4:2	who are already dead M fortunate than the living
	6:11	The M words, the more vanity, and what is
	6:11	The more words, the M vanity, and what is
	7:19	to the wise man M than ten rulers that
	7:26	And I found M bitter than death the woman
	9:5	and they have no M reward; but the memory
	9:6	and they have no M for ever any share
	10:10	he must put forth M strength; but wisdom helps
Song	1:4	will extol your love M than wine; rightly do
	5:9	What is your beloved M than another beloved, O
	5:9	What is your beloved M than another beloved, that
Wis	7:10	I loved her M than health and beauty, and
	7:24	For wisdom is M mobile than any motion; because
	7:29	For she is M beautiful than the sun, and
	8:6	is effective, who M than she is fashioner
	8:7	nothing in life is M profitable for men than
	10:12	learn that godliness is M powerful than anything.
	12:22	enemies ten thousand times M, so that we may
	13:4	from them how much M powerful is he who
	14:1	a piece of wood M fragile than the ship
	14:19	the likeness to take M beautiful form,
	15:13	For this man, M than all others, knows that
	15:14	But most foolish, and M miserable than an infant,
	16:19	of water it burned M intensely than fire, to
	19:13	for they practiced a M bitter hatred of strangers.
Sir	3:18	greater you are, the M you must humble yourself;
	4:10	he will love you M than does your mother.
	7:19	her charm is worth M than gold.
	10:30	in poverty, how much M in wealth!
	10:30	in wealth, how much M in poverty!
	11:11	is so much the M in want.
	13:9	will invite you the M often.
	13:16	No M has a sinner with a godly man.
	16:5	ear has heard things M striking than these.
	19:13	anything, so that he may do it no M
	21:1	Do so no M, but pray about your former
	24:20	me will hunger for M, and those who drink
	24:20	and those who drink me will thirst for M
	24:27	for her thought is M abundant than the sea,
	29:11	it will profit you M than gold.
	29:13	you from all affliction; M than a mighty shield
	29:13	a mighty shield and M than a heavy spear,
	31:13	What has been created M greedy than the eye?
	32:7	of you, but no M than twice, and only
	34:11	travels, and I understand M than I can express.
	37:13	for no one is M faithful to you than
	39:12	I have yet M to say, which I have
	40:8	upon sinners seven times M,
	40:22	green shoots of grain M than both.
	40:25	good counsel is esteemed M than both.
Is	1:13	Bring no M vain offerings; incense is an abomination
	2:4	against nation, neither shall they learn war any M
	5:4	What M was there to do for my vineyard,
	5:8	until there is no M room, and you are
	10:20	of Jacob will no M lean upon him that
	13:12	I will make men M rare than fine gold,
	15:6	the new growth fails, the verdure is no M
	15:9	bring upon Dibon even M, a lion for those
	16:4	the oppressor is no M, and destruction has ceased,
	17:14	Before morning, they are no M
	19:7	dry up, be driven away, and be no M
	23:10	daughter of Tarshish; there is no restraint any M
	23:12	said: "You will no M exult, O oppressed virgin
	24:9	No M do they drink wine with singing; strong
	25:2	is a city no M, it will never be
	26:21	her, and will no M cover her slain.
	29:22	Jacob: "Jacob shall no M be ashamed, no more
	29:22	more be ashamed, no M shall his face grow
	30:11	let us hear no M of the Holy One
	30:19	who dwell at Jerusalem; you shall weep no M
	30:20	not hide himself any M, but your eyes shall
	32:5	The fool will no M be called noble, nor
	32:10	In little M than a year you will shudder,
	33:19	You will see no M the insolent people, the
	38:11	look upon man no M among the inhabitants of
	47:1	For you shall no M be called tender and
	47:5	for you shall no M be called the mistress
	51:22	you shall drink no M;
	52:1	for there shall no M come into you the
	54:1	desolate one will be M than the children of

54:4 of your widowhood you will remember no M
54:9 of Noah should no M go over the earth,
60:18 Violence shall no M be heard in your land,
60:19 sun shall be no M your light by day,
60:20 Your sun shall no M go down, nor your
62:4 You shall no M be termed Forsaken, and your
62:4 your land shall no M be termed Desolate; but
65:19 in my people; no M shall be heard in
65:20 No M shall there be in it an infant
Jer 2:31 we will come no M to thee?
3:16 LORD, they shall no M say, "The ark of
3:17 and they shall no M stubbornly follow their own
7:32 when it will no M be called Topheth, or
11:19 the living, that his name be remembered no M
15:8 have made their widows M in number than the
19:6 this place shall no M be called Topheth, or
20:9 him, or speak any M in his name," there
22:10 he shall return no M to see his native
22:11 shall return here no M,
23:4 they shall fear no M, nor be dismayed, neither
23:36 you shall mention no M, for the burden is
25:27 fall and rise no M, because of the sword
30:8 and strangers shall no M make servants of them.
31:12 a watered garden, and they shall languish no M
31:23 God of Israel: "Once M they shall use these
31:34 iniquity, and I will remember their sin no M
31:40 uprooted or overthrown any M for ever."
42:18 You shall see this place no M
44:26 my name shall no M be invoked by the
46:23 because they are M numerous than locusts; they
48:2 broken down; the renown of Moab is no M
48:32 M than for Jazer I weep for you, O
49:7 hosts: "Is wisdom no M in Teman?
49:10 brothers, and his neighbors; and he is no M
50:39 shall be peopled no M for ever, nor inhabited
51:64 sink, to rise no M, because of the evil
Lam 2:9 the law is no M, and her prophets obtain
4:7 milk; their bodies were M ruddy than coral, the
4:16 will regard them no M; no honor was shown
5:7 sinned, and are no M; and we bear their
Bar 6:19 They light lamps, even M than they light for
Ezek 5:6 rebelled against my ordinances M than the nations,
5:6 and against my statutes M than the countries round
5:7 GOD: Because you are M turbulent than the nations
5:16 and when I bring M and more famine upon
5:16 I bring more and M famine upon you, and
12:23 and they shall no M use it as a
12:24 there shall be no M any false vision or
13:15 The wall is no M, nor those who daubed
13:21 they shall be no M in your hand as
13:23 therefore you shall no M see delusive visions nor
14:11 Israel may go no M astray from me, nor
14:11 defile themselves any M with all their transgressions,
14:21 Lord GOD: How much M when I send upon
16:41 harlot, and you shall also give hire no M
16:42 calm, and will no M be angry.
16:47 little time you were M corrupt than they in
16:51 sins; you have committed M abominations than they,
16:52 in which you acted M abominably than they, they
16:52 than they, they are M in the right than
18:3 this proverb shall no M be used by you
19:9 his voice should no M be heard upon the
20:39 name you shall no M profane with your gifts
21:32 you shall be no M remembered; for I the
23:11 this, yet she was M corrupt than she in
23:27 eyes to the Egyptians or remember them any M
24:13 not be cleansed any M till I have satisfied
25:10 may be remembered no M among the nations,
26:13 sound of your lyres shall be heard no M
26:21 you shall be no M; though you be sought
27:36 and shall be no M for ever.'"
28:19 and shall be no M for ever."
28:24 there shall be no M a brier to prick
32:13 shall trouble them any M, nor shall the hoofs
34:28 They shall no M be a prey to the
34:29 that they shall no M be consumed with hunger
36:11 times, and will do M good to you than
36:15 let you hear any M the reproach of the
37:23 not defile themselves any M with their idols and
39:7 name be profaned any M; and the nations shall
39:28 among the nations any M;
39:29 hide my face any M from them, when I
42:5 for the galleries took M away from them than
42:6 back from the ground M than the lower and
43:7 of Israel shall no M defile my holy name,
45:8 my princes shall no M oppress my people; but

MORE

Dan 2:30 wisdom that I have M than all the living
3:19 furnace heated seven times M than it was wont
4:36 my kingdom, and still M greatness was added to
11:2 Behold, three M kings shall arise in Persia; and
Hos 1:6 for I will no M have pity on the
2:17 and they shall be mentioned by name no M
4:7 The M they increased, the more they sinned against
4:7 more they increased, the M they sinned against me;
4:18 harlotry; they love shame M than their glory.
9:15 will love them no M; all their princes are
10:1 The M his fruit increased the more altars he
10:1 his fruit increased the M altars he built; as
11:2 The M I called them, the more they went
11:2 I called them, the M they went from me;
13:2 And now they sin M and more, and make
13:2 they sin more and M, and make for themselves
14:3 we will say no M, 'Our God,' to the
Joel 2:19 and I will no M make you a reproach
Amos 5:2 of Israel: "Fallen, no M to rise, is the
Jon 1:11 For the sea grew M and more tempestuous.
1:11 sea grew more and M tempestuous.
1:13 for the sea grew M and more tempestuous against
1:13 sea grew more and M tempestuous against them.
4:11 in which there are M than a hundred and
Mic 4:3 they learn war any M;
5:12 you shall have no M soothsayers;
5:13 shall bow down no M to the work of
Nah 1:12 have afflicted you, I will afflict you no M
1:14 commandment about you: "No M shall your name be
2:13 your messengers shall no M be heard.
3:16 You increased your merchants M than the stars of
Hab 1:8 are swifter than leopards, M fierce than the evening
1:13 swallows up the man M righteous than he?
Zeph 1:11 the traders are no M; all who weigh out
3:7 her.' But all the M they were eager to
3:15 in your midst; you shall fear evil no M
Zech 11:15 to me, "Take once M the implements of a
13:2 shall be remembered no M; and also I will
14:11 there shall be no M curse; Jerusalem shall dwell
Mal 3:18 Then once M you shall distinguish between the
1Mac 3:30 he used to give M lavishly than preceding kings.
7:23 of Israel; it was M than the Gentiles had
9:6 the camp, until no M than eight hundred of
9:72 land, and came no M into their territory.
10:88 he honored Jonathan still M;
15:31 tribute money of the cities, five hundred talents M
2Mac 4:9 one hundred and fifty M if permission were given
5:22 Phrygian and in character M barbarous than the
8:8 was pushing ahead with M frequent successes, he
8:24 their ally, they slew M than nine thousand of
8:30 and Bacchides they killed M than twenty thousand of
9:7 insolence, but was even M filled with arrogance,
9:28 blasphemer, having endured the M intense suffering,
10:19 places where he was M urgently needed.
10:23 he undertook, he destroyed M than twenty thousand
12:10 When they had gone M than a mile from
12:19 left in the stronghold, M than ten thousand men.
14:11 hostile to Judas, quickly inflamed Demetrius still M
14:30 noticing that Nicanor was M austere in his dealings
14:30 and was meeting him M rudely than had been
14:39 for the Jews, sent M than five hundred soldiers
15:9 he made them the M eager.
Mt 2:18 refused to be consoled, because they were no M
5:37 'Yes' or 'No'; anything M than this comes from
5:47 only your brethren, what M are you doing than
6:25 Is not life M than food, and the body
6:25 food, and the body M than clothing?
6:26 Are you not of M value than they?
6:30 will he not much M clothe you, O men
7:11 your children, how much M will your Father who
10:15 you, it shall be M tolerable on the day
10:25 house Be-elzebul, how much M will they malign
10:31 therefore; you are of M value than many sparrows.
10:37 loves father or mother M than me is not
10:37 loves son or daughter M than me is not
11:9 I tell you, and M than a prophet.
11:22 you, it shall be M tolerable on the day
11:24 that it shall be M tolerable on the day
12:12 Of how much M value is a man than
12:45 him seven other spirits M evil than himself, and
13:12 him who has will M be given, and he
18:12 he rejoices over it M than over the ninety-nine
20:10 thought they would receive M; but each of them
20:31 they cried out the M, "Lord, have mercy on
21:36 he sent other servants, M than the first; and
22:46 to ask him any M questions.

M

25:16 traded with them; and he made five talents M
25:17 who had the two talents made two talents M
25:20 forward, bringing five talents M, saying, 'Master, you
25:20 have made five talents M
25:22 have made two talents M
25:29 one who has will M be given, and he
26:53 at once send me M than twelve legions of
27:23 they shouted all the M, "Let him be crucified."
Mk 4:24 you get, and still M will be given you.
4:25 him who has will M be given; and from
5:3 could bind him any M, even with a chain;
7:35 no one; but the M he charged them, the
7:35 he charged them, the M zealously they proclaimed it.
10:48 cried out all the M, "Son of David, have
12:33 as oneself, is much M than all whole burnt
12:43 widow has put in M than all those who
14:5 have been sold for M than three hundred denarii,
15:14 they shouted all the M, "Crucify him."
Lk 3:13 to them, "Collect no M than is appointed you."
5:15 But so much the M the report went abroad
7:26 I tell you, and M than a prophet.
7:42 Now which of them will love him M
7:43 "The one, I suppose, to whom he forgave M
8:18 him who has will M be given, and from
8:49 is dead; do not trouble the Teacher any M
9:13 said, "We have no M than five loaves and
10:12 you, it shall be M tolerable on that day
10:14 But it shall be M tolerable in the judgment
10:35 of him; and whatever M you spend, I will
11:13 your children, how much M will the heavenly Father
11:26 brings seven other spirits M evil than himself, and
12:4 after that have no M that they can do.
12:7 not; you are of M value than many sparrows.
12:23 For life is M than food, and the body
12:23 food, and the body M than clothing.
12:24 Of how much M value are you than the
12:28 the oven, how much M will he clothe you,
12:48 whom men commit much they will demand the M
14:8 of honor, lest a M eminent man than you
15:7 you, there will be M joy in heaven over
16:8 of this world are M shrewd in dealing with
18:30 will not receive manifold M in this time, and
18:39 cried out all the M, "Son of David, have
19:16 has made ten pounds M
19:26 one who has will M be given; but from
20:36 they cannot die any M, because they are equal
21:3 widow has put in M than all of them;
22:49 But Jesus said, "No M of this!" And he
23:19 Pilate addressed them once M, desiring to release
Jn 4:1 was making and baptizing M disciples than John
4:41 And many M believed because of his word.
5:13 Sin no M, that nothing worse befall you."
5:17 Jews sought all the M to kill him, because
7:31 appears, will he do M signs than this man
8:8 And once M he bent down and wrote with
12:43 the praise of men M than the praise of
14:19 will see me no M, but you will see
15:2 that it may bear M fruit.
16:10 will see me no M;
16:16 will see me no M; again a little while,
17:11 now I am no M in the world, but
19:8 words, he was the M afraid;
21:15 do you love me M than these?" He said
Acts 4:17 them to speak no M to any one in
4:22 healing was performed was M than forty years old.
5:14 And M than ever believers were added to the
8:38 eunuch saw him no M, and went on his
9:22 Saul increased all the M in strength, and confounded
13:34 from the dead, no M to return to corruption,
17:11 Now these Jews were M noble than those in
18:26 the way of God M accurately.
20:25 preaching the kingdom will see my face no M
20:35 he said, 'It is M blessed to give than
20:38 spoken, that they should see his face no M
22:2 language, they were the M quiet.
23:13 There were M than forty who made this conspiracy.
23:15 to determine his case M exactly.
23:20 going to inquire somewhat M closely about him.
23:21 yield to them; for M than forty of their
24:10 ascertain, it is not M than twelve days since
25:6 stayed among them not M than eight or ten
27:11 But the centurion paid M attention to the captain
Rom 5:3 M than that, we rejoice in our sufferings, knowing
5:9 by his blood, much M shall we be saved
5:10 of his Son, much M, now that we are
5:15 one man's trespass, much M have the grace of
5:17 that one man, much M will those who receive
5:20 grace abounded all the M,
8:37 these things we are M than conquerors through him
11:12 the Gentiles, how much M will their full inclusion
11:24 olive tree, how much M will these natural branches
12:3 to think of himself M highly than he ought
14:13 Then let us no M pass judgment on one
1Cor 6:3 How much M, matters pertaining to this life!
9:12 rightful claim upon you, do not we still M
9:19 slave to all, that I might win the M
12:24 greater modesty, which our M presentable parts do
12:31 show you a still M excellent way.
14:5 in tongues, but even M to prophesy.
14:18 I speak in tongues M than you all;
15:6 Then he appeared to M than five hundred brethren
15:34 Come to your right mind, and sin no M
2Cor 1:12 the world, and still M toward you, with holiness
3:11 permanent must have much M splendor.
4:15 as grace extends to M and more people it
4:15 extends to more and M people it may increase
7:7 zeal for me, so that I rejoiced still M
7:13 comfort we rejoiced still M at the joy of
7:15 goes out all the M to you, as he
8:22 but who is now M earnest than ever because
11:23 greater labors, far M imprisonments, with countless
12:6 no one may think M of me than he
12:9 I will all the M gladly boast of my
12:15 I love you the M, am I to be
Gal 3:20 Now an intermediary implies M than one; but God
4:9 spirits, whose slaves you want to be once M
4:27 desolate one are many M than the children of
Eph 3:20 able to do far M abundantly than all that
Phil 1:9 your love may abound M and more, with knowledge
1:9 may abound more and M, with knowledge and all
1:14 imprisonment, and are much M bold to speak the
1:24 in the flesh is M necessary on your account.
2:12 my presence but much M in my absence, work
2:28 I am the M eager to send him, therefore,
3:4 the flesh, I have M:
4:18 received full payment, and M; I am filled, having
1Thes 2:17 heart, we endeavored the M eagerly and with great
4:1 doing, you do so M and more.
4:1 you are doing, you do so more and M
4:10 brethren, to do so M and more,
4:10 do so more and M,
2Tim 2:16 will lead people into M and more ungodliness,
2:16 people into more and M ungodliness,
Tit 3:10 or twice, have nothing M to do with him,
Philem 1:16 as a slave but M than a slave, as
1:16 me but how much M to you, both in
1:21 you will do even M than I say.
Heb 1:4 he has obtained is M excellent than theirs.
3:3 worthy of as much M glory than Moses as
3:3 of a house has M honor than the house.
6:17 God desired to show M convincingly to the heirs
7:15 This becomes even M evident when another priest
8:6 which is as much M excellent than the old
8:12 iniquities, and I will remember their sins no M
9:11 through the greater and M perfect tent (not made
9:14 the flesh, how much M shall the blood of
10:17 will remember their sins and their misdeeds no M
10:25 another, and all the M as you see the
11:4 offered to God a M acceptable sacrifice than Cain,
11:32 And what M shall I say?
12:9 Shall we not much M be subject to the
12:24 sprinkled blood that speaks M graciously than the
12:26 has promised, "Yet once M I will shake not
12:27 This phrase, "Yet once M
13:19 I urge you the M earnestly to do this
Jas 3:12 No M can salt water yield fresh.
4:6 But he gives M grace; therefore it says, "God
1Pet 1:7 genuineness of your faith, M precious than gold
2Pet 1:10 Therefore, brethren, be the M zealous to confirm
1:19 the prophetic word made M sure.
Rev 7:16 They shall hunger no M, neither thirst any more;
7:16 more, neither thirst any M; the sun shall not
10:6 there should be no M delay,
18:11 buys their cargo any M,
18:21 shall be found no M;
18:22 heard in thee no M; and a craftsman of
18:22 found in thee no M; and the sound of
18:22 heard in thee no M;
18:23 shine in thee no M; and the voice of
18:23 heard in thee no M; for thy merchants were
19:3 Once M they cried, "Hallelujah!
20:3 deceive the nations no M, till the thousand years

21:1 had passed away, and the sea was no M
21:4 death shall be no M, neither shall there be
21:4 crying nor pain any M, for the former things
22:3 There shall no M be anything accursed, but the
22:5 night shall be no M; they need no light

MOREH (3)

Gen 12:6 the place at Shechem, to the oak of M
Deut 11:30 Arabah, over against Gilgal, beside the oak of M
Judg 7:1 by the hill of M, in the valley.

MOREOVER (91)

Gen 17:16 will bless her, and M I will give you
22:24 M, his concubine, whose name was Reumah, bore
32:18 my lord Esau; and M he is behind us.'"
32:20 and you shall say, M your servant Jacob is
38:24 played the harlot; and M she is with child
41:44 M Pharaoh said to Joseph, "I am Pharaoh, and
41:57 M, all the earth came to Egypt to Joseph
48:22 M I have given to you rather than to
Ex 5:2 know the LORD, and M I will not let
6:5 M I have heard the groaning of the people
11:3 M, the man Moses was very great in the
18:21 M choose able men from all the people, such
26:1 M you shall make the tabernacle with ten curtains
30:22 M, the LORD said to Moses,
Lev 7:26 M you shall eat no blood whatever, whether of
14:46 M he who enters the house while it is
Num 16:14 M you have not brought us into a land
18:26 LORD said to Moses, M you shall say to
35:31 M you shall accept no ransom for the life
Deut 1:28 up to heaven; and M we have seen the
1:39 M your little ones, who you said would become
7:20 M the LORD your God will send hornets among
26:13 of my house, and M I have given it
Josh 2:24 into our hands; and M all the inhabitants of
1Sam 2:15 M, before the fat was burned, the priest's servant
12:23 M as for me, far be it from me
28:19 M the LORD will give Israel also with you
2Sam 7:11 M the LORD declares to you that the LORD
12:27 have fought against Rabbah; M, I have taken the
15:4 Absalom said M, "Oh that I were judge in
17:1 M Ahithophel said to Absalom, "Let me choose
17:8 Hushai said M, "You know that your father and
1Kgs 1:47 M the king's servants came to congratulate our lord
2:5 the throne of Israel.' M you know also what
7:30 M each stand had four bronze wheels and axles
10:11 M the fleet of Hiram, which brought gold from
14:14 M the LORD will raise up for himself a
16:7 M the word of the LORD came by the
2Kgs 18:25 M, is it without the LORD that I have
21:16 M Manasseh shed very much innocent blood, till he
23:15 M the altar at Bethel, the high place erected
23:24 M Josiah put away the mediums and the wizards
1Chr 16:4 M he appointed certain of the Levites as ministers
17:10 M I declare to you that the LORD will
29:3 M, in addition to all that I have provided
2Chr 1:5 for it in Jerusalem.) M the bronze altar that
9:10 M the servants of Huram and the servants of
12:12 a complete destruction; M, conditions were good in
19:8 M in Jerusalem Jehoshaphat appointed certain
21:11 M he made high places in the hill country
26:9 M Uzziah built towers in Jerusalem at the Corner
26:11 M Uzziah had an army of soldiers, fit for
27:4 M he built cities in the hill country of
Ezra 6:8 M I make a decree regarding what you shall
Neh 5:10 M I and my brethren and my servants are
5:14 M from the time that I was appointed to
5:17 M there were at my table a hundred and
6:17 M in those days the nobles of Judah sent
Esth 7:9 attendance on the king, M, the gallows which Haman
Ps 19:11 M by them is thy servant warned; in keeping
Eccl 3:16 M I saw under the sun that in the
6:5 its name is covered; M it has not seen
Is 30:26 M the light of the moon will be as
36:10 M, is it without the LORD that I have
Jer 2:16 M, the men of Memphis and Tahpanhes have broken
20:5 M, I will give all the wealth of the
25:10 M, I will banish from them the voice of
Ezek 3:10 M he said to me, "Son of man, all
4:16 M he said to me, "Son of man, behold,
5:14 M I will make you a desolation and an
12:17 M the word of the LORD came to me:
20:12 M I gave them my sabbaths, as a sign
20:15 M I swore to them in the wilderness that
20:23 M I swore to them in the wilderness that
20:25 M I gave them statutes that were not good
22:1 M the word of the LORD came to me,
23:38 M this they have done to me: they have
28:11 M the word of the LORD came to me:
Hab 2:5 M, wine is treacherous; the arrogant man shall not
Zech 4:8 M the word of the LORD came to me,
1Mac 6:24 became hostile to us; M, they have put to
10:42 M, the five thousand shekels of silver which my
2Mac 6:23 even from childhood, and M according to the holy
8:19 M, he told them of the times when help
9:25 M, I understand how the princes along the borders
Lk 16:21 the rich man's table; M the dogs came and
24:22 M, some women of our company amazed us.
Acts 2:26 and my tongue rejoiced; M my flesh will dwell
21:28 law and this place; M he also brought Greeks
1Cor 4:2 M it is required of stewards that they be
1Tim 3:7 condemnation of the devil; M he must be well

MORESHETH (2)

Jer 26:18 people, saying, "Micah of M prophesied in the days
Mic 1:1 came to Micah of M in the days of

MORESHETH-GATH

Mic 1:14 give parting gifts to M; the houses of Achzib

MORIAH (2)

Gen 22:2 to the land of M, and offer him there
2Chr 3:1 in Jerusalem on Mount M, where the LORD had

MORNING (244)

Gen 1:5 evening and there was M, one day.
1:8 evening and there was M, a second day.
1:13 evening and there was M, a third day.
1:19 evening and there was M, a fourth day.
1:23 evening and there was M, a fifth day.
1:31 evening and there was M, a sixth day.
19:15 M dawned, the angels urged Lot, saying, "Arise,
19:27 went early in the M to the place where
20:8 rose early in the M, and called all his
21:14 rose early in the M, and took bread and
22:3 rose early in the M, saddled his ass, and
24:54 they arose in the M, he said, "Send me
26:31 In the M they rose early and took oath
28:18 rose early in the M, and he took the
29:25 maid.) And in the M, behold, it was Leah;
31:55 Early in the M Laban arose, and kissed his
40:6 to them in the M and saw them, they
41:8 So in the M his spirit was troubled; and
44:3 As soon as the M was light, the men
49:27 ravenous wolf, in the M devouring the prey, and
Ex 7:15 to Pharaoh in the M, as he is going
8:20 up early in the M and wait for Pharaoh,
9:13 up early in the M and stand before Pharaoh,
10:13 and when it was M the east wind had
12:10 it remain until the M, anything that remains until
12:10 that remains until the M you shall burn.
12:22 of the door of his house until the M
14:24 And in the M watch the LORD in the
14:27 flow when the M appeared; and the Egyptians
16:7 Egypt, and in the M you shall see the
16:8 eat and in the M bread to the full,
16:12 flesh, and in the M you shall be filled
16:13 camp; and in the M dew lay round about
16:19 no man leave any of it till the M
16:20 of it till the M, and it bred worms
16:21 M by morning they gathered it, each as much
16:21 Morning by M they gathered it, each as much
16:23 over lay by to be kept till the M
16:24 it by till the M, as Moses bade them;
18:13 stood about Moses from M till evening.
18:14 stand about you from M till evening?"
19:16 On the M of the third day there were
23:18 the fat of my feast remain until the M
24:4 rose early in the M, and built an altar
27:21 it from evening to M before the LORD.
29:34 bread, remain until the M, then you shall burn
29:39 shall offer in the M, and the other lamb
29:41 libation, as in the M, for a pleasing odor,
30:7 incense on it; every M when he dresses the
34:2 Be ready in the M, and come up in
34:2 come up in the M to Mount Sinai, and
34:4 rose early in the M and went up on
34:25 feast of the passover be left until the M
36:3 him freewill offerings every M,
Lev 6:9 all night until the M, and the fire of
6:12 wood on it every M, and he shall lay

M

6:20 of it in the M and half in the
7:15 shall not leave any of it until the M
9:17 the altar, besides the burnt offering of the M
19:13 not remain with you all night until the M
22:30 none of it until M: I am the LORD.
24:3 order from evening to M before the LORD
Num 9:12 of it until the M, nor break a bone
9:15 the tabernacle like the appearance of fire until M
9:21 remained from evening until M; and when the cloud
9:21 taken up in the M, they set out, or
14:40 rose early in the M, and went up to
16:5 his company, "In the M the LORD will show
22:13 Balaam rose in the M, and said to the
22:21 Balaam rose in the M, and saddled his ass,
28:4 shall offer in the M, and the other lamb
28:8 cereal offering of the M, and like its drink
28:23 burnt offering of the M, which is for a
Deut 16:4 of the first day remain all night until M
16:7 choose; and in the M you shall turn and
28:67 In the M you shall say, 'Would it were
28:67 say, 'Would it were M because of the dread
Josh 3:1 Early in the M Joshua rose and set out
6:12 rose early in the M, and the priests took
7:14 In the M therefore you shall be brought near
7:16 rose early in the M, and brought Israel near
8:10 arose early in the M and mustered the people,
Judg 6:28 rose early in the M, behold, the altar of
6:31 for him shall be put to death by M
6:38 he rose early next M and squeezed the fleece,
9:33 Then in the M, as soon as the sun
16:2 the light of the M; then we will kill
19:5 arose early in the M, and he prepared to
19:8 arose early in the M to depart; and the
19:9 arise early in the M for your journey, and
19:25 her, and abused her all night until the M
19:26 And as M appeared, the woman came and fell
19:27 rose up in the M, and when he opened
20:19 Israel rose in the M, and encamped against Gibe-ah.
Ruth 2:7 has continued from early M until now, without
3:13 night, and in the M, if he will do
3:13 Lie down until the M
3:14 his feet until the M, but arose before one
1Sam 1:19 rose early in the M and worshiped before the
3:15 Samuel lay until M; then he opened the doors
5:4 early on the next M, behold, Dagon had fallen
9:19 me, and in the M I will let you
11:11 the camp in the M watch, and cut down
14:36 despoil them until the M light; let us not
15:12 meet Saul in the M; and it was told
17:16 and took his stand, M and evening.
17:20 rose early in the M, and left the sheep
19:2 to yourself in the M, stay in a secret
19:11 him, that he might kill him in the M
20:35 In the M Jonathan went out into the field
25:22 more also, if by M I leave so much
25:34 meet me, truly by M there had not been
25:36 at all until the M light.
25:37 And in the M, when the wine had gone
29:10 rise early in the M with the servants of
29:10 start early in the M, and depart as soon
29:11 men early in the M, to return to the
2Sam 2:27 up the pursuit of their brethren in the M
11:14 In the M David wrote a letter to Joab,
13:4 are you so haggard M after morning?
13:4 king, why are you so haggard morning after M
23:4 on them like the M light, like the sun
23:4 forth upon a cloudless M, like rain that makes
24:11 David arose in the M, the word of the
24:15 upon Israel from the M until the appointed time;
1Kgs 3:21 I rose in the M to nurse my child,
3:21 it closely in the M, behold, it was not
17:6 and meat in the M, and bread and meat
18:26 name of Baal from M until noon, saying, "O
2Kgs 3:20 The next M, about the time of offering the
3:22 rose early in the M, and the sun shone
6:15 rose early in the M and went out, behold,
7:9 and wait until the M light, punishment will overtake
10:8 at the entrance of the gate until the M
10:9 Then in the M, when he went out, he
16:15 great altar burn the M burnt offering, and the
19:35 arose early in the M, behold, these were all
1Chr 9:27 and they had charge of opening it every M
16:40 burnt offering continually M and evening, according
23:30 they shall stand every M, thanking and praising the
2Chr 2:4 and for burnt offerings M and evening, on the
13:11 to the LORD every M and every evening burnt
20:20 rose early in the M and went out into
31:3 the burnt offerings of M and evening, and the
Ezra 3:3 the LORD, burnt offerings M and evening.
Neh 8:3 Water Gate from early M until midday, in the
Tob 9:6 In the M they both got up early and
Jud 12:5 Along toward the M watch she arose
14:2 And as soon as M comes and the sun
Esth 2:14 went, and in the M she came back to
5:14 made, and in the M tell the king to
Job 1:5 rise early in the M and offer burnt offerings
3:9 the eyelids of the M;
4:20 Between M and evening they are destroyed; they
7:18 dost visit him every M, and test him every
11:17 the noonday; its darkness will be like the M
24:17 For deep darkness is M to all of them;
38:7 its cornerstone, when the M stars sang together, and
38:12 "Have you commanded the M since your days began,
Ps 5:3 O LORD, in the M thou dost hear my
5:3 my voice; in the M I prepare a sacrifice
30:5 for the night, but joy comes with the M
55:17 Evening and M and at noon I utter my
59:16 sing aloud of thy steadfast love in the M
65:8 the outgoings of the M and the evening to
73:14 long I have been stricken, and chastened every M
88:13 to thee; in the M my prayer comes before
90:5 is renewed in the M:
90:6 the morning: in the M it flourishes and is
90:14 Satisfy us in the M with thy steadfast love,
92:2 steadfast love in the M, and thy faithfulness by
101:8 M by morning I will destroy all the wicked
101:8 Morning by M I will destroy all the wicked
110:3 the womb of the M like dew your youth
130:6 than watchmen for the M, more than watchmen for
130:6 for the morning, more than watchmen for the M
139:9 the wings of the M and dwell in the
143:8 me hear in the M of thy steadfast love,
Prov 7:18 fill of love till M; let us delight ourselves
27:14 rising early in the M, will be counted as
Eccl 10:16 a child, and your princes feast in the M
11:6 In the M sow your seed, and at evening
Wis 11:22 like a drop of M dew that falls upon
Sir 18:25 From M to evening conditions change, and all things
47:10 name, and the sanctuary resounded from early M
50:6 Like the M star among the clouds, like the
Is 5:11 rise early in the M, that they may run
17:11 them blossom in the M that you sow; yet
17:14 Before M, they are no more!
21:12 The watchman says: M comes, and also the night.
28:19 will take you; for M by morning it will
28:19 you; for morning by M it will pass through,
33:2 Be our arm every M, our salvation in the
37:36 arose early in the M, behold, these were all
38:13 cry for help until M; like a lion he
50:4 M by morning he wakens, he wakens my ear
50:4 Morning by M he wakens, he wakens my ear
Jer 20:16 a cry in the M and an alarm at
21:12 "'Execute justice in the M, and deliver from the
Lam 3:23 they are new every M; great is thy faithfulness.
Ezek 12:8 In the M the word of the LORD came
24:18 the people in the M, and at evening my
24:18 And on the next M I did as I
33:22 to me in the M; so my mouth was
46:13 to the LORD daily; M by morning he shall
46:13 LORD daily; morning by M he shall provide it.
46:14 cereal offering with it M by morning, one sixth
46:14 with it morning by M, one sixth of an
46:15 oil shall be provided, M by morning, for a
46:15 be provided, morning by M, for a continual burnt
Dan 14:12 you return in the M, if you do not
14:16 Early in the M the king rose and came,
Hos 6:4 love is like a M cloud, like the dew
7:7 anger smolders; in the M it blazes like a
13:3 shall be like the M mist or like the
Amos 4:4 bring your sacrifices every M, your tithes every three
4:13 thought; who makes the M darkness, and treads on
5:8 deep darkness into the M, and darkens the day
Mic 2:1 When the M dawns, they perform it, because it
Zeph 3:3 are evening wolves that leave nothing till the M
3:5 does no wrong; every M he shows forth his
1Mac 3:58 ready early in the M to fight with these
4:52 Early in the M on the twenty-fifth day of
6:33 Early in the M the king rose and took
9:13 the battle raged from M till evening.
10:80 his men from early M till late afternoon.
11:67 Early in the M they marched to the plain
12:29 not know it until M, for they saw the

16:5 Early in the M they arose and marched into
Mt 16:3 red.' And in the M, 'It will be stormy
20:1 out early in the M to hire laborers for
21:18 In the M, as he was returning to the
27:1 When M came, all the chief priests and the
Mk 1:35 And in the M, a great while before day,
11:20 passed by in the M, they saw the fig
13:35 cockcrow, or in the M --
15:1 soon as it was M the chief priests, with
Lk 21:38 And early in the M all the people came
24:22 tomb early in the M
Jn 8:2 Early in the M he came again to the
Acts 28:23 matter to them from M till evening, testifying to
2Pet 1:19 day dawns and the M star rises in your
Rev 2:28 will give him the M star.
22:16 of David, the bright M star."

MORNINGS (2)
Dan 8:14 three hundred evenings and M; then the sanctuary
8:26 the evenings and the M which has been told

MORROW (29)
Ex 9:6 And on the M the LORD did this thing;
18:13 On the M Moses sat to judge the people,
32:6 up early on the M, and offered burnt offerings
32:30 On the M Moses said to the people, "You
Lev 7:16 sacrifice, and on the M what remains of it
19:6 it, or on the M; and anything left over
23:11 find acceptance; on the M after the sabbath the
23:15 shall count from the M after the sabbath, from
23:16 fifty days to the M after the seventh sabbath;
Num 16:41 But on the M all the congregation of the
17:8 And on the M Moses went into the tent
22:41 And on the M Balak took Balaam and brought
Josh 5:11 And on the M after the passover, on that
5:12 manna ceased on the M, when they ate of
Judg 21:4 And on the M the people rose early, and
1Sam 11:11 And on the M Saul put the people in
18:10 And on the M an evil spirit from God
20:27 the second day, the M after the new moon,
31:8 On the M, when the Philistines came to strip
2Kgs 8:15 But on the M he took the coverlet and
1Chr 10:8 On the M, when the Philistines came to strip
Jer 20:3 On the M, when Pashhur released Jeremiah from
Acts 4:3 in custody until the M, for it was already
4:5 On the M their rulers and elders and scribes
20:7 to depart on the M; and he prolonged his
21:8 On the M we departed and came to Caesarea;
22:30 But on the M, desiring to know the real
23:32 And on the M they returned to the barracks,
25:23 So on the M Agrippa and Bernice came with

MORSEL (13)
Gen 18:5 while I fetch a M of bread, that you
Judg 19:5 your heart with a M of bread, and after
Ruth 2:14 bread, and dip your M in the wine." So
1Sam 2:36 I may eat a M of bread.'"
28:22 let me set a M of bread before you;
2Sam 12:3 to eat of his M, and drink from his
1Kgs 17:11 said, "Bring me a M of bread in your
Job 31:17 or have eaten my M alone, and the fatherless
Prov 17:1 Better is a dry M with quiet than a
Jn 13:26 I shall give this M when I have dipped
13:26 he had dipped the M, he gave it to
13:27 Then after the M, Satan entered into him.
13:30 So, after receiving the M, he immediately went out;

MORSELS (4)
Ps 147:17 forth his ice like M; who can stand before
Prov 18:8 whisperer are like delicious M; they go down into
23:8 will vomit up the M which you have eaten,
26:22 whisperer are like delicious M; they go down into

MORTAL (22)
Esth 14:10 magnify for ever a M king.
Job 4:17 heard a voice: 'Can M man be righteous before
Wis 7:1 I also am M, like all men, a descendant
15:17 He is M, and what he makes with lawless
Ezek 31:14 the nether world among M men, with those who
2Mac 7:16 have authority among men, M though you are, you
9:12 to God, and no M should think that he
Rom 1:23 God for images resembling M man or birds or
6:12 therefore reign in your M bodies, to make you
8:11 give life to your M bodies also through his
1Cor 15:53 the imperishable, and this M nature must put on
15:54 the imperishable, and the M puts on immortality,
2Cor 4:11 be manifested in our M flesh.
5:4 so that what is M may be swallowed up
Heb 7:8 tithes are received by M men; there, by one
1Jn 5:16 what is not a M sin, he will ask,
5:16 him life for those whose sin is not M
5:16 is sin which is M; I do not say
5:17 sin, but there is sin which is not M
Rev 13:3 seemed to have a M wound, but its mortal
13:3 mortal wound, but its M wound was healed, and
13:12 the first beast, whose M wound was healed.

MORTALLY (3)
Deut 19:6 long, and wound him M, though the man did
19:11 him, and wounds him M so that he dies,
Ezek 30:24 him like a man M wounded.

MORTALS
Wis 9:14 For the reasoning of M is worthless, and our

MORTAR (7)
Gen 11:3 they had brick for stone, and bitumen for M
Ex 1:13 with hard service, in M and brick, and in
Prov 27:22 a fool in a M with a pestle along
Is 41:25 on rulers as on M, as the potter treads
Jer 43:9 hide them in the M in the pavement which
Nah 3:14 the clay, tread the M, take hold of the
Zeph 1:11 Wail, O inhabitants of the M

MORTARS
Num 11:8 or beat it in M, and boiled it in

MORTGAGING
Neh 5:3 who said, "We are M our fields, our vineyards,

MOSAIC
Esth 1:6 and silver on a M pavement of porphyry, marble,

MOSERAH
Deut 10:6 of Israel journeyed from Be-eroth Bene-jaakan to M

MOSEROTH (2)
Num 33:30 they set out from Hashmonah, and encamped at M
33:31 they set out from M, and encamped at Bene-jaakan.

MOSES (858)
Ex 2:10 and she named him M, for she said, "Because
2:11 One day, when M had grown up, he went
2:14 Then M was afraid, and thought, "Surely the thing
2:15 Pharaoh heard of it, he sought to kill M
2:15 But M fled from Pharaoh, and stayed in the
2:17 drove them away; but M stood up and helped
2:21 And M was content to dwell with the man,
2:21 man, and he gave M his daughter Zipporah.
3:1 Now M was keeping the flock of his father-in-law,
3:3 And M said, "I will turn aside and see
3:4 out of the bush, M, Moses!" And he said,
3:4 called to him out of the bush, "Moses, M
3:6 And M hid his face, for he was afraid
3:11 But M said to God, "Who am I that
3:13 Then M said to God, "If I come to
3:14 God said to M, "I AM WHO AM." And
3:15 God also said to M, "Say this to the
4:1 Then M answered, "But behold, they will not believe
4:3 became a serpent; and M fled from it.
4:4 the LORD said to M, "Put out your hand,
4:10 But M said to the LORD, "Oh, my Lord,
4:14 LORD was kindled against M and he said, "Is
4:18 M went back to Jethro his father-in-law and said
4:18 And Jethro said to M, "Go in peace."
4:19 the LORD said to M in Midian, "Go back
4:20 So M took his wife and his sons and
4:20 and in his hand M took the rod of
4:21 the LORD said to M, "When you go back
4:25 son's foreskin, and touched M feet with it, and
4:27 to Aaron, "Go into the wilderness to meet M
4:28 And M told Aaron all the words of the
4:29 Then M and Aaron went and gathered together all
4:30 LORD had spoken to M, and did the signs
5:1 Afterward M and Aaron went to Pharaoh and said,
5:4 Egypt said to them, M and Aaron, why do
5:20 They met M and Aaron, who were waiting for
5:22 Then M turned again to the LORD and said,
6:1 the LORD said to M, "Now you shall see
6:2 And God said to M, "I am the LORD.
6:9 M spoke thus to the people of Israel; but
6:9 did not listen to M, because of their broken

6:10 the LORD said to M,
6:12 But M said to the LORD, "Behold, the people
6:13 the LORD spoke to M and Aaron, and gave
6:20 bore him Aaron and M, the years of the
6:26 are the Aaron and M to whom the LORD
6:27 Israel from Egypt, this M and this Aaron.
6:28 the LORD spoke to M in the land of
6:29 the LORD said to M, "I am the LORD;
6:30 But M said to the LORD, "Behold, I am
7:1 the LORD said to M, "See, I make you
7:6 And M and Aaron did so; they did as
7:7 Now M was eighty years old, and Aaron eighty-three
7:8 the LORD said to M and Aaron,
7:10 So M and Aaron went to Pharaoh and did
7:14 the LORD said to M, "Pharaoh's heart is hardened,
7:19 the LORD said to M, "Say to Aaron, 'Take
7:20 M and Aaron did as the LORD commanded; in
8:1 the LORD said to M, "Go in to Pharaoh
8:5 the LORD said to M, "Say to Aaron, 'Stretch
8:8 Pharaoh called M and Aaron, and said, "Entreat
8:9 M said to Pharaoh, "Be pleased to command me
8:10 M said, "Be it as you say, that you
8:12 So M and Aaron went out from Pharaoh; and
8:12 out from Pharaoh; and M cried to the LORD
8:13 to the word of M; the frogs died out
8:16 the LORD said to M, "Say to Aaron, 'Stretch
8:20 the LORD said to M, "Rise up early in
8:25 Then Pharaoh called M and Aaron, and said, "Go,
8:26 But M said, "It would not be right to
8:29 Then M said, "Behold, I am going out from
8:30 So M went out from Pharaoh and prayed to
8:31 the LORD did as M asked, and removed the
9:1 the LORD said to M, "Go in to Pharaoh,
9:8 the LORD said to M and Aaron, "Take handfuls
9:8 the kiln, and let M throw them toward heaven
9:10 before Pharaoh, and M threw them toward heaven,
9:11 could not stand before M because of the boils,
9:12 to them; as the LORD had spoken to M
9:13 the LORD said to M, "Rise up early in
9:22 the LORD said to M, "Stretch forth your hand
9:23 Then M stretched forth his rod toward heaven; and
9:27 Pharaoh sent, and called M and Aaron, and said
9:29 M said to him, "As soon as I have
9:33 in coming up.) So M went out of the
9:35 Israel go; as the LORD had spoken through M
10:1 the LORD said to M, "Go in to Pharaoh;
10:3 So M and Aaron went in to Pharaoh, and
10:8 So M and Aaron were brought back to Pharaoh;
10:9 And M said, "We will go with our young
10:12 the LORD said to M, "Stretch out your hand
10:13 So M stretched forth his rod over the land
10:16 Then Pharaoh called M and Aaron in haste, and
10:21 the LORD said to M, "Stretch out your hand
10:22 So M stretched out his hand toward heaven, and
10:24 Then Pharaoh called M, and said, "Go, serve the
10:25 But M said, "You must also let us have
10:29 M said, "As you say!
11:1 The LORD said to M, "Yet one plague more
11:3 Moreover, the man M was very great in the
11:4 And M said, "Thus says the LORD: About midnight
11:9 the LORD said to M, "Pharaoh will not listen
11:10 M and Aaron did all these wonders before Pharaoh;
12:1 The LORD said to M and Aaron in the
12:21 Then M called all the elders of Israel, and
12:28 the LORD had commanded M and Aaron, so they
12:31 And he summoned M and Aaron by night, and
12:35 had also done as M told them, for they
12:43 the LORD said to M and Aaron, "This is
12:50 as the LORD commanded M and Aaron, so they
13:1 The LORD said to M,
13:3 And M said to the people, "Remember this day,
13:19 And M took the bones of Joseph with him;
14:1 the LORD said to M,
14:11 and they said to M, "Is it because there
14:13 And M said to the people, "Fear not, stand
14:15 The LORD said to M, "Why do you cry
14:21 Then M stretched out his hand over the sea;
14:26 the LORD said to M, "Stretch out your hand
14:27 So M stretched forth his hand over the sea,
14:31 believed in the LORD and in his servant M
15:1 Then M and the people of Israel sang this
15:22 Then M led Israel onward from the Red Sea,
15:24 the people murmured against M, saying, "What shall
16:2 of Israel murmured against M and Aaron in the
16:4 the LORD said to M, "Behold, I will rain
16:6 So M and Aaron said to all the people
16:8 And M said, "When the LORD gives you in
16:9 And M said to Aaron, "Say to the whole
16:11 the LORD said to M,
16:15 And M said to them, "It is the bread
16:19 And M said to them, "Let no man leave
16:20 did not listen to M; some left part of
16:20 and became foul; and M was angry with them.
16:22 congregation came and told M,
16:24 till the morning, as M bade them; and it
16:25 M said, "Eat it today, for today is a
16:28 the LORD said to M, "How long do you
16:32 And M said, "This is what the LORD has
16:33 And M said to Aaron, "Take a jar, and
16:34 As the LORD commanded M, so Aaron placed it
17:2 people found fault with M, and said, "Give us
17:2 And M said to them, "Why do you find
17:3 the people murmured against M, and said, "Why did
17:4 So M cried to the LORD, "What shall I
17:5 the LORD said to M, "Pass on before the
17:6 And M did so, in the sight of the
17:9 And M said to Joshua, "Choose for us men,
17:10 So Joshua did as M told him, and fought
17:10 fought with Amalek; and M, Aaron, and Hur went
17:11 Whenever M held up his hand, Israel prevailed; and
17:12 But M hands grew weary; so they took a
17:14 the LORD said to M, "Write this as a
17:15 And M built an altar and called the name
18:1 the priest of Midian, M father-in-law, heard of all
18:1 God had done for M and for Israel his
18:2 Jethro, M father-in-law, had taken Zipporah, Moses'
18:2 father-in-law, had taken Zipporah, M wife, after he
18:5 And Jethro, M father-in-law, came with his sons and
18:5 and his wife to M in the wilderness where
18:6 And when one told M, "Lo, your father-in-law Jethro
18:7 M went out to meet his father-in-law, and did
18:8 Then M told his father-in-law all that the LORD
18:12 And Jethro, M father-in-law, offered a burnt offering
18:12 to eat bread with M father-in-law before God.
18:13 On the morrow M sat to judge the people,
18:13 the people stood about M from morning till evening.
18:14 When M father-in-law saw all that he was doing
18:15 And M said to his father-in-law, "Because the people
18:17 M father-in-law said to him, "What you are doing
18:24 So M gave heed to the voice of his
18:25 M chose able men out of all Israel, and
18:26 cases they brought to M, but any small matter
18:27 Then M let his father-in-law depart, and he went
19:3 And M went up to God, and the LORD
19:7 So M came and called the elders of the
19:8 And M reported the words of the people to
19:9 the LORD said to M, "Lo, I am coming
19:9 Then M told the words of the people to
19:10 the LORD said to M, "Go to the people
19:14 So M went down from the mountain to the
19:17 Then M brought the people out of the camp
19:19 grew louder and louder, M spoke, and God answered
19:20 and the LORD called M to the top of
19:20 of the mountain, and M went up.
19:21 the LORD said to M, "Go down and warn
19:23 And M said to the LORD, "The people cannot
19:25 So M went down to the people and told
20:19 off, and said to M, "You speak to us,
20:20 And M said to the people, "Do not fear;
20:21 stood afar off, while M drew near to the
20:22 the LORD said to M, "Thus you shall say
24:1 And he said to M, "Come up to the
24:2 M alone shall come near to the LORD; but
24:3 M came and told the people all the words
24:4 And M wrote all the words of the LORD.
24:6 And M took half of the blood and put
24:8 And M took the blood and threw it upon
24:9 Then M and Aaron, Nadab, and Abihu, and seventy
24:12 The LORD said to M, "Come up to me
24:13 So M rose with his servant Joshua, and Moses
24:13 his servant Joshua, and M went up into the
24:15 Then M went up on the mountain, and the
24:16 day he called to M out of the midst
24:18 And M entered the cloud, and went up on
24:18 And M was on the mountain forty days and
25:1 The LORD said to M,
30:11 The LORD said to M,
30:17 The LORD said to M,
30:22 the LORD said to M,
30:34 the LORD said to M, "Take sweet spices, stacte,
31:1 The LORD said to M,
31:12 the LORD said to M,

31:18 And he gave to M, when he had made
32:1 the people saw that M delayed to come down
32:1 us; as for this M, the man who brought
32:7 the LORD said to M, "Go down; for your
32:9 the LORD said to M, "I have seen this
32:11 But M besought the LORD his God, and said,
32:15 And M turned, and went down from the mountain
32:17 shouted, he said to M, "There is a noise
32:19 calf and the dancing, M anger burned hot, and
32:21 And M said to Aaron, "What did this people
32:23 us; as for this M, the man who brought
32:25 And when M saw that the people had broken
32:26 among their enemies), then M stood in the gate
32:28 to the word of M; and there fell of
32:29 And M said, "Today you have ordained yourselves for
32:30 On the morrow M said to the people, "You
32:31 So M returned to the LORD and said, "Alas,
32:33 the LORD said to M, "Whoever has sinned against
33:1 The LORD said to M, "Depart, go up hence,
33:5 LORD had said to M, "Say to the people
33:7 Now M used to take the tent and pitch
33:8 Whenever M went out to the tent, all the
33:8 door, and looked after M, until he had gone
33:9 When M entered the tent, the pillar of cloud
33:9 the tent, and the LORD would speak with M
33:11 used to speak to M face to face, as
33:11 When M turned again into the camp, his servant
33:12 M said to the LORD, "See, thou sayest to
33:17 the LORD said to M, "This very thing that
33:18 M said, "I pray thee, show me thy glory."
34:1 The LORD said to M, "Cut two tables of
34:4 So M cut two tables of stone like the
34:8 And M made haste to bow his head toward
34:27 the LORD said to M, "Write these words; in
34:29 When M came down from Mount Sinai, with the
34:29 down from the mountain, M did not know that
34:30 people of Israel saw M, behold, the skin of
34:31 But M called to them; and Aaron and all
34:31 returned to him, and M talked with them.
34:33 And when M had finished speaking with them, he
34:34 his face; but whenever M went in before the
34:35 saw the face of M, that the skin of
34:35 that the skin of M face shone; and Moses
34:35 Moses' face shone; and M would put the veil
35:1 M assembled all the congregation of the people of
35:4 M said to all the congregation of the people
35:20 people of Israel departed from the presence of M
35:29 LORD had commanded by M to be done, brought
35:30 And M said to the people of Israel, "See,
36:2 And M called Bezalel and Oholiab and every able
36:3 and they received from M all the freewill offering
36:5 doing, and said to M, "The people bring much
36:6 So M gave command, and word was proclaimed
38:21 at the commandment of M, for the work of
38:22 that the LORD commanded M;
39:1 for Aaron; as the LORD had commanded M
39:5 fine twined linen; as the LORD had commanded M
39:7 sons of Israel; as the LORD had commanded M
39:21 from the ephod; as the LORD had commanded M
39:26 for ministering; as the LORD had commanded M
39:29 with needlework; as the LORD had commanded M
39:31 the turban above; as the LORD had commanded M
39:32 the LORD had commanded M; so had they done.
39:33 brought the tabernacle to M, the tent and all
39:42 the LORD had commanded M, so the people of
39:43 And M saw all the work, and behold, they
39:43 And M blessed them.
Lev 1:1 The LORD called M, and spoke to him
4:1 the LORD said to M,
5:14 The LORD said to M,
6:1 The LORD said to M,
6:8 The LORD said to M,
6:19 The LORD said to M,
6:24 The LORD said to M,
7:22 The LORD said to M,
7:28 The LORD said to M,
7:38 which the LORD commanded M on Mount Sinai, on
8:1 The LORD said to M,
8:4 And M did as the LORD commanded him; and
8:5 And M said to the congregation, "This is the
8:6 And M brought Aaron and his sons, and washed
8:9 plate, the holy crown, as the LORD commanded M
8:10 Then M took the anointing oil, and anointed the
8:13 And M brought Aaron's sons, and clothed them with
8:13 bound caps on them, as the LORD commanded M
8:15 And M killed it, and took the blood, and
8:16 with their fat, and M burned them on the
8:17 fire outside the camp, as the LORD commanded M
8:19 And M killed it, and threw the blood upon
8:20 was cut into pieces, M burned the head and
8:21 were washed with water, M burned the whole ram
8:21 fire to the LORD, as the LORD commanded M
8:23 And M killed it, and took some of its
8:24 sons were brought, and M put some of the
8:24 their right feet; and M threw the blood upon
8:28 Then M took them from their hands, and burned
8:29 And M took the breast, and waved it for
8:29 the LORD; it was M portion of the ram
8:29 the ram of ordination, as the LORD commanded M
8:30 Then M took some of the anointing oil and
8:31 And M said to Aaron and his sons, "Boil
8:36 all the things which the LORD commanded by M
9:1 On the eighth day M called Aaron and his
9:5 they brought what M commanded before the tent
9:6 And M said, "This is the thing which the
9:7 Then M said to Aaron, "Draw near to the
9:10 burned upon the altar, as the LORD commanded M
9:21 before the LORD; as M commanded.
9:23 And M and Aaron went into the tent of
10:3 Then M said to Aaron, "This is what the
10:4 And M called Mishael and Elzaphan, the sons of
10:5 of the camp, as M had said.
10:6 And M said to Aaron and to Eleazar and
10:7 And they did according to the word of M
10:11 which the LORD has spoken to them by M
10:12 And M said to Aaron and to Eleazar and
10:16 Now M diligently inquired about the goat of the
10:19 And Aaron said to M, "Behold, today they have
10:20 And when M heard that, he was content.
11:1 the LORD said to M and Aaron,
12:1 The LORD said to M,
13:1 The LORD said to M and Aaron,
14:1 The LORD said to M,
14:33 The LORD said to M and Aaron,
15:1 The LORD said to M and Aaron,
16:1 The LORD spoke to M, after the death of
16:2 the LORD said to M, "Tell Aaron your brother
16:34 And M did as the LORD commanded him.
17:1 the LORD said to M,
18:1 the LORD said to M,
19:1 the LORD said to M,
20:1 The LORD said to M,
21:1 the LORD said to M, "Speak to the priests,
21:16 the LORD said to M,
21:24 So M spoke to Aaron and to his sons
22:1 the LORD said to M,
22:17 the LORD said to M,
22:26 the LORD said to M,
23:1 The LORD said to M,
23:9 the LORD said to M,
23:23 the LORD said to M,
23:26 the LORD said to M,
23:33 the LORD said to M,
23:44 Thus M declared to the people of Israel the
24:1 The LORD said to M,
24:11 And they brought him to M
24:13 the LORD said to M,
24:23 So M spoke to the people of Israel; and
24:23 people of Israel did as the LORD commanded M
25:1 The LORD said to M on Mount Sinai,
26:46 the people of Israel on Mount Sinai by M
27:1 The LORD said to M,
27:34 which the LORD commanded M for the people of
Num 1:1 The LORD spoke to M in the wilderness of
1:17 M and Aaron took these men who have been
1:19 upward, head by head, as the LORD commanded M
1:44 who were numbered, whom M and Aaron numbered
1:48 the LORD said to M,
1:54 did according to all that the LORD commanded M
2:1 The LORD said to M and Aaron,
2:33 the people of Israel, as the LORD commanded M
2:34 that the LORD commanded M, so they encamped by
3:1 generations of Aaron and M at the time when
3:1 the LORD spoke with M on Mount Sinai.
3:5 the LORD said to M,
3:11 the LORD said to M,
3:14 the LORD said to M in the wilderness of
3:16 So M numbered them according to the word of
3:38 toward the sunrise, were M and Aaron and his
3:39 of the Levites, whom M and Aaron numbered at
3:40 the LORD said to M, "Number all the first-born
3:42 So M numbered all the first-born among the people

30:16 which the LORD commanded M, as between a man
31:1 The LORD said to M,
31:3 And M said to the people, "Arm men from
31:6 And M sent them to the war, a thousand
31:7 as the LORD commanded M, and slew every male.
31:12 and the spoil to M, and to Eleazar the
31:13 M, and Eleazar the priest, and all the leaders
31:14 And M was angry with the officers of the
31:15 M said to them, "Have you let all the
31:21 the LORD has commanded M:
31:25 The LORD said to M,
31:31 And M and Eleazar the priest did as the
31:31 Eleazar the priest did as the LORD commanded M
31:41 And M gave the tribute, which was the offering
31:41 to Eleazar the priest, as the LORD commanded M
31:42 of Israel's half, which M separated from that of
31:47 people of Israel's half M took one of every
31:47 of the LORD; as the LORD commanded M
31:48 hundreds, came near to M,
31:49 Moses, and said to M, "Your servants have counted
31:51 And M and Eleazar the priest received from them
31:54 man for himself.) And M and Eleazar the priest
32:2 came and said to M and to Eleazar the
32:6 But M said to the sons of Gad and
32:20 So M said to them, "If you will do
32:25 of Reuben said to M, "Your servants will do
32:28 So M gave command concerning them to Eleazar
32:29 And M said to them, "If the sons of
32:33 And M gave to them, to the sons of
32:40 And M gave Gilead to Machir the son of
33:1 under the leadership of M and Aaron.
33:2 M wrote down their starting places, stage by stage,
33:50 the LORD said to M in the plains of
34:1 The LORD said to M,
34:13 M commanded the people of Israel, saying, "This is
34:16 The LORD said to M,
35:1 The LORD said to M in the plains of
35:9 the LORD said to M,
36:1 near and spoke before M and before the leaders,
36:5 And M commanded the people of Israel according to
36:10 as the LORD commanded M;
36:13 the LORD commanded by M to the people of
Deut 1:1 are the words that M spoke to all Israel
1:3 of the eleventh month, M spoke to the people
1:5 the land of Moab, M undertook to explain this
4:41 Then M set apart three cities in the east
4:44 is the law which M set before the children
4:45 and the ordinances, which M spoke to the children
4:46 lived at Heshbon, whom M and the children of
5:1 And M summoned all Israel, and said to them,
27:1 Now M and the elders of Israel commanded the
27:9 And M and the Levitical priests said to all
27:11 And M charged the people the same day, saying,
29:1 which the LORD commanded M to make with the
29:2 And M summoned all Israel and said to them:
31:1 So M continued to speak these words to all
31:7 Then M summoned Joshua, and said to him in
31:9 And M wrote this law, and gave it to
31:10 And M commanded them, "At the end of every
31:14 the LORD said to M, "Behold, the days approach
31:14 And M and Joshua went and presented themselves
31:16 the LORD said to M, "Behold, you are about
31:22 So M wrote this song the same day, and
31:24 When M had finished writing the words of this
31:25 to the very end, M commanded the Levites who
31:30 Then M spoke the words of this song until
32:44 M came and recited all the words of this
32:45 And when M had finished speaking all these words
32:48 the LORD said to M that very day,
33:1 the blessing with which M the man of God
33:4 direction from thee, when M commanded us a law,
34:1 And M went up from the plains of Moab
34:5 So M the servant of the LORD died there
34:7 M was a hundred and twenty years old when
34:8 of Israel wept for M in the plains of
34:8 weeping and mourning for M were ended.
34:9 spirit of wisdom, for M had laid his hands
34:9 him, and did as the LORD had commanded M
34:10 since in Israel like M, whom the LORD knew
34:12 and terrible deeds which M wrought in the sight
Josh 1:1 After the death of M the servant of the
1:1 the son of Nun, M minister,
1:2 of Nun, Moses' minister, M my servant is dead;
1:3 have given to you, as I promised to M
1:5 as I was with M, so I will be
1:7 all the law which M my servant commanded you;
1:13 "Remember the word which M the servant of the
1:14 in the land which M gave you beyond the
1:15 it, the land which M the servant of the
1:17 Just as we obeyed M in all things, so
1:17 God be with you, as he was with M
3:7 as I was with M, so I will be
4:10 according to all that M had commanded Joshua.
4:12 people of Israel, as M had bidden them;
4:14 stood in awe of M, all the days of
8:31 God of Israel, as M the servant of the
8:31 of the law of M, "an altar of unhewn
8:32 of the law of M, which he had written.
8:33 of Mount Ebal, as M the servant of the
8:35 word of all that M commanded which Joshua did
9:24 had commanded his servant M to give you all
11:12 utterly destroying them, as M the servant of the
11:15 the LORD had commanded M his servant, so Moses
11:15 Moses his servant, so M commanded Joshua, and so
11:15 undone of all that the LORD had commanded M
11:20 but be exterminated, as the LORD commanded M
11:23 LORD had spoken to M; and Joshua gave it
12:6 M, the servant of the LORD, and the people
12:6 Israel defeated them; and M the servant of the
13:8 received their inheritance, which M gave them,
13:8 the Jordan eastward, as M the servant of the
13:12 of the Rephaim); these M had defeated and driven
13:14 tribe of Levi alone M gave no inheritance; the
13:15 And M gave an inheritance to the tribe of
13:21 reigned in Heshbon, whom M defeated with the
13:24 And M gave an inheritance also to the tribe
13:29 And M gave an inheritance to the half-tribe of
13:32 are the inheritances which M distributed in the
13:33 the tribe of Levi M gave no inheritance; the
14:2 the LORD had commanded M for the nine and
14:3 For M had given an inheritance to the two
14:5 as the LORD commanded M; they allotted the land.
14:6 the LORD said to M the man of God
14:7 forty years old when M the servant of the
14:9 And M swore on that day, saying, 'Surely the
14:10 spoke this word to M, while Israel walked in
14:11 in the day that M sent me; my strength
17:4 said, "The LORD commanded M to give us an
18:7 the Jordan eastward, which M the servant of the
20:2 spoke to you through M,
21:2 "The LORD commanded through M that we be
21:8 Levites, as the LORD had commanded through M
22:2 have kept all that M the servant of the
22:4 your possession lies, which M the servant of the
22:5 and the law which M the servant of the
22:7 the tribe of Manasseh M had given a possession
22:9 themselves by command of the LORD through M
23:6 of the law of M, turning aside from it
24:5 And I sent M and Aaron, and I plagued
Judg 1:16 descendants of the Kenite, M father-in-law, went up
1:20 given to Caleb, as M had said; and he
3:4 the LORD, which he commanded their fathers by M
4:11 Hobab the father-in-law of M, and had pitched his
18:30 of Gershom, son of M, and his sons were
1Sam 12:6 is witness, who appointed M and Aaron and brought
12:8 and the LORD sent M and Aaron, who brought
1Kgs 2:3 in the law of M, that you may prosper
8:9 tables of stone which M put there at Horeb,
8:53 thou didst declare through M, thy servant, when thou
8:56 which he uttered by M his servant.
2Kgs 14:6 of the law of M, where the LORD commanded,
18:4 the bronze serpent that M had made, for until
18:6 the commandments which the LORD commanded M
18:12 covenant, even all that M the servant of the
21:8 law that my servant M commanded them."
23:25 all the law of M; nor did any like
1Chr 6:3 children of Amram: Aaron, M, and Miriam.
6:49 according to all that M the servant of God
15:15 with the poles, as M had commanded according to
21:29 of the LORD, which M had made in the
22:13 which the LORD commanded M for Israel.
23:13 The sons of Amram: Aaron and M
23:14 But the sons of M the man of God
23:15 The sons of M: Gershom and Eliezer.
26:24 of Gershom, son of M, was chief officer in
2Chr 1:3 meeting of God, which M the servant of the
5:10 the two tables which M put there at Horeb,
8:13 to the commandment of M for the sabbaths, the
23:18 in the law of M, with rejoicing and with
24:6 the tax levied by M, the servant of the
24:9 LORD the tax that M the servant of God
25:4 in the book of M, where the LORD commanded,

30:16 to the law of M the man of God;
33:8 the statutes, and the ordinances given through M
34:14 of the law of the LORD given through M
35:6 according to the word of the LORD by M
35:12 as it is written in the book of M
Ezra 3:2 in the law of M the man of God.
6:18 as it is written in the book of M
7:6 in the law of M which the LORD the
Neh 1:7 ordinances which thou didst command thy servant M
1:8 didst command thy servant M, saying, 'If you are
8:1 of the law of M which the LORD had
8:14 LORD had commanded by M that the people of
9:14 and a law by M thy servant.
10:29 which was given by M the servant of God,
13:1 from the book of M in the hearing of
Tob 6:12 to the law of M, cannot give her to
7:13 to the law of M, and take her with
Ps 77:20 by the hand of M and Aaron.
99:6 M and Aaron were among his priests, Samuel also
103:7 known his ways to M, his acts to the
105:26 He sent M his servant, and Aaron whom he
106:16 camp were jealous of M and Aaron, the holy
106:23 them– had not M, his chosen one, stood
106:32 it went ill with M on their account;
Sir 24:22 God, the law which M commanded us as an
45:1 by God and man, M, whose memory is blessed.
45:6 Aaron, the brother of M, a holy man like
45:15 M ordained him, and anointed him with holy oil;
46:1 was the successor of M in prophesying.
46:7 in the days of M he did a loyal
Is 63:11 days of old, of M his servant.
63:12 the right hand of M, who divided the waters
Jer 15:1 said to me, "Though M and Samuel stood before
Bar 1:20 the Lord declared through M his servant at the
2:2 in the law of M,
2:28 speak by thy servant M on the day when
Dan 9:11 in the law of M the servant of God
9:13 in the law of M, all this calamity has
13:3 taught their daughter according to the law of M
13:62 with the law of M, they put them to
Mic 6:4 I sent before you M, Aaron, and Miriam.
Mal 4:4 law of my servant M, the statutes and ordinances
2Mac 1:29 thy holy place, as M said.
2:4 to the mountain where M had gone up and
2:8 in the case of M, and as Solomon asked
2:10 Just as M prayed to the Lord, and fire
2:11 And M said, "They were consumed because the sin
7:6 compassion on us, as M declared in his song
7:30 law that was given to our fathers through M
Mt 8:4 offer the gift that M commanded, for a proof
17:3 there appeared to them M and Elijah, talking with
17:4 you and one for M and one for Elijah."
19:7 him, "Why then did M command one to give
19:8 your hardness of heart M allowed you to divorce
22:24 a question, saying, "Teacher, M said, 'If a man
23:2 the Pharisees sit on M seat;
Mk 1:44 for your cleansing what M commanded, for a proof
7:10 For M said, 'Honor your father and your mother';
9:4 to them Elijah with M; and they were talking
9:5 you and one for M and one for Elijah."
10:3 answered them, "What did M command you?"
10:4 They said, M allowed a man to write a
12:19 a question, saying, "Teacher, M wrote for us that
12:26 in the book of M, in the passage about
Lk 2:22 to the law of M, they brought him up
5:14 for your cleansing, as M commanded, for a proof
9:30 men talked with him, M and Elijah,
9:33 you and one for M and one for Elijah"–
16:29 Abraham said, 'They have M and the prophets; let
16:31 they do not hear M and the prophets, neither
20:28 a question, saying, "Teacher, M wrote for us that
20:37 dead are raised, even M showed, in the passage
24:27 And beginning with M and all the prophets, he
24:44 in the law of M and the prophets and
Jn 1:17 law was given through M; grace and truth came
1:45 found him of whom M in the law and
3:14 And as M lifted up the serpent in the
5:44 the Father; it is M who accuses you, on
5:45 If you believed M, you would believe me, for
6:32 you, it was not M who gave you the
7:19 Did not M give you the law?
7:22 M gave you circumcision (not that it is from
7:22 that it is from M, but from the fathers),
7:23 that the law of M may not be broken,
8:5 Now in the law M commanded us to stone
9:28 are his disciple, but we are disciples of M
9:29 God has spoken to M, but as for this
Acts 3:22 M said, 'The Lord God will raise up for
6:11 speak blasphemous words against M and God."
6:14 change the customs which M delivered to us."
7:20 At this time M was born, and was beautiful
7:22 And M was instructed in all the wisdom of
7:29 yesterday?' At this retort M fled, and became an
7:31 When M saw it he wondered at the sight;
7:32 and of Jacob.' And M trembled and did not
7:35 you to Egypt.' "This M whom they refused, saying,
7:37 This is the M who said to the Israelites,
7:40 us; as for this M who led us out
7:44 he who spoke to M directed him to make
13:39 could not be freed by the law of M
15:1 to the custom of M, you cannot be saved."
15:5 to charge them to keep the law of M
15:21 For from early generations M has had in every
21:21 the Gentiles to forsake M, telling them not to
26:22 what the prophets and M said would come to
28:23 from the law of M and from the prophets.
Rom 5:14 reigned from Adam to M, even over those whose
9:15 For he says to M, "I will have mercy
10:5 M writes that the man who practices the
10:19 First M says, "I will make you jealous of
1Cor 9:9 in the law of M, "You shall not muzzle
10:2 all were baptized into M in the cloud and
2Cor 3:7 could not look at M face because of its
3:13 very bold, not like M, who put a veil
3:15 to this day whenever M is read a veil
2Tim 3:8 Jannes and Jambres opposed M, so these men also
Heb 3:2 appointed him, just as M also was faithful in
3:3 much more glory than M as the builder of
3:5 things is God.) Now M was faithful in all
3:16 those who left Egypt under the leadership of M
7:14 connection with that tribe M said nothing about
8:5 heavenly sanctuary; for when M was about to erect
9:19 had been declared by M to all the people,
10:28 violated the law of M dies without mercy at
11:23 By faith M, when he was born, was hid
11:24 By faith M, when he was grown up, refused
12:21 was the sight that M said, "I tremble with
Jude 1:9 about the body of M, he did not presume
Rev 15:3 sing the song of M, the servant of God,

MOST (229)

Gen 14:18 was priest of God M High.
14:19 be Abram by God M High, maker of heaven
14:20 and blessed be God M High, who has delivered
14:22 to the LORD God M High, maker of heaven
34:19 Now he was the M honored of all his
Ex 26:33 holy place from the M holy.
26:34 the testimony in the M holy place.
29:37 the altar shall be M holy; whatever touches the
30:10 your generations; it is M holy to the LORD."
30:29 that they may be M holy; whatever touches them
30:36 shall be for you M holy.
Lev 2:3 sons; it is a M holy part of the
2:10 sons; it is a M holy part of the
6:17 it is a thing M holy, like the sin
6:25 the LORD; it is M holy.
6:29 of it; it is M holy.
7:1 It is M holy;
7:6 holy place; it is M holy.
10:12 altar, for it is M holy;
10:17 it is a thing M holy and has been
14:13 the priest; it is M holy.
21:22 God, both of the M holy and of the
24:9 is for him a M holy portion out of
27:28 every devoted thing is M holy to the LORD.
Num 4:4 tent of meeting: the M holy things.
4:19 come near to the M holy things: Aaron and
18:9 be yours of the M holy things, reserved from
18:9 to me, shall be M holy to you and
18:10 In a M holy place shall you eat of
24:16 the knowledge of the M High, who sees the
Deut 28:54 man who is the M tender and delicately bred
28:56 The M tender and delicately bred woman among
32:8 When the M High gave to the nations their
Judg 5:24 M blessed of women be Jael, the wife of
5:24 Kenite, of tent-dwelling women M blessed.
Ruth 2:13 she said, "You are M gracious to me, my
2Sam 22:14 from heaven, and the M High uttered his voice.
23:19 He was the M renowned of the thirty, and
1Kgs 6:16 inner sanctuary, as the M holy place.
7:50 of the house, the M holy place, and for
8:6 the house, in the M holy place, underneath the

1Chr 6:49 the work of the M holy place, and to
11:21 He was the M renowned of the thirty, and
23:13 apart to consecrate the M holy things, that he
2Chr 3:8 And he made the M holy place; its length,
3:10 In the M holy place he made two cherubim
4:22 inner doors to the M holy place and for
5:7 the house, in the M holy place, underneath the
31:14 the LORD and the M holy offerings.
Ezra 2:63 to partake of the M holy food, until there
Neh 7:65 to partake of the M holy food, until a
Tob 1:4 the dwelling of the M High was consecrated and
1:13 Then the M High gave me favor and good
4:11 the presence of the M High.
Jud 4:7 only wide enough for two men at the M
13:18 are blessed by the M High God above all
Esth 4:3 weeping and lamenting, and M of them lay in
6:9 one of the king's M noble princes; let him
15:6 And he was M terrifying.
16:15 but are governed by M righteous laws
16:16 are sons of the M High, the most mighty
16:16 the Most High, the M mighty living God, who
16:16 our fathers in the M excellent order.
16:24 for men, but also M hateful for all time
Ps 7:17 of the LORD, the M High.
9:2 to thy name, O M High.
18:13 the heavens, and the M High uttered his voice,
21:6 thou dost make him M blessed for ever; thou
21:7 steadfast love of the M High he shall not
28:2 my hands toward thy M holy sanctuary.
46:4 holy habitation of the M High.
47:2 For the LORD, the M High, is terrible, a
50:14 your vows to the M High;
57:2 I cry to God M High, to God who
73:11 there knowledge in the M High?"
77:10 right hand of the M High has changed."
78:17 him, rebelling against the M High in the desert.
78:35 was their rock, the M High God their redeemer.
78:56 and rebelled against the M High God, and did
82:6 gods, sons of the M High, all of you;
83:18 the LORD, art the M High over all the
87:5 in her"; for the M High himself will establish
91:1 the shelter of the M High, who abides in
91:9 LORD your refuge, the M High your habitation,
92:1 to thy name, O M High;
97:9 thou, O LORD, art M high over all the
106:7 but rebelled against the M High at the Red
107:11 the counsel of the M High.
Song 5:16 His speech is M sweet, and he is altogether
8:6 flashes of fire, a M vehement flame.
Wis 5:15 with the Lord; the M High takes care of
6:3 your sovereignty from the M High, who will search
6:17 of wisdom is the M sincere desire for instruction,
7:23 intelligent and pure and M subtle.
12:7 fathers, that the land M precious of all to
15:14 But M foolish, and more miserable than an infant,
15:18 people worship even the M hateful animals, which
16:17 For-- M incredible of all--in the water, which
17:19 the sound of the M savage roaring beasts, or
18:12 in one instant their M valued children had been
Sir 4:10 a son of the M High, and he will
7:9 an offering to the M High God he will
7:15 were created by the M High.
9:15 the law of the M High.
12:2 him, certainly by the M High.
12:6 For the M High also hates sinners and will
16:19 man can see, so M of his works are
17:21 Return to the M High and turn away from
17:22 sing praises to the M High in Hades, as
19:17 the law of the M High take its course.
23:18 The M High will not take notice of my
23:23 the law of the M High; second, she has
24:2 the assembly of the M High she will open
24:3 the mouth of the M High, and covered the
24:22 the covenant of the M High God, the law
28:7 the covenant of the M High, and overlook ignorance.
29:11 the commandments of the M High, and it will
33:15 the works of the M High; they likewise are
34:6 are sent from the M High as a visitation,
34:19 The M High is not pleased with the offerings
35:6 odor rises before the M High.
35:10 Give to the M High as he has given,
35:17 not desist until the M High visits him, and
37:15 this pray to the M High that he may
38:2 healing comes from the M High, and he will
39:1 the law of the M High will seek out
39:5 make supplication before the M High; he will open
41:4 good pleasure of the M High?
41:8 the law of the M High God!
42:2 the law of the M High and his covenant,
42:18 For the M High knows all that may be
43:2 the work of the M High.
43:12 the hands of the M High have stretched it
44:21 the law of the M High, and was taken
46:5 He called upon the M High, the Mighty One,
47:5 to the Lord, the M High, and he gave
47:8 the Holy One, the M High, with ascriptions of
48:5 the word of the M High;
49:4 the law of the M High; the kings of
50:7 the temple of the M High, and like the
50:14 the offering to the M High, the Almighty,
50:15 pleasing odor to the M High, the King of
50:16 for remembrance before the M High.
50:17 Lord, the Almighty, God M High.
50:19 people besought the Lord M High in prayer before
50:21 the blessing from the M High.
Is 14:14 make myself like the M High.'
Jer 3:19 pleasant land, a heritage M beauteous of all nations.
6:26 for an only son, M bitter lamentation; for suddenly
Lam 3:35 the presence of the M High,
3:38 the mouth of the M High that good and
Ezek 20:6 milk and honey, the M glorious of all lands.
20:15 milk and honey, the M glorious of all lands,
28:7 strangers upon you, the M terrible of the nations;
29:15 It shall be the M lowly of the kingdoms,
30:11 people with him, the M terrible of the nations,
31:12 Foreigners, the M terrible of the nations, will cut
32:12 ones, all of them M terrible among the nations.
41:4 me, This is the M holy place.
42:13 LORD shall eat the M holy offerings; there they
42:13 they shall put the M holy offerings--the cereal
43:12 the mountain shall be M holy.
44:13 the things that are M sacred; but they shall
45:3 be the sanctuary, the M holy place.
48:12 of the land, a M holy place, adjoining the
Dan 3:32 hands of lawless enemies, M hateful rebels, and to
3:32 an unjust king, the M wicked in all the
3:94 Abednego, servants of the M High God, come forth,
4:2 and wonders that the M High God has wrought
4:17 may know that the M High rules the kingdom
4:24 a decree of the M High, which has come
4:25 you know that the M High rules the kingdom
4:32 have learned that the M High rules the kingdom
4:34 and I blessed the M High, and praised and
5:18 O king, the M High God gave Nebuchadnezzar your
5:21 he knew that the M High God rules the
7:18 the saints of the M High shall receive the
7:22 the saints of the M High, and the time
7:25 speak words against the M High, and shall wear
7:25 the saints of the M High, and shall think
7:27 the saints of the M High; their kingdom shall
9:24 and to anoint a M holy place.
13:4 because he was the M honored of them all.
14:2 king, and was the M honored of his friends.
Mic 7:4 like a brier, the M upright of them a
1Mac 1:6 So he summoned his M honored officers, who had
2Mac 1:14 his friends, to secure M of its treasures as
1:36 means purification, but by M people it is called
3:31 to call upon the M High and to grant
5:15 dared to enter the M holy temple in all
6:11 their regard for that M holy day.
7:34 you, unholy wretch, you M defiled of all men,
8:7 found the nights M advantageous for such attacks.
8:24 and wounded and disabled M of Nicanor's army, and
8:32 of Timothy's forces, a M unholy man, and one
9:25 entrusted and commended to M of you when I
9:28 his life by a M pitiable fate, among the
11:12 M of them got away stripped and wounded, and
12:14 of provisions, behaved M insolently toward Judas and
12:24 held the parents of M of them and the
Mt 11:20 upbraid the cities where M of his mighty works
21:8 M of the crowd spread their garments on the
24:12 because wickedness is multiplied, M men's love will
Mk 5:7 Jesus, Son of the M High God?
9:26 a corpse; so that M of them said, "He
Lk 1:3 orderly account for you, M excellent Theophilus,
1:32 the Son of the M High; and the Lord
1:35 the power of the M High will overshadow you;
1:76 the prophet of the M High; for you will
6:35 be sons of the M High; for he is
8:28 Jesus, Son of the M High God?
Acts 7:48 Yet the M High does not dwell in houses
16:17 are servants of the M High God, who proclaim

	19:32	was in confusion, and M of them did not
	20:38	and kissed him, sorrowing M of all because of
	24:2	since by your provision, M excellent Felix, reforms
	26:25	"I am not mad, M excellent Festus, but I
1Cor	10:5	Nevertheless with M of them God was not pleased;
	14:27	only two or at M three, and each in
	15:6	brethren at one time, M of whom are still
	15:19	are of all men M to be pitied.
2Cor	9:2	zeal has stirred up M of them.
	12:15	I will M gladly spend and be spent for
Eph	5:16	as wise, making the M of the time, because
Phil	1:14	is for Christ; and M of the brethren have
Col	4:5	toward outsiders, making the M of the time.
Heb	7:1	Salem, priest of the M High God, met Abraham
Jude	1:20	yourselves up on your M holy faith; pray in
Rev	21:11	its radiance like a M rare jewel, like a

MOTH (9)

Job	4:19	in the dust, who are crushed before the M
Ps	39:11	dost consume like a M what is dear to
Sir	42:13	from garments comes the M, and from a woman
Is	50:9	like a garment; the M will eat them up.
	51:8	For the M will eat them up like a
Hos	5:12	I am like a M to Ephraim, and like
Mt	6:19	treasures on earth, where M and rust consume and
	6:20	in heaven, where neither M nor rust consumes and
Lk	12:33	thief approaches and no M destroys.

MOTH-EATEN (2)

Job	13:28	a rotten thing, like a garment that is M
Jas	5:2	Your riches have rotted and your garments are M

MOTHER (334)

Gen	2:24	his father and his M and cleaves to his
	3:20	because she was the M of all living.
	17:16	she shall be a M of nations; kings of
	20:12	the daughter of my M; and she became my
	21:21	of Paran; and his M took a wife for
	24:28	ran and told her M's household about these things.
	24:53	brother and to her M costly ornaments.
	24:55	Her brother and her M said, "Let the maiden
	24:60	"Our sister, be the M of thousands of ten
	24:67	was comforted after his M's death.
	27:11	said to Rebekah his M, "Behold, my brother Esau
	27:13	His M said to him, "Upon me be your
	27:14	brought them to his M; and his mother prepared
	27:14	his mother; and his M prepared savory food, such
	27:29	brothers, and may your M's sons bow down to
	28:2	house of Bethuel your M's father; and take as
	28:2	daughters of Laban your M's brother.
	28:5	the brother of Rebekah, Jacob's and Esau's M
	28:7	his father and his M and gone to Paddan-aram.
	29:10	daughter of Laban his M's brother, and the sheep
	29:10	sheep of Laban his M's brother, Jacob went up
	29:10	flock of Laban his M's brother.
	30:14	brought them to his M Leah.
	37:10	Shall I and your M and your brothers indeed
	43:29	his brother Benjamin, his M's son, and said, "Is
	44:20	is left of his M's children; and his father
Ex	2:8	So the girl went and called the child's M
	20:12	your father and your M, that your days may
	21:15	his father or his M shall be put to
	21:17	his father or his M shall be put to
	23:19	a kid in its M's milk.
	34:26	a kid in its M's milk."
Lev	18:7	the nakedness of your M; she is your mother,
	18:7	mother; she is your M, you shall not uncover
	18:9	the daughter of your M, whether born at home
	18:13	the nakedness of your M's sister, for she is
	18:13	for she is your M's near kinswoman.
	19:3	you shall revere his M and his father, and
	20:9	his father or his M shall be put to
	20:9	his father or his M, his blood is upon
	20:14	a wife and her M also, it is wickedness;
	20:17	a daughter of his M, and sees her nakedness,
	20:19	the nakedness of your M's sister or of your
	21:2	nearest of kin, his M, his father, his son,
	21:11	father or for his M;
	22:27	seven days with its M; and from the eighth
	22:28	And whether the M is a cow or a
	24:11	His M's name was Shelomith, the daughter of Dibri,
Num	6:7	father nor for his M, nor for brother or
	12:12	comes out of his M's womb."
Deut	5:16	your father and your M, as the LORD your
	13:6	the son of your M, or your son, or
	14:21	a kid in its M's milk.
	21:13	her father and her M a full month; after
	21:18	the voice of his M, and, though they chastise
	21:19	his father and his M shall take hold of
	22:6	or eggs and the M sitting upon the young
	22:6	shall not take the M with the young;
	22:7	you shall let the M go, but the young
	22:15	young woman and her M shall take and bring
	27:16	his father or his M And all the people
	27:22	the daughter of his M And all the people
	33:9	of his father and M, 'I regard them not';
Josh	2:13	alive my father and M, my brothers and sisters,
	2:18	house your father and M, your brothers, and all
	6:23	and her father and M and brothers and all
Judg	5:7	Deborah, arose as a M in Israel.
	5:28	window she peered, the M of Sisera gazed through
	8:19	the sons of my M; as the LORD lives,
	9:1	to Shechem to his M's kinsmen and said to
	9:1	whole clan of his M's family,
	9:3	And his M's kinsmen spoke all these words on
	14:2	told his father and M, "I saw one of
	14:3	But his father and M said to him, "Is
	14:4	His father and M did not know that it
	14:5	with his father and M to Timnah, and he
	14:6	his father or his M what he had done.
	14:9	to his father and M, and gave some to
	14:16	my father nor my M, and shall I tell
	16:17	to God from my M's womb.
	17:2	he said to his M, "The eleven hundred pieces
	17:2	And his M said, "Blessed be my son by
	17:3	of silver to his M; and his mother said,
	17:3	his mother; and his M said, "I consecrate the
	17:4	the money to his M, his mother took two
	17:4	to his mother, his M took two hundred pieces
Ruth	1:8	of you to her M's house.
	2:11	left your father and M and your native land
1Sam	2:19	And his M used to make for him a
	15:33	so shall your M be childless among women."
	20:30	the shame of your M's nakedness?
	22:3	my father and my M stay with you, till
2Sam	17:25	the daughter of Nahash, sister of Zeruiah, Joab's M
	19:37	near the grave of my father and my M
	20:19	city which is a M in Israel; why will
1Kgs	1:11	said to Bathsheba the M of Solomon, "Have you
	2:13	came to Bathsheba the M of Solomon.
	2:19	brought for the king's M; and she sat on
	2:20	"Make your request, my M; for I will not
	2:22	King Solomon answered his M, "And why do you
	3:27	by no means slay it; she is its M
	11:26	servant of Solomon, whose M's name was Zeruah, a
	14:21	His M's name was Naamah the Ammonitess.
	14:31	His M's name was Naamah the Ammonitess.
	15:2	M's name was Maacah the daughter of Abishalom.
	15:10	His M's name was Maacah the daughter of
	15:13	also removed Maacah his M from being queen
	15:13	mother from being queen M because she had an
	17:23	delivered him to his M; and Elijah said, "See,
	19:20	my father and my M, and then I will
	22:42	His M's name was Azubah the daughter of Shilhi.
	22:52	the way of his M, and in the way
2Kgs	3:2	like his father and M, for he put away
	3:13	of your father and the prophets of your M
	4:19	said to his servant, "Carry him to his M
	4:20	brought him to his M, the child sat on
	4:30	Then the M of the child said, "As the
	8:26	His M's name was Athaliah; she was a
	9:22	the sorceries of your M Jezebel are so many?"
	10:13	royal princes and the sons of the queen M
	11:1	Now when Athaliah the M of Ahaziah saw that
	12:1	His M's name was Zibiah of Beer-sheba.
	14:2	His M's name was Jeho-addin of Jerusalem.
	15:2	His M's name was Jecoliah of Jerusalem.
	15:33	His M's name was Jerusha the daughter of Zadok.
	18:2	His M's name was Abi the daughter of Zechariah.
	21:1	His M's name was Hephzibah.
	21:19	His M's name was Meshullemeth the daughter of
	22:1	His M's name was Jedidah the daughter of Adaiah
	23:31	His M's name was Hamutal the daughter of
	23:36	His M's name was Zebidah the daughter of Pedaiah
	24:8	M's name was Nehushta the daughter of Elnathan
	24:12	Babylon, himself, and his M, and his servants, and
	24:15	to Babylon; the king's M, the king's wives, his
	24:18	M's name was Hamutal the daughter of Jeremiah
1Chr	2:26	Atarah; she was the M of Onam.
	3:2	the third Absalom, whose M was Maacah, the
	3:2	the fourth Adonijah, whose M was Haggith;
	4:9	his brothers; and his M called his name Jabez,

M

2Chr 12:13 His M's name was Naamah the Ammonitess.
13:2 His M's name was Micaiah the daughter of Uriel
15:16 Even Maacah, his M, King Asa removed from being
15:16 removed from being queen M because she had made
20:31 His M's name was Azubah the daughter of Shilhi.
22:2 His M's name was Athaliah, the granddaughter of.
22:3 of Ahab, for his M was his counselor in
22:10 Now when Athaliah the M of Ahaziah saw that
24:1 years in Jerusalem; his M's name was Zibiah of
25:1 His M's name was Jeho-addan of Jerusalem.
26:3 His M's name was Jecoliah of Jerusalem.
27:1 His M's name was Jerushah the daughter of Zadok.
29:1 His M's name was Abijah the daughter of Zechariah.
Tob 1:8 as Deborah my father's M had commanded me, for
4:3 die, bury me, and do not neglect your M
4:13 because shiftlessness is the M of famine.
5:17 But Anna, his M, began to weep, and said
6:14 of my father and M to the grave in
7:17 But the M comforted her daughter in her tears,
10:7 for my father and M have given up hope
11:17 us, and blessed are your father and your M
14:10 me properly, and your M with me.
Jud 8:26 sheep of Laban, his M's brother.
Esth 2:7 had neither father nor M; the maiden was beautiful
2:7 her father and her M died, Mordecai adopted her
Job 1:21 I came from my M's womb, and naked shall
3:10 the doors of my M's womb, nor hide trouble
17:14 to the worm, 'My M or 'My sister,'
19:17 wife, loathsome to the sons of my own M
31:18 father, and from his M's womb I guided him);
Ps 22:9 me safe upon my M's breasts.
22:10 birth, and since my M bore me thou hast
27:10 my father and my M have forsaken me, but
35:14 one who laments his M, bowed down and in
50:20 you slander your own M's son.
51:5 in sin did my M conceive me.
69:8 an alien to my M's sons.
71:6 took me from my M's womb.
109:14 the sin of his M be blotted out!
113:9 making her the joyous M of children.
131:2 child quieted at its M's breast; like a child
139:13 me together in my M's womb.
Prov 1:8 and reject not your M's teaching;
4:4 the sight of my M,
6:20 and forsake not your M's teaching.
10:1 a foolish son is a sorrow to his M
15:20 glad father, but a foolish man despises his M
19:26 and chases away his M is a son who
20:20 his father or his M, his lamp will be
23:22 do not despise your M when she is old.
23:25 Let your father and M be glad, let her
28:24 his father or his M and says, "That is
29:15 child left to himself brings shame to his M
30:17 scorns to obey a M will be picked out
31:1 of Massa, which his M taught him:
Eccl 5:15 he came from his M's womb he shall go
Song 1:6 My M's sons were angry with me, they made
3:4 brought him into my M's house, and into the
3:11 crown with which his M crowned him on the
6:9 the darling of her M, flawless to her that
8:1 that nursed at my M's breast!
8:2 the house of my M, and into the chamber
8:5 There your M was in travail with you, there
Wis 7:1 the womb of a M I was molded into
7:12 I did not know that she was their M
Sir 3:2 the right of the M over her sons.
3:4 and whoever glorifies his M is like one who
3:6 Lord will refresh his M;
3:9 children, but a M's curse uproots their foundations.
3:11 a disgrace for children not to respect their M
3:16 and whoever angers his M is cursed by the
4:10 a husband to their M; you will then be
4:10 he will love you more than does your M
7:27 and do not forget the birth-pangs of your M
15:2 meet him like a M, and like the wife
23:14 Remember your father and M when you sit among
40:1 come forth from their M's womb till the day
40:1 they return to the M of all.
41:17 before your father or M; and of a lie,
Is 8:4 'My father' or 'My M the wealth of Damascus
49:1 the body of my M he named my name.
50:1 LORD: "Where is your M's bill of divorce, with
50:1 for your transgressions your M was put away.
66:13 As one whom his M comforts, so I will
Jer 13:18 king and the queen M: "Take a lowly seat,
15:10 Woe is me, my M, that you bore me,
16:7 consolation to drink for his father or his M
20:14 The day when my M bore me, let it
20:17 the womb; so my M would have been my
22:26 hurl you and the M who bore you into
29:2 Jeconiah, and the queen M, the eunuchs, the princes
50:12 neigh like stallions, your M shall be utterly shamed,
52:1 M's name was Hamutal the daughter of Jeremiah
Ezek 16:3 an Amorite, and your M a Hittite.
16:44 proverb about you, 'Like M, like daughter.'
16:45 the daughter of your M, who loathed her husband
16:45 Your M was a Hittite and your father an
19:2 a lioness was your M among lions!
19:10 Your M was like a vine in a vineyard
22:7 Father and M are treated with contempt in you;
23:2 the daughters of one M;
44:25 however, for father or M, for son or daughter,
Hos 2:2 "Plead with your M, plead-- for she is
2:5 For their M has played the harlot; she that
4:5 you by night; and I will destroy your M
Mic 7:6 rises up against her M, the daughter-in-law against
Zech 13:3 prophet, his father and M who bore him will
13:3 and his father and M who bore him shall
1Mac 13:28 for his father and M and four brothers.
2Mac 7:1 seven brothers and their M were arrested and were
7:4 the brothers and the M looked on.
7:5 the brothers and their M encouraged one another to
7:20 The M was especially admirable and worthy of
7:25 the king called the M to him and urged
7:41 Last of all, the M died, after her sons.
Mt 1:18 When his M Mary had been betrothed to Joseph,
2:11 child with Mary his M, and they fell down
2:13 the child and his M, and flee to Egypt,
2:14 the child and his M by night, and departed
2:20 the child and his M, and go to the
2:21 the child and his M, and went to the
10:35 a daughter against her M, and a daughter-in-law
10:37 who loves father or M more than me is
12:46 the people, behold, his M and his brethren stood
12:47 him, "Who is my M, and who are my
12:48 said, "Here are my M and my brethren!
12:49 in heaven is my brother, and sister, and M
13:55 Is not his M called Mary?
14:8 Prompted by her M, she said, "Give me the
14:11 the girl, and she brought it to her M
15:4 your father and your M and, 'He who speaks
15:4 evil of father or M, let him surely die.'
15:5 his father or his M, What you would have
19:5 leave his father and M and be joined to
19:19 Honor your father and M, and, You shall love
19:29 sisters or father or M or children or lands,
20:20 Then the M of the sons of Zebedee came
27:56 Magdalene, and Mary the M of James and Joseph,
27:56 and Joseph, and the M of the sons of
Mk 3:31 And his M and his brethren came; and standing
3:32 said to him, "Your M and your brethren are
3:33 replied, "Who are my M and my brethren?"
3:34 said, "Here are my M and my brethren!
3:35 of God is my brother, and sister, and M
5:40 the child's father and M and those who were
6:24 and said to her M, "What shall I ask?"
6:28 girl; and the girl gave it to her M
7:10 your father and your M; and, 'He who speaks
7:10 evil of father or M, let him surely die';
7:11 his father or his M, What you would have
7:12 for his father or M,
10:7 leave his father and M and be joined to
10:19 witness, Do not defraud, Honor your father and M
10:29 brothers or sisters or M or father or children
15:39 Magdalene, and Mary the M of James the younger
15:46 Magdalene and Mary the M of Joses saw where
16:1 Magdalene, and Mary the M of James, and Salome,
Lk 1:15 Spirit, even from his M's womb.
1:43 granted me, that the M of my Lord should
1:60 his father, but his M said, "Not so; he
2:33 his father and his M marveled at what was
2:34 said to Mary his M, "Behold, this child is
2:48 were astonished; and his M said to him, "Son,
2:51 to them; and his M kept all these things
7:12 only son of his M, and she was a
7:15 And he gave him to his M
8:19 Then his M and his brethren came to him,
8:20 he was told, "Your M and your brrethren are
8:21 said to them, "My M and my brethren are
8:51 and the father and M of the child.
12:53 son against father, M against daughter and daughter
12:53 daughter against her M, mother-in-law against her

M

14:26 his own father and M and wife and children
18:20 not bear false witness, Honor your father and M
24:10 Jo-anna and Mary the M of James and the
Jn 2:1 in Galilee, and the M of Jesus was there;
2:3 the wine failed, the M of Jesus said to
2:5 His M said to the servants, "Do whatever he
2:12 to Caperna-um, with his M and his brothers and
3:4 second time into his M's womb and be born?"
6:42 Joseph, whose father and M we know?
19:25 of Jesus were his M, and his mother's sister,
19:25 his mother, and his M's sister, Mary the wife
19:26 When Jesus saw his M, and the disciple whom
19:26 he said to his M, "Woman, behold, your son!"
19:27 Then he said to the disciple, "Behold, your M
Acts 1:14 women and Mary the M of Jesus, and with
12:12 house of Mary, the M of John whose other
Rom 16:13 the Lord, also his M and mine.
Gal 4:26 Jerusalem above is free, and she is our M
Eph 5:31 leave his father and M and be joined to
6:2 "Honor your father and M
2Tim 1:5 grandmother Lois and your M Eunice and now, I
Heb 7:3 is without father or M or genealogy, and has
Rev 17:5 mystery: "Babylon the great, M of harlots and of

MOTHER-IN-LAW (20)
Deut 27:23 who lies with his M And all the people
Ruth 1:14 and Orpah kissed her M, but Ruth clung to
2:11 have done for your M since the death of
2:18 city; she showed her M what she had gleaned,
2:19 And her M said to her, "Where did you
2:19 So she told her M with whom she had
2:23 and wheat harvests; and she lived with her M
3:1 Then Naomi her M said to her, "My daughter,
3:6 did just as her M had told her.
3:16 she came to her M, she said, "How did
3:17 'You must not go back empty-handed to your M
Tob 10:12 your father-in-law and your M; they are now your
14:13 gave his father-in-law and M magnificent funerals.
Mic 7:6 the daughter-in-law against her M; a man's enemies
Mt 8:14 house, he saw his M lying sick with a
10:35 a daughter-in-law against her M;
Mk 1:30 Now Simon's M lay sick with a fever, and
Lk 4:38 Now Simon's M was ill with a high fever,
12:53 her mother, M against her daughter-in-law and
12:53 mother-in-law against her daughter-in-law and

MOTHER-OF-PEARL
Esth 1:6 pavement of porphyry, marble, M and precious

MOTHERS (13)
Gen 32:11 slay us all, the M with the children.
Prov 30:11 curse their fathers and do not bless their M
Is 49:23 your foster fathers, and their queens your nursing M
Jer 15:8 have brought against the M of young men a
16:3 place, and concerning the M who bore them and
Lam 2:12 They cry to their M, "Where is bread and
2:12 poured out on their M bosom.
5:3 become orphans, fatherless; our M are like widows.
Hos 10:14 the day of battle; M were dashed in pieces
1Mac 1:61 the infants from their M necks.
Mk 10:30 brothers and sisters and M and children and lands,
1Tim 1:9 fathers and murderers of M, for manslayers,
5:2 brothers, older women like M, younger women like

MOTION
Wis 7:24 more mobile than any M; because of her pureness

MOTIONED (3)
Acts 19:33 And Alexander M with his hand, wishing to make
21:40 standing on the steps, M with his hand to
24:9 when the governor had M to him to speak,

MOTIONING (2)
Acts 12:17 But M to them with his hand to be
13:16 Paul stood up, and M with his hand said:

MOTIVES
2Mac 14:30 this austerity did not spring from the best M

MOTTLED (2)
Gen 31:10 leaped upon the flock were striped, spotted, and M
31:12 are striped, spotted, and M; for I have seen

MOULDS
Sir 38:30 He M the clay with his arm and makes

MOUND (9)
2Sam 20:15 they cast up a M against the city, and
2Kgs 19:32 cast up a siege M against it.
Sir 21:8 like one who gathers stones for his burial M
Is 37:33 cast up a siege M against it.
Jer 6:6 cast up a siege M against Jerusalem.
30:18 be rebuilt upon its M, and the palace shall
49:2 shall become a desolate M, and its villages shall
Ezek 4:2 and cast up a M against it; set camps
26:8 and throw up a M against you, and raise

MOUNDS (5)
Josh 11:13 cities that stood on M did Israel burn, except
Jer 32:24 Behold, the siege M have come up to the
33:4 defense against the siege M and before the sword:
Ezek 17:17 him in war, when M are cast up and
21:22 gates, to cast up M, to build siege towers.

MOUNT (167)
Gen 14:6 the Horites in their M Seir as far as
22:14 this day, "On the M of the LORD it
Ex 19:11 will come down upon M Sinai in the sight
19:18 And M Sinai was wrapped in smoke, because the
19:20 LORD came down upon M Sinai, to the top
19:23 cannot come up to M Sinai; for thou thyself
24:16 the LORD settled on M Sinai, and the cloud
31:18 speaking with him upon M Sinai, the two tables
33:6 of their ornaments, from M Horeb onward.
34:2 in the morning to M Sinai, and present yourself
34:4 and went up on M Sinai, as the LORD
34:29 Moses came down from M Sinai, with the two
34:32 spoken with him in M Sinai.
Lev 7:38 LORD commanded Moses on M Sinai, on the day
25:1 said to Moses on M Sinai,
26:46 people of Israel on M Sinai by Moses.
27:34 people of Israel on M Sinai.
Num 3:1 spoke with Moses on M Sinai.
10:33 set out from the M of the LORD three
20:22 whole congregation, came to M Hor.
20:23 Moses and Aaron at M Hor, on the border
20:25 bring them up to M Hor;
20:27 and they went up M Hor in the sight
21:4 From M Hor they set out by the way
28:6 which was ordained at M Sinai for a pleasing
33:23 Kehelathah, and encamped at M Shepher.
33:24 they set out from M Shepher, and encamped at
33:37 Kadesh, and encamped at M Hor, on the edge
33:38 the priest went up M Hor at the command
33:39 when he died on M Hor.
33:41 they set out from M Hor, and encamped at
34:7 out your line to M Hor;
34:8 to Mount Hor; from M Hor you shall mark
Deut 1:2 by the way of M Seir to Kadesh-barnea.
2:1 days we went about M Seir.
2:5 because I have given M Seir to Esau as
3:8 of the Arnon to M Hermon
4:48 Arnon, as far as M Sirion (that is, Hermon),
11:29 set the blessing on M Gerizim and the curse
11:29 and the curse on M Ebal.
27:4 you this day, on M Ebal, and you shall
27:12 these shall stand upon M Gerizim to bless the
27:13 these shall stand upon M Ebal for the curse:
28:43 is among you shall M above you higher and
32:49 mountain of the Abarim, M Nebo, which is in
32:50 your brother died in M Hor and was gathered
33:2 he shone forth from M Paran, he came from
34:1 plains of Moab to M Nebo, to the top
Josh 8:30 built an altar in M Ebal to the LORD,
8:33 them in front of M Gerizim and half of
8:33 them in front of M Ebal, as Moses the
11:17 and its lowland from M Halak, that rises toward
11:17 valley of Lebanon below M Hermon.
12:1 of the Arnon to M Hermon, with all the
12:5 Edre-i and ruled over M Hermon and Salecah and
12:7 valley of Lebanon to M Halak, that rises toward
13:5 sunrising, from Baal-gad below M Hermon to the
13:11 and Ma-acathites, and all M Hermon, and all Bashan
15:9 to the cities of M Ephron; then the boundary
15:10 west of Baalah to M Seir, passes along to
15:10 northern shoulder of M Jearim (that is, Chesalon),
15:11 and passes along to M Baalah, and goes out
Judg 3:3 who dwelt on M Lebanon, from Mount Baal-hermon
3:3 on Mount Lebanon, from M Baal-hermon as far as
4:6 gather your men at M Tabor, taking ten thousand
4:12 had gone up to M Tabor,
4:14 Barak went down from M Tabor with ten thousand

M

9:7 on the top of M Gerizim, and cried aloud
9:48 Abimelech went up to M Zalmon, he and all
1Sam 31:1 and fell slain on M Gilboa.
31:8 three sons fallen on M Gilboa.
2Sam 1:6 happened to be on M Gilboa; and there was
15:30 the ascent of the M of Olives, weeping as
1Kgs 12:18 Rehoboam made haste to M his chariot, to flee
18:19 Israel to me at M Carmel, and the four
18:20 the prophets together at M Carmel.
19:8 nights to Horeb the M of God.
19:11 and stand upon the M before the LORD." And
2Kgs 2:25 he went on to M Carmel, and thence he
4:25 man of God at M Carmel.
19:31 remnant, and out of M Zion a band of
23:13 the south of the M of corruption, which Solomon
23:16 tombs there on the M; and he sent and
1Chr 4:42 the Simeonites, went to M Seir, having as their
5:23 to Baal-hermon, Senir, and M Hermon.
10:1 and fell slain on M Gilboa.
10:8 his sons fallen on M Gilboa.
2Chr 3:1 LORD in Jerusalem on M Moriah, where the LORD
10:18 Rehoboam made haste to M his chariot, to flee
13:4 Abijah stood up on M Zemaraim which is in
20:10 Ammon and Moab and M Seir, whom thou wouldest
20:22 of Ammon, Moab, and M Seir, who had come
20:23 the inhabitants of M Seir, destroying them utterly,
Neh 9:13 didst come down upon M Sinai, and speak with
Job 20:6 Though his height M up to the heavens, and
Ps 42:6 and of Hermon, from M Mizar.
48:2 of all the earth, M Zion, in the far
48:11 filled with victory; let M Zion be glad!
68:16 many-peaked mountain, at the M which God desired
68:18 didst ascend the high M, leading captives in thy
74:2 Remember M Zion, where thou hast dwelt.
78:68 the tribe of Judah, M Zion, which he loves.
87:1 On the holy M stands the city he founded;
125:1 the LORD are like M Zion, which cannot be
Sir 50:26 Those who live on M Seir, and the Philistines,
Is 4:5 the whole site of M Zion and over her
8:18 hosts, who dwells on M Zion.
10:12 all his work on M Zion and on Jerusalem
10:32 his fist at the M of the daughter of
14:13 will sit on the M of assembly in the
16:1 the desert, to the M of the daughter of
18:7 the rivers divide, to M Zion, the place of
24:23 hosts will reign on M Zion and in Jerusalem
28:21 rise up as on M Perazim, he will be
29:8 be that fight against M Zion.
31:4 down to fight upon M Zion and upon its
37:32 remnant, and out of M Zion a band of
40:31 their strength, they shall M up with wings like
Jer 4:15 and proclaims evil from M Ephraim.
46:4 Harness the horses; M, O horsemen!
49:22 Behold, one shall M up and fly swiftly like
51:53 Though Babylon should M up to heaven, and though
Lam 5:18 have grown dim, for M Zion which lies desolate;
Ezek 10:16 up their wings to M up from the earth,
35:2 set your face against M Seir, and prophesy against
35:3 I am against you, M Seir, and I will
35:7 I will make M Seir a waste and a
35:15 you shall be desolate, M Seir, and all Edom,
Joel 2:32 be delivered; for in M Zion and in Jerusalem
Obad 1:8 and understanding out of M Esau?
1:9 that every man from M Esau will be cut
1:17 But in M Zion there shall be those that
1:19 the Negeb shall possess M Esau, and those of
1:21 shall go up to M Zion to rule Mount
1:21 Mount Zion to rule M Esau; and the kingdom
Mic 4:7 reign over them in M Zion from this time
Hab 3:3 the Holy One from M Paran.
Zech 14:4 shall stand on the M of Olives which lies
14:4 the east; and the M of Olives shall be
14:4 one half of the M shall withdraw northward, and
1Mac 4:37 they went up to M Zion.
4:60 that time they fortified M Zion with high walls
5:54 they went up to M Zion with gladness and
6:48 in Judea and at M Zion.
6:62 when the king entered M Zion and saw what
7:33 Nicanor went up to M Zion.
9:15 them as far as M Azotus.
10:11 the walls and encircle M Zion with squared stones,
14:27 it upon pillars on M Zion.
Mt 21:1 to Bethphage, to the M of Olives, then Jesus
24:3 he sat on the M of Olives, the disciples
26:30 went out to the M of Olives.
Mk 11:1 and Bethany, at the M of Olives, he sent
13:3 he sat on the M of Olives opposite the
14:26 went out to the M of Olives.
Lk 19:29 and Bethany, at the M that is called Olivet,
19:37 the descent of the M of Olives, the whole
21:37 and lodged on the M called Olivet.
22:39 his custom, to the M of Olives; and the
Jn 8:1 Jesus went to the M of Olives.
Acts 1:12 to Jerusalem from the M called Olivet, which is
7:30 in the wilderness of M Sinai, in a flame
7:38 spoke to him at M Sinai, and with our
Gal 4:24 One is from M Sinai, bearing children for slavery;
4:25 Now Hagar is M Sinai in Arabia; she corresponds
Heb 12:22 you have come to M Zion and to the
Rev 14:1 looked, and lo, on M Zion stood the Lamb,

MOUNTAIN (194)

Gen 12:8 he removed to the M on the east of
14:10 into them, and the rest fled to the M
31:54 a sacrifice on the M and called his kinsmen
31:54 ate bread and tarried all night on the M
48:22 to your brothers one M slope which I took
Ex 3:1 came to Horeb, the M of God.
3:12 of Egypt, you shall serve God upon this M
4:27 met him at the M of God and kissed
15:17 them on thy own M, the place, O LORD,
18:5 was encamped at the M of God.
19:2 wilderness; and there Israel encamped before the M
19:3 him out of the M, saying, "Thus you shall
19:12 go up into the M or touch the border
19:12 it; whoever touches the M shall be put to
19:13 long blast, they shall come up to the M
19:14 went down from the M to the people, and
19:16 thick cloud upon the M, and a very loud
19:17 took their stand at the foot of the M
19:18 kiln, and the whole M quaked greatly.
19:20 the top of the M; and the LORD called
19:20 the top of the M, and Moses went up.
19:23 'Set bounds about the M, and consecrate it.'"
20:18 the trumpet and the M smoking, the people were
24:4 the foot of the M, and twelve pillars, according
24:12 to me on the M, and wait there; and
24:13 went up into the M of God.
24:15 went up on the M, and the cloud covered
24:15 on the mountain, and the cloud covered the M
24:17 the top of the M in the sight of
24:18 entered the cloud, and went up on the M
24:18 Moses was on the M forty days and forty
25:40 them, which is being shown you on the M
26:30 it which has been shown you on the M
27:8 shown you on the M, so shall it be
32:1 come down from the M, the people gathered
32:15 went down from the M with the two tables
32:19 and broke them at the foot of the M
34:2 there to me on the top of the M
34:3 seen throughout all the M; let no flocks or
34:3 let no flocks or herds feed before that M
34:29 came down from the M, Moses did not know
Num 20:28 Aaron died there on the top of the M
20:28 Then Moses and Eleazar came down from the M
27:12 "Go up into this M of Abarim, and see
Deut 1:6 long enough at this M;
2:3 been going about this M country long enough; turn
4:11 the foot of the M, while the mountain burned
4:11 the mountain, while the M burned with fire to
5:4 to face at the M, out of the midst
5:5 and you did not go up into the M
5:22 your assembly at the M out of the midst
5:23 the darkness, while the M was burning with fire,
9:9 I went up the M to receive the tables
9:9 I remained on the M forty days and forty
9:10 with you on the M out of the midst
9:15 came down from the M, and the mountain was
9:15 the mountain, and the M was burning with fire;
9:21 into the brook that descended out of the M
10:1 to me on the M, and make an ark
10:3 and went up the M with the two tables
10:4 to you on the M out of the midst
10:5 came down from the M, and put the tables
10:10 "I stayed on the M, as at the first
32:49 very day, "Ascend this M of the Abarim, Mount
32:50 and die on the M which you ascend, and
33:19 call peoples to their M; there they offer right
Josh 15:8 the top of the M that lies over against
15:9 the top of the M to the spring of
18:13 to Ataroth-addar, upon the M that lies south of
18:14 side southward from the M that lies to the

M

18:16 the border of the M that overlooks the valley
24:30 Ephraim, north of the M of Gaash.
Judg 2:9 Ephraim, north of the M of Gaash.
9:25 against him on the M tops, and they robbed
9:36 coming down from the M tops!" And Zebul said
1Sam 17:3 Philistines stood on the M on the one side,
17:3 Israel stood on the M on the other side,
23:26 one side of the M, and David and his
23:26 other side of the M; and David was making
25:20 under cover of the M, behold, David and his
26:13 the top of the M, with a great space
2Sam 13:34 the Horonaim road by the side of the M
21:6 at Gibeon on the M of the LORD." And
21:9 hanged them on the M before the LORD, and
1Kgs 11:7 the Ammonites, on the M east of Jerusalem.
2Kgs 2:16 cast him upon some M or into some valley."
4:27 she came to the M to the man of
6:17 saw; and behold, the M was full of horses
2Chr 33:15 had built on the M of the house of
Jud 2:21 opposite Bectileth near the M which is to the
5:5 dwells in the nearby M district.
7:12 the foot of the M –
10:10 had gone down the M and passed through the
13:10 and went up the M to Bethulia and came
Job 14:18 "But the M falls and crumbles away, and the
39:1 you know when the M goats bring forth?
Ps 30:7 me as a strong M; thou didst hide thy
48:1 His holy M,
68:15 O mighty M, mountain of Bashan; O many-peaked
68:15 O mighty mountain, M of Bashan; O many-peaked
68:15 of Bashan; O many-peaked M, mountain of Bashan!
68:15 Bashan; O many-peaked mountain, M of Bashan!
68:16 with envy, O many-peaked M, at the mount which
78:54 holy land, to the M which his right hand
99:9 worship at his holy M; for the LORD our
Song 4:6 hie me to the M of myrrh and the
Wis 9:8 temple on thy holy M, and an altar in
Is 2:2 latter days that the M of the house of
2:3 go up to the M of the LORD, to
11:9 in all my holy M; for the earth shall
25:6 On this M the LORD of hosts will make
25:7 will destroy on this M the covering that is
25:10 will rest on this M, and Moab shall be
27:13 LORD on the holy M at Jerusalem.
30:17 the top of a M, like a signal on
30:25 And upon every lofty M and every high hill
30:29 to go to the M of the LORD, to
40:4 lifted up, and every M and hill be made
40:9 up to a high M, O Zion, herald of
56:7 bring to my holy M, and make them joyful
57:7 a high and lofty M you have set your
57:13 possess the land, and shall inherit my holy M
65:11 who forget my holy M, who set a table
65:25 in all my holy M, says the LORD."
66:20 dromedaries, to my holy M Jerusalem, says the
Jer 16:16 hunt them from every M and every hill, and
18:14 Do the M waters run dry, the cold flowing
26:18 of ruins, and the M of the house a
50:6 on the mountains; from M to hill they have
51:25 against you, O destroying M, says the LORD, which
51:25 from the crags, and make you a burnt M
Bar 5:7 ordered that every high M and the everlasting hills
6:39 like stones from the M, and those who serve
Ezek 6:13 hill, on all the M tops, under every green
11:23 and stood upon the M which is on the
17:22 a high and lofty M;
17:23 lofty mountain; on the M height of Israel will
20:40 "For on my holy M, the mountain height of
20:40 my holy mountain, the M height of Israel, says
28:14 were on the holy M of God; in the
28:16 profane thing from the M of God, and the
34:14 pasture, and upon the M heights of Israel shall
40:2 upon a very high M, on which was a
43:12 the top of the M shall be most holy.
Dan 2:35 image became a great M and filled the whole
2:45 was cut from a M by no human hand,
11:45 and the glorious holy M; yet he shall come
Joel 2:1 in Zion; sound the alarm on my holy M
3:17 your God, who dwell in Zion, my holy M
Amos 4:1 who are in the M of Samaria, who oppress
6:1 feel secure on the M of Samaria, the notable
Obad 1:16 drunk upon my holy M, all the nations round
Mic 3:12 of ruins, and the M of the house a
4:1 latter days that the M of the house of
4:2 go up to the M of the LORD, to
7:12 to sea and from M to mountain.
7:12 from sea to sea and from mountain to M
Zeph 3:11 shall no longer be haughty in my holy M
Zech 4:7 What are you, O great M
8:3 faithful city, and the M of the LORD of
8:3 mountain of the LORD of hosts, the holy M
1Mac 9:38 went up and hid under cover of the M
9:40 rest fled to the M; and they took all
11:37 up in a conspicuous place on the holy M
2Mac 2:4 went out to the M where Moses had gone
Mt 4:8 to a very high M, and showed him all
5:1 went up on the M, and when he sat
8:1 came down from the M, great crowds followed him;
14:23 went up on the M by himself to pray.
15:29 went up on the M, and sat down there.
17:1 them up a high M apart.
17:9 coming down the M, Jesus commanded them, "Tell
17:20 will say to this M, 'Move from here to
21:21 you say to this M, 'Be taken up and
28:16 to Galilee, to the M to which Jesus had
Mk 3:13 went up on the M, and called to him
6:46 went up on the M to pray.
9:2 them up a high M apart by themselves; and
9:9 were coming down the M, he charged them to
11:23 whoever says to this M, 'Be taken up and
Lk 3:5 be filled, and every M and hill shall be
6:12 went out to the M to pray; and all
9:28 went up on the M to pray.
9:37 come down from the M, a great crowd met
Jn 4:20 fathers worshiped on this M; and you say that
4:21 when neither on this M nor in Jerusalem will
6:3 went up on the M, and there sat down
6:15 withdrew again to the M by himself.
Heb 8:5 the pattern which was shown you on the M
12:20 a beast touches the M, it shall be stoned."
2Pet 1:18 for we were with him on the holy M
Rev 6:14 rolled up, and every M and island was removed
8:8 something like a great M, burning with fire, was
21:10 to a great, high M, and showed me the

MOUNTAIN-SHEEP

Deut 14:5 wild goat, the ibex, the antelope, and the M

MOUNTAINS (187)

Gen 7:19 that all the high M under the whole heaven
7:20 waters prevailed above the M, covering them fifteen
8:4 to rest upon the M of Ararat.
8:5 the tops of the M were seen.
22:2 upon one of the M of which I shall
49:26 blessings of the eternal M, the bounties of the
Ex 32:12 slay them in the M, and to consume them
Num 23:7 Moab from the eastern M: 'Come, curse Jacob for
23:9 the top of the M I see him, from
33:47 and encamped in the M of Abarim, before Nebo.
33:48 set out from the M of Abarim, and encamped
Deut 12:2 gods, upon the high M and upon the hills
32:22 and sets on fire the foundations of the M
33:15 produce of the ancient M, and the abundance of
Judg 5:5 The M quaked before the LORD, yon Sinai before
6:2 which are in the M, and the caves and
9:36 the shadow of the M as if they were
11:37 and wander on the M, and bewail my virginity,
11:38 companions, and bewailed her virginity upon the M
1Sam 26:20 like one who hunts a partridge in the M
2Sam 1:21 "Ye M of Gilboa, let there be no dew
1Kgs 19:11 strong wind rent the M, and broke in pieces
22:17 Israel scattered upon the M, as sheep that have
2Kgs 19:23 the heights of the M, to the far recesses
1Chr 12:8 as gazelles upon the M:
2Chr 18:16 Israel scattered upon the M, as sheep that have
Tob 1:21 they fled to the M of Ararat.
Jud 1:15 captured Arphaxad in the M of Ragae and struck
6:4 them up, and their M will be drunk with
7:4 land; neither the high M nor the valleys nor
7:10 the height of the M where they live, for
7:10 not easy to reach the tops of their M
7:13 tops of the nearby M and camp there to
14:11 out in companies to the passes in the M
16:4 came down from the M of the north; he
16:15 For the M shall be shaken to their foundations
Job 9:5 he who removes M, and they know it
24:8 the rain of the M, and cling to the
28:9 flinty rock, and overturns M by the roots.
39:8 He ranges the M as his pasture, and he
40:20 For the M yield food for him where all
Ps 11:1 a bird to the M;
18:7 foundations also of the M trembled and quaked,

M

36:6 righteousness is like the M of God, thy judgments
46:2 should change, though the M shake in the heart
46:3 and foam, though the M tremble with its tumult.
65:6 strength hast established the M, being girded with
72:3 Let the M bear prosperity for the people, and
72:16 the tops of the M may it wave; may
76:4 art thou, more majestic than the everlasting M
80:10 The M were covered with its shade, the mighty
83:14 the flame sets the M ablaze,
90:2 Before the M were brought forth, or ever thou
95:4 the heights of the M are his also.
97:5 The M melt like wax before the LORD, before
104:6 with a garment; the waters stood above the M
104:8 The M rose, the valleys sank down to the
104:13 abode thou waterest the M; the earth is satisfied
104:18 The high M are for the wild goats; the
104:32 trembles, who touches the M and they smoke!
110:3 day you lead your host upon the holy M
114:4 The M skipped like rams, the hills like lambs.
114:6 O M, that you skip like rams?
125:2 As the M are round about Jerusalem, so the
133:3 which falls on the M of Zion!
144:5 Touch the M that they smoke!
148:9 M and all hills, fruit trees and all cedars!
Prov 8:25 Before the M had been shaped, before the hills,
27:25 the herbage of the M is gathered,
Song 2:8 comes, leaping upon the M, bounding over the hills.
2:17 a gazelle, or a young stag upon rugged M
4:8 of lions, from the M of leopards.
8:14 young stag upon the M of spices.
Wis 17:19 a hollow of the M, it paralyzed them with
Sir 16:17 The M also and the foundations of the earth
43:4 the sun burns the M three times as much;
43:16 At his appearing the M are shaken; at his
43:21 He consumes the M and burns up the wilderness,
Is 2:2 the highest of the M, and shall be raised
2:14 against all the high M, and against all the
5:25 smote them, and the M quaked; and their corpses
13:4 a tumult on the M as of a great
14:25 land, and upon my M trample him under foot;
17:13 like chaff on the M before the wind and
18:3 is raised on the M, look!
18:6 of prey of the M and to the beasts
22:5 down of walls and a shouting to the M
34:3 corpses shall rise; the M shall flow with their
37:24 the heights of the M, to the far recesses
40:12 measure and weighed the M in scales and the
41:15 you shall thresh the M and crush them, and
42:11 let them shout from the top of the M
42:15 I will lay waste M and hills, and dry
44:23 forth into singing, O M, O forest, and every
45:2 you and level the M, I will break in
49:11 will make all my M a way, and my
49:13 earth; break forth, O M, into singing!
52:7 How beautiful upon the M are the feet of
54:10 For the M may depart and the hills be
55:12 forth in peace; the M and the hills before
64:1 come down, that the M might quake at thy
64:3 thou camest down, the M quaked at thy presence.
65:7 burned incense upon the M and reviled me upon
65:9 Judah inheritors of my M; my chosen shall inherit
Jer 3:23 hills are a delusion, the orgies on the M
4:24 I looked on the M, and lo, they were
9:10 and wailing for the M, and a lamentation for
13:16 stumble on the twilight M, and while you look
17:3 high hills, on the M in the open country.
31:5 plant vineyards upon the M of Samaria; the planters
46:18 like Tabor among the M, and like Carmel by
50:6 them away on the M; from mountain to hill
Lam 4:19 chased us on the M, they lay in wait
Bar 6:63 from above to consume M and woods does what
Ezek 6:2 your face toward the M of Israel, and prophesy
6:3 them, and say, You M of Israel, hear the
6:3 Lord GOD to the M and the hills, to
7:7 tumult, and not of joyful shouting upon the M
7:16 will be on the M, like doves of the
18:6 not eat upon the M or lift up his
18:11 but eats upon the M, defiles his neighbor's wife,
18:15 not eat upon the M or lift up his
19:9 be heard upon the M of Israel.
22:9 who eat upon the M; men commit lewdness in
31:12 On the M and in all the valleys its
32:5 your flesh upon the M, and fill the valleys
32:6 land even to the M with your flowing blood;
33:28 an end; and the M of Israel shall be
34:6 wandered over all the M and on every high
34:13 feed them on the M of Israel, by the
34:14 shall feed on the M of Israel.
35:8 I will fill your M with the slain; on
35:12 you uttered against the M of Israel, saying, 'They
36:1 man, prophesy to the M of Israel, and say,
36:1 Israel, and say, O M of Israel, hear the
36:4 the people; therefore, O M of Israel, hear the
36:4 Lord GOD to the M and the hills, the
36:6 and say to the M and hills, to the
36:8 "But you, O M of Israel, shall shoot forth
37:22 the land, upon the M of Israel; and one
38:8 many nations upon the M of Israel, which had
38:20 my presence, and the M shall be thrown down,
39:2 lead you against the M of Israel;
39:4 shall fall upon the M of Israel, you and
39:17 sacrificial feast upon the M of Israel, and you
Dan 3:76 Bless the Lord, M and hills, sing praise to
Hos 4:13 the tops of the M, and make offerings upon
10:8 shall say to the M, Cover us, and to
Joel 2:2 is spread upon the M a great and powerful
2:5 the tops of the M, like the crackling of
3:18 in that day the M shall drip sweet wine,
Amos 3:9 "Assemble yourselves upon the M of Samaria, and
4:13 he who forms the M, and creates the wind,
9:13 sows the seed; the M shall drip sweet wine,
Jon 2:6 about my head at the roots of the M
Mic 1:4 And the M will melt under him and the
4:1 the highest of the M, and shall be raised
6:1 your case before the M, and let the hills
6:2 Hear, you M, the controversy of the LORD, and
Nah 1:5 The M quake before him, the hills melt; the
1:15 Behold, on the M the feet of him who
3:18 are scattered on the M with none to gather
Hab 3:6 nations; then the eternal M were scattered, the
3:10 The M saw thee, and writhed; the raging waters
Zech 6:1 out from between two M; and the mountains were
6:1 mountains; and the M were mountains of bronze.
6:1 and the mountains were M of bronze.
14:5 the valley of my M shall be stopped up,
14:5 the valley of the M shall touch the side
1Mac 4:38 a thicket, or as on one of the M
11:68 against him in the M, but they themselves met
2Mac 5:27 companions alive in the M as wild animals do;
9:8 could weigh the high M in a balance, was
9:28 pitiable fate, among the M in a strange land.
10:6 been wandering in the M and caves like wild
Mt 18:11 the ninety-nine on the M and go in search
24:16 Judea flee to the M;
Mk 5:5 tombs and on the M he was always crying
13:14 Judea flee to the M;
Lk 21:21 Judea flee to the M, and let those who
23:29 to say to the M, 'Fall on us'; and
1Cor 13:2 so as to remove M, but have not love,
Heb 11:38 wandering over deserts and M, and in dens and
Rev 6:15 the rocks of the M,
6:16 mountains, calling to the M and rocks, "Fall on
16:20 fled away, and no M were to be found;
17:9 seven heads are seven M on which the woman

MOUNTED (16)

1Sam 25:42 haste and rose and M on an ass, and
30:17 hundred young men, who M camels and fled.
2Sam 13:29 sons arose, and each M his mule and fled.
1Kgs 13:13 for him and he M it.
2Kgs 7:14 So they took two M men, and the king
9:16 Then Jehu M his chariot, and went to Jezreel,
Ezra 9:6 and our guilt has M up to the heavens.
Esth 8:10 letters were sent by M couriers riding on swift
8:14 So the couriers, M on their swift horses that
Ps 78:21 against Jacob, his anger M against Israel;
107:26 They M up to heaven, they went down to
Ezek 10:15 And the cherubim M up.
10:17 still, and when they M up, these mounted up
10:17 they mounted up, these M up with them; for
10:19 up their wings and M up from the earth
Mt 21:5 to you, humble, and M on an ass, and

MOUNTS (2)

Job 39:27 command that the eagle M up and makes his
Acts 23:24 Also provide M for Paul to ride, and bring

MOURN (46)

Gen 23:2 Abraham went in to M for Sarah and to
2Sam 3:31 gird on sackcloth, and M before Abner." And King
1Kgs 13:29 to the city, to M and to bury him.
14:13 And all Israel shall M for him, and bury

Neh	8:9	your God; do not M or weep." For all
Tob	10:4	Then she began to M for him, and said,
Job	5:11	lowly, and those who M are lifted to safety.
Eccl	3:4	laugh; a time to M, and a time to
Sir	7:34	those who weep, but M with those who mourn.
	7:34	those who weep, but mourn with those who M
Is	3:26	gates shall lament and M; ravaged, she shall sit
	16:7	M, utterly stricken, for the raisin-cakes of
	19:8	The fishermen will M and lament, all who cast
	61:2	to comfort all who M;
	61:3	grant to those who M in Zion– to
	66:10	joy, all you who M over her;
Jer	4:28	this the earth shall M, and the heavens above
	8:21	my heart wounded, I M, and dismay has taken
	12:4	long will the land M, and the grass of
	48:31	all Moab; for the men of Kir-heres I M
Lam	1:4	The roads to Zion M, for none come to
Ezek	7:12	rejoice, nor the seller M, for wrath is upon
	24:16	yet you shall not M or weep nor shall
	24:23	feet; you shall not M or weep, but you
	31:15	will make the deep M for it, and restrain
Dan	14:40	the king came to M for Daniel.
Hos	10:5	Its people shall M for it, and its idolatrous
Joel	1:9	The priests M, the ministers of the LORD.
Amos	1:2	pastures of the shepherds M, and the top of
	8:8	account, and every one M who dwells in it,
	9:5	who dwell in it M, and all of it
Zech	7:3	the prophets, "Should I M and fast in the
	12:10	have pierced, they shall M for him, as one
	12:12	The land shall M, each family by itself; the
1Mac	3:51	profaned, and thy priests M in humiliation.
2Mac	5:10	had no one to M for him; he had
Mt	5:4	"Blessed are those who M, for they shall be
	9:15	"Can the wedding guests M as long as the
	11:17	and you did not M
	24:30	of the earth will M, and they will see
Lk	6:25	now, for you shall M and weep.
1Cor	5:2	Ought you not rather to M
	7:30	none, and those who M as though they were
2Cor	12:21	I may have to M over many of those
Jas	4:9	Be wretched and M and weep.
Rev	18:11	the earth weep and M for her, since no

MOURNED (27)

Gen	37:34	upon his loins, and M for his son many
Ex	33:4	these evil tidings, they M; and no man put
Num	14:39	Israel, and the people M greatly.
1Sam	6:19	them, and the people M because the LORD had
	25:1	all Israel assembled and M for him, and they
	28:3	and all Israel had M for him and buried
2Sam	1:12	with him; and they M and wept and fasted
	13:37	And David M for his son day after day.
1Kgs	13:30	own grave; and they M over him, saying, "Alas,
	14:18	Israel buried him and M for him, according to
1Chr	7:22	And Ephraim their father M many days, and his
2Chr	35:24	All Judah and Jerusalem M for Josiah.
Neh	1:4	down and wept, and M for days; and I
Jud	16:24	the house of Israel M for her seven days.
Sir	48:24	and comforted those who M in Zion.
Zech	7:5	When you fasted and M in the fifth month
1Mac	1:25	Israel M deeply in every community,
	2:14	put on sackcloth, and M greatly.
	2:39	learned of it, they M for them deeply.
	2:70	And all Israel M for him with great lamentation.
	4:39	rent their clothes, and M with great lamentation, and
	9:20	lamentation for him; they M many days and said,
	12:52	Judah safely, and they M for Jonathan and his
	12:52	fear; and all Israel M deeply.
	13:26	with great lamentation, and M for him many days.
Mk	16:10	with him, as they M and wept.
Rev	18:19	as they wept and M, crying out, "Alas, alas,

MOURNER (2)

2Sam	14:2	"Pretend to be a M, and put on mourning
Jer	16:7	break bread for the M, to comfort him for

MOURNERS (6)

Job	29:25	king among his troops, like one who comforts M
Eccl	12:5	eternal home, and the M go about the streets;
Is	57:18	comfort, creating for his M the fruit of the
Ezek	24:17	cover your lips, nor eat the bread of M
	24:22	cover your lips, nor eat the bread of M
Hos	9:4	bread shall be like M bread; all who eat

MOURNING (68)

Gen	27:41	himself, "The days of M for my father are
	37:35	shall go down to Sheol to my son, M
	50:10	and he made a M for his father seven
	50:11	the Canaanites, saw the M on the threshing floor
	50:11	"This is a grievous M to the Egyptians." Therefore
Deut	26:14	tithe while I was M, or removed any of
	34:8	days of weeping and M for Moses were ended.
2Sam	11:27	And when the M was over, David sent and
	14:2	mourner, and put on M garments; do not anoint
	14:2	woman who has been M many days for the
	19:1	king is weeping and M for Absalom."
	19:2	day was turned into M for all the people;
Ezra	10:6	water; for he was M over the faithlessness of
Tob	2:6	shall be turned into M, and all your festivities
	10:7	nights she never stopped M for her son Tobias,
Jud	16:8	took off her widow's M to exalt the oppressed
Esth	4:3	came, there was great M among the Jews, with
	6:12	hurried to his house, M and with his head
	9:22	into gladness and from M into a holiday; that
	13:17	thy inheritance; turn our M into feasting, that we
	14:2	garments of distress and M, and instead of costly
Job	30:31	lyre is turned to M, and my pipe to
Ps	30:11	turned for me my M into dancing; thou hast
	35:14	who laments his mother, bowed down and in M
	38:6	and prostrate; all the day I go about M
	42:9	Why go I M because of the oppression of
	43:2	Why go I M because of the oppression of
Eccl	7:2	to the house of M than to go to
	7:4	in the house of M; but the heart of
Wis	19:3	were still busy at M, and were lamenting at
Sir	19:23	rascal bowed down in M, but inwardly he is
	22:6	Like music in M is a tale told at
	22:10	M for the dead lasts seven days, but for
	38:17	wailing fervent; observe the M according to his
	41:11	The M of men is about their bodies, but
Is	22:12	called to weeping and M, to baldness and girding
	60:20	and your days of M shall be ended.
	61:3	of gladness instead of M, the mantle of praise
Jer	6:26	roll in ashes; make M as for an only
	9:17	and call for the M women to come; send
	16:5	enter the house of M, or go to lament,
	31:13	I will turn their M into joy, I will
Lam	2:5	the daughter of Judah M and lamentation.
	5:15	has ceased; our dancing has been turned to M
Ezek	2:10	words of lamentation and M and woe.
	24:17	not aloud; make no M for the dead.
	27:31	over you in bitterness of soul, with bitter M
Dan	10:2	days I, Daniel, was M for three weeks.
Joel	2:12	with weeping, and with M;
Amos	5:16	call the farmers to M and to wailing those
	8:10	turn your feasts into M, and all your songs
	8:10	make it like the M for an only son,
Mic	1:8	like the jackals, and M like the ostriches.
Zech	12:11	On that day the M in Jerusalem will be
	12:11	as great as the M for Hadadrimmon in the
Mal	3:14	of walking as in M before the LORD of
1Mac	1:27	she who sat in the bridal chamber was M
	1:39	feasts were turned into M, her sabbaths into a
	1:40	as her glory; her exaltation was turned into M
	9:41	wedding was turned into M and the voice of
1Cor	7:30	though they were not M, and those who rejoice
2Cor	7:7	of your longing, your M, your zeal for me,
Jas	4:9	laughter be turned to M and your joy to
Rev	18:7	give her a like measure of torment and M
	18:7	I am no widow, M I shall never see,'
	18:8	single day, pestilence and M and famine, and she
	18:15	her torment, weeping and M aloud,
	21:4	neither shall there be M nor crying nor pain

MOURNS (11)

Job	14:22	own body, and he M only for himself."
Is	24:4	The earth M and withers, the world languishes and
	24:7	wine M, the vine languishes, all the merry-hearted
	33:9	The land M and languishes; Lebanon is confounded
Jer	12:11	a desolation; desolate, it M to me.
	14:2	concerning the drought: "Judah M and her gates
	23:10	the curse the land M, and the pastures of
Ezek	7:27	The king M, the prince is wrapped in despair,
Hos	4:3	Therefore the land M, and all who dwell in
Joel	1:10	laid waste, the ground M; because the grain is
Zech	12:10	for him, as one M for an only child,

MOUSE

Lev	11:29	earth: the weasel, the M, the great lizard according

MOUTH (379)

Gen	4:11	which has opened its M to receive your brother's

8:11 and lo, in her M a freshly plucked olive
29:2 stone on the well's M was large,
29:3 the stone from the M of the well, and
29:3 its place upon the M of the well.
29:8 is rolled from the M of the well; then
29:10 stone from the well's M, and watered the flock
42:27 his money in the M of his sack;
42:28 it is in the M of my sack!" At
43:12 was returned in the M of your sacks; perhaps
43:21 man's money in the M of his sack, our
44:1 man's money in the M of his sack,
44:2 silver cup, in the M of the sack of
44:8 we found in the M of our sacks, we
45:12 that it is my M that speaks to you.
Ex 4:11 LORD said to him, "Who has made man's M
4:12 will be with your M and teach you what
4:15 the words in his M; and I will be
4:15 will be with your M and with his mouth,
4:15 mouth and with his M, and will teach you
4:16 he shall be a M for you, and you
13:9 may be in your M; for with a strong
23:13 nor let such be heard out of your M
Num 12:8 With him I speak M to mouth, clearly, and
12:8 I speak mouth to M, clearly, and not in
16:30 the ground opens its M, and swallows them up,
16:32 the earth opened its M and swallowed them up,
22:28 the LORD opened the M of the ass, and
22:38 God puts in my M, that must I speak."
23:5 a word in Balaam's M, and said, "Return to
23:12 to speak what the LORD puts in my M
23:16 a word in his M, and said, "Return to
26:10 the earth opened its M and swallowed them up
30:2 according to all that proceeds out of his M
Deut 8:3 proceeds out of the M of the LORD.
11:6 the earth opened its M and swallowed them up,
18:18 my words in his M, and he shall speak
23:23 your God what you have promised with your M
30:14 it is in your M and in your heart,
32:1 let the earth hear the words of my M
Josh 1:8 depart out of your M, but you shall meditate
6:10 go out of your M, until the day I
10:18 great stones against the M of the cave, and
10:22 Joshua said, "Open the M of the cave, and
10:27 great stones against the M of the cave, which
15:5 Salt Sea, to the M of the Jordan.
15:5 the sea at the M of the Jordan;
Judg 9:38 him, "Where is your M now, you who said,
11:35 I have opened my M to the LORD, and
11:36 you have opened your M to the LORD, do
11:36 gone forth from your M, now that the LORD
18:19 your hand upon your M, and come with us,
1Sam 1:12 praying before the LORD, Eli observed her M
2:1 My M derides my enemies, because I rejoice in
2:3 arrogance come from your M; for the LORD is
14:26 his hand to his M; for the people feared
14:27 his hand to his M; and his eyes became
17:35 it out of his M; and if he arose
2Sam 1:16 head; for your own M has testified against you,
14:3 So Joab put the words in her M
14:19 these words in the M of your handmaid.
17:19 covering over the well's M, and scattered grain upon
18:25 he is alone, there are tidings in his M
22:9 devouring fire from his M; glowing coals flamed
1Kgs 8:15 he promised with his M to David my father,
8:24 didst speak with thy M, and with thy hand
17:24 the LORD in your M is truth."
19:18 to Baal, and every M that has not kissed
22:22 lying spirit in the M of all his prophets.'
22:23 lying spirit in the M of all these your
2Kgs 4:34 the child, putting his M upon his mouth, his
4:34 his mouth upon his M, his eyes upon his
19:28 my bit in your M, and I will turn
2Chr 6:4 he promised with his M to David my father,
6:15 didst speak with thy M, and with thy hand
18:21 lying spirit in the M of all his prophets.'
18:22 lying spirit in the M of these your prophets;
35:22 of Neco from the M of God, but joined
36:12 who spoke from the M of the LORD.
36:21 the LORD by the M of Jeremiah, until the
36:22 the LORD by the M of Jeremiah might be
Ezra 1:1 the LORD by the M of Jeremiah might be
Neh 9:20 thy manna from their M, and gavest them water
Jud 5:5 a word from the M of your servant, and
5:5 No falsehood shall come from your servant's M
11:19 much as open its M to growl at you.
Esth 7:8 the words left the M of the king, they
13:17 do not destroy the M of those who praise
14:9 to abolish what thy M has ordained and to
14:13 eloquent speech in my M before the lion, and
Job 3:1 this Job opened his M and cursed the day
5:15 the fatherless from their M, the needy from the
5:16 the poor have hope, and injustice shuts her M
7:11 will not restrain my M; I will speak in
8:2 the words of your M be a great wind?
8:21 will yet fill your M with laughter, and your
9:20 am innocent, my own M would condemn me; though
15:5 your iniquity teaches your M, and you choose the
15:6 Your own M condemns you, and not I; your
15:13 and let such words go out of your M
16:5 strengthen you with my M, and the solace of
16:10 at me with their M, they have struck me
19:16 no answer; I must beseech him with my M
20:12 is sweet in his M, though he hides it
20:13 holds it in his M,
21:5 be appalled, and lay your hand upon your M
22:22 Receive instruction from his M, and lay up his
23:4 him and fill my M with arguments.
23:12 treasured in my bosom the words of his M
29:9 their hand on their M;
29:10 their tongue cleaved to the roof of their M
31:27 secretly enticed, and my M has kissed my hand;
31:30 have not let my M sin by asking for
32:5 no answer in the M of these three men,
33:2 Behold, I open my M; the tongue in my
33:2 the tongue in my M speaks.
35:16 transgression, Job opens his M in empty talk, he
37:2 voice and the rumbling that comes from his M
40:4 I lay my hand on my M
40:23 he is confident though Jordan rushes against his M
41:19 Out of his M go flaming torches; sparks of
41:21 coals, and a flame comes forth from his M
Ps 5:9 no truth in their M; their heart is destruction,
8:2 is chanted by the M of babes and infants,
10:7 His M is filled with cursing and deceit and
17:3 wickedness in me; my M does not transgress.
18:8 devouring fire from his M; glowing coals flamed
19:14 the words of my M and the meditation of
22:21 Save me from the M of the lion, my
33:6 all their host by the breath of his M
34:1 times; his praise shall continually be in my M
36:3 The words of his M are mischief and deceit;
37:30 The M of the righteous utters wisdom, and his
38:13 a dumb man who does not open his M
38:14 hear, and in whose M are no rebukes.
39:1 I will bridle my M, so long as the
39:9 do not open my M; for it is thou
40:3 new song in my M, a song of praise
49:3 My M shall speak wisdom; the meditation of my
50:19 "You give your M free rein for evil, and
51:15 my lips, and my M shall show forth thy
54:2 God; give ear to the words of my M
63:5 and fat, and my M praises thee with joyful
66:14 lips uttered and my M promised when I was
69:15 the pit close its M over me.
71:8 My M is filled with thy praise, and with
71:15 My M will tell of thy righteous acts, of
78:1 incline your ears to the words of my M
78:2 I will open my M in a parable; I
81:10 Open your M wide, and I will fill it.
89:1 for ever; with my M I will proclaim thy
107:42 and are glad; and all wickedness stops its M
109:30 With my M I will give great thanks to
119:13 lips I declare all the ordinances of thy M
119:43 utterly out of my M, for my hope is
119:72 The law of thy M is better to me
119:88 that I may keep the testimonies of thy M
119:103 to my taste, sweeter than honey to my M
119:131 With open M I pant, because I long for
126:2 Then our M was filled with laughter, and our
137:6 the roof of my M, if I do not
138:4 the words of thy M;
141:3 a guard over my M, O LORD, keep watch
141:7 be strewn at the M of Sheol.
145:21 My M will speak the praise of the LORD,
Prov 2:6 gives wisdom; from his M come knowledge and
4:6 not turn away from the words of my M
5:7 do not depart from the words of my M
6:2 the words of your M;
7:24 and be attentive to the words of my M
8:7 is right; for my M will utter truth; wickedness
8:8 the words of my M are righteous; there is
10:6 the righteous, but the M of the wicked conceals

M

M

	11:8	has ever entered my M
	15:7	you, that by my M the Gentiles should hear
	15:27	tell you the same things by word of M
	18:14	about to open his M, Gallio said to the
	22:14	a voice from his M;
	23:2	stood by him to strike him on the M
Rom	3:14	"Their M is full of curses and bitterness."
	3:19	law, so that every M may be stopped, and
2Cor	6:11	Our M is open to you, Corinthians; our heart
Eph	6:19	me in opening my M boldly to proclaim the
Col	3:8	wrath, malice, slander, and foul talk from your M
2Thes	2:8	the breath of his M and destroy him by
	2:15	either by word of M or by letter.
2Tim	4:17	So I was rescued from the lion's M
Jas	3:10	From the same M come blessing and cursing.
Rev	1:16	seven stars, from his M issued a sharp two-edged
	2:16	war against them with the sword of my M
	3:16	hot, I will spew you out of my M
	10:9	your stomach, but sweet as honey in your M
	10:10	as honey in my M, but when I had
	11:5	pours out from their M and consumes their foes;
	12:15	river out of his M after the woman, to
	12:16	the earth opened its M and swallowed the river
	12:16	river which the dragon had poured from his M
	13:2	a bears, and its M was like a lion's
	13:2	bears, and its mouth was like a lion's M
	13:5	beast was given a M uttering haughty and
	13:6	months; it opened its M to utter blasphemies against
	14:5	Lamb, and in their M no lie was found,
	16:13	saw, issuing from the M of the dragon and
	16:13	dragon and from the M of the beast and
	16:13	beast and from the M of the false prophet,
	19:15	From his M issues a sharp sword with which
	19:21	that issues from his M; and all the birds

MOUTHS (42)

Deut	31:19	put it in their M, that this song may
	31:21	live unforgotten in the M of their descendants); for
Judg	7:6	their hands to their M, was three hundred men;
Esth	14:9	inheritance, to stop the M of those who praise
	14:10	house, to open the M of the nations for
Job	29:23	and they opened their M as for the spring
Ps	17:10	to pity; with their M they speak arrogantly.
	22:7	at me, they make M at me, they wag
	22:13	they open wide their M at me, like a
	35:21	They open wide their M against me; they say,
	58:6	the teeth in their M; tear out the fangs
	59:7	are, bellowing with their M, and snarling with their
	59:12	the sin of their M, the words of their
	62:4	They bless with their M, but inwardly they curse.
	63:11	shall glory; for the M of liars will be
	73:9	They set their M against the heavens, and their
	78:30	was still in their M,
	78:36	flattered him with their M; they lied to him
	109:2	For wicked and deceitful M are opened against me,
	115:5	They have M, but do not speak; eyes, but
	135:16	They have M, but they speak not, they have
	135:17	not, nor is there any breath in their M
	144:8	hand of aliens, whose M speak lies, and whose
	144:11	hand of aliens, whose M speak lies, and whose
Prov	15:2	dispenses knowledge, but the M of fools pour out
	15:14	seeks knowledge, but the M of fools feed on
Wis	8:12	length they will put their hands on their M
Is	52:15	kings shall shut their M because of him; for
Jer	44:25	have declared with your M, and have fulfilled it
Ezek	34:10	my sheep from their M, that they may not
Dan	3:33	we cannot open our M; shame and disgrace have
	6:22	and shut the lions' M, and they have not
	13:61	out of their own M Daniel had convicted them
Mic	3:5	war against him who puts nothing into their M
	7:16	their hands on their M; their ears shall be
Zech	14:12	sockets, and their tongues shall rot in their M
Eph	4:29	come out of your M, but only such as
Heb	11:33	received promises, stopped the M of lions,
Jas	3:3	put bits into the M of horses that they
Rev	9:17	fire and smoke and sulphur issued from their M
	9:18	fire and smoke and sulphur issuing from their M
	9:19	horses is in their M and in their tails;

MOVE (16)

2Kgs	23:18	be; let no man M his bones." So they
1Chr	12:1	while he could not M about freely because of
Jud	7:1	to break camp and M against Bethulia, and to
Ps	80:13	it, and all that M in the field feed
Eccl	4:15	all the living who M about under the sun,
Sir	18:25	change, and all things M swiftly before the Lord.
Is	40:20	to set up an image that will not M
	46:7	stands there; it cannot M from its place.
Jer	10:4	with hammer and nails so that it cannot M
Bar	6:27	them upright, it cannot M itself; and if it
Dan	3:80	and all creatures that M in the waters, sing
Mt	17:20	say to this mountain, M from here to there,'
	17:20	there,' and it will M; and nothing will be
	23:4	they themselves will not M them with their finger.
Acts	17:28	him we live and M and have our being';
2Cor	6:16	live in them and M among them, and I

MOVED (53)

Gen	7:21	all flesh died that M upon the earth, birds,
	13:12	of the valley and M his tent as far
	13:18	So Abram M his tent, and came and dwelt
	26:22	And he M from there and dug another well,
Ex	13:20	And they M on from Succoth, and encamped at
	14:19	the host of Israel M and went behind them;
	14:19	the pillar of cloud M from before them and
	17:1	the people of Israel M on from the wilderness
	35:21	every one whose spirit M him, and brought the
	35:26	women whose hearts were M with ability spun the
	35:29	of Israel, whose heart M them to bring anything
Josh	10:21	Makkedah; not a man M his tongue against any
Judg	2:18	for the LORD was M to pity by their
	9:26	the son of Ebed M into Shechem with his
	20:37	the men in ambush M out and smote all
1Sam	1:13	heart; only her lips M, and her voice was
2Sam	7:7	places where I have M with all the people
	18:33	the king was deeply M, and went up to
1Chr	16:30	yea, the world stands firm, never to be M
	17:6	places where I have M with all Israel, did
Jud	7:2	So all their warriors M their camp that day;
	7:17	army of the Ammonites M forward, together with
	12:16	her and he was M with great desire to
Job	2:3	his integrity, although you M me against him, to
Ps	10:6	"I shall not be M; throughout all generations I
	15:5	He who does these things shall never be M
	16:8	at my right hand, I shall not be M
	21:7	of the Most High he shall not be M
	30:6	said in my prosperity, "I shall never be M
	46:5	she shall not be M; God will help her
	55:22	he will never permit the righteous to be M
	62:2	salvation, my fortress; I shall not be greatly M
	78:58	their high places; they M him to jealousy with
	93:1	it shall never be M;
	96:10	it shall never be M; he will judge the
	112:6	righteous will never be M; he will be remembered
	121:3	let your foot be M, he who keeps you
	125:1	Zion, which cannot be M, but abides for ever.
Prov	12:3	the root of the righteous will never be M
Wis	19:19	and creatures that swim M over to the land.
Is	10:14	there was none that M a wing, or opened
	41:7	it with nails so that it cannot be M
Jer	4:24	and all the hills M to and fro.
Dan	11:11	king of the south, M with anger, shall come
1Mac	2:1	the sons of Joarib, M from Jerusalem and settled
	4:1	cavalry, and this division M out by night
	4:3	and his mighty men M out to attack the
Mk	1:41	M with pity, he stretched out his hand and
Jn	11:33	weeping, he was deeply M in spirit and troubled;
	11:38	Then Jesus, deeply M again, came to the tomb;
1Cor	12:2	to dumb idols, however you may have been M
1Thes	3:3	that no one be M by these afflictions.
2Pet	1:21	of man, but men M by the Holy Spirit

MOVEMENT

Wis	5:11	is traversed by the M of its wings, and

MOVES (7)

Gen	1:21	every living creature that M, with which the waters
	1:28	every living thing that M upon the earth."
	8:19	every bird, everything that M upon the earth, went
Lev	11:46	every living creature that M through the waters and
Job	9:11	see him not; he M on, but I do
Ps	50:11	air, and all that M in the field is
	69:34	seas and everything that M therein.

MOVING (7)

Gen	1:2	Spirit of God was M over the face of
	9:3	Every M thing that lives shall be food for
2Sam	7:6	but I have been M about in a tent
Job	31:26	shone, or the moon M in splendor,
Song	4:1	a flock of goats, M down the slopes of
	6:5	a flock of goats, M down the slopes of
Ezek	1:13	of fire, like torches M to and fro among

MOWED (2)
Ex 17:13 And Joshua M down Amalek and his people with
Jas 5:4 of the laborers who M your fields, which you

MOWINGS
Amos 7:1 it was the latter growth after the king's M

MOWN
Ps 72:6 that falls on the M grass, like showers that

MOZA (5)
1Chr 2:46 Caleb's concubine, bore Haran, M, and Gazez; and
8:36 Azmaveth, and Zimri; Zimri was the father of M
8:37 M was the father of Bine-a; Raphah was his
9:42 and Zimri; and Zimri was the father of M
9:43 M was the father of Bine-a; and Rephaiah was

MOZAH
Josh 18:26 Ramah, Be-eroth, Mizpeh, Chephirah, M,

MUCH (260)
Gen 20:8 the men were very M afraid.
26:16 us; for you are M mightier than we."
34:12 of me ever so M as marriage present and
43:34 was five times as M as any of theirs.
44:1 sacks with food, as M as they can carry,
Ex 14:28 the sea; not so M as one of them
16:5 will be twice as M as they gather daily."
16:16 man of you, as M as he can eat;
16:18 omer, he that gathered M had nothing over, and
16:21 gathered it, each as M as he could eat;
16:22 they gathered twice as M bread, two omers apiece;
30:23 sweet-smelling cinnamon half as M, that is, two
36:5 Moses, "The people bring M more than enough for
Lev 14:21 and cannot afford so M, then he shall take
Deut 2:5 land, no, not so M as for the sole
12:15 of your towns, as M as you desire, according
12:20 you may eat as M flesh as you desire.
12:21 within your towns as M as you desire.
28:38 You shall carry M seed into the field, and
31:27 against the LORD; how M more after my death!
Josh 13:1 there remains yet very M land to be possessed.
22:8 to your homes with M wealth, and with very
22:8 and iron, and with M clothing; divide the spoil
1Sam 2:16 and then take as M as you wish," he
14:30 How M better if the people had eaten freely
17:24 from him, and were M afraid.
19:1 Jonathan, Saul's son, delighted M in David.
21:5 a common journey; how M more today will their
21:12 to heart, and was M afraid of Achish the
22:15 nothing of all this, M or little."
23:3 here in Judah; how M more then if we
25:22 morning I leave so M as one male of
25:34 left to Nabal so M as one male."
2Sam 3:22 from a raid, bringing M spoil with them.
4:11 How M more, when wicked men have slain a
8:8 King David took very M bronze.
12:8 add to you as M more.
14:25 was no one so M to be praised for
16:11 seeks my life; how M more now may this
1Kgs 8:27 cannot contain thee; how M less this house which
9:11 timber and gold, as M as he desired, King
10:2 bearing spices, and very M gold, and precious stones;
10:25 horses, and mules, so M year by year.
2Kgs 5:13 How M rather, then, when he says to you,
10:18 Baal a little; but Jehu will serve him M
12:10 saw that there was M money in the chest,
21:6 He did M evil in the sight of the
21:16 Moreover Manasseh shed very M innocent blood, till
1Chr 18:8 David took very M bronze; with it Solomon
22:8 saying, 'You have shed M blood and have waged
22:8 you have shed so M blood before me upon
22:14 for there is so M of it; timber and
2Chr 6:18 cannot contain thee; how M less this house which
9:1 bearing spices and very M gold and precious stones.
9:24 horses, and mules, so M year by year.
14:13 Judah carried away very M booty.
14:14 cities, for there was M plunder in them.
20:25 days in taking the spoil, it was so M
24:11 saw that there was M money in it, the
25:9 able to give you M more than this."
25:13 in them, and took M spoil.
27:3 the LORD, and did M building on the wall
28:8 daughters; they also took M spoil from them and
32:4 Assyria come and find M water?"
32:15 How M less will your God deliver you out
33:6 He did M evil in the sight of the
Ezra 7:22 baths of oil, and salt without prescribing how M
Neh 2:2 Then I was very M afraid.
4:10 failing, and there is M rubbish; we are not
Tob 7:2 his wife Edna, "How M the young man resembles
12:8 righteousness is better than M with wrongdoing.
Jud 4:9 they humbled themselves with M fasting.
5:9 settled, and prospered, with M gold and silver and
11:13 of the people so M as to touch these
11:19 a dog will so M as open its mouth
12:20 great quantity of wine, M more than he had
Esth 16:7 be seen not so M from the more ancient
Job 4:19 charges with error; how M more those who dwell
7:17 thou dost make so M of him, and that
15:16 in his sight; how M less one who is
16:6 if I forbear, how M of it leaves me?
25:6 in his sight; how M less man, who is
31:25 my hand had gotten M;
35:14 How M less when you say that you do
42:10 gave Job twice as M as he had before.
Ps 19:10 they than gold, even M fine gold; sweeter also
119:14 testimonies I delight as M as in all riches.
Prov 7:21 With M seductive speech she persuades him; with
11:31 requited on earth, how M more the wicked and
13:23 of the poor yields M food, but it is
15:6 the righteous there is M treasure, but trouble befalls
15:11 before the LORD, how M more the hearts of
19:7 brothers hate him; how M more do his friends
19:10 to live in luxury, M less for a slave
21:27 is an abomination; how M more when he brings
25:27 not good to eat M honey, so be sparing
29:22 given to anger causes M transgression.
Eccl 1:18 For in M wisdom is much vexation, and he
1:18 in much wisdom is M vexation, and he who
5:3 a dream comes with M business, and a fool's
5:12 he eats little or M; but the surfeit of
5:17 darkness and grief, in M vexation and sickness and
5:20 For he will not M remember the days of
8:17 However M man may toil in seeking, he will
9:18 but one sinner destroys M good.
12:12 is no end, and M study is a weariness
Song 4:10 how M better is your love than wine, and
Wis 7:28 God loves nothing so M as the man who
13:3 let them know how M better than these is
13:4 perceive from them how M more powerful is he
13:9 power to know so M that they could investigate
Sir 9:14 As M as you can, aim to know your
10:30 honored in poverty, how M more in wealth!
10:30 dishonored in wealth, how M more in poverty!
11:11 on, but is so M the more in want.
11:17 does not know how M time will pass until
12:5 will receive twice as M evil for all the
12:18 his hands, and whisper M, and change his expression.
13:11 will test you through M talk, and while he
14:13 give to him as M as you can.
20:2 How M better it is to reprove than to
20:11 a man who buys M for a little, but
20:14 gives little and upbraids M, he opens his mouth
22:11 Do not talk M with a foolish man, and
29:23 Be content with little or M
31:12 say, "There is certainly M upon it!"
32:8 Speak concisely, say M in few words; be as
33:27 idle, for idleness teaches M evil.
34:9 things, and one with M experience will speak with
34:10 that has traveled acquires M cleverness.
38:11 on your offering, as M as you can afford.
40:1 M labor was created for every man, and a
42:4 weights, and of acquiring M or little;
42:5 with merchants, and of M discipline of children, and
43:4 mountains three times as M; it breathes out fiery
43:27 Though we speak M we cannot reach the end,
43:30 Lord, exalt him as M as you can; for
46:19 one's property, not so M as a pair of
51:16 I found for myself M instruction.
51:27 little and found myself M rest.
51:28 will gain by it M gold.
Jer 2:22 with lye and use M soap, the stain of
Ezek 14:21 the Lord GOD: How M more when I send
15:5 used for nothing; how M less, when the fire
17:7 with great wings and M plumage; and behold, this
23:32 derision, for it contains M;
33:31 their lips they show M love, but their heart
46:5 lambs shall be as M as he is able,
46:7 with the lambs as M as he is able,
46:11 with the lambs as M as one is able
Dan 6:14 heard these words, was M distressed, and set his

	7:5	was told, 'Arise, devour M flesh.'
	14:6	you not see how M he eats and drinks
Jon	4:11	their left, and also M cattle?"
Hag	1:6	You have sown M, and harvested little; you eat,
	1:9	You have looked for M, and, lo, it came
1Mac	4:23	camp, and they seized M gold and silver, and
	9:39	procession with M baggage; and the bridegroom
	10:87	returned to Jerusalem with M booty.
	11:48	the city and seized M spoil on that day,
	11:51	returned to Jerusalem with M spoil.
	15:26	silver and gold and M military equipment.
	16:11	Jericho, and he had M silver and gold,
2Mac	2:32	narrative, adding only so M to what has already
	6:6	his fathers, nor so M as confess himself to
	7:26	After M urging on his part, she undertook to
	8:20	twenty thousand and took M booty.
	8:30	and they divided very M plunder, giving to those
	9:11	he began to lose M of his arrogance and
	15:11	of them not so M with confidence in shields
	15:14	the brethren and prays M for the people and
Mt	6:30	oven, will he not M more clothe you, O
	7:11	to your children, how M more will your Father
	10:25	the house Be-elzebul, how M more will they malign
	12:12	Of how M more value is a man than
	13:5	where they had not M soil, and immediately they
	23:14	make him twice as M a child of hell
	25:21	will set you over M; enter into the joy
	25:23	will set you over M; enter into the joy
	27:19	for I have suffered M over him today in
Mk	4:5	where it had not M soil, and immediately it
	5:19	and tell them how M the Lord has done
	5:20	in the Decapolis how M Jesus had done for
	5:26	and who had suffered M under many physicians, and
	6:20	heard him, he was M perplexed; and yet he
	12:33	neighbor as oneself, is M more than all whole
Lk	5:15	But so M the more the report went abroad
	6:34	sinners, to receive as M again.
	7:47	forgiven, for she loved M; but he who is
	8:39	home, and declare how M God has done for
	8:39	the whole city how M Jesus had done for
	10:40	Martha was distracted with M serving; and she went
	11:13	to your children, how M more will the heavenly
	12:24	Of how M more value are you than the
	12:28	into the oven, how M more will he clothe
	12:48	Every one to whom M is given, of him
	12:48	given, of him will M be required; and of
	12:48	to whom men commit M they will demand the
	16:5	to the first, 'How M do you owe my
	16:7	to another, 'And how M do you owe?' He
	16:10	is faithful also in M; and he who is
	16:10	in a very little is dishonest also in M
Jn	3:23	Salim, because there was M water there; and people
	6:10	Now there was M grass in the place; so
	6:11	also the fish, as M as they wanted.
	7:12	And there was M muttering about him among the
	8:26	I have M to say about you and much
	8:26	say about you and M to judge; but he
	12:24	it dies, it bears M fruit.
	14:30	will no longer talk M with you, for the
	15:5	it is that bears M fruit, for apart from
	15:8	glorified, that you bear M fruit, and so prove
Acts	5:8	me whether you sold the land for so M
	5:8	And she said, "Yes, for so M
	5:24	these words, they were M perplexed about them,
	8:8	So there was M joy in that city.
	9:13	about this man, how M evil he has done
	9:16	will show him how M he must suffer for
	15:7	after there had been M debate, Peter rose and
	16:16	and brought her owners M gain by soothsaying.
	20:2	and had given them M encouragement, he came to
	24:2	through you we enjoy M peace, and since by
	27:9	As M time had been lost, and the voyage
	27:10	be with injury and M loss, not only of
Rom	3:2	M in every way.
	5:9	justified by his blood, M more shall we be
	5:10	death of his Son, M more, now that we
	5:15	through one man's trespass, M more have the grace
	5:17	through that one man, M more will those who
	9:22	power, has endured with M patience the vessels of
	11:12	for the Gentiles, how M more will their full
	11:24	cultivated olive tree, how M more will these natural
1Cor	2:3	in weakness and in M fear and trembling;
	6:3	How M more, matters pertaining to this life!
	9:11	you, is it too M if we reap your
2Cor	2:4	wrote you out of M affliction and anguish of
	3:11	is permanent must have M more splendor.
	8:15	written, "He who gathered M had nothing over, and
	10:8	boast a little too M of our authority, which
Gal	4:17	They make M of you, but for no good
	4:17	that you may make M of them.
	4:18	good to be made M of, and not only
Phil	1:14	my imprisonment, and are M more bold to speak
	2:12	in my presence but M more in my absence,
1Thes	1:6	received the word in M affliction, with joy inspired
1Tim	3:8	double-tongued, not addicted to M wine, not greedy
Philem	1:7	For I have derived M joy and comfort from
	1:16	to me but how M more to you, both
Heb	1:4	high, having become as M superior to angels as
	3:3	counted worthy of as M more glory than Moses
	5:11	About this we have M to say which is
	8:6	ministry which is as M more excellent than the
	9:14	of the flesh, how M more shall the blood
	10:29	How M worse punishment do you think will be
	12:9	Shall we not M more be subject to the
	12:25	warned them on earth, M less shall we escape
2Jn	1:12	Though I have M to write to you, I
3Jn	1:13	I had M to write to you, but I
Rev	5:4	it, and I wept M that no one was
	8:3	and he was given M incense to mingle with

MUD

Zech	10:5	the foe in the M of the streets; they

MUDDIED

Prov	25:26	Like a M spring or a polluted fountain is

MULBERRIES

1Mac	6:34	juice of grapes and M, to arouse them for

MULE (9)

2Sam	13:29	and each mounted his M and fled.
	18:9	was riding upon his M, and the mule went
	18:9	his mule, and the M went under the thick
	18:9	and earth, while the M that was under him
1Kgs	1:33	ride on my own M, and bring him down
	1:38	ride on King David's M, and brought him to
	1:44	ride on the king's M;
Jud	15:11	them and loaded her M and hitched up her
Ps	32:9	a horse or a M, without understanding, which must

MULES (11)

1Kgs	10:25	myrrh, spices, horses, and M, so much year by
	18:5	save the horses and M alive, and not lose
2Kgs	5:17	to your servant two M burden of earth; for
1Chr	12:40	on camels and on M and on oxen, abundant
2Chr	9:24	myrrh, spices, horses, and M, so much year by
Ezra	2:66	hundred and thirty-six, their M were two hundred
Neh	7:68	and thirty-six, their M two hundred and forty-five,
Jud	2:17	camels and asses and M for transport, and
Is	66:20	in litters, and upon M, and upon dromedaries, to
Ezek	27:14	exchanged for your wares horses, war horses, and M
Zech	14:15	on the horses, the M, the camels, the asses,

MULTIPLIED (37)

Gen	47:27	and were fruitful and M exceedingly.
Ex	1:6	greatly; they M and grew exceedingly strong;
	1:11	oppressed, the more they M and the more they
	1:19	midwives; and the people M and grew very strong.
	11:9	my wonders may be M in the land of
Deut	1:10	LORD your God has M you, and behold, you
	8:13	silver and gold is M, and all that you
	8:13	that you have is M,
	11:21	your children may be M in the land which
1Chr	5:9	because their cattle had M in the land of
Job	27:14	If his children are M, it is for the
	35:6	if your transgressions are M, what do you do
Ps	40:5	Thou hast M, O LORD my God, thy wondrous
Prov	9:11	your days will be M, and years will be
Sir	23:3	mistakes may not be M, and my sins may
	48:16	to God, but others M sins.
Is	9:3	Thou hast M the nation, thou hast increased its
	57:9	Molech with oil and M your perfumes; you sent
	59:12	For our transgressions are M before thee, and our
Jer	3:16	And when you have M and increased in the
Lam	2:5	strongholds; and he has M in the daughter of
Ezek	11:6	You have M your slain in this city, and
	16:29	You M your harlotry also with the trading land
	35:13	with your mouth, and M your words against me;
Dan	4:1	the earth: Peace be M to you!
	6:25	the earth: "Peace be M to you.
Hos	8:11	Because Ephraim has M altars for sinning, they have
	8:14	palaces; and Judah has M fortified cities; but I

M

	12:10	it was I who M visions, and through the
Mt	24:12	And because wickedness is M, most men's love will
Acts	6:7	number of the disciples M greatly in Jerusalem, and
	7:17	the people grew and M in Egypt
	9:31	the comfort of the Holy Spirit it was M
	12:24	But the word of God grew and M
1Pet	1:2	grace and peace be M to you.
2Pet	1:2	grace and peace be M to you in the
Jude	1:2	peace, and love be M to you.

MULTIPLIES (6)

Job	9:17	with a tempest, and M my wounds without cause;
	34:37	hands among us, and M his words against God."
	35:16	in empty talk, he M words without knowledge."
Eccl	10:14	A fool M words, though no man knows what
Sir	6:5	A pleasant voice M friends, and a gracious tongue
	6:5	and a gracious tongue M courtesies.

MULTIPLY (57)

Gen	1:22	saying, "Be fruitful and M and fill the waters
	1:22	seas, and let birds M on the earth."
	1:28	them, "Be fruitful and M, and fill the earth
	3:16	said, "I will greatly M your pain in childbearing;
	6:1	When men began to M on the face of
	8:17	and be fruitful and M upon the earth."
	9:1	them, "Be fruitful and M, and fill the earth.
	9:7	you, be fruitful and M, bring forth abundantly on
	9:7	on the earth and M in it."
	16:10	"I will so greatly M your descendants that they
	17:2	and you, and will M you exceedingly."
	17:20	make him fruitful and M him exceedingly; he shall
	22:17	you, and I will M your descendants as the
	26:4	I will M your descendants as the stars of
	26:24	will bless you and M your descendants for my
	28:3	make you fruitful and M you, that you may
	35:11	Almighty: be fruitful and M; a nation and a
	48:4	make you fruitful, and M you, and I will
Ex	1:9	with them, lest they M, and, if war befall
	7:3	heart, and though I M my signs and wonders
	23:29	and the wild beasts M against you.
	32:13	to them, 'I will M your descendants as the
Lev	26:9	make you fruitful and M you, and will confirm
Deut	6:3	and that you may M greatly, as the LORD,
	7:13	you, bless you, and M you; he will also
	8:1	you may live and M, and go in and
	8:13	your herds and flocks M, and your silver and
	13:17	compassion on you, and M you, as he swore
	17:16	Only he must not M horses for himself, or
	17:16	Egypt in order to M horses, since the LORD
	17:17	And he shall not M wives for himself, lest
	17:17	nor shall he greatly M for himself silver and
	30:16	you shall live and M, and the LORD your
1Chr	4:27	did all their family M like the men of
Neh	9:23	Thou didst M their descendants as the stars of
Job	29:18	nest, and I shall M my days as the
Ps	16:4	choose another god M their sorrows; their libations
	107:38	By his blessing they M greatly; and he does
Prov	6:35	be appeased though you M gifts.
Sir	11:10	many matters; if you M activities you will not
	16:2	If they M, do not rejoice in them,
	23:16	Two sorts of men M sins, and a third
	44:22	posterity; that he would M him like the dust
Jer	23:3	their fold, and they shall be fruitful and M
	29:6	bear sons and daughters; M there, and do not
	30:19	I will M them, and they shall not be
	33:22	measured, so I will M the descendants of David
Ezek	36:10	sown; and I will M men upon you, the
	36:11	rebuilt; and I will M upon you man and
	37:26	will bless them and M them, and will set
Hos	4:10	the harlot, but not M; because they have forsaken
	12:1	all day long; they M falsehood and violence; they
Amos	4:4	to Gilgal, and M transgression; bring your sacrifices
Nah	3:15	M yourselves like the locust, multiply like the
	3:15	yourselves like the locust, M like the grasshopper!
2Cor	9:10	food will supply and M your resources and increase
Heb	6:14	will bless you and M you."

MULTIPLYING (3)

Deut	28:63	doing you good and M you, so the LORD
Ezek	16:25	to any passer-by, and M your harlotry.
	16:26	Egyptians, your lustful neighbors, M your harlotry, to

MULTITUDE (135)

Gen	16:10	descendants that they cannot be numbered for M
	17:4	the father of a M of nations.
	17:5	the father of a M of nations.
	32:12	of the sea, which cannot be numbered for M
	48:16	them grow into a M in the midst of
	48:19	descendants shall become a M of nations."
Ex	12:38	A mixed M also went up with them, and
	23:2	shall not follow a M to do evil; nor
	23:2	turning aside after a M, so as to pervert
Num	32:1	had a very great M of cattle; and they
Deut	1:10	this day as the stars of heaven for M
	10:22	made you as the stars of heaven for M
	28:62	stars of heaven for M, you shall be left
Judg	7:12	valley like locusts for M; and their camels were
	7:12	the sand which is upon the seashore for M
1Sam	13:5	on the seashore in M; they came up and
	14:16	looked; and behold, the M was surging hither and
2Sam	6:19	the people, the whole M of Israel, both men
	17:11	by the sea for M, and that you go
1Kgs	3:8	people, that cannot be numbered or counted for M
	20:13	the LORD, Have you seen all this great M
	20:28	give all this great M into your hand, and
2Kgs	7:13	fare like the whole M of Israel that have
	25:11	the rest of the M, Nebuzaradan the captain of
2Chr	13:8	you are a great M and have with you
	14:11	in thy name we have come against this M
	20:2	told Jehoshaphat, "A great M is coming against you
	20:12	powerless against this great M that is coming against
	20:15	dismayed at this great M; for the battle is
	20:24	they looked toward the M; and behold, they were
	30:18	For a M of the people, many of them
	31:18	their daughters, the whole M; for they were faithful
Jud	2:20	of the earth--a M that could not be
	5:10	they became a great M -- so great that
	7:2	the foot soldiers handling it, a very great M
	7:18	in great number, and they formed a vast M
	16:4	of his warriors; their M blocked up the valleys,
Esth	10:3	and popular with the M of his brethren, for
Job	11:2	Naamathite answered: "Should a M of words go
	31:34	great fear of the M, and the contempt of
	35:9	"Because of the M of oppressions people cry out;
Ps	42:4	songs of thanksgiving, a M keeping festival.
Prov	14:28	In a M of people is the glory of
Wis	6:24	A M of wise men is the salvation of
	11:15	send upon them a M of irrational creatures to
	11:17	send upon them a M of bears, or bold
	14:20	beautiful form, and the M, attracted by the charm
	16:1	were tormented by a M of animals.
	18:5	punishment take away a M of their children; and
	18:20	plague came upon the M in the desert, but
Sir	5:6	he will forgive the M of my sins," for
	7:9	"He will consider the M of my gifts, and
	16:1	Do not desire a M of useless children, nor
	16:3	not rely on their M; for one is better
	34:19	for sins by a M of sacrifices.
	35:18	he takes away the M of the insolent, and
	42:11	and put you to shame before the great M
	44:20	great father of a M of nations, and no
Is	1:11	to me is the M of your sacrifices?
	5:13	of hunger, and their M is parched with thirst.
	5:14	of Jerusalem and her M go down, her throng
	13:4	tumult on the mountains as of a great M
	16:14	of all his great M, and those who survive
	29:5	But the M of your foes shall be like
	29:5	small dust, and the M of the ruthless like
	29:7	And the M of all the nations that fight
	29:8	quenched, so shall the M of all the nations
	60:6	A M of camels shall cover you, the young
Jer	46:16	Your M stumbled and fell, and they said one
Lam	1:5	her suffer for the M of her transgressions; her
Bar	2:29	voice, this very great M will surely turn into
	6:5	when you see the M before and behind them
Ezek	7:12	seller mourn, for wrath is upon all their M
	7:13	is upon all their M; it shall not turn
	7:14	battle, for my wrath is upon all their M
	14:4	myself because of the M of his idols,
	23:42	sound of a carefree M was with her; and
	28:18	By the M of your iniquities, in the unrighteousness
	30:15	and cut off the M of Thebes.
	31:2	Egypt and to his M: "Whom are you like
	31:18	Pharaoh and all his M, says the Lord GOD."
	32:12	I will cause your M to fall by the
	32:12	Egypt, and all its M shall perish.
	32:16	and over all her M, shall they chant it,
	32:18	man, wail over the M of Egypt, and send
	32:24	there, and all her M about her grave; all
	32:25	slain with all her M, their graves round about
	32:26	there, and all their M, their graves round about
	32:31	himself for all his M, Pharaoh and all his

32:32 Pharaoh and all his M, says the Lord GOD."
39:11 Gog and all his M will be buried; it
Dan 10:6 of his words like the noise of a M
11:10 war and assemble a M of great forces, which
11:11 shall raise a great M, but it shall be
11:12 And when the M is taken, his heart shall
11:13 shall again raise a M, greater than the former;
Hos 10:13 chariots and in the M of your warriors,
Mic 2:12 its pasture, a noisy M of men.
Zech 2:4 walls, because of the M of men and cattle
1Mac 3:17 are, fight against so great and strong a M
6:41 noise made by their M, by the marching of
6:41 the marching of the M and the clanking of
9:35 as leader of the M and begged the Nabateans,
2Mac 8:16 to fear the great M of Gentiles who were
Mt 21:26 are afraid of the M; for all hold that
Mk 3:7 sea, and a great M from Galilee followed; also
3:8 and Sidon a great M, hearing all that he
7:32 him aside from the M privately, he put his
8:34 called to him the M with his disciples, and
10:46 disciples and a great M, Bartimaeus, a blind beggar,
11:18 him, because all the M was astonished at his
12:12 him, but feared the M, for they perceived that
12:41 treasury, and watched the M putting money into the
Lk 1:10 And the whole M of the people were praying
2:13 with the angel a M of the heavenly host
6:17 disciples and a great M of people from all
7:9 and said to the M that followed him, "I
12:1 many thousands of the M had gathered together that
12:13 One of the M said to him, "Teacher, bid
18:36 begging and hearing a M going by, he inquired
19:37 of Olives, the whole M of the disciples began
19:39 the Pharisees in the M said to him, "Teacher,
22:6 him to them in the absence of the M
23:26 followed him a great M of the people, and
Jn 5:3 In these lay a M of invalids, blind, lame,
6:2 And a M followed him, because they saw the
6:5 and seeing that a M was coming to him,
Acts 2:6 at this sound the M came together, and they
6:5 said pleased the whole M, and they chose Stephen,
14:14 rushed out among the M, crying,
Jas 5:20 and will cover a M of sins.
1Pet 4:8 since love covers a M of sins.
Rev 7:9 and behold, a great M which no man could
19:1 voice of a great M in heaven, crying, "Hallelujah!
19:6 voice of a great M, like the sound of

MULTITUDES (19)

Wis 6:2 you that rule over M, and boast of many
8:10 have glory among the M and honor in the
Ezek 32:20 sword, and with her shall lie all her M
Joel 3:14 M, multitudes, in the valley of decision!
3:14 Multitudes, M, in the valley of decision!
2Mac 12:27 where Lysias dwelt with M of people of all
Mt 21:46 him, they feared the M, because they held him
Lk 3:7 said therefore to the M that came out to
3:10 And the M asked him, "What then shall we
5:15 concerning him; and great M gathered to hear and
8:45 Peter said, "Master, the M surround you and press
12:54 also said to the M, "When you see a
14:25 Now great M accompanied him; and he turned and
23:4 chief priests and the M, "I find no crime
23:47 And all the M who assembled to see the
Acts 5:14 added to the Lord, M both of men and
8:6 And the M with one accord gave heed to
13:45 the Jews saw the M, they were filled with
Rev 17:15 seated, are peoples and M and nations and tongues.

MUPPIM

Gen 46:21 Gera, Naaman, Ehi, Rosh, M, Huppim, and Ard

MURDER (20)

Ps 94:6 and the sojourner, and M the fatherless;
Wis 12:6 cult, these parents who M helpless lives, thou didst
14:25 riot of blood and M, theft and deceit, corruption,
Sir 34:22 neighbor's living is to M him; to deprive an
Jer 7:9 Will you steal, M, commit adultery, swear falsely,
41:4 the day after the M of Gedaliah, before any
Hos 4:2 break all bounds and M follows murder.
4:2 they break all bounds and murder follows M
6:9 are banded together; they M on the way to
1Mac 1:24 He committed deeds of M, and spoke with great
2Mac 4:35 displeased at the unjust M of the man.
4:36 regard to the unreasonable M of Onias, and the
Mt 15:19 come evil thoughts, M, adultery, fornication, theft,
Mk 7:20 evil thoughts, fornication, theft, M, adultery,
15:7 prison, who had committed M in the insurrection,
Lk 23:18 an insurrection started in the city, and for M
23:24 prison for insurrection and M, whom they asked for;
Acts 9:1 still breathing threats and M against the disciples of
Rom 1:29 Full of envy, M, strife, deceit, malignity, they are
1Jn 3:12 And why did he M him?

MURDERED (6)

Judg 20:4 the woman who was M, answered and said, "I
1Kgs 2:5 of Jether, whom he M, avenging in time of
Mt 23:30 sons of those who M the prophets.
23:34 of Barachiah, whom you M between the sanctuary
Acts 7:52 have now betrayed and M,
1Jn 3:12 the evil one and M his brother.

MURDERER (21)

Num 35:16 died, he is a M; the murderer shall be
35:16 is a murderer; the M shall be put to
35:17 died, he is a M; the murderer shall be
35:17 is a murderer; the M shall be put to
35:18 died, he is a M; the murderer shall be
35:18 is a murderer; the M shall be put to
35:19 shall himself put the M to death; when he
35:21 death; he is a M; the avenger of blood
35:21 blood shall put the M to death, when he
35:30 kills a person, the M shall be put to
35:31 the life of a M, who is guilty of
2Kgs 6:32 you see how this M has sent to take
9:31 it peace, you Zimri, M of your master?"
Job 24:14 The M rises in the dark, that he may
2Mac 9:28 So the M and blasphemer, having endured the more
Jn 8:44 He was a M from the beginning, and has
Acts 3:14 and asked for a M to be granted to
28:4 one another, "No doubt this man is a M
1Pet 4:15 you suffer as a M, or a thief, or
1Jn 3:15 his brother is a M, and you know that
3:15 you know that no M has eternal life abiding

MURDERERS (9)

2Kgs 14:6 the children of the M; according to what is
Is 1:21 Righteousness lodged in her, but now M
Jer 4:31 I am fainting before M
2Mac 12:6 righteous Judge, attacked the M of his brethren.
Mt 22:7 troops and destroyed those M and burned their city.
1Tim 1:9 unholy and profane, for M of fathers and murderers
1:9 of fathers and M of mothers, for manslayers,
Rev 21:8 the polluted, as for M, fornicators, sorcerers,
22:15 sorcerers and fornicators and M and idolaters, and

MURDERING

Deut 22:26 a man attacking and M his neighbor;

MURDERS (3)

Ps 10:8 in hiding places he M the innocent.
2Mac 4:3 a degree that even M were committed by one
Rev 9:21 they repent of their M or their sorceries or

MURMUR (9)

Ex 16:7 are we, that you M against us?"
16:8 your murmurings which you M against him--what
Num 14:27 shall this wicked congregation M against me?
14:27 of Israel, which they M against me.
14:36 all the congregation to M against him by bringing
16:11 is Aaron that you M against him?"
17:5 of Israel, which they M against you."
Is 29:24 understanding, and those who M will accept
Jn 6:43 answered them, "Do not M among yourselves.

MURMURED (15)

Ex 15:24 And the people M against Moses, saying, "What
16:2 the people of Israel M against Moses and Aaron
17:3 water, and the people M against Moses, and said,
Num 14:2 the people of Israel M against Moses and Aaron;
14:29 and upward, who have M against me,
16:41 the people of Israel M against Moses and against
Deut 1:27 your God; and you M in your tents, and
Josh 9:18 Then all the congregation M against the leaders.
Ps 106:25 They M in their tents, and did not obey
Lk 5:30 Pharisees and their scribes M against his disciples,
15:2 Pharisees and the scribes M, saying, "This man
19:7 saw it they all M, "He has gone in
Jn 6:41 The Jews then M at him, because he said,
6:61 himself that his disciples M at it, said to
Acts 6:1 in number, the Hellenists M against the Hebrews

	49:12	go unpunished, but you M drink.
	51:49	Babylon M fall for the slain of Israel, as
Lam	5:4	We M pay for the water we drink, the
	5:4	the wood we get M be bought.
Bar	6:6	O Lord, whom we M worship."
	6:40	Why then M any one think that they are
	6:44	Why then M any one think that they are
	6:56	Why then M any one admit or think that
	6:64	Therefore one M not think that they are gods
Ezek	12:4	as men do who M go into exile.
	34:18	good pasture, that you M tread down with your
	34:18	clear water, that you M foul the rest with
	34:19	And M my sheep eat what you have trodden
Dan	9:2	to Jeremiah the prophet, M pass before the end
Hos	3:3	said to her, "You M dwell as mine for
	9:13	for a prey; Ephraim M lead forth his sons
	10:2	is false; now they M bear their guilt.
	10:11	to the yoke, Judah M plow, Jacob must harrow
	10:11	Judah must plow, Jacob M harrow for himself.
Amos	6:10	We M not mention the name of the LORD."
	7:11	the sword, and Israel M go into exile away
2Mac	2:29	of a new house M be concerned with the
	3:13	said that this money M in any case be
	6:17	as a reminder; we M go on briefly with
Mt	5:48	You, therefore, M be perfect, as your heavenly Father
	6:5	when you pray, you M not be like the
	16:21	his disciples that he M go to Jerusalem and
	17:10	say that first Elijah M come?"
	19:16	"Teacher, what good deed M I do, to have
	20:26	be great among you M be your servant,
	20:27	be first among you M be your slave;
	22:24	no children, his brother M marry the widow, and
	24:6	not alarmed; for this M take place, but the
	24:44	Therefore you also M be ready; for the Son
	26:35	him, "Even if I M die with you, I
	26:54	be fulfilled, that it M be so?"
Mk	8:31	the Son of man M suffer many things, and
	9:11	say that first Elijah M come?"
	9:35	would be first, he M be last of all
	10:17	him, "Good Teacher, what M I do to inherit
	10:43	be great among you M be your servant,
	10:44	be first among you M be slave of all.
	12:19	no child, the man M take the wife, and
	13:7	not be alarmed; this M take place, but the
	13:10	And the gospel M first be preached to all
	14:31	said vehemently, "If I M die with you, I
Lk	2:49	not know that I M be in my Father's
	4:43	said to them, "I M preach the good news
	5:38	But new wine M be put into fresh wineskins.
	9:22	"The Son of man M suffer many things, and
	12:40	You also M be ready; for the Son of
	13:33	Nevertheless I M go on my way today and
	14:18	a field, and I M go out and see
	17:4	says, 'I repent,' you M forgive him."
	17:25	But first he M suffer many things and be
	19:5	come down; for I M stay at your house
	20:28	no children, the man M take the wife and
	21:9	be terrified; for this M first take place, but
	22:37	you that this scripture M be fulfilled in me,
	24:7	the Son of man M be delivered into the
	24:44	prophets and the psalms M be fulfilled."
Jn	3:7	said to you, 'You M be born anew.'
	3:14	in the wilderness, so M the Son of man
	3:30	He M increase, but I must decrease."
	3:30	must increase, but I M decrease."
	4:24	those who worship him M worship in spirit and
	6:28	said to him, "What M we do, to be
	9:4	We M work the works of him who sent
	10:16	of this fold; I M bring them also, and
	12:26	one serves me, he M follow me; and where
	12:34	the Son of man M be lifted up?
	20:9	the scripture, that he M rise from the dead.
Acts	1:22	one of these men M become with us a
	3:21	you, Jesus, whom heaven M receive until the time
	4:12	men by which we M be saved."
	4:19	than to God, you M judge;
	5:29	the apostles answered, "We M obey God rather than
	9:16	him how much he M suffer for the sake
	10:15	God has cleansed, you M not call common."
	11:9	God has cleansed you M not call common.'
	14:22	through many tribulations we M enter the kingdom
	16:30	and said, "Men, what M I do to be
	19:21	have been there, I M also see Rome."
	20:35	by so toiling one M help the weak, remembering
	23:11	at Jerusalem, so you M bear witness also at
	26:23	pass: that the Christ M suffer, and that, by
	27:24	be afraid, Paul; you M stand before Caesar; and
Rom	2:22	who say that one M not commit adultery, do
	6:11	So you also M consider yourselves dead to sin
	13:5	Therefore one M be subject, not only to avoid
1Cor	10:8	We M not indulge in immorality as some of
	10:9	We M not put the Lord to the test,
	11:19	believe it, for there M be factions among you
	15:25	For he M reign until he has put all
	15:53	this perishable nature M put on the imperishable,
	15:53	and this mortal nature M put on immortality.
2Cor	1:11	You also M help us by prayer, so that
	3:9	the dispensation of righteousness M far exceed it in
	3:11	splendor, what is permanent M have much more
	5:10	For we M all appear before the judgment seat
	9:7	Each one M do as he has made up
	11:21	To my shame, I M say, we were too
	11:30	If I M boast, I will boast of the
	12:1	I M boast; there is nothing to be gained
	13:1	Any charge M be sustained by the evidence of
Eph	4:17	the Lord, that you M no longer live as
	5:3	all impurity or covetousness M not even be named
Col	3:13	you, so you also M forgive.
1Tim	3:2	Now a bishop M be above reproach, the husband
	3:4	He M manage his own household well, keeping his
	3:6	He M not be a recent convert, or he
	3:7	the devil; moreover he M be well thought of
	3:8	Deacons likewise M be serious, not double-tongued,
	3:9	greedy for gain; they M hold the mystery of
	3:11	The women likewise M be serious, no slanderers, but
	5:10	one husband; and she M be well attested for
	6:2	who have believing masters M not be disrespectful
	6:2	are brethren; rather they M serve all the better
2Tim	2:24	And the Lord's servant M not be quarrelsome but
Tit	1:6	bishop, as God's steward, M be blameless; he must
	1:6	must be blameless; he M not be arrogant or
	1:8	holy, and self-controlled; he M hold firm to the
	1:10	the circumcision party; they M be silenced, since
Heb	2:1	Therefore we M pay the closer attention to what
	9:16	one who made it M be established.
	11:6	draw near to God M believe that he exists
Jas	1:7	For that person M not suppose that a double-minded
2Pet	1:20	First of all you M understand this, that no
	3:3	First of all you M understand this, that scoffers
Jude	1:17	But you M remember, beloved, the predictions of the
Rev	1:1	to his servants what M soon take place; and
	4:1	will show you what M take place after this."
	10:11	I was told, "You M again prophesy about many
	13:10	sword, with the sword M he be slain.
	17:10	when he comes he M remain only a little
	19:10	said to me, "You M not do that!
	20:3	After that he M be loosed for a little
	22:6	show his servants what M soon take place.
	22:9	said to me, "You M not do that!

MUSTARD (5)

Mt	13:31	like a grain of M seed which a man
	17:20	as a grain of M seed, you will say
Mk	4:31	like a grain of M seed, which, when sown
Lk	13:19	like a grain of M seed which a man
	17:6	as a grain of M seed, you could say

MUSTER (4)

1Kgs	20:25	in their places; and M an army like the
2Chr	17:14	This was the M of them by fathers' houses:
	26:11	the numbers in the M made by Je-iel the
Neh	3:31	the merchants, opposite the M Gate, and to the

MUSTERED (24)

Josh	8:10	in the morning and M the people, and went
Judg	20:15	And the Benjaminites M out of their cities on
	20:15	inhabitants of Gibe-ah, who M seven hundred picked.
	20:17	Israel, apart from Benjamin, M four hundred
	21:9	when the people were M, behold, not one of
1Sam	11:8	When he M them at Bezek, the men of
	13:5	And the Philistines M to fight with Israel, thirty
	13:11	that the Philistines had M at Michmash,
2Sam	18:1	Then David M the men who were with him,
1Kgs	20:15	Then he M the servants of the governors of
	20:15	and after them he M all the people of
	20:26	In the spring Ben-hadad M the Syrians, and went
	20:27	people of Israel were M, and were provisioned, and
2Kgs	3:6	at that time and M all Israel.
	6:24	Ben-hadad king of Syria M his entire army, and
	25:19	of the army who M the people of the
1Chr	19:7	And the Ammonites were M from their cities and
2Chr	25:5	He M those twenty years old and upward, and

49:13 I have sworn by M, says the LORD, that
Ezek 4:14 I have never defiled M; from my youth up
5:13 upon them and satisfy M; and they shall know
14:3 faces; should I let M be inquired of at
14:4 LORD will answer him M because of the multitude
14:7 LORD will answer him M;
17:22 the Lord GOD: "I M will take a sprig
17:22 tender one, and I M will plant it upon
20:5 house of Jacob, making M known to them in
20:9 whose sight I made M known to them in
24:12 vain I have wearied M; its thick rust does
34:11 GOD: Behold, I, I M will search for my
34:15 I M will be the shepherd of my sheep,
34:20 them: Behold, I, I M will judge between the
35:11 and I will make M known among you, when
38:23 my holiness and make M known in the eyes
Dan 10:3 nor did I anoint M at all, for the
Hos 2:23 will sow him for M in the land.
12:8 have gained wealth for M: but all his riches
Mic 6:6 the LORD, and bow M before God on high?
Hab 2:1 to watch, and station M on the tower, and
1Mac 3:14 make a name for M and win honor in
6:11 I said to M, 'To what distress I have
2Mac 6:27 now, I will show M worthy of my old
15:38 that is what I M desired; if it is
Lk 24:39 that it is I M; handle me, and see;
Jn 1:31 was before me.' I M did not know him;
1:33 I M did not know him; but he who
5:30 I bear witness to M, my testimony is not
8:14 do bear witness to M, my testimony is true,
8:18 I bear witness to M, and the Father who
8:54 answered, "If I glorify M, my glory is nothing;
12:32 from the earth, will draw all men to M
14:3 will take you to M, that where I am
14:21 love him and manifest M to him."
17:19 their sake I consecrate M, that they also may
Acts 20:24 nor as precious to M, if only I may
25:22 Festus, "I should like to hear the man M
26:2 his defense: "I think M fortunate that it is
26:9 "I M was convinced that I ought to do
Rom 7:25 So then, I of M serve the law of
9:3 could wish that I M were accursed and cut
10:20 me; I have shown M to those who did
11:1 I M am an Israelite, a descendant of Abraham,
11:4 "I have kept for M seven thousand men who
15:14 I M am satisfied about you, my brethren, that
16:2 of many and of M as well.
1Cor 4:3 I do not even judge M
4:4 aware of anything against M, but I am not
4:6 applied all this to M and Apollos for your
7:7 all were as I M am.
9:19 men, I have made M a slave to all,
9:20 law--though not being M under the law--that
9:27 preaching to others I M should be disqualified.
2Cor 10:1 I, Paul, M entreat you, by the meekness and
11:7 a sin in abasing M so that you might
12:13 churches, except that I M did not burden you?
12:16 But granting that I M did not burden you,
Gal 2:18 down, then I prove M a transgressor.
Phil 2:24 Lord that shortly I M shall come also.
3:4 Though I M have reason for confidence in the
Rev 2:27 pieces, even as I M have received power from
3:21 my throne, as I M conquered and sat down

MYSIA (2)

Acts 16:7 they had come opposite M, they attempted to go
16:8 them; so, passing by M, they went down to

MYSIANS

2Mac 5:24 the captain of the M, with an army of

MYSTERIES (7)

Wis 14:23 initiations, or celebrate secret M, or hold frenzied
Dan 2:28 in heaven who reveals M, and he has made
2:29 and he who reveals M made known to you
2:47 and a revealer of M, for you have been
1Cor 4:1 and stewards of the M of God.
13:2 powers, and understand all M and all knowledge, and
14:2 him, but he utters M in the Spirit.

MYSTERIOUS

Dan 2:22 he reveals deep and M things; he knows what

MYSTERY (26)

Dan 2:18 of heaven concerning this M, so that Daniel and
2:19 Then the M was revealed to Daniel in a
2:27 to the king the M which the king has
2:30 the living has this M been revealed to me,
2:47 for you have been able to reveal this M
4:9 you and that no M is difficult for you,
Rom 11:25 you to understand this M, brethren: a hardening has
16:24 the revelation of the M which was kept secret
1Cor 15:51 I tell you a M
Eph 1:9 wisdom and insight the M of his will, according
3:3 for you, how the M was made known to
3:4 my insight into the M of Christ,
3:9 the plan of the M hidden for ages in
5:32 This M is a profound one, and I am
6:19 boldly to proclaim the M of the gospel,
Col 1:26 God fully known, the M hidden for ages and
1:27 the glory of this M, which is Christ in
2:2 the knowledge of God's M, of Christ,
4:3 word, to declare the M of Christ, on account
2Thes 2:7 For the M of lawlessness is already at work;
1Tim 3:9 they must hold the M of the faith with
3:16 we confess, is the M of our religion: He
Rev 1:20 As for the M of the seven stars which
10:7 the seventh angel, the M of God, as he
17:5 written a name of M: "Babylon the great, mother
17:7 will tell you the M of the woman, and

MYTHS (5)

1Tim 1:4 occupy themselves with M and endless genealogies
4:7 Have nothing to do with godless and silly M
2Tim 4:4 from listening to the truth and wander into M
Tit 1:13 giving heed to Jewish M or to commands of
2Pet 1:16 not follow cleverly devised M when we made known

N

NAAM

1Chr 4:15 Jephunneh: Iru, Elah, and N; and the sons of

NAAMAH (5)

Gen 4:22 The sister of Tubal-cain was N
Josh 15:41 Lahmam, Chitlish, Gederoth, Beth-dagon, N, and
1Kgs 14:21 His mother's name was N the Ammonitess.
14:31 His mother's name was N the Ammonitess.
2Chr 12:13 His mother's name was N the Ammonitess.

NAAMAN (19)

Gen 46:21 Ashbel, Gera, N, Ehi, Rosh, Muppim, Huppim,
Num 26:40 Bela were Ard and N: of Ard, the family
26:40 of the Ardites; of N, the family of the
2Kgs 5:1 N, commander of the army of the king of
5:2 and she waited on N's wife.
5:4 So N went in and told his lord, "Thus
5:6 have sent to you N my servant, that you
5:9 So N came with his horses and chariots, and
5:11 But N was angry, and went away, saying, "Behold,
5:17 Then N said, "If not, I pray you, let
5:19 But when N had gone from him a short
5:20 master has spared this N the Syrian, in not
5:21 So Gehazi followed N
5:21 And when N saw some one running after him,
5:23 And N said, "Be pleased to accept two talents."
5:27 Therefore the leprosy of N shall cleave to you,
1Chr 8:4 Addar, Gera, Abihud, Abishua, N, Ahoah,
8:7 into exile to Manahath): N, Ahijah, and Gera, that
Lk 4:27 was cleansed, but only N the Syrian."

NAAMATHITE (4)

Job 2:11 the Temanite, Bildad the Shuhite, and Zophar the N
11:1 Then Zophar the N answered:
20:1 Then Zophar the N answered:
42:9 Shuhite and Zophar the N went and did what

NAAMITES

Num 26:40 the Ardites; of Naaman, the family of the N

NAARAH (4)

Josh 16:7 to Ataroth and to N, and touches Jericho, ending
1Chr 4:5 two wives, Helah and N;
4:6 wives, Helah and Naarah; N bore him Ahuzzam,
4:6 These were the sons of N

NAARAI

1Chr 11:37 Pelonite, Hezro of Carmel, N the son of Ezbai,

NAARAN
1Chr 7:28 its towns, and eastward N, and westward Gezer and

NABAL (22)
1Sam 25:3 of the man was N, and the name of
25:4 in the wilderness that N was shearing his sheep.
25:5 Carmel, and go to N, and greet him in
25:9 said all this to N in the name of
25:10 And N answered David's servants, "Who is David?
25:14 young men told Abigail, N's wife, "Behold, David sent
25:19 But she did not tell her husband N
25:25 regard this ill-natured fellow, N; for as his name
25:25 is, so is he; N is his name, and
25:26 to do evil to my lord be as N
25:34 not been left to N so much as one
25:36 And Abigail came to N; and, lo, he was
25:36 And N's heart was merry within him, for he
25:37 had gone out of N, his wife told him
25:38 later the LORD smote N; and he died.
25:39 When David heard that N was dead, he said,
25:39 at the hand of N, and has kept back
25:39 returned the evil-doing of N upon his own head."
27:3 and Abigail of Carmel, N's widow.
30:5 Abigail the widow of N of Carmel.
2Sam 2:2 Abigail the widow of N of Carmel.
3:3 Abigail the widow of N of Carmel; and the

NABATEANS (2)
1Mac 5:25 They encountered the N, who met them peaceably
9:35 multitude and begged the N, who were his friends,

NABOTH (22)
1Kgs 21:1 Now N the Jezreelite had a vineyard in Jezreel,
21:2 this Ahab said to N, "Give me your vineyard,
21:3 But N said to Ahab, "The LORD forbid that
21:4 sullen because of what N the Jezreelite had said
21:6 "Because I spoke to N the Jezreelite, and said
21:7 you the vineyard of N the Jezreelite."
21:8 nobles who dwelt with N in his city.
21:9 a fast, and set N on high among the
21:12 a fast, and set N on high among the
21:13 brought a charge against N, in the presence of
21:13 of the people, saying, N cursed God and the
21:14 sent to Jezebel, saying, N has been stoned; he
21:15 as Jezebel heard that N had been stoned and
21:15 of the vineyard of N the Jezreelite, which he
21:15 you for money; for N is not alive, but
21:16 as Ahab heard that N was dead, Ahab arose
21:16 to the vineyard of N the Jezreelite, to take
21:18 in the vineyard of N, where he has gone
21:19 up the blood of N shall dogs lick your
2Kgs 9:21 at the property of N the Jezreelite.
9:25 of ground belonging to N the Jezreelite; for
9:26 yesterday the blood of N and the blood of

NACON
2Sam 6:6 the threshing floor of N, Uzzah put out his

NADAB (24)
Ex 6:23 and she bore him N, Abihu, Eleazar, and Ithamar.
24:1 LORD, you and Aaron, N, and Abihu, and seventy
24:9 Then Moses and Aaron, N, and Abihu, and seventy
28:1 Aaron and Aaron's sons, N and Abihu, Eleazar and
Lev 10:1 Now N and Abihu, the sons of Aaron, each
Num 3:2 the sons of Aaron: N the first-born, and Abihu,
3:4 But N and Abihu died before the LORD when
26:60 to Aaron were born N, Abihu, Eleazar and Ithamar.
26:61 But N and Abihu died when they offered unholy
1Kgs 14:20 with his fathers, and N his son reigned in
15:25 N the son of Jeroboam began to reign over
15:27 to the Philistines; for N and all Israel were
15:31 of the acts of N, and all that he
1Chr 2:28 The sons of Shammai: N and Abishur.
2:30 The sons of N: Seled and Appa-im; and Seled
6:3 The sons of Aaron: N, Abihu, Eleazar, and Ithamar.
8:30 then Zur, Kish, Baal, N,
9:36 Zur, Kish, Baal, Ner, N,
24:1 The sons of Aaron: N, Abihu, Eleazar, and Ithamar.
24:2 But N and Abihu died before their father, and
Tob 11:18 Ahikar and his nephew N came,
14:10 See, my son, what N did to Ahikar who
14:10 escaped the deathtrap which N had set for him;
14:10 set for him; but N fell into the trap

NADABATH
1Mac 9:37 nobles of Canaan, from N with a large escort."

NAGGAI
Lk 3:25 Esli, the son of N,

NAHALAL (2)
Josh 19:15 and Kattath, N, Shimron, Idalah, and Bethlehem–
21:35 with its pasture lands, N with its pasture lands–

NAHALIEL (2)
Num 21:19 and from Mattanah to N, and from Nahaliel to
21:19 to Nahaliel, and from N to Bamoth,

NAHALOL
Judg 1:30 or the inhabitants of N; but the Canaanites dwelt

NAHAM
1Chr 4:19 Hodiah, the sister of N, were the fathers of

NAHAMANI
Neh 7:7 Jeshua, Nehemiah, Azariah, Raamiah, N, Mordecai,

NAHARAI (2)
2Sam 23:37 Gadite, Zelek the Ammonite, N of Be-eroth, the
1Chr 11:39 Hagri, Zelek the Ammonite, N of Be-eroth, the

NAHASH (9)
1Sam 11:1 Then N the Ammonite went up and besieged
11:1 of Jabesh said to N, "Make a treaty with
11:2 But N the Ammonite said to them, "On this
12:12 when you saw that N the king of the
2Sam 10:2 Hanun the son of N, as his father dealt
17:25 Abigal the daughter of N, sister of Zeruiah, Joab's
17:27 Shobi the son of N from Rabbah of the
1Chr 19:1 Now after this N the king of the Ammonites
19:2 Hanun the son of N, for his father dealt

NAHATH (5)
Gen 36:13 the sons of Reuel: N, Zerah, Shammah, and Mizzah.
36:17 Esau's son: the chiefs N, Zerah, Shammah, and
1Chr 1:37 The sons of Reuel: N, Zerah, Shammah, and Mizzah.
6:26 son, Zophai his son, N his son,
2Chr 31:13 second; while Jehiel, Azaziah, N, Asahel, Jerimoth,

NAHBI
Num 13:14 the tribe of Naphtali, N the son of Vophsi;

NAHOR (19)
Gen 11:22 became the father of N;
11:23 after the birth of N two hundred years, and
11:24 When N had lived twenty-nine years, he became the
11:25 father of Terah; and N lived after the birth
11:26 the father of Abram, N, and Haran.
11:27 the father of Abram, N, and Haran; and Haran
11:29 And Abram and N took wives; the name of
11:29 and the name of N's wife, Milcah, the daughter
22:20 children to your brother N:
22:23 eight Milcah bore to N, Abraham's brother.
24:10 and went to Mesopotamia, to the city of N
24:15 Milcah, the wife of N, Abraham's brother, came out
24:24 the son of Milcah, whom she bore to N
24:47 The daughter of Bethuel, N's son, whom Milcah bore
29:5 them, "Do you know Laban the son of N
31:53 and the God of N, the God of their
Josh 24:2 of Abraham and of N; and they served other
1Chr 1:26 Eber, Peleg, Reu; Serug, N, Terah;
Lk 3:34 Terah, the son of N,

NAHSHON (13)
Ex 6:23 and the sister of N; and she bore him
Num 1:7 Zurishaddai; from Judah, N the son of Amminadab;
2:3 people of Judah being N the son of Amminadab,
7:12 the first day was N the son of Amminadab,
7:17 was the offering of N the son of Amminadab.
10:14 over their host was N the son of Amminadab.
Ruth 4:20 Amminadab, Amminadab of N, N of Salmon,
1Chr 2:10 was the father of N, prince of the sons
2:11 N was the father of Salma, Salma of Boaz,
Mt 1:4 Amminadab the father of N, and Nahshon the father
1:4 father of Nahshon, and N the father of Salmon,
Lk 3:32 Sala, the son of N,
Nah 1:1 of the vision of N of Elkosh.
Lk 3:25 Amos, the son of N, the son of Esli,

NAILING
Col 2:14 this he set aside, N it to the cross.

NAILS (9)

Deut 21:12 she shall shave her head and pare her N
1Chr 22:3 stores of iron for N for the doors of
2Chr 3:9 The weight of the N was one shekel to
Eccl 12:11 like goads, and like N firmly fixed are the
Is 41:7 they fasten it with N so that it cannot
Jer 10:4 it with hammer and N so that it cannot
Dan 4:33 eagles' feathers, and his N were like birds' claws.
Jn 20:25 the print of the N, and place my finger
20:25 the mark of the N, and place my hand

NAIN

Lk 7:11 to a city called N, and his disciples and

NAIOTH (6)

1Sam 19:18 And he and Samuel went and dwelt at N
19:19 "Behold, David is at N in Ramah."
19:22 "Behold, they are at N in Ramah."
19:23 went from there to N in Ramah; and the
19:23 until he came to N in Ramah.
20:1 Then David fled from N in Ramah, and came

NAKED (41)

Gen 2:25 his wife were both N, and were not ashamed.
3:7 knew that they were N; and they sewed fig
3:10 afraid, because I was N; and I hid myself."
3:11 He said, "Who told you that you were N
Ex 28:42 breeches to cover their N flesh; from the loins
Lev 20:18 nakedness, he has made N her fountain, and she
20:19 that is to make N one's near kin; they
1Sam 19:24 before Samuel, and lay N all that day and
2Chr 28:15 clothed all that were N among them; they clothed
Tob 1:17 my clothing to the N; and if I saw
4:16 the hungry, and of your clothing to the N
Job 1:21 And he said, N I came from my mother's
1:21 my mother's womb, and N shall I return; the
22:6 nothing, and stripped the N of their clothing.
24:7 They lie all night N, without clothing, and have
24:10 poor.) They go about N, without clothing; hungry,
26:6 Sheol is N before God, and Abaddon has no
Eccl 5:15 he shall go again, N as he came, and
Is 20:2 had done so, walking N and barefoot—
20:3 servant Isaiah has walked N and barefoot for three
20:4 young and the old, N and barefoot, with buttocks
58:7 when you see the N, to cover him, and
Ezek 16:7 grown; yet you were N and bare.
16:22 youth, when you were N and bare, weltering in
16:39 jewels, and leave you N and bare.
18:7 hungry and covers the N with a garment,
18:16 hungry and covers the N with a garment,
23:29 labor, and leave you N and bare, and the
Hos 2:3 lest I strip her N and make her as
Amos 2:16 mighty shall flee away N in that day," says
Mic 1:8 will go stripped and N; I will make lamentation
Mt 25:36 welcomed me, I was N and you clothed me,
25:38 and welcome thee, or N and clothe thee?
25:43 did not welcome me, N and you did not
25:44 or a stranger or N or sick or in
Mk 14:52 he left the linen cloth and ran away N
Acts 19:16 out of that house N and wounded.
2Cor 5:3 putting it on we may not be found N
Rev 3:17 that you are wretched, pitiable, poor, blind, and N
16:15 he may not go N and be seen exposed!")
17:16 make her desolate and N, and devour her flesh

NAKEDNESS (53)

Gen 9:22 of Canaan, saw the N of his father, and
9:23 backward and covered the N of their father; their
9:23 away, and they did not see their father's N
Ex 20:26 my altar, that your N be not exposed on
Lev 18:6 one near of kin to him to uncover N
18:7 shall not uncover the N of your father, which
18:7 father, which is the N of your mother; she
18:7 is your mother, you shall not uncover her N
18:8 shall not uncover the N of your father's wife;
18:8 of your father's wife; it is your father's N
18:9 shall not uncover the N of your sister, the
18:10 shall not uncover the N of your son's daughter
18:10 daughter's daughter, for their N is your own N.
18:11 shall not uncover the N of your father's wife's
18:12 shall not uncover the N of your father's sister;
18:13 shall not uncover the N of your mother's sister,
18:14 shall not uncover the N of your father's brother,
18:15 shall not uncover the N of your daughter-in-law; she
18:15 your son's wife, you shall not uncover her N
18:16 shall not uncover the N of your brother's wife;
18:16 of your brother's wife; she is your brother's N
18:17 shall not uncover the N of a woman and
18:17 daughter to uncover her N; they are your near
18:18 her sister, uncovering her N while her sister is
18:19 woman to uncover her N while she is in
20:11 has uncovered his father's N; both of them shall
20:17 mother, and sees her N, and she sees his
20:17 and she sees his N, it is a shameful
20:17 has uncovered his sister's N, he shall bear his
20:18 sickness, and uncovers her N, he has made naked
20:19 shall not uncover the N of your mother's sister
20:20 has uncovered his uncle's N; they shall bear their
20:21 has uncovered his brother's N, they shall be childless.
Deut 28:48 hunger and thirst, in N, and in want of
1Sam 20:30 shame, and to the shame of your mother's N
Sir 29:21 and clothing and a house to cover one's N
Is 47:3 Your N shall be uncovered, and your shame shall
57:8 have loved their bed, you have looked on N
Lam 1:8 they have seen her N; yea, she herself groans,
Ezek 16:8 you, and covered your N: yea, I plighted my
16:36 laid bare and your N uncovered in your harlotries
16:37 and will uncover your N to them, that they
16:37 to them, that they may see all your N
22:10 men uncover their fathers' N; in you they humble
23:10 These uncovered her N; they seized her sons and
23:18 openly and flaunted her N, I turned in disgust
23:29 and bare, and the N of your harlotry shall
Hos 2:9 and my flax, which were to cover her N
Mic 1:11 inhabitants of Shaphir, in N and shame; the
Nah 3:5 nations look on your N and kingdoms on your
Rom 8:35 persecution, or famine, or N, or peril, or sword?
Rev 3:18 the shame of your N from being seen, and

NAME (1,005)

Gen 2:11 The N of the first is Pishon; it is
2:13 The N of the second river is Gihon; it
2:14 And the N of the third river is Tigris,
2:19 man called every living creature, that was its N
3:20 man called his wife's N Eve, because she was
4:17 city, and called the N of the city after
4:17 the city after the N of his son, Enoch.
4:19 took two wives; the N of the one was
4:19 was Adah, and the N of the other Zillah.
4:21 His brother's N was Jubal; he was the father
4:25 son and called his N Seth, for she said,
4:26 and he called his N Enosh.
4:26 to call upon the N of the LORD.
5:29 son, and called his N Noah, saying, "Out of
10:25 born two sons: the N of the one was
10:25 divided, and his brother's N was Joktan.
11:4 let us make a N for ourselves, lest we
11:9 Therefore its N was called Babel, because there the
11:29 Nahor took wives; the N of Abram's wife was
11:29 was Sarai, and the N of Nahor's wife, Milcah,
12:2 you, and make your N great, so that you
12:8 and called on the N of the LORD.
13:4 Abram called on the N of the LORD.
16:1 an Egyptian maid whose N was Hagar;
16:11 you shall call his N Ishmael; because the LORD
16:13 So she called the N of the LORD who
16:15 and Abram called the N of his son, whom
17:5 No longer shall your N be Abram, but your
17:5 be Abram, but your N shall be Abraham; for
17:15 shall not call her N Sarai, but Sarah shall
17:15 her name Sarai, but Sarah shall be her N
17:19 you shall call his N Isaac.
19:22 Therefore the N of the city was called Zoar.
19:37 son, and called his N Moab; he is the
19:38 son, and called his N Ben-ammi; he is the
21:3 Abraham called the N of his son who was
21:33 called there on the N of the LORD, the
22:14 So Abraham called the N of that place The
22:24 his concubine, whose N was Reumah, bore Tebah,
24:29 had a brother whose N was Laban; and Laban
25:1 took another wife, whose N was Keturah.
25:25 so they called his N Esau.
25:26 Esau's heel; so his N was called Jacob.
25:30 (Therefore his N was called Edom.
26:20 So he called the N of the well Esek,
26:21 so he called its N Sitnah.
26:22 so he called its N Rehoboth, saying, "For now
26:25 and called upon the N of the LORD, and
26:33 it Shibah; therefore the N of the city is
28:19 He called the N of that place Bethel; but
28:19 place Bethel; but the N of the city was
29:16 had two daughters; the N of the older was

	29:16	was Leah, and the N of the younger was
	29:32	and she called his N Reuben; for she said,
	29:33	and she called his N Simeon.
	29:34	three sons"; therefore his N was called Levi.
	29:35	therefore she called his N Judah; then she ceased
	30:6	therefore she called his N Dan.
	30:8	so she called his N Naphtali.
	30:11	so she called his N Gad.
	30:13	so she called his N Asher.
	30:18	so she called his N Issachar.
	30:20	so she called his N Zebulun.
	30:21	daughter, and called her N Dinah.
	30:24	and she called his N Joseph, saying, "May the
	30:28	me because of you; N your wages, and I
	32:2	So he called the N of that place Mahanaim.
	32:27	And he said to him, "What is your N
	32:28	Then he said, "Your N shall no more be
	32:29	Jacob asked him, "Tell me, I pray, your N
	32:29	said, "Why is it that you ask my N
	32:30	So Jacob called the N of the place Peniel,
	33:17	his cattle; therefore the N of the place is
	35:8	below Bethel; so the N of it was called
	35:10	said to him, "Your N is Jacob; no longer
	35:10	no longer shall your N be called Jacob, but
	35:10	be called Jacob, but Israel shall be your N
	35:10	So his N was called Israel.
	35:15	So Jacob called the N of the place where
	35:18	died), she called his N Ben-oni; but his father
	35:18	his father called his N Benjamin.
	36:32	reigned in Edom, the N of his city being
	36:35	in his stead, the N of his city being
	36:39	in his stead, the N of his city being
	36:39	being Pau; his wife's N was Mehetabel, the daughter
	38:1	a certain Adullamite, whose N was Hirah.
	38:2	a certain Canaanite whose N was Shua; he married
	38:3	and he called his N Er.
	38:4	and she called his N Onan.
	38:5	and she called his N Shelah.
	38:6	his first-born, and her N was Tamar.
	38:29	Therefore his N was called Perez.
	38:30	his hand; and his N was called Zerah.
	41:45	Pharaoh called Joseph's N Zaphenath-paneah; and
	41:51	Joseph called the N of the first-born Manasseh,
	41:52	The N of the second he called Ephraim, "For
	48:6	be called by the N of their brothers in
	48:16	in them let my N be perpetuated, and the
	48:16	be perpetuated, and the N of my fathers Abraham
	49:24	of Jacob (by the N of the Shepherd, the
Ex	2:22	and he called his N Gershom; for he said,
	3:13	me, 'What is his N what shall I say
	3:15	you: this is my N for ever, and thus
	5:23	to speak in thy N, he has done evil
	6:3	Almighty, but by my N the LORD I did
	9:16	power, so that my N may be declared throughout
	15:3	a man of war; the LORD is his N
	16:31	of Israel called its N manna; it was like
	17:7	And he called the N of the place Massah
	17:15	altar and called the N of it, The LORD
	18:3	sons, of whom the N of the one was
	18:4	foreign land"), and the N of the other, Eliezer
	20:7	shall not take the N of the LORD your
	20:7	guiltless who takes his N in vain.
	20:24	where I cause my N to be remembered I
	23:21	your transgression; for my N is in him.
	28:21	each engraved with its N, for the twelve tribes.
	31:2	I have called by N Bezalel the son of
	33:12	'I know you by N, and you have also
	33:17	in my sight, and I know you by N
	33:19	proclaim before you my N 'The LORD'; and I
	34:5	there, and proclaimed the N of the LORD.
	34:14	for the LORD, whose N is Jealous, is a
	35:30	LORD has called by N Bezalel the son of
	39:14	each engraved with its N, for the twelve tribes.
Lev	18:21	and so profane the N of your God: I
	19:12	not swear by my N falsely, and so profane
	19:12	and so profane the N of your God: I
	20:3	defiling my sanctuary and profaning my holy N
	21:6	and not profane the N of their God; for
	22:2	not profane my holy N; I am the LORD.
	22:32	not profane my holy N, but I will be
	24:11	woman's son blasphemed the N, and cursed.
	24:11	His mother's N was Shelomith, the daughter of Dibri,
	24:16	He who blasphemes the N of the LORD shall
	24:16	when he blasphemes the N, shall be put to
Num	4:32	you shall assign by N the objects which they
	6:27	shall they put my N upon the people of
	11:3	So the N of that place was called Taberah,
	11:34	the N of that place was called Kibroth-hattaavah,
	17:2	Write each man's N upon his rod,
	17:3	rod, and write Aaron's N upon the rod of
	21:3	their cities; so the N of the place was
	25:14	The N of the slain man of Israel, who
	25:15	And the N of the Midianite woman who was
	26:46	And the N of the daughter of Asher was
	26:59	The N of Amram's wife was Jochebed the daughter
	27:4	Why should the N of our father be taken
	32:42	villages, and called it Nobah, after his own N
Deut	3:14	villages after his own N, Havvoth-jair, as it is
	5:11	shall not take the N of the LORD your
	5:11	guiltless who takes his N in vain.
	6:13	you shall serve him, and swear by his N
	7:24	you shall make their N perish from under heaven;
	9:14	and blot out their N from under heaven; and
	10:8	to bless in his N, to this day.
	10:20	him, and by his N you shall swear.
	12:3	gods, and destroy their N out of that place.
	12:5	tribes to put his N and make his habitation
	12:11	choose, to make his N dwell there, thither you
	12:21	choose to put his N there is too far
	14:23	choose, to make his N dwell there, you shall
	14:24	chooses, to set his N there,
	16:2	choose, to make his N dwell there.
	16:6	choose, to make his N dwell in it, there
	16:11	choose, to make his N dwell there.
	18:5	and minister in the N of the LORD, him
	18:7	may minister in the N of the LORD his
	18:19	shall speak in my N, I myself will require
	18:20	a word in my N which I have not
	18:20	who speaks in the N of other gods, that
	18:22	prophet speaks in the N of the LORD, if
	21:5	to bless in the N of the LORD, and
	22:14	and brings an evil N upon her, saying, 'I
	22:19	has brought an evil N upon a virgin of
	25:6	shall succeed to the N of his brother who
	25:6	is dead, that his N may not be blotted
	25:7	to perpetuate his brother's N in Israel; he will
	25:10	brother's house.' And the N of his house shall
	26:2	choose, to make his N to dwell there.
	28:10	are called by the N of the LORD; and
	28:58	this glorious and awful N, the LORD your God,
	29:20	would blot out his N from under heaven.
	32:3	I will proclaim the N of the LORD.
Josh	2:1	of a harlot whose N was Rahab, and lodged
	5:9	And so the N of that place is called
	7:9	and cut off our N from the earth; and
	7:9	and what wilt thou do for thy great N
	7:26	to this day the N of that place is
	9:9	come, because of the N of the LORD your
	14:15	Now the N of Hebron formerly was Kiriath-arba; this
	15:15	of Debir; now the N of Debir formerly was
	19:47	Leshem, Dan, after the N of Dan their ancestor.
	21:9	following cities mentioned by N,
Judg	1:10	in Hebron (now the N of Hebron was formerly
	1:11	The N of Debir was formerly Kiriath-sepher.
	1:17	So the N of the city was called Hormah.
	1:23	(Now the N of the city was formerly Luz.)
	1:26	city, and called its N Luz; that is its
	1:26	Luz; that is its N to this day.
	2:5	And they called the N of that place Bochim;
	8:31	and he called his N Abimelech.
	13:2	of the Danites, whose N was Manoah; and his
	13:6	not tell me his N;
	13:17	LORD, "What is your N, so that, when your
	13:18	do you ask my N, seeing it is wonderful?"
	13:24	son, and called his N Samson; and the boy
	15:19	Therefore the N of it was called En-hakkore; it
	16:4	valley of Sorek, whose N was Delilah.
	17:1	country of Ephraim, whose N was Micah.
	18:29	city Dan, after the N of Dan their ancestor,
	18:29	to Israel; but the N of the city was
Ruth	1:2	The N of the man was Elimelech and the
	1:2	was Elimelech and the N of his wife Naomi,
	1:4	took Moabite wives; the N of the one was
	1:4	was Orpah and the N of the other Ruth.
	2:1	family of Elimelech, whose N was Boaz.
	2:19	and said, "The man's N with whom I worked
	4:5	order to restore the N of the dead to
	4:10	wife, to perpetuate the N of the dead in
	4:10	his inheritance, that the N of the dead may
	4:14	kin; and may his N be renowned in Israel!
	4:17	neighborhood gave him a N, saying, "A son has
1Sam	1:1	country of Ephraim, whose N was Elkanah the son

1:2 had two wives; the N of the one was
1:2 was Hannah, and the N of the other Peninnah.
1:20 and she called his N Samuel, for she said,
7:12 Jeshanah, and called its N Ebenezer; for he said,
8:2 The N of his first-born son was Joel, and
8:2 was Joel, and the N of his second, Abijah;
9:1 man of Benjamin whose N was Kish, the son
9:2 had a son whose N was Saul, a handsome
12:22 people, for his great N's sake, because it has
14:4 the other side; the N of the one was
14:4 was Bozez, and the N of the other Seneh.
14:49 daughters were these: the N of the first-born was
14:49 was Merab, and the N of the younger Michal;
14:50 younger Michal; and the N of Saul's wife was
14:50 And the N of the commander of his army
16:3 me him whom I N to you."
17:23 of Gath, Goliath by N, came up out of
17:45 to you in the N of the LORD of
18:30 Saul; so that his N was highly esteemed.
20:16 earth, let not the N of Jonathan be cut
20:42 of us in the N of the LORD, saying,
21:7 before the LORD; his N was Doeg the Edomite,
24:21 will not destroy my N out of my father's
25:3 Now the N of the man was Nabal, and
25:3 was Nabal, and the N of his wife Abigail.
25:5 go to Nabal, and greet him in my N
25:9 to Nabal in the N of David; and then
25:25 Nabal; for as his N is, so is he;
25:25 he; Nabal is his N, and folly is with
28:8 me whomever I shall N to you."
2Sam 3:7 had a concubine, whose N was Rizpah, the daughter
4:2 of raiding bands; the N of the one was
4:2 was Baanah, and the N of the other Rechab,
4:4 And his N was Mephibosheth.
5:20 Therefore the N of that place is called Baal-perazim.
6:2 is called by the N of the LORD of
6:18 the people in the N of the LORD of
7:9 for you a great N, like the name of
7:9 great name, like the N of the great ones
7:13 a house for my N, and I will establish
7:23 people, making himself a N, and doing for them
7:26 hast spoken; and thy N will be magnified for
8:13 And David won a N for himself.
9:2 house of Saul whose N was Ziba, and they
9:12 a young son, whose N was Mica.
12:24 and he called his N Solomon.
12:25 so he called his N Jedidiah, because of the
12:28 the city, and it be called by my N
13:1 a beautiful sister, whose N was Tamar; and after
13:3 had a friend, whose N was Jonadab, the son
14:7 to my husband neither N nor remnant upon the
14:27 and one daughter whose N was Tamar; she was
16:5 house of Saul, whose N was Shimei, the son
18:18 son to keep my N in remembrance"; he called
18:18 pillar after his own N, and it is called
20:1 a worthless fellow, whose N was Sheba, the son
22:50 among the nations, and sing praises to thy N
23:18 them, and won a N beside the three.
23:22 Jehoiada, and won a N beside the three mighty
1Kgs 1:47 'Your God make the N of Solomon more famous
3:2 been built for the N of the LORD.
5:3 a house for the N of the LORD his
5:5 a house for the N of the LORD my
5:5 the house for my N
7:21 south and called its N Jachin; and he set
7:21 north and called its N Boaz.
8:16 a house, that my N might be there; but
8:17 a house for the N of the LORD, the
8:18 a house for my N, you did well that
8:19 the house for my N
8:20 the house for the N of the LORD, the
8:29 thou hast said, 'My N shall be there,' that
8:33 thee, and acknowledge thy N, and pray and make
8:35 place, and acknowledge thy N, and turn from their
8:41 far country for thy N's sake
8:42 hear of thy great N, and thy mighty hand,
8:43 earth may know thy N and fear thee, as
8:43 which I have built is called by thy N
8:44 have built for thy N,
8:48 have built for thy N;
9:3 built, and put my N there for ever; my
9:7 have consecrated for my N I will cast out
10:1 of Solomon concerning the N of the LORD, she
11:26 of Solomon, whose mother's N was Zeruah, a widow,
11:36 city where I have chosen to put my N
13:2 of David, Josiah by N; and he shall sacrifice
14:21 Israel, to put his N there.
14:21 His mother's N was Naamah the Ammonitess.
14:31 His mother's N was Naamah the Ammonitess.
15:2 mother's N was Maacah the daughter of Abishalom.
15:10 mother's N was Maacah the daughter of Abishalom.
16:24 hill, and called the N of the city which
16:24 built, Samaria, after the N of Shemer, the owner
18:24 you call on the N of your god and
18:24 will call on the N of the LORD; and
18:25 and call on the N of your god, but
18:26 and called on the N of Baal from morning
18:31 "Israel shall be your N;
18:32 an altar in the N of the LORD.
21:8 wrote letters in Ahab's N and sealed them with
22:16 the truth in the N of the LORD?"
22:42 His mother's N was Azubah the daughter of Shilhi.
2Kgs 2:24 cursed them in the N of the LORD.
5:11 and call on the N of the LORD his
8:26 mother's N was Athaliah; she was a granddaughter
12:1 His mother's N was Zibiah of Beer-sheba.
14:2 His mother's N was Jeho-addin of Jerusalem.
14:7 Joktheel, which is its N to this day.
14:27 would blot out the N of Israel from under
15:2 His mother's N was Jecoliah of Jerusalem.
15:33 His mother's N was Jerusha the daughter of Zadok.
18:2 His mother's N was Abi the daughter of Zechariah.
21:1 His mother's N was Hephzibah.
21:4 had said, "In Jerusalem will I put my N
21:7 I will put my N for ever;
21:19 His mother's N was Meshullemeth the daughter of
22:1 His mother's N was Jedidah the daughter of Adaiah
23:27 which I said, My N shall be there."
23:31 His mother's N was Hamutal the daughter of
23:34 father, and changed his N to Jehoiakim.
23:36 His mother's N was Zebidah the daughter of Pedaiah
24:8 mother's N was Nehushta the daughter of Elnathan
24:17 stead, and changed his N to Zedekiah.
24:18 mother's N was Hamutal the daughter of Jeremiah
1Chr 1:19 born two sons: the N of the one was
1:19 was divided), and the N of his brother Joktan.
1:43 son of Beor, the N of whose city was
1:46 his stead; and the N of his city was
1:50 his stead; and the N of his city was
1:50 Pai, and his wife's N Mehetabel the daughter of
2:26 had another wife, whose N was Atarah; she was
2:29 The N of Abishur's wife was Abihail, and she
2:34 an Egyptian slave, whose N was Jarha.
4:3 and Idbash; and the N of their sister was
4:9 his mother called his N Jabez, saying, "Because I
4:38 these mentioned by N were princes in their
4:41 These, registered by N, came in the days of
6:65 and Benjamin these cities which are mentioned by N
7:15 The N of his sister was Maacah.
7:15 And the N of the second was Zelophehad; and
7:16 and she called his N Peresh; and the name
7:16 name Peresh; and the N of his brother was
7:23 and he called his N Beriah, because evil had
8:29 in Gibeon, and the N of his wife was
9:35 Gibeon, Je-iel, and the N of his wife was
11:20 them, and won a N beside the three.
11:24 Jehoiada, and won a N beside the three mighty
13:6 is called by the N of the LORD who
14:11 Therefore the N of that place is called Baal-perazim.
16:2 the people in the N of the LORD,
16:8 LORD, call on his N, make known his deeds
16:10 Glory in his holy N; let the hearts of
16:29 the glory due his N; bring an offering, and
16:35 thanks to thy holy N, and glory in thy
17:8 make for you a N, like the name of
17:8 a name, like the N of the great ones
17:21 making for thyself a N for great and terrible
17:24 hast spoken; and thy N will be established and
21:19 had spoken in the N of the LORD.
22:7 a house to the N of the LORD my
22:8 a house to my N, because you have shed
22:9 round about; for his N shall be Solomon, and
22:10 He shall build a house for my N
22:19 house built for the N of the LORD."
23:13 pronounce blessings in his N for ever.
28:3 a house for my N, for you are a
29:13 thank thee, our God, and praise thy glorious N
29:16 house for thy holy N comes from thy hand
2Chr 2:1 a temple for the N of the LORD, and
2:4 a house for the N of the LORD my
6:5 a house, that my N might be there, and
6:6 chosen Jerusalem that my N may be there and

6:7 a house for the N of the LORD, the
6:8 a house for my N, you did well that
6:9 the house for my N
6:10 the house for the N of the LORD, the
6:20 promised to set thy N, that thou mayest hearken
6:24 again and acknowledge thy N, and pray and make
6:26 place, and acknowledge thy N, and turn from their
6:32 sake of thy great N, and thy mighty hand,
6:33 earth may know thy N and fear thee, as
6:33 which I have built is called by thy N
6:34 have built for thy N,
6:38 have built for thy N,
7:14 are called by my N humble themselves, and pray
7:16 this house that my N may be there for
7:20 have consecrated for my N, I will cast out
12:13 Israel to put his N there.
12:13 His mother's N was Naamah the Ammonitess.
13:2 His mother's N was Micaiah the daughter of Uriel
14:11 thee, and in thy N we have come against
18:15 the truth in the N of the LORD?"
20:8 a sanctuary for thy N, saying,
20:9 before thee, for thy N is in this house,
20:26 the LORD; therefore the N of that place has
20:31 His mother's N was Azubah the daughter of Shilhi.
22:2 mother's N was Athaliah, the granddaughter of Omri.
24:1 Jerusalem; his mother's N was Zibiah of Beer-sheba.
25:1 His mother's N was Jeho-addan of Jerusalem.
26:3 His mother's N was Jecoliah of Jerusalem.
27:1 His mother's N was Jerushah the daughter of Zadok.
28:9 LORD was there, whose N was Oded; and he
28:15 have been mentioned by N rose and took the
29:1 mother's N was Abijah the daughter of Zechariah.
31:19 who were designated by N to distribute portions to
33:4 "In Jerusalem shall my N be for ever."
33:7 I will put my N for ever;
33:18 to him in the N of the LORD the
36:4 Jerusalem, and changed his N to Jehoiakim; but
Ezra 2:61 Barzillai the Gileadite, and was called by their N
5:1 and Jerusalem, in the N of the God of
5:14 delivered to one whose N was Shesh-bazzar, whom
6:12 who has caused his N to dwell there overthrow
8:20 These were all mentioned by N
10:16 their fathers' houses, each of them designated by N
Neh 1:9 chosen, to make my N dwell there.'
1:11 delight to fear thy N; and give success to
6:13 give me an evil N, in order to taunt
7:63 Barzillai the Gileadite and was called by their N
9:5 Blessed be thy glorious N which is exalted above
9:7 and give him the N Abraham;
9:10 didst get thee a N, as it is to
13:25 take oath in the N of God, saying, "You
Tob 3:11 thy holy and honored N for ever.
3:15 did not stain my N or the name of
3:15 my name or the N of my father in
5:11 to know, my brother, your people and your N
8:5 thy holy and glorious N for ever.
11:14 and blessed is thy N for ever, and blessed
12:6 and to exalt his N, worthily declaring the works
13:11 from afar to the N of the Lord God,
Jud 9:7 Lord who crushest wars; the Lord is thy N
9:8 tabernacle where thy glorious N rests, and to cast
14:7 those who hear your N will be alarmed.
16:2 new psalm; exalt him, and call upon his N
Esth 2:5 Susa the capital whose N was Mordecai, the son
2:14 delighted in her and she was summoned by N
2:22 the king in the N of Mordecai.
3:12 was written in the N of King Ahasuerus and
8:8 the Jews, in the N of the king, and
8:8 edict written in the N of the king and
8:10 writing was in the N of King Ahasuerus and
10:8 gathered to destroy the N of the Jews.
13:17 sing praise to thy N, O Lord; do not
Job 1:1 land of Uz, whose N was Job; and that
1:21 away; blessed be the N of the LORD."
18:17 and he has no N in the street.
24:20 town forget them; their N is no longer remembered;
42:14 And he called the N of the first Jemimah;
42:14 first Jemimah; and the N of the second Keziah;
42:14 second Keziah; and the N of the third
Ps 5:11 those who love thy N may exult in thee.
7:17 sing praise to the N of the LORD, the
8:1 how majestic is thy N in all the earth!
8:9 how majestic is thy N in all the earth!
9:2 sing praise to thy N, O Most High.
9:5 hast blotted out their N for ever and ever.
9:10 those who know thy N put their trust in

18:49 among the nations, and sing praises to thy N
20:1 The N of the God of Jacob protect you!
20:5 victory, and in the N of our God set
20:7 we boast of the N of the LORD our
22:22 will tell of thy N to my brethren; in
23:3 of righteousness for his N's sake.
25:11 For thy N's sake, O LORD, pardon my guilt,
29:2 the glory of his N; worship the LORD in
30:4 his saints, and give thanks to his holy N
31:3 my fortress; for thy N's sake lead me and
33:21 in him, because we trust in his holy N
34:3 let us exalt his N together!
41:5 he die, and his N perish?"
44:5 our foes; through thy N we tread down our
44:8 give thanks to thy N for ever.
44:20 we had forgotten the N of our God, or
45:17 I will cause your N to be celebrated in
48:10 As thy N, O God, so thy praise reaches
52:9 I will proclaim thy N, for it is good,
54:1 O God, by thy N, and vindicate me by
54:6 give thanks to thy N, O LORD, for it
61:5 me the heritage of those who fear thy N
61:8 sing praises to thy N, as I pay my
63:4 lift up my hands and call on thy N
66:2 the glory of his N; give to him glorious
66:4 sing praises to thee, sing praises to thy N
68:4 sing praises to his N; lift up a song
68:4 upon the clouds; his N is the LORD, exult
69:30 I will praise the N of God with a
69:36 those who love his N shall dwell in it.
72:17 May his N endure for ever, his fame continue
72:19 Blessed be his glorious N for ever; may his
74:7 ground they desecrated the dwelling place of thy N
74:10 enemy to revile thy N for ever?
74:18 enemy scoffs, and an impious people reviles thy N
74:21 shame; let the poor and needy praise thy N
75:1 we call on thy N and recount thy wondrous
76:1 God is known, his N is great in Israel.
79:6 the kingdoms that do not call on thy N
79:9 the glory of thy N; deliver us, and forgive
79:9 our sins, for thy N's sake!
80:18 us life, and we will call on thy N
83:4 a nation; let the N of Israel be remembered
83:16 they may seek thy N, O LORD.
83:18 that thou alone, whose N is the LORD, art
86:9 before thee, O Lord, and shall glorify thy N
86:11 thy truth; unite my heart to fear thy N
86:12 I will glorify thy N for ever.
89:12 them; Tabor and Hermon joyously praise thy N
89:16 who exult in thy N all the day, and
89:24 him, and in my N shall his horn be
91:14 I will protect him, because he knows my N
92:1 sing praises to thy N, O Most High;
96:2 the LORD, bless his N; tell of his salvation
96:8 the glory due his N; bring an offering, and
97:12 you righteous, and give thanks to his holy N
99:3 Let them praise thy great and terrible N
99:6 also was among those who called on his N
100:4 Give thanks to him, bless his N
102:8 deride me use my N for a curse.
102:12 enthroned for ever; thy N endures to all generations.
102:15 nations will fear the N of the LORD, and
102:21 declare in Zion the N of the LORD, and
103:1 all that is within me, bless his holy N
105:1 LORD, call on his N, make known his deeds
105:3 Glory in his holy N; let the hearts of
106:8 saved them for his N's sake, that he might
106:47 thanks to thy holy N and glory in thy
109:13 cut off; may his N be blotted out in
109:21 my behalf for thy N's sake; because thy steadfast
111:9 Holy and terrible is his N
113:1 the LORD, praise the N of the LORD!
113:2 Blessed be the N of the LORD from this
113:3 to its setting the N of the LORD is
115:1 us, but to thy N give glory, for the
116:4 I called on the N of the LORD: "O
116:13 and call on the N of the LORD,
116:17 and call on the N of the LORD.
118:10 surrounded me; in the N of the LORD I
118:11 every side; in the N of the LORD I
118:12 of thorns; in the N of the LORD I
118:26 who enters in the N of the LORD!
119:55 I remember thy N in the night, O LORD,
119:132 is thy wont toward those who love thy N
122:4 give thanks to the N of the LORD.
124:8 help is in the N of the LORD, who

N

129:8 bless you in the N of the LORD!"
135:1 Praise the N of the LORD, give praise, O
135:3 good; sing to his N, for he is gracious!
135:13 Thy N, O LORD, endures for ever, thy renown,
138:2 give thanks to thy N for thy steadfast love
138:2 exalted above everything thy N and thy word.
140:13 give thanks to thy N; the upright shall dwell
142:7 prison, that I may give thanks to thy N
143:11 For thy N's sake, O LORD, preserve my life!
145:1 King, and bless thy N for ever and ever.
145:2 thee, and praise thy N for ever and ever.
145:21 flesh bless his holy N for ever and ever.
148:5 Let them praise the N of the LORD!
148:13 Let them praise the N of the LORD, for
148:13 the LORD, for his N alone is exalted; his
149:3 Let them praise his N with dancing, making melody
Prov 10:7 a blessing, but the N of the wicked will
18:10 The N of the LORD is a strong tower;
21:24 is the N of the proud, haughty man who
22:1 A good N is to be chosen rather than
30:4 What is his N, and what is his son's
30:4 is his name, and what is his son's N
30:9 steal, and profane the N of my God.
Eccl 6:4 and in darkness its N is covered;
7:1 A good N is better than precious ointment; and
Song 1:3 oils are fragrant, your N is oil poured out;
Wis 2:4 Our N will be forgotten in time and no
10:20 Lord, to thy holy N, and praised with one
13:10 men who give the N "gods" to the works
14:21 stone or wood the N that ought not to
Sir 6:1 for a bad N incurs shame and reproach: so
6:22 wisdom is like her N, and is not manifest
15:6 crown of rejoicing, and will acquire an everlasting N
17:8 will praise his holy N, to proclaim the grandeur
22:12 And what is its N except "Fool"?
23:9 not habitually utter the N of the Holy One;
23:10 swears and utters the N will not be cleansed
36:12 people called by thy N, upon Israel, whom thou
36:15 beginning, and fulfil the prophecies spoken in thy N
37:1 friend"; but some friends are friends only in N
37:26 inherit confidence, and his N will live for ever.
39:9 not disappear, and his N will live through all
39:11 he will leave a N greater than a thousand,
39:15 ascribe majesty to his N and give thanks to
39:35 voice, and bless the N of the Lord.
40:19 city establish a man's N, but a blameless wife
41:11 bodies, but the evil N of sinners will be
41:12 Have regard for your N, since it will remain
41:13 numbered, but a good N endures for ever.
44:9 who have left a N, so that men declare
44:15 in peace, and their N lives to all generations.
45:15 as priest and bless his people in his N
46:1 in accordance with his N, a great savior of
46:12 lie, and may the N of those who have
47:10 they praised God's holy N, and the sanctuary
47:13 a house for his N and prepare a sanctuary
47:16 Your N reached to far-off islands, and you were
47:18 In the N of the Lord God, who is
50:20 to glory in his N;
51:1 give thanks to thy N,
51:3 mercy and of thy N, from the gnashings of
51:11 I will praise thy N continually, and will sing
51:12 I will bless the N of the Lord.
Is 4:1 be called by your N; take away our reproach."
7:14 and shall call his N Immanu-el.
8:3 to me, "Call his N Maher-shalal-hash-baz;
9:6 his shoulder, and his N will be called "Wonderful
12:4 LORD, call upon his N; make known his deeds
12:4 nations, proclaim that his N is exalted.
14:22 cut off from Babylon N and remnant, offspring and
18:7 the place of the N of the LORD of
24:15 the sea, to the N of the LORD, the
25:1 I will praise thy N; for thou hast done
26:8 for thee; thy memorial N is the desire of
26:13 over us, but thy N alone we acknowledge.
29:23 they will sanctify my N; they will sanctify the
30:27 Behold, the N of the LORD comes from far,
34:12 They shall N it No Kingdom There, and all
40:26 calling them all by N; by the greatness of
41:25 shall call on my N; he shall trample on
42:8 LORD, that is my N; my glory I give
43:1 have called you by N, you are mine.
43:7 is called by my N, whom I created for
44:5 call himself by the N of Jacob, and another
44:5 surname himself by the N of Israel."
45:3 God of Israel, who call you by your N
45:4 call you by your N, I surname you, though
47:4 of hosts is his N -- is the Holy
48:1 are called by the N of Israel, and who
48:1 who swear by the N of the LORD, and
48:2 of Israel; the LORD of hosts is his N
48:9 "For my N's sake I defer my anger, for
48:11 for how should my N be profaned?
48:19 like its grains; their N would never be cut
49:1 the body of my mother he named my N
50:10 yet trusts in the N of the LORD and
51:15 roar-- the LORD of hosts is his N
52:5 all the day my N is despised.
52:6 people shall know my N; therefore in that day
54:5 of hosts is his N; and the Holy One
56:5 a monument and a N better than sons and
56:5 give them an everlasting N which shall not be
56:6 him, to love the N of the LORD, and
57:15 who inhabits eternity, whose N is Holy: "I dwell
59:19 they shall fear the N of the LORD from
60:9 with them, for the N of the LORD your
62:2 called by a new N which the mouth of
63:12 for himself an everlasting N,
63:14 thy people, to make for thyself a glorious N
63:16 Father, our Redeemer from of old is thy N
63:19 like those who are not called by thy N
64:2 to make thy N known to thy adversaries,
64:7 that calls upon thy N, that bestirs himself to
65:1 a nation that did not call on my N
65:15 You shall leave your N to my chosen for
65:15 his servants he will call by a different N
66:5 you out for my N's sake have said, 'Let
66:22 your descendants and your N remain.
Jer 7:10 is called by my N, and say, 'We are
7:11 is called by my N, become a den of
7:12 where I made my N dwell at first, and
7:14 is called by my N, and in which you
7:30 is called by my N, to defile it.
10:6 art great, and thy N is great in might.
10:16 his inheritance; the LORD of hosts is his N
10:25 call not on thy N; for they have devoured
11:19 the living, that his N be remembered no more."
11:21 not prophesy in the N of the LORD, or
12:16 to swear by my N, 'As the LORD lives,'
13:11 me a people, a N, a praise, and a
14:7 O LORD, for thy N's sake; for our backslidings
14:9 are called by thy N; leave us not."
14:14 prophesying lies in my N; I did not send
14:15 who prophesy in my N although I did not
14:21 spurn us, for thy N's sake; do not dishonor
15:16 am called by thy N, O LORD, God of
16:21 shall know that my N is the LORD."
20:3 does not call your N Pashhur, but Terror on
20:9 mention him, or speak any more in his N
23:6 And this is the N by which he will
23:25 prophesy lies in my N, saying, 'I have dreamed,
23:27 my people forget my N by their dreams which
23:27 their fathers forgot my N for Baal?
25:29 is called by my N, and shall you go
26:9 you prophesied in the N of the LORD, saying,
26:16 to us in the N of the LORD our
26:20 who prophesied in the N of the LORD, Uriah
27:15 prophesying falsely in my N, with the result that
29:9 to you in my N; I did not send
29:21 to you in my N: Behold, I will deliver
29:23 have spoken in my N lying words which I
29:25 sent letters in your N to all the people
31:35 of hosts is his N:
32:18 and mighty God whose N is the LORD of
32:20 hast made thee a N, as at this day.
32:34 is called by my N, to defile it.
33:2 the LORD is his N:
33:9 be to me a N of joy, a praise
33:16 And this is the N by which it will
34:15 is called by my N;
34:16 around and profaned my N when each of you
44:16 to us in the N of the LORD, we
44:26 sworn by my great N, says the LORD, that
44:26 the LORD, that my N shall no more be
46:17 the oppressor.' Call the N of Pharaoh, king of
46:18 says the King, whose N is the LORD of
48:15 says the King, whose N is the LORD of
48:17 all who know his N; say, 'How the mighty
50:34 is strong; the LORD of hosts is his N
51:19 his inheritance; the LORD of hosts is his N
51:57 says the King, whose N is the LORD of
52:1 mother's N was Hamutal the daughter of Jeremiah

Lam 3:55 "I called on thy N, O LORD, from the
Bar 2:11 hast made thee a N, as at this day,
2:15 Israel and his descendants are called by thy N
2:26 is called by thy N thou hast made as
2:32 and will remember my N,
3:5 in this crisis remember thy power and thy N
3:7 should call upon thy N; and we will praise
5:4 For your N will for ever be called by
Ezek 20:9 the sake of my N, that it should not
20:14 the sake of my N, that it should not
20:22 the sake of my N, that it should not
20:29 So its N is called Bamah to this day.)
20:39 me; but my holy N you shall no more
20:44 with you for my N's sake, not according to
23:4 Oholah was the N of the elder and Oholibah
23:4 elder and Oholibah the N of her sister.
24:2 man, write down the N of this day, this
36:20 they profaned my holy N, in that men said
36:21 concern for my holy N, which the house of
36:22 sake of my holy N, which you have profaned
36:23 holiness of my great N, which has been profaned
39:7 "And my holy N I will make known in
39:7 not let my holy N be profaned any more;
39:25 and I will be jealous for my holy N
43:7 more defile my holy N, neither they, nor their
43:8 have defiled my holy N by their abominations which
48:35 And the N of the city henceforth shall be,
Dan 2:20 said: "Blessed be the N of God for ever
2:26 said to Daniel, whose N was Belteshazzar, "Are you
3:26 of praise; and thy N is glorified for ever.
3:34 For thy N's sake do not give us up
3:43 give glory to thy N, O Lord!
3:53 is thy glorious, holy N and to be highly
4:8 named Belteshazzar after the N of my god, and
4:19 Daniel, whose N was Belteshazzar, was dismayed for
9:6 who spoke in thy N to our kings, our
9:15 hast made thee a N, as at this day,
9:18 is called by thy N; for we do not
9:19 city and thy people are called by thy N
12:1 delivered, every one whose N shall be found written
13:1 living in Babylon whose N was Joakim.
Hos 1:4 to him, "Call his N Jezreel; for yet a
1:6 to him, "Call her N Not pitied, for I
1:9 LORD said, "Call his N Not my people, for
2:17 shall be mentioned by N no more.
12:5 the LORD is his N:
Joel 2:26 satisfied, and praise the N of the LORD your
2:32 who call upon the N of the LORD shall
Amos 2:7 so that my holy N is profaned;
4:13 the LORD, the God of hosts, is his N
5:8 the LORD is his N,
5:27 says the LORD, whose N is the God of
6:10 must not mention the N of the LORD."
9:6 of the earth-- the LORD is his N
9:12 all the nations who are called by my N
Mic 4:5 walk each in the N of its god, but
4:5 will walk in the N of the LORD our
5:4 the majesty of the N of the LORD his
6:9 wisdom to fear thy N: "Hear, O tribe and
Nah 1:14 "No more shall your N be perpetuated; from the
Zeph 1:4 of Baal and the N of the idolatrous priests;
3:9 may call on the N of the LORD and
3:12 seek refuge in the N of the LORD,
Zech 5:4 swears falsely by my N; and it shall abide
6:12 "Behold, the man whose N is the Branch: for
10:12 the LORD and they shall glory in his N
13:3 speak lies in the N of the LORD'; and
13:9 will call on my N, and I will answer
14:9 be one and his N one.
Mal 1:6 hosts to you, O priests, who despise my N
1:6 have we despised thy N
1:11 to its setting my N is great among the
1:11 is offered to my N, and a pure offering;
1:11 pure offering; for my N is great among the
1:14 of hosts, and my N is feared among the
2:2 give glory to my N, says the LORD of
2:5 feared me, he stood in awe of my N
3:16 who feared the LORD and thought on his N
4:2 you who fear my N the sun of righteousness
1Mac 2:51 and receive great honor and an everlasting N
3:14 "I will make a N for myself and win
4:33 all who know thy N praise thee with hymns."
5:57 us also make a N for ourselves; let us
5:63 the Gentiles, wherever their N was heard.
6:44 people and to win for himself an everlasting N
7:37 be called by thy N, and to be for
14:43 be written in his N, and that he should
2Mac 8:4 blasphemies committed against his N, and to show
8:15 had called them by his holy and glorious N
12:13 Its N was Caspin.
Mt 1:21 you shall call his N Jesus, for he will
1:23 a son, and his N shall be called Emmanuel"
1:25 and he called his N Jesus.
6:9 Father who art in heaven, Hallowed be thy N
7:22 not prophesy in your N, and cast out demons
7:22 out demons in your N, and do many mighty
7:22 mighty works in your N
10:22 by all for my N's sake.
12:21 victory; and in his N will the Gentiles hope."
18:5 such child in my N receives me;
18:19 are gathered in my N, there am I in
19:29 or lands, for my N's sake, will receive a
21:9 who comes in the N of the Lord!
23:38 who comes in the N of the Lord.'"
24:5 will come in my N, saying, 'I am the
24:9 all nations for my N's sake.
27:32 of Cyrene, Simon by N; this man they compelled
28:19 baptizing them in the N of the Father and
Mk 5:9 And Jesus asked him, "What is your N
5:9 He replied, "My N is Legion; for we are
5:22 the synagogue, Jairus by N; and seeing him, he
6:14 of it; for Jesus' N had become known.
9:37 such child in my N receives me; and whoever
9:38 out demons in your N, and we forbade him,
9:39 mighty work in my N will be able soon
9:41 because you bear the N of Christ, will by
11:9 who comes in the N of the Lord!
13:6 will come in my N, saying, 'I am he!'
13:13 by all for my N's sake.
16:17 who believe: in my N they will cast out
Lk 1:5 of Aaron, and her N was Elizabeth.
1:13 you shall call his N John.
1:27 to a man whose N was Joseph, of the
1:27 David; and the virgin's N was Mary.
1:31 you shall call his N Jesus.
1:49 great things for me, and holy is his N
1:61 "None of your kindred is called by this N
1:63 tablet, and wrote, "His N is John." And they
2:21 was called Jesus, the N given by the angel
2:25 man in Jerusalem, whose N was Simeon, and this
6:22 and cast out your N as evil, on account
8:30 desert.) Jesus then asked him, "What is your N
9:48 this child in my N receives me, and whoever
9:49 out demons in your N, and we forbade him,
10:17 the demons are subject to us in your N
11:2 "When you pray, say: "Father, hallowed be thy N
13:35 who comes in the N of the Lord!'"
19:38 who comes in the N of the Lord!
21:8 will come in my N, saying, 'I am he!'
21:12 and governors for my N's sake.
21:17 by all for my N's sake.
24:47 be preached in his N to all nations, beginning
Jn 1:6 sent from God, whose N was John.
1:12 who believed in his N, he gave power to
2:23 many believed in his N when they saw the
3:18 not believed in the N of the only Son
5:42 come in my Father's N, and you do not
5:42 comes in his own N, him you will receive.
10:3 his own sheep by N and leads them out.
10:25 do in my Father's N, they bear witness to
12:13 who comes in the N of the Lord, even
12:28 Father, glorify thy N
14:13 you ask in my N, I will do it,
14:14 ask anything in my N, I will do it.
14:26 will send in my N, he will teach you
15:16 the Father in my N, he may give it
16:23 he will give it to you in my N
16:24 asked nothing in my N; ask, and you will
16:26 will ask in my N; and I do not
17:6 "I have manifested thy N to the men whom
17:11 keep them in thy N, which thou hast given
17:12 kept them in thy N, which thou hast given
17:26 known to them thy N, and I will make
18:10 The slave's N was Malchus.
20:31 that believing you may have life in his N
Acts 2:21 whoever calls on the N of the Lord shall
2:38 of you in the N of Jesus Christ for
3:6 I have; in the N of Jesus Christ of
3:16 And his N, by faith in his name, has
3:16 by faith in his N, has made this man
4:7 power or by what N did you do this?"
4:10 Israel, that by the N of Jesus Christ of

4:12 there is no other N under heaven given among
4:17 speak no more to any one in this N
4:18 at all in the N of Jesus.
4:30 are performed through the N of thy holy servant
5:28 to teach in this N, yet here you have
5:40 to speak in the N of Jesus, and let
5:41 were counted worthy to suffer dishonor for the N
8:12 of God and the N of Jesus Christ, they
8:16 been baptized in the N of the Lord Jesus.
9:14 priests to bind all who call upon thy N
9:15 mine to carry my N before the Gentiles and
9:16 he must suffer for the sake of my N
9:21 in Jerusalem of those who called on this N
9:27 preached boldly in the N of Jesus.
9:29 preaching boldly in the N of the Lord.
10:43 in him receives forgiveness of sins through his N
10:48 be baptized in the N of Jesus Christ.
12:12 of John whose other N was Mark, where many
12:25 them John whose other N was Mark.
13:8 the meaning of his N withstood them, seeking to
15:14 take out of them a people for his N
15:17 are called by my N,
16:18 charge you in the N of Jesus Christ to
19:5 were baptized in the N of the Lord Jesus.
19:13 undertook to pronounce the N of the Lord Jesus
19:17 them all; and the N of the Lord Jesus
21:13 at Jerusalem for the N of the Lord Jesus."
22:16 sins, calling on his N
26:9 things in opposing the N of Jesus of Nazareth.
Rom 1:5 the sake of his N among all the nations,
2:24 it is written, "The N of God is blasphemed
9:17 you, so that my N may be proclaimed in
10:13 who calls upon the N of the Lord will
15:9 and sing to thy N;
1Cor 1:2 place call on the N of our Lord Jesus
1:10 you, brethren, by the N of our Lord Jesus
1:13 you baptized in the N of Paul?
1:15 should say that you were baptized in my N
5:4 pronounced judgment in the N of the Lord Jesus
5:11 one who bears the N of brother if he
6:11 were justified in the N of the Lord Jesus
Eph 1:21 dominion, and above every N that is named, not
5:20 giving thanks in the N of our Lord Jesus
Phil 2:9 bestowed on him the N which is above every
2:9 which is above every N,
2:10 name, that at the N of Jesus every knee
Col 3:17 do everything in the N of the Lord Jesus,
2Thes 1:12 power, so that the N of our Lord Jesus
3:6 you, brethren, in the N of our Lord Jesus
1Tim 6:1 honor, so that the N of God and the
2Tim 2:19 one who names the N of the Lord depart
Heb 1:4 to angels as the N he has obtained is
2:12 "I will proclaim thy N to my brethren, in
7:2 by translation of his N, king of righteousness, and
13:15 is, the fruit of lips that acknowledge his N
Jas 2:7 who blaspheme that honorable N which was invoked
5:10 who spoke in the N of the Lord.
5:14 with oil in the N of the Lord;
1Pet 4:14 are reproached for the N of Christ, you are
4:16 ashamed, but under that N let him glorify God.
1Jn 3:23 should believe in the N of his Son Jesus
5:13 who believe in the N of the Son of
Rev 2:3 bearing up for my N's sake, and you have
2:13 you hold fast my N and you did not
2:17 stone, with a new N written on the stone
3:1 works; you have the N of being alive, and
3:5 will not blot his N out of the book
3:5 I will confess his N before my Father and
3:8 kept my word and have not denied my N
3:12 write on him the N of my God, and
3:12 my God, and the N of the city of
3:12 God out of heaven, and my own new N
6:8 horse, and its rider's N was Death, and Hades
8:11 The N of the star is Wormwood.
9:11 the bottomless pit; his N in Hebrew is Abaddon,
11:18 those who fear thy N, both small and great,
13:1 horns and a blasphemous N upon its heads.
13:6 against God, blaspheming his N and his dwelling, that
13:8 it, every one whose N has not been written
13:17 mark, that is, the N of the beast or
13:17 of the beast or the number of its N
14:1 thousand who had his N and his Father's name
14:1 name and his Father's N written on their foreheads.
14:11 image, and whoever receives the mark of its N
15:2 the number of its N, standing beside the sea
15:4 fear and glorify thy N, O Lord?
16:9 and they cursed the N of God who had
17:5 forehead was written a N of mystery: "Babylon the
19:12 and he has a N inscribed which no one
19:13 in blood, and the N by which he is
19:16 thigh he has a N inscribed, King of kings
20:15 and if any one's N was not found written
22:4 his face, and his N shall be on their

NAMED (92)

Gen 5:2 he blessed them and N them Man when they
5:3 after his image, and N him Seth.
21:12 you, for through Isaac shall your descendants be N
23:16 silver which he had N in the hearing of
25:13 the sons of Ishmael, N in the order of
27:36 "Is he not rightly N Jacob?
31:48 Therefore he N it Galeed,
50:11 Therefore the place was N Abel-mizraim; it is
Ex 1:14 one of whom was N Shiphrah and the other
2:10 her son; and she N him Moses, for she
15:23 bitter; therefore it was N Marah.
Num 1:17 men who have been N,
11:26 in the camp, one N Eldad, and the other
11:26 Eldad, and the other N Medad, and the spirit
Judg 18:29 And they N the city Dan, after the name
Ruth 4:17 They N him Obed; he was the father of
1Sam 4:21 And she N the child Ichabod, saying, "The glory
17:4 the Philistines a champion N Goliath, of Gath, whose
17:12 of Bethlehem in Judah, N Jesse, who had eight
22:20 the son of Ahitub, N Abiathar, escaped and fled
2Sam 17:25 son of a man N Ithra the Ishmaelite, who
2Kgs 17:34 of Jacob, whom he N Israel.
1Chr 12:31 thousand, who were expressly N to come and make
16:41 those chosen and expressly N to give thanks to
23:14 man of God were N among the tribe of
Tob 6:10 has an only daughter N Sarah.
Ps 49:11 all generations, though they N lands their own.
Eccl 6:10 be has already been N, and it is known
Wis 14:8 the perishable thing was N a god.
14:27 idols not to be N is the beginning and
Sir 43:8 The month is N for the moon, increasing marvelously
Is 14:20 "May the descendants of evildoers nevermore be N
49:1 of my mother he N my name.
Jer 37:13 Gate, a sentry there N Irijah the son of
Bar 4:30 Jerusalem, for he who N you will comfort you.
Ezek 48:31 of the city being N after the tribes of
Dan 4:8 me--he who was N Belteshazzar after the name
5:12 Daniel, whom the king N Belteshazzar.
10:1 to Daniel, who was N Belteshazzar.
13:2 he took a wife N Susanna, the daughter of
13:45 of a young lad N Daniel;
Zech 11:7 two staffs; one I N Grace, the other I
11:7 Grace, the other I N Union.
1Mac 6:17 a boy, and he N him Eupator.
2Mac 3:4 But a man N Simon, of the tribe of
Mt 27:57 rich man from Arimathea, N Joseph, who also was
Lk 1:5 there was a priest N Zechariah, of the division
1:26 a city of Galilee N Nazareth,
1:59 and they would have N him Zechariah after his
5:27 saw a tax collector, N Levi, sitting at the
6:13 them twelve, whom he N apostles;
6:14 apostles; Simon, whom he N Peter, and Andrew his
8:41 there came a man N Jairus, who was a
10:38 village; and a woman N Martha received him into
16:20 lay a poor man N Lazarus, full of sores,
19:2 there was a man N Zacchaeus; he was a
23:49 there was a man N Joseph from the Jewish
24:13 going to a village N Emmaus, about seven miles
24:18 Then one of them, N Cleopas, answered him, "Are
Jn 3:1 man of the Pharisees, N Nicodemus, a ruler of
Acts 5:1 But a man N Ananias with his wife Sapphira
5:34 Pharisee in the council N Gamali-el, a teacher of
7:58 of a young man N Saul.
8:9 there was a man N Simon who had previously
9:10 a disciple at Damascus N Ananias.
9:11 a man of Tarsus N Saul; for behold, he
9:12 has seen a man N Ananias come in and
9:33 he found a man N Aeneas, who had been
9:36 at Joppa a disciple N Tabitha, which means Dorcas.
10:1 there was a man N Cornelius, a centurion of
11:28 And one of them N Agabus stood up and
12:13 the gateway, a maid N Rhoda came to answer.
13:6 a Jewish false prophet, N Bar-Jesus.
16:1 A disciple was there, N Timothy, the son of
16:14 us was a woman N Lydia, from the city
17:34 Are-opagite and a woman N Damaris and others
18:2 he found a Jew N Aquila, a native of

18:7 house of a man N Titius Justus, a worshiper
18:24 Now a Jew N Apollos, a native of Alexandria,
19:14 a Jewish high priest N Sceva were doing this.
19:24 For a man N Demetrius, a silversmith, who made
20:9 And a young man N Eutychus was sitting in
21:10 some days, a prophet N Agabus came down from
27:1 of the Augustan Cohort, N Julius.
28:7 man of the island, N Publius, who received us
Rom 9:7 but "Through Isaac shall your descendants be N
15:20 Christ has already been N, lest I build on
Eph 1:21 every name that is N, not only in this
3:15 and on earth is N,
5:3 must not even be N among you, as is
Heb 7:11 Melchizedek, rather than one N after the order of
11:18 said, "Through Isaac shall your descendants be N

NAMELY (15)
Num 1:32 the people of Joseph, N, of the people of
2Kgs 25:23 to Gedaliah at Mizpah, N, Ishmael the son of
1Chr 5:26 he carried them away, N, the Reubenites, the
6:39 on his right hand, N, Asaph the son of
7:2 of their fathers' houses, N of Tola, mighty warriors
Ezra 2:6 The sons of Pahath-moab, N the sons of Jeshua
2:16 The sons of Ater, N of Hezekiah, ninety-eight.
8:17 at the place Casiphia, N, to send us ministers
8:18 Levi, son of Israel, N Sherebiah with his sons
Neh 7:11 The sons of Pahath-moab, N the sons of Jeshua
7:21 The sons of Ater, N of Hezekiah, ninety-eight.
7:39 the sons of Jedaiah, N the house of Jeshua,
7:43 the sons of Jeshua, N of Kadmi-el of the
Dan 9:2 the desolations of Jerusalem, N, seventy years.
Rom 1:20 world his invisible nature, N, his eternal power and

NAMES (88)
Gen 2:20 The man gave N to all cattle, and to
25:13 These are the N of the sons of Ishmael,
25:16 and these are their N, by their villages and
26:18 he gave them the N which his father had
36:10 These are the N of Esau's sons: Eliphaz the
36:40 These are the N of the chiefs of Esau,
36:40 dwelling places, by their N: the chiefs Timna, Alvah,
46:8 Now these are the N of the descendants of
Ex 1:1 THESE are the N of the sons of
6:16 These are the N of the sons of Levi
23:13 no mention of the N of other gods, nor
28:9 engrave on them the N of the sons of
28:10 Israel, six of their N on the one stone,
28:10 one stone, and the N of the remaining six
28:11 two stones with the N of the sons of
28:12 Aaron shall bear their N before the LORD upon
28:21 twelve stones with their N according to the names
28:21 names according to the N of the sons of
28:29 Aaron shall bear the N of the sons of
39:6 signet, according to the N of the sons of
39:14 twelve stones with their N according to the names
39:14 names according to the N of the sons of
Num 1:2 to the number of N, every male, head by
1:5 And these are the N of the men who
1:18 to the number of N from twenty years old
1:20 to the number of N, head by head, every
1:22 to the number of N, head by head, every
1:24 the number of the N, from twenty years old
1:26 to the number of N, from twenty years old
1:28 to the number of N, from twenty years old
1:30 to the number of N, from twenty years old
1:32 to the number of N, from twenty years old
1:34 to the number of N, from twenty years old
1:36 to the number of N, from twenty years old
1:38 to the number of N, from twenty years old
1:40 to the number of N, from twenty years old
1:42 to the number of N, from twenty years old
3:2 These are the N of the sons of Aaron:
3:3 Ithamar; these are the N of the sons of
3:17 of Levi by their N: Gershon and Kohath and
3:18 And these are the N of the sons of
3:40 month old and upward, taking their number by N
3:43 to the number of N, from a month old
13:4 And these were their N: From the tribe of
13:16 These were the N of the men whom Moses
26:33 but daughters: and the N of the daughters of
26:53 divided for inheritance according to the number of N
26:55 lot; according to the N of the tribes of
27:1 The N of his daughters were: Mahlah, Noah, Hoglah,
32:38 Nebo, and Baal-meon (their N to be changed), and
32:38 and they gave other N to the cities which
34:17 Moses, "These are the N of the men who
34:19 These are the N of the men: Of the
Josh 17:3 and these are the N of his daughters: Mahlah,
23:7 make mention of the N of their gods, or
Ruth 1:2 wife Naomi, and the N of his two sons
1Sam 14:49 and Malchishua; and the N of his two daughters
17:13 the battle; and the N of his three sons
2Sam 5:14 And these are the N of those who were
23:8 These are the N of the mighty men whom
1Kgs 4:8 These were their N: Ben-hur, in the hill country
1Chr 6:17 And these are the N of the sons of
8:38 are their N: Azrikam, Bocheru, Ishmael, She-ariah,
9:44 are their N: Azrikam, Bocheru, Ishmael, She-ariah,
14:4 These are the N of the children whom he
23:24 the number of the N of the individuals from
Ezra 5:4 this, "What are the N of the men who
5:10 also asked them their N, for your information, that
5:10 might write down the N of the men at
8:13 who came later, their N being Eliphelet, Jeuel, and
Ps 16:4 out or take their N upon my lips.
147:4 stars, he gives to all of them their N
Sir 46:11 also, with their respective N, those whose hearts did
Ezek 23:4 As for their N, Oholah is Samaria, and Oholibah
48:1 "These are the N of the tribes: Beginning at
Dan 1:7 eunuchs gave them N: Daniel he called Belteshazzar,
Hos 2:17 I will remove the N of the Baals from
Zech 13:2 will cut off the N of the idols from
Mt 10:2 The N of the twelve apostles are these: first,
Lk 10:20 but rejoice that your N are written in heaven."
Acts 18:15 questions about words and N and your own law,
Phil 4:3 my fellow workers, whose N are in the book
2Tim 2:19 "Let every one who N the name of the
Rev 3:4 have still a few N in Sardis, people who
17:3 was full of blasphemous N, and it had seven
17:8 dwellers on earth whose N have not been written
21:12 on the gates the N of the twelve tribes
21:14 on them the twelve N of the twelve apostles

NANEA (3)
2Mac 1:13 in the temple of N by a deception employed
1:13 by a deception employed by the priests of N
1:15 of the temple of N had set out the

NAOMI (22)
Ruth 1:2 name of his wife N, and the names of
1:3 Elimelech, the husband of N, died, and she was
1:8 But N said to her two daughters-in-law, "Go, return
1:11 But N said, "Turn back, my daughters, why will
1:18 And when N saw that she was determined to
1:19 of them; and the women said, "Is this N
1:20 "Do not call me N, call me Mara, for
1:21 Why call me N, when the LORD has afflicted
1:22 So N returned, and Ruth the Moabitess her
2:1 Now N had a kinsman of her husbands, a
2:2 the Moabitess said to N, "Let me go to
2:6 who came back with N from the country of
2:20 And N said to her daughter-in-law, "Blessed be he
2:20 N also said to her, "The man is a
2:22 And N said to Ruth, her daughter-in-law, "It is
3:1 Then N her mother-in-law said to her, "My daughter,
4:3 the next of kin, N, who has come back
4:5 from the hand of N, you are also buying
4:9 from the hand of N all that belonged to
4:14 the women said to N, "Blessed be the LORD,
4:16 Then N took the child and laid him in
4:17 name, saying, "A son has been born to N

NAPH-TUHIM (2)
Gen 10:13 of Ludim, Anamim, Lehabim, N,
1Chr 1:11 of Ludim, Anamim, Lehabim, N,

NAPHATH
Josh 17:11 of Megiddo and its villages; the third is N

NAPHATH-DOR (2)
Josh 12:23 king of Dor in N, one; the king of
1Kgs 4:11 Hepher); Ben-abinadab, in all N (he had Taphath the

NAPHISH (3)
Gen 25:15 Massa, Hadad, Tema, Jetur, N, and Kedemah.
1Chr 1:31 Massa, Hadad, Tema, Jetur, N, and Kedemah.
5:19 upon the Hagrites, Jetur, N, and Nodab;

NAPHOTH-DOR
Josh 11:2 the lowland, and in N on the west,

N

NAPHTALI (59)

Book	Ref	Context
Gen	30:8	and have prevailed"; so she called his name N
	35:25	The sons of Bilhah, Rachel's maid: Dan and N
	46:24	The sons of N: Jahzeel, Guni, Jezer, and Shillem
	49:21	N is a hind let loose, that bears comely
Ex	1:3	and Benjamin, Dan and N, Gad and Asher.
Num	1:15	son of Deuel; from N, Ahira the son of
	1:42	Of the people of N, their generations, by their
	1:43	of the tribe of N was fifty-three thousand four
	2:29	Then the tribe of N, the leader of the
	2:29	of the people of N being Ahira the son
	7:78	of the men of N:
	10:27	of the men of N was Ahira the son
	13:14	from the tribe of N, Nahbi the son of
	26:48	The sons of N according to their families: of
	26:50	are the families of N according to their families;
	34:28	of the sons of N a leader, Pedahel the
Deut	27:13	the curse: Reuben, Gad, Asher, Zebulun, Dan, and N
	33:23	And of N he said, "O Naphtali, satisfied with
	33:23	Naphtali he said, "O N, satisfied with favor, and
	34:2	far as Dan, all N, the land of Ephraim
Josh	19:32	for the tribe of N, for the tribe of
	19:32	for the tribe of N, according to its families.
	19:39	of the tribe of N according to its families–
	20:7	the hill country of N, and Shechem in the
	21:6	from the tribe of N, and from the half-tribe
	21:32	of the tribe of N, Kedesh in Galilee with
Judg	1:33	N did not drive out the inhabitants of Beth-shemesh,
	4:6	Abino-am from Kedesh in N, and said to him,
	4:6	from the tribe of N and the tribe of
	4:10	Barak summoned Zebulun and N to Kedesh; and ten
	5:18	lives to the death; N too, on the heights
	6:35	to Asher, Zebulun, and N; and they went up
	7:23	were called out from N and from Asher and
1Kgs	4:15	Mahanaim; Ahima-az, in N (he had taken Basemath
	7:14	of the tribe of N, and his father was
	15:20	and all Chinneroth, with all the land of N
2Kgs	15:29	all the land of N; and he carried the
1Chr	2:2	Zebulun, Dan, Joseph, Benjamin, N, Gad, and Asher.
	6:62	tribes of Issachar, Asher, N, and Manasseh in Bashan.
	6:76	of the tribe of N: Kedesh in Galilee with
	7:13	The sons of N: Jahzi-el, Guni, Jezer, and Shallum,
	12:34	Of N a thousand commanders with whom were
	12:40	Issachar and Zebulun and N, came bringing food on
	27:19	son of Obadiah; for N, Jeremoth the son of
2Chr	16:4	Ijon, Dan, Abel-maim, and all the store-cities of N
	34:6	and as far as N, in their ruins round
Tob	1:1	and the tribe of N,
	1:2	the south of Kedesh N in Galilee above Asher.
	1:4	the whole tribe of N my forefather deserted the
	1:5	did the house of N my forefather.
	7:3	to the sons of N, who are captives in
Ps	68:27	throng, the princes of Zebulun, the princes of N
Is	9:1	and the land of N, but in the latter
Ezek	48:3	side to the west, N, one portion.
	48:4	Adjoining the territory of N, from the east side
	48:34	the gate of Asher, and the gate of N
Mt	4:13	territory of Zebulun and N,
	4:15	and the land of N, toward the sea, across
Rev	7:6	of the tribe of N, twelve thousand of the

NAPHTHA (2)

Book	Ref	Context
Dan	3:46	the furnace fires with N, pitch, tow, and brush.
2Mac	1:36	purification, but by most people it is called N

NAPKIN (2)

Book	Ref	Context
Lk	19:20	laid away in a N;
Jn	20:7	cloths lying, and the N, which had been on

NARCISSUS

Book	Ref	Context
Rom	16:11	the Lord who belong to the family of N

NARD (5)

Book	Ref	Context
Song	1:12	on his couch, my N gave forth its fragrance.
	4:13	choicest fruits, henna with N,
	4:14	fruits, henna with nard, N and saffron, calamus and
Mk	14:3	of ointment of pure N, very costly, and she
Jn	12:3	costly ointment of pure N and anointed the feet

NARRATION

Book	Ref	Context
Sir	21:16	A fool's N is like a burden on a

NARRATIVE (4)

Book	Ref	Context
Sir	6:35	to listen to every N, and do not let
2Mac	2:31	one who recasts the N should be allowed to
	2:32	let us begin our N, adding only so much
Lk	1:1	undertaken to compile a N of the things which

NARRATIVES

Book	Ref	Context
2Mac	2:24	to enter upon the N of history because of

NARROW (11)

Book	Ref	Context
Num	22:24	LORD stood in a N path between the vineyards,
	22:26	and stood in a N place, where there was
Josh	17:15	of Ephraim is too N for you."
Jud	4:7	for the approach was N, only wide enough for
Prov	23:27	an adventuress is a N well.
Is	28:20	and the covering too N to wrap oneself in
	49:19	you will be too N for your inhabitants, and
	49:20	'The place is too N for me; make room
Mt	7:13	"Enter by the N gate; for the gate is
	7:14	For the gate is N and the way is
Lk	13:24	to enter by the N door; for many, I

NARROWER

Book	Ref	Context
Ezek	42:5	the upper chambers were N, for the galleries took

NARROWING

Book	Ref	Context
Ezek	40:16	windows round about, N inwards into their jambs

NARROWNESS

Book	Ref	Context
2Mac	12:21	access because of the N of all the approaches.

NATHAN (43)

Book	Ref	Context
2Sam	5:14	in Jerusalem: Shammua, Shobab, N, Solomon,
	7:2	the king said to N the prophet, "See now,
	7:3	And N said to the king, "Go, do all
	7:4	the LORD came to N,
	7:17	with all this vision, N spoke to David.
	12:1	And the LORD sent N to David.
	12:5	and he said to N, "As the LORD lives,
	12:7	N said to David, "You are the man.
	12:13	David said to N, "I have sinned against the
	12:13	And N said to David, "The LORD also has
	12:15	Then N went to his house.
	12:25	sent a message by N the prophet; so he
	23:36	Igal the son of N of Zobah, Bani the
1Kgs	1:8	son of Jehoiada, and N the prophet, and Shimei,
	1:10	he did not invite N the prophet or Benaiah
	1:11	Then N said to Bathsheba the mother of Solomon,
	1:22	speaking with the king, N the prophet came in.
	1:23	the king, "Here is N the prophet." And when
	1:24	And N said, "My lord the king, have you
	1:32	me Zadok the priest, N the prophet, and Benaiah
	1:34	Zadok the priest and N the prophet there anoint
	1:38	So Zadok the priest, N the prophet, and Benaiah
	1:44	him Zadok the priest, N the prophet, and Benaiah
	1:45	Zadok the priest and N the prophet have anointed
	4:5	Azariah the son of N was over the officers;
	4:5	Zabud the son of N was priest and king's
1Chr	2:36	was the father of N and Nathan of Zabad.
	2:36	father of Nathan and N of Zabad.
	3:5	in Jerusalem: Shimea, Shobab, N and Solomon, four
	11:38	Joel the brother of N, Mibhar the son of
	14:4	in Jerusalem: Shammua, Shobab, N, Solomon,
	17:1	house, David said to N the prophet, "Behold, I
	17:2	And N said to David, "Do all that is
	17:3	the LORD came to N,
	17:15	with all this vision, N spoke to David.
	29:29	in the Chronicles of N the prophet, and in
2Chr	9:29	in the history of N the prophet, and in
	29:25	king's seer and of N the prophet; for the
Ezra	8:16	Elnathan, Jarib, Elnathan, N, Zechariah, and Meshul
	10:39	of Binnui: Shimei, Shelemiah, N, Adaiah,
Sir	47:1	And after him N rose up to prophesy in
Zech	12:12	of the house of N by itself, and their
Lk	3:31	Mattatha, the son of N, the son of David,

NATHAN-MELECH

Book	Ref	Context
2Kgs	23:11	by the chamber of N the chamberlain, which was

NATHANAEL (7)

Book	Ref	Context
Jud	8:1	of Eliab, son of N, son of Salamiel, son
Jn	1:45	Philip found N, and said to him, "We have
	1:46	N said to him, "Can anything good come out
	1:47	Jesus saw N coming to him, and said of
	1:48	N said to him, "How do you know me?"
	1:49	N answered him, "Rabbi, you are the Son of
	21:2	Thomas called the Twin, N of Cana in Galilee,

NATION (234)

Book	Ref	Context
Gen	12:2	of you a great N, and I will bless

15:14 bring judgment on the N which they serve, and
17:20 princes, and I will make him a great N
18:18 a great and mighty N, and all the nations
21:13 I will make a N of the son of
21:18 hand; for I will make him a great N
35:11 fruitful and multiply; a N and a company of
46:3 I will there make of you a great N
Ex 9:24 the land of Egypt since it became a N
19:6 me a kingdom of priests and a holy N
32:10 but of you I will make a great N
33:13 Consider too that this N is thy people."
34:10 earth or in any N; and all the people
Lev 18:28 it vomited out the N that was before you.
20:23 the customs of the N which I am casting
Num 14:12 make of you a N greater and mightier than
Deut 4:6 say, 'Surely this great N is a wise and
4:7 people.' For what great N is there that has
4:8 And what great N is there, that has statutes
4:34 go and take a N for himself from the
4:34 the midst of another N, by trials, by signs,
9:14 make of you a N mightier and greater than
26:5 there he became a N, great, mighty, and populous.
28:33 A N which you have not known shall eat
28:36 over you, to a N that neither you nor
28:49 LORD will bring a N against you from afar,
28:49 the eagle flies, a N whose language you do
28:50 do not understand, a N of stern countenance, who
32:21 people; I will provoke them with a foolish N
32:28 "For they are a N void of counsel, and
Josh 3:17 Jordan, until all the N finished passing over the
4:1 When all the N had finished passing over the
5:6 wilderness, till all the N, the men of war
5:8 circumcising of all the N was done, they remained
10:13 moon stayed, until the N took vengeance on their
2Sam 7:23 What other N on earth is like thy people
7:23 before his people a N and its gods?
1Kgs 18:10 lives, there is no N or kingdom whither my
18:10 of the kingdom or N, that they had not
2Kgs 17:29 But every N still made gods of its own,
17:29 Samaritans had made, every N in the cities in
1Chr 16:20 in it, wandering from N to nation, from one
16:20 wandering from nation to N, from one kingdom to
17:21 What other N on earth is like thy people
2Chr 15:6 were broken in pieces, N against nation and city
15:6 in pieces, nation against N and city against city,
32:15 no god of any N or kingdom has been
Tob 13:6 and majesty to a N of sinners.
Jud 5:21 no transgression in their N, then let my lord
8:20 will not disdain us or any of our N
9:14 And cause thy whole N and every tribe to
11:10 it is true: our N cannot be punished, nor
13:20 own life when our N was brought low, but
14:7 In every N those who hear your name will
15:9 Israel, you are the great pride of our N
Esth 10:9 And my N, this is Israel, who cried out
11:7 at their roaring every N prepared for war, to
11:7 to fight against the N of the righteous.
11:9 And the whole righteous N was troubled; they feared
13:4 to those of every N and continually disregard the
16:11 we have for every N that he was called
16:13 partner of our kingdom, together with their whole N
Job 34:29 whether it be a N or a man?—
Ps 33:12 Blessed is the N whose God is the LORD,
83:4 them out as a N; let the name of
105:13 in it, wandering from N to nation, from one
105:13 wandering from nation to N, from one kingdom to
106:5 the gladness of thy N, that I may glory
147:20 thus with any other N; they do not know
Prov 14:34 Righteousness exalts a N, but sin is a reproach
Wis 10:15 wisdom delivered from a N of oppressors.
17:2 they held the holy N in their power they
19:8 passed through as one N, after gazing on marvelous
Sir 10:8 Sovereignty passes from N to nation on account of
10:8 passes from nation to N on account of injustice
16:6 and in a disobedient N wrath was kindled.
16:9 no pity for a N devoted to destruction, for
17:14 a ruler for every N, but Israel is the
24:6 in every people and N I have gotten a
28:14 and scattered them from N to nation, and destroyed
28:14 them from nation to N, and destroyed strong cities,
46:6 down war upon that N, and at the descent
49:5 glory to a foreign N,
50:25 the third is no N:
Is 1:4 Ah, sinful N, a people laden with iniquity, offspring
2:4 spears into pruning hooks; N shall not lift up
2:4 lift up sword against N, neither shall they learn
5:26 a signal for a N afar off, and whistle
9:3 Thou hast multiplied the N, thou hast increased its
10:6 Against a godless N I send him, and against
14:32 What will one answer the messengers of the N
18:2 swift messengers, to a N, tall and smooth, to
18:2 near and far, a N mighty and conquering, whose
18:7 near and far, a N mighty and conquering, whose
26:2 gates, that the righteous N which keeps faith may
26:15 thou hast increased the N, O LORD, thou hast
26:15 thou hast increased the N; thou art glorified; thou
51:4 ear to me, my N; for a law will
58:2 if they were a N that did righteousness and
60:12 For the N and kingdom that will not serve
60:22 smallest one a mighty N; I am the LORD;
65:1 to a N that did not call on my
66:8 Shall a N be brought forth in one moment?
Jer 2:11 Has a N changed its gods, even though they
5:9 avenge myself on a N such as this?
5:15 bringing upon you a N from afar, O house
5:15 It is an enduring N, it is an ancient
5:15 it is an ancient N, a nation whose language
5:15 an ancient nation, a N whose language you do
5:29 avenge myself on a N such as this?"
6:22 north country, a great N is stirring from the
7:28 them, 'This is the N that did not obey
9:9 avenge myself on a N such as this?
12:17 But if any N will not listen, then I
18:7 I declare concerning a N or a kingdom, that
18:8 it, and if that N, concerning which I have
18:9 I declare concerning a N or a kingdom that
25:12 of Babylon and that N, the land of the
25:32 is going forth from N to nation, and a
25:32 forth from nation to N, and a great tempest
27:8 "'"But if any N or kingdom will not serve
27:8 I will punish that N with the sword, with
27:11 But any N which will bring its neck under
27:13 has spoken concerning any N which will not serve
31:36 cease from being a N before me for ever."
33:24 are no longer a N in their sight.
48:2 off from being a N You also, O Madmen,
49:31 up, advance against a N at ease, that dwells
49:36 there shall be no N to which those driven
50:3 of the north a N has come up against
50:41 the north; a mighty N and many kings are
Lam 4:17 we watched for a N which could not save.
Bar 4:15 brought against them a N from afar, a shameless
4:15 from afar, a shameless N, of a strange language,
Ezek 2:3 of Israel, to a N of rebels, who have
36:13 and you bereave your N of children,'
36:14 no longer bereave your N of children, says the
36:15 no longer cause your N to stumble, says the
37:22 will make them one N in the land, upon
Dan 3:37 become fewer than any N, and are brought low
3:97 a decree: Any people, N, or language that speaks
8:22 shall arise from his N, but not with his
12:1 since there was a N till that time; but
Joel 1:6 For a N has come up against my land,
3:8 the Sabeans, to a N far-off; for the LORD
Amos 6:14 up against you a N, O house of Israel,"
Mic 4:3 spears into pruning hooks; N shall not lift up
4:3 lift up sword against N, neither shall they learn
4:7 cast off, a strong N; and the LORD will
Hab 1:6 that bitter and hasty N, who march through the
Zeph 2:1 hold assembly, O shameless N,
2:5 of the seacoast, you N of the Cherethites!
2:9 the survivors of my N shall possess them."
Hag 2:14 people, and with this N before me, says the
Mal 3:9 robbing me; the whole N of you.
1Mac 2:10 What N has not inherited her palaces and has
3:59 the misfortunes of our N and of the sanctuary.
6:58 and with all their N,
8:23 Romans and with the N of the Jews at
8:25 all their dominion, the N of the Jews shall
8:27 comes first to the N of the Jews, the
9:29 with those of our N who hate us.
10:5 to him and to his brothers and his N
10:20 high priest of your N; you are to be
10:25 "King Demetrius to the N of the Jews, greeting.
11:21 men who hated their N went to the king
11:25 lawless men of his N kept making complaints against
11:30 brother and to the N of the Jews, greeting.
11:33 To the N of the Jews, who are our
11:42 for you and your N, but I will confer
11:42 on you and your N, if I find an
12:3 priest and the Jewish N have sent us to
12:6 the senate of the N, the priests, and the

13:6 I will avenge my N and the sanctuary and
13:36 to the elders and N of the Jews, greeting.
14:4 the good of his N; his rule was pleasing
14:6 the borders of his N, and gained full control
14:28 the rulers of the N and the elders of
14:29 the enemies of their N, in order that their
14:29 perserved; and they brought great glory to their N
14:30 Jonathan rallied the N, and became their high priest,
14:32 then Simon rose up and fought for his N
14:32 the men of his N's forces and paid them
14:35 to win for his N, and they made him
14:35 and loyalty which he had maintained toward his N
15:1 and to all the N;
15:2 ethnarch and to the N of the Jews, greeting.
15:9 upon you and your N and the temple, so
16:3 and fight for our N, and may the help
2Mac 5:19 did not choose the N for the sake of
5:19 but the place for the sake of the N
5:20 misfortunes that befell the N and afterward
6:31 young but to the great body of his N
7:37 mercy soon to our N and by afflictions and
7:38 Almighty which has justly fallen on our whole N
10:8 vote that the whole N of the Jews should
11:25 we choose that this N also be free from
11:27 To the N the king's letter was as follows:
14:8 have mentioned our whole N is now in no
14:9 and our hard-pressed N with the gracious kindness
14:34 constant Defender of our N, in these words:
Mt 21:43 and given to a N producing the fruits of
24:7 For N will rise against N, and kingdom against
Mk 13:8 For N will rise against N, and kingdom against
Lk 7:5 for he loves our N, and he built us
21:10 "N will rise against N, and kingdom against
23:2 this man perverting our N, and forbidding us to
Jn 11:48 and destroy both our holy place and our N
11:50 and that the whole N should not perish."
11:51 should die for the N,
11:52 and not for the N only, but to gather
18:35 Your own N and the chief priests have handed
Acts 2:5 devout men from every N under heaven.
7:7 I will judge the N which they serve,' said
8:9 city and amazed the N of Samaria, saying that
10:22 by the whole Jewish N, was directed by a
10:28 any one of another N; but God has shown
10:35 partiality, but in every N any one who fears
17:26 made from one every N of men to live
24:2 on behalf of this N,
24:9 been judge over this N, I cheerfully make my
24:16 to bring to my N alms and offerings.
26:4 beginning among my own N and at Jerusalem, is
28:19 I had no charge to bring against my N
Rom 10:19 who are not a N; with a foolish nation
10:19 nation; with a foolish N I will make you
1Pet 2:9 royal priesthood, a holy N, God's own people, that
Rev 5:9 tongue and people and N,
7:9 could number, from every N, from all tribes and
13:7 people and tongue and N,
14:6 on earth, to every N and tribe and tongue

NATIONALITIES

2Mac 12:27 Lysias dwelt with multitudes of people of all N

NATIONS (544)

Gen 10:5 his own language, by their families, in their N
10:20 families, their languages, their lands, and their N
10:31 families, their languages, their lands, and their N
10:32 their genealogies, in their N; and from these the
10:32 and from these the N spread abroad on the
17:4 shall be the father of a multitude of N
17:5 made you the father of a multitude of N
17:6 and I will make N of you, and kings
17:16 be a mother of N; kings of peoples shall
18:18 nation, and all the N of the earth shall
22:18 descendants shall all the N of the earth bless
25:23 said to her, "Two N are in your womb,
26:4 your descendants all the N of the earth shall
27:29 peoples serve you, and N bow down to you.
35:11 and a company of N shall come from you,
48:19 and his descendants shall become a multitude of N
Ex 34:24 I will cast out N before you, and enlarge
Lev 18:24 by all these the N I am casting out
25:44 slaves from among the N that are round about
26:33 scatter you among the N, and I will unsheathe
26:38 shall perish among the N, and the land of
26:45 the sight of the N, that I might be
Num 14:15 one man, then the N who have heard thy
23:9 dwelling alone, and not reckoning itself among the N
24:8 shall eat up the N his adversaries, and shall
24:20 the first of the N, but in the end
Deut 4:27 in number among the N where the LORD will
4:38 driving out before you N greater and mightier than
7:1 and clears away many N before you, the Hittites,
7:1 and the Jebusites, seven N greater and mightier than
7:17 in your heart, 'These N are greater than I;
7:22 will clear away these N before you little by
8:20 Like the N that the LORD makes to perish
9:1 go in to dispossess N greater and mightier than
9:4 the wickedness of these N that the LORD is
9:5 the wickedness of these N the LORD your God
11:23 drive out all these N before you, and you
11:23 and you will dispossess N greater and mightier than
12:2 the places where the N whom you shall dispossess
12:29 off before you the N whom you go in
12:30 saying, 'How did these N serve their gods?—that
15:6 shall lend to many N, but you shall not
15:6 shall rule over many N, but they shall not
17:14 me, like all the N that are round about
18:9 learn to follow the abominable practices of those N
18:14 For these N, which you are about to dispossess,
19:1 God cuts off the N whose land the LORD
20:15 not cities of the N here.
26:19 you high above all N that he has made,
28:1 high above all the N of the earth.
28:12 shall lend to many N, but you shall not
28:65 And among these N you shall find no ease,
29:16 the midst of the N through which you passed;
29:18 the gods of those N; lest there be among
29:24 yea, all the N would say, 'Why has
30:1 mind among all the N where the LORD your
31:3 he will destroy these N before you, so that
32:8 High gave to the N their inheritance, when he
32:43 his people, O you N; for he avenges the
Josh 23:3 done to all these N for your sake, for
23:4 for your tribes those N that remain, along with
23:4 along with all the N that I have already
23:7 be mixed with these N left here among you,
23:9 you great and strong N; and as for you,
23:12 the remnant of these N left here among you,
23:13 to drive out these N before you; but they
Judg 2:21 them any of the N that Joshua left when
2:23 the LORD left those N, not driving them out
3:1 Now these are the N which the LORD left,
3:3 These are the N: the five lords of the
1Sam 8:5 a king to govern us like all the N
8:20 be like all the N, and that our king
2Sam 8:11 dedicated from all the N he subdued,
22:44 the head of the N; people whom I had
22:50 O LORD, among the N, and sing praises to
1Kgs 4:31 was in all the N round about.
11:2 women, from the N concerning which the LORD
14:24 the abominations of the N which the LORD drove
2Kgs 16:3 abominable practices of the N whom the LORD
17:8 the customs of the N whom the LORD drove
17:11 high places, as the N did whom the LORD
17:15 and they followed the N that were round about
17:26 Assyria was told, "The N which you have carried
17:33 the manner of the N from among whom they
17:41 So these N feared the LORD, and also served
18:33 the gods of the N ever delivered his land
19:12 the gods of the N delivered them, the nations
19:12 delivered them, the N which my fathers destroyed,
19:17 have laid waste the N and their lands,
21:2 abominable practices of the N whom the LORD
21:9 more evil than the N had done whom the
1Chr 14:17 LORD brought the fear of him upon all N
16:24 his glory among the N, his marvelous works among
16:31 them say among the N, "The LORD reigns!"
16:35 us from among the N, that we may give
17:21 things, in driving out N before thy people whom
18:11 off from all the N, from Edom, Moab, the
2Chr 20:6 not rule over all the kingdoms of the N
28:3 abominable practices of the N whom the LORD
32:13 the gods of the N of those lands at
32:14 the gods of those N which my fathers utterly
32:17 the gods of the N of the lands who
32:23 the sight of all N from that time onward.
33:2 abominable practices of the N whom the LORD
33:9 more evil than the N whom the LORD destroyed
36:14 the abominations of the N; and they polluted the
Ezra 4:10 the rest of the N whom the great and
Neh 5:8 been sold to the N; but you even sell
5:9 the taunts of the N our enemies?

5:17 to us from the N which were about us.
6:6 is reported among the N, and Geshem also says
6:16 of it, all the N round about us were
13:26 Among the many N there was no king like
Tob 3:4 reproach in all the N among which we have
4:19 For none of the N has understanding; but the
13:3 Acknowledge him before the N, O sons of Israel;
13:5 us from all the N among whom you have
13:11 Many N will come from afar to the name
Jud 1:6 Many N joined the forces of the Chaldeans.
1:8 and those among the N of Carmel and Gilead,
3:8 land, so that all N should worship Nebuchadnezzar
4:1 had done to the N, and how he had
16:17 Woe to the N that rise up against my
Esth 10:8 The N are those that gathered to destroy the
10:9 and wonders, which have not occurred among the N
10:10 people of God and one for all the N
10:11 of decision before God and among all the N
13:2 become ruler of many N and master of the
13:4 that among all the N in the world there
14:5 out of all the N, and our fathers from
14:10 the mouths of the N for the praise of
Job 12:23 He makes N great, and he destroys them: he
12:23 destroys them: he enlarges N, and leads them away.
Ps 2:1 Why do the N conspire, and the peoples plot
2:8 I will make the N your heritage, and the
9:5 Thou hast rebuked the N, thou hast destroyed the
9:15 The N have sunk in the pit which they
9:17 to Sheol, all the N that forget God.
9:19 man prevail; let the N be judged before thee!
9:20 Let the N know that they are but men!
10:16 ever and ever; the N shall perish from his
18:43 the head of the N; people whom I had
18:49 O LORD, among the N, and sing praises to
22:27 the families of the N shall worship before him.
22:28 to the LORD, and he rules over the N
33:10 the counsel of the N to nought; he frustrates
44:2 didst drive out the N, but them thou didst
44:11 for slaughter, and hast scattered us among the N
44:14 a byword among the N, a laughingstock among the
46:6 The N rage, the kingdoms totter; he utters his
46:10 am exalted among the N, I am exalted in
47:3 peoples under us, and N under our feet.
47:8 God reigns over the N; God sits on his
57:9 I will sing praises to thee among the N
59:5 to punish all the N; spare none of those
59:8 dost hold all the N in derision.
66:7 keep watch on the N – let not the
67:2 known upon earth, thy saving power among all N
67:4 Let the N be glad and sing for joy,
67:4 equity and guide the N upon earth.
72:11 down before him, all N serve him!
72:17 themselves by him, all N call him blessed!
78:55 He drove out N before them; he apportioned them
79:6 thy anger on the N that do not know
79:10 Why should the N say, "Where is their God?"
79:10 be known among the N before our eyes!
80:8 didst drive out the N and plant it.
82:8 the earth; for to thee belong all the N
86:9 All the N thou hast made shall come and
94:10 He who chastens the N, does he not chastise?
96:3 his glory among the N, his marvelous works among
96:10 Say among the N, "The LORD reigns!
98:2 revealed his vindication in the sight of the N
102:15 The N will fear the name of the LORD,
105:44 the lands of the N; and they took possession
106:27 their descendants among the N, scattering them over
106:35 they mingled with the N and learned to do
106:41 the hand of the N, so that those who
106:47 us from among the N, that we may give
108:3 I will sing praises to thee among the N
110:6 execute judgment among the N, filling them with
111:6 works, in giving them the heritage of the N
113:4 is high above all N, and his glory above
115:2 Why should the N say, "Where is their God?"
117:1 Praise the LORD, all N
118:10 All N surrounded me; in the name of the
126:2 they said among the N, "The LORD has done
135:10 servants; who smote many N and slew mighty kings,
135:15 The idols of the N are silver and gold,
149:7 wreak vengeance on the N and chastisement on the
Prov 24:24 by peoples, abhorred by N;
Wis 3:8 They will govern N and rule over peoples, and
6:2 that rule over multitudes, and boast of many N
8:14 shall govern peoples, and N will be subject to
10:5 Wisdom also, when the N in wicked agreement had

12:12 for the destruction of N which thou didst make?
Sir 4:15 her will judge the N, and whoever gives heed
10:15 the roots of the N, and has planted the
10:16 the lands of the N, and has destroyed them
29:18 into exile, and they have wandered among foreign N
35:18 repays vengeance on the N; till he takes away
36:2 fear of thee to fall upon all the N
36:3 thy hand against foreign N and let them see
39:4 the lands of foreign N, for he tests the
39:10 N will declare his wisdom, and the congregation will
39:23 The N will incur his wrath, just as he
44:20 of a multitude of N, and no one has
44:22 an oath that the N would be blessed through
46:6 resisted, so that the N might know his armament,
50:25 With two N my soul is vexed, and the
Is 2:2 hills; and all the N shall flow to it,
2:4 shall judge between the N, and shall decide for
9:1 the land beyond the Jordan, Galilee of the N
10:7 and to cut off N not a few;
11:10 peoples; him shall the N seek, and his dwellings
11:12 an ensign for the N, and will assemble the
12:4 his deeds among the N, proclaim that his name
13:4 uproar of kingdoms, of N gathering together!
14:6 blows, that ruled the N in anger with unrelenting
14:9 their thrones all who were kings of the N
14:12 you who laid the N low!
14:18 the kings of the N lie in glory, each
14:26 hand that is stretched out over all the N
16:8 the lords of the N have struck down its
17:12 Ah, the roar of N, they roar like the
17:13 The N roar like the roaring of many waters,
23:3 the Nile; you were the merchant of the N
24:13 the earth among the N, as when an olive
25:3 thee; cities of ruthless N will fear thee.
25:7 peoples, the veil that is spread over all N
29:7 multitude of all the N that fight against Ariel,
29:8 multitude of all the N be that fight against
30:28 neck; to sift the N with the sieve of
33:3 lifting up of thyself N are scattered;
34:1 Draw near, O N, to hear, and hearken, O
34:2 enraged against all the N, and furious against all
36:18 the gods of the N delivered his land out
37:12 the gods of the N delivered them, the nations
37:12 nations delivered them, the N which my fathers
37:18 laid waste all the N and their lands,
40:15 Behold, the N are like a drop from a
40:17 All the N are as nothing before him, they
41:2 He gives up N before him, so that he
42:1 him, he will bring forth justice to the N
42:6 a light to the N,
43:9 Let all the N gather together, and let the
45:1 have grasped, to subdue N before him and ungird
45:20 come, draw near together, you survivors of the N
49:6 a light to the N, that my salvation may
49:7 despised, abhorred by the N, the servant of rulers:
49:22 my hand to the N, and raise my signal
52:10 eyes of all the N; and all the ends
52:15 shall he startle many N; kings shall shut their
54:3 descendants will possess the N and will people the
55:5 Behold, you shall call N that you know not,
55:5 you know not, and N that knew you not
60:3 And N shall come to your light, and kings
60:5 the wealth of the N shall come to you.
60:11 the wealth of the N, with their kings led
60:12 you shall perish; those N shall be utterly laid
60:16 suck the milk of N, you shall suck the
61:6 the wealth of the N, and in their riches
61:9 be known among the N, and their offspring in
61:11 and praise to spring forth before all the N
62:2 The N shall see your vindication, and all the
64:2 adversaries, and that the N might tremble at thy
66:12 the wealth of the N like an overflowing stream;
66:18 coming to gather all N and tongues; and they
66:19 send survivors to the N, to Tarshish, Put, and
66:19 and they shall declare my glory among the N
66:20 brethren from all the N as an offering to
Jer 1:5 you; I appointed you a prophet to the N
1:10 you this day over N and over kingdoms, to
3:17 the LORD, and all N shall gather to it,
3:19 pleasant land, a heritage most beauteous of all N
4:2 and in uprightness, then N shall bless themselves in
4:7 thicket, a destroyer of N has set out; he
4:16 Warn the N that he is coming; announce to
6:18 heed.' Therefore hear, O N, and know, O
9:16 scatter them among the N whom neither they nor
9:26 hair; for all these N are uncircumcised, and all

N

10:2 the way of the N, nor be dismayed at
10:2 the heavens because the N are dismayed at them,
10:7 would not fear thee, O King of the N
10:7 wise ones of the N and in all their
10:10 earth quakes, and the N cannot endure his
10:25 thy wrath upon the N that know thee not,
14:22 false gods of the N that can bring rain?
16:19 to thee shall the N come from the ends
18:13 LORD: Ask among the N, who has heard the
22:8 "And many N will pass by this city, and
25:9 and against all these N round about; I will
25:11 a waste, and these N shall serve the king
25:13 book, which Jeremiah prophesied against all the N
25:14 For many N and great kings shall make slaves
25:15 and make all the N to whom I send
25:17 and made all the N to whom the Lord
25:31 an indictment against the N; he is entering into
26:6 curse for all the N of the earth.'"
27:7 All the N shall serve him and his son
27:7 land comes; then many N and great kings shall
28:11 neck of all the N within two years." But
28:14 neck of all these N an iron yoke of
29:14 you from all the N and all the places
29:18 reproach among all the N where I have driven
30:11 end of all the N among whom I scattered
31:7 the chief of the N; proclaim, give praise, and
31:10 of the LORD, O N, and declare it in
33:9 glory before all the N of the earth who
36:2 Judah and all the N, from the day I
43:5 Judah from all the N to which they had
44:8 taunt among all the N of the earth?
46:1 came to Jeremiah the prophet concerning the N
46:12 The N have heard of your shame, and the
46:28 end of all the N to which I have
49:14 been sent among the N: "Gather yourselves together
49:15 you small among the N, despised among men.
50:2 prophet: "Declare among the N and proclaim, set up
50:9 a company of great N, from the north country;
50:12 the last of the N, a wilderness dry and
50:23 How Babylon has become a horror among the N
50:46 and her cry shall be heard among the N
51:7 the earth drunken; the N drank of her wine,
51:7 her wine, therefore the N went mad.
51:20 with you I break N in pieces; with you
51:27 the trumpet among the N; prepare the nations for
51:27 the nations; prepare the N for war against her,
51:28 Prepare the N for war against her, the kings
51:41 How Babylon has become a horror among the N
51:44 The N shall no longer flow to him; the
51:58 for nought, and the N weary themselves only for
Lam 1:1 she become, she that was great among the N
1:3 dwells now among the N, but finds no resting
1:10 she has seen the N invade her sanctuary, those
2:9 princes are among the N; the law is no
4:15 men said among the N, "They shall stay with
4:20 "Under his shadow we shall live among the N
Bar 2:13 in number, among the N where thou hast scattered
2:29 small number among the N, where I will scatter
3:16 the princes of the N, and those who rule
4:6 were sold to the N, but you were handed
6:51 manifest to all the N and kings that they
6:67 heavens and among the N, or shine like the
Ezek 4:13 bread unclean, among the N whither I will drive
5:5 the center of the N, with countries round about
5:6 ordinances more than the N, and against my statutes
5:7 more turbulent than the N that are round about
5:7 the ordinances of the N that are round about
5:8 midst of you in the sight of the N
5:14 of reproach among the N round about you and
5:15 a horror, to the N round about you, when
6:8 you have among the N some who escape the
6:9 remember me among the N where they are carried
7:24 the worst of the N to take possession of
11:12 the ordinances of the N that are round about
11:16 them far-off among the N, and though I scattered
12:15 disperse them among the N and scatter them
12:16 their abominations among the N where they go, and
16:14 went forth among the N because of your beauty,
19:4 The N sounded an alarm against him; he was
19:8 Then the N set against him snares on every
20:9 the sight of the N among whom they dwelt,
20:14 the sight of the N, in whose sight I
20:22 the sight of the N, in whose sight I
20:23 scatter them among the N and disperse them
20:32 us be like the N, like the tribes of
20:41 holiness among you in the sight of the N
22:4 a reproach to the N, and a mocking to
22:15 scatter you among the N and disperse you through
22:16 the sight of the N; and you shall know
23:30 the harlot with the N, and polluted yourself with
25:7 as spoil to the N; and I will cut
25:8 like all the other N,
25:10 no more among the N,
26:3 will bring up many N against you, as the
26:5 a spoil to the N;
28:7 most terrible of the N; and they shall draw
28:25 the sight of the N, then they shall dwell
29:12 the Egyptians among the N, and disperse them
29:15 exalt itself above the N; and I will make
29:15 that they will never again rule over the N
30:3 of clouds, a time of doom for the N
30:11 most terrible of the N, shall be brought in
30:23 the Egyptians among the N, and disperse them
30:26 the Egyptians among the N and disperse them
31:6 young; and under its shadow dwelt all great N
31:11 mighty one of the N; he shall surely deal
31:12 most terrible of the N, will cut it down
31:16 I will make the N quake at the sound
31:17 its shadow among the N shall perish.
32:2 a lion among the N, but you are like
32:9 you captive among the N, into the countries which
32:12 ones, all of them most terrible among the N
32:16 the daughters of the N shall chant it; over
32:18 the daughters of majestic N, to the nether world,
34:28 a prey to the N, nor shall the beasts
34:29 and no longer suffer the reproach of the N
35:10 you said, 'These two N and these two countries
36:3 the rest of the N, and you became the
36:4 the rest of the N round about;
36:5 the rest of the N, and against all Edom,
36:6 the reproach of the N;
36:7 I swear that the N that are round about
36:15 the reproach of the N, and you shall no
36:19 scattered them among the N, and they were
36:20 they came to the N, wherever they came, they
36:21 be profaned among the N to which they came.
36:22 have profaned among the N to which you came.
36:23 been profaned among the N, and which you have
36:23 among them; and the N will know that I
36:24 take you from the N, and gather you from
36:30 again suffer the disgrace of famine among the N
36:36 and fortified.' Then the N that are left round
37:21 of Israel from the N among which they have
37:22 be no longer two N, and no longer divided
37:28 Then the N will know that I the LORD
38:8 were gathered from many N upon the mountains of
38:8 brought out from the N and now dwell securely,
38:12 were gathered from the N, who have gotten cattle
38:16 my land, that the N may know me, when
38:23 make myself known in the eyes of many N
39:7 any more; and the N shall know that I
39:21 my glory among the N; and all the nations
39:21 nations; and all the N shall see my judgment
39:23 And the N shall know that the house of
39:27 vindicated my holiness in the sight of many N
39:28 into exile among the N, and then gathered them
39:28 them remaining among the N any more;
Dan 3:4 are commanded, O peoples, N, and languages,
3:7 music, all the peoples, N, and languages fell down
4:1 Nebuchadnezzar to all peoples, N, and languages,
5:19 gave him, all peoples, N, and languages trembled and
6:25 to all the peoples, N, and languages that dwell
7:14 kingdom, that all peoples, N, and languages should
Hos 8:8 they are among the N as a useless vessel.
8:10 hire allies among the N, I will soon gather
9:17 to him; they shall be wanderers among the N
10:10 to chastise them; and N shall be gathered against
Joel 2:17 thy heritage a reproach, a byword among the N
2:19 no more make you a reproach among the N
3:2 will gather all the N and bring them down
3:2 scattered them among the N, and have divided up
3:9 Proclaim this among the N: Prepare war, stir up
3:11 and come, all you N round about, gather yourselves
3:12 Let the N bestir themselves, and come up to
3:12 to judge all the N round about.
Amos 6:1 the first of the N, to whom the house
9:9 Israel among all the N as one shakes with
9:12 Edom and all the N who are called by
Obad 1:1 been sent among the N: "Rise up!
1:2 you small among the N, you shall be utterly
1:15 of the LORD is near upon all the N
1:16 holy mountain, all the N round about shall drink;

Mic 4:2 to it, and many N shall come, and say:
4:3 shall decide for strong N afar off; and they
4:11 Now many N are assembled against you, saying,
5:8 shall be among the N, in the midst of
5:15 execute vengeance upon the N that did not obey.
7:16 The N shall see and be ashamed of all
Nah 3:4 deadly charms, who betrays N with her harlotries,
3:5 and I will let N look on your nakedness
Hab 1:5 Look among the N, and see; wonder and be
1:17 net, and mercilessly slaying N for ever?
2:5 gathers for himself all N, and collects as his
2:8 you have plundered many N, all the remnant of
2:13 only for fire, and N weary themselves for nought?
3:6 looked and shook the N; then the eternal mountains
3:12 thou didst trample the N in anger.
Zeph 2:11 in its place, all the lands of the N
3:6 "I have cut off N; their battlements are in
3:8 decision is to gather N, to assemble kingdoms, to
Hag 2:7 I will shake all N, so that the treasures
2:7 the treasures of all N shall come in, and
2:22 the kingdoms of the N, and overthrow the chariots
Zech 1:15 very angry with the N that are at ease;
1:21 the horns of the N who lifted up their
2:8 sent me to the N who plundered you, for
2:11 And many N shall join themselves to the LORD
7:14 whirlwind among all the N which they had not
8:13 of cursing among the N, O house of Judah
8:22 Many peoples and strong N shall come to seek
8:23 ten men from the N of every tongue shall
9:10 command peace to the N; his dominion shall be
10:9 scattered them among the N, yet in far countries
12:3 And all the N of the earth will come
12:9 to destroy all the N that come against Jerusalem.
14:2 will gather all the N against Jerusalem to battle,
14:3 and fight against those N as when he fights
14:14 wealth of all the N round about shall be
14:16 survives of all the N that have come against
14:18 the LORD afflicts the N that do not go
14:19 punishment to all the N that do not go
Mal 1:11 is great among the N, and in every place
1:11 is great among the N, says the LORD of
1:14 hosts, and my name is feared among the N
3:12 Then all N will call you blessed, for you
1Mac 1:3 the ends of the earth, and plundered many N
1:4 and ruled over countries, N, and princes, and they
2:19 "Even if all the N that live under the
11:38 he had recruited from the islands of the N
12:53 And all the N round about them tried to
13:6 children, for all the N have gathered together out
2Mac 4:35 many also of other N, were grieved and displeased
6:14 case of the other N the Lord waits patiently
8:9 thousand Gentiles of all N, to wipe out the
10:4 not be handed over to blasphemous and barbarous N
11:3 places of the other N, and to put up
Mt 24:9 be hated by all N for my name's sake.
24:14 a testimony to all N; and then the end
25:32 be gathered all the N, and he will separate
28:19 make disciples of all N, baptizing them in the
Mk 11:17 called a house of prayer for all the N
13:10 the gospel must first be preached to all N
Lk 12:30 For all the N of the world seek these
21:24 led captive among all N; and Jerusalem will be
21:25 the earth distress of N in perplexity at the
24:47 his name to all N, beginning from Jerusalem.
Acts 7:45 when they dispossessed the N which God thrust out
13:19 he had destroyed seven N in the land of
14:16 he allowed all the N to walk in their
Rom 1:5 name among all the N,
4:17 "I have made you the father of many N
4:18 the father of many N; as he had been
16:25 made known to all N, according to the command
Gal 3:8 you shall all the N be blessed."
1Tim 3:16 angels, preached among the N, believed on in the
Rev 2:26 him power over the N,
10:11 about many peoples and N and tongues and kings."
11:2 given over to the N, and they will trample
11:9 tribes and tongues and N gaze at their dead
11:18 The N raged, but thy wrath came, and the
12:5 to rule all the N with a rod of
14:8 she who made all N drink the wine of
15:4 All N shall come and worship thee, for thy
16:19 the cities of the N fell, and God remembered
17:15 peoples and multitudes and N and tongues.
18:3 hateful bird; for all N have drunk the wine
18:23 the earth, and all N were deceived by thy
19:15 which to smite the N, and he will rule
20:3 he should deceive the N no more, till the
20:8 out to deceive the N which are at the
21:24 its light shall the N walk; and the kings
21:26 it the glory and the honor of the N
22:2 the tree were for the healing of the N

NATIVE (24)

Ex 12:19 a sojourner or a N of the land.
12:48 shall be as a N of the land.
12:49 one law for the N and for the stranger
Lev 16:29 no work, either the N or the stranger who
17:15 whether he is a N or a sojourner, shall
18:26 these abominations, either the N or the stranger who
19:34 to you as the N among you, and you
23:42 days; all that are N in Israel shall dwell
24:16 as well as the N, when he blasphemes the
24:22 sojourner and for the N; for I am the
Num 9:14 statute, both for the sojourner and for the N
15:13 All who are N shall do these things in
15:29 for him who is N among the people of
15:30 hand, whether he is N or a sojourner, reviles
Ruth 2:11 and mother and your N land and came to
4:10 the gate of his N place; you are witnesses
Wis 16:23 fed, even forgot its N power.
Jer 22:10 more to see his N land.
Ezek 23:15 picture of Babylonians whose N land was Chaldea.
2Mac 7:27 she spoke in their N tongue as follows, deriding
Acts 2:8 us in his own N language?
4:36 encouragement), a Levite, a N of Cyprus,
18:2 Jew named Aquila, a N of Pontus, lately come
18:24 Jew named Apollos, a N of Alexandria, came to

NATIVE-BORN

Ezek 47:22 be to you as N sons of Israel; with

NATIVES (2)

Acts 28:2 And the N showed us unusual kindness, for they
28:4 When the N saw the creature hanging from his

NATURAL (8)

Deut 34:7 not dim, nor his N force abated.
2Mac 6:20 taste, even for the N love of life.
Rom 1:26 Their women exchanged N relations for unnatural,
1:27 men likewise gave up N relations with women and
6:19 terms, because of your N limitations.
11:21 did not spare the N branches, neither will he
11:24 much more will these N branches be grafted back
Jas 1:22 man who observes his N face in a mirror;

NATURE (28)

Wis 8:19 child I was by N well endowed, and a
13:1 God were foolish by N; and they were unable
19:6 whole creation in its N was fashioned anew,
19:18 the notes vary the N of the rhythm, while
19:20 normal power, and water forgot its fire-quenching N
Jn 8:44 according to his own N, for he is a
Acts 14:15 are men, of like N with you, and bring
Rom 1:20 the world his invisible N, namely, his eternal power
2:14 the law do by N what the law requires,
11:24 from what is by N a wild olive tree,
11:24 and grafted, contrary to N, into a cultivated olive
1Cor 11:14 Does not N itself teach you that for a
15:53 For this perishable N must put on the imperishable,
15:53 imperishable, and this mortal N must put on
2Cor 4:16 Though our outer N is wasting away, our inner
4:16 wasting away, our inner N is being renewed every
Gal 4:8 to beings that by N are no gods;
Eph 2:3 so we were by N children of wrath, like
4:22 Put off your old N which belongs to your
4:24 put on the new N, created after the likeness
Col 3:9 put off the old N with its practices
3:10 put on the new N, which is being renewed
Heb 1:3 very stamp of his N, upholding the universe by
2:14 partook of the same N, that through death he
Jas 3:6 fire the cycle of N, and set on fire
5:17 a man of like N with ourselves and he
2Pet 1:4 of passion, and become partakers of the divine N
1Jn 3:9 commits sin; for God's N abides in him, and

NATURES (2)

Esth 16:6 trickery of their evil N beguile the sincere good
Wis 7:20 of the stars, the N of animals and the

NAUSEA (2)

Sir 31:20 of sleeplessness and of N and colic are with
37:30 overeating brings sickness, and gluttony leads to N

N

NAVE (17)

1Kgs 6:3 in front of the N of the house was
6:5 the house, both the N and the inner sanctuary;
6:17 house, that is, the N in front of the
6:33 the entrance to the N doorposts of olivewood, in
7:50 the doors of the N of the temple.
2Chr 3:4 in front of the N of the house was
3:5 The N he lined with cypress, and covered it
3:13 the cherubim stood on their feet, facing the N
4:22 the doors of the N of the temple were
Ezek 41:1 brought me to the N, and measured the jambs;
41:2 the length of the N forty cubits, and its
41:4 cubits, and its breadth, twenty cubits, beyond the N
41:15 The N of the temple and the inner room
41:17 inner room and the N were carved likenesses
41:21 The doorposts of the N were squared; and in
41:23 The N and the holy place had each a
41:25 the doors of the N were carved cherubim and

NAVEL (2)

Song 7:2 Your N is a rounded bowl that never lacks
Ezek 16:4 you were born your N string was not cut,

NAY (6)

Josh 22:24 N, but we did it from fear that in
24:21 people said to Joshua, N; but we will serve
Judg 5:29 wisest ladies make answer, N, she gives answer to
Ps 44:22 N, for thy sake we are slain all the
58:2 N, in your hearts you devise wrongs; your hands
Is 28:11 N, but by men of strange lips and with

NAZARENE (2)

Mt 2:23 might be fulfilled, "He shall be called a N
Mk 14:67 also were with the N, Jesus."

NAZARENES

Acts 24:5 and a ringleader of the sect of the N

NAZARETH (28)

Mt 2:23 in a city called N, that what was spoken
4:13 into Galilee; and leaving N he went and dwelt
21:11 the prophet Jesus from N of Galilee."
26:71 the bystanders, "This man was with Jesus of N
Mk 1:9 days Jesus came from N of Galilee and was
1:24 have you to do with us, Jesus of N
10:47 it was Jesus of N, he began to cry
16:6 you seek Jesus of N, who was crucified.
Lk 1:26 city of Galilee named N,
2:4 from the city of N, to Judea, to the
2:39 they returned into Galilee, to their own city, N
2:51 them and came to N, and was obedient to
4:16 And he came to N, where he had been
4:34 have you to do with us, Jesus of N
18:37 told him, "Jesus of N is passing by."
24:19 him, "Concerning Jesus of N, who was a prophet
Jn 1:45 prophets wrote, Jesus of N, the son of Joseph."
1:46 to him, "Can anything good come out of N
18:5 They answered him, "Jesus of N
18:7 And they said, "Jesus of N
19:19 it read, "Jesus of N, the King of the
Acts 2:22 these words: Jesus of N, a man attested to
3:6 of Jesus Christ of N, walk."
4:10 of Jesus Christ of N, whom you crucified, whom
6:14 that this Jesus of N will destroy this place,
10:38 God anointed Jesus of N with the Holy Spirit
22:8 'I am Jesus of N whom you are persecuting.'
26:9 things in opposing the name of Jesus of N

NAZIRITE (11)

Num 6:2 the vow of a N, to separate himself to
6:13 the law for the N, when the time of
6:18 And the N shall shave his consecrated head at
6:19 the hands of the N, after he has shaven
6:20 and after that the N may drink wine.
6:21 the law for the N who takes a vow.
6:21 his vow as a N, apart from what else
6:21 to the law for his separation as a N
Judg 13:5 boy shall be a N to God from birth;
13:7 boy shall be a N to God from birth
16:17 I have been a N to God from my

NAZIRITES (3)

Amos 2:11 prophets, and some of your young men for N
2:12 "But you made the N drink wine, and commanded
1Mac 3:49 they stirred up the N who had completed their

NE-APOLIS

Acts 16:11 the following day to N,

NEAH

Josh 19:13 Rimmon it bends toward N;

NEARBY (2)

Jud 5:5 that dwells in the N mountain district.
7:13 the tops of the N mountains and camp there

NEARER (2)

Ruth 3:12 there is a kinsman N than I.
Rom 13:11 For salvation is N to us now than when

NEAREST (7)

Lev 21:2 people, except for his N of kin, his mother,
Num 22:41 there he saw the N of the people.
23:13 shall see only the N of them, and shall
Deut 21:3 the city which is N to the slain man
21:6 elders of that city N to the slain man
Ruth 2:20 ours, one of our N kin."
Jud 16:24 and to her own N kindred.

NEARIAH (3)

1Chr 3:22 Shemaiah: Hattush, Igal, Bariah, N, and Shaphat,
3:23 The sons of N: Eli-o-enai, Hizkiah, and Azrikam,
4:42 as their leaders Pelatiah, N, Rephaiah, and Uzziel,

NEARING

Acts 27:27 suspected that they were N land.

NEARLY

Phil 2:30 such men, for he N died for the work

NEBAI

Neh 10:19 Hashum, Bezai, Hariph, Anathoth, N,

NEBAIOTH (5)

Gen 25:13 order of their birth: N, the first-born of Ishmael;
28:9 daughter of Ishmael Abraham's son, the sister of N
36:3 and Basemath, Ishmael's daughter, the sister of N
1Chr 1:29 the first-born of Ishmael, N; and Kedar, Adbeel,
Is 60:7 you, the rams of N shall minister to you;

NEBALLAT

Neh 11:34 Ramah, Gittaim, Hadid, Zeboim, N,

NEBAT (26)

1Kgs 11:26 Jeroboam the son of N, an Ephraimite of Zeredah,
12:2 Jeroboam the son of N heard of it (for
12:15 Ahijah the Shilonite to Jeroboam the son of N
15:1 Jeroboam the son of N, Abijam began to reign
16:3 like the house of Jeroboam the son of N
16:26 Jeroboam the son of N, and in the sins
16:31 Jeroboam the son of N, he took for wife
21:22 Jeroboam the son of N, and like the house
22:52 Jeroboam the son of N, who made Israel to
2Kgs 3:3 Jeroboam the son of N, which he made Israel
9:9 Jeroboam the son of N, and like the house
10:29 Jeroboam the son of N, which he made Israel
13:2 Jeroboam the son of N, which he made Israel
13:11 Jeroboam the son of N, which he made Israel
14:24 Jeroboam the son of N, which he made Israel
15:9 Jeroboam the son of N, which he made Israel
15:18 Jeroboam the son of N, which he made Israel
15:24 Jeroboam the son of N, which he made Israel
15:28 Jeroboam the son of N, which he made Israel
17:21 Jeroboam the son of N king.
23:15 Jeroboam the son of N, who made Israel to
2Chr 9:29 Iddo the seer concerning Jeroboam the son of N
10:2 Jeroboam the son of N heard of it (for
10:15 Ahijah the Shilonite to Jeroboam the son of N
13:6 Jeroboam the son of N, a servant of Solomon
Sir 47:23 Jeroboam the son of N, who caused Israel to

NEBO (13)

Num 32:3 Nimrah, Heshbon, Elealeh, Sebam, N, and Beon,
32:38 built Heshbon, Elealeh, Kiriathaim, N, and
33:47 and encamped in the mountains of Abarim, before N
Deut 32:49 of the Abarim, Mount N, which is in the
34:1 of Moab to Mount N, to the top of
1Chr 5:8 Aroer, as far as N and Baal-meon.
Ezra 2:29 The sons of N, fifty-two.
10:43 Of the sons of N: Je-iel, Mattithiah, Zabad, Zebina,
Neh 7:33 men of the other N, fifty-two.
Is 15:2 places to weep; over N and over Medeba Moab

46:1 Bel bows down, N stoops, their idols are on
Jer 48:1 of Israel: "Woe to N, for it is laid
48:22 Mephaath, and Dibon, and N, and Beth-diblathaim,

NEBUCHADNEZZAR (84)

2Kgs 24:1 In his days N king of Babylon came up,
24:10 time the servants of N king of Babylon came
24:11 And N king of Babylon came to the city,
25:1 day of the month, N king of Babylon came
25:8 nineteenth year of King N, king of Babylon–
25:22 land of Judah, whom N king of Babylon had
1Chr 6:15 and Jerusalem into exile by the hand of N
2Chr 36:6 Against him came up N king of Babylon, and
36:7 N also carried part of the vessels of the
36:10 of the year King N sent and brought him
36:13 also rebelled against King N, who had made him
Ezra 1:7 of the LORD which N had carried away from
2:1 of those exiles whom N the king of Babylon
5:12 into the hand of N king of Babylon, the
5:14 house of God, which N had taken out of
6:5 house of God, which N took out of the
Neh 7:6 of those exiles whom N the king of Babylon
Tob 14:15 destruction of Nineveh, which N and Ahasuerus had
Jud 1:1 of the reign of N, who ruled over the
1:5 those days that King N made war against King
1:7 Then N king of the Assyrians sent to all
1:11 disregarded the orders of N king of the Assyrians,
1:12 Then N was very angry with this whole region,
2:1 in the palace of N king of the Assyrians
2:4 setting forth his plan, N king of the Assyrians
2:19 go ahead of King N and to cover the
3:2 we the servants of N, the Great King, lie
3:8 all nations should worship N only, and all their
4:1 Holofernes, the general of N the king of the
6:2 Who is God except N
6:4 So says King N, the lord of the whole
11:1 who chose to serve N, the king of all
11:4 they do the servants of my lord King N
11:7 N the king of the whole earth lives, and
11:7 by your power under N and all his house.
11:23 the house of King N and be renowned throughout
12:13 the Assyrians who serve in the house of N
14:18 has brought disgrace upon the house of King N
Esth 2:6 king of Judah, whom N king of Babylon had
11:4 of the captives whom N king of Babylon had
Jer 27:6 into the hand of N, the king of Babylon,
27:8 will not serve this N king of Babylon, and
27:20 in this city, which N king of Babylon did
28:3 the LORD's house, which N king of Babylon took
28:11 break the yoke of N king of Babylon from
28:14 yoke of servitude to N king of Babylon, and
29:1 all the people, whom N had taken into exile
29:3 sent to Babylon to N king of Babylon.
Bar 1:9 Judah, had made, after N king of Babylon had
1:11 for the life of N king of Babylon, and
1:12 under the protection of N king of Babylon, and
6:2 Babylon as captives by N, king of the Babylonians.
Dan 1:1 Jehoiakim king of Judah, N king of Babylon came
1:18 chief of the eunuchs brought them in before N
2:1 of the reign of N, Nebuchadnezzar had dreams; and
2:1 the reign of Nebuchadnezzar, N had dreams; and his
2:28 made known to King N what will be in
2:46 Then King N fell upon his face, and did
3:1 King N made an image of gold, whose height
3:2 Then King N sent to assemble the satraps, the
3:2 the image which King N had set up.
3:3 the image that King N had set up; and
3:3 before the image that N had set up.
3:5 golden image that King N has set up;
3:7 golden image which King N had set up.
3:9 They said to King N, "O king, live for
3:13 Then N in furious rage commanded that Shadrach,
3:14 N said to them, "Is it true, O Shadrach,
3:16 answered the king, "O N, we have no need
3:19 Then N was full of fury, and the expression
3:92 Then King N was astonished and rose up in
3:94 Then N came near to the door of the
3:96 N said, "Blessed be the God of Shadrach, Meshach,
4:1 King N to all peoples, nations, and languages, that
4:4 I, N, was at ease in my house and
4:18 This dream I, King N, saw.
4:28 All this came upon King N
4:31 from heaven, "O King N, to you it is
4:33 Immediately the word was fulfilled upon N
4:34 of the days I, N, lifted my eyes to
4:37 Now I, N, praise and extol and honor the
5:2 and of silver which N his father had taken
5:11 in him, and King N, your father, made him
5:18 Most High God gave N your father kingship and

NEBUCHADREZZAR (33)

Jer 21:2 LORD for us, for N king of Babylon is
21:7 into the hand of N king of Babylon and
22:25 into the hand of N king of Babylon and
24:1 After N king of Babylon had taken into exile
25:1 the first year of N king of Babylon),
25:9 the LORD, and for N the king of Babylon,
29:21 into the hand of N king of Babylon, and
32:1 of Judah, which was the eighteenth year of N
32:28 into the hand of N king of Babylon, and
34:1 from the LORD, when N king of Babylon and
35:11 But when N king of Babylon came up against
37:1 son of Josiah, whom N king of Babylon made
39:1 in the tenth month, N king of Babylon and
39:5 brought him up to N king of Babylon, at
39:11 N king of Babylon gave command concerning
43:10 will send and take N the king of Babylon,
44:30 into the hand of N king of Babylon, who
46:2 at Carchemish and which N king of Babylon
46:13 about the coming of N king of Babylon to
46:26 into the hand of N king of Babylon and
49:28 kingdoms of Hazor which N king of Babylon smote.
49:30 For N king of Babylon has made a plan
50:17 and now at last N king of Babylon has
51:34 N the king of Babylon has devoured me, he
52:4 day of the month, N king of Babylon came
52:12 nineteenth year of King N, king of Babylon–
52:28 of the people whom N carried away captive: in
52:29 the eighteenth year of N he carried away captive
52:30 the twenty-third year of N, Nebuzaradan the captain
Ezek 26:7 Tyre from the north N king of Babylon, king
29:18 me: "Son of man, N king of Babylon made
29:19 land of Egypt to N king of Babylon; and
30:10 by the hand of N king of Babylon.

NEBUSHAZBAN

Jer 39:13 captain of the guard, N the Rabsaris,

NEBUZARADAN (15)

2Kgs 25:8 Nebuchadnezzar, king of Babylon– N, the captain of
25:11 rest of the multitude, N the captain of the
25:20 And N the captain of the guard took them,
Jer 39:9 Then N, the captain of the guard, carried into
39:10 N, the captain of the guard, left in the
39:11 concerning Jeremiah through N, the captain of the
39:13 So N the captain of the guard, Nebushazban the
40:1 from the LORD after N the captain of the
41:10 left at Mizpah, whom N, the captain of the
43:6 and every person whom N the captain of the
52:12 Nebuchadrezzar, king of Babylon– N the captain of
52:15 And N the captain of the guard carried away
52:16 But N the captain of the guard left some
52:26 And N the captain of the guard took them,
52:30 twenty-third year of Nebuchadrezzar, N the captain

NECESSARILY

Heb 7:12 the priesthood, there is N a change in the

NECESSARY (19)

Wis 16:4 For it was N that upon those oppressors inexorable
1Mac 10:39 Jerusalem, to meet the N expenses of the sanctuary.
14:34 those cities whatever was N for their restoration.
2Mac 1:18 temple, we thought it N to notify you, in
9:21 I have deemed it N to take thought for
12:39 time it had become N, Judas and his men
13:20 Judas sent in to the garrison whatever was N
Mt 18:7 For it is N that temptations come, but woe
Lk 24:26 Was it not N that the Christ should suffer
Acts 13:46 boldly, saying, "It was N that the word of
15:5 and said, "It is N to circumcise them, and
15:28 greater burden than these N things:
17:3 proving that it was N for the Christ to
2Cor 9:5 So I thought it N to urge the brethren
Phil 1:24 the flesh is more N on your account.
2:25 I have thought it N to send to you
Heb 8:3 sacrifices; hence it is N for this priest also
9:23 Thus it was N for the copies of the
Jude 1:3 salvation, I found it N to write appealing to

NECESSITIES

Acts 20:34 hands ministered to my N, and to those who

N

NECESSITY (4)

Tob	4:9	good treasure for yourself against the day of N
Esth	14:16	Thou knowest my N _ that I abhor the
1Cor	7:37	heart, being under no N but having his desire
	9:16	For N is laid upon me.

NECK (70)

Gen	27:16	smooth part of his N;
	27:40	loose you shall break his yoke from your N
	33:4	and fell on his N and kissed him, and
	41:42	gold chain about his N;
	45:14	upon his brother Benjamin's N and wept; and
	45:14	neck and wept; and Benjamin wept upon his N
	46:29	and fell on his N, and wept on his
	46:29	and wept on his N a good while.
	49:8	shall be on the N of your enemies; your
Ex	13:13	will not redeem it you shall break its N
	34:20	will not redeem it you shall break its N
Lev	5:8	its head from its N, but shall not sever
Deut	21:4	shall break the heifer's N there in the valley.
	21:6	over the heifer whose N was broken in the
	28:48	of iron upon your N, until he has destroyed
Judg	5:30	work embroidered for my N as spoil?'
1Sam	4:18	the gate; and his N was broken and he
2Chr	36:13	God; he stiffened his N and hardened his heart
Neh	9:16	presumptuously and stiffened their N and did not
	9:17	but they stiffened their N and appointed a leader
	9:29	shoulder and stiffened their N and would not obey.
Jud	13:8	And she struck his N twice with all her
	16:9	captivated his mind, and the sword severed his N
Esth	15:11	touched it to her N;
Job	16:12	seized me by the N and dashed me to
	39:19	Do you clothe his N with strength?
	41:22	In his N abides strength, and terror dances before
Ps	69:1	For the waters have come up to my N
	75:5	your horn on high, or speak with insolent N
	105:18	hurt with fetters, his N was put in a
Prov	1:9	garland for your head, and pendants for your N
	3:3	bind them about your N, write them on the
	3:22	life for your soul and adornment for your N
	6:21	upon your heart always; tie them about your N
	29:1	reproved, yet stiffens his N will suddenly be broken
Song	1:10	comely with ornaments, your N with strings of
	4:4	Your N is like the tower of David, built
	7:4	Your N is like an ivory tower.
Sir	6:24	her fetters, and your N into her collar.
	30:12	Bow down his N in his youth, and beat
	33:26	thong will bow the N, and for a wicked
	51:26	Put your N under the yoke, and let your
Is	8:8	reaching even to the N; and its outspread wings
	10:27	and his yoke will be destroyed from your N
	30:28	reaches up to the N; to sift the nations
	48:4	are obstinate, and your N is an iron sinew
	52:2	the bonds from your N, O captive daughter of
	66:3	who breaks a dog's N; he who presents a
Jer	7:26	me, or incline their ear, but stiffened their N
	17:23	ear, but stiffened their N, that they might not
	19:15	they have stiffened their N, refusing to hear my
	27:2	thongs and yoke-bars, and put them on your N
	27:8	Babylon, and put its N under the yoke of
	27:11	which will bring its N under the yoke of
	28:10	the yoke-bars from the N of Jeremiah the prophet,
	28:11	of Babylon from the N of all the nations
	28:12	yoke-bars from off the N of Jeremiah the prophet,
	28:14	have put upon the N of all these nations
	30:8	yoke from off their N, and I will burst
Lam	1:14	were set upon my N; he caused my strength
Ezek	16:11	on your arms, and a chain on your N
Dan	5:7	of gold about his N, and shall be the
	5:16	of gold about your N, and shall be the
	5:29	was put about his N, and proclamation was made
Hos	10:11	I spared her fair N; but I will put
Hab	3:13	the wicked, laying him bare from thigh to N
Mt	18:6	millstone fastened round his N and to be drowned
Mk	9:42	were hung round his N and he were thrown
Lk	17:2	were hung round his N and he were cast
Acts	15:10	a yoke upon the N of the disciples which

NECKLACE (3)

2Chr	3:16	made chains like a N and put them on
Ps	73:6	Therefore pride is their N; violence covers them as
Song	4:9	of your eyes, with one jewel of your N

NECKS (13)

Josh	10:24	your feet upon the N of these kings." Then
	10:24	came near, and put their feet on their N
Judg	8:21	that were on the N of their camels.
	8:26	that were about the N of their camels.
Neh	3:5	did not put their N to the work of
Is	3:16	walk with outstretched N, glancing wantonly with
Jer	27:12	like manner: "Bring your N under the yoke of
Lam	5:5	a yoke on our N we are hard driven;
Bar	4:25	see their destruction and will tread upon their N
Ezek	21:29	be laid on the N of the unhallowed wicked,
Mic	2:3	you cannot remove your N; and you shall not
1Mac	1:61	and they hung the infants from their mothers' N
Rom	16:4	Jesus, who risked their N for my life, to

NECO (9)

2Kgs	23:29	In his days Pharaoh N king of Egypt went
	23:29	meet him; and Pharaoh N slew him at Megiddo,
	23:33	And Pharaoh N put him in bonds at Riblah
	23:34	And Pharaoh N made Eliakim the son of Josiah
	23:35	to his assessment, to give it to Pharaoh N
2Chr	35:20	had prepared the temple, N king of Egypt went
	35:22	to the words of N from the mouth of
	36:4	name to Jehoiakim; but N took Jehoahaz his brother
Jer	46:2	the army of Pharaoh N, king of Egypt, which

NECROMANCER

Deut	18:11	or a medium, or a wizard, or a N

NECTAR

Song	4:11	Your lips distil N, my bride; honey and milk

NEDABIAH

1Chr	3:18	Shenazzar, Jekamiah, Hoshama, and N;

NEED (90)

Gen	33:15	But he said, "What N is there?
Lev	13:36	the skin, the priest N not seek for the
Deut	15:8	him sufficient for his N, whatever it may be.
	18:22	spoken it presumptuously, you N not be afraid of
2Kgs	12:5	the house wherever any N of repairs is discovered."
1Chr	23:26	the Levites no longer N to carry the tabernacle
2Chr	2:16	cut whatever timber you N from Lebanon, and bring
	20:17	You will not N to fight in this battle;
	35:3	of Israel, built; you N no longer carry it
	35:15	gate; they did not N to depart from their
Job	33:7	no fear of me N terrify you; my pressure
Wis	11:5	punished, they themselves received benefit in their N
	13:16	an image and has N of help.
	16:25	of those who had N,
Sir	3:21	for you do not N what is hidden.
	8:9	how to give an answer in time of N
	11:21	say, "What do I N, and what prosperity could
	13:4	if you are in N he will forsake you.
	13:6	to you kindly and say, "What do you N
	14:1	with his lips and N not suffer grief for
	15:12	for he had no N of a sinful man.
	18:24	the days of wealth think of poverty and N
	29:2	the time of his N; and in turn, repay
	29:3	on every occasion you will find what you N
	29:9	and because of his N do not send him
	29:27	stay with me; I N my house."
	32:7	man, if there is N of you, but no
	33:31	own soul you will N him.
	38:1	him, according to your N of him, for the
	38:12	you, for there is N of him.
	39:33	he will supply every N in its hour.
	40:26	it there is no N to seek for help.
	41:2	one who is in N and is failing in
	42:23	for ever for every N, and are all obedient.
Jer	2:24	None who seek her N weary themselves; in her
Bar	6:59	that serves its owner's N, than to be these
Ezek	39:10	that they will not N to take wood out
Dan	3:16	Nebuchadnezzar, we have no N to answer you in
1Mac	3:28	and ordered them to be ready for any N
	12:9	though we have no N of these things, since
2Mac	2:15	So if you have N of them, send people
	14:35	of all, who hast N of nothing, thou wast
Mt	3:14	prevented him, saying, "I N to be baptized by
	6:8	Father knows what you N before you ask him.
	6:32	Father knows that you N them all.
	9:12	are well have no N of a physician, but
	14:16	Jesus said, "They N not go away; you give
	15:5	given to God, he N not honor his father.'
	21:3	say, 'The Lord has N of them,' and he
	26:65	Why do we still N witnesses?
Mk	2:17	are well have no N of a physician, but
	2:25	when he was in N and was hungry, he
	11:3	say, 'The Lord has N of it and will

N

14:63 "Why do we still N witnesses?
Lk 5:31 are well have no N of a physician, but
9:11 cured those who had N of healing.
12:30 Father knows that you N them.
15:7 ninety-nine righteous persons who N no repentance.
19:31 this, 'The Lord has N of it.'"
19:34 said, "The Lord has N of it."
22:69 And they said, "What further testimony do we N
Jn 13:10 has bathed does not N to wash, except for
13:29 him, "Buy what we N for the feast"; or,
16:30 know all things, and N none to question you;
Acts 2:45 and distributed them to all, as any had N
4:35 distribution was made to each as any had N
1Cor 5:10 since then you would N to go out of
12:21 hand, "I have no N of you," nor again
12:21 feet, "I have no N of you."
16:2 prosper, so that contributions N not be made when
2Cor 3:1 Or do we N, as some do, letters of
Eph 4:28 may be able to give to those in N
Phil 2:25 and minister to my N,
4:19 God will supply every N of yours according to
1Thes 1:8 everywhere, so that we N not say anything.
4:9 brethren you have no N to have any one
5:1 brethren, you have no N to have anything written
2Tim 2:15 workman who has no N to be ashamed, rightly
Tit 3:14 help cases of urgent N, and not to be
Heb 4:16 and find grace to help in time of N
5:12 to be teachers, you N some one to teach
5:12 You N milk, not solid food;
7:11 the law), what further N would there have been
7:27 He has no N, like those high priests, to
10:36 For you have N of endurance, so that you
1Jn 2:27 and you have no N that any one should
3:17 sees his brother in N, yet closes his heart
Rev 3:17 have prospered, and I N nothing; not knowing that
21:23 the city has no N of sun or moon
22:5 be no more; they N no light of lamp

NEEDED (7)

Ezra 6:9 And whatever is N -- young bulls, rams, or
2Mac 10:19 off for places where he was more urgently N
11:18 king of everything that N to be brought before
Jn 2:25 knew all men and N no one to bear
Acts 17:25 hands, as though he N anything, since he himself
28:10 we sailed, they put on board whatever we N
Jas 2:16 giving them the things N for the body, what

NEEDFUL (2)

Prov 30:8 the food that is N for me,
Lk 10:42 and troubled about many things; one thing is N

NEEDLE (3)

Mt 19:24 the eye of a N than for a rich
Mk 10:25 the eye of a N than for a rich
Lk 18:25 the eye of a N than for a rich

NEEDLESSLY (4)

Sir 20:22 to a friend, and N make him an enemy.
23:11 if he has sworn N, he will not be
29:6 money, and he has N made him his enemy;
29:7 lend; they have been afraid of being defrauded N

NEEDLEWORK (6)

Ex 26:36 stuff and fine twined linen, embroidered with N
27:16 twined linen, embroidered with N; it shall have four
28:39 and you shall make a girdle embroidered with N
36:37 twined linen, embroidered with N;
38:18 court was embroidered with N in blue and purple
39:29 scarlet stuff, embroidered with N; as the LORD had

NEEDS (11)

Num 4:26 shall do all that N to be done with
Wis 13:11 vessel that serves life's N,
Sir 11:12 who is slow and N help, who lacks strength
13:6 When he N you he will deceive you, he
39:26 Basic to all the N of man's life are
42:21 taken away, and he N no one to be
1Mac 16:14 and attending to their N, and he went down
Lk 11:8 he will rise and give him whatever he N
Acts 24:22 friends should be prevented from attending to his N
Rom 12:13 Contribute to the N of the saints, practice hospitality.
2Cor 11:9 any one, for my N were supplied by the

NEEDY (52)

Deut 15:11 your brother, to the N and to the poor,
24:14 who is poor and N, whether he is one
1Sam 2:8 dust; he lifts the N from the ash heap,
Job 5:15 from their mouth, the N from the hand of
24:14 kill the poor and N; and in the night
Ps 9:18 For the N shall not always be forgotten, and
12:5 are despoiled, because the N groan, I will now
35:10 him, the weak and N from him who despoils
37:14 down the poor and N, to slay those who
40:17 I am poor and N; but the Lord takes
68:10 goodness, O God, thou didst provide for the N
69:33 the LORD hears the N, and does not despise
70:5 I am poor and N; hasten to me, O
72:4 give deliverance to the N, and crush the oppressor!
72:12 For he delivers the N when he calls, the
72:13 the weak and the N, and saves the lives
72:13 the needy, and saves the lives of the N
74:21 let the poor and N praise thy name.
82:4 the weak and the N; deliver them from the
86:1 and answer me, for I am poor and N
107:41 he raises up the N out of affliction, and
109:16 pursued the poor and N and the brokenhearted to
109:22 I am poor and N, and my heart is
109:31 right hand of the N, to save him from
113:7 dust, and lifts the N from the ash heap,
140:12 of the afflicted, and executes justice for the N
Prov 14:31 is kind to the N honors him.
30:14 off the earth, the N from among men.
31:9 righteously, maintain the rights of the poor and N
31:20 poor, and reaches out her hands to the N
Sir 4:1 and do not keep N eyes waiting.
4:5 your eye from the N, nor give a man
31:4 diminishes, and when he rests he becomes N
34:21 The bread of the N is the life of
Is 10:2 to turn aside the N from justice and to
14:30 will feed, and the N lie down in safety;
25:4 a stronghold to the N in his distress, a
26:6 feet of the poor, the steps of the N
32:7 the plea of the N is right.
41:17 When the poor and N seek water, and there
Jer 5:28 they do not defend the rights of the N
20:13 the life of the N from the hand of
22:16 of the poor and N; then it was well.
Ezek 16:49 ease, but did not aid the poor and N
18:12 oppresses the poor and N, commits robbery, does not
22:29 oppressed the poor and N, and have extorted from
Amos 2:6 for silver, and the N for a pair of
4:1 poor, who crush the N, who say to their
5:12 and turn aside the N in the gate.
8:4 who trample upon the N, and bring the poor
8:6 for silver and the N for a pair of
Acts 4:34 There was not a N person among them, for

NEGEB (40)

Gen 12:9 And Abram journeyed on, still going toward the N
13:1 he had, and Lot with him, into the N
13:3 journeyed on from the N as far as Bethel,
20:1 the territory of the N, and dwelt between Kadesh
24:62 come from Beer-lahai-roi, and was dwelling in the N
Num 13:17 "Go up into the N yonder, and go up
13:22 went up into the N, and came to Hebron;
13:29 the land of the N; the Hittites, the Jebusites,
21:1 who dwelt in the N, heard that Israel was
33:40 who dwelt in the N in the land of
Deut 1:7 lowland, and in the N, and by the seacoast,
34:3 the Western Sea, the N, and the Plain, that
Josh 10:40 hill country and the N and the lowland and
11:16 country and all the N and all the land
12:8 wilderness, and in the N, the land of the
15:19 the land of the N, give me also springs
19:8 cities as far as Baalath-beer, Ramah of the N
Judg 1:9 hill country, in the N, and in the lowland.
1:15 the land of the N, give me also springs
1:16 which lies in the N near Arad; and they
1Sam 27:10 would say, "Against the N of Judah," or "Against
27:10 or "Against the N of the Jerahmeelites," or, "Against
27:10 or, "Against the N of the Kenites."
30:1 a raid upon the N and upon Ziklag.
30:14 a raid upon the N of the Cherethites and
30:14 Judah and upon the N of Caleb; and we
30:27 in Ramoth of the N, in Jattir,
2Sam 24:7 went out to the N of Judah at Beer-sheba.
2Chr 28:18 the Shephelah and the N of Judah, and had
Ps 126:4 fortunes, O LORD, like the watercourses in the N
Is 21:1 As whirlwinds in the N sweep on, it comes
30:6 An oracle on the beasts of the N
Jer 13:19 The cities of the N are shut up, with
17:26 country, and from the N, bringing burnt offerings and

32:44 the cities of the N; for I will restore
33:13 the cities of the N, in the land of
Ezek 20:46 forest land in the N;
20:47 the forest of the N, Hear the word of
Obad 1:19 Those of the N shall possess Mount Esau, and
1:20 in Sepharad shall possess the cities of the N

NEGLECT (11)

Neh 10:39 We will not N the house of our God.
Tob 4:3 me, and do not N your mother.
Esth 13:16 Do not N thy portion, which thou didst redeem
Prov 8:33 wise, and do not N it.
Sir 7:10 in your prayer, nor N to give alms.
38:16 him, and do not N his burial.
Lk 11:42 and every herb, and N justice and the love
1Tim 4:14 Do not N the gift you have, which was
Heb 2:3 we escape if we N such a great salvation?
13:2 Do not N to show hospitality to strangers, for
13:16 Do not N to do good and to share

NEGLECTED (4)

1Chr 13:3 to us; for we N it in the days
Wis 19:22 and thou hast not N to help them at
Mt 23:22 and cummin, and have N the weightier matters of
Acts 6:1 their widows were N in the daily distribution.

NEGLECTING (4)

2Mac 4:14 Despising the sanctuary and N the sacrifices, they
Mt 23:22 to have done, without N the others.
Lk 11:42 to have done, without N the others.
Heb 10:25 and good works, not N to meet together, as

NEGLIGENT (3)

2Chr 29:11 do not now be N, for the LORD has
Sir 38:9 sick do not be N, but pray to the
Bar 1:19 and we have been N, in not heeding his

NEGOTIATED

2Mac 13:22 The king N a second time with the people

NEHELAM (3)

Jer 29:24 To Shemaiah of N you shall say:
29:31 LORD concerning Shemaiah of N: Because
29:32 will punish Shemaiah of N and his descendants; he

NEHEMIAH (17)

Ezra 2:2 came with Zerubbabel, Jeshua, N, Seraiah,
Neh 1:1 The words of N the son of Hacaliah.
3:16 After him N the son of Azbuk, ruler of
7:7 came with Zerubbabel, Jeshua, N, Azariah, Raamiah,
8:9 And N, who was the governor, and Ezra the
10:1 set their seal are N the governor, the son
12:26 in the days of N the governor and of
12:47 in the days of N gave the daily portions
Sir 49:13 The memory of N also is lasting; he raised
2Mac 1:18 the fire given when N, who built the temple
1:20 when it pleased God, N, having been commissioned
1:21 the sacrifices were presented, N ordered the priests
1:23 Jonathan led, and the rest responded, as did N
1:31 the sacrifice were consumed, N ordered that the
1:33 had appeared with which N and his associates had
1:36 N and his associates called this "nephthar," which
2:13 in the memoirs of N, and also that he

NEHUM

Neh 7:7 Mordecai, Bilshan, Mispereth, Bigvai, N, Baanah.

NEHUSHTA

2Kgs 24:8 His mother's name was N the daughter of Elnathan

NEHUSHTAN

2Kgs 18:4 had burned incense to it; it was called N

NEIEL

Josh 19:27 northward to Beth-emek and N; then it continues in

NEIGH

Jer 50:11 heifer at grass, and N like stallions,

NEIGHBOR (157)

Ex 3:22 shall ask of her N, and of her who
11:2 every man of his N and every woman of
11:2 every woman of her N, jewelry of silver and
12:4 a man and his N next to his house
18:16 a man and his N, and I make them
20:16 "You shall not bear false witness against your N
20:17 shall not covet your N's house; you shall not
20:17 shall not covet your N's wife, or his manservant,
22:7 man delivers to his N money or goods to
22:8 his hand to his N's goods.
22:9 God shall condemn shall pay double to his N
22:10 man delivers to his N an ass or an
22:11 his hand to his N's property; and the owner
22:14 borrows anything of his N, and it is hurt
22:26 ever you take your N's garment in pledge, you
32:27 every man his companion, and every man his N
Lev 6:2 LORD by deceiving his N in a matter of
6:2 he has oppressed his N
18:20 lie carnally with your N's wife, and defile yourself
19:13 shall not oppress your N or rob him.
19:15 great, but in righteousness shall you judge your N
19:16 the life of your N: I am the LORD.
19:17 shall reason with your N, lest you bear sin
19:18 you shall love your N as yourself: I am
20:10 the wife of his N, both the adulterer and
24:19 a disfigurement in his N, as he has done
25:14 you sell to your N or buy from your
25:14 or buy from your N, you shall not wrong
25:15 shall buy from your N, and according to the
Deut 4:42 there, who kills his N unintentionally, without being
5:20 "'Neither shall you bear false witness against your N
5:21 shall you covet your N's wife; and you shall
5:21 shall not desire your N's house, his field, or
15:2 has lent to his N; he shall not exact
15:2 exact it of his N, his brother, because the
19:4 any one kills his N unintentionally without having
19:5 the forest with his N to cut wood, and
19:5 handle and strikes his N so that he dies--
19:6 at enmity with his N in time past.
19:11 any man hates his N, and lies in wait
19:14 shall not remove your N's landmark, which the men
22:24 because he violated his N's wife; so you shall
22:26 attacking and murdering his N;
23:24 you go into your N's vineyard, you may eat
23:25 you go into your N's standing grain, you may
23:25 a sickle to your N's standing grain.
24:10 "When you make your N a loan of any
27:17 he who removes his N's landmark.' And all the
27:24 he who slays his N in secret.' And all
Josh 20:5 because he killed his N unwittingly, having had no
1Sam 15:28 given it to a N of yours, who is
28:17 given it to your N, David.
2Sam 12:11 give them to your N, and he shall lie
1Kgs 8:31 man sins against his N and is made to
2Chr 6:22 man sins against his N and is made to
Jud 7:4 one said to his N, "These men will now
10:19 one said to his N, "Who can despise these
Job 16:21 God, like that of a man with his N
31:9 in wait at my N's door;
Ps 12:2 utters lies to his N; with flattering lips and
15:3 a reproach against his N;
101:5 Him who slanders his N secretly I will destroy.
Prov 3:24 Love Your N
3:28 not say to your N, "Go, and come again,
3:29 plan evil against your N who dwells trustingly beside
6:1 become surety for your N, have given your pledge
6:3 have come into your N's power: go, hasten, and
6:3 neighbor's power: go, hasten, and importune your N
6:29 goes in to his N's wife; none who touches
11:9 man would destroy his N, but by knowledge the
11:12 He who belittles his N lacks sense, but a
14:20 disliked even by his N, but the rich has
14:21 He who despises his N is a sinner, but
16:29 of violence entices his N and leads him in
17:18 and becomes surety in the presence of his N
21:10 wicked desires evil; his N finds no mercy in
24:28 a witness against your N without cause, and do
25:8 the end, when your N puts you to shame?
25:9 your case with your N himself, and do not
25:17 be seldom in your N's house, lest he become
25:18 false witness against his N is like a war
26:19 man who deceives his N and says, "I am
27:10 Better is a N who is near than a
27:14 He who blesses his N with a loud voice,
29:5 man who flatters his N spreads a net for
Eccl 4:4 work come from a man's envy of his N
Sir 5:12 have understanding, answer your N; but if not, put
6:17 is, so is his N also.
10:6 be angry with your N for any injury, and
13:14 and every person his N;
17:12 commandment to each of them concerning his N
18:12 man is for his N, but the compassion of

N

19:14 Question a N, perhaps he did not say it;
19:17 Question your N before you threaten him; and let
22:21 the trust of your N in his poverty, that
27:18 so you have destroyed the friendship of your N
27:19 you have let your N go, and will not
28:2 Forgive your N the wrong he has done, and
28:7 be angry with your N; remember the covenant of
29:1 will lend to his N, and he that strengthens
29:2 Lend to your N in the time of his
29:2 in turn, repay your N promptly.
29:5 in speaking of his N's money; but at the
29:14 be surety for his N, but a man who
29:20 Assist your N according to your ability, but take
31:14 do not crowd your N at the dish.
31:15 Judge your N's feelings by your own, and in
31:31 Do not reprove your N at a banquet of
34:22 To take away a N's living is to murder
Is 3:5 and every man his N; the youth will be
9:20 satisfied; each devours his N's flesh,
19:2 every man against his N, city against city, kingdom
41:6 Every one helps his N, and says to his
Jer 5:8 each neighing for his N's wife.
6:21 fathers and sons together, N and friend shall perish.'"
9:4 one beware of his N, and put no trust
9:4 a supplanter, and every N goes about as a
9:5 Every one deceives his N, and no one speaks
9:8 speaks peaceably to his N, but in his heart
9:20 and each to her N a dirge.
19:9 the flesh of his N in the siege and
22:8 will say to his N, "Why has the LORD
22:13 injustice; who makes his N serve him for nothing,
23:35 every one to his N and every one to
31:34 each man teach his N and each his brother,
34:15 liberty, each to his N, and you made a
34:17 brother and to his N; behold, I proclaim to
49:18 and Gomorrah and their N cities were overthrown,
50:40 and Gomorrah and their N cities, says the LORD,
Ezek 18:6 does not defile his N's wife or approach a
18:11 the mountains, defiles his N's wife,
18:15 does not defile his N's wife,
22:11 abomination with his N's wife; another lewdly defiles
33:26 of you defiles his N's wife; shall you then
Dan 13:62 to do to their N; acting in accordance with
Mic 7:5 no trust in a N, have no confidence in
Zech 3:10 you will invite his N under his vine and
1Mac 2:40 each said to his N: "If we all do
Mt 5:43 'You shall love your N and hate your enemy.'
19:19 You shall love your N as yourself."
22:39 You shall love your N as yourself.
Mk 12:31 'You shall love your N as yourself.' There is
12:33 and to love one's N as oneself, is much
Lk 10:27 your mind; and your N as yourself."
10:29 himself, said to Jesus, "And who is my N
10:36 do you think, proved N to the man who
Acts 7:27 who was wronging his N thrust him aside, saying,
Rom 13:8 he who loves his N has fulfilled the law.
13:9 "You shall love your N as yourself."
13:10 no wrong to a N; therefore love is the
15:2 of us please his N for his good, to
1Cor 10:24 his own good, but the good of his N
Gal 5:14 "You shall love your N as yourself."
6:4 be in himself alone and not in his N
Eph 4:25 the truth with his N, for we are members
Jas 2:8 "You shall love your N as yourself," you do
4:12 But who are you that you judge your N

NEIGHBORHOOD (8)

Judg 6:4 as far as the N of Gaza, and leave
11:33 from Aroer to the N of Minnith, twenty cities,
Ruth 4:17 the women of the N gave him a name,
Sir 21:28 his own soul and is hated in his N
Mt 8:34 saw him, they begged him to leave their N
Mk 5:17 began to beg Jesus to depart from their N
6:55 ran about the whole N and began to bring
Acts 28:7 Now in the N of that place were lands

NEIGHBORING (3)

1Mac 12:33 as Askalon and the N strongholds.
2Mac 4:32 to Tyre and the N cities.
6:8 was issued to the N Greek cities, that they

NEIGHBORS (39)

Ex 20:17 or his ass, or anything that is your N
Deut 1:7 and to all their N in the Arabah, in
5:21 anything that is your N
Josh 9:16 that they were their N, and that they dwelt
2Kgs 4:3 vessels of all your N, empty vessels and not
1Chr 12:40 And also their N, from as far as Issachar
Tob 2:8 And my N laughed at me and said, "He
Ps 28:3 speak peace with their N, while mischief is in
31:11 a horror to my N, an object of dread
44:13 the taunt of our N, the derision and scorn
79:4 a taunt to our N, mocked and derided by
79:12 the bosom of our N the taunts with which
80:6 the scorn of our N; and our enemies laugh
89:41 him; he has become the scorn of his N
Sir 9:14 aim to know your N, and consult with the
15:5 exalt him above his N, and will open his
16:8 did not spare the N of Lot, whom he
25:1 between brothers, friendship between N, and a wife
25:17 his meals among the N, and he cannot help
Jer 12:14 concerning all my evil N who touch the heritage
29:23 committed adultery with their N wives, and they
49:10 his brothers, and his N; and he is no
Lam 1:17 against Jacob that his N should be his foes;
Bar 4:9 she said: "Hearken, you N of Zion, God has
4:14 Let the N of Zion come; remember the capture
4:24 For as the N of Zion have now seen
Ezek 16:26 Egyptians, your lustful N, multiplying your harlotry,
16:57 Edom and all her N, and for the daughters
22:12 make gain of your N by extortion; and you
28:24 them among all their N who have treated them
28:26 judgments upon all their N who have treated them
Hab 2:15 him who makes his N drink of the cup
2Mac 9:25 the borders and the N to my kingdom keep
Lk 1:58 And her N and kinsfolk heard that the Lord
1:65 And fear came on all their N
14:12 your kinsmen or rich N, lest they also invite
15:6 his friends and his N, saying to them, 'Rejoice
15:9 together her friends and N, saying, 'Rejoice with me,
Jn 9:8 The N and those who had seen him before

NEIGHING (2)

Jer 5:8 well-fed lusty stallions, each N for his neighbor's
8:16 the sound of the N of their stallions the

NEIGHINGS

Jer 13:27 your adulteries and N, your lewd harlotries, on

NEIGHS

Sir 33:6 a mocking friend; he N under every one who

NEITHER (209)

Gen 3:3 midst of the garden, N shall you touch it,
8:21 evil from his youth; N will I ever again
31:29 you speak to Jacob N good nor bad.'
45:6 which there will be N plowing nor harvest.
Ex 10:6 all the Egyptians; as N your fathers nor your
10:15 a green thing remained, N tree nor plant of
12:39 and could not tarry, N had they prepared for
34:24 and enlarge your borders; N shall any man desire
34:25 my sacrifice with leaven; N shall the sacrifice of
34:28 and forty nights; he N ate bread nor drank
36:6 throughout the camp, "Let N man nor woman do
Lev 3:17 places, that you eat N fat nor blood."
7:18 shall not be accepted, N shall it be credited
17:12 you shall eat blood, N shall any stranger who
18:23 defile yourself with it, N shall any woman give
19:9 to its very border, N shall you gather the
19:10 strip your vineyard bare, N shall you gather the
21:7 who has been defiled; N shall they marry a
21:12 or for his mother; N shall he go out
22:25 sacrifice within your land; N shall you offer as
23:14 And you shall eat N bread nor grain parched
25:11 in it you shall N sow, nor reap what
26:44 will not spurn them, N will I abhor them
27:33 is good or bad, N shall he exchange it;
Num 6:7 N for his father nor for his mother, nor
14:44 the hill country, although N the ark of the
18:20 inheritance in their land, N shall you have any
20:17 through field or vineyard, N will we drink water
23:25 Balak said to Balaam, N curse them at all,
Deut 2:27 I will turn aside N to the right nor
4:28 of men's hands, that N see, nor hear, nor
5:18 N shall you commit adultery.
5:19 N shall you steal.
5:20 N shall you bear false witness against your neighbor.
5:21 N shall you covet your neighbor's wife; and you
7:16 shall not pity them; N shall you serve their
9:9 and forty nights; I N ate bread nor drank
9:18 and forty nights; I N ate bread nor drank
13:6 serve other gods,' which N you nor your fathers

21:4 running water, which is N plowed nor sown, and
21:7 not shed this blood, N did our eyes see
23:17 the daughters of Israel, N shall there be a
26:13 any of thy commandments, N have I forgotten them;
28:36 to a nation that N you nor your fathers
28:39 them, but you shall N drink of the wine
28:64 wood and stone, which N you nor your fathers
30:11 too hard for you, N is it far-off.
30:13 it and do it?' N is it beyond the
Josh 1:9 courage; be not frightened, N be dismayed; for the
6:10 your voice be heard, N shall any word go
23:6 turning aside from it N to the right hand
Judg 11:34 beside her he had N son nor daughter.
13:14 comes from the vine, N let her drink wine
21:22 his wife in battle, N did you give them
1Sam 1:15 troubled; I have drunk N wine nor strong drink,
6:12 they went; they turned N to the right nor
13:22 the battle there was N sword nor spear found
16:8 And he said, N has the LORD chosen this
16:9 And he said, N has the LORD chosen this
20:31 lives upon the earth, N you nor your kingdom
21:8 For I have brought N my sword nor my
27:9 the land, and left N man nor woman alive,
27:11 And David saved N man nor woman alive, to
2Sam 2:19 he went he turned N to the right hand
13:22 Absalom spoke to Amnon N good nor bad; for
14:7 leave to my husband N name nor remnant upon
19:24 the king; he had N dressed his feet, nor
21:4 Saul or his house; N is it for us
1Kgs 3:26 said, "It shall be N mine nor yours; divide
5:4 every side; there is N adversary nor misfortune.
6:7 the quarry; so that N hammer nor axe nor
11:2 into marriage with them, N shall they with you,
13:9 LORD, saying, 'You shall N eat bread, nor drink
13:16 go in with you; N will I eat bread
13:17 the LORD, 'You shall N eat bread nor drink
17:1 stand, there shall be N dew nor rain these
17:16 meal was not spent, N did the cruse of
22:31 his chariots, "Fight with N small nor great, but
2Kgs 2:21 this water wholesome; henceforth N death nor
3:14 of Judah, I would N look at you, nor
4:23 It is N new moon nor sabbath." She said,
18:12 the LORD commanded; they N listened nor obeyed.
2Chr 18:30 his chariots, "Fight with N small nor great, but
Ezra 9:12 daughters to their sons, N take their daughters for
10:6 he spent the night, N eating bread nor drinking
Neh 4:23 So N I nor my brethren nor my servants
5:14 the king, twelve years, N I nor my brethren
Jud 7:4 of the whole land; N the high mountains nor
Esth 2:7 uncle, for she had N father nor mother; the
4:16 on my behalf, and N eat nor drink for
5:9 king's gate, that he N rose nor trembled before
Ps 82:5 have N knowledge nor understanding, they walk
121:4 who keeps Israel will N slumber nor sleep.
Prov 30:8 and lying; give me N poverty nor riches; feed
Eccl 7:17 Be not wicked overmuch, N be a fool; why
8:13 well with the wicked, N will he prolong his
8:16 done on earth, how N day nor night one's
Song 8:7 waters cannot quench love, N can floods drown it.
Wis 6:23 pass by the truth; N will I travel in
7:9 N did I liken to her any priceless gem,
12:13 For N is there any god besides thee, whose
14:13 corruption of life, for N have they existed from
15:4 For N has the evil intent of human art
15:15 gods, though these have N the use of their
16:12 For N herb nor poultice cured them, but it
Sir 16:25 for all generations; they N hunger nor grow weary,
23:6 Let N gluttony nor lust overcome me, and do
30:19 For it can N eat nor smell.
35:18 Lord will not delay, N will he be patient
38:32 established, and men can N sojourn nor live there.
Is 2:4 up sword against nation, N shall they learn war
3:7 my house there is N bread nor mantle; you
23:4 sea, saying: "I have N travailed nor given birth,
23:4 given birth, I have N reared young men nor
30:5 profit them, that brings N help nor profit, but
44:9 not profit; their witnesses N see nor know, that
49:10 not hunger or thirst, N scorching wind nor sun
51:14 down to the Pit, N shall his bread fail.
55:8 are not your thoughts, N are your ways my
Jer 9:16 among the nations whom N they nor their fathers
10:5 they cannot do evil, N is it in them
16:13 into a land which N you nor your fathers
19:4 to other gods whom N they nor their fathers
23:4 more, nor be dismayed, N shall any be missing,
25:4 You have N listened nor inclined your ears to
35:6 shall not drink wine, N you nor your sons
36:24 Yet N the king, nor any of his servants
37:2 But N he nor his servants nor the people
44:3 that they knew not, N they, nor you, nor
51:62 shall dwell in it, N man nor beast, and
Bar 6:66 For they can N curse nor bless kings;
Ezek 7:11 nor their wealth; N shall there be pre-eminence
14:16 GOD, they would deliver N sons nor daughters; they
14:18 GOD, they would deliver N sons nor daughters, but
14:20 GOD, they would deliver N son nor daughter; they
22:26 holy and the common, N have they taught the
29:18 was rubbed bare; yet N he nor his army
43:7 defile my holy name, N they, nor their kings,
Dan 11:20 he shall be broken, N in anger nor in
11:24 he shall do what N his fathers nor his
Hos 1:10 sea, which can be N measured nor numbered; and
Jon 3:7 and his nobles: Let N man nor beast, herd
Mic 4:3 up sword against nation, N shall they learn war
Zeph 1:18 N their silver nor their gold shall be able
Zech 8:10 any wage for beast, N was there any safety
14:6 day there shall be N cold nor frost.
Mal 4:1 it will leave them N root nor branch.
1Mac 12:36 that its garrison could N buy nor sell.
15:33 this reply: "We have N taken foreign land nor
2Mac 6:6 A man could N keep the sabbath, nor observe
Mt 6:15 forgive men their trespasses, N will your Father
6:20 treasures in heaven, where N moth nor rust
6:26 of the air: they N sow nor reap nor
6:28 how they grow; they N toil nor spin;
9:17 N is new wine put into old wineskins; if
11:18 mourn.' For John came N eating nor drinking, and
21:27 he said to them, N will I tell you
22:29 wrong, because you know N the scriptures nor the
22:30 in the resurrection they N marry nor are given
23:10 N be called masters, for you have one master,
23:13 against men; for you N enter yourselves, nor allow
25:13 therefore, for you know N the day nor the
Mk 11:32 Jesus said to them, N will I tell you
12:24 wrong, that you know N the scriptures nor the
12:25 from the dead, they N marry nor are given
14:68 denied it, saying, "I N know nor understand what
Lk 12:24 Consider the ravens: they N sow nor reap, they
12:24 nor reap, they have N storehouse nor barn, and
12:27 how they grow; they N toil nor spin; yet
14:35 It is fit N for the land nor for
16:31 Moses and the prophets, N will they be convinced
18:2 was a judge who N feared God nor regarded
18:4 to himself, 'Though I N fear God nor regard
20:8 Jesus said to them, N will I tell you
20:35 resurrection from the dead N marry nor are given
23:15 your charges against him; N did Herod, for he
Jn 1:25 baptizing, if you are N the Christ, nor Elijah,
4:21 hour is coming when N on this mountain nor
8:11 And Jesus said, N do I condemn you; go,
8:19 Jesus answered, "You know N me nor my Father;
14:17 cannot receive, because it N sees him nor knows
14:27 your hearts be troubled, N let them be afraid.
15:4 abides in the vine, N can you, unless you
Acts 8:21 You have N part nor lot in this matter,
9:9 was without sight, and N ate nor drank.
15:10 of the disciples which N our fathers nor we
19:37 men here who are N sacrilegious nor blasphemers of
23:12 themselves by an oath N to eat nor drink
23:21 themselves by an oath N to eat nor drink
24:12 N can they prove to you what they now
25:8 said in his defense, N against the law of
27:20 And when N sun nor stars appeared for many
Rom 8:38 I am sure that N death, nor life, nor
11:21 spare the natural branches, N will he spare you.
1Cor 3:7 So N he who plants nor he who waters
6:9 Do not be deceived; N the immoral, nor idolaters,
7:19 For N circumcision counts for anything nor
11:9 N was man created for woman, but woman for
Gal 3:28 There is N Jew nor Greek, there is neither
3:28 nor Greek, there is N slave nor free, there
3:28 nor free, there is N male nor female; for
5:6 in Christ Jesus N circumcision nor uncircumcision
6:15 For N circumcision counts for anything, nor
Heb 7:3 or genealogy, and has N beginning of days nor
10:8 said above, "Thou hast N desired nor taken pleasure
Rev 3:15 your works: you are N cold nor hot.
3:16 you are lukewarm, and N cold nor hot, I
7:16 shall hunger no more, N thirst any more; the
21:4 shall be no more, N shall there be mourning

N

NEKODA (4)
Ezra 2:48 Rezin, the sons of N, the sons of Gazzam,
2:60 and the sons of N, six hundred and fifty-two.
Neh 7:50 Rezin, the sons of N,
7:62 Tobiah, the sons of N, six hundred and forty-two.

NEMUEL (3)
Num 26:9 The sons of Eliab: N, Dathan, and Abiram.
26:12 to their families: of N, the family of the
1Chr 4:24 The sons of Simeon: N, Jamin, Jarib, Zerah, Shaul;

NEMUELITES
Num 26:12 the family of the N; of Jamin, the family

NEPHEG (4)
Ex 6:21 sons of Izhar: Korah, N, and Zichri.
2Sam 5:15 Nathan, Solomon, Ibhar, Elishu-a, N, Japhia,
1Chr 3:7 Ibhar, Elishama, Eliphelet, Nogah, N, Japhia,
14:6 Ibhar, Elishu-a, Elpelet, Nogah, N, Japhia,

NEPHEW (2)
Tob 1:22 He was my N
11:18 Ahikar and his N Nadab came,

NEPHILIM (3)
Gen 6:4 The N were on the earth in those days,
Num 13:33 there we saw the N (the sons of Anak,
13:33 who come from the N; and we seemed to

NEPHISIM
Ezra 2:50 Me-unim, the sons of N,

NEPHTHAR
2Mac 1:36 Nehemiah and his associates called this N

NEPHTOAH (2)
Josh 15:9 of the Waters of N, and from there to
18:15 of the Waters of N;

NEPHUSHESIM
Neh 7:52 Me-unim, the sons of N,

NER (16)
1Sam 14:50 Abner the son of N, Saul's uncle;
14:51 father of Saul, and N the father of Abner
26:5 Abner the son of N, the commander of his
26:14 Abner the son of N, saying, "Will you not
2Sam 2:8 Abner the son of N, commander of Saul's army,
2:12 Abner the son of N, and the servants of
3:23 "Abner the son of N came to the king,
3:25 Abner the son of N came to deceive you,
3:28 for the blood of Abner the son of N
3:37 king's will to slay Abner the son of N
1Kgs 2:5 Abner the son of N, and Amasa the son
2:32 Abner the son of N, commander of the army
1Chr 8:33 N was the father of Kish, Kish of Saul,
9:36 then Zur, Kish, Baal, N, Nadab,
9:39 N was the father of Kish, Kish of Saul,
26:28 Abner the son of N, and Joab the son

NERAIAH
Bar 1:1 Baruch the son of N, son of Mahseiah, son

NEREUS
Rom 16:15 Greet Philologus, Julia, N and his sister, and

NERGAL
2Kgs 17:30 men of Cuth made N, the men of Hamath

NERGAL-SHAREZER (3)
Jer 39:3 in the middle gate: N, Samgar-nebo, Sarsechim the
39:3 Sarsechim the Rabsaris, N the Rabmag, with all
39:13 guard, Nebushazban the Rabsaris, N the Rabmag,

NERI
Lk 3:27 Shealtiel, the son of N,

NERIAH (10)
Jer 32:12 Baruch the son of N son of Mahseiah, in
32:16 Baruch the son of N, I prayed to the
36:4 Baruch the son of N, and Baruch wrote upon
36:8 Baruch the son of N did all that Jeremiah
36:14 Baruch the son of N took the scroll in
36:32 scribe, the son of N, who wrote on it
43:3 Baruch the son of N has set you against
43:6 Jeremiah the prophet and Baruch the son of N
45:1 Baruch the son of N, when he wrote these
51:59 Seraiah the son of N, son of Mahseiah, when

NEST (13)
Num 24:21 dwelling place, and your N is set in the
Deut 22:6 come upon a bird's N, in any tree or
32:11 that stirs up its N, that flutters over its
Job 29:18 shall die in my N, and I shall multiply
39:27 up and makes his N on high?
Ps 84:3 and the swallow a N for herself, where she
Prov 27:8 that strays from its N, is a man who
Is 10:14 has found like a N the wealth of the
34:15 There shall the owl N and lay and hatch
Jer 49:16 Though you make your N as high as the
Ezek 17:23 of its branches birds of every sort will N
Obad 1:4 the eagle, though your N is set among the
Hab 2:9 house, to set his N on high, to be

NESTED
Jer 22:23 O inhabitant of Lebanon, N among the cedars, how

NESTLINGS
Is 16:2 birds, like scattered N, so are the daughters

NESTS (8)
Ps 104:17 the birds build their N; the stork has her
Jer 48:28 like the dove that N in the sides of
Ezek 31:6 the air made their N in its boughs; under
Mt 8:20 of the air have N; but the Son of
13:32 air come and make N in its branches."
Mk 4:32 the air can make N in its shade."
Lk 9:58 of the air have N; but the Son of
13:19 of the air made N in its branches."

NET (37)
Ex 27:4 bronze; and upon the N you shall make four
27:5 altar so that the N shall extend halfway down
1Kgs 7:17 of the pillars; a N for the one capital,
7:17 one capital, and a N for the other capital.
Job 18:8 is cast into a N by his own feet,
19:6 wrong, and closed his N about me.
Ps 9:15 they made; in the N which they hid has
10:9 the poor when he draws him into his N
25:15 he will pluck my feet out of the N
31:4 me out of the N which is hidden for
35:7 cause they hid their N for me; without cause
35:8 And let the N which they hid ensnare them;
57:6 They set a N for my steps; my soul
66:11 bring us into the N; thou didst lay affliction
140:5 they have spread a N, by the wayside they
Prov 1:17 in vain is a N spread in the sight
29:5 his neighbor spreads a N for his feet.
Eccl 9:12 taken in an evil N, and like birds which
Is 51:20 an antelope in a N; they are full of
Lam 1:13 descend; he spread a N for my feet; he
Ezek 12:13 I will spread my N over him, and he
17:20 I will spread my N over him, and he
19:8 side; they spread their N over him; he was
32:3 I will throw my N over you with a
Hos 5:1 at Mizpah, and a N spread upon Tabor.
7:13 spread over them my N; I will bring them
Mic 7:2 blood, and each hunts his brother with a N
Hab 1:15 them out with his N, he gathers them in
1:16 he sacrifices to his N and burns incense to
1:17 keep on emptying his N, and mercilessly slaying
Mt 4:18 his brother, casting a N into the sea; for
13:47 heaven is like a N which was thrown into
Mk 1:16 of Simon casting a N in the sea; for
Jn 21:6 to them, "Cast the N on the right side
21:8 the boat, dragging the N full of fish, for
21:11 aboard and hauled the N ashore, full of large
21:11 were so many, the N was not torn.

NETAIM
1Chr 4:23 potters and inhabitants of N and Gederah; they dwelt

NETHANEL (14)
Num 1:8 of Amminadab; from Issachar, N the son of Zuar;
2:5 people of Issachar being N the son of Zuar,
7:18 On the second day N the son of Zuar,
7:23 was the offering of N the son of Zuar.
10:15 men of Issachar was N the son of Zuar.
1Chr 2:14 second, Shimea the third, N the fourth, Raddai the
15:24 Joshaphat, N, Amasai, Zechariah, Benaiah, and
24:6 Shemaiah the son of N, a Levite, recorded them
26:4 third, Sachar the fourth, N the fifth,

N

2Chr 17:7 princes, Ben-hail, Obadiah, Zechariah, N, and
35:9 and Shemaiah and N his brothers, and Hashabiah
Ezra 10:22 Eli-o-enai, Ma-aseiah, Ishmael, N, Jozabad, and
Neh 12:21 Eber; of Hilkiah, Hashabiah; of Jedaiah, N
12:36 Milalai, Gilalai, Maai, N, Judah, and Hanani,

NETHANIAH (20)

2Kgs 25:23 Ishmael the son of N, and Johanan the son
25:25 Ishmael the son of N, son of Elishama, of
1Chr 25:2 of Asaph: Zaccur, Joseph, N, and Asharelah, sons of
25:12 twelve; the fifth to N, his sons and his
2Chr 17:8 them the Levites, Shemaiah, N, Zebadiah, Asahel,
Jer 36:14 Jehudi the son of N, son of Shelemiah, son
40:8 Ishmael the son of N, Johanan the son of
40:14 Ishmael the son of N to take your life?"
40:15 Ishmael the son of N, and no one will
41:1 Ishmael the son of N, son of Elishama, of
41:2 Ishmael the son of N and the ten men
41:6 Ishmael the son of N came out from Mizpah
41:7 Ishmael the son of N and the men with
41:9 Ishmael the son of N filled it with the
41:10 Ishmael the son of N took them captive and
41:11 Ishmael the son of N had done,
41:12 went to fight against Ishmael the son of N
41:15 Ishmael the son of N escaped from Johanan with
41:16 Ishmael the son of N had carried away captive
41:18 Ishmael the son of N had slain Gedaliah the

NETHER (11)

Job 41:24 stone, hard as the N millstone.
Ezek 26:20 to dwell in the N world, among primeval ruins,
31:14 to death, to the N world among mortal men,
31:16 be comforted in the N world.
31:18 of Eden to the N world; you shall lie
32:18 majestic nations, to the N world, to those who
32:24 uncircumcised into the N world, who spread terror
2Pet 2:4 them to pits of N gloom to be kept
2:17 storm; for them the N gloom of darkness has
Jude 1:6 eternal chains in the N gloom until the judgment
1:13 stars for whom the N gloom of darkness has

NETOPHAH (7)

2Sam 23:28 the Ahohite, Maharai of N,
23:29 son of Baanah of N, Ittai the son of
1Chr 11:30 the Ahohite, Maharai of N, Heled the son of
11:30 son of Baanah of N,
27:13 month, was Maharai of N, of the Zerahites; in
Ezra 2:22 The men of N, fifty-six.
Neh 7:26 men of Bethlehem and N, a hundred and

NETOPHATHITE (3)

2Kgs 25:23 son of Tanhumeth the N, and Ja-azaniah the son
1Chr 27:15 month, was Heldai the N, of Othni-el; in his
Jer 40:8 sons of Ephai the N, Jezaniah the son of

NETOPHATHITES (3)

1Chr 2:54 Salma: Bethlehem, the N, Atroth-beth-joab, and half
9:16 Elkanah, who dwelt in the villages of the N
Neh 12:28 the villages of the N;

NETS (15)

1Kgs 7:17 Then he made two N of checker work with
Ps 141:10 fall into their own N, while I escape.
Eccl 7:26 heart is snares and N, and whose hands are
Is 19:8 will languish who spread N upon the water.
Ezek 26:5 for the spreading of N; for I have spoken,
26:14 for the spreading of N; you shall never be
47:10 for the spreading of N; its fish will be
Mt 4:20 Immediately they left their N and followed him.
4:21 their father, mending their N, and he called them.
Mk 1:18 immediately they left their N and followed him.
1:19 brother, who were in their boat mending the N
Lk 5:2 gone out of them and were washing their N
5:4 and let down your N for a catch."
5:5 at your word I will let down the N
5:6 fish; and as their N were breaking,

NETTLES (5)

Job 30:7 they bray; under the N they huddle together.
Prov 24:31 ground was covered with N, and its stone wall
Is 34:13 grow over its strongholds, N and thistles in its
Hos 9:6 N shall possess their precious things of silver; thorns
Zeph 2:9 a land possessed by N and salt pits, and

NETWORK (10)

Ex 27:4 it a grating, a N of bronze; and upon
38:4 altar a grating, a N of bronze, under its
1Kgs 7:18 about upon the one N, to cover the capital
7:20 which was beside the N; there were two hundred
7:42 of pomegranates for each N, to cover the two
2Kgs 25:17 was three cubits; a N and pomegranates, all of
25:17 the second pillar had the like, with the N
2Chr 4:13 of pomegranates for each N, to cover the two
Jer 52:22 was five cubits; a N and pomegranates, all of
52:23 a hundred upon the N round about.

NETWORKS (4)

1Kgs 7:41 pillars, and the two N to cover the two
7:42 pomegranates for the two N, two rows of
2Chr 4:12 pillars; and the two N to cover the two
4:13 pomegranates for the two N, two rows of

NEVER (255)

Gen 8:21 his heart, "I will N again curse the ground
9:11 covenant with you, that N again shall all flesh
9:11 of a flood, and N again shall there be
9:15 and the waters shall N again become a flood
41:19 such as I had N seen in all the
44:28 pieces; and I have N seen him since.
Ex 9:18 to fall, such as N has been in Egypt
9:24 hail, such as had N been in all the
10:14 of locusts as had N been before, nor ever
10:28 take heed to yourself; N see my face again;
11:6 such as there has N been, nor ever shall
14:13 see today, you shall N see again.
Lev 18:30 So keep my charge N to practice any of
18:30 practiced before you, and N to defile yourselves by
Num 19:2 which a yoke has N come.
Deut 13:11 hear, and fear, and N again do any such
15:11 For the poor will N cease out of the
17:16 to you, 'You shall N return that way again.'
19:20 and fear, and shall N again commit any such
21:3 a heifer which has N been worked and which
28:68 promised that you should N make again; and there
32:17 to gods they had N known, to new gods
32:17 whom your fathers had N dreaded.
Judg 2:1 I said, 'I will N break my covenant with
11:39 She had N known a man.
16:17 her, "A razor has N come upon my head;
19:30 "Such a thing has N happened or been seen
1Sam 6:7 upon which there has N come a yoke, and
2Sam 3:29 the house of Joab N be without one who
12:10 therefore the sword shall N depart from your house,
14:10 me, and he shall N touch you again."
1Kgs 1:6 His father had N at any time displeased him
8:25 him, saying, 'There shall N fail you a man
10:10 spices, and precious stones; N again came such an
10:20 like of it was N made in any kingdom.
22:8 hate him, for he N prophesies good concerning me,
1Chr 16:30 the world stands firm, N to be moved.
2Chr 6:16 him, saying, 'There shall N fail you a man
9:11 for the singers; there N was seen the like
9:19 like of it was N made in any kingdom.
18:7 hate him, for he N prophesies good concerning me,
Ezra 9:12 for your sons, and N seek their peace or
Tob 3:9 May we N see a son or daughter of
6:7 and that person will N be troubled again.
6:17 flee away, and will N again return.
10:7 throughout the nights she N stopped mourning for
Jud 8:13 test--but you will N know anything!
8:18 "For N in our generation, nor in these present
11:1 heart, for I have N hurt any one who
11:2 slighted me, I would N have lifted my spear
13:19 Your hope will N depart from the hearts of
Esth 9:28 days of Purim should N fall into disuse among
Job 3:16 birth, as infants that N see the light?
7:7 breath; my eye will N again see good.
8:18 him, saying, 'I have N seen you.'
21:25 in bitterness of soul, N having tasted of good.
24:1 those who know him N see his days?
30:27 in turmoil, and is N still; days of affliction
Ps 10:11 his face, he will N see it."
15:5 does these things shall N be moved.
30:6 my prosperity, "I shall N be moved."
31:1 seek refuge; let me N be put to shame;
34:5 so your faces shall N be ashamed.
49:8 is costly, and can N suffice,
49:9 on for ever, and N see the Pit.
49:19 his fathers, who will N more see the light.
55:22 sustain you; he will N permit the righteous to
58:8 the untimely birth that N sees the sun.
71:1 take refuge; let me N be put to shame!

77:7 spurn for ever, and N again be favorable?
80:18 Then we will N turn back from thee; give
89:48 man can live and N see death?
93:1 is established; it shall N be moved;
96:10 is established, it shall N be moved; he will
104:5 so that it should N be shaken.
112:6 For the righteous will N be moved; he will
119:93 I will N forget thy precepts; for by them
141:5 oil of the wicked N anoint my head; for
Prov 10:30 The righteous will N be removed, but the wicked
12:3 of the righteous will N be moved.
27:20 Sheol and Abaddon are N satisfied, and never
27:20 are never satisfied, and N satisfied are the eyes
30:15 Three things are N satisfied; four never say,
30:15 are never satisfied; four N say, "Enough":
30:16 and the fire which N says, "Enough."
Eccl 4:8 and his eyes are N satisfied with riches, so
4:8 riches, so that he N asks, "For whom am
7:20 who does good and N sins.
Song 7:2 a rounded bowl that N lacks mixed wine.
Wis 2:2 as though we had N been; because the breath
7:10 light, because her radiance N ceases.
10:8 that their failures could N go unnoticed.
12:10 way of thinking would N change.
15:17 has life, but they N have.
Sir 4:25 N speak against the truth, but be mindful of
7:1 evil, and evil will N befall you.
7:36 and then you will N sin.
9:9 N dine with another man's wife, nor revel with
11:5 but one who was N thought of has worn
12:10 N trust your enemy, for like the rusting of
15:8 pride, and liars will N think of her.
16:26 aside, and they will N disobey his word.
19:7 N repeat a conversation, and you will lose nothing
19:16 Who has N sinned with his tongue?
22:11 rest, and you will N be wearied by his
23:7 who observes it will N be caught.
23:12 to death; may it N be found in the
23:14 wish that you had N been born, and you
23:15 use insulting words will N become disciplined all his
23:16 near of kin will N cease until the fire
23:17 tastes sweet; he will N cease until he dies.
27:16 confidence, and he will N find a congenial friend.
38:8 His works will N be finished; and from him
39:9 understanding, and it will N be blotted out; his
40:23 friend or a companion N meets one amiss, but
43:10 stand as ordered, they N relax in their watches.
45:13 Before his time there N were such beautiful things.
47:22 But the Lord will N give up his mercy,
47:22 to perish; he will N blot out the descendants
51:18 good; and I shall N be put to shame.
Is 13:20 It will N be inhabited or dwelt in for
25:2 no more, it will N be rebuilt.
33:20 tent, whose stakes will N be plucked up, nor
48:7 before today you have N heard of them, lest
48:8 knew them.' You have N heard, you have never
48:8 never heard, you have N known, from of old
48:19 grains; their name would N be cut off or
51:6 and my deliverance will N be ended.
56:11 a mighty appetite; they N have enough.
62:6 the night they shall N be silent.
63:19 over whom thou hast N ruled, like those who
Jer 19:11 so that it can N be mended.
20:11 Their eternal dishonor will N be forgotten.
22:12 die, and he shall N see this land again."
33:17 the LORD: David shall N lack a man to
33:18 the Levitical priests shall N lack a man in
35:19 son of Rechab shall N lack a man to
50:5 everlasting covenant which will N be forgotten.'
Lam 3:22 love of the LORD N ceases, his mercies never
3:22 never ceases, his mercies N come to an end;
Bar 2:35 people; and I will N again remove my people
Ezek 4:14 behold, I have N defiled myself; from my youth
4:14 till now I have N eaten what died of
5:9 you what I have N yet done, and the
5:9 of which I will N do again.
16:16 harlot; the like has N been, nor ever shall
16:63 and be confounded, and N open your mouth again
20:32 in your mind shall N happen—the thought, 'Let
26:14 of nets; you shall N be rebuilt; for I
26:21 sought for, you will N be found again, says
29:15 of the kingdoms, and N again exalt itself above
29:15 small that they will N again rule over the
29:16 And it shall N again be the reliance of
36:30 abundant, that you may N again suffer the disgrace
Dan 2:44 a kingdom which shall N be destroyed, nor shall
6:26 ever; his kingdom shall N be destroyed, and his
12:1 of trouble, such as N has been since there
14:7 brass outside, and it N ate or drank anything."
14:35 said, "Sir, I have N seen Babylon, and I
Hos 12:8 all his riches can N offset the guilt he
Joel 2:2 people; their like has N been from of old,
2:26 And my people shall N again be put to
2:27 And my people shall N again be put to
3:17 holy and strangers shall N again pass through it.
Amos 7:8 people Israel; I will N again pass by them;
7:13 and prophesy there; but N again prophesy at Bethel,
8:2 people Israel; I will N again pass by them.
8:7 Jacob: "Surely I will N forget any of their
8:14 they shall fall, and N rise again."
9:15 land, and they shall N again be plucked up
Nah 1:15 fulfil your vows, for N again shall the wicked
Hab 1:4 is slacked and justice N goes forth.
2:5 like death he has N enough.
Hag 1:6 you eat, but you N have enough; you drink,
1:6 you drink, but you N have your fill; you
1Mac 2:48 and kings, and they N let the sinner gain
6:36 with it, and they N left it.
2Mac 6:16 Therefore he N withdraws his mercy from us.
10:4 Lord that they might N again fall into such
15:36 decreed by public vote N to let this day
Mt 5:20 and Pharisees, you will N enter the kingdom of
5:26 to you, you will N get out till you
7:23 declare to them, 'I N knew you; depart from
9:33 the crowds marveled, saying, N was anything like
13:14 shall indeed hear but N understand, and you shall
13:14 shall indeed see but N perceive.
16:22 This shall N happen to you."
18:3 like children, you will N enter the kingdom of
18:12 over the ninety-nine that N went astray.
21:16 them, "Yes; have you N read, 'Out of the
21:21 you have faith and N doubt, you will not
21:42 to them, "Have you N read in the scriptures:
24:21 until now, no, and N will be.
26:33 of you, I will N fall away."
Mk 2:12 glorified God, saying, "We N saw anything like this!"
2:25 to them, "Have you N read what David did,
3:29 against the Holy Spirit N has forgiveness, but is
9:25 out of him, and N enter him again."
13:19 created until now, and N will be.
Lk 12:59 tell you, you will N get out till you
15:29 served you, and I N disobeyed your command; yet
15:29 your command; yet you N gave me a kid,
23:28 and the wombs that N bore, and the breasts
23:28 and the breasts that N gave suck!'
Jn 4:14 shall give him will N thirst; the water that
5:36 His voice you have N heard, his form you
5:36 his form you have N seen;
6:35 believes in me shall N thirst.
7:15 learning, when he has N studied?"
8:33 of Abraham, and have N been in bondage to
8:51 my word, he will N see death."
8:52 my word, he will N taste death.'
9:32 N since the world began has it been heard
10:28 life, and they shall N perish, and no one
11:26 believes in me shall N die.
13:8 to him, "You shall N wash my feet." Jesus
Acts 6:13 who said, "This man N ceases to speak words
10:14 Lord; for I have N eaten anything that is
13:41 a deed you will N believe, if one declares
14:8 from birth, who had N walked.
19:2 said, "No, we have N even heard that there
28:26 shall indeed hear but N understand, and you shall
28:26 shall indeed see but N perceive.
Rom 6:9 from the dead will N die again; death no
10:14 of whom they have N heard?
12:11 N flag in zeal, be aglow with the Spirit,
12:16 associate with the lowly; N be conceited.
12:19 Beloved, N avenge yourselves, but leave it to the
14:13 another, but rather decide N to put a stumbling
15:21 shall see who have N been told of him,
15:21 shall understand who have N heard of him."
1Cor 6:15 N! Do you not know
7:21 N mind.
8:13 brother's falling, I will N eat meat, lest I
13:8 Love N ends; as for prophecies, they will pass
1Thes 2:5 For we N used either words of flattery, as
1Tim 5:19 N admit any charge against an elder except on
2Tim 3:7 to anybody and can N arrive at a knowledge
Tit 1:2 life which God, who N lies, promised ages ago
Heb 1:12 and thy years will N end."
3:11 my wrath, 'They shall N enter my rest.'"

3:18 swear that they should N enter his rest, but
4:3 my wrath, 'They shall N enter my rest,'' although
4:5 he said, ''They shall N enter my rest.''
10:1 these realities, it can N, by the same sacrifices
10:11 same sacrifices, which can N take away sins.
13:5 has said, ''I will N fail you nor forsake
2Pet 1:10 do this you will N fall;
2:21 been better for them N to have known the
Rev 3:12 temple of my God; N shall he go out
4:8 day and night they N cease to sing, ''Holy,
16:18 earthquake such as had N been since men were
18:7 widow, mourning I shall N see,'
18:14 are lost to thee, N to be found again!''
21:25 and its gates shall N be shut by day–

NEVER-ENDING

Ezek 25:15 heart to destroy in N enmity;

NEVERMORE

Is 14:20 the descendants of evildoers N be named!

NEVERTHELESS (59)

Gen 48:19 also shall be great; N his younger brother shall
Ex 32:34 N, in the day when I visit, I will
Lev 11:4 N among those that chew the cud or part
11:36 N a spring or a cistern holding water shall
25:32 N the cities of the Levites, the houses in
Num 18:15 LORD, shall be yours; N the first-born of man
24:22 set in the rock; N Kain shall be wasted.
25:9 N those that died by the plague were twenty-four
31:23 N it shall also be purified with the water
Deut 23:5 N the LORD your God would not hearken to
Judg 1:33 of the land; N the inhabitants of Beth-shemesh
4:9 surely go with you; N, the road on which
1Sam 29:6 N the lords do not approve of you.
29:9 an angel of God; N the commanders of the
2Sam 5:7 N David took the stronghold of Zion, that is,
12:14 N, because by this deed you have utterly scorned
1Kgs 8:19 was in your heart; N you shall not build
11:34 N I will not take the whole kingdom out
15:4 N for David's sake the LORD his God gave
15:14 N the heart of Asa was wholly true to
20:6 wives and your children''; N I will send my
2Kgs 3:3 N he clung to the sin of Jeroboam the
12:3 N the high places were not taken away; the
13:6 N they did not depart from the sins of
15:4 N the high places were not taken away; the
15:35 N the high places were not removed; the people
1Chr 11:5 N David took the stronghold of Zion, that is,
2Chr 6:9 was in your heart; N you shall not build
12:8 N they shall be servants to him, that they
15:17 N the heart of Asa was blameless all his
19:3 N some good is found in you, for you
33:17 N the people still sacrificed at the high places,
35:22 N Josiah would not turn away from him, but
Neh 9:26 N they were disobedient and rebelled against thee
9:31 N in thy great mercies thou didst not make
13:26 king over all Israel; N foreign women made even
Esth 5:10 N Haman restrained himself, and went home; and he
Ps 73:23 N I am continually with thee; thou dost hold
82:7 High, all of you; N, you shall die like
106:44 N he regarded their distress, when he heard their
Sir 29:8 N, be patient with a man in humble circumstances,
Ezek 3:21 N if you warn the righteous man not to
20:17 N my eye spared them, and I did not
Dan 5:17 your rewards to another; N I will read the
Jon 1:13 N the men rowed hard to bring the ship
2Mac 14:18 N Nicanor, hearing of the valor of Judas and
15:5 N, he did not succeed in carrying out his
Mt 26:39 cup pass from me; N, not as I will,
Lk 10:11 wipe off against you; N know this, that the
10:20 N do not rejoice in this, that the spirits
13:33 N I must go on my way today and
18:8 N, when the Son of man comes, will he
22:42 this cup from me; N not my will, but
Jn 12:42 N many even of the authorities believed in him,
16:7 N I tell you the truth: it is to
1Cor 9:12 N, we have not made use of this right,
10:5 N with most of them God was not pleased;
11:11 N, in the Lord woman is not independent of
14:19 more than you all; N, in church I would

NEW (159)

Ex 1:7 Now there arose a N king over Egypt, who
19:1 On the third N moon after the people of
Lev 2:14 your first fruits crushed N grain from fresh ears,
23:16 a cereal offering of N grain to the LORD.
26:10 out the old to make way for the N
Num 16:30 LORD creates something N, and the ground opens
28:26 a cereal offering of N grain to the LORD
29:6 burnt offering of the N moon, and its cereal
Deut 20:5 that has built a N house and has not
22:8 ''When you build a N house, you shall make
32:17 had never known, to N gods that had come
Josh 9:13 moldy; these wineskins were N when we filled them,
Judg 5:8 When N gods were chosen, then war was in
15:13 bound him with two N ropes, and brought him
16:11 they bind me with N ropes that have not
16:12 So Delilah took N ropes and bound him with
1Sam 6:7 take and prepare a N cart and two milch
20:5 ''Behold, tomorrow is the N moon, and I should
20:18 him, ''Tomorrow is the N moon; and you will
20:24 field; and when the N moon came, the king
20:27 the morrow after the N moon, David's place was
2Sam 6:3 of God upon a N cart, and brought it
6:3 Abinadab, were driving the N cart
21:16 was girded with a N sword, thought to kill
1Kgs 11:29 clad himself with a N garment; and the two
11:30 laid hold of the N garment that was on
2Kgs 2:20 said, ''Bring me a N bowl, and put salt
4:23 It is neither N moon nor sabbath.'' She said,
1Chr 13:7 of God upon a N cart, from the house
23:31 the LORD on sabbaths, N moons, and feast days,
2Chr 2:4 the sabbaths and the N moons and the appointed
8:13 for the sabbaths, the N moons, and the three
20:5 the LORD, before the N court,
31:3 for the sabbaths, the N moons, and the appointed
Ezra 3:5 the offerings at the N moon and at all
Neh 10:33 offering, the sabbaths, the N moons, the appointed
Jud 8:6 the day before the N moon and the day
8:6 the day of the N moon, and the feasts
16:2 Raise to him a N psalm; exalt him, and
16:13 to my God a N song: O Lord, thou
Job 29:20 and my bow ever N in my hand.'
32:19 has no vent; like N wineskins, it is ready
Ps 33:3 Sing to him a N song, play skilfully on
40:3 He put a N song in my mouth, a
51:10 God, and put a N and right spirit within
81:3 the trumpet at the N moon, at the full
96:1 to the LORD a N song; sing to the
98:1 to the LORD a N song, for he has
144:9 I will sing a N song to thee, O
149:1 to the LORD a N song, his praise in
Prov 19:4 Wealth brings many N friends, but a poor man
27:25 is gone, and the N growth appears, and the
Eccl 1:9 and there is nothing N under the sun.
1:10 of which it is said, ''See, this is N
Song 7:13 are all choice fruits, N as well as old,
Wis 14:6 the seed of a N generation.
19:11 they saw also a N kind of birds, when
Sir 9:10 old friend, for a N one does not compare
9:10 A N friend is like new wine; when it
9:10 new friend is like N wine; when it has
Is 1:13 N moon and sabbath and the calling of assemblies–
1:14 Your N moons and your appointed feasts my soul
15:6 grass is withered, the N growth fails, the verdure
41:15 you a threshing sledge, N, sharp, and having teeth;
42:9 come to pass, and N things I now declare;
42:10 to the LORD a N song, his praise from
43:19 I am doing a N thing; now it springs
47:13 stars, who at the N moons predict what shall
48:6 I make you hear N things, hidden things which
57:10 is hopeless''; you found N life for your strength,
62:2 be called by a N name which the mouth
65:17 ''For behold, I create N heavens and a new
65:17 new heavens and a N earth; and the former
66:22 ''For as the N heavens and the new earth
66:22 new heavens and the N earth which I will
66:23 From N moon to new moon, and from sabbath
66:23 From new moon to N moon, and from sabbath
Jer 26:10 the entry of the N Gate of the house
31:22 LORD has created a N thing on the earth:
31:31 I will make a N covenant with the house
36:10 the entry of the N Gate of the LORD's
Lam 3:23 an end; they are N every morning; great is
Ezek 11:19 heart, and put a N spirit within them; I
18:31 and get yourselves a N heart and a new
18:31 new heart and a N spirit!
36:26 A N heart I will give you, and a
36:26 give you, and a N spirit I will put
45:17 at the feasts, the N moons, and the sabbaths,
46:1 the day of the N moon it shall be

46:3 sabbaths and on the N moons.
46:6 the day of the N moon he shall offer
Hos 2:11 mirth, her feasts, her N moons, her sabbaths, and
4:11 Wine and N wine take away the understanding.
5:7 Now the N moon shall devour them with their
9:2 feed them, and the N wine shall fail them.
Amos 8:5 saying, "When will the N moon be over, that
Hag 1:11 upon the grain, the N wine, the oil, upon
Zech 9:17 young men flourish, and N wine the maidens.
1Mac 4:47 directs, and built a N altar like the former
4:49 made N holy vessels, and brought the lampstand,
4:53 law directs, on the N altar of burnt offering
10:34 feasts and sabbaths and N moons and appointed
2Mac 2:29 master builder of a N house must be concerned
4:11 of living and introduced N customs contrary to the
Mt 9:17 Neither is N wine put into old wineskins; if
9:17 skins are destroyed; but N wine is put into
13:52 his treasure what is N and what is old."
19:28 to you, in the N world, when the Son
26:29 when I drink it N with you in my
27:60 it in his own N tomb, which he had
Mk 1:27 A N teaching!
2:21 away from it, the N from the old, and
2:22 And no one puts N wine into old wineskins;
2:22 are the skins; but N wine is for fresh
14:25 when I drink it N in the kingdom of
16:17 they will speak in N tongues;
Lk 5:36 a piece from a N garment and puts it
5:36 he will tear the N, and the piece from
5:36 the piece from the N will not match the
5:37 And no one puts N wine into old wineskins;
5:37 if he does, the N wine will burst the
5:38 But N wine must be put into fresh wineskins.
5:39 drinking old wine desires N; for he says, 'The
22:20 for you is the N covenant in my blood.
Jn 13:34 you cannot come.' A N commandment I give to
19:41 in the garden a N tomb where no one
Acts 2:13 "They are filled with N wine."
17:19 we know what this N teaching is which you
17:21 in nothing except telling or hearing something N
Rom 7:6 code but in the N life of the Spirit.
1Cor 5:7 you may be a N lump, as you really
11:25 "This cup is the N covenant in my blood.
2Cor 3:6 be ministers of a N covenant, not in a
5:17 Christ, he is a N creation; the old has
5:17 passed away, behold, the N has come.
Gal 6:15 nor uncircumcision, but a N creation.
Eph 2:15 create in himself one N man in place of
4:24 and put on the N nature, created after the
Col 2:16 a festival or a N moon or a sabbath.
3:10 have put on the N nature, which is being
Heb 8:8 I will establish a N covenant with the house
8:13 In speaking of a N covenant he treats the
9:15 the mediator of a N covenant, so that those
10:20 of Jesus, by the N and living way which
12:24 the mediator of a N covenant, and to the
2Pet 3:13 promise we wait for N heavens and a new
3:13 new heavens and a N earth in which righteousness
1Jn 2:7 am writing you no N commandment, but an old
2:8 am writing you a N commandment, which is true
2Jn 1:5 were writing you a N commandment, but the one
Rev 2:17 white stone, with a N name written on the
3:12 of my God, the N Jerusalem which comes down
3:12 heaven, and my own N name.
5:9 and they sang a N song, saying, "Worthy art
14:3 and they sing a N song before the throne
21:1 Then I saw a N heaven and a new
21:1 new heaven and a N earth; for the first
21:2 saw the holy city, N Jerusalem, coming down out
21:5 the throne said, "Behold, I make all things N

NEWBORN (2)

Jer 14:5 the field forsakes her N calf because there is
1Pet 2:2 Like N babes, long for the pure spiritual milk,

NEWLY (3)

Deut 24:5 "When a man is N married, he shall not
Jud 4:3 people of Judea were N gathered together, and the
Wis 11:18 or bold lions, or N created unknown beasts full

NEWNESS

Rom 6:4 too might walk in N of life.

NEWS (46)

1Sam 4:13 city and told the N, all the city cried
31:9 to carry the good N to their idols and
2Sam 4:4 years old when the N about Saul and Jonathan
4:10 he was bringing good N, I seized him and
4:10 was the reward I gave him for his N
11:18 told David all the N about the fighting;
11:19 finished telling all the N about the fighting to
1Kgs 1:42 you are a worthy man and bring good N
2:28 When the N came to Joab --for Joab
2Kgs 7:9 a day of good N; if we are silent
9:15 go and tell the N in Jezreel."
1Chr 10:9 to carry the good N to their idols and
Ps 40:9 have told the glad N of deliverance in the
Prov 15:30 the heart, and good N refreshes the bones.
25:25 soul, so is good N from a far country.
Jer 20:15 man who brought the N to my father, "A
37:5 besieging Jerusalem heard N of them, they withdrew
Ezek 24:26 come to you to report to you the N
Nah 3:19 All who hear the N of you clap their
1Mac 6:8 the king heard this N, he was astounded and
2Mac 5:11 When N of what had happened reached the king,
9:3 he was in Ecbatana, N came to him of
9:24 happened or any unwelcome N came, the people
Mt 11:5 the poor have good N preached to them.
Mk 1:45 and to spread the N, so that Jesus could
Lk 1:19 to you, and to bring you this good N
2:10 I bring you good N of a great joy
3:18 exhortations, he preached good N to the people.
4:18 me to preach good N to the poor.
4:43 must preach the good N of the kingdom of
7:22 the poor have good N preached to them.
8:1 and bringing the good N of the kingdom of
16:16 since then the good N of the kingdom of
Acts 8:12 as he preached good N about the kingdom of
8:35 told him the good N of Jesus.
10:36 to Israel, preaching good N of peace by Jesus
11:22 N of this came to the ears of the
13:32 bring you the good N that what God promised
14:15 and bring you good N, that you should turn
Rom 10:15 are the feet of those who preach good N
Phil 2:19 may be cheered by N of you.
1Thes 3:6 brought us the good N of your faith and
Heb 4:2 For good N came to us just as to
4:6 formerly received the good N failed to enter because
1Pet 1:12 who preached the good N to you through the
1:25 word is the good N which was preached to

NEXT (99)

Gen 17:21 you at this season N year."
19:34 And on the N day, the first-born said to
Ex 2:13 he went out the N day, behold, two Hebrews
12:4 man and his neighbor N to his house shall
28:26 on its inside edge N to the ephod.
39:19 on its inside edge N to the ephod.
Lev 25:25 his property, then his N of kin shall come
Num 2:5 Those to encamp N to him shall be the
2:12 And those to encamp N to him shall be
2:20 And N to him shall be the tribe of
2:27 And those to encamp N to him shall be
11:32 night, and all the N day, and gathered the
27:11 his kinsman that is N to him of his
Judg 6:38 When he rose early N morning and squeezed the
Ruth 3:9 maidservant, for you are N of kin."
3:13 the part of the N of kin for you,
3:13 the part of the N of kin for you,
3:13 the part of the N of kin for you.
4:1 there; and behold, the N of kin, of whom
4:3 he said to the N of kin, "Naomi, who
4:6 Then the N of kin said, "I cannot redeem
4:8 So when the N of kin said to Boaz,
4:14 you this day without N of kin; and may
1Sam 5:3 Ashdod rose early the N day, behold, Dagon had
5:4 rose early on the N morning, behold, Dagon had
17:13 Eliab the first-born, and N to him Abinadab, and
23:17 and I shall be N to you; Saul my
30:17 the evening of the N day; and not a
2Sam 11:12 Uriah remained in Jerusalem that day, and the N
14:30 "See, Joab's field is N to mine, and he
23:9 And N to him among the three mighty men
23:11 And N to him was Shammah, the son of
1Kgs 1:6 and he was born N after Absalom.
2Kgs 3:20 The N morning, about the time of offering the
6:29 And on the N day I said to her,
1Chr 11:12 And N to him among the three mighty men
29:21 LORD, and on the N day offered burnt offerings
2Chr 17:15 men of valor, and N to him Jehohanan the
17:16 and eighty thousand, and N to him Amasiah the
17:18 bow and shield, and N to him Jehozabad with

28:7 palace and Elkanah the N in authority to the
Neh 3:2 And N to him the men of Jericho built.
3:2 And N to them Zaccur the son of Imri
3:4 And N to them Meremoth the son of Uriah,
3:4 And N to them Meshullam the son of Berechiah,
3:4 And N to them Zadok the son of Baana
3:5 And N to them the Tekoites repaired; but their
3:7 And N to them repaired Melatiah the Gibeonite and
3:8 N to them Uzziel the son of Harhaiah, goldsmiths,
3:8 N to him Hananiah, one of the perfumers, repaired;
3:9 N to them Rephaiah the son of Hur, ruler
3:10 N to them Jedaiah the son of Harumaph repaired
3:10 opposite his house; and N to him Hattush the
3:12 N to him Shallum the son of Hallohesh, ruler
3:17 the son of Bani; N to him Hashabiah, ruler
3:19 the district of Keilah; N to him Ezer the
Tob 4:14 hold over till the N day the wages of
7:14 N he called his wife Edna, and took a
Jud 7:1 The N day Holofernes ordered his whole army, and
16:24 all those who were N of kin to her
Esth 1:14 and judgment, the men N to him being Carshena,
4:8 because Haman, who is N to the king, spoke
10:3 Mordecai the Jew was N in rank to King
Ps 48:13 you may tell the N generation
78:6 their children; that the N generation might know
Sir 12:12 Do not put him N to you, lest he
Bar 6:43 she derides the woman N to her, because she
Ezek 24:18 And on the N morning I did as I
Dan 13:28 The N day, when the people gathered at the
Jon 4:7 dawn came up the N day, God appointed a
Zech 13:7 the man who stands N to me," says the
1Mac 4:28 But the N year he mustered sixty thousand picked
5:35 N he turned aside to Alema, and fought against
2Mac 7:15 N they brought forward the fifth and maltreated him.
12:39 On the N day, as by that time it
Mt 10:23 town, flee to the N; for truly, I say
27:62 N day, that is, after the day of Preparation,
Mk 1:38 go on to the N towns, that I may
Lk 9:37 On the N day, when they had come down
10:35 And the N day he took out two denarii
13:9 if it bears fruit N year, well and good;
Jn 1:29 The N day he saw Jesus coming toward him,
1:35 The N day again John was standing with two
1:43 The N day Jesus decided to go to Galilee.
6:22 On the N day the people who remained on
12:12 The N day a great crowd who had come
Acts 10:9 The N day, as they were on their journey
10:23 The N day he rose and went off with
13:42 be told them the N sabbath.
13:44 The N sabbath almost the whole city gathered
14:20 city; and on the N day he went on
18:7 God; his house was N door to the synagogue.
20:15 day opposite Chios; the N day we touched at
21:1 to Cos, and the N day to Rhodes, and
21:26 the men, and the N day he purified himself
25:6 to Caesarea; and the N day he took his
25:17 delay, but on the N day took my seat
27:3 The N day we put in at Sidon; and
27:18 violently storm-tossed, they began N day to throw

NEZIAH (2)
Ezra 2:54 Temah, the sons of N, and the sons of
Neh 7:56 Temah, the sons of N, the sons of Hatipha.

NEZIB
Josh 15:43 Ether, Ashan, Iphtah, Ashnah, N,

NIBHAZ
2Kgs 17:31 and the Avvites made N and Tartak; and the

NIBSHAN
Josh 15:62 Beth-arabah, Middin, Secacah, N, the City of Salt,

NICANOR (45)
1Mac 3:38 son of Dorymenes, and N and Gorgias, mighty men
7:26 Then the king sent N, one of his honored
7:27 So N came to Jerusalem with a large force,
7:30 known to Judas that N had come to him
7:31 When N learned that his plan had been disclosed,
7:32 of the army of N fell, and the rest
7:33 After these events N went up to Mount Zion.
7:39 Now N went out from Jerusalem and encamped in
7:42 the rest learn that N has spoken wickedly against
7:43 The army of N was crushed, and he himself
7:44 his army saw that N had fallen, they threw
7:47 and they cut off N's head and the right
9:1 When Demetrius heard that N and his army had
2Mac 8:9 And Ptolemy promptly appointed N the son of
8:10 N determined to make up for the king the
8:12 came to Judas concerning N's invasion; and when he
8:14 sold by the ungodly N before he ever met
8:23 the first division himself, he joined battle with N
8:24 and disabled most of N's army, and forced them
8:34 thrice-accursed N, who had brought the thousand
9:3 what had happened to N and the forces of
12:2 in addition to these N the governor of Cyprus,
14:12 And he immediately chose N, who had been in
14:14 Judas, flocked to join N, thinking that the
14:15 the Jews heard of N's coming and the gathering
14:17 of Judas, had encountered N, but had been
14:18 Nevertheless N, hearing of the valor of Judas and
14:23 N stayed on in Jerusalem and did nothing out
14:26 He told him that N was disloyal to the
14:27 depraved man, wrote to N, stating that he was
14:28 this message came to N, he was troubled and
14:30 But Maccabeus, noticing that N was more austere in
14:30 of his men, and went into hiding from N
14:37 Jerusalem, was denounced to N as a man who
14:39 N, wishing to exhibit the enmity which he had
15:1 When N heard that Judas and his men were
15:6 This N in his utter boastfulness and arrogance had
15:25 N and his men advanced with trumpets and battle
15:28 with joy, they recognized N, lying dead, in full
15:30 them to cut off N's head and arm and
15:32 showed them the vile N's head and that profane
15:33 tongue of the ungodly N and said that he
15:35 And he hung N's head from the citadel, a
15:37 This, then, is how matters turned out with N
Acts 6:5 Philip, and Prochorus, and N, and Timon, and

NICHE
Wis 13:15 makes for it a N that befits it, and

NICODEMUS (5)
Jn 3:1 of the Pharisees, named N, a ruler of the
3:4 N said to him, "How can a man be
3:9 N said to him, "How can this be?"
7:50 N, who had gone to him before, and who
19:39 N also, who had at first come to him

NICOLAITANS (2)
Rev 2:6 the works of the N, which I also hate.
2:15 have some who hold the teaching of the N

NICOLAUS
Acts 6:5 Timon, and Parmenas, and N, a proselyte of Antioch.

NICOPOLIS
Tit 3:12 come to me at N, for I have decided

NIGER
Acts 13:1 Simeon who was called N, Lucius of Cyrene,

NIGGARDLINESS
Sir 31:24 their testimony to his N is accurate.

NIGGARDLY
Sir 31:24 the one who is N with food, and their

NIGH (3)
Num 24:17 behold him, but not N: a star shall come
Ps 73:2 my steps had well N slipped.
Eccl 12:1 and the years draw N, when you will say,

NIGHT (344)
Gen 1:5 the light Day, and the darkness he called N
1:14 the day from the N; and let them be
1:16 light to rule the N; he made the stars
1:18 day and over the N, and to separate the
8:22 and winter, day and N, shall not cease."
14:15 forces against them by N, he and his servants,
19:2 house and spend the N, and wash your feet;
19:2 we will spend the N in the street."
19:33 father drink wine that N; and the first-born went
19:34 "Behold, I lay last N with my father; let
19:35 father drink wine that N also; and the younger
20:3 in a dream by N, and said to him,
24:54 and they spent the N there.
26:24 to him the same N and said, "I am
28:11 and stayed there that N, because the sun had
30:16 So he lay with her that N
31:24 in a dream by N, and said to him,

N

31:29 spoke to me last N, saying, 'Take heed that
31:39 it, whether stolen by day or stolen by N
31:40 and the cold by N, and my sleep fled
31:42 labor of my hands, and rebuked you last N
31:54 bread and tarried all N on the mountain.
32:13 he lodged there that N, and took from what
32:21 he himself lodged that N in the camp.
32:22 The same N he arose and took his two
40:5 And one N they both dreamed—the butler and
41:11 dreamed on the same N, he and I, each
46:2 in visions of the N, and said, "Jacob, Jacob."
Ex 10:13 day and all that N; and when it was
12:8 eat the flesh that N, roasted; with unleavened bread
12:12 land of Egypt that N, and I will smite
12:30 rose up in the N, he, and all his
12:31 Moses and Aaron by N, and said, "Rise up,
12:42 It was a N of watching by the LORD,
12:42 Egypt; so this same N is a night of
12:42 same night is a N of watching kept to
13:21 the way, and by N in a pillar of
13:21 by day and by N;
13:22 pillar of fire by N did not depart from
14:20 the darkness; and the N passed without one coming
14:20 passed without one coming near the other all N
14:21 strong east wind all N, and made the sea
Lev 6:9 upon the altar all N until the morning, and
8:35 shall remain day and N for seven days, performing
19:13 remain with you all N until the morning.
Num 9:16 by day, and the appearance of fire by N
9:21 a day and a N, when the cloud was
11:9 the camp in the N, the manna fell with
11:32 that day, and all N, and all the next
14:1 a loud cry; and the people wept that N
14:14 day and in a pillar of fire by N
22:8 them, "Lodge here this N, and I will bring
22:19 now, tarry here this N also, that I may
22:20 came to Balaam at N and said to him,
Deut 1:33 tents, in fire by N, to show you by
16:1 your God brought you out of Egypt by N
16:4 first day remain all N until morning.
21:23 shall not remain all N upon the tree, but
23:10 chances to him by N, then he shall go
28:66 in doubt before you; N and day you shall
Josh 1:8 on it day and N, that you may be
6:11 camp, and spent the N in the camp.
8:3 men of valor, and sent them forth by N
8:9 but Joshua spent that N among the people.
8:13 But Joshua spent that N in the valley.
10:9 having marched up all N from Gilgal.
Judg 6:25 That N the LORD said to him, "Take your
6:27 do it by day, he did it by N
6:40 God did so that N; for it was dry
7:9 That same N the LORD said to him, "Arise,
9:32 Now therefore, go by N, you and the men
9:34 him rose up by N, and laid wait against
16:2 wait for him all N at the gate of
16:2 They kept quiet all N, saying, "Let us wait
19:6 pleased to spend the N, and let your heart
19:9 day has waned toward evening; pray tarry all N
19:10 would not spend the N; he rose up and
19:11 Jebusites, and spend the N in it."
19:13 places, and spend the N at Gibe-ah or at
19:15 in and spend the N at Gibe-ah.
19:15 took them into his house to spend the N
19:20 do not spend the N in the square."
19:25 and abused her all N until the morning.
20:4 Benjamin, I and my concubine, to spend the N
20:5 round about me by N; they meant to kill
Ruth 1:12 have a husband this N and should bear sons,
3:13 Remain this N, and in the morning, if he
1Sam 14:34 ox with him that N, and slew them there.
14:36 after the Philistines by N and despoil them until
15:11 angry; and he cried to the LORD all N
15:16 you what the LORD said to me this N
19:11 That N Saul sent messengers to David's house to
19:24 lay naked all that day and all that N
25:16 to us both by N and by day, all
26:7 to the army by N; and there lay Saul
28:8 him; and they came to the woman by N
28:20 he had eaten nothing all day and all N
28:25 Then they rose and went away that N
31:12 arose, and went all N, and took the body
2Sam 2:29 men went all that N through the Arabah; they
2:32 his men marched all N, and the day broke
4:7 of the Arabah all N,
7:4 But that same N the word of the LORD
12:16 in and lay all N upon the ground.
17:8 will not spend the N with the people.
19:7 stay with you this N; and this will be
21:10 day, or the beasts of the field by N
1Kgs 3:5 in a dream by N; and God said, "Ask
3:19 son died in the N, because she lay on
8:29 eyes may be open N and day toward this
8:59 our God day and N, and may he maintain
2Kgs 6:14 and they came by N, and surrounded the city.
7:12 king rose in the N, and said to his
8:21 chariots, and rose by N, and he and his
19:35 And that N the angel of the LORD went
25:4 of war fled by N by the way of
1Chr 9:33 service, for they were on duty day and N
17:3 But that same N the word of the LORD
2Chr 1:7 In that N God appeared to Solomon, and said
6:20 be open day and N toward this house, the
7:12 to Solomon in the N and said to him:
21:9 and he rose by N and smote the Edomites
35:14 the fat parts until N; so the Levites prepared
Ezra 10:6 where he spent the N, neither eating bread nor
Neh 1:6 before thee day and N for the people of
2:12 I arose in the N, I and a few
2:13 I went out by N by the Valley Gate
2:15 went up in the N by the valley and
4:9 guard as a protection against them day and N
4:22 his servant pass the N within Jerusalem, that they
4:22 guard for us by N and may labor by
6:10 to kill you, at N they are coming to
9:12 of fire in the N to light for them
9:19 pillar of fire by N which lighted for them
Tob 2:9 On the same N I returned from burying him,
6:15 demon, for this very N she will be given
7:11 each came to her he died in the N
8:9 Then they both went to sleep for the N
9:5 journey and stayed over N with Gabael.
Jud 6:21 elders; and all that N they called on the
7:5 their towers they remained on guard all that N
11:5 will tell nothing false to my lord this N
11:17 of heaven day and N; therefore, my lord, I
11:17 with you, and every N your servant will go
12:7 and went out each N to the valley of
13:14 destroyed our enemies by my hand this very N
Esth 4:16 drink for three days, N or day.
6:1 On that N the king could not sleep; and
Job 3:3 was born, and the N which said, 'A man-child
3:6 That N—let thick darkness seize it!
3:7 Yea, let that N be barren; let no joyful
4:13 from visions of the N, when deep sleep falls
5:14 daytime, and grope at noonday as in the N
7:4 I arise?' But the N is long, and I
17:12 They make N into day; 'The light,' they say,
20:8 be chased away like a vision of the N
24:7 They lie all N naked, without clothing, and have
24:14 needy; and in the N he is as a
27:20 a flood; in the N a whirlwind carries him
29:19 with the dew all N on my branches,
30:17 The N racks my bones, and the pain that
33:15 a vision of the N, when deep sleep falls
34:25 overturns them in the N, and they are crushed.
35:10 gives songs in the N,
36:20 not long for the N, when peoples are cut
39:9 Will he spend the N at your crib?
Ps 1:2 and on his law he meditates day and N
6:6 with my moaning; every N I flood my bed
16:7 me counsel; in the N also my heart instructs
17:3 thou visitest me by N, if thou testest me,
19:2 forth speech, and N to night declares knowledge.
19:2 speech, and night to N declares knowledge.
22:2 not answer; and by N, but find no rest.
30:5 may tarry for the N, but joy comes with
32:4 For day and N thy hand was heavy upon
42:3 my food day and N, while men say to
42:8 steadfast love; and at N his song is with
55:10 Day and N they go around it on its
63:6 the watches of the N;
74:16 day, thine also the N; thou hast established the
77:2 the Lord; in the N my hand is stretched
77:6 my heart in the N; I meditate and search
78:14 cloud, and all the N with a fiery light.
88:1 cry out in the N before thee.
90:4 is past, or as a watch in the N
91:5 the terror of the N, nor the arrow that
92:2 and thy faithfulness by N,
104:20 darkness, and it is N, when all the beasts
105:39 a covering, and fire to give light by N

119:55 thy name in the N, O LORD, and keep
119:148 the watches of the N, that I may meditate
121:6 smite you by day, nor the moon by N
134:1 LORD, who stand by N in the house of
136:9 to rule over the N, for his steadfast love
139:11 cover me, and the light about me be N
139:12 dark to thee, the N is bright as the
Prov 7:9 at the time of N and darkness.
31:15 while it is yet N and provides food for
31:18 Her lamp does not go out at N
Eccl 2:23 vexation; even in the N his mind does not
8:16 how neither day nor N one's eyes see sleep;
Song 3:1 Upon my bed by N I sought him whom
3:8 his sword at his thigh, against alarms by N
5:2 dew, my locks with the drops of the N
Wis 7:30 is succeeded by the N, but against wisdom evil
10:17 by day, and a starry flame through the N
17:2 and prisoners of long N, shut in under their
17:5 of the stars avail to illumine that hateful N
17:14 But throughout the N, which was really powerless,
17:21 those men alone heavy N was spread, an image
18:6 That N was made known beforehand to our fathers,
18:14 enveloped all things, and N in its swift course
Sir 36:26 home, and lodges wherever N finds him?
38:27 workman who labors by N as well as by
40:5 bed, his sleep at N confuses his mind.
Is 4:5 a flaming fire by N; for over all the
10:29 they lodge for the N; Ramah trembles, Gibe-ah of
15:1 laid waste in a N Moab is undone; because
15:1 laid waste in a N Moab is undone.
16:3 make your shade like N at the height of
21:11 to me from Seir, "Watchman, what of the N
21:11 Watchman, what of the N
21:12 watchman says: "Morning comes, and also the N
26:9 for thee in the N, my spirit within me
27:3 it, I guard it N and day;
28:19 by day and by N; and it will be
29:7 be like a dream, a vision of the N
30:29 song as in the N when a holy feast
34:10 N and day it shall not be quenched; its
34:14 yea, there shall the N hag alight, and find
38:12 loom; from day to N thou dost bring me
38:13 bones; from day to N thou dost bring me
60:11 open continually; day and N they shall not be
60:19 light to you by N; but the LORD will
62:6 day and all the N they shall never be
65:4 tombs, and spend the N in secret places; who
Jer 6:5 let us attack by N, and destroy her palaces!"
9:1 might weep day and N for the slain of
14:8 wayfarer who turns aside to tarry for a N
14:17 run down with tears N and day, and let
16:13 other gods day and N, for I will show
31:35 stars for light by N, who stirs up the
33:20 my covenant with the N, so that day and
33:20 so that day and N will not come at
33:25 covenant with day and N and the ordinances of
36:30 the heat by day and the frost by N
39:4 of the city at N by way of the
49:9 If thieves came by N, would they not destroy
52:7 from the city by N by the way of
Lam 1:2 weeps bitterly in the N, tears on her cheeks;
2:18 tears stream down like a torrent day and N
2:19 cry out in the N, at the beginning of
Bar 2:25 the heat of day and the frost of N
Dan 2:19 revealed to Daniel in a vision of the N
5:30 That very N Belshazzar the Chaldean king was slain.
6:18 palace, and spent the N fasting; no diversions were
7:2 in my vision by N, and behold, the four
7:7 I saw in the N visions, and behold, a
7:13 I saw in the N visions, and behold, with
14:15 In the N the priests came with their wives
Hos 4:5 stumble with you by N; and I will destroy
7:7 burn with intrigue; all N their anger smolders; in
Joel 1:12 Go in, pass the N in sackcloth, O ministers
Amos 5:8 darkens the day into N, who calls for the
Obad 1:5 you, if plunderers by N –how you have been
Jon 4:10 into being in a N, and perished in a
4:10 being in a night, and perished in a N
Mic 3:6 Therefore it shall be N to you, without vision,
Zech 1:8 "I saw in the N, and behold, a man
14:7 not day and not N, for at evening time
1Mac 4:1 division moved out by N
4:5 camp of Judas by N, he found no one
5:29 departed from there at N, and they went all
5:50 day and all the N, and the city was
9:58 and he will capture them all in one N
11:6 another and spent the N there.
12:26 in formation to fall upon the Jews by N
12:27 to be ready all N for battle, and he
13:22 to go, but that N a very heavy snow
16:4 and camped for the N in Modein.
2Mac 12:6 to the harbor by N, and burned the boats,
12:9 people of Jamnia by N and set fire to
13:10 the Lord day and N, now if ever to
13:15 the king's pavilion at N and slew as many
Mt 2:14 and his mother by N, and departed to Egypt,
14:25 fourth watch of the N he came to them,
24:43 what part of the N the thief was coming,
26:31 because of me this N; for it is written,
26:34 to you, this very N, before the cock crows,
28:13 'His disciples came by N and stole him away
Mk 4:27 should sleep and rise N and day, and the
5:5 N and day among the tombs and on the
6:48 fourth watch of the N he came to them,
14:30 to you, this very N, before the cock crows
Lk 2:8 the field, keeping watch over their flock by N
2:37 with fasting and prayer N and day.
5:5 "Master, we toiled all N and took nothing!
6:12 to pray; and all N he continued in prayer
12:20 This N your soul is required of you; and
17:34 tell you, in that N there will be two
18:7 his elect, who cry to him day and N
21:37 the temple, but at N he went out and
Jn 3:2 came to Jesus by N and said to him,
9:4 while it is day; N comes, when no one
11:10 one walks in the N, he stumbles, because the
13:30 morsel, he immediately went out; and it was N
19:39 come to him by N, came bringing a mixture
21:3 the boat; but that N they caught nothing.
Acts 5:19 But at N an angel of the Lord opened
9:24 the gates day and N, to kill him;
9:25 disciples took him by N and let him down
12:6 The very N when Herod was about to bring
16:9 to Paul in the N: a man of Macedonia
16:33 same hour of the N, and washed their wounds,
17:10 and Silas away by N to Beroea; and when
18:9 said to Paul one N in a vision, "Do
20:31 I did not cease N or day to admonish
23:11 The following N the Lord stood by him and
23:23 third hour of the N get ready two hundred
23:31 and brought him by N to Antipatris.
26:7 as they earnestly worship N and day.
27:23 For this very N there stood by me an
27:27 When the fourteenth N had come, as we were
Rom 13:12 we first believed; the N is far gone, the
1Cor 11:23 Lord Jesus on the N when he was betrayed
2Cor 11:25 have been shipwrecked; a N and a day I
11:27 through many a sleepless N, in hunger and thirst,
1Thes 2:9 toil, brethren; we worked N and day, that we
3:10 our God, praying earnestly N and day that we
5:2 Lord will come like a thief in the N
5:5 are not of the N or of darkness.
5:7 who sleep sleep at N, and those who get
5:7 and those who get drunk are drunk at N
2Thes 3:8 and labor we worked N and day, that we
1Tim 5:5 in supplications and prayers N and day;
2Tim 1:4 your tears, I long N and day to see
Rev 4:8 within, and day and N they never cease to
7:15 serve him day and N within his temple; and
8:12 from shining, and likewise a third of the N
12:10 accuses them day and N before our God.
14:11 no rest, day or N, these worshipers of the
20:10 be tormented day and N for ever and ever.
21:25 there shall be no N there;
22:5 And N shall be no more; they need no

NIGHTHAWK (2)

Lev 11:16 kind, the ostrich, the N, the sea gull, the
Deut 14:15 kind; the ostrich, the N, the sea gull, the

NIGHTS (21)

Gen 7:4 forty days and forty N; and every living thing
7:12 fell upon the earth forty days and forty N
Ex 24:18 was on the mountain forty days and forty N
34:28 forty days and forty N; he neither ate bread
Deut 9:9 forty days and forty N; I neither ate bread
9:11 forty days and forty N the LORD gave me
9:18 forty days and forty N; I neither ate bread
9:25 forty days and forty N, because the LORD had
10:10 forty days and forty N, and the LORD hearkened
1Sam 30:12 or drunk water for three days and three N
1Kgs 19:8 forty days and forty N to Horeb the mount

N

Tob 10:7 daytime, and throughout the N she never stopped
Job 2:13 seven days and seven N, and no one spoke
7:3 months of emptiness, and N of misery are
Is 21:8 and at my post I am stationed whole N
Dan 3:70 Bless the Lord, N and days, sing praise to
Jon 1:17 belly of the fish three days and three N
2Mac 8:7 He found the N most advantageous for such attacks.
Mt 4:2 forty days and forty N, and afterward he was
12:40 three days and three N in the belly of
12:40 three days and three N in the heart of

NILE (46)

Gen 41:1 was standing by the N,
41:2 up out of the N seven cows sleek and
41:3 up out of the N after them, and stood
41:3 the other cows on the bank of the N
41:17 the banks of the N;
41:18 up out of the N and fed in the
Ex 1:21 shall cast into the N, but you shall let
4:9 some water from the N and pour it upon
4:9 shall take from the N will become blood upon
7:17 that is in the N with the rod that
7:18 the fish in the N shall die, and the
7:18 shall die, and the N shall become foul, and
7:18 Egyptians will loathe to drink water from the N
7:20 that was in the N, and all the water
7:20 that was in the N turned to blood.
7:21 the fish in the N died; and the Nile
7:21 Nile died; and the N became foul, so that
7:21 drink water from the N; and there was blood
7:24 dug round about the N for water to drink,
7:24 they could not drink the water of the N
7:25 days passed after the LORD had struck the N
8:3 country with frogs; the N shall swarm with frogs
8:9 your houses and be left only in the N
8:11 people; they shall be left only in the N
17:5 which you struck the N, and go.
Is 18:2 sends ambassadors by the N, in vessels of papyrus
19:5 the waters of the N will be dried up,
19:6 the branches of Egypt's N will diminish and dry
19:7 bare places by the N, on the brink of
19:7 the brink of the N, and all that is
19:7 is sown by the N will dry up, be
19:8 cast hook in the N; and they will languish
23:3 the harvest of the N; you were the merchant
23:10 your land like the N, O daughter of Tarshish;
Jer 2:18 to Egypt, to drink the waters of the N
46:7 this, rising like the N, like rivers whose waters
46:8 Egypt rises like the N, like rivers whose waters
Ezek 29:3 streams, that says, 'My N is my own; I
29:9 "Because you said, 'The N is mine, and I
30:12 will dry up the N, and will sell the
Amos 8:8 it rise like the N, and be tossed about
8:8 sink again, like the N of Egypt?"
9:5 it rises like the N, and sinks again, like
9:5 sinks again, like the N of Egypt;
Nah 3:8 that sat by the N, with water around her,
Zech 10:11 the depths of the N dried up.

NIMBLE

Sir 36:26 who will trust a N robber that skips from

NIMRAH

Num 32:3 congregation, "Ataroth, Dibon, Jazer, N, Heshbon,

NIMRIM (2)

Is 15:6 destruction; the waters of N are a desolation; the
Jer 48:34 For the waters of N also have become desolate.

NIMROD (4)

Gen 10:8 became the father of N; he was the first
10:9 it is said, "Like N a mighty hunter before
1Chr 1:10 was the father of N; he began to be
Mic 5:6 and the land of N with the drawn sword;

NIMSHI (5)

1Kgs 19:16 Jehu the son of N you shall anoint to
2Kgs 9:2 of Jehoshaphat, son of N; and go in and
9:14 Jehoshaphat the son of N conspired against Joram.
9:20 Jehu the son of N; for he drives furiously."
2Chr 22:7 Jehu the son of N, whom the LORD had

NINE (34)

Gen 5:5 that Adam lived were N hundred and thirty years;
5:8 days of Seth were N hundred and twelve years;
5:11 days of Enosh were N hundred and five years;
5:14 days of Kenan were N hundred and ten years;
5:20 days of Jared were N hundred and sixty-two years;
5:27 days of Methuselah were N hundred and sixty-nine
9:29 days of Noah were N hundred and fifty years;
11:19 Reu two hundred and N years, and had other
Num 29:26 "On the fifth day N bulls, two rams, fourteen
34:13 to give to the N tribes and to the
Deut 3:11 N cubits was its length, and four cubits its
Josh 13:7 an inheritance to the N tribes and half the
14:2 commanded Moses for the N and one-half tribes.
15:44 Keilah, Achzib, and Mareshah: N cities with their
15:54 is, Hebron), and Zior: N cities with their villages.
21:16 with its pasture lands— N cities out of these
Judg 4:3 help; for he had N hundred chariots of iron,
4:13 out all his chariots, N hundred chariots of iron,
2Sam 24:8 at the end of N months and twenty days.
2Kgs 17:1 Israel, and he reigned N years.
1Chr 3:8 Nogah, Nepheg, Japhia, Elishama, Eliada, and
9:9 according to their generations, N hundred and
Ezra 2:8 The sons of Zattu, N hundred and forty-five.
2:36 the house of Jeshua, N hundred and seventy-three.
Neh 7:38 of Senaah, three thousand N hundred and thirty.
7:39 the house of Jeshua, N hundred and seventy-three.
11:1 the holy city, while N tenths remained in the
11:8 after him Gabbai, Sallai, N hundred and
Sir 25:7 With N thoughts I have gladdened my heart, and
2Mac 5:27 Judas Maccabeus, with about N others, got away to
7:27 I carried you N months in my womb, and
8:24 they slew more than N thousand of the enemy,
10:18 When no less than N thousand took refuge in
Lk 17:17 Where are the N

NINETEEN (3)

Gen 11:25 Terah a hundred and N years, and had other
Josh 19:38 Beth-anath, and Beth-shemesh— N cities with their
2Sam 2:30 missing of David's servants N men besides Asahel.

NINETEENTH (4)

2Kgs 25:8 which was the N year of King Nebuchadnezzar,
1Chr 24:16 eighteenth to Happizzez, the N to Pethahiah, the
25:26 brethren, twelve; to the N, to Mallothi, his sons
Jer 52:12 which was the N year of King Nebuchadrezzar,

NINETIETH

2Mac 6:24 that Eleazar in his N year has gone over

NINETY (8)

Gen 5:9 When Enosh had lived N years, he became the
17:17 Shall Sarah, who is N years old, bear a
1Chr 9:6 Zerah: Jeuel and their kinsmen, six hundred and N
Ezek 4:5 days, three hundred and N days, equal to the
4:9 side, three hundred and N days, you shall eat
41:12 about, and its length N cubits.
Dan 12:11 thousand two hundred and N days.
2Mac 8:11 promising to hand over N slaves for a talent,

NINETY-EIGHT (3)

1Sam 4:15 Now Eli was N years old and his eyes
Ezra 2:16 The sons of Ater, namely of Hezekiah, N
Neh 7:21 The sons of Ater, namely of Hezekiah, N

NINETY-FIVE (5)

Gen 5:17 were eight hundred and N years; and he died.
5:30 Noah five hundred and N years, and had other
Ezra 2:20 The sons of Gibbar, N
Neh 7:25 The sons of Gibeon, N
2Mac 12:17 When they had gone N miles from there, they

NINETY-NINE (6)

Gen 17:1 When Abram was N years old the LORD appeared
17:24 Abraham was N years old when he was circumcised
Mt 18:11 he not leave the N on the mountains and
18:12 more than over the N that never went astray.
Lk 15:4 does not leave the N in the wilderness, and
15:7 who repents than over N righteous persons who need

NINETY-SIX (2)

Ezra 8:35 bulls for all Israel, N rams, seventy-seven lambs, and
Jer 52:23 There were N pomegranates on the sides; all the

NINETY-TWO (2)

Ezra 2:58 of Solomon's servants were three hundred and N
Neh 7:60 of Solomon's servants were three hundred and N

NINEVEH (37)

Gen 10:11 into Assyria, and built N, Rehoboth-Ir, Calah, and

	10:12	Calah, and Resen between N and Calah; that is
2Kgs	19:36	Assyria departed, and went home, and dwelt at N
Tob	1:3	me into the land of the Assyrians, to N
	1:10	carried away captive to N, all my brethren and
	1:17	behind the wall of N, I would bury him.
	1:19	of the men of N went and informed the
	1:22	Ahikar interceded for me, and I returned to N
	7:3	the sons of Naphtali, who are captives in N
	11:1	on his way until they came near to N
	11:16	at the gate of N, rejoicing and praising God.
	11:17	there was rejoicing among all his brethren in N
	14:4	the prophet said about N, that it will be
	14:8	now, my son, leave N, because what the prophet
	14:10	do not live in N any longer.
	14:15	of the destruction of N, which Nebuchadnezzar and
	14:15	Before his death he rejoiced over N
Jud	1:1	the great city of N, in the days of
	1:16	returned with them to N, he and all his
	2:21	for three days from N to the plain of
Is	37:37	Assyria departed, and went home and dwelt at N
Jon	1:2	saying, "Arise, go to N, that great city, and
	3:2	saying, "Arise, go to N, that great city, and
	3:3	arose and went to N, according to the word
	3:3	Now N was an exceedingly great city, three days'
	3:4	"Yet forty days, and N shall be overthrown!"
	3:5	And the people of N believed God; they proclaimed
	3:6	reached the king of N, and he arose from
	3:7	proclamation and published through N, "By the
	4:11	should not I pity N, that great city, in
Nah	1:1	An oracle concerning N
	2:8	N is like a pool whose waters run away.
	3:7	and say, Wasted is N; who will bemoan her?
Zeph	2:13	and he will make N a desolation, a dry
Mt	12:41	The men of N will arise at the judgment
Lk	11:30	to the men of N, so will the Son
	11:32	The men of N will arise at the judgment

NINTH (34)

Lev	23:32	afflict yourselves; on the N day of the month
	25:22	old produce; until the N year, when its produce
Num	7:60	On the N day Abidan the son of Gideoni,
2Kgs	17:6	In the N year of Hoshea the king of
	18:10	Hezekiah, which was the N year of Hoshea king
	25:1	And in the N year of his reign, in
	25:3	On the N day of the fourth month the
1Chr	12:12	seventh, Johanan eighth, Elzabad N,
	24:11	eighth to Abijah, the N to Jeshua, the tenth
	25:16	his brethren, twelve; the N to Mattaniah, his sons
	27:12	N, for the ninth month, was Abi-ezer of Anathoth,
	27:12	Ninth, for the N month, was Abi-ezer of Anathoth,
Ezra	10:9	days; it was the N month, on the twentieth
Jer	36:9	of Judah, in the N month, all the people
	36:22	It was the N month, and the king was
	39:1	In the N year of Zedekiah king of Judah,
	39:2	fourth month, on the N day of the month,
	52:4	And in the N year of his reign, in
	52:6	On the N day of the fourth month the
Ezek	24:1	In the N year, in the tenth month, on
Hag	2:10	twenty-fourth day of the N month, in the second
	2:18	twenty-fourth day of the N month.
Zech	7:1	fourth day of the N month, which is Chislev.
1Mac	4:52	twenty-fifth day of the N month, which is the
Mt	20:5	sixth hour and the N hour, he did the
	27:45	the land until the N hour.
	27:46	And about the N hour Jesus cried with a
Mk	15:32	whole land until the N hour.
	15:33	And at the N hour Jesus cried with a
Lk	23:43	whole land until the N hour,
Acts	3:1	hour of prayer, the N hour.
	10:3	About the N hour of the day he saw
	10:30	I was keeping the N hour of prayer in
Rev	21:20	the eighth beryl, the N topaz, the tenth chrysoprase,

NISAN (3)

Neh	2:1	In the month of N, in the twentieth year
Esth	3:7	is the month of N, in the twelfth year
	11:2	the first day of N, Mordecai the son of

NISROCH (2)

2Kgs	19:37	in the house of N his god, Adrammelech and
Is	37:38	in the house of N his god, Adrammelech and

NO-ADIAH (2)

Ezra	8:33	son of Jeshua and N the son of Binnui.
Neh	6:14	and also the prophetess N and the rest of

NOAH (59)

Gen	5:29	and called his name N, saying, "Out of the
	5:30	after the birth of N five hundred and ninety-five
	5:32	After N was five hundred years old, Noah became
	5:32	five hundred years old, N became the father of
	6:8	But N found favor in the eyes of the
	6:9	These are the generations of N
	6:9	N was a righteous man, blameless in his generation;
	6:9	blameless in his generation; N walked with God.
	6:10	And N had three sons, Shem, Ham, and Japheth.
	6:13	And God said to N, "I have determined to
	6:22	N did this; he did all that God commanded
	7:1	the LORD said to N, "Go into the ark,
	7:5	And N did all that the LORD had commanded
	7:6	N was six hundred years old when the flood
	7:7	And N and his sons and his wife and
	7:9	into the ark with N, as God had commanded
	7:9	the ark with Noah, as God had commanded N
	7:11	six hundredth year of N's life, in the second
	7:13	the very same day N and his sons, Shem
	7:13	Ham and Japheth, and N's wife and the three
	7:15	into the ark with N, two and two of
	7:23	Only N was left, and those that were with
	8:1	But God remembered N and all the beasts and
	8:6	end of forty days N opened the window of
	8:11	plucked olive leaf; so N knew that the waters
	8:13	off the earth; and N removed the covering of
	8:15	Then God said to N,
	8:18	So N went forth, and his sons and his
	8:20	Then N built an altar to the LORD, and
	9:1	And God blessed N and his sons, and said
	9:8	Then God said to N and to his sons
	9:17	God said to N, "This is the sign of
	9:18	The sons of N who went forth from the
	9:19	were the sons of N; and from these the
	9:20	N was the first tiller of the soil.
	9:24	When N awoke from his wine and knew what
	9:28	After the flood N lived three hundred and fifty
	9:29	All the days of N were nine hundred and
	10:1	of the sons of N, Shem, Ham, and Japheth;
	10:32	of the sons of N, according to their genealogies,
Num	26:33	of Zelophehad were Mahlah, N, Hoglah, Milcah, and
	27:1	his daughters were: Mahlah, N, Hoglah, Milcah, and
	36:11	Tirzah, Hoglah, Milcah, and N, the daughters of
Josh	17:3	of his daughters: Mahlah, N, Hoglah, Milcah, and
1Chr	1:4	Enoch, Thuselah, Lamech, N, Shem, Ham, and
Tob	4:12	Remember, my son, that N, Abraham, Isaac, and,
Sir	44:18	N was found perfect and righteous; in the time
Is	54:9	like the days of N to me: as I
	54:9	that the waters of N should no more go
Ezek	14:14	if these three men, N, Daniel, and Job, were
	14:20	and beast; even if N, Daniel, and Job were
Mt	24:37	were the days of N, so will be the
	24:38	until the day when N entered the ark,
Lk	3:36	Shem, the son of N, the son of Lamech,
	17:26	in the days of N, so will it be
	17:27	until the day when N entered the ark, and
Heb	11:7	By faith N, being warned by God concerning events
1Pet	3:20	in the days of N, during the building of
2Pet	2:5	world, but preserved N, a herald of righteousness,

NOB (6)

1Sam	21:1	Then came David to N to Ahimelech the priest;
	22:9	of Jesse coming to N, to Ahimelech the son
	22:11	priests who were at N; and all of them
	22:19	And N, the city of the priests, he put
Neh	11:32	and its villages, Anathoth, N, Ananiah,
Is	10:32	he will halt at N, he will shake his

NOBAH (3)

Num	32:42	And N went and took Kenath and its villages,
	32:42	villages, and called it N, after his own name.
Judg	8:11	caravan route east of N and Jogbehah, and attacked

NOBILITY (3)

Is	5:14	beyond measure, and the N of Jerusalem and her
Dan	1:3	family and of the N,
2Mac	6:31	death an example of N and a memorial of

NOBLE (29)

Judg	5:13	the remnant of the N; the people of the
Ezra	4:10	whom the great and N Osnappar deported and
Tob	5:13	of a good and N lineage.
	7:7	of that good and N man!" When he heard
Esth	6:9	of the king's most N princes; let him array
Ps	16:3	land, they are the N, in whom is all

N

Prov 8:6 for I will speak N things, and from my
17:26 not good; to flog N men is wrong.
Wis 8:3 She glorifies her N birth by living with God,
Is 32:5 no more be called N, nor the knave said
32:8 But he who is N devises noble things, and
32:8 who is noble devises N things, and by noble
32:8 noble things, and by N things he stands.
Ezek 17:8 fruit, and become a N vine.
17:23 fruit, and become a N cedar; and under it
2Mac 6:18 in age and of N presence, was being forced
6:28 to the young a N example of how to
7:21 Filled with a N spirit, she fired her woman's
12:42 And the N Judas exhorted the people to keep
14:42 outrages unworthy of his N birth.
15:12 been high priest, a N and good man, of
15:17 words of Judas, so N and so effective in
Lk 21:5 it was adorned with N stones and offerings, he
Acts 17:11 these Jews were more N than those in Thessalonica,
Rom 12:17 thought for what is N in the sight of
1Cor 1:26 not many were of N birth;
1Tim 3:1 bishop, he desires a N task.
2Tim 2:20 earthenware, and some for N use, some for ignoble.
2:21 be a vessel for N use, consecrated and useful

NOBLEMAN (2)
Sir 10:23 The N, and the judge, and the ruler will
Lk 19:12 He said therefore, "A N went into a far

NOBLES (28)
Num 21:18 princes dug, which the N of the people delved,
1Kgs 21:8 the elders and the N who dwelt with Naboth
21:11 the elders and the N who dwelt in his
2Chr 23:20 took the captains, the N, the governors of the
Neh 2:16 Jews, the priests, the N, the officials, and the
3:5 Tekoites repaired; but their N did not put their
4:14 and said to the N and to the officials
4:19 I said to the N and to the officials
5:7 brought charges against the N and the officials.
6:17 in those days the N of Judah sent many
7:5 mind to assemble the N and the officials and
10:29 with their brethren, their N, and enter into a
13:17 I remonstrated with the N of Judah and said
Jud 2:2 officers and all his N and set forth to
Esth 1:3 and Media and the N and governors of the
Job 29:10 the voice of the N was hushed, and their
34:18 'Worthless one,' and to N, 'Wicked man';
Ps 83:11 Make their N like Oreb and Zeeb, all their
149:8 with chains and their N with fetters of iron,
Prov 8:16 me princes rule, and N govern the earth.
Is 13:2 for them to enter the gates of the N
34:11 it, and the plummet of chaos over its N
Jer 14:3 Her N send their servants for water; they come
27:20 Judah, and all the N of Judah and Jerusalem—
39:6 Babylon slew all the N of Judah.
Jon 3:7 the king and his N: Let neither man nor
Nah 3:18 king of Assyria; your N slumber.
1Mac 9:37 one of the great N of Canaan, from Nadabath

NOBLEST
2Mac 4:12 and he induced the N of the young men

NOBLY (7)
1Mac 4:35 live or to die N, he departed to Antioch
2Mac 6:28 good death willingly and N for the revered and
7:5 one another to die N, saying,
7:11 his hands, and said N, "I got these from
8:16 them, but to fight N,
13:14 his men to fight N to the death for
14:42 sword, preferring to die N rather than to fall

NOBODY (2)
Judg 19:18 to my home; and N takes me into his
1Thes 4:12 the respect of outsiders, and be dependent on N

NOD (2)
Gen 4:16 in the land of N, east of Eden.
2Mac 8:18 able with a single N to strike down those

NODAB
1Chr 5:19 Hagrites, Jetur, Naphish, and N;

NOGAH (2)
1Chr 3:7 then Ibhar, Elishama, Eliphelet, N, Nepheg, Japhia,
14:6 Ibhar, Elishu-a, Elpelet, N, Nepheg, Japhia,

NOHAH (2)
Judg 20:43 trod them down from N as far as opposite
1Chr 8:2 second, Aharah the third, N the fourth, and Rapha

NOISE (36)
Ex 32:17 When Joshua heard the N of the people as
32:17 Moses, "There is a N of war in the
1Sam 4:6 the Philistines heard the N of the shouting, they
1Kgs 1:40 so that the earth was split by their N
1:45 This is the N that you have heard.
2Kgs 11:13 When Athaliah heard the N of the guard and
2Chr 23:12 When Athaliah heard the N of the people running
Jud 14:9 and made a joyful N in their city.
Esth 11:5 was his dream: Behold, N and confusion, thunders
Ps 55:3 am distraught by the N of the enemy, because
66:1 Make a joyful N to God, all the earth;
95:1 us make a joyful N to the rock of
95:2 us make a joyful N to him with songs
98:4 Make a joyful N to the LORD, all the
98:6 horn make a joyful N before the King, the
100:1 Make a joyful N to the LORD, all the
Sir 50:16 they made a great N to be heard for
Is 24:8 timbrels is stilled, the N of the jubilant has
25:5 Thou dost subdue the N of the aliens; as
29:6 with earthquake and great N, with whirlwind and
31:4 or daunted at their N, so the LORD of
33:3 At the thunderous N peoples flee, at the lifting
Jer 4:29 At the N of horseman and archer every city
47:3 At the N of the stamping of the hoofs
50:22 The N of battle is in the land, and
51:54 The N of great destruction from the land of
51:55 like many waters, the N of their voice is
Ezek 26:10 will shake at the N of the horsemen and
37:7 prophesied, there was a N, and behold, a rattling;
Dan 10:6 his words like the N of a multitude.
Amos 5:23 away from me the N of your songs; to
1Mac 6:41 All who heard the N made by their multitude,
9:13 was shaken by the N of the armies, and
2Pet 3:10 away with a loud N, and the elements will
Rev 9:9 iron breastplates, and the N of their wings was
9:9 wings was like the N of many chariots with

NOISY (4)
Prov 9:13 A foolish woman is N; she is wanton and
Jer 46:17 Pharaoh, king of Egypt, N one who lets the
Mic 2:12 in its pasture, a N multitude of men.
1Cor 13:1 love, I am a N gong or a clanging

NOMADS
2Mac 12:11 defeated N besought Judas to grant them pledges

NONE (302)
Gen 23:6 choicest of our sepulchres; N of us will withhold
28:17 This is N other than the house of God,
39:11 do his work and N of the men of
41:8 dream, but there was N who could interpret it
41:39 all this, there is N so discreet and wise
Ex 9:14 know that there is N like me in all
12:10 And you shall let N of it remain until
12:22 in the basin; and N of you shall go
15:26 statutes, I will put N of the diseases upon
16:26 day, which is a sabbath, there will be N
16:27 people went out to gather, and they found N
23:15 N shall appear before me empty-handed.
23:26 N shall cast her young or be barren in
34:20 And N shall appear before me empty.
Lev 18:6 N of you shall approach any one near of
18:26 my ordinances and do N of these abominations,
21:1 say to them that N of them shall defile
21:17 Moses, "Say to Aaron, N of your descendants
22:4 N of the line of Aaron who is a
22:30 day, you shall leave N of it until morning:
26:6 shall lie down, and N shall make you afraid;
26:17 you shall flee when N pursues you.
26:36 they shall fall when N pursues.
26:37 escape a sword, though N pursues; and you shall
Num 7:9 of Kohath he gave N, because they were charged
9:12 They shall leave N of it until the morning,
14:22 glory of the LORD, N of the men who
14:23 to their fathers; and N of those who despised
32:11 he swore, saying, 'Surely N of the men who
32:12 not wholly followed me; N except Caleb the son
Deut 2:34 and children; we left N remaining;
7:15 you all sickness; and N of the evil diseases
13:17 N of the devoted things shall cleave to your
23:2 to the tenth generation N of his descendants shall

N

23:3 to the tenth generation N belonging to them shall
32:36 gone, and there is N remaining, bond or free.
32:39 heal; and there is N that can deliver out
33:26 "There is N like God, O Jeshurun, who rides
34:11 knew face to face, N like him for all
Josh 6:1 the people of Israel; N went out, and none
6:1 none went out, and N came in.
8:22 until there was left N that survived or escaped.
10:28 in it, he left N remaining; and he did
10:30 in it; he left N remaining in it; and
10:33 people, until he left N remaining.
10:37 in it; he left N remaining, as he had
10:39 in it; he left N remaining; as he had
10:40 kings; he left N remaining, but utterly destroyed
11:8 them, until they left N remaining.
11:11 destroying them; there was N left that breathed, and
11:13 But N of the cities that stood on mounds
11:22 There was N of the Anakim left in the
Judg 20:8 to his tent, and N of us will return
1Sam 2:2 "There is N holy like the LORD, there is
2:2 the LORD, there is N besides thee; there is
3:19 with him and let N of his words fall
10:24 There is N like him among all the people."
14:24 So N of the people tasted food.
21:9 it, for there is N but that here." And
21:9 David said, "There is N like that; give it
22:8 the son of Jesse, N of you is sorry
2Sam 7:22 God; for there is N like thee, and there
22:42 looked, but there was N to save; they cried
1Kgs 3:12 discerning mind, so that N like you has been
3:12 been before you and N like you shall arise
10:21 were of pure gold; N were of silver, it
12:20 There was N that followed the house of David,
15:22 proclamation to all Judah, N was exempt, and they
21:25 (There was N who sold himself to do what
2Kgs 5:16 LORD lives, whom I serve, I will receive N
6:12 of his servants said, N, my lord, O king;
9:10 territory of Jezreel, and N shall bury her." Then
10:11 until he left him N remaining.
10:14 persons, and he spared N of them.
10:19 all his priests; let N be missing, for I
14:26 bitter, for there was N left, bond or free,
14:26 free, and there was N to help Israel.
17:18 out of his sight; N was left but the
18:5 so that there was N like him among all
24:14 and the smiths; N remained, except the poorest
1Chr 17:20 There is N like thee, O LORD, and there
2Chr 1:12 and honor, such as N of the kings had
1:12 were before you, and N after you shall have
14:11 "O LORD, there is N like thee to help,
14:13 the Ethiopians fell until N remained alive; for they
20:6 and might, so that N is able to withstand
20:24 lying on the ground; N had escaped.
35:18 of Samuel the prophet; N of the kings of
Ezra 8:15 priests, I found there N of the sons of
9:15 in our guilt, for N can stand before thee
Neh 4:23 guard who followed me, N of us took off
Tob 4:17 the righteous, but give N to sinners.
4:19 For N of the nations has understanding; but the
Jud 6:4 For he has spoken; N of his words shall
6:9 I have spoken and N of my words shall
12:3 For N of your people is here with us."
16:14 formed them; there is N that can resist thy
Esth 10:5 concerning these matters, and N of them has failed
Job 1:8 Job, that there is N like him on the
2:3 Job, that there is N like him on the
3:9 for light, but have N, nor see the eyelids
10:7 guilty, and there is N to deliver out of
11:19 will lie down, and N will make you afraid;
12:14 If he tears down, N can rebuild; if he
12:14 shuts a man in, N can open.
18:15 dwells that which is N of his; brimstone is
29:12 the fatherless who had N to help him.
32:12 and, behold, there was N that confuted Job, or
33:13 saying, 'He will answer N of my words'?
35:10 But N says, 'Where is God my Maker, who
Ps 7:2 dragging me away, with N to rescue.
10:15 evildoer; seek out his wickedness till thou find N
14:1 abominable deeds, there is N that does good.
14:3 alike corrupt; there is N that does good, no,
18:41 help, but there was N to save, they cried
22:11 near and there is N to help.
25:3 Yea, let N that wait for thee be put
34:22 life of his servants; N of those who take
40:5 thy thoughts toward us; N can compare with thee!
50:22 rend, and there be N to deliver!
53:1 abominable iniquity; there is N that does good.
53:3 alike depraved; there is N that does good, no,
59:5 all the nations; spare N of those who treacherously
69:20 pity, but there was N; and for comforters, but
69:20 was none; and for comforters, but I found N
71:11 him, for there is N to deliver him."
74:9 prophet, and there is N among us who knows
79:3 Jerusalem, and there was N to bury them.
81:11 voice; Israel would have N of me.
86:8 There is N like thee among the gods, O
105:37 gold, and there was N among his tribes who
107:12 they fell down, with N to help.
109:12 Let there be N to extend kindness to him,
139:16 as yet there was N of them.
142:4 watch, but there is N who takes notice of
Prov 1:25 counsel and would have N of my reproof,
1:30 the LORD, would have N of my counsel, and
2:19 paths to the shades; N who go to her
6:29 to his neighbor's wife; N who touches her will
Song 8:1 would kiss you, and N would despise me.
Wis 2:9 Let N of us fail to share in our
4:3 of no use, and N of their illegitimate seedlings
11:24 and hast loathing for N of the things which
Sir 10:23 will be honored, but N of them is greater
18:3 To N has he given power to proclaim his
27:24 hated many things, but N to be compared to
39:18 him is done, and N can limit his saving
51:7 for the assistance of men, and there was N
Is 1:31 shall burn together, with N to quench them.
5:27 N is weary, none stumbles, none slumbers or sleeps,
5:27 None is weary, N stumbles, none slumbers or sleeps,
5:27 is weary, none stumbles, N slumbers or sleeps, not
5:29 carry it off, and N can rescue.
10:14 earth; and there was N that moved a wing,
13:14 or like sheep with N to gather them, every
17:2 will lie down, and N will make them afraid.
22:22 he shall open, and N shall shut; and he
22:22 he shall shut, and N shall open.
24:10 shut up so that N can enter.
33:1 treacherous one, with whom N has dealt
34:10 it shall lie waste; N shall pass through it
34:16 these shall be missing; N shall be without her
41:17 water, and there is N, and their tongue is
41:26 There was N who declared it, none who proclaimed,
41:26 none who declared it, N who proclaimed, none who
41:26 it, none who proclaimed, N who heard your words.
42:22 become a prey with N to rescue, a spoil
42:22 rescue, a spoil with N to say, "Restore!"
43:13 am He; there is N who can deliver from
45:6 west, that there is N besides me; I am
45:21 a Savior; there is N besides me.
46:9 God, and there is N like me,
51:18 There is N to guide her among all the
51:18 has borne; there is N to take her by
59:11 justice, but there is N; for salvation, but it
Jer 2:6 in a land that N passes through, where no
2:24 N who seek her need weary themselves; in her
4:4 fire, and burn with N to quench it, because
7:33 of the earth; and N will frighten them away.
9:22 after the reaper, and N shall gather them.'"
10:6 There is N like thee, O LORD; thou art
10:7 their kingdoms there is N like thee.
11:23 die by famine; and N of them shall be
13:19 are shut up, with N to open them; all
14:16 famine and sword, with N to bury them--them,
21:12 fire, and burn with N to quench it, because
22:30 in his days; for N of his offspring shall
30:7 so great there is N like it; it is
30:10 quiet and ease, and N shall make him afraid.
30:13 There is N to uphold your cause, no medicine
35:14 kept; and they drink N to this day, for
36:30 Judah, He shall have N to sit upon the
44:14 with pestilence, so that N of the remnant of
46:27 quiet and ease, and N shall make him afraid.
49:5 straight before him, with N to gather the fugitives.
50:3 land a desolation, and N shall dwell in it;
50:20 and there shall be N; and sin in Judah,
50:20 sin in Judah, and N shall be found; for
50:32 stumble and fall, with N to raise him up,
Lam 1:2 her lovers she has N to comfort her; all
1:4 to Zion mourn, for N come to the appointed
1:7 foe, and there was N to help her, the
1:17 hands, but there is N to comfort her; the
1:21 I groan; there is N to comfort me.
2:22 anger of the LORD N escaped or survived; those
4:14 defiled with blood that N could touch their garments.

	5:8	over us; there is N to deliver us from
Bar	6:19	their gods can see N of them.
	6:28	with salt, but give N to the poor or
Ezek	7:11	a rod of wickedness; N of them shall remain,
	7:13	because of his iniquity, N can maintain his life.
	7:14	made all ready; but N goes to battle, for
	7:25	they will seek peace, but there shall be N
	12:28	says the Lord GOD: N of my words will
	16:34	women in your harlotries: N solicited you to play
	18:11	of blood, who does N of these duties, but
	18:22	N of the transgressions which he has committed shall
	18:24	N of the righteous deeds which he has done
	22:30	I should not destroy it; but I found N
	33:13	and commits iniquity, N of his righteous deeds
	33:16	N of the sins that he has committed shall
	33:28	be so desolate that N will pass through.
	34:6	of the earth, with N to search or seek
	34:28	shall dwell securely, and N shall make them afraid.
	39:26	in their land with N to make them afraid,
	39:28	I will leave N of them remaining among the
	46:18	own property, so that N of my people shall
Dan	1:19	and among them all N was found like Daniel,
	2:11	asks is difficult, and N can show it to
	4:35	of the earth; and N can stay his hand
	10:21	of truth: there is N who contends by my
	11:16	his own will, and N shall stand before him;
	11:45	to his end, with N to help him.
	12:10	shall do wickedly; and N of the wicked shall
	13:43	Yet I have done N of the things that
	14:18	there is no deceit, N at all."
Hos	4:4	one contend, and let N accuse, for with you
	5:14	will carry off, and N shall rescue.
	7:8	kings have fallen; and N of them calls upon
	9:12	will bereave them till N is left.
	11:7	to the yoke, and N shall remove it.
Joel	2:27	God and there is N else.
Amos	5:2	on her land, with N to raise her up."
	5:6	and it devour, with N to quench it for
Mic	2:5	Therefore you will have N to cast the line
	4:4	his fig tree, and N shall make them afraid;
	5:8	pieces, and there is N to deliver.
	7:2	earth, and there is N upright among men; they
Nah	2:8	they cry; but N turns back.
	2:11	his cubs were, with N to disturb?
	3:18	on the mountains with N to gather them.
Zeph	2:15	am and there is N else." What a desolation
	3:6	their streets so that N walks in them; their
	3:13	and lie down, and N shall make them afraid."
Zech	7:10	the poor; and let N of you devise evil
	9:8	a guard, so that N shall march to and
	11:6	and I will deliver N from their hand."
Mal	2:15	to yourselves, and let N be faithless to the
1Mac	2:61	generation to generation, that N who put their trust
	7:17	Jerusalem, and there was N to bury them."
	14:7	it; and there was N to oppose him.
	14:12	tree, and there was N to make them afraid.
	14:44	"And N of the people or priests shall be
2Mac	11:31	just as formerly, and N of them shall be
Mt	12:43	through waterless places seeking rest, but he finds N
	26:60	death, but they found N, though many false witnesses
Mk	14:55	to put him to death; but they found N
Lk	1:61	they said to her, N of your kindred is
	3:11	with him who has N; and he who has
	4:26	Elijah was sent to N of them but only
	4:27	the prophet Elisha; and N of them was cleansed,
	7:28	those born of women N is greater than John;
	11:24	seeking rest; and finding N he says, 'I will
	13:6	he came seeking fruit on it and found N
	13:7	fruit on this fig tree, and I find N
	14:24	For I tell you, N of those men who
	16:26	not be able, and N may cross from there
	18:34	But they understood N of these things; this saying
	21:15	mouth and wisdom, which N of your adversaries will
Jn	4:27	with a woman, but N said, "What do you
	7:19	Yet N of you keeps the law.
	16:5	who sent me; yet N of you asks me,
	16:30	all things, and need N to question you; by
	17:12	have guarded them, and N of them is lost
	21:12	Now N of the disciples dared ask him, "Who
Acts	5:13	N of the rest dared join them, but the
	11:19	speaking the word to N except Jews.
	24:22	some liberty, and that N of his friends should
	26:26	I am persuaded that N of these things has
	28:21	Judea about you, and N of the brethren coming
Rom	3:10	as it is written: N is righteous, no, not
	14:7	N of us lives to himself, and none of
	14:7	lives to himself, and N of us dies to
1Cor	1:14	thankful that I baptized N of you except Crispus
	2:8	N of the rulers of this age understood this;
	4:6	what is written, that N of you may be
	7:29	as though they had N,
	14:10	in the world, and N is without meaning;
Gal	1:19	But I saw N of the other apostles except
1Thes	5:15	See that N of you repays evil for evil,
Heb	3:13	that N of you may be hardened by the
1Pet	4:15	But let N of you suffer as a murderer,

NONSENSE

Zech	10:2	For the teraphim utter N, and the diviners see

NOON (17)

Gen	43:16	the men are to dine with me at N
	43:25	for Joseph's coming at N, for they heard that
1Kgs	18:26	Baal from morning until N, saying, "O Baal, answer
	18:27	And at N Elijah mocked them, saying, "Cry aloud,
	20:16	they went out at N, while Ben-hadad was drinking
2Kgs	4:20	on her lap till N, and then he died.
Ps	55:17	and morning and at N I utter my complaint
Song	1:7	it lie down at N; for why should I
Sir	43:3	At N it parches the land; and who can
Is	16:3	at the height of N; hide the outcasts, betray
	59:10	eyes; we stumble at N as in the twilight,
Jer	6:4	against her; up, and let us attack at N
	20:16	and an alarm at N,
Dan	13:7	the people departed at N, Susanna would go into
Amos	8:9	sun go down at N, and darken the earth
Zeph	2:4	be driven out at N, and Ekron shall be
Acts	22:6	near to Damascus, about N a great light from

NOONDAY (9)

Deut	28:29	you shall grope at N, as the blind grope
2Sam	4:5	he was taking his N rest.
Job	5:14	daytime, and grope at N as in the night.
	11:17	be brighter than the N; its darkness will be
Ps	37:6	as the light, and your right as the N
	91:6	in darkness, nor the destruction that wastes at N
Sir	34:16	and a shade from N sun, a guard against
Is	58:10	the darkness and your gloom be as the N
Jer	15:8	men a destroyer at N; I have made anguish

NOONTIDE

Is	38:10	I said, In the N of my days I

NORMAL

Wis	19:20	in water retained its N power, and water forgot

NORTH (151)

Gen	14:15	pursued them to Hobah, N of Damascus.
	28:14	east and to the N and to the south;
Ex	26:20	the tabernacle, on the N side twenty frames,
	26:35	the table on the N side.
	27:11	its length on the N side there shall be
	36:25	the tabernacle, on the N side, he made twenty
	38:11	And for the N side a hundred cubits, their
Lev	1:11	kill it on the N side of the altar
Num	2:25	"On the N side shall be the standard of
	3:35	to encamp on the N side of the tabernacle.
	35:5	cubits, and for the N side two thousand cubits,
Josh	8:11	and encamped on the N side of Ai, with
	8:13	main encampment which was N of the city and
	15:5	the boundary on the N side runs from the
	15:6	Beth-hoglah, and passes along N of Beth-arabah;
	15:11	shoulder of the hill N of Ekron, then the
	16:6	the sea; on the N is Mich-methath; then on
	17:9	Manasseh goes on the N side of the brook
	17:10	and that to the N being Manassehs, with the
	17:10	its boundary; on the N Asher is reached, and
	18:5	house of Joseph in their territory on the N
	18:12	On the N side their boundary began at the
	18:12	up to the shoulder N of Jericho, then up
	18:16	which is at the N end of the valley
	18:18	passing on to the N of the shoulder of
	18:19	passes on to the N of the shoulder of
	19:14	Neah; then on the N the boundary turns about
	19:27	it continues in the N to Cabul,
	24:30	hill country of Ephraim, N of the mountain of
Judg	2:9	hill country of Ephraim, N of the mountain of
	7:1	camp of Midian was N of them, by the
	21:19	at Shiloh, which is N of Bethel, on the
1Sam	14:5	crag rose on the N in front of Michmash,
1Kgs	7:21	the pillar on the N and called its name
	7:25	twelve oxen, three facing N, three facing west, three

7:39 and five on the N side of the house;
7:49 and five on the N, before the inner sanctuary;
2Kgs 11:11 the house to the N side of the house,
16:14 put it on the N side of his altar.
1Chr 9:24 four sides, east, west, N, and south;
26:14 counselor, and his lot came out for the N
26:17 each day, on the N four each day, on
2Chr 3:17 the other on the N; that on the south
3:17 and that on the N Boaz.
4:4 twelve oxen, three facing N, three facing west, three
4:6 and five on the N side.
4:7 on the south side and five on the N
4:8 on the south side and five on the N
23:10 the house to the N side of the house,
Jud 2:21 which is to the N of Upper Cilicia.
16:4 the mountains of the N; he came with myriads
Job 26:7 He stretches out the N over the void, and
37:22 Out of the N comes golden splendor; God is
Ps 48:2 Zion, in the far N, the city of the
89:12 The N and the south, thou hast created them;
107:3 the west, from the N and from the south.
Prov 25:23 The N wind brings forth rain; and a backbiting
Eccl 1:6 goes round to the N; round and round goes
11:3 south or to the N, in the place where
Song 4:16 Awake, O N wind, and come, O south wind!
Sir 43:17 the tempest from the N and the whirlwind.
43:20 The cold N wind blows, and ice freezes over
Is 14:13 assembly in the far N;
14:31 comes out of the N, and there is no
41:25 up one from the N, and he has come,
43:6 will say to the N, Give up, and to
49:12 lo, these from the N and from the west,
Jer 1:13 see a boiling pot, facing away from the N
1:14 me, "Out of the N evil shall break forth
1:15 the kingdoms of the N, says the LORD; and
3:12 these words toward the N, and say, 'Return, faithless
3:18 the land of the N to the land that
4:6 bring evil from the N, and great destruction.
6:1 looms out of the N, and great destruction.
6:22 is coming from the N country, a great nation
10:22 commotion out of the N country to make the
13:20 eyes and see those who come from the N
15:12 iron, iron from the N, and bronze?
16:15 Israel out of the N country and out of
23:8 Israel out of the N country and out of
25:9 the tribes of the N, says the LORD, and
25:26 the kings of the N, far and near, one
31:8 bring them from the N country, and gather them
46:6 warrior escape; in the N by the river Euphrates
46:10 a sacrifice in the N country by the river
46:20 a gadfly from the N has come upon her.
46:24 into the hand of a people from the N
47:2 rising out of the N, and shall become an
50:3 "For out of the N a nation has come
50:9 great nations, from the N country; and they shall
50:41 people comes from the N; a mighty nation and
51:48 them out of the N, says the LORD.
Ezek 1:4 came out of the N, and a great cloud,
8:3 inner court that faces N, where was the seat
8:5 your eyes now in the direction of the N
8:5 my eyes toward the N, and behold, north of
8:5 the north, and behold, N of the altar gate,
8:14 the entrance of the N gate of the house
9:2 upper gate, which faces N, every man with his
16:46 her daughters to the N of you; and your
20:47 faces from south to N shall be scorched by
21:4 flesh from south to N;
23:24 against you from the N with chariots and wagons
26:7 Tyre from the N Nebuchadrezzar king of Babylon,
32:30 "The princes of the N are there, all of
38:6 uttermost parts of the N with all his hordes--
38:15 uttermost parts of the N, you and many peoples
39:2 uttermost parts of the N, and lead you against
40:19 before me to the N,
40:20 which faced toward the N, belonging to the outer
40:23 the gate on the N, as on the east,
40:35 brought me to the N gate, and he measured
40:40 the entrance of the N gate were two tables;
40:44 the side of the N gate facing south, the
40:44 at the side of the south gate facing N
40:46 the chamber which faces N is for the priests
41:11 one door toward the N, and another door toward
42:1 inner court, toward the N, and he brought me
42:1 temple yard and opposite the building on the N
42:2 which was on the N side was a hundred
42:4 cubits long, and their doors were on the N
42:11 the chambers on the N, of the same length
42:13 said to me, "The N chambers and the south
42:17 turned and measured the N side, five hundred cubits
44:4 by way of the N gate to the front
46:9 who enters by the N gate to worship shall
46:9 go out by the N gate: no one shall
46:19 the gate, to the N row of the holy
47:2 by way of the N gate, and led me
47:15 the land: On the N side, from the Great
47:17 Damascus, with the border of Hamath to the N
47:17 This shall be the N side.
48:16 be its dimensions: the N side four thousand five
48:17 open land: on the N two hundred and fifty
48:30 the city: On the N side, which is to
Dan 11:6 the king of the N to make peace; but
11:7 the king of the N, and he shall deal
11:8 shall refrain from attacking the king of the N
11:11 the king of the N; and he shall raise
11:13 the king of the N shall again raise a
11:15 the king of the N shall come and throw
11:40 the king of the N shall rush upon him
11:44 the east and the N shall alarm him, and
Amos 8:12 to sea, and from N to east; they shall
Zeph 2:13 his hand against the N, and destroy Assyria; and
Zech 2:6 the land of the N, says the LORD; for
6:6 horses goes toward the N country, the white ones
6:8 who go toward the N country have set my
6:8 at rest in the N country."
Lk 13:29 and west, and from N and south, and sit
Rev 21:13 three gates, on the N three gates, on the

NORTHEAST

Acts 27:12 harbor of Crete, looking N and southeast, and winter

NORTHEASTER

Acts 27:14 tempestuous wind, called the N, struck down from

NORTHERLY

Josh 18:17 it bends in a N direction going on to

NORTHERN (10)

Num 34:7 "This shall be your N boundary: from the Great
34:9 this shall be your N boundary.
Josh 11:2 who were in the N hill country, and in
15:8 the west, at the N end of the valley
15:10 passes along to the N shoulder of Mount Jearim
18:19 boundary ends at the N bay of the Salt
Ezek 47:17 which is on the N border of Damascus, with
48:1 tribes: Beginning at the N border, from the sea
48:1 (which is on the N border of Damascus over
48:10 thousand cubits on the N side, ten thousand cubits

NORTHERNER

Joel 2:20 "I will remove the N far from you, and

NORTHWARD (8)

Gen 13:14 place where you are, N and southward and eastward
Deut 2:3 about this mountain country long enough; turn N
3:27 your eyes westward and N and southward and
Josh 13:3 is east of Egypt, N to the boundary of
15:7 of Achor, and so N, turning toward Gilgal, which
19:27 the valley of Iphtahel N to Beth-emek and Neiel;
Dan 8:4 ram charging westward and N and southward; no
Zech 14:4 the Mount shall withdraw N, and the other half

NOSE (11)

Gen 24:47 the ring on her N, and the bracelets on
2Kgs 19:28 my hook in your N and my bit in
Job 40:24 hooks, or pierce his N with a snare?
41:2 a rope in his N, or pierce his jaw
Prov 30:33 produces curds, pressing the N produces blood, and
Song 7:4 Your N is like a tower of Lebanon, overlooking
Is 3:21 the signet rings and N rings;
37:29 my hook in your N and my bit in
Ezek 8:17 Lo, they put the branch to their N
16:12 a ring on your N, and earrings in your
23:25 shall cut off your N and your ears, and

NOSES

Ps 115:6 but do not hear; N, but do not smell.

NOSTRILS (16)

Gen 2:7 and breathed into his N the breath of life;
7:22 dry land in whose N was the breath of
Ex 15:8 the blast of thy N the waters piled up,
Num 11:20 comes out at your N and becomes loathsome to

N

2Sam 22:9 went up from his N, and devouring fire from
22:16 at the blast of the breath of his N
Job 27:3 God is in my N;
41:20 Out of his N comes forth smoke, as from
Ps 18:8 went up from his N, and devouring fire from
18:15 at the blast of the breath of thy N
Wis 2:2 the breath in our N is smoke, and reason
15:15 to see with, nor N with which to draw
Is 2:22 from man in whose N is breath, for of
65:5 a smoke in my N, a fire that burns
Lam 4:20 The breath of our N, the LORD's anointed, was
Amos 4:10 go up into your N; yet you did not

NOTABLE (4)
Esth 16:22 good cheer as a N day among your commemorative
Sir 39:2 preserve the discourse of N men and penetrate the
Amos 6:1 mountain of Samaria, the N men of the first
Acts 4:16 For that a N sign has been performed through

NOTE (8)
1Sam 23:23 See therefore, and take N of all the lurking
Ps 10:14 see; yea, thou dost N trouble and vexation, that
Wis 19:18 the rhythm, while each N remains the same.
Jer 5:1 through the streets of Jerusalem, look and take N
Rom 11:22 N then the kindness and the severity of God:
16:7 they are men of N among the apostles, and
16:17 you, brethren, to take N of those who create
2Thes 3:14 say in this letter, N that man, and have

NOTED
Jud 10:7 they saw her, and N how her face was

NOTES (2)
Wis 19:18 on a harp the N vary the nature of
1Cor 14:7 do not give distinct N, how will any one

NOTHING (326)
Gen 11:6 they will do; and N that they propose to
14:24 rich.' I will take N but what the young
19:8 you please; only do N to these men, for
19:22 for I can do N till you arrive there."
26:29 have done to you N but good and have
29:15 my kinsman, should you therefore serve me for N
40:15 also I have done N that they should put
47:18 my lords; there is N left in the sight
Ex 9:4 of Egypt, so that N shall die of all
12:20 You shall eat N leavened; in all your dwellings
16:18 that gathered much had N over, and he that
21:2 the seventh he shall go out free, for N
21:11 shall go out for N, without payment of money.
22:1 restitution; if he has N, then he shall be
Num 6:4 separation he shall eat N that is produced by
11:5 ate in Egypt for N, the cucumbers, the melons,
11:6 up, and there is N at all but this
16:26 wicked men, and touch N of theirs, lest you
20:19 pass through on foot, N more."
22:16 son of Zippor: 'Let N hinder you from coming
23:11 behold, you have done N but bless them."
30:4 bound herself, and says N to her; then all
30:7 of it, and says N to her on the
30:11 of it, and said N to her, and did
30:14 if her husband says N to her from day
30:14 them, because he said N to her on the
Deut 2:7 you; you have lacked N
8:9 which you will lack N, a land whose stones
15:9 and you give him N, and he cry to
20:16 you shall save alive N that breathes,
22:26 woman you shall do N; in the young woman
28:55 eating, because he has N left him, in the
29:23 waste, unsown, and growing N, where no grass can
Josh 2:22 made search all along the way and found N
11:15 Joshua did; he left N undone of all that
Judg 13:4 strong drink, and eat N unclean,
13:7 strong drink, and eat N unclean, for the boy
14:6 kid; and he had N in his hand.
18:7 quiet and unsuspecting, lacking N that is in the
18:9 And will you do N
1Sam 3:18 him everything and hid N from him.
4:7 For N like this has happened before.
14:6 work for us; for N can hinder the LORD
20:2 Behold, my father does N either great or small
20:39 But the lad knew N; only Jonathan and David
22:15 your servant has known N of all this, much
25:7 harm, and they missed N, all the time they
25:21 the wilderness, so that N was missed of all
25:36 so she told him N at all until the
27:1 of Saul; there is N better for me than
28:20 for he had eaten N all day and all
29:6 for I have found N wrong in you from
30:19 N was missing, whether small or great, sons or
2Sam 12:3 the poor man had N but one little ewe
15:11 and they went in their simplicity, and knew N
17:19 grain upon it; and N was known of it.
18:13 life (and there is N hidden from the king),
19:6 commanders and servants are N to you; for today
19:10 why do you say N about bringing the king
24:24 to the LORD my God which cost me N
1Kgs 4:27 his month; they let N be lacking.
8:9 There was N in the ark except the two
10:3 her questions; there was N hidden from the king
17:12 God lives, I have N baked, only a handful
18:43 went up and looked, and said, "There is N
22:16 you speak to me N but the truth in
2Kgs 4:2 said, "Your maidservant has N in the house, except
7:10 seen or heard there, N but the horses tied,
10:10 fall to the earth N of the word of
20:13 his storehouses; there was N in his house or
20:15 my house; there is N in my storehouses that
20:17 be carried to Babylon; N shall be left, says
1Chr 21:24 yours, nor offer burnt offerings which cost me N
2Chr 5:10 There was N in the ark except the two
9:2 her questions; there was N hidden from Solomon
18:15 you speak to me N but the truth in
30:26 Israel there had been N like this in Jerusalem.
Ezra 4:3 to them, "You have N to do with us
Neh 2:2 This is N else but sadness of the heart."
5:12 restore these and require N from them.
8:10 to him for whom N is prepared; for this
9:21 wilderness, and they lacked N; their clothes did not
Tob 1:20 property was confiscated and N was left to me
7:11 said, "I will eat N here until you make
10:7 had left; she ate N in the daytime, and
10:12 daughter to you; do N to grieve her."
Jud 11:5 and I will tell N false to my lord
Esth 2:15 king, she asked for N except what Hegai the
6:3 who attended him said, N has been done for
6:10 Leave out N that you have mentioned."
16:4 of those who know N of goodness they suppose
Job 5:24 and you shall inspect your fold and miss N
8:9 of yesterday, and know N, for our days on
20:21 There was N left after he had eaten; therefore
21:34 There is N left of your answers but falsehood."
22:6 of your brothers for N, and stripped the naked
24:25 show that there is N in what I say?"
26:7 over the void, and hangs the earth upon N
34:9 'It profits a man N that he should take
Ps 19:6 them; and there is N hid from its heat.
39:5 my lifetime is as N in thy sight.
49:17 dies he will carry N away; his glory will
73:25 And there is N upon earth that I desire
101:4 me; I will know N of evil.
119:165 who love thy law; N can make them stumble.
Prov 3:15 precious than jewels, and N you desire can compare
8:8 are righteous; there is N twisted or crooked in
13:4 sluggard craves, and gets N, while the soul of
13:7 be rich, yet has N; another pretends to be
20:4 autumn; he will seek at harvest and have N
22:27 If you have N with which to pay, why
29:24 own life; he hears the curse, but discloses N
Eccl 1:9 done; and there is N new under the sun.
2:11 wind, and there was N to be gained under
2:24 There is N better for a man than that
3:12 know that there is N better for them than
3:14 does endures for ever; N can be added to
3:22 saw that there is N better than that a
5:14 son, but he has N in his hand.
5:15 came, and shall take N for his toil, which
6:2 so that he lacks N of all that he
9:5 but the dead know N, and they have no
Wis 4:5 not ripe enough to eat, and good for N
7:8 I accounted wealth as N in comparison with her.
7:25 of the Almighty; therefore N defiled gains entrance
7:28 prophets; for God loves N so much as the
8:7 prudence, justice and courage; N in life is more
9:6 comes from thee he will be regarded as N
13:13 among them, useful for N, a stick crooked and
17:6 N was shining through to them except a dreadful,
17:9 For even if N disturbing frightened them, yet, scared
17:12 For fear is N but surrender of the helps
Sir 6:15 There is N so precious as a faithful friend,
8:16 because blood is as N in his sight, and
8:18 of a stranger do N that is to be

18:21 Let N hinder you from paying a vow promptly,
18:32 money, when you have N in your purse.
19:7 and you will lose N at all.
20:9 gift that profits you N, and there is a
20:13 gift will profit you N, for he has many
23:27 her will recognize that N is better than the
23:27 of the Lord, and N sweeter than to heed
25:3 You have gathered N in your youth; how then
26:14 Lord, and there is N so precious as a
32:19 Do N without deliberation; and when you have acted,
33:29 toward anybody, and do N without discretion.
39:19 are before him, and N can be hid from
39:20 he beholds them, and N is marvelous to him.
40:7 up, and wonders that his fear came to N
42:21 N can be added or taken away, and he
42:24 and he has made N incomplete.
48:13 N was too hard for him, and when he
Is 10:4 N remains but to crouch among the prisoners or
19:15 And there will be N for Egypt which head
34:12 Kingdom There, and all its princes shall be N
39:2 There was N in his house or in all
39:4 my house; there is N in my storehouses that
39:6 be carried to Babylon; N shall be left, says
40:17 the nations are as N before him, they are
40:17 him as less than N and emptiness.
40:23 and makes the rulers of the earth as N
41:11 you shall be as N and shall perish.
41:12 you shall be as N at all.
41:24 Behold, you are N, and your work is nought;
41:29 delusion; their works are N; their molten images are
44:9 who make idols are N, and the things they
44:10 or casts an image, that is profitable for N
47:11 come on you suddenly, of which you know N
49:4 spent my strength for N and vanity; yet surely
52:3 "You were sold for N, and you shall be
52:4 sojourn there, and the Assyrian oppressed them for N
52:5 seeing that my people are taken away for N
Jer 5:12 said, 'He will do N; no evil will come
6:6 be punished; there is N but oppression within her.
10:24 in thy anger, lest thou bring me to N
12:13 thorns, they have tired themselves out but profit N
13:7 the waistcloth was spoiled; it was good for N
13:10 be like this waistcloth, which is good for N
22:13 neighbor serve him for N, and does not give
30:14 forgotten you; they care N for you; for I
32:17 N is too hard for thee,
32:23 thy law; they did N of all thou didst
32:30 of Judah have done N but evil in my
32:30 of Israel have done N but provoke me to
38:5 the king can do N against you."
38:14 you a question; hide N from me."
38:25 said to you; hide N from us and we
39:10 poor people who owned N, and gave them vineyards
42:4 you; I will keep N back from you."
48:38 the squares there is N but lamentation; for I
50:26 destroy her utterly; let N be left of her.
51:62 it off, so that N shall dwell in it,
Lam 1:12 "Is it N to you, all you who pass
Bar 6:45 goldsmiths; they can be N but what the craftsmen
6:70 cucumber bed, that guards N, so are their gods
Ezek 13:3 who follow their own spirit, and have seen N
15:5 it was used for N; how much less, when
31:8 plane trees were as N compared with its branches;
44:17 garments; they shall have N of wool on them,
Dan 4:35 earth are accounted as N; and he does according
6:17 of his lords, that N might be changed concerning
9:26 off, and shall have N; and the people of
13:27 were greatly ashamed, for N like this had ever
13:63 all her kindred, because N shameful was found in
14:35 Babylon, and I know N about the den."
Joel 2:3 a desolate wilderness, and N escapes them.
Amos 3:4 out from his den, if he has taken N
3:5 up from the ground, when it has taken N
3:7 the Lord GOD does N, without revealing his secret
Mic 3:5 against him who puts N into their mouths.
Zeph 3:3 evening wolves that leave N till the morning.
Hag 2:3 Is it not in your sight as N
2:19 the pomegranate, and the olive tree still yield N
1Mac 3:17 for we have eaten N today."
2Mac 7:12 man's spirit, for he regarded his sufferings as N
12:4 live peaceably and suspected N, the men of Joppa
14:23 in Jerusalem and did N out of the way,
14:35 who hast need of N, thou wast pleased that
Mt 8:4 "See that you say N to any one; but
10:26 fear of them; for N is covered that will
13:34 parables; indeed he said N to them without a
15:32 three days, and have N to eat; and I
17:20 it will move; and N will be impossible to
21:19 to it, and found N on it but leaves
23:15 the temple, it is N; but if any one
23:17 the altar, it is N; but if any one
27:19 word to him, "Have N to do with that
27:24 that he was gaining N, but rather that a
Mk 1:44 "See that you say N to any one; but
4:22 For there is N hid, except to be made
6:8 charged them to take N for their journey except
7:15 and understand: there is N outside a man which
8:1 gathered, and they had N to eat, he called
8:2 three days, and have N to eat;
11:13 to it, he found N but leaves, for it
14:51 man followed him, with N but a linen cloth
16:8 them; and they said N to any one, for
Lk 1:37 For with God N will be impossible."
4:2 And he ate N in those days; and when
5:5 answered, "Master, we toiled all night and took N
6:35 good, and lend, expecting N in return; and your
8:17 For N is hid that shall not be made
9:3 said to them, "Take N for your journey, no
10:19 of the enemy; and N shall hurt you.
11:6 journey, and I have N to set before him';
12:2 N is covered up that will not be revealed,
22:35 They said, N
23:15 Behold, N deserving death has been done by him;
23:40 this man has done N wrong."
Jn 4:11 him, "Sir, you have N to draw with, and
5:13 Sin no more, that N worse befall you."
5:18 the Son can do N of his own accord,
5:29 "I can do N on my own authority; as
6:12 fragments left over, that N may be lost."
6:39 that I should lose N of all that he
7:26 openly, and they say N to him!
8:28 and that I do N on my own authority
8:44 the beginning, and has N to do with the
8:54 myself, my glory is N; it is my Father
9:33 man were not from God, he could do N
10:13 a hireling and cares N for the sheep.
11:49 to them, "You know N at all;
12:19 that you can do N; look, the world has
15:5 fruit, for apart from me you can do N
16:23 day you will ask N of me.
16:24 Hitherto you have asked N in my name; ask,
18:20 together; I have said N secretly.
21:3 into the boat; but that night they caught N
Acts 4:14 beside them, they had N to say in opposition.
5:36 who followed him were dispersed and came to N
8:24 to the Lord, that N of what you have
9:8 opened, he could see N; so they led him
11:8 said, 'No, Lord; for N common or unclean has
13:28 could charge him with N deserving death, yet they
17:21 spent their time in N except telling or hearing
19:27 Artemis may count for N, and that she may
19:36 be quiet and do N rash.
21:24 know that there is N in what they have
23:9 and contended, "We find N wrong in this man.
23:29 charged with N deserving death or imprisonment.
25:11 but if there is N in their charges against
25:25 that he had done N deserving death; and as
25:26 But I have N definite to write to my
26:22 small and great, saying N but what the prophets
26:31 "This man is doing N to deserve death or
27:33 in suspense and without food, having taken N
28:17 though I had done N against the people or
Rom 7:18 For I know that N good dwells within me,
9:11 born and had done N either good or bad,
14:14 the Lord Jesus that N is unclean in itself;
1Cor 1:28 not, to bring to N things that are,
2:2 I decided to know N among you except Jesus
11:22 church of God and humiliate those who have N
13:2 remove mountains, but have not love, I am N
13:3 be burned, but have not love, I gain N
2Cor 1:13 For we write you N but what you can
6:10 many rich; as having N, and yet possessing
6:17 the Lord, and touch N unclean; then I will
8:15 who gathered much had N over, and he who
9:4 be humiliated–to say N of you–for being
12:1 must boast; there is N to be gained by
12:11 to these superlative apostles, even though I am N
Gal 2:6 were of repute added N to me;
6:3 something, when he is N, he deceives himself.
Phil 2:3 Do N from selfishness or conceit, but in humility
2Thes 3:14 that man, and have N to do with him,
1Tim 4:4 God is good, and N is to be rejected

4:7 Have N to do with godless and silly myths.
5:21 rules without favor, doing N from partiality.
6:4 with conceit, he knows N; he has a morbid
6:7 contentment; for we brought N into the world, and
2Tim 2:23 Have N to do with stupid, senseless controversies;
Tit 1:14 the corrupt and unbelieving N is pure; their very
2:8 put to shame, having N evil to say of
3:10 once or twice, have N more to do with
3:13 Apollos on their way; see that they lack N
Philem 1:14 I preferred to do N without your consent in
1:19 repay it--to say N of your owing me
Heb 2:8 to him, he left N outside his control.
7:14 that tribe Moses said N about priests.
7:19 (for the law made N perfect); on the other
Jas 1:4 you may be perfect and complete, lacking in N
1Pet 3:6 do right and let N terrify you.
3Jn 1:7 sake and have accepted N from the heathen.
Rev 3:17 prospered, and I need N; not knowing that you
21:27 But N unclean shall enter it, nor any one

NOTHINGS
Job 21:34 How then will you comfort me with empty N

NOTICE (13)
Ruth 2:10 that you should take N of me, when I
2:19 the man who took N of you." So she
2Sam 3:36 all the people took N of it, and it
Ps 142:4 is none who takes N of me; no refuge
Wis 1:8 unrighteous things will escape N, and justice, when it
Sir 23:18 High will not take N of my sins."
Bar 6:20 They do not N
Dan 14:19 at the floor, and N whose footsteps these are."
Mt 7:3 eye, but do not N the log that is
Lk 6:41 eye, but do not N the log that is
Acts 21:26 the temple, to give N when the days of
23:15 with the council, give N now to the tribune
26:26 things has escaped his N, for this was not

NOTICED (2)
2Mac 14:26 But when Alcimus N their good will for one
Acts 27:39 the land, but they N a bay with a

NOTICES
Sir 19:24 but where no one N, he will forestall you.

NOTICING
2Mac 14:30 But Maccabeus, N that Nicanor was more austere in

NOTIFY (2)
Ezra 7:24 We also N you that it shall not be
2Mac 1:18 thought it necessary to N you, in order that

NOTION
2Mac 3:32 king might get the N that some foul play

NOTORIOUS (3)
Sir 42:11 in the city and N among the people, and
2Mac 13:6 guilty of sacrilege or N for other crimes.
Mt 27:16 they had then a N prisoner, called Barabbas.

NOTWITHSTANDING
Num 26:11 N, the sons of Korah did not die.

NOUGHT (18)
Job 1:9 answered the LORD, "Does Job fear God for N
Ps 33:10 of the nations to N; he frustrates the plans
39:6 Surely for N are they in turmoil; man heaps
112:10 the desire of the wicked man comes to N
Prov 10:28 but the expectation of the wicked comes to N
11:7 and the expectation of the godless comes to N
Is 8:10 it will come to N; speak a word, but
29:20 ruthless shall come to N and the scoffer cease,
40:23 who brings princes to N, and makes the rulers
41:24 and your work is N; an abomination is he
Jer 16:19 "Our fathers have inherited N but lies, worthless
51:58 The peoples labor for N, and the nations weary
Ezek 12:22 days grow long, and every vision comes to N
32:12 "They shall bring to N the pride of Egypt,
Dan 3:96 him, and set at N the king's command, and
Hos 12:11 shall surely come to N; if in Gilgal they
Amos 5:5 go into exile, and Bethel shall come to N
Hab 2:13 only for fire, and nations weary themselves for N

NOURISH
Zech 11:16 heal the maimed, or N the sound, but devours

NOURISHED (5)
Ezek 31:4 The waters N it, the deep made it grow
Col 2:19 whom the whole body, N and knit together through
1Tim 4:6 minister of Christ Jesus, N on the words of
Rev 12:6 in which to be N for one thousand two
12:14 she is to be N for a time, and

NOURISHER
Ruth 4:15 of life and a N of your old age;

NOURISHES (2)
Is 44:14 cedar and the rain N it.
Eph 5:29 his own flesh, but N and cherishes it, as

NOWADAYS
1Sam 25:10 There are many servants N who are breaking away

NOWHERE (6)
2Kgs 5:25 And he said, "Your servant went N
Wis 17:10 the air, though it N could be avoided.
Mt 8:20 Son of man has N to lay his head."
10:5 out, charging them, "Go N among the Gentiles, and
Lk 9:58 Son of man has N to lay his head."
12:17 do, for I have N to store my crops?'

NULL (3)
Num 30:12 her husband makes them N and void on the
30:15 if he makes them N and void after he
Rom 4:14 the heirs, faith is N and the promise is

NULLIFIES
1Mac 14:45 to these decisions or N any of them shall

NULLIFY (3)
1Mac 14:44 shall be permitted to N any of these decisions
Rom 3:3 Does their faithlessness N the faithfulness of God?
Gal 2:21 I do not N the grace of God; for

NUMBER (245)
Gen 15:5 "Look toward heaven, and N the stars, if you
15:5 you are able to N them." Then he said
47:12 food, according to the N of their dependents.
Ex 5:8 But the N of bricks which they made heretofore
5:18 shall deliver the same N of bricks."
5:19 means lessen your daily N of bricks."
12:4 take according to the N of persons; according to
16:16 apiece, according to the N of the persons whom
23:26 I will fulfil the N of your days.
30:12 the LORD when you N them, that there be
30:12 among them when you N them.
Lev 25:15 According to the N of years after the jubilee,
25:15 and according to the N of years for crops
25:16 for it is the N of the crops that
25:50 be according to the N of years; the time
26:22 make you few in N, so that your ways
Num 1:2 houses, according to the N of names, every male,
1:3 you and Aaron shall N them, company by company.
1:18 houses, according to the N of names from twenty
1:20 houses, according to the N of names, head by
1:21 forth to war: the N of the tribe of
1:22 numbered, according to the N of names, head by
1:23 forth to war: the N of the tribe of
1:24 houses, according to the N of the names, from
1:25 forth to war: the N of the tribe of
1:26 houses, according to the N of names, from twenty
1:27 forth to war: the N of the tribe of
1:28 houses, according to the N of names, from twenty
1:29 forth to war: the N of the tribe of
1:30 houses, according to the N of names, from twenty
1:31 forth to war: the N of the tribe of
1:32 houses, according to the N of names, from twenty
1:33 forth to war: the N of the tribe of
1:34 houses, according to the N of names, from twenty
1:35 forth to war: the N of the tribe of
1:36 houses, according to the N of names, from twenty
1:37 forth to war: the N of the tribe of
1:38 houses, according to the N of names, from twenty
1:39 forth to war: the N of the tribe of
1:40 houses, according to the N of names, from twenty
1:41 forth to war: the N of the tribe of
1:42 houses, according to the N of names, from twenty
1:43 forth to war: the N of the tribe of
1:45 So the whole N of the people of Israel,
1:46 Israel-- their whole N was six hundred and
1:49 Levi you shall not N, and you shall not
2:9 The whole N of the camp of Judah, by

	2:16	The whole N of the camp of Reuben, by
	2:24	The whole N of the camp of Ephraim, by
	2:31	The whole N of the camp of Dan is
	3:15	the wilderness of Sinai, N the sons of Levi,
	3:15	from a month old and upward you shall N
	3:22	Their N according to the number of all the
	3:22	number according to the N of all the males
	3:28	According to the N of all the males, from
	3:34	Their N according to the number of all the
	3:34	number according to the N of all the males
	3:40	LORD said to Moses, N all the first-born males
	3:40	and upward, taking their N by names.
	3:43	males, according to the N of names, from a
	3:46	over and above the N of the male Levites,
	3:48	by which the excess N of them is redeemed
	4:23	years old, you shall N them, all who can
	4:29	of Merari, you shall N them by their families
	4:30	years old, you shall N them, every one that
	4:36	of meeting; and their N by families was two
	4:37	This was the N of the families of the
	4:38	The N of the sons of Gershon, by their
	4:40	of meeting-- their N by their families and
	4:41	This was the N of the families of the
	4:42	The N of the families of the sons of
	4:44	of meeting-- their N by families was three
	11:21	among whom I am N six hundred thousand on
	14:29	and of all your N, numbered from twenty years
	14:34	According to the N of the days in which
	15:12	According to the N that you prepare, so shall
	15:12	you do with every one according to their N
	16:2	before Moses, with a N of the people of
	22:15	sent princes, more in N and more honorable than
	23:10	dust of Jacob, or N the fourth part of
	26:7	Reubenites; and their N was forty-three thousand
	26:18	Gad according to their N, forty thousand five
	26:22	Judah according to their N, seventy-six thousand five
	26:25	Issachar according to their N, sixty-four thousand
	26:27	Zebulunites according to their N, sixty thousand five
	26:34	of Manasseh; and their N was fifty-two thousand
	26:37	Ephraim according to their N, thirty-two thousand
	26:41	their families; and their N was forty-five thousand six
	26:43	Shuhamites, according to their N, were sixty-four
	26:47	Asher according to their N, fifty-three thousand four
	26:50	their families; and their N was forty-five thousand
	26:51	This was the N of the people of Israel,
	26:53	inheritance according to the N of names.
	29:18	for the lambs, by N, according to the ordinance;
	29:21	for the lambs, by N, according to the ordinance;
	29:24	for the lambs, by N, according to the ordinance;
	29:27	for the lambs, by N, according to the ordinance;
	29:30	for the lambs, by N, according to the ordinance;
	29:33	for the lambs, by N, according to the ordinance;
	29:37	for the lambs, by N, according to the ordinance;
	31:36	to war, was in N three hundred and thirty-seven
Deut	4:27	be left few in N among the nations where
	7:7	you were more in N than any other people
	25:2	his presence with a N of stripes in proportion
	26:5	sojourned there, few in N; and there he became
	28:62	be left few in N; because you did not
	32:8	peoples according to the N of the sons of
Josh	4:5	shoulder, according to the N of the tribes of
	4:8	Jordan, according to the N of the tribes of
	11:4	a great host, in N like the sand that
Judg	6:5	coming like locusts for N; both they and their
	7:6	And the N of those that lapped, putting their
	7:12	their camels were without N, as the sand which
	18:2	men from the whole N of their tribe, from
	21:23	wives, according to their N, from the dancers whom
1Sam	6:4	mice, according to the N of the lords of
	6:18	mice, according to the N of all the cities
	14:17	who were with him, N and see who has
	18:27	were given in full N to the king, that
	27:7	And the N of the days that David dwelt
2Sam	2:15	and passed over by N, twelve for Benjamin and
	21:20	each foot, twenty-four in N; and he also was
	24:1	against them, saying, "Go, N Israel and Judah."
	24:2	Dan to Beer-sheba, and N the people, that I
	24:2	I may know the N of the people."
	24:4	of the king to N the people of Israel.
1Kgs	18:31	stones, according to the N of the tribes of
1Chr	7:2	of their generations, their N in the days of
	7:40	Their N enrolled by genealogies, for service in war,
	16:19	they were few in N, and of little account,
	20:6	each foot, twenty-four in N; and he also was
	21:1	and incited David to N Israel.
	21:2	of the army, "Go, N Israel, from Beer-sheba to
	21:2	me a report, that I may know their N
	21:17	who gave command to N the people?
	22:4	and cedar timbers without N; for the Sidonians and
	22:15	kinds of craftsmen without N, skilled in working
	23:24	registered according to the N of the names of
	23:27	David these were the N of the Levites from
	23:31	days, according to the N required of them,
	25:7	The N of them along with their brethren, who
	27:23	David did not N those below twenty years of
	27:24	of Zeruiah began to N, but did not finish;
	27:24	for this, and the N was not entered in
2Chr	12:3	the people were without N who came with him
	26:12	The whole N of the heads of fathers' houses
	28:5	took captive a great N of his people and
	29:32	The N of the burnt offerings which the assembly
	29:35	Besides the great N of burnt offerings there was
	30:3	sanctified themselves in sufficient N, nor had the
	35:7	the flock to the N of thirty thousand, and
Ezra	1:9	And this was the N of them: a thousand
	2:2	The N of the men of the people of
	3:4	daily burnt offerings by N according to the ordinance,
	6:17	he-goats, according to the N of the tribes of
Neh	7:7	The N of the men of the people of
Jud	2:5	their strength, to the N of one hundred and
	2:17	He collected a vast N of camels and asses
	7:18	spread out in great N, and they formed a
	10:17	They chose from their N a hundred men to
Esth	5:11	of his riches, the N of his sons, all
	9:11	That very day the N of those slain in
Job	1:5	offerings according to the N of them all; for
	3:6	not come into the N of the months.
	5:9	unsearchable, marvelous things without N:
	9:10	understanding, and marvelous things without N
	14:5	are determined, and the N of his months is
	14:16	For then thou wouldest N my steps, thou wouldest
	21:21	after them, when the N of their months is
	25:3	Is there any N to his armies?
	31:4	see my ways, and N all my steps?
	36:26	know him not; the N of his years is
	38:21	born then, and the N of your days is
	38:37	Who can N the clouds by wisdom?
	39:2	Can you N the months that they fulfil, and
Ps	40:12	have encompassed me without N; my iniquities have
	48:12	go round about her, N her towers,
	69:4	More in N than the hairs of my head
	71:15	the day, for their N is past my knowledge.
	90:12	So teach us to N our days that we
	105:12	they were few in N, of little account, and
	105:34	and young locusts without N;
	147:4	He determines the N of the stars, he gives
Song	6:8	and eighty concubines, and maidens without N
Wis	4:8	time, nor measured by N of years;
	11:20	things by measure and N and weight.
Sir	18:8	The N of a man's days is great if
	26:1	a good wife; the N of his days will
	37:25	days, but the days of Israel are without N
	38:29	his work, and all his output is by N
	42:7	let it be by N and weight, and make
	45:11	letters, according to the N of the tribes of
	48:2	by his zeal he made them few in N
	48:15	left very few in N, but with rulers from
Is	40:26	out their host by N, calling them all by
Jer	2:32	Yet my people have forgotten me days without N
	15:8	their widows more in N than the sand of
	44:28	of Judah, few in N; and all the remnant
	46:23	are more numerous than locusts; they are without N
	52:28	This is the N of the people whom Nebuchadrezzar
Bar	2:13	are left, few in N, among the nations where
	2:29	turn into a small N among the nations, where
Ezek	4:4	upon you; for the N of the days that
	4:5	assign to you a N of days, three hundred
	4:5	days, equal to the N of the years of
	4:9	During the N of days that you lie upon
	5:3	from these a small N, and bind them in
	20:37	and I will let you go in by N
Dan	9:2	in the books the N of years which, according
Hos	1:10	Yet the N of the people of Israel shall
Joel	1:6	land, powerful and without N; its teeth are lions'
1Mac	2:38	and cattle, to the N of a thousand persons.
	6:30	The N of his forces was a hundred thousand
	9:6	they saw the huge N of the enemy forces,
	10:36	king's forces to the N of thirty thousand men,
	10:37	be of their own N, and let them live
	10:85	The N of those who fell by the sword,
	11:45	the city, to the N of a hundred and
2Mac	2:21	that though few in N they seized the whole

8:16 men together, to the N six thousand, and exhorted
10:24 collected the cavalry from Asia in no small N
Lk 22:3 who was of the N of the twelve;
Jn 6:10 men sat down, in N about five thousand.
Acts 2:47 Lord added to their N day by day those
4:4 word believed; and the N of the men came
5:36 be somebody, and a N of men, about four
6:1 disciples were increasing in N, the Hellenists
6:7 God increased; and the N of the disciples multiplied
11:21 them, and a great N that believed turned to
19:19 And a N of those who practiced magic arts
27:7 sailed slowly for a N of days, and arrived
Rom 9:27 concerning Israel: "Though the N of the sons of
11:25 Israel, until the full N of the Gentiles come
Heb 7:23 priests were many in N, because they were
Rev 6:11 little longer, until the N of their fellow servants
7:4 And I heard the N of the sealed, a
7:9 which no man could N, from every nation, from
9:16 The N of the troops of cavalry was twice
9:16 ten thousand times ten thousand; I heard their N
13:17 the beast or the N of its name.
13:18 has understanding reckon the N of the beast, for
13:18 it is a human N, its number is six
13:18 a human number, its N is six hundred and
15:2 its image and the N of its name, standing
20:8 them for battle; their N is like the sand

NUMBERED (73)

Gen 16:10 that they cannot be N for multitude."
32:12 sea, which cannot be N for multitude.'"
46:15 sons and his daughters N thirty-three).
Ex 30:13 Each who is N in the census shall give
30:14 Every one who is N in the census, from
38:25 the congregation who were N was a hundred talents
38:26 every one who was N in the census, from
Num 1:19 So he N them in the wilderness of Sinai.
1:22 of them that were N, according to the number
1:44 are those who were N, whom Moses and Aaron
1:44 whom Moses and Aaron N with the help of
1:47 the Levites were not N by their ancestral tribe
2:4 Amminadab, his host as N being seventy-four
2:6 Zuar, his host as N being fifty-four thousand four
2:8 Helon, his host as N being fifty-seven thousand four
2:11 Shedeur, his host as N being forty-six thousand five
2:13 Zurishaddai, his host as N being fifty-nine thousand
2:15 Reuel, his host as N being forty-five thousand six
2:19 Ammihud, his host as N being forty thousand five
2:21 Pedahzur, his host as N being thirty-two thousand
2:23 Gideoni, his host as N being thirty-five thousand four
2:26 Ammishaddai, his host as N being sixty-two thousand
2:28 Ochran, his host as N being forty-one thousand five
2:30 Enan, his host as N being fifty-three thousand four
2:32 people of Israel as N by their fathers' houses;
2:32 the camps who were N by their companies were
2:33 the Levites were not N among the people of
3:16 So Moses N them according to the word of
3:39 All who were N of the Levites, whom Moses
3:39 whom Moses and Aaron N at the commandment of
3:42 So Moses N all the first-born among the people
3:43 old and upward as N were twenty-two thousand two
4:34 leaders of the congregation N the sons of the
4:37 whom Moses and Aaron N according to the
4:41 Moses and Aaron N according to the commandment
4:45 are those who were N of the families of
4:45 whom Moses and Aaron N according to the
4:46 All those who were N of the Levites, whom
4:46 the leaders of Israel N, by their families and
4:48 meeting, those who were N of them were eight
4:49 carrying; thus they were N by him, as the
7:2 over those who were N,
14:29 of all your number, N from twenty years old
26:57 are the Levites as N according to their families:
26:62 And those N of them were twenty-three thousand,
26:62 for they were not N among the people of
26:63 These were those N by Moses and Eleazar the
26:63 Eleazar the priest, who N the people of Israel
26:64 a man of those N by Moses and Aaron
26:64 the priest, who had N the people of Israel
1Sam 13:15 And Saul N the people who were present with
14:17 And when they had N, behold, Jonathan and his
15:4 summoned the people, and N them in Telaim, two
2Sam 24:10 him after he had N the people.
1Kgs 3:8 people, that cannot be N or counted for multitude.
5:13 Israel; and the levy N thirty thousand men.
8:5 oxen that they could not be counted or N
1Chr 23:3 old and upward, were N, and the total was
2Chr 5:6 oxen that they could not be counted or N
Ps 40:5 them, they would be more than can be N
Eccl 1:15 made straight, and what is lacking cannot be N
Wis 5:5 Why has he been N among the sons of
Sir 37:25 of a man is N by days, but the
41:13 a good life are N, but a good name
Is 53:12 to death, and was N with the transgressors; yet
Jer 33:22 of heaven cannot be N and the sands of
Lam 4:18 near; our days were N; for our end had
Dan 5:26 matter: MENE, God has N the days of your
Hos 1:10 be neither measured nor N; and in the place
1Mac 2:18 your sons will be N among the friends of
Mt 10:30 even the hairs of your head are all N
Lk 12:7 even the hairs of your head are all N
Acts 1:17 For he was N among us, and was allotted

NUMBERING (6)

2Sam 24:9 the sum of the N of the people to
1Chr 21:5 the sum of the N of the people to
21:6 and Benjamin in the N, for the king's command
27:1 the year, each division N twenty-four thousand:
Mk 5:13 swine; and the herd, N about two thousand, rushed
Rev 5:11 voice of many angels, N myriads of myriads and

NUMBERS (17)

Gen 34:30 and the Perizzites; my N are few, and if
Num 26:54 shall be given its inheritance according to its N
1Chr 12:23 These are the N of the divisions of the
2Chr 15:9 with them, for great N had deserted to him
20:25 found cattle in great N, goods, clothing, and precious
26:11 divisions according to the N in the muster made
30:5 kept it in great N as prescribed.
30:24 And the priests sanctified themselves in great N
Jud 7:4 Israelites saw their vast N they were greatly
9:11 power depends not upon N, nor thy might upon
Wis 19:10 river spewed out vast N of frogs.
1Mac 4:8 "Do not fear their N or be afraid when
2Mac 2:24 considering the flood of N involved and the difficulty
5:26 men and killed great N of people.
12:16 God, and slaughtered untold N, so that the adjoining
Acts 16:5 and they increased in N daily.
28:23 came to him at his lodging in great N

NUMENIUS (4)

1Mac 12:16 We therefore have chosen N the son of Antiochus
14:22 public decrees, as follows, N the son of Antiochus
14:24 After this Simon sent N to Rome with a
15:15 Then N and his companions arrived from Rome, with

NUMEROUS (9)

Deut 7:22 wild beasts grow too N for you.
30:5 you more prosperous and N than your fathers.
Josh 17:14 although I am a N people, since hitherto the
17:15 "If you are a N people, go up to
17:17 Manasseh, "You are a N people, and have great
1Chr 5:23 land; they were very N from Bashan to Baal-hermon,
Jer 46:23 because they are more N than locusts; they are
1Mac 11:24 gold and clothing and N other gifts.
16:7 for the cavalry of the enemy were very N

NUN (31)

Ex 33:11 Joshua the son of N, a young man, did
Num 11:28 Joshua the son of N, the minister of Moses,
13:8 Hoshea the son of N;
13:16 Hoshea the son of N Joshua.
14:6 Joshua the son of N and Caleb the son
14:30 son of Jephunneh and Joshua the son of N
14:38 Joshua the son of N and Caleb the son
26:65 son of Jephunneh and Joshua the son of N
27:18 Joshua the son of N, a man in whom
32:12 Joshua the son of N, for they have wholly
32:28 Joshua the son of N, and to the heads
34:17 Eleazar the priest and Joshua the son of N
Deut 1:38 Joshua the son of N, who stands before you,
31:23 Joshua the son of N and said, "Be strong
32:44 the people, he and Joshua the son of N
34:9 Joshua the son of N was full of the
Josh 1:1 Joshua the son of N, Moses' minister,
2:1 Joshua the son of N sent two men secretly
2:23 Joshua the son of N; and they told him
6:6 Joshua the son of N called the priests and
14:1 Joshua the son of N, and the heads of
17:4 Joshua the son of N and the leaders, and
19:49 inheritance among them to Joshua the son of N
19:51 Joshua the son of N and the heads of
21:1 Joshua the son of N and to the heads

24:29 Joshua the son of N, the servant of the
Judg 2:8 Joshua the son of N, the servant of the
1Kgs 16:34 which he spoke by Joshua the son of N
1Chr 7:27 son, Elishama his son, N his son, Joshua his
Neh 8:17 Jeshua the son of N to that day the
Sir 46:1 Joshua the son of N was mighty in war,

NURSE (14)

Gen 24:59 their sister and her N, and Abraham's servant and
35:8 And Deborah, Rebekah's N, died, and she was buried
Ex 2:7 and call you a N from the Hebrew women
2:7 the Hebrew women to N the child for you?"
2:9 this child away, and N him for me, and
Num 11:12 your bosom, as a N carries the sucking child,
Ruth 4:16 laid him in her bosom, and became his N
2Sam 4:4 from Jezreel; and his N took him up, and
1Kgs 1:2 king, and be his N; let her lie in
1:4 she became the king's N and ministered to him;
3:21 in the morning to N my child, behold, it
2Kgs 11:2 put him and his N in a bedchamber.
2Chr 22:11 put him and his N in a bedchamber.
1Thes 2:7 among you, like a N taking care of her

NURSED (5)

Ex 2:9 took the child and N him.
1Sam 1:23 the woman remained and N her son, until she
Song 8:1 brother to me, that N at my mother's breast!
Wis 7:4 I was N with care in swaddling cloths.
2Mac 7:27 in my womb, and N you for three years,

NURSING (2)

Is 49:23 and their queens your N mothers.
Joel 2:16 gather the children, even N infants.

NURSLING

Lam 4:4 The tongue of the N cleaves to the roof

NURTURED

Bar 4:11 With joy I N them, but I sent them

NUT

Song 6:11 went down to the N orchard, to look at

NUTS

Gen 43:11 honey, gum, myrrh, pistachio N, and almonds.

NYMPHA

Col 4:15 at La-odicea, and to N and the church in

O

OAK (24)

Gen 12:6 at Shechem, to the O of Moreh.
35:4 hid them under the O which was near Shechem.
35:8 was buried under an O below Bethel; so the
Deut 11:30 against Gilgal, beside the O of Moreh?
Josh 19:33 from Heleph, from the O in Za-anannim, and
24:26 up there under the O in the sanctuary of
Judg 4:11 far away as the O in Za-anannim, which is
6:11 and sat under the O at Ophrah, which belonged
6:19 to him under the O and presented them.
9:6 Abimelech king, by the O of the pillar at
9:37 is coming from the direction of the Diviners' O
1Sam 10:3 and come to the O of Tabor; three men
2Sam 18:9 branches of a great O, and his head caught
18:9 caught fast in the O, and he was left
18:10 Joab, "Behold, I saw Absalom hanging in an O
18:14 Absalom, while he was still alive in the O
1Kgs 13:14 him sitting under an O; and he said to
1Chr 10:12 their bones under the O in Jabesh, and fasted
Is 1:30 shall be like an O whose leaf withers, and
6:13 a terebinth or an O, whose stump remains standing
44:14 holm tree or an O and lets it grow
Ezek 6:13 under every leafy O, wherever they offered pleasing
Dan 13:58 He answered, "Under an evergreen O
Hos 4:13 upon the hills, under O, poplar, and terebinth, because

OAKS (11)

Gen 13:18 and dwelt by the O of Mamre, which are
14:13 was living by the O of Mamre the Amorite,
18:1 to him by the O of Mamre, as he
Ps 29:9 the LORD makes the O to whirl, and strips
Is 1:29 be ashamed of the O in which you delighted;
2:13 and against all the O of Bashan;
57:5 with lust among the O, under every green tree;
61:3 they may be called O of righteousness, the planting
Ezek 27:6 Of O of Bashan they made your oars; they
Amos 2:9 as strong as the O; I destroyed his fruit
Zech 11:2 Wail, O of Bashan, for the thick forest has

OAR

Ezek 27:29 from their ships come all that handle the O

OARS (2)

Is 33:21 where no galley with O can go, nor stately
Ezek 27:6 Bashan they made your O; they made your deck

OATH (86)

Gen 21:31 Beer-sheba; because there both of them swore an O
24:8 be free from this O of mine; only you
24:41 be free from my O, when you come to
24:41 be free from my O
26:3 I will fulfil the O which I swore to
26:28 let there be an O between you and us,
26:31 rose early and took O with one another; and
50:25 Then Joseph took an O of the sons of
Ex 22:11 one seeing it, an O by the LORD shall
22:11 owner shall accept the O, and he shall not
Lev 5:4 his lips a rash O to do evil or
5:4 any sort of rash O that men swear, and
Num 5:19 make her take an O, saying, 'If no man
5:21 the woman take the O of the curse, and
5:21 an execration and an O among your people, when
30:2 LORD, or swears an O to bind himself by
30:10 a pledge with an O,
30:13 vow and any binding O to afflict herself, her
Deut 7:8 and is keeping the O which he swore to
Josh 2:17 with respect to this O of yours which you
2:20 with respect to your O which you have made
6:26 Joshua laid an O upon them at that time,
9:20 us, because of the O which we swore to
Judg 21:5 had taken a great O concerning him who did
1Sam 14:24 for Saul laid an O on the people, saying,
14:26 to his mouth; for the people feared the O
14:27 the people with the O; so he put forth
14:28 the people with an O, saying, 'Cursed be the
2Sam 19:23 And the king gave him his O
21:7 Jonathan, because of the O of the LORD which
1Kgs 2:43 you not kept your O to the LORD and
8:31 made to take an O, and comes and swears
8:31 comes and swears his O before thine altar in
18:10 he would take an O of the kingdom or
2Kgs 11:4 and put them under O in the house of
2Chr 6:22 made to take an O, and comes and swears
6:22 comes and swears his O before thy altar in
15:14 They took O to the LORD with a loud
15:15 Judah rejoiced over the O; for they had sworn
Ezra 10:5 and all Israel take O that they would do
10:5 So they took the O
Neh 5:12 priests, and took an O of them to do
6:18 Judah were bound by O to him, because he
10:29 a curse and an O to walk in God's
13:25 I made them take O in the name of
Tob 8:20 over, Raguel declared by O to Tobias that he
Jud 8:9 he promised them under O to surrender the city
8:11 sworn and pronounced this O between God and you,
8:30 made us take an O which we cannot break.
Ps 119:106 I have sworn an O and confirmed it, to
132:11 to David a sure O from which he will
Eccl 8:2 because of your sacred O be not dismayed;
9:2 who swears is as he who shuns an O
Sir 44:22 assured him by an O that the nations would
Is 65:16 he who takes an O in the land shall
Jer 11:5 I may perform the O which I swore to
Ezek 16:59 who have despised the O in breaking the covenant,
17:13 made a covenant with him, putting him under O
17:16 made him king, whose O he despised, and whose
17:18 Because he despised the O and broke the covenant,
17:19 I live, surely my O which he despised, and
Dan 9:11 And the curse and O which are written in
Zech 8:17 and love no false O, for all these things
1Mac 6:61 the king and the commanders gave them their O
6:62 was, he broke the O he had sworn and
7:15 them and swore this O to them, "We will
7:18 the agreement and the O which they swore."
7:35 anger he swore this O, "Unless Judas and his
2Mac 14:32 when they declared on O that they did not
14:33 sanctuary, and swore this O: "If you do not
Mt 14:7 he promised with an O to give her whatever
23:15 is bound by his O

	23:17	is bound by his O
	26:72	denied it with an O, "I do not know
Lk	1:73	his holy covenant, the O which he swore to
Acts	2:30	had sworn with an O to him that he
	23:12	bound themselves by an O neither to eat nor
	23:14	bound ourselves by an O to taste no food
	23:21	bound themselves by an O neither to eat nor
Heb	6:16	all their disputes an O is final for confirmation.
	6:17	he interposed with an O,
	7:20	And it was not without an O
	7:21	their office without an O, but this one was
	7:21	was addressed with an O, "The Lord has sworn
	7:28	the word of the O, which came later than
Jas	5:12	or with any other O, but let your yes

OATHS (12)

Wis	12:21	whose fathers thou gavest O and covenants full of
	14:29	idols they swear wicked O and expect to suffer
	18:6	sure knowledge of the O in which they trusted.
	18:22	punisher, appealing to the O and covenants given to
Sir	23:9	accustom your mouth to O, and do not habitually
	23:11	man who swears many O will be filled with
Ezek	21:23	they have sworn solemn O; but he brings their
Hos	10:4	mere words; with empty O they make covenants; so
2Mac	7:24	words, but promised with O that he would make
	15:10	perfidy of the Gentiles and their violation of O
Mt	14:9	but because of his O and his guests he
Mk	6:26	but because of his O and his guests he

OBADIAH (21)

1Kgs	18:3	And Ahab called O, who was over the household.
	18:3	(Now O revered the LORD greatly;
	18:4	prophets of the LORD, O took a hundred prophets
	18:5	And Ahab said to O, "Go through the land
	18:6	direction by himself, and O went in another direction
	18:7	And as O was on the way, behold, Elijah
	18:7	Elijah met him; and O recognized him, and fell
	18:16	So O went to meet Ahab, and told him;
1Chr	3:21	son Arnan, his son O, his son Shecaniah.
	7:3	sons of Izrahiah: Michael, O, Joel, and Isshiah, five,
	8:38	Azrikam, Bocheru, Ishmael, She-ariah, O, and
	9:16	son of Asaph; and O the son of Shemaiah,
	9:44	Bocheru, Ishmael, She-ariah, O, and Hanan; these
	12:9	mountains: Ezer the chief, O second, Eliab third,
	27:19	Ishmaiah the son of O; for Naphtali, Jeremoth the
2Chr	17:7	sent his princes, Ben-hail, O, Zechariah, Nethanel,
	34:12	were set Jahath and O the Levites, of the
Ezra	8:9	the sons of Joab, O the son of Jehiel,
Neh	10:5	Shebaniah, Malluch, Harim, Meremoth, O,
	12:25	Bakbukiah, O, Meshullam, Talmon, and Akkub were
Obad	1:1	The vision of O

OBAL

Gen	10:28	Hadoram, Uzal, Diklah, O, Abima-el, Sheba,

OBED (13)

Ruth	4:17	They named him O; he was the father of
	4:21	of Boaz, Boaz of O,
	4:22	Boaz, Boaz of Obed, O of Jesse, and Jesse
1Chr	2:12	of Boaz, Boaz of O, Obed of Jesse.
	2:12	Boaz, Boaz of Obed, O of Jesse.
	2:37	was the father of Ephlal, and Ephlal of O
	2:38	O was the father of Jehu, and Jehu of
	11:47	Moabite, Eliel, and O, and Jaasiel the Mezoba-ite.
	26:7	Othni, Repha-el, O, and Elzabad, whose brethren
2Chr	23:1	Azariah the son of O, Ma-aseiah the son of
Mt	1:5	Boaz the father of O by Ruth, and Obed
	1:5	Obed by Ruth, and O the father of Jesse,
Lk	3:32	Jesse, the son of O, the son of Boaz,

OBED-EDOM (20)

2Sam	6:10	to the house of O the Gittite.
	6:11	in the house of O the Gittite three months;
	6:11	and the LORD blessed O and all his household.
	6:12	blessed the household of O and all that belongs
	6:12	from the house of O to the city of
1Chr	13:13	to the house of O the Gittite.
	13:14	with the household of O in his house three
	13:14	blessed the household of O and all that he
	15:18	Mikneiah, and the gatekeepers O and Je-iel.
	15:21	but Mattithiah, Eliphelehu, Mikneiah, O, Je-iel, and
	15:24	O and Jehiah also were to be gatekeepers for
	15:25	from the house of O with rejoicing.
	16:5	Jehiel, Mattithiah, Eliab, Benaiah, O, and Je-iel, who
	16:38	day required, and also O and his sixty-eight brethren;
	16:38	his sixty-eight brethren; while O, the son of Jeduthun,
	26:4	And O had sons: Shemaiah the first-born, Jehozabad
	26:8	of the sons of O with their sons and
	26:8	able men qualified for the service; sixty-two of O
	26:15	O's came out for the south, and to his
2Chr	25:24	house of God, and O with them; he seized

OBEDIENCE (14)

Gen	49:10	him shall be the O of the peoples.
Rom	1:5	to bring about the O of faith for the
	5:19	so by one man's O many will be made
	6:16	to death, or of O, which leads to righteousness?
	15:18	through me to win O from the Gentiles, by
	16:19	For while your O is known to all, so
	16:25	to bring about the O of faith--
2Cor	7:15	as he remembers the O of you all, and
	9:13	glorify God by your O in acknowledging the gospel
	10:6	every disobedience, when your O is complete.
Philem	1:21	Confident of your O, I write to you, knowing
Heb	5:8	a Son, he learned O through what he suffered;
1Pet	1:2	by the Spirit for O to Jesus Christ and
	1:22	your souls by your O to the truth for

OBEDIENT (14)

Ex	24:7	spoken we will do, and we will be O
Sir	7:23	them, and make them O from their youth.
	42:23	for ever for every need, and are all O
Is	1:19	you are willing and O, you shall eat the
Bar	6:60	stars, shining and sent forth for service, are O
Lk	2:51	to Nazareth, and was O to them; and his
Acts	6:7	of the priests were O to the faith.
Rom	6:16	to any one as O slaves, you are slaves
	6:17	of sin have become O from the heart to
2Cor	2:9	know whether you are O in everything.
Eph	6:5	Slaves, be O to those who are your earthly
Phil	2:8	humbled himself and became O unto death, even
Tit	3:1	and authorities, to be O, to be ready for
1Pet	1:14	As O children, do not be conformed to the

OBEISANCE (22)

Gen	43:28	And they bowed their heads and made O
Ex	18:7	his father-in-law, and did O and kissed him; and
1Sam	24:8	with his face to the earth, and did O
	28:14	with his face to the ground, and did O
2Sam	1:2	David, he fell to the ground and did O
	9:6	David, and fell on his face and did O
	9:8	And he did O, and said, "What is your
	14:4	the ground, and did O, and said, "Help, O
	14:22	the ground, and did O, and blessed the king;
	15:5	came near to do O to him, he would
	16:4	Ziba said, "I do O; let me ever find
	24:20	went forth, and did O to the king with
1Kgs	1:16	Bathsheba bowed and did O to the king, and
	1:31	the ground, and did O to the king, and
	1:53	he came and did O to King Solomon; and
1Chr	21:21	threshing floor, and did O to David with his
	29:20	the LORD, and did O to the king.
2Chr	24:17	Judah came and did O to the king; then
Jud	10:23	prostrated herself and made O to him, and his
Esth	3:2	bowed down and did O to Haman; for the
	3:2	But Mordecai did not bow down or do O
	3:5	bow down or do O to him, Haman was

OBELISKS

Jer	43:13	He shall break the O of Heliopolis which is

OBEY (106)

Gen	27:8	Now therefore, my son, O my word as I
	27:13	curse, my son; only O my word, and go,
	27:43	Now therefore, my son, O my voice; arise, flee
Ex	19:5	therefore, if you will O my voice and keep
Num	27:20	the congregation of the people of Israel may O
Deut	4:30	LORD your God and O his voice,
	8:20	because you would not O the voice of the
	9:23	not believe him or O his voice.
	11:13	"And if you will O my commandments which I
	11:27	the blessing, if you O the commandments of the
	11:28	if you do not O the commandments of the
	13:4	keep his commandments and O his voice, and you
	13:18	your fathers, if you O the voice of the
	15:5	if only you will O the voice of the
	21:18	son, who will not O the voice of his
	21:20	rebellious, he will not O our voice; he is
	26:17	his ordinances, and will O his voice;
	27:10	You shall therefore O the voice of the LORD
	28:1	'Amen.' "And if you O the voice of the
	28:2	overtake you, if you O the voice of the

O

28:13 not downward; if you O the commandments of the
28:15 if you will not O the voice of the
28:45 because you did not O the voice of the
28:62 because you did not O the voice of the
30:2 and your children, and O his voice in all
30:8 And you shall again O the voice of the
30:10 your fathers, if you O the voice of the
30:16 If you O the commandments of the LORD your
Josh 1:17 things, so we will O you; only may the
24:24 we will serve, and his voice we will O
Judg 3:4 know whether Israel would O the commandments of
1Sam 15:19 then did you not O the voice of the
15:22 Behold, to O is better than sacrifice, and to
28:18 Because you did not O the voice of the
1Kgs 2:42 say is good; I O
6:12 in my statutes and O my ordinances and keep
2Kgs 10:6 you are ready to O me, take the heads
18:12 because they did not O the voice of the
Ezra 7:26 Whoever will not O the law of your God
Neh 9:16 neck and did not O thy commandments;
9:17 commandments; they refused to O, and were not
9:29 presumptuously and did not O thy commandments,
9:29 shoulder and stiffened their neck and would not O
Ps 106:25 tents, and did not O the voice of the
Prov 30:17 father and scorns to O a mother will be
Sir 33:28 if he does not O, make his fetters heavy.
Is 11:14 and the Ammonites shall O them.
42:24 not walk, and whose law they would not O
Jer 7:23 command I gave them, O my voice, and I
7:24 But they did not O or incline their ear,
7:28 nation that did not O the voice of the
11:7 to this day, saying, O my voice.
11:8 Yet they did not O or incline their ear,
22:4 if you will indeed O this word, then there
26:13 and your doings, and O the voice of the
32:23 But they did not O thy voice or walk
38:20 O now the voice of the LORD in what
40:3 LORD, and did not O his voice, this thing
42:6 or evil, we will O the voice of the
42:6 with us when we O the voice of the
43:4 the people did not O the voice of the
43:7 for they did not O the voice of the
44:23 LORD and did not O the voice of the
Bar 2:22 if you will not O the voice of the
2:24 "'But we did not O thy voice, to serve
2:29 "If you will not O my voice, this very
2:30 that they will not O me, for they are
Ezek 11:20 keep my ordinances and O them; and they shall
Dan 7:27 dominions shall serve and O them.'
9:11 turned aside, refusing to O thy voice.
Mic 5:15 execute vengeance upon the nations that did not O
Zech 6:15 if you will diligently O the voice of the
1Mac 1:50 "And whoever does not O the command of the
2:19 rule of the king O him, and have chosen
2:22 We will not O the king's words by turning
10:38 under one ruler and O no other authority but
12:43 and his troops to O him as they would
2Mac 7:30 I will not O the king's command, but I
7:30 king's command, but I O the command of the
Mt 8:27 even winds and sea O him?"
Mk 1:27 unclean spirits, and they O him."
4:41 even wind and sea O him?"
Lk 8:25 and water, and they O him?"
17:6 sea,' and it would O you.
Jn 3:36 he who does not O the Son shall not
Acts 5:29 apostles answered, "We must O God rather than
5:32 given to those who O him."
7:39 Our fathers refused to O him, but thrust him
Rom 2:8 factious and do not O the truth, but obey
2:8 obey the truth, but O wickedness, there will be
2:25 of value if you O the law; but if
6:12 bodies, to make you O their passions.
6:16 the one whom you O, either of sin, which
2Cor 10:5 every thought captive to O Christ,
Eph 6:1 Children, O your parents in the Lord, for this
Col 3:20 Children, O your parents in everything, for this
3:22 Slaves, O in everything those who are your earthly
2Thes 1:8 those who do not O the gospel of our
3:14 any one refuses to O what we say in
Heb 5:9 salvation to all who O him,
13:17 O your leaders and submit to them; for they
Jas 3:3 horses that they may O us, we guide their
1Pet 3:1 though they do not O the word, may be
3:20 who formerly did not O, when God's patience waited
4:17 those who do not O the gospel of God?
1Jn 5:2 we love God and O his commandments.

OBEYED (46)

Gen 22:18 themselves, because you have O my voice."
26:5 bless themselves: because Abraham O my voice and
28:7 and that Jacob had O his father and his
Ex 7:16 the wilderness; and behold, you have not yet O
Deut 26:14 the dead; I have O the voice of the
34:9 the people of Israel O him, and did as
Josh 1:17 Just as we O Moses in all things, so
22:2 commanded you, and have O my voice in all
Judg 2:2 But you have not O my command.
2:17 had walked, who had O the commandments of the
2:20 fathers, and have not O my voice,
1Sam 15:20 to Samuel, "I have O the voice of the
15:24 feared the people and O their voice.
2Sam 22:45 heard of me, they O me.
1Kgs 20:36 "Because you have not O the voice of the
2Kgs 18:12 the LORD commanded; they neither listened nor O
22:13 our fathers have not O the words of this
1Chr 29:23 prospered, and all Israel O him.
Jud 2:3 one who had not O his command should be
Esth 2:20 charged her; for Esther O Mordecai just as when
Ps 18:44 heard of me they O me; foreigners came cringing
Jer 3:13 that you have not O my voice, says the
3:25 and we have not O the voice of the
9:13 them, and have not O my voice, or walked
22:21 that you have not O my voice.
25:8 Because you have not O my words,
34:10 And they O, all the princes and all the
34:10 be enslaved again; they O and set them free.
34:17 LORD: You have not O me by proclaiming liberty,
35:8 you sojourn.' We have O the voice of Jonadab
35:10 in tents, and have O and done all that
35:14 day, for they have O their father's command.
35:16 this people has not O me.
35:18 Israel: Because you have O the command of Jonadab
42:21 but you have not O the voice of the
Bar 2:10 Yet we have not O his voice, to walk
3:33 called it, and it O him in fear;
Dan 3:29 things and have not O thy commandments;
9:10 him, and have not O the voice of the
9:14 and we have not O his voice.
Hag 1:12 remnant of the people, O the voice of the
1Mac 14:43 that he should be O by all, and that
Rom 10:16 they have not all O the gospel; for Isaiah
Phil 2:12 as you have always O, so now, not only
Heb 11:8 By faith Abraham O when he was called to
1Pet 3:6 husbands, as Sarah O Abraham, calling him lord.

OBEYING (4)

Deut 17:12 acts presumptuously, by not O the priest who stands
30:20 the LORD your God, O his voice, and cleaving
1Sam 15:22 and sacrifices, as in O the voice of the
Gal 5:7 who hindered you from O the truth?

OBEYS (6)

Eccl 8:5 He who O a command will meet no harm,
Sir 3:6 long life, and whoever O the Lord will refresh
4:15 He who O her will judge the nations, and
24:21 Whoever O me will not be put to shame,
Is 50:10 fears the LORD and O the voice of his
Bar 2:31 them a heart that O and ears that hear;

OBIL

1Chr 27:30 Over the camels was O the Ishmaelite; and over

OBJECT (10)

2Chr 29:8 has made them an O of horror, of astonishment,
Ps 31:11 to my neighbors, an O of dread to my
109:25 I am an O of scorn to my accusers;
Wis 14:20 now regarded as an O of worship the one
Sir 38:28 his eyes are on the pattern of the O
Jer 6:10 is to them an O of scorn, they take
Ezek 5:14 a desolation and an O of reproach among the
16:57 become like her an O of reproach for the
23:46 and make them an O of terror and a
2Thes 2:4 every so-called god or O of worship, so that

OBJECTED

Acts 28:19 But when the Jews O, I was compelled to

OBJECTION

Acts 10:29 when I was sent for, I came without O

OBJECTS (6)

Ex 35:22 all sorts of gold O, every man dedicating an
Num 4:32 assign by name the O which they are required

O

Wis	14:21	royal authority, bestowed on O of stone or wood
	15:6	and fit for such O of hope are those
	15:17	is better than the O he worships, since he
Acts	17:23	along, and observed the O of your worship, I

OBLATION (3)

1Kgs	18:29	the offering of the O, but there was no
	18:36	the offering of the O, Elijah the prophet came
Dan	3:38	offering, or sacrifice, or O, or incense, no place

OBLIGATE

Neh	10:35	We O ourselves to bring the first fruits of

OBLIGATION (3)

Num	32:22	and be free of O to the LORD and
Neh	10:32	lay upon ourselves the O to charge ourselves yearly
Rom	1:14	I am under O both to Greeks and to

OBLIGATIONS (3)

1Mac	8:26	they shall keep their O without receiving any return.
	8:28	they shall keep these O and do so without
	11:33	friends and fulfil their O to us, we have

OBLIGED (2)

1Chr	9:25	in their villages were O to come in every
2Mac	8:25	some distance, they were O to return because the

OBOTH (4)

Num	21:10	people of Israel set out, and encamped in O
	21:11	they set out from O, and encamped at Iye-abarim,
	33:43	they set out from Punon, and encamped at O
	33:44	they set out from O, and encamped at Iye-abarim,

OBSCURE (2)

Prov	22:29	will not stand before O men.
Is	33:19	the people of an O speech which you cannot

OBSCURES

Wis	4:12	the fascination of wickedness O what is good, and

OBSCURITIES

Sir	39:3	at home with the O of parables.

OBSERVANCE (6)

Neh	9:29	thy ordinances, by the O of which a man
Ezek	20:11	my ordinances, by whose O man shall live.
	20:13	my ordinances, by whose O man shall live; and
	20:21	my ordinances, by whose O man shall live; they
Acts	16:4	delivered to them for O the decisions which had
	21:24	you yourself live in O of the law.

OBSERVE (60)

Ex	12:14	your generations you shall O it as an ordinance
	12:17	And you shall O the feast of unleavened bread,
	12:17	Egypt: therefore you shall O this day, throughout your
	12:24	You shall O this rite as an ordinance for
	34:11	O what I command you this day.
	34:22	And you shall O the feast of weeks, the
Lev	19:37	And you shall O all my statutes and all
	23:24	the month, you shall O a day of solemn
	26:3	in my statutes and O my commandments and do
Num	15:22	err, and do not O all these commandments which
Deut	5:12	O the sabbath day, to keep it holy, as
	16:1	O the month of Abib, and keep the passover
	16:12	shall be careful to O these statutes.
Josh	22:5	Take good care to O the commandment and the
Judg	13:14	thing; all that I commanded her let her O
Ruth	3:4	when he lies down, O the place where he
2Sam	20:10	But Amasa did not O the sword which was
1Chr	22:13	you are careful to O the statutes and the
	28:8	hearing of our God, O and seek out all
Neh	10:29	of God, and to O and do all the
Esth	10:13	So they will O these days in the month
	16:22	'Therefore you shall O this with all good cheer
Job	39:1	Do you O the calving of the hinds?
Ps	78:56	God, and did not O his testimonies,
	105:45	keep his statutes, and O his laws.
	106:3	Blessed are they who O justice, who do righteousness
	119:8	I will O thy statutes; O forsake me not
	119:17	I may live and O thy word.
	119:34	keep thy law and O it with my whole
	119:106	and confirmed it, to O thy righteous ordinances.
	119:146	me, that I may O thy testimonies.
Prov	23:1	eat with a ruler, O carefully what is before
	23:26	and let your eyes O my ways.
Wis	6:10	be made holy who O holy things in holiness,
Sir	4:20	O the right time, and beware of evil; and
	24:32	O that I have not labored for myself alone,
	38:17	and your wailing fervent; O the mourning according
	41:14	My children, O instruction and be at peace; hidden
Is	42:20	things, but does not O them; his ears are
Ezek	18:9	and is careful to O my ordinances --he
	18:19	has been careful to O all my statutes, he
	20:18	of your fathers, nor O their ordinances, nor defile
	20:19	and be careful to O my ordinances,
	20:21	were not careful to O my ordinances, by whose
	36:27	and be careful to O my ordinances.
	37:24	and be careful to O my statutes.
	43:11	so that they may O and perform all its
1Mac	1:13	He authorized them to O the ordinances of the
	2:61	"And so O, from generation to generation, that none
	2:67	about you all who O the law, and avenge
2Mac	6:6	keep the sabbath, nor O the feasts of his
	6:11	caves near by, to O the seventh day secretly,
	10:8	of the Jews should O these days every year.
	13:23	yielded and swore to O all their rights, settled
	15:4	who ordered us to O the seventh day,"
Mt	23:3	seat; so practice and O whatever they tell you,
	28:20	Spirit, teaching them to O all that I have
Mk	7:4	other traditions which they O, the washing of cups
Acts	21:21	circumcise their children or O the customs.
Gal	4:10	You O days, and months, and seasons, and years!

OBSERVED (22)

Ex	3:16	me, saying, "I have O you and what has
	27:21	for ever to be O throughout their generations by
Deut	33:9	For they O thy word, and kept thy covenant.
1Sam	1:12	before the LORD, Eli O her mouth.
Jud	10:14	heard her words, and O her face--she was
Esth	9:31	of Purim should be O at their appointed seasons,
Eccl	8:9	All this I O while applying my mind to
Jer	33:24	Jeremiah: "Have you not O what these people are
Dan	1:13	king's rich food be O by you, and according
	3:30	commandments; we have not O them or done them,
1Mac	4:35	of his troops and O the boldness which inspired
	4:59	the altar should be O with gladness and joy
	13:48	in it men who O the law.
2Mac	3:1	laws were very well O because of the piety
	9:23	my illness, but I O that my father, on
Mt	19:20	"All these I have O; what do I still
Mk	10:20	all these I have O from my youth."
Lk	17:20	with signs to be O;
	18:21	"All these I have O from my youth."
Acts	11:6	at it closely I O animals and beasts of
	17:23	I passed along, and O the objects of your
2Tim	3:10	Now you have O my teaching, my conduct, my

OBSERVER

Wis	1:6	feelings, and a true O of his heart, and

OBSERVES (10)

Ps	33:15	of them all, and O all their deeds.
Prov	21:12	The righteous O the house of the wicked; the
Eccl	11:4	He who O the wind will not sow; and
Sir	11:28	like a spy he O your weakness;
	23:7	speech; the one who O it will never be
Ezek	18:17	no interest or increase, O my ordinances, and walks
Rom	14:6	He who O the day, observes it in honor
	14:6	who observes the day, O it in honor of
Jas	1:22	like a man who O his natural face in
	1:23	a mirror; for he O himself and goes away

OBSERVING (2)

Ex	31:16	shall keep the sabbath, O the sabbath throughout
Mk	7:3	they wash their hands, O the tradition of the

OBSOLETE (2)

Heb	8:13	a new covenant he treats the first as O
	8:13	And what is becoming O and growing old is

OBSTACLE (3)

1Cor	9:12	rather than put an O in the way of
2Cor	6:3	We put no O in any one's way, so
	10:5	arguments and every proud O to the knowledge of

OBSTACLES

Sir	39:24	just as they are O to the wicked.

OBSTINACY

Sir	28:10	in proportion to the O of strife will be

OBSTINATE (2)
Deut 2:30 and made his heart O, that he might give
Is 48:4 know that you are O, and your neck is

OBSTRUCTION
Is 57:14 the way, remove every O from my people's way."

OBTAIN (29)
Gen 16:2 be that I shall O children by her." And
Tob 5:2 but how can I O the money when I
Prov 28:13 and forsakes them will O mercy.
29:23 lowly in spirit will O honor.
Wis 7:14 those who get it O friendship with God, commended
Sir 4:13 holds her fast will O glory, and the Lord
4:16 in her he will O her; and his descendants
15:1 to the law will O wisdom.
15:7 Foolish men will not O her, and sinful men
Is 29:19 The meek shall O fresh joy in the LORD,
35:10 their heads; they shall O joy and gladness, and
51:11 their heads; they shall O joy and gladness, and
Lam 2:9 more, and her prophets O no vision from the
Dan 11:21 in without warning and O the kingdom by flatteries.
1Mac 9:70 peace with him and O release of the captives.
Mt 5:7 merciful, for they shall O mercy.
Acts 8:20 you thought you could O the gift of God
Rom 8:21 bondage to decay and O the glorious liberty of
11:7 Israel failed to O what it sought.
1Cor 9:24 run that you may O it.
1Thes 5:9 for wrath, but to O salvation through our Lord
2Thes 2:14 so that you may O the glory of our
2Tim 2:10 that they also may O salvation in Christ Jesus
Heb 1:14 those who are to O salvation?
12:15 no one fail to O the grace of God;
Jas 4:2 you covet and cannot O; so you fight and
1Pet 1:9 of your faith you O the salvation of your
3:9 called, that you may O a blessing.
5:4 is manifested you will O the unfading crown of

OBTAINED (17)
Josh 19:9 the tribe of Simeon O an inheritance in the
Tob 12:3 cured my wife, he O the money for me,
Sir 34:18 has been wrongfully O, the offering is blemished;
46:9 country, and his children O it for an inheritance;
Hos 2:1 your sister, "She has O pity."
2Mac 4:7 brother of Onias O the high-priesthood by corruption,
4:32 Menelaus, thinking he had O a suitable opportunity,
Acts 20:28 the LORD which he O with the blood of
27:13 supposing that they had O their purpose, they
Rom 5:2 Through him we have O access to this grace
11:7 The elect O it, but the rest were hardened,
Phil 3:12 that I have already O this or am already
Heb 1:4 the name he has O is more excellent than
6:15 Abraham, having patiently endured, O the promise.
8:6 it is, Christ has O a ministry which is
2Pet 1:1 To those who have O a faith of equal
1Jn 5:15 know that we have O the requests made of

OBTAINS (4)
Prov 8:35 me finds life and O favor from the LORD;
12:2 A good man O favor from the LORD, but
18:22 a good thing, and O favor from the LORD.
Sir 22:4 A sensible daughter O her husband, but one who

OCCASION (13)
Gen 43:18 that he may seek O against us and fall
Judg 9:33 do to them as O offers."
14:4 he was seeking an O against the Philistines.
Ezra 7:20 God, which you have O to provide, you may
Tob 4:19 Lord God on every O; ask him that your
Sir 4:5 nor give a man O to curse you;
29:3 him, and on every O you will find what
1Mac 8:25 allies wholeheartedly, as the O may indicate to them.
8:27 their allies, as the O may indicate to them.
12:11 you constantly on every O, both in our feasts
Eph 4:29 edifying, as fits the O, that it may impart
1Tim 5:14 give the enemy no O to revile us.
Heb 8:7 would have been no O for a second.

OCCASIONED
1Sam 22:22 I have O the death of all the persons

OCCASIONS (2)
Job 33:10 Behold, he finds O against me, he counts me
2Mac 9:23 my father, on the O when he made expeditions

OCCUPANTS
1Mac 13:11 he drove out its O and remained there.

OCCUPATION (4)
Gen 46:33 says, 'What is your O
47:3 Pharaoh said to his brothers, "What is your O
Jon 1:8 What is your O
Acts 19:25 the workmen of like O, and said, "Men, you

OCCUPIED (6)
Jud 5:19 were scattered, and have O Jerusalem, where their
Eccl 5:20 because God keeps him O with joy in his
Sir 38:25 drives oxen and is O with their work, and
1Mac 10:1 of Antiochus, landed and O Ptolemais.
2Mac 10:36 the force, and they O the city.
Acts 18:5 from Macedonia, Paul was O with preaching,

OCCUPY (7)
Num 13:30 up at once, and O it; for we are
Deut 2:31 possession, that you may O his land.'
3:20 you, and they also O the land which the
Neh 2:8 city, and for the house which I shall O
Ps 131:1 high; I do not O myself with things too
2Mac 2:30 the original historian to O the ground and to
1Tim 1:4 different doctrine, nor to O themselves with myths

OCCUR (2)
Sir 20:17 of the wicked will O speedily.
48:25 revealed what was to O to the end of

OCCURRED (6)
Esth 10:9 wonders, which have not O among the nations.
Wis 11:12 a groaning at the memory of what had O
1Mac 9:24 a very great famine O, and the country deserted
14:29 us: "Since wars often O in the country, Simon
Acts 13:12 he saw what had O, for he was astonished
Heb 9:15 since a death has O which redeems them from

OCHRAN (5)
Num 1:13 Pagiel the son of O;
2:27 Pagiel the son of O,
7:72 Pagiel the son of O, the leader of the
7:77 was the offering of Pagiel the son of O
10:26 men of Asher was Pagiel the son of O

OCINA
Jud 2:28 lived in Sur and O and all who lived

ODED (3)
2Chr 15:1 Azariah the son of O,
15:8 Azariah the son of O, he took courage, and
28:9 there, whose name was O; and he went out

ODIOUS (6)
Gen 34:30 me by making me O to the inhabitants of
1Sam 13:4 that Israel had become O to the Philistines.
2Sam 10:6 that they had become O to David, the Ammonites
16:21 you have made yourself O to your father, and
1Chr 19:6 they had made themselves O to David, Hanun and
Wis 16:3 appetite because of the O creatures sent to them,

ODOMERA
1Mac 9:66 He struck down O and his brothers and the

ODOR (48)
Gen 8:21 LORD smelled the pleasing O, the LORD said in
Ex 29:18 it is a pleasing O, an offering by fire
29:25 offering, as a pleasing O before the LORD; it
29:41 morning, for a pleasing O, an offering by fire
Lev 1:9 by fire, a pleasing O to the LORD.
1:13 by fire, a pleasing O to the LORD.
1:17 by fire, a pleasing O to the LORD.
2:2 by fire, a pleasing O to the LORD.
2:9 by fire, a pleasing O to the LORD.
2:12 be offered on the altar for a pleasing O
3:5 by fire, a pleasing O to the LORD.
3:16 as food offered by fire for a pleasing O
4:31 altar for a pleasing O to the LORD; and
6:15 the altar, a pleasing O to the LORD.
6:21 it for a pleasing O to the LORD.
8:21 burnt offering, a pleasing O, an offering by fire
8:28 ordination offering, a pleasing O, an offering by fire
17:6 fat for a pleasing O to the LORD.
23:13 the LORD, a pleasing O; and the drink offering
23:18 by fire, a pleasing O to the LORD.
Num 15:3 to make a pleasing O to the LORD,

O

15:7 of wine, a pleasing O to the LORD.
15:10 by fire, a pleasing O to the LORD.
15:13 by fire, a pleasing O to the LORD.
15:14 by fire, a pleasing O to the LORD, he
15:24 burnt offering, a pleasing O to the LORD, with
18:17 by fire, a pleasing O to the LORD;
28:2 by fire, my pleasing O, you shall take heed
28:6 Sinai for a pleasing O, an offering by fire
28:8 by fire, a pleasing O to the LORD.
28:13 burnt offering of pleasing O, an offering by fire
28:24 by fire, a pleasing O to the LORD; it
28:27 burnt offering, a pleasing O to the LORD; two
29:2 burnt offering, a pleasing O to the LORD: one
29:6 for them, a pleasing O, an offering by fire
29:8 the LORD, a pleasing O: one young bull, one
29:13 by fire, a pleasing O to the LORD, thirteen
29:36 by fire, a pleasing O to the LORD: one
Tob 8:3 the demon smelled the O he fled to the
Eccl 10:1 give off an evil O; so a little folly
Sir 24:15 I spread a pleasant O, like galbanum, onycha, and
35:6 altar, and its pleasing O rises before the Most
45:16 incense and a pleasing O as a memorial portion,
50:15 the altar, a pleasing O to the Most High,
Ezek 6:13 wherever they offered pleasing O to all their idols.
16:19 them for a pleasing O, says the Lord GOD.
20:41 As a pleasing O I will accept you, when
Jn 11:39 there will be an O, for he has been

ODORS (2)

Lev 26:31 desolate, and I will not smell your pleasing O
Ezek 20:28 sent up their soothing O, and there they poured

OFF (463)

Gen 8:13 waters were dried from O the earth; and Noah
9:11 all flesh be cut O by the waters of
11:8 earth, and they left O building the city.
17:14 foreskin shall be cut O from his people; he
21:16 him a good way O, about the distance of
22:4 up his eyes and saw the place afar O
37:18 They saw him afar O, and before he came
38:14 she put O her widow's garments, and put on
38:19 went away, and taking O her veil she put
Ex 3:5 not come near; put O your shoes from your
4:25 a flint and cut O her son's foreskin, and
9:15 would have been cut O from the earth;
12:15 person shall be cut O from Israel.
12:19 person shall be cut O from the congregation of
20:18 and they stood afar O,
20:21 the people stood afar O, while Moses drew near
24:1 of the elders of Israel, and worship afar O
30:33 outsider shall be cut O from his people.'"
30:38 perfume shall be cut O from his people."
31:14 soul shall be cut O from among his people.
32:2 said to them, "Take O the rings of gold
32:3 all the people took O the rings of gold
32:24 have gold take it O; so they gave it
33:5 So now put O your ornaments from you, that
34:34 he took the veil O, until he came out;
Lev 1:15 the altar and wring O its head, and burn
6:11 Then he shall put O his garments, and put
7:20 person shall be cut O from his people.
7:21 person shall be cut O from his people."
7:25 LORD shall be cut O from his people.
7:27 person shall be cut O from his people."
14:8 his clothes, and shave O all his hair, and
14:9 shave all his hair O his head; he shall
14:9 head; he shall shave O his beard and his
14:41 plaster that they scrape O they shall pour into
16:23 meeting, and shall put O the linen garments which
17:4 man shall be cut O from among his people.
17:9 man shall be cut O from his people.
17:10 and will cut him O from among his people.
17:14 its blood; whoever eats it shall be cut O
18:29 them shall be cut O from among their people.
19:8 person shall be cut O from his people.
19:27 You shall not round O the hair on your
20:3 and will cut him O from among his people,
20:5 and will cut them O from among their people,
20:6 and will cut him O from among his people.
20:17 they shall be cut O in the sight of
20:18 them shall be cut O from among their people.
21:5 their heads, nor shave O the edges of their
22:3 person shall be cut O from my presence: I
23:29 day shall be cut O from his people.
Num 5:23 book, and wash them O into the water of
9:10 body, or is afar O on a journey, he
9:13 person shall be cut O from his people, because
15:30 person shall be cut O from among his people.
15:31 shall be utterly cut O; his iniquity shall be
16:46 put fire therein from O the altar, and lay
19:13 person shall be cut O from Israel; because the
19:20 person shall be cut O from the midst of
Deut 6:15 he destroy you from O the face of the
11:17 and you perish quickly O the good land which
12:29 LORD your God cuts O before you the nations
19:1 LORD your God cuts O the nations whose land
21:13 And she shall put O her captive's garb, and
23:1 male member is cut O shall not enter the
25:9 and pull his sandal O his foot, and spit
25:10 house of him that had his sandal pulled O
25:12 then you shall cut O her hand; your eye
25:18 and weary, and cut O at your rear all
28:21 he has consumed you O the land which you
28:40 with the oil; for your olives shall drop O
28:63 you shall be plucked O the land which you
29:5 sandals have not worn O your feet;
Josh 3:16 Sea, were wholly cut O; and the people passed
4:7 the Jordan were cut O before the ark of
4:7 Jordan, the waters of the Jordan were cut O
5:15 said to Joshua, "Put O your shoes from your
7:9 surround us, and cut O our name from the
23:4 I have already cut O, from the Jordan to
23:13 till you perish from O this good land which
23:15 have destroyed you from O this good land which
23:16 shall perish quickly from O the good land which
Judg 1:6 caught him, and cut O his thumbs and his
1:7 their great toes cut O used to pick up
6:13 LORD has cast us O, and given us into
8:11 for the army was O its guard.
15:14 and his bonds melted O his hands.
16:12 he snapped the ropes O his arms like a
16:19 and had him shave O the seven locks of
21:6 "One tribe is cut O from Israel this day.
21:23 dancers whom they carried O; then they went and
Ruth 4:7 transaction, the one drew O his sandal and gave
4:8 he drew O his sandal.
4:10 may not be cut O from among his brethren
1Sam 2:9 wicked shall be cut O in darkness; for not
2:31 when I will cut O your strength and the
2:33 I shall not cut O from my altar shall
5:4 hands were lying cut O upon the threshold; only
6:5 lighten his hand from O you and your gods
6:8 Then send it O, and let it go its
17:39 And David put them O
17:46 you down, and cut O your head; and I
17:51 killed him, and cut O his head with it.
19:24 And he too stripped O his clothes, and he
20:15 and do not cut O your loyalty from my
20:15 When the LORD cuts O every one of the
20:16 of Jonathan be cut O from the house of
24:4 arose and stealthily cut O the skirt of Saul's
24:5 because he had cut O Saul's skirt.
24:11 fact that I cut O the skirt of your
24:21 you will not cut O my descendants after me,
26:13 side, and stood afar O on the top of
28:9 how he has cut O the mediums and the
30:2 one, but carried them O, and went their way.
31:9 And they cut O his head, and stripped off
31:9 his head, and stripped O his armor, and sent
2Sam 4:12 killed them, and cut O their hands and feet,
5:6 lame will ward you O —thinking, "David cannot come
7:9 went, and have cut O all your enemies from
10:4 David's servants, and shaved O half the beard of
10:4 of each, and cut O their garments in the
16:9 go over and take O his head."
17:23 his ass, and went O home to his own
20:22 And they cut O the head of Sheba the
1Kgs 9:7 then I will cut O Israel from the land
11:16 until he had cut O every male in Edom);
13:34 as to cut it O and to destroy it
14:10 Jeroboam, and will cut O from Jeroboam every
14:14 Israel, who shall cut O the house of Jeroboam
18:4 and when Jezebel cut O the prophets of the
20:11 armor boast himself as he that puts it O
21:21 away, and will cut O from Ahab every male,
2Kgs 5:2 their raids had carried O a little maid from
6:6 the place, he cut O a stick, and threw
6:32 has sent to take O my head?
7:8 drank, and they carried O silver and gold and
7:8 another tent, and carried O things from it, and
9:8 and I will cut O from Ahab every male,
10:32 LORD began to cut O parts of Israel.

	11:5	you, those who come O duty on the sabbath
	11:9	who were to go O duty on the sabbath,
	16:17	And King Ahaz cut O the frames of the
	16:17	down the sea from O the bronze oxen that
	21:14	And I will cast O the remnant of my
	23:27	and I will cast O this city which I
	24:13	his reign, and carried O all the treasures of
	25:29	So Jehoiachin put O his prison garments.
1Chr	5:21	They carried O their livestock: fifty thousand of their
	17:8	went, and have cut O all your enemies from
	18:11	which he had carried O from all the nations,
	19:4	shaved them, and cut O their garments in the
	28:9	he will cast you O for ever.
2Chr	4:6	they were to rinse O what was used for
	23:4	and Levites who come O duty on the sabbath,
	23:8	who were to go O duty on the sabbath,
	32:21	an angel, who cut O all the mighty warriors
Neh	4:23	none of us took O our clothes; each kept
	5:10	Let us leave O this interest.
	12:43	And the joy of Jerusalem was heard afar O
Tob	11:13	the white films scaled O from the corners of
Jud	10:3	been wearing, and took O her widow's garments, and
	13:9	she tumbled his body O the bed and pulled
	14:15	with his head cut O and missing.
	16:8	For she took O her widow's mourning to exalt
Esth	4:4	that he might take O his sackcloth, but he
	8:2	and the king took O his signet ring, which
	14:2	the Lord; she took O her splendid apparel and
	15:1	her prayer, she took O the garments in which
Job	4:7	Or where were the upright cut O
	6:9	would let loose his hand and cut me O
	9:27	complaint, I will put O my sad countenance, and
	15:33	He will shake O his unripe grape, like the
	15:33	the vine, and cast O his blossom, like the
	17:11	my plans are broken O, the desires of my
	20:28	be carried away, dragged O in the day of
	21:21	when the number of their months is cut O
	22:20	our adversaries are cut O, and what they left
	24:4	They thrust the poor O the road; the poor
	24:24	mallow; they are cut O like the heads of
	27:8	when God cuts him O, when God takes away
	27:20	flood; in the night a whirlwind carries him O
	30:11	me, they have cast O restraint in my presence.
	33:17	his deed, and cut O pride from man;
	35:3	How am I better O than if I had
	36:20	when peoples are cut O in their place.
	39:29	out the prey; his eyes behold it afar O
	41:13	Who can strip O his outer garment?
Ps	10:1	dost thou stand afar O, O LORD?
	12:3	May the LORD cut O all flattering lips, the
	27:9	Cast me not O, forsake me not, O God
	28:3	Take me not O with the wicked, with those
	34:16	against evildoers, to cut O the remembrance of them
	37:9	wicked shall be cut O; but those who wait
	37:22	but those cursed by him shall be cut O
	37:28	the children of the wicked shall be cut O
	37:38	the posterity of the wicked shall be cut O
	38:11	from my plague, and my kinsmen stand afar O
	43:2	I take refuge; why hast thou cast me O
	44:9	thou hast cast us O and abased us, and
	44:23	Do not cast us O for ever!
	71:9	Do not cast me O in the time of
	74:1	dost thou cast us O for ever?
	75:10	wicked he will cut O, but the horns of
	76:12	be feared, who cuts O the spirit of princes,
	88:5	for they are cut O from thy hand.
	88:14	O LORD, why dost thou cast me O
	89:38	now thou hast cast O and rejected, thou art
	101:8	in the land, cutting O all the evildoers from
	109:13	his posterity be cut O; may his name be
	109:15	his memory be cut O from the earth!
	109:23	evening; I am shaken O like a locust.
	118:10	the name of the LORD I cut them O
	118:11	the name of the LORD I cut them O
	118:12	the name of the LORD I cut them O
	143:12	thy steadfast love cut O my enemies, and destroy
Prov	2:22	wicked will be cut O from the land, and
	10:31	wisdom, but the perverse tongue will be cut O
	14:16	but a fool throws O restraint and is careless.
	23:18	future, and your hope will not be cut O
	24:14	future, and your hope will not be cut O
	25:20	like one who takes O a garment on a
	26:6	of a fool cuts O his own feet and
	29:18	prophecy the people cast O restraint, but blessed is
	30:14	devour the poor from O the earth, the needy
Eccl	6:3	untimely birth is better O than he.
	10:1	the perfumer's ointment give O an evil odor; so
Song	5:3	I had put O my garment, how could I
Wis	4:5	branches will be broken O before they come to
	11:3	their enemies and fought O their foes.
	13:11	handle and skilfully strip O all its bark, and
	17:8	who promised to drive O the fears and disorders
	18:23	the wrath, and cut O its way to the
Sir	6:21	he will not be slow to cast her O
	22:2	up will shake it O his hand.
	22:11	when he shakes himself O; avoid him and you
	22:18	a friend will break O the friendship.
	30:14	Better O is a poor man who is well
	31:2	a severe illness carries O sleep.
	40:18	finds treasure is better O than both.
Is	5:26	for a nation afar O, and whistle for it
	5:29	prey, they carry it O, and none can rescue.
	9:14	So the LORD cut O from Israel head and
	10:7	destroy, and to cut O nations not a few;
	11:13	Judah shall be cut O; Ephraim shall not be
	14:22	hosts, "and will cut O from Babylon name and
	18:5	grape, he will cut O the shoots with pruning
	20:2	your loins and take O your shoes from your
	22:25	it will be cut O, for the LORD has
	29:20	evil shall be cut O,
	33:9	Bashan and Carmel shake O their leaves.
	38:12	life; he cuts me O from the loom; from
	40:12	his hand and marked O the heavens with a
	40:24	the tempest carries them O like stubble.
	41:9	and not cast you O;
	47:2	and grind meal, put O your veil, strip off
	47:2	off your veil, strip O your robe, uncover your
	48:9	for you, that I may not cut you O
	48:19	would never be cut O or destroyed from before
	53:8	that he was cut O out of the land
	54:6	when she is cast O, says your God.
	55:13	an everlasting sign which shall not be cut O
	56:5	an everlasting name which shall not be cut O
	57:13	wind will carry them O, a breath will take
	59:14	and righteousness stands afar O; for truth has fallen
	66:19	to the coastlands afar O, that have not heard
Jer	7:28	perished; it is cut O from their lips.
	7:29	Cut O your hair and cast it away; raise
	9:21	entered our palaces, cutting O the children from the
	11:19	let us cut him O from the land of
	22:24	I would tear you O
	23:23	says the LORD, and not a God afar O
	23:33	I will cast you O, says the LORD.'
	28:12	broken the yoke-bars from O the neck of Jeremiah
	30:8	break the yoke from O their neck, and I
	31:10	in the coastlands afar O; say, 'He who scattered
	31:37	then I will cast O all the descendants of
	36:23	king would cut them O with a penknife and
	36:29	land, and will cut O from it man and
	38:27	So they left O speaking with him, for the
	44:7	against yourselves, to cut O from you man and
	44:8	you may be cut O and become a curse
	44:11	for evil, to cut O all Judah.
	44:18	But since we left O burning incense to the
	47:4	the Philistines, to cut O from Tyre and Sidon
	48:2	let us cut her O from being a nation!'
	48:25	of Moab is cut O, and his arm is
	48:37	and every beard cut O; upon all the hands
	50:16	Cut O from Babylon the sower, and the one
	51:6	Be not cut O in her punishment, for this
	51:62	thou wilt cut it O, so that nothing shall
	52:33	So Jehoiachin put O his prison garments.
Lam	2:8	Zion; he marked it O by the line; he
	3:11	hiding; he led me O my way and tore
	3:31	Lord will not cast O for ever,
Bar	4:20	I have taken O the robe of peace and
	4:26	like a flock carried O by the enemy.
	5:1	Take O the garment of your sorrow and affliction,
	6:24	unless some one wipes O the rust; for even
	6:43	of them is led O by one of the
	6:58	they wear, and go O with this booty, and
Ezek	13:21	also I will tear O, and deliver my people
	14:8	byword and cut him O from the midst of
	14:13	upon it, and cut O from it man and
	14:17	land; and I cut O from it man and
	14:19	with blood, to cut O from it man and
	14:21	and pestilence, to cut O from it man and
	16:9	with water and washed O your blood from you,
	17:4	the cedar; he broke O the topmost of its
	17:9	its roots and cut O its branches, so that
	17:17	walls built to cut O many lives.
	17:22	out; I will break O from the topmost of

19:12 its fruit was stripped O, its strong stem was
21:3 sheath, and will cut O from you both righteous
21:4 Because I will cut O from you both righteous
21:26 the turban, and take O the crown; things shall
23:25 They shall cut O your nose and your ears,
25:7 I will cut you O from the peoples and
25:13 against Edom, and cut O from it man and
25:16 and I will cut O the Cherethites, and destroy
26:16 their robes, and strip O their embroidered garments;
29:8 you, and will cut O from you man and
29:19 and he shall carry O its wealth and despoil
30:15 of Egypt, and cut O the multitude of Thebes.
35:7 and I will cut O from it all who
37:11 we are clean cut O
38:12 seize spoil and carry O plunder; to assail the
38:13 your hosts to carry O plunder, to carry away
44:19 people, they shall put O the garments in which
45:3 district you shall measure O a section twenty-five
Dan 4:14 the tree and cut O its branches, strip off
4:14 off its branches, strip O its leaves and scatter
4:27 acceptable to you; break O your sins by practicing
7:4 its wings were plucked O, and it was lifted
9:26 one shall be cut O, and shall have nothing;
11:8 He shall also carry O to Egypt their gods
Hos 5:14 away, I will carry O, and none shall rescue.
9:17 God will cast them O, because they have not
10:15 the king of Israel shall be utterly cut O
Joel 1:5 for it is cut O from your mouth.
1:7 trees; it has stripped O their bark and thrown
1:9 drink offering are cut O from the house of
1:15 not the food cut O before our eyes, joy
Amos 1:5 of Damascus, and cut O the inhabitants from the
1:8 I will cut O the inhabitants from Ashdod, and
1:11 the sword, and cast O all pity, and his
2:3 trumpet; I will cut O the ruler from its
3:14 altar shall be cut O and fall to the
Obad 1:9 Esau will be cut O by slaughter.
1:10 you shall be cut O for ever.
1:11 day that strangers carried O his wealth, and
1:14 the ways to cut O his fugitives; you should
Mic 1:16 yourselves bald and cut O your hair, for the
3:2 tear the skin from O my people, and their
3:2 and their flesh from O their bones;
3:3 flay their skin from O them, and break their
4:3 for strong nations afar O; and they shall beat
4:7 those who were cast O, a strong nation; and
5:9 adversaries, and all your enemies shall be cut O
5:10 LORD, I will cut O your horses from among
5:11 and I will cut O the cities of your
5:12 and I will cut O sorceries from your hand,
5:13 and I will cut O your images and your
Nah 1:12 they will be cut O and pass away.
1:13 break his yoke from O you and will burst
1:14 gods I will cut O the graven image and
1:15 wicked come against you, he is utterly cut O
2:7 stripped, she is carried O, her maidens lamenting,
2:13 lions; I will cut O your prey from the
3:15 fire devour you, the sword will cut you O
Hab 2:10 your house by cutting O many peoples; you have
3:17 the flock be cut O from the fold and
Zeph 1:3 wicked; I will cut O mankind from the face
1:4 and I will cut O from this place the
1:11 more; all who weigh out silver are cut O
3:6 "I have cut O nations; their battlements are in
Zech 5:3 steals shall be cut O henceforth according to it,
5:3 falsely shall be cut O henceforth according to it.
6:7 were impatient to get O and patrol the earth.
9:10 I will cut O the chariot from Ephraim and
9:10 bow shall be cut O, and he shall command
11:13 which I was paid O by them.
11:16 the fat ones, tearing O even their hoofs.
13:2 hosts, I will cut O the names of the
13:8 thirds shall be cut O and perish, and one
14:2 shall not be cut O from the city.
Mal 2:12 May the LORD cut O from the tents of
1Mac 1:22 front of the temple; he stripped it all O
5:66 Then he marched O to go into the land
7:47 plunder, and they cut O Nicanor's head and the
9:4 Jerusalem; then they marched O and went to Berea
10:62 gave orders to take O Jonathan's garments and to
11:17 Zabdiel the Arab cut O the head of Alexander
11:55 that Demetrius had cast O gathered around him, and
13:22 He marched O and went into the land of
2Mac 1:16 dismembered them and cut O their heads and threw
3:35 Onias farewell, he marched O with his forces to
4:38 anger, he immediately stripped O the purple robe
4:38 robe from Andronicus, tore O his garments, and led
5:21 So Antiochus carried O eighteen hundred talents
7:4 scalp him and cut O his hands and feet,
7:7 They tore O the skin of his head with
8:13 of God's justice ran O and got away.
8:35 the least account, took O his splendid uniform and
9:25 you when I hastened O to the upper provinces;
10:17 the places, and beat O all who fought upon
10:19 and he himself set O for places where he
11:7 Then they eagerly rushed O together.
12:21 of Judas, he sent O the women and the
12:22 things; and they rushed O in flight and were
12:35 cloak was dragging him O by main strength, wishing
12:35 upon him and cut O his arm; so Gorgias
14:12 Judea, and sent him O
15:30 ordered them to cut O Nicanor's head and arm
Mt 5:30 to sin, cut it O and throw it away;
10:14 to your words, shake O the dust from your
18:8 to sin, cut it O and throw it away;
22:5 of it and went O, one to his farm,
26:51 high priest, and cut O his ear.
Mk 6:11 when you leave, shake O the dust that is
9:43 to sin, cut it O; it is better for
9:44 to sin, cut it O; it is better for
10:50 And throwing O his mantle he sprang up and
14:47 high priest and cut O his ear.
Lk 9:5 leave that town shake O the dust from your
10:11 our feet, we wipe O against you; nevertheless know
14:32 yet a great way O, he sends an embassy
22:48 high priest and cut O his right ear.
Jn 11:18 Jerusalem, about two miles O,
18:10 priest's slave and cut O his right ear.
18:26 ear Peter had cut O, asked, "Did I not
21:8 from the land, but about a hundred yards O
Acts 7:33 said to him, 'Take O the shoes from your
8:3 after house, he dragged O men and women and
9:30 Caesarea, and sent him O to Tarsus.
10:23 he rose and went O with them, and some
12:7 And the chains fell O his hands.
13:3 laid their hands on them and sent them O
13:51 But they shook O the dust from their feet
15:30 when they were sent O, they went down to
15:33 time, they were sent O in peace by the
16:22 magistrates tore the garments O them and gave
17:14 brethren immediately sent Paul O on his way to
24:21 the Way, put them O, saying, "When Lysias the
27:5 the sea which is O Cilicia and Pamphylia, we
27:7 and arrived with difficulty O Cnidus, and as the
27:7 the lee of Crete O Salmone.
27:40 So they cast O the anchors and left them
28:5 He, however, shook O the creature into the fire
Rom 3:9 Are we Jews any better O
9:3 were accursed and cut O from Christ for the
11:17 the branches were broken O, and you, a wild
11:19 say, "Branches were broken O so that I might
11:20 They were broken O because of their unbelief, but
11:22 his kindness; otherwise you too will be cut O
13:12 Let us then cast O the works of darkness
1Cor 8:8 We are no worse O if we do not
8:8 eat, and no better O if we do.
11:6 then she should cut O her hair; but if
Eph 4:22 Put O your old nature which belongs to your
Col 2:11 without hands, by putting O the body of flesh
3:9 that you have put O the old nature with
2Pet 1:14 know that the putting O of my body will
Rev 12:17 the woman, and went O to make war on

OFFENCES

Tob 3:3 and for my unwitting O and those which my

OFFEND (2)

Job 34:31 chastisement; I will not O any more;
Sir 7:7 Do not O against the public, and do not

OFFENDED (8)

Gen 40:1 Egypt and his baker O their lord the king
Job 4:2 ventures a word with you, will you be O
Sir 25:2 and I am greatly O at their life: a
30:13 you may not be O by his shamelessness.
Bar 6:18 a man who has O a king, as though
Ezek 25:12 Judah and has grievously O in taking vengeance upon
Mt 15:12 that the Pharisees were O when they heard this
Acts 25:8 against Caesar have I O at all."

OFFENDER

Is 29:21 out to be an O, and lay a snare

O

2Kgs 5:17 your servant will not O burnt offering or sacrifice
10:19 a great sacrifice to O to Baal; whoever is
10:24 he went in to O sacrifices and burnt offerings.
1Chr 16:40 was at Gibeon, to O burnt offerings to the
21:10 LORD, Three things I O you; choose one of
21:24 what is yours, nor O burnt offerings which cost
23:5 and four thousand shall O praises to the LORD
29:5 Who then will O willingly, consecrating himself today
29:14 be able thus to O willingly?
2Chr 13:11 They O to the LORD every morning and every
23:18 of the LORD, to O burnt offerings to the
29:21 sons of Aaron to O them on the altar
35:12 the lay people, to O to the LORD, as
35:16 the passover and to O burnt offerings on the
Ezra 3:2 God of Israel, to O burnt offerings upon it,
3:6 month they began to O burnt offerings to the
6:10 fail, that they may O pleasing sacrifices to the
7:17 offerings, and you shall O them upon the altar
Job 1:5 in the morning and O burnt offerings according to
6:22 Or, 'From your wealth O a bribe for me?
42:8 my servant Job, and O up for yourselves a
Ps 4:5 [Selah] O right sacrifices, and put your trust in
27:6 me; and I will O in his tent sacrifices
32:6 one who is godly O prayer to thee; at
50:14 O to God a sacrifice of thanksgiving, and pay
66:15 I will O to thee burnt offerings of fatlings,
107:22 And let them O sacrifices of thanksgiving, and tell
110:3 Your people will O themselves freely on the day
116:17 I will O to thee the sacrifice of thanksgiving
Prov 7:14 him: "I had to O sacrifices, and today I
Eccl 5:1 is better than to O the sacrifice of fools;
Sir 35:12 Do not O him a bribe, for he will
38:11 O a sweet-smelling sacrifice, and a memorial portion
45:16 all the living to O sacrifice to the Lord,
Is 57:7 you went up to O sacrifice.
Jer 14:12 cry, and though they O burnt offering and cereal
32:35 son of Hinnom, to O up their sons and
33:18 in my presence to O burnt offerings, to burn
35:2 of the chambers; then O them wine to drink."
Bar 1:10 a cereal offering, and O them upon the altar
6:56 Besides, they can O no resistance to a king
Ezek 20:26 gifts in making them O by fire all their
20:31 When you O your gifts and sacrifice your sons
43:22 second day you shall O a he-goat without blemish
43:23 cleansing it, you shall O a bull without blemish
43:24 salt upon them and O them up as a
43:27 onward the priests shall O upon the altar your
44:7 profaning it, when you O to me my food,
44:15 attend on me to O me the fat and
44:27 holy place, he shall O his sin offering, says
46:2 The priests shall O his burnt offering and his
46:6 new moon he shall O a young bull without
46:12 him; and he shall O his burnt offering or
Amos 4:5 tithes every three days; O a sacrifice of thanksgiving
5:22 Even though you O me your burnt offerings and
8:5 sabbath, that we may O wheat for sale, that
Hag 2:14 hands; and what they O there is unclean.
Mal 1:8 When you O blind animals in sacrifice, is that
1:8 And when you O those that are lame or
1Mac 1:51 cities of Judah to O sacrifice, city by city.
2:15 Modein to make them O sacrifice.
2:23 sight of all to O sacrifice upon the altar
6:60 to the Jews an O of peace, and they
11:34 To all those who O sacrifice in Jerusalem, we
12:11 the sacrifices which we O and in our prayers,
Mt 5:24 and then come and O your gift.
8:4 to the priest, and O the gift that Moses
Mk 1:44 to the priest, and O for your cleansing what
Lk 2:24 the Lord") and to O a sacrifice according to
5:33 John fast often and O prayers, and so do
6:29 you on the cheek, O the other also; and
Acts 7:42 the prophets: 'Did you O to me slain beasts
14:13 gates and wanted to O sacrifice with the people.
1Cor 10:20 what pagans sacrifice they O to demons and not
Heb 5:1 relation to God, to O gifts and sacrifices for
5:3 he is bound to O sacrifice for his own
7:27 those high priests, to O sacrifices daily, first for
8:3 priest is appointed to O gifts and sacrifices; hence
8:3 for this priest also to have something to O
8:4 there are priests who O gifts according to the
9:25 Nor was it to O himself repeatedly, as the
11:17 promises was ready to O up his only son,
12:28 and thus let us O to God acceptable worship,
13:15 then let us continually O up a sacrifice of
1Pet 2:5 a holy priesthood, to O spiritual sacrifices acceptable

OFFERED (158)

Gen 8:20 every clean bird, and O burnt offerings on the
22:13 took the ram, and O it up as a
31:54 father Isaac, and Jacob O a sacrifice on the
46:1 came to Beer-sheba, and O sacrifices to the God
Ex 18:12 And Jethro, Moses' father-in-law, O a burnt offering
24:5 people of Israel, who O burnt offerings and sacrificed
29:27 waved, and which is O from the ram of
29:28 priests' portion to be O by the people of
32:6 on the morrow, and O burnt offerings and brought
Lev 2:12 they shall not be O on the altar for
3:11 the altar as food O by fire to the
3:16 the altar as food O by fire for a
7:3 its fat shall be O, the fat tail, the
7:8 skin of the burnt offering which he has O
7:34 the thigh that is O I have taken from
9:15 and killed it, and O it for sin, like
9:16 the burnt offering, and O it according to the
10:1 incense on it, and O unholy fire before the
10:14 the thigh that is O you shall eat in
10:15 The thigh that is O and the breast that
10:19 "Behold, today they have O their sin offering and
22:18 freewill offering which is O to the LORD as
23:13 with oil, to be O by fire to the
24:7 memorial portion to be O by fire to the
27:11 such as is not O as an offering to
Num 3:4 the LORD when they O unholy fire before the
6:20 the thigh that is O; and after that the
7:3 who were numbered, O and brought their offerings
7:3 one an ox; they O them before the tabernacle.
7:10 And the leaders O offerings for the dedication of
7:10 anointed; and the leaders O their offering before the
7:12 He who O his offering the first day was
7:19 made an offering; he O for his offering one
8:15 have cleansed them and O them as a wave
8:21 their clothes; and Aaron O them as a wave
16:38 the altar, for they O them before the LORD;
16:39 who were burned had O; and they were hammered
18:30 them, 'When you have O from it the best
18:32 it, when you have O the best of it.
23:2 and Balak and Balaam O on each altar a
23:4 altars, and I have O upon each altar a
23:14 built seven altars, and O a bull and a
23:30 Balaam had said, and O a bull and a
26:61 Abihu died when they O unholy fire before the
28:15 LORD; it shall be O besides the continual burnt
28:24 LORD; it shall be O besides the continual burnt
31:52 the offering that they O to the LORD, from
Deut 26:14 I was unclean, or O any of it to
Josh 8:31 iron tool"; and they O on it burnt offerings
Judg 5:2 Israel, that the people O themselves willingly, bless
5:9 commanders of Israel who O themselves willingly
6:28 the second bull was O upon the altar which
13:19 the cereal offering, and O it upon the rock
20:26 day until evening, and O burnt offerings and peace
21:4 there an altar, and O burnt offerings and peace
1Sam 2:13 that when any man O sacrifice, the priest's servant
6:14 of the cart and O the cows as a
6:15 of Beth-shemesh O burnt offerings and sacrificed
7:9 a sucking lamb and O it as a whole
13:9 And he O the burnt offering.
13:12 I forced myself, and O the burnt offering."
2Sam 6:17 for it; and David O burnt offerings and peace
24:25 to the LORD, and O burnt offerings and peace
1Kgs 3:15 of the LORD, and O up burnt offerings and
8:62 all Israel with him, O sacrifice before the LORD.
8:63 Solomon O as peace offerings to the LORD twenty-
8:64 LORD; for there he O the burnt offering and
10:5 burnt offerings which he O at the house of
12:32 in Judah, and he O sacrifices upon the altar;
2Kgs 3:27 in his stead, and O him for a burnt
17:4 king of Egypt, and O no tribute to the
1Chr 16:1 for it; and they O burnt offerings and peace
23:31 whenever burnt offerings are O to the LORD on
29:9 whole heart they had O freely to the LORD;
29:17 heart I have freely O all these things, and
29:21 on the next day O burnt offerings to the
2Chr 1:6 tent of meeting, and O a thousand burnt offerings
7:4 and all the people O sacrifice before the LORD.
7:5 King Solomon O as a sacrifice twenty-two thousand
7:6 for ever—whenever David O praises by their ministry;
7:7 LORD; for there he O the burnt offering and
8:12 Then Solomon O up burnt offerings to the LORD
9:4 burnt offerings which he O at the house of
24:14 And they O burnt offerings in the house of
29:7 not burned incense or O burnt offerings in the

29:27 the burnt offering be O on the altar.
33:16 of the LORD and O upon it sacrifices of
Ezra 1:6 with costly wares, besides all that was freely O
3:3 the lands, and they O burnt offerings upon it
3:4 it is written, and O the daily burnt offerings
6:3 place where sacrifices are O and burnt offerings are
6:17 They O at the dedication of this house of
7:15 his counselors have freely O to the God of
8:25 Israel there present had O;
8:35 captivity, the returned exiles, O burnt offerings to the
Neh 11:2 the men who willingly O to live in Jerusalem.
12:43 And they O great sacrifices that day and rejoiced,
Tob 5:13 Jerusalem to worship and O the first-born of our
Jud 4:14 loins girded with sackcloth, O the continual burnt
9:1 evening's incense was being O in the house of
16:18 people were purified, they O their burnt offerings,
Ps 51:19 then bulls will be O on thy altar.
106:28 Peor, and ate sacrifices O to the dead;
Song 8:7 If a man O for love all the wealth
Wis 18:9 children of good men O sacrifices, and with one
Sir 46:16 every side, and he O in sacrifice a sucking
Jer 32:29 roofs incense has been O to Baal and drink
44:15 that their wives had O incense to other gods,
Bar 6:28 the sacrifices that are O to these gods and
Ezek 3:1 man, eat what is O to you; eat this
6:13 leafy oak, wherever they O pleasing odor to all
20:28 leafy tree, there they O their sacrifices and presented
23:37 and they have even O up to them for
Dan 2:46 offering and incense be O up to him.
3:25 Then Azariah stood and O this prayer; in the
Jon 1:16 LORD exceedingly, and they O a sacrifice to the
Mal 1:11 every place incense is O to my name, and
1Mac 1:59 of the month they O sacrifice on the altar
2:42 Israel, every one who O himself willingly for the
4:53 year, they rose and O sacrifice, as the law
4:56 for eight days, and O burnt offerings with gladness;
4:56 offerings with gladness; they O a sacrifice of
5:54 gladness and joy, and O burnt offerings, because not
7:33 offering that was being O for the king.
2Mac 1:8 were heard, and we O sacrifice and cereal offering,
1:18 temple and the altar, O sacrifices.
1:23 being consumed, the priests O prayer – the
2:9 possessed of wisdom Solomon O sacrifice for the
3:32 with regard to Heliodorus, O sacrifice for the man's
3:35 Then Heliodorus O sacrifice to the Lord and made
4:34 and resorting to treachery O him sworn pledges and
10:3 out of flint, they O sacrifices, after a lapse
10:7 fronds of palm, they O hymns of thanksgiving to
13:23 settled with them and O sacrifice, honored the
Mt 2:11 opening their treasures, they O him gifts, gold and
27:34 of a skull), they O him wine to drink,
Mk 15:23 And they O him wine mingled with myrrh; but
Acts 7:41 in those days, and O a sacrifice to the
8:18 the apostles' hands, he O them money,
Rom 11:16 If the dough O as first fruits is holy,
1Cor 8:1 Now concerning food O to idols: we know that
8:4 the eating of food O to idols, we know
8:7 eat food as really O to an idol; and
8:10 weak, to eat food O to idols?
10:19 That food O to idols is anything, or that
10:28 you, "This has been O in sacrifice," then out
Heb 5:7 of his flesh, Jesus O up prayers and supplications,
7:27 for all when he O up himself.
9:9 gifts and sacrifices are O which cannot perfect the
9:14 through the eternal Spirit O himself without blemish
9:28 so Christ, having been O once to bear the
10:1 sacrifices which are continually O year after year,
10:2 Otherwise, would they not have ceased to be O
10:8 (these are O according to the law),
10:12 But when Christ had O for all time a
11:4 By faith Abel O to God a more acceptable
11:17 when he was tested, O up Isaac, and he
Jas 2:21 by works, when he O his son Isaac upon

OFFERING (820)

Gen 4:3 to the LORD an O of the fruit of
4:4 for Abel and his O,
4:5 for Cain and his O he had no regard.
22:2 there as a burnt O upon one of the
22:3 wood for the burnt O, and arose and went
22:6 wood of the burnt O, and laid it on
22:7 but where is the lamb for a burnt O
22:8 lamb for a burnt O, my son." So they
22:13 up as a burnt O instead of his son.
35:14 poured out a drink O on it, and poured
Ex 18:12 father-in-law, offered a burnt O and sacrifices to God;
25:2 take for me an O; from every man whose
25:2 you shall receive the O for me.
25:3 And this is the O which you shall receive
28:38 incurred in the holy O which the people of
29:14 fire outside the camp; it is a sin O
29:18 it is a burnt O to the LORD; it
29:18 a pleasing odor, an O by fire to the
29:24 them for a wave O before the LORD.
29:25 addition to the burnt O, as a pleasing odor
29:25 LORD; it is an O by fire to the
29:26 it for a wave O before the LORD; and
29:27 breast of the wave O, and the thigh of
29:28 offerings; it is their O to the LORD.
29:36 bull as a sin O for atonement.
29:36 shall offer a sin O for the altar, when
29:41 with it a cereal O and its libation, as
29:41 a pleasing odor, an O by fire to the
29:42 be a continual burnt O throughout your generations
30:9 incense thereon, nor burnt O, nor cereal offering; and
30:9 burnt offering, nor cereal O; and you shall pour
30:10 blood of the sin O of atonement he shall
30:13 a shekel as an O to the LORD.
30:14 years old and upward, shall give the LORD's O
30:15 you give the LORD's O to make atonement for
30:20 minister, to burn an O by fire to the
30:28 the altar of burnt O with all its utensils
31:9 the altar of burnt O with all its utensils,
35:5 from among you an O to the LORD; whoever
35:5 him bring the LORD's O: gold, silver, and bronze;
35:16 the altar of burnt O, with its grating of
35:21 and brought the LORD's O to be used for
35:22 every man dedicating an O of gold to the
35:24 who could make an O of silver or bronze
35:24 it as the LORD's O; and every man with
35:29 it as their freewill O to the LORD.
36:3 Moses all the freewill O which the people of
36:6 anything more for the O for the sanctuary." So
38:1 the altar of burnt O also of acacia wood;
38:24 the gold from the O, was twenty-nine talents and
Lev 1:2 of you brings an O to the LORD, you
1:2 you shall bring your O of cattle from the
1:3 "If his O is a burnt offering from the
1:3 offering is a burnt O from the herd, he
1:4 head of the burnt O, and it shall be
1:6 shall flay the burnt O and cut it into
1:9 altar, as a burnt O, an offering by fire,
1:9 a burnt offering, an O by fire, a pleasing
1:10 gift for a burnt O is from the flock,
1:13 it is a burnt O, an offering by fire,
1:13 a burnt offering, an O by fire, a pleasing
1:14 "If his O to the LORD is a burnt
1:14 LORD is a burnt O of birds, then he
1:14 he shall bring his O of turtledoves or of
1:17 it is a burnt O, an offering by fire,
1:17 a burnt offering, an O by fire, a pleasing
2:1 one brings a cereal O as an offering to
2:1 cereal offering as an O to the LORD, his
2:1 to the LORD, his O shall be of fine
2:2 upon the altar, an O by fire, a pleasing
2:3 left of the cereal O shall be for Aaron
2:4 you bring a cereal O baked in the oven
2:4 the oven as an O, it shall be unleavened
2:5 And if your O is a cereal offering baked
2:5 offering is a cereal O baked on a griddle,
2:6 pour oil on it; it is a cereal O
2:7 And if your O is a cereal offering cooked
2:7 offering is a cereal O cooked in a pan,
2:8 shall bring the cereal O that is made of
2:9 take from the cereal O its memorial portion and
2:9 on the altar, an O by fire, a pleasing
2:10 left of the cereal O shall be for Aaron
2:11 "No cereal O which you bring to the LORD
2:11 any honey as an O by fire to the
2:12 As an O of first fruits you may bring
2:13 lacking from your cereal O; with all your offerings
2:14 you offer a cereal O of first fruits to
2:14 offer for the cereal O of your first fruits
2:15 lay frankincense on it; it is a cereal O
2:16 frankincense; it is an O by fire to the
3:1 "If a man's O is a sacrifice of peace
3:1 a sacrifice of peace O, if he offers an
3:2 the head of his O and kill it at
3:3 sacrifice of the peace O, as an offering by
3:3 peace offering, as an O by fire to the
3:5 altar upon the burnt O, which is upon the
3:5 fire; it is an O by fire, a pleasing

O

14:31 along with a cereal O; and the priest shall
15:15 one for a sin O and the other for
15:15 other for a burnt O; and the priest shall
15:30 one for a sin O and the other for
15:30 other for a burnt O; and the priest shall
16:3 bull for a sin O and a ram for
16:3 sin offering and a ram for a burnt O
16:5 goats for a sin O, and one ram for
16:5 sin offering, and one ram for a burnt O
16:6 bull as a sin O for himself, and shall
16:9 it as a sin O;
16:11 bull as a sin O for himself, and shall
16:11 bull as a sin O for himself.
16:15 goat of the sin O which is for the
16:24 and offer his burnt O and the burnt offering
16:24 offering and the burnt O of the people, and
16:25 fat of the sin O he shall burn upon
16:27 bull for the sin O and the goat for
16:27 goat for the sin O, whose blood was brought
17:8 who offers a burnt O or sacrifice,
19:21 shall bring a guilt O for himself to the
19:21 tent of meeting, a ram for a guilt O
19:22 ram of the guilt O before the LORD for
19:24 shall be holy, an O of praise to the
22:12 not eat of the O of the holy things.
22:18 in Israel presents his O, whether in payment of
22:18 or as a freewill O which is offered to
22:18 LORD as a burnt O,
22:21 or as a freewill O, from the herd or
22:22 make of them an O by fire upon the
22:23 present for a freewill O; but for a votive
22:23 but for a votive O it cannot be accepted.
22:27 be acceptable as an O by fire to the
23:8 you shall present an O by fire to the
23:12 blemish as a burnt O to the LORD.
23:13 And the cereal O with it shall be two
23:13 odor; and the drink O with it shall be
23:14 you have brought the O of your God: it
23:15 sheaf of the wave O; seven full weeks shall
23:16 shall present a cereal O of new grain to
23:18 shall be a burnt O to the LORD, with
23:18 LORD, with their cereal O and their drink offerings,
23:18 their drink offerings, an O by fire, a pleasing
23:19 goat for a sin O, and two male lambs
23:20 fruits as a wave O before the LORD, with
23:25 you shall present an O by fire to the
23:27 yourselves and present an O by fire to the
23:36 convocation and present an O by fire to the
27:9 men offer as an O to the LORD, all
27:11 not offered as an O to the LORD, then
Num 4:7 flagons for the drink O; the continual bread also
4:16 incense, the continual cereal O, and the anointing oil,
5:9 And every O, all the holy things of the
5:15 priest, and bring the O required of her, a
5:15 it is a cereal O of jealousy, a cereal
5:15 of jealousy, a cereal O of remembrance, bringing
5:18 her hands the cereal O of remembrance, which is
5:18 which is the cereal O of jealousy.
5:25 shall take the cereal O of jealousy out of
5:25 shall wave the cereal O before the LORD and
5:26 handful of the cereal O, as its memorial portion,
6:11 one for a sin O and the other for
6:11 other for a burnt O, and make atonement for
6:12 old for a guilt O; but the former time
6:14 blemish for a burnt O, and one ewe lamb
6:14 blemish as a sin O, and one ram without
6:14 blemish as a peace O,
6:15 oil, and their cereal O and their drink offerings.
6:16 and offer his sin O and his burnt offering,
6:16 offering and his burnt O,
6:17 a sacrifice of peace O to the LORD, with
6:17 offer also its cereal O and its drink offering.
6:17 offer also its cereal offering and its drink O
6:18 which is under the sacrifice of the peace O
6:20 them for a wave O before the LORD; they
6:21 His O to the LORD shall be according to
7:10 the leaders offered their O before the altar.
7:12 He who offered his O the first day was
7:13 of Judah; and his O was one silver plate
7:13 oil for a cereal O;
7:15 old, for a burnt O;
7:16 goat for a sin O;
7:17 This was the O of Nahshon the son of
7:18 of Issachar, made an O;
7:19 he offered for his O one silver plate, whose
7:19 oil for a cereal O;
7:21 old, for a burnt O;
7:22 goat for a sin O;
7:23 This was the O of Nethanel the son of
7:25 men of Zebulun: his O was one silver plate,
7:25 oil for a cereal O;
7:27 old, for a burnt O;
7:28 goat for a sin O;
7:29 This was the O of Eliab the son of
7:31 men of Reuben: his O was one silver plate
7:31 oil for a cereal O;
7:33 old, for a burnt O;
7:34 goat for a sin O;
7:35 This was the O of Elizur the son of
7:37 men of Simeon: his O was one silver plate,
7:37 oil for a cereal O;
7:39 old, for a burnt O;
7:40 goat for a sin O;
7:41 This was the O of Shelumi-el the son of
7:43 men of Gad: his O was one silver plate,
7:43 oil for a cereal O;
7:45 old, for a burnt O;
7:46 goat for a sin O;
7:47 This was the O of Eliasaph the son of
7:49 men of Ephraim: his O was one silver plate,
7:49 oil for a cereal O;
7:51 old, for a burnt O;
7:52 goat for a sin O;
7:53 This was the O of Elishama the son of
7:55 men of Manasseh: his O was one silver plate,
7:55 oil for a cereal O;
7:57 old, for a burnt O;
7:58 goat for a sin O;
7:59 This was the O of Gamaliel the son of
7:61 men of Benjamin: his O was one silver plate,
7:61 oil for a cereal O;
7:63 old, for a burnt O;
7:64 goat for a sin O;
7:65 This was the O of Abidan the son of
7:67 men of Dan: his O was one silver plate,
7:67 oil for a cereal O;
7:69 old, for a burnt O;
7:70 goat for a sin O;
7:71 This was the O of Ahiezer the son of
7:73 men of Asher: his O was one silver plate,
7:73 oil for a cereal O;
7:75 old, for a burnt O;
7:76 goat for a sin O;
7:77 This was the O of Pagiel the son of
7:79 men of Naphtali: his O was one silver plate,
7:79 oil for a cereal O;
7:81 old, for a burnt O;
7:82 goat for a sin O;
7:83 This was the O of Ahira the son of
7:84 This was the dedication O for the altar, on
7:87 cattle for the burnt O twelve bulls, twelve rams,
7:87 old, with their cereal O; and twelve male goats
7:87 goats for a sin O;
7:88 This was the dedication O for the altar, after
8:8 bull and its cereal O of fine flour mixed
8:8 shall take another young bull for a sin O
8:11 LORD as a wave O from the people of
8:12 one for a sin O and the other for
8:12 other for a burnt O to the LORD, to
8:13 them as a wave O to the LORD.
8:15 cleansed them and offered them as a wave O
8:21 them as a wave O before the LORD, and
9:7 are we kept from O the LORD's offering at
9:7 from offering the LORD's O at its appointed time
9:13 not offer the LORD's O at its appointed time;
15:3 from the flock an O by fire or a
15:3 fire or a burnt O or a sacrifice, to
15:3 or as a freewill O or at your appointed
15:4 he who brings his O shall offer to the
15:4 the LORD a cereal O of a tenth of
15:5 wine for the drink O, a fourth of a
15:5 prepare with the burnt O, or for the sacrifice,
15:6 prepare for a cereal O two tenths of an
15:7 and for the drink O you shall offer a
15:8 bull for a burnt O, or for a sacrifice,
15:9 the bull a cereal O of three tenths of
15:10 offer for the drink O half a hin of
15:10 of wine, as an O by fire, a pleasing
15:13 in this way, in O an offering by fire,
15:13 way, in offering an O by fire, a pleasing
15:14 wishes to offer an O by fire, a pleasing
15:19 you shall present an O to the LORD.

15:20 a cake as an O; as an offering from
15:20 an offering; as an O from the threshing floor,
15:21 to the LORD an O throughout your generations.
15:24 bull for a burnt O, a pleasing odor to
15:24 LORD, with its cereal O and its drink offering,
15:24 offering and its drink O, according to the ordinance,
15:24 ordinance, and one male goat for a sin O
15:25 they have brought their O, an offering by fire
15:25 brought their offering, an O by fire to the
15:25 LORD, and their sin O before the LORD, for
15:27 female goat a year old for a sin O
16:15 said to the LORD, "Do not respect their O
16:35 hundred and fifty men O the incense.
18:9 from the fire; every O of theirs, every cereal
18:9 of theirs, every cereal O of theirs and every
18:9 theirs and every sin O of theirs and every
18:9 theirs and every guilt O of theirs, which they
18:11 also is yours, the O of their gift, all
18:17 their fat as an O by fire, a pleasing
18:24 they present as an O to the LORD, I
18:26 you shall present an O from it to the
18:27 And your O shall be reckoned to you as
18:28 you also present an O to the LORD from
18:28 shall give the LORD's O to Aaron the priest.
18:29 you shall present every O due to the LORD,
19:17 of the burnt sin O, and running water shall
23:3 "Stand beside your burnt O, and I will go;
23:6 princes of Moab were standing beside his burnt O
23:15 here beside your burnt O, while I meet the
23:17 standing beside his burnt O, and the princes of
28:2 say to them, 'My O, my food for my
28:3 them, This is the O by fire which you
28:3 without blemish, day by day, as a continual O
28:5 flour for a cereal O, mixed with a fourth
28:6 is a continual burnt O, which was ordained at
28:6 a pleasing odor, an O by fire to the
28:7 Its drink O shall be a fourth of a
28:7 pour out a drink O of strong drink to
28:8 evening; like the cereal O of the morning, and
28:8 and like its drink O, you shall offer it
28:8 offer it as an O by fire, a pleasing
28:9 flour for a cereal O, mixed with oil, and
28:9 oil, and its drink O:
28:10 this is the burnt O of every sabbath, besides
28:10 besides the continual burnt O and its drink offering.
28:10 besides the continual burnt offering and its drink O
28:11 shall offer a burnt O to the LORD: two
28:12 flour for a cereal O, mixed with oil, for
28:12 flour for a cereal O, mixed with oil, for
28:13 oil as a cereal O for every lamb; for
28:13 lamb; for a burnt O of pleasing odor, an
28:13 of pleasing odor, an O by fire to the
28:14 this is the burnt O of each month throughout
28:15 goat for a sin O to the LORD; it
28:15 besides the continual burnt O and its drink offering.
28:15 besides the continual burnt offering and its drink O
28:19 work, but offer an O by fire, a burnt
28:19 by fire, a burnt O to the LORD: two
28:20 blemish; also their cereal O of fine flour mixed
28:22 goat for a sin O, to make atonement for
28:23 these besides the burnt O of the morning, which
28:23 the morning, which is for a continual burnt O
28:24 the food of an O by fire, a pleasing
28:24 besides the continual burnt O and its drink offering.
28:24 besides the continual burnt offering and its drink O
28:26 you offer a cereal O of new grain to
28:27 but offer a burnt O, a pleasing odor to
28:28 old; also their cereal O of fine flour mixed
28:31 Besides the continual burnt O and its cereal offering,
28:31 offering and its cereal O, you shall offer them
28:31 offering, you shall offer them and their drink O
29:2 shall offer a burnt O, a pleasing odor to
29:3 blemish; also their cereal O of fine flour mixed
29:5 goat for a sin O, to make atonement for
29:6 you; besides the burnt O of the new moon,
29:6 moon, and its cereal O, and the continual burnt
29:6 and the continual burnt O and its cereal offering,
29:6 offering and its cereal O, and their drink offering,
29:6 and their drink O, according to the ordinance
29:6 a pleasing odor, an O by fire to the
29:8 shall offer a burnt O to the LORD, a
29:9 blemish; and their cereal O of fine flour mixed
29:11 goat for a sin O, besides the sin offering
29:11 offering, besides the sin O of atonement, and the
29:11 and the continual burnt O and its cereal offering,
29:11 offering and its cereal O, and their drink offerings.
29:13 shall offer a burnt O, an offering by fire,
29:13 a burnt offering, an O by fire, a pleasing
29:14 blemish; and their cereal O of fine flour mixed
29:16 goat for a sin O, besides the continual burnt
29:16 besides the continual burnt O, its cereal offering and
29:16 burnt offering, its cereal O and its drink offering.
29:16 burnt offering, its cereal offering and its drink O
29:18 blemish, with the cereal O and the drink offerings
29:19 goat for a sin O, besides the continual burnt
29:19 besides the continual burnt O and its cereal offering,
29:19 offering and its cereal O, and their drink offerings.
29:21 blemish, with the cereal O and the drink offerings
29:22 goat for a sin O, besides the continual burnt
29:22 besides the continual burnt O and its cereal offering
29:22 offering and its cereal O and its drink offering.
29:22 offering and its cereal offering and its drink O
29:24 blemish, with the cereal O and the drink offerings
29:25 goat for a sin O, besides the continual burnt
29:25 besides the continual burnt O, its cereal offering and
29:25 burnt offering, its cereal O and its drink offering.
29:25 burnt offering, its cereal offering and its drink O
29:27 blemish, with the cereal O and the drink offerings
29:28 goat for a sin O; besides the continual burnt
29:28 besides the continual burnt O and its cereal offering
29:28 offering and its cereal O and its drink offering.
29:28 offering and its cereal offering and its drink O
29:30 blemish, with the cereal O and the drink offerings
29:31 goat for a sin O; besides the continual burnt
29:31 besides the continual burnt O, its cereal offering, and
29:31 burnt offering, its cereal O, and its drink offerings.
29:33 blemish, with the cereal O and the drink offerings
29:34 goat for a sin O; besides the continual burnt
29:34 besides the continual burnt O, its cereal offering, and
29:34 burnt offering, its cereal O, and its drink offering.
29:34 burnt offering, its cereal offering, and its drink O
29:36 shall offer a burnt O, an offering by fire,
29:36 a burnt offering, an O by fire, a pleasing
29:37 blemish, and the cereal O and the drink offerings
29:38 goat for a sin O; besides the continual burnt
29:38 besides the continual burnt O and its cereal offering
29:38 offering and its cereal O and its drink offering.
29:38 offering and its cereal offering and its drink O
31:29 the priest as an O to the LORD.
31:41 tribute, which was the O for the LORD, to
31:50 have brought the LORD's O, what each man found,
31:52 the gold of the O that they offered to
Deut 12:6 your tithes and the O that you present, your
12:11 your tithes and the O that you present, and
12:17 freewill offerings, or the O that you present;
13:16 as a whole burnt O to the LORD your
16:10 tribute of a freewill O from your hand, which
18:3 the people, from those O a sacrifice, whether it
18:10 his daughter as an O, any one who practices
32:38 sacrifices, and drank the wine of their drink O
33:10 thee, and whole burnt O upon thy altar.
Josh 22:26 altar, not for burnt O, nor for sacrifice,
22:29 an altar for burnt O, cereal offering, or sacrifice,
22:29 for burnt offering, cereal O, or sacrifice, other than
Judg 6:26 it as a burnt O with the wood of
11:31 I will offer him up for a burnt O
13:16 make ready a burnt O, then offer it to
13:19 kid with the cereal O, and offered it upon
13:23 have accepted a burnt O and a cereal offering
13:23 offering and a cereal O at our hands, or
1Sam 2:17 the men treated the O of the LORD with
2:29 choicest parts of every O of my people Israel?'
3:14 expiated by sacrifice or O for ever."
6:3 but by all means return him a guilt O
6:4 "What is the guilt O that we shall return
6:8 you are returning to him as a guilt O
6:14 cows as a burnt O to the LORD.
6:17 returned as a guilt O to the LORD: one
7:9 as a whole burnt O to the LORD; and
7:10 As Samuel was O up the burnt offering, the
7:10 offering up the burnt O, the Philistines drew near
13:9 said, "Bring the burnt O here to me, and
13:9 And he offered the burnt O
13:10 as he had finished O the burnt offering, behold,
13:10 finished offering the burnt O, behold, Samuel came;
13:12 so I forced myself, and offered the burnt O
26:19 may he accept an O; but if it is
2Sam 6:18 when David had finished O the burnt offerings and
15:12 And while Absalom was O the sacrifices, he sent
24:22 oxen for the burnt O, and the threshing sledges
1Kgs 8:54 Now as Solomon finished O all this prayer and
8:64 he offered the burnt O and the cereal offering

O

	2:14	behind him, a cereal O and a drink offering
	2:14	offering and a drink O for the LORD, your
Zeph	3:10	daughter of my dispersed ones, shall bring my O
Mal	1:7	despised thy name?' By O polluted food upon my
	1:10	will not accept an O from your hand.
	1:11	name, and a pure O; for my name is
	1:13	or sick, and this you bring as your O
	2:12	or to bring an O to the LORD of
	2:13	no longer regards the O or accepts it with
	3:4	Then the O of Judah and Jerusalem will be
1Mac	1:54	a desolating sacrilege upon the altar of burnt O
	1:59	altar which was upon the altar of burnt O
	4:44	the altar of burnt O, which had been profaned.
	4:53	new altar of burnt O which they had built.
	7:33	show him the burnt O that was being offered
2Mac	1:8	offered sacrifice and cereal O, and we lighted the
	2:11	consumed because the sin O had not been eaten."
	3:33	priest was making the O of atonement, the same
	12:43	it to Jerusalem to provide for a sin O
	14:31	while the priests were O the customary sacrifices,
Mt	5:23	So if you are O your gift at the
Lk	5:14	priest, and make an O for your cleansing, as
	23:35	him, coming up and O him vinegar,
Jn	16:2	will think he is O service to God.
Acts	14:18	restrained the people from O sacrifice to them.
	21:26	be fulfilled and the O presented for every one
Rom	15:16	God, so that the O of the Gentiles may
2Cor	9:1	to you about the O for the saints,
Eph	5:2	for us, a fragrant O and sacrifice to God.
Phil	2:17	libation upon the sacrificial O of your faith, I
	4:18	you sent, a fragrant O, a sacrifice acceptable and
Heb	10:10	been sanctified through the O of the body of
	10:11	daily at his service, O repeatedly the same sacrifices,
	10:14	For by a single O he has perfected for
	10:18	is no longer any O for sin.

OFFERINGS (326)

Gen	8:20	bird, and offered burnt O on the altar.
Ex	8:26	the LORD our God O abominable to the Egyptians.
	8:26	If we sacrifice O abominable to the Egyptians before
	10:25	have sacrifices and burnt O, that we may sacrifice
	20:24	on it your burnt O and your peace offerings,
	20:24	offerings and your peace O, your sheep and your
	24:5	Israel, who offered burnt O and sacrificed peace
	24:5	offerings and sacrificed peace O of oxen to the
	29:28	Israel from their peace O; it is their offering
	32:6	morrow, and offered burnt O and brought peace
	32:6	offerings and brought peace O; and the people sat
	36:3	kept bringing him freewill O every morning,
Lev	2:3	holy part of the O by fire to the
	2:10	holy part of the O by fire to the
	2:13	season all your cereal O with salt; you shall
	2:13	offering; with all your O you shall offer salt.
	4:10	sacrifice of the peace O, and the priest shall
	4:26	the sacrifice of peace O; so the priest shall
	4:31	removed from the peace O, and the priest shall
	4:35	the sacrifice of peace O, and the priest shall
	4:35	the altar, upon the O by fire to the
	5:12	the altar, upon the O by fire to the
	6:12	burn on it the fat of the peace O
	6:17	their portion of my O by fire; it is
	6:18	generations, from the LORD's O by fire; whoever
	7:11	the sacrifice of peace O which one may offer
	7:13	sacrifice of his peace O for thanksgiving he shall
	7:14	priest who throws the blood of the peace O
	7:15	sacrifice of his peace O for thanksgiving shall be
	7:20	of the LORD's peace O while an uncleanness is
	7:21	of the LORD's peace O, that person shall be
	7:29	sacrifice of his peace O to the LORD shall
	7:29	sacrifice of his peace O
	7:30	his own hands the O by fire to the
	7:32	sacrifice of your peace O;
	7:33	blood of the peace O and the fat shall
	7:34	sacrifices of their peace O, and have given them
	7:35	his sons from the O made by fire to
	7:37	and of the peace O,
	7:38	Israel to bring their O to the LORD, in
	8:31	the basket of ordination O, as I commanded, saying,
	9:4	a ram for peace O, to sacrifice before the
	9:18	the sacrifice of peace O for the people; and
	9:22	offering and the burnt offering and the peace O
	10:12	that remains of the O by fire to the
	10:13	sons' due, from the O by fire to the
	10:14	sacrifices of the peace O of the people of
	10:15	shall bring with the O by fire of the
	14:32	who cannot afford the O for his cleansing."
	17:5	as sacrifices of peace O to the LORD;
	19:5	a sacrifice of peace O to the LORD, you
	21:6	for they offer the O by fire to the
	21:21	to offer the LORD's O by fire; since he
	22:21	a sacrifice of peace O to the LORD, to
	23:18	offering and their drink O, an offering by fire,
	23:19	a year old as a sacrifice of peace O
	23:36	days you shall present O by fire to the
	23:37	presenting to the LORD O by fire, burnt offerings
	23:37	offerings by fire, burnt O and cereal offerings,
	23:37	burnt offerings and cereal O, sacrifices and drink
	23:37	offerings, sacrifices and drink O, each on its proper
	23:38	besides all your votive O, and besides all your
	23:38	besides all your freewill O, which you give to
	24:9	portion out of the O by fire to the
Num	6:15	oil, and their cereal offering and their drink O
	7:3	offered and brought their O before the LORD, six
	7:10	And the leaders offered O for the dedication of
	7:11	"They shall offer their O, one leader each day,
	7:17	the sacrifice of peace O, two oxen, five rams,
	7:23	the sacrifice of peace O, two oxen, five rams,
	7:29	the sacrifice of peace O, two oxen, five rams,
	7:35	the sacrifice of peace O, two oxen, five rams,
	7:41	the sacrifice of peace O, two oxen, five rams,
	7:47	the sacrifice of peace O, two oxen, five rams,
	7:53	the sacrifice of peace O, two oxen, five rams,
	7:59	the sacrifice of peace O, two oxen, five rams,
	7:65	the sacrifice of peace O, two oxen, five rams,
	7:71	the sacrifice of peace O, two oxen, five rams,
	7:77	the sacrifice of peace O, two oxen, five rams,
	7:83	the sacrifice of peace O, two oxen, five rams,
	7:88	the sacrifice of peace O twenty-four bulls, the rams
	10:10	trumpets over your burnt O and over the sacrifices
	10:10	sacrifices of your peace O; they shall serve you
	15:8	vow, or for peace O to the LORD,
	18:8	is kept of the O made to me, all
	18:11	gift, all the wave O of the people of
	18:19	All the holy O which the people of Israel
	28:2	my food for my O by fire, my pleasing
	28:14	Their drink O shall be half a hin of
	29:11	offering and its cereal offering, and their drink O
	29:18	offering and the drink O for the bulls, for
	29:19	offering and its cereal offering, and their drink O
	29:21	offering and the drink O for the bulls, for
	29:24	offering and the drink O for the bulls, for
	29:27	offering and the drink O for the bulls, for
	29:30	offering and the drink O for the bulls, for
	29:31	burnt offering, its cereal offering, and its drink O
	29:33	offering and the drink O for the bulls, for
	29:37	offering and the drink O for the bull, for
	29:39	addition to your votive O and your freewill offerings,
	29:39	offerings and your freewill O, for your burnt
	29:39	offerings, for your burnt O, and for your cereal
	29:39	and for your cereal O, and for your drink
	29:39	and for your drink O, and for your peace
	29:39	for your drink offerings, and for your peace O
Deut	12:6	shall bring your burnt O and your sacrifices, your
	12:6	you present, your votive O, your freewill offerings,
	12:6	votive offerings, your freewill O, and the firstlings of
	12:11	command you: your burnt O and your sacrifices, your
	12:11	and all your votive O which you vow to
	12:13	not offer your burnt O at every place that
	12:14	shall offer your burnt O, and there you shall
	12:17	any of your votive O which you vow, or
	12:17	vow, or your freewill O, or the offering that
	12:26	you, and your votive O, you shall take, and
	12:27	and offer your burnt O, the flesh and the
	18:1	they shall eat the O by fire to the
	27:6	you shall offer burnt O on it to the
	27:7	you shall sacrifice peace O, and shall eat there;
Josh	8:31	offered on it burnt O to the LORD, and
	8:31	burnt offerings to the LORD, and sacrificed peace O
	13:14	gave no inheritance; the O by fire to the
	22:23	so to offer burnt O or cereal offerings or
	22:23	burnt offerings or cereal O or peace offerings on
	22:23	cereal offerings or peace O on it, may the
	22:27	presence with our burnt O and sacrifices and peace
	22:27	and sacrifices and peace O; lest your children say
	22:28	made, not for burnt O, nor for sacrifice, but
Judg	20:26	evening, and offered burnt O and peace offerings
	20:26	burnt offerings and peace O before the LORD.
	21:4	altar, and offered burnt O and peace offerings.
	21:4	an altar, and offered burnt offerings and peace O
1Sam	2:28	your father all my O by fire from the
	2:29	my sacrifices and my O which I commanded, and
	6:15	of Beth-shemesh offered burnt O and sacrificed

10:8 you to offer burnt O and to sacrifice peace
10:8 to offer burnt offerings and to sacrifice peace O
11:15 There they sacrificed peace O before the LORD, and
13:9 burnt offering here to me, and the peace O
15:22 great delight in burnt O and sacrifices, as in
2Sam 6:17 and David offered burnt O and peace offerings
6:17 burnt offerings and peace O before the LORD.
6:18 finished offering the burnt O and the peace offerings,
6:18 offerings and the peace O, he blessed the people
24:24 will not offer burnt O to the LORD my
24:25 LORD, and offered burnt O and peace offerings.
24:25 the LORD, and offered burnt offerings and peace O
1Kgs 3:4 offer a thousand burnt O upon that altar.
3:15 and offered up burnt O and peace offerings, and
3:15 burnt offerings and peace O, and made a feast
8:63 Solomon offered as peace O to the LORD twenty-
8:64 pieces of the peace O, because the bronze altar
8:64 offering and the fat pieces of the peace O
9:25 to offer up burnt O and peace offerings upon
9:25 burnt offerings and peace O upon the altar which
10:5 cupbearers, and his burnt O which he offered at
2Kgs 10:24 he went in to offer sacrifices and burnt O
12:16 money from the guilt O and the money from
12:16 money from the sin O was not brought into
16:13 blood of his peace O upon the altar.
17:17 and their daughters as O, and used divination and
1Chr 6:49 and his sons made O upon the altar of
16:1 and they offered burnt O and peace offerings before
16:1 burnt offerings and peace O before God.
16:2 finished offering the burnt O and the peace offerings,
16:2 offerings and the peace O, he blessed the people
16:40 Gibeon, to offer burnt O to the LORD upon
21:23 the oxen for burnt O, and the threshing sledges
21:24 yours, nor offer burnt O which cost me nothing."
21:26 LORD and presented burnt O and peace offerings,
21:26 burnt offerings and peace O, and called upon the
23:31 evening, and whenever burnt O are offered to the
29:6 houses made their freewill O, as did also the
29:21 next day offered burnt O to the LORD, a
29:21 lambs, with their drink O, and sacrifices in abundance
2Chr 1:6 offered a thousand burnt O upon it.
2:4 showbread, and for burnt O morning and evening, on
7:7 fat of the peace O, because the bronze altar
8:12 Solomon offered up burnt O to the LORD upon
9:4 clothing, and his burnt O which he offered at
13:11 and every evening burnt O and incense of sweet
23:18 LORD, to offer burnt O to the LORD, as
24:14 and for the burnt O, and dishes for incense,
24:14 And they offered burnt O in the house of
25:14 and worshiped them, making O to them.
29:7 incense or offered burnt O in the holy place
29:31 bring sacrifices and thank O to the house of
29:31 brought sacrifices and thank O; and all who were
29:31 who were of a willing heart brought burnt O
29:32 number of the burnt O which the assembly brought
29:33 And the consecrated O were six hundred bulls and
29:34 flay all the burnt O, so until other priests
29:35 great number of burnt O there was the fat
29:35 fat of the peace O, and there were the
29:35 and there were the libations for the burnt O
30:15 themselves, and brought burnt O into the house of
30:22 seven days, sacrificing peace O and giving thanks to
30:24 seven thousand sheep for O, and the princes gave
31:2 the Levites, for burnt O and peace offerings, to
31:2 burnt offerings and peace O, to minister in the
31:3 was for the burnt O: the burnt offerings of
31:3 burnt offerings: the burnt O of morning and evening,
31:3 evening, and the burnt O for the sabbaths, the
31:14 was over the freewill O to God, to apportion
31:14 reserved for the LORD and the most holy O
33:16 it sacrifices of peace O and of thanksgiving; and
35:7 lay people, as passover O for all that were
35:8 priests for the passover O two thousand six hundred
35:9 Levites for the passover O five thousand lambs and
35:12 set aside the burnt O that they might distribute
35:13 they boiled the holy O in pots, in caldrons,
35:14 in offering the burnt O and the fat parts
35:16 and to offer burnt O on the altar of
Ezra 1:4 with beasts, besides freewill O for the house of
2:68 in Jerusalem, made freewill O for the house of
3:2 Israel, to offer burnt O upon it, as it
3:3 and they offered burnt O upon it to the
3:3 to the LORD, burnt O morning and evening.
3:4 offered the daily burnt O by number according to
3:5 that the continual burnt O, the offerings at the
3:5 continual burnt offerings, the O at the new moon
3:5 the LORD, and the O of every one who
3:6 began to offer burnt O to the LORD.
6:3 are offered and burnt O are brought; its height
6:9 or sheep for burnt O to the God of
7:16 and with the freewill O of the people and
7:17 lambs, with their cereal O and their drink offerings,
7:17 offerings and their drink O, and you shall offer
8:35 returned exiles, offered burnt O to the God of
Neh 10:33 things, and the sin O to make atonement for
Jud 4:14 offered the continual burnt O and the vows and
4:14 the vows and freewill O of the people.
16:16 all fat for burnt O to thee is a
16:18 they offered their burnt O, their freewill offerings,
16:18 burnt offerings, their freewill O, and their gifts.
Job 1:5 morning and offer burnt O according to the number
Ps 20:3 he remember all your O, and regard with favor
50:8 your sacrifices; your burnt O are continually before
51:19 right sacrifices, in burnt O and whole burnt offerings;
51:19 offerings and whole burnt O; then bulls will be
56:12 I will render thank O to thee.
66:13 thy house with burnt O; I will pay thee
66:15 offer to thee burnt O of fatlings, with the
119:108 Accept my O of praise, O LORD, and teach
Sir 14:11 means, and present worthy O to the Lord.
30:18 is closed are like O of food placed upon
34:19 not pleased with the O of the ungodly; and
35:1 the law makes many O; he who heeds the
Is 1:11 had enough of burnt O of rams and the
1:13 Bring no more vain O; incense is an abomination
43:23 your sheep for burnt O, or honored me with
43:23 not burdened you with O, or wearied you with
56:7 of prayer; their burnt O and their sacrifices will
Jer 6:20 Your burnt O are not acceptable, nor your sacrifices
7:18 they pour out drink O to other gods, to
7:21 Israel: "Add your burnt O to your sacrifices, and
7:22 command them concerning burnt O and sacrifices.
17:26 the Negeb, bringing burnt O and sacrifices, cereal
17:26 offerings and sacrifices, cereal O and frankincense,
17:26 frankincense, and bringing thank O to the house of
19:5 the fire as burnt O to Baal, which I
19:13 of heaven, and drink O have been poured out
32:29 to Baal and drink O have been poured out
33:11 as they bring thank O to the house of
33:18 presence to offer burnt O, to burn cereal offerings,
33:18 offerings, to burn cereal O, and to make sacrifices
41:5 bodies gashed, bringing cereal O and incense to
Bar 1:10 with the money burnt O and sin offerings and
1:10 burnt offerings and sin O and incense, and prepare
Ezek 20:28 odors, and there they poured out their drink O
20:40 choicest of your gifts, with all your sacred O
40:42 with which the burnt O and the sacrifices were
42:13 eat the most holy O; there they shall put
42:13 put the most holy O --the cereal offering, the
43:18 erected for offering burnt O upon it and for
43:27 the altar your burnt O and your peace offerings;
43:27 offerings and your peace O; and I will accept
44:30 kinds from all your O, shall belong to the
45:15 the offering for cereal O, burnt offerings, and peace
45:15 for cereal offerings, burnt O, and peace offerings, to
45:15 burnt offerings, and peace O, to make atonement for
45:17 to furnish the burnt O, cereal offerings, and drink
45:17 the burnt offerings, cereal O, and drink offerings, at
45:17 cereal offerings, and drink O, at the feasts, the
45:17 shall provide the sin O, cereal offerings, burnt
45:17 the sin offerings, cereal O, burnt offerings, and peace
45:17 offerings, cereal offerings, burnt O, and peace
45:17 burnt offerings, and peace O, to make atonement for
45:25 same provision for sin O, burnt offerings, and cereal
45:25 for sin offerings, burnt O, and cereal offerings, and
45:25 burnt offerings, and cereal O, and for the oil.
46:2 offering and his peace O, and he shall worship
46:12 burnt offering or peace O as a freewill offering
46:12 offering or his peace O as he does on
Dan 3:39 it were with burnt O of rams and bulls,
Hos 4:13 the mountains, and make O upon the hills, under
6:6 sacrifice, the knowledge of God, rather than burnt O
Amos 4:5 leavened, and proclaim freewill O, publish them; for
5:22 offer me your burnt O and cereal offerings, I
5:22 burnt offerings and cereal O, I will not accept
5:22 them, and the peace O of your fatted beasts
5:25 to me sacrifices and O the forty years in
Mic 6:6 before him with burnt O, with calves a year
Mal 2:3 the dung of your O, and I will put
3:3 till they present right O to the LORD.
3:8 are we robbing thee?' In your tithes and O
1Mac 1:22 the cups for drink O, the bowls, the golden

O

1:45 land, to forbid burnt O and sacrifices and drink
1:45 and sacrifices and drink O in the sanctuary, to
4:56 days, and offered burnt O with gladness; they offered
5:54 joy, and offered burnt O, because not one of
2Mac 2:10 fire came down and consumed the whole burnt O
2:13 of David, and letters of kings about votive O
5:16 profane hands the votive O which other kings had
6:5 covered with abominable O which were forbidden by
9:16 adorn with the finest O; and the holy vessels
Mk 12:33 than all whole burnt O and sacrifices."
Lk 21:5 with noble stones and O, he said,
Acts 24:16 came to bring to my nation alms and O
1Cor 9:13 serve at the altar share in the sacrificial O
Heb 10:5 he said, "Sacrifices and O thou hast not desired,
10:6 for me; in burnt O and sin offerings thou
10:6 burnt offerings and sin O thou hast taken no
10:8 pleasure in sacrifices and O and burnt offerings and
10:8 and offerings and burnt O and sin offerings" (these
10:8 sacrifices and offerings and burnt offerings and sin O

OFFERS (23)

Lev 3:1 peace offering, if he O an animal from the
3:7 If he O a lamb for his offering, then
6:26 The priest who O it for sin shall eat
7:8 And the priest who O any man's burnt offering
7:9 to the priest who O it.
7:12 If he O it for a thanksgiving, then he
7:16 the day that he O his sacrifice, and on
7:18 third day, he who O it shall not be
7:29 of Israel, He that O the sacrifice of his
7:33 sons of Aaron who O the blood of the
17:8 sojourn among them, who O a burnt offering or
21:8 consecrate him, for he O the bread of your
22:21 And when any one O a sacrifice of peace
Judg 9:33 you, you may do to them as occasion O
1Kgs 8:29 prayer which thy servant O toward this place.
2Chr 6:20 prayer which thy servant O toward this place.
Ezra 7:13 my kingdom, who freely O to go to Jerusalem,
Sir 34:20 is the man who O a sacrifice from the
35:2 who returns a kindness O fine flour, and he
Is 66:3 offering, like him who O swine's blood; he who
Jer 48:35 the LORD, him who O sacrifice in the high
Ezek 46:4 offering that the prince O to the LORD on
Heb 9:7 taking blood which he O for himself and for

OFFICE (24)

Gen 40:13 restore you to your O; and you shall place
41:13 was restored to my O, and the baker was
Num 3:3 whom he ordained to minister in the priest's O
Deut 17:9 judge who is in O in those days, you
19:17 judges who are in O in those days;
26:3 priest who is in O at that time, and
1Chr 9:22 established them in their O of trust.
Sir 7:4 the Lord the highest O, nor the seat of
Is 22:19 thrust you from your O, and you will be
1Mac 11:63 a large army, intending to remove him from O
2Mac 4:10 and Jason came to O, he at once shifted
4:27 And Menelaus held the O, but he did not
4:50 in power, remained in O, growing in wickedness,
10:13 the respect due his O, he took poison and
13:3 he thought that he would be established in O
Mt 9:9 sitting at the tax O; and he said to
Mk 2:14 sitting at the tax O, and he said to
Lk 5:27 sitting at the tax O; and he said to
Acts 1:20 in it'; and 'His O let another take.'
Col 1:25 according to the divine O which was given to
1Tim 3:1 one aspires to the O of bishop, he desires
Heb 7:5 who receive the priestly O have a commandment in
7:21 became priests took their O without an oath, but
7:23 death from continuing in O;

OFFICER (20)

Gen 37:36 Egypt to Potiphar, an O of Pharaoh, the captain
39:1 Egypt, and Potiphar, an O of Pharaoh, the captain
Judg 9:28 Jerubbaal and Zebul his O serve the men of
1Kgs 4:19 And there was one O in the land of
22:9 of Israel summoned an O and said, "Bring quickly
2Kgs 25:19 city he took an O who had been in
1Chr 9:11 of Ahitub, the chief O of the house of
26:24 of Moses, was chief O in charge of the
27:16 of Zichri was chief O; for the Simeonites, Shephatiah
2Chr 18:8 of Israel summoned an O and said, "Bring quickly
24:11 king's secretary and the O of the chief priest
26:11 secretary and Ma-aseiah the O, under the direction
31:12 The chief O in charge of them was Conaniah
31:13 and Azariah the chief O of the house of
Prov 6:7 Without having any chief, O or ruler,
Jer 20:1 Immer, who was chief O in the house of
52:25 city he took an O who had been in
1Mac 2:25 he killed the king's O who was forcing them
Lk 12:58 you over to the O, and the officer put
12:58 the officer, and the O put you in prison.

OFFICERS (86)

Gen 40:2 angry with his two O, the chief butler and
40:7 So he asked Pharaoh's O who were with him
Ex 14:7 chariots of Egypt with O over all of them.
15:4 sea; and his picked O are sunk in the
Num 11:16 of the people and O over them; and bring
31:14 was angry with the O of the army, the
31:48 Then the O who were over the thousands of
Deut 1:15 commanders of tens, and O, throughout your tribes.
16:18 shall appoint judges and O in all your towns
20:5 the victory.' Then the O shall speak to the
20:8 take her.' And the O shall speak further to
20:9 heart.' And when the O have made an end
29:10 your elders, and your O, all the men of
31:28 your tribes, and your O, that I may speak
Josh 1:10 Then Joshua commanded the O of the people,
3:2 of three days the O went through the camp
8:33 with their elders and O and their judges, stood
23:2 heads, their judges and O, and said to them,
24:1 the judges, and the O of Israel; and they
1Sam 8:15 give it to his O and to his servants.
1Kgs 4:5 Nathan was over the O; Zabud the son of
4:7 Solomon had twelve O over all Israel, who provided
4:27 And those O supplied provisions for King Solomon,
5:16 thousand three hundred chief O who were over the
9:23 These were the chief O who were over Solomon's
14:27 the hands of the O of the guard, who
2Kgs 10:25 guard and to the O, "Go in and slay
10:25 the guard and the O cast them out and
1Chr 12:14 These Gadites were O of the army, the lesser
12:18 them, and made them O of his troops.
23:4 six thousand shall be O and judges,
24:5 alike, for there were O of the sanctuary and
24:5 of the sanctuary and O of God among both
26:26 fathers' houses, and the O of the thousands and
26:29 duties for Israel, as O and judges.
27:1 and hundreds, and their O who served the king
28:1 of the tribes, the O of the divisions that
28:21 of service; also the O and all the people
29:6 of hundreds, and the O over the king's work.
2Chr 8:9 were soldiers, and his O, the commanders of his
8:10 these were the chief O of King Solomon, two
12:10 the hands of the O of the guard, who
19:11 matters; and the Levites will serve you as O
24:11 brought to the king's O by the Levites, when
32:3 he planned with his O and his mighty men
32:21 warriors and commanders and O in the camp of
35:8 and Jehiel, the chief O of the house of
Ezra 7:28 his counselors, and before all the king's mighty O
Neh 2:9 had sent with me O of the army and
Jud 2:2 called together all his O and all his nobles
2:14 the commanders, generals, and O of the Assyrian
5:22 began to complain; Holofernes' O and all the men
12:10 only, and did not invite any of his O
14:3 camp and rouse the O of the Assyrian army;
14:12 generals and the captains and to all their O
Esth 2:3 let the king appoint O in all the provinces
Is 31:9 in terror, and his O desert the standard in
Jer 39:3 the rest of the O of the king of
39:13 and all the chief O of the king of
41:1 one of the chief O of the king, came
46:26 hand of Nebuchadrezzar king of Babylon and his O
Ezek 23:15 of them looking like O, a picture of Babylonians
23:23 commanders all of them, O and warriors, all of
Nah 2:5 The O are summoned, they stumble as they go,
1Mac 1:6 summoned his most honored O, who had been
1:8 Then his O began to rule, each in his
2:15 Then the king's O who were enforcing the apostasy
2:17 Then the king's O spoke to Mattathias as follows:
2:31 reported to the king's O, and to the troops
5:40 Timothy said to the O of his forces, "If
10:37 Let their O and leaders be of their own
10:63 he said to his O, "Go forth with him
11:63 Jonathan heard that the O of Demetrius had come
Mk 6:21 for his courtiers and O and the leading men
Lk 22:4 the chief priests and O how he might betray
22:50 the chief priests and O of the temple and
Jn 7:32 priests and Pharisees sent O to arrest him.
7:45 The O then went back to the chief priests

7:46 The O answered, "No man ever spoke like this
18:3 of soldiers and some O from the chief priests
18:12 their captain and the O of the Jews seized
18:18 Now the servants and O had made a charcoal
18:22 this, one of the O standing by struck Jesus
19:6 chief priests and the O saw him, they cried
Acts 5:22 But when the O came, they did not find
5:26 the captain with the O went and brought them,

OFFICES (5)
2Chr 8:14 the Levites for their O of praise and ministry
31:16 service according to their O, by their divisions.
31:17 was according to their O, by their divisions.
35:2 the priests to their O and encouraged them in
1Mac 13:15 in connection with the O he held, that we

OFFICIAL (4)
2Kgs 8:6 the king appointed an O for her, saying, "Restore
Eccl 5:8 matter; for the high O is watched by a
Jn 4:46 Caperna-um there was an O whose son was ill.
4:49 The O said to him, "Sir, come down before

OFFICIALS (46)
Ex 23:8 a bribe blinds the O, and subverts the cause
Judg 8:6 And the O of Succoth said, "Are Zebah and
8:14 down for him the O and elders of Succoth,
1Kgs 1:9 and all the royal O of Judah,
4:2 these were his high O: Azariah the son of
9:22 soldiers, they were his O, his commanders, his
10:5 the seating of his O, and the attendance of
2Kgs 24:12 his servants, and his princes, and his palace O
24:15 the king's wives, his O, and the chief men
25:24 because of the Chaldean O; dwell in the land,
1Chr 18:17 sons were the chief O in the service of
28:1 at Jerusalem all the O of Israel, the officials
28:1 officials of Israel, the O of the tribes, the
28:1 together with the palace O, the mighty men, and
2Chr 9:4 the seating of his O, and the attendance of
29:20 early and gathered the O of the city, and
34:13 Levites were scribes, and O, and gatekeepers.
Ezra 4:9 judges, the governors, the O, the Persians, the men
8:20 whom David and his O had set apart to
9:1 had been done, the O approached me and said,
9:2 the hand of the O and chief men has
10:8 by order of the O and the elders all
10:14 Let our O stand for the whole assembly; let
Neh 2:16 And the O did not know where I had
2:16 priests, the nobles, the O, and the rest that
4:14 nobles and to the O and to the rest
4:19 nobles and to the O and to the rest
5:7 I brought charges against the nobles and the O
5:17 fifty men, Jews and O, besides those who came
7:5 the nobles and the O and the people to
12:40 and half of the O with me;
13:11 I remonstrated with the O and said, "Why is
Esth 1:8 orders to all the O of his palace to
9:3 governors and the royal O also helped the Jews,
Prov 29:12 to falsehood, all his O will be wicked.
Sir 10:2 people, so are his O; and like the ruler
Is 30:4 For though his O are at Zoan and his
Dan 3:2 magistrates, and all the O of the provinces to
3:3 magistrates, and all the O of the provinces, were
Zeph 1:8 "I will punish the O and the king's sons
3:3 Her O within her are roaring lions; her judges
1Mac 10:33 payment; and let all O cancel also the taxes
10:41 funds which the government O have not paid as
10:42 of silver which my O have received every year
12:45 troops and all the O, and will turn round
13:37 to write to our O to grant you release

OFFSCOURING (2)
Lam 3:45 Thou hast made us O and refuse among the
1Cor 4:13 of the world, the O of all things.

OFFSET (2)
Ezek 41:7 the enlargement of the O from story to story
Hos 12:8 his riches can never O the guilt he has

OFFSETS (2)
1Kgs 6:6 the house he made O on the wall in
Ezek 41:6 There were O all around the wall of the

OFFSPRING (69)
Gen 15:3 hast given me no O; and a slave born
17:12 is not of your O,
19:32 that we may preserve O through our father."
19:34 that we may preserve O through our father."
21:13 the slave woman also, because he is your O
21:23 me or with my O or with my posterity,
38:8 her, and raise up O for your brother."
38:9 Onan knew that the O would not be his;
38:9 lest he should give O to his brother.
46:6 Jacob and all his O with him,
46:7 sons' daughters; all his O he brought with him
46:26 who were his own O, not including Jacob's sons'
48:6 And the O born to you after them shall
Ex 1:4 All the O of Jacob were seventy persons; Joseph
Num 18:19 you and for your O with you."
Deut 28:51 and shall eat the O of your cattle and
28:53 you shall eat the O of your own body,
28:59 you and your O extraordinary afflictions,
30:6 the heart of your O, so that you will
Josh 24:3 Canaan, and made his O many.
Judg 8:30 seventy sons, his own O, for he had many
2Sam 4:8 king this day on Saul and on his O
7:12 will raise up your O after you, who shall
1Kgs 1:48 granted one of my O to sit on my
1Chr 7:13 Jezer, and Shallum, the O of Bilhah.
16:13 judgments he uttered, O O of Abraham his servant,
17:11 will raise up your O after you, one of
Job 5:25 be many, and your O as the grass of
18:19 He has no O or descendant among his people,
21:8 their presence, and their O before their eyes.
27:14 the sword; and his O have not enough to
39:3 crouch, bring forth their O, and are delivered of
Ps 21:10 You will destroy their O from the earth, and
105:6 judgments he uttered, O O of Abraham his servant,
Wis 3:13 their children evil; their O are accursed.
3:16 to maturity, and the O of an unlawful union
Is 1:4 people laden with iniquity, O of evildoers, sons who
14:22 Babylon name and remnant, O and posterity, says the
22:24 his father's house, the O and issue, every small
41:8 I have chosen, the O of Abraham, my friend;
43:5 I will bring your O from the east, and
44:3 upon your descendants, and my blessing on your O
45:19 not say to the O of Jacob, 'Seek me
45:25 the LORD all the O of Israel shall triumph
48:19 of the sea; your O would have been like
53:10 he shall see his O, he shall prolong his
57:3 sons of the sorceress, O of the adulterer and
57:4 children of transgression, the O of deceit,
61:9 the nations, and their O in the midst of
65:23 they shall be the O of the blessed of
Jer 7:15 your kinsmen, all the O of Ephraim.
22:30 for none of his O shall succeed in sitting
30:10 from afar, and your O from the land of
36:31 punish him and his O and his servants for
46:27 from afar, and your O from the land of
Lam 2:20 Should women eat their O, the children of their
Dan 11:6 and he and his O shall not endure; but
13:56 said to him, "You O of Canaan and not
Mal 2:3 I will rebuke your O, and spread dung upon
2:15 Godly O
1Mac 1:38 became strange to her O, and her children forsook
Acts 17:28 we are indeed his O
17:29 offspring.' Being then God's O, we ought not to
Gal 3:16 promises were made to Abraham and to his O
3:16 many; but, referring to one, "And to your O
3:19 of transgressions, till the O should come to whom
3:29 you are Abraham's O, heirs according to promise.
Rev 12:17 the rest of her O, on those who keep
22:16 the root and the O of David, the bright

OFFSPRINGS
Gal 3:16 It does not say, "And to O

OFTEN (45)
1Sam 1:7 year by year; as O as she went up
18:30 to battle, and as O as they came out
2Sam 8:10 him; for Hadadezer had O been at war with
1Kgs 14:28 And as O as the king went into the
1Chr 18:10 him; for Hadadezer had O been at war with
2Chr 12:11 And as O as the king went into the
Tob 1:6 But I alone went O to Jerusalem for the
Esth 16:2 "The more O they are honored by the too
16:5 And O many of those who are set in
Job 21:17 "How O is it that the lamp of the
Ps 78:38 he restrained his anger O, and did not stir
78:40 How O they rebelled against him in the wilderness
Prov 29:1 He who is O reproved, yet stiffens his neck
Sir 13:9 reserved; and he will invite you the more O
19:15 Question a friend, for O it is slander; so

O

20:16 How many will ridicule him, and how O
30:1 son will whip him O, in order that he
34:12 I have O been in danger of death, but
Is 28:19 As O as it passes through it will take
Jer 31:20 For as O as I speak against him, I
1Mac 14:29 to us: "Since wars O occurred in the country,
2Mac 9:25 king, whom I have O entrusted and commended to
12:22 and that, so that O they were injured by
Mt 17:15 he suffers terribly; for O he falls into the
17:15 into the fire, and O into the water.
18:20 to him, "Lord, how O shall my brother sin
23:36 How O would I have gathered your children together
Mk 5:4 chain; for he had O been bound with fetters
9:22 And it has O cast him into the fire
Lk 5:33 disciples of John fast O and offer prayers, and
13:34 How O would I have gathered your children together
Jn 18:2 the place; for Jesus O met there with his
Acts 24:25 he sent for him O and conversed with him.
26:11 And I punished them O in all the synagogues
Rom 1:13 brethren, that I have O intended to come to
15:22 why I have so O been hindered from coming
1Cor 11:25 Do this, as O as you drink it, in
11:26 For as O as you eat this bread and
2Cor 8:22 brother whom we have O tested and found earnest
11:23 with countless beatings, and O near death.
11:27 in hunger and thirst, O without food, in cold
Phil 3:18 of whom I have O told you and now
2Tim 1:16 of Onesiphorus, for he O refreshed me; he was
Heb 6:7 drunk the rain that O falls upon it, and
Rev 11:6 with every plague, as O as they desire.

OG (22)
Num 21:33 way to Bashan; and O the king of Bashan
32:33 and the kingdom of O king of Bashan, the
Deut 1:4 lived in Heshbon, and O the king of Bashan,
3:1 way to Bashan; and O the king of Bashan
3:3 gave into our hand O also, the king of
3:4 Argob, the kingdom of O in Bashan.
3:10 of the kingdom of O in Bashan.
3:11 (For only O the king of Bashan was left
3:13 Bashan, the kingdom of O, that is, all the
4:47 and the land of O the king of Bashan,
29:7 king of Heshbon and O the king of Bashan
31:4 did to Sihon and O, the kings of the
Josh 2:10 Jordan, to Sihon and O, whom you utterly destroyed.
9:10 king of Heshbon, and O king of Bashan, who
12:4 slopes of Pisgah; and O king of Bashan, one
13:12 all the kingdom of O in Bashan, who reigned
13:30 the whole kingdom of O king of Bashan, and
13:31 of the kingdom of O in Bashan; these were
1Kgs 4:19 the Amorites and of O king of Bashan.
Neh 9:22 and the land of O king of Bashan.
Ps 135:11 of the Amorites, and O, king of Bashan, and
136:20 endures for ever; and O, king of Bashan, for

OHAD (2)
Gen 46:10 of Simeon: Jemuel, Jamin, O, Jachin, Zohar, and
Ex 6:15 of Simeon: Jemuel, Jamin, O, Jachin, Zohar, and

OHEL
1Chr 3:20 their sister; and Hashubah, O, Berechiah, Hasadiah,

OHOLAH (5)
Ezek 23:4 O was the name of the elder and Oholibah
23:4 As for their names, O is Samaria, and Oholibah
23:5 O played the harlot while she was mine; and
23:36 man, will you judge O and Oholibah?
23:44 they went in to O and to Oholibah to

OHOLIAB (5)
Ex 31:6 have appointed with him O, the son of Ahisamach,
35:34 teach, both him and O the son of Ahisamach
36:1 Bezalel and O and every able man in whom
36:2 Moses called Bezalel and O and every able man
38:23 and with him was O the son of Ahisamach,

OHOLIBAH (6)
Ezek 23:4 of the elder and O the name of her
23:4 Oholah is Samaria, and O is Jerusalem.
23:11 "Her sister O saw this, yet she was more
23:22 Therefore, O O, thus says the Lord GOD: "Behold,
23:36 "Son of man, will you judge Oholah and O
23:44 to Oholah and to commit lewdness.

OHOLIBAMAH (8)
Gen 36:2 of Elon the Hittite, O the daughter of Anah
36:5 Basemath bore Reuel; and O bore Jeush, Jalam, and
36:14 are the sons of O the daughter of Anah
36:18 are the sons of O, Esau's wife: the chiefs
36:18 the chiefs born of O the daughter of Anah,
36:25 of Anah: Dishon and O the daughter of Anah.
36:41 chiefs Timna, Alvah, Jetheth, O, Elah, Pinon,
1Chr 1:52 chiefs Timna, Aliah, Jetheth, O, Elah, Pinon,

OIL (215)
Gen 28:18 a pillar and poured O on the top of
35:14 on it, and poured O on it.
Ex 25:6 skins, goatskins, acacia wood, O for the lamps, spices
25:6 spices for the anointing O and for the fragrant
27:20 you pure beaten olive O for the light, that
29:2 unleavened cakes mixed with O, and unleavened
29:2 mixed with oil, and unleavened wafers spread with O
29:7 shall take the anointing O, and pour it on
29:21 and of the anointing O, and sprinkle it upon
29:23 cake of bread with O, and one wafer, out
29:40 a hin of beaten O, and a fourth of
30:24 sanctuary, and of olive O a hin;
30:25 these a sacred anointing O blended as by the
30:25 perfumer; a holy anointing O it shall be.
30:31 be my holy anointing O throughout your generations.
31:11 priests, and the anointing O and the fragrant incense
35:8 and goatskins; acacia wood, O for the light, spices
35:8 spices for the anointing O and for the fragrant
35:14 its lamps, and the O for the light;
35:15 poles, and the anointing O and the fragrant incense,
35:28 breastpiece, and spices and O for the light, and
35:28 and for the anointing O, and for the fragrant
37:29 made the holy anointing O also, and the pure
39:37 its utensils, and the O for the light;
39:38 golden altar, the anointing O and the fragrant
Lev 2:1 flour; he shall pour O upon it, and put
2:2 the fine flour and O, with all of its
2:4 fine flour mixed with O, or unleavened wafers spread
2:4 mixed with oil, or unleavened wafers spread with O
2:5 flour unleavened, mixed with O;
2:6 in pieces, and pour O on it; it is
2:7 it shall be made of fine flour with O
2:15 And you shall put O upon it, and lay
2:16 grain and of the O with all of its
5:11 he shall put no O upon it, and shall
6:15 cereal offering with its O and all the frankincense
6:21 shall be made with O on a griddle; you
7:10 cereal offering, mixed with O or dry, shall be
7:12 unleavened cakes mixed with O, unleavened wafers
7:12 unleavened wafers spread with O, and cakes of fine
7:12 and cakes of fine flour well mixed with O
8:2 garments, and the anointing O, and the bull of
8:10 Moses took the anointing O, and anointed the
8:12 some of the anointing O on Aaron's head, and
8:26 cake of bread with O, and one wafer, and
8:30 some of the anointing O and of the blood
9:4 cereal offering mixed with O; for today the LORD
10:7 die; for the anointing O of the LORD is
14:10 fine flour mixed with O, and one log of
14:10 flour mixed with oil, and one log of O
14:12 with the log of O, and wave them for
14:15 of the log of O, and pour it into
14:16 right finger in the O that is in his
14:16 hand, and sprinkle some O with his finger seven
14:17 And some of the O that remains in his
14:18 the rest of the O that is in the
14:21 fine flour mixed with O for a cereal offering,
14:21 and a log of O;
14:24 and the log of O, and the priest shall
14:26 pour some of the O into the palm of
14:27 finger some of the O that is in his
14:28 put some of the O that is in his
14:29 the rest of the O that is in the
21:10 whose head the anointing O is poured, and who
21:12 consecration of the anointing O of his God is
23:13 fine flour mixed with O, to be offered by
24:2 to bring you pure O from beaten olives for
Num 4:9 all the vessels for O with which it is
4:16 have charge of the O for the light, the
4:16 offering, and the anointing O, with the oversight of
5:15 he shall pour no O upon it and put
6:15 fine flour mixed with O, and unleavened wafers
6:15 unleavened wafers spread with O, and their cereal
7:13 fine flour mixed with O for a cereal offering;
7:19 fine flour mixed with O for a cereal offering;
7:25 fine flour mixed with O for a cereal offering;
7:31 fine flour mixed with O for a cereal offering;

7:37 fine flour mixed with O for a cereal offering;
7:43 fine flour mixed with O for a cereal offering;
7:49 fine flour mixed with O for a cereal offering;
7:55 fine flour mixed with O for a cereal offering;
7:61 fine flour mixed with O for a cereal offering;
7:67 fine flour mixed with O for a cereal offering;
7:73 fine flour mixed with O for a cereal offering;
7:79 fine flour mixed with O for a cereal offering;
8:8 fine flour mixed with O, and you shall take
11:8 was like the taste of cakes baked with O
15:4 of a hin of O;
15:6 of a hin of O;
15:9 half a hin of O,
18:12 the best of the O, and all the best
28:5 with a fourth of a hin of beaten O
28:9 cereal offering, mixed with O, and its drink offering:
28:12 cereal offering, mixed with O, for each bull; and
28:12 cereal offering, mixed with O, for the one ram;
28:13 fine flour mixed with O as a cereal offering
28:20 fine flour mixed with O; three tenths of an
28:28 fine flour mixed with O, three tenths of an
29:3 fine flour mixed with O, three tenths of an
29:9 fine flour mixed with O, three tenths of an
29:14 fine flour mixed with O, three tenths of an
35:25 high priest who was anointed with the holy O
Deut 7:13 your wine and your O, the increase of your
11:14 in your grain and your wine and your O
12:17 wine or of your O, or the firstlings of
14:23 wine, and of your O, and the firstlings of
18:4 wine and of your O, and the first of
28:40 anoint yourself with the O; for your olives shall
28:51 you grain, wine, or O, the increase of your
32:13 of the rock, and O out of the flinty
33:24 brothers, and let him dip his foot in O
1Sam 10:1 took a vial of O and poured it on
16:1 Fill your horn with O, and go; I will
16:13 took the horn of O, and anointed him in
2Sam 1:21 defiled, the shield of Saul, not anointed with O
14:2 not anoint yourself with O, but behave like a
1Kgs 1:39 took the horn of O from the tent, and
5:11 his household, and twenty thousand cors of beaten O
17:12 jar, and a little O in a cruse; and
17:14 and the cruse of O shall not fail, until
17:16 did the cruse of O fail, according to the
2Kgs 4:2 nothing in the house, except a jar of O
4:6 Then the O stopped flowing.
4:7 said, "Go, sell the O and pay your debts,
9:1 take this flask of O in your hand, and
9:3 take the flask of O, and pour it on
9:6 young man poured the O on his head, saying
20:13 the spices, the precious O, his armory, all that
1Chr 9:29 flour, the wine, the O, the incense, and the
12:40 raisins, and wine and O, oxen and sheep, for
23:29 the offering mixed with O, and all measures of
27:28 over the stores of O was Joash.
2Chr 2:10 baths of wine, and twenty thousand baths of O
2:15 the wheat and barley, O and wine, of which
11:11 and stores of food, O, and wine.
31:5 fruits of grain, wine, O, honey, and of all
32:28 of grain, wine, and O; and stalls for all
Ezra 3:7 and food, drink, and O to the Sidonians and
6:9 wheat, salt, wine, or O, as the priests at
7:22 a hundred baths of O, and salt without prescribing
Neh 5:11 money, grain, wine, and O which you have been
10:37 the wine and the O, to the priests, to
10:39 of grain, wine, and O to the chambers, where
13:5 of grain, wine, and O, which were given by
13:12 the grain, wine, and O into the storehouses.
Jud 10:5 and a flask of O, and filled a bag
11:13 of the wine and O, which they had consecrated
Esth 2:12 beautifying, six months with O of myrrh and six
Job 24:11 the wicked they make O; they tread the wine
29:6 the rock poured out for me streams of O
Ps 23:5 anointest my head with O, my cup overflows.
45:7 anointed you with the O of gladness above your
55:21 words were softer than O, yet they were drawn
89:20 servant; with my holy O I have anointed him;
92:10 wild ox; thou hast poured over me fresh O
104:15 the heart of man, O to make his face
109:18 body like water, like O into his bones!
133:2 is like the precious O upon the head, running
141:5 kindness, but let the O of the wicked never
Prov 5:3 speech is smoother than O;
21:17 who loves wine and O will not be rich.
27:9 O and perfume make the heart glad, but the
27:16 wind or to grasp O in his right hand.
Eccl 9:8 always white; let not O be lacking on your
Song 1:3 fragrant, your name is O poured out; therefore the
Sir 38:11 fine flour, and pour O on your offering, as
39:26 of the grape, and O and clothing.
45:15 anointed him with holy O; it was an everlasting
Is 1:6 pressed out, or bound up, or softened with O
21:5 Arise, O princes, O the shield!
39:2 the spices, the precious O, his whole armory, all
57:9 to Molech with O and multiplied your perfumes;
61:3 instead of ashes, the O of gladness instead of
Jer 31:12 the wine, and the O, and over the young
40:10 and summer fruits and O, and store them in
41:8 stores of wheat, barley, O, and honey hidden in
Ezek 16:9 your blood from you, and anointed you with O
16:13 cloth; you ate fine flour and honey and O
16:18 them, and set my O and my incense before
16:19 with fine flour and O and honey--you set
23:41 which you had placed my incense and my O
27:17 and early figs, honey, O, and balm.
32:14 rivers to run like O, says the Lord GOD.
45:14 the fixed portion of O, one tenth of a
45:24 and a hin of O to each ephah.
45:25 burnt offerings, and cereal offerings, and for the O
46:5 with a hin of O to each ephah.
46:7 with a hin of O to each ephah.
46:11 with a hin of O to an ephah.
46:14 of a hin of O to moisten the flour,
46:15 meal offering and the O shall be provided, morning
Dan 13:17 her maids, "Bring me O and ointments, and shut
Hos 2:5 and my flax, my O and my drink.'
2:8 the wine, and the O, and who lavished upon
2:22 the wine, and the O, and they shall answer
12:1 bargain with Assyria, and O is carried to Egypt.
Joel 1:10 the wine fails, the O languishes.
2:19 you grain, wine, and O, and you will be
2:24 grain, the vats shall overflow with wine and O
Mic 6:7 of rams, with ten thousands of rivers of O
6:15 not anoint yourselves with O; you shall tread grapes,
Hag 1:11 the new wine, the O, upon what the ground
2:12 pottage, or wine, or O, or any kind of
Zech 4:12 pipes from which the O is poured out?"
Mt 25:3 lamps, they took no O with them;
25:4 wise took flasks of O with their lamps.
25:8 us some of your O, for our lamps are
Mk 6:13 demons, and anointed with O many that were sick
Lk 7:46 anoint my head with O, but she has anointed
10:34 his wounds, pouring on O and wine; then he
16:6 'A hundred measures of O And he said to
Heb 1:9 anointed thee with the O of gladness beyond thy
Jas 5:14 him, anointing him with O in the name of
Rev 6:6 but do not harm O and wine!"
18:13 incense, myrrh, frankincense, wine, O, fine flour and

OILS (3)

Song 1:3 than wine, your anointing O are fragrant, your name
4:10 the fragrance of your O than any spice!
Amos 6:6 themselves with the finest O, but are not grieved

OINTMENT (18)

Jud 10:3 anointed herself with precious O, and combed her
16:8 anointed her face with O and fastened her hair
Job 41:31 he makes the sea like a pot of O
Eccl 7:1 is better than precious O; and the day of
10:1 flies make the perfumer's O give off an evil
Mt 26:7 flask of very expensive O, and she poured it
26:9 For this O might have been sold for a
26:12 In pouring this O on my body she has
Mk 14:3 an alabaster flask of O of pure nard, very
14:4 indignantly, "Why was the O thus wasted?
14:5 For this O might have been sold for more
Lk 7:37 an alabaster flask of O,
7:38 kissed his feet, and anointed them with the O
7:46 oil, but she has anointed my feet with O
Jn 11:2 anointed the Lord with O and wiped his feet
12:3 a pound of costly O of pure nard and
12:3 house was filled with the fragrance of the O
12:5 said, "Why was this O not sold for three

OINTMENTS (5)

Esth 2:3 the women; let their O be given them.
2:9 provided her with her O and her portion of
2:12 months with spices and O for women--
Dan 13:17 "Bring me oil and O, and shut the garden
Lk 23:55 laid; then they returned, and prepared spices and O

O

OLD (451)

Gen 5:32 was five hundred years O, Noah became the father
6:4 men that were of O, the men of renown.
7:6 was six hundred years O when the flood of
11:10 was a hundred years O, he became the father
12:4 Abram was seventy-five years O when he departed
15:9 a heifer three years O, a she-goat three years
15:9 a she-goat three years O, a ram three years
15:9 a ram three years O, a turtledove, and a
15:15 buried in a good O age.
16:16 Abram was eighty-six years O when Hagar bore
17:1 Abram was ninety-nine years O the LORD appeared
17:12 that is eight days O among you shall be
17:17 to a man who is a hundred years O
17:17 who is ninety years O, bear a child?"
17:24 Abraham was ninety-nine years O when he was
17:25 son was thirteen years O when he was circumcised
18:11 Abraham and Sarah were O, advanced in age; it
18:12 "After I have grown O, and my husband is
18:12 and my husband is O, shall I have pleasure?"
18:13 now that I am O
19:4 Sodom, both young and O, all the people to
19:31 younger, "Our father is O, and there is not
21:2 a son in his O age at the time
21:4 he was eight days O, as God had commanded
21:5 was a hundred years O when his son Isaac
21:7 a son in his O age."
24:1 Now Abraham was O, well advanced in years; and
24:36 master when she was O; and to him he
25:8 died in a good O age, an old man
25:8 good old age, an O man and full of
25:20 Isaac was forty years O when he took to
25:26 Isaac was sixty years O when she bore them.
26:34 Esau was forty years O, he took to wife
27:1 When Isaac was O and his eyes were dim
27:2 said, "Behold, I am O; I do not know
35:29 gathered to his people, O and full of days;
37:2 Joseph, being seventeen years O, was shepherding
37:3 the son of his O age; and he made
41:46 Joseph was thirty years O when he entered the
43:27 your father well, the O man of whom you
44:20 have a father, an O man, and a young
44:20 the child of his O age; and his brother
50:26 hundred and ten years O; and they embalmed him,
Ex 7:7 Moses was eighty years O, and Aaron eighty-three
7:7 and Aaron eighty-three years O, when they spoke to
10:9 our young and our O; we will go with
12:5 a male a year O; you shall take it
29:38 two lambs a year O day by day continually.
30:14 census, from twenty years O and upward, shall give
38:26 census, from twenty years O and upward, for six
Lev 9:3 lamb, both a year O without blemish, for a
12:6 a lamb a year O for a burnt offering,
14:10 ewe lamb a year O without blemish, and a
19:32 the face of an O man, and you shall
23:12 male lamb a year O without blemish as a
23:18 seven lambs a year O without blemish, and one
23:19 male lambs a year O as a sacrifice of
25:22 you will be eating O produce; until the ninth
25:22 its produce comes in, you shall eat the O
26:10 And you shall eat O store long kept, and
26:10 shall clear out the O to make way for
27:3 male from twenty years O up to sixty years
27:3 up to sixty years O shall be fifty shekels
27:5 is from five years O up to twenty years
27:5 up to twenty years O, your valuation shall be
27:6 is from a month O up to five years
27:6 up to five years O, your valuation shall be
27:7 person is sixty years O and upward, then your
Num 1:3 head; from twenty years O and upward, all in
1:18 names from twenty years O and upward, head by
1:20 male from twenty years O and upward, all who
1:22 male from twenty years O and upward, all who
1:24 names, from twenty years O and upward, all who
1:26 names, from twenty years O and upward, every man
1:28 names, from twenty years O and upward, every man
1:30 names, from twenty years O and upward, every man
1:32 names, from twenty years O and upward, every man
1:34 names, from twenty years O and upward, every man
1:36 names, from twenty years O and upward, every man
1:38 names, from twenty years O and upward, every man
1:40 names, from twenty years O and upward, every man
1:42 names, from twenty years O and upward, every man
1:45 houses, from twenty years O and upward, every man
3:15 male from a month O and upward you shall
3:22 males from a month O and upward was seven
3:28 males, from a month O and upward, there were
3:34 males from a month O and upward was six
3:39 males from a month O and upward, were twenty-two
3:40 Israel, from a month O and upward, taking their
3:43 names, from a month O and upward as numbered
4:3 houses, from thirty years O up to fifty years
4:3 up to fifty years O, all who can enter
4:23 houses; from thirty years O up to fifty years
4:23 up to fifty years O, you shall number them,
4:30 houses; from thirty years O up to fifty years
4:30 up to fifty years O, you shall number them,
4:35 houses, from thirty years O up to fifty years
4:35 up to fifty years O, every one that could
4:39 houses, from thirty years O up to fifty years
4:39 up to fifty years O, every one that could
4:43 houses, from thirty years O up to fifty years
4:43 up to fifty years O, every one that could
4:47 houses, from thirty years O up to fifty years
4:47 up to fifty years O, every one that could
6:12 male lamb a year O for a guilt offering;
6:14 male lamb a year O without blemish for a
6:14 ewe lamb a year O without blemish as a
7:15 male lamb a year O, for a burnt offering;
7:17 male goats, and five male lambs a year O
7:21 male lamb a year O, for a burnt offering;
7:23 male goats, and five male lambs a year O
7:27 male lamb a year O, for a burnt offering;
7:29 male goats, and five male lambs a year O
7:33 male lamb a year O, for a burnt offering;
7:35 male goats, and five male lambs a year O
7:39 male lamb a year O, for a burnt offering;
7:41 male goats, and five male lambs a year O
7:45 male lamb a year O, for a burnt offering;
7:47 male goats, and five male lambs a year O
7:51 male lamb a year O, for a burnt offering;
7:53 male goats, and five male lambs a year O
7:57 male lamb a year O, for a burnt offering;
7:59 male goats, and five male lambs a year O
7:63 male lamb a year O, for a burnt offering;
7:65 male goats, and five male lambs a year O
7:69 male lamb a year O, for a burnt offering;
7:71 male goats, and five male lambs a year O
7:75 male lamb a year O, for a burnt offering;
7:77 male goats, and five male lambs a year O
7:81 male lamb a year O, for a burnt offering;
7:83 male goats, and five male lambs a year O
7:87 male lambs a year O, with their cereal offering;
7:88 male lambs a year O sixty.
8:24 Levites: from twenty-five years O and upward they
14:29 numbered from twenty years O and upward, who
15:27 female goat a year O for a sin offering.
18:16 price (at a month O you shall redeem them)
26:2 Israel, from twenty years O and upward, by their
26:4 people, from twenty years O and upward," as the
26:62 male from a month O and upward; for they
28:3 male lambs a year O without blemish, day by
28:9 male lambs a year O without blemish, and two
28:11 male lambs a year O without blemish;
28:19 male lambs a year O; see that they are
28:27 male lambs a year O;
29:2 male lambs a year O without blemish;
29:8 male lambs a year O; they shall be to
29:13 male lambs a year O; they shall be without
29:17 male lambs a year O without blemish,
29:20 male lambs a year O without blemish,
29:23 male lambs a year O without blemish,
29:26 male lambs a year O without blemish,
29:29 male lambs a year O without blemish,
29:32 male lambs a year O without blemish,
29:36 male lambs a year O without blemish,
32:11 Egypt, from twenty years O and upward, shall see
33:39 hundred and twenty-three years O when he died on
Deut 4:25 children, and have grown O in the land, if
19:14 which the men of O have set.
28:50 the person of the O or show favor to
31:2 hundred and twenty years O this day; I am
32:7 Remember the days of O, consider the years of
34:7 hundred and twenty years O when he died; his
Josh 6:21 and women, young and O, oxen, sheep, and asses,
13:1 Now Joshua was O and advanced in years; and
13:1 to him, "You are O and advanced in years,
14:7 I was forty years O when Moses the servant
14:10 now, lo, I am this day eighty-five years O
23:1 about, and Joshua was O and well advanced in
23:2 them, "I am now O and well advanced in
24:2 "Your fathers lived of O beyond the Euphrates, Terah,

O

24:29 LORD, died, being a hundred and ten years O
Judg 6:25 second bull seven years O, and pull down the
8:32 died in a good O age, and was buried
19:16 And behold, an O man was coming from his
19:17 the city; and the O man said, "Where are
19:20 And the O man said, "Peace be to you;
19:22 they said to the O man, the master of
Ruth 1:12 for I am too O to have a husband.
4:15 a nourisher of your O age; for your daughter-in-law
1Sam 2:22 Now Eli was very O, and he heard all
2:31 will not be an O man in your house.
2:32 shall not be an O man in your house
4:15 Eli was ninety-eight years O and his eyes were
4:18 for he was an O man, and heavy.
5:9 city, both young and O, so that tumors broke
8:1 When Samuel became O, he made his sons judges
8:5 him, "Behold, you are O and your sons do
12:2 you; and I am O and gray, and behold,
13:1 years O when he began to reign; and he
17:12 the man was already O and advanced in years.
27:8 the land from of O, as far as Shur,
28:14 And she said, "An O man is coming up;
2Sam 2:10 son, was forty years O when he began to
4:4 He was five years O when the news about
5:4 David was thirty years O when he began to
13:18 the virgin daughters of the king clad of O
19:32 aged man, eighty years O; and he had provided
19:35 this day eighty years O; can I discern what
20:18 wont to say in O time, 'Let them but
1Kgs 1:1 Now King David was O and advanced in years,
1:15 the king was very O, and Abishag the Shunammite
11:4 For when Solomon was O his wives turned away
12:6 took counsel with the O men, who had stood
12:8 the counsel which the O men gave him, and
12:13 the counsel which the O men had given him,
13:11 Now there dwelt an O prophet in Bethel.
13:25 the city where the O prophet dwelt.
14:21 Rehoboam was forty-one years O when he began to
15:23 But in his O age he was diseased in
22:42 Jehoshaphat was thirty-five years O when he began
2Kgs 4:14 she has no son, and her husband is O
8:17 He was thirty-two years O when he became king,
8:26 Ahaziah was twenty-two years O when he began to
11:21 Jehoash was seven years O when he began to
14:2 He was twenty-five years O when he began to
14:21 who was sixteen years O, and made him king
15:2 He was sixteen years O when he began to
15:33 He was twenty-five years O when he began to
16:2 Ahaz was twenty years O when he began to
18:2 He was twenty-five years O when he began to
19:25 planned from days of O what now I bring
21:1 Manasseh was twelve years O when he began to
21:19 Amon was twenty-two years O when he began to
22:1 Josiah was eight years O when he began to
23:31 Jehoahaz was twenty-three years O when he began
23:36 Jehoiakim was twenty-five years O when he began to
24:8 Jehoiachin was eighteen years O when he became
24:18 Zedekiah was twenty-one years O when he became
1Chr 2:21 he was sixty years O; and she bore him
23:1 When David was O and full of days, he
23:3 The Levites, thirty years O and upward, were
23:24 individuals from twenty years O and upward who
23:27 Levites from twenty years O and upward--
29:28 died in a good O age, full of days,
2Chr 3:3 in cubits of the O standard, was sixty cubits,
10:6 took counsel with the O men, who had stood
10:8 the counsel which the O men gave him, and
10:13 the counsel of the O men,
12:13 Rehoboam was forty-one years O when he began to
15:13 death, whether young or O, man or woman.
20:31 He was thirty-five years O when he began to
21:5 Jehoram was thirty-two years O when he became
21:20 He was thirty-two years O when he began to
22:2 Ahaziah was forty-two years O when he began to
24:1 Joash was seven years O when he began to
24:15 But Jehoiada grew O and full of days, and
24:15 hundred and thirty years O at his death.
25:1 Amaziah was twenty-five years O when he began to
25:5 mustered those twenty years O and upward, and
26:1 who was sixteen years O, and made him king
26:3 Uzziah was sixteen years O when he began to
27:1 Jotham was twenty-five years O when he began to
27:8 He was twenty-five years O when he began to
28:1 Ahaz was twenty years O when he began to
29:1 was twenty-five years O, and he reigned twenty-nine
31:15 portions to their brethren, O and young alike, by
31:16 males from three years O and upwards, all who
31:17 Levites from twenty years O and upwards was
33:1 Manasseh was twelve years O when he began to
33:21 Amon was twenty-two years O when he began to
34:1 Josiah was eight years O when he began to
36:2 Jehoahaz was twenty-three years O when he began
36:5 Jehoiakim was twenty-five years O when he began to
36:9 Jehoiachin was eight years O when he began to
36:11 Zedekiah was twenty-one years O when he began to
36:17 young man or virgin, O man or aged; he
Ezra 3:8 Levites, from twenty years O and upward, to have
3:12 heads of fathers' houses, O men who had seen
4:15 sedition was stirred up in it from of O
4:19 this city from of O has risen against kings,
Neh 3:6 of Besodeiah repaired the O Gate; they laid its
12:39 Ephraim, and by the O Gate, and by the
12:46 David and Asaph of O there was a chief
Tob 3:10 I shall bring his O age down in sorrow
4:12 Jacob, our fathers of O, all took wives from
8:7 mercy and may grow O together with her."
12:4 The O man said, "He deserves it."
14:2 He was fifty-eight years O when he lost his
14:3 he had grown very O he called his son
14:3 behold, I have grown O and am about to
14:11 hundred and fifty-eight years O; and Tobias gave him
14:13 He grew O with honor, and he gave his
Jud 16:23 more famous, and grew O in her husband's house,
16:23 until she was one hundred and five years O
Esth 3:13 all Jews, young and O, women and children, in
Job 5:26 your grave in ripe O age, as a shock
14:8 Though its root grow O in the earth, and
20:4 know this from of O, since man was placed
21:7 the wicked live, reach O age, and grow mighty
22:15 you keep to the O way which wicked men
29:2 in the months of O, as in the days
32:9 It is not the O that are wise, nor
42:17 And Job died, an O man, and full of
Ps 25:6 steadfast love, for they have been from of O
37:25 young, and now am O; yet I have not
44:1 in the days of O:
55:19 is enthroned from of O; because they keep no
71:9 in the time of O age; forsake me not
71:18 So even to O age and gray hairs, O
74:2 thou hast gotten of O, which thou hast redeemed
74:12 King is from of O, working salvation in the
77:5 consider the days of O, I remember the years
77:11 LORD; yea, I will remember thy wonders of O
78:2 dark sayings from of O,
89:19 Of O thou didst speak in a vision to
89:49 thy steadfast love of O, which by thy faithfulness
92:14 bring forth fruit in O age, they are ever
93:2 is established from of O; thou art from everlasting.
102:25 Of O thou didst lay the foundation of the
119:52 thy ordinances from of O, I take comfort, O
143:5 remember the days of O, I meditate on all
148:12 men and maidens together, O men and children!
Prov 8:22 his work, the first of his acts of O
20:29 but the beauty of O men is their gray
22:6 and when he is O he will not depart
23:22 do not despise your mother when she is O
Eccl 4:13 wise youth than an O and foolish king, who
Song 7:13 new as well as O, which I have laid
Wis 3:17 account, and finally their O age will be without
4:8 For O age is not honored for length of
4:9 blameless life is ripe O age.
4:16 will condemn the prolonged O age of the unrighteous
8:8 knows the things of O, and infers the things
12:3 Those who dwelt of O in thy holy land
Sir 3:12 your father in his O age, and do not
6:18 and until you are O you will keep finding
8:6 man when he is O, for some of us
8:6 is old, for some of us are growing O
9:10 Forsake not an O friend, for a new one
11:18 to it, and grow O in your work.
14:17 All living beings become O like a garment, for
14:17 the decree from of O is, "You must surely
25:2 liar, and an adulterous O man who lacks good
25:3 find anything in your O age?
30:24 and anxiety brings on O age too soon.
41:2 failing in strength, very O and distracted over
46:9 remained with him to O age, so that he
50:23 days in Israel, as in the days of O
51:8 thy work from of O, that thou dost deliver
Is 20:4 the young and the O, naked and barefoot, with
22:11 the water of the O pool.
23:7 is from days of O, whose feet carried her

OLDER (13)

OLDEST (2)

OLIVE (44)

Rev	11:4	These are the two O trees and the two

OLIVES (17)

Lev	24:2	pure oil from beaten O for the lamp, that
Deut	28:40	the oil; for your O shall drop off.
2Sam	15:30	of the Mount of O, weeping as he went,
Ezek	27:17	for your merchandise wheat, O and early figs, honey,
Mic	6:15	reap; you shall tread O, but not anoint yourselves
Zech	14:4	on the Mount of O which lies before Jerusalem
	14:4	and the Mount of O shall be split in
Mt	21:1	to the Mount of O, then Jesus sent two
	24:3	on the Mount of O, the disciples came to
	26:30	hymn, they went out to the Mount of O
Mk	11:1	at the Mount of O, he sent two of
	13:3	on the Mount of O opposite the temple, Peter
	14:26	hymn, they went out to the Mount of O
Lk	19:37	of the Mount of O, the whole multitude of
	22:39	to the Mount of O; and the disciples followed
Jn	8:1	But Jesus went to the Mount of O
Jas	3:12	tree, my brethren, yield O, or a grapevine figs?

OLIVET (3)

Lk	19:29	mount that is called O, he sent two of
	21:37	went out and lodged on the mount called O
Acts	1:12	from the mount called O, which is near Jerusalem,

OLIVEWOOD (4)

1Kgs	6:23	made two cherubim of O, each ten cubits high.
	6:31	he made doors of O; the lintel and the
	6:32	the two doors of O with carvings of cherubim,
	6:33	the nave doorposts of O, in the form of

OLIVEYARDS

Josh	24:13	fruit of vineyards and O which you did not

OLYMPAS

Rom	16:15	and his sister, and O, and all the saints

OLYMPIAN

2Mac	6:2	it the temple of O Zeus, and to call

OMAR (3)

Gen	36:11	of Eliphaz were Teman, O, Zepho, Gatam, and Kenaz.
	36:15	Esau: the chiefs Teman, O, Zepho, Kenaz,
1Chr	1:36	sons of Eliphaz: Teman, O, Zephi, Gatam, Kenaz,

OMEGA (3)

Rev	1:8	"I am the Alpha and the O
	21:6	the Alpha and the O, the beginning and the
	22:13	the Alpha and the O, the first and the

OMEN (4)

1Kgs	20:33	were watching for an O, and they quickly took
Zech	3:8	are men of good O: behold, I will bring
2Mac	5:4	apparition might prove to have been a good O
Phil	1:28	This is a clear O to them of their

OMENS (3)

Num	24:1	times, to look for O, but set his face
Sir	34:5	Divinations and O and dreams are folly, and like
Is	44:25	who frustrates the O of liars, and makes

OMER (5)

Ex	16:16	you shall take an O apiece, according to the
	16:18	measured it with an O, he that gathered much
	16:32	has commanded: 'Let an O of it be kept
	16:33	jar, and put an O of manna in it,
	16:36	(An O is the tenth part of an ephah.)

OMERS

Ex	16:22	as much bread, two O apiece; and when all

OMRI (18)

1Kgs	16:16	therefore all Israel made O, the commander of the
	16:17	So O went up from Gibbethon, and all Israel
	16:21	Ginath, to make him king, and half followed O
	16:22	the people who followed O overcame the people who
	16:22	so Tibni died, and O became king.
	16:23	Asa king of Judah, O began to reign over
	16:25	O did what was evil in the sight of
	16:27	of the acts of O which he did, and
	16:28	And O slept with his fathers, and was buried
	16:29	Ahab the son of O began to reign over
	16:29	Ahab the son of O reigned over Israel in
	16:30	Ahab the son of O did evil in the
2Kgs	8:26	was a granddaughter of O king of Israel.
1Chr	7:8	Zemirah, Joash, Eliezer, Eli-o-enai, O, Jeremoth,
	9:4	of Ammihud, son of O, son of Imri, son
	27:18	David's brothers; for Issachar, O the son of Michael;
2Chr	22:2	mother's name was Athaliah, the granddaughter of O
Mic	6:16	kept the statutes of O, and all the works

ONAM (4)

Gen	36:23	of Shobal: Alvan, Manahath, Ebal, Shepho, and O
1Chr	1:40	sons of Shobal: Alian, Manahath, Ebal, Shephi, and O
	2:26	name was Atarah; she was the mother of O
	2:28	The sons of O: Shammai and Jada.

ONAN (8)

Gen	38:4	bore a son, and she called his name O
	38:8	Then Judah said to O, "Go in to your
	38:9	But O knew that the offspring would not be
	46:12	sons of Judah: Er, O, Shelah, Perez, and Zerah
	46:12	Zerah (but Er and O died in the land
Num	26:19	Judah were Er and O; and Er and Onan
	26:19	Onan; and Er and O died in the land
1Chr	2:3	sons of Judah: Er, O, and Shelah; these three

ONE-HALF (2)

Josh	14:2	for the nine and O tribes.
	14:3	to the two and O tribes beyond the Jordan;

ONES (103)

Gen	34:29	wealth, all their little O and their wives, all
	43:8	both we and you and also our little O
	45:19	Egypt for your little O and for your wives,
	46:5	their father, their little O, and their wives, in
	47:24	your households, and as food for your little O
	50:21	I will provide for you and your little O
Ex	10:10	you and your little O go!
Num	1:16	These were the O chosen from the congregation, the
	14:3	wives and our little O will become a prey;
	14:31	But your little O, who you said would become
	16:27	with their wives, their sons, and their little O
	31:9	Midian and their little O; and they took as
	31:17	male among the little O, and kill every woman
	32:16	cities for our little O,
	32:17	place; and our little O shall live in the
	32:24	cities for your little O, and folds for your
	32:26	Our little O, our wives, our flocks, and all
Deut	1:39	Moreover your little O, who you said would become
	3:19	your wives, your little O, and your cattle (I
	14:12	But these are the O which you shall not
	20:14	women and the little O, the cattle, and everything
	22:6	the ground, with young O or eggs and the
	29:11	of Israel, your little O, your wives, and the
	31:12	men, women, and little O, and the sojourner within
	33:2	ten thousands of holy O, with flaming fire at
Josh	1:14	Your wives, your little O, and your cattle shall
	8:35	women, and the little O, and the sojourners who
Judg	18:21	departed, putting the little O and the cattle and
	21:10	the sword; also the women and the little O
1Sam	2:9	feet of his faithful O; but the wicked shall
2Sam	7:9	name of the great O of the earth.
	15:22	and all the little O who were with him.
2Kgs	8:12	in pieces their little O, and rip up their
1Chr	16:13	Abraham his servant, sons of Jacob, his chosen O
	16:22	"Touch not my anointed O, do my prophets no
	17:8	name of the great O of the earth.
2Chr	20:13	LORD, with their little O, their wives, and their
Neh	4:2	of rubbish, and burned O at that?"
Job	5:1	which of the holy O will you turn?
	15:15	trust in his holy O, and the heavens are
	21:11	send forth their little O like a flock, and
	38:41	prey, when its young O cry to God, and
	39:4	Their young O become strong, they grow up in
	39:30	His young O suck up blood; and where the
Ps	50:5	to me my faithful O, who made a covenant
	83:3	people; they consult together against thy protected O
	89:5	thy faithfulness in the assembly of the holy O
	89:7	council of the holy O, great and terrible above
	103:20	his angels, you mighty O who do his word,
	105:6	Abraham his servant, sons of Jacob, his chosen O
	105:15	"Touch not my anointed O, do my prophets no
	105:43	with joy, his chosen O with singing.
	106:5	prosperity of thy chosen O, that I may rejoice
	119:21	rebuke the insolent, accursed O, who wander from
	137:9	who takes your little O and dashes them against
	149:9	This is glory for all his faithful O
Prov	1:22	"How long, O simple O, will you love being
	8:5	O simple O, learn prudence; O foolish men, pay
Eccl	5:8	there are yet higher O over them.

O

Wis 3:9 his elect, and he watches over his holy O
4:15 his elect, and he watches over his holy O
18:1 But for thy holy O there was very great
18:2 thankful that thy holy O, though previously wronged,
18:5 babes of thy holy O, and one child had
Sir 42:17 not enabled his holy O to recount all his
45:2 glory to the holy O, and made him great
Is 13:3 commanded my consecrated O, have summoned my
13:3 men to execute my anger, my proudly exulting O
32:11 ease, shudder, you complacent O; strip, and make
33:7 Behold, the valiant O cry without; the envoys of
Jer 10:7 among all the wise O of the nations and
49:20 Teman: Even the little O of the flock shall
50:45 Chaldeans: Surely the little O of their flock shall
Ezek 32:12 the swords of mighty O, all of them most
42:6 ground more than the lower and the middle O
Dan 4:17 word of the holy O, to the end that
7:24 different from the former O, and shall put down
Hos 13:16 the sword, their little O shall be dashed in
Nah 3:10 into captivity; her little O were dashed in pieces
Zeph 3:10 daughter of my dispersed O, shall bring my offering.
3:11 midst your proudly exultant O, and you shall no
Zech 6:6 north country, the white O go toward the west
6:6 country, and the dappled O go toward the south
11:16 flesh of the fat O, tearing off even their
13:7 I will turn my hand against the little O
14:5 and all the holy O with him.
Mt 10:42 one of these little O even a cup of
18:6 one of these little O who believe in me
18:10 one of these little O; for I tell you
18:13 one of these little O should perish.
Mk 4:15 And these are the O along the path, where
4:16 like manner are the O sown upon rocky ground,
4:18 And others are the O sown among thorns; they
4:20 good soil are the O who hear the word
9:42 one of these little O who believe in me
Lk 8:12 The O along the path are those who have
8:13 And the O on the rock are those who,
12:18 barns, and build larger O; and there I will
17:2 one of these little O to sin.
1Cor 14:36 are you the only O it has reached?
Col 3:12 as God's chosen O, holy and beloved, compassion,
2Pet 2:10 to revile the glorious O,
Jude 1:8 the flesh, reject authority, and revile the glorious O

ONESELF (5)

Is 28:20 too short to stretch O on it, and the
28:20 too narrow to wrap O in it.
47:14 No coal for warming O is this, no fire
Mk 12:33 love one's neighbor as O, is much more than
Jas 1:26 affliction, and to keep O unstained from the world.

ONESIMUS (2)

Col 4:9 hearts, and with him O, the faithful and beloved
Philem 1:10 you for my child, O, whose father I have

ONESIPHORUS (2)

2Tim 1:16 to the household of O, for he often refreshed
4:19 Greet Prisca and Aquila, and the household of O

ONIAS (21)

Sir 50:1 high priest, son of O, who in his life
1Mac 12:7 letter was sent to O the high priest from
12:8 O welcomed the envoy with honor, and received the
12:19 which they sent to O:
12:20 of the Spartans, to O the high priest, greeting.
2Mac 3:1 of the high priest O and his hatred of
3:5 could not prevail over O he went to Apollonius
3:31 of Heliodorus' friends asked O to call upon the
3:33 "Be very grateful to O the high priest, since
3:35 life, and having bidden O farewell, he marched off
4:1 his own country, slandered O, saying that it was
4:4 of Simon's approved agents, O recognized that the
4:7 Jason the brother of O obtained the high-priesthood
4:33 When O became fully aware of these acts he
4:34 taking Andronicus aside, urged him to kill O
4:34 Andronicus came to O, and resorting to treachery
4:34 of his suspicion persuaded O to come out from
4:36 the unreasonable murder of O, and the Greeks
4:38 committed the outrage against O, and there he
15:12 he saw was this: O, who had been high
15:14 And O spoke, saying, "This is a man who

ONIONS

Num 11:5 melons, the leeks, the O, and the garlic;

ONLY (387)

Gen 6:5 of his heart was O evil continually.
7:23 O Noah was left, and those that were with
9:4 O you shall not eat flesh with its life,
11:6 language; and this is O the beginning of what
19:8 them as you please; O do nothing to these
22:2 "Take your son, your O son Isaac, whom you
22:12 withheld your son, your O son, from me."
22:16 withheld your son, your O son,
24:8 this oath of mine; O you must not take
27:13 your curse, my son; O obey my word, and
32:10 thy servant, for with O my staff I crossed
34:12 you say to me; O give me the maiden
34:15 O on this condition will we consent to you:
34:22 O on this condition will the men agree to
34:23 O let us agree with them, and they will
37:5 to his brothers they O hated him the more.
41:40 themselves as you command; O as regards the throne
42:38 is dead, and he O is left.
44:17 O the man in whose hand the cup was
47:22 O the land of the priests he did not
50:8 his father's household; O their children, their flocks,
Ex 8:9 houses and be left O in the Nile."
8:11 they shall be left O in the Nile."
8:28 God in the wilderness; O you shall not go
8:29 from his people, tomorrow; O let not Pharaoh deal
9:26 O in the land of Goshen, where the people
10:17 sin, I pray you, O this once, and entreat
10:17 the LORD your God O to remove this death
10:24 may go with you; O let your flocks and
12:16 one must eat, that O may be prepared by
14:14 you, and you have O to be still."
21:19 him shall be clear; O he shall pay for
22:20 save to the LORD O, shall be utterly destroyed.
22:27 for that is his O covering, it is his
Lev 13:6 him clean; it is O an eruption; and he
Num 1:49 LORD said to Moses, O the tribe of Levi
10:4 But if they blow O one, then the leaders,
12:2 the LORD indeed spoken O through Moses?
14:9 O, do not rebel against the LORD; and do
20:19 for it; let me O pass through on foot,
22:20 go with them; but O what I bid you,
22:35 with the men; but O the word which I
23:13 them; you shall see O the nearest of them,
31:22 LORD has commanded Moses: O the gold, the silver,
36:6 whom they think best; O, they shall marry within
Deut 2:27 land; I will go O by the road, I
2:28 that I may drink; O let me pass through
2:35 we left none remaining; O the cattle we took
2:37 O to the land of the sons of Ammon
3:11 (For O Og the king of Bashan was left
3:24 Lord GOD, thou hast O begun to show thy
4:9 O take heed, and keep your soul diligently, lest
4:12 no form; there was O a voice.
12:16 O you shall not eat the blood; you shall
12:23 O be sure that you do not eat the
15:5 inheritance to possess), if O you will obey the
15:23 O you shall not eat its blood; you shall
16:20 Justice, and O justice, you shall follow, that you
17:16 O he must not multiply horses for himself, or
19:15 that he has committed; O on the evidence of
20:20 O the trees which you know are not trees
22:25 lies with her, then O the man who lay
28:13 you shall tend upward O, and not downward; if
28:29 and you shall be O oppressed and robbed continually,
28:33 and you shall be O oppressed and crushed
29:14 is it with you O that I make this
Josh 1:7 O be strong and very courageous, being careful to
1:17 we will obey you; O may the LORD your
1:18 O be strong and of good courage."
6:15 seven times: it was O on that day that
6:17 the LORD for destruction; O Rahab the harlot and
6:24 and all within it; O the silver and gold,
8:2 Jericho and its king; O its spoil and its
8:27 O the cattle and the spoil of that city
11:13 Israel burn, except Hazor O; that Joshua burned.
11:22 the people of Israel; O in Gaza, in Gath,
13:6 the people of Israel; O allot the land to
14:4 in the land, but O cities to dwell in,
17:3 had no sons, but O daughters; and these are
17:17 not have one lot O,
22:19 a possession among us; O do not rebel against
Judg 3:2 in Canaan; it was O that the generations of
3:24 they thought, "He is O relieving himself in the
6:39 let me make trial O this once with the
6:39 let it be dry O on the fleece, and

	6:40	dry on the fleece O, and on all the
	10:15	seems good to thee; O deliver us, we pray
	11:34	dances; she was his O child; beside her he
	14:16	him, and said, "You O hate me, you do
	15:13	him, "No; we will O bind you and give
	16:28	me, I pray thee, O this once, O God,
	19:20	for all your wants; O, do not spend the
1Sam	1:5	he would give Hannah O one portion, because the
	1:13	speaking in her heart; O her lips moved, and
	1:23	you have weaned him; O, may the LORD establish
	5:4	off upon the threshold; O the trunk of Dagon
	7:3	LORD, and serve him O, and he will deliver
	7:4	and the Ashtaroth, and they served the LORD O
	8:9	hearken to their voice; O, you shall solemnly warn
	12:24	O fear the LORD, and serve him faithfully with
	18:17	you for a wife; O be valiant for me
	20:39	the lad knew nothing; O Jonathan and David knew
	21:4	is holy bread; if O the young men have
2Sam	15:20	You came O yesterday, and shall I today make
	17:2	strike down the king O,
	17:3	seek the life of O one man, and all
	23:10	men returned after him O to strip the slain.
1Kgs	3:3	of David his father; O, he sacrificed and burnt
	3:18	us in the house, O we two were in
	8:25	throne of Israel, if O your sons take heed
	8:39	ways (for thou, thou O, knowest the hearts of
	11:22	he said to him, O let me go."
	12:20	house of David, but the tribe of Judah O
	14:8	all his heart, doing O that which was right
	14:13	bury him; for he O of Jeroboam shall come
	17:12	I have nothing baked, O a handful of meal
	18:22	people, "I, even I O, am left a prophet
	19:10	and I, even I O, am left; and they
	19:14	and I, even I O, am left; and they
	22:31	small nor great, but O with the king of
2Kgs	3:25	the good trees; till O its stones were left
	5:7	O consider, and see how he is seeking a
	10:23	here among you, but O the worshipers of Baal."
	13:19	will strike down Syria O three times."
	17:18	none was left but the tribe of Judah O
	21:8	to their fathers, if O they will be careful
1Chr	2:34	Sheshan had no sons, O daughters; but Sheshan had
	22:12	O, may the LORD grant you discretion and
	23:22	having no sons, but O daughters; their kinsmen, the
2Chr	6:16	throne of Israel, if O your sons take heed
	6:30	ways (for thou, thou O, knowest the hearts of
	18:30	small nor great, but O with the king of
	27:2	father Uzziah had done-- O he did not invade
	30:11	O a few men of Asher, of Manasseh, and
	33:8	for your fathers, if O they will be careful
	33:17	the high places, but O to the LORD their
Ezra	10:15	O Jonathan the son of Asahel and Jahzeiah the
Tob	3:10	said, "I am the O child of my father;
	3:15	I am my father's O child, and he has
	6:10	and he has an O daughter named Sarah.
	6:11	for you are her O eligible kinsman.
	6:14	Now I am the O son my father has,
	8:17	had compassion on two O children.
Jud	1:11	looked upon him as O one man, and they
	2:4	of his army, second O to himself, and said
	3:8	nations should worship Nebuchadnezzar O, and all
	4:3	For they had O recently returned from the captivity,
	4:7	the approach was narrow, O wide enough for two
	7:12	your forces with you; O let your servants take
	8:34	O, do not try to find out what I
	11:7	every living soul, not O do men serve him
	11:23	You are not O beautiful in appearance, but wise
	12:10	banquet for his slave O, and did not invite
	14:2	against the Assyrian outpost; O do not go down.
Esth	1:16	and the princes, "Not O to the king has
	14:3	"O my Lord, thou O art our King; help
	15:10	for our law applies O to the people.
	16:3	They not O seek to injure our subjects, but
	16:4	They not O take away thankfulness from among
	16:24	shall be made not O impassable for men, but
Job	1:12	is in your power; O upon himself do not
	2:6	is in your power; O spare his life."
	13:20	O grant two things to me, then I will
	14:22	He feels O the pain of his own body,
	14:22	body, and he mourns O for himself."
Ps	37:8	not yourself; it tends O to evil.
	38:16	For I pray, O let them not rejoice over
	51:4	Against thee, thee O, have I sinned, and done
	62:2	He O is my rock and my salvation, my
	62:4	They O plan to thrust him down from his
	62:6	He O is my rock and my salvation, my
	91:8	You will O look with your eyes and see
	139:11	If I say, "Let O darkness cover me, and
Prov	4:4	my father, tender, the O one in the sight
	11:23	of the righteous ends O in good; the expectation
	11:24	he should give, and O suffers want.
	14:23	but mere talk tends O to want.
	17:11	An evil man seeks O rebellion, and a cruel
	18:2	pleasure in understanding, but O in expressing his
	19:19	deliver him, you will O have to do it
	19:27	son, to hear instruction O to stray from the
	20:25	and to reflect O after making his vows.
	21:5	who is hasty comes O to want.
	22:16	to the rich, will O come to want.
	25:16	have found honey, eat O enough for you, lest
	26:19	and says, "I am O joking!"
	29:9	a fool, the fool O rages and laughs, and
Eccl	2:12	O what he has already done.
	2:26	of gathering and heaping, O to give to one
Song	6:9	my perfect one, is O one, the darling of
Wis	10:8	wisdom by, they not O were hindered from
	11:19	from their eyes; not O could their damage
	13:16	itself, for it is O an image and has
	19:15	And not O so, but punishment of some sort
Sir	16:11	Even if there is O one stiff-necked person, it
	32:7	more than twice, and O if asked.
	37:1	some friends are friends O in name.
	45:13	put them on, but O his sons and his
	45:25	from son to son O; so the heritage of
Is	4:1	wear our own clothes, O let us be called
	10:22	sand of the sea, O a remnant of them
	45:14	'God is with you O, and there is no
	45:24	every tongue shall swear.' O in the LORD, it
	58:4	Behold, you fast O to quarrel and to fight
Jer	1:6	speak, for I am O a youth."
	1:7	not say, 'I am O a youth'; for to
	3:13	O acknowledge your guilt, that you rebelled against
	5:4	I said, "These are O the poor, they have
	6:26	mourning as for an O son, most bitter lamentation;
	7:10	say, 'We are delivered!'-- O to go on doing
	22:17	have eyes and heart O for your dishonest gain,
	26:15	O know for certain that if you put me
	34:7	for these were the O fortified cities of Judah
	37:10	there remained of them O wounded men, every man
	38:6	in the cistern, but O mire, and Jeremiah sank
	49:9	would they not destroy O enough for themselves?
	51:58	the nations weary themselves O for fire."
Bar	6:47	They have left O lies and reproach for those
Ezek	33:24	keep saying, 'Abraham was O one man, yet he
	43:8	beside my doorposts, with O a wall between me
	44:3	O the prince may sit in it to eat
	44:20	grow long; they shall O trim the hair of
	44:22	a divorced woman, but O a virgin of the
	46:17	revert to the prince; O his sons may keep
Dan	3:45	art the Lord, the O God, glorious over the
	11:24	plans against strongholds, but O for a time.
	13:15	in as before with O two maids, and wished
Hos	9:4	be for their hunger O; it shall not come
Amos	3:2	land of Egypt: "You O have I known of
	8:10	the mourning for an O son, and the end
Obad	1:5	would they not steal O enough for themselves?
Hab	2:13	hosts that peoples labor O for fire, and nations
Zech	12:10	one mourns for an O child, and weep bitterly
Mal	3:15	arrogant blessed; evildoers not O prosper but when
1Mac	9:55	But he O began to tear it down, for
	9:65	and he went with O a few men.
	10:14	O in Bethzur did some remain who had forsaken
	10:70	priest: "You are the O one to rise up
	11:42	message to Jonathan, "Not O will I do these
	15:33	seized foreign property, but O the inheritance of our
2Mac	2:29	decoration has to consider O what is suitable for
	2:32	begin our narrative, adding O so much to what
	4:35	For this reason not O Jews, but many also
	5:7	in the end got O disgrace from his conspiracy,
	6:31	memorial of courage, not O to the young but
	7:24	still alive, Antiochus not O appealed to him in
	10:28	success and victory not O their valor but their
	11:9	ready to assail not O men but the wildest
Mt	4:10	your God and him O shall you serve.'"
	5:47	And if you salute O your brethren, what more
	8:8	under my roof; but O say the word, and
	9:21	to herself, "If I O touch his garment, I
	12:4	were with him, but O for the priests?
	12:24	they said, "It is O by Be-elzebul, the prince
	14:17	to him, "We have O five loaves here and
	14:36	him that they might O touch the fringe of
	15:24	answered, "I was sent O to the lost sheep

17:8 their eyes, they saw no one but Jesus O
19:11 receive this saying, but O those to whom it
20:12 saying, 'These last worked O one hour, and you
21:19 it, and found nothing on it but leaves O
21:21 doubt, you will not O do what has been
24:36 of heaven, nor the Son, but the Father O
Mk 5:36 synagogue, "Do not fear, O believe."
8:14 bread; and they had O one loaf with them
9:8 longer saw any one with them but Jesus O
13:32 nor the Son, but O the Father.
Lk 4:8 your God, and him O shall you serve."'
4:26 none of them but O to Zarephath, in the
4:27 them was cleansed, but O Naaman the Syrian."
5:21 Who can forgive sins but God O
7:12 being carried out, the O son of his mother,
8:42 for he had an O daughter, about twelve years
8:50 him, "Do not fear; O believe, and she shall
9:38 for he is my O child;
17:10 unworthy servants; we have O done what was our
24:18 him, "Are you the O visitor to Jerusalem who
Jn 1:14 glory as of the O Son from the Father.
1:18 ever seen God; the O Son, who is in
3:16 that he gave his O Son, that whoever believes
3:18 the name of the O Son of God.
4:2 did not baptize, but O his disciples),
5:17 him, because he not O broke the sabbath but
5:18 his own accord, but O what he sees the
5:43 that comes from the O God?
6:22 that there had been O one boat there, and
10:10 The thief comes O to steal and kill and
11:52 not for the nation O, but to gather into
12:9 there, they came, not O on account of Jesus
13:9 "Lord, not my feet O but also my hands
17:3 they know thee the O true God, and Jesus
17:20 not pray for these O, but also for those
Acts 2:15 suppose, since it is O the third hour of
5:2 the proceeds, and brought O a part and laid
8:16 them, but they had O been baptized in the
18:25 Jesus, though he knew O the baptism of John.
19:26 and hear that not O at Ephesus but almost
19:27 there is danger not O that this trade of
20:24 precious to myself, if O I may accomplish my
21:13 I am ready not O to be imprisoned but
26:10 in Jerusalem; I not O shut up many of
26:29 to God that not O you but also all
27:10 and much loss, not O of the cargo and
27:22 life among you, but O of the ship.
Rom 1:32 to die, they not O do them but approve
3:29 Or is God the God of Jews O
4:9 Is this blessing pronounced O upon the circumcised,
4:16 his descendants-- not O to the adherents of
5:11 Not O so, but we also rejoice in God
7:1 binding on a person O during his life?
8:23 until now; and not O the creation, but we
9:10 And not O so, but also when Rebecca had
9:24 not from the Jews O but also from the
9:27 sand of the sea, O a remnant of them
11:20 but you stand fast O through faith.
13:5 must be subject, not O to avoid God's wrath
14:2 the weak man eats O vegetables.
16:4 life, to whom not O I but also all
16:26 faith-- to the O wise God be glory
1Cor 3:7 waters is anything, but O God who gives the
3:15 will be saved, but O as through fire.
7:17 O, let every one lead the life which the
7:39 to whom she wishes, O in the Lord.
8:9 O take care lest this liberty of yours somehow
9:6 Or is it O Barnabas and I who have
9:24 the runners compete, but O one receives the prize?
14:27 tongue, let there be O two or at most
14:36 or are you the O ones it has reached?
15:19 If for this life O we have hoped in
2Cor 3:14 veil remains unlifted, because O through Christ is it
4:3 veiled, it is veiled O to those who are
7:7 of Titus, and not O by his coming but
7:8 letter grieved you, though O for a while.
8:10 ago you began not O to do but to
8:17 For he not O accepted our appeal, but being
8:19 the gospel; and not O that, but he has
8:21 what is honorable not O in the Lord's sight
9:12 of this service not O supplies the wants of
13:8 against the truth, but O for the truth.
Gal 1:23 Christ in Judea; they O heard it said, "He
2:10 they to the circumcised; O they would have us
3:2 Let me ask you O this: Did you receive
4:18 much of, and not O when I am present
5:13 called to freedom, brethren; O do not use your
6:12 to be circumcised, and O in order that they
Eph 1:21 that is named, not O in this age but
4:29 of your mouths, but O such as is good
Phil 1:18 O that in every way, whether in pretense or
1:27 O let your manner of life be worthy of
1:29 Christ you should not O believe in him but
2:4 of you look not O to his own interests,
2:12 obeyed, so now, not O as in my presence
2:27 on him, and not O on him but on
3:16 O let us hold true to what we have
4:15 and receiving except you O;
Col 2:17 These are O a shadow of what is to
4:11 These are the O men of the circumcision among
1Thes 1:5 came to you not O in word, but also
1:8 For not O has the word of the Lord
2:8 share with you not O the gospel of God
2Thes 2:7 is already at work; O he who now restrains
1Tim 1:17 ages, immortal, invisible, the O God, be honor and
5:13 to house, and not O idlers but gossips and
5:23 No longer drink O water, but use a little
6:15 by the blessed and O Sovereign, the King of
2Tim 2:14 does no good, but O ruins the hearers.
2:20 house there are not O vessels of gold and
4:8 that Day, and not O to me but also
Heb 3:14 share in Christ, if O we hold our first
9:7 but into the second O the high priest goes,
9:10 the worshiper, but deal O with food and drink
9:17 a will takes effect O at death, since it
11:17 to offer up his O son,
12:26 I will shake not O the earth but also
Jas 1:21 word, and not hearers O, deceiving yourselves.
1Pet 2:18 with all respect, not O to the kind and
2Pet 2:22 the sow is washed O to wallow in the
1Jn 2:2 and not for ours O but also for the
4:9 that God sent his O Son into the world,
5:6 not with the water O but with the water
2Jn 1:1 the truth, and not O I but also all
Jude 1:4 and deny our O Master and Lord, Jesus
1:25 with rejoicing, to the O God, our Savior through
Rev 2:25 you any other burden; O hold fast what you
9:4 or any tree, but O those of mankind who
17:10 comes he must remain O a little while.
21:27 abomination or falsehood, but O those who are

ONO (5)

1Chr 8:12 and Shemed, who built O and Lod with its
Ezra 2:33 of Lod, Hadid, and O, seven hundred and twenty-five.
Neh 6:2 one of the villages in the plain of O
7:37 of Lod, Hadid, and O, seven hundred and twenty-one.
11:35 Neballat, Lod, and O, the valley of craftsmen.

ONRUSHING

Judg 5:21 swept them away, the O torrent, the torrent Kishon.

ONS

Rom 9:26 they will be called O'sons of the living God.'"

ONSLAUGHT

2Mac 6:3 utterly grievous was the O of evil.

ONWARD (9)

Ex 15:22 Then Moses led Israel O from the Red Sea,
33:6 themselves of their ornaments, from Mount Horeb O
Num 15:23 LORD gave commandment, and O throughout your
2Chr 32:23 the sight of all nations from that time O
Neh 11:31 also lived from Geba O, at Michmash, Aija, Bethel
Ezek 43:27 from the eighth day O the priests shall offer
Dan 13:64 And from that day O Daniel had a great
Hag 2:15 what will come to pass from this day O
2:18 Consider from this day O, from the twenty-fourth day

ONYCHA (2)

Ex 30:34 sweet spices, stacte, and O, and galbanum, sweet
Sir 24:15 pleasant odor, like galbanum, O, and stacte, and like

ONYX (12)

Gen 2:12 is good; bdellium and O stone are there.
Ex 25:7 for the fragrant incense, O stones, and stones for
28:9 you shall take two O stones, and engrave on
28:20 row a beryl, an O, and a jasper; they
35:9 the fragrant incense, and O stones and stones for
35:27 And the leaders brought O stones and stones to
39:6 The O stones were prepared, enclosed in settings of
39:13 row, a beryl, an O, and a jasper; they
1Chr 29:2 besides great quantities of O and stones for setting,

Job 28:16 of Ophir, in precious O or sapphire.
Ezek 28:13 jasper, chrysolite, beryl, and O, sapphire, carbuncle,
Rev 21:20 fourth emerald, the fifth O, the sixth carnelian, the

OPEN (194)

Gen 34:10 the land shall be O to you; dwell and
Ex 13:2 is the first to O the womb among the
13:15 the males that first O the womb; but all
21:33 man leaves a pit O, or when a man
Lev 14:7 bird go into the O field.
14:53 the city into the O field; so he shall
17:5 they slay in the O field, that they may
Num 8:16 instead of all that O the womb, the first-born
19:15 And every O vessel, which has no cover fastened
19:16 Whoever in the O field touches one who is
Deut 13:16 the midst of its O square, and burn the
15:8 brother, but you shall O your hand to him,
15:11 command you, You shall O wide your hand to
21:1 slain, lying in the O country, and it is
22:25 "But if in the O country a man meets
22:27 upon her in the O country, and though the
28:12 The LORD will O to you his good treasury
32:25 In the O the sword shall bereave, and in
Josh 8:17 they left the city O, and pursued Israel.
8:24 of Ai in the O wilderness where they pursued
10:22 Then Joshua said, O the mouth of the cave,
Judg 3:25 he still did not O the doors of the
15:19 And God split O the hollow place that is
19:15 sat down in the O square of the city;
19:17 the wayfarer in the O square of the city;
20:31 Gibe-ah, and in the O country, about thirty men
1Sam 30:11 an Egyptian in the O country, and brought him
2Sam 10:8 by themselves in the O country.
11:11 are camping in the O field; shall I then
1Kgs 6:18 form of gourds and O flowers; all was cedar,
6:29 and palm trees and O flowers, in the inner
6:32 cherubim, palm trees, and O flowers; he overlaid
6:35 and palm trees and O flowers; and he overlaid
8:29 thy eyes may be O night and day toward
8:52 Let thy eyes be O to the supplication of
11:29 were alone in the O country.
14:11 who dies in the O country the birds of
21:24 who dies in the O country the birds of
2Kgs 6:17 LORD, I pray thee, O his eyes that he
6:20 Elisha said, "O LORD, O the eyes of these
7:12 hide themselves in the O country, thinking, 'When
9:3 king over Israel.' Then O the door and flee;
13:17 And he said, O the window eastward"; and he
15:16 because they did not O it to him, therefore
19:16 O LORD, and hear; O thy eyes, O LORD,
25:23 the forces in the O country and their men
1Chr 19:9 by themselves in the O country.
2Chr 6:20 thy eyes may be O day and night toward
6:40 let thy eyes be O and thy ears attentive
7:15 my eyes will be O and my ears attentive
Ezra 10:9 people sat in the O square before the house
10:13 of heavy rain; we cannot stand in the O
Neh 1:6 attentive, and thy eyes O, to hear the prayer
4:13 behind the wall, in O places, I stationed the
6:5 to me with an O letter in his hand.
Tob 2:10 droppings fell into my O eyes and white films
6:4 said to him, "Cut O the fish and take
11:7 that your father will O his eyes.
Jud 10:9 the young men to O the gate for her,
11:19 will so much as O its mouth to growl
13:11 watchmen at the gates, O, open the gate!
13:11 at the gates, "Open, O the gate!
Esth 4:6 to Mordecai in the O square of the city
6:9 on horseback through the O square of the city,
6:11 him ride through the O square of the city,
9:19 who live in the O towns, hold the fourteenth
13:2 my kingdom peaceable and O to travel throughout all
14:10 of thy house, to O the mouths of the
Job 11:5 God would speak, and O his lips to you,
12:14 if he shuts a man in, none can O
14:3 And dost thou O thy eyes upon such a
16:13 He slashes O my kidneys, and does not spare;
28:4 They O shafts in a valley away from where
32:20 find relief; I must O my lips and answer.
33:2 Behold, I O my mouth; the tongue in my
39:4 grow up in the O; they go forth, and
41:14 Who can O the doors of his face?
Ps 5:9 their throat is an O sepulchre, they flatter with
22:13 Bashan surround me; they O wide their mouths at
35:21 They O wide their mouths against me; they say,
38:13 man who does not O his mouth.
39:9 dumb, I do not O my mouth; for it
40:6 hast given me an O ear.
51:15 O Lord, O thou my lips, and my mouth
60:2 thou hast rent it O; repair its breaches, for
74:15 Thou didst cleave O springs and brooks; thou didst
78:2 I will O my mouth in a parable; I
81:10 O your mouth wide, and I will fill it.
118:19 O to me the gates of righteousness, that I
119:18 O my eyes, that I may behold wondrous things
119:131 With O mouth I pant, because I long for
Prov 15:11 Sheol and Abaddon lie O before the LORD, how
20:13 you come to poverty; O your eyes, and you
24:7 gate he does not O his mouth.
27:5 Better is O rebuke than hidden love.
31:8 O your mouth for the dumb, for the rights
31:9 O your mouth, judge righteously, maintain the rights
Song 5:2 O to me, my sister, my love, my dove,
5:5 I arose to O to my beloved, and my
Sir 15:5 his neighbors, and will O his mouth in the
24:2 Most High she will O her mouth, and in
26:12 of every post and O her quiver to the
29:24 stranger you may not O your mouth;
39:5 Most High; he will O his mouth in prayer
Is 9:12 west devour Israel with O mouth.
22:22 of David; he shall O, and none shall shut;
22:22 shut; and he shall shut, and none shall O
26:2 O the gates, that the righteous nation which keeps
28:24 does he continually O and harrow his ground?
37:17 O LORD, and hear; O thy eyes, O LORD,
41:18 I will O rivers on the bare heights, and
42:7 to the nations, to O the eyes that are
42:20 them; his ears are O, but he does not
45:1 loins of kings, to O doors before him that
45:8 righteousness; let the earth O, that salvation may
57:4 Against whom do you O your mouth wide and
60:11 Your gates shall be O continually; day and night
Jer 5:16 quiver is like an O tomb, they are all
9:22 like dung upon the O field, like sheaves after
13:19 up, with none to O them; all Judah is
17:3 the mountains in the O country.
32:11 and conditions, and the O copy;
32:14 of purchase and this O deed, and put them
32:19 deed; whose eyes are O to all the ways
40:7 the forces in the O country and their men
40:13 the forces in the O country came to Gedaliah
50:26 her from every quarter; O her granaries; pile her
Bar 2:17 O Lord, and hear; O thy eyes, O Lord,
Ezek 2:8 like that rebellious house; O your mouth, and eat
3:27 with you, I will O your mouth, and you
16:5 cast out on the O field, for you were
16:63 be confounded, and never O your mouth again
21:22 lot for Jerusalem, to O the mouth with a
25:9 therefore I will lay O the flank of Moab
26:2 broken, it has swung O to me; I shall
29:5 shall fall upon the O field, and not be
29:21 Israel, and I will O your lips among them.
32:4 the ground, on the O field I will fling
33:27 that is in the O field I will give
37:12 GOD: Behold, I will O your graves, and raise
37:13 the LORD, when I O your graves, and raise
39:5 shall fall in the O field; for I have
45:2 fifty cubits for an O space around it.
48:15 for dwellings and for O country.
48:17 the city shall have O land: on the north
Dan 3:33 And now we cannot O our mouths; shame and
6:10 in his upper chamber O toward Jerusalem; and he
9:18 thy ear and hear; O thy eyes and behold
14:27 The dragon ate them, and burst O
Hos 13:8 cubs, I will tear O their breast, and there
13:16 in pieces, and their pregnant women ripped O
Mic 1:6 a heap in the O country, a place for
4:10 and dwell in the O country; you shall go
Nah 3:13 your land are wide O to your foes; fire
Zech 11:1 O your doors, O Lebanon, that the fire may
12:4 of Judah I will O my eyes, when I
Mal 3:10 if I will not O the windows of heaven
1Mac 5:48 But they refused to O to him.
2Mac 1:4 May he O your heart to his law and
6:18 was being forced to O his mouth to eat
10:36 Others broke O the gates and let in the
15:19 the encounter in the O country.
Mt 13:35 the prophet: "I will O my mouth in parables,
17:26 up, and when you O its mouth you will
25:11 also, saying, 'Lord, lord, O to us.'
Mk 11:4 door out in the O street; and they untied
Lk 12:36 so that they may O to him at once

13:25 the door, saying, 'Lord, O to us.' He will
Jn 9:26 How did he O your eyes?"
10:21 Can a demon O the eyes of the blind?"
Acts 1:18 falling headlong he burst O in the middle and
12:14 joy she did not O the gate but ran
16:27 the prison doors were O, he drew his sword
18:14 Paul was about to O his mouth, Gallio said
19:38 one, the courts are O, and there are proconsuls;
26:18 I send you to O their eyes, that they
Rom 3:13 "Their throat is an O grave, they use their
2Cor 4:2 word, but by the O statement of the truth
6:11 Our mouth is O to you, Corinthians; our heart
7:2 O your hearts to us; we have wronged no
Col 4:3 also, that God may O to us a door
Tit 1:5 are believers and not O to the charge of
Heb 4:13 hidden, but all are O and laid bare to
Jas 3:17 pure, then peaceable, gentle, O to reason, full of
1Pet 3:12 and his ears are O to their prayer.
Rev 3:8 set before you an O door, which no one
4:1 lo, in heaven an O door!
5:2 "Who is worthy to O the scroll and break
5:3 earth was able to O the scroll or to
5:4 was found worthy to O the scroll or to
5:5 so that he can O the scroll and its
5:9 the scroll and to O its seals, for thou
10:2 had a little scroll O in his hand.
10:8 the scroll which is O in the hand of

OPEN-MOUTHED

Sir 19:27 A man's attire and O laughter, and a man's

OPENED (144)

Gen 3:5 your eyes will be O, and you will be
3:7 eyes of both were O, and they knew that
4:11 the ground, which has O its mouth to receive
7:11 forth, and the windows of the heavens were O
8:6 of forty days Noah O the window of the
21:19 Then God O her eyes, and she saw a
29:31 Leah was hated, he O her womb; but Rachel
30:22 hearkened to her and O her womb.
41:56 all the land, Joseph O all the storehouses, and
42:27 as one of them O his sack to give
43:21 the lodging place we O our sacks, and there
44:11 ground, and every man O his sack.
Ex 2:6 When she O it she saw the child; and
Num 16:32 asunder; and the earth O its mouth and swallowed
22:28 Then the LORD O the mouth of the ass,
22:31 Then the LORD O the eyes of Balaam, and
24:3 man whose eye is O,
24:15 man whose eye is O,
26:10 LORD, and the earth O its mouth and swallowed
Deut 11:6 Reuben; how the earth O its mouth and swallowed
Judg 3:25 took the key and O them; and there lay
4:19 So she O a skin of milk and gave
11:35 me; for I have O my mouth to the
11:36 father, if you have O your mouth to the
19:27 morning, and when he O the doors of the
1Sam 3:15 until morning; then he O the doors of the
2Kgs 4:35 times, and the child O his eyes.
6:17 So the LORD O the eyes of the young
6:20 So the LORD O their eyes, and they saw;
9:10 Then he O the door, and fled.
13:17 window eastward"; and he O it.
2Chr 29:3 the first month, he O the doors of the
Neh 7:3 gates of Jerusalem be O until the sun is
8:5 And Ezra O the book in the sight of
8:5 people; and when he O it all the people
13:19 they should not be O until after the sabbath.
Tob 8:13 So the maid O the door and went in,
Jud 10:9 the city to be O for me, and I
13:13 she had returned; they O the gate and admitted
14:15 no one answered, he O it and went into
Job 3:1 After this Job O his mouth and cursed the
29:23 the rain; and they O their mouths as for
31:32 the street; I have O my doors to the
Ps 78:23 the skies above, and O the doors of heaven;
105:41 He O the rock, and water gushed forth; it
106:17 the LORD, the earth O and swallowed up Dathan,
109:2 and deceitful mouths are O against me, speaking
Song 5:6 I O to my beloved, but my beloved had
7:12 the grape blossoms have O and the pomegranates
Wis 10:21 defending hand, because wisdom O the mouth of the
Sir 22:20 If you have O your mouth against your friend,
43:14 Therefore the storehouses are O, and the clouds fly
51:25 I O my mouth and said, Get these things
Is 5:14 enlarged its appetite and O its mouth beyond
10:14 moved a wing, or O the mouth, or chirped."
24:18 windows of heaven are O, and the foundations of
35:5 the blind shall be O, and the ears of
48:8 from of old your ear has not been O
50:5 The Lord GOD has O my ear, and I
53:7 was afflicted, yet he O not his mouth; like
53:7 is dumb, so he O not his mouth.
Jer 50:25 The LORD has O his armory, and brought out
Ezek 1:1 Chebar, the heavens were O, and I saw visions
3:2 So I O my mouth, and he gave me
24:27 your mouth will be O to the fugitive, and
33:22 came; and he had O my mouth by the
33:22 so my mouth was O, and I was no
41:11 of the side chambers O on the part of
44:2 it shall not be O, and no one shall
46:1 day it shall be O and on the day
46:1 day of the new moon it shall be O
46:12 facing east shall be O for him; and he
Dan 3:25 of the fire he O his mouth and said:
7:10 court sat in judgment, and the books were O
10:16 my lips; then I O my mouth and spoke.
13:25 of them ran and O the garden doors.
13:39 for us, and he O the doors and dashed
14:18 as the doors were O, the king looked at
Nah 2:6 The river gates are O, the palace is in
Zech 13:1 shall be a fountain O for the house of
1Mac 3:28 And he O his coffers and gave a year's
3:48 And they O the book of the law to
10:76 city became afraid and O the gates, and Jonathan
11:2 people of the cities O their gates to him
14:5 for a harbor, and O a way to the
2Mac 14:44 drew back, a space O and he fell in
Mt 3:16 behold, the heavens were O and he saw the
5:2 And he O his mouth and taught them, saying:
7:7 and it will be O to you.
7:8 and to him who knocks it will be O
9:30 And their eyes were O
20:33 said to him, "Lord, let our eyes be O
27:52 the tombs also were O, and many bodies of
Mk 1:10 he saw the heavens O and the Spirit descending
7:33 that is, "Be O
7:34 And his ears were O, his tongue was released,
Lk 1:64 immediately his mouth was O and his tongue loosed,
3:21 praying, the heaven was O,
4:17 He O the book and found the place where
11:9 and it will be O to you.
11:10 and to him who knocks it will be O
24:31 And their eyes were O and they recognized him;
24:32 the road, while he O to us the scriptures?"
24:45 Then he O their minds to understand the scriptures,
Jn 1:51 you will see heaven O, and the angels of
9:10 said to him, "Then how were your eyes O
9:14 made the clay and O his eyes.
9:17 him, since he has O your eyes?" He said,
9:21 do we know who O his eyes.
9:30 from, and yet he O my eyes.
9:32 heard that any one O the eyes of a
11:37 "Could not he who O the eyes of the
Acts 5:19 angel of the Lord O the prison doors and
5:23 doors, but when we O it we found no
7:56 I see the heavens O, and the Son of
8:35 Then Philip O his mouth, and beginning with this
9:8 when his eyes were O, he could see nothing;
9:40 And she O her eyes, and when she saw
10:11 and saw the heaven O, and something descending,
10:34 And Peter O his mouth and said: "Truly I
12:10 It O to them of its own accord, and
12:16 knocking; and when they O, they saw him and
14:27 and how he had O a door of faith
16:14 The Lord O her heart to give heed to
16:26 all the doors were O and every one's fetters
1Cor 16:9 for effective work has O to me, and there
2Cor 2:12 Christ, a door was O for me in the
Heb 9:8 sanctuary is not yet O as long as the
10:20 living way which he O for us through the
Rev 6:1 saw when the Lamb O one of the seven
6:3 When he O the second seal, I heard the
6:5 When he O the third seal, I heard the
6:7 When he O the fourth seal, I heard the
6:9 When he O the fifth seal, I saw under
6:12 When he O the sixth seal, I looked, and
8:1 When the Lamb O the seventh seal, there was
9:2 the bottomless pit; he O the shaft of the
11:19 temple in heaven was O, and the ark of
12:16 woman, and the earth O its mouth and swallowed
13:6 for forty-two months; it O its mouth to utter

O

OPPOSED (8)
Num 30:5 her, because her father O her.
Ezra 10:15 the son of Tikvah O this, and Meshullum and
1Mac 8:11 as many as ever O them, they destroyed and
Acts 18:6 And when they O and reviled him, he shook
Gal 2:11 came to Antioch I O him to his face,
5:17 flesh; for these are O to each other, to
2Tim 3:8 As Jannes and Jambres O Moses, so these men
4:15 yourself, for he strongly O our message.

OPPOSES (4)
Wis 2:12 inconvenient to us and O our actions; he reproaches
2Thes 2:4 son of perdition, who O and exalts himself against
Jas 4:6 therefore it says, "God O the proud, but gives
1Pet 5:5 one another, for "God O the proud, but gives

OPPOSING (4)
1Sam 15:2 did to Israel in O them on the way,
2Chr 35:21 Cease O God, who is with me, lest he
Acts 5:39 might even be found O God!"
26:9 do many things in O the name of Jesus

OPPOSITE (86)
Gen 25:18 to Shur, which is O Egypt in the direction
Ex 26:5 the loops shall be O one another.
26:35 side of the tabernacle O the table; and you
30:4 its molding on two O sides of it shall
36:12 set; the loops were O one another.
37:27 its molding, on two O sides of it, as
Num 21:11 the wilderness which is O Moab, toward the sunrise.
22:5 and they are dwelling O me.
Deut 3:29 remained in the valley O Beth-peor.
4:46 Jordan in the valley O Beth-peor, in the land
32:49 the land of Moab, O Jericho; and view the
34:1 of Pisgah, which is O Jericho.
34:6 the land of Moab O Beth-peor; but no man
Josh 3:16 the people passed over O Jericho.
8:33 their judges, stood on O sides of the ark
15:7 toward Gilgal, which is O the ascent of Adummim,
18:14 lies to the south, O Beth-horon, and it ends
18:17 to Geliloth, which is O the ascent of Adummim;
Judg 19:10 departed, and arrived O Jebus (that is, Jerusalem).
20:43 Nohah as far as O Gibe-ah on the east.
1Sam 20:25 the wall; Jonathan sat O, and Abner sat by
2Sam 5:23 and come upon them O the balsam trees.
16:13 along on the hillside O him and cursed as
1Kgs 7:4 three rows, and window O window in three tiers.
7:5 frames, and window was O window in three tiers.
20:29 And they encamped O one another seven days.
21:10 set two base fellows O him, and let them
21:13 came in and sat O him; and the base
2Kgs 3:22 Moabites saw the water O them as red as
3:26 swordsmen to break through, O the king of Edom;
1Chr 8:32 Now these also dwelt O their kinsmen in Jerusalem,
9:38 and these also dwelt O their kinsmen in Jerusalem,
14:14 and come upon them O the balsam trees.
2Chr 7:6 praises by their ministry; O them the priests sounded
Neh 3:10 son of Harumaph repaired O his house; and next
3:16 repaired to a point O the sepulchres of David,
3:19 Mizpah, repaired another section O the ascent to the
3:23 Benjamin and Hasshub repaired O their house.
3:25 son of Uzai repaired O the Angle and the
3:26 repaired to a point O the Water Gate on
3:27 Tekoites repaired another section O the great
3:28 priests repaired, each one O his own house.
3:29 son of Immer repaired O his own house.
3:30 son of Berechiah repaired O his chamber.
3:31 and of the merchants, O the Muster Gate, and
7:3 his station and each O his own house."
12:9 Unno their brethren stood O them in the service.
Jud 2:21 and camped O Bectileth near the mountain
4:6 Betomesthaim, which faces Esdraelon O the plain
7:18 in the hill country O Dothan; and they sent
Esth 5:1 of the king's palace, O the king's hall.
5:1 throne inside the palace O the entrance to the
Sir 33:14 Good is the O of evil, and life the
33:14 evil, and life the O of death; so the
33:14 the sinner is the O of the godly.
33:15 in pairs, one the O of the other.
42:24 things are twofold, one O the other, and he
Ezek 40:2 structure like a city O me.
40:23 And O the gate on the north, as on
42:1 the chambers which were O the temple yard and
42:1 the temple yard and O the building on the
42:7 toward the outer court, O the chambers, fifty cubits
42:8 cubits long, while those O the temple were a
42:10 On the south also, O the yard and opposite
42:10 opposite the yard and O the building, there were
42:12 enters the passage, and O them was a dividing
42:13 and the south chambers O the yard are the
47:20 boundary to a point O the entrance of Hamath.
Dan 5:5 of the king's palace, O the lampstand; and the
1Mac 2:32 overtook them; they encamped O them and prepared
3:46 and went to Mizpah, O Jerusalem, because Israel
5:37 another army and encamped O Raphon, on the other
6:32 and encamped at Beth-zechariah, O the camp of the
10:48 large forces and encamped O Demetrius.
13:20 army kept marching along O him to every place
13:28 also erected seven pyramids, O one another, for his
2Mac 15:33 rewards of his folly O the sanctuary.
Mt 21:2 "Go into the village O you, and immediately you
27:61 Mary were there, sitting O the sepulchre.
Mk 11:2 "Go into the village O you, and immediately as
12:41 And he sat down O the treasury, and watched
13:3 the Mount of Olives O the temple, Peter and
Lk 8:26 the Gerasenes, which is O Galilee.
19:30 "Go into the village O, where on entering you
Acts 16:7 when they had come O Mysia, they attempted to
20:15 came the following day O Chios; the next day

OPPOSITION (5)
Esth 13:5 alone, stands constantly in O to all men, perversely
1Mac 11:38 that there was no O to him, he dismissed
Acts 4:14 beside them, they had nothing to say in O
Rom 16:17 dissensions and difficulties, in O to the doctrine which
1Thes 2:2 gospel of God in the face of great O

OPPRESS (26)
Ex 3:9 with which the Egyptians O them.
22:21 wrong a stranger or O him, for you were
23:9 "You shall not O a stranger; you know the
Lev 19:13 "You shall not O your neighbor or rob him.
Deut 23:16 best; you shall not O him.
24:14 "You shall not O a hired servant who is
1Chr 16:21 allowed no one to O them; he rebuked kings
Job 10:3 good to thee to O, to despise the work
Ps 56:1 all day long foemen O me;
105:14 allowed no one to O them; he rebuked kings
119:122 let not the godless O me.
Wis 2:10 Let us O the righteous poor man; let us
Is 3:5 And the people will O one another, every man
58:3 your own pleasure, and O all your workers.
Jer 7:6 if you do not O the alien, the fatherless
30:20 will punish all who O them.
Ezek 18:7 of impurity, does not O any one, but restores
45:8 princes shall no more O my people; but they
Hos 12:7 whose hands are false balances, he loves to O
Amos 4:1 mountain of Samaria, who O the poor, who crush
6:14 hosts; "and they shall O you from the entrance
Mic 2:2 take them away; they O a man and his
Zech 7:10 his brother, do not O the widow, the fatherless,
Mal 3:5 falsely, against those who O the hireling in his
2Mac 1:28 Afflict those who O and are insolent with pride.
Jas 2:6 not the rich who O you, is it not

OPPRESSED (46)
Gen 15:13 and they will be O for four hundred years;
Ex 1:11 the more they were O, the more they multiplied
Lev 6:2 or if he has O his neighbor
Deut 28:29 you shall be only O and robbed continually, and
28:33 you shall be only O and crushed continually;
Judg 2:18 those who afflicted and O them.
4:3 chariots of iron, and O the people of Israel
6:9 hand of all who O you, and drove them
10:8 and they crushed and O the children of Israel
10:8 For eighteen years they O all the people of
10:12 Amalekites, and the Maonites, O you; and you cried
1Sam 12:3 Whom have I O
12:4 not defrauded us or O us or taken anything
12:8 Egypt and the Egyptians O them, then your fathers
2Kgs 13:4 the king of Syria O them.
13:22 Hazael king of Syria O Israel all the days
Jud 9:11 lowly, helper of the O, upholder of the weak,
16:8 mourning to exalt the O in Israel.
16:11 Then my O people shouted for joy; my weak
Ps 9:9 a stronghold for the O, a stronghold in times
10:18 the fatherless and the O, so that man who
69:32 Let the O see it and be glad; you
76:9 to save all the O of the earth.
103:6 works vindication and justice for all who are O
106:42 Their enemies O them, and they were brought into
146:7 executes justice for the O; who gives food to

Eccl 4:1 the tears of the O, and they had no
5:8 a province the poor O and justice and right
Wis 15:14 all the enemies who O thy people.
Is 14:2 rule over those who O them.
23:12 no more exult, O O virgin daughter of Sidon;
38:14 O Lord, I am O; be thou my security!
52:4 there, and the Assyrian O them for nothing.
53:7 He was O, and he was afflicted, yet he
58:6 yoke, to let the O go free, and to
60:14 sons of those who O you shall come bending
Jer 50:33 people of Israel are O, and the people of
Ezek 22:29 committed robbery; they have O the poor and needy,
Dan 4:27 showing mercy to the O, that there may perhaps
Hos 5:11 Ephraim is O, crushed in judgment, because he was
1Mac 10:46 how he had greatly O them.
11:53 had done him, but O him greatly.
2Mac 8:2 the people who were O by all, and to
Lk 4:18 liberty those who are O,
Acts 7:24 wronged, he defended the O man and avenged him
10:38 healing all that were O by the devil, for

OPPRESSES (5)

Num 10:9 against the adversary who O you, then you shall
Prov 14:31 He who O a poor man insults his Maker,
22:16 He who O the poor to increase his own
28:3 A poor man who O the poor is a
Ezek 18:12 defiles his neighbor's wife, O the poor and needy,

OPPRESSING (2)

1Sam 10:18 the kingdoms that were O you.'
Zeph 3:1 rebellious and defiled, the O city!

OPPRESSION (26)

Ex 3:9 I have seen the O with which the Egyptians
Lev 6:4 what he got by O, or the deposit which
Deut 26:7 our toil, and our O;
2Kgs 13:4 for he saw the O of Israel, how the
Ps 10:7 cursing and deceit and O; under his tongue are
42:9 mourning because of the O of the enemy?"
43:2 mourning because of the O of the enemy?
44:24 Why dost thou forget our affliction and O
55:3 enemy, because of the O of the wicked.
55:11 is in its midst; O and fraud do not
72:14 From O and violence he redeems their life; and
73:8 scoff and speak with malice; loftily they threaten O
107:39 and brought low through O, trouble, and sorrow,
119:134 Redeem me from man's O, that I may keep
Eccl 7:7 Surely O makes the wise man foolish, and a
Is 1:17 good; seek justice, correct O; defend the fatherless,
10:1 writers who keep writing O,
30:12 word, and trust in O and perverseness, and rely
53:8 By O and judgment he was taken away; and
54:14 shall be far from O, for you shall not
59:13 following our God, speaking O and revolt, conceiving
Jer 6:6 there is nothing but O within her.
9:6 Heaping O upon oppression, and deceit upon deceit,
9:6 Heaping oppression upon O, and deceit upon deceit,
22:17 blood, and for practicing O and violence."
Ezek 45:9 Put away violence and O, and execute justice and

OPPRESSIONS (4)

Job 35:9 of the multitude of O people cry out; they
Eccl 4:1 I saw all the O that are practiced under
Is 33:15 despises the gain of O, who shakes his hands,
Amos 3:9 within her, and the O in her midst."

OPPRESSOR (14)

Ps 72:4 give deliverance to the needy, and crush the O
Prov 28:16 understanding is a cruel O; but he who hates
29:13 poor man and the O meet together; the LORD
Is 9:4 the rod of his O, thou hast broken as
14:4 of Babylon: "How the O has ceased, the insolent
16:4 When the O is no more, and destruction has
51:13 the fury of the O, when he sets himself
51:13 And where is the fury of the O
Jer 21:12 the hand of the O him who has been
22:3 the hand of the O him who has been
25:38 the sword of the O, and because of his
46:16 the sword of the O
50:16 the sword of the O, every one shall turn
Zech 9:8 to and fro; no O shall again overrun them,

OPPRESSORS (11)

Job 6:23 Or, 'Ransom me from the hand of O
27:13 and the heritage which O receive from the Almighty:
Ps 119:121 and right; do not leave me to my O

Eccl 4:1 the side of their O there was power, and
Wis 10:11 When his O were covetous, she stood by him
10:15 blameless race wisdom delivered from a nation of O
16:4 necessary that upon those O inexorable want should
Is 3:12 children are their O, and women rule over
19:20 the LORD because of O he will send them
49:26 I will make your O eat their own flesh,
Zeph 3:19 that time I will deal with all your O

ORACLE (29)

Num 24:3 discourse, and said, "The O of Balaam the son
24:3 son of Beor, the O of the man whose
24:4 eye is opened, the O of him who hears
24:15 discourse, and said, "The O of Balaam the son
24:15 son of Beor, the O of the man whose
24:16 eye is opened, the O of him who hears
2Sam 16:23 if one consulted the O of God; so was
23:1 words of David: The O of David, the son
23:1 son of Jesse, the O of the man who
2Kgs 9:25 the LORD uttered this O against him:
Sir 45:10 an embroiderer; with the O of judgment, Urim and
Is 13:1 The O concerning Babylon which Isaiah the son of
14:28 Ahaz died came this O:
15:1 An O concerning Moab.
17:1 An O concerning Damascus.
19:1 An O concerning Egypt.
21:1 The O concerning the wilderness of the sea.
21:11 The O concerning Dumah.
21:13 The O concerning Arabia.
22:1 The O concerning the valley of vision.
23:1 The O concerning Tyre.
30:6 An O on the beasts of the Negeb.
Ezek 12:10 the Lord GOD: This O concerns the prince in
Nah 1:1 An O concerning Nineveh.
Hab 1:1 The O of God which Habakkuk
Zech 9:1 An O The word of the LORD is against
12:1 An O The word of the LORD concerning Israel:
Mal 1:1 The O of the word of
2Mac 2:4 prophet, having received an O, ordered that the tent

ORACLES (7)

2Chr 24:27 and of the many O against him, and of
Wis 16:11 remind them of thy O they were bitten, and
Lam 2:14 have seen for you O false and misleading.
Hos 4:12 thing of wood, and their staff gives them O
Acts 7:38 and he received living O to give to us.
Rom 3:2 are entrusted with the O of God.
1Pet 4:11 as one who utters O of God; whoever renders

ORATION

Acts 12:21 throne, and made an O to them.

ORCHARD (4)

Ex 23:11 likewise with your vineyard, and with your olive O
Song 4:13 Your shoots are an O of pomegranates with all
6:11 down to the nut O, to look at the
Sir 24:29 "I will water my O and drench my garden

ORCHARDS (5)

Judg 15:5 the standing grain, as well as the olive O
1Sam 8:14 and vineyards and olive O and give them to
2Kgs 5:26 money and garments, olive O and vineyards, sheep
Neh 5:11 their vineyards, their olive O, and their houses, and
9:25 hewn out, vineyards, olive O and fruit trees in

ORDAIN (6)

Ex 28:41 shall anoint them and O them and consecrate them,
29:9 Thus you shall O Aaron and his sons.
29:33 atonement was made, to O and consecrate them, but
29:35 seven days shall you O them,
Lev 8:33 take seven days to O you.
Is 26:12 O LORD, thou wilt O peace for us, thou

ORDAINED (22)

Ex 29:29 anointed in them and O in them.
32:29 said, "Today you have O yourselves for the service
Num 3:3 anointed priests, whom he O to minister in the
28:6 burnt offering, which was O at Mount Sinai for
2Sam 17:14 For the LORD had O to defeat the good
1Kgs 12:33 own heart; and he O a feast for the
2Kgs 23:5 kings of Judah had O to burn incense in
1Chr 15:13 care for it in the way that is O
2Chr 2:4 LORD our God, as O for ever for Israel.
22:7 But it was O by God that the downfall
Tob 1:6 feasts, as it is O for all Israel by
Esth 9:27 befallen them, the Jews O and took it upon

O

14:9 what thy mouth has O and to destroy thy
Sir 42:21 He has O the splendors of his wisdom, and
45:15 Moses O him, and anointed him with holy oil;
Lam 2:17 his threat; as he O long ago, he has
3:37 unless the Lord has O it?
Hab 1:12 O LORD, thou hast O them as a judgment;
2Mac 8:36 they followed the laws O by him.
Acts 10:42 he is the one O by God to be
13:48 as many as were O to eternal life believed.
Gal 3:19 made; and it was O by angels through an

ORDAINEST

Ps 44:4 and my God, who O victories for Jacob.

ORDEAL

1Pet 4:12 surprised at the fiery O which comes upon you

ORDER (156)

Gen 22:9 laid the wood in O, and bound Isaac his
25:13 Ishmael, named in the O of their birth: Nebaioth,
32:5 tell my lord, in O that I may find
41:40 all my people shall O themselves as you command;
46:34 and our fathers,' in O that you may dwell
Ex 28:10 other stone, in the O of their birth.
Lev 1:7 and lay wood in O upon the fire;
1:8 and the fat, in O upon the wood that
1:12 shall lay them in O upon the wood that
6:12 the burnt offering in O upon it, and shall
24:3 shall keep it in O from evening to morning
24:4 keep the lamps in O upon the lampstand of
24:8 shall set it in O before the LORD continually
Num 10:28 This was the O of march of the people
Deut 17:16 return to Egypt in O to multiply horses, since
20:19 war against it in O to take it, you
Josh 2:6 she had laid in O on the roof.
11:20 Israel in battle, in O that they should be
Judg 6:26 stones laid in due O; then take the second
Ruth 4:5 of the dead, in O to restore the name
2Sam 14:20 In O to change the course of affairs your
17:23 set his house in O, and hanged himself; and
24:21 floor of you, in O to build an altar
1Kgs 5:17 great, costly stones in O to lay the foundation
6:6 on the wall in O that the supporting beams
8:43 calls to thee; in O that all the peoples
18:33 put the wood in O, and cut the bull
2Kgs 1:11 this is the king's O, 'Come down quickly!'"
10:19 it with cunning in O to destroy the worshipers
20:1 'Set your house in O; for you shall die,
23:4 priests of the second O, and the keepers of
1Chr 6:32 and they performed their service in due O
12:38 war, arrayed in battle O, came to Hebron with
15:18 brethren of the second O, Zechariah, Ja-aziel,
25:6 Heman were under the O of the king.
2Chr 6:33 calls to thee; in O that all the peoples
23:18 singing, according to the O of David.
25:20 was of God, in O that he might give
32:18 and terrify them, in O that they might take
32:31 him to himself, in O to try him and
35:22 but disguised himself in O to fight with him.
Ezra 4:15 inform the king, in O that search may be
10:8 within three days, by O of the officials and
Neh 6:13 an evil name, in O to taunt me.
8:13 Ezra the scribe in O to study the words
9:26 had warned them in O to turn them back
9:29 didst warn them in O to turn them back
Tob 12:13 leave your dinner in O to go and lay
Jud 3:10 a whole month in O to assemble all the
4:8 of Israel, in session at Jerusalem, had given O
8:27 near to him, in O to admonish them."
10:9 she said to them, O the gate of the
11:11 "And now, in O that my lord may not
14:13 to give battle, in O to be destroyed completely."
Esth 1:11 her royal crown, in O to show the peoples
1:19 king, let a royal O go forth from him,
2:8 So when the king's O and his edict were
3:4 they told Haman, in O to see whether Mordecai's
3:15 went in haste by O of the king, and
8:5 his eyes, let an O be written to revoke
13:2 lasting tranquillity and, in O to make my kingdom
16:16 an for our fathers in the most excellent O
Job 33:5 set your words in O before me; take your
Ps 110:4 for ever after the O of Melchizedek."
119:101 every evil way, in O to keep thy word.
Eccl 3:14 made it so, in O that men should fear
Wis 16:3 desire of appetite; in O that those men, when
16:23 whereas the fire, in O that the righteous might
19:4 what had happened, in O that they might fill
Sir 16:25 works in an eternal O, and their dominion for
23:3 by my sins; in O that my mistakes may
30:1 whip him often, in O that he may rejoice
38:5 with a tree in O that his power might
50:19 is merciful, till the O of worship of the
Is 38:1 Set your house in O; for you shall die,
Jer 31:35 day and the fixed O of the moon and
31:36 name: "If this fixed O departs from before me,
44:29 in this place, in O that you may know
Bar 3:7 in our hearts in O that we should call
6:18 locks and bars, in O that they may not
Ezek 3:18 his wicked way, in O to save his life,
22:20 fire upon it in O to melt it; so
31:14 All this is in O that no trees by
39:12 be burying them, in O to cleanse the land.
40:4 were brought here in O that I might show
46:20 the cereal offering, in O not to bring them
Dan 2:30 to me, but in O that the interpretation may
3:22 Because the king's O was strict and the furnace
11:14 lift themselves up in O to fulfil the vision;
Zech 13:4 a hairy mantle in O to deceive,
1Mac 6:40 plain, and they advanced steadily and in good O
12:36 from the city, in O to isolate it so
14:29 of their nation, in O that their sanctuary and
2Mac 1:18 to notify you, in O that you also may
6:15 way with us, in O that he may not
7:22 I who set in O the elements within each
11:10 They advanced in battle O, having their heavenly ally,
Mt 6:1 piety before men in O to be seen by
12:44 he finds it empty, swept, and put in O
26:4 took counsel together in O to arrest Jesus by
27:64 will rise again.' Therefore O the sepulchre to be
Mk 7:9 commandment of God, in O to keep your tradition!
10:2 came up and in O to test him asked,
14:10 the chief priests in O to betray him to
Lk 11:25 comes he finds it swept and put in O
16:26 has been fixed, in O that those who would
Jn 19:31 day of Preparation, in O to prevent the bodies
Acts 4:17 But in O that it may spread no further
11:4 explained to them in O:
23:3 to the law you O me to be struck?"
Rom 1:13 have been prevented), in O that I may reap
4:16 depends on faith, in O that the promise may
7:4 from the dead in O that we may bear
7:13 what is good, in O that sin might be
8:4 in the flesh, in O that the just requirement
8:17 suffer with him in O that we may also
8:29 of his Son, in O that he might be
9:11 good or bad, in O that God's purpose of
9:23 made for destruction, in O to make known the
11:14 magnify my ministry in O to make my fellow
11:31 now been disobedient in O that by the mercy
15:8 show God's truthfulness, in O to confirm the promises
15:9 the patriarchs, and in O that the Gentiles might
1Cor 7:35 but to promote good O and to secure your
9:20 as a Jew, in O to win Jews; to
11:19 factions among you in O that those who are
14:19 with my mind, in O to instruct others, than
14:40 all things should be done decently and in O
15:23 each in his own O: Christ the first fruits,
2Cor 7:12 the wrong, but in O that your zeal for
11:8 support from them in O to serve you.
11:12 continue to do, in O to undermine the claim
11:32 city of Damascus in O to seize me,
13:10 away from you, in O that when I come
Gal 1:16 Son to me, in O that I might preach
2:16 in Christ Jesus, in O to be justified by
6:12 circumcised, and only in O that they may not
Phil 3:8 them as refuse, in O that I may gain
Col 1:22 by his death, in O to present you holy
2:4 I say this in O that no one may
2:5 to see your good O and the firmness of
Philem 1:13 him with me, in O that he might serve
1:14 without your consent in O that your goodness might
Heb 5:6 for ever, after the O of Melchizedek."
5:10 high priest after the O of Melchizedek.
6:20 for ever after the O of Melchizedek.
7:11 to arise after the O of Melchizedek, rather than
7:11 one named after the O of Aaron?
7:17 for ever, after the O of Melchizedek."
10:9 abolishes the first in O to establish the second.
12:20 could not endure the O that was given, "If
12:27 has been made, in O that what cannot be
13:12 outside the gate in O to sanctify the people
13:19 to do this in O that I may be

1Pet 3:7 grace of life, in O that your prayers may
4:11 which God supplies; in O that in everything God

ORDERED (56)

2Sam 18:5 And the king O Joab and Abishai and Ittai,
23:5 me an everlasting covenant, O in all things and
2Kgs 10:20 And Jehu O, "Sanctify a solemn assembly for Baal."
2Chr 27:6 became mighty, because he O his ways before the
Ezra 6:13 with all diligence what Darius the king had O
Tob 8:18 Then he O his servants to fill in the
Jud 2:13 just as I have O you; and do not
2:15 as his lord had O him to do, one
6:10 Then Holofernes O his slaves, who waited on him
7:1 The next day Holofernes O his whole army, and
10:9 So they O the young men to open the
12:1 dishes were kept, and O them to set a
Esth 4:5 to attend her, and O him to go to
4:17 everything as Esther had O him.
12:5 And the king O Mordecai to serve in the
Prov 20:24 A man's steps are O by the LORD; how
Sir 43:10 One they stand as O, they never relax in
Jer 36:5 And Jeremiah O Baruch, saying, "I am debarred
36:8 that Jeremiah the prophet O him about reading from
Bar 5:7 For God has O that every high mountain and
6:63 consume mountains and woods does what it is O
Dan 3:19 He O the furnace heated seven times more than
3:20 And he O certain mighty men of his army
13:32 veiled, the wicked men O her to be unveiled,
14:14 Then Daniel O his servants to bring ashes and
1Mac 3:28 to his forces, and O them to be ready
5:49 Then Judas O proclamation to be made to the
15:41 as the king had O him.
2Mac 1:20 but thick liquid, he O them to dip it
1:21 sacrifices were presented, Nehemiah O the priests to
1:31 sacrifice were consumed, Nehemiah O that the liquid
2:1 that Jeremiah the prophet O those who were being
2:4 having received an oracle, O that the tent and
5:25 not at work, he O his men to parade
7:5 utterly helpless, the king O them to take him
9:4 to flight; so he O his charioteer to drive
11:20 their details, I have O these men and my
13:4 all the trouble, he O them to take him
13:10 heard of this, he O the people to call
13:12 Judas exhorted them and O them to stand ready.
14:41 of the courtyard, they O that fire be brought
15:4 Sovereign in heaven, who O us to observe the
15:30 will toward his countrymen, O them to cut off
Mt 12:16 healed them all, and O them not to make
14:19 Then he O the crowds to sit down on
18:24 not pay, his lord O him to be sold,
27:58 Then Pilate O it to be given to him.
Mk 3:12 And he strictly O them not to make him
Acts 5:34 people, stood up and O the men to be
12:19 examined the sentries and O that they should be
21:33 and arrested him, and O him to be bound
21:34 of the uproar, he O him to be brought
22:24 into the barracks, and O him to be examined
25:6 on the tribunal and O Paul to be brought.
25:17 on the tribunal and O the man to be
27:43 He O those who could swim to throw themselves

ORDERING (2)

Jud 4:7 the plain near Dothan, O them to seize the
Acts 23:30 to you at once, O his accusers also to

ORDERLY

Lk 1:3 past, to write an O account for you, most

ORDERS (36)

Gen 12:20 And Pharaoh gave men O concerning him; and they
42:25 And Joseph gave O to fill their bags with
Num 32:27 before the LORD to battle, as my lord O
2Sam 14:8 and I will give O concerning you."
18:5 when the king gave O to all the commanders
Neh 13:9 Then I gave O and they cleansed the chambers;
13:19 be shut and gave O that they should not
Jud 1:11 whole region disregarded the O of Nebuchadnezzar
2:6 whole west country, because they disobeyed my O
7:16 servants, and he gave O to do as they
Esth 1:8 the king had given O to all the officials
6:1 sleep; and he gave O to bring the book
9:25 the king, he gave O in writing that his
Ps 50:23 me; to him who O his way aright I
Wis 8:1 the other, and she O all things well.
Jer 37:21 King Zedekiah gave O, and they committed Jeremiah
1Mac 3:34 elephants, and gave him O about all that he
5:58 And they issued O to the men of the
6:57 So he quickly gave O to depart, and said
6:62 had sworn and gave O to tear down the
9:54 second month, Alcimus gave O to tear down the
9:63 his forces, and sent O to the men of
10:62 The king gave O to take off Jonathan's garments
11:23 heard this, he gave O to continue the siege;
14:48 And they gave O to inscribe this decree upon
2Mac 4:25 After receiving the king's O he returned, possessing
7:3 a rage, and gave O that pans and caldrons
9:7 the Jews, and giving O to hasten the journey.
12:5 his countrymen, he gave O to his men
14:13 sent him off with O to kill Judas and
15:10 courage, he gave his O, at the same time
Mt 8:18 around him, he gave O to go over to
Mk 6:27 the guard and gave O to bring his head.
Jn 11:57 the Pharisees had given O that if any one
Acts 16:22 off them and gave O to beat them with
24:22 Then he gave O to the centurion that he

ORDINANCE (34)

Ex 12:14 observe it as an O for ever.
12:17 your generations, as an O for ever.
12:24 this rite as an O for you and for
12:43 Aaron, "This is the O of the passover: no
13:10 shall therefore keep this O at its appointed time
15:25 a statute and an O and there he proved
Lev 5:10 offering according to the O; and the priest shall
9:16 burnt offering, and offered it according to the O
Num 9:14 and according to its O, so shall he do;
15:16 One law and one O shall be for you
15:24 offering, according to the O, and one male goat
27:11 Israel a statute and O, as the LORD commanded
29:6 offering, according to the O for them, a pleasing
29:18 number, according to the O;
29:21 number, according to the O;
29:24 number, according to the O;
29:27 number, according to the O;
29:30 number, according to the O;
29:33 number, according to the O;
29:37 number, according to the O;
35:29 for a statute and O to you throughout your
1Sam 30:25 a statute and an O for Israel to this
2Chr 8:14 According to the O of David his father, he
35:13 fire according to the O; and they boiled the
35:25 They made these an O in Israel; behold, they
Ezra 3:4 number according to the O, as each day required,
Neh 8:18 there was a solemn assembly, according to the O
Ps 81:4 statute for Israel, an O of the God of
Is 58:2 did not forsake the O of their God; they
Jer 8:7 people know not the O of the LORD.
Ezek 46:14 LORD; this is the O for the continual burnt
Dan 6:7 king should establish an O and enforce an interdict,
6:15 that no interdict or O which the king establishes
2Mac 10:8 They decreed by public O and vote that the

ORDINANCES (107)

Ex 21:1 "Now these are the O which you shall set
24:3 LORD and all the O; and all the people
Lev 18:4 You shall do my O and keep my statutes
18:5 my statutes and my O, by doing which a
18:26 my statutes and my O and do none of
19:37 statutes and all my O, and do them: I
20:22 statutes and all my O, and do them; that
25:18 statutes, and keep my O and perform them; so
26:15 your soul abhors my O, so that you will
26:43 because they spurned my O, and their soul abhorred
26:46 are the statutes and O and laws which the
Num 9:3 statutes and all its O you shall keep it."
35:24 in accordance with these O;
36:13 the commandments and the O which the LORD
Deut 4:1 the statutes and the O which I teach you,
4:5 taught you statutes and O, as the LORD my
4:8 that has statutes and O so righteous as all
4:14 teach you statutes and O, that you might do
4:45 the statutes, and the O, which Moses spoke to
5:1 the statutes and the O which I speak in
5:31 the statutes and the O which you shall teach
6:1 the statutes and the O which the LORD your
6:20 the statutes and the O which the LORD our
7:11 the statutes, and the O, which I command you
7:12 you hearken to these O, and keep and do
8:11 his commandments and his O and his statutes, which
11:1 charge, his statutes, his O, and his commandments.
11:32 the statutes and the O which I set before
12:1 are the statutes and O which you shall be

26:16 do these statutes and O; you shall therefore be
26:17 his commandments and his O, and will obey his
30:16 his statutes and his O, then you shall live
33:10 shall teach Jacob thy O, and Israel thy law;
Josh 24:25 and made statutes and O for them at Shechem.
2Sam 22:23 For all his O were before me, and from
1Kgs 2:3 his commandments, his O, and his testimonies, as
6:12 statutes and obey my O and keep all my
8:58 his statutes, and his O, which he commanded our
9:4 my statutes and my O,
11:33 my statutes and my O, as David his father
2Kgs 17:34 the statutes or the O or the law or
17:37 the statutes and the O and the law and
1Chr 22:13 the statutes and the O which the LORD commanded
28:7 my commandments and my O, as he is today.'
2Chr 7:17 my statutes and my O,
19:10 or commandment, statutes or O, then you shall
33:8 the statutes, and the O given through Moses."
Ezra 7:10 teach his statutes and O in Israel.
Neh 1:7 the statutes, and the O which thou didst command
9:13 and give them right O and true laws, good
9:29 but sinned against thy O, by the observance of
10:29 our Lord and his O and his statutes.
Esth 13:4 and continually disregard the O of the kings, so
Job 38:33 Do you know the O of the heavens?
Ps 18:22 For all his O were before me, and his
19:9 enduring for ever; the O of the LORD are
89:30 walk according to my O,
119:7 an upright heart, when I learn thy righteous O
119:13 I declare all the O of thy mouth.
119:20 with longing for thy O at all times.
119:30 faithfulness, I set thy O before me.
119:39 I dread; for thy O are good.
119:43 my mouth, for my hope is in thy O
119:52 I think of thy O from of old, I
119:62 rise to praise thee, because of thy righteous O
119:102 turn aside from thy O, for thou hast taught
119:106 oath and confirmed it, to observe thy righteous O
119:108 of praise, O LORD, and teach me thy O
119:160 one of thy righteous O endures for ever.
119:164 a day I praise thee for thy righteous O
119:175 thee, and let thy O help me.
147:19 Jacob, his statutes and O to Israel.
147:20 any other nation; they do not know his O
Sir 4:17 him, and she will test him with her O
Jer 33:25 and night and the O of heaven and earth,
Bar 2:12 wrong, O Lord our God, against all thy O
Ezek 5:6 wickedly rebelled against my O more than the
5:6 her, by rejecting my O and not walking in
5:7 statutes or kept my O, but have acted according
5:7 acted according to the O of the nations that
11:12 statutes, nor executed my O, but have acted
11:12 acted according to the O of the nations that
11:20 statutes and keep my O and obey them; and
18:9 careful to observe my O —he is righteous,
18:17 or increase, observes my O, and walks in my
20:11 and showed them my O, by whose observance man
20:13 statutes but rejected my O, by whose observance
20:16 because they rejected my O and did not walk
20:18 fathers, nor observe their O, nor defile yourselves
20:19 careful to observe my O,
20:21 careful to observe my O, by whose observance man
20:24 had not executed my O, but had rejected my
20:25 were not good and O by which they could
36:27 my statutes and be careful to observe my O
37:24 They shall follow my O and be careful to
43:11 to them all its O and all its laws;
43:11 and perform all its laws and all its O
43:18 GOD: These are the O for the altar: On
44:5 you concerning all the O of the temple of
Dan 9:5 from thy commandments and O;
Mal 4:4 Moses, the statutes and O that I commanded him
1Mac 1:13 them to observe the O of the Gentiles.
1:49 should forget the law and change all the O
2:21 from us to desert the law and the O
2:40 lives and for our O, they will quickly destroy
Lk 1:6 all the commandments and O of the Lord blameless.
Eph 2:15 law of commandments and O, that he might create

ORDINARY (4)
Ex 30:32 upon the bodies of O men, and you shall
Sir 33:9 of them he made O days.
Ezek 48:15 length, shall be for O use for the city,
1Cor 3:3 flesh, and behaving like O men?

ORDINATION (10)
Ex 29:22 is a ram of O,
29:26 the ram of Aaron's O and wave it for
29:27 from the ram of O, since it is for
29:31 take the ram of O, and boil its flesh
29:34 the flesh for the O, or of the bread,
Lev 8:22 ram, the ram of O; and Aaron and his
8:28 burnt offering, as an O offering, a pleasing odor,
8:29 of the ram of O, as the LORD commanded
8:31 in the basket of O offerings, as I commanded,
8:33 the days of your O are completed, for it

ORE (2)
Job 28:2 the earth, and copper is smelted from the O
28:3 the farthest bound the O in gloom and deep

OREB (7)
Judg 7:25 two princes of Midian, O and Zeeb; they killed
7:25 and Zeeb; they killed O at the rock of
7:25 at the rock of O, and Zeeb they killed
7:25 brought the heads of O and Zeeb to Gideon
8:3 the princes of Midian, O and Zeeb; what have
Ps 83:11 Make their nobles like O and Zeeb, all their
Is 10:26 at the rock of O; and his rod will

OREN
1Chr 2:25 Ram, his first-born, Bunah, O, Ozem, and Ahijah.

ORGAN
1Cor 12:19 all were a single O, where would the body

ORGANIZED (8)
1Chr 23:6 And David O them in divisions corresponding to the
24:3 sons of Ithamar, David O them according to the
24:4 sons of Ithamar, they O them under sixteen heads
24:5 They O them by lot, all alike, for there
2Chr 23:18 Levites whom David had O to be in charge
Jud 2:16 on horseback, and he O them as a great
1Mac 2:44 They O an army, and struck down sinners in
2Mac 8:5 Maccabeus got his army O, the Gentiles could not

ORGANS
1Cor 12:18 is, God arranged the O in the body, each

ORGIES
Jer 3:23 are a delusion, the O on the mountains.

ORIGIN (8)
Wis 12:10 not unaware that their O was evil and their
Is 23:7 your exultant city whose O is from days of
Ezek 16:3 GOD to Jerusalem: Your O and your birth are
21:30 the land of your O, I will judge you.
29:14 the land of their O; and there they shall
Mic 5:2 ruler in Israel, whose O is from of old,
2Mac 7:23 man and devised the O of all things, will
Heb 2:11 and those who are sanctified have all one O

ORIGINAL
2Mac 2:30 the duty of the O historian to occupy the

ORIGINATE
1Cor 14:36 the word of God O with you, or are

ORION (3)
Job 9:9 made the Bear and O, the Pleiades and the
38:31 of the Pleiades, or loose the cords of O
Amos 5:8 made the Pleiades and O, and turns deep darkness

ORNAMENT (5)
Prov 25:12 gold ring or an O of gold is a
Sir 6:30 yoke is a golden O, and her bonds are
21:21 is like a golden O, and like a bracelet
Is 49:18 all on as an O, you shall bind them
Ezek 7:20 Their beautiful O they used for vainglory, and they

ORNAMENTS (13)
Gen 24:53 to her brother and to her mother costly O
Ex 33:4 they mourned; and no man put on his O
33:5 now put off your O from you, that I
33:6 stripped themselves of their O, from Mount Horeb
2Sam 1:24 in scarlet, who put O of gold upon your
Jud 10:4 earrings and all her O, and made herself very
Song 1:10 cheeks are comely with O, your neck with strings
1:11 We will make you O of gold, studded with
Jer 2:32 a maiden forget her O, or a bride her
4:30 you deck yourself with O of gold, that you

O

7:18 out drink offerings to O gods, to provoke me
11:10 they have gone after O gods to serve them;
12:12 the land to the O; no flesh has peace.
13:10 and have gone after O gods to serve them
16:11 and have gone after O gods and have served
16:13 there you shall serve O gods day and night,
19:4 incense in it to O gods whom neither they
19:13 been poured out to O gods–shall be defiled
22:9 their God, and worshiped O gods and served them.'"'"
24:2 first-ripe figs, but the O basket had very bad
25:6 do not go after O gods to serve and
25:33 from one end of the earth to the O
32:29 been poured out to O gods, to provoke me
35:15 do not go after O gods to serve them,
40:11 in Edom and in O lands heard that the
44:3 burn incense and serve O gods that they knew
44:5 burn no incense to O gods.
44:8 hands, burning incense to O gods in the land
44:15 had offered incense to O gods, and all the
Bar 1:21 wicked heart by serving O gods and doing what
3:35 is our God; no O can be compared to
Ezek 4:8 one side to the O, till you have completed
13:18 my people, and keep O souls alive for your
16:34 you were different from O women in your harlotries:
25:8 is like all the O nations,
40:13 the back of the O, a breadth of five
40:40 tables; and on the O side of the vestibule
40:44 gate facing south, the O at the side of
41:19 palm tree on the O side.
42:14 they shall put on O garments before they go
44:19 they shall put on O garments, lest they communicate
47:7 trees on the one side and on the O
Dan 3:21 their hats, and their O garments, and they were
3:97 for there is no O god who is able
6:3 distinguished above all the O presidents and satraps,
7:20 its head, and the O horn which came up
8:3 was higher than the O, and the higher one
11:37 give heed to any O god, for he shall
13:10 did not tell each O of their distress,
13:13 They said to each O, "Let us go home,
13:14 when they went out, they parted from each O
13:14 when each pressed the O for the reason, they
13:51 them far from each O, and I will examine
13:52 were separated from each O, he summoned one of
13:54 did you see them being intimate with each O
13:56 him aside, and commanded them to bring the O
13:58 did you catch them being intimate with each O
14:41 and there is no O besides thee."
Hos 3:1 though they turn to O gods and love cakes
Zech 4:3 the bowl and the O on its left."
11:7 I named Grace, the O I named Union.
14:4 withdraw northward, and the O half southward.
14:13 the hand of the O;
1Mac 5:14 still being read, behold, O messengers, with their
5:27 shut up in the O cities of Gilead; the
5:36 and Bosor, and the O cities of Gilead.
5:37 opposite Raphon, on the O side of the stream.
5:41 and camps on the O side of the river,
6:20 built siege towers and O engines of war.
6:29 came to him from O kingdoms and from islands
9:48 swam across to the O side, and the enemy
10:38 ruler and obey no O authority but the high
10:71 match strength with each O there, for I have
11:9 a covenant with each O, and I will give
11:24 and clothing and numerous O gifts.
11:27 and in as many O honors as he had
11:35 And the O payments henceforth due to us of
12:2 the Spartans and to O places.
12:11 our feasts and on O appropriate days, at the
12:14 annoy you and our O allies and friends with
12:45 as well as the O strongholds and the remaining
13:39 you owe; and whatever O tax has been collected
15:5 release from all the O payments from which they
16:19 He sent O men to Gazara to do away
16:20 gifts; and he sent O men to take possession
2Mac 2:3 And with O similar words he exhorted them that
4:32 gave them to Andronicus; O vessels, as it happened,
4:35 but many also of O nations, were grieved and
5:16 the votive offerings which O kings had made to
6:14 the case of the O nations the Lord waits
10:28 the Lord, while the O made rage their leader
11:3 sacred places of the O nations, and to put
11:27 Jews and to the O Jews, greeting.
12:11 his people in all O ways.
13:6 sacrilege or notorious for O crimes.
15:2 honored and hallowed above O days,"

Mt 4:21 there he saw two O brothers, James the son
5:39 turn to him the O also;
6:24 one and love the O, or he will be
6:24 be devoted to the one and despise the O
8:18 go over to the O side.
8:28 he came to the O side, to the country
12:13 out, and it was restored, whole like the O
12:45 brings with him seven O spirits more evil than
13:5 O seeds fell on rocky ground, where they had
13:7 O seeds fell upon thorns, and the thorns grew
13:8 O seeds fell on good soil and brought forth
14:22 before him to the O side, while he dismissed
16:5 the disciples reached the O side, they had forgotten
21:36 Again he sent O servants, more than the first;
21:41 out the vineyard to O tenants who will give
22:4 Again he sent O servants, saying, 'Tell those who
24:31 winds, from one end of heaven to the O
25:11 Afterward the O maidens came also, saying, 'Lord,
27:61 Mary Magdalene and the O Mary were there, sitting
28:1 Mary Magdalene and the O Mary went to see
Mk 4:5 O seed fell on rocky ground, where it had
4:7 O seed fell among thorns and the thorns grew
4:8 And O seeds fell into good soil and brought
4:19 and the desire for O things, enter in and
4:35 go across to the O side."
4:36 And O boats were with him.
5:1 They came to the O side of the sea,
5:21 the boat to the O side, a great crowd
6:45 before him to the O side, to Beth-saida, while
7:4 and there are many O traditions which they observe,
8:13 he departed to the O side.
12:6 He had still one O, a beloved son; finally
12:31 yourself.' There is no O commandment greater than
12:32 and there is no O but he;
15:40 him; and also many O women who came up
Lk 3:18 So, with many O exhortations, he preached good
4:43 of God to the O cities also; for I
5:7 their partners in the O boat to come and
6:29 the cheek, offer the O also; and from him
7:41 hundred denarii, and the O fifty.
8:22 go across to the O side of the lake."
10:31 passed by on the O side.
10:32 passed by on the O side.
11:26 goes and brings seven O spirits more evil than
13:2 sinners than all the O Galileans, because they
14:32 if not, while the O is yet a great
16:13 one and love the O, or he will be
16:13 be devoted to the one and despise the O
17:24 one side to the O, so will the Son
17:34 be taken and the O left.
17:35 be taken and the O left."
18:10 a Pharisee and the O a tax collector.
18:11 I am not like O men, extortioners, unjust, adulterers,
18:14 justified rather than the O; for every one who
22:63 And they spoke many O words against him, reviling
23:12 became friends with each O that very day, for
23:12 this they had been at enmity with each O
23:39 But the O rebuked him, saying, "Do you not
24:10 of James and the O women with them who
24:14 and talking with each O about all these things
24:17 are holding with each O as you walk?" And
24:32 They said to each O, "Did not our hearts
Jn 6:1 Jesus went to the O side of the Sea
6:22 who remained on the O side of the sea
6:25 found him on the O side of the sea,
10:16 And I have O sheep, that are not of
18:16 So the O disciple, who was known to the
19:32 first, and of the O who had been crucified
20:2 Simon Peter and the O disciple, the one whom
20:3 came out with the O disciple, and they went
20:4 both ran, but the O disciple outran Peter and
20:8 Then the O disciple, who reached the tomb first,
20:25 So the O disciples told him, "We have seen
20:30 Now Jesus did many O signs in the presence
21:8 But the O disciples came in the boat, dragging
21:25 there are also many O things which Jesus did;
Acts 2:4 began to speak in O tongues, as the Spirit
2:40 he testified with many O words and exhorted them,
4:12 for there is no O name under heaven given
7:26 do you wrong each O
9:39 and showing tunics and O garments which Dorcas
12:12 mother of John whose O name was Mark, where
12:25 with them John whose O name was Mark.
15:38 they separated from each O; Barnabas took Mark
23:6 were Sadducees and the O Pharisees, he cried out
27:1 delivered Paul and some O prisoners to a centurion

Rom 1:12 mutually encouraged by each O's faith, both yours
13:9 and any O commandment, are summed up in this
1Cor 3:11 For no O foundation can any one lay than
6:13 and God will destroy both one and the O
6:18 Every O sin which a man commits is outside
9:5 a wife, as the O apostles and the brothers
11:16 contentious, we recognize no O practice, nor do the
11:34 About the O things I will give directions when
14:3 On the O hand, he who prophesies speaks to
14:17 well enough, but the O man is not edified.
15:37 wheat or of some O grain.
16:12 visit you with the O brethren, but it was
2Cor 2:16 to death, to the O a fragrance from life
10:15 boast beyond limit, in O men's labors; but our
11:8 I robbed O churches by accepting support from them
11:28 And, apart from O things, there is the daily
Gal 1:19 saw none of the O apostles except James the
5:10 you will take no O view than mine; and
5:17 are opposed to each O, to prevent you from
Eph 3:5 sons of men in O generations as it has
Phil 3:4 If any O man thinks he has reason for
Col 3:13 against another, forgiving each O; as the Lord has
Heb 7:19 nothing perfect); on the O hand, a better hope
Jas 5:12 earth or with any O oath, but let your
2Pet 2:5 of righteousness, with seven O persons, when he
3:16 as they do the O scriptures.
Rev 2:24 lay upon you any O burden;
8:13 the blasts of the O trumpets which the three
17:10 fallen, one is, the O has not yet come,

OTHERS (134)

Gen 42:5 to buy among the O who came, for the
Ex 24:2 the LORD; but the O shall not come near,
Josh 8:22 And the O came forth from the city against
Judg 7:7 and let all the O go every man to
1Chr 9:29 O of them were appointed over the furniture, and
9:30 O, of the sons of the priests, prepared the
Job 8:19 out of the earth O will spring.
31:10 for another, and let O bow down upon her.
34:24 without investigation, and sets O in their place.
Ps 49:10 alike must perish and leave their wealth to O
Prov 5:9 give your honor to O and your years to
Eccl 7:22 knows that many times you have yourself cursed O
Wis 2:15 is unlike that of O, and his ways are
15:13 man, more than all O, knows that he sins
15:18 are worse than all O, when judged by their
19:14 O had refused to receive strangers when they came
Sir 11:6 and illustrious men have been handed over to O
11:17 he leaves them to O and dies.
14:4 depriving himself, accumulates for O; and others will
14:4 accumulates for others; and O will live in luxury
14:18 some and puts forth O, so are the generations
19:4 One who trusts O too quickly is lightminded, and
48:16 pleasing to God, but O multiplied sins.
49:5 gave their power to O, and their glory to
Is 56:8 I will gather yet O to him besides those
Jer 6:12 be turned over to O, their fields and wives
8:10 give their wives to O and their fields to
26:22 son of Achbor and O with him,
Bar 3:19 down to Hades, and O have arisen in their
Ezek 9:5 And to the O he said in my hearing,
10:11 front wheel faced the O followed without turning as
40:24 vestibule; they had the same size as the O
40:25 the windows of the O; its length was fifty
40:28 same size as the O;
40:29 same size as the O; and there were windows
40:32 it was of the same size as the O
40:33 same size as the O; and there were windows
40:35 it; it had the same size as the O
40:36 same size as the O; and it had windows
Dan 8:22 place of which four O arose, four kingdoms shall
11:4 up and go to O besides these.
12:5 looked, and behold, two O stood, one on this
1Mac 6:43 taller than all the O, and he supposed that
8:5 the Macedonians, and the O who rose up against
10:72 am and who the O are that are helping
2Mac 2:27 prepares a banquet and seeks the benefit of O
3:19 to the walls, while O peered out of the
4:41 blocks of wood, and O took handfuls of the
5:23 citizens worse than the O did.
5:27 Maccabeus, with about nine O, got away to the
6:11 O who had assembled in the caves near by,
7:39 him worse than the O, being exasperated at his
8:14 O sold all their remaining property, and at the
8:33 gates, Callisthenes and some O, who had fled into
9:6 tortured the bowels of O with many and strange
9:28 he had inflicted on O, came to the end
10:36 O who came up in the same way wheeled
10:36 O broke open the gates and let in the
11:7 and he urged the O to risk their lives
Mt 5:47 your brethren, what more are you doing than O
15:30 the dumb, and many O, and they put them
16:14 say John the Baptist, O say Elijah, and others
16:14 others say Elijah, and O Jeremiah or one of
17:24 From their sons or from O
17:25 And when he said, "From O
18:15 take one or two O along with you, that
20:3 third hour he saw O standing idle in the
20:6 went out and found O standing; and he said
21:8 on the road, and O cut branches from the
23:22 you ought to have done, without neglecting the O
27:42 him, saying, "He saved O; he cannot save himself.
27:49 But the O said, "Wait, let us see whether
Mk 4:18 And O are the ones sown among thorns; they
6:15 But O said, "It is Elijah." And others said,
6:15 And O said, "It is a prophet, like one
8:28 "John the Baptist; and O say, Elijah; and others
8:28 others say, Elijah; and O one of the prophets."
11:8 on the road, and O spread leafy branches which
12:5 and so with many O, some they beat and
12:9 destroy the tenants, and give the vineyard to O
15:30 scribes, saying, "He saved O; he cannot save himself.
Lk 5:29 of tax collectors and O sitting at table with
8:3 and Susanna, and many O, who provided for them
8:10 of God; but for O they are in parables,
9:8 had appeared, and by O that one of the
9:19 "John the Baptist; but O say, Elijah; and others,
9:19 others say, Elijah; and O, that one of the
10:1 the Lord appointed seventy O, and sent them on
11:16 prince of demons"; while O, to test him, sought
11:42 you ought to have done, without neglecting the O
13:4 offenders than all the O who dwelt in Jerusalem?
18:9 were righteous and despised O:
20:16 destroy those tenants, and give the vineyard to O
23:31 Two O also, who were criminals, were led away
23:34 him, saying, "He saved O; let him save himself,
Jn 4:38 you did not labor; O have labored, and you
7:12 O said, "No, he is leading the people astray."
7:41 O said, "This is the Christ." But some said,
9:9 said, "It is he"; O said, "No, but he
9:16 But O said, "How can a man who is
10:21 O said, "These are not the sayings of one
12:29 O said, "An angel has spoken to him."
18:34 own accord, or did O say it to you
19:18 and with him two O, one on either side,
21:2 of Zebedee, and two O of his disciples were
Acts 2:13 But O mocking said, "They are filled with new
7:6 a land belonging to O, who would enslave them
15:2 and some of the O were appointed to go
15:34 the Lord, with many O also.
17:18 O said, "He seems to be a preacher of
17:32 dead, some mocked; but O said, "We will hear
17:34 woman named Damaris and O with them.
28:24 what he said, while O disbelieved.
Rom 2:21 you then who teach O, will you not teach
11:23 And even the O, if they do not persist
14:20 any one to make O fall by what he
1Cor 9:2 If to O I am not an apostle, at
9:12 If O share this rightful claim upon you, do
9:27 lest after preaching to O I myself should be
14:19 in order to instruct O, than ten thousand words
14:29 speak, and let the O weigh what is said.
2Cor 8:8 by the earnestness of O that your love also
8:13 do not mean that O should be eased and
9:13 them and for all O;
13:2 before and all the O, and I warn them
Phil 1:15 envy and rivalry, but O from good will.
2:3 but in humility count O better than yourselves.
2:4 own interests, but also to the interests of O
1Thes 2:6 from you or from O, though we might have
4:13 may not grieve as O do who have no
5:6 us not sleep, as O do, but let us
1Tim 5:24 but the sins of O appear later.
2Tim 2:2 be able to teach O also.
Heb 11:36 O suffered mocking and scourging, and even chains

OTHERWISE (12)

1Kgs 1:21 O it will come to pass, when my lord
2Chr 30:18 they ate the passover O than as prescribed.
1Mac 15:31 O we will come and conquer you."
Lk 14:29 O, when he has laid a foundation, and is
Rom 11:6 the basis of works; O grace would no longer

11:22 continue in his kindness; O you too will be
1Cor 7:14 O, your children would be unclean, but as it
14:16 O, if you bless with the spirit, how can
15:29 O, what do people mean by being baptized on
Phil 3:15 in anything you are O minded, God will reveal
1Tim 6:3 If any one teaches O and does not agree
Heb 10:2 O, would they not have ceased to be offered?

OTHNI
1Chr 26:7 The sons of Shemaiah: O, Repha-el, Obed, and

OTHNI-EL (7)
Josh 15:17 And O the son of Kenaz, the brother of
Judg 1:13 And O the son of Kenaz, Caleb's younger brother,
3:9 Israel, who delivered them, O the son of Kenaz,
3:11 Then O the son of Kenaz died.
1Chr 4:13 The sons of Kenaz: O and Seraiah; and the
4:13 and the sons of O: Hathath and Meonothai.
27:15 Heldai the Netophathite, of O; in his division were

OUGHT (52)
Gen 20:9 to me things that O not to be done."
34:7 for such a thing O not to be done.
Lev 10:18 You certainly O to have eaten it in the
1Kgs 2:9 will know what you O to do to him,
1Chr 12:32 to know what Israel O to do, two hundred
2Chr 13:5 O you not to know that the LORD God
Neh 5:9 O you not to walk in the fear of
Wis 14:21 wood the name that O not to be shared.
2Mac 6:20 the flesh, as men O to go who have
Mt 23:22 and faith; these you O to have done, without
25:27 Then you O to have invested my money with
Mk 13:14 set up where it O not to be (let
Lk 11:42 of God; these you O to have done, without
12:12 very hour what you O to say."
13:14 days on which work O to be done; come
13:16 And O not this woman, a daughter of Abraham
18:1 the effect that they O always to pray and
Jn 4:20 the place where men O to worship."
13:14 your feet, you also O to wash one another's
19:7 by that law he O to die, because he
Acts 17:29 then God's offspring, we O not to think that
19:36 cannot be contradicted, you O to be quiet and
22:22 For he O not to live."
24:18 from Asia-- they O to be here before
25:10 Caesar's tribunal, where I O to be tried; to
25:24 here, shouting that he O not to live any
26:9 was convinced that I O to do many things
Rom 8:26 to pray as we O, but the Spirit himself
12:3 more highly than he O to think, but to
15:1 We who are strong O to bear with the
15:27 their spiritual blessings, they O also to be of
1Cor 5:2 O you not rather to mourn?
8:2 yet know as he O to know.
11:7 For a man O not to cover his head,
11:10 is why a woman O to have a veil
2Cor 12:11 to it, for I O to have been commended
12:14 but you; for children O not to lay up
Eph 6:20 it boldly, as I O to speak.
Col 4:4 it clear, as I O to speak.
4:6 may know how you O to answer every one.
1Thes 4:1 from us how you O to live and to
2Thes 3:7 yourselves know how you O to imitate us; we
1Tim 3:15 may know how one O to behave in the
2Tim 2:6 the hard-working farmer who O to have the first
Heb 5:12 by this time you O to be teachers, you
Jas 3:10 My brethren, this O not to be so.
4:15 Instead you O to say, "If the Lord wills,
2Pet 3:11 what sort of persons O you to be in
1Jn 2:6 he abides in him O to walk in the
3:16 for us; and we O to lay down our
4:11 loved us, we also O to love one another.
3Jn 1:8 So we O to support such men, that we

OURSELVES (62)
Gen 11:4 "Come, let us build O a city, and a
11:4 make a name for O, lest we be scattered
34:16 take your daughters to O, and we will dwell
37:10 indeed come to bow O to the ground before
43:7 questioned us carefully about O and our kindred,
44:16 Or how can we clear O
Num 13:33 and we seemed to O like grasshoppers, and so
31:50 to make atonement for O before the LORD."
Deut 2:35 took as spoil for O, with the booty of
Josh 22:17 we have not cleansed O, and for which there
1Sam 11:3 us, we will give O up to you."
11:10 "Tomorrow we will give O up to you, and
12:19 evil, to ask for O a king."
14:8 and we will show O to them.
Ezra 8:21 that we might humble O before our God, to
8:21 a straight way for O, our children, and all
Neh 10:32 We also lay upon O the obligation to charge
10:32 the obligation to charge O yearly with the third
10:35 We obligate O to bring the first fruits of
Job 34:4 let us determine among O what is good.
Ps 83:12 us take possession for O of the pastures of
Prov 7:18 morning; let us delight O with love.
Wis 2:8 Let us crown O with rosebuds before they wither.
Sir 36:10 enemy, who say, "There is no one but O
Is 7:6 us conquer it for O, and set up the
56:12 wine, let us fill O with strong drink; and
58:3 Why have we humbled O, and thou takest no
Jer 26:19 we are about to bring great evil upon O
35:8 wine all our days, O, our wives, our sons,
50:5 'Come, let us join O to the LORD in
Amos 6:13 not by our own strength taken Karnaim for O
1Mac 5:57 make a name for O; let us go and
12:13 But as for O, many afflictions and many wars
Lk 11:4 our sins, for we O forgive every one who
22:69 We have heard it O from his own lips."
Jn 4:42 we have heard for O, and we know that
Acts 6:4 But we will devote O to prayer and to
23:14 "We have strictly bound O by an oath to
Rom 8:23 the creation, but we O, who have the first
13:13 light; let us conduct O becomingly as in the
15:1 and not to please O;
1Cor 11:31 But if we judged O truly, we should not
2Cor 1:4 comfort with which we O are comforted by God.
1:9 us rely not on O but on God who
3:1 we beginning to commend O again?
3:5 we are competent of O to claim anything as
4:2 truth we would commend O to every man's
4:5 we preach is not O, but Jesus Christ as
4:5 Christ as Lord, with O as your servants for
5:12 We are not commending O to you again but
5:13 if we are beside O, it is for God;
6:4 of God we commend O in every way: through
7:1 beloved, let us cleanse O from every defilement of
10:12 to class or compare O with some of those
10:14 we are not overextending O, as though we did
12:19 we have been defending O before you?
Gal 2:15 We O, who are Jews by birth and not
2:17 justified in Christ, we O were found to be
2Thes 1:4 Therefore we O boast of you in the churches
Tit 3:3 For we O were once foolish, disobedient, led astray,
Jas 5:17 of like nature with O and he prayed fervently
1Jn 1:8 no sin, we deceive O, and the truth is

OUT-FLANKED (2)
Jud 15:5 Gilead and in Galilee O them with great slaughter,
1Mac 7:46 round about, and they O the enemy and drove

OUTBIDDING
2Mac 4:24 the high-priesthood for himself, O Jason by three

OUTCAST (3)
2Sam 14:14 means not to keep his banished one an O
Jer 30:17 have called you an O: 'It is Zion, for
Zeph 3:19 lame and gather the O, and I will change

OUTCASTS (6)
Deut 30:4 If your O are in the uttermost parts of
Ps 147:2 Jerusalem; he gathers the O of Israel.
Is 11:12 and will assemble the O of Israel, and gather
16:3 of noon; hide the O, betray not the fugitive;
16:4 the fugitive; let the O of Moab sojourn among
56:8 GOD, who gathers the O of Israel, I will

OUTCOME (5)
Wis 8:8 wonders and of the O of seasons and times.
Is 41:22 we may know their O; or declare to us
2Mac 3:40 This was the O of the episode of Heliodorus
Heb 13:7 of God; consider the O of their life, and
1Pet 1:9 As the O of your faith you obtain the

OUTCRY (7)
Gen 18:20 LORD said, "Because the O against Sodom and
18:21 altogether according to the O which has come to
19:13 this place, because the O against its people has
1Sam 4:14 the sound of the O, he said, "What is
Neh 5:1 there arose a great O of the people and
5:6 when I heard their O and these words.

O

Is 24:11 There is an O in the streets for lack

OUTDO

Rom 12:10 another with brotherly affection; O one another in

OUTER (33)

1Kgs 6:29 in the inner and O rooms.
6:30 in the inner and O rooms.
2Kgs 16:18 the palace, and the O entrance for the king
2Chr 33:14 Afterwards he built an O wall for the city
Esth 6:4 had just entered the O court of the king's
Job 41:13 can strip off his O garment?
Ezek 10:5 as far as the O court, like the voice
40:17 brought me into the O court; and behold, there
40:19 lower gate to the O front of the inner
40:20 north, belonging to the O court.
40:31 Its vestibule faced the O court, and palm trees
40:34 Its vestibule faced the O court, and it had
40:37 Its vestibule faced the O court, and it had
41:9 The thickness of the O wall of the side
41:15 inner room and the O vestibule
42:3 which belonged to the O court, was gallery against
42:6 the pillars of the O court; hence the upper
42:7 the chambers, toward the O court, opposite the
42:8 the chambers on the O court were fifty cubits
42:9 enters them from the O court,
42:14 of it into the O court without laying there
44:1 me back to the O gate of the sanctuary,
44:19 go out into the O court to the people,
46:20 them out into the O court and so communicate
46:21 me forth to the O court, and led me
47:2 the outside to the O gate, that faces toward
Mt 8:12 be thrown into the O darkness; there men will
22:13 cast him into the O darkness; there men will
25:30 worthless servant into the O darkness; there men
2Cor 4:16 Though our O nature is wasting away, our inner
Heb 9:2 tent was prepared, the O one, in which were
9:6 go continually into the O tent, performing their ritual
9:8 as long as the O tent is still standing

OUTFIT

Ezek 12:7 the dark, carrying my O upon my shoulder in

OUTFLOW

Ex 22:29 harvest and from the O of your presses.

OUTGOINGS

Ps 65:8 signs; thou makest the O of the morning and

OUTLAY

2Kgs 12:12 LORD, and for any O upon the repairs of

OUTLET (2)

2Chr 32:30 Hezekiah closed the upper O of the waters of
Sir 25:24 Allow no O to water, and no boldness of

OUTLINES

2Mac 2:28 to arriving at the O of the condensation.

OUTLIVED (2)

Josh 24:31 of the elders who O Joshua and had known
Judg 2:7 of the elders who O Joshua, who had seen

OUTLYING

Num 11:1 them, and consumed some O parts of the camp.

OUTMOST (7)

Ex 26:4 the edge of the O curtain in the first
26:4 the edge of the O curtain in the second
26:10 the curtain that is O in one set, and
26:10 the curtain which is O in the second set.
36:11 the edge of the O curtain of the first
36:11 the edge of the O curtain of the second
36:17 the edge of the O curtain of the one

OUTPOST

Jud 14:2 plain against the Assyrian O; only do not go

OUTPOSTS (2)

Judg 7:11 his servant to the O of the armed men
1Mac 12:27 battle, and he stationed O around the camp.

OUTPOURED

Ps 79:10 the avenging of the O blood of thy servants

OUTPOURING

Ezek 9:8 of Israel in the O of thy wrath upon

OUTPUT

Sir 38:29 work, and all his O is by number.

OUTRAGE (3)

Wis 4:18 dishonored corpses, and an O among the dead for
2Mac 4:38 he had committed the O against Onias, and there
8:17 their eyes the lawless O which the Gentiles had

OUTRAGED

Heb 10:29 he was sanctified, and O the Spirit of grace?

OUTRAGEOUS

Sir 10:7 men, and injustice is O to both.

OUTRAGES

2Mac 14:42 of sinners and suffer O unworthy of his noble

OUTRAN (2)

2Sam 18:23 of the plain, and O the Cushite.
Jn 20:4 but the other disciple O Peter and reached the

OUTRIGHT

Ezek 9:6 pity; slay old men O, young men and maidens,

OUTSIDE (115)

Gen 9:22 of his father, and told his two brothers O
15:5 And he brought him O and said, "Look toward
19:16 forth and set him O the city.
24:11 the camels kneel down O the city by the
24:31 blessed of the LORD; why do you stand O
Ex 12:46 any of the flesh O the house; and you
26:35 shall set the table O the veil, and the
27:21 the tent of meeting, O the veil which is
29:14 shall burn with fire O the camp; it is
33:7 tent and pitch it O the camp, far-off from
33:7 of meeting, which was O the camp.
Lev 4:12 he shall carry forth O the camp to a
4:21 carry forth the bull O the camp, and burn
6:11 carry forth the ashes O the camp to a
8:17 he burned with fire O the camp, as the
9:11 he burned with fire O the camp.
13:46 alone in a habitation O the camp.
14:8 camp, but shall dwell O his tent seven days.
14:40 into an unclean place O the city;
14:41 into an unclean place O the city;
16:27 shall be carried forth O the camp; their skin
17:3 camp, or kills it O the camp,
24:3 O the veil of the testimony, in the tent
Num 5:3 and female, putting them O the camp, that they
5:4 so, and drove them O the camp; as the
12:14 her be shut up O the camp seven days,
12:15 Miriam was shut up O the camp seven days;
15:35 stone him with stones O the camp."
15:36 congregation brought him O the camp, and stoned
19:3 she shall be taken O the camp and slaughtered
19:9 heifer, and deposit them O the camp in a
31:13 forth to meet them O the camp.
31:19 Encamp O the camp seven days; whoever of you
35:5 And you shall measure, O the city, for the
35:27 of blood finds him O the bounds of his
Deut 23:10 then he shall go O the camp, he shall
23:12 shall have a place O the camp and you
23:13 when you sit down O, you shall dig a
24:11 You shall stand O, and the man to whom
25:5 shall not be married O the family to a
Josh 6:23 kindred, and set them O the camp of Israel.
Judg 12:9 he gave in marriage O his clan, and thirty
12:9 he brought in from O for his sons.
1Kgs 6:6 broad; for around the O of the house he
8:8 not be seen from O; and they are there
21:13 So they took him O the city, and stoned
2Kgs 4:3 Then he said, "Go O, borrow vessels of all
10:24 had stationed eighty men O, and said, "The man
23:4 heaven; he burned them O Jerusalem in the fields
23:6 house of the LORD, O Jerusalem, to the brook
1Chr 26:29 sons were appointed to O duties for Israel, as
2Chr 5:9 not be seen from O; and they are there
24:8 chest, and set it O the gate of the
32:3 the springs that were O the city; and they
32:5 towers upon it, and O it he built another
33:15 and he threw them O of the city.
Neh 11:16 who were over the O work of the house
13:20 kinds of wares lodged O Jerusalem once or twice.

Jud 6:1 made by the men O the council died down,
10:18 her as she waited O the tent of Holofernes
13:1 closed the tent from O and shut out the
13:3 her maid to stand O the bedchamber and to
Prov 22:13 The sluggard says, "There is a lion O
24:27 Prepare your work O, get everything ready for you
Song 8:1 If I met you O, I would kiss you,
Sir 21:23 from the door, but a cultivated man remains O
Jer 21:4 who are besieging you O the walls; and I
Ezek 40:5 wall all around the O of the temple area,
40:40 And on the O of the vestibule at the
40:41 four tables on the O of the side of
41:17 even to the inner room, and on the O
41:25 canopy of wood in front of the vestibule O
42:7 there was a wall O parallel to the chambers,
42:10 outer court, where the O wall begins.
43:21 belonging to the temple, O the sacred area.
47:2 me round on the O to the outer gate,
Dan 14:7 clay inside and brass O, and it never ate
14:11 "Behold, we are going O; you yourself, O king,
1Mac 7:47 and displayed them just O Jerusalem.
15:30 which you have conquered O the borders of Judea;
2Mac 1:16 their heads and threw them to the people O
Mt 9:25 crowd had been put O, he went in and
12:46 and his brethren stood O, asking to speak to
23:24 for you cleanse the O of the cup and
23:25 the plate, that the O also may be clean.
26:69 Now Peter was sitting O in the courtyard.
Mk 3:31 brethren came; and standing O they sent to him
3:32 and your brethren are O, asking for you."
4:11 God, but for those O everything is in parables;
5:40 he put them all O, and took the child's
7:15 understand: there is nothing O a man which by
7:17 into a man from O cannot defile him,
Lk 1:10 the people were praying O at the hour of
8:20 your brrethren are standing O, desiring to see you."
11:39 you Pharisees cleanse the O of the cup and
11:40 he who made the O make the inside also?
13:25 will begin to stand O and to knock at
Jn 18:16 Jesus, while Peter stood O at the door.
20:11 But Mary stood weeping O the tomb, and as
Acts 5:34 men to be put O for a while.
9:40 Peter put them all O and knelt down and
16:13 sabbath day we went O the gate to the
21:5 way till we were O the city; and kneeling
1Cor 5:13 God judges those O
6:18 a man commits is O the body; but the
9:21 To those O the law I became as one
9:21 I became as one O the law—not being
9:21 I might win those O the law.
Heb 2:8 him, he left nothing O his control.
13:11 for sin are burned O the camp.
13:12 So Jesus also suffered O the gate in order
13:13 go forth to him O the camp and bear
Rev 11:2 not measure the court O the temple; leave that
14:20 wine press was trodden O the city, and blood
22:15 O are the dogs and sorcerers and fornicators and

OUTSIDER (8)
Ex 29:33 consecrate them, but an O shall not eat of
30:33 of it on an O shall be cut off
Lev 22:10 "An O shall not eat of a holy thing.
22:12 is married to an O she shall not eat
22:13 father's food; yet no O shall eat of it.
Sir 45:13 No O ever put them on, but only his
1Cor 14:16 the position of an O say the "Amen" to
14:24 and an unbeliever or O enters, he is convicted

OUTSIDERS (6)
Sir 45:18 O conspired against him, and envied him in the
1Cor 5:12 For what have I to do with judging O
14:23 speak in tongues, and O or unbelievers enter, will
Col 4:5 Conduct yourselves wisely toward O, making the
1Thes 4:12 command the respect of O, and be dependent on
1Tim 3:7 well thought of by O, or he may fall

OUTSKIRTS (6)
Josh 18:15 side begins at the O of Kiriath-jearim; and the
Judg 7:17 I come to the O of the camp, do
7:19 him came to the O of the camp at
1Sam 9:27 going down to the O of the city, Samuel
14:2 was staying in the O of Gibe-ah under the
Job 26:14 these are but the O of his ways; and

OUTSPREAD
Is 8:8 the neck; and its O wings will fill the

OUTSTRETCHED (21)
Ex 6:6 redeem you with an O arm and with great
Deut 4:34 mighty hand and an O arm, and by great
5:15 mighty hand and an O arm; therefore the LORD
7:19 mighty hand, and the O arm, by which the
9:29 power and by thy O arm.'
11:2 mighty hand and his O arm,
26:8 mighty hand and an O arm, with great terror,
1Kgs 8:42 hand, and of thy O arm), when he comes
8:54 had knelt with hands O toward heaven;
2Kgs 17:36 power and with an O arm; you shall bow
2Chr 6:32 mighty hand, and thy O arm, when he comes
Ps 136:12 strong hand and an O arm, for his steadfast
Is 3:16 haughty and walk with O necks, glancing wantonly
Jer 21:5 fight against you with O hand and strong arm,
27:5 great power and my O arm have made the
32:17 power and by thy O arm!
32:21 a strong hand and O arm, and with great
Bar 2:11 with great power and O arm, and hast made
Ezek 20:33 mighty hand and an O arm, and with wrath
20:34 mighty hand and an O arm, and with wrath
2Mac 15:12 excellence, was praying with O hands for the whole

OUTSTRIP
Is 49:17 Your builders O your destroyers, and those who laid

OUTWARD (3)
Num 35:4 wall of the city O a thousand cubits all
1Sam 16:7 man looks on the O appearance, but the LORD
1Pet 3:3 not yours be the O adorning with braiding of

OUTWARDLY (3)
Mt 23:26 like whitewashed tombs, which O appear beautiful,
23:27 So you also O appear righteous to men, but
Rom 2:28 Jew who is one O, nor is true circumcision

OUTWEIGH
Sir 8:2 man, lest his resources O yours; for gold has

OUTWEIGHS
Eccl 10:1 so a little folly O wisdom and honor.

OUTWIT
Ps 89:22 The enemy shall not O him, the wicked shall

OUTWITTED (2)
Gen 31:20 And Jacob O Laban the Aramean, in that he
2Mac 14:31 he had been cleverly O by the man, he

OVEN (12)
Lev 2:4 offering baked in the O as an offering, it
7:9 offering baked in the O and all that is
11:35 shall be unclean; whether O or stove, it shall
26:26 your bread in one O, and shall deliver your
Ps 21:9 them as a blazing O when you appear.
Lam 5:10 is hot as an O with the burning heat
Hos 7:5 are like a heated O, whose baker ceases to
7:7 For like an O their hearts burn with intrigue;
7:8 are hot as an O, and they devour their
Mal 4:1 comes, burning like an O, when all the arrogant
Mt 6:30 is thrown into the O, will he not much
Lk 12:28 is thrown into the O, how much more will

OVENS (3)
Ex 8:3 people, and into your O and your kneading bowls;
Neh 3:11 repaired another section and the Tower of the O
12:38 the Tower of the O, to the Broad Wall,

OVERBEARING (2)
Ps 37:35 seen a wicked man O, and towering like a
1Pet 2:18 the kind and gentle but also to the O

OVERBOARD (2)
Acts 27:18 to throw the cargo O;
27:43 swim to throw themselves O first and make for

OVERCAME
1Kgs 16:22 people who followed Omri O the people who

OVERCOME (22)
Num 13:30 are well able to O it."
22:3 were many; Moab was O with fear of the
1Sam 30:1 They had O Ziklag, and burned it with fire,
Jud 8:3 the field, he was O by the burning heat,
13:2 bed, for he was O with wine.
Ps 55:2 answer me; I am O by my trouble.

O

Wis	2:4	of the sun and O by its heat.
Sir	23:6	neither gluttony nor lust O me, and do not
Is	28:1	rich valley of those O with wine!
Jer	20:10	deceived, then we can O him, and take our
	20:11	stumble, they will not O me.
	23:9	man, like a man O by wine, because of
Dan	8:27	And I, Daniel, was O and lay sick for
Mk	5:42	and they were immediately O with amazement.
Jn	1:5	the darkness has not O it.
	16:33	good cheer, I have O the world."
Acts	20:9	still longer; and being O by sleep, he fell
Rom	12:21	Do not be O by evil, but overcome evil
	12:21	overcome by evil, but O evil with good.
1Jn	2:13	men, because you have O the evil one.
	2:14	you, and you have O the evil one.
	4:4	of God, and have O them; for he who

OVERCOMES (5)

Lk	11:22	he assails him and O him, he takes away
2Pet	2:19	of corruption; for whatever O a man, to that
1Jn	5:4	is born of God O the world; and this
	5:4	is the victory that O the world, our faith.
	5:5	Who is it that O the world but he

OVERCONFIDENT

Sir	32:21	Do not be O on a smooth way,

OVERDRIVEN

Gen	33:13	and if they are O for one day, all

OVEREATING

Sir	37:30	up to food; for O brings sickness, and gluttony

OVEREXTENDING

2Cor	10:14	For we are not O ourselves, as though we

OVERFLOW (11)

Deut	11:4	of the Red Sea O them as they pursued
Jud	2:8	with their dead, and O;
Ps	73:7	with fatness, their hearts O with follies.
Is	8:8	into Judah, it will O and pass on, reaching
	23:10	O your land like the Nile, O daughter of
Jer	47:2	overflowing torrent; they shall O the land and all
Dan	11:10	shall come on and O and pass through, and
	11:40	into countries and shall O and pass through.
Joel	2:24	grain, the vats shall O with wine and oil.
	3:13	The vats O, for their wickedness is great.
Zech	1:17	My cities shall again O with prosperity, and the

OVERFLOWED (5)

Josh	4:18	to their place and O all its banks, as
Ps	78:20	rock so that water gushed out and streams O
Sir	47:14	You O like a river with understanding.
2Cor	8:2	their extreme poverty have O in a wealth of
1Tim	1:14	grace of our Lord O for me with the

OVERFLOWING (9)

1Chr	12:15	month, when it was O all its banks, and
Is	10:22	Destruction is decreed, O with righteousness.
	28:2	a storm of mighty, O waters, he will cast
	30:28	breath is like an O stream that reaches up
	54:8	In O wrath for a moment I hid my
	66:12	the nations like an O stream; and you shall
Jer	47:2	and shall become an O torrent; they shall overflow
Nah	1:8	But with an O flood he will make a
Mal	3:10	down for you an O blessing.

OVERFLOWINGS

Job	40:11	Pour forth the O of your anger, and look

OVERFLOWS (4)

Josh	3:15	the water (the Jordan O all its banks throughout
Ps	23:5	thou anointest my head with oil, my cup O
	45:1	My heart O with a goodly theme; I address
2Cor	9:12	the saints but also O in many thanksgivings to

OVERGROWN (2)

Prov	15:19	of a sluggard is O with thorns, but the
	24:31	lo, it was all O with thorns; the ground

OVERHEARD (2)

Esth	12:2	He O their conversation their conversation and
Jer	38:27	with him, for the conversation had not been O

OVERJOYED

2Cor	7:4	With all our affliction, I am O

OVERLAID (39)

Ex	26:32	four pillars of acacia O with gold, with hooks
	36:34	And he O the frames with gold, and made
	36:34	for the bars, and O the bars with gold.
	36:36	pillars of acacia, and O them with gold; their
	36:38	He O their capitals, and their fillets were of
	37:2	And he O it with pure gold within and
	37:4	of acacia wood, and O them with gold,
	37:11	its height; and he O it with pure gold,
	37:15	carry the table, and O them with gold.
	37:26	He O it with pure gold, its top, and
	37:28	of acacia wood, and O them with gold.
	38:2	with it, and he O it with bronze.
	38:6	of acacia wood, and O them with bronze.
	38:28	for the pillars, and O their capitals and made
1Kgs	6:20	cubits high; and he O it with pure gold.
	6:21	And Solomon O the inside of the house with
	6:21	the inner sanctuary, and O it with gold.
	6:22	And he O the whole house with gold, until
	6:22	the inner sanctuary he O with gold.
	6:28	And he O the cherubim with gold.
	6:30	of the house he O with gold in the
	6:32	and open flowers; he O them with gold, and
	6:35	open flowers; and he O them with gold evenly
	10:18	great ivory throne, and O it with the finest
2Kgs	18:16	king of Judah had O and gave it to
2Chr	3:4	He O it on the inside with pure gold.
	3:8	was twenty cubits; he O it with six hundred
	3:9	And he O the upper chambers with gold.
	3:10	cherubim of wood and O them with gold.
	4:9	for the court, and O their doors with bronze;
	9:17	great ivory throne, and O it with pure gold.
Bar	6:8	and they themselves are O with gold and silver;
	6:39	made of wood and O with gold and silver
	6:50	made of wood and O with gold and silver,
	6:55	temple of wooden gods O with gold or silver,
	6:57	made of wood and O with silver and gold
	6:70	their gods of wood, O with gold and silver.
	6:71	their gods of wood, O with gold and silver,
Hab	2:19	Behold, it is O with gold and silver, and

OVERLAY (12)

Ex	25:11	And you shall O it with pure gold, within
	25:11	and without shall you O it, and you shall
	25:13	of acacia wood, and O them with gold.
	25:24	You shall O it with pure gold, and make
	25:28	of acacia wood, and O them with gold, and
	26:29	You shall O the frames with gold, and shall
	26:29	bars; and you shall O the bars with gold.
	26:37	pillars of acacia, and O them with gold; their
	27:2	it, and you shall O it with bronze.
	27:6	of acacia wood, and O them with bronze;
	30:3	And you shall O it with pure gold, its
	30:5	of acacia wood, and O them with gold.

OVERLAYING (3)

Ex	38:17	were of silver; the O of their capitals was
	38:19	of silver, and the O of their capitals and
1Chr	29:4	of refined silver, for O the walls of the

OVERLAYS

Is	40:19	it, and a goldsmith O it with gold, and

OVERLOOK (5)

Prov	19:11	is his glory to O an offense.
Wis	11:23	things, and thou dost O men's sins, that they
Sir	28:7	the Most High, and O ignorance.
	32:18	of judgment will not O an idea, and an
Heb	6:10	so unjust as to O your work and the

OVERLOOKED (2)

Sir	2:10	Or who ever called upon him and was O
Acts	17:30	times of ignorance God O, but now he commands

OVERLOOKING

Song	7:4	a tower of Lebanon, O Damascus.

OVERLOOKS (2)

Num	23:28	top of Peor, that O the desert.
Josh	18:16	of the mountain that O the valley of the

OVERMUCH (2)

Eccl	7:16	Be not righteous O, and do not make yourself
	7:17	Be not wicked O, neither be a fool; why

OVERPAYMENT
Lev 25:27 and pay back the O to the man to

OVERPOWER
Judg 16:5 what means we may O him, that we may

OVERPOWERED (3)
Dan 6:24 the den the lions O them and broke all
Acts 19:16 all of them, and O them, so that they
2Pet 2:20 entangled in them and O, the last state has

OVERRUN
Zech 9:8 no oppressor shall again O them, for now I

OVERSEE
2Chr 2:2 thousand six hundred to O them.

OVERSEEING (2)
Jud 8:3 For as he stood O the men who were
Wis 7:23 free from anxiety, all-powerful, O all, and penetrating

OVERSEER (5)
Gen 39:4 and he made him O of his house and
39:5 that he made him O in his house and
Neh 11:9 of Zichri was their O; and Judah the son
11:14 hundred and twenty-eight; their O was Zabdiel the
11:22 The O of the Levites in Jerusalem was Uzzi

OVERSEERS (6)
Gen 41:34 Pharaoh proceed to appoint O over the land, and
2Chr 2:18 thousand six hundred as O to make the people
31:13 Mahath, and Benaiah were O assisting Conaniah and
34:17 the hand of the O and the workmen."
Is 60:17 I will make your O peace and your taskmasters
Acts 20:28 Spirit has made you O, to care for the

OVERSHADOW
Lk 1:35 the Most High will O you; therefore the child

OVERSHADOWED (3)
Mt 17:5 lo, a bright cloud O them, and a voice
Mk 9:7 And a cloud O them, and a voice came
Lk 9:34 a cloud came and O them; and they were

OVERSHADOWING (4)
Ex 25:20 out their wings above, O the mercy seat with
37:9 out their wings above, O the mercy seat with
Wis 19:7 The cloud was seen O the camp, and dry
Heb 9:5 the cherubim of glory O the mercy seat.

OVERSIGHT (14)
Gen 43:12 mouth of your sacks; perhaps it was an O
Num 3:32 Levites, and to have O of those who had
4:16 anointing oil, with the O of all the tabernacle
4:28 to be under the O of Ithamar the son
2Kgs 12:11 workmen who had the O of the house of
22:5 workmen who have the O of the house of
22:9 workmen who have the O of the house of
1Chr 26:30 of ability, had the O of Israel westward of
26:32 houses, to have the O of the Reubenites, the
2Chr 34:10 workmen who had the O of the house of
34:12 of the sons of the Kohathites, to have O
Ezra 3:8 upward, to have the O of the work of
3:9 Judah, together took the O of the workmen in
Ezek 44:11 in my sanctuary, having O at the gates of

OVERSTUFFED
Sir 31:21 If you are O with food, get up in

OVERTAKE (30)
Gen 19:19 hills, lest the disaster O me, and I die.
44:4 men; and when you O them, say to them,
Ex 15:9 will pursue, I will O, I will divide the
Deut 19:6 pursue the manslayer and O him, because the way
28:2 come upon you and O you, if you obey
28:15 come upon you and O you.
28:45 and pursue you and O you, till you are
Josh 2:5 quickly, for you will O them."
1Sam 30:8 Shall I O them?" He answered him, "Pursue; for
30:8 for you shall surely O and shall surely rescue."
2Sam 15:14 in haste, lest he O us quickly, and bring
2Kgs 7:9 morning light, punishment will O us; now therefore
Tob 12:7 and evil will not O you.
Job 27:20 Terrors O him like a flood; in the night
Ps 7:5 enemy pursue me and O me, and let him
69:24 let thy burning anger O them.
Wis 14:30 But just penalties will O them on two counts:
Sir 11:10 pursue you will not O, and by fleeing you
31:22 and no sickness will O you.
Is 59:9 and righteousness does not O us; we look for
Jer 42:16 which you fear shall O you there in the
Hos 2:7 her lovers, but not O them; and she shall
10:9 Shall not war O them in Gibe-ah?
Amos 9:10 say, 'Evil shall not O or meet us.'
9:13 "when the plowman shall O the reaper and the
Mic 2:6 things; disgrace will not O us."
Zech 1:6 prophets, did they not O your fathers?
1Mac 12:30 but he did not O them, for they had
2Mac 8:11 that was about to O him.
Jn 12:35 light, lest the darkness O you; he who walks

OVERTAKEN (7)
Jud 11:11 for a sin has O them by which they
Ps 40:12 number; my iniquities have O me, till I cannot
Sir 23:8 The sinner is O through his lips, the reviler
Lam 1:3 her pursuers have all O her in the midst
Bar 4:25 Your enemy has O you, but you will soon
1Cor 10:13 No temptation has O you that is not common
Gal 6:1 if a man is O in any trespass, you

OVERTAKES
1Chr 21:12 sword of your enemies O you; or else three

OVERTHREW (14)
Gen 19:25 of heaven; and he O those cities, and all
19:29 the overthrow, when he O the cities in which
Deut 29:23 Zeboiim, which the LORD O in his anger and
2Kgs 3:25 And they O the cities, and on every good
1Chr 20:1 Joab smote Rabbah, and O it.
Jud 1:13 him in battle, and O the whole army of
Ps 136:15 endures for ever; but O Pharaoh and his host
Is 13:19 and Gomorrah when God O them.
14:17 like a desert and O its cities, who did
Jer 20:16 cities which the LORD O without pity; let him
50:40 As when God O Sodom and Gomorrah and their
Amos 4:11 "I O some of you, as when God overthrew
4:11 you, as when God O Sodom and Gomorrah, and
2Mac 12:15 or engines of war O Jericho in the days

OVERTHROW (19)
Gen 19:21 that I will not O the city of which
19:29 the midst of the O, when he overthrew the
Ex 23:24 but you shall utterly O them and break their
Deut 29:23 grass can sprout, an O like that of Sodom
2Sam 10:3 it out, and to O it?"
11:25 upon the city, and O it.' And encourage him."
1Chr 19:3 to search and to O and to spy out
Ezra 6:12 name to dwell there O any king or people
Ps 17:13 confront them, O them!
Sir 12:12 to you, lest he O you and take your
29:16 A sinner will O the prosperity of his surety,
Jer 1:10 to destroy and to O, to build and to
31:28 and break down, to O, destroy, and bring evil,
Zeph 1:3 I will O the wicked; I will cut off
Hag 2:22 the earth, and to O the throne of kingdoms;
2:22 of the nations, and O the chariots and their
2Mac 8:17 city, and besides, the O of their ancestral way
Acts 5:39 not be able to O them.
Rom 3:31 Do we then O the law by this faith?

OVERTHROWEST
Ex 15:7 of thy majesty thou O thy adversaries; thou sendest

OVERTHROWN (17)
Tob 14:4 prophet said about Nineveh, that it will be O
Prov 11:11 exalted, but it is O by the mouth of
12:7 The wicked are O and are no more, but
14:32 The wicked is O through his evil-doing, but the
24:16 but the wicked are O by calamity.
Sir 10:16 The Lord has O the lands of the nations,
27:3 of the Lord, his house will be quickly O
Is 1:7 it is desolate, as O by aliens.
Jer 6:15 time that I punish them, they shall be O
8:12 them, they shall be O, says the LORD.
18:23 Let them be O before thee; deal with them
31:40 not be uprooted or O any more for ever."
49:18 their neighbor cities were O, says the LORD, no
Lam 4:6 of Sodom, which was O in a moment, no
Dan 8:11 him, and the place of his sanctuary was O
Jon 3:4 cried, "Yet forty days, and Nineveh shall be O
1Cor 10:5 pleased; for they were O in the wilderness.

O

OVERTHROWS (3)
Job 12:19 priests away stripped, and O the mighty.
Prov 13:6 is upright, but sin O the wicked.
22:12 over knowledge, but he O the words of the

OVERTOOK (14)
Gen 31:25 And Laban O Jacob.
44:6 When he O them, he spoke to them these
Ex 14:9 and his army, and O them encamped at the
Judg 18:22 called out, and they O the Danites.
20:42 wilderness; but the battle O them, and those who
1Sam 31:2 And the Philistines O Saul and his sons; and
2Kgs 25:5 pursued the king, and O him in the plains
1Chr 10:2 And the Philistines O Saul and his sons; and
Job 31:29 or exulted when evil O him
Ps 18:37 pursued my enemies and O them; and did not
Jer 39:5 Chaldeans pursued them, and O Zedekiah in the
52:8 pursued the king, and O Zedekiah in the plains
1Mac 2:32 Many pursued them, and O them; they encamped
2Mac 4:16 this reason heavy disaster O them, and those whose

OVERTURN
Wis 5:23 earth, and evil-doing will O the thrones of rulers.

OVERTURNED (4)
Sir 28:14 destroyed strong cities, and O the houses of great
Mt 21:12 the temple, and he O the tables of the
Mk 11:15 the temple, and he O the tables of the
Jn 2:15 of the money-changers and O their tables.

OVERTURNS (3)
Job 9:5 it not, when he O them in his anger;
28:9 the flinty rock, and O mountains by the roots.
34:25 knowing their works, he O them in the night,

OVERWHELM (7)
Job 12:15 sends them out, they O the land.
Ps 88:7 me, and thou dost O me with all thy
140:9 mischief of their lips O them!
Wis 5:22 and rivers will relentlessly O them;
Is 28:17 lies, and waters will O the shelter."
43:2 rivers, they shall not O you; when you walk
Hab 2:17 done to Lebanon will O you; the destruction of

OVERWHELMED (7)
Ps 78:53 afraid; but the sea O their enemies.
90:7 by thy anger; by thy wrath we are O
Wis 17:15 sudden and unexpected fear O them.
Ezek 3:15 And I sat there O among them seven days.
Dan 13:10 Both were O with passion for her, but they
1Mac 10:82 was exhausted); they were O by him and fled,
2Cor 2:7 or he may be O by excessive sorrow.

OVERWHELMING (3)
Prov 27:4 is cruel, anger is O; but who can stand
Is 28:15 an agreement; when the O scourge passes through it
28:18 not stand; when the O scourge passes through you

OVERWHELMS (2)
Job 22:10 you, and sudden terror O you;
Ps 55:5 upon me, and horror O me.

OVERWISE
Eccl 7:16 do not make yourself O; why should you destroy

OWE (6)
1Mac 13:39 crown tax which you O; and whatever other tax
15:8 Every debt you O to the royal treasury and
Mt 18:28 said, 'Pay what you O
Lk 16:5 'How much do you O my master?'
16:7 how much do you O He said, 'A hundred
Rom 13:8 O no one anything, except to love one another;

OWED (4)
1Mac 13:15 that Jonathan your brother O the royal treasury, in
Mt 18:23 brought to him who O him ten thousand talents;
18:27 his fellow servants who O him a hundred denarii;
Lk 7:41 had two debtors; one O five hundred denarii, and

OWES (2)
1Mac 10:43 its precincts, because he O money to the king
Philem 1:18 you at all, or O you anything, charge that

OWING
Philem 1:19 say nothing of your O me even your own

OWL (7)
Lev 11:17 to its kind, the O, the cormorant, the ibis,
Deut 14:16 their kinds; the little O and the great owl,
14:16 owl and the great O, the water hen
Ps 102:6 the wilderness, like an O of the waste places;
Is 34:11 shall possess it, the O and the raven shall
34:15 There shall the O nest and lay and hatch
Zeph 2:14 in her capitals; the O shall hoot in the

OWN (677)
Gen 1:12 seed according to their O kinds, and trees bearing
1:27 created man in his O image, in the image
5:3 a son in his O likeness, after his image,
9:6 made man in his O image.
10:5 lands, each with his O language, by their families,
15:4 be your heir; your O son shall be your
30:25 may go to my O home and country.
30:30 I provide for my O household also?"
30:40 and he put his O droves apart, and did
37:27 is our brother, our O flesh." And his brothers
38:23 the things as her O, lest we be laughed
40:5 the prison—each his O dream, and each dream
40:5 each dream with its O meaning.
41:11 a dream with its O meaning.
46:26 Egypt, who were his O offspring, not including
47:24 fifths shall be your O, as seed for the
Ex 5:16 fault is in your O people."
15:17 plant them on thy O mountain, the place, O
18:27 his way to his O country.
19:5 you shall be my O possession among all peoples;
22:5 the best in his O field and in his
22:5 field and in his O vineyard.
32:13 didst swear by thine O self, and didst say
Lev 7:30 shall bring with his O hands the offerings by
14:15 the palm of his O left hand,
14:26 the palm of his O left hand;
18:10 their nakedness is your O nakedness.
19:18 the sons of your O people, but you shall
21:14 a virgin of his O people,
25:41 go back to his O family, and return to
Num 1:52 every man by his O camp and every man
1:52 every man by his O standard;
2:2 encamp each by his O standard, with the ensigns
3:13 I consecrated for my O all the first-born in
10:30 will depart to my O land and to my
15:39 to follow after your O heart and your own
15:39 own heart and your O eyes, which you are
16:28 not been of my O accord.
22:13 Balak, "Go to your O land; for the LORD
24:13 or bad of my O will; what the LORD
27:3 but died for his O sin; and he had
32:42 it Nobah, after his O name.
36:9 shall cleave to its O inheritance.'"
Deut 3:14 the villages after his O name, Havvoth-jair, as it
4:20 a people of his O possession, as at this
4:37 of Egypt with his O presence, by his great
7:6 a people for his O possession, out of all
12:8 is right in his O eyes;
13:6 who is as your O soul, entices you secretly,
14:2 a people for his O possession, out of all
20:1 army larger than your O, you shall not be
24:16 to death for his O sin.
26:18 a people for his O possession, as he has
28:53 the offspring of your O body, the flesh of
Josh 7:11 put them among their O stuff.
20:6 go again to his O town and his own
20:6 own town and his O home, to the town
22:9 land of Gilead, their O land of which they
24:30 buried him in his O inheritance at Timnath-serah,
Judg 3:6 for wives, and their O daughters they gave to
7:2 against me, saying, 'My O hand has delivered me.'
8:29 and dwelt in his O house.
8:30 had seventy sons, his O offspring, for he had
17:6 was right in his O eyes.
21:25 was right in his O eyes.
Ruth 4:6 lest I impair my O inheritance.
1Sam 3:2 lying down in his O place;
5:11 it return to its O place, that it may
6:9 the way to its O land, to Beth-shemesh, then
13:14 a man after his O heart; and the LORD
14:46 Philistines went to their O place.
15:17 are little in your O eyes, are you not
18:1 loved him as his O soul.
18:3 loved him as his O soul.
20:17 as he loved his O soul.
20:30 of Jesse to your O shame, and to the

O

3:7 not wise in your O eyes; fear the LORD,
5:15 Drink water from your O cistern, flowing water from
5:15 flowing water from your O well.
11:5 wicked falls by his O wickedness.
12:15 is right in his O eyes, but a wise
14:1 but folly with her O hands tears it down.
14:10 The heart knows its O bitterness, and no stranger
16:2 are pure in his O eyes, but the LORD
20:6 a man proclaims his O loyalty, but a faithful
21:2 is right in his O eyes, but the LORD
22:16 poor to increase his O wealth, or gives to
26:5 be wise in his O eyes.
26:6 fool cuts off his O feet and drinks violence.
26:12 is wise in his O eyes?
26:16 is wiser in his O eyes than seven men
26:17 a quarrel not his O is like one who
27:2 you, and not your O mouth; a stranger, and
27:2 stranger, and not your O lips.
28:10 will fall into his O pit; but the blameless
28:11 is wise in his O eyes, but a poor
28:26 who trusts in his O mind is a fool;
29:24 a thief hates his O life; he hears the
30:12 are pure in their O eyes but are not
Eccl 4:5 hands, and eats his O flesh.
4:14 throne or in his O kingdom had been born
Song 1:6 the vineyards; but, my O vineyard I have not
8:12 My vineyard, my very O, is for myself; you,
Wis 2:23 the image of his O eternity,
11:13 heard that through their O punishments the righteous
12:23 didst torment through their O abominations.
17:11 condemned by its O testimony; distressed by
19:17 the way through his O door.
Sir 3:5 be gladdened by his O children, and when he
4:22 show partiality, to your O harm, or deference, to
6:8 is such at his O convenience, but will not
9:1 evil lesson to your O hurt.
10:28 man that dishonors his O life?
13:5 If you O something, he will live with you;
13:13 walking about with your O downfall.
14:5 will not enjoy his O riches.
15:14 the power of his O inclination.
15:15 a matter of your O choice.
17:3 with strength like his O, and made them in
17:3 made them in his O image.
17:14 Israel is the Lord's O portion.
21:27 adversary, he curses his O soul.
21:28 A whisperer defiles his O soul and is hated
27:23 speech and with your O words he will give
27:25 throws it on his O head; and a treacherous
28:4 yet pray for his O sins?
31:15 neighbor's feelings by your O, and in every matter
33:31 brother, for as your O soul you will need
37:7 give counsel in their O interest.
37:13 the counsel of your O heart, for no one
37:22 be wise to his O advantage, and the fruits
37:23 man will instruct his O people, and the fruits
38:31 is skilful in his O work.
Is 2:8 hands, to what their O fingers have made.
4:1 "We will eat our O bread and wear our
4:1 bread and wear our O clothes, only let us
5:21 are wise in their O eyes, and shrewd in
5:21 and shrewd in their O sight!
13:14 will turn to his O people, and every man
13:14 will flee to his O land.
14:1 set them in their O land, and aliens will
14:18 glory, each in his O tomb;
17:8 look to what their O fingers have made, either
36:12 you to eat their O dung and drink their
36:12 dung and drink their O urine?"
36:16 will eat of his O vine, and every one
36:16 every one of his O fig tree, and every
36:16 the water of his O cistern;
36:17 a land like your O land, a land of
37:7 and return to his O land; and I will
37:7 the sword in his O land.'"
37:35 save it, for my O sake and for the
39:7 And some of your O sons, who are born
43:25 your transgressions for my O sake, and I will
47:15 about each in his O direction; there is no
48:11 For my O sake, for my own sake, I
48:11 own sake, for my O sake, I do it,
49:26 your oppressors eat their O flesh, and they shall
49:26 be drunk with their O blood as with wine.
53:6 every one to his O way; and the LORD
56:11 all turned to their O way, each to his
56:11 way, each to his O gain, one and all.
57:17 the way of his O heart.
58:3 fast you seek your O pleasure, and oppress all
58:7 hide yourself from your O flesh?
58:13 it, not going your O ways, or seeking your
58:13 ways, or seeking your O pleasure, or talking idly;
59:16 to intervene; then his O arm brought him victory,
63:5 to uphold; so my O arm brought me victory,
65:2 not good, following their O devices;
66:3 These have chosen their O ways, and their soul
Jer 1:16 the works of their O hands.
2:30 no correction; your O sword devoured your prophets
3:15 you shepherds after my O heart, who will feed
3:17 more stubbornly follow their O evil heart.
7:6 other gods to your O hurt,
7:19 not themselves, to their O confusion?
7:24 but walked in their O counsels and the stubbornness
8:6 one turns to his O course, like a horse
9:14 have stubbornly followed their O hearts and have
13:10 who stubbornly follow their O heart and have gone
14:14 the deceit of their O minds.
16:15 them back to their O land which I gave
18:12 We will follow our O plans, and will every
23:8 shall dwell in their O land."
23:16 speak visions of their O minds, not from the
23:17 who stubbornly follows his O heart, they say, 'No
23:26 the deceit of their O heart,
23:36 burden is every man's O word, and you pervert
25:7 your hands to your O harm.
26:11 have heard with your O ears."
27:7 the time of his O land comes; then many
27:11 will leave on its O land, to till it
31:17 come back to their O country.
31:30 shall die for his O sin; each man who
32:39 for ever, for their O good and the good
37:7 to Egypt, to its O land.
42:12 you remain in your O land.
44:9 of their wives, your O wickedness, and the
46:16 go back to our O people and to the
50:16 shall turn to his O people, and every one
50:16 shall flee to his O land.
51:9 go each to his O country; for her judgment
Lam 4:10 women have boiled their O children; they became
Bar 1:21 the intent of his O wicked heart by serving
2:14 supplication, and for thy O sake deliver us, and
4:33 be grieved at her O desolation.
6:54 They cannot judge their O cause or deliver one
Ezek 6:9 be loathsome in their O sight for the evils
7:27 and according to their O judgments I will judge
11:21 their deeds upon their O heads, says the Lord
12:7 the wall with my O hands; I went forth
13:2 prophesy out of their O minds: 'Hear the word
13:3 prophets who follow their O spirit, and have seen
13:17 prophesy out of their O minds; prophesy against them
14:14 would deliver but their O lives by their righteousness,
14:20 would deliver but their O lives by their righteousness.
16:53 I will restore your O fortunes in the midst
27:15 many coastlands were your O special markets, they
28:25 shall dwell in their O land which I gave
29:3 'My Nile is my O; I made it.'
32:10 every one for his O life, on the day
33:4 shall be upon his O head.
33:17 when it is their O way that is not
34:13 bring them into their O land; and I will
36:17 Israel dwelt in their O land, they defiled it
36:24 bring you into your O land.
37:14 place you in your O land; then you shall
37:21 bring them to their O land;
39:28 gathered them into their O land.
46:18 inheritance out of his O property, so that none
Dan 1:10 who are of your O age.
3:96 any god except their O God.
6:17 sealed it with his O signet and with the
8:25 hand, and in his O mind he shall magnify
9:17 supplications, and for thy O sake, O Lord, cause
9:19 delay not, for thy O sake, O my God,
11:9 shall return into his O land.
11:14 of violence among your O people shall lift themselves
11:16 do according to his O will, and none shall
11:19 the fortresses of his O land; but he shall
11:28 and return to his O land.
13:55 have lied against your O head, for the angel
13:59 have lied against your O head, for the angel
13:61 for out of their O mouths Daniel had convicted
14:4 But Daniel worshiped his O God.
14:39 returned Habakkuk to his O place.
Hos 8:4 made idols for their O destruction.

 OWN

Joel	3:4	your deed upon your O head swiftly and speedily.
	3:6	them far from their O border.
	3:7	your deed upon your O head.
Amos	6:13	we not by our O strength taken Karnaim for
Obad	1:15	shall return on your O head.
	1:17	Jacob shall possess their O possessions.
Mic	7:6	the men of his O house.
Hab	1:6	of the earth, to seize habitations not their O
	1:11	on, guilty men, whose O might is their god!
	2:5	and collects as his O all peoples."
	2:6	what is not his O--for how long?--and
	2:18	workman trusts in his O creation when he makes
Hag	1:9	yourselves each with his O house.
Zech	9:8	I see with my O eyes.
	11:5	become rich'; and their O shepherds have no pity
Mal	1:5	Your O eyes shall see this, and you shall
1Mac	1:8	rule, each in his O place.
	1:24	he departed to his O land.
	6:54	scattered, each to his O place.
	9:9	us rather save our O lives now, and let
	9:69	to depart to his O land.
	9:72	and departed to his O land, and came no
	10:13	and departed to his O land.
	10:32	it men of his O choice to guard it.
	10:37	leaders be of their O number, and let them
	10:37	them live by their O laws, just as the
	10:72	to flight in their O land.
	11:1	add it to his O kingdom.
	11:38	each man to his O place, except the foreign
	12:25	opportunity to invade his O country.
	13:24	and departed to his O land.
	14:32	great sums of his O money; he armed the
	15:6	you to mint your O coinage as money for
2Mac	3:3	Asia, defrayed from his O revenues all the expenses
	3:30	acted marvelously for his O place.
	3:36	had seen with his O eyes.
	4:1	the money against his O country, slandered Onias,
	4:21	took measures for his O security.
	4:26	who after supplanting his O brother was supplanted
	4:29	Menelaus left his O brother Lysimachus as deputy in
	5:9	driven many from their O country into exile died
	6:16	does not forsake his O people.
	6:19	the rack of his O accord, spitting out the
	6:21	bring meat of his O providing, proper for him
	7:18	these things on our O account, because of our
	7:18	our sins against our O God.
	7:32	suffering because of our O sins.
	7:33	be reconciled with his O servants.
	8:15	if not for their O sake, yet for the
	8:30	also to the aged, shares equal to their O
	8:35	the destruction of his O army!
	9:12	could not endure his O stench, he uttered these
	9:16	would provide from his O revenues;
	10:7	the purifying of his O holy place.
	10:30	protecting him with their O armor and weapons, they
	11:23	in caring for their O affairs.
	11:24	customs but prefer their O way of living and
	11:24	and ask that their O customs be allowed them.
	11:26	the conduct of their O affairs."
	11:29	and look after your O affairs.
	11:31	Jews to enjoy their O food and laws, just
	12:22	were injured by their O men and pierced by
	12:42	had seen with their O eyes what had happened
	14:15	him who established his O people for ever and
	14:15	and always upholds his O heritage by manifesting
	14:41	Razis fell upon his O sword,
	15:34	who has kept his O place undefiled."
Mt	2:12	they departed to their O country by another way.
	6:34	Let the day's O trouble be sufficient for the
	7:3	that is in your O eye?
	7:4	the log in your O eye?
	7:5	log out of your O eye, and then you
	8:22	dead to bury their O dead."
	9:1	and came to his O city.
	10:36	be those of his O household.
	13:54	and coming to his O country he taught them
	13:57	honor except in his O country and in his
	13:57	country and in his O house."
	25:27	received what was my O with interest.
	27:31	robe, and put his O clothes on him, and
	27:60	laid it in his O new tomb, which he
Mk	4:34	but privately to his O disciples he explained
	6:1	and came to his O country; and his disciples
	6:4	honor, except in his O country, and among his
	6:4	country, and among his O kin, and in his
	6:4	kin, and in his O house."
	15:20	cloak, and put his O clothes on him.
Lk	2:3	enrolled, each to his O city.
	2:35	will pierce through your O soul also), that thoughts
	2:39	into Galilee, to their O city, Nazareth.
	4:23	here also in your O country.'"
	4:24	is acceptable in his O country.
	6:41	that is in your O eye?
	6:42	that is in your O eye?
	6:42	log out of your O eye, and then you
	6:44	is known by its O fruit.
	9:60	dead to bury their O dead; but as for
	10:34	set him on his O beast and brought him
	11:21	fully armed, guards his O palace, his goods are
	14:26	does not hate his O father and mother and
	14:26	yes, and even his O life, he cannot be
	14:27	does not bear his O cross and come after
	16:8	in dealing with their O generation than the sons
	16:12	who will give you that which is your O
	19:22	you out of your O mouth, you wicked servant!
	22:69	it ourselves from his O lips."
Jn	1:11	He came to his O home, and his own
	1:11	own home, and his O people received him not.
	4:44	no honor in his O country.
	5:18	do nothing of his O accord, but only what
	5:29	do nothing on my O authority; as I hear,
	5:29	I seek not my O will but the will
	5:42	another comes in his O name, him you will
	6:38	not to do my O will, but the will
	7:17	am speaking on my O authority.
	7:18	who speaks on his O authority seeks his own
	7:18	own authority seeks his O glory; but he who
	7:28	not come of my O accord; he who sent
	7:53	went each to his O house.
	8:28	do nothing on my O authority but speak thus
	8:42	came not of my O accord, but he sent
	8:44	speaks according to his O nature, for he is
	8:50	do not seek my O glory; there is One
	10:3	and he calls his O sheep by name and
	10:4	brought out all his O, he goes before them,
	10:12	not a shepherd, whose O the sheep are not,
	10:14	shepherd; I know my O and my own know
	10:14	my own and my O know me,
	10:18	it down of my O accord.
	11:51	say this of his O accord, but being high
	12:49	not spoken on my O authority; the Father who
	13:1	Father, having loved his O who were in the
	14:10	not speak on my O authority; but the Father
	15:19	world would love its O; but because you are
	16:13	not speak on his O authority, but whatever he
	17:5	thou me in thy O presence with the glory
	18:31	judge him by your O law." The Jews said
	18:34	say this of your O accord, or did others
	18:35	Your O nation and the chief priests have handed
	19:17	went out, bearing his O cross, to the place
	19:27	took her to his O home.
Acts	1:7	has fixed by his O authority.
	1:25	to go to his O place."
	2:6	them speaking in his O language.
	2:8	of us in his O native language?
	2:11	them telling in our O tongues the mighty works
	3:12	as though by our O power or piety we
	4:32	he possessed was his O, but they had everything
	5:4	it remained unsold, did it not remain your O
	7:21	him up as her O son.
	12:10	to them of its O accord, and they went
	13:36	of God in his O generation, fell asleep, and
	14:16	to walk in their O ways;
	18:15	and names and your O law, see to it
	20:28	which he obtained with the blood of his O
	20:30	and from among your O selves will arise men
	21:11	girdle and bound his O feet and hands, and
	25:19	with him about their O superstition and about one
	26:4	the beginning among my O nation and at Jerusalem,
	27:19	cast out with their O hands the tackle of
	28:29	whole years at his O expense, and welcomed all
Rom	1:27	and receiving in their O persons the due penalty
	4:19	when he considered his O body, which was as
	7:15	do not understand my O actions.
	8:3	not do: sending his O Son in the likeness
	8:20	futility, not of its O will but by the
	8:32	did not spare his O Son but gave him
	10:3	seeking to establish their O, they did not submit
	11:24	grafted back into their O olive tree.
	11:25	be wise in your O conceits, I want you
	14:4	It is before his O master that he stands
	14:5	fully convinced in his O mind.

O

O

28:31 Your O shall be slain before your eyes, and
33:17 horns of a wild O; with them he shall
Judg 6:4 and no sheep or O or ass.
1Sam 12:3 Whose O have I taken?
14:34 every man bring his O or his sheep, and
14:34 the people brought his O with him that night,
15:3 woman, infant and suckling, O and sheep, camel and
2Sam 6:13 paces, he sacrificed an O and a fatling.
Neh 5:18 one day was one O and six choice sheep;
Jud 8:1 Merari the son of O, son of Joseph, son
Job 6:5 has grass, or the O low over his fodder?
24:3 they take the widow's O for a pledge.
39:9 "Is the wild O willing to serve you?
40:15 I made you; he eats grass like an O
Ps 29:6 a calf, and Sirion like a young wild O
69:31 LORD more than an O or a bull with
92:10 that of the wild O; thou hast poured over
106:20 the image of an O that eats grass.
Prov 7:22 follows her, as an O goes to the slaughter,
14:4 abundant crops come by the strength of the O
15:17 is than a fatted O and hatred with it.
Sir 26:7 evil wife is an O yoke which chafes; taking
Is 1:3 The O knows its owner, and the ass its
11:7 and the lion shall eat straw like the O
32:20 the feet of the O and the ass range
65:25 eat straw like the O; and dust shall be
66:3 "He who slaughters an O is like him who
Ezek 1:10 the face of an O on the left side,
Dan 4:25 eat grass like an O, and you shall be
4:32 eat grass like an O; and seven times shall
4:33 ate grass like an O, and his body was
5:21 fed grass like an O, and his body was
Lk 13:15 the sabbath untie his O or his ass from
14:5 an ass or an O that has fallen into
1Cor 9:9 shall not muzzle an O when it is treading
1Tim 5:18 shall not muzzle an O when it is treading
Rev 4:7 living creature like an O, the third living creature

OXEN (89)
Gen 12:16 had sheep, O, he-asses, menservants, maidservants,
20:14 Abimelech took sheep and O, and male and female
21:27 Abraham took sheep and O and gave them to
32:5 now; and I have O, asses, flocks, menservants, and
49:6 slay men, and in their wantonness they hamstring O
Ex 20:24 your sheep and your O; in every place where
22:1 he shall pay five O for an ox, and
22:30 do likewise with your O and with your sheep:
24:5 sacrificed peace offerings of O to the LORD.
Num 7:3 covered wagons and twelve O, a wagon for every
7:6 the wagons and the O, and gave them to
7:7 Two wagons and four O he gave to the
7:8 four wagons and eight O he gave to the
7:17 of peace offerings, two O, five rams, five male
7:23 of peace offerings, two O, five rams, five male
7:29 of peace offerings, two O, five rams, five male
7:35 of peace offerings, two O, five rams, five male
7:41 of peace offerings, two O, five rams, five male
7:47 of peace offerings, two O, five rams, five male
7:53 of peace offerings, two O, five rams, five male
7:59 of peace offerings, two O, five rams, five male
7:65 of peace offerings, two O, five rams, five male
7:71 of peace offerings, two O, five rams, five male
7:77 of peace offerings, two O, five rams, five male
7:83 of peace offerings, two O, five rams, five male
22:40 And Balak sacrificed O and sheep, and sent to
31:28 persons and of the O and of the asses
31:30 the persons, of the O, of the asses, and
Deut 14:26 for whatever you desire, O, or sheep, or wine
Josh 6:21 women, young and old, O, sheep, and asses, with
7:24 and daughters, and his O and asses and sheep,
1Sam 11:5 the field behind the O; and Saul said, "What
11:7 took a yoke of O, and cut them in
11:7 Samuel, so shall it be done to his O
14:32 and took sheep and O and calves, and slew
15:9 sheep and of the O and of the fatlings,
15:14 the lowing of the O which I hear?"
15:15 sheep and of the O, to sacrifice to the
15:21 the spoil, sheep and O, the best of the
22:19 women, children and sucklings, O, asses and sheep,
27:9 away the sheep, the O, the asses, the camels,
2Sam 6:6 of it, for the O stumbled.
24:22 him; here are the O for the burnt offering,
24:22 the yokes of the O for the wood.
24:24 threshing floor and the O for fifty shekels of
1Kgs 1:9 Adonijah sacrificed sheep, O, and fatlings by the
1:19 He has sacrificed O, fatlings, and sheep in abundance,
1:25 day, and has sacrificed O, fatlings, and sheep in
4:23 of meal, ten fat O, and twenty pasture-fed cattle,
7:25 It stood upon twelve O, three facing north, three
7:29 the frames were lions, O, and cherubim.
7:29 below the lions and O, there were wreaths of
7:44 sea, and the twelve O underneath the sea.
8:5 so many sheep and O that they could not
8:63 the LORD twenty-two thousand O and a hundred and
19:19 with twelve yoke of O before him, and he
19:20 And he left the O, and ran after Elijah,
19:21 took the yoke of O, and slew them, and
19:21 the yokes of the O, and gave it to
2Kgs 5:26 and vineyards, sheep and O, menservants and
16:17 from off the bronze O that were under it,
1Chr 12:40 on mules and on O, abundant provisions of meal,
12:40 and wine and oil, O and sheep, for there
13:9 the ark, for the O stumbled.
21:23 see, I give the O for burnt offerings, and
2Chr 4:4 It stood upon twelve O, three facing north, three
4:15 sea, and the twelve O underneath it.
5:6 so many sheep and O that they could not
7:5 a sacrifice twenty-two thousand O and a hundred and
15:11 had brought, seven hundred O and seven thousand
18:2 abundance of sheep and O for him and for
Jud 2:17 and innumerable sheep and O and goats for
Job 1:3 five hundred yoke of O, and five hundred she-asses,
1:14 Job, and said, "The O were plowing and the
42:12 a thousand yoke of O, and a thousand she-asses.
Ps 8:7 feet, all sheep and O, and also the beasts
22:21 afflicted soul from the horns of the wild O
Prov 14:4 Where there are no O, there is no grain;
Sir 38:25 a goad, who drives O and is occupied with
Is 22:13 joy and gladness, slaying O and killing sheep, eating
30:24 large pastures; and the O and the asses that
34:7 Wild O shall fall with them, and young steers
Amos 6:12 Does one plow the sea with O
Mt 22:4 ready my dinner, my O and my fat calves
Lk 14:19 bought five yoke of O, and I go to
Jn 2:14 those who were selling O and sheep and pigeons,
2:15 with the sheep and O, out of the temple;
Acts 14:13 of the city, brought O and garlands to the
1Cor 9:9 Is it for O that God is concerned?

OXGOAD
Judg 3:31 the Philistines with an O; and he too delivered

OZEM (2)
1Chr 2:15 fourth, Raddai the fifth, O the sixth, David the
2:25 his first-born, Bunah, Oren, O, and Ahijah.

OZIEL
Jud 8:1 of Joseph, son of O, son of Elkiah, son

OZNI
Num 26:16 of the Shunites; of O, the family of the

OZNITES
Num 26:16 the family of the O; of Eri, the family

P

PAARAI
2Sam 23:35 Gilo, Hezro of Carmel, P the Arbite,

PACE (3)
Gen 33:14 slowly, according to the P of the cattle which
33:14 and according to the P of the children, until
2Kgs 4:24 do not slacken the P for me unless I

PACES
2Sam 6:13 LORD had gone six P, he sacrificed an ox

PADDAN
Gen 48:7 when I came from P, Rachel to my sorrow

PADDAN-ARAM (10)
Gen 25:20 Bethuel the Aramean of P, the sister of Laban
28:2 Arise, go to P to the house of Bethuel
28:5 and he went to P to Laban, the son
28:6 sent him away to P to take a wife
28:7 his father and his mother and gone to P
31:18 he had acquired in P, to go to the
33:18 on his way from P; and he camped before
35:9 when he came from P, and blessed him.

35:26 of Jacob who were born to him in P
46:15 bore to Jacob in P, together with his daughter

PADON (2)

Ezra 2:44 Siaha, the sons of P,
Neh 7:47 Sia, the sons of P,

PAGANS (2)

1Cor 5:1 not found even among P; for a man is
10:20 I imply that what P sacrifice they offer to

PAGIEL (5)

Num 1:13 of Ammishaddai; from Asher, P the son of Ochran;
2:27 people of Asher being P the son of Ochran,
7:72 On the eleventh day P the son of Ochran,
7:77 was the offering of P the son of Ochran.
10:26 men of Asher was P the son of Ochran.

PAHATH-MOAB (6)

Ezra 2:6 The sons of P, namely the sons of Jeshua
8:4 Of the sons of P, Eli-e-ho-enai the son of
10:30 Of the sons of P: Adna, Chelal, Benaiah, Ma-aseiah,
Neh 3:11 Hasshub the son of P repaired another section and
7:11 The sons of P, namely the sons of Jeshua
10:14 of the people: Parosh, P, Elam, Zattu, Bani,

PAI

1Chr 1:50 of his city was P, and his wife's name

PAID (33)

Gen 39:23 keeper of the prison P no heed to anything
Lev 25:51 out of the price P for him the price
2Kgs 12:11 the LORD; and they P it out to the
17:3 became his vassal, and P him tribute.
1Chr 21:25 So David P Ornan six hundred shekels of gold
2Chr 26:8 The Ammonites P tribute to Uzziah, and his fame
27:5 The Ammonites P him the same amount in the
Ezra 4:20 River, to whom tribute, custom, and toll were P
6:4 let the cost be P from the royal treasury.
6:8 cost is to be P to these men in
Tob 2:12 Once when they P her wages, they also gave
Job 15:32 It will be P in full before his time,
Prov 7:14 and today I have P my vows;
Jon 1:3 to Tarshish; so he P the fare, and went
Zech 11:13 at which I was P off by them.
1Mac 7:11 But they P no attention to their words, for
8:4 upon them; the rest P them tribute every year.
10:41 government officials have not P as they did in
10:44 of the sanctuary be P from the revenues of
10:45 in Judea, also be P from the revenues of
10:61 him; but the king P no attention to them.
10:64 the honor that was P him, in accordance with
11:60 city met him and P him honor.
14:32 his nation's forces and P them wages.
14:39 the king's friends and P him high honors.
Mt 5:26 out till you have P the last penny.
26:15 And they P him thirty pieces of silver.
Lk 12:59 out till you have P the very last copper."
Acts 18:17 But Gallio P no attention to this.
27:11 But the centurion P more attention to the captain
Col 3:25 the wrongdoer will be P back for the wrong
Heb 7:9 who receives tithes, P tithes through Abraham,
8:9 covenant, and so I P no heed to them,

PAIN (45)

Gen 3:16 will greatly multiply your P in childbearing; in pain
3:16 pain in childbearing; in P you shall bring forth
Num 5:24 curse shall enter into her and cause bitter P
5:27 her and cause bitter P, and her body shall
1Chr 4:9 name Jabez, saying, "Because I bore him in P
Jud 16:17 they shall weep in P for ever.
Job 6:10 would even exult in P unsparing; for I have
14:22 He feels only the P of his own body,
15:20 wicked man writhes in P all his days, through
16:5 the solace of my lips would assuage your P
16:6 "If I speak, my P is not assuaged, and
30:17 my bones, and the P that gnaws me takes
33:19 is also chastened with P upon his bed, and
Ps 13:2 long must I bear P in my soul, and
38:17 to fall, and my P is ever with me.
69:29 am afflicted and in P; let thy salvation, O
Eccl 2:23 days are full of P, and his work is
11:10 mind, and put away P from your body; for
Wis 8:16 with her has no P, but gladness and joy.
Sir 27:29 in a snare, and P will consume them before
38:7 heals and takes away P;
Is 14:3 you rest from your P and turmoil and the
17:11 away in a day of grief and incurable P
65:14 shall cry out for P of heart, and shall
66:7 gave birth; before her P came upon her she
Jer 4:19 I writhe in P
6:24 taken hold of us, P as of a woman
15:18 Why is my P unceasing, my wound incurable,
22:23 pangs come upon you, P as of a woman
30:15 Your P is incurable.
45:3 added sorrow to my P; I am weary with
50:43 helpless; anguish seized him, P as of a woman
51:8 Take balm for her P; perhaps she may be
51:29 trembles and writhes in P, for the LORD's purposes
2Mac 3:17 looked at him the P lodged in his heart.
9:5 was seized with a P in his bowels for
9:9 living in anguish and P, his flesh rotted away,
9:11 he was tortured with P every moment.
2Cor 2:2 if I cause you P, who is there to
2:3 I might not suffer P from those who should
2:4 not to cause you P but to let you
2:5 any one has caused P, he has caused it
1Pet 2:19 of God, he endures P while suffering unjustly.
Rev 16:11 of heaven for their P and sores, and did
21:4 mourning nor crying nor P any more, for the

PAINED

2Cor 2:2 me glad but the one whom I have P

PAINFUL (3)

Sir 13:25 to devise proverbs requires P thinking.
2Cor 2:1 to make you another P visit.
Heb 12:11 moment all discipline seems P rather than pleasant;

PAINFULLY

Mk 6:48 they were making headway P, for the wind was

PAINS (7)

1Sam 4:19 gave birth; for her P came upon her.
1Chr 22:14 With great P I have provided for the house
Job 21:17 That God distributes P in his anger?
Sir 30:13 your son and take P with him, that you
Dan 10:16 reason of the vision P have come upon me,
Mt 4:24 various diseases and P, demoniacs, epileptics,
Acts 24:15 So I always take P to have a clear

PAINT (3)

Wis 13:14 a coat of red P and coloring its surface
13:14 blemish in it with P;
Jer 4:30 of gold, that you enlarge your eyes with P

PAINTED (2)

2Kgs 9:30 of it; and she P her eyes, and adorned
Ezek 23:40 them you bathed yourself, P your eyes, and decked

PAINTERS

Wis 15:4 the fruitless toil of P, a figure stained with

PAINTING (3)

Sir 38:27 sets his heart on P a lifelike image, and
Jer 22:14 it with cedar, and P it with vermilion.
2Mac 2:29 one who undertakes its P and decoration has to

PAIR (8)

Gen 7:2 his mate; and a P of the animals that
Ex 25:35 with it under each P of the six branches
37:21 with it under each P of the six branches
Judg 15:4 a torch between each P of tails.
Sir 46:19 so much as a P of shoes." And no
Amos 2:6 the needy for a P of shoes—
8:6 the needy for a P of sandals, and sell
Lk 2:24 of the Lord, "a P of turtledoves, or two

PAIRS (5)

Gen 7:2 Take with you seven P of all clean animals,
7:3 his mate; and seven P of the birds of
Sir 33:15 they likewise are in P, one the opposite of
Is 21:7 sees riders, horsemen in P, riders on asses, riders
21:9 And, behold, here come riders, horsemen in P

PALACE (51)

1Kgs 4:6 in charge of the P; and Adoniram the son
21:1 in Jezreel, beside the P of Ahab king of
2Kgs 10:5 who was over the P, and he who was
11:6 guards), shall guard the P;
16:18 been built inside the P, and the outer entrance
20:18 be eunuchs in the P of the king of

P

24:12 his princes, and his P officials.
1Chr 28:1 sons, together with the P officials, the mighty men,
29:1 is great; for the P will not be for
29:19 he may build the P for which I have
2Chr 2:1 LORD, and a royal P for himself.
2:12 LORD, and a royal P for himself.
28:7 the commander of the P and Elkanah the next
36:7 put them in his P in Babylon.
Ezra 4:14 the salt of the P and it is not
Jud 2:1 was talk in the P of Nebuchadnezzar king of
2:18 amount of gold and silver from the royal P
Esth 1:5 the court of the garden of the king's P
1:8 the officials of his P to do as every
1:9 the women in the P which belonged to King
2:8 taken into the king's P and put in custody
2:9 maids from the king's P, and advanced her and
2:13 with her from the harem to the king's P
2:16 Ahasuerus into his royal P in the tenth month,
4:13 that in the king's P you will escape any
5:1 court of the king's P, opposite the king's hall.
5:1 royal throne inside the P opposite the entrance to
5:1 the entrance to the P;
6:4 court of the king's P to speak to the
7:7 and went into the P garden; but Haman stayed
7:8 king returned from the P garden to the place
Ps 45:15 as they enter the P of the king.
144:12 the structure of a P;
Is 25:2 city a ruin; the P of aliens is a
32:14 For the P will be forsaken, the populous city
39:7 be eunuchs in the P of the king of
Jer 30:18 its mound, and the P shall stand where it
32:2 which was in the P of the king of
43:9 the entrance to Pharaoh's P in Tahpanhes, in the
Bar 6:59 wooden pillar in a P, than these false gods.
Dan 1:4 serve in the king's P, and to teach them
4:4 ease in my house and prospering in my P
4:29 roof of the royal P of Babylon,
5:5 wall of the king's P, opposite the lampstand; and
6:18 king went to his P, and spent the night
Nah 2:6 gates are opened, the P is in dismay;
1Mac 7:2 was entering the royal P of his fathers, the
11:46 But the king fled into the P
Mt 26:3 people gathered in the P of the high priest,
Mk 15:16 him away inside the P (that is, the praetorium);
Lk 11:21 armed, guards his own P, his goods are in

PALACES (12)

2Chr 36:19 and burned all its P with fire, and destroyed
Ps 45:8 From ivory P stringed instruments make you glad;
Prov 30:28 in your hands, yet it is in kings' P
Is 13:22 jackals in the pleasant P; its time is close
23:13 siegetowers, they razed her P, they made her a
Jer 6:5 let us attack by night, and destroy her P
9:21 it has entered our P, cutting off the children
17:27 it shall devour the P of Jerusalem and shall
Lam 2:5 has destroyed all its P, laid in ruins its
2:7 the walls of her P; a clamor was raised
Hos 8:14 his Maker, and built P; and Judah has multiplied
1Mac 2:10 has not inherited her P and has not seized

PALAL

Neh 3:25 P the son of Uzai repaired opposite the Angle

PALANQUIN

Song 3:9 Solomon made himself a P from the wood of

PALATE (3)

Job 12:11 try words as the P tastes food?
34:3 tests words as the P tastes food.
Sir 36:19 As the P tastes the kinds of game, so

PALATIAL

Dan 11:45 he shall pitch his P tents between the sea

PALE (6)

Esth 15:7 queen faltered, and turned P and faint, and collapsed
Is 29:22 be ashamed, no more shall his face grow P
Jer 30:6 Why has every face turned P
Joel 2:6 them peoples are in anguish, all faces grow P
Nah 2:10 anguish is on all loins, all faces grow P
Rev 6:8 saw, and behold, a P horse, and its rider's

PALL

Wis 11:18 belch forth a thick P of smoke, or flash

PALLET (9)

Mk 2:4 they let down the P on which the paralytic
2:9 Rise, take up your P and walk?
2:11 rise, take up your P and go home."
2:12 immediately took up the P and went out before
Jn 5:7 "Rise, take up your P, and walk."
5:8 he took up his P and walked.
5:9 is not lawful for you to carry your P
5:10 me, 'Take up your P, and walk.'"
5:11 you, 'Take up your P, and walk'?"

PALLETS (2)

Mk 6:55 sick people on their P to any place where
Acts 5:15 them on beds and P, that as Peter came

PALLU (5)

Gen 46:9 sons of Reuben: Hanoch, P, Hezron, and Carmi.
Ex 6:14 first-born of Israel: Hanoch, P, Hezron, and Carmi;
Num 26:5 of the Hanochites; of P, the family of the
26:8 And the sons of P: Eliab.
1Chr 5:3 first-born of Israel: Hanoch, P, Hezron, and Carmi.

PALLUITES

Num 26:5 the family of the P;

PALM (41)

Ex 15:27 of water and seventy P trees; and they encamped
Lev 14:15 pour it into the P of his own left
14:26 the oil into the P of his own left
23:40 goodly trees, branches of P trees, and boughs of
Num 33:9 of water and seventy P trees, and they encamped
Deut 34:3 Jericho the city of P trees, as far as
Judg 4:5 to sit under the P of Deborah between Ramah
1Kgs 6:29 figures of cherubim and P trees and open flowers,
6:32 with carvings of cherubim, P trees, and open flowers;
6:32 cherubim and upon the P trees.
6:35 he carved cherubim and P trees and open flowers;
7:36 carved cherubim, lions, and P trees, according to the
2Chr 28:15 Jericho, the city of P trees.
Neh 8:15 olive, wild olive, myrtle, P, and other leafy trees
Ps 92:12 righteous flourish like the P tree, and grow like
Song 7:7 are stately as a P tree, and your breasts
7:8 I will climb the P tree and lay hold
Sir 24:14 grew tall like a P tree in En-ge'di, and
50:12 like the trunks of P trees,
Is 9:14 Israel head and tail, P branch and reed in
19:15 which head or tail, P branch or reed, may
Ezek 40:16 on the jambs were P trees.
40:22 its vestibule, and its P trees were of the
40:26 inside; and it had P trees on its jambs,
40:31 the outer court, and P trees were on its
40:34 court, and it had P trees on its jambs,
40:37 court, and it had P trees on its jambs,
41:18 likenesses of cherubim and P trees, a palm tree
41:18 and palm trees, a P tree between cherub and
41:19 a man toward the P tree on the one
41:19 young lion toward the P tree on the other
41:20 the door cherubim and P trees were carved on
41:25 were carved cherubim and P trees, such as were
41:26 were recessed windows and P trees on either side,
Joel 1:11 Pomegranate, P, and apple, all the trees of the
1Mac 13:37 gold crown and the P branch which you sent,
13:51 it with praise and P branches, and with harps
2Mac 10:7 and also fronds of P, they offered hymns of
14:4 of gold and a P, and besides these some
Jn 12:13 they took branches of P trees and went out
Rev 7:9 in white robes, with P branches in their hands,

PALMS (5)

Judg 1:16 from the city of P into the wilderness of
3:13 and they took possession of the city of P
2Kgs 9:35 the feet and the P of her hands.
2Chr 3:5 fine gold, and made P and chains on it.
Is 49:16 graven you on the P of my hands; your

PALSIED

Ezek 7:27 of the land are P by terror.

PALTI (2)

Num 13:9 the tribe of Benjamin, P the son of Raphu;
1Sam 25:44 daughter, David's wife, to P the son of Laish,

PALTIEL (2)

Num 34:26 of Issachar a leader, P the son of Azzan.
2Sam 3:15 her from her husband P the son of Laish.

P

PALTITE
2Sam 23:26 of Harod, Helez the P, Ira the son of

PALTRY
Wis 10:4 righteous man by a P piece of wood.

PAMPER
Sir 30:9 P a child, and he will frighten you; play

PAMPERS
Prov 29:21 He who P his servant from childhood, will in

PAMPHYLIA (6)
1Mac 15:23 to Samos, and to P, and to Lycia, and
Acts 2:10 and Asia, Phrygia and P, Egypt and the parts
13:13 sail from Paphos, and came to Perga in P
14:24 Then they passed through Pisidia, and came to P
15:37 withdrawn from them in P, and had not gone
27:5 is off Cilicia and P, we came to Myra

PAN (6)
Lev 2:7 offering cooked in a P, it shall be made
7:9 is prepared on a P or a griddle shall
1Sam 2:14 thrust it into the P, or kettle, or caldron,
2Sam 13:9 And she took the P and emptied it out
2Mac 7:5 still breathing, and to fry him in a P
7:5 The smoke from the P spread widely, but the

PANELED (3)
Ezek 41:16 the outer vestibule were P and round about all
41:16 threshold the temple was P with wood round about,
Hag 1:4 to dwell in your P houses, while this house

PANELING
Jer 22:14 out windows for it, P it with cedar, and

PANELS (7)
1Kgs 7:28 the stands: they had P, and the panels were
7:28 had panels, and the P were set in the
7:29 frames and on the P that were set in
7:31 were carvings; and its P were square, not round.
7:32 wheels were underneath the P; the axles of the
7:35 its stays and its P were of one piece
7:36 stays and on its P, he carved cherubim, lions,

PANGS (19)
Ex 15:14 have heard, they tremble; P have seized on the
1Sam 25:31 cause of grief, or P of conscience, for having
Ps 32:10 Many are the P of the wicked; but steadfast
73:4 For they have no P; their bodies are sound
116:3 death encompassed me; the P of Sheol laid hold
Sir 19:11 a fool will suffer P like a woman in
Is 13:8 P and agony will seize them; they will be
21:3 are filled with anguish; P have seized me, like
21:3 seized me, like the P of a woman in
26:17 cries out in her P, when she is near
Jer 13:21 Will not P take hold of you, like those
22:23 you will groan when P come upon you, pain
48:41 a woman in her P;
49:22 like the heart of a woman in her P
Hos 13:13 The P of childbirth come for him, but he
Mic 4:9 your counselor perished, that P have seized you like
Acts 2:24 up, having loosed the P of death, because it
1Tim 6:10 the faith and pierced their hearts with many P
Rev 12:2 cried out in her P of birth, in anguish

PANIC (18)
Josh 10:10 threw them into a P before Israel, who slew
Judg 8:12 and he threw all the army into a P
1Sam 5:9 causing a very great P, and he afflicted the
5:11 there was a deathly P throughout the whole city.
14:15 And there was a P in the camp, in
14:15 earth quaked; and it became a very great P
2Sam 17:2 throw him into a P; and all the people
Ps 48:5 astounded, they were in P, they took to flight;
Prov 1:26 I will mock when P strikes you,
1:27 panic strikes you, when P strikes you like a
3:25 be afraid of sudden P, or of the ruin
Is 31:9 terror, and his officers desert the standard in P
Jer 30:5 heard a cry of P, of terror, and no
49:24 turned to flee, and P seized her; anguish and
51:32 burned with fire, and the soldiers are in P
Lam 3:47 enemies rail against us; P and pitfall have come
Zech 12:4 strike every horse with P, and its rider with
14:13 that day a great P from the LORD shall

PANS (2)
2Chr 35:13 in caldrons, and in P, and carried them quickly
2Mac 7:3 and gave orders that P and caldrons be heated.

PANT (4)
Job 5:5 thorns; and the thirsty P after his wealth.
Ps 119:131 With open mouth I P, because I long for
Is 42:14 a woman in travail, I will gasp and P
Jer 14:6 the bare heights, they P for air like jackals;

PAPER
2Jn 1:12 would rather not use P and ink, but I

PAPHOS (2)
Acts 13:6 island as far as P, they came upon a
13:13 company set sail from P, and came to Perga

PAPYRUS (2)
Job 8:11 "Can P grow where there is no marsh?
Is 18:2 Nile, in vessels of P upon the waters!

PAR-SHAN-DATHA
Esth 9:7 men, and also slew P and Dalphon and Aspatha

PARABLE (31)
Ps 78:2 my mouth in a P; I will utter dark
Sir 3:27 man will ponder a P, and an attentive ear
Mt 13:18 "Hear then the P of the sower.
13:24 Another P he put before them, saying, "The kingdom
13:31 Another P he put before them, saying, "The kingdom
13:33 He told them another P
13:34 indeed he said nothing to them without a P
13:36 "Explain to us the P of the weeds of
15:15 to him, "Explain the P to us."
21:33 "Hear another P
Mk 4:13 said to them, "Do you not understand this P
4:30 of God, or what P shall we use for
4:34 to them without a P, but privately to his
7:16 the people, his disciples asked him about the P
12:12 he had told the P against them; so they
Lk 5:36 He told them a P also: "No one tears
6:39 also told them a P: "Can a blind man
8:4 he said in a P:
8:9 asked him what this P meant,
8:11 Now the P is this: The seed is the
12:16 he told them a P, saying, "The land of
12:41 are you telling this P for us or for
13:6 And he told this P: "A man had a
14:7 Now he told a P to those who were
15:3 he told them this P:
18:1 he told them a P, to the effect that
18:9 He also told this P to some who trusted
19:11 proceeded to tell a P, because he was near
20:9 tell the people this P: "A man planted a
20:19 he had told this P against them.
21:29 he told them a P: "Look at the fig

PARABLES (21)
Sir 39:2 penetrate the subtleties of P;
39:3 and be at home with the obscurities of P
47:15 you filled it with P and riddles.
47:17 songs and proverbs and P, and for your
Hos 12:10 multiplied visions, and through the prophets gave P
Mt 13:3 them many things in P, saying: "A sower went
13:10 him, "Why do you speak to them in P
13:13 speak to them in P, because seeing they do
13:34 to the crowds in P; indeed he said nothing
13:35 open my mouth in P, I will utter what
13:53 Jesus had finished these P, he went away from
21:45 the Pharisees heard his P, they perceived that he
22:1 spoke to them in P, saying,
Mk 3:23 said to them in P, "How can Satan cast
4:2 them many things in P, and in his teaching
4:10 him with the twelve asked him concerning the P
4:11 outside everything is in P;
4:13 How then will you understand all the P
4:33 With many such P he spoke the word to
12:1 And he began to speak to them in P
Lk 8:10 others they are in P, so that seeing they

PARADE
2Mac 5:25 ordered his men to P under arms.

PARADED
2Mac 6:10 These women they publicly P about the city, with

PARADISE (3)
Lk 23:42 you, today you will be with me in P
2Cor 12:3 was caught up into P --whether in the body
Rev 2:7 which is in the P of God.'

PARAH
Josh 18:23 Beth-arabah, Zemaraim, Bethel, Avvim, P, Ophrah,

PARALLEL (2)
Ezek 42:7 was a wall outside P to the chambers, toward
48:21 to the west border, P to the tribal portions,

PARALYTIC (8)
Mt 9:2 brought to him a P, lying on his bed;
9:2 he said to the P, "Take heart, my son;
9:6 then said to the P --"Rise, take up your
Mk 2:3 bringing to him a P carried by four men.
2:4 pallet on which the P lay.
2:5 he said to the P, "My son, your sins
2:9 to say to the P, 'Your sins are forgiven,'
2:10 he said to the P --

PARALYTICS
Mt 4:24 pains, demoniacs, epileptics, and P, and he healed

PARALYZED (9)
Wis 17:15 specters, and now were P by their souls' surrender,
17:19 of the mountains, it P them with terror.
1Mac 9:55 stopped and he was P, so that he could
Mt 8:6 my servant is lying P at home, in terrible
Lk 5:18 a man who was P, and they sought to
5:24 the man who was P --"I say to you,
Jn 5:3 these lay a multitude of invalids, blind, lame, P
Acts 8:7 and many who were P or lame were healed.
9:33 had been bedridden for eight years and was P

PARAMOUR
Hos 3:1 is beloved of a P and is an adulteress;

PARAMOURS
Ezek 23:20 and doted upon her P there, whose members were

PARAN (11)
Gen 21:21 in the wilderness of P; and his mother took
Num 10:12 the cloud settled down in the wilderness of P
12:16 from Hazeroth, and encamped in the wilderness of P
13:3 from the wilderness of P, according to the command
13:26 in the wilderness of P, at Kadesh; they brought
Deut 1:1 against Suph, between P and Tophel, Laban,
33:2 shone forth from Mount P, he came from the
1Sam 25:1 rose and went down to the wilderness of P
1Kgs 11:18 Midian and came to P, and took men with
11:18 men with them from P and came to Egypt,
Hab 3:3 from Teman, and the Holy One from Mount P

PARAPET (2)
Deut 22:8 you shall make a P for your roof, that
Jud 14:1 hang it upon the P of your wall.

PARBAR (2)
1Chr 26:18 storehouse; and for the P on the west there
26:18 four at the road and two at the P

PARCEL
Ruth 4:3 Moab, is selling the P of land which belonged

PARCELED
Amos 7:17 your land shall be P out by line; you

PARCHED (20)
Lev 2:14 grain from fresh ears, P with fire.
23:14 neither bread nor grain P or fresh until this
Josh 5:11 land, unleavened cakes and P grain.
Ruth 2:14 he passed to her P grain; and she ate
1Sam 17:17 an ephah of this P grain, and these ten
25:18 and five measures of P grain, and a hundred
2Sam 17:28 vessels, wheat, barley, meal, P grain, beans and
Jud 10:5 filled a bag with P grain and a cake
Ps 68:6 rebellious dwell in a P land.
69:3 am weary with my crying; my throat is P
107:35 pools of water, a P land into springs of
143:6 for thee like a P land.
Is 5:13 and their multitude is P with thirst.
19:5 the river will be P and dry;
41:17 and their tongue is P with thirst, I the
Jer 17:6 shall dwell in the P places of the wilderness,
48:18 and sit on the P ground, O inhabitant of
Hos 2:3 set her like a P land, and slay her
13:15 his spring shall be P; it shall strip his
Joel 2:20 drive him into a P and desolate land, his

PARCHES
Sir 43:3 At noon it P the land; and who can

PARCHMENTS
2Tim 4:13 Troas, also the books, and above all the P

PARDON (18)
Ex 23:21 for he will not P your transgression; for my
34:9 a stiff-necked people; and P our iniquity and our
Num 14:19 upon the fourth generation.' P the iniquity of this
Deut 29:20 The LORD would not P him, but rather the
1Sam 15:25 Now therefore, I pray, P my sin, and return
2Kgs 5:18 matter may the LORD P your servant: when my
5:18 of Rimmon, the LORD P your servant in this
24:4 with innocent blood, and the LORD would not P
2Chr 30:18 saying, "The good LORD P every one
Job 7:21 Why dost thou not P my transgression and take
Ps 25:11 name's sake, O LORD, P my guilt, for it
85:2 thy people; thou didst P all their sin.
Wis 18:2 and they begged their P for having been at
Is 55:7 and to our God, for he will abundantly P
Jer 5:1 truth; that I may P her.
5:7 "How can I P you?
50:20 found; for I will P those whom I leave
1Mac 13:39 We P any errors and offenses committed to this

PARDONED (4)
Num 14:20 LORD said, "I have P, according to your word;
Wis 6:6 lowliest man may be P in mercy, but mighty
Sir 28:2 your sins will be P when you pray.
Is 40:2 that her iniquity is P, that she has received

PARDONING
Mic 7:18 a God like thee, P iniquity and passing over

PARE
Deut 21:12 shave her head and P her nails.

PARENT
1Jn 5:1 one who loves the P loves the child.

PARENTS (31)
Tob 10:12 and your mother-in-law; they are now your P
Wis 4:6 of evil against their P when God examines them.
12:6 a heathen cult, these P who murder helpless lives,
Sir 3:7 he will serve his P as his masters.
7:28 Remember that through your P you were born; and
Dan 13:3 Her P were righteous, and had taught their daughter
13:30 she came, with her P, her children, and all
1Mac 10:9 to Jonathan, and he returned them to their P
2Mac 12:24 because he held the P of most of them
Mt 10:21 children will rise against P and have them put
Mk 13:12 children will rise against P and have them put
Lk 2:27 temple; and when the P brought in the child
2:41 Now his P went to Jerusalem every year at
2:43 His P did not know it,
8:56 And her P were amazed; but he charged them
18:29 wife or brothers or P or children, for the
21:16 delivered up even by P and brothers and kinsmen
Jn 9:2 this man or his P, that he was born
9:3 man sinned, or his P, but that the works
9:18 until they called the P of the man who
9:20 His P answered, "We know that this is our
9:22 His P said this because they feared the Jews,
9:23 Therefore his P said, "He is of age, ask
Rom 1:30 of evil, disobedient to P,
2Cor 12:14 lay up for their P, but parents for their
12:14 for their parents, but P for their children.
Eph 6:1 Children, obey your P in the Lord, for this
Col 3:20 Children, obey your P in everything, for this pleases
1Tim 5:4 some return to their P; for this is acceptable
2Tim 3:2 abusive, disobedient to their P, ungrateful, unholy,
Heb 11:23 three months by his P, because they saw that

PARKS
Eccl 2:5 made myself gardens and P, and planted in them

PARMASHTA
Esth 9:9 Adalia and Aridatha and P and Arisai and Aridai

PARMENAS

Acts 6:5 Nicanor, and Timon, and P, and Nicolaus, a proselyte

PARNACH

Num 34:25 of Zebulun a leader, Eli-zaphan the son of P

PAROSH (6)

Ezra 2:3 Israel: the sons of P, two thousand one hundred
8:3 Of the sons of P, Zechariah, with whom were
10:25 of the sons of P: Ramiah, Izziah, Malchijah, Mijamin,
Neh 3:25 Pedaiah the son of P
7:8 Israel: the sons of P, two thousand a hundred
10:14 chiefs of the people: P, Pahath-moab, Elam, Zattu,

PARSIN

Dan 5:25 was inscribed: MENE, MENE, TEKEL, and P

PART (100)

Gen 27:16 and upon the smooth P of his neck;
41:34 and take the fifth P of the produce of
Ex 16:20 to Moses; some left P of it till the
16:36 omer is the tenth P of an ephah.)
26:12 And the P that remains of the curtains of
28:27 front to the lower P of the two shoulder-pieces
29:12 meeting, and shall take P of the blood of
29:20 the ram, and take P of its blood and
29:21 Then you shall take P of the blood that
30:34 there be an equal P,
30:36 very small, and put P of it before the
39:20 front to the lower P of the two shoulder-pieces
Lev 2:3 is a most holy P of the offerings by
2:10 is a most holy P of the offerings by
2:16 as its memorial portion P of the crushed grain
4:6 the blood and sprinkle P of the blood seven
10:18 brought into the inner P of the sanctuary.
11:4 chew the cud or P the hoof, you shall
11:4 cud but does not P the hoof, is unclean
11:5 cud but does not P the hoof, is unclean
11:6 cud but does not P the hoof, is unclean
11:25 and whoever carries any P of their carcass shall
11:35 everything upon which any P of their carcass falls
11:37 And if any P of their carcass falls upon
11:38 the seed and any P of their carcass falls
22:23 lamb which has a P too long or too
25:25 becomes poor, and sells P of his property, then
27:16 dedicates to the LORD P of the land which
27:22 which is not a P of his possession by
Num 18:29 them, giving the hallowed P from them.'
23:10 or number the fourth P of Israel?
Deut 14:7 cud but do not P the hoof, are unclean
Josh 9:4 Ai, they on their P acted with cunning, and
19:9 tribe of Simeon formed P of the territory of
Ruth 2:3 to come to the P of the field belonging
3:13 he will do the P of the next of
3:13 willing to do the P of the next of
3:13 I will do the P of the next of
1Sam 9:8 with me the fourth P of a shekel of
23:20 come down; and our P shall be to surrender
30:26 to Ziklag, he sent P of the spoil to
2Sam 14:6 was no one to P them, and one struck
1Kgs 6:19 prepared in the innermost P of the house, to
6:27 cherubim in the innermost P of the house; and
7:50 doors of the innermost P of the house, the
2Kgs 6:25 silver, and the fourth P of a kab of
18:23 are able on your P to set riders upon
2Chr 29:16 went into the inner P of the house of
35:5 be for each a P of a father's house
36:7 Nebuchadnezzar also carried P of the vessels of the
Neh 10:32 yearly with the third P of a shekel for
Tob 12:18 a favor on my P, but by the will
Esth 14:2 her body, and every P that she loved to
16:5 have been made in P responsible for the shedding
Wis 14:11 heathen idols, because, though P of what God
Sir 45:3 people, and showed him P of his glory.
Is 36:8 are able on your P to set riders upon
44:15 man; he takes a P of it and warms
Ezek 4:11 by measure, the sixth P of a hin; once
5:2 A third P you shall burn in the fire
5:2 completed; and a third P you shall take and
5:2 city; and a third P you shall scatter to
5:12 A third P of you shall die of pestilence
5:12 of you; a third P shall fall by the
5:12 you; and a third P I will scatter to
41:9 five cubits; and the P of the platform which
41:11 chambers opened on the P of the platform that
41:11 the breadth of the P that was left free
Dan 11:41 Moab and the main P of the Ammonites.
Amos 3:12 of a couch and P of a bed."
Jon 1:5 down into the inner P of the ship and
1Mac 6:40 Now a P of the king's army was spread
10:33 of Judah into any P of my kingdom, I
12:23 welfare; we on our P write to you that
12:37 build up the city; P of the wall on
2Mac 4:14 they hastened to take P in the unlawful proceedings
7:26 much urging on his P, she undertook to persuade
14:22 sudden treachery on the P of the enemy; they
Mt 23:29 would not have taken P with them in shedding
24:43 had known in what P of the night the
Lk 11:36 of light, having no P dark, it will be
Jn 13:8 you, you have no P in me."
Acts 5:2 and brought only a P and laid it at
5:3 and to keep back P of the proceeds of
8:21 You have neither P nor lot in this matter,
23:6 Paul perceived that one P were Sadducees and the
Rom 9:14 Is there injustice on God's P
11:25 hardening has come upon P of Israel, until the
1Cor 12:15 it any less a P of the body.
12:16 it any less a P of the body.
12:24 honor to the inferior P,
13:12 Now I know in P; then I shall understand
2Cor 1:14 you have understood in P, that you can be
8:2 overflowed in a wealth of liberality on their P
8:4 the favor of taking P in the relief of
Eph 4:16 is supplied, when each P is working properly, makes
5:11 Take no P in the unfruitful works of darkness,
2Tim 4:16 no one took my P; all deserted me.
Heb 7:2 Abraham apportioned a tenth P of everything.
Rev 18:4 people, lest you take P in her sins, lest

PARTAKE (9)

Ezra 2:63 they were not to P of the most holy
Neh 7:65 they were not to P of the most holy
Wis 16:3 a short time, might P of delicacies.
2Mac 6:7 under bitter constraint, to P of the sacrifices; and
6:8 Jews and make them P of the sacrifices,
7:1 whips and cords, to P of unlawful swine's flesh.
1Cor 10:17 body, for we all P of the one bread.
10:21 You cannot P of the table of the Lord
10:30 If I P with thankfulness, why am I denounced

PARTAKER

1Pet 5:1 as well as a P in the glory that

PARTAKERS (4)

Eph 3:6 the same body, and P of the promise in
Phil 1:7 for you are all P with me of grace,
Heb 6:4 gift, and have become P of the Holy Spirit,
2Pet 1:4 of passion, and become P of the divine nature.

PARTED (8)

2Kgs 2:8 and the water was P to the one side
2:14 water, the water was P to the one side
Dan 13:14 they went out, they P from each other.
1Mac 6:45 and left, and they P before him on both
Lk 24:51 he blessed them, he P from them, and was
Jn 19:24 fulfill the scripture, "They P my garments among
Acts 21:1 And when we had P from them and set
Philem 1:15 is why he was P from you for a

PARTHIANS

Acts 2:9 P and Medes and Elamites and residents of

PARTIAL (6)

Ex 23:3 nor shall you be P to a poor man
Lev 19:15 you shall not be P to the poor or
Deut 1:17 You shall not be P in judgment; you shall
10:17 God, who is not P and takes no bribe.
Prov 18:5 not good to be P to a wicked man,
Sir 7:6 iniquity, lest you be P to a powerful man,

PARTIALITY (25)

Deut 16:19 you shall not show P; and you shall not
2Chr 19:7 LORD our God, or P, or taking bribes."
Job 13:8 Will you show P toward him, will you plead
13:10 surely rebuke you if in secret you show P
32:21 I will not show P to any person or
34:19 man'; who shows no P to princes, nor regards
Ps 82:2 judge unjustly and show P to the wicked?
Prov 24:23 P in judging is not good.
28:21 To show P is not good; but for a
Sir 4:22 Do not show P, to your own harm, or
4:27 foolish fellow, nor show P to a ruler.

35:12 is the judge, and with him is no P
35:13 He will not show P in the case of
42:1 and do not let P lead you to sin:
Is 3:9 Their P witnesses against them; they proclaim their
Mal 2:9 ways but have shown P in your instruction."
Lk 20:21 rightly, and show no P, but truly teach the
Acts 10:34 that God shows no P,
Rom 2:11 For God shows no P.
Gal 2:6 me; God shows no P –those, I say, who
Eph 6:9 that there is no P with him.
Col 3:25 wrong he has done, and there is no P
1Tim 5:21 keep these rules without favor, doing nothing from P
Jas 2:1 My brethren, show no P as you hold the
2:9 But if you show P, you commit sin, and

PARTICIPATE

1Tim 5:22 on of hands, nor P in another man's sins;

PARTICIPATED (2)

2Mac 5:20 the nation and afterward P in its benefits; and
Heb 12:8 in which all have P, then you are illegitimate

PARTICIPATION (3)

1Cor 10:16 is it not a P in the blood of
10:16 is it not a P in the body of
Phil 2:1 incentive of love, any P in the Spirit, any

PARTIES (3)

Ex 22:9 the case of both P shall come before God;
Deut 19:17 of wrongdoing, then both P to the dispute shall
1Mac 8:30 are in effect both P shall determine to add

PARTING (5)

Josh 22:9 of Manasseh returned home, P from the people of
Ezek 21:21 Babylon stands at the P of the way, at
Obad 1:14 have stood at the P of the ways to
Mic 1:14 Therefore you shall give P gifts to Moresheth-gath;
Lk 9:33 as the men were P from him, Peter said

PARTISANSHIP

Phil 1:17 proclaim Christ out of P, not sincerely but thinking

PARTLY (9)

Dan 2:33 of iron, its feet P of iron and partly
2:33 partly of iron and P of clay.
2:41 the feet and toes P of potter's clay and
2:41 of potter's clay and P of iron, it shall
2:42 of the feet were P iron and partly clay,
2:42 were partly iron and P clay, so the kingdom
2:42 the kingdom shall be P strong and partly brittle.
2:42 be partly strong and P brittle.
1Cor 11:18 among you; and I P believe it,

PARTNER (7)

Esth 16:13 of Esther, the blameless P of our kingdom, together
Prov 29:24 The P of a thief hates his own life;
Sir 41:18 unjust dealing, before your P or friend;
42:3 accounts with a P or with traveling companions,
1Cor 7:15 But if the unbelieving P desires to separate, let
2Cor 8:23 Titus, he is my P and fellow worker in
Philem 1:17 you consider me your P, receive him as you

PARTNERS (5)

Lk 5:7 they beckoned to their P in the other boat
5:10 of Zebedee, who were P with Simon.
1Cor 10:18 who eat the sacrifices P in the altar?
10:20 want you to be P with demons.
Heb 10:33 affliction, and sometimes being P with those so

PARTNERSHIP (3)

2Cor 6:14 For what P have righteousness and iniquity?
Phil 1:5 joy, thankful for your P in the gospel from
4:15 no church entered into P with me in giving

PARTOOK (3)

Josh 9:14 So the men P of their provisions, and did
Acts 2:46 in their homes, they P of food with glad
Heb 2:14 blood, he himself likewise P of the same nature,

PARTRIDGE (3)

1Sam 26:20 one who hunts a P in the mountains."
Sir 11:28 Like a decoy P in a cage, so is
Jer 17:11 Like the P that gathers a brood which she

PARTS (59)

Ex 12:9 its head with its legs and its inner P
Lev 11:3 Whatever P the hoof and is cloven-footed and chews
11:7 the swine, because it P the hoof and is
11:26 Every animal which P the hoof but is not
Num 11:1 and consumed some outlying P of the camp.
31:27 the booty into two P, between the warriors who
Deut 14:6 Every animal that P the hoof and has the
14:8 the swine, because it P the hoof but does
19:3 and divide into three P the area of the
25:11 him by the private P,
30:4 are in the uttermost P of heaven, from there
Judg 19:1 sojourning in the remote P of the hill country
19:18 Judah to the remote P of the hill country
Ruth 1:17 also if even death P me from you."
1Sam 2:29 yourselves upon the choicest P of every offering of
24:3 sitting in the innermost P of the cave.
1Kgs 6:38 finished in all its P, and according to all
7:25 and all their hinder P were inward.
16:21 were divided into two P; half of the people
2Kgs 10:32 began to cut off P of Israel.
2Chr 4:4 and all their hinder P were inward.
35:14 offerings and the fat P until night; so the
Neh 4:13 So in the lowest P of the space behind
Tob 8:3 fled to the remotest P of Egypt, and the
Ps 139:9 dwell in the uttermost P of the sea,
139:13 didst form my inward P, thou didst knit me
Prov 18:8 down into the inner P of the body.
20:27 lamp of the LORD, searching all his innermost P
20:30 away evil; strokes make clean the innermost P
26:22 down into the inner P of the body.
Is 3:17 and the LORD will lay bare their secret P
Jer 6:22 stirring from the farthest P of the earth.
25:32 stirring from the farthest P of the earth!
31:8 them from the farthest P of the earth, among
34:18 and passed between its P –
34:19 who passed between the P of the calf;
50:41 stirring from the farthest P of the earth.
Ezek 32:23 set in the uttermost P of the Pit, and
38:6 Beth-togarmah from the uttermost P of the north
38:15 out of the uttermost P of the north, you
39:2 up from the uttermost P of the north, and
Dan 11:24 come into the richest P of the province; and
Amos 6:10 is in the innermost P of the house, "Is
Mic 6:14 hunger in your inward P; you shall put away,
1Mac 7:24 into all the surrounding P of Judea, and took
9:23 lawless emerged in all P of Israel; all the
9:62 wilderness; he rebuilt the P of it that had
2Mac 8:21 country; then he divided his army into four P
Jn 19:23 garments and made four P, one for each soldier;
Acts 2:10 Pamphylia, Egypt and the P of Libya belonging to
13:47 salvation to the uttermost P of the earth.'"
20:2 had gone through these P and had given them
1Cor 12:20 is, there are many P, yet one body.
12:22 On the contrary, the P of the body which
12:23 are indispensable, and those P of the body which
12:23 honor, and our unpresentable P are treated with
12:24 which our more presentable P do not require.
Eph 4:9 descended into the lower P of the earth?
Rev 16:19 was split into three P, and the cities of

PARTY (10)

Wis 1:16 because they are fit to belong to his P
2:24 who belong to his P experience it.
Acts 5:17 him, that is, the P of the Sadducees, and
11:2 to Jerusalem, the circumcision P criticized him,
15:5 who belonged to the P of the Pharisees rose
23:9 scribes of the Pharisees' P stood up and contended,
26:5 according to the strictest P of our religion I
Gal 2:12 and separated himself, fearing the circumcision P
5:20 jealousy, anger, selfishness, dissension, P spirit,
Tit 1:9 deceivers, especially the circumcision P;

PARUAH

1Kgs 4:17 Jehoshaphat the son of P, in Issachar;

PARVAIM

2Chr 3:6 The gold was gold of P

PAS-DAMMIM

1Chr 11:13 was with David at P when the Philistines were

PASACH

1Chr 7:33 The sons of Japhlet: P, Bimhal, and Ashvath.

PASCHAL

1Cor 5:7 For Christ, our P lamb, has been sacrificed.

PASEAH (4)

1Chr	4:12	the father of Bethrapha, P, and Tehinnah the father
Ezra	2:49	Uzza, the sons of P, the sons of Besai,
Neh	3:6	Joiada the son of P and Meshullam the son
	7:51	Uzza, the sons of P,

PASHHUR (14)

1Chr	9:12	of Jeroham, son of P, son of Malchijah, and
Ezra	2:38	The sons of P, one thousand two hundred and
	10:22	Of the sons of P: Eli-o-enai, Ma-aseiah, Ishmael,
Neh	7:41	The sons of P, a thousand two hundred and
	10:3	Seraiah, Azariah, Jeremiah, P, Amariah, Malchijah,
	11:12	of Zechariah, son of P, son of Malchijah,
Jer	20:1	Now P the priest, the son of Immer, who
	20:2	Then P beat Jeremiah the prophet, and put him
	20:3	On the morrow, when P released Jeremiah from the
	20:3	not call your name P, but Terror on every
	20:6	And you, P, and all who dwell in your
	21:1	Zedekiah sent to him P the son of Malchiah
	38:1	Gedaliah the son of P, Jucal the son of
	38:1	son of Shelemiah, and P the son of Malchiah

PASS (238)

Gen	18:3	your sight, do not P by your servant.
	18:5	after that you may P on--since you have
	30:32	keep it: let me P through all your flock
	31:52	that I will not P over this heap to
	31:52	and you will not P over this heap and
	32:16	said to his servants, P on before me, and
	33:14	Let my lord P on before his servant, and
	41:13	so it came to P; I was restored to
	41:32	God, and God will shortly bring it to P
Ex	12:12	For I will P through the land of Egypt
	12:13	the blood, I will P over you, and no
	12:23	For the LORD will P through to slay the
	12:23	doorposts, the LORD will P over the door, and
	15:16	thy people, O LORD, P by, till the people
	15:16	by, till the people P by whom thou hast
	17:5	LORD said to Moses, P on before the people,
	26:28	up the frames, shall P through from end to
	33:19	make all my goodness P before you, and will
	36:33	the middle bar to P through from end to
Lev	27:32	animal of all that P under the herdsman's staff,
Num	5:22	that brings the curse P into your bowels and
	20:17	Now let us P through your land.
	20:17	We will not P through field or vineyard, neither
	20:18	him, "You shall not P through, lest I come
	20:19	it; let me only P through on foot, nothing
	20:20	said, "You shall not P through." And Edom came
	21:22	Amorites, saying, "Let me P through your land; we
	21:23	not allow Israel to P through his territory.
	27:7	of their father to P to them.
	27:8	cause his inheritance to P to his daughter.
	31:23	the fire, you shall P through the fire, and
	31:23	the fire, you shall P through the water.
	32:21	man of you will P over the Jordan before
	32:27	but your servants will P over, every man who
	32:29	before the LORD, will P with you over the
	32:30	if they will not P over with you armed,
	32:32	We will P over armed before the LORD into
	33:51	of Israel, When you P over the Jordan into
	34:4	on to Hazar-addar, and P along to Azmon;
Deut	2:4	You are about to P through the territory of
	2:18	day you are to P over the boundary of
	2:27	peace, saying, 'Let me P through your land; I
	2:28	drink; only let me P through on foot,
	2:30	would not let us P by him; for the
	3:18	men of valor shall P over armed before your
	9:1	Israel; you are to P over the Jordan this
	11:31	For you are to P over the Jordan to
	13:2	tells you comes to P, and if he says,
	18:22	does not come to P or come true, that
	27:2	on the day you P over the Jordan to
	27:3	this law, when you P over to enter the
Josh	1:11	officers of the people, P through the camp, and
	1:11	days you are to P over this Jordan, to
	1:14	valor among you shall P over armed before your
	3:6	of the covenant, and P on before the people."
	3:11	the earth is to P over before you into
	3:14	from their tents, to P over the Jordan with
	4:5	Joshua said to them, P on before the ark
	6:7	let the armed men P on before the ark
	21:45	house of Israel had failed; all came to P
	22:19	your land is unclean, P over into the LORD's
	23:14	all have come to P for you, not one
Judg	3:28	not a man to P over.
	11:17	Edom, saying, 'Let us P, we pray, through your
	11:19	to him, 'Let us P, we pray, through your
	11:20	not trust Israel to P through his territory; so
	19:12	Israel; but we will P on to Gibe-ah."
	20:3	"Tell us, how was this wickedness brought to P
	21:3	has this come to P in Israel, that there
1Sam	9:27	"Tell the servant to P on before us, and
	10:9	these signs came to P that day.
	13:23	went out to the P of Michmash.
	14:4	In the P, by which Jonathan sought to go
	16:8	Abinadab, and made him P before Samuel.
	16:9	Then Jesse made Shammah P by.
	16:10	seven of his sons P before Samuel.
2Sam	15:22	to Ittai, "Go then, P on." So Ittai the
	17:16	but by all means P over; lest the king
1Kgs	1:21	it will come to P, when my lord the
	13:32	the cities of Samaria, shall surely come to P
	18:6	land between them to P through it; Ahab went
2Kgs	6:9	that you do not P this place, for the
	15:12	so it came to P
	19:25	now I bring to P, that you should turn
Neh	2:7	they may let me P through until I come
	2:14	for the beast that was under me to P
	4:22	man and his servant P the night within Jerusalem,
Jud	5:21	then let my lord P them by; for their
	7:32	But if these days P by, and no help
	9:5	didst intend came to P,
Job	6:15	torrent-bed, as freshets that P away,
	14:5	bounds that he cannot P,
	19:8	so that I cannot P, and he has set
	34:20	people are shaken and P away, and the mighty
Ps	57:1	the storms of destruction P by.
	78:13	sea and let them P through it, and made
	80:12	so that all who P along the way pluck
	89:41	All that P by despoil him; he has become
	90:9	For all our days P away under thy wrath,
	102:3	For my days P away like smoke, and my
	102:26	like raiment, and they P away;
	104:9	which they should not P, so that they might
	105:19	had said came to P the word of the
	129:8	bosom, while those who P by do not say,
	136:14	ever; and made Israel P through the midst of
Prov	4:16	away from it and P on.
	9:15	calling to those who P by, who are going
	16:30	he who compresses his lips brings evil to P
Wis	1:8	it punishes, will not P him by.
	2:4	works; our life will P away like the traces
	2:7	no flower of spring P by us.
	6:22	and I will not P by the truth;
Sir	11:17	how much time will P until he leaves them
	14:14	share of desired good P by you.
	14:19	who made it will P away with it.
	23:2	that it may not P by my sins;
	48:25	and the hidden things before they came to P
Is	2:2	It shall come to P in the latter days
	2:18	the idols shall utterly P away.
	7:7	not stand, and it shall not come to P
	8:8	it will overflow and P on, reaching even to
	8:21	They will P through the land, greatly distressed and
	10:29	have crossed over the P, at Geba they lodge
	23:6	P over to Tarshish, wail, O inhabitants of the
	23:12	daughter of Sidon; arise, P over to Cyprus, even
	28:19	by morning it will P through, by day and
	31:9	His rock shall P away in terror, and his
	33:21	with oars can go, nor stately ship can P
	34:10	lie waste; none shall P through it for ever
	35:8	the unclean shall not P over it, and fools
	37:26	now I bring to P, that you should make
	42:9	things have come to P, and new things I
	43:2	When you P through the waters I will be
	46:11	will bring it to P; I have purposed, and
	47:2	robe, uncover your legs, P through the rivers.
	48:3	suddenly I did them and they came to P
	48:5	before they came to P I announced them to
	51:10	for the redeemed to P over?
	51:23	down, that we may P over'; and you have
	51:23	street for them to P over."
Jer	5:22	barrier which it cannot P; though the waves toss,
	5:22	they roar, they cannot P over it.
	6:9	Israel; like a grape-gatherer P your hand again over
	12:16	it shall come to P, if they will diligently
	22:8	"'And many nations will P by this city, and
	28:9	that prophet comes to P, then it will be
	30:8	it shall come to P in that day, says
	31:28	it shall come to P that as I have
	32:24	speak has come to P, and behold, thou seest

P

33:13 Judah, flocks shall again P under the hands of
52:3 came to such a P in Jerusalem and Judah
Lam 1:12 you, all you who P by?
2:15 All who P along the way clap their hands
3:37 and it came to P, unless the Lord has
3:44 that no prayer can P through.
4:21 also the cup shall P; you shall become drunk
Ezek 5:1 a barber's razor and P it over your head
5:14 sight of all that P by.
5:17 pestilence and blood shall P through you; and I
9:5 said in my hearing, P through the city after
11:13 And it came to P, while I was prophesying,
14:15 cause wild beasts to P through the land, and
14:15 that no man may P through because of the
20:37 I will make you P under the rod, and
23:45 But righteous men shall P judgment on them with
24:14 it shall come to P, I will do it;
29:11 foot of man shall P through it, and no
29:11 foot of beast shall P through it; it shall
33:28 desolate that none will P through.
39:14 set apart men to P through the land continually
39:15 And when these P through the land and any
47:5 that I could not P through, for the water
Dan 4:16 and let seven times P over him.
4:23 field, till seven times P over him';
4:25 and seven times shall P over you, till you
4:32 and seven times shall P over you, until you
7:14 dominion, which shall not P away, and his kingdom
9:2 Jeremiah the prophet, must P before the end of
11:10 on and overflow and P through, and again shall
11:40 and shall overflow and P through.
Joel 1:12 Go in, P the night in sackcloth, O ministers
2:28 it shall come to P afterward, that I will
2:32 it shall come to P that all who call
3:17 strangers shall never again P through it.
Amos 5:17 wailing, for I will P through the midst of
6:2 P over to Calneh, and see; and thence go
6:7 who stretch themselves shall P away."
7:8 I will never again P by them;
8:2 I will never again P by them.
Mic 1:11 P on your way, inhabitants of Shaphir, in nakedness
2:8 peaceful, from those who P by trustingly with no
2:13 will break through and P the gate, going out
2:13 Their king will P on before them, the LORD
4:1 It shall come to P in the latter days
Nah 1:12 be cut off and P away.
Hag 2:15 what will come to P from this day onward.
Zech 6:15 this shall come to P, if you will diligently
10:11 They shall P through the sea of Egypt, and
1Mac 5:48 friendly message, "Let us P through your land to
5:48 harm; we will simply P by on foot." But
Mt 5:18 till heaven and earth P away, not an iota,
5:18 not a dot, will P from the law until
8:28 that no one could P that way.
24:34 this generation will not P away till all these
24:35 Heaven and earth will P away, but my words
24:35 my words will not P away.
26:39 possible, let this cup P from me; nevertheless, not
26:42 Father, if this cannot P unless I drink it,
Mk 6:48 He meant to P by them,
11:23 says will come to P, it will be done
13:30 this generation will not P away before all these
13:31 Heaven and earth will P away, but my words
13:31 my words will not P away.
14:35 possible, the hour might P from him.
Lk 1:20 these things come to P, because you did not
16:17 heaven and earth to P away, than for one
16:26 that those who would P from here to you
19:4 for he was to P that way.
21:32 this generation will not P away till all has
21:33 Heaven and earth will P away, but my words
21:33 my words will not P away.
Jn 4:4 He had to P through Samaria.
Acts 19:21 in the Spirit to P through Macedonia and Achaia
26:22 said would come to P:
Rom 14:3 not him who abstains P judgment on him who
14:4 Who are you to P judgment on the servant
14:10 Why do you P judgment on your brother?
14:13 let us no more P judgment on one another,
1Cor 2:6 who are doomed to P away.
13:8 for prophecies, they will P away; as for tongues,
13:8 for knowledge, it will P away.
13:10 comes, the imperfect will P away.
15:54 then shall come to P the saying that is
16:5 for I intend to P through Macedonia,
Col 2:16 Therefore let no one P judgment on you in
1Thes 3:4 it has come to P, and as you know.
Jas 1:9 the grass he will P away.
2Pet 3:10 then the heavens will P away with a loud

PASSAGE (8)

Num 20:21 refused to give Israel P through his territory; so
Wis 5:11 no evidence of its P is found; the light
Ezek 42:4 the chambers was a P inward, ten cubits wide
42:11 were chambers with a P in front of them;
42:12 where one enters the P, and opposite them was
Mk 12:26 of Moses, in the P about the bush, how
Lk 20:37 Moses showed, in the P about the bush, where
Acts 8:32 Now the P of the scripture which he was

PASSAGES

Jud 7:23 city and in the P through the gates; there

PASSAGEWAYS

Bar 6:43 them, sit along the P, burning bran for incense;

PASSED (143)

Gen 12:6 land of Canaan, Abram P through the land to
15:17 and a flaming torch P between these pieces.
32:21 So the present P on before him; and he
32:31 upon him as he P Penuel, limping because of
37:28 Then Midianite traders P by; and they drew Joseph
Ex 7:25 Seven days P after the LORD had struck the
12:27 LORD's passover, for he P over the houses of
14:20 darkness; and the night P without one coming near
33:22 hand until I have P by;
34:6 The LORD P before him, and proclaimed, "The
Num 14:7 "The land, which we P through to spy it
20:17 left, until we have P through your territory."
21:22 Highway, until we have P through your territory."
33:8 from before Hahiroth, and P through the midst of
Deut 23:23 to perform what has P your lips, for you
27:4 And when you have P over the Jordan, you
27:12 saying, "When you have P over the Jordan, these
29:16 nations through which you P;
Josh 2:23 from the hills, and P over and came to
3:1 lodged there before they P over.
3:4 for you have not P this way before.
3:16 off; and the people P over opposite Jericho.
4:7 the LORD; when it P over the Jordan, the
4:10 The people P over in haste;
4:11 LORD and the priests P over before the people.
4:12 the half-tribe of Manasseh P over armed before the
4:13 ready armed for war P over before the LORD
4:22 your children know, 'Israel P over this Jordan on
4:23 for you until you P over, as the LORD
4:23 for us until we P over,
6:13 ark of the LORD P on, blowing the trumpets
10:29 Then Joshua P on from Makkedah, and all Israel
10:31 And Joshua P on from Libnah, and all Israel
10:34 And Joshua P on with all Israel from Lachish
18:9 the men went and P up and down in
24:17 peoples through whom we P;
Judg 3:26 while they delayed, and P beyond the sculptured
8:4 to the Jordan and P over, he and the
9:25 they robbed all who P by them along that
11:29 Jephthah, and he P through Gilead and Manasseh,
11:29 Gilead and Manasseh, and P on to Mizpah of
11:29 Mizpah of Gilead he P on to the Ammonites.
18:13 And they P on from there to the hill
19:14 So they P on and went their way; and
Ruth 2:14 the reapers, and he P to her parched grain;
1Sam 7:2 Kiriath-jearim, a long time P, some twenty years, and
9:4 And they P through the hill country of Ephraim
9:4 country of Ephraim and P through the land of
9:4 And they P through the land of Shaalim, but
9:4 Then they P through the land of Benjamin, but
9:27 and when he has P on stop here yourself
14:23 day; and the battle P beyond Beth-aven.
15:12 himself and turned, and P on, and went down
2Sam 2:15 Then they arose and P over by number, twelve
15:18 And all his servants P by him; and all
15:18 followed him from Gath, P on before the king.
15:22 So Ittai the Gittite P on, with all his
15:23 as all the people P by, and the king
15:23 and all the people P on toward the wilderness.
15:24 the people had all P out of the city.
16:1 When David had P a little beyond the summit,
20:14 And Sheba P through all the tribes of Israel
1Kgs 13:25 And behold, men P by, and saw the body
18:29 And as midday P, they raved on until the
19:11 And behold, the LORD P by, and a great

P

	19:19	Elijah P by him and cast his mantle upon
	20:39	And as the king P, he cried to the
2Kgs	4:8	So whenever he P that way, he would turn
	8:21	Then Joram P over to Zair with all his
	14:9	wild beast of Lebanon P by and trampled down
	25:6	Babylon at Riblah, who P sentence upon him.
2Chr	21:9	Then Jehoram P over with his commanders and all
	25:18	wild beast of Lebanon P by and trampled down
Tob	1:21	But not fifty days P before two of Sennacherib's
Jud	2:24	followed the Euphrates and P through Mesopotamia
	10:10	down the mountain and P through the valley and
	13:10	for prayer; and they P through the camp and
Job	11:16	as waters that have P away.
	15:19	given, and no stranger P among them).
	28:8	the lion has not P over it.
	30:15	and my prosperity has P away like a cloud.
	37:21	when the wind has P and cleared them.
Ps	31:12	I have P out of mind like one who
	37:36	Again I P by, and, lo, he was no
	66:6	into dry land; men P through the river on
	148:6	ever; he fixed their bounds which cannot be P
Prov	24:30	I P by the field of a sluggard, by
Song	3:4	Scarcely had I P them, when I found him
Wis	5:10	and when it has P no trace can be
	10:8	For because they P wisdom by, they not only
	19:8	protected by thy hand P through as one nation,
Is	10:28	to Aiath; he has P through Migron, at Michmash
	16:8	shoots spread abroad and P over the sea.
	23:2	of Sidon; your messengers P over the sea
Jer	8:13	I gave them has P away from them."
	34:18	cut in two and P between its parts—
	34:19	of the land who P between the parts of
	39:5	of Hamath; and he P sentence upon him.
	48:32	Your branches P over the sea, reached as far
	52:9	of Hamath, and he P sentence upon him.
Ezek	16:6	"And when I P by you, and saw you
	16:8	"When I P by you again and looked upon
	36:34	sight of all who P by.
	47:5	that could not be P through.
Jon	2:3	waves and thy billows P over me.
1Mac	5:51	Then he P through the city over the slain.
	5:66	of the Philistines, and P through Marisa.
	11:62	And he P through the country as far as
	12:10	for considerable time has P since you sent your
2Mac	1:20	after many years had P, when it pleased God,
	1:22	and some time had P and the sun, which
Mt	9:9	As Jesus P on from there, he saw a
	9:27	And as Jesus P on from there, two blind
	15:29	on from there and P along the Sea of
	27:39	And those who P by derided him, wagging their
Mk	2:14	And as he P on, he saw Levi the
	9:30	on from there and P through Galilee.
	11:20	As they P by in the morning, they saw
	15:28	And those who P by derided him, wagging their
Lk	10:31	he saw him he P by on the other
	10:32	place and saw him, P by on the other
Jn	5:23	into judgment, but has P from death to life.
	9:1	As he P by, he saw a man blind
Acts	7:30	when forty years had P, an angel appeared to
	9:23	When many days had P, the Jews plotted to
	12:10	When they had P the first and the second
	12:10	they went out and P on through one street;
	13:14	to Jerusalem; but they P on from Perga and
	14:24	they P through Pisidia, and came to Pamphylia.
	15:3	by the church, they P through both Phoenicia and
	17:1	when they had P through Amphipolis and Apollonia,
	17:23	For as I P along, and observed the objects
	19:1	was at Corinth, Paul P through the upper country
	25:13	when some days had P, Agrippa the king and
Rom	3:25	divine forbearance he had P over former sins;
1Cor	10:1	the cloud, and all P through the sea,
2Cor	5:17	creation; the old has P away, behold, the new
Heb	4:14	high priest who has P through the heavens, Jesus,
1Jn	3:14	know that we have P out of death into
Rev	9:12	The first woe has P; behold, two woes are
	11:14	The second woe has P; behold, the third woe
	21:1	the first earth had P away, and the sea
	21:4	the former things have P away."

PASSER-BY (3)

Ezek	16:15	your renown, and lavished your harlotries on any P
	16:25	yourself to any P, and multiplying your harlotry.
Mk	15:21	And they compelled a P, Simon of Cyrene, who

PASSERS-BY

Bar	6:43	by one of the P and is lain with,

PASSES (50)

Ex	33:22	and while my glory P by I will put
Josh	15:3	the ascent of Akrabbim, P along to Zin, and
	15:4	turns about to Karka, P along to Azmon, goes
	15:6	to Beth-hoglah, and P along north of Beth-arabah;
	15:7	valley; and the boundary P along to the waters
	15:10	Baalah to Mount Seir, P along to the northern
	15:10	down to Beth-shemesh, and P along by Timnah;
	15:11	round to Shikkeron, and P along to Mount Baalah,
	16:2	Bethel to Luz, it P along to Ataroth, the
	16:6	round toward Taanath-shiloh, and P along beyond it
	18:13	From there the boundary P along southward in the
	18:19	Arabah; then the boundary P on to the north
	19:13	Japhia; from there it P along on the east
Jud	4:7	them to seize the P up into the hills,
	5:1	and had closed the P in the hills and
	6:7	the cities beside the P,
	7:1	and to seize the P up into the hill
	14:11	in companies to the P in the mountains.
Job	9:11	Lo, he P by me, and I see him
	11:10	If he P through, and imprisons, and calls to
	14:20	against him, and he P; thou changest his
Ps	8:8	of the sea, whatever P along the paths of
	78:39	flesh, a wind that P and comes not again.
	103:16	field; for the wind P over it, and it
Prov	10:25	When the tempest P, the wicked is no more,
Eccl	6:12	vain life, which he P like a shadow?
Wis	5:9	like a rumor that P by;
	5:14	the wind, and it P like the remembrance of
	7:27	in every generation she P into holy souls and
Sir	10:8	Sovereignty P from nation to nation on account of
Is	28:15	when the overwhelming scourge P through it will not
	28:18	when the overwhelming scourge P through you will
	28:19	As often as it P through it will take
	41:3	He pursues them and P on safely, by paths
Jer	2:6	a land that none P through, where no man
	9:10	so that no one P through, and the lowing
	9:12	so that no one P through?
	18:16	Every one who P by it is horrified and
	19:8	at; every one who P by it will be
	49:17	horror; every one who P by it will be
	50:13	desolation; every one who P by Babylon shall be
	51:43	dwells, and through which no son of man P
Zeph	2:15	Every one who P by her hisses and shakes
Mt	12:43	of a man, he P through waterless places seeking
	15:17	goes into the mouth P into the stomach, and
	15:17	the stomach, and so P on?
Mk	7:18	his stomach, and so P on?" (Thus he declared
Lk	11:24	of a man, he P through waterless places seeking
Phil	4:7	peace of God, which P all understanding, will keep
1Jn	2:17	And the world P away, and the lust of

PASSING (41)

Josh	3:17	while all Israel were P over on dry ground,
	3:17	all the nation finished P over the Jordan.
	4:1	the nation had finished P over the Jordan, the
	4:11	the people had finished P over, the ark of
	18:18	son of Reuben; and P on to the north
Judg	19:18	to him, "We are P from Bethlehem in Judah
1Sam	29:2	of the Philistines were P on by hundreds and
	29:2	and his men were P on in the rear
2Sam	1:26	to me was wonderful, P the love of women.
1Kgs	9:8	heap of ruins; everyone P by it will be
2Kgs	4:9	God, who is continually P our way.
	6:26	king of Israel was P by upon the wall,
	6:30	clothes—now he was P by upon the wall—
2Chr	7:21	is exalted, every one P by will be astonished,
Ps	39:12	For I am thy P guest, a sojourner, like
	144:4	days are like a P shadow.
Prov	7:8	young man without sense, P along the street near
	26:10	he who hires a P fool or drunkard.
	26:17	one who takes a P dog by the ears.
Wis	2:5	allotted time is the P of a shadow, and
	14:5	piece of wood, and P through the billows on
	17:9	yet, scared by the P of beasts and the
Is	29:5	of the ruthless like P chaff.
	60:15	hated, with no one P through, I will make
Ezek	26:18	are dismayed at your P
Mic	7:18	thee, pardoning iniquity and P over transgression for
Mt	20:30	heard that Jesus was P by, cried out, "Have
Mk	1:16	And P along by the Sea of Galilee, he
Lk	4:30	But P through the midst of them he went
	17:11	to Jerusalem he was P along between Samaria and
	18:37	"Jesus of Nazareth is P by."
	19:1	entered Jericho and was P through.
Acts	8:39	found at Azotus, and P on he preached the

P

16:8 not allow them; so, P by Mysia, they went
Rom 2:1 judge another; for in P judgment upon him you
15:24 to see you in P as I go to
1Cor 7:31 of this world is P away.
16:5 will visit you after P through Macedonia, for I
16:7 you now just in P; I hope to spend
Tit 3:3 various passions and pleasures, P our days in malice
1Jn 2:8 because the darkness is P away and the true

PASSION (12)

Prov 14:30 to the flesh, but P makes the bones rot.
Sir 9:8 beauty, and by it P is kindled like a
Dan 13:10 Both were overwhelmed with P for her, but they
Acts 1:3 himself alive after his P by many proofs, appearing
Rom 1:27 and were consumed with P for one another, men
1Cor 7:9 better to marry than to be aflame with P
Col 3:5 fornication, impurity, P, evil desire, and covetousness,
1Thes 4:5 honor, not in the P of lust like heathen
2Pet 1:4 the world because of P, and become partakers of
2:10 the lust of defiling P and despise authority.
Rev 14:8 all nations drink the wine of her impure P
18:3 wine of her impure P, and the kings of

PASSIONS (19)

Rom 1:26 this reason God gave them up to dishonorable P
6:12 your mortal bodies, to make you obey their P
7:5 the flesh, our sinful P, aroused by the law,
1Cor 7:36 his betrothed, if his P are strong, and it
Gal 5:24 the flesh with its P and desires.
Eph 2:3 once lived in the P of our flesh, following
2Tim 2:22 So shun youthful P and aim at righteousness, faith,
Tit 2:12 renounce irreligion and worldly P, and to live sober,
3:3 astray, slaves to various P and pleasures, passing our
Jas 4:1 Is it not your P that are at war
4:3 you ask wrongly, to spend it on your P
1Pet 1:14 be conformed to the P of your former ignorance,
2:11 to abstain from the P of the flesh that
4:2 no longer by human P but by the will
4:3 do, living in licentiousness, P, drunkenness, revels,
2Pet 2:18 they entice with licentious P of the flesh men
3:3 scoffing, following their own P
Jude 1:16 malcontents, following their own P, loud-mouthed
1:18 there will be scoffers, following their own ungodly P

PASSOVER (77)

Ex 12:11 It is the LORD'S P.
12:21 families, and kill the P lamb.
12:27 sacrifice of the LORD's P, for he passed over
12:43 the ordinance of the P: no foreigner shall eat
12:48 and would keep the P to the LORD, let
34:25 the feast of the P be left until the
Lev 23:5 the month in the evening, is the LORD's P
Num 9:2 of Israel keep the P at its appointed time.
9:4 people of Israel that they should keep the P
9:5 And they kept the P in the first month,
9:6 could not keep the P on that day; and
9:10 shall still keep the P to the LORD.
9:12 the statute for the P they shall keep it.
9:13 refrains from keeping the P, that person shall be
9:14 and will keep the P to the LORD, according
9:14 the statute of the P and according to its
28:16 day of the first month is the LORD's P
33:3 the day after the P the people of Israel
Deut 16:1 Abib, and keep the P to the LORD your
16:2 you shall offer the P sacrifice to the LORD
16:5 may not offer the P sacrifice within any of
16:6 you shall offer the P sacrifice, in the evening
Josh 5:10 Gilgal they kept the P on the fourteenth day
5:11 the morrow after the P, on that very day,
2Kgs 23:21 the people, "Keep the P to the LORD your
23:22 For no such P had been kept since the
23:23 of King Josiah this P was kept to the
2Chr 30:1 Jerusalem, to keep the P to the LORD the
30:2 counsel to keep the P in the second month—
30:5 come and keep the P to the LORD the
30:15 And they killed the P lamb on the fourteenth
30:17 had to kill the P lamb for every one
30:18 yet they ate the P otherwise than as prescribed.
35:1 Josiah kept a P to the LORD in Jerusalem;
35:1 and they killed the P lamb on the fourteenth
35:6 And kill the P lamb, and sanctify yourselves, and
35:7 the lay people, as P offerings for all that
35:8 the priests for the P offerings two thousand six
35:9 the Levites for the P offerings five thousand lambs
35:11 And they killed the P lamb, and the priests
35:13 And they roasted the P lamb with fire according
35:16 day, to keep the P and to offer burnt
35:17 were present kept the P at that time, and
35:18 No P like it had been kept in Israel
35:18 had kept such a P as was kept by
35:19 reign of Josiah this P was kept.
Ezra 6:19 the first month the returned exiles kept the P
6:20 So they killed the P lamb for all the
Ezek 45:21 the feast of the P, and for seven days
Mt 26:2 after two days the P is coming, and the
26:17 have us prepare for you to eat the P
26:18 I will keep the P at your house with
26:19 Jesus had directed them, and they prepared the P
Mk 14:1 two days before the P and the feast of
14:12 when they sacrificed the P lamb, his disciples said
14:12 go and prepare for you to eat the P
14:14 am to eat the P with my disciples?'
14:16 he had told them; and they prepared the P
Lk 2:41 Jerusalem every year at the feast of the P
22:1 Unleavened Bread drew near, which is called the P
22:7 Bread, on which the P lamb had to be
22:8 "Go and prepare the P for us, that we
22:11 am to eat the P with my disciples?'
22:13 he had told them; and they prepared the P
22:15 desired to eat this P with you before I
Jn 2:13 The P of the Jews was at hand, and
2:23 in Jerusalem at the P feast, many believed in
6:4 Now the P, the feast of the Jews, was
11:55 Now the P of the Jews was at hand,
11:55 to Jerusalem before the P, to purify themselves.
12:1 Six days before the P, Jesus came to Bethany,
13:1 the feast of the P, when Jesus knew that
18:28 might not be defiled, but might eat the P
18:39 for you at the P; will you have me
19:14 of Preparation of the P; it was about the
Acts 12:4 him, intending after the P to bring him out
Heb 11:28 faith he kept the P and sprinkled the blood,

PAST (32)

Gen 50:4 weeping for him were P, Joseph spoke to the
Ex 21:29 to gore in the P, and its owner has
21:36 to gore in the P, and its owner has
Deut 4:32 the days that are P, which were before you,
4:42 with him in time P, and that by fleeing
19:4 with him in time P –
19:6 not at enmity with his neighbor in time P
Josh 20:5 having had no enmity against him in times P
1Sam 15:32 Agag said, "Surely the bitterness of death is P
2Sam 3:17 saying, "For some time P you have been seeking
5:2 In times P, when Saul was king over us,
15:34 father's servant in time P, so now I will
1Chr 9:20 over them in time P; the LORD was with
11:2 In times P, even when Saul was king, it
Job 4:15 A spirit glided P my face; the hair of
14:13 until thy wrath be P, that thou wouldest appoint
17:11 My days are P, my plans are broken off,
Ps 71:15 for their number is P my knowledge.
90:4 yesterday when it is P, or as a watch
Song 2:11 lo, the winter is P, the rain is over
Is 16:13 which the LORD spoke concerning Moab in the P
26:20 for a little while until the wrath is P
Jer 8:20 "The harvest is P, the summer is ended, and
Dan 13:52 have committed in the P,
1Mac 12:7 Already in time P a letter was sent to
Mk 16:1 the sabbath was P, Mary Magdalene, and Mary
Lk 1:3 closely for some time P, to write an orderly
Acts 14:16 In P generations he allowed all the nations to
20:16 had decided to sail P Ephesus, so that he
2Tim 2:18 that the resurrection is P already.
Heb 11:11 even when she was P the age, since she
1Pet 4:3 the time that is P suffice for doing what

PASTORS

Eph 4:11 prophets, some evangelists, some P and teachers,

PASTURE (146)

Gen 29:7 the sheep, and go, P them."
37:12 his brothers went to P their father's flock near
47:4 for there is no P for your servants' flocks,
Num 35:2 give to the Levites P lands round about the
35:3 dwell in, and their P lands shall be for
35:4 The P lands of the cities, which you shall
35:5 belong to them as P land for their cities.
35:7 be forty-eight, with their P lands.
Josh 14:4 dwell in, with their P lands for their cattle
21:2 in, along with their P lands for our cattle."
21:3 the following cities and P lands out of their

P

21:8 These cities and their P lands the people of
21:11 Judah, along with the P lands round about it.
21:13 the slayer, with its P lands, Libnah with its
21:13 lands, Libnah with its P lands,
21:14 lands, Jattir with its P lands, Eshtemoa with its
21:14 lands, Eshtemoa with its P lands,
21:15 lands, Holon with its P lands, Debir with its
21:15 lands, Debir with its P lands,
21:16 lands, Ain with its P lands, Juttah with its
21:16 lands, Juttah with its P lands, Beth-shemesh with its
21:16 lands, Beth-shemesh with its P lands--nine cities out
21:17 Benjamin, Gibeon with its P lands, Geba with its
21:17 lands, Geba with its P lands,
21:18 lands, Anathoth with its P lands, and Almon with
21:18 and Almon with its P lands--four cities.
21:19 thirteen cities with their P lands.
21:21 the slayer, with its P lands in the hill
21:21 Ephraim, Gezer with its P lands,
21:22 lands, Kibza-im with its P lands, Beth-horon with its
21:22 lands, Beth-horon with its P lands--four cities;
21:23 Dan, Elteke with its P lands, Gibbethon with its
21:23 lands, Gibbethon with its P lands,
21:24 lands, Aijalon with its P lands, Gath-rimmon with its
21:24 lands, Gath-rimmon with its P lands--four cities;
21:25 Manasseh, Taanach with its P lands, and
21:25 and Gath-rimmon with its P lands--two cities.
21:26 in all with their P lands.
21:27 in Bashan with its P lands, the city of
21:27 and Beeshterah with its P lands--two cities;
21:28 Issachar, Kishion with its P lands, Daberath with its
21:28 lands, Daberath with its P lands,
21:29 lands, Jarmuth with its P lands, En-gannim with its
21:29 lands, En-gannim with its P lands--four cities;
21:30 Asher, Mishal with its P lands, Abdon with its
21:30 lands, Abdon with its P lands,
21:31 lands, Helkath with its P lands, and Rehob with
21:31 and Rehob with its P lands--four cities;
21:32 in Galilee with its P lands, the city of
21:32 slayer, Hammoth-dor with its P lands, and Kartan
21:32 and Kartan with its P lands--three cities.
21:33 thirteen cities with their P lands.
21:34 Zebulun, Jokne-am with its P lands, Kartah with its
21:34 lands, Kartah with its P lands,
21:35 lands, Dimnah with its P lands, Nahalal with its
21:35 lands, Nahalal with its P lands--four cities;
21:36 Reuben, Bezer with its P lands, Jahaz with its
21:36 lands, Jahaz with its P lands,
21:37 lands, Kedemoth with its P lands, and Mephaath
21:37 and Mephaath with its P lands--four cities;
21:38 in Gilead with its P lands, the city of
21:38 slayer, Mahanaim with its P lands,
21:39 lands, Heshbon with its P lands, Jazer with its
21:39 lands, Jazer with its P lands--four cities in
21:41 forty-eight cities with their P lands.
21:42 cities had each its P lands round about it;
2Sam 7:8 took you from the P, from following the sheep,
1Chr 4:39 the valley, to seek P for their flocks,
4:40 they found rich, good P, and the land was
4:41 place, because there was P there for their flocks.
5:16 and in all the P lands of Sharon to
6:55 Judah and its surrounding P lands,
6:57 Hebron, Libnah with its P lands, Jattir, Eshtemoa
6:57 Jattir, Eshtemoa with its P lands,
6:58 lands, Hilen with its P lands, Debir with its
6:58 lands, Debir with its P lands,
6:59 lands, Ashan with its P lands, and Beth-shemesh with
6:59 and Beth-shemesh with its P lands;
6:60 Benjamin, Geba with its P lands, Alemeth with its
6:60 lands, Alemeth with its P lands, and Anathoth with
6:60 and Anathoth with its P lands.
6:64 the cities with their P lands.
6:67 refuge: Shechem with its P lands in the hill
6:67 Ephraim, Gezer with its P lands,
6:68 lands, Jokmeam with its P lands, Beth-horon with its
6:68 lands, Beth-horon with its P lands,
6:69 lands, Aijalon with its P lands, Gath-rimmon with its
6:69 lands, Gath-rimmon with its P lands,
6:70 Manasseh, Aner with its P lands, and Bile-am with
6:70 and Bile-am with its P lands, for the rest
6:71 in Bashan with its P lands and Ashtaroth with
6:71 and Ashtaroth with its P lands;
6:72 Issachar: Kedesh with its P lands, Daberath with its
6:72 lands, Daberath with its P lands,
6:73 lands, Ramoth with its P lands, and Anem with
6:73 and Anem with its P lands;
6:74 Asher: Mashal with its P lands, Abdon with its
6:74 lands, Abdon with its P lands,
6:75 lands, Hukok with its P lands, and Rehob with
6:75 and Rehob with its P lands;
6:76 in Galilee with its P lands, Hammon with its
6:76 lands, Hammon with its P lands, and Kiriathaim with
6:76 and Kiriathaim with its P lands.
6:77 Zebulun: Rimmono with its P lands, Tabor with its
6:77 lands, Tabor with its P lands,
6:78 the steppe with its P lands, Jahzah with its
6:78 lands, Jahzah with its P lands,
6:79 lands, Kedemoth with its P lands, and Mephaath
6:79 and Mephaath with its P lands;
6:80 in Gilead with its P lands, Mahanaim with its
6:80 lands, Mahanaim with its P lands,
6:81 lands, Heshbon with its P lands, and Jazer with
6:81 and Jazer with its P lands.
13:2 the cities that have P lands, that they may
17:7 took you from the P, from following the sheep,
Job 24:2 they seize flocks and P them.
39:8 the mountains as his P, and he searches after
Ps 74:1 thy anger smoke against the sheep of thy P
79:13 the flock of thy P, will give thanks to
95:7 the people of his P, and the sheep of
100:3 are his people, and the sheep of his P
Song 1:7 soul loves, where you P your flock, where you
1:8 of the flock, and P your kids beside the
6:2 beds of spices, to P his flock in the
Is 5:17 graze as in their P, fatlings and kids shall
32:14 of wild asses, a P of flocks;
49:9 heights shall be their P;
65:10 Sharon shall become a P for flocks, and the
Jer 6:3 around her, they shall P, each in his place.
23:1 who destroy and scatter the sheep of my P
25:36 LORD is despoiling their P,
50:19 restore Israel to his P, and he shall feed
Lam 1:6 harts that find no P; they fled without strength
Ezek 25:5 will make Rabbah a P for camels and the
34:14 feed them with good P, and upon the mountain
34:14 Israel shall be their P; there they shall lie
34:14 land, and on fat P they shall feed on
34:18 feed on the good P, that you must tread
34:18 the rest of your P; and to drink of
34:31 the sheep of my P, and I am your
Hos 4:16 feed them like a lamb in a broad P
Joel 1:17 because there is no P for them; even the
Mic 2:12 a flock in its P, a noisy multitude of
Zeph 2:7 on which they shall P, and in the houses
3:13 For they shall P and lie down, and none
Jn 10:9 and will go in and out and find P

PASTURE-FED

1Kgs 4:23 fat oxen, and twenty P cattle, a hundred sheep,

PASTURED (2)

Gen 36:24 the wilderness, as he P the asses of Zibeon
1Chr 27:29 Over the herds that P in Sharon was Shitrai

PASTURES (16)

Ps 23:2 want; he makes me lie down in green P
37:20 the glory of the P, they vanish--like smoke
65:12 The P of the wilderness drip, the hills gird
83:12 for ourselves of the P of God."
Song 2:16 I am his, he P his flock among the
6:3 beloved is mine; he P his flock among the
Sir 13:18 likewise the poor are P for the rich.
Is 7:19 on all the thornbushes, and on all the P
30:23 will graze in large P;
Jer 9:10 a lamentation for the P of the wilderness, because
23:10 land mourns, and the P of the wilderness are
Joel 1:18 fire has devoured the P of the wilderness, and
1:19 fire has devoured the P of the wilderness.
2:22 the field, for the P of the wilderness are
Amos 1:2 voice from Jerusalem; the P of the shepherds mourn
Zeph 2:6 O seacoast, shall be P, meadows for shepherds and

PASTURING (2)

Gen 37:13 "Are not your brothers P the flock at Shechem?
37:16 you, where they are P the flock."

PATARA

Acts 21:1 next day to Rhodes, and from there to P

PATCH (2)

Mt 9:16 old garment, for the P tears away from the
Mk 2:21 if he does, the P tears away from it,

P

PATCHED

Josh 9:5 and mended, with worn-out, P sandals on their feet,

PATE

Ps 7:16 and on his own P his violence descends.

PATH (46)

Gen 49:17 a viper by the P, that bites the horse's
Num 22:24 stood in a narrow P between the vineyards, with
Jud 13:20 walking in the straight P before our God." And
15:2 and fled by every P across the plain and
Job 18:10 the ground, a trap for him in the P
28:7 "That P no bird of prey knows, and the
30:13 They break up my P, they promote my calamity;
Ps 16:11 dost show me the P of life; in thy
27:11 me on a level P because of my enemies.
77:19 through the sea, thy P through the great waters;
78:50 He made a P for his anger; he did
119:35 Lead me in the P of thy commandments, for
119:105 to my feet and a light to my P
139:3 Thou searchest out my P and my lying down,
142:3 In the P where I walk they have hidden
143:10 thy good spirit lead me on a level P
Prov 1:7 Beware of the P of Greed and Violence
2:9 and equity, every good P;
4:15 Do not enter the P of the wicked, and
4:19 But the P of the righteous is like the
4:27 Take heed to the P of your feet, then
5:5 her steps follow the P to Sheol;
5:6 take heed to the P of life; her ways
10:17 instruction is on the P to life, but he
12:28 In the P of righteousness is life, but the
15:19 with thorns, but the P of the upright is
15:24 The wise man's P leads upward to life, that
Wis 14:3 hast given it a P in the sea, and
Sir 5:9 wind, nor follow every P: the double-tongued sinner
32:20 not go on a P full of hazards, and
50:29 for the light of the Lord is his P
51:15 entered upon the straight P; from my youth I
Is 26:7 dost make smooth the P of the righteous.
26:8 In the P of thy judgments, O LORD, we
30:11 turn aside from the P, let us hear no
40:14 who taught him the P of justice, and taught
43:16 in the sea, a P in the mighty waters,
Jer 31:9 water, in a straight P in which they shall
Bar 3:31 is concerned about the P to her.
Joel 2:8 each marches in his P; they burst through the
Mt 13:4 seeds fell along the P, and the birds came
13:19 heart; this is what was sown along the P
Mk 4:4 seed fell along the P, and the birds came
4:15 the ones along the P, where the word is
Lk 8:5 some fell along the P, and was trodden under
8:12 The ones along the P are those who have

PATHLESS

Job 12:24 them wander in a P waste.

PATHROS (5)

Is 11:11 Assyria, from Egypt, from P, from Ethiopia, from
Jer 44:1 in the land of P,
44:15 people who dwelt in P in the land of
Ezek 29:14 to the land of P, the land of their
30:14 I will make P a desolation, and will set

PATHRUSIM (2)

Gen 10:14 Anamim, Lehabim, Naph-tuhim, P, Casluhim
1Chr 1:12 Ludim, Anamim, Lehabim, Naph-tuhim, P, Casluhim

PATHS (54)

Tob 4:19 and that all your P and plans may prosper.
Job 8:13 Such are the P of all who forget God;
13:27 and watchest all my P; thou settest a bound
19:8 pass, and he has set darkness upon my P
24:13 its ways, and do not stay in its P
33:11 and watches all my P
38:20 you may discern the P to its home?
Ps 8:8 whatever passes along the P of the sea.
17:5 held fast to thy P, my feet have not
23:3 He leads me in P of righteousness for his
25:4 know thy ways, O LORD; teach me thy P
25:10 All the P of the LORD are steadfast love
Prov 1:15 your foot from their P;
2:8 in integrity, guarding the P of justice and preserving
2:13 speech, who forsake the P of uprightness to walk
2:15 of evil; men whose P are crooked, and who
2:18 to death, and her P to the shades;
2:19 do they regain the P of life.
2:20 and keep to the P of the righteous.
3:6 acknowledge him, and he will make straight your P
3:17 pleasantness, and all her P are peace.
4:12 led you in the P of uprightness.
5:21 of the LORD, and he watches all his P
7:25 not stray into her P;
8:2 the way, in the P she takes her stand;
8:20 of righteousness, in the P of justice,
Wis 5:7 our fill of the P of lawlessness and destruction,
6:16 to them in their P, and meets them in
9:18 And thus the P of those on earth were
10:10 guided him on straight P; she showed him the
12:24 far astray on the P of error, accepting as
Sir 4:17 with him on tortuous P, she will bring fear
14:22 a hunter, and lie in wait on her P
32:22 smooth way, and give good heed to your P
Is 2:3 ways and that we may walk in his P
3:12 mislead you, and confuse the course of your P
41:3 passes on safely, by P his feet have not
42:16 they know not, in P that they have not
59:8 no justice in their P; they have made their
Jer 6:16 ask for the ancient P, where the good way
23:12 to them like slippery P in the darkness, into
Lam 3:9 he has made my P crooked.
Bar 3:20 knowledge, nor understood her P, nor laid hold of
3:23 way to wisdom, nor given thought to her P
4:13 commandments, nor tread the P of discipline in his
Hos 2:6 against her, so that she cannot find her P
Joel 2:7 his way, they do not swerve from their P
Mic 4:2 his ways and we may walk in his P
Mt 3:3 the Lord, make his P straight."
Mk 1:3 the Lord, make his P straight--"
Lk 3:4 the Lord, make his P straight.
Acts 13:10 making crooked the straight P of the Lord?
Rom 3:16 shed blood, in their P are ruin and misery,
Heb 12:13 knees, and make straight P for your feet, so

PATHWAY

Wis 5:12 at once, so that no one knows its P

PATIENCE (23)

Prov 25:15 With P a ruler may be persuaded, and a
Sir 16:13 his plunder, and the P of the godly will
41:2 one who is contrary, and has lost his P
Bar 4:25 My children, endure with P the wrath that has
1Mac 8:4 by their planning and P, even though the place
Mt 18:25 imploring him, 'Lord, have P with me, and I
18:28 and besought him, 'Have P with me, and I
Lk 8:15 and good heart, and bring forth fruit with P
Rom 2:4 the riches of his kindness and forbearance and P
2:7 to those who by P in well-doing seek for
8:25 do not see, we wait for it with P
9:22 has endured with much P the vessels of wrath
2Cor 12:12 among you in all P, with signs and wonders
Gal 5:22 is love, joy, peace, P, kindness, goodness, faithfulness,
Eph 4:2 lowliness and meekness, with P, forbearing one
Col 1:11 for all endurance and P with joy,
3:12 kindness, lowliness, meekness, and P,
1Tim 1:16 might display his perfect P for an example to
2Tim 3:10 life, my faith, my P, my love, my steadfastness,
4:2 exhort, be unfailing in P and in teaching.
Heb 6:12 who through faith and P inherit the promises.
Jas 5:10 example of suffering and P, brethren, take the
1Pet 3:20 not obey, when God's P waited in the days

PATIENT (19)

Job 6:11 what is my end, that I should be P
Prov 14:17 acts foolishly, but a man of discretion is P
Eccl 7:8 its beginning; and the P in spirit is better
Wis 15:1 art kind and true, P, and ruling all things
Sir 1:20 A P man will endure until the right moment,
2:4 you, and in changes that humble you be P
18:10 Therefore the Lord is P with them and pours
29:8 Nevertheless, be P with a man in humble
35:18 neither will he be P with them, till he
Rom 12:12 in your hope, be P in tribulation, be constant
1Cor 13:4 Love is P and kind; love is not jealous
1Thes 5:14 help the weak, be P with them all.
Jas 5:7 Be P, therefore, brethren, until the coming of the
5:7 of the earth, being P over it until it
5:8 You also be P
Rev 1:9 the kingdom and the P endurance, was on the
2:2 your toil and your P endurance, and how you
2:19 faith and service and P endurance, and that your
3:10 kept my word of P endurance, I will keep

PATIENTLY (9)
Ps 37:7 the LORD, and wait P for him; fret not
40:1 I waited P for the LORD; he inclined to
2Mac 6:14 nations the Lord waits P to punish them until
Acts 26:3 therefore I beg you to listen to me P
2Cor 1:6 experience when you P endure the same sufferings
Heb 6:15 Abraham, having P endured, obtained the promise.
1Pet 2:20 and are beaten for it you take it P
2:20 it you take it P, you have God's approval.
Rev 2:3 know you are enduring P and bearing up for

PATMOS
Rev 1:9 on the island called P on account of the

PATRIARCH (2)
Acts 2:29 you confidently of the P David that he both
Heb 7:4 Abraham the P gave him a tithe of the

PATRIARCHS (4)
Acts 7:8 father of Jacob, and Jacob of the twelve P
7:9 "And the P, jealous of Joseph, sold him into
Rom 9:5 to them belong the P, and of their race,
15:8 promises given to the P,

PATRIMONY
Deut 18:8 what he receives from the sale of his P

PATROBAS
Rom 16:14 Greet Asyncritus, Phlegon, Hermes, P, Hermas, and

PATROCLUS
2Mac 8:9 Nicanor the son of P, one of the king's

PATROL (4)
Jud 10:11 valley; and an Assyrian P met her
Zech 1:10 LORD has sent to P the earth.'
6:7 to get off and P the earth.
6:7 And he said, "Go, P the earth." So they

PATROLLED (2)
Zech 1:11 myrtle trees, 'We have P the earth, and behold,
6:7 So they P the earth.

PATTERN (8)
Ex 25:9 show you concerning the P of the tabernacle, and
25:40 make them after the P for them, which is
Num 8:4 work; according to the P which the LORD had
2Kgs 16:10 the altar, and its P, exact in all its
Sir 38:28 eyes are on the P of the object.
Acts 7:44 it, according to the P that he had seen.
2Tim 1:13 Follow the P of the sound words which you
Heb 8:5 everything according to the P which was shown you

PAU
Gen 36:39 of his city being P; his wife's name was

PAUL (161)
Acts 13:9 who is also called P, filled with the Holy
13:13 Now P and his company set sail from Paphos,
13:16 So P stood up, and motioning with his hand
13:43 converts to Judaism followed P and Barnabas, who
13:45 what was spoken by P, and reviled him.
13:46 And P and Barnabas spoke out boldly, saying, "It
13:50 stirred up persecution against P and Barnabas, and
14:9 He listened to P speaking; and Paul, looking intently
14:9 to Paul speaking; and P, looking intently at him
14:11 the crowds saw what P had done, they lifted
14:12 they called Zeus, and P, because he was the
14:14 the apostles Barnabas and P heard of it, they
14:19 the people, they stoned P and dragged him out
15:2 And when P and Barnabas had no small dissension
15:2 and debate with them, P and Barnabas and some
15:12 listened to Barnabas and P as they related what
15:22 them to Antioch with P and Barnabas.
15:25 our beloved Barnabas and P,
15:34 But P and Barnabas remained in Antioch, teaching
15:35 And after some days P said to Barnabas, "Come,
15:37 But P thought best not to take with them
15:39 away to Cyprus, but P chose Silas and departed,
16:3 P wanted Timothy to accompany him; and he took
16:9 a vision appeared to P in the night: a
16:14 to give heed to what was said by P
16:17 She followed P and us, crying, "These men are
16:18 But P was annoyed, and turned and said to
16:19 was gone, they seized P and Silas and dragged
16:25 But about midnight P and Silas were praying and
16:28 But P cried with a loud voice, "Do not
16:29 he fell down before P and Silas,
16:36 reported the words to P, saying, "The magistrates
16:37 But P said to them, "They have beaten us
17:2 And P went in, as was his custom, and
17:4 were persuaded, and joined P and Silas; as did
17:10 The brethren immediately sent P and Silas away by
17:13 God was proclaimed by P at Beroea also, they
17:14 the brethren immediately sent P off on his way
17:15 Those who conducted P brought him as far as
17:16 Now while P was waiting for them at Athens,
17:22 So P, standing in the middle of the Are-opagus,
17:33 So P went out from among them.
18:5 Timothy arrived from Macedonia, P was occupied
18:8 Corinthians hearing P believed and were baptized.
18:9 the Lord said to P one night in a
18:12 a united attack upon P and brought him before
18:14 But when P was about to open his mouth,
18:18 After this P stayed many days longer, and then
19:1 Apollos was at Corinth, P passed through the upper
19:4 And P said, "John baptized with the baptism of
19:6 And when P had laid his hands upon them,
19:11 by the hands of P,
19:13 by the Jesus whom P preaches."
19:15 "Jesus I know, and P I know; but who
19:21 Now after these events P resolved in the Spirit
19:26 throughout all Asia this P has persuaded and turned
19:29 Macedonians who were P's companions in travel.
19:30 P wished to go in among the crowd, but
20:1 After the uproar ceased, P sent for the disciples
20:7 together to break bread, P talked with them,
20:9 a deep sleep as P talked still longer; and
20:10 But P went down and bent over him, and
20:11 And when P had gone up and had broken
20:13 Assos, intending to take P aboard there; for so
20:16 For P had decided to sail past Ephesus, so
20:37 all wept and embraced P and kissed him,
21:4 the Spirit they told P not to go on
21:11 to us he took P's girdle and bound his
21:13 Then P answered, "What are you doing, weeping
21:18 On the following day P went in with us
21:26 Then P took the men, and the next day
21:29 and they supposed that P had brought him into
21:30 ran together; they seized P and dragged him out
21:32 the tribune and the soldiers, they stopped beating P
21:37 As P was about to be brought into the
21:39 P replied, "I am a Jew, from Tarsus in
21:40 had given him leave, P, standing on the steps,
22:25 up with the thongs, P said to the centurion
22:28 P said, "But I was born a citizen."
22:29 for he realized that P was a Roman citizen
22:30 meet, and he brought P down and set him
23:1 P, looking intently at the council, said, "Brethren,
23:3 Then P said to him, "God shall strike you,
23:5 And P said, "I did not know, brethren, that
23:6 But when P perceived that one part were Sadducees
23:10 the tribune, afraid that P would be torn in
23:12 to eat nor drink till they had killed P
23:14 to taste no food till we have killed P
23:16 Now the son of P's sister heard of their
23:16 he went and entered the barracks and told P
23:17 And P called one of the centurions and said,
23:18 the tribune and said, P the prisoner called me
23:20 ask you to bring P down to the council
23:24 Also provide mounts for P to ride, and bring
23:31 to their instructions, took P and brought him by
23:33 the governor, they presented P also before him.
24:1 governor their case against P;
24:9 to him to speak, P replied: "Realizing that for
24:23 and he sent for P and heard him speak
24:25 hoped that money would be given him by P
24:26 a favor, Felix left P in prison.
25:2 Jews informed him against P; and they urged him,
25:4 Festus replied that P was being kept at Caesarea,
25:6 the tribunal and ordered P to be brought.
25:8 P said in his defense, "Neither against the law
25:9 a favor, said to P, "Do you wish to
25:10 But P said, "I am standing before Caesar's tribunal,
25:14 many days, Festus laid P's case before the king,
25:19 was dead, but whom P asserted to be alive.
25:21 But when P had appealed to be kept in
25:23 by command of Festus P was brought in.
26:1 Agrippa said to P, "You have permission to speak
26:1 Then P stretched out his hand and made his
26:24 with a loud voice, P, you are mad; your
26:25 But P said, "I am not mad, most excellent

26:28 And Agrippa said to P, "In a short time
26:29 And P said, "Whether short or long, I would
27:1 for Italy, they delivered P and some other prisoners
27:3 Sidon; and Julius treated P kindly, and gave him
27:9 had already gone by, P advised them,
27:11 ship than to what P said.
27:21 been long without food, P then came forward among
27:24 'Do not be afraid, P; you must stand before
27:31 anchors from the bow, P said to the centurion
27:33 was about to dawn, P urged them all to
27:43 centurion, wishing to save P, kept them from carrying
28:3 P had gathered a bundle of sticks and put
28:8 fever and dysentery; and P visited him and prayed,
28:15 On seeing them P thanked God and took courage.
28:16 we came into Rome, P was allowed to stay
28:25 themselves, they departed, after P had made one
Rom 1:1 P, a servant of Jesus
1Cor 1:1 P, called by the will
1:12 each one of you says, "I belong to P
1:13 Was P crucified for you?
1:13 Or were you baptized in the name of P
3:4 For when one says, "I belong to P
3:5 What is P
3:22 things are yours, whether P or Apollos or Cephas
16:21 I, P, write this greeting with my own hand.
2Cor 1:1 P, an apostle of Christ
10:1 I, P, myself entreat you, by the meekness and
Gal 1:1 P an apostle--not from
5:2 Now I, P, say to you that if you
Eph 1:1 P, an apostle of Christ
3:1 For this reason I, P, a prisoner for Christ
Phil 1:1 P and Timothy, servants of
Col 1:1 P, an apostle of Christ
1:23 and of which I, P, became a minister.
4:18 I, P, write this greeting with my own hand.
1Thes 1:1 P, Silvanus, and Timothy, to
2:18 come to you--I, P, again and again--but
2Thes 1:1 P, Silvanus, and Timothy, to
3:17 I, P, write this greeting with my own hand.
1Tim 1:1 P, an apostle of Christ
2Tim 1:1 P, an apostle of Christ
Tit 1:1 P, a servant of God
Philem 1:1 P, a prisoner for Christ
1:9 appeal to you--I, P, an ambassador and now
1:19 I, P, write this with my own hand, I
2Pet 3:15 also our beloved brother P wrote to you according

PAULUS
Acts 13:7 with the proconsul, Sergius P, a man of intelligence,

PAVED (2)
Tob 13:17 of Jerusalem will be P with beryl and ruby
Sir 21:10 of sinners is smoothly P with stones, but at

PAVEMENT (11)
Ex 24:10 as it were a P of sapphire stone, like
2Chr 7:3 the earth on the P, and worshiped and gave
Esth 1:6 on a mosaic P of porphyry, marble, mother-of-pearl
Sir 20:17 A slip on the P is better than a
Jer 43:9 the mortar in the P which is at the
Ezek 40:17 were chambers and a P, round about the court;
40:17 about the court; thirty chambers fronted on the P
40:18 And the P ran along the side of the
40:18 length of the gates; this was the lower P
42:3 court, and facing the P which belonged to the
Jn 19:13 a place called The P, and in Hebrew, Gabbatha.

PAVILION (3)
Job 36:29 spreading of the clouds, the thunderings of his P
Is 4:5 glory there will be a canopy and a P
2Mac 13:15 he attacked the king's P at night and slew

PAW (2)
1Sam 17:37 delivered me from the P of the lion and
17:37 lion and from the P of the bear, will

PAWS (2)
Lev 11:27 that go on their P, among the animals that
Job 39:21 He P in the valley, and exults in his

PAY (80)
Gen 50:15 will hate us and P us back for all
Ex 5:9 labor at it and P no regard to lying
21:19 clear; only he shall P for the loss of
21:22 him; and he shall P as the judges determine.
21:36 it in, he shall P ox for ox, and
22:1 sells it, he shall P five oxen for an
22:2 a sheep, he shall P double.
22:7 is found, he shall P double.
22:9 God shall condemn shall P double to his neighbor.
22:17 to him, he shall P money equivalent to the
Lev 25:27 he sold it and P back the overpayment to
27:8 is too poor to P your valuation, then he
Num 20:19 cattle, then I will P for it; let me
Deut 23:21 not be slack to P it; for the LORD
Judg 6:10 God; you shall not P reverence to the gods
1Sam 1:21 yearly sacrifice, and to P his vow.
2Sam 15:7 let me go and P my vow, which I
1Kgs 5:6 servants, and I will P you for your servants
20:39 or else you shall P a talent of silver.'
2Kgs 4:7 sell the oil and P your debts, and you
12:15 delivered the money to P out to the workmen,
Ezra 4:13 finished, they will not P tribute, custom, or toll,
Tob 4:14 works for you, but P him at once; and
5:3 you and I will P him wages as long
5:11 man whom you will P to go with your
5:14 wages am I to P you--a drachma a
Jud 7:15 So you will P them back with evil, because
Esth 3:9 destroyed, and I will P ten thousand talents of
4:7 Haman had promised to P into the king's treasuries
Job 22:27 you; and you will P your vows.
Ps 22:25 my vows I will P before those who fear
31:6 Thou hatest those who P regard to vain idols;
37:21 wicked borrows, and cannot P back, but the
50:14 sacrifice of thanksgiving, and P your vows to the
61:8 thy name, as I P my vows day after
66:13 burnt offerings; I will P thee my vows,
116:14 the LORD, I will P my vows to the
116:18 I will P my vows to the LORD in
Prov 6:31 is caught, he will P sevenfold; he will give
8:5 prudence; O foolish men, P attention.
19:19 of great wrath will P the penalty; for if
22:27 nothing with which to P, why should your bed
24:29 to me; I will P the man back for
Eccl 5:4 P what you vow.
5:5 vow than that you should vow and not P
Sir 8:13 give surety, be concerned as one who must P
16:22 and acquire knowledge, and P close attention to my
29:5 will delay, and will P in words of unconcern,
36:20 man of experience will P him back.
37:11 a big task-- P no attention to these
Lam 5:4 We must P for the water we drink, the
Ezek 29:18 anything from Tyre to P for the labor that
Dan 3:12 These men, O king, P no heed to you;
Jon 2:8 Those who P regard to vain idols forsake their
2:9 to thee; what I have vowed I will P
1Mac 2:68 P back the Gentiles in full, and heed what
3:28 and gave a year's P to his forces, and
8:2 and forced them to P tribute,
8:7 reign after him should P a heavy tribute and
2Mac 4:9 this he promised to P one hundred and fifty
4:27 but he did not P regularly any of the
Mt 10:8 You received without paying, give without P
17:23 "Does not your teacher P the tax?"
18:24 as he could not P, his lord ordered him
18:25 me, and I will P you everything.'
18:27 the throat he said, P what you owe.'
18:28 me, and I will P you.'
18:29 prison till he should P the debt.
18:33 jailers, till he should P all his debt.
20:8 'Call the laborers and P them their wages, beginning
22:17 Is it lawful to P taxes to Caesar, or
Mk 12:14 Is it lawful to P taxes to Caesar, or
12:15 Should we P them, or should we not?" But
Lk 7:42 When they could not P, he forgave them both.
Acts 21:24 along with them and P their expenses, so that
Rom 13:6 same reason you also P taxes, for the authorities
13:7 P all of them their dues, taxes to whom
Heb 2:1 Therefore we must P the closer attention to what
Jas 2:3 comes in, and you P attention to the one
2Pet 1:19 will do well to P attention to this as

PAYING (8)
Deut 26:12 "When you have finished P all the tithe of
Eccl 5:4 God, do not delay P it; for he has
Wis 13:1 recognize the craftsman while P heed to his works;
Sir 18:21 nothing hinder you from P a vow promptly, and
Joel 3:4 Are you P me back for something?
3:4 If you are P me back, I will requite
Mt 10:8 You received without P, give without pay.
2Thes 3:8 any one's bread without P, but with toil and

PAYMENT (13)

Ex 21:11 out for nothing, without P of money.
Lev 22:18 his offering, whether in P of a vow or
Deut 23:18 LORD your God in P for any vow; for
Tob 4:14 and if you serve God you will receive P
Job 31:39 eaten its yield without P, and caused the death
Is 65:7 measure into their bosom P for their former doings."
Ezek 27:15 they brought you in P ivory tusks and ebony.
1Mac 10:29 all the Jews from P of tribute and salt
10:33 I set free without P; and let all officials
2Mac 4:28 the citadel kept requesting P, for the collection of
Mt 18:24 that he had, and P to be made.
Phil 4:18 I have received full P, and more; I am
Rev 21:6 the fountain of the water of life without P

PAYMENTS (2)

1Mac 11:35 And the other P henceforth due to us of
15:5 from all the other P from which they have

PAYS (4)

Job 24:12 for help; yet God P no attention to their
Sir 20:11 for a little, but P for it seven times
28:16 Whoever P heed to slander will not find rest,
Dan 6:13 the exiles from Judah, P no heed to you,

PE-ULLETHAI

1Chr 26:5 sixth, Issachar the seventh, P the eighth; for God

PEACE (419)

Gen 15:15 to your fathers in P; you shall be buried
26:29 but good and have sent you away in P
26:31 their way, and they departed from him in P
28:21 my father's house in P, then the LORD shall
34:5 so Jacob held his P until they came.
44:17 you, go up in P to your father."
Ex 4:18 And Jethro said to Moses, "Go in P
18:23 people also will go to their place in P
20:24 burnt offerings and your P offerings, your sheep and
24:5 burnt offerings and sacrificed P offerings of oxen to
29:28 of Israel from their P offerings; it is their
32:6 burnt offerings and brought P offerings; and the
Lev 3:1 is a sacrifice of P offering, if he offers
3:3 the sacrifice of the P offering, as an offering
3:6 for a sacrifice of P offering to the LORD
3:9 the sacrifice of the P offering as an offering
4:10 the sacrifice of the P offerings), and the priest
4:26 of the sacrifice of P offerings; so the priest
4:31 is removed from the P offerings, and the priest
4:35 from the sacrifice of P offerings, and the priest
6:12 the fat of the P offerings.
7:11 of the sacrifice of P offerings which one may
7:13 the sacrifice of his P offerings for thanksgiving he
7:14 the blood of the P offerings.
7:15 the sacrifice of his P offerings for thanksgiving shall
7:18 the sacrifice of his P offering is eaten on
7:20 sacrifice of the LORD's P offerings while an
7:21 sacrifice of the LORD's P offerings, that person shall
7:29 the sacrifice of his P offerings to the LORD
7:29 the sacrifice of his P offerings
7:32 the sacrifice of your P offerings;
7:33 the blood of the P offerings and the fat
7:34 the sacrifices of their P offerings, and have given
7:37 consecration, and of the P offerings,
9:4 and a ram for P offerings, to sacrifice before
9:18 ram, the sacrifice of P offerings for the people;
9:22 burnt offering and the P offerings.
10:3 And Aaron held his P
10:14 the sacrifices of the P offerings of the people
17:5 them as sacrifices of P offerings to the LORD;
19:5 offer a sacrifice of P offerings to the LORD,
22:21 offers a sacrifice of P offerings to the LORD,
23:19 as a sacrifice of P offerings.
26:6 And I will give P in the land, and
Num 6:14 without blemish as a P offering,
6:17 as a sacrifice of P offering to the LORD,
6:18 the sacrifice of the P offering.
6:26 up his countenance upon you, and give you P
7:17 for the sacrifice of P offerings, two oxen, five
7:23 for the sacrifice of P offerings, two oxen, five
7:29 for the sacrifice of P offerings, two oxen, five
7:35 for the sacrifice of P offerings, two oxen, five
7:41 for the sacrifice of P offerings, two oxen, five
7:47 for the sacrifice of P offerings, two oxen, five
7:53 for the sacrifice of P offerings, two oxen, five
7:59 for the sacrifice of P offerings, two oxen, five
7:65 for the sacrifice of P offerings, two oxen, five
7:71 for the sacrifice of P offerings, two oxen, five
7:77 for the sacrifice of P offerings, two oxen, five
7:83 for the sacrifice of P offerings, two oxen, five
7:88 for the sacrifice of P offerings twenty-four bulls, the
10:10 the sacrifices of your P offerings; they shall serve
15:8 a vow, or for P offerings to the LORD,
25:12 him my covenant of P;
29:39 offerings, and for your P offerings."
Deut 2:26 Heshbon, with words of P, saying,
20:10 it, offer terms of P to it.
20:11 answer to you is P and it opens to
20:12 if it makes no P with you, but makes
23:6 shall not seek their P or their prosperity all
27:7 and you shall sacrifice P offerings, and shall eat
Josh 8:31 the LORD, and sacrificed P offerings.
9:15 And Joshua made P with them, and made a
10:1 of Gibeon had made P with Israel and were
10:4 for it has made P with Joshua and with
11:19 a city that made P with the people of
22:23 or cereal offerings or P offerings on it, may
22:27 offerings and sacrifices and P offerings; lest your
Judg 4:17 Kenite; for there was P between Jabin the king
6:23 LORD said to him, P be to you; do
6:24 the LORD, and called it, The LORD is P
8:9 I come again in P, I will break down
18:6 And the priest said to them, "Go in P
19:20 the old man said, P be to you; I
20:26 burnt offerings and P offerings before the LORD.
21:4 offered burnt offerings and P offerings.
21:13 of Rimmon, and proclaimed P to them.
1Sam 1:17 Eli answered, "Go in P, and the God of
7:14 There was P also between Israel and the Amorites.
10:8 offerings and to sacrifice P offerings.
10:27 But he held his P
11:15 There they sacrificed P offerings before the LORD,
13:9 to me, and the P offerings." And he offered
20:42 to David, "Go in P, forasmuch as we have
25:6 you shall salute him: P be to you, and
25:6 be to you, and P be to your house,
25:6 to your house, and P be to all that
25:35 her, "Go up in P to your house; see,
2Sam 3:21 David sent Abner away; and he went in P
3:22 sent him away, and he had gone in P
3:23 let him go, and he has gone in P
6:17 burnt offerings and P offerings before the LORD.
6:18 burnt offerings and the P offerings, he blessed the
10:19 by Israel, they made P with Israel, and became
13:20 Now hold your P, my sister; he is your
15:9 The king said to him, "Go in P
15:27 to the city in P, you and Abiathar, with
17:3 man, and all the people will be at P
24:25 offered burnt offerings and P offerings.
1Kgs 2:5 avenging in time of P blood which had been
2:6 his gray head go down to Sheol in P
2:33 throne, there shall be P from the LORD for
3:15 up burnt offerings and P offerings, and made a
4:24 Euphrates; and he had P on all sides round
5:12 him; and there was P between Hiram and Solomon;
8:63 Solomon offered as P offerings to the LORD twenty-
8:64 fat pieces of the P offerings, because the bronze
8:64 fat pieces of the P offerings.
9:25 up burnt offerings and P offerings upon the altar
20:18 have come out for P, take them alive; or
22:17 master; let each return to his home in P
22:27 of bread and water, until I come in P
22:28 "If you return in P, the LORD has not
22:44 Jehoshaphat also made P with the king of Israel.
2Kgs 2:3 he said, "Yes, I know it; hold your P
2:5 he answered, "Yes, I know it; hold your P
5:19 He said to him, "Go in P
9:17 meet them, and let him say, 'Is it P
9:18 and said, "Thus says the king, 'Is it P
9:18 Jehu said, "What have you to do with P
9:19 said, "Thus the king has said, 'Is it P
9:19 Jehu answered, "What have you to do with P
9:22 he said, "Is it P, Jehu?" He answered, "What
9:22 He answered, "What P can there be, so long
9:31 she said, "Is it P, you Zimri, murderer of
16:13 the blood of his P offerings upon the altar.
18:31 of Assyria: 'Make your P with me and come
20:19 if there will be P and security in my
22:20 to your grave in P, and your eyes shall
1Chr 12:18 P, peace to you, and peace to your helpers!
12:18 Peace, P to you, and peace to your helpers!
12:18 peace to you, and P to your helpers!
16:1 offered burnt offerings and P offerings before God.

PEACE

	16:2	burnt offerings and the P offerings, he blessed the
	19:19	by Israel, they made P with David, and became
	21:26	presented burnt offerings and P offerings, and called
	22:9	to you; he shall be a man of P
	22:9	I will give him P from all his enemies
	22:9	and I will give P and quiet to Israel
	22:18	he not given you P on every side?
	23:25	of Israel, has given P to his people; and
2Chr	7:7	the fat of the P offerings, because the bronze
	14:6	in those years, for the LORD gave him P
	14:7	he has given us P on every side." So
	15:5	times there was no P to him who went
	18:16	master; let each return to his home in P
	18:26	of bread and water, until I return in P
	18:27	"If you return in P, the LORD has not
	29:35	the fat of the P offerings, and there were
	30:22	for seven days, sacrificing P offerings and giving
	31:2	for burnt offerings and P offerings, to minister in
	33:16	upon it sacrifices of P offerings and of thanksgiving;
	34:28	to your grave in P, and your eyes shall
Ezra	5:7	written as follows: "To Darius the king, all P
	9:12	and never seek their P or prosperity, that you
Tob	13:14	They will rejoice in your P
	14:4	Media there will be P for a time.
Jud	3:1	messengers to sue for P, and said,
	7:25	injury in not making P with the Assyrians.
	8:35	to her, "Go in P, and may the Lord
Esth	7:4	would have held my P; for our affliction is
	9:30	Ahasuerus, in words of P and truth,
	10:3	his people and spoke P to all his people.
	13:2	extent, to re-establish the P which all men desire.
Job	5:23	field shall be at P with you.
	12:6	of robbers are at P, and those who provoke
	21:13	in prosperity, and in P they go down to
	22:21	God, and be at P; thereby good will come
	25:2	with God; he makes P in his high heaven.
Ps	4:8	In P I will both lie down and sleep;
	28:3	of evil, who speak P with their neighbors, while
	29:11	May the LORD bless his people with P
	34:14	and do good; seek P, and pursue it.
	35:20	they do not speak P, but against those who
	37:37	for there is posterity for the man of P
	39:2	silent, I held my P to no avail; my
	39:12	cry; hold not thy P at my tears!
	72:7	may righteousness flourish, and P abound, till the
	83:1	do not hold thy P or be still, O
	85:8	for he will speak P to his people, to
	85:10	will meet; righteousness and P will kiss each other.
	119:165	Great P have those who love thy law; nothing
	120:6	I had my dwelling among those who hate P
	120:7	I am for P; but when I speak, they
	122:6	Pray for the P of Jerusalem!
	122:7	P be within your walls, and security within your
	122:8	sake I will say, P be within you!"
	125:5	P be in Israel!
	128:6	P be upon Israel!
	147:14	He makes P in your borders; he fills you
Prov	3:17	ways of pleasantness, and all her paths are P
	10:10	causes trouble, but he who boldly reproves makes P
	16:7	enemies to be at P with him.
Eccl	3:8	a time for war, and a time for P
Song	8:10	was in his eyes as one who brings P
Wis	3:3	to be their destruction; but they are at P
	14:22	to ignorance, and they call such great evils P
Sir	1:16	crown of wisdom, making P and perfect health to
	6:6	those that are at P with you be many,
	13:17	What P is there between a hyena and a
	13:17	And what P between a rich man and a
	26:2	husband, and he will complete his years in P
	28:9	and inject enmity among those who are at P
	28:13	for he has destroyed many who were at P
	28:16	find rest, nor will he settle down in P
	35:1	the commandments sacrifices a P offering.
	41:1	one who lives at P among his possessions, to
	41:14	instruction and be at P; hidden wisdom and unseen
	44:15	bodies were buried in P, and their name lives
	45:24	Therefore a covenant of P was established with him,
	47:2	is selected from the P offering, so David was
	47:13	reigned in days of P, and God gave him
	47:16	far-off islands, and you were loved for your P
	50:23	heart, and grant that P may be in our
Is	9:6	Mighty God, Everlasting Father, Prince of P
	9:7	his government and of P there will be no
	26:3	keep him in perfect P, whose mind is stayed
	26:12	LORD, thou wilt ordain P for us, thou hast
	27:5	protection, let them make P with me, let them
	27:5	me, let them make P with me."
	32:17	of righteousness will be P, and the result of
	33:7	without; the envoys of P weep bitterly.
	36:16	of Assyria: Make your P with me and come
	39:8	thought, "There will be P and security in my
	42:14	I have held my P, I have kept still
	48:18	Then your P would have been like a river,
	48:22	"There is no P
	52:7	good tidings, who publishes P, who brings good
	54:10	and my covenant of P shall not be removed,
	55:12	be led forth in P; the mountains and the
	57:2	calamity, he enters into P; they rest in their
	57:11	I not held my P, even for a long
	57:19	P, peace, to the far and to the near,
	57:19	Peace, P, to the far and to the near,
	57:21	There is no P, says my God, for the
	59:8	The way of P they know not, and there
	59:8	crooked, no one who goes in them knows P
	60:17	overseers P and your taskmasters righteousness.
Jer	6:14	my people lightly, saying, P, peace,' when there is
	6:14	people lightly, saying, 'Peace, P when there is no
	6:14	lightly, saying, 'Peace, peace,' when there is no P
	8:11	my people lightly, saying, P, peace,' when there is
	8:11	people lightly, saying, 'Peace, P when there is no
	8:11	lightly, saying, 'Peace, peace,' when there is no P
	8:15	We looked for P, but no good came, for
	12:12	the land to the other; no flesh has P
	14:13	will give you assured P in this place.'"
	14:19	We looked for P, but no good came; for
	16:5	have taken away my P from this people, says
	28:9	the prophet who prophesies P, when the word of
	30:5	a cry of panic, of terror, and no P
	34:5	You shall die in P
	43:12	and he shall go away from there in P
Lam	3:17	soul is bereft of P, I have forgotten what
Bar	3:13	would be dwelling in P for ever.
	3:14	where there is light for the eyes, and P
	4:20	off the robe of P and put on the
	5:4	be called by God, P of righteousness and glory
	6:3	I will bring you away from there in P
Ezek	7:25	comes, they will seek P, but there shall be
	13:10	misled my people, saying, P when there is no
	13:10	when there is no P; and because, when the
	13:16	and saw visions of P for her, when there
	13:16	when there was no P, says the Lord GOD.
	34:25	them a covenant of P and banish wild beasts
	37:26	make a covenant of P with them; it shall
	43:27	burnt offerings and your P offerings; and I will
	45:15	offerings, burnt offerings, and P offerings, to make
	45:17	burnt offerings, and P offerings, to make atonement
	46:2	burnt offering and his P offerings, and he shall
	46:12	a burnt offering or P offerings as a freewill
	46:12	burnt offering or his P offerings as he does
Dan	4:1	in all the earth: P be multiplied to you!
	6:25	in all the earth: P be multiplied to you.
	10:19	greatly beloved, fear not, P be with you; be
	11:6	the north to make P; but she shall not
	11:17	shall bring terms of P and perform them.
Amos	5:22	accept them, and the P offerings of your fatted
Mic	3:5	prophets who lead my people astray, who cry P
	5:5	And this shall be P, when the Assyrian comes
Nah	1:15	of him who brings good tidings, who proclaims P
Zech	8:12	be a sowing of P; the vine shall yield
	8:16	true and make for P,
	8:19	and cheerful feasts; therefore love truth and P
	9:10	and he shall command P to the nations; his
Mal	2:5	covenant of life and P, and I gave them
	2:6	walked with me in P and uprightness, and he
1Mac	6:49	He made P with the men of Bethzur, and
	6:58	these men, and make P with them and with
	6:60	Jews an offer of P, and they accepted it.
	7:13	of Israel to seek P from them,
	7:28	men to see you face to face in P
	8:20	to establish alliance and P with you, that we
	8:22	as a memorial of P and alliance:
	9:70	to him to make P with him and obtain
	10:4	act first to make P with him before he
	10:4	him before he makes P with Alexander against us,
	10:66	returned to Jerusalem in P and gladness.
	11:50	this entreaty, "Grant us P, and make the Jews
	11:51	And they threw down their arms and made P
	11:62	Jonathan, and he made P with them, and took
	11:66	grant them terms of P, and he did so.
	13:37	to make a general P with you and to
	13:40	and let there be P between us."
	13:45	asking Simon to make P with them;

13:50 to Simon to make P with them, and he
14:8 tilled their land in P; the ground gave its
14:11 He established P in the land, and Israel rejoiced
2Mac 1:1 their Jewish brethren in Egypt, Greeting, and good P
1:4 law and his commandments, and may he bring P
3:1 was inhabited in unbroken P and the laws were
12:2 would not let them live quietly and in P
12:12 ways, agreed to make P with them; and after
14:10 it is impossible for the government to find P
Mt 10:13 is worthy, let your P come upon it; but
10:13 not worthy, let your P return to you.
10:34 have come to bring P on earth; I have
10:34 not come to bring P, but a sword.
Mk 4:39 rebuked the wind, and said to the sea, P
5:34 you well; go in P, and be healed of
9:48 yourselves, and be at P with one another."
Lk 1:79 to guide our feet into the way of P
2:14 highest, and on earth P among men with whom
2:29 thy servant depart in P, according to thy word;
7:50 woman, "Your faith has saved you; go in P
8:48 your faith has made you well; go in P
10:5 you enter, first say, P be to this house!'
10:6 if a son of P is there, your peace
10:6 peace is there, your P shall rest upon him;
11:21 his goods are in P;
12:51 have come to give P on earth?
14:32 he sends an embassy and asks terms of P
19:38 P in heaven and glory in the highest!"
19:42 today you knew the things that make for P
24:36 and said to them, P to you."
Jn 14:27 P I leave with you; my peace I give
14:27 leave with you; my P I give to you;
16:33 to you, that in me you may have P
20:19 and said to them, P be with you."
20:21 said to them again, P be with you.
20:26 among them, and said, P be with you."
Acts 9:31 Galilee and Samaria had P and was built up;
10:36 preaching good news of P by Jesus Christ (he
12:20 chamberlain, they asked for P, because their country
15:33 were sent off in P by the brethren to
16:36 go; now therefore come out and go in P
24:2 you we enjoy much P, and since by your
Rom 1:7 Grace to you and P from God our Father
2:10 glory and honor and P for every one who
3:17 and the way of P they do not know."
5:1 by faith, we have P with God through our
8:6 the mind on the Spirit is life and P
14:17 drink but righteousness and P and joy in the
14:19 pursue what makes for P and for mutual upbuilding.
15:13 with all joy and P in believing, so that
15:33 The God of P be with you all.
16:20 then the God of P will soon crush Satan
1Cor 1:3 Grace to you and P from God our Father
7:15 For God has called us to P
14:33 is not a God of confusion but of P
16:11 on his way in P, that he may return
2Cor 1:2 Grace to you and P from God our Father
13:11 one another, live in P, and the God of
13:11 God of love and P will be with you.
Gal 1:3 Grace to you and P from God the Father
5:22 Spirit is love, joy, P, patience, kindness, goodness,
6:16 P and mercy be upon all who walk by
Eph 1:2 Grace to you and P from God our Father
2:14 For he is our P, who has made us
2:15 the two, so making P,
2:17 he came and preached P to you who were
2:17 who were far-off and P to those who were
4:3 unity of the Spirit in the bond of P
6:15 of the gospel of P;
6:23 P be to the brethren, and love with faith,
Phil 1:2 Grace to you and P from God our Father
4:7 And the P of God, which passes all understanding,
4:9 and the God of P will be with you.
Col 1:2 Grace to you and P from God our Father.
1:20 or in heaven, making P by the blood of
3:15 And let the P of Christ rule in your
1Thes 1:1 the Lord Jesus Christ: Grace to you and P
5:3 people say, "There is P and security," then sudden
5:13 Be at P among yourselves.
5:23 May the God of P himself sanctify you wholly;
2Thes 1:2 Grace to you and P from God the Father
3:16 may the Lord of P himself give you peace
3:16 peace himself give you P at all times in
1Tim 1:2 faith: Grace, mercy, and P from God the Father
2Tim 1:2 child: Grace, mercy, and P from God the Father
2:22 righteousness, faith, love, and P, along with those
Tit 1:3 common faith: Grace and P from God the Father
Philem 1:3 Grace to you and P from God our Father
Heb 7:2 also king of Salem, that is, king of P
12:14 Strive for P with all men, and for the
13:20 may the God of P who brought again from
Jas 2:16 to them, "Go in P, be warmed and filled,"
3:18 righteousness is sown in P by those who make
3:18 is sown in peace by those who make P
1Pet 1:2 blood: May grace and P be multiplied to you.
3:11 right; let him seek P and pursue it.
5:14 P to all of you that are in Christ.
2Pet 1:2 Christ: May grace and P be multiplied to you
3:14 by him without spot or blemish, and at P
2Jn 1:3 ever: Grace, mercy, and P will be with us,
3Jn 1:15 P be to you.
Jude 1:2 Jesus Christ: May mercy, P, and love be multiplied
Rev 1:4 Grace to you and P from him who is
6:4 was permitted to take P from the earth, so

PEACEABLE (12)

2Sam 20:19 of those who are P and faithful in Israel;
Esth 13:2 to make my kingdom P and open to travel
16:8 our kingdom quiet and P for all men,
1Mac 1:30 Deceitfully he spoke P words to them, and they
7:10 and his brothers with P but treacherous words.
7:15 And he spoke P words to them and swore
7:27 and his brothers this P message,
10:3 Jonathan a letter in P words to honor him;
10:47 the first to speak P words to them, and
11:2 out for Syria with P words, and the people
1Tim 2:2 lead a quiet and P life, godly and respectful
Jas 3:17 is first pure, then P, gentle, open to reason,

PEACEABLY (17)

Gen 37:4 and could not speak P to him.
Judg 11:13 and to the Jordan; now therefore restore it P
1Sam 16:4 meet him trembling, and said, "Do you come P
16:5 And he said, P; I have come to sacrifice
29:7 back now; and go P, that you may not
1Kgs 2:13 And she said, "Do you come P
2:13 He said, P
Jud 7:15 because they rebelled and did not receive you P
Sir 4:8 poor, and answer him P and gently.
44:7 furnished with resources, living P in their
Jer 9:8 his mouth each speaks P to his neighbor, but
1Mac 5:25 Nabateans, who met them P and told them all
7:29 came to Judas, and they greeted one another P
7:33 people, to greet him P and to show him
2Mac 5:25 he pretended to be P disposed and waited until
12:4 they wished to live P and suspected nothing, the
Rom 12:18 depends upon you, live P with all.

PEACEFUL (8)

1Chr 4:40 very broad, quiet, and P; for the former inhabitants
Is 32:18 will abide in a P habitation, in secure dwellings,
Jer 25:37 their pasture, and the P folds are devastated,
Mic 2:8 the robe from the P, from those who pass
Zech 6:13 by his throne, and P understanding shall be between
2Mac 4:6 not again reach a P settlement, and that Simon
10:12 and attempted to maintain P relations with them.
Heb 12:11 later it yields the P fruit of righteousness to

PEACEMAKERS

Mt 5:9 "Blessed are the P, for they shall be called

PEACOCKS (2)

1Kgs 10:22 to come bringing gold, silver, ivory, apes, and P
2Chr 9:21 to come bringing gold, silver, ivory, apes, and P

PEAK (2)

Song 4:8 Depart from the P of Amana, from the peak
4:8 of Amana, from the P of Senir and Hermon,

PEALS (4)

Rev 4:5 lightning, and voices and P of thunder, and before
8:5 earth; and there were P of thunder, voices, flashes
11:19 flashes of lightning, voices, P of thunder, and
16:18 flashes of lightning, voices, P of thunder, and a

PEARL (2)

Mt 13:46 who, on finding one P of great value, went
Rev 21:21 made of a single P, and the street of

PEARLS (8)

Job 28:18 of crystal; the price of wisdom is above P
Mt 7:6 do not throw your P before swine, lest they

	13:45	in search of fine P,
1Tim	2:9	hair or gold or P or costly attire
Rev	17:4	gold and jewels and P, holding in her hand
	18:12	gold, silver, jewels and P, fine linen, purple, silk
	18:16	scarlet, bedecked with gold, with jewels, and with P
	21:21	twelve gates were twelve P, each of the gates

PEASANTRY (2)

Judg	5:7	The P ceased in Israel, they ceased until you
	5:11	the triumphs of his P in Israel."Then down to

PEBBLE (3)

2Sam	17:13	until not even a P is to be found
Amos	9:9	a sieve, but no P shall fall upon the
1Mac	10:73	is no stone or P, or place to flee."

PEDAHEL

Num	34:28	of Naphtali a leader, P the son of Ammihud.

PEDAHZUR (5)

Num	1:10	Gamaliel the son of P;
	2:20	Gamaliel the son of P,
	7:54	Gamaliel the son of P, the leader of the
	7:59	was the offering of Gamaliel the son of P
	10:23	men of Manasseh was Gamaliel the son of P

PEDAIAH (8)

2Kgs	23:36	Zebidah the daughter of P of Rumah.
1Chr	3:18	his son, Malchiram, P, Shenazzar, Jekamiah, Hosha
	3:19	and the sons of P: Zerubbabel and Shimei; and
	27:20	Joel the son of P;
Neh	3:25	After him P the son of Parosh
	8:4	and P, Mishael, Malchijah, Hashum, Hash-baddanah,
	11:7	of Joed, son of P, son of Kolaiah, son
	13:13	Zadok the scribe, and P of the Levites, and

PEDDLERS

2Cor	2:17	not, like so many, P of God's word; but

PEDESTAL

1Kgs	7:31	was round, as a P is made, a cubit

PEDIMENT

2Kgs	16:17	put it upon a P of stone.

PEELED (2)

Gen	30:37	almond and plane, and P white streaks in them,
	30:38	rods which he had P in front of the

PEERED (2)

Judg	5:28	of the window she P, the mother of Sisera
2Mac	3:19	the walls, while others P out of the windows.

PEERS (2)

Sir	14:23	He who P through her windows will also listen
	21:23	A boor P into the house from the door,

PEG (9)

Judg	4:21	Heber took a tent P, and took a hammer
	4:21	him and drove the P into his temple, till
	4:22	dead, with the tent P in his temple.
	5:26	hand to the tent P and her right hand
Sir	14:24	also fasten his tent P to her walls;
Is	22:23	fasten him like a P in a sure place,
	22:25	LORD of hosts, the P that was fastened in
Ezek	15:3	Do men take a P from it to hang
Zech	10:4	of them the tent P, out of them the

PEGS (10)

Ex	27:19	use, and all its P and all the pegs
	27:19	pegs and all the P of the court, shall
	35:18	of the court; the P of the tabernacle and
	35:18	the tabernacle and the P of the court, and
	38:20	And all the P for the tabernacle and for
	38:31	the court, all the P of the tabernacle, and
	38:31	tabernacle, and all the P round about the court.
	39:40	its cords, and its P; and all the utensils
Num	3:37	with their bases and P and cords.
	4:32	about with their bases, P, and cords, with all

PEKAH (11)

2Kgs	15:25	And P the son of Remaliah, his captain, conspired
	15:27	Azariah king of Judah P the son of Remaliah
	15:29	In the days of P king of Israel Tiglath-pileser
	15:30	made a conspiracy against P the son of Remaliah,
	15:31	of the acts of P, and all that he
	15:32	the second year of P the son of Remaliah,
	15:37	king of Syria and P the son of Remaliah
	16:1	the seventeenth year of P the son of Remaliah,
	16:5	king of Syria and P the son of Remaliah,
2Chr	28:6	For P the son of Remaliah slew a hundred
Is	7:1	king of Syria and P the son of Remaliah

PEKAHIAH (3)

2Kgs	15:22	with his fathers, and P his son reigned in
	15:23	Azariah king of Judah P the son of Menahem
	15:26	of the deeds of P, and all that he

PEKOD (2)

Jer	50:21	land of Merathaim, and against the inhabitants of P
Ezek	23:23	and all the Chaldeans, P and Shoa and Koa,

PELAIAH (3)

1Chr	3:24	of Eli-o-enai: Hodaviah, Eliashib, P, Akkub, Johanan,
Neh	8:7	Kelita, Azariah, Jozabad, Hanan, P, the Levites,
	10:10	brethren, Shebaniah, Hodiah, Kelita, P, Hanan,

PELALIAH

Neh	11:12	of Jeroham, son of P, son of Amzi, son

PELATIAH (5)

1Chr	3:21	The sons of Hananiah: P and Jeshaiah, his son
	4:42	having as their leaders P, Neariah, Rephaiah, and
Neh	10:22	Meshezabel, Zadok, Jaddu-a, P, Hanan, Anaiah,
Ezek	11:1	son of Azzur, and P the son of Benaiah,
	11:13	I was prophesying, that P the son of Benaiah

PELEG (8)

Gen	10:25	of the one was P, for in his days
	11:16	became the father of P;
	11:17	after the birth of P four hundred and thirty
	11:18	When P had lived thirty years, he became the
	11:19	father of Reu; and P lived after the birth
1Chr	1:19	of the one was P (for in his days
	1:25	Shem, Arpachshad, Shelah; Eber, P, Reu;
Lk	3:35	Reu, the son of P, the son of Eber,

PELET (2)

1Chr	2:47	Jahdai: Regem, Jotham, Geshan, P, Ephah, and
	12:3	Gibe-ah; also Jezi-el and P the sons of Azmaveth;

PELETH (2)

Num	16:1	On the son of P, sons of Reuben,
1Chr	2:33	The sons of Jonathan: P and Zaza.

PELETHITES (7)

2Sam	8:18	the Cherethites and the P; and David's sons were
	15:18	Cherethites, and all the P, and all the six
	20:7	the Cherethites and the P, and all the mighty
	20:23	the Cherethites and the P;
1Kgs	1:38	the Cherethites and the P, went down and caused
	1:44	the Cherethites and the P; and they have caused
1Chr	18:17	the Cherethites and the P; and David's sons were

PELICAN (2)

Lev	11:18	the water hen, the P, the carrion vulture,
Deut	14:17	water hen and the P, the carrion vulture and

PELONITE (3)

1Chr	11:27	of Harod, Helez the P,
	11:36	the Mecherathite, Ahijah the P,
	27:10	month, was Helez the P, of the sons of

PELUSIUM (2)

Ezek	30:15	pour my wrath upon P, the stronghold of Egypt,
	30:16	set fire to Egypt; P shall be in great

PEN (5)

Job	19:24	that with an iron P and lead they were
Ps	45:1	tongue is like the P of a ready scribe.
Jer	8:8	But, behold, the false P of the scribes has
	17:1	is written with a P of iron; with a
3Jn	1:13	rather not write with P and ink

PENALTIES (2)

Wis	14:30	But just P will overtake them on two counts:
Sir	9:5	you stumble and incur P for her.

PENALTY (11)

Tob	3:5	are true in exacting P from me for my
	6:12	man without incurring the P of death, because you
Jud	8:21	exact of us the P for its desecration.

P

9:1 the Hebrews, "Let my P go, that they may
9:4 that belongs to the P of Israel.'"
9:6 the cattle of the P of Israel not one
9:7 did not let the P go.
9:13 the Hebrews, "Let my P go, that they may
9:14 your servants and your P, that you may know
9:15 struck you and your P with pestilence, and you
9:17 exalting yourself against my P, and will not let
9:26 of Goshen, where the P of Israel were, there
9:27 and I and my P are in the wrong.
9:35 did not let the P of Israel go; as
10:3 Let my P go, that they may serve me.
10:4 refuse to let my P go, behold, tomorrow I
10:23 days; but all the P of Israel had light
11:2 the hearing of the P, that they ask, every
11:3 the LORD gave the P favor in the sight
11:3 Pharaoh's servants and in the sight of the P
11:7 against any of the P of Israel, either man
11:8 out, and all the P who follow you.' And
11:10 did not let the P of Israel go out
12:27 the houses of the P of Israel in Egypt,
12:27 And the P bowed their heads and worshiped.
12:28 Then the P of Israel went and did so;
12:31 forth from among my P, both you and the
12:31 both you and the P of Israel; and go,
12:33 were urgent with the P, to send them out
12:34 So the P took their dough before it was
12:35 The P of Israel had also done as Moses
12:36 LORD had given the P favor in the sight
12:37 And the P of Israel journeyed from Rameses to
12:40 The time that the P of Israel dwelt in
12:42 LORD by all the P of Israel throughout their
12:50 Thus did all the P of Israel; as the
12:51 the LORD brought the P of Israel out of
13:2 the womb among the P of Israel, both of
13:3 Moses said to the P, "Remember this day, in
13:17 When Pharaoh let the P go, God did not
13:17 God said, "Lest the P repent when they see
13:18 But God led the P round by the way
13:18 And the P of Israel went up out of
13:19 had solemnly sworn the P of Israel, saying, "God
13:22 by night did not depart from before the P
14:2 to Moses, "Tell the P of Israel to turn
14:3 will say of the P of Israel, 'They are
14:5 was told that the P had fled, the mind
14:5 was changed toward the P, and they said, "What
14:8 and he pursued the P of Israel as they
14:10 Pharaoh drew near, the P of Israel lifted up
14:10 And the P of Israel cried out to the
14:13 Moses said to the P, "Fear not, stand firm,
14:15 Tell the P of Israel to go forward.
14:16 divide it, that the P of Israel may go
14:22 And the P of Israel went into the midst
14:29 But the P of Israel walked on dry ground
14:31 the Egyptians, and the P feared the LORD; and
15:1 Then Moses and the P of Israel sang this
15:13 thy steadfast love the P whom thou hast redeemed,
15:16 a stone, till thy P, O LORD, pass by,
15:16 pass by, till the P pass by whom thou
15:19 upon them; but the P of Israel walked on
15:24 And the P murmured against Moses, saying, "What
16:1 the congregation of the P of Israel came to
16:2 whole congregation of the P of Israel murmured
16:4 for you; and the P shall go out and
16:6 said to all the P of Israel, "At evening
16:9 whole congregation of the P of Israel, 'Come near
16:10 whole congregation of the P of Israel, they looked
16:12 the murmurings of the P of Israel; say to
16:15 When the P of Israel saw it, they said
16:17 And the P of Israel did so; they gathered,
16:27 day some of the P went out to gather,
16:30 So the P rested on the seventh day.
16:35 And the P of Israel ate the manna forty
17:1 the congregation of the P of Israel moved on
17:1 no water for the P to drink.
17:2 Therefore the P found fault with Moses, and said,
17:3 But the P thirsted there for water, and the
17:3 for water, and the P murmured against Moses, and
17:4 the LORD, "What shall I do with this P
17:5 "Pass on before the P, taking with you some
17:6 of it, that the P may drink." And Moses
17:13 down Amalek and his P with the edge of
18:1 and for Israel his P, how the LORD had
18:11 because he delivered the P from under the hand
18:13 sat to judge the P, and the people stood
18:13 the people, and the P stood about Moses from
18:14 was doing for the P, he said, "What is
18:14 is this that you are doing for the P
18:14 alone, and all the P stand about you from
18:15 his father-in-law, "Because the P come to me to
18:18 You and the P with you will wear yourselves
18:19 You shall represent the P before God, and bring
18:21 men from all the P, such as fear God,
18:21 such men over the P as rulers of thousands,
18:22 let them judge the P at all times; every
18:23 endure, and all this P also will go to
18:25 them heads over the P, rulers of thousands, of
18:26 And they judged the P at all times; hard
19:1 new moon after the P of Israel had gone
19:3 Jacob, and tell the P of Israel:
19:7 the elders of the P, and set before them
19:8 And all the P answered together and said, "All
19:8 the words of the P to the LORD.
19:9 thick cloud, that the P may hear when I
19:9 the words of the P to the LORD.
19:10 Moses, "Go to the P and consecrate them today
19:11 Mount Sinai in the sight of all the P
19:12 set bounds for the P round about, saying, 'Take
19:14 the mountain to the P, and consecrated the people;
19:14 people, and consecrated the P; and they washed
19:15 he said to the P, "Be ready by the
19:16 so that all the P who were in the
19:17 Then Moses brought the P out of the camp
19:21 down and warn the P, lest they break through
19:23 to the LORD, "The P cannot come up to
19:24 the priests and the P break through to come
19:25 went down to the P and told them.
20:18 Now when all the P perceived the thunderings and
20:18 the mountain smoking, the P were afraid and
20:20 Moses said to the P, "Do not fear; for
20:21 And the P stood afar off, while Moses drew
20:22 shall say to the P of Israel: 'You have
21:8 her to a foreign P, since he has dealt
22:25 to any of my P with you who is
22:28 revile God, nor curse a ruler of your P
23:11 the poor of your P may eat; and what
23:27 into confusion all the P against whom you shall
24:2 come near, and the P shall not come up
24:3 came and told the P all the words of
24:3 ordinances; and all the P answered with one voice,
24:5 young men of the P of Israel, who offered
24:7 the hearing of the P; and they said, "All
24:8 threw it upon the P, and said, "Behold the
24:11 chief men of the P of Israel; they beheld
24:17 the sight of the P of Israel.
25:2 Moses, "Speak to the P of Israel, that they
25:22 in commandment for the P of Israel.
27:20 you shall command the P of Israel that they
27:21 their generations by the P of Israel.
28:1 him, from among the P of Israel, to serve
28:30 the judgment of the P of Israel upon his
28:38 holy offering which the P of Israel hallow as
29:28 perpetual due from the P of Israel, for it
29:28 be offered by the P of Israel from their
29:43 will meet with the P of Israel, and it
29:45 will dwell among the P of Israel, and will
30:12 the census of the P of Israel, then each
30:16 atonement money from the P of Israel, and shall
30:16 it may bring the P of Israel to remembrance
30:31 shall say to the P of Israel, 'This shall
30:33 an outsider shall be cut off from his P
30:38 as perfume shall be cut off from his P
31:13 Moses, "Say to the P of Israel, 'You shall
31:14 soul shall be cut off from among his P
31:16 Therefore the P of Israel shall keep the sabbath,
31:17 between me and the P of Israel that in
32:1 When the P saw that Moses delayed to come
32:1 from the mountain, the P gathered themselves
32:3 So all the P took off the rings of
32:6 peace offerings; and the P sat down to eat
32:7 "Go down; for your P, whom you brought up
32:9 "I have seen this P, and behold, it is
32:9 it is a stiff-necked P;
32:11 burn hot against thy P, whom thou hast brought
32:12 wrath, and repent of this evil against thy P
32:14 evil which he thought to do to his P
32:17 the noise of the P as they shouted, he
32:20 water, and made the P of Israel drink it.
32:21 Aaron, "What did this P do to you that
32:22 hot; you know the P, that they are set
32:25 Moses saw that the P had broken loose (for
32:28 there fell of the P that day about three

32:30 Moses said to the P, "You have sinned a
32:31 and said, "Alas, this P have sinned a great
32:34 now go, lead the P to the place of
32:35 a plague upon the P, because they made the
33:1 hence, you and the P whom you have brought
33:3 in the way, for you are a stiff-necked P
33:4 When the P heard these evil tidings, they mourned;
33:5 Moses, "Say to the P of Israel, 'You are
33:5 'You are a stiff-necked P; if for a single
33:6 Therefore the P of Israel stripped themselves of
33:8 the tent, all the P rose up, and every
33:10 And when all the P saw the pillar of
33:10 the tent, all the P would rise up and
33:12 me, 'Bring up this P; but thou hast not
33:13 Consider too that this nation is thy P
33:16 found favor in thy sight, I and thy P
33:16 distinct, I and thy P, from all other people
33:16 people, from all other P that are upon the
34:9 it is a stiff-necked P; and pardon our iniquity
34:10 Before all your P I will do marvels, such
34:10 nation; and all the P among whom you are
34:30 Aaron and all the P of Israel saw Moses,
34:32 And afterward all the P of Israel came near,
34:34 out, and told the P of Israel what he
34:35 he was commanded, the P of Israel saw the
35:1 the congregation of the P of Israel, and said
35:4 the congregation of the P of Israel, "This is
35:20 the congregation of the P of Israel departed from
35:29 men and women, the P of Israel, whose heart
35:30 Moses said to the P of Israel, "See, the
36:3 freewill offering which the P of Israel had brought
36:5 said to Moses, "The P bring much more than
36:6 So the P were restrained from bringing;
39:32 was finished; and the P of Israel had done
39:42 commanded Moses, so the P of Israel had done
Lev 1:2 saying, "Speak to the P of Israel, and say
4:2 Moses, "Say to the P of Israel, If any
4:3 bringing guilt on the P, then let him offer
4:27 one of the common P sins unwittingly in doing
7:20 that person shall be cut off from his P
7:21 that person shall be cut off from his P
7:23 Moses, "Say to the P of Israel, You shall
7:25 the LORD shall be cut off from his P
7:27 that person shall be cut off from his P
7:29 Moses, "Say to the P of Israel, He that
7:34 have taken from the P of Israel, out of
7:34 perpetual due from the P of Israel.
7:36 given them by the P of Israel, on the
7:38 that he commanded the P of Israel to bring
9:3 And say to the P of Israel, 'Take a
9:7 yourself and for the P; and bring the offering
9:7 the offering of the P, and make atonement for
9:15 Then he presented the P's offering, and took the
9:15 which was for the P, and killed it, and
9:18 peace offerings for the P; and Aaron's sons delivered
9:22 his hands toward the P and blessed them; and
9:23 out they blessed the P, and the glory of
9:23 glory of the LORD appeared to all the P
9:24 and when all the P saw it, they shouted,
10:3 and before all the P I will be glorified.'"
10:11 are to teach the P of Israel all the
10:14 peace offerings of the P of Israel.
11:2 Aaron, "Say to the P of Israel, These are
12:2 Moses, "Say to the P of Israel, If a
15:2 Aaron, "Say to the P of Israel, When any
15:31 you shall keep the P of Israel separate from
16:5 the congregation of the P of Israel two male
16:15 which is for the P, and bring its blood
16:16 the uncleannesses of the P of Israel, and because
16:19 the uncleannesses of the P of Israel.
16:21 the iniquities of the P of Israel, and all
16:24 burnt offering of the P, and make atonement for
16:24 and make atonement for himself and for the P
16:33 and for all the P of the assembly.
16:34 be made for the P of Israel once in
17:2 and to all the P of Israel, This is
17:4 man shall be cut off from among his P
17:5 the end that the P of Israel may bring
17:9 that man shall be cut off from his P
17:10 and will cut him off from among his P
17:12 have said to the P of Israel, No person
17:13 man also of the P of Israel, or of
17:14 have said to the P of Israel, You shall
18:2 Moses, "Say to the P of Israel, I am
18:29 them shall be cut off from among their P
19:2 the congregation of the P of Israel, You shall
19:8 that person shall be cut off from his P
19:16 a slanderer among your P, and you shall not
19:18 sons of your own P, but you shall love
20:2 Moses, "Say to the P of Israel, Any man
20:2 Any man of the P of Israel, or of
20:2 put to death; the P of the land shall
20:3 off from among his P, because he has given
20:4 And if the P of the land do at
20:5 off from among their P, him and all who
20:6 and will cut him off from among his P
20:17 the children of their P; he has uncovered his
20:18 them shall be cut off from among their P
21:1 the dead among his P,
21:4 a husband among his P and so profane himself.
21:14 virgin of his own P,
21:15 his children among his P; for I am the
21:24 and to all the P of Israel.
22:2 holy things of the P of Israel, which they
22:3 holy things, which the P of Israel dedicate to
22:15 holy things of the P of Israel, which they
22:18 sons and all the P of Israel, When any
22:32 be hallowed among the P of Israel; I am
23:2 Moses, "Say to the P of Israel, The appointed
23:10 Moses, "Say to the P of Israel, When you
23:24 Moses, "Say to the P of Israel, In the
23:29 same day shall be cut off from his P
23:30 that person I will destroy from among his P
23:34 Moses, "Say to the P of Israel, On the
23:43 that I made the P of Israel dwell in
23:44 Moses declared to the P of Israel the appointed
24:2 to Moses, "Command the P of Israel to bring
24:8 on behalf of the P of Israel as a
24:10 went out among the P of Israel; and the
24:15 And say to the P of Israel, Whoever curses
24:23 Moses spoke to the P of Israel; and they
24:23 Thus the P of Israel did as the LORD
25:2 Sinai, "Say to the P of Israel, When you
25:33 their possession among the P of Israel.
25:46 over your brethren the P of Israel you shall
25:55 For to me the P of Israel are servants,
26:12 be your God, and you shall be my P
26:46 between him and the P of Israel on Mount
27:2 Moses, "Say to the P of Israel, When a
27:34 commanded Moses for the P of Israel on Mount
Num 1:2 the congregation of the P of Israel, by families,
1:20 The P of Reuben, Israel's first-born, their
1:22 Of the P of Simeon, their generations, by their
1:24 Of the P of Gad, their generations, by their
1:26 Of the P of Judah, their generations, by their
1:28 Of the P of Issachar, their generations, by their
1:30 Of the P of Zebulun, their generations, by their
1:32 Of the P of Joseph, namely, of the people
1:32 Joseph, namely, of the P of Ephraim, their
1:34 Of the P of Manasseh, their generations, by their
1:36 Of the P of Benjamin, their generations, by their
1:38 Of the P of Dan, their generations, by their
1:40 Of the P of Asher, their generations, by their
1:42 Of the P of Naphtali, their generations, by their
1:45 whole number of the P of Israel, by their
1:49 of them among the P of Israel;
1:52 The P of Israel shall pitch their tents by
1:53 the congregation of the P of Israel; and the
1:54 Thus did the P of Israel; they did according
2:2 Moses and Aaron, "The P of Israel shall encamp
2:3 the leader of the P of Judah being Nahshon
2:5 the leader of the P of Issachar being Nethanel
2:7 the leader of the P of Zebulun being Eliab
2:10 the leader of the P of Reuben being Elizur
2:12 the leader of the P of Simeon being Shelumi-el
2:14 the leader of the P of Gad being Eliasaph
2:18 the leader of the P of Ephraim being Elishama
2:20 the leader of the P of Manasseh being Gamaliel
2:22 the leader of the P of Benjamin being Abidan
2:25 the leader of the P of Dan being Ahiezer
2:27 the leader of the P of Asher being Pagiel
2:29 the leader of the P of Naphtali being Ahira
2:32 These are the P of Israel as numbered by
2:33 not numbered among the P of Israel, as the
2:34 Thus did the P of Israel.
3:8 the duties for the P of Israel as they
3:9 him from among the P of Israel.
3:12 Levites from among the P of Israel instead of
3:12 the womb among the P of Israel.
3:38 be done for the P of Israel; and any
3:40 first-born males of the P of Israel, from a
3:41 the first-born among the P of Israel, and the

3:41 the cattle of the P of Israel."
3:42 the first-born among the P of Israel, as the
3:45 the first-born among the P of Israel, and the
3:46 the first-born of the P of Israel, over and
3:50 the first-born of the P of Israel he took
5:2 to Moses, "Command the P of Israel that they
5:4 And the P of Israel did so, and drove
5:4 to Moses, so the P of Israel did.
5:6 Moses, "Say to the P of Israel, When a
5:9 holy things of the P of Israel, which they
5:12 Moses, "Say to the P of Israel, If any
5:21 an oath among your P, when the LORD makes
5:27 the woman shall become an execration among her P
6:2 Moses, "Say to the P of Israel, When either
6:23 you shall bless the P of Israel: you shall
6:27 my name upon the P of Israel, and I
8:6 Levites from among the P of Israel, and cleanse
8:9 whole congregation of the P of Israel.
8:10 before the LORD, the P of Israel shall lay
8:11 wave offering from the P of Israel, that it
8:14 Levites from among the P of Israel, and the
8:16 me from among the P of Israel; instead of
8:16 first-born of all the P of Israel, I have
8:17 the first-born among the P of Israel are mine,
8:18 the first-born among the P of Israel.
8:19 sons from among the P of Israel, to do
8:19 the service for the P of Israel at the
8:19 make atonement for the P of Israel, that there
8:19 no plague among the P of Israel in case
8:19 Israel in case the P of Israel should come
8:20 the congregation of the P of Israel to the
8:20 concerning the Levites, the P of Israel did to
9:2 Egypt, saying, "Let the P of Israel keep the
9:4 So Moses told the P of Israel that they
9:5 commanded Moses, so the P of Israel did.
9:7 appointed time among the P of Israel?"
9:10 Moses, "Say to the P of Israel, If any
9:13 cut off from his P, because he did not
9:17 tent, after that the P of Israel set out;
9:17 settled down, there the P of Israel encamped.
9:18 of the LORD the P of Israel set out,
9:19 tabernacle many days, the P of Israel kept the
9:22 tabernacle, abiding there, the P of Israel remained
10:12 the testimony, and the P of Israel set out
10:28 of march of the P of Israel according to
11:1 And the P complained in the hearing of the
11:2 Then the P cried to Moses; and Moses prayed
11:4 strong craving; and the P of Israel also wept
11:8 The P went about and gathered it, and ground
11:10 Moses heard the P weeping throughout their
11:11 burden of all this P upon me?
11:12 Did I conceive all this P
11:13 to get meat to give to all this P
11:14 to carry all this P alone, the burden is
11:16 the elders of the P and officers over them;
11:17 the burden of the P with you, that you
11:18 And say to the P, 'Consecrate yourselves for
11:21 But Moses said, "The P among whom I am
11:24 out and told the P the words of the
11:24 the elders of the P, and placed them round
11:29 that all the LORD's P were prophets, that the
11:32 And the P rose all that day, and all
11:33 was kindled against the P, and the LORD smote
11:33 the LORD smote the P with a very great
11:34 there they buried the P who had the craving.
11:35 Kibroth-hattaavah the P journeyed to Hazeroth; and
12:15 seven days; and the P did not set out
12:16 After that the P set out from Hazeroth, and
13:2 I give to the P of Israel; from each
13:3 were heads of the P of Israel.
13:18 is, and whether the P who dwell in it
13:26 the congregation of the P of Israel in the
13:28 Yet the P who dwell in the land are
13:30 But Caleb quieted the P before Moses, and said,
13:31 go up against the P; for they are stronger
13:32 they brought to the P of Israel an evil
13:32 inhabitants; and all the P that we saw in
14:1 loud cry; and the P wept that night.
14:2 And all the P of Israel murmured against Moses
14:5 the congregation of the P of Israel.
14:7 the congregation of the P of Israel, "The land,
14:9 do not fear the P of the land, for
14:10 meeting to all the P of Israel.
14:11 "How long will this P despise me?
14:13 didst bring up this P in thy might from
14:14 the midst of this P; for thou, O LORD,
14:15 thou dost kill this P as one man, then
14:16 able to bring this P into the land which
14:19 the iniquity of this P, I pray thee, according
14:19 thou hast forgiven this P, from Egypt even until
14:27 the murmurings of the P of Israel, which they
14:39 words to all the P of Israel, and the
14:39 of Israel, and the P mourned greatly.
15:2 Moses, "Say to the P of Israel, When you
15:18 Moses, "Say to the P of Israel, When you
15:25 the congregation of the P of Israel, and they
15:26 the congregation of the P of Israel shall be
15:29 is native among the P of Israel, and for
15:30 person shall be cut off from among his P
15:32 While the P of Israel were in the wilderness,
15:38 Moses, "Speak to the P of Israel, and bid
16:2 a number of the P of Israel, two hundred
16:38 a sign to the P of Israel."
16:40 a reminder to the P of Israel, so that
16:41 the congregation of the P of Israel murmured
16:41 "You have killed the P of the LORD."
16:47 already begun among the P; and he put on
16:47 on the incense, and made atonement for the P
17:2 Moses, "Speak to the P of Israel, and get
17:5 the murmurings of the P of Israel, which they
17:6 Moses spoke to the P of Israel; and all
17:9 LORD to all the P of Israel; and they
17:12 And the P of Israel said to Moses, "Behold,
18:5 no more upon the P of Israel.
18:6 Levites from among the P of Israel; they are
18:8 consecrated things of the P of Israel; I have
18:11 wave offerings of the P of Israel; I have
18:19 holy offerings which the P of Israel present to
18:20 your inheritance among the P of Israel.
18:22 And henceforth the P of Israel shall not come
18:23 generations; and among the P of Israel they shall
18:24 the tithe of the P of Israel, which they
18:24 no inheritance among the P of Israel."
18:26 you take from the P of Israel the tithe
18:28 you receive from the P of Israel; and from
18:32 holy things of the P of Israel, lest you
19:2 has commanded: Tell the P of Israel to bring
19:9 the congregation of the P of Israel for the
19:10 shall be to the P of Israel, and to
20:1 And the P of Israel, the whole congregation, came
20:1 first month, and the P stayed in Kadesh; and
20:3 And the P contended with Moses, and said, "Would
20:12 the eyes of the P of Israel, therefore you
20:13 of Meribah, where the P of Israel contended with
20:19 And the P of Israel said to him, "We
20:22 from Kadesh, and the P of Israel, the whole
20:24 be gathered to his P; for he shall not
20:24 have given to the P of Israel, because you
20:26 be gathered to his P, and shall die there."
21:2 wilt indeed give this P into my hand, then
21:4 of Edom; and the P became impatient on the
21:5 And the P spoke against God and against Moses,
21:6 fiery serpents among the P, and they bit the
21:6 and they bit the P, so that many people
21:6 people, so that many P of Israel died.
21:7 And the P came to Moses, and said, "We
21:7 So Moses prayed for the P
21:10 And the P of Israel set out, and encamped
21:16 to Moses, "Gather the P together, and I will
21:18 the nobles of the P delved, with the scepter
21:29 You are undone, O P of Chemosh!
21:33 he and all his P, to battle at Edre-i.
21:34 hand, and all his P, and his land; and
21:35 sons, and all his P, until there was not
22:1 Then the P of Israel set out, and encamped
22:3 great dread of the P, because they were many;
22:3 with fear of the P of Israel.
22:5 him, saying, "Behold, a P has come out of
22:6 Come now, curse this P for me, since they
22:11 me, saying, 'Behold, a P has come out of
22:12 shall not curse the P, for they are blessed."
22:17 do; come, curse this P for me.'"
22:41 from there he saw the nearest of the P
23:9 behold him; lo, a P dwelling alone, and not
23:24 and Israel, 'What has God wrought!' Behold, a P
24:14 am going to my P; come, I will let
24:14 you know what this P will do to your
24:14 will do to your P in the latter days."
25:1 dwelt in Shittim the P began to play the
25:2 These invited the P to the sacrifices of their
25:2 their gods, and the P ate, and bowed down
25:4 the chiefs of the P, and hang them in

25:6 behold, one of the P of Israel came and
25:6 whole congregation of the P of Israel, while they
25:8 was stayed from the P of Israel.
25:11 my wrath from the P of Israel, in that
25:11 did not consume the P of Israel in my
25:13 made atonement for the P of Israel.'"
25:15 the head of the P of a fathers' house
26:2 the congregation of the P of Israel, from twenty
26:4 a census of the P, from twenty years old
26:4 The P of Israel, who came forth out of
26:51 the number of the P of Israel, six hundred
26:62 not numbered among the P of Israel, because there
26:62 to them among the P of Israel.
26:63 priest, who numbered the P of Israel in the
26:64 who had numbered the P of Israel in the
27:8 shall say to the P of Israel, 'If a
27:11 shall be to the P of Israel a statute
27:12 have given to the P of Israel.
27:13 be gathered to your P, as your brother Aaron
27:20 the congregation of the P of Israel may obey.
27:21 he and all the P of Israel with him,
28:2 to Moses, "Command the P of Israel, and say
29:40 And Moses told the P of Israel everything just
30:1 the tribes of the P of Israel, "This is
31:2 to Moses, "Avenge the P of Israel on the
31:2 afterward you shall be gathered to your P
31:3 Moses said to the P, "Arm men from among
31:9 And the P of Israel took captive the women
31:12 the congregation of the P of Israel, at the
31:16 Behold, these caused the P of Israel, by the
31:30 And from the P of Israel's half you shall
31:42 From the P of Israel's half, which Moses separated
31:47 persons-- from the P of Israel's half Moses
31:54 a memorial for the P of Israel before the
32:7 the heart of the P of Israel from going
32:9 the heart of the P of Israel from going
32:15 the wilderness; and you will destroy all this P
32:17 to go before the P of Israel, until we
32:18 our homes until the P of Israel have inherited
32:28 the tribes of the P of Israel.
33:1 the stages of the P of Israel, when they
33:3 after the passover the P of Israel went out
33:5 So the P of Israel set out from Rameses,
33:14 no water for the P to drink.
33:38 fortieth year after the P of Israel had come
33:40 the coming of the P of Israel.
33:51 Jericho, "Say to the P of Israel, When you
34:2 to Moses, "Command the P of Israel, and say
34:13 Moses commanded the P of Israel, saying, "This is
34:29 the inheritance for the P of Israel in the
35:2 at Jericho, "Command the P of Israel, that they
35:8 the possession of the P of Israel, from the
35:10 Moses, "Say to the P of Israel, When you
35:15 for refuge for the P of Israel, and for
35:34 the midst of the P of Israel."
36:1 fathers' houses of the P of Israel;
36:2 by lot to the P of Israel; and my
36:3 other tribes of the P of Israel then their
36:4 the jubilee of the P of Israel comes, then
36:5 And Moses commanded the P of Israel according to
36:7 The inheritance of the P of Israel shall not
36:7 every one of the P of Israel shall cleave
36:8 any tribe of the P of Israel shall be
36:8 every one of the P of Israel may possess
36:9 the tribes of the P of Israel shall cleave
36:13 by Moses to the P of Israel in the
Deut 1:3 Moses spoke to the P of Israel according to
1:28 hearts melt, saying, "The P are greater and taller
2:4 And command the P, You are about to pass
2:10 formerly lived there, a P great and many, and
2:16 dead from among the P,
2:21 call them Zamzummim, a P great and many, and
2:32 he and all his P, to battle at Jahaz.
2:33 defeated him and his sons and all his P
3:1 he and all his P, to battle at Edre-i.
3:2 him and all his P and his land into
3:3 Bashan, and all his P; and we smote him
3:18 before your brethren the P of Israel.
3:28 the head of this P, and he shall put
4:6 a wise and understanding P
4:10 to me, 'Gather the P to me, that I
4:20 Egypt, to be a P of his own possession,
4:33 Did any P ever hear the voice of a
5:28 the words of this P, which they have spoken
7:6 "For you are a P holy to the LORD
7:6 you to be a P for his own possession,
7:7 number than any other P that the LORD set
9:2 up to heaven, a P great and tall, the
9:6 of your righteousness; for you are a stubborn P
9:12 from here; for your P whom you have brought
9:13 'I have seen this P, and behold, it is
9:13 it is a stubborn P;
9:26 GOD, destroy not thy P and thy heritage, whom
9:27 the stubbornness of this P, or their wickedness, or
9:29 For they are thy P and thy heritage, whom
10:6 (The P of Israel journeyed from Be-eroth
10:11 the head of the P, that they may go
13:9 death, and afterwards the hand of all the P
14:2 For you are a P holy to the LORD
14:2 you to be a P for his own possession,
14:21 for you are a P holy to the LORD
16:18 they shall judge the P with righteous judgment.
17:7 death, and afterward the hand of all the P
17:13 And all the P shall hear, and fear, and
17:16 himself, or cause the P to return to Egypt
18:3 priests' due from the P, from those offering a
20:2 and speak to the P,
20:5 shall speak to the P, saying, 'What man is
20:8 speak further to the P, and say, What man
20:9 of speaking to the P, then commanders shall be
20:9 shall be appointed at the head of the P
20:11 you, then all the P who are found in
21:8 Forgive, O LORD, thy P Israel, whom thou hast
21:8 the midst of thy P Israel; but let the
24:7 of his brethren, the P of Israel, and if
26:15 heaven, and bless thy P Israel and the ground
26:18 that you are a P for his own possession,
26:19 you shall be a P holy to the LORD
27:1 of Israel commanded the P, saying, "Keep all the
27:9 you have become the P of the LORD your
27:11 And Moses charged the P the same day, saying,
27:12 Gerizim to bless the P: Simeon, Levi, Judah,
27:15 secret.' And all the P shall answer and say,
27:16 mother.' And all the P shall say, 'Amen.'
27:17 landmark.' And all the P shall say, 'Amen.'
27:18 road.' And all the P shall say, 'Amen.'
27:19 widow.' And all the P shall say, 'Amen.'
27:20 ' And all the P shall say, 'Amen.'
27:21 beast.' And all the P shall say, 'Amen.'
27:22 mother.' And all the P shall say, 'Amen.'
27:23 mother-in-law.' And all the P shall say, 'Amen.'
27:24 secret.' And all the P shall say, 'Amen.'
27:25 person.' And all the P shall say, 'Amen.'
27:26 them.' And all the P shall say, 'Amen.'
28:9 establish you as a P holy to himself, as
28:32 be given to another P, while your eyes look
29:1 to make with the P of Israel in the
29:13 this day as his P, and that he may
31:7 shall go with this P into the land which
31:12 Assemble the P, men, women, and little ones, and
31:16 your fathers; then this P will rise and play
31:19 teach it to the P of Israel; put it
31:19 for me against the P of Israel.
31:22 taught it to the P of Israel.
32:6 thus requite the LORD, you foolish and senseless P
32:9 LORD's portion is his P, Jacob his allotted heritage.
32:21 those who are no P; I will provoke them
32:36 LORD will vindicate his P and have compassion on
32:43 the enemy.' "Praise his P, O you nations; for
32:43 and makes expiation for the land of his P
32:44 the hearing of the P, he and Joshua the
32:49 I give to the P of Israel for a
32:50 be gathered to your P, as Aaron your brother
32:50 was gathered to his P;
32:51 the midst of the P of Israel at the
32:51 the midst of the P of Israel.
32:52 I give to the P of Israel."
33:3 Yea, he loved his P; all those consecrated to
33:5 the heads of the P were gathered, all the
33:7 of Judah, and bring him in to his P
33:21 the heads of the P, with Israel he executed
33:29 is like you, a P saved by the LORD,
34:8 And the P of Israel wept for Moses in
34:9 upon him; so the P of Israel obeyed him,
Josh 1:2 you and all this P, into the land which
1:2 to them, to the P of Israel.
1:6 you shall cause this P to inherit the land
1:10 the officers of the P,
1:11 camp, and command the P, 'Prepare your provisions;
3:1 Shittim, with all the P of Israel; and they
3:3 camp and commanded the P, "When you see the
3:5 Joshua said to the P, "Sanctify yourselves; for

6:33 the Amalekites and the P of the East came
7:1 Gideon) and all the P who were with him
7:2 said to Gideon, "The P with you are too
7:3 the ears of the P, saying, 'Whoever is fearful
7:4 said to Gideon, "The P are still too many;
7:5 So he brought the P down to the water;
7:6 the rest of the P knelt down to drink
7:8 the jars of the P from their hands, and
7:12 Amalekites and all the P of the East lay
8:5 of bread to the P who follow me; for
8:10 the army of the P of the East; for
8:28 was subdued before the P of Israel, and they
8:33 as Gideon died, the P of Israel turned again
8:34 And the P of Israel did not remember the
9:29 Would that this P were under my hand!
9:45 city, and killed the P that were in it;
9:46 When all the P of the Tower of Shechem
9:47 told that all the P of the Tower of
9:49 every one of the P cut down his bundle
9:49 so that all the P of the Tower of
9:51 city, and all the P of the city fled
10:6 And the P of Israel again did what was
10:8 they oppressed all the P of Israel that were
10:10 And the P of Israel cried to the LORD,
10:11 LORD said to the P of Israel, "Did I
10:15 And the P of Israel said to the LORD,
10:17 in Gilead; and the P of Israel came together,
10:18 And the P, the leaders of Gilead, said one
11:11 of Gilead, and the P made him head and
11:20 Sihon gathered all his P together, and encamped at
11:21 Sihon and all his P into the hand of
11:23 Amorites from before his P Israel; and are you
11:27 this day between the P of Israel and the
11:27 of Israel and the P of Ammon."
11:33 were subdued before the P of Israel.
12:2 them, "I and my P had a great feud
13:1 And the P of Israel again did what was
14:3 or among all our P, that you must go
14:11 And when the P saw him, they brought thirty
16:24 And when the P saw him, they praised their
16:30 and upon all the P that were in it.
18:7 Laish, and saw the P who were there, how
18:10 you go, you will come to an unsuspecting P
18:20 image, and went in the midst of the P
18:27 to Laish, to a P quiet and unsuspecting, and
19:12 not belong to the P of Israel; but we
19:30 the day that the P of Israel came up
20:1 Then all the P of Israel came out, from
20:2 chiefs of all the P, of all the tribes
20:2 the assembly of the P of God, four hundred
20:3 Benjaminites heard that the P of Israel had gone
20:3 to Mizpah.) And the P of Israel said, "Tell
20:7 Behold, you P of Israel, all of you, give
20:8 And all the P arose as one man, saying,
20:10 bring provisions for the P, that when they come
20:13 of their brethren, the P of Israel.
20:14 to battle against the P of Israel.
20:18 The P of Israel arose and went up to
20:19 Then the P of Israel rose in the morning,
20:22 But the P, the men of Israel, took courage,
20:23 And the P of Israel went up and wept
20:24 So the P of Israel came near against the
20:25 thousand men of the P of Israel; all these
20:26 Then all the P of Israel, the whole army,
20:27 And the P of Israel inquired of the LORD
20:30 And the P of Israel went up against the
20:31 went out against the P, and were drawn away
20:31 kill some of the P, in the highways, one
21:2 And the P came to Bethel, and sat there
21:4 on the morrow the P rose early, and built
21:5 And the P of Israel said, "Which of all
21:6 And the P of Israel had compassion for Benjamin
21:9 For when the P were mustered, behold, not one
21:15 And the P had compassion on Benjamin because the
21:18 For the P of Israel had sworn, "Cursed be
21:24 And the P of Israel departed from there at
Ruth 1:6 LORD had visited his P and given them food.
1:10 "No, we will return with you to your P
1:15 gone back to her P and to her gods;
1:16 I will lodge; your P shall be my people,
1:16 people shall be my P, and your God my
2:11 and came to a P that you did not
4:4 in the presence of the elders of my P
4:9 elders and all the P, "You are witnesses this
4:11 Then all the P who were at the gate,
1Sam 2:13 the priests with the P was that when any
2:23 hear of your evil dealings from all the P
2:24 that I hear the P of the LORD spreading
2:28 by fire from the P of Israel.
2:29 every offering of my P Israel?'
4:4 So the P sent to Shiloh, and brought from
4:17 great slaughter among the P; your two sons also,
5:3 And when the P of Ashdod rose early the
5:6 was heavy upon the P of Ashdod, and he
5:10 came to Ekron, the P of Ekron cried out,
5:10 God of Israel to slay us and our P
5:11 that it may not slay us and our P
6:6 not they let the P go, and they departed?
6:13 Now the P of Beth-shemesh were reaping their
6:19 of them, and the P mourned because the LORD
6:19 LORD had made a great slaughter among the P
7:6 And Samuel judged the P of Israel at Mizpah.
7:7 Philistines heard that the P of Israel had gathered
7:7 And when the P of Israel heard of it
7:8 And the P of Israel said to Samuel, "Do
8:7 the voice of the P in all that they
8:10 the LORD to the P who were asking a
8:19 But the P refused to listen to the voice
8:21 the words of the P, he repeated them in
9:2 a man among the P of Israel more handsome
9:2 upward he was taller than any of the P
9:12 the city, because the P have a sacrifice today
9:13 to eat; for the P will not eat till
9:16 be prince over my P Israel.
9:16 He shall save my P from the hand of
9:16 the affliction of my P, because their cry has
9:17 He it is who shall rule over my P
10:1 be prince over his P Israel?
10:1 shall reign over the P of the LORD and
10:11 with the prophets, the P said to one another,
10:17 Now Samuel called the P together to the LORD
10:18 he said to the P of Israel, "Thus says
10:23 he stood among the P, he was taller than
10:23 than any of the P from his shoulders upward.
10:24 said to all the P, "Do you see him
10:24 There is none like him among all the P
10:24 And all the P shouted, "Long live the king!"
10:25 Then Samuel told the P the rights and duties
10:25 Samuel sent all the P away, each one to
11:4 the ears of the P; and all the people
11:4 people; and all the P wept aloud.
11:5 said, "What ails the P, that they are weeping?"
11:7 LORD fell upon the P, and they came out
11:11 morrow Saul put the P in three companies; and
11:12 Then the P said to Samuel, "Who is it
11:14 Samuel said to the P, "Come, let us go
11:15 So all the P went to Gilgal, and there
12:6 Samuel said to the P, "The LORD is witness,
12:18 day; and all the P greatly feared the LORD
12:19 And all the P said to Samuel, "Pray for
12:20 Samuel said to the P, "Fear not; you have
12:22 not cast away his P, for his great name's
12:22 to make you a P for himself.
13:2 the rest of the P he sent home, every
13:4 And the P were called out to join Saul
13:6 in straits (for the P were hard-pressed), the people
13:6 were hard-pressed), the P hid themselves in caves
13:7 Gilgal, and all the P followed him trembling.
13:8 to Gilgal, and the P were scattering from him.
13:11 I saw that the P were scattering from me,
13:14 be prince over his P, because you have not
13:15 And Saul numbered the P who were present with
13:16 his son, and the P who were present with
13:22 of any of the P with Saul and Jonathan;
14:2 is at Migron; the P who were with him
14:3 And the P did not know that Jonathan had
14:15 and among all the P; the garrison and even
14:17 Saul said to the P who were with him,
14:18 that time with the P of Israel.
14:20 Saul and all the P who were with him
14:24 an oath on the P, saying, "Cursed be the
14:24 So none of the P tasted food.
14:25 And all the P came into the forest; and
14:26 And when the P entered the forest, behold, the
14:26 his mouth; for the P feared the oath.
14:27 his father charge the P with the oath; so
14:28 Then one of the P said, "Your father strictly
14:28 father strictly charged the P with an oath, saying,
14:28 And the P were faint.
14:30 much better if the P had eaten freely today
14:31 And the P were very faint;
14:32 were very faint; the P flew upon the spoil,

P

14:32 the ground; and the P ate them with the
14:33 told Saul, "Behold, the P are sinning against the
14:34 "Disperse yourselves among the P, and say to them,
14:34 every one of the P brought his ox with
14:38 you leaders of the P; and know and see
14:39 man among all the P that answered him.
14:40 And the P said to Saul, "Do what seems
14:41 guilt is in thy P Israel, give Thummim." And
14:41 were taken, but the P escaped.
14:45 Then the P said to Saul, "Shall Jonathan die,
14:45 So the P ransomed Jonathan, that he did not
15:1 you king over his P Israel; now therefore hearken
15:4 So Saul summoned the P, and numbered them in
15:6 kindness to all the P of Israel when they
15:8 utterly destroyed all the P with the edge of
15:9 But Saul and the P spared Agag, and the
15:15 the Amalekites; for the P spared the best of
15:21 But the P took of the spoil, sheep and
15:24 because I feared the P and obeyed their voice.
15:30 the elders of my P and before Israel, and
17:27 And the P answered him in the same way,
17:30 same way; and the P answered him again as
18:5 sight of all the P and also in the
18:13 he went out and came in before the P
23:8 Saul summoned all the P to war, to go
26:15 For one of the P came in to destroy
27:12 utterly abhorred by his P Israel; therefore he shall
30:4 Then David and the P who were with him
30:6 greatly distressed; for the P spoke of stoning him,
30:6 him, because all the P were bitter in soul,
30:20 and herds; and the P drove those cattle before
30:21 and to meet the P who were with him;
30:21 drew near to the P he saluted them.
31:9 good news to their idols and to the P
2Sam 1:4 And he answered, "The P have fled from the
1:4 and many of the P also have fallen and
1:12 son and for the P of the LORD and
1:18 be taught to the P of Judah; behold, it
2:26 before you bid your P turn from the pursuit
2:30 had gathered all the P together, there were missing
3:18 I will save my P Israel from the hand
3:31 and to all the P who were with him,
3:32 Abner; and all the P wept.
3:34 And all the P wept again over him.
3:35 Then all the P came to persuade David to
3:36 And all the P took notice of it, and
3:36 everything that the king did pleased all the P
3:37 So all the P and all Israel understood that
5:2 be shepherd of my P Israel, and you shall
5:12 the sake of his P Israel.
6:2 went with all the P who were with him
6:18 offerings, he blessed the P in the name of
6:19 distributed among all the P, the whole multitude of
6:19 Then all the P departed, each to his house.
6:21 prince over Israel, the P of the LORD--and
7:6 I brought up the P of Israel from Egypt
7:7 moved with all the P of Israel, did I
7:7 commanded to shepherd my P Israel, saying, "Why
7:8 be prince over my P Israel;
7:10 a place for my P Israel, and will plant
7:11 appointed judges over my P Israel; and I will
7:23 earth is like thy P Israel, whom God went
7:23 redeem to be his P, making himself a name,
7:23 driving out before his P a nation and its
7:24 establish for thyself thy P Israel to be thy
7:24 Israel to be thy P for ever; and thou,
8:15 David administered justice and equity to all his P
10:12 the man for our P, and for the cities
10:13 So Joab and the P who were with him
11:7 doing, and how the P fared, and how the
11:17 of David among the P fell.
12:28 the rest of the P together, and encamp against
12:29 David gathered all the P together and went to
12:31 he brought forth the P who were in it,
12:31 David and all the P returned to Jerusalem.
13:34 looked, and behold, many P were coming from the
14:13 a thing against the P of God?
14:15 the king because the P have made me afraid;
15:12 grew strong, and the P with Absalom kept
15:17 forth, and all the P after him; and they
15:23 aloud as all the P passed by, and the
15:23 Kidron, and all the P passed on toward the
15:24 of God, until the P had all passed out
15:30 covered; and all the P who were with him
16:6 David; and all the P and all the mighty
16:14 king, and all the P who were with him,
16:15 Absalom and all the P, the men of Israel,
16:18 the LORD and this P and all the men
17:2 panic; and all the P who are with him
17:3 will bring all the P back to you as
17:3 man, and all the P will be at peace."
17:8 he will not spend the night with the P
17:9 when some of the P fall at the first
17:9 a slaughter among the P who follow Absalom.'
17:16 king and all the P who are with him
17:22 arose, and all the P who were with him,
17:29 for David and the P with him to eat;
17:29 for they said, "The P are hungry and weary
18:5 And all the P heard when the king gave
18:8 the forest devoured more P that day than the
19:2 mourning for all the P; for the people heard
19:2 the people; for the P heard that day, "The
19:3 And the P stole into the city that day
19:3 city that day as P steal in who are
19:8 And the P were all told, "Behold, the king
19:8 gate"; and all the P came before the king.
19:9 And all the P were at strife throughout all
19:39 Then all the P went over the Jordan, and
19:40 with him; all the P of Judah, and also
19:40 and also half the P of Israel, brought the
20:12 saw that all the P stopped, he carried Amasa
20:13 the highway, all the P went on after Joab
20:22 went to all the P in her wisdom.
21:2 were not of the P of Israel, but of
21:2 the Amorites; although the P of Israel had sworn
21:2 his zeal for the P of Israel and Judah.
22:28 dost deliver a humble P, but thy eyes are
22:44 head of the nations; P whom I had not
24:2 Beer-sheba, and number the P, that I may know
24:2 that I may know the number of the P
24:3 God add to the P a hundred times as
24:4 king to number the P of Israel.
24:9 the numbering of the P to the king: in
24:10 heart smote him after he had numbered the P
24:15 there died of the P from Dan to Beer-sheba
24:16 working destruction among the P, "It is enough; now
24:17 who was smiting the P, and said, "Lo, I
24:21 that the plague may be averted from the P
1Kgs 1:39 trumpet; and all the P said, "Long live King
1:40 And all the P went up after him, playing
3:2 The P were sacrificing at the high places, however,
3:8 the midst of thy P whom thou hast chosen,
3:8 hast chosen, a great P, that cannot be numbered
3:9 mind to govern thy P, that I may discern
3:9 who is able to govern this thy great P
4:30 wisdom of all the P of the east, and
5:7 a wise son to be over this great P
5:16 had charge of the P who carried on the
6:1 eightieth year after the P of Israel came out
6:13 will not forsake my P Israel."
8:1 fathers' houses of the P of Israel, before King
8:9 a covenant with the P of Israel, when they
8:16 that I brought my P Israel out of Egypt,
8:16 to be over my P Israel.'
8:30 servant and of thy P Israel, when they pray
8:33 "When thy P Israel are defeated before the enemy
8:34 the sin of thy P Israel, and bring them
8:36 of thy servants, thy P Israel, when thou dost
8:36 hast given to thy P as an inheritance.
8:38 or by all thy P Israel, each knowing the
8:41 is not of thy P Israel, comes from a
8:43 thee, as do thy P Israel, and that they
8:44 "If thy P go out to battle against their
8:50 cause and forgive thy P who have sinned against
8:51 (for they are thy P, and thy heritage, which
8:52 the supplication of thy P Israel, giving ear to
8:56 given rest to his P Israel, according to all
8:59 the cause of his P Israel, as each day
8:63 king and all the P of Israel dedicated the
8:66 day he sent the P away; and they blessed
8:66 to David his servant and to Israel his P
9:20 All the P who were left of the Amorites,
9:20 were not of the P of Israel--
9:21 the land, whom the P of Israel were unable
9:22 But of the P of Israel Solomon made no
9:23 had charge of the P who carried on the
11:2 had said to the P of Israel, "You shall
12:5 So the P went away.
12:6 "How do you advise me to answer this P
12:7 a servant to this P today and serve them,
12:9 that we answer this P who have said to
12:10 you speak to this P who said to you,

12:12 Jeroboam and all the P came to Rehoboam the
12:13 the king answered the P harshly, and forsaking the
12:15 not hearken to the P; for it was a
12:16 hearken to them, the P answered the king, "What
12:17 Rehoboam reigned over the P of Israel who dwelt
12:23 the rest of the P,
12:24 against your kinsmen the P of Israel.
12:27 of David; if this P go up to offer
12:27 the heart of this P will turn again to
12:28 he said to the P, "You have gone up
12:30 a sin, for the P went to the one
12:31 from among all the P, who were not of
12:33 a feast for the P of Israel, and went
13:33 from among all the P; any who would, he
14:2 me that I should be king over this P
14:7 you from among the P, and made you leader
14:7 you leader over my P Israel,
14:24 drove out before the P of Israel.
16:2 you leader over my P Israel, and you have
16:2 and have made my P Israel to sin, provoking
16:21 Then the P of Israel were divided into two
16:21 parts; half of the P followed Tibni the son
16:22 But the P who followed Omri overcame the people
16:22 followed Omri overcame the P who followed Tibni
18:20 sent to all the P of Israel, and gathered
18:21 near to all the P, and said, "How long
18:21 And the P did not answer him a word.
18:22 Elijah said to the P, "I, even I only,
18:24 And all the P answered, "It is well spoken."
18:30 said to all the P, "Come near to me";
18:30 me"; and all the P came near to him.
18:37 answer me, that this P may know that thou,
18:39 And when all the P saw it, they fell
19:10 of hosts; for the P of Israel have forsaken
19:14 of hosts; for the P of Israel have forsaken
19:21 gave it to the P, and they ate.
20:8 elders and all the P said to him, "Do
20:10 handfuls for all the P who follow me."
20:15 he mustered all the P of Israel, seven thousand.
20:27 And the P of Israel were mustered, and were
20:27 went against them; the P of Israel encamped before
20:29 was joined; and the P of Israel smote of
20:42 his life, and your P for his people.'"
20:42 for his life, and your people for his P
21:9 on high among the P;
21:12 fast, and set Naboth on high among the P
21:13 the presence of the P, saying, "Naboth cursed God
21:26 cast out before the P of Israel.)
22:4 as you are, my P as your people, my
22:4 my people as your P, my horses as your
22:43 taken away, and the P still sacrificed and burned
2Kgs 3:7 as you are, my P as your people, my
3:7 my people as your P, my horses as your
4:13 She answered, "I dwell among my own P
6:18 and said, "Strike this P, I pray thee, with
6:30 the wall--and the P looked, and behold, he
7:16 Then the P went out, and plundered the camp
7:17 the gate; and the P trod upon him in
7:20 to him, for the P trod upon him in
8:12 will do to the P of Israel; you will
9:6 you king over the P of the LORD, over
10:9 said to all the P, "You are innocent.
10:18 Jehu assembled all the P, and said to them,
11:13 guard and of the P, she went into the
11:13 the LORD to the P;
11:14 king, and all the P of the land rejoicing
11:17 and the king and P, that they should be
11:17 should be the LORD's P; and also between the
11:17 people; and also between the king and the P
11:18 Then all the P of the land went to
11:19 guards, and all the P of the land; and
11:20 So all the P of the land rejoiced; and
12:3 not taken away; the P continued to sacrifice and
12:8 more money from the P, and that they should
13:5 the Syrians; and the P of Israel dwelt in
14:4 were not removed; the P still sacrificed and burned
14:21 And all the P of Judah took Azariah, who
15:4 not taken away; the P still sacrificed and burned
15:5 the household, governing the P of the land.
15:29 and he carried the P captive to Assyria.
15:35 were not removed; the P still sacrificed and burned
16:3 drove out before the P of Israel.
16:9 took it, carrying its P captive to Kir, and
16:15 offering of all the P of the land, and
17:7 was so, because the P of Israel had sinned
17:8 drove out before the P of Israel, and in
17:9 And the P of Israel did secretly against the
17:22 The P of Israel walked in all the sins
17:24 king of Assyria brought P from Babylon, Cuthah,
17:24 Samaria instead of the P of Israel; and they
17:32 themselves all sorts of P as priests of the
18:4 until those days the P of Israel had burned
18:26 the hearing of the P who are on the
18:36 But the P were silent and answered him not
19:12 Haran, Rezeph, and the P of Eden who were
20:5 the prince of my P, Thus says the LORD,
21:2 drove out before the P of Israel.
21:9 LORD destroyed before the P of Israel.
21:24 But the P of the land slew all those
21:24 King Amon, and the P of the land made
22:4 have collected from the P;
22:13 me, and for the P, and for all Judah,
23:2 the prophets, all the P, both small and great;
23:3 book; and all the P joined in the covenant.
23:6 of it upon the graves of the common P
23:21 king commanded all the P, "Keep the passover to
23:30 And the P of the land took Jehoahaz the
23:35 the gold of the P of the land, from
24:14 remained, except the poorest P of the land.
25:3 no food for the P of the land.
25:11 the rest of the P who were left in
25:19 army who mustered the P of the land; and
25:19 sixty men of the P of the land who
25:22 And over the P who remained in the land
25:26 Then all the P, both small and great, and
1Chr 6:64 So the P of Israel gave the Levites the
9:3 And some of the P of Judah, Benjamin, Ephraim,
10:9 good news to their idols and to the P
11:2 be shepherd of my P Israel, and you shall
11:2 be prince over my P Israel.'"
13:4 was right in the eyes of all the P
14:2 the sake of his P Israel.
16:2 offerings, he blessed the P in the name of
16:20 one kingdom to another P,
16:36 Then all the P said "Amen!" and praised the
16:43 Then all the P departed each to his house,
17:6 commanded to shepherd my P, saying, "Why have
17:7 be prince over my P Israel;
17:9 a place for my P Israel, and will plant
17:10 appointed judges over my P Israel; and I will
17:21 earth is like thy P Israel, whom God went
17:21 redeem to be his P, making for thyself a
17:21 out nations before thy P whom thou didst redeem
17:22 thou didst make thy P Israel to be thy
17:22 Israel to be thy P for ever; and thou,
18:14 he administered justice and equity to all his P
19:13 the man for our P, and for the cities
19:14 So Joab and the P who were with him
20:3 he brought forth the P who were in it,
20:3 David and all the P returned to Jerusalem.
21:3 LORD add to his P a hundred times as
21:5 the numbering of the P to David.
21:17 not I who gave command to number the P
21:17 but let not the plague be upon thy P
21:22 that the plague may be averted from the P
22:18 land is subdued before the LORD and his P
23:25 given peace to his P; and he dwells in
27:1 the list of the P of Israel, the heads
28:2 and said: "Hear me, my brethren and my P
28:21 officers and all the P will be wholly at
29:9 Then the P rejoiced because these had given
29:14 and what is my P, that we should be
29:17 I have seen thy P, who are present here,
29:18 the hearts of thy P, and direct their hearts
2Chr 1:9 me king over a P as many as the
1:10 come in before this P, for who can rule
1:10 can rule this thy P, that is so great?"
1:11 you may rule my P over whom I have
2:11 the LORD loves his P he has made you
2:18 overseers to make the P work.
5:2 fathers' houses of the P of Israel, in Jerusalem,
5:10 a covenant with the P of Israel, when they
6:5 that I brought my P out of the land
6:5 as prince over my P Israel;
6:6 to be over my P Israel.'
6:11 he made with the P of Israel."
6:21 servant and of thy P Israel, when they pray
6:24 "If thy P Israel are defeated before the enemy
6:25 the sin of thy P Israel, and bring them
6:27 of thy servants, thy P Israel, when thou dost
6:27 hast given to thy P as an inheritance.
6:29 or by all thy P Israel, each knowing his

P

Book	Ref	Context
	8:14	by Moses that the P of Israel should dwell
	8:16	So the P went out and brought them and
	8:17	to that day the P of Israel had not
	9:1	of this month the P of Israel were assembled
	9:10	servants and all the P of his land, for
	9:32	fathers, and all thy P, since the time of
	10:14	The chiefs of the P: Parosh, Pahath-moab, Elam,
	10:28	The rest of the P, the priests, the Levites,
	10:34	the Levites, and the P, for the wood offering,
	10:39	For the P of Israel and the sons of
	11:1	the leaders of the P lived in Jerusalem; and
	11:1	the rest of the P cast lots to bring
	11:2	And the P blessed all the men who willingly
	11:24	the king's hand in all matters concerning the P
	11:25	fields, some of the P of Judah lived in
	11:31	The P of Benjamin also lived from Geba onward,
	12:30	and they purified the P and the gates and
	12:38	with half of the P, upon the wall, above
	13:1	the hearing of the P; and in it was
	13:3	When the P heard the law, they separated from
	13:16	the sabbath to the P of Judah, and in
	13:24	language of Judah, but the language of each P
Tob	1:17	any one of my P dead and thrown out
	2:3	"Father, one of our P has been strangled and
	4:13	and daughters of your P by refusing to take
	5:11	know, my brother, your P and your name."
	6:15	to take a wife from among your own P
	8:15	angels and thy chosen P bless thee for ever.
	14:7	the Lord, and his P will give thanks to
	14:7	to God, and the Lord will exalt his P
Jud	1:6	joined by all the P of the hill country
	1:12	of Moab, and the P of Ammon, and all
	2:23	and plundered all the P of Rassis and the
	2:28	fell upon all the P who lived along the
	3:7	And these P and all in the country round
	4:1	By this time the P of Israel living in
	4:3	captivity, and all the P of Judea were newly
	4:6	time, wrote to the P of Bethulia and Betomesthaim,
	4:8	senate of the whole P of Israel, in session
	4:13	their affliction; for the P fasted many days
	4:14	and the vows and freewill offerings of the P
	5:1	army, heard that the P of Israel had prepared
	5:3	me, you Canaanites, what P is this that lives
	5:5	the truth about this P that dwells in the
	5:6	This P is descended from the Chaldeans.
	5:14	drove out all the P of the wilderness.
	5:20	unwitting error in this P and they sin against
	5:23	Israelites; they are a P with no strength or
	6:2	make war against the P of Israel because their
	6:16	midst of all their P, and Uzziah asked him
	6:18	Then the P fell down and worshiped God, and
	6:19	the humiliation of our P, and look this day
	7:8	the chieftains of the P of Esau and all
	7:10	For these P, the Israelites, do not rely on
	7:13	is where all the P of Bethulia get their
	7:13	We and our P will go up to the
	7:19	The P of Israel cried out to the Lord
	7:24	Then all the P, the young men, the women,
	7:33	Then he dismissed the P to their various posts,
	8:9	words spoken by the P against the ruler, because
	8:11	me, rulers of the P of Bethulia!
	8:11	have said to the P today is not right;
	8:18	tribe or family or P or city of ours
	8:29	your life all the P have recognized your
	8:30	But the P were very thirsty, and they compelled
	9:14	other who protects the P of Israel but thou
	10:8	your plans, that the P of Israel may glory
	10:12	asked her, "To what P do you belong, and
	10:19	"Who can despise these P, who have women like
	11:2	even now, if your P who live in the
	11:13	for any of the P so much as to
	11:14	Jerusalem, because even the P living there have
	11:22	send you before the P, to lend strength to
	12:3	For none of your P is here with us."
	12:8	her way for the raising up of her P
	13:17	All the P were greatly astonished, and bowed down
	13:17	into contempt this day the enemies of thy P
	13:20	And all the P said, "So be it, so
	14:6	the gathering of the P, he fell down on
	14:8	the presence of the P all that she had
	14:9	she had finished, the P raised a great shout
	14:17	rushed out to the P and shouted,
	15:6	The rest of the P of Bethulia fell upon
	15:8	the senate of the P of Israel who lived
	15:10	And all the P said, "So be it!"
	15:11	So all the P plundered the camp for thirty
	15:13	went before all the P in the dance, leading
	16:1	Israel, and all the P loudly sang this song
	16:3	to his camp, in the midst of the P
	16:11	Then my oppressed P shouted for joy; my weak
	16:11	for joy; my weak P shouted and the enemy
	16:17	to the nations that rise up against my P
	16:18	As soon as the P were purified, they offered
	16:19	of Holofernes, which the P had given her; and
	16:20	So the P continued feasting in Jerusalem before the
	16:22	her husband died and was gathered to his P
	16:25	spread terror among the P of Israel in the
Esth	1:5	gave for all the P present in Susa the
	1:22	script and to every P in its own language,
	1:22	and speak according to the language of his P
	2:10	not made known her P or kindred, for Mordecai
	2:20	her kindred or her P, as Mordecai had charged
	3:6	known to him the P of Mordecai, Haman sought
	3:6	all the Jews, the P of Mordecai, throughout the
	3:8	"There is a certain P scattered abroad and
	3:8	those of every other P, and they do not
	3:11	given to you, the P also, to do with
	3:12	own script and every P in its own language;
	4:8	supplication to him and entreat him for her P
	4:11	king's servants and the P of the king's provinces
	6:13	is of the Jewish P, you will not prevail
	7:3	my petition, and my P at my request.
	7:4	sold, I and my P, to be destroyed, to
	8:6	see the calamity that is coming to my P
	8:9	script and to every P in its own language,
	8:11	armed force of any P or province that might
	10:3	the welfare of his P and spoke peace to
	10:3	his people and spoke peace to all his P
	10:9	Lord has saved his P; the Lord has delivered
	10:10	lots, one for the P of God and one
	10:12	And God remembered his P and vindicated his
	10:13	for ever among his P Israel."
	12:6	injure Mordecai and his P because of the two
	13:4	scattered a certain hostile P, who have laws contrary
	13:5	We understand that this P, and it alone, stands
	13:15	of Abraham, spare thy P; for the eyes of
	15:10	die, for our law applies only to the P
	16:21	joy to his chosen P instead of a day
Job	1:3	greatest of all the P of the east.
	1:19	fell upon the young P, and they are dead;
	12:2	doubt you are the P, and wisdom will die
	12:24	the chiefs of the P of the earth, and
	18:19	or descendant among his P, and no survivor where
	34:20	die; at midnight the P are shaken and pass
	34:30	not reign, that he should not ensnare the P
	35:9	the multitude of oppressions P cry out; they call
Ps	3:6	of ten thousands of P who have set themselves
	3:8	to the LORD; thy blessing be upon thy P
	14:4	who eat up my P as they eat bread,
	14:7	the fortunes of his P, Jacob shall rejoice, Israel
	18:27	dost deliver a humble P; but the haughty eyes
	18:43	head of the nations; P whom I had not
	22:6	man; scorned by men, and despised by the P
	22:31	his deliverance to a P yet unborn, that he
	28:8	the strength of his P, he is the saving
	28:9	O save thy P, and bless thy heritage; be
	29:11	May the LORD give strength to his P
	29:11	the LORD bless his P with peace!
	33:12	is the LORD, the P whom he has chosen
	43:1	cause against an ungodly P; from deceitful and
	44:12	Thou hast sold thy P for a trifle, demanding
	45:10	your ear; forget your P and your father's house;
	45:12	bow to him; the P of Tyre will sue
	45:12	the richest of the P
	47:9	peoples gather as the P of the God of
	50:4	he may judge his P:
	50:7	[Selah] "Hear, O my P, and I will speak,
	53:4	who eat up my P as they eat bread,
	53:6	the fortunes of his P, Jacob will rejoice and
	59:11	them not, lest my P forget; make them totter
	60:3	Thou hast made thy P suffer hard things; thou
	62:8	at all times, O P; pour out your heart
	68:7	go forth before thy P, when thou didst march
	68:35	Israel, he gives power and strength to his P
	72:2	May he judge thy P with righteousness, and thy
	72:3	bear prosperity for the P, and the hills, in
	72:4	the poor of the P, give deliverance to the
	73:10	Therefore the P turn and praise them; and find
	74:18	scoffs, and an impious P reviles thy name.
	77:15	thy arm redeem thy P, the sons of Jacob
	77:20	Thou didst lead thy P like a flock by
	78:1	Give ear, O my P, to my teaching; incline

78:20 also give bread, or provide meat for his P
78:52 he led forth his P like sheep, and guided
78:62 He gave his P over to the sword, and
78:71 shepherd of Jacob his P, of Israel his inheritance.
79:13 Then we thy P, the flock of thy pasture,
80:4 be angry with thy P's prayers?
81:8 [Selah] Hear, O my P, while I admonish you!
81:11 "But my P did not listen to my voice;
81:13 O that my P would listen to me, that
83:3 crafty plans against thy P; they consult together
85:2 the iniquity of thy P; thou didst pardon all
85:6 us again, that thy P may rejoice in thee?
85:8 speak peace to his P, to his saints, to
89:15 Blessed are the P who know the festal shout,
89:19 mighty, I have exalted one chosen from the P
94:5 They crush thy P, O LORD, and afflict thy
94:8 Understand, O dullest of the P
94:14 will not forsake his P; he will not abandon
95:7 and we are the P of his pasture, and
95:10 said, "They are a P who err in heart,
100:3 his; we are his P, and the sheep of
102:18 come, so that a P yet unborn may praise
103:7 his acts to the P of Israel.
105:13 one kingdom to another P,
105:24 the LORD made his P very fruitful, and made
105:25 hearts to hate his P, to deal craftily with
105:43 he led forth his P with joy, his chosen
106:4 showest favor to thy P; help me when thou
106:40 was kindled against his P, and he abhorred his
106:48 And let all the P say, "Amen!" Praise the
107:32 the congregation of the P, and praise him in
110:3 Your P will offer themselves freely on the day
111:6 He has shown his P the power of his
111:9 sent redemption to his P; he has commanded his
113:8 sit with princes, with the princes of his P
114:1 of Jacob from a P of strange language,
116:14 the LORD in the presence of all his P
116:18 presence of all his P,
125:2 is round about his P, from this time forth
135:12 a heritage to his P Israel.
135:14 LORD will vindicate his P, and have compassion on
136:16 him who led his P through the wilderness, for
144:15 Happy the P to whom such blessings fall!
144:15 Happy the P whose God is the LORD!
148:14 a horn for his P, praise for all his
148:14 his saints, for the P of Israel who are
149:4 takes pleasure in his P; he adorns the humble
Prov 11:14 is no guidance, a P falls; but in an
11:26 The P curse him who holds back grain, but
14:28 In a multitude of P is the glory of
14:28 a king, but without P a prince is ruined.
14:34 nation, but sin is a reproach to any P
28:15 bear is a wicked ruler over a poor P
29:2 are in authority, the P rejoice; but when the
29:2 the wicked rule, the P groan.
29:18 is no prophecy the P cast off restraint, but
30:25 the ants are a P not strong, yet they
30:26 the badgers are a P not mighty, yet they
30:31 the he-goat, and a king striding before his P
Eccl 4:16 end of all the P; he was over all
12:9 Preacher also taught the P knowledge, weighing and
Wis 6:24 a sensible king is the stability of his P
8:15 of me; among the P I shall show myself
9:7 be king of thy P and to be judge
9:12 I shall judge thy P justly, and shall be
10:15 A holy P and blameless race wisdom delivered from
12:19 thou has taught thy P that the righteous man
15:14 infant, are all the enemies who oppressed thy P
15:18 The enemies of thy P worship even the most
16:2 show kindness to thy P, and thou didst prepare
16:3 to them, while thy P, after suffering want a
16:5 beasts came upon thy P and they were being
16:20 thou didst give thy P food of angels, and
18:3 a guide for thy P's unknown journey, and a
18:7 destruction of their enemies were expected by thy P
18:13 destroyed, they acknowledged thy P to be God's son.
19:2 themselves had permitted thy P to depart and hastily
19:5 lacked, and that thy P might experience an
19:22 exalted and glorified thy P; and thou hast not
Sir 7:7 public, and do not disgrace yourself among the P
9:17 the craftsmen; so a P's leader is proved wise
10:1 magistrate will educate his P, and the rule of
10:2 the magistrate of the P, so are his officials;
10:3 king will ruin his P, but a city will
14:8 grudging eye; he averts his face and disregards P
16:4 will be filled with P, but through a tribe
16:15 Among so many P I shall not be known,
19:22 unjust, and there are P who distort kindness to
21:8 his house with other P's money is like one
24:1 and will glory in the midst of her P
24:6 earth, and in every P and nation I have
24:12 root in an honored P, in the portion of
27:12 Among stupid P watch for a chance to leave,
27:12 leave, but among thoughtful P stay on.
31:9 for he has done wonderful things among his P
33:18 are great among the P, and you leaders of
35:19 the case of his P and makes them rejoice
36:8 appointed time, and let P recount thy mighty deeds.
36:9 those who harm thy P meet destruction.
36:12 O Lord, upon the P called by thy name,
36:17 of Aaron for thy P, and all who are
37:23 will instruct his own P, and the fruits of
37:26 is wise among his P will inherit confidence, and
38:33 the council of the P, nor do they attain
39:25 were created for good P, just as evil things
41:18 a congregation or the P; of unjust dealing, before
42:11 and notorious among the P, and put you to
44:4 prophecies; leaders of the P in their deliberations
44:4 of learning for the P, wise in their words
45:3 him commands for his P, and showed him part
45:7 him, and gave him the priesthood of the P
45:9 the sons of his P;
45:15 priest and bless his P in his name.
45:16 a memorial portion, to make atonement for the P
45:22 the land of the P he has no inheritance,
45:22 no portion among the P; for the Lord himself
45:23 stood fast, when the P turned away, in the
45:24 sanctuary and of his P, that he and his
45:26 heart to judge his P in righteousness, so that
46:7 the congregation, restrained the P from sin, and
46:8 of six hundred thousand P on foot, to bring
46:13 the kingdom and anointed rulers over his P
46:18 the leaders of the P of Tyre and all
46:20 prophecy, to blot out the wickedness of the P
47:4 away reproach from the P, when he lifted his
47:5 in war, to exalt the power of his P
47:23 whose policy caused the P to revolt.
48:15 For all this the P did not repent, and
48:15 all the earth; the P were left very few
49:2 aright in converting the P, and took away the
49:10 for they comforted the P of Jacob and delivered
50:1 the pride of his P was Simon the high
50:4 how to save his P from ruin, and fortified
50:5 he was when the P gathered round him as
50:17 Then all the P together made haste and fell
50:19 And the P besought the Lord Most High in
50:26 Philistines, and the foolish P that dwell in Shechem.
Is 1:3 does not know, my P does not understand."
1:4 Ah, sinful nation, a P laden with iniquity, offspring
1:10 of our God, you P of Gomorrah!
2:6 thou hast rejected thy P, the house of Jacob,
3:5 And the P will oppress one another, every man
3:7 you shall not make me leader of the P
3:12 My P — children are their oppressors, and women
3:12 O my P, your leaders mislead you, and confuse
3:13 place to contend, he stands to judge his P
3:14 and princes of his P: "It is you who
3:15 mean by crushing my P, by grinding the face
5:13 Therefore my P go into exile for want of
5:25 was kindled against his P, and he stretched out
6:5 the midst of a P of unclean lips; for
6:9 and say to this P: 'Hear and hear, but
6:10 the heart of this P fat, and their ears
7:2 the heart of his P shook as the trees
7:8 no longer be a P
7:17 you and upon your P and upon your father's
8:6 me again: "Because this P have refused the waters
8:11 the way of this P, saying:
8:12 conspiracy all that this P call conspiracy, and do
8:19 should not a P consult their God?
9:2 The P who walked in darkness have seen a
9:9 Israel; and all the P will know, Ephraim and
9:13 The P did not turn to him who smote
9:16 those who lead this P lead them astray, and
9:19 is burned, and the P are like fuel for
10:2 the poor of my P of their right, that
10:6 him, and against the P of my wrath I
10:22 For though your P Israel be as the sand
10:24 of hosts: "O my P, who dwell in Zion,
11:11 is left of his P, from Assyria, from Egypt,
11:14 they shall plunder the P of the east.
11:16 is left of his P, as there was for

13:14 turn to his own P, and every man will
14:20 have destroyed your land, you have slain your P
14:32 the afflicted of his P find refuge."
18:2 and smooth, to a P feared near and far,
18:7 of hosts from a P tall and smooth, from
18:7 and smooth, from a P feared near and far,
19:25 "Blessed be Egypt my P, and Assyria the work
22:4 for the destruction of the daughter of my P
23:13 This is the P; it was not Assyria.
24:2 be, as with the P, so with the priest;
25:8 the reproach of his P he will take away
26:11 thy zeal for thy P, and be ashamed.
26:20 Come, my P, enter your chambers, and shut your
27:11 For this is a P without discernment; therefore he
27:12 one by one, O P of Israel.
28:5 the remnant of his P;
28:11 will speak to this P,
28:14 scoffers, who rule this P in Jerusalem!
29:13 Lord said: "Because this P draw near with their
29:14 marvelous things with this P, wonderful and
30:5 to shame through a P that cannot profit them,
30:6 of camels, to a P that cannot profit them.
30:9 they are a rebellious P, lying sons, sons who
30:19 Yea, O P in Zion who dwell at Jerusalem;
30:26 the hurt of his P, and heals the wounds
31:6 have deeply revolted, O P of Israel.
32:13 the soil of my P growing up in thorns
32:18 My P will abide in a peaceful habitation, in
33:19 no more the insolent P, the people of an
33:19 the insolent people, the P of an obscure speech
33:24 "I am sick"; the P who dwell there will
34:5 upon Edom, upon the P I have doomed.
36:11 the hearing of the P who are on the
37:12 Haran, Rezeph, and the P of Eden who were
40:1 Comfort, comfort my P, says your God.
40:7 upon it; surely the P is grass.
42:5 gives breath to the P upon it and spirit
42:6 a covenant to the P, a light to the
42:22 But this is a P robbed and plundered, they
43:8 Bring forth the P who are blind, yet have
43:20 drink to my chosen P,
43:21 my chosen people, the P whom I formed for
47:6 was angry with my P, I profaned my heritage;
49:8 a covenant to the P, to establish the land,
49:13 LORD has comforted his P, and will have compassion
51:4 "Listen to me, my P, and give ear to
51:7 who know righteousness, the P in whose heart is
51:16 earth, and saying to Zion, 'You are my P
51:22 the cause of his P: "Behold, I have taken
52:4 the Lord GOD: My P went down at the
52:5 LORD, seeing that my P are taken away for
52:6 Therefore my P shall know my name; therefore in
52:9 LORD has comforted his P, he has redeemed
53:8 the living, stricken for the transgression of my P
54:3 the nations and will P the desolate cities.
56:3 separate me from his P; and let not the
57:14 every obstruction from my P's way."
58:1 trumpet; declare to my P their transgression, to the
60:21 Your P shall all be righteous; they shall possess
61:9 that they are a P whom the LORD has
62:10 the way for the P; build up, build up
62:12 be called The holy P, The redeemed of the
63:8 Surely they are my P, sons who will not
63:14 thou didst lead thy P, to make for thyself
63:18 Thy holy P possessed thy sanctuary a little while;
64:9 Behold, consider, we are all thy P
65:2 day to a rebellious P, who walk in a
65:3 their own devices; a P who provoke me to
65:10 lie down, for my P who have sought me.
65:18 a rejoicing, and her P a joy.
65:19 be glad in my P; no more shall be
65:22 the days of my P be, and my chosen
Jer 1:18 its priests, and the P of the land.
2:11 But my P have changed their glory for that
2:13 the LORD, for my P have committed two evils:
2:31 Why then do my P say, 'We are free,
2:32 Yet my P have forgotten me days without number.
4:10 hast utterly deceived this P and Jerusalem, saying, 'It
4:11 be said to this P and to Jerusalem, "A
4:11 the daughter of my P, not to winnow or
4:22 "For my P are foolish, they know me not;
5:14 a fire, and this P wood, and the fire
5:19 And when your P say, 'Why has the LORD
5:21 O foolish and senseless P, who have eyes, but
5:23 But this P has a stubborn and rebellious heart;
5:26 are found among my P; they lurk like fowlers
5:31 at their direction; my P love to have it
6:1 Flee for safety, O P of Benjamin, from the
6:14 the wound of my P lightly, saying, 'Peace, peace,'
6:19 bringing evil upon this P, the fruit of their
6:21 will lay before this P stumbling blocks against which
6:22 the LORD: "Behold, a P is coming from the
6:26 O daughter of my P, gird on sackcloth, and
6:27 and tester among my P, that you may know
7:12 the wickedness of my P Israel.
7:16 not pray for this P, or lift up cry
7:23 you shall be my P; and walk in all
7:33 dead bodies of this P will be food for
8:5 Why then has this P turned away in perpetual
8:7 their coming; but my P know not the ordinance
8:11 the wound of my P lightly, saying, 'Peace, peace,'
8:19 the daughter of my P from the length and
8:21 the daughter of my P is my heart wounded,
8:22 the daughter of my P not been restored?
9:1 for the slain of the daughter of my P
9:2 I might leave my P and go away from
9:7 what else can I do, because of my P
9:15 I will feed this P with wormwood, and give
11:4 shall you be my P, and I will be
11:14 not pray for this P, or lift up a
12:14 I have given my P Israel to inherit: "Behold,
12:16 the ways of my P, to swear by my
12:16 as they taught my P to swear by Baal,
12:16 be built up in the midst of my P
13:10 This evil P, who refuse to hear my words,
13:11 be for me a P, a name, a praise,
14:2 her gates languish; her P lament on the ground,
14:10 the LORD concerning this P: "They have loved to
14:11 "Do not pray for the welfare of this P
14:16 And the P to whom they prophesy shall be
14:17 virgin daughter of my P is smitten with a
15:1 yet my heart would not turn toward this P
15:7 I have destroyed my P; they did not turn
15:20 make you to this P a fortified wall of
16:5 my peace from this P, says the LORD, my
16:10 when you tell this P all these words, and
16:14 who brought up the P of Israel out of
16:15 who brought up the P of Israel out of
17:26 And P shall come from the cities of Judah
18:15 But my P have forgotten me, they burn incense
19:1 the elders of the P and some of the
19:4 Because the P have forsaken me, and have profaned
19:7 and will cause their P to fall by the
19:11 will I break this P and this city, as
19:14 said to all the P:
21:7 his servants, and the P in this city who
21:8 compassion.' "And to this P you shall say: 'Thus
22:2 your servants, and your P who enter these gates.
22:4 on horses, they, and their servants, and their P
23:2 who care for my P: "You have scattered my
23:7 who brought up the P of Israel out of
23:13 Baal and led my P Israel astray.
23:22 my words to my P, and they would have
23:27 think to make my P forget my name by
23:32 them and lead my P astray by their lies
23:32 do not profit this P at all, says the
23:33 "When one of this P, or a prophet, or
23:34 or one of the P who says, 'The burden
24:7 they shall be my P and I will be
25:1 Jeremiah concerning all the P of Judah, in the
25:2 spoke to all the P of Judah and all
25:19 his princes, all his P,
26:7 prophets and all the P heard Jeremiah speaking
26:8 speak to all the P, then the priests and
26:8 prophets and all the P laid hold of him,
26:9 And all the P gathered about Jeremiah in the
26:11 and to all the P, "This man deserves the
26:12 princes and all the P, saying, "The LORD sent
26:16 princes and all the P said to the priests
26:17 to all the assembled P, saying,
26:18 said to all the P of Judah: 'Thus says
26:23 body into the burial place of the common P
26:24 given over to the P to be put to
27:12 serve him and his P, and live.
27:13 will you and your P die by the sword,
27:16 and to all this P, saying, "Thus says the
28:1 priests and all the P, saying,
28:5 priests and all the P who were standing in
28:7 hearing and in the hearing of all the P
28:11 presence of all the P, saying, "Thus says the
28:15 you have made this P trust in a lie.
29:1 prophets, and all the P, whom Nebuchadnezzar had

	29:16	and concerning all the P who dwell in this
	29:25	name to all the P who are in Jerusalem,
	29:32	one living among this P to see the good
	29:32	will do to my P, says the LORD, for
	30:3	the fortunes of my P, Israel and Judah, says
	30:22	you shall be my P, and I will be
	31:1	families of Israel, and they shall be my P
	31:2	says the LORD: "The P who survived the sword
	31:7	LORD has saved his P, the remnant of Israel.'
	31:14	with abundance, and my P shall be satisfied with
	31:33	be their God, and they shall be my P
	32:21	Thou didst bring thy P Israel out of the
	32:38	they shall be my P, and I will be
	32:42	great evil upon this P, so I will bring
	33:24	not observed what these P are saying, 'The LORD
	33:24	they have despised my P so that they are
	34:8	covenant with all the P in Jerusalem to make
	34:10	princes and all the P who had entered into
	34:19	priests, and all the P of the land who
	35:16	gave them, but this P has not obeyed me.
	36:6	hearing of all the P in the LORD's house
	36:7	wrath that the LORD has pronounced against this P
	36:9	ninth month, all the P in Jerusalem and all
	36:9	Jerusalem and all the P who came from the
	36:10	hearing of all the P, Baruch read the words
	36:13	read the scroll in the hearing of the P
	36:14	the hearing of the P, and come." So Baruch
	37:2	his servants nor the P of the land listened
	37:4	and out among the P, for he had not
	37:12	Benjamin to receive his portion there among the P
	37:18	your servants or this P, that you have put
	38:1	saying to all the P,
	38:4	hands of all the P, by speaking such words
	38:4	the welfare of this P, but their harm."
	39:8	the house of the P, and broke down the
	39:9	the rest of the P who were left in
	39:9	to him, and the P who remained.
	39:10	some of the poor P who owned nothing, and
	39:14	So he dwelt among the P
	40:5	with him among the P; or go wherever you
	40:6	with him among the P who were left in
	41:10	the rest of the P who were in Mizpah,
	41:10	daughters and all the P who were left at
	41:13	And when all the P who were with Ishmael
	41:14	So all the P whom Ishmael had carried away
	41:16	the rest of the P whom Ishmael the son
	42:1	Hoshaiah, and all the P from the least to
	42:8	him, and all the P from the least to
	43:1	speaking to all the P all these words of
	43:4	forces and all the P did not obey the
	44:15	great assembly, all the P who dwelt in Pathros
	44:20	said to all the P, men and women, all
	44:20	and women, all the P who had given him
	44:21	your princes, and the P of the land, did
	44:24	said to all the P and all the women,
	46:16	back to our own P and to the land
	46:24	the hand of a P from the north."
	48:42	be no longer a P, because he magnified himself
	48:46	The P of Chemosh is undone; for your sons
	49:1	dispossessed Gad, and his P settled in its cities?
	49:28	Destroy the P of the east!
	50:4	says the LORD, the P of Israel and the
	50:4	of Israel and the P of Judah shall come
	50:6	never be forgotten.' "My P have been lost sheep;
	50:16	turn to his own P, and every one shall
	50:33	LORD of hosts: The P of Israel are oppressed,
	50:33	are oppressed, and the P of Judah with them;
	50:41	"Behold, a P comes from the north; a mighty
	51:45	"Go out of the midst of her, my P
	52:6	no food for the P of the land.
	52:15	the poorest of the P and the rest of
	52:15	the rest of the P who were left in
	52:25	army who mustered the P of the land; and
	52:25	sixty men of the P of the land, who
	52:28	the number of the P whom Nebuchadrezzar carried
Lam	1:1	lonely sits the city that was full of P
	1:7	When her P fell into the hand of the
	1:11	All her P groan as they search for bread;
	2:11	the daughter of my P, because infants and babes
	3:48	of the destruction of the daughter of my P
	4:3	the daughter of my P has become cruel, like
	4:6	the daughter of my P has been greater than
	4:10	in the destruction of the daughter of my P
Bar	1:3	hearing of all the P who came to hear
	1:4	hearing of all the P, small and great, all
	1:7	and to all the P who were present with
	1:9	mighty men and the P of the land, and
	2:11	who didst bring thy P out of the land
	2:28	the presence of the P of Israel, saying,
	2:30	not obey me, for they are a stiff-necked P
	2:35	they shall be my P; and I will never
	2:35	never again remove my P Israel from the land
	4:3	to another, or your advantages to an alien P
	4:5	Take courage, my P, O memorial of Israel!
	6:9	P take gold and make crowns for the heads
Ezek	2:3	send you to the P of Israel, to a
	2:4	The P also are impudent and stubborn: I send
	3:5	not sent to a P of foreign speech and
	3:11	the exiles, to your P, and say to them,
	3:25	go out among the P;
	4:13	said, "Thus shall the P of Israel eat their
	6:5	dead bodies of the P of Israel before their
	7:27	the hands of the P of the land are
	11:1	Pelatiah the son of Benaiah, princes of the P
	11:20	they shall be my P, and I will be
	12:19	and say of the P of the land, Thus
	13:9	the council of my P, nor be enrolled in
	13:10	they have misled my P, saying, 'Peace,' when there
	13:10	and because, when the P build a wall, these
	13:17	the daughters of your P, who prophesy out of
	13:18	souls belonging to my P, and keep other souls
	13:19	profaned me among my P for handfuls of barley
	13:19	your lies to my P, who listen to lies.
	13:21	off, and deliver my P out of your hand,
	13:23	I will deliver my P out of your hand.
	14:8	the midst of my P; and you shall know
	14:9	the midst of my P Israel.
	14:11	they may be my P and I may be
	17:9	strong arm or many P to pull it from
	18:18	not good among his P, behold, he shall die
	21:12	it is against my P; it is against all
	21:12	are delivered over to the sword with my P
	22:29	The P of the land have practiced extortion and
	24:18	I spoke to the P in the morning, and
	24:19	And the P said to me, "Will you not
	25:4	you over to the P of the East for
	25:10	the Ammonites to the P of the East as
	25:14	the hand of my P Israel; and they shall
	26:11	he will slay your P with the sword; and
	26:20	the Pit, to the P of old, and I
	30:5	and Libya, and the P of the land that
	30:11	He and his P with him, the most terrible
	33:2	man, speak to your P and say to them,
	33:2	a land, and the P of the land take
	33:3	trumpet and warns the P;
	33:6	trumpet, so that the P are not warned, and
	33:12	man, say to your P, The righteousness of the
	33:17	"Yet your P say, 'The way of the Lord
	33:30	son of man, your P who talk together about
	33:31	come to you as P come, and they sit
	33:31	before you as my P, and they hear what
	34:30	of Israel, are my P, says the Lord GOD.
	35:5	and gave over the P of Israel to the
	36:3	evil gossip of the P;
	36:8	your fruit to my P Israel; for they will
	36:12	upon you, even my P Israel; and they shall
	36:20	them, 'These are the P of the LORD, and
	36:28	you shall be my P, and I will be
	37:12	your graves, O my P; and I will bring
	37:13	and raise you from your graves, O my P
	37:18	And when your P say to you, 'Will you
	37:21	I will take the P of Israel from the
	37:23	they shall be my P, and I will be
	37:27	be their God, and they shall be my P
	38:8	war, the land where P were gathered from many
	38:8	a continual waste; its P were brought out from
	38:11	fall upon the quiet P who dwell securely, all
	38:12	now inhabited, and the P who were gathered from
	38:14	that day when my P Israel are dwelling securely,
	38:16	come up against my P Israel, like a cloud
	39:7	the midst of my P Israel; and I will
	39:13	All the P of the land will bury them;
	42:14	go near to that which is for the P
	43:7	the midst of the P of Israel for ever.
	44:9	who are among the P of Israel, shall enter
	44:11	the sacrifice for the P, and they shall attend
	44:11	shall attend on the P, to serve them.
	44:15	my sanctuary when the P of Israel went astray
	44:19	outer court to the P, they shall put off
	44:19	communicate holiness to the P with their garments.
	44:23	They shall teach my P the difference between the
	45:8	no more oppress my P; but they shall let

45:9 your evictions of my P, says the Lord GOD.
45:16 All the P of the land shall give this
45:22 himself and all the P of the land a
46:3 The P of the land shall worship at the
46:9 "When the P of the land come before the
46:18 the inheritance of the P, thrusting them out of
46:18 that none of my P shall be dispossessed of
46:20 outer court and so communicate holiness to the P
46:24 the temple shall boil the sacrifices of the P
48:11 go astray when the P of Israel went astray,
Dan 1:3 bring some of the P of Israel, both of
2:44 nor shall its sovereignty be left to another P
3:97 make a decree: Any P, nation, or language that
7:27 be given to the P of the saints of
8:24 mighty men and the P of the saints.
9:6 and to all the P of the land.
9:15 who didst bring thy P out of the land
9:16 fathers, Jerusalem and thy P have become a byword
9:19 thy city and thy P are called by thy
9:20 the sin of my P Israel, and presenting my
9:24 are decreed concerning your P and your holy city,
9:26 have nothing; and the P of the prince who
10:14 is to befall your P in the latter days.
11:14 violence among your own P shall lift themselves up
11:23 and he shall become strong with a small P
11:32 the covenant; but the P who know their God
11:33 And those among the P who are wise shall
12:1 the great prince who has charge of your P
12:1 at that time your P shall be delivered, every
12:7 power of the holy P comes to an end
13:5 two elders from the P were appointed as judges.
13:5 were judges, who were supposed to govern the P
13:7 When the P departed at noon, Susanna would go
13:28 next day, when the P gathered at the house
13:29 They said before the P, "Send for Susanna, the
13:34 the midst of the P, and laid their hands
13:41 were elders of the P and judges; and they
13:47 All the P turned to him, and said, "What
13:50 Then all the P returned in haste.
13:64 onward Daniel had a great reputation among the P
Hos 1:9 his name Not my P, for you are not
1:9 you are not my P and I am not
1:10 the number of the P of Israel shall be
1:10 was said to them, "You are not my P
1:11 And the P of Judah and the people of
1:11 of Judah and the P of Israel shall be
2:1 Say to your brother, "My P
2:23 say to Not my P, 'You are my people';
2:23 people, 'You are my P; and he shall say
3:1 the LORD loves the P of Israel, though they
4:1 of the LORD, O P of Israel; for the
4:6 My P are destroyed for lack of knowledge; because
4:8 the sin of my P; they are greedy for
4:9 it shall be like P, like priest; I will
4:12 My P inquire of a thing of wood, and
4:14 cult prostitutes, and a P without understanding shall
7:1 the fortunes of my P,
9:8 watchman of Ephraim, the P of my God, yet
10:5 Its P shall mourn for it, and its idolatrous
10:10 come against the wayward P to chastise them; and
10:14 shall arise among your P, and all your fortresses
11:7 My P are bent on turning away from me;
Joel 2:2 a great and powerful P; their like has never
2:16 a fast; call a solemn assembly; gather the P
2:17 and say, "Spare thy P, O LORD, and make
2:18 for his land, and had pity on his P
2:19 and said to his P, "Behold, I am sending
2:26 And my P shall never again be put to
2:27 And my P shall never again be put to
3:2 on account of my P and my heritage Israel,
3:3 cast lots for my P, and have given a
3:6 You have sold the P of Judah and Jerusalem
3:16 a refuge to his P, a stronghold to the
3:16 a stronghold to the P of Israel.
3:19 violence done to the P of Judah, because they
Amos 1:5 from Beth-eden; and the P of Syria shall go
1:6 into exile a whole P to deliver them up
1:9 delivered up a whole P to Edom, and did
2:11 not indeed so, O P of Israel?" says the
3:1 spoken against you, O P of Israel, against the
3:6 a city, and the P are not afraid?
3:12 ear, so shall the P of Israel who dwell
4:5 love to do, O P of Israel!" says the
7:8 the midst of my P Israel; I will never
7:15 'Go, prophesy to my P Israel.'
8:2 has come upon my P Israel; I will never
9:1 heads of all the P; and what are left
9:7 Ethiopians to me, O P of Israel?" says the
9:10 the sinners of my P shall die by the
9:14 the fortunes of my P Israel, and they shall
Obad 1:12 have rejoiced over the P of Judah in the
1:13 the gate of my P in the day of
1:20 who are of the P of Israel shall possess
Jon 1:8 And of what P are you?"
3:5 And the P of Nineveh believed God; they proclaimed
Mic 1:9 the gate of my P, to Jerusalem.
2:4 the portion of my P; how he removes it
2:8 you rise against my P as an enemy; you
2:9 The women of my P you drive out from
2:11 he would be the preacher for this P
3:2 skin from off my P, and their flesh from
3:3 the flesh of my P, and flay their skin
3:5 prophets who lead my P astray, who cry "Peace"
5:3 shall return to the P of Israel.
6:2 a controversy with his P, and he will contend
6:3 "O my P, what have I done to you?
6:5 O my P, remember what Balak king of Moab
7:14 Shepherd thy P with thy staff, the flock of
Nah 3:18 Your P are scattered on the mountains with none
Hab 3:13 the salvation of thy P, for the salvation of
3:16 trouble to come upon P who invade us.
Zeph 2:4 become a desolation; Ashdod's P shall be driven out
2:8 they have taunted my P and made boasts against
2:9 The remnant of my P shall plunder them, and
2:10 and boasted against the P of the LORD of
3:12 midst of you a P humble and lowly.
Hag 1:2 LORD of hosts: This P say the time has
1:12 the remnant of the P, obeyed the voice of
1:12 sent him; and the P feared before the LORD.
1:13 LORD, spoke to the P with the LORD's message,
1:14 the remnant of the P; and they came and
2:2 the remnant of the P, and say,
2:4 take courage, all you P of the land, says
2:14 is it with this P, and with this nation
Zech 2:11 and shall be my P; and I will dwell
7:2 Now the P of Bethel had sent Sharezer and
7:5 "Say to all the P of the land and
8:6 the remnant of this P in these days, should
8:7 I will save my P from the east country
8:8 they shall be my P and I will be
8:11 the remnant of this P as in the former
8:12 the remnant of this P to possess all these
9:6 be uninhabited; a mongrel P shall dwell in Ashdod;
9:16 the flock of his P; for like the jewels
10:2 Therefore the P wander like sheep; they are
13:9 say, 'They are my P; and they will say,
14:2 the rest of the P shall not be cut
Mal 1:4 the wicked country, the P with whom the LORD
2:9 abased before all the P, inasmuch as you have
1Mac 1:13 and some of the P eagerly went to the
1:30 blow, and destroyed many P of Israel.
1:34 stationed there a sinful P, lawless men.
1:41 all should be one P,
1:51 inspectors over all the P and commanded the cities
1:52 Many of the P, every one who forsook the
2:7 the ruin of my P, the ruin of the
2:67 law, and avenge the wrong done to your P
3:3 He extended the glory of his P
3:5 the lawless; he burned those who troubled his P
3:42 to do to the P to cause their final
3:43 the destruction of our P, and fight for our
3:43 and fight for our P and the sanctuary."
3:55 appointed leaders of the P, in charge of thousands
4:17 he said to the P, "Do not be greedy
4:31 the hand of thy P Israel, and let them
4:55 All the P fell on their faces and worshiped
4:58 great gladness among the P, and the reproach of
4:61 Bethzur, so that the P might have a stronghold
5:2 they began to kill and destroy among the P
5:4 a snare to the P and ambushed them on
5:6 strong band and many P with Timothy as their
5:16 When Judas and the P heard these messages, a
5:18 a leader of the P, with the rest of
5:19 "Take charge of this P, but do not engage
5:42 the scribes of the P at the stream and
5:53 laggards and encouraging the P all the way till
5:60 two thousand of the P of Israel fell that
5:61 Thus the P suffered a great rout because, thinking
6:19 and assembled all the P to besiege them.
6:24 the sons of our P besieged the citadel and
6:44 life to save his P and to win for
7:6 accusation against the P: "Judas and his brothers

7:18 fell upon all the P, for they said, "There
7:19 and some of the P, and killed them and
7:22 who were troubling their P joined him.
7:26 Israel, and he commanded him to destroy the P
7:33 the elders of the P, to greet him peaceably
7:37 to be for thy P a house of prayer
7:48 The P rejoiced greatly and celebrated that day as
8:15 deliberate concerning the P, to govern them well.
8:20 his brothers and the P of the Jews have
8:29 the Romans make a treaty with the Jewish P
9:2 Arbela, and they took it and killed many P
9:73 began to judge the P, and he destroyed the
10:7 hearing of all the P and of the men
10:46 When Jonathan and the P heard these words, they
11:2 peaceable words, and the P of the cities opened
11:14 that time, because the P of that region were
11:51 and of all the P in his kingdom, and
11:60 came to Askalon, the P of the city met
11:62 Then the P of Gaza pleaded with Jonathan, and
12:4 them letters to the P in every place, asking
12:6 rest of the Jewish P to their brethren the
12:35 the elders of the P and planned with them
12:44 you wearied all these P when we are not
13:2 he saw that the P were trembling and fearful.
13:2 Jerusalem, and gathering the P together
13:7 The spirit of the P was rekindled when they
13:17 great hostility among the P, who might say,
13:42 from Israel, and the P began to write in
14:14 the humble of his P; he sought out the
14:20 rest of the Jewish P, our brethren, greeting.
14:21 were sent to our P have told us about
14:23 It has pleased our P to receive these men
14:23 archives, so that the P of the Spartans may
14:25 When the P heard these things they said, "How
14:28 the priests and the P and the rulers of
14:30 their high priest, and was gathered to his P
14:35 "The P saw Simon's faithfulness and the glory which
14:35 He sought in every way to exalt his P
14:44 "And none of the P or priests shall be
14:46 And all the P agreed to grant Simon the
15:17 priest and by the P of the Jews,
15:35 great damage among the P and to our land;
15:39 make war on the P; but the king pursued
15:40 began to provoke the P and invade Judea and
15:40 Judea and take the P captive and kill them.
2Mac 1:16 threw them to the P outside.
1:26 behalf of all thy P Israel and preserve thy
1:27 Gather together our scattered P, set free those who
1:29 Plant thy P in thy holy place, as Moses
1:36 purification, but by most P it is called naphtha.
2:7 until God gathers his P together again and shows
2:15 need of them, send P to get them for
2:17 has saved all his P, and has returned the
3:12 be done to those P who had trusted in
3:18 P also hurried out of their houses in crowds
4:5 welfare, both public and private, of all the P
4:30 it happened that the P of Tarsus and of
5:22 governors to afflict the P: at Jerusalem, Philip, by
5:26 his armed men and killed great numbers of P
6:2 Strangers, as did the P who dwelt in that
6:12 designed not to destroy but to discipline our P
6:16 with calamities, he does not forsake his own P
7:6 bore witness against the P to their faces, when
7:16 do not think that God has forsaken our P
8:2 to look upon the P who were oppressed by
8:36 the capture of the P of Jerusalem proclaimed that
9:2 Therefore the P rushed to the rescue with arms,
9:24 unwelcome news came, the P throughout the realm
10:21 the leaders of the P, and accused these men
11:6 they and all the P, with lamentations and tears,
11:16 effect: "Lysias to the P of the Jews, greeting.
11:34 the Romans, to the P of the Jews, greeting.
12:9 them, he attacked the P of Jamnia by night
12:11 and to help his P in all other ways.
12:26 of Atargatis, and slaughtered twenty-five thousand P
12:27 dwelt with multitudes of P of all nationalities.
12:30 good will which the P of Scythopolis had shown
12:42 noble Judas exhorted the P to keep themselves free
13:10 this, he ordered the P to call upon the
13:11 not to let the P who had just begun
13:22 second time with the P in Bethzur, gave pledges,
13:25 The P of Ptolemais were indignant over the treaty;
14:15 who established his own P for ever and always
14:20 leader had informed the P, and it had appeared
14:23 dismissed the flocks of P that had gathered.
15:14 prays much for the P and the holy city,
15:24 come against thy holy P be struck down." With
Mt 1:21 he will save his P from their sins."
2:4 and scribes of the P, he inquired of them
2:6 who will govern my P Israel.'"
4:16 the Gentiles– the P who sat in darkness
4:23 every disease and every infirmity among the P
8:4 that Moses commanded, for a proof to the P
12:23 And all the P were amazed, and said, "Can
12:46 still speaking to the P, behold, his mother and
13:15 For this P's heart has grown dull, and their
14:5 death, he feared the P, because they held him
15:8 when he said: 'This P honors me with their
15:10 And he called the P to him and said
19:13 The disciples rebuked the P;
21:23 the elders of the P came up to him
26:3 the elders of the P gathered in the palace
26:5 feast, lest there be a tumult among the P
26:47 the chief priests and the elders of the P
27:1 the elders of the P took counsel against Jesus
27:20 the elders persuaded the P to ask for Barabbas
27:25 And all the P answered, "His blood be on
27:64 away, and tell the P, 'He has risen from
28:13 soldiers and said, "Tell P, 'His disciples came by
Mk 1:5 Judea, and all the P of Jerusalem; and they
1:44 what Moses commanded, for a proof to the P
1:45 in the country; and P came to him from
2:18 Pharisees were fasting; and P came and said to
3:21 to seize him, for P were saying, "He is
5:14 And P came to see what it was that
5:38 saw a tumult, and P weeping and wailing loudly.
6:5 upon a few sick P and healed them.
6:41 to set before the P; and he divided the
6:54 the boat, immediately the P recognized him,
6:55 began to bring sick P on their pallets to
7:6 it is written, 'This P honors me with their
7:14 And he called the P to him again, and
7:16 house, and left the P, his disciples asked him
8:6 to set before the P; and they set them
8:9 And there were about four thousand P
8:22 And some P brought to him a blind man,
11:31 were afraid of the P, for all held that
12:41 Many rich P put in large sums.
14:2 feast, lest there be a tumult of the P
Lk 1:10 whole multitude of the P were praying outside at
1:17 for the Lord a P prepared."
1:21 And the P were waiting for Zechariah, and they
1:68 visited and redeemed his P,
1:77 of salvation to his P in the forgiveness of
2:10 come to all the P;
2:32 for glory to thy P Israel."
3:15 As the P were in expectation, and all men
3:18 other exhortations, he preached good news to the P
3:21 Now when all the P were baptized, and when
4:42 And the P sought him and came to him,
5:1 While the P pressed upon him to hear the
5:3 down and taught the P from the boat.
5:14 as Moses commanded, for a proof to the P
6:17 a great multitude of P from all Judea and
7:1 the hearing of the P he entered Caperna-um.
7:16 and "God has visited his P
7:29 heard this all the P and the tax collectors
8:4 crowd came together and P from town after town
8:35 Then P went out to see what had happened,
8:37 Then all the P of the surrounding country of
8:42 As he went, the P pressed round him.
8:47 presence of all the P why she had touched
9:13 to go and buy food for all these P
9:18 them, "Who do the P say that I am?"
9:53 for him; but the P would not receive him,
11:14 man spoke, and the P marveled.
13:14 sabbath, said to the P, "There are six days
13:17 shame; and all the P rejoiced at all the
14:23 and hedges, and compel P to come in, that
16:4 to do, so that P may receive me into
18:43 God; and all the P, when they saw it,
19:47 principal men of the P sought to destroy him;
19:48 do, for all the P hung upon his words.
20:1 he was teaching the P in the temple and
20:6 'From men,' all the P will stone us; for
20:9 began to tell the P this parable: "A man
20:19 but they feared the P; for they perceived that
20:26 the presence of the P to catch him by
20:45 hearing of all the P he said to his
21:23 and wrath upon this P;
21:38 the morning all the P came to him in
22:2 put him to death; for they feared the P

P

	22:64	the elders of the P gathered together, both chief
	23:5	"He stirs up the P, teaching throughout all Judea,
	23:13	the rulers and the P,
	23:14	who was perverting the P; and after examining him
	23:26	great multitude of the P, and of women who
	23:34	And the P stood by, watching; but the rulers
	24:19	God and all the P,
Jn	1:11	home, and his own P received him not.
	3:23	much water there; and P came and were baptized.
	4:28	and said to the P,
	6:5	bread, so that these P may eat?"
	6:10	Jesus said, "Make the P sit down." Now there
	6:14	When the P saw the sign which he had
	6:22	the next day the P who remained on the
	6:24	So when the P saw that Jesus was not
	7:12	there was much muttering about him among the P
	7:12	he is leading the P astray."
	7:20	The P answered, "You have a demon!
	7:25	Some of the P of Jerusalem therefore said, "Is
	7:31	Yet many of the P believed in him; they
	7:40	words, some of the P said, "This is really
	7:43	a division among the P over him.
	8:2	the temple; all the P came to him, and
	11:42	on account of the P standing by, that they
	11:50	should die for the P, and that the whole
	18:14	expedient that one man should die for the P
Acts	2:47	praising God and having favor with all the P
	3:9	And all the P saw him walking and praising
	3:11	and John, all the P ran together to them
	3:12	it he addressed the P, "Men of Israel, why
	3:23	be destroyed from the P
	4:1	were speaking to the P, the priests and the
	4:2	they were teaching the P and proclaiming in Jesus
	4:8	them, "Rulers of the P and elders,
	4:10	and to all the P of Israel, that by
	4:17	no further among the P, let us warn them
	4:21	them, because of the P; for all men praised
	5:12	were done among the P by the hands of
	5:13	join them, but the P held them in high
	5:16	The P also gathered from the towns around
	5:20	and speak to the P all the words of
	5:25	are standing in the temple and teaching the P
	5:26	they were afraid of being stoned by the P
	5:34	honor by all the P, stood up and ordered
	5:37	away some of the P after him; he also
	6:8	power, did great wonders and signs among the P
	6:12	they stirred up the P and the elders and
	7:17	granted to Abraham, the P grew and multiplied in
	7:34	the ill-treatment of my P that are in Egypt
	7:51	things?' "You stiff-necked P, uncircumcised in heart
	10:2	alms liberally to the P, and prayed constantly to
	10:41	not to all the P but to us who
	10:42	to preach to the P, and to testify that
	10:47	water for baptizing these P who have received the
	11:26	a large company of P; and in Antioch the
	12:4	the Passover to bring him out to the P
	12:11	all that the Jewish P were expecting."
	12:20	was angry with the P of Tyre and Sidon;
	12:22	And the P shouted, "The voice of a god,
	13:11	he went about seeking P to lead him by
	13:15	of exhortation for the P, say it."
	13:17	The God of this P Israel chose our fathers
	13:17	fathers and made the P great during their stay
	13:24	repentance to all the P of Israel.
	13:31	Jerusalem, who are now his witnesses to the P
	13:42	they went out, the P begged that these things
	14:4	But the P of the city were divided; some
	14:13	gates and wanted to offer sacrifice with the P
	14:18	they scarcely restrained the P from offering sacrifice
	14:19	and having persuaded the P, they stoned Paul and
	15:14	out of them a P for his name.
	17:5	Jason, seeking to bring them out to the P
	17:8	And the P and the city authorities were disturbed
	18:10	for I have many P in this city."
	19:4	of repentance, telling the P to believe in the
	19:26	a considerable company of P, saying that gods made
	19:33	hand, wishing to make a defense to the P
	21:12	this, we and the P there begged him not
	21:28	men everywhere against the P and the law and
	21:30	was aroused, and the P ran together; they seized
	21:36	the mob of the P followed, crying, "Away with
	21:39	I beg you, let me speak to the P
	21:40	his hand to the P; and when there was
	23:5	not speak evil of a ruler of your P
	25:24	whom the whole Jewish P petitioned me, both at
	26:17	delivering you from the P and from the Gentiles--
	26:23	light both to the P and to the Gentiles."
	28:9	the rest of the P on the island who
	28:17	done nothing against the P or the customs of
	28:26	prophet: 'Go to this P, and say, You shall
	28:27	For this P's heart has grown dull, and their
Rom	3:8	may come?--as some P slanderously charge us with
	9:25	who were not my P I will call 'my
	9:25	I will call 'my P and her who was
	9:26	'You are not my P they will be called
	10:21	out my hands to a disobedient and contrary P
	11:1	I ask, then, has God rejected his P
	11:2	has not rejected his P whom he foreknew.
	15:10	O Gentiles, with his P;
1Cor	1:11	to me by Chloe's P that there is quarreling
	4:19	talk of these arrogant P but their power.
	10:7	it is written, "The P sat down to eat
	10:18	Consider the P of Israel; are not those who
	14:21	I speak to this P, and even then they
	15:29	Otherwise, what do P mean by being baptized on
	15:29	at all, why are P baptized on their behalf?
2Cor	4:15	to more and more P it may increase thanksgiving,
	6:16	be their God, and they shall be my P
	9:2	about you to the P of Macedonia, saying that
	10:11	Let such P understand that what we say by
	11:26	danger from my own P, danger from Gentiles, danger
Gal	1:14	own age among my P, so extremely zealous was
Phil	3:5	eighth day, of the P of Israel, of the
1Thes	5:3	When P say, "There is peace and security," then
2Tim	2:16	for it will lead P into more and more
	3:5	Avoid such P
	4:3	time is coming when P will not endure sound
Tit	2:14	purify for himself a P of his own who
	3:14	And let our P learn to apply themselves to
Heb	2:17	to make expiation for the sins of the P
	4:9	sabbath rest for the P of God;
	5:3	sins as well as for those of the P
	7:5	take tithes from the P, that is, from their
	7:11	(for under it the P received the law), what
	7:27	for those of the P; he did this once
	8:10	be their God, and they shall be my P
	9:7	for himself and for the errors of the P
	9:19	Moses to all the P, he took the blood
	9:19	itself and all the P,
	10:30	And again, "The Lord will judge his P
	11:14	For P who speak thus make it clear that
	11:25	share ill-treatment with the P of God than to
	11:29	By faith the P crossed the Red Sea as
	13:12	order to sanctify the P through his own blood.
1Pet	2:9	holy nation, God's own P, that you may declare
	2:10	Once you were no P but now you are
	2:10	now you are God's P; once you had not
2Pet	2:1	also arose among the P, just as there will
Jude	1:5	he who saved a P out of the land
	1:16	passions, loud-mouthed boasters, flattering P to gain
	1:19	set up divisions, worldly P, devoid of the Spirit.
Rev	3:4	few names in Sardis, P who have not soiled
	5:9	tribe and tongue and P and nation,
	11:13	city fell; seven thousand P were killed in the
	13:7	over every tribe and P and tongue and nation,
	14:6	tribe and tongue and P;
	18:4	out of her, my P, lest you take part
	21:3	they shall be his P, and God himself will

PEOPLED (2)

Gen	9:19	Noah; and from these the whole earth was P
Jer	50:39	her; she shall be P no more for ever,

PEOPLES (243)

Gen	10:5	From these the coastland P spread.
	17:16	of nations; kings of P shall come from her."
	25:23	your womb, and two P, born of you, shall
	27:29	Let P serve you, and nations bow down to
	28:3	you, that you may become a company of P
	48:4	you a company of P, and will give this
	49:10	to him shall be the obedience of the P
Ex	15:14	The P have heard, they tremble; pangs have seized
	19:5	own possession among all P; for all the earth
Lev	20:24	your God, who have separated you from the P
	20:26	separated you from the P, that you should be
Deut	2:25	of you upon the P that are under the
	4:6	the sight of the P, who, when they hear
	4:19	allotted to all the P under the whole heaven.
	4:27	scatter you among the P, and you will be
	6:14	the gods of the P who are round about
	7:6	out of all the P that are on the
	7:7	the fewest of all P;

32:3 a host of many P; and I will haul
32:9 the hearts of many P, when I carry you
32:10 I will make many P appalled at you, and
34:13 them out from the P, and gather them from
36:15 the disgrace of the P and no longer cause
38:6 all his hordes–many P are with you.
38:9 your hordes, and many P with you.
38:15 north, you and many P with you, all of
38:22 hordes and the many P that are with him,
39:4 your hordes and the P that are with you;
39:27 them back from the P and gathered them from
Dan 3:4 "You are commanded, O P, nations, and languages,
3:7 soon as all the P heard the sound of
3:7 of music, all the P, nations, and languages fell
4:1 King Nebuchadnezzar to all P, nations, and
5:19 he gave him, all P, nations, and languages trembled
6:25 wrote to all the P, nations, and languages that
7:14 and kingdom, that all P, nations, and languages
Hos 7:9 mixes himself with the P; Ephraim is a cake
9:1 Exult not like the P; for you have played
Joel 2:6 Before them P are in anguish, all faces grow
2:17 they say among the P, 'Where is their God?"
Mic 1:2 Hear, you P, all of you; hearken, O earth,
4:1 above the hills; and P shall flow to it,
4:3 shall judge between many P, and shall decide for
4:5 For all the P walk each in the name
4:13 beat in pieces many P, and shall devote their
5:7 the midst of many P like dew from the
5:8 the midst of many P, like a lion among
6:16 so you shall bear the scorn of the P
Nah 3:4 with her harlotries, and P with her charms.
Hab 2:5 all nations, and collects as his own all P
2:8 the remnant of the P shall plunder you, for
2:10 by cutting off many P; you have forfeited your
2:13 LORD of hosts that P labor only for fire,
Zeph 3:9 the speech of the P to a pure speech,
Zech 8:20 the LORD of hosts: P shall yet come, even
8:22 I am going.' Many P and strong nations shall
11:10 covenant which I had made with all the P
12:2 reeling to all the P round about; it will
12:3 stone for all the P; all who lift it
12:4 every horse of the P with blindness.
12:6 the left all the P round about, while Jerusalem
14:12 will smite all the P that wage war against
1Mac 2:66 for you and fight the battle against the P
Lk 2:31 the presence of all P,
Acts 4:25 Gentiles rage, and the P imagine vain things?
4:27 the Gentiles and the P of Israel,
Rom 15:11 and let all the P praise him";
Rev 7:9 from all tribes and P and tongues, standing before
10:11 prophesy about many P and nations and tongues
11:9 half men from the P and tribes and tongues
17:15 harlot is seated, are P and multitudes and nations

PEOR (9)
Num 23:28 to the top of P, that overlooks the desert.
25:3 So Israel yoked himself to Baal of P
25:5 men who have yoked themselves to Baal of P
25:18 in the matter of P, and in the matter
25:18 the day of the plague on account of P
31:16 in the matter of P, and so the plague
Deut 4:3 followed the Baal of P;
Josh 22:17 of the sin at P from which even yet
Ps 106:28 to the Baal of P, and ate sacrifices offered

PERAZIM
Is 28:21 up as on Mount P, he will be wroth

PERCEIVE (30)
2Sam 19:6 you; for today I P that if Absalom were
2Kgs 4:9 husband, "Behold now, I P that this is a
Job 9:11 but I do not P him.
23:8 backward, but I cannot P him;
33:14 though man does not P it.
Ps 94:7 not see; the God of Jacob does not P
Prov 24:12 who weighs the heart P it?
Wis 13:4 and working, let them P from them how much
Sir 23:19 ways of men, and P even the hidden places.
Is 6:9 see, but do not P
43:19 forth, do you not P it?
Jer 23:18 of the LORD to P and to hear his
Bar 6:42 Yet they themselves cannot P this and abandon them,
2Mac 5:17 spirit, and did not P that the Lord was
Mt 13:14 understand, and you shall indeed see but never P
13:15 closed, lest they should P with their eyes, and
16:9 Do you not yet P
16:11 that you fail to P that I did not
Mk 4:12 indeed see but not P, and may indeed hear
8:17 Do you not yet P or understand?
Lk 8:46 touched me; for I P that power has gone
9:45 that they should not P it; and they were
Jn 4:19 to him, "Sir, I P that you are a
12:40 with their eyes and P with their heart, and
Acts 10:34 and said: "Truly I P that God shows no
17:22 "Men of Athens, I P that in every way
27:10 them, saying, "Sirs, I P that the voyage will
28:26 understand, and you shall indeed see but never P
28:27 closed; lest they should P with their eyes, and
Eph 3:4 read this you can P my insight into the

PERCEIVED (31)
Ex 20:18 when all the people P the thunderings and the
Judg 6:22 Then Gideon P that he was the angel of
1Sam 3:8 Then Eli P that the LORD was calling the
2Sam 5:12 And David P that the LORD had established him
12:19 were whispering together, David P that the child was
14:1 the son of Zeruiah P that the king's heart
1Kgs 3:28 the king, because they P that the wisdom of
1Chr 14:2 And David P that the LORD had established him
Neh 6:16 own esteem; for they P that this work had
Ps 73:17 of God; then I P their end.
Prov 7:7 the simple, I have P among the youths, a
Eccl 1:17 I P that this also is but a striving
2:14 darkness; and yet I P that one fate comes
Wis 8:21 But I P that I would not possess wisdom
11:13 had received benefit, they P it was the Lord's
Is 64:4 one has heard or P by the ear, no
Dan 9:2 his reign, I, Daniel, P in the books the
1Mac 1:5 he fell sick and P that he was dying.
4:21 When they P this they were greatly frightened, and
Mt 21:45 heard his parables, they P that he was speaking
Mk 12:12 the multitude, for they P that he had told
15:10 For he P that it was out of envy
Lk 1:22 to them, and they P that he had seen
5:22 When Jesus P their questionings, he answered them,
9:47 But when Jesus P the thought of their hearts,
20:19 the people; for they P that he had told
20:23 But he P their craftiness, and said to them,
Acts 4:13 Peter and John, and P that they were uneducated,
23:6 But when Paul P that one part were Sadducees
Rom 1:20 deity, has been clearly P in the things that
Gal 2:9 Gentiles), and when they P the grace that was

PERCEIVES (2)
Job 14:21 brought low, and he P it not.
Prov 31:18 She P that her merchandise is profitable.

PERCEIVING (4)
2Mac 15:21 on the flanks, Maccabeus, P the hosts that were
Mk 2:8 And immediately Jesus, P in his spirit that they
5:30 And Jesus, P in himself that power had gone
Jn 6:15 P then that they were about to come and

PERCEPTION
Wis 13:5 things comes a corresponding P of their Creator.

PERDITION (6)
2Sam 22:5 me, the torrents of P assailed me;
Ps 18:4 me, the torrents of P assailed me;
Jn 17:12 but the son of P, that the scripture might
2Thes 2:3 revealed, the son of P,
Rev 17:8 pit and go to P; and the dwellers on
17:11 belongs to the seven, and it goes to P

PERES
Dan 5:28 balances and found wanting; P, your kingdom is

PERESH
1Chr 7:16 she called his name P; and the name of

PEREZ (18)
Gen 38:29 Therefore his name was called P
46:12 Judah: Er, Onan, Shelah, P, and Zerah (but Er
46:12 and the sons of P were Hezron and Hamul.
Num 26:20 of the Shelanites; of P, the family of the
26:21 And the sons of P were: of Hezron, the
Ruth 4:12 like the house of P, whom Tamar bore to
4:18 are the descendants of P: Perez was the father
4:18 the descendants of Perez: P was the father of
1Chr 2:4 Tamar also bore him P and Zerah.
2:5 The sons of P: Hezron and Hamul.
4:1 The sons of Judah: P, Hezron, Carmi, Hur, and

Jn 11:47 For this man P many signs.

PERFUME (4)

Ex 30:38 it to use as P shall be cut off
Prov 27:9 Oil and P make the heart glad, but the
Is 3:20 armlets, the sashes, the P boxes, and the amulets;
3:24 Instead of P there will be rottenness; and instead

PERFUMED (2)

Prov 7:17 Egyptian linen; I have P my bed with myrrh,
Song 3:6 a column of smoke, P with myrrh and frankincense,

PERFUMER (6)

Ex 30:25 blended as by the P; a holy anointing oil
30:35 blended as by the P, seasoned with salt, pure
37:29 the pure fragrant incense, blended as by the P
2Chr 16:14 spices prepared by the P's art; and they made
Eccl 10:1 Dead flies make the P's ointment give off an
Sir 49:1 the art of the P; it is sweet as

PERFUMERS (2)

1Sam 8:13 your daughters to be P and cooks and bakers.
Neh 3:8 Hananiah, one of the P, repaired; and they restored

PERFUMES (3)

Esth 14:2 and instead of costly P she covered her head
Wis 2:7 of costly wine and P, and let no flower
Is 57:9 oil and multiplied your P; you sent your envoys

PERGA (3)

Acts 13:13 Paphos, and came to P in Pamphylia.
13:14 they passed on from P and came to Antioch
14:25 spoken the word in P, they went down to

PERGAMUM (2)

Rev 1:11 to Smyrna and to P and to Thyatira and
2:12 of the church in P write: 'The words of

PERHAPS (41)

Gen 24:5 servant said to him, P the woman may not
24:39 said to my master, P the woman will not
27:12 P my father will feel me, and I shall
32:20 shall see his face; P he will accept me."
43:12 mouth of your sacks; P it was an oversight.
Ex 32:30 up to the LORD; P I can make atonement
Num 22:6 too mighty for me; P I shall be able
22:11 curse them for me; P I shall be able
23:3 and I will go; P the LORD will come
23:27 you to another place; P it will please God
Josh 9:7 said to the Hivites, P you live among us;
1Sam 6:5 the God of Israel; P he will lighten his
9:6 Let us go there; P he can tell us
1Kgs 18:5 to all the valleys; P we may find grass
18:27 on a journey, or P he is asleep and
20:31 the king of Israel; P he will spare your
Tob 8:10 grave, with the thought, P he too will die."
Wis 13:6 to be blamed, for P they go astray while
14:19 For he, P wishing to please his ruler, skilfully
Sir 19:13 Question a friend, P he did not do it;
19:14 Question a neighbor, P he did not say it;
Is 47:12 labored from your youth; P you may be able
47:12 be able to succeed, P you may inspire terror.
Jer 20:10 P he will be deceived, then we can overcome
21:2 making war against us; P the LORD will deal
51:8 balm for her pain; P she may be healed.
Ezek 12:3 P they will understand, though they are a rebellious
Dan 4:27 oppressed, that there may P be a lengthening of
Jon 1:6 P the god will give a thought to us,
Zeph 2:3 seek righteousness, seek humility; P you may be
Mt 25:9 But the wise replied, P there will not be
Lk 3:15 concerning John, whether P he were the Christ,
Rom 2:15 conflicting thoughts accuse or P excuse them
5:7 a righteous man—though P for a good man
1Cor 7:5 refuse one another except P by agreement for a
15:37 but a bare kernel, P of wheat or of
16:6 pass through Macedonia, and P I will stay with
2Cor 12:20 For I fear that P I may come and
12:20 what you wish; that P there may be quarreling,
2Tim 2:25 God may P grant that they will repent and
Philem 1:15 P this is why he was parted from you

PERIDA

Neh 7:57 Sophereth, the sons of P,

PERIL (5)

1Chr 12:19 him away, saying, "At P to our heads he
Lam 5:9 our bread at the P of our lives, because
Rom 8:35 famine, or nakedness, or P, or sword?
1Cor 15:30 Why am I in P every hour?
2Cor 1:10 from so deadly a P, and he will deliver

PERIOD (4)

Esth 2:12 this was the regular P of their beautifying, six
Wis 7:2 into flesh, within the P of ten months, compacted
2Mac 4:23 After a P of three years Jason sent Menelaus,
Acts 18:20 stay for a longer P, he declined;

PERIODS

Acts 17:26 having determined allotted P and the boundaries of

PERISH (121)

Gen 41:36 the land may not P through the famine."
Ex 19:21 the LORD to gaze and many of them P
Lev 26:38 And you shall P among the nations, and the
Num 17:12 to Moses, "Behold, we P, we are undone, we
17:13 Are we all to P
Deut 4:26 you will soon utterly P from the land which
7:24 shall make their name P from under heaven; not
8:19 warn you this day that you shall surely P
8:20 the LORD makes to P before you, so shall
8:20 you, so shall you P, because you would not
9:3 out, and make them P quickly, as the LORD
11:17 no fruit, and you P quickly off the good
28:20 you are destroyed and P quickly, on account of
28:22 with mildew; they shall pursue you until you P
28:51 your flock, until they have caused you to P
30:18 day, that you shall P; you shall not live
Josh 22:20 And he did not P alone for his iniquity.'"
23:13 your eyes, till you P from off this good
23:16 you, and you shall P quickly from off the
Judg 5:31 neck as spoil?' "So P all thine enemies, O
1Sam 26:10 or he shall go down into battle and P
27:1 heart, "I shall now P one day by the
2Kgs 9:8 house of Ahab shall P; and I will cut
Jud 6:4 They cannot withstand us, but will utterly P
6:8 not die until you P along with them.
Esth 4:14 quarter, but you and your father's house will P
4:16 law; and if I P, I perish."
4:16 against the law; and if I perish, I P
11:9 evils that threatened them, and were ready to P
Job 3:3 said: "Let the day P wherein I was born,
4:9 breath of God they P, and by the blast
4:20 they are destroyed; they P for ever without any
6:18 course; they go up into the waste, and P
8:13 God; the hope of the godless man shall P
20:7 the clouds, he will P for ever like his
29:13 who was about to P came upon me, and
31:19 have seen any one P for lack of clothing,
34:15 breath, all flesh would P together, and man would
36:12 do not hearken, they P by the sword, and
Ps 1:6 righteous, but the way of the wicked will P
2:12 be angry, and you P in the way; for
9:18 the poor shall not P for ever.
10:16 ever; the nations shall P from his land.
37:20 But the wicked P; the enemies of the LORD
41:5 malice: "When will he die, and his name P
49:10 the stupid alike must P and leave their wealth
49:12 his pomp, he is like the beasts that P
49:20 his pomp, he is like the beasts that P
68:2 fire, let the wicked P before God!
73:27 far from thee shall P; thou dost put an
80:16 it down; may they P at the rebuke of
83:17 for ever; let them P in disgrace.
92:9 lo, thy enemies shall P; all evildoers shall be
102:26 They will P, but thou dost endure; they will
146:4 his earth; on that very day his plans P
Prov 11:10 and when the wicked P there are shouts of
19:9 go unpunished, and he who utters lies will P
21:28 A false witness will P, but the word of
28:28 themselves, but when they P, the righteous increase.
Wis 3:16 and the offspring of an unlawful union will P
4:19 suffer anguish, and the memory of them will P
18:19 that they might not P without knowing why they
Sir 3:24 whoever loves danger will P by it.
5:7 and at the time of punishment you will P
8:15 his folly you will P with him.
41:6 children of sinners will P, and on their posterity
47:22 of his works to P; he will never blot
Is 29:14 their wise men shall P, and the discernment of
31:3 and they will all P together.
41:11 against you shall be as nothing and shall P
60:12 not serve you shall P; those nations shall be

Jer	6:21	and sons together, neighbor and friend shall P
	8:14	the fortified cities and P there; for the LORD
	8:14	has doomed us to P, and has given us
	10:11	and the earth shall P from the earth and
	10:15	at the time of their punishment they shall P
	16:4	They shall P by the sword and by famine,
	18:18	the law shall not P from the priest, nor
	27:10	I will drive you out, and you will P
	27:15	out and you will P, you and the prophets
	40:15	be scattered, and the remnant of Judah would P
	48:8	escape; the valley shall P, and the plain shall
	51:18	at the time of their punishment they shall P
Lam	4:5	who feasted on dainties P in the streets; those
Ezek	13:14	it falls, you shall P in the midst of
	25:7	and will make you P out of the countries;
	31:17	dwelt under its shadow among the nations shall P
	32:12	pride of Egypt, and all its multitude shall P
Dan	2:18	his companions might not P with the rest of
Hos	10:7	Samaria's king shall P, like a chip on the
Amos	1:8	Ekron; and the remnant of the Philistines shall P
	2:14	Flight shall P from the swift, and the strong
	3:15	houses of ivory shall P, and the great houses
Jon	1:6	a thought to us, that we do not P
	1:14	LORD, let us not P for this man's life,
	3:9	anger, so that we P not?"
Zech	9:5	The king shall P from Gaza; Ashkelon shall be
	13:8	be cut off and P, and one third shall
1Mac	2:63	returned to the dust, and his plans will P
2Mac	7:20	saw her seven sons P within a single day,
Mt	18:13	heaven that one of these little ones should P
	26:52	take the sword will P by the sword.
Mk	4:38	him, "Teacher, do you not care if we P
Lk	13:3	but unless you repent you will all likewise P
	13:5	but unless you repent you will all likewise P
	13:33	that a prophet should P away from Jerusalem.'
	15:17	to spare, but I P here with hunger!
	21:18	But not a hair of your head will P
Jn	3:16	in him should not P but have eternal life.
	10:28	and they shall never P, and no one shall
	11:50	people, and that the whole nation should not P
Acts	8:20	to him, "Your silver P with you, because you
	13:41	scoffers, and wonder, and P; for I do a
	27:34	a hair is to P from the head of
Rom	2:12	the law will also P without the law, and
Col	2:22	to things which all P as they are used),
2Thes	2:10	those who are to P, because they refused to
Heb	1:11	thy hands; they will P, but thou remainest; they
	11:31	the harlot did not P with those who were
2Pet	3:9	wishing that any should P, but that all should
Jude	1:11	to Balaam's error, and P in Korah's rebellion.

PERISHABLE (11)

Wis	9:15	to fail, for a P body weighs down the
	14:8	the work, and the P thing was named a
	19:21	consume the flesh of P creatures that walked among
1Cor	9:25	it to receive a P wreath, but we an
	15:42	What is sown is P, what is raised is
	15:50	God, nor does the P inherit the imperishable.
	15:53	For this P nature must put on the imperishable,
	15:54	When the P puts on the imperishable, and the
1Pet	1:7	than gold which though P is tested by fire,
	1:18	your fathers, not with P things such as silver
	1:23	born anew, not of P seed but of imperishable,

PERISHED (44)

Num	16:33	over them, and they P from the midst of
	21:30	So their posterity P from Heshbon, as far as
Deut	2:14	men of war, had P from the camp, as
	2:15	destroy them from the camp, until they had P
	2:16	men of war had P and were dead from
Josh	5:6	forth out of Egypt, P, because they did not
2Sam	1:27	the mighty fallen, and the weapons of war P
	21:9	the seven of them P together.
2Kgs	7:13	Israel that have already P; let us send and
Tob	10:4	him, "The lad has P; his long delay proves
	10:7	still and stop deceiving me; my child has P
	14:10	him; but Nadab fell into the trap and P
Jud	16:12	children of fugitives, they P before the army of
Job	4:7	"Think now, who that was innocent ever P
Ps	9:3	back, they stumbled and P before thee.
	9:6	rooted out; the very memory of them has P
	119:92	delight, I should have P in my affliction.
Eccl	9:6	their envy have already P, and they have no
Wis	10:3	in his anger, he P because in rage he
	17:10	hissing of serpents, they P in trembling fear, refusing
Sir	44:10	no memorial, who have P as though they had
Jer	7:28	accept discipline; truth has P; it is cut off
	47:5	Baldness has come upon Gaza, Ashkelon has P
	48:36	of Kir-heres; therefore the riches they gained have P
	49:7	Has counsel P from the prudent?
Lam	1:19	my priests and elders P in the city, while
Bar	2:25	They P in great misery, by famine and sword
	3:28	to knowledge; so they P because they had no
	3:28	had no wisdom, they P through their folly.
Joel	1:10	barley; because the harvest of the field has P
Jon	4:10	in a night, and P in a night.
Mic	4:9	Has your counselor P, that pangs have seized you
	7:2	The godly man has P from the earth, and
1Mac	12:50	been seized and had P along with his men,
	13:4	all my brothers have P for the sake of
	13:18	send him the money and the sons, he P
	13:49	and many of them P from famine.
	16:21	father and brothers had P, and that "he has
2Mac	8:19	hundred and eighty-five thousand P,
Mt	8:32	into the sea, and P in the waters.
Lk	11:51	blood of Zechariah, who P between the altar and
Acts	5:37	after him; he also P, and all who followed
1Cor	15:18	also who have fallen asleep in Christ have P
2Pet	3:6	that then existed was deluged with water and P

PERISHES (8)

Job	4:11	The strong lion P for lack of prey, and
	18:17	His memory P from the earth, and he has
Prov	11:7	wicked dies, his hope P, and the expectation of
Eccl	7:15	a righteous man who P in his righteousness, and
Is	57:1	The righteous man P, and no one lays it
Ezek	7:26	prophet, but the law P from the priest, and
Jn	6:27	for the food which P, but for the food
Jas	1:10	the grass; its flower falls, and its beauty P

PERISHING (13)

Job	33:18	Pit, his life from P by the sword.
Prov	31:6	to him who is P, and wine to those
Wis	10:6	when the ungodly were P; he escaped the fire
	14:6	when arrogant giants were P, the hope of the
Bar	3:3	ever, and we are P for ever.
Zech	11:16	not care for the P, or seek the wandering,
1Mac	3:9	the earth; he gathered in those who were P
	6:13	and behold, I am P of deep grief in
Mt	8:25	and woke him, saying, "Save, Lord; we are P
Lk	8:24	and woke him, saying, "Master, Master, we are P
1Cor	1:18	to those who are P, but to us who
2Cor	2:15	among those who are P,
	4:3	it is veiled only to those who are P

PERIZZITE

Neh	9:8	Hittite, the Amorite, the P, the Jebusite, and the

PERIZZITES (23)

Gen	13:7	the Canaanites and the P dwelt in the land.
	15:20	Kadmonites, the Hittites, the P, the Rephaim,
	34:30	the Canaanites and the P; my numbers are few,
Ex	3:8	Hittites, the Amorites, the P, the Hivites, and the
	3:17	Hittites, the Amorites, the P, the Hivites, and the
	23:23	the Hittites, and the P, and the Canaanites, the
	33:2	Amorites, the Hittites, the P, the Hivites, and the
	34:11	Canaanites, the Hittites, the P, the Hivites, and the
Deut	7:1	Amorites, the Canaanites, the P, the Hivites, and the
	20:17	the Canaanites and the P, the Hivites and the
Josh	3:10	the Hivites, the P, the Girgashites, the Amorites,
	9:1	Amorites, the Canaanites, the P, the Hivites, and the
	11:3	Amorites, the Hittites, the P, and the Jebusites in
	12:8	Amorites, the Canaanites, the P, the Hivites, and the
	17:15	the land of the P and the Rephaim, since
	24:11	also the Amorites, the P, the Canaanites, the Hittites,
Judg	1:4	the Canaanites and the P into their hand; and
	1:5	against him, and defeated the Canaanites and the P
	3:5	Hittites, the Amorites, the P, the Hivites, and the
1Kgs	9:20	Amorites, the Hittites, the P, the Hivites, and the
2Chr	8:7	Hittites, the Amorites, the P, the Hivites, and the
Ezra	9:1	Canaanites, the Hittites, the P, the Jebusites, the
Jud	5:16	the Canaanites and the P and the Jebusites and

PERJURERS

1Tim	1:10	sodomites, kidnapers, liars, P, and whatever else is

PERJURY (2)

Wis	14:25	deceit, corruption, faithlessness, tumult, P,
	14:28	unrighteously, or readily commit P;

PERMANENT (3)

Esth	12:4	The king made a P record of these things,

1Mac 13:29 of armor for a P memorial, and beside the
2Cor 3:11 with splendor, what is P must have much more

PERMANENTLY

Heb 7:24 he holds his priesthood P, because he continues for

PERMISSION (9)

Jud 11:14 bring back to them P from the senate.
Sir 15:20 not given any one P to sin.
Dan 14:26 king, will give me P, I will slay the
14:26 The king said, "I give you P
1Mac 9:35 were his friends, for P to store with them
14:44 the country without his P, or to be clothed
2Mac 4:9 and fifty more if P were given to establish
11:30 of friendship and full P
Acts 26:1 to Paul, "You have P to speak for yourself."

PERMIT (16)

Gen 31:7 but God did not P him to harm me.
31:28 why did you not P me to kiss my
Ex 22:18 "You shall not P a sorceress to live.
Num 35:6 refuge, where you shall P the manslayer to flee,
1Sam 24:7 words, and did not P them to attack Saul.
1Kgs 15:17 Ramah, that he might P no one to go
2Chr 16:1 Ramah, that he might P no one to go
Esth 16:19 in every place, and P the Jews to live
Ps 55:22 you; he will never P the righteous to be
Hos 5:4 Their deeds do not P them to return to
1Mac 5:42 gave them this command, P no man to encamp,
12:40 that Jonathan might not P him to do so,
15:6 I P you to mint your own coinage as
Mk 1:34 and he would not P the demons to speak,
7:12 then you no longer P him to do anything
1Tim 2:12 I P no woman to teach or to have

PERMITS (2)

1Cor 16:7 spend some time with you, if the Lord P
Heb 6:3 And this we will do if God P

PERMITTED (7)

Jud 12:6 that your servant be P to go out and
Wis 19:2 though they themselves had P thy people to depart
1Mac 14:44 or priests shall be P to nullify any of
15:14 land and sea, and P no one to leave
Lk 8:51 to the house, he P no one to enter
1Cor 14:34 For they are not P to speak, but should
Rev 6:4 red; its rider was P to take peace from

PERPETRATED

2Mac 3:32 foul play had been P by the Jews with

P

PERPETUAL (32)

Ex 28:43 This shall be a P statute for him and
29:9 be theirs by a P statute.
29:28 his sons as a P due from the people
30:8 shall burn it, a P incense before the LORD
31:16 their generations, as a P covenant.
Lev 3:17 It shall be a P statute throughout your generations,
7:34 his sons, as a P due from the people
7:36 anointed; it is a P due throughout their generations."
24:9 to the LORD, a P due."
25:34 for that is their P possession.
Num 10:8 to you for a P statute throughout your generations.
15:15 sojourns with you, a P statute throughout your
18:8 your sons as a P due.
18:11 with you, as a P due; every one who
18:19 with you, as a P due; it is a
18:23 it shall be a P statute throughout your generations;
19:10 sojourns among them, a P statute.
19:21 it shall be a P statute for them.
25:13 the covenant of a P priesthood, because he was
Jud 13:20 this to be a P honor to you, and
Esth 16:13 Mordecai, our savior and P benefactor, and of Esther,
Ps 74:3 thy steps to the P ruins; the enemy has
Sir 41:6 posterity will be a P reproach.
Jer 5:22 for the sea, a P barrier which it cannot
8:5 people turned away in P backsliding?
23:40 you everlasting reproach and P shame, which shall
49:13 her cities shall be P wastes."
51:26 you shall be a P waste, says the LORD.
51:39 away and sleep a P sleep and not wake,
51:57 they shall sleep a P sleep and not wake,
Ezek 35:5 Because you cherished P enmity, and gave over the
35:9 will make you a P desolation, and your cities

PERPETUALLY (2)

Sir 45:13 on, but only his sons and his descendants P
Amos 1:11 and his anger tore P, and he kept his

PERPETUATE (2)

Deut 25:7 husband's brother refuses to P his brother's name in
Ruth 4:10 be my wife, to P the name of the

PERPETUATED (2)

Gen 48:16 let my name be P, and the name of
Nah 1:14 shall your name be P; from the house of

PERPETUITY (2)

Lev 25:23 not be sold in P, for the land is
25:30 be made sure in P to him who bought

PERPLEXED (13)

Esth 3:15 to drink; but the city of Susa was P
Dan 5:9 and his color changed; and his lords were P
Joel 1:17 herds of cattle are P because there is no
1Mac 3:31 He was greatly P in mind, and determined to
4:27 heard it, he was P and discouraged, for things
Mk 6:20 him, he was much P; and yet he heard
Lk 9:7 done, and he was P, because it was said
24:4 While they were P about this, behold, two men
Acts 2:12 all were amazed and P, saying to one another,
5:24 words, they were much P about them, wondering
10:17 while Peter was inwardly P as to what the
2Cor 4:8 way, but not crushed; P, but not driven to
Gal 4:20 tone, for I am P about you.

PERPLEXITIES

Sir 40:2 Their P and fear of heart-- their anxious

PERPLEXITY

Lk 21:25 distress of nations in P at the roaring of

PERSECUTE (19)

Job 30:21 thy hand thou dost P me.
Ps 69:26 For they P him whom thou hast smitten, and
119:84 thou judge those who P me?
119:86 commandments are sure; they P me with falsehood;
119:150 They draw near who P me with evil purpose;
119:161 Princes P me without cause, but my heart stands
Jer 17:18 put to shame who P me, but let me
Mt 5:11 men revile you and P you and utter all
5:44 pray for those who P you,
10:23 When they P you in one town, flee to
23:33 in your synagogues and P from town to town,
Lk 11:49 they will kill and P
21:12 hands on you and P you, delivering you up
Jn 15:20 persecuted me, they will P you; if they kept
Acts 7:52 Which of the prophets did not your fathers P
9:4 Saul, why do you P me?"
22:7 Saul, why do you P me?'
26:14 Saul, why do you P me?
Rom 12:14 Bless those who P you; bless and do not

PERSECUTED (17)

Deut 30:7 foes and enemies who P you.
Mt 5:10 are those who are P for righteousness' sake, for
5:12 heaven, for so men P the prophets who were
Jn 5:15 was why the Jews P Jesus, because he did
15:20 his master.' If they P me, they will persecute
Acts 22:4 I P this Way to the death, binding and
26:11 fury against them, I P them even to foreign
1Cor 4:12 reviled, we bless; when P, we endure;
15:9 an apostle, because I P the church of God.
2Cor 4:9 not driven to despair; P, but not forsaken; struck
Gal 1:13 in Judaism, how I P the church of God
1:23 said, "He who once P us is now preaching
4:29 according to the flesh P him who was born
5:11 brethren, still preach circumcision, why am I still P
6:12 they may not be P for the cross of
1Tim 1:13 I formerly blasphemed and P and insulted him; but
2Tim 3:12 Christ Jesus will be P,

PERSECUTING (3)

Acts 9:5 Jesus, whom you are P;
22:8 Nazareth whom you are P
26:15 Lord said, 'I am Jesus whom you are P

PERSECUTION (7)

Is 14:6 that ruled the nations in anger with unrelenting P
Mt 13:21 and when tribulation or P arises on account of
Mk 4:17 then, when tribulation or P arises on account of

Acts 8:1 that day a great P arose against the church
11:19 scattered because of the P that arose over Stephen
13:50 city, and stirred up P against Paul and Barnabas,
Rom 8:35 tribulation, or distress, or P, or famine, or nakedness,

PERSECUTIONS (5)

Mk 10:30 children and lands, with P, and in the age
2Cor 12:10 with weaknesses, insults, hardships, P, and calamities;
2Thes 1:4 faith in all your P and in the afflictions
2Tim 3:11 love, my steadfastness, my P, my sufferings, what
3:11 and at Lystra, what P I endured; yet from

PERSECUTOR

Phil 3:6 as to zeal a P of the church, as

PERSECUTORS (6)

Ps 31:15 me from the hand of my enemies and P
49:5 the iniquity of my P surrounds me,
119:157 Many are my P and my adversaries, but I
142:6 Deliver me from my P; for they are too
Jer 15:15 me, and take vengeance for me on my P
20:11 dread warrior; therefore my P will stumble, they will

PERSEPOLIS

2Mac 9:2 entered the city called P, and attempted to rob

PERSERVED

1Mac 14:29 the law might be P; and they brought great

PERSEUS

1Mac 8:5 Philip, and P king of the Macedonians, and the

PERSEVERANCE (2)

Eph 6:18 keep alert with all P, making supplication for all
Heb 12:1 let us run with P the race that is

PERSEVERED

Sir 2:10 Or who ever P in the fear of the

PERSEVERES

Jas 1:24 law of liberty, and P, being no hearer that

PERSIA (40)

2Chr 36:20 of the kingdom of P,
36:22 of Cyrus king of P, that the word of
36:22 of Cyrus king of P so that he made
36:23 says Cyrus king of P, 'The LORD, the God
Ezra 1:1 of Cyrus King of P, that the word of
1:1 of Cyrus king of P so that he made
1:2 says Cyrus king of P: The LORD, the God
1:8 Cyrus king of P brought these out in charge
3:7 grant which they had from Cyrus king of P
4:3 Cyrus the king of P has commanded us."
4:5 of Cyrus king of P, even until the reign
4:5 even until the reign of Darius king of P
4:7 to Artaxerxes king of P; the letter was written
4:24 year of the reign of Darius king of P
6:14 and Artaxerxes king of P;
7:1 of Artaxerxes king of P, Ezra the son of
9:9 before the kings of P, to grant us some
Jud 1:7 all who lived in P and to all who
Esth 1:3 the army chiefs of P and Media and the
1:14 the seven princes of P and Media, who saw
1:18 day the ladies of P and Media who have
10:2 the Chronicles of the kings of Media and P
Ezek 27:10 P and Lud and Put were in your army
38:5 and shield, wielding swords; P, Cush, and Put are
Dan 8:20 horns, these are the kings of Media and P
10:1 of Cyrus king of P a word was revealed
10:13 of the kingdom of P withstood me twenty-one days;
10:13 of the kingdom of P
10:20 against the prince of P; and when I am
11:2 kings shall arise in P; and a fourth shall
1Mac 3:31 determined to go to P and collect the revenues
6:1 heard that Elymais in P was a city famed
6:5 came to him in P and reported that the
6:56 king, had returned from P and Media with the
14:2 Arsaces the king of P and Media heard that
2Mac 1:13 when the leader reached P with a force that
1:19 being led captive to P, the pious priests of
1:20 by the king of P, sent the descendants of
9:1 had retreated in disorder from the region of P
9:21 from the region of P I suffered an annoying

PERSIAN (4)

Neh 12:22 the priests until the reign of Darius the P
Esth 16:10 an alien to the P blood, and quite devoid
Dan 6:28 of Darius and the reign of Cyrus the P
14:1 his fathers, Cyrus the P received his kingdom.

PERSIANS (11)

Ezra 4:9 governors, the officials, the P, the men of Erech,
Jud 16:10 The P trembled at her boldness, the Medes were
Esth 1:19 the laws of the P and the Medes so
16:14 the kingdom of the P to the Macedonians.
16:23 us and the loyal P, but that for those
Dan 5:28 is divided and given to the Medes and P
6:8 the Medes and the P, which cannot be revoked."
6:12 of the Medes and P, which cannot be revoked."
6:15 of the Medes and P that no interdict or
1Mac 1:1 Darius, king of the P and the Medes, he
2Mac 1:33 the king of the P that, in the place

PERSIS

Rom 16:12 Greet the beloved P, who has worked hard in

PERSIST (2)

Rom 11:23 if they do not P in their unbelief, will
1Tim 5:20 As for those who P in sin, rebuke them

PERSISTED (3)

Josh 17:12 cities; but the Canaanites P in dwelling in that
Judg 1:27 villages; but the Canaanites P in dwelling in that
1:35 the plain; the Amorites P in dwelling in Har-heres,

PERSISTENTLY (11)

2Chr 36:15 of their fathers, sent P to them by his
Jer 7:13 I spoke to you P you did not listen,
7:25 this day, I have P sent all my servants
11:7 of Egypt, warning them P, even to this day,
25:3 and I have spoken P to you, but you
25:4 hear, although the LORD P sent to you all
29:19 the LORD, which I P sent to you by
32:33 I have taught them P they have not listened
35:14 have spoken to you P, but you have not
35:15 the prophets, sending them P, saying, 'Turn now every
44:4 Yet I P sent to you all my servants

PERSISTS (2)

Deut 25:8 him: and if he P, saying, 'I do not
Sir 12:3 to the man who P in evil or to

PERSON (93)

Ex 4:13 "Oh, my Lord, send, I pray, some other P
12:15 the seventh day, that P shall be cut off
12:19 what is leavened, that P shall be cut off
12:48 But no uncircumcised P shall eat of it.
Lev 7:20 eat flesh, but the P who eats of the
7:20 is on him, that P shall be cut off
7:21 LORD's peace offerings, that P shall be cut off
7:25 For every P who eats of the fat of
7:27 eats any blood, that P shall be cut off
13:4 shut up the diseased P for seven days;
13:12 skin of the diseased P from head to foot,
13:17 shall pronounce the diseased P clean; he is clean.
13:31 shall shut up the P with the itching disease
13:33 shall shut up the P with the itching disease
17:10 my face against that P who eats blood, and
17:12 people of Israel, No P among you shall eat
17:15 And every P that eats what dies of itself
19:8 the LORD; and that P shall be cut off
20:6 "If a P turns to mediums and wizards, playing
20:6 my face against that P, and will cut him
22:3 has an uncleanness, that P shall be cut off
22:6 may be– the P who touches any such
23:30 this same day, that P I will destroy from
27:4 If the P is a female, your valuation shall
27:5 If the P is from five years old up
27:6 If the P is from a month old up
27:7 And if the P is sixty years old and
27:8 he shall bring the P before the priest, and
Num 5:6 the LORD, and that P is guilty,
9:13 keeping the passover, that P shall be cut off
15:27 "If one P sins unwittingly, he shall offer a
15:28 the LORD for the P who commits an error,
15:30 But the P who does anything with a high
15:30 the LORD, and that P shall be cut off
15:31 broken his commandment, that P shall be utterly cut
19:11 dead body of any P shall be unclean seven
19:13 Whoever touches a dead P, the body of any
19:13 the LORD, and that P shall be cut off
19:18 vessel; then a clean P shall take hyssop, and

P

19:19 grave; and the clean P shall sprinkle upon the
19:20 not cleanse himself, that P shall be cut off
19:22 And whatever the unclean P touches shall be
31:19 you has killed any P, and whoever has touched
35:11 manslayer who kills any P without intent may flee
35:15 one who kills any P without intent may flee
35:30 any one kills a P, the murderer shall be
35:30 of witnesses; but no P shall be put to
Deut 17:6 put to death; a P shall not be put
27:25 to slay an innocent P And all the people
28:50 shall not regard the P of the old or
Josh 10:28 he utterly destroyed every P in it, he left
10:30 the sword, and every P in it; he left
10:32 the sword, and every P in it, as he
10:35 the sword; and every P in it he utterly
10:37 its towns, and every P in it; he left
10:37 destroyed it with every P in it.
10:39 and utterly destroyed every P in it; he left
20:3 manslayer who kills any P without intent or
20:9 one who killed a P without intent could flee
2Sam 17:11 multitude, and that you go to battle in P
Tob 6:7 or woman, and that P will never be troubled
Esth 16:11 by all as the P second to the royal
Job 32:21 show partiality to any P or use flattery toward
Prov 6:12 A worthless P, a wicked man, goes about with
19:15 sleep, and an idle P will suffer hunger.
Eccl 4:8 under the sun: a P who has no one,
Sir 8:4 jest with an ill-bred P, lest your ancestors be
10:5 his honor upon the P of the scribe.
13:14 its like, and every P his neighbor;
16:11 is only one stiff-necked P, it will be a
17:17 he will keep a P's kindness like the apple
19:16 A P may make a slip without intending it.
29:27 stranger, to an honored P; my brother has come
37:28 one, and not every P enjoys everything.
Jer 43:6 the princesses, and every P whom Nebuzaradan the
Bar 2:18 the Lord, but the P that is greatly distressed,
2:18 are failing, and the P that hungers, will ascribe
Ezek 44:25 near to a dead P; however, for father or
Dan 11:21 shall arise a contemptible P to whom royal majesty
13:53 an innocent and righteous P
2Mac 3:37 Heliodorus what sort of P would be suitable to
Acts 4:34 was not a needy P among them, for as
Rom 7:1 is binding on a P only during his life?
13:1 Let every P be subject to the governing authorities.
1Cor 2:11 For what P knows a man's thoughts except the
5:13 "Drive out the wicked P from among you."
7:26 is well for a P to remain as he
1Thes 2:17 a short time, in P not in heart, we
Tit 3:11 knowing that such a P is perverted and sinful;
Jas 1:7 For that P must not suppose that a double-minded
1:13 no one; but each P is tempted when he
1Pet 1:11 salvation; they inquired what P or time was
3:4 it be the hidden P of the heart with

PERSONAL (2)

Jud 12:11 had charge of his P affairs, "Go now and
14:13 charge of all his P affairs, "Wake up our

PERSONS (59)

Gen 12:5 had gathered, and the P that they had gotten
14:21 Abram, "Give me the P, but take the goods
46:18 daughter; and these she bore to Jacob--sixteen P
46:22 born to Jacob--fourteen P in all).
46:25 bore to Jacob--seven P in all).
46:26 All the P belonging to Jacob who came into
46:26 sons' wives, were sixty-six P in all;
46:27 were two; all the P of the house of
Ex 1:4 of Jacob were seventy P; Joseph was already in
12:4 to the number of P; according to what each
16:16 the number of the P whom each of you
Lev 18:29 of these abominations, the P that do them shall
27:2 a special vow of P to the LORD at
Num 19:18 furnishings, and upon the P who were there, and
31:28 five hundred, of the P and of the oxen
31:30 every fifty, of the P, of the oxen, of
31:35 asses, and thirty-two thousand P in all, women who
31:40 The P were sixteen thousand, of which the LORD's
31:40 of which the LORD's tribute was thirty-two P
31:46 asses, and sixteen thousand P --
31:47 every fifty, both of P and of beasts, and
Deut 10:22 down to Egypt seventy P; and now the LORD
1Sam 9:22 who had been invited, who were about thirty P
22:18 on that day eighty-five P who wore the linen
22:22 death of all the P of your father's house.
2Kgs 10:6 the king's sons, seventy P, were with the great
10:7 and slew them, seventy P, and put their heads
10:14 pit of Beth-eked, forty-two P, and he spared none
12:4 from the assessment of P --and the money which
Sir 29:4 Many P regard a loan as a windfall, and
31:18 are seated among many P, do not reach out
Jer 52:29 eight hundred and thirty-two P;
52:30 seven hundred and forty-five P; all the persons were
52:30 forty-five persons; all the P were four thousand and
Ezek 13:18 for the heads of P of every stature, in
13:19 bread, putting to death P who should not die
13:19 die and keeping alive P who should not live,
27:13 you; they exchanged the P of men and vessels
Jon 4:11 hundred and twenty thousand P who do not know
1Mac 2:38 and cattle, to the number of a thousand P
2Mac 1:35 And with those P whom the king favored he
Lk 15:7 ninety-nine righteous P who need no repentance.
Acts 1:15 brethren (the company of P was in all about
10:27 in and found many P gathered;
15:24 have heard that some P from us have troubled
17:17 Jews and the devout P, and in the market
27:37 two hundred and seventy-six P in the ship.)
Rom 1:27 receiving in their own P the due penalty for
16:18 For such P do not serve our Lord Christ,
2Thes 3:12 Now such P we command and exhort in the
1Tim 1:3 you may charge certain P not to teach any
1:6 Certain P by swerving from these have wandered
1:10 manslayers, immoral P, sodomites, kidnapers, liars,
1:19 rejecting conscience, certain P have made shipwreck
Heb 9:13 the sprinkling of defiled P with the blood of
1Pet 3:20 few, that is, eight P, were saved through water.
2Pet 2:5 righteousness, with seven other P, when he brought a
3:11 dissolved, what sort of P ought you to be
Jude 1:4 this condemnation, ungodly P who pervert the grace

PERSUADE (5)

2Sam 3:35 the people came to P David to eat bread
Jud 12:11 affairs, "Go now and P the Hebrew woman who
2Mac 7:26 part, she undertook to P her son.
11:14 promising that he would P the king, constraining him
2Cor 5:11 of the Lord, we P men; but what we

PERSUADED (13)

1Sam 24:7 So David P his men with these words, and
Prov 25:15 a ruler may be P, and a soft tongue
2Mac 4:34 spite of his suspicion P Onias to come out
11:14 sent to them and P them to settle everything
Mt 27:20 priests and the elders P the people to ask
Acts 12:20 a body, and having P Blastus, the king's chamberlain,
14:19 and Iconium; and having P the people, they stoned
17:4 some of them were P, and joined Paul and
18:4 synagogue every sabbath, and P Jews and Greeks.
19:26 Asia this Paul has P and turned away a
21:14 he would not be P, we ceased and said,
26:26 freely; for I am P that none of these
Rom 14:14 I know and am P in the Lord Jesus

PERSUADES

Prov 7:21 much seductive speech she P him; with her smooth

PERSUADING

Acts 18:13 saying, "This man is P men to worship God

PERSUASION (2)

Esth 16:5 irremediable calamities, by the P of friends who
Gal 5:8 This P is not from him who calls you.

PERSUASIVENESS (2)

Prov 16:21 of discernment, and pleasant speech increases P
16:23 speech judicious, and adds P to his lips.

PERTAIN

2Pet 1:3 us all things that P to life and godliness,

PERTAINING (6)

Lev 11:46 This is the law P to beast and bird
Num 3:26 cords; all the service P to these.
3:31 screen; all the service P to these.
3:36 accessories; all the service P to these;
1Chr 26:32 the Manassites for everything P to God and for
1Cor 6:3 How much more, matters P to this life!

PERTAINS (5)

Num 8:24 Moses, "This is what P to the Levites: from
Deut 22:5 not wear anything that P to a man, nor
Dan 8:19 the indignation; for it P to the appointed time
8:26 the vision, for it P to many days hence."

Hos 5:1 For the judgment P to you; for you have

PERUDA

Ezra 2:55 Hassophereth, the sons of P,

PERVADES

Wis 7:24 of her pureness she P and penetrates all things.

PERVERSE (27)

Num 22:32 because your way is P before me;
Deut 32:5 blemish; they are a P and crooked generation.
32:20 for they are a P generation, children in whom
1Sam 20:30 "You son of a P, rebellious woman, do I
2Sam 22:27 and with the crooked thou dost show thyself P
Job 9:20 though I am blameless, he would prove me P
Ps 18:26 and with the crooked thou dost show thyself P
Prov 3:32 his ways; for the P man is an abomination
10:31 forth wisdom, but the P tongue will be cut
10:32 but the mouth of the wicked, what is P
11:20 Men of P mind are an abomination to the
12:8 sense, but one of P mind is despised.
14:14 A P man will be filled with the fruit
16:28 A P man spreads strife, and a whisperer separates
16:30 winks his eyes plans P things, he who compresses
17:20 and one with a P tongue falls into calamity.
19:1 a man who is P in speech, and is
22:5 the way of the P; he who guards himself
23:33 and your mind utter P things.
28:6 rich man who is P in his ways.
28:18 but he who is P in his ways will
Wis 1:3 For P thoughts separate men from God, and when
Sir 36:20 A P mind will cause grief, but a man
Mt 17:17 answered, "O faithless and P generation, how long
Lk 9:41 answered, "O faithless and P generation, how long
Acts 20:30 will arise men speaking P things, to draw away
Phil 2:15 of a crooked and P generation, among whom you

PERVERSELY (4)

1Kgs 8:47 sinned, and have acted P and wickedly';
2Chr 6:37 sinned, and have acted P and wickedly';
Esth 13:5 opposition to all men, P following a strange manner
Is 26:10 of uprightness he deals P and does not see

PERVERSENESS (4)

Ps 101:4 P of heart shall be far from me; I
Prov 2:14 and delight in the P of evil;
15:4 tree of life, but P in it breaks the
Is 30:12 trust in oppression and P, and rely on them;

PERVERSION (3)

Lev 18:23 a beast to lie with it: it is P
2Chr 19:7 for there is no P of justice with the
Wis 14:26 pollution of souls, sex P, disorder in marriage,

PERVERT (13)

Ex 23:2 multitude, so as to P justice;
23:6 "You shall not P the justice due to your
Deut 16:19 You shall not P justice; you shall not show
24:17 "You shall not P the justice due to the
Job 8:3 Does God P justice?
8:3 Or does the Almighty P the right?
34:12 the Almighty will not P justice.
Prov 17:23 from the bosom to P the ways of justice.
31:5 has been decreed, and P the rights of all
Jer 23:36 own word, and you P the words of the
Mic 3:9 who abhor justice and P all equity,
Gal 1:7 you and want to P the gospel of Christ.
Jude 1:4 condemnation, ungodly persons who P the grace of

PERVERTED (11)

1Sam 8:3 they took bribes and P justice.
Job 33:27 says: 'I sinned, and P what was right, and
Prov 2:12 evil, from men of P speech,
6:14 with his finger, with P heart devises evil, continually
8:13 way of evil and P speech I hate.
Sir 8:2 ruined many, and has P the minds of kings.
Jer 3:21 sons, because they have P their way, they have
Dan 13:9 And they P their minds and turned away their
13:56 you and lust has P your heart.
Hab 1:4 surround the righteous, so justice goes forth P
Tit 3:11 such a person is P and sinful; he is

PERVERTING (2)

Lk 23:2 "We found this man P our nation, and forbidding
23:14 as one who was P the people; and after

PERVERTS (3)

Deut 27:19 "'Cursed be he who P the justice due to
Prov 10:9 securely, but he who P his ways will be
Wis 4:12 good, and roving desire P the innocent mind.

PESTILENCE (57)

Ex 5:3 fall upon us with P or with the sword."
9:15 and your people with P, and you would have
Lev 26:25 cities I will send P among you, and you
Num 14:12 strike them with the P and disinherit them, and
Deut 28:21 LORD will make the P cleave to you until
32:24 burning heat and poisonous P; and I will send
2Sam 24:13 there be three days' P in your land?
24:15 the LORD sent a P upon Israel from the
1Kgs 8:37 land, if there is P or blight or mildew
1Chr 21:12 sword of the LORD, P upon the land, and
21:14 the LORD sent a P upon Israel; and there
2Chr 6:28 land, if there is P or blight or mildew
7:13 the land, or send P among my people,
20:9 the sword, judgment, or P, or famine, we will
Job 27:15 who survive him the P buries, and their widows
Ps 91:3 and from the deadly P;
91:6 by day, nor the P that stalks in darkness,
Sir 39:29 hail and famine and P, all these have been
Jer 14:12 them by the sword, by famine, and by P
15:2 "Those who are for P, to pestilence, and those
15:2 are for pestilence, to P, and those who are
18:21 men meet death by P, their youths be slain
21:6 and beast; they shall die of a great P
21:7 city who survive the P, sword, and famine, into
21:9 by famine, and by P; but he who goes
24:10 send sword, famine, and P upon them, until they
27:8 with famine, and with P, says the LORD, until
27:13 by famine, and by P, as the LORD has
28:8 prophesied war, famine, and P against many
29:17 them sword, famine, and P, and I will make
29:18 with sword, famine, and P, and will make them
32:24 sword and famine and P the city is given
32:36 by famine, and by P:
34:17 to the sword, to P, and to famine, says
38:2 by famine, and by P; but he who goes
42:17 by famine, and by P; they shall have no
42:22 by famine, and by P in the place where
43:11 Egypt, giving to the P those who are doomed
43:11 are doomed to the P, to captivity those who
44:13 with famine, and with P,
Bar 2:25 in great misery, by famine and sword and P
Ezek 5:12 you shall die of P and be consumed with
5:17 you of your children; P and blood shall pass
6:11 fall by the sword, by famine, and by P
6:12 far-off shall die of P; and he that is
7:15 The sword is without, P and famine are within;
7:15 the city famine and P devour.
12:16 sword, from famine and P, that they may confess
14:19 if I send a P into that land, and
14:21 famine, evil beasts, and P, to cut off from
28:23 for I will send P into her, and blood
33:27 in strongholds and in caves shall die by P
38:22 With P and bloodshed I will enter into judgment
Amos 4:10 sent among you a P after the manner of
Hab 3:5 Before him went P, and plague followed close behind.
Rev 6:8 with famine and with P and by wild beasts
18:8 in a single day, P and mourning and famine,

PESTILENCES

Lk 21:11 various places famines and P; and there will be

PESTILENT (5)

Esth 16:7 wickedly accomplished through the P behavior of
1Mac 10:61 A group of P men from Israel, lawless men,
15:3 Whereas certain P men have gained control of the
15:21 Therefore if any P men have fled to you
Acts 24:5 found this man a P fellow, an agitator among

PESTLE

Prov 27:22 a mortar with a P along with crushed grain,

PETER (156)

Mt 4:18 Simon who is called P and Andrew his brother,
8:14 And when Jesus entered P's house, he saw his
10:2 Simon, who is called P, and Andrew his brother;
14:28 And P answered him, "Lord, if it is you,
14:29 So P got out of the boat and walked
15:15 But P said to him, "Explain the parable to
16:16 Simon P replied, "You are the Christ, the Son
16:18 tell you, you are P, and on this rock

	16:22	And P took him and began to rebuke him,
	16:23	turned and said to P, "Get behind me, Satan!
	17:1	Jesus took with him P and James and John
	17:4	And P said to Jesus, "Lord, it is well
	17:23	tax went up to P and said, "Does not
	18:20	Then P came up and said to him, "Lord,
	19:27	Then P said in reply, "Lo, we have left
	26:33	P declared to him, "Though they all fall away
	26:35	P said to him, "Even if I must die
	26:37	And taking with him P and the two sons
	26:40	and he said to P, "So, could you not
	26:58	But P followed him at a distance, as far
	26:69	Now P was sitting outside in the courtyard.
	26:73	up and said to P, "Certainly you are also
	26:75	And P remembered the saying of Jesus, "Before the
Mk	3:16	Simon whom he surnamed P;
	5:37	to follow him except P and James and John
	8:29	P answered him, "You are the Christ."
	8:32	And P took him, and began to rebuke him.
	8:33	his disciples, he rebuked P, and said, "Get behind
	9:2	Jesus took with him P and James and John,
	9:5	And P said to Jesus, "Master, it is well
	10:28	P began to say to him, "Lo, we have
	11:21	And P remembered and said to him, "Master, look!
	13:3	Olives opposite the temple, P and James and John
	14:29	P said to him, "Even though they all fall
	14:33	he took with him P and James and John,
	14:37	and he said to P, "Simon, are you asleep?
	14:54	And P had followed him at a distance, right
	14:66	And as P was below in the courtyard, one
	14:67	priest came; and seeing P warming himself, she
	14:70	the bystanders said to P, "Certainly you are one
	14:72	And P remembered how Jesus had said to him,
	16:7	tell his disciples and P that he is going
Lk	5:8	But when Simon P saw it, he fell down
	6:14	Simon, whom he named P, and Andrew his brother,
	8:45	When all denied it, P said, "Master, the multitudes
	8:51	enter with him, except P and John and James,
	9:20	And P answered, "The Christ of God."
	9:28	he took with him P and John and James,
	9:32	Now P and those who were with him were
	9:33	were parting from him, P said to Jesus, "Master,
	12:41	P said, "Lord, are you telling this parable for
	18:28	And P said, "Lo, we have left our homes
	22:8	So Jesus sent P and John, saying, "Go and
	22:34	said, "I tell you, P, the cock will not
	22:52	P followed at a distance;
	22:53	and sat down together, P sat among them.
	22:56	But P said, "Man, I am not."
	22:58	But P said, "Man, I do not know what
	22:59	And the Lord turned and looked at P
	22:59	And P remembered the word of the Lord, how
	24:12	But P rose and ran to the tomb; stooping
Jn	1:40	him, was Andrew, Simon P's brother.
	1:42	(which means P).
	1:44	was from Beth-saida, the city of Andrew and P
	6:8	his disciples, Andrew, Simon P's brother, said to him,
	6:68	Simon P answered him, "Lord, to whom shall we
	13:6	He came to Simon P; and Peter said to
	13:6	to Simon Peter; and P said to him, "Lord,
	13:8	P said to him, "You shall never wash my
	13:9	Simon P said to him, "Lord, not my feet
	13:24	of Jesus; so Simon P beckoned to him and
	13:36	Simon P said to him, "Lord, where are you
	13:37	P said to him, "Lord, why cannot I follow
	18:10	Then Simon P, having a sword, drew it and
	18:11	Jesus said to P, "Put your sword into its
	18:15	Simon P followed Jesus, and so did another disciple.
	18:16	along with Jesus, while P stood outside at the
	18:16	the door, and brought P in.
	18:17	the door said to P, "Are not you also
	18:18	standing and warming themselves; P also was with
	18:25	Now Simon P was standing and warming himself.
	18:26	the man whose ear P had cut off, asked,
	18:27	P again denied it; and at once the cock
	20:2	and went to Simon P and the other disciple,
	20:3	P then came out with the other disciple, and
	20:4	the other disciple outran P and reached the tomb
	20:6	Then Simon P came, following him, and went into
	21:2	Simon P, Thomas called the Twin, Nathanael of Cana
	21:3	Simon P said to them, "I am going fishing."
	21:7	Jesus loved said to P, "It is the Lord!"
	21:7	When Simon P heard that it was the Lord,
	21:11	So Simon P went aboard and hauled the net
	21:15	Jesus said to Simon P, "Simon, son of John,
	21:17	P was grieved because he said to him the
	21:20	P turned and saw following them the disciple whom
	21:21	When P saw him, he said to Jesus, "Lord,
Acts	1:13	where they were staying, P and John and James
	1:15	In those days P stood up among the brethren
	2:14	But P, standing with the eleven, lifted up his
	2:37	heart, and said to P and the rest of
	2:38	And P said to them, "Repent, and be baptized
	3:1	Now P and John were going up to the
	3:3	Seeing P and John about to go into the
	3:4	And P directed his gaze at him, with John,
	3:6	But P said, "I have no silver and gold,
	3:11	While he clung to P and John, all the
	3:12	And when P saw it he addressed the people,
	4:8	Then P, filled with the Holy Spirit, said to
	4:13	saw the boldness of P and John, and perceived
	4:19	But P and John answered them, "Whether it is
	5:3	But P said, "Ananias, why has Satan filled your
	5:8	And P said to her, "Tell me whether you
	5:9	But P said to her, "How is it that
	5:15	and pallets, that as P came by at least
	5:29	But P and the apostles answered, "We must obey
	8:14	they sent to them P and John,
	8:20	But P said to him, "Your silver perish with
	9:32	Now as P went here and there among them
	9:34	And P said to him, "Aeneas, Jesus Christ heals
	9:38	the disciples, hearing that P was there, sent two
	9:39	So P rose and went with them.
	9:40	But P put them all outside and knelt down
	9:40	and when she saw P she sat up.
	10:5	Simon who is called P;
	10:9	coming near the city, P went up on the
	10:13	voice to him, "Rise, P; kill and eat."
	10:14	But P said, "No, Lord; for I have never
	10:17	Now while P was inwardly perplexed as to what
	10:18	Simon who was called P was lodging there.
	10:19	And while P was pondering the vision, the Spirit
	10:21	And P went down to the men and said,
	10:25	When P entered, Cornelius met him and fell down
	10:26	But P lifted him up, saying, "Stand up; I
	10:32	Simon who is called P; he is lodging in
	10:34	And P opened his mouth and said: "Truly I
	10:44	While P was still saying this, the Holy Spirit
	10:45	circumcised who came with P were amazed,
	10:46	Then P declared,
	11:2	So when P went up to Jerusalem, the circumcision
	11:4	But P began and explained to them in order:
	11:7	saying to me, 'Rise, P; kill and eat.'
	11:13	and bring Simon called P;
	12:3	he proceeded to arrest P also.
	12:5	So P was kept in prison; but earnest prayer
	12:6	to bring him out, P was sleeping between two
	12:7	cell; and he struck P on the side and
	12:11	And P came to himself, and said, "Now I
	12:14	Recognizing P's voice, in her joy she did not
	12:14	in and told that P was standing at the
	12:16	But P continued knocking; and when they opened,
	12:18	among the soldiers over what had become of P
	15:7	had been much debate, P rose and said to
Gal	2:7	the uncircumcised, just as P had been entrusted with
	2:8	he who worked through P for the mission to
1Pet	1:1	P, an apostle of Jesus
2Pet	1:1	Simeon P, a servant and apostle

PETHAHIAH (4)

1Chr	24:16	Happizzez, the nineteenth to P, the twentieth to
Ezra	10:23	Kelaiah (that is, Kelita), P, Judah, and Eliezer.
Neh	9:5	Sherebiah, Hodiah, Shebaniah, and P, said, "Stand up
	11:24	And P the son of Meshezabel, of the sons

PETHOR (2)

Num	22:5	son of Beor at P, which is near the
Deut	23:4	son of Beor from P of Mesopotamia, to curse

PETHUEL

Joel	1:1	Joel, the son of P:

PETITION (14)

1Sam	1:17	of Israel grant your P which you have made
	1:27	has granted me my P which I made to
	25:35	to your voice, and I have granted your P
Esth	5:6	the king said to Esther, "What is your P
	5:7	But Esther said, "My P and my request is:
	5:8	king to grant my P and fulfil my request,
	7:2	Esther, "What is your P, Queen Esther?
	7:3	given me at my P, and my people at
	9:12	Now what is your P

P

Dan 6:7 interdict, that whoever makes P to any god or
6:11 and found Daniel making P and supplication before
6:12 any man who makes P to any god or
6:13 signed, but makes his P three times a day."
2Mac 13:12 joined in the same P and had besought the

PETITIONED

Acts 25:24 the whole Jewish people P me, both at Jerusalem

PETITIONS

Ps 20:5 May the LORD fulfil all your P

PHALANX (3)

1Mac 6:45 the midst of the P to reach it; he
9:12 the two companies, the P advanced to the sound
10:82 force and engaged the P in battle (for the

PHALANXES (2)

1Mac 6:35 the beasts among the P; with each elephant they
6:38 enemy while being themselves protected by the P

PHANTOMS (2)

Ps 73:20 when one awakes, on awaking you despise their P
Wis 17:4 around them, and dismal P with gloomy faces

PHANU-EL

Lk 2:36 Anna, the daughter of P, of the tribe of

PHARAOH (279)

Gen 12:15 when the princes of P saw her, they praised
12:15 of Pharaoh saw her, they praised her to P
12:15 woman was taken into P's house.
12:17 But the LORD afflicted P and his house with
12:18 So P called Abram, and said, "What is this
12:20 And P gave men orders concerning him; and they
37:36 Potiphar, an officer of P, the captain of the
39:1 Potiphar, an officer of P, the captain of the
40:2 And P was angry with his two officers, the
40:7 So he asked P's officers who were with him
40:11 P's cup was in my hand; and I took
40:11 and pressed them into P's cup, and placed the
40:11 placed the cup in P's hand."
40:13 days; within three days P will lift up your
40:13 and you shall place P's cup in his hand
40:14 mention of me to P, and so get me
40:17 of baked food for P, but the birds were
40:19 days; within three days P will lift up your
40:20 third day, which was P's birthday, he made a
40:21 placed the cup in P's hand;
41:1 After two whole years, P dreamed that he was
41:4 And P awoke.
41:7 And P awoke, and behold, it was a dream.
41:8 its wise men; and P told them his dream,
41:8 there was none who could interpret it to P
41:9 chief butler said to P, "I remember my faults
41:10 When P was angry with his servants, and put
41:14 Then P sent and called Joseph, and they brought
41:14 and changed his clothes, he came in before P
41:15 And P said to Joseph, "I have had a
41:16 Joseph answered P, "It is not in me; God
41:16 me; God will give P a favorable answer."
41:17 Then P said to Joseph, "Behold, in my dream
41:25 Then Joseph said to P, "The dream of Pharaoh
41:25 Pharaoh, "The dream of P is one; God has
41:25 God has revealed to P what he is about
41:28 is as I told P, God has shown to
41:28 God has shown to P what he is about
41:32 And the doubling of P's dream means that the
41:33 Now therefore let P select a man discreet and
41:34 Let P proceed to appoint overseers over the land,
41:35 under the authority of P for food in the
41:37 proposal seemed good to P and to all his
41:38 And P said to his servants, "Can we find
41:39 So P said to Joseph, "Since God has shown
41:41 And P said to Joseph, "Behold, I have set
41:42 Then P took his signet ring from his hand
41:44 Moreover P said to Joseph, "I am Pharaoh, and
41:44 to Joseph, "I am P, and without your consent
41:45 And P called Joseph's name Zaphenath-paneah; and
41:46 entered the service of P king of Egypt.
41:46 from the presence of P, and went through all
41:55 the people cried to P for bread; and Pharaoh
41:55 Pharaoh for bread; and P said to all the
42:15 by the life of P, you shall not go
42:16 by the life of P, surely you are spies."
44:18 for you are like P himself.
45:2 and the household of P heard it.
45:8 me a father to P, and lord of all
45:16 report was heard in P's house, "Joseph's brothers
45:16 it pleased P and his servants well.
45:17 And P said to Joseph, "Say to your brothers,
45:21 to the command of P, and gave them provisions
46:5 in the wagons which P had sent to carry
46:31 go up and tell P, and will say to
46:33 that they have.' When P calls you, and says,
47:1 went in and told P, "My father and my
47:2 he took five men and presented them to P
47:3 P said to his brothers, "What is your occupation?"
47:3 And they said to P, "Your servants are shepherds,
47:4 They said to P, "We have come to sojourn
47:5 Then P said to Joseph, "Your father and your
47:7 and set him before P, and Jacob blessed Pharaoh.
47:7 and set him before Pharaoh, and Jacob blessed P
47:8 And P said to Jacob, "How many are the
47:9 And Jacob said to P, "The days of the
47:10 And Jacob blessed P, and went out from the
47:10 Pharaoh, and went out from the presence of P
47:11 land of Rameses, as P had commanded.
47:14 brought the money into P's house.
47:19 will be slaves to P; and give us seed,
47:20 land of Egypt for P; for all the Egyptians
47:22 a fixed allowance from P, and lived on the
47:22 on the allowance which P gave them; therefore they
47:23 this day bought you and your land for P
47:24 give a fifth to P, and four fifths shall
47:25 please my lord, we will be slaves to P
47:26 to this day, that P should have the fifth;
50:4 to the household of P, saying, "If now I
50:4 in the ears of P, saying,
50:6 And P answered, "Go up, and bury your father,
50:7 all the servants of P, the elders of his

Ex 1:10 and they built for P store-cities, Pithom and
1:18 The midwives said to P, "Because the Hebrew
1:21 Then P commanded all his people, "Every son that
2:5 Now the daughter of P came down to bathe
2:7 his sister said to P's daughter, "Shall I go
2:8 And P's daughter said to her, "Go." So the
2:9 And P's daughter said to her, "Take this child
2:10 she brought him to P's daughter, and he became
2:15 When P heard of it, he sought to kill
2:15 But Moses fled from P, and stayed in the
3:10 will send you to P that you may bring
3:11 I should go to P, and bring the sons
4:21 that you do before P all the miracles which
4:22 you shall say to P, 'Thus says the LORD,
5:1 and Aaron went to P and said, "Thus says
5:2 But P said, "Who is the LORD, that I
5:5 And P said, "Behold, the people of the land
5:6 The same day P commanded the taskmasters of the
5:10 the people, "Thus says P, 'I will not give
5:14 people of Israel, whom P's taskmasters had set over
5:15 came and cried to P, "Why do you deal
5:20 they came forth from P;
5:21 in the sight of P and his servants, and
5:23 since I came to P to speak in thy
6:1 I will do to P; for with a strong
6:11 Moses, "Go in, tell P king of Egypt to
6:12 me; how then shall P listen to me, who
6:13 of Israel and to P king of Egypt to
6:27 they who spoke to P king of Egypt about
6:29 am the LORD; tell P king of Egypt all
6:30 lips; how then shall P listen to me?"
7:1 you as God to P; and Aaron your brother
7:2 your brother shall tell P to let the people
7:3 But I will harden P's heart, and though I
7:4 the land of Egypt, P will not listen to
7:7 Aaron eighty-three years old, when they spoke to P
7:9 Moses and Aaron, "When P says to you, 'Prove
7:9 cast it down before P, that it may become
7:10 and Aaron went to P and did as the
7:10 down his rod before P and his servants, and
7:11 Then P summoned the wise men and the sorcerers;
7:13 Still P's heart was hardened, and he would not
7:14 LORD said to Moses, P's heart is hardened, he
7:15 Go to P in the morning, as he is
7:20 in the sight of P and in the sight
7:22 their secret arts; so P's heart remained hardened,
7:23 P turned and went into his house, and he
8:1 Moses, "Go in to P and say to him,
8:8 Then P called Moses and Aaron, and said, "Entreat
8:9 Moses said to P, "Be pleased to command me
8:12 Aaron went out from P; and Moses cried to

P

	8:12	concerning the frogs, as he had agreed with P
	8:15	But when P saw that there was a respite,
	8:19	the magicians said to P, "This is the finger
	8:19	But P's heart was hardened, and he would not
	8:20	morning and wait for P, as he goes out
	8:24	into the house of P and into his servants'
	8:25	Then P called Moses and Aaron, and said, "Go,
	8:28	So P said, "I will let you go, to
	8:29	flies may depart from P, from his servants, and
	8:29	tomorrow; only let not P deal falsely again by
	8:30	Moses went out from P and prayed to the
	8:31	swarms of flies from P, from his servants, and
	8:32	But P hardened his heart this time also, and
	9:1	Moses, "Go in to P, and say to him,
	9:7	And P sent, and behold, not one of the
	9:7	But the heart of P was hardened, and he
	9:8	throw them toward heaven in the sight of P
	9:10	kiln, and stood before P, and Moses threw them
	9:12	hardened the heart of P, and he did not
	9:13	morning and stand before P, and say to him,
	9:20	among the servants of P made his slaves and
	9:27	Then P sent, and called Moses and Aaron, and
	9:33	of the city from P, and stretched out his
	9:34	But when P saw that the rain and the
	9:35	So the heart of P was hardened, and he
	10:1	Moses, "Go in to P; for I have hardened
	10:3	Aaron went in to P, and said to him,
	10:6	Then he turned and went out from P
	10:7	And P's servants said to him, "How long shall
	10:8	were brought back to P; and he said to
	10:11	were driven out from P's presence.
	10:16	Then P called Moses and Aaron in haste, and
	10:18	he went out from P, and entreated the LORD.
	10:20	But the LORD hardened P's heart, and he did
	10:24	Then P called Moses, and said, "Go, serve the
	10:27	But the LORD hardened P's heart, and he would
	10:28	Then P said to him, "Get away from me;
	11:1	I will bring upon P and upon Egypt; afterwards
	11:3	in the sight of P's servants and in the
	11:5	from the first-born of P who sits upon his
	11:8	he went out from P in hot anger.
	11:9	LORD said to Moses, P will not listen to
	11:10	all these wonders before P; and the LORD hardened
	11:10	and the LORD hardened P's heart, and he did
	12:29	from the first-born of P who sat on his
	12:30	And P rose up in the night, he, and
	13:15	For when P stubbornly refused to let us go,
	13:17	When P let the people go, God did not
	14:3	For P will say of the people of Israel,
	14:4	And I will harden P's heart, and he will
	14:4	will get glory over P and all his host;
	14:5	fled, the mind of P and his servants was
	14:8	hardened the heart of P king of Egypt and
	14:9	Egyptians pursued them, all P's horses and chariots
	14:10	When P drew near, the people of Israel lifted
	14:17	will get glory over P and all his host,
	14:18	have gotten glory over P, his chariots, and his
	14:23	of the sea, all P's horses, his chariots, and
	14:28	all the host of P that had followed them
	15:4	P's chariots and his host he cast into the
	15:19	when the horses of P with his chariots and
	18:4	help, and delivered me from the sword of P
	18:8	LORD had done to P and to the Egyptians
	18:10	the Egyptians and out of the hand of P
Deut	6:21	your son, 'We were P's slaves in Egypt; and
	6:22	against Egypt and against P and all his household,
	7:8	from the hand of P king of Egypt.
	7:18	your God did to P and to all Egypt,
	11:3	did in Egypt to P the king of Egypt
	29:2	land of Egypt, to P and to all his
	34:11	land of Egypt, to P and to all his
1Sam	2:27	were in Egypt subject to the house of P
	6:6	as the Egyptians and P hardened their hearts?
1Kgs	3:1	a marriage alliance with P king of Egypt; he
	3:1	of Egypt; he took P's daughter, and brought her
	7:8	like this hall for P's daughter whom he had
	9:16	and Megiddo and Gezer P king of Egypt had
	9:24	But P's daughter went up from the city of
	11:1	women: the daughter of P, and Moabite, Ammonite,
	11:18	came to Egypt, to P king of Egypt, who
	11:19	in the sight of P, so that he gave
	11:20	whom Tahpenes weaned in P's house; and Genubath
	11:20	and Genubath was in P's house among the sons
	11:20	was in Pharaoh's house among the sons of P
	11:21	dead, Hadad said to P, "Let me depart, that
	11:22	But P said to him, "What have you lacked
2Kgs	17:7	under the hand of P king of Egypt, and
	18:21	Such is P king of Egypt to all who
	23:29	In his days P Neco king of Egypt went
	23:29	to meet him; and P Neco slew him at
	23:33	And P Neco put him in bonds at Riblah
	23:34	And P Neco made Eliakim the son of Josiah
	23:35	and the gold to P, but he taxed the
	23:35	give the money according to the command of P
	23:35	to give it to P Neco.
1Chr	4:17	Bithi-ah, the daughter of P, whom Mered married;
2Chr	8:11	Solomon brought P's daughter up from the city of
Neh	9:10	signs and wonders against P and all his servants
Ps	135:9	signs and wonders against P and all his servants;
	136:15	for ever; but overthrew P and his host in
Song	1:9	to a mare of P's chariots.
Is	19:11	the wise counselors of P give stupid counsel.
	19:11	can you say to P, "I am a son
	30:2	in the protection of P, and to seek shelter
	30:3	shall the protection of P turn to your shame,
	36:6	Such is P king of Egypt to all who
Jer	25:19	as at this day; P king of Egypt, his
	37:5	The army of P had come out of Egypt;
	37:7	inquire of me, 'Behold, P's army which came to
	37:11	at the approach of P's army,
	43:9	at the entrance to P's palace in Tahpanhes, in
	44:30	Behold, I will give P Hophra king of Egypt
	46:2	Concerning the army of P Neco, king of Egypt,
	46:17	Call the name of P, king of Egypt, 'Noisy
	46:25	Amon of Thebes, and P, and Egypt and her
	46:25	and her kings, upon P and those who trust
	47:1	concerning the Philistines, before P smote Gaza.
Ezek	17:17	P with his mighty army and great company will
	29:2	set your face against P king of Egypt, and
	29:3	I am against you, P king of Egypt, the
	30:21	broken the arm of P king of Egypt; and
	30:22	Behold, I am against P king of Egypt, and
	30:24	break the arms of P, and he will groan
	30:25	but the arms of P shall fall; and they
	31:2	of man, say to P king of Egypt and
	31:18	"This is P and all his multitude, says the
	32:2	raise a lamentation over P king of Egypt, and
	32:31	"When P sees them, he will comfort himself for
	32:31	for all his multitude, P and all his army,
	32:32	slain by the sword, P and all his multitude,
1Mac	4:9	the Red Sea, when P with his forces pursued
Acts	7:10	favor and wisdom before P, king of Egypt, who
	7:13	his brothers, and Joseph's family became known to P
	7:21	when he was exposed, P's daughter adopted him and
Rom	9:17	the scripture says to P, "I have raised you
Heb	11:24	called the son of P's daughter,

PHARAOHS (2)

Gen	47:20	The land became P;
	47:26	land of the priests alone did not become P

PHARATHON

1Mac	9:50	Bethel, and Timnath, and P, and Tephon, with high

PHARISEE (12)

Mt	23:25	You blind P
Lk	7:36	he went into the P's house, and took his
	7:37	at table in the P's house, brought an alabaster
	7:39	Now when the P who had invited him saw
	11:37	he was speaking, a P asked him to dine
	11:38	The P was astonished to see that he did
	18:10	to pray, one a P and the other a
	18:11	The P stood and prayed thus with himself, 'God,
Acts	5:34	But a P in the council named Gamali-el, a
	23:6	"Brethren, I am a P, a son of Pharisees;
	26:5	of our religion I have lived as a P
Phil	3:5	to the law a P,

PHARISEES (86)

Mt	3:7	saw many of the P and Sadducees coming for
	5:20	of the scribes and P, you will never enter
	9:11	And when the P saw this, they said to
	9:14	do we and the P fast, but your disciples
	9:34	But the P said, "He casts out demons by
	12:2	But when the P saw it, they said to
	12:14	But the P went out and took counsel against
	12:24	But when the P heard it they said, "It
	12:38	of the scribes and P said to him, "Teacher,
	15:1	Then P and scribes came to Jesus from Jerusalem
	15:12	you know that the P were offended when they
	16:1	And the P and Sadducees came, and to test
	16:6	the leaven of the P and Sadducees."

16:11 the leaven of the P and Sadducees."
16:12 the teaching of the P and Sadducees.
19:3 And P came up to him and tested him
21:45 chief priests and the P heard his parables, they
22:15 Then the P went and took counsel how to
22:34 But when the P heard that he had silenced
22:41 Now while the P were gathered together, Jesus
23:2 "The scribes and the P sit on Moses' seat;
23:13 to you, scribes and P, hypocrites!
23:14 to you, scribes and P, hypocrites!
23:22 to you, scribes and P, hypocrites!
23:24 to you, scribes and P, hypocrites!
23:26 to you, scribes and P, hypocrites!
23:28 to you, scribes and P, hypocrites!
27:62 chief priests and the P gathered before Pilate
Mk 2:16 the scribes of the P, when they saw that
2:18 John's disciples and the P were fasting; and people
2:18 the disciples of the P fast, but your disciples
2:24 And the P said to him, "Look, why are
3:6 The P went out, and immediately held counsel with
7:1 Now when the P gathered together to him, with
7:3 (For the P, and all the Jews, do not
7:5) And the P and the scribes asked him,
8:11 The P came and began to argue with him,
8:15 the leaven of the P and the leaven of
10:2 And P came up and in order to test
12:13 him some of the P and some of the
Lk 5:17 was teaching, there were P and teachers of the
5:21 the scribes and the P began to question, saying,
5:30 And the P and their scribes murmured against his
5:33 the disciples of the P, but yours eat and
6:2 But some of the P said, "Why are you
6:7 the scribes and the P watched him, to see
7:30 of John; but the P and the lawyers rejected
7:36 One of the P asked him to eat with
11:39 to him, "Now you P cleanse the outside of
11:42 "But woe to you P
11:43 Woe to you P
11:53 the scribes and the P began to press him
12:1 the leaven of the P, which is hypocrisy.
13:31 that very hour some P came, and said to
14:1 who belonged to the P, they were watching him.
14:3 to the lawyers and P, saying, "Is it lawful
15:2 And the P and the scribes murmured, saying, "This
16:14 The P, who were lovers of money, heard all
17:20 Being asked by the P when the kingdom of
19:39 And some of the P in the multitude said
Jn 1:24 Now they had been sent from the P
3:1 a man of the P, named Nicodemus, a ruler
4:1 Lord knew that the P had heard that Jesus
7:32 The P heard the crowd thus muttering about him,
7:32 the chief priests and P sent officers to arrest
7:45 the chief priests and P, who said to them,
7:47 The P answered them, "Are you led astray, you
7:48 authorities or of the P believed in him?
8:3 The scribes and the P brought a woman who
8:13 The P then said to him, "You are bearing
9:13 They brought to the P the man who had
9:15 The P again asked him how he had received
9:16 Some of the P said, "This man is not
9:40 Some of the P near him heard this, and
11:46 them went to the P and told them what
11:47 chief priests and the P gathered the council, and
11:57 chief priests and the P had given orders that
12:19 The P then said to one another, "You see
12:42 for fear of the P they did not confess
18:3 chief priests and the P, went there with lanterns
Acts 15:5 the party of the P rose up, and said,
23:6 Sadducees and the other P, he cried out in
23:6 Pharisee, a son of P; with respect to the
23:7 dissension arose between the P and the Sadducees;
23:8 nor spirit; but the P acknowledge them all.
23:9 the scribes of the P party stood up and

PHARMACIST

Sir 38:8 takes away pain; the P makes of them a

PHARPAR

2Kgs 5:12 Are not Abana and P, the rivers of Damascus,

PHASELIS

1Mac 15:23 to Rhodes, and to P, and to Cos, and

PHASES

Sir 43:8 increasing marvelously in its P, an instrument of the

PHASIRON

1Mac 9:66 and the sons of P in their tents.

PHICOL (3)

Gen 21:22 that time Abimelech and P the commander of his
21:32 Then Abimelech and P the commander of his army
26:26 Ahuzzath his adviser and P the commander of his

PHILADELPHIA (2)

Rev 1:11 to Sardis and to P and to La-odicea."
3:7 of the church in P write: 'The words of

PHILEMON

Philem 1:1 Timothy our brother, To P our beloved fellow worker

PHILETUS

2Tim 2:17 them are Hymenaeus and P,

PHILIP (45)

1Mac 1:1 After Alexander son of P, the Macedonian, who came
6:2 Alexander, the son of P, the Macedonian king who
6:14 Then he called for P, one of his friends,
6:55 Then Lysias heard that P, whom King Antiochus
6:63 He found P in control of the city, but
8:5 P, and Perseus king of the Macedonians, and the
2Mac 5:22 the people: at Jerusalem, P, by birth a Phrygian
6:11 secretly, were betrayed to P and were all burned
8:8 When P saw that the man was gaining ground
9:29 And P, one of his courtiers, took his body
13:23 he got word that P, who had been left
Mt 10:3 and John his brother; P and Bartholomew; Thomas
14:3 of Herodi-as, his brother P's wife;
Mk 3:18 of thunder; Andrew, and P, and Bartholomew, and
6:17 of Herodi-as, his brother P's wife; because he had
Lk 3:1 Galilee, and his brother P tetrarch of the region
6:14 James and John, and P, and Bartholomew,
Jn 1:43 And he found P and said to him, "Follow
1:44 Now P was from Beth-saida, the city of Andrew
1:45 P found Nathanael, and said to him, "We have
1:46 P said to him, "Come and see."
1:48 Jesus answered him, "Before P called you, when you
6:5 him, Jesus said to P, "How are we to
6:7 P answered him, "Two hundred denarii would not
12:21 So these came to P, who was from Beth-saida
12:22 P went and told Andrew; Andrew went with Philip
12:22 Andrew; Andrew went with P and they told Jesus.
14:8 P said to him, "Lord, show us the Father,
14:9 long, and yet you do not know me, P
Acts 1:13 James and Andrew, P and Thomas, Bartholomew
6:5 the Holy Spirit, and P, and Prochorus, and Nicanor,
8:5 P went down to a city of Samaria, and
8:6 what was said by P, when they heard him
8:12 But when they believed P as he preached good
8:13 and after being baptized he continued with P
8:26 the Lord said to P, "Rise and go toward
8:29 the Spirit said to P, "Go up and join
8:30 So P ran to him, and heard him reading
8:31 And he invited P to come up and sit
8:34 the eunuch said to P, "About whom, pray, does
8:35 Then P opened his mouth, and beginning with this
8:37 down into the water, P and the eunuch, and
8:38 the Lord caught up P; and the eunuch saw
8:39 But P was found at Azotus, and passing on
21:8 entered the house of P the evangelist, who was

PHILIPPI (6)

Mt 16:13 the district of Caesarea P, he asked his disciples,
Mk 8:27 the villages of Caesarea P; and on the way
Acts 16:12 and from there to P, which is the leading
20:6 we sailed away from P after the days of
Phil 1:1 Jesus who are at P, with the bishops and
1Thes 2:2 been shamefully treated at P, as you know, we

PHILIPPIANS

Phil 4:15 And you P yourselves know that in the beginning

PHILISTIA (9)

Ex 15:14 tremble; pangs have seized on the inhabitants of P
Ps 60:8 cast my shoe; over P I shout in triumph."
83:7 and Ammon and Amalek, P with the inhabitants of
87:4 and Babylon; behold, P and Tyre, with Ethiopia--
108:9 cast my shoe; over P I shout in triumph."
Is 14:29 oracle: "Rejoice not, O P, all of you, that
14:31 melt in fear, O P, all of you!
Joel 3:4 Tyre and Sidon, and all the regions of P
Zech 9:6 will make an end of the pride of P

P

PHILISTINE (36)

1Sam 14:1 go over to the P garrison on yonder side."
14:4 go over to the P garrison, there was a
17:8 Am I not a P, and are you not
17:10 And the P said, "I defy the ranks of
17:11 these words of the P, they were dismayed and
17:16 For forty days the P came forward and took
17:23 behold, the champion, the P of Gath, Goliath by
17:26 man who kills this P, and takes away the
17:26 who is this uncircumcised P, that he should defy
17:32 your servant will go and fight with this P
17:33 to go against this P to fight with him;
17:36 bears; and this uncircumcised P shall be like one
17:37 will deliver me from the hand of this P
17:40 his hand, and he drew near to the P
17:41 And the P came on and drew near to
17:42 And when the P looked, and saw David, he
17:43 And the P said to David, "Am I a
17:43 And the P cursed David by his gods.
17:44 The P said to David, "Come to me, and
17:45 David said to the P, "You come to me
17:48 When the P arose and came and drew near
17:48 quickly toward the battle line to meet the P
17:49 it, and struck the P on his forehead; the
17:50 David prevailed over the P with a sling and
17:50 stone, and struck the P, and killed him; there
17:51 and stood over the P, and took his sword
17:54 the head of the P and brought it to
17:55 go forth against the P, he said to Abner,
17:57 the slaughter of the P, Abner took him, and
17:57 the head of the P in his hand.
18:6 returned from slaying the P, the women came out
19:5 and he slew the P, and the LORD wrought
21:9 sword of Goliath the P, whom you killed in
22:10 and gave him the sword of Goliath the P
2Sam 21:17 aid, and attacked the P and killed him.
1Chr 14:16 and they smote the P army from Gibeon to

PHILISTINES (261)

Gen 10:14 Casluhim (whence came the P, and Caphtorim.
21:32 up and returned to the land of the P
21:34 sojourned many days in the land of the P
26:1 went to Gerar, to Abimelech king of the P
26:8 Abimelech king of the P looked out of a
26:14 household, so that the P envied him.
26:15 (Now the P had stopped and filled with earth
26:18 his father; for the P had stopped them after
Ex 13:17 the land of the P, although that was near;
23:31 the sea of the P, and from the wilderness
Josh 13:2 the regions of the P, and all those of
13:3 five rulers of the P, those of Gaza, Ashdod,
Judg 3:3 five lords of the P, and all the Canaanites,
3:31 six hundred of the P with an oxgoad; and
10:6 the gods of the P; and they forsook the
10:7 the hand of the P and into the hand
10:11 the Amorites, from the Ammonites and from the P
13:1 the hand of the P for forty years.
13:5 to deliver Israel from the hand of the P
14:1 he saw one of the daughters of the P
14:2 the daughters of the P at Timnah; now get
14:3 go to take a wife from the uncircumcised P
14:4 for he was seeking an occasion against the P
14:4 At that time the P had dominion over Israel.
15:3 in regard to the P, when I do them
15:5 standing grain of the P, and burned up the
15:6 Then the P said, "Who has done this?" And
15:6 And the P came up, and burned her and
15:9 Then the P came up and encamped in Judah,
15:11 not know that the P are rulers over us?
15:12 may give you into the hands of the P
15:14 came to Lehi, the P came shouting to meet
15:20 the days of the P twenty years.
16:5 the lords of the P came to her and
16:8 the lords of the P brought her seven fresh
16:9 said to him, "The P are upon you, Samson!"
16:12 said to him, "The P are upon you, Samson!"
16:14 said to him, "The P are upon you, Samson!"
16:18 the lords of the P, saying, "Come up this
16:18 the lords of the P came up to her,
16:20 And she said, "The P are upon you, Samson!"
16:21 And the P seized him and gouged out his
16:23 the lords of the P gathered to offer a
16:27 the lords of the P were there, and on
16:28 be avenged upon the P for one of my
16:30 And Samson said, "Let me die with the P
1Sam 4:1 to battle against the P; they encamped at Ebenezer,
4:1 at Ebenezer, and the P encamped at Aphek.
4:2 The P drew up in line against Israel, and
4:2 was defeated by the P, who slew about four
4:3 LORD put us to rout today before the P
4:6 And when the P heard the noise of the
4:7 to the camp, the P were afraid; for they
4:9 yourselves like men, O P, lest you become slaves
4:10 So the P fought, and Israel was defeated, and
4:17 has fled before the P, and there has also
5:1 When the P captured the ark of God, they
5:2 to Ashdod; then the P took the ark of
5:8 the lords of the P, and said, "What shall
5:11 the lords of the P, and said, "Send away
6:1 the country of the P seven months.
6:2 And the P called for the priests and the
6:4 the lords of the P; for the same plague
6:12 the lords of the P went after them as
6:16 five lords of the P saw it, they returned
6:17 golden tumors, which the P returned as a guilt
6:18 the cities of the P belonging to the five
6:21 Kiriath-jearim, saying, "The P have returned the ark
7:3 deliver you out of the hand of the P
7:7 Now when the P heard that the people of
7:7 the lords of the P went up against Israel.
7:7 heard of it they were afraid of the P
7:8 may save us from the hand of the P
7:10 the burnt offering, the P drew near to attack
7:10 that day against the P and threw them into
7:11 Mizpah and pursued the P, and smote them, as
7:13 So the P were subdued and did not again
7:13 LORD was against the P all the days of
7:14 The cities which the P had taken from Israel
7:14 rescued their territory from the hand of the P
9:16 the hand of the P; for I have seen
10:5 a garrison of the P; and there, as you
12:9 the hand of the P, and into the hand
13:3 the garrison of the P which was at Geba;
13:3 at Geba; and the P heard of it.
13:4 the garrison of the P, and also that Israel
13:4 also that Israel had become odious to the P
13:5 And the P mustered to fight with Israel, thirty
13:11 appointed, and that the P had mustered at
13:12 I said, 'Now the P will come down upon
13:16 of Benjamin; but the P encamped in Michmash.
13:17 the camp of the P in three companies; one
13:19 of Israel; for the P said, "Lest the Hebrews
13:20 went down to the P to sharpen his plowshare,
13:23 the garrison of the P went out to the
14:11 the garrison of the P; and the Philistines said,
14:11 the Philistines; and the P said, "Look, Hebrews are
14:19 the camp of the P increased more and more;
14:21 had been with the P before that time and
14:22 Ephraim heard that the P were fleeing, they too
14:30 the slaughter among the P has not been great."
14:31 They struck down the P that day from Michmash
14:36 go down after the P by night and despoil
14:37 of God, "Shall I go down after the P
14:46 up from pursuing the P; and the Philistines went
14:46 the Philistines; and the P went to their own
14:47 Zobah, and against the P; wherever he turned he
14:52 hard fighting against the P all the days of
17:1 Now the P gathered their armies for battle; and
17:2 drew up in line of battle against the P
17:3 And the P stood on the mountain on the
17:4 the camp of the P a champion named Goliath,
17:19 in the valley of Elah, fighting with the P
17:21 And Israel and the P drew up for battle,
17:23 the ranks of the P, and spoke the same
17:46 the host of the P this day to the
17:51 When the P saw that their champion was dead,
17:52 shout and pursued the P as far as Gath
17:52 so that the wounded P fell on the way
17:53 back from chasing the P, and they plundered their
18:17 the hand of the P be upon him."
18:21 the hand of the P may be against him."
18:25 hundred foreskins of the P, that he may be
18:25 make David fall by the hand of the P
18:27 two hundred of the P; and David brought their
18:30 the princes of the P came out to battle,
19:8 and fought with the P, and made a great
23:1 told David, "Behold, the P are fighting against
23:2 the LORD, "Shall I go and attack these P
23:2 "Go and attack the P and save Keilah."
23:3 go to Keilah against the armies of the P
23:4 I will give the P into your hand."
23:5 and fought with the P, and brought away their

23:27 and come; for the P have made a raid
23:28 and went against the P; therefore that place was
24:1 returned from following the P, he was told, "Behold,
27:1 the land of the P; then Saul will despair
27:7 the country of the P was a year and
27:11 while he dwelt in the country of the P
28:1 In those days the P gathered their forces for
28:4 The P assembled, and came and encamped at
28:5 the army of the P, he was afraid, and
28:15 great distress; for the P are warring against me,
28:19 the hand of the P; and tomorrow you and
28:19 of Israel also into the hand of the P
29:1 Now the P gathered all their forces at Aphek;
29:2 the lords of the P were passing on by
29:3 the commanders of the P said, "What are these
29:3 the commanders of the P, "Is not this David,
29:4 the commanders of the P were angry with him;
29:4 the commanders of the P said to him, "Send
29:7 you may not displease the lords of the P
29:9 the commanders of the P have said, 'He shall
29:11 morning, to return to the land of the P
29:11 But the P went up to Jezreel.
30:16 the land of the P and from the land
31:1 Now the P fought against Israel; and the men
31:1 Israel fled before the P, and fell slain on
31:2 And the P overtook Saul and his sons; and
31:2 his sons; and the P slew Jonathan and Abinadab
31:7 and fled; and the P came and dwelt in
31:8 the morrow, when the P came to strip the
31:9 the land of the P, to carry the good
31:11 Jabesh-gilead heard what the P had done to Saul,
2Sam 1:20 the daughters of the P rejoice, lest the daughters
3:14 the price of a hundred foreskins of the P
3:18 the hand of the P, and from the hand
5:17 When the P heard that David had been anointed
5:17 over Israel, all the P went up in search
5:18 Now the P had come and spread out in
5:19 the LORD, "Shall I go up against the P
5:19 will certainly give the P into your hand."
5:21 And the P left their idols there, and David
5:22 And the P came up yet again, and spread
5:24 before you to smite the army of the P
5:25 him, and smote the P from Geba to Gezer.
8:1 this David defeated the P and subdued them, and
8:1 took Metheg-ammah out of the hand of the P
8:12 Moab, the Ammonites, the P, Amalek, and from the
19:9 the hand of the P; and now he has
21:12 of Beth-shan, where the P had hanged them, on
21:12 on the day the P killed Saul on Gilboa;
21:15 The P had war again with Israel, and David
21:15 they fought against the P; and David grew weary.
21:18 again war with the P at Gob; then Sibbecai
21:19 again war with the P at Gob; and Elhanan
23:9 when they defied the P who were gathered there
23:10 and struck down the P until his hand was
23:11 The P gathered together at Lehi, where there was
23:11 of lentils; and the men fled from the P
23:12 it, and slew the P; and the LORD wrought
23:13 when a band of P was encamped in the
23:14 the garrison of the P was then at Bethlehem.
23:16 the camp of the P, and drew water out
1Kgs 4:21 the land of the P and to the border
15:27 which belonged to the P; for Nadab and all
16:15 which belonged to the P,
2Kgs 8:2 the land of the P seven years.
8:3 the land of the P, she went forth to
18:8 He smote the P as far as Gaza and
1Chr 1:12 Casluhim (whence came the P, and Caphtorim.
10:1 Now the P fought against Israel; and the men
10:1 Israel fled before the P, and fell slain on
10:2 And the P overtook Saul and his sons; and
10:2 his sons; and the P slew Jonathan and Abinadab
10:7 and fled; and the P came and dwelt in
10:8 the morrow, when the P came to strip the
10:9 the land of the P, to carry the good
10:11 heard all that the P had done to Saul,
11:13 at Pas-dammim when the P were gathered there for
11:13 of barley, and the men fled from the P
11:14 it, and slew the P; and the LORD saved
11:15 when the army of P was encamped in the
11:16 the garrison of the P was then at Bethlehem.
11:18 the camp of the P, and drew water out
12:19 he came with the P for the battle against
12:19 the rulers of the P took counsel and sent
14:8 When the P heard that David had been anointed
14:8 all Israel, all the P went up in search
14:9 Now the P had come and made a raid
14:10 of God, "Shall I go up against the P
14:13 And the P yet again made a raid in
14:15 before you to smite the army of the P
18:1 this David defeated the P and subdued them, and
18:1 its villages out of the hand of the P
18:11 Moab, the Ammonites, the P, and Amalek.
20:4 arose war with the P at Gezer; then Sibbecai
20:4 the giants; and the P were subdued.
20:5 again war with the P; and Elhanan the son
2Chr 9:26 the land of the P, and to the border
17:11 Some of the P brought Jehoshaphat presents, and
21:16 the anger of the P and of the Arabs
26:6 made war against the P, and broke down the
26:6 the territory of Ashdod and elsewhere among the P
26:7 helped him against the P, and against the Arabs
28:18 And the P had made raids on the cities
Sir 46:18 of Tyre and all the rulers of the P
47:7 annihilated his adversaries the P; he crushed their
50:26 Mount Seir, and the P, and the foolish people
Is 2:6 of soothsayers like the P, and they strike hands
9:12 the east and the P on the west devour
11:14 the shoulder of the P in the west, and
Jer 25:20 the land of the P (Ashkelon, Gaza, Ekron, and
47:1 the prophet concerning the P, before Pharaoh smote
47:4 to destroy all the P, to cut off from
47:4 LORD is destroying the P, the remnant of the
Ezek 16:27 the daughters of the P, who were ashamed of
16:57 the daughters of the P, those round about who
25:15 Lord GOD: Because the P acted revengefully and
25:16 my hand against the P, and I will cut
Amos 1:8 the remnant of the P shall perish," says the
6:2 great; then go down to Gath of the P
9:7 of Egypt, and the P from Caphtor and the
Obad 1:19 the land of the P; they shall possess the
Zeph 2:5 Canaan, land of the P; and I will destroy
1Mac 3:24 the rest fled into the land of the P
3:41 the land of the P joined with them.
4:22 they all fled into the land of the P
4:30 the camp of the P into the hands of
5:66 the land of the P, and passed through Marisa.
5:68 the land of the P; he tore down their

PHILOLOGUS

Rom 16:15 Greet P, Julia, Nereus and his sister, and Olympas,

PHILOMETOR (4)

2Mac 4:21 for the coronation of P as king, Antiochus learned
4:21 king, Antiochus learned that P had become hostile to
9:29 betook himself to Ptolemy P in Egypt.
10:13 had abandoned Cyprus, which P had entrusted to

PHILOSOPHERS

Acts 17:18 the Epicurean and Stoic P met him.

PHILOSOPHY

Col 2:8 prey of you by P and empty deceit, according

PHINEHAS (28)

Ex 6:25 the daughters of Puti-el; and she bore him P
Num 25:7 When P the son of Eleazar, son of Aaron
25:11 LORD said to Moses, P the son of Eleazar,
31:6 each tribe, together with P the son of Eleazar
Josh 22:13 the land of Gilead, P the son of Eleazar
22:30 When P the priest and the chiefs of the
22:31 And P the son of Eleazar the priest said
22:32 Then P the son of Eleazar the priest, and
24:33 Gibe-ah, the town of P his son, which had
Judg 20:28 in those days, and P the son of Eleazar,
1Sam 1:3 of Eli, Hophni and P, were priests of the
2:34 two sons, Hophni and P, shall be the sign
4:4 of Eli, Hophni and P, were there with the
4:11 of Eli, Hophni and P, were slain.
4:17 sons also, Hophni and P, are dead, and the
4:19 daughter-in-law, the wife of P, was with child, about
14:3 Ichabod's brother, son of P, son of Eli, the
1Chr 6:4 was the father of P, Phinehas of Abishua,
6:4 the father of Phinehas, P of Abishua,
6:50 Aaron: Eleazar his son, P his son, Abishua his
9:20 And P the son of Eleazar was the ruler
Ezra 7:5 of Abishua, son of P, son of Eleazar, son
8:2 Of the sons of P, Gershom.
8:33 Eleazar the son of P, and with them were
Ps 106:30 Then P stood up and interposed, and the plague
Sir 45:23 P the son of Eleazar is the third in
1Mac 2:26 for the law, as P did against Zimri the

2:54 P our father, because he was deeply zealous,

PHLEGON

Rom 16:14 Greet Asyncritus, P, Hermes, Patrobas, Hermas, and

PHOEBE

Rom 16:1 to you our sister P, a deaconess of the

PHOENICIA (10)

Obad 1:20 of Israel shall possess P as far as Zarephath;
2Mac 3:5 at that time was governor of Coelesyria and P
3:8 cities of Coelesyria and P, but in fact to
4:4 governor of Coelesyria and P, was intensifying the
4:22 Then he marched into P
8:8 governor of Coelesyria and P, for aid to the
10:11 and to be chief governor of Coelesyria and P
Acts 11:19 traveled as far as P and Cyprus and Antioch,
15:3 they passed through both P and Samaria, reporting
21:2 a ship crossing to P, we went aboard, and

PHOENIX

Acts 27:12 somehow they could reach P, a harbor of Crete,

PHRASE

Heb 12:27 This P, "Yet once more," indicates the removal of

PHRASES

Mt 6:7 not heap up empty P as the Gentiles do;

PHRYGIA (3)

Acts 2:10 Pontus and Asia, P and Pamphylia, Egypt
16:6 through the region of P and Galatia, having been
18:23 of Galatia and P, strengthening all the disciples.

PHRYGIAN

2Mac 5:22 Philip, by birth a P and in character more

PHYGELUS

2Tim 1:15 me, and among them P and Hermogenes.

PHYLACTERIES

Mt 23:5 for they make their P broad and their fringes

PHYSICAL (4)

Rom 2:28 nor is true circumcision something external and P
1Cor 15:44 It is sown a P body, it is raised
15:44 If there is a P body, there is also
15:46 is first but the P, and then the spiritual.

PHYSICALLY

Rom 2:27 Then those who are P uncircumcised but keep the

PHYSICIAN (11)

Sir 10:10 long illness baffles the P; the king of today
38:1 Honor the P with the honor due him, according
38:3 The skill of the P lifts up his head,
38:12 And give the P his place, for the Lord
38:15 may he fall into the care of a P
Jer 8:22 Is there no P there?
Mt 9:12 no need of a P, but those who are
Mk 2:17 no need of a P, but those who are
Lk 4:23 to me this proverb, P, heal yourself; what we
5:31 no need of a P, but those who are
Col 4:14 Luke the beloved P and Demas greet you.

PHYSICIANS (8)

Gen 50:2 commanded his servants the P to embalm his father.
50:2 So the P embalmed Israel;
2Chr 16:12 not seek the LORD, but sought help from P
Tob 2:10 I went to P, but they did not help
Job 13:4 whitewash with lies; worthless P are you all.
Sir 38:13 in the hands of P,
Mk 5:26 suffered much under many P, and had spent all
Lk 8:43 all her living upon P, and could not be

PI-HA-HIROTH (2)

Ex 14:2 encam in front of P, between Migdol and the
14:9 at the sea, by P, in front of Baal-zephon.

PI-HAHIROTH

Num 33:7 and turned back to P, which is east of

PIBESETH

Ezek 30:17 of On and of P shall fall by the

PICK (6)

Judg 1:7 cut off used to P up scraps under my
Job 30:4 and desolate ground; they P mallow and the leaves
Ezek 17:21 And all the P of his troops shall fall
2Mac 9:15 for the birds to P, he would make, all
Mk 16:18 new tongues; they will P up serpents, and if
Acts 6:3 Therefore, brethren, P out from among you seven

PICKED (26)

Ex 14:7 and took six hundred P chariots and all the
15:4 the sea; and his P officers are sunk in
Judg 20:15 who mustered seven hundred P men.
20:16 were seven hundred P men who were left-handed;
20:34 against Gibe-ah ten thousand P men out of all
2Sam 10:9 chose some of the P men of Israel, and
1Chr 19:10 chose some of the P men of Israel, and
2Chr 13:3 war, four hundred thousand P men; and Jeroboam
13:3 with eight hundred thousand P mighty warriors.
13:17 Israel five hundred thousand P men.
25:5 were three hundred thousand P men, fit for war,
Jud 2:15 army, and mustered the P troops by divisions as
2:19 chariots and horsemen and P troops of infantry.
3:6 hilltop cities and took P men from them as
Ps 78:31 and laid low the P men of Israel.
Prov 30:17 a mother will be P out by the ravens
Dan 11:15 stand, or even his P troops, for there shall
1Mac 4:1 infantry and a thousand P cavalry, and this division
4:28 he mustered sixty thousand P infantrymen and five
6:35 heads; and five hundred P horsemen were assigned
9:5 him were three thousand P men.
12:41 him with forty thousand P fighting men, and he
15:26 to Antiochus two thousand P men, to fight for
2Mac 4:41 of Lysimachus' attack, some P up stones, some
13:15 and with a P force of the bravest young
Lk 6:44 thorns, nor are grapes P from a bramble bush.

PICKS (3)

2Sam 12:31 with saws and iron P and iron axes, and
1Chr 20:3 with saws and iron P and axes; and thus
Sir 22:2 dunghills; any one that P it up will shake

PICTURE

Ezek 23:15 looking like officers, a P of Babylonians whose

PICTURES

Ezek 8:12 the dark, every man in his room of P

PIECE (42)

Gen 23:15 listen to me; a P of land worth four
33:19 pieces of money the P of land on which
Ex 25:19 other end; of one P with the mercy seat
25:31 shall be of one P with it;
25:35 a capital of one P with it under each
25:36 shall be of one P with it, the whole
25:36 whole of it one P of hammered work of
27:2 shall be of one P with it, and you
30:2 shall be of one P with it.
37:8 other end; of one P with the mercy seat
37:17 flowers were of one P with it.
37:21 a capital of one P with it under each
37:22 branches were of one P with it; the whole
37:22 of it was one P of hammered work of
37:25 horns were of one P with it.
38:2 horns were of one P with it, and he
Lev 9:13 burnt offering to him, P by piece, and the
9:13 to him, piece by P, and the head; and
1Sam 2:36 implore him for a P of silver or a
30:12 they gave him a P of a cake of
1Kgs 7:32 wheels were of one P with the stands; and
7:34 supports were of one P with the stands.
7:35 panels were of one P with it.
2Kgs 3:19 and ruin every good P of land with stones."
3:25 and on every good P of land every man
Job 33:6 was formed from a P of clay.
42:11 them gave him a P of money and a
Prov 28:21 good; but for a P of bread a man
Wis 10:4 man by a paltry P of wood.
13:13 But a castoff P from among them, useful for
14:1 waves calls upon a P of wood more fragile
14:5 even to the smallest P of wood, and passing
Sir 22:13 Sand, salt, and a P of iron are easier
Ezek 24:6 Take out of it P after piece, without making
24:6 of it piece after P, without making any choice.
Amos 3:12 two legs, or a P of an ear, so
Mt 9:16 no one puts a P of unshrunk cloth on
Mk 2:21 No one sews a P of unshrunk cloth on

Lk 5:36 "No one tears a P from a new garment
5:36 the new, and the P from the new will
24:42 They gave him a P of broiled fish,
Acts 5:1 wife Sapphira sold a P of property,

PIECEMEAL

2Mac 15:33 he would give it P to the birds and

PIECES (128)

Gen 15:17 pot and a flaming torch passed between these P
20:16 your brother a thousand P of silver; it is
33:19 bought for a hundred P of money the piece
37:33 devoured him; Joseph is without doubt torn to P
44:28 has been torn to P; and I have never
Ex 23:24 utterly overthrow them and break their pillars in P
29:17 cut the ram into P, and wash its entrails
29:17 put them with its P and its head,
Lev 1:6 and cut it into P;
1:8 priests shall lay the P, the head, and the
1:12 shall cut it into P, with its head and
2:6 shall break it in P, and pour oil on
6:21 well mixed, in baked P like a cereal offering,
8:20 ram was cut into P, Moses burned the head
8:20 the head and the P and the fat.
11:35 shall be broken in P; they are unclean, and
Num 24:8 break their bones in P, and pierce them through
Deut 7:5 altars, and dash in P their pillars, and hew
12:3 altars, and dash in P their pillars, and burn
Josh 24:32 Shechem for a hundred P of money; it became
Judg 5:30 dyed stuffs embroidered, two P of dyed work
9:4 they gave him seventy P of silver out of
16:5 give you eleven hundred P of silver."
17:2 mother, "The eleven hundred P of silver which were
17:3 restored the eleven hundred P of silver to his
17:4 mother took two hundred P of silver, and gave
17:10 will give you ten P of silver a year,
19:29 by limb, into twelve P, and sent her throughout
20:6 and cut her in P, and sent her throughout
1Sam 2:10 shall be broken to P; against them he will
11:7 and cut them in P and sent them throughout
15:33 Samuel hewed Agag in P before the LORD in
2Sam 18:11 to give you ten P of silver and a
18:12 weight of a thousand P of silver, I would
1Kgs 8:64 offering and the fat P of the peace offerings,
8:64 offering and the fat P of the peace offerings.
11:30 was on him, and tore it into twelve P
11:31 "Take for yourself ten P; for thus says the
18:23 and cut it in P and lay it on
18:33 cut the bull in P and laid it on
19:11 mountains, and broke in P the rocks before the
2Kgs 2:12 his own clothes and rent them in two P
8:12 sword, and dash in P their little ones, and
11:18 images they broke in P, and they slew Mattan
18:4 And he broke in P the bronze serpent that
23:12 down and broke in P, and cast the dust
23:14 And he broke in P the pillars, and cut
23:15 and he broke in P its stones, crushing them
24:13 house, and cut in P all the vessels of
25:13 the Chaldeans broke in P, and carried the bronze
2Chr 15:6 They were broken in P, nation against nation and
23:17 images they broke in P, and they slew Mattan
25:12 the rock; and they were all dashed to P
28:24 God and cut in P the vessels of the
31:1 Judah and broke in P the pillars and hewed
34:4 and he broke in P the Asherim and the
Job 16:12 and dashed me to P; he set me up
19:2 and break me in P with words?
Ps 2:9 and dash them in P like a potter's vessel."
119:72 to me than thousands of gold and silver P
Song 8:11 its fruit a thousand P of silver.
Wis 13:12 and burn the castoff P of his work to
Sir 6:2 soul be torn in P like a bull.
43:15 the clouds, and the hailstones are broken in P
Is 7:8 will be broken to P so that it will
13:16 will be dashed in P before their eyes; their
27:9 like chalkstones crushed to P, no Asherim or incense
45:2 I will break in P the doors of bronze
51:9 didst cut Rahab in P, that didst pierce the
Jer 5:6 shall be torn in P; because their transgressions are
23:29 like a hammer which breaks the rock in P
48:12 empty his vessels, and break his jars in P
51:20 I break nations in P; with you I destroy
51:21 you I break in P the horse and his
51:21 you I break in P the chariot and the
51:22 you I break in P man and woman; with
51:22 you I break in P the old man and
51:22 you I break in P the young man and
51:23 you I break in P the shepherd and his
51:23 you I break in P the farmer and his
51:23 you I break in P governors and commanders.
51:56 bows are broken in P; for the LORD is
52:17 the Chaldeans broke in P, and carried all the
Lam 3:11 and tore me to P; he has made me
Ezek 13:19 of barley and for P of bread, putting to
16:40 and cut you to P with their swords.
24:4 put in it the P of flesh, all the
24:4 flesh, all the good P, the thigh and the
24:5 under it; boil its P, seethe also its bones
Dan 2:34 and broke them in P;
2:35 together were broken in P, and became like the
2:40 because iron breaks to P and shatters all things;
2:44 It shall break in P all these kingdoms and
2:45 that it broke in P the iron, the bronze,
6:24 overpowered them and broke all their bones in P
7:7 devoured and broke in P, and stamped the residue
7:19 devoured and broke in P, and stamped the residue
7:23 and trample it down, and break it to P
Hos 8:6 The calf of Samaria shall be broken to P
10:14 mothers were dashed in P with their children.
13:16 shall be dashed in P, and their pregnant women
Mic 1:7 shall be beaten to P, all her hires shall
3:3 break their bones in P, and chop them up
4:13 you shall beat in P many peoples, and shall
5:8 down and tears in P, and there is none
Nah 3:10 ones were dashed in P at the head of
1Mac 1:56 found they tore to P and burned with fire.
2Mac 1:13 they were cut to P in the temple of
10:30 they were thrown into disorder and cut to P
Mt 14:20 full of the broken P left over.
15:37 full of the broken P left over.
21:44 will be broken to P; but when it falls
26:15 they paid him thirty P of silver.
27:3 brought back the thirty P of silver to the
27:5 And throwing down the P of silver in the
27:6 chief priests, taking the P of silver, said, "It
27:9 they took the thirty P of silver, the price
Mk 5:4 fetters he broke in P; and no one had
6:43 baskets full of broken P and of the fish.
8:8 took up the broken P left over, seven baskets
8:19 baskets full of broken P did you take up?"
8:20 baskets full of broken P did you take up?"
Lk 9:17 what was left over, twelve baskets of broken P
20:18 will be broken to P; but when it falls
Acts 19:19 came to fifty thousand P of silver.
23:10 would be torn in P by them, commanded the
27:44 on planks or on P of the ship.
Rev 2:27 pots are broken in P, even as I myself

PIERCE (10)

Num 24:8 bones in pieces, and P them through with his
2Kgs 18:21 a staff, which will P the hand of any
Jud 6:6 of my servants shall P your sides, and you
Job 40:24 him with hooks, or P his nose with a
41:2 in his nose, or P his jaw with a
Is 36:6 a staff, which will P the hand of any
51:9 in pieces, that didst P the dragon?
Hab 3:14 Selah Thou didst P with thy shafts the head
Zech 13:3 who bore him shall P him through when he
Lk 2:35 (and a sword will P through your own soul

PIERCED (14)

Num 25:8 the inner room, and P both of them, the
Judg 5:26 head, she shattered and P his temple.
2Kgs 9:24 so that the arrow P his heart, and he
Jud 16:12 sons of maidservants have P them through; they
Job 26:13 made fair; his hand P the fleeing serpent.
Ps 22:16 encircle me; they have P my hands and feet--
Wis 5:11 of its pinions and P by the force of
Is 14:19 with the slain, those P by the sword, who
Zech 12:10 him whom they have P, they shall mourn for
2Mac 12:22 their own men and P by the points of
Jn 19:34 one of the soldiers P his side with a
19:37 "They shall look on him whom they have P
1Tim 6:10 from the faith and P their hearts with many
Rev 1:7 him, every one who P him; and all tribes

PIERCES (2)

Prov 7:23 fast till an arrow P its entrails; as a
Sir 35:17 prayer of the humble P the clouds, and he

PIERCING

Heb 4:12 than any two-edged sword, P to the division of

P

PIETY (4)

2Mac 3:1 observed because of the P of the high priest
6:11 burned together, because their P kept them from
Mt 6:1 "Beware of practicing your P before men in order
Acts 3:12 our own power or P we had made him

PIGEON (2)

Gen 15:9 three years old, a turtledove, and a young P
Lev 12:6 offering, and a young P or a turtledove for

PIGEONS (14)

Lev 1:14 bring his offering of turtledoves or of young P
5:7 turtledoves or two young P, one for a sin
5:11 turtledoves or two young P, then he shall bring,
12:8 turtledoves or two young P, one for a burnt
14:22 turtledoves or two young P, such as he can
14:30 the turtledoves or young P such as he can
15:14 turtledoves or two young P, and come before the
15:29 turtledoves or two young P, and bring them to
Num 6:10 turtledoves or two young P to the priest to
Mt 21:12 money-changers and the seats of those who sold P
Mk 11:15 of those who sold P;
Lk 2:24 Lord, "a pair of turtledoves, or two young P
Jn 2:14 oxen and sheep and P, and the money-changers at
2:16 those who sold the P, "Take these things away;

PILATE (56)

Mt 27:2 and delivered him to P the governor.
27:13 Then P said to him, "Do you not hear
27:17 when they had gathered, P said to them, "Whom
27:22 P said to them, "Then what shall I do
27:24 So when P saw that he was gaining nothing,
27:58 He went to P and asked for the body
27:58 Then P ordered it to be given to him.
27:62 the Pharisees gathered before P
27:65 P said to them, "You have a guard of
Mk 15:1 and led him away and delivered him to P
15:2 And P asked him, "Are you the King of
15:4 And P again asked him, "Have you no answer
15:5 further answer, so that P wondered.
15:8 and began to ask P to do as he
15:12 And P again said to them, "Then what shall
15:14 And P said to them, "Why, what evil has
15:15 So P, wishing to satisfy the crowd, released for
15:42 courage and went to P, and asked for the
15:43 And P wondered if he were already dead; and
Lk 3:1 of Tiberi-us Caesar, Pontius P being governor of
13:1 the Galileans whose blood P had mingled with their
23:1 company of them arose, and brought him before P
23:3 And P asked him, "Are you the King of
23:4 And P said to the chief priests and the
23:6 When P heard this, he asked whether the man
23:11 in gorgeous apparel, he sent him back to P
23:12 And Herod and P became friends with each other
23:13 P then called together the chief priests and the
23:19 P addressed them once more, desiring to release
23:23 So P gave sentence that their demand should be
23:51 This man went to P and asked for the
Jn 18:29 So P went out to them and said, "What
18:31 P said to them, "Take him yourselves and judge
18:33 P entered the praetorium again and called Jesus,
18:35 P answered, "Am I a Jew?
18:37 P said to him, "So you are a king?"
18:38 P said to him, "What is truth?" After he
19:1 Then P took Jesus and scourged him.
19:4 P went out again, and said to them, "See,
19:5 P said to them, "Behold the man!"
19:6 P said to them, "Take him yourselves and crucify
19:8 When P heard these words, he was the more
19:10 P therefore said to him, "You will not speak
19:12 Upon this P sought to release him, but the
19:13 When P heard these words, he brought Jesus out
19:15 P said to them, "Shall I crucify your King?"
19:19 P also wrote a title and put it on
19:21 Jews then said to P, "Do not write, 'The
19:22 P answered, "What I have written I have written."
19:31 day), the Jews asked P that their legs might
19:38 of the Jews, asked P that he might take
19:38 body of Jesus, and P gave him leave.
Acts 3:13 in the presence of P, when he had decided
4:27 both Herod and Pontius P, with the Gentiles and
13:28 death, yet they asked P to have him killed.
1Tim 6:13 his testimony before Pontius P made the good

PILDASH

Gen 22:22 of Aram, Chesed, Hazo, P, Jidlaph, and Bethuel."

PILE (6)

2Chr 31:7 month they began to P up the heaps, and
Job 27:16 silver like dust, and P up clothing like clay;
27:17 like clay; he may P it up, but the
Jer 50:26 quarter; open her granaries; P her up like heaps
Ezek 24:5 one of the flock, P the logs under it;
24:9 also will make the P great.

PILED (3)

Ex 15:8 thy nostrils the waters P up, the floods stood
Jud 15:11 up her carts and P the things on them.
1Mac 11:4 war, for they had P them in heaps along

PILFER

Tit 2:10 be refractory, nor to P, but to show entire

PILGRIMAGE

Ps 119:54 been my songs in the house of my P

PILHA

Neh 10:24 Hoshea, Hananiah, Hasshub, Hallohesh, P, Shobek,

PILLAGED

Obad 1:6 How Esau has been P, his treasures sought out!

PILLAR (61)

Gen 19:26 and she became a P of salt.
28:18 it up for a P and poured oil on
28:22 set up for a P, shall be God's house;
31:13 where you anointed a P and made a vow
31:45 a stone, and set it up as a P
31:49 it Galeed, and the P Mizpah, for he said,
31:51 this heap and the P, which I have set
31:52 a witness, and the P is a witness, that
31:52 this heap and this P to me, for harm.
35:14 Jacob set up a P in the place where
35:14 spoken with him, a P of stone; and he
35:20 Jacob set up a P upon her grave; it
35:20 grave; it is the P of Rachel's tomb, which
Ex 13:21 by day in a P of cloud to lead
13:21 by night in a P of fire to give
13:22 and by night; the P of cloud by day
13:22 by day and the P of fire by night
14:19 behind them; and the P of cloud moved from
14:24 the LORD in the P of fire and of
33:9 entered the tent, the P of cloud would descend
33:10 the people saw the P of cloud standing at
Lev 26:1 no graven image or P, and you shall not
Num 12:5 came down in a P of cloud, and stood
14:14 before them, in a P of cloud by day
14:14 day and in a P of fire by night.
Deut 16:22 not set up a P, which the LORD your
31:15 the tent in a P of cloud; and the
31:15 of cloud; and the P of cloud stood by
Judg 9:6 the oak of the P at Shechem.
2Sam 18:18 up for himself the P which is in the
18:18 remembrance"; he called the P after his own name,
1Kgs 7:15 the height of one P, and a line of
7:15 four fingers; the second P was the same.
7:18 the top of the P; and he did the
7:21 he set up the P on the south and
7:21 he set up the P on the north and
2Kgs 3:2 he put away the P of Baal which his
10:26 they brought out the P that was in the
10:27 And they demolished the P of Baal, and demolished
11:14 king standing by the P, according to the custom,
23:3 king stood by the P and made a covenant
25:17 height of the one P was eighteen cubits, and
25:17 And the second P had the like, with the
2Chr 23:13 king standing by his P at the entrance, and
Neh 9:12 By a P of cloud thou didst lead them
9:12 day, and by a P of fire in the
9:19 in the wilderness; the P of cloud which led
9:19 by day, nor the P of fire by night
Ps 99:7 to them in the P of cloud; they kept
Wis 10:7 not ripen, and a P of salt standing as
18:3 didst provide a flaming P of fire as a
Sir 24:4 throne was in a P of cloud.
36:24 for him and a P of support.
Is 19:19 of Egypt, and a P to the LORD at
Jer 1:18 fortified city, an iron P, and bronze walls, against
52:21 height of the one P was eighteen cubits, its
52:22 And the second P had the like, with pomegranates.
Bar 6:59 better also a wooden P in a palace, than
Hos 3:4 prince, without sacrifice or P, without ephod or
1Tim 3:15 the living God, the P and bulwark of the

P

Rev 3:12 will make him a P in the temple of

PILLARS (98)

Ex 23:24 them and break their P in pieces.
24:4 the mountain, and twelve P, according to the twelve
26:32 hang it upon four P of acacia overlaid with
26:37 for the screen five P of acacia, and overlay
27:10 for one side; their P shall be twenty and
27:10 the hooks of the P and their fillets shall
27:11 hundred cubits long, their P twenty and their bases
27:11 the hooks of the P and their fillets shall
27:12 fifty cubits, with ten P and ten bases.
27:14 fifteen cubits, with three P and three bases.
27:15 fifteen cubits, with three P and three bases.
27:16 it shall have four P and with them four
27:17 All the P around the court shall be filleted
34:13 altars, and break their P, and cut down their
35:11 frames, its bars, its P, and its bases;
35:17 of the court, its P and its bases, and
36:36 it he made four P of acacia, and overlaid
36:38 needlework; and its five P with their hooks.
38:10 a hundred cubits; their P were twenty and their
38:10 the hooks of the P and their fillets were
38:11 a hundred cubits, their P twenty, their bases twenty,
38:11 the hooks of the P and their fillets were
38:12 of fifty cubits, their P ten, and their sockets
38:12 the hooks of the P and their fillets were
38:14 fifteen cubits, with three P and three bases.
38:15 fifteen cubits, with three P and three bases.
38:17 the bases for the P were of bronze, but
38:17 the hooks of the P and their fillets were
38:17 silver, and all the P of the court were
38:19 And their P were four; their four bases were
38:28 made hooks for the P, and overlaid their capitals
39:33 frames, its bars, its P, and its bases;
39:40 of the court, its P, and its bases, and
Num 3:36 tabernacle, the bars, the P, the bases, and all
3:37 to these; also the P of the court round
4:31 tabernacle, with its bars, P, and bases,
4:32 and bases, and the P of the court round
Deut 7:5 dash in pieces their P, and hew down their
12:3 dash in pieces their P, and burn their Asherim
Judg 16:25 him stand between the P;
16:26 "Let me feel the P on which the house
16:29 grasped the two middle P upon which the house
1Sam 2:8 For the P of the earth are the LORDS,
1Kgs 7:2 three rows of cedar P, with cedar beams upon
7:2 of cedar pillars, with cedar beams upon the P
7:3 were upon the forty-five P, fifteen in each row.
7:6 made the Hall of P; its length was fifty
7:6 porch in front with P, and a canopy before
7:15 He cast two P of bronze.
7:16 the tops of the P; the height of the
7:17 the tops of the P; a net for the
7:19 the tops of the P in the vestibule were
7:20 were upon the two P and also above the
7:21 He set up the P at the vestibule of
7:22 the tops of the P was lily-work.
7:22 the work of the P was finished.
7:41 the LORD: the two P, the two bowls of
7:41 the tops of the P, and the two networks
7:41 the tops of the P;
7:42 that were upon the P;
14:23 themselves high places, and P, and Asherim on every
2Kgs 17:10 set up for themselves P and Asherim on every
18:4 places, and broke the P, and cut down the
23:14 broke in pieces the P, and cut down the
25:13 And the P of bronze that were in the
25:16 As for the two P, the one sea, and
1Chr 18:8 bronze sea and the P and the vessels of
2Chr 3:15 house he made two P thirty-five cubits high, with
3:16 the tops of the P; and he made a
3:17 He set up the P in front of the
4:12 of God: the two P, the bowls, and the
4:12 the top of the P; and the two networks
4:12 the top of the P;
4:13 bowls of the capitals that were upon the P
14:3 and broke down the P and hewed down the
31:1 broke in pieces the P and hewed down the
Esth 1:6 silver rings and marble P, and also couches of
Job 9:6 its place, and its P tremble;
26:11 The P of heaven tremble, and are astounded at
Ps 75:3 inhabitants, it is I who keep steady its P
144:12 our daughters like corner P cut for the structure
Prov 9:1 her house, she has set up her seven P
Sir 26:18 Like P of gold on a base of silver,
Is 19:10 Those who are the P of the land will
Jer 27:19 of hosts concerning the P, the sea, the stands,
52:17 And the P of bronze that were in the
52:20 As for the two P, the one sea, the
52:21 As for the P, the height of the one
Ezek 26:11 sword; and your mighty P will fall to the
40:49 it; and there were P beside the jambs on
42:6 and they had no P like the pillars of
42:6 no pillars like the P of the outer court;
Hos 10:1 built; as his country improved he improved his P
10:2 will break down their altars, and destroy their P
Mic 5:13 your images and your P from among you, and
1Mac 14:27 and put it upon P on Mount Zion.
Gal 2:9 were reputed to be P, gave to me and
Rev 10:1 and his legs like P of fire.

PILLOW (2)

1Sam 19:13 bed and put a P of goats' hair at
19:16 the bed, with the P of goats' hair at

PILOT

Jas 3:4 the will of the P directs.

PILOTS (4)

Ezek 27:8 of Zemer were in you, they were your P
27:27 your mariners and your P, your caulkers, your dealers
27:28 the cry of your P the countryside shakes,
27:29 mariners and all the P of the sea stand

PILTAI

Neh 12:17 of Miniamin, of Moadiah, P;

PIM

1Sam 13:21 the charge was a P for the plowshares and

PIN (6)

Judg 16:13 it tight with the P, then I shall become
16:14 them tight with the P, and said to him,
16:14 and pulled away the P, the loom, and the
1Sam 18:11 he thought, "I will P David to the wall."
19:10 And Saul sought to P David to the wall
26:8 now therefore let me P him to the earth

PINE (9)

Lev 26:16 and cause life to P away.
26:39 that are left shall P away in your enemies'
26:39 their fathers they shall P away like them.
Song 1:17 of our house are cedar, our rafters are P
Is 24:16 But I say, "I P away, I pine away.
24:16 "I pine away, I P away.
41:19 the plane and the P together;
60:13 the plane, and the P, to beautify the place
Ezek 24:23 weep, but you shall P away in your iniquities

PINED (2)

Wis 1:16 him a friend, they P away, and they made
Lam 4:9 victims of hunger, who P away, stricken by want

PINES

Ezek 27:6 made your deck of P from the coasts of

PINIONS (6)

Deut 32:11 bearing them on its P,
Job 39:13 but are they the P and plumage of love?
Ps 68:13 covered with silver, its P with green gold.
91:4 cover you with his P, and under his wings
Wis 5:11 the beat of its P and pierced by the
Ezek 17:3 great wings and long P, rich in plumage of

PINNACLE (2)

Mt 4:5 set him on the P of the temple,
Lk 4:9 set him on the P of the temple, and

PINNACLES

Is 54:12 I will make your P of agate, your gates

PINON (2)

Gen 36:41 Alvah, Jetheth, Oholibamah, Elah, P,
1Chr 1:52 Aliah, Jetheth, Oholibamah, Elah, P,

PIONEER (2)

Heb 2:10 glory, should make the P of their salvation perfect
12:2 looking to Jesus the P and perfecter of our

PIOUS (2)

2Mac 1:19 captive to Persia, the P priests of that time

P

12:45 was a holy and P thought.

PIPE (8)

Gen 4:21 of all those who play the lyre and P
Job 21:12 lyre, and rejoice to the sound of the P
30:31 to mourning, and my P to the voice of
Ps 150:4 timbrel and dance; praise him with strings and P
Dan 3:5 sound of the horn, P, lyre, trigon, harp, bagpipe,
3:7 sound of the horn, P, lyre, trigon, harp, bagpipe,
3:10 sound of the horn, P, lyre, trigon, harp, bagpipe,
3:15 sound of the horn, P, lyre, trigon, harp, bagpipe,

PIPED (2)

Mt 11:17 to their playmates, 'We P to you, and you
Lk 7:32 to one another, 'We P to you, and you

PIPES (2)

1Kgs 1:40 after him, playing on P, and rejoicing with great
Zech 4:12 beside the two golden P from which the oil

PIPING

Judg 5:16 sheepfolds, to hear the P for the flocks?

PIRAM

Josh 10:3 king of Hebron, to P king of Jarmuth, to

PIRATHON (4)

Judg 12:15 and was buried at P in the land of
2Sam 23:30 the Benjaminites, Benaiah of P, Hiddai of the brooks
1Chr 11:31 the Benjaminites, Benaiah of P,
27:14 month, was Benaiah of P, of the sons of

PIRATHONITE (2)

Judg 12:13 son of Hillel the P judged Israel.
12:15 son of Hillel the P died, and was buried

PISGAH (8)

Num 21:20 by the top of P which looks down upon
23:14 to the top of P, and built seven altars,
Deut 3:17 under the slopes of P on the east.
3:27 to the top of P, and lift up your
4:49 Sea of the Arabah, under the slopes of P
34:1 to the top of P, which is opposite Jericho.
Josh 12:3 of the slopes of P;
13:20 and the slopes of P, and Beth-jeshimoth,

PISHON (2)

Gen 2:11 of the first is P; it is the one
Sir 24:23 with wisdom, like the P, and like the Tigris

P

PISIDIA (2)

Acts 13:14 on from Perga and came to Antioch of P
14:24 Then they passed through P, and came to Pamphylia.

PISPA

1Chr 7:38 sons of Jether: Jephunneh, P, and Ara.

PISTACHIO

Gen 43:11 little honey, gum, myrrh, P nuts, and almonds.

PIT (91)

Gen 37:22 cast him into this P here in the wilderness,
37:24 they took him and cast him into a P
37:24 The P was empty, there was no water in
37:28 him out of the P, and sold him to
37:29 Reuben returned to the P and saw that Joseph
37:29 was not in the P, he rent his clothes
Ex 21:33 a man leaves a P open, or when a
21:33 a man digs a P and does not cover
21:34 the owner of the P shall make it good;
2Sam 18:17 him into a great P in the forest, and
23:20 a lion in a P on a day when
2Kgs 10:14 slew them at the P of Beth-eked, forty-two persons,
1Chr 11:22 a lion in a P on a day when
Job 9:31 plunge me into a P, and my own clothes
17:14 I say to the P, 'You are my father,'
33:18 his soul from the P, his life from perishing
33:22 soul draws near the P, and his life to
33:24 going down into the P, I have found a
33:28 going down into the P, and my life shall
33:30 his soul from the P, that he may see
Ps 7:15 He makes a P, digging it out, and falls
9:15 have sunk in the P which they made; in
16:10 Sheol, or let thy godly one see the P
28:1 become like those who go down to the P
30:3 life from among those gone down to the P
30:9 my death, if I go down to the P
35:7 cause they dug a P for my life.
40:2 up from the desolate P, out of the miry
49:9 live on for ever, and never see the P
55:23 down into the lowest P; men of blood and
57:6 They dug a P in my way, but they
69:15 me up, or the P close its mouth over
88:4 go down to the P; I am a man
88:6 the depths of the P, in the regions dark
94:13 of trouble, until a P is dug for the
103:4 your life from the P, who crowns you with
143:7 be like those who go down to the P
Prov 1:12 go down to the P;
22:14 woman is a deep P; he with whom the
23:27 harlot is a deep P; an adventuress is a
26:27 He who digs a P will fall into it,
28:10 fall into his own P; but the blameless will
28:18 perverse in his ways will fall into a P
Eccl 10:8 He who digs a P will fall into it;
Sir 12:16 throw you into a P; an enemy will weep
21:10 its end is the P of Hades.
27:26 He who digs a P will fall into it,
Is 14:15 down to Sheol, to the depths of the P
14:19 the stones of the P, like a dead body
24:17 Terror, and the P, and the snare are upon
24:18 shall fall into the P; and he who climbs
24:18 climbs out of the P shall be caught in
24:22 as prisoners in a P; they will be shut
38:17 my life from the P of destruction, for thou
38:18 go down to the P cannot hope for thy
51:14 go down to the P, neither shall his bread
Jer 18:20 they have dug a P for my life.
18:22 they have dug a P to take me, and
48:43 Terror, P, and snare are before you, O inhabitant
48:44 shall fall into the P, and he who climbs
48:44 climbs out of the P shall be caught in
Lam 3:53 me alive into the P and cast stones on
3:55 the depths of the P;
Ezek 19:4 was taken in their P; and they brought him
19:8 net over him; he was taken in their P
26:20 who descend into the P, to the people of
26:20 go down to the P, so that you will
28:8 you down into the P, and you shall die
31:14 men, with those who go down to the P
31:16 go down to the P; and all the trees
32:18 gone down to the P:
32:23 uttermost parts of the P, and her company is
32:24 shame with those who go down to the P
32:25 go down to the P; they are placed among
32:29 uncircumcised, with those who go down to the P
32:30 shame with those who go down to the P
Hos 5:2 have made deep the P of Shittim; but I
Jon 2:6 my life from the P, O LORD my God.
Zech 9:11 will set your captives free from the waterless P
1Mac 7:19 killed them and threw them into a great P
Mt 12:11 it falls into a P on the sabbath, will
15:14 a blind man, both will fall into a P
Mk 12:1 it, and dug a P for the wine press,
Lk 6:39 Will they not both fall into a P
Rev 9:1 shaft of the bottomless P;
9:2 shaft of the bottomless P, and from the shaft
9:11 angel of the bottomless P; his name in Hebrew
11:7 ascends from the bottomless P will make war upon
17:8 ascend from the bottomless P and go to perdition;
20:1 key of the bottomless P and a great chain.
20:3 threw him into the P, and shut it and

PITCH (14)

Gen 6:14 ark, and cover it inside and out with P
Ex 2:3 it with bitumen and P; and she put the
33:7 take the tent and P it outside the camp,
Num 1:52 people of Israel shall P their tents by their
Deut 1:33 out a place to P your tents, in fire
Sir 13:1 Whoever touches P will be defiled, and whoever
14:25 her walls; he will P his tent near her,
Is 13:20 generations; no Arab will P his tent there, no
34:9 shall be turned into P, and her soil into
34:9 soil into brimstone; her land shall become burning P
Jer 6:3 against her; they shall P their tents around her,
Dan 3:46 furnace fires with naphtha, P, tow, and brush.
11:45 And he shall P his palatial tents between the
14:27 Then Daniel took P, fat, and hair, and boiled

PITCHED (14)

Gen 12:8 east of Bethel, and P his tent, with Bethel
26:25 of the LORD, and P his tent there.

31:25 Now Jacob had P his tent in the hill
33:19 on which he had P his tent.
35:21 Israel journeyed on, and P his tent beyond the
Num 1:51 tabernacle is to be P, the Levites shall set
Judg 4:11 of Moses, and had P his tent as far
2Sam 6:17 tent which David had P for it; and David
16:22 So they P a tent for Absalom upon the
1Chr 15:1 ark of God, and P a tent for it.
16:1 tent which David had P for it; and they
2Chr 1:4 it, for he had P a tent for it
Wis 11:2 an uninhabited wilderness, and P their tents in
2Mac 13:14 country, and commonwealth, he P his camp near

PITCHER
Eccl 12:6 is broken, or the P is broken at the

PITCHERS
Jer 35:5 set before the Rechabites P full of wine, and

PITEOUS
Wis 18:10 echoed back, and their P lament for their children

PITFALL (3)
Job 18:8 his own feet, and he walks on a P
Lam 3:47 against us; panic and P have come upon us,
Rom 11:9 and a trap, a P and a retribution for

PITFALLS
Ps 119:85 Godless men have dug P for me, men who

PITHOM
Ex 1:10 built for Pharaoh store-cities, P and Raamses.

PITHON (2)
1Chr 8:35 The sons of Micah: P, Melech, Tarea, and Ahaz.
9:41 The sons of Micah: P, Melech, Tahre-a, and Ahaz;

PITIABLE (3)
2Mac 3:21 There was something P in the prostration of the
9:28 life by a most P fate, among the mountains
Rev 3:17 that you are wretched, P, poor, blind, and naked.

PITIED (6)
Ps 106:46 caused them to be P by all those who
Ezek 16:5 No eye P you, to do any of these
Hos 1:6 "Call her name Not P, for I will no
1:8 she had weaned Not P, she conceived and bore
2:23 have pity on Not P, and I will say
1Cor 15:19 we are of all men most to be P

PITIES (2)
Ps 103:13 As a father P his children, so the LORD
103:13 children, so the LORD P those who fear him.

PITILESS
Wis 19:1 to the end by P anger, for God knew

PITS (9)
Gen 14:10 was full of bitumen P; and as the kings
37:20 into one of the P; then we shall say
2Sam 17:9 in one of the P, or in some other
Ps 140:10 them be cast into P, no more to rise!
Jer 2:6 land of deserts and P, in a land of
Lam 4:20 was taken in their P, he of whom we
Zeph 2:9 by nettles and salt P, and a waste for
1Mac 11:35 us, and the salt P and the crown taxes
2Pet 2:4 and committed them to P of nether gloom to

PITY (61)
Ex 2:6 She took P on him and said, "This is
Deut 7:16 your eye shall not P them; neither shall you
13:8 nor shall your eye P him, nor shall you
19:13 Your eye shall not P him, but you shall
19:21 Your eye shall not P; it shall be life
25:12 off her hand; your eye shall have no P
Judg 2:18 LORD was moved to P by their groaning because
2Sam 12:6 did this thing, and because he had no P
Tob 3:15 shown to me and P be taken upon me,
Jud 6:19 their arrogance, and have P on the humiliation of
Esth 13:6 of their enemies, without P or mercy, on the
Job 19:21 Have P on me, have pity on me, O
19:21 pity on me, have P on me, O you
27:22 hurls at him without P; he flees from its
Ps 17:10 close their hearts to P; with their mouths they
69:20 I looked for P, but there was none; and
72:13 He has P on the weak and the needy,
86:16 to me and take P on me; give thy
90:13 Have P on thy servants!
102:13 wilt arise and have P on Zion; it is
102:14 stones dear, and have P on her dust.
109:12 him, nor any to P his fatherless children!
Sir 12:13 Who will P a snake charmer bitten by a
12:14 So no one will P a man who associates
16:9 He showed no P for a nation devoted to
36:13 Have P on the city of thy sanctuary, Jerusalem,
Is 13:18 their eyes will not P children.
49:10 for he who has P on them will lead
63:9 love and in his P he redeemed them; he
Jer 13:14 I will not P or spare or have compassion,
15:5 "Who will have P on you, O Jerusalem, or
20:16 the LORD overthrew without P; let him hear a
21:7 sword; he shall not P them, or spare them,
Lam 2:17 he has demolished without P; he has made the
3:43 pursued us, slaying without P;
Bar 4:15 man, and had no P for a child.
6:38 They cannot take P on a widow or do
Ezek 5:11 will not spare, and I will have no P
7:4 nor will I have P; but I will punish
7:9 nor will I have P; I will punish you
8:18 nor will I have P; and though they cry
9:5 you shall show no P;
9:10 nor will I have P, but I will requite
Hos 1:6 will no more have P on the house of
1:7 But I will have P on the house of
2:1 and to your sister, "She has obtained P
2:4 I will have no P, because they are children
2:23 And I will have P on Not pitied, and
Joel 2:18 his land, and had P on his people.
Amos 1:11 and cast off all P, and his anger tore
Jon 4:10 the LORD said, "You P the plant, for which
4:11 And should not I P Nineveh, that great city,
Zech 11:5 own shepherds have no P on them.
11:6 will no longer have P on the inhabitants of
2Mac 4:37 heart and filled with P, and wept because of
7:27 tyrant: "My son, have P on me.
8:2 all, and to have P on the temple which
Mt 18:26 everything.' And out of P for him the lord
20:34 And Jesus in P touched their eyes, and immediately
Mk 1:41 Moved with P, he stretched out his hand and
9:22 can do anything, have P on us and help

PLACE (845)
Gen 1:9 gathered together into one P, and let the dry
2:21 and closed up its P with flesh;
8:9 the dove found no P to set her foot,
12:6 the land to the P at Shechem, to the
13:3 as Bethel, to the P where his tent had
13:4 and Ai, to the P where he had made
13:14 and look from the P where you are, northward
18:24 thou then destroy the P and not spare it
18:26 will spare the whole P for their sake."
18:33 to Abraham; and Abraham returned to his P
19:12 them out of the P;
19:13 about to destroy this P, because the outcry against
19:14 get out of this P; for the LORD is
19:27 the morning to the P where he had stood
20:11 at all in this P, and they will kill
20:13 do me: at every P to which we come,
21:31 Therefore that P was called Beer-sheba; because
22:3 and went to the P of which God had
22:4 eyes and saw the P afar off.
22:9 they came to the P of which God had
22:14 the name of that P The LORD will provide;
23:4 you for a burying P, that I may bury
23:9 your presence as a possession for a burying P
23:20 possession for a burying P by the Hittites.
24:31 the house and a P for the camels."
26:7 the men of the P asked him about his
26:7 the men of the P should kill me for
28:11 came to a certain P, and stayed there that
28:11 the stones of the P, he put it under
28:11 lay down in that P to sleep.
28:16 LORD is in this P; and I did not
28:17 was afraid, and said, "How awesome is this P
28:19 the name of that P Bethel; but the name
29:3 stone back in its P upon the mouth of
29:22 the men of the P, and made a feast.
30:2 "Am I in the P of God, who has
32:2 the name of that P Mahanaim.
32:30 the name of the P Peniel, saying, "For I
33:17 the name of the P is called Succoth.
35:7 altar, and called the P El-bethel, because there God

P

35:13 from him in the P where he had spoken
35:14 a pillar in the P where he had spoken
35:15 the name of the P where God had spoken
38:21 the men of the P, "Where is the harlot
38:22 the men of the P said, 'No harlot has
39:20 into the prison, the P where the king's prisoners
40:13 office; and you shall P Pharaoh's cup in his
42:15 not go from this P unless your youngest brother
42:27 provender at the lodging P, he saw his money
43:21 came to the lodging P we opened our sacks,
43:30 and he sought a P to weep.
47:30 of Egypt and bury me in their burying P
49:15 saw that a resting P was good, and that
49:30 Ephron the Hittite to possess as a burying P
50:11 Therefore the P was named Abel-mizraim; it is
50:13 Ephron the Hittite, to possess as a burying P
50:19 am I in the P of God?
Ex 3:5 your feet, for the P on which you are
3:8 and honey, to the P of the Canaanites, the
4:24 At a lodging P on the way the LORD
10:23 any rise from his P for three days; but
13:3 you out from this P; no leavened bread shall
15:17 thy own mountain, the P, O LORD, which thou
16:29 of you in his P, let no man go
16:29 go out of his P on the seventh day."
16:33 manna in it, and P it before the LORD,
17:7 the name of the P Massah and Meribah, because
18:21 hate a bribe; and P such men over the
18:23 will go to their P in peace."
20:24 your oxen; in every P where I cause my
21:13 appoint for you a P to which he may
23:20 bring you to the P which I have prepared.
26:33 for you the holy P from the most holy.
26:34 ark of the testimony in the most holy P
28:29 goes into the holy P, to bring them to
28:35 goes into the holy P before the LORD, and
28:43 minister in the holy P; lest they bring guilt
29:30 is priest in his P shall wear them seven
29:30 tent of meeting to minister in the holy P
29:31 flesh in a holy P;
31:11 oil and the fragrant incense for the holy P
32:34 the people to the P of which I have
33:21 "Behold, there is a P by me where you
35:19 ministering in the holy P, the holy garments for
39:1 ministering in the holy P; they made the holy
39:41 ministering in the holy P, the holy garments for
Lev 1:16 east side, in the P for ashes;
4:12 camp to a clean P, where the ashes are
4:24 kill it in the P where they kill the
4:29 sin offering in the P of burnt offering.
4:33 sin offering in the P where they kill the
6:11 the ashes outside the camp to a clean P
6:16 unleavened in a holy P; in the court of
6:25 In the P where the burnt offering is killed
6:26 it; in a holy P it shall be eaten,
6:27 on which it was sprinkled in a holy P
6:30 atonement in the holy P; it shall be burned
7:2 most holy; in the P where they kill the
7:6 eaten in a holy P; it is most holy.
10:13 it in a holy P, because it is your
10:14 eat in any clean P, you and your sons
10:17 sin offering in the P of the sanctuary, since
13:19 healed, and in the P of the boil there
13:23 spot remains in one P and does not spread,
13:28 spot remains in one P and does not spread
14:13 the lamb in the P where they kill the
14:13 offering, in the holy P; for the guilt offering,
14:28 right foot, in the P where the blood of
14:40 them into an unclean P outside the city;
14:41 pour into an unclean P outside the city;
14:42 put them in the P of those stones, and
14:45 forth out of the city to an unclean P
16:2 times into the holy P within the veil, before
16:3 come into the holy P: with a young bull
16:16 atonement for the holy P, because of the
16:17 atonement in the holy P until he comes out
16:20 atoning for the holy P and the tent of
16:23 went into the holy P, and shall leave them
16:24 water in a holy P, and put on his
16:27 atonement in the holy P, shall be carried forth
16:32 priest in his father's P shall make atonement,
24:9 it in a holy P, since it is for
Num 5:18 the woman's head, and P in her hands the
9:17 out; and in the P where the cloud settled
10:29 setting out for the P of which the LORD
10:33 seek out a resting P for them.
11:3 the name of that P was called Taberah, because
11:34 the name of that P was called Kibroth-hattaavah,
13:24 That P was called the Valley of Eshcol, because
14:40 go up to the P which the LORD has
18:10 In a most holy P shall you eat of
18:31 eat it in any P, you and your households;
19:9 camp in a clean P; and they shall be
20:5 of Egypt, to bring us to this evil P
20:5 It is no P for grain, or figs, or
21:3 the name of the P was called Hormah.
22:26 stood in a narrow P, where there was no
23:13 with me to another P, from which you may
23:27 take you to another P; perhaps it will please
24:11 now flee to your P; I said, 'I will
24:21 "Enduring is your dwelling P, and your nest is
24:25 went back to his P; and Balak also went
28:7 lamb; in the holy P you shall pour out
32:1 Gilead, and behold, the P was a place for
32:1 the place was a P for cattle.
32:17 brought them to their P; and our little ones
Deut 1:31 you came to this P
1:33 seek you out a P to pitch your tents,
9:7 you came to this P, you have been rebellious
11:5 you came to this P;
11:24 Every P on which the sole of your foot
12:3 gods, and destroy their name out of that P
12:5 you shall seek the P which the LORD your
12:11 safety, then to the P which the LORD your
12:13 burnt offerings at every P that you see;
12:14 see; but at the P which the LORD will
12:18 your God in the P which the LORD your
12:21 If the P which the LORD your God will
12:26 shall go to the P which the LORD will
14:23 your God, in the P which he will choose,
14:24 blesses you, because the P is too far from
14:25 and go to the P which the LORD your
15:20 by year at the P which the LORD will
16:2 the herd, at the P which the LORD will
16:6 you; but at the P which the LORD your
16:7 eat it at the P which the LORD your
16:11 among you, at the P which the LORD your
16:15 your God at the P which the LORD will
16:16 your God at the P which he will choose:
17:8 go up to the P which the LORD your
17:10 to you from that P which the LORD will
18:6 he desires—to the P which the LORD will
21:19 the gate of the P where he lives,
23:12 "You shall have a P outside the camp and
23:16 your midst, in the P which he shall choose
26:2 shall go to the P which the LORD your
26:9 brought us into this P and gave us this
29:7 you came to this P, Sihon the king of
31:11 your God at the P which he will choose,
33:27 God is your dwelling P, and underneath are the
34:6 no man knows the P of his burial to
Josh 1:3 Every P that the sole of your foot will
1:13 is providing you a P of rest, and will
3:3 set out from your P and follow it,
4:3 Jordan, from the very P where the priests' feet
4:3 them down in the P where you lodge tonight.'"
4:8 with them to the P where they lodged, and
4:9 the Jordan, in the P where the feet of
4:18 Jordan returned to their P and overflowed all its
5:9 the name of that P is called Gilgal to
5:15 your feet; for the P where you stand is
7:26 the name of that P is called the Valley
8:9 they went to the P of ambush, and lay
8:19 quickly out of their P, and as soon as
9:27 this day, in the P which he should choose.
20:4 and give him a P, and he shall remain
Judg 2:5 the name of that P Bochim; and they sacrificed
7:21 every man in his P round about the camp,
15:17 his hand; and that P was called Ramathlehi.
15:19 split open the hollow P that is at Lehi,
16:2 and they surrounded the P and lay in wait
17:8 he could find a P; and as he journeyed,
17:9 going to sojourn where I may find a P
18:3 What are you doing in this P
18:10 into your hands, a P where there is no
18:12 On this account that P is called Mahaneh-dan to
19:16 the men of the P were Benjaminites.
20:12 this that has taken P among you?
20:22 line in the same P where they had formed
20:33 up out of their P, and set themselves in
20:33 rushed out of their P west of Geba.
Ruth 1:7 set out from the P where she was, with

P

3:4 lies down, observe the P where he lies; then,
4:10 gate of his native P; you are witnesses this
1Sam 3:2 down in his own P;
3:9 So Samuel went and lay down in his P
5:3 took Dagon and put him back in his P
5:11 return to its own P, that it may not
6:2 with what we shall send it to its P
6:8 of the LORD and P it on the cart,
9:12 people have a sacrifice today on the high P
9:13 up to the high P to eat; for the
9:14 them on his way up to the high P
9:19 me to the high P, for today you shall
9:22 and gave them a P at the head of
9:25 down from the high P into the city, a
10:5 down from the high P with harp, tambourine, flute,
10:12 a man of the P answered, "And who is
10:13 had finished prophesying, he came to the high P
12:8 of Egypt, and made them dwell in this P
14:9 stand still in our P, and we will not
14:46 Philistines; and the Philistines went to their own P
19:2 stay in a secret P and hide yourself;
20:19 then go to the P where you hid yourself
20:25 Saul's side, but David's P was empty.
20:27 the new moon, David's P was empty.
20:37 lad came to the P of the arrow which
21:2 the young men for such and such a P
23:22 know and see the P where his haunt is,
23:28 the Philistines; therefore that P was called the Rock
26:5 and came to the P where Saul had encamped;
26:5 and David saw the P where Saul lay, with
26:25 went his way, and Saul returned to his P
27:5 your eyes, let a P be given me in
29:4 may return to the P to which you have
2Sam 2:16 Therefore that P was called Helkath-hazzurim,
2:23 who came to the P where Asahel had fallen
5:20 the name of that P is called Baal-perazim.
6:8 upon Uzzah; and that P is called Perez-uzzah, to
6:17 set it in its P, inside the tent which
7:10 I will appoint a P for my people Israel,
7:10 dwell in their own P, and be disturbed no
11:16 assigned Uriah to the P where he knew there
16:8 of Saul, in whose P you have reigned; and
17:9 one of the pits, or in some other P
17:12 upon him in some P where he is to
19:13 my army henceforth in P of Joab.'"
21:5 we should have no P in all the territory
22:20 forth into a broad P; he delivered me, because
22:37 didst give a wide P for my steps under
1Kgs 2:35 over the army in P of Joab, and the
2:35 the priest in the P of Abiathar.
2:36 from there to any P whatever.
2:42 and go to any P whatever, you shall die?
3:4 was the great high P; Solomon used to offer
3:7 thy servant king in P of David my father,
4:28 they brought to the P where it was required,
5:1 anointed him king in P of his father; for
5:5 your throne in your P, shall build the house
5:9 by sea to the P you direct, and I
6:16 as an inner sanctuary, as the most holy P
7:50 house, the most holy P, and for the doors
8:6 the LORD to its P, in the inner sanctuary
8:6 in the most holy P, underneath the wings of
8:7 their wings over the P of the ark, so
8:8 seen from the holy P before the inner sanctuary;
8:10 out of the holy P, a cloud filled the
8:13 an exalted house, a P for thee to dwell
8:20 have risen in the P of David my father,
8:21 I have provided a P for the ark, in
8:29 toward this house, the P of which thou hast
8:29 the prayer which thy servant offers toward this P
8:30 they pray toward this P; yea, hear thou in
8:30 in heaven thy dwelling P; and when thou hearest,
8:35 they pray toward this P, and acknowledge thy name,
8:39 in heaven thy dwelling P, and forgive, and act,
8:43 in heaven thy dwelling P, and do according to
8:49 in heaven thy dwelling P their prayer and their
11:7 Solomon built a high P for Chemosh the abomination
13:8 drink water in this P;
13:16 with you in this P;
13:22 drunk water in the P of which he said
19:16 you shall anoint to be prophet in your P
21:19 the LORD: "In the P where dogs licked up
2Kgs 5:11 his hand over the P, and cure the leper.
6:1 to Elisha, "See, the P where we dwell under
6:2 let us make a P for us to dwell
6:6 he showed him the P, he cut off a
6:8 such and such a P shall be my camp."
6:9 do not pass this P, for the Syrians are
6:10 Israel sent to the P of which the man
16:14 the house, from the P between his altar and
18:25 come up against this P to destroy it?
22:16 bring evil upon this P and upon its inhabitants,
22:17 be kindled against this P, and it will not
22:19 I spoke against this P, and against its inhabitants,
22:20 the evil which I will bring upon this P
23:15 at Bethel, the high P erected by Jeroboam the
23:15 altar with the high P he pulled down and
23:34 Josiah king in the P of Josiah his father,
1Chr 4:41 and settled in their P, because there was pasture
5:22 they dwelt in their P until the exile.
6:49 of the most holy P, and to make atonement
13:11 upon Uzzah; and that P is called Perez-uzza to
14:11 the name of that P is called Baal-perazim.
15:1 and he prepared a P for the ark of
15:3 the LORD to its P, which he had prepared
15:12 of Israel, to the P that I have prepared
16:27 before him; strength and joy are in his P
16:39 LORD in the high P that was at Gibeon,
17:9 I will appoint a P for my people Israel,
17:9 dwell in their own P, and be disturbed no
21:29 time in the high P at Gibeon;
2Chr 1:3 went to the high P that was at Gibeon;
1:4 from Kiriath-jearim to the P that David had
1:13 came from the high P at Gibeon, from before
2:6 him, except as a P to burn incense before
3:1 his father, at the P that David had appointed,
3:8 made the most holy P; its length, corresponding to
3:10 In the most holy P he made two cherubim
4:22 to the most holy P and for the doors
5:7 the LORD to its P, in the inner sanctuary
5:7 in the most holy P, underneath the wings of
5:8 their wings over the P of the ark, so
5:9 seen from the holy P before the inner sanctuary;
5:11 out of the holy P (for all the priests
6:2 an exalted house, a P for thee to dwell
6:10 have risen in the P of David my father,
6:20 toward this house, the P where thou hast promised
6:20 the prayer which thy servant offers toward this P
6:21 they pray toward this P; yea, hear thou from
6:21 from heaven thy dwelling P; and when thou hearest,
6:26 they pray toward this P, and acknowledge thy name,
6:30 from heaven thy dwelling P, and forgive, and render
6:33 from heaven thy dwelling P, and do according to
6:39 from heaven thy dwelling P their prayer and their
6:40 thy ears attentive to a prayer of this P
6:41 go to thy resting P, thou and the ark
7:12 and have chosen this P for myself as a
7:15 to the prayer that is made in this P
20:26 the name of that P has been called the
24:11 and take it and return it to its P
29:5 and carry out the filth from the holy P
29:7 offerings in the holy P to the God of
34:24 bring evil upon this P and upon its inhabitants,
34:25 poured out upon this P and will not be
34:27 his words against this P and its inhabitants, and
34:28 will bring upon this P and its inhabitants.'" And
34:31 king stood in his P and made a covenant
35:5 stand in the holy P according to the groupings
35:10 priests stood in their P, and the Levites in
35:15 Asaph, were in their P according to the command
36:15 and on his dwelling P;
Ezra 1:4 each survivor, in whatever P he sojourns, be assisted
1:4 the men of his P with silver and gold,
3:3 the altar in its P, for fear was upon
6:3 house be rebuilt, the P where sacrifices are offered
6:5 Jerusalem, each to its P; you shall put them
8:17 leading man at the P Casiphia, telling them what
8:17 temple servants at the P Casiphia, namely, to send
9:8 hold within his holy P, that our God may
Neh 1:9 bring them to the P which I have chosen,
2:3 when the city, the P of my fathers' sepulchres,
2:14 but there was no P for the beast that
4:20 In the P where you hear the sound of
9:3 stood up in their P and read from the
13:6 While this was taking P I was not in
Tob 1:4 This was the P which had been chosen from
1:15 son reigned in his P; and under him the
1:21 son, reigned in his P; and he appointed Ahikar,
2:3 has been strangled and thrown into the market P
2:4 the body to a P of shelter until sunset.
4:17 P your bread on the grave of the righteous,
7:18 grant you joy in P of this sorrow of

Jud 5:9 them to leave the P where they were living
6:17 them what had taken P at the council of
8:12 yourselves up in the P of God among the
15:4 tell what had taken P and to urge all
Esth 2:9 maids to the best P in the harem.
7:8 palace garden to the P where they were drinking
13:3 has attained the second P in the kingdom,
16:19 letter publicly in every P, and permit the Jews
Job 2:11 each from his own P, Eliphaz the Temanite, Bildad
6:17 when it is hot, they vanish from their P
7:10 house, nor does his P know him any more.
8:18 is destroyed from his P, then it will deny
9:6 earth out of its P, and its pillars tremble;
14:18 is removed from its P;
16:4 you were in my P; I could join words
16:18 blood, and let my cry find no resting P
18:4 or the rock be removed out of its P
18:21 ungodly, such is the P of him who knows
20:9 more, nor will his P any more behold him.
27:21 is gone; it sweeps him out of his P
27:23 at him, and hisses at him from its P
28:1 for silver, and a P for gold which they
28:6 Its stones are the P of sapphires, and it
28:12 And where is the P of understanding?
28:20 And where is the P of understanding?
28:23 the way to it, and he knows its P
34:24 without investigation, and sets others in their P
36:16 distress into a broad P where there was no
36:20 night, when peoples are cut off in their P
37:1 my heart trembles, and leaps out of its P
38:12 dawn to know its P,
38:19 and where is the P of darkness,
38:24 the way to the P where the light is
39:6 home, and the salt land for his dwelling P
Ps 12:5 the LORD; "I will P him in the safety
18:19 forth into a broad P; he delivered me, because
18:36 didst give a wide P for my steps under
24:3 And who shall stand in his holy P
26:8 thy house, and the P where thy glory dwells.
31:8 thou hast set my feet in a broad P
32:7 Thou art a hiding P for me, thou preservest
37:10 look well at his P, he will not be
44:19 broken us in the P of jackals, and covered
55:11 and fraud do not depart from its market P
66:12 thou hast brought us forth to a spacious P
68:17 the Lord came from Sinai into the holy P
74:4 midst of thy holy P; they set up their
74:7 they desecrated the dwelling P of thy name.
76:2 in Salem, his dwelling P in Zion.
81:7 you in the secret P of thunder; I tested
82:1 God has taken his P in the divine council;
84:1 lovely is thy dwelling P, O LORD of hosts!
84:6 they make it a P of springs; the early
90:1 hast been our dwelling P in all generations.
103:16 is gone, and its P knows it no more.
104:8 sank down to the P which thou didst appoint
119:114 Thou art my hiding P and my shield; I
132:5 until I find a P for the LORD, a
132:5 the LORD, a dwelling P for the Mighty One
132:7 go to his dwelling P; let us worship at
132:8 go to thy resting P, thou and the ark
132:14 "This is my resting P for ever; here I
134:2 hands to the holy P, and bless the LORD!
Prov 4:10 She will P on your head a fair garland;
15:3 LORD are in every P, keeping watch on the
25:6 or stand in the P of the great;
Eccl 1:5 and hastens to the P where it rises.
1:7 not full; to the P where the streams flow,
3:16 sun that in the P of justice, even there
3:16 wickedness, and in the P of righteousness, even
3:20 All go to one P; all are from the
4:15 to stand in his P;
6:6 good--do not all go to the one P
8:10 out of the holy P, and were praised in
8:14 a vanity which takes P on earth, that there
10:4 do not leave your P, for deference will make
10:6 places, and the rich sit in a low P
11:3 the north, in the P where the tree falls,
Wis 3:14 his faithfulness, and a P of great delight in
19:18 clearly inferred from the sight of what took P
Sir 4:13 Lord will bless the P she enters.
10:14 rulers, and has seated the lowly in their P
10:15 nations, and has planted the humble in their P
12:12 you and take your P; do not have him
14:25 in an excellent lodging P;
14:26 lodging place; he will P his children under her
22:16 set on a high P will not stand firm
24:7 I sought a resting P; I sought in whose
24:8 created me assigned a P for my tent.
24:11 gave me a resting P, and in Jerusalem was
29:27 "Give P, stranger, to an honored person; my brother
32:2 your duties, take your P, that you may be
33:12 low, and he turned them out of their P
33:20 you, do not let any one take your P
36:13 thy sanctuary, Jerusalem, the P of thy rest.
38:12 give the physician his P, for the Lord created
41:19 of theft, in the P where you live.
Is 3:13 LORD has taken his P to contend, he stands
7:23 In that day every P where there used to
7:25 they will become a P where cattle are let
9:10 down, but we will put cedars in their P
13:13 shaken out of its P, at the wrath of
14:2 bring them to their P, and the house of
16:12 himself upon the high P, when he comes to
18:7 to Mount Zion, the P of the name of
22:22 And I will P on his shoulder the key
22:23 peg in a sure P, and he will become
22:25 fastened in a sure P will give way; and
25:5 against a wall, like heat in a dry P
25:10 trodden down in his P, as straw is trodden
26:21 forth out of his P to punish the inhabitants
28:8 full of vomit, no P is without filthiness.
28:25 barley in its proper P, and spelt as the
30:28 of destruction, and to P on the jaws of
30:33 For a burning P has long been prepared; yea,
32:2 be like a hiding P from the wind, a
32:2 water in a dry P, like the shade of
33:16 on the heights; his P of defense will be
33:21 be for us a P of broad rivers and
33:23 mast firm in its P, or keep the sail
34:14 hag alight, and find for herself a resting P
46:7 set it in its P, and it stands there;
46:7 it stands there; it cannot move from its P
49:20 in your ears: 'The P is too narrow for
54:2 Enlarge the P of your tent, and let the
57:15 the high and holy P, and also with him
60:13 pine, to beautify the P of my sanctuary; and
60:13 I will make the P of my feet glorious.
65:10 Valley of Achor a P for herds to lie
66:1 and what is the P of my rest?
Jer 4:7 gone forth from his P to make your land
6:3 around her, they shall pasture, each in his P
7:3 and I will let you dwell in this P
7:6 innocent blood in this P, and if you do
7:7 you dwell in this P, in the land that
7:12 Go now to my P that was in Shiloh,
7:14 trust, and to the P which I gave to
7:20 poured out on this P, upon man and beast,
7:31 have built the high P of Topheth, which is
9:2 desert a wayfarers' lodging P, that I might leave
13:7 the waistcloth from the P where I had hidden
14:13 I will give you assured peace in this P
16:2 shall you have sons or daughters in this P
16:3 are born in this P, and concerning the mothers
16:9 to cease from this P, before your eyes and
17:12 the beginning is the P of our sanctuary.
19:3 such evil upon this P that the ears of
19:4 and have profaned this P by burning incense in
19:4 they have filled this P with the blood of
19:6 the LORD, when this P shall no more be
19:7 And in this P I will make void the
19:11 there will be no P else to bury.
19:12 I do to this P, says the LORD, and
19:13 be defiled like the P of Topheth.'"
22:3 the widow, nor shed innocent blood in this P
22:11 went away from this P: "He shall return here
22:12 more, but in the P where they have carried
24:5 sent away from this P to the land of
26:23 body into the burial P of the common people.
27:22 bring them back and restore them to this P
28:3 bring back to this P all the vessels of
28:3 took away from this P and carried to Babylon.
28:4 bring back to this P Jeconiah the son of
28:6 bring back to this P from Babylon the vessels
28:13 will make in their P bars of iron.
29:10 my promise and bring you back to this P
29:14 you back to the P from which I sent
32:37 them back to this P, and I will make
33:10 the LORD: In this P of which you say,
33:12 of hosts: In this P which is waste, without
40:2 this evil against this P;
42:18 You shall see this P no more.

P

6:35 "This is a lonely P, and the hour is
6:55 their pallets to any P where they heard he
7:4 come from the market P, they do not eat
13:7 alarmed; this must take P, but the end is
13:29 see these things taking P, you know that he
13:30 not pass away before all these things take P
14:32 they went to a P which was called Gethsemane;
15:22 brought him to the P called Golgotha (which means
15:22 Golgotha (which means the P of a skull).
16:6 not here; see the P where they laid him.
Lk 2:7 because there was no P for them in the
4:17 book and found the P where it was written,
4:37 went out into every P in the surrounding region.
4:42 day he departed and went into a lonely P
6:17 stood on a level P, with a great crowd
7:32 sitting in the market P and calling to one
7:36 house, and took his P at table.
9:12 provisions; for we are here in a lonely P
10:1 into every town and P where he himself was
10:32 he came to the P and saw him, passed
11:1 praying in a certain P, and when he ceased,
14:8 sit down in a P of honor, lest a
14:9 say to you, 'Give P to this man,' and
14:9 will begin with shame to take the lowest P
14:10 sit in the lowest P, so that when your
16:28 also come into this P of torment.'
19:5 Jesus came to the P, he looked up and
21:7 the sign when this is about to take P
21:9 this must first take P, but the end will
21:28 things begin to take P, look up and raise
21:31 see these things taking P, you know that the
21:32 will not pass away till all has taken P
21:36 things that will take P, and to stand before
22:40 he came to the P he said to them,
23:5 throughout all Judea, from Galilee even to this P
23:32 they came to the P which is called The
23:46 saw what had taken P, he praised God, and
23:47 saw what had taken P, returned home beating their
Jn 1:28 This took P in Bethany beyond the Jordan, where
4:20 in Jerusalem is the P where men ought to
5:12 withdrawn, as there was a crowd in the P
6:10 much grass in the P; so the men sat
6:23 Tiberi-as came near the P where they ate the
8:37 my word finds no P in you.
10:40 the Jordan to the P where John at first
11:6 days longer in the P where he was.
11:30 was still in the P where Martha had met
11:48 destroy both our holy P and our nation."
13:12 garments, and resumed his P, he said to them,
13:19 now, before it takes P, that when it does
13:19 when it does take P you may believe that
14:2 go to prepare a P for you?
14:3 go and prepare a P for you, I will
14:29 you before it takes P, so that when it
14:29 when it does take P, you may believe.
18:2 him, also knew the P; for Jesus often met
19:13 judgment seat at a P called The Pavement, and
19:17 own cross, to the P called the place of
19:17 the place called the P of a skull, which
19:20 this title, for the P where Jesus was crucified
19:36 For these things took P that the scripture might
19:41 Now in the P where he was crucified there
20:7 rolled up in a P by itself.
20:25 of the nails, and P my finger in the
20:25 of the nails, and P my hand in his
20:27 out your hand, and P it in my side;
Acts 1:25 chosen to take the P in this ministry and
1:25 Judas turned aside, to go to his own P
2:1 had come, they were all together in one P
4:28 hand and thy plan had predestined to take P
4:31 they had prayed, the P in which they were
6:13 words against this holy P and the law;
6:14 Nazareth will destroy this P, and will change the
7:7 worship me in this P
7:33 your feet, for the P where you are standing
7:49 or what is the P of my rest?
11:28 world; and this took P in the days of
12:17 Then he departed and went to another P
16:13 supposed there was a P of prayer; and we
16:16 were going to the P of prayer, we were
16:19 them into the market P before the rulers;
17:17 and in the market P every day with those
18:23 departed and went from P to place through the
18:23 went from place to P through the region of
21:28 the law and this P; moreover he also brought
21:28 the temple, and he has defiled this holy P

26:18 of sins and a P among those who are
27:8 we came to a P called Fair Havens, near
28:7 the neighborhood of that P were lands belonging to
28:9 when this had taken P, the rest of the
Rom 9:26 "And in the very P where it was said
11:17 were grafted in their P to share the richness
1Cor 1:2 those who in every P call on the name
11:18 For, in the first P, when you assemble as
Eph 2:15 one new man in P of the two, so
2:22 it for a dwelling P of God in the
Col 4:9 everything that has taken P here.
1Tim 2:8 then that in every P the men should pray,
Heb 4:5 And again in this P he said, "They shall
5:6 says also in another P, "Thou art a priest
9:2 of the Presence; it is called the Holy P
9:12 all into the Holy P, taking not the blood
9:25 priest enters the Holy P yearly with blood not
11:8 go out to a P which he was to
2Pet 1:19 shining in a dark P, until the day dawns
Rev 1:1 what must soon take P; and he made it
1:19 what is to take P hereafter.
2:5 your lampstand from its P, unless you repent.
4:1 you what must take P after this."
6:14 every mountain and island was removed from its P
12:6 where she has a P prepared by God, in
12:8 was no longer any P for them in heaven.
12:14 the wilderness, to the P where she is to
16:16 assembled them at the P which is called in
18:2 has become a dwelling P of demons, a haunt
20:11 fled away, and no P was found for them.
22:6 to show his servants what must soon take P

PLACED (43)

Gen 3:24 garden of Eden he P the cherubim, and a
40:11 into Pharaoh's cup, and P the cup in Pharaoh's
40:21 his butlership, and he P the cup in Pharaoh's
Ex 2:3 child in it and P it among the reeds
16:34 commanded Moses, so Aaron P it before the
Lev 8:8 And he P the breastpiece on him, and in
8:26 and one wafer, and P them on the fat
Num 11:24 of the people, and P them round about the
2Sam 12:30 stone; and it was P on David's head.
1Kgs 2:24 has established me, and P me on the throne
12:32 And he P in Bethel the priests of the
2Kgs 17:6 away to Assyria, and P them in Halah, and
17:24 Hamath, and Sepharvaim, and P them in the cities
17:26 have carried away and P in the cities of
1Chr 20:2 stone; and it was P on David's head.
2Chr 4:8 made ten tables, and P them in the temple,
17:2 He P forces in all the fortified cities of
17:19 whom the king had P in the fortified cities
Ezra 1:7 away from Jerusalem and P in the house of
Jud 6:14 him into Bethulia and P him before the magistrates
13:10 to her maid, who P it in her food
Job 20:4 old, since man was P upon earth,
Sir 15:16 He has P before you fire and water: stretch
17:4 He P the fear of them in all living
30:18 like offerings of food P upon a grave.
47:9 He P singers before the altar, to make sweet
Jer 5:22 I P the sand as the bound for the
24:1 two baskets of figs P before the temple of
Bar 6:27 itself; but gifts are P before them just as
Ezek 3:25 behold, cords will be P upon you, and you
17:5 in fertile soil; he P it beside abundant waters.
23:41 on which you had P my incense and my
28:14 anointed guardian cherub I P you; you were on
32:25 the Pit; they are P among the slain.
Dan 1:2 of his god, and P the vessels in the
7:9 I looked, thrones were P and one that was
Hag 2:15 Before a stone was P upon a stone in
1Mac 4:51 They P the bread on the table and hung
7:20 He P Alcimus in charge of the country and
9:51 And he P garrisons in them to harass Israel.
14:33 been stored, and he P there a garrison of
16:7 divided the army and P the horsemen in the
Rev 11:9 to let them be P in a tomb,

PLACES (184)

Gen 36:40 families and their dwelling P, by their names: the
36:43 according to their dwelling P in the land of
Lev 3:17 in all your dwelling P, that you eat neither
26:30 will destroy your high P, and cut down your
Num 31:10 their cities in the P where they dwelt, and
33:2 wrote down their starting P, stage by stage, by
33:2 these are their stages according to their starting P
33:52 demolish all their high P;

Deut 12:2 surely destroy all the P where the nations whom
32:13 ride on the high P of the earth, and
33:29 you; and you shall tread upon their high P
Josh 5:8 they remained in their P in the camp till
Judg 5:11 musicians at the watering P, there they repeat the
19:13 to one of these P, and spend the night
1Sam 2:36 one of the priest's P, that I may eat
7:16 Mizpah; and he judged Israel in all these P
23:23 of all the lurking P where he hides, and
30:31 Hebron, for all the P where David and his
2Sam 1:19 glory, O Israel, is slain upon thy high P
1:25 "Jonathan lies slain upon thy high P
7:7 In all P where I have moved with all
1Kgs 3:2 sacrificing at the high P, however, because no house
3:3 he sacrificed and burnt incense at the high P
12:31 made houses on high P, and appointed priests from
12:32 priests of the high P that he had made.
13:2 priests of the high P who burn incense upon
13:32 houses of the high P which are in the
13:33 priests for the high P again from among all
13:33 he consecrated to be priests of the high P
14:23 built for themselves high P, and pillars, and Asherim
15:14 But the high P were not taken away.
20:24 put commanders in their P;
22:43 LORD; yet the high P were not taken away,
22:43 still sacrificed and burned incense on the high P
2Kgs 12:3 Nevertheless the high P were not taken away; the
12:3 to sacrifice and burn incense on the high P
14:4 But the high P were not removed; the people
14:4 still sacrificed and burned incense on the high P
15:4 Nevertheless the high P were not taken away; the
15:4 still sacrificed and burned incense on the high P
15:35 Nevertheless the high P were not removed; the
15:35 still sacrificed and burned incense on the high P
16:4 incense on the high P, and on the hills,
17:9 built for themselves high P at all their towns,
17:11 on all the high P, as the nations did
17:29 shrines of the high P which the Samaritans had
17:32 priests of the high P, who sacrificed for them
17:32 for them in the shrines of the high P
18:4 He removed the high P, and broke the pillars,
18:22 not he whose high P and altars Hezekiah has
21:3 he rebuilt the high P which Hezekiah his father
23:5 incense in the high P at the cities of
23:8 and defiled the high P where the priests had
23:8 broke down the high P of the gates that
23:9 priests of the high P did not come up
23:13 king defiled the high P that were east of
23:14 Asherim, and filled their P with the bones of
23:19 also of the high P that were in the
23:20 priests of the high P who were there, upon
1Chr 6:54 These are their dwelling P according to their
17:6 In all P where I have moved with all
2Chr 8:11 of Israel, for the P to which the ark
11:13 to him from all P where they lived.
11:15 priests for the high P, and for the satyrs,
14:3 altars and the high P, and broke down the
14:5 of Judah the high P and the incense altars.
15:17 But the high P were not taken out of
17:6 he took the high P and the Asherim out
20:33 The high P, however, were not taken away; the
21:11 Moreover he made high P in the hill country
28:4 incense on the high P, and on the hills,
28:25 Judah he made high P to burn incense to
31:1 broke down the high P and the altars throughout
32:12 taken away his high P and his altars and
33:3 he rebuilt the high P which his father Hezekiah
33:17 sacrificed at the high P, but only to the
33:19 which he built high P and set up the
34:3 Jerusalem of the high P, the Asherim, and the
Neh 4:12 times, "From all the P where they live they
4:13 the wall, in open P, I stationed the people
8:7 the law, while the people remained in their P
12:27 Levites in all their P, to bring them to
Tob 14:5 will return from the P of their captivity, and
Jud 5:19 come back from the P to which they were
Esth 16:5 who are set in P of authority have been
Ps 10:8 the villages; in hiding P he murders the innocent.
16:6 for me in pleasant P; yea, I have a
49:11 for ever, their dwelling P to all generations, though
73:18 set them in slippery P; thou dost make them
74:8 burned all the meeting P of God in the
74:20 covenant; for the dark P of the land are
78:58 anger with their high P; they moved him to
87:2 than all the dwelling P of Jacob.
102:6 owl of the waste P;
103:22 his works, in all P of his dominion.
Prov 9:3 call from the highest P in the town,
9:14 seat on the high P of the town,
Eccl 10:6 set in many high P, and the rich sit
Wis 6:5 because severe judgment falls on those in high P
11:2 wilderness, and pitched their tents in untrodden P
19:18 For the elements changed P with one another, as
19:22 help them at all times and in all P
Sir 23:19 ways of men, and perceive even the hidden P
24:4 I dwelt in high P, and my throne was
Is 6:12 away, and the forsaken P are many in the
15:2 up to the high P to weep; over Nebo
17:9 be like the deserted P of the Hivites and
19:7 There will be bare P by the Nile, on
32:18 habitation, in secure dwellings, and in quiet resting P
36:7 not he whose high P and altars Hezekiah has
40:4 level, and the rough P a plain.
42:16 into light, the rough P into level ground.
45:3 the hoards in secret P, that you may know
49:19 waste and your desolate P and your devastated
51:3 comfort all her waste P, and will make her
52:9 into singing, you waste P of Jerusalem; for the
64:11 and all our pleasant P have become ruins.
65:4 the night in secret P; who eat swine's flesh,
Jer 8:3 family in all the P where I have driven
17:6 dwell in the parched P of the wilderness, in
17:26 of Judah and the P round about Jerusalem, from
19:5 have built the high P of Baal to burn
23:24 hide himself in secret P so that I cannot
24:9 curse in all the P where I shall drive
29:14 nations and all the P where I have driven
32:35 They built the high P of Baal in the
32:44 of Benjamin, in the P about Jerusalem, and in
33:13 land of Benjamin, the P about Jerusalem, and in
40:12 returned from all the P to which they had
45:5 of war in all P to which you may
49:10 have uncovered his hiding P, and he is not
51:51 come into the holy P of the LORD's house.'
Ezek 6:3 upon you, and I will destroy your high P
6:6 waste and your high P ruined, so that your
7:24 might, and their holy P shall be profaned.
16:39 break down your lofty P; they shall strip you
33:24 inhabitants of these waste P in the land of
33:27 are in the waste P shall fall by the
34:12 rescue them from all P where they have been
34:13 in all the inhabited P of the country.
34:26 make them and the P round about my hill
36:10 inhabited and the waste P rebuilt;
36:33 inhabited, and the waste P shall be rebuilt.
36:36 have rebuilt the ruined P, and replanted that which
38:12 to assail the waste P which are now inhabited,
Hos 10:8 The high P of Aven, the sin of Israel,
Amos 4:6 bread in all your P, yet you did not
7:9 by them; the high P of Isaac shall be
Mic 1:3 tread upon the high P of the earth.
Hab 3:19 feet, he makes me tread upon my high P
1Mac 2:31 down to the hiding P in the wilderness.
2:36 block up their hiding P,
2:41 die as our brethren died in their hiding P
10:40 yearly out of the king's revenues from appropriate P
11:69 ambush emerged from their P and joined battle.
12:2 same effect to the Spartans and to other P
15:29 taken possession of many P in my kingdom.
15:30 tribute money of the P which you have conquered
2Mac 8:31 all carefully in strategic P, and carried the rest
10:17 gained possession of the P, and beat off all
10:19 himself set off for P where he was more
11:3 did on the sacred P of the other nations,
12:2 the governors in various P, Timothy and Apollonius
14:22 in readiness at key P to prevent sudden treachery
Mt 11:16 sitting in the market P and calling to their
12:43 he passes through waterless P seeking rest, but he
23:7 salutations in the market P, and being called rabbi
24:7 and earthquakes in various P:
Mk 6:56 sick in the market P, and besought him that
12:38 salutations in the market P
12:39 the synagogues and the P of honor at feasts,
13:8 be earthquakes in various P, there will be famines;
Lk 11:24 he passes through waterless P seeking rest; and
11:43 in the synagogues and salutations in the market P
14:7 how they chose the P of honor, saying to
20:46 salutations in the market P and the best seats
20:46 the synagogues and the P of honor at feasts,
21:11 earthquakes, and in various P famines and
Acts 16:3 that were in those P, for they all knew
Eph 1:3 blessing in the heavenly P,

P

1:20 hand in the heavenly P,
2:6 him in the heavenly P in Christ Jesus,
3:10 to the principalities and powers in the heavenly P
6:12 the spiritual hosts of wickedness in the heavenly P

PLACING

Jn 8:3 caught in adultery, and P her in the midst

PLAGUE (43)

Ex 8:2 go, behold, I will P all your country with
9:3 with a very severe P upon your cattle which
11:1 to Moses, "Yet one P more I will bring
12:13 over you, and no P shall fall upon you
30:12 that there be no P among them when you
32:35 the LORD sent a P upon the people, because
Num 8:19 there may be no P among the people of
11:33 LORD smote the people with a very great P
14:37 the land, died by P before the LORD.
16:46 from the LORD, the P has begun."
16:47 assembly; and behold, the P had already begun
16:48 the living; and the P was stopped.
16:49 who died by the P were fourteen thousand seven
16:50 of meeting, when the P was stopped.
25:8 Thus the P was stayed from the people of
25:9 that died by the P were twenty-four thousand.
25:18 the day of the P on account of Peor."
26:1 After the P the LORD said to Moses and
31:16 Peor, and so the P came among the congregation
Josh 22:17 which there came a P upon the congregation of
1Sam 4:8 with every sort of P in the wilderness.
6:4 Philistines; for the same P was upon all of
2Sam 24:21 the LORD, that the P may be averted from
24:25 the land, and the P was averted from Israel.
1Kgs 8:37 of their cities; whatever P, whatever sickness there
1Chr 21:17 but let not the P be upon thy people."
21:22 full price--that the P may be averted from
2Chr 6:28 of their cities; whatever P, whatever sickness there
21:14 will bring a great P on your people, your
Ps 38:11 stand aloof from my P, and my kinsmen stand
78:50 death, but gave their lives over to the P
106:29 their doings, and a P broke out among them.
106:30 and interposed, and the P was stayed.
Wis 18:20 the righteous, and a P came upon the multitude
Sir 40:9 and sword, calamities, famine and affliction and P
Hab 3:5 him went pestilence, and P followed close behind.
Zech 14:12 this shall be the P with which the LORD
14:15 And a P like this plague shall fall on
14:15 a plague like this P shall fall on the
14:18 them shall come the P with which the LORD
Rev 11:6 the earth with every P, as often as they
16:21 cursed God for the P of the hail, so
16:21 plague of the hail, so fearful was that P

PLAGUED

Josh 24:5 and Aaron, and I P Egypt with what I

PLAGUES (17)

Gen 12:17 his house with great P because of Sarai, Abram's
Ex 9:14 will send all my P upon your heart, and
Lev 26:21 I will bring more P upon you, sevenfold as
Jud 5:12 of Egypt with incurable P; and so the Egyptians
Hos 13:14 O Death, where are your P
2Mac 7:37 and by afflictions and P to make you confess
Lk 7:21 many of diseases and P and evil spirits, and
Rev 9:18 By these three P a third of mankind was
9:20 not killed by these P, did not repent of
15:1 seven angels with seven P, which are the last,
15:6 angels with the seven P, robed in pure bright
15:8 temple until the seven P of the seven angels
16:9 had power over these P, and they did not
18:4 you share in her P;
18:8 see,' so shall her P come in a single
21:9 of the seven last P, and spoke to me,
22:18 add to him the P described in this book,

PLAIN (62)

Gen 11:2 east, they found a P in the land of
Num 15:34 had not been made P what should be done
Deut 34:3 the Negeb, and the P, that is, the valley
Josh 17:16 who dwell in the P have chariots of iron,
Judg 1:19 the inhabitants of the P, because they had chariots
1:34 come down to the P;
2Sam 18:23 the way of the P, and outran the Cushite.
1Kgs 7:46 In the P of the Jordan the king cast
20:23 against them in the P, and surely we shall
20:25 against them in the P, and surely we shall
2Chr 4:17 In the P of the Jordan the king cast
26:10 Shephelah and in the P, and he had farmers
35:22 joined battle in the P of Megiddo.
Neh 3:22 the men of the P, repaired.
6:2 the villages in the P of Ono." But they
Jud 1:5 Arphaxad in the great P which is on the
1:6 Hydaspes and in the P where Arioch ruled the
1:8 Galilee and the great P of Esdraelon,
2:21 from Nineveh to the P of Bectileth, and camped
2:27 went down into the P of Damascus during the
4:6 faces Esdraelon opposite the P near Dothan,
6:11 the camp into the P, and from the plain
6:11 plain, and from the P they went up into
7:18 army encamped in the P, and covered the whole
14:2 going down to the P against the Assyrian outpost;
15:2 every path across the P and through the hill
15:7 country and in the P got a great amount
Wis 19:7 Sea, and a grassy P out of the raging
Is 40:4 shall become level, and the rough places a P
Jer 21:13 O rock of the P, says the LORD; you
48:8 shall perish, and the P shall be destroyed, as
Ezek 3:22 go forth into the P, and there I will
3:23 went forth into the P; and, lo, the glory
8:4 like the vision that I saw in the P
Dan 3:1 it up on the P of Dura, in the
Hab 2:2 the vision; make it P upon tablets, so he
Zech 4:7 you shall become a P; and he shall bring
12:11 for Hadadrimmon in the P of Megiddo.
14:10 be turned into a P from Geba to Rimmon
1Mac 3:24 of Beth-horon to the P; eight hundred of them
3:40 they arrived they encamped near Emmaus in the P
4:6 Judas appeared in the P with three thousand men,
4:14 and fled into the P,
4:21 drawn up in the P for battle,
5:52 Jordan into the large P before Beth-shan.
6:40 troops were on the P, and they advanced steadily
10:71 come down to the P to meet us, and
10:73 an army in the P, where there is no
10:77 he advanced into the P, for he had a
10:83 fled, and the cavalry was dispersed in the P
11:67 they marched to the P of Hazor,
11:68 met him in the P; they had set an
12:49 Galilee and the Great P to destroy all Jonathan's
13:13 And Simon encamped in Adida, facing the P
16:5 and marched into the P, and behold, a large
16:11 appointed governor over the P of Jericho, and he
Rom 1:19 known about God is P to them, because God
1Cor 15:27 it is P that he is excepted who put
2Cor 11:6 we have made this P to you in all
Gal 5:19 the flesh are P: fornication, impurity, licentiousness,
2Tim 3:9 their folly will be P to all, as was
1Jn 2:19 that it might be P that they all are

PLAINLY (12)

Gen 26:28 They said, "We see P that the LORD is
Ex 21:5 But if the slave P says, 'I love my
Deut 27:8 stones all the words of this law very P
1Sam 10:16 uncle, "He told us P that the asses had
Ezra 4:18 to us has been P read before me.
2Mac 3:17 over the man, which P showed to those who
Mk 7:34 opened, his tongue was released, and he spoke P
8:32 And he said this P
Jn 10:24 If you are the Christ, tell us P
11:14 Then Jesus told them P, "Lazarus is dead;
16:25 figures but tell you P of the Father.
16:29 now you are speaking P, not in any figure!

PLAINS (20)

Num 22:1 and encamped in the P of Moab beyond the
26:3 with them in the P of Moab by the
26:63 of Israel in the P of Moab by the
31:12 the camp on the P of Moab by the
33:48 and encamped in the P of Moab by the
33:49 as Abel-shittim in the P of Moab.
33:50 to Moses in the P of Moab by the
35:1 to Moses in the P of Moab by the
36:13 of Israel in the P of Moab by the
Deut 34:1 went up from the P of Moab to Mount
34:8 for Moses in the P of Moab thirty days;
Josh 4:13 for battle, to the P of Jericho.
5:10 at evening in the P of Jericho.
13:32 Moses distributed in the P of Moab, beyond the
2Kgs 25:5 overtook him in the P of Jericho; and all
Jud 5:1 up barricades in the P,
Jer 39:5 overtook Zedekiah in the P of Jericho; and when
52:8 overtook Zedekiah in the P of Jericho; and all

P

1Mac 4:15 Gazara, and to the P of Idumea, and to
14:8 the trees of the P their fruit.

PLAITED

Jn 19:2 And the soldiers P a crown of thorns, and

PLAITING (2)

Mt 27:29 robe upon him, and P a crown of thorns
Mk 15:17 a purple cloak, and P a crown of thorns

PLAN (37)

Ex 26:30 tabernacle according to the P for it which has
1Chr 28:9 hearts, and understands every P and thought.
28:11 Solomon his son the P of the vestibule of
28:12 mercy seat; and the P of all that he
28:18 its weight; also his P for the golden chariot
28:19 the work to be done according to the P
2Chr 30:4 Jerusalem– and the P seemed right to the
Neh 4:15 God had frustrated their P, we all returned to
Tob 6:12 Now listen to my P
Jud 2:2 to them his secret P and recounted fully, with
2:4 finished setting forth his P, Nebuchadnezzar king of
8:34 find out what I P; for I will not
9:9 a widow, the strength to do what I P
Esth 14:11 downfall; but turn their P against themselves, and
Ps 21:11 If they P evil against you, if they devise
62:4 They only P to thrust him down from his
140:2 from violent men, who P evil things in their
Prov 3:29 Do not P evil against your neighbor who dwells
12:20 evil, but those who P good have joy.
Sir 12:16 his mind he will P to throw you into
Is 30:1 "who carry out a P, but not mine; and
Jer 18:11 you and devising a P against you.
49:20 Therefore hear the P which the LORD has made
49:30 Babylon has made a P against you, and formed
50:45 Therefore hear the P which the LORD has made
Ezek 43:10 and its appearance and P, that they may be
Mic 4:12 do not understand his P, that he has gathered
1Mac 6:3 could not, because his P became known to the
7:31 Nicanor learned that his P had been disclosed, he
9:60 do it, because their P became known.
9:68 him greatly, for his P and his expedition had
Acts 2:23 according to the definite P and foreknowledge of
4:28 thy hand and thy P had predestined to take
5:38 alone; for if this P or this undertaking is
27:42 The soldiers' P was to kill the prisoners, lest
Eph 1:10 in Christ as a P for the fullness of
3:9 see what is the P of the mystery hidden

PLANE (5)

Gen 30:37 poplar and almond and P, and peeled white streaks
Sir 24:14 field, and like a P tree I grew tall.
Is 41:19 desert the cypress, the P and the pine together;
60:13 you, the cypress, the P, and the pine, to
Ezek 31:8 equal its boughs; the P trees were as nothing

PLANES

Is 44:13 he fashions it with P, and marks it with

PLANKS (3)

1Kgs 6:9 house of beams and P of cedar.
Ezek 27:5 They made all your P of fir trees from
Acts 27:44 and the rest on P or on pieces of

PLANNED (24)

2Sam 14:13 "Why then have you P such a thing against
21:5 who consumed us and P to destroy us, so
2Kgs 19:25 I P from days of old what now I
2Chr 7:11 all that Solomon had P to do in the
32:3 fight against Jerusalem, he P with his officers and
Jud 9:13 stripe, for they have P cruel things against thy
11:12 given out, they have P to kill their cattle
Ps 140:4 violent men, who have P to trip up my
Wis 14:2 desire for gain that P that vessel, and wisdom
14:14 world, and therefore their speedy end has been P
Is 14:24 sworn: "As I have P, so shall it be,
22:11 regard for him who P it long ago.
37:26 I P from days of old what now I
Jer 48:2 In Heshbon they P evil against her: 'Come, let
51:12 the LORD has both P and done what he
Dan 6:3 him; and the king P to set him over
13:62 as they had wickedly P to do to their
1Mac 5:9 in their territory, and P to destroy them.
6:8 not turned out for him as he had P
8:9 The Greeks P to come and destroy them,
12:35 of the people and P with them to build

2Mac 9:15 worth burying but had P to throw out with
Jn 12:10 So the chief priests P to put Lazarus also
Acts 27:39 beach, on which they P if possible to bring

PLANNING (3)

Gen 27:42 Esau comforts himself by P to kill you.
1Mac 8:4 whole region by their P and patience, even though
Acts 25:3 man sent to Jerusalem, P an ambush to kill

PLANS (33)

Tob 4:19 all your paths and P may prosper.
Jud 10:8 favor and fulfill your P, that the people of
Job 17:11 days are past, my P are broken off, the
Ps 14:6 You would confound the P of the poor, but
20:4 you your heart's desire, and fulfil all your P
33:10 nought; he frustrates the P of the peoples.
55:9 Destroy their P, O Lord, confuse their tongues; for
83:3 They lay crafty P against thy people; they consult
146:4 that very day his P perish.
Prov 6:18 heart that devises wicked P, feet that make haste
15:22 Without counsel P go wrong, but with many advisers
16:1 The P of the mind belong to man, but
16:3 the LORD, and your P will be established.
16:9 A man's mind P his way, but the LORD
16:30 who winks his eyes P perverse things, he who
19:21 Many are the P in the mind of a
20:18 P are established by counsel; by wise guidance wage
21:5 The P of the diligent lead surely to abundance,
24:8 He who P to do evil will be called
Wis 6:3 search out your works and inquire into your P
Sir 27:22 Whoever winks his eye P evil deeds, and no
Is 19:3 I will confound their P; and they will consult
25:1 hast done wonderful things, P formed of old, faithful
Jer 9:8 in his heart he P an ambush for him.
18:12 will follow our own P, and will every one
19:7 will make void the P of Judah and Jerusalem,
29:11 For I know the P I have for you,
29:11 you, says the LORD, P for welfare and not
Dan 11:24 He shall devise P against strongholds, but only for
1Mac 2:63 the dust, and his P will perish.
16:13 country, and made treacherous P against Simon and
2Mac 15:1 of Samaria, he made P to attack them with
2Cor 1:17 Do I make my P like a worldly man,

PLANT (58)

Gen 1:29 have given you every P yielding seed which is
1:30 have given every green P for food." And it
2:5 the heavens, when no P of the field was
Ex 9:22 and beast and every P of the field, throughout
9:25 hail struck down every P of the field, and
10:12 Egypt, and eat every P in the land, all
10:15 remained, neither tree nor P of the field, through
15:17 bring them in, and P them on thy own
Lev 19:23 into the land and P all kinds of trees
Deut 6:11 which you did not P, and when you eat
16:21 "You shall not P any tree as an Asherah
28:30 in it; you shall P a vineyard, and you
28:39 You shall P vineyards and dress them, but you
Josh 24:13 which you did not P
2Sam 7:10 people Israel, and will P them, that they may
2Kgs 19:29 sow, and reap, and P vineyards, and eat their
1Chr 17:9 people Israel, and will P them, that they may
Job 8:12 not cut down, they wither before any other P
14:9 bud and put forth branches like a young P
Ps 44:2 but them thou didst P; thou didst afflict the
80:8 out the nations and P it.
107:37 they sow fields, and P vineyards, and get a
Eccl 3:2 die; a time to P, and a time to
Sir 3:26 no healing, for a P of wickedness has taken
49:7 and destroy, and likewise to build and to P
Is 17:10 refuge; therefore, though you P pleasant plants and
17:11 the day that you P them, and make them
37:30 sow and reap, and P vineyards, and eat their
53:2 him like a young P, and like a root
65:21 inhabit them; they shall P vineyards and eat their
65:22 inhabit; they shall not P and another eat; for
Jer 1:10 destroy and to overthrow, to build and to P
18:9 I will build and P it,
24:6 them down; I will P them, and not uproot
29:5 and live in them; P gardens and eat their
29:28 live in them, and P gardens and eat their
31:5 Again you shall P vineyards upon the mountains of
31:5 Samaria; the planters shall P, and shall enjoy the
31:28 to build and to P, says the LORD.
32:41 good, and I will P them in this land
35:7 seed; you shall not P or have a vineyard;

42:10 you down; I will P you, and not pluck
Ezek 4:2 also against it, and P battering-rams against it round
16:7 grow up like a P of the field.' And
17:22 and I myself will P it upon a high
17:23 of Israel will I P it, that it may
28:26 shall build houses and P vineyards.
Hos 13:15 flourish as the reed P, the east wind, the
Amos 9:14 inhabit them; they shall P vineyards and drink their
9:15 I will P them upon their land, and they
Jon 4:6 LORD God appointed a P, and made it come
4:6 So Jonah was exceedingly glad because of the P
4:7 worm which attacked the P, so that it withered.
4:9 you do well to be angry for the P
4:10 said, "You pity the P, for which you did
Zeph 1:13 inhabit them; though they P vineyards, they shall not
2Mac 1:29 P thy people in thy holy place, as Moses
Mt 15:13 He answered, "Every P which my heavenly Father

PLANTATIONS

Ezek 34:29 provide for them prosperous P so that they shall

PLANTED (32)

Gen 2:8 And the LORD God P a garden in Eden,
9:20 He P a vineyard;
21:33 Abraham P a tamarisk tree in Beer-sheba, and
Num 24:6 that the LORD has P, like cedar trees beside
Deut 20:6 is there that has P a vineyard and has
Ps 1:3 is like a tree P by streams of water,
80:15 this vine, the stock which thy right hand P
92:13 They are P in the house of the LORD,
94:9 He who P the ear, does he not hear?
104:16 abundantly, the cedars of Lebanon which he P
Eccl 2:4 I built houses and P vineyards for myself;
2:5 gardens and parks, and P in them all kinds
3:2 pluck up what is P;
Sir 10:15 the nations, and has P the humble in their
43:23 the great deep and P islands in it.
Is 5:2 it of stones, and P it with choice vines;
40:24 Scarcely are they P, scarcely sown, scarcely has their
Jer 2:21 Yet I P you a choice vine, wholly of
11:17 LORD of hosts, who P you, has pronounced evil
17:8 is like a tree P by water, that sends
45:4 and what I have P I am plucking up—
Ezek 17:5 of the land and P it in fertile soil;
17:7 bed where it was P
Amos 5:11 in them; you have P pleasant vineyards, but you
Mt 15:13 heavenly Father has not P will be rooted up.
21:33 was a householder who P a vineyard, and set
Mk 12:1 "A man P a vineyard, and set a hedge
Lk 13:6 had a fig tree P in his vineyard; and
17:6 rooted up, and be P in the sea,' and
17:28 bought, they sold, they P, they built,
20:9 this parable: "A man P a vineyard, and let
1Cor 3:6 I P, Apollos watered, but God gave the growth.

PLANTERS

Jer 31:5 mountains of Samaria; the P shall plant, and shall

PLANTEST

Jer 12:2 Thou P them, and they take root; they grow

PLANTING (6)

Is 5:7 Judah are his pleasant P; and he looked for
60:21 the shoot of my P, the work of my
61:3 oaks of righteousness, the P of the LORD, that
Ezek 31:4 the place of its P, sending forth its streams
Mic 1:6 country, a place for P vineyards; and I will
1Mac 3:56 were betrothed, or were P vineyards, or were

PLANTS (21)

Gen 1:11 earth put forth vegetation, P yielding seed, and fruit
1:12 earth brought forth vegetation, P yielding seed
3:18 you shall eat the P of the field.
9:3 gave you the green P, I give you everything.
Ex 10:15 they ate all the P in the land and
2Kgs 19:26 and have become like P of the field, and
Job 12:8 tell you; or the P of the earth, and
40:21 Under the lotus P he lies, in the covert
Ps 104:14 for the cattle, and P for man to cultivate,
144:12 their youth be like P full-grown, our daughters like
Prov 31:16 of her hands she P a vineyard.
Wis 7:20 men, the varieties of P and the virtues of
10:7 a continually smoking wasteland, P bearing fruit that
Sir 24:14 En-ge'di, and like rose P in Jericho; like a
Is 17:10 though you plant pleasant P and set out slips
37:27 and have become like P of the field and
44:14 of the forest; he P a cedar and the
Mt 13:26 So when the P came up and bore grain,
1Cor 3:7 So neither he who P nor he who waters
3:8 He who P and he who waters are equal,
9:7 Who P a vineyard without eating any of its

PLASTER (9)

Lev 14:41 round about, and the P that they scrape off
14:42 he shall take other P and plaster the house.
14:42 take other plaster and P the house.
14:45 timber and all the P of the house; and
Deut 27:2 up large stones, and P them with plaster;
27:2 and plaster them with P;
27:4 Ebal, and you shall P them with plaster.
27:4 Mount Ebal, and you shall plaster them with P
Dan 5:5 and wrote on the P of the wall of

PLASTERED (2)

Lev 14:43 scraped the house and P it,
14:48 after the house was P, then the priest shall

PLATE (21)

Ex 28:36 you shall make a P of pure gold, and
39:30 And they made the P of the holy crown
Lev 8:9 he set the golden P, the holy crown, as
Num 7:13 offering was one silver P whose weight was a
7:19 his offering one silver P, whose weight was a
7:25 offering was one silver P, whose weight was a
7:31 offering was one silver P whose weight was a
7:37 offering was one silver P, whose weight was a
7:43 offering was one silver P, whose weight was a
7:49 offering was one silver P, whose weight was a
7:55 offering was one silver P, whose weight was a
7:61 offering was one silver P, whose weight was a
7:67 offering was one silver P, whose weight was a
7:73 offering was one silver P, whose weight was a
7:79 offering was one silver P, whose weight was a
7:85 golden dishes, each silver P weighing a hundred and
Ezek 4:3 And take an iron P, and place it as
1Mac 11:58 he sent him gold P and a table service,
15:32 its gold and silver P, and his great magnificence,
Mt 23:24 cup and of the P, but inside they are
23:25 cup and of the P, that the outside also

PLATES (5)

Ex 25:29 you shall make its P and dishes for incense,
37:16 upon the table, its P and dishes for incense,
Num 4:7 put upon it the P, the dishes for incense,
7:84 of Israel: twelve silver P, twelve silver basins, twelve
16:38 be made into hammered P as a covering for

PLATFORM (7)

2Chr 6:13 had made a bronze P five cubits long, five
Jud 14:15 thrown down on the P dead, with his head
Ezek 41:8 temple had a raised P round about; the foundations
41:9 the part of the P which was left free
41:9 Between the P of the temple and the
41:11 the part of the P that was left free,
2Mac 13:26 Lysias took the public P, made the best possible

PLATTER (4)

Mt 14:8 head of John the Baptist here on a P
14:11 was brought on a P and given to the
Mk 6:25 the head of John the Baptist on a P
6:28 his head on a P, and gave it to

PLAUSIBLE

1Cor 2:4 message were not in P words of wisdom, but

PLAY (36)

Gen 4:21 of all those who P the lyre and pipe.
19:9 sojourn, and he would P the judge!
Ex 32:6 to eat and drink, and rose up to P
34:15 land, and when they P the harlot after their
34:16 sons, and their daughters P the harlot after their
34:16 and make your sons P the harlot after their
Lev 17:7 satyrs, after whom they P the harlot.
Num 25:1 the people began to P the harlot with the
Deut 31:16 people will rise and P the harlot after the
1Sam 16:16 upon you, he will P it, and you will
16:17 a man who can P well, and bring him
21:15 brought this fellow to P the madman in my
2Sam 2:14 young men arise and P before us." And Joab
10:12 courage, and let us P the man for our
1Chr 15:16 singers who should P loudly on musical instruments,
15:20 and Benaiah were to P harps according to Alamoth;

P

16:5 Je-iel, who were to P harps and lyres; Asaph
19:13 courage, and let us P the man for our
Job 40:20 food for him where all the wild beasts P
41:5 Will you P with him as with a bird,
Ps 33:3 him a new song, P skilfully on the strings,
144:9 ten-stringed harp I will P to thee,
Sir 29:25 your mouth; you will P the host and provide
30:9 he will frighten you; P with him, and he
34:14 not be timid, nor P the coward, for he
Is 11:8 The sucking child shall P over the hole of
23:17 her hire, and will P the harlot with all
Ezek 16:34 none solicited you to P the harlot; and you
Hos 3:3 days; you shall not P the harlot, or belong
4:10 be satisfied; they shall P the harlot, but not
4:12 left their God to P the harlot.
4:13 your daughters P the harlot, and your brides
4:14 your daughters when they P the harlot, nor your
4:15 Though you P the harlot, O Israel, let not
1Mac 3:45 Jacob; the flute and the harp ceased to P
2Mac 3:32 notion that some foul P had been perpetrated by

PLAYED (29)

Gen 38:24 "Tamar your daughter-in-law has P the harlot; and
Judg 2:17 their judges; for they P the harlot after other
8:27 Ophrah; and all Israel P the harlot after it
8:33 Israel turned again and P the harlot after the
1Sam 16:23 took the lyre and P it with his hand;
26:21 day; behold, I have P the fool, and have
2Kgs 3:15 And when the minstrel P, the power of the
1Chr 5:25 of their fathers, and P the harlot after the
Ps 106:39 by their acts, and P the harlot in their
Sir 47:3 He P with lions as with young goats, and
Jer 3:1 You have P the harlot with many lovers; and
3:6 green tree, and there P the harlot?
3:8 she too went and P the harlot.
Ezek 16:15 in your beauty, and P the harlot because of
16:16 shrines, and on them P the harlot; the like
16:17 men, and with them P the harlot;
16:26 You also P the harlot with the Egyptians, your
16:28 You P the harlot also with the Assyrians, because
16:28 were insatiable; yea, you P the harlot with them,
23:3 of one mother; they P the harlot in Egypt;
23:3 harlot in Egypt; they P the harlot in their
23:5 "Oholah P the harlot while she was mine; and
23:19 her youth, when she P the harlot in the
23:30 upon you, because you P the harlot with the
Hos 2:5 For their mother has P the harlot; she that
5:3 O Ephraim, you have P the harlot, Israel is
9:1 peoples; for you have P the harlot, forsaking your
1Cor 14:7 notes, how will any one know what is P
Rev 18:7 she glorified herself and P the wanton, so give

PLAYERS (2)

Mt 9:23 and saw the flute P, and the crowd making
Rev 18:22 and minstrels, of flute P and trumpeters, shall be

PLAYING (14)

Gen 21:9 had borne to Abraham, P with her son Isaac.
Lev 20:5 who follow him in P the harlot after Molech.
20:6 to mediums and wizards, P the harlot after them,
21:9 she profanes herself by P the harlot, profanes her
Deut 22:21 folly in Israel by P the harlot in her
1Sam 16:16 who is skilful in P the lyre; and when
16:18 who is skilful in P, a man of valor,
18:10 house, while David was P the lyre, as he
19:9 hand; and David was P the lyre.
1Kgs 1:40 went up after him, P on pipes, and rejoicing
Ps 68:25 last, between them maidens P timbrels:
Ezek 16:41 will make you stop P the harlot, and you
Zech 8:5 of boys and girls P in its streets.
Rev 14:2 the sound of harpers P on their harps,

PLAYMATES

Mt 11:16 and calling to their P,

PLAYS (2)

Prov 12:9 himself than one who P the great man but
Ezek 33:32 a beautiful voice and P well on an instrument,

PLEA (6)

Is 29:21 and with an empty P turn aside him who
32:7 words, even when the P of the needy is
Jer 18:19 to me, O LORD, and hearken to my P
37:20 king: let my humble P come before you, and
38:26 'I made a humble P to the king that
Lam 3:56 thou didst hear my P, 'Do not close thine

PLEAD (15)

1Sam 12:7 still, that I may P with you before the
24:15 see to it, and P my cause, and deliver
Job 13:8 toward him, will you P the case for God?
Ps 74:22 Arise, O God, P thy cause; remember how the
119:154 P my cause and redeem me; give me life
Prov 22:23 for the LORD will P their cause and despoil
23:11 is strong; he will P their cause against you.
Wis 12:12 come before thee to P as an advocate for
Is 1:17 oppression; defend the fatherless, P for the widow.
Jer 12:1 thee; yet I would P my case before thee.
50:34 He will surely P their cause, that he may
51:36 LORD: "Behold, I will P your cause and take
Hos 2:2 P with your mother, plead— for she is
2:2 "Plead with your mother, P – for she is
Mic 6:1 the LORD says: Arise, P your case before the

PLEADED (3)

Jer 15:11 if I have not P with thee on behalf
1Mac 11:62 the people of Gaza P with Jonathan, and he
2Mac 4:47 uncondemned if they had P even before Scythians.

PLEADING (3)

Jud 8:16 a human being, to be won over by P
Jer 3:21 heard, the weeping and P of Israel's sons, because
Acts 19:8 spoke boldly, arguing and P about the kingdom of

PLEADINGS

Job 13:6 and listen to the P of my lips.

PLEADS (3)

Is 51:22 LORD, your God who P the cause of his
Mic 7:9 against him, until he P my cause and executes
Rom 11:2 of Elijah, how he P with God against Israel?

PLEAS

Is 59:4 they rely on empty P, they speak lies, they

PLEASANT (35)

Gen 2:9 every tree that is P to the sight and
49:15 that the land was P; so he bowed his
2Sam 1:26 my brother Jonathan; very P have you been to
19:35 I discern what is P and what is not?
2Kgs 2:19 of this city is P, as my lord sees;
Ps 16:6 fallen for me in P places; yea, I have
106:24 Then they despised the P land, having no faith
133:1 Behold, how good and P it is when brothers
Prov 2:10 and knowledge will be P to your soul;
9:17 is sweet, and bread eaten in secret is P
16:21 man of discernment, and P speech increases
16:24 P words are like a honeycomb, sweetness to the
22:18 for it will be P if you keep them
23:8 eaten, and waste your P words.
24:4 with all precious and P riches.
Eccl 11:7 sweet, and it is P for the eyes to
Song 7:6 How fair and P you are, O loved one,
Sir 6:5 A P voice multiplies friends, and a gracious tongue
24:15 myrrh I spread a P odor, like galbanum, onycha,
40:21 and the harp make P melody, but a pleasant
40:21 pleasant melody, but a P voice is better than
Is 5:7 of Judah are his P planting; and he looked
13:22 and jackals in the P palaces; its time is
17:10 therefore, though you plant P plants and set out
27:2 In that day: "A P vineyard, sing of it!
32:12 your breasts for the P fields, for the fruitful
64:11 fire, and all our P places have become ruins.
Jer 3:19 and give you a P land, a heritage most
12:10 they have made my P portion a desolate wilderness.
31:26 and my sleep was P to me.
Ezek 26:12 walls and destroy your P houses; your stones and
Amos 5:11 them; you have planted P vineyards, but you shall
Mic 2:9 drive out from their P houses; from their young
Zech 7:14 and fro, and the P land was made desolate."
Heb 12:11 seems painful rather than P; later it yields the

PLEASANTNESS (2)

Job 36:11 their days in prosperity, and their years in P
Prov 3:17 ways are ways of P, and all her paths

PLEASE (55)

Gen 16:6 in your power; do to her as you P
19:8 to them as you P; only do nothing to
28:8 Canaanite women did not P Isaac his father,
47:25 our lives; may it P my lord, we will
Ex 21:8 If she does not P her master, who has
Num 23:27 place; perhaps it will P God that you may

P

Judg	16:6	Delilah said to Samson, P tell me wherein your
	16:10	and told me lies; P tell me how you
1Sam	20:13	But should it P my father to do you
2Sam	7:29	now therefore may it P thee to bless the
1Kgs	9:12	him, they did not P him.
	21:6	or else, if it P you, I will give
1Chr	17:27	now therefore may it P thee to bless the
2Chr	10:7	to this people and P them, and speak good
Jud	3:3	lie before you; do with them whatever you P
	12:13	"This beautiful maidservant will P come to my lord
Esth	1:19	If it P the king, let a royal order
	3:9	If it P the king, let it be decreed
	5:4	Esther said, "If it P the king, let the
	5:8	king, and if it P the king to grant
	7:3	king, and if it P the king, let my
	8:5	she said, "If it P the king, and if
	8:8	may write as you P with regard to the
	9:13	Esther said, "If it P the king, let the
Job	6:9	desire; that it would P God to crush me,
Ps	69:31	This will P the LORD more than an ox
Prov	16:7	When a man's ways P the LORD, he makes
Song	2:7	stir not up nor awaken love until it P
	3:5	stir not up nor awaken love until it P
	8:4	stir not up nor awaken love until it P
Wis	14:19	he, perhaps wishing to P his ruler, skilfully forced
Sir	20:26	a sensible man will P great men.
Is	56:4	choose the things that P me and hold fast
Hos	9:4	and they shall not P him with their sacrifices.
1Mac	12:18	And now P send us a reply to this."
	12:22	we have learned this, P write us concerning your
2Mac	2:16	Will you therefore P keep the days?
	2:25	we have aimed to P those who wish to
	7:16	mortal though you are, you do what you P
Acts	9:38	to him entreating him, P come to us without
Rom	8:8	in the flesh cannot P God.
	15:1	weak, and not to P ourselves;
	15:2	let each of us P his neighbor for his
	15:3	For Christ did not P himself; but, as it
1Cor	7:32	the Lord, how to P the Lord;
	7:33	worldly affairs, how to P his wife,
	7:34	worldly affairs, how to P her husband.
	10:33	as I try to P all men in everything
2Cor	5:9	it our aim to P him.
Gal	1:10	am I trying to P men?
1Thes	2:4	we speak, not to P men, but to please
	2:4	please men, but to P God who tests our
	4:1	to live and to P God, just as you
Heb	11:6	it is impossible to P him.
Jas	2:3	fine clothing and say, "Have a seat here, P

PLEASED (71)

Gen	34:18	Their words P Hamor and Hamor's son Shechem.
	45:16	it P Pharaoh and his servants well.
Ex	8:9	said to Pharaoh, "Be P to command me when
Num	24:1	Balaam saw that it P the LORD to bless
Josh	22:30	the Manassites spoke, it P them well.
	22:33	And the report P the people of Israel; and
Judg	14:7	the woman; and she P Samson well.
	19:6	to the man, "Be P to spend the night,
1Sam	12:22	sake, because it has P the LORD to make
	18:20	Saul, and the thing P him.
	18:26	David these words, it P David well to be
2Sam	3:36	of it, and it P them; as everything that
	3:36	that the king did P all the people.
	17:4	And the advice P Absalom and all the elders
	19:6	us were dead today, then you would be P
1Kgs	3:10	It P the Lord that Solomon had asked this.
2Kgs	5:23	And Naaman said, "Be P to accept two talents."
	6:3	of them said, "Be P to go with your
Neh	2:6	So it P the king to send me; and
Jud	7:16	These words P Holofernes and all his servants, and
	11:20	Her words P Holofernes and all his servants, and
	12:20	And Holofernes was greatly P with her, and drank
	15:10	and God is well P with it.
Esth	1:21	This advice P the king and the princes, and
	2:4	This P the king, and he did so.
	2:9	And the maiden P him and won his favor;
	5:14	This counsel P Haman, and he had the gallows
	9:5	and did as they P to those who hated
Job	6:28	"But now, be P to look at me; for
Ps	40:13	Be P, O LORD, to deliver me!
	41:11	know that thou art P with me, in that
	49:13	of those who are P with their portion.
	51:16	give a burnt offering, thou wouldst not be P
	70:1	Be P, O God, to deliver me!
Wis	4:10	There was one who P God and was loved
Sir	34:19	Most High is not P with the offerings of
	44:17	Enoch P the Lord, and was taken up; he
	45:19	it and was not P, and in the wrath
Is	42:21	The LORD was P, for his righteousness' sake, to
Dan	6:1	It P Darius to set over the kingdom a
	8:4	he did as he P and magnified himself.
Jon	1:14	hast done as it P thee."
Mic	6:7	Will the LORD be P with thousands of rams,
Mal	1:8	governor; will he be P with you or show
1Mac	1:12	This proposal P them,
	6:60	The speech P the king and the commanders, and
	8:21	The proposal P them,
	11:49	the city as they P, their courage failed and
	14:23	It has P our people to receive these men
2Mac	1:20	had passed, when it P God, Nehemiah, having been
	14:35	of nothing, thou wast P that there be a
Mt	3:17	my beloved Son, with whom I am well P
	12:18	my beloved with whom my soul is well P
	14:6	before the company, and P Herod,
	17:5	whom I am well P; listen to him."
	17:12	know him, but did to him whatever they P
Mk	1:11	my beloved Son; with thee I am well P
	6:22	in and danced, she P Herod and his guests;
	9:13	to him whatever they P, as it is written
Lk	2:14	earth peace among men with whom he is P
	3:22	my beloved Son; with thee I am well P
Acts	6:5	And what they said P the whole multitude, and
	12:3	he saw that it P the Jews, he proceeded
Rom	15:26	and Achaia have been P to make some contribution
	15:27	at Jerusalem; they were P to do it, and
1Cor	1:21	God through wisdom, it P God through the folly
	10:5	them God was not P; for they were overthrown
Gal	1:16	through his grace, was P to reveal his Son
Col	1:19	fulness of God was P to dwell,
Heb	11:5	was attested as having P God.
2Pet	1:17	my beloved Son, with whom I am well P

PLEASES (25)

Gen	20:15	you; dwell where it P you."
Deut	23:16	your towns, where it P him best; you shall
Judg	14:3	for me; for she P me well."
1Kgs	20:6	lay hands on whatever P them, and take it
Neh	2:5	the king, "If it P the king, and if
	2:7	the king, "If it P the king, let letters
Jud	8:15	within any time he P, or even to destroy
	8:17	our voice, if it P him.
	12:14	Surely whatever P him I will do at once,
Esth	2:4	let the maiden who P the king be queen
Ps	115:3	is in the heavens; he does whatever he P
	135:6	Whatever the LORD P he does, in heaven and
Eccl	2:26	to the man who P him God gives wisdom
	2:26	give to one who P God.
	7:26	are fetters; he who P God escapes her, but
	8:3	matter is unpleasant, for he does whatever he P
Wis	9:18	men were taught what P thee, and were saved
Sir	7:26	have a wife who P you, do not cast
	8:15	will act as he P, and through his folly
	9:12	not delight in what P the ungodly; remember that
	20:27	his harvest, and whoever P great men will atone
	33:13	ways are as he P – so men are
	39:18	At his command whatever P him is done, and
Col	3:20	in everything, for this P the Lord.
1Jn	3:22	commandments and do what P him.

PLEASING (73)

Gen	8:21	the LORD smelled the P odor, the LORD said
Ex	29:18	LORD; it is a P odor, an offering by
	29:25	burnt offering, as a P odor before the LORD;
	29:41	the morning, for a P odor, an offering by
Lev	1:9	offering by fire, a P odor to the LORD.
	1:13	offering by fire, a P odor to the LORD.
	1:17	offering by fire, a P odor to the LORD.
	2:2	offering by fire, a P odor to the LORD.
	2:9	offering by fire, a P odor to the LORD.
	2:12	the altar for a P odor.
	3:5	offering by fire, a P odor to the LORD.
	3:16	by fire for a P odor.
	4:31	the altar for a P odor to the LORD;
	6:15	on the altar, a P odor to the LORD.
	6:21	offer it for a P odor to the LORD.
	8:21	a burnt offering, a P odor, an offering by
	8:28	an ordination offering, a P odor, an offering by
	17:6	the fat for a P odor to the LORD.
	23:13	to the LORD, a P odor; and the drink
	23:18	offering by fire, a P odor to the LORD.
	26:31	will not smell your P odors.

Num 15:3 feasts, to make a P odor to the LORD,
15:7 hin of wine, a P odor to the LORD.
15:10 offering by fire, a P odor to the LORD.
15:13 offering by fire, a P odor to the LORD.
15:14 offering by fire, a P odor to the LORD,
15:24 a burnt offering, a P odor to the LORD,
18:17 offering by fire, a P odor to the LORD;
28:2 offerings by fire, my P odor, you shall take
28:6 Mount Sinai for a P odor, an offering by
28:8 offering by fire, a P odor to the LORD.
28:13 a burnt offering of P odor, an offering by
28:24 offering by fire, a P odor to the LORD;
28:27 a burnt offering, a P odor to the LORD;
29:2 a burnt offering, a P odor to the LORD:
29:6 ordinance for them, a P odor, an offering by
29:8 to the LORD, a P odor: one young bull,
29:13 offering by fire, a P odor to the LORD,
29:36 offering by fire, a P odor to the LORD:
1Kgs 14:13 there is found something P to the LORD, the
Ezra 6:10 that they may offer P sacrifices to the God
Tob 3:15 if it be not P to thee to take
4:3 life; do what is P to her, and do
4:21 and do what is P in his sight."
Esth 8:5 king, and I be P in his eyes, let
Ps 104:34 May my meditation be P to him, for I
Prov 15:26 of the pure are P to him.
Eccl 12:10 Preacher sought to find P words, and uprightly he
Wis 4:14 for his soul was P to the Lord, therefore
9:9 who understand what is P in thy sight and
9:10 may learn what is P to thee.
13:11 bark, and then with P workmanship make a useful
Sir 35:3 keep from wickedness is P to the Lord, and
35:6 the altar, and its P odor rises before the
35:16 He whose service is P to the Lord will
45:16 Lord, incense and a P odor as a memorial
48:16 them did what was P to God, but others
48:22 Hezekiah did what was P to the Lord, and
50:15 of the altar, a P odor to the Most
Jer 6:20 acceptable, nor your sacrifices P to me.
Bar 4:4 we know what is P to God.
Ezek 6:13 oak, wherever they offered P odor to all their
16:19 before them for a P odor, says the Lord
20:41 As a P odor I will accept you, when
Mal 3:4 and Jerusalem will be P to the LORD as
1Mac 14:4 nation; his rule was P to them, as was
Jn 8:29 always do what is P to him."
Gal 1:10 If I were still P men, I should not
Eph 5:10 to learn what is P to the Lord.
Phil 4:18 a sacrifice acceptable and P to God.
Col 1:10 of the Lord, fully P to him, bearing fruit
Heb 13:16 for such sacrifices are P to God.
13:21 you that which is P in his sight, through

PLEASURE (54)

Gen 18:12 and my husband is old, shall I have P
2Sam 15:26 says, 'I have no P in you,' behold, here
19:18 over the king's household, and to do his P
1Chr 28:4 father's sons he took P in me to make
29:17 the heart, and hast P in uprightness; in the
Ezra 5:17 king send us his P in this matter."
Neh 9:37 our cattle at their P, and we are in
Tob 3:6 me according to thy P; command my spirit to
Job 22:3 Is it any P to the Almighty if you
Ps 51:18 Zion in thy good P; rebuild the walls of
62:4 They take P in falsehood.
105:22 his princes at his P, and to teach his
111:2 by all who have P in them.
147:10 the horse, nor his P in the legs of
147:11 but the LORD takes P in those who fear
149:4 For the LORD takes P in his people; he
Prov 10:23 but wise conduct is P to a man of
18:2 A fool takes no P in understanding, but only
21:17 He who loves P will be a poor man;
Eccl 2:1 make a test of P; enjoy yourself." But behold,
2:2 and of P, "What use is it?"
2:10 my heart from no P, for my heart found
2:10 for my heart found P in all my toil,
3:13 and drink and take P in all his toil.
4:8 whom am I toiling and depriving myself of P
5:4 for he has no P in fools.
12:1 say, "I have no P in them";
Wis 7:2 a man and the P of marriage.
16:20 to eat, providing every P and suited to every
Sir 9:10 it has aged you will drink it with P
18:30 your soul to take P in base desire, it
25:1 My soul takes P in three things, and they
41:4 you reject the good P of the Most High?
Is 58:3 you seek your own P, and oppress all your
58:13 sabbath, from doing your P on my holy day,
58:13 or seeking your own P, or talking idly;
Jer 6:10 scorn, they take no P in it.
Ezek 16:37 with whom you took P, all those you loved
18:23 Have I any P in the death of the
18:32 For I have no P in the death of
33:11 GOD, I have no P in the death of
Hag 1:8 that I may take P in it and that
Mal 1:10 I have no P in you, says the LORD
Lk 12:32 is your Father's good P to give you the
2Cor 1:15 might have a double P;
Phil 2:13 to will and to work for his good P
2Thes 2:12 the truth but had P in unrighteousness.
2Tim 3:4 with conceit, lovers of P rather than lovers of
Heb 10:6 offerings and sin offerings thou hast taken no P
10:8 neither desired nor taken P in sacrifices and
10:38 my soul has no P in him."
12:10 short time at their P, but he disciplines us
Jas 5:5 in luxury and in P; you have fattened your
2Pet 2:13 They count it P to revel in the daytime.

PLEASURES (5)

Ps 16:11 thy right hand are P for evermore.
Is 47:8 this, you lover of P, who sit securely, who
Lk 8:14 cares and riches and P of life, and their
Tit 3:3 to various passions and P, passing our days in
Heb 11:25 to enjoy the fleeting P of sin.

PLEDGE (34)

Gen 38:17 you give me a P, till you send it?"
38:18 He said, "What P shall I give you?" She
38:20 Adullamite, to receive the P from the woman's hand,
Ex 22:26 your neighbor's garment in P, you shall restore it
Num 30:2 bind himself by a P, he shall not break
30:3 binds herself by a P, while within her father's
30:4 vow and of her P by which she has
30:4 shall stand, and every P by which she has
30:5 vow of hers, no P by which she has
30:10 bound herself by a P with an oath,
30:11 shall stand, and every P by which she bound
30:12 vows, or concerning her P of herself, shall not
Deut 24:6 an upper millstone in P; for he would be
24:6 for he would be taking a life in P
24:10 not go into his house to fetch his P
24:11 loan shall bring the P out to you.
24:12 not sleep in his P;
24:13 restore to him the P that he may sleep
24:17 a widow's garment in P;
Job 17:3 "Lay down a P for me with thyself; who
24:3 fatherless; they take the widow's ox for a P
24:9 breast, and take in P the infant of the
Prov 6:1 neighbor, have given your P for a stranger;
17:18 without sense gives a P, and becomes surety in
20:16 and hold him in P when he gives surety
27:13 and hold him in P when he gives surety
Ezek 18:7 to the debtor his P, commits no robbery, gives
18:12 does not restore the P, lifts up his eyes
18:16 any one, exacts no P, commits no robbery, but
33:15 the wicked restores the P, gives back what he
Amos 2:8 upon garments taken in P; and in the house
2Mac 10:28 the one having as P of success and victory
11:30 Xanthicus will have our P of friendship and full
1Tim 5:12 incur condemnation for having violated their first P

PLEDGED (3)

1Chr 29:24 sons of King David, P their allegiance to King
Ezra 10:19 They P themselves to put away their wives, and
1Mac 8:1 with them, that they P friendship to those who

PLEDGES (11)

Num 30:7 shall stand, and her P by which she has
30:14 vows, or all her P, that are upon her;
Job 22:6 For you have exacted P of your brothers for
Prov 22:26 of those who give P, who become surety for
Hab 2:6 own--for how long?--and loads himself with P
2Mac 4:34 treachery offered him sworn P and gave him his
11:26 them and give them P of friendship, so that
12:11 Judas to grant them P of friendship, promising to
12:12 and after receiving his P they departed to their
13:22 people in Bethzur, gave P, received theirs, withdrew,
14:19 to give and receive P of friendship.

PLEIADES (3)

Job 9:9 Bear and Orion, the P and the chambers of

P

31:28 watched over them to P up and break down,
42:10 plant you, and not P you up; for I
Ezek 23:34 drain it out, and P out your hair, and
Mt 5:29 causes you to sin, P it out and throw
12:1 and they began to P heads of grain and
18:9 causes you to sin, P it out and throw
Mk 2:23 his disciples began to P heads of grain.
9:45 causes you to sin, P it out; it is

PLUCKED (17)

Gen 8:11 her mouth a freshly P olive leaf; so Noah
Deut 28:63 and you shall be P off the land which
Job 4:21 If their tent-cord is P up within them, do
Sir 10:15 The Lord has P up the roots of the
40:16 river bank will be P up before any grass.
Is 33:20 stakes will never be P up, nor will any
38:12 My dwelling is P up and removed from me
Jer 12:15 And after I have P them up, I will
Ezek 19:12 But the vine was P up in fury, cast
Dan 7:4 looked its wings were P off, and it was
7:8 the first horns were P up by the roots;
11:4 his kingdom shall be P up and go to
Amos 4:11 were as a brand P out of the burning;
9:15 shall never again be P up out of the
Zech 3:2 not this a brand P from the fire?"
Lk 6:1 the grainfields, his disciples P and ate some heads
Gal 4:15 possible, you would have P out your eyes and

PLUCKING

Jer 45:4 have planted I am P up—that is, the

PLUMAGE (3)

Job 39:13 they the pinions and P of love?
Ezek 17:3 long pinions, rich in P of many colors, came
17:7 great wings and much P; and behold, this vine

PLUMB (5)

Jud 8:14 You cannot P the depths of the human heart,
Amos 7:7 wall built with a P line, with a plumb
7:7 plumb line, with a P line in his hand.
7:8 And I said, "A P line." Then the Lord
7:8 I am setting a P line in the midst

PLUMMET (4)

2Kgs 21:13 of Samaria, and the P of the house of
Is 28:17 line, and righteousness the P; and hail will sweep
34:11 over it, and the P of chaos over its
Zech 4:10 and shall see the P in the hand of

PLUMP (2)

Gen 41:5 seven ears of grain, P and good, were growing
41:7 swallowed up the seven P and full ears.

PLUNDER (39)

2Chr 14:14 for there was much P in them.
Tob 3:4 gavest us over to P, captivity, and death; thou
Jud 2:11 over to slaughter and P throughout your whole
Esth 3:13 of Adar, and to P their goods.
8:11 and women, and to P their goods,
9:10 Jews; but they laid no hand on the P
9:15 Susa; but they laid no hands on the P
9:16 them; but they laid no hands on the P
Ps 109:11 he has; may strangers P the fruits of his
Sir 16:13 not escape with his P, and the patience of
Is 10:6 take spoil and seize P, and to tread them
11:14 and together they shall P the people of the
17:14 lot of those who P us.
Jer 20:5 their enemies, who shall P them, and seize them,
50:10 be plundered; all who P her shall be sated,
Ezek 29:19 and despoil it and P it; and it shall
36:5 might possess it and P it.
38:12 spoil and carry off P; to assail the waste
38:13 hosts to carry off P, to carry away silver
39:10 who despoiled them, and P those who plundered
Dan 11:24 done, scattering among them P, spoil, and goods.
11:33 flame, by captivity and P, for some days.
Nah 2:9 P the silver, plunder the gold!
2:9 Plunder the silver, P the gold!
3:1 of lies and booty—no end to the P
Hab 2:8 of the peoples shall P you, for the blood
Zeph 2:9 of my people shall P them, and the survivors
Zech 2:9 and they shall become P for those who served
1Mac 4:17 not be greedy for P, for there is a
4:18 and afterward seize the P boldly."
4:23 Then Judas returned to P the camp, and they
6:3 take the city and P it, but he could
7:47 the spoils and the P, and they cut off
13:34 country, for all that Trypho did was to P
2Mac 8:30 they divided very much P, giving to those who
Mt 12:29 strong man's house and P his goods, unless he
12:29 Then indeed he may P his house.
Mk 3:27 strong man's house and P his goods, unless he
3:27 then indeed he may P his house.

PLUNDERED (44)

Gen 34:27 upon the slain, and P the city, because their
Judg 2:14 over to plunderers, who P them; and he sold
2:16 power of those who P them.
1Sam 14:48 hands of those who P them.
17:53 the Philistines, and they P their camp.
2Kgs 7:16 people went out, and P the camp of the
2Chr 14:14 They P all the cities, for there was much
Neh 4:4 them up to be P in a land where
Jud 1:14 Ecbatana, captured its towers, P its markets, and
2:7 them over to be P by my troops,
2:23 Put and Lud, and P all the people of
2:26 burned their tents and P their sheepfolds.
4:1 and how he had P and destroyed all their
7:27 Holofernes and to all his forces, to be P
8:19 sword, and to be P, and so they suffered
8:21 our sanctuary will be P; and he will exact
15:6 the Assyrian camp and P it, and were greatly
15:11 So all the people P the camp for thirty
Ps 7:4 friend with evil or P my enemy without cause,
Wis 10:20 Therefore the righteous P the ungodly; they sang
Sir 36:25 the property will be P; and where there is
Is 10:13 of peoples, and have P their treasures; like a
13:16 their houses will be P and their wives ravished.
42:22 a people robbed and P, they are all of
Jer 50:10 Chaldea shall be P; all who plunder her shall
50:37 upon all her treasures, that they may be P
Bar 6:18 they may not be P by robbers.
Ezek 39:10 and plunder those who P them, says the Lord
Amos 3:11 defenses from you, and your strongholds shall be P
Hab 2:8 Because you have P many nations, all the remnant
Zeph 1:13 Their goods shall be P, and their houses laid
Zech 2:8 to the nations who P you, for he who
14:2 taken and the houses P and the women ravished;
1Mac 1:3 of the earth, and P many nations.
1:19 of Egypt, and he P the land of Egypt.
1:31 He P the city, burned it with fire, and
5:35 every male in it, P it, and burned it
5:51 sword, and razed and P the city.
5:68 burned with fire; he P the cities and returned
8:10 wives and children; they P them, conquered the land,
10:84 the surrounding towns and P them; and the temple
11:61 suburbs with fire and P them.
12:31 he crushed them and P them.
2Mac 9:16 which he had formerly P, he would adorn with

PLUNDERER

Is 21:2 told to me; the P plunders, and the destroyer

PLUNDERERS (4)

Judg 2:14 gave them over to P, who plundered them; and
Jer 50:11 though you exult, O P of my heritage, though
Obad 1:5 came to you, if P by night—how you
Nah 2:2 majesty of Israel, for P have stripped them and

PLUNDERING (2)

Ezra 9:7 sword, to captivity, to P, and to utter shame,
Heb 10:34 you joyfully accepted the P of your property, since

PLUNDERS

Is 21:2 to me; the plunderer P, and the destroyer destroys.

PLUNGE (2)

Job 9:31 lye, yet thou wilt P me into a pit,
1Tim 6:9 and hurtful desires that P men into ruin and

PLUNGED (2)

Sir 9:9 in blood you be P into destruction.
1Mac 6:11 into what a great flood I now am P

PLUNGES

Prov 13:17 A bad messenger P men into trouble, but a

PLUNGING

Jer 8:6 course, like a horse P headlong into battle.

PLY

Jer 14:18 both prophet and priest P their trade through the

P

POCHERETH-HAZZEBAIM (2)
Ezra 2:57 Hattil, the sons of P, and the sons of
Neh 7:59 Hattil, the sons of P, the sons of Amon.

PODS
Lk 15:16 have fed on the P that the swine ate;

POETS
Acts 17:28 even some of your P have said, 'For we

POINT (29)
Gen 31:32 presence of our kinsmen P out what I have
2Kgs 20:1 and was at the P of death.
24:20 it came to the P in Jerusalem and Judah
2Chr 32:24 and was at the P of death, and he
Neh 3:16 Bethzur, repaired to a P opposite the sepulchres of
3:26 Ophel repaired to a P opposite the Water Gate
Job 20:25 his body, the glittering P comes out of his
Prov 5:14 I was at the P of utter ruin in
Sir 18:20 you are on the P of sinning, turn back.
Is 38:1 and was at the P of death.
Jer 17:1 of iron; with a P of diamond it is
Ezek 47:20 the boundary to a P opposite the entrance of
2Mac 2:32 At this P therefore let us begin our narrative,
7:27 you up to this P in your life, and
13:10 who were on the P of being deprived of
15:38 told and to the P, that is what I
Mt 24:1 his disciples came to P out to him the
Mk 5:23 daughter is at the P of death.
Lk 7:2 sick and at the P of death.
Jn 4:47 he was at the P of death.
2Cor 5:16 one from a human P of view; even though
5:16 Christ from a human P of view, we regard
7:11 At every P you have proved yourselves guiltless in
9:6 The P is this: he who sows sparingly will
2Tim 4:6 am already on the P of being sacrificed; the
Heb 8:1 Now the P in what we are saying is
12:4 yet resisted to the P of shedding your blood.
Jas 2:10 but fails in one P has become guilty of
Rev 3:2 and is on the P of death, for I

POINTED (3)
Esth 13:4 place in the kingdom, P out to us that
Sir 43:19 it freezes, it becomes P thorns.
1Tim 1:18 the prophetic utterances which P to you, that

POINTING (3)
Is 58:9 you the yoke, the P of the finger, and
2Mac 15:10 at the same time P out the perfidy of
1Tim 5:24 some men are conspicuous, P to judgment, but the

POINTS (4)
Prov 6:13 scrapes with his feet, P with his finger,
2Mac 12:22 and pierced by the P of their swords.
Acts 25:19 but they had certain P of dispute with him
Rom 15:15 But on some P I have written to you

POISON (10)
Deut 32:32 grapes are grapes of P, their clusters are bitter;
32:33 their wine is the P of serpents, and the
Job 6:4 my spirit drinks their P; the terrors of God
20:16 He will suck the P of asps; the tongue
Ps 69:21 They gave me P for food, and for my
140:3 their lips is the P of vipers.
Wis 1:14 there is no destructive P in them; and the
Amos 6:12 have turned justice into P and the fruit of
2Mac 10:13 his office, he took P and ended his life.
Jas 3:8 the tongue—a restless evil, full of deadly P

POISONED (3)
Jer 8:14 and has given us P water to drink, because
23:15 wormwood, and give them P water to drink; for
Acts 14:2 up the Gentiles and P their minds against the

POISONOUS (4)
Deut 29:18 you a root bearing P and bitter fruit,
32:24 with burning heat and P pestilence; and I will
Jer 9:15 wormwood, and give them P water to drink.
Hos 10:4 judgment springs up like P weeds in the furrows

POLE (3)
Num 13:23 carried it on a P between two of them;
21:8 set it on a P; and every one who
21:9 set it on a P; and if a serpent

POLES (37)
Ex 25:13 You shall make P of acacia wood, and overlay
25:14 you shall put the P into the rings on
25:15 The P shall remain in the rings of the
25:27 as holders for the P to carry the table.
25:28 You shall make the P of acacia wood, and
27:6 And you shall make P for the altar, poles
27:6 poles for the altar, P of acacia wood, and
27:7 with bronze; and the P shall be put through
27:7 rings, so that the P shall be upon the
30:4 shall be holders for P with which to carry
30:5 You shall make the P of acacia wood, and
35:12 the ark with its P, the mercy seat, and
35:13 the table with its P and all its utensils,
35:15 of incense, with its P, and the anointing oil
35:16 grating of bronze, its P, and all its utensils,
37:4 And he made P of acacia wood, and overlaid
37:5 gold, and put the P into the rings on
37:14 as holders for the P to carry the table.
37:15 He made the P of acacia wood to carry
37:27 as holders for the P with which to carry
37:28 And he made the P of acacia wood, and
38:5 as holders for the P;
38:6 poles; he made the P of acacia wood, and
38:7 And he put the P through the rings on
39:35 the testimony with its P and the mercy seat;
39:39 grating of bronze, its P, and all its utensils;
Num 4:6 all of blue, and shall put in its P
4:8 covering of goatskin, and shall put in its P
4:11 shall put in its P;
4:14 covering of goatskin, and shall put in its P
1Kgs 8:7 made a covering above the ark and its P
8:8 And the P were so long that the ends
8:8 the ends of the P were seen from the
1Chr 15:15 their shoulders with the P, as Moses had commanded
2Chr 5:8 made a covering above the ark and its P
5:9 And the P were so long that the ends
5:9 the ends of the P were seen from the

POLICE (2)
Acts 16:35 the magistrates sent the P, saying, "Let those men
16:38 The P reported these words to the magistrates, and

POLICY (4)
Sir 47:23 in understanding, Rehoboam, whose P caused the
2Mac 6:8 should adopt the same P toward the Jews and
9:27 he will follow my P and will treat you
11:26 they may know our P and be of good

POLISH
Jer 46:4 stations with your helmets, P your spears, put on

POLISHED (9)
Sir 12:11 like one who has P a mirror, and you
Is 49:2 he made me a P arrow, in his quiver
Ezek 21:9 is sharpened and also P,
21:10 sharpened for slaughter, P to flash like lightning!
21:11 is given to be P, that it may be
21:11 it is sharpened and P to be given into
21:15 like lightning, it is P for slaughter.
21:28 the slaughter, it is P to glitter and to
1Mac 13:27 might be seen, with P stone at the front

POLLUTE (3)
Num 35:33 You shall not thus P the land in which
Jud 9:8 thy sanctuary, and to P the tabernacle where thy
2Mac 6:2 God, and also to P the temple in Jerusalem

POLLUTED (19)
1Chr 5:1 first-born; but because he P his father's couch, his
2Chr 36:14 the nations; and they P the house of the
Jud 9:2 her to shame, and P her womb to disgrace
Ps 106:38 and the land was P with blood.
Prov 25:26 muddied spring or a P fountain is a righteous
Is 24:5 The earth lies P under its inhabitants; for they
64:6 deeds are like a P garment.
Jer 3:1 Would not that land be greatly P
3:2 You have P the land with your vile harlotry.
3:9 light to her, she P the land, committing adultery
16:18 sin, because they have P my land with the
Ezek 20:43 with which you have P yourselves; and you shall
23:17 and after she was P by them, she turned
23:30 with the nations, and P yourself with their idols.
Mal 1:7 thy name?' By offering P food upon my altar.
1:7 say, 'How have we P it?' By thinking that
1:12 the LORD's table is P, and the food for

2Mac	5:16	holy vessels with his P hands, and swept away
Rev	21:8	cowardly, the faithless, the P, as for murderers,

POLLUTES (2)

Num	35:33	you live; for blood P the land, and no
Sir	40:29	He P himself with another man's food, but a

POLLUTION (3)

Jud	9:4	thee, and abhorred the P of their blood, and
Wis	14:26	good, forgetfulness of favors, P of souls, sex
2Mac	6:19	rather than life with P, went up to the

POLLUTIONS (4)

Ezra	6:21	separated himself from the P of the peoples of
	9:11	land unclean with the P of the peoples of
1Mac	13:50	from there and cleansed the citadel from its P
Acts	15:20	to abstain from the P of idols and from

POMEGRANATE (9)

Ex	28:34	golden bell and a P, a golden bell and
	28:34	golden bell and a P, round about on the
	39:26	a bell and a P, a bell and a
	39:26	a bell and a P round about upon the
1Sam	14:2	of Gibe-ah under the P tree which is at
Song	4:3	like halves of a P behind your veil.
	6:7	like halves of a P behind your veil.
Joel	1:11	P, palm, and apple, all the trees of the
Hag	2:19	the fig tree, the P, and the olive tree

POMEGRANATES (24)

Ex	28:33	skirts you shall make P of blue and purple
	39:24	the robe they made P of blue and purple
	39:25	the bells between the P upon the skirts of
	39:25	round about, between the P;
Num	13:23	they brought also some P and figs.
	20:5	figs, or vines, or P; and there is no
Deut	8:8	and fig trees and P, a land of olive
1Kgs	7:18	Likewise he made P; in two rows round about
	7:20	there were two hundred P, in two rows round
	7:42	and the four hundred P for the two networks,
	7:42	networks, two rows of P for each network, to
2Kgs	25:17	cubits; a network and P, all of bronze, were
2Chr	3:16	he made a hundred P, and put them on
	4:13	and the four hundred P for the two networks,
	4:13	networks, two rows of P for each network, to
Song	4:13	are an orchard of P with all choicest fruits,
	6:11	had budded, whether the P were in bloom.
	7:12	have opened and the P are in bloom.
	8:2	spiced wine to drink, the juice of my P
Sir	45:9	he encircled him with P, with very many golden
Jer	52:22	cubits; a network and P, all of bronze, were
	52:22	And the second pillar had the like, with P
	52:23	There were ninety-six P on the sides; all the
	52:23	the sides; all the P were a hundred upon

POMMEL

1Cor	9:27	the air; but I P my body and subdue

POMP (9)

Esth	1:4	and the splendor and P of his majesty for
Ps	49:12	cannot abide in his P, he is like the
	49:20	cannot abide in his P, he is like the
Is	14:11	become like us!' Your P is brought down to
1Mac	10:58	at Ptolemais with great P, as kings do.
	10:60	So he went with P to Ptolemais and met
	10:86	city came out to meet him with great P
	11:6	king at Joppa with P, and they greeted one
Acts	25:23	Bernice came with great P, and they entered the

PONDER (6)

Ps	64:9	God has wrought, and P what he has done.
Sir	3:27	the intelligent man will P a parable, and an
	14:21	her ways will also P her secrets.
	16:18	Who will P his ways?
	21:17	assembly, and they will P his words in their
Is	14:16	stare at you, and P over you: 'Is this

PONDERED

2Mac	11:13	not without intelligence, he P over the defeat which

PONDERING (2)

Lk	2:19	kept all these things, P them in her heart.
Acts	10:19	And while Peter was P the vision, the Spirit

PONDERS

Prov	15:28	mind of the righteous P how to answer, but

PONDS

Ex	7:19	their canals, and their P, and all their pools

PONTIUS (3)

Lk	3:1	reign of Tiberi-us Caesar, P Pilate being governor of
Acts	4:27	anoint, both Herod and P Pilate, with the Gentiles
1Tim	6:13	in his testimony before P Pilate made the good

PONTUS (3)

Acts	2:9	Mesopotamia, Judea and Cappadocia, P and Asia,
	18:2	Aquila, a native of P, lately come from Italy
1Pet	1:1	of the dispersion in P, Galatia, Cappadocia, Asia, and

POOL (24)

2Sam	2:13	met them at the P of Gibeon; and they
	2:13	one side of the P, and the other on
	2:13	the other on the other side of the P
	4:12	hanged them beside the P at Hebron.
1Kgs	22:38	the chariot by the P of Samaria, and the
2Kgs	18:17	conduit of the upper P, which is on the
	20:20	how he made the P and the conduit and
Neh	2:14	and to the King's P; but there was no
	3:15	the wall of the P of Shelah of the
	3:16	David, to the artificial P, and to the house
Ps	114:8	the rock into a P of water, the flint
Sir	43:20	it rests upon every P of water, and the
Is	7:3	conduit of the upper P on the highway to
	22:9	waters of the lower P,
	22:11	two walls for the water of the old P
	35:7	sand shall become a P, and the thirsty ground
	36:2	conduit of the upper P on the highway to
	41:18	make the wilderness a P of water, and the
Jer	41:12	him at the great P which is in Gibeon.
Nah	2:8	Nineveh is like a P whose waters run away.
1Mac	9:33	the water of the P of Asphar.
Jn	5:2	the Sheep Gate a P, in Hebrew called Beth-zatha,
	5:6	put me into the P when the water is
	9:7	"Go, wash in the P of Siloam" (which means

POOLS (10)

Ex	7:19	ponds, and all their P of water, that they
	8:5	canals, and over the P, and cause frogs to
2Kgs	3:16	dry stream-bed full of P
Ps	84:6	springs; the early rain also covers it with P
	107:35	turns a desert into P of water, a parched
Eccl	2:6	I made myself P from which to water the
Song	7:4	Your eyes are P in Heshbon, by the gate
Sir	48:17	with iron and built P for water.
Is	14:23	of the hedgehog, and P of water, and I
	42:15	the rivers into islands, and dry up the P

POOR (204)

Gen	41:19	came up after them, P and very gaunt and
Ex	22:25	with you who is P, you shall not be
	23:3	be partial to a P man in his suit.
	23:6	justice due to your P in his suit.
	23:11	lie fallow, that the P of your people may
	30:15	give more, and the P shall not give less,
Lev	14:21	"But if he is P and cannot afford so
	19:10	leave them for the P and for the sojourner:
	19:15	be partial to the P or defer to the
	23:22	leave them for the P and for the stranger:
	25:25	"If your brother becomes P, and sells part of
	25:35	if your brother becomes P, and cannot maintain
	25:39	if your brother becomes P beside you, and sells
	25:47	brother beside him becomes P and sells himself to
	27:8	a man is too P to pay your valuation,
Num	13:20	land is rich or P, and whether there is
Deut	15:4	there will be no P among you (for the
	15:7	is among you a P man, one of your
	15:7	your hand against your P brother,
	15:9	be hostile to your P brother, and you give
	15:11	For the P will never cease out of the
	15:11	needy and to the P, in the land.
	24:12	if he is a P man, you shall not
	24:14	hired servant who is P and needy, whether he
	24:15	down (for he is P, and sets his heart
Ruth	3:10	after young men, whether P or rich.
1Sam	2:7	The LORD makes P and makes rich; he brings
	2:8	He raises up the P from the dust; he
	18:23	that I am a P man and of no
2Sam	12:1	certain city, the one rich and the other P
	12:3	and herds; but the P man had nothing but
	12:4	but he took the P man's lamb, and prepared
Tob	2:2	"Go and bring whatever P man of our brethren
	4:7	face away from any P man, and the face

P

	4:21	be afraid, my son, because we have become P
Esth	9:22	portions to one another and gifts to the P
Job	5:16	So the P have hope, and injustice shuts her
	20:10	the favor of the P, and his hands will
	20:19	crushed and abandoned the P, he has seized a
	24:4	They thrust the P off the road; the poor
	24:4	off the road; the P of the earth all
	24:9	the infant of the P
	24:14	he may kill the P and needy; and in
	29:12	because I delivered the P who cried, and the
	29:16	a father to the P, and I searched out
	30:25	Was not my soul grieved for the P
	31:16	withheld anything that the P desired, or have caused
	31:19	of clothing, or a P man without covering;
	34:19	rich more than the P, for they are all
	34:28	the cry of the P to come to him,
Ps	9:18	the hope of the P shall not perish for
	10:2	wicked hotly pursue the P; let them be caught
	10:9	he may seize the P, he seizes the poor
	10:9	poor, he seizes the P when he draws him
	12:5	"Because the P are despoiled, because the needy
	14:6	the plans of the P, but the LORD is
	34:6	This P man cried, and the LORD heard him,
	37:14	to bring down the P and needy, to slay
	40:17	for me, I am P and needy; but the
	41:1	Blessed is he who considers the P
	49:2	and high, rich and P together!
	70:5	But I am P and needy; hasten to me,
	72:2	with righteousness, and thy P with justice!
	72:4	the cause of the P of the people, give
	72:12	when he calls, the P and him who has
	74:19	the life of thy P for ever.
	74:21	to shame; let the P and needy praise thy
	86:1	me, for I am P and needy.
	109:16	kindness, but pursued the P and needy and the
	109:22	For I am P and needy, and my heart
	112:9	has given to the P; his righteousness endures for
	113:7	He raises the P from the dust, and lifts
	132:15	I will satisfy her P with bread.
Prov	10:15	the poverty of the P is their ruin.
	13:7	another pretends to be P, yet has great wealth.
	13:8	his wealth, but a P man has no means
	13:23	fallow ground of the P yields much food, but
	14:20	The P is disliked even by his neighbor, but
	14:21	happy is he who is kind to the P
	14:31	He who oppresses a P man insults his Maker,
	16:19	lowly spirit with the P than to divide the
	17:5	He who mocks the P insults his Maker; he
	18:23	The P use entreaties, but the rich answer roughly.
	19:1	Better is a P man who walks in his
	19:4	new friends, but a P man is deserted by
	19:7	All a P man's brothers hate him; how much
	19:17	is kind to the P lends to the LORD,
	19:22	is loyalty, and a P man is better than
	21:13	the cry of the P will himself cry out
	21:17	pleasure will be a P man; he who loves
	22:2	The rich and the P meet together; the LORD
	22:7	rich rules over the P, and the borrower is
	22:9	blessed, for he shares his bread with the P
	22:16	He who oppresses the P to increase his own
	22:22	Do not rob the P, because he is poor,
	22:22	poor, because he is P, or crush the afflicted
	28:3	A P man who oppresses the poor is a
	28:3	man who oppresses the P is a beating rain
	28:6	Better is a P man who walks in his
	28:8	it for him who is kind to the P
	28:11	own eyes, but a P man who has understanding
	28:15	wicked ruler over a P people.
	28:27	who gives to the P will not want, but
	29:7	the rights of the P; a wicked man does
	29:13	The P man and the oppressor meet together; the
	29:14	a king judges the P with equity his throne
	30:9	or lest I be P, and steal, and profane
	30:14	knives, to devour the P from off the earth,
	31:9	the rights of the P and needy.
	31:20	her hand to the P, and reaches out her
Eccl	4:13	Better is a P and wise youth than an
	4:14	or in his own kingdom had been born P
	5:8	in a province the P oppressed and justice and
	6:8	And what does the P man have who knows
	9:15	found in it a P wise man, and he
	9:15	no one remembered that P man.
	9:16	than might, though the P man's wisdom is despised,
Wis	2:10	us oppress the righteous P man; let us not
Sir	4:1	son, deprive not the P of his living, and
	4:4	suppliant, nor turn your face away from the P
	4:8	your ear to the P, and answer him peaceably
	7:32	your hand to the P, so that your blessing
	10:21	the eminent, and the P – their glory is
	10:22	to despise an intelligent P man, nor is it
	10:29	A P man is honored for his knowledge, while
	11:19	Lord to enrich a P man quickly and suddenly.
	13:3	even adds reproaches; a P man suffers wrong, and
	13:17	rich man and a P man?
	13:18	of lions; likewise the P are pastures for the
	13:19	proud man; likewise a P man is an abomination
	13:22	When the P man speaks they say, "Who is
	21:5	The prayer of a P man goes from his
	26:4	Whether rich or P, his heart is glad, and
	29:9	Help a P man for the commandment's sake, and
	29:22	the life of a P man under the shelter
	30:14	Better off is a P man who is well
	31:4	The P man toils as his livelihood diminishes, and
	34:20	offers a sacrifice from the property of the P
	34:21	the life of the P; whoever deprives them of
	35:13	the case of a P man; and he will
	38:19	the life of the P man weighs down his
Is	3:14	the spoil of the P is in your houses.
	3:15	my people, by grinding the face of the P
	10:2	and to rob the P of my people of
	11:4	he shall judge the P, and decide with equity
	14:30	the first-born of the P will feed, and the
	25:4	a stronghold to the P, a stronghold to the
	26:6	the feet of the P, the steps of the
	29:19	the LORD, and the P among men shall exult
	32:7	devices to ruin the P with lying words, even
	41:17	When the P and needy seek water, and there
	58:7	and bring the homeless P into your house; when
Jer	2:34	the lifeblood of guiltless P; you did not find
	5:4	"These are only the P, they have no sense;
	22:16	the cause of the P and needy; then it
	39:10	Judah some of the P people who owned nothing,
Bar	6:28	give none to the P or helpless.
Ezek	16:49	did not aid the P and needy.
	18:12	neighbor's wife, oppresses the P and needy, commits
	22:29	they have oppressed the P and needy, and have
Amos	2:7	the head of the P into the dust of
	4:1	Samaria, who oppress the P, who crush the needy,
	5:11	you trample upon the P and take from him
	8:4	needy, and bring the P of the land to
	8:6	we may buy the P for silver and the
Hab	3:14	if to devour the P in secret.
Zech	7:10	the sojourner, or the P; and let none of
Mt	5:3	saying: "Blessed are the P in spirit, for theirs
	11:5	raised up, and the P have good news preached
	19:21	and give to the P, and you will have
	26:9	for a large sum, and given to the P
	26:11	you always have the P with you, but you
Mk	10:21	and give to the P, and you will have
	12:42	And a P widow came, and put in two
	12:43	say to you, this P widow has put in
	14:5	than three hundred denarii, and given to the P
	14:7	you always have the P with you, and whenever
Lk	4:18	anointed me to preach good news to the P
	6:20	said: "Blessed are you P, for yours is the
	7:22	are raised up, the P have good news preached
	14:13	a feast, invite the P, the maimed, the lame,
	14:21	and bring in the P and maimed and blind
	16:20	his gate lay a P man named Lazarus, full
	16:22	The P man died and was carried by the
	18:22	and distribute to the P, and you will have
	19:8	I give to the P; and if I have
	21:2	and he saw a P widow put in two
	21:3	I tell you, this P widow has put in
Jn	2:10	drunk freely, then the P wine; but you have
	12:5	for three hundred denarii and given to the P
	12:6	he cared for the P but because he was
	12:8	The P you always have with you, but you
	13:29	or, that he should give something to the P
Rom	15:26	some contribution for the P among the saints at
2Cor	6:10	yet always rejoicing; as P, yet making many rich;
	8:9	your sake he became P, so that by his
	9:9	he gives to the P; his righteousness endures for
Gal	2:10	have us remember the P, which very thing I
Jas	2:2	your assembly, and a P man in shabby clothing
	2:3	you say to the P man, "Stand there," or,
	2:5	chosen those who are P in the world to
	2:6	you have dishonored the P man.
Rev	3:17	you are wretched, pitiable, P, blind, and naked.
	13:16	great, both rich and P, both free and slave,

POORER
Dan 1:10 that you were in P condition than the youths

POOREST (5)
2Kgs 24:14 none remained, except the P people of the land.
25:12 left some of the P of the land to
Jer 40:7 children, those of the P of the land who
52:15 captive some of the P of the people and
52:16 left some of the P of the land to

POORLY
2Mac 15:38 desired; if it is P done and mediocre, that

POPLAR (3)
Gen 30:37 took fresh rods of P and almond and plane,
Hos 4:13 the hills, under oak, P, and terebinth, because their
14:5 strike root as the P;

POPULACE (2)
2Mac 3:21 prostration of the whole P and the anxiety of
4:39 spread abroad, the P gathered against Lysimachus,

POPULAR
Esth 10:3 among the Jews and P with the multitude of

POPULATION (2)
Num 15:26 them, because the whole P was involved in the
Bar 4:34 pride in her great P, and her insolence will

POPULOUS (2)
Deut 26:5 there he became a nation, great, mighty, and P
Is 32:14 will be forsaken, the P city deserted; the hill

PORATHA
Esth 9:8 Dalphon and Aspatha and P and Adalia and Aridatha

PORCH (3)
1Kgs 7:6 cubits; there was a P in front with pillars,
Ezek 8:16 the LORD, between the P and the altar, were
Mt 26:71 went out to the P, another maid saw him,

PORCIUS
Acts 24:26 Felix was succeeded by P Festus; and desiring to

PORCUPINE
Is 34:11 the hawk and the P shall possess it, the

PORPHYRY
Esth 1:6 a mosaic pavement of P, marble, mother-of-pearl and

PORTALS
Prov 8:3 the entrance of the P she cries aloud:

PORTENT (5)
Ps 71:7 have been as a P to many; but thou
Is 20:3 a sign and a P against Egypt and Ethiopia,
Rev 12:1 And a great P appeared in heaven, a woman
12:3 And another P appeared in heaven; behold, a great
15:1 Then I saw another P in heaven, great and

PORTENTS (2)
Is 8:18 me are signs and P in Israel from the
Joel 2:30 "And I will give P in the heavens and

PORTICO (3)
Jn 10:23 the temple, in the P of Solomon.
Acts 3:11 to them in the P called Solomons, astounded.
5:12 And they were all together in Solomon's P

PORTICOES
Jn 5:2 pool, in Hebrew called Beth-zatha, which has five P

PORTION (131)
Gen 31:14 him, "Is there any P or inheritance left to
43:34 Joseph's table, but Benjamin's P was five times as
Ex 16:4 and gather a day's P every day, that I
29:26 before the LORD; and it shall be your P
29:27 thigh of the priests' P, which is waved, and
29:28 it is the priests' P to be offered by
Lev 2:2 this as its memorial P upon the altar, an
2:9 cereal offering its memorial P and burn this on
2:16 burn as its memorial P part of the crushed
5:12 it as its memorial P and burn this on
6:15 this as its memorial P on the altar, a
6:17 given it as their P of my offerings by
7:33 fat shall have the right thigh for a P
7:35 This is the P of Aaron and of his
8:29 LORD; it was Moses' P of the ram of
24:7 bread as a memorial P to be offered by
24:9 him a most holy P out of the offerings
Num 5:26 offering, as its memorial P, and burn it upon
6:20 they are a holy P for the priest, together
18:8 to you as a P, and to your sons
18:20 shall you have any P among them; I am
18:20 them; I am your P and your inheritance among
31:36 And the half, the P of those who had
Deut 10:9 Therefore Levi has no P or inheritance with his
12:12 since he has no P or inheritance with you.
14:27 for he has no P or inheritance with you.
14:29 because he has no P or inheritance with you,
18:1 Levi, shall have no P or inheritance with Israel;
21:17 giving him a double P of all that he
26:13 have removed the sacred P out of my house,
32:9 For the LORD's P is his people, Jacob his
33:21 for there a commander's P was reserved; and he
Josh 14:4 and Ephraim; and no P was given to the
15:13 son of Jephunneh a P among the people of
17:14 one lot and one P as an inheritance, although
18:7 The Levites have no P among you, for the
18:10 to the people of Israel, to each his P
19:9 of Judah; because the P of the tribe of
22:25 Gadites; you have no P in the LORD.' So
22:27 come, "You have no P in the LORD."'
24:32 at Shechem, in the P of ground which Jacob
1Sam 1:5 give Hannah only one P, because the LORD had
9:23 the cook, "Bring the P I gave you, of
9:24 leg and the upper P and set them before
2Sam 6:19 cake of bread, a P of meat, and a
20:1 said, "We have no P in David, and we
1Kgs 12:16 answered the king, "What P have we in David?
2Kgs 25:30 king, every day a P, as long as he
1Chr 16:3 loaf of bread, a P of meat, and a
16:18 of Canaan, as your P for an inheritance."
2Chr 10:16 answered the king, "What P have we in David?
31:4 Jerusalem to give the P due to the priests
Neh 2:20 but you have no P or right or memorial
Esth 2:9 her ointments and her P of food, and with
13:16 Do not neglect thy P, which thou didst redeem
Job 20:29 is the wicked man's P from God, the heritage
24:18 of the waters; their P is cursed in the
27:13 "This is the P of a wicked man with
31:2 What would be my P from God above, and
Ps 11:6 wind shall be the P of their cup.
16:5 LORD is my chosen P and my cup; thou
17:14 LORD, from men whose P in life is of
49:13 end of those who are pleased with their P
60:6 divide up Shechem and P out the Vale of
68:23 dogs may have their P from the foe."
73:26 my heart and my P for ever.
105:11 of Canaan as your P for an inheritance."
108:7 divide up Shechem, and P out the Vale of
119:57 The LORD is my P; I promise to keep
142:5 art my refuge, my P in the land of
Eccl 9:9 because that is your P in life and in
11:2 Give a P to seven, or even to eight,
Wis 2:9 because this is our P, and this our lot.
Sir 7:31 and give him his P, as is commanded you:
14:9 not satisfied with a P, and mean injustice withers
17:14 every nation, but Israel is the Lord's own P
24:12 honored people, in the P of the Lord, who
38:11 sacrifice, and a memorial P of fine flour, and
41:21 taking away some one's P or gift, and of
45:16 odor as a memorial P, to make atonement for
45:22 and he has no P among the people; for
45:22 Lord himself is his P and inheritance.
Is 17:14 This is the P of those who despoil us,
53:12 will divide him a P with the great, and
57:6 the valley is your P; they, they, are your
61:7 shall have a double P, instead of dishonor you
61:7 shall possess a double P; yours shall be everlasting
Jer 10:16 he who is the P of Jacob, for he
12:10 have trampled down my P, they have made my
12:10 have made my pleasant P a desolate wilderness.
13:25 is your lot, the P I have measured out
37:12 Benjamin to receive his P there among the people.
51:19 he who is the P of Jacob, for he
Lam 3:24 "The LORD is my P
Ezek 16:27 and diminished your allotted P, and delivered you to
45:1 for the LORD a P of the land as
45:4 shall be the holy P of the land; it
45:6 "Alongside the P set apart as the holy district
45:14 and as the fixed P of oil, one tenth

P

48:1 the east side to the west, Dan, one P
48:2 the east side to the west, Asher, one P
48:3 the east side to the west, Naphtali, one P
48:4 the east side to the west, Manasseh, one P
48:5 the east side to the west, Ephraim, one P
48:6 the east side to the west, Reuben, one P
48:7 the east side to the west, Judah, one P
48:8 west, shall be the P which you shall set
48:9 The P which you shall set apart for the
48:10 allotments of the holy P: the priests shall have
48:12 them as a special P from the holy portion
48:12 portion from the holy P of the land, a
48:14 not alienate this choice P of the land, for
48:18 length alongside the holy P shall be ten thousand
48:18 west, and it shall be alongside the holy P
48:20 The whole P which you shall set apart shall
48:20 that is, the holy P together with the property
48:21 sides of the holy P and of the property
48:21 cubits of the holy P to the east border,
48:21 The holy P with the sanctuary of the temple
48:22 The P of the prince shall lie between the
48:23 the east side to the west, Benjamin, one P
48:24 the east side to the west, Simeon, one P
48:25 the east side to the west, Issachar, one P
48:26 the east side to the west, Zebulun, one P
48:27 the east side to the west, Gad, one P
Dan 1:5 assigned them a daily P of the rich food
Mic 2:4 ruined; he changes the P of my people; how
Zech 2:12 inherit Judah as his P in the holy land,
2Mac 1:26 Israel and preserve thy P and make it holy.
Lk 10:42 has chosen the good P, which shall not be
12:42 to give them their P of food at the

PORTIONED

Is 34:17 them, his hand has P it out to them

PORTIONS (22)

Gen 4:4 firstlings of his flock and of their fat P
43:34 P were taken to them from Joseph's table, but
Deut 18:8 They shall have equal P to eat, besides what
Josh 17:5 fell to Manasseh ten P, besides the land of
18:5 divide it into seven P, Judah continuing in his
1Sam 1:4 sacrificed, he would give P to Peninnah his wife
2Chr 31:15 priests, to distribute the P to their brethren, old
31:19 by name to distribute P to every male among
Neh 8:10 sweet wine and send P to him for whom
8:12 drink and to send P and to make great
12:44 gather into them the P required by the law
12:47 Nehemiah gave the daily P for the singers and
13:10 found out that the P of the Levites had
Esth 9:19 which they send choice P to one another.
9:22 days for sending choice P to one another and
Sir 44:24 inheritance; he determined his P, and distributed
50:12 when he received the P from the hands of
Ezek 45:7 one of the tribal P, and extending from the
47:13 Joseph shall have two P
48:8 one of the tribal P, from the east side
48:21 parallel to the tribal P, it shall belong to
48:29 these are their several P, says the Lord GOD.

PORTRAY (2)

Ezek 4:1 it before you, and P upon it a city,
43:11 that they have done, P the temple, its arrangement,

PORTRAYED (4)

Ezek 8:10 and saw; and there, P upon the wall round
23:14 further; she saw men P upon the wall, the
23:14 images of the Chaldeans P in vermilion,
Gal 3:1 Jesus Christ was publicly P as crucified?

PORTS

Acts 27:2 to sail to the P along the coast of

POSIDONIUS

2Mac 14:19 Therefore he sent P and Theodotus and Mattathias

POSITION (14)

Num 2:17 set out, each in P, standard by standard.
2Chr 20:17 this battle; take your P, stand still, and see
Esth 1:19 king give her royal P to another who is
14:16 sign of my proud P, which is upon my
1Mac 1:34 These strengthened their P;
6:36 These took their P beforehand wherever the beast
10:54 you and to her in keeping with your P
2Mac 3:11 man of very prominent P, and that it totaled
6:18 the scribes in high P, a man now advanced
Mt 22:16 do not regard the P of men.
Mk 12:14 do not regard the P of men, but truly
1Cor 14:16 any one in the P of an outsider say
2Cor 5:12 themselves on a man's P and not on his
Jude 1:6 not keep their own P but left their proper

POSITIONS (6)

1Kgs 20:12 booths, he said to his men, "Take your P
20:12 And they took their P against the city.
1Mac 10:37 them be put in P of trust in the
2Mac 8:6 He captured strategic P and put to flight not
13:18 of the Jews, tried strategy in attacking their P
1Tim 2:2 who are in high P, that we may lead

POSSESS (98)

Gen 15:7 the Chaldeans, to give you this land to P
15:8 know that I shall P it?"
22:17 And your descendants shall P the gate of their
24:60 and may your descendants P the gate of those
47:1 and all that they P, have come from the
49:30 Ephron the Hittite to P as a burying place.
50:13 Ephron the Hittite, to P as a burying place.
Ex 23:30 you are increased and P the land.
Lev 20:24 it to you to P, a land flowing with
25:24 all the country you P, you shall grant a
Num 14:24 and his descendants shall P it.
27:11 family, and he shall P it.
33:53 land to you to P it.
36:8 people of Israel may P the inheritance of his
Deut 1:39 it, and they shall P it.
3:18 you this land to P; all your men of
4:14 the land which you are going over to P
4:26 over the Jordan to P; you will not live
5:31 I give them to P
5:33 live long in the land which you shall P
6:1 are going over, to P it;
8:1 and go in and P the land which the
9:4 brought me in to P this land'; whereas it
9:5 you going in to P their land; but because
9:6 this good land to P because of your righteousness;
10:11 may go in and P the land, which I
11:8 are going over to P,
11:11 are going over to P is a land of
11:31 you; and when you P it and live in
12:1 has given you to P, all the days that
15:4 for an inheritance to P,
17:14 gives you, and you P it and dwell in
19:2 which the LORD your God gives you to P
19:14 God gives you to P, you shall not remove
21:1 God gives you to P, any one is found
25:19 for an inheritance to P, you shall blot out
28:42 the fruit of your ground the locust shall P
30:5 possessed, that you may P it; and he will
30:18 are going over the Jordan to enter and P
31:13 which you are going over the Jordan to P
32:47 which you are going over the Jordan to P
33:23 blessing of the LORD, P the lake and the
Josh 1:11 which the LORD your God gives you to P
1:15 your possession, and shall P it, the land which
17:18 shall clear it and P it to its farthest
23:5 sight; and you shall P their land, as the
24:4 country of Seir to P, but Jacob and his
Judg 11:24 Will you not P what Chemosh your god gives
11:24 possess what Chemosh your god gives you to P
11:24 our God has dispossessed before us, we will P
18:9 and enter in and P the land.
1Chr 28:8 God; that you may P this good land, and
Neh 9:15 to go in to P the land which thou
9:23 thou hadst told their fathers to enter and P
Tob 3:17 Tobias was entitled to P her.
Jud 12:16 with great desire to P her; for he had
Ps 25:13 and his children shall P the land.
37:9 for the LORD shall P the land.
37:11 But the meek shall P the land, and delight
37:22 by the LORD shall P the land, but those
37:29 The righteous shall P the land, and dwell upon
37:34 will exalt you to P the land; you will
69:35 shall dwell there and P it;
Wis 8:21 that I would not P wisdom unless God gave
Sir 25:4 for the aged to P good counsel!
27:30 the sinful man will P them.
Is 14:2 house of Israel will P them in the LORD's
14:21 lest they rise and P the earth, and fill
34:11 and the porcupine shall P it, the owl and
34:17 the line; they shall P it for ever, from
54:3 and your descendants will P the nations and will

P

57:13 refuge in me shall P the land, and shall
60:21 be righteous; they shall P the land for ever,
61:7 your land you shall P a double portion; yours
Bar 6:5 fear for these gods P you, when you see
Ezek 33:24 surely given us to P
33:25 blood; shall you then P the land?
33:26 wife; shall you then P the land?
36:5 contempt, that they might P it and plunder it.
36:12 Israel; and they shall P you, and you shall
Dan 7:18 receive the kingdom, and P the kingdom for ever,
13:11 their lustful desire to P her.
Hos 9:6 Nettles shall P their precious things of silver; thorns
Amos 2:10 in the wilderness, to P the land of the
9:12 old; that they may P the remnant of Edom
Obad 1:17 house of Jacob shall P their own possessions.
1:19 of the Negeb shall P Mount Esau, and those
1:19 the Philistines; they shall P the land of Ephraim
1:19 Samaria and Benjamin shall P Gilead.
1:20 people of Israel shall P Phoenicia as far as
1:20 are in Sepharad shall P the cities of the
Zeph 2:9 of my nation shall P them."
Zech 8:12 of this people to P all these things.
Mt 19:21 go, sell what you P and give to the
1Cor 2:13 truths to those who P the Spirit.
8:1 that "all of us P knowledge." "Knowledge" puffs up,
8:7 However, not all P this knowledge.
12:30 Do all P gifts of healing?

POSSESSED (22)

Num 21:35 to him; and they P his land.
Deut 30:5 land which your fathers P, that you may possess
Josh 13:1 there remains yet very much land to be P
22:9 of which they had P themselves by command of
Neh 9:24 descendants went in and P the land, and thou
Jud 8:10 charge of all she P, to summon Chabris and
9:13 and against the house P by thy children.
Job 22:8 The man with power P the land, and the
Wis 11:12 for a twofold grief P them, and a groaning
Is 63:18 Thy holy people P thy sanctuary a little while;
Zeph 2:9 like Gomorrah, a land P by nettles and salt
1Mac 5:23 children, and all they P, and led them to
2Mac 2:9 made clear that being P of wisdom Solomon offered
Mt 8:16 him many who were P with demons; and he
15:22 my daughter is severely P by a demon."
Mk 1:32 who were sick or P with demons.
3:22 Jerusalem said, "He is P by Be-elzebul, and by
5:18 man who had been P with demons begged him
7:24 whose little daughter was P by an unclean spirit,
Lk 8:36 he who had been P with demons was healed.
Acts 4:32 the things which he P was his own, but
8:7 of many who were P, crying with a loud

POSSESSES (2)

Num 36:8 And every daughter who P an inheritance in any
Bar 3:24 And how vast the territory that he P

POSSESSING (3)

Judg 18:7 in the earth, and P wealth, and how they
2Mac 4:25 king's orders he returned, P no qualification for the
2Cor 6:10 having nothing, and yet P everything.

POSSESSION (162)

Gen 17:8 Canaan, for an everlasting P; and I will be
23:9 your presence as a P for a burying place."
23:18 to Abraham as a P in the presence of
23:20 to Abraham as a P for a burying place
28:4 that you may take P of the land of
31:18 the cattle in his P which he had acquired
36:43 their dwelling places in the land of their P
47:11 and gave them a P in the land of
48:4 you for an everlasting P
Ex 6:8 I will give it to you for a P
19:5 shall be my own P among all peoples; for
21:16 or is found in P of him, shall be
22:2 found alive in his P, whether it is an
Lev 14:34 give you for a P, and I put a
14:34 the land of your P,
25:32 the cities of their P, the Levites may redeem
25:33 a city of their P shall be released in
25:33 the Levites are their P among the people of
25:34 not be sold; for that is their perpetual P
25:41 and return to the P of his fathers.
25:46 to inherit as a P for ever; you may
27:21 priest shall be in P of it.
27:22 a part of his P by inheritance,
27:24 land belongs as a P by inheritance.
Num 21:24 the sword, and took P of his land from
27:4 Give to us a P among our father's brethren."
27:7 you shall give them P of an inheritance among
32:5 your servants for a P; do not take us
32:22 land shall be your P before the LORD.
32:29 of Gilead for a P;
32:32 of Canaan, and the P of our inheritance shall
33:53 and you shall take P of the land and
35:2 the inheritance of their P, cities to dwell in;
35:8 shall give from the P of the people of
35:28 manslayer may return to the land of his P
Deut 1:8 go in and take P of the land which
1:21 you; go up, take P, as the LORD, the
2:5 have given Mount Seir to Esau as a P
2:9 their land for a P, because I have given
2:9 of Lot for a P
2:12 the land of their P, which the LORD gave
2:19 of Ammon as a P, because I have given
2:19 of Lot for a P
2:24 land; begin to take P, and contend with him
2:31 you; begin to take P, that you may occupy
3:12) "When we took P of this land at
3:20 every man to his P which I have given
3:28 shall put them in P of the land which
4:1 go in and take P of the land which
4:5 are entering to take P of it.
4:20 people of his own P, as at this day.
4:22 go over and take P of that good land.
4:47 And they took P of his land and the
6:18 go in and take P of the good land
7:1 are entering to take P of it, and clears
7:6 people for his own P, out of all the
9:23 'Go up and take P of the land which
11:8 go in and take P of the land which
11:10 are entering to take P of it is not
11:29 are entering to take P of it, you shall
11:31 go in to take P of the land which
14:2 people for his own P, out of all the
19:3 gives you as a P, so that any manslayer
23:20 are entering to take P of it.
26:1 inheritance, and have taken P of it, and live
26:18 people for his own P, as he has promised
28:21 are entering to take P of it.
28:63 are entering to take P of it.
30:16 are entering to take P of it.
31:7 shall put them in P of it.
32:49 of Israel for a P;
33:4 a law, as a P for the assembly of
Josh 1:11 go in to take P of the land which
1:15 and they also take P of the land which
1:15 the land of your P, and shall possess it,
12:1 Israel defeated, and took P of their land beyond
12:6 their land for a P to the Reubenites and
12:7 of Israel as a P according to their allotments,
17:12 Manasseh could not take P of those cities; but
18:3 go in and take P of the land, which
19:47 the sword they took P of it and settled
21:12 to Caleb the son of Jephunneh as his P
21:41 the midst of the P of the people of
21:43 fathers; and having taken P of it, they settled
22:4 the land where your P lies, which Moses the
22:7 Moses had given a P in Bashan; but to
22:7 Joshua had given a P beside their brethren in
22:19 take for yourselves a P among us; only do
24:8 hand, and you took P of their land, and
Judg 1:19 Judah, and he took P of the hill country,
2:6 his inheritance to take P of the land.
3:13 Israel; and they took P of the city of
6:34 of the LORD took P of Gideon; and he
11:21 them; so Israel took P of all the land
11:22 And they took P of all the territory of
11:23 are you to take P of them?
1Kgs 21:15 to Ahab, "Arise, take P of the vineyard of
21:16 the Jezreelite, to take P of it.
21:18 of Naboth, where he has gone to take P
21:19 killed, and also taken P And you shall say
2Kgs 17:24 Israel; and they took P of Samaria, and dwelt
2Chr 20:11 us out of thy P, which thou hast given
24:20 Spirit of God took P of Zechariah the son
31:1 returned to their cities, every man to his P
Ezra 4:16 will then have no P in the province Beyond
9:11 are entering, to take P of it, is a
Neh 9:22 corner; so they took P of the land of
9:25 rich land, and took P of houses full of
Jud 1:14 Thus he took P of his cities, and came
5:15 the Jordan they took P of all the hill

P

7:12 let your servants take P of the spring of
15:7 from the slaughter, took P of what remained, and
Ps 2:8 heritage, and the ends of the earth your P
78:55 apportioned them for a P and settled the tribes
83:12 said, "Let us take P for ourselves of the
105:44 nations; and they took P of the fruit of
135:4 chosen Jacob for himself, Israel as his own P
Wis 8:5 riches are a desirable P in life, what is
Sir 4:16 descendants will remain in P of her.
24:6 every people and nation I have gotten a P
36:24 wife gets his best P, a helper fit for
51:21 seek her, therefore I have gained a good P
Is 14:23 will make it a P of the hedgehog, and
Jer 30:3 and they shall take P of it."
32:8 for the right of P and redemption is yours;
32:23 they entered and took P of it.
Ezek 7:24 the nations to take P of their houses; I
11:15 is given for a P
25:4 the East for a P, and they shall set
25:10 the East as a P, that it may be
33:24 man, yet he got P of the land; but
35:10 and we will take P of them,--although the
36:2 heights have become our P
36:3 that you became the P of the rest of
36:5 to themselves as a P with wholehearted joy and
44:28 shall give them no P in Israel; I am
44:28 them no possession in Israel; I am their P
45:1 the land as a P, you shall set apart
45:5 the temple, as their P for cities to live
45:6 shall assign for the P of the city an
Dan 11:6 and he who got P of her.
Zeph 2:7 seacoast shall become the P of the remnant of
Zech 13:5 land has been my P since my youth.'
Mal 3:17 of hosts, my special P on the day when
1Mac 1:57 was found in the P of any one, or
10:76 gates, and Jonathan gained P of Joppa.
10:89 him Ekron and all its environs as his P
11:1 he tried to get P of Alexander's kingdom by
11:34 have confirmed as their P both the territory of
11:66 them from there, took P of the city, and
13:38 the strongholds that you have built be your P
15:29 and you have taken P of many places in
16:20 other men to take P of Jerusalem and the
2Mac 2:14 come upon us, and they are in our P
8:30 of them and got P of some exceedingly high
10:17 them vigorously, they gained P of the places, and
13:13 enter Judea and get P of the city.
14:2 fleet, and had taken P of the country, having
15:37 has been in the P of the Hebrews.
Acts 7:5 it to him in P and to his posterity
Eph 1:14 inheritance until we acquire P of it, to the
Heb 10:34 yourselves had a better P and an abiding one.

POSSESSIONS (38)

Gen 12:5 son, and all their P which they had gathered,
13:6 dwelling together; for their P were so great that
15:14 and afterward they shall come out with great P
26:14 He had P of flocks and herds, and a
36:7 For their P were too great for them to
47:27 Goshen; and they gained P in it, and were
Num 32:30 armed, they shall have P among you in the
Deut 21:16 when he assigns his P as an inheritance to
1Chr 7:28 Their P and settlements were Bethel and its towns,
9:2 dwell again in their P in their cities were
2Chr 1:11 you have not asked P, wealth, honor, or the
1:12 also give you riches, P, and honor, such as
21:3 silver, gold, and valuable P, together with fortified
21:14 wives, and all your P,
21:17 carried away all the P they found that belonged
31:3 king from his own P was for the burnt
32:29 abundance; for God had given him very great P
35:7 three thousand bulls; these were from the king's P
Tob 4:7 Give alms from your P to all who live
4:8 If you have many P, make your gift from
Job 1:10 his hands, and his P have increased in the
20:28 The P of his house will be carried away,
Ps 105:21 ruler of all his P,
Eccl 2:7 I had also great P of herds and flocks,
5:19 has given wealth and P and power to enjoy
6:2 whom God gives wealth, P, and honor, so that
Wis 13:17 When he prays about P and his marriage and
Sir 25:20 and do not desire a woman for her P
41:1 at peace among his P, to a man without
Obad 1:17 the house of Jacob shall possess their own P
Zech 9:4 strip her of her P and hurl her wealth
Mt 19:22 he went away sorrowful; for he had great P
24:47 you, he will set him over all his P
Mk 10:22 he went away sorrowful; for he had great P
Lk 12:15 does not consist in the abundance of his P
12:33 Sell your P, and give alms; provide yourselves with
12:44 you, he will set him over all his P
Acts 2:45 and they sold their P and goods and distributed

POSSESSORS (2)

Prov 1:19 violence; it takes away the life of its P
Acts 4:34 as many as were P of lands or houses

POSSIBLE (28)

Tob 10:2 he said, "Is it P that he has been
10:2 Or is it P that Gabael has died and
Sir 18:5 It is not P to diminish or increase them,
18:5 them, nor is it P to trace the wonders
22:19 not despair, for a renewal of friendship is P
22:20 worry, for reconciliation is P; but as for reviling,
1Mac 11:22 for a conference at Ptolemais as quickly as P
2Mac 3:6 but that it was P for them to fall
11:18 him, and he has agreed to what was P
13:26 platform, made the best P defense, convinced them,
14:29 Since it was not P to oppose the king,
Mt 19:26 is impossible, but with God all things are P
24:24 to lead astray, if P, even the elect.
26:39 Father, if it be P, let this cup pass
Mk 9:23 All things are P to him who believes."
10:27 for all things are P with God."
13:22 to lead astray, if P, the elect.
14:35 that, if it were P, the hour might pass
14:36 Father, all things are P to thee; remove this
Lk 18:27 impossible with men is P with God."
Acts 2:24 because it was not P for him to be
8:22 the Lord that, if P, the intent of your
17:15 him as soon as P, they departed.
20:16 be at Jerusalem, if P, on the day of
27:39 which they planned if P to bring the ship
Rom 12:18 If P, so far as it depends upon you,
Gal 4:15 you witness that, if P, you would have plucked
Phil 3:11 his death, that if P I may attain the

POST (6)

1Kgs 20:24 kings, each from his P, and put commanders in
Jud 13:6 went up to the P at the end of
Esth 16:19 'Therefore P a copy of this letter publicly in
Sir 26:12 in front of every P and open her quiver
Is 21:8 day, and at my P I am stationed whole
Ezek 46:2 his stand by the P of the gate.

POSTED (3)

2Kgs 11:18 And the priest P watchmen over the house of
2Chr 23:18 And Jehoiada P watchmen for the house of the
2Mac 14:22 set in place; Judas P armed men in readiness

POSTERITY (21)

Gen 21:23 offspring or with my P, but as I have
Num 21:30 So their P perished from Heshbon, as far as
Tob 4:12 their children, and their P will inherit the land.
Ps 22:30 P shall serve him; men shall tell of the
37:37 upright, for there is P for the man of
37:38 be altogether destroyed; the P of the wicked shall
102:28 shall dwell secure; their P shall be established
109:13 May his P be cut off; may his name
Sir 41:6 perish, and on their P will be a perpetual
44:14 Their P will continue for ever, and their glory
44:22 be blessed through his P; that he would multiply
44:22 earth, and exalt his P like the stars, and
47:20 honor, and defiled your P, so that you brought
47:22 one, nor destroy the P of him who loved
Is 14:22 and remnant, offspring and P, says the LORD.
Dan 11:4 but not to his P, nor according to the
Lk 1:55 Abraham and to his P for ever."
Acts 3:25 Abraham, 'And in your P shall all the families
7:5 possession and to his P after him, though he
7:6 this effect, that his P would be aliens in
13:23 will.' Of this man's P God has brought to

POSTPONE

Sir 5:7 to the Lord, nor P it from day to

POSTS (8)

Judg 16:3 city and the two P, and pulled them up,
2Chr 7:6 priests stood at their P; the Levites also, with
30:16 They took their accustomed P according to the law
Jud 7:33 people to their various P, and they went up
8:36 returned from the tent and went to their P

	13:9	the canopy from the P; after a moment she
Song	3:10	He made its P of silver, its back of
Ezek	45:19	the altar, and the P of the gate of

POT (20)

Gen	15:17	behold, a smoking fire P and a flaming torch
Judg	6:19	he put in a P, and brought them to
1Sam	2:14	kettle, or caldron, or P; all that the fork
2Kgs	4:38	"Set on the great P, and boil pottage for
	4:39	them up into the P of pottage, not knowing
	4:40	man of God, there is death in the P
	4:41	threw it into the P, and said, "Pour out
	4:41	And there was no harm in the P
Job	41:20	as from a boiling P and burning rushes.
	41:31	deep boil like a P; he makes the sea
	41:31	the sea like a P of ointment.
Eccl	7:6	of thorns under a P, so is the laughter
Sir	13:2	How can the clay P associate with the iron
	13:2	The P will strike against it, and will itself
Jer	1:13	"I see a boiling P, facing away from the
	22:28	Coniah a despised, broken P, a vessel no one
Ezek	24:3	GOD: Set on the P, set it on, pour
	24:6	bloody city, to the P whose rust is in
Zech	12:6	Judah like a blazing P in the midst of
	14:21	the altar; and every P in Jerusalem and Judah

POTIPHAR (2)

Gen	37:36	him in Egypt to P, an officer of Pharaoh,
	39:1	down to Egypt, and P, an officer of Pharaoh,

POTIPHERA (3)

Gen	41:45	Asenath, the daughter of P priest of On.
	41:50	Asenath, the daughter of P priest of On, bore
	46:20	Asenath, the daughter of P the priest of On,

POTS (16)

Ex	27:3	You shall make P for it to receive its
	38:3	of the altar, the P, the shovels, the basins,
Num	11:8	and boiled it in P, and made cakes of
1Kgs	7:40	Hiram also made the P, the shovels, and the
	7:45	Now the P, the shovels, and the basins, all
2Kgs	25:14	they took away the P, and the shovels, and
2Chr	4:11	Huram also made the P, the shovels, and the
	4:16	The P, the shovels, the forks, and all the
	35:13	the holy offerings in P, in caldrons, and in
Ps	58:9	Sooner than your P can feel the heat of
Jer	52:18	they took away the P, and the shovels, and
	52:19	the basins, and the P, and the lampstands, and
Lam	4:2	are reckoned as earthen P, the work of a
Zech	14:20	And the P in the house of the LORD
Mk	7:4	washing of cups and P and vessels of bronze.
Rev	2:27	iron, as when earthen P are broken in pieces,

POTSHERD (3)

Job	2:8	And he took a P with which to scrape
Ps	22:15	dried up like a P, and my tongue cleaves
Jer	19:2	the entry of the P Gate, and proclaim there

POTSHERDS (2)

Job	41:30	underparts are like sharp P; he spreads himself like
Sir	22:7	like one who glues P together, or who rouses

POTTAGE (8)

Gen	25:29	when Jacob was boiling P, Esau came in from
	25:30	some of that red P, for I am famished!"
	25:34	gave Esau bread and P of lentils, and he
2Kgs	4:38	great pot, and boil P for the sons of
	4:39	into the pot of P, not knowing what they
	4:40	were eating of the P, they cried out, "O
Dan	14:33	He had boiled P and had broken bread into
Hag	2:12	his skirt bread, or P, or wine, or oil,

POTTER (23)

Ps	2:9	in pieces like a P's vessel."
Wis	15:7	For when a P kneads the soft earth and
Sir	27:5	The kiln tests the P's vessels; so the test
	33:13	the hand of the P — for all his
	38:29	So too is the P sitting at his work
Is	29:16	Shall the P be regarded as the clay; that
	30:14	like that of a P's vessel which is smashed
	41:25	on mortar, as the P treads clay.
	45:9	with his Maker, an earthen vessel with the P
	64:8	and thou art our P; we are all the
Jer	18:2	go down to the P's house, and there I
	18:3	went down to the P's house, and there he
	18:4	was spoiled in the P's hand, and he reworked
	18:4	seemed good to the P to do.
	18:6	with you as this P has done?
	18:6	the clay in the P's hand, so are you
	19:1	LORD, "Go, buy a P's earthen flask, and take
	19:11	as one breaks a P's vessel, so that it
Lam	4:2	the work of a P's hands!
Dan	2:41	and toes partly of P's clay and partly of
Mt	27:7	bought with them the P's field, to bury strangers
	27:10	gave them for the P's field, as the Lord
Rom	9:21	Has the P no right over the clay, to

POTTERS

1Chr	4:23	These were the P and inhabitants of Netaim and

POULTICE

Wis	16:12	For neither herb nor P cured them, but it

POUND (5)

Lk	19:16	him, saying, 'Lord, your P has made ten pounds
	19:18	came, saying, 'Lord, your P has made five pounds.'
	19:20	'Lord, here is your P, which I kept laid
	19:24	stood by, 'Take the P from him, and give
Jn	12:3	Mary took a P of costly ointment of pure

POUNDS (6)

Lk	19:13	he gave them ten P, and said to them,
	19:16	pound has made ten P more.'
	19:18	pound has made five P
	19:24	who has the ten P
	19:25	'Lord, he has ten P
Jn	19:39	aloes, about a hundred P weight.

POUR (81)

Ex	4:9	from the Nile and P it upon the dry
	25:29	bowls with which to P libations; of pure gold
	29:7	the anointing oil, and P it on his head
	29:12	the blood you shall P out at the base
	30:9	offering; and you shall P no libation thereon.
	37:16	flagons with which to P libations.
Lev	2:1	fine flour; he shall P oil upon it, and
	2:6	it in pieces, and P oil on it; it
	4:7	the bull he shall P out at the base
	4:18	the blood he shall P out at the base
	4:25	of burnt offering, and P out the rest of
	4:30	of burnt offering, and P out the rest of
	4:34	of burnt offering, and P out the rest of
	14:15	log of oil, and P it into the palm
	14:26	And the priest shall P some of the oil
	14:41	scrape off they shall P into an unclean place
	17:13	may be eaten shall P out its blood and
Num	5:15	barley meal; he shall P no oil upon it
	28:7	holy place you shall P out a drink offering
Deut	12:16	the blood; you shall P it out upon the
	12:24	eat it; you shall P it out upon the
	15:23	its blood; you shall P it out on the
Judg	6:20	on this rock, and P the broth over them."
1Kgs	18:33	jars with water, and P it on the burnt
2Kgs	4:4	and your sons, and P into all these vessels;
	4:41	the pot, and said, P out for the men,
	9:3	flask of oil, and P it on his head,
Job	10:10	Didst thou not P me out like milk and
	36:28	rain which the skies P down, and drop upon
	40:11	P forth the overflowings of your anger, and look
Ps	16:4	blood I will not P out or take their
	42:4	I remember, as I P out my soul: how
	62:8	all times, O people; P out your heart before
	69:24	P out thy indignation upon them, and let thy
	75:8	mixed; and he will P a draught from it,
	79:6	P out thy anger on the nations that do
	94:4	They P out their arrogant words, they boast, all
	119:171	My lips will P forth praise that thou dost
	142:2	to the LORD, I P out my complaint before
	145:7	They shall P forth the fame of thy abundant
Prov	1:23	reproof; behold, I will P out my thoughts to
	15:2	the mouths of fools P out folly.
Sir	18:28	become skilled themselves, and P forth apt proverbs.
	24:31	afar; I will again P out teaching like prophecy,
	32:4	is entertainment, do not P out talk; do not
	36:7	Rouse thy anger and P out thy wrath; destroy
	38:11	of fine flour, and P oil on your offering,
	39:6	of understanding; he will P forth words of wisdom
	39:28	of consummation they will P out their strength and
Is	44:3	For I will P water on the thirsty land,
	44:3	dry ground; I will P my Spirit upon your
	58:10	speaking wickedness, if you P yourself out for the
Jer	6:11	P it out upon the children in the street,

7:18 of heaven; and they P out drink offerings to
10:25 P out thy wrath upon the nations that know
14:16 For I will P out their wickedness upon them.
44:17 queen of heaven and P out libations to her,
44:25 of heaven and to P out libations to her.'
Lam 2:19 P out your heart like water before the presence
Ezek 7:8 Now I will soon P out my wrath upon
14:19 into that land, and P out my wrath upon
20:8 I thought I would P out my wrath upon
20:13 I thought I would P out my wrath upon
20:21 I thought I would P out my wrath upon
21:31 And I will P out my indignation upon you;
24:3 pot, set it on, P in water also;
24:7 rock, she did not P it upon the ground
30:15 And I will P my wrath upon Pelusium, the
39:29 from them, when I P out my Spirit upon
Hos 5:10 upon them I will P out my wrath like
9:4 They shall not P libations of wine to the
Joel 2:28 afterward, that I will P out my spirit on
2:29 those days, I will P out my spirit.
Mic 1:6 vineyards; and I will P down her stones into
Zeph 3:8 to assemble kingdoms, to P out upon them my
Zech 12:10 "And I will P out on the house of
Mal 3:10 heaven for you and P down for you an
Acts 2:17 declares, that I will P out my Spirit upon
2:18 those days I will P out my Spirit; and
Jas 3:11 Does a spring P forth from the same opening
Rev 16:1 seven angels, "Go and P out on the earth

POURED (99)

Gen 28:18 for a pillar and P oil on the top
35:14 of stone; and he P out a drink offering
35:14 offering on it, and P oil on it.
Ex 9:33 the rain no longer P upon the earth.
30:32 It shall not be P upon the bodies of
Lev 4:12 where the ashes are P out, and shall burn
4:12 where the ashes are P out it shall be
8:12 And he P some of the anointing oil on
8:15 purified the altar, and P out the blood at
9:9 of the altar, and P out the blood at
21:10 the anointing oil is P, and who has been
Deut 12:27 your sacrifices shall be P out on the altar
1Sam 7:6 and drew water and P it out before the
10:1 vial of oil and P it on his head,
2Sam 23:16 drink of it; he P it out to the
1Kgs 13:3 upon it shall be P out.'"
13:5 down, and the ashes P out from the altar,
2Kgs 3:11 Shaphat is here, who P water on the hands
4:5 sons; and as she P they brought the vessels
4:40 And they P out for the men to eat.
9:6 and the young man P the oil on his
16:13 his cereal offering, and P his drink offering, and
1Chr 11:18 drink of it; he P it out to the
2Chr 12:7 wrath shall not be P out upon Jerusalem by
34:21 the LORD that is P out on us, because
34:25 my wrath will be P out upon this place
Job 3:24 and my groanings are P out like water.
29:6 milk, and the rock P out for me streams
30:16 now my soul is P out within me; days
Ps 22:14 I am P out like water, and all my
45:2 of men; grace is P upon your lips; therefore
68:8 earth quaked, the heavens P down rain, at the
77:17 The clouds P out water; the skies gave forth
79:3 They have P out their blood like water round
92:10 wild ox; thou hast P over me fresh oil.
106:38 to the demons; they P out innocent blood, the
Song 1:3 your name is oil P out; therefore the maidens
Sir 1:7 and apportioned her, he P her out upon all
30:18 Good things P out upon a mouth that is
50:15 to the cup and P a libation of the
50:15 of the grape; he P it out at the
50:27 out of his heart P forth wisdom.
Is 26:16 they sought thee, they P out a prayer when
29:10 For the LORD has P out upon you a
32:15 until the Spirit is P upon us from on
42:25 So he P upon him the heat of his
53:12 the strong; because he P out his soul to
57:6 to them you have P out a drink offering,
63:6 my wrath, and I P out their lifeblood on
Jer 7:20 my wrath will be P out on this place,
19:13 drink offerings have been P out to other gods—
32:29 drink offerings have been P out to other gods,
42:18 and my wrath were P out on the inhabitants
42:18 my wrath will be P out on you when
44:6 and my anger were P forth and kindled in
44:19 queen of heaven and P out libations to her,
44:19 bearing her image and P out libations to her?"
Lam 2:4 of Zion; he has P out his fury like
2:11 tumult; my heart is P out in grief because
2:12 as their life is P out on their mothers'
4:11 to his wrath, he P out his hot anger;
Ezek 20:28 odors, and there they P out their drink offerings.
20:33 arm, and with wrath P out, I will be
20:34 arm, and with wrath P out;
22:22 I the LORD have P out my wrath upon
22:31 Therefore I have P out my indignation upon them;
23:8 her virgin bosom and P out their lust upon
36:18 So I P out my wrath upon them for
Dan 9:11 of God have been P out upon us, because
9:27 the decreed end is P out on the desolator."
Joel 2:23 your vindication, he has P down for you abundant
Mic 1:4 the fire, like waters P down a steep place.
Nah 1:6 His wrath is P out like fire, and the
Zeph 1:17 their blood shall be P out like dust, and
Zech 4:12 which the oil is P out?"
1Mac 7:17 and their blood they P out round about Jerusalem,
2Mac 1:31 was left should be P upon large stones.
Mt 26:7 expensive ointment, and she P it on his head,
26:28 the covenant, which is P out for many for
Mk 14:3 broke the flask and P it over his head.
14:24 the covenant, which is P out for many.
Lk 22:20 "This cup which is P out for you is
Jn 2:15 the temple; and he P out the coins of
13:5 Then he P water into a basin, and began
Acts 2:33 Holy Spirit, he has P out this which you
10:45 Holy Spirit had been P out even on the
Rom 5:5 God's love has been P into our hearts through
Phil 2:17 I am to be P as a libation upon
Tit 3:6 Holy Spirit, which he P out upon us richly
Rev 12:15 The serpent P water like a river out of
12:16 which the dragon had P from his mouth.
14:10 wine of God's wrath, P unmixed into the cup
16:2 first angel went and P his bowl on the
16:3 The second angel P his bowl into the sea,
16:4 The third angel P his bowl into the rivers
16:8 The fourth angel P his bowl on the sun,
16:10 The fifth angel P his bowl on the throne
16:12 The sixth angel P his bowl on the great
16:17 The seventh angel P his bowl into the air,

POURING (4)

1Sam 1:15 but I have been P out my soul before
Jer 44:18 queen of heaven and P out libations to her,
Mt 26:12 In P this ointment on my body she has
Lk 10:34 bound up his wounds, P on oil and wine;

POURS (14)

Job 12:21 He P contempt on princes, and looses the belt
16:13 does not spare; he P out my gall on
16:20 scorn me; my eye P out tears to God,
Ps 19:2 Day to day P forth speech, and night to
107:40 trouble, and sorrow, he P contempt upon princes and
Prov 15:28 mouth of the wicked P out evil things.
Sir 10:13 who clings to it P out abominations.
16:11 to forgive, and he P out wrath.
18:10 patient with them and P out his mercy upon
35:14 the widow when she P out her story.
43:19 He P the hoarfrost upon the earth like salt,
Amos 5:8 of the sea, and P them out upon the
9:6 of the sea, and P them out upon the
Rev 11:5 would harm them, fire P out from their mouth

POVERTY (25)

Gen 45:11 you have, come to P
Prov 6:11 hands to rest, and P will come upon you
10:4 A slack hand causes P, but the hand of
10:15 his strong city; the P of the poor is
13:18 P and disgrace come to him who ignores instruction,
20:13 lest you come to P; open your eyes, and
23:21 glutton will come to P, and drowsiness will clothe
24:34 hands to rest, and P will come upon you
28:19 who follows worthless pursuits will have plenty of P
30:8 lying; give me neither P nor riches; feed me
31:7 drink and forget their P, and remember their misery
Sir 10:30 A man honored in P, how much more in
10:30 man dishonored in wealth, how much more in P
11:12 strength and abounds in P; but the eyes of
11:14 bad, life and death, P and wealth, come from
13:23 free from sin, and P is evil in the
18:24 of wealth think of P and need.
20:20 from sinning by his P, so when he rests
22:21 your neighbor in his P, that you may rejoice

26:19 warrior in want through P, and intelligent men who
Mk 12:44 she out of her P has put in everything
Lk 21:4 she out of her P put in all the
2Cor 8:2 joy and their extreme P have overflowed in a
8:9 so that by his P you might become rich.
Rev 2:9 your tribulation and your P (but you are rich)

POWDER (3)

Ex 32:20 and ground it to P, and scattered it upon
Deut 28:24 rain of your land P and dust; from heaven
2Chr 34:7 and the images into P, and hewed down all

POWDERS

Song 3:6 with all the fragrant P of the merchant?

POWER (320)

Gen 16:6 maid is in your P; do to her as
31:29 It is in my P to do you harm;
49:3 strength, pre-eminent in pride and pre-eminent in P
Ex 4:21 have put in your P; but I will harden
9:16 to show you my P, so that my name
15:6 O LORD, glorious in P, thy right hand, O
32:11 of Egypt with great P and with a mighty
Lev 26:19 the pride of your P, and I will make
26:37 you shall have no P to stand before your
Num 14:17 pray thee, let the P of the LORD be
22:38 Have I now any P at all to speak
Deut 4:37 presence, by his great P,
8:17 in your heart, 'My P and the might of
8:18 he who gives you P to get wealth; that
9:29 out by thy great P and by thy outstretched
28:32 not be in the P of your hand to
32:36 he sees that their P is gone, and there
34:12 for all the mighty P and all the great
Josh 8:20 and they had no P to flee this way
17:17 people, and have great P; you shall not have
Judg 2:14 sold them into the P of their enemies round
2:16 them out of the P of those who plundered
2:23 give them into the P of Joshua.
1Sam 2:10 king, and exalt the P of his anointed."
4:3 save us from the P of our enemies."
4:8 deliver us from the P of these mighty gods?
2Sam 8:3 went to restore his P at the river Euphrates.
18:19 delivered him from the P of his enemies."
18:31 this day from the P of all who rose
2Kgs 3:15 the minstrel played, the P of the LORD came
14:5 soon as the royal P was firmly in his
15:19 him to confirm his hold of the royal P
17:36 of Egypt with great P and with an outstretched
18:20 words are strategy and P for war?
1Chr 29:11 the greatness, and the P, and the glory, and
29:12 In thy hand are P and might; and in
2Chr 13:20 did not recover his P in the days of
20:6 In thy hand are P and might, so that
25:3 soon as the royal P was firmly in his
25:8 enemy; for God has P to help or to
26:13 make war with mighty P, to help the king
Ezra 4:23 and by force and P made them cease.
8:22 seek him, and the P of his wrath is
Neh 1:10 redeemed by thy great P and by thy strong
5:5 is not in our P to help it, for
9:37 our sins; they have P also over our bodies
Tob 13:6 and I show his P and majesty to a
Jud 2:12 live, and by the P of my kingdom, what
5:3 in what does their P or strength consist?
5:23 with no strength or P for making war.
8:15 five days, he has P to protect us within
9:8 and bring down their P in thy anger; for
9:11 "For thy P depends not upon numbers, nor thy
9:14 the God of all P and might, and that
11:7 lives, and as his P endures, who had sent
11:7 will live by your P under Nebuchadnezzar and all
13:11 us, to show his P in Israel, and his
13:19 as they remember the P of God.
Esth 10:2 the acts of his P and might, and the
13:9 universe is in thy P and there is no
Job 1:12 has is in your P; only upon himself do
2:6 he is in your P; only spare his life."
5:20 in war from the P of the sword.
8:4 delivered them into the P of their transgression.
21:7 live, reach old age, and grow mighty in P
22:8 The man with P possessed the land, and the
23:6 contend with me in the greatness of his P
24:22 the mighty by his P; they rise up when
26:2 "How you have helped him who has no P
26:12 By his P he stilled the sea; by his
26:14 the thunder of his P who can understand?"
27:22 he flees from its P in headlong flight.
36:22 is exalted in his P; who is a teacher
37:23 he is great in P and justice, and abundant
40:16 his loins, and his P in the muscles of
Ps 21:13 We will sing and praise thy P
22:20 my life from the P of the dog!
37:33 abandon him to his P, or let him be
49:15 my soul from the P of Sheol, for he
59:11 them totter by thy P, and bring them down,
62:11 I heard this: that P belongs to God;
63:2 the sanctuary, beholding thy P and glory.
63:10 given over to the P of the sword, they
66:3 So great is thy P that thy enemies cringe
67:2 upon earth, thy saving P among all nations.
68:34 Ascribe P to God, whose majesty is over Israel,
68:34 over Israel, and his P is in the skies.
68:35 of Israel, he gives P and strength to his
71:18 Thy P
78:22 in God, and did not trust his saving P
78:26 heavens, and by his P he led out the
78:42 keep in mind his P, or the day when
78:61 men, and delivered his P to captivity, his glory
79:11 according to thy great P preserve those doomed to
89:48 his soul from the P of Sheol?
90:11 Who considers the P of thy anger, and thy
90:16 servants, and thy glorious P to their children.
106:8 sake, that he might make known his mighty P
106:10 delivered them from the P of the enemy.
106:42 and they were brought into subjection under their P
111:6 shown his people the P of his works, in
145:11 and tell of thy P,
147:5 LORD, and abundant in P; his understanding is
Prov 3:27 it is in your P to do it.
6:3 into your neighbor's P: go, hasten, and importune
18:21 life are in the P of the tongue, and
Eccl 4:1 their oppressors there was P, and there was no
5:19 wealth and possessions and P to enjoy them, and
6:2 does not give him P to enjoy them, but
8:8 No man has P to retain the spirit, or
Wis 1:3 God, and when his P is tested, it convicts
7:25 a breath of the P of God, and a
11:20 justice and scattered by the breath of thy P
11:21 is always in thy P to show great strength,
12:15 it alien to thy P to condemn him who
12:17 the completeness of thy P, and dost rebuke any
12:18 us; for thou hast P to act whenever thou
13:4 were amazed at their P and working, let them
13:9 if they had the P to know so much
14:31 it is not the P of the things by
15:2 are thine, knowing thy P; but we will not
15:3 and to know thy P is the root of
16:13 For thou hast P over life and death; thou
16:23 righteous might be fed, even forgot its native P
17:2 holy nation in their P they themselves lay as
17:5 And no P of fire was able to give
19:20 water retained its normal P, and water forgot its
Sir 3:20 for you, nor investigate what is beyond your P
5:3 say, "Who will have P over me?" for the
9:13 man who has the P to kill, and you
15:14 left him in the P of his own inclination.
15:18 he is mighty in P and sees everything;
18:3 none has he given P to proclaim his works;
18:4 Who can measure his majestic P
28:23 will fall into its P; it will burn among
29:18 has driven men of P into exile, and they
31:10 Who has had the P to transgress and did
33:19 friend, do not give P over yourself, as long
38:5 in order that his P might be known?
39:18 is done, and none can limit his saving P
43:29 Lord and very great, and marvelous is his P
44:3 men renowned for their P, giving counsel by their
46:6 Lord answered him with hailstones of mighty P
47:5 war, to exalt the P of his people.
47:7 Philistines; he crushed their P even to this day.
47:11 sins, and exalted his P for ever; he gave
49:5 for they gave their P to others, and their
Is 10:33 the boughs with terrifying P; the great in height
36:5 words are strategy and P for war?
40:26 he is strong in P not one is missing.
40:29 He gives P to the faint, and to him
47:9 sorceries and the great P of your enchantments.
47:14 deliver themselves from the P of the flame.
50:2 Or have I no P to deliver?
Jer 10:12 the earth by his P, who established the world
16:21 make them know my P and my might, and

P

18:21 them over to the P of the sword, let
27:5 who by my great P and my outstretched arm
32:17 earth by thy great P and by thy outstretched
51:15 the earth by his P, who established the world
Bar 2:11 wonders and with great P and outstretched arm, and
3:5 this crisis remember thy P and thy name.
4:21 deliver you from the P and hand of the
6:54 for they have no P; they are like crows
6:63 to be compared with them in appearance or P
Ezek 22:6 one according to his P, have been bent on
24:21 the pride of your P, the delight of your
35:5 of Israel to the P of the sword at
Dan 2:37 given the kingdom, the P, and the might, and
3:44 and deprived of all P and dominion, and let
3:95 had not had any P over the bodies of
4:30 built by my mighty P as a royal residence
6:27 saved Daniel from the P of the lions."
8:4 could rescue from his P; he did as he
8:7 the ram had no P to stand before him,
8:7 one who could rescue the ram from his P
8:22 arise from his nation, but not with his P
8:24 His P shall be great, and he shall cause
11:16 and all of it shall be in his P
11:25 shall stir up his P and his courage against
12:7 the shattering of the P of the holy people
Hos 13:14 ransom them from the P of Sheol?
Mic 2:1 it is in the P of their hand.
3:8 I am filled with P, with the Spirit of
Hab 3:4 from his hand; and there he veiled his P
Zech 4:6 by might, nor by P, but by my Spirit,
1Mac 6:11 and beloved in my P
10:71 have with me the P of the cities.
2Mac 3:24 were astounded by the P of God, and became
3:28 recognized clearly the sovereign P of God.
3:34 all men the majestic P of God." Having said
3:38 about the place some P of God.
4:50 cupidity of those in P, remained in office, growing
7:17 see how his mighty P will torture you and
9:8 a litter, making the P of God manifest to
9:17 place to proclaim the P of God.
11:4 account whatever of the P of God, but was
12:28 the Sovereign who with P shatters the might of
Mt 22:29 the scriptures nor the P of God.
24:30 clouds of heaven with P and great glory;
26:64 the right hand of P, and coming on the
Mk 5:30 perceiving in himself that P had gone forth from
9:1 that the kingdom of God has come with P
12:24 the scriptures nor the P of God?
13:26 in clouds with great P and glory.
14:62 the right hand of P, and coming with the
Lk 1:17 in the spirit and P of Elijah, to turn
1:35 upon you, and the P of the Most High
4:14 Jesus returned in the P of the Spirit into
4:36 For with authority and P he commands the unclean
5:17 from Jerusalem; and the P of the Lord was
6:19 to touch him, for P came forth from him
8:46 for I perceive that P has gone forth from
9:1 together and gave them P and authority over all
10:19 and over all the P of the enemy; and
12:5 he has killed, has P to cast into hell;
19:12 to receive a kingly P and then return.
19:15 having received the kingly P, he commanded these
21:27 in a cloud with P and great glory.
22:51 your hour, and the P of darkness."
22:67 right hand of the P of God."
24:49 you are clothed with P from on high."
Jn 1:12 his name, he gave P to become children of
10:18 I have P to lay it down, and I
10:18 down, and I have P to take it again;
14:30 He has no P over me;
17:2 thou hast given him P over all flesh, to
19:10 know that I have P to release you, and
19:10 to release you, and P to crucify you?"
19:11 "You would have no P over me unless it
Acts 1:8 But you shall receive P when the Holy Spirit
3:12 though by our own P or piety we had
4:7 they inquired, "By what P or by what name
4:33 And with great P the apostles gave their testimony
6:8 full of grace and P, did great wonders and
8:10 "This man is that P of God which is
8:19 "Give me also this P, that any one on
10:38 Holy Spirit and with P; how he went about
26:18 light and from the P of Satan to God,
Rom 1:4 Son of God in P according to the Spirit
1:16 gospel: it is the P of God for salvation
1:20 nature, namely, his eternal P and deity, has been
3:9 Greeks, are under the P of sin,
9:17 purpose of showing my P in you, so that
9:22 to make known his P, has endured with much
11:23 for God has the P to graft them in
15:13 so that by the P of the Holy Spirit
15:19 and deed, by the P of signs and wonders,
15:19 and wonders, by the P of the Holy Spirit,
1Cor 1:17 the cross of Christ be emptied of its P
1:18 saved it is the P of God.
1:24 and Greeks, Christ the P of God and the
2:4 the Spirit and of P,
2:5 men but in the P of God.
4:19 the talk of these arrogant people but their P
4:20 God does not consist in talk but in P
5:4 is present, with the P of our Lord Jesus,
6:14 and will also raise us up by his P
14:13 should pray for the P to interpret.
15:24 after destroying every rule and every authority and P
15:43 is sown in weakness, it is raised in P
15:56 is sin, and the P of sin is the
2Cor 4:7 show that the transcendent P belongs to God and
6:7 truthful speech, and the P of God; with the
10:4 worldly but have divine P to destroy strongholds.
12:9 for you, for my P is made perfect in
12:9 my weaknesses, that the P of Christ may rest
13:4 but lives by the P of God.
13:4 with him by the P of God.
Eph 1:19 immeasurable greatness of his P in us who believe,
1:21 rule and authority and P and dominion, and above
2:2 the prince of the P of the air, the
3:7 was given me by the working of his P
3:18 in love, may have P to comprehend with all
3:20 him who by the P at work within us
Phil 3:10 know him and the P of his resurrection, and
3:21 glorious body, by the P which enables him even
Col 1:11 be strengthened with all P, according to his glorious
1Thes 1:5 word, but also in P and in the Holy
2Thes 1:11 of faith by his P,
2:9 will be with all P and with pretended signs
2Tim 1:7 but a spirit of P and love and self-control.
1:8 the gospel in the P of God,
3:5 religion but denying the P of it.
Heb 1:3 nature, upholding the universe by his word of P
2:14 him who has the P of death, that is,
7:16 descent but by the P of an indestructible life.
11:11 faith Sarah herself received P to conceive, even
Jas 5:16 righteous man has great P in its effects.
1Pet 1:5 you, who by God's P are guarded through faith
2Pet 1:3 His divine P has granted to us all things
1:16 known to you the P and coming of our
2:11 greater in might and P, do not pronounce a
1Jn 5:19 world is in the P of the evil one.
Rev 2:26 I will give him P over the nations,
2:27 I myself have received P from my Father;
3:8 you have but little P, and yet you have
4:11 glory and honor and P, for thou didst create
5:12 was slain, to receive P and wealth and wisdom
6:8 and they were given P over a fourth of
7:2 who had been given P to harm earth and
7:12 thanksgiving and honor and P and might be to
9:3 and they were given P like the power of
9:3 given power like the P of scorpions of the
9:10 and stings, and their P of hurting men for
9:19 For the P of the horses is in their
11:3 grant my two witnesses P to prophesy for one
11:6 They have P to shut the sky, that no
11:6 prophesying, and they have P over the waters to
11:17 hast taken thy great P and begun to reign.
12:10 the salvation and the P and the kingdom of
13:2 the dragon gave his P and his throne and
14:18 the angel who has P over fire, and he
15:8 God and from his P, and no one could
16:9 of God who had P over these plagues, and
17:12 not yet received royal P, but they are to
17:13 and give over their P and authority to the
17:17 giving over their royal P to the beast, until
19:1 Salvation and glory and P belong to our God,
20:6 second death has no P, but they shall be

POWERFUL (15)

Esth 9:4 for the man Mordecai grew more and more P
Ps 29:4 of the LORD is P, the voice of the
Prov 18:18 disputes and decides between P contenders.
Wis 10:12 that godliness is more P than anything.
13:4 them how much more P is he who formed
Sir 7:6 be partial to a P man, and thus put

P

8:1 not contend with a P man, lest you fall
13:9 When a P man invites you, be reserved; and
Dan 2:10 for no great and P king has asked such
Joel 1:6 up against my land, P and without number; its
2:2 mountains a great and P people; their like has
2:5 the stubble, like a P army drawn up for
2:11 exceedingly great; he that executes his word is P
1Cor 1:26 standards, not many were P, not many were of
2Cor 13:3 with you, but is P in you.

POWERFULLY
Acts 18:28 had believed, for he P confuted the Jews in

POWERLESS (3)
2Chr 20:12 For we are P against this great multitude that
Wis 17:14 night, which was really P, and which beset them
17:14 from the recesses of P Hades, they all slept

POWERS (15)
Wis 7:20 of wild beasts, the P of spirits and the
Dan 3:62 Bless the Lord, all P, sing praise to him
Mt 14:2 that is why these P are at work in
16:18 my church, and the P of death shall not
24:29 from heaven, and the P of the heavens will
Mk 6:14 that is why these P are at work in
13:25 from heaven, and the P in the heavens will
Lk 21:26 the world; for the P of the heavens will
Rom 8:38 things to come, nor P,
1Cor 13:2 if I have prophetic P, and understand all mysteries
Eph 3:10 to the principalities and P in the heavenly places.
6:12 the principalities, against the P, against the world
Col 2:15 disarmed the principalities and P and made a public
Heb 6:5 of God and the P of the age to
1Pet 3:22 with angels, authorities, and P subject to him.

PRACTICE (25)
Lev 18:30 my charge never to P any of these abominable
19:26 You shall not P augury or witchcraft.
Ezra 9:14 with the peoples who P these abominations?
Tob 4:11 and for all who P it charity is an
Ps 111:10 have all those who P it.
Sir 27:9 returns to those who P it.
38:34 prayer is in the P of their trade.
Is 32:6 mind plots iniquity: to P ungodliness, to utter error
Jer 9:24 am the LORD who P steadfast love, justice, and
Ezek 13:23 see delusive visions nor P divination; I will deliver
23:43 commit adultery when they P harlotry with her?
Mt 23:3 on Moses' seat; so P and observe whatever they
23:3 they do; for they preach, but do not P
Acts 16:21 not lawful for us Romans to accept or P
Rom 1:32 but approve those who P them.
12:13 needs of the saints, P hospitality.
1Cor 11:16 we recognize no other P, nor do the churches
2Cor 4:2 ways; we refuse to P cunning or to tamper
Eph 4:19 to licentiousness, greedy to P every kind of
1Tim 4:15 P these duties, devote yourself to them, so that
Heb 5:14 their faculties trained by P to distinguish good from
Jas 3:16 exist, there will be disorder and every vile P
1Pet 4:9 P hospitality ungrudgingly to one another.
Rev 2:14 sacrificed to idols and P immorality.
2:20 beguiling my servants to P immorality and to eat

PRACTICED (13)
Lev 18:30 abominable customs which were P before you, and
2Kgs 21:6 as an offering, and P soothsaying and augury, and
2Chr 33:6 son of Hinnom, and P soothsaying and augury and
Jud 9:3 the deceit they had P, to be stained with
Eccl 4:1 the oppressions that are P under the sun.
Wis 19:13 wicked acts; for they P a more bitter hatred
Ezek 18:18 his father, because he P extortion, robbed his brother,
22:29 of the land have P extortion and committed robbery;
23:8 harlotry which she had P since her days in
39:26 the treachery they have P against me, when they
Acts 8:9 Simon who had previously P magic in the city
19:19 number of those who P magic arts brought their
2Cor 12:21 impurity, immorality, and licentiousness which they

PRACTICES (19)
Deut 18:9 to follow the abominable P of those nations.
18:10 offering, any one who P divination, a soothsayer, or
18:12 because of these abominable P the LORD your God
20:18 to all their abominable P which they have done
32:16 strange gods; with abominable P they provoked him
Judg 2:19 drop any of their P or their stubborn ways.
2Kgs 16:3 according to the abominable P of the nations whom
21:2 according to the abominable P of the nations whom
2Chr 27:2 But the people still followed corrupt P
28:3 according to the abominable P of the nations whom
33:2 according to the abominable P of the nations whom
Esth 9:32 Queen Esther fixed these P of Purim, and it
Ps 101:7 No man who P deceit shall dwell in my
Wis 12:4 hate for their detestable P, their works of sorcery
Acts 19:18 now believers came, confessing and divulging their P
Rom 10:5 that the man who P the righteousness which is
Col 3:9 old nature with its P
Rev 21:27 nor any one who P abomination or falsehood, but
22:15 one who loves and P falsehood.

PRACTICING (3)
Jer 22:17 innocent blood, and for P oppression and violence."
Dan 4:27 off your sins by P righteousness, and your iniquities
Mt 6:1 "Beware of P your piety before men in order

PRAETORIAN
Phil 1:13 known throughout the whole P guard and to all

PRAETORIUM (7)
Mt 27:27 took Jesus into the P, and they gathered the
Mk 15:16 palace (that is, the P; and they called together
Jn 18:28 Jesus from the house of Caiaphas to the P
18:28 did not enter the P, so that they might
18:33 Pilate entered the P again and called Jesus, and
19:9 afraid; he entered the P again and said to
Acts 23:35 he commanded him to be guarded in Herod's P

PRAISE (301)
Gen 29:35 "This time I will P the LORD"; therefore she
49:8 Judah, your brothers shall P you; your hand shall
Ex 15:2 God, and I will P him, my father's God,
Lev 19:24 holy, an offering of P to the LORD.
Deut 10:21 He is your P; he is your God, who
26:19 he has made, in P and in fame and
32:43 heads of the enemy.' P his people, O you
Josh 7:19 of Israel, and render P to him; and tell
1Chr 16:4 to thank, and to P the LORD, the God
16:35 to thy holy name, and glory in thy P
23:5 with the instruments which I have made for P
25:3 lyre in thanksgiving and P to the LORD.
29:13 thee, our God, and P thy glorious name.
2Chr 5:13 heard in unison in P and thanksgiving to the
5:13 other musical instruments, in P to the LORD, "For
8:14 for their offices of P and ministry before the
20:19 Korahites, stood up to P the LORD, the God
20:21 to the LORD and P him in holy array,
20:22 began to sing and P, the LORD set an
31:2 of the LORD and to give thanks and P
Ezra 3:10 Asaph, with cymbals, to P the LORD, according to
Neh 9:5 name which is exalted above all blessing and P
12:24 over against them, to P and to give thanks,
12:46 there were songs of P and thanksgiving to God.
Tob 3:11 May all thy works P thee for ever.
12:6 and said to them: P God and give thanks
12:6 It is good to P God and to exalt
12:17 But P God for ever.
12:18 Therefore P him for ever.
13:6 P the Lord of righteousness, and exalt the King
13:10 to the Lord, and P the King of the
13:11 Generations of generations will give you joyful P
13:13 gathered together, and will P the Lord of the
13:15 Let my soul P God the great King.
13:18 'Hallelujah!' and will give P, saying, 'Blessed is God,
14:1 Here Tobit ended his words of P
14:2 Lord God and to P him.
14:7 All the Gentiles will P the Lord, and his
Jud 13:14 with a loud voice, P God, O praise him!
13:14 voice, "Praise God, O P him!
13:14 P God, who has not withdrawn his mercy from
16:1 all the people loudly sang this song of P
Esth 13:17 may live and sing P to thy name, O
13:17 mouth of those who P thee."
14:9 mouths of those who P thee and to quench
14:10 the nations for the P of vain idols, and
Ps 6:5 of thee; in Sheol who can give thee P
7:17 and I will sing P to the name of
9:2 thee, I will sing P to thy name, O
21:13 We will sing and P thy power.
22:22 the congregation I will P thee:
22:23 who fear the LORD, P him!
22:25 From thee comes my P in the great congregation;
22:26 who seek him shall P the LORD!
30:9 Will the dust P thee?
30:12 that my soul may P thee and not be

P

P

31:7 the nations; proclaim, give P, and say, 'The LORD
33:9 name of joy, a P and a glory before
51:41 Babylon is taken, the P of the whole earth
Bar 2:32 hear; and they will P me in the land
3:6 our God, and thee, O Lord, will we P
3:7 name; and we will P thee in our exile,
Dan 2:23 I give thanks and P, for thou hast given
3:26 fathers, and worthy of P; and thy name is
3:58 of the Lord, sing P to him and highly
3:59 Lord, you heavens, sing P to him and highly
3:60 of the Lord, sing P to him and highly
3:61 above the heaven, sing P to him and highly
3:62 Lord, all powers, sing P to him and highly
3:63 sun and moon, sing P to him and highly
3:64 stars of heaven, sing P to him and highly
3:65 rain and dew, sing P to him and highly
3:66 Lord, all winds, sing P to him and highly
3:67 fire and heat, sing P to him and highly
3:68 and summer heat, sing P to him and highly
3:69 dews and snows, sing P to him and highly
3:70 nights and days, sing P to him and highly
3:71 light and darkness, sing P to him and highly
3:72 ice and cold, sing P to him and highly
3:73 frosts and snows, sing P to him and highly
3:74 lightnings and clouds, sing P to him and highly
3:75 Lord; let it sing P to him and highly
3:76 mountains and hills, sing P to him and highly
3:77 on the earth, sing P to him and highly
3:78 Lord, you springs, sing P to him and highly
3:79 seas and rivers, sing P to him and highly
3:80 in the waters, sing P to him and highly
3:81 of the air, sing P to him and highly
3:82 beasts and cattle, sing P to him and highly
3:83 sons of men, sing P to him and highly
3:84 Lord, O Israel, sing P to him and highly
3:85 of the Lord, sing P to him and highly
3:86 of the Lord, sing P to him and highly
3:87 of the righteous, sing P to him and highly
3:88 humble in heart, sing P to him and highly
3:89 Azariah, and Mishael, sing P to him and highly
3:91 God of gods, sing P to him and give
4:37 Now I, Nebuchadnezzar, P and extol and honor the
Joel 2:26 and be satisfied, and P the name of the
Hab 3:3 heavens, and the earth was full of his P
Zeph 3:19 change their shame into P and renown in all
1Mac 4:33 who know thy name P thee with hymns."
4:56 they offered a sacrifice of deliverance and P
13:47 were, and then entered it with hymns and P
13:51 Jews entered it with P and palm branches, and
2Mac 8:27 the sabbath, giving great P and thanks to the
Mt 21:16 of babes and sucklings thou hast brought perfect P
Lk 17:18 to return and give P to God except this
18:43 they saw it, gave P to God.
19:37 began to rejoice and P God with a loud
Jn 9:24 him, "Give God the P; we know that this
12:43 for they loved the P of men more than
12:43 men more than the P of God.
Rom 2:29 His P is not from men but from God.
14:11 every tongue shall give P to God."
15:9 written, "Therefore I will P thee among the
15:11 his people"; and again, P the Lord, all Gentiles,
15:11 let all the peoples P him";
Eph 1:6 his will, to the P of his glorious grace
1:12 to live for the P of his glory.
1:14 of it, to the P of his glory.
Phil 1:11 to the glory and P of God.
4:8 is anything worthy of P, think about these things.
Heb 2:12 the congregation I will P thee."
13:15 up a sacrifice of P to God, that is,
Jas 5:13 Let him sing P
1Pet 1:7 fire, may redound to P and glory and honor
2:14 do wrong and to P those who do right.
Rev 19:5 came a voice crying, P our God, all you

PRAISED (39)

Gen 12:15 Pharaoh saw her, they P her to Pharaoh.
Judg 16:24 people saw him, they P their god; for they
2Sam 14:25 so much to be P for his beauty as
22:4 is worthy to be P, and I am saved
1Chr 16:25 and greatly to be P, and he is to
16:36 and P the LORD.
2Chr 30:21 Levites and the priests P the LORD day by
Ezra 3:11 great shout, when they P the LORD, because the
Neh 5:13 and P the LORD.
Jud 6:20 they consoled Achior, and P him greatly.
Ps 18:3 is worthy to be P, and I am saved
48:1 and greatly to be P in the city of
96:4 and greatly to be P; he is to be
113:3 the name of the LORD is to be P
145:3 and greatly to be P, and his greatness is
Prov 31:30 woman who fears the LORD is to be P
Eccl 8:10 holy place, and were P in the city where
Song 6:9 concubines also, and they P her.
Wis 10:20 thy holy name, and P with one accord thy
Sir 9:17 A work will be P for the skill of
47:6 his ten thousands, and P him for the blessings
47:10 the year, while they P God's holy name, and
50:18 And the singers P him with their voices in
Is 64:11 house, where our fathers P thee, has been burned
Dan 3:51 as with one mouth, P and glorified and blessed
3:52 fathers, and to be P and highly exalted for
3:53 and to be highly P and highly exalted for
3:55 deeps, and to be P and highly exalted for
4:34 the Most High, and P and honored him who
5:4 They drank wine, and P the gods of gold
5:23 them; and you have P the gods of silver
13:63 Hilkiah and his wife P God for their daughter
1Mac 5:64 gathered to them and P them.
2Mac 3:30 hope of recovery, they P the Lord who had
11:9 And they all together P the merciful God, and
Mt 6:2 that they may be P by men.
Lk 13:13 made straight, and she P God.
23:46 had taken place, he P God, and said, "Certainly
Acts 4:21 people; for all men P God for what had

PRAISES (45)

2Sam 22:50 the nations, and sing P to thy name.
1Chr 16:9 Sing to him, sing P to him, tell of
23:5 four thousand shall offer P to the LORD with
2Chr 7:6 ever--whenever David offered P by their ministry;
29:30 the Levites to sing P to the LORD with
29:30 And they sang P with gladness, and they bowed
Ps 9:11 Sing P to the LORD, who dwells in Zion!
9:14 may recount all thy P, that in the gates
18:49 the nations, and sing P to thy name.
22:3 holy, enthroned on the P of Israel.
30:4 Sing P to the LORD, O you his saints,
47:6 Sing P to God, sing praises!
47:6 Sing praises to God, sing P
47:6 Sing P to our King, sing praises!
47:6 Sing praises to our King, sing P
47:7 all the earth; sing P with a psalm!
57:9 peoples; I will sing P to thee among the
59:9 Strength, I will sing P to thee; for thou,
59:17 Strength, I will sing P to thee, for thou,
61:8 will I ever sing P to thy name, as
63:5 fat, and my mouth P thee with joyful lips,
66:4 worships thee; they sing P to thee, sing praises
66:4 praises to thee, sing P to thy name." [Selah]
68:4 Sing to God, sing P to his name; lift
68:32 of the earth; sing P to the Lord, [Selah]
71:22 God; I will sing P to thee with the
71:23 joy, when I sing P to thee; my soul
75:9 ever, I will sing P to the God of
92:1 the LORD, to sing P to thy name, O
98:4 earth; break forth into joyous song and sing P
98:5 Sing P to the LORD with the lyre, with
105:2 Sing to him, sing P to him, tell of
108:3 peoples, I will sing P to thee among the
146:2 live; I will sing P to my God while
147:1 is good to sing P to our God; for
149:6 Let the high P of God be in their
Prov 31:28 husband also, and he P her:
Wis 18:9 they were singing the P of the fathers.
Sir 17:22 Who will sing P to the Most High in
17:23 who is alive and well sings the Lord's P
18:27 knows wisdom, and he P the one who finds
37:7 Every counselor P counsel, but some give counsel in
Is 12:5 "Sing P to the LORD, for he has done
63:7 of the LORD, the P of the LORD, according
1Mac 4:24 they sang hymns and P to Heaven, for he

PRAISING (12)

1Chr 23:30 every morning, thanking and P the LORD, and
2Chr 23:12 the people running and P the king, she went
Ezra 3:11 and they sang responsively, P and giving thanks to
Tob 11:1 went on his way, P God because he had
11:16 of Nineveh, rejoicing and P God.
Wis 19:9 and leaped like lambs, P thee, O Lord, who
Lk 2:13 of the heavenly host P God and saying,
2:20 shepherds returned, glorifying and P God for all they
17:15 was healed, turned back, P God with a loud

P

Acts 2:47 glad and generous hearts, P God and having favor
3:8 walking and leaping and P God.
3:9 saw him walking and P God,

PRANCE

Nah 2:3 like flame when mustered in array; the chargers P

PRASIE

Ps 111:1 P the LORD.

PRATING (2)

Prov 10:8 heed commandments, but a P fool will come to
3Jn 1:10 what he is doing, P against me with evil

PRATTLE

Sir 7:14 Do not P in the assembly of the elders,

PRAY (219)

Gen 19:2 lords, turn aside, I P you, to your servant's
20:7 prophet, and he will P for you, and you
24:12 me success today, I P thee, and show steadfast
24:14 whom I shall say, P let down your jar
24:17 meet her, and said, P give me a little
24:43 whom I shall say, P give me a little
24:45 I said to her, P let me drink.'
30:14 Leah, "Give me, I P, some of your son's
32:11 Deliver me, I P thee, from the hand of
32:29 him, "Tell me, I P, your name." But he
33:10 Jacob said, "No, I P you, if I have
33:11 Accept, I P you, my gift that is brought
34:8 for your daughter; I P you, give her to
37:16 said, "tell me, I P you, where they are
38:25 she said, "Mark, I P you, whose these are,
40:8 them to me, I P you."
40:14 me the kindness, I P you, to make mention
44:18 let your servant, I P you, speak a word
44:33 let your servant, I P you, remain instead of
45:4 near to me, I P you." And they came
47:4 Canaan; and now, we P you, let your servants
48:9 them to me, I P you, that I may
50:4 your eyes, speak, I P you, in the ears
50:5 me go up, I P you, and bury my
50:17 to Joseph, Forgive, I P you, the transgression of
50:17 you.' And now, we P you, forgive the transgression
Ex 3:18 us; and now, we P you, let us go
4:13 my Lord, send, I P, some other person."
4:18 me go back, I P, to my kinsmen in
5:3 let us go, we P, a three days' journey
8:29 you and I will P to the LORD that
10:17 forgive my sin, I P you, only this once,
32:32 not, blot me, I P thee, out of thy
33:13 sight.' Now therefore, I P thee, if I have
33:18 Moses said, "I P thee, show me thy glory."
34:9 let the Lord, I P thee, go in the
Num 10:31 not leave us, I P you, for you know
14:17 wilderness.' And now, I P thee, let the power
14:19 of this people, I P thee, according to the
16:26 the congregation, "Depart, I P you, from the tents
21:7 LORD and against you; P to the LORD, that
22:19 P, now, tarry here this night also, that I
Deut 3:25 me go over, I P, and see the good
Judg 1:24 they said to him, P, show us the way
4:19 he said to her, P, give me a little
6:13 Gideon said to him, P, sir, if the LORD
6:15 he said to him, P, Lord, how can I
6:18 depart from here, I P thee, until I come
6:39 speak but this once; P, let me make trial
6:39 once with the fleece; P, let it be dry
8:5 the men of Succoth, P, give loaves of bread
10:15 only deliver us, we P thee, this day."
11:17 'Let us pass, we P, through your land'; but
11:19 'Let us pass, we P, through your land to
13:8 said, "O, LORD, I P thee, let the man
13:15 angel of the LORD, P, let us detain you,
15:2 P take her instead."
16:28 GOD, remember me, I P thee, and strengthen me,
16:28 and strengthen me, I P thee, only this once,
18:5 "Inquire of God, we P thee, that we may
19:9 has waned toward evening; P tarry all night.
Ruth 2:7 She said, P, let me glean and gather among
1Sam 2:36 say, 'Put me, I P you, in one of
7:5 Mizpah, and I will P to the LORD for
10:15 And Saul's uncle said, P, tell me what Samuel
12:19 people said to Samuel, P for your servants to
12:23 LORD by ceasing to P for you; and I
15:25 Now therefore, I P, pardon my sin, and return
22:3 the king of Moab, P let my father and
25:8 P, give whatever you have at hand to your
25:24 lord, be the guilt; P let your handmaid speak
25:28 P forgive the trespass of your handmaid; for the
2Sam 7:27 has found courage to P this prayer to thee.
13:6 said to the king, P let my sister Tamar
13:13 Now therefore, I P you, speak to the king;
13:24 your servant has sheepshearers; P let the king and
13:26 Absalom said, "If not, P let my brother Amnon
14:11 Then she said, P let the king invoke the
14:12 Then the woman said, P let your handmaid speak
15:7 said to the king, P let me go and
15:31 said, "O LORD, I P thee, turn the counsel
19:37 P let your servant return, that I may die
24:10 now, O LORD, I P thee, take away the
24:17 Let thy hand, I P thee, be against me
1Kgs 2:17 And he said, P ask King Solomon–he will
8:30 people Israel, when they P toward this place; yea,
8:33 acknowledge thy name, and P and make supplication
8:35 against thee, if they P toward this place, and
8:44 send them, and they P to the LORD toward
8:48 carried them captive, and P to thee toward their
13:6 LORD your God, and P for me, that my
20:32 "Your servant Ben-hadad says, P, let me live.'" And
20:35 the command of the LORD, "Strike me, I P
20:37 found another man, and said, "Strike me, I P
2Kgs 1:13 man of God, I P you, let my life,
2:2 Elisha, "Tarry here, I P you; for the LORD
2:4 "Elisha, tarry here, I P you; for the LORD
2:6 him, "Tarry here, I P you; for the LORD
2:9 And Elisha said, "I P you, let me inherit
2:16 servants fifty strong men; P, let them go, and
5:17 said, "If not, I P you, let there be
5:22 sons of the prophets; P, give them a talent
6:17 said, "O LORD, I P thee, open his eyes
6:18 "Strike this people, I P thee, with blindness." So
18:26 said to the Rabshakeh, P, speak to your servants
1Chr 17:25 has found courage to P before thee.
21:8 But now, I P thee, take away the iniquity
21:17 Let thy hand, I P thee, O LORD my
2Chr 6:21 people Israel, when they P toward this place; yea,
6:24 acknowledge thy name, and P and make supplication
6:26 against thee, if they P toward this place, and
6:34 send them, and they P to thee toward this
6:38 were carried captive, and P toward their land, which
7:14 name humble themselves, and P and seek my face,
Ezra 6:10 God of heaven, and P for the life of
Neh 1:6 servant which I now P before thee day and
Tob 8:4 up, and let us P that the Lord may
8:5 And Tobias began to P, "Blessed art thou, O
Jud 8:31 So P for us, since you are a devout
11:17 valley, and I will P to God and he
12:6 your servant be permitted to go out and P
Job 6:29 Turn, I P, let no wrong be done.
8:8 "For inquire, I P you, of bygone ages, and
21:15 we get if we P to him?'
42:8 my servant Job shall P for you, for I
Ps 5:2 and my God, for to thee do I P
38:16 For I P, "Only let them not rejoice over
122:6 P for the peace of Jerusalem!
Wis 16:28 thee thanks, and must P to thee at the
Sir 17:20 and forsake your sins; P in his presence and
21:1 so no more, but P about your former sins.
28:2 then your sins will be pardoned when you P
28:4 like himself, and yet P for his own sins?
37:15 And besides all this P to the Most High
38:9 not be negligent, but P to the Lord, and
38:14 for they too will P to the Lord that
Is 5:3 of Judah, judge, I P you, between me and
16:12 to his sanctuary to P, he will not prevail.
36:11 said to the Rabshakeh, P, speak to your servants
Jer 7:16 for you, do not P for this people, or
11:14 "Therefore do not P for this people, or lift
14:11 to me: "Do not P for the welfare of
29:7 you into exile, and P to the LORD on
29:12 me and come and P to me, and I
37:3 Jeremiah the prophet, saying, P for us to the
37:20 Now hear, I P you, O my lord the
42:2 come before you, and P to the LORD your
42:4 you; behold, I will P to the LORD your
42:20 LORD your God, saying, P for us to the
Bar 1:11 Lord our God; and P for the life of
1:13 And P for us to the Lord our God,
6:41 they bring him and P Bel that the man
Jon 4:2 LORD and said, "I P thee, LORD, is not
Hag 2:15 P now, consider what will come to pass from

1Mac	3:44	for battle, and to P and ask for mercy
2Mac	12:44	superfluous and foolish to P for the dead.
Mt	5:44	Love your enemies and P for those who persecute
	6:5	"And when you P, you must not be like
	6:5	love to stand and P in the synagogues and
	6:6	But when you P, go into your room and
	6:6	shut the door and P to your Father who
	6:9	P then like this: Our Father who art in
	9:38	the laborers are few; P therefore the Lord of
	14:23	went up on the mountain by himself to P
	19:13	he might lay his hands on them and P
	24:20	P that your flight may not be in winter
	26:36	disciples, "Sit here, while I go yonder and P
	26:41	Watch and P that you may not enter into
Mk	6:46	them, he went up on the mountain to P
	13:18	P that it may not happen in winter.
	13:33	Take heed, watch and P; for you do not
	14:32	said to his disciples, "Sit here, while I P
	14:38	Watch and P that you may not enter into
Lk	6:12	to the mountain to P; and all night he
	6:28	those who curse you, P for those who abuse
	9:28	James, and went up on the mountain to P
	10:2	the laborers are few; P therefore the Lord of
	11:1	"Lord, teach us to P, as John taught his
	11:2	to them, "When you P, say: "Father, hallowed be
	14:18	and see it; I P you, have me excused.'
	14:19	to examine them; I P you, have me excused.'
	18:1	they ought always to P and not lose heart.
	18:10	into the temple to P, one a Pharisee and
	22:40	he said to them, P that you may not
	22:44	Rise and P that you may not enter into
Jn	14:16	And I will P the Father, and he will
	16:26	you that I shall P the Father for you;
	17:15	I do not P that thou shouldst take them
	17:20	"I do not P for these only, but also
Acts	8:22	wickedness of yours, and P to the Lord that,
	8:24	And Simon answered, P for me to the Lord,
	8:34	to Philip, "About whom, P, does the prophet say
	10:9	on the housetop to P, about the sixth hour.
Rom	8:26	not know how to P as we ought, but
1Cor	11:13	for a woman to P to God with her
	14:13	in a tongue should P for the power to
	14:14	For if I P in a tongue, my spirit
	14:15	I will P with the spirit and I will
	14:15	spirit and I will P with the mind also;
2Cor	9:14	long for you and P for you, because of
	13:7	But we P God that you may not do
	13:9	What we P for is your improvement.
Eph	6:18	P at all times in the Spirit, with all
Col	1:3	Jesus Christ, when we P for you,
	1:9	have not ceased to P for you, asking that
	4:3	it with thanksgiving; and P for us also, that
1Thes	5:17	Rejoice always, P constantly,
	5:25	Brethren, P for us.
2Thes	1:11	this end we always P for you, that our
	3:1	Finally, brethren, P for us, that the word of
1Tim	2:8	place the men should P, lifting holy hands without
Philem	1:6	the saints, and I P that the sharing of
Heb	13:18	P for us, for we are sure that we
Jas	5:13	Let him P
	5:14	church, and let them P over him, anointing him
	5:16	to one another, and P for one another, that
1Jn	5:16	that one is to P for that.
3Jn	1:2	Beloved, I P that all may go well with
Jude	1:20	your most holy faith; P in the Holy Spirit;

PRAYED (72)

Gen	20:17	Then Abraham P to God; and God healed Abimelech,
	25:21	And Isaac P to the LORD for his wife,
Ex	8:30	out from Pharaoh and P to the LORD.
Num	11:2	to Moses; and Moses P to the LORD, and
	21:7	So Moses P for the people.
Deut	9:20	destroy him; and I P for Aaron also at
	9:26	And I P to the LORD, 'O Lord GOD,
1Sam	1:10	was deeply distressed and P to the LORD, and
	1:27	For this child I P; and the LORD has
	2:1	Hannah also P and said, "My heart exults in
	8:6	And Samuel P to the LORD.
2Kgs	4:33	two of them, and P to the LORD.
	6:17	Then Elisha P, and said, "O LORD, I pray
	6:18	down against him, Elisha P to the LORD, and
	19:15	And Hezekiah P before the LORD, and said: "O
	20:2	to the wall, and P to the LORD, saying,
2Chr	30:18	For Hezekiah had P for them, saying, "The good
	32:20	the son of Amoz, P because of this and
	32:24	of death, and he P to the LORD; and
	33:13	He P to him, and God received his entreaty
Ezra	10:1	While Ezra P and made confession, weeping and
Neh	2:4	So I P to the God of heaven.
	4:9	And we P to our God, and set a
Tob	3:1	I wept, and I P in anguish, saying,
	3:11	So she P by her window and said, "Blessed
	12:12	and your daughter-in-law Sarah P, I brought a
Jud	12:8	from the spring she P the Lord God of
Esth	13:8	Then Mordecai P to the Lord, calling to
	14:3	And she P to the Lord God of Israel,
Job	42:10	Job, when he had P for his friends; and
Ps	35:13	I P with head bowed on my bosom,
Wis	7:7	Therefore I P, and understanding was given me; I
Sir	51:9	from the earth, and P for deliverance from death.
Is	37:15	And Hezekiah P to the LORD:
	37:21	Israel: Because you have P to me concerning
	38:2	to the wall, and P to the LORD,
Jer	32:16	son of Neriah, I P to the LORD, saying:
Bar	1:5	wept, and fasted, and P before the Lord;
Dan	6:10	times a day and P and gave thanks before
	9:4	I P to the LORD my God and made
Jon	2:1	Then Jonah P to the LORD his God from
	4:2	And he P to the LORD and said, "I
1Mac	4:30	army was strong, he P, saying, "Blessed art thou,
	7:40	Then Judas P and said,
	11:71	garments and put dust on his head, and P
2Mac	2:10	Just as Moses P to the Lord, and fire
	2:10	sacrifices, so also Solomon P, and the fire came
	5:4	Therefore all men P that the apparition might prove
	14:15	upon their heads and P to him who established
Mt	26:39	on his face and P, "My Father, if it
	26:42	he went away and P, "My Father, if this
	26:44	he went away and P for the third time,
Mk	1:35	out to a lonely place, and there he P
	14:35	on the ground and P that, if it were
	14:39	he went away and P, saying the same words.
Lk	5:16	But he withdrew to the wilderness and P
	18:11	The Pharisee stood and P thus with himself, 'God,
	22:32	wheat, but I have P for you that your
	22:41	and knelt down and P,
Acts	1:24	And they P and said, "Lord, who knowest the
	4:31	And when they had P, the place in which
	6:6	the apostles, and they P and laid their hands
	7:59	were stoning Stephen, he P, "Lord Jesus, receive my
	8:15	who came down and P for them that they
	9:40	and knelt down and P; then turning to the
	10:2	to the people, and P constantly to God.
	20:36	he knelt down and P with them all.
	21:5	on the beach we P and bade one another
	27:29	from the stern, and P for day to come.
	28:8	Paul visited him and P, and putting his hands
Jas	5:17	with ourselves and he P fervently that it might
	5:18	Then he P again and the heaven gave rain,

PRAYER (147)

Gen	25:21	the LORD granted his P, and Rebekah his wife
2Sam	7:27	courage to pray this P to thee.
1Kgs	8:28	have regard to the P of thy servant and
	8:28	cry and to the P which thy servant prays
	8:29	mayest hearken to the P which thy servant offers
	8:38	sickness there is; whatever P, whatever supplication
	8:45	thou in heaven their P and their supplication, and
	8:49	thy dwelling place their P and their supplication, and
	8:54	finished offering all this P and supplication to the
	9:3	"I have heard your P and your supplication, which
2Kgs	6:18	in accordance with the P of Elisha.
	19:4	therefore lift up your P for the remnant that
	19:20	God of Israel: Your P to me about Sennacherib
	20:5	I have heard your P, I have seen your
2Chr	6:19	have regard to the P of thy servant and
	6:19	cry and to the P which thy servant prays
	6:20	mayest hearken to the P which thy servant offers
	6:29	there is; whatever P, whatever supplication is made
	6:35	thou from heaven their P and their supplication, and
	6:39	thy dwelling place their P and their supplications,
	6:40	ears attentive to a P of this place.
	7:1	Solomon had ended his P, fire came down from
	7:12	"I have heard your P, and have chosen this
	7:15	ears attentive to the P that is made in
	30:27	was heard, and their P came to his holy
	33:18	of Manasseh, and his P to his God, and
	33:19	And his P, and how God received his entreaty,
Neh	1:6	open, to hear the P of thy servant which
	1:11	be attentive to the P of thy servant, and
	1:11	servant, and to the P of thy servants who
	11:17	begin the thanksgiving in P, and Bakbukiah, the

Tob 3:16 The P of both was heard in the presence
12:8 P is good when accompanied by fasting, almsgiving,
12:12 a reminder of your P before the Holy One;
13:1 Then Tobit wrote a P of rejoicing, and said:
Jud 9:12 waters, King of all thy creation, hear my P
13:10 accustomed to go for P; and they passed through
Esth 13:17 Hear my P, and have mercy upon thy inheritance;
15:1 when she ended her P, she took off the
Job 16:17 my hands, and my P is pure.
22:27 You will make your P to him, and he
24:12 help; yet God pays no attention to their P
42:8 I will accept his P not to deal with
42:9 had told them; and the LORD accepted Job's P
Ps 4:1 Be gracious to me, and hear my P
6:9 has heard my supplication; the LORD accepts my P
17:1 Give ear to my P from lips free of
32:6 who is godly offer P to thee; at a
39:12 [Selah] "Hear my P, O LORD, and give ear
42:8 is with me, a P to the God of
54:2 Hear my P, O God; give ear to the
55:1 Give ear to my P, O God; and hide
61:1 God, listen to my P;
65:2 shall vows be performed, O thou who hearest P
66:19 has given heed to the voice of my P
66:20 has not rejected my P or removed his steadfast
69:13 as for me, my P is to thee, O
72:15 May P be made for him continually, and blessings
84:8 of hosts, hear my P; give ear, O God
86:6 O LORD, to my P; hearken to my cry
88:2 Let my P come before thee, incline thy ear
88:13 in the morning my P comes before thee.
102:1 Hear my P, O LORD; let my cry come
102:17 he will regard the P of the destitute, and
109:4 even as I make P for them.
109:7 forth guilty; let his P be counted as sin!
141:2 Let my P be counted as incense before thee,
141:5 my head; for my P is continually against their
143:1 Hear my P, O LORD; give ear to my
Prov 15:8 the LORD, but the P of the upright is
15:29 but he hears the P of the righteous.
28:9 the law, even his P is an abomination.
Wis 18:21 shield of his ministry, P and propitiation by incense;
Sir 4:6 curse upon you, his Creator will hear his P
7:10 be fainthearted in your P, nor neglect to give
7:14 of the elders, nor repeat yourself in your P
21:5 The P of a poor man goes from his
34:26 the same things, who will listen to his P
35:13 will listen to the P of one who is
35:16 be accepted, and his P will reach to the
35:17 The P of the humble pierces the clouds, and
36:17 O Lord, to the P of thy servants, according
38:34 the world, and their P is in the practice
39:5 open his mouth in P and make supplication for
39:6 wisdom and give thanks to the Lord in P
50:19 Lord Most High in P before him who is
51:11 My P was heard,
51:13 my travels, I sought wisdom openly in my P
Is 26:16 they poured out a P when thy chastening was
37:4 therefore lift up your P for the remnant that
38:5 I have heard your P, I have seen your
56:7 in my house of P; their burnt offerings and
56:7 called a house of P for all peoples.
Jer 7:16 lift up cry or P for them, and do
11:14 up a cry or P on their behalf, for
Lam 3:8 he shuts out my P;
3:44 cloud so that no P can pass through.
Bar 2:14 Hear, O Lord, our P and our supplication, and
2:19 bring before thee our P for mercy, O Lord
3:4 Israel, hear now the P of the dead of
Dan 3:25 stood and offered this P; in the midst of
9:3 God, seeking him by P and supplications with fasting
9:17 God, hearken to the P of thy servant and
9:21 I was speaking in P, the man Gabriel, whom
Jon 2:7 the LORD; and my P came to thee, into
Hab 3:1 A P of Habakkuk the prophet, according to
1Mac 3:46 had a place of P in Mizpah.
5:33 who sounded their trumpets and cried aloud in P
7:37 people a house of P and supplication.
2Mac 1:23 consumed, the priests offered P -- the priests
1:24 The P was to this effect: "O Lord, Lord
10:27 And rising from their P they took up their
12:42 and they turned to P, beseeching that the sin
15:24 With these words he ended his P
Mt 21:13 called a house of P; but you make it
21:22 whatever you ask in P, you will receive, if
Mk 9:29 out by anything but P and fasting."
11:17 called a house of P for all the nations?
11:24 whatever you ask in P, believe that you have
Lk 1:13 afraid, Zechariah, for your P is heard, and your
2:37 worshiping with fasting and P night and day.
6:12 night he continued in P to God.
19:46 be a house of P; but you have made
22:43 when he rose from P, he came to the
Acts 1:14 accord devoted themselves to P, together with the
3:1 at the hour of P, the ninth hour.
6:4 will devote ourselves to P and to the ministry
10:30 the ninth hour of P in my house; and
10:31 apparel, saying, 'Cornelius, your P has been heard
12:5 in prison; but earnest P for him was made
14:23 in every church, with P and fasting they committed
16:13 was a place of P; and we sat down
16:16 to the place of P, we were met by
Rom 10:1 my heart's desire and P to God for them
12:12 hope, be patient in tribulation, be constant in P
1Cor 7:5 may devote yourselves to P; but then come together
2Cor 1:11 must help us by P, so that many will
Eph 6:18 the Spirit, with all P and supplication.
Phil 1:4 you, always in every P of mine for you
1:4 you all making my P with joy,
1:9 And it is my P that your love may
4:6 but in everything by P and supplication with
Col 4:2 Continue steadfastly in P, being watchful in it with
1Tim 4:5 is consecrated by the word of God and P
Jas 5:15 the Lord; and the P of faith will save
5:16 The P of a righteous man has great power
1Pet 3:12 righteous, and his ears are open to their P

PRAYERS (32)

Tob 12:15 angels who present the P of the saints and
Jud 4:13 the Lord heard their P and looked upon their
13:3 said she would be going out for her P
Ps 72:20 The P of David, the son of Jesse, are
80:4 long wilt thou be angry with thy people's P
Is 1:15 though you make many P, I will not listen;
1Mac 12:11 offer and in our P, as it is right
2Mac 1:5 May he hear your P and be reconciled to
15:26 enemy in battle with invocation to God and P
Mk 12:40 widows' houses and for a pretense make long P
Lk 5:33 fast often and offer P, and so do the
20:47 widows' houses and for a pretense make long P
Acts 2:42 fellowship, to the breaking of bread and the P
10:4 said to him, "Your P and your alms have
Rom 1:9 you always in my P,
15:30 with me in your P to God on my
2Cor 1:11 the blessing granted us in answer to many P
Eph 1:16 remembering you in my P,
Phil 1:19 know that through your P and the help of
Col 4:12 you earnestly in his P, that you may stand
1Thes 1:2 for you all, constantly mentioning you in our P
1Tim 2:1 I urge that supplications, P, intercessions, and
5:5 continues in supplications and P night and day;
2Tim 1:3 fathers, when I remember you constantly in my P
Philem 1:4 remember you in my P,
1:22 am hoping through your P to be granted to
Heb 5:7 flesh, Jesus offered up P and supplications, with loud
1Pet 3:7 in order that your P may not be hindered.
4:7 hand; therefore keep sane and sober for your P
Rev 5:8 incense, which are the P of the saints;
8:3 to mingle with the P of all the saints
8:4 incense rose with the P of the saints from

PRAYING (26)

1Sam 1:12 As she continued P before the LORD, Eli observed
1:26 here in your presence, P to the LORD.
Neh 1:4 I continued fasting and P before the God of
Jud 4:12 cried out in unison, P earnestly to the God
Is 45:20 idols, and keep on P to a god that
Dan 9:20 I was speaking and P, confessing my sin and
2Mac 1:6 We are now P for you here.
15:12 belongs to excellence, was P with outstretched
15:27 with their hands and P to God in their
Mt 6:7 "And in P do not heap up empty phrases
Mk 11:25 And whenever you stand P, forgive, if you have
Lk 1:10 of the people were P outside at the hour
3:21 been baptized and was P, the heaven was opened,
9:18 that as he was P alone the disciples were
9:29 And as he was P, the appearance of his
11:1 He was P in a certain place, and when
21:36 watch at all times, P that you may have
Jn 17:9 I am P for them; I am not praying
17:9 them; I am not P for the world but
Acts 9:11 for behold, he is P,

P

11:5 the city of Joppa P; and in a trance
12:12 where many were gathered together and were P
13:3 Then after fasting and P they laid their hands
16:25 Paul and Silas were P and singing hymns to
22:17 to Jerusalem and was P in the temple, I
1Thes 3:10 sake before our God, P earnestly night and day

PRAYS (14)

1Kgs 8:28 prayer which thy servant P before thee this day;
8:42 when he comes and P toward this house,
2Chr 6:19 prayer which thy servant P before thee;
6:32 when he comes and P toward this house,
Job 33:26 youthful vigor'; then man P to God, and he
Wis 13:17 When he P about possessions and his marriage and
13:18 weak; for life he P to a thing that
Sir 3:5 children, and when he P he will be heard.
34:24 When one P and another curses, to whose voice
Is 44:17 and worships it; he P to it and says,
2Mac 15:14 loves the brethren and P much for the people
1Cor 11:4 Any man who P or prophesies with his head
11:5 but any woman who P or prophesies with her
14:14 a tongue, my spirit P but my mind is

PRE-EMINENCE (2)

Gen 49:4 you shall not have P because you went up
Ezek 7:11 neither shall there be P among them.

PRE-EMINENT (3)

Gen 49:3 fruits of my strength, P in pride and pre-eminent
49:3 pre-eminent in pride and P in power.
Col 1:18 the dead, that in everything he might be P

PREACH (42)

Ezek 20:46 face toward the south, P against the south, and
21:2 toward Jerusalem and P against the sanctuaries;
Amos 7:16 Israel, and do not P against the house of
Mic 2:6 "Do not P --thus they preach--"one should not
2:6 not preach"--thus they P --"one should not preach
2:6 preach--"one should not P of such things; disgrace
2:11 lies, saying, "I will P to you of wine
Mt 4:17 time Jesus began to P, saying, "Repent, for the
10:7 And P as you go, saying, 'The kingdom of
11:1 there to teach and P in their cities.
23:3 they do; for they P, but do not practice.
Mk 1:38 towns, that I may P there also; for that
3:14 be sent out to P
16:15 all the world and P the gospel to the
Lk 4:18 has anointed me to P good news to the
4:43 to them, "I must P the good news of
9:2 sent them out to P the kingdom of God
Acts 10:42 he commanded us to P to the people, and
15:21 every city those who P him, for he is
16:10 had called us to P the gospel to them.
Rom 1:15 I am eager to P the gospel to you
2:21 While you P against stealing, do you steal?
10:8 of faith which we P;
10:15 And how can men P unless they are sent?
10:15 feet of those who P good news!"
15:20 it my ambition to P the gospel, not where
1Cor 1:17 to baptize but to P the gospel, and not
1:21 folly of what we P to save those who
1:23 seek wisdom, but we P Christ crucified, a stumbling
9:16 For if I P the gospel, that gives me
9:16 if I do not P the gospel!
15:11 or they, so we P and so you believed.
2Cor 2:12 came to Troas to P the gospel of Christ,
4:5 For what we P is not ourselves, but Jesus
10:16 so that we may P the gospel in lands
Gal 1:8 angel from heaven, should P to you a gospel
1:16 order that I might P him among the Gentiles,
2:2 the gospel which I P among the Gentiles, lest
5:11 if I, brethren, still P circumcision, why am I
Eph 3:8 grace was given, to P to the Gentiles the
Phil 1:15 Some indeed P Christ from envy and rivalry, but
2Tim 4:2 appearing and his kingdom: P the word, be urgent

PREACHED (39)

Mt 11:5 poor have good news P to them.
24:14 the kingdom will be P throughout the whole world,
26:13 wherever this gospel is P in the whole world,
Mk 1:7 And he P, saying, "After me comes he who
6:12 they went out and P that men should repent.
13:10 gospel must first be P to all nations.
14:9 wherever the gospel is P in the whole world,
16:20 they went forth and P everywhere, while the Lord
Lk 3:18 many other exhortations, he P good news to the
7:22 poor have good news P to them.
16:16 kingdom of God is P, and every one enters
24:47 of sins should be P in his name to
Acts 8:12 believed Philip as he P good news about the
8:39 and passing on he P the gospel to all
9:27 at Damascus he had P boldly in the name
10:37 the baptism which John P:
13:24 his coming John had P a baptism of repentance
14:7 country; and there they P the gospel.
14:21 When they had P the gospel to that city
17:18 divinities"--because he P Jesus and the resurrection.
Rom 15:19 Illyricum I have fully P the gospel of Christ,
1Cor 15:1 in what terms I P to you the gospel,
15:12 Now if Christ is P as raised from the
2Cor 1:19 Jesus Christ, whom we P among you, Silvanus and
11:4 than the one we P, or if you receive
11:7 be exalted, because I P God's gospel without cost
Gal 1:8 to that which we P to you, let him
1:11 the gospel which was P by me is not
3:8 the Gentiles by faith, P the gospel beforehand to
4:13 bodily ailment that I P the gospel to you
Eph 2:17 And he came and P peace to you who
Col 1:23 heard, which has been P to every creature under
1Thes 2:9 of you, while we P to you the gospel
1Tim 3:16 Spirit, seen by angels, P among the nations, believed
2Tim 2:8 descended from David, as P in my gospel,
1Pet 1:12 you by those who P the good news to
1:25 good news which was P to you.
3:19 which he went and P to the spirits in
4:6 why the gospel was P even to the dead,

PREACHER (12)

Eccl 1:1 The words of the P, the son of David,
1:2 of vanities, says the P, vanity of vanities!
1:12 I the P have been king over Israel in
7:27 I found, says the P, adding one thing to
12:8 of vanities, says the P; all is vanity.
12:9 Besides being wise, the P also taught the people
12:10 The P sought to find pleasing words, and uprightly
Mic 2:11 he would be the P for this people!
Acts 17:18 seems to be a P of foreign divinities"--because
Rom 10:14 And how are they to hear without a P
1Tim 2:7 I was appointed a P and apostle (I am
2Tim 1:11 I was appointed a P and apostle and teacher,

PREACHES (2)

Acts 19:13 "I adjure you by the Jesus whom Paul P
2Cor 11:4 some one comes and P another Jesus than the

PREACHING (36)

Mt 3:1 came John the Baptist, P in the wilderness of
4:23 in their synagogues and P the gospel of the
9:35 in their synagogues and P the gospel of the
12:41 they repented at the P of Jonah, and behold,
Mk 1:4 appeared in the wilderness, P a baptism of
1:14 Jesus came into Galilee, P the gospel of God,
1:39 went throughout all Galilee, P in their synagogues
2:2 door; and he was P the word to them.
Lk 3:3 region about the Jordan, P a baptism of repentance
4:44 And he was P in the synagogues of Judea.
8:1 through cities and villages, P and bringing the good
9:6 went through the villages, P the gospel and healing
11:32 they repented at the P of Jonah, and behold,
20:1 in the temple and P the gospel, the chief
Acts 5:42 not cease teaching and P Jesus as the Christ.
6:2 we should give up P the word of God
8:4 were scattered went about P the word.
8:25 they returned to Jerusalem, P the gospel to many
9:29 among them at Jerusalem, P boldly in the name
10:36 he sent to Israel, P good news of peace
11:20 to the Greeks also, P the Lord Jesus.
15:34 in Antioch, teaching and P the word of the
18:5 Paul was occupied with P, testifying to the Jews
20:25 whom I have gone P the kingdom will see
28:30 who came to him, P the kingdom of God
Rom 10:17 heard comes by the P of Christ.
16:24 my gospel and the P of Jesus Christ, according
1Cor 9:18 this: that in my P I may make the
9:27 subdue it, lest after P to others I myself
15:14 been raised, then our P is in vain and
2Cor 8:18 the churches for his P of the gospel;
Gal 1:9 If any one is P to you a gospel
1:23 persecuted us is now P the faith he once
1Tim 4:13 reading of scripture, to P, to teaching.
5:17 those who labor in P and teaching;
Tit 1:3 his word through the P with which I have

PRECAUTIONS
2Mac 1:19 where they took such P that the place was

PRECEDE (3)
Sir 22:22 smoke of the furnace P the fire; so insults
22:22 the fire; so insults P bloodshed.
1Thes 4:15 the Lord, shall not P those who have fallen

PRECEDED
Jer 28:8 The prophets who P you and me from ancient

PRECEDES (2)
Sir 32:10 the thunder, and approval P a modest man.
37:16 every work, and counsel P every undertaking.

PRECEDING (2)
Esth 11:1 brought to Egypt the P Letter of Purim, which
1Mac 3:30 give more lavishly than P kings.

PRECEPT (8)
Is 28:10 For it is P upon precept, precept upon precept,
28:10 it is precept upon P, precept upon precept, line
28:10 is precept upon precept, P upon precept, line upon
28:10 upon precept, precept upon P, line upon line, line
28:13 will be to them P upon precept, precept upon
28:13 to them precept upon P, precept upon precept, line
28:13 them precept upon precept, P upon precept, line
28:13 upon precept, precept upon P, line upon line, line

PRECEPTS (29)
Ps 19:8 wise the simple; the P of the LORD are
111:7 and just; all his P are trustworthy,
119:4 Thou hast commanded thy P to be kept diligently.
119:15 will meditate on thy P, and fix my eyes
119:27 the way of thy P, and I will meditate
119:40 I long for thy P; in thy righteousness give
119:45 walk at liberty, for I have sought thy P
119:56 fallen to me, that I have kept thy P
119:63 who fear thee, of those who keep thy P
119:69 heart I keep thy P;
119:78 as for me, I will meditate on thy P
119:87 on earth; but I have not forsaken thy P
119:93 will never forget thy P; for by them thou
119:94 thine, save me; for I have sought thy P
119:100 more than the aged, for I keep thy P
119:104 Through thy P I get understanding; therefore I hate
119:110 me, but I do not stray from thy P
119:128 steps by all thy P; I hate every false
119:134 from man's oppression, that I may keep thy P
119:141 and despised, yet I do not forget thy P
119:159 Consider how I love thy P
119:168 I keep thy P and testimonies, for all my
119:173 to help me, for I have chosen thy P
Prov 4:3 I give you good P: do not forsake my
Jer 35:18 and kept all his P, and done all that
Mt 15:9 teaching as doctrines the P of men.'"
Mk 7:7 teaching as doctrines the P of men.'
Rom 2:26 is uncircumcised keeps the P of the law, will
Col 2:22 used), according to human P and doctrines?

PRECINCT (2)
2Mac 1:15 wall of the sacred P, they closed the temple
14:33 I will level this P of God to the

PRECINCTS (8)
2Kgs 23:11 which was in the P; and he burned the
1Mac 1:47 build altars and sacred P and shrines for idols,
5:43 fled into the sacred P at Carnaim.
5:44 and burned the sacred P with fire, together with
10:43 in any of its P, because he owes money
14:48 conspicuous place in the P of the sanctuary,
2Mac 6:4 women within the sacred P, and besides brought in
10:2 by the foreigners, and also destroyed the sacred P

PRECIOUS (77)
1Sam 26:21 because my life was P in your eyes this
26:24 as your life was P this day in my
26:24 may my life be P in the sight of
2Sam 12:30 in it was a P stone; and it was
1Kgs 10:2 very much gold, and P stones; and when she
10:10 quantity of spices, and P stones; never again came
10:11 of almug wood and P stones.
2Kgs 1:13 servants of yours, be P in your sight.
1:14 let my life be P in your sight."
20:13 gold, the spices, the P oil, his armory, all
1Chr 20:2 in it was a P stone; and it was
29:2 stones, all sorts of P stones, and marble.
29:8 And whoever had P stones gave them to the
2Chr 3:6 house with settings of P stones.
9:1 very much gold and P stones.
9:9 quantity of spices, and P stones: there were no
9:10 brought algum wood and P stones.
20:25 numbers, goods, clothing, and P things, which they
32:23 LORD to Jerusalem and P things to Hezekiah king
32:27 silver, for gold, for P stones, for spices, for
36:10 to Babylon, with the P vessels of the house
36:19 and destroyed all its P vessels.
Ezra 8:27 fine bright bronze as P as gold.
Tob 13:16 emeralds, her walls with P stones, and her towers
Jud 10:3 and anointed herself with P ointment, and combed
10:21 gold and emeralds and P stones.
Esth 1:6 porphyry, marble, mother-of-pearl and P stones.
15:6 covered with gold and P stones.
Job 22:25 your gold, and your P silver;
28:10 his eye sees every P thing.
28:16 gold of Ophir, in P onyx or sapphire.
Ps 36:7 How P is thy steadfast love, O God!
72:14 redeems their life; and P is their blood in
116:15 P in the sight of the LORD is the
133:2 It is like the P oil upon the head,
139:17 How P to me are thy thoughts, O God!
Prov 1:13 we shall find all P goods, we shall fill
3:15 She is more P than jewels, and nothing you
12:27 diligent man will get P wealth.
20:15 of knowledge are a P jewel.
21:20 P treasure remains in a wise man's dwelling, but
24:4 are filled with all P and pleasant riches.
31:10 She is far more P than jewels.
Eccl 7:1 name is better than P ointment; and the day
Wis 12:7 that the land most P of all to thee
Sir 6:15 There is nothing so P as a faithful friend,
26:14 there is nothing so P as a disciplined soul.
45:11 of a craftsman; with P stones engraved like signets,
50:9 with all kinds of P stones;
Is 28:16 a tested stone, a P cornerstone, of a sure
39:2 gold, the spices, the P oil, his whole armory,
43:4 Because you are P in my eyes, and honored,
54:12 all your wall of P stones.
Jer 15:19 you utter what is P, and not what is
Lam 1:7 and bitterness all the P things that were hers
1:10 hands over all her P things; yea, she has
4:2 The P sons of Zion, worth their weight in
Ezek 7:22 they may profane my P place; robbers shall enter
22:25 have taken treasure and P things; they have made
27:22 of spices, and all P stones, and gold.
28:13 garden of God; every P stone was your covering,
Dan 11:8 images and with their P vessels of silver and
11:38 gold and silver, with P stones and costly gifts.
11:43 silver, and all the P things of Egypt; and
Hos 9:6 Nettles shall possess their P things of silver; thorns
13:15 his treasury of every P thing.
Nah 2:9 or wealth of every P thing.
Acts 20:24 any value nor as P to myself, if only
1Cor 3:12 foundation with gold, silver, P stones, wood, hay,
Jas 5:7 farmer waits for the P fruit of the earth,
1Pet 1:7 of your faith, more P than gold which though
1:19 gold, but with the P blood of Christ, like
2:4 God's sight chosen and P;
2:6 a cornerstone chosen and P, and he who believes
2:7 who believe, he is P, but for those who
3:4 quiet spirit, which in God's sight is very P
2Pet 1:4 granted to us his P and very great promises,

PRECIPITOUSLY
2Mac 13:5 on all sides inclines P into the ashes.

PREDECESSORS
1Mac 11:26 treated him as his P had treated him; he

PREDESTINED (3)
Acts 4:28 and thy plan had P to take place.
Rom 8:29 he foreknew he also P to be conformed to
8:30 And those whom he P he also called; and

PREDICT
Is 47:13 at the new moons P what shall befall you.

PREDICTED (3)
2Kgs 23:16 God proclaimed, who had P these things.
23:17 came from Judah and P these things which you
Rom 9:29 And as Isaiah P, "If the Lord of hosts

PREDICTING
1Pet 1:11 Christ within them when P the sufferings of Christ

PREDICTIONS (2)
2Pet 3:2 you should remember the P of the holy prophets
Jude 1:17 must remember, beloved, the P of the apostles of

PREFACE
2Mac 2:32 foolish to lengthen the P while cutting short the

PREFECT
Dan 2:48 of Babylon, and chief P over all the wise

PREFECTS (4)
Dan 3:2 assemble the satraps, the P, and the governors, the
3:3 Then the satraps, the P, and the governors, the
3:95 And the satraps, the P, the governors, and the
6:7 of the kingdom, the P and the satraps, the

PREFER (2)
2Mac 11:24 to Greek customs but P their own way of
Philem 1:9 for love's sake I P to appeal to you–

PREFERABLE (2)
Sir 20:24 A thief is P to a habitual liar, but
28:21 death, and Hades is P to it.

PREFERENCE
Deut 21:16 as the first-born in P to the son of

PREFERRED (3)
Wis 7:8 I P her to scepters and thrones, and I
Jer 8:3 Death shall be P to life by all the
Philem 1:14 the gospel; but I P to do nothing without

PREFERRING
2Mac 14:42 upon his own sword, P to die nobly rather

PREFERS
Wis 17:13 of help, being weak, P ignorance of what causes

PREGNANCY
Hos 9:11 bird--no birth, no P, no conception!

PREGNANT (3)
Ps 7:14 conceives evil, and is P with mischief, and brings
Sir 42:10 be defiled or become P in her father's house;
Hos 13:16 in pieces, and their P women ripped open.

PREPARATION (9)
1Chr 12:39 their brethren had made P for them.
22:5 I will therefore make P for it." So David
Jud 4:5 stored up food in P for war--since their
Mt 27:62 after the day of P, the chief priests and
Mk 15:41 was the day of P, that is, the day
Lk 23:53 was the day of P, and the sabbath was
Jn 19:14 was the day of P of the Passover; it
19:31 was the day of P, in order to prevent
19:42 the Jewish day of P, as the tomb was

PREPARATIONS (3)
1Chr 28:2 God; and I made P for building.
Tob 5:16 his son made the P for the journey.
Heb 9:6 These P having thus been made, the priests go

PREPARE (79)
Gen 18:7 servant, who hastened to P it.
27:4 game for me, and P for me savory food,
27:7 'Bring me game, and P for me savory food,
27:9 kids, that I may P from them savory food
Ex 16:5 sixth day, when they P what they bring in,
Num 15:5 a hin, you shall P with the burnt offering,
15:6 a ram, you shall P for a cereal offering
15:8 And when you P a bull for a burnt
15:12 the number that you P, so shall you do
Deut 19:3 You shall P the roads, and divide into three
Josh 1:11 and command the people, P your provisions; for
Judg 13:15 us detain you, and P a kid for you."
1Sam 6:7 Now then, take and P a new cart and
2Sam 12:4 flock or herd to P for the wayfarer who
13:5 bread to eat, and P the food in my
13:7 brother Amnon's house, and P food for him."
1Kgs 17:12 may go in and P it for myself and
18:23 it; and I will P the other bull and
18:25 yourselves one bull and P it first, for you
18:44 up, say to Ahab, P your chariot and go
1Chr 9:32 of the showbread, to P it every sabbath.
22:2 he set stonecutters to P dressed stones for building
2Chr 2:9 with your servants, to P timber for me in
31:11 Hezekiah commanded them to P chambers in the
35:4 P yourselves according to your fathers' houses by
35:6 and sanctify yourselves, and P for your brethren, to
Tob 11:3 of your wife and P the house.
Jud 2:7 Tell them to P earth and water, for I
Esth 5:8 dinner which I will P for them, and tomorrow
Ps 5:3 in the morning I P a sacrifice for thee,
Prov 24:27 P your work outside, get everything ready for you
Wis 9:8 tent which thou didst P from the beginning.
13:12 of his work to P his food, and eat
16:2 people, and thou didst P quails to eat, a
Sir 2:1 to serve the Lord, P yourself for temptation.
2:17 fear the Lord will P their hearts, and will
18:22 Before making a vow, P yourself; and do not
26:19 the Lord will P him for the sword!
29:26 words: "Come here, stranger, P the table, and if
33:4 P what to say, and thus you will be
47:13 for his name and P a sanctuary to stand
Is 14:21 P slaughter for his sons because of the guilt
21:5 They P the table, they spread the rugs, they
40:3 cries: "In the wilderness P the way of the
57:14 "Build up, build up, P the way, remove every
62:10 go through the gates, P the way for the
Jer 6:4 P war against her; up, and let us attack
22:7 I will P destroyers against you, each with his
46:3 Josiah, king of Judah: P buckler and shield, and
46:19 P yourselves baggage for exile, O inhabitants of
51:12 strong; set up watchmen; P the ambushes; for the
51:27 trumpet among the nations; P the nations for war
51:28 P the nations for war against her, the kings
51:39 are inflamed I will P them a feast and
Bar 1:10 offerings and incense, and P a cereal offering, and
Ezek 4:15 on which you may P your bread."
12:3 Therefore, son of man, P for yourself an exile's
35:6 Lord GOD, I will P you for blood, and
Joel 3:9 this among the nations: P war, stir up the
Amos 4:12 do this to you, P to meet your God,
Mal 3:1 send my messenger to P the way before me,
Mt 3:3 crying in the wilderness: P the way of the
11:10 thy face, who shall P thy way before thee.'
26:12 has done it to P me for burial.
26:17 will you have us P for you to eat
Mk 1:2 thy face, who shall P thy way;
1:3 crying in the wilderness: P the way of the
14:12 have us go and P for you to eat
14:15 furnished and ready; there P for us."
Lk 1:76 before the Lord to P his ways,
3:4 crying in the wilderness: P the way of the
7:27 thy face, who shall P thy way before thee.'
17:8 rather say to him, P supper for me, and
22:8 John, saying, "Go and P the passover for us,
22:9 will you have us P it?"
Jn 14:2 that I go to P a place for you?
14:3 when I go and P a place for you,
Philem 1:22 At the same time, P a guest room for
Rev 16:12 was dried up, to P the way for the

PREPARED (91)
Gen 18:8 calf which he had P, and set it before
24:31 For I have P the house and a place
27:14 mother; and his mother P savory food, such as
27:17 bread, which she had P, into the hand of
27:31 He also P savory food, and brought it to
Ex 12:16 that only may be P by you.
12:39 tarry, neither had they P for themselves any
23:20 bring you to the place which I have P
39:6 The onyx stones were P, enclosed in settings of
Lev 7:9 and all that is P on a pan or
Num 23:4 to him, "I have P the seven altars, and
Judg 6:19 into his house and P a kid, and unleavened
19:5 the morning, and he P to go; but the
2Sam 12:4 poor man's lamb, and P it for the man
1Kgs 1:5 be king"; and he P for himself chariots and
5:18 did the hewing and P the timber and the
6:7 it was with stone P at the quarry; so
6:19 The inner sanctuary he P in the innermost part
18:26 given them, and they P it, and called on
2Kgs 6:23 So he P for them a great feast; and
7:12 what the Syrians have P against us.
1Chr 9:30 sons of the priests, P the mixing of the
15:1 of David; and he P a place for the
15:3 place, which he had P for it.
15:12 place that I have P for it.

P

2Chr 1:4 place that David had P for it, for he
16:14 various kinds of spices P by the perfumer's art;
26:14 And Uzziah P for all the army shields, spears,
31:11 the LORD; and they P them.
35:10 the service had been P for, the priests stood
35:14 And afterward they P for themselves and for the
35:14 night; so the Levites P for themselves and for
35:15 their brethren the Levites P for them.
35:16 of the LORD was P that day, to keep
35:20 this, when Josiah had P the temple, Neco king
Neh 5:18 Now that which was P for one day was
5:18 sheep; fowls likewise were P for me, and every
8:10 for whom nothing is P; for this day is
13:5 was connected with Tobiah, P for Tobiah a large
Tob 2:1 a good dinner was P for me and I
Jud 5:1 people of Israel had P for war and had
9:6 all they ways are P in advance, and thy
12:19 and drank before him what her maid had P
Esth 5:4 dinner that I have P for the king."
5:5 Haman came to the dinner that Esther had P
5:12 to the banquet she P but myself.
6:4 gallows that he had P for him.
6:14 in haste to the banquet that Esther had P
7:9 gallows which Haman has P for Mordecai, whose
7:10 gallows which he had P for Mordecai.
11:7 their roaring every nation P for war, to fight
Job 13:18 Behold, I have P my case; I know that
15:24 him, like a king P for battle.
29:7 the city, when I P my seat in the
Ps 7:13 his bow; he has P his deadly weapons, making
65:9 for so thou hast P it.
132:17 for David; I have P a lamp for my
Sir 45:20 the first fruits, he P bread of first fruits
49:1 a blending of incense P by the art of
49:12 holy to the Lord, P for everlasting glory.
Is 30:33 place has long been P; yea, for the king
Jer 46:14 'Stand ready and be P, for the sword shall
Bar 3:32 He who P the earth for all time filled
Ezek 28:13 the day that you were created they were P
Zeph 1:7 hand; the LORD has P a sacrifice and consecrated
Zech 5:11 and when this is P, they will set the
1Mac 2:32 encamped opposite them and P for battle against
12:28 and his men were P for battle, they were
15:7 weapons which you have P and the strongholds
Mt 20:23 whom it has been P by my Father."
25:34 Father, inherit the kingdom P for you from the
25:41 into the eternal fire P for the devil and
26:19 directed them, and they P the passover.
Mk 10:40 is for those for whom it has been P
14:16 told them; and they P the passover.
Lk 1:17 to make ready for the Lord a people P
2:31 salvation which thou hast P in the presence of
12:20 the things you have P, whose will they be?'
22:13 told them; and they P the passover.
23:55 then they returned, and P spices and ointments.
24:1 the tomb, taking the spices which they had P
Rom 9:23 mercy, which he has P beforehand for glory,
1Cor 2:9 conceived, what God has P for those who love
2Cor 5:5 He who has P us for this very thing
Eph 2:10 good works, which God P beforehand, that we should
Heb 9:2 For a tent was P, the outer one, in
10:5 a body hast thou P for me;
11:16 God, for he has P for them a city.
1Pet 3:15 Always be P to make a defense to any
Rev 12:6 she has a place P by God, in which
21:2 of heaven from God, P as a bride adorned

PREPARES (4)

Job 15:35 evil and their heart P deceit."
Ps 147:8 heavens with clouds, he P rain for the earth,
Prov 6:8 officer or ruler, she P her food in summer,
2Mac 2:27 easy for one who P a banquet and seeks

PREPAREST

Ps 23:5 Thou P a table before me in the presence

PREPARING (8)

Neh 13:7 had done for Tobiah, P for him a chamber
Esth 12:2 learned that they were P to lay hands upon
Wis 14:1 Again, one P to sail and about to voyage
Ezek 39:17 feast which I am P for you, a great
39:19 feast which I am P for you.
1Mac 5:11 They are P to come and capture the stronghold
Acts 10:10 but while they were P it, he fell into
2Cor 4:17 slight momentary affliction is P for us an eternal

PRESCRIBED (6)

2Chr 4:7 ten golden lampstands as P, and set them in
4:20 the inner sanctuary, as P;
30:5 had not kept it in great numbers as P
30:18 yet they ate the passover otherwise than as P
Job 36:23 Who has P for him his way, or who
38:10 its swaddling band, and P bounds for it, and

PRESCRIBING

Ezra 7:22 oil, and salt without P how much.

PRESENCE (215)

Gen 3:8 hid themselves from the P of the LORD God
4:16 went away from the P of the LORD, and
23:9 to me in your P as a possession for
23:11 in it; in the P of the sons of
23:18 a possession in the P of the Hittites, before
27:30 gone out from the P of Isaac his father,
31:32 In the P of our kinsmen point out what
41:46 went out from the P of Pharaoh, and went
45:3 answer him, for they were dismayed at his P
47:10 went out from the P of Pharaoh.
Ex 10:11 And they were driven out from Pharaoh's P
25:30 the bread of the P on the table before
33:14 And he said, "My P will go with you,
33:15 to him, "If thy P will not go with
35:13 the bread of the P;
35:20 Israel departed from the P of Moses.
39:36 the bread of the P;
Lev 10:2 came forth from the P of the LORD and
22:3 cut off from my P: I am the LORD.
Num 4:7 the bread of the P they shall spread a
20:6 Aaron went from the P of the assembly to
Deut 4:37 Egypt with his own P, by his great power,
25:2 be beaten in his P with a number of
25:9 to him in the P of the elders, and
Josh 8:32 And there, in the P of the people of
22:27 the LORD in his P with our burnt offerings
Judg 3:19 And all his attendants went out from his P
Ruth 4:4 Buy it in the P of those sitting here,
4:4 here, and in the P of the elders of
1Sam 1:22 may appear in the P of the LORD, and
1:26 standing here in your P, praying to the LORD.
2:11 the LORD, in the P of Eli the priest.
2:21 Samuel grew in the P of the LORD.
16:18 a man of good P; and the LORD is
18:13 removed him from his P, and made him a
19:7 he was in his P as before.
21:6 the bread of the P, which is removed from
21:15 this fellow to play the madman in my P
26:20 earth away from the P of the LORD; for
2Sam 3:26 came out from David's P, he sent messengers after
11:13 he ate in his P and drank, so that
13:17 woman out of my P, and bolt the door
14:24 house; he is not to come into my P
14:24 house, and did not come into the king's P
14:28 years in Jerusalem, without coming into the king's P
14:32 me go into the P of the king; and
24:4 went out from the P of the king to
1Kgs 1:28 came into the king's P, and stood before the
7:48 the bread of the P,
8:22 the LORD in the P of all the assembly
10:24 whole earth sought the P of Solomon to hear
21:13 against Naboth, in the P of the people, saying,
2Kgs 5:27 went out from his P a leper, as white
6:32 a man from his P; but before the messenger
13:23 cast them from his P until now.
24:20 Judah that he cast them out from his P
1Chr 16:11 his strength, seek his P continually!
24:6 recorded them in the P of the king, and
24:31 of Aaron, in the P of King David, Zadok,
29:10 the LORD in the P of all the assembly;
2Chr 4:19 the bread of the P,
6:12 the LORD in the P of all the assembly
6:13 his knees in the P of all the assembly
9:23 the earth sought the P of Solomon to hear
26:19 his forehead, in the P of the priests in
29:11 to stand in his P, to minister to him,
34:4 the Baals in his P; and he hewed down
Neh 2:1 Now I had not been sad in his P
4:2 he said in the P of his brethren and
6:19 good deeds in my P, and reported my words
8:3 until midday, in the P of the men and
Tob 3:16 was heard in the P of the glory of
4:11 excellent offering in the P of the Most High.
12:6 to him in the P of all the living

	12:15	and enter into the P of the glory of
	13:4	exalt him in the P of all the living;
Jud	2:5	When you leave my P, take with you men
	2:14	So Holofernes left the P of his master, and
	5:8	them out from the P of their gods; and
	6:1	the Moabites in the P of all the foreign
	6:17	had said in the P of the Assyrian leaders,
	8:15	destroy us in the P of our enemies.
	10:13	my way to the P of Holofernes the commander
	10:15	hurrying down to the P of our lord.
	10:23	Judith came into the P of Holofernes and his
	11:5	maidservant speak in your P, and I will tell
	11:13	who minister in the P of our God at
	12:13	went out from the P of Holofernes, and approached
	12:13	be honored in his P, and drink wine and
	13:1	attendants from his master's P; and they went to
	14:8	to him in the P of the people all
	16:15	the waters; at thy P the rocks shall melt
Esth	1:16	Then Memucan said in P of the king and
	2:23	the Chronicles in the P of the king.
	7:8	the queen in my P, in my own house?"
	8:15	went out from the P of the king in
Job	1:12	went forth from the P of the LORD.
	2:7	went forth from the P of the LORD, and
	21:8	are established in their P, and their offspring before
	23:15	am terrified at his P; when I consider, I
	30:11	me, they have cast off restraint in my P
	33:26	he comes into his P with joy.
Ps	16:11	of life; in thy P there is fulness of
	21:6	make him glad with the joy of thy P
	23:5	before me in the P of my enemies; thou
	31:20	the covert of thy P thou hidest them from
	39:1	so long as the wicked are in my P
	41:12	set me in thy P for ever.
	51:11	not away from thy P, and take not thy
	52:9	is good, in the P of the godly.
	68:8	down rain, at the P of God; yon Sinai
	68:8	Sinai quaked at the P of God, the God
	95:2	us come into his P with thanksgiving; let us
	100:2	Come into his P with singing!
	101:7	man who utters lies shall continue in my P
	105:4	his strength, seek his P continually!
	114:7	O earth, at the P of the LORD, at
	114:7	the LORD, at the P of the God of
	116:14	the LORD in the P of all his people.
	116:18	the LORD in the P of all his people,
	139:7	Or whither shall I flee from thy P
	140:13	thy name; the upright shall dwell in thy P
Prov	14:7	Leave the P of a fool, for there you
	17:18	becomes surety in the P of his neighbor.
	25:5	the wicked from the P of the king, and
	25:6	forward in the king's P or stand in the
	25:7	put lower in the P of the prince.
Eccl	8:3	dismayed; go from his P, do not delay when
Wis	5:1	great confidence in the P of those who have
	8:10	and honor in the P of the elders, though
	14:17	honor monarchs in their P, since they lived at
Sir	6:12	against you, and will hide himself from your P
	8:18	In the P of a stranger do nothing that
	17:20	sins; pray in his P and lessen your offenses.
	23:14	be forgetful in their P, and be deemed a
	24:2	mouth, and in the P of his host she
	27:23	In your P his mouth is all sweetness, and
	30:3	in him in the P of friends.
	38:3	head, and in the P of great men he
	45:3	glorified him in the P of kings.
Is	1:7	fire; in your very P aliens devour your land;
	3:8	deeds are against the LORD, defying his glorious P
	19:1	will tremble at his P, and the heart of
	63:9	the angel of his P saved them; in his
	64:1	might quake at thy P --
	64:2	and that the nations might tremble at thy P
	64:3	thou camest down, the mountains quaked at thy P
Jer	3:17	to it, to the P of the LORD in
	4:1	your abominations from my P, and do not waver,
	23:39	you away from my P, you and the city
	28:1	the LORD, in the P of the priests and
	28:5	the prophet in the P of the priests and
	28:11	Hananiah spoke in the P of all the people,
	32:12	of Mahseiah, in the P of Hanamel my cousin,
	32:12	my cousin, in the P of the witnesses who
	32:12	purchase, and in the P of all the Jews
	32:13	charged Baruch in their P, saying,
	33:18	a man in my P to offer burnt offerings,
	52:3	Judah that he cast them out from his P
Lam	2:19	like water before the P of the Lord!
	3:35	a man in the P of the Most High,
Bar	2:28	thy law in the P of the people of
Ezek	28:9	a god,' in the P of those who slay
	38:20	shall quake at my P, and the mountains shall
Dan	5:24	"Then from his P the hand was sent, and
	14:14	whole temple in the P of the king alone.
Jon	1:3	to Tarshish from the P of the LORD.
	1:3	Tarshish, away from the P of the LORD.
	1:10	was fleeing from the P of the LORD, because
	2:4	cast out from thy P; how shall I again
Mal	2:3	and I will put you out of my P
1Mac	1:22	the bread of the P, the cups for drink
	11:26	exalted him in the P of all his friends.
2Mac	6:18	age and of noble P, was being forced to
	10:3	lamps and set out the bread of the P
	14:24	Judas always in his P; he was warmly attached
Mt	12:4	the bread of the P, which it was not
Mk	2:26	the bread of the P, which it is not
Lk	1:19	who stand in the P of God; and I
	2:31	hast prepared in the P of all peoples,
	6:4	the bread of the P, which it is not
	8:47	him declared in the P of all the people
	13:26	and drank in your P, and you taught in
	14:10	be honored in the P of all who sit
	20:26	not able in the P of the people to
Jn	17:5	me in thy own P with the glory which
	20:30	other signs in the P of the disciples, which
Acts	2:28	of gladness with thy P
	3:13	and denied in the P of Pilate, when he
	3:16	perfect health in the P of you all.
	3:19	may come from the P of the Lord,
	5:41	Then they left the P of the council, rejoicing
	27:35	to God in the P of all he broke
Rom	4:17	--in the P of the God in whom
1Cor	1:29	might boast in the P of God.
2Cor	2:10	your sake in the P of Christ,
	4:14	Jesus and bring us with you into his P
	10:10	strong, but his bodily P is weak, and his
Phil	2:12	only as in my P but much more in
2Thes	1:9	and exclusion from the P of the Lord and
1Tim	5:20	rebuke them in the P of all, so that
	5:21	In the P of God and of Christ Jesus
	6:12	good confession in the P of many witnesses.
	6:13	In the P of God who gives life to
2Tim	4:1	charge you in the P of God and of
Heb	9:2	the bread of the P; it is called the
	9:24	to appear in the P of God on our
Jude	1:24	without blemish before the P of his glory with
Rev	7:15	upon the throne will shelter them with his P
	13:12	first beast in its P, and makes the earth
	13:14	to work in the P of the beast, it
	14:10	and sulphur in the P of the holy angels
	14:10	angels and in the P of the Lamb.
	19:20	prophet who in its P had worked the signs
	20:11	upon it; from his P earth and sky fled

PRESENT (144)

Gen	32:13	had with him a P for his brother Esau,
	32:18	Jacob; they are a P sent to my lord
	32:20	appease him with the P that goes before me,
	32:21	So the P passed on before him; and he
	33:10	sight, then accept my P from my hand; for
	34:12	so much as marriage P and gift, and I
	43:11	to the man a P, a little balm and
	43:15	the men took the P, and they took double
	43:25	they made ready the P for Joseph's coming at
	43:26	house to him the P which they had with
Ex	22:16	shall give the marriage P for her, and make
	22:17	equivalent to the marriage P for virgins.
	34:2	to Mount Sinai, and P yourself there to me
Lev	1:5	sons the priests shall P the blood, and throw
	16:9	And Aaron shall P the goat on which the
	16:11	"Aaron shall P the bull as a sin offering
	16:20	the altar, he shall P the live goat;
	22:23	too short you may P for a freewill offering;
	23:8	But you shall P an offering by fire to
	23:16	sabbath; then you shall P a cereal offering of
	23:18	And you shall P with the bread seven lambs
	23:25	work; and you shall P an offering by fire
	23:27	shall afflict yourselves and P an offering by fire
	23:36	Seven days you shall P offerings by fire to
	23:36	a holy convocation and P an offering by fire
Num	6:16	And the priest shall P them before the LORD
	8:9	And you shall P the Levites before the tent
	8:10	When you P the Levites before the LORD, the
	15:19	the land, you shall P an offering to the

P

15:20 coarse meal you shall P a cake as an
15:20 floor, so shall you P it.
16:16 said to Korah, "Be P, you and all your
18:19 the people of Israel P to the LORD I
18:24 of Israel, which they P as an offering to
18:26 inheritance, then you shall P an offering from it
18:28 So shall you also P an offering to the
18:29 to you, you shall P every offering due to
Deut 12:6 the offering that you P, your votive offerings, your
12:11 the offering that you P, and all your votive
12:17 the offering that you P;
31:14 die; call Joshua, and P yourselves in the tent
Josh 15:19 him, "Give me a P; since you have set
Judg 1:15 him, "Give me a P; since you have set
6:18 and bring out my P, and set it before
1Sam 9:7 and there is no P to bring to the
10:19 us.' Now therefore P yourselves before the LORD
10:27 And they despised him, and brought him no P
13:15 the people who were P with him, about six
13:16 the people who were P with them, stayed in
18:25 desires no marriage P except a hundred foreskins
25:27 And now let this P which your servant has
30:26 saying, "Here is a P for you from the
2Sam 11:8 there followed him a P from the king.
1Kgs 10:25 of them brought his P, articles of silver and
15:19 sending to you a P of silver and gold;
2Kgs 5:15 so accept now a P from your servant."
8:8 to Hazael, "Take a P with you and go
8:9 him, and took a P with him, all kinds
16:8 house, and sent a P to the king of
20:12 with letters and a P to Hezekiah; for he
1Chr 29:17 thy people, who are P here, offering freely and
2Chr 5:11 the priests who were P had sanctified themselves,
9:24 of them brought his P, articles of silver and
28:13 in addition to our P sins and guilt.
29:29 and all who were P with him bowed themselves
30:21 of Israel that were P at Jerusalem kept the
31:1 all Israel who were P went out to the
34:32 made all who were P in Jerusalem and in
35:7 for all that were P, lambs and kids from
35:17 of Israel who were P kept the passover at
35:18 and Israel who were P, and the inhabitants of
Ezra 8:25 and all Israel there P had offered;
Tob 7:11 But for the P be merry." And Tobias said,
12:12 dead, I was likewise P with you.
12:15 seven holy angels who P the prayers of the
Jud 8:18 generation, nor in these P days, has there been
Esth 1:5 for all the people P in Susa the capital,
13:6 month, Adar, of this P year,
Job 1:6 of God came to P themselves before the LORD,
2:1 of God came to P themselves before the LORD,
2:1 came among them to P himself before the LORD.
Ps 46:1 and strength, a very P help in trouble.
Wis 4:2 When it is P, men imitate it, and they
9:9 thy works and was P when thou didst make
11:11 Whether absent or P, they were equally distressed,
14:17 they might flatter the absent one as though P
Sir 14:11 to your means, and P worthy offerings to the
18:14 your words when you P a gift.
Is 39:1 with letters and a P to Hezekiah, for he
45:21 Declare and P your case; let them take counsel
Jer 40:5 of food and a P, and let him go.
41:5 offerings and incense to P at the temple of
42:9 you sent me to P your supplication before him:
Bar 1:7 the people who were P with him in Jerusalem.
Ezek 43:24 You shall P them before the LORD, and the
Dan 9:18 for we do not P our supplications before thee
Hos 13:13 now he does not P himself at the mouth
Zech 14:18 not go up and P themselves, then upon them
Mal 1:8 P that to your governor; will he be pleased
3:3 and silver, till they P right offerings to the
2Mac 4:18 and the king was P,
4:30 been given as a P to Antiochis, the king's
6:26 even if for the P I should avoid the
7:9 dismiss us from this P life, but the King
9:26 and to maintain your P good will, each of
Lk 2:22 up to Jerusalem to P him to the Lord
12:56 how to interpret the P time?
13:1 There were some P at that very time who
Acts 5:38 So in the P case I tell you, keep
10:33 we are all here P in the sight of
17:19 know what this new teaching is which you P
21:18 us to James; and all the elders were P
24:24 "Go away for the P; when I have an
25:24 and all who are P with us, you see
Rom 3:26 to prove at the P time that he himself
8:18 the sufferings of this P time are not worth
8:38 nor principalities, nor things P, nor things to come,
11:5 So too at the P time there is a
12:1 mercies of God, to P your bodies as a
15:25 At P, however, I am going to Jerusalem with
1Cor 3:22 or death or the P or the future, all
4:11 To the P hour we hunger and thirst, we
5:3 in body I am P in spirit, and as
5:3 spirit, and as if P, I have already pronounced
5:4 and my spirit is P, with the power of
7:26 in view of the P distress it is well
2Cor 8:14 your abundance at the P time should supply their
10:2 that when I am P I may not have
10:11 say by letter when absent, we do when P
11:2 you to Christ to P you as a pure
13:2 as I did when P on my second visit,
Gal 1:4 deliver us from the P evil age, according to
4:18 only when I am P with you.
4:20 could wish to be P with you now and
4:25 she corresponds to the P Jerusalem, for she is
Eph 5:27 word, that he might P the church to himself
6:12 world rulers of this P darkness, against the spiritual
Col 1:22 death, in order to P you holy and blameless
1:28 wisdom, that we may P every man mature in
1Tim 4:8 holds promise for the P life and also for
2Tim 2:15 Do your best to P yourself to God as
4:10 in love with this P world, has deserted me
Heb 9:9 is symbolic for the P age).
Jude 1:24 from falling and to P you without blemish before

PRESENTABLE

1Cor 12:24 modesty, which our more P parts do not require.

PRESENTED (28)

Gen 46:29 in Goshen; and he P himself to him, and
47:2 took five men and P them to Pharaoh.
Lev 2:8 and when it is P to the priest, he
7:35 the day they were P to serve as priests
8:18 Then he P the ram of the burnt offering;
8:22 Then he P the other ram, the ram of
9:9 the sons of Aaron P the blood to him,
9:15 Then he P the people's offering, and took the
9:16 And he P the burnt offering, and offered it
9:17 And he P the cereal offering, and filled his
16:10 for Azazel shall be P alive before the LORD
Deut 31:14 and Joshua went and P themselves in the tent
Josh 24:1 of Israel; and they P themselves before God.
Judg 3:17 And he P the tribute to Eglon king of
6:19 under the oak and P them.
20:2 the tribes of Israel, P themselves in the assembly
1Chr 21:26 to the LORD and P burnt offerings and peace
Jud 9:6 things thou didst will P themselves and said, 'Lo,
Ezek 20:28 offered their sacrifices and P the provocation of their
Dan 7:13 of Days and was P before him.
2Mac 1:21 the sacrifices were P, Nehemiah ordered the priests
4:24 But he, when P to the king, extolled him
4:44 sent by the senate P the case before him.
Acts 1:3 To them he P himself alive after his passion
9:41 saints and widows he P her alive.
21:26 fulfilled and the offering P for every one of
23:33 to the governor, they P Paul also before him.
28:10 They P many gifts to us; and when we

PRESENTING (5)

Lev 23:37 of holy convocation, for P to the LORD offerings
Judg 3:18 when Ehud had finished P the tribute, he sent
Dan 9:20 my people Israel, and P my supplication before the
Zech 6:5 of heaven, after P themselves before the LORD
2Mac 14:4 hundred and fifty-first year, P to him a crown

PRESENTS (7)

Lev 22:18 the sojourners in Israel P his offering, whether in
2Chr 17:11 the Philistines brought Jehoshaphat P, and silver for
Sir 20:28 P and gifts blind the eyes of the wise;
Is 16:12 And when Moab P himself, when he wearies himself
66:3 dog's neck; he who P a cereal offering, like
2Mac 3:2 temple with the finest P,
Rev 11:10 make merry and exchange P, because these two

PRESERVE (25)

Gen 19:32 him, that we may P offspring through our father."
19:34 him, that we may P offspring through our father."
45:5 me before you to P life.
45:7 me before you to P for you a remnant
Deut 6:24 always, that he might P us alive, as at
Ps 16:1 P me, O God, for in thee I take

25:21 May integrity and uprightness P me, for I wait
40:11 and thy faithfulness ever P me!
64:1 God, in my complaint; P my life from dread
79:11 to thy great power P those doomed to die!
86:2 P my life, for I am godly; save thy
119:149 LORD, in thy justice P my life.
119:159 P my life according to thy steadfast love.
138:7 of trouble, thou dost P my life; thou dost
140:1 LORD, from evil men; P me from violent men,
140:4 hands of the wicked; P me from violent men,
143:11 name's sake, O LORD, P my life!
Prov 6:24 way of life, to P you from the evil
7:5 your intimate friend; to P you from the loose
14:3 of the wise will P them.
20:28 Loyalty and faithfulness P the king, and his throne
Sir 39:2 with prophecies; he will P the discourse of notable
Bar 6:28 and likewise their wives P some with salt, but
2Mac 1:26 thy people Israel and P thy portion and make
Lk 17:33 loses his life will P it.

PRESERVED (15)

Gen 32:30 face to face, and yet my life is P
Josh 24:17 in our sight, and P us in all the
1Sam 30:23 given us; he has P us and given into
Job 10:12 and thy care has P my spirit.
Ps 37:28 The righteous shall be P for ever, but the
Wis 10:5 the righteous man and P him blameless before God,
11:25 anything not called forth by thee have been P
Sir 46:8 these two alone were P out of six hundred
Is 49:6 and to restore the P of Israel; I will
Ezek 6:12 is left and is P shall die of famine.
Hos 12:13 from Egypt, and by a prophet he was P
2Mac 8:27 the Lord, who had P them for that day
Mt 9:17 put into fresh wineskins, and so both are P
Gal 2:5 the gospel might be P for you.
2Pet 2:5 the ancient world, but P Noah, a herald of

PRESERVES (8)

Ps 31:23 The LORD P the faithful, but abundantly requites
97:10 who hate evil; he P the lives of his
116:6 The LORD P the simple; when I was brought
145:20 The LORD P all who love him; but all
Prov 13:3 who guards his mouth P his life; he who
16:17 who guards his way P his life.
Eccl 7:12 knowledge is that wisdom P the life of him
Wis 16:26 but that thy word P those who trust in

PRESERVEST (2)

Neh 9:6 in them; and thou P all of them; and
Ps 32:7 place for me, thou P me from trouble; thou

PRESERVING (2)

Prov 2:8 paths of justice and P the way of his
Sir 38:14 for the sake of P life.

PRESIDENTS (5)

Dan 6:2 and over them three P, of whom Daniel was
6:3 above all the other P and satraps, because an
6:4 Then the P and the satraps sought to find
6:6 Then these P and satraps came by agreement to
6:7 All the P of the kingdom, the prefects and

PRESS (29)

Num 18:27 floor, and as the fulness of the wine P
18:30 produce of the wine P;
Deut 15:14 out of your wine P; as the LORD your
16:13 floor and your wine P;
Judg 6:11 wheat in the wine P, to hide it from
7:25 killed at the wine P of Zeeb, as they
2Kgs 6:27 From the threshing floor, or from the wine P
Job 41:1 with a fishhook, or P down his tongue with
Sir 33:16 and like a grape-gatherer I filled my wine P
Is 21:15 bow, and from the P of battle.
63:2 garments like his that treads in the wine P
63:3 have trodden the wine P alone, and from the
Lam 1:15 as in a wine P the virgin daughter of
Ezek 4:3 state of siege, and P the siege against it.
Hos 6:3 us know, let us P on to know the
Joel 3:13 tread, for the wine P is full.
Amos 2:13 prophesy.' "Behold, I will P you down in your
Hab 1:8 evening wolves; their horsemen P proudly on.
1Mac 6:57 affairs of the kingdom P urgently upon us.
Mt 21:33 and dug a wine P in it, and built
Mk 12:1 pit for the wine P, and built a tower,
Lk 8:45 multitudes surround you and P upon you!"
11:53 the Pharisees began to P him hard, and to
Phil 3:12 already perfect; but I P on to make it
3:14 what lies ahead, I P on toward the goal
Rev 14:19 into the great wine P of the wrath of
14:20 God; and the wine P was trodden outside the
14:20 flowed from the wine P, as high as a
19:15 will tread the wine P of the fury of

PRESSED (26)

Gen 19:9 Then they P hard against the man Lot, and
40:11 took the grapes and P them into Pharaoh's cup,
Num 22:25 against the wall, and P Balaam's foot against the
Judg 1:34 The Amorites P the Danites back into the hill
14:17 told her, because she P him hard.
16:16 And when she P him hard with her words
1Sam 31:3 The battle P hard upon Saul, and the archers
2Sam 13:25 He P him, but he would not go but
13:27 But Absalom P him until he let Amnon and
1Chr 10:3 The battle P hard upon Saul, and the archers
Sir 46:5 Mighty One, when enemies P him on every side,
46:16 One, when his enemies P him on every side,
Is 1:6 wounds; they are not P out, or bound up,
Jer 17:16 I have not P thee to send evil, nor
Ezek 23:3 there their breasts were P and their virgin bosoms
23:21 handled your bosom and P your young breasts."
Dan 13:14 again; and when each P the other for the
1Mac 2:30 their cattle, because evils P heavily upon them.
10:50 He P the battle strongly until the sun set,
15:14 from the sea; he P the city hard from
2Mac 11:5 leagues from Jerusalem, and P it hard.
12:23 And Judas P the pursuit with the utmost vigor,
Mk 3:10 all who had diseases P upon him to touch
Lk 5:1 While the people P upon him to hear the
6:38 you; good measure, P down, shaken together, running
8:42 he went, the people P round him.

PRESSES (8)

Ex 22:29 your harvest and from the outflow of your P
Neh 13:15 Judah men treading wine P on the sabbath, and
Job 24:11 they tread the wine P, but suffer thirst.
Sir 11:11 works, and toils, and P on, but is so
Is 16:10 out wine in the P; the vintage shout is
Jer 48:33 cease from the wine P; no one treads them
Amos 2:13 cart full of sheaves P down.
Zech 14:10 the Tower of Hananel to the king's wine P

PRESSING (5)

Prov 30:33 For P milk produces curds, pressing the nose
30:33 pressing milk produces curds, P the nose produces
30:33 nose produces blood, and P anger produces strife.
Dan 14:30 saw that they were P him hard, and under
Mk 5:31 "You see the crowd P around you, and yet

PRESSURE (3)

Job 33:7 need terrify you; my P will not be heavy
Sir 29:6 If the lender exert P, he will hardly get
2Cor 11:28 there is the daily P upon me of my

PRESTIGE

2Mac 4:15 putting the highest value upon Greek forms of P

PRESUME (5)

Esth 7:5 is he, that would P to do this?"
Mt 3:9 repentance, and do not P to say to yourselves,
Lk 7:7 therefore I did not P to come to you.
Rom 2:4 Or do you P upon the riches of his
Jude 1:9 Moses, he did not P to pronounce a reviling

PRESUMED

Num 14:44 But they P to go up to the heights

PRESUMES

Deut 18:20 But the prophet who P to speak a word

PRESUMPTION (2)

1Sam 17:28 I know your P, and the evil of your
Esth 13:2 world, not elated with P of authority but always

PRESUMPTUOUS (2)

Deut 1:43 the LORD, and were P and went up into
Ps 19:13 thy servant also from P sins; let them not

PRESUMPTUOUSLY (5)

Deut 17:12 The man who acts P, by not obeying the
17:13 fear, and not act P again.
18:22 prophet has spoken it P, you need not be
Neh 9:16 and our fathers acted P and stiffened their neck

9:29 Yet they acted P and did not obey thy

PRETEND (5)
2Sam 13:5 on your bed, and P to be ill; and
14:2 and said to her, P to be a mourner,
1Kgs 14:6 Jeroboam; why do you P to be another?
Prov 18:24 There are friends who P to be friends, but
2Mac 6:21 him to use, and P that he was eating

PRETENDED (5)
2Sam 13:6 Amnon lay down, and P to be ill; and
1Kgs 14:5 When she came, she P to be another woman.
2Mac 5:25 arrived in Jerusalem, he P to be peaceably disposed
Lk 20:20 and sent spies, who P to be sincere, that
2Thes 2:9 all power and with P signs and wonders,

PRETENDING
Sir 12:17 of you; and while P to help you, he

PRETENDS (3)
Prov 13:7 One man P to be rich, yet has nothing;
13:7 yet has nothing; another P to be poor, yet
Sir 19:24 hides his face and P not to hear; but

PRETENSE (8)
Josh 8:15 all Israel made a P of being beaten before
Jer 3:10 whole heart, but in P, says the LORD."
2Mac 6:24 "Such P is not worthy of our time of
6:25 religion, and through my P, for the sake of
Mk 12:40 houses and for a P make long prayers.
Lk 20:47 houses and for a P make long prayers.
Acts 27:30 into the sea, under P of laying out anchors
Phil 1:18 every way, whether in P or in truth, Christ

PRETENSIONS
1Tim 4:2 of demons, through the P of liars whose consciences

PRETEXT (2)
2Mac 1:14 For under P of intending to marry her, Antiochus
1Pet 2:16 your freedom as a P for evil; but live

PRETEXTS
Prov 18:1 who is estranged seeks P to break out against

PREVAIL (22)
Gen 32:25 that he did not P against Jacob, he touched
Deut 19:15 single witness shall not P against a man for
1Sam 2:9 darkness; for not by might shall a man P
17:9 servants; but if I P against him and kill
2Chr 14:11 God; let not man P against thee."
Jud 11:10 nor can the sword P against them, unless they
Esth 6:13 people, you will not P against him but will
Job 15:24 anguish terrify him; they P against him, like a
Ps 9:19 Let not man P; let the nations be judged
12:4 our tongue we will P, our lips are with
65:3 When our transgressions P over us, thou dost forgive
Eccl 4:12 though a man might P against one who is
Wis 7:30 the night, but against wisdom evil does not P
Is 16:12 to his sanctuary to pray, he will not P
Jer 1:19 but they shall not P against you, for I
5:22 waves toss, they cannot P, though they roar, they
15:20 but they shall not P over you, for I
Dan 11:7 and he shall deal with them and shall P
11:12 down tens of thousands, but he shall not P
2Mac 3:5 when he could not P over Onias he went
Mt 16:18 of death shall not P against it.
Rom 3:4 in thy words, and P when thou art judged."

PREVAILED (28)
Gen 7:18 The waters P and increased greatly upon the earth;
7:19 And the waters P so mightily upon the earth
7:20 were covered; the waters P above the mountains,
7:24 And the waters P upon the earth a hundred
30:8 my sister, and have P; so she called his
32:28 striven with God and with men, and have P
41:53 years of plenty that P in the land of
Ex 17:11 up his hand, Israel P; and whenever he lowered
17:11 and whenever he lowered his hand, Amalek P
Judg 3:10 hand; and his hand P over Cushan-rishathaim.
6:2 the hand of Midian P over Israel; and because
1Sam 17:50 So David P over the Philistine with a sling
2Sam 24:4 But the king's word P against Joab and the
1Chr 21:4 But the king's word P against Joab.
2Chr 13:18 the men of Judah P, because they relied upon
27:5 of the Ammonites and P against them.
Ps 13:4 enemy say, "I have P over him"; lest my
129:2 yet they have not P against me.
Jer 20:7 thou art stronger than I, and thou hast P
38:22 have deceived you and P against you; now that
Lam 1:16 my children are desolate, for the enemy has P
Dan 7:21 with the saints, and P over them,
Hos 12:4 with the angel and P, he wept and sought
Obad 1:7 border; your confederates have P against you; your
1Mac 6:54 sanctuary, because famine had P over the rest and
Lk 23:22 And their voices P
Acts 16:15 And she P upon us.
19:20 the Lord grew and P mightily.

PREVAILEST
Job 14:20 Thou P for ever against him, and he passes;

PREVENT (7)
Deut 28:32 of your hand to P it.
Neh 5:9 of our God to P the taunts of the
1Mac 6:27 and unless you quickly P them, they will do
2Mac 14:22 at key places to P sudden treachery on the
Jn 19:31 Preparation, in order to P the bodies from remaining
Acts 8:36 What is to P my being baptized?"
Gal 5:17 to each other, to P you from doing what

PREVENTED (9)
Gen 16:2 now, the LORD has P me from bearing children;
Sir 19:25 of strength he is P from sinning, he will
20:20 A man may be P from sinning by his
1Mac 7:24 had deserted, and he P those in the city
13:49 citadel at Jerusalem were P from going out to
Mt 3:14 John would have P him, saying, "I need to
Acts 24:22 his friends should be P from attending to his
Rom 1:13 thus far have been P, in order that I
Heb 7:23 number, because they were P by death from

PREVENTS
Sir 31:2 Wakeful anxiety P slumber, and a severe illness

PREVIOUSLY (9)
Neh 13:5 chamber where they had P put the cereal offering,
Wis 18:2 thy holy ones, though P wronged, were doing them
Dan 6:10 thanks before his God, as he had done P
1Mac 1:1 (He had P become king of Greece.)
2Mac 4:1 The P mentioned Simon, who had informed about
4:23 the brother of the P mentioned Simon, to carry
Acts 8:9 named Simon who had P practiced magic in the
21:29 For they had P seen Trophimus the Ephesian with
Gal 3:17 not annul a covenant P ratified by God, so

PREY (64)
Gen 15:11 And when birds of P came down upon the
34:29 in the houses, they captured and made their P
49:9 lion's whelp; from the P, my son, you have
49:27 the morning devouring the P, and at even dividing
Num 14:3 ones will become a P; would it not be
14:31 said would become a P, I will bring in,
23:24 till it devours the P, and drinks the blood
Deut 1:39 said would become a P, and your children, who
2Kgs 21:14 they shall become a P and a spoil to
Jud 4:12 up their infants as P and their wives as
9:4 their wives for a P and their daughters to
16:5 seize my children as P, and take my virgins
Job 4:11 perishes for lack of P, and the whelps of
9:26 of reed, like an eagle swooping on the P
24:5 to their toil, seeking P in the wilderness as
28:7 path no bird of P knows, and the falcon's
29:17 made him drop his P from his teeth.
38:39 "Can you hunt the P for the lion, or
38:41 for the raven its P, when its young ones
39:29 he spies out the P; his eyes behold it
Ps 63:10 sword, they shall be P for jackals.
104:21 lions roar for their P, seeking their food from
124:6 not given us as P to their teeth!
Prov 12:27 will not catch his P, but the diligent man
Sir 13:18 the wilderness are the P of lions; likewise the
27:10 lies in wait for P; so does sin for
Is 5:29 growl and seize their P, they carry it off,
10:2 and that they may make the fatherless their P
18:6 to the birds of P of the mountains and
18:6 And the birds of P will summer upon them,
31:4 lion growls over his P, and when a band
33:23 Then P and spoil in abundance will be divided;
33:23 be divided; even the lame will take the P
42:22 they have become a P with none to rescue,
46:11 calling a bird of P from the east, the
49:24 Can the P be taken from the mighty, or

49:25 be taken, and the P of the tyrant be
59:15 he who departs from evil makes himself a P
Jer 2:14 Why then has he become a P
12:9 heritage to me like a speckled bird of P
12:9 Are the birds of P against her round about?
30:16 spoil, and all who P on you I will
30:16 who prey on you I will make a P
Ezek 7:21 of foreigners for a P, and to the wicked
13:21 in your hand as P; and you shall know
19:3 he learned to catch P; he devoured men.
19:6 he learned to catch P; he devoured men.
22:25 roaring lion tearing the P; they have devoured
22:27 like wolves tearing the P, shedding blood, destroying
26:12 your riches and a P of your merchandise; they
34:8 sheep have become a P, and my sheep have
34:22 no longer be a P; and I will judge
34:28 no more be a P to the nations, nor
36:4 which have become a P and derision to the
39:4 you to birds of P of every sort and
Hos 9:13 are destined for a P; Ephraim must lead forth
Amos 3:4 roar in the forest, when he has no P
Nah 2:11 the lion brought his P, where his cubs were,
2:12 his whelps and strangled P for his lionesses; he
2:12 filled his caves with P and his dens with
2:13 will cut off your P from the earth, and
1Mac 3:4 his deeds, like a lion's cub roaring for P
Acts 11:6 animals and beasts of P and reptiles and birds
Col 2:8 no one makes a P of you by philosophy

PREYS

2Cor 11:20 slaves of you, or P upon you, or takes

PRICE (34)

Gen 23:9 For the full P let him give it to
23:13 I will give the P of the field; accept
Ex 21:35 ox and divide the P of it; and the
Lev 5:18 by you at the P for a guilt offering,
6:6 by you at the P for a guilt offering;
25:16 you shall increase the P, and if the years
25:16 you shall diminish the P, for it is the
25:50 of jubilee, and the P of his release shall
25:51 refund out of the P paid for him the
25:51 paid for him the P for his redemption.
Num 18:16 And their redemption P (at a month old you
2Sam 3:14 I betrothed at the P of a hundred foreskins
24:24 of you for a P; I will not offer
1Kgs 10:28 king's traders received them from Kue at a P
1Chr 21:22 me at its full P --that the plague may
21:24 it for the full P; I will not take
2Chr 1:16 king's traders received them from Kue for a P
Job 28:15 gold, and silver cannot be weighed as its P
28:18 or of crystal; the P of wisdom is above
Ps 44:12 trifle, demanding no high P for them.
49:7 give to God the P of his life,
Prov 17:16 a fool have a P in his hand to
27:26 and the goats the P of a field;
Is 45:13 exiles free, not for P or reward," says the
55:1 buy wine and milk without money and without P
Jer 15:13 give as spoil, without P, for all your sins,
17:3 for spoil as the P of your sin throughout
Dan 11:39 many and shall divide the land for a P
Zech 11:13 --the lordly P at which I was paid
Mt 27:9 pieces of silver, the P of him on whom
27:9 him on whom a P had been set by
1Cor 6:20 not your own; you were bought with a P
7:23 were bought with a P; do not become slaves
Rev 22:17 who desires take the water of life without P

PRICELESS

Wis 7:9 liken to her any P gem, because all gold

PRICK

Ezek 28:24 more a brier to P or a thorn to

PRICKED

Ps 73:21 embittered, when I was P in heart,

PRICKS (3)

Num 33:55 remain shall be as P in your eyes and
Sir 22:17 A man who P an eye will make tears
22:17 fall, and one who P the heart makes it

PRIDE (71)

Gen 49:3 my strength, pre-eminent in P and pre-eminent in
Lev 26:19 I will break the P of your power, and
2Chr 32:26 humbled himself for the P of his heart, both
Tob 4:13 For in P there is ruin and great confusion;
Jud 9:9 Behold their P, and send thy wrath upon their
15:9 you are the great P of our nation!
Esth 13:12 to in insolence or P or for any love
13:14 and I will not do these things in P
Job 33:17 deed, and cut off P from man;
35:12 answer, because of the P of evil men.
41:34 he is king over all the sons of P
Ps 10:4 In the P of his countenance the wicked does
31:18 against the righteous in P and contempt.
47:4 heritage for us, the P of Jacob whom he
59:12 their lips, let them be trapped in their P
73:6 Therefore P is their necklace; violence covers them
Prov 8:13 P and arrogance and the way of evil and
11:2 When P comes, then comes disgrace; but with the
16:18 P goes before destruction, and a haughty spirit
21:24 the proud, haughty man who acts with arrogant P
29:23 A man's P will bring him low, but he
Sir 10:12 The beginning of man's P is to depart from
10:13 For the beginning of P is sin, and the
10:18 P was not created for men, nor fierce anger
15:8 far from men of P, and liars will never
43:1 The P of the heavenly heights is the clear
50:1 his brethren and the P of his people was
Is 2:11 brought low, and the P of men shall be
2:17 be humbled, and the P of men shall be
4:2 land shall be the P and glory of the
9:9 Samaria, who say in P and in arrogance of
10:12 of the king of Assyria and his haughty P
13:11 an end to the P of the arrogant, and
13:19 kingdoms, the splendor and P of the Chaldeans, will
16:6 have heard of the P of Moab, how proud
16:6 of his arrogance, his P, and his insolence--
23:9 it, to defile the P of all glory, to
25:11 will lay low his P together with the skill
Jer 13:9 will I spoil the P of Judah and the
13:9 Judah and the great P of Jerusalem.
13:17 in secret for your P; my eyes will weep
48:29 have heard of the P of Moab--he is
48:29 of his loftiness, his P, and his arrogance, and
49:16 deceived you, and the P of your heart, you
Lam 2:4 has slain all the P of our eyes in
Bar 4:34 will take away her P in her great population,
Ezek 7:10 come, injustice has blossomed, P has budded.
16:49 and her daughters had P, surfeit of food, and
16:56 the day of your P,
24:21 profane my sanctuary, the P of your power, the
32:12 bring to nought the P of Egypt, and all
Dan 4:37 those who walk in P he is able to
Hos 5:5 The P of Israel testifies to his face; Ephraim
7:11 The P of Israel witnesses against him; yet they
Amos 6:8 hosts): "I abhor the P of Jacob, and hate
8:7 has sworn by the P of Jacob: "Surely I
Obad 1:3 The P of your heart has deceived you, you
Zeph 2:10 in return for their P, because they scoffed and
Zech 9:6 an end of the P of Philistia.
10:11 The P of Assyria shall be laid low, and
1Mac 3:20 against us in great P and lawlessness to destroy
8:14 as a mark of P,
2Mac 1:28 Afflict those who oppress and are insolent with P
Mk 7:21 deceit, licentiousness, envy, slander, P, foolishness.
1Cor 11:15 a woman has long hair, it is her P
15:31 protest, brethren, by my P in you which I
2Cor 5:12 to answer those who P themselves on a man's
7:4 you; I have great P in you; I am
7:14 expressed to him some P in you, I was
Heb 3:6 fast our confidence and P in our hope.
1Jn 2:16 the eyes and the P of life, is not

PRIEST (569)

Gen 14:18 and wine; he was P of God Most High.
41:45 the daughter of Potiphera P of On.
41:50 the daughter of Potiphera P of On, bore to
46:20 daughter of Potiphera the P of On, bore to
Ex 2:16 Now the P of Midian had seven daughters; and
3:1 his father-in-law, Jethro, the P of Midian; and he
18:1 Jethro, the P of Midian, Moses' father-in-law, heard
29:30 The son who is P in his place shall
31:10 garments for Aaron the P and the garments of
35:19 garments for Aaron the P, and the garments of
38:21 direction of Ithamar the son of Aaron the P
39:41 garments for Aaron the P, and the garments of
Lev 1:7 sons of Aaron the P shall put fire on
1:9 And the P shall burn the whole on the
1:12 its fat, and the P shall lay them in
1:13 And the P shall offer the whole, and burn

1:15 And the P shall bring it to the altar
1:17 And the P shall burn it on the altar,
2:2 its frankincense; and the P shall burn this as
2:8 is presented to the P, he shall bring it
2:9 And the P shall take from the cereal offering
2:16 And the P shall burn as its memorial portion
3:11 And the P shall burn it on the altar
3:16 And the P shall burn them on the altar
4:3 it is the anointed P who sins, thus bringing
4:5 And the anointed P shall take some of the
4:6 of meeting; and the P shall dip his finger
4:7 And the P shall put some of the blood
4:10 peace offerings), and the P shall burn them upon
4:16 Then the anointed P shall bring some of the
4:17 of meeting, and the P shall dip his finger
4:20 with this; and the P shall make atonement for
4:25 Then the P shall take some of the blood
4:26 peace offerings; so the P shall make atonement for
4:30 And the P shall take some of its blood
4:31 peace offerings, and the P shall burn it upon
4:31 the LORD; and the P shall make atonement for
4:34 Then the P shall take some of the blood
4:35 peace offerings, and the P shall burn it on
4:35 the LORD; and the P shall make atonement for
5:6 sin offering; and the P shall make atonement for
5:8 bring them to the P, who shall offer first
5:10 the ordinance; and the P shall make atonement for
5:12 bring it to the P, and the priest shall
5:12 the priest, and the P shall take a handful
5:13 Thus the P shall make atonement for him for
5:13 shall be for the P, as in the cereal
5:16 give it to the P; and the priest shall
5:16 the priest; and the P shall make atonement for
5:18 shall bring to the P a ram without blemish
5:18 guilt offering, and the P shall make atonement for
6:6 shall bring to the P his guilt offering to
6:7 guilt offering; and the P shall make atonement for
6:10 And the P shall put on his linen garment,
6:12 not go out; the P shall burn wood on
6:22 The P from among Aaron's sons, who is anointed
6:23 cereal offering of a P shall be wholly burned;
6:26 The P who offers it for sin shall eat
7:5 with the kidneys; the P shall burn them on
7:7 law for them; the P who makes atonement with
7:8 And the P who offers any man's burnt offering
7:9 shall belong to the P who offers it.
7:14 shall belong to the P who throws the blood
7:31 The P shall burn the fat on the altar,
7:32 shall give to the P as an offering from
7:34 them to Aaron the P and to his sons,
12:6 shall bring to the P at the door of
12:8 sin offering; and the P shall make atonement for
13:2 brought to Aaron the P or to one of
13:3 the priests, and the P shall examine the diseased
13:3 leprous disease; when the P has examined him he
13:4 not turned white, the P shall shut up the
13:5 seven days; and the P shall examine him on
13:5 the skin, then the P shall shut him up
13:6 days more; and the P shall examine him again
13:6 the skin, then the P shall pronounce him clean;
13:7 shown himself to the P for his cleansing, he
13:7 appear again before the P;
13:8 the priest; and the P shall make an examination,
13:8 the skin, then the P shall pronounce him unclean;
13:9 be brought to the P;
13:10 the priest; and the P shall make an examination,
13:11 his body, and the P shall pronounce him unclean;
13:12 so far as the P can see,
13:13 can see, then the P shall make an examination,
13:15 And the P shall examine the raw flesh, and
13:16 shall come to the P,
13:17 the priest, and the P shall examine him, and
13:17 turned white, then the P shall pronounce the
13:19 be shown to the P;
13:20 the priest; and the P shall make an examination,
13:20 turned white, then the P shall pronounce him
13:21 But if the P examines it, and the hair
13:21 is dim, then the P shall shut him up
13:22 the skin, then the P shall pronounce him unclean;
13:23 the boil; and the P shall pronounce him clean.
13:25 reddish-white or white, the P shall examine it, and
13:25 the burn, and the P shall pronounce him unclean;
13:26 But if the P examines it, and the hair
13:26 but is dim, the P shall shut him up
13:27 seven days, and the P shall examine him the
13:27 the skin, then the P shall pronounce him unclean;
13:28 the burn, and the P shall pronounce him clean;
13:30 or the beard, the P shall examine the disease;
13:30 and thin, then the P shall pronounce him unclean;
13:31 And if the P examines the itching disease, and
13:31 in it, then the P shall shut up the
13:32 the seventh day the P shall examine the disease;
13:33 not shave; and the P shall shut up the
13:34 the seventh day the P shall examine the itch,
13:34 the skin, then the P shall pronounce him clean;
13:36 his cleansing, then the P shall examine him, and
13:36 in the skin, the P need not seek for
13:37 is clean; and the P shall pronounce him clean.
13:39 body, white spots, the P shall make an examination,
13:43 Then the P shall examine him, and if the
13:44 he is unclean; the P must pronounce him unclean;
13:49 leprous disease and shall be shown to the P
13:50 And the P shall examine the disease, and shut
13:53 "And if the P examines, and the disease has
13:54 of skin, then the P shall command that they
13:55 days more; and the P shall examine the diseased
13:56 "But if the P examines, and the disease is
14:2 be brought to the P;
14:3 the priest; and the P shall go out of
14:3 the camp, and the P shall make an examination.
14:4 in the leper, the P shall command them to
14:5 and hyssop; and the P shall command them to
14:11 And the P who cleanses him shall set the
14:12 And the P shall take one of the male
14:13 offering, belongs to the P; it is most holy.
14:14 The P shall take some of the blood of
14:14 guilt offering, and the P shall put it on
14:15 Then the P shall take some of the log
14:17 in his hand the P shall put on the
14:18 that is in the P's hand he shall put
14:18 Then the P shall make atonement for him before
14:19 The P shall offer the sin offering, to make
14:20 burnt offering; and the P shall offer the burnt
14:20 Thus the P shall make atonement for him, and
14:23 his cleansing to the P, to the door of
14:24 the LORD; and the P shall take the lamb
14:24 of oil, and the P shall wave them for
14:25 guilt offering; and the P shall take some of
14:26 And the P shall pour some of the oil
14:28 the LORD; and the P shall put some of
14:29 that is in the P's hand he shall put
14:31 cereal offering; and the P shall make atonement
14:35 come and tell the P, 'There seems to me
14:36 my house.' Then the P shall command that they
14:36 the house before the P goes to examine the
14:36 unclean; and afterward the P shall go in to
14:38 the surface, then the P shall go out of
14:39 And the P shall come again on the seventh
14:40 the house, then the P shall command that they
14:44 plastered it, then the P shall go and look;
14:48 "But if the P comes and makes an examination,
14:48 was plastered, then the P shall pronounce the house
15:14 give them to the P;
15:15 the priest; and the P shall offer them, one
15:15 burnt offering; and the P shall make atonement for
15:29 bring them to the P, to the door of
15:30 And the P shall offer one for a sin
15:30 burnt offering; and the P shall make atonement for
16:32 And the P who is anointed and consecrated as
16:32 anointed and consecrated as P in his father's place
17:5 the LORD, to the P at the door of
17:6 the LORD; and the P shall sprinkle the blood
19:22 And the P shall make atonement for him with
21:7 her husband; for the P is holy to his
21:9 the daughter of any P, if she profanes herself
21:10 "The P who is chief among his brethren, upon
21:21 descendants of Aaron the P who has a blemish
22:10 A sojourner of the P's or a hired servant
22:11 thing; but if a P buys a slave as
22:12 If a P's daughter is married to an outsider
22:13 But if a P's daughter is a widow or
22:14 it, and give the holy thing to the P
23:10 your harvest to the P;
23:11 after the sabbath the P shall wave it.
23:20 And the P shall wave them with the bread
23:20 shall be holy to the LORD for the P
27:8 the person before the P, and the priest shall
27:8 the priest, and the P shall value him; according
27:8 him who vowed the P shall value him.
27:11 the animal before the P,
27:12 the priest, and the P shall value it as
27:12 bad; as you, the P, value it, so it

27:14 to the LORD, the P shall value it as
27:14 or bad; as the P values it, so it
27:18 jubilee, then the P shall compute the money-value
27:21 has been devoted; the P shall be in possession
27:23 by inheritance, then the P shall compute the
Num 3:3 to minister in the P's office.
3:6 them before Aaron the P, that they may minister
3:32 son of Aaron the P was to be chief
4:16 son of Aaron the P shall have charge of
4:28 oversight of Ithamar the son of Aaron the P
4:33 hand of Ithamar the son of Aaron the P
5:8 the LORD for the P, in addition to the
5:9 they bring to the P, shall be his;
5:10 man gives to the P shall be his."
5:15 his wife to the P, and bring the offering
5:16 "And the P shall bring her near, and set
5:17 the LORD; and the P shall take holy water
5:18 And the P shall set the woman before the
5:18 in his hand the P shall have the water
5:19 Then the P shall make her take an oath,
5:21 you, then' (let the P make the woman take
5:23 'Amen, Amen.' "Then the P shall write these curses
5:25 And the P shall take the cereal offering of
5:26 the altar; and the P shall take a handful
5:30 the LORD, and the P shall execute upon her
6:10 young pigeons to the P to the door of
6:11 of meeting, and the P shall offer one for
6:16 And the P shall present them before the LORD
6:17 of unleavened bread; the P shall offer also its
6:19 And the P shall take the shoulder of the
6:20 his consecration, and the P shall wave them for
6:20 holy portion for the P, together with the breast
7:8 direction of Ithamar the son of Aaron the P
15:25 And the P shall make atonement for all the
15:28 And the P shall make atonement before the LORD
16:37 son of Aaron the P to take up the
16:39 So Eleazar the P took the bronze censers, which
16:40 who is not a P, who is not of
18:28 shall give the LORD's offering to Aaron the P
19:3 her to Eleazar the P, and she shall be
19:4 him; and Eleazar the P shall take some of
19:6 be burned; and the P shall take cedarwood and
19:7 Then the P shall wash his clothes and bathe
19:7 the camp; and the P shall be unclean until
25:7 son of Aaron the P, saw it, he rose
25:11 son of Aaron the P, has turned back my
26:1 son of Aaron, the P,
26:3 Moses and Eleazar the P spoke with them in
26:63 Moses and Eleazar the P, who numbered the people
26:64 Moses and Aaron the P, who had numbered the
27:2 and before Eleazar the P, and before the leaders
27:19 stand before Eleazar the P and all the congregation,
27:21 stand before Eleazar the P, who shall inquire for
27:22 stand before Eleazar the P and the whole
31:6 son of Eleazar the P, with the vessels of
31:12 and to Eleazar the P, and to the congregation
31:13 Moses, and Eleazar the P, and all the leaders
31:21 And Eleazar the P said to the men of
31:26 you and Eleazar the P and the heads of
31:29 it to Eleazar the P as an offering to
31:31 Moses and Eleazar the P did as the LORD
31:41 LORD, to Eleazar the P, as the LORD commanded
31:51 Moses and Eleazar the P received from them the
31:54 Moses and Eleazar the P received the gold from
32:2 and to Eleazar the P and to the leaders
32:28 them to Eleazar the P, and to Joshua the
33:38 And Aaron the P went up Mount Hor at
34:17 for inheritance: Eleazar the P and Joshua the son
35:25 death of the high P who was anointed with
35:28 death of the high P; but after the death
35:28 death of the high P the manslayer may return
35:32 the land before the death of the high P
Deut 10:6 son Eleazar ministered as P in his stead.
17:12 by not obeying the P who stands to minister
18:3 shall give to the P the shoulder and the
20:2 to the battle, the P shall come forward and
26:3 shall go to the P who is in office
26:4 give us.' Then the P shall take the basket
Josh 14:1 Canaan, which Eleazar the P, and Joshua the son
17:4 came before Eleazar the P and Joshua the son
19:51 inheritances which Eleazar the P and Joshua the son
20:6 him who is high P at the time: then
21:1 came to Eleazar the P and to Joshua the
21:4 descendants of Aaron the P received by lot from
21:13 descendants of Aaron the P they gave Hebron, the
22:13 son of Eleazar the P,
22:30 When Phinehas the P and the chiefs of the
22:31 son of Eleazar the P said to the Reubenites
22:32 son of Eleazar the P, and the chiefs, returned
Judg 17:5 installed one of his sons, who became his P
17:10 a father and a P, and I will give
17:12 young man became his P, and was in the
17:13 prosper me, because I have a Levite as P
18:4 has hired me, and I have become his P
18:6 And the P said to them, "Go in peace.
18:17 molten image, while the P stood by the entrance
18:18 the molten image, the P said to them, "What
18:19 and be to us a father and a P
18:19 for you to be P to the house of
18:19 man, or to be P to a tribe and
18:20 And the P's heart was glad; he took the
18:24 I made, and the P, and go away, and
18:27 had made, and the P who belonged to him,
1Sam 1:9 Now Eli the P was sitting on the seat
2:11 the LORD, in the presence of Eli the P
2:13 man offered sacrifice, the P's servant would come,
2:14 fork brought up the P would take for himself.
2:15 fat was burned, the P's servant would come and
2:15 "Give meat for the P to roast; for he
2:28 Israel to be my P, to go up to
2:35 for myself a faithful P, who shall do according
2:36 in one of the P's places, that I may
14:3 son of Eli, the P of the LORD in
14:19 was talking to the P, the tumult in the
14:19 Saul said to the P, "Withdraw your hand."
14:36 But the P said, "Let us draw near hither
21:1 Nob to Ahimelech the P; and Ahimelech came to
21:2 said to Ahimelech the P, "The king has charged
21:4 And the P answered David, "I have no common
21:5 And David answered the P, "Of a truth women
21:6 So the P gave him the holy bread; for
21:9 And the P said, "The sword of Goliath the
22:11 to summon Ahimelech the P, the son of Ahitub,
23:9 said to Abiathar the P, "Bring the ephod here."
30:7 said to Abiathar the P, the son of Ahimelech,
2Sam 15:27 said to Zadok the P, "Look, go back to
20:26 priests; and Ira the Jairite was also David's P
1Kgs 1:7 and with Abiathar the P; and they followed Adonijah
1:8 But Zadok the P, and Benaiah the son of
1:19 the king, Abiathar the P, and Joab the commander
1:25 army, and Abiathar the P; and behold, they are
1:26 servant, and Zadok the P, and Benaiah the son
1:32 to me Zadok the P, Nathan the prophet, and
1:34 and let Zadok the P and Nathan the prophet
1:38 So Zadok the P, Nathan the prophet, and Benaiah
1:39 There Zadok the P took the horn of oil
1:42 son of Abiathar the P came; and Adonijah said,
1:44 with him Zadok the P, Nathan the prophet, and
1:45 mule; and Zadok the P and Nathan the prophet
2:22 side are Abiathar the P and Joab the son
2:26 And to Abiathar the P the king said, "Go
2:27 expelled Abiathar from being P to the LORD, thus
2:35 king put Zadok the P in the place of
4:2 of Zadok was the P;
4:5 son of Nathan was P and king's friend;
2Kgs 11:9 all that Jehoiada the P commanded, and each
11:9 on the sabbath, and came to Jehoiada the P
11:10 And the P delivered to the captains the spears
11:15 Then Jehoiada the P commanded the captains who
11:15 For the P said, "Let her not be slain
11:18 they slew Mattan the P of Baal before the
11:18 And the P posted watchmen over the house of
12:2 days, because Jehoiada the P instructed him.
12:7 Jehoash summoned Jehoiada the P and the other
12:9 Then Jehoiada the P took a chest, and bored
12:10 secretary and the high P came up and they
16:10 sent to Uriah the P a model of the
16:11 And Uriah the P built the altar; in accordance
16:11 Damascus, so Uriah the P made it, before King
16:15 Ahaz commanded Uriah the P, saying, "Upon the
16:16 Uriah the P did all this, as King Ahaz
22:4 to Hilkiah the high P, that he may reckon
22:8 And Hilkiah the high P said to Shaphan the
22:10 the king, "Hilkiah the P has given me a
22:12 king commanded Hilkiah the P, and Ahikam the son
22:14 So Hilkiah the P, and Ahikam, and Achbor, and
23:4 commanded Hilkiah, the high P, and the priests of
23:24 book that Hilkiah the P found in the house
25:18 took Seraiah the chief P, and Zephaniah the second
25:18 and Zephaniah the second P, and the three keepers
1Chr 6:10 he who served as P in the house that
16:39 he left Zadok the P and his brethren the

	24:6	princes, and Zadok the P, and Ahimelech the son
	27:5	son of Jehoiada the P, as chief; in his
	29:22	as prince for the LORD, and Zadok as P
2Chr	13:9	seven rams becomes a P of what are no
	15:3	and without a teaching P, and without law;
	19:11	behold, Amariah the chief P is over you in
	22:11	wife of Jehoiada the P, because she was a
	23:8	all that Jehoiada the P commanded.
	23:8	sabbath; for Jehoiada the P did not dismiss the
	23:9	And Jehoiada the P delivered to the captains the
	23:14	Then Jehoiada the P brought out the captains who
	23:14	For the P said, "Do not slay her in
	23:17	they slew Mattan the P of Baal before the
	24:2	the LORD all the days of Jehoiada the P
	24:11	officer of the chief P would come and empty
	24:20	son of Jehoiada the P; and he stood above
	24:25	son of Jehoiada the P, and slew him on
	26:17	But Azariah the P went in after him, with
	26:20	And Azariah the chief P, and all the priests,
	31:10	Azariah the chief P, who was of the house
	34:9	to Hilkiah the high P and delivered the money
	34:14	the LORD, Hilkiah the P found the book of
	34:18	the king, "Hilkiah the P has given me a
Ezra	2:63	there should be a P to consult Urim and
	7:5	of Aaron the chief P –
	7:11	gave to Ezra the P, the scribe, learned in
	7:12	kings, to Ezra the P, the scribe of the
	7:21	River: Whatever Ezra the P, the scribe of the
	8:33	hands of Meremoth the P, son of Uriah, and
	10:10	And Ezra the P stood up and said to
	10:16	Ezra the P selected men, heads of fathers' houses,
Neh	3:1	Then Eliashib the high P rose up with his
	3:20	door of the house of Eliashib the high P
	7:65	holy food, until a P with Urim and Thummim
	8:2	And Ezra the P brought the law before the
	8:9	governor, and Ezra the P and scribe, and the
	10:38	And the P, the son of Aaron, shall be
	12:26	and of Ezra the P the scribe.
	13:4	before this, Eliashib the P, who was appointed over
	13:13	the storehouses Shelemiah the P, Zadok the scribe,
	13:28	of Eliashib the high P, was the son-in-law of
Jud	4:6	And Joakim, the high P, who was in Jerusalem
	4:8	as Joakim the high P and the senate of
	4:14	And Joakim the high P and all the priests
	15:8	Then Joakim the high P, and the senate of
Esth	11:1	that he was a P and a Levite, and
Ps	110:4	mind, "You are a P for ever after the
Sir	7:31	Lord and honor the P, and give him his
	45:15	Lord and serve as P and bless his people
	50:1	was Simon the high P, son of Onias, who
Is	8:2	reliable witnesses, Uriah the P and Zechariah the
	24:2	people, so with the P; as with the slave,
	28:7	with strong drink; the P and the prophet reel
Jer	6:13	and from prophet to P, every one deals falsely.
	8:10	gain; from prophet to P every one deals falsely.
	14:18	For both prophet and P ply their trade through
	18:18	not perish from the P, nor counsel from the
	20:1	Now Pashhur the P, the son of Immer, who
	21:1	Malchiah and Zephaniah the P, the son of Ma-aseiah,
	23:11	"Both prophet and P are ungodly; even in my
	23:33	a prophet, or a P asks you, 'What is
	23:34	as for the prophet, P, or one of the
	29:25	son of Ma-aseiah the P, and to all the
	29:26	LORD has made you P instead of Jehoiada the
	29:26	instead of Jehoiada the P, to have charge in
	29:29	Zephaniah the P read this letter in the hearing
	37:3	and Zephaniah the P, the son of Ma-aseiah,
	52:24	took Seraiah the chief P, and Zephaniah the second
	52:24	and Zephaniah the second P, and the three keepers
Lam	2:6	in his fierce indignation has spurned king and P
	2:20	Should P and prophet be slain in the sanctuary
Bar	1:7	to Jehoiakim the high P, the son of Hilkiah,
Ezek	1:3	came to Ezekiel the P, the son of Buzi,
	7:26	law perishes from the P, and counsel from the
	44:13	to serve me as P, nor come near any
	44:21	No P shall drink wine, when he enters the
	44:22	a widow who is the widow of a P
	45:19	The P shall take some of the blood of
Hos	4:4	accuse, for with you is my contention, O P
	4:6	you from being a P to me.
	4:9	be like people, like P; I will punish them
Amos	7:10	Then Amaziah the P of Bethel sent to Jeroboam
Hag	1:1	of Jehozadak, the high P,
	1:12	of Jehozadak, the high P, with all the remnant
	1:14	of Jehozadak, the high P, and the spirit of
	2:2	of Jehozadak, the high P, and to all the
	2:4	of Jehozadak, the high P; take courage, all you
Zech	3:1	me Joshua the high P standing before the angel
	3:8	O Joshua the high P, you and your friends
	6:11	of Jehozadak, the high P;
	6:13	there shall be a P by his throne, and
Mal	2:7	the lips of a P should guard knowledge, and
1Mac	2:1	son of Simeon, a P of the sons of
	7:5	led by Alcimus, who wanted to be high P
	7:9	whom he made high P; and he commanded him
	7:14	for they said, "A P of the line of
	10:20	to be the high P of your nation; you
	10:32	it to the high P, that he may station
	10:38	and obey no other authority but the high P
	10:69	to Jonathan the high P:
	12:3	said, "Jonathan the high P and the Jewish nation
	12:6	Spartans: "Jonathan the high P, the senate of the
	12:7	to Onias the high P from Arius, who was
	12:20	to Onias the high P, greeting.
	13:36	to Simon, the high P and friend of kings,
	13:42	Simon the great high P and commander and leader
	14:17	brother had become high P in his place, and
	14:20	to Simon the high P and to the elders
	14:23	a copy of this to Simon the high P
	14:27	Simon the great high P,
	14:29	son of Mattathias, a P of the sons of
	14:30	and became their high P, and was gathered to
	14:35	their leader and high P, because he had done
	14:41	their leader and high P for ever, until a
	14:47	agreed to be high P, to be commander and
	15:1	sea to Simon, the P and ethnarch of the
	15:2	to Simon the high P and ethnarch and to
	15:17	by Simon the high P and by the people
	15:21	to Simon the high P, that he may punish
	15:24	copy of these things to Simon the high P
	16:12	gold, for he was son-in-law of the high P
	16:24	that he became high P after his father.
2Mac	3:1	piety of the high P Onias and his hatred
	3:4	disagreement with the high P about the
	3:9	welcomed by the high P of the city, he
	3:10	The high P explained that there were some deposits
	3:16	appearance of the high P was to be wounded
	3:21	anxiety of the high P in his great anguish.
	3:32	And the high P, fearing that the king might
	3:33	While the high P was making the offering of
	3:33	to Onias the high P, since for his sake
	4:13	ungodly and no high P,
	14:3	had formerly been high P but had wilfully defiled
	14:13	up Alcimus as high P of the greatest temple.
	15:12	who had been high P, a noble and good
Mt	8:4	show yourself to the P, and offer the gift
	26:3	palace of the high P, who was called Caiaphas,
	26:51	slave of the high P, and cut off his
	26:57	to Caiaphas the high P, where the scribes and
	26:58	courtyard of the high P, and going inside he
	26:62	And the high P stood up and said, "Have
	26:63	And the high P said to him, "I adjure
	26:65	Then the high P tore his robes, and said,
Mk	1:44	show yourself to the P, and offer for your
	2:26	when Abiathar was high P, and ate the bread
	14:47	slave of the high P and cut off his
	14:53	Jesus to the high P; and all the chief
	14:54	courtyard of the high P; and he was sitting
	14:60	And the high P stood up in the midst,
	14:61	Again the high P asked him, "Are you the
	14:63	And the high P tore his garments, and said,
	14:66	maids of the high P came;
Lk	1:5	Judea, there was a P named Zechariah, of the
	1:8	he was serving as P before God when his
	5:14	show yourself to the P, and make an offering
	10:31	Now by chance a P was going down that
	22:48	slave of the high P and cut off his
	22:52	him into the high P's house.
Jn	11:49	Caiaphas, who was high P that year, said to
	11:51	accord, but being high P that year he prophesied
	18:10	and struck the high P's slave and cut off
	18:13	Caiaphas, who was high P that year.
	18:15	known to the high P, he entered the court
	18:15	court of the high P along with Jesus,
	18:16	known to the high P, went out and spoke
	18:19	The high P then questioned Jesus about his disciples
	18:22	saying, "Is that how you answer the high P
	18:24	then sent him bound to Caiaphas the high P
	18:26	servants of the high P, a kinsman of the
Acts	4:6	with Annas the high P and Caiaphas and John
	5:17	But the high P rose up and all who
	5:21	Now the high P came and those who were

5:27 And the high P questioned them,
7:1 And the high P said, "Is this so?"
9:1 went to the high P
14:13 And the P of Zeus, whose temple was in
19:14 of a Jewish high P named Sceva were doing
22:5 women, as the high P and the whole council
23:2 And the high P Ananias commanded those who stood
23:4 stood by said, "Would you revile God's high P
23:5 he was the high P; for it is written,
24:1 five days the high P Ananias came down with
Heb 2:17 merciful and faithful high P in the service of
3:1 the apostle and high P of our confession.
4:14 have a great high P who has passed through
4:15 have not a high P who is unable to
5:1 For every high P chosen from among men is
5:5 be made a high P, but was appointed by
5:6 place, "Thou art a P for ever, after the
5:10 by God a high P after the order of
6:20 having become a high P for ever after the
7:1 Melchizedek, king of Salem, P of the Most High
7:3 God he continues a P for ever.
7:11 have been for another P to arise after the
7:15 more evident when another P arises in the likeness
7:16 who has become a P, not according to a
7:17 him, "Thou art a P for ever, after the
7:21 mind, 'Thou art a P for ever.'"
7:26 have such a high P, holy, blameless, unstained,
8:1 have such a high P, one who is seated
8:3 For every high P is appointed to offer gifts
8:3 is necessary for this P also to have something
8:4 would not be a P at all, since there
9:7 second only the high P goes, and he but
9:11 appeared as a high P of the good things
9:25 repeatedly, as the high P enters the Holy Place
10:11 And every P stands daily at his service, offering
10:21 we have a great P over the house of
13:11 sanctuary by the high P as a sacrifice for

PRIESTHOOD (24)

Ex 28:3 make Aaron's garments to consecrate him for my P
29:9 on them; and the P shall be theirs by
Num 3:10 shall attend to their P; but if any one
16:10 would you seek the P also?
18:1 you shall bear iniquity in connection with your P
18:7 shall attend to your P for all that concerns
18:7 I give your P as a gift, and any
25:13 covenant of a perpetual P, because he was jealous
Josh 18:7 among you, for the P of the LORD is
Ezra 2:62 were excluded from the P as unclean;
Neh 7:64 were excluded from the P as unclean;
13:29 they have defiled the P and the covenant of
13:29 the covenant of the P and the Levites.
Sir 45:7 and gave him the P of the people.
45:24 the dignity of the P for ever.
1Mac 2:54 zealous, received the covenant of everlasting P
3:49 the garments of the P and the first fruits
2Mac 2:17 and the kingship and P and consecration,
Lk 1:9 the custom of the P, it fell to him
Heb 7:11 attainable through the Levitical P (for under it the
7:12 a change in the P, there is necessarily a
7:24 but he holds his P permanently, because he continues
1Pet 2:5 to be a holy P, to offer spiritual sacrifices
2:9 chosen race, a royal P, a holy nation, God's

PRIESTLY (3)

2Mac 3:15 the altar in their P garments and called toward
Rom 15:16 the Gentiles in the P service of the gospel
Heb 7:5 Levi who receive the P office have a commandment

PRIESTS (472)

Gen 47:22 the land of the P he did not buy;
47:22 not buy; for the P had a fixed allowance
47:26 the land of the P alone did not become
Ex 19:6 me a kingdom of P and a holy nation.
19:22 And also let the P who come near to
19:24 do not let the P and the people break
28:1 to serve me as P --Aaron and Aaron's sons,
28:4 brother and his sons to serve me as P
28:41 consecrate them, that they may serve me as P
29:1 consecrate them, that they may serve me as P
29:27 the thigh of the P portion, which is waved,
29:28 for it is the P portion to be offered
29:44 sons I will consecrate, to serve me as P
30:30 consecrate them, that they may serve me as P
31:10 for their service as P,
35:19 garments of his sons, for their service as P
39:41 the garments of his sons to serve as P
Lev 1:5 and Aaron's sons the P shall present the blood,
1:8 and Aaron's sons the P shall lay the pieces,
1:11 and Aaron's sons the P shall throw its blood
2:2 it, and bring it to Aaron's sons the P
3:2 and Aaron's sons the P shall throw the blood
6:29 Every male among the P may eat of it;
7:6 Every male among the P may eat of it;
7:35 presented to serve as P of the LORD;
13:2 of his sons the P,
16:33 make atonement for the P and for all the
21:1 Moses, "Speak to the P, the sons of Aaron,
22:15 The P shall not profane the holy things of
Num 3:3 of Aaron, the anointed P, whom he ordained to
3:4 and Ithamar served as P in the lifetime of
3:31 sanctuary with which the P minister, and the screen;
10:8 sons of Aaron, the P, shall blow the trumpets.
Deut 17:9 coming to the Levitical P, and to the judge
17:18 charge of the Levitical P;
18:1 "The Levitical P, that is, all the tribe of
18:3 this shall be the P due from the people,
19:17 the LORD, before the P and the judges who
21:5 And the P the sons of Levi shall come
24:8 all that the Levitical P shall direct you; as
27:9 Moses and the Levitical P said to all Israel,
31:9 gave it to the P the sons of Levi,
Josh 3:3 carried by the Levitical P, then you shall set
3:6 Joshua said to the P, "Take up the ark
3:8 you shall command the P who bear the ark
3:13 the feet of the P who bear the ark
3:14 the Jordan with the P bearing the ark of
3:15 the feet of the P bearing the ark were
3:17 on dry ground, the P who bore the ark
4:3 very place where the P feet stood, and carry
4:9 the feet of the P bearing the ark of
4:10 For the P who bore the ark stood in
4:11 the LORD and the P passed over before the
4:16 to Joshua, "Command the P who bear the ark
4:17 Joshua therefore commanded the P, "Come up out of
4:18 And when the P bearing the ark of the
4:18 the soles of the P feet were lifted up
6:4 And seven P shall bear seven trumpets of rams'
6:4 city seven times, the P blowing the trumpets.
6:6 of Nun called the P and said to them,
6:6 covenant, and let seven P bear seven trumpets of
6:8 the people, the seven P bearing the seven trumpets
6:9 men went before the P who blew the trumpets,
6:12 the morning, and the P took up the ark
6:13 And the seven P bearing the seven trumpets of
6:16 seventh time, when the P had blown the trumpets,
8:33 ark before the Levitical P who carried the ark
21:19 descendants of Aaron, the P, were in all thirteen
Judg 18:30 and his sons were P to the tribe of
1Sam 1:3 Hophni and Phinehas, were P of the LORD.
2:13 The custom of the P with the people was
5:5 This is why the P of Dagon and all
6:2 Philistines called for the P and the diviners and
22:11 his father's house, the P who were at Nob;
22:17 "Turn and kill the P of the LORD; because
22:17 to fall upon the P of the LORD.
22:18 to Doeg, "You turn and fall upon the P
22:18 and fell upon the P, and he killed on
22:19 the city of the P, he put to the
22:21 Saul had killed the P of the LORD.
2Sam 8:17 son of Abiathar were P; and Seraiah was secretary;
8:18 and the Pelethites; and David's sons were P
15:35 Zadok and Abiathar the P with you there?
15:35 house, tell it to Zadok and Abiathar the P
17:15 Zadok and Abiathar the P, "Thus and so did
19:11 Zadok and Abiathar the P, "Say to the elders
20:25 Zadok and Abiathar were P;
1Kgs 4:4 Zadok and Abiathar were P;
8:3 Israel came, and the P took up the ark.
8:4 in the tent; the P and the Levites brought
8:6 Then the P brought the ark of the covenant
8:10 And when the P came out of the holy
8:11 LORD, so that the P could not stand to
12:31 high places, and appointed P from among all the
12:32 placed in Bethel the P of the high places
13:2 sacrifice upon you the P of the high places
13:33 evil way, but made P for the high places
13:33 he consecrated to be P of the high places.
2Kgs 10:11 familiar friends, and his P, until he left him
10:19 worshipers and all his P; let none be missing,
12:4 Jehoash said to the P, "All the money of
12:5 the LORD, let the P take, each from his

12:6 of King Jehoash the P had made no repairs
12:7 priest and the other P and said to them,
12:8 So the P agreed that they should take no
12:9 the LORD; and the P who guarded the threshold
12:16 house of the LORD; it belonged to the P
17:27 there one of the P whom you carried away
17:28 So one of the P whom they had carried
17:32 sorts of people as P of the high places,
19:2 secretary, and the senior P, covered with sackcloth,
23:2 of Jerusalem, and the P and the prophets, all
23:4 high priest, and the P of the second order,
23:5 he deposed the idolatrous P whom the kings of
23:8 he brought all the P out of the cities
23:8 high places where the P had burned incense, from
23:9 However, the P of the high places did not
23:20 he slew all the P of the high places
1Chr 9:2 cities were Israel, the P, the Levites, and the
9:10 Of the P: Jedaiah, Jehoiarib, Jachin,
9:30 the sons of the P, prepared the mixing of
13:2 with them to the P and Levites in the
15:11 Then David summoned the P Zadok and Abiathar,
15:14 So the P and the Levites sanctified themselves to
15:24 Benaiah, and Eliezer, the P, should blow the trumpets
16:6 Benaiah and Jahaziel the P were to blow trumpets
16:39 and his brethren the P before the tabernacle of
18:16 son of Abiathar were P; and Shavsha was secretary;
23:2 of Israel and the P and the Levites.
24:2 no children, so Eleazar and Ithamar became the P
24:6 fathers' houses of the P and of the Levites;
24:31 fathers' houses of the P and of the Levites.
28:13 the divisions of the P and of the Levites,
28:21 the divisions of the P and the Levites for
2Chr 4:6 sea was for the P to wash in.
4:9 the court of the P, and the great court,
5:5 in the tent; the P and the Levites brought
5:7 So the P brought the ark of the covenant
5:11 Now when the P came out of the holy
5:11 place (for all the P who were present had
5:12 a hundred and twenty P who were trumpeters;
5:14 cloud, so that the P could not stand to
6:41 Let thy P, O LORD God, be clothed with
7:2 And the P could not enter the house of
7:6 The P stood at their posts; the Levites also,
7:6 ministry; opposite them the P sounded trumpets; and
8:14 the divisions of the P for their service, and
8:14 and ministry before the P as the duty of
8:15 king had commanded the P and Levites concerning
11:13 And the P and the Levites that were in
11:14 out from serving as P of the LORD,
11:15 he appointed his own P for the high places,
13:9 not driven out the P of the LORD, the
13:9 the Levites, and made P for yourselves like the
13:10 We have P ministering to the LORD who are
13:12 our head, and his P with their battle trumpets
13:14 the LORD, and the P blew the trumpets.
17:8 with these Levites, the P Elishama and Jehoram.
19:8 appointed certain Levites and P and heads of
23:4 shall do: of you P and Levites who come
23:6 the LORD except the P and ministering Levites; they
23:18 direction of the Levitical P and the Levites whom
24:5 And he gathered the P and the Levites, and
26:17 after him, with eighty P of the LORD who
26:18 LORD, but for the P the sons of Aaron,
26:19 became angry with the P leprosy broke out on
26:19 the presence of the P in the house of
26:20 priest, and all the P, looked at him, and
29:4 He brought in the P and the Levites, and
29:16 The P went into the inner part of the
29:21 And he commanded the P the sons of Aaron
29:22 the bulls, and the P received the blood and
29:24 upon them, and the P killed them and made
29:26 of David, and the P with the trumpets.
29:34 But the P were too few and could not
29:34 offerings, so until other P had sanctified themselves
29:34 in heart than the P in sanctifying themselves.
30:3 its time because the P had not sanctified themselves
30:15 And the P and the Levites were put to
30:16 man of God; the P sprinkled the blood which
30:21 the Levites and the P praised the LORD day
30:24 And the P sanctified themselves in great numbers.
30:25 of Judah, and the P and the Levites, and
30:27 Then the P and the Levites arose and blessed
31:2 the divisions of the P and of the Levites,
31:2 to his service, the P and the Levites, for
31:4 portion due to the P and the Levites, that
31:9 And Hezekiah questioned the P and the Levites
31:15 the cities of the P, to distribute the portions
31:17 The enrollment of the P was according to their
31:18 The P were enrolled with all their little children,
31:19 sons of Aaron, the P, who were in the
31:19 every male among the P and to every one
34:5 the bones of the P on their altars, and
34:30 of Jerusalem and the P and the Levites, all
35:2 He appointed the P to their offices and encouraged
35:8 the people, to the P, and to the Levites.
35:8 God, gave to the P for the passover offerings
35:10 been prepared for, the P stood in their place,
35:11 passover lamb, and the P sprinkled the blood which
35:14 themselves and for the P, because the priests the
35:14 the priests, because the P the sons of Aaron
35:14 themselves and for the P the sons of Aaron.
35:18 by Josiah, and the P and the Levites, and
36:14 All the leading P and the people likewise were
Ezra 1:5 and Benjamin, and the P and the Levites, every
2:36 The P: the sons of Jedaiah, of the house
2:61 the sons of the P: the sons of Habaiah,
2:69 silver, and one hundred P garments.
2:70 The P, the Levites, and some of the people
3:2 Jozadak, with his fellow P, and Zerubbabel the son
3:8 of their brethren, the P and the Levites and
3:10 of the LORD, the P in their vestments came
3:12 But many of the P and Levites and heads
6:9 or oil, as the P at Jerusalem require–
6:16 people of Israel, the P and the Levites, and
6:18 And they set the P in their divisions and
6:20 For the P and the Levites had purified themselves
6:20 exiles, for their fellow P, and for themselves;
7:7 and some of the P and Levites, the singers
7:13 of Israel or their P or Levites in my
7:16 the people and the P, vowed willingly for the
7:24 any one of the P, the Levites, the singers,
8:15 the people and the P, I found there none
8:24 twelve of the leading P: Sherebiah, Hashabiah, and
8:29 them before the chief P and the Levites and
8:30 So the P and the Levites took over the
9:1 of Israel and the P and the Levites have
9:7 our kings, and our P have been given into
10:5 and made the leading P and Levites and all
10:18 the sons of the P who had married foreign
Neh 2:16 told the Jews, the P, the nobles, the officials,
3:1 with his brethren the P and they built the
3:22 After him the P, the men of the Plain,
3:28 the Horse Gate the P repaired, each one opposite
5:12 And I called the P, and took an oath
7:39 The P: the sons of Jedaiah, namely the house
7:63 Also, of the P: the sons of Hobaiah, the
7:70 five hundred and thirty P garments.
7:72 of silver, and sixty-seven P garments.
7:73 So the P, the Levites, the gatekeepers, the singers,
8:13 the people, with the P and the Levites, came
9:32 kings, our princes, our P, our prophets, our fathers,
9:34 kings, our princes, our P, and our fathers have
9:38 our Levites, and our P set their seal to
10:8 Ma-aziah, Bilgai, Shemaiah; these are the P
10:28 of the people, the P, the Levites, the gatekeepers,
10:34 likewise cast lots, the P, the Levites, and the
10:36 our God, to the P who minister in the
10:37 the oil, to the P, to the chambers of
10:39 the sanctuary, and the P that minister, and the
11:3 their towns: Israel, the P, the Levites, the temple
11:10 Of the P: Jedaiah the son of Joiarib, Jachin,
11:20 Israel, and of the P and the Levites, were
12:1 These are the P and the Levites who came
12:7 the chiefs of the P and of their brethren
12:12 days of Joiakim were P, heads of fathers' houses:
12:22 fathers' houses; also the P until the reign of
12:30 And the P and the Levites purified themselves; and
12:35 and certain of the P sons with trumpets: Zechariah
12:41 with me; and the P Eliakim, Ma-aseiah, Miniamin,
12:44 the law for the P and for the Levites
12:44 Judah rejoiced over the P and the Levites who
13:5 and gatekeepers, and the contributions for the P
13:30 the duties of the P and Levites, each in
Tob 1:6 give these to the P, the sons of Aaron,
Jud 4:14 priest and all the P who stood before the
11:13 set aside for the P who minister in the
Job 12:19 He leads P away stripped, and overthrows the
Ps 78:64 Their P fell by the sword, and their widows
99:6 Aaron were among his P, Samuel also was among
132:9 Let thy P be clothed with righteousness, and let
132:16 Her P I will clothe with salvation, and her
Sir 7:29 your soul fear the Lord, and honor his P

50:12 the hands of the P, as he stood by
Is 37:2 secretary, and the senior P, clothed with sackcloth, to
61:6 shall be called the P of the LORD, men
66:21 I will take for P and for Levites, says
Jer 1:1 of Hilkiah, of the P who were in Anathoth
1:18 Judah, its princes, its P, and the people of
2:8 The P did not say, 'Where is the LORD?'
2:26 kings, their princes, their P, and their prophets,
4:9 king and princes; the P shall be appalled and
5:31 prophesy falsely, and the P rule at their direction;
8:1 the bones of the P, the bones of the
13:13 on David's throne, the P, the prophets, and all
19:1 some of the senior P,
26:7 The P and the prophets and all the people
26:8 the people, then the P and the prophets and
26:11 Then the P and the prophets said to the
26:16 people said to the P and the prophets, "This
27:16 I spoke to the P and to all this
28:1 the presence of the P and all the people,
28:5 the presence of the P and all the people
29:1 exiles, and to the P, the prophets, and all
29:25 and to all the P, saying,
31:14 the soul of the P with abundance, and my
32:32 and their princes, their P and their prophets, the
33:18 Israel, and the Levitical P shall never lack a
33:21 covenant with the Levitical P my ministers.
33:22 servant, and the Levitical P who minister to me."
34:19 Jerusalem, the eunuchs, the P, and all the people
48:7 into exile, with his P and his princes.
49:3 into exile, with his P and his princes.
Lam 1:4 gates are desolate, her P groan; her maidens have
1:19 they deceived me; my P and elders perished in
4:13 the iniquities of her P, who shed in the
4:16 was shown to the P, no favor to the
Bar 1:7 Shallum, and to the P, and to all the
1:16 our princes and our P and our prophets and
6:10 ornaments; and sometimes the P secretly take gold
6:18 to death, so the P make their temples secure
6:28 The P sell the sacrifices that are offered to
6:31 in their temples the P sit with their clothes
6:33 The P take some of the clothing of their
6:48 comes upon them, the P consult together as to
6:55 gold or silver, their P will flee and escape,
Ezek 22:26 Her P have done violence to my law and
40:45 south is for the P who have charge of
40:46 north is for the P who have charge of
42:13 chambers, where the P who approach the LORD
42:14 When the P enter the holy place, they shall
43:19 give to the Levitical P of the family of
43:24 the LORD, and the P shall sprinkle salt upon
43:27 eighth day onward the P shall offer upon the
44:15 "But the Levitical P, the sons of Zadok, who
44:30 shall belong to the P; you shall also give
44:30 also give to the P the first of your
44:31 The P shall not eat of anything, whether bird
45:4 shall be for the P, who minister in the
46:2 The P shall offer his burnt offering and his
46:19 holy chambers for the P; and there I saw
46:20 the place where the P shall boil the guilt
48:10 the holy portion: the P shall have an allotment
48:11 be for the consecrated P, the sons of Zadok,
48:13 the territory of the P, the Levites shall have
Dan 3:85 Bless the Lord, you P of the Lord, sing
14:8 and he called his P and said to them,
14:10 Now there were seventy P of Bel, besides their
14:11 And the P of Bel said, "Behold, we are
14:15 In the night the P came with their wives
14:21 and he seized the P and their wives and
14:28 Bel, and slain the dragon, and slaughtered the P
Hos 5:1 Hear this, O P
6:9 a man, so the P are banded together; they
10:5 it, and its idolatrous P shall wail over it,
Joel 1:9 The P mourn, the ministers of the LORD.
1:12 sackcloth and lament, O P, wail, O ministers of
2:17 the altar let the P, the ministers of the
Mic 3:11 for a bribe, its P teach for hire, its
Zeph 1:4 name of the idolatrous P;
3:4 wanton, faithless men; her P profane what is sacred,
Hag 2:11 of hosts: Ask the P to decide this question,
2:12 The P answered, "No."
2:13 The P answered, "It does become unclean."
Zech 7:3 and to ask the P of the house of
7:5 the land and the P, When you fasted and
Mal 1:6 hosts to you, O P, who despise my name.
2:1 "And now, O P, this command is for you.
1Mac 1:46 the sanctuary and the P,
3:51 and profaned, and thy P mourn in humiliation.
4:38 the chambers of the P in ruins.
4:42 He chose blameless P devoted to the law,
4:57 the chambers for the P, and furnished them with
5:67 On that day some P, who wished to do
7:33 Some of the P came out of the sanctuary,
7:36 Then the P went in and stood before the
10:42 it belongs to the P who minister there.
11:23 and some of the P, and put himself in
12:6 of the nation, the P, and the rest of
14:20 the elders and the P and the rest of
14:28 great assembly of the P and the people and
14:41 the Jews and their P decided that Simon should
14:44 of the people or P shall be permitted to
14:47 of the Jews and P, and to be protector
2Mac 1:10 family of the anointed P, teacher of Ptolemy the
1:13 deception employed by the P of Nanea.
1:15 When the P of the temple of Nanea had
1:19 to Persia, the pious P of that time took
1:20 the descendants of the P who had hidden the
1:21 presented, Nehemiah ordered the P to sprinkle the
1:23 was being consumed, the P offered prayer –
1:23 prayer – the P and every one.
1:30 Then the P sang the hymns.
1:33 place where the exiled P had hidden the fire,
3:15 The P prostrated themselves before the altar in their
4:14 high priest, that the P were no longer intent
14:31 holy temple while the P were offering the customary
14:34 Then the P stretched forth their hands toward
15:31 together and stationed the P before the altar, he
Mt 2:4 assembling all the chief P and scribes of the
12:4 who were with him, but only for the P
12:5 on the sabbath the P in the temple profane
16:21 the elders and chief P and scribes, and be
20:18 delivered to the chief P and scribes, and they
21:15 But when the chief P and the scribes saw
21:23 the temple, the chief P and the elders of
21:45 When the chief P and the Pharisees heard his
26:3 Then the chief P and the elders of the
26:14 went to the chief P
26:47 clubs, from the chief P and the elders of
26:59 Now the chief P and the whole council sought
27:1 came, all the chief P and the elders of
27:3 silver to the chief P and the elders,
27:6 But the chief P, taking the pieces of silver,
27:12 accused by the chief P and elders, he made
27:20 Now the chief P and the elders persuaded the
27:41 So also the chief P, with the scribes and
27:62 of Preparation, the chief P and the Pharisees
28:11 and told the chief P all that had taken
Mk 2:26 for any but the P to eat, and also
8:31 elders and the chief P and the scribes, and
10:33 delivered to the chief P and the scribes, and
11:18 And the chief P and the scribes heard it
11:26 the temple, the chief P and the scribes and
14:1 And the chief P and the scribes were seeking
14:10 went to the chief P in order to betray
14:43 clubs, from the chief P and the scribes and
14:53 and all the chief P and the elders and
14:55 Now the chief P and the whole council sought
15:1 was morning the chief P, with the elders and
15:3 And the chief P accused him of many things.
15:10 envy that the chief P had delivered him up.
15:11 But the chief P stirred up the crowd to
15:30 So also the chief P mocked him to one
Lk 6:4 for any but the P to eat, and also
9:22 the elders and chief P and scribes, and be
17:14 to them, "Go and show yourselves to the P
19:47 The chief P and the scribes and the principal
20:1 the gospel, the chief P and the scribes with
20:19 scribes and the chief P tried to lay hands
22:2 And the chief P and the scribes were seeking
22:4 conferred with the chief P and officers how he
22:50 said to the chief P and officers of the
22:64 gathered together, both chief P and scribes; and they
23:4 said to the chief P and the multitudes, "I
23:10 The chief P and the scribes stood by, vehemently
23:13 called together the chief P and the rulers and
24:20 and how our chief P and rulers delivered him
Jn 1:19 when the Jews sent P and Levites from Jerusalem
7:32 him, and the chief P and Pharisees sent officers
7:45 back to the chief P and Pharisees, who said
11:47 So the chief P and the Pharisees gathered the
11:57 Now the chief P and the Pharisees had given
12:10 So the chief P planned to put Lazarus also
18:3 officers from the chief P and the Pharisees, went

18:35 nation and the chief P have handed you over
19:6 When the chief P and the officers saw him,
19:15 The chief P answered, "We have no king but
19:21 The chief P of the Jews then said to
Acts 4:1 to the people, the P and the captain of
4:23 reported what the chief P and the elders had
5:24 temple and the chief P heard these words, they
6:7 great many of the P were obedient to the
9:14 authority from the chief P to bind all who
9:21 purpose, to bring them bound before the chief P
22:30 and commanded the chief P and all the council
23:14 went to the chief P and elders, and said,
25:2 And the chief P and the principal men of
25:15 at Jerusalem, the chief P and the elders of
26:10 authority from the chief P, but when they were
26:12 with the authority and commission of the chief P
Heb 7:14 with that tribe Moses said nothing about P
7:21 Those who formerly became P took their office
7:23 The former P were many in number, because they
7:27 need, like those high P, to offer sacrifices daily,
7:28 their weakness as high P, but the word of
8:4 all, since there are P who offer gifts according
9:6 thus been made, the P go continually into the
Rev 1:6 made us a kingdom, P to his God and
5:10 them a kingdom and P to our God, and
20:6 but they shall be P of God and of

PRIMEVAL

Ezek 26:20 the nether world, among P ruins, with those who

PRINCE (84)

Gen 23:6 you are a mighty P among us.
34:2 Hamor the Hivite, the P of the land, saw
Ex 2:14 "Who made you a P and a judge over
Num 16:13 also make yourself a P over us?
25:18 the daughter of the P of Midian, their sister,
Deut 33:16 of him that is P among his brothers.
1Sam 9:16 anoint him to be P over my people Israel.
10:1 anointed you to be P over his people Israel?
10:1 anointed you to be P over his heritage.
13:14 appointed him to be P over his people, because
25:30 and has appointed you P over Israel,
2Sam 3:38 not know that a P and a great man
5:2 and you shall be P over Israel.'"
6:21 to appoint me as P over Israel, the people
7:8 that you should be P over my people Israel;
2Kgs 20:5 say to Hezekiah the P of my people, Thus
1Chr 2:10 the father of Nahshon, P of the sons of
5:2 his brothers and a P was from him, yet
11:2 and you shall be P over my people Israel.'"
12:27 The P Jehoiada, of the house of Aaron, and
17:7 that you should be P over my people Israel;
29:22 they anointed him as P for the LORD, and
2Chr 6:5 chose no man as P over my people Israel;
11:22 of Maacah as chief P among his brothers, for
Ezra 1:8 out to Shesh-bazzar the P of Judah.
Jud 9:10 the slave with the P and the prince with
9:10 the prince and the P with his servant; crush
Job 21:28 you say, 'Where is the house of the P
31:37 my steps; like a P I would approach him.
Ps 82:7 shall die like men, and fall like any P
Prov 14:28 but without people a P is ruined.
17:7 fool; still less is false speech to a P
25:7 be put lower in the presence of the P
Song 6:12 fancy set me in a chariot beside my P
Sir 41:17 a lie, before a P or a ruler;
Is 9:6 Mighty God, Everlasting Father, P of Peace."
Jer 30:21 Their P shall be one of themselves, their ruler
Ezek 7:27 The king mourns, the P is wrapped in despair,
12:10 This oracle concerns the P in Jerusalem and all
12:12 into captivity.' And the P who is among them
21:25 O unhallowed wicked one, P of Israel, whose day
28:2 man, say to the P of Tyre, Thus says
30:13 no longer be a P in the land of
34:24 servant David shall be P among them; I, the
37:25 servant shall be their P for ever.
38:2 of Magog, the chief P of Meshech and Tubal,
38:3 you, O Gog, chief P of Meshech and Tubal;
39:1 you, O Gog, chief P of Meshech and Tubal;
44:3 Only the P may sit in it to eat
45:7 "And to the P shall belong the land on
45:16 this offering to the P in Israel.
45:17 It shall be the P's duty to furnish the
45:22 On that day the P shall provide for himself
46:2 The P shall enter by the vestibule of the
46:4 burnt offering that the P offers to the LORD
46:8 When the P enters, he shall go in by
46:10 they go in, the P shall go in with
46:12 When the P provides a freewill offering, either a
46:16 Lord GOD: If the P makes a gift to
46:17 shall revert to the P; only his sons may
46:18 The P shall not take any of the inheritance
48:21 property of the city shall belong to the P
48:21 the tribal portions, it shall belong to the P
48:22 the midst of that which belongs to the P
48:22 The portion of the P shall lie between the
Dan 3:38 time there is no P, or prophet, or leader,
8:11 even up to the P of the host; and
8:25 rise up against the P of princes; but, by
9:25 an anointed one, a P, there shall be seven
9:26 the people of the P who is to come
10:13 The P of the kingdom of Persia withstood me
10:13 him there with the P of the kingdom of
10:20 to fight against the P of Persia; and when
10:20 with him, lo, the P of Greece will come.
10:21 by my side against these except Michael, your P
11:22 and broken, and the P of the covenant also.
12:1 arise Michael, the great P who has charge of
Hos 3:4 days without king or P, without sacrifice or pillar,
Mic 7:3 do it diligently; the P and the judge ask
Mt 9:34 out demons by the P of demons."
12:24 only by Be-elzebul, the P of demons, that this
Mk 3:22 Be-elzebul, and by the P of demons he casts
Lk 11:15 demons by Be-elzebul, the P of demons";
Eph 2:2 this world, following the P of the power of

PRINCES (194)

Gen 12:15 And when the P of Pharaoh saw her, they
17:20 the father of twelve P, and I will make
25:16 by their encampments, twelve P according to their
Num 21:18 the well which the P dug, which the nobles
22:8 to me"; so the P of Moab stayed with
22:13 and said to the P of Balak, "Go to
22:14 So the P of Moab rose and went to
22:15 Once again Balak sent P, more in number and
22:21 and went with the P of Moab.
22:35 went on with the P of Balak.
22:40 Balaam and to the P who were with him.
23:6 he and all the P of Moab were standing
23:17 burnt offering, and the P of Moab with him.
Josh 13:21 Hur and Reba, the P of Sihon, who dwelt
Judg 5:3 kings; give ear, O P; to the LORD I
5:15 the marshal's staff; the P of Issachar came with
7:25 they took the two P of Midian, Oreb and
8:3 into your hands the P of Midian, Oreb and
1Sam 2:8 make them sit with P and inherit a seat
18:30 Then the P of the Philistines came out to
2Sam 10:3 But the P of the Ammonites said to Hanun
2Kgs 10:13 to visit the royal P and the sons of
24:12 his servants, and his P, and his palace officials.
24:14 Jerusalem, and all the P, and all the mighty
1Chr 4:38 mentioned by name were P in their families, and
7:40 houses, approved, mighty warriors, chief of the P
19:3 But the P of the Ammonites said to Hanun,
24:6 the king, and the P, and Zadok the priest,
2Chr 12:5 Rehoboam and to the P of Judah, who had
12:6 Then the P of Israel and the king humbled
17:7 reign he sent his P, Ben-hail, Obadiah, Zechariah,
21:4 also some of the P of Israel.
22:8 Ahab, he met the P of Judah and the
24:10 And all the P and all the people rejoiced
24:17 death of Jehoiada the P of Judah came and
24:23 and destroyed all the P of the people from
28:14 the spoil before the P and all the assembly.
28:21 king and of the P, and gave tribute to
29:30 the king and the P commanded the Levites to
30:2 the king and his P and all the assembly
30:6 the king and his P, as the king had
30:12 the king and the P commanded by the word
30:24 for offerings, and the P gave the assembly a
31:8 When Hezekiah and the P came and saw the
32:31 the envoys of the P of Babylon, who had
35:8 And his P contributed willingly to the people, to
36:18 king and of his P, all these he brought
Neh 9:32 upon our kings, our P, our priests, our prophets,
9:34 wickedly; our kings, our P, our priests, and our
9:38 write it, and our P, our Levites, and our
12:31 I brought up the P of Judah upon the
12:32 and half of the P of Judah,
Jud 5:2 called together all the P of Moab and the
9:3 down slaves along with P, and princes on their
9:3 along with princes, and P on their thrones;

Esth 1:3 banquet for all his P and servants, the army
1:11 the peoples and the P her beauty; for she
1:14 and Memucan, the seven P of Persia and Media,
1:16 the king and the P, "Not only to the
1:16 also to all the P and all the peoples
1:18 to all the king's P, and there will be
1:21 the king and the P, and the king did
2:18 banquet to all his P and servants; it was
3:1 seat above all the P who were with him.
3:12 provinces and to the P of all the peoples,
5:11 advanced him above the P and the servants of
6:9 the king's most noble P; let him array the
8:9 the governors and the P of the provinces from
9:3 All the P of the provinces and the satraps
Job 3:15 for themselves, or with P who had gold, who
12:21 He pours contempt on P, and looses the belt
29:9 rose and stood; the P refrained from talking, and
34:19 shows no partiality to P, nor regards the rich
Ps 45:16 you will make them P in all the earth.
47:9 The P of the peoples gather as the people
68:27 in the lead, the P of Judah in their
68:27 in their throng, the P of Zebulun, the princes
68:27 princes of Zebulun, the P of Naphtali.
76:12 off the spirit of P, who is terrible to
83:11 and Zeeb, all their P like Zebah and Zalmunna,
105:22 possessions, to instruct his P at his pleasure, and
107:40 he pours contempt upon P and makes them wander
113:8 make them sit with P, with the princes of
113:8 with princes, with the P of his people.
118:9 in the LORD than to put confidence in P
119:23 Even though P sit plotting against me, thy servant
119:161 P persecute me without cause, but my heart stands
146:3 not your trust in P, in a son of
148:11 earth and all peoples, P and all rulers of
Prov 8:16 is just; by me P rule, and nobles govern
19:10 much less for a slave to rule over P
Eccl 10:7 slaves on horses, and P walking on foot like
10:16 a child, and your P feast in the morning!
10:17 free men, and your P feast at the proper
Is 1:23 Your P are rebels and companions of thieves.
3:4 will make boys their P, and babes shall rule
3:14 with the elders and P of his people: "It
19:11 The P of Zoan are utterly foolish; the wise
19:13 The P of Zoan have become fools, and the
19:13 become fools, and the P of Memphis are deluded;
21:5 Arise, O P, oil the shield!
23:8 crowns, whose merchants were P, whose traders
32:1 reign in righteousness, and P will rule in justice.
34:12 There, and all its P shall be nothing.
40:23 dwell in; who brings P to nought, and makes
43:28 Therefore I profaned the P of the sanctuary, I
49:7 shall see and arise; P, and they shall prostrate
Jer 1:18 kings of Judah, its P, its priests, and the
2:26 they, their kings, their P, their priests, and their
4:9 fail both king and P; the priests shall be
8:1 the bones of its P, the bones of the
17:25 horses, they and their P, the men of Judah
24:1 Judah, together with the P of Judah, the craftsmen,
24:8 king of Judah, his P, the remnant of Jerusalem
25:18 Judah, its kings and P, to make them a
25:19 Egypt, his servants, his P, all his people,
26:10 When the P of Judah heard these things, they
26:11 prophets said to the P and to all the
26:12 spoke to all the P and all the people,
26:16 Then the P and all the people said to
26:21 warriors and all the P, heard his words, the
29:2 mother, the eunuchs, the P of Judah and Jerusalem,
32:32 their kings and their P, their priests and their
34:10 they obeyed, all the P and all the people
34:19 its parts– the P of Judah, the princes
34:19 princes of Judah, the P of Jerusalem, the eunuchs,
34:21 of Judah, and his P I will give into
35:4 the chamber of the P, above the chamber of
36:12 chamber; and all the P were sitting there: Elishama
36:12 Zedekiah the son of Hananiah, and all the P
36:14 Then all the P sent Jehudi the son of
36:19 Then the P said to Baruch, "Go and hide,
36:21 king and all the P who stood beside the
37:14 and seized Jeremiah and brought him to the P
37:15 And the P were enraged at Jeremiah, and they
38:4 Then the P said to the king, "Let this
38:17 will surrender to the P of the king of
38:18 not surrender to the P of the king of
38:22 led out to the P of the king of
38:25 If the P hear that I have spoken with
38:27 Then all the P came to Jeremiah and asked
39:3 was taken, all the P of the king of
44:17 our kings and our P, in the cities of
44:21 your kings and your P, and the people of
48:7 forth into exile, with his priests and his P
49:3 go into exile, with his priests and his P
49:38 destroy their king and P, says the LORD.
50:35 Babylon, and upon her P and her wise men!
51:57 will make drunk her P and her wise men,
52:10 also slew all the P of Judah at Riblah.
Lam 1:6 Her P have become like harts that find no
2:9 bars; her king and P are among the nations;
4:7 Her P were purer than snow, whiter than milk;
5:12 P are hung up by their hands; no respect
Bar 1:4 mighty men and the P, and in the hearing
1:9 Jerusalem Jeconiah and the P and the prisoners and
1:16 our kings and our P and our priests and
2:1 kings and against our P and against the men
3:16 Where are the P of the nations, and those
Ezek 11:1 the son of Benaiah, P of the people.
17:12 her king and her P and brought them to
19:1 a lamentation for the P of Israel,
21:12 is against all the P of Israel; they are
22:6 "Behold, the P of Israel in you, every one
22:25 Her P in the midst of her are like
22:27 Her P in the midst of her are like
26:16 Then all the P of the sea will step
27:21 Arabia and all the P of Kedar were your
32:29 kings and all her P, who for all their
32:30 "The P of the north are there, all of
39:18 the blood of the P of the earth–of
45:8 And my P shall no more oppress my people;
45:9 Lord GOD: Enough, O P of Israel!
Dan 8:25 against the Prince of P; but, by no human
9:6 to our kings, our P, and our fathers, and
9:8 our kings, to our P, and to our fathers,
10:13 one of the chief P, came to help me,
11:5 but one of his P shall be stronger than
Hos 5:10 The P of Judah have become like those who
7:4 king glad, and the P by their treachery.
7:6 of our king the P became sick with the
7:17 a treacherous bow, their P shall fall by the
8:4 They set up P, but without my knowledge.
8:10 for a little while from anointing king and P
9:15 no more; all their P are rebels.
13:10 where are all your P, to defend you –
13:10 whom you said, "Give me a king and P
Amos 1:15 exile, he and his P together," says the LORD.
2:3 will slay all its P with him," says the
Mic 5:5 seven shepherds and eight P of men;
Nah 3:17 Your P are like grasshoppers, your scribes like clouds
1Mac 1:4 over countries, nations, and P, and they became
7:26 one of his honored P, who hated and detested
2Mac 9:25 I understand how the P along the borders and

PRINCESS (2)

Ps 45:13 The P is decked in her chamber with gold-woven
Lam 1:1 She that was a P among the cities has

PRINCESSES (2)

1Kgs 11:3 hundred wives, P, and three hundred concubines;
Jer 43:6 women, the children, the P, and every person whom

PRINCIPAL (3)

2Mac 10:10 brief summary of the P calamities of the wars.
Lk 19:47 the scribes and the P men of the people
Acts 25:2 chief priests and the P men of the Jews

PRINCIPALITIES (5)

Rom 8:38 life, nor angels, nor P, nor things present, nor
Eph 3:10 made known to the P and powers in the
6:12 blood, but against the P, against the powers, against
Col 1:16 thrones or dominions or P or authorities–all things
2:15 He disarmed the P and powers and made a

PRINCIPLE (3)

Rom 3:27 On what P
3:27 On the P of works?
3:27 No, but on the P of faith.

PRINCIPLES

Heb 5:12 you again the first P of God's word.

PRINT

Jn 20:25 in his hands the P of the nails, and

P

PRIOR

Wis 19:13 upon the sinners without P signs in the violence

PRISCA (3)

Rom 16:3 Greet P and Aquila, my fellow workers in Christ
1Cor 16:19 Aquila and P, together with the church in their
2Tim 4:19 Greet P and Aquila, and the household of

PRISCILLA (3)

Acts 18:2 Italy with his wife P, because Claudius had
18:18 Syria, and with him P and Aquila.
18:26 the synagogue; but when P and Aquila heard him,

PRISON (77)

Gen 39:20 put him into the P, the place where the
39:20 prisoners were confined, and he was there in P
39:21 in the sight of the keeper of the P
39:22 the keeper of the P committed to Joseph's care
39:22 who were in the P; and whatever was done
39:23 the keeper of the P paid no heed to
40:3 the guard, in the P where Joseph was confined.
40:5 were confined in the P --each his own dream,
42:16 while you remain in P, that your words may
42:17 them all together in P for three days.
42:19 remain confined in your P, and let the rest
Judg 16:21 and he ground at the mill in the P
16:25 Samson out of the P, and he made sport
1Kgs 22:27 "Put this fellow in P, and feed him with
2Kgs 17:4 Assyria shut him up, and bound him in P
25:27 king of Judah from P;
25:29 Jehoiachin put off his P garments.
2Chr 16:10 in the stocks, in P, for he was in
18:26 Put this fellow in P, and feed him with
Ps 142:7 Bring me out of P, that I may give
Eccl 4:14 he had gone from P to the throne or
Wis 10:14 when he was in P she did not leave
17:16 shut up in a P not made of iron;
Is 24:22 shut up in a P, and after many days
42:7 the dungeon, from the P those who sit in
61:1 the opening of the P to those who are
Jer 37:4 for he had not yet been put in P
37:15 the secretary, for it had been made a P
37:18 this people, that you have put me in P
52:11 and put him in P till the day of
52:31 brought him out of P;
52:33 Jehoiachin put off his P garments.
2Mac 13:21 he was sought for, caught, and put in P
Mt 5:25 you be put in P;
11:2 when John heard in P about the deeds of
14:3 and put him in P, for the sake of
14:10 John beheaded in the P,
18:29 and put him in P till he should pay
25:36 me, I was in P and you came to
25:39 thee sick or in P and visit thee?'
25:43 me, sick and in P and you did not
25:44 or sick or in P, and did not minister
Mk 6:17 and bound him in P for the sake of
6:27 beheaded him in the P,
15:7 among the rebels in P, who had committed murder
Lk 3:20 them all, that he shut up John in P
12:58 the officer, and the officer put you in P
22:33 go with you to P and to death."
23:18 had been thrown into P for an insurrection started
23:24 had been thrown into P for insurrection and murder,
Jn 3:24 For John had not yet been put in P
Acts 5:18 the apostles and put them in the common P
5:19 the Lord opened the P doors and brought them
5:21 and sent to the P to have them brought.
5:22 find them in the P, and they returned and
5:23 reported, "We found the P securely locked and the
5:25 whom you put in P are standing in the
8:3 off men and women and committed them to P
12:4 he put him in P, and delivered him to
12:5 Peter was kept in P; but earnest prayer for
12:6 door were guarding the P;
12:17 the Lord had brought him out of the P
16:23 they threw them into P, charging the jailer to
16:24 them into the inner P and fastened their feet
16:26 the foundations of the P were shaken; and
16:27 and saw that the P doors were open, he
16:37 have thrown us into P; and do they now
16:40 went out of the P, and visited Lydia; and
22:4 binding and delivering to P both men and women,
24:26 the Jews a favor, Felix left Paul in P
26:10 of the saints in P, by authority from the
Col 4:3 which I am in P,
Heb 13:3 those who are in P, as though in prison
13:3 prison, as though in P with them; and those
1Pet 3:19 to the spirits in P,
Rev 2:10 some of you into P, that you may be
20:7 be loosed from his P

PRISONER (17)

2Kgs 24:12 of Babylon took him P in the eighth year
2Mac 14:27 to Antioch as a P without delay.
14:33 to me as a P, I will level this
Mt 27:15 the crowd any one P whom they wanted.
27:16 had then a notorious P, called Barabbas.
Mk 15:6 release for them one P for whom they asked.
Acts 23:18 and said, "Paul the P called me and asked
25:14 is a man left P by Felix;
25:27 unreasonable, in sending a P, not to indicate the
28:17 yet I was delivered P from Jerusalem into the
Eph 3:1 reason I, Paul, a P for Christ Jesus on
4:1 I therefore, a P for the Lord, beg you
Col 4:10 Aristarchus my fellow P greets you, and Mark the
2Tim 1:8 nor of me his P, but share in suffering
Philem 1:1 Paul, a P for Christ Jesus, and
1:9 ambassador and now a P also for Christ Jesus--
1:23 Epaphras, my fellow P in Christ Jesus, sends

PRISONERS (23)

Gen 39:20 place where the king's P were confined, and he
39:22 Joseph's care all the P who were in the
Job 3:18 There the P are at ease together; they hear
Ps 68:6 he leads out the P to prosperity; but the
79:11 the groans of the P come before thee; according
102:20 the groans of the P, to set free those
107:10 darkness and in gloom, P in affliction and in
146:7 The LORD sets the P free;
Wis 17:2 captives of darkness and P of long night, shut
Is 10:4 to crouch among the P or fall among the
14:17 did not let his P go home?'
24:22 be gathered together as P in a pit; they
42:7 to bring out the P from the dungeon, from
49:9 heritages; saying to the P, 'Come forth,' to those
Lam 3:34 under foot all the P of the earth,
Bar 1:9 the princes and the P and the mighty men
Zech 9:12 to your stronghold, O P of hope; today I
Acts 16:25 to God, and the P were listening to them,
16:27 himself, supposing that the P had escaped.
27:1 Paul and some other P to a centurion of
27:42 was to kill the P, lest any should swim
Rom 16:7 kinsmen and my fellow P; they are men of
Heb 10:34 had compassion on the P, and you joyfully accepted

PRISONS (2)

Is 42:22 holes and hidden in P; they have become a
Lk 21:12 to the synagogues and P, and you will be

PRIVATE (6)

Deut 25:11 seizes him by the P parts,
1Sam 18:22 "Speak to David in P and say, 'Behold, the
2Mac 4:5 welfare, both public and P, of all the people.
9:26 remember the public and P services rendered to you
Lk 12:3 you have whispered in P rooms shall be proclaimed
Jn 7:10 he also went up, not publicly but in P

PRIVATELY (13)

2Sam 3:27 to speak with him P, and there he smote
Tob 12:6 the two of them P and said to them:
2Mac 6:21 acquaintance with him, and P urged him to bring
13:13 After consulting P with the elders, he determined to
Mt 17:19 disciples came to Jesus P and said, "Why could
24:3 disciples came to him P, saying, "Tell us, when
Mk 4:34 without a parable, but P to his own disciples
7:32 aside from the multitude P, he put his fingers
9:28 his disciples asked him P, "Why could we not
13:3 and Andrew asked him P,
Lk 10:23 the disciples he said P, "Blessed are the eyes
Acts 23:19 going aside asked him P, "What is it that
Gal 2:2 laid before them (but P before those who were

PRIZE (8)

Prov 4:9 P her highly, and she will exalt you; she
Wis 2:22 holiness, nor discern the P for blameless souls;
Jer 21:9 his life as a P of war.
38:2 his life as a P of war, and live.
39:18 your life as a P of war, because you
45:5 your life as a P of war in all
1Cor 9:24 the runners compete, but only one receives the P
Phil 3:14 the goal for the P of the upward call

PRIZED (3)
Sir 45:12 a distinction to be P, the work of an
Jer 20:5 its gains, all its P belongings, and all the
2Mac 4:15 discus, disdaining the honors P by their fathers and

PRIZES
Wis 4:2 in the contest for P that are undefiled.

PROBLEMS (2)
Dan 5:12 explain riddles, and solve P were found in this
5:16 heard that you can give interpretations and solve P

PROCEDURE (2)
1Chr 24:19 LORD according to the P established for them by
Esth 1:13 this was the king's P toward all who were

PROCEED (7)
Gen 41:34 Let Pharaoh P to appoint overseers over the land,
Jud 11:15 reaches them and they P to do this, on
Job 40:5 twice, but I will P no further."
Jer 9:3 the land; for they P from evil to evil,
Hab 1:7 their justice and dignity P from themselves.
1Mac 15:4 so that I may P against those who have
Rom 14:23 for whatever does not P from faith is sin.

PROCEEDED (6)
Tob 6:1 Now as they P on their way they came
2Mac 4:21 arriving at Joppa he P to Jerusalem.
Lk 4:22 the gracious words which P out of his mouth;
19:11 heard these things, he P to tell a parable,
Jn 8:42 love me, for I P and came forth from
Acts 12:3 pleased the Jews, he P to arrest Peter also.

PROCEEDING
Eccl 10:5 it were an error P from the ruler:

PROCEEDINGS
2Mac 4:14 part in the unlawful P in the wrestling arena

PROCEEDS (11)
Num 30:2 according to all that P out of his mouth.
30:12 hears them, then whatever P out of her lips
Deut 8:3 lives by everything that P out of the mouth
Tob 1:7 go and spend the P each year at Jerusalem;
Is 57:16 angry; for from me P the spirit, and I
Mt 4:4 by every word that P from the mouth of
15:18 out of the mouth P from the heart, and
Jn 15:26 Spirit of truth, who P from the Father, he
Acts 4:34 them, and brought the P of what was sold
5:2 back some of the P, and brought only a
5:3 back part of the P of the land?

PROCESSION (6)
Neh 12:31 great companies which gave thanks and went in P
Ps 42:4 and led them in P to the house of
118:27 Bind the festal P with branches, up to the
Is 60:11 of the nations, with their kings led in P
1Mac 9:39 and saw a tumultuous P with much baggage; and
2Mac 6:7 to walk in the P in honor of Dionysus,

PROCESSIONS (2)
Ps 68:24 Thy solemn P are seen, O God, the processions
68:24 seen, O God, the P of my God, my

PROCHORUS
Acts 6:5 Spirit, and Philip, and P, and Nicanor, and Timon,

PROCLAIM (69)
Ex 33:19 before you, and will P before you my name
Lev 23:2 LORD which you shall P as holy convocations, my
23:4 convocations, which you shall P at the time
23:37 LORD, which you shall P as times of holy
25:10 the fiftieth year, and P liberty throughout the land
Deut 32:3 For I will P the name of the LORD.
Judg 7:3 delivered me.' Now therefore P in the ears of
1Kgs 21:9 wrote in the letters, P a fast, and set
Neh 6:7 set up prophets to P concerning you in Jerusalem,
8:15 they should publish and P in all their towns
Ps 22:31 the coming generation, and P his deliverance to a
40:5 Were I to P and tell of them, they
52:9 I will P thy name, for it is good,
71:17 me, and I still P thy wondrous deeds.
71:18 forsake me, till I P thy might to all
89:1 my mouth I will P thy faithfulness to all
97:6 The heavens P his righteousness; and all the peoples
145:6 Men shall P the might of thy terrible acts,
Prov 12:23 his knowledge, but fools P their folly.
Sir 17:8 his holy name, to P the grandeur of his
18:3 he given power to P his works; and who
39:10 and the congregation will P his praise;
Is 3:9 witnesses against them; they P their sin like Sodom,
12:4 deeds among the nations, P that his name is
44:7 Let him P it, let him declare and set
48:20 a shout of joy, P it, send it forth
60:6 and frankincense, and shall P the praise of the
61:1 up the brokenhearted, to P liberty to the captives,
61:2 who are bound; to P the year of the
Jer 2:2 me, saying, "Go and P in the hearing of
3:12 Go, and P these words toward the north, and
4:5 Declare in Judah, and P in Jerusalem, and say,
5:20 the house of Jacob, P it in Judah:
7:2 the LORD's house, and P there this word, and
11:6 LORD said to me, P all these words in
19:2 the Potsherd Gate, and P there the words that
31:7 chief of the nations; P, give praise, and say,
34:17 his neighbor; behold, I P to you liberty to
46:14 "Declare in Egypt, and P in Migdol; proclaim in
46:14 and proclaim in Migdol; P in Memphis and
50:2 among the nations and P, set up a banner
50:2 up a banner and P, conceal it not, and
Joel 3:9 P this among the nations: Prepare war, stir up
Amos 3:9 P to the strongholds in Assyria, and to the
4:5 which is leavened, and P freewill offerings, publish
Jon 3:2 that great city, and P to it the message
1Mac 10:63 of the city and P that no one is
2Mac 9:17 every inhabited place to P the power of God.
Mt 10:27 what you hear whispered, P upon the housetops.
12:18 him, and he shall P justice to the Gentiles.
Mk 5:20 away and began to P in the Decapolis how
Lk 4:18 has sent me to P release to the captives
4:19 who are oppressed, to P the acceptable year of
9:60 for you, go and P the kingdom of God."
Acts 16:17 Most High God, who P to you the way
17:3 "This Jesus, whom I P to you, is the
17:23 as unknown, this I P to you.
26:23 the dead, he would P light both to the
1Cor 9:14 commanded that those who P the gospel should get
11:26 drink the cup, you P the Lord's death until
Eph 6:19 my mouth boldly to P the mystery of the
Phil 1:17 the gospel; the former P Christ out of partisanship,
Col 1:28 Him we P, warning every man and teaching every
2Tim 4:17 gave me strength to P the message fully, that
Heb 2:12 brethren, saying, "I will P thy name to my
1Jn 1:2 testify to it, and P to you the eternal
1:3 seen and heard we P also to you, so
1:5 heard from him and P to you, that God
Rev 14:6 an eternal gospel to P to those who dwell

PROCLAIMED (41)
Ex 34:5 with him there, and P the name of the
34:6 passed before him, and P, "The LORD, the LORD,
36:6 command, and word was P throughout the camp,
Lev 23:24 solemn rest, a memorial P with blast of trumpets,
Deut 15:2 his brother, because the LORD's release has been P
Judg 21:13 rock of Rimmon, and P peace to them.
1Kgs 21:12 sent to them, they P a fast, and set
2Kgs 9:13 blew the trumpet, and P, "Jehu is king."
10:20 So they P it.
11:12 the testimony; and they P him king, and anointed
23:16 the man of God P, who had predicted these
2Chr 20:3 seek the LORD, and P a fast throughout all
23:11 the testimony; and they P him king, and Jehoiada
Ezra 8:21 Then I P a fast there, at the river
Esth 1:20 by the king is P throughout all his kingdom,
2:8 and his edict were P, and when many maidens
Is 41:26 declared it, none who P, none who heard your
43:12 declared and saved and P, when there was no
62:11 Behold, the LORD has P to the end of
Jer 23:22 then they would have P my words to my
36:9 of Judah to Jerusalem P a fast before the
Dan 3:4 And the herald P aloud, "You are commanded, O
Jon 3:5 Nineveh believed God; they P a fast, and put
Zech 7:7 words which the LORD P by the former prophets?"
1Mac 14:28 country, the following was P to us:
2Mac 8:36 the people of Jerusalem P that the Jews had
Mk 7:35 the more zealously they P it.
Lk 12:3 private rooms shall be P upon the housetops.
Jn 7:28 So Jesus P, as he taught in the temple,
7:37 Jesus stood up and P, "If any one thirst,
Acts 3:24 who came afterwards, also P these days.
8:5 city of Samaria, and P to them the Christ.
9:20 the synagogues immediately he P Jesus, saying, "He

10:37 the word which was P throughout all Judea,
13:5 arrived at Salamis, they P the word of God
13:38 forgiveness of sins is P to you,
15:35 every city where we P the word of the
17:13 word of God was P by Paul at Beroea
Rom 1:8 because your faith is P in all the world.
9:17 my name may be P in all the earth."
Phil 1:18 in truth, Christ is P; and in that I

PROCLAIMING (10)

Esth 6:9 square of the city, P before him: 'Thus shall
6:11 square of the city, P, "Thus shall it be
Sir 44:3 by their understanding, and P prophecies;
Jer 34:15 in my eyes by P liberty, each to his
34:17 not obeyed me by P liberty, every one to
Lk 8:39 And he went away, P throughout the whole city
Acts 4:2 teaching the people and P in Jesus the resurrection
1Cor 2:1 I did not come P to you the testimony
2Thes 2:4 the temple of God, P himself to be God.
Rev 5:2 saw a strong angel P with a loud voice,

PROCLAIMS (5)

Ps 19:1 God; and the firmament P his handiwork.
Prov 20:6 Many a man P his own loyalty, but a
Sir 44:16 wisdom, and the congregation P their praise.
Jer 4:15 declares from Dan and P evil from Mount Ephraim.
Nah 1:15 brings good tidings, who P peace!

PROCLAMATION (16)

Ex 32:5 it; and Aaron made P and said, "Tomorrow shall
Lev 23:21 And you shall make P on the same day;
1Kgs 15:22 King Asa made a P to all Judah, none
2Chr 24:9 And P was made throughout Judah and Jerusalem,
30:5 decreed to make a P throughout all Israel, from
36:22 that he made a P throughout all his kingdom
Ezra 1:1 that he made a P throughout all his kingdom
10:7 And a P was made throughout Judah and Jerusalem
Esth 3:14 in every province by P to all the peoples
8:13 every province, and by P to all peoples, and
Sir 43:2 when it appears, making P as it goes forth,
Jer 34:8 Jerusalem to make a P of liberty to them,
Dan 5:29 about his neck, and P was made concerning him,
Jon 3:7 And he made P and published through Nineveh, "By
1Mac 5:49 Then Judas ordered P to be made to the
10:64 in accordance with the P, and saw him clothed

PROCONSUL (4)

Acts 13:7 He was with the P, Sergius Paulus, a man
13:8 to turn away the P from the faith.
13:12 Then the P believed, when he saw what had
18:12 But when Gallio was P of Achaia, the Jews

PROCONSULS

Acts 19:38 open, and there are P; let them bring charges

PROCURED

2Chr 11:23 them abundant provisions, and P wives for them.

PROCURING

Jn 18:3 So Judas, P a band of soldiers and some

PRODUCE (33)

Gen 41:34 fifth part of the P of the land of
Lev 23:39 have gathered in the P of the land, you
25:22 will be eating old P; until the ninth year,
25:22 ninth year, when its P comes in, you shall
Num 18:30 to the Levites as P of the threshing floor,
18:30 threshing floor, and as P of the wine press;
Deut 14:28 the tithe of your P in the same year,
16:15 you in all your P and in all the
26:12 the tithe of your P in the third year,
32:13 and he ate the P of the field; and
33:15 months, with the finest P of the ancient mountains,
Josh 5:11 they ate of the P of the land, unleavened
5:12 they ate of the P of the land; and
Judg 6:4 them and destroy the P of the land, as
2Sam 9:10 shall bring in the P, that your master's son
2Kgs 8:6 together with all the P of the fields from
1Chr 27:27 Ramathite; and over the P of the vineyards for
2Chr 31:5 and of all the P of the field; and
Tob 1:6 the tithes of my P and the first shearings,
1:7 Of all my P I would give a tenth
5:13 of our flocks and the tithes of our P
Prov 3:9 fruits of all your P;
Sir 1:15 desirable goods, and their storehouses with her P
6:19 while, and soon you will eat of her P
24:18 desire me, and eat your fill of my P
Is 30:23 ground, and grain, the P of the ground, which
Jer 29:5 live in them; plant gardens and eat their P
29:28 in them, and plant gardens and eat their P
Ezek 48:18 Its P shall be food for the workers of
Hab 3:17 on the vines, the P of the olive fail
Hag 1:10 the dew, and the earth has withheld its P
2Cor 9:11 which through us will P thanksgiving to God;
1Tim 6:4 disputes about words, which P envy, dissension,

PRODUCED (3)

Num 6:4 eat nothing that is P by the grapevine, not
17:8 put forth buds, and P blossoms, and it bore
2Cor 7:11 this godly grief has P in you, what eagerness

PRODUCES (13)

Prov 30:33 For pressing milk P curds, pressing the nose
30:33 curds, pressing the nose P blood, and pressing anger
30:33 blood, and pressing anger P strife.
Is 54:16 fire of coals, and P a weapon for its
Mk 4:28 The earth P of itself, first the blade, then
Lk 6:45 treasure of his heart P good, and the evil
6:45 of his evil treasure P evil; for out of
Rom 5:3 sufferings, knowing that suffering P endurance,
5:4 produces endurance, and endurance P character, and
5:4 produces character, and character P hope,
2Cor 7:10 For godly grief P a repentance that leads to
7:10 regret, but worldly grief P death.
Jas 1:3 testing of your faith P steadfastness.

PRODUCING (2)

Wis 19:10 sojourn, how instead of P animals the earth brought
Mt 21:43 given to a nation P the fruits of it.

PRODUCT (3)

Tob 2:12 used to send the P to the owners.
Sir 11:3 flying creatures, but her P is the best of
14:19 Every P decays and ceases to exist, and the

PRODUCTION

Wis 16:26 it is not the P of crops that feeds

PRODUCTS

Hag 2:17 you and all the P of your toil with

PROFANATION

Jud 4:3 and the temple had been consecrated after their P

PROFANE (35)

Ex 20:25 tool upon it you P it.
Lev 18:21 to Molech, and so P the name of your
19:12 name falsely, and so P the name of your
19:29 "Do not P your daughter by making her a
21:4 his people and so P himself.
21:6 their God, and not P the name of their
21:12 of the sanctuary, nor P the sanctuary of his
21:15 that he may not P his children among his
21:23 that he may not P my sanctuaries; for I
22:2 that they may not P my holy name; I
22:9 die thereby when they P it: I am the
22:15 The priests shall not P the holy things of
22:32 And you shall not P my holy name, but
Num 18:32 And you shall not P the holy things of
Prov 30:9 poor, and steal, and P the name of my
Is 56:6 sabbath, and does not P it, and holds fast
Ezek 7:21 spoil; and they shall P it.
7:22 them, that they may P my precious place; robbers
7:22 robbers shall enter and P it,
20:39 you shall no more P with your gifts and
23:39 into my sanctuary to P it.
24:21 GOD: Behold, I will P my sanctuary, the pride
28:16 cast you as a P thing from the mountain
Dan 11:31 him shall appear and P the temple and fortress,
Zeph 3:4 faithless men; her priests P what is sacred, they
Mal 1:12 But you P it when you say that the
1Mac 1:45 in the sanctuary, to P sabbaths and feasts,
1:48 by everything unclean and P,
1:63 by food or to P the holy covenant; and
2:34 king commands and so P the sabbath day."
2Mac 5:16 and swept away with P hands the votive offerings
15:32 Nicanor's head and that P man's arm, which had
Mt 12:5 priests in the temple P the sabbath, and are
Acts 24:6 He even tried to P the temple, but we
1Tim 1:9 for the unholy and P, for murderers of fathers

PROFANED (41)

Lev 19:8 iniquity, because he has P a holy thing of
Jud 4:12 the sanctuary to be P and desecrated to the
Is 43:28 Therefore I P the princes of the sanctuary, I
47:6 with my people, I P my heritage; I gave
48:11 do it, for how should my name be P
Jer 19:4 forsaken me, and have P this place by burning
34:16 you turned around and P my name when each
Ezek 7:24 proud might, and their holy places shall be P
13:19 You have P me among my people for handfuls
20:9 it should not be P in the sight of
20:13 man shall live; and my sabbaths they greatly P
20:14 it should not be P in the sight of
20:16 in my statutes, and P my sabbaths; for their
20:21 man shall live; they P my sabbaths.
20:22 it should not be P in the sight of
20:24 rejected my statutes and P my sabbaths, and their
22:8 my holy things, and P my sabbaths.
22:16 And I shall be P through you in the
22:26 my law and have P my holy things; they
22:26 so that I am P among them.
23:38 the same day and P my sabbaths.
25:3 sanctuary when it was P, and over the land
28:18 of your trade you P your sanctuaries; so I
36:20 wherever they came, they P my holy name, in
36:21 Israel caused to be P among the nations to
36:22 name, which you have P among the nations to
36:23 name, which has been P among the nations, and
36:23 and which you have P among them; and the
39:7 my holy name be P any more; and the
Amos 2:7 my holy name is P;
Mic 4:11 saying, "Let her be P, and let our eyes
Mal 2:11 Jerusalem; for Judah has P the sanctuary of the
1Mac 1:43 sacrificed to idols and P the sabbath.
2:12 waste; the Gentiles have P it.
3:51 is trampled down and P, and thy priests mourn
4:38 sanctuary desolate, the altar P, and the gates burned.
4:44 the altar of burnt offering, which had been P
4:54 that the Gentiles had P it, it was dedicated
2Mac 8:2 temple which had been P by ungodly men,
10:5 the sanctuary had been P by the foreigners, the
Heb 10:29 Son of God, and P the blood of the

PROFANES (3)

Ex 31:14 you; every one who P it shall be put
Lev 21:9 any priest, if she P herself by playing the
21:9 by playing the harlot, P her father; she shall

PROFANING (7)

Lev 20:3 defiling my sanctuary and P my holy name.
Neh 13:17 which you are doing, P the sabbath day?
13:18 wrath upon Israel by P the sabbath."
Is 56:2 keeps the sabbath, not P it, and keeps his
Ezek 44:7 be in my sanctuary, P it, when you offer
Mal 2:10 faithless to one another, P the covenant of our
1Cor 11:27 will be guilty of P the body and blood

PROFESS (2)

1Tim 2:10 as befits women who P religion.
Tit 1:15 They P to know God, but they deny him

PROFESSES

Wis 2:13 He P to have knowledge of God, and calls

PROFESSING

1Tim 6:21 called knowledge, for by P it some have missed

PROFIT (36)

Gen 37:26 to his brothers, "What P is it if we
Lev 25:37 at interest, nor give him your food for P
1Sam 12:21 vain things which cannot P or save, for they
Esth 3:8 not for the king's P to tolerate them.
Job 20:18 it down; from the P of his trading he
21:15 And what P do we get if we pray
Ps 30:9 I made supplication: "What P is there in my
Prov 3:14 from silver and its P better than gold.
10:2 by wickedness do not P, but righteousness delivers
11:4 Riches do not P in the day of wrath,
14:23 all toil there is P, but mere talk tends
Wis 6:25 be instructed by my words, and you will P
15:12 a festival held for P, for he says one
Sir 20:13 A fool's gift will P you nothing, for he
29:11 High, and it will P you more than gold.
30:2 disciplines his son will P by him, and will
30:23 and there is no P in it.
42:5 much or little; of P from dealing with merchants,
Is 30:5 a people that cannot P them, that brings neither
30:5 brings neither help nor P, but shame and disgrace."
30:6 a people that cannot P them.
44:9 delight in do not P; their witnesses neither see
48:17 who teaches you to P, who leads you in
Jer 2:8 Baal, and went after things that do not P
2:11 changed their glory for that which does not P
12:13 tired themselves out but P nothing.
16:19 lies, worthless things in which there is no P
23:32 so they do not P this people at all,
Ezek 13:18 people, and keep other souls alive for your P
Hab 2:18 What P is an idol when its maker has
2Mac 2:25 to memorize, and to P all readers.
Mt 16:26 For what will it P a man, if he
Mk 8:36 For what does it P a man, to gain
Lk 9:25 For what does it P a man if he
Jas 2:14 What does it P, my brethren, if a man
2:16 things needed for the body, what does it P

PROFITABLE (9)

Job 22:2 "Can a man be P to God?
22:2 who is wise is P to himself.
Prov 31:18 She perceives that her merchandise is P
Wis 8:7 in life is more P for men than these.
Sir 7:22 them; if they are P to you, keep them.
Is 44:10 an image, that is P for nothing?
Acts 20:20 you anything that was P, and teaching you in
2Tim 3:16 inspired by God and P for teaching, for reproof,
Tit 3:8 these are excellent and P to men.

PROFITED

Wis 5:8 What has our arrogance P us?

PROFITS (2)

Job 34:9 he has said, 'It P a man nothing that
Sir 20:9 is a gift that P you nothing, and there

PROFLIGACY

1Pet 4:4 in the same wild P, and they abuse you;

PROFLIGATE

Tit 1:5 the charge of being P or insubordinate.

PROFLIGATES

2Tim 3:3 unholy, inhuman, implacable, slanderers, P, fierce,

PROFOUND

Eph 5:32 This mystery is a P one, and I am

PROFUSE

Prov 27:6 wounds of a friend; P are the kisses of

PROGRESS (3)

Sir 51:17 I made P therein; to him who gives wisdom
Phil 1:25 you all, for your P and joy in the
1Tim 4:15 to them, so that all may see your P

PROGRESSED

2Mac 4:3 When his hatred P to such a degree that

PROJECTED

1Kgs 7:31 within a crown which P upward one cubit; its

PROJECTING (4)

Neh 3:25 Angle and the tower P from the upper house
3:26 the east and the P tower.
3:27 section opposite the great P tower as far as
Ezek 43:15 from the altar hearth P upward, four horns, one

PROJECTION

1Kgs 7:20 also above the rounded P which was beside the

PROLIFIC

Wis 4:3 But the P brood of the ungodly will be

PROLONG (6)

Deut 4:40 and that you may P your days in the
Ps 61:6 P the life of the king; may his years
85:5 Wilt thou P thy anger to all generations?
Prov 28:16 hates unjust gain will P his days.
Eccl 8:13 wicked, neither will he P his days like a
Is 53:10 his offspring, he shall P his days; the will

PROLONGED (7)

Deut 5:16 your days may be P, and that it may
6:2 your life; and that your days may be P

P

25:15 your days may be P in the land which
Wis 4:16 perfected will condemn the P old age of the
Is 13:22 at hand and its days will not be P
Dan 7:12 but their lives were P for a season and
Acts 20:7 the morrow; and he P his speech until midnight.

PROLONGS (5)

Job 24:22 Yet God P the life of the mighty by
Prov 10:27 fear of the LORD P life, but the years
Eccl 7:15 a wicked man who P his life in his
8:12 a hundred times and P his life, yet I
Sir 37:31 careful to avoid it P his life.

PROMINENT (2)

2Mac 3:11 a man of very P position, and that it
Acts 25:23 military tribunes and the P men of the city.

PROMISE (74)

Gen 47:29 under my thigh, and P to deal loyally and
Ex 3:17 in Egypt; and I P that I will bring
2Sam 7:21 Because of thy P, and according to thy own
22:31 way is perfect; the P of the LORD proves
1Kgs 8:20 LORD has fulfilled his P which he made; for
8:56 of all his good P, which he uttered by
2Kgs 15:12 (This was the P of the LORD which he
1Chr 16:16 with Abraham, his sworn P to Isaac,
25:5 seer, according to the P of God to exalt
2Chr 1:9 LORD God, let thy P to David my father
6:10 LORD has fulfilled his P which he made; for
Neh 5:13 from his labor who does not perform this P
9:8 thou hast fulfilled thy P, for thou art righteous.
Esth 14:5 didst do for them all that thou didst P
Ps 18:30 way is perfect; the P of the LORD proves
105:9 with Abraham, his sworn P to Isaac,
105:42 he remembered his holy P, and Abraham his servant.
106:24 the pleasant land, having no faith in his P
119:38 to thy servant thy P, which is for those
119:41 salvation according to thy P;
119:50 my affliction that thy P gives me life.
119:57 is my portion; I P to keep thy words.
119:58 heart; be gracious to me according to thy P
119:76 me according to thy P to thy servant.
119:82 with watching for thy P; I ask, "When wilt
119:116 me according to thy P, that I may live,
119:123 salvation, and for the fulfilment of thy righteous P
119:133 steps according to thy P, and let no iniquity
119:140 Thy P is well tried, and thy servant loves
119:148 the night, that I may meditate upon thy P
119:154 redeem me; give me life according to thy P
Jer 29:10 fulfil to you my P and bring you back
32:42 the good that I P them.
33:14 I will fulfil the P I made to the
Dan 3:36 to whom thou didst P to make their descendants
Hag 2:5 hosts, according to the P that I made you
1Mac 10:24 words of encouragement and P them honor and
2Mac 12:25 had confirmed his solemn P to restore them
Lk 24:49 behold, I send the P of my Father upon
Acts 1:4 to wait for the P of the Father, which,
2:33 from the Father the P of the Holy Spirit,
2:39 For the P is to you and to your
7:17 the time of the P drew near, which God
23:21 ready, waiting for the P from you."
26:6 for hope in the P made by God to
Rom 4:13 The P to Abraham and his descendants, that they
4:14 is null and the P is void.
4:16 in order that the P may rest on grace
4:20 him waver concerning the P of God, but he
9:8 the children of the P are reckoned as descendants.
9:9 this is what the P said, "About this time
Gal 3:14 we might receive the P of the Spirit through
3:17 as to make the P void.
3:18 is no longer by P; but God gave it
3:18 but God gave it to Abraham by a P
3:19 come to whom the P had been made; and
3:29 you are Abraham's offspring, heirs according to P
4:23 flesh, the son of the free woman through P
4:28 Now we, brethren, like Isaac, are children of P
Eph 2:12 to the covenants of P, having no hope and
3:6 and partakers of the P in Christ Jesus through
6:2 first commandment with a P,
1Tim 4:8 way, as it holds P for the present life
2Tim 1:1 God according to the P of the life which
Heb 4:1 Therefore, while the P of entering his rest remains,
6:13 when God made a P to Abraham, since he
6:15 Abraham, having patiently endured, obtained the P
6:17 the heirs of the P the unchangeable character of
11:9 in the land of P, as in a foreign
11:9 and Jacob, heirs with him of the same P
2Pet 2:19 They P them freedom, but they themselves are
3:4 saying, "Where is the P of his coming?
3:9 not slow about his P as some count slowness,
3:13 But according to his P we wait for new

PROMISED (88)

Gen 18:19 Abraham what he has P him."
21:1 the LORD did to Sarah as he had P
Ex 12:25 you, as he has P, you shall keep this
32:13 land that I have P I will give to
Num 10:29 for the LORD has P good to Israel."
14:17 great as thou hast P, saying,
14:40 which the LORD has P; for we have sinned."
32:24 for your sheep; and do what you have P
Deut 1:11 you, as he has P you!
6:3 of your fathers, has P you, in a land
6:19 enemies from before you, as the LORD has P
9:3 as the LORD has P you.
9:28 the land which he P them, and because he
11:25 shall tread, as he P you.
12:20 territory, as he has P you, and you say,
15:6 bless you, as he P you, and you shall
18:2 their inheritance, as he P them.
19:8 the land which he P to give to your
23:23 God what you have P with your mouth.
26:18 possession, as he has P you, and that you
27:3 of your fathers, has P you.
28:68 a journey which I P that you should never
29:13 your God, as he P you, and as he
Josh 1:3 to you, as I P to Moses.
22:4 your brethren, as he P them; therefore turn and
23:5 the LORD your God P you.
23:10 for you, as he P you.
23:14 the LORD your God P concerning you; all have
23:15 the LORD your God P concerning you have been
1Sam 2:30 of Israel declares: 'I P that your house and
2Sam 3:18 for the LORD has P David, saying, 'By the
7:28 true, and thou hast P this good thing to
1Kgs 2:24 a house, as he P, Adonijah shall be put
5:12 Solomon wisdom, as he P him; and there was
8:15 has fulfilled what he P with his mouth to
8:20 Israel, as the LORD P, and I have built
8:25 father what thou hast P him, saying, 'There shall
8:56 to all that he P; not one word has
9:5 for ever, as I P David your father, saying,
2Kgs 8:19 his servant, since he P to give a lamp
20:9 thing that he has P: shall the shadow go
1Chr 17:26 God, and thou hast P this good thing to
27:23 for the LORD had P to make Israel as
2Chr 6:4 has fulfilled what he P with his mouth to
6:10 Israel, as the LORD P, and I have built
6:16 father what thou hast P him, saying, 'There shall
6:20 place where thou hast P to set thy name,
21:7 and since he had P to give a lamp
Neh 5:12 oath of them to do as they had P
5:13 And the people did as they had P
Jud 8:9 them, and how he P them under oath to
8:30 them what we have P, and made us take
8:33 after which you have P to surrender the city
Esth 4:7 money that Haman had P to pay into the
Ps 66:14 uttered and my mouth P when I was in
108:7 God has P in his sanctuary: "With exultation I
Wis 17:8 For those who P to drive off the fears
Is 38:7 thing that he has P:
1Mac 11:28 Samaria from tribute, and P him three hundred
11:53 all that he had P; and he became estranged
2Mac 2:18 and consecration, as he P through the law.
4:9 addition to this he P to pay one hundred
4:27 any of the money P to the king.
4:45 as good as beaten, P a substantial bribe to
7:24 him in words, but P with oaths that he
Mt 14:7 Herod, so that he P with an oath to
Mk 14:11 they were glad, and P to give him money.
Lk 1:72 to perform the mercy P to our fathers, and
Acts 7:5 a foot's length, but P to give it to
13:23 brought to Israel a Savior, Jesus, as he P
13:32 news that what God P to the fathers,
Rom 1:2 which he P beforehand through his prophets in the
4:21 God was able to do what he had P
7:10 the very commandment which P life proved to be
2Cor 9:5 this gift you have P, so that it may
Gal 3:22 sin, that what was P to faith in Jesus
Eph 1:13 were sealed with the P Holy Spirit,
Tit 1:2 God, who never lies, P ages ago

Heb 9:15 called may receive the P eternal inheritance, since a
10:23 wavering, for he who P is faithful;
10:36 the will of God and receive what is P
11:11 age, since she considered him faithful who had P
11:13 having received what was P, but having seen it
11:39 not receive what was P,
12:26 but now he has P, "Yet once more I
Jas 1:11 life which God has P to those who love
2:5 kingdom which he has P to those who love
1Jn 2:25 is what he has P us, eternal life.

PROMISES (19)

Josh 21:45 of all the good P which the LORD had
Ps 12:6 The P of the LORD are promises that are
12:6 of the LORD are P that are pure, silver
77:8 Are his P at an end for all time?
Wis 12:21 thou gavest oaths and covenants full of good P
Sir 20:22 may for shame make P to a friend, and
1Mac 10:15 heard of all the P which Demetrius had sent
Rom 9:4 the worship, and the P;
15:8 order to confirm the P given to the patriarchs,
2Cor 1:20 For all the P of God find their Yes
7:1 Since we have these P, beloved, let us cleanse
Gal 3:16 Now the P were made to Abraham and to
3:21 law then against the P of God?
Heb 6:12 those who through faith and patience inherit the P
7:6 from Abraham and blessed him who had the P
8:6 is better, since it is enacted on better P
11:17 who had received the P was ready to offer
11:33 enforced justice, received P, stopped the mouths of
2Pet 1:4 precious and very great P, that through these you

PROMISING (7)

2Kgs 19:10 rely deceive you by P that Jerusalem will not
Jud 8:11 between God and you, P to surrender the city
Is 37:10 rely deceive you by P that Jerusalem will not
2Mac 4:8 the high-priesthood by corruption, P the king at an
8:11 buy Jewish slaves and P to hand over ninety
11:14 everything on just terms, P that he would persuade
12:11 them pledges of friendship, P to give him cattle

PROMOTE (5)

Job 30:13 up my path, they P my calamity; no one
2Mac 11:19 the future to help P your welfare.
1Cor 7:35 upon you, but to P good order and to
1Tim 1:4 endless genealogies which P speculations rather
Philem 1:6 of your faith may P the knowledge of all

PROMOTED (2)

Esth 3:1 these things King Ahasuerus P Haman the Agagite,
Dan 3:98 Then the king P Shadrach, Meshach, and Abednego

PROMOTING

Col 2:23 appearance of wisdom in P rigor of devotion and

PROMOTIONS

Esth 5:11 his sons, all the P with which the king

PROMPTED (2)

Mt 14:8 P by her mother, she said, "Give me the
Acts 19:33 Some of the crowd P Alexander, whom the Jews

PROMPTLY (4)

Sir 18:21 from paying a vow P, and do not wait
29:2 his need; and in turn, repay your neighbor P
2Mac 8:9 And Ptolemy P appointed Nicanor the son of
11:36 them, send some one P, so that we may

PROMPTS

2Kgs 12:4 which a man's heart P him to bring into

PRONOUNCE (31)

Gen 48:20 "By you Israel will P blessings, saying, 'God make
Lev 13:3 examined him he shall P him unclean.
13:6 then the priest shall P him clean; it is
13:8 then the priest shall P him unclean; it is
13:11 and the priest shall P him unclean; he shall
13:13 his body, he shall P him clean of the
13:15 the raw flesh, and P him unclean; raw flesh
13:17 then the priest shall P the diseased person clean;
13:20 then the priest shall P him unclean; it is
13:22 then the priest shall P him unclean; it is
13:23 and the priest shall P him clean.
13:25 and the priest shall P him unclean; it is
13:27 then the priest shall P him unclean; it is
13:28 and the priest shall P him clean; for it
13:30 then the priest shall P him unclean; it is
13:34 then the priest shall P him clean; and he
13:37 and the priest shall P him clean.
13:44 unclean; the priest must P him unclean; his disease
14:7 leprosy; then he shall P him clean, and shall
14:48 then the priest shall P the house clean, for
Deut 17:11 the decision which they P to you, you shall
Judg 12:6 for he could not P it right; then they
1Kgs 7:7 where he was to P judgment, even the Hall
1Chr 23:13 minister to him and P blessings in his name
Wis 9:3 and righteousness, and P judgment in uprightness of
Sir 50:20 sons of Israel, to P the blessing of the
Mt 7:2 with the judgment you P you will be judged,
Acts 19:13 Jewish exorcists undertook to P the name of the
1Cor 4:5 Therefore do not P judgment before the time, before
2Pet 2:11 and power, do not P a reviling judgment upon
Jude 1:9 did not presume to P a reviling judgment upon

PRONOUNCED (13)

Neh 6:12 him, but he had P the prophecy against me
Jud 8:11 have even sworn and P this oath between God
Jer 11:17 who planted you, has P evil against you, because
16:10 'Why has the LORD P all this great evil
19:15 evil that I have P against it, because they
26:13 evil which he has P against you.
26:19 evil which he had P against them?
35:17 evil that I have P against them; because I
36:7 that the LORD has P against this people."
36:31 evil that I have P against them, but they
40:2 "The LORD your God P this evil against this
Rom 4:9 Is this blessing P only upon the circumcised, or
1Cor 5:3 present, I have already P judgment

PRONOUNCES

Rom 4:6 So also David P a blessing upon the man

PRONOUNCING

Dan 13:53 in the past, P unjust judgments, condemning the

PROOF (9)

Ex 17:2 Why do you put the LORD to the P
17:7 the LORD to the P by saying, "Is the
Num 14:22 put me to the P these ten times and
Ps 95:9 put me to the P, though they had seen
Mt 8:4 Moses commanded, for a P to the people."
Mk 1:44 Moses commanded, for a P to the people."
Lk 5:14 Moses commanded, for a P to the people."
2Cor 8:24 So give P, before the churches, of your love
13:3 since you desire P that Christ is speaking

PROOFS (2)

Is 41:21 the LORD; bring your P, says the King of
Acts 1:3 his passion by many P, appearing to them during

PROPER (18)

Lev 23:37 offerings, each on its P day;
2Chr 24:13 of God to its P condition and strengthened it.
Eccl 10:17 princes feast at the P time, for strength, and
Sir 10:22 man, nor is it P to honor a sinful
20:19 tell it at its P time.
41:23 Then you will show P shame, and will find
Is 28:25 and barley in its P place, and spelt as
1Mac 12:11 it is right and P to remember brethren.
2Mac 6:21 of his own providing, P for him to use,
8:33 so these received the P recompense for their impiety.
14:22 enemy; they held the P conference.
Mt 24:45 their food at the P time?
Lk 12:42 of food at the P time?
1Cor 11:13 for yourselves; is it P for a woman to
1Tim 2:6 was borne at the P time.
6:15 made manifest at the P time by the blessed
Tit 1:3 ago and at the P time manifested in his
Jude 1:6 position but left their P dwelling have been kept

PROPERLY (3)

Tob 14:10 Bury me P, and your mother with me.
1Cor 7:36 he is not behaving P toward his betrothed, if
Eph 4:16 each part is working P, makes bodily growth and

PROPERTY (50)

Gen 23:4 among you; give me P among you for a
31:16 All the P which God has taken away from
34:10 in it, and get P in it."
34:23 not their cattle, their P and all their beasts
36:6 beasts, and all his P which he had acquired
Ex 22:11 hand to his neighbor's P; and the owner shall

29:2 king of Egypt, and P against him and against
30:2 me: "Son of man, P, and say, Thus says
34:2 me: "Son of man, P against the shepherds of
34:2 the shepherds of Israel, P, and say to them,
35:2 against Mount Seir, and P against it,
36:1 you, son of man, P to the mountains of
36:3 become our possession,' therefore P, and say, Thus
36:6 Therefore P concerning the land of Israel, and say
37:4 he said to me, P to these bones, and
37:9 he said to me, P to the breath, prophesy,
37:9 "Prophesy to the breath, P, son of man, and
37:12 clean cut off.' Therefore P, and say to them,
38:2 Meshech and Tubal, and P against him
38:14 "Therefore, son of man, P, and say to Gog,
39:1 you, son of man, P against Gog, and say,
Joel 2:28 and your daughters shall P, your old men shall
Amos 2:12 saying, 'You shall not P
3:8 The Lord GOD has spoken; who can but P
7:12 eat bread there, and P there;
7:13 there; but never again P at Bethel, for it
7:15 said to me, 'Go, P to my people Israel.'
7:16 You say, 'Do not P against Israel, and do
Mt 7:22 Lord, did we not P in your name, and
15:7 Well did Isaiah P of you, when he said:
26:68 some slapped him, saying, P to us, you Christ!
Mk 7:6 them, "Well did Isaiah P of you hypocrites, as
14:65 face, and to strike him, saying to him, P
Lk 22:62 him; they also blindfolded him and asked him, P
Acts 2:17 and your daughters shall P, and your young men
2:18 will pour out my Spirit; and they shall P
1Cor 14:1 desire the spiritual gifts, especially that you may P
14:5 to speak in tongues, but even more to P
14:24 But if all P, and an unbeliever or outsider
14:31 For you can all P one by one, so
14:39 brethren, earnestly desire to P, and do not forbid
Rev 10:11 told, "You must again P about many peoples and
11:3 two witnesses power to P for one thousand two

PROPHESYING (23)

Num 11:27 "Eldad and Medad are P in the camp."
1Sam 10:5 with harp, tambourine, flute, and lyre before them, P
10:13 When he had finished P, he came to the
19:20 company of the prophets P, and Samuel standing as
1Kgs 22:10 all the prophets were P before them.
2Chr 18:9 all the prophets were P before them.
Ezra 6:14 and prospered, through the P of Haggai the prophet
Sir 46:1 war, and was the successor of Moses in P
Jer 14:14 me: "The prophets are P lies in my name;
14:14 They are P to you a lying vision, worthless
20:1 the LORD, heard Jeremiah P these things.
27:10 lie which they are P to you, with the
27:14 lie which they are P to you.
27:15 LORD, but they are P falsely in my name,
27:15 the prophets who are P to you."
27:16 your prophets who are P to you, saying, 'Behold,
27:16 lie which they are P to you.
29:9 lie which they are P to you in my
29:21 of Ma-aseiah, who are P a lie to you
29:27 of Anathoth who is P to you?
Ezek 11:13 pass, while I was P, that Pelatiah the son
1Thes 5:20 Spirit, do not despise P,
Rev 11:6 the days of their P, and they have power

PROPHET (252)

Gen 20:7 for he is a P, and he will pray
Ex 7:1 Pharaoh; and Aaron your brother shall be your P
Num 12:6 If there is a P among you, I the
Deut 13:1 "If a P arises among you, or a dreamer
13:3 the words of that P or to that dreamer
13:5 But that P or that dreamer of dreams shall
18:15 up for you a P like me from among
18:18 up for them a P like you from among
18:20 But the P who presumes to speak a word
18:20 other gods, that same P shall die.'
18:22 spoken?— when a P speaks in the name
18:22 has not spoken; the P has spoken it presumptuously,
34:10 has not arisen a P since in Israel like
Judg 6:8 the LORD sent a P to the people of
1Sam 3:20 was established as a P of the LORD.
9:9 is now called a P was formerly called a
22:5 Then the P Gad said to David, "Do not
2Sam 7:2 said to Nathan the P, "See now, I dwell
12:25 message by Nathan the P; so he called his
24:11 LORD came to the P Gad, David's seer, saying,
1Kgs 1:8 Jehoiada, and Nathan the P, and Shimei, and Rei,
1:10 not invite Nathan the P or Benaiah or the
1:22 the king, Nathan the P came in.
1:23 they told the king, "Here is Nathan the P
1:32 the priest, Nathan the P, and Benaiah the son
1:34 priest and Nathan the P there anoint him king
1:38 the priest, Nathan the P, and Benaiah the son
1:44 the priest, Nathan the P, and Benaiah the son
1:45 priest and Nathan the P have anointed him king
11:29 out of Jerusalem, the P Ahijah the Shilonite found
13:11 there dwelt an old P in Bethel.
13:18 "I also am a P as you are, and
13:20 LORD came to the P who had brought him
13:23 the ass for the P whom he had brought
13:25 city where the old P dwelt.
13:26 And when the P who had brought him back
13:29 And the P took up the body of the
14:2 Shiloh; behold, Ahijah the P is there, who said
14:18 which he spoke by his servant Ahijah the P
16:7 LORD came by the P Jehu the son of
16:12 Baasha by Jehu the P,
18:22 only, am left a P of the LORD; but
18:36 the oblation, Elijah the P came near and said,
19:16 shall anoint to be P in your place.
20:13 And behold, a P came near to Ahab king
20:22 Then the P came near to the king of
20:38 So the P departed, and waited for the king
22:7 there not here another P of the LORD of
2Kgs 3:11 said, "Is there no P of the LORD here,
5:3 lord were with the P who is in Samaria!
5:8 that there is a P in Israel."
5:13 "My father, if the P had commanded you to
6:12 king; but Elisha, the P who is in Israel,
9:1 Then Elisha the P called one of the sons
9:4 the young man, the P, went to Ramoth-gilead.
14:25 son of Amittai, the P, who was from Gath-hepher.
17:13 and Judah by every P and every seer, saying,
19:2 with sackcloth, to the P Isaiah the son of
20:1 And Isaiah the P the son of Amoz came
20:11 And Isaiah the P cried to the LORD; and
20:14 Then Isaiah the P came to King Hezekiah, and
23:18 the bones of the P who came out of
1Chr 17:1 said to Nathan the P, "Behold, I dwell in
29:29 Chronicles of Nathan the P, and in the Chronicles
2Chr 9:29 history of Nathan the P, and in the prophecy
12:5 Then Shemaiah the P came to Rehoboam and to
12:15 chronicles of Shemaiah the P and of Iddo the
13:22 the story of the P Iddo.
18:6 there not here another P of the LORD of
21:12 him from Elijah the P, saying, "Thus says the
25:15 sent to him a P, who said to him,
25:16 So the P stopped, but said, "I know that
26:22 to last, Isaiah the P the son of Amoz
28:9 But a P of the LORD was there, whose
29:25 and of Nathan the P; for the commandment was
32:20 king and Isaiah the P, the son of Amoz,
32:32 vision of Isaiah the P the son of Amoz,
35:18 days of Samuel the P; none of the kings
36:12 himself before Jeremiah the P, who spoke from the
Ezra 6:14 prophesying of Haggai the P and Zechariah the son
Tob 14:4 believe what Jonah the P said about Nineveh, that
14:8 Nineveh, because what the P Jonah said will surely
Ps 74:9 is no longer any P, and there is none
Wis 11:1 their works by the hand of a holy P
Sir 46:13 by his Lord, a P of the Lord, established
46:15 proved to be a P, and by his words
48:1 Then the P Elijah arose like a fire, and
48:22 father, which Isaiah the P commanded, who was
49:7 in the womb as P, to pluck up and
Is 3:2 the judge and the P, the diviner and the
9:15 the head, and the P who teaches lies is
28:7 the priest and the P reel with strong drink,
37:2 with sackcloth, to the P Isaiah the son of
38:1 And Isaiah the P the son of Amoz came
39:3 Then Isaiah the P came to King Hezekiah, and
Jer 1:5 I appointed you a P to the nations."
6:13 unjust gain; and from P to priest, every one
8:10 for unjust gain; from P to priest every one
14:18 For both P and priest ply their trade through
18:18 from the wise, nor the word from the P
20:2 Pashhur beat Jeremiah the P, and put him in
23:11 "Both P and priest are ungodly; even in my
23:28 Let the P who has a dream tell the
23:33 this people, or a P, or a priest asks
23:34 And as for the P, priest, or one of
23:37 shall say to the P, 'What has the LORD
25:2 Babylon), which Jeremiah the P spoke to all the
28:1 son of Azzur, the P from Gibeon, spoke to

P

28:5 Then the P Jeremiah spoke to Hananiah the prophet
28:5 spoke to Hananiah the P in the presence of
28:6 the LORD; and the P Jeremiah said, "Amen!
28:9 As for the P who prophesies peace, when the
28:9 the word of that P comes to pass, then
28:9 known that the LORD has truly sent the P
28:10 Then the P Hananiah took the yoke-bars from the
28:10 neck of Jeremiah the P, and broke them.
28:11 But Jeremiah the P went his way.
28:12 after the P Hananiah had broken the yoke-bars
28:12 neck of Jeremiah the P, the word of the
28:15 And Jeremiah the P said to the prophet Hananiah,
28:15 prophet said to the P Hananiah, "Listen, Hananiah,
28:17 the seventh month, the P Hananiah died.
29:1 letter which Jeremiah the P sent from Jerusalem to
29:29 this letter in the hearing of Jeremiah the P
32:2 Jerusalem, and Jeremiah the P was shut up in
34:6 Then Jeremiah the P spoke all these words to
36:8 all that Jeremiah the P ordered him about reading
36:26 secretary and Jeremiah the P, but the LORD hid
37:2 the LORD which he spoke through Jeremiah the P
37:3 Ma-aseiah, to Jeremiah the P, saying, "Pray for us
37:6 came to Jeremiah the P:
37:13 Hananiah, seized Jeremiah the P, saying, "You are
38:9 did to Jeremiah the P by casting him into
38:10 and lift Jeremiah the P out of the cistern
38:14 sent for Jeremiah the P and received him at
42:2 said to Jeremiah the P, "Let our supplication come
42:4 Jeremiah the P said to them, "I have heard
43:6 Shaphan; also Jeremiah the P and Baruch the son
45:1 word that Jeremiah the P spoke to Baruch the
46:1 came to Jeremiah the P concerning the nations.
46:13 spoke to Jeremiah the P about the coming of
47:1 came to Jeremiah the P concerning the Philistines,
49:34 came to Jeremiah the P concerning Elam, in the
50:1 Chaldeans, by Jeremiah the P:
51:59 word which Jeremiah the P commanded Seraiah the
Lam 2:20 Should priest and P be slain in the sanctuary
Ezek 2:5 there has been a P among them.
7:26 a vision from the P, but the law perishes
14:4 yet comes to the P, I the LORD will
14:7 yet comes to a P to inquire for himself
14:9 And if the P be deceived and speak a
14:9 LORD, have deceived that P, and I will stretch
14:10 the punishment of the P and the punishment of
33:33 will know that a P has been among them."
Dan 3:38 is no prince, or P, or leader, no burnt
9:2 LORD to Jeremiah the P, must pass before the
9:24 seal both vision and P, and to anoint a
14:33 Now the P Habakkuk was in Judea.
Hos 4:5 stumble by day, the P also shall stumble with
9:7 The P is a fool, the man of the
9:8 The P is the watchman of Ephraim, the people
12:13 herded sheep.) By a P the LORD brought Israel
12:13 Egypt, and by a P he was preserved.
Amos 7:14 Amaziah, "I am no P, nor a prophet's son;
7:14 no prophet, nor a P's son; but I am
Hab 1:1 God which Habakkuk the P saw.
3:1 prayer of Habakkuk the P, according to Shigionoth.
Hag 1:1 came by Haggai the P to Zerubbabel the son
1:3 came by Haggai the P,
1:12 words of Haggai the P, as the LORD their
2:1 came by Haggai the P,
2:10 came by Haggai the P,
Zech 1:1 son of Iddo, the P, saying,
1:7 son of Iddo, the P; and Zechariah said,
13:3 again appears as a P, his father and mother
13:4 On that day every P will be ashamed of
13:5 say, 'I am no P, I am a tiller
Mal 4:5 send you Elijah the P before the great and
1Mac 4:46 there should come a P to tell what to
14:41 ever, until a trustworthy P should arise,
2Mac 2:1 records that Jeremiah the P ordered those who
2:2 told, and that the P after giving them the
2:4 the writing that the P, having received an oracle,
15:14 holy city, Jeremiah, the P of God."
Mt 1:22 had spoken by the P:
2:5 is written by the P:
2:15 had spoken by the P, "Out of Egypt have
2:17 was spoken by the P Jeremiah:
3:3 spoken of by the P Isaiah when he said,
4:14 was spoken by the P Isaiah might be fulfilled:
8:17 was spoken by the P Isaiah, "He took our
10:41 He who receives a P because he is a
10:41 because he is a P shall receive a prophet's
10:41 prophet shall receive a P's reward, and he who
11:9 To see a P
11:9 Yes, I tell you, and more than a P
12:17 was spoken by the P Isaiah:
12:39 the sign of the P Jonah.
13:35 was spoken by the P: "I will open my
13:57 said to them, "A P is not without honor
14:5 people, because they held him to be a P
21:4 was spoken by the P, saying,
21:11 said, "This is the P Jesus from Nazareth of
21:26 multitude; for all hold that John was a P
21:46 multitudes, because they held him to be a P
24:15 spoken of by the P Daniel, standing in the
27:9 been spoken by the P Jeremiah, saying, "And they
Mk 1:2 written in Isaiah the P, "Behold, I send my
6:4 said to them, "A P is not without honor,
6:15 said, "It is a P, like one of the
11:31 for all held that John was a real P
Lk 1:76 will be called the P of the Most High;
3:4 words of Isaiah the P, "The voice of one
4:17 the book of the P Isaiah.
4:24 say to you, no P is acceptable in his
4:27 the time of the P Elisha; and none of
7:16 God, saying, "A great P has arisen among us!"
7:26 A P
7:26 Yes, I tell you, and more than a P
7:39 this man were a P, he would have known
13:33 cannot be that a P should perish away from
20:6 for they are convinced that John was a P
24:19 Nazareth, who was a P mighty in deed and
Jn 1:21 "Are you the P
1:23 the Lord,' as the P Isaiah said."
1:25 are neither the Christ, nor Elijah, nor the P
4:19 him, "Sir, I perceive that you are a P
4:44 himself testified that a P has no honor in
6:14 "This is indeed the P who is to come
7:40 of the people said, "This is really the P
7:52 will see that no P is to rise from
9:17 He said, "He is a P
12:38 word spoken by the P Isaiah might be fulfilled:
Acts 2:16 was spoken by the P Joel:
2:30 Being therefore a P, and knowing that God had
3:22 up for you a P from your brethren as
3:23 not listen to that P shall be destroyed from
7:37 up for you a P from your brethren as
7:48 with hands; as the P says,
8:28 he was reading the P Isaiah.
8:30 him reading Isaiah the P, and asked, "Do you
8:34 whom, pray, does the P say this, about himself
13:6 magician, a Jewish false P, named Bar-Jesus.
13:20 that he gave them judges until Samuel the P
21:10 for some days, a P named Agabus came down
28:25 fathers through Isaiah the P:
1Cor 14:37 that he is a P, or spiritual, he should
Tit 1:11 One of themselves, a P of their own, said,
2Pet 2:16 voice and restrained the P's madness.
Rev 16:13 mouth of the false P, three foul spirits like
19:20 with it the false P who in its presence
20:10 beast and the false P were, and they will

PROPHETESS (8)

Ex 15:20 Then Miriam, the P, the sister of Aaron, took
Judg 4:4 Now Deborah, a P, the wife of Lappidoth, was
2Kgs 22:14 went to Huldah the P, the wife of Shallum
2Chr 34:22 went to Huldah the P, the wife of Shallum
Neh 6:14 did, and also the P No-adiah and the rest
Is 8:3 I went to the P, and she conceived and
Lk 2:36 And there was a P, Anna, the daughter of
Rev 2:20 who calls herself a P and is teaching and

PROPHETIC (5)

Rom 16:25 disclosed and through the P writings is made known
1Cor 13:2 And if I have P powers, and understand all
1Tim 1:18 in accordance with the P utterances which pointed
4:14 was given you by P utterance when the council
2Pet 1:19 And we have the P word made more sure.

PROPHETS (248)

Num 11:29 the LORD's people were P, that the LORD would
1Sam 10:5 meet a band of P coming down from the
10:10 behold, a band of P met him; and the
10:11 he prophesied with the P, the people said to
10:11 Is Saul also among the P
10:12 became a proverb, "Is Saul also among the P
19:20 the company of the P prophesying, and Samuel
19:24 it is said, "Is Saul also among the P
28:6 either by dreams, or by Urim, or by P

28:15 no more, either by P or by dreams; therefore
1Kgs 18:4 Jezebel cut off the P of the LORD, Obadiah
18:4 Obadiah took a hundred P and hid them by
18:13 when Jezebel killed the P of the LORD, how
18:13 men of the LORD's P by fifties in a
18:19 four hundred and fifty P of Baal and the
18:19 and the four hundred P of Asherah, who eat
18:20 Israel, and gathered the P together at Mount
18:22 the LORD; but Baal's P are four hundred and
18:25 Elijah said to the P of Baal, "Choose for
18:40 to them, "Seize the P of Baal; let not
19:1 had slain all the P with the sword.
19:10 altars, and slain thy P with the sword; and
19:14 altars, and slain thy P with the sword; and
20:35 the sons of the P said to his fellow
20:41 of Israel recognized him as one of the P
22:6 of Israel gathered the P together, about four hundred
22:10 Samaria; and all the P were prophesying before
22:12 And all the P prophesied so, and said, "Go
22:13 the words of the P with one accord are
22:22 mouth of all his P And he said, 'You
22:23 of all these your P; the LORD has spoken
2Kgs 2:3 the sons of the P who were in Bethel
2:5 The sons of the P who were at Jericho
2:7 the sons of the P also went, and stood
2:15 the sons of the P who were at Jericho
3:13 Go to the P of your father and the
3:13 your father and the P of your mother." But
4:1 the sons of the P cried to Elisha, "Your
4:38 the sons of the P were sitting before him,
4:38 and boil pottage for the sons of the P
5:22 the sons of the P; pray, give them a
6:1 the sons of the P said to Elisha, "See,
9:1 the sons of the P and said to him,
9:7 of my servants the P, and the blood of
10:19 to me all the P of Baal, all his
17:13 I sent to you by my servants the P
17:23 he had spoken by all his servants the P
21:10 by his servants the P,
23:2 the priests and the P, all the people, both
24:2 LORD which he spoke by his servants the P
1Chr 16:22 anointed ones, do my P no harm!"
2Chr 18:5 of Israel gathered the P together, four hundred men,
18:9 Samaria; and all the P were prophesying before
18:11 And all the P prophesied so, and said, "Go
18:12 the words of the P with one accord are
18:21 mouth of all his P And he said, 'You
18:22 mouth of these your P; the LORD has spoken
20:20 be established; believe his P, and you will succeed."
24:19 Yet he sent P among them to bring them
29:25 commandment was from the LORD through his P
36:16 and scoffing at his P, till the wrath of
Ezra 5:1 Now the P, Haggai and Zechariah the son of
5:2 with them were the P of God, helping them.
9:11 by thy servants the P, saying, 'The land which
Neh 6:7 have also set up P to proclaim concerning you
6:14 the rest of the P who wanted to make
9:26 back and killed thy P, who had warned them
9:30 thy Spirit through thy P; yet they would not
9:32 princes, our priests, our P, our fathers, and all
Tob 4:12 tribe; for we are the sons of the P
14:5 ever, just as the P said of it.
Ps 105:15 anointed ones, do my P no harm!"
Wis 7:27 friends of God, and P;
Sir 36:16 thee, and let thy P be found trustworthy.
48:8 to inflict retribution, and P to succeed you.
49:10 bones of the twelve P revive from where they
Is 29:10 closed your eyes, the P, and covered your heads,
30:10 not"; and to the P, "Prophesy not to us
Jer 2:8 transgressed against me; the P prophesied by Baal,
2:26 their priests, and their P,
2:30 own sword devoured your P like a ravening lion.
4:9 be appalled and the P astounded."
5:13 The P will become wind; the word is not
5:31 in the land: the P prophesy falsely, and the
7:25 all my servants the P to them, day after
8:1 the bones of the P, and the bones of
13:13 throne, the priests, the P, and all the inhabitants
14:13 Lord GOD, behold, the P say to them, 'You
14:14 said to me: "The P are prophesying lies in
14:15 the LORD concerning the P who prophesy in my
14:15 sword and famine those P shall be consumed.
23:9 Concerning the P: My heart is broken within me,
23:13 In the P of Samaria I saw an unsavory
23:14 But in the P of Jerusalem I have seen
23:15 of hosts concerning the P: "Behold, I will feed
23:15 drink; for from the P of Jerusalem ungodliness has
23:16 the words of the P who prophesy to you,
23:21 did not send the P, yet they ran; I
23:25 have heard what the P have said who prophesy
23:26 the heart of the P who prophesy lies, and
23:30 I am against the P, says the LORD, who
23:31 I am against the P, says the LORD, who
25:4 all his servants the P,
26:5 of my servants the P whom I send to
26:7 The priests and the P and all the people
26:8 the priests and the P and all the people
26:11 the priests and the P said to the princes
26:16 the priests and the P, "This man does not
27:9 not listen to your P, your diviners, your dreamers,
27:14 the words of the P who are saying to
27:15 perish, you and the P who are prophesying to
27:16 the words of your P who are prophesying to
27:18 If they are P, and if the word of
28:8 The P who preceded you and me from ancient
29:1 to the priests, the P, and all the people,
29:8 Do not let your P and your diviners who
29:15 LORD has raised up P for us in Babylon,--
29:19 by my servants the P, but you would not
32:32 their priests and their P, the men of Judah
35:15 all my servants the P, sending them persistently,
37:19 Where are your P who prophesied to you, saying,
44:4 all my servants the P, saying, Oh, do not
Lam 2:9 no more, and her P obtain no vision from
2:14 Your P have seen for you false and deceptive
4:13 the sins of her P and the iniquities of
Bar 1:16 our priests and our P and our fathers,
1:21 the words of the P whom he sent to
2:20 by thy servants the P, saying:
2:24 by thy servants the P, that the bones of
Ezek 13:2 man, prophesy against the P of Israel, prophesy and
13:3 Woe to the foolish P who follow their own
13:4 Your P have been like foxes among ruins, O
13:9 will be against the P who see delusive visions
13:10 build a wall, these P daub it with whitewash;
13:16 who daubed it, the P of Israel who prophesied
22:28 And her P have daubed for them with whitewash,
38:17 by my servants the P of Israel, who in
Dan 9:6 to thy servants the P, who spoke in thy
9:10 he set before us by his servants the P
Hos 6:5 hewn them by the P, I have slain them
12:10 I spoke to the P; it was I who
12:10 visions, and through the P gave parables.
Amos 2:11 of your sons for P, and some of your
2:12 wine, and commanded the P, saying, 'You shall not
3:7 without revealing his secret to his servants the P
Mic 3:5 the LORD concerning the P who lead my people
3:6 go down upon the P, and the day shall
3:11 teach for hire, its P divine for money; yet
Zeph 3:4 Her P are wanton, faithless men; her priests profane
Zech 1:4 to whom the former P cried out, 'Thus says
1:5 And the P, do they live for ever?
1:6 commanded my servants the P, did they not overtake
7:3 of hosts and the P, "Should I mourn and
7:7 words which the LORD proclaimed by the former P
7:12 had sent by his Spirit through the former P
8:9 the mouth of the P, since the day that
13:2 from the land the P and the unclean spirit.
1Mac 9:27 since the time that P ceased to appear among
9:54 He tore down the work of the P
2Mac 2:13 about the kings and P, and the writings of
15:9 the law and the P, and reminding them also
Mt 2:23 was spoken by the P might be fulfilled, "He
5:12 so men persecuted the P who were before you.
5:17 the law and the P; I have come not
7:12 them; for this is the law and the P
7:15 "Beware of false P, who come to you in
11:13 For all the P and the law prophesied until
13:17 say to you, many P and righteous men longed
16:14 Elijah, and others Jeremiah or one of the P
22:40 two commandments depend all the law and the P
23:28 the tombs of the P and adorn the monuments
23:29 the blood of the P
23:30 you are sons of those who murdered the P
23:33 Therefore I send you P and wise men and
23:36 Jerusalem, killing the P and stoning those who
24:11 And many false P will arise and lead many
24:24 false Christs and false P will arise and show
26:56 the scriptures of the P might be fulfilled." Then
Mk 6:15 like one of the P of old."
8:28 others say, Elijah; and others one of the P
13:22 False Christs and false P will arise and show

Lk 1:70 mouth of his holy P from of old,
6:23 heaven; for so their fathers did to the P
6:26 for so their fathers did to the false P
9:8 one of the old P had risen.
9:19 one of the old P has risen."
10:24 tell you that many P and kings desired to
11:47 the tombs of the P whom your fathers killed.
11:49 'I will send them P and apostles, some of
11:50 blood of all the P, shed from the foundation
13:28 Jacob and all the P in the kingdom of
13:34 Jerusalem, Jerusalem, killing the P and stoning
16:16 "The law and the P were until John; since
16:29 have Moses and the P; let them hear them.'
16:31 hear Moses and the P, neither will they be
18:31 of man by the P will be accomplished.
24:25 believe all that the P have spoken!
24:27 Moses and all the P, he interpreted to them
24:44 of Moses and the P and the psalms must
Jn 1:45 law and also the P wrote, Jesus of Nazareth,
6:45 is written in the P, 'And they shall all
8:52 died, as did the P; and you say, 'If
8:53 And the P died!
Acts 3:18 mouth of all the P, that his Christ should
3:21 mouth of his holy P from of old.
3:24 people.' And all the P who have spoken, from
3:25 the sons of the P and of the covenant
7:42 the book of the P: 'Did you offer to
7:52 Which of the P did not your fathers persecute?
10:43 To him all the P bear witness that every
11:27 Now in these days P came down from Jerusalem
13:1 at Antioch there were P and teachers, Barnabas,
13:15 the law and the P, the rulers of the
13:27 the utterances of the P which are read every
13:40 is said in the P:
15:15 the words of the P agree, as it is
15:32 Silas, who were themselves P, exhorted the brethren
24:13 or written in the P,
26:22 nothing but what the P and Moses said would
26:27 King Agrippa, do you believe the P
28:23 from the law of Moses and from the P
Rom 1:2 promised beforehand through his P in the holy
3:21 the law and the P bear witness to it,
11:3 they have killed thy P, they have demolished thy
1Cor 12:28 church first apostles, second P, third teachers, then
12:29 Are all P
14:29 Let two or three P speak, and let the
14:32 and the spirits of P are subject to prophets.
14:32 and the spirits of prophets are subject to P
Eph 2:20 of the apostles and P, Christ Jesus himself being
3:5 his holy apostles and P by the Spirit;
4:11 should be apostles, some P, some evangelists, some
1Thes 2:15 Lord Jesus and the P, and drove us out,
Heb 1:1 our fathers by the P,
11:32 and Samuel and the P --
Jas 5:10 patience, brethren, take the P who spoke in the
1Pet 1:10 The P who prophesied of the grace that was
2Pet 2:1 But false P also arose among the people, just
3:2 predictions of the holy P and the commandment of
1Jn 4:1 God; for many false P have gone out into
Rev 10:7 to his servants the P, should be fulfilled.
11:10 presents, because these two P had been a torment
11:18 rewarding thy servants, the P and saints, and those
16:6 blood of saints and P, and thou hast given
18:20 saints and apostles and P, for God has given
18:24 found the blood of P and of saints, and
22:6 the spirits of the P, has sent his angel
22:9 and your brethren the P, and with those who

PROPITIATED (2)

Sir 16:7 He was not P for the ancient giants who
34:19 and he is not P for sins by a

PROPITIATION

Wis 18:21 his ministry, prayer and P by incense; he withstood

PROPORTION (8)

Num 35:8 take few; each, in P to the inheritance which
Deut 25:2 number of stripes in P to his offense.
Tob 4:8 gift from them in P; if few, do not
Sir 28:10 In P to the fuel for the fire, so
28:10 the burning, and in P to the obstinacy of
28:10 be the burning; in P to the strength of
28:10 his anger, and in P to his wealth he
Rom 12:6 them: if prophecy, in P to our faith;

PROPOSAL (4)

Gen 41:37 This P seemed good to Pharaoh and to all
Tob 7:9 So he communicated the P to Raguel.
1Mac 1:12 This P pleased them,
8:21 The P pleased them,

PROPOSALS

2Mac 11:36 that we may make P appropriate for you.

PROPOSE (2)

Gen 11:6 and nothing that they P to do will now
2Chr 28:13 in here, for you P to bring upon us

PROPOSED

Esth 1:21 king did as Memucan P;

PROPOUND

Ezek 17:2 me: "Son of man, P a riddle, and speak

PROPPED (2)

1Kgs 22:35 and the king was P up in his chariot
2Chr 18:34 the king of Israel P himself up in his

PROSELYTE (3)

Mt 23:14 to make a single P, and when he becomes
23:14 when he becomes a P, you make him twice
Acts 6:5 Parmenas, and Nicolaus, a P of Antioch.

PROSELYTES

Acts 2:10 Rome, both Jews and P,

PROSPECT

Heb 10:27 sins, but a fearful P of judgment, and a

PROSPER (39)

Gen 24:40 angel with you and P your way; and you
24:42 if now thou wilt P the way which I
39:3 that he did to P in his hands.
39:23 and whatever he did, the LORD made it P
Deut 28:29 and you shall not P in your ways; and
29:9 covenant, that you may P in all that you
Judg 17:13 that the LORD will P me, because I have
Ruth 4:11 May you P in Ephrathah and be renowned in
2Sam 23:5 he not cause to P all my help and
1Kgs 2:3 Moses, that you may P in all that you
1Chr 22:13 Then you will P if you are careful to
2Chr 24:20 commandments of the LORD, so that you cannot P
26:5 as he sought the LORD, God made him P
Neh 2:20 heaven will make us P, and we his servants
Tob 4:6 true, your ways will P through your deeds.
4:19 and that all your paths and plans may P
5:16 dwells in heaven will P your way, and may
10:11 God of heaven will P you, my children, before
Ps 10:5 His ways P at all times; thy judgments are
122:6 "May they P who love you!
Prov 16:20 to the word will P, and happy is he
17:20 crooked mind does not P, and one with a
19:8 loves himself; he who keeps understanding will P
28:13 his transgressions will not P, but he who confesses
Eccl 11:6 not know which will P, this or that, or
Sir 15:10 and the Lord will P it.
Is 48:15 him, and he will P in his way.
52:13 Behold, my servant shall P, he shall be exalted
53:10 of the LORD shall P in his hand;
54:17 fashioned against you shall P, and you shall confute
55:11 which I purpose, and P in the thing for
Jer 2:37 and you will not P by them.
5:28 fatherless, to make it P, and they do not
12:1 Why does the way of the wicked P
Lam 1:5 the head, her enemies P, because the LORD has
Dan 8:25 he shall make deceit P under his hand, and
11:36 He shall P till the indignation is accomplished; for
Mal 3:15 blessed; evildoers not only P but when they put
1Cor 16:2 up, as he may P, so that contributions need

PROSPERED (23)

Gen 24:21 whether the LORD had P his journey or not.
24:56 since the LORD has P my way; let me
2Sam 11:7 how the people fared, and how the war P
2Kgs 18:7 was with him; wherever he went forth, he P
1Chr 29:23 his father; and he P, and all Israel obeyed
2Chr 14:7 So they built and P
31:21 God, he did with all his heart, and P
32:30 And Hezekiah P in all his works.
Ezra 6:14 the Jews built and P, through the prophesying of
Jud 5:9 There they settled, and P, with much gold and

5:17 against their God they P, for the God who
Wis 10:10 knowledge of angels; she P him in his labors,
11:1 Wisdom P their works by the hand of a
Jer 10:21 therefore they have not P, and all their flock
44:17 plenty of food, and P, and saw no evil.
Dan 6:28 So this Daniel P during the reign of Darius
8:12 to the ground, and the horn acted and P
1Mac 2:47 men, and the work P in their hands.
3:6 were confounded; and deliverance P by his hand.
4:55 blessed Heaven, who had P them.
14:36 in his days things P in his hands, so
16:2 day, and things have P in our hands so
Rev 3:17 am rich, I have P, and I need nothing;

PROSPERING (2)
Deut 30:9 again take delight in P you, as he took
Dan 4:4 in my house and P in my palace.

PROSPERITY (44)
Deut 23:6 their peace or their P all your days for
28:11 make you abound in P, in the fruit of
1Sam 2:32 eye on all the P which shall be bestowed
1Kgs 10:7 me; your wisdom and P surpass the report which
Ezra 9:12 seek their peace or P, that you may be
Esth 16:3 their inability to stand P they even undertake to
Job 15:21 in his ears; in P the destroyer will come
20:21 had eaten; therefore his P will not endure.
21:13 spend their days in P, and in peace they
21:16 Behold, is not their P in their hand?
21:23 One dies in full P, being wholly at ease
30:15 the wind, and my P has passed away like
36:11 complete their days in P, and their years in
Ps 25:13 himself shall abide in P, and his children shall
30:6 I said in my P, "I shall never be
37:11 the land, and delight themselves in abundant P
68:6 out the prisoners to P; but the rebellious dwell
72:3 Let the mountains bear P for the people, and
73:3 when I saw the P of the wicked.
106:5 I may see the P of thy chosen ones,
128:5 May you see the P of Jerusalem all the
Prov 8:18 and honor are with me, enduring wealth and P
13:21 Misfortune pursues sinners, but P rewards the
Eccl 7:14 In the day of P be joyful, and in
Sir 6:11 In P he will make himself your equal, and
11:21 I need, and what P could be mine in
11:23 In the day of P, adversity is forgotten, and
11:23 the day of adversity, P is not remembered.
12:8 not be known in P, nor will an enemy
22:21 with him in his P; stand by him in
29:16 sinner will overthrow the P of his surety,
31:11 His P will be established, and the assembly will
44:12 not been forgotten; their P will remain with their
45:26 righteousness, so that their P may not vanish, and
Is 54:13 great shall be the P of your sons.
66:12 "Behold, I will extend P to her like a
Jer 22:21 to you in your P, but you said, 'I
33:6 to them abundance of P and security.
33:9 good and all the P I provide for it.
Hag 2:9 place I will give P, says the LORD of
Zech 1:17 shall again overflow with P, and the LORD will
7:7 was inhabited and in P, with her cities round
2Mac 9:19 greetings and good wishes for their health and P
14:14 the Jews would mean P for themselves.

PROSPEROUS (9)
Lev 25:26 and then himself becomes P and finds sufficient
Deut 30:5 will make you more P and numerous than your
30:9 will make you abundantly P in all the work
Josh 1:8 shall make your way P, and then you shall
Wis 13:18 utterly inexperienced; for a P journey, a thing that
Sir 29:18 many men who were P, and has shaken them
41:1 without distractions, who is P in everything, and who
Ezek 16:49 surfeit of food, and P ease, but did not
34:29 will provide for them P plantations so that they

PROSPERS (5)
Ezra 5:8 goes on diligently and P in their hands.
Ps 1:3 In all that he does, he P
37:7 yourself over him who P in his way, over
Prov 17:8 him who gives it; wherever he turns he P
Sir 12:9 are grieved when he P, and in his adversity

PROSTITUTE (4)
Deut 23:17 shall be no cult P of the daughters of
23:17 there be a cult P of the sons of
1Cor 6:15 of Christ and make them members of a P
6:16 joins himself to a P becomes one body with

PROSTITUTED
Ezek 16:25 your lofty place and P your beauty, offering yourself

PROSTITUTES (5)
1Kgs 14:24 were also male cult P in the land.
15:12 away the male cult P out of the land,
22:46 of the male cult P who remained in the
2Kgs 23:7 of the male cult P which were in the
Hos 4:14 and sacrifice with cult P, and a people without

PROSTRATE (10)
Deut 9:18 Then I lay P before the LORD as before,
9:25 "So I lay P before the LORD for these
Jud 3:2 the Great King, lie P before you.
10:2 from where she lay P and called her maid
Ps 36:12 There the evildoers lie P, they are thrust down,
38:6 utterly bowed down and P; all the day I
Is 49:7 princes, and they shall P themselves; because of the
2Mac 3:29 While he lay P, speechless because of the divine
10:4 done this, they fell P and besought the Lord
13:12 and fasting and lying P for three days without

PROSTRATED (3)
Jud 4:11 children, living at Jerusalem, P themselves before
10:23 her face; and she P herself and made obeisance
2Mac 3:15 The priests P themselves before the altar in their

PROSTRATION
2Mac 3:21 something pitiable in the P of the whole populace

PROTECT (12)
2Sam 18:12 Ittai, 'For my sake P the young man Absalom.'
Ezra 8:22 soldiers and horsemen to P us against the enemy
Jud 5:21 and their God will P them, and we shall
8:15 he has power to P us within any time
Ps 12:7 Do thou, O LORD, P us, guard us ever
20:1 the God of Jacob P you!
59:1 enemies, O my God, P me from those who
91:14 deliver him; I will P him, because he knows
Sir 22:23 not be ashamed to P a friend, and I
Is 31:5 LORD of hosts will P Jerusalem; he will protect
31:5 protect Jerusalem; he will P and deliver it, he
Zech 9:15 LORD of hosts will P them, and they shall

PROTECTED (11)
Jud 13:16 Lord lives, who has P me in the way
Job 11:18 hope; you will be P and take your rest
Ps 83:3 consult together against thy P ones.
Wis 2:20 according to what he says, he will be P
10:1 Wisdom P the first-formed father of the world, when
10:12 She P him from his enemies, and kept him
17:4 chamber that held them P them from fear, but
19:8 raging waves, where those P by thy hand passed
Sir 28:19 the man who is P from it, who has
1Mac 6:38 enemy while being themselves P by the phalanxes.
2Mac 13:17 because the Lord's help P him.

PROTECTING (3)
Prov 18:11 like a high wall P him.
1Mac 3:3 war and waged battles, P the host by his
2Mac 10:30 Surrounding Maccabeus and P him with their own

PROTECTION (16)
Num 14:9 bread for us; their P is removed from them,
Deut 32:38 up and help you, let them be your P
Ezra 9:9 and to give us P in Judea and Jerusalem.
Neh 4:9 a guard as a P against them day and
Eccl 7:12 For the P of wisdom is like the protection
7:12 wisdom is like the P of money; and the
Sir 6:29 for you a strong P, and her collar a
34:16 love him, a mighty P and strong support, a
Is 27:5 lay hold of my P, let them make peace
30:2 take refuge in the P of Pharaoh, and to
30:3 Therefore shall the P of Pharaoh turn to your
Bar 1:12 shall live under the P of Nebuchadnezzar king of
1:12 Babylon, and under the P of Belshazzar his son,
1Mac 11:16 into Arabia to find P there, and King Ptolemy
2Mac 3:40 of Heliodorus and the P of the treasury.
5:9 in hope of finding P because of their kinship.

PROTECTOR (5)
Jud 9:11 upholder of the weak, P of the forlorn, savior
Ps 68:5 of the fatherless and P of widows is God
Sir 51:2 thou hast been my P and helper and hast

P

1Mac 14:47 priests, and to be P of them all.
2Mac 4:2 of the city, the P of his fellow countrymen,

PROTECTS (4)

Jud 9:14 is no other who P the people of Israel
Ps 41:2 of trouble; the LORD P him and keeps him
Jer 31:22 the earth: a woman P a man."
Bar 6:59 of a house that P its contents, than these

PROTEST

1Cor 15:31 I P, brethren, by my pride in you which

PROUD (59)

2Chr 26:16 was strong he grew P, to his destruction.
32:25 benefit done to him, for his heart was P
Esth 13:12 bow down to this P Haman.
14:16 the sign of my P position, which is upon
16:2 their benefactors, the more P do many men become.
Job 22:29 For God abases the P, but he saves the
28:8 The P beasts have not trodden it; the lion
38:11 and here shall your P waves be stayed?
40:11 every one that is P, and abase him.
40:12 every one that is P, and bring him low;
Ps 22:29 him shall all the P of the earth bow
40:4 not turn to the P, to those who go
94:2 earth; render to the P their deserts!
123:4 who are at ease, the contempt of the P
Prov 15:25 the house of the P, but maintains the widow's
16:19 poor than to divide the spoil with the P
21:4 Haughty eyes and a P heart, the lamp of
21:24 the name of the P, haughty man who acts
Eccl 7:8 is better than the P in spirit.
Sir 3:26 The affliction of the P has no healing, for
10:9 can he who is dust and ashes be P
11:28 the mind of a P man, and like a
13:1 whoever associates with a P man will become like
13:19 an abomination to a P man; likewise a poor
21:4 the house of the P will be laid waste.
25:2 a beggar who is P, a rich man who
27:15 The strife of the P leads to bloodshed, and
27:28 abuse issue from the P man, but vengeance lies
31:26 wine tests hearts in the strife of the P
32:12 do not sin through P speech.
32:18 and an insolent and P man will not cower
51:10 time when there is no help against the P
Is 2:12 against all that is P and lofty, against all
16:6 pride of Moab, how P he was; of his
28:1 Woe to the P crown of the drunkards of
28:3 The P crown of the drunkards of Ephraim will
Jer 13:15 give ear; be not P, for the LORD has
48:29 Moab--he is very P--of his loftiness, his
50:31 am against you, O P one, says the Lord
50:32 The P one shall stumble and fall, with none
Ezek 7:24 an end to their P might, and their holy
28:2 "Because your heart is P, and you have said,
28:5 your heart has become P in your wealth--
28:17 Your heart was P because of your beauty; you
30:6 shall fall, and her P might shall come down;
30:18 of Egypt, and her P might shall come to
31:10 and its heart was P of its height,
33:28 a waste; and her P might shall come to
Zech 10:3 make them like his P steed in battle.
Lk 1:51 he has scattered the P in the imagination of
Rom 11:20 So do not become P, but stand in awe.
15:17 have reason to be P of my work for
2Cor 1:14 that you can be P of us as we
5:12 you cause to be P of us, so that
10:5 destroy arguments and every P obstacle to the
Phil 2:16 Christ I may be P that I did not
2Tim 3:2 self, lovers of money, P, arrogant, abusive, disobedient
Jas 4:6 says, "God opposes the P, but gives grace to
1Pet 5:5 for "God opposes the P, but gives grace to

PROUDLY (8)

1Sam 2:3 no more so very P, let not arrogance come
Job 39:13 of the ostrich wave P; but are they the
Ps 56:2 all day long, for many fight against me P
Is 13:3 execute my anger, my P exulting ones.
Jer 50:29 done; for she has P defied the LORD, the
Dan 5:20 so that he dealt P, he was deposed from
Hab 1:8 wolves; their horsemen press P on.
Zeph 3:11 from your midst your P exultant ones, and you

PROVE (27)

Ex 7:9 Pharaoh says to you, P yourselves by working a
16:4 day, that I may P them, whether they will
20:20 God has come to P you, and that the
1Kgs 1:52 Solomon said, "If he P to be a worthy
Ezra 2:59 though they could not P their fathers' houses or
Neh 7:61 but they could not P their fathers' houses nor
Job 9:20 am blameless, he would P me perverse.
24:25 not so, who will P me a liar, and
Ps 26:2 P me, O LORD, and try me; test my
Wis 12:13 to whom thou shouldst P that thou hast not
Sir 31:26 Fire and water P the temper of steel, so
39:34 for all things will P good in their season.
42:10 a husband, lest she P unfaithful, or, though married,
Dan 14:9 But if you P that Bel is eating them,
2Mac 5:4 that the apparition might P to have been a
7:29 fear this butcher, but P worthy of your brothers.
Jn 15:8 much fruit, and so P to be my disciples.
Acts 24:12 Neither can they P to you what they now
25:7 him many serious charges which they could not P
Rom 3:26 sins; it was to P at the present time
12:2 mind, that you may P what is the will
2Cor 8:8 a command, but to P by the earnestness of
9:3 about you may not P vain in this case,
Gal 2:18 tore down, then I P myself a transgressor.
1Tim 3:10 first; then if they P themselves blameless let them
Heb 6:18 impossible that God should P false, we who have
1Pet 4:12 comes upon you to P you, as though something

PROVED (9)

Ex 15:25 ordinance and there he P them,
Sir 9:17 a people's leader is P wise by his words.
46:15 his faithfulness he was P to be a prophet,
Is 43:26 that you may be P right.
Lk 10:36 three, do you think, P neighbor to the man
Rom 7:10 commandment which promised life P to be death to
2Cor 7:11 every point you have P yourselves guiltless in the
7:14 boasting before Titus has P true.
1Thes 1:5 kind of men we P to be among you

PROVENDER (7)

Gen 24:25 have both straw and P enough, and room to
24:32 gave him straw and P for the camels, and
42:27 to give his ass P at the lodging place,
43:24 had given their asses P,
Judg 19:19 We have straw and P for our asses, with
19:21 and gave the asses P; and they washed their
Is 30:24 ground will eat salted P, which has been winnowed

PROVERB (18)

Deut 28:37 become a horror, a P, and a byword, among
1Sam 10:12 Therefore it became a P, "Is Saul also among
24:13 As the P of the ancients says, 'Out of
1Kgs 9:7 Israel will become a P and a byword among
2Chr 7:20 will make it a P and a byword among
Ps 49:4 my ear to a P; I will solve my
Prov 1:6 skill, to understand a P and a figure, the
26:7 hang useless, is a P in the mouth of
26:9 a drunkard is a P in the mouth of
Sir 20:19 A P from a fool's lips will be rejected,
Ezek 12:22 man, what is this P that you have about
12:23 an end to this P, and they shall no
12:23 use it as a P in Israel.' But say
16:44 proverbs will use this P about you, 'Like mother,
18:2 mean by repeating this P concerning the land of
18:3 the Lord GOD, this P shall no more be
Lk 4:23 quote to me this P, 'Physician, heal yourself; what
2Pet 2:22 according to the true P, The dog turns back

PROVERBS (13)

1Kgs 4:32 also uttered three thousand P; and his songs were
Job 13:12 Your maxims are P of ashes, your defenses are
Prov 1:1 The P of Solomon, son of
10:1 The P of Solomon.
25:1 These also are P of Solomon which the men
Eccl 12:9 and studying and arranging P with great care.
Sir 6:35 do not let wise P escape you.
13:25 face, but to devise P requires painful thinking.
18:28 become skilled themselves, and pour forth apt P
38:33 or judgment, and they are not found using P
39:3 the hidden meanings of P and be at home
47:17 For your songs and P and parables, and for
Ezek 16:44 every one who uses P will use this proverb

PROVES (7)

2Sam 22:31 promise of the LORD P true; he is a
Tob 10:4 perished; his long delay P it." Then she began
Ps 18:30 promise of the LORD P true; he is a
Prov 30:5 Every word of God P true; he is a

P

Wis 2:11 for what is weak P itself to be useless.
Mt 13:22 the word, and it P unfruitful.
Mk 4:19 the word, and it P unfruitful.

PROVIDE (40)

Gen 22:8 Abraham said, "God will P himself the lamb for
22:14 place The LORD will P; as it is said
30:30 now when shall I P for my own household
45:11 and there I will P for you, for there
50:21 not fear; I will P for you and your
Lev 25:6 of the land shall P food for you, for
Num 23:1 here seven altars, and P for me here seven
23:29 here seven altars, and P for me here seven
Josh 18:4 P three men from each tribe, and I will
1Sam 16:17 said to his servants, P for me a man
2Sam 19:33 me, and I will P for you with me
Ezra 7:20 you have occasion to P, you may provide it
7:20 to provide, you may P it out of the
Ps 68:10 O God, thou didst P for the needy.
78:20 also give bread, or P meat for his people?"
Prov 27:26 gathered, the lambs will P your clothing, and the
30:25 not strong, yet they P their food in the
Wis 18:3 Therefore thou didst P a flaming pillar of fire
Sir 29:25 play the host and P drink without being thanked,
Jer 33:9 all the prosperity I P for it.
Ezek 34:29 And I will P for them prosperous plantations so
43:25 seven days you shall P daily a goat for
45:17 of Israel: he shall P the sin offerings, cereal
45:22 day the prince shall P for himself and all
45:23 the festival he shall P as a burnt offering
45:24 And he shall P as a cereal offering an
46:7 cereal offering he shall P an ephah with the
46:13 "He shall P a lamb a year old without
46:13 by morning he shall P it.
46:14 And he shall P a cereal offering with it
1Mac 12:4 place, asking them to P for the envoys safe
2Mac 9:16 the sacrifices he would P from his own revenues;
12:43 it to Jerusalem to P for a sin offering.
Lk 10:7 and drinking what they P, for the laborer deserves
12:33 possessions, and give alms; P yourselves with purses
Acts 23:24 Also P mounts for Paul to ride, and bring
1Cor 10:13 the temptation will also P the way of escape,
2Cor 9:8 God is able to P you with every blessing
9:8 of everything and may P in abundance for every
1Tim 5:8 any one does not P for his relatives, and

PROVIDED (32)

Gen 22:14 the mount of the LORD it shall be P
47:12 And Joseph P his father, his brothers, and all
Num 31:5 So there were P, out of the thousands of
Deut 19:9 to your fathers— P you are careful to
1Sam 16:1 Bethlehemite, for I have P for myself a king
2Sam 19:32 old; and he had P the king with food
20:3 house under guard, and P for them, but did
1Kgs 4:7 over all Israel, who P food for the king
8:21 And there I have P a place for the
1Chr 22:3 David also P great stores of iron for nails
22:5 So David P materials in great quantity before his
22:14 great pains I have P for the house of
22:14 of it; timber and stone too I have P
29:2 So I have P for the house of my
29:3 all that I have P for the holy house,
29:16 abundance that we have P for building thee a
2Chr 2:7 in Judah and Jerusalem, whom David my father P
28:15 them, gave them sandals, P them with food and
32:29 He likewise P cities for himself, and flocks and
Neh 13:31 his work; and I P for the wood offering,
Jud 12:2 but I will be P from the things I
Esth 2:9 favor; and he quickly P her with her ointments
Ezek 43:25 ram from the flock, without blemish, shall be P
46:15 the oil shall be P, morning by morning, for
1Mac 14:34 settled Jews there, and P in those cities whatever
2Mac 4:49 hatred of the crime, P magnificently for their
12:3 boats which they had P, as though there were
Lk 8:3 and many others, who P for them out of
Rom 8:17 fellow heirs with Christ, P we suffer with him
11:22 God's kindness to you, P you continue in his
Col 1:23 and irreproachable before him, P that you continue
2Pet 1:11 there will be richly P for you an entrance

PROVIDENCE (2)

Wis 14:3 but it is thy P, O Father, that steers
17:2 shut in under their roofs, exiles from eternal P

PROVIDES (5)

Job 38:41 Who P for the raven its prey, when its
Ps 111:5 He P food for those who fear him; he
Prov 31:15 is yet night and P food for her household
Sir 23:22 leaves her husband and P an heir by a
Ezek 46:12 When the prince P a freewill offering, either a

PROVIDEST

Ps 65:9 full of water; thou P their grain, for so

PROVIDING (5)

Josh 1:13 LORD your God is P you a place of
1Kgs 5:9 meet my wishes by P food for my household."
Ps 144:13 our garners be full, P all manner of store;
Wis 16:20 bread ready to eat, P every pleasure and suited
2Mac 6:21 meat of his own P, proper for him to

PROVINCE (46)

Ezra 2:1 the people of the P who came up out
4:10 the rest of the P Beyond the River, and
4:11 the men of the P Beyond the River, send
4:16 no possession in the P Beyond the River."
4:17 the rest of the P Beyond the River, greeting.
4:20 ruled over the whole P Beyond the River, to
5:3 the governor of the P Beyond the River and
5:6 the governor of the P Beyond the River and
5:6 who were in the P Beyond the River sent
5:8 we went to the P of Judah, to the
6:2 which is in the P of Media, a scroll
6:6 governor of the P Beyond the River, Shethar-
6:6 who are in the P Beyond the River, keep
6:8 the tribute of the P from Beyond the River.
6:13 the governor of the P Beyond the River,
7:16 find in the whole P of Babylonia, and with
7:21 the treasurers in the P Beyond the River: Whatever
7:25 the people in the P Beyond the River, all
8:36 the governors of the P Beyond the River; and
Neh 1:3 survivors there in the P who escaped exile are
2:7 the governors of the P Beyond the River, that
2:9 the governors of the P Beyond the River, and
3:7 the governor of the P Beyond the River.
7:6 the people of the P who came up out
11:3 the chiefs of the P who lived in Jerusalem;
Esth 1:22 royal provinces, to every P in its own script
3:12 the peoples, to every P in its own script
3:14 a decree in every P by proclamation to all
4:3 And in every P, wherever the king's command and
8:9 twenty-seven provinces, to every P in its own script
8:11 of any people or P that might attack them,
8:13 a decree in every P, and by proclamation to
8:17 And in every P and in every city, wherever
9:28 generation, in every family, P, and city, and that
Eccl 5:8 you see in a P the poor oppressed and
Dan 2:48 ruler over the whole P of Babylon, and chief
2:49 the affairs of the P of Babylon; but Daniel
3:1 of Dura, in the P of Babylon.
3:12 the affairs of the P of Babylon: Shadrach, Meshach,
3:98 and Abednego in the P of Babylon.
8:2 which is in the P of Elam; and I
11:24 richest parts of the P; and he shall do
1Mac 7:8 friends, governor of the P Beyond the River; he
10:65 and made him general and governor of the P
Acts 23:34 he asked to what P he belonged.
25:1 had come into his P, after three days he

PROVINCES (31)

Ezra 4:15 hurtful to kings and P, and that sedition was
Esth 1:1 one hundred and twenty-seven P,
1:3 and governors of the P being before him,
1:16 are in all the P of King Ahasuerus.
1:22 to all the royal P, to every province in
2:3 officers in all the P of his kingdom to
2:18 of taxes to the P and gave gifts with
3:8 peoples in all the P of your kingdom; their
3:12 governors over all the P and to the princes
3:13 to all the king's P, to destroy, to slay,
4:11 people of the king's P know that if any
8:5 are in all the P of the king.
8:9 the princes of the P from India to Ethiopia,
8:9 a hundred and twenty-seven P, to every province in
8:12 day throughout all the P of King Ahasuerus, on
9:2 cities throughout all the P of King Ahasuerus to
9:3 the princes of the P and the satraps and
9:4 spread throughout all the P; for the man Mordecai
9:12 they done in the rest of the king's P
9:16 were in the king's P also gathered to defend
9:20 were in all the P of King Ahasuerus, both
9:30 the hundred and twenty-seven P of the kingdom of

13:1 hundred and twenty-seven P from India to Ethiopia
16:1 the rulers of the P from India to Ethiopia,
Eccl 2:8 treasure of kings and P; I got singers, both
Dan 3:2 the officials of the P to come to the
3:3 the officials of the P, were assembled for the
1Mac 3:37 the Euphrates river and went through the upper P
6:1 going through the upper P when he heard that
8:7 some of their best P,
2Mac 9:25 off to the upper P; and I have written

PROVING (2)
Acts 9:22 lived in Damascus by P that Jesus was the
17:3 the scriptures, explaining and P that it was necessary

PROVISION (11)
Gen 45:23 with grain, bread, and P for his father on
Deut 19:4 "This is the P for the manslayer, who by
1Kgs 4:7 man had to make P for one month in
4:22 Solomon's P for one day was thirty cors of
1Chr 29:19 build the palace for which I have made P
Neh 11:23 them, and a settled P for the singers, as
Jud 2:17 oxen and goats for P;
Ezek 45:25 shall make the same P for sin offerings, burnt
Acts 24:2 and since by your P, most excellent Felix, reforms
Rom 13:14 Christ, and make no P for the flesh, to
1Cor 9:15 am I writing this to secure any such P

PROVISIONED
1Kgs 20:27 were mustered, and were P, and went against them;

PROVISIONS (22)
Gen 14:11 Gomorrah, and all their P, and went their way;
42:25 and to give them P for the journey.
45:21 Pharaoh, and gave them P for the journey.
Ex 12:39 neither had they prepared for themselves any P
Josh 1:11 the people, 'Prepare your P; for within three days
9:4 went and made ready P, and took worn-out sacks
9:5 clothes; and all their P were dry and moldy.
9:11 said to us, 'Take P in your hand for
9:14 men partook of their P, and did not ask
Judg 20:10 ten thousand, to bring P for the people, that
1Sam 17:20 keeper, and took the P, and went, as Jesse
22:10 him, and gave him P, and gave him the
1Kgs 4:27 And those officers supplied P for King Solomon, and
1Chr 12:40 and on oxen, abundant P of meal, cakes of
2Chr 11:23 he gave them abundant P, and procured wives for
Tob 1:13 of Shalmaneser, and I was his buyer of P
Ps 132:15 will abundantly bless her P; I will satisfy her
Dan 14:8 who is eating these P, you shall die.
14:13 used to go in regularly and consume the P
1Mac 6:49 because they had no P there to withstand a
2Mac 12:14 on their supply of P, behaved most insolently toward
Lk 9:12 to lodge and get P; for we are here

PROVOCATION (7)
Deut 32:19 them, because of the P of his sons and
32:27 had I not feared P by the enemy, lest
Job 17:2 about me, and my eye dwells on their P
Prov 27:3 weighty, but a fool's P is heavier than both.
Sir 31:29 bitterness of soul, with P and stumbling.
Ezek 20:28 sacrifices and presented the P of their offering;
Hos 12:14 Ephraim has given bitter P; so his LORD will

PROVOCATIONS
2Kgs 23:26 because of all the P with which Manasseh had

PROVOKE (29)
Deut 4:25 God, so as to P him to anger,
9:18 of the LORD, to P him to anger.
32:21 no people; I will P them with a foolish
1Sam 1:6 her rival used to P her sorely, to irritate
1:7 LORD, she used to P her.
1Kgs 16:33 Ahab did more to P the LORD, the God
2Kgs 14:10 for why should you P trouble so that you
22:17 gods, that they might P me to anger with
2Chr 25:19 home; why should you P trouble so that you
34:25 gods, that they might P me to anger with
Jud 8:14 my brethren, do not P the Lord our God
11:11 they are about to P their God to anger
Job 12:6 peace, and those who P God are secure, who
Is 65:3 devices; a people who P me to my face
Jer 7:18 to other gods, to P me to anger.
7:19 Is it I whom they P
25:6 and worship them, or P me to anger with
25:7 LORD, that you might P me to anger with
32:29 to other gods, to P me to anger.
32:30 have done nothing but P me to anger by
32:32 which they did to P me to anger--their
44:8 Why do you P me to anger with the
Ezek 8:17 land with violence, and P me further to anger?
16:26 multiplying your harlotry, to P me to anger.
1Mac 15:40 Jamnia and began to P the people and invade
Lk 11:53 him hard, and to P him to speak of
1Cor 10:22 Shall we P the Lord to jealousy?
Eph 6:4 Fathers, do not P your children to anger, but
Col 3:21 Fathers, do not P your children, lest they become

PROVOKED (23)
Deut 9:7 not forget how you P the LORD your God
9:8 Even at Horeb you P the LORD to wrath,
9:22 and at Kibroth-hattaavah, you P the LORD to wrath.
32:16 with abominable practices they P him to anger.
32:21 no god; they have P me with their idols.
Judg 2:12 to them; and they P the LORD to anger.
1Kgs 14:22 the LORD, and they P him to jealousy with
15:30 anger to which he P the LORD, the God
21:22 to which you have P me, and because you
22:53 and worshiped him, and P the LORD, the God
2Kgs 21:15 my sight and have P me to anger, since
23:26 with which Manasseh had P him.
Neh 4:5 sight; for they have P thee to anger before
Ps 78:41 again and again, and P the Holy One of
78:58 For they P him to anger with their high
106:29 to the dead; they P the LORD to anger
Jer 8:19 "Why have they P me to anger with their
Bar 4:7 For you P him who made you, by sacrificing
Zech 8:14 you, when your fathers P me to wrath, and
2Mac 14:27 king became excited and, P by the false accusations
Acts 17:16 Athens, his spirit was P within him as he
Heb 3:10 Therefore I was P with that generation, and said,
3:17 with whom was he P forty years?

PROVOKES (3)
Job 16:3 Or what P you that you answer?
Prov 20:2 a lion; he who P him to anger forfeits
Ezek 8:3 image of jealousy, which P to jealousy.

PROVOKING (16)
Deut 31:29 sight of the LORD, P him to anger through
1Kgs 14:9 gods, and molten images, P me to anger, and
14:15 have made their Asherim, P the LORD to anger.
16:2 people Israel to sin, P me to anger with
16:7 sight of the LORD, P him to anger with
16:13 made Israel to sin, P the LORD God of
16:26 made Israel to sin, P the LORD, the God
2Kgs 17:11 they did wicked things, P the LORD to anger,
17:17 sight of the LORD, P him to anger.
21:6 sight of the LORD, P him to anger.
23:19 of Israel had made, P the LORD to anger,
2Chr 28:25 incense to other gods, P to anger the LORD,
33:6 sight of the LORD, P him to anger.
Jer 11:17 of Judah have done, P me to anger by
44:3 wickedness which they committed, P me to anger, in
Gal 5:26 have no self-conceit, no P of one another, no

PROWL (2)
Ps 12:8 every side the wicked P, as vileness is exalted
Lam 5:18 which lies desolate; jackals P over it.

PROWLED
Ezek 19:6 He P among the lions; he became a young

PROWLING (2)
Ps 59:6 howling like dogs and P about the city.
59:14 howling like dogs and P about the city.

PROWLS
1Pet 5:8 Your adversary the devil P around like a roaring

PRUDENCE (8)
Prov 1:4 justice, and equity; that P may be given to
8:5 O simple ones, learn P; O foolish men, pay
8:12 I, wisdom, dwell in P, and I find knowledge
19:25 the simple will learn P; reprove a man of
Wis 8:7 she teaches self-control and P, justice and courage;
Sir 19:19 wisdom, nor is there P where sinners take counsel.
22:25 and a seal of P upon my lips, that
Dan 2:14 Then Daniel replied with P and discretion to Arioch,

PRUDENT (18)
1Sam 16:18 a man of war, P in speech, and a
Prov 10:5 gathers in summer is P, but a son who

P

	10:19	lacking, but he who restrains his lips is P
	12:16	at once, but the P man ignores an insult.
	12:23	A P man conceals his knowledge, but fools proclaim
	13:16	In everything a P man acts with knowledge, but
	14:8	The wisdom of a P man is to discern
	14:15	believes everything, but the P looks where he is
	14:18	acquire folly, but the P are crowned with knowledge.
	15:5	instruction, but he who heeds admonition is P
	19:14	from fathers, but a P wife is from the
	22:3	A P man sees danger and hides himself; but
	27:12	A P man sees danger and hides himself; but
Sir	1:4	before all things, and P understanding from eternity.
	19:21	intelligence, than the highly P man who transgresses
	21:25	the words of the P will be weighed in
Jer	49:7	Has counsel perished from the P
Amos	5:13	Therefore he who is P will keep silent in

PRUNE (2)

Lev	25:3	six years you shall P your vineyard, and gather
	25:4	sow your field or P your vineyard.

PRUNED

Is	5:6	it shall not be P or hoed, and briers

PRUNES

Jn	15:2	does bear fruit he P, that it may bear

PRUNING (4)

Is	2:4	and their spears into P hooks; nation shall not
	18:5	off the shoots with P hooks, and the spreading
Joel	3:10	into swords, and your P hooks into spears; let
Mic	4:3	and their spears into P hooks; nation shall not

PSALM (4)

Jud	16:2	to him a new P; exalt him, and call
Ps	47:7	of all the earth; sing praises with a P
Acts	13:33	written in the second P, 'Thou art my Son,
	13:35	says also in another P, 'Thou wilt not let

PSALMIST

2Sam	23:1	of Jacob, the sweet P of Israel:

PSALMS (5)

Lk	20:42	in the Book of P, 'The Lord said to
	24:44	the prophets and the P must be fulfilled."
Acts	1:20	in the book of P, 'Let his habitation become
Eph	5:19	addressing one another in P and hymns and spiritual
Col	3:16	all wisdom, and sing P and hymns and spiritual

PTOLEMAIS (20)

1Mac	5:15	gathered together men of P and Tyre and Sidon,
	5:22	to the gate of P, and as many as
	5:55	was in Galilee before P,
	10:1	the son of Antiochus, landed and occupied P
	10:39	P and the land adjoining it I have given
	10:56	but meet me at P, so that we may
	10:57	daughter, and came to P in the one hundred
	10:58	celebrated her wedding at P with great pomp, as
	10:60	went with pomp to P and met the two
	11:22	out and came to P; and he wrote Jonathan
	11:22	for a conference at P as quickly as possible.
	11:24	to the king at P, taking silver and gold
	12:45	stay with you, and come with me to P
	12:48	But when Jonathan entered P, the men of Ptolemais
	12:48	Ptolemais, the men of P closed the gates and
	13:12	Then Trypho departed from P with a large army
2Mac	13:24	Hegemonides as governor from P to Gerar,
	13:25	governor from Ptolemais to Gerar, and went to P
	13:25	The people of P were indignant over the treaty;
Acts	21:7	Tyre, we arrived at P; and we greeted the

PTOLEMY (29)

Esth	11:1	of the reign of P and Cleopatra, Dositheus, who
	11:1	and a Levite, and P his son brought to
	11:1	Lysimachus the son of P, one of the residents
1Mac	1:18	He engaged P king of Egypt in battle, and
	1:18	Egypt in battle, and P turned and fled before
	3:38	Lysias chose P the son of Dorymenes, and Nicanor
	10:51	Alexander sent ambassadors to P king of Egypt with
	10:55	P the king replied and said, "Happy was the
	10:57	So P set out from Egypt, he and Cleopatra
	10:58	king met him, and P gave him Cleopatra his
	11:3	But when P entered the cities he stationed forces
	11:8	So King P gained control of the coastal cities
	11:13	Then P entered Antioch and put on the crown
	11:15	P marched out and met him with a strong
	11:16	protection there, and King P was exalted.
	11:17	the head of Alexander and sent it to P
	11:18	But King P died three days later, and his
	15:16	the Romans, to King P, greeting.
	16:11	Now P the son of Abubus had been appointed
	16:16	his sons were drunk, P and his men rose
	16:18	Then P wrote a report about these things and
2Mac	1:10	anointed priests, teacher of P the king, and to
	4:45	a substantial bribe to P son of Dorymenes to
	4:46	Therefore P, taking the king aside into a colonnade
	6:8	At the suggestion of P a decree was issued
	8:8	successes, he wrote to P, the governor of Coelesyria
	8:9	And P promptly appointed Nicanor the son of
	9:29	he betook himself to P Philometor in Egypt.
	10:12	P, who was called Macron, took the lead in

PUAH (3)

Ex	1:14	Shiphrah and the other P,
Judg	10:1	Tola the son of P, son of Dodo, a
1Chr	7:1	sons of Issachar: Tola, P, Jashub, and Shimron, four.

PUBLIC (23)

Lev	5:1	that he hears a P adjuration to testify and
2Sam	21:12	stolen them from the P square of Beth-shan, where
Esth	14:16	head on the days when I appear in P
	16:5	with the administration of P affairs,
Sir	7:7	not offend against the P, and do not disgrace
	38:33	attain eminence in the P assembly.
Is	59:14	has fallen in the P squares, and uprightness cannot
1Mac	14:22	recorded in our P decrees, as follows, 'Numenius
	14:23	their words in the P archives, so that the
2Mac	4:5	view the welfare, both P and private, of all
	4:6	without the king's attention P affairs could not again
	7:24	and entrust him with P affairs.
	9:26	you to remember the P and private services
	10:2	been built in the P square by the foreigners,
	10:8	They decreed by P ordinance and vote that the
	12:4	this was done by P vote of the city.
	13:26	Lysias took the P platform, made the best possible
	15:6	determined to erect a P monument of victory over
	15:36	they all decreed by P vote never to let
Acts	18:28	confuted the Jews in P, showing by the scriptures
	20:20	and teaching you in P and from house to
Col	2:15	powers and made a P example of them, triumphing
1Tim	4:13	come, attend to the P reading of scripture, to

PUBLICLY (7)

Esth	16:19	copy of this letter P in every place, and
2Mac	4:33	of these acts he P exposed them, having first
	6:10	These women they P paraded about the city, with
Jn	7:10	also went up, not P but in private.
Acts	16:37	"They have beaten us P, uncondemned, men who are
Gal	3:1	eyes Jesus Christ was P portrayed as crucified?
Heb	10:33	with sufferings, sometimes being P exposed to abuse

PUBLISH (3)

2Sam	1:20	it not in Gath, P it not in the
Neh	8:15	and that they should P and proclaim in all
Amos	4:5	and proclaim freewill offerings, P them; for so you

PUBLISHED

Jon	3:7	he made proclamation and P through Nineveh, "By

PUBLISHES (2)

Is	52:7	brings good tidings, who P peace, who brings good
	52:7	tidings of good, who P salvation, who says to

PUBLIUS (2)

Acts	28:7	of the island, named P, who received us and
	28:8	that the father of P lay sick with fever

PUDENS

2Tim	4:21	to you, as do P and Linus and Claudia

PUFFED (5)

2Mac	7:34	elated in vain and P up by uncertain hopes,
1Cor	4:6	of you may be P up in favor of
Col	2:18	his stand on visions, P up without reason by
1Tim	3:6	or he may be P up with conceit and
	6:4	with godliness, he is P up with conceit, he

PUFFS (2)

Ps	10:5	all his foes, he P at them.
1Cor	8:1	P up, but love builds up.

P

PUL (3)

2Kgs 15:19 P the king of Assyria came against the land;
15:19 land; and Menahem gave P a thousand talents of
1Chr 5:26 up the spirit of P king of Assyria, the

PULL (9)

Deut 25:9 of the elders, and P his sandal off his
Judg 6:25 seven years old, and P down the altar of
Ruth 2:16 And also P out some from the bundles for
Jer 12:3 P them out like sheep for the slaughter, and
42:10 you up and not P you down; I will
Ezek 17:9 Will he not P up its roots and cut
17:9 or many people to P it from its roots.
Lk 12:18 do this: I will P down my barns, and
14:5 well, will not immediately P him out on a

PULLED (16)

Deut 21:3 and which has not P in the yoke.
25:10 that had his sandal P off.
Judg 6:30 die, for he has P down the altar of
6:31 his altar has been P down."
6:32 because he P down his altar.
16:3 the two posts, and P them up, bar and
16:14 from his sleep, and P away the pin, the
2Kgs 23:12 of the LORD, he P down and broke in
23:15 the high place he P down and he broke
Ezra 6:11 a beam shall be P out of his house,
9:3 and my mantle, and P hair from my head
Neh 13:25 some of them and P out their hair; and
Jud 13:9 off the bed and P down the canopy from
Job 19:10 my hope has he P up like a tree.
Is 50:6 cheeks to those who P out the beard; I
Dan 14:42 And he P Daniel out, and threw into the

PULPIT

Neh 8:4 stood on a wooden P which they had made

PUNISH (67)

Num 12:11 my lord, do not P us because we have
1Sam 3:13 I am about to P his house for ever,
15:2 of hosts, 'I will P what Amalek did to
Tob 3:3 upon me; do not P me for my sins
Job 35:15 his anger does not P, and he does not
Ps 59:5 Awake to P all the nations; spare none of
89:32 commandments, then I will P their transgression
Wis 11:8 time how thou didst P their enemies.
11:15 of irrational creatures to P them,
12:20 For if thou didst P with such great care
16:24 it, exerts itself to P the unrighteous, and in
18:8 by which thou didst P our enemies thou didst
Sir 5:3 the Lord will surely P you.
Is 10:12 on Jerusalem he will P the arrogant boasting of
13:11 I will P the world for its evil, and
24:21 day the LORD will P the host of heaven,
26:21 of his place to P the inhabitants of the
27:1 strong sword will P Leviathan the fleeing serpent,
Jer 5:9 Shall I not P them for these things?
5:29 Shall I not P them for these things?
6:15 the time that I P them, they shall be
8:12 the fallen; when I P them, they shall be
9:9 Shall I not P them for these things?
9:25 LORD, when I will P all those who are
11:22 hosts: "Behold, I will P them; the young men
14:10 remember their iniquity and P their sins."
21:14 our habitations?' I will P you according to the
23:34 the LORD,' I will P that man and his
25:12 are completed, I will P the king of Babylon
27:8 of Babylon, I will P that nation with the
29:32 LORD: Behold, I will P Shemaiah of Nehelam and
30:20 me; and I will P all who oppress them.
36:31 And I will P him and his offspring and
44:13 I will P those who dwell in the land
44:29 LORD, that I will P you in this place,
49:8 the time when I P him.
50:31 time when I will P you.
51:44 And I will P Bel in Babylon, and take
51:47 coming when I will P the images of Babylon;
Lam 4:22 of Edom, he will P, he will uncover your
Ezek 7:3 ways; and I will P you for all your
7:4 pity; but I will P you for your ways,
7:8 ways; and I will P you for all your
7:9 have pity; I will P you according to your
Hos 1:4 while, and I will P the house of Jehu
2:13 And I will P her for the feast days
4:9 like priest; I will P them for their ways,
4:14 I will not P your daughters when they play
8:13 remember their iniquity, and P their sins; they shall
9:9 their iniquity, he will P their sins.
12:2 against Judah, and will P Jacob according to his
Amos 3:2 earth; therefore I will P you for all your
3:14 on the day I P Israel for his transgressions,
3:14 his transgressions, I will P the altars of Bethel,
Zeph 1:8 LORD's sacrifice--"I will P the officials and the
1:9 that day I will P every one who leaps
1:12 lamps, and I will P the men who are
Zech 10:3 shepherds, and I will P the leaders; for the
1Mac 7:7 king, and let him P them and all who
15:21 priest, that he may P them according to their
2Mac 6:13 for long, but to P them immediately, is a
6:14 Lord waits patiently to P them until they have
Mt 24:51 not know, and will P him, and put him
Lk 12:46 not know, and will P him, and put him
Acts 4:21 finding no way to P them, because of the
2Cor 10:6 Christ, being ready to P every disobedience, when
1Pet 2:14 sent by him to P those who do wrong

PUNISHABLE (2)

Deut 21:22 has committed a crime P by death and he
22:26 there is no offense P by death, for this

PUNISHED (31)

Ex 21:20 slave dies under his hand, he shall be P
21:21 is not to be P; for the slave is
Lev 18:25 defiled, so that I P its iniquity, and the
Ezra 9:13 thou, our God, hast P us less than our
Jud 11:10 our nation cannot be P, nor can the sword
Job 31:11 an iniquity to be P by the judges;
31:28 an iniquity to be P by the judges, for
Prov 21:11 When a scoffer is P, the simple becomes wise;
Wis 3:4 of men they were P, their hope is full
3:10 the ungodly will be P as their reasoning deserves,
11:5 enemies were P, they themselves received benefit
11:16 learn that one is P by the very things
12:14 confront thee about those whom thou hast P
12:15 condemn him who does not deserve to be P
12:27 to be gods, being P by means of them,
14:10 was done will be P together with him who
16:1 men were deservedly P through such creatures, and
16:9 they deserved to be P by such things;
18:11 The slave was P with the same penalty as
Sir 23:21 This man will be P in the streets of
Is 24:22 prison, and after many days they will be P
Jer 6:6 city which must be P; there is nothing but
44:13 Egypt, as I have P Jerusalem, with the sword,
50:18 his land, as I P the king of Assyria.
Bar 3:8 reproached and cursed and P for all the iniquities
2Mac 4:16 became their enemies and P them.
7:7 than have your body P limb by limb?"
Acts 22:5 bring them in bonds to Jerusalem to be P
26:11 And I P them often in all the synagogues
2Cor 6:9 behold we live; as P, and yet not killed;
Heb 12:5 courage when you are P by him.

PUNISHER

Wis 18:22 word he subdued the P, appealing to the oaths

PUNISHES (4)

Jud 7:29 of our fathers, who P us according to our
Wis 1:8 and justice, when it P, will not pass him
Sir 2:14 do when the Lord P you?
39:30 and the sword that P the ungodly with destruction;

PUNISHMENT (73)

Gen 4:13 to the LORD, "My P is greater than I
19:15 be consumed in the P of the city."
1Sam 28:10 the LORD lives, no P shall come upon you
2Kgs 7:9 until the morning light, P will overtake us; now
Jud 2:10 them for me till the day of their P
Esth 16:18 inflicted on him the P he deserved.
Job 19:29 for wrath brings the P of the sword, that
Ps 69:27 Add to them P upon punishment; may they have
69:27 to them punishment upon P; may they have no
Wis 16:2 Instead of this P thou didst show kindness to
18:5 rescued, thou didst in P take away a multitude
19:4 might fill up the P which their torments still
19:15 not only so, but P of some sort will
Sir 5:7 at the time of P you will perish.
7:17 yourself greatly, for the P of the ungodly is
8:5 away from sin; remember that we all deserve P
12:6 sinners and will inflict P on the ungodly.
23:24 before the assembly, and P will fall on her
Is 10:3 on the day of P, in the storm which

P

30:32 of the staff of P which the LORD lays
Jer 10:15 the time of their P they shall perish.
11:23 the men of Anathoth, the year of their P
23:12 the year of their P, says the LORD.
30:14 of an enemy, the P of a merciless foe,
46:21 has come upon them, the time of their P
46:25 "Behold, I am bringing P upon Amon of Thebes,
48:44 the year of their P, says the LORD.
50:18 Behold, I am bringing P on the king of
50:27 their day has come, the time of their P
51:6 cut off in her P, for this is the
51:18 the time of their P they shall perish.
Lam 3:39 a man, about the P of his sins?
4:6 been greater than the P of Sodom, which was
4:22 The P of your iniquity, O daughter of Zion,
Ezek 4:4 I will lay the P of the house of
4:4 you lie upon it, you shall bear their P
4:5 the years of their P; so long shall you
4:5 shall you bear the P of the house of
4:6 side, and bear the P of the house of
4:17 another in dismay, and waste away under their P
14:10 they shall bear their P --the punishment of the
14:10 bear their punishment--the P of the prophet and
14:10 the prophet and the P of the inquirer shall
21:25 time of your final P,
21:29 day has come, the time of their final P
35:5 time of their final P;
44:10 idols when Israel went astray, shall bear their P
44:12 the Lord GOD, that they shall bear their P
Hos 5:9 in the day of P; among the tribes of
9:7 The days of P have come, the days of
Amos 1:3 will not revoke the P; because they have threshed
1:6 will not revoke the P; because they carried into
1:9 will not revoke the P; because they delivered up
1:11 will not revoke the P; because he pursued his
1:13 will not revoke the P; because they have ripped
2:1 will not revoke the P; because he burned to
2:4 will not revoke the P; because they have rejected
2:6 will not revoke the P; because they sell the
Mic 7:4 their watchmen, of their P, has come; now their
Zech 14:19 This shall be the P to Egypt and the
14:19 to Egypt and the P to all the nations
1Mac 14:45 nullifies any of them shall be liable to P
2Mac 4:38 repaid him with the P he deserved.
6:26 I should avoid the P of men, yet whether
7:36 God, will receive just P for your arrogance.
Mt 25:46 go away into eternal P, but the righteous into
2Cor 2:6 such a one this P by the majority is
7:11 what alarm, what longing, what zeal, what P
2Thes 1:9 They shall suffer the P of eternal destruction and
Heb 10:29 How much worse P do you think will be
2Pet 2:9 keep the unrighteous under P until the day of
1Jn 4:18 has to do with P, and he who fears
Jude 1:7 example by undergoing a P of eternal fire.

PUNISHMENTS (3)
Wis 11:13 that through their own P the righteous had received
19:13 The P did not come upon the sinners without
2Mac 6:12 to recognize that these P were designed not to

PUNITES
Num 26:23 the family of the P;

PUNON (2)
Num 33:42 they set out from Zalmonah, and encamped at P
33:43 they set out from P, and encamped at Oboth.

PUPIL
1Chr 25:8 and great, teacher and P alike.

PUR (3)
Esth 3:7 King Ahasuerus, they cast P, that is the lot,
9:24 them, and had cast P, that is the lot,
9:26 they called these days Purim, after the term P

PURAH (2)
Judg 7:10 to the camp with P your servant;
7:11 he went down with P his servant to the

PURCHASE (7)
Deut 2:6 You shall P food from them for money, that
Jer 32:7 right of redemption by P is yours.'
32:11 the sealed deed of P, containing the terms and
32:12 gave the deed of P to Baruch the son
32:12 signed the deed of P, and in the presence
32:14 this sealed deed of P and this open deed,
32:16 given the deed of P to Baruch the son

PURCHASED (4)
Gen 25:10 the field which Abraham P from the Hittites.
49:32 is in it were P from the Hittites."
Ex 15:16 till the people pass by whom thou hast P
Jud 4:10 and hired laborer and P slave--they all girded

PURE (103)
Ex 25:11 shall overlay it with P gold, within and without
25:17 a mercy seat of P gold; two cubits and
25:24 shall overlay it with P gold, and make a
25:29 to pour libations; of P gold you shall make
25:31 make a lampstand of P gold.
25:36 of hammered work of P gold.
25:38 trays shall be of P gold.
25:39 Of a talent of P gold shall it be
27:20 they bring to you P beaten olive oil for
28:14 and two chains of P gold, twisted like cords;
28:22 chains like cords, of P gold;
28:36 make a plate of P gold, and engrave on
30:3 shall overlay it with P gold, its top and
30:34 galbanum, sweet spices with P frankincense (of each
30:35 perfumer, seasoned with salt, P and holy;
31:8 its utensils, and the P lampstand with all its
37:2 he overlaid it with P gold within and without,
37:6 a mercy seat of P gold; two cubits and
37:11 he overlaid it with P gold, and made a
37:16 made the vessels of P gold which were to
37:17 made the lampstand of P gold.
37:22 of hammered work of P gold.
37:23 and its trays of P gold.
37:24 of a talent of P gold.
37:26 He overlaid it with P gold, its top, and
37:29 oil also, and the P fragrant incense, blended as
39:15 chains like cords, of P gold;
39:25 also made bells of P gold, and put the
39:30 the holy crown of P gold, and wrote upon
39:37 Presence; the lampstand of P gold and its lamps
Lev 24:2 Israel to bring you P oil from beaten olives
24:4 upon the lampstand of P gold before the LORD
24:6 upon the table of P gold.
24:7 And you shall put P frankincense with each row,
2Sam 22:27 thyself blameless; with the P thou dost show thyself
22:27 thou dost show thyself P, and with the crooked
1Kgs 6:20 he overlaid it with P gold.
6:21 of the house with P gold, and he drew
7:49 Presence, the lampstands of P gold, five on the
7:50 incense, and firepans, of P gold; and the sockets
10:21 of Lebanon were of P gold; none were of
1Chr 28:17 the silver tables, and P gold for the forks,
2Chr 3:4 on the inside with P gold.
4:20 and their lamps of P gold to burn before
4:22 incense, and firepans, of P gold; and the sockets
9:17 and overlaid it with P gold.
9:20 of Lebanon were of P gold; silver was not
13:11 on the table of P gold, and care for
Tob 8:15 O God, with every P and holy blessing.
13:16 towers and battlements with P gold.
Job 4:17 Can a man be P before his Maker?
8:6 Almighty, if you are P and upright, surely then
11:4 say, 'My doctrine is P, and I am clean
16:17 violence in my hands, and my prayer is P
28:19 it be valued in P gold.
33:9 without transgression; I am P, and there is no
Ps 12:6 are promises that are P, silver refined in a
18:26 thyself blameless; with the P thou dost show thyself
18:26 thou God dost show thyself P; and with the crooked
19:8 of the LORD is P, enlightening the eyes;
24:4 clean hands and a P heart, who does not
73:1 to those who are P in heart.
119:9 How can a young man keep his way P
Prov 15:26 the words of the P are pleasing to him.
16:2 of a man are P in his own eyes,
20:9 heart clean; I am P from my sin"?
20:11 what he does is P and right.
21:8 the conduct of the P is right.
30:12 are those who are P in their own eyes
Wis 7:23 that are intelligent and P and most subtle.
7:25 of God, and a P emanation of the glory
8:18 in friendship with her, P delight, and in the
14:24 or their marriages P, but they either treacherously
Jer 2:21 choice vine, wholly of P seed.
Lam 4:1 grown dim, how the P gold is changed!
Bar 3:30 will buy her for P gold?
Dan 7:9 of his head like P wool; his throne was

Hos 8:5 be till they are P
Zeph 3:9 the peoples to a P speech, that all of
Mal 1:11 my name, and a P offering; for my name
Mt 5:8 "Blessed are the P in heart, for they shall
Mk 14:3 flask of ointment of P nard, very costly, and
Jn 12:3 of costly ointment of P nard and anointed the
2Cor 11:2 present you as a P bride to her one
11:3 from a sincere and P devotion to Christ.
Phil 1:10 excellent, and may be P and blameless for the
4:8 is just, whatever is P, whatever is lovely, whatever
1Tim 1:5 that issues from a P heart and a good
5:22 participate in another man's sins; keep yourself P
2Tim 2:22 the Lord from a P heart.
Tit 1:14 To the P all things are pure, but to the
1:14 pure all things are P, but to the corrupt
1:14 and unbelieving nothing is P; their very minds and
Heb 10:22 our bodies washed with P water.
Jas 1:26 Religion that is P and undefiled before God and
3:17 from above is first P, then peaceable, gentle, open
1Pet 2:2 babes, long for the P spiritual milk, that by
1Jn 3:3 hopes in him purifies himself as he is P
Rev 15:6 seven plagues, robed in P bright linen, and their
19:8 fine linen, bright and P – for the fine
19:14 fine linen, white and P, followed him on white
21:18 while the city was P gold, clear as glass.
21:21 of the city was P gold, transparent as glass.

PURENESS
Wis 7:24 motion; because of her P she pervades and

PURER (2)
Lam 4:7 Her princes were P than snow, whiter than milk;
Hab 1:13 Thou who art of P eyes than to behold

PUREST
2Chr 4:21 and the tongs, of P gold;

PURGE (15)
Deut 13:5 So you shall P the evil from the midst
17:7 So you shall P the evil from the midst
17:12 die; so you shall P the evil from Israel.
19:13 him, but you shall P the guilt of innocent
19:19 brother; so you shall P the evil from the
21:9 them.' So you shall P the guilt of innocent
21:21 stones; so you shall P the evil from your
22:21 house; so you shall P the evil from the
22:22 woman; so you shall P the evil from Israel.
22:24 wife; so you shall P the evil from the
24:7 die; so you shall P the evil from the
2Chr 34:3 year he began to P Judah and Jerusalem of
Tob 12:9 death, and it will P away every sin.
Ps 51:7 P me with hyssop, and I shall be clean;
Ezek 20:38 I will P out the rebels from among you,

PURGED (2)
2Chr 34:5 on their altars, and P Judah and Jerusalem.
34:8 reign, when he had P the land and the

PURIFICATION (12)
Neh 12:45 and the service of P, as did the singers
Sir 51:20 to her, and through P I found her.
2Mac 1:18 we shall celebrate the P of the temple, we
1:36 which means P, but by most people it is
2:16 about to celebrate the P, we write to you.
2:19 his brothers, and the P of the great temple,
10:5 by the foreigners, the P of the sanctuary took
Lk 2:22 time came for their P according to the law
Jn 2:6 the Jewish rites of P, each holding twenty or
Acts 21:26 when the days of P would be fulfilled and
Heb 1:3 When he had made P for sins, he sat
9:13 heifer sanctifies for the P of the flesh,

PURIFIED (17)
Lev 8:15 altar round about, and P the altar, and poured
Num 8:21 And the Levites P themselves from sin, and washed
31:23 it shall also be P with the water of
Ezra 6:20 and the Levites had P themselves together; all of
Neh 12:30 priests and the Levites P themselves; and they
12:30 purified themselves; and they P the people and the
Jud 16:18 as the people were P, they offered their burnt
Ps 12:6 furnace on the ground, P seven times.
2Mac 2:18 great evils and has P the place.
10:3 They P the sanctuary, and made another altar of
12:38 was coming on, they P themselves according to the
14:36 ever this house that has been so recently P
Acts 21:26 the next day he P himself with them and
24:17 this, they found me P in the temple, without
Heb 9:22 law almost everything is P with blood, and without
9:23 heavenly things to be P with these rites, but
1Pet 1:22 Having P your souls by your obedience to the

PURIFIER
Mal 3:3 as a refiner and P of silver, and he

PURIFIES (2)
2Tim 2:21 If any one P himself from what is ignoble,
1Jn 3:3 thus hopes in him P himself as he is

PURIFY (15)
Gen 35:2 are among you, and P yourselves, and change your
Num 31:19 has touched any slain, P yourselves and your captives
31:20 You shall P every garment, every article of skin,
Neh 13:22 Levites that they should P themselves and come and
Is 52:11 the midst of her, P yourselves, you who bear
66:17 "Those who sanctify and P themselves to go into
Ezek 43:26 for the altar and P it, and so consecrate
Dan 12:10 shall P themselves, and make themselves white, and
Mal 3:3 silver, and he will P the sons of Levi
Mk 7:4 not eat unless they P themselves; and there are
Jn 11:55 before the Passover, to P themselves.
Acts 21:24 take these men and P yourself along with them
Tit 2:14 all iniquity and to P for himself a people
Heb 9:14 without blemish to God, P your conscience from
Jas 4:8 hands, you sinners, and P your hearts, you men

PURIFYING (7)
Lev 12:4 the blood of her P; she shall not touch
12:4 the days of her P are completed.
12:5 the blood of her P for sixty-six days.
12:6 the days of her P are completed, whether for
2Sam 11:4 (Now she was P herself from her uncleanness.) Then
2Mac 10:7 given success to the P of his own holy
Jn 3:25 arose between John's disciples and a Jew over P

PURIM (6)
Esth 9:26 they called these days P, after the term Pur.
9:28 that these days of P should never fall into
9:29 authority, confirming this second letter about P
9:31 that these days of P should be observed at
9:32 fixed these practices of P, and it was recorded
11:1 the preceding Letter of P, which they said was

PURITY (5)
Prov 22:11 He who loves P of heart, and whose speech
1Mac 14:36 the sanctuary and do great damage to its P
2Cor 6:6 watching, hunger; by P, knowledge, forbearance,
1Tim 4:12 speech and conduct, in love, in faith, in P
5:2 like mothers, younger women like sisters, in all P

PURPLE (67)
Ex 25:4 and bronze, blue and P and scarlet stuff and
26:1 linen and blue and P and scarlet stuff; with
26:31 veil of blue and P and scarlet stuff and
26:36 tent, of blue and P and scarlet stuff and
27:16 long, of blue and P and scarlet stuff and
28:5 receive gold, blue and P and scarlet stuff, and
28:6 gold, of blue and P and scarlet stuff, and
28:8 of gold, blue and P and scarlet stuff, and
28:15 of gold, blue and P and scarlet stuff, and
28:33 pomegranates of blue and P and scarlet stuff, around
35:6 and bronze; blue and P and scarlet stuff and
35:23 was found blue or P or scarlet stuff or
35:25 spun in blue and P and scarlet stuff and
35:35 embroiderer in blue and P and scarlet stuff and
36:8 linen and blue and P and scarlet stuff, with
36:35 veil of blue and P and scarlet stuff and
36:37 tent, of blue and P and scarlet stuff and
38:18 needlework in blue and P and scarlet stuff and
38:23 embroiderer in blue and P and scarlet stuff and
39:1 of the blue and P and scarlet stuff they
39:2 of gold, blue and P and scarlet stuff, and
39:3 into the blue and P and the scarlet stuff,
39:5 of gold, blue and P and scarlet stuff, and
39:8 of gold, blue and P and scarlet stuff, and
39:24 pomegranates of blue and P and scarlet stuff and
39:29 and of blue and P and scarlet stuff, embroidered
Num 4:13 altar, and spread a P cloth over it;
Judg 8:26 the pendants and the P garments worn by the
2Chr 2:7 and iron, and in P, crimson, and blue fabrics,
2:14 and wood, and in P, blue, and crimson fabrics
3:14 veil of blue and P and crimson fabrics and
Jud 10:21 which was woven with P and gold and emeralds

Esth 1:6 of fine linen and P to silver rings and
8:15 of fine linen and P, while the city of
Prov 31:22 herself coverings; her clothing is fine linen and P
Song 3:10 gold, its seat of P; it was lovingly wrought
7:5 flowing locks are like P; a king is held
Sir 40:4 the man who wears P and a crown to
45:10 gold and blue and P, the work of an
Jer 10:9 clothing is violet and P; they are all the
Lam 4:5 were brought up in P lie on ash heaps.
Bar 6:12 have been dressed in P robes,
6:72 By the P and linen that rot upon them
Ezek 23:6 Assyrians, warriors clothed in P, governors and
27:7 your ensign; blue and P from the coasts of
27:16 for your wares emeralds, P, embroidered work, fine
Dan 5:7 shall be clothed with P, and have a chain
5:16 shall be clothed with P, and have a chain
5:29 Daniel was clothed with P, a chain of gold
1Mac 4:23 dyed blue and sea P, and great riches.
8:14 a crown or worn P as a mark of
10:20 he sent him a P robe and a golden
10:62 to clothe him in P, and they did so.
10:64 saw him clothed in P, they all fled.
11:58 cups and dress in P and wear a gold
14:43 should be clothed in P and wear gold.
14:44 to be clothed in P or put on a
2Mac 4:38 stripped off the P robe from Andronicus, tore
Mk 15:17 clothed him in a P cloak, and plaiting a
15:20 stripped him of the P cloak, and put his
Lk 16:19 who was clothed in P and fine linen and
Jn 19:2 arrayed him in a P robe;
19:5 of thorns and the P robe.
Acts 16:14 Thyatira, a seller of P goods, who was a
Rev 17:4 woman was arrayed in P and scarlet, and bedecked
18:12 and pearls, fine linen, P, silk and scarlet, all
18:16 in fine linen, in P and scarlet, bedecked with

PURPORTING

2Thes 2:2 word, or by letter P to be from us,

PURPOSE (61)

Ex 9:16 earth; but for this P have I let you
10:10 you have some evil P in mind.
Lev 11:32 is used for any P; it must be put
1Kgs 5:5 And so I P to build a house for
1Chr 12:33 of war, to help David with singleness of P
Ezra 4:5 them to frustrate their P, all the days of
Neh 6:13 For this P he was hired, that I should
8:4 had made for the P; and beside him stood
Jud 11:11 be defeated and his P frustrated, death will fall
Esth 10:10 For this P he made two lots, one for
Job 10:13 thy heart; I know that this was thy P
42:2 things, and that no P of thine can be
Ps 57:2 God who fulfils his P for me.
64:5 fast to their evil P; they talk of laying
119:150 persecute me with evil P; they are far from
138:8 LORD will fulfil his P for me; thy steadfast
Prov 16:4 made everything for its P, even the wicked for
19:21 but it is the P of the LORD that
20:5 The P in a man's mind is like deep
Wis 6:4 walk according to the P of God,
Sir 22:16 heart with a fool's P will not stand firm
Is 5:19 see it; let the P of the Holy One
14:26 This is the P that is purposed concerning the
19:17 fear because of the P which the LORD of
44:28 shall fulfil all my P; saying of Jerusalem, 'She
46:10 will accomplish all my P
48:14 he shall perform his P on Babylon, and his
54:16 of coals, and produces a weapon for its P
55:11 accomplish that which I P, and prosper in the
Jer 6:20 To what P does frankincense come to me from
49:30 you, and formed a P against you.
51:11 the Medes, because his P concerning Babylon is to
2Mac 3:8 but in fact to carry out the king's P
4:19 was inappropriate, but to expend it for another P
14:5 that furthered his mad P when he was invited
Lk 4:43 cities also; for I was sent for this P
7:30 the lawyers rejected the P of God for themselves,
23:50 not consented to their P and deed, and he
Jn 12:27 No, for this P I have come to this
Acts 9:21 come here for this P, to bring them bound
11:23 the Lord with steadfast P;
26:16 to you for this P, to appoint you to
27:13 they had obtained their P, they weighed anchor and
27:43 save Paul, kept them from carrying out their P
Rom 4:11 The P was to make him the father of
8:28 love him, who are called according to his P
9:11 in order that God's P of election might continue,
9:17 up for the very P of showing my power
Gal 2:21 through the law, then Christ died to no P
4:17 but for no good P; they want to shut
4:18 For a good P it is always good to
Eph 1:5 Christ, according to the P of his will,
1:9 will, according to his P which he set forth
1:11 him, according to the P of him who accomplishes
3:11 according to the eternal P which he has realized
6:22 you for this very P, that you may know
Col 4:8 you for this very P, that you may know
2Tim 1:9 virtue of his own P and the grace which
Heb 6:17 unchangeable character of his P, he interposed with
Jas 5:11 you have seen the P of the Lord, how
Rev 17:17 to carry out his P by being of one

PURPOSED (16)

2Chr 2:1 Now Solomon P to build a temple for the
Wis 4:17 understand what the Lord P for him, and for
Is 14:24 and as I have P, so shall it stand,
14:26 the purpose that is P concerning the whole earth;
14:27 LORD of hosts has P, and who will annul
19:12 LORD of hosts has P against Egypt.
19:17 LORD of hosts has P against them.
23:8 Who has P this against Tyre, the bestower of
23:9 LORD of hosts has P it, to defile the
46:11 to pass; I have P, and I will do
Jer 4:28 have spoken, I have P; I have not relented
Lam 2:17 has done what he P, has carried out his
Bar 4:28 For just as you P to go astray from
Zech 1:6 the LORD of hosts P to deal with us
8:14 of hosts: "As I P to do evil to
8:15 so again have I P in these days to

PURPOSES (11)

Deut 31:21 for I know the P which they are already
1Chr 29:18 keep for ever such P and thoughts in the
Jud 8:16 try to bind the P of the Lord our
11:6 my lord will not fail to achieve his P
Esth 12:2 and inquired into their P, and learned that they
Ps 106:43 were rebellious in their P, and were brought low
Wis 2:22 not know the secret P of God, nor hope
Jer 49:20 against Edom and the P which he has formed
50:45 against Babylon, and the P which he has formed
51:29 pain, for the LORD's P against Babylon stand, to
1Cor 4:5 and will disclose the P of the heart.

PURSE (6)

Prov 1:14 will all have one P –
Sir 18:32 borrowed money, when you have nothing in your P
Is 46:6 lavish gold from the P, and weigh out silver
Lk 10:4 Carry no P, no bag, no sandals; and salute
22:35 you out with no P or bag or sandals,
22:36 him who has a P take it, and likewise

PURSES

Lk 12:33 alms; provide yourselves with P that do not grow

PURSLANE

Job 6:6 there any taste in the slime of the P

PURSUE (45)

Gen 35:5 that they did not P the sons of Jacob.
Ex 14:4 heart, and he will P them and I will
15:9 enemy said, 'I will P, I will overtake, I
Deut 19:6 blood in hot anger P the manslayer and overtake
28:22 with mildew; they shall P you until you perish.
28:45 come upon you and P you and overtake you,
Josh 2:5 I do not know; P them quickly, for you
8:16 were called together to P them, and as they
10:19 not stay there yourselves, P your enemies, fall upon
1Sam 24:14 After whom do you P
25:29 men rise up to P you and to seek
26:18 "Why does my lord P after his servant?
30:8 the LORD, "Shall I P after this band?
30:8 He answered him, P; for you shall surely overtake
2Sam 17:1 will set out and P David tonight.
20:6 your lord's servants and P him, lest he get
20:7 out from Jerusalem to P Sheba the son of
20:13 on after Joab to P Sheba the son of
24:13 your foes while they P you?
Jud 14:4 borders of Israel shall P them and cut them
Job 13:25 a driven leaf and P dry chaff?
19:22 do you, like God, P me?
19:28 say, 'How we will P him!' and, 'The root
Ps 7:5 cause, let the enemy P me and overtake me,

P

P

PUSHING

2Mac 8:8 and that he was P ahead with more frequent

PUT (1,065)

Gen 1:11 said, "Let the earth P forth vegetation, plants
2:8 east; and there he P the man whom he
2:15 took the man and P him in the garden
3:15 I will P enmity between you and the woman,
3:22 and now, lest he P forth his hand and
4:15 And the LORD P a mark on Cain, lest
8:9 So he P forth his hand and took her
10:6 of Ham: Cush, Egypt, P, and Canaan.
19:10 But the men P forth their hands and brought
22:10 Then Abraham P forth his hand, and took the
24:2 all that he had, P your hand under my
24:9 So the servant P his hand under the thigh
24:47 to him.' So I P the ring on her
26:11 his wife shall be P to death."
27:15 in the house, and P them on Jacob her
27:16 of the kids she P upon his hands and
28:11 of the place, he P it under his head
28:18 stone which he had P under his head and
29:3 water the sheep, and P the stone back in
30:35 that was black, and P them in charge of
30:40 of Laban; and he P his own droves apart,
30:40 apart, and did not P them with Laban's flock.
31:34 the household gods and P them in the camel's
32:16 on before me, and P a space between drove
32:25 and Jacob's thigh was P out of joint as
33:2 And he P the maids with their children in
35:2 who were with him, P away the foreign gods
37:34 rent his garments, and P sackcloth upon his loins,
38:14 she P off her widow's garments, and put on
38:14 her widow's garments, and P on a veil, wrapping
38:19 off her veil she P on the garments of
38:28 was in labor, one P out a hand; and
39:4 of his house and P him in charge of
39:8 house, and he has P everything that he has
39:20 master took him and P him into the prison,
40:3 chief baker, and he P them in custody in
40:15 nothing that they should P me into the dungeon."
41:10 with his servants, and P me and the chief
41:42 from his hand and P it on Joseph's hand,
41:42 of fine linen, and P a gold chain about
42:17 And he P them all together in prison for
42:28 "My money has been P back; here it is
42:37 him back to you; P him in my hands,
43:22 do not know who P our money in our
43:23 your father must have P treasure in your sacks
44:1 they can carry, and P each man's money in
44:2 of his sack, and P my cup, the silver
47:6 able men among them, P them in charge of
47:29 favor in your sight, P your hand under my
48:18 one is the first-born; P your right hand upon
48:20 Manasseh"; and thus he P Ephraim before
50:26 him, and he was P in a coffin in
Ex 2:3 and pitch; and she P the child in it
3:5 "Do not come near; P off your shoes from
3:22 clothing, and you shall P them on your sons
4:4 LORD said to Moses, P out your hand, and
4:4 tail"– so he P out his hand and
4:6 LORD said to him, P your hand into your
4:6 And he P his hand into his bosom; and
4:7 Then God said, P your hand back into your
4:7 So he P his hand back into his bosom;
4:15 speak to him and P the words in his
4:21 miracles which I have P in your power; but
5:21 his servants, and have P a sword in their
8:23 Thus I will P a division between my people
9:15 now I could have P forth my hand and
12:7 of the blood, and P it on the two
12:15 first day you shall P away leaven out of
15:26 his statutes, I will P none of the diseases
15:26 upon you which I P upon the Egyptians; for
16:33 "Take a jar, and P an omer of manna
17:2 Why do you P the LORD to the proof?"
17:7 Israel, and because they P the LORD to the
17:12 took a stone and P it under him, and
19:12 the mountain shall be P to death;
21:12 he dies shall be P to death.
21:15 his mother shall be P to death.
21:16 of him, shall be P to death.
21:17 his mother shall be P to death.
21:29 owner also shall be P to death.
22:8 or not he has P his hand to his
22:11 whether he has not P his hand to his
22:19 a beast shall be P to death.
24:6 of the blood and P it in basins, and
25:12 gold for it and P them on its four
25:14 And you shall P the poles into the rings
25:16 And you shall P into the ark the testimony
25:21 And you shall P the mercy seat on the
25:21 the ark you shall P the testimony that I
26:11 clasps of bronze, and P the clasps into the
26:34 You shall P the mercy seat upon the ark
26:35 table; and you shall P the table on the
27:7 the poles shall be P through the rings, so
28:23 rings of gold, and P the two rings on
28:24 And you shall P the two cords of gold
28:26 rings of gold, and P them at the two
28:30 of judgment you shall P the Urim and the
28:41 And you shall P them upon Aaron your brother,
29:3 And you shall P them in one basket and
29:5 take the garments, and P on Aaron the coat
29:6 on his head, and P the holy crown upon
29:8 bring his sons, and P coats on them,
29:12 of the bull and P it upon the horns
29:17 and its legs, and P them with its pieces
29:20 of its blood and P it upon the tip
29:24 LORD; and you shall P all these in the
30:6 And you shall P it before the veil that
30:18 And you shall P it between the tent of
30:18 altar, and you shall P water in it,
30:36 it very small, and P part of it before
31:14 profanes it shall be P to death; whoever does
31:15 sabbath day shall be P to death.
32:27 LORD God of Israel, P every man his sword
33:4 mourned; and no man P on his ornaments.
33:5 So now P off your ornaments from you, that
33:22 passes by I will P you in a cleft
34:33 speaking with them, he P a veil on his
34:35 shone; and Moses would P the veil upon his
35:2 on it shall be P to death;
36:1 whom the LORD has P ability and intelligence to
36:2 mind the LORD had P ability, every one whose
37:5 them with gold, and P the poles into the
38:7 And he P the poles through the rings on
39:16 two gold rings, and P the two rings on
39:17 the breastpiece; and they P the two cords of
39:19 rings of gold, and P them at the two
39:25 of pure gold, and P the bells between the
Lev 1:7 Aaron the priest shall P fire on the altar,
2:1 oil upon it, and P frankincense on it,
2:15 And you shall P oil upon it, and lay
4:7 And the priest shall P some of the blood
4:18 And he shall P some of the blood on
4:25 with his finger and P it on the horns
4:30 with his finger and P it on the horns
4:34 with his finger and P it on the horns
5:11 sin offering; he shall P no oil upon it,
5:11 upon it, and shall P no frankincense on it,
6:10 And the priest shall P on his linen garment,
6:10 his linen garment, and P his linen breeches upon
6:10 on the altar, and P them beside the altar.
6:11 Then he shall P off his garments, and put
6:11 off his garments, and P on other garments, and
7:24 by beasts, may be P to any other use,
8:7 And he P on him the coat, and girded
8:7 with the robe, and P the ephod upon him,
8:8 in the breastpiece he P the Urim and the
8:15 and with his finger P it on the horns
8:23 of its blood and P it on the tip
8:24 were brought, and Moses P some of the blood
8:27 right thigh; and he P all these in the
9:9 in the blood and P it on the horns
9:20 the liver; and they P the fat upon the
10:1 took his censer, and P fire in it, and
11:32 purpose; it must be P into water, and it
11:38 but if water is P on the seed and
14:14 and the priest shall P it on the tip
14:17 hand the priest shall P on the tip of
14:18 priest's hand he shall P on the head of
14:25 the guilt offering, and P it on the tip
14:28 and the priest shall P some of the oil
14:28 the guilt offering was P;
14:29 priest's hand he shall P on the head of
14:34 a possession, and I P a leprous disease in
14:42 take other stones and P them in the place
16:4 He shall P on the holy linen coat, and
16:4 in water, and then P them on.
16:13 within the veil and P the incense on the
16:18 of the goat, and P it on the horns

P

	16:21	sins; and he shall P them upon the head
	16:23	of meeting, and shall P off the linen garments
	16:23	linen garments which he P on when he went
	16:24	a holy place, and P on his garments, and
	19:14	curse the deaf or P a stumbling block before
	19:20	They shall not be P to death, because she
	20:2	to Molech shall be P to death; the people
	20:4	Molech, and do not P him to death,
	20:9	his mother shall be P to death; he has
	20:10	the adulteress shall be P to death.
	20:11	of them shall be P to death, their blood
	20:12	of them shall be P to death; they have
	20:13	abomination; they shall be P to death, their blood
	20:15	beast, he shall be P to death; and you
	20:16	beast; they shall be P to death, their blood
	20:27	a wizard shall be P to death; they shall
	24:7	And you shall P pure frankincense with each row,
	24:12	And they P him in custody, till the will
	24:16	the LORD shall be P to death; all the
	24:16	the Name, shall be P to death.
	24:17	a man shall be P to death.
	24:21	a man shall be P to death.
	26:36	a driven leaf shall P them to flight, and
	27:29	ransomed; he shall be P to death.
Num	1:51	near, he shall be P to death.
	3:10	near, he shall be P to death."
	3:38	near was to be P to death.
	4:6	it; then they shall P on it a covering
	4:6	of blue, and shall P in its poles.
	4:7	cloth of blue, and P upon it the plates,
	4:8	of goatskin, and shall P in its poles.
	4:10	supplied: and they shall P it with all its
	4:10	covering of goatskin and P it upon the carrying
	4:11	of goatskin, and shall P in its poles;
	4:12	in the sanctuary, and P them in a cloth
	4:12	covering of goatskin, and P them on the carrying
	4:14	it; and they shall P on it all the
	4:14	of goatskin, and shall P in its poles.
	5:2	of Israel that they P out of the camp
	5:3	the dead; you shall P out both male and
	5:15	oil upon it and P no frankincense on it,
	5:17	of the tabernacle and P it into the water.
	6:18	his consecrated head and P it on the fire
	6:19	unleavened wafer, and shall P them upon the hands
	6:27	"So shall they P my name upon the people
	11:17	is upon you and P it upon them; and
	11:25	was upon him and P it upon the seventy
	11:29	that the LORD would P his spirit upon them!"
	14:22	wilderness, and yet have P me to the proof
	15:34	They P him in custody, because it had not
	15:35	"The man shall be P to death; all the
	15:38	their generations, and to P upon the tassel of
	16:7	and all his company; P fire in them and
	16:7	fire in them and P incense upon them before
	16:14	Will you P out the eyes of these men?
	16:17	take his censer, and P incense upon it, and
	16:18	his censer, and they P fire in them and
	16:46	"Take your censer, and P fire therein from off
	16:47	the people; and he P on the incense, and
	17:8	Levi had sprouted and P forth buds, and produced
	17:10	LORD said to Moses, P back the rod of
	18:7	comes near shall be P to death."
	20:26	of his garments, and P them upon Eleazar his
	20:28	of his garments, and P them upon Eleazar his
	23:5	And the LORD P a word in Balaam's mouth,
	23:16	LORD met Balaam, and P a word in his
	35:16	the murderer shall be P to death.
	35:17	the murderer shall be P to death.
	35:18	the murderer shall be P to death.
	35:19	of blood shall himself P the murderer to death;
	35:19	meets him, he shall P him to death.
	35:21	the blow shall be P to death; he is
	35:21	avenger of blood shall P the murderer to death,
	35:30	the murderer shall be P to death on the
	35:30	no person shall be P to death on the
	35:31	but he shall be P to death.
Deut	2:25	I will begin to P the dread and fear
	3:28	people, and he shall P them in possession of
	6:16	"You shall not P the LORD your God to
	10:2	broke, and you shall P them in the ark.'
	10:5	from the mountain, and P the tables in the
	12:5	all your tribes to P his name and make
	12:21	God will choose to P his name there is
	13:5	of dreams shall be P to death, because he
	13:9	first against him to P him to death, and
	13:15	you, you shall surely P the inhabitants of that
	16:9	the time you first P the sickle to the
	17:6	to die shall be P to death; a person
	17:6	person shall not be P to death on the
	17:7	first against him to P him to death, and
	17:15	you; you may not P a foreigner over you,
	18:18	brethren; and I will P my words in his
	20:13	your hand you shall P all its males to
	21:13	And she shall P off her captive's garb, and
	21:22	death and he is P to death, and you
	22:5	nor shall a man P on a woman's garment;
	22:19	wife; he may not P her away all his
	22:29	her; he may not P her away all his
	23:24	but you shall not P any in your vessel.
	23:25	but you shall not P a sickle to your
	24:16	fathers shall not be P to death for the
	24:16	shall the children be P to death for the
	24:16	every man shall be P to death for his
	26:2	you, and you shall P it in a basket,
	28:48	things; and he will P a yoke of iron
	30:7	LORD your God will P all these curses upon
	31:7	them; and you shall P them in possession of
	31:19	the people of Israel; P it in their mouths,
	31:26	of the law, and P it by the side
	32:30	a thousand, and two P ten thousand to flight,
	33:10	thy law; they shall P incense before thee, and
Josh	1:18	command him, shall be P to death.
	5:15	army said to Joshua, P off your shoes from
	6:24	and of iron, they P into the treasury of
	7:6	of Israel; and they P dust upon their heads.
	7:11	stolen, and lied, and P them among their own
	10:24	with him, "Come near, P your feet upon the
	10:24	they came near, and P their feet on their
	10:26	Joshua smote them and P them to death, and
	11:11	And they P to the sword all who were
	11:17	and smote them, and P them to death.
	17:13	Israel grew strong, they P the Canaanites to forced
	24:7	to the LORD, he P darkness between you and
	24:14	sincerity and in faithfulness; P away the gods which
	24:23	He said, "Then P away the foreign gods which
Judg	1:28	Israel grew strong, they P the Canaanites to forced
	5:26	She P her hand to the tent peg and
	6:3	For whenever the Israelites P in seed the Midianites
	6:19	flour; the meat he P in a basket, and
	6:19	and the broth he P in a pot, and
	6:20	the unleavened cakes, and P them on this rock,
	6:31	for him shall be P to death by morning.
	7:16	into three companies, and P trumpets into the hands
	8:27	ephod of it and P it in his city,
	9:25	the men of Shechem P men in ambush against
	9:26	the men of Shechem P confidence in him.
	9:49	bundle and following Abimelech P it against the
	10:16	So they P away the foreign gods from among
	14:12	them, "Let me now P a riddle to you;
	14:13	they said to him, P your riddle, that we
	14:16	love me; you have P a riddle to my
	15:4	tail to tail, and P a torch between each
	15:15	of an ass, and P out his hand and
	16:3	bar and all, and P them on his shoulders
	18:19	to him, "Keep quiet, P your hand upon your
	19:25	seized his concubine, and P her out to them;
	19:28	Then he P her upon the ass; and the
	20:13	Gibe-ah, that we may P them to death, and
	20:13	them to death, and P away evil from Israel."
	21:5	saying, "He shall be P to death."
Ruth	3:3	and anoint yourself, and P on your best clothes
1Sam	1:14	P away your wine from you."
	2:36	bread, and shall say, P me, I pray you,
	4:3	"Why has the LORD P us to rout today
	5:3	they took Dagon and P him back in his
	6:8	on the cart, and P in a box at
	6:11	And they P the ark of the LORD on
	7:3	all your heart, then P away the foreign gods
	7:4	So Israel P away the Baals and the Ashtaroth,
	8:16	and your asses, and P them to his work.
	9:23	I said to you, P it aside.'"
	11:2	right eyes, and thus P disgrace upon all Israel."
	11:11	on the morrow Saul P the people in three
	11:12	men, that we may P them to death."
	11:13	a man shall be P to death this day,
	14:26	dropping, but no man P his hand to his
	14:27	the oath; so he P forth the tip of
	14:27	in the honeycomb, and P his hand to his
	14:47	wherever he turned he P them to the worse.
	17:38	with his armor; he P a helmet of bronze
	17:39	And David P them off.
	17:40	from the brook, and P them in his shepherd's

17:49 And David P his hand in his bag and
17:54 to Jerusalem; but he P his armor in his
19:6 he shall not be P to death."
19:13 on the bed and P a pillow of goats'
20:32 "Why should he be P to death?
20:33 father was determined to P David to death.
22:17 the king would not P forth their hand to
22:19 of the priests, he P to the sword; both
22:19 asses and sheep, he P to the sword.
24:6 the LORD's anointed, to P forth my hand against
24:10 said, 'I will not P forth my hand against
24:18 me when the LORD P me into your hands.
26:9 him; for who can P forth his hand against
26:11 forbid that I should P forth my hand against
26:23 and I would not P forth my hand against
28:3 And Saul had P the mediums and the wizards
28:8 Saul disguised himself and P on other garments, and
28:25 of it, and she P it before Saul and
31:10 They P his armor in the temple of Ashtaroth;
2Sam 1:14 were not afraid to P forth your hand to
1:24 daintily in scarlet, who P ornaments of gold upon
6:6 floor of Nacon, Uzzah P out his hand to
6:7 him there because he P forth his hand to
7:15 from Saul, whom I P away from before you.
8:2 he measured to be P to death, and one
8:6 Then David P garrisons in Aram of Damascus; and
8:14 And he P garrisons in Edom; throughout all Edom
8:14 throughout all Edom he P garrisons, and all the
10:10 of his men he P in the charge of
12:13 "The LORD also has P away your sin; you
13:17 served him and said, P this woman out of
13:18 So his servant P her out, and bolted the
13:19 And Tamar P ashes on her head, and rent
14:2 be a mourner, and P on mourning garments; do
14:3 So Joab P the words in her mouth.
14:19 it was he who P all these words in
15:5 to him, he would P out his hand, and
18:12 silver, I would not P forth my hand against
19:21 "Shall not Shimei be P to death for this,
19:22 Shall any one be P to death in Israel
20:3 for the house, and P them in a house
21:1 his house, because he P the Gibeonites to death."
21:4 it for us to P any man to death
21:9 They were P to death in the first days
1Kgs 2:8 saying, 'I will not P you to death with
2:24 promised, Adonijah shall be P to death this day."
2:26 not at this time P you to death, because
2:35 The king P Benaiah the son of Jehoiada over
2:35 Joab, and the king P Zadok the priest in
5:3 him, until the LORD P them under the soles
6:27 He P the cherubim in the innermost part of
8:9 of stone which Moses P there at Horeb, where
9:3 you have built, and P my name there for
10:17 shield; and the king P them in the House
10:24 wisdom, which God had P into his mind.
11:36 I have chosen to P my name.
12:9 yoke that your father P upon us'?"
12:29 and the other he P in Dan.
14:21 tribes of Israel, to P his name there.
15:12 He P away the male cult prostitutes out of
18:23 on the wood, but P no fire to it;
18:23 on the wood, and P no fire to it.
18:25 of your god, but P no fire to it."
18:33 And he P the wood in order, and cut
18:42 upon the earth, and P his face between his
20:24 from his post, and P commanders in their places;
20:31 merciful kings; let us P sackcloth on our loins
20:32 on their loins, and P ropes on their heads,
21:27 rent his clothes, and P sackcloth upon his flesh,
22:23 behold, the LORD has P a lying spirit in
22:27 'Thus says the king, P this fellow in prison,
2Kgs 2:20 a new bowl, and P salt in it." So
3:2 and mother, for he P away the pillar of
3:21 who were able to P on armor, from the
4:10 chamber with walls, and P there for him a
5:24 from their hand, and P them in the house;
9:13 took his garment, and P it under him on
10:7 them, seventy persons, and P their heads in baskets,
10:25 So when they P them to the sword, the
11:2 be slain, and she P him and his nurse
11:4 covenant with them and P them under oath in
11:12 the king's son, and P the crown upon him,
12:9 who guarded the threshold P in it all the
14:6 But he did not P to death the children
14:6 fathers shall not be P to death for the
14:6 or the children be P to death for the

16:14 of the LORD, and P it on the north
16:17 were under it, and P it upon a pediment
17:29 of its own, and P them in the shrines
18:11 away to Assyria, and P them in Halah, and
19:7 Behold, I will P a spirit in him, so
19:28 my ears, I will P my hook in your
21:4 "In Jerusalem will I P my name."
21:7 of Israel, I will P my name for ever;
23:24 Moreover Josiah P away the mediums and the
23:33 And Pharaoh Neco P him in bonds at Riblah
25:7 before his eyes, and P out the eyes of
25:21 Babylon smote them, and P them to death at
25:29 So Jehoiachin P off his prison garments.
1Chr 1:8 of Ham: Cush, Egypt, P, and Canaan.
6:31 the men whom David P in charge of the
8:13 inhabitants of Aijalon, who P to flight the inhabitants
10:10 And they P his armor in the temple of
12:15 all its banks, and P to flight all those
13:9 floor of Chidon, Uzzah P out his hand to
13:10 smote him because he P forth his hand to
18:6 Then David P garrisons in Syria of Damascus; and
18:13 And he P garrisons in Edom; and all the
19:11 of his men he P in the charge of
21:27 the angel; and he P his sword back into
2Chr 3:16 like a necklace and P them on the tops
3:16 a hundred pomegranates, and P them on the chains.
5:10 two tables which Moses P there at Horeb, where
9:16 shield; and the king P them in the House
9:23 wisdom, which God had P into his mind.
10:9 yoke that your father P upon us'?"
11:11 the fortresses strong, and P commanders in them,
11:12 And he P shields and spears in all the
12:13 tribes of Israel to P his name there.
15:8 he took courage, and P away the abominable idols
15:13 of Israel, should be P to death, whether young
16:10 with the seer, and P him in the stocks,
18:22 behold, the LORD has P a lying spirit in
18:26 'Thus says the king, P this fellow in prison,
22:9 brought to Jehu and P to death.
22:11 be slain, and she P him and his nurse
23:11 the king's son, and P the crown upon him,
25:4 But he did not P their children to death,
25:4 fathers shall not be P to death for the
25:4 or the children be P to death for the
25:16 Why should you be P to death?" So the
29:7 of the vestibule and P out the lamps, and
30:15 and the Levites were P to shame, so that
33:7 of Israel, I will P my name for ever;
33:14 great height; he also P commanders of the army
35:3 holy to the LORD, P the holy ark in
36:7 LORD to Babylon and P them in his palace
36:22 his kingdom and also P it in writing:
Ezra 1:1 his kingdom and also P it in writing:
5:15 these vessels, go and P them in the temple
6:5 its place; you shall P them in the house
6:12 or people that shall P forth a hand to
7:27 of our fathers, who P such a thing as
10:3 with our God to P away all these wives
10:19 They pledged themselves to P away their wives, and
10:44 foreign women, and they P them away with their
Neh 2:12 what my God had P into my heart to
3:5 their nobles did not P their necks to the
7:5 Then God P it into my mind to assemble
13:5 where they had previously P the cereal offering, the
Tob 1:18 if Sennacherib the king P to death any who
1:18 in his anger he P many to death.
1:19 searched for, to be P to death, I left
2:8 that he will be P to death for doing
6:4 liver and gall and P them away safely."
8:2 ashes of incense and P the heart and liver
Jud 2:23 hill country and ravaged P and Lud, and plundered
2:27 ravaged their lands and P to death all their
4:11 before the temple and P ashes on their heads
5:21 and we shall be P to shame before the
5:22 that he must be P to death.
6:7 the hill country and P you in one of
8:12 are you, that have P God to the test
9:1 upon her face, and P ashes on her head,
9:2 uncovered her thigh to P her to shame, and
10:3 combed her hair and P on a tiara, and
10:4 And she P sandals on her feet, and put
10:4 on her feet, and P on her anklets and
16:8 with a tiara and P on a linen gown
Esth 2:8 the king's palace and P in custody of Hegai
3:9 business, that they may P it into the king's
4:1 rent his clothes and P on sackcloth and ashes,

P

4:11 alike are to be P to death, except the
5:1 the third day Esther P on her royal robes
14:2 her splendid apparel and P on the garments of
14:13 P eloquent speech in my mouth before the lion,
16:17 do well not to P in execution the letters
Job 1:10 Hast thou not P a hedge about him and
1:11 But P forth thy hand now, and touch all
1:12 upon himself do not P forth your hand." So
2:5 But P forth thy hand now, and touch his
9:27 my complaint, I will P off my sad countenance,
11:14 is in your hand, P it far away, and
13:14 in my teeth, and P my life in my
14:9 it will bud and P forth branches like a
18:5 of the wicked is P out, and the flame
18:6 lamp above him is P out.
19:6 then that God has P me in the wrong,
19:13 "He has P my brethren far from me, and
21:17 of the wicked is P out?
27:5 die I will not P away my integrity from
28:3 Men P an end to darkness, and search out
29:14 I P on righteousness, and it clothed me; my
32:22 would my Maker soon P an end to me.
38:27 to make the ground P forth grass?
38:36 Who has P wisdom in the clouds, or given
40:8 Will you even P me in the wrong?
41:2 Can you P a rope in his nose, or
41:5 bird, or will you P him on leash for
Ps 4:5 Offer right sacrifices, and P your trust in the
4:7 Thou hast P more joy in my heart than
6:10 turn back, and be P to shame in a
8:6 thy hands; thou hast P all things under his
9:10 who know thy name P their trust in thee,
9:20 P them in fear, O LORD!
15:5 change; who does not P out his money at
18:22 statutes I did not P away from me.
21:12 For you will P them to flight; you will
25:2 let me not be P to shame; let not
25:3 wait for thee be P to shame; let them
25:20 let me not be P to shame, for I
31:1 let me never be P to shame; in thy
31:17 Let me not be P to shame, O LORD,
31:17 let the wicked be P to shame, let them
33:7 in a bottle; he P the deeps in storehouses.
35:4 Let them be P to shame and dishonor who
35:26 Let them be P to shame and confusion altogether
37:19 ever; they are not P to shame in evil
40:3 He P a new song in my mouth, a
40:3 see and fear, and P their trust in the
40:14 Let them be P to shame and confusion altogether
44:7 our foes, and hast P to confusion those who
51:10 heart, O God, and P a new and right
53:5 ungodly; they will be P to shame, for God
54:5 evil; in thy faithfulness P an end to them.
56:3 I am afraid, I P my trust in thee.
56:8 count of my tossings; P thou my tears in
57:3 save me, he will P to shame those who
62:10 P no confidence in extortion, set no vain hopes
69:6 hope in thee be P to shame through me,
70:2 Let them be P to shame and confusion who
71:1 let me never be P to shame!
71:13 May my accusers be P to shame and consumed;
71:24 for they have been P to shame and disgraced
73:27 shall perish; thou dost P an end to those
74:21 not the downtrodden be P to shame; let the
78:66 And he P his adversaries to rout; he put
78:66 adversaries to rout; he P them to everlasting shame.
83:17 Let them be P to shame and dismayed for
85:4 of our salvation, and P away thy indignation toward
86:17 may see and be P to shame because thou,
88:6 Thou hast P me in the depths of the
95:9 fathers tested me, and P me to the proof,
97:7 worshipers of images are P to shame, who make
105:18 fetters, his neck was P in a collar of
106:14 in the wilderness, and P God to the test
109:28 Let my assailants be P to shame; may thy
115:10 O house of Aaron, P your trust in the
118:8 the LORD than to P confidence in man.
118:9 the LORD than to P confidence in princes.
119:6 I shall not be P to shame, having my
119:29 P false ways far from me; and graciously teach
119:31 let me not be P to shame!
119:46 and shall not be P to shame;
119:78 Let the godless be P to shame, because they
119:80 I may not be P to shame!
119:116 let me not be P to shame in my
125:3 righteous, lest the righteous P forth their hands to
127:5 He shall not be P to shame when he
129:5 who hate Zion be P to shame and turned
143:8 for in thee I P my trust.
146:3 P not your trust in princes, in a son
Prov 4:25 P away from you crooked speech, and put devious
4:25 you crooked speech, and P devious talk far from
12:24 the slothful will be P to forced labor.
13:9 the wicked will be P out.
20:20 his lamp will be P out in utter darkness.
23:2 is before you; and P a knife to your
24:20 the wicked will be P out.
25:6 Do not P yourself forward in the king's presence
25:7 than to be P lower in the presence of
30:32 have been devising evil, P your hand on your
Eccl 3:11 time; also he has P eternity into man's mind,
10:10 the edge, he must P forth more strength; but
11:10 from your mind, and P away pain from your
Song 5:3 I had P off my garment, how could I
5:3 garment, how could I P it on?
5:4 My beloved P his hand to the latch, and
Wis 1:2 those who do not P him to the test,
4:4 For even if they P forth boughs for a
5:18 his enemies; he will P on righteousness as a
8:12 greater length they will P their hands on their
12:2 freed from wickedness and P their trust in thee,
14:4 lacks skill, he may P to sea.
18:21 withstood the anger and P an end to the
Sir 2:10 the Lord and was P to shame?
5:12 neighbor; but if not, P your hand on your
6:24 P your feet into her fetters, and your neck
6:25 P your shoulder under her and carry her, and
6:31 a glorious robe, and P her on like a
7:6 powerful man, and thus P a blot on your
12:12 Do not P him next to you, lest he
15:4 and will not be P to shame.
24:21 me will not be P to shame, and those
28:12 it, it will be P out; and both come
28:23 and will not be P out.
33:27 P him to work, that he may not be
34:7 many, and those who P their hope in them
39:14 fragrance like frankincense, and P forth blossoms
40:15 the ungodly will not P forth many branches; they
42:11 among the people, and P you to shame before
43:30 When you exalt him, P forth all your strength,
45:7 with splendid vestments, and P a glorious robe upon
45:13 No outsider ever P them on, but only his
47:20 You P stain upon your honor, and defiled your
50:11 When he P on his glorious robe and clothed
51:18 I shall never be P to shame.
51:26 P your neck under the yoke, and let your
51:29 may you not be P to shame when you
Is 5:20 and good evil, who P darkness for light and
5:20 light for darkness, who P bitter for sweet and
7:12 and I will not P the LORD to the
9:10 down, but we will P cedars in their place."
11:8 the weaned child shall P his hand on the
11:14 They shall P forth their hand against Edom and
13:11 their iniquity; I will P an end to the
27:6 Israel shall blossom and P forth shoots, and fill
28:25 dill, sow cummin, and P in wheat in rows
31:8 young men shall be P to forced labor.
37:7 Behold, I will P a spirit in him, so
37:29 my ears, I will P my hook in your
41:11 against you shall be P to shame and confounded;
41:19 I will P in the wilderness the cedar, the
42:1 soul delights; I have P my Spirit upon him,
42:17 turned back and utterly P to shame, who trust
43:26 P me in remembrance, let us argue together; set
44:9 that they may be P to shame.
44:11 his fellows shall be P to shame, and the
44:11 terrified, they shall be P to shame together.
45:16 All of them are P to shame and confounded,
45:17 you shall not be P to shame or confounded
46:13 not tarry; I will P salvation in Zion, for
47:2 millstones and grind meal, P off your veil, strip
49:18 the LORD, you shall P them all on as
49:21 and barren, exiled and P away, but who has
49:23 me shall not be P to shame."
50:1 divorce, with which I P her away?
50:1 transgressions your mother was P away.
50:7 I shall not be P to shame;
51:9 Awake, awake, P on strength, O arm of the
51:16 And I have P my words in your mouth,
51:23 more; and I will P it into the hand
52:1 Awake, awake, P on your strength, O Zion; put
52:1 your strength, O Zion; P on your beautiful garments,

	53:10	bruise him; he has P him to grief; when
	54:4	you will not be P to shame; for you
	57:4	your mouth wide and P out your tongue?
	59:17	He P on righteousness as a breastplate, and a
	59:17	upon his head; he P on garments of vengeance
	59:21	words which I have P in your mouth, shall
	62:6	You who P the LORD in remembrance, take no
	63:11	Where is he who P in the midst of
	65:13	but you shall be P to shame;
	66:5	they who shall be P to shame.
	66:19	the nations, to Tarshish, P, and Lud, who draw
Jer	1:9	Then the LORD P forth his hand and touched
	1:9	me, "Behold, I have P my words in your
	2:36	You shall be P to shame by Egypt as
	2:36	Egypt as you were P to shame by Assyria.
	8:9	wise men shall be P to shame, they shall
	9:4	of his neighbor, and P no trust in any
	10:14	knowledge; every goldsmith is P to shame by his
	13:1	a linen waistcloth, and P it on your loins,
	13:2	of the LORD, and P it on my loins.
	17:13	forsake thee shall be P to shame; those who
	17:18	Let those be P to shame who persecute me,
	17:18	let me not be P to shame; let them
	20:2	Jeremiah the prophet, and P him in the stocks
	25:31	the wicked he will P to the sword, says
	26:15	certain that if you P me to death, you
	26:19	Judah and all Judah P him to death?
	26:21	the king sought to P him to death; but
	26:24	the people to be P to death.
	27:2	thongs and yoke-bars, and P them on your neck.
	27:8	king of Babylon, and P its neck under the
	28:14	of Israel: I have P upon the neck of
	29:26	madman who prophesies, to P him in the stocks
	31:33	the LORD: I will P my law within them,
	32:14	this open deed, and P them in an earthenware
	32:40	them; and I will P the fear of me
	36:20	to the king, having P the scroll in the
	37:4	had not yet been P in prison.
	37:18	people, that you have P me in prison?
	38:4	"Let this man be P to death, for he
	38:7	heard that they had P Jeremiah into the cistern—
	38:12	Ethiopian said to Jeremiah, P the rags and clothes
	38:15	not be sure to P me to death?
	38:16	souls, I will not P you to death or
	38:25	and we will not P you to death,'
	39:7	He P out the eyes of Zedekiah, and bound
	39:18	war, because you have P your trust in me,
	46:4	helmets, polish your spears, P on your coats of
	46:9	men of Ethiopia and P who handle the shield,
	46:24	of Egypt shall be P to shame, she shall
	47:6	P yourself into your scabbard, rest and be still!
	48:1	Kiriathaim is P to shame, it is taken; the
	48:1	taken; the fortress is P to shame and broken
	48:20	has happened?' Moab is P to shame, for it
	50:2	is taken, Bel is P to shame, Merodach is
	50:2	Her images are P to shame, her idols are
	51:17	knowledge; every goldsmith is P to shame by his
	51:47	whole land shall be P to shame, and all
	51:51	your mind: 'We are P to shame, for we
	52:11	He P out the eyes of Zedekiah, and bound
	52:11	him to Babylon, and P him in prison till
	52:27	Babylon smote them, and P them to death at
	52:33	So Jehoiachin P off his prison garments.
Lam	2:10	on their heads and P on sackcloth; the maidens
	3:7	cannot escape; he has P heavy chains on me;
	3:29	on him; let him P his mouth in the
Bar	3:7	For thou hast P the fear of thee in
	3:7	exile, for we have P away from our hearts
	4:20	robe of peace and P on the sackcloth of
	4:22	For I have P my hope in the Everlasting
	5:1	affliction, O Jerusalem, and P on for ever the
	5:2	P on the robe of the righteousness from God;
	5:2	the righteousness from God; P on your head the
	6:39	serve them will be P to shame.
Ezek	4:2	city, even Jerusalem; and P siegeworks against it,
	4:8	And, behold, I will P cords upon you, so
	4:9	millet and spelt, and P them into a single
	7:24	their houses; I will P an end to their
	8:3	He P forth the form of a hand, and
	8:17	Lo, they P the branch to their nose.
	9:4	city, through Jerusalem, and P a mark upon the
	10:7	some of it, and P it into the hands
	11:19	them one heart, and P a new spirit within
	12:23	Lord GOD: I will P an end to this
	16:11	you with ornaments, and P bracelets on your arms,
	16:12	And I P a ring on your nose, and
	17:6	brought forth branches and P forth foliage.
	19:9	With hooks they P him in a cage, and
	22:20	wrath, and I will P you in and melt
	23:27	Thus I will P an end to your lewdness
	23:42	the wilderness; and they P bracelets upon the hands
	23:48	Thus will I P an end to lewdness in
	24:4	pour in water also; P in it the pieces
	24:7	midst of her; she P it on the bare
	24:17	on your turban, and P your shoes on your
	27:10	"Persia and Lud and P were in your army
	29:4	made it.' I will P hooks in your jaws,
	30:5	Ethiopia, and P, and Lud, and all Arabia, and
	30:10	Lord GOD: I will P an end to the
	30:13	destroy the idols, and P an end to the
	30:13	Egypt; so I will P fear in the land
	30:24	king of Babylon, and P my sword in his
	30:25	When I P my sword into the hand of
	32:8	dark over you, and P darkness upon your land,
	34:10	at their hand, and P a stop to their
	36:26	new spirit I will P within you; and I
	36:27	And I will P my spirit within you, and
	37:6	you with skin, and P breath in you, and
	37:14	And I will P my Spirit within you, and
	38:4	turn you about, and P hooks into your jaws,
	38:5	swords; Persia, Cush, and P are with them, all
	42:13	offerings; there they shall P the most holy offerings—
	42:14	are holy; they shall P on other garments before
	43:9	Now let them P away their idolatry and the
	43:20	of its blood, and P it on the four
	44:19	the people, they shall P off the garments in
	44:19	chambers; and they shall P on other garments, lest
	45:9	P away violence and oppression, and execute justice
	45:19	the sin offering and P it on the doorposts
Dan	3:42	Do not P us to shame, but deal with
	3:43	to thy servants be P to shame;
	5:19	whom he would he P down.
	5:29	chain of gold was P about his neck, and
	7:24	former ones, and shall P down three kings.
	9:24	finish the transgression, to P an end to sin,
	11:18	but a commander shall P an end to his
	13:28	plot to have Susanna P to death.
	13:45	led away to be P to death, God aroused
	13:53	Lord said, 'Do not P to death an innocent
	13:56	Then he P him aside, and commanded them to
	13:62	law of Moses, they P them to death.
	14:22	Therefore the king P them to death, and gave
Hos	1:4	Jezreel, and I will P an end to the
	2:2	her husband—that she P away her harlotry from
	2:11	And I will P an end to all her
	10:6	Ephraim shall be P to shame, and Israel shall
	10:11	neck; but I will P Ephraim to the yoke,
Joel	2:26	shall never again be P to shame.
	2:27	shall never again be P to shame.
	3:13	P in the sickle, for the harvest is ripe.
Amos	6:3	territory, O you who P far away the evil
Jon	3:5	proclaimed a fast, and P on sackcloth, from the
Mic	3:7	disgraced, and the diviners P to shame; they shall
	6:14	inward parts; you shall P away, but not save,
	7:5	P no trust in a neighbor, have no confidence
Nah	3:9	and that without limit; P and the Libyans were
Hab	3:9	from thy bow, and P the arrows to the
Zeph	3:11	you shall not be P to shame because of
Hag	1:6	wages earns wages to P them into a bag
Zech	3:5	I said, "Let them P a clean turban on
	3:5	So they P a clean turban on his head
	12:8	day the LORD will P a shield about the
	13:4	prophesies; he will not P on a hairy mantle
	13:9	And I will P this third into the fire,
Mal	2:3	offerings, and I will P you out of my
	3:10	my house; and thereby P me to the test,
	3:15	prosper but when they P God to the test
1Mac	1:2	battles, conquered strongholds, and P to death the
	1:9	They all P on crowns after his death, and
	1:60	to the decree, they P to death the women
	2:14	sons rent their clothes, P on sackcloth, and mourned
	2:61	generation, that none who P their trust in him
	3:3	Like a giant he P on his breastplate; he
	3:47	They fasted that day, P on sackcloth and sprinkled
	4:20	their army had been P to flight, and that
	6:24	us; moreover, they have P to death as many
	8:14	one of them has P on a crown or
	9:25	chose the ungodly and P them in charge of
	9:52	and in them he P troops and stores of
	9:53	land as hostages and P them under guard in
	10:21	So Jonathan P on the holy garments in the
	10:37	some of them be P in positions of trust

P

10:72 your fathers were twice P to flight in their
10:77 troop of cavalry and P confidence in it.
11:13 Ptolemy entered Antioch and P on the crown of
11:13 Thus he P two crowns upon his head, the
11:15 a strong force, and P him to flight.
11:23 of the priests, and P himself in danger,
11:37 given to Jonathan and P up in a conspicuous
11:54 began to reign and P on the crown.
11:71 rent his garments and P dust on his head,
12:39 king in Asia and P on the crown, and
13:29 upon the columns he P suits of armor for
14:3 him to Arsaces, who P him under guard.
14:23 with honor and to P a copy of their
14:27 on bronze tablets and P it upon pillars on
14:36 that the Gentiles were P out of the country,
14:44 clothed in purple or P on a gold buckle.
14:48 upon bronze tablets, to P them up in a
16:8 and his army were P to flight, and many
2Mac 3:27 took him up and P him on a stretcher
4:34 for justice, he immediately P him out of the
4:42 and killed some, and P them all to flight;
5:26 He P to the sword all those who came
7:10 was demanded, he quickly P out his tongue and
8:6 captured strategic positions and P to flight not a
9:2 result that Antiochus was P to flight by the
9:4 by those who had P him to flight; so
11:3 other nations, and to P up the high-priesthood for
12:37 not expecting it, and P them to flight.
13:4 to Beroea and to P him to death by
13:21 sought for, caught, and P in prison.
Mt 1:19 man and unwilling to P her to shame, resolved
5:15 light a lamp and P it under a bushel,
5:25 guard, and you be P in prison;
6:25 body, what you shall P on.
9:17 Neither is new wine P into old wineskins; if
9:17 but new wine is P into fresh wineskins, and
9:25 the crowd had been P outside, he went in
10:21 parents and have them P to death;
12:18 I will P my Spirit upon him, and he
12:44 it empty, swept, and P in order.
13:24 Another parable he P before them, saying, "The
13:31 parable he P before them, saying, "The kingdom
14:3 and bound him and P him in prison, for
14:5 though he wanted to P him to death, he
15:30 many others, and they P them at his feet,
18:2 him a child, he P him in the midst
18:29 refused and went and P him in prison till
19:6 together, let not man P asunder."
19:7 of divorce, and to P her away?"
21:7 and the colt, and P their garments on them,
21:41 to him, "He will P those wretches to a
22:18 their malice, said, "Why P me to the test,
22:44 right hand, till I P thy enemies under thy
24:9 up to tribulation, and P you to death; and
24:51 will punish him, and P him with the hypocrites;
26:52 Jesus said to him, P your sword back into
26:59 Jesus that they might P him to death,
27:1 counsel against Jesus to P him to death;
27:6 is not lawful to P them into the treasury,
27:28 they stripped him and P a scarlet robe upon
27:29 crown of thorns they P it on his head,
27:29 on his head, and P a reed in his
27:31 of the robe, and P his own clothes on
27:37 over his head they P the charge against him,
27:48 it with vinegar, and P it on a reed,
Mk 4:21 brought in to be P under a bushel, or
5:40 But he P them all outside, and took the
6:9 wear sandals and not P on two tunics.
7:32 the multitude privately, he P his fingers into his
9:36 took a child, and P him in the midst
10:4 of divorce, and to P her away."
10:9 together, let not man P asunder."
12:15 said to them, "Why P me to the test?
12:36 right hand, till I P thy enemies under thy
12:41 Many rich people P in large sums.
12:42 poor widow came, and P in two copper coins,
12:43 this poor widow has P in more than all
12:44 of her poverty has P in everything she had,
13:12 parents and have them P to death;
14:55 testimony against Jesus to P him to death; but
15:17 crown of thorns they P it on him.
15:20 the purple cloak, and P his own clothes on
15:35 sponge full of vinegar, P it on a reed
Lk 1:52 their hearts, he has P down the mighty from
4:29 they rose up and P him out of the
5:3 he asked him to P out a little from
5:4 he said to Simon, P out into the deep
5:38 new wine must be P into fresh wineskins.
6:38 running over, will be P into your lap.
9:47 took a child and P him by his side,
10:25 lawyer stood up to P him to the test,
11:25 finds it swept and P in order.
12:22 body, what you shall P on.
12:46 will punish him, and P him with the unfaithful.
12:58 officer, and the officer P you in prison.
13:8 dig about it and P on manure.
13:17 all his adversaries were P to shame; and all
15:22 the best robe, and P it on him; and
15:22 it on him; and P a ring on his
16:4 houses when I am P out of the stewardship.'
19:23 then did you not P my money into the
21:2 saw a poor widow P in two copper coins.
21:3 this poor widow has P in more than all
21:4 out of her poverty P in all the living
21:16 of you they will P to death;
22:2 were seeking how to P him to death; for
23:31 led away to be P to death with him.
Jn 3:24 had not yet been P in prison.
5:6 have no man to P me into the pool
9:15 said to them, "He P clay on my eyes,
9:22 he was to be P out of the synagogue.
11:53 took counsel how to P him to death.
12:6 to take what was P into it.
12:10 chief priests planned to P Lazarus also to death,
12:42 lest they should be P out of the synagogue:
13:2 the devil had already P it into the heart
16:2 They will P you out of the synagogues; indeed,
18:11 Jesus said to Peter, P your sword into its
18:31 lawful for us to P any man to death."
19:2 crown of thorns, and P it on his head,
19:19 wrote a title and P it on the cross;
19:29 stood there; so they P a sponge full of
20:27 he said to Thomas, P your finger here, and
20:27 see my hands; and P out your hand, and
21:7 was the Lord, he P on his clothes, for
Acts 1:23 And they P forward two, Joseph called Barsabbas,
4:3 they arrested them and P them in custody until
5:18 arrested the apostles and P them in the common
5:25 "The men whom you P in prison are standing
5:34 the men to be P outside for a while.
9:40 But Peter P them all outside and knelt down
10:39 They P him to death by hanging him on
12:4 had seized him, he P him in prison, and
12:8 him, "Dress yourself and P on your sandals." And
12:19 that they should be P to death.
12:21 an appointed day Herod P on his royal robes,
16:24 received this charge, he P them into the inner
19:33 whom the Jews had P forward.
24:21 knowledge of the Way, P them off, saying, "When
26:10 but when they were P to death I cast
27:2 coast of Asia, we P to sea, accompanied by
27:3 The next day we P in at Sidon; and
27:6 sailing for Italy, and P us on board.
27:12 the majority advised to P to sea from there,
28:3 bundle of sticks and P them on the fire,
28:10 when we sailed, they P on board whatever we
Rom 3:25 Christ Jesus, whom God P forward as an expiation
4:25 our Lord, who was P to death for our
8:13 by the Spirit you P to death the deeds
9:33 him will not be P to shame."
10:11 in him will be P to shame."
13:12 works of darkness and P on the armor of
13:14 But P on the Lord Jesus Christ, and make
14:13 rather decide never to P a stumbling block or
1Cor 9:12 endure anything rather than P an obstacle in the
10:9 We must not P the Lord to the test,
15:25 reign until he has P all his enemies under
15:27 "For God has P all things in subjection under
15:27 says, "All things are P in subjection under him,"
15:27 he is excepted who P all things under him.
15:28 subjected to him who P all things under him,
15:53 this perishable nature must P on the imperishable,
15:53 this mortal nature must P on immortality.
16:2 of you is to P something aside and store
16:10 comes, see that you P him at ease among
2Cor 1:22 commissioned us; he has P his seal upon us
2:5 some measure--not to P it too severely--
3:13 not like Moses, who P a veil over his
5:2 groan, and long to P on our heavenly dwelling,
6:3 We P no obstacle in any one's way, so
7:14 you, I was not P to shame; but just
10:8 I shall not be P to shame.

Gal 3:27 baptized into Christ have P on Christ.
Eph 1:22 come; and he has P all things under his
4:22 P off your old nature which belongs to your
4:24 of your minds, and P on the new nature,
4:31 clamor and slander be P away from you, with
6:11 P on the whole armor of God, that you
6:14 with truth, and having P on the breastplate of
Phil 1:16 knowing that I am P here for the defense
3:3 in Christ Jesus, and P no confidence in the
Col 3:5 P to death therefore what is earthly in you:
3:8 But now P them all away: anger, wrath, malice,
3:9 seeing that you have P off the old nature
3:10 its practices and have P on the new nature,
3:12 P on then, as God's chosen ones, holy and
3:14 And above all these P on love, which binds
1Thes 5:8 us be sober, and P on the breastplate of
1Tim 4:6 If you P these instructions before the brethren, you
Tit 2:8 an opponent may be P to shame, having nothing
Heb 2:13 And again, "I will P my trust in him."
3:9 wilderness, where your fathers P me to the test
8:10 the Lord: I will P my laws into their
9:26 of the age to P away sin by the
10:16 the Lord: I will P my laws on their
11:34 became mighty in war, P foreign armies to flight.
12:13 lame may not be P out of joint but
Jas 1:20 Therefore P away all filthiness and rank growth of
3:3 If we P bits into the mouths of horses
1Pet 2:1 So P away all malice and all guile and
2:6 him will not be P to shame."
2:15 doing right you should P to silence the ignorance
3:16 in Christ may be P to shame.
3:18 us to God, being P to death in the
3Jn 1:9 Diotrephes, who likes to P himself first, does not
Rev 2:14 who taught Balak to P a stumbling block before
14:15 sat upon the cloud, P in your sickle, and
14:18 had the sharp sickle, P in your sickle, and
17:17 fire, for God has P it into their hearts

PUTEOLI

Acts 28:13 and on the second day we came to P

PUTHITES

1Chr 2:53 Kiriath-jearim: the Ithrites, the P, the Shumathites,

PUTI-EL

Ex 6:25 of the daughters of P; and she bore him

PUTS (39)

Ex 30:33 like it or whoever P any of it on
Num 22:38 The word that God P in my mouth, that
23:12 speak what the LORD P in my mouth?"
Deut 24:1 bill of divorce and P it in her hand
24:3 bill of divorce and P it in her hand
25:11 is beating him, and P out her hand and
Josh 23:10 One man of you P to flight a thousand,
1Kgs 20:11 himself as he that P it off.'"
Job 4:18 in his servants he P no trust, and his
15:15 Behold, God P no trust in his holy ones,
28:9 "Man P his hand to the flinty rock, and
33:11 as his enemy; he P my feet in the
Prov 18:18 The lot P an end to disputes and decides
21:29 A wicked man P on a bold face, but
25:8 end, when your neighbor P you to shame?
31:19 She P her hands to the distaff, and her
Song 2:13 The fig tree P forth its figs, and the
Sir 14:18 which sheds some and P forth others, so are
26:13 husband, and her skill P fat on his bones.
43:20 water, and the water P it on like a
Mic 3:5 war against him who P nothing into their mouths.
Mt 9:16 And no one P a piece of unshrunk cloth
24:32 branch becomes tender and P forth its leaves, you
Mk 2:22 And no one P new wine into old wineskins;
4:29 ripe, at once he P in the sickle, because
4:32 of all shrubs, and P forth large branches, so
13:28 branch becomes tender and P forth its leaves, you
13:34 he leaves home and P his servants in charge,
Lk 5:36 a new garment and P it upon an old
5:37 And no one P new wine into old wineskins;
8:16 with a vessel, or P it under a bed,
8:16 under a bed, but P it on a stand,
9:62 him, "No one who P his hand to the
11:33 after lighting a lamp P it in a cellar
1Cor 15:54 When the perishable P on the imperishable, and the
15:54 imperishable, and the mortal P on immortality, then
2Cor 8:16 be to God who P the same earnest care
11:20 advantage of you, or P on airs, or strikes

3Jn 1:10 to welcome them and P them out of the

PUTTEST

Job 13:27 Thou P my feet in the stocks, and watchest

PUTTING (31)

Gen 21:14 gave it to Hagar, P it on her shoulder,
Num 5:3 both male and female, P them outside the camp,
Josh 19:47 after capturing it and P it to the sword
Judg 7:6 of those that lapped, P their hands to their
18:21 they turned and departed, P the little ones and
1Kgs 2:5 shed in war, and P innocent blood upon the
2Kgs 4:34 lay upon the child, P his mouth upon his
Jud 8:13 You are P the Lord Almighty to the test--
8:25 our God, who is P us to the test
Ps 75:7 God who executes judgment, P down one and lifting
Sir 50:10 like an olive tree P forth its fruit, and
Ezek 13:19 for pieces of bread, P to death persons who
14:7 into his heart and P the stumbling block of
17:13 a covenant with him, P him under oath.
1Mac 13:32 king in his place, P on the crown of
2Mac 4:15 by their fathers and P the highest value upon
7:40 died in his integrity, P his whole trust in
8:22 to command a division, P fifteen hundred men under
12:23 with the utmost vigor, P the sinners to the
Mk 12:41 and watched the multitude P money into the
Lk 21:1 and saw the rich P their gifts into the
Acts 15:10 trial of God by P a yoke upon the
27:4 And P to sea from there we sailed under
28:8 him and prayed, and P his hands on him
28:12 P in at Syracuse, we stayed there for three
2Cor 5:3 dwelling, so that by P it on we may
Eph 4:25 Therefore, P away falsehood, let every one speak the
Col 2:11 made without hands, by P off the body of
Heb 2:8 with glory and honor, P everything in subjection
2:8 Now in P everything in subjection to him, he
2Pet 1:14 I know that the P off of my body

PUVAH (2)

Gen 46:13 sons of Issachar: Tola, P, Iob, and Shimron.
Num 26:23 of the Tolaites; of P, the family of the

PYRAMIDS (2)

1Mac 13:28 He also erected seven P, opposite one another, for
13:29 And for the P he devised an elaborate setting,

PYRE

Is 30:33 is made ready, its P made deep and wide,

PYRRHUS

Acts 20:4 Beroea, the son of P, accompanied him; and of

Q

QUADRENNIAL

2Mac 4:18 When the Q games were being held at Tyre

QUAILS (6)

Ex 16:13 In the evening Q came up and covered the
Num 11:31 LORD, and it brought Q from the sea, and
11:32 day, and gathered the Q; he who gathered least
Ps 105:40 asked, and he brought Q, and gave them bread
Wis 16:2 and thou didst prepare Q to eat, a delicacy
19:12 to give them relief, Q came up from the

QUAKE (6)

Ps 60:2 made the land to Q, thou hast rent it
99:1 sits enthroned upon the cherubim; let the earth Q
Is 64:1 that the mountains might Q at thy presence--
Ezek 31:16 will make the nations Q at the sound of
38:20 of the earth, shall Q at my presence, and
Nah 1:5 The mountains Q before him, the hills melt; the

QUAKED (9)

Ex 19:18 and the whole mountain Q greatly.
Judg 5:5 The mountains Q before the LORD, yon Sinai before
1Sam 14:15 raiders trembled; the earth Q; and it became a
2Sam 22:8 the heavens trembled and Q, because he was angry.
Ps 18:7 the mountains trembled and Q, because he was
68:8 wilderness, [Selah] the earth Q, the heavens poured
68:8 of God; yon Sinai Q at the presence of
Is 5:25 them, and the mountains Q; and their corpses were
64:3 camest down, the mountains Q at thy presence.

QUAKES (3)

Jer 8:16 the neighing of their stallions the whole land Q
10:10 his wrath the earth Q, and the nations cannot
Joel 2:10 The earth Q before them, the heavens tremble.

QUAKING (2)

Jer 4:24 and lo, they were Q, and all the hills
Ezek 12:18 eat your bread with Q, and drink water with

QUALIFICATION

2Mac 4:25 he returned, possessing no Q for the high-priesthood,

QUALIFIED (3)

1Chr 26:8 and brethren, able men Q for the service; sixty-two
1Mac 13:40 any of you are Q to be enrolled in
Col 1:12 the Father, who has Q us to share in

QUANTITIES (4)

1Chr 22:3 well as bronze in Q beyond weighing,
22:4 and Tyrians brought great Q of cedar to David.
29:2 of wood, besides great Q of onyx and stones
2Chr 4:18 these things in great Q, so that the weight

QUANTITY (8)

Lev 19:35 judgment, in measures of length or weight or Q
1Kgs 10:10 and a very great Q of spices, and precious
1Chr 22:5 provided materials in great Q before his death.
23:29 and all measures of Q or size.
2Chr 9:9 and a very great Q of spices, and precious
Jud 12:20 and drank a great Q of wine, much more
15:7 there was a vast Q of it.
Jn 21:6 it in, for the Q of fish.

QUARREL (10)

Gen 26:22 that they did not Q; so he called its
45:24 to them, "Do not Q on the way."
Ex 21:18 "When men Q and one strikes the other with
2Kgs 5:7 he is seeking a Q with me."
Prov 17:14 so quit before the Q breaks out.
26:17 who meddles in a Q not his own is
Sir 6:9 and will disclose a Q to your disgrace.
8:2 Do not Q with a rich man, lest his
28:11 A hasty Q kindles fire, and urgent strife sheds
Is 58:4 you fast only to Q and to fight and

QUARRELED (4)

Gen 26:20 the herdsmen of Gerar Q with Isaac's herdsmen,
26:21 another well, and they Q over that also; so
Lev 24:10 a man of Israel Q in the camp,
2Sam 14:6 two sons, and they Q with one another in

QUARRELING (11)

Prov 18:19 a strong city, but Q is like the bars
19:13 father, and a wife's Q is a continual dripping
20:3 aloof from strife; but every fool will be Q
22:10 will go out, and Q and abuse will cease.
26:20 there is no whisperer, Q ceases.
Acts 7:26 them as they were Q and would have reconciled
Rom 13:13 and licentiousness, not in Q and jealousy.
1Cor 1:11 people that there is Q among you, my brethren.
2Cor 12:20 there may be Q, jealousy, anger, selfishness, slander,
1Tim 2:8 hands without anger or Q;
Tit 3:2 no one, to avoid Q, to be gentle, and

QUARRELS (4)

Sir 27:14 on end, and their Q make a man stop
42:8 the aged man who Q with the young.
2Tim 2:23 senseless controversies; you know that they breed Q
Tit 3:9 genealogies, dissensions, and Q over the law, for

QUARRELSOME (3)

Prov 26:21 fire, so is a Q man for kindling strife.
1Tim 3:3 violent but gentle, not Q, and no lover of
2Tim 2:24 servant must not be Q but kindly to every

QUARRIED (5)

1Kgs 5:17 the king's command, they Q out great, costly stones
2Kgs 12:12 to buy timber and Q stone for making repairs
22:6 for buying timber and Q stone to repair the
2Chr 34:11 the builders to buy Q stone, and timber for
Sir 50:3 cistern for water was Q out, a reservoir like

QUARRIES

Eccl 10:9 He who Q stones is hurt by them; and

QUARRY (4)

1Kgs 6:7 stone prepared at the Q; so that neither hammer
2Chr 2:2 and eighty thousand to Q in the hill country,
2:18 burdens, eighty thousand to Q in the hill country,
Is 51:1 hewn, and to the Q from which you were

QUART

Rev 6:6 living creatures saying, "A Q of wheat for a

QUARTER (7)

2Kgs 22:14 Jerusalem in the Second Q; and they talked with
2Chr 34:22 Jerusalem in the Second Q and spoke to her
Esth 4:14 the Jews from another Q, but you and your
Jer 50:26 against her from every Q; open her granaries; pile
Zeph 1:10 wail from the Second Q, a loud crash from
2Mac 12:16 the adjoining lake, a Q of a mile wide,
Mk 1:45 country; and people came to him from every Q

QUARTERMASTER

Jer 51:59 Seraiah was the Q

QUARTERS

Jer 49:36 winds from the four Q of heaven; and I

QUARTS

Rev 6:6 a denarius, and three Q of barley for a

QUARTUS

Rom 16:23 treasurer, and our brother Q, greet you.

QUEEN (58)

1Kgs 10:1 Now when the Q of Sheba heard of the
10:4 And when the Q of Sheba had seen all
10:10 as these which the Q of Sheba gave to
10:13 Solomon gave to the Q of Sheba all that
11:19 his own wife, the sister of Tahpenes the Q
15:13 his mother from being Q mother because she had
2Kgs 10:13 the sons of the Q mother."
2Chr 9:1 Now when the Q of Sheba heard of the
9:3 And when the Q of Sheba had seen the
9:9 as those which the Q of Sheba gave to
9:12 Solomon gave to the Q of Sheba all that
15:16 Asa removed from being Q mother because she had
Neh 2:6 said to me (the Q sitting beside him), "How
Esth 1:9 Q Vashti also gave a banquet for the women
1:11 as chamberlains, to bring Q Vashti before the king
1:12 But Q Vashti refused to come at the king's
1:15 to be done to Q Vashti, because she has
1:16 to the king has Q Vashti done wrong, but
1:17 this deed of the Q will be made known
1:17 say, 'King Ahasuerus commanded Q Vashti to be
1:18 have heard of the Q's behavior will be telling
2:4 pleases the king be Q instead of Vashti." This
2:17 head and made her Q instead of Vashti.
2:22 he told it to Q Esther, and Esther told
4:4 and told her, the Q was deeply distressed; she
5:2 when the king saw Q Esther standing in the
5:3 her, "What is it, Q Esther?
5:12 And Haman added, "Even Q Esther let no one
7:1 in to feast with Q Esther.
7:2 "What is your petition, Q Esther?
7:3 Then Q Esther answered, "If I have found favor
7:5 King Ahasuerus said to Q Esther, "Who is he,
7:6 was in terror before the king and the Q
7:7 beg his life from Q Esther, for he saw
7:8 he even assault the Q in my presence, in
8:1 King Ahasuerus gave to Q Esther the house of
8:7 King Ahasuerus said to Q Esther and to Mordecai
9:12 the king said to Q Esther, "In Susa the
9:29 Q Esther, the daughter of Abihail, and Mordecai
9:31 Mordecai the Jew and Q Esther enjoined upon the
9:32 The command of Q Esther fixed these practices of
10:6 is Esther, whom the king married and made Q
14:1 And Esther the Q, seized with deathly anxiety, fled
15:7 And the Q faltered, and turned pale and faint,
Ps 45:9 right hand stands the Q in gold of Ophir.
Jer 7:18 make cakes for the Q of heaven; and they
13:18 the king and the Q mother: "Take a lowly
29:2 King Jeconiah, and the Q mother, the eunuchs, the
44:17 burn incense to the Q of heaven and pour
44:18 burning incense to the Q of heaven and pouring
44:19 burned incense to the Q of heaven and poured
44:25 burn incense to the Q of heaven and to
Dan 5:10 The Q, because of the words of the king
5:10 banqueting hall; and the Q said, "O king, live
Mt 12:42 The Q of the South will arise at the

Lk 11:31 The Q of the South will arise at the
Acts 8:27 minister of the Candace, Q of the Ethiopians, in
Rev 18:7 heart she says, 'A Q I sit, I am

QUEENLY

Song 7:1 feet in sandals, O Q maiden!

QUEENS (3)

Song 6:8 There are sixty Q and eighty concubines, and
6:9 called her happy; the Q and concubines also, and
Is 49:23 foster fathers, and their Q your nursing mothers.

QUENCH (13)

2Sam 14:7 Thus they would Q my coal which is left,
21:17 to battle, lest you Q the lamp of Israel."
Esth 14:9 praise thee and to Q thy altar and the
Ps 104:11 field; the wild asses Q their thirst.
Song 8:7 Many waters cannot Q love, neither can floods drown
Is 1:31 together, with none to Q them.
42:3 wick he will not Q; he will faithfully bring
Jer 4:4 burn with none to Q it, because of the
21:12 burn with none to Q it, because of your
Amos 5:6 devour, with none to Q it for Bethel,
Mt 12:20 a bruised reed or Q a smoldering wick, till
Eph 6:16 with which you can Q all the flaming darts
1Thes 5:19 Do not Q the Spirit,

QUENCHED (13)

2Kgs 22:17 against this place, and it will not be Q
2Chr 34:25 out upon this place and will not be Q
Sir 23:16 fire will not be Q until it is consumed;
Is 29:8 with his thirst not Q, so shall the multitude
34:10 it shall not be Q; its smoke shall go
43:17 rise, they are extinguished, Q like a wick:
66:24 fire shall not be Q, and they shall be
Jer 7:20 the ground; it will burn and not be Q
17:27 the palaces of Jerusalem and shall not be Q
Ezek 20:47 flame shall not be Q, and all faces from
20:48 LORD have kindled it; it shall not be Q
Mk 9:46 does not die, and the fire is not Q
Heb 11:34 the mouths of lions, Q raging fire, escaped the

QUENCHES

Wis 16:17 in the water, which Q all things, the fire

QUESTION (29)

Job 38:3 a man, I will Q you, and you shall
40:7 a man; I will Q you, and you declare
42:4 will speak; I will Q you, and you declare
Sir 19:13 Q a friend, perhaps he did not do it;
19:14 Q a neighbor, perhaps he did not say it;
19:15 Q a friend, for often it is slander; so
19:17 Q your neighbor before you threaten him; and let
Is 45:11 his Maker: "Will you Q me about my children,
Jer 38:14 will ask you a Q; hide nothing from me."
Hag 2:11 priests to decide this Q,
1Mac 9:10 leave no cause to Q our honor."
Mt 21:24 will ask you a Q; and if you tell
22:23 they asked him a Q,
22:35 lawyer, asked him a Q, to test him.
22:41 Jesus asked them a Q,
Mk 2:8 them, "Why do you Q thus in your hearts?
11:28 will ask you a Q; answer me, and I
12:18 they asked him a Q, saying,
12:34 that no one dared to ask him any Q
Lk 5:21 the Pharisees began to Q, saying, "Who is this
5:22 them, "Why do you Q in your hearts?
20:3 will ask you a Q; now tell me,
20:28 they asked him a Q, saying, "Teacher, Moses wrote
20:40 they no longer dared to ask him any Q
22:23 And they began to Q one another, which of
Jn 16:30 and need none to Q you; by this we
Acts 15:2 to the apostles and the elders about this Q
1Cor 10:25 market without raising any Q on the ground of
10:27 you without raising any Q on the ground of

QUESTIONED (10)

Gen 43:7 They replied, "The man Q us carefully about
Judg 8:14 man of Succoth, and Q him; and he wrote
2Chr 31:9 And Hezekiah Q the priests and the Levites about
Jer 37:17 The king Q him secretly in his house, and
Mk 1:27 amazed, so that they Q among themselves, saying,
2:8 spirit that they thus Q within themselves, said to
Lk 3:15 expectation, and all men Q in their hearts concerning
23:9 So he Q him at some length; but he
Jn 18:19 The high priest then Q Jesus about his disciples
Acts 5:27 And the high priest Q them,

QUESTIONING (3)

Mk 2:6 scribes were sitting there, Q in their hearts,
9:10 the matter to themselves, Q what the rising from
Phil 2:14 things without grumbling or Q,

QUESTIONINGS (2)

Lk 5:22 When Jesus perceived their Q, he answered them,
24:38 troubled, and why do Q rise in your hearts?

QUESTIONS (11)

Gen 43:7 in answer to these Q; could we in any
1Kgs 10:1 LORD, she came to test him with hard Q
10:3 Solomon answered all her Q; there was nothing
2Chr 9:1 test him with hard Q, having a very great
9:2 Solomon answered all her Q; there was nothing
Mt 22:46 any one dare to ask him any more Q
Lk 2:46 them and asking them Q;
Acts 18:15 is a matter of Q about words and names
23:29 he was accused about Q of their law, but
25:20 how to investigate these Q, I asked whether he
Col 2:16 judgment on you in Q of food and drink

QUICK (7)

Lev 13:10 white, and there is Q raw flesh in the
Job 5:13 are brought to a Q end.
Prov 14:17 A man of Q temper acts foolishly, but a
Eccl 7:9 Be not Q to anger, for anger lodges in
Wis 18:21 a blameless man was Q to act as their
Sir 5:11 Be Q to hear, and be deliberate in answering.
Jas 1:18 Let every man be Q to hear, slow to

QUICK-TEMPERED

Tit 1:6 not be arrogant or Q or a drunkard or

QUICKLY (72)

Gen 18:6 and said, "Make ready Q three measures of fine
24:18 my lord"; and she Q let down her jar
24:20 So she Q emptied her jar into the trough
24:46 let me drink.' She Q let down her jar
27:20 have found it so Q, my son?" He answered,
44:11 Then every man Q lowered his sack to the
Ex 32:8 they have turned aside Q out of the way
Num 16:46 it, and carry it Q to the congregation, and
Deut 7:4 kindled against you, and he would destroy you Q
9:3 and make them perish Q, as the LORD has
9:12 me, 'Arise, go down Q from here; for your
9:12 they have turned aside Q out of the way
9:16 you had turned aside Q from the way which
11:17 fruit, and you perish Q off the good land
28:20 are destroyed and perish Q, on account of the
Josh 2:5 not know; pursue them Q, for you will overtake
8:19 And the ambush rose Q out of their place,
10:6 come up to us Q, and save us, and
23:16 and you shall perish Q from off the good
1Sam 17:17 loaves, and carry them Q to the camp to
17:48 meet David, David ran Q toward the battle line
28:24 the house, and she Q killed it, and she
2Sam 15:14 lest he overtake us Q, and bring down evil
17:16 Now therefore send Q and tell David, 'Do not
17:18 of them went away Q, and came to the
17:21 David, "Arise, and go Q over the water; for
1Kgs 20:33 an omen, and they Q took it up from
22:9 officer and said, "Bring Q Micaiah the son of
2Kgs 1:11 God, this is the king's order, 'Come down Q
4:22 asses, that I may Q go to the man
2Chr 18:8 officer and said, "Bring Q Micaiah the son of
26:20 they thrust him out Q, and he himself hastened
35:13 pans, and carried them Q to all the lay
Jud 13:1 evening came, his slaves Q withdrew, and Bagoas
Esth 2:9 his favor; and he Q provided her with her
5:5 the king, "Bring Haman Q, that we may do
Ps 2:12 for his wrath is Q kindled.
Eccl 4:12 threefold cord is not Q broken.
Wis 4:14 therefore he took him Q from the midst of
4:16 and youth that is Q perfected will condemn the
16:11 bitten, and then were Q delivered, lest they should
Sir 11:19 enrich a poor man Q and suddenly.
11:20 of the godly, and Q God causes his blessing
19:4 who trusts others too Q is lightminded, and one
27:3 his house will be Q overthrown.
32:11 the last; go home Q and do not linger.
43:22 A mist Q heals all things; when the dew
48:20 and the Holy One Q heard them from heaven,
1Mac 2:40 our ordinances, they will Q destroy us from the

Q

5:28 Judas and his army Q turned back by the
6:27 Bethzur; and unless you Q prevent them, they will
6:57 So he Q gave orders to depart, and said
11:22 conference at Ptolemais as Q as possible.
2Mac 3:31 Q some of Heliodorus' friends asked Onias to call
4:48 and the holy vessels Q suffered the unjust penalty.
6:23 law, he declared himself Q, telling them to send
7:10 it was demanded, he Q put out his tongue
14:11 were hostile to Judas, Q inflamed Demetrius still
14:44 But as they Q drew back, a space opened
Mt 5:25 Make friends Q with your accuser, while you are
28:7 Then go Q and tell his disciples that he
28:8 So they departed Q from the tomb with fear
Lk 14:21 his servant, 'Go out Q to the streets and
15:22 to his servants, 'Bring Q the best robe, and
16:6 bill, and sit down Q and write fifty.'
Jn 11:29 heard it, she rose Q and went to him.
11:31 her, saw Mary rise Q and go out, they
13:27 him, "What you are going to do, do Q
Acts 12:7 the side and woke him, saying, "Get up Q
22:18 'Make haste and get Q out of Jerusalem, because
Gal 1:6 that you are so Q deserting him who called
2Thes 2:2 brethren, not to be Q shaken in mind or

QUIET (43)

Gen 25:27 while Jacob was a Q man, dwelling in tents.
Judg 16:2 They kept Q all night, saying, "Let us wait
18:7 manner of the Sidonians, Q and unsuspecting, lacking
18:19 said to him, "Keep Q, put your hand upon
18:27 Laish, to a people Q and unsuspecting, and smote
1Kgs 22:3 us, and we keep Q and do not take
2Kgs 11:20 and the city was Q after Athaliah had been
1Chr 4:40 land was very broad, Q, and peaceful; for the
22:9 will give peace and Q to Israel in his
2Chr 20:30 realm of Jehoshaphat was Q, for his God gave
23:21 and the city was Q, after Athaliah had been
Neh 8:11 the people, saying, "Be Q, for this day is
Esth 16:8 to render our kingdom Q and peaceable for all
Job 3:13 lain down and been Q; I should have slept;
3:26 ease, nor am I Q; I have no rest;
34:29 When he is Q, who can condemn?
Ps 35:20 against those who are Q in the land they
107:30 glad because they had Q, and he brought them
Prov 17:1 a dry morsel with Q than a house full
29:9 only rages and laughs, and there is no Q
Eccl 9:17 the wise heard in Q are better than the
Sir 25:19 garrulous wife for a Q husband.
Is 7:4 him, 'Take heed, be Q, do not fear, and
14:7 is at rest and Q; they break forth into
32:18 secure dwellings, and in Q resting places.
33:20 will see Jerusalem, a Q habitation, an immovable
Jer 30:10 shall return and have Q and ease, and none
46:27 shall return and have Q and ease, and none
47:6 How long till you are Q
47:7 How can it be Q, when the LORD has
49:23 are troubled like the sea which cannot be Q
Ezek 38:11 will fall upon the Q people who dwell securely,
Jon 1:11 that the sea may Q down for us?" For
1:12 then the sea will Q down for you; for
1Mac 1:3 When the earth became Q before him, he was
9:58 men are living in Q and confidence.
11:38 that the land was Q before him and that
11:52 and the land was Q before him.
2Mac 14:4 During that day he kept Q
Acts 19:36 you ought to be Q and do nothing rash.
22:2 in the Hebrew language, they were the more Q
1Tim 2:2 we may lead a Q and peaceable life, godly
1Pet 3:4 of a gentle and Q spirit, which in God's

QUIETED (5)

Num 13:30 But Caleb Q the people before Moses, and said,
Ps 131:2 I have calmed and Q my soul, like a
131:2 soul, like a child Q at its mother's breast;
131:2 a child that is Q is my soul.
Acts 19:35 the town clerk had Q the crowd, he said,

QUIETLY (8)

Prov 29:11 but a wise man Q holds it back.
Sir 21:20 when he laughs, but a clever man smiles Q
Is 18:4 to me: "I will Q look from my dwelling
Lam 3:26 that one should wait Q for the salvation of
Hab 3:16 I will Q wait for the day of trouble
2Mac 12:2 not let them live Q and in peace.
Jn 11:28 her sister Mary, saying Q, "The Teacher is here
1Thes 4:11 to aspire to live Q, to mind your own

QUIETNESS (4)

Eccl 4:6 is a handful of Q than two hands full
Is 30:15 shall be saved; in Q and in trust shall
32:17 the result of righteousness, Q and trust for ever.
2Thes 3:12 do their work in Q and to earn their

QUIETS

Prov 15:18 is slow to anger Q contention.

QUINTUS

2Mac 11:34 letter, which read thus: Q Memmius and Titus

QUIRINIUS

Lk 2:2 the first enrollment, when Q was governor of Syria.

QUIT (3)

Judg 15:7 avenged upon you, and after that I will Q
Prov 17:14 letting out water; so Q before the quarrel breaks
Lam 5:14 The old men have Q the city gate, the

QUITE (4)

Esth 16:10 the Persian blood, and Q devoid of our kindliness),
2Mac 3:31 one who was lying Q at his last breath.
Mk 12:27 the living; you are Q wrong."
Acts 28:30 the Lord Jesus Christ Q openly and unhindered.

QUIVER (9)

Gen 27:3 take your weapons, your Q and your bow, and
Job 39:23 Upon him rattle the Q, the flashing spear and
Ps 127:5 man who has his Q full of them!
Sir 26:12 post and open her Q to the arrow.
Is 22:6 And Elam bore the Q with chariots and horsemen,
49:2 polished arrow, in his Q he hid me away.
Jer 5:16 Their Q is like an open tomb, they are
Lam 3:13 the arrows of his Q;
Hab 3:16 body trembles, my lips Q at the sound; rottenness

QUOTE

Lk 4:23 them, "Doubtless you will Q to me this proverb,

QUOTED

Heb 4:7 in the words already Q, "Today, when you hear

R

RAAMA

1Chr 1:9 Cush: Seba, Havilah, Sabta, R, and Sabteca.

RAAMAH (4)

Gen 10:7 Cush: Seba, Havilah, Sabtah, R, and Sabteca.
10:7 The sons of R: Sheba and Dedan.
1Chr 1:9 The sons of R: Sheba and Dedan.
Ezek 27:22 traders of Sheba and R traded with you; they

RAAMIAH

Neh 7:7 Jeshua, Nehemiah, Azariah, R, Nahamani, Mordecai,

RAAMSES (2)

Ex 1:10 and they built for Pharaoh store-cities, Pithom and R
Jud 1:9 Egypt, and Tahpanhes and R and the whole land

RAB-BONI

Jn 20:16 She turned and said to him in Hebrew, R

RABBAH (15)

Deut 3:11 is it not in R of the Ammonites?
Josh 13:25 which is east of R,
15:60 (that is, Kiriath-jearim), and R: two cities with their
2Sam 11:1 and they ravaged the Ammonites, and besieged R
12:26 Now Joab fought against R of the Ammonites, and
12:27 "I have fought against R; moreover, I have taken
12:29 together and went to R, and fought against it
17:27 son of Nahash from R of the Ammonites, and
1Chr 20:1 country of the Ammonites, and came and besieged R
20:1 And Joab smote R, and overthrew it.
Jer 49:2 to be heard against R of the Ammonites; it
49:3 Cry, O daughters of R
Ezek 21:20 sword to come to R of the Ammonites and
25:5 I will make R a pasture for camels and
Amos 1:14 in the wall of R, and it shall devour

RABBI (10)

Mt 23:7 places, and being called R by men.
23:8 not to be called R, for you have one

Jn 1:38 And they said to him, R
1:49 Nathanael answered him, R, you are the Son of
3:2 and said to him, R, we know that you
3:26 and said to him, R, he who was with
4:31 disciples besought him, saying, R, eat."
6:25 they said to him, R, when did you come
9:2 his disciples asked him, R, who sinned, this man
11:8 disciples said to him, R, the Jews were but

RABBITH

Josh 19:20 Haphara-im, Shion, Anaharath, R, Kishion, Ebez,

RABBLE (3)

Num 11:4 Now the R that was among them had a
Job 30:12 my right hand the R rise, they drive me
Acts 17:5 wicked fellows of the R, they gathered a crowd,

RABMAG (2)

Jer 39:3 the Rabsaris, Nergal-sharezer the R, with all the rest
39:13 the Rabsaris, Nergal-sharezer the R, and all the

RABSARIS (3)

2Kgs 18:17 sent the Tartan, the R, and the Rabshakeh with
Jer 39:3 Nergal-sharezer, Samgar-nebo, Sarsechim the R,
39:13 the guard, Nebushazban the R, Nergal-sharezer the

RABSHAKEH (17)

2Kgs 18:17 the Rabsaris, and the R with a great army
18:19 And the R said to them, "Say to Hezekiah,
18:26 Joah, said to the R, "Pray, speak to your
18:27 But the R said to them, "Has my master
18:28 Then the R stood and called out in a
18:37 rent, and told him the words of the R
19:4 the words of the R, whom his master the
19:8 The R returned, and found the king of Assyria
Sir 48:18 up, and sent the R; he lifted up his
Is 36:2 of Assyria sent the R from Lachish to King
36:4 And the R said to them, "Say to Hezekiah,
36:11 Joah said to the R, "Pray, speak to your
36:12 But the R said, "Has my master sent me
36:13 Then the R stood and called out in a
36:22 rent, and told him the words of the R
37:4 the words of the R, whom his master the
37:8 The R returned, and found the king of Assyria

RACAL

1Sam 30:29 Siphmoth, in Eshtemoa, in R, in the cities of

RACE (21)

Ezra 9:2 so that the holy R has mixed itself with
Tob 8:6 From them the R of mankind has sprung.
Jud 6:5 take revenge on this R that came out of
Eccl 9:11 under the sun the R is not to the
Wis 10:15 holy people and blameless R wisdom delivered from
12:11 they were an accursed R from the beginning, and
Sir 10:19 What R is worthy of honor?
10:19 The human R
10:19 What R is worthy of honor?
10:19 What R is unworthy of honor?
10:19 The human R
10:19 What R is unworthy of honor?
2Mac 8:9 wipe out the whole R of Judea.
12:31 be well-disposed to their R in the future also.
Acts 7:19 dealt craftily with our R and forced our fathers
Rom 9:3 the sake of my brethren, my kinsmen by R
9:5 patriarchs, and of their R, according to the flesh,
1Cor 9:24 know that in a R all the runners compete,
2Tim 4:7 I have finished the R, I have kept the
Heb 12:1 run with perseverance the R that is set before
1Pet 2:9 you are a chosen R, a royal priesthood, a

RACED

Jer 12:5 "If you have R with men on foot, and

RACHEL (46)

Gen 29:6 is well; and see, R his daughter is coming
29:9 still speaking with them, R came with her father's
29:10 Now when Jacob saw R the daughter of Laban
29:11 Then Jacob kissed R, and wept aloud.
29:12 And Jacob told R that he was her father's
29:16 Leah, and the name of the younger was R
29:17 eyes were weak, but R was beautiful and lovely.
29:18 Jacob loved R; and he said, "I will serve
29:18 serve you seven years for your younger daughter R
29:20 served seven years for R, and they seemed to
29:25 Did I not serve with you for R
29:28 gave him his daughter R to wife.
29:29 Bilhah to his daughter R to be her maid.)
29:30 Jacob went in to R also, and he loved
29:30 also, and he loved R more than Leah, and
29:31 opened her womb; but R was barren.
30:1 When R saw that she bore Jacob no children,
30:2 anger was kindled against R, and he said, "Am
30:6 Then R said, "God has judged me, and has
30:7 R's maid Bilhah conceived again and bore Jacob a
30:8 Then R said, "With mighty wrestlings I have
30:14 Then R said to Leah, "Give me, I pray,
30:15 R said, "Then he may lie with you tonight
30:22 Then God remembered R, and God hearkened to her
30:25 When R had borne Joseph, Jacob said to Laban,
31:4 Jacob sent and called R and Leah into the
31:14 Then R and Leah answered him, "Is there any
31:19 shear his sheep, and R stole her father's household
31:32 did not know that R had stolen them.
31:34 Now R had taken the household gods and put
33:1 children among Leah and R and the two maids.
33:2 with her children, and R and Joseph last of
33:7 and last Joseph and R drew near, and they
35:16 some distance from Ephrath, R travailed, and she
35:19 So R died, and she was buried on the
35:20 is the pillar of R's tomb, which is there
35:24 The sons of R: Joseph and Benjamin.
35:25 The sons of Bilhah, R's maid: Dan and Naphtali.
46:19 The sons of R, Jacob's wife: Joseph and Benjamin.
46:22 are the sons of R, who were born to
46:25 whom Laban gave to R his daughter, and these
48:7 I came from Paddan, R to my sorrow died
Ruth 4:11 into your house, like R and Leah, who together
1Sam 10:2 meet two men by R's tomb in the territory
Jer 31:15 R is weeping for her children; she refuses to
Mt 2:18 and loud lamentation, R weeping for her children;

RACHELS

Gen 31:33 he went out of Leah's tent, and entered R

RACK (2)

2Mac 6:19 up to the the R of his own accord,
6:28 said this, he went at once to the R

RACKS (2)

Job 30:17 The night R my bones, and the pain that
Sir 33:26 wicked servant there are R and tortures.

RADDAI

1Chr 2:14 third, Nethanel the fourth, R the fifth,

RADIANCE (2)

Wis 7:10 than light, because her R never ceases.
Rev 21:11 glory of God, its R like a most rare

RADIANT (7)

Esth 15:5 She was R with perfect beauty, and she looked
Ps 34:5 to him, and be R; so your faces shall
Song 5:10 My beloved is all R and ruddy, distinguished among
Wis 6:12 Wisdom is R and unfading, and she is easily
Is 60:5 shall see and be R, your heart shall thrill
Jer 31:12 and they shall be R over the goodness of
Dan 10:8 left in me; my R appearance was fearfully changed,

RAFT (2)

Wis 14:5 the billows on a R they come safely to
14:6 took refuge on a R, and guided by thy

RAFTERS (4)

1Kgs 6:15 the house to the R of the ceiling, he
6:16 the floor to the R, and he built this
7:7 it was finished with cedar from floor to R
Song 1:17 house are cedar, our R are pine.

RAFTS (2)

1Kgs 5:9 will make it into R to go by sea
2Chr 2:16 it to you in R by sea to Joppa,

RAG

Esth 14:16 it like a menstruous R, and I do not

RAGAE (2)

Jud 1:5 great plain which is on the borders of R
1:15 in the mountains of R and struck him down

RAGE (21)

2Kgs 5:12 So he turned and went away in a R

Q
R

2Chr 16:10 he was in a R with him because of
28:9 slain them in a R which has reached up
Job 39:24 With fierceness and R he swallows the ground; he
Ps 46:6 The nations R, the kingdoms totter; he utters his
Wis 5:22 of the sea will R against them, and rivers
10:3 he perished because in R he slew his brother.
11:18 unknown beasts full of R, or such as breathe
16:5 For when the terrible R of wild beasts came
Jer 46:9 Advance, O horses, and R, O chariots!
Dan 3:13 Then Nebuchadnezzar in furious R commanded that
Hos 11:6 The sword shall R against their cities, consume the
Nah 2:4 The chariots R in the streets, they rush to
2Mac 4:25 cruel tyrant and the R of a savage wild
7:3 king fell into a R, and gave orders that
7:39 king fell into a R, and handled him worse
9:4 Transported with R, he conceived the idea of turning
9:7 breathing fire in his R against the Jews, and
10:28 while the other made R their leader in the
Mt 2:16 was in a furious R, and he sent and
Acts 4:25 'Why did the Gentiles R, and the peoples imagine

RAGED (4)

2Kgs 19:28 Because you have R against me and your arrogance
Is 37:29 Because you have R against me and your arrogance
1Mac 9:13 armies, and the battle R from morning till evening.
Rev 11:18 The nations R, but thy wrath came, and the

RAGES (8)

Tob 1:14 Media, and once at R in Media I left
4:1 trust with Gabael at R in Media, and he
4:20 son of Gabrias at R in Media.
5:5 go with me to R in Media?
6:12 as we return from R we will celebrate the
9:2 go to Gabael at R in Media and get
Prov 19:3 to ruin, his heart R against the LORD.
29:9 fool, the fool only R and laughs, and there

RAGING (14)

2Kgs 19:27 coming in, and your R against me.
Ps 55:8 a shelter from the R wind and tempest."
89:9 Thou dost rule the R of the sea; when
124:5 would have gone the R waters.
Wis 14:1 about to voyage over R waves calls upon a
14:25 and all is a R riot of blood and
19:7 plain out of the R waves,
Is 37:28 coming in, and your R against me.
Jon 1:15 the sea; and the sea ceased from its R
Hab 3:10 thee, and writhed; the R waters swept on; the
2Mac 5:11 So, R inwardly, he left Egypt and took the
Lk 8:24 the wind and the R waves; and they ceased,
Acts 26:11 them blaspheme; and in R fury against them, I
Heb 11:34 mouths of lions, quenched R fire, escaped the edge

RAGS (3)

Prov 23:21 poverty, and drowsiness will clothe a man with R
Jer 38:11 took from there old R and worn-out clothes, which
38:12 to Jeremiah, "Put the R and clothes between your

RAGUEL (24)

Tob 3:7 Sarah, the daughter of R, was reproached by her
3:17 Sarah the daughter of R in marriage to Tobias
3:17 Sarah the daughter of R came down from her
6:10 young man, "Brother, today we shall stay with R
6:12 For I know that R, according to the law
7:1 at the house of R, Sarah met them and
7:2 Then R said to his wife Edna, "How much
7:3 And R asked them, "Where are you from, brethren?"
7:6 Then R sprang up and kissed him and wept.
7:9 So he communicated the proposal to R
7:9 And R said to Tobias, "Eat, drink, and be
7:12 So R said, "Take her right now, in accordance
7:16 And R called his wife Edna and said to
8:9 But R arose and went and dug a grave,
8:11 Then R went into his house
8:15 Then R blessed God and said, "Blessed art thou,
8:20 the feast were over, R declared by oath to
8:21 should take half of R's property and return in
9:3 For R has sworn that I should not leave;
10:7 feast had expired which R had sworn that he
10:7 time Tobias said to R, "Send me back, for
10:10 So R arose and gave him his wife Sarah
11:1 And he blessed R and his wife Edna.
14:12 sons to Ecbatana, to R his father-in-law.

RAHAB (14)

Josh 2:1 harlot whose name was R, and lodged there.
2:3 of Jericho sent to R, saying, "Bring forth the
6:17 LORD for destruction; only R the harlot and all
6:23 in, and brought out R, and her father and
6:25 But R the harlot, and her father's household, and
Job 9:13 his anger; beneath him bowed the helpers of R
26:12 stilled the sea; by his understanding he smote R
Ps 87:4 know me I mention R and Babylon; behold, Philistia
89:10 Thou didst crush R like a carcass, thou didst
Is 30:7 I have called her R who sits still."
51:9 thou that didst cut R in pieces, that didst
Mt 1:5 father of Boaz by R, and Boaz the father
Heb 11:31 By faith R the harlot did not perish with
Jas 2:25 way was not also R the harlot justified by

RAHAM

1Chr 2:44 was the father of R, the father of Jorke-am;

RAID (13)

Gen 49:19 Raiders shall R Gad, but he shall raid at
49:19 Gad, but he shall R at their heels.
Judg 15:9 Judah, and made a R on Lehi.
1Sam 23:27 Philistines have made a R upon the land."
27:10 have you made a R today?" David would say,
30:1 Amalekites had made a R upon the Negeb and
30:14 We had made a R upon the Negeb of
2Sam 3:22 with Joab from a R, bringing much spoil with
1Chr 7:21 they came down to R their cattle.
14:9 come and made a R in the valley of
14:13 yet again made a R in the valley.
Job 1:17 companies, and made a R upon the camels and
Hos 7:2 in, and the bandits R without.

RAIDERS (4)

Gen 49:19 R shall raid Gad, but he shall raid at
1Sam 13:17 And R came out of the camp of the
14:15 garrison and even the R trembled; the earth quaked;
1Chr 12:21 against the band of R; for they were all

RAIDING (2)

Judg 11:3 round Jephthah, and went R with him.
2Sam 4:2 who were captains of R bands; the name of

RAIDS (5)

1Sam 27:8 went up, and made R upon the Geshurites, the
2Kgs 5:2 on one of their R had carried off a
6:23 came no more on R into the land of
2Chr 28:18 the Philistines had made R on the cities in
1Mac 15:41 go out and make R along the highways of

RAIL (2)

Lam 2:16 All your enemies R against you; they hiss, they
3:46 "All our enemies R against us;

RAILED (2)

1Sam 25:14 our master; and he R at them.
Lk 23:38 criminals who were hanged R at him, saying, "Are

RAILING

2Mac 12:14 Judas and his men, R at them and even

RAIMENT (10)

Gen 24:53 and of gold, and R, and gave them to
Ps 22:18 them, and for my R they cast lots.
102:26 Thou changest them like R, and they pass away;
Is 63:3 my garments, and I have stained all my R
Ezek 16:13 and silver; and your R was of fine linen,
Dan 7:9 took his seat; his R was white as snow,
Mt 11:8 To see a man clothed in soft R
11:8 those who wear soft R are in kings' houses.
28:3 like lightning, and his R white as snow.
Lk 9:29 was altered, and his R became dazzling white.

RAIN (112)

Gen 2:5 not caused it to R upon the earth, and
7:4 days I will send R upon the earth forty
7:12 And R fell upon the earth forty days and
8:2 heavens were closed, the R from the heavens was
Ex 9:33 hail ceased, and the R no longer poured upon
9:34 Pharaoh saw that the R and the hail and
16:4 Moses, "Behold, I will R bread from heaven for
Deut 11:11 drinks water by the R from heaven,
11:14 he will give the R for your land in
11:14 its season, the early R and the later rain,
11:14 rain and the later R, that you may gather
11:17 that there be no R, and the land yield
28:12 heavens, to give the R of your land in

28:24 LORD will make the R of your land powder
32:2 teaching drop as the R, my speech distil as
32:2 dew, as the gentle R upon the tender grass,
1Sam 12:17 may send thunder and R; and you shall know
12:18 LORD sent thunder and R that day; and all
2Sam 1:21 be no dew or R upon you, nor upsurging
21:10 beginning of harvest until R fell upon them from
23:4 a cloudless morning, like R that makes grass to
1Kgs 8:35 and there is no R because they have sinned
8:36 should walk; and grant R upon thy land, which
17:1 be neither dew nor R these years, except by
17:7 because there was no R in the land.
17:14 that the LORD sends R upon the earth.'"
18:1 and I will send R upon the earth."
18:41 there is a sound of the rushing of R
18:44 go down, lest the R stop you.'"
18:45 clouds and wind, and there was a great R
2Kgs 3:17 not see wind or R, but that stream-bed shall
2Chr 6:26 and there is no R because they have sinned
6:27 should walk; and grant R upon thy land, which
7:13 that there is no R, or command the locust
Ezra 10:9 of this matter and because of the heavy R
10:13 a time of heavy R; we cannot stand in
Jud 8:31 Lord will send us R to fill our cisterns
Job 5:10 without number: he gives R upon the earth and
20:23 anger into him, and R it upon him as
24:8 are wet with the R of the mountains, and
28:26 a decree for the R, and a way for
29:23 me as for the R; and they opened their
29:23 they opened their mouths as for the spring R
36:27 distils his mist in R
37:6 the shower and the R, 'Be strong.'
38:25 for the torrents of R, and a way for
38:26 the thunderbolt, to bring R on a land where
38:28 "Has the R a father, or who has begotten
Ps 11:6 the wicked he will R coals of fire and
68:8 the heavens poured down R, at the presence of
68:9 R in abundance, O God, thou didst shed abroad;
72:6 May he be like R that falls on the
84:6 of springs; the early R also covers it with
105:32 gave them hail for R, and lightning that flashed
135:7 makes lightnings for the R and brings forth the
147:8 with clouds, he prepares R for the earth, he
Prov 16:15 is like the clouds that bring the spring R
19:13 a wife's quarreling is a continual dripping of R
25:14 clouds and wind without R is a man who
25:23 north wind brings forth R; and a backbiting tongue,
26:1 snow in summer or R in harvest, so honor
28:3 poor is a beating R that leaves no food.
Eccl 11:3 clouds are full of R, they empty themselves on
12:2 clouds return after the R;
Song 2:11 winter is past, the R is over and gone.
Wis 16:22 in the showers of R;
Sir 1:2 sea, the drops of R, and the days of
35:20 them as clouds of R in the time of
40:13 like a loud clap of thunder in a R
Is 4:6 refuge and a shelter from the storm and R
5:6 the clouds that they R no rain upon it.
5:6 that they rain no R upon it.
30:23 And he will give R for the seed with
44:14 a cedar and the R nourishes it.
45:8 and let the skies R down righteousness; let the
55:10 "For as the R and the snow come down
Jer 3:3 withheld, and the spring R has not come; yet
5:24 God, who gives the R in its season, the
5:24 its season, the autumn R and the spring rain,
5:24 rain and the spring R, and keeps for us
10:13 makes lightnings for the R, and he brings forth
14:4 since there is no R on the land, the
14:22 false gods of the nations that can bring R
51:16 makes lightnings for the R, and he brings forth
Bar 6:53 a country or give R to men.
Ezek 1:28 on the day of R, so was the appearance
13:11 be a deluge of R, great hailstones will fall,
13:13 be a deluge of R in my anger, and
38:22 him; and I will R upon him and his
Dan 3:65 Bless the Lord, all R and dew, sing praise
Hos 10:12 he may come and R salvation upon you.
Joel 2:23 has given the early R for your vindication, he
2:23 down for you abundant R, the early and the
2:23 early and the latter R, as before.
Amos 4:7 I also withheld the R from you when there
4:7 harvest; I would send R upon one city, and
4:7 city, and send no R upon another city; one
4:7 which it did not R withered;
Zech 10:1 Ask R from the LORD in the season of
10:1 season of the spring R, from the LORD who
10:1 gives men showers of R, to every one the
14:17 there will be no R upon them.
Mt 5:45 the good, and sends R on the just and
7:25 the rock; and the R fell, and the floods
7:27 the sand; and the R fell, and the floods
Acts 28:2 it had begun to R and was cold.
Heb 6:7 which has drunk the R that often falls upon
Jas 5:7 until it receives the early and the late R
5:17 that it might not R, and for three years
5:17 months it did not R on the earth.
5:18 and the heaven gave R, and the earth brought
Rev 11:6 the sky, that no R may fall during the

RAINBOW (4)

Sir 43:11 Look upon the R, and praise him who made
50:7 High, and like the R gleaming in glorious clouds;
Rev 4:3 the throne was a R that looked like an
10:1 a cloud, with a R over his head, and

RAINED (8)

Gen 19:24 Then the LORD R on Sodom and Gomorrah
Ex 9:23 And the LORD R hail upon the land of
Ps 78:24 of heaven; and he R down upon them manna
78:27 the south wind; he R flesh upon them like
Sir 1:17 and apportioned her; he R down knowledge and
Ezek 22:24 is not cleansed, or R upon in the day
Amos 4:7 one field would be R upon, and the field
Lk 17:29 Sodom fire and sulphur R from heaven and

RAINS (5)

Lev 26:4 will give you your R in their season, and
Wis 16:16 arm, pursued by unusual R and hail and relentless
Ezek 38:22 are with him, torrential R and hailstones, fire and
Hos 6:3 showers, as the spring R that water the earth."
Acts 14:17 gave you from heaven R and fruitful seasons,

RAINY

Prov 27:15 continual dripping on a R day and a contentious

RAISE (77)

Gen 38:8 brother-in-law to her, and R up offspring for your
Deut 18:15 LORD your God will R up for you a
18:18 I will R up for them a prophet like
1Sam 2:35 And I will R up for myself a faithful
2Sam 7:12 your fathers, I will R up your offspring after
12:11 LORD, 'Behold, I will R up evil against you
12:17 stood beside him, to R him from the ground;
1Kgs 14:14 Moreover the LORD will R up for himself a
1Chr 15:16 lyres and cymbals, to R sounds of joy.
17:11 your fathers, I will R up your offspring after
Jud 16:2 R to him a new psalm; exalt him, and
Ps 41:10 gracious to me, and R me up, that I
81:2 R a song, sound the timbrel, the sweet lyre
Prov 2:3 out for insight and R your voice for understanding,
8:1 call, does not understanding R her voice?
Sir 10:4 over it he will R up the right man
Is 5:26 He will R a signal for a nation afar
11:12 He will R an ensign for the nations, and
13:2 On a bare hill R a signal, cry aloud
15:5 road to Horonaim they R a cry of destruction;
29:3 towers and I will R siegeworks against you.
44:26 built, and I will R up their ruins';
49:6 be my servant to R up the tribes of
49:22 to the nations, and R my signal to the
58:12 be rebuilt; you shall R up the foundations of
61:4 ancient ruins, they shall R up the former
Jer 4:6 into the fortified cities!' R a standard toward Zion,
6:1 trumpet in Tekoa, and R a signal on Beth-haccherem;
7:29 and cast it away; R a lamentation on the
9:18 them make haste and R a wailing over us,
23:5 LORD, when I will R up for David a
30:9 king, whom I will R up for them.
31:7 gladness for Jacob, and R shouts for the chief
50:15 R a shout against her round about, she has
50:32 fall, with none to R him up, and I
51:14 locusts, and they shall R the shout of victory
Ezek 26:8 mound against you, and R a roof of shields
26:17 And they will R a lamentation over you, and
27:2 you, son of man, R a lamentation over Tyre,
27:32 In their wailing they R a lamentation for you,
28:12 me: "Son of man, R a lamentation over the
32:2 me: "Son of man, R a lamentation over Pharaoh
37:12 open your graves, and R you from your graves,
37:13 open your graves, and R you from your graves,
Dan 11:11 north; and he shall R a great multitude, but

11:13 the north shall again R a multitude, greater than
Hos 6:2 third day he will R us up, that we
Amos 5:2 land, with none to R her up."
6:14 "For behold, I will R up against you a
9:11 that day I will R up the booth of
9:11 repair its breaches, and R up its ruins, and
Mic 5:5 soil, that we will R against him seven shepherds
1Mac 3:31 from those regions and R a large fund.
12:39 the crown, and to R his hand against Antiochus
12:42 he was afraid to R his hand against him.
2Mac 7:9 of the universe will R us up to an
7:34 uncertain hopes, when you R your hand against the
Mt 3:9 from these stones to R up children to Abraham.
10:8 hand.' Heal the sick, R the dead, cleanse lepers,
22:24 marry the widow, and R up children for his
Mk 12:19 take the wife, and R up children for his
Lk 3:8 from these stones to R up children to Abraham.
20:28 take the wife and R up children for his
21:28 place, look up and R your heads, because your
Jn 2:19 three days I will R it up."
2:20 temple, and will you R it up in three
6:39 has given me, but R it up at the
6:40 life; and I will R him up at the
6:44 him; and I will R him up at the
6:54 life, and I will R him up at the
Acts 3:22 'The Lord God will R up for you a
7:37 the Israelites, 'God will R up for you a
1Cor 6:14 Lord and will also R us up by his
15:15 whom he did not R if it is true
2Cor 4:14 the Lord Jesus will R us also with Jesus
Heb 11:19 God was able to R men even from the
Jas 5:15 and the Lord will R him up; and if

RAISED (137)

Gen 33:5 And when Esau R his eyes and saw the
Num 14:1 Then all the congregation R a loud cry; and
Josh 5:7 their children, whom he R up in their stead,
6:20 the trumpet, the people R a great shout, and
7:26 And they R over him a great heap of
8:29 of the city, and R over it a great
Judg 2:16 Then the LORD R up judges, who saved them
2:18 Whenever the LORD R up judges for them, the
3:9 the LORD, the LORD R up a deliverer for
3:15 the LORD, the LORD R up for them a
1Sam 30:4 who were with him R their voices and wept,
2Sam 18:17 in the forest, and R over him a very
18:28 up the men who R their hand against my
23:1 the man who was R on high, the anointed
1Kgs 5:13 King Solomon R a levy of forced labor out
11:14 And the LORD R up an adversary against Solomon,
11:23 God also R up as an adversary to him,
2Kgs 19:22 Against whom have you R your voice and haughtily
2Chr 5:13 when the song was R, with trumpets and cymbals
13:15 the men of Judah R the battle shout.
32:5 was broken down, and R towers upon it, and
33:14 it round Ophel, and R it to a very
Tob 13:10 his tent may be R for you again with
Jud 10:23 him, and his slaves R her up.
14:7 And when they R him up he fell at
14:9 had finished, the people R a great shout and
Esth 15:11 Then he R the golden scepter and touched it
Job 2:12 recognize him; and they R their voices and wept;
31:21 sheep; if I have R my hand against the
Ps 83:2 who hate thee have R their heads.
106:26 Therefore he R his hand and swore to them
107:25 For he commanded, and R the stormy wind, which
131:1 my eyes are not R too high; I do
148:14 He has R up a horn for his people,
Sir 20:10 are men who have R their heads from humble
48:5 You who R a corpse from death and from
49:12 built the house and R a temple holy to
49:13 also is lasting; he R for us the walls
Is 2:2 mountains, and shall be R above the hills; and
16:10 sung, no shouts are R; no treader treads out
18:3 when a signal is R on the mountains, look!
37:23 Against whom have you R your voice and haughtily
49:11 my highways shall be R up.
Jer 29:15 said, 'The LORD has R up prophets for us
51:55 of their voice is R;
Lam 2:7 palaces; a clamor was R in the house of
Bar 2:5 brought low and not R up, because we sinned
6:17 full of the dust R by the feet of
Ezek 41:8 the temple had a R platform round about; the
Dan 5:19 whom he would he R up, and whom he
7:5 It was R up on one side; it had
8:3 I R my eyes and saw, and behold, a

12:7 waters of the stream, R his right hand and
Amos 2:11 And I R up some of your sons for
Mic 4:1 mountains, and shall be R up above the hills;
Zech 1:21 so that no man R his head; and these
14:13 the one will be R against the hand of
1Mac 9:39 They R their eyes and looked, and saw a
2Mac 7:14 God gives of being R again by him.
12:37 of their fathers he R the battle cry, with
Mt 11:5 and the dead are R up, and the poor
14:2 Baptist, he has been R from the dead; that
16:21 be killed, and on the third day be R
17:9 Son of man is R from the dead."
17:22 and he will be R on the third day."
20:19 and he will be R on the third day."
26:32 But after I am R up, I will go
27:52 had fallen asleep were R,
Mk 6:14 the baptizer has been R from the dead; that
6:16 he said, "John, whom I beheaded, has been R
12:26 for the dead being R, have you not read
14:28 But after I am R up, I will go
Lk 1:69 his people, and has R up a horn of
7:22 hear, the dead are R up, the poor have
9:7 that John had been R from the dead,
9:22 be killed, and on the third day be R
11:27 woman in the crowd R her voice and said
20:37 that the dead are R, even Moses showed, in
Jn 2:22 When therefore he was R from the dead, his
12:1 was, whom Jesus had R from the dead.
12:9 Lazarus, whom he had R from the dead.
12:17 of the tomb and R him from the dead
21:14 disciples after he was R from the dead.
Acts 2:24 But God R him up, having loosed the pangs
2:32 This Jesus God R up, and of that we
3:7 the right hand and R him up; and immediately
3:15 of life, whom God R from the dead.
3:22 your brethren as he R me up.
3:26 be blessed.' God, having R up his servant, sent
4:10 you crucified, whom God R from the dead, by
5:30 God of our fathers R Jesus whom you killed
7:37 your brethren as he R me up.'
10:40 a tree; but God R him on the third
13:22 had removed him, he R up David to be
13:30 But God R him from the dead;
13:34 the fact that he R him from the dead,
13:37 but he whom God R up saw no corruption.
Rom 4:24 believe in him that R from the dead Jesus
4:25 for our trespasses and R for our justification.
6:4 that as Christ was R from the dead by
6:9 know that Christ being R from the dead will
7:4 him who has been R from the dead in
8:11 Spirit of him who R Jesus from the dead
8:11 in you, he who R Christ Jesus from the
8:34 died, yes, who was R from the dead, who
9:17 to Pharaoh, "I have R you up for the
10:9 your heart that God R him from the dead,
15:28 them what has been R, I shall go on
1Cor 6:14 And God R the Lord and will also raise
15:4 buried, that he was R on the third day
15:12 Christ is preached as R from the dead, how
15:13 Christ has not been R;
15:14 Christ has not been R, then our preaching is
15:15 of God that he R Christ, whom he did
15:15 it is true that the dead are not R
15:16 the dead are not R, then Christ has not
15:16 are not raised, then Christ has not been R
15:17 Christ has not been R, your faith is futile
15:20 fact Christ has been R from the dead, the
15:29 the dead are not R at all, why are
15:32 the dead are not R, "Let us eat and
15:35 some one will ask, "How are the dead R
15:42 is perishable, what is R is imperishable.
15:43 in dishonor, it is R in glory.
15:43 in weakness, it is R in power.
15:44 physical body, it is R a spiritual body.
15:52 the dead will be R imperishable, and we shall
2Cor 4:14 knowing that he who R the Lord Jesus will
5:15 him who for their sake died and was R
Gal 1:1 God the Father, who R him from the dead—
Eph 1:20 in Christ when he R him from the dead
2:6 have been saved), and R us up with him,
Col 2:12 which you were also R with him through faith
2:12 working of God, who R him from the dead.
3:1 then you have been R with Christ, seek the
1Thes 1:10 from heaven, whom he R from the dead, Jesus
1Pet 1:21 confidence in God, who R him from the dead

R

RAISES (15)

1Sam 2:6 down to Sheol and R up.
2:8 He R up the poor from the dust; he
Job 41:25 When he R himself up the mighty are afraid;
Ps 107:41 trackless wastes; but he R up the needy out
113:7 He R the poor from the dust, and lifts
145:14 who are falling, and R up all who are
Prov 1:20 in the markets she R her voice;
Sir 11:13 his low estate and R up his head, so
21:20 A fool R his voice when he laughs, but
28:17 blow of a whip R a welt, but a
Is 9:11 So the LORD R adversaries against them, and stirs
14:9 of the earth; it R from their thrones all
Jn 5:20 For as the Father R the dead and gives
Acts 26:8 of you that God R the dead?
2Cor 1:9 but on God who R the dead;

RAISIN-CAKES

Is 16:7 utterly stricken, for the R of Kir-hareseth.

RAISING (6)

Jud 12:8 her way for the R up of her people.
Zech 11:16 For lo, I am R up in the land
Acts 13:33 us their children by R Jesus; as also it
17:31 to all men by R him from the dead."
1Cor 10:25 the meat market without R any question on the
10:27 set before you without R any question on the

RAISINS (8)

1Sam 25:18 a hundred clusters of R, and two hundred cakes
30:12 a cake of figs and two clusters of R
2Sam 6:19 a portion of meat, and a cake of R
16:1 a hundred bunches of R, a hundred of summer
1Chr 12:40 of figs, clusters of R, and wine and oil,
16:3 a portion of meat, and a cake of R
Song 2:5 Sustain me with R, refresh me with apples; for
Hos 3:1 turn to other gods and love cakes of R

RAKEM

1Chr 7:16 was Sheresh; and his sons were Ulam and R

RAKKATH

Josh 19:35 are Ziddim, Zer, Hammath, R, Chinnereth,

RAKKON

Josh 19:46 Gath-rimmon, and Me-jarkon and R with the

RALLIED (4)

1Sam 14:20 who were with him R and went into the
1Mac 11:47 aid, and they all R about him and then
14:30 Jonathan R the nation, and became their high priest,
15:10 All the troops R to him, so that there

RALLY (3)

Neh 4:20 sound of the trumpet, R to us there.
Ps 60:4 who fear thee, to R to it from the
1Mac 2:67 You shall R about you all who observe the

RALLYING

1Mac 5:53 And Judas kept R the laggards and encouraging the

RAM (99)

Gen 15:9 three years old, a R three years old, a
22:13 behind him was a R, caught in a thicket
22:13 went and took the R, and offered it up
Ex 29:15 the head of the R,
29:16 you shall slaughter the R, and shall take its
29:17 you shall cut the R into pieces, and wash
29:18 and burn the whole R upon the altar; it
29:19 shall take the other R; and Aaron and his
29:19 the head of the R,
29:20 you shall kill the R, and take part of
29:22 the fat of the R, and the fat tail,
29:22 (for it is a R of ordination),
29:26 the breast of the R of Aaron's ordination and
29:27 is offered from the R of ordination, since it
29:31 "You shall take the R of ordination, and boil
29:32 the flesh of the R and the bread that
Lev 5:15 to the LORD, a R without blemish out of
5:16 for him with the R of the guilt offering,
5:18 to the priest a R without blemish out of
6:6 to the LORD, a R without blemish out of
8:18 Then he presented the R of the burnt offering;
8:18 laid their hands on the head of the R
8:20 And when the R was cut into pieces, Moses
8:21 Moses burned the whole R on the altar, as
8:22 he presented the other R, the ram of ordination;
8:22 the other ram, the R of ordination; and Aaron
8:22 laid their hands on the head of the R
8:29 Moses' portion of the R of ordination, as the
9:2 sin offering, and a R for a burnt offering,
9:4 an ox and a R for peace offerings, to
9:18 ox also and the R, the sacrifice of peace
9:19 ox and of the R, the fat tail, and
16:3 sin offering and a R for a burnt offering.
16:5 sin offering, and one R for a burnt offering.
19:21 tent of meeting, a R for a guilt offering.
19:22 for him with the R of the guilt offering
Num 5:8 in addition to the R of atonement with which
6:14 sin offering, and one R without blemish as a
6:17 he shall offer the R as a sacrifice of
6:19 the shoulder of the R, when it is boiled,
7:15 one young bull, one R, one male lamb a
7:21 one young bull, one R, one male lamb a
7:27 one young bull, one R, one male lamb a
7:33 one young bull, one R, one male lamb a
7:39 one young bull, one R, one male lamb a
7:45 one young bull, one R, one male lamb a
7:51 one young bull, one R, one male lamb a
7:57 one young bull, one R, one male lamb a
7:63 one young bull, one R, one male lamb a
7:69 one young bull, one R, one male lamb a
7:75 one young bull, one R, one male lamb a
7:81 one young bull, one R, one male lamb a
15:6 Or for a R, you shall prepare for a
15:11 for each bull or R, or for each of
23:2 offered on each altar a bull and a R
23:4 offered upon each altar a bull and a R
23:14 a bull and a R on each altar.
23:30 a bull and a R on each altar.
28:11 two young bulls, one R, seven male lambs a
28:12 oil, for the one R;
28:14 a hin for a R, and a fourth of
28:19 two young bulls, one R, and seven male lambs
28:20 two tenths for a R;
28:27 two young bulls, one R, seven male lambs a
28:28 two tenths for one R,
29:2 one young bull, one R, seven male lambs a
29:3 two tenths for the R,
29:8 one young bull, one R, seven male lambs a
29:9 tenths for the one R,
29:36 LORD: one bull, one R, seven male lambs a
29:37 the bull, for the R, and for the lambs,
Josh 6:5 long blast with the R's horn, as soon as
Ruth 4:19 of Hezron, Hezron of R, Ram of Amminadab,
4:19 Hezron, Hezron of Ram, R of Amminadab,
1Chr 2:9 born to him: Jerahmeel, R, and Chelubai.
2:10 R was the father of Amminadab, and Amminadab
2:25 the first-born of Hezron: R, his first-born, Bunah,
2:27 The sons of R, the first-born of Jerahmeel: Maaz,
Ezra 10:19 guilt offering was a R of the flock for
Tob 7:8 and they killed a R from the flock and
Job 32:2 of the family of R, became angry.
Ezek 43:23 without blemish and a R from the flock without
43:25 a bull and a R from the flock, without
45:24 an ephah for each R, and a hin of
46:4 without blemish and a R without blemish;
46:5 cereal offering with the R shall be an ephah,
46:6 six lambs and a R, which shall be without
46:7 an ephah with the R, and with the lambs
46:11 ephah, and with a R an ephah, and with
Dan 8:3 saw, and behold, a R standing on the bank
8:4 I saw the R charging westward and northward and
8:6 He came to the R with the two horns,
8:7 come close to the R, and he was enraged
8:7 him and struck the R and broke his two
8:7 two horns; and the R had no power to
8:7 who could rescue the R from his power.
8:20 As for the R which you saw with the
Mt 1:3 Hezron the father of R,
1:4 father of Ram, and R the father of Amminadab,

RAMAH (37)

Josh 18:25 with their villages: Gibeon, R, Be-eroth,
19:8 as far as Baalath-beer, R of the Negeb.
19:29 the boundary turns to R, reaching to the fortified
19:36 Hammath, Rakkath, Chinnereth, Adamah, R, Hazor,
Judg 4:5 palm of Deborah between R and Bethel in the
19:13 and spend the night at Gibe-ah or at R
1Sam 1:19 then they went back to their house at R
2:11 Then Elkanah went home to R
7:17 would come back to R, for his home was

R

8:4 came to Samuel at R,
15:34 Then Samuel went to R; and Saul went up
16:13 And Samuel rose up, and went to R
19:18 came to Samuel at R, and told him all
19:19 told Saul, "Behold, David is at Naioth in R
19:22 he himself went to R, and came to the
19:22 one said, "Behold, they are at Naioth in R
19:23 there to Naioth in R; and the Spirit of
19:23 he prophesied, until he came to Naioth in R
20:1 fled from Naioth in R, and came and said
25:1 and they buried him in his house at R
28:3 and buried him in R, his own city.
1Kgs 15:17 against Judah, and built R, that he might permit
15:21 it, he stopped building R, and he dwelt in
15:22 away the stones of R and its timber, with
2Kgs 8:29 had given him at R, when he fought against
2Chr 16:1 against Judah, and built R, that he might permit
16:5 it, he stopped building R, and let his work
16:6 away the stones of R and its timber, with
22:6 he had received at R, when he fought against
Ezra 2:26 The sons of R and Geba, six hundred and
Neh 7:30 The men of R and Geba, six hundred and
11:33 Anathoth, Nob, Ananiah, Hazor, R, Gittaim,
Is 10:29 lodge for the night; R trembles, Gibe-ah of Saul
Jer 31:15 voice is heard in R, lamentation and bitter weeping.
40:1 let him go from R, when he took him
Hos 5:8 Blow the horn in Gibe-ah, the trumpet in R
Mt 2:18 voice was heard in R, wailing and loud lamentation,

RAMATH-MIZPEH

Josh 13:26 and from Heshbon to R and Betonim, and from

RAMATHAIM-ZOPHIM

1Sam 1:1 a certain man of R of the hill country

RAMATHITE

1Chr 27:27 vineyards was Shimei the R; and over the produce

RAMATHLEHI

Judg 15:17 of his hand; and that place was called R

RAMESES (4)

Gen 47:11 in the land of R, as Pharaoh had commanded.
Ex 12:37 of Israel journeyed from R to Succoth, about six
Num 33:3 They set out from R in the first month,
33:5 Israel set out from R, and encamped at Succoth.

RAMIAH

Ezra 10:25 the sons of Parosh: R, Izziah, Malchijah, Mijamin,

RAMOTH (6)

Deut 4:43 for the Reubenites, and R in Gilead for the
Josh 20:8 tribe of Reuben, and R in Gilead, from the
21:38 the tribe of Gad, R in Gilead with its
1Sam 30:27 those in Bethel, in R of the Negeb, in
1Chr 6:73 with its pasture lands, R with its pasture lands,
6:80 the tribe of Gad: R in Gilead with its

RAMOTH-GILEAD (20)

1Kgs 4:13 of Jokmeam; Ben-geber, in R (he had the villages
22:3 "Do you know that R belongs to us, and
22:4 "Will you go with me to battle at R
22:6 go to battle against R, or shall I forbear?"
22:12 said, "Go up to R and triumph; the LORD
22:15 shall we go to R to battle, or shall
22:20 up and fall at R And one said one
22:29 Jehoshaphat the king of Judah went up to R
2Kgs 8:28 king of Syria at R, where the Syrians wounded
9:1 of oil in your hand, and go to R
9:4 So the young man, the prophet, went to R
9:14 been on guard at R against Hazael king of
2Chr 18:2 him, and induced him to go up against R
18:3 of Judah, "Will you go with me to R
18:5 go to battle against R, or shall I forbear?"
18:11 said, "Go up to R and triumph; the LORD
18:14 shall we go to R to battle, or shall
18:19 up and fall at R And one said one
18:28 Jehoshaphat the king of Judah went up to R
22:5 make war against Hazael king of Syria at R

RAMPART (4)

2Sam 20:15 it stood against the R; and they were battering
Lam 2:8 from destroying; he caused R and wall to lament,
Nah 3:8 water around her, her R a sea, and water
Zech 9:3 has built herself a R, and heaped up silver

RAMPARTS (2)

Ps 48:13 towers, consider well her R, go through her citadels;
Nah 2:1 Man the R; watch the road; gird your loins;

RAMS (76)

Gen 31:38 have not eaten the R of your flocks.
32:14 hundred ewes and twenty R,
Ex 25:5 linen, goats' hair, tanned R skins, goatskins, acacia
26:14 a covering of tanned R skins and goatskins.
29:1 young bull and two R without blemish,
29:3 basket, and bring the bull and the two R
29:15 take one of the R, and Aaron and his
35:7 linen; goats' hair, tanned R skins, and goatskins;
35:23 goats' hair or tanned R skins or goatskins, brought
36:19 a covering of tanned R skins and goatskins.
39:34 the covering of tanned R skins and goatskins, and
Lev 8:2 offering, and the two R, and the basket of
23:18 young bull, and two R; they shall be a
Num 7:17 offerings, two oxen, five R, five male goats, and
7:23 offerings, two oxen, five R, five male goats, and
7:29 offerings, two oxen, five R, five male goats, and
7:35 offerings, two oxen, five R, five male goats, and
7:41 offerings, two oxen, five R, five male goats, and
7:47 offerings, two oxen, five R, five male goats, and
7:53 offerings, two oxen, five R, five male goats, and
7:59 offerings, two oxen, five R, five male goats, and
7:65 offerings, two oxen, five R, five male goats, and
7:71 offerings, two oxen, five R, five male goats, and
7:77 offerings, two oxen, five R, five male goats, and
7:83 offerings, two oxen, five R, five male goats, and
7:87 offering twelve bulls, twelve R, twelve male lambs a
7:88 offerings twenty-four bulls, the R sixty, the male
23:1 provide for me here seven bulls and seven R
23:29 provide for me here seven bulls and seven R
29:13 thirteen young bulls, two R, fourteen male lambs a
29:14 each of the two R,
29:17 twelve young bulls, two R, fourteen male lambs a
29:18 the bulls, for the R, and for the lambs,
29:20 day eleven bulls, two R, fourteen male lambs a
29:21 the bulls, for the R, and for the lambs,
29:23 day ten bulls, two R, fourteen male lambs a
29:24 the bulls, for the R, and for the lambs,
29:26 day nine bulls, two R, fourteen male lambs a
29:27 the bulls, for the R, and for the lambs,
29:29 day eight bulls, two R, fourteen male lambs a
29:30 the bulls, for the R, and for the lambs,
29:32 day seven bulls, two R, fourteen male lambs a
29:33 the bulls, for the R, and for the lambs,
Deut 32:14 fat of lambs and R, herds of Bashan and
Josh 6:4 bear seven trumpets of R horns before the ark;
6:6 bear seven trumpets of R horns before the ark
6:8 the seven trumpets of R horns before the LORD
6:13 the seven trumpets of R horns before the ark
1Sam 15:22 sacrifice, and to hearken than the fat of R
2Kgs 3:4 lambs, and the wool of a hundred thousand R
1Chr 15:26 the LORD, they sacrificed seven bulls and seven R
29:21 thousand bulls, a thousand R, and a thousand lambs,
2Chr 13:9 young bull or seven R becomes a priest of
17:11 seven thousand seven hundred R and seven thousand
29:21 brought seven bulls, seven R, seven lambs, and seven
29:22 and they killed the R and their blood was
29:32 seventy bulls, a hundred R, and two hundred lambs;
Ezra 6:9 needed-- young bulls, R, or sheep for burnt
6:17 hundred bulls, two hundred R, four hundred lambs,
7:17 all diligence buy bulls, R, and lambs, with their
8:35 for all Israel, ninety-six R, seventy-seven lambs, and
Job 42:8 seven bulls and seven R, and go to my
Ps 66:15 of the sacrifice of R; I will make an
114:4 The mountains skipped like R, the hills like lambs.
114:6 O mountains, that you skip like R
Is 1:11 of burnt offerings of R and the fat of
34:6 goats, with the fat of the kidneys of R
60:7 gathered to you, the R of Nebaioth shall minister
Jer 25:34 have come, and you shall fall like choice R
51:40 to the slaughter, like R and he-goats.
Ezek 27:21 favored dealers in lambs, R, and goats; in these
34:17 between sheep and sheep, R and he-goats.
39:18 of the earth--of R, of lambs, and of
45:23 young bulls and seven R without blemish, on each
Dan 3:39 with burnt offerings of R and bulls, and with
Mic 6:7 pleased with thousands of R, with ten thousands of

RAN (73)

Gen 18:2 he saw them, he R from the tent door
18:7 And Abraham R to the herd, and took a
24:17 Then the servant R to meet her, and said,

	24:20	into the trough and R again to the well
	24:28	Then the maiden R and told her mother's household
	24:29	was Laban; and Laban R out to the man,
	29:12	Rebekah's son; and she R and told her father.
	29:13	his sister's son, he R to meet him, and
	33:4	But Esau R to meet him, and embraced him,
Ex	9:23	and hail, and fire R down to the earth.
Num	11:27	And a young man R and told Moses, "Eldad
	16:47	as Moses said, and R into the midst of
Josh	7:22	sent messengers, and they R to the tent; and
	8:19	out his hand, they R and entered the city
	15:2	And their south boundary R from the end of
	19:33	And its boundary R from Heleph, from the oak
Judg	1:36	border of the Amorites R from the ascent of
	7:21	and all the army R; they cried out and
	9:21	And Jotham R away and fled, and went to
	13:10	And the woman R in haste and told her
1Sam	3:5	and R to Eli, and said, "Here I am,
	4:12	A man of Benjamin R from the battle line,
	10:23	Then they R and fetched him from there; and
	17:22	of the baggage, and R to the ranks, and
	17:48	to meet David, David R quickly toward the battle
	17:51	Then David R and stood over the Philistine, and
	20:36	As the lad R, he shot an arrow beyond
2Sam	18:21	The Cushite bowed before Joab, and R
	18:23	Then Ahima-az R by the way of the plain,
1Kgs	2:39	two of Shimei's slaves R away to Achish, son
	18:35	And the water R round about the altar, and
	18:46	up his loins and R before Ahab to the
	19:20	left the oxen, and R after Elijah, and said,
Tob	2:8	doing this; he once R away, and here he
	11:9	Then Anna R to meet them, and embraced her
	11:10	But his son R to him
Jud	6:12	up their weapons and R out of the city
	6:16	men and their women R to the assembly; and
	13:13	They all R together, both small and great, for
Jer	23:21	the prophets, yet they R; I did not speak
Ezek	40:18	And the pavement R along the side of the
Dan	8:6	the river, and he R at him in his
	13:19	two elders rose and R to her, and said:
	13:25	And one of them R and opened the garden
	13:38	saw this wickedness we R to them.
1Mac	2:24	to righteous anger; he R and killed him upon
	6:45	He courageously R into the midst of the phalanx
	16:21	But some one R ahead and reported to John
2Mac	3:19	who were kept indoors R together to the gates,
	8:13	distrustful of God's justice R off and got away.
	11:22	The king's letter R thus: "King Antiochus to his
	14:43	He bravely R up on the wall, and manfully
	14:45	wounds were severe he R through the crowd; and
Mt	27:48	of them at once R and took a sponge,
	28:8	and great joy, and R to tell his disciples.
Mk	5:6	Jesus from afar, he R and worshiped him;
	6:33	knew them, and they R there on foot from
	6:55	people recognized him, and R about the whole
	9:15	were greatly amazed, and R up to him and
	10:17	his journey, a man R up and knelt before
	14:52	the linen cloth and R away naked.
	15:35	And one R and, filling a sponge full of
Lk	15:20	and had compassion, and R and embraced him and
	19:4	So he R on ahead and climbed up into
	24:12	But Peter rose and R to the tomb; stooping
Jn	20:2	So she R, and went to Simon Peter and
	20:4	They both R, but the other disciple outran Peter
Acts	3:11	John, all the people R together to them in
	8:30	So Philip R to him, and heard him reading
	12:14	open the gate but R in and told that
	21:30	aroused, and the people R together; they seized Paul
	21:32	soldiers and centurions, and R down to them; and
	27:41	striking a shoal they R the vessel aground; the

RANG

Wis	17:4	fear, but terrifying sounds R out around them, and

RANGE (2)

Is	32:20	ox and the ass R free.
Zech	4:10	of the LORD, which R through the whole earth."

RANGED

Wis	19:9	For they R like horses, and leaped like lambs,

RANGES

Job	39:8	He R the mountains as his pasture, and he

RANK (5)

Esth	10:3	Jew was next in R to King Ahasuerus, and
Prov	30:27	of them march in R;
Is	3:3	and the man of R, the counselor and the
2Mac	4:31	a man of high R, to act as his
Jas	1:20	away all filthiness and R growth of wickedness and

RANKS (12)

1Sam	17:8	and shouted to the R of Israel, "Why have
	17:10	said, "I defy the R of Israel this day;
	17:22	and ran to the R, and went and greeted
	17:23	up out of the R of the Philistines, and
2Kgs	11:8	and whoever approaches the R is to be slain.
	11:15	her out between the R; and slay with the
2Chr	23:14	her out between the R; any one who follows
Jud	1:4	his infantry form their R —
Is	14:31	north, and there is no straggler in his R
2Mac	13:21	a man from the R of the Jews, gave
Jn	1:15	who comes after me R before me, for he
	1:30	comes a man who R before me, for he

RANSOM (18)

Ex	21:30	If a R is laid on him, then he
	30:12	each shall give a R for himself to the
Num	35:31	you shall accept no R for the life of
	35:32	you shall accept no R for him who has
Job	6:23	Or, R me from the hand of oppressors?
	33:24	I have found a R;
	36:18	the greatness of the R turn you aside.
Ps	49:7	Truly no man can R himself, or give to
	49:8	his life, for the R of his life is
	49:15	But God will R my soul from the power
Prov	13:8	The R of a man's life is his wealth,
	21:18	The wicked is a R for the righteous, and
Is	43:3	give Egypt as your R, Ethiopia and Seba in
Hos	13:14	Shall I R them from the power of Sheol?
Mt	20:28	his life as a R for many."
Mk	10:45	his life as a R for many."
1Tim	2:6	gave himself as a R for all, the testimony
Rev	5:9	by thy blood didst R men for God from

RANSOMED (7)

Lev	19:20	man and not yet R or given her freedom,
	27:29	among men, shall be R; he shall be put
1Sam	14:45	So the people R Jonathan, that he did not
Is	35:10	And the R of the LORD shall return, and
	51:11	And the R of the LORD shall return, and
Jer	31:11	For the LORD has R Jacob, and has redeemed
1Pet	1:18	know that you were R from the futile ways

RAPACITY

Mt	23:24	but inside they are full of extortion and R

RAPHA

1Chr	8:2	Nohah the fourth, and R the fifth.

RAPHAEL (9)

Tob	3:17	And R was sent to heal the two of
	5:4	man; and he found R, who was an angel,
	7:8	Then Tobias said to R, "Brother Azarias, speak of
	8:2	remembered the words of R, and he took the
	9:1	Then Tobias called R and said to him,
	9:5	So R made the journey and stayed over night
	11:2	Then R said to Tobias, "Are you not aware,
	11:7	R said, "I know, Tobias, that your father will
	12:15	I am R, one of the seven holy angels

RAPHAH

1Chr	8:37	the father of Bine-a; R was his son, Ele-asah

RAPHAIM

Jud	8:1	of Gideon, son of R, son of Ahitub, son

RAPHON

1Mac	5:37	army and encamped opposite R, on the other side

RAPHU

Num	13:9	Palti the son of R;

RARE (3)

1Sam	3:1	of the LORD was R in those days; there
Is	13:12	will make men more R than fine gold, and
Rev	21:11	radiance like a most R jewel, like a jasper,

RASCAL

Sir	19:23	There is a R bowed down in mourning, but

RASE (2)
Ps 137:7 Jerusalem, how they said, R it, rase it!
137:7 they said, "Rase it, R it!

RASH (9)
Lev 5:4 with his lips a R oath to do evil
5:4 good, any sort of R oath that men swear,
Job 6:3 of the sea; therefore my words have been R
Ps 106:33 spirit bitter, and he spoke words that were R
Prov 12:18 There is one whose R words are like sword
Eccl 5:2 Be not R with your mouth, nor let your
Is 32:4 The mind of the R will have good judgment,
2Mac 5:18 turned back from his R act as soon as
Acts 19:36 you ought to be quiet and do nothing R

RASHLY
Prov 20:25 a man to say R, "It is holy," and

RASSIS
Jud 2:23 all the people of R and the Ishmaelites who

RATED
Lev 25:50 his owner shall be R as the time of

RATHAMIN
1Mac 11:34 Aphairema and Lydda and R; the latter, with all

RATHER (64)
Gen 48:22 have given to you R than to your brothers
Deut 29:20 not pardon him, but R the anger of the
2Kgs 5:13 How much R, then, when he says to you,
20:10 to lengthen ten steps; R let the shadow go
Tob 6:12 of death, because you R than any other man
Job 7:15 choose strangling and death R than my bones.
32:2 because he justified himself R than God;
36:21 this you have chosen R than affliction.
Ps 84:10 I would R be a doorkeeper in the house
Prov 8:10 of silver, and knowledge R than choice gold;
16:16 is to be chosen R than silver.
17:12 robbed of her cubs, R than a fool in
22:1 is to be chosen R than great riches, and
Eccl 6:5 yet it finds rest R than he.
Wis 7:10 chose to have her R than light, because her
8:20 to my lot; or R, being good, I entered
Sir 25:15 I would R dwell with a lion and a
Ezek 18:23 Lord GOD, and not R that he should turn
Dan 3:96 yielded up their bodies R than serve and worship
13:23 fall into your hands, R than to sin in
Hos 6:6 the knowledge of God, R than burnt offerings.
1Mac 1:63 They chose to die R than to be defiled
9:9 Let us R save our own lives now, and
2Mac 6:19 welcoming death with honor R than life with
7:2 are ready to die R than transgress the laws
7:7 him, "Will you eat R than have your body
14:42 preferring to die nobly R than to fall into
Mt 10:6 the Samaritans, but go R to the lost sheep
10:28 cannot kill the soul; R fear him who can
25:9 and for you; go R to the dealers and
27:24 was gaining nothing, but R that a riot was
Mk 5:26 was no better but R grew worse.
Lk 11:28 But he said, "Blessed R are those who hear
12:51 I tell you, but R division;
17:8 Will he not R say to him, 'Prepare supper
18:14 to his house justified R than the other; for
22:26 not so with you; R let the greatest among
Jn 3:19 and men loved darkness R than light, because their
Acts 4:19 to listen to you R than to God, you
5:29 "We must obey God R than men.
24:21 But Felix, having a R accurate knowledge of the
Rom 1:25 and served the creature R than the Creator, who
14:13 on one another, but R decide never to put
1Cor 5:2 Ought you not R to mourn?
5:11 But R I wrote to you not to associate
6:7 Why not R suffer wrong?
6:7 Why not R be defrauded?
9:12 but we endure anything R than put an obstacle
9:15 For I would R die than have any one
14:19 in church I would R speak five words with
2Cor 2:7 enough; so you should R turn to forgive and
5:8 courage, and we would R be away from the
Gal 4:9 to know God, or R to be known by
Eph 4:15 R, speaking the truth in love, we are to
4:28 no longer steal, but R let him labor, doing
1Tim 1:4 genealogies which promote speculations R than the
6:2 that they are brethren; R they must serve all
2Tim 3:4 conceit, lovers of pleasure R than lovers of God,
Heb 7:11 the order of Melchizedek, R than one named after
11:25 Pharaoh's daughter, choosing R to share
12:11 all discipline seems painful R than pleasant; later it
12:13 out of joint but R be healed.
2Jn 1:12 to you, I would R not use paper and
3Jn 1:13 you, but I would R not write with pen

RATIFIED (3)
Gal 3:15 or adds to it, once it has been R
3:17 annul a covenant previously R by God, so as
Heb 9:18 first covenant was not R without blood.

RATTLE (2)
Job 39:23 Upon him R the quiver, the flashing spear and
41:29 he laughs at the R of javelins.

RATTLING
Ezek 37:7 noise, and behold, a R; and the bones came

RAVAGE (2)
1Sam 6:5 of your mice that R the land, and give
Ezek 14:15 the land, and they R it, and it be

RAVAGED (6)
2Sam 11:1 all Israel; and they R the Ammonites, and besieged
1Chr 20:1 out the army, and R the country of the
Jud 2:23 the hill country and R Put and Lud, and
2:27 sacked their cities and R their lands and put
Is 3:26 shall lament and mourn; R, she shall sit upon
Ezek 19:7 And he R their strongholds, and laid waste their

RAVAGER (2)
Judg 16:24 into our hand, the R of our country, who
Is 54:16 have also created the R to destroy;

RAVAGES (2)
Ps 35:17 Rescue me from their R, my life from the
80:13 boar from the forest R it, and all that

RAVAGING
Acts 8:3 But Saul was R the church, and entering house

RAVE
Wis 14:28 For their worshippers either R in exultation, or

RAVED (2)
1Sam 18:10 upon Saul, and he R within his house, while
1Kgs 18:29 as midday passed, they R on until the time

RAVEN (7)
Gen 8:7 and sent forth a R; and it went to
Lev 11:15 to its kind, every R according to its kind,
Deut 14:14 after their kinds; every R after its kind;
Job 38:41 Who provides for the R its prey, when its
Song 5:11 gold; his locks are wavy, black as a R
Is 34:11 the owl and the R shall dwell in it.
Zeph 2:14 in the window, the R croak on the threshold;

RAVENING (2)
Ps 22:13 at me, like a R and roaring lion.
Jer 2:30 your prophets like a R lion.

RAVENOUS (3)
Gen 49:27 Benjamin is a R wolf, in the morning devouring
Is 35:9 there, nor shall any R beast come up on
Mt 7:15 clothing but inwardly are R wolves.

RAVENS (5)
1Kgs 17:4 I have commanded the R to feed you there."
17:6 And the R brought him bread and meat in
Ps 147:9 and to the young R which cry.
Prov 30:17 picked out by the R of the valley and
Lk 12:24 Consider the R: they neither sow nor reap, they

RAVINE
Josh 8:11 of Ai, with a R between them and Ai.

RAVINES (5)
Is 7:19 settle in the steep R, and in the clefts
Ezek 6:3 the hills, to the R and the valleys: Behold,
35:8 and in all your R those slain with the
36:4 and the hills, the R and the valleys, the
36:6 and hills, to the R and valleys, Thus says

RAVISH
Judg 19:24 R them and do with them what seems good

RAVISHED (8)

Judg 20:5 kill me, and they R my concubine, and she
Jud 12:16 and Holofernes' heart was R with her and he
16:9 Her sandal R his eyes, her beauty captivated his
Song 4:9 You have R my heart, my sister, my bride,
4:9 my bride, you have R my heart with a
Is 13:16 their houses will be plundered and their wives R
Lam 5:11 Women are R in Zion, virgins in the towns
Zech 14:2 plundered and the women R; half of the city

RAW (8)

Ex 12:9 eat any of it R or boiled with water,
Lev 13:10 and there is quick R flesh in the swelling,
13:14 But when R flesh appears on him, he shall
13:15 priest shall examine the R flesh, and pronounce him
13:15 and pronounce him unclean; R flesh is unclean, for
13:16 But if the R flesh turns again and is
13:24 its skin and the R flesh of the burn
1Sam 2:15 will not accept boiled meat from you, but R

RAY

Wis 16:27 warmed by a fleeting R of the sun,

RAYS (3)

Wis 2:4 is chased by the R of the sun and
Hab 3:4 was like the light, R flashed from his hand;
Lk 11:36 a lamp with its R gives you light."

RAZED (4)

Judg 9:45 in it; and he R the city and sowed
Jud 5:18 of their God was R to the ground, and
Is 23:13 erected their siegetowers, they R her palaces, they
1Mac 5:51 of the sword, and R and plundered the city.

RAZIS (2)

2Mac 14:37 A certain R, one of the elders of Jerusalem,
14:41 Being surrounded, R fell upon his own sword,

RAZOR (8)

Num 6:5 vow of separation no R shall come upon his
8:7 them go with a R over all their body,
Judg 13:5 No R shall come upon his head, for the
16:17 said to her, "A R has never come upon
1Sam 1:11 his life, and no R shall touch his head."
Ps 52:2 is like a sharp R, you worker of treachery.
Is 7:20 will shave with a R which is hired beyond
Ezek 5:1 it as a barber's R and pass it over

RE-AIAH (4)

1Chr 4:2 R the son of Shobal was the father of
5:5 son, Micah his son, R his son, Baal his
Ezra 2:47 Gahar, the sons of R,
Neh 7:50 Gahar, the sons of R, the sons of Rezin,

RE-EL-AIAH

Ezra 2:2 Jeshua, Nehemiah, Seraiah, R, Mordecai,

RE-ESTABLISH

Esth 13:2 all its extent, to R the peace which all

REACH (26)

Ex 28:42 the thighs they shall R;
Num 34:11 shall go down, and R to the shoulder of
35:4 to the Levites, shall R from the wall of
Ezra 5:5 till a report should R Darius and then answer
Jud 7:10 is not easy to R the tops of their
Job 20:6 heavens, and his head R to the clouds,
21:7 do the wicked live, R old age, and grow
Ps 32:6 waters, they shall not R him.
71:19 thy righteousness, O God, R the high heavens.
Sir 14:13 before you die, and R out and give to
31:14 Do not R out your hand for everything you
31:18 many persons, do not R out your hand before
35:16 and his prayer will R to the clouds.
43:27 speak much we cannot R the end, and the
Is 30:4 Zoan and his envoys R Hanes,
49:6 that my salvation may R to the end of
Ezek 31:14 that drink water may R up to them in
Hab 2:9 be safe from the R of harm!
1Mac 6:45 of the phalanx to R it; he killed men
2Mac 4:6 affairs could not again R a peaceful settlement, and
Lk 8:19 but they could not R him for the crowd.
Acts 27:12 that somehow they could R Phoenix, a harbor of
2Cor 10:13 has apportioned us, to R even to you.
10:14 though we did not R you; we were the
Heb 4:1 to have failed to R it.
2Pet 3:9 but that all should R repentance.

REACHED (54)

Gen 28:12 the top of it R to heaven; and behold,
Josh 9:17 Israel set out and R their cities on the
15:1 according to their families R southward to the
17:7 territory of Manasseh R from Asher to Mich-
17:10 the north Asher is R, and on the east
19:10 territory of its inheritance R as far as Sarid;
Judg 3:21 And Ehud R with his left hand, took the
6:21 angel of the LORD R out the tip of
2Sam 22:17 "He R from on high, he took me, he
2Kgs 6:7 So he R out his hand and took it.
9:18 reported, saying, "The messenger R them, but he is
9:20 the watchman reported, "He R them, but he is
2Chr 28:9 a rage which has R up to heaven.
Tob 7:1 When they R Ecbatana and arrived at the house
Ps 18:6 my cry to him R his ears.
18:16 He R from on high, he took me, he
107:7 straight way, till they R a city to dwell
Wis 19:3 of their dead, they R another foolish decision, and
Sir 43:7 wanes when it has R the full.
47:16 Your name R to far-off islands, and you were
50:15 High, the Almighty, he R out his hand to
Is 10:10 As my hand has R to the kingdoms of
16:8 down its branches, which R to Jazer and strayed
24:11 wine; all joy has R its eventide; the gladness
Jer 4:10 whereas the sword has R their very life."
4:18 is bitter; it has R your very heart."
48:32 passed over the sea, R as far as Jazer,
51:9 for her judgment has R up to heaven and
Dan 4:11 strong, and its top R to heaven, and it
4:20 so that its top R to heaven, and it
6:24 wives; and before they R the bottom of the
8:23 when the transgressors have R their full measure, a
Jon 3:6 Then tidings R the king of Nineveh, and he
Mic 1:9 to Judah, it has R to the gate of
1Mac 3:26 His fame R the king, and the Gentiles talked
12:52 So they all R the land of Judah safely,
13:47 So Simon R an agreement with them and stopped
13:53 John his son had R manhood, so he made
16:9 pursued them until Cendebeus R Kedron, which he
2Mac 1:13 For when the leader R Persia with a force
5:11 of what had happened R the king, he took
6:14 them until they have R the full measure of
6:15 when our sins have R their height.
6:23 hairs which he had R with distinction and his
8:35 the country till he R Antioch, having succeeded
12:1 this agreement had been R, Lysias returned to the
12:35 so Gorgias escaped and R Marisa.
Mt 14:31 Jesus immediately R out his hand and caught him,
16:5 When the disciples R the other side, they had
Jn 20:4 disciple outran Peter and R the tomb first;
20:8 the other disciple, who R the tomb first, also
Acts 16:4 decisions which had been R by the apostles and
1Cor 14:36 or are you the only ones it has R
Jas 5:4 of the harvesters have R the ears of the

REACHES (14)

2Kgs 5:6 read, "When this letter R you, know that I
Jud 7:14 and before the sword R them they will be
11:15 When the word R them and they proceed to
Job 41:26 Though the sword R him, it does not avail;
Ps 48:10 God, so thy praise R to the ends of
108:4 the heavens, thy faithfulness R to the clouds.
Prov 31:20 to the poor, and R out her hands to
Wis 8:1 She R mightily from one end of the earth
Sir 18:8 is great if he R a hundred years.
35:17 be consoled until it R the Lord; he will
Is 15:8 of Moab; the wailing R to Eglaim, the wailing
15:8 to Eglaim, the wailing R to Beer-elim.
30:28 an overflowing stream that R up to the neck;
Dan 4:22 greatness has grown and R to heaven, and your

REACHING (2)

Josh 19:29 boundary turns to Ramah, R to the fortified city
Is 8:8 overflow and pass on, R even to the neck;

READ (83)

Ex 24:7 of the covenant, and R it in the hearing
Deut 17:19 him, and he shall R in it all the
31:11 will choose, you shall R this law before all
Josh 8:34 And afterward he R all the words of the
8:35 which Joshua did not R before all the assembly
2Kgs 5:6 king of Israel, which R, "When this letter reaches
5:7 the king of Israel R the letter, he rent

R

	19:14	of the messengers, and R it; and Hezekiah went
	22:8	to Shaphan, and he R it.
	22:10	And Shaphan R it before the king.
	22:16	the book which the king of Judah has R
	23:2	and great; and he R in their hearing all
2Chr	34:18	And Shaphan R it before the king.
	34:24	the book which was R before the king of
	34:30	and small; and he R in their hearing all
Ezra	4:18	us has been plainly R before me.
	4:23	King Artaxerxes' letter was R before Rehum and
Neh	8:3	And he R from it facing the square before
	8:8	And they R from the book, from the law
	8:18	the last day, he R from the book of
	9:3	in their place and R from the book of
	13:1	On that day they R from the book of
Esth	6:1	chronicles, and they were R before the king.
Is	29:11	to one who can R, saying, "Read this," he
	29:11	who can read, saying, R this," he says, "I
	29:12	to one who cannot R, saying, "Read this," he
	29:12	who cannot read, saying, R this," he says, "I
	29:12	he says, "I cannot R
	34:16	Seek and R from the book of the LORD:
	37:14	of the messengers, and R it; and Hezekiah went
Jer	29:29	Zephaniah the priest R this letter in the hearing
	36:6	LORD's house you shall R the words of the
	36:6	You shall R them also in the hearing of
	36:10	all the people, Baruch R the words of Jeremiah
	36:13	had heard, when Baruch R the scroll in the
	36:14	the scroll that you R in the hearing of
	36:15	him, "Sit down and R it." So Baruch read
	36:15	So Baruch R it to them.
	36:21	the secretary; and Jehudi R it to the king
	36:23	As Jehudi R three or four columns, the king
	51:61	Babylon, see that you R all these words,
Bar	1:3	And Baruch R the words of this book in
	1:14	And you shall R this book which we are
Dan	5:8	but they could not R the writing or make
	5:15	in before me to R this writing and make
	5:16	Now if you can R the writing and make
	5:17	another; nevertheless I will R the writing to the
1Mac	5:14	letter was still being R, behold, other messengers,
	10:7	came to Jerusalem and R the letter in the
	14:19	And these were R before the assembly in Jerusalem.
2Mac	2:25	those who wish to R, to make it easy
	6:12	I urge those who R this book not to
	8:23	he appointed Eleazar to R aloud from the holy
	11:34	them a letter, which R thus: "Quintus Memmius and
	15:39	ears of those who R the work.
Mt	12:3	them, "Have you not R what David did, when
	12:5	Or have you not R in the law how
	19:4	answered, "Have you not R that he who made
	21:16	"Yes; have you never R, 'Out of the mouth
	21:42	them, "Have you never R in the scriptures: 'The
	22:31	dead, have you not R what was said to
	27:37	charge against him, which R, "This is Jesus the
Mk	2:25	them, "Have you never R what David did, when
	12:10	Have you not R this scripture: 'The very stone
	12:26	raised, have you not R in the book of
	15:26	the charge against him R, "The King of the
Lk	4:16	he stood up to R;
	6:3	answered, "Have you not R what David did when
	10:26	How do you R
Jn	19:19	on the cross; it R, "Jesus of Nazareth, the
	19:20	Many of the Jews R this title, for the
Acts	13:27	the prophets which are R every sabbath, fulfilled
	15:21	him, for he is R every sabbath in the
	15:31	And when they R it, they rejoiced at the
2Cor	1:13	but what you can R and understand; I hope
	3:2	to be known and R by all men;
	3:14	this day, when they R the old covenant, that
	3:15	day whenever Moses is R a veil lies over
Eph	3:4	When you R this you can perceive my insight
Col	4:16	this letter has been R among you, have it
	4:16	among you, have it R also in the church
	4:16	and see that you R also the letter from
1Thes	5:27	that this letter be R to all the brethren.

READER (2)

Mt	24:15	holy place (let the R understand),
Mk	13:14	to be (let the R understand), then let those

READERS

2Mac	2:25	are inclined to memorize, and to profit all R

READILY (3)

Wis	14:28	or live unrighteously, or R commit perjury;
Is	32:4	the stammerers will speak R and distinctly.
2Cor	11:4	you submit to it R enough.

READINESS (6)

Lev	16:21	the hand of a man who is in R
Josh	8:4	hold yourselves all in R;
2Mac	14:22	posted armed men in R at key places to
2Cor	8:11	desire, so that your R in desiring it may
	8:12	For if the R is there, it is acceptable
	9:2	for I know your R, of which I boast

READING (10)

Neh	8:8	the sense, so that the people understood the R
Jer	36:8	prophet ordered him about R from the scroll the
	51:63	ever.' When you finish R this book, bind a
Acts	8:28	his chariot, he was R the prophet Isaiah.
	8:30	him, and heard him R Isaiah the prophet, and
	8:30	and asked, "Do you understand what you are R
	8:32	scripture which he was R was this: "As a
	13:15	After the R of the law and the prophets,
	23:34	On R the letter, he asked to what province
1Tim	4:13	attend to the public R of scripture, to preaching,

READS (3)

Dan	5:7	men of Babylon, "Whoever R this writing, and shows
Hab	2:2	he may run who R it.
Rev	1:3	Blessed is he who R aloud the words of

READY (118)

Gen	18:6	Sarah, and said, "Make R quickly three measures of
	43:16	an animal and make R, for the men are
	43:25	provender, they made R the present for Joseph's
	46:29	Then Joseph made R his chariot and went up
Ex	14:6	So he made R his chariot and took his
	17:4	They are almost R to stone me."
	19:11	their garments, and be R by the third day;
	19:15	to the people, "Be R by the third day;
	34:2	Be R in the morning, and come up in
Num	32:17	will take up arms, R to go before the
Deut	9:8	you that he was R to destroy you.
	9:19	so that he was R to destroy you.
	9:20	Aaron that he was R to destroy him; and
Josh	4:13	them; about forty thousand R armed for war passed
	9:4	and went and made R provisions, and took worn-out
Judg	13:16	but if you make R a burnt offering, then
1Sam	25:18	wine, and five sheep R dressed, and five measures
2Sam	15:15	"Behold, your servants are R to do whatever my
1Kgs	5:8	to me; I am R to do all you
2Kgs	9:21	Joram said, "Make R
	9:21	And they made R his chariot.
	10:6	and if you are R to obey me, take
1Chr	5:18	seven hundred and sixty, R for service.
	7:11	thousand and two hundred, R for service in war.
	12:36	forty thousand seasoned troops R for battle.
2Chr	29:19	faithless, we have made R and sanctified; and behold,
Neh	9:17	thou art a God R to forgive, gracious and
Tob	5:16	said to Tobias, "Get R for the journey, and
	11:9	child; now I am R to die." And they
Esth	3:14	the peoples to be R for that day.
	8:13	Jews were to be R on that day to
	11:6	dragons came forward, both R to fight, and they
	11:9	threatened them, and were R to perish.
Job	12:5	for misfortune; it is R for those whose feet
	15:23	day of darkness is R at his hand;
	17:1	extinct, the grave is R for me.
	18:12	hunger-bitten, and calamity is R for his stumbling.
	32:19	new wineskins, it is R to burst.
Ps	38:17	For I am R to fall, and my pain
	45:1	the pen of a R scribe.
	59:4	no fault of mine, they run and make R
	119:76	thy steadfast love be R to comfort me according
	119:173	Let thy hand be R to help me, for
Prov	19:29	Condemnation is R for scoffers, and flogging for the
	21:31	The horse is made R for the day of
	22:18	all of them are R on your lips.
	24:27	work outside, get everything R for you in the
Wis	16:20	from heaven with bread R to eat, providing every
Sir	6:35	Be R to listen to every narrative, and do
	39:31	commands, and be made R on earth for their
	45:23	turned away, in the R goodness of his soul,
	48:10	fire; you who are R at the appointed time,
Is	30:33	king it is made R, its pyre made deep
	65:1	I was R to be sought by those who
	65:1	for me; I was R to be found by
Jer	46:14	and Tahpanhes; Say, 'Stand R and be prepared, for
Bar	2:9	has kept the calamities R, and the Lord has

Ezek 7:14 trumpet and made all R; but none goes to
38:7 "Be R and keep ready, you and all the
38:7 "Be ready and keep R, you and all the
Dan 3:15 Now if you are R when you hear the
9:14 the LORD has kept R the calamity and has
1Mac 3:28 ordered them to be R for any need.
3:44 congregation assembled to be R for battle, and to
3:58 Be R early in the morning to fight with
4:35 of Judas, and how R they were either to
5:27 the enemy are getting R to attack the strongholds
5:39 encamped across the stream, R to come and fight
6:33 and his troops made R for battle and sounded
7:29 But the enemy were R to seize Judas.
12:27 so as to be R all night for battle,
12:34 heard that they were R to hand over the
12:50 marching in close formation, R for battle.
13:22 got all his cavalry R to go, but that
13:37 sent, and we are R to make a general
2Mac 7:2 For we are R to die rather than transgress
8:21 courage and made them R to die for their
11:9 were strengthened in heart, R to assail not only
13:12 Judas exhorted them and ordered them to stand R
Mt 22:4 Behold, I have made R my dinner, my oxen
22:4 killed, and everything is R; come to the marriage
22:8 servants, 'The wedding is R, but those invited were
24:44 you also must be R; for the Son of
25:10 and those who were R went in with him
Mk 3:9 to have a boat R for him because of
14:15 upper room furnished and R; there prepare for us."
Lk 1:17 the just, to make R for the Lord a
9:52 the Samaritans, to make R for him;
12:40 You also must be R; for the Son of
12:47 but did not make R or act according to
14:17 for all is now R
22:12 you a large upper room furnished; there make R
22:33 him, "Lord, I am R to go with you
Acts 21:13 For I am R not only to be imprisoned
21:15 these days we made R and went up to
23:15 And we are R to kill him before he
23:21 and now they are R, waiting for the promise
23:23 of the night get R two hundred soldiers with
1Cor 3:2 for you were not R for it; and even
3:2 yet you are not R,
14:8 sound, who will get R for battle?
2Cor 1:17 like a worldly man, R to say Yes and
9:2 that Achaia has been R since last year; and
9:3 that you may be R, as I said you
9:4 that you are not R, we be humiliated–to
9:5 that it may be R not as an exaction
10:6 to obey Christ, being R to punish every disobedience,
12:14 third time I am R to come to you.
1Thes 2:8 of you, we were R to share with you
2Tim 2:21 master of the house, R for any good work.
Tit 3:1 be obedient, to be R for any honest work,
Heb 8:13 and growing old is R to vanish away.
11:17 received the promises was R to offer up his
1Pet 1:5 faith for a salvation R to be revealed in
4:5 to him who is R to judge the living
Rev 8:6 the seven trumpets made R to blow them.
9:15 who had been held R for the hour, the
19:7 Bride has made herself R;

REAFFIRM

2Cor 2:8 I beg you to R your love for him.

REAL (11)

Sir 7:18 for money, or a R brother for the gold
2Mac 4:1 and had been the R cause of the misfortune.
Mk 11:31 that John was a R prophet.
Acts 12:9 by the angel was R, but thought he was
22:30 desiring to know the R reason why the Jews
Rom 2:28 he is not a R Jew who is one
2:29 is one inwardly, and R circumcision is a matter
1Cor 8:4 "an idol has no R existence," and that "there
1Tim 5:3 Honor widows who are R widows.
5:5 She who is a R widow, and is left
5:16 assist those who are R widows.

REALITIES

Heb 10:1 true form of these R, it can never, by

REALIZE (3)

Sir 12:12 at last you will R the truth of my
23:19 and he does not R that the eyes of
2Cor 13:5 Do you not R that Jesus Christ is in

REALIZED (8)

1Mac 5:34 the army of Timothy R that it was Maccabeus,
7:25 had grown strong, and R that he could not
12:50 But they R that Jonathan had been seized and
2Mac 11:13 had befallen him, and R that the Hebrews were
14:3 the times of separation, R that there was no
Acts 12:12 When he R this, he went to the house
22:29 was afraid, for he R that Paul was a
Eph 3:11 purpose which he has R in Christ Jesus our

REALIZING (3)

2Mac 5:6 his fellow citizens, not R that success at the
Acts 24:9 to speak, Paul replied: R that for many years
Heb 6:11 the same earnestness in R the full assurance of

REALLY (19)

Gen 16:13 she said, "Have I R seen God and remained
27:21 know whether you are R my son Esau or
27:24 He said, "Are you R my son Esau?" He
Judg 15:2 her father said, "I R thought that you utterly
Jud 6:9 If you R hope in your heart that they
Esth 16:10 of Hammedatha, a Macedonian R an alien to the
Wis 17:14 the night, which was R powerless, and which beset
Dan 13:54 Now then, if you R saw her, tell me
2Mac 3:9 he inquired whether this R was the situation.
12:12 thinking that they might R be useful in many
Jn 7:26 be that the authorities R know that this is
7:40 people said, "This is R the prophet."
1Cor 5:7 new lump, as you R are unleavened.
8:7 idols, eat food as R offered to an idol;
14:25 declare that God is R among you.
Gal 3:4 in vain?–if it R is in vain.
Phil 1:12 happened to me has R served to advance the
1Thes 2:13 but as what it R is, the word of
Jas 2:8 If you R fulfil the royal law, according to

REALM (7)

2Kgs 20:13 or in all his R that Hezekiah did not
2Chr 20:30 So the R of Jehoshaphat was quiet, for his
Ezra 7:23 wrath be against the R of the king and
Is 39:2 or in all his R that Hezekiah did not
Dan 9:1 became king over the R of the Chaldeans–
11:9 shall come into the R of the king of
2Mac 9:24 the people throughout the R would not be troubled,

REAP (34)

Lev 19:9 "When you R the harvest of your land, you
19:9 land, you shall not R your field to its
23:10 I give you and R its harvest, you shall
23:22 "And when you R the harvest of your land,
23:22 land, you shall not R your field to its
25:5 harvest you shall not R, and the grapes of
25:11 shall neither sow, nor R what grows of itself,
Deut 24:19 "When you R your harvest in your field, and
1Sam 8:12 his ground and to R his harvest, and to
2Kgs 19:29 third year sow, and R, and plant vineyards, and
Job 4:8 iniquity and sow trouble R the same.
Ps 126:5 who sow in tears R with shouts of joy!
Prov 22:8 who sows injustice will R calamity, and the rod
Eccl 11:4 and he who regards the clouds will not R
Sir 7:3 and you will not R a sevenfold crop.
Is 37:30 third year sow and R, and plant vineyards, and
Hos 8:7 wind, and they shall R the whirlwind.
10:12 Sow for yourselves righteousness, R the fruit of
Mic 6:15 shall sow, but not R; you shall tread olives,
Mt 6:26 they neither sow nor R nor gather into barns,
25:26 You knew that I R where I have not
Lk 12:24 they neither sow nor R, they have neither storehouse
19:21 not lay down, and R what you did not
Jn 4:38 I sent you to R that for which you
Rom 1:13 order that I may R some harvest among you
1Cor 9:11 too much if we R your material benefits?
2Cor 9:6 sows sparingly will also R sparingly, and he who
9:6 sows bountifully will also R bountifully.
Gal 6:7 whatever a man sows, that he will also R
6:8 will from the flesh R corruption; but he who
6:8 will from the Spirit R eternal life.
6:9 due season we shall R, if we do not
Rev 14:15 in your sickle, and R, for the hour to
14:15 for the hour to R has come, for the

REAPED (4)

Gen 26:12 in that land, and R in the same year
Jer 12:13 sown wheat and have R thorns, they have tired
Hos 10:13 plowed iniquity, you have R injustice, you have eaten
Rev 14:16 sickle on the earth, and the earth was R

REAPER (5)
Ps 129:7 up, with which the R does not fill his
Is 17:5 be as when the R gathers standing grain and
Jer 9:22 like sheaves after the R, and none shall gather
Amos 9:13 plowman shall overtake the R and the treader of
Jn 4:36 so that sower and R may rejoice together.

REAPERS (10)
Ruth 2:3 the field after the R; and she happened to
2:4 he said to the R, "The LORD be with
2:5 in charge of the R, "Whose maiden is this?"
2:6 in charge of the R answered, "It is the
2:7 the sheaves after the R So she came, and
2:14 she sat beside the R, and he passed to
2Kgs 4:18 out one day to his father among the R
Dan 14:33 into the field to take it to the R
Mt 13:30 I will tell the R, Gather the weeds first
13:39 the age, and the R are angels.

REAPING (4)
Ruth 2:9 field which they are R, and go after them.
1Sam 6:13 people of Beth-shemesh were R their wheat harvest
Mt 25:24 be a hard man, R where you did not
Lk 19:22 not lay down and R what I did not

REAPS (2)
Jn 4:36 He who R receives wages, and gathers fruit for
4:37 'One sows and another R

REAR (24)
Ex 26:22 frame; and for the R of the tabernacle westward
26:23 the tabernacle in the R;
26:27 the tabernacle at the R westward.
36:27 And for the R of the tabernacle westward he
36:28 frames for corners of the tabernacle in the R
36:32 the tabernacle at the R westward.
Num 10:25 Dan, acting as the R guard of all the
Deut 25:18 cut off at your R all who lagged behind
Josh 6:9 the trumpets, and the R guard came after the
6:13 before them, and the R guard came after the
8:13 the city and its R guard west of the
10:19 enemies, fall upon their R, do not let them
1Sam 29:2 passing on in the R with Achish,
2Sam 5:23 go around to their R, and come upon them
10:9 front and in the R, he chose some of
24:18 to him, "Go up, R an altar to the
1Kgs 6:16 twenty cubits of the R of the house with
1Chr 19:10 front and in the R, he chose some of
21:18 should go up and R an altar to the
Is 52:12 Israel will be your R guard.
58:8 LORD shall be your R guard.
Joel 2:20 eastern sea, and his R into the western sea;
1Mac 4:15 all those in the R fell by the sword.
9:47 but he eluded him and went to the R

REARED (7)
Tob 14:10 to Ahikar who had R him, how he brought
Job 31:18 from his youth I R him as a father,
Is 1:2 spoken: "Sons have I R and brought up, but
23:4 birth, I have neither R young men nor brought
Lam 2:22 whom I dandled and R my enemy destroyed.
Bar 4:8 you grieved Jerusalem, who R you.
2Mac 7:27 three years, and have R you and brought you

REARING
Ezek 19:2 midst of young lions, R her whelps.

REASON (63)
Gen 41:31 in the land by R of that famine which
47:13 of Canaan languished by R of the famine.
Ex 8:24 land was ruined by R of the flies.
Lev 17:11 that makes atonement, by R of the life.
19:17 heart, but you shall R with your neighbor, lest
Num 6:11 because he sinned by R of the dead body.
18:32 bear no sin by R of it, when you
Deut 23:10 is not clean by R of what chances to
28:47 gladness of heart, by R of the abundance of
Josh 5:4 And this is the R why Joshua circumcised them:
1Sam 20:29 my brothers.' For this R he has not come
1Kgs 11:27 And this was the R why he lifted up
Job 23:7 an upright man could R with him, and I
Ps 90:10 ten, or even by R of strength fourscore; yet
Prov 3:30 a man for no R, when he has done
Wis 2:2 nostrils is smoke, and R is a spark kindled
17:12 helps that come from R;
Sir 27:7 before you hear him R, for this is the
37:16 R is the beginning of every work, and counsel
Is 1:18 "Come now, let us R together, says the LORD:
Ezek 19:10 full of branches by R of abundant water.
Dan 4:34 to heaven, and my R returned to me, and
4:36 the same time my R returned to me; and
10:16 "O my lord, by R of the vision pains
13:14 the other for the R, they confessed their lust.
1Mac 6:12 to destroy the inhabitants of Judah without good R
6:24 For this R the sons of our people besieged
10:63 and let no one annoy him for any R
13:4 By R of this all my brothers have perished
2Mac 4:16 For this R heavy disaster overtook them, and those
4:35 For this R not only Jews, but many also
8:26 sabbath, and for that R they did not continue
Mt 19:5 and said, 'For this R a man shall leave
Mk 10:7 and female.' 'For this R a man shall leave
Jn 8:47 words of God; the R why you do not
10:17 For this R the Father loves me, because I
12:18 The R why the crowd went to meet him
Acts 10:21 for; what is the R for your coming?"
18:14 crime, I should have R to bear with you,
22:30 to know the real R why the Jews accused
26:21 For this R the Jews seized me in the
28:18 because there was no R for the death penalty
28:20 For this R therefore I have asked to see
Rom 1:26 For this R God gave them up to dishonorable
13:6 For the same R you also pay taxes, for
14:22 he who has no R to judge himself for
15:17 Jesus, then, I have R to be proud of
15:22 This is the R why I have so often
Gal 6:4 work, and then his R to boast will be
Eph 1:15 For this R, because I have heard of your
3:1 For this R I, Paul, a prisoner for Christ
3:14 For this R I bow my knees before the
5:31 "For this R a man shall leave his father
Phil 3:4 Though I myself have R for confidence in the
3:4 man thinks he has R for confidence in the
Col 2:18 visions, puffed up without R by his sensuous mind,
1Thes 3:5 For this R, when I could bear it no
3:7 you-- for this R, brethren, in all our
1Tim 1:16 received mercy for this R, that in me, as
Jas 3:17 peaceable, gentle, open to R, full of mercy and
2Pet 1:5 For this very R make every effort to supplement
1Jn 3:1 The R why the world does not know us
3:8 The R the Son of God appeared was to

REASONABLE
Sir 22:14 firmly fixed on a R counsel will not be

REASONABLY
Esth 13:2 authority but always acting R and with kindness, I

REASONED (3)
Wis 2:1 For they R unsoundly, saying to themselves, "Short
2:21 Thus they R, but they were led astray, for
1Cor 13:11 like a child, I R like a child; when

REASONING (5)
Job 13:6 Hear now my R, and listen to the pleadings
Wis 3:10 be punished as their R deserves, who disregarded the
9:14 For the R of mortals is worthless, and our
Sir 27:5 the test of a man is in his R
2Mac 7:21 she fired her woman's R with a man's courage,

REASONINGS
Wis 7:20 of spirits and the R of men, the varieties

REASONS
Sir 14:20 on wisdom and who R intelligently.

REASSURE
1Jn 3:19 of the truth, and R our hearts before him

REASSURED
Gen 50:21 Thus he R them and comforted them.

REBA (2)
Num 31:8 Rekem, Zur, Hur, and R, the five kings of
Josh 13:21 Zur and Hur and R, the princes of Sihon,

REBECCA
Rom 9:10 so, but also when R had conceived children by

REBEKAH (30)
Gen 22:23 Bethuel became the father of R
24:15 had done speaking, behold, R, who was born to

24:29 R had a brother whose name was Laban; and
24:30 heard the words of R his sister, "Thus the
24:45 in my heart, behold, R came out with her
24:51 Behold, R is before you, take her and go,
24:53 and gave them to R; he also gave to
24:58 And they called R, and said to her, "Will
24:59 So they sent away R their sister and her
24:60 And they blessed R, and said to her, "Our
24:61 Then R and her maids arose, and rode upon
24:61 thus the servant took R, and went his way.
24:64 And R lifted up her eyes, and when she
24:67 the tent, and took R, and she became his
25:20 he took to wife R, the daughter of Bethuel
25:21 granted his prayer, and R his wife conceived.
25:28 of his game; but R loved Jacob.
26:7 for the sake of R; because she was fair
26:8 and saw Isaac fondling R his wife.
26:35 and they made life bitter for Isaac and R
27:5 Now R was listening when Isaac spoke to his
27:6 game and bring it, R said to her son
27:11 But Jacob said to R his mother, "Behold, my
27:15 Then R took the best garments of Esau her
27:42 son were told to R; so she sent and
27:46 Then R said to Isaac, "I am weary of
28:5 Aramean, the brother of R, Jacob's and Esau's
29:12 and that he was R's son; and she ran
35:8 And Deborah, R's nurse, died, and she was buried
49:31 they buried Isaac and R his wife; and there

REBEL (14)

Ex 23:21 his voice, do not R against him, for he
Num 14:9 Only, do not R against the LORD; and do
Josh 22:18 And if you R against the LORD today he
22:19 us; only do not R against the LORD, or
22:29 us that we should R against the LORD, and
1Sam 12:14 his voice and not R against the commandment of
12:15 of the LORD, but R against the commandment of
Neh 6:6 the Jews intend to R; that is why you
Job 24:13 "There are those who R against the light, who
Is 1:5 you still be smitten, that you continue to R
1:20 if you refuse and R, you shall be devoured
48:8 and that from birth you were called a R
Hos 7:15 they gash themselves, they R against me.
2Mac 5:8 men, hated as a R against the laws, and

REBELLED (45)

Gen 14:4 Ched-or-laomer, but in the thirteenth year they R
Num 20:24 of Israel, because you R against my command at
27:14 was gathered, because you R against my word in
Deut 1:26 not go up, but R against the command of
1:43 not hearken; but you R against the command of
9:23 given you,' then you R against the commandment of
2Kgs 1:1 death of Ahab, Moab R against Israel.
3:5 the king of Moab R against the king of
3:7 king of Moab has R against me; will you
18:7 He R against the king of Assyria, and would
18:20 rely, that you have R against me?
24:1 then he turned and R against him.
24:20 And Zedekiah R against the king of Babylon.
2Chr 13:6 David, rose up and R against his lord;
36:13 He also R against King Nebuchadnezzar, who had
Neh 9:26 they were disobedient and R against thee and cast
Jud 7:15 with evil, because they R and did not receive
Ps 5:10 out, for they have R against thee.
78:40 How often they R against him in the wilderness
78:56 Yet they tested and R against the Most High
105:28 the land dark; they R against his words.
106:7 thy steadfast love, but R against the Most High
107:11 irons, for they had R against the words of
Wis 3:10 the righteous man and R against the Lord;
Is 1:2 up, but they have R against me.
36:5 rely, that you have R against me?
63:10 But they R and grieved his holy Spirit; therefore
66:24 the men that have R against me; for their
Jer 2:29 You have all R against me, says the LORD.
3:13 your guilt, that you R against the LORD your
4:17 about, because she has R against me, says the
52:3 And Zedekiah R against the king of Babylon.
Lam 1:18 right, for I have R against his word; but
3:42 "We have transgressed and R, and thou hast not
Ezek 2:3 of rebels, who have R against me; they and
5:6 And she has wickedly R against my ordinances more
17:15 might stand.) But he R against him by sending
20:8 But they R against me and would not listen
20:13 the house of Israel R against me in the
20:21 But the children R against me; they did not
Dan 9:5 and acted wickedly and R, turning aside from thy
9:9 forgiveness; because we have R against him,
Hos 7:14 them, for they have R against me!
13:16 guilt, because she has R against her God; they
Zeph 3:11 by which you have R against me; for then

REBELLING (2)

Neh 2:19 Are you R against the king?"
Ps 78:17 still more against him, R against the Most High

REBELLION (16)

Deut 13:5 because he has taught R against the LORD your
Josh 22:16 altar this day in R against the LORD?
22:22 If it was in R or in breach of
1Sam 15:23 For R is as the sin of divination, and
1Kgs 12:19 Israel has been in R against the house of
2Chr 10:19 Israel has been in R against the house of
Ezra 4:19 against kings, and that R and sedition have been
Job 34:37 For he adds R to his sin; he claps
Prov 17:11 evil man seeks only R, and a cruel messenger
Jer 28:16 because you have uttered R against the LORD.'"
29:32 for he has talked R against the LORD.'"
33:8 of their sin and R against me.
2Thes 2:3 not come, unless the R comes first, and the
Heb 3:8 hearts as in the R, on the day of
3:15 do not harden your hearts as in the R
Jude 1:11 gain to Balaam's error, and perish in Korah's R

REBELLIOUS (39)

Deut 9:7 place, you have been R against the LORD.
9:24 You have been R against the LORD from the
21:18 has a stubborn and R son, who will not
21:20 son is stubborn and R, he will not obey
31:27 For I know how R and stubborn you are;
31:27 today you have been R against the LORD; how
1Sam 20:30 son of a perverse, R woman, do I not
Ezra 4:12 They are rebuilding that R and wicked city; they
4:15 this city is a R city, hurtful to kings
Ps 66:7 let not the R exalt themselves.
68:6 to prosperity; but the R dwell in a parched
68:18 men, even among the R, that the LORD God
78:8 fathers, a stubborn and R generation, a generation
106:43 them, but they were R in their purposes, and
Is 30:1 "Woe to the R children," says the LORD, "who
30:9 For they are a R people, lying sons, sons
50:5 and I was not R, I turned not backward.
65:2 the day to a R people, who walk in
Jer 5:23 has a stubborn and R heart; they have turned
6:28 They are all stubbornly R, going about with slanders;
Lam 1:20 wrung within me, because I have been very R
Ezek 2:5 (for they are a R house) they will know
2:6 for they are a R house.
2:7 for they are a R house.
2:8 to you; be not R like that rebellious house;
2:8 not rebellious like that R house; open your mouth,
3:9 for they are a R house."
3:26 for they are a R house.
3:27 for they are a R house.
12:2 the midst of a R house, who have eyes
12:3 for they are a R house.
12:3 though they are a R house.
12:9 house of Israel, the R house, said to you,
12:25 in your days, O R house, I will speak
17:12 "Say now to the R house, Do you not
24:3 an allegory to the R house and say to
44:6 And say to the R house, to the house
Zeph 3:1 to her that is R and defiled, the oppressing
Heb 3:16 Who were they that heard and yet were R

REBELLIOUSLY

Sir 16:10 men on foot, who R assembled in their stubbornness.

REBELS (11)

Num 17:10 a sign for the R, that you may make
20:10 them, "Hear now, you R; shall we bring forth
Josh 1:18 Whoever R against your commandment and disobeys
22:19 or make us as R by building yourselves an
Is 1:23 Your princes are R and companions of thieves.
1:28 But R and sinners shall be destroyed together, and
Ezek 2:3 to a nation of R, who have rebelled against
20:38 will purge out the R from among you, and
Dan 3:32 lawless enemies, most hateful R, and to an unjust
Hos 9:15 love them no more; all their princes are R
Mk 15:7 And among the R in prison, who had committed

REBUILD (18)
Ezra 1:3 is in Judah, and R the house of the
1:5 to go up to R the house of the
5:2 arose and began to R the house of God
6:7 elders of the Jews R this house of God
Neh 2:5 sepulchres, that I may R it."
Tob 14:5 land; and they will R the house of God,
14:5 their captivity, and will R Jerusalem in splendor.
Job 12:14 tears down, none can R; if he shuts a
Ps 51:18 in thy good pleasure; R the walls of Jerusalem,
69:35 will save Zion and R the cities of Judah;
Jer 33:7 fortunes of Israel, and R them as they were
Amos 9:11 up its ruins, and R it as in the
9:14 Israel, and they shall R the ruined cities and
Hag 1:2 not yet come to R the house of the
Mal 1:4 shattered but we will R the ruins," the LORD
1Mac 10:10 Jerusalem and began to R and restore the city.
Acts 15:16 return, and I will R the dwelling of David,
15:16 has fallen; I will R its ruins, and I

REBUILDING (8)
2Chr 24:27 him, and of the R of the house of
Ezra 4:12 They are R that rebellious and wicked city; they
5:11 earth, and we are R the house that was
5:17 the king for the R of this house of
6:8 the Jews for the R of this house of
1Mac 10:44 "Let the cost of R and restoring the structures
10:45 let the cost of R the walls of Jerusalem
10:45 and the cost of R the walls in Judea,

REBUILDS
Josh 6:26 that rises up and R this city, Jericho.

REBUILT (29)
Josh 19:50 of Ephraim; and he R the city, and settled
Judg 18:28 And they R the city, and dwelt in it.
21:23 to their inheritance, and R the towns, and dwelt
1Kgs 9:17 Solomon's wife; so Solomon R Gezer) and Lower
2Kgs 21:3 For he R the high places which Hezekiah his
2Chr 8:2 his own house, Solomon R the cities which Huram
33:3 For he R the high places which his father
Ezra 4:13 if this city is R and the walls finished,
4:16 if this city is R and its walls finished,
4:21 this city be not R, until a decree is
5:13 decree that this house of God should be R
5:15 house of God be R on its site."
6:3 let the house be R, the place where sacrifices
Neh 3:13 the Valley Gate; they R it and set its
3:14 the Dung Gate; he R it and set its
3:15 the Fountain Gate; he R it and covered it
Tob 14:5 of God will be R there with a glorious
Job 3:14 of the earth who R ruins for themselves,
Sir 49:13 gates and bars and R our ruined houses.
Is 25:2 a city no more, it will never be R
58:12 ancient ruins shall be R; you shall raise up
Jer 30:18 the city shall be R upon its mound, and
31:38 the city shall be R for the LORD from
Ezek 26:14 you shall never be R; for I the LORD
36:10 and the waste places R;
36:33 be inhabited, and the waste places shall be R
36:36 I, the LORD, have R the ruined places, and
1Mac 4:48 They also R the sanctuary and the interior of
9:62 in the wilderness; he R the parts of it

REBUKE (47)
Ruth 2:16 glean, and do not R her."
2Sam 22:16 laid bare, at the R of the LORD, at
2Kgs 19:3 day of distress, of R, and of disgrace; children
19:4 living God, and will R the words which the
1Chr 12:17 our fathers see and R you."
Job 13:10 He will surely R you if in secret you
26:11 of heaven tremble, and are astounded at his R
Ps 6:1 O LORD, R me not in thy anger, nor
18:15 laid bare, at thy R, O LORD, at the
38:1 O LORD, R me not in thy anger, nor
50:21 But now I R you, and lay the charge
68:30 R the beasts that dwell among the reeds, the
76:6 At thy R, O God of Jacob, both rider
80:16 they perish at the R of thy countenance!
104:7 At thy R they fled; at the sound of
119:21 Thou dost R the insolent, accursed ones, who wander
141:5 good man strike or R me in kindness, but
Prov 13:1 instruction, but a scoffer does not listen to R
17:10 A R goes deeper into a man of understanding
24:25 nations; but those who R the wicked will have
27:5 Better is open R than hidden love.
30:6 his words, lest he R you, and you be
Eccl 7:5 man to hear the R of the wise than
Wis 11:7 defiled with blood in R for the decree to
12:17 thy power, and dost R any insolence among those
Sir 48:7 their beds; who heard R at Sinai and judgments
Is 17:13 waters, but he will R them, and they will
37:3 day of distress, of R, and of disgrace; children
37:4 living God, and will R the words which the
50:2 Behold, by my R I dry up the sea,
51:20 of the LORD, the R of your God.
54:9 you and will not R you.
66:15 in fury, and his R with flames of fire.
Zech 3:2 to Satan, "The LORD R you, O Satan!
3:2 who has chosen Jerusalem R you!
Mal 2:3 Behold, I will R your offspring, and spread dung
3:11 I will R the devourer for you, so that
2Mac 7:33 a little while, to R and discipline us, he
Mt 16:22 him and began to R him, saying, "God forbid,
Mk 8:32 him, and began to R him.
Lk 17:3 if your brother sins, R him, and if he
19:39 said to him, "Teacher, R your disciples."
1Tim 5:1 Do not R an older man but exhort him
5:20 who persist in sin, R them in the presence
2Tim 4:2 out of season, convince, R, and exhort, be unfailing
Tit 1:12 Therefore R them sharply, that they may be sound
Jude 1:9 but said, "The Lord R you."

REBUKED (29)
Gen 31:42 of my hands, and R you last night."
37:10 his brothers, his father R him, and said to
1Chr 16:21 to oppress them; he R kings on their account,
Ps 9:5 Thou hast R the nations, thou hast destroyed the
105:14 to oppress them; he R kings on their account,
106:9 He R the Red Sea, and it became dry;
Wis 17:7 humbled, and their boasted wisdom was scornfully R
Jer 29:27 why have you not R Jeremiah of Anathoth who
2Mac 2:7 learned of it, he R them and declared: "The
Mt 8:26 Then he rose and R the winds and the
17:18 And Jesus R him, and the demon came out
19:13 The disciples R the people;
20:31 The crowd R them, telling them to be silent;
Mk 1:25 But Jesus R him, saying, "Be silent, and come
4:39 And he awoke and R the wind, and said
8:33 seeing his disciples, he R Peter, and said, "Get
9:25 came running together, he R the unclean spirit,
10:13 them; and the disciples R them.
10:48 And many R him, telling him to be silent;
Lk 4:35 But Jesus R him, saying, "Be silent, and come
4:39 stood over her and R the fever, and it
4:41 But he R them, and would not allow them
8:24 And he awoke and R the wind and the
9:42 But Jesus R the unclean spirit, and healed the
9:55 But he turned and R them.
18:15 disciples saw it, they R them.
18:39 who were in front R him, telling him to
23:39 But the other R him, saying, "Do you not
2Pet 2:16 from wrongdoing, but was R for his own

REBUKES (7)
Ps 38:14 not hear, and in whose mouth are no R
39:11 dost chasten man with R for sin, thou dost
Prov 28:23 He who R a man will afterward find more
Wis 12:26 the warning of light R will experience the deserved
Sir 18:12 He R and trains and teaches them, and turns
43:17 voice of his thunder R the earth; so do
Nah 1:4 He R the sea and makes it dry, he

RECAH
1Chr 4:12 These are the men of R

RECALL (3)
Is 46:8 "Remember this and consider, R it to mind, you
Heb 10:32 But R the former days when, after you were
2Pet 1:15 at any time to R these things.

RECALLED
Wis 19:10 For they still R the events of their sojourn,

RECALLING
Ezek 29:16 the house of Israel, R their iniquity, when they

RECASTS
2Mac 2:31 but the one who R the narrative should be

RECEDED
Gen 8:3 restrained, and the waters R from the earth

RECEIPT (2)

Tob 5:3 Tobit gave him the R, and said to him,
9:5 He gave him the R, and Gabael brought out

RECEIVE (156)

Gen 4:11 opened its mouth to R your brother's blood from
38:20 friend the Adullamite, to R the pledge from the
Ex 25:2 him willing you shall R the offering for me.
25:3 offering which you shall R from them: gold, silver,
27:3 pots for it to R its ashes, and shovels
28:5 "They shall R gold, blue and purple and scarlet
Num 18:28 your tithes, which you R from the people of
Deut 9:9 up the mountain to R the tables of stone,
Josh 11:20 utterly destroyed, and should R no mercy but be
1Kgs 5:9 there, and you shall R it; and you shall
8:64 was too small to R the burnt offering and
2Kgs 5:16 I serve, I will R none." And he urged
Neh 10:38 Levites when the Levites R the tithes; and the
Tob 4:14 serve God you will R payment.
Jud 7:15 rebelled and did not R you peaceably."
Job 2:10 Shall we R good at the hand of God,
2:10 and shall we not R evil?" In all this
3:12 Why did the knees R me?
22:22 R instruction from his mouth, and lay up his
27:13 the heritage which oppressors R from the Almighty:
35:7 or what does he R from your hand?
Ps 24:5 He will R blessing from the LORD, and vindication
49:15 Sheol, for he will R me.
73:24 and afterward thou wilt R me to glory.
Prov 1:3 understand words of insight, R instruction in wise
2:1 My son, if you R my words and treasure
Wis 3:5 a little, they will R great good, because God
5:16 Therefore they will R a glorious crown and a
12:7 all to thee might R a worthy colony of
17:21 that was destined to R them; but still heavier
19:14 Others had refused to R strangers when they came
Sir 4:31 hand be extended to R, but withdrawn when it
11:32 R a stranger into your home and he will
12:5 you; for you will R twice as much evil
16:14 mercy; every one will R in accordance with his
24:8 Jacob, and in Israel R your inheritance.'
32:2 on their account and R a wreath for your
38:2 High, and he will R a gift from the
50:21 a second time, to R the blessing from the
51:26 and let your souls R instruction; it is to
Jer 9:20 and let your ear R the word of his
17:23 might not hear and R instruction.
32:33 have not listened to R instruction.
35:13 Jerusalem, Will you not R instruction and listen to
37:12 land of Benjamin to R his portion there among
Ezek 3:10 shall speak to you R in your heart, and
Dan 2:6 its interpretation, you shall R from me gifts and
7:18 the Most High shall R the kingdom, and possess
11:34 they fall, they shall R a little help.
1Mac 2:51 in their generations; and R great honor and an
10:30 trees that I should R, I release them from
10:43 him be released and R back all his property
14:23 pleased our people to R these men with honor
15:27 But he refused to R them, and he broke
2Mac 7:36 judgment of God, will R just punishment for your
14:19 Mattathias to give and R pledges of friendship.
Mt 10:14 any one will not R you or listen to
10:41 is a prophet shall R a prophet's reward, and
10:41 a righteous man shall R a righteous man's reward.
11:5 and see: the blind R their sight and the
19:11 "Not all men can R this saying, but only
19:12 who is able to R this, let him receive
19:12 receive this, let him R it."
19:29 my name's sake, will R a hundredfold, and inherit
20:10 they thought they would R more; but each of
21:22 in prayer, you will R, if you have faith."
Mk 4:16 hear the word, immediately R it with joy;
6:11 any place will not R you and they refuse
10:15 you, whoever does not R the kingdom of God
10:30 gospel, who will not R a hundredfold now in
10:51 him, "Master, let me R my sight."
12:40 They will R the greater condemnation."
Lk 6:34 whom you hope to R, what credit is that
6:34 lend to sinners, to R as much again.
7:22 and heard: the blind R their sight, the lame
8:13 they hear the word, R it with joy; but
9:5 wherever they do not R you, when you leave
9:53 the people would not R him, because his face
10:8 a town and they R you, eat what is
10:10 and they do not R you, go into its
12:47 to his will, shall R a severe beating.
12:48 deserved a beating, shall R a light beating.
16:4 so that people may R me into their houses
16:9 it fails they may R you into the eternal
18:17 you, whoever does not R the kingdom of God
18:30 God, who will not R manifold more in this
18:41 said, "Lord, let me R my sight."
18:42 Jesus said to him, R your sight; your faith
19:12 a far country to R a kingly power and
20:47 They will R the greater condemnation."
Jn 3:11 but you do not R our testimony.
3:27 answered, "No one can R anything except what is
5:33 the testimony which I R is from man; but
5:40 I do not R glory from men.
5:42 and you do not R me; if another comes
5:42 comes in his own name, him you will R
5:43 can you believe, who R glory from one another
7:39 in him were to R; for as yet the
12:48 me and does not R my sayings has a
14:17 whom the world cannot R, because it neither sees
16:24 ask, and you will R, that your joy may
20:22 and said to them, R the Holy Spirit.
Acts 1:8 But you shall R power when the Holy Spirit
2:38 sins; and you shall R the gift of the
3:5 upon them, expecting to R something from them.
3:21 Jesus, whom heaven must R until the time for
7:59 he prayed, "Lord Jesus, R my spirit."
8:15 them that they might R the Holy Spirit;
8:19 lay my hands may R the Holy Spirit."
18:27 to the disciples to R him.
19:2 to them, "Did you R the Holy Spirit when
20:35 'It is more blessed to give than to R
22:13 to me, 'Brother Saul, R your sight.' And in
26:18 God, that they may R forgiveness of sins and
Rom 5:17 more will those who R the abundance of grace
8:15 For you did not R the spirit of slavery
11:31 you they also may R mercy.
13:3 good, and you will R his approval,
16:2 Cenchre-ae, that you may R her in the Lord
1Cor 2:14 unspiritual man does not R the gifts of the
3:8 equal, and each shall R his wages according to
3:14 foundation survives, he will R a reward.
4:5 Then every man will R his commendation from God.
4:7 What have you that you did not R
9:25 They do it to R a perishable wreath, but
2Cor 5:10 that each one may R good or evil, according
11:4 preached, or if you R a different spirit from
Gal 1:12 For I did not R it from man, nor
3:2 only this: Did you R the Spirit by works
3:14 Gentiles, that we might R the promise of the
4:5 so that we might R adoption as sons.
5:2 you that if you R circumcision, Christ will be
6:13 For even those who R circumcision do not
Eph 6:8 one does, he will R the same again from
Phil 2:29 So R him in the Lord with all joy;
Col 3:24 the Lord you will R the inheritance as your
4:10 he comes to you, R him),
Philem 1:17 consider me your partner, R him as you would
1:17 him as you would R me.
Heb 4:16 grace, that we may R mercy and find grace
7:5 descendants of Levi who R the priestly office have
9:15 who are called may R the promised eternal
10:36 will of God and R what is promised.
11:8 which he was to R as an inheritance; and
11:19 figuratively speaking, he did R him back.
11:39 their faith, did not R what was promised,
Jas 1:7 all his ways, will R anything from the Lord.
1:11 the test he will R the crown of life
1:20 growth of wickedness and R with meekness the
4:3 ask and do not R, because you ask wrongly,
1Jn 3:22 before God; and we R from him whatever we
5:9 If we R the testimony of men, the testimony
2Jn 1:10 this doctrine, do not R him into the house
Rev 4:11 Lord and God, to R glory and honor and
5:12 who was slain, to R power and wealth and
17:12 but they are to R authority as kings for

RECEIVED (169)

Gen 33:10 such favor have you R me.
43:23 sacks for you; I R your money." Then he
Ex 32:4 And he R the gold at their hand, and
36:3 the work; and they R from Moses all the
Num 23:20 Behold, I R a command to bless: he has
31:51 and Eleazar the priest R from them the gold,
31:54 and Eleazar the priest R the gold from the
34:14 their fathers' houses have R their inheritance, and
34:15 and the half-tribe have R their inheritance beyond

Josh 13:8 and the Gadites R their inheritance, which Moses
14:1 the people of Israel R in the land of
16:4 Joseph, Manasseh and Ephraim, R their inheritance.
17:6 the daughters of Manasseh R an inheritance along
18:7 tribe of Manasseh have R their inheritance beyond
21:4 of Aaron the priest R by lot from the
21:5 rest of the Kohathites R by lot from the
21:6 The Gersonites R by lot from the families of
21:7 according to their families R from the tribe of
1Sam 25:35 Then David R from her hand what she had
25:39 avenged the insult I R at the hand of
1Kgs 10:28 and the king's traders R them from Kue at
2Kgs 19:14 Hezekiah R the letter from the hand of the
1Chr 5:20 Nodab; and when they R help against them, the
12:18 Then David R them, and made them officers of
2Chr 1:16 and the king's traders R them from Kue for
22:6 wounds which he had R at Ramah, when he
29:22 bulls, and the priests R the blood and threw
30:16 the blood which they R from the hand of
33:13 to him, and God R his entreaty and heard
33:19 prayer, and how God R his entreaty, and all
35:11 the blood which they R from them while the
Tob 7:8 They R them very warmly; and they killed a
14:10 saved, and the other R repayment as he himself
Jud 12:15 fleeces which she had R from Bagoas for her
Job 4:12 me stealthily, my ear R the whisper of it.
Prov 24:32 it; I looked and R instruction.
Wis 7:15 of what I have R, for he is the
11:5 were punished, they themselves R benefit in their
11:13 punishments the righteous had R benefit, they
16:6 as a warning, and R a token of deliverance
Sir 50:12 And when he R the portions from the hands
51:16 ear a little and R her, and I found
Is 37:14 Hezekiah R the letter from the hand of the
40:2 pardoned, that she has R from the LORD's hand
Jer 37:17 sent for him, and R him.
38:14 Jeremiah the prophet and R him at the third
Bar 4:32 be the city which R your sons.
Dan 5:31 And Darius the Mede R the kingdom, being about
7:22 came when the saints R the kingdom.
13:55 angel of God has R the sentence from God
14:1 fathers, Cyrus the Persian R his kingdom.
Zech 13:6 say, 'The wounds I R in the house of
1Mac 2:54 he was deeply zealous, R the covenant of everlasting
2:56 testified in the assembly, R an inheritance in the
10:42 which my officials have R every year from the
11:34 which the king formerly R from them each year,
12:8 envoy with honor, and R the letter, which contained
12:43 So he R him with honor and commended him
13:37 We have R the gold crown and the palm
14:40 that the Romans had R the envoys of Simon
16:15 The son of Abubus R them treacherously in the
2Mac 2:4 that the prophet, having R an oracle, ordered that
8:33 little house; so these R the proper recompense for
10:15 harassing the Jews; they R those who were banished
13:22 gave pledges, R theirs, withdrew, attacked Judas
13:24 He R Maccabeus, left Hegemonides as governor
Mt 6:2 to you, they have R their reward.
6:5 to you, they have R their reward.
6:16 to you, they have R their reward.
10:8 You R without paying, give without pay.
20:9 came, each of them R a denarius.
20:10 each of them also R a denarius.
20:34 eyes, and immediately they R their sight and
25:16 He who had R the five talents went at
25:18 But he who had R the one talent went
25:20 And he who had R the five talents came
25:24 He also who had R the one talent came
25:27 coming I should have R what was my own
Mk 10:52 And immediately he R his sight and followed him
11:24 believe that you have R it, and it will
14:65 And the guards R him with blows.
Lk 6:24 rich, for you have R your consolation.
9:51 for him to be R up, he set his
10:38 a woman named Martha R him into her house.
15:27 calf, because he has R him safe and sound.'
16:25 you in your lifetime R your good things, and
18:43 And immediately he R his sight and followed him,
19:6 and came down, and R him joyfully.
19:15 When he returned, having R the kingly power, he
Jn 1:11 and his own people R him not.
1:12 But to all who R him, who believed in
1:16 fulness have we all R, grace upon grace.
9:11 went and washed and R my sight."
9:15 him how he had R his sight.
9:18 been blind and had R his sight, until they
9:18 the man who had R his sight,
10:18 this charge I have R from my Father."
17:8 me, and they have R them and know in
19:30 When Jesus had R the vinegar, he said, "It
Acts 2:33 of God, and having R from the Father the
2:41 So those who R his word were baptized, and
7:38 our fathers; and he R living oracles to give
7:53 and murdered, you who R the law as delivered
8:14 heard that Samaria had R the word of God,
8:17 on them and they R the Holy Spirit.
10:47 these people who have R the Holy Spirit just
11:1 the Gentiles also had R the word of God.
16:24 Having R this charge, he put them into the
17:7 also, and Jason has R them; and they are
17:11 in Thessalonica, for they R the word with all
20:24 the ministry which I R from the Lord Jesus,
21:17 to Jerusalem, the brethren R us gladly.
22:5 From them I R letters to the brethren, and
22:13 that very hour I R my sight and saw
28:7 island, named Publius, who R us and entertained us
28:21 to him, "We have R no letters from Judea
Rom 1:5 through whom we have R grace and apostleship to
3:25 his blood, to be R by faith.
4:11 He R circumcision as a sign or seal of
5:11 whom we have now R our reconciliation.
8:15 fear, but you have R the spirit of sonship.
11:30 God but now have R mercy because of their
1Cor 2:12 Now we have R not the spirit of the
4:7 If then you R it, why do you boast
11:23 For I R from the Lord what I also
15:1 the gospel, which you R, in which you stand,
15:3 importance what I also R, that Christ died for
2Cor 1:9 felt that we had R the sentence of death;
7:15 trembling with which you R him.
11:4 from the one you R, or if you accept
11:24 Five times I have R at the hands of
Gal 1:9 to that which you R, let him be accursed.
4:14 or despise me, but R me as an angel
Phil 4:9 you have learned and R and heard and seen
4:18 I have R full payment, and more; I am
4:18 I am filled, having R from Epaphroditus the gifts
Col 2:6 As therefore you R Christ Jesus the Lord, so
4:10 (concerning whom you have R instructions--if he
4:17 ministry which you have R in the Lord."
1Thes 1:6 the Lord, for you R the word in much
2:13 this, that when you R the word of God
2Thes 3:6 the tradition that you R from us.
1Tim 1:13 insulted him; but I R mercy because I had
1:16 of sinners; but I R mercy for this reason,
4:3 God created to be R with thanksgiving by those
4:4 rejected if it is R with thanksgiving;
Heb 2:2 every transgression or disobedience R a just
4:6 and those who formerly R the good news failed
7:6 has not their genealogy R tithes from Abraham and
7:8 Here tithes are R by mortal men; there, by
7:11 under it the people R the law), what further
11:2 the men of old R divine approval.
11:4 Cain, through which he R approval as righteous, God
11:11 By faith Sarah herself R power to conceive, even
11:13 in faith, not having R what was promised, but
11:17 and he who had R the promises was ready
11:33 conquered kingdoms, enforced justice, R promises,
11:35 Women R their dead by resurrection.
Jas 2:25 by works when she R the messengers and sent
1Pet 2:10 once you had not R mercy but now you
2:10 but now you have R mercy.
4:10 As each has R a gift, employ it for
2Pet 1:17 For when he R honor and glory from God
1Jn 2:27 the anointing which you R from him abides in
Rev 2:27 as I myself have R power from my Father;
3:3 Remember then what you R and heard; keep that,
17:12 who have not yet R royal power, but they
19:20 deceived those who had R the mark of the
20:4 image and had not R its mark on their

RECEIVES (41)

Deut 18:8 eat, besides what he R from the sale of
Sir 13:21 he speaks sensibly, and R no attention.
Ezek 16:32 Adulterous wife, who R strangers instead of her
Mt 7:8 every one who asks R, and he who seeks
10:40 "He who R you receives me, and he who
10:40 "He who receives you R me, and he who
10:40 me, and he who R me receives him who
10:40 he who receives me R him who sent me.
10:41 He who R a prophet because he is a
10:41 reward, and he who R a righteous man because

13:20 the word and immediately R it with joy;
18:5 "Whoever R one such child in my name receives
18:5 child in my name R me;
Mk 9:37 said to them, "Whoever R one such child in
9:37 child in my name R me; and whoever receives
9:37 receives me; and whoever R me, receives not me
9:37 and whoever receives me, R not me but him
Lk 9:48 said to them, "Whoever R this child in my
9:48 child in my name R me, and whoever receives
9:48 receives me, and whoever R me receives him who
9:48 and whoever receives me R him who sent me;
11:10 every one who asks R, and he who seeks
15:2 murmured, saying, "This man R sinners and eats
Jn 3:32 heard, yet no one R his testimony;
3:33 his testimony; he who R his testimony sets his
4:36 He who reaps R wages, and gathers fruit for
7:23 the sabbath a man R circumcision, so that the
13:20 to you, he who R any one whom I
13:20 one whom I send R me; and he who
13:20 me; and he who R me receives him who
13:20 he who receives me R him who sent me."
Acts 10:43 who believes in him R forgiveness of sins through
1Cor 9:24 compete, but only one R the prize?
Gal 5:3 to every man who R circumcision that he is
Heb 6:7 sake it is cultivated, R a blessing from God.
7:9 that Levi himself, who R tithes, paid tithes through
12:6 he loves, and chastises every son whom he R
Jas 5:7 over it until it R the early and the
Rev 2:17 knows except him who R it.'
14:9 and its image, and R a mark on his
14:11 its image, and whoever R the mark of its

RECEIVING (16)

Deut 33:3 followed in thy steps, R direction from thee,
Ps 68:18 in thy train, and R gifts among men, even
Wis 19:16 but the latter, after R them with festal celebrations,
Sir 41:19 meals, of surliness in R and giving,
1Mac 8:26 keep their obligations without R any return.
2Mac 4:25 After R the king's orders he returned, possessing no
10:20 the towers, and on R seventy thousand drachmas let
12:12 with them; and after R his pledges they departed
Mt 20:11 And on R it they grumbled at the householder,
Lk 23:40 justly; for we are R the due reward of
Jn 13:30 So, after R the morsel, he immediately went out;
Acts 17:15 far as Athens; and R a command for Silas
Rom 1:27 acts with men and R in their own persons
Phil 4:15 me in giving and R except you only;
Heb 10:26 we sin deliberately after R the knowledge of the
12:28 us be grateful for R a kingdom that cannot

RECENT

1Tim 3:6 must not be a R convert, or he may

RECENTLY (5)

Jud 4:3 For they had only R returned from the captivity,
4:5 since their fields had R been harvested.
Jer 34:15 You R repented and did what was right in
2Mac 14:36 that has been so R purified."
Acts 21:38 the Egyptian, then, who R stirred up a revolt

RECEPTION

Wis 19:15 former for their hostile R of the aliens;

RECESSED (3)

1Kgs 6:4 the house windows with R frames.
Ezek 41:16 three had windows with R frames.
41:26 And there were R windows and palm trees on

RECESSES (4)

2Kgs 19:23 mountains, to the far R of Lebanon; I felled
Job 38:16 or walked in the R of the deep?
Wis 17:14 beset them from the R of powerless Hades, they
Is 37:24 mountains, to the far R of Lebanon; I felled

RECHAB (13)

2Sam 4:2 name of the other R, sons of Rimmon a
4:5 of Rimmon the Be-erothite, R and Baanah, set out,
4:6 drowsy and slept; so R and Baanah his brother
4:9 But David answered R and Baanah his brother, the
2Kgs 10:15 Jehonadab the son of R coming to meet him;
10:23 Jehonadab the son of R; and he said to
1Chr 2:55 from Hammath, the father of the house of R
Neh 3:14 Malchijah the son of R, ruler of the district
Jer 35:6 Jonadab the son of R, our father, commanded us,
35:8 Jonadab the son of R, our father, in all
35:14 Jonadab the son of R gave to his sons,
35:16 Jonadab the son of R have kept the command
35:19 Jonadab the son of R shall never lack a

RECHABITES (4)

Jer 35:2 the house of the R, and speak with them,
35:3 his sons, and the whole house of the R
35:5 I set before the R pitchers full of wine,
35:18 the house of the R Jeremiah said, "Thus says

RECITE (2)

Ex 17:14 in a book and R it in the ears
Ps 50:16 right have you to R my statutes, or take

RECITED

Deut 32:44 Moses came and R all the words of this

RECKLESS (6)

Judg 9:4 Abimelech hired worthless and R fellows, who.
Sir 4:29 Do not be R in your speech, or sluggish
9:18 the man who is R in speech will be
19:2 the man who consorts with harlots is very R
19:3 inherit him, and the R soul will be snatched
2Tim 3:4 haters of good, treacherous, R, swollen with conceit,

RECKLESSNESS

Jer 23:32 their lies and their R, when I did not

RECKON (5)

Lev 25:27 redeem it, let him R the years since he
25:50 He shall R with him who bought him from
2Kgs 22:4 priest, that he may R the amount of the
Rom 4:8 the Lord will not R his sin."
Rev 13:18 him who has understanding R the number of the

RECKONED (27)

Gen 15:6 the LORD; and he R it to him as
Lev 25:31 around them shall be R with the fields of
Num 3:50 hundred and sixty-five shekels, R by the shekel of
18:27 your offering shall be R to you as though
18:30 the rest shall be R to the Levites as
Josh 13:3 of Ekron, it is R as Canaanite; there are
2Sam 4:2 (for Be-eroth also is R to Benjamin;
1Chr 5:7 of their generations was R: the chief, Je-iel, and
Ps 88:4 I am R among those who go down to
106:31 And that has been R to him as righteousness
Wis 4:20 when their sins are R up, and their lawless
Lam 4:2 gold, how they are R as earthen pots, the
1Mac 2:52 tested, and it was R to him as righteousness?
2Mac 3:6 funds could not be R, and that they did
Lk 22:37 me, 'And he was R with transgressors'; for what
Rom 4:3 God, and it was R to him as righteousness."
4:4 his wages are not R as a gift but
4:5 ungodly, his faith is R as righteousness.
4:9 say that faith was R to Abraham as righteousness.
4:10 How then was it R to him?
4:11 who thus have righteousness R to them,
4:22 why his faith was R to him as righteousness."
4:23 the words, "it was R to him," were written
4:24 It will be R to us who believe in
9:8 of the promise are R as descendants.
Gal 3:6 God, and it was R to him as righteousness."
Jas 2:23 God, and it was R to him as righteousness";

RECKONING (8)

Gen 9:5 will surely require a R; of every beast I
42:22 now there comes a R for his blood."
Lev 25:52 he shall make a R with him; according to
Num 3:47 take five shekels apiece; R by the shekel of
23:9 dwelling alone, and not R itself among the nations!
1Chr 23:11 therefore they became a father's house in one R
Prov 23:7 for he is like one who is inwardly R
Mt 18:23 When he began the R, one was brought to

RECKONS

Rom 4:6 man to whom God R righteousness apart from

RECLINE

Jud 12:15 so that she might R on them when she

RECOGNITION

1Cor 16:18 Give R to such men.

RECOGNIZE (12)

Gen 27:23 And he did not R him, because his hands
Ruth 3:14 arose before one could R another; and he said,
Jud 14:5 let him see and R the man who despised

R

Job 2:12 afar, they did not R him; and they raised
Wis 13:1 exists, nor did they R the craftsman while paying
Sir 23:27 who survive her will R that nothing is better
2Mac 6:12 such calamities, but to R that these punishments
7:28 is in them, and R that God did not
Acts 13:27 because they did not R him nor understand the
27:39 day, they did not R the land, but they
1Cor 11:16 to be contentious, we R no other practice, nor
14:38 any one does not R this, he is not

RECOGNIZED (20)

Gen 37:33 And he R it, and said, "It is my
Judg 18:3 house of Micah, they R the voice of the
1Sam 26:17 Saul R David's voice, and said, "Is this your
1Kgs 18:7 met him; and Obadiah R him, and fell on
20:41 the king of Israel R him as one of
Jud 8:29 all the people have R your understanding, for your
Wis 10:5 had been confounded, R the righteous man and
12:27 them, they saw and R as the true God
Lam 4:8 soot, they are not R in the streets; their
2Mac 3:28 help himself; and they R clearly the sovereign power
4:4 Simon's approved agents, Onias R that the rivalry
15:28 returning with joy, they R Nicanor, lying dead, in
Mt 14:35 men of that place R him, they sent round
Mk 6:54 boat, immediately the people R him,
Lk 24:31 were opened and they R him; and he vanished
Acts 3:10 and praising God, and R him as the one
4:13 they wondered; and they R that they had been
19:34 But when they R that he was a Jew,
1Cor 11:19 those who are genuine among you may be R
14:38 one does not recognize this, he is not R

RECOGNIZES

Sir 18:11 He sees and R that their end will be

RECOGNIZING (3)

Wis 10:8 only were hindered from R the good, but also
Lk 24:16 eyes were kept from R him.
Acts 12:14 R Peter's voice, in her joy she did not

RECOILS

Hos 11:8 My heart R within me, my compassion grows warm

RECOMMENDATION (2)

2Cor 3:1 some do, letters of R to you, or from
3:2 are our letter of R, written on your hearts,

RECOMPENSE (23)

Deut 32:35 Vengeance is mine, and R, for the time when
Ruth 2:12 The LORD R you for what you have done,
2Sam 19:36 Why should the king R me with such a
Job 15:31 deceiving himself; for emptiness will be his R
21:19 their sons.' Let him R it to themselves, that
Ps 56:7 for my life, so R them for their crime;
91:8 eyes and see the R of the wicked.
Sir 17:18 he will bring their R on their heads.
Is 34:8 vengeance, a year of R for the cause of
35:4 with vengeance, with the R of God.
40:10 with him, and his R before him.
49:4 the LORD, and my R with my God."
61:8 faithfully give them their R, and I will make
62:11 with him, and his R before him."
66:6 of the LORD, rendering R to his enemies!
Jer 16:18 And I will doubly R their iniquity and their
18:20 Is evil a R for good?
25:14 them; and I will R them according to their
51:56 is a God of R, he will surely requite.
Ezek 29:20 of Egypt as his R for which he labored,
Hos 9:7 come, the days of R have come; Israel shall
2Mac 8:33 these received the proper R for their impiety.
Rev 22:12 coming soon, bringing my R, to repay every one

RECOMPENSED (4)

2Sam 22:21 of my hands he R me.
22:25 Therefore the LORD has R me according to my
Ps 18:20 of my hands he R me.
18:24 Therefore the LORD has R me according to my

RECONCILE (3)

1Sam 29:4 how could this fellow R himself to his lord?
Eph 2:16 making peace, and might R us both to God
Col 1:20 and through him to R to himself all things,

RECONCILED (12)

2Mac 1:5 your prayers and be R to you, and may
5:20 all its glory when the great Lord became R
7:33 he will again be R with his own servants.
8:29 Lord to be wholly R with his servants.
Mt 5:24 and go; first be R to your brother, and
Acts 7:26 quarreling and would have R them, saying, 'Men, you
Rom 5:10 were enemies we were R to God by the
5:10 now that we are R, shall we be saved
1Cor 7:11 single or else be R to her husband)–and
2Cor 5:18 God, who through Christ R us to himself and
5:20 behalf of Christ, be R to God.
Col 1:22 deeds, he has now R in his body of

RECONCILIATION (6)

Sir 22:20 do not worry, for R is possible; but as
27:21 bandaged, and there is R after abuse, but whoever
Rom 5:11 Christ, through whom we have now received our R
11:15 their rejection means the R of the world, what
2Cor 5:18 us the ministry of R;
5:19 them, and entrusting to us the message of R

RECONCILING

2Cor 5:19 in Christ God was R the world to himself,

RECORD (6)

1Chr 4:33 their settlements, and they kept a genealogical R
Ezra 6:2 was found on which this was written: "A R
Esth 12:4 king made a permanent R of these things, and
Sir 42:7 weight, and make a R of all that you
1Mac 14:23 Spartans may have a R of them.
14:27 So they made a R on bronze tablets and

RECORDED (12)

Deut 28:61 affliction which is not R in the book of
1Chr 24:6 of Nethanel, a Levite, R them in the presence
2Chr 20:34 of Hanani, which are R in the Book of
Ezra 8:34 and weighed, and the weight of everything was R
Neh 12:22 and Jaddu-a, there were R the heads of fathers'
Esth 2:23 And it was R in the Book of the
9:20 And Mordecai R these things, and sent letters to
9:32 Purim, and it was R in writing.
Ps 102:18 Let this be R for a generation to come,
Is 4:3 one who has been R for life in Jerusalem,
1Mac 9:22 greatness, have not been R, for they were very
14:22 they said we have R in our public decrees,

RECORDER (9)

2Sam 8:16 son of Ahilud was R;
20:24 of Ahilud was the R;
1Kgs 4:3 son of Ahilud was R;
2Kgs 18:18 secretary, and Joah the son of Asaph, the R
18:37 son of Asaph, the R, came to Hezekiah with
1Chr 18:15 son of Ahilud was R;
2Chr 34:8 son of Joahaz, the R, to repair the house
Is 36:3 secretary, and Joah the son of Asaph, the R
36:22 son of Asaph, the R, came to Hezekiah with

RECORDS (8)

1Chr 4:22 to Lehem (now the R are ancient).
Ezra 4:15 the book of the R of your fathers.
4:15 the book of the R and learn that this
Esth 16:7 from the more ancient R which we hand on
Ps 87:6 The LORD R as he registers the peoples, "This
2Mac 2:1 One finds in the R that Jeremiah the prophet
2:13 are reported in the R and in the memoirs
4:23 and to complete the R of essential business.

RECOUNT (8)

Ps 9:14 death, that I may R all thy praises, that
75:1 on thy name and R thy wondrous deeds.
79:13 to generation we will R thy praise.
118:17 I shall live, and R the deeds of the
Sir 18:4 And who can fully R his mercies?
36:8 time, and let people R thy mighty deeds.
42:17 his holy ones to R all his marvelous works,
Is 63:7 I will R the steadfast love of the LORD,

RECOUNTED (3)

Judg 6:13 deeds which our fathers R to us, saying, 'Did
Jud 2:2 his secret plan and R fully, with his own
Esth 5:11 And Haman R to them the splendor of his

RECOUNTS

Job 33:26 He R to men his salvation,

RECOVER (14)

Judg 11:26 why did you not R them within that time?
2Kgs 1:2 Ekron, whether I shall R from this sickness."

R

9:26 heritage, whom thou hast R through thy greatness,
13:5 land of Egypt and R you out of the
15:15 the LORD your God R you; therefore I command
21:8 Israel, whom thou hast R, and set not the
24:18 the LORD your God R you from there; therefore
2Sam 4:9 LORD lives, who has R my life out of
1Kgs 1:29 LORD lives, who has R my soul out of
Neh 1:10 people, whom thou hast R by thy great power
Job 33:28 He has R my soul from going down into
Ps 31:5 my spirit; thou hast R me, O LORD, faithful
74:2 old, which thou hast R to be the tribe
78:42 the day when he R them from the foe;
107:2 Let the R of the LORD say so, whom
107:2 so, whom he has R from trouble
Is 1:27 Zion shall be R by justice, and those in
29:22 says the LORD, who R Abraham, concerning the
35:9 found there, but the R shall walk there.
43:1 not, for I have R you; I have called
44:22 me, for I have R you.
44:23 For the LORD has R Jacob, and will be
48:20 say, "The LORD has R his servant Jacob!"
51:10 a way for the R to pass over?
52:3 and you shall be R without money.
52:9 his people, he has R Jerusalem.
62:12 The holy people, The R of the LORD; and
63:9 in his pity he R them; he lifted them
Jer 31:11 ransomed Jacob, and has R him from hands too
Lam 3:58 O Lord, thou hast R my life.
Mic 6:4 land of Egypt, and R you from the house
Zech 10:8 in, for I have R them, and they shall
Lk 1:68 he has visited and R his people,
Gal 3:13 Christ R us from the curse of the law,
Rev 14:3 thousand who had been R from the earth.
14:4 goes; these have been R from mankind as first

REDEEMER (18)

Job 19:25 I know that my R lives, and at last
Ps 19:14 thy sight, O LORD, my rock and my R
78:35 was their rock, the Most High God their R
Prov 23:11 the fatherless; for their R is strong; he will
Is 41:14 says the LORD; your R is the Holy One
43:14 says the LORD, your R, the Holy One of
44:6 of Israel and his R, the LORD of hosts:
44:24 says the LORD, your R, who formed you from
47:4 Our R -- the LORD of hosts is his
48:17 says the LORD, your R, the Holy One of
49:7 says the LORD, the R of Israel and his
49:26 your Savior, and your R, the Mighty One of
54:5 of Israel is your R, the God of the
54:8 have compassion on you, says the LORD, your R
59:20 come to Zion as R, to those in Jacob
60:16 your Savior and your R, the Mighty One of
63:16 art our Father, our R from of old is
Jer 50:34 Their R is strong; the LORD of hosts is

REDEEMING

Ruth 4:7 times in Israel concerning R and exchanging: to

REDEEMS (5)

Ps 34:22 The LORD R the life of his servants; none
72:14 oppression and violence he R their life; and precious
103:4 all your diseases, who R your life from the
1Mac 4:11 there is one who R and saves Israel."
Heb 9:15 death has occurred which R them from the

REDEMPTION (26)

Ex 21:30 shall give for the R of his life whatever
Lev 25:24 you shall grant a R of the land.
25:29 full year he shall have the right of R
25:33 exercise his right of R, then the house that
25:51 price paid for him the price for his R
25:52 him he shall refund the money for his R
Num 3:46 And for the R of the two hundred and
3:49 So Moses took the R money from those who
3:51 and Moses gave the R money to Aaron and
18:16 And their R price (at a month old you
Ruth 4:6 Take my right of R yourself, for I cannot
Ps 111:9 He sent R to his people; he has commanded
130:7 is steadfast love, and with him is plenteous R
Prov 13:8 but a poor man has no means of R
Is 63:4 and my year of R has come.
Jer 32:7 for the right of R by purchase is yours.'
32:8 right of possession and R is yours; buy it
Lk 2:38 were looking for the R of Jerusalem.
21:28 your heads, because your R is drawing near."
Rom 3:24 a gift, through the R which is in Christ
8:23 adoption as sons, the R of our bodies.
1Cor 1:30 righteousness and sanctification and R;
Eph 1:7 In him we have R through his blood, the
4:30 whom you were sealed for the day of R
Col 1:14 in whom we have R, the forgiveness of sins.
Heb 9:12 but his own blood, thus securing an eternal R

REDNESS

Prov 23:29 Who has R of eyes?

REDOUND (2)

Ezek 39:13 them; and it will R to their honor on
1Pet 1:7 tested by fire, may R to praise and glory

REDRESS

Ezek 22:29 and have extorted from the sojourner without R

REDUCING

Sir 31:30 fool to his injury, R his strength and adding

REED (33)

Gen 41:2 they fed in the R grass.
41:18 and fed in the R grass;
1Kgs 14:15 smite Israel, as a R is shaken in the
2Kgs 18:21 on Egypt, that broken R of a staff, which
Job 9:26 by like skiffs of R, like an eagle swooping
Is 9:14 tail, palm branch and R in one day--
19:15 tail, palm branch or R, may do.
36:6 on Egypt, that broken R of a staff, which
42:3 the street; a bruised R he will not break,
Ezek 29:6 been a staff of R to the house of
40:3 flax and a measuring R in his hand; and
40:5 length of the measuring R in the man's hand
40:5 of the wall, one R; and the height, one
40:5 the wall, one reed; and the height, one R
40:6 of the gate, one R deep;
40:7 the side rooms, one R long, and one reed
40:7 reed long, and one R broad; and the space
40:7 of the gate at the inner end, one R
41:8 chambers measured a full R of six long cubits.
42:16 side with the measuring R, five hundred cubits by
42:16 reed, five hundred cubits by the measuring R
42:17 north side, five hundred cubits by the measuring R
42:18 south side, five hundred cubits by the measuring R
42:19 measured, five hundred cubits by the measuring R
Hos 13:15 may flourish as the R plant, the east wind,
Mt 11:7 A R shaken by the wind?
12:20 not break a bruised R or quench a smoldering
27:29 head, and put a R in his right hand.
27:30 him, and took the R and struck him on
27:48 put it on a R, and gave it to
Mk 15:19 his head with a R, and spat upon him,
15:35 put it on a R and gave it to
Lk 7:24 A R shaken by the wind?

REEDS (8)

Ex 2:3 placed it among the R at the river's brink.
2:5 the basket among the R and sent her maid
Job 8:11 Can R flourish where there is no water?
40:21 the covert of the R and in the marsh.
Ps 68:30 that dwell among the R, the herd of bulls
Sir 40:16 The R by any water or river bank will
Is 19:6 diminish and dry up, R and rushes will rot
35:7 the grass shall become R and rushes.

REEL (3)

Ps 60:3 given us wine to drink that made us R
Is 28:7 These also R with wine and stagger with strong
28:7 priest and the prophet R with strong drink, they

REELED (3)

2Sam 22:8 "Then the earth R and rocked; the foundations of
Ps 18:7 Then the earth R and rocked; the foundations also
107:27 their evil plight; they R and staggered like drunken

REELING

Zech 12:2 Jerusalem a cup of R to all the peoples

REELS

Is 21:4 My mind R, horror has appalled me; the twilight

REFERRED

2Mac 11:36 decided are to be R to the king, as

REFERRING (3)

Gal 3:16 R to many; but, referring to one, "And to

3:16 referring to many; but, R to one, "And to
Col 2:22 R to things which all perish as they are

REFERS

Eph 5:32 am saying that it R to Christ and the

REFINE (5)

Job 28:1 silver, and a place for gold which they R
Jer 9:7 hosts: "Behold, I will R them and test them,
Dan 11:35 wise shall fall, to R and to cleanse them
Zech 13:9 into the fire, and R them as one refines
Mal 3:3 sons of Levi and R them like gold and

REFINED (8)

1Chr 28:18 of incense made of R gold, and its weight;
29:4 seven thousand talents of R silver, for overlaying the
Ps 12:6 that are pure, silver R in a furnace on
Is 25:6 of marrow, of wine on the lees well R
48:10 Behold, I have R you, but not like silver;
Dan 12:10 themselves white, and be R; but the wicked shall
Rev 1:15 were like burnished bronze, R as in a furnace,
3:18 buy from me gold R by fire, that you

REFINEMENT

Dan 13:31 a woman of great R, and beautiful in appearance.

REFINER (2)

Mal 3:2 he is like a R's fire and like fullers'
3:3 will sit as a R and purifier of silver,

REFINES

Zech 13:9 refine them as one R silver, and test them

REFINING

Jer 6:29 fire; in vain the R goes on, for the

REFLECT (4)

Prov 20:25 and to R only after making his vows.
Sir 3:21 R upon what has been assigned to you, for
6:37 R on the statutes of the Lord, and meditate
16:18 And no mind will R on this.

REFLECTION

Wis 7:26 For she is a R of eternal light, a

REFLECTS (3)

Prov 27:19 the mind of man R the man.
Sir 14:21 He who R in his mind on her ways
Heb 1:3 He R the glory of God and bears the

REFORMATION

Heb 9:10 for the body imposed until the time of R

REFORMS

Acts 24:2 provision, most excellent Felix, R are introduced on

REFRACTORY

Tit 2:9 are not to be R,

REFRAIN (12)

Ex 23:5 its burden, you shall R from leaving him with
Deut 23:22 But if you R from vowing, it shall be
Ruth 1:13 Would you therefore R from marrying?
Tob 4:21 you fear God and R from every sin and
Ps 37:8 R from anger, and forsake wrath!
Eccl 3:5 and a time to R from embracing;
Sir 4:23 Do not R from speaking at the crucial time,
28:8 R from strife, and you will lessen sins; for
Dan 11:8 some years he shall R from attacking the king
1Cor 9:6 have no right to R from working for a
2Cor 11:9 I refrained and will R from burdening you in
12:6 But I R from it, so that no one

REFRAINED (4)

Job 29:9 and stood; the princes R from talking, and laid
Jer 41:8 So he R and did not kill them with
2Cor 1:23 spare you that I R from coming to Corinth.
11:9 So I R and will refrain from burdening you

REFRAINS (2)

Num 9:13 on a journey, yet R from keeping the passover,
1Cor 7:38 well; and he who R from marriage will do

REFRESH (5)

Gen 18:5 bread, that you may R yourselves, and after that
1Kgs 13:7 home with me, and R yourself, and I will
Song 2:5 Sustain me with raisins, R me with apples; for
Sir 3:6 obeys the Lord will R his mother;
Philem 1:20 R my heart in Christ.

REFRESHED (8)

Ex 23:12 of your bondmaid, and the alien, may be R
31:17 on the seventh day he rested, and was R
1Sam 16:23 hand; so Saul was R, and was well, and
2Sam 16:14 Jordan; and there he R himself.
Rom 15:32 with joy and be R in your company.
1Cor 16:18 your absence; for they R my spirit as well
2Tim 1:16 Onesiphorus, for he often R me; he was not
Philem 1:7 the saints have been R through you.

REFRESHES (3)

Prov 15:30 heart, and good news R the bones.
25:13 who send him, he R the spirit of his
Sir 43:22 the dew appears, it R from the heat.

REFRESHING

Acts 3:19 out, that times of R may come from the

REFRESHMENT (2)

Prov 3:8 to your flesh and R to your bones.
2Mac 4:46 colonnade as if for R, induced the king to

REFUGE (103)

Num 35:6 the six cities of R, where you shall permit
35:11 to be cities of R for you, that the
35:12 be for you a R from the avenger, that
35:13 you give shall be your six cities of R
35:14 the land of Canaan, to be cities of R
35:15 cities shall be for R for the people of
35:25 to his city of R, to which he had
35:26 of his city of R to which he fled,
35:27 of his city of R, and the avenger of
35:28 in his city of R until the death of
35:32 to his city of R, that he may return
Deut 32:37 in which they took R,
Josh 20:2 'Appoint the cities of R, of which I spoke
20:3 be for you a R from the avenger of
21:13 Hebron, the city of R for the slayer, with
21:21 Shechem, the city of R for the slayer, with
21:27 lands, the city of R for the slayer, and
21:32 lands, the city of R for the slayer, Hammoth-dor
21:38 lands, the city of R for the slayer, Mahanaim
Judg 9:15 then come and take R in my shade; but
Ruth 2:12 under whose wings you have come to take R
2Sam 22:3 in whom I take R, my shield and the
22:3 my stronghold and my R, my savior; thou savest
22:31 all those who take R in him.
22:33 God is my strong R, and has made my
1Chr 6:57 gave the cities of R: Hebron, Libnah with its
6:67 given the cities of R: Shechem with its pasture
Ps 2:12 are all who take R in him.
5:11 let all who take R in thee rejoice, let
7:1 thee do I take R; save me from all
11:1 the LORD I take R; how can you say
14:6 of the poor, but the LORD is his R
16:1 me, O God, for in thee I take R
17:7 of those who seek R from their adversaries at
18:2 in whom I take R, my shield, and the
18:30 all those who take R in him.
25:20 shame, for I take R in thee.
28:8 he is the saving R of his anointed.
31:1 LORD, do I seek R; let me never be
31:2 thou a rock of R for me, a strong
31:4 is hidden for me, for thou art my R
31:19 for those who take R in thee, in the
34:8 the man who takes R in him!
34:22 of those who take R in him will be
36:7 children of men take R in the shadow of
37:39 LORD; he is their R in the time of
37:40 them, because they take R in him.
43:2 in whom I take R; why hast thou cast
46:1 God is our R and strength, a very present
46:7 with us; the God of Jacob is our R
46:11 with us; the God of Jacob is our R
52:7 not make God his R, but trusted in the
52:7 his riches, and sought R in his wealth!"
57:1 thee my soul takes R; in the shadow of
57:1 wings I will take R, till the storms of
59:16 a fortress and a R in the day of
61:3 for thou art my R, a strong tower against
62:7 my mighty rock, my R is God.
62:8 him; God is a R for us.

R

64:10 the LORD, and take R in him!
71:1 LORD, do I take R; let me never be
71:3 me a rock of R, a strong fortress, to
71:7 portent to many; but thou art my strong R
73:28 the Lord GOD my R, that I may tell
91:2 to the LORD, "My R and my fortress; my
91:4 wings you will find R; his faithfulness is a
91:9 made the LORD your R, the Most High your
94:22 stronghold, and my God the rock of my R
104:18 the rocks are a R for the badgers.
118:8 is better to take R in the LORD than
118:9 is better to take R in the LORD than
141:8 in thee I seek R; leave me not defenseless!
142:4 notice of me; no R remains to me, no
142:5 say, Thou art my R, my portion in the
143:9 I have fled to thee for R
144:2 in whom I take R, who subdues the peoples
Prov 14:26 strong confidence, and his children will have a R
14:32 but the righteous finds R through his integrity.
30:5 to those who take R in him.
Wis 14:6 of the world took R on a raft, and
Is 4:6 heat, and for a R and a shelter from
14:32 in her the afflicted of his people find R
16:4 among you; be a R to them from the
17:10 the Rock of your R; therefore, though you plant
28:15 have made lies our R, and in falsehood we
28:17 will sweep away the R of lies, and waters
30:2 my counsel, to take R in the protection of
57:13 But he who takes R in me shall possess
Jer 16:19 and my stronghold, my R in the day of
17:17 me; thou art my R in the day of
25:35 No R will remain for the shepherds, nor escape
Joel 3:16 the LORD is a R to his people, a
Nah 1:7 knows those who take R in him.
3:11 you will seek a R from the enemy.
Zeph 3:12 They shall seek R in the name of the
1Mac 1:53 in every place of R they had.
10:14 commandments, for it served as a place of R
10:43 And whoever takes R at the temple in Jerusalem,
10:84 those who had taken R in it he burned
2Mac 5:5 being taken, Menelaus took R in the citadel.
10:18 than nine thousand took R in two very strong
12:6 those who had taken R there.
Heb 6:18 have fled for R might have strong encouragement

REFUND (2)

Lev 25:51 to them he shall R out of the price
25:52 from him he shall R the money for his

REFUSE (51)

Ex 4:23 serve me"; if you R to let him go,
8:2 But if you R to let them go, behold,
9:2 For if you R to let them go and
10:3 'How long will you R to humble yourself before
10:4 For if you R to let my people go,
16:28 "How long do you R to keep my commandments
1Kgs 2:16 of you; do not R me." She said to
2:17 Solomon–he will not R you–to give me
2:20 of you; do not R me." And the king
2:20 for I will not R you."
20:7 and I did not R him."
Tob 4:5 days, my son, and R to sin or to
Jud 2:11 But if they R, your eye shall not spare
12:14 "Who am I, to R my lord?
Prov 21:7 them away, because they R to do what is
21:25 him for his hands R to labor.
Sir 7:13 R to utter any lie, for the habit of
27:4 sieve is shaken, the R remains; so a man's
Is 1:20 land; But if you R and rebel, you shall
5:25 their corpses were as R in the midst of
7:15 he knows how to R the evil and choose
7:16 child knows how to R the evil and choose
Jer 3:3 a harlot's brow, you R to be ashamed.
6:30 R silver they are called, for the LORD has
8:5 fast to deceit, they R to return.
9:6 deceit upon deceit, they R to know me, says
13:10 This evil people, who R to hear my words,
25:28 you.' "And if they R to accept the cup
38:21 But if you R to surrender, this is the
50:33 held them fast, they R to let them go.
Lam 3:45 made us offscouring and R among the peoples.
Ezek 2:5 whether they hear or R to hear (for they
2:7 whether they hear or R to hear; for they
3:11 whether they hear or R to hear."
3:27 and he that will R to hear, let him
3:27 to hear, let him R; for they are a
Dan 13:21 If you R, we will testify against you that
Amos 8:6 sandals, and sell the R of the wheat?"
1Mac 2:40 brethren have done and R to fight with the
2Mac 6:20 have the courage to R things that it is
Mt 5:42 you, and do not R him who would borrow
Mk 6:11 receive you and they R to hear you, when
Jn 5:39 to me; yet you R to come to me
Acts 18:15 to it yourselves; I R to be a judge
1Cor 4:13 are now, as the R of the world, the
7:5 Do not R one another except perhaps by agreement
2Cor 4:2 disgraceful, underhanded ways; we R to practice
Phil 3:8 and count them as R, in order that I
1Tim 5:11 But R to enrol younger widows; for when they
Heb 12:25 that you do not R him who is speaking.
Rev 11:9 their dead bodies and R to let them be

REFUSED (41)

Gen 37:35 comfort him; but he R to be comforted, and
39:8 But he R and said to his master's wife,
48:19 But his father R, and said, "I know, my
Ex 13:15 For when Pharaoh stubbornly R to let us go,
Num 20:21 Thus Edom R to give Israel passage through his
22:13 for the LORD has R to let me go
1Sam 8:19 But the people R to listen to the voice
28:23 He R, and said, "I will not eat." But
2Sam 2:23 But he R to turn aside; therefore Abner smote
13:9 before him, but he R to eat.
1Kgs 20:35 But the man R to strike him.
21:15 the Jezreelite, which he R to give you for
2Kgs 5:16 he urged him to take it, but he R
Neh 9:17 obey thy commandments; they R to obey, and were
Jud 1:11 of the Assyrians, and R to join him in
5:4 live in the west, R to come out and
Esth 1:12 But Queen Vashti R to come at the king's
13:12 I did this, and R to bow down to
Ps 78:10 keep God's covenant, but R to walk according to
Prov 1:24 have called and you R to listen, have stretched
Wis 12:27 whom they had before R to know.
19:14 Others had R to receive strangers when they came
Sir 29:7 wickedness, therefore, many have R to lend; they
Is 8:6 "Because this people have R the waters of Shiloah
Jer 5:3 consumed them, but they R to take correction.
5:3 than rock; they have R to repent.
11:10 of their forefathers, who R to hear my words;
Hos 11:5 king, because they have R to return to me.
Zech 7:11 But they R to hearken, and turned a stubborn
1Mac 5:48 But they R to open to him.
15:27 But he R to receive them, and he broke
Mt 2:18 for her children; she R to be consoled, because
18:29 will pay you.' He R and went and put
Mk 5:19 But he R, and said to him, "Go home
Lk 15:28 he was angry and R to go in.
18:4 For a while he R; but afterward he said
Acts 7:35 "This Moses whom they R, saying, 'Who made you
7:39 Our fathers R to obey him, but thrust him
2Thes 2:10 to perish, because they R to love the truth
Heb 11:24 he was grown up, R to be called the
12:25 not escape when they R him who warned them

REFUSES (12)

Ex 7:14 heart is hardened, he R to let the people
22:17 If her father utterly R to give her to
Num 22:14 Balak, and said, "Balaam R to come with us."
Deut 25:7 say, 'My husband's brother R to perpetuate his
Job 6:7 My appetite R to touch them; they are as
Ps 77:2 without wearying; my soul R to be comforted.
Jer 31:15 for her children; she R to be comforted for
Mt 18:16 If he R to listen to them, tell it
18:16 church; and if he R to listen even to
2Thes 3:14 If any one R to obey what we say
3Jn 1:10 content with that, he R himself to welcome the
Rev 2:21 to repent, but she R to repent of her

REFUSING (8)

Tob 4:13 of your people by R to take a wife
Wis 16:16 impossible; for the ungodly, R to know thee, were
17:10 perished in trembling fear, R to look even at
Jer 15:18 unceasing, my wound incurable, R to be healed?
16:12 his stubborn evil will, R to listen to me;
19:15 have stiffened their neck, R to hear my words."
Dan 9:11 law and turned aside, R to obey thy voice.
Heb 11:35 Some were tortured, R to accept release, that they

REGAIN (3)

Prov 2:19 back nor do they R the paths of life.
Acts 9:12 so that he might R his sight."

9:17 me that you may R your sight and be

REGAINED (2)

Tob 14:2 after eight years he R it.
Acts 9:18 his eyes and he R his sight.

REGAL

Ezek 16:13 beautiful, and came to R estate.

REGARD (73)

Gen 4:4 And the LORD had R for Abel and his
4:5 for Cain and his offering he had no R
31:2 that Laban did not R him with favor as
31:5 your father does not R me with favor as
Ex 5:9 it and pay no R to lying words."
9:21 he who did not R the word of the
Lev 26:9 And I will have R for you and make
Num 4:26 to be done with R to them.
Deut 9:27 and Jacob; do not R the stubbornness of this
28:50 countenance, who shall not R the person of the
33:9 father and mother, 'I R them not'; he disowned
Josh 7:1 Israel broke faith in R to the devoted things;
Judg 15:3 shall be blameless in R to the Philistines, when
1Sam 1:16 Do not R your maidservant as a base woman,
2:12 men; they had no R for the LORD.
25:25 Let not my lord R this ill-natured fellow, Nabal;
1Kgs 8:28 Yet have R to the prayer of thy servant
2Kgs 3:14 not that I have R for Jehoshaphat the king
2Chr 5:11 had sanctified themselves, without R to their
6:19 Yet have R to the prayer of thy servant
Esth 8:8 as you please with R to the Jews, in
9:31 for their descendants, with R to their fasts and
Job 9:21 I am blameless; I R not myself; I loathe
34:27 him, and had no R for any of his
35:13 nor does the Almighty R it.
37:24 him; he does not R any who are wise
Ps 17:4 With R to the works of men, by the
20:3 all your offerings, and R with favor your burnt
28:5 Because they do not R the works of the
31:6 hatest those who pay R to vain idols; but
74:20 Have R for thy covenant; for the dark places
80:14 heaven, and see; have R for this vine,
95:10 and they do not R my ways."
102:17 his glory; he will R the prayer of the
119:117 be safe and have R for thy statutes continually!
144:3 man that thou dost R him, or the son
Prov 12:10 A righteous man has R for the life of
Eccl 3:18 in my heart with R to the sons of
Wis 2:10 spare the widow nor R the gray hairs of
Sir 29:4 Many persons R a loan as a windfall, and
29:6 back half, and will R that as a windfall.
41:12 Have R for your name, since it will remain
Is 5:12 but they do not R the deeds of the
8:13 hosts, him you shall R as holy; let him
13:17 them, who have no R for silver and do
17:7 that day men will R their Maker, and their
17:8 they will not have R for the altars, the
22:11 did it, or have R for him who planned
33:8 despised, there is no R for man.
Jer 24:5 figs, so I will R as good the exiles
Lam 4:16 scattered them, he will R them no more; no
Bar 4:13 They had no R for his statutes; they did
Dan 6:4 complaint against Daniel with R to the kingdom; but
Jon 2:8 Those who pay R to vain idols forsake their
2Mac 3:32 by the Jews with R to Heliodorus, offered sacrifice
4:34 sanctuary; then, with no R for justice, he immediately
4:36 appealed to him with R to the unreasonable murder
6:11 in view of their R for that most holy
11:15 Maccabeus, having R for the common good, agreed
11:35 With R to what Lysias the kinsman of the
14:8 second because I have R also for my fellow
Mt 22:16 for you do not R the position of men.
Mk 12:14 for you do not R the position of men,
Lk 18:4 neither fear God nor R man,
Acts 28:22 views are; for with R to this sect we
Rom 6:20 you were free in R to righteousness.
1Cor 4:1 is how one should R us, as servants of
2Cor 5:16 now on, therefore, we R no one from a
5:16 point of view, we R him thus no longer.
Col 2:16 and drink or with R to a festival or
1Tim 6:1 the yoke of slavery R their masters as worthy
Heb 12:5 "My son, do not R lightly the discipline of
1Pet 5:12 faithful brother as I R him, I have written

REGARDED (16)

Gen 31:15 Are we not R by him as foreigners?
Ps 106:44 Nevertheless he R their distress, when he heard their
Wis 9:6 thee he will be R as nothing.
14:20 of his work, now R as an object of
Is 29:16 Shall the potter be R as the clay; that
29:17 fruitful field shall be R as a forest?
Hos 8:12 thousands, they would be R as a strange thing.
1Mac 11:27 made him to be R as one of his
2Mac 7:12 man's spirit, for he R his sufferings as nothing.
8:35 by opponents whom he R as of the least
Lk 1:48 Savior, for he has R the low estate of
18:2 neither feared God nor R man;
22:24 them was to be R as the greatest.
Rom 2:26 not his uncircumcision be R as circumcision?
8:36 day long; we are R as sheep to be
2Cor 5:16 even though we once R Christ from a human

REGARDING (5)

2Kgs 22:18 the God of Israel: R the words which you
2Chr 34:26 the God of Israel: R the words which you
Ezra 6:8 I make a decree R what you shall do
Job 4:20 for ever without any R it.
Acts 25:20 and be tried there R them.

REGARDS (8)

Gen 41:40 you command; only as R the throne will I
Job 34:19 partiality to princes, nor R the rich more than
Ps 138:6 LORD is high, he R the lowly; but the
Eccl 11:4 sow; and he who R the clouds will not
Mal 2:13 because he no longer R the offering or accepts
Rom 11:28 As R the gospel they are enemies of God,
11:28 your sake; but as R election they are beloved
1Tim 6:21 missed the mark as R the faith.

REGEM

1Chr 2:47 The sons of Jahdai: R, Jotham, Geshan, Pelet,

REGEM-MELECH

Zech 7:2 had sent Sharezer and R and their men, to

REGENERATION

Tit 3:5 by the washing of R and renewal in the

REGION (55)

Num 21:20 valley lying in the R of Moab by the
Deut 3:4 sixty cities, the whole R of Argob, the kingdom
3:13 that is, all the R of Argob, I gave
3:14 Manassite took all the R of Argob, that is,
Josh 13:11 and Gilead, and the R of the Geshurites and
13:30 Their R extended from Mahanaim, through all
22:10 they came to the R about the Jordan, that
22:11 of Canaan, in the R about the Jordan, on
24:15 fathers served in the R beyond the River, or
Judg 5:4 didst march from the R of Edom, the earth
1Kgs 4:13 and he had the R of Argob, which is
4:24 dominion over all the R west of the Euphrates
1Chr 5:10 tents throughout all the R east of Gilead.
Neh 12:29 Beth-gilgal and from the R of Geba and Azmaveth;
Tob 5:5 Are you acquainted with that R
Jud 1:11 lived in the whole R disregarded the orders of
1:12 angry with this whole R, and swore by his
2:1 revenge on the whole R, just as he said.
2:2 the wickedness of the R;
2:11 to slaughter and plunder throughout your whole R
Bar 2:23 Judah and from the R about Jerusalem the voice
Ezek 47:8 flows toward the eastern R and goes down into
1Mac 3:41 the traders of the R heard what was said
8:4 control of the whole R by their planning and
11:14 the people of that R were in revolt.
11:34 latter, with all the R bordering them, were added
12:25 met them in the R of Hamath, for he
12:32 went to Damascus, and marched through all that R
2Mac 4:36 king returned from the R of Cilicia, the Jews
9:1 in disorder from the R of Persia.
9:21 way back from the R of Persia I suffered
10:14 became governor of the R, he maintained a force
12:18 find Timothy in that R, for he had by
12:18 then departed from the R without accomplishing
15:1 men were in the R of Samaria, he made
Mt 2:16 and in all that R who were two years
3:5 Judea and all the R about the Jordan,
4:16 who sat in the R and shadow of death
14:35 round to all that R and brought to him
15:22 Canaanite woman from that R came out and cried,
15:39 and went to the R of Magadan.
19:1 Galilee and entered the R of Judea beyond the
Mk 1:28 throughout all the surrounding R of Galilee.

7:23 went away to the R of Tyre and Sidon.
7:30 he returned from the R of Tyre, and went
7:30 of Galilee, through the R of the Decapolis.
10:1 and went to the R of Judea and beyond
Lk 2:8 And in that R there were shepherds out in
3:1 Philip tetrarch of the R of Ituraea and Trachonitis,
3:3 went into all the R about the Jordan, preaching
4:37 went out into every place in the surrounding R
Acts 8:1 scattered throughout the R of Judea and Samaria,
13:49 word of the Lord spread throughout all the R
16:6 they went through the R of Phrygia and Galatia,
18:23 to place through the R of Galatia and Phrygia,

REGIONS (7)
Josh 13:2 yet remains: all the R of the Philistines, and
Ps 88:6 the Pit, in the R dark and deep.
Joel 3:4 Sidon, and all the R of Philistia?
1Mac 3:31 the revenues from those R and raise a large
Rom 15:23 for work in these R, and since I have
2Cor 11:10 be silenced in the R of Achaia.
Gal 1:21 I went into the R of Syria and Cilicia.

REGISTER
Ezek 13:9 be enrolled in the R of the house of

REGISTERED (5)
Num 1:18 congregation together, who R themselves by families,
11:26 they were among those R, but they had not
1Chr 4:41 These, R by name, came in the days of
23:24 houses as they were R according to the number
Ezra 8:3 Zechariah, with whom were R one hundred and fifty

REGISTERS
Ps 87:6 LORD records as he R the peoples, "This one

REGISTRATION (2)
Ezra 2:62 These sought their R among those enrolled in the
Neh 7:64 These sought their R among those enrolled in the

REGRET (6)
2Chr 21:20 in Jerusalem; and he departed with no one's R
Sir 32:19 have acted, do not R it.
1Mac 11:10 For I now R that I gave him my
2Cor 7:8 letter, I do not R it (though I did
7:8 it (though I did R it), for I see
7:10 salvation and brings no R, but worldly grief produces

REGULAR (6)
Lev 6:20 fine flour as a R cereal offering, half of
15:19 blood which is her R discharge from her body,
2Kgs 25:30 for his allowance, a R allowance was given him
Esth 2:12 since this was the R period of their beautifying,
Jer 52:34 for his allowance, a R allowance was given him
Acts 19:39 be settled in the R assembly.

REGULARLY (4)
2Kgs 25:29 his life he dined R at the king's table;
Jer 52:33 his life he dined R at the king's table;
Dan 14:13 used to go in R and consume the provisions.
2Mac 4:27 he did not pay R any of the money

REGULATIONS (4)
Esth 2:12 twelve months under the R for the women, since
Col 2:20 do you submit to R,
Heb 9:1 the first covenant had R for worship and an
9:10 drink and various ablutions, R for the body imposed

REHABIAH (5)
1Chr 23:17 The sons of Eliezer: R the chief; Eliezer had
23:17 but the sons of R were very many.
24:21 Of R: of the sons of Rehabiah, Isshiah the
24:21 of the sons of R, Isshiah the chief.
26:25 Eliezer were his son R, and his son Jeshaiah,

REHOB (10)
Num 13:21 wilderness of Zin to R, near the entrance of
Josh 19:28 north to Cabul, Ebron, R, Hammon, Kanah, as far
19:30 Achzib, Ummah, Aphek and R --twenty-two cities
21:31 its pasture lands, and R with its pasture lands--
Judg 1:31 of Aphik, or of R;
2Sam 8:3 Hadadezer the son of R, king of Zobah, as
8:12 Hadadezer the son of R, king of Zobah.
10:8 of Zobah and of R, and the men of
1Chr 6:75 its pasture lands, and R with its pasture lands;
Neh 10:11 Kelita, Pelaiah, Hanan, Mica, R, Hashabiah,

REHOBOAM (53)
1Kgs 11:43 David his father; and R his son reigned in
12:1 R went to Shechem, for all Israel had come
12:3 came and said to R,
12:6 Then King R took counsel with the old men,
12:12 the people came to R the third day, as
12:17 But R reigned over the people of Israel who
12:18 Then King R sent Adoram, who was taskmaster over
12:18 And King R made haste to mount his chariot,
12:21 When R came to Jerusalem, he assembled all the
12:21 restore the kingdom to R the son of Solomon.
12:23 of God: "Say to R the son of Solomon,
12:27 to their lord, to R king of Judah, and
12:27 me and return to R king of Judah."
14:21 Now R the son of Solomon reigned in Judah.
14:21 R was forty-one years old when he began to
14:25 fifth year of King R, Shishak king of Egypt
14:27 had made; and King R made in their stead
14:29 of the acts of R, and all that he
14:30 there was war between R and Jeroboam continually.
14:31 And R slept with his fathers and was buried
15:6 there was war between R and Jeroboam all the
1Chr 3:10 The descendants of Solomon: R, Abijah his son, Asa
2Chr 9:31 David his father; and R his son reigned in
10:1 R went to Shechem, for all Israel had come
10:3 came and said to R,
10:6 Then King R took counsel with the old men,
10:12 the people came to R the third day, as
10:14 the old men, King R spoke to them according
10:17 But R reigned over the people of Israel who
10:18 Then King R sent Hadoram, who was taskmaster
10:18 And King R made haste to mount his chariot,
11:1 When R came to Jerusalem, he assembled the house
11:1 fight against Israel, to restore the kingdom to R
11:3 of God: "Say to R the son of Solomon
11:5 R dwelt in Jerusalem, and he built cities for
11:17 three years they made R the son of Solomon
11:18 R took as wife Mahalath the daughter of Jerimoth
11:21 R loved Maacah the daughter of Absalom above all
11:22 and sixty daughters); and R appointed Abijah the son
12:1 When the rule of R was established and was
12:2 fifth year of King R, because they had been
12:5 the prophet came to R and to the princes
12:10 had made; and King R made in their stead
12:13 So King R established himself in Jerusalem and
12:13 R was forty-one years old when he began to
12:15 Now the acts of R, from first to last,
12:15 were continual wars between R and Jeroboam.
12:16 And R slept with his fathers, and was buried
13:7 about him and defied R the son of Solomon,
13:7 son of Solomon, when R was young and irresolute
Sir 47:23 and lacking in understanding, R, whose policy caused
Mt 1:7 Solomon the father of R, and Rehoboam the father
1:7 father of Rehoboam, and R the father of Abijah,

REHOBOTH (3)
Gen 26:22 he called its name R, saying, "For now the
36:37 died, and Shaul of R on the Euphrates reigned
1Chr 1:48 Samlah died, Shaul of R on the Euphrates reigned

REHOBOTH-IR
Gen 10:11 Assyria, and built Nineveh, R, Calah, and

REHUM (8)
Ezra 2:2 Mordecai, Bilshan, Mispar, Bigvai, R, and Baanah.
4:8 R the commander and Shimshai the scribe wrote a
4:9 follows-- then wrote R the commander, Shimshai the
4:17 sent an answer: "To R the commander and Shimshai
4:23 letter was read before R and Shimshai the scribe
Neh 3:17 him the Levites repaired: R the son of Bani;
10:25 Hallohesh, Pilha, Shobek, R, Hashabnah, Ma-aseiah,
12:3 Malluch, Hattush, Shecaniah, R, Meremoth,

REI
1Kgs 1:8 prophet, and Shimei, and R, and David's mighty men

REIGN (162)
Gen 37:8 "Are you indeed to R over us?
Ex 15:18 The LORD will R for ever and ever."
Judg 9:8 to the olive tree, R over us.'
9:10 tree, 'Come you, and R over us.'
9:12 vine, 'Come you, and R over us.'
9:14 bramble, 'Come you, and R over us.'
1Sam 8:9 the king who shall R over them."
8:11 the king who will R over you: he will
10:1 And you shall R over the people of the

11:12 that said, 'Shall Saul R over us?' Bring the
12:12 but a king shall R over us,' when the
13:1 when he began to R; and he reigned .
2Sam 2:10 when he began to R over Israel, and he
3:21 and that you may R over all that your
5:4 when he began to R, and he reigned forty
1Kgs 1:13 "Solomon your son shall R after me, and he
1:17 'Solomon your son shall R after me, and he
1:24 you said, 'Adonijah shall R after me, and he
1:30 'Solomon your son shall R after me, and he
2:15 fully expected me to R; however the kingdom has
6:1 fourth year of Solomon's R over Israel, in the
11:37 you, and you shall R over all that your
14:21 when he began to R, and he reigned seventeen
15:1 Nebat, Abijam began to R over Judah.
15:9 Israel Asa began to R over Judah,
15:25 of Jeroboam began to R over Israel in the
15:33 of Ahijah began to R over all Israel at
16:8 of Baasha began to R over Israel in Tirzah,
16:11 When he began to R, as soon as he
16:23 Judah, Omri began to R over Israel, and reigned
16:29 of Omri began to R over Israel, and Ahab
22:41 of Asa began to R over Judah in the
22:42 when he began to R, and he reigned twenty-five
22:51 of Ahab began to R over Israel in Samaria
2Kgs 3:27 son who was to R in his stead, and
8:16 son of Jehoshaphat, king of Judah, began to R
8:25 son of Jehoram, king of Judah, began to R
8:26 when he began to R, and he reigned one
9:29 Ahab, Ahaziah began to R over Judah.
11:21 was seven years old when he began to R
12:1 Jehu Jehoash began to R, and he reigned forty
13:1 of Jehu began to R over Israel in Samaria,
13:10 of Jehoahaz began to R over Israel in Samaria,
14:1 son of Joash, king of Judah, began to R
14:2 when he began to R, and he reigned twenty-nine
14:23 of Israel, began to R in Samaria, and he
15:1 son of Amaziah, king of Judah, began to R
15:2 when he began to R, and he reigned fifty-two
15:13 of Jabesh began to R in the thirty-ninth year
15:17 of Gadi began to R over Israel, and he
15:23 of Menahem began to R over Israel in Samaria,
15:27 of Remaliah began to R over Israel in Samaria,
15:32 son of Uzziah, king of Judah, began to R
15:33 when he began to R, and he reigned sixteen
16:1 son of Jotham, king of Judah, began to R
16:2 when he began to R, and he reigned sixteen
17:1 of Elah began to R in Samaria over Israel,
18:1 son of Ahaz, king of Judah, began to R
18:2 when he began to R, and he reigned twenty-nine
21:1 when he began to R, and he reigned fifty-five
21:19 when he began to R, and he reigned two
22:1 when he began to R, and he reigned thirty-one
23:31 when he began to R, and he reigned three
23:33 that he might not R in Jerusalem, and laid
23:36 when he began to R, and he reigned eleven
24:12 eighth year of his R,
25:1 ninth year of his R, in the tenth month,
25:27 that he began to R, graciously freed Jehoiachin king
1Chr 26:31 fortieth year of David's R search was made and
2Chr 3:2 second month of the fourth year of his R
12:13 when he began to R, and he reigned seventeen
13:1 Jeroboam Abijah began to R over Judah.
15:10 fifteenth year of the R of Asa.
15:19 thirty-fifth year of the R of Asa.
16:1 thirty-sixth year of the R of Asa, Baasha king
16:12 thirty-ninth year of his R Asa was diseased in
16:13 fathers, dying in the forty-first year of his R
17:7 third year of his R he sent his princes,
20:31 when he began to R, and he reigned twenty-five
21:20 when he began to R, and he reigned eight
22:2 when he began to R, and he reigned one
23:3 Let him R, as the LORD spoke concerning the
24:1 when he began to R, and he reigned forty
25:1 when he began to R, and he reigned twenty-nine
26:3 when he began to R, and he reigned fifty-two
27:1 when he began to R, and he reigned sixteen
27:8 when he began to R, and he reigned sixteen
28:1 when he began to R, and he reigned sixteen
29:1 Hezekiah began to R when he was twenty-five years
29:3 first year of his R, in the first month,
29:19 Ahaz discarded in his R when he was faithless,
33:1 when he began to R, and he reigned fifty-five
33:21 when he began to R, and he reigned two
34:1 when he began to R, and he reigned thirty-one
34:3 eighth year of his R, while he was yet
34:8 eighteenth year of his R, when he had purged
35:19 eighteenth year of the R of Josiah this passover
36:2 when he began to R; and he reigned three
36:5 when he began to R, and he reigned eleven
36:9 when he began to R, and he reigned three
36:11 when he began to R, and he reigned eleven
Ezra 4:5 Persia, even until the R of Darius king of
4:6 And in the R of Ahasuerus, in the beginning
4:6 the beginning of his R, they wrote an accusation
4:24 second year of the R of Darius king of
6:15 sixth year of the R of Darius the king.
7:1 after this, in the R of Artaxerxes king of
8:1 from Babylonia, in the R of Artaxerxes the king:
Neh 12:22 the priests until the R of Darius the Persian.
Jud 1:1 twelfth year of the R of Nebuchadnezzar, who ruled
Esth 1:3 third year of his R he gave a banquet
2:16 seventh year of his R,
11:1 fourth year of the R of Ptolemy and Cleopatra,
11:2 second year of the R of Artaxerxes the Great,
Job 34:30 godless man should not R, that he should not
Ps 146:10 The LORD will R for ever, thy God, O
Prov 8:15 By me kings R, and rulers decree what is
Wis 3:8 and the Lord will R over them for ever.
6:21 wisdom, that you may R for ever.
Is 24:23 LORD of hosts will R on Mount Zion and
32:1 Behold, a king will R in righteousness, and princes
Jer 1:2 of Judah, in the thirteenth year of his R
23:5 Branch, and he shall R as king and deal
26:1 the beginning of the R of Jehoiakim the son
27:1 the beginning of the R of Zedekiah the son
28:1 the beginning of the R of Zedekiah king of
33:21 have a son to R on his throne, and
49:34 the beginning of the R of Zedekiah king of
51:59 to Babylon, in the fourth year of his R
52:4 ninth year of his R, in the tenth month,
Lam 5:19 thou, O LORD, dost R for ever; thy throne
Dan 1:1 third year of the R of Jehoiakim king of
2:1 second year of the R of Nebuchadnezzar,
6:28 Daniel prospered during the R of Darius and the
6:28 of Darius and the R of Cyrus the Persian.
8:1 third year of the R of King Belshazzar a
9:2 first year of his R, I, Daniel, perceived in
Mic 4:7 and the LORD will R over them in Mount
1Mac 1:10 He began to R in the one hundred and
1:16 Egypt, that he might R over both kingdoms.
6:17 he set up Antiochus the king's son to R
7:1 city by the sea, and there began to R
8:7 and those who should R after him should pay
10:1 They welcomed him, and there he began to R
11:9 wife, and you shall R over your father's kingdom.
11:54 Antiochus who began to R and put on the
2Mac 1:7 In the R of Demetrius, in the one hundred
Lk 1:33 David, and he will R over the house of
3:1 fifteenth year of the R of Tiberi-us Caesar, Pontius
19:14 want this man to R over us.'
19:27 not want me to R over them, bring them
Rom 5:17 free gift of righteousness R in life through the
5:21 death, grace also might R through righteousness to
6:12 Let not sin therefore R in your mortal bodies,
1Cor 4:8 would that you did R, so that we might
15:25 For he must R until he has put all
2Tim 2:12 endure, we shall also R with him; if we
Rev 5:10 God, and they shall R on earth."
11:15 Christ, and he shall R for ever and ever."
11:17 hast taken thy great power and begun to R
20:6 Christ, and they shall R with him a thousand
22:5 light, and they shall R for ever and ever.

REIGNED (171)

Gen 36:31 are the kings who R in the land of
36:31 Edom, before any king R over the Israelites.
36:32 the son of Beor R in Edom, the name
36:33 of Zerah of Bozrah R in his stead.
36:34 land of the Temanites R in his stead.
36:35 the country of Moab, R in his stead, the
36:36 and Samlah of Masrekah R in his stead.
36:37 Rehoboth on the Euphrates R in his stead.
36:38 the son of Achbor R in his stead.
36:39 Achbor died, and Hadar R in his stead, the
Josh 13:10 of the Amorites, who R in Heshbon, as far
13:12 Og in Bashan, who R in Ashtaroth and in
13:21 of the Amorites, who R in Heshbon, whom Moses
Judg 4:2 king of Canaan, who R in Hazor; the commander
1Sam 13:1 to reign; and he R .
2Sam 2:10 over Israel, and he R two years.
5:4 to reign, and he R forty years.

R

5:5 At Hebron he R over Judah seven years and
5:5 and at Jerusalem he R over all Israel and
8:15 So David R over all Israel; and David administered
10:1 and Hanun his son R in his stead.
16:8 whose place you have R; and the LORD has
1Kgs 2:11 the time that David R over Israel was forty
2:11 was forty years; he R seven years in Hebron,
11:25 he abhorred Israel, and R over Syria.
11:42 the time that Solomon R in Jerusalem over all
11:43 and Rehoboam his son R in his stead.
12:17 But Rehoboam R over the people of Israel who
14:19 warred and how he R, behold, they are written
14:20 the time that Jeroboam R was twenty-two years; an
14:20 and Nadab his son R in his stead.
14:21 the son of Solomon R in Judah.
14:21 to reign, and he R seventeen years in Jerusalem,
14:31 And Abijam his son R in his stead.
15:2 He R for three years in Jerusalem.
15:8 And Asa his son R in his stead.
15:10 over Judah, and he R forty-one years in Jerusalem.
15:24 and Jehoshaphat his son R in his stead.
15:25 of Judah; and he R over Israel two years.
15:28 king of Judah, and R in his stead.
15:33 Israel at Tirzah, and R twenty-four years.
16:6 and Elah his son R in his stead.
16:8 Israel in Tirzah, and R two years.
16:10 king of Judah, and R in his stead.
16:15 king of Judah, Zimri R seven days in Tirzah.
16:23 reign over Israel, and R for twelve years; six
16:23 years; six years he R in Tirzah.
16:28 and Ahab his son R in his stead.
16:29 the son of Omri R over Israel in Samaria
22:40 and Ahaziah his son R in his stead.
22:42 to reign, and he R twenty-five years in Jerusalem.
22:50 and Jehoram his son R in his stead.
22:51 of Judah, and he R two years over Israel.
2Kgs 3:1 in Samaria, and he R twelve years.
8:17 became king, and he R eight years in Jerusalem.
8:24 and Ahaziah his son R in his stead.
8:26 to reign, and he R one year in Jerusalem.
10:35 And Jehoahaz his son R in his stead.
10:36 The time that Jehu R over Israel in Samaria
11:3 the LORD, while Athaliah R over the land.
12:1 to reign, and he R forty years in Jerusalem.
12:21 and Amaziah his son R in his stead.
13:1 in Samaria, and he R seventeen years.
13:9 and Joash his son R in his stead.
13:10 in Samaria, and he R sixteen years.
14:2 to reign, and he R twenty-nine years in Jerusalem.
14:16 and Jeroboam his son R in his stead.
14:23 in Samaria, and he R forty-one years.
14:29 and Zechariah his son R in his stead.
15:2 to reign, and he R fifty-two years in Jerusalem.
15:7 and Jotham his son R in his stead.
15:8 the son of Jeroboam R over Israel in Samaria
15:10 and killed him, and R in his stead.
15:13 of Judah, and he R one month in Samaria.
15:14 and slew him, and R in his stead.
15:17 over Israel, and he R ten years in Samaria.
15:22 and Pekahiah his son R in his stead.
15:23 in Samaria, and he R two years.
15:25 he slew him, and R in his stead.
15:27 Israel in Samaria, and R twenty years.
15:30 and slew him, and R in his stead, in
15:33 to reign, and he R sixteen years in Jerusalem.
15:38 and Ahaz his son R in his stead.
16:2 to reign, and he R sixteen years in Jerusalem.
16:20 and Hezekiah his son R in his stead.
17:1 over Israel, and he R nine years.
18:2 to reign, and he R twenty-nine years in Jerusalem.
19:37 And Esarhaddon his son R in his stead.
20:21 and Manasseh his son R in his stead.
21:1 to reign, and he R fifty-five years in Jerusalem.
21:18 and Amon his son R in his stead.
21:19 to reign, and he R two years in Jerusalem.
21:26 and Josiah his son R in his stead.
22:1 to reign, and he R thirty-one years in Jerusalem.
23:31 to reign, and he R three months in Jerusalem.
23:36 to reign, and he R eleven years in Jerusalem.
24:6 and Jehoiachin his son R in his stead.
24:8 became king, and he R three months in Jerusalem.
24:18 became king, and he R eleven years in Jerusalem.
1Chr 1:43 are the kings who R in the land of
1:43 Edom before any king R over the Israelites: Bela
1:44 of Zerah of Bozrah R in his stead.
1:45 land of the Temanites R in his stead.
1:46 the country of Moab, R in his stead; and
1:47 died, Samlah of Masrekah R in his stead.
1:48 Rehoboth on the Euphrates R in his stead.
1:49 the son of Achbor, R in his stead.
1:50 When Baal-hanan died, Hadad R in his stead; and
3:4 in Hebron, where he R for seven years and
3:4 And he R thirty-three years in Jerusalem.
4:31 These were their cities until David R
18:14 So David R over all Israel; and he administered
19:1 died, and his son R in his stead.
29:26 the son of Jesse R over all Israel.
29:27 The time that he R over Israel was forty
29:27 was forty years; he R seven years in Hebron,
29:28 and Solomon his son R in his stead.
2Chr 1:13 And he R over Israel.
9:30 Solomon R in Jerusalem over all Israel forty years.
9:31 and Rehoboam his son R in his stead.
10:17 But Rehoboam R over the people of Israel who
12:13 Rehoboam established himself in Jerusalem and R
12:13 to reign, and he R seventeen years in Jerusalem,
12:16 and Abijah his son R in his stead.
13:2 He R for three years in Jerusalem.
14:1 and Asa his son R in his stead.
17:1 Jehoshaphat his son R in his stead, and strengthened
20:31 Thus Jehoshaphat R over Judah.
20:31 to reign, and he R twenty-five years in Jerusalem.
21:1 and Jehoram his son R in his stead.
21:5 became king, and he R eight years in Jerusalem.
21:20 to reign, and he R eight years in Jerusalem;
22:1 Ahaziah the son of Jehoram king of Judah R
22:2 to reign, and he R one year in Jerusalem.
22:12 of God, while Athaliah R over the land.
24:1 to reign, and he R forty years in Jerusalem;
24:27 And Amaziah his son R in his stead.
25:1 to reign, and he R twenty-nine years in Jerusalem.
26:3 to reign, and he R fifty-two years in Jerusalem.
26:23 And Jotham his son R in his stead.
27:1 to reign, and he R sixteen years in Jerusalem.
27:8 to reign, and he R sixteen years in Jerusalem.
27:9 and Ahaz his son R in his stead.
28:1 to reign, and he R sixteen years in Jerusalem.
28:27 And Hezekiah his son R in his stead.
29:1 years old, and he R twenty-nine years in Jerusalem.
32:33 And Manasseh his son R in his stead.
33:1 to reign, and he R fifty-five years in Jerusalem.
33:20 and Amon his son R in his stead.
33:21 to reign, and he R two years in Jerusalem.
34:1 to reign, and he R thirty-one years in Jerusalem.
36:2 to reign; and he R three months in Jerusalem.
36:5 to reign, and he R eleven years in Jerusalem.
36:8 and Jehoiachin his son R in his stead.
36:9 to reign, and he R three months and ten
36:11 to reign, and he R eleven years in Jerusalem.
Tob 1:15 died, Sennacherib his son R in his place; and
1:21 Then Esarhaddon, his son, R in his place; and
Esth 1:1 the Ahasuerus who R from India to Ethiopia
Sir 47:13 because of him; Solomon R in days of peace,
Is 37:38 And Esarhaddon his son R in his stead.
Jer 22:11 king of Judah, who R instead of Josiah his
37:1 the land of Judah, R instead of Coniah the
52:1 became king; and he R eleven years in Jerusalem.
1Mac 1:7 And after Alexander had R twelve years, he died.
6:2 Macedonian king who first R over the Greeks.
Mt 2:22 he heard that Archelaus R over Judea in place
Rom 5:14 Yet death R from Adam to Moses, even over
5:17 one man's trespass, death R through that one man,
5:21 so that, as sin R in death, grace also
Rev 20:4 came to life, and R with Christ a thousand

REIGNS (9)

1Sam 12:14 and the king who R over you will follow
1Chr 16:31 let them say among the nations, "The LORD R
Ps 47:8 God R over the nations; God sits on his
93:1 The LORD R; he is robed in majesty; the
96:10 Say among the nations, "The LORD R
97:1 The LORD R; let the earth rejoice; let the
99:1 The LORD R; let the peoples tremble!
Is 52:7 publishes salvation, who says to Zion, "Your God R
Rev 19:6 For the Lord our God the Almighty R

REIN

Ps 50:19 give your mouth free R for evil, and your

REINED

2Kgs 9:23 Then Joram R about and fled, saying to Ahaziah,

REINFORCED

1Mac 2:43 troubles joined them and R them.

REINFORCEMENTS

Esth 16:20 And give them R, so that on the thirteenth

REJECT (12)

Job 8:20 "Behold, God will not R a blameless man, nor
34:33 suit you, because you R it?
Prov 1:8 your father's instruction, and R not your mother's
Wis 9:4 throne, and do not R me from among thy
Sir 4:4 Do not R an afflicted suppliant, nor turn your
6:23 my judgment; do not R my counsel.
41:4 and how can you R the good pleasure of
Jer 33:26 earth, then I will R the descendants of Jacob
Hos 4:6 have rejected knowledge, I R you from being a
Tit 1:13 commands of men who R the truth.
Heb 12:25 we escape if we R him who warns from
Jude 1:8 dreamings defile the flesh, R authority, and revile the

REJECTED (57)

Num 11:20 you, because you have R the LORD who is
1Sam 8:7 for they have not R you, but they have
8:7 you, but they have R me from being king
10:19 you have this day R your God, who saves
15:23 Because you have R the word of the LORD,
15:23 LORD, he has also R you from being king."
15:26 you; for you have R the word of the
15:26 and the LORD has R you from being king
16:1 Saul, seeing I have R him from being king
16:7 stature, because I have R him; for the LORD
2Kgs 17:20 And the LORD R all the descendants of Israel,
Job 31:13 "If I have R the cause of my manservant
Ps 53:5 shame, for God has R them.
60:1 O God, thou hast R us, broken our defenses;
60:10 Hast thou not R us, O God?
66:20 because he has not R my prayer or removed
78:59 wrath, and he utterly R Israel.
78:67 He R the tent of Joseph, he did not
89:38 hast cast off and R, thou art full of
108:11 Hast thou not R us, O God?
118:22 stone which the builders R has become the head
Wis 11:14 though they had mockingly R him who long before
Sir 20:19 fool's lips will be R, for he does not
Is 2:6 For thou hast R thy people, the house of
5:24 dust; for they have R the law of the
53:3 He was despised and R by men; a man
Jer 2:37 for the LORD has R those in whom you
6:19 my law, they have R it.
6:30 for the LORD has R them."
7:29 for the LORD has R and forsaken the generation
8:9 taken; lo, they have R the word of the
14:19 Hast thou utterly R Judah?
15:6 You have R me, says the LORD, you keep
33:24 saying, 'The LORD has R the two families which
Lam 5:22 Or hast thou utterly R us?
Ezek 20:13 in my statutes but R my ordinances, by whose
20:16 all lands, because they R my ordinances and did
20:24 my ordinances, but had R my statutes and profaned
Hos 4:6 knowledge; because you have R knowledge, I reject
Amos 2:4 punishment; because they have R the law of the
Zech 10:6 though I had not R them; for I am
1Mac 2:31 that men who had R the king's command had
2Mac 1:27 upon those who are R and despised, and let
Mt 21:42 stone which the builders R has become the head
Mk 8:31 many things, and be R by the elders and
12:10 stone which the builders R has become the head
Lk 7:30 Pharisees and the lawyers R the purpose of God
9:22 many things, and be R by the elders and
17:25 many things and be R by this generation.
20:17 stone which the builders R has become the head
Acts 4:11 the stone which was R by you builders, but
Rom 11:1 ask, then, has God R his people?
11:2 God has not R his people whom he foreknew.
1Tim 4:4 nothing is to be R if it is received
Heb 12:17 the blessing, he was R, for he found no
1Pet 2:4 to that living stone, R by men but in
2:7 stone which the builders R has become the head

REJECTING (4)

Sir 41:21 a harlot, and of R the appeal of a
Ezek 5:6 round about her, by R my ordinances and not
Mk 7:9 a fine way of R the commandment of God,
1Tim 1:19 By R conscience, certain persons have made

REJECTION

Rom 11:15 For if their R means the reconciliation of the

REJECTS (6)

Prov 10:17 life, but he who R reproof goes astray.
Lk 10:16 me, and he who R you rejects me, and
10:16 he who rejects you R me, and he who
10:16 me, and he who R me rejects him who
10:16 he who rejects me R him who sent me."
Jn 12:48 He who R me and does not receive my

REJOICE (178)

Lev 23:40 brook; and you shall R before the LORD your
Deut 12:7 God, and you shall R, you and your households,
12:12 And you shall R before the LORD your God,
12:18 towns; and you shall R before the LORD your
14:26 LORD your God and R, you and your household.
16:11 you; and you shall R before the LORD your
16:14 wine press; you shall R in your feast, you
26:11 God; and you shall R in all the good
27:7 there; and you shall R before the LORD your
33:18 of Zebulun he said, R, Zebulun, in your going
Judg 9:19 house this day, then R in Abimelech, and let
9:19 and let him also R in you;
16:23 their god, and to R; for they said, "Our
1Sam 2:1 my enemies, because I R in thy salvation.
2Sam 1:20 daughters of the Philistines R, lest the daughters of
1Chr 16:10 the hearts of those who seek the LORD R
16:31 and let the earth R, and let them say
2Chr 6:41 and let thy saints R in thy goodness.
20:27 LORD had made them R over their enemies.
Neh 12:43 God had made them R with great joy; the
Tob 10:12 Sarah, that I may R before the Lord.
13:7 of heaven, and will R in his majesty.
13:13 R and be glad for the sons of the
13:14 They will R in your peace.
13:14 afflictions; for they will R for you upon seeing
14:7 truth and righteousness will R, showing mercy to our
Job 3:6 let it not R among the days of the
3:22 for hid treasures; who R exceedingly, and are glad,
21:12 and the lyre, and R to the sound of
Ps 5:11 take refuge in thee R, let them ever sing
9:14 of Zion I may R in thy deliverance.
13:4 him"; lest my foes R because I am shaken.
13:5 love; my heart shall R in thy salvation.
14:7 his people, Jacob shall R, Israel shall be glad.
30:1 not let my foes R over me.
31:7 I will R and be glad for thy steadfast
32:11 in the LORD, and R, O righteous, and shout
33:1 R in the LORD, O you righteous!
35:9 Then my soul shall R in the LORD, exulting
35:19 Let not those R over me who are wrongfully
35:24 and let them not R over me!
35:26 and confusion altogether who R at my calamity!
38:16 "Only let them not R over me, who boast
40:16 all who seek thee R and be glad in
48:11 the daughters of Judah R because of thy judgments!
51:8 gladness; let the bones which thou hast broken R
53:6 his people, Jacob will R and Israel be glad.
58:10 The righteous will R when he sees the vengeance;
63:11 But the king shall R in God; all who
64:10 Let the righteous R in the LORD, and take
66:6 There did we R in him,
70:4 all who seek thee R and be glad in
75:9 But I will R for ever, I will sing
85:6 that thy people may R in thee?
89:42 his foes; thou hast made all his enemies R
90:14 love, that we may R and be glad all
96:11 and let the earth R; let the sea roar,
97:1 reigns; let the earth R; let the many coastlands
97:8 the daughters of Judah R, because of thy judgments,
97:12 R in the LORD, O you righteous, and give
104:31 ever, may the LORD R in his works,
104:34 to him, for I R in the LORD.
105:3 the hearts of those who seek the LORD R
106:5 ones, that I may R in the gladness of
118:24 has made; let us R and be glad in
119:74 shall see me and R, because I have hoped
119:162 I R at thy word like one who finds
149:2 the sons of Zion R in their King!
Prov 2:14 ways of darkness, who R in doing evil and
5:18 fountain be blessed, and R in the wife of
23:16 My soul will R when your lips speak what
23:24 the righteous will greatly R; he who begets a
23:25 mother be glad, let her who bore you R
24:17 Do not R when your enemy falls, and let

R

	29:2	in authority, the people R; but when the wicked
Eccl	4:16	come later will not R in him.
	11:8	many years, let him R in them all; but
	11:9	R, O young man, in your youth, and let
Song	1:4	We will exult and R in you; we will
Wis	18:6	so that they might R in sure knowledge of
Sir	8:7	Do not R over any one's death; remember that
	16:1	of useless children, nor R in ungodly sons.
	16:2	multiply , do not R in them, unless the
	22:21	poverty, that you may R with him in his
	23:3	my enemy will not R over me.
	27:29	Those who R in the fall of the godly
	30:1	order that he may R at the way he
	35:19	people and makes them R in his mercy.
	37:4	Some companions R in the happiness of a friend,
	39:31	with destruction; they will R in his commands, and
	51:29	May your soul R in his mercy, and may
Is	9:3	increased its joy; they R before thee as with
	9:3	the harvest, as men R when they divide the
	9:17	the Lord does not R over their young men,
	14:8	The cypresses R at you, the cedars of Lebanon,
	14:29	died came this oracle: R not, O Philistia, all
	25:9	us be glad and R in his salvation."
	35:1	glad, the desert shall R and blossom; like the
	35:2	shall blossom abundantly, and R with joy and singing.
	41:16	And you shall R in the LORD; in the
	60:5	heart shall thrill and R; because the abundance of
	61:7	of dishonor you shall R in your lot; therefore
	61:10	I will greatly R in the LORD, my soul
	62:5	so shall your God R over you.
	65:13	behold, my servants shall R, but you shall be
	65:18	But be glad and R for ever in that
	65:19	I will R in Jerusalem, and be glad in
	66:10	R with Jerusalem, and be glad for her, all
	66:10	you who love her; R with her in joy,
	66:14	and your heart shall R; your bones shall flourish
Jer	15:17	merrymakers, nor did I R; I sat alone, because
	31:13	Then shall the maidens R in the dance, and
	32:41	I will R in doing them good, and I
	50:11	"Though you R, though you exult, O plunderers of
Lam	2:17	has made the enemy R over you, and exalted
	4:21	R and be glad, O daughter of Edom, dweller
Bar	4:12	Let no one R over me, a widow and
Ezek	7:12	Let not the buyer R, nor the seller mourn,
Hos	9:1	R not, O Israel!
Joel	2:21	land; be glad and R, for the LORD has
	2:23	sons of Zion, and R in the LORD, your
Amos	6:13	wormwood-- you who R in Lo-debar, who say,
Mic	7:8	R not over me, O my enemy; when I
Hab	3:18	stalls, yet I will R in the LORD, I
Zeph	3:14	R and exult with all your heart, O daughter
	3:17	gives victory; he will R over you with gladness,
Zech	2:10	Sing and R, O daughter of Zion; for lo,
	4:10	of small things shall R, and shall see the
	9:9	R greatly, O daughter of Zion!
	10:7	shall see it and R, their hearts shall exult
1Mac	12:12	And we R in your glory.
Mt	5:12	R and be glad, for your reward is great
Lk	1:14	gladness, and many will R at his birth;
	6:23	R in that day, and leap for joy, for
	10:20	Nevertheless do not R in this, that the spirits
	10:20	subject to you; but R that your names are
	15:6	neighbors, saying to them, R with me, for I
	15:9	friends and neighbors, saying, R with me, for I
	19:37	the disciples began to R and praise God with
Jn	4:36	sower and reaper may R together.
	5:34	you were willing to R for a while in
	16:20	but the world will R; you will be sorrowful,
	16:22	and your hearts will R, and no one will
Rom	5:2	we stand, and we R in our hope of
	5:3	More than that, we R in our sufferings, knowing
	5:11	so, but we also R in God through our
	12:12	R in your hope, be patient in tribulation, be
	12:15	R with those who rejoice, weep with those who
	12:15	Rejoice with those who R, weep with those who
	15:10	again it is said, R, O Gentiles, with his
	16:19	all, so that I R over you, I would
1Cor	7:30	mourning, and those who R as though they were
	12:26	member is honored, all R together.
	13:6	resentful; it does not R at wrong, but rejoices
	16:17	I R at the coming of Stephanas and Fortunatus
2Cor	2:3	should have made me R, for I felt sure
	7:9	As it is, I R, not because you were
	7:16	I R, because I have perfect confidence in you.
Gal	4:27	For it is written, R, O barren one who
Phil	1:18	truth, Christ is proclaimed; and in that I R
	1:19	Yes, and I shall R
	2:17	I am glad and R with you all.
	2:18	should be glad and R with me.
	2:28	therefore, that you may R at seeing him again,
	3:1	Finally, my brethren, R in the Lord.
	4:4	R in the Lord always; again I will say,
	4:4	in the Lord always; again I will say, R
	4:10	I R in the Lord greatly that now at
Col	1:24	Now I R in my sufferings for your sake,
1Thes	5:16	R always,
1Pet	1:6	In this you R, though now for a little
	1:8	believe in him and R with unutterable and exalted
	4:13	But R in so far as you share Christ's
	4:13	that you may also R and be glad when
Rev	11:10	on the earth will R over them and make
	12:12	R then, O heaven and you that dwell therein!
	18:20	R over her, O heaven, O saints and apostles
	19:7	Let us R and exult and give him the

REJOICED (47)

Ex	18:9	And Jethro R for all the good which the
1Sam	6:13	saw the ark, they R to see it.
	11:15	the men of Israel R greatly.
	19:5	You saw it, and R; why then will you
1Kgs	5:7	words of Solomon, he R greatly, and said, "Blessed
2Kgs	11:20	people of the land R; and the city was
1Chr	29:9	Then the people R because these had given willingly,
	29:9	David the king also R greatly.
2Chr	15:15	And all Judah R over the oath; for they
	23:21	people of the land R; and the city was
	24:10	and all the people R and brought their tax
	29:36	and all the people R because of what God
	30:25	Israel, and the sojourners who dwelt in Judah, R
Neh	12:43	sacrifices that day and R, for God had made
	12:43	with great joy; the women and children also R
	12:44	the towns; for Judah R over the priests and
Tob	14:15	Before his death he R over Nineveh.
Esth	8:15	purple, while the city of Susa shouted and R
Job	31:25	confidence; if I have R because my wealth was
	31:29	"If I have R at the ruin of him
Wis	7:12	I R in them all, because wisdom leads them;
Sir	30:5	alive he saw and R, and when he died
Jer	41:13	the leaders of the forces with him, they R
Bar	4:31	who afflicted you and R at your fall.
	4:33	For just as she R at your fall and
Ezek	25:6	stamped your feet and R with all the malice
	35:15	As you R over the inheritance of the house
Obad	1:12	you should not have R over the people of
1Mac	7:48	The people R greatly and celebrated that day as
	10:26	our enemies, we have heard of it and R
	11:44	the king, the king R at their arrival.
	14:11	the land, and Israel R with great joy.
	14:21	and honor, and we R at their coming.
Mt	2:10	saw the star, they R exceedingly with great joy;
Lk	1:58	to her, and they R with her.
	10:21	that same hour he R in the Holy Spirit
	13:17	and all the people R at all the glorious
Jn	8:56	Your father Abraham R that he was to see
	14:28	me, you would have R, because I go to
Acts	2:26	glad, and my tongue R; moreover my flesh will
	7:41	to the idol and R in the works of
	15:31	they read it, they R at the exhortation.
	16:34	before them; and he R with all his household
2Cor	7:7	me, so that I R still more.
	7:13	our own comfort we R still more at the
2Jn	1:4	I R greatly to find some of your children
3Jn	1:3	For I greatly R when some of the brethren

REJOICES (14)

Ps	16:9	glad, and my soul R; my body also dwells
	21:1	thy strength the king R, O LORD; and in
Prov	11:10	the righteous, the city R; and when the wicked
	13:9	light of the righteous R, but the lamp of
	15:30	light of the eyes R the heart, and good
	29:6	his transgression, but a righteous man sings and R
Sir	19:5	One who R in wickedness will be condemned,
	26:2	A loyal wife R her husband, and he will
Is	62:5	and as the bridegroom R over the bride, so
Hab	1:15	his seine; so he R and exults.
Mt	18:12	say to you, he R over it more than
Lk	1:47	Lord, and my spirit R in God my Savior,
Jn	3:29	stands and hears him, R greatly at the bridegroom's
1Cor	13:6	rejoice at wrong, but R in the right.

REJOICING (37)

2Sam	6:12	city of David with R;

R

40:5 If you R, then return to Gedaliah the son
42:10 him: If you will R in this land, then
42:12 you and let you R in your own land.
42:13 say, 'We will not R in this land,' disobeying
43:4 of the LORD, to R in the land of
51:30 have ceased fighting, they R in their strongholds;
Bar 2:21 Babylon, and you will R in the land which
6:3 to Babylon you will R there for many years,
Ezek 7:11 none of them shall R, nor their abundance, nor
21:26 crown; things shall not R as they are; exalt
44:2 me, "This gate shall R shut; it shall not
44:2 it; therefore it shall R shut.
Hos 9:3 They shall not R in the land of the
Amos 6:9 And if ten men R in one house, they
Zech 14:10 But Jerusalem shall R aloft upon its site from
1Mac 8:22 sent to Jerusalem to R with them there as
10:14 in Bethzur did some R who had forsaken the
13:38 have made to you R valid, and let the
15:7 and now hold shall R yours.
2Mac 15:19 those who had to R in the city were
Mt 2:13 flee to Egypt, and R there till I tell
26:38 sorrowful, even to death; R here, and watch with
Mk 14:34 sorrowful, even to death; R here, and watch."
Lk 10:7 And R in the same house, eating and drinking
Jn 1:33 the Spirit descend and R, this is he who
12:46 in me may not R in darkness.
21:22 my will that he R until I come, what
21:23 my will that he R until I come, what
Acts 5:4 unsold, did it not R your own?
10:48 they asked him to R for some days.
11:23 exhorted them all to R faithful to the Lord
1Cor 7:8 well for them to R single as I do.
7:11 she does, let her R single or else be
7:20 Every one should R in the state in which
7:24 called, there let him R with God.
7:26 for a person to R as he is.
Phil 1:24 But to R in the flesh is more necessary
1:25 know that I shall R and continue with you
1Tim 1:3 was going to Macedonia, R at Ephesus that you
5:25 are not, they cannot R hidden.
Heb 12:27 in order that what cannot be shaken may R
Rev 17:10 he comes he must R only a little while.

REMAINDER (6)

Ex 29:34 you shall burn the R with fire; it shall
Lev 5:13 And the R shall be for the priest, as
Josh 21:40 families, that is, the R of the families of
Is 21:17 an end; and the R of the archers of
Ezek 48:15 "The R, five thousand cubits in breadth and
48:18 The R of the length alongside the holy portion

REMAINED (91)

Gen 16:13 really seen God and R alive after seeing him?"
49:24 sorely; yet his bow R unmoved, his arms were
Ex 7:22 arts; so Pharaoh's heart R hardened, and he would
8:31 his servants, and from his people; not one R
10:15 not a green thing R, neither tree nor plant
14:28 sea; not so much as one of them R
Num 9:18 over the tabernacle, they R in camp.
9:20 of the LORD they R in camp; then according
9:21 And sometimes the cloud R from evening until
9:22 the people of Israel R in camp and did
11:26 Now two men R in the camp, one named
11:35 to Hazeroth; and they R at Hazeroth.
14:38 the son of Jephunneh R alive, of those men
36:12 Joseph, and their inheritance R in the tribe of
Deut 1:46 So you R at Kadesh many days, the days
1:46 the days that you R there.
3:29 shall see.' So we R in the valley opposite
9:9 made with you, I R on the mountain forty
Josh 2:22 into the hills, and R there three days, until
5:8 nation was done, they R in their places in
10:20 when the remnant which R of them had entered
18:2 There R among the people of Israel seven tribes
Judg 7:3 twenty-two thousand returned, and en thousand R
11:17 So Israel R at Kadesh.
19:4 him stay, and he R with him three days;
Ruth 1:2 country of Moab and R there.
1Sam 1:23 So the woman R and nursed her son, until
23:14 And David R in the strongholds in the wilderness,
23:18 before the LORD; David R at Horesh, and Jonathan
25:13 David, while two hundred R with the baggage.
26:3 But David R in the wilderness; and when he
2Sam 1:1 of the Amalekites, David R two days in Ziklag;
6:11 ark of the LORD R in the house of
11:1 But David R at Jerusalem.
11:12 So Uriah R in Jerusalem that day, and the
15:29 to Jerusalem; and they R there.
1Kgs 11:16 Joab and all Israel R there six months, until
22:46 male cult prostitutes who R in the days of
2Kgs 10:11 Jehu slew all that R of the house of
10:17 he slew all that R to Ahab in Samaria,
11:3 not slain; and he R with her six years,
13:6 and the Asherah also R in Samaria.)
24:14 and the smiths; none R, except the poorest people
25:22 over the people who R in the land of
1Chr 13:14 the ark of God R with the household of
20:1 But David R at Jerusalem.
2Chr 14:13 Ethiopians fell until none R alive; for they were
22:12 slay him; and he R with them six years,
Ezra 8:32 Jerusalem, and there we R three days.
Neh 8:7 law, while the people R in their places.
11:1 city, while nine tenths R in the other towns.
Jud 3:10 Geba and Scythopolis, and R for a whole month
7:5 on their towers they R on guard all that
12:7 And she R in the camp for three days,
15:7 took possession of what R, and the villages and
16:20 three months, and Judith R with them.
16:21 went to Bethulia, and R on her estate, and
16:22 marry her, but she R a widow all the
Eccl 2:9 Jerusalem; also my wisdom R with me.
Sir 46:9 gave Caleb strength, which R with him to old
Jer 34:7 were the only fortified cities of Judah that R
37:10 against you, and there R of them only wounded
37:16 the dungeon cells, and R there many days,
37:21 So Jeremiah R in the court of the guard.
38:13 And Jeremiah R in the court of the guard.
38:28 And Jeremiah R in the court of the guard
39:9 had deserted to him, and the people who R
Ezek 17:6 him, and its roots R where it stood.
Dan 2:49 of Babylon; but Daniel R at the king's court.
1Mac 10:47 to them, and they R his allies all his
13:11 out its occupants and R there.
2Mac 4:50 of those in power, R in office, growing in
Mt 2:15 departed to Egypt, and R there until the death
11:23 Sodom, it would have R until this day.
Lk 1:22 signs to them and R dumb.
1:56 And Mary R with her about three months, and
Jn 1:32 from heaven, and it R on him.
3:22 of Judea; there he R with them and baptized.
6:22 day the people who R on the other side
7:9 So saying, he R in Galilee.
10:40 where John at first baptized, and there he R
Acts 5:4 While it R unsold, did it not remain your
12:19 Judea to Caesarea, and R there.
14:3 So they R for a long time, speaking boldly
14:28 And they R no little time with the disciples.
15:34 But Paul and Barnabas R in Antioch, teaching and
16:12 We R in this city some days;
17:14 but Silas and Timothy R there.
27:41 the bow stuck and R immovable, and the stern
Gal 1:18 to visit Cephas, and R with him fifteen days.
2Tim 4:20 Erastus R at Corinth; Trophimus I left ill at

REMAINEST

Heb 1:11 will perish, but thou R; they will all grow

REMAINING (22)

Ex 28:10 the names of the R six on the other
Num 31:32 Now the booty R of the spoil that the
Deut 2:34 children; we left none R;
32:36 and there is none R, bond or free.
Josh 10:28 it, he left none R; and he did to
10:30 it; he left none R in it; and he
10:33 him and his people, until he left none R
10:37 it; he left none R, as he had done
10:39 it; he left none R; as he had done
10:40 kings; he left none R, but utterly destroyed all
11:8 and they smote them, until they left none R
2Kgs 7:13 take five of the R horses, seeing that those
10:11 and his priests, until he left him none R
Jud 14:10 the house of Israel, R so to this day.
Wis 7:27 all things, and while R in herself, she renews
Ezek 39:14 continually and bury those R upon the face of
39:28 leave none of them R among the nations any
1Mac 3:37 the king took the R half of his troops
8:11 The R kingdoms and islands, as many as ever
12:45 other strongholds and the R troops and all the
2Mac 8:14 Others sold all their R property, and at the
Jn 19:31 prevent the bodies from R on the cross on

REMAINS (53)

Gen	8:22	While the earth R, seedtime and harvest, cold and
Ex	12:10	the morning, anything that R until the morning you
	26:12	And the part that R of the curtains of
	26:12	the half curtain that R, shall hang over the
	26:13	other side, of what R in the length of
Lev	7:16	on the morrow what R of it shall be
	7:17	be eaten, but what R of the flesh of
	8:32	eat it'; and what R of the flesh and
	10:12	the cereal offering that R of the offerings by
	13:23	But if the spot R in one place and
	13:28	But if the spot R in one place and
	14:17	of the oil that R in his hand the
Josh	7:26	heap of stones that R to this day; then
	13:1	in years, and there R yet very much land
	13:2	the land that yet R: all the regions of
1Sam	16:11	And he said, "There R yet the youngest, but
2Sam	16:3	the king, "Behold, he R in Jerusalem; for he
2Kgs	6:31	the son of Shaphat R on his shoulders today."
Job	19:4	have erred, my error R with myself.
Ps	142:4	of me; no refuge R to me, no man
Prov	11:12	a man of understanding R silent.
	21:20	Precious treasure R in a wise man's dwelling, but
Eccl	1:4	comes, but the earth R for ever.
Wis	10:7	wickedness still R: a continually smoking wasteland,
	19:18	rhythm, while each note R the same.
Sir	16:11	a wonder if he R unpunished.
	21:23	but a cultivated man R outside.
	23:11	he offends, his sin R on him, and if
	27:4	is shaken, the refuse R; so a man's filth
	27:4	so a man's filth R in his thoughts.
Is	4:3	left in Zion and R in Jerusalem will be
	6:13	an oak, whose stump R standing when it is
	10:4	Nothing R but to crouch among the prisoners or
Jer	8:3	all the remnant that R of this evil family
	47:4	off from Tyre and Sidon every helper that R
	48:11	exile; so his taste R in him, and his
Ezek	9:8	thou destroy all that R of Israel in the
	19:14	fruit, so that there R in it no strong
	48:21	"What R on both sides of the holy portion
Dan	10:17	For now no strength R in me, and no
Zech	1:11	behold, all the earth R at rest.'
1Mac	13:30	built in Modein; it R to this day.
Jn	9:41	now that you say, 'We see,' your guilt R
	12:24	earth and dies, it R alone; but if it
	12:34	law that the Christ R for ever.
1Cor	7:40	is happier if she R as she is.
2Cor	3:14	covenant, that same veil R unlifted, because only
2Tim	2:13	we are faithless, he R faithful-- for he
Heb	4:1	of entering his rest R, let us fear lest
	4:6	Since therefore it R for some to enter it,
	4:9	So then, there R a sabbath rest for the
	10:26	truth, there no longer R a sacrifice for sins,
Rev	3:2	Awake, and strengthen what R and is on the

REMALIAH (13)

2Kgs	15:25	Pekah the son of R, his captain, conspired against
	15:27	Pekah the son of R began to reign over
	15:30	Pekah the son of R, and struck him down,
	15:32	Pekah the son of R, king of Israel, Jotham
	15:37	Pekah the son of R against Judah.
	16:1	Pekah the son of R, Ahaz the son of
	16:5	Pekah the son of R, king of Israel, came
2Chr	28:6	Pekah the son of R slew a hundred and
Is	7:1	Pekah the son of R the king of Israel
	7:4	of Rezin and Syria and the son of R
	7:5	and the son of R, has devised evil against
	7:9	the head of Samaria is the son of R
	8:6	and the son of R;

REMARKABLY

2Mac	3:26	also appeared to him, R strong, gloriously beautiful

REMEDY (2)

2Chr	36:16	rose against his people, till there was no R
Wis	2:1	and there is no R when a man comes

REMEMBER (202)

Gen	9:15	the clouds, I will R my covenant which is
	9:16	look upon it and R the everlasting covenant between
	31:50	man is with us, R, God is witness between
	40:14	But R me, when it is well with you,
	40:23	chief butler did not R Joseph, but forgot him.
	41:9	said to Pharaoh, "I R my faults today.
Ex	13:3	said to the people, R this day, in which
	20:8	R the sabbath day, to keep it holy.
	32:13	R Abraham, Isaac, and Israel, thy servants, to whom
Lev	26:42	iniquity; then I will R my covenant with Jacob,
	26:42	Jacob, and I will R my covenant with Isaac
	26:42	Abraham, and I will R the land.
	26:45	will for their sake R the covenant with their
Num	11:5	We R the fish we ate in Egypt for
	15:39	to look upon and R all the commandments of
	15:40	So you shall R and do all my commandments,
Deut	5:15	You shall R that you were a servant in
	7:18	them, but you shall R what the LORD your
	8:2	And you shall R all the way which the
	8:18	this wealth.' You shall R the LORD your God,
	9:7	R and do not forget how you provoked the
	9:27	R thy servants, Abraham, Isaac, and Jacob; do not
	15:15	You shall R that you were a slave in
	16:3	your life you may R the day when you
	16:12	You shall R that you were a slave in
	24:9	R what the LORD your God did to Miriam
	24:18	pledge; but you shall R that you were a
	24:22	You shall R that you were a slave in
	25:17	R what Amalek did to you on the way
	32:7	R the days of old, consider the years of
Josh	1:13	of Manasseh Joshua said, R the word which Moses
Judg	8:34	of Israel did not R the LORD their God,
	9:2	one rule over you?' R also that I am
	16:28	said, "O Lord GOD, R me, I pray thee,
1Sam	1:11	of thy maidservant, and R me, and not forget
	25:31	with my lord, then R your handmaid."
2Sam	19:19	hold me guilty or R how your servant did
2Kgs	9:25	Naboth the Jezreelite; for R, when you and I
	20:3	to the LORD, saying, R now, O LORD, I
1Chr	16:12	R the wonderful works that he has done, the
2Chr	6:42	R thy steadfast love for David thy servant."
	24:22	the king did not R the kindness which Jehoiada,
Neh	1:8	R the word which thou didst command thy servant
	4:14	R the Lord, who is great and terrible, and
	5:19	R for my good, O my God, all that
	6:14	R Tobiah and Sanballat, O my God, according to
	13:14	R me, O my God, concerning this, and wipe
	13:22	R this also in my favor, O my God,
	13:29	R them, O my God, because they have defiled
	13:31	R me, O my God, for good.
Tob	3:3	R me and look favorably upon me; do not
	4:4	R, my son, that she faced many dangers for
	4:5	R the Lord our God all your days, my
	4:12	R, my son, that Noah, Abraham, Isaac, and Jacob,
	4:19	"So, my son, R my commands, and do not
	6:15	him, "Do you not R the words with which
Jud	8:26	R what he did with Abraham, and how he
	13:19	of men, as they R the power of God.
Esth	10:5	For I R the dream that I had concerning
	14:12	R, O Lord; make thyself known in this time
Job	7:7	R that my life is a breath; my eye
	10:9	R that thou hast made me of clay; and
	11:16	your misery; you will R it as waters that
	14:13	a set time, and R me!
	36:24	R to extol his work, of which men have
Ps	20:3	May he R all your offerings, and regard with
	22:27	of the earth shall R and turn to the
	25:7	R not the sins of my youth, or my
	25:7	to thy steadfast love R me, for thy goodness'
	42:4	These things I R, as I pour out my
	42:6	within me, therefore I R thee from the land
	74:2	R thy congregation, which thou hast gotten of old,
	74:2	R Mount Zion, where thou hast dwelt.
	74:18	R this, O LORD, how the enemy scoffs, and
	74:22	God, plead thy cause; R how the impious scoff
	77:5	days of old, I R the years long ago.
	77:11	LORD; yea, I will R thy wonders of old.
	79:8	Do not R against us the iniquities of our
	88:5	those whom thou dost R no more, for they
	89:47	R, O Lord, what the measure of life is,
	89:50	R, O Lord, how thy servant is scorned; how
	103:18	keep his covenant and R to do his commandments.
	105:5	R the wonderful works that he has done, his
	106:4	R me, O LORD, when thou showest favor to
	106:7	works; they did not R the abundance of thy
	109:16	For he did not R to show kindness, but
	119:49	R thy word to thy servant, in which thou
	119:55	I R thy name in the night, O LORD,
	132:1	R, O LORD, in David's favor, all the hardships
	137:6	if I do not R you, if I do
	137:7	R, O LORD, against the Edomites the day of
	143:5	I R the days of old, I meditate on
Prov	31:7	forget their poverty, and R their misery no more.
Eccl	5:20	he will not much R the days of his

11:8 all; but let him R that the days of
12:1 R also your Creator in the days of your
Wis 2:4 and no one will R our works; our life
Sir 7:16 the crowd of sinners; R that wrath does not
7:28 R that through your parents you were born; and
7:36 In all you do, R the end of your
8:5 turning away from sin; R that we all deserve
8:7 over any one's death; R that we all must
9:12 what pleases the ungodly; R that they will not
14:12 R that death will not delay, and the decree
16:15 from on high will R me?
23:14 R your father and mother when you sit among
28:6 R the end of your life, and cease from
28:6 and cease from enmity, R destruction and death, and
28:7 R the commandments, and do not be angry with
28:7 angry with your neighbor; R the covenant of the
31:13 R that a greedy eye is a bad thing.
36:8 Hasten the day, and R the appointed time, and
38:22 R my doom, for yours is like it: yesterday
41:3 the sentence of death; R your former days and
Is 38:3 the LORD, and said, R now, O LORD, I
43:18 quenched like a wick: R not the former things,
43:25 and I will not R your sins.
44:21 R these things, O Jacob, and Israel, for you
46:8 R this and consider, recall it to mind, you
46:9 to mind, you transgressors, R the former things of
47:7 things to heart or R their end.
54:4 your widowhood you will R no more.
57:11 lied, and did not R me, did not give
64:5 works righteousness, those that R thee in thy ways.
64:9 angry, O LORD, and R not iniquity for ever.
Jer 2:2 says the LORD, I R the devotion of your
14:10 them, now he will R their iniquity and punish
14:21 dishonor thy glorious throne; R and do not break
15:15 O LORD, thou knowest; R me and visit me,
17:2 altars, while their children R their altars and their
18:20 R how I stood before thee to speak good
31:20 against him, I do R him still.
31:34 iniquity, and I will R their sin no more."
44:21 did not the LORD R it?
51:50 R the LORD from afar, and let Jerusalem come
Lam 3:19 R my affliction and my bitterness, the wormwood
5:1 R, O LORD, what has befallen us; behold, and
Bar 2:32 their exile, and will R my name,
2:33 deeds; for they will R the ways of their
3:5 R not the iniquities of our fathers, but in
3:5 but in this crisis R thy power and thy
4:14 neighbors of Zion come; R the capture of my
Ezek 6:9 you who escape will R me among the nations
16:22 harlotries you did not R the days of your
16:60 covenant, yet I will R my covenant with you
16:61 Then you will R your ways, and be ashamed
16:63 LORD, that you may R and be confounded, and
20:43 And there you shall R your ways and all
23:27 to the Egyptians or R them any more.
36:31 Then you will R your evil ways, and your
Hos 7:3 not consider that I R all their evil works.
8:13 Now he will R their iniquity, and punish their
9:9 of Gibe-ah: he will R their iniquity, he will
Amos 1:9 Edom, and did not R the covenant of brotherhood.
Mic 6:5 O my people, R what Balak king of Moab
Hab 3:2 it known; in wrath R mercy.
Zech 10:9 far countries they shall R me, and with their
Mal 4:4 R the law of my servant Moses, the statutes
1Mac 2:51 R the deeds of the fathers, which they did
4:9 R how our fathers were saved at the Red
4:10 will favor us and R his covenant with our
6:12 power.' But now I R the evils I did
7:38 fall by the sword; R their blasphemies, and let
10:5 us, for he will R all the wrongs which
12:11 We therefore R you constantly on every occasion,
12:11 right and proper to R brethren.
2Mac 1:2 you, and may he R his covenant with Abraham
8:4 to him, and to R also the lawless destruction
9:21 is in heaven, I R with affection your esteem
9:26 and beseech you to R the public and private
Mt 5:23 the altar, and there R that your brother has
16:9 Do you not R the five loaves of the
27:63 and said, "Sir, we R how that impostor said,
Mk 8:18 And do you not R
Lk 1:72 our fathers, and to R his holy covenant,
16:25 But Abraham said, 'Son, R that you in your
17:32 R Lot's wife.
23:41 And he said, "Jesus, R me when you come
24:6 R how he told you, while he was still
Jn 15:20 R the word that I said to you, 'A
16:4 hour comes you may R that I told you
Rom 11:18 If you do boast, R it is not you
1Cor 11:2 commend you because you R me in everything and
Gal 2:10 they would have us R the poor, which very
Eph 2:11 Therefore R that at one time you Gentiles in
2:12 flesh by hands-- R that you were at
Col 4:18 R my fetters.
1Thes 2:9 For you R our labor and toil, brethren; we
3:6 reported that you always R us kindly and long
2Thes 2:5 Do you not R that when I was still
2Tim 1:3 my fathers, when I R you constantly in my
1:4 As I R your tears, I long night and
2:8 R Jesus Christ, risen from the dead, descended from
Philem 1:4 God always when I R you in my prayers,
Heb 8:12 iniquities, and I will R their sins no more."
10:17 he adds, "I will R their sins and their
13:3 R those who are in prison, as though in
13:7 R your leaders, those who spoke to you the
2Pet 3:2 reminder; that you should R the predictions of the
Jude 1:17 But you must R, beloved, the predictions of the
Rev 2:5 R then from what you have fallen, repent and
3:3 R then what you received and heard; keep that,

REMEMBERED (70)

Gen 8:1 But God R Noah and all the beasts and
19:29 of the valley, God R Abraham, and sent Lot
30:22 Then God R Rachel, and God hearkened to her
42:9 And Joseph R the dreams which he had dreamed
Ex 2:24 groaning, and God R his covenant with Abraham,
3:15 I am to be R throughout all generations.
6:5 bondage and I have R my covenant.
20:24 my name to be R I will come to
Num 10:9 that you may be R before the LORD your
1Sam 1:19 wife, and the LORD R her;
Tob 1:12 eating it, because I R God with all my
2:6 Then I R the prophecy of Amos, how he
4:1 On that day Tobit R the money which he
8:2 As he went he R the words of Raphael,
Esth 2:1 Ahasuerus had abated, he R Vashti and what she
9:28 these days should be R and kept throughout every
10:12 And God R his people and vindicated his inheritance.
Job 24:20 name is no longer R; so wickedness is broken
Ps 78:35 They R that God was their rock, the Most
78:39 He R that they were but flesh, a wind
83:4 name of Israel be R no more!"
98:3 He has R his steadfast love and faithfulness to
105:42 For he R his holy promise, and Abraham his
106:45 He R for their sake his covenant, and relented
109:14 of his fathers be R before the LORD, and
111:4 wonderful works to be R; the LORD is gracious
112:6 moved; he will be R for ever.
136:23 It is he who R us in our low
137:1 and wept, when we R Zion.
Eccl 9:15 Yet no one R that poor man.
Sir 3:15 affliction it will be R in your favor; as
11:23 in the day of adversity, prosperity is not R
49:9 For God R his enemies with storm, and did
51:8 Then I R thy mercy, O Lord, and thy
Is 17:10 salvation, and have not R the Rock of your
23:16 melody, sing many songs, that you may be R
63:11 Then he R the days of old, of Moses
65:17 things shall not be R or come into mind.
Jer 3:16 to mind, or be R, or missed; it shall
11:19 that his name be R no more."
Lam 2:1 Israel; he has not R his footstool in the
Bar 4:27 for you will be R by him who brought
5:5 rejoicing that God has R them.
Ezek 3:20 done shall not be R; but his blood I
16:43 Because you have not R the days of your
18:22 has committed shall be R against him; for the
18:24 has done shall be R; for the treachery of
21:24 your guilt to be R, in that your transgressions
21:32 shall be no more R; for I the LORD
25:10 that it may be R no more among the
33:13 righteous deeds shall be R; but in the iniquity
33:16 has committed shall be R against him; he has
Dan 14:38 Daniel said, "Thou hast R me, O God, and
Jon 2:7 fainted within me, I R the LORD; and my
Zech 13:2 that they shall be R no more; and also
1Mac 5:4 He also R the wickedness of the sons of
9:38 And they R the blood of John their brother,
10:46 accept them, because they R the great wrongs which
Mt 26:75 And Peter R the saying of Jesus, "Before the
Mk 11:21 And Peter R and said to him, "Master, look!
14:72 And Peter R how Jesus had said to him,
Lk 22:59 And Peter R the word of the Lord, how

24:8 And they R his words,
Jn 2:17 His disciples R that it was written, "Zeal for
2:22 the dead, his disciples R that he had said
12:16 was glorified, then they R that this had been
Acts 10:31 your alms have been R before God.
11:16 And I R the word of the Lord, how
Rev 16:19 nations fell, and God R great Babylon, to make
18:5 heaven, and God has R her iniquities.

REMEMBERING (10)

Esth 4:8 R the days of your lowliness, when you were
Sir 38:20 sorrow; drive it away, R the end of life.
Ezek 23:19 she increased her harlotry, R the days of her
Dan 13:9 looking to Heaven or R righteous judgments.
2Mac 10:6 the feast of booths, R how not long before,
Acts 20:31 Therefore be alert, R that for three years I
20:35 must help the weak, R the words of the
Eph 1:16 give thanks for you, R you in my prayers,
Col 4:12 Jesus, greets you, always R you earnestly in his
1Thes 1:3 R before our God and Father your work of

REMEMBERS (4)

Ps 103:14 knows our frame; he R that we are dust.
Lam 1:7 Jerusalem R in the days of her affliction and
Jn 16:21 child, she no longer R the anguish, for joy
2Cor 7:15 to you, as he R the obedience of you

REMEMBRANCE (37)

Ex 17:14 utterly blot out the R of Amalek from under
28:12 ephod, as stones of R for the sons of
28:12 before the LORD upon his two shoulders for R
28:29 bring them to continual R before the LORD.
30:16 people of Israel to R before the LORD, so
39:7 to be stones of R for the sons of
Num 5:15 a cereal offering of R, bringing iniquity to
5:15 offering of remembrance, bringing iniquity to R
5:18 the cereal offering of R, which is the cereal
10:10 shall serve you for R before your God: I
Deut 25:19 shall blot out the R of Amalek from under
32:26 I will make the R of them cease from
2Sam 18:18 keep my name in R; he called the pillar
1Kgs 17:18 bring my sin to R, and to cause the
Esth 13:8 the Lord, calling to R all the works of
Ps 6:5 death there is no R of thee; in Sheol
34:16 to cut off the R of them from the
Eccl 1:11 There is no R of former things, nor will
1:11 will there be any R of later things yet
2:16 there is no enduring R, seeing that in the
Wis 5:14 it passes like the R of a guest who
8:13 and leave an everlasting R to those who come
Sir 24:19 For the R of me is sweeter than honey,
38:23 at rest, let his R cease, and be comforted
50:16 to be heard for R before the Most High.
Is 26:14 and wiped out all R of them.
43:26 Put me in R, let us argue together; set
62:6 put the LORD in R, take no rest,
Ezek 21:23 brings their guilt to R, that they may be
21:24 you have come to R, you shall be taken
Mal 3:16 and a book of R was written before him
Lk 1:54 his servant Israel, in R of his mercy,
22:19 Do this in R of me."
Jn 14:26 and bring to your R all that I have
1Cor 11:24 Do this in R of me."
11:25 you drink it, in R of me."
Phil 1:3 God in all my R of you,

REMETH

Josh 19:21 Rabbith, Kishion, Ebez, R, En-gannim, En-haddah,

REMIND (11)

Wis 12:2 who trespass, and dost R and warn them of
16:6 token of deliverance to R them of thy law's
16:11 To R them of thy oracles they were bitten,
1Cor 4:17 in the Lord, to R you of my ways
15:1 Now I would R you, brethren, in what terms
2Cor 10:7 is Christs, let him R himself that as he
2Tim 1:6 Hence I R you to rekindle the gift of
2:14 R them of this, and charge them before the
Tit 3:1 R them to be submissive to rulers and authorities,
2Pet 1:12 I intend always to R you of these things,
Jude 1:5 Now I desire to R you, though you were

REMINDED

2Tim 1:5 I am R of your sincere faith, a faith

REMINDER (13)

Num 16:40 altar, to be a R to the people of
Tob 12:12 prayed, I brought a R of your prayer before
Esth 16:23 it may be a R of destruction.
Wis 10:8 left for mankind a R of their folly, so
Sir 41:1 how bitter is the R of you to one
45:9 the temple as a R to the sons of
45:11 a jeweler, for a R, in engraved letters, according
Zech 6:14 the LORD as a R to Heldai, Tobijah, Jedaiah,
2Mac 6:17 said serve as a R; we must go on
Rom 15:15 boldly by way of R, because of the grace
Heb 10:3 sacrifices there is a R of sin year after
2Pet 1:13 you by way of R,
3:1 mind by way of R;

REMINDING

2Mac 15:9 and the prophets, and R them also of the

REMISS

Sir 4:29 speech, or sluggish and R in your deeds.

REMISSION

Esth 2:18 He also granted a R of taxes to the

REMISSIONS

1Mac 15:5 you all the tax R that the kings before

REMNANT (83)

Gen 45:7 preserve for you a R on earth, and to
Deut 3:11 was left of the R of the Rephaim; behold,
Josh 10:20 out, and when the R which remained of them
12:4 Bashan, one of the R of the Rephaim, who
13:12 was left of the R of the Rephaim); these
23:12 back, and join the R of these nations left
Judg 5:13 Then down marched the R of the noble; the
2Sam 14:7 husband neither name nor R upon the face of
21:2 Israel, but of the R of the Amorites; although
1Kgs 22:46 And the R of the male cult prostitutes who
2Kgs 19:4 your prayer for the R that is left."
19:30 And the surviving R of the house of Judah
19:31 shall go forth a R, and out of Mount
21:14 will cast off the R of my heritage, and
1Chr 4:43 and they destroyed the R of the Amalekites that
2Chr 30:6 turn again to the R of you who have
34:9 and from all the R of Israel and from
Ezra 9:8 to leave us a R, and to give us
9:13 given us such a R as this,
9:14 there should be no R, nor any to escape?
9:15 we are left a R that has escaped, as
Wis 16:3 might lose the least R of appetite because of
Sir 44:18 in exchange; therefore a R was left to the
47:22 so he gave a R to Jacob, and to
Is 10:19 The R of the trees of his forest will
10:20 In that day the R of Israel and the
10:21 A R will return, the remnant of Jacob, to
10:21 remnant will return, the R of Jacob, to the
10:22 the sea, only a R of them will return.
11:11 time to recover the R which is left of
11:16 from Assyria for the R which is left of
14:22 from Babylon name and R, offspring and posterity,
14:30 with famine, and your R I will slay.
15:9 who escape, for the R of the land.
17:3 from Damascus; and the R of Syria will be
28:5 of beauty, to the R of his people;
37:4 your prayer for the R that is left.'"
37:31 And the surviving R of the house of Judah
37:32 shall go forth a R, and out of Mount
46:3 of Jacob, all the R of the house of
Jer 6:9 as a vine the R of Israel; like a
8:3 life by all the R that remains of this
23:3 I will gather the R of my flock out
24:8 Judah, his princes, the R of Jerusalem who remain
25:20 Gaza, Ekron, and the R of Ashdod);
31:7 saved his people, the R of Israel.'
40:11 Babylon had left a R in Judah and had
40:15 be scattered, and the R of Judah would perish?"
42:2 us, for all this R (for we are left
42:15 of the LORD, O R of Judah.
42:17 they shall have no R or survivor from the
42:19 said to you, O R of Judah, 'Do not
43:5 forces took all the R of Judah who had
44:7 from the midst of Judah, leaving you no R
44:12 I will take the R of Judah who have
44:14 that none of the R of Judah who have
44:28 number; and all the R of Judah, who came
47:4 destroying the Philistines, the R of the coastland of

47:5 O R of the Anakim, how long will you
50:20 will pardon those whom I leave as a R
Ezek 11:13 full end of the R of Israel?"
Amos 1:8 against Ekron; and the R of the Philistines shall
5:15 be gracious to the R of Joseph.
9:12 they may possess the R of Edom and all
Mic 2:12 I will gather the R of Israel; I will
4:7 I will make the R; and those who were
5:7 Then the R of Jacob shall be in the
5:8 And the R of Jacob shall be among the
7:18 over transgression for the R of his inheritance?
Hab 2:8 many nations, all the R of the peoples shall
Zeph 1:4 from this place the R of Baal and the
2:7 the possession of the R of the house of
2:9 The R of my people shall plunder them, and
Hag 1:12 priest, with all the R of the people, obeyed
1:14 spirit of all the R of the people; and
2:2 and to all the R of the people, and
Zech 8:6 the sight of the R of this people in
8:11 not deal with the R of this people as
8:12 I will cause the R of this people to
9:7 too shall be a R for our God; it
1Mac 3:35 of Israel and the R of Jerusalem; he was
Rom 9:27 the sea, only a R of them will be
11:5 time there is a R, chosen by grace.

REMONSTRATED (2)
Neh 13:11 So I R with the officials and said, "Why
13:17 Then I R with the nobles of Judah and

REMORSE
Sir 20:20 poverty, so when he rests he feels no R

REMOTE (2)
Judg 19:1 was sojourning in the R parts of the hill
19:18 in Judah to the R parts of the hill

REMOTEST (2)
Tob 8:3 he fled to the R parts of Egypt, and
Is 37:24 I came to its R height, its densest forest.

REMOVAL (5)
Num 19:9 for impurity, for the R of sin.
Is 27:9 full fruit of the R of his sin: when
2Mac 3:7 commands to effect the R of the aforesaid money.
Heb 12:27 indicates the R of what is shaken, as of
1Pet 3:21 you, not as a R of dirt from the

REMOVE (54)
Gen 48:17 his father's hand, to R it from Ephraim's head
Ex 10:17 your God only to R this death from me."
Lev 4:31 its fat he shall R, as the fat is
4:35 its fat he shall R as the fat of
26:6 afraid; and I will R evil beasts from the
Deut 19:14 possess, you shall not R your neighbor's landmark,
Judg 9:29 then I would R Abimelech.
1Kgs 20:24 And do this: R the kings, each from his
2Kgs 23:27 LORD said, "I will R Judah also out of
24:3 of the LORD, to R them out of his
2Chr 33:8 I will no more R the foot of Israel
Job 22:23 humble yourself, if you R unrighteousness far from
24:2 Men R landmarks; they seize flocks and pasture
Ps 39:10 R thy stroke from me; I am spent by
89:33 but I will not R from him my steadfast
103:12 so far does he R our transgressions from us.
Prov 22:28 R not the ancient landmark which your fathers have
23:10 Do not R an ancient landmark or enter the
30:8 me before I die: R far from me falsehood
Eccl 11:10 R vexation from your mind, and put away pain
Sir 7:6 you be unable to R iniquity, lest you be
23:5 me haughty eyes, and R from me evil desire.
30:23 comfort your heart, and R sorrow far from you,
47:24 many, so as to R them from their land.
Is 1:16 yourselves; make yourselves clean; R the evil of your
1:25 as with lye and R all your alloy.
5:5 I will R its hedge, and it shall be
57:14 up, prepare the way, R every obstruction from my
Jer 4:1 If you R your abominations from my presence, and
4:4 yourselves to the LORD, R the foreskin of your
28:16 LORD: 'Behold, I will R you from the face
32:31 so that I will R it from my sight
Bar 2:35 I will never again R my people Israel from
Ezek 11:18 come there, they will R from it all its
21:26 says the Lord GOD: R the turban, and take
26:16 from their thrones, and R their robes, and strip
Hos 2:17 Baal.' For I will R the names of the
5:10 become like those who R the landmark; upon them
11:7 yoke, and none shall R it.
Joel 2:20 "I will R the northerner far from you, and
Mic 2:3 from which you cannot R your necks; and you
Zeph 3:11 for then I will R from your midst your
3:18 "I will R disaster from you, so that you
Zech 3:4 were standing before him, R the filthy garments
3:9 hosts, and I will R the guilt of this
13:2 and also I will R from the land the
1Mac 11:41 the request that he R the troops of the
11:63 large army, intending to R him from office.
Mk 14:36 are possible to thee; R this cup from me;
Lk 22:42 if thou art willing, R this cup from me;
Acts 7:43 worship; and I will R you beyond Babylon.'
1Cor 7:18 him not seek to R the marks of circumcision.
13:2 faith, so as to R mountains, but have not
Rev 2:5 come to you and R your lampstand from its

REMOVED (62)
Gen 8:13 the earth; and Noah R the covering of the
12:8 Thence he R to the mountain on the east
30:35 But that day Laban R the he-goats that were
48:12 Then Joseph R them from his knees, and he
Ex 8:31 as Moses asked, and R the swarms of flies
Lev 4:31 as the fat is R from the peace offerings,
4:35 of the lamb is R from the sacrifice of
Num 12:10 and when the cloud R from over the tent,
14:9 us; their protection is R from them, and the
Deut 26:13 your God, 'I have R the sacred portion out
26:14 I was mourning, or R any of it while
1Sam 18:13 So Saul R him from his presence, and made
21:6 the Presence, which is R from before the LORD,
1Kgs 15:12 of the land, and R all the idols that
15:13 He also R Maacah his mother from being queen
2Kgs 14:4 high places were not R; the people still sacrificed
15:35 high places were not R; the people still sacrificed
16:14 before the LORD he R from the front of
16:17 of the stands, and R the laver from them,
16:18 for the king he R from the house of
17:18 angry with Israel, and R them out of his
17:23 them, until the LORD R Israel out of his
18:4 He R the high places, and broke the pillars,
18:22 and altars Hezekiah has R, saying to Judah and
23:11 And he R the horses that the kings of
23:19 LORD to anger, Josiah R; he did to them
23:27 sight, as I have R Israel, and I will
2Chr 15:16 his mother, King Asa R from being queen mother
30:14 set to work and R the altars that were
Tob 2:4 I sprang up and R the body to a
Jud 10:3 feast days; and she R the sackcloth which she
Job 14:18 and the rock is R from its place;
18:4 or the rock be R out of its place?
Ps 66:20 rejected my prayer or R his steadfast love from
89:44 Thou hast R the scepter from his hand, and
Prov 10:30 righteous will never be R, but the wicked will
Sir 10:17 He has R some of them and destroyed them,
Is 10:13 understanding; I have R the boundaries of peoples,
27:8 contend with them; he R them with his fierce
36:7 and altars Hezekiah has R, saying to Judah and
38:12 is plucked up and R from me like a
54:10 and the hills be R, but my steadfast love
54:10 peace shall not be R, says the LORD, who
Jer 6:29 refining goes on, for the wicked are not R
27:10 that you will be R far from your land,
Ezek 11:16 Lord GOD: Though I R them far-off among the
16:50 before me; therefore I R them, when I saw
Jon 3:6 arose from his throne, R his robe, and covered
1Mac 1:15 to Gentile custom, and R the marks of circumcision,
4:43 cleansed the sanctuary and R the defiled stones to
4:58 people, and the reproach of the Gentiles was R
11:66 He R them from there, took possession of the
13:41 of the Gentiles was R from Israel,
13:51 had been crushed and R from Israel.
14:7 the citadel, and he R its uncleanness from it;
Mk 2:4 of the crowd, they R the roof above him;
Acts 7:4 his father died, God R him from there into
13:22 And when he had R him, he raised up
1Cor 5:2 has done this be R from among you.
2Cor 3:16 man turns to the Lord the veil is R
Gal 5:11 the stumbling block of the cross has been R
Rev 6:14 mountain and island was R from its place.

REMOVES (6)
Deut 27:17 "Cursed be he who R his neighbor's landmark.' And
Job 9:5 succeeded?– he who R mountains, and they know
Sir 31:1 and anxiety about it R sleep.

Is 6:12 desolate, and the LORD R men far away, and
Dan 2:21 times and seasons; he R kings and sets up
Mic 2:4 my people; how he R it from me!

REMOVING (2)

Gen 30:32 all your flock today, R from it every speckled
Joel 3:6 Jerusalem to the Greeks, R them far from their

REND (11)

Lev 10:6 loose, and do not R your clothes, lest you
21:10 head hang loose, nor R his clothes;
2Sam 3:31 who were with him, R your clothes, and gird
Ps 7:2 like a lion they R me, dragging me away,
50:22 forget God, lest I R, and there be none
Eccl 3:7 away; a time to R, and a time to
Is 64:1 O that thou wouldst R the heavens and come
Jer 36:24 afraid, nor did they R their garments.
Hos 5:14 I, even I, will R and go away, I
13:8 a wild beast would R them.
Joel 2:13 and with mourning; and R your hearts and not

RENDER (26)

Num 18:9 of theirs, which they R to me, shall be
Josh 7:19 God of Israel, and R praise to him; and
1Kgs 3:28 was in him, to R justice.
8:39 forgive, and act, and R to each whose heart
2Chr 6:30 place, and forgive, and R to each whose heart
Tob 3:2 truth, and thou dost R true and righteous judgment
Esth 16:8 will take care to R our kingdom quiet and
Ps 28:4 work of their hands; R them their due reward.
38:20 Those who R me evil for good are my
56:12 O God; I will R thank offerings to thee.
72:10 and of the isles R him tribute, may the
94:2 judge of the earth; R to the proud their
116:12 What shall I R to the LORD for all
Is 59:18 the coastlands he will R requital.
66:15 like the stormwind, to R his anger in fury,
Hos 14:2 good and we will R the fruit of our
Zech 7:9 the LORD of hosts, R true judgments, show kindness
8:16 truth to one another, R in your gates judgments
Mt 12:36 of judgment men will R account for every careless
22:21 he said to them, R therefore to Caesar the
Mk 12:17 Jesus said to them, R to Caesar the things
Lk 20:25 said to them, "Then R to Caesar the things
Rom 2:6 For he will R to every man according to
1Thes 3:9 what thanksgiving can we R to God for you,
3Jn 1:5 you do when you R any service to the
Rev 18:6 R to her as she herself has rendered, and

RENDERED (4)

1Kgs 3:28 which the king had R; and they stood in
2Mac 9:26 public and private services R to you and to
2Tim 1:18 all the service he R at Ephesus.
Rev 18:6 as she herself has R, and repay her double

RENDERING (5)

Sir 42:2 his covenant, and of R judgment to acquit the
Is 66:6 voice of the LORD, R recompense to his enemies!
Jer 51:6 the requital he is R her.
2Cor 9:12 to God; for the R of this service not
Eph 6:7 God from the heart, R service with a good

RENDERS (2)

1Pet 4:11 oracles of God; whoever R service, as one who
4:11 service, as one who R it by the strength

RENEW (14)

1Sam 11:14 to Gilgal and there R the kingdom."
Job 10:17 against me; thou dost R thy witnesses against me,
Is 40:31 for the LORD shall R their strength, they shall
41:1 coastlands; let the peoples R their strength; let them
Lam 5:21 R our days as of old!
Hab 3:2 midst of the years R it; in the midst
Zeph 3:17 with gladness, he will R you in his love;
1Mac 12:1 Rome to confirm and R the friendship with them.
12:3 have sent us to R the former friendship and
12:10 undertaken to send to R our brotherhood and
12:16 them to Rome to R our former friendship and
14:18 on bronze tablets to R with him the friendship
14:22 come to us to R their friendship with us.
15:17 friends and allies to R our ancient friendship and

RENEWAL (5)

Sir 22:19 not despair, for a R of friendship is possible.
1Mac 12:17 from us concerning the R of our brotherhood.
2Mac 7:9 up to an everlasting R of life, because we

Rom 12:2 be transformed by the R of your mind, that
Tit 3:5 washing of regeneration and R in the Holy Spirit,

RENEWED (6)

Ps 90:5 like grass which is R in the morning:
90:6 it flourishes and is R; in the evening it
103:5 that your youth is R like the eagles.
2Cor 4:16 inner nature is being R every day.
Eph 4:23 deceitful lusts, and be R in the spirit of
Col 3:10 nature, which is being R in knowledge after the

RENEWEST

Ps 104:30 are created; and thou R the face of the

RENEWS

Wis 7:27 remaining in herself, she R all things; in every

RENOUNCE (3)

Ps 10:13 Why does the wicked R God, and say in
Lk 14:33 of you does not R all that he has
Tit 2:12 men, training us to R irreligion and worldly passions,

RENOUNCED (2)

Ps 89:39 Thou hast R the covenant with thy servant; thou
2Cor 4:2 We have R disgraceful, underhanded ways; we

RENOUNCES

Ps 10:3 for gain curses and R the LORD.

RENOWN (8)

Gen 6:4 men that were of old, the men of R
Ps 135:13 endures for ever, thy R, O LORD, throughout all
Wis 8:18 her company, understanding, and R in sharing her
Jer 48:2 and broken down; the R of Moab is no
Ezek 16:14 And your R went forth among the nations because
16:15 harlot because of your R, and lavished your harlotries
Zeph 3:19 shame into praise and R in all the earth.
1Mac 14:10 of defense, till his R spread to the ends

RENOWNED (11)

Ruth 4:11 in Ephrathah and be R in Bethlehem;
4:14 may his name be R in Israel!
2Sam 23:19 He was the most R of the thirty, and
23:23 He was R among the thirty, but he did
1Chr 11:21 He was the most R of the thirty, and
11:25 He was R among the thirty, but he did
Jud 11:23 Nebuchadnezzar and be R throughout the whole
Wis 3:15 of good labors is R, and the root of
Sir 44:3 kingdoms, and were men R for their power, giving
Ezek 26:17 the seas, O city R, that was mighty on
1Mac 3:9 He was R to the ends of the earth;

RENT (47)

Gen 37:29 in the pit, he R his clothes
37:34 Then Jacob R his garments, and put sackcloth upon
44:13 Then they R their clothes, and every man loaded
Num 14:6 spied out the land, R their clothes,
Josh 7:6 Then Joshua R his clothes, and fell to the
Judg 11:35 he saw her, he R his clothes, and said,
1Sam 4:12 day, with his clothes R and with earth upon
2Sam 1:2 camp, with his clothes R and earth upon his
1:11 of his clothes, and R them; and so did
13:19 on her head, and R the long robe which
13:31 the king arose, and R his garments, and lay
13:31 who were standing by R their garments.
15:32 him with his coat R and earth upon his
1Kgs 19:11 great and strong wind R the mountains, and broke
21:27 heard those words, he R his clothes, and put
2Kgs 2:12 his own clothes and R them in two pieces.
5:7 read the letter, he R his clothes and said,
5:8 king of Israel had R his clothes, he sent
5:8 saying, "Why have you R your clothes?
6:30 of the woman he R his clothes--now he
11:14 And Athaliah R her clothes, and cried, "Treason!
18:37 Hezekiah with their clothes R, and told him the
19:1 Hezekiah heard it, he R his clothes, and covered
22:11 of the law, he R his clothes.
22:19 curse, and you have R your clothes and wept
2Chr 23:13 And Athaliah R her clothes, and cried, "Treason!
34:19 of the law he R his clothes.
34:27 before me, and have R your clothes and wept
Ezra 9:3 I heard this, I R my garments and my
9:5 garments and my mantle R, and fell upon my
Jud 14:16 groaned and shouted, and R his garments.
14:19 army heard this, they R their tunics and were
Esth 4:1 had been done, Mordecai R his clothes and put

R

Job 1:20 Then Job arose, and R his robe, and shaved
2:12 and wept; and they R their robes and sprinkled
26:8 the cloud is not R under them.
Ps 60:2 to quake, thou hast R it open; repair its
Is 24:19 broken, the earth is R asunder, the earth is
36:22 Hezekiah with their clothes R, and told him the
37:1 Hezekiah heard it, he R his clothes, and covered
Bar 6:31 sit with their clothes R, their heads and beards
1Mac 2:14 Mattathias and his sons R their clothes, put on
3:47 on their heads, and R their clothes.
4:39 Then they R their clothes, and mourned with great
5:14 with their garments R, came from Galilee and
11:71 Jonathan R his garments and put dust on his
13:45 wall with their clothes R, and they cried out

REPAID (8)

1Sam 24:17 I; for you have R me good, whereas I
24:17 good, whereas I have R you evil.
Tob 14:10 and with what he R him.
Sir 12:2 and you will be R – if not by
2Mac 4:38 The Lord thus R him with the punishment he
Lk 14:12 also invite you in return, and you be R
14:14 You will be R at the resurrection of the
Rom 11:35 a gift to him that he might be R

REPAIR (12)

2Kgs 12:5 acquaintance; and let them R the house wherever
12:7 it over for the R of the house."
12:8 that they should not R the house.
22:6 and quarried stone to R the house.
2Chr 24:5 all Israel money to R the house of your
24:12 iron and bronze to R the house of the
34:8 Joahaz, the recorder, to R the house of the
Ezra 9:9 of our God, to R its ruins, and to
Ps 60:2 hast rent it open; R its breaches, for it
Is 61:4 former devastations; they shall R the ruined cities,
Amos 9:11 that is fallen and R its breaches, and raise
1Mac 3:43 one another, "Let us R the destruction of our

REPAIRED (44)

1Kgs 18:30 And he R the altar of the LORD that
1Chr 11:8 complete circuit; and Joab R the rest of the
2Chr 15:8 of Ephraim, and he R the altar of the
29:3 of the LORD, and R them.
Neh 3:4 Meremoth the son of Uriah, son of Hakkoz R
3:4 the son of Berechiah, son of Meshezabel R
3:4 next to them Zadok the son of Baana R
3:5 to them the Tekoites R; but their nobles did
3:6 the son of Besodeiah R the Old Gate; they
3:7 And next to them R Melatiah the Gibeonite and
3:8 to them Uzziel the son of Harhaiah, goldsmiths, R
3:8 of the perfumers, R; and they restored Jerusalem
3:9 Hur, ruler of half the district of Jerusalem, R
3:10 the son of Harumaph R opposite his house; and
3:10 next to him Hattush the son of Hashabneiah R
3:11 the son of Pahath-moab R another section and the
3:12 the district of Jerusalem, R, he and his daughters.
3:13 the inhabitants of Zanoah R the Valley Gate; they
3:13 and its bars, and R a thousand cubits of
3:14 the district of Beth-haccherem, R the Dung Gate; he
3:15 the district of Mizpah, R the Fountain Gate; he
3:16 the district of Bethzur, R to a point opposite
3:17 After him the Levites R: Rehum the son of
3:17 the district of Keilah, R for his district.
3:18 After him their brethren R: Bavvai the son of
3:19 Jeshua, ruler of Mizpah, R another section opposite
3:20 the son of Zabbai R another section from the
3:21 Uriah, son of Hakkoz R another section from the
3:22 him the priests, the men of the Plain, R
3:23 them Benjamin and Hasshub R opposite their house.
3:23 Ma-aseiah, son of Ananiah R beside his own house.
3:24 the son of Henadad R another section, from the
3:25 the son of Uzai R opposite the Angle and
3:26 servants living on Ophel R to a point opposite
3:27 After him the Tekoites R another section opposite
3:28 Horse Gate the priests R, each one opposite his
3:29 the son of Immer R opposite his own house.
3:29 of Shecaniah, the keeper of the East Gate, R
3:30 sixth son of Zalaph R another section.
3:30 the son of Berechiah R opposite his chamber.
3:31 one of the goldsmiths, R as far as the
3:32 the Sheep Gate the goldsmiths and the merchants R
Sir 50:1 who in his life R the house, and in
1Mac 12:37 had fallen, and he R the section called Chaphenatha.

REPAIRER

Is 58:12 shall be called the R of the breach, the

REPAIRING (7)

2Kgs 12:7 "Why are you not R the house?
12:14 the workmen who were R the house of the
22:5 house of the LORD, R the house,
2Chr 24:13 work labored, and the R went forward in their
34:10 LORD gave it for R and restoring the house.
Ezra 4:12 finishing the walls and R the foundations.
Neh 4:7 Ashdodites heard that the R of the walls of

REPAIRS (4)

2Kgs 12:5 wherever any need of R is discovered."
12:6 priests had made no R on the house.
12:12 quarried stone for making R on the house of
12:12 any outlay upon the R of the house.

REPAY (26)

2Sam 16:12 that the LORD will R me with good for
Job 41:11 me, that I should R him?
Prov 19:17 LORD, and he will R him for his deed.
20:22 not say, "I will R evil"; wait for the
Sir 4:31 receive, but withdrawn when it is time to R
29:2 need; and in turn, R your neighbor promptly.
29:6 his enemy; he will R him with curses and
29:6 instead of glory will R him with dishonor.
30:6 enemies, and one to R the kindness of his
35:11 repays, and he will R you sevenfold.
Is 59:18 deeds, so will he R, wrath to his adversaries,
65:6 silent, but I will R, yea, I will repay
65:6 repay, yea, I will R into their bosom
Bar 6:34 not be able to R it.
1Mac 10:27 us, and we will R you with good for
11:53 Jonathan and did not R the favors which Jonathan
Mt 16:27 and then he will R every man for what
Lk 10:35 you spend, I will R you when I come
14:14 blessed, because they cannot R you.
Rom 12:17 R no one evil for evil, but take thought
12:19 is mine, I will R, says the Lord."
2Thes 1:6 deems it just to R with affliction those who
Philem 1:19 own hand, I will R it--to say nothing
Heb 10:30 him who said, "Vengeance is mine, I will R
Rev 18:6 herself has rendered, and R her double for her
22:12 bringing my recompense, to R every one for what

REPAYMENT (2)

Tob 14:10 and the other received R as he himself went
Sir 29:5 at the time for R he will delay, and

REPAYS (4)

Sir 35:11 is the one who R, and he will repay
35:18 of the unmerciful and R vengeance on the nations;
35:19 the unrighteous; till he R the man according to
1Thes 5:15 that none of you R evil for evil, but

REPEAT (4)

Judg 5:11 watering places, there they R the triumphs of the
Sir 7:14 of the elders, nor R yourself in your prayer.
19:7 Never R a conversation, and you will lose nothing
2Cor 11:16 I R, let no one think me foolish; but

REPEATED (3)

1Sam 8:21 of the people, he R them in the ears
17:31 spoke were heard, they R them before Saul; and
2Kgs 4:43 So he R, "Give them to the men, that

REPEATEDLY (4)

Eccl 7:28 my mind has sought R, but I have not
Heb 9:25 it to offer himself R, as the high priest
9:26 have had to suffer R since the foundation of
10:11 at his service, offering R the same sacrifices, which

REPEATING (2)

Sir 41:23 making a gift; of R and telling what you
Ezek 18:2 do you mean by R this proverb concerning the

REPEATS (2)

Prov 17:9 love, but he who R a matter alienates a
26:11 is a fool that R his folly.

REPEL

Wis 5:17 arm all creation to R his enemies;

REPENT (60)

Ex 13:17 said, "Lest the people R when they see war,

R

32:12 thy fierce wrath, and R of this evil against
Num 23:19 or a son of man, that he should R
1Sam 15:11 came to Samuel: "I R that I have made
15:29 will not lie or R; for he is not
15:29 he is not a man, that he should R
1Kgs 8:47 been carried captive, and R, and make supplication
8:48 and wickedly'; if they R with all their mind
2Chr 6:37 been carried captive, and R, and make supplication
6:38 and wickedly'; if they R with all their mind
Job 42:6 I despise myself, and R in dust and ashes."
Ps 7:12 a man does not R, God will whet his
Wis 11:23 thou dost overlook men's sins, that they may R
12:10 them a chance to R, though thou wast not
Sir 17:19 Yet to those who R he grants a return,
21:6 fears the Lord will R in his heart.
48:15 the people did not R, and they did not
Is 1:27 those in her who R, by righteousness.
Jer 5:3 faces harder than rock; they have refused to R
9:5 they commit iniquity and are too weary to R
18:8 its evil, I will R of the evil that
18:10 voice, then I will R of the good which
26:3 way, that I may R of the evil which
26:13 and the LORD will R of the evil which
26:19 did not the LORD R of the evil which
42:10 you up; for I R of the evil which
Ezek 14:6 says the Lord GOD: R and turn away from
18:30 R and turn from all your transgressions, lest iniquity
24:14 spare, I will not R; according to your ways
Joel 2:14 will not turn and R, and leave a blessing
Jon 3:9 knows, God may yet R and turn from his
Mt 3:2 the wilderness of Judea, R, for the kingdom of
4:17 began to preach, saying, R, for the kingdom of
11:20 works had been done, because they did not R
21:32 you did not afterward R and believe him.
Mk 1:15 God is at hand; R, and believe in the
6:12 they went out and preached that men should R
Lk 13:3 No; but unless you R you will all likewise
13:5 No; but unless you R you will all likewise
16:30 the dead, they will R
17:4 times, and says, 'I R you must forgive him."
Acts 2:38 Peter said to them, R, and be baptized every
3:19 R therefore, and turn again, that your sins may
8:22 R therefore of this wickedness of yours, and pray
17:30 all men everywhere to R,
26:20 Gentiles, that they should R and turn to God
2Tim 2:25 grant that they will R and come to know
Heb 12:17 found no chance to R, though he sought it
Rev 2:5 what you have fallen, R and do the works
2:5 remove your lampstand from its place, unless you R
2:16 R then.
2:21 gave her time to R, but she refuses to
2:21 but she refuses to R of her immorality.
2:22 great tribulation, unless they R of her doings;
3:3 what you received and heard; keep that, and R
3:19 I reprove and chasten; so be zealous and R
9:20 these plagues, did not R of the works of
9:21 walk; nor did they R of their murders or
16:9 and they did not R and give him glory.
16:11 sores, and did not R of their deeds.

REPENTANCE (22)

Wis 5:3 to one another in R, and in anguish of
12:19 hope, because thou givest R for sins.
Sir 44:17 was an example of R to all generations.
Mt 3:8 Bear fruit that befits R,
3:11 you with water for R, but he who is
Mk 1:4 preaching a baptism of R for the forgiveness of
Lk 3:3 preaching a baptism of R for the forgiveness of
3:8 Bear fruits that befit R, and do not begin
5:32 come to call the righteous, but sinners to R
15:7 over ninety-nine righteous persons who need no R
24:47 the dead, and that R and forgiveness of sins
Acts 5:31 and Savior, to give R to Israel and forgiveness
11:18 also God has granted R unto life."
13:24 preached a baptism of R to all the people
19:4 with the baptism of R, telling the people to
20:21 and to Greeks of R to God and of
26:20 to God and perform deeds worthy of their R
Rom 2:4 God's kindness is meant to lead you to R
2Cor 7:10 godly grief produces a R that leads to salvation
Heb 6:1 again a foundation of R from dead works and
6:4 to restore again to R those who have once
2Pet 3:9 any should perish, but that all should reach R

REPENTED (18)

Ex 32:14 And the LORD R of the evil which he
1Sam 15:35 And the LORD R that he had made Saul
2Sam 24:16 destroy it, the LORD R of the evil, and
1Chr 21:15 LORD saw, and he R of the evil; and
Ps 78:34 sought for him; they R and sought God earnestly.
Jer 31:19 had turned away I R; and after I was
34:15 You recently R and did what was right in
Amos 7:3 The LORD R concerning this; "It shall not be,"
7:6 The LORD R concerning this; "This also shall not
Jon 3:10 their evil way, God R of the evil which
Zech 1:6 So they R and said, As the LORD of
Mt 11:21 Sidon, they would have R long ago in sackcloth
12:41 condemn it; for they R at the preaching of
21:29 not'; but afterward he R and went.
27:3 he was condemned, he R and brought back the
Lk 10:13 Sidon, they would have R long ago, sitting in
11:32 condemn it; for they R at the preaching of
2Cor 12:21 before and have not R of the impurity, immorality,

REPENTEST

Jon 4:2 in steadfast love, and R of evil.

REPENTING

2Cor 7:9 you were grieved into R; for you felt a

REPENTS (5)

Jer 8:6 spoken aright; no man R of his wickedness, saying,
Joel 2:13 in steadfast love, and R of evil.
Lk 15:7 one sinner who R than over ninety-nine righteous
15:10 the angels of God over one sinner who R
17:3 him, and if he R, forgive him;

REPHA-EL

1Chr 26:7 sons of Shemaiah: Othni, R, Obed, and Elzabad,

REPHAH

1Chr 7:25 R was his son, Resheph his son, Telah his

REPHAIAH (5)

1Chr 3:21 and Jeshaiah, his son R, his son Arnan, his
4:42 their leaders Pelatiah, Neariah, R, and Uzziel, the
7:2 sons of Tola: Uzzi, R, Jeri-el, Jahmai, Ibsam, and
9:43 father of Bine-a; and R was his son, Ele-asah
Neh 3:9 Next to them R the son of Hur, ruler

REPHAIM (18)

Gen 14:5 came and subdued the R in Ashteroth-karnaim, the
15:20 Hittites, the Perizzites, the R,
Deut 2:11 are also known as R, but the Moabites call
2:20 as a land of R; Rephaim formerly lived there,
2:20 a land of Rephaim; R formerly lived there, but
3:11 the remnant of the R; behold, his bedstead was
3:13 of that Bashan is called the land of R
Josh 12:4 the remnant of the R, who dwelt at Ashtaroth
13:12 the remnant of the R; these Moses had defeated
15:8 of the valley of R;
17:15 the Perizzites and the R, since the hill country
18:16 of the valley of R; and it then goes
2Sam 5:18 come and spread out in the valley of R
5:22 again, and spread out in the valley of R
23:13 of Philistines was encamped in the valley of R
1Chr 11:15 of Philistines was encamped in the valley of R
14:9 and made a raid in the valley of R
Is 17:5 the ears of grain in the Valley of R

REPHAN

Acts 7:43 star of the god R, the figures which you

REPHIDIM (5)

Ex 17:1 LORD, and camped at R; but there was no
17:8 Then came Amalek and fought with Israel at R
19:2 they set out from R and came into the
Num 33:14 Alush, and encamped at R, where there was no
33:15 they set out from R, and encamped in the

REPLACE

Gen 42:25 with grain, and to R every man's money in

REPLACED (2)

Gen 43:18 the money, which was R in our sacks the
1Sam 21:6 the LORD, to be R by hot bread on

REPLANTED

Ezek 36:36 the ruined places, and R that which was desolate;

REPLENISH

Jer 31:25 weary soul, and every languishing soul I will R

REPLENISHED

Ezek	26:2	me; I shall be R, now that she is

REPLIED (39)

Gen	38:18	She R, "Your signet and your cord, and your
	38:23	And Judah R, "Let her keep the things as
	43:7	They R, "The man questioned us carefully about
	43:23	He R, "Rest assured, do not be afraid; your
Ruth	3:5	And she R, "All that you say I will
	3:18	She R, "Wait, my daughter, until you learn how
1Sam	20:3	But David R, "Your father knows well that I
1Kgs	2:31	The king R to him, "Do as he has
Neh	2:20	Then I R to them, "The God of heaven
Tob	2:14	Then she R to me, "Where are your charities
	5:6	The angel R, "I will go with you; I
	5:12	He R, "I am Azarias the son of the
	6:7	He R, "As for the heart and liver, if
	7:5	They R, "He is alive and in good health."
	10:9	Tobias R, "No, send me back to my father."
	12:2	He R, "Father, it would do me no harm
Jud	10:12	She R, "I am a daughter of the Hebrews,
	11:5	Judith R to him, "Accept the words of your
	12:4	Judith R, "As your soul lives, my lord, your
Dan	2:14	Then Daniel R with prudence and discretion to
1Mac	3:18	Judas R, "It is easy for many to be
	10:55	Ptolemy the king R and said, "Happy was the
2Mac	3:37	mission to Jerusalem, he R,
	7:8	He R in the language of his fathers, and
	15:5	he R, "And I am a sovereign also, on
Mt	12:47	But he R to the man who told him,
	16:16	Simon Peter R, "You are the Christ, the Son
	17:11	He R, "Elijah does come, and he is to
	20:13	scorching heat.' But he R to one of them,
	25:9	out.' But the wise R, 'Perhaps there will not
	25:12	to us.' But he R, 'Truly, I say to
Mk	3:33	And he R, "Who are my mother and my
	5:9	He R, "My name is Legion; for we are
Lk	10:30	Jesus R, "A man was going down from Jerusalem
Jn	7:52	They R, "Are you from Galilee too?
Acts	15:13	they finished speaking, James R, "Brethren, listen to
	21:39	Paul R, "I am a Jew, from Tarsus in
	24:9	him to speak, Paul R: "Realizing that for many
	25:4	Festus R that Paul was being kept at Caesarea,

REPORT (44)

Gen	37:2	Joseph brought an ill R of them to their
	45:16	When the R was heard in Pharaoh's house, "Joseph's
Ex	23:1	"You shall not utter a false R
Num	13:32	of Israel an evil R of the land which
	14:36	bringing up an evil R against the land,
	14:37	brought up an evil R of the land, died
Deut	2:25	who shall hear the R of you and shall
Josh	9:9	we have heard a R of him, and all
	22:33	And the R pleased the people of Israel; and
Judg	18:8	their brethren said to them, "What do you R
1Sam	2:24	it is no good R that I hear the
1Kgs	10:6	to the king, "The R was true which I
	10:7	and prosperity surpass the R which I heard.
1Chr	21:2	and bring me a R, that I may know
2Chr	9:5	to the king, "The R was true which I
	9:6	me; you surpass the R which I heard.
Ezra	5:5	stop them till a R should reach Darius and
	5:7	they sent him a R, in which was written
Neh	6:6	wish to become their king, according to this R
Tob	10:12	me hear a good R of you.
Jud	10:13	give him a true R; and I will show
Wis	1:9	ungodly man, and a R of his words will
Sir	19:8	or foe do not R it, and unless it
Is	23:5	When the R comes to Egypt, they will be
	23:5	in anguish over the R about Tyre.
Jer	6:24	We have heard the R of it, our hands
	36:16	to Baruch, "We must R all these words to
	50:43	of Babylon heard the R of them, and his
	51:46	not fearful at the R heard in the land,
	51:46	the land, when a R comes in one year
	51:46	year and afterward a R in another year, and
Ezek	24:26	come to you to R to you the news.
Hab	3:2	I have heard the R of thee, and thy
1Mac	5:14	and made a similar R;
	12:23	command that our envoys R to you accordingly."
	16:18	Then Ptolemy wrote a R about these things and
2Mac	3:34	been scourged by heaven, R to all men the
	4:39	of Menelaus, and when R of them had spread
Mt	9:26	And the R of this went through all that
Lk	4:14	into Galilee, and a R concerning him went out
	5:15	much the more the R went abroad concerning him;
	7:17	And this R concerning him spread through the whole
Jn	12:38	who has believed our R, and to whom has
1Thes	1:9	For they themselves R concerning us what a

REPORTED (43)

Ex	19:8	And Moses R the words of the people to
1Sam	11:4	Gibe-ah of Saul, they R the matter in the
1Kgs	20:17	out scouts, and they R to him, "Men are
2Kgs	9:18	the watchman R, saying, "The messenger reached
	9:20	Again the watchman R, "He reached them, but he
	22:9	to the king, and R to the king, "Your
2Chr	34:16	the king, and further R to the king, "All
Neh	6:1	Now when it was R to Sanballat and Tobiah
	6:6	was written, "It is R among the nations, and
	6:7	now it will be R to the king according
	6:19	in my presence, and R my words to him.
Tob	11:15	in rejoicing, and he R to his father the
Jud	10:18	for her arrival was R from tent to tent,
	11:8	skill, and it is R throughout the whole world
Esth	9:11	Susa the capital was R to the king.
Jer	36:20	the secretary; and they R all the words to
1Mac	2:31	And it was R to the king's officers, and
	4:26	who escaped went and R to Lysias all that
	5:38	the camp, and they R to him, "All the
	6:5	him in Persia and R that the armies which
	9:37	these things it was R to Jonathan and Simon
	11:21	to the king and R to him that Jonathan
	11:40	He also R to Imalkue what Demetrius had done
	12:26	and they returned and R to him that the
	15:32	He R to him the words of the king,
	15:36	to the king and R to him these words
	16:1	up from Gazara and R to Simon his father
	16:21	one ran ahead and R to John at Gazara
2Mac	1:20	And when they R to us that they had
	1:33	known, and it was R to the king of
	2:13	The same things are R in the records and
	3:6	He R to him that the treasury in Jerusalem
Mt	18:30	and they went and R to their lord all
Mk	2:1	some days, it was R that he was at
Lk	14:21	the servant came and R this to his master.
Acts	4:23	to their friends and R what the chief priests
	5:22	and they returned and R,
	16:36	And the jailer R the words to Paul, saying,
	16:38	The police R these words to the magistrates, and
	28:21	brethren coming here has R or spoken any evil
1Cor	1:11	For it has been R to me by Chloe's
	5:1	It is actually R that there is immorality among
1Thes	3:6	faith and love and R that you always remember

REPORTING

Acts	15:3	both Phoenicia and Samaria, R the conversion of the

REPORTS (5)

1Kgs	10:7	did not believe the R until I came and
2Chr	9:6	did not believe the R until I came and
1Mac	3:27	king Antiochus heard these R, he was greatly
Mk	5:27	She had heard the R about Jesus, and came
Lk	4:37	And R of him went out into every place

REPOSE

Is	28:12	weary; and this is R; yet they would not

REPRESENT

Ex	18:19	You shall R the people before God, and bring

REPRESENTATION

Acts	17:29	silver, or stone, a R by the art and

REPRESENTATIVES

2Mac	11:20	these men and my R to confer with you.

REPRESENTING

Num	1:44	Israel, twelve men, each R his fathers' house.

REPROACH (65)

Gen	30:23	has taken away my R;
Josh	5:9	have rolled away the R of Egypt from you."
Ruth	2:15	sheaves, and do not R her.
1Sam	17:26	and takes away the R from Israel?
Tob	3:4	us a byword of R in all the nations
	3:13	and that I hear R no more.
	3:15	and that I hear R no more."
Jud	8:22	an offense and a R in the eyes of
Job	19:3	times you have cast R upon me; are you
	27:6	my heart does not R me for any of
Ps	15:3	nor takes up a R against his neighbor;

R

R

REQUEST (22)
Judg 8:24 "Let me make a R of you; give me
2Sam 14:15 king will perform the R of his servant.
14:22 king has granted the R of his servant."
1Kgs 2:16 now I have one R to make of you;
2:20 "I have one small R to make of you;
2:20 to her, "Make your R, my mother; for I
Neh 2:4 said to me, "For what do you make R
Esth 5:3 What is your R
5:6 And what is your R
5:7 "My petition and my R is:
5:8 petition and fulfil my R, let the king and
7:2 And what is your R
7:3 at my petition, and my people at my R
9:12 And what further is your R
Job 6:8 I might have my R, and that God would
Ps 21:2 hast not withheld the R of his lips.
Jer 42:4 God according to your R, and whatever the LORD
Dan 2:49 Daniel made R of the king, and he appointed
1Mac 11:41 Demetrius the king the R that he remove the
13:34 the king with a R to grant relief to
13:35 favorable reply to this R, and wrote him a
2Mac 11:15 the king granted every R in behalf of the

REQUESTED
Judg 8:26 golden earrings that he R was one thousand seven

REQUESTING
2Mac 4:28 of the citadel kept R payment, for the collection

REQUESTS (2)
Phil 4:6 with thanksgiving let your R be made known to
1Jn 5:15 we have obtained the R made of him.

REQUIRE (22)
Gen 9:5 lifeblood I will surely R a reckoning; of every
9:5 every beast I will R it and of man;
9:5 man's brother I will R the life of man.
43:9 my hand you shall R him.
Deut 10:12 the LORD your God R of you, but to
18:19 name, I myself will R it of him.
23:21 your God will surely R it of you, and
2Sam 3:13 but one thing I R of you; that is,
4:11 shall I not now R his blood at your
1Chr 21:3 then should my lord R this?
Ezra 6:9 the priests at Jerusalem R -- let that be
Neh 5:12 will restore these and R nothing from them.
Bar 6:35 it, they will not R it.
Ezek 3:18 his blood I will R at your hand.
3:20 his blood I will R at your hand.
20:40 and there I will R your contributions and the
33:6 his blood I will R at the watchman's hand.
33:8 his blood I will R at your hand.
34:10 shepherds; and I will R my sheep at their
Mic 6:8 what does the LORD R of you but to
Rom 16:2 in whatever she may R from you, for she
1Cor 12:24 modesty, which our more presentable parts do not R

REQUIRED (29)
Gen 31:39 of my hand you R it, whether stolen by
50:3 Israel; forty days were R for it, for so
50:3 for so many are R for embalming.
Num 4:32 objects which they are R to carry.
5:15 and bring the offering R of her, a tenth
1Sam 21:8 because the king's business R haste."
1Kgs 4:28 place where it was R, each according to his
2Kgs 18:14 the king of Assyria R of Hezekiah king of
1Chr 9:28 service, for they were R to count them when
16:37 ark as each day R,
23:31 according to the number R of them, continually
2Chr 8:13 duty of each day R, offering according to the
8:14 duty of each day R, and the gatekeepers in
24:6 "Why have you not R the Levites to bring
31:16 duty of each day R, for their service according
Ezra 3:4 ordinance, as each day R,
7:20 And whatever else is R for the house of
Neh 11:23 settled provision for the singers, as every day R
12:44 into them the portions R by the law for
Ps 40:6 Burnt offering and sin offering thou hast not R
137:3 For there our captors R of us songs, and
Wis 15:8 taken, when he is R to return the soul
Lk 11:50 the world, may be R of this generation,
11:51 you, it shall be R of this generation.
12:20 night your soul is R of you; and the
12:48 him will much be R; and of him to
1Cor 4:2 Moreover it is R of stewards that they be

Philem 1:8 to do what is R,
1Pet 5:9 experience of suffering is R of your brotherhood

REQUIREMENT (2)
Rom 8:4 order that the just R of the law might
Heb 7:16 according to a legal R concerning bodily descent but

REQUIRES (6)
1Kgs 8:59 Israel, as each day R;
Ezra 7:21 the God of heaven, R of you, be it
Sir 13:25 but to devise proverbs R painful thinking.
Is 1:12 appear before me, who R of you this trampling
Rom 2:14 nature what the law R, they are a law
2:15 that what the law R is written on their

REQUIRING
Deut 17:8 "If any case arises R decision between one kind

REQUITAL (4)
Job 34:33 Will he then make R to suit you, because
Is 59:18 wrath to his adversaries, R to his enemies; to
59:18 his enemies; to the coastlands he will render R
Jer 51:6 the LORD's vengeance, the R he is rendering her.

REQUITE (31)
Deut 7:10 hates him, he will R him to his face.
32:6 Do you thus R the LORD, you foolish and
32:41 my adversaries, and will R those who hate me.
Judg 20:10 they come they may R Gibe-ah of Benjamin, for
2Sam 3:39 LORD R the evildoer according to his wickedness!"
2Kgs 9:26 the LORD--I will R you on this plot
Job 34:11 a man he will R him, and according to
Ps 28:4 R them according to their work, and according to
28:4 evil of their deeds; R them according to the
35:12 They R me evil for good; my soul is
41:10 up, that I may R them!
54:5 He will R my enemies with evil; in thy
62:12 For thou dost R a man according to his
103:10 to our sins, nor R us according to our
Prov 24:12 and will he not R man according to his
Sir 17:18 he will arise and R them, and he will
Is 57:18 will lead him and R him with comfort, creating
Jer 32:18 to thousands, but dost R the guilt of fathers
50:29 R her according to her deeds, do to her
51:24 "I will R Babylon and all the inhabitants of
51:56 is a God of recompense, he will surely R
Lam 3:64 "Thou wilt R them, O LORD, according to the
Ezek 9:10 pity, but I will R their deeds upon their
11:21 their abominations, I will R their deeds upon their
16:43 therefore, behold, I will R your deeds upon your
17:19 he broke, I will R upon his head.
Hos 4:9 for their ways, and R them for their deeds.
12:2 to his ways, and R him according to his
Joel 3:4 me back, I will R your deed upon your
3:7 them, and I will R your deed upon your
2Tim 4:14 harm; the Lord will R him for his deeds.

REQUITED (7)
Judg 1:7 done, so God has R me." And they brought
9:56 Thus God R the crime of Abimelech, which he
Job 33:27 and it was not R to me.
Ps 7:4 hands, if I have R my friend with evil
Prov 11:31 If the righteous is R on earth, how much
Ezek 22:31 their way have I R upon their heads, says
23:49 your lewdness shall be R upon you, and you

REQUITES (5)
Deut 7:10 a thousand generations, and R to their face those
Job 21:31 his face, and who R him for what he
Ps 31:23 the faithful, but abundantly R him who acts haughtily.
137:8 shall he be who R you with what you
Sir 3:29 Whoever R favors gives thought to the future; at

REQUITING
2Chr 6:23 and judge thy servants, R the guilty by bringing

RESCUE (40)
Gen 37:22 him"--that he might R him out of their
Num 35:25 and the congregation shall R the manslayer from the
Deut 22:27 was no one to R her.
25:11 one draws near to R her husband from the
1Sam 30:8 for you shall surely overtake and shall surely R
2Kgs 16:7 Come up, and R me from the hand of
Ps 7:2 rend me, dragging me away, with none to R
22:8 deliver him, let him R him, for he delights
31:2 thy ear to me, R me speedily!

R

35:17 R me from their ravages, my life from the
69:14 With thy faithful help R me from sinking in
71:2 righteousness deliver me and R me; incline thy ear
71:4 R me, O my God, from the hand of
82:4 R the weak and the needy; deliver them from
91:15 in trouble, I will R him and honor him.
144:7 hand from on high, R me and deliver me
144:11 R me from the cruel sword, and deliver me
Prov 24:11 R those who are being taken away to death;
Sir 29:12 treasury, and it will R you from all affliction;
40:7 the moment of his R he wakes up, and
51:12 me from destruction and R me from an evil
Is 5:29 prey, they carry it off, and none can R
31:5 he will spare and R it.
42:22 prey with none to R, a spoil with none
Bar 6:36 man from death or R the weak from the
6:37 blind man; they cannot R a man who is
Ezek 34:10 I will R my sheep from their mouths, that
34:12 sheep; and I will R them from all places
Dan 6:14 sun went down to R him.
8:4 no one who could R from his power; he
8:7 no one who could R the ram from his
Hos 2:10 and no one shall R her out of my
5:14 away, I will carry off, and none shall R
1Mac 5:12 Now then come and R us from their hands,
5:17 men and go and R your brethren in Galilee;
2Mac 1:25 and eternal, who dost R Israel from every evil,
8:14 besought the Lord to R those who had been
9:2 people rushed to the R with arms, and Antiochus
2Tim 4:18 The Lord will R me from every evil and
2Pet 2:9 Lord knows how to R the godly from trial,

RESCUED (23)
Judg 8:34 their God, who had R them from the hand
9:17 risked his life, and R you from the hand
1Sam 7:14 to Gath; and Israel R their territory from the
30:18 had taken; and David R his two wives.
Job 21:30 calamity, that he is R in the day of
Ps 71:23 to thee; my soul also, which thou hast R
136:24 endures for ever; and R us from our foes,
Wis 10:6 Wisdom R a righteous man when the ungodly were
10:9 Wisdom R from troubles those who served her.
18:5 had been exposed and R, thou didst in punishment
Is 49:24 mighty, or the captives of a tyrant be R
49:25 of the tyrant be R, for I will contend
Dan 3:89 ever; for he has R us from Hades and
Amos 3:12 dwell in Samaria be R, with the corner of
Mic 4:10 There you shall be R, there the LORD will
1Mac 2:48 They R the law out of the hands of
2Mac 2:18 place, for he has R us from great evils
Acts 7:10 was with him, and R him out of all
12:11 sent his angel and R me from the hand
23:27 with the soldiers and R him, having learned that
2Tim 3:11 them all the Lord R me.
4:17 So I was R from the lion's mouth.
2Pet 2:7 ungodly; and if he R righteous Lot, greatly distressed

RESCUER
Sir 29:17 who does not feel grateful will abandon his R

RESCUES (3)
Sir 40:24 of trouble, but almsgiving R better than both.
Dan 6:27 He delivers and R, he works signs and wonders
Amos 3:12 LORD: "As the shepherd R from the mouth of

RESCUEST
Ps 144:10 victory to kings, who R David thy servant.

RESEMBLED
Judg 8:18 one of them; they R the sons of a

RESEMBLES
Tob 7:2 much the young man R my cousin Tobit!"

RESEMBLING (4)
Ezek 10:1 a sapphire, in form R a throne.
41:21 holy place was something R
Rom 1:23 immortal God for images R mortal man or birds
Heb 7:3 end of life, but R the Son of God

RESEN
Gen 10:12 Nineveh, Rehoboth-Ir, Calah, and R between

RESENTFUL (2)
1Kgs 20:43 went to his house R and sullen, and came
1Cor 13:5 is not irritable or R;

RESENTMENT
Eccl 5:17 and grief, in much vexation and sickness and R

RESERVE
Gen 41:36 food shall be a R for the land against

RESERVED (8)
Gen 27:36 said, "Have you not R a blessing for me?"
Num 18:9 the most holy things, R from the fire; every
Deut 33:21 a commander's portion was R; and he came to
2Chr 31:14 to apportion the contribution R for the LORD and
Job 38:23 hail, which I have R for the time of
Sir 13:9 man invites you, be R; and he will invite
2Pet 2:17 them the nether gloom of darkness has been R
Jude 1:13 of darkness has been R for ever.

RESERVOIR (2)
Sir 50:3 was quarried out, a R like the sea in
Is 22:11 You made a R between the two walls for

RESERVOIRS
Sir 39:17 a heap, and the R of water at the

RESHEPH
1Chr 7:25 Rephah was his son, R his son, Telah his

RESIDE
Ezek 47:22 for the aliens who R among you and have

RESIDENCE
Dan 4:30 power as a royal R and for the glory

RESIDENT
Jud 4:10 their cattle and every R alien and hired laborer

RESIDENTS (7)
Esth 11:1 Ptolemy, one of the R of Jerusalem.
1Mac 1:38 Because of them the R of Jerusalem fled; she
3:34 As for the R of Judea and Jerusalem,
Acts 2:9 Medes and Elamites and R of Mesopotamia, Judea
9:35 And all the R of Lydda and Sharon saw
19:10 so that all the R of Asia heard the
19:17 became known to all R of Ephesus, both Jews

RESIDES
Ezek 47:23 whatever tribe the alien R, there you shall assign

RESIDUE (4)
Ps 76:10 shall praise thee; the R of wrath thou wilt
Is 44:19 shall I make the R of it an abomination?
Dan 7:7 pieces, and stamped the R with its feet.
7:19 pieces, and stamped the R with its feet;

RESIST (12)
Jud 6:3 They cannot R the might of our cavalry.
16:14 is none that can R thy voice.
Esth 13:11 no one who can R thee, who art the
Wis 12:12 Or will R thy judgment?
1Mac 5:40 not be able to R him, for he will
Mt 5:39 to you, Do not R one who is evil.
Acts 7:51 and ears, you always R the Holy Spirit.
Rom 9:19 For who can R his will?"
13:2 appointed, and those who R will incur judgment.
Jas 4:7 R the devil and he will flee from you.
5:6 man; he does not R you.
1Pet 5:9 R him, firm in your faith, knowing that the

RESISTANCE
Bar 6:56 they can offer no R to a king or

RESISTED (4)
Jud 2:25 killed every one who R him, and came to
Sir 46:6 he destroyed those who R, so that the nations
1Mac 14:29 themselves to danger and R the enemies of their
Heb 12:4 you have not yet R to the point of

RESISTS (2)
Rom 13:2 Therefore he who R the authorities resists what God
13:2 who resists the authorities R what God has

RESOLUTE
1Chr 28:7 ever if he continues R in keeping my commandment

RESOLUTELY
2Chr 32:5 He set to work R and built up all

RESOLVE (2)
2Mac 6:23 But making a high R, worthy of his years
2Thes 1:11 may fulfil every good R and work of faith

RESOLVED (7)
Wis 18:5 When they had R to kill the babes of
Sir 51:18 For I R to live according to wisdom, and
Dan 1:8 But Daniel R that he would not defile himself
1Mac 1:62 stood firm and were R in their hearts not
14:35 glory which he had R to win for his
Mt 1:19 put her to shame, R to send her away.
Acts 19:21 after these events Paul R in the Spirit to

RESORT
Ezek 33:26 You R to the sword, you commit abominations and

RESORTED (2)
2Chr 11:13 were in all Israel R to him from all
25:15 him, "Why have you R to the gods of

RESORTING
2Mac 4:34 came to Onias, and R to treachery offered him

RESOUND
Jer 25:31 The clamor will R to the ends of the

RESOUNDED (2)
1Sam 4:5 gave a mighty shout, so that the earth R
Sir 47:10 name, and the sanctuary R from early morning.

RESOURCE
Job 6:13 in me, and any R is driven from me.

RESOURCES (4)
Sir 8:2 rich man, lest his R outweigh yours; for gold
13:5 he will drain your R and he will not
44:6 rich men furnished with R,
2Cor 9:10 supply and multiply your R and increase the harvest

RESPECT (23)
Num 16:15 the LORD, "Do not R their offering.
Josh 2:17 will be guiltless with R to this oath of
2:20 shall be guiltless with R to your oath which
Tob 3:15 my life, command that R be shown to me
Sir 3:11 for children not to R their mother.
41:16 Therefore show R for my words: For it is
Lam 5:12 by their hands; no R is shown to the
Bar 4:15 language, who had no R for an old man,
2Mac 10:13 Unable to command the R due his office, he
15:2 and barbarously, but show R for the day which
Mt 21:37 them, saying, 'They will R my son.'
Mk 12:6 them, saying, 'They will R my son.'
Lk 20:13 may be they will R him.'
Acts 23:6 son of Pharisees; with R to the hope and
24:20 standing among them, 'With R to the resurrection of
Rom 13:7 whom revenue is due, R to whom respect is
13:7 due, respect to whom R is due, honor to
1Thes 4:12 you may command the R of outsiders, and be
5:12 beseech you, brethren, to R those who labor among
Tit 2:9 give satisfaction in every R; they are not to
Heb 2:17 his brethren in every R, so that he might
4:15 one who in every R has been tempted as
1Pet 2:18 your masters with all R, not only to the

RESPECTED (2)
Mk 15:42 Joseph of Arimathea, a R member of the council,
Heb 12:9 discipline us and we R them.

RESPECTFUL (2)
1Tim 2:2 peaceable life, godly and R in every way.
3:4 his children submissive and R in every way;

RESPECTFULLY
Sir 21:22 man of experience stands R before it.

RESPECTIVE
Sir 46:11 judges also, with their R names, those whose hearts

RESPECTS (3)
Prov 13:13 himself, but he who R the commandment will be
Eph 5:33 wife see that she R her husband.
Tit 2:7 Show yourself in all R a model of good

RESPITE (5)
Ex 8:15 that there was a R, he hardened his heart,
1Sam 11:3 "Give us seven days R that we may send
Ps 94:13 law to give him R from days of trouble,
Lam 2:18 Give yourself no rest, your eyes no R
3:49 flow without ceasing, without R,

RESPLENDENT
2Mac 10:29 enemy from heaven five R men on horses with

RESPOND
Hab 2:11 the wall, and the beam from the woodwork R

RESPONDED
2Mac 1:23 led, and the rest R, as did Nehemiah.

RESPONSE
Deut 26:5 "And you shall make R before the LORD your

RESPONSIBILITY (2)
2Mac 2:28 uncomfortable toil, leaving the R for exact details to
4:28 the revenue was his R, the two of them

RESPONSIBLE
Esth 16:5 been made in part R for the shedding of

RESPONSIVELY
Ezra 3:11 Israel; and they sang R, praising and giving thanks

REST (346)
Gen 8:4 the ark came to R upon the mountains of
14:10 into them, and the R fled to the mountain.
18:4 wash your feet, and R yourselves under the tree,
30:36 and Jacob fed the R of Laban's flock.
42:19 prison, and let the R go and carry grain
43:23 He replied, R assured, do not be afraid; your
44:10 my slave, and the R of you shall be
Ex 4:7 was restored like the R of his flesh.
5:5 and you make them R from their burdens!"
16:23 a day of solemn R, a holy sabbath to
23:11 you shall let it R and lie fallow, that
23:12 seventh day you shall R; that your ox and
23:12 your ass may have R, and the son of
29:12 your finger, and the R of the blood you
29:20 feet, and throw the R of the blood against
31:15 a sabbath of solemn R, holy to the LORD;
33:14 go with you, and I will give you R
34:21 seventh day you shall R; in plowing time and
34:21 in plowing time and in harvest you shall R
35:2 holy sabbath of solemn R to the LORD; whoever
Lev 4:7 of meeting, and the R of the blood of
4:18 the LORD; and the R of the blood he
4:25 and pour out the R of its blood at
4:30 and pour out the R of its blood at
4:34 and pour out the R of its blood at
5:9 the altar, while the R of the blood shall
6:16 And the R of it Aaron and his sons
14:18 guilt offering; and the R of the oil that
14:29 was put; and the R of the oil that
16:31 a sabbath of solemn R to you, and you
23:3 a sabbath of solemn R, a holy convocation; you
23:24 a day of solemn R, a memorial proclaimed with
23:32 a sabbath of solemn R, and you shall afflict
23:39 shall be a solemn R, and on the eighth
23:39 on the eighth day shall be a solemn R
25:4 a sabbath of solemn R for the land, a
25:5 a year of solemn R for the land.
26:34 then the land shall R, and enjoy its sabbaths.
26:35 desolate it shall have R, the rest which it
26:35 shall have rest, the R which it had not
Num 18:30 of it, then the R shall be reckoned to
31:8 of Midian with the R of their slain, Evi,
Deut 3:13 with its cities; the R of Gilead, and all
3:20 until the LORD gives R to your brethren, as
5:14 and your maidservant may R as well as you.
12:9 yet come to the R and to the inheritance
12:10 when he gives you R from all your enemies
19:20 And the R shall hear, and fear, and shall
25:19 God has given you R from all your enemies
28:65 there shall be no R for the sole of
Josh 1:13 you a place of R, and will give you
1:15 until the LORD gives R to your brethren as
3:13 all the earth, shall R in the waters of
11:23 And the land had R from war.
13:22 the sword among the R of their slain.
13:27 Succoth, and Zaphon, the R of the kingdom of
14:15 And the land had R from war.
17:2 were made to the R of the tribe of
17:6 was allotted to the R of the Manassites.

R

	21:5	And the R of the Kohathites received by lot
	21:20	As to the R of the Kohathites belonging to
	21:26	the families of the R of the Kohathites were
	21:34	And to the R of the Levites, the Merarite
	21:44	the LORD gave them R on every side just
	22:4	your God has given R to your brethren, as
	23:1	the LORD had given R to Israel from all
Judg	3:11	So the land had R forty years.
	3:30	And the land had R for eighty years.
	5:31	And the land had R for forty years.
	7:6	men; but all the R of the people knelt
	7:8	he sent all the R of Israel every man
	8:28	And the land had R forty years in the
Ruth	3:18	the man will not R, but will settle the
1Sam	13:2	Gibe-ah of Benjamin; the R of the people he
	15:15	your God; and the R we have utterly destroyed."
2Sam	4:5	of Ish-bosheth, as he was taking his noonday R
	7:1	LORD had given him R from all his enemies
	7:11	I will give you R from all your enemies.
	10:10	against the Syrians; the R of his men he
	12:28	Now, then, gather the R of the people together,
	14:17	will set me at R; for my lord the
1Kgs	5:4	God has given me R on every side; there
	8:56	LORD who has given R to his people Israel,
	11:41	Now the R of the acts of Solomon, and
	12:23	Benjamin, and to the R of the people,
	14:19	Now the R of the acts of Jeroboam, how
	14:29	Now the R of the acts of Rehoboam, and
	15:7	The R of the acts of Abijam, and all
	15:23	Now the R of all the acts of Asa,
	15:31	Now the R of the acts of Nadab, and
	16:5	Now the R of the acts of Baasha, and
	16:14	Now the R of the acts of Elah, and
	16:20	Now the R of the acts of Zimri, and
	16:27	Now the R of the acts of Omri which
	20:30	And the R fled into the city of Aphek;
	22:39	Now the R of the acts of Ahab, and
	22:45	Now the R of the acts of Jehoshaphat, and
2Kgs	1:18	Now the R of the acts of Ahaziah which
	4:7	you and your sons can live on the R
	8:23	Now the R of the acts of Joram, and
	10:34	Now the R of the acts of Jehu, and
	12:19	Now the R of the acts of Joash, and
	13:8	Now the R of the acts of Jehoahaz and
	13:12	Now the R of the acts of Joash, and
	14:15	Now the R of the acts of Jehoash which
	14:18	Now the R of the deeds of Amaziah, are
	14:28	Now the R of the acts of Jeroboam, and
	15:6	Now the R of the acts of Azariah, and
	15:11	Now the R of the deeds of Zechariah, behold,
	15:15	Now the R of the deeds of Shallum, and
	15:21	Now the R of the deeds of Menahem, and
	15:26	Now the R of the deeds of Pekahiah, and
	15:31	Now the R of the acts of Pekah, and
	15:36	Now the R of the acts of Jotham, and
	16:19	Now the R of the acts of Ahaz which
	18:19	On what do you R this confidence of yours?
	20:20	The R of the deeds of Hezekiah, and all
	21:17	Now the R of the acts of Manasseh, and
	21:25	Now the R of the acts of Amon which
	23:28	Now the R of the acts of Josiah, and
	24:5	Now the R of the deeds of Jehoiakim, and
	25:11	And the R of the people who were left
	25:11	Babylon, together with the R of the multitude,
1Chr	6:61	To the R of the Kohathites were given by
	6:70	pasture lands, for the R of the families of
	6:77	To the R of the Merarites were allotted out
	11:8	and Joab repaired the R of the city.
	12:38	Israel; likewise all the R of Israel were of
	16:41	and Jeduthun, and the R of those chosen and
	19:11	against the Syrians; the R of his men he
	24:20	And of the R of the sons of Levi:
	28:2	build a house of R for the ark of
2Chr	9:29	Now the R of the acts of Solomon, from
	13:22	The R of the acts of Abijah, his ways
	14:1	days the land had R for ten years.
	14:5	And the kingdom had R under him.
	14:6	fortified cities in Judah, for the land had R
	15:15	the LORD gave them R round about.
	20:30	his God gave him R round about.
	20:34	Now the R of the acts of Jehoshaphat, from
	24:14	finished, they brought the R of the money before
	25:26	Now the R of the deeds of Amaziah, from
	26:22	Now the R of the acts of Uzziah, from
	27:7	Now the R of the acts of Jotham, and
	28:26	Now the R of his acts and all his
	32:22	and he gave them R on every side.
	32:32	Now the R of the acts of Hezekiah, and
	33:18	Now the R of the acts of Manasseh, and
	35:26	Now the R of the acts of Josiah, and
	36:8	Now the R of the acts of Jehoiakim, and
Ezra	3:8	beginning, together with the R of their brethren, the
	4:3	Zerubbabel, Jeshua, and the R of the heads of
	4:7	and Tabeel and the R of their associates wrote
	4:9	the scribe, and the R of their associates, the
	4:10	the Elamites, and the R of the nations whom
	4:10	Samaria and in the R of the province Beyond
	4:17	the scribe and the R of their associates who
	4:17	Samaria and in the R of the province Beyond
	6:16	the Levites, and the R of the returned exiles,
	7:18	to do with the R of the silver and
Neh	2:16	the officials, and the R that were to do
	4:14	officials and to the R of the people, "Do
	4:19	officials and to the R of the people, "The
	6:1	Arab and to the R of our enemies that
	6:14	prophetess No-adiah and the R of the prophets who
	7:72	And what the R of the people gave was
	9:28	But after they had R they did evil again
	10:28	The R of the people, the priests, the Levites,
	11:1	in Jerusalem; and the R of the people cast
	11:20	And the R of Israel, and of the priests
Tob	8:21	father, and that the R would be his "when
Jud	7:18	The R of the Assyrian army encamped in the
	8:24	temple and the altar R upon us.
	15:6	The R of the people of Bethulia fell upon
Esth	9:12	they done in the R of the king's provinces!
	12:1	Now Mordecai took his R in the courtyard with
Job	3:13	should have been at R,
	3:17	from troubling, and there the weary are at R
	3:26	quiet; I have no R; but trouble comes."
	11:18	protected and take your R in safety.
	20:20	his greed knew no R, he will not save
	30:17	and the pain that gnaws me takes no R
Ps	22:2	not answer; and by night, but find no R
	55:6	away and be at R;
	95:11	my anger that they should not enter my R
	116:7	my soul, to your R; for the LORD has
	125:3	of wickedness shall not R upon the land allotted
	127:2	and go late to R, eating the bread of
Prov	6:10	of the hands to R,
	21:16	way of understanding will R in the assembly of
	24:33	of the hands to R,
	29:17	he will give you R; he will give delight
Eccl	2:23	even in the night his mind does not R
	6:5	anything; yet it finds R rather than he.
Wis	4:7	man, though he die early, will be at R
	8:16	house, I shall find R with her, for companionship
Sir	6:28	you will find the R she gives, and she
	11:17	says, "I have found R, and now I shall
	22:9	for he has attained R; but the life of
	22:11	and you will find R, and you will never
	28:16	slander will not find R, nor will he settle
	30:17	miserable life, and eternal R than chronic sickness.
	33:25	and you will find R; leave his hands idle,
	36:13	of thy sanctuary, Jerusalem, the place of thy R
	38:23	the dead is at R, let his remembrance cease,
	39:11	if he goes to R, it is enough for
	40:6	gets little or no R, and afterward in his
	44:24	covenant he made to R upon the head of
	47:13	and God gave him R on every side, that
	51:27	I have labored little and found myself much R
Is	11:2	of the LORD shall R upon him, the spirit
	14:3	LORD has given you R from your pain and
	14:7	whole earth is at R and quiet; they break
	23:12	to Cyprus, even there you will have no R
	25:10	of the LORD will R on this mountain, and
	28:12	has said, "This is R; give rest to the
	28:12	"This is rest; give R to the weary; and
	30:15	Israel, "In returning and R you shall be saved;
	36:4	On what do you R this confidence of yours?
	38:10	of Sheol for the R of my years.
	44:17	And the R of it he makes into a
	57:2	enters into peace; they R in their beds who
	57:20	sea; for it cannot R, and its waters toss
	62:1	sake I will not R, until her vindication goes
	62:6	in remembrance, take no R,
	62:7	and give him no R until he establishes Jerusalem
	63:14	valley, the Spirit of the LORD gave them R
	66:1	me, and what is the place of my R
Jer	6:16	in it, and find R for your souls.
	15:9	And the R of them I will give to
	27:19	the stands, and the R of the vessels which

31:2 when Israel sought for R,
39:3 Rabmag, with all the R of the officers of
39:9 exile to Babylon the R of the people who
41:10 took captive all the R of the people who
41:16 him took all the R of the people whom
45:3 and I find no R
47:6 yourself into your scabbard, R and be still!
50:34 that he may give R to the earth, but
52:15 the people and the R of the people who
52:15 Babylon, together with the R of the artisans.
Lam 2:18 Give yourself no R, your eyes no respite!
5:5 driven; we are weary, we are given no R
Ezek 25:16 Cherethites, and destroy the R of the seacoast.
34:18 with your feet the R of your pasture; and
34:18 you must foul the R with your feet?
36:3 the possession of the R of the nations, and
36:4 and derision to the R of the nations round
36:5 hot jealousy against the R of the nations, and
44:30 that a blessing may R on your house.
48:23 "As for the R of the tribes: from the
Dan 2:18 not perish with the R of the wise men
7:12 As for the R of the beasts, their dominion
7:19 different from all the R, exceedingly terrible, with its
12:13 end; and you shall R, and shall stand in
Mic 2:10 is no place to R; because of uncleanness that
5:3 brought forth; then the R of his brethren shall
Zech 1:11 the earth remains at R
6:8 set my Spirit at R in the north country."
9:1 of Hadrach and will R upon Damascus.
14:2 into exile, but the R of the people shall
1Mac 3:11 and fell, and the R fled.
3:12 it in battle the R of his life.
3:24 them fell, and the R fled into the land
5:18 the people, with the R of the forces, in
6:38 The R of the horsemen were stationed on either
6:54 had prevailed over the R and they had been
7:32 Nicanor fell, and the R fled into the city
7:42 us today; let the R learn that Nicanor has
7:50 land of Judah had R for a few days.
8:4 disaster upon them; the R paid them tribute every
9:18 also fell, and the R fled.
9:22 Now the R of the acts of Judas, and
9:40 and fell, and the R fled to the mountain;
9:57 land of Judah had R for two years.
12:6 the priests, and the R of the Jewish people
14:4 The land had R all the days of Simon.
14:20 the priests and the R of the Jewish people,
16:8 wounded and fell; the R fled into the stronghold.
16:23 The R of the acts of John and his
2Mac 1:23 Jonathan led, and the R responded, as did Nehemiah.
7:4 and feet, while the R of the brothers and
8:28 orphans, and distributed the R among themselves
8:31 places, and carried the R of the spoils to
10:36 and let in the R of the force, and
11:11 and forced all the R to flee.
14:11 had said this, the R of the king's friends,
15:1 them with complete safety on the day of R
Mt 2:9 till it came to R over the place where
11:28 are heavy laden, and I will give you R
11:29 and you will find R for your souls.
12:43 through waterless places seeking R, but he finds.
22:6 his business, while the R seized his servants, treated
26:45 them, "Are you still sleeping and taking your R
Mk 6:31 a lonely place, and R a while." For many
14:41 them, "Are you still sleeping and taking your R
16:13 back and told the R, but they did not
Lk 10:6 there, your peace shall R upon him; but if
11:24 through waterless places seeking R; and finding none
12:26 as that, why are you anxious about the R
24:9 this to the eleven and to all the R
Jn 11:13 that he meant taking R in sleep.
Acts 2:37 to Peter and the R of the apostles, "Brethren,
5:13 None of the R dared join them, but the
7:49 Lord, or what is the place of my R
15:17 it up, that the R of men may seek
17:9 from Jason and the R, they let them go.
27:44 the land, and the R on planks or on
28:9 had taken place, the R of the people on
Rom 1:13 well as among the R of the Gentiles.
4:16 that the promise may R on grace and be
11:7 obtained it, but the R were hardened,
1Cor 2:5 your faith might not R in the wisdom of
7:12 To the R I say, not the Lord, that
2Cor 2:13 my mind could not R because I did not
7:5 our bodies had no R but we were afflicted
7:13 has been set at R by you all.
12:9 power of Christ may R upon me.
12:13 less favored than the R of the churches, except
Gal 2:13 And with him the R of the Jews acted
3:12 the law does not R on faith, for "He
Eph 2:3 of wrath, like the R of mankind.
Phil 1:13 and to all the R that my imprisonment is
4:3 with Clement and the R of my fellow workers,
2Thes 1:7 you, and to grant R with us to you
1Tim 5:20 all, so that the R may stand in fear.
Heb 3:11 in my wrath, 'They shall never enter my R
3:18 should never enter his R, but to those who
4:1 promise of entering his R remains, let us fear
4:3 have believed enter that R, as he has said,
4:3 in my wrath, 'They shall never enter my R
4:5 place he said, "They shall never enter my R
4:8 Joshua had given them R, God would not speak
4:9 there remains a sabbath R for the people of
4:10 for whoever enters God's R also ceases from his
4:11 strive to enter that R, that no one fall
1Pet 4:2 to live for the R of the time in
Rev 2:24 But to the R of you in Thyatira, who
6:11 robe and told to R a little longer, until
9:20 The R of mankind, who were not killed by
11:13 the earthquake, and the R were terrified and gave
12:17 make war on the R of her offspring, on
14:11 and they have no R, day or night, these
14:13 Spirit, "that they may R from their labors, for
19:21 And the R were slain by the sword of
20:5 The R of the dead did not come to

RESTED (20)

Gen 2:2 had done, and he R on the seventh day
2:3 because on it God R from all his work
Ex 16:30 So the people R on the seventh day.
20:11 is in them, and R the seventh day; therefore
31:17 the seventh day he R, and was refreshed.'"
Num 9:18 long as the cloud R over the tabernacle, they
10:36 And when it R, he said, "Return, O LORD,
11:25 and when the spirit R upon them, they prophesied.
11:26 Medad, and the spirit R upon them; they were
Judg 1:35 the house of Joseph R heavily upon them, and
16:29 upon which the house R, and he leaned his
2Kgs 4:11 into the chamber and R there.
1Chr 6:31 LORD, after the ark R there.
Jud 1:16 he and his forces R and feasted for one
Esth 9:17 the fourteenth day they R and made that a
9:18 on the fourteenth, and R on the fifteenth day,
Sir 47:23 Solomon R with his fathers, and left behind him
Ezek 9:3 cherubim on which it R to the threshold of
Lk 23:55 On the sabbath they R according to the
Heb 4:4 this way, "And God R on the seventh day

RESTING (15)

Gen 49:15 he saw that a R place was good, and
Num 10:33 to seek out a R place for them.
Ruth 2:7 morning until now, without R even for a moment."
2Chr 6:41 and go to thy R place, thou and the
Jud 10:21 Holofernes was R on his bed, under a canopy
Job 16:18 my cry find no R place.
Ps 132:8 and go to thy R place, thou and the
132:14 habitation: "This is my R place for ever; here
Sir 24:7 these I sought a R place; I sought in
24:11 he gave me a R place, and in Jerusalem
Is 32:18 dwellings, and in quiet R places.
34:14 find for herself a R place.
Jer 33:12 be habitations of shepherds R their flocks.
Lam 1:3 nations, but finds no R place; her pursuers have
Acts 2:3 of fire, distributed and R on each one of

RESTITUTION (12)

Ex 22:1 He shall make R; if he has nothing, then
22:5 field, he shall make R from the best in
22:6 he that kindled the fire shall make full R
22:11 accept the oath, and he shall not make R
22:12 him, he shall make R to its owner.
22:13 he shall not make R for what has been
22:14 not being with it, he shall make full R
22:15 he shall not make R; if it was hired,
Lev 5:16 He shall also make R for what he has
Num 5:7 he shall make full R for his wrong, adding
5:8 no kinsman to whom R may be made for
5:8 for the wrong, the R for wrong shall go

RESTIVE

Jer 2:23 you have done—a R young camel interlacing her

RESTLESS

Jas 3:8 tame the tongue--a R evil, full of deadly

RESTORATION

1Mac 14:34 in those cities whatever was necessary for their R

RESTORE (83)

Gen 20:7 Now then R the man's wife; for he is
20:7 if you do not R her, know that you
37:22 of their hand, to R him to his father.
40:13 up your head and R you to your office;
Ex 22:26 in pledge, you shall R it to him before
Lev 6:4 become guilty, he shall R what he took by
6:5 sworn falsely; he shall R it in full, and
Num 35:25 and the congregation shall R him to his city
Deut 22:2 it; then you shall R it to him.
24:13 goes down, you shall R to him the pledge
30:3 LORD your God will R your fortunes, and have
Judg 11:13 the Jordan; now therefore R it peaceably."
17:3 now therefore I will R it to you."
Ruth 4:5 dead, in order to R the name of the
1Sam 12:3 me and I will R it to you."
2Sam 8:3 as he went to R his power at the
9:7 Jonathan, and I will R to you all the
12:6 die; and he shall R the lamb fourfold, because
1Kgs 12:21 house of Israel, to R the kingdom to Rehoboam
20:34 your father I will R; and you may establish
2Kgs 8:6 official for her, saying, R all that was hers,
2Chr 11:1 fight against Israel, to R the kingdom to Rehoboam.
24:4 this Joash decided to R the house of the
24:12 masons and carpenters to R the house of the
Neh 4:2 Will they R things?
5:12 they said, "We will R these and require nothing
Jud 7:31 Lord our God will R to us his mercy,
Ps 51:12 R to me the joy of thy salvation, and
60:1 hast been angry; oh, R us.
68:9 shed abroad; thou didst R thy heritage as it
69:4 What I did not steal must I now R
80:3 R us, O God; let thy face shine, that
80:7 R us, O God of hosts; let thy face
80:19 R us, O LORD God of hosts!
85:1 thy land; thou didst R the fortunes of Jacob.
85:4 R us again, O God of our salvation, and
126:4 R our fortunes, O LORD, like the watercourses in
Sir 48:10 the son, and to R the tribes of Jacob.
Is 1:26 And I will R your judges as at the
38:16 Oh, R me to health and make me live!
42:22 to rescue, a spoil with none to say, R
49:6 of Jacob and to R the preserved of Israel;
Jer 15:19 you return, I will R you, and you shall
27:22 bring them back and R them to this place."
29:14 LORD, and I will R your fortunes and gather
30:3 LORD, when I will R the fortunes of my
30:17 For I will R health to you, and your
30:18 LORD: Behold, I will R the fortunes of the
31:23 its cities, when I R their fortunes: 'The LORD
32:44 Negeb; for I will R their fortunes, says the
33:7 I will R the fortunes of Judah and the
33:11 ever!' For I will R the fortunes of the
33:26 For I will R their fortunes, and will have
48:47 Yet I will R the fortunes of Moab in
49:6 But afterward I will R the fortunes of the
49:39 latter days I will R the fortunes of Elam,
50:19 I will R Israel to his pasture, and he
Lam 2:13 your ruin; who can R you?
2:14 exposed your iniquity to R your fortunes, but have
5:21 R us to thyself, O LORD, that we may
Bar 6:37 They cannot R sight to a blind man; they
Ezek 16:53 "I will R their fortunes, both the fortunes of
16:53 daughters, and I will R your own fortunes in
18:12 commits robbery, does not R the pledge, lifts up
29:14 scattered; and I will R the fortunes of Egypt,
39:25 GOD: Now I will R the fortunes of Jacob,
Dan 9:25 of the word to R and build Jerusalem to
Hos 7:1 When I would R the fortunes of my people,
Joel 2:25 I will R to you the years which the
3:1 that time, when I R the fortunes of Judah
Amos 9:14 I will R the fortunes of my people Israel,
Zeph 2:7 mindful of them and R their fortunes.
Zech 9:12 declare that I will R to you double.
1Mac 10:10 began to rebuild and R the city.
15:3 so that I may R it as it formerly
2Mac 12:25 his solemn promise to R them unharmed, they let
Mt 17:11 and he is to R all things;
Mk 9:12 does come first to R all things; and how
Lk 19:8 one of anything, I R it fourfold."
Acts 1:6 you at this time R the kingdom to Israel?"
Gal 6:1 who are spiritual should R him in a spirit
Heb 6:4 it is impossible to R again to repentance those
1Pet 5:10 in Christ, will himself R, establish, and strengthen

RESTORED (45)

Gen 20:14 them to Abraham, and R Sarah his wife to
40:21 He R the chief butler to his butlership, and
41:13 to pass; I was R to my office, and
Ex 4:7 out, behold, it was R like the rest of
Deut 28:31 and shall not be R to you; your sheep
Judg 17:3 And he R the eleven hundred pieces of silver
17:4 So when he R the money to his mother,
1Sam 7:14 taken from Israel were R to Israel, from Ekron
1Kgs 13:6 my hand may be R to me." And the
13:6 the king's hand was R to him, and became
2Kgs 5:10 your flesh shall be R, and you shall be
5:14 and his flesh was R like the flesh of
8:1 whose son he had R to life, "Arise, and
8:5 king how Elisha had R the dead to life,
8:5 whose son he had R to life appealed to
8:5 her son whom Elisha R to life."
14:22 He built Elath and R it to Judah, after
14:25 He R the border of Israel from the entrance
2Chr 24:13 their hands, and they R the house of God
26:2 He built Eloth and R it to Judah, after
29:35 service of the house of the LORD was R
33:16 He also R the altar of the LORD and
Ezra 6:5 brought to Babylon, be R and brought back to
Neh 3:8 perfumers, repaired; and they R Jerusalem as far as
Tob 2:1 my son Tobias were R to me, at the
Job 42:10 And the LORD R the fortunes of Job, when
Ps 30:3 my soul from Sheol, R me to life from
126:1 When the LORD R the fortunes of Zion, we
Jer 8:22 of the daughter of my people not been R
31:18 that I may be R, for thou art the
Lam 5:21 to thyself, O LORD, that we may be R
Ezek 38:8 the land that is R from war, the land
Dan 8:14 the sanctuary shall be R to its rightful state."
1Mac 4:57 and small shields; they R the gates and the
9:72 He R to him the captives whom he had
2Mac 2:22 freed the city and R the laws that were
5:20 of the Almighty was R again in all its
11:25 that their temple be R to them and that
Mt 5:13 lost its taste, how shall its saltness be R
12:13 out, and it was R, whole like the other.
Mk 3:5 He stretched it out, and his hand was R
8:25 looked intently and was R, and saw everything
Lk 6:10 And he did so, and his hand was R
14:34 lost its taste, how shall its saltness be R
Heb 13:19 that I may be R to you the sooner.

RESTORER (2)

Ruth 4:15 be to you a R of life and a
Is 58:12 of the breach, the R of streets to dwell

RESTORES (5)

Ps 14:7 When the LORD R the fortunes of his people,
23:3 beside still waters; he R my soul.
53:6 When God R the fortunes of his people, Jacob
Ezek 18:7 oppress any one, but R to the debtor his
33:15 right, if the wicked R the pledge, gives back

RESTORING (3)

2Chr 34:10 it for repairing and R the house.
Nah 2:2 (For the LORD is R the majesty of Jacob
1Mac 10:44 cost of rebuilding and R the structures of the

RESTRAIN (11)

1Sam 3:13 and he did not R them.
Esth 16:12 But, unable to R his arrogance, he undertook to
Job 7:11 "Therefore I will not R my mouth; I will
37:4 and he does not R the lightnings when his
Prov 27:16 woman are alike; to R her is to restrain
27:16 restrain her is to R the wind or to
Sir 18:29 your base desires, but R your appetites.
Is 48:9 of my praise I R it for you, that
64:12 Wilt thou R thyself at these things, O LORD?
Jer 2:24 Who can R her lust?
Ezek 31:15 mourn for it, and R its rivers, and many

RESTRAINED (16)

Gen 8:2 from the heavens was R,
Ex 36:6 So the people were R from bringing;
1Sam 25:26 seeing the LORD has R you from bloodguilt, and
25:34 Israel lives, who has R me from hurting you,

2Sam 18:16 pursuing Israel; for Joab R them.
Esth 5:10 Nevertheless Haman R himself, and went home; and
Ps 40:9 lo, I have not R my lips, as thou
78:38 not destroy them; he R his anger often, and
Wis 16:18 time the flame was R, so that it might
Sir 46:7 they withstood the congregation, R the people from
Is 42:14 have kept still and R myself; now I will
Jer 14:10 thus, they have not R their feet; therefore the
Lam 2:8 by the line; he R not his hand from
Dan 14:19 Then Daniel laughed, and R the king from going
Acts 14:18 these words they scarcely R the people from offering
2Pet 2:16 with human voice and R the prophet's madness.

RESTRAINING

2Thes 2:6 you know what is R him now so that

RESTRAINS (4)

Job 30:13 my calamity; no one R them.
Prov 10:19 lacking, but he who R his lips is prudent.
17:27 He who R his words has knowledge, and he
2Thes 2:7 only he who now R it will do so

RESTRAINT (6)

Job 30:11 they have cast off R in my presence.
Prov 14:16 a fool throws off R and is careless.
29:18 the people cast off R, but blessed is he
Is 23:10 Tarshish; there is no R any more.
1Cor 7:35 not to lay any R upon you, but to
Gal 3:23 the law, kept under R until faith should be

RESTRICTED (2)

2Cor 6:12 You are not R by us, but you are
6:12 us, but you are R in your own affections.

RESTS (17)

Judg 16:26 on which the house R, that I may lean
1Kgs 10:19 the seat were arm R and two lions standing
10:19 standing beside the arm R,
2Kgs 2:15 "The spirit of Elijah R on Elisha." And they
2Chr 9:18 the seat were arm R and two lions standing
9:18 standing beside the arm R,
Jud 9:8 where thy glorious name R, and to cast down
Ps 62:7 On God R my deliverance and my honor; my
Prov 19:23 he who has it R satisfied; he will not
Sir 5:6 him, and his anger R on sinners.
20:20 poverty, so when he R he feels no remorse.
31:3 accumulates, and when he R he fills himself with
31:4 diminishes, and when he R he becomes needy.
40:5 And when one R upon his bed, his sleep
43:20 over the water; it R upon every pool of
Jn 3:36 the wrath of God R upon him.
1Pet 4:14 glory and of God R upon you.

RESULT (9)

Wis 1:11 secret word is without R, and a lying mouth
Sir 20:8 and a windfall may R in a loss.
Is 32:17 be peace, and the R of righteousness, quietness and
Jer 27:10 to you, with the R that you will be
27:15 my name, with the R that I will drive
2Mac 4:42 As a R, they wounded many of them, and
7:12 As a R the king himself and those with
9:2 were defeated, with the R that Antiochus was put
10:13 As a R he was accused before Eupator by

RESULTS

Sir 38:18 For sorrow R in death, and sorrow of heart

RESUMED

Jn 13:12 taken his garments, and R his place, he said

RESURRECTION (43)

2Mac 7:14 there will be no R to life!"
12:43 very well and honorably, taking account of the R
Mt 22:23 that there is no R; and they asked him
22:28 In the R, therefore, to which of the seven
22:30 For in the R they neither marry nor are
22:31 And as for the R of the dead, have
27:53 the tombs after his R they went into the
Mk 12:18 that there is no R; and they asked him
12:23 In the R whose wife will she be?
Lk 14:14 be repaid at the R of the just."
20:27 that there is no R,
20:33 In the R, therefore, whose wife will the woman
20:35 age and to the R from the dead neither
20:36 are sons of God, being sons of the R
Jn 5:28 done good, to the R of life, and those
5:28 done evil, to the R of judgment.
11:24 rise again in the R at the last day."
11:25 her, "I am the R and the life; he
Acts 1:22 must become with us a witness to his R
2:31 and spoke of the R of the Christ, that
4:2 proclaiming in Jesus the R from the dead.
4:33 their testimony to the R of the Lord Jesus,
17:18 divinities"—because he preached Jesus and the R
17:32 they heard of the R of the dead, some
23:6 the hope and the R of the dead I
23:8 that there is no R, nor angel, nor spirit;
24:14 there will be a R of both the just
24:20 'With respect to the R of the dead I
Rom 1:4 of holiness by his R from the dead, Jesus
6:5 with him in a R like his.
1Cor 15:12 that there is no R of the dead?
15:13 if there is no R of the dead, then
15:21 has come also the R of the dead.
15:42 is it with the R of the dead.
Phil 3:10 the power of his R, and may share his
3:11 I may attain the R from the dead.
2Tim 2:18 by holding that the R is past already.
Heb 6:2 on of hands, the R of the dead, and
11:35 Women received their dead by R
1Pet 1:3 living hope through the R of Jesus Christ from
3:21 clear conscience, through the R of Jesus Christ,
Rev 20:5 This is the first R
20:6 holy is he who shares in the first R

RETAIN (7)

Eccl 8:8 man has power to R the spirit, or authority
Sir 41:16 it is good to R every kind of shame,
Dan 10:16 upon me, and I R no strength.
11:6 but she shall not R the strength of her
Amos 2:14 the strong shall not R his strength, nor shall
Mic 7:18 He does not R his anger for ever because
Jn 20:23 are forgiven; if you R the sins of any,

RETAINED (4)

Judg 7:8 to his tent, but R the three hundred men;
Wis 19:20 Fire even in water R its normal power, and
Dan 10:8 fearfully changed, and I R no strength.
Jn 20:23 you retain the sins of any, they are R

RETAINING

Sir 50:2 double walls, the high R walls for the temple

RETINUE (3)

1Kgs 10:2 with a very great R, with camels bearing spices,
2Chr 9:1 having a very great R and camels bearing spices
2Mac 3:28 treasury with a great R and all his bodyguard

RETORT

Acts 7:29 Egyptian yesterday?' At this R Moses fled, and

RETREAT (2)

2Kgs 19:23 I entered its farthest R, its densest forest.
2Mac 9:2 flight by the inhabitants and beat a shameful R

RETREATED

2Mac 9:1 it happened, Antiochus had R in disorder from the

RETRIBUTION (4)

Sir 14:6 and this is the R for his baseness;
48:8 anointed kings to inflict R, and prophets to succeed
Rom 11:9 a pitfall and a R for them;
Heb 2:2 disobedience received a just R,

RETURN (268)

Gen 3:19 eat bread till you R to the ground, for
3:19 you are dust, and to dust you shall R
8:12 and she did not R to him any more.
14:17 After his R from the defeat of Ched-or-laomer and
16:9 LORD said to her, R to your mistress, and
18:10 said, "I will surely R to you in the
18:14 appointed time I will R to you, in the
29:27 the other also in R for serving me another
31:3 LORD said to Jacob, R to the land of
31:13 from this land, and R to the land of
32:9 didst say to me, R to your country and
50:5 you, and bury my father; then I will R
Ex 13:17 they see war, and R to Egypt."
Lev 25:10 each of you shall R to his property and
25:10 each of you shall R to his family.
25:13 each of you shall R to his property.
25:27 it; and he shall R to his property.

	25:28	released, and he shall R to his property.
	25:41	his own family, and R to the possession of
	27:24	jubilee the field shall R to him from whom
Num	10:36	it rested, he said, R, O LORD, to the
	18:21	for an inheritance, in R for their service which
	18:31	is your reward in R for your service in
	23:5	Balaam's mouth, and said, R to Balak, and thus
	23:16	his mouth, and said, R to Balak, and thus
	32:18	We will not R to our homes until the
	32:22	after that you shall R and be free of
	35:28	priest the manslayer may R to the land of
	35:32	refuge, that he may R to dwell in the
Deut	3:20	Jordan; then you shall R every man to his
	4:30	latter days, you will R to the LORD your
	5:30	and say to them, R to your tents."
	17:16	cause the people to R to Egypt in order
	17:16	you, 'You shall never R that way again.'
	30:2	has driven you, and R to the LORD your
Josh	1:15	them; then you shall R to the land of
Judg	6:18	And he said, "I will stay till you R
	7:3	and trembling, let him R home.'" And Gideon tested
	8:35	(that is, Gideon) in R for all the good
	11:31	meet me, when I R victorious from the Ammonites,
	20:8	none of us will R to his house.
Ruth	1:6	with her daughters-in-law to R from the country of
	1:7	on the way to R to the land of
	1:8	her two daughters-in-law, "Go, R each of you to
	1:10	her, "No, we will R with you to your
	1:15	and to her gods; R after your sister-in-law."
	1:16	leave you or to R from following you; for
1Sam	2:20	so then they would R to their home.
	5:11	Israel, and let it R to its own place,
	6:3	but by all means R him a guilt offering.
	6:4	offering that we shall R to him?" They answered,
	15:25	pardon my sin, and R with me, that I
	15:26	Saul, "I will not R with you; for you
	15:30	and before Israel, and R with me, that I
	18:2	would not let him R to his father's house.
	26:21	"I have done wrong; R, my son David, for
	29:4	back, that he may R to the place to
	29:11	in the morning, to R to the land of
2Sam	3:16	said to him, "Go, R; and he returned.
	10:5	Jericho until your beards have grown, and then R
	12:23	but he will not R to me."
	15:34	But if you R to the city, and say
	19:14	word to the king, R, both you and all
	19:37	Pray let your servant R, that I may die
	24:13	what answer I shall R to him who sent
1Kgs	12:24	R every man to his home, for this thing
	12:27	will kill me and R to Rehoboam king of
	13:9	nor drink water, nor R by the way that
	13:10	way, and did not R by the way that
	13:16	said, "I may not R with you, or go
	13:17	drink water there, nor R by the way that
	19:15	said to him, "Go, R on your way to
	22:17	no master; let each R to his home in
	22:28	Micaiah said, "If you R in peace, the LORD
2Kgs	19:7	hear a rumor and R to his own land;
	19:33	the same he shall R, and he shall not
1Chr	19:5	Jericho until your beards have grown, and then R
	21:12	what answer I shall R to him who sent
2Chr	11:4	R every man to his home, for this thing
	18:16	no master; let each R to his home in
	18:26	and water, until I R in peace.'"
	18:27	Micaiah said, "If you R in peace, the LORD
	24:11	and take it and R it to its place.
	30:6	"O people of Israel, R to the LORD, the
	30:9	For if you R to the LORD, your brethren
	30:9	with their captors, and R to this land.
	30:9	from you, if you R to him."
	32:25	Hezekiah did not make R according to the benefit
Neh	1:9	peoples; but if you R to me and keep
	2:6	will you be gone, and when will you R
	5:11	R to them this very day their fields, their
	9:17	appointed a leader to R to their bondage in
Tob	2:13	R it to the owners; for it is not
	2:14	and told her to R it to the owners;
	5:15	wages if you both R safe and sound." So
	5:20	my sister; he will R safe and sound, and
	6:12	as soon as we R from Rages we will
	6:17	it and flee away, and will never again R
	8:21	of Raguel's property and R in safety to his
	14:5	After this they will R from the places of
Jud	6:6	you shall fall among their wounded, when I R
Esth	4:13	Mordecai told them to R answer to Esther, "Think
Job	1:21	and naked shall I R; the LORD gave, and
	10:21	whence I shall not R, to the land of
	15:22	believe that he will R out of darkness, and
	16:22	shall go the way whence I shall not R
	22:23	If you R to the Almighty and humble yourself,
	33:25	with youth; let him R to the days of
	34:15	together, and man would R to dust.
	36:10	and commands that they R from iniquity.
	39:4	forth, and do not R to them.
	39:12	him that he will R, and bring your grain
Ps	51:13	ways, and sinners will R to thee.
	79:12	R sevenfold into the bosom of our neighbors the
	90:13	R, O LORD!
	94:15	heritage; for justice will R to the righteous, and
	104:29	breath, they die and R to their dust.
	109:4	In R for my love they accuse me, even
	116:7	R, O my soul, to your rest; for the
Eccl	12:2	darkened and the clouds R after the rain;
Song	6:13	R, return, O Shulammite, return, return, that we may
	6:13	Return, R, O Shulammite, return, return, that we
	6:13	Return, return, O Shulammite, R, return, that we
	6:13	return, O Shulammite, return, R, that we may look
Wis	2:1	has been known to R from Hades.
	2:5	and there is no R from our death, because
	11:15	In R for their foolish and wicked thoughts, which
	15:8	he is required to R the soul that was
Sir	16:28	he covered its surface, and to it they R
	17:19	repent he grants a R, and he encourages those
	17:21	R to the Most High and turn away from
	20:9	there is a gift that brings a double R
	40:1	till the day they R to the mother of
Is	10:21	A remnant will R, the remnant of Jacob, to
	10:22	the sea, only a remnant of them will R
	19:22	healing, and they will R to the LORD, and
	23:17	Tyre, and she will R to her hire, and
	35:10	of the LORD shall R, and come to Zion
	37:7	hear a rumor, and R to his own land;
	37:34	the same he shall R, and he shall not
	43:4	I give men in R for you, peoples in
	44:22	your sins like mist; R to me, for I
	45:23	word that shall not R: 'To me every knee
	51:11	of the LORD shall R, and come to Zion
	52:8	eye they see the R of the LORD to
	55:7	his thoughts; let him R to the LORD, that
	55:10	down from heaven, and R not thither but water
	55:11	mouth; it shall not R to me empty, but
	63:17	R for the sake of thy servants, the tribes
Jer	3:1	man's wife, will he R to her?
	3:1	lovers; and would you R to me?
	3:7	all this she will R to me'; but she
	3:7	but she did not R, and her false sister
	3:10	sister Judah did not R to me with her
	3:12	the north, and say, R, faithless Israel, says the
	3:14	R, O faithless children, says the LORD; for I
	3:22	R, O faithless sons, I will heal your faithlessness."
	4:1	"If you R, O Israel, says the LORD, to
	4:1	Israel, says the LORD, to me you should R
	8:4	If one turns away, does he not R
	8:5	They hold fast to deceit, they refuse to R
	14:3	find no water, they R with their vessels empty;
	15:19	the LORD: "If you R, I will restore you,
	18:11	R, every one from his evil way, and amend
	22:10	away, for he shall R no more to see
	22:11	this place: "He shall R here no more,
	22:27	they will long to R, there they shall not
	22:27	will long to return, there they shall not R
	24:7	God, for they shall R to me with their
	30:10	Jacob shall R and have quiet and ease, and
	31:8	great company, they shall R here.
	31:21	R, O virgin Israel, return to these your cities.
	31:21	Return, O virgin Israel, R to these your cities.
	37:7	you is about to R to Egypt, to its
	40:5	If you remain, then R to Gedaliah the son
	44:14	escape or survive or R to the land of
	44:14	which they desire to R to dwell there; for
	44:14	for they shall not R, except some fugitives."
	44:28	escape the sword shall R from the land of
	46:27	Jacob shall R and have quiet and ease, and
	50:9	warrior who does not R empty-handed.
Lam	3:40	examine our ways, and R to the LORD!
Bar	1:8	from the temple, to R them to the land
	4:28	go astray from God, R with tenfold zeal to
Ezek	7:13	the seller shall not R to what he has
	16:55	and her daughters shall R to their former estate,
	16:55	and her daughters shall R to their former estate;
	16:55	and your daughters shall R to your former estate.
	21:30	R it to its sheath.

46:9 gate: no one shall R by way of the
Dan 10:20 But now I will R to fight against the
11:9 the south but shall R into his own land.
11:28 And he shall R to his land with great
11:28 work his will, and R to his own land.
11:29 time appointed he shall R and come into the
13:49 R to the place of judgment.
14:12 And when you R in the morning, if you
Hos 2:7 'I will go and R to my first husband,
3:5 children of Israel shall R and seek the LORD
5:4 not permit them to R to their God.
5:15 I will R again to my place, until they
6:1 saying, "Come, let us R to the LORD; for
7:11 yet they do not R to the LORD their
8:13 their sins; they shall R to Egypt.
9:3 LORD; but Ephraim shall R to Egypt, and they
11:5 They shall R to the land of Egypt, and
11:5 they have refused to R to me.
11:11 Assyria; and I will R them to their homes,
12:6 help of your God, R, hold fast to love
14:1 R, O Israel, to the LORD your God, for
14:2 with you words and R to the LORD; say
14:7 They shall R and dwell beneath my shadow, they
Joel 2:12 says the LORD, R to me with all your
2:13 R to the LORD, your God, for he is
Amos 4:6 yet you did not R to me," says the
4:8 yet you did not R to me," says the
4:9 yet you did not R to me," says the
4:10 yet you did not R to me," says the
4:11 yet you did not R to me," says the
Obad 1:15 you, your deeds shall R on your own head.
Mic 1:7 to the hire of a harlot they shall R
5:3 of his brethren shall R to the people of
Zeph 2:10 be their lot in R for their pride, because
Hag 2:17 yet you did not R to me, says the
Zech 1:3 the LORD of hosts: R to me, says the
1:3 hosts, and I will R to you, says the
1:4 the LORD of hosts, R from your evil ways
8:3 the LORD: I will R to Zion, and will
9:12 R to your stronghold, O prisoners of hope; today
10:9 and with their children they shall live and R
Mal 3:7 R to me, and I will return to you,
3:7 me, and I will R to you, says the
3:7 say, 'How shall we R
1Mac 3:56 fainthearted, that each should R to his home,
4:24 On their R they sang hymns and praises to
5:19 engage in battle with the Gentiles until we R
6:4 departed from there to R to Babylon.
7:35 time, then if I R safely I will burn
8:26 shall keep their obligations without receiving any R
2Mac 8:25 they were obliged to R because the hour was
11:29 that you wish to R home and look after
Mt 2:12 a dream not to R to Herod, they departed
10:13 worthy, let your peace R to you.
12:44 he says, 'I will R to my house from
16:26 a man give in R for his life?
Mk 8:37 a man give in R for his life?
Lk 6:35 lend, expecting nothing in R; and your reward will
8:39 sent him away, saying, R to your home, and
9:10 On their R the apostles told him what they
10:6 if not, it shall R to you.
11:24 he says, 'I will R to my house from
14:12 also invite you in R, and you be repaid.
17:18 no one found to R and give praise to
19:12 country to receive a kingly power and then R
Acts 13:34 dead, no more to R to corruption, he spoke
15:16 'After this I will R, and I will rebuild
15:35 Barnabas, "Come, let us R and visit the brethren
18:21 he said, "I will R to you if God
20:3 Syria, he determined to R through Macedonia.
Rom 6:21 But then what R did you get from the
6:22 slaves of God, the R you get is sanctification
9:9 this time I will R and Sarah shall have
1Cor 16:11 peace, that he may R to me; for I
2Cor 6:13 In R --I speak as to children--widen your
1Tim 5:4 family and make some R to their parents; for
Heb 11:15 gone out, they would have had opportunity to R
1Pet 2:23 did not revile in R; when he suffered, he
3:9 Do not R evil for evil or reviling for

RETURNED (210)

Gen 8:9 her foot, and she R to him to the
18:33 to Abraham; and Abraham R to his place.
21:32 army rose up and R to the land of
22:19 So Abraham R to his young men, and they
31:55 then he departed and R home.
32:6 And the messengers R to Jacob, saying, "We came
33:16 So Esau R that day on his way to
37:29 When Reuben R to the pit and saw that
37:30 rent his clothes and R to his brothers, and
38:22 So he R to Judah, and said, "I have
42:24 and wept; and he R to them and spoke
43:10 we would now have R twice."
43:12 the money that was R in the mouth of
44:4 them, 'Why have you R evil for good?
44:13 his ass, and they R to the city.
50:14 buried his father, Joseph R to Egypt with his
Ex 14:27 sea, and the sea R to its wonted flow
14:28 The waters R and covered the chariots and the
32:31 So Moses R to the LORD and said, "Alas,
34:31 leaders of the congregation R to him, and Moses
Num 11:30 the elders of Israel R to the camp.
13:25 of forty days they R from spying out the
14:36 the land, and who R and made all the
16:50 And Aaron R to Moses at the entrance of
23:6 And he R to him, and lo, he and
Deut 1:45 And you R and wept before the LORD; but
Josh 2:16 until the pursuers have R; then afterward you may
2:22 days, until the pursuers R; for the pursuers had
4:18 waters of the Jordan R to their place and
6:14 the city once, and R into the camp.
7:3 And they R to Joshua, and said to him,
8:24 the sword, all Israel R to Ai, and smote
10:15 Then Joshua R, and all Israel with him, to
10:21 cities, all the people R safe to Joshua in
10:43 Then Joshua R, and all Israel with him, to
22:9 the half-tribe of Manasseh R home, parting from the
22:32 priest, and the chiefs, R from the Reubenites and
Judg 7:3 tested them; twenty-two thousand R, and
7:15 he worshiped; and he R to the camp of
8:13 the son of Joash R from the battle by
11:39 of two months, she R to her father, who
14:8 after a while he R to take her; and
15:19 he drank, his spirit R, and he revived.
21:14 And Benjamin R at that time; and they gave
21:23 then they went and R to their inheritance, and
Ruth 1:22 So Naomi R, and Ruth the Moabitess her
1:22 daughter-in-law with her, who R from the country of
1Sam 6:16 Philistines saw it, they R that day to Ekron.
6:17 tumors, which the Philistines R as a guilt offering
6:21 saying, "The Philistines have R the ark of the
17:57 And as David R from the slaughter of the
18:6 coming home, when David R from slaying the
23:28 So Saul R from pursuing after David, and went
24:1 When Saul R from following the Philistines, he was
25:21 him; and he has R me evil for good.
25:39 evil; the LORD has R the evil-doing of Nabal
26:25 his way, and Saul R to his place.
2Sam 1:1 Saul, when David had R from the slaughter of
1:22 the sword of Saul R not empty.
2:30 Joab R from the pursuit of Abner; and when
3:16 Abner said to him, "Go, return"; and he R
3:27 And when Abner R to Hebron, Joab took him
6:20 And David R to bless his household.
8:13 When he R, he slew eighteen thousand Edomites in
10:14 Then Joab R from fighting against the Ammonites,
11:4 her uncleanness.) Then she R to her house.
12:31 and all the people R to Jerusalem.
17:20 not find them, they R to Jerusalem.
19:39 blessed him, and he R to his own home.
20:22 And Joab R to Jerusalem to the king.
23:10 day; and the men R after him only to
1Kgs 2:41 Jerusalem to Gath and R,
12:2 King Solomon), then Jeroboam R from Egypt.
12:20 heard that Jeroboam had R, they sent and called
19:21 And he R from following him, and took the
2Kgs 1:5 The messengers R to the king, and he said
1:5 and he said to them, "Why have you R
2:25 Carmel, and thence he R to Samaria.
3:27 withdrew from him and R to their own land.
4:31 Therefore he R to meet him, and told him,
5:15 Then he R to the man of God, he
7:15 And the messengers R, and told the king.
8:3 years, when the woman R from the land of
8:29 And King Joram R to be healed in Jezreel
9:15 but King Joram had R to be healed in
14:14 also hostages, and he R to Samaria.
19:8 The Rabshakeh R, and found the king of Assyria
23:20 Then he R to Jerusalem.
1Chr 4:22 ruled in Moab and R to Lehem (now the
20:3 and all the people R to Jerusalem.
2Chr 10:2 King Solomon), then Jeroboam R from Egypt.

11:4 of the LORD, and R and did not go
14:15 Then they R to Jerusalem.
19:1 the king of Judah R in safety to his
20:27 Then they R, every man of Judah and Jerusalem,
22:6 wounded Joram, and he R to be healed in
25:10 angry with Judah, and R home in fierce anger.
25:24 and hostages, and he R to Samaria.
28:15 Then they R to Samaria.
31:1 the people of Israel R to their cities, every
32:21 So he R with shame of face to his
34:7 Then he R to Jerusalem.
Ezra 2:1 captive to Babylonia; they R to Jerusalem and
4:1 Benjamin heard that the R exiles were building a
5:5 and then answer be R by letter concerning it.
6:16 the rest of the R exiles, celebrated the dedication
6:19 the first month the R exiles kept the passover.
6:20 lamb for all the R exiles, for their fellow
6:21 of Israel who had R from exile, and also
8:35 come from captivity, the R exiles, offered burnt
9:4 the faithlessness of the R exiles, gathered round me
10:7 Jerusalem to all the R exiles that they should
10:16 Then the R exiles did so.
Neh 2:15 and entered by the Valley Gate, and so R
4:15 their plan, we all R to the wall, each
7:6 carried into exile; they R to Jerusalem and Judah,
8:17 of those who had R from the captivity made
Tob 1:22 for me, and I R to Nineveh.
2:5 And when I R I washed myself and ate
2:9 the same night I R from burying him, and
2:13 kid; and when she R to me it began
3:17 that very moment Tobit R and entered his house
7:1 They R her greeting, and she brought them into
14:12 Then Tobias R with his wife and his sons
Jud 1:16 Then he R with them to Nineveh, he and
4:3 they had only recently R from the captivity, and
5:19 But now they have R to their God, and
6:13 of the hill, and R to their master.
7:7 over them, and then R to his army.
8:36 So they R from the tent and went to
12:9 So she R clean and stayed in the tent
13:13 unbelievable that she had R; they opened the gate
15:7 the Israelites, when they R from the slaughter, took
16:21 After this every one R home to his own
Esth 6:12 Then Mordecai R to the king's gate.
7:8 And the king R from the palace garden to
Is 37:8 The Rabshakeh R, and found the king of Assyria
Jer 40:12 then all the Jews R from all the places
43:5 of Judah who had R to live in the
Dan 4:34 heaven, and my reason R to me, and I
4:36 same time my reason R to me; and for
4:36 my majesty and splendor R to me.
13:50 Then all the people R in haste.
14:39 angel of God immediately R Habakkuk to his own
Zech 1:16 the LORD, I have R to Jerusalem with compassion;
1Mac 1:20 After subduing Egypt, Antiochus R in the one
2:63 found, because he has R to the dust, and
3:33 take care of Antiochus his son until he R
4:23 Then Judas R to plunder the camp, and they
5:8 its villages; then he R to Judea.
5:54 had fallen before they R in safety.
5:68 plundered the cities and R to the land of
6:56 to be king, had R from Persia and Media
6:63 departed with haste and R to Antioch.
7:25 not withstand them, he R to the king and
9:42 of their brother, they R to the marshes of
9:50 Bacchides then R to Jerusalem and built strong
9:57 Alcimus was dead, he R to the king, and
10:9 to Jonathan, and he R them to their parents.
10:52 message: "Since I have R to my kingdom and
10:55 day on which you R to the land of
10:66 And Jonathan R to Jerusalem in peace and gladness.
10:68 was greatly grieved and R to Antioch.
10:87 and those with him R to Jerusalem with much
11:7 called Eleutherus; then he R to Jerusalem.
11:51 his kingdom, and they R to Jerusalem with much
11:54 After this Trypho R, and with him the young
11:73 fleeing saw this, they R to him and joined
11:74 And Jonathan R to Jerusalem.
12:24 commanders of Demetrius had R, with a larger force
12:26 their camp, and they R and reported to him
12:35 When Jonathan R he convened the elders of the
12:46 the troops, and they R to the land of
15:36 him a word, but R in wrath to the
16:10 And he R to Judea safely.
16:17 of great treachery and R evil for good.
2Mac 2:17 his people, and has R the inheritance to all,
4:25 the king's orders he R, possessing no qualification for
4:36 When the king R from the region of Cilicia,
12:1 had been reached, Lysias R to the king, and
Mk 2:1 And when he R to Caperna-um after some days,
6:30 The apostles R to Jesus, and told him all
7:30 Then he R from the region of Tyre, and
Lk 1:56 about three months, and R to her home.
2:20 And the shepherds R, glorifying and praising God for
2:39 of the Lord, they R into Galilee, to their
2:45 not find him, they R to Jerusalem, seeking him.
4:1 of the Holy Spirit, R from the Jordan, and
4:14 And Jesus R in the power of the Spirit
7:10 who had been sent R to the house, they
8:37 fear; so he got into the boat and R
8:40 Now when Jesus R, the crowd welcomed him, for
8:55 And her spirit R, and she got up at
10:17 The seventy R with joy, saying, "Lord, even the
19:15 over us.' When he R, having received the kingly
23:47 what had taken place, R home beating their breasts.
23:55 was laid; then they R, and prepared spices and
24:33 that same hour and R to Jerusalem; and they
24:52 they worshipped him, and R to Jerusalem with great
Acts 1:12 Then they R to Jerusalem from the mount called
5:22 the prison, and they R and reported,
8:25 of the Lord, they R to Jerusalem, preaching the
12:25 And Barnabas and Saul R from Jerusalem when
13:13 John left them and R to Jerusalem;
14:21 made many disciples, they R to Lystra and to
21:6 the ship, and they R home.
22:17 name.' "When I had R to Jerusalem and was
23:32 on the morrow they R to the barracks, leaving
Gal 1:17 Arabia; and again I R to Damascus.
1Pet 2:25 sheep, but have now R to the Shepherd and

RETURNING (10)

1Sam 6:8 gold, which you are R to him as a
7:3 Israel, "If you are R to the LORD with
2Chr 20:27 Jehoshaphat at their head, R to Jerusalem with joy,
Is 30:15 One of Israel, "In R and rest you shall
2Mac 15:28 over and they were R with joy, they recognized
Mt 21:18 morning, as he was R to the city, he
Lk 2:43 ended, as they were R, the boy Jesus stayed
24:9 remembered his words, and R from the tomb they
Acts 8:28 to worship and was R; seated in his chariot,
Heb 7:1 High God, met Abraham R from the slaughter of

RETURNS (13)

Lev 22:13 has no child, and R to her father's house,
Job 7:10 not come up; he R no more to his
Ps 7:16 His mischief R upon his own head, and on
146:4 his breath departs he R to his earth; on
Prov 17:13 If a man R evil for good, evil will
26:11 Like a dog that R to his vomit is
Eccl 1:6 the wind, and on its circuits the wind R
12:7 cistern, and the dust R to the earth as
12:7 was, and the spirit R to God who gave
Sir 27:9 their kind; so truth R to those who practice
35:2 He who R a kindness offers fine flour, and
40:11 is from the waters R to the sea.
41:10 is from the dust R to dust; so the

REU (6)

Gen 11:18 became the father of R;
11:19 after the birth of R two hundred and nine
11:20 When R had lived thirty-two years, he became the
11:21 father of Serug; and R lived after the birth
1Chr 1:25 Arpachshad, Shelah; Eber, Peleg, R;
Lk 3:35 Serug, the son of R, the son of Peleg,

REUBEN (59)

Gen 29:32 she called his name R; for she said, "Because
30:14 days of wheat harvest R went and found mandrakes
35:22 dwelt in that land R went and lay with
35:23 The sons of Leah: R (Jacob's first-born), Simeon,
37:21 But when R heard it, he delivered him out
37:22 And R said to them, "Shed no blood; cast
37:29 When R returned to the pit and saw that
42:22 And R answered them, "Did I not tell you
42:37 Then R said to his father, "Slay my two
46:8 R, Jacob's first-born,
46:9 and the sons of R: Hanoch, Pallu, Hezron, and
48:5 shall be mine, as R and Simeon are.
49:3 R, you are my first-born, my might, and the
Ex 1:2 each with his household: R, Simeon, Levi, and Judah,
6:14 houses: the sons of R, the first-born of Israel:
6:14 Hezron, and Carmi; these are the families of R

Num 1:5 From R, Elizur the son of Shedeur;
1:20 The people of R, Israel's first-born, their generations,
1:21 of the tribe of R was forty-six thousand five
2:10 of the camp of R by their companies, the
2:10 of the people of R being Elizur the son
2:16 of the camp of R, by their companies, is
7:30 of the men of R:
10:18 of the camp of R set out by their
13:4 From the tribe of R, Shammua the son of
16:1 of Peleth, sons of R,
26:5 land of Egypt, were: R, the first-born of Israel;
26:5 Israel; the sons of R: of Hanoch, the family
32:1 Now the sons of R and the sons of
32:2 and the sons of R came and said to
32:6 to the sons of R, "Shall your brethren go
32:25 and the sons of R said to Moses, "Your
32:29 and the sons of R, every man who is
32:31 and the sons of R answered, "As the LORD
32:33 to the sons of R and to the half-tribe
32:37 And the sons of R built Heshbon, Elealeh,
34:14 of the sons of R by fathers' houses and
Deut 11:6 of Eliab, son of R; how the earth opened
27:13 Ebal for the curse: R, Gad, Asher, Zebulun, Dan,
33:6 "Let R live, and not die, nor let his
Josh 4:12 The sons of R and the sons of Gad
13:23 of the people of R was the Jordan as
15:6 Bohan the son of R;
18:7 heritage; and Gad and R and half the tribe
18:17 Bohan the son of R;
20:8 from the tribe of R, and Ramoth in Gilead,
21:7 from the tribe of R, the tribe of Gad,
21:36 of the tribe of R, Bezer with its pasture
Judg 5:15 Among the clans of R there were great searchings
5:16 Among the clans of R there were great searchings
1Chr 2:1 the sons of Israel: R, Simeon, Levi, Judah, Issachar,
5:1 The sons of R the first-born of Israel (for
5:3 Joseph), the sons of R, the first-born of Israel:
6:63 of the tribes of R, Gad, and Zebulun.
6:78 of the tribe of R: Bezer in the steppe
Ezek 48:6 side to the west, R, one portion.
48:7 Adjoining the territory of R, from the east side
48:31 gates, the gate of R, the gate of Judah,
Rev 7:5 of the tribe of R, twelve thousand of the

REUBENITE

1Chr 11:42 son of Shiza the R, a leader of the

REUBENITES (31)

Num 26:7 the families of the R; and their number was
Deut 3:12 I gave to the R and the Gadites the
3:16 Gilead, and to the R and the Gadites I
4:43 the tableland for the R, and Ramoth in Gilead
29:8 an inheritance to the R, the Gadites, and the
Josh 1:12 And to the R, the Gadites, and the half-tribe
12:6 a possession to the R and the Gadites and
13:8 tribe of Manasseh the R and the Gadites received
13:15 the tribe of the R according to their families.
13:23 the inheritance of the R, according to their families
22:1 Then Joshua summoned the R, and the Gadites, and
22:9 So the R and the Gadites and the half-tribe
22:10 land of Canaan, the R and the Gadites and
22:11 heard say, "Behold, the R and the Gadites and
22:13 Israel sent to the R and the Gadites and
22:15 they came to the R, the Gadites, and the
22:21 Then the R, the Gadites, and the half-tribe of
22:25 us and you, you R and Gadites; you have
22:30 the words that the R and the Gadites and
22:31 priest said to the R and the Gadites and
22:32 chiefs, returned from the R and the Gadites in
22:33 the land where the R and the Gadites were
22:34 The R and the Gadites called the altar Witness;
2Kgs 10:33 the Gadites, and the R, and the Manassites, from
1Chr 5:6 into exile; he was a chieftain of the R
5:18 The R, the Gadites, and the half-tribe of Manasseh
5:26 them away, namely, the R, the Gadites, and the
11:42 a leader of the R, and thirty with him,
12:37 Of the R and Gadites and the half-tribe of
26:32 the oversight of the R, the Gadites, and the
27:16 of Israel, for the R Eliezer the son of

REUEL (11)

Gen 36:4 Esau, Eliphaz; Basemath bore R;
36:10 the wife of Esau, R the son of Basemath
36:13 are the sons of R: Nahath, Zerah, Shammah, and
36:17 are the sons of R, Esau's son: the chiefs
36:17 are the chiefs of R in the land of
Ex 2:18 came to their father R, he said, "How is
Num 2:14 Eliasaph the son of R,
10:29 the son of R the Midianite, Moses' father-in-law,
1Chr 1:35 sons of Esau: Eliphaz, R, Jeush, Jalam, and Korah.
1:37 The sons of R: Nahath, Zerah, Shammah, and
9:8 of Shephatiah, son of R, son of Ibnijah;

REUMAH

Gen 22:24 concubine, whose name was R, bore Tebah, Gaham,

REVEAL (13)

Tob 12:7 king, but gloriously to R the works of God.
12:11 king, but gloriously to R the works of God.'
Job 20:27 The heavens will R his iniquity, and the earth
Sir 1:27 The Lord will R your secrets and cast you
4:18 gladden him, and will R her secrets to him.
8:19 will divulge Do not R your thoughts to every
39:8 He will R instruction in his teaching, and will
Jer 33:6 will heal them and R to them abundance of
Dan 2:47 have been able to R this mystery."
Mt 11:27 the Son chooses to R him.
Lk 10:22 the Son chooses to R him."
Gal 1:16 grace, was pleased to R his Son to me,
Phil 3:15 otherwise minded, God will R that also to you.

REVEALED (54)

Gen 35:7 because there God had R himself to him when
41:25 is one; God has R to Pharaoh what he
Deut 29:29 the things that are R belong to us and
1Sam 2:27 LORD has said, 'I R myself to the house
3:7 had not yet been R to him.
3:21 Shiloh, for the LORD R himself to Samuel at
9:15 came, the LORD had R to Samuel:
1Chr 17:25 thou, my God, hast R to thy servant that
Job 38:17 gates of death been R to you, or have
Ps 98:2 his victory, he has R his vindication in the
Sir 1:5 root of wisdom--to whom has it been R
11:25 of a man's life his deeds will be R
46:20 asleep he prophesied and R to the king his
48:25 He R what was to occur to the end
Is 22:14 LORD of hosts has R himself in my ears:
23:1 of Cyprus it is R to them.
40:5 the LORD shall be R, and all flesh shall
53:1 whom has the arm of the LORD been R
56:1 my salvation will come, and my deliverance be R
Dan 2:19 Then the mystery was R to Daniel in a
2:30 has this mystery been R to me, but in
10:1 Persia a word was R to Daniel, who was
Hos 7:2 corruption of Ephraim is R, and the wicked deeds
Mt 10:26 that will not be R, or hidden that will
11:25 wise and understanding and R them to babes;
16:17 and blood has not R this to you, but
Lk 2:26 And it had been R to him by the
2:35 that thoughts out of many hearts may be R
10:21 wise and understanding and R them to babes; yea,
12:2 that will not be R, or hidden that will
17:30 the day when the Son of man is R
Jn 1:31 that he might be R to Israel."
12:38 whom has the arm of the Lord been R
21:1 After this Jesus R himself again to the disciples
21:1 of Tiberi-as; and he R himself in this way.
21:14 time that Jesus was R to the disciples after
Rom 1:17 righteousness of God is R through faith for faith;
1:18 wrath of God is R from heaven against all
2:5 of wrath when God's righteous judgment will be R
8:18 that is to be R to us.
1Cor 2:10 God has R to us through the Spirit.
3:13 because it will be R with fire, and the
2Cor 7:12 for us might be R to you in the
Gal 3:23 law, kept under restraint until faith should be R
Eph 3:5 it has now been R to his holy apostles
2Thes 1:7 the Lord Jesus is R from heaven with his
2:3 man of lawlessness is R, the son of perdition,
2:6 that he may be R in his time.
2:8 lawless one will be R, and the Lord Jesus
1Pet 1:5 salvation ready to be R in the last time.
1:12 It was R to them that they were serving
4:13 rejoice and be glad when his glory is R
5:1 partaker in the glory that is to be R
Rev 15:4 and worship thee, for thy judgments have been R

REVEALER

Dan 2:47 of kings, and a R of mysteries, for you

REVEALING (5)

Sir 41:23 you hear, and of R secrets.

R

Bar 6:26 carried on men's shoulders, R to mankind their
Amos 3:7 GOD does nothing, without R his secret to his
Rom 8:19 eager longing for the R of the sons of
1Cor 1:7 you wait for the R of our Lord Jesus

REVEALS (7)
Prov 11:13 about as a talebearer R secrets, but he who
20:19 who goes about gossiping R secrets; therefore do not
Sir 42:19 to be, and he R the tracks of hidden
Dan 2:22 who have understanding; he R deep and mysterious
2:28 God in heaven who R mysteries, and he has
2:29 hereafter, and he who R mysteries made known to
2Mac 12:41 the righteous Judge, who R the things that are

REVEL (3)
Sir 9:9 another man's wife, nor R with her at wine;
18:31 Do not R in great luxury, lest you become
2Pet 2:13 count it pleasure to R in the daytime.

REVELATION (14)
2Sam 7:27 Israel, hast made this R to thy servant, saying,
Hab 2:19 Can this give R
Lk 2:32 peoples, a light for R to the Gentiles, and
Rom 16:24 Christ, according to the R of the mystery which
1Cor 14:6 I bring you some R or knowledge or prophecy
14:26 hymn, a lesson, a R, a tongue, or an
14:30 If a R is made to another sitting by,
Gal 1:12 it came through a R of Jesus Christ.
2:2 I went up by R; and I laid before
Eph 1:17 of wisdom and of R in the knowledge of
3:3 known to me by R, as I have written
1Pet 1:7 and honor at the R of Jesus Christ.
1:13 to you at the R of Jesus Christ.
Rev 1:1 THE R of Jesus Christ, which

REVELATIONS (2)
2Cor 12:1 on to visions and R of the Lord.
12:7 by the abundance of R, a thorn was given

REVELER
Sir 21:15 to it; when a R hears it, he dislikes

REVELING (3)
2Mac 6:4 filled with debauchery and R by the Gentiles, who
Rom 13:13 the day, not in R and drunkenness, not in
2Pet 2:13 are blots and blemishes, R in their dissipation,

REVELRY (2)
Wis 2:9 to share in our R, everywhere let us leave
Amos 6:7 into exile, and the R of those who stretch

REVELS (2)
Wis 14:23 mysteries, or hold frenzied R with strange customs,
1Pet 4:3 in licentiousness, passions, drunkenness, R, carousing,

REVENGE (8)
Jud 1:12 he would surely take R on the whole territory
2:1 about carrying out his R on the whole region,
6:5 day until I take R on this race that
8:27 nor has he taken R upon us; but the
8:35 before you, to take R upon our enemies."
9:2 a sword to take R on the strangers who
Prov 6:34 and he will not spare when he takes R
Jer 20:10 him, and take our R on him."

REVENGEFULLY (2)
Ezek 25:12 GOD: Because Edom acted R against the house of
25:15 Because the Philistines acted R and took vengeance

REVENUE (7)
Ezra 4:13 toll, and the royal R will be impaired.
6:8 delay from the royal R, the tribute of the
Is 23:3 on many waters; your R was the grain of
2Mac 4:8 from another source of R, eighty talents.
4:28 the collection of the R was his responsibility, the
Rom 13:7 whom taxes are due, R to whom revenue is
13:7 due, revenue to whom R is due, respect to

REVENUES (9)
Prov 16:8 with righteousness than great R with injustice.
1Mac 3:29 exhausted, and that the R from the country were
3:31 Persia and collect the R from those regions and
10:31 her tithes and her R, be holy and free
10:40 out of the king's R from appropriate places.
10:44 be paid from the R of the king.
10:45 be paid from the R of the king."

2Mac 3:3 defrayed from his own R all the expenses connected
9:16 provide from his own R;

REVERE (4)
Lev 19:3 one of you shall R his mother and his
Deut 32:51 because you did not R me as holy in
Ps 119:48 I R thy commandments, which I love, and I
Dan 14:5 "Because I do not R man-made idols, but the

REVERED (5)
1Kgs 18:3 (Now Obadiah R the LORD greatly;
18:12 I your servant have R the LORD from my
Dan 14:4 The king R it and went every day to
14:23 was also a great dragon, which the Babylonians R
2Mac 6:28 and nobly for the R and holy laws." When

REVERENCE (7)
Lev 19:30 keep my sabbaths and R my sanctuary: I am
26:2 keep my sabbaths and R my sanctuary: I am
Judg 6:10 you shall not pay R to the gods of
Eph 5:21 one another out of R for Christ.
Heb 12:28 God acceptable worship, with R and awe;
1Pet 3:15 but in your hearts R Christ as Lord.
3:15 it with gentleness and R;

REVERENT (2)
Tit 2:3 women likewise to be R in behavior, not to
1Pet 3:2 when they see your R and chaste behavior.

REVERT
Ezek 46:17 liberty; then it shall R to the prince; only

REVIEWED
Ezra 8:15 As I R the people and the priests, I

REVILE (11)
Ex 22:28 "You shall not R God, nor curse a ruler
Ps 74:10 Is the enemy to R thy name for ever?
Mt 5:11 are you when men R you and persecute you
Lk 6:22 they exclude you and R you, and cast out
Acts 23:4 by said, "Would you R God's high priest?"
1Tim 5:14 enemy no occasion to R us.
1Pet 2:23 reviled, he did not R in return; when he
3:16 are abused, those who R your good behavior in
2Pet 2:10 are not afraid to R the glorious ones,
Jude 1:8 flesh, reject authority, and R the glorious ones.
1:10 But these men R whatever they do not understand,

REVILED (14)
Judg 9:27 ate and drank and R Abimelech.
2Kgs 19:6 king of Assyria have R me.
19:22 "Whom have you mocked and R
Is 37:6 king of Assyria have R me.
37:23 'Whom have you mocked and R
65:7 upon the mountains and R me upon the hills,
Mt 27:44 crucified with him also R him in the same
Mk 15:31 crucified with him also R him.
Jn 9:28 And they R him, saying, "You are his disciple,
Acts 13:45 spoken by Paul, and R him.
18:6 when they opposed and R him, he shook out
1Cor 4:12 When R, we bless; when persecuted, we endure;
1Pet 2:23 When he was R, he did not revile in
2Pet 2:2 of them the way of truth will be R

REVILER (2)
Sir 23:8 through his lips, the R and the arrogant are
1Cor 5:11 or is an idolater, R, drunkard, or robber—not

REVILERS (2)
Ps 44:16 of the taunters and R, at the sight of
1Cor 6:10 greedy, nor drunkards, nor R, nor robbers will inherit

REVILES (3)
Num 15:30 native or a sojourner, R the LORD, and that
Ps 74:18 and an impious people R thy name.
Sir 22:18 away, and one who R a friend will break

REVILING (8)
Sir 22:20 possible; but as for R, arrogance, disclosure of
Is 43:28 delivered Jacob to utter destruction and Israel to R
Lk 22:63 other words against him, R him.
1Pet 3:9 evil for evil or R for reviling; but on
3:9 evil or reviling for R; but on the contrary
2Pet 2:11 do not pronounce a R judgment upon them before
2:12 be caught and killed, R in matters of which
Jude 1:9 presume to pronounce a R judgment upon him, but

REVILINGS (3)
Is 51:7 of men, and be not dismayed at their R
Ezek 35:12 have heard all the R which you uttered against
Zeph 2:8 of Moab and the R of the Ammonites, how

REVIVE (14)
Neh 4:2 Will they R the stones out of the heaps
Ps 69:32 glad; you who seek God, let your hearts R
71:20 many sore troubles wilt R me again; from the
85:6 Wilt thou not R us again, that thy people
119:25 cleaves to the dust; R me according to thy
Sir 46:12 May their bones R from where they lie, and
49:10 of the twelve prophets R from where they lie,
Is 57:15 and humble spirit, to R the spirit of the
57:15 the humble, and to R the heart of the
Lam 1:11 treasures for food to R their strength.
1:16 from me, one to R my courage; my children
1:19 they sought food to R their strength.
Hos 6:2 two days he will R us; on the third
2Mac 13:11 had just begun to R fall into the hands

REVIVED (7)
Gen 45:27 of their father Jacob R;
Judg 15:19 when he drank, his spirit returned, and he R
1Sam 30:12 had eaten, his spirit R; for he had not
1Kgs 17:22 the child came into him again, and he R
2Kgs 13:21 bones of Elisha, he R, and stood on his
Rom 7:9 the commandment came, sin R and I died;
Phil 4:10 at length you have R your concern for me;

REVIVING (3)
Ezra 9:8 grant us a little R in our bondage.
9:9 to grant us some R to set up the
Ps 19:7 the LORD is perfect, R the soul; the testimony

REVOKE (10)
Num 23:20 blessed, and I cannot R it.
Esth 8:5 order be written to R the letters devised by
Amos 1:3 four, I will not R the punishment; because they
1:6 four, I will not R the punishment; because they
1:9 four, I will not R the punishment; because they
1:11 four, I will not R the punishment; because he
1:13 four, I will not R the punishment; because they
2:1 four, I will not R the punishment; because he
2:4 four, I will not R the punishment; because they
2:6 four, I will not R the punishment; because they

REVOKED (3)
Esth 8:8 and sealed with the king's ring cannot be R
Dan 6:8 the Medes and the Persians, which cannot be R
6:12 of the Medes and Persians, which cannot be R

REVOLT (7)
Sir 47:23 Rehoboam, whose policy caused the people to R
Is 59:13 God, speaking oppression and R, conceiving and
Jer 11:9 to me, "There is R among the men of
1Mac 11:14 because the people of that region were in R
13:16 released he will not R against us, and we
2Mac 5:11 took it to mean that Judea was in R
Acts 21:38 recently stirred up a R and led the four

REVOLTED (12)
2Kgs 8:20 In his days Edom R from the rule of
8:22 So Edom R from the rule of Judah to
8:22 Then Libnah R at the same time.
2Chr 21:8 In his days Edom R from the rule of
21:10 So Edom R from the rule of Judah to
21:10 that time Libnah also R from his rule, because
Sir 16:7 the ancient giants who R in their might.
Is 31:6 whom you have deeply R, O people of Israel.
1Mac 11:43 will help me, for all my troops have R
2Mac 1:7 Jason and his company R from the holy land
4:30 Tarsus and of Mallus R because their cities had
13:23 of the government, had R in Antioch; he was

REVULSION
2Mac 9:9 the whole army felt R at his decay.

REWARD (59)
Gen 15:1 am your shield; your R shall be very great."
Num 18:31 for it is your R in return for your
Ruth 2:12 done, and a full R be given you by
1Sam 24:19 So may the LORD R you with good for
2Sam 4:10 Ziklag, which was the R I gave him for
18:22 you will have no R for the tidings?"
19:36 should the king recompense me with such a R
1Kgs 13:7 refresh yourself, and I will give you a R
2Chr 20:11 destroy– behold, they R us by coming to
Job 8:6 himself for you and R you with a rightful
Ps 19:11 servant warned; in keeping them there is great R
28:4 work of their hands; render them their due R
58:11 "Surely there is a R for the righteous; surely
109:5 So they R me evil for good, and hatred
109:20 May this be the R of my accusers from
127:3 the LORD, the fruit of the womb a R
Prov 11:18 but one who sows righteousness gets a sure R
22:4 The R for humility and fear of the LORD
25:22 and the LORD will R you.
Eccl 2:10 and this was my R for all my toil.
4:9 they have a good R for their toil.
9:5 they have no more R; but the memory of
Wis 5:15 for ever, and their R is with the Lord;
10:17 gave holy men the R of their labors; she
Sir 2:8 in him, and your R will not fail;
11:16 and this is the R allotted to him:
11:20 the Lord is the R of the godly, and
11:24 of the Lord to R a man on the
36:16 R those who wait for thee, and let thy
51:22 a tongue as my R, and I will praise
51:30 in God's time he will give you your R
Is 40:10 for him; behold, his R is with him, and
45:13 set my exiles free, not for price or R
62:11 salvation comes; behold, his R is with him, and
2Mac 12:45 looking to the splendid R that is laid up
Mt 5:12 be glad, for your R is great in heaven,
5:46 who love you, what R have you?
6:1 you will have no R from your Father who
6:2 I say to you, they have received their R
6:4 sees in secret will R you.
6:5 I say to you, they have received their R
6:6 sees in secret will R you.
6:16 I say to you, they have received their R
6:18 sees in secret will R you.
10:41 shall receive a prophet's R, and he who receives
10:41 a righteous man shall receive a righteous man's R
10:42 say to you, he shall not lose his R
Mk 9:41 of Christ, will by no means lose his R
Lk 6:23 joy, for behold, your R is great in heaven;
6:35 in return; and your R will be great, and
23:40 are receiving the due R of our deeds; but
Acts 1:18 a field with the R of his wickedness; and
1Cor 3:14 on the foundation survives, he will receive a R
9:17 will, I have a R; but if not of
9:18 What then is my R
Col 3:24 the inheritance as your R; you are serving the
Heb 10:35 throw away your confidence, which has a great R
11:26 treasures of Egypt, for he looked to the R
2Jn 1:8 have worked for, but may win a full R

REWARDED (6)
2Sam 22:21 "The LORD R me according to my righteousness;
2Chr 15:7 hands be weak, for your work shall be R
Esth 12:5 in the court and R him for these things.
Ps 18:20 The LORD R me according to my righteousness;
Prov 13:13 but he who respects the commandment will be R
Jer 31:16 your work shall be R, says the LORD, and

REWARDING (4)
1Kgs 8:32 vindicating the righteous by R him according to his
2Chr 6:23 vindicating the righteous by R him according to his
Jer 32:19 the ways of men, R every man according to
Rev 11:18 to be judged, for R thy servants, the prophets

REWARDS (6)
1Sam 26:23 The LORD R every man for his righteousness and
Prov 13:21 pursues sinners, but prosperity R the righteous.
Dan 2:6 from me gifts and R and great honor.
5:17 yourself, and give your R to another; nevertheless I
2Mac 15:33 and hang up these R of his folly opposite
Heb 11:6 exists and that he R those who seek him.

REWORKED
Jer 18:4 potter's hand, and he R it into another vessel,

REZEPH (2)
2Kgs 19:12 fathers destroyed, Gozan, Haran, R, and the people
Is 37:12 fathers destroyed, Gozan, Haran, R, and the people

REZIN (9)
2Kgs 15:37 LORD began to send R the king of Syria
16:5 Then R king of Syria and Pekah the son
16:9 its people captive to Kir, and he killed R

Ezra 2:48 Re-aiah, the sons of R, the sons of Nekoda,
Neh 7:50 Re-aiah, the sons of R, the sons of Nekoda,
Is 7:1 Uzziah, king of Judah, R the king of Syria
7:4 the fierce anger of R and Syria and the
7:8 is Damascus, and the head of Damascus is R
8:6 melt in fear before R and the son of

REZON

1Kgs 11:23 an adversary to him, R the son of Eliada,

RHEGIUM

Acts 28:13 circuit and arrived at R; and after one day

RHESA

Lk 3:27 Jo-anan, the son of R, the son of Zerubbabel,

RHODA

Acts 12:13 gateway, a maid named R came to answer.

RHODES (3)

Ezek 27:15 The men of R traded with you; many coastlands
1Mac 15:23 to Halicarnassus, and to R, and to Phaselis, and
Acts 21:1 the next day to R, and from there to

RHODOCUS

2Mac 13:21 But R, a man from the ranks of the

RHYTHM (2)

Wis 17:18 wide-spreading branches, or the R of violently
19:18 the nature of the R, while each note remains

RIB

Gen 2:22 with flesh; and the R which the LORD God

RIBAI (2)

2Sam 23:29 Ittai the son of R of Gibe-ah of the
1Chr 11:31 Ithai the son of R of Gibe-ah of the

RIBLAH (12)

Num 34:11 down from Shepham to R on the east side
2Kgs 23:33 him in bonds at R in the land of
25:6 king of Babylon at R, who passed sentence upon
25:20 brought them to the king of Babylon at R
25:21 them to death at R in the land of
Jer 39:5 king of Babylon, at R, in the land of
39:6 sons of Zedekiah at R before his eyes; and
52:9 king of Babylon at R in the land of
52:10 also slew all the princes of Judah at R
52:26 brought them to the king of Babylon at R
52:27 them to death at R in the land of
Ezek 6:14 all their habitations, from the wilderness to R

RIBS (2)

Gen 2:21 took one of his R and closed up its
Dan 7:5 side; it had three R in its mouth between

RICH (129)

Gen 13:2 Now Abram was very R in cattle, in silver,
14:23 'I have made Abram R
26:13 and the man became R, and gained more and
30:43 the man grew exceedingly R, and had large flocks,
49:20 Asher's food shall be R, and he shall yield
Ex 30:15 The R shall not give more, and the poor
Lev 25:47 sojourner with you becomes R, and your brother
25:49 or if he grows R he may redeem himself.
Num 13:20 whether the land is R or poor, and whether
Deut 33:14 the sun, and the R yield of the months,
Judg 5:10 you who sit on R carpets and you who
Ruth 3:10 not gone after young men, whether poor or R
1Sam 2:7 makes poor and makes R; he brings low, he
25:2 The man was very R; he had three thousand
2Sam 12:1 certain city, the one R and the other poor.
12:2 The R man had very many flocks and herds;
12:4 a traveler to the R man, and he was
1Chr 4:40 flocks, where they found R, good pasture, and the
Neh 9:25 fortified cities and a R land, and took possession
9:35 in the large and R land which thou didst
9:37 And its R yield goes to the kings whom
Job 15:29 he will not be R, and his wealth will
27:19 He goes to bed R, but will do so
34:19 princes, nor regards the R more than the poor,
Ps 49:2 both low and high, R and poor together!
49:16 afraid when one becomes R, when the glory of
Prov 10:4 poverty, but the hand of the diligent makes R
10:15 A R man's wealth is his strong city; the
10:22 of the LORD makes R, and he adds no
13:7 man pretends to be R, yet has nothing; another
14:20 his neighbor, but the R has many friends.
18:11 A R man's wealth is his strong city, and
18:23 use entreaties, but the R answer roughly.
21:17 who loves wine and oil will not be R
22:2 The R and the poor meet together; the LORD
22:7 The R rules over the poor, and the borrower
22:16 or gives to the R, will only come to
28:6 his integrity than a R man who is perverse
28:11 A R man is wise in his own eyes,
28:20 who hastens to be R will not go unpunished.
Eccl 5:12 the surfeit of the R will not let him
10:6 high places, and the R sit in a low
10:20 your bedchamber curse the R; for a bird of
Wis 10:11 covetous, she stood by him and made him R
Sir 8:2 not quarrel with a R man, lest his resources
10:21 The R, and the eminent, and the poor--
10:29 his knowledge, while a R man is honored for
11:16 a man who is R through his diligence and
13:3 A R man does wrong, and he even adds
13:4 A R man will exploit you if you can
13:17 what peace between a R man and a poor
13:18 lions; likewise the poor are pastures for the R
13:19 an abomination to a R one.
13:20 When a R man totters, he is steadied by
13:21 If a R man slips, his helpers are many;
13:22 When the R man speaks all are silent, and
19:1 drunkard will not become R; he who despises small
25:2 who is proud, a R man who is a
25:6 R experience is the crown of the aged, and
26:4 Whether R or poor, his heart is glad, and
27:1 whoever seeks to get R will avert his eyes.
30:14 in constitution than a R man who is severely
31:3 The R man toils as his wealth accumulates, and
31:8 Blessed is the R man who is found blameless,
32:6 of emerald in a R setting of gold is
44:6 forth verses in writing; R men furnished with
Is 3:24 and instead of a R robe, a girding of
28:1 the head of the R valley of those overcome
28:4 the head of the R valley, will be like
30:23 ground, which will be R and plenteous.
34:7 and their soil made R with fat.
53:9 wicked and with a R man in his death,
Jer 5:27 have become great and R,
9:23 might, let not the R man glory in his
51:13 dwell by many waters, R in treasures, your end
Ezek 17:3 wings and long pinions, R in plumage of many
Dan 1:5 daily portion of the R food which the king
1:8 himself with the king's R food, or with the
1:13 who eat the king's R food be observed by
1:15 who ate the king's R food.
1:16 steward took away their R food and the wine
11:26 those who eat his R food shall be his
13:4 Joakim was very R, and had a spacious garden
Hos 12:8 "Ah, but I am R, I have gained wealth
Joel 3:5 and have carried my R treasures into your temples.
Mic 6:12 Your R men are full of violence; your inhabitants
Hab 1:16 he lives in luxury, and his food is R
Zech 3:4 will clothe you with R apparel."
11:5 LORD, I have become R; and their own shepherds
1Mac 6:2 Its temple was very R, containing golden shields,
2Mac 7:24 he would make him R and enviable if he
Mt 19:23 be hard for a R man to enter the
19:24 needle than for a R man to enter the
27:57 evening, there came a R man from Arimathea,
Mk 10:25 needle than for a R man to enter the
12:41 Many R people put in large sums.
Lk 1:53 good things, and the R he has sent empty
6:24 to you that are R, for you have received
12:16 "The land of a R man brought forth plentifully;
12:21 himself, and is not R toward God."
14:12 or your kinsmen or R neighbors, lest they also
16:1 disciples, "There was a R man who had a
16:19 "There was a R man, who was clothed in
16:21 what fell from the R man's table; moreover the
16:22 The R man also died and was buried;
18:23 this he became sad, for he was very R
18:25 needle than for a R man to enter the
19:2 Zacchaeus; he was a chief tax collector, and R
21:1 up and saw the R putting their gifts into
1Cor 4:8 Already you have become R
2Cor 6:10 poor, yet making many R; as having nothing, and
8:9 that though he was R, yet for your sake
8:9 so that by his poverty you might become R
Eph 2:4 But God, who is R in mercy, out of
1Tim 6:9 who desire to be R fall into temptation, into

6:17 As for the R in this world, charge them
6:18 do good, to be R in good deeds, liberal
Jas 1:9 his exaltation, and the R in his humiliation, because
1:10 So will the R man fade away in the
2:5 the world to be R in faith and heirs
2:6 Is it not the R who oppress you, is
5:1 Come now, you R, weep and howl for the
Rev 2:9 poverty (but you are R and the slander of
3:17 you say, I am R, I have prospered, and
3:18 that you may be R, and white garments to
6:15 the generals and the R and the strong, and
13:16 small and great, both R and poor, both free
18:3 the earth have grown R with the wealth of
18:19 ships at sea grew R by her wealth!

RICHER (4)

Prov 11:24 yet grows all the R; another withholds what he
Wis 8:5 in life, what is R than wisdom who effects
Sir 13:2 a man mightier and R than you.
Dan 11:2 fourth shall be far R than all of them;

RICHES (74)

1Sam 17:25 will enrich with great R, and will give him
1Kgs 3:11 yourself long life or R or the life of
3:13 have not asked, both R and honor, so that
10:23 of the earth in R and in wisdom.
1Chr 29:12 Both R and honor come from thee, and thou
29:28 age, full of days, R, and honor; and Solomon
2Chr 1:12 will also give you R, possessions, and honor, such
9:22 of the earth in R and in wisdom.
17:5 and he had great R and honor.
18:1 Now Jehoshaphat had great R and honor; and he
32:27 Hezekiah had very great R and honor; and he
Esth 1:4 while he showed the R of his royal glory
5:11 the splendor of his R, the number of his
Job 20:15 He swallows down R and vomits them up again;
Ps 49:6 wealth and boast of the abundance of their R
52:7 the abundance of his R, and sought refuge in
62:10 hopes on robbery; if R increase, set not your
73:12 the wicked; always at ease, they increase in R
112:3 Wealth and R are in his house; and his
119:14 testimonies I delight as much as in all R
Prov 3:16 her left hand are R and honor.
8:18 R and honor are with me, enduring wealth and
11:4 R do not profit in the day of wrath,
11:16 gracious woman gets honor, and violent men get R
11:28 who trusts in his R will wither, but the
22:1 chosen rather than great R, and favor is better
22:4 of the LORD is R and honor and life.
24:4 rooms are filled with all precious and pleasant R
27:24 to your herds; for R do not last for
30:8 me neither poverty nor R; feed me with the
Eccl 4:8 are never satisfied with R, so that he never
5:13 seen under the sun: R were kept by their
5:14 his hurt, and those R were lost in a
9:11 to the wise, nor R to the intelligent, nor
Wis 8:5 If R are a desirable possession in life, what
Sir 13:23 R are good if they are free from sin,
14:3 R are not seemly for a stingy man; and
14:5 He will not enjoy his own R
21:4 violence will lay waste R; thus the house of
30:15 all gold, and a robust body than countless R
40:26 R and strength lift up the heart, but the
Is 30:6 serpent, they carry their R on the backs of
61:6 nations, and in their R you shall glory.
Jer 9:23 man glory in his R;
17:11 is he who gets R but not by right;
48:36 of Kir-heres; therefore the R they gained have
Ezek 26:12 a spoil of your R and a prey of
27:27 Your R, your wares, your merchandise, your mariners
Dan 11:2 become strong through his R, he shall stir up
Hos 12:8 myself": but all his R can never offset the
1Mac 4:23 cloth dyed blue and sea purple, and great R
Mt 13:22 and the delight in R choke the word, and
Mk 4:19 and the delight in R, and the desire for
10:23 those who trust in R to enter the kingdom
10:24 those who trust in R to enter the kingdom
Lk 8:14 by the cares and R and pleasures of life,
16:11 mammon, who will entrust to you the true R
18:24 for those who have R to enter the kingdom
Rom 2:4 you presume upon the R of his kindness and
9:23 to make known the R of his glory for
10:12 all and bestows his R upon all who call
11:12 if their trespass means R for the world, and
11:12 if their failure means R for the Gentiles, how
11:33 the depth of the R and wisdom and knowledge
Eph 1:7 trespasses, according to the R of his grace
1:18 you, what are the R of his glorious inheritance
2:7 might show the immeasurable R of his grace in
3:8 the Gentiles the unsearchable R of Christ,
3:16 that according to the R of his glory he
Phil 4:19 yours according to his R in glory in Christ
Col 1:27 the Gentiles are the R of the glory of
2:2 to have all the R of assured understanding and
1Tim 6:17 their hopes on uncertain R but on God who
Jas 5:2 Your R have rotted and your garments are moth-

RICHEST (2)

Ps 45:12 favor with gifts, the R of the people
Dan 11:24 shall come into the R parts of the province;

RICHLY (7)

Lev 19:25 they may yield more R for you: I am
Prov 13:4 of the diligent is R supplied.
Sir 45:12 delight of the eyes, R adorned.
Col 3:16 Christ dwell in you R, teach and admonish one
1Tim 6:17 but on God who R furnishes us with everything
Tit 3:6 poured out upon us R through Jesus Christ our
2Pet 1:11 so there will be R provided for you an

RICHNESS

Rom 11:17 place to share the R of the olive tree,

RIDDEN (2)

Num 22:30 upon which you have R all your life long
Esth 6:8 which the king has R, and on whose head

RIDDLE (10)

Judg 14:12 me now put a R to you; if you
14:13 to him, "Put your R, that we may hear
14:14 days tell what the R was.
14:15 tell us what the R is, lest we burn
14:16 you have put a R to my countrymen, and
14:17 Then she told the R to her countrymen.
14:18 heifer, you would not have found out my R
14:19 festal garments to those who had told the R
Ps 49:4 I will solve my R to the music of
Ezek 17:2 of man, propound a R, and speak an allegory

RIDDLES (5)

Prov 1:6 figure, the words of the wise and their R
Wis 8:8 and the solutions of R; she has foreknowledge of
Sir 47:15 earth, and you filled it with parables and R
Dan 5:12 to interpret dreams, explain R, and solve problems
8:23 countenance, one who understands R, shall arise.

RIDE (22)

Gen 41:43 he made him to R in his second chariot;
Deut 32:13 He made him R on the high places of
Judg 5:10 of it, you who R on tawny asses, you
2Sam 16:2 the king's household to R on, the bread and
19:26 me, that I may R upon it and go
1Kgs 1:33 Solomon my son to R on my own mule,
1:38 and caused Solomon to R on King David's mule,
1:44 have caused him to R on the king's mule;
2Kgs 9:18 Turn round and R behind me." And the watchman
9:19 Turn round and R behind me."
10:16 So he had him R in his chariot.
Esth 6:11 Mordecai and made him R through the open square
Job 30:22 wind, thou makest me R on it, and thou
Ps 45:4 In your majesty R forth victoriously for the cause
66:12 thou didst let men R over our heads; we
Is 30:16 away; and, "We will R upon swift steeds," therefore
58:14 I will make you R upon the heights of
Jer 6:23 the roaring sea; they R upon horses, set in
50:42 of the sea; they R upon horses, arrayed as
Hos 14:3 us, we will not R upon horses; and we
Hab 3:8 sea, when thou didst R upon thy horses, upon
Acts 23:24 mounts for Paul to R, and bring him safely

RIDER (14)

Gen 49:17 heels so that his R falls backward.
Ex 15:1 the horse and his R he has thrown into
15:21 the horse and his R he has thrown into
Job 39:18 flee, she laughs at the horse and his R
Ps 76:6 God of Jacob, both R and horse lay stunned.
Jer 51:21 the horse and his R; with you I break
Zech 12:4 with panic, and its R with madness.
2Mac 3:25 caparisoned horse, with a R of frightening mien, and
3:25 Its R was seen to have armor and weapons
13:15 He stabbed the leading elephant and its R
Rev 6:2 white horse, and its R had a bow; and

6:4 horse, bright red; its R was permitted to take
6:5 black horse, and its R had a balance in
6:8 pale horse, and its R's name was Death, and

RIDERS (13)

2Kgs 18:23 your part to set R upon them.
Jud 9:7 with their horses and R; they glory in the
Is 21:7 When he sees R, horsemen in pairs, riders on
21:7 riders, horsemen in pairs, R on asses, riders on
21:7 pairs, riders on asses, R on camels, let him
21:9 And, behold, here come R, horsemen in pairs!" And
36:8 your part to set R upon them.
Ezek 39:20 table with horses and R, with mighty men and
Hag 2:22 the chariots and their R; and the horses and
2:22 the horses and their R shall go down, every
Zech 10:5 they shall confound the R on horses.
Rev 9:17 in my vision: the R wore breastplates the color
19:18 of horses and their R, and the flesh of

RIDES (5)

Lev 15:9 who has the discharge R shall be unclean.
Deut 33:26 God, O Jeshurun, who R through the heavens to
Ps 68:4 song to him who R upon the clouds; his
68:33 [Selah] to him who R in the heavens, the
Amos 2:15 nor shall he who R the horse save his

RIDEST

Ps 104:3 clouds thy chariot, who R on the wings of

RIDGE

Jud 3:9 Dothan, fronting the great R of Judea;

RIDGES

Ps 65:10 furrows abundantly, settling its R, softening it with

RIDICULE (2)

Sir 7:11 Do not R a man who is bitter in
20:16 How many will R him, and how often!

RIDICULED

Neh 4:1 greatly enraged, and he R the Jews.

RIDICULOUS

Wis 17:8 were sick themselves with R fear.

RIDING (13)

Num 22:22 Now he was R on the ass, and his
2Sam 18:9 Absalom was R upon his mule, and the mule
Esth 8:10 sent by mounted couriers R on swift horses that
Is 19:1 Behold, the LORD is R on a swift cloud
Jer 17:25 the throne of David, R in chariots and on
22:4 the throne of David, R in chariots and on
Ezek 23:6 desirable young men, horsemen R on horses.
23:12 in full armor, horsemen R on horses, all of
23:23 warriors, all of them R on horses.
27:20 Dedan traded with you in saddlecloths for R
38:15 you, all of them R on horses, a great
Zech 1:8 and behold, a man R upon a red horse!
9:9 is he, humble and R on an ass, on

RIGHT (458)

Gen 13:9 will go to the R; or if you take
13:9 if you take the R hand, then I will
18:25 not the Judge of all the earth do R
24:48 led me by the R way to take the
24:49 may turn to the R hand or to the
48:13 both, Ephraim in his R hand toward Israel's left
48:13 left hand toward Israel's R hand, and brought them
48:14 Israel stretched out his R hand and laid it
48:17 his father laid his R hand upon the head
48:18 the first-born; put your R hand upon his head."
Ex 8:26 "It would not be R to do so; for
9:27 LORD is in the R, and I and my
14:22 to them on their R hand and on their
14:29 to them on their R hand and on their
15:6 Thy R hand, O LORD, glorious in power, thy
15:6 glorious in power, thy R hand, O LORD, shatters
15:12 didst stretch out thy R hand, the earth swallowed
15:26 do that which is R in his eyes, and
21:8 he shall have no R to sell her to
23:8 the cause of those who are in the R
29:20 the tip of the R ear of Aaron and
29:20 the tips of the R ears of his sons,
29:20 the thumbs of their R hands, and upon the
29:20 great toes of their R feet, and throw the
29:22 on them, and the R thigh (for it is
Lev 7:32 And the R thigh you shall give to the
7:33 fat shall have the R thigh for a portion.
8:23 the tip of Aaron's R ear and on the
8:23 the thumb of his R hand and on the
8:23 great toe of his R foot.
8:24 the tips of their R ears and on the
8:24 the thumbs of their R hands and on the
8:24 great toes of their R feet; and Moses threw
8:25 their fat, and the R thigh;
8:26 fat and on the R thigh;
9:21 the breasts and the R thigh Aaron waved for
14:14 the tip of the R ear of him who
14:14 the thumb of his R hand, and on the
14:14 great toe of his R foot.
14:16 hand, and dip his R finger in the oil
14:17 the tip of the R ear of him who
14:17 the thumb of his R hand, and on the
14:17 great toe of his R foot, upon the blood
14:25 the tip of the R ear of him who
14:25 the thumb of his R hand, and on the
14:25 great toe of his R foot.
14:27 shall sprinkle with his R finger some of the
14:28 the tip of the R ear of him who
14:28 the thumb of his R hand, and the great
14:28 great toe of his R foot, in the place
25:29 he shall have the R of redemption.
25:33 does not exercise his R of redemption, then the
Num 18:18 waved and as the R thigh are yours.
20:17 turn aside to the R hand or to the
22:26 turn either to the R or to the left.
27:7 daughters of Zelophehad are R; you shall give them
36:5 "The tribe of the sons of Joseph is R
Deut 2:27 aside neither to the R nor to the left.
5:32 turn aside to the R hand or to the
6:18 shall do what is R and good in the
12:8 man doing whatever is R in his own eyes;
12:25 you do what is R in the sight of
12:28 what is good and R in the sight of
13:18 and doing what is R in the sight of
17:8 one kind of legal R and another, or one
17:11 you, either to the R hand or to the
17:20 commandment, either to the R hand or to the
21:9 you do what is R in the sight of
21:17 of his strength; the R of the first-born is
28:14 this day, to the R hand or to the
32:4 without iniquity, just and R is he.
33:2 flaming fire at his R hand.
33:19 mountain; there they offer R sacrifices; for they suck
Josh 1:7 from it to the R hand or to the
9:25 it seems good and R in your sight to
23:6 it neither to the R hand nor to the
Judg 3:16 girded it on his R thigh under his clothes.
3:21 the sword from his R thigh, and thrust it
5:26 tent peg and her R hand to the workmen's
7:20 torches, and in their R hands the trumpets to
12:6 could not pronounce it R; then they seized him
16:29 weight upon them, his R hand on the one
17:6 man did what was R in his own eyes.
21:25 man did what was R in his own eyes.
Ruth 4:6 Take my R of redemption yourself, for I cannot
1Sam 6:12 turned neither to the R nor to the left,
11:2 gouge out all your R eyes, and thus put
12:23 the good and the R way.
29:6 to me it seems R that you should march
2Sam 2:19 turned neither to the R hand nor to the
2:21 "Turn aside to your R hand or to your
14:19 cannot turn to the R hand or to the
15:3 claims are good and R; but there is no
16:6 men were on his R hand and on his
19:28 What further R have I, then, to cry to
20:9 the beard with his R hand to kiss him.
1Kgs 2:19 the king's mother; and she sat on his R
3:11 to discern what is R,
11:33 ways, doing what is R in my sight and
11:38 and do what is R in my eyes by
14:8 only that which was R in my eyes,
15:5 David did what was R in the eyes of
15:11 Asa did what was R in the eyes of
22:19 beside him on his R hand and on his
22:43 it, doing what was R in the sight of
2Kgs 7:9 said to one another, "We are not doing R
10:30 carrying out what is R in my eyes, and
12:2 Jehoash did what was R in the eyes of
12:9 the altar on the R side as one entered
14:3 he did what was R in the eyes of
15:3 he did what was R in the eyes of

15:34 he did what was R in the eyes of
16:2 not do what was R in the eyes of
17:9 the LORD their God things that were not R
18:3 he did what was R in the eyes of
22:2 he did what was R in the eyes of
22:2 turn aside to the R hand or to the
1Chr 6:39 who stood on his R hand, namely, Asaph the
12:2 stones with either the R or the left hand;
13:4 for the thing was R in the eyes of
2Chr 14:2 what was good and R in the eyes of
18:18 heaven standing on his R hand and on his
20:32 he did what was R in the sight of
24:2 Joash did what was R in the eyes of
25:2 he did what was R in the eyes of
26:4 he did what was R in the eyes of
27:2 he did what was R in the eyes of
28:1 not do what was R in the eyes of
29:2 he did what was R in the eyes of
30:4 and the plan seemed R to the king and
31:20 what was good and R and faithful before the
34:2 He did what was R in the eyes of
34:2 turn aside to the R or to the left.
Neh 2:20 have no portion or R or memorial in Jerusalem."
8:4 and Ma-aseiah on his R hand; and Pedaiah, Mishael,
9:13 heaven and give them R ordinances and true laws,
12:31 One went to the R upon the wall to
Tob 2:13 for it is not R to eat what is
7:10 for it is your R to take my child.
7:12 Raguel said, "Take her R now, in accordance with
13:6 you sinners, and do R before him; who knows
Jud 8:11 people today is not R; you have even sworn
8:29 your understanding, for your heart's disposition is R
Esth 8:5 if the thing seem R before the king, and
Job 8:3 Or does the Almighty pervert the R
16:21 he would maintain the R of a man with
23:9 I turn to the R hand, but I cannot
27:2 has taken away my R, and the Almighty, who
27:5 say that you are R; till I die I
30:12 On my R hand the rabble rise, they drive
32:9 wise, nor the aged that understand what is R
33:12 my paths.' "Behold, in this you are not R
33:23 to man what is R for him;
33:27 and perverted what was R, and it was not
34:4 us choose what is R; let us determine among
34:5 has taken away my R;
34:6 in spite of my R I am counted a
35:2 say, 'It is my R before God,'
36:6 the wicked alive, but gives the afflicted their R
40:14 you, that your own R hand can give you
42:7 of me what is R, as my servant Job
42:8 of me what is R, as my servant Job
Ps 4:1 me when I call, O God of my R
4:5 [Selah] Offer R sacrifices, and put your trust in
15:2 and does what is R, and speaks truth from
16:8 he is at my R hand, I shall not
16:11 of joy, in thy R hand are pleasures for
17:2 Let thy eyes see the R
17:7 their adversaries at thy R hand.
18:35 thy salvation, and thy R hand supported me, and
19:8 of the LORD are R, rejoicing the heart; the
20:6 mighty victories by his R hand.
21:8 all your enemies; your R hand will find out
25:9 humble in what is R, and teaches the humble
26:10 evil devices, and whose R hands are full of
35:23 and awake for my R, for my cause, my
37:6 the light, and your R as the noonday.
44:3 them victory; but thy R hand, and thy arm,
45:4 and to defend the R; let your right hand
45:4 the right; let your R hand teach you dread
45:9 of honor; at your R hand stands the queen
46:5 God will help her R early.
48:10 Thy R hand is filled with victory;
50:16 wicked God says: "What R have you to recite
51:10 put a new and R spirit within me.
51:19 wilt thou delight in R sacrifices, in burnt offerings
58:1 indeed decree what is R, you gods?
60:5 give victory by thy R hand and answer us!
63:8 clings to thee; thy R hand upholds me.
73:23 thou dost hold my R hand.
74:11 dost thou keep thy R hand in thy bosom?
77:10 my grief that the R hand of the Most
78:54 the mountain which his R hand had won.
80:15 the stock which thy R hand planted.
80:17 the man of thy R hand, the son of
82:3 the fatherless; maintain the R of the afflicted and
89:13 thy hand, high thy R hand.
89:25 the sea and his R hand on the rivers.
89:42 Thou hast exalted the R hand of his foes;
91:7 ten thousand at your R hand; but it will
98:1 His R hand and his holy arm have gotten
108:6 give help by thy R hand, and answer me!
109:31 he stands at the R hand of the needy,
110:1 lord: "Sit at my R hand, till I make
110:5 Lord is at your R hand; he will shatter
118:15 of the righteous: "The R hand of the LORD
118:16 LORD does valiantly, the R hand of the LORD
118:16 LORD is exalted, the R hand of the LORD
119:75 that thy judgments are R, and that in faithfulness
119:121 what is just and R; do not leave me
119:137 thou, O LORD, and R are thy judgments.
119:172 of thy word, for all thy commandments are R
121:5 your shade on your R hand.
137:5 O Jerusalem, let my R hand wither!
138:7 my enemies, and thy R hand delivers me.
139:10 lead me, and thy R hand shall hold me.
139:14 Thou knowest me R well;
142:4 I look to the R and watch, but there
144:8 speak lies, and whose R hand is a right
144:8 right hand is a R hand of falsehood.
144:11 speak lies, and whose R hand is a right
144:11 right hand is a R hand of falsehood.
Prov 3:16 life is in her R hand; in her left
4:28 not swerve to the R or to the left;
8:6 will come what is R;
8:9 him who understands and R to those who find
12:15 of a fool is R in his own eyes,
14:12 a way which seems R to a man, but
16:13 and he loves him who speaks what is R
16:25 a way which seems R to a man, but
18:17 his case first seems R, until the other comes
20:11 acts, whether what he does is pure and R
21:2 of a man is R in his own eyes,
21:8 crooked, but the conduct of the pure is R
22:21 show you what is R and true, that you
23:16 will rejoice when your lips speak what is R
24:26 He who gives a R answer kisses the lips.
27:16 grasp oil in his R hand.
Eccl 5:8 oppressed and justice and R violently taken away, do
10:2 inclines him toward the R, but a fool's heart
Song 2:6 head, and that his R hand embraced me!
8:3 head, and that his R hand embraced me!
Wis 2:11 be our law of R, for what is weak
5:16 Lord, because with his R hand he will cover
9:9 sight and what is R according to thy commandments.
9:18 on earth were set R, and men were taught
Sir 1:20 will endure until the R moment, and then joy
1:21 his words until the R moment, and the lips
2:2 Set your heart R and be steadfast, and do
3:2 and he confirmed the R of the mother over
4:20 Observe the R time, and beware of evil; and
10:4 will raise up the R man for the time.
10:22 It is not R to despise an intelligent poor
12:12 him sit at your R, lest he try to
15:11 Lord I left the R way"; for he will
20:6 be silent until the R moment, but a braggart
20:6 fool goes beyond the R moment.
20:7 and whoever usurps the R to speak will be
21:19 like manacles on his R hand.
21:21 a bracelet on the R arm.
36:6 thy hand and thy R arm glorious.
47:5 him strength in his R hand to slay a
48:4 And who has the R to boast which you
49:11 a signet on the R hand,
Is 5:23 a bribe, and deprive the innocent of his R
9:20 They snatch on the R, but are still hungry,
10:2 my people of their R, that widows may be
29:21 plea turn aside him who is in the R
30:10 to us what is R; speak to us smooth
30:21 you turn to the R or when you turn
32:7 even when the plea of the needy is R
40:27 the LORD, and my R is disregarded by my
41:10 you with my victorious R hand.
41:13 your God, hold your R hand; it is I
41:26 and beforetime, that we might say, "He is R
43:26 forth your case, that you may be proved R
44:20 a lie in my R hand?"
45:1 anointed, to Cyrus, whose R hand I have grasped,
45:19 LORD speak the truth, I declare what is R
48:1 God of Israel, but not in truth or R
48:13 the earth, and my R hand spread out the
49:4 vanity; yet surely my R is with the LORD,
54:3 spread abroad to the R and to the left,

62:8 has sworn by his R hand and by his
63:12 to go at the R hand of Moses, who
Jer 11:15 What R has my beloved in my house, when
17:11 riches but not by R; in the midst of
22:24 signet ring on my R hand, yet I would
23:10 course is evil, and their might is not R
26:14 as seems good and R to you.
27:5 to whomever it seems R to me.
32:7 at Anathoth, for the R of redemption by purchase
32:8 of Benjamin, for the R of possession and redemption
34:15 and did what was R in my eyes by
40:4 think it good and R to go.
40:5 wherever you think it R to go." So the
Lam 1:18 LORD is in the R, for I have rebelled
2:3 withdrawn from them his R hand in the face
2:4 an enemy, with his R hand set like a
3:35 to turn aside the R of a man in
Bar 6:15 a dagger in its R hand, and has an
Ezek 1:10 a lion on the R side, the four had
4:6 time, but on your R side, and bear the
16:52 are more in the R than you.
18:5 what is lawful and R –
18:19 what is lawful and R, and has been careful
18:21 what is lawful and R, he shall surely live;
18:27 what is lawful and R, he shall save his
21:16 Cut sharply to R and left where your edge
21:22 Into his R hand comes the lot for Jerusalem,
21:27 until he comes whose R it is; and to
33:14 what is lawful and R,
33:16 what is lawful and R, he shall surely live.
33:19 what is lawful and R, he shall live by
39:3 drop out of your R hand.
Dan 3:27 true and thy ways R, and all thy judgments
4:37 all his works are R and his ways are
12:7 the stream, raised his R hand and his left
13:50 inform us, for God has given you that R
14:36 him down in Babylon, R over the den, with
Hos 14:9 of the LORD are R, and the upright walk
Amos 3:10 "They do not know how to do R
Jon 4:11 do not know their R hand from their left,
Hab 2:16 cup in the LORD's R hand will come around
Zech 3:1 Satan standing at his R hand to accuse him.
3:7 will give you the R of access among those
4:3 it, one on the R of the bowl and
4:11 olive trees on the R and the left of
11:12 them, "If it seems R to you, give me
11:17 his arm and his R eye!
11:17 be wholly withered, his R eye utterly blinded!"
12:6 shall devour to the R and to the left
Mal 3:3 silver, till they present R offerings to the LORD.
1Mac 2:22 our religion to the R hand or to the
5:46 round it to the R or to the left;
6:45 it; he killed men R and left, and they
7:47 Nicanor's head and the R hand which he so
9:1 and with them the R wing of the army.
9:12 Bacchides was on the R wing.
9:14 army were on the R; then all the stouthearted
9:15 and they crushed the R wing, and he pursued
9:16 wing saw that the R wing was crushed, they
11:58 and granted him the R to drink from gold
12:11 prayers, as it is R and proper to remember
14:46 to grant Simon the R to act in accord
2Mac 4:12 he founded a gymnasium R under the citadel, and
4:34 and gave him his R hand, and in spite
6:20 that it is not R to taste, even for
9:12 these words: "It is R to be subject to
14:33 he stretched out his R hand toward the sanctuary,
15:15 Jeremiah stretched out his R hand and gave to
Mt 5:29 If your R eye causes you to sin, pluck
5:30 And if your R hand causes you to sin,
5:39 strikes you on the R cheek, turn to him
6:3 hand know what your R hand is doing,
20:4 too, and whatever is R I will give you.'
20:21 sit, one at your R hand and one at
20:23 to sit at my R hand and at my
22:44 Lord, Sit at my R hand, till I put
25:33 the sheep at his R hand, but the goats
25:34 to those at his R hand, 'Come, O blessed
26:64 man seated at the R hand of Power, and
27:29 a reed in his R hand.
27:38 him, one on the R and one on the
Mk 5:15 clothed and in his R mind, the man who
7:26 for it is not R to take the children's
10:37 sit, one at your R hand and one at
10:40 to sit at my R hand or at my
12:32 to him, "You are R, Teacher; you have truly
12:36 Lord, Sit at my R hand, till I put
14:54 him at a distance, R into the courtyard of
14:62 man seated at the R hand of Power, and
15:27 robbers, one on his R and one on his
16:5 man sitting on the R side, dressed in a
16:19 sat down at the R hand of God.
Lk 1:11 Lord standing on the R side of the altar
6:6 man was there whose R hand was withered.
8:35 clothed and in his R mind; and they were
10:28 him, "You have answered R; do this, and you
12:57 do you not judge for yourselves what is R
20:42 Lord, Sit at my R hand,
22:48 and cut off his R ear.
22:67 be seated at the R hand of the power
23:32 criminals, one on the R and one on the
Jn 4:17 to her, "You are R in saying, 'I have
7:24 appearances, but judge with R judgment."
8:48 him, "Are we not R in saying that you
13:13 Lord; and you are R, for so I am.
18:10 and cut off his R ear.
21:6 the net on the R side of the boat,
Acts 2:25 he is at my R hand that I may
2:33 therefore exalted at the R hand of God, and
2:34 Lord, Sit at my R hand,
3:7 took him by the R hand and raised him
4:19 them, "Whether it is R in the sight of
5:31 exalted him at his R hand as Leader and
6:2 said, "It is not R that we should give
7:55 Jesus standing at the R hand of God;
7:56 man standing at the R hand of God."
8:21 your heart is not R before God.
10:35 and does what is R is acceptable to him.
28:25 "The Holy Spirit was R in saying to your
Rom 5:6 still weak, at the R time Christ died for
7:18 can will what is R, but I cannot do
7:21 I want to do R, evil lies close at
8:34 who is at the R hand of God, who
9:21 Has the potter no R over the clay, to
14:21 he eats; it is R not to eat meat
1Cor 9:4 we not have the R to our food and
9:5 we not have the R to be accompanied by
9:6 I who have no R to refrain from working
9:12 made use of this R, but we endure anything
9:18 full use of my R in the gospel.
13:6 not rejoice at wrong, but rejoices in the R
15:34 Come to your R mind, and sin no more.
2Cor 5:13 we are in our R mind, it is for
6:7 of righteousness for the R hand and for the
13:7 may do what is R, though we may seem
Gal 2:9 me and Barnabas the R hand of fellowship, that
Eph 1:20 him sit at his R hand in the heavenly
5:9 that is good and R and true),
6:1 your parents in the Lord, for this is R
Phil 1:7 It is R for me to feel thus about
Col 3:1 is, seated at the R hand of God.
2Thes 3:9 we have not that R, but to give you
Tit 1:10 what they have no R to teach.
Heb 1:3 sat down at the R hand of the Majesty
1:13 said, "Sit at my R hand, till I make
8:1 is seated at the R hand of the throne
10:12 sat down at the R hand of God,
12:2 is seated at the R hand of the throne
13:10 the tent have no R to eat.
Jas 4:17 Whoever knows what is R to do and fails
1Pet 2:14 do wrong and to praise those who do R
2:15 will that by doing R you should put to
2:20 if when you do R and suffer for it
3:6 children if you do R and let nothing terrify
3:11 from evil and do R; let him seek peace
3:13 you if you are zealous for what is R
3:17 to suffer for doing R, if that should be
3:22 and is at the R hand of God, with
4:19 to God's will do R and entrust their souls
2Pet 1:13 I think it R, as long as I am
2:15 Forsaking the R way they have gone astray; they
1Jn 2:29 every one who does R is born of him.
3:7 He who does R is righteous, as he is
3:10 whoever does not do R is not of God,
Rev 1:16 many waters; in his R hand he held seven
1:17 But he laid his R hand upon me, saying,
1:20 you saw in my R hand, and the seven
2:1 seven stars in his R hand, who walks among
5:1 I saw in the R hand of him who
5:7 the scroll from the R hand of him who
10:2 And he set his R foot on the sea,
10:5 land lifted up his R hand to heaven

21:26 wicked covets, but the R gives and does not
23:24 The father of the R will greatly rejoice; he
24:15 the dwelling of the R; do not violence to
24:16 his home; for a R man falls seven times,
25:26 polluted fountain is a R man who gives way
28:1 one pursues, but the R are bold as a
28:12 When the R triumph, there is great glory; but
28:28 when they perish, the R increase.
29:2 When the R are in authority, the people rejoice;
29:6 his transgression, but a R man sings and rejoices.
29:7 A R man knows the rights of the poor;
29:16 transgression increases; but the R will look upon
29:27 an abomination to the R, but he whose way
Eccl 3:17 God will judge the R and the wicked, for
7:15 everything; there is a R man who perishes in
7:16 Be not R overmuch, and do not make yourself
7:20 there is not a R man on earth who
8:14 earth, that there are R men to whom it
8:14 it happens according to the deeds of the R
9:1 it all, how the R and the wise and
9:2 to all, to the R and the wicked, to
Wis 2:10 Let us oppress the R poor man; let us
2:12 in wait for the R man, because he is
2:16 last end of the R happy, and boasts that
2:18 life; for if the R man is God's son,
3:1 the souls of the R are in the hand
3:10 deserves, who disregarded the R man and rebelled
4:7 But the R man, though he die early, will
4:16 The R man who had died will condemn the
5:1 Then the R man will stand with great confidence
5:15 But the R live for ever, and their reward
10:4 saved it, steering the R man by a paltry
10:5 confounded, recognized the R man and preserved
10:6 Wisdom rescued a R man when the ungodly were
10:10 When a R man fled from his brother's wrath,
10:13 When a R man was sold, wisdom did not
10:20 the R plundered the ungodly; they sang hymns,
11:13 their own punishments the R had received benefit,
11:14 their thirst was not like that of the R
12:9 the hands of the R in battle, or to
12:15 Thou art R and rulest all things righteously, deeming
12:19 thy people that the R man must be kind,
16:17 still greater effect, for the universe defends the R
16:23 in order that the R might be fed, even
18:7 The deliverance of the R and the destruction of
18:20 death touched also the R, and a plague came
19:17 the door of the R man-- when, surrounded
Sir 9:16 Let R men be your dinner companions, and let
18:2 whole universe; the Lord alone will be declared R
32:16 light they will kindle R deeds.
35:6 The offering of a R man anoints the altar,
35:7 The sacrifice of a R man is acceptable, and
35:17 does justice for the R, and executes judgment.
44:11 men of mercy, whose R deeds have not been
44:18 was found perfect and R; in the time of
Is 3:10 Tell the R that it shall be well with
24:16 of glory to the R One.
26:2 the gates, that the R nation which keeps faith
26:7 The way of the R is level; thou dost
26:7 thou dost make smooth the path of the R
45:21 god besides me, a R God and a Savior;
53:11 his knowledge shall the R one, my servant, make
53:11 many to be accounted R; and he shall bear
57:1 The R man perishes, and no one lays it
57:1 For the R man is taken away from calamity,
58:2 they ask of me R judgments, they delight to
60:21 people shall all be R; they shall possess the
64:6 unclean, and all our R deeds are like a
Jer 12:1 R art thou, O LORD, when I complain to
20:12 hosts, who triest the R, who seest the heart
23:5 up for David a R Branch, and he shall
33:15 I will cause a R Branch to spring forth
Lam 4:13 the midst of her the blood of the R
Bar 2:9 for the Lord is R in all his works
2:19 not because of any R deeds of our fathers
Ezek 3:20 Again, if a R man turns from his righteousness
3:20 his sin, and his R deeds which he has
3:21 if you warn the R man not to sin,
13:22 you have disheartened the R falsely, although I have
16:51 made your sisters appear R by all the abominations
16:52 disgrace, for you have made your sisters appear R
18:5 "If a man is R and does what is
18:9 ordinances --he is R, he shall surely live,
18:20 the righteousness of the R shall be upon himself,
18:24 But when a R man turns away from his
18:24 None of the R deeds which he has done
18:26 When a R man turns away from his righteousness
21:3 off from you both R and wicked.
21:4 off from you both R and wicked, therefore my
23:45 But R men shall pass judgment on them with
33:12 The righteousness of the R shall not deliver him
33:12 his wickedness; and the R shall not be able
33:13 I say to the R that he shall surely
33:13 iniquity, none of his R deeds shall be remembered;
33:18 When the R turns from his righteousness, and
Dan 3:87 and souls of the R, sing praise to him
9:14 LORD our God is R in all the works
9:16 according to all thy R acts, let thy anger
13:3 Her parents were R, and had taught their daughter
13:9 to Heaven or remembering R judgments.
13:53 death an innocent and R person.'
Amos 2:6 because they sell the R for silver, and the
5:12 you who afflict the R, who take a bribe,
Hab 1:4 the wicked surround the R, so justice goes forth
1:13 up the man more R than he?
2:4 shall fail, but the R shall live by his
Zeph 3:5 LORD within her is R, he does no wrong;
Mal 3:18 shall distinguish between the R and the wicked,
1Mac 2:24 He gave vent to R anger; he ran and
2Mac 12:6 calling upon God the R Judge, attacked the
12:41 of the Lord, the R Judge, who reveals the
Mt 9:13 not to call the R, but sinners."
10:41 he who receives a R man because he is
10:41 because he is a R man shall receive a
10:41 man shall receive a R man's reward.
13:17 you, many prophets and R men longed to see
13:43 Then the R will shine like the sun in
13:49 the evil from the R,
23:27 you also outwardly appear R to men, but within
23:28 the monuments of the R,
23:34 may come all the R blood shed on earth,
25:37 to me.' Then the R will answer him, 'Lord,
25:46 eternal punishment, but the R into eternal life."
27:19 to do with that R man, for I have
27:24 am innocent of this R man's blood; see to
Mk 2:17 not to call the R, but sinners."
6:20 that he was a R and holy man, and
Lk 1:6 And they were both R before God, walking in
2:25 and this man was R and devout, looking for
5:32 come to call the R, but sinners to repentance."
15:7 repents than over ninety-nine R persons who need no
18:9 themselves that they were R and despised others:
23:49 council, a good and R man,
Jn 17:25 O R Father, the world has not known thee,
Acts 3:14 denied the Holy and R One, and asked for
7:52 the coming of the R One, whom you have
Rom 1:17 who through faith is R shall live."
2:5 of wrath when God's R judgment will be revealed.
2:13 the law who are R before God, but the
3:10 is written: "None is R, no, not one;
3:26 that he himself is R and that he justifies
5:7 hardly die for a R man--though perhaps for
5:19 by one man's obedience many will be made R
Gal 3:11 who through faith is R shall live";
1Thes 2:10 also, how holy and R and blameless was our
2Thes 1:5 is evidence of the R judgment of God, that
2Tim 4:8 which the Lord, the R judge, will award to
Heb 1:8 ever and ever, the R scepter is the scepter
10:38 not tarry; but my R one shall live by
11:4 he received approval as R, God bearing witness by
Jas 5:6 you have killed the R man; he does not
5:16 The prayer of a R man has great power
1Pet 3:12 Lord are upon the R, and his ears are
3:18 once for all, the R for the unrighteous, that
4:18 And "If the R man is scarcely saved, where
2Pet 2:7 and if he rescued R Lot, greatly distressed by
2:8 (for by what that R man saw and heard
2:8 was vexed in his R soul day after day
1Jn 2:1 Father, Jesus Christ the R;
2:29 know that he is R, you may be sure
3:7 who does right is R, as he is righteous.
3:7 who does right is righteous, as he is R
3:12 his own deeds were evil and his brother's R
Rev 19:8 fine linen is the R deeds of the saints.
22:11 be filthy, and the R still do right, and

RIGHTEOUSLY (5)

Deut 1:16 your brethren, and judge R between a man and
Prov 31:9 Open your mouth, judge R, maintain the rights of
Wis 12:15 and rulest all things R, deeming it alien to
Is 33:15 He who walks R and speaks uprightly, who despises
Jer 11:20 of hosts, who judgest R, who triest the heart

R

33:12 to live by his R when he sins.
33:13 he trusts in his R and commits iniquity, none
33:18 righteous turns from his R, and commits iniquity, he
45:9 and execute justice and R; cease your evictions of
Dan 4:27 your sins by practicing R, and your iniquities by
9:7 thee, O Lord, belongs R, but to us confusion
9:18 the ground of our R, but on the ground
9:24 to bring in everlasting R, to seal both vision
12:3 who turn many to R, like the stars for
Hos 2:19 you to me in R and in justice, in
10:12 Sow for yourselves R, reap the fruit of steadfast
Amos 5:7 wormwood, and cast down R to the earth!
5:24 down like waters, and R like an ever-flowing stream.
6:12 and the fruit of R into wormwood—
Zeph 2:3 do his commands; seek R, seek humility; perhaps you
Zech 8:8 will be their God, in faithfulness and in R
Mal 4:2 name the sun of R shall rise, with healing
1Mac 2:29 many who were seeking R and justice went down
2:52 tested, and it was reckoned to him as R
Mt 3:15 it is fitting for us to fulfil all R
5:6 hunger and thirst for R, for they shall be
5:10 who are persecuted for R sake, for theirs is
5:20 tell you, unless your R exceeds that of the
6:33 his kingdom and his R, and all these things
21:32 in the way of R, and you did not
Lk 1:75 fear, in holiness and R before him all the
Jn 16:8 world concerning sin and R and judgment:
16:10 believe in me; concerning R, because I go to
Acts 13:10 you enemy of all R, full of all deceit
17:31 judge the world in R by a man whom
Rom 1:17 For in it the R of God is revealed
3:21 But now the R of God has been manifested
3:22 witness to it, the R of God through faith
3:25 was to show God's R, because in his divine
4:3 God, and it was reckoned to him as R
4:5 justifies the ungodly, his faith is reckoned as R
4:6 to whom God reckons R apart from works:
4:9 say that faith was reckoned to Abraham as R
4:11 or seal of the R which he had by
4:11 and who thus have R reckoned to them,
4:13 law but through the R of faith.
4:22 why his faith was "reckoned to him as R
5:17 the free gift of R reign in life through
5:18 one man's act of R leads to acquittal and
5:21 also might reign through R to eternal life through
6:13 and your members to God as instruments of R
6:16 to death, or of obedience, which leads to R
6:18 set free from sin, have become slaves of R
6:19 yield your members to R for sanctification.
6:20 of sin, you were free in regard to R
8:10 of sin, your spirits are alive because of R
9:30 who did not pursue R have attained it, that
9:30 attained it, that is, R through faith;
9:31 Israel who pursued the R which is based on
10:3 being ignorant of the R that comes from God,
10:3 their own, they did not submit to God's R
10:5 man who practices the R which is based on
10:6 But the R based on faith says, Do not
14:17 food and drink but R and peace and joy
1Cor 1:30 wisdom, our R and sanctification and redemption;
2Cor 3:9 condemnation, the dispensation of R must far exceed
5:21 we might become the R of God.
6:7 with the weapons of R for the right hand
6:14 For what partnership have R and iniquity?
9:9 to the poor; his R endures for ever."
9:10 your resources and increase the harvest of your R
11:15 his servants also disguise themselves as servants of R
Gal 3:6 God, and it was reckoned to him as R
3:21 could make alive, then R would indeed be by
5:5 by faith, we wait for the hope of R
Eph 4:24 of God in true R and holiness.
6:14 on the breastplate of R,
Phil 1:11 with the fruits of R which come through Jesus
3:6 the church, as to R under the law blameless.
3:9 him, not having a R of my own, based
3:9 faith in Christ, the R from God that depends
1Tim 6:11 all this; aim at R, godliness, faith, love, steadfastness,
2Tim 2:22 passions and aim at R, faith, love, and peace,
3:16 and for training in R,
4:8 me the crown of R, which the Lord, the
Tit 3:5 done by us in R, but in virtue of
Heb 1:9 hast loved R and hated lawlessness; therefore God,
5:13 in the word of R, for he is a
7:2 his name, king of R, and then he is
11:7 an heir of the R which comes by faith.
12:11 the peaceful fruit of R to those who have
Jas 1:19 does not work the R of God.
2:23 reckoned to him as R; and he was called
3:18 And the harvest of R is sown in peace
1Pet 2:24 we might die to sin and live to R
3:14 you do suffer for R sake, you will be
2Pet 1:1 with ours in the R of our God and
2:5 Noah, a herald of R, with seven other persons,
2:21 known the way of R than after knowing it
3:13 new earth in which R dwells.
Rev 19:11 and True, and in R he judges and makes

RIGHTFUL (4)
Deut 18:1 the LORD, and his R dues.
Job 8:6 reward you with a R habitation.
Dan 8:14 be restored to its R state."
1Cor 9:12 If others share this R claim upon you, do

RIGHTLY (10)
Gen 27:36 said, "Is he not R named Jacob?
Deut 5:28 to you; they have R said all that they
18:17 to me, 'They have R said all that they
Song 1:4 love more than wine; R do they love you.
Wis 6:4 you did not rule R, nor keep the law,
Lk 7:43 And he said to him, "You have judged R
20:21 you speak and teach R, and show no partiality,
Jn 18:23 if I have spoken R, why do you strike
Rom 2:2 the judgment of God R falls upon those who
2Tim 2:15 need to be ashamed, R handling the word of

RIGHTS (12)
Ex 21:10 diminish her food, her clothing, or her marital R
1Sam 10:25 told the people the R and duties of the
Prov 29:7 righteous man knows the R of the poor; a
31:5 decreed, and pervert the R of all the afflicted.
31:8 the dumb, for the R of all who are
31:9 judge righteously, maintain the R of the poor and
Wis 19:16 sufferings those who had already shared the same R
Jer 5:28 do not defend the R of the needy.
1Mac 8:32 we will defend their R and fight you on
2Mac 13:23 to observe all their R, settled with them and
1Cor 7:3 his wife her conjugal R, and likewise the wife
9:15 of any of these R, nor am I writing

RIGID
Mk 9:18 his teeth and becomes R; and I asked your

RIGOR (4)
Ex 1:12 of Israel serve with R,
1:13 all their work they made them serve with R
Rom 9:28 upon the earth with R and dispatch."
Col 2:23 of wisdom in promoting R of devotion and self-

RIM (4)
Ezek 43:13 cubit broad, with a R of one span around
43:17 fourteen broad, with a R around it half a
43:20 ledge, and upon the R round about; thus you
2Mac 13:5 and it has a R running around it which

RIMMON (15)
Josh 15:32 Lebaoth, Shilhim, Ain, and R: in all, twenty-nine
19:13 and going on to R it bends toward Neah;
Judg 20:45 to the rock of R; five thousand men of
20:47 to the rock of R, and abode at the
20:47 at the rock of R four months.
21:13 at the rock of R, and proclaimed peace to
2Sam 4:2 other Rechab, sons of R a man of Benjamin
4:5 Now the sons of R the Be-erothite, Rechab and
4:9 brother, the sons of R the Be-erothite, "As the
2Kgs 5:18 into the house of R to worship there, leaning
5:18 in the house of R, when I bow myself
5:18 in the house of R, the LORD pardon your
1Chr 4:32 villages were Etam, Ain, R, Tochen, and Ashan, five
Is 10:27 has gone up from R,
Zech 14:10 plain from Geba to R south of Jerusalem.

RIMMON-PEREZ (2)
Num 33:19 they set out from Rithmah, and encamped at R
33:20 they set out from R, and encamped at Libnah.

RIMMONO
1Chr 6:77 the tribe of Zebulun: R with its pasture lands,

RIMS (4)
1Kgs 7:33 wheel; their axles, their R, their spokes, and their
Ezek 1:18 The four wheels had R and they had spokes;
1:18 had spokes; and their R were full of eyes

R

10:12 And their R, and their spokes, and the wheels

RING (20)

Gen 24:22 man took a gold R weighing a half-shekel, and
24:30 When he saw the R, and the bracelets on
24:47 So I put the R on her nose, and
41:42 Pharaoh took his signet R from his hand and
Ex 26:24 top, at the first R; thus shall it be
36:29 top, at the first R; he made two of
Esth 3:10 king took his signet R from his hand and
3:12 of King Ahasuerus and sealed with the king's R
8:2 took off his signet R, which he had taken
8:8 it with the king's R; for an edict written
8:8 sealed with the king's R cannot be revoked."
8:10 sealed with the king's R, and letters were sent
Job 42:11 of money and a R of gold.
Prov 11:22 Like a gold R in a swine's snout is
25:12 Like a gold R or an ornament of gold
Jer 22:24 Judah, were the signet R on my right hand,
Ezek 16:12 And I put a R on your nose, and
Hos 2:13 decked herself with her R and jewelry, and went
Hag 2:23 you like a signet R; for I have chosen
Lk 15:22 him; and put a R on his hand, and

RINGING

Sir 45:9 walked, to make their R heard in the temple

RINGLEADER

Acts 24:5 the world, and a R of the sect of

RINGS (47)

Gen 35:4 they had, and the R that were in their
Ex 25:12 you shall cast four R of gold for it
25:12 its four feet, two R on the one side
25:12 of it, and two R on the other side
25:14 the poles into the R on the sides of
25:15 shall remain in the R of the ark; they
25:26 make for it four R of gold, and fasten
25:26 gold, and fasten the R to the four corners
25:27 to the frame the R shall lie, as holders
26:29 and shall make their R of gold for holders
27:4 shall make four bronze R at its four corners.
27:7 be put through the R, so that the poles
28:23 for the breastpiece two R of gold, and put
28:23 and put the two R on the two edges
28:24 gold in the two R at the edges of
28:26 you shall make two R of gold, and put
28:27 you shall make two R of gold, and attach
28:28 the breastpiece by its R to the rings of
28:28 its rings to the R of the ephod with
30:4 And two golden R shall you make for it;
32:2 them, "Take off the R of gold which are
32:3 people took off the R of gold which were
35:22 and earrings and signet R and armlets, all sorts
36:34 gold, and made their R of gold for holders
37:3 cast for it four R of gold for its
37:3 its four corners, two R on its one side
37:3 one side and two R on its other side.
37:5 the poles into the R on the sides of
37:13 cast for it four R of gold, and fastened
37:13 gold, and fastened the R to the four corners
37:14 the frame were the R, as holders for the
37:27 it, and made two R of gold on it
38:5 He cast four R on the four corners of
38:7 the poles through the R on the sides of
39:16 filigree and two gold R, and put the two
39:16 and put the two R on the two edges
39:17 gold in the two R at the edges of
39:19 Then they made two R of gold, and put
39:20 And they made two R of gold, and attached
39:21 the breastpiece by its R to the rings of
39:21 its rings to the R of the ephod with
Num 31:50 armlets and bracelets, signet R, earrings, and beads,
Jud 10:4 anklets and bracelets and R, and her earrings and
Esth 1:6 and purple to silver R and marble pillars, and
Is 3:21 the amulets; the signet R and nose rings;
3:21 signet rings and nose R;
Jas 2:2 a man with gold R and in fine clothing

RINNAH

1Chr 4:20 sons of Shimon: Amnon, R, Ben-hanan, and Tilon.

RINSE

2Chr 4:6 these they were to R off what was used

RINSED (4)

Lev 6:28 shall be scoured, and R in water.
15:11 discharge touches without having R his hands in
15:12 of wood shall be R in water.
Jer 51:34 my delicacies, he has R me out.

RIOT (2)

Wis 14:25 all is a raging R of blood and murder,
Mt 27:24 but rather that a R was beginning, he took

RIOTING

Acts 19:40 of being charged with R today, there being no

RIP

2Kgs 8:12 their little ones, and R up their women with

RIPE (8)

Num 17:8 blossoms, and it bore R almonds.
Job 5:26 to your grave in R old age, as a
Wis 4:5 will be useless, not R enough to eat, and
4:9 a blameless life is R old age.
Joel 3:13 Put in the sickle, for the harvest is R
Mk 4:29 when the grain is R, at once he puts
Rev 14:15 for the harvest of the earth is fully R
14:18 vine of the earth, for its grapes are R

RIPEN

Wis 10:7 fruit that does not R, and a pillar of

RIPENED

Gen 40:10 forth, and the clusters R into grapes.

RIPENING (2)

Sir 51:15 From blossom to R grape my heart delighted in
Is 18:5 the flower becomes a R grape, he will cut

RIPHATH

Gen 10:3 sons of Gomer: Ashkenaz, R, and Togarmah.

RIPPED (3)

2Kgs 15:16 sacked it, and he R up all the women
Hos 13:16 and their pregnant women R open.
Amos 1:13 punishment; because they have R up women with child

RISE (164)

Gen 19:2 feet; then you may R up early and go
31:35 angry that I cannot R before you, for the
Ex 8:20 LORD said to Moses, R up early in the
9:13 LORD said to Moses, R up early in the
10:23 another, nor did any R from his place for
12:31 by night, and said, R up, go forth from
33:10 all the people would R up and worship, every
Lev 19:32 "You shall R up before the hoary head, and
Num 22:20 come to call you, R, go with them; but
23:18 his discourse, and said, R, Balak, and hear; hearken
24:17 and a scepter shall R out of Israel; it
Deut 2:13 gave to them.) 'Now R up, and go over
2:24 settled in their stead.) R up, take your journey,
6:7 and when you lie down, and when you R
11:19 and when you lie down, and when you R
28:7 cause your enemies who R against you to be
29:22 come, your children who R up after you, and
31:16 then this people will R and play the harlot
32:38 Let them R up and help you, let them
33:11 hate him, that they R not again."
Josh 8:7 them; then you shall R up from the ambush,
Judg 8:20 to Jether his first-born, R, and slay them." But
8:21 Zebah and Zalmunna said, R yourself, and fall upon
9:33 the sun is up, R early and rush upon
20:38 great cloud of smoke R up out of the
20:40 the signal began to R out of the city
1Sam 25:29 If men R up to pursue you and to
29:10 the battle.' Now then R early in the morning
2Sam 15:2 And Absalom used to R early and stand beside
18:32 king, and all who R up against you for
22:39 that they did not R; they fell under my
2Kgs 9:2 in and bid him R from among his fellows,
Neh 2:18 they said, "Let us R up and build." So
Tob 6:17 when you approach her, R up, both of you,
12:13 did not hesitate to R and leave your dinner
Jud 16:17 to the nations that R up against my people!
Esth 4:14 relief and deliverance will R for the Jews from
Job 1:5 them, and he would R early in the morning
9:7 and it does not R; who seals up the
19:18 despise me; when I R they talk against me.

R

27:7 and let him that R up against me be
31:14 I do when God R up?
Ps 94:16 Who R up for me against the wicked?
104:22 When the sun R, they get them away and
112:4 Light R in the darkness for the upright; the
Prov 24:16 falls seven times, and R again; but the wicked
31:15 She R while it is yet night and provides
Eccl 1:5 The sun R and the sun goes down, and
1:5 down, and hastens to the place where it R
10:4 anger of the ruler R against you, do not
12:4 is low, and one R up at the voice
Wis 6:14 He who R early to seek her will have
Sir 31:20 on moderate eating; he R early, and feels fit.
35:6 and its pleasing odor R before the Most High.
Is 2:19 his majesty, when he R to terrify the earth.
2:21 his majesty, when he R to terrify the earth.
54:17 confute every tongue that R against you in judgment.
Jer 46:8 Egypt R like the Nile, like rivers whose waters
Amos 9:5 and all of it R like the Nile, and
Mic 7:6 contempt, the daughter R up against her mother,
Nah 3:17 cold--when the sun R, they fly away; no
Rom 15:12 shall come, he who R to rule the Gentiles;
Jas 1:10 For the sun R with its scorching heat and
2Pet 1:19 and the morning star R in your hearts.

RISING (24)

1Kgs 18:44 a man's hand is R out of the sea."
Ps 3:1 Many are R against me;
19:6 Its R is from the end of the heavens,
50:1 the earth from the R of the sun to
113:3 From the R of the sun to its setting
Prov 27:14 with a loud voice, R early in the morning,
Sir 26:16 Like the sun R in the heights of the
Is 13:10 be dark at its R and the moon will
30:27 anger, and in thick R smoke; his lips are
41:25 has come, from the R of the sun, and
45:6 may know, from the R of the sun and
59:19 his glory from the R of the sun; for
60:3 light, and kings to the brightness of your R
Jer 46:7 "Who is this, R like the Nile, like rivers
47:2 LORD: Behold, waters are R out of the north,
Lam 3:63 their sitting and their R; I am the burden
Hos 13:15 the LORD, shall come, R from the wilderness; and
Mal 1:11 For from the R of the sun to its
2Mac 10:27 And R from their prayer they took up their
Mk 9:10 themselves, questioning what the R from the dead
Lk 2:34 for the fall and R of many in Israel,
12:54 you see a cloud R in the west, you
Rev 7:2 angel ascend from the R of the sun, with
13:1 I saw a beast R out of the sea,

RISK (3)

2Sam 23:17 who went at the R of their lives?" Therefore
1Chr 11:19 For at the R of their lives they brought
2Mac 11:7 urged the others to R their lives with him

RISKED (4)

Judg 9:17 fought for you, and R his life, and rescued
2Mac 14:38 had with all zeal R body and life.
Acts 15:26 Paul, men who have R their lives for the
Rom 16:4 in Christ Jesus, who R their necks for my

RISKING

Phil 2:30 the work of Christ, R his life to complete

RISSAH (2)

Num 33:21 they set out from Libnah, and encamped at R
33:22 they set out from R, and encamped at Kehelathah.

RITE

Ex 12:24 You shall observe this R as an ordinance for

RITES (5)

Num 3:38 having charge of the R within the sanctuary,
Wis 12:4 of sorcery and unholy R,
14:15 to his dependents secret R and initiations.
Jn 2:6 there, for the Jewish R of purification, each holding
Heb 9:23 be purified with these R, but the heavenly things

RITHMAH (2)

Num 33:18 they set out from Hazeroth, and encamped at R
33:19 set out from R, and encamped at Rimmon-perez.

RITUAL

Heb 9:6 outer tent, performing their R duties;

RIVAL (5)

Lev 18:18 a woman as a R wife to her sister,
1Sam 1:6 And her R used to provoke her sorely, to
Sir 26:6 is envious of a R, and a tongue-lashing makes
37:11 a woman about her R or with a coward
Ezek 31:8 of God could not R it, nor the fir

RIVALRY (2)

2Mac 4:4 Onias recognized that the R was serious and that
Phil 1:15 Christ from envy and R, but others from good

RIVER (130)

Gen 2:10 A R flowed out of Eden to water the
2:13 name of the second R is Gihon; it is
2:14 name of the third R is Tigris, which flows
2:14 And the fourth R is the Euphrates.
15:18 this land, from the R of Egypt to the
15:18 Egypt to the great R, the river Euphrates,
15:18 the great river, the R Euphrates,
Ex 2:3 the reeds at the R's brink.
2:5 to bathe at the R, and her maidens walked
2:5 maidens walked beside the R; she saw the basket
7:15 for him by the R's brink, and take in
Num 22:5 which is near the R, in the land of
24:6 like gardens beside a R, like aloes that the
Deut 1:7 far as the great R, the river Euphrates.
1:7 the great river, the R Euphrates.
2:37 the banks of the R Jabbok and the cities
3:16 far over as the R Jabbok, the boundary of
11:24 Lebanon and from the R, the river Euphrates, to
11:24 from the River, the R Euphrates, to the western
Josh 1:4 far as the great R, the river Euphrates, all
1:4 the great river, the R Euphrates, all the land
12:2 as far as the R Jabbok, the boundary of
24:3 Abraham from beyond the R and led him through
24:14 fathers served beyond the R, and in Egypt, and
24:15 the region beyond the R, or the gods of
Judg 4:7 meet you by the R Kishon with his chariots
4:13 from Harosheth-ha-goiim to the R Kishon.
2Sam 8:3 his power at the R Euphrates.
2Kgs 17:6 on the Habor, the R of Gozan, and in
18:11 on the Habor, the R of Gozan, and in
23:29 of Assyria to the R Euphrates.
24:7 of Egypt to the R Euphrates.
1Chr 5:26 Habor, Hara, and the R Gozan, to this day.
18:3 his monument at the R Euphrates.
Ezra 4:10 the province Beyond the R, and now
4:11 the province Beyond the R, send greeting.
4:16 have no possession in the province Beyond the R
4:17 the province Beyond the R, greeting.
4:20 whole province Beyond the R, to whom tribute,
5:3 the province Beyond the R and Shethar-bozenai and
5:6 the province Beyond the R and Shethar-bozenai and
5:6 the province Beyond the R sent to Darius the
6:6 Beyond the R, Shethar-bozenai, and your associates
6:6 the province Beyond the R, keep away;
6:8 the tribute of the province from Beyond the R
6:13 province Beyond the R, Shethar-bozenai, and their
7:21 the province Beyond the R: Whatever Ezra the
7:25 the province Beyond the R, all such as know
8:15 gathered them to the R that runs to Ahava,
8:21 fast there, at the R Ahava, that we might
8:31 we departed from the R Ahava on the twelfth
8:36 the province Beyond the R; and they aided the
Neh 2:7 the province Beyond the R, that they may let
2:9 the province Beyond the R, and gave them the
3:7 of the governor of the province Beyond the R
Tob 6:1 evening to the Tigris R and camped there.
6:2 leaped up from the R and would have swallowed
Jud 1:9 and Kadesh and the R of Egypt, and Tahpanhes
2:8 and every brook and R shall be filled with
Esth 10:6 spring which became a R, and there was light
10:6 abundant water _ the R is Esther, whom the
11:10 there came a great R, with abundant water;
Job 14:11 a lake, and a R wastes away and dries
40:23 Behold, if the R is turbulent he is not
Ps 36:8 them drink from the R of thy delights.
46:4 [Selah] There is a R whose streams make glad
65:9 greatly enrichest it; the R of God is full
66:6 men passed through the R on foot.
72:8 sea, and from the R to the ends of
80:11 to the sea, and its shoots to the R
83:9 and Jabin at the R Kishon,
105:41 forth; it flowed through the desert like a R
Wis 11:6 fountain of an ever-flowing R, stirred up and defiled
19:10 instead of fish the R spewed out vast numbers

R

Sir 4:26 not try to stop the current of a R
24:28 a canal from a R and like a water
24:29 my canal became a R, and my river became
24:29 a river, and my R became a sea.
39:22 dry land like a R, and drenches it like
40:16 by any water or R bank will be plucked
44:22 sea and from the R to the ends of
47:14 You overflowed like a R with understanding.
Is 7:20 is hired beyond the R — with the king
8:7 the waters of the R, mighty and many, the
11:15 his hand over the R with his scorching wind,
19:5 dried up, and the R will be parched and
27:12 that day from the R Euphrates to the Brook
48:18 have been like a R, and your righteousness like
66:12 to her like a R, and the wealth of
Jer 46:2 which was by the R Euphrates at Carchemish and
46:6 the north by the R Euphrates they have stumbled
46:10 north country by the R Euphrates.
Bar 1:4 in Babylon by the R Sud.
Ezek 1:1 the exiles by the R Chebar, the heavens were
1:3 the Chaldeans by the R Chebar; and the hand
3:15 who dwelt by the R Chebar.
3:23 had seen by the R Chebar; and I fell
10:15 I saw by the R Chebar.
10:20 of Israel by the R Chebar; and I knew
10:22 had seen by the R Chebar.
43:3 had seen by the R Chebar; and I fell
47:5 and it was a R that I could not
47:5 to swim in, a R that could not be
47:6 led me back along the bank of the R
47:7 the bank of the R very many trees on
47:9 And wherever the R goes every living creature which
47:9 will live where the R goes.
47:12 both sides of the R, there will grow all
Dan 8:2 I was at the R Ulai.
8:3 a ram standing on the bank of the R
8:6 the bank of the R, and he ran at
10:4 bank of the great R, that is, the Tigris,
Mic 7:12 from Egypt to the R, from sea to sea
Nah 2:6 The R gates are opened, the palace is in
Zech 9:10 sea, and from the R to the ends of
1Mac 3:32 king's affairs from the R Euphrates to the borders
3:37 He crossed the Euphrates R and went through the
5:41 other side of the R, we will cross over
7:8 the province Beyond the R; he was a great
11:7 as far as the R called Eleutherus; then he
11:60 and traveled beyond the R and among the cities,
12:30 them, for they had crossed the Eleutherus R
Mt 3:6 by him in the R Jordan, confessing their sins.
Mk 1:5 by him in the R Jordan, confessing their sins.
Rev 9:14 bound at the great R Euphrates."
12:15 poured water like a R out of his mouth
12:16 mouth and swallowed the R which the dragon had
16:12 bowl on the great R Euphrates, and its water
22:1 he showed me the R of the water of
22:2 either side of the R, the tree of life

RIVERS (44)

Gen 2:10 garden, and there it divided and became four R
Ex 7:19 of Egypt, over their R, their canals, and their
8:5 your rod over the R, over the canals, and
Lev 11:9 seas or in the R, you may eat.
11:10 the seas or the R that has not fins
2Kgs 5:12 Abana and Pharpar, the R of Damascus, better than
Job 20:17 not look upon the R, the streams flowing with
Ps 24:2 upon the seas, and established it upon the R
78:16 rock, and caused waters to flow down like R
78:44 He turned their R to blood, so that they
89:25 the sea and his right hand on the R
107:33 He turns R into a desert, springs of water
Wis 5:22 rage against them, and R will relentlessly overwhelm
Is 18:1 which is beyond the R of Ethiopia;
18:2 conquering, whose land the R divide.
18:7 conquering, whose land the R divide, to Mount Zion,
33:21 a place of broad R and streams, where no
41:18 I will open R on the bare heights, and
42:15 I will turn the R into islands, and dry
43:2 you; and through the R, they shall not overwhelm
43:19 in the wilderness and R in the desert.
43:20 water in the wilderness, R in the desert, to
44:27 will dry up your R;
47:2 your robe, uncover your legs, pass through the R
50:2 sea, I make the R a desert; their fish
Jer 46:7 like the Nile, like R whose waters surge?
46:8 like the Nile, like R whose waters surge.
Lam 3:48 my eyes flow with R of tears because of
Ezek 31:4 grow tall, making its R flow round the place
31:15 it, and restrain its R, and many waters shall
32:2 burst forth in your R, trouble the waters with
32:2 the waters with your feet, and foul their R
32:14 clear, and cause their R to run like oil,
Dan 3:79 the Lord, seas and R, sing praise to him
Mic 6:7 with ten thousands of R of oil?
Nah 1:4 dries up all the R; Bashan and Carmel wither,
Hab 3:8 thy wrath against the R, O LORD?
3:8 thy anger against the R, or thy indignation against
3:9 Selah Thou didst cleave the earth with R
Zeph 3:10 From beyond the R of Ethiopia my suppliants, the
Jn 7:38 his heart shall flow R of living water.'"
2Cor 11:26 journeys, in danger from R, danger from robbers,
Rev 8:10 a third of the R and on the fountains
16:4 his bowl into the R and the fountains of

RIVERSIDE

Acts 16:13 the gate to the R, where we supposed there

RIZIA

1Chr 7:39 The sons of Ulla: Arah, Hanniel, and R

RIZPAH (4)

2Sam 3:7 concubine, whose name was R, the daughter of Aiah;
21:8 the two sons of R the daughter of Aiah,
21:10 Then R the daughter of Aiah took sackcloth, and
21:11 David was told what R the daughter of Aiah,

ROAD (52)

Gen 38:14 which is on the R to Timnah; for she
38:16 to her at the R side, and said, "Come,
Num 22:23 LORD standing in the R, with a drawn sword
22:23 aside out of the R, and went into the
22:23 struck the ass, to turn her into the R
22:34 didst stand in the R against me.
Deut 2:8 away from the Arabah R from Elath and
2:27 go only by the R, I will turn aside
11:30 Jordan, west of the R, toward the going down
27:18 blind man on the R And all the people
Judg 4:9 with you; nevertheless, the R on which you are
1Sam 4:13 his seat by the R watching, for his heart
26:3 which is beside the R on the east of
2Sam 13:34 coming from the Horonaim R by the side of
16:13 men went on the R, while Shimei went along
1Kgs 11:29 prophet Ahijah the Shilonite found him on the R
13:24 met him on the R and killed him.
13:24 was thrown in the R, and the ass stood
13:25 body thrown in the R, and the lion standing
13:28 body thrown in the R, and the ass and
1Chr 26:16 of Shallecheth on the R that goes up.
26:18 were four at the R and two at the
Tob 10:7 every day to the R by which they had
11:5 looking intently down the R for her son.
Job 24:4 the poor off the R; the poor of the
Prov 7:8 her corner, taking the R to her house
26:13 sluggard says, "There is a lion in the R
Eccl 10:3 fool walks on the R, he lacks sense, and
Sir 8:15 not travel on the R with a foolhardy fellow,
Is 15:5 up weeping; on the R to Horonaim they raise
Jer 6:25 nor walk on the R; for the enemy has
31:21 well the highway, the R by which you went.
Nah 2:1 the ramparts; watch the R; gird your loins; collect
1Mac 5:28 back by the wilderness R to Bozrah; and he
5:46 strong city on the R, and they could not
6:33 forced march along the R to Beth-zechariah, and his
9:2 They went by the R which leads to Gilgal
Mt 21:8 their garments on the R, and others cut branches
21:8 from the trees and spread them on the R
Mk 10:32 they were on the R, going up to Jerusalem,
11:8 their garments on the R, and others spread leafy
Lk 9:57 were going along the R, a man said to
10:4 no sandals; and salute no one on the R
10:31 was going down that R; and when he saw
19:36 rode along, they spread their garments on the R
24:32 to us on the R, while he opened to
24:35 had happened on the R, and how he was
Acts 8:26 the south to the R that goes down from
8:26 This is a desert R
8:36 they went along the R they came to some
9:17 to you on the R by which you came,
9:27 them how on the R he had seen the

ROADS (7)

Deut 19:3 You shall prepare the R, and divide into three
Job 21:29 those who travel the R, and do you not

Is 59:8 they have made their R crooked, no one who
Jer 6:16 LORD: "Stand by the R, and look, and ask
18:15 ways, in the ancient R, and have gone into
Lam 1:4 The R to Zion mourn, for none come to
Bar 4:26 sons have traveled rough R; they were taken away

ROADSIDE (3)

Mt 20:30 men sitting by the R, when they heard that
Mk 10:46 the son of Timaeus, was sitting by the R
Lk 18:35 was sitting by the R begging

ROAM

Ps 59:15 They R about for food, and growl if they

ROAMED

1Sam 30:31 the places where David and his men had R

ROAR (24)

1Chr 16:32 Let the sea R, and all that fills it,
Job 4:10 The R of the lion, the voice of the
30:22 me about in the R of the storm.
Ps 46:3 sea; though its waters R and foam, though the
96:11 rejoice; let the sea R, and all that fills
98:7 Let the sea R, and all that fills it;
104:21 The young lions R for their prey, seeking their
Is 5:29 like young lions they R; they growl and seize
17:12 Ah, the R of nations, they roar like the
17:12 roar of nations, they R like the roaring of
17:13 The nations R like the roaring of many waters,
42:10 Let the sea R and all that fills it,
51:15 so that its waves R – the LORD of
Jer 5:22 cannot prevail, though they R, they cannot pass over
11:16 fruit'; but with the R of a great tempest
25:30 them: 'The LORD will R from on high, and
25:30 his voice; he will R mightily against his fold,
31:35 so that its waves R –the LORD of hosts
51:38 "They shall R together like lions; they shall growl
51:55 Their waves R like many waters, the noise of
Hos 11:10 the LORD, he will R like a lion; yea,
11:10 lion; yea, he will R, and his sons shall
Amos 3:4 Does a lion R in the forest, when he
Zech 11:3 Hark, the R of the lions, for the jungle

ROARED (6)

Judg 14:5 behold, a young lion R against him;
Esth 11:6 to fight, and they R terribly.
Ps 74:4 Thy foes have R in the midst of thy
Jer 2:15 The lions have R against him, they have roared
2:15 against him, they have R loudly.
Amos 3:8 The lion has R; who will not fear?

ROARING (20)

Esth 11:7 And at their R every nation prepared for war,
Ps 22:13 like a ravening and R lion.
65:7 who dost still the R of the seas, the
65:7 of the seas, the R of their waves, the
93:3 up their voice, the floods lift up their R
Prov 28:15 Like a R lion or a charging bear is
Wis 17:19 of the most savage R beasts, or an echo
Is 5:29 Their R is like a lion, like young lions
5:30 that day, like the R of the sea.
17:12 they roar like the R of mighty waters!
17:13 nations roar like the R of many waters, but
Jer 6:23 them is like the R sea; they ride upon
50:42 them is like the R of the sea; they
Ezek 19:7 were in it at the sound of his R
22:25 her are like a R lion tearing the prey;
Zeph 3:3 officials within her are R lions; her judges are
1Mac 3:4 like a lion's cub R for prey.
Lk 21:25 in perplexity at the R of the sea and
1Pet 5:8 prowls around like a R lion, seeking some one
Rev 10:3 voice, like a lion R; when he called out,

ROARS (3)

Job 37:4 After it his voice R; he thunders with his
Joel 3:16 And the LORD R from Zion, and utters his
Amos 1:2 he said: "The LORD R from Zion, and utters

ROAST

1Sam 2:15 for the priest to R; for he will not

ROASTED (6)

Ex 12:8 the flesh that night, R; with unleavened bread and
12:9 boiled with water, but R, its head with its
2Chr 35:13 And they R the passover lamb with fire according
Tob 6:5 told him; and they R and ate the fish.

Is 44:19 on its coals, I R flesh and have eaten;
Jer 29:22 the king of Babylon R in the fire,"

ROASTS

Is 44:16 he eats flesh, he R meat and is satisfied;

ROB (10)

Lev 19:13 oppress your neighbor or R him.
26:22 among you, which shall R you of your children,
Prov 22:22 Do not R the poor, because he is poor,
Sir 9:13 no misstep, lest he R you of your life.
Is 10:2 from justice and to R the poor of my
Ezek 5:17 you, and they will R you of your children;
Mal 3:8 we return?' Will man R God?
2Mac 9:2 Persepolis, and attempted to R the temples and
Lk 3:14 he said to them, R no one by violence
Rom 2:22 abhor idols, do you R temples?

ROBBED (12)

Deut 28:29 be only oppressed and R continually, and there shall
Judg 9:25 mountain tops, and they R all who passed by
2Sam 17:8 enraged, like a bear R of her cubs in
Prov 4:17 done wrong; they are R of sleep unless they
17:12 man meet a she-bear R of her cubs, rather
Sir 29:6 not, the borrower has R him of his money,
Is 42:22 this is a people R and plundered, they are
Jer 21:12 him who has been R, lest my wrath go
22:3 hand of the oppressor him who has been R
Ezek 18:18 because he practiced extortion, R his brother, and did
Hos 13:8 them like a bear R of her cubs, I
2Cor 11:8 I R other churches by accepting support from them

ROBBER (11)

Prov 23:28 in wait like a R and increases the faithless
24:34 upon you like a R, and want like an
Sir 36:26 will trust a nimble R that skips from city
Ezek 18:10 son who is a R, a shedder of blood,
2Mac 4:42 flight; and the temple R himself they killed close
Mt 26:55 out as against a R, with swords and clubs
Mk 14:48 out as against a R, with swords and clubs
Lk 22:50 out as against a R, with swords and clubs?
Jn 10:1 a thief and a R;
18:40 Now Barabbas was a R
1Cor 5:11 idolater, reviler, drunkard, or R –not even to eat

ROBBERS (20)

Job 12:6 The tents of R are at peace, and those
Is 42:24 Jacob to the spoiler, and Israel to the R
Jer 7:11 become a den of R in your eyes?
Bar 6:15 but it cannot save itself from war and R
6:18 order that they may not be plundered by R
6:57 not able to save themselves from thieves and R
Ezek 7:22 profane my precious place; R shall enter and profane
Hos 6:9 As R lie in wait for a man, so
Mt 21:13 prayer'; but you make it a den of R
27:38 Then two R were crucified with him, one on
27:44 And the R who were crucified with him also
Mk 11:17 But you have made it a den of R
15:27 him they crucified two R, one on his right
Lk 10:30 and he fell among R, who stripped him and
10:36 neighbor to the man who fell among the R
19:46 but you have made it a den of R
Jn 10:8 me are thieves and R; but the sheep did
1Cor 5:10 or the greedy and R, or idolaters, since then
6:10 nor revilers, nor R will inherit the kingdom
2Cor 11:26 from rivers, danger from R, danger from my own

ROBBERY (10)

Lev 6:2 or security, or through R, or if he has
6:4 what he took by R, or what he got
Ps 62:10 no vain hopes on R; if riches increase, set
Is 61:8 love justice, I hate R and wrong; I will
Ezek 18:7 his pledge, commits no R, gives his bread to
18:12 poor and needy, commits R, does not restore the
18:16 no pledge, commits no R, but gives his bread
22:29 extortion and committed R; they have oppressed the
33:15 he has taken by R, and walks in the
Amos 3:10 store up violence and R in their strongholds."

ROBBING (4)

1Sam 23:1 against Keilah, and are R the threshing floors."
Mal 3:8 Yet you are R me.
3:8 say, 'How are we R thee?' In your tithes
3:9 curse, for you are R me; the whole nation

R

ROBE (60)

Gen 37:3 made him a long R with sleeves.
37:23 stripped him of his R, the long robe with
37:23 his robe, the long R with sleeves that he
37:31 Then they took Joseph's R, and killed a goat,
37:31 goat, and dipped the R in the blood;
37:32 they sent the long R with sleeves and brought
37:32 it is your son's R or not."
37:33 "It is my son's R; a wild beast has
Ex 28:4 breastpiece, an ephod, a R, a coat of checker
28:31 you shall make the R of the ephod all
28:34 pomegranate, round about on the skirts of the R
29:5 the coat and the R of the ephod, and
39:22 He also made the R of the ephod woven
39:23 the opening of the R in it was like
39:24 the skirts of the R they made pomegranates of
39:25 the skirts of the R round about, between the
39:26 the skirts of the R for ministering; as the
Lev 8:7 clothed him with the R, and put the ephod
1Sam 2:19 for him a little R and take it to
15:27 the skirt of his R, and it tore.
18:4 stripped himself of the R that was upon him,
24:4 and stealthily cut off the skirt of Saul's R
24:11 the skirt of your R in my hand; for
24:11 the skirt of your R, and did not kill
28:14 coming up; and he is wrapped in a R
2Sam 13:18 was wearing a long R with sleeves; for thus
13:19 and rent the long R which she wore; and
1Chr 15:27 was clothed with a R of fine linen, as
Job 1:20 arose, and rent his R, and shaved his head,
29:14 justice was like a R and a turban.
Wis 18:24 For upon his long R the whole world was
Sir 6:29 a strong protection, and her collar a glorious R
6:31 her like a glorious R, and put her on
27:8 attain it and wear it as a glorious R
45:7 and put a glorious R upon him.
45:8 linen breeches, the long R, and the ephod.
50:11 put on his glorious R and clothed himself with
Is 3:24 instead of a rich R, a girding of sackcloth;
22:21 clothe him with your R, and will bind your
47:2 veil, strip off your R, uncover your legs, pass
61:10 covered me with the R of righteousness, as a
Bar 4:20 have taken off the R of peace and put
5:2 Put on the R of the righteousness from God;
Ezek 5:3 and bind them in the skirts of your R
Jon 3:6 his throne, removed his R, and covered himself with
Mic 2:8 enemy; you strip the R from the peaceful, from
Zech 8:23 take hold of the R of a Jew, saying,
1Mac 6:15 the crown and his R and the signet, that
10:20 sent him a purple R and a golden crown)
2Mac 4:38 stripped off the purple R from Andronicus, tore off
Mt 27:28 and put a scarlet R upon him,
27:31 stripped him of the R, and put his own
Mk 16:5 dressed in a white R; and they were amazed.
Lk 15:22 'Bring quickly the best R, and put it on
Jn 19:2 him in a purple R;
19:5 wearing the crown of thorns and the purple R
Rev 1:13 clothed with a long R and with a golden
6:11 each given a white R and told to rest
19:13 is clad in a R dipped in blood, and
19:16 On his R and on his thigh he has

ROBED (3)

Ps 93:1 LORD reigns; he is R in majesty; the LORD
93:1 majesty; the LORD is R, he is girded with
Rev 15:6 with the seven plagues, R in pure bright linen,

ROBES (29)

1Kgs 22:10 thrones, arrayed in their R, at the threshing floor
22:30 and go into battle, but you wear your R
2Chr 18:9 thrones, arrayed in their R; and they were sitting
18:29 and go into battle, but you wear your R
Esth 5:1 put on her royal R and stood in the
6:8 to honor, let royal R be brought, which the
6:9 set; and let the R and the horse be
6:10 "Make haste, take the R and the horse, as
6:11 So Haman took the R and the horse, and
8:15 the king in royal R of blue and white,
Job 2:12 and they rent their R and sprinkled dust upon
Ps 45:8 above your fellows; your R are all fragrant with
45:13 her chamber with gold-woven R;
45:14 gold-woven robes; in many-colored R she is led to
133:2 Aaron, running down on the collar of his R
Is 3:22 nose rings; the festal R, the mantles, the cloaks,
Bar 6:12 been dressed in purple R,
6:20 worms from the earth devour them and their R
6:58 silver and of the R they wear, and go
Ezek 26:16 thrones, and remove their R, and strip off their
Mt 26:65 high priest tore his R, and said, "He has
Mk 12:38 go about in long R, and to have salutations
Lk 20:46 go about in long R, and love salutations in
Acts 1:10 by them in white R,
12:21 put on his royal R, took his seat upon
Rev 7:9 Lamb, clothed in white R, with palm branches in
7:13 these, clothed in white R, and whence have they
7:14 they have washed their R and made them white
22:14 those who wash their R, that they may have

ROBS (2)

Prov 28:24 He who R his father or his mother and
Sir 42:9 and worry over her R him of sleep; when

ROBUST

Sir 30:15 all gold, and a R body than countless riches.

ROCK (129)

Gen 49:24 of the Shepherd, the R of Israel),
Ex 17:6 you there on the R at Horeb; and you
17:6 you shall strike the R, and water shall come
33:21 shall stand upon the R;
33:22 a cleft of the R, and I will cover
Lev 11:5 And the R badger, because it chews the cud
Num 20:8 brother, and tell the R before their eyes to
20:8 water out of the R for them; so you
20:10 assembly together before the R, and he said to
20:10 bring forth water for you out of this R
20:11 hand and struck the R with his rod twice;
24:21 is set in the R;
Deut 8:15 out of the flinty R,
14:7 the hare, and the R badger, because they chew
32:4 "The R, his work is perfect; for all his
32:13 honey out of the R, and oil out of
32:13 the rock, and oil out of the flinty R
32:15 and scoffed at the R of his salvation.
32:18 were unmindful of the R that begot you, and
32:30 to flight, unless their R had sold them, and
32:31 For their R is not as our Rock, even
32:31 is not as our R, even our enemies themselves
32:37 are their gods, the R in which they took
Judg 6:20 put them on this R, and pour the broth
6:21 up fire from the R and consumed the flesh
7:25 killed Oreb at the R of Oreb, and Zeeb
13:19 offered it upon the R to the LORD, to
15:8 the cleft of the R of Etam.
15:11 the cleft of the R of Etam, and said
15:13 new ropes, and brought him up from the R
20:45 the wilderness to the R of Rimmon; five thousand
20:47 the wilderness to the R of Rimmon, and abode
20:47 and abode at the R of Rimmon four months.
21:13 who were at the R of Rimmon, and proclaimed
1Sam 2:2 thee; there is no R like our God.
23:25 went down to the R which is in the
23:28 place was called the R of Escape.
2Sam 21:10 for herself on the R, from the beginning of
22:2 "The LORD is my R, and my fortress, and
22:3 deliverer, my God, my R, in whom I take
22:32 And who is a R, except our God?
22:47 and blessed be my R, and exalted be my
22:47 be my God, the R of my salvation,
23:3 Israel has spoken, the R of Israel has said
1Chr 11:15 went down to the R to David at the
2Chr 25:12 the top of a R and threw them down
25:12 the top of the R; and they were all
Neh 9:15 for them from the R for their thirst, and
Job 14:18 crumbles away, and the R is removed from its
18:4 for you, or the R be removed out of
19:24 were graven in the R for ever!
24:8 and cling to the R for want of shelter.
28:9 hand to the flinty R, and overturns mountains by
29:6 with milk, and the R poured out for me
39:28 On the R he dwells and makes his home
Ps 18:2 The LORD is my R, and my fortress, and
18:2 deliverer, my God, my R, in whom I take
18:31 And who is a R, except our God?–
18:46 and blessed be my R, and exalted be the
19:14 sight, O LORD, my R and my redeemer.
27:5 tent, he will set me high upon a R
28:1 LORD, I call; my R, be not deaf to
31:2 Be thou a R of refuge for me, a
31:3 Yea, thou art my R and my fortress; for
40:2 my feet upon a R, making my steps secure.
42:9 say to God, my R: "Why hast thou forgotten

61:2 thou me to the R that is higher than
62:2 He only is my R and my salvation, my
62:6 He only is my R and my salvation, my
62:7 my honor; my mighty R, my refuge is God.
71:3 thou to me a R of refuge, a strong
71:3 for thou art my R and my fortress.
78:16 come out of the R, and caused waters to
78:20 He smote the R so that water gushed out
78:35 that God was their R, the Most High God
81:16 with honey from the R I would satisfy you."
89:26 my God, and the R of my salvation.'
92:15 upright; he is my R, and there is no
94:22 and my God the R of my refuge.
95:1 joyful noise to the R of our salvation!
105:41 He opened the R, and water gushed forth; it
114:8 Jacob, who turns the R into a pool of
137:9 your little ones and dashes them against the R
141:7 As a R which one cleaves and shatters on
144:1 be the LORD, my R, who trains my hands
144:2 fingers for battle; my R and my fortress, my
Prov 30:19 a serpent on a R, the way of a
Song 2:14 the clefts of the R, in the covert of
Wis 11:4 them out of flinty R, and slaking of thirst
Sir 40:15 branches; they are unhealthy roots upon sheer R
48:17 he tunneled the sheer R with iron and built
Is 2:10 Enter into the R, and hide in the dust
8:14 of offense, and a R of stumbling to both
10:26 smote Midian at the R of Oreb; and his
17:10 have not remembered the R of your refuge;
22:16 and carve a habitation for yourself in the R
26:4 ever, for the LORD GOD is an everlasting R
30:29 the LORD, to the R of Israel.
31:9 His R shall pass away in terror, and his
32:2 shade of a great R in a weary land.
44:8 There is no R; I know not any."
48:21 for them from the R; he cleft the rock
48:21 rock; he cleft the R and the water gushed
51:1 LORD; look to the R from which you were
Jer 5:3 their faces harder than R; they have refused to
13:4 hide it there in a cleft of the R
21:13 of the valley, O R of the plain, says
23:29 hammer which breaks the R in pieces?
48:28 and dwell in the R, O inhabitants of Moab!
49:16 the clefts of the R, who hold the height
Ezek 24:7 it on the bare R, she did not pour
24:8 set on the bare R the blood she has
26:4 soil from her, and make her a bare R
26:14 make you a bare R; you shall be a
Obad 1:3 the clefts of the R, whose dwelling is high,
Hab 1:12 judgment; and thou, O R, hast established them for
2Mac 14:45 standing upon a steep R,
Mt 7:24 his house upon the R;
7:25 fall, because it had been founded on the R
16:18 Peter, and on this R I will build my
27:60 had hewn in the R; and he rolled a
Mk 15:45 hewn out of the R; and he rolled a
Lk 6:48 laid the foundation upon R; and when a flood
8:6 some fell on the R; and as it grew
8:13 the ones on the R are those who, when
Rom 9:33 make men stumble, a R that will make them
1Cor 10:4 drank from the supernatural R which followed them,
10:4 followed them, and the R was Christ.
1Pet 2:8 make men stumble, a R that will make them

ROCK-HEWN

Lk 23:52 laid him in a R tomb, where no one

ROCKED (2)

2Sam 22:8 the earth reeled and R; the foundations of the
Ps 18:7 the earth reeled and R; the foundations also of

ROCKS (24)

1Sam 13:6 in holes and in R and in tombs and
24:2 and his men in front of the Wildgoats' R
1Kgs 19:11 broke in pieces the R before the LORD, but
Jud 16:15 at thy presence the R shall melt like wax,
Job 8:17 twine about the stoneheap; he lives among the R
28:10 out channels in the R, and his eye sees
30:6 in holes of the earth and of the R
Ps 78:15 He cleft R in the wilderness, and gave them
104:18 the wild goats; the R are a refuge for
Prov 30:26 their homes in the R;
Wis 17:19 the harsh crash of R hurled down, or the
Is 2:19 the caves of the R and the holes of
2:21 the caverns of the R and the clefts of
7:19 the clefts of the R, and on all the
33:16 be the fortresses of R; his bread will be
57:5 in the valleys, under the clefts of the R
Jer 4:29 thickets; they climb among R; all the cities are
16:16 hill, and out of the clefts of the R
Amos 6:12 Do horses run upon R
Nah 1:6 like fire, and the R are broken asunder by
Mt 27:51 earth shook, and the R were split;
Acts 27:29 might run on the R, they let out four
Rev 6:15 caves and among the R of the mountains,
6:16 to the mountains and R, "Fall on us and

ROCKY (7)

1Sam 14:4 garrison, there was a R crag on the one
14:4 one side and a R crag on the other
Job 39:28 the fastness of the R crag.
Mt 13:5 Other seeds fell on R ground, where they had
13:20 what was sown on R ground, this is he
Mk 4:5 Other seed fell on R ground, where it had
4:16 the ones sown upon R ground, who, when they

ROD (71)

Ex 4:2 He said, "A R
4:4 and it became a R in his hand--
4:17 in your hand this R, with which you shall
4:20 hand Moses took the R of God.
7:9 to Aaron, 'Take your R and cast it down
7:10 Aaron cast down his R before Pharaoh and his
7:12 man cast down his R, and they became serpents.
7:12 But Aaron's R swallowed up their rods.
7:15 in your hand the R which was turned into
7:17 the Nile with the R that is in my
7:19 to Aaron, 'Take your R and stretch out your
7:20 he lifted up the R and struck the water
8:5 your hand with your R over the rivers, over
8:16 Aaron, 'Stretch out your R and strike the dust
8:17 his hand with his R, and struck the dust
9:23 Moses stretched forth his R toward heaven; and the
10:13 Moses stretched forth his R over the land of
14:16 Lift up your R, and stretch out your hand
17:5 in your hand the R with which you struck
17:9 the hill with the R of God in my
21:20 or female, with a R and the slave dies
Num 17:2 man's name upon his R,
17:3 Aaron's name upon the R of Levi.
17:3 there shall be one R for the head of
17:5 And the R of the man whom I choose
17:6 twelve rods; and the R of Aaron was among
17:8 testimony; and behold, the R of Aaron for the
17:9 and they looked, and each man took his R
17:10 Moses, "Put back the R of Aaron before the
20:8 Moses, "Take the R, and assemble the congregation,
20:9 And Moses took the R from before the LORD,
20:11 the rock with his R twice; and water came
2Sam 7:14 chasten him with the R of men, with the
Job 9:34 Let him take his R away from me, and
21:9 from fear, and no R of God is upon
Ps 2:9 break them with a R of iron, and dash
23:4 art with me; thy R and thy staff, they
89:32 their transgression with the R and their iniquity with
Prov 10:13 is found, but a R is for the back
13:24 He who spares the R hates his son, but
14:3 a fool is a R for his back, but
22:8 reap calamity, and the R of his fury will
22:15 a child, but the R of discipline drives it
23:13 beat him with a R, he will not die.
23:14 beat him with the R you will save his
26:3 the ass, and a R for the back of
29:15 The R and reproof give wisdom, but a child
Is 9:4 for his shoulder, the R of his oppressor, thou
10:5 Ah, Assyria, the R of my anger, the staff
10:15 As if a R should wield him who lifts
10:24 they smite with the R and lift up their
10:26 of Oreb; and his R will be over the
11:4 the earth with the R of his mouth, and
14:29 of you, that the R which smote you is
28:27 out with a stick, and cummin with a R
30:31 of the LORD, when he smites with his R
Jer 1:11 said, "I see a R of almond."
Lam 3:1 seen affliction under the R of his wrath;
Ezek 7:11 grown up into a R of wickedness; none of
20:37 you pass under the R, and I will let
21:10 You have despised the R, my son, with everything
21:13 what could it do if you despise the R
Mic 5:1 against us; with a R they strike upon the
1Cor 4:21 to you with a R, or with love in
Heb 9:4 the manna, and Aaron's R that budded, and the

Rev 2:27 rule them with a R of iron, as when
11:1 was given a measuring R like a staff, and
12:5 the nations with a R of iron, but her
19:15 rule them with a R of iron; he will
21:15 me had a measuring R of gold to measure
21:16 the city with his R, twelve thousand stadia; its

RODANIM
1Chr 1:7 The sons of Javan: Elishah, Tarshish, Kittim, and R

RODE (12)
Gen 24:61 her maids arose, and R upon the camels and
Judg 10:4 had thirty sons who R on thirty asses; and
12:14 and thirty grandsons, who R on seventy asses; and
1Sam 25:20 And as she R on the ass, and came
2Sam 22:11 He R on a cherub, and flew; he was
1Kgs 18:45 And Ahab R and went to Jezreel.
2Kgs 9:25 when you and I R side by side behind
Neh 2:12 with me but the beast on which I R
Esth 8:14 in the king's service, R out in haste, urged
Ps 18:10 He R on a cherub, and flew; he came
2Mac 9:4 the judgment of heaven R with him!
Lk 19:36 And as he R along, they spread their garments

RODS (16)
Gen 30:37 Then Jacob took fresh R of poplar and almond
30:37 streaks in them, exposing the white of the R
30:38 He set the R which he had peeled in
30:39 in front of the R and so the flocks
30:41 breeding Jacob laid the R in the runnels before
30:41 might breed among the R,
Ex 7:12 But Aaron's rod swallowed up their R
Num 17:2 and get from them R, one for each fathers'
17:2 leaders according to their fathers' houses, twelve R
17:6 their leaders gave him R, one for each leader,
17:6 their fathers' houses, twelve R; and the rod of
17:6 and the rod of Aaron was among their R
17:7 And Moses deposited the R before the LORD in
17:9 brought out all the R from before the LORD
Acts 16:22 them and gave orders to beat them with R
2Cor 11:25 have been beaten with R; once I was stoned.

ROEBUCK
Deut 14:5 hart, the gazelle, the R, the wild goat, the

ROEBUCKS
1Kgs 4:23 sheep, besides harts, gazelles, R, and fatted fowl.

ROGELIM (2)
2Sam 17:27 Barzillai the Gileadite from R,
19:31 had come down from R; and he went on

ROHGAH
1Chr 7:34 of Shemer his brother: R, Jehubbah, and Aram.

ROLL (16)
Gen 29:3 there, the shepherds would R the stone from the
Josh 10:18 And Joshua said, R great stones against the mouth
1Sam 14:33 "You have dealt treacherously; R a great stone to
Job 30:14 amid the crash they R on.
Ps 40:7 I come; in the R of the book it
Sir 27:27 does evil, it will R back upon him, and
Is 9:18 the forest, and they R upward in a column
34:4 away, and the skies R up like a scroll.
Jer 6:26 gird on sackcloth, and R in ashes; make mourning
25:34 shepherds, and cry, and R in ashes, you lords
51:25 hand against you, and R you down from the
Amos 5:24 But let justice R down like waters, and righteousness
Mic 1:10 at all; in Beth-le-aphrah R yourselves in the dust.
Mk 16:3 one another, "Who will R away the stone for
Heb 1:12 a mantle thou wilt R them up, and they
10:7 of me in the R of the book."

ROLLED (15)
Gen 29:8 and the stone is R from the mouth of
29:10 Jacob went up and R the stone from the
Josh 5:9 "This day I have R away the reproach of
2Kgs 2:8 took his mantle, and R it up, and struck
Is 9:5 tumult and every garment R in blood will be
28:27 is a cart wheel R over cummin; but dill
38:12 a weaver I have R up my life; he
Mt 27:60 the rock; and he R a great stone to
28:2 heaven and came and R back the stone, and
Mk 9:20 on the ground and R about, foaming at the
15:45 the rock; and he R a stone against the
16:4 that the stone was R back;—it was

Lk 24:2 they found the stone R away from the tomb,
Jn 20:7 the linen cloths but R up in a place
Rev 6:14 a scroll that is R up, and every mountain

ROLLING
Prov 26:27 will come back upon him who starts it R

ROMAMTI-EZER (2)
1Chr 25:4 Hanani, Eliathah, Giddalti, and R, Joshbekashah,
25:31 to the twenty-fourth, to R, his sons and his

ROMAN (8)
Acts 16:12 of Macedonia, and a R colony.
16:37 uncondemned, men who are R citizens, and have
16:38 heard that they were R citizens;
22:25 man who is a R citizen, and uncondemned?"
22:26 this man is a R citizen."
22:27 me, are you a R citizen?" And he said,
22:29 that Paul was a R citizen and that he
23:27 that he was a R citizen.

ROMANS (19)
1Mac 8:1 the fame of the R, that they were very
8:10 and fell, and the R took captive their wives
8:23 go well with the R and with the nation
8:27 of the Jews, the R shall willingly act as
8:29 on these terms the R make a treaty with
12:4 And the R gave them letters to the people
14:24 thousand minas, to confirm the alliance with the R
14:40 were addressed by the R as friends and allies
14:40 brethren, and that the R had received the envoys
15:16 "Lucius, consul of the R, to King Ptolemy, greeting.
2Mac 4:11 and alliance with the R; and he destroyed the
8:10 tribute due to the R, two thousand talents, by
8:36 secure tribute for the R by the capture of
11:34 The R also sent them a letter, which read
11:34 Manius, envoys of the R, to the people of
Jn 11:48 in him, and the R will come and destroy
Acts 16:21 not lawful for us R to accept or practice."
25:16 the custom of the R to give up any
28:17 prisoner from Jerusalem into the hands of the R

ROME (22)
1Mac 1:10 the king; he had been a hostage in R
7:1 Seleucus set forth from R, sailed with a few
8:17 and sent them to R to establish friendship and
8:19 They went to R, a very long journey; and
8:24 war comes first to R or to any of
8:26 money, or ships, as R has decided; and they
8:28 money, or ships, as R has decided; and they
12:1 and sent them to R to confirm and renew
12:3 So they went to R and entered the senate
12:16 have sent them to R to renew our former
14:16 It was heard in R, and as far away
14:24 Simon sent Numenius to R with a large gold
15:15 his companions arrived from R, with letters to the
Acts 2:10 and visitors from R, both Jews and proselytes,
18:2 Claudius had commanded all the Jews to leave R
19:21 I have been there, I must also see R
23:11 Jerusalem, so you must bear witness also at R
28:14 And so we came to R
28:16 when we came into R, Paul was allowed to
Rom 1:7 all God's beloved in R, who are called to
1:15 the gospel to you also who are in R
2Tim 1:17 when he arrived in R he searched for me

ROOF (34)
Gen 6:16 Make a R for the ark, and finish it
19:8 they have come under the shelter of my R
Deut 22:8 a parapet for your R, that you may not
Josh 2:6 them up to the R, and hid them with
2:6 which she had laid in order on the R
2:8 to them on the R,
Judg 3:20 alone in his cool R chamber.
3:23 the doors of the R chamber upon him, and
3:24 the doors of the R chamber were locked, they
3:25 the doors of the R chamber, they took the
9:51 they went to the R of the tower.
16:27 there, and on the R there were about three
1Sam 9:25 for Saul upon the R, and he lay down
9:26 to Saul upon the R, "Up, that I may
2Sam 11:2 was walking upon the R of the king's house,
11:2 he saw from the R a woman bathing; and
16:22 for Absalom upon the R; and Absalom went in
18:24 went up to the R of the gate by
2Kgs 4:10 us make a small R chamber with walls, and

23:12 the altars on the R of the upper chamber
Neh 8:16 themselves, each on his R, and in their courts
Jud 8:5 for herself on the R of her house, and
Job 29:10 tongue cleaved to the R of their mouth.
Ps 137:6 tongue cleave to the R of my mouth, if
Eccl 10:18 Through sloth the R sinks in, and through indolence
Sir 29:22 the shelter of his R than sumptuous food in
Lam 4:4 nursling cleaves to the R of its mouth for
Ezek 3:26 tongue cleave to the R of your mouth, so
26:8 you, and raise a R of shields against you.
Dan 4:29 was walking on the R of the royal palace
Mt 8:8 you come under my R; but only say the
Mk 2:4 crowd, they removed the R above him; and when
Lk 5:19 went up on the R and let him down
7:6 you come under my R;

ROOFS (4)
Wis 17:2 shut in under their R, exiles from eternal providence.
Jer 19:13 the houses upon whose R incense has been burned
32:29 the houses on whose R incense has been offered
Zeph 1:5 bow down on the R to the host of

ROOM (35)
Gen 24:23 Is there R in your father's house for us
24:25 and provender enough, and R to lodge in."
26:22 the LORD has made R for us, and we
Num 25:8 Israel into the inner R, and pierced both of
2Kgs 10:25 went into the inner R of the house of
1Chr 28:11 chambers, and of the R for the mercy seat;
Tob 3:17 daughter of Raguel came down from her upper R
7:16 make up the other R, and take her into
Ps 4:1 Thou hast given me R when I was in
Prov 18:16 A man's gift makes R for him and brings
Sir 16:14 He will make R for every act of mercy;
Is 5:8 there is no more R, and you are made
49:20 narrow for me; make R for me to dwell
Jer 7:32 because there is no R elsewhere.
Ezek 8:12 every man in his R of pictures?
40:13 of the one side R to the back of
41:3 went into the inner R and measured the jambs
41:4 the length of the R, twenty cubits, and its
41:15 temple and the inner R and the outer vestibule
41:17 even to the inner R, and on the outside.
41:17 about in the inner R and the nave were
Joel 2:16 the bridegroom leave his R, and the bride her
Zech 10:10 till there is no R for them.
Mt 6:6 pray, go into your R and shut the door
Mk 2:2 there was no longer R for them, not even
14:14 Where is my guest R, where I am to
14:15 you a large upper R furnished and ready; there
Lk 14:22 and still there is R
22:11 Where is the guest R, where I am to
22:12 you a large upper R furnished; there make ready."
Acts 1:13 up to the upper R, where they were staying,
9:37 washed her, they laid her in an upper R
9:39 had come, they took him to the upper R
Rom 15:23 no longer have any R for work in these
Philem 1:22 time, prepare a guest R for me, for I

ROOMS (20)
Gen 6:14 of gopher wood; make R in the ark, and
1Kgs 6:29 and open flowers, in the inner and outer R
6:30 overlaid with gold in the inner and outer R
1Chr 28:11 its treasuries, its upper R, and its inner chambers,
Prov 24:4 established; by knowledge the R are filled with all
Jer 22:13 unrighteousness, and his upper R by injustice; who
22:14 house with spacious upper R and cuts out windows
Ezek 40:7 deep; and the side R, one reed long, and
40:7 space between the side R, five cubits; and the
40:10 there were three side R on either side of
40:12 barrier before the side R, one cubit on either
40:12 side; and the side R were six cubits on
40:16 jambs in the side R, and likewise the vestibule
40:21 Its side R, three on either side, and its
40:29 the others; Its side R, its jambs, and its
40:33 Its side R, its jambs, and its vestibule were
40:36 Its side R, its jambs, and its vestibule were
Mt 24:26 is in the inner R do not believe it.
Lk 12:3 have whispered in private R shall be proclaimed
Jn 14:2 Father's house are many R; if it were not

ROOT (51)
Deut 29:18 be among you a R bearing poisonous and bitter
1Kgs 14:15 in the water, and R up Israel out of
2Kgs 19:30 Judah shall again take R downward, and bear fruit
Job 5:3 seen the fool taking R, but suddenly I cursed
14:8 Though its R grow old in the earth, and
15:29 nor will he strike R in the earth;
19:28 pursue him!' and, 'The R of the matter is
31:12 would burn to the R all my increase.
Ps 80:9 it; it took deep R and filled the land.
Prov 12:3 by wickedness, but the R of the righteous will
12:12 to ruin, but the R of the righteous stands
Wis 3:15 is renowned, and the R of understanding does not
4:3 will strike a deep R or take a firm
15:3 thy power is the R of immortality.
Sir 1:5 The R of wisdom—to whom has it been
1:18 the Lord is the R of wisdom, and her
3:26 of wickedness has taken R in him.
23:25 children will not take R, and her branches will
24:12 So I took R in an honored people, in
47:22 and to David a R of his stock.
Is 5:24 the flame, so their R will be as rottenness,
11:10 In that day the R of Jesse shall stand
14:29 for from the serpent's R will come forth an
14:30 I will kill your R with famine, and your
27:6 come Jacob shall take R, Israel shall blossom and
37:31 Judah shall again take R downward, and bear fruit
40:24 has their stem taken R in the earth, when
53:2 plant, and like a R out of dry ground;
Jer 12:2 them, and they take R; they grow and bring
Hos 9:16 Ephraim is stricken, their R is dried up, they
14:5 lily, he shall strike R as the poplar;
Mic 5:14 hands; and I will R out your Asherim from
Mal 4:1 will leave them neither R nor branch.
1Mac 1:10 came forth a sinful R, Antiochus Epiphanes, son of
2Mac 12:7 to come again and R out the whole community
Mt 3:10 is laid to the R of the trees; every
13:6 since they had no R they withered away.
13:21 yet he has no R in himself, but endures
13:29 gathering the weeds you R up the wheat along
Mk 4:6 since it had no R it withered away.
4:17 and they have no R in themselves, but endure
Lk 3:9 is laid to the R of the trees; every
8:13 but these have no R, they believe for a
Rom 11:16 lump; and if the R is holy, so are
11:18 you that support the R, but the root that
11:18 the root, but the R that supports you.
15:12 further Isaiah says, "The R of Jesse shall come,
1Tim 6:10 of money is the R of all evils; it
Heb 12:15 of God; that no R of bitterness" spring up
Rev 5:5 tribe of Judah, the R of David, has conquered,
22:16 I am the R and the offspring of David,

ROOTED (7)
Job 31:8 grows for me be R out.
Ps 9:6 their cities thou hast R out; the very memory
Prov 2:22 the treacherous will be R out of it.
Mt 15:13 not planted will be R up.
Lk 17:6 this sycamine tree, 'Be R up, and be planted
Eph 3:17 faith; that you, being R and grounded in love,
Col 2:7 so live in him, R and built up in

ROOTS (24)
Job 8:17 His R twine about the stoneheap; he lives among
18:16 His R dry up beneath, and his branches wither
28:9 the flinty rock, and overturns mountains by the R
29:19 as the sand, my R spread out to the
30:4 to warm themselves the R of the broom.
36:30 him, and covers the R of the sea.
Wis 7:20 and the virtues of R;
Sir 10:15 has plucked up the R of the nations, and
40:15 branches; they are unhealthy R upon sheer rock.
Is 11:1 and a branch shall grow out of his R
Jer 17:8 that sends out its R by the stream, and
Ezek 17:6 toward him, and its R remained where it stood.
17:7 this vine bent its R toward him, and shot
17:9 not pull up its R and cut off its
17:9 or many people to pull it from its R
31:7 its branches; for its R went down to abundant
Dan 4:15 the stump of its R in the earth, bound
4:23 the stump of its R in the earth, bound
4:26 the stump of the R of the tree, your
7:8 plucked up by the R; and behold, in this
11:7 a branch from her R shall arise in his
Amos 2:9 fruit above, and his R beneath.
Jon 2:6 my head at the R of the mountains.
Mk 11:20 saw the fig tree withered away to its R

ROPE (4)
Josh 2:15 them down by a R through the window, for
Job 18:10 A R is hid for him in the ground,

R

	41:2	Can you put a R in his nose, or
Is	3:24	of a girdle, a R; and instead of well-set

ROPES (16)

Judg	15:13	him with two new R, and brought him up
	15:14	upon him, and the R which were on his
	16:11	bind me with new R that have not been
	16:12	So Delilah took new R and bound him with
	16:12	But he snapped the R off his arms like
2Sam	17:13	all Israel will bring R to that city, and
1Kgs	20:31	on our loins and R upon our heads, and
	20:32	their loins, and put R on their heads, and
Job	39:10	in the furrow with R, or will he harrow
Is	5:18	sin as with cart R,
Jer	38:6	court of the guard, letting Jeremiah down by R
	38:11	let down to Jeremiah in the cistern by R
	38:12	rags and clothes between your armpits and the R
	38:13	drew Jeremiah up with R and lifted him out
Acts	27:32	soldiers cut away the R of the boat, and
	27:40	same time loosening the R that tied the rudders;

ROSE (170)

Gen	4:8	in the field, Cain R up against his brother
	7:17	the ark, and it R high above the earth.
	19:1	Lot saw them, he R to meet them, and
	20:8	So Abimelech R early in the morning, and called
	21:14	So Abraham R early in the morning, and took
	21:32	commander of his army R up and returned to
	22:3	So Abraham R early in the morning, saddled his
	23:3	And Abraham R up from before his dead, and
	23:7	Abraham R and bowed to the Hittites, the people
	25:34	ate and drank, and R and went his way.
	26:31	In the morning they R early and took oath
	28:18	So Jacob R early in the morning, and he
	32:31	The sun R upon him as he passed Penuel,
	37:35	and all his daughters R up to comfort him;
Ex	12:30	And Pharaoh R up in the night, he, and
	24:4	And he R early in the morning, and built
	24:13	So Moses R with his servant Joshua, and Moses
	32:6	And they R up early on the morrow, and
	32:6	eat and drink, and R up to play.
	33:8	tent, all the people R up, and every man
	34:4	the first; and he R early in the morning
Num	11:32	And the people R all that day, and all
	14:40	And they R early in the morning, and went
	16:2	took men; and they R up before Moses, with
	16:25	Then Moses R and went to Dathan and Abiram;
	22:13	So Balaam R in the morning, and said to
	22:14	the princes of Moab R and went to Balak,
	22:21	So Balaam R in the morning, and saddled his
	24:25	Then Balaam R, and went back to his place;
	25:7	priest, saw it, he R and left the congregation,
Josh	3:1	in the morning Joshua R and set out from
	3:16	from above stood and R up in a heap
	6:12	Then Joshua R early in the morning, and the
	6:15	the seventh day they R early at the dawn
	7:16	So Joshua R early in the morning, and brought
	8:19	And the ambush R quickly out of their place,
Judg	6:28	men of the town R early in the morning,
	6:38	When he R early next morning and squeezed the
	7:1	who were with him R early and encamped beside
	9:34	that were with him R up by night, and
	9:35	that were with him R from the ambush.
	9:43	the city, and he R against them and slew
	19:7	And when the man R up to go, his
	19:9	concubine and his servant R up to depart, his
	19:10	spend the night; he R up and departed, and
	19:27	And her master R up in the morning, and
	19:28	ass; and the man R up and went away
	20:5	the men of Gibe-ah R against me, and beset
	20:19	the people of Israel R in the morning, and
	20:33	the men of Israel R up out of their
	21:4	the morrow the people R early, and built there
Ruth	2:15	When she R to glean, Boaz instructed his young
1Sam	1:9	they had eaten and drunk in Shiloh, Hannah R
	1:19	They R early in the morning and worshiped before
	5:3	the people of Ashdod R early the next day,
	5:4	But when they R early on the next morning,
	14:5	The one crag R on the north in front
	15:12	And Samuel R early to meet Saul in the
	16:13	And Samuel R up, and went to Ramah.
	17:20	And David R early in the morning, and left
	17:52	of Israel and Judah R with a shout and
	20:34	And Jonathan R from the table in fierce anger
	20:41	lad had gone, David R from beside the stone
	20:42	And he R and departed; and Jonathan went into
	21:10	And David R and fled that day from Saul,
	23:16	And Jonathan, Saul's son, R, and went to David
	24:7	And Saul R up and left the cave, and
	25:1	Then David R and went down to the wilderness
	25:41	And she R and bowed with her face to
	25:42	Abigail made haste and R and mounted on an
	26:5	Then David R and came to the place where
	28:25	Then they R and went away that night.
2Sam	18:31	power of all who R up against you."
	23:10	He R and struck down the Philistines until his
1Kgs	1:49	of Adonijah trembled, and R, and each went his
	2:19	And the king R to meet her, and bowed
	3:21	When I R in the morning to nurse my
2Kgs	3:22	And when they R early in the morning, and
	3:24	of Israel, the Israelites R and attacked the Moabites,
	6:15	the man of God R early in the morning
	7:12	And the king R in the night, and said
	8:21	all his chariots, and R by night, and he
1Chr	28:2	Then King David R to his feet and said:
2Chr	13:6	the son of David, R up and rebelled against
	20:20	And they R early in the morning and went
	20:23	of Ammon and Moab R against the inhabitants of
	21:9	his chariots, and he R by night and smote
	28:15	been mentioned by name R and took the captives,
	29:20	Then Hezekiah the king R early and gathered the
	36:16	wrath of the LORD R against his people, till
Ezra	1:5	Then R up the heads of the fathers' houses
	9:5	the evening sacrifice I R from my fasting, with
Neh	3:1	Eliashib the high priest R up with his brethren
Jud	10:2	all these words, she R from where she lay
Esth	5:9	gate, that he neither R nor trembled before him,
	7:7	And the king R from the feast in wrath
	8:5	to Esther, and Esther R and stood before the
	11:11	came, and the sun R, and the lowly were
Job	29:8	withdrew, and the aged R and stood;
Ps	78:31	the anger of God against them and he
	104:8	The mountains R, the valleys sank down to the
	124:2	our side, when men R up against us,
Song	2:1	I am a R of Sharon, a lily of
Sir	24:14	in En-ge'di, and like R plants in Jericho; like
	39:13	and bud like a R growing by a stream
	46:1	on the enemies that R against them, so that
	47:1	And after him Nathan R up to prophesy in
	47:12	After him R up a wise son who fared
Jer	41:2	ten men with him R up and struck down
Ezek	1:19	when the living creatures R from the earth, the
	1:19	living creatures rose from the earth, the wheels R
	1:20	went, and the wheels R along with them; for
	1:21	stood; and when those R from the earth, the
	1:21	the earth, the wheels R along with them; for
	41:7	became broader as they R from story to story,
Dan	3:92	Nebuchadnezzar was astonished and R up in haste.
	8:27	some days; then I R and went about the
	13:19	out, the two elders R and ran to her,
	13:61	And they R against the two elders, for out
	14:16	the morning the king R and came, and Daniel
Jon	1:3	But Jonah R to flee to Tarshish from the
	4:8	When the sun R, God appointed a sultry east
1Mac	4:53	and forty-eighth year, they R and offered sacrifice, as
	6:33	the morning the king R and took his army
	8:5	and the others who R up against them, they
	14:32	their sanctuary, then Simon R up and fought for
	16:16	Ptolemy and his men R up, took their weapons,
2Mac	14:45	aflame with anger, he R, and though his blood
Mt	2:14	And he R and took the child and his
	2:21	And he R and took the child and his
	8:15	left her, and she R and served him.
	8:26	Then he R and rebuked the winds and the
	9:7	And he R and went home.
	9:9	And he R and followed him.
	9:19	And Jesus R and followed him, with his disciples.
	13:6	but when the sun R they were scorched; and
	25:7	Then all those maidens R and trimmed their lamps.
Mk	1:35	while before day, he R and went out to
	2:12	And he R, and immediately took up the pallet
	2:14	And he R and followed him.
	4:6	and when the sun R it was scorched, and
	16:9	Now when he R early on the first day
Lk	4:29	And they R up and put him out of
	4:39	her; and immediately she R and served them.
	5:25	And immediately he R before them, and took up
	5:28	he left everything, and R and followed him.
	6:8	And he R and stood there.
	22:43	And when he R from prayer, he came to
	24:12	But Peter R and ran to the tomb; stooping
	24:33	And they R that same hour and returned to

R

Jn 6:18 The sea R because a strong wind was blowing.
11:29 she heard it, she R quickly and went to
13:4 was going to God, R from supper, laid aside
Acts 5:6 The young men R and wrapped him up and
5:17 But the high priest R up and all who
8:27 And he R and went.
9:18 Then he R and was baptized,
9:34 And immediately he R
9:39 So Peter R and went with them.
10:23 The next day he R and went off with
10:41 with him after he R from the dead.
14:20 gathered about him, he R up and entered the
15:5 party of the Pharisees R up, and said, "It
15:7 been much debate, Peter R and said to them,
26:30 Then the king R, and the governor and Bernice
1Cor 10:7 eat and drink and R up to dance."
1Thes 4:14 that Jesus died and R again, even so, through
Rev 8:4 smoke of the incense R with the prayers of
9:2 and from the shaft R smoke like the smoke
13:11 saw another beast which R out of the earth;

ROSEBUDS
Wis 2:8 us crown ourselves with R before they wither.

ROSES
Sir 50:8 in glorious clouds; like R in the days of

ROSH
Gen 46:21 Ashbel, Gera, Naaman, Ehi, R, Muppim, Huppim,

ROT (10)
Prov 10:7 blessing, but the name of the wicked will R
14:30 to the flesh, but passion makes the bones R
Is 19:6 reeds and rushes will R away.
34:4 host of heaven shall R away, and the skies
40:20 wood that will not R; he seeks out a
Bar 6:72 purple and linen that R upon them you will
Hos 5:12 Ephraim, and like dry R to the house of
Zech 14:12 Jerusalem: their flesh shall R while they are still
14:12 feet, their eyes shall R in their sockets, and
14:12 and their tongues shall R in their mouths.

ROTE
Is 29:13 of men learned by R;

ROTTED (2)
2Mac 9:9 and pain, his flesh R away, and because of
Jas 5:2 riches have R and your garments are moth-eaten.

ROTTEN (2)
Job 13:28 wastes away like a R thing, like a garment
41:27 straw, and bronze as R wood.

ROTTENNESS (4)
Prov 12:4 brings shame is like R in his bones.
Is 3:24 perfume there will be R; and instead of a
5:24 root will be as R, and their blossom go
Hab 3:16 quiver at the sound; R enters into my bones,

ROUGH (4)
Is 40:4 become level, and the R places a plain.
42:16 them into light, the R places into level ground.
Bar 4:26 tender sons have traveled R roads; they were taken
Lk 3:5 made straight, and the R ways shall be made

ROUGHLY (4)
Gen 42:7 like strangers and spoke R to them.
42:30 of the land, spoke R to us, and took
1Sam 20:10 will tell me if your father answers you R
Prov 18:23 The poor use entreaties, but the rich answer R

ROUND (261)
Gen 35:5 the cities that were R about them, so that
37:7 behold, your sheaves gathered R it, and bowed down
Ex 7:24 all the Egyptians dug R about the Nile for
13:18 God led the people R by the way of
16:13 the morning dew lay R about the camp.
19:12 bounds for the people R about, saying, 'Take heed
25:11 a molding of gold R about.
28:34 bell and a pomegranate, R about on the skirts
29:16 it against the altar R about.
29:20 blood against the altar R about.
30:3 top and its sides R about and its horns;
30:3 a molding of gold R about.
37:26 top, and its sides R about, and its horns;
37:26 a molding of gold R about it,
38:16 All the hangings R about the court were of
38:20 and for the court R about were of bronze.
38:31 the altar, the bases R about the court, and
38:31 and all the pegs R about the court.
39:25 of the robe R about, between the pomegranates;
39:26 bell and a pomegranate R about upon the skirts
Lev 1:5 and throw the blood R about against the altar
1:11 blood against the altar R about.
3:2 blood against the altar R about.
3:8 blood against the altar R about.
3:13 blood against the altar R about.
7:2 thrown on the altar R about.
8:15 horns of the altar R about, and purified the
8:19 blood upon the altar R about.
8:24 blood upon the altar R about.
9:12 it on the altar R about.
9:18 threw upon the altar R about,
14:41 house to be scraped R about, and the plaster
16:18 horns of the altar R about.
19:27 You shall not R off the hair on your
25:44 the nations that are R about you.
Num 3:37 pillars of the court R about, with their bases
4:32 pillars of the court R about with their bases,
11:24 people, and placed them R about the tent.
11:31 on the other side, R about the camp, and
16:34 all Israel that were R about them fled at
22:4 up all that is R about us, as the
34:12 shall be your land with its boundaries all R
35:2 the Levites pasture lands R about the cities.
35:4 of the city outward a thousand cubits all R
Deut 6:14 the peoples who are R about you;
12:10 from all your enemies R about, so that you
13:7 the peoples that are R about you, whether near
17:14 the nations that are R about me';
25:19 from all your enemies R about, in the land
Josh 15:9 then the boundary bends R to Baalah (that is,
15:11 then the boundary bends R to Shikkeron, and passes
15:12 This is the boundary R about the people of
16:6 east the boundary turns R toward Taanath-shiloh,
18:20 families, boundary by boundary R about.
19:8 with all the villages R about these cities as
21:11 with the pasture lands R about it.
21:42 each its pasture lands R about it; so it
23:1 from all their enemies R about, and Joshua was
Judg 2:12 the peoples who were R about them, and bowed
2:14 power of their enemies R about, so that they
7:21 man in his place R about the camp, and
11:3 worthless fellows collected R Jephthah, and went
18:23 the Danites, who turned R and said to Micah,
19:22 fellows, beset the house R about, beating on the
20:5 and beset the house R about me by night;
20:29 set men in ambush R about Gibe-ah.
1Sam 10:1 hand of their enemies R about.
2Sam 5:9 David built the city R about from the Millo
7:1 from all his enemies R about,
1Kgs 4:24 peace on all sides R about him.
4:31 in all the nations R about.
6:5 of the house, running R the walls of the
6:29 walls of the house R about with carved figures
7:12 courses of hewn stone R about, and a course
7:18 pomegranates; in two rows R about upon the one
7:20 pomegranates, in two rows R about; and so with
7:23 molten sea; it was R, ten cubits from brim
7:24 cubits, compassing the sea R about; the gourds were
7:31 cubit; its opening was R, as a pedestal is
7:31 were carvings; and its panels were square, not R
7:35 stand there was a R band half a cubit
7:36 of each, with wreaths R about.
18:35 And the water ran R about the altar, and
2Kgs 4:16 when the time comes R, you shall embrace a
6:15 horses and chariots was R about the city.
6:17 and chariots of fire R about Elisha.
9:18 Turn R and ride behind me." And the watchman
9:19 Turn R and ride behind me."
17:15 the nations that were R about them, concerning
23:5 cities of Judah and R about Jerusalem; those also
25:1 built siegeworks against it R about.
25:17 were upon the capital R about.
1Chr 4:33 their villages which were R about these cities as
9:27 And they lodged R about the house of God;
11:8 he built the city R about from the Millo
22:9 from all his enemies R about; for his name
2Chr 4:2 molten sea; it was R, ten cubits from brim
4:3 cubits, compassing the sea R about; the gourds were
14:14 smote all the cities R about Gerar, for the
15:15 LORD gave them rest R about.

R

17:10 the lands that were R about Judah, and they
20:30 God gave him rest R about.
33:14 Gate, and carried it R Ophel, and raised it
34:6 Naphtali, in their ruins R about,
Ezra 9:4 the returned exiles, gathered R me while I sat
Neh 6:16 it, all the nations R about us were afraid
12:28 together from the circuit R Jerusalem and from the
Jud 3:7 all in the country R about welcomed him with
Job 19:12 against me, and encamp R about my tent.
22:10 Therefore snares are R about you, and sudden terror
37:12 They turn R and round by his guidance, to
37:12 They turn round and R by his guidance, to
41:14 R about his teeth is terror.
Ps 3:6 set themselves against me R about.
22:16 Yea, dogs are R about me; a company of
27:6 up above my enemies R about me; and I
48:12 Walk about Zion, go R about her, number her
50:3 is a devouring fire, R about him a mighty
79:3 their blood like water R about Jerusalem, and there
79:4 and derided by those R about us.
89:7 above all that are R about him?
89:8 LORD, with thy faithfulness R about thee?
97:2 and thick darkness are R about him; righteousness
97:3 burns up his adversaries R about.
109:19 garment which he wraps R him, like a belt
125:2 As the mountains are R about Jerusalem, so the
125:2 so the LORD is R about his people, from
Eccl 1:6 the south, and goes R to the north; round
1:6 round to the north; R and round goes the
1:6 the north; round and R goes the wind, and
Sir 45:9 very many golden bells R about, to send forth
50:5 when the people gathered R him as he came
Is 15:8 a cry has gone R the land of Moab;
22:18 you, and whirl you R and round, and throw
22:18 whirl you round and R, and throw you like
29:1 year to year; let the feasts run their R
29:3 will encamp against you R about, and will besiege
42:25 set him on fire R about, but he did
49:18 Lift up your eyes R about and see; they
60:4 Lift up your eyes R about, and see; they
Jer 1:15 against all its walls R about, and against all
4:17 are they against her R about, because she has
12:9 of prey against her R about?
17:26 Judah and the places R about Jerusalem, from the
21:14 devour all that is R about her."
25:9 against all these nations R about; I will utterly
46:14 the sword shall devour R about you.'
48:17 all you who are R about him, and all
48:39 to all that are R about him."
49:5 from all who are R about you, and you
50:14 in array against Babylon R about, all you that
50:15 a shout against her R about, she has surrendered;
50:29 Encamp R about her; let no one escape.
50:32 devour all that is R about him.
52:4 built siegeworks against it R about.
52:7 while the Chaldeans were R about the city.
52:14 down all the walls R about Jerusalem.
52:22 were upon the capital R about.
52:23 hundred upon the network R about.
Ezek 1:4 great cloud, with brightness R about it, and fire
1:18 were full of eyes R about.
1:27 appearance of fire enclosed R about; and downward
1:27 and there was brightness R about him.
1:28 appearance of the brightness R about.
4:2 plant battering-rams against it R about.
5:2 strike with the sword R about the city; and
5:5 the nations, with countries R about her.
5:6 more than the countries R about her, by rejecting
5:7 the nations that are R about you, and have
5:7 the nations that are R about you;
5:12 fall by the sword R about you; and a
5:14 reproach among the nations R about you and in
5:15 horror, to the nations R about you, when I
6:5 will scatter your bones R about your altars.
6:13 lie among their idols R about their altars, upon
8:10 portrayed upon the wall R about, were all kinds
10:12 were full of eyes R about--the wheels that
11:12 the nations that are R about you."
12:14 wind all who are R about him, his helpers
16:57 of the Philistines, those R about who despise you.
27:11 were upon your walls R about, and men of
27:11 shields upon your walls R about; they made perfect
31:4 making its rivers flow R the place of its
32:22 her company, their graves R about her, all of
32:23 and her company is R about her grave; all
32:25 her multitude, their graves R about her, all of
32:26 their multitude, their graves R about them, all of
34:26 them and the places R about my hill a
36:4 rest of the nations R about;
36:7 the nations that are R about you shall themselves
36:36 nations that are left R about you shall know
37:2 And he led me R among them; and behold,
40:14 vestibule, twenty cubits; and R about the vestibule of
40:16 gateway had windows R about, narrowing inwards
40:16 the vestibule had windows R about inside, and on
40:17 chambers and a pavement, R about the court; thirty
40:25 And there were windows R about in it and
40:29 and there were windows R about in it and
40:30 there were vestibules R about, twenty-five cubits
40:33 and there were windows R about in it and
40:36 and it had windows R about; its length was
40:43 handbreadth long, were fastened R about within.
41:5 side chambers, four cubits, R about the temple.
41:7 from story to story R about the temple; on
41:8 had a raised platform R about; the foundations of
41:10 breadth of twenty cubits R about the temple on
41:11 free was five cubits R about.
41:12 was five cubits thick R about, and its length
41:16 vestibule were paneled and R about all three had
41:16 was paneled with wood R about, from the floor
41:17 on all the walls R about in the inner
41:19 on the whole temple R about;
42:15 measured the temple area R about.
43:12 temple: the whole territory R about upon the top
43:17 its base one cubit R about.
43:20 and upon the rim R about; thus you shall
46:23 bottom of the rows R about.
47:2 gate, and led me R on the outside to
Dan 9:16 among all who are R about us.
Joel 3:11 come, all you nations R about, gather yourselves
3:12 judge all the nations R about.
Obad 1:16 mountain, all the nations R about shall drink; they
Jon 2:3 and the flood was R about me; all thy
2:5 me, the deep was R about me; weeds were
Zech 2:5 a wall of fire R about, says the LORD,
7:7 prosperity, with her cities R about her, and the
12:2 to all the peoples R about; it will be
12:6 left all the peoples R about, while Jerusalem shall
14:14 of all the nations R about shall be collected,
1Mac 1:11 covenant with the Gentiles R about us, for since
3:25 fell upon the Gentiles R about them.
4:7 and fortified, with cavalry R about it; and these
4:60 walls and strong towers R about, to keep the
5:1 When the Gentiles R about heard that the altar
5:46 they could not go R it to the right
5:65 and burned its towers R about.
7:17 blood they poured out R about Jerusalem, and there
7:46 the villages of Judea R about, and they out-flanked
10:45 Jerusalem and fortifying it R about, and the cost
12:13 encircled us; the kings R about us have waged
12:45 officials, and will turn R and go home.
12:53 And all the nations R about them tried to
Mt 14:35 recognized him, they sent R to all that region
18:6 a great millstone fastened R his neck and to
Mk 6:36 the country and villages R about and buy themselves
9:42 great millstone were hung R his neck and he
11:11 when he had looked R at everything, as it
Lk 8:42 went, the people pressed R him.
9:12 the villages and country R about, to lodge and
17:2 a millstone were hung R his neck and he
Jn 10:24 So the Jews gathered R him and said to
20:14 Saying this, she turned R and saw Jesus standing,
Acts 26:13 than the sun, shining R me and those who
Rom 15:19 Jerusalem and as far R as Illyricum I have
Rev 1:13 with a golden girdle R his breast;
4:3 jasper and carnelian, and R the throne was a
4:4 R the throne were twenty-four thrones, and seated
4:6 And R the throne, on each side of the
4:8 full of eyes all R and within, and day
7:11 all the angels stood R the throne and round
7:11 round the throne and R the elders and the

ROUNDED (4)

1Kgs 7:20 and also above the R projection which was beside
Song 5:14 His arms are R gold, set with jewels.
7:1 Your R thighs are like jewels, the work of
7:2 Your navel is a R bowl that never lacks

ROUSE (12)

Gen 49:9 a lioness; who dares R him up?
Num 24:9 a lioness; who will R him up?
Jud 14:3 into the camp and R the officers of the

Job 3:8 who are skilled to R up Leviathan.
8:6 surely then he will R himself for you and
Ps 44:23 R thyself!
59:4 R thyself, come to my help, and see!
Sir 36:7 R thy anger and pour out thy wrath; destroy
Is 51:17 R yourself, rouse yourself, stand up, O Jerusalem, you
51:17 Rouse yourself, R yourself, stand up, O Jerusalem,
Ezek 23:22 GOD: "Behold, I will R against you your lovers
24:8 To R my wrath, to take vengeance, I have

ROUSED (4)
Job 14:12 not awake, or be R out of his sleep.
Ps 76:7 stand before thee when once thy anger is R
Ezek 38:18 says the Lord GOD, my wrath will be R
Zech 2:13 LORD; for he has R himself from his holy

ROUSES (3)
Job 39:18 When she R herself to flee, she laughs at
Sir 22:7 potsherds together, or who R a sleeper from deep
Is 14:9 when you come, it R the shades to greet

ROUSING
Hab 1:6 For lo, I am R the Chaldeans, that bitter

ROUT (6)
1Sam 4:3 LORD put us to R today before the Philistines?
Ps 78:66 put his adversaries to R; he put them to
144:6 out thy arrows and R them!
1Mac 4:35 when Lysias saw the R of his troops and
5:61 people suffered a great R because, thinking to do
2Mac 12:27 After the R and destruction of these, he marched

ROUTE (2)
Judg 8:11 up by the caravan R east of Nobah and
1Mac 11:4 they had piled them in heaps along his R

ROUTED (12)
Gen 14:15 and his servants, and R them and pursued them
Ex 14:27 it, and the LORD R the Egyptians in the
Judg 4:15 And the LORD R Sisera and all his chariots
20:32 Benjaminites said, "They are R before us, as at
1Sam 7:10 confusion; and they were R before Israel.
2Sam 22:15 scattered them; lightning, and R them.
2Chr 20:22 had come against Judah, so that they were R
Ps 18:14 flashed forth lightnings, and R them.
1Mac 5:60 Joseph and Azariah were R, and were pursued to
6:5 of Judah had been R;
11:55 fought against Demetrius, and he fled and was R
11:72 against the enemy and R them, and they fled.

ROVING
Wis 4:12 what is good, and R desire perverts the innocent

ROW (15)
Ex 28:17 A R of sardius, topaz, and carbuncle shall be
28:17 shall be the first R;
28:18 row; and the second R an emerald, a sapphire,
28:19 diamond; and the third R a jacinth, an agate,
28:20 amethyst; and the fourth R a beryl, an onyx,
39:10 A R of sardius, topaz, and carbuncle was the
39:10 carbuncle was the first R;
39:11 row; and the second R, an emerald, a sapphire,
39:12 diamond; and the third R, a jacinth, an agate,
39:13 amethyst; and the fourth R, a beryl, an onyx,
Lev 24:6 rows, six in a R, upon the table of
24:7 pure frankincense with each R, that it may go
1Kgs 7:3 were upon the forty-five pillars, fifteen in each R
Ezek 46:19 gate, to the north R of the holy chambers
46:23 four courts was a R of masonry, with hearths

ROWED (2)
Jon 1:13 Nevertheless the men R hard to bring the ship
Jn 6:19 When they had R about three or four miles,

ROWERS (2)
Ezek 27:8 and Arvad were your R; skilled men of Zemer
27:26 Your R have brought you out into the high

ROWS (16)
Ex 28:17 set in it four R of stones.
39:10 set in it four R of stones.
Lev 24:6 set them in two R, six in a row,
1Kgs 7:2 was built upon three R of cedar pillars, with
7:4 window frames in three R, and window opposite
7:18 made pomegranates; in two R round about upon the
7:20 hundred pomegranates, in two R round about; and so
7:24 gourds were in two R, cast with it when
7:42 the two networks, two R of pomegranates for each
2Chr 4:3 gourds were in two R, cast with it when
4:13 the two networks, two R of pomegranates for each
Job 24:11 sheaves; among the olive R of the wicked they
41:15 back is made of R of shields, shut up
Wis 18:24 engraved on the four R of stones, and thy
Is 28:25 put in wheat in R and barley in its
Ezek 46:23 the bottom of the R round about.

ROYAL (74)
Gen 49:20 and he shall yield R dainties.
Josh 10:2 like one of the R cities, and because it
1Sam 27:5 servant dwell in the R city with you?"
2Sam 12:26 Ammonites, and took the R city.
1Kgs 1:9 sons, and all the R officials of Judah,
1:46 Solomon sits upon the R throne.
9:5 I will establish your R throne over Israel for
11:14 he was of the R house in Edom.
2Kgs 10:13 down to visit the R princes and the sons
11:1 and destroyed all the R family.
14:5 as soon as the R power was firmly in
15:19 his hold of the R power.
25:25 of Elishama, of the R family, came with ten
1Chr 22:10 I will establish his R throne in Israel for
29:25 bestowed upon him such R majesty as had not
2Chr 2:1 the LORD, and a R palace for himself.
2:12 the LORD, and a R palace for himself.
7:18 I will establish your R throne, as I covenanted
22:10 and destroyed all the R family of house of
23:20 the king upon the R throne.
25:3 as soon as the R power was firmly in
25:16 we made you a R counselor?
Ezra 4:13 or toll, and the R revenue will be impaired.
5:17 be made in the R archives there in Babylon,
6:4 be paid from the R treasury.
6:8 without delay from the R revenue, the tribute of
Jud 2:18 and silver from the R palace.
Esth 1:2 Ahasuerus sat on his R throne in Susa the
1:4 the riches of his R glory and the splendor
1:7 different kinds, and the R wine was lavished
1:11 the king with her R crown, in order to
1:19 the king, let a R order go forth from
1:19 the king give her R position to another who
1:22 letters to all the R provinces, to every province
2:16 King Ahasuerus into his R palace in the tenth
2:17 that he set the R crown on her head
2:18 and gave gifts with R liberality.
5:1 Esther put on her R robes and stood in
5:1 was sitting on his R throne inside the palace
6:8 delights to honor, let R robes be brought, which
6:8 on whose head a R crown is set;
8:10 service, bred from the R stud.
8:15 of the king in R robes of blue and
9:3 the governors and the R officials also helped the
15:6 was seated on his R throne, clothed in the
16:11 person second to the R throne.
Ps 45:6 Your R scepter is a scepter of equity;
72:1 thy righteousness to the R son!
Wis 14:21 to misfortune or to R authority, bestowed on objects
18:15 from heaven, from the R throne, into the midst
Is 62:3 the LORD, and a R diadem in the hand
Jer 41:1 of Elishama, of the R family, one of the
43:10 he will spread his R canopy over them.
Bar 5:6 glory, as on a R throne.
Ezek 17:13 one of the seed R and made a covenant
Dan 1:3 Israel, both of the R family and of the
4:29 the roof of the R palace of Babylon,
4:30 mighty power as a R residence and for the
6:26 that in all my R dominion men tremble and
11:21 contemptible person to whom R majesty has not
Zech 6:13 LORD, and shall bear R honor, and shall sit
1Mac 3:32 a distinguished man of R lineage, in charge of
6:43 beasts was equipped with R armor.
6:47 the Jews saw the R might and the fierce
7:2 he was entering the R palace of his fathers,
11:34 granted release from the R taxes which the king
13:15 your brother owed the R treasury, in connection with
15:8 you owe to the R treasury and any such
2Mac 4:11 set aside the existing R concessions to the Jews,
Acts 12:21 Herod put on his R robes, took his seat
Jas 2:8 you really fulfil the R law, according to the
1Pet 2:9 a chosen race, a R priesthood, a holy nation,
Rev 17:12 have not yet received R power, but they are
17:17 and giving over their R power to the beast,

R

RUB

Tob 11:8 they smart he will R them, and will cause

RUBBED (3)

Tob 11:12 began to smart he R them,
Ezek 16:4 to cleanse you, nor R with salt, nor swathed
29:18 and every shoulder was R bare; yet neither he

RUBBING

Lk 6:1 some heads of grain, R them in their hands.

RUBBISH (3)

Neh 4:2 of the heaps of R, and burned ones at
4:10 and there is much R; we are not able
Tob 5:18 but consider it as R as compared to our

RUBY (2)

Tob 13:17 paved with beryl and R and stones of Ophir;
Sir 32:5 A R seal in a setting of gold is

RUDDER

Jas 3:4 by a very small R wherever the will of

RUDDERS

Acts 27:40 ropes that tied the R; then hoisting the foresail

RUDDY (4)

1Sam 16:12 Now he was R, and had beautiful eyes, and
17:42 was but a youth, R and comely in appearance.
Song 5:10 is all radiant and R, distinguished among ten
Lam 4:7 their bodies were more R than coral, the beauty

RUDE

1Cor 13:5 jealous or boastful; it is not arrogant or R

RUDELY

2Mac 14:30 was meeting him more R than had been his

RUE

Lk 11:42 you tithe mint and R and every herb, and

RUFUS (2)

Mk 15:21 father of Alexander and R, to carry his cross.
Rom 16:13 Greet R, eminent in the Lord, also his mother

RUG

Judg 4:18 the tent, and she covered him with a R

RUGGED

Song 2:17 a young stag upon R mountains.

RUGS

Is 21:5 table, they spread the R, they eat, they drink.

RUIN (62)

Deut 28:63 take delight in bringing R upon you and destroying
2Sam 16:8 See, your R is on you; for you are
2Kgs 3:19 springs of water, and R every good piece of
2Chr 28:23 But they were the R of him, and of
34:11 the kings of Judah had let go to R
Tob 4:13 in pride there is R and great confusion; and
Jud 13:20 but have avenged our R, walking in the straight
Job 31:29 have rejoiced at the R of him that hated
Ps 35:8 Let R come upon them unawares!
35:8 hid ensnare them; let them fall therein to R
38:12 my hurt speak of R, and meditate treachery all
55:11 trouble are within it, R is in its midst;
64:8 will bring them to R; all who see them
73:18 slippery places; thou dost make them fall to R
146:9 the way of the wicked he brings to R
Prov 3:25 panic, or of the R of the wicked, when
5:14 the point of utter R in the assembled congregation."
10:8 commandments, but a prating fool will come to R
10:14 of a fool brings R near.
10:15 city; the poverty of the poor is their R
12:12 the wicked comes to R, but the root of
13:3 he who opens wide his lips comes to R
13:15 but the way of the faithless is their R
18:7 fool's mouth is his R, and his lips are
19:3 brings his way to R, his heart rages against
19:13 A foolish son is R to his father, and
21:12 the wicked; the wicked are cast down to R
24:22 and who knows the R that will come from
26:28 hates its victims, and a flattering mouth works R
Sir 1:19 a man's anger tips the scale to his R
4:19 forsake him, and hand him over to his R
10:3 An undisciplined king will R his people, but a
20:24 habitual liar, but the lot of both is R
31:6 Many have come to R because of gold, and
50:4 save his people from R, and fortified the city
Is 23:13 they razed her palaces, they made her a R
25:2 the fortified city a R; the palace of aliens
32:7 devises wicked devices to R the poor with lying
47:11 able to expiate; and R shall come on you
Jer 25:11 land shall become a R and a waste, and
46:19 become a waste, a R, without inhabitant.
Lam 2:13 the sea is your R; who can restore you?
Bar 4:33 was glad for your R, so she will be
Ezek 18:30 from all your transgressions, lest iniquity be your R
21:27 A R, ruin, ruin I will make it; there
21:27 A ruin, R, ruin I will make it; there
21:27 A ruin, ruin, R I will make it; there
27:27 of the seas on the day of your R
31:13 Upon its R will dwell all the birds of
Hos 4:14 and a people without understanding shall come to R
Amos 6:6 not grieved over the R of Joseph!
Obad 1:12 the day of their R; you should not have
Nah 2:10 Desolation and R
Zeph 1:15 anguish, a day of R and devastation, a day
1Mac 2:7 to see this, the R of my people, the
2:7 of my people, the R of the holy city,
2:49 is a time of R and furious anger.
7:7 and see all the R which Judas has brought
Lk 6:49 it fell, and the R of that house was
Rom 3:16 in their paths are R and misery,
14:15 you eat cause the R of one for whom
1Tim 6:9 that plunge men into R and destruction.

RUINED (22)

Ex 8:24 Egypt the land was R by reason of the
9:31 and the barley were R, for the barley was
9:32 the spelt were not R, for they are late
10:7 do you not yet understand that Egypt is R
Prov 14:28 a king, but without people a prince is R
Sir 8:2 yours; for gold has R many, and has perverted
29:18 Being surety has R many men who were prosperous,
49:13 bars and rebuilt our R houses.
Is 61:4 they shall repair the R cities, the devastations of
Jer 4:13 eagles– woe to us, for we are R
9:12 Why is the land R and laid waste like
9:19 wailing is heard from Zion: 'How we are R
Lam 2:9 the ground; he has R and broken her bars;
Ezek 6:6 and your high places R, so that your altars
6:6 will be waste and R, your idols broken and
36:35 waste and desolate and R cities are now inhabited
36:36 LORD, have rebuilt the R places, and replanted that
Joel 1:16 desolate; the granaries are R because the grain has
Amos 9:14 they shall rebuild the R cities and inhabit them;
Mic 2:4 say, "We are utterly R; he changes the portion
Nah 2:2 have stripped them and R their branches.)
Zech 11:2 cedar has fallen, for the glorious trees are R

RUINS (48)

Josh 8:28 ever a heap of R, as it is to
1Kgs 9:8 become a heap of R; everyone passing by it
2Kgs 19:25 cities into heaps of R,
2Chr 34:6 as Naphtali, in their R round about,
Ezra 9:9 God, to repair its R, and to give us
Neh 2:17 how Jerusalem lies in R with its gates burned.
Tob 14:4 and will be in R for a time.
Job 3:14 the earth who rebuilt R for themselves,
15:28 to become heaps of R;
30:24 in a heap of R stretch out his hand,
Ps 9:6 have vanished in everlasting R; their cities thou hast
74:3 steps to the perpetual R; the enemy has destroyed
79:1 thy holy temple; they have laid Jerusalem in R
89:40 his walls; thou hast laid his strongholds in R
109:10 driven out of the R they inhabit!
Prov 29:4 one who exacts gifts R it.
Is 3:6 and this heap of R shall be under your
5:17 pasture, fatlings and kids shall feed among the R
17:1 a city, and will become a heap of R
24:12 in the city, the gates are battered into R
37:26 crash into heaps of R,
44:26 will raise up their R;
58:12 And your ancient R shall be rebuilt; you shall
61:4 build up the ancient R, they shall raise up
64:11 fire, and all our pleasant places have become R
Jer 2:15 his cities are in R, without inhabitant.
4:7 your cities will be R without inhabitant.
4:26 cities were laid in R before the LORD, before
9:11 Jerusalem a heap of R, a lair of jackals;

26:18 become a heap of R, and the mountain of
51:37 become a heap of R, the haunt of jackals,
Lam 2:5 its palaces, laid in R its strongholds; and he
2:6 a garden, laid in R the place of his
2:8 determined to lay in R the wall of the
Ezek 13:4 been like foxes among R, O Israel.
26:20 nether world, among primeval R, with those who go
Dan 2:5 limb, and your houses shall be laid in R
3:97 their houses laid in R; for there is no
Amos 9:11 and raise up its R, and rebuild it as
Mic 3:12 become a heap of R, and the mountain of
Zeph 3:6 their battlements are in R; I have laid waste
Hag 1:4 your paneled houses, while this house lies in R
1:9 house that lies in R, while you busy yourselves
Mal 1:4 "We are shattered but we will rebuild the R
1Mac 4:38 saw also the chambers of the priests in R
Acts 15:16 I will rebuild its R, and I will set
1Cor 15:33 be deceived: "Bad company R good morals."
2Tim 2:14 no good, but only R the hearers.

RULE (90)

Gen 1:16 the greater light to R the day, and the
1:16 the lesser light to R the night; he made
1:18 upon the earth, to R over the day and
3:16 husband, and he shall R over you."
Ex 21:31 shall be dealt with according to this same R
Lev 25:43 You shall not R over him with harshness, but
25:46 Israel you shall not R, one over another, with
25:53 him; he shall not R with harshness over him
26:17 who hate you shall R over you, and you
Deut 15:6 borrow; and you shall R over many nations, but
15:6 but they shall not R over you.
Judg 8:22 Israel said to Gideon, R over us, you and
8:23 them, "I will not R over you, and my
8:23 my son will not R over you; the LORD
8:23 you; the LORD will R over you."
9:2 the sons of Jerubbaal R over you, or that
9:2 you, or that one R over you?' Remember also
1Sam 9:17 it is who shall R over my people."
2Kgs 8:20 Edom revolted from the R of Judah, and set
8:22 Edom revolted from the R of Judah to this
1Chr 29:30 accounts of all his R and his might and
2Chr 1:10 people, for who can R this thy people, that
1:11 yourself that you may R my people over whom
7:18 you a man to R Israel.'
12:1 When the R of Rehoboam was established and was
20:6 Dost thou not R over all the kingdoms of
21:8 Edom revolted from the R of Judah, and set
21:10 Edom revolted from the R of Judah to this
21:10 also revolted from his R, because he had forsaken
22:9 no one able to R the kingdom.
Job 38:33 Can you establish their R on the earth?
Ps 89:9 Thou dost R the raging of the sea; when
110:2 R in the midst of your foes!
136:8 ever; the sun to R over the day, for
136:9 moon and stars to R over the night, for
Prov 8:16 just; by me princes R, and nobles govern the
12:24 of the diligent will R, while the slothful will
17:2 who deals wisely will R over a son who
19:10 for a slave to R over princes.
29:2 but when the wicked R, the people groan.
Wis 3:8 will govern nations and R over peoples, and the
6:2 Give ear, you that R over multitudes, and boast
6:4 kingdom you did not R rightly, nor keep the
9:3 thou hast made, and R the world in holiness
10:2 gave him strength to R all things.
13:2 were the gods that R the world.
Sir 10:1 his people, and the R of an understanding man
Is 3:4 princes, and babes shall R over them.
3:6 shall be under your R;
3:12 their oppressors, and women R over them.
14:2 were their captors, and R over those who oppressed
19:4 a fierce king will R over them, says the
28:14 LORD, you scoffers, who R this people in Jerusalem!
32:1 righteousness, and princes will R in justice.
51:5 and my arms will R the peoples; the coastlands
Jer 5:31 falsely, and the priests R at their direction; my
33:26 of his descendants to R over the seed of
Lam 5:8 Slaves R over us; there is none to deliver
Bar 2:34 Jacob, and they will R over it; and I
3:16 nations, and those who R over the beasts on
Ezek 29:15 they will never again R over the nations.
Dan 2:38 the air, making you R over them all--you
2:39 of bronze, which shall R over all the earth.
8:23 latter end of their R, when the transgressors have
11:3 shall arise, who shall R with great dominion and
Obad 1:21 to Mount Zion to R Mount Esau; and the
Mic 5:6 of men; they shall R the land of Assyria
Zech 3:7 charge, then you shall R my house and have
6:13 and shall sit and R upon his throne.
1Mac 1:8 his officers began to R, each in his own
2:19 that live under the R of the king obey
8:16 man each year to R over them and to
10:52 fathers, and established my R -- for I
14:4 of his nation; his R was pleasing to them,
Mk 10:42 who are supposed to R over the Gentiles lord
Rom 15:12 he who rises to R the Gentiles; in him
1Cor 4:8 we might share the R with you!
7:4 the wife does not R over her own body,
7:4 the husband does not R over his own body,
7:17 This is my R in all the churches.
15:24 Father after destroying every R and every authority
Gal 6:16 who walk by this R, upon the Israel of
Eph 1:21 places, far above all R and authority and power
Col 2:10 the head of all R and authority.
3:15 the peace of Christ R in your hearts, to
1Tim 5:14 widows marry, bear children, R their households, and
5:17 Let the elders who R well be considered worthy
Rev 2:27 nations, and he shall R them with a rod
12:5 one who is to R all the nations with
19:15 nations, and he will R them with a rod

RULED (21)

Josh 12:2 dwelt at Heshbon, and R from Aroer, which is
12:5 and at Edre-i and R over Mount Hermon and
Judg 9:22 Abimelech R over Israel three years.
Ruth 1:1 days when the judges R there was a famine
1Kgs 4:21 Solomon R over all the kingdoms from the
1Chr 4:22 Joash, and Saraph, who R in Moab and returned
2Chr 9:26 And he R over all the kings from the
Ezra 4:20 been over Jerusalem, who R over the whole province
Jud 1:1 reign of Nebuchadnezzar, who R over the Assyrians
1:1 days of Arphaxad, who R over the Medes in
1:6 the plain where Arioch R the Elymaeans.
Ps 106:41 those who hated them R over them.
Sir 44:3 There were those who R in their kingdoms, and
Is 14:6 with unceasing blows, that R the nations in anger
26:13 lords besides thee have R over us, but thy
63:19 whom thou hast never R, like those who are
Ezek 34:4 and harshness you have R them.
Dan 9:12 against our rulers who R us, by bringing upon
11:4 dominion with which he R; for his kingdom shall
1Mac 1:4 very strong army and R over countries, nations, and
14:7 host of captives; he R over Gazara and Bethzur

RULER (84)

Gen 45:8 all his house and R over all the land
45:26 alive, and he is R over all the land
49:10 from Judah, nor the R's staff from between his
Ex 22:28 God, nor curse a R of your people.
Lev 4:22 "When a R sins, doing unwittingly any one of
Judg 9:30 When Zebul the R of the city heard the
1Kgs 1:35 appointed him to be R over Israel and over
11:34 I will make him R all the days of
1Chr 9:20 of Eleazar was the R over them in time
Neh 3:9 the son of Hur, R of half the district
3:12 the son of Hallohesh, R of half the district
3:14 the son of Rechab, R of the district of
3:15 the son of Colhozeh, R of the district of
3:16 the son of Azbuk, R of half the district
3:17 next to him Hashabiah, R of half the district
3:18 the son of Henadad, R of half the district
3:19 the son of Jeshua, R of Mizpah, repaired another
11:11 Meraioth, son of Ahitub, R of the house of
Jud 8:9 the people against the R, because they were faint
Esth 13:2 writes thus: "Having become R of many nations and
Ps 105:20 and released him, the R of the peoples set
105:21 of his house, and R of all his possessions,
Prov 6:7 any chief, officer or R,
23:1 to eat with a R, observe carefully what is
25:15 With patience a R may be persuaded, and a
28:15 bear is a wicked R over a poor people.
28:16 A R who lacks understanding is a cruel oppressor;
29:12 If a R listens to falsehood, all his officials
29:26 the favor of a R, but from the LORD
Eccl 9:17 the shouting of a R among fools.
10:4 the anger of the R rises against you, do
10:5 error proceeding from the R:
Wis 14:19 wishing to please his R, skilfully forced the likeness
Sir 4:27 a foolish fellow, nor show partiality to a R
10:2 officials; and like the R of the city, so
10:23 the judge, and the R will be honored, but

R

17:14 He appointed a R for every nation, but Israel
23:1 O Lord, Father and R of my life, do
41:17 a prince or a R;
48:12 not tremble before any R, and no one brought
Is 16:1 sent lambs to the R of the land, from
33:22 the LORD is our R, the LORD is our
Jer 30:21 one of themselves, their R shall come forth from
51:46 in the land, and R is against ruler.
51:46 is in the land, and ruler is against R
Bar 6:14 Like a local R the god holds a scepter,
Ezek 19:11 strongest stem became a R's scepter; it towered aloft
19:14 it no strong stem, no scepter for a R
Dan 2:48 gifts, and made him R over the whole province
5:7 shall be the third R in the kingdom."
5:16 shall be the third R in the kingdom.
5:29 should be the third R in the kingdom.
11:43 He shall become R of the treasures of gold
Amos 2:3 will cut off the R from its midst, and
Mic 5:1 upon the cheek the R of Israel.
5:2 who is to be R in Israel, whose origin
Hab 1:14 the sea, like crawling things that have no R
Zech 10:4 them the battle bow, out of them every R
1Mac 6:14 friends, and made him R over all his kingdom.
9:30 his place as our R and leader, to fight
10:38 to be under one R and obey no other
2Mac 5:8 Accused before Aretas the R of the Arabs, fleeing
Mt 2:6 you shall come a R who will govern my
9:18 to them, behold, a R came in and knelt
9:23 Jesus came to the R's house, and saw the
Mk 5:35 there came from the R's house some who said,
5:36 Jesus said to the R of the synagogue, "Do
5:38 the house of the R of the synagogue, he
Lk 8:41 Jairus, who was a R of the synagogue; and
8:49 a man from the R's house came and said,
13:14 But the R of the synagogue, indignant because Jesus
14:1 the house of a R who belonged to the
18:18 And a R asked him, "Good Teacher, what shall
Jn 3:1 Pharisees, named Nicodemus, a R of the Jews.
12:31 world, now shall the R of this world be
14:30 with you, for the R of this world is
16:11 concerning judgment, because the R of this world is
Acts 7:27 'Who made you a R and a judge over
7:35 'Who made you a R and a judge?' God
7:35 God sent as both R and deliverer by the
18:8 Crispus, the R of the synagogue, believed in the
18:17 all seized Sosthenes, the R of the synagogue, and
23:5 speak evil of a R of your people.'"
Rev 1:5 the dead, and the R of kings on earth.

RULERS (71)

Ex 18:21 over the people as R of thousands, of hundreds,
18:25 heads over the people, R of thousands, of hundreds,
Josh 13:3 Canaanite; there are five R of the Philistines, those
Judg 15:11 that the Philistines are R over us?
2Kgs 10:1 to Samaria, to the R of the city, to
1Chr 12:19 help them, for the R of the Philistines took
26:6 sons born who were R in their fathers' houses,
Jud 7:24 about Uzziah and the R of the city and
8:11 them, "Listen to me, R of the people of
8:35 Uzziah and the R said to her, "Go in
9:3 thou gavest up their R to be slain, and
Esth 13:1 King, Artaxerxes, to the R of the hundred and
16:1 King, Artaxerxes, to the R of the provinces from
Ps 2:2 set themselves, and the R take counsel together,
2:10 wise; be warned, O R of the earth.
94:20 Can wicked R be allied with thee, who frame
148:11 peoples, princes and all R of the earth!
Prov 8:15 me kings reign, and R decree what is just;
28:2 transgresses it has many R; but with men of
31:4 drink wine, or for R to desire strong drink;
Eccl 7:19 man more than ten R that are in a
Wis 1:1 Love righteousness, you R of the earth, think
5:23 earth, and evil-doing will overturn the thrones of R
8:11 in the sight of R I shall be admired.
Sir 10:3 city will grow through the understanding of its R
10:14 down the thrones of R, and has seated the
11:6 Many R have been greatly disgraced, and illustrious
36:10 the heads of the R of the enemy, who
39:4 men and appear before R; he will travel through
46:13 the kingdom and anointed R over his people.
46:18 Tyre and all the R of the Philistines.
48:15 in number, but with R from the house of
Is 1:10 of the LORD, you R of Sodom!
14:5 wicked, the scepter of R,
22:3 All your R have fled together, without the bow
40:23 nought, and makes the R of the earth as
41:25 he shall trample on R as on mortar, as
49:7 nations, the servant of R: "Kings shall see and
52:5 Their R wail, says the LORD, and continually all
Jer 2:8 not know me; the R transgressed against me; the
Lam 2:2 the ground in dishonor the kingdom and its R
Dan 9:12 us and against our R who ruled us, by
11:39 He shall make them R over many and shall
Hos 7:8 hot as an oven, and they devour their R
Mic 3:1 heads of Jacob and R of the house of
3:9 house of Jacob and R of the house of
Hab 1:10 they scoff, and of R they make sport.
1Mac 1:26 in every community, R and elders groaned, maidens
11:62 the sons of their R as hostages and sent
14:20 the Spartans sent: "The R and the city of
14:28 the people and the R of the nation and
Mt 2:6 means least among the R of Judah; for from
20:25 "You know that the R of the Gentiles lord
Mk 5:22 came one of the R of the synagogue, Jairus
Lk 12:11 the synagogues and the R and the authorities, do
23:13 chief priests and the R and the people,
23:34 by, watching; but the R scoffed at him, saying,
24:20 our chief priests and R delivered him up to
Acts 3:17 you acted in ignorance, as did also your R
4:5 On the morrow their R and elders and scribes
4:8 Spirit, said to them, R of the people and
4:26 in array, and the R were gathered together, against
13:15 and the prophets, the R of the synagogue sent
13:27 in Jerusalem and their R, because they did not
14:5 and Jews, with their R, to molest them and
16:19 market place before the R;
Rom 13:3 For R are not a terror to good conduct,
1Cor 2:6 age or of the R of this age, who
2:8 None of the R of this age understood this;
Eph 6:12 powers, against the world R of this present darkness,
Tit 3:1 to be submissive to R and authorities, to be

RULES (20)

2Sam 23:3 to me: When one R justly over men, ruling
2Chr 30:19 according to the sanctuary's R of cleanness."
Jud 5:3 Who R over them as king, leading their army?
Esth 16:18 For God, who R over all things, has speedily
16:21 For God, who R over all things, has made
Ps 22:28 the LORD, and he R over the nations.
59:13 may know that God R over Jacob to the
66:7 rejoice in him, who R by his might for
103:19 heavens, and his kingdom R over all.
Prov 16:32 mighty, and he who R his spirit than he
22:7 The rich R over the poor, and the borrower
Sir 37:18 the tongue that continually R them.
Is 40:10 might, and his arm R for him; behold, his
Dan 4:17 that the Most High R the kingdom of men,
4:25 that the Most High R the kingdom of men,
4:26 from the time that you know that Heaven R
4:32 that the Most High R the kingdom of men
5:21 the Most High God R the kingdom of men,
1Tim 5:21 you to keep these R without favor, doing nothing
2Tim 2:5 not crowned unless he competes according to the R

RULEST (3)

1Chr 29:12 from thee, and thou R over all.
Esth 13:9 Lord, Lord, King who R over all things, for
Wis 12:15 Thou art righteous and R all things righteously,

RULING (4)

2Sam 23:3 rules justly over men, R in the fear of
Wis 15:1 and true, patient, and R all things in mercy.
Jer 22:30 throne of David, and R again in Judah."
1Mac 14:17 and that he was R over the country and

RUMAH

2Kgs 23:36 name was Zebidah the daughter of Pedaiah of R

RUMBLE

Nah 3:2 crack of whip, and R of wheel, galloping horse

RUMBLING (3)

Job 37:2 his voice and the R that comes from his
Jer 47:3 his chariots, at the R of their wheels, the
Joel 2:5 As with the R of chariots, they leap on

RUMOR (8)

2Kgs 19:7 he shall hear a R and return to his
Job 28:22 'We have heard a R of it with our
Wis 5:9 shadow, and like a R that passes by;
Is 37:7 he shall hear a R, and return to his
Jer 10:22 Hark, a R

R

Ezek 7:26 Disaster comes upon disaster, R follows rumor; they
7:26 upon disaster, rumor follows R; they seek a vision
2Mac 5:5 When a false R arose that Antiochus was dead,

RUMORS (2)
Mt 24:6 hear of wars and R of wars; see that
Mk 13:7 hear of wars and R of wars, do not

RUN (61)
Gen 49:22 a spring; his branches R over the wall.
1Sam 8:11 his horsemen, and to R before his chariots;
20:6 leave of me to R to Bethlehem his city;
20:36 said to his lad, R and find the arrows
21:13 and let his spittle R down his beard.
2Sam 15:1 and fifty men to R before him.
18:19 of Zadok, "Let me R, and carry tidings to
18:22 may, let me also R after the Cushite." And
18:22 said, "Why will you R, my son, seeing that
18:23 he said, "I will R
18:23 So he said to him, R
1Kgs 1:5 and fifty men to R before him.
2Kgs 4:26 yonder is the Shunammite; R at once to meet
5:20 LORD lives, I will R after him, and get
2Chr 16:9 eyes of the LORD R to and fro throughout
Tob 11:3 Let us R ahead of your wife and prepare
Job 1:5 of the feast had R their course, Job would
Ps 59:4 fault of mine, they R and make ready.
119:32 I will R in the way of thy commandments
Prov 1:16 paths; for their feet R to evil, and they
4:13 hampered; and if you R, you will not stumble.
6:18 that make haste to R to evil,
Eccl 1:7 All streams R to the sea, but the sea
Wis 3:7 shine forth, and will R like sparks through the
Sir 27:17 his secrets, do not R after him.
35:15 tears of the widow R down her cheek as
Is 5:11 morning, that they may R after strong drink, who
29:1 year; let the feasts R their round.
40:31 like eagles, they shall R and not be weary,
55:5 knew you not shall R to you, because of
59:7 Their feet R to evil, and they make haste
Jer 5:1 R to and fro through the streets of Jerusalem,
9:18 that our eyes may R down with tears, and
13:17 will weep bitterly and R down with tears, because
14:17 word: 'Let my eyes R down with tears night
18:14 Do the mountain waters R dry, the cold flowing
49:3 with sackcloth, lament, and R to and fro among
49:19 will suddenly make them R away from her; and
50:44 will suddenly make them R away from her; and
Ezek 24:16 nor shall your tears R down.
32:14 cause their rivers to R like oil, says the
47:17 So the boundary shall R from the sea to
47:18 side, the boundary shall R from Hazar-enon between
47:19 south side, it shall R from Tamar as far
48:28 south, the boundary shall R from Tamar to the
Dan 12:4 Many shall R to and fro, and knowledge shall
Joel 2:4 appearance of horses, and like war horses they R
2:9 upon the city, they R upon the walls; they
Amos 6:12 Do horses R upon rocks?
8:12 to east; they shall R to and fro, to
Nah 2:8 a pool whose waters R away.
Hab 2:2 tablets, so he may R who reads it.
Zech 2:4 and said to him, R, say to that young
Acts 27:17 fearing that they should R on the Syrtis, they
27:26 we shall have to R on some island."
27:29 fearing that we might R on the rocks, they
1Cor 9:24 So R that you may obtain it.
9:26 Well, I do not R aimlessly, I do not
Gal 2:2 be running or had R in vain.
Phil 2:16 that I did not R in vain or labor
Heb 12:1 closely, and let us R with perseverance the race

RUNAWAY
2Mac 8:35 way alone like a R slave across the country

RUNNELS (2)
Gen 30:38 the flocks in the R, that is, the watering
30:41 the rods in the R before the eyes of

RUNNER (2)
Job 9:25 are swifter than a R; they flee away, they
Jer 51:31 One R runs to meet another, and one messenger

RUNNERS
1Cor 9:24 a race all the R compete, but only one

RUNNING (28)
Lev 14:5 an earthen vessel over R water.
14:6 was killed over the R water;
14:50 an earthen vessel over R water,
14:51 killed and in the R water, and sprinkle the
14:52 bird, and with the R water, and with the
15:13 bathe his body in R water, and shall be
Num 19:17 burnt sin offering, and R water shall be added
Deut 21:4 to a valley with R water, which is neither
2Sam 18:24 he saw a man R alone.
18:26 watchman saw another man R; and the watchman
18:26 said, "See, another man R alone!" The king said,
18:27 said, "I think the R of the foremost is
18:27 foremost is like the R of Ahima-az the son
1Kgs 6:5 wall of the house, R round the walls of
2Kgs 5:21 Naaman saw some one R after him, he alighted
2Chr 23:12 noise of the people R and praising the king,
Job 15:26 defiance to the Almighty, R stubbornly against him
Ps 133:2 oil upon the head, R down upon the beard,
133:2 the beard of Aaron, R down on the collar
Wis 17:19 down, or the unseen R of leaping animals, or
Is 30:25 there will be brooks R with water, in the
2Mac 12:16 wide, appeared to be R over with blood.
13:5 it has a rim R around it which on
Mk 9:25 that a crowd came R together, he rebuked the
Lk 6:38 pressed down, shaken together, R over, will be put
Acts 27:16 And R under the lee of a small island
Gal 2:2 somehow I should be R or had run in
5:7 You were R well; who hindered you from obeying

RUNS (13)
Lev 15:3 discharge: whether his body R with his discharge, or
Josh 15:5 on the north side R from the bay of
Ezra 8:15 to the river that R to Ahava, and there
Jud 12:3 her, "If your supply R out, where can we
Job 16:14 breach upon breach; he R upon me like a
38:38 heavens, when the dust R into a mass and
Ps 19:5 like a strong man R its course with joy.
58:7 vanish like water that R away; like grass let
147:15 the earth; his word R swiftly.
Prov 18:10 tower; the righteous man R into it and is
Sir 33:31 and he leaves and R away, which way will
Is 1:23 loves a bribe and R after gifts.
Jer 51:31 One runner R to meet another, and one messenger

RURAL
Neh 10:37 tithes in all our R towns.

RUSH (8)
Judg 9:33 up, rise early and R upon the city; and
Jud 14:3 army; and they will R into the tent of
15:4 to urge all to R out upon their enemies
Ps 32:6 of distress, in the R of great waters, they
Is 58:5 his head like a R, and to spread sackcloth
Dan 11:40 of the north shall R upon him like a
Nah 2:4 in the streets, they R to and fro through
Acts 2:2 from heaven like the R of a mighty wind,

RUSHED (28)
Judg 5:15 into the valley they R forth at his heels.
9:44 that was with him R forward and stood at
9:44 while the two companies R upon all who were
20:33 who were in ambush R out of their place
20:37 ambush made haste and R upon Gibe-ah; the men
1Sam 18:10 evil spirit from God R upon Saul, and he
2Sam 19:17 and his twenty servants, R down to the Jordan
Jud 14:17 not find her he R out to the people
15:2 with one impulse all R out and fled by
15:3 that was a soldier, R out upon them.
Dan 13:26 in the garden, they R in at the side
1Mac 3:23 he finished speaking, he R suddenly against Seron
9:40 Then they R upon them from the ambush and
16:16 took their weapons, and R in against Simon in
2Mac 3:25 frightening mien, and it R furiously at Heliodorus
5:26 to see them, then R into the city with
9:2 Therefore the people R to the rescue with arms,
10:16 fight on their side, R to the strongholds of
11:7 Then they eagerly R off together.
12:15 the days of Joshua, R furiously upon the walls.
12:22 all things; and they R off in flight and
Mt 8:32 behold, the whole herd R down the steep bank
Mk 5:13 numbering about two thousand, R down the steep
Lk 8:33 swine, and the herd R down the steep bank
Acts 7:57 stopped their ears and R together upon him.
14:14 tore their garments and R out among the multitude,
16:29 called for lights and R in, and trembling with

19:29 the confusion; and they R together into the theater,

RUSHES (6)

Job 40:23 is confident though Jordan R against his mouth.
41:20 smoke, as from a boiling pot and burning R
Prov 7:23 entrails; as a bird R into a snare; he
Sir 21:22 foot of a fool R into a house, but
Is 19:6 dry up, reeds and R will rot away.
35:7 a swamp, the grass shall become reeds and R

RUSHING (9)

1Kgs 18:41 a sound of the R of rain."
Wis 5:11 the force of its R flight, is traversed by
17:18 the rhythm of violently R water,
Is 59:19 will come like a R stream, which the wind
Jer 47:3 his stallions, at the R of his chariots, at
Dan 14:36 the den, with the R sound of the wind
2Mac 9:7 chariot as it was R along, and the fall
14:43 the crowd was now R in through the doors.
Rev 9:9 many chariots with horses R into battle.

RUST (11)

Sir 29:10 do not let it R under a stone and
Bar 6:12 cannot save themselves from R and corrosion.
6:24 one wipes off the R; for even when they
Ezek 24:6 to the pot whose R is in it, and
24:6 in it, and whose R has not gone out
24:11 melted in it, its R consumed.
24:12 wearied myself; its thick R does not go out
24:13 Its R is your filthy lewdness.
Mt 6:19 where moth and R consume and where thieves
6:20 where neither moth nor R consumes and where
Jas 5:3 have rusted, and their R will be evidence against

RUSTED

Jas 5:3 gold and silver have R, and their rust will

RUSTING

Sir 12:10 enemy, for like the R of copper, so is

RUTH (13)

Ruth 1:4 was Orpah and the name of the other R
1:14 kissed her mother-in-law, but R clung to her.
1:16 But R said, "Entreat me not to leave you
1:22 So Naomi returned, and R the Moabitess her
2:2 And R the Moabitess said to Naomi, "Let me
2:8 Then Boaz said to R, "Now, listen, my daughter,
2:21 And R the Moabitess said, "Besides, he said to
2:22 And Naomi said to R, her daughter-in-law, "It is
3:9 she answered, "I am R, your maidservant; spread
4:5 you are also buying R the Moabitess, the widow
4:10 Also R the Moabitess, the widow of Mahlon, I
4:13 So Boaz took R and she became his wife;
Mt 1:5 father of Obed by R, and Obed the father

RUTHLESS (11)

Job 15:20 the years that are laid up for the R
Ps 54:3 have risen against me, R men seek my life;
86:14 me; a band of R men seek my life,
Is 13:11 arrogant, and lay low the haughtiness of the R
25:3 glorify thee; cities of R nations will fear thee.
25:4 the blast of the R is like a storm
25:5 the song of the R is stilled.
29:5 the multitude of the R like passing chaff.
29:20 For the R shall come to nought and the
Jer 15:21 and redeem you from the grasp of the R
Rom 1:31 disobedient to parents, foolish, faithless, heartless, R

RUTHLESSLY

Is 30:14 which is smashed so R that among its fragments

S

SABACH-THANI (2)

Mt 27:46 cried with a loud voice, "Eli, Eli, lama S
Mk 15:33 cried with a loud voice, "Elo-i, Elo-i, lama S

SABBATH (152)

Ex 16:23 solemn rest, a holy S to the LORD; bake
16:25 for today is a S to the LORD; today
16:26 day, which is a S, there will be none."
16:29 has given you the S, therefore on the sixth
20:8 "Remember the S day, to keep it holy.
20:10 seventh day is a S to the LORD your
20:11 the LORD blessed the S day and hallowed it.
31:14 You shall keep the S, because it is holy
31:15 seventh day is a S of solemn rest, holy
31:15 any work on the S day shall be put
31:16 the S, observing the S throughout their generations,
35:2 shall have a holy S of solemn rest to
35:3 your habitations on the S day."
Lev 16:31 It is a S of solemn rest to you,
23:3 seventh day is a S of solemn rest, a
23:3 work; it is a S to the LORD in
23:11 the morrow after the S the priest shall wave
23:15 the morrow after the S, from the day that
23:16 morrow after the seventh S; then you shall present
23:32 be to you a S of solemn rest, and
23:32 from evening to evening shall you keep your S
24:8 Every S day Aaron shall set it in order
25:2 land shall keep a S to the LORD.
25:4 there shall be a S of solemn rest for
25:4 for the land, a S to the LORD; you
25:6 The S of the land shall provide food for
Num 15:32 gathering sticks on the S day.
28:9 "On the S day two male lambs a year
28:10 burnt offering of every S, besides the continual burnt
Deut 5:12 "'Observe the S day, to keep it holy, as
5:14 seventh day is a S to the LORD your
5:15 you to keep the S day.
2Kgs 4:23 It is neither new moon nor S
11:5 off duty on the S and guard the king's
11:7 in force on the S and guard the house
11:9 off duty on the S, with those who were
11:9 on duty on the S, and came to Jehoiada
16:18 covered way for the S which had been built
1Chr 9:32 charge of the showbread, to prepare it every S
2Chr 23:4 off duty on the S, one third shall be
23:8 off duty on the S, with those who were
23:8 on duty on the S; for Jehoiada the priest
36:21 lay desolate it kept S, to fulfil seventy years.
Neh 9:14 them thy holy S and command them
10:31 any grain on the S day to sell, we
10:31 from them on the S or on a holy
13:15 wine presses on the S, and bringing in heaps
13:15 into Jerusalem on the S day; and I warned
13:16 sold them on the S to the people of
13:17 are doing, profaning the S day?
13:18 bring more wrath upon Israel by profaning the S
13:19 of Jerusalem before the S, I commanded that the
13:19 they should not be opened until after the S
13:19 brought in on the S day.
13:21 time on they did not come on the S
13:22 gates, to keep the S day holy.
Jud 8:6 the day before the S and the sabbath itself,
8:6 the sabbath and the S itself, the day before
Is 1:13 New moon and S and the calling of assemblies—
56:2 fast, who keeps the S, not profaning it, and
56:6 one who keeps the S, and does not profane
58:13 your foot from the S, from doing your pleasure
58:13 day, and call the S a delight and the
66:23 new moon, and from S to sabbath, all flesh
66:23 and from sabbath to S, all flesh shall come
Jer 17:21 a burden on the S day or bring it
17:22 your houses on the S or do any work,
17:22 work, but keep the S day holy, as I
17:24 this city on the S day, but keep the
17:24 day, but keep the S day holy and do
17:27 me, to keep the S day holy, and not
17:27 of Jerusalem on the S day, then I will
Lam 2:6 Zion appointed feast and S, and in his fierce
Ezek 46:1 days; but on the S day it shall be
46:4 the LORD on the S day shall be six
46:12 he does on the S day.
Amos 8:5 And the S, that we may offer wheat for
1Mac 1:43 religion; they sacrificed to idols and profaned the S
2:32 against them on the S day.
2:34 and so profane the S day."
2:38 attacked them on the S, and they died, with
2:41 attack us on the S day; let us not
9:34 this out on the S day, and he with
9:43 large force on the S day to the banks
2Mac 5:25 waited until the holy S day; then, finding the
6:6 could neither keep the S, nor observe the feasts
8:26 the day before the S, and for that reason
8:27 spoils, they kept the S, giving great praise and
8:28 After the S they gave some of the spoils
12:38 and they kept the S there.
15:3 the keeping of the S day.
Mt 12:1 the grainfields on the S; his disciples were hungry,

12:2 what is not lawful to do on the S
12:5 law how on the S the priests in the
12:5 the temple profane the S, and are guiltless?
12:8 the Son of man is lord of the S
12:10 him, "Is it lawful to heal on the S
12:11 a pit on the S, will not lay hold
12:12 it is lawful to do good on the S
24:20 may not be in winter or on a S
28:1 Now after the S, toward the dawn of the
Mk 1:21 and immediately on the S he entered the synagogue
2:23 One S he was going through the grainfields; and
2:24 they doing what is not lawful on the S
2:27 said to them, "The S was made for man,
2:27 not man for the S;
2:28 Son of man is lord even of the S
3:2 heal him on the S, so that they might
3:4 it lawful on the S to do good or
6:2 And on the S he began to teach in
15:41 the day before the S,
16:1 And when the S was past, Mary Magdalene, and
Lk 4:16 custom was, on the S day.
4:31 teaching them on the S;
6:1 On a S, while he was going through the
6:2 what is not lawful to do on the S
6:5 "The Son of man is lord of the S
6:6 On another S, when he entered the synagogue and
6:7 would heal on the S, so that they might
6:9 it lawful on the S to do good or
13:10 teaching in one of the synagogues on the S
13:14 had healed on the S, said to the people,
13:14 and not on the S day."
13:15 of you on the S untie his ox or
13:16 this bond on the S day?"
14:1 One S when he went to dine at the
14:3 to heal on the S, or not?"
14:5 him out on a S day?"
23:53 of Preparation, and the S was beginning.
23:55 On the S they rested according to the commandment.
Jn 5:8 Now that day was the S
5:9 cured, "It is the S, it is not lawful
5:15 persecuted Jesus, because he did this on the S
5:17 not only broke the S but also called God
7:22 fathers), and you circumcise a man upon the S
7:23 If on the S a man receives circumcision, so
7:23 me because on the S I made a man's
9:14 Now it was a S day when Jesus made
9:16 from God, for he does not keep the S
19:31 the cross on the S (for that sabbath was
19:31 the sabbath (for that S was a high day),
Acts 1:12 is near Jerusalem, a S day's journey away;
13:14 And on the S day they went into the
13:27 are read every S, fulfilled these by condemning
13:42 these things might be told them the next S
13:44 The next S almost the whole city gathered together
15:21 he is read every S in the synagogues."
16:13 days; and on the S day we went outside
18:4 in the synagogue every S, and persuaded Jews and
Col 2:16 a festival or a new moon or a S
Heb 4:9 then, there remains a S rest for the people

SABBATHS (33)

Ex 31:13 'You shall keep my S, for this is a
Lev 19:3 you shall keep my S: I am the LORD
19:30 You shall keep my S and reverence my sanctuary:
23:38 proper day; besides the S of the LORD, and
26:2 You shall keep my S and reverence my sanctuary:
26:34 land shall enjoy its S as long as it
26:34 then the land shall rest, and enjoy its S
26:35 had not in your S when you dwelt upon
26:43 them, and enjoy its S while it lies desolate
1Chr 23:31 to the LORD on S, new moons, and feast
2Chr 2:4 and evening, on the S and the new moons
8:13 of Moses for the S, the new moons, and
31:3 burnt offerings for the S, the new moons, and
36:21 of Jeremiah, until the land had enjoyed its S
Neh 10:33 continual burnt offering, the S, the new moons, the
Jud 10:2 where she lived on S and on her feast
Is 56:4 eunuchs who keep my S, who choose the things
Ezek 20:12 I gave them my S, as a sign between
20:13 shall live; and my S they greatly profaned.
20:16 statutes, and profaned my S; for their heart went
20:20 ordinances, and hallow my S that they may be
20:21 observance man shall live; they profaned my S
20:24 statutes and profaned my S, and their eyes were
22:8 have despised my holy things, and profaned my S
22:26 they have disregarded my S, so that I am
23:38 sanctuary on the same day and profaned my S
44:24 they shall keep my S holy.
45:17 new moons, and the S, all the appointed feasts
46:3 the LORD on the S and on the new
Hos 2:11 her new moons, her S, and all her appointed
1Mac 1:39 turned into mourning, her S into a reproach, her
1:45 the sanctuary, to profane S and feasts,
10:34 all the feasts and S and new moons and

SABBATICAL

1Mac 6:49 since it was a S year for the land.

SABEANS (3)

Job 1:15 beside them; and the S fell upon them and
Is 45:14 of Ethiopia, and the S, men of stature, shall
Joel 3:8 sell them to the S, to a nation far-off;

SABTA

1Chr 1:9 of Cush: Seba, Havilah, S, Raama, and Sabteca.

SABTAH

Gen 10:7 of Cush: Seba, Havilah, S, Raamah, and Sabteca.

SABTECA (2)

Gen 10:7 sons of Cush: Seba, Havilah, Sabtah, Raamah, and S
1Chr 1:9 sons of Cush: Seba, Havilah, Sabta, Raama, and S

SACHAR (2)

1Chr 11:35 Ahiam the son of S the Hararite, Eliphal the
26:4 second, Joah the third, S the fourth, Nethanel the

SACHIA

1Chr 8:10 Zibi-a, Mesha, Malcam, Jeuz, S, and Mirmah.

SACK (13)

Gen 42:25 man's money in his S, and to give them
42:27 of them opened his S to give his ass
42:27 the mouth of his S;
42:28 here it is in the mouth of my S
42:35 money was in his S; and when they and
43:21 the mouth of his S, our money in full
44:1 the mouth of his S,
44:2 the mouth of the S of the youngest, with
44:11 man quickly lowered his S to the ground, and
44:11 to the ground, and every man opened his S
44:12 youngest; and the cup was found in Benjamin's S
Lev 11:32 a skin or a S, any vessel that is
2Kgs 4:42 barley, and fresh ears of grain in his S

SACKCLOTH (60)

Gen 37:34 his garments, and put S upon his loins, and
2Sam 3:31 clothes, and gird on S, and mourn before Abner."
21:10 daughter of Aiah took S, and spread it for
1Kgs 20:31 kings; let us put S on our loins and
20:32 So they girded S on their loins, and put
21:27 his clothes, and put S upon his flesh, and
21:27 fasted and lay in S, and went about dejectedly.
2Kgs 6:30 and behold, he had S beneath upon his body--
19:1 and covered himself with S, and went into the
19:2 senior priests, covered with S, to the prophet Isaiah
1Chr 21:16 the elders, clothed in S, fell upon their faces.
Neh 9:1 with fasting and in S, and with earth upon
Jud 4:10 purchased slave--they all girded themselves with S
4:11 and spread out their S before the Lord.
4:12 surrounded the altar with S and cried out in
4:14 their loins girded with S, offered the continual burnt
8:5 her house, and girded S about her loins and
9:1 head, and uncovered the S she was wearing; and
10:3 and she removed the S which she had been
Esth 4:1 clothes and put on S and ashes, and went
4:2 one might enter the king's gate clothed with S
4:3 of them lay in S and ashes.
4:4 might take off his S, but he would not
Job 16:15 I have sewed S upon my skin, and have
Ps 30:11 thou hast loosed my S and girded me with
35:13 sick-- I wore S, I afflicted myself with
69:11 When I made S my clothing, I became a
Is 3:24 robe, a girding of S; instead of beauty, shame.
15:3 streets they gird on S; on the housetops and
20:2 "Go, and loose the S from your loins and
22:12 baldness and girding with S;
32:11 yourselves bare, and gird S upon your loins.
37:1 and covered himself with S, and went into the
37:2 senior priests, clothed with S, to the prophet Isaiah
50:3 with blackness, and make S their covering."
58:5 rush, and to spread S and ashes under him?

S

Jer 4:8 this gird you with S, lament and wail; for
6:26 my people, gird on S, and roll in ashes;
48:37 hands are gashes, and on the loins is S
49:3 Gird yourselves with S, lament, and run to and
Lam 2:10 heads and put on S; the maidens of Jerusalem
Bar 4:20 and put on the S of my supplication; I
Ezek 7:18 They gird themselves with S, and horror covers
27:31 and gird themselves with S, and they weep over
Dan 9:3 supplications with fasting and S and ashes.
Joel 1:8 a virgin girded with S for the bridegroom of
1:12 Gird on S and lament, O priests, wail, O
1:12 pass the night in S, O ministers of my
Amos 8:10 lamentation; I will bring S upon all loins, and
Jon 3:5 fast, and put on S, from the greatest of
3:6 and covered himself with S, and sat in ashes.
3:8 beast be covered with S, and let them cry
1Mac 2:14 their clothes, put on S, and mourned greatly.
3:47 that day, put on S and sprinkled ashes on
2Mac 3:19 Women, girded with S under their breasts, thronged
10:25 girded their loins with S, in supplication to God.
Mt 11:21 repented long ago in S and ashes.
Lk 10:13 long ago, sitting in S and ashes.
Rev 6:12 sun became black as S, the full moon became
11:3 thousand two hundred and sixty days, clothed in S

SACKED (3)

2Kgs 15:16 At that time Menahem S Tappuah and all who
15:16 to him, therefore he S it, and he ripped
Jud 2:27 flocks and herds and S their cities and ravaged

SACKS (10)

Gen 42:35 As they emptied their S, behold, every man's bundle
43:12 the mouth of your S; perhaps it was an
43:18 was replaced in our S the first time, that
43:21 place we opened our S, and there was every
43:22 not know who put our money in our S
43:23 put treasure in your S for you; I received
44:1 house, "Fill the men's S with food, as much
44:8 the mouth of our S, we brought back to
Josh 9:4 provisions, and took worn-out S upon their asses, and
1Sam 9:7 the bread in our S is gone, and there

SACRED (30)

Ex 30:25 make of these a S anointing oil blended as
Deut 26:13 'I have removed the S portion out of my
Josh 6:19 bronze and iron, are S to the LORD; they
1Sam 20:8 your servant into a S covenant with you.
1Chr 16:42 music and instruments for S song.
Tob 2:1 Pentecost, which is the S festival of the seven
Jud 3:8 and cut down their S groves; for it had
4:3 gathered together, and the S vessels and the altar
Eccl 8:2 and because of your S oath be not dismayed;
Jer 31:40 the east, shall be S to the LORD.
Ezek 20:40 gifts, with all your S offerings.
43:21 the temple, outside the S area.
44:13 near any of my S things and the things
44:13 things that are most S; but they shall bear
Zeph 3:4 priests profane what is S, they do violence to
Zech 14:21 and Judah shall be S to the LORD of
1Mac 1:47 to build altars and S precincts and shrines for
5:43 and fled into the S precincts at Carnaim.
5:44 city and burned the S precincts with fire, together
2Mac 1:15 the wall of the S precinct, they closed the
1:34 matter, and enclosed the place and made it S
6:4 with women within the S precincts, and besides
8:33 set fire to the S gates, Callisthenes and some
10:2 and also destroyed the S precincts.
11:3 he did on the S places of the other
12:40 the dead they found S tokens of the idols
Mt 23:16 or the temple that has made the gold S
23:18 gift or the altar that makes the gift S
Acts 19:35 Artemis, and of the S stone that fell from
2Tim 3:15 been acquainted with the S writings which are able

SACRIFICE (213)

Gen 31:54 and Jacob offered a S on the mountain and
Ex 3:18 wilderness, that we may S to the LORD our
5:3 into the wilderness, and S to the LORD our
5:8 us go and offer S to our God.'
5:17 'Let us go and S to the LORD.'
8:8 the people go to S to the LORD."
8:25 Aaron, and said, "Go, S to your God within
8:26 so; for we shall S to the LORD our
8:26 If we S offerings abominable to the Egyptians before
8:27 into the wilderness and S to the LORD our
8:28 let you go, to S to the LORD your
8:29 the people go to S to the LORD."
10:25 offerings, that we may S to the LORD our
12:27 say, 'It is the S of the LORD's passover,
13:15 Therefore I S to the LORD all the males
20:24 make for me and S on it your burnt
23:18 the blood of my S with leavened bread, or
34:15 after their gods and S to their gods and
34:15 you eat of his S,
34:25 the blood of my S with leaven; neither shall
34:25 leaven; neither shall the S of the feast of
Lev 3:1 man's offering is a S of peace offering, if
3:3 And from the S of the peace offering, as
3:6 his offering for a S of peace offering to
3:9 Then from the S of the peace offering as
4:10 the ox of the S of the peace offerings),
4:26 the fat of the S of peace offerings; so
4:35 is removed from the S of peace offerings, and
7:11 the law of the S of peace offerings which
7:13 With the S of his peace offerings for thanksgiving
7:15 the flesh of the S of his peace offerings
7:16 But if the S of his offering is a
7:16 that he offers his S, and on the morrow
7:17 the flesh of the S on the third day
7:18 the flesh of the S of his peace offering
7:20 the flesh of the S of the LORD's peace
7:21 the flesh of the S of the LORD's peace
7:29 He that offers the S of his peace offerings
7:29 the LORD; from the S of his peace offerings
7:32 an offering from the S of your peace offerings;
9:4 for peace offerings, to S before the LORD, and
9:18 and the ram, the S of peace offerings for
17:8 a burnt offering or S,
17:9 tent of meeting, to S it to the LORD;
19:5 "When you offer a S of peace offerings to
22:21 any one offers a S of peace offerings to
22:24 to the LORD or S within your land;
22:29 And when you S a sacrifice of thanksgiving to
22:29 when you sacrifice a S of thanksgiving to the
22:29 the LORD, you shall S it so that you
23:19 year old as a S of peace offerings.
Num 6:17 the ram as a S of peace offering to
6:18 which is under the S of the peace offering.
7:17 offering; and for the S of peace offerings, two
7:23 offering; and for the S of peace offerings, two
7:29 offering; and for the S of peace offerings, two
7:35 offering; and for the S of peace offerings, two
7:41 offering; and for the S of peace offerings, two
7:47 offering; and for the S of peace offerings, two
7:53 offering; and for the S of peace offerings, two
7:59 offering; and for the S of peace offerings, two
7:65 offering; and for the S of peace offerings, two
7:71 offering; and for the S of peace offerings, two
7:77 offering; and for the S of peace offerings, two
7:83 offering; and for the S of peace offerings, two
7:88 the cattle for the S of peace offerings twenty-four
15:3 burnt offering or a S, to fulfil a vow
15:5 offering, or for the S, for each lamb.
15:8 offering, or for a S, to fulfil a vow,
Deut 15:21 whatever, you shall not S it to the LORD
16:2 shall offer the passover S to the LORD your
16:4 the flesh which you S on the evening of
16:5 not offer the passover S within any of your
16:6 shall offer the passover S, in the evening at
17:1 "You shall not S to the LORD your God
18:3 from those offering a S, whether it be ox
27:7 God; and you shall S peace offerings, and shall
Josh 22:26 burnt offering, nor for S,
22:28 burnt offerings, nor for S, but to be a
22:29 offering, cereal offering, or S, other than the altar
Judg 16:23 to offer a great S to Dagon their god,
1Sam 1:3 to worship and to S to the LORD of
1:21 the LORD the yearly S, and to pay his
2:13 when any man offered S, the priest's servant would
2:19 up with her husband to offer the yearly S
3:14 not be expiated by S or offering for ever."
9:12 the people have a S today on the high
9:13 he must bless the S; afterward those eat who
10:8 burnt offerings and to S peace offerings.
15:15 of the oxen, to S to the LORD your
15:21 devoted to destruction, to S to the LORD your
15:22 obey is better than S, and to hearken than
16:2 'I have come to S to the LORD.'
16:3 invite Jesse to the S, and I will show
16:5 I have come to S to the LORD; consecrate
16:5 consecrate yourselves, and come with me to the S
16:5 and his sons, and invited them to the S

S

20:6 there is a yearly S there for all the
20:29 our family holds a S in the city, and
1Kgs 3:4 went to Gibeon to S there, for that was
8:62 Israel with him, offered S before the LORD.
13:2 name; and he shall S upon you the priests
2Kgs 3:20 time of offering the S, behold, water came from
5:17 offer burnt offering or S to any god but
10:19 I have a great S to offer to Baal;
12:3 the people continued to S and burn incense on
16:15 the blood of the S; but the bronze altar
17:35 or serve them or S to them;
17:36 yourselves to him, and to him you shall S
2Chr 7:4 all the people offered S before the LORD.
7:5 Solomon offered as a S twenty-two thousand oxen
7:12 this place for myself as a house of S
11:16 Israel to Jerusalem to S to the LORD, the
28:23 helped them, I will S to them that they
Ezra 9:4 me while I sat appalled until the evening S
9:5 And at the evening S I rose from my
Neh 4:2 Will they S
Tob 1:4 all the tribes should S and where the temple
1:5 in apostasy used to S to the calf Baal,
Jud 16:16 For every S as a fragrant offering is a
Ps 5:3 morning I prepare a S for thee, and watch.
40:6 S and offering thou dost not desire; but thou
50:5 ones, who made a covenant with me by S
50:14 Offer to God a S of thanksgiving, and pay
50:23 brings thanksgiving as his S honors me; to him
51:16 hast no delight in S; were I to give
51:17 The S acceptable to God is a broken spirit;
54:6 freewill offering I will S to thee; I will
66:15 the smoke of the S of rams; I will
116:17 offer to thee the S of thanksgiving and call
141:2 lifting up of my hands as an evening S
Prov 15:8 The S of the wicked is an abomination to
21:3 justice is more acceptable to the LORD than S
21:27 The S of the wicked is an abomination; how
Eccl 5:1 than to offer the S of fools; for they
9:2 him who sacrifices and him who does not S
Sir 7:31 of the shoulders, the S of sanctification, and the
34:20 man who offers a S from the property of
35:7 The S of a righteous man is acceptable, and
35:12 trust to an unrighteous S; for the Lord is
38:11 Offer a sweet-smelling S, and a memorial portion of
45:16 the living to offer S to the Lord, incense
46:16 and he offered in S a sucking lamb.
Is 19:21 day and worship with S and burnt offering, and
34:6 the LORD has a S in Bozrah, a great
57:7 bed, and thither you went up to offer S
Jer 46:10 of hosts holds a S in the north country
48:35 LORD, him who offers S in the high place
Ezek 20:31 offer your gifts and S your sons by fire,
23:39 slaughtered their children in S to their idols, on
44:11 burnt offering and the S for the people, and
Dan 3:38 no burnt offering, or S, or oblation, or incense,
3:40 lambs; such may our S be in thy sight
9:21 swift flight at the time of the evening S
9:27 week he shall cause S and offering to cease;
Hos 3:4 king or prince, without S or pillar, without ephod
4:13 They S on the tops of the mountains, and
4:14 aside with harlots, and S with cult prostitutes, and
6:6 steadfast love and not S, the knowledge of God,
8:13 They love S; they sacrifice flesh and eat it;
8:13 They love sacrifice; they S flesh and eat it;
12:11 if in Gilgal they S bulls, their altars also
13:2 S to these, they say.
Amos 4:5 three days; offer a S of thanksgiving of that
Jon 1:16 and they offered a S to the LORD and
2:9 voice of thanksgiving will S to thee; what I
Zeph 1:7 LORD has prepared a S and consecrated his guests.
1:8 day of the LORD's S —"I will punish the
Zech 14:21 so that all who S may come and take
14:21 the flesh of the S in them.
Mal 1:8 offer blind animals in S, is that no evil?
1Mac 1:47 shrines for idols, to S swine and unclean animals,
1:51 of Judah to offer S, city by city.
1:59 the month they offered S on the altar which
2:15 the city of Modein to make them offer S
2:23 of all to offer S upon the altar in
2:25 was forcing them to S, and he tore down
4:53 they rose and offered S, as the law directs,
4:56 gladness; they offered a S of deliverance and praise.
11:34 all those who offer S in Jerusalem, we have
2Mac 1:8 heard, and we offered S and cereal offering, and
1:23 And while the S was being consumed, the priests
1:26 consecrate them, accept this S on behalf of all
1:31 the materials of the S were consumed, Nehemiah
1:33 the materials of the S,
2:9 of wisdom Solomon offered S for the dedication and
3:32 regard to Heliodorus, offered S for the man's
3:35 Then Heliodorus offered S to the Lord and made
4:19 silver drachmas for the S to Hercules.
4:19 to use it for S, because that was inappropriate,
4:20 the sender for the S to Hercules, but by
6:4 brought in things for S that were unfit.
6:21 charge of that unlawful S took the man aside,
10:3 made another altar of S; then, striking fire out
13:23 with them and offered S, honored the sanctuary and
Mt 9:13 desire mercy, and not S For I came not
12:7 desire mercy, and not S you would not have
Lk 2:24 and to offer a S according to what is
Acts 7:41 days, and offered a S to the idol and
14:13 and wanted to offer S with the people.
14:18 the people from offering S to them.
Rom 12:1 bodies as a living S, holy and acceptable to
1Cor 10:20 imply that what pagans S they offer to demons
10:28 says to you, "This has been offered in S
Eph 5:2 a fragrant offering and S to God.
Phil 4:18 a fragrant offering, a S acceptable and pleasing to
Heb 5:3 is bound to offer S for his own sins
9:26 away sin by the S of himself.
10:12 all time a single S for sins, he sat
10:26 no longer remains a S for sins,
11:4 God a more acceptable S than Cain, through which
13:11 high priest as a S for sin are burned
13:15 continually offer up a S of praise to God,

SACRIFICED (40)

Ex 24:5 offered burnt offerings and S peace offerings of oxen
32:8 have worshiped it and S to it, and said,
Num 22:40 And Balak S oxen and sheep, and sent to
Deut 32:17 They S to demons which were no gods, to
Josh 8:31 to the LORD, and S peace offerings.
Judg 2:5 place Bochim; and they S there to the LORD.
1Sam 1:4 the day when Elkanah S, he would give portions
6:15 offered burnt offerings and S sacrifices on that day
11:15 There they S peace offerings before the LORD, and
2Sam 6:13 gone six paces, he S an ox and a
1Kgs 1:9 Adonijah S sheep, oxen, and fatlings by the Serpent's
1:19 He has S oxen, fatlings, and sheep in abundance,
1:25 this day, and has S oxen, fatlings, and sheep
3:3 his father; only, he S and burnt incense at
11:8 who burned incense and S to their gods.
22:43 and the people still S and burned incense on
2Kgs 14:4 removed; the people still S and burned incense on
15:4 away; the people still S and burned incense on
15:35 removed; the people still S and burned incense on
16:4 And he S and burned incense on the high
17:32 the high places, who S for them in the
1Chr 15:26 of the LORD, they S seven bulls and seven
2Chr 15:11 They S to the LORD on that day, from
28:4 And he S and burned incense on the high
28:23 For he S to the gods of Damascus which
33:17 Nevertheless the people still S at the high places,
33:22 Amon S to all the images that Manasseh his
34:4 of those who had S to them.
Ps 106:37 They S their sons and their daughters to the
106:38 and daughters, whom they S to the idols of
Ezek 16:20 me, and these you S to them to be
1Mac 1:43 adopted his religion; they S to idols and profaned
Mk 14:12 Unleavened Bread, when they S the passover lamb,
Lk 22:7 on which the passover lamb had to be S
Acts 15:29 from what has been S to idols and from
21:25 from what has been S to idols and from
1Cor 5:7 For Christ, our paschal lamb, has been S
2Tim 4:6 the point of being S; the time of my
Rev 2:14 they might eat food S to idols and practice
2:20 and to eat food S to idols.

SACRIFICES (104)

Gen 46:1 to Beer-sheba, and offered S to the God of
Ex 10:25 also let us have S and burnt offerings, that
18:12 a burnt offering and S to God; and Aaron
22:20 "Whoever S to any god, save to the LORD
Lev 7:34 Israel, out of the S of their peace offerings,
10:14 sons' due, from the S of the peace offerings
17:5 Israel may bring their S which they slay in
17:5 and slay them as S of peace offerings to
17:7 no more slay their S for satyrs, after whom
23:37 offerings and cereal offerings, S and drink offerings,
Num 10:10 offerings and over the S of your peace offerings;
25:2 the people to the S of their gods, and

S

Deut 12:6 burnt offerings and your S, your tithes and the
12:11 burnt offerings and your S, your tithes and the
12:27 the blood of your S shall be poured out
32:38 the fat of their S, and drank the wine
33:19 there they offer right S; for they suck the
Josh 22:27 our burnt offerings and S and peace offerings; lest
1Sam 2:29 greedy eye at my S and my offerings which
6:15 burnt offerings and sacrificed S on that day to
15:22 in burnt offerings and S, as in obeying the
2Sam 15:12 Absalom was offering the S, he sent for Ahithophel
1Kgs 12:27 go up to offer S in the house of
12:32 Judah, and he offered S upon the altar; so
2Kgs 10:24 went in to offer S and burnt offerings.
1Chr 21:28 Jebusite, he made his S there.
29:21 And they performed S to the LORD, and on
29:21 their drink offerings, and S in abundance for all
2Chr 7:1 burnt offering and the S, and the glory of
29:31 LORD; come near, bring S and thank offerings to
29:31 And the assembly brought S and thank offerings; and
32:12 worship, and upon it you shall burn your S
33:16 and offered upon it S of peace offerings and
Ezra 6:3 rebuilt, the place where S are offered and burnt
6:10 they may offer pleasing S to the God of
Neh 12:43 And they offered great S that day and rejoiced,
Ps 4:5 [Selah] Offer right S, and put your trust in
20:3 your offerings, and regard with favor your burnt S
27:6 offer in his tent S with shouts of joy;
50:8 reprove you for your S; your burnt offerings are
51:19 thou delight in right S, in burnt offerings and
106:28 of Peor, and ate S offered to the dead;
107:22 And let them offer S of thanksgiving, and tell
Prov 7:14 "I had to offer S, and today I have
Eccl 9:2 unclean, to him who S and him who does
Wis 18:9 of good men offered S, and with one accord
Sir 34:18 If one S from what has been wrongfully obtained,
34:19 not propitiated for sins by a multitude of S
35:1 who heeds the commandments S a peace offering.
35:2 he who gives alms S a thank offering.
45:14 His S shall be wholly burned twice every day
45:21 for they eat the S to the Lord, which
Is 1:11 "What to me is the multitude of your S
43:23 for burnt offerings, or honored me with your S
43:24 or satisfied me with the fat of your S
56:7 burnt offerings and their S will be accepted on
66:3 a man; he who S a lamb, like him
Jer 6:20 not acceptable, nor your S pleasing to me.
7:21 burnt offerings to your S, and eat the flesh.
7:22 or command them concerning burnt offerings and S
17:26 bringing burnt offerings and S, cereal offerings and
33:18 offerings, and to make S for ever."
Bar 6:28 The priests sell the S that are offered to
6:29 S to them may be touched by women in
Ezek 20:28 they offered their S and presented the provocation
36:38 Like the flock for S, like the flock at
40:41 tables, on which the S were to be slaughtered.
40:42 burnt offerings and the S were slaughtered.
46:24 temple shall boil the S of the people."
Hos 9:4 and they shall not please him with their S
Amos 4:4 multiply transgression; bring your S every morning,
5:25 you bring to me S and offerings the forty
Hab 1:16 Therefore he S to his net and burns incense
Mal 1:14 vows it, and yet S to the Lord what
1Mac 1:45 forbid burnt offerings and S and drink offerings in
12:11 appropriate days, at the S which we offer and
2Mac 1:18 who built the temple and the altar, offered S
1:21 the materials for the S were presented, Nehemiah
2:10 heaven and devoured the S, so also Solomon prayed,
3:3 the expenses connected with the service of the S
3:6 the account of the S, but that it was
4:14 sanctuary and neglecting the S, they hastened to
6:7 to partake of the S; and when the feast
6:8 them partake of the S,
7:42 about the eating of S and the extreme tortures.
9:16 expenses incurred for the S he would provide from
10:3 of flint, they offered S, after a lapse of
14:31 offering the customary S, and commanded them to
Mk 12:33 much more than all whole burnt offerings and S
Lk 13:1 whose blood Pilate had mingled with their S
Acts 7:42 me slain beasts and S, forty years in the
1Cor 10:18 those who eat the S partners in the altar?
Heb 5:1 to offer gifts and S for sins.
7:27 high priests, to offer S daily, first for his
8:3 to offer gifts and S; hence it is necessary
9:9 this arrangement, gifts and S are offered which
9:23 things themselves with better S than these.
10:1 never, by the same S which are continually offered
10:3 But in these S there is a reminder of
10:5 the world, he said, S and offerings thou hast
10:8 nor taken pleasure in S and offerings and burnt
10:11 offering repeatedly the same S, which can never
13:16 you have, for such S are pleasing to God.
1Pet 2:5 priesthood, to offer spiritual S acceptable to God

SACRIFICIAL (10)

Ps 69:22 a snare; let their S feasts be a trap.
Wis 3:6 them, and like a S burnt offering he accepted
12:5 of children, and their S feasting on human flesh
Jer 11:15 Can vows and S flesh avert your doom?
Ezek 39:17 all sides to the S feast which I am
39:17 for you, a great S feast upon the mountains
39:19 are drunk, at the S feast which I am
2Mac 6:21 the flesh of the S meal which had been
1Cor 9:13 altar share in the S offerings?
Phil 2:17 a libation upon the S offering of your faith,

SACRIFICING (10)

1Sam 2:15 the man who was S, "Give meat for the
1Kgs 3:2 The people were S at the high places, however,
8:5 him before the ark, S so many sheep and
12:32 he did in Bethel, S to the calves that
2Chr 5:6 were before the ark, S so many sheep and
30:22 festival for seven days, S peace offerings and giving
Ezra 4:2 and we have been S to him ever since
Is 65:3 to my face continually, S in gardens and burning
Bar 4:7 who made you, by S to demons and not
Hos 11:2 from me; they kept S to the Baals, and

SACRILEGE (5)

1Mac 1:54 they erected a desolating S upon the altar of
2Mac 4:39 When many acts of S had been committed in
13:6 any man guilty of S or notorious for other
Mt 24:15 you see the desolating S spoken of by the
Mk 13:14 you see the desolating S set up where it

SACRILEGIOUS

Acts 19:37 here who are neither S nor blasphemers of our

SAD (9)

1Sam 1:8 And why is your heart S
1:18 and ate, and her countenance was no longer S
Neh 2:1 I had not been S in his presence.
2:2 "Why is your face S, seeing you are not
2:3 not my face be S, when the city, the
Job 9:27 will put off my S countenance, and be of
Prov 14:13 laughter the heart is S, and the end of
Lk 18:23 heard this he became S, for he was very
24:17 And they stood still, looking S

SADDLE (5)

Gen 31:34 them in the camel's S, and sat upon them.
Lev 15:9 And any S on which he who has the
2Sam 19:26 servant said to him, S an ass for me,
1Kgs 13:13 said to his sons, S the ass for me."
13:27 said to his sons, S the ass for me."

SADDLECLOTHS

Ezek 27:20 traded with you in S for riding.

SADDLED (10)

Gen 22:3 early in the morning, S his ass, and took
Num 22:21 in the morning, and S his ass, and went
Judg 19:10 him a couple of S asses, and his concubine
2Sam 16:1 a couple of asses S, bearing two hundred loaves
17:23 was not followed, he S his ass, and went
1Kgs 2:40 Shimei arose and S an ass, and went to
13:13 So they S the ass for him and he
13:23 bread and drunk, he S the ass for the
13:27 And they S it.
2Kgs 4:24 Then she S the ass, and she said to

SADDUCEES (14)

Mt 3:7 of the Pharisees and S coming for baptism, he
16:1 And the Pharisees and S came, and to test
16:6 beware of the leaven of the Pharisees and S
16:11 Beware of the leaven of the Pharisees and S
16:12 but of the teaching of the Pharisees and S
22:23 The same day S came to him, who say
22:34 he had silenced the S, they came together.
Mk 12:18 And S came to him, who say that there
Lk 20:27 came to him some S, those who say that
Acts 4:1 the temple and the S came upon them,
5:17 the party of the S, and filled with jealousy

S

23:6 that one part were S and the other Pharisees,
23:7 the Pharisees and the S; and the assembly was
23:8 For the S say that there is no resurrection,

SADLY

Heb 13:17 this joyfully, and not S, for that would be

SADNESS (2)

Neh 2:2 is nothing else but S of the heart." Then
Eccl 7:3 than laughter, for by S of countenance the heart

SAFE (31)

Ex 9:19 in the field into S shelter; for the hail
Deut 29:19 saying, 'I shall be S, though I walk in
Josh 10:21 all the people returned S to Joshua in the
1Sam 20:21 LORD lives, it is S for you and there
24:19 his enemy, will he let him go away S
2Sam 22:33 my strong refuge, and has made my way S
Tob 5:15 if you both return S and sound." So they
5:20 sister; he will return S and sound, and your
5:21 he will come back S and sound." So she
12:17 them, "Do not be afraid; you will be S
Job 5:24 that your tent is S, and you shall inspect
21:9 Their houses are S from fear, and no rod
Ps 18:32 girded me with strength, and made my way S
22:9 thou didst keep me S upon my mother's breasts.
31:20 men; thou holdest them S under thy shelter from
61:4 Oh to be S under the shelter of thy
119:117 that I may be S and have regard for
Prov 18:10 the righteous man runs into it and is S
29:25 but he who trusts in the LORD is S
Wis 4:17 for him, and for what he kept him S
10:12 enemies, and kept him S from those who lay
14:3 the sea, and a S way through the waves,
Jer 12:5 And if in a S land you fall down,
Hab 2:9 on high, to be S from the reach of
1Mac 12:4 provide for the envoys S conduct to the land
2Mac 3:15 he should keep them S for those who had
3:22 what had been entrusted S and secure for those
14:3 for him to be S or to have access
Mk 6:20 a righteous and holy man, and kept him S
Lk 15:27 he has received him S and sound.'
Phil 3:1 to me, and is S for you.

SAFEKEEPING

1Sam 22:23 your life; with me you shall be in S

SAFELY (13)

Gen 33:18 And Jacob came S to the city of Shechem,
2Sam 19:30 the king has come S home."
Tob 6:4 and liver and gall and put them away S
10:12 heaven bring you back S, dear brother, and grant
12:3 me back to you S, he cured my wife,
Wis 14:5 a raft they come S to land.
Is 41:3 them and passes on S, by paths his feet
Bar 5:7 that Israel may walk S in the glory of
1Mac 7:35 then if I return S I will burn up
12:52 the land of Judah S, and they mourned for
16:10 And he returned to Judea S
Acts 16:23 into prison, charging the jailer to keep them S
23:24 ride, and bring him S to Felix the governor."

SAFETY (33)

Deut 12:10 that you live in S,
33:12 LORD, he dwells in S by him; he encompasses
33:28 So Israel dwelt in S, the fountain of Jacob
1Sam 12:11 enemies on every side; and you dwelt in S
20:13 send you away, that you may go in S
2Sam 19:24 departed until the day he came back in S
1Kgs 4:25 and Israel dwelt in S, from Dan even to
2Chr 19:1 of Judah returned in S to his house in
Tob 8:21 property and return in S to his father, and
Jud 11:3 over to us--since you have come to S
Job 5:4 sons are far from S, they are crushed in
5:11 lowly, and those who mourn are lifted to S
11:18 will be protected and take your rest in S
Ps 4:8 thou alone, O LORD, makest me dwell in S
12:5 place him in the S for which he longs."
55:18 deliver my soul in S from the battle that
78:53 He led them in S, so that they were
Prov 11:14 but in an abundance of counselors there is S
Sir 3:1 act accordingly, that you may be kept in S
Is 10:31 in flight, the inhabitants of Gebim flee for S
14:30 needy lie down in S; but I will kill
Jer 4:6 toward Zion, flee for S, stay not, for I
6:1 Flee for S, O people of Benjamin, from the
32:37 place, and I will make them dwell in S
Hos 2:18 and I will make you lie down in S
Zech 8:10 neither was there any S from the foe for
1Mac 2:44 wrath; the survivors fled to the Gentiles for S
5:54 of them had fallen before they returned in S
6:53 year; those who found S in Judea from the
10:83 entered Beth-dagon, the temple of their idol, for S
14:37 fortified it for the S of the country and
2Mac 12:24 let him go in S, because he held the
15:1 attack them with complete S on the day of

SAFFRON

Song 4:14 with nard, nard and S, calamus and cinnamon, with

SAGES

Sir 8:8 the discourse of the S, but busy yourself with

SAIL (19)

Wis 14:1 Again, one preparing to S and about to voyage
Sir 43:24 Those who S the sea tell of its dangers,
Is 33:23 place, or keep the S spread out.
Ezek 27:7 from Egypt was your S, serving as your ensign;
1Mac 13:29 seen by all who S the sea.
2Mac 5:21 arrogance that he could S on the land and
Acts 13:13 and his company set S from Paphos, and came
16:11 Setting S therefore from Troas, we made a direct
18:21 and he set S from Ephesus.
20:3 was about to set S for Syria, he determined
20:13 the ship, we set S for Assos, intending to
20:16 Paul had decided to S past Ephesus, so that
21:1 from them and set S, we came by a
21:2 crossing to Phoenicia, we went aboard, and set S
27:1 decided that we should S for Italy, they delivered
27:2 which was about to S to the ports along
27:21 should not have set S from Crete and incurred
27:24 you all those who S with you.'
28:11 three months we set S in a ship which

SAILED (15)

1Mac 7:1 set forth from Rome, S with a few men
2Mac 14:1 son of Seleucus, had S into the harbor of
Lk 8:23 out, and as they S he fell asleep.
Acts 13:4 and from there they S to Cyprus.
14:26 and from there they S to Antioch, where they
15:38 Mark with him and S away to Cyprus,
18:18 of the brethren and S for Syria, and with
20:6 at Troas, but we S away from Philippi after
21:3 on the left we S to Syria, and landed
27:4 sea from there we S under the lee of
27:5 And when we had S across the sea which
27:7 We S slowly for a number of days, and
27:7 to go on, we S under the lee of
27:13 they weighed anchor and S along Crete, close.
28:10 us; and when we S, they put on board

SAILING (2)

Acts 20:15 And S from there we came the following day
27:6 a ship of Alexandria S for Italy, and put

SAILORS (3)

Acts 27:27 Adria, about midnight the S suspected that they
27:30 And as the S were seeking to escape from
Rev 18:17 shipmasters and seafaring men, S and all whose

SAILS

Wis 5:10 like a ship that S through the billowy water,

SAINT

Phil 4:21 Greet every S in Christ Jesus.

SAINTS (88)

2Chr 6:41 salvation, and let thy S rejoice in thy goodness.
Tob 8:15 Let thy S and all thy creatures bless thee;
12:15 the prayers of the S and enter into the
Ps 16:3 As for the S in the land, they are
30:4 LORD, O you his S, and give thanks to
31:23 Love the LORD, all you his S
34:9 the LORD, you his S, for those who fear
37:28 LORD loves justice; he will not forsake his S
79:2 the flesh of thy S to the beasts of
85:8 his people, to his S, to those who turn
97:10 the lives of his S; he delivers them from
116:15 of the LORD is the death of his S
132:9 righteousness, and let thy S shout for joy.
132:16 with salvation, and her S will shout for joy.
145:10 LORD, and all thy S shall bless thee!

S

	148:14	praise for all his S, for the people of
Prov	2:8	of justice and preserving the way of his S
Wis	5:5	And why is his lot among the S
	18:9	divine law, that the S would share alike the
Dan	7:18	But the S of the Most High shall receive
	7:21	made war with the S, and prevailed over them,
	7:22	was given for the S of the Most High,
	7:22	time came when the S received the kingdom.
	7:25	shall wear out the S of the Most High,
	7:27	the people of the S of the Most High;
	8:24	destroy mighty men and the people of the S
1Mac	7:17	"The flesh of thy S and their blood they
Mt	27:52	many bodies of the S who had fallen asleep
Acts	9:13	has done to thy S at Jerusalem;
	9:32	down also to the S that lived at Lydda.
	9:41	Then calling the S and widows he presented her
	26:10	up many of the S in prison, by authority
Rom	1:7	are called to be S: Grace to you and
	8:27	Spirit intercedes for the S according to the will
	12:13	the needs of the S, practice hospitality.
	15:25	am going to Jerusalem with aid for the S
	15:26	the poor among the S at Jerusalem;
	15:31	be acceptable to the S,
	16:2	Lord as befits the S, and help her in
	16:15	Olympas, and all the S who are with them.
1Cor	1:2	Jesus, called to be S together with all those
	6:1	to law before the unrighteous instead of the S
	6:2	not know that the S will judge the world?
	14:33	the churches of the S,
	16:1	the contribution for the S: as I directed the
	16:15	the service of the S;
2Cor	1:1	Corinth, with all the S who are in the
	8:4	the relief of the S —
	9:1	the offering for the S,
	9:12	the wants of the S but also overflows in
	13:13	All the S greet you.
Eph	1:1	of God, To the S who are also faithful
	1:15	love toward all the S,
	1:18	glorious inheritance in the S,
	2:19	fellow citizens with the S and members of the
	3:8	least of all the S, this grace was given,
	3:18	comprehend with all the S what is the breadth
	4:12	teachers, to equip the S for the work of
	5:3	be named among you, as is fitting among S
	6:18	supplication for all the S,
Phil	1:1	Jesus, To all the S in Christ Jesus who
	4:22	All the S greet you, especially those of Caesar's
Col	1:2	our brother, To the S and faithful brethren in
	1:4	have for all the S,
	1:12	the inheritance of the S in light.
	1:26	and generations but now made manifest to his S
1Thes	3:13	coming of our Lord Jesus with all his S
2Thes	1:10	be glorified in his S, and to be marveled
1Tim	5:10	the feet of the S, relieved the afflicted, and
Philem	1:5	Jesus and all the S,
	1:7	the hearts of the S have been refreshed through
Heb	6:10	sake in serving the S, as you still do.
	13:24	Greet all your leaders and all the S
Jude	1:3	which was once for all delivered to the S
Rev	5:8	the prayers of the S;
	8:3	prayers of all the S upon the golden altar
	8:4	the prayers of the S from the hand of
	11:18	servants, the prophets and S, and those who fear
	13:7	make war on the S and to conquer them.
	13:10	call for the endurance and faith of the S
	14:12	the endurance of the S, those who keep the
	16:6	shed the blood of S and prophets, and thou
	17:6	the blood of the S and the blood of
	18:20	her, O heaven, O S and apostles and prophets,
	18:24	of prophets and of S, and of all who
	19:8	fine linen is the righteous deeds of the S
	20:9	the camp of the S and the beloved city;
	22:21	of the Lord Jesus be with all the S

SAKE (174)

Gen	12:16	And for her S he dealt well with Abram;
	18:26	I will spare the whole place for their S
	18:29	He answered, "For the S of forty I will
	18:31	He answered, "For the S of twenty I will
	18:32	He answered, "For the S of ten I will
	26:7	kill me for the S of Rebekah"; because she
	26:24	your descendants for my servant Abraham's S
	39:5	Egyptian's house for Joseph's S; the blessing of the
Ex	18:8	the Egyptians for Israel's S, all the hardship that
	21:26	let the slave go free for the eye's S
	21:27	let the slave go free for the tooth's S
Lev	26:45	I will for their S remember the covenant with
Num	11:29	said to him, "Are you jealous for my S
Josh	23:3	these nations for your S, for it is the
Ruth	1:13	to me for your S that the hand of
1Sam	12:22	for his great name's S, because it has pleased
2Sam	5:12	his kingdom for the S of his people Israel.
	9:1	that I may show him kindness for Jonathan's S
	9:7	you kindness for the S of your father Jonathan,
	18:5	"Deal gently for my S with the young man
	18:12	and Ittai, 'For my S protect the young man
1Kgs	8:41	country for thy name's S
	11:12	Yet for the S of David your father I
	11:13	your son, for the S of David my servant
	11:13	servant and for the S of Jerusalem which I
	11:32	one tribe, for the S of my servant David
	11:32	David and for the S of Jerusalem, the city
	11:34	his life, for the S of David my servant
	15:4	Nevertheless for David's S the LORD his God gave
2Kgs	8:19	destroy Judah, for the S of David his servant,
	19:34	it, for my own S and for the sake
	19:34	sake and for the S of my servant David."
	20:6	city for my own S and for my servant
	20:6	my own sake and for my servant David's S
1Chr	14:2	highly exalted for the S of his people Israel.
	17:19	For thy servant's S, O LORD, and according to
2Chr	6:32	far country for the S of thy great name,
Ps	6:4	deliver me for the S of thy steadfast love.
	23:3	me in paths of righteousness for his name's S
	25:7	me, for thy goodness' S, O LORD!
	25:11	For thy name's S, O LORD, pardon my guilt,
	31:3	fortress; for thy name's S lead me and guide
	44:22	Nay, for thy S we are slain all the
	44:26	Deliver us for the S of thy steadfast love!
	69:7	it is for thy S that I have borne
	79:9	us, and forgive our sins, for thy name's S
	106:8	them for his name's S, that he might make
	106:45	He remembered for their S his covenant, and
	109:21	behalf for thy name's S; because thy steadfast love
	115:1	give glory, for the S of thy steadfast love
	122:8	my brethren and companions' S I will say, "Peace
	122:9	For the S of the house of the LORD
	132:10	For thy servant David's S do not turn away
	143:11	For thy name's S, O LORD, preserve my life!
Sir	29:9	man for the commandment's S, and because of his
	29:10	your silver for the S of a brother or
	31:17	stop eating, for the S of good manners, and
	37:5	friend for their stomach's S, and in the face
	38:14	in healing, for the S of preserving life.
	44:13	by the covenants; their children also, for their S
	44:23	same assurance for the S of Abraham his father.
Is	37:35	it, for my own S and for the sake
	37:35	sake and for the S of my servant David."
	42:21	pleased, for his righteousness' S, to magnify his law
	43:14	of Israel: "For your S I will send to
	43:25	transgressions for my own S, and I will not
	45:4	For the S of my servant Jacob, and Israel
	48:9	"For my name's S I defer my anger, for
	48:9	my anger, for the S of my praise I
	48:11	For my own S, for my own sake, I
	48:11	sake, for my own S, I do it, for
	62:1	For Zion's S I will not keep silent, and
	62:1	silent, and for Jerusalem's S I will not rest,
	63:17	Return for the S of thy servants, the tribes
	65:8	do for my servants' S, and not destroy them
	66:5	out for my name's S have said, 'Let the
Jer	14:7	LORD, for thy name's S; for our backslidings are
	14:21	us, for thy name's S; do not dishonor thy
	15:15	know that for thy S I bear reproach.
	17:21	Take heed for the S of your lives, and
Bar	2:14	and for thy own S deliver us, and grant
Ezek	20:9	I acted for the S of my name, that
	20:14	I acted for the S of my name, that
	20:22	and acted for the S of my name, that
	20:44	you for my name's S, not according to your
	28:17	your wisdom for the S of your splendor.
	36:22	is not for your S, O house of Israel,
	36:22	act, but for the S of my holy name,
	36:32	is not for your S that I will act,
Dan	3:34	For thy name's S do not give us up
	3:35	from us, for the S of Abraham thy beloved
	3:35	beloved and for the S of Isaac thy servant
	9:17	and for thy own S, O Lord, cause thy
	9:19	not, for thy own S, O my God, because
1Mac	13:4	have perished for the S of Israel, and I
2Mac	3:33	priest, since for his S the Lord has granted
	5:19	the nation for the S of the holy place,

	5:19	the place for the S of the nation.
	6:25	my pretense, for the S of living a brief
	7:23	forget yourselves for the S of his laws."
	8:15	not for their own S, yet for the sake
	8:15	sake, yet for the S of the covenants made
	12:25	him go, for the S of saving their brethren.
	13:3	on, not for the S of his country's welfare,
Mt	5:10	are persecuted for righteousness' S, for theirs is the
	10:18	and kings for my S, to bear testimony before
	10:22	will be hated by all for my name's S
	10:39	his life for my S will find it.
	14:3	in prison, for the S of Herodi-as, his brother
	15:3	of God for the S of your tradition?
	15:6	father.' So, for the S of your tradition, you
	16:25	his life for my S will find it.
	19:12	themselves eunuchs for the S of the kingdom of
	19:29	lands, for my name's S, will receive a hundredfold,
	24:9	be hated by all nations for my name's S
	24:22	saved; but for the S of the elect those
Mk	6:17	in prison for the S of Herodi-as, his brother
	8:35	his life for my S and the gospel's will
	10:29	or lands, for my S and for the gospel,
	13:9	and kings for my S, to bear testimony before
	13:13	will be hated by all for my name's S
	13:20	saved; but for the S of the elect, whom
Lk	9:24	his life for my S, he will save it.
	18:29	or children, for the S of the kingdom of
	21:12	brought before kings and governors for my name's S
	21:17	will be hated by all for my name's S
Jn	11:15	dead; and for your S I am glad that
	12:30	has come for your S, not for mine.
	14:11	believe me for the S of the works themselves.
	17:19	And for their S I consecrate myself, that they
Acts	9:16	must suffer for the S of my name."
	15:26	their lives for the S of our Lord Jesus
Rom	1:5	of faith for the S of his name among
	4:23	written not for his S alone,
	8:36	is written, "For thy S we are being killed
	9:3	from Christ for the S of my brethren, my
	11:28	of God, for your S; but as regards election
	11:28	are beloved for the S of their forefathers.
	13:5	but also for the S of conscience.
	14:20	Do not, for the S of food, destroy the
1Cor	4:10	are fools for Christ's S, but you are wise
	9:10	Does he not speak entirely for our S
	9:10	was written for our S, because the plowman should
	9:23	it all for the S of the gospel, that
	10:28	you, and for conscience' S —
2Cor	2:10	has been for your S in the presence of
	4:5	Lord, with ourselves as your servants for Jesus' S
	4:11	to death for Jesus' S, so that the life
	4:15	is all for your S, so that as grace
	5:15	him who for their S died and was raised.
	5:21	For our S he made him to be sin
	8:9	rich, yet for your S he became poor, so
	12:10	For the S of Christ, then, I am content
Phil	1:29	you that for the S of Christ you should
	1:29	also suffer for his S,
	3:7	as loss for the S of Christ.
	3:8	For his S I have suffered the loss of
Col	1:24	my sufferings for your S, and in my flesh
	1:24	Christ's afflictions for the S of his body, that
1Thes	1:5	we proved to be among you for your S
	3:9	we feel for your S before our God,
1Tim	5:23	little wine for the S of your stomach and
2Tim	2:10	endure everything for the S of the elect, that
Philem	1:9	required, yet for love's S I prefer to appeal
Heb	1:14	to serve, for the S of those who are
	6:7	to those for whose S it is cultivated, receives
	6:10	you showed for his S in serving the saints,
1Pet	1:20	at the end of the times for your S
	2:13	subject for the Lord's S to every human institution,
	3:14	do suffer for righteousness' S, you will be blessed.
1Jn	2:12	children, because your sins are forgiven for his S
3Jn	1:7	set out for his S and have accepted nothing
Jude	1:11	abandon themselves for the S of gain to Balaam's
Rev	2:3	up for my name's S, and you have not

SAKKUTH

Amos	5:26	You shall take up S your king, and Kaiwan

SALA

Lk	3:32	Boaz, the son of S, the son of Nahshon,

SALAMIEL

Jud	8:1	of Nathanael, son of S, son of Sarasadai, son

SALAMIS

Acts	13:5	When they arrived at S, they proclaimed the word

SALE (5)

Lev	25:29	whole year after its S; for a full year
Deut	18:8	he receives from the S of his patrimony.
	28:68	shall offer yourselves for S to your enemies as
Amos	8:5	may offer wheat for S, that we may make
2Mac	11:3	up the high-priesthood for S every year.

SALECAH (4)

Deut	3:10	Bashan, as far as S and Edre-i, cities of
Josh	12:5	over Mount Hermon and S and all Bashan to
	13:11	and all Bashan to S;
1Chr	5:11	Bashan as far as S:

SALEM (5)

Gen	14:18	And Melchizedek king of S brought out bread and
Jud	4:4	and the valley of S,
Ps	76:2	has been established in S, his dwelling place in
Heb	7:1	this Melchizedek, king of S, priest of the Most
	7:2	is also king of S, that is, king of

SALIM

Jn	3:23	baptizing at Aenon near S, because there was much

SALLAI (2)

Neh	11:8	after him Gabbai, S, nine hundred and twenty-eight.
	12:20	of Jedaiah, Uzzi; of S, Kallai; of Amok, Eber;

SALLIED (2)

1Mac	6:31	war; but the Jews S out and burned these
	9:67	Simon and his men S out from the city

SALLU (3)

1Chr	9:7	Of the Benjaminites: S the son of Meshullam, son
Neh	11:7	the sons of Benjamin: S the son of Meshullam,
	12:7	Shemaiah, Joiarib, Jedaiah, S, Amok, Hilkiah,

SALLY

1Mac	14:36	which they used to S forth and defile the

SALMA (4)

1Chr	2:11	was the father of S, Salma of Boaz,
	2:11	the father of Salma, S of Boaz,
	2:51	father of Kiriath-jearim, S, the father of Bethelem,
	2:54	The sons of S: Bethlehem, the Netophathites,

SALMON (4)

Ruth	4:20	of Nahshon, Nahshon of S,
	4:21	Nahshon, Nahshon of Salmon, S of Boaz, Boaz of
Mt	1:4	Nahshon the father of S,
	1:5	father of Salmon, and S the father of Boaz

SALMONE

Acts	27:7	we sailed under the lee of Crete off S

SALOME (2)

Mk	15:39	and of Joses, and S,
	16:1	mother of James, and S, bought spices, so that

SALT (52)

Gen	14:3	Siddim (that is, the S Sea).
	19:26	looked back, and she became a pillar of S
Ex	30:35	the perfumer, seasoned with S, pure and holy;
Lev	2:13	your cereal offerings with S; you shall not let
	2:13	shall not let the S of the covenant with
	2:13	offering; with all your offerings you shall offer S
Num	18:19	is a covenant of S for ever before the
	34:3	the end of the S Sea on the east;
	34:12	shall be at the S Sea.
Deut	3:17	of the Arabah, the S Sea, under the slopes
	29:23	whole land brimstone and S, and a burnt-out waste,
Josh	3:16	of the Arabah, the S Sea, were wholly cut
	12:3	of the Arabah, the S Sea, southward to the
	15:2	the end of the S Sea, from the bay
	15:5	east boundary is the S Sea, to the mouth
	15:62	Nibshan, the City of S, and Engedi: six cities
	18:19	northern bay of the S Sea, at the south
Judg	9:45	he razed the city and sowed it with S
2Sam	8:13	slew eighteen thousand Edomites in the Valley of S
2Kgs	2:20	new bowl, and put S in it." So they
	2:21	of water and threw S in it, and said,
	14:7	in the Valley of S and took Sela by
1Chr	18:12	slew eighteen thousand Edomites in the Valley of S
2Chr	13:5	David and his sons by a covenant of S
	25:11	to the Valley of S and smote ten thousand

S

Ezra 4:14 because we eat the S of the palace and
6:9 God of heaven, wheat, S, wine, or oil, as
7:22 baths of oil, and S without prescribing how much.
Job 6:6 tasteless be eaten without S, or is there any
39:6 his home, and the S land for his dwelling
Wis 10:7 and a pillar of S standing as a monument
Sir 22:13 Sand, S, and a piece of iron are easier
39:23 wrath, just as he turns fresh water into S
39:26 fire and iron and S and wheat flour and
43:19 upon the earth like S, and when it freezes,
Jer 17:6 wilderness, in an uninhabited S land.
Bar 6:28 wives preserve some with S, but give none to
Ezek 16:4 you, nor rubbed with S, nor swathed with bands.
43:24 the priests shall sprinkle S upon them and offer
47:11 become fresh; they are to be left for S
Zeph 2:9 possessed by nettles and S pits, and a waste
1Mac 10:29 payment of tribute and S tax and crown levies,
11:35 to us, and the S pits and the crown
Mt 5:13 "You are the S of the earth; but if
5:13 the earth; but if S has lost its taste,
Mk 9:48 S is good; but if the salt has lost
9:48 good; but if the S has lost its saltness,
9:48 Have S in yourselves, and be at peace with
Lk 14:34 S is good; but if salt has lost its
14:34 is good; but if S has lost its taste,
Col 4:6 be gracious, seasoned with S, so that you may
Jas 3:12 No more can S water yield fresh.

SALTED (2)

Is 30:24 the ground will eat S provender, which has been
Mk 9:47 every one will be S with fire.

SALTNESS (3)

Mt 5:13 taste, how shall its S be restored?
Mk 9:48 salt has lost its S, how will you season
Lk 14:34 taste, how shall its S be restored?

SALTY

Ps 107:34 fruitful land into a S waste, because of the

SALU (2)

Num 25:14 Zimri the son of S, head of a fathers'
1Mac 2:26 as Phinehas did against Zimri the son of S

SALUTATIONS (4)

Mt 23:7 in the synagogues, and S in the market places,
Mk 12:38 robes, and to have S in the market places
Lk 11:43 in the synagogues and S in the market places.
20:46 long robes, and love S in the market places

SALUTE (8)

1Sam 13:10 to meet him and S him.
25:6 And thus you shall S him: 'Peace be to
25:14 of the wilderness to S our master; and he
2Kgs 4:29 any one, do not S him; and if any
Mt 5:47 And if you S only your brethren, what more
10:12 you enter the house, S it.
Mk 15:18 And they began to S him, "Hail, King of
Lk 10:4 bag, no sandals; and S no one on the

SALUTED

1Sam 30:21 to the people he S them.

SALUTES

2Kgs 4:29 and if any one S you, do not reply;

SALVATION (136)

Gen 49:18 I wait for thy S, O LORD.
Ex 14:13 firm, and see the S of the LORD, which
15:2 he has become my S; this is my God,
Deut 32:15 him, and scoffed at the Rock of his S
1Sam 2:1 derides my enemies, because I rejoice in thy S
2Sam 22:3 the horn of my S, my stronghold and my
22:36 the shield of thy S, and thy help made
22:47 the rock of my S,
1Chr 16:23 Tell of his S from day to day.
16:35 O God of our S, and gather and save
2Chr 6:41 God, be clothed with S, and let thy saints
Esth 16:23 hereafter it may mean S for us and the
Job 13:16 This will be my S, that a godless man
33:26 recounts to men his S,
Ps 13:5 steadfast love; my heart shall rejoice in thy S
18:2 the horn of my S, my stronghold.
18:35 the shield of thy S, and thy right hand
18:46 the God of my S,
24:5 LORD, and vindication from the God of his S
25:5 the God of my S; for thee I wait
27:1 my light and my S; whom shall I fear?
27:9 off, forsake me not, O God of my S
36:10 know thee, and thy S to the upright of
37:39 The S of the righteous is from the LORD;
38:22 Make haste to help me, O Lord, my S
40:10 thy faithfulness and thy S; I have not concealed
40:16 those who love thy S say continually, "Great is
50:23 I will show the S of God!"
51:12 the joy of thy S, and uphold me with
51:14 thou God of my S, and my tongue will
62:1 soul waits in silence; from him comes my S
62:2 my rock and my S, my fortress; I shall
62:6 my rock and my S, my fortress; I shall
65:5 O God of our S, who art the hope
68:19 who daily bears us up; God is our S
68:20 is a God of S; and to GOD, the
69:29 in pain; let thy S, O God, set me
70:4 those who love thy S say evermore, "God is
71:15 of thy deeds of S all the day, for
74:12 from of old, working S in the midst of
79:9 O God of our S, for the glory of
85:4 O God of our S, and put away thy
85:7 steadfast love, O LORD, and grant us thy S
85:9 Surely his S is at hand for those who
89:26 the Rock of my S
91:16 I will satisfy him, and show him my S
95:1 a joyful noise to the rock of our S
96:2 name; tell of his S from day to day.
116:13 up the cup of S and call on the
118:14 strength and my song; he has become my S
118:21 thou hast answered me and hast become my S
119:41 me, O LORD, thy S according to thy promise;
119:81 soul languishes for thy S; I hope in thy
119:123 with watching for thy S, and for the fulfilment
119:155 S is far from the wicked, for they do
119:166 I hope for thy S, O LORD, and I
119:174 I long for thy S, O LORD, and thy
132:16 I will clothe with S, and her saints will
Wis 5:2 and they will be amazed at his unexpected S
6:24 wise men is the S of the world, and
Is 12:2 "Behold, God is my S; I will trust, and
12:2 and my song, and he has become my S
12:3 you will draw water from the wells of S
17:10 the God of your S, and have not remembered
25:9 let us be glad and rejoice in his S
26:1 city; he sets up S as walls and bulwarks.
33:2 arm every morning, our S in the time of
33:6 your times, abundance of S, wisdom, and knowledge;
45:8 the earth open, that S may sprout forth, and
45:17 the LORD with everlasting S; you shall not be
46:13 not far-off, and my S will not tarry; I
46:13 tarry; I will put S in Zion, for Israel
49:6 the nations, that my S may reach to the
49:8 in a day of S I have helped you;
51:5 draws near speedily, my S has gone forth, and
51:6 like gnats; but my S will be for ever,
51:8 for ever, and my S to all generations."
52:7 of good, who publishes S, who says to Zion,
52:10 earth shall see the S of our God.
56:1 righteousness, for soon my S will come, and my
59:11 there is none; for S, but it is far
59:17 and a helmet of S upon his head; he
60:18 shall call your walls S, and your gates Praise.
61:10 with the garments of S, he has covered me
62:1 as brightness, and her S as a burning torch.
62:11 of Zion, "Behold, your S comes; behold, his reward
Jer 3:23 our God is the S of Israel.
Lam 3:26 wait quietly for the S of the LORD.
Bar 4:24 soon will see your S by God, which will
4:29 you will bring you everlasting joy with your S
Hos 10:12 may come and rain S upon you.
Mic 7:7 the God of my S; my God will hear
Hab 3:13 wentest forth for the S of thy people, for
3:13 thy people, for the S of thy anointed.
3:18 I will joy in the God of my S
Lk 1:69 up a horn of S for us in the
1:77 to give knowledge of S to his people in
2:30 eyes have seen thy S
3:6 flesh shall see the S of God."
19:9 said to him, "Today S has come to this
Jn 4:22 what we know, for S is from the Jews.
Acts 4:12 And there is S in no one else, for
13:26 us has been sent the message of this S
13:47 that you may bring S to the uttermost parts
16:17 God, who proclaim to you the way of S

28:28 you then that this S of God has been
Rom 1:16 power of God for S to every one who
11:11 But through their trespass S has come to the
13:11 For S is nearer to us now than when
2Cor 1:6 for your comfort and S; and if we are
6:2 you, and helped you on the day of S
6:2 acceptable time; behold, now is the day of S
7:10 repentance that leads to S and brings no regret,
Eph 1:13 the gospel of your S, and have believed in
6:17 take the helmet of S, and the sword of
Phil 1:28 destruction, but of your S, and that from God.
2:12 work out your own S with fear and trembling;
1Thes 5:8 love, and for a helmet the hope of S
5:9 wrath, but to obtain S through our Lord Jesus
2Tim 2:10 they also may obtain S in Christ Jesus with
3:15 to instruct you for S through faith in Christ
Tit 2:11 has appeared for the S of all men,
Heb 1:14 the sake of those who are to obtain S
2:3 we escape if we neglect such a great S
2:10 the pioneer of their S perfect through suffering.
5:9 the source of eternal S to all who obey
6:9 feel sure of better things that belong to S
1Pet 1:5 through faith for a S ready to be revealed
1:9 faith you obtain the S of your souls.
1:10 and inquired about this S;
2:2 may grow up to S;
2Pet 3:15 And count the forbearance of our Lord as S
Jude 1:3 you of our common S, I found it necessary
Rev 7:10 with a loud voice, S belongs to our God
12:10 heaven, saying, "Now the S and the power and
19:1 S and glory and power belong to our God,

SALVE

Rev 3:18 from being seen, and S to anoint your eyes,

SAMARIA (131)

1Kgs 13:32 in the cities of S, shall surely come to
16:24 bought the hill of S from Shemer for two
16:24 city which he built, S, after the name of
16:28 and was buried in S; and Ahab his son
16:29 reigned over Israel in S twenty-two years.
16:32 the house of Baal, which he built in S
18:2 Now the famine was severe in S
20:1 went up and besieged S, and fought against it.
20:10 if the dust of S shall suffice for handfuls
20:17 reported to him, "Men are coming out from S
20:34 yourself in Damascus, as my father did in S
20:43 his house resentful and sullen, and came to S
21:1 Jezreel, beside the palace of Ahab king of S
21:18 Israel, who is in S; behold, he is in
22:10 of the gate of S; and all the prophets
22:37 and was brought to S; and they buried the
22:37 to Samaria; and they buried the king in S
22:38 by the pool of S, and the dogs licked
22:51 reign over Israel in S in the seventeenth year
2Kgs 1:2 his upper chamber in S, and lay sick; so
1:3 of the king of S, and say to them,
2:25 to Mount Carmel, and thence he returned to S
3:1 king over Israel in S, and he reigned twelve
3:6 Jehoram marched out of S at that time and
5:3 lord were with the prophet who is in S
6:19 And he led them to S
6:20 soon as they entered S, Elisha said, "O LORD,
6:20 and lo, they were in the midst of S
6:24 his entire army, and went up, and besieged S
6:25 a great famine in S, as they besieged it,
7:1 barley for a shekel, at the gate of S
7:18 about this time tomorrow in the gate of S
10:1 Now Ahab had seventy sons in S
10:1 and sent them to S, to the rulers of
10:12 Then he set out and went to S
10:17 when he came to S, he slew all that
10:17 remained to Ahab in S, till he had wiped
10:35 with his fathers, and they buried him in S
10:36 reigned over Israel in S was twenty-eight years.
13:1 reign over Israel in S, and he reigned seventeen
13:6 Asherah also remained in S
13:9 they buried him in S; and Joash his son
13:10 reign over Israel in S, and he reigned sixteen
13:13 Joash was buried in S with the kings of
14:14 king's house, also hostages, and he returned to S
14:16 and was buried in S with the kings of
14:23 began to reign in S, and he reigned forty-one
15:8 reigned over Israel in S six months.
15:13 of Judah, and he reigned one month in S
15:14 Tirzah and came to S, and he struck down
15:14 son of Jabesh in S and slew him, and
15:17 over Israel, and he reigned ten years in S
15:23 reign over Israel in S, and he reigned two
15:25 and slew him in S, in the citadel of
15:27 reign over Israel in S, and reigned twenty years.
17:1 began to reign in S over Israel, and he
17:5 land and came to S, and for three years
17:6 king of Assyria captured S, and he carried the
17:24 in the cities of S instead of the people
17:24 they took possession of S, and dwelt in its
17:26 in the cities of S do not know the
17:28 had carried away from S came and dwelt in
18:9 Assyria came up against S and besieged it
18:10 Hoshea king of Israel, S was taken.
18:34 Have they delivered S out of my hand?
21:13 the measuring line of S, and the plummet of
23:18 bones of the prophet who came out of S
23:19 in the cities of S, which kings of Israel
2Chr 18:2 some years he went down to Ahab in S
18:9 of the gate of S; and all the prophets
22:9 captured while hiding in S, and he was brought
25:13 cities of Judah, from S to Beth-horon, and killed
25:24 king's house, and hostages, and he returned to S
28:8 spoil from them and brought the spoil to S
28:9 army that came to S, and said to them,
28:15 Then they returned to S
Ezra 4:10 in the cities of S and in the rest
4:17 associates who live in S and in the rest
Neh 4:2 of the army of S, "What are these feeble
Jud 1:9 all who were in S and its surrounding towns,
4:4 to every district of S, and to Kona and
Is 7:9 head of Ephraim is S, and the head of
7:9 and the head of S is the son of
8:4 and the spoil of S will be carried away
9:9 and the inhabitants of S, who say in pride
10:9 Is not S like Damascus?
10:10 those of Jerusalem and S,
10:11 I have done to S and her images?"
36:19 Have they delivered S out of my hand?
Jer 23:13 In the prophets of S I saw an unsavory
31:5 upon the mountains of S; the planters shall plant,
41:5 Shechem and Shiloh and S, with their beards shaved
Ezek 16:46 your elder sister is S, who lived with her
16:51 S has not committed half your sins; you have
16:53 and the fortunes of S and her daughters, and
16:55 their former estate, and S and her daughters shall
23:4 their names, Oholah is S, and Oholibah is Jerusalem.
23:33 cup of your sister S;
Hos 7:2 the wicked deeds of S; for they deal falsely,
8:5 I have spurned your calf, O S
8:6 The calf of S shall be broken to pieces.
10:5 The inhabitants of S tremble for the calf of
10:7 S's king shall perish, like a chip on the
13:16 S shall bear her guilt, because she has rebelled
Amos 3:9 upon the mountains of S, and see the great
3:12 Israel who dwell in S be rescued, with the
4:1 in the mountain of S, who oppress the poor,
6:1 on the mountain of S, the notable men of
8:14 swear by Ashimah of S, and say, 'As thy
Obad 1:19 and the land of S and Benjamin shall possess
Mic 1:1 which he saw concerning S and Jerusalem.
1:5 Is it not S
1:6 Therefore I will make S a heap in the
1Mac 3:10 a large force from S to fight against Israel.
10:30 added to it from S and Galilee, from this
10:38 from the country of S, let them be so
11:28 the three districts of S from tribute, and promised
11:34 region bordering them, were added to Judea from S
2Mac 15:1 in the region of S, he made plans to
Lk 17:11 was passing along between S and Galilee.
Jn 4:4 He had to pass through S
4:5 to a city of S, called Sychar, near the
4:7 came a woman of S to draw water.
4:9 ask a drink of me, a woman of S
Acts 1:8 in all Judea and S and to the end
8:1 region of Judea and S, except the apostles.
8:5 to a city of S, and proclaimed to them
8:9 amazed the nation of S, saying that he himself
8:14 at Jerusalem heard that S had received the word
9:31 Judea and Galilee and S had peace and was
15:3 both Phoenicia and S, reporting the conversion of

SAMARITAN (4)

Lk 10:33 But a S, as he journeyed, came to where
17:16 Now he was a S
Jn 4:9 The S woman said to him, "How is it

8:48 that you are a S and have a demon?"

SAMARITANS (7)

2Kgs 17:29 high places which the S had made, every nation
Mt 10:5 no town of the S,
Lk 9:52 a village of the S, to make ready for
Jn 4:9 For Jews have no dealings with S
4:39 Many S from that city believed in him because
4:40 So when the S came to him, they asked
Acts 8:25 preaching the gospel to many villages of the S

SAME (229)

Gen 7:13 On the very S day Noah and his sons,
26:12 and reaped in the S year a hundredfold.
26:24 appeared to him the S night and said, "I
26:32 That S day Isaac's servants came and told him
32:19 "You shall say the S thing to Esau when
32:22 The S night he arose and took his two
39:17 she told him the S story, saying, "The Hebrew
41:11 we dreamed on the S night, he and I,
Ex 5:6 The S day Pharaoh commanded the taskmasters of
5:18 you shall deliver the S number of bricks."
7:11 of Egypt, did the S by their secret arts.
7:22 of Egypt did the S by their secret arts;
8:7 the magicians did the S by their secret arts,
12:42 of Egypt; so this S night is a night
21:31 with according to this S rule.
26:8 curtains shall have the S measure.
28:8 shall be of the S workmanship and materials, of
36:9 the curtains had the S measure.
36:15 eleven curtains had the S measure.
39:5 on, was of the S materials and workmanship, of
Lev 19:6 shall be eaten the S day you offer it,
22:30 be eaten on the S day, you shall leave
23:6 fifteenth day of the S month is the feast
23:14 or fresh until this S day, until you have
23:21 make proclamation on the S day; you shall hold
23:28 no work on this S day; for it is
23:29 not afflicted on this S day shall be cut
23:30 any work on this S day, that person I
Num 4:8 scarlet, and cover the S with a covering of
6:11 consecrate his head that S day,
10:32 do to us, the S will we do to
28:24 In the S way you shall offer daily, for
Deut 9:20 Aaron also at the S time.
14:28 your produce in the S year, and lay it
18:20 of other gods, that S prophet shall die.'
21:23 shall bury him the S day, for a hanged
27:11 charged the people the S day, saying,
31:22 wrote this song the S day, and taught it
Josh 6:15 the city in the S manner seven times: it
18:13 shoulder of Luz (the S is Bethel), then the
Judg 7:9 That S night the LORD said to him, "Arise,
8:8 to them in the S way; and the men
20:22 battle line in the S place where they had
1Sam 2:34 shall die on the S day.
4:12 came to Shiloh the S day, with his clothes
6:4 the Philistines; for the S plague was upon all
17:23 Philistines, and spoke the S words as before.
17:27 answered him in the S way, "So shall it
17:30 and spoke in the S way; and the people
31:6 his men, on the S day together.
2Sam 7:4 But that S night the word of the LORD
1Kgs 3:17 I dwell in the S house; and I gave
6:25 both cherubim had the S measure and the same
6:25 same measure and the S form.
7:15 was four fingers; the second pillar was the S
7:18 and he did the S with the other capital.
7:37 cast alike, of the S measure and the same
7:37 same measure and the S form.
8:64 The S day the king consecrated the middle of
13:3 gave a sign the S day, saying, "This is
2Kgs 8:22 Libnah revolted at the S time.
19:29 what springs of the S; then in the third
19:33 he came, by the S he shall return, and
1Chr 17:3 But that S night the word of the LORD
2Chr 16:10 the people at the S time.
27:5 Ammonites paid him the S amount in the second
28:22 to the LORD—this S King Ahaz.
32:12 Has not this S Hezekiah taken away his high
32:30 This S Hezekiah closed the upper outlet of the
Ezra 5:3 At the S time Tattenai the governor of the
Neh 6:4 answered them in the S manner.
6:5 In the S way Sanballat for the fifth time
Tob 2:9 On the S night I returned from burying him,
3:7 On the S day, at Ecbatana in Media, it
4:4 beside me in the S grave.
Jud 13:3 she had said the S thing to Bagoas.
Esth 9:1 thirteenth day of the S, when the king's command
9:21 fifteenth day of the S, year by year,
Job 4:8 who plow iniquity and sow trouble reap the S
Ps 102:27 but thou art the S, and thy years have
Eccl 3:19 of beasts is the S; as one dies, so
3:19 They all have the S breath, and man has
Wis 15:7 fashions out of the S clay both the vessels
15:8 futile god from the S clay— this man
17:14 they all slept the S sleep,
18:8 For by the S means by which thou didst
18:9 would share alike the S things, both blessings and
18:11 was punished with the S penalty as the master,
18:11 common man suffered the S loss as the king;
19:16 had already shared the S rights.
19:18 of the rhythm, while each note remains the S
Sir 34:26 again and does the S things, who will listen
44:23 also he gave the S assurance for the sake
Is 37:30 what springs of the S; then in the third
37:34 he came, by the S he shall return, and
Jer 28:1 In that S year, at the beginning of the
28:17 In that S year, in the seventh month, the
39:10 and fields at the S time.
Bar 1:8 At the S time, on the tenth day of
3:14 you may at the S time discern where there
6:71 In the S way, their gods of wood, overlaid
Ezek 1:16 the four had the S likeness, their construction being
10:10 the four had the S likeness, as if a
18:24 iniquity and does the S abominable things that the
21:19 come forth from the S land.
23:13 they both took the S way.
23:38 my sanctuary on the S day and profaned my
23:39 their idols, on the S day they came into
40:10 three were of the S size; and the jambs
40:10 side were of the S size.
40:21 vestibule were of the S size as those of
40:22 trees were of the S size as those of
40:24 vestibule; they had the S size as the others.
40:28 it was of the S size as the others;
40:29 vestibule were of the S size as the others;
40:32 it was of the S size as the others.
40:33 vestibule were of the S size as the others;
40:35 it; it had the S size as the others.
40:36 vestibule were of the S size as the others;
42:11 the north, of the S length and breadth, with
42:11 and breadth, with the S exits and arrangements and
44:3 go out by the S way."
45:11 shall be of the S measure, the bath containing
45:20 You shall do the S on the seventh day
45:25 he shall make the S provision for sin offerings,
46:8 go out by the S way.
46:22 four were of the S size.
Dan 4:36 At the S time my reason returned to me;
11:27 speak lies at the S table, but to no
Amos 2:7 go in to the S maiden, so that my
Zech 6:10 Babylon; and go the S day to the house
1Mac 2:25 At the S time he killed the king's officer
8:27 In the S way, if war comes first to
10:77 At the S time he advanced into the plain,
12:2 sent letters to the S effect to the Spartans
15:22 The consul wrote the S thing to Demetrius the
2Mac 2:13 The S things are reported in the records and
2:14 In the S way Judas also collected all the
3:33 offering of atonement, the S young men appeared
3:33 Heliodorus dressed in the S clothing, and they stood
6:8 they should adopt the S policy toward the Jews
7:13 the fourth in the S way.
8:14 property, and at the S time besought the Lord
10:5 happened that on the S day on which the
10:5 twenty-fifth day of the S month, which was Chislev.
10:36 came up in the S way wheeled around against
12:8 Jamnia meant in the S way to wipe out
13:12 all joined in the S petition and had besought
15:10 his orders, at the S time pointing out the
Mt 5:46 Do not even the tax collectors do the S
5:47 Do not even the Gentiles do the S
13:1 That S day Jesus went out of the house
18:27 But that S servant, as he went out, came
20:5 hour and the ninth hour, he did the S
21:30 second and said the S; and he answered, 'I
21:36 and they did the S to them.
22:23 The S day Sadducees came to him, who say
26:44 third time, saying the S words.
27:44 reviled him in the S way.
Mk 14:31 And they all said the S

S

	14:39	and prayed, saying the S words.
Lk	6:33	For even sinners do the S
	10:7	And remain in the S house, eating and drinking
	10:21	In that S hour he rejoiced in the Holy
	23:39	you are under the S sentence of condemnation?
	24:33	And they rose that S hour and returned to
Acts	1:11	will come in the S way as you saw
	11:17	then God gave the S gift to them as
	15:27	will tell you the S things by word of
	16:33	he took them the S hour of the night,
	18:3	he was of the S trade he stayed with
	24:25	At the S time he hoped that money would
	27:40	the sea, at the S time loosening the ropes
Rom	2:1	are doing the very S things.
	9:21	make out of the S lump one vessel for
	10:12	Jew and Greek; the S Lord is Lord of
	12:4	do not have the S function,
	13:6	For the S reason you also pay taxes, for
1Cor	1:10	be united in the S mind and the same
	1:10	same mind and the S judgment.
	9:8	Does not the law say the S
	9:14	In the S way, the Lord commanded that those
	10:3	and all ate the S supernatural food
	10:4	and all drank the S supernatural drink.
	11:5	head--it is the S as if her head
	11:25	In the S way also the cup, after supper,
	12:4	of gifts, but the S Spirit;
	12:5	of service, but the S Lord;
	12:6	but it is the S God who inspires them
	12:8	knowledge according to the S Spirit,
	12:9	another faith by the S Spirit, to another gifts
	12:11	by one and the S Spirit, who apportions to
	12:25	members may have the S care for one another.
2Cor	1:6	you patiently endure the S sufferings that we suffer.
	3:14	the old covenant, that S veil remains unlifted,
	4:13	Since we have the S spirit of faith as
	8:16	God who puts the S earnest care for you
	11:12	they work on the S terms as we do.
	12:18	not act in the S spirit?
	12:18	we not take the S steps?
Eph	3:6	heirs, members of the S body, and partakers of
	6:8	he will receive the S again from the Lord,
	6:9	Masters, do the S to them, and forbear threatening,
Phil	1:30	sake, engaged in the S conflict which you saw
	2:2	by being of the S mind, having the same
	2:2	same mind, having the S love, being in full
	3:1	To write the S things to you is not
1Thes	2:14	for you suffered the S things from your own
Philem	1:22	At the S time, prepare a guest room for
Heb	1:12	But thou art the S, and thy years will
	2:14	likewise partook of the S nature, that through death
	4:11	one fall by the S sort of disobedience.
	6:11	you to show the S earnestness in realizing the
	9:21	And in the S way he sprinkled with the
	10:1	can never, by the S sacrifices which are continually
	10:11	service, offering repeatedly the S sacrifices, which
	11:9	with him of the S promise.
	11:29	attempted to do the S, were drowned.
	13:8	Jesus Christ is the S yesterday and today and
Jas	2:25	And in the S way was not also Rahab
	3:10	From the S mouth come blessing and cursing.
	3:11	pour forth from the S opening fresh water and
1Pet	4:1	arm yourselves with the S thought, for whoever has
	4:4	join them in the S wild profligacy, and they
	5:9	faith, knowing that the S experience of suffering is
2Pet	2:12	be destroyed in the S destruction with them,
	3:7	But by the S word the heavens and earth
1Jn	2:6	to walk in the S way in which he
Rev	21:16	foursquare, its length the S as its breadth; and

SAMGAR-NEBO

Jer	39:3	the middle gate: Nergal-sharezer, S, Sarsechim the

SAMLAH (4)

Gen	36:36	Hadad died, and S of Masrekah reigned in his
	36:37	S died, and Shaul of Rehoboth on the Euphrates
1Chr	1:47	When Hadad died, S of Masrekah reigned in his
	1:48	When S died, Shaul of Rehoboth on the Euphrates

SAMOS (2)

1Mac	15:23	to Caria, and to S, and to Pamphylia, and
Acts	20:15	day we touched at S; and the day after

SAMOTHRACE

Acts	16:11	a direct voyage to S, and the following day

SAMPSAMES

1Mac	15:23	the countries, and to S, and to the Spartans,

SAMSON (39)

Judg	13:24	and called his name S; and the boy grew,
	14:1	S went down to Timnah, and at Timnah he
	14:3	But S said to his father, "Get her for
	14:5	Then S went down with his father and mother
	14:7	woman; and she pleased S well.
	14:10	to the woman, and S made a feast there;
	14:12	And S said to them, "Let me now put
	14:15	day they said to S's wife, "Entice your husband
	14:16	And S's wife wept before him, and said, "You
	14:20	And S's wife was given to his companion, who
	15:1	time of wheat harvest, S went to visit his
	15:3	And S said to them, "This time I shall
	15:4	So S went and caught three hundred foxes, and
	15:6	And they said, S, the son-in-law of the Timnite,
	15:7	And S said to them, "If this is what
	15:10	come up to bind S, to do to him
	15:11	Etam, and said to S, "Do you not know
	15:12	And S said to them, "Swear to me that
	15:16	And S said, "With the jawbone of an ass,
	16:1	S went to Gaza, and there he saw a
	16:2	The Gazites were told, S has come here," and
	16:3	But S lay till midnight, and at midnight he
	16:6	And Delilah said to S, "Please tell me wherein
	16:7	And S said to her, "If they bind me
	16:9	said to him, "The Philistines are upon you, S
	16:10	And Delilah said to S, "Behold, you have mocked
	16:12	said to him, "The Philistines are upon you, S
	16:13	And Delilah said to S, "Until now you have
	16:14	said to him, "The Philistines are upon you, S
	16:20	And she said, "The Philistines are upon you, S
	16:23	"Our god has given S our enemy into our
	16:25	merry, they said, "Call S, that he may make
	16:25	So they called S out of the prison, and
	16:26	between the pillars; and S said to the lad
	16:27	who looked on while S made sport.
	16:28	Then S called to the LORD and said, "O
	16:29	And S grasped the two middle pillars upon which
	16:30	And S said, "Let me die with the Philistines."
Heb	11:32	tell of Gideon, Barak, S, Jephthah, of David and

SAMUEL (145)

1Sam	1:20	she called his name S, for she said, "I
	2:18	S was ministering before the LORD, a boy girded
	2:21	And the boy S grew in the presence of
	2:26	Now the boy S continued to grow both in
	3:1	Now the boy S was ministering to the LORD
	3:3	yet gone out, and S was lying down within
	3:4	Then the LORD called, S! S!
	3:6	And the LORD called again, S
	3:6	And S arose and went to Eli, and said,
	3:7	Now S did not yet know the LORD, and
	3:8	And the LORD called S again the third time.
	3:9	Therefore Eli said to S, "Go, lie down; and
	3:9	So S went and lay down in his place.
	3:10	and stood forth, calling as at other times, S
	3:10	S! And S said, "Speak,
	3:10	And S said, "Speak, for thy servant hears."
	3:11	the LORD said to S, "Behold, I am about
	3:15	S lay until morning; then he opened the doors
	3:15	And S was afraid to tell the vision to
	3:16	But Eli called S and said, "Samuel, my son."
	3:16	called Samuel and said, S, my son." And he
	3:18	So S told him everything and hid nothing from
	3:19	And S grew, and the LORD was with him
	3:20	to Beer-sheba knew that S was established as a
	3:21	LORD revealed himself to S at Shiloh by the
	4:1	And the word of S came to all Israel.
	7:3	Then S said to all the house of Israel,
	7:5	Then S said, "Gather all Israel at Mizpah, and
	7:6	And S judged the people of Israel at Mizpah.
	7:8	of Israel said to S, "Do not cease to
	7:9	So S took a sucking lamb and offered it
	7:9	to the LORD; and S cried to the LORD
	7:10	As S was offering up the burnt offering, the
	7:12	Then S took a stone and set it up
	7:13	was against the Philistines all the days of S
	7:15	S judged Israel all the days of his life.
	8:1	When S became old, he made his sons judges
	8:4	together and came to S at Ramah,
	8:6	But the thing displeased S when they said, "Give
	8:6	And S prayed to the LORD.
	8:7	the LORD said to S, "Hearken to the voice

S

	8:10	So S told all the words of the LORD
	8:19	to the voice of S; and they said, "No!
	8:21	And when S had heard all the words of
	8:22	the LORD said to S, "Hearken to their voice,
	8:22	S then said to the men of Israel, "Go
	9:14	the city, they saw S coming out toward them
	9:15	LORD had revealed to S:
	9:17	When S saw Saul, the LORD told him, "Here
	9:18	Then Saul approached S in the gate, and said,
	9:19	S answered Saul, "I am the seer; go up
	9:22	Then S took Saul and his servant and brought
	9:23	And S said to the cook, "Bring the portion
	9:24	them before Saul; and S said, "See, what was
	9:24	So Saul ate with S that day.
	9:26	the break of dawn S called to Saul upon
	9:26	and both he and S went out into the
	9:27	outskirts of the city, S said to Saul, "Tell
	10:1	Then S took a vial of oil and poured
	10:9	his back to leave S, God gave him another
	10:14	were not to be found, we went to S
	10:15	"Pray, tell me what S said to you."
	10:16	the kingdom, of which S had spoken, he did
	10:17	Now S called the people together to the LORD
	10:20	Then S brought all the tribes of Israel near,
	10:24	And S said to all the people, "Do you
	10:25	Then S told the people the rights and duties
	10:25	Then S sent all the people away, each one
	11:7	out after Saul and S, so shall it be
	11:12	the people said to S, "Who is it that
	11:14	Then S said to the people, "Come, let us
	12:1	And S said to all Israel, "Behold, I have
	12:6	And S said to the people, "The LORD is
	12:11	Barak, and Jephthah, and S, and delivered you out
	12:18	So S called upon the LORD, and the LORD
	12:18	all the people greatly feared the LORD and S
	12:19	the people said to S, "Pray for your servants
	12:20	And S said to the people, "Fear not; you
	13:8	the time appointed by S; but Samuel did not
	13:8	appointed by Samuel; but S did not come to
	13:10	the burnt offering, behold, S came; and Saul went
	13:11	S said, "What have you done?" And Saul said,
	13:13	And S said to Saul, "You have done foolishly;
	13:15	And S arose, and went up from Gilgal to
	15:1	And S said to Saul, "The LORD sent me
	15:10	the LORD came to S:
	15:11	And S was angry; and he cried to the
	15:12	And S rose early to meet Saul in the
	15:12	and it was told S, "Saul came to Carmel,
	15:13	And S came to Saul, and Saul said to
	15:14	And S said, "What then is this bleating of
	15:16	Then S said to Saul, "Stop!
	15:17	And S said, "Though you are little in your
	15:20	And Saul said to S, "I have obeyed the
	15:22	And S said, "Has the LORD as great delight
	15:24	And Saul said to S, "I have sinned; for
	15:26	And S said to Saul, "I will not return
	15:27	As S turned to go away, Saul laid hold
	15:28	And S said to him, "The LORD has torn
	15:31	So S turned back after Saul; and Saul worshiped
	15:32	Then S said, "Bring here to me Agag the
	15:33	And S said, "As your sword has made women
	15:33	And S hewed Agag in pieces before the LORD
	15:34	Then S went to Ramah; and Saul went up
	15:35	And S did not see Saul again until the
	15:35	of his death, but S grieved over Saul.
	16:1	The LORD said to S, "How long will you
	16:2	And S said, "How can I go?
	16:4	S did what the LORD commanded, and came to
	16:7	the LORD said to S, "Do not look on
	16:8	Jesse called Abinadab, and made him pass before S
	16:10	Jesse made seven of his sons pass before S
	16:10	And S said to Jesse, "The LORD has not
	16:11	And S said to Jesse, "Are all your sons
	16:11	And S said to Jesse, "Send and fetch him;
	16:13	Then S took the horn of oil, and anointed
	16:13	And S rose up, and went to Ramah.
	19:18	and he came to S at Ramah, and told
	19:18	And he and S went and dwelt at Naioth.
	19:20	the prophets prophesying, and S standing as head
	19:22	he asked, "Where are S and David?" And one
	19:24	he too prophesied before S, and lay naked all
	25:1	Now S died; and all Israel assembled and mourned
	28:3	Now S had died, and all Israel had mourned
	28:11	He said, "Bring up S for me."
	28:12	When the woman saw S, she cried out with
	28:14	knew that it was S, and he bowed with
	28:15	Then S said to Saul, "Why have you disturbed
	28:16	And S said, "Why then do you ask me,
	28:20	of the words of S; and there was no
1Chr	6:28	The sons of S: Joel his first-born, the second
	6:33	of Joel, son of S,
	9:22	David and S the seer established them in their
	11:3	according to the word of the LORD by S
	26:28	Also all that S the seer, and Saul the
	29:29	in the Chronicles of S the seer, and in
2Chr	35:18	since the days of S the prophet; none of
Ps	99:6	were among his priests, S also was among those
Sir	46:13	S, beloved by his Lord, a prophet of the
	46:19	of his eternal sleep, S called men to witness
Jer	15:1	me, "Though Moses and S stood before me, yet
Acts	3:24	who have spoken, from S and those who came
	13:20	gave them judges until S the prophet.
Heb	11:32	Jephthah, of David and S and the prophets—

SANBALLAT (10)

Neh	2:10	But when S the Horonite and Tobiah the servant,
	2:19	But when S the Horonite and Tobiah the servant,
	4:1	Now when S heard that we were building the
	4:7	But when S and Tobiah and the Arabs and
	6:1	it was reported to S and Tobiah and to
	6:2	doors in the gates), S and Geshem sent to
	6:5	In the same way S for the fifth time
	6:12	me because Tobiah and S had hired him.
	6:14	Remember Tobiah and S, O my God, according to
	13:28	was the son-in-law of S the Horonite; therefore I

SANCTIFICATION (6)

Sir	7:31	shoulders, the sacrifice of S, and the first fruits
Rom	6:19	so now yield your members to righteousness for S
	6:22	return you get is S and its end, eternal
1Cor	1:30	wisdom, our righteousness and S and redemption;
1Thes	4:3	will of God, your S: that you abstain from
2Thes	2:13	to be saved, through S by the Spirit and

SANCTIFIED (24)

Ex	29:43	and it shall be S by my glory;
1Chr	15:14	priests and the Levites S themselves to bring up
2Chr	5:11	who were present had S themselves, without regard
	29:15	gathered their brethren, and S themselves, and went
	29:17	for eight days they S the house of the
	29:19	have made ready and S; and behold, they are
	29:34	until other priests had S themselves their brethren
	30:3	the priests had not S themselves in sufficient number,
	30:8	sanctuary, which he has S for ever, and serve
	30:15	shame, so that they S themselves, and brought burnt
	30:17	who had not S themselves; therefore the Levites
	30:24	And the priests S themselves in great numbers.
Sir	36:4	us thou hast been S before them, so in
	45:4	He S him through faithfulness and meekness; he
Acts	20:32	you the inheritance among all those who are S
	26:18	among those who are S by faith in me.'
Rom	15:16	Gentiles may be acceptable, S by the Holy Spirit.
1Cor	1:2	at Corinth, to those S in Christ Jesus, called
	6:11	were washed, you were S, you were justified in
Heb	2:11	and those who are S have all one origin.
	10:10	will we have been S through the offering of
	10:14	has perfected for all time those who are S
	10:29	by which he was S, and outraged the Spirit
1Pet	1:2	God the Father and S by the Spirit for

SANCTIFIES (2)

Heb	2:11	For he who S and those who are sanctified
	9:13	ashes of a heifer S for the purification of

SANCTIFY (32)

Ex	31:13	that I, the LORD, S you.
Lev	20:8	am the LORD who S you.
	21:8	I the LORD, who S you, am holy.
	21:15	am the LORD who S him."
	21:23	am the LORD who S them."
	22:9	am the LORD who S them.
	22:16	am the LORD who S them."
	22:32	am the LORD who S you,
Num	20:12	believe in me, to S me in the eyes
	27:14	of the congregation, to S me at the waters
Josh	3:5	said to the people, S yourselves; for tomorrow the
	7:13	Up, S the people, and say, 'Sanctify yourselves for
	7:13	the people, and say, S yourselves for tomorrow; for
2Kgs	10:20	And Jehu ordered, S a solemn assembly for Baal."
1Chr	15:12	houses of the Levites; S yourselves, you and your
2Chr	29:5	Now S yourselves, and sanctify the house of the
	29:5	Now sanctify yourselves, and S the house of the

44:16 they shall enter my S, and they shall approach
45:2 shall be for the S, with fifty cubits for
45:3 which shall be the S, the most holy place.
45:4 who minister in the S and approach the LORD
45:4 their houses and a holy place for the S
45:18 a young bull without blemish, and cleanse the S
47:12 because the water for them flows from the S
48:8 the west, with the S in the midst of
48:10 southern side, with the S of the LORD in
48:21 holy portion with the S of the temple in
Dan 8:11 the place of his S was overthrown.
8:13 giving over of the S and host to be
8:14 and mornings; then the S shall be restored to
9:17 to shine upon thy S, which is desolate.
9:26 to come shall destroy the city and the S
Amos 7:13 it is the king's S, and it is a
Mal 2:11 Judah has profaned the S of the LORD, which
1Mac 1:21 He arrogantly entered the S and took the golden
1:36 an ambush against the S, an evil adversary of
1:37 every side of the S they shed innocent blood;
1:37 they shed innocent blood; they even defiled the S
1:39 Her S became desolate as a desert; her feasts
1:45 drink offerings in the S, to profane sabbaths and
1:46 feasts, to defile the S and the priests,
2:7 to the enemy, the S given over to aliens?
3:43 people, and fight for our people and the S
3:45 The S was trampled down, and the sons of
3:51 Thy S is trampled down and profaned, and thy
3:58 assembled against us to destroy us and our S
3:59 the misfortunes of our nation and of the S
4:36 up to cleanse the S and dedicate it."
4:38 And they saw the S desolate, the altar profaned,
4:41 in the citadel until he had cleansed the S
4:43 and they cleansed the S and removed the defiled
4:48 They also rebuilt the S and the interior of
5:1 been built and the S dedicated as it was
6:7 they had surrounded the S with high walls as
6:18 the citadel kept hemming Israel in around the S
6:26 have fortified both the S and Bethzur;
6:51 he encamped before the S for many days.
6:54 were left in the S, because famine had prevailed
7:33 came out of the S, and some of the
7:42 spoken wickedly against the S, and judge him
9:54 the wall of the inner court of the S
10:39 a gift to the S in Jerusalem, to meet
10:39 Jerusalem, to meet the necessary expenses of the S
10:44 the structures of the S be paid from the
13:3 the laws and the S; you know also the
13:6 my nation and the S and your wives and
14:15 He made the S glorious, and added to the
14:15 glorious, and added to the vessels of the S
14:29 in order that their S and the law might
14:31 lay hands on their S,
14:36 the environs of the S and do great damage
14:42 take charge of the S and appoint men over
14:42 take charge of the S,
14:48 the precincts of the S,
15:7 and I grant freedom to Jerusalem and the S
2Mac 4:14 Despising the S and neglecting the sacrifices, they
4:33 to a place of S at Daphne near Antioch.
4:34 from the place of S; then, with no regard
9:16 Athens; and the holy S, which he had formerly
10:3 They purified the S, and made another altar of
10:5 day on which the S had been profaned by
10:5 the purification of the S took place, that is,
13:23 offered sacrifice, honored the S and showed
14:33 right hand toward the S, and swore this oath:
15:17 the city and the S and the temple were
15:18 greatest and first fear was for the consecrated S
15:33 up these rewards of his folly opposite the S
Mt 23:34 you murdered between the S and the altar.
Lk 11:51 who perished between the altar and the S
Heb 8:2 a minister in the S and the true tent
8:5 shadow of the heavenly S; for when Moses was
9:1 had regulations for worship and an earthly S
9:8 the way into the S is not yet opened
9:24 entered, not into a S made with hands, a
10:19 confidence to enter the S by the blood of
13:11 is brought into the S by the high priest

SAND (35)

Gen 22:17 heaven and as the S which is on the
32:12 your descendants as the S of the sea, which
41:49 great abundance, like the S of the sea, until
Ex 2:12 killed the Egyptian and hid him in the S
Lev 11:30 crocodile, the lizard, the S lizard, and the chameleon.
Deut 33:19 the seas and the hidden treasures of the S
Josh 11:4 in number like the S that is upon the
Judg 7:12 without number, as the S which is upon the
1Sam 13:5 and troops like the S on the seashore in
2Sam 17:11 to Beer-sheba, as the S by the sea for
1Kgs 4:20 as many as the S by the sea; they
4:29 of mind like the S on the seashore,
Job 6:3 be heavier than the S of the sea; therefore
29:18 my days as the S,
Ps 78:27 winged birds like the S of the seas;
139:18 would count them, they are more than the S
Prov 27:3 stone is heavy, and S is weighty, but a
Wis 7:9 is but a little S in her sight, and
Sir 1:2 The S of the sea, the drops of rain,
18:9 and a grain of S so are a few
22:13 S, salt, and a piece of iron are easier
Is 10:22 Israel be as the S of the sea, only
35:7 the desert; the burning S shall become a pool,
48:19 have been like the S, and your descendants like
Jer 5:22 I placed the S as the bound for the
15:8 in number than the S of the seas; I
Dan 3:36 heaven and as the S on the shore of
Hos 1:10 shall be like the S of the sea, which
Hab 1:9 They gather captives like S
1Mac 11:1 great forces, like the S by the seashore, and
Mt 7:26 his house upon the S;
Rom 9:27 Israel be as the S of the sea, only
Heb 11:12 the innumerable grains of S by the seashore.
Rev 12:17 he stood on the S of the sea.
20:8 number is like the S of the sea.

SANDAL (6)

Deut 25:9 elders, and pull his S off his foot, and
25:10 him that had his S pulled off.
Ruth 4:7 one drew off his S and gave it to
4:8 he drew off his S
Jud 16:9 Her S ravished his eyes, her beauty captivated his
Jn 1:27 the thong of whose S I am not worthy

SANDAL-THONG (2)

Gen 14:23 a thread or a S or anything that is
Is 5:27 is loose, not a S broken;

SANDALS (17)

Ex 12:11 your loins girded, your S on your feet, and
Deut 29:5 upon you, and your S have not worn off
Josh 9:5 mended, with worn-out, patched S on their feet, and
1Kgs 2:5 loins, and upon the S on my feet.
2Chr 28:15 clothed them, gave them S, provided them with food
Jud 10:4 And she put S on her feet, and put
Song 7:1 are your feet in S, O queenly maiden!
Amos 8:6 for a pair of S, and sell the refuse
Mt 3:11 mightier than I, whose S I am not worthy
10:10 nor two tunics, nor S, nor a staff; for
Mk 1:7 the thong of whose S I am not worthy
6:9 belts; but to wear S and not put on
Lk 3:16 the thong of whose S I am not worthy
10:4 purse, no bag, no S; and salute no one
22:35 purse or bag or S, did you lack anything?"
Acts 12:8 to him, "Dress yourself and put on your S
13:25 one is coming, the S of whose feet I

SANDS

Jer 33:22 be numbered and the S of the sea cannot

SANDY

Sir 25:19 A S ascent for the feet of the aged–

SANE

1Pet 4:7 at hand; therefore keep S and sober for your

SANG (17)

Ex 15:1 the people of Israel S this song to the
15:21 And Miriam S to them: "Sing to the LORD,
Num 21:17 Then Israel S this song: "Spring up, O well!–
Judg 5:1 Then S Deborah and Barak the son of Abino-am
1Sam 18:7 And the women S to one another as they
2Chr 29:28 worshiped, and the singers S, and the trumpeters
29:30 And they S praises with gladness, and they bowed
Ezra 3:11 of Israel; and they S responsively, praising and giving
Neh 12:42 And the singers S with Jezrahiah as their leader.
Jud 16:1 all the people loudly S this song of praise.
Job 38:7 when the morning stars S together, and all the
Ps 106:12 believed his words; they S his praise.
Wis 10:20 plundered the ungodly; they S hymns, O Lord, to
Sir 47:8 ascriptions of glory; he S praise with all his

1Mac 4:24 On their return they S hymns and praises to
2Mac 1:30 Then the priests S the hymns.
Rev 5:9 the saints; and they S a new song, saying,

SANK (11)

Ex 15:10 sea covered them; they S as lead in the
Judg 5:27 He S, he fell, he lay still at her
5:27 at her feet he S, he fell; where he
5:27 he fell; where he S, there he fell dead.
1Sam 17:49 his forehead; the stone S into his forehead, and
2Kgs 9:24 his heart, and he S in his chariot.
Ps 76:5 of their spoil; they S into sleep; all the
104:8 mountains rose, the valleys S down to the place
Jer 38:6 only mire, and Jeremiah S in the mire.
Hab 3:6 scattered, the everlasting hills S low.
Acts 20:9 He S into a deep sleep as Paul talked

SANSANNAH

Josh 15:31 Chesil, Hormah, Ziklag, Madmannah, S,

SAP

Ps 92:14 are ever full of S and green,

SAPH

2Sam 21:18 Sibbecai the Hushathite slew S, who was one of

SAPPHIRA

Acts 5:1 Ananias with his wife S sold a piece of

SAPPHIRE (10)

Ex 24:10 were a pavement of S stone, like the very
28:18 row an emerald, a S, and a diamond;
39:11 row, an emerald, a S, and a diamond;
Job 28:16 the gold of Ophir, in precious onyx or S
Lam 4:7 coral, the beauty of their form was like S
Ezek 1:26 throne, in appearance like S; and seated above the
10:1 them something like a S, in form resembling a
28:13 chrysolite, beryl, and onyx, S, carbuncle, and
Rev 9:17 of fire and of S and of sulphur, and
21:19 was jasper, the second S, the third agate, the

SAPPHIRES (4)

Tob 13:16 will be built with S and emeralds, her walls
Job 28:6 are the place of S, and it has dust
Song 5:14 His body is ivory work, encrusted with S
Is 54:11 stones in antimony, and lay your foundations with S

SAPS

Sir 38:18 and sorrow of heart S one's strength.

SARAH (53)

Gen 17:15 her name Sarai, but S shall be her name.
17:17 Shall S, who is ninety years old, bear a
17:19 God said, "No, but S your wife shall bear
17:21 covenant with Isaac, whom S shall bear to you
18:6 into the tent to S, and said, "Make ready
18:9 to him, "Where is S your wife?" And he
18:10 in the spring, and S your wife shall have
18:10 And S was listening at the tent door behind
18:11 Now Abraham and S were old, advanced in age;
18:11 ceased to be with S after the manner of
18:12 So S laughed to herself, saying, "After I have
18:13 to Abraham, "Why did S laugh, and say, 'Shall
18:14 in the spring, and S shall have a son."
18:15 But S denied, saying, "I did not laugh"; for
20:2 And Abraham said of S his wife, "She is
20:2 And Abimelech king of Gerar sent and took S
20:14 to Abraham, and restored S his wife to him.
20:16 To S he said, "Behold, I have given your
20:18 of Abimelech because of S, Abraham's wife.
21:1 The LORD visited S as he had said, and
21:1 the LORD did to S as he had promised.
21:2 And S conceived, and bore Abraham a son in
21:3 born to him, whom S bore him, Isaac.
21:6 And S said, "God has made laughter for me;
21:7 said to Abraham that S would suckle children?
21:9 But S saw the son of Hagar the Egyptian,
21:12 your slave woman; whatever S says to you, do
23:1 S lived a hundred and twenty-seven years; these
23:1 these were the years of the life of S
23:2 And S died at Kiriath-arba (that is, Hebron) in
23:2 in to mourn for S and to weep for
23:19 After this, Abraham buried S his wife in the
24:36 And S my master's wife bore a son to
25:10 Abraham was buried, with S his wife.
25:12 Hagar the Egyptian, S's maid, bore to Abraham.
49:31 they buried Abraham and S his wife; there they
Tob 3:7 it also happened that S, the daughter of Raguel,
3:17 Tobit's eyes; to give S the daughter of Raguel
3:17 entered his house and S the daughter of Raguel
6:10 relative, and he has an only daughter named S
7:1 the house of Raguel, S met them and greeted
7:8 Edna and his daughter S wept.
7:13 he called his daughter S, and taking her by
10:10 gave him his wife S and half of his
10:12 children by my daughter S, that I may rejoice
11:17 Tobit came near to S his daughter-in-law, he blessed
12:12 you and your daughter-in-law S prayed, I brought a
12:14 sent me to heal you and your daughter-in-law S
Is 51:2 your father and to S who bore you; for
Rom 4:19 considered the barrenness of S's womb.
9:9 I will return and S shall have a son."
Heb 11:11 By faith S herself received power to conceive, even
1Pet 3:6 to their husbands, as S obeyed Abraham, calling him

SARAI (17)

Gen 11:29 of Abram's wife was S, and the name of
11:30 Now S was barren; she had no child.
11:31 Haran, his grandson, and S his daughter-in-law, his
12:5 And Abram took S his wife, and Lot his
12:11 Egypt, he said to S his wife, "I know
12:17 great plagues because of S, Abram's wife.
16:1 Now S, Abram's wife, bore him no children.
16:2 name was Hagar; and S said to Abram, "Behold
16:2 And Abram hearkened to the voice of S
16:3 the land of Canaan, S, Abram's wife, took Hagar
16:5 And S said to Abram, "May the wrong done
16:6 But Abram said to S, "Behold, your maid is
16:6 Then S dealt harshly with her, and she fled
16:8 said, "Hagar, maid of S, where have you come
16:8 She said, "I am fleeing from my mistress S
17:15 to Abraham, "As for S your wife, you shall
17:15 not call her name S, but Sarah shall be

SARAPH

1Chr 4:22 Cozeba, and Joash, and S, who ruled in Moab

SARASADAI

Jud 8:1 of Salamiel, son of S, son of Israel.

SARDIS (3)

Rev 1:11 to Thyatira and to S and to Philadelphia and
3:1 of the church in S write: 'The words of
3:4 a few names in S, people who have not

SARDIUS (2)

Ex 28:17 A row of S, topaz, and carbuncle shall be
39:10 A row of S, topaz, and carbuncle was the

SARGON

Is 20:1 who was sent by S the king of Assyria,

SARID (2)

Josh 19:10 reached as far as S;
19:12 east of Jokne-am; from S it goes in the

SARSECHIM

Jer 39:3 middle gate: Nergal-sharezer, Samgar-nebo, S the

SASHES

Is 3:20 headdresses, the armlets, the S, the perfume boxes,

SAT (143)

Gen 18:1 of Mamre, as he S at the door of
21:16 Then she went, and S down over against him
21:16 And as she S over against him, the child
31:34 the camel's saddle, and S upon them.
37:25 Then they S down to eat; and looking up
38:14 wrapping herself up, and S at the entrance to
43:33 And they S before him, the first-born according to
48:2 summoned his strength, and S up in bed.
Ex 2:15 of Midian; and he S down by a well.
12:29 first-born of Pharaoh who S on his throne to
16:3 of Egypt, when we S by the fleshpots and
17:12 under him, and he S upon it, and Aaron
18:13 On the morrow Moses S to judge the people,
32:6 offerings; and the people S down to eat and
Lev 15:6 has the discharge has S shall wash his clothes,
Judg 5:17 Asher S still at the coast of the sea,
6:11 the LORD came and S under the oak at
13:9 the woman as she S in the field; but
19:6 So the two men S and ate and drank

S

19:15 he went in and S down in the open
20:26 Bethel and wept; they S there before the LORD,
21:2 came to Bethel, and S there till evening before
Ruth 2:14 So she S beside the reapers, and he passed
4:1 to the gate aside and S down there; and behold,
4:1 he turned aside and S down.
4:2 down here"; so they S down.
1Sam 19:9 upon Saul, as he S in his house with
20:24 moon came, the king S down to eat food.
20:25 The king S upon his seat, as at other
20:25 by the wall; Jonathan S opposite, and Abner sat
20:25 sat opposite, and Abner S by Saul's side, but
28:23 from the earth, and S upon the bed.
2Sam 2:13 of Gibeon; and they S down, the one on
7:18 David went in and S before the LORD, and
1Kgs 2:12 So Solomon S upon the throne of David his
2:19 to her; then he S on his throne, and
2:19 king's mother; and she S on his right.
13:20 And as they S at the table, the word
19:4 wilderness, and came and S down under a broom
21:13 fellows came in and S opposite him; and the
2Kgs 4:20 his mother, the child S on her lap till
13:13 his fathers, and Jeroboam S upon his throne; and
1Chr 17:16 David went in and S before the LORD, and
29:23 Then Solomon S on the throne of the LORD
Ezra 9:3 head and beard, and S appalled.
9:4 round me while I S appalled until the evening
10:9 And all the people S in the open square
10:16 the tenth month they S down to examine the
Neh 1:4 heard these words I S down and wept, and
Tob 2:1 for me and I S down to eat.
11:5 Now Anna S looking intently down the road for
Esth 1:2 days when King Ahasuerus S on his royal throne
1:14 the king's face, and S first in the kingdom--
3:15 the king and Haman S down to drink; but
Job 2:8 to scrape himself, and S among the ashes.
2:13 And they S with him on the ground seven
29:25 chose their way, and S as chief, and I
Ps 9:4 just cause; thou hast S on the throne giving
107:10 Some S in darkness and in gloom, prisoners in
137:1 of Babylon, there we S down and wept, when
Song 2:3 With great delight I S in his shadow, and
Is 10:13 brought down those who S on thrones.
Jer 3:2 the waysides you have S awaiting lovers like an
15:17 did I rejoice; I S alone, because thy hand
39:3 of Babylon came and S in the middle gate:
Ezek 3:15 And I S there overwhelmed among them seven days.
8:1 the month, as I S in my house, with
8:14 LORD; and behold, there S women weeping for
14:1 Israel to me; and S before me.
20:1 of the LORD, and S before me.
23:41 yourself with ornaments; you S upon a stately couch,
Dan 7:10 before him; the court S in judgment, and the
14:40 looked in, and there S Daniel.
Jon 3:6 himself with sackcloth, and S in ashes.
4:5 of the city and S to the east of
4:5 He S under it in the shade, till he
Nah 3:8 better than Thebes that S by the Nile, with
1Mac 1:27 the lament; she who S in the bridal chamber
11:52 So Demetrius the king S on the throne of
14:9 Old men S in the streets; they all talked
14:12 Each man S under his vine and his fig
Mt 4:16 the people who S in darkness have seen
4:16 and for those who S in the region and
5:1 mountain, and when he S down his disciples came
9:10 And as he S at table in the house,
9:10 and sinners came and S down with Jesus and
13:1 of the house and S beside the sea.
13:2 into a boat and S there; and the whole
13:48 drew it ashore and S down and sorted the
15:29 on the mountain, and S down there.
21:7 on them, and he S thereon.
24:3 As he S on the Mount of Olives, the
26:7 his head, as he S at table.
26:20 it was evening, he S at table with the
26:55 Day after day I S in the temple teaching,
26:58 and going inside he S with the guards to
27:36 casting lots; then they S down and kept watch
28:2 back the stone, and S upon it.
Mk 2:15 And as he S at table in his house,
3:34 around on those who S about him, he said,
4:1 into a boat and S in it on the
6:40 So they S down in groups, by hundreds and
9:35 And he S down and called the twelve; and
11:2 no one has ever S; untie it and bring
11:7 on it; and he S upon it.
12:41 And he S down opposite the treasury, and watched
13:3 And as he S on the Mount of Olives
14:3 the leper, as he S at table, a woman
16:14 eleven themselves as they S at table; and he
16:19 up into heaven, and S down at the right
Lk 4:20 to the attendant, and S down; and the eyes
5:3 And he S down and taught the people from
7:15 And the dead man S up, and began to
10:39 sister called Mary, who S at the Lord's feet
11:37 he went in and S at table.
14:15 one of those who S at table with him
19:30 one has ever yet S; untie it and bring
22:14 the hour came, he S at table, and the
22:53 of the courtyard and S down together, Peter sat
22:53 sat down together, Peter S among them.
22:54 seeing him as he S in the light and
Jn 4:6 was with his journey, S down beside the well.
6:3 the mountain, and there S down with his disciples.
6:10 place; so the men S down, in number about
8:2 to him, and he S down and taught them.
11:20 met him, while Mary S in the house.
12:14 a young ass and S upon it; as it
19:13 brought Jesus out and S down on the judgment
Acts 3:10 as the one who S for alms at the
6:15 at him, all who S in the council saw
9:40 she saw Peter she S up.
13:14 into the synagogue and S down.
16:13 of prayer; and we S down and spoke to
1Cor 10:7 is written, "The people S down to eat and
Heb 1:3 purification for sins, he S down at the right
10:12 sacrifice for sins, he S down at the right
Rev 3:21 I myself conquered and S down with my Father
4:3 And he who S there appeared like jasper and
14:15 voice to him who S upon the cloud, "Put
14:16 So he who S upon the cloud swung his
19:11 He who S upon it is called Faithful and
20:11 throne and him who S upon it; from his
21:5 And he who S upon the throne said, "Behold,

SATAN (54)

1Chr 21:1 S stood up against Israel, and incited David to
Job 1:6 before the LORD, and S also came among them.
1:7 The LORD said to S, "Whence have you come?"
1:7 S answered the LORD, "From going to and fro
1:8 the LORD said to S, "Have you considered my
1:9 Then S answered the LORD, "Does Job fear God
1:12 the LORD said to S, "Behold, all that he
1:12 So S went forth from the presence of the
2:1 before the LORD, and S also came among them
2:2 the LORD said to S, "Whence have you come?"
2:2 S answered the LORD, "From going to and fro
2:3 the LORD said to S, "Have you considered my
2:4 Then S answered the LORD, "Skin for skin!
2:6 the LORD said to S, "Behold, he is in
2:7 So S went forth from the presence of the
Zech 3:1 of the LORD, and S standing at his right
3:2 the LORD said to S, "The LORD rebuke you,
3:2 said to Satan, "The LORD rebuke you, O S
Mt 4:10 Then Jesus said to him, "Begone, S
12:26 will stand; and if S casts out Satan, he
12:26 if Satan casts out S, he is divided against
16:23 turned and said to Peter, "Get behind me, S
Mk 1:13 forty days, tempted by S; and he was with
3:23 in parables, "How can S cast out Satan?
3:23 them in parables, "How can Satan cast out S
3:26 And if S has risen up against himself and
4:15 sown; when they hear, S immediately comes and
8:33 he rebuked Peter, and said, "Get behind me, S
Lk 10:18 to them, "I saw S fall like lightning from
11:18 And if S also is divided against himself, how
13:16 daughter of Abraham whom S bound for eighteen
22:3 Then S entered into Judas called Iscariot, who was
22:31 "Simon, Simon, behold, S demanded to have you,
Jn 13:27 Then after the morsel, S entered into him.
Acts 5:3 said, "Ananias, why has S filled your heart to
26:18 from the power of S to God, that they
Rom 16:20 peace will soon crush S under your feet.
1Cor 5:5 deliver this man to S for the destruction of
7:5 come together again, lest S tempt you through lack
2Cor 2:11 of Christ, to keep S from gaining the advantage
11:14 no wonder, for even S disguises himself as an
12:7 flesh, a messenger of S, to harass me, to
1Thes 2:18 again and again--but S hindered us.
2Thes 2:9 by the activity of S will be with all
1Tim 1:20 I have delivered to S that they may learn
5:15 For some have already strayed after S

Rev 2:9 and are not, but are a synagogue of S
2:13 where you dwell, where S's throne is; you hold
2:13 killed among you, where S dwells.
2:24 the deep things of S, to you I say,
3:9 of the synagogue of S who say that they
12:9 called the Devil and S, the deceiver of the
20:2 is the Devil and S, and bound him for
20:7 thousand years are ended, S will be loosed from

SATED (10)

Ps 78:30 But before they had S their craving, while the
123:4 our soul has been S with the scorn of
Prov 1:31 their way and be S with their own devices.
25:16 you, lest you be S with it and vomit
27:7 He who is S loathes honey, but to one
Is 34:6 a sword; it is S with blood, it is
Jer 46:10 shall devour and be S, and drink its fill
50:10 plunder her shall be S, says the LORD.
Lam 3:15 with bitterness, he has S me with wormwood.
Hab 2:16 You will be S with contempt instead of glory.

SATISFACTION (2)

Gal 4:15 has become of the S you felt?
Tit 2:9 masters and to give S in every respect; they

SATISFIED (48)

Lev 26:26 weight; and you shall eat, and not be S
Deut 33:23 he said, "O Naphtali, S with favor, and full
Ruth 2:14 ate until she was S, and she had some
2:18 what food she had left over after being S
Esth 14:8 now they are not S that we are in
Job 19:22 Why are you not S with my flesh?
Ps 17:15 awake, I shall be S with beholding thy form.
22:26 shall eat and be S; those who seek him
65:4 We shall be S with the goodness of thy
104:13 mountains; the earth is S with the fruit of
Prov 12:14 words a man is S with good, and the
18:20 mouth a man is S; he is satisfied by
18:20 is satisfied; he is S by the yield of
19:23 who has it rests S; he will not be
27:20 and Abaddon are never S, and never satisfied are
27:20 never satisfied, and never S are the eyes of
30:15 Three things are never S; four never say, "Enough":
Eccl 1:8 the eye is not S with seeing, nor the
4:8 his eyes are never S with riches, so that
5:10 money will not be S with money; nor he
6:7 for his mouth, yet his appetite is not S
Sir 14:9 man's eye is not S with a portion, and
Is 9:20 left, but are not S; each devours his neighbor's
29:8 with his hunger not S, or as when a
43:24 cane with money, or S me with the fat
44:16 roasts meat and is S; also he warms himself
53:11 his soul and be S; by his knowledge shall
66:11 may suck and be S with her consoling breasts;
Jer 31:14 my people shall be S with my goodness, says
50:19 his desire shall be S on the hills of
Ezek 16:28 harlot with them, and still you were not S
16:29 Chaldea; and even with this you were not S
24:13 more till I have S my fury upon you.
27:33 from the seas, you S many peoples; with your
Hos 4:10 eat, but not be S; they shall play the
Joel 2:19 and you will be S; and I will no
2:26 in plenty and be S, and praise the name
Amos 4:8 water, and were not S; yet you did not
Mic 6:14 eat, but not be S, and there shall be
Mt 5:6 and thirst for righteousness, for they shall be S
14:20 And they all ate and were S
15:37 all ate and were S; and they took up
Mk 6:42 And they all ate and were S
8:8 they ate, and were S; and they took up
Lk 6:21 you that hunger now, for you shall be S
9:17 And all ate and were S
Jn 14:8 show us the Father, and we shall be S
Rom 15:14 I myself am S about you, my brethren, that

SATISFIES (4)

Ps 103:5 love and mercy, who S you with good as
107:9 For he S him who is thirsty, and the
Sir 1:14 wisdom's full measure; she S men with her fruits;
32:13 who made you and S you with his good

SATISFIEST

Ps 145:16 openest thy hand, thou S the desire of every

SATISFY (20)

Job 38:27 is no man; to S the waste and desolate
38:39 for the lion, or S the appetite of the
Ps 81:16 the rock I would S you."
90:14 S us in the morning with thy steadfast love,
91:16 long life I will S him, and show him
132:15 her provisions; I will S her poor with bread.
Prov 6:30 if he steals to S his appetite when he
13:25 righteous has enough to S his appetite, but the
Wis 16:2 eat, a delicacy to S the desire of appetite;
Is 55:2 and your labor for that which does not S
58:10 for the hungry and S the desire of the
58:11 guide you continually, and S your desire with good
Jer 31:25 For I will S the weary soul, and every
Ezek 5:13 fury upon them and S myself; and they shall
7:19 the LORD; they cannot S their hunger or fill
16:42 So will I S my fury on you, and
21:17 hands, and I will S my fury; I the
Mt 28:14 governor's ears, we will S him and keep you
Mk 15:15 So Pilate, wishing to S the crowd, released for
2Tim 2:4 his aim is to S the one who enlisted

SATISFYING

Acts 14:17 rains and fruitful seasons, S your hearts with food

SATRAPIES

Esth 16:1 one hundred and twenty-seven S, and to those who

SATRAPS (13)

Ezra 8:36 commissions to the king's S and to the governors
Esth 3:12 written to the king's S and to the governors
8:9 the Jews to the S and the governors and
9:3 the provinces and the S and the governors and
Dan 3:2 sent to assemble the S, the prefects, and the
3:3 Then the S, the prefects, and the governors, the
3:95 And the S, the prefects, the governors, and the
6:1 a hundred and twenty S, to be throughout the
6:2 one, to whom these S should give account, so
6:3 other presidents and S, because an excellent spirit
6:4 the presidents and the S sought to find a
6:6 Then these presidents and S came by agreement to
6:7 the prefects and the S, the counselors and the

SATYR

Is 34:14 meet with hyenas, the S shall cry to his

SATYRS (3)

Lev 17:7 slay their sacrifices for S, after whom they play
2Chr 11:15 places, and for the S, and for the calves
Is 13:21 will dwell, and there S will dance.

SAUL (417)

1Sam 9:2 son whose name was S, a handsome young man.
9:3 the asses of Kish, S's father, were lost.
9:3 So Kish said to S his son, "Take one
9:5 the land of Zuph, S said to his servant
9:7 Then S said to his servant, "But if we
9:8 The servant answered S again, "Here, I have with
9:10 called a seer.) And S said to his servant,
9:15 Now the day before S came, the LORD had
9:17 When Samuel saw S, the LORD told him, "Here
9:18 Then S approached Samuel in the gate, and said,
9:19 Samuel answered S, "I am the seer; go up
9:21 S answered, "Am I not a Benjaminite, from the
9:22 Then Samuel took S and his servant and brought
9:24 and set them before S; and Samuel said, "See,
9:24 So S ate with Samuel that day.
9:25 bed was spread for S upon the roof, and
9:26 dawn Samuel called to S upon the roof, "Up,
9:26 So S arose, and both he and Samuel went
9:27 city, Samuel said to S, "Tell the servant to
10:11 Is S also among the prophets?"
10:12 became a proverb, "Is S also among the prophets?"
10:14 S's uncle said to him and to his servant,
10:15 And S's uncle said, "Pray, tell me what Samuel
10:16 And S said to his uncle, "He told us
10:21 man by man, and S the son of Kish
10:26 S also went to his home at Gibe-ah, and
11:4 came to Gibe-ah of S, they reported the matter
11:5 Now S was coming from the field behind the
11:5 behind the oxen; and S said, "What ails the
11:6 God came mightily upon S when he heard these
11:7 not come out after S and Samuel, so shall
11:11 And on the morrow S put the people in
11:12 it that said, 'Shall S reign over us?' Bring
11:13 But S said, "Not a man shall be put
11:15 and there they made S king before the LORD
11:15 the LORD, and there S and all the men

S

S

22:13 And S said to him, "Why have you conspired
22:21 Abiathar told David that S had killed the priests
22:22 Edomite was there, that he would surely tell S
23:7 Now it was told S that David had come
23:7 And S said, "God has given him into my
23:8 And S summoned all the people to war, to
23:9 David knew that S was plotting evil against him;
23:10 has surely heard that S seeks to come to
23:11 Will S come down, as thy servant has heard?
23:12 me and my men into the hand of S
23:13 When S was told that David had escaped from
23:14 And S sought him every day, but God did
23:15 David was afraid because S had come out to
23:16 And Jonathan, S's son, rose, and went to David
23:17 for the hand of S my father shall not
23:17 be next to you; S my father also knows
23:19 Ziphites went up to S at Gibe-ah, saying, "Does
23:21 And S said, "May you be blessed by the
23:24 they arose, and went to Ziph ahead of S
23:25 And S and his men went to seek him.
23:25 And when S heard that, he pursued after David
23:26 S went on one side of the mountain, and
23:26 to get away from S, as Saul and his
23:26 away from Saul, as S and his men were
23:27 a messenger came to S, saying, "Make haste and
23:28 So S returned from pursuing after David, and went
24:1 When S returned from following the Philistines, he
24:2 Then S took three thousand chosen men out of
24:3 was a cave; and S went in to relieve
24:4 off the skirt of S's robe.
24:5 he had cut off S's skirt.
24:7 words, and did not permit them to attack S
24:7 And S rose up and left the cave, and
24:8 cave, and called after S, "My lord the king!"
24:8 And when S looked behind him, David bowed with
24:9 And David said to S, "Why do you listen
24:16 speaking these words to S, Saul said, "Is this
24:16 these words to Saul, S said, "Is this your
24:16 And S lifted up his voice and wept.
24:22 And David swore this to S
24:22 Then S went home; but David and his men
25:44 S had given Michal his daughter, David's wife, to
26:1 the Ziphites came to S at Gibe-ah, saying, "Is
26:2 So S arose and went down to the wilderness
26:3 And S encamped on the hill of Hachilah, which
26:3 when he saw that S came after him into
26:4 of a certainty that S had come.
26:5 to the place where S had encamped; and David
26:5 saw the place where S lay, with Abner the
26:5 commander of his army; S was lying within the
26:6 go down with me into the camp to S
26:7 and there lay S sleeping within the encampment,
26:12 jar of water from S's head; and they went
26:17 S recognized David's voice, and said, "Is this your
26:21 Then S said, "I have done wrong; return, my
26:25 Then S said to David, "Blessed be you, my
26:25 went his way, and S returned to his place.
27:1 by the hand of S; there is nothing better
27:1 of the Philistines; then S will despair of seeking
27:4 when it was told S that David had fled
28:3 And S had put the mediums and the wizards
28:4 encamped at Shunem; and S gathered all Israel, and
28:5 When S saw the army of the Philistines, he
28:6 And when S inquired of the LORD, the LORD
28:7 Then S said to his servants, "Seek out for
28:8 So S disguised himself and put on other garments,
28:9 "Surely you know what S has done, how he
28:10 But S swore to her by the LORD, "As
28:12 the woman said to S, "Why have you deceived
28:12 You are S
28:13 the woman said to S, "I see a god
28:14 And S knew that it was Samuel, and he
28:15 Then Samuel said to S, "Why have you disturbed
28:15 S answered, "I am in great distress; for the
28:20 Then S fell at once full length upon the
28:21 the woman came to S, and when she saw
28:25 she put it before S and his servants; and
29:3 David, the servant of S, king of Israel, who
29:5 one another in dances, S has slain his thousands,
31:2 And the Philistines overtook S and his sons; and
31:2 and Abinadab and Malchishua, the sons of S
31:3 battle pressed hard upon S, and the archers found
31:4 Then S said to his armor-bearer, "Draw your sword,
31:4 Therefore S took his own sword, and fell upon
31:5 his armor-bearer saw that S was dead, he also
31:6 Thus S died, and his three sons, and his
31:7 had fled and that S and his sons were
31:8 the slain, they found S and his three sons
31:11 Philistines had done to S,
31:12 took the body of S and the bodies of
2Sam 1:1 After the death of S, when David had returned
1:2 a man came from S's camp, with his clothes
1:4 and are dead; and S and his son Jonathan
1:5 do you know that S and his son Jonathan
1:6 Gilboa; and there was S leaning upon his spear;
1:12 fasted until evening for S and for Jonathan his
1:17 with this lamentation over S and Jonathan his son,
1:21 defiled, the shield of S, not anointed with oil.
1:22 and the sword of S returned not empty.
1:23 S and Jonathan, beloved and lovely!
1:24 of Israel, weep over S, who clothed you daintily
2:4 "It was the men of Jabesh-gilead who buried S
2:5 showed this loyalty to S your lord, and buried
2:7 and be valiant; for S your lord is dead,
2:8 of Ner, commander of S's army, had taken
2:8 Ish-bosheth the son of S, and brought him over
2:10 Ish-bosheth, S's son, was forty years old when he
2:12 Ish-bosheth the son of S, went out from Mahanaim
2:15 Ish-bosheth the son of S, and twelve of the
3:1 between the house of S and the house of
3:1 while the house of S became weaker and weaker.
3:6 between the house of S and the house of
3:6 was making himself strong in the house of S
3:7 Now S had a concubine, whose name was Rizpah,
3:8 to the house of S your father, to his
3:10 from the house of S, and set up the
3:13 you first bring Michal, S's daughter, when you come
3:14 sent messengers to Ish-bosheth S's son, saying, "Give
4:1 Ish-bosheth, S's son, heard that Abner had died
4:2 Now S's son had two men who were captains
4:4 Jonathan, the son of S, had a son who
4:4 when the news about S and Jonathan came from
4:8 Ish-bosheth, the son of S, your enemy, who sought
4:8 king this day on S and on his offspring."
4:10 one told me, 'Behold, S is dead,' and thought
5:2 In times past, when S was king over us,
6:16 Michal the daughter of S looked out of the
6:20 Michal the daughter of S came out to meet
6:23 Michal the daughter of S had no child to
7:15 I took it from S, whom I put away
9:1 of the house of S, that I may show
9:2 of the house of S whose name was Ziba,
9:3 of the house of S, that I may show
9:6 of Jonathan, son of S, came to David, and
9:7 all the land of S your father; and you
9:9 the king called Ziba, S's servant, and said to
9:9 "All that belonged to S and to all his
12:7 of the hand of S;
16:5 of the house of S, whose name was Shimei,
16:8 of the house of S, in whose place you
19:17 of the house of S, with his fifteen sons
19:24 Mephibosheth the son of S came down to meet
21:1 "There is bloodguilt on S and on his house,
21:2 sworn to spare them, S had sought to slay
21:4 gold between us and S or his house; neither
21:7 Mephibosheth, the son of S's son Jonathan, because
21:7 them, between David and Jonathan the son of S
21:8 whom she bore to S, Armoni and Mephibosheth; and
21:8 Merab the daughter of S, whom she bore to
21:11 Aiah, the concubine of S, had done,
21:12 took the bones of S and the bones of
21:12 day the Philistines killed S on Gilboa;
21:13 there the bones of S and the bones of
21:14 buried the bones of S and his son Jonathan
22:1 all his enemies, and from the hand of S
1Chr 5:10 in the days of S they made war on
8:33 of Kish, Kish of S, Saul of Jonathan, Malchishua,
8:33 Kish of Saul, S of Jonathan, Malchishua, Abinadab,
9:39 of Kish, Kish of S, Saul of Jonathan, Malchishua,
9:39 Kish of Saul, S of Jonathan, Malchishua, Abinadab,
10:2 And the Philistines overtook S and his sons; and
10:2 and Abinadab and Malchishua, the sons of S
10:3 battle pressed hard upon S, and the archers found
10:4 Then S said to his armor-bearer, "Draw your sword,
10:4 Therefore S took his own sword, and fell upon
10:5 his armor-bearer saw that S was dead, he also
10:6 Thus S died; he and his three sons and
10:7 had fled and that S and his sons were
10:8 the slain, they found S and his sons fallen
10:11 Philistines had done to S,
10:12 away the body of S and the bodies of
10:13 So S died for his unfaithfulness; he was unfaithful

S

11:2 times past, even when S was king, it was
12:1 about freely because of S the son of Kish;
12:2 hand; they were Benjaminites, S's kinsmen.
12:19 came with the Philistines for the battle against S
12:19 desert to his master S
12:23 turn the kingdom of S over to him, according
12:29 Benjaminites, the kinsmen of S, three thousand, of
12:29 hitherto kept their allegiance to the house of S
13:3 for we neglected it in the days of S
15:29 Michal the daughter of S looked out of the
26:28 Samuel the seer, and S the son of Kish,
Is 10:29 Ramah trembles, Gibe-ah of S has fled.
1Mac 4:30 Jonathan, the son of S, and of the man
Acts 7:58 at the feet of a young man named S
8:1 And S was consenting to his death.
8:3 But S was ravaging the church, and entering house
9:1 But S, still breathing threats and murder against the
9:4 voice saying to him, S, Saul, why do you
9:4 saying to him, "Saul, S, why do you persecute
9:8 S arose from the ground; and when his eyes
9:11 man of Tarsus named S; for behold, he is
9:17 him he said, "Brother S, the Lord Jesus who
9:22 But S increased all the more in strength, and
9:24 kill him, but their plot became known to S
11:25 Tarsus to look for S;
11:30 the elders by the hand of Barnabas and S
12:25 And Barnabas and S returned from Jerusalem when
13:1 of the court of Herod the tetrarch, and S
13:2 for me Barnabas and S for the work to
13:7 who summoned Barnabas and S and sought to hear
13:9 But S, who is also called Paul, filled with
13:21 and God gave them S the son of Kish,
22:7 voice saying to me, S, Saul, why do you
22:7 saying to me, 'Saul, S, why do you persecute
22:13 said to me, 'Brother S, receive your sight.' And
26:14 in the Hebrew language, S, Saul, why do you
26:14 the Hebrew language, 'Saul, S, why do you persecute

SAVAGE (3)
Wis 17:19 sound of the most S roaring beasts, or an
2Mac 4:25 the rage of a S wild beast.
10:35 the wall and with S fury cut down every

SAVAGELY
2Mac 15:2 "Do not destroy so S and barbarously, but show

SAVAGERY
2Mac 15:21 of arms and the S of the elephants, stretched

SAVE (167)
Ex 22:20 sacrifices to any god, S to the LORD only,
Deut 4:42 these cities he might S his life:
19:4 by fleeing there may S his life.
19:5 of these cities and S his life;
20:16 inheritance, you shall S alive nothing that breathes,
23:14 of your camp, to S you and to give
Josh 2:13 a sure sign, and S alive my father and
10:6 to us quickly, and S us, and help us;
1Sam 4:3 come among us and S us from the power
7:8 us, that he may S us from the hand
9:16 He shall S my people from the hand of
10:1 LORD and you will S them from the hand
10:27 "How can this man S us?" And they despised
11:3 is no one to S us, we will give
12:21 which cannot profit or S, for they are vain.
19:11 "If you do not S your life tonight, tomorrow
23:2 attack the Philistines and S Keilah."
2Sam 3:18 servant David I will S my people Israel from
22:42 there was none to S; they cried to the
1Kgs 1:12 counsel, that you may S your own life and
18:5 may find grass and S the horses and mules
2Kgs 19:19 O LORD our God, S us, I beseech thee,
19:34 defend this city to S it, for my own
1Chr 16:35 salvation, and gather and S us from among the
2Chr 20:9 thou wilt hear and S
Tob 6:17 God, and he will S you and have mercy
6:17 You will S her, and she will go with
Esth 13:9 is thy will to S Israel.
13:13 of his feet, to S Israel!
14:14 But S us by thy hand, and help me,
14:19 of the despairing, and S us from the hands
14:19 And S me from my fear!"
Job 20:20 rest, he will not S anything in which he
Ps 6:4 Turn, O LORD, S my life; deliver me for
7:1 do I take refuge; S me from all my
18:41 there was none to S, they cried to the
22:21 S me from the mouth of the lion, my
28:9 O S thy people, and bless thy heritage; be
31:2 a strong fortress to S me!
31:16 shine on thy servant; S me in thy steadfast
33:17 victory, and by its great might it cannot S
44:6 nor can my sword S me.
54:1 S me, O God, by thy name, and vindicate
55:16 and the LORD will S me.
57:3 send from heaven and S me, he will put
59:2 who work evil, and S me from bloodthirsty men.
69:1 S me, O God!
69:35 For God will S Zion and rebuild the cities
71:2 ear to me, and S me!
71:3 a strong fortress, to S me, for thou art
76:9 to establish judgment to S all the oppressed of
80:2 might, and come to S us!
86:2 for I am godly; S thy servant who trusts
86:16 to thy servant, and S the son of thy
106:47 S us, O LORD our God, and gather us
109:26 S me according to thy steadfast love!
109:31 of the needy, to S him from those who
116:4 LORD, I beseech thee, S my life!"
118:25 S us, we beseech thee, O LORD!
119:94 I am thine, S me; for I have sought
119:146 I cry to thee; S me, that I may
Prov 6:3 this, my son, and S yourself, for you have
6:5 your eyelids no slumber; S yourself like a gazelle
23:14 the rod you will S his life from Sheol.
Wis 14:4 showing that thou canst S from every danger, so
Sir 50:4 He considered how to S his people from ruin,
51:8 for thee and dost S them from the hand
51:12 heard, for thou didst S me from destruction and
Is 25:9 him, that he might S us.
33:22 our king; he will S us.
35:4 He will come and S you."
37:20 O LORD our God, S us from his hand,
37:35 defend this city to S it, for my own
38:20 The LORD will S me, and we will sing
45:20 keep on praying to a god that cannot S
46:2 down together, they cannot S the burden, but
46:4 I will bear; I will carry and will S
46:7 does not answer or S him from his trouble.
47:13 them stand forth and S you, those who divide
47:15 is no one to S you.
49:25 you, and I will S your children.
59:1 shortened, that it cannot S, or his ear dull,
63:1 "It is I, announcing vindication, mighty to S
Jer 2:27 they say, 'Arise and S us!'
2:28 arise, if they can S you, in your time
11:12 incense, but they cannot S them in the time
14:9 man confused, like a mighty man who cannot S
15:20 am with you to S you and deliver you,
17:14 I shall be healed; S me, and I shall
30:10 for lo, I will S you from afar, and
30:11 am with you to S you, says the LORD;
39:18 For I will surely S you, and you shall
42:11 am with you, to S you and to deliver
46:27 for lo, I will S you from afar, and
48:6 S yourselves!
51:6 Babylon, let every man S his life!
51:45 Let every man S his life from the fierce
Lam 4:17 we watched for a nation which could not S
Bar 4:22 in the Everlasting to S you, and joy has
6:12 and wood, which cannot S themselves from rust and
6:15 axe; but it cannot S itself from war and
6:36 They cannot S a man from death or rescue
6:49 gods, for they cannot S themselves from war or
6:57 are not able to S themselves from thieves and
Ezek 3:18 way, in order to S his life, that wicked
13:22 his wicked way to S his life;
18:27 and right, he shall S his life.
34:22 them abroad, I will S my flock, they shall
37:23 transgressions; but I will S them from all the
Hos 13:10 is your king, to S you; where are all
14:3 Assyria shall not S us, we will not ride
Amos 2:14 nor shall the mighty S his life;
2:15 of foot shall not S himself, nor shall he
2:15 who rides the horse S his life;
Jon 4:6 over his head, to S him from his discomfort.
Mic 6:14 put away, but not S, and what you save
6:14 save, and what you S I will give to
Hab 1:2 and thou wilt not S
Zeph 3:19 And I will S the lame and gather the
Zech 8:7 hosts: Behold, I will S my people from the
8:13 Israel, so will I S you and you shall
9:16 LORD their God will S them for they are

S

10:6 Judah, and I will S the house of Joseph.
1Mac 6:44 gave his life to S his people and to
9:9 Let us rather S our own lives now, and
2Mac 7:25 advise the youth to S himself.
11:6 a good angel to S Israel.
Mt 1:21 Jesus, for he will S his people from their
8:25 and woke him, saying, S, Lord; we are perishing."
14:30 he cried out, "Lord, S me."
16:25 For whoever would S his life will lose it,
27:40 it in three days, S yourself!
27:42 saved others; he cannot S himself.
27:49 Elijah will come to S him."
Mk 3:4 to do harm, to S life or to kill?"
8:35 For whoever would S his life will lose it;
8:35 and the gospel's will S it.
15:29 it in three days, S yourself, and come down
15:30 saved others; he cannot S himself.
Lk 6:9 to do harm, to S life or to destroy
9:24 For whoever would S his life will lose it;
9:24 my sake, he will S it.
19:10 to seek and to S the lost."
23:34 saved others; let him S himself, if he is
23:36 King of the Jews, S yourself!"
23:38 S yourself and us!"
Jn 12:27 'Father, S me from this hour?
12:47 the world but to S the world.
Acts 2:40 and exhorted them, saying, S yourselves from this
27:43 the centurion, wishing to S Paul, kept them from
Rom 11:14 Jews jealous, and thus S some of them.
1Cor 1:21 what we preach to S those who believe.
7:16 know whether you will S your husband?
7:16 know whether you will S your wife?
9:22 might by all means S some.
1Tim 1:15 into the world to S sinners.
4:16 so doing you will S both yourself and your
2Tim 4:18 from every evil and S me for his heavenly
Heb 5:7 who was able to S him from death, and
7:25 for all time to S those who draw near
9:28 with sin but to S those who are eagerly
Jas 1:20 which is able to S your souls.
2:14 Can his faith S him?
4:12 who is able to S and to destroy.
5:15 prayer of faith will S the sick man, and
5:20 of his way will S his soul from death
Jude 1:23 convince some, who doubt; S some, by snatching

SAVED (124)

Gen 19:20 a little one?--and my life will be S
47:25 they said, "You have S our lives; may it
Ex 14:30 Thus the LORD S Israel that day from the
Num 10:9 and you shall be S from your enemies.
Deut 33:29 like you, a people S by the LORD, the
Josh 6:25 belonged to her, Joshua S alive; and she dwelt
22:31 LORD; now you have S the people of Israel
Judg 2:16 raised up judges, who S them out of the
2:18 the judge, and he S them from the hand
8:19 lives, if you had S them alive, I would
21:14 women whom they had S alive of the women
1Sam 27:11 And David S neither man nor woman alive, to
2Sam 19:5 who have this day S your life, and the
19:9 of our enemies, and S us from the hand
22:4 praised, and I am S from my enemies.
2Kgs 6:10 him, so that he S himself there more than
14:27 under heaven, so he S them by the hand
1Chr 11:14 Philistines; and the LORD S them by a great
2Chr 32:22 So the LORD S Hezekiah and the inhabitants of
Neh 9:27 give them saviors who S them from the hand
Tob 14:10 But Ahikar was S, and the other received repayment
Jud 10:15 to her, "You have S your life by hurrying
Esth 7:9 for Mordecai, whose word S the king, is standing
10:9 Israel, who cried out to God and were S
10:9 The Lord has S his people; the Lord has
Job 26:2 How you have S the arm that has no
Ps 18:3 praised, and I am S from my enemies.
22:5 they cried, and were S; in thee they trusted,
33:16 A king is not S by his great army;
34:6 LORD heard him, and S him out of all
44:7 But thou hast S us from our foes, and
80:3 let thy face shine, that we may be S
80:7 let thy face shine, that we may be S
80:19 let thy face shine, that we may be S
106:8 Yet he S them for his name's sake, that
106:10 So he S them from the hand of the
116:6 was brought low, he S me.
Prov 2:16 You will be S from the loose woman, from
Wis 9:18 pleases thee, and were S by wisdom."
10:4 of him, wisdom again S it, steering the righteous
16:7 turned toward it was S, not by what he
Is 30:15 rest you shall be S; in quietness and in
43:12 I declared and S and proclaimed, when there was
45:17 But Israel is S by the LORD with everlasting
45:22 to me and be S, all the ends of
63:9 angel of his presence S them; in his love
64:5 been a long time, and shall we be S
Jer 4:14 your heart from wickedness, that you may be S
8:20 the summer is ended, and we are not S
17:14 and I shall be S; for thou art my
23:6 days Judah will be S, and Israel will dwell
30:7 yet he shall be S out of it.
31:7 say, 'The LORD has S his people, the remnant
33:16 days Judah will be S and Jerusalem will dwell
Ezek 3:19 but you will have S your life.
3:21 and you will have S your life."
33:5 warning, he would have S his life.
33:9 but you will have S your life.
Dan 3:89 us from Hades and S us from the hand
6:27 earth, he who has S Daniel from the power
13:62 Thus innocent blood was S that day.
1Mac 2:59 Mishael believed and were S from the flame.
4:9 how our fathers were S at the Red Sea,
11:48 that day, and they S the king.
2Mac 1:11 Having been S by God out of grave dangers
2:17 is God who has S all his people, and
6:22 this he might be S from death, and be
6:30 I might have been S from death, I am
Mt 10:22 he who endures to the end will be S
19:25 were greatly astonished, saying, "Who then can be S
24:13 he who endures to the end will be S
24:22 human being would be S; but for the sake
27:42 mocked him, saying, "He S others; he cannot save
Mk 10:26 and said to him, "Then who can be S
13:13 he who endures to the end will be S
13:20 human being would be S; but for the sake
15:30 the scribes, saying, "He S others; he cannot save
16:16 is baptized will be S; but he who does
Lk 1:71 that we should be S from our enemies, and
7:50 woman, "Your faith has S you; go in peace."
8:12 hearts, that they may not believe and be S
13:23 will those who are S be few?" And he
18:26 who heard it said, "Then who can be S
23:34 at him, saying, "He S others; let him save
Jn 3:17 the world might be S through him.
5:33 but I say this that you may be S
10:9 me, he will be S, and will go in
Acts 2:21 the Lord shall be S
2:47 number day by day those who were being S
4:12 given among men by which we must be S
11:14 which you will be S, you and all your
15:1 to the custom of Moses, you cannot be S
15:11 that we shall be S through the grace of
16:30 said, "Men, what must I do to be S
16:31 and you will be S, you and your household."
27:20 hope of our being S was at last abandoned.
27:31 men stay in the ship, you cannot be S
Rom 5:9 more shall we be S by him from the
5:10 reconciled, shall we be S by his life.
8:24 For in this hope we were S
9:27 of them will be S;
10:1 God for them is that they may be S
10:9 raised him from the dead, you will be S
10:10 he confesses with his lips and so is S
10:13 upon the name of the Lord will be S
11:26 all Israel will be S; as it is written,
1Cor 1:18 us who are being S it is the power
3:15 he himself will be S, but only as through
5:5 his spirit may be S in the day of
10:33 but that of many, that they may be S
15:2 by which you are S, if you hold it
2Cor 2:15 those who are being S and among those who
Eph 2:5 grace you have been S,
2:8 grace you have been S through faith; and this
1Thes 2:16 that they may be S --so as always to
2Thes 2:10 refused to love the truth and so be S
2:13 the beginning to be S, through sanctification by the
1Tim 2:4 all men to be S and to come to
2:15 Yet woman will be S through bearing children, if
2Tim 1:9 power of God, who S us and called us
Tit 3:5 our Savior appeared, he S us, not because of
1Pet 3:20 is, eight persons, were S through water.
4:18 righteous man is scarcely S, where will the impious
Jude 1:5 informed, that he who S a people out of

SAVES (16)

1Sam 10:19 rejected your God, who S you from all your
14:39 the LORD lives who S Israel, though it be
17:47 know that the LORD S not with sword and
Job 5:15 But he S the fatherless from their mouth, the
22:29 the proud, but he S the lowly.
Ps 7:10 is with God, who S the upright in heart.
34:18 to the brokenhearted, and S the crushed in spirit.
37:40 from the wicked, and S them, because they take
72:13 and the needy, and S the lives of the
145:19 hears their cry, and S them.
Prov 14:25 A truthful witness S lives, but one who utters
Sir 2:11 he forgives sins and S in time of affliction.
34:13 is in him who S them.
Dan 13:60 and blessed God, who S those who hope in
1Mac 4:11 one who redeems and S Israel."
1Pet 3:21 corresponds to this, now S you, not as a

SAVEST (2)

2Sam 22:3 refuge, my savior; thou S me from violence.
Ps 36:6 man and beast thou S, O LORD.

SAVING (13)

Gen 19:19 me great kindness in S my life; but I
1Sam 12:7 LORD concerning all the S deeds of the LORD
14:6 hinder the LORD from S by many or by
Ps 28:8 people, he is the S refuge of his anointed.
40:10 have not hid thy S help within my heart,
67:2 known upon earth, thy S power among all nations.
78:22 did not trust his S power.
88:12 the darkness, or thy S help in the land
Sir 39:18 none can limit his S power.
Mic 6:5 you may know the S acts of the LORD."
1Mac 3:18 is no difference between S by many or by
2Mac 12:25 for the sake of S their brethren.
Heb 11:7 an ark for the S of his household; by

SAVIOR (48)

2Sam 22:3 and my refuge, my S; thou savest me from
2Kgs 13:5 LORD gave Israel a S, so that they escaped
Jud 9:11 protector of the forlorn, S of those without hope.
Esth 15:2 the all-seeing God and S, she took her two
16:13 destruction of Mordecai, our S and perpetual
Ps 17:7 thy steadfast love, O S of those who seek
106:21 They forgot God, their S, who had done great
Wis 16:7 but by thee, the S of all.
Sir 46:1 his name, a great S of God's elect, to
51:1 King, and will praise thee as God my S
Is 19:20 will send them a S, and will defend and
43:3 your God, the Holy One of Israel, your S
43:11 the LORD, and besides me there is no S
45:15 who hidest thyself, O God of Israel, the S
45:21 righteous God and a S; there is none besides
49:26 am the LORD your S, and your Redeemer, the
60:16 the LORD, am your S and your Redeemer, the
63:8 will not deal falsely; and he became their S
Jer 14:8 hope of Israel, its S in time of trouble,
Bar 4:22 soon will come to you from your everlasting S
Hos 13:4 but me, and besides me there is no S
1Mac 4:30 "Blessed art thou, O S of Israel, who didst
9:21 the mighty fallen, the S of Israel!"
2Mac 3:35 great vows to the S of his life, and
Lk 1:47 rejoices in God my S,
2:11 city of David a S, who is Christ the
Jn 4:42 this is indeed the S of the world."
Acts 5:31 hand as Leader and S, to give repentance to
13:23 brought to Israel a S, Jesus, as he promised.
Eph 5:23 the church, his body, and is himself its S
Phil 3:20 it we await a S, the Lord Jesus Christ,
1Tim 1:1 command of God our S and of Christ Jesus
2:3 sight of God our S,
4:10 God, who is the S of all men, especially
2Tim 1:10 the appearing of our S Christ Jesus, who abolished
Tit 1:3 command of God our S; To Titus, my true
1:3 from God the Father and Christ Jesus our S
2:10 they may adorn the doctrine of God our S
2:13 our great God and S Jesus Christ,
3:4 kindness of God our S appeared,
3:6 through Jesus Christ our S,
2Pet 1:1 of our God and S Jesus Christ:
1:11 of our Lord and S Jesus Christ.
2:20 of our Lord and S Jesus Christ, they are
3:2 of the Lord and S through your apostles.
3:18 of our Lord and S Jesus Christ.
1Jn 4:14 his Son as the S of the world.
Jude 1:25 the only God, our S through Jesus Christ our

SAVIORS (2)

Neh 9:27 thou didst give them S who saved them from
Obad 1:21 S shall go up to Mount Zion to rule

SAVORY (6)

Gen 27:4 and prepare for me S food, such as I
27:7 and prepare for me S food, that I may
27:9 may prepare from them S food for your father,
27:14 and his mother prepared S food, such as his
27:17 and she gave the S food and the bread,
27:31 He also prepared S food, and brought it to

SAWED

1Kgs 7:9 hewn according to measure, S with saws, back and

SAWN

Heb 11:37 were stoned, they were S in two, they were

SAWS (3)

2Sam 12:31 them to labor with S and iron picks and
1Kgs 7:9 to measure, sawed with S, back and front, even
1Chr 20:3 them to labor with S and iron picks and

SAYEST (2)

Ex 33:12 the LORD, "See, thou S to me, 'Bring up
Ps 90:3 to the dust, and S, "Turn back, O children

SAYINGS (18)

2Chr 13:22 his ways and his S, are written in the
Job 32:11 listened for your wise S, while you searched out
Ps 78:2 I will utter dark S from of old,
Prov 4:21 to my words; incline your ear to my S
22:20 written for you thirty S of admonition and
24:23 These also are S of the wise.
Eccl 12:11 The S of the wise are like goads, and
12:11 fixed are the collected S which are given by
Sir 1:22 of wisdom are wise S, but godliness is an
18:28 who understand S become skilled themselves, and
Mt 7:28 Jesus finished these S, the crowds were astonished
19:1 Jesus had finished these S, he went away from
26:1 had finished all these S, he said to his
Lk 7:1 had ended all his S in the hearing of
9:28 eight days after these S he took with him
Jn 10:21 "These are not the S of one who has
12:47 any one hears my S and does not keep
12:48 does not receive my S has a judge; the

SCAB

Is 3:17 will smite with a S the heads of the

SCABBARD

Jer 47:6 Put yourself into your S, rest and be still!

SCABS (2)

Lev 21:20 an itching disease or S or crushed testicles;
22:22 or an itch or S, you shall not offer

SCALE (5)

1Kgs 22:34 of Israel between the S armor and the breastplate;
2Chr 18:33 of Israel between the S armor and the breastplate;
Tob 3:17 two of them: to S away the white films
Sir 1:19 man's anger tips the S to his ruin.
Joel 2:7 charge, like soldiers they S the wall.

SCALED

Tob 11:13 and the white films S off from the corners

SCALES (21)

Lev 11:9 that has fins and S, whether in the seas
11:10 has not fins and S, of the swarming creatures
11:12 has not fins and S is an abomination to
Deut 14:9 whatever has fins and S you may eat.
14:10 not have fins and S you shall not eat;
Prov 16:11 A just balance and S are the LORDs; all
20:23 the LORD, and false S are not good.
21:22 A wise man S the city of the mighty
Wis 11:22 speck that tips the S, and like a drop
Sir 6:15 faithful friend, and no S can measure his excellence.
28:25 gold, make balances and S for your words, and
42:4 friends; of accuracy with S and weights, and of
Is 40:12 weighed the mountains in S and the hills in
40:15 the dust on the S; behold, he takes up
46:6 out silver in the S, hire a goldsmith, and
Jer 32:10 it, got witnesses, and weighed the money on S
Ezek 29:4 streams stick to your S; and I will draw
29:4 fish of your streams which stick to your S

S

Mic 6:11 the man with wicked S and with a bag
Acts 9:18 And immediately something like S fell from his eyes
Rev 9:9 lions' teeth; they had S like iron breastplates, and

SCALP

2Mac 7:4 out and that they S him and cut off

SCANT (4)

1Kgs 22:27 and feed him with S fare of bread and
2Chr 18:26 and feed him with S fare of bread and
Mic 6:10 the wicked, and the S measure that is accursed?
1Mac 6:57 our food supply is S, the place against which

SCAR (2)

Lev 13:23 spread, it is the S of the boil; and
13:28 for it is the S of the burn.

SCARCELY (7)

Gen 27:30 Jacob, when Jacob had S gone out from the
Song 3:4 S had I passed them, when I found him
Is 40:24 S are they planted, scarcely sown, scarcely has their
40:24 Scarcely are they planted, S sown, scarcely has their
40:24 they planted, scarcely sown, S has their stem taken
Acts 14:18 With these words they S restrained the people from
1Pet 4:18 the righteous man is S saved, where will the

SCARCITY

Deut 8:9 will eat bread without S, in which you will

SCARE

Job 7:14 complaint,' then thou dost S me with dreams and

SCARECROW

Bar 6:70 Like a S in a cucumber bed, that guards

SCARECROWS

Jer 10:5 Their idols are like S in a cucumber field,

SCARED

Wis 17:9 disturbing frightened them, yet, S by the passing of

SCARES

Sir 22:18 a stone at birds S them away, and one

SCARFS

Is 3:19 the bracelets, and the S;

SCARLET (50)

Gen 38:28 on his hand a S thread, saying, "This came
38:30 came out with the S thread upon his hand;
Ex 25:4 blue and purple and S stuff and fine twined
26:1 blue and purple and S stuff; with cherubim skilfully
26:31 blue and purple and S stuff and fine twined
26:36 blue and purple and S stuff and fine twined
27:16 blue and purple and S stuff and fine twined
28:5 blue and purple and S stuff, and fine twined
28:6 blue and purple and S stuff, and of fine
28:8 blue and purple and S stuff, and fine twined
28:15 blue and purple and S stuff, and fine twined
28:33 blue and purple and S stuff, around its skirts,
35:6 blue and purple and S stuff and fine twined
35:23 blue or purple or S stuff or fine linen
35:25 blue and purple and S stuff and fine twined
35:35 blue and purple and S stuff and fine twined
36:8 blue and purple and S stuff, with cherubim skilfully
36:35 blue and purple and S stuff and fine twined
36:37 blue and purple and S stuff and fine twined
38:18 blue and purple and S stuff and fine twined
38:23 blue and purple and S stuff and fine twined
39:1 blue and purple and S stuff they made finely
39:2 blue and purple and S stuff, and fine twined
39:3 and purple and the S stuff, and into the
39:5 blue and purple and S stuff, and fine twined
39:8 blue and purple and S stuff, and fine twined
39:24 blue and purple and S stuff and fine twined
39:29 purple and S stuff, embroidered with needlework;
Lev 14:4 birds and cedarwood and S stuff and hyssop;
14:6 the cedarwood and the S stuff and the hyssop,
14:49 birds, with cedarwood and S stuff and hyssop,
14:51 the hyssop and the S stuff, along with the
14:52 cedarwood and hyssop and S stuff;
Num 4:8 them a cloth of S, and cover the same
19:6 cedarwood and hyssop and S stuff, and cast them
Josh 2:18 you shall bind this S cord in the window
2:21 and she bound the S cord in the window.
2Sam 1:24 clothed you daintily in S, who put ornaments of
Prov 31:21 household, for all her household are clothed in S
Song 4:3 lips are like a S thread, and your mouth
Sir 45:11 and Thummim; with twisted S, the work of a
Is 1:18 your sins are like S, they shall be as
Jer 4:30 that you dress in S, that you deck yourself
Nah 2:3 men is red, his soldiers are clothed in S
Mt 27:28 him and put a S robe upon him,
Heb 9:19 goats, with water and S wool and hyssop, and
Rev 17:3 woman sitting on a S beast which was full
17:4 arrayed in purple and S, and bedecked with gold
18:12 linen, purple, silk and S, all kinds of scented
18:16 linen, in purple and S, bedecked with gold, with

SCATTER (42)

Gen 49:7 them in Jacob and S them in Israel.
Lev 26:33 And I will S you among the nations, and
Num 16:37 of the blaze; then S the fire far and
Deut 4:27 And the LORD will S you among the peoples,
28:64 And the LORD will S you among all peoples,
32:26 have said, "I will S them afar, I will
1Kgs 14:15 to their fathers, and S them beyond the Euphrates,
Neh 1:8 are unfaithful, I will S you among the peoples;
Job 37:11 with moisture; the clouds S his lightning.
Ps 53:5 For God will S the bones of the ungodly;
68:30 who lust after tribute; S the peoples who delight
89:10 a carcass, thou didst S thy enemies with thy
144:6 forth the lightning and S them, send out thy
Sir 39:14 S the fragrance, and sing a hymn of praise;
Is 24:1 twist its surface and S its inhabitants.
28:25 surface, does he not S dill, sow cummin, and
30:22 You will S them as unclean things; you will
41:16 and the tempest shall S them.
Jer 9:16 I will S them among the nations whom neither
13:24 I will S you like chaff driven by the
18:17 east wind I will S them before the enemy.
23:1 shepherds who destroy and S the sheep of my
49:32 I will S to every wind those who cut
49:36 heaven; and I will S them to all those
Bar 2:29 nations, where I will S them.
Ezek 5:2 third part you shall S to the wind, and
5:10 who survive I will S to all the winds.
5:12 third part I will S to all the winds
6:5 idols; and I will S your bones round about
10:2 between the cherubim, and S them over the city."
12:14 And I will S toward every wind all who
12:15 among the nations and S them through the countries.
20:23 wilderness that I would S them among the nations
22:15 I will S you among the nations and disperse
29:12 I will S the Egyptians among the nations, and
30:23 I will S the Egyptians among the nations, and
30:26 Egypt; and I will S the Egyptians among the
Dan 4:14 off its leaves and S its fruit; let the
Hab 3:14 like a whirlwind to S me, rejoicing as if
Zech 1:21 land of Judah to S it."
2Mac 14:13 to kill Judas and S his men, and to
Mk 4:26 if a man should S seed upon the ground,

SCATTERED (81)

Gen 11:4 ourselves, lest we be S abroad upon the face
11:8 So the LORD S them abroad from there over
11:9 from there the LORD S them abroad over the
Ex 5:12 So the people were S abroad throughout all the
32:20 it to powder, and S it upon the water,
Num 10:35 let thy enemies be S; and let them that
Deut 30:3 LORD your God has S you.
1Sam 11:11 those who survived were S, so that no two
2Sam 17:19 the well's mouth, and S grain upon it; and
22:15 sent out arrows, and S them; lightning, and routed
1Kgs 22:17 "I saw all Israel S upon the mountains, as
2Kgs 25:5 all his army was S from him.
2Chr 18:16 "I saw all Israel S upon the mountains, as
Tob 13:3 Israel; for he has S us among them.
13:5 all the nations among whom you have been S
14:4 Our brethren will be S over the earth from
Jud 5:19 to which they were S, and have occupied Jerusalem,
Esth 3:8 is a certain people S abroad and dispersed among
13:4 the world there is S a certain hostile people,
Job 4:11 prey, and the whelps of the lioness are S
18:15 of his; brimstone is S upon his habitation.
38:24 the east wind is S upon the earth?
Ps 18:14 out his arrows, and S them; he flashed forth
44:11 for slaughter, and hast S us among the nations.
68:1 let his enemies be S; let those who hate
68:14 When the Almighty S kings there, snow fell on
92:9 thy enemies shall perish; all evildoers shall be S
Prov 5:16 Should your springs be S abroad, streams of water

S

SCOFFING (6)
2Chr 36:16 despising his words, and S at his prophets, till
Job 34:7 Job, who drinks up S like water,
36:18 wrath entice you into S; and let not the
Prov 1:22 scoffers delight in their S and fools hate knowledge?
Hab 2:6 taunt against him, in S derision of him, and
2Pet 3:3 the last days with S, following their own passions

SCOFFS
Ps 74:18 LORD, how the enemy S, and an impious people

SCOLDING
Sir 29:28 man who has feeling: S about lodging and the

SCORCH
Rev 16:8 it was allowed to S men with fire;

SCORCHED (7)
Prov 6:28 upon hot coals and his feet not be S
Song 1:6 because the sun has S me.
Is 24:6 of the earth are S, and few men are
Ezek 20:47 to north shall be S by it.
Mt 13:6 sun rose they were S; and since they had
Mk 4:6 sun rose it was S, and since it had
Rev 16:9 with fire; men were S by the fierce heat,

SCORCHING (9)
Ps 11:6 fire and brimstone; a S wind shall be the
Prov 16:27 speech is like a S fire.
Sir 18:15 the dew assuage the S heat?
Is 11:15 the River with his S wind, and smite it
49:10 hunger or thirst, neither S wind nor sun shall
Mt 20:12 the day and the S heat.'
Lk 12:55 say, 'There will be S heat'; and it happens.
Jas 1:10 sun rises with its S heat and withers the
Rev 7:16 strike them, nor any S heat.

SCORN (18)
2Chr 30:10 they laughed them to S, and mocked them.
Job 16:20 My friends S me; my eye pours out tears
22:19 innocent laugh them to S,
Ps 31:11 I am the S of all my adversaries, a
39:8 Make me not the S of the fool!
44:13 neighbors, the derision and S of those about us.
71:13 shame and consumed; with S and disgrace may they
80:6 dost make us the S of our neighbors; and
89:41 he has become the S of his neighbors.
109:25 am an object of S to my accusers; when
119:22 away from me their S and contempt, for I
123:4 been sated with the S of those who are
Wis 4:18 him, but the Lord will laugh them to S
Jer 6:10 them an object of S, they take no pleasure
Mic 6:16 you shall bear the S of the peoples."
1Mac 3:14 and his companions, who S the king's command."
2Mac 7:39 worse than the others, being exasperated at his S
Gal 4:14 you, you did not S or despise me, but

SCORNED (6)
2Sam 12:14 deed you have utterly S the LORD, the child
Ps 22:6 worm, and no man; S by men, and despised
89:50 how thy servant is S; how I bear in
Song 8:7 wealth of his house, it would be utterly S
Lam 2:7 The Lord has S his altar, disowned his sanctuary;
Ezek 16:31 a harlot, because you S hire.

SCORNERS
Prov 3:34 Toward the S he is scornful, but to the

SCORNFUL
Prov 3:34 the scorners he is S, but to the humble

SCORNFULLY
Wis 17:7 their boasted wisdom was S rebuked.

SCORNS (5)
2Kgs 19:21 "She despises you, she S you--the virgin daughter
Job 39:7 He S the tumult of the city; he hears
Prov 14:9 God S the wicked, but the upright enjoy his
30:17 mocks a father and S to obey a mother
Is 37:22 'She despises you, she S you-- the virgin

SCORPION (3)
Sir 26:7 taking hold of her is like grasping a S
Lk 11:12 asks for an egg, will give him a S
Rev 9:5 the torture of a S, when it stings a

SCORPIONS (10)
Deut 8:15 its fiery serpents and S and thirsty ground where
1Kgs 12:11 with whips, but I will chastise you with S
12:14 with whips, but I will chastise you with S
2Chr 10:11 with whips, but I will chastise you with S
10:14 with whips, but I will chastise you with S
Sir 39:30 of wild beasts, and S and vipers, and the
Ezek 2:6 and you sit upon S; be not afraid of
Lk 10:19 tread upon serpents and S, and over all the
Rev 9:3 like the power of S of the earth;
9:10 They have tails like S, and stings, and their

SCOUNDREL (2)
Sir 11:31 Beware of a S, for he devises evil, lest
2Mac 13:4 Antiochus against the S; and when Lysias informed

SCOUNDRELS
2Chr 13:7 lord; and certain worthless S gathered about him

SCOURED
Lev 6:28 vessel, that shall be S, and rinsed in water.

SCOURGE (13)
Josh 23:13 trap for you, a S on your sides, and
Job 5:21 be hid from the S of the tongue, and
Ps 91:10 shall befall you, no S come near your tent.
Sir 23:11 with iniquity, and the S will not leave his
39:28 in their anger they S heavily; in the time
Is 10:26 wield against them a S, as when he smote
28:15 when the overwhelming S passes through it will
28:18 stand; when the overwhelming S passes through you
2Mac 9:11 his senses under the S of God, for he
Mt 23:33 and some you will S in your synagogues and
Mk 10:34 spit upon him, and S him, and kill him;
Lk 18:33 spit upon; they will S him and kill him,
Acts 22:25 lawful for you to S a man who is

SCOURGED (9)
Wis 16:16 to know thee, were S by the strength of
2Mac 3:26 side of him and S him continuously, inflicting many
3:34 you, who have been S by heaven, report to
3:38 get him back thoroughly S, if he escapes at
5:18 man would have been S and turned back from
Mt 20:19 to be mocked and S and crucified, and he
27:26 them Barabbas, and having S Jesus, delivered him to
Mk 15:15 them Barabbas; and having S Jesus, he delivered
Jn 19:1 Pilate took Jesus and S him.

SCOURGES (2)
Jud 8:27 us; but the Lord S those who draw near
Ps 89:32 and their iniquity with S;

SCOURGEST
Wis 12:22 while chastening us thou S our enemies ten thousand

SCOURGING (2)
Acts 22:24 to be examined by S, to find out why
Heb 11:36 Others suffered mocking and S, and even chains and

SCOUTS
1Kgs 20:17 And Ben-hadad sent out S, and they reported to

SCRAPE (3)
Lev 14:41 the plaster that they S off they shall pour
Job 2:8 potsherd with which to S himself, and sat among
Ezek 26:4 towers; and I will S her soil from her,

SCRAPED (3)
Lev 14:41 the house to be S round about, and the
14:43 out the stones and S the house and plastered
Judg 14:9 He S it out into his hands, and went

SCRAPES
Prov 6:13 winks with his eyes, S with his feet, points

SCRAPS
Judg 1:7 used to pick up S under my table; as

SCREEN (17)
Ex 26:36 you shall make a S for the door of
26:37 shall make for the S five pillars of acacia,
27:16 there shall be a S twenty cubits long, of
35:12 the veil of the S;
35:15 fragrant incense, and the S for the door, at
35:17 its bases, and the S for the gate of
36:37 He also made a S for the door of

38:18 And the S for the gate of the court
39:34 the veil of the S;
39:38 fragrant incense, and the S for the door of
39:40 its bases, and the S for the gate of
Num 3:25 with its covering, the S for the door of
3:26 of the court, the S for the door of
3:31 priests minister, and the S; all the service pertaining
4:5 the veil of the S, and cover the ark
4:25 of it, and the S for the door of
4:26 the court, and the S for the entrance of

SCRIBE (25)

1Chr 24:6 And the S Shemaiah the son of Nethanel, a
27:32 of understanding and a S; he and Jehiel the
Ezra 4:8 commander and Shimshai the S wrote a letter
4:9 the commander, Shimshai the S, and the rest of
4:17 commander and Shimshai the S and the rest of
4:23 Rehum and Shimshai the S and their associates, they
7:6 He was a S skilled in the law of
7:11 Ezra the priest, the S, learned in matters of
7:12 Ezra the priest, the S of the law of
7:21 Ezra the priest, the S of the law of
Neh 8:1 they told Ezra the S to bring the book
8:4 And Ezra the S stood on a wooden pulpit
8:9 Ezra the priest and S, and the Levites who
8:13 together to Ezra the S in order to study
12:26 the governor and of Ezra the priest the S
12:36 God; and Ezra the S went before them.
13:13 the priest, Zadok the S, and Pedaiah of the
Ps 45:1 tongue is like the pen of a ready S
Sir 10:5 confers his honor upon the person of the S
38:24 The wisdom of the S depends on the opportunity
Jer 36:32 it to Baruch the S, the son of Neriah,
Mt 8:19 And a S came up and said to him,
13:52 to them, "Therefore every S who has been trained
Mk 12:32 And the S said to him, "You are right,
1Cor 1:20 Where is the S

SCRIBES (65)

1Chr 2:55 families also of the S that dwelt at Jabez:
2Chr 34:13 of the Levites were S, and officials, and gatekeepers.
Jer 8:8 false pen of the S has made it into
Nah 3:17 are like grasshoppers, your S like clouds of locusts
1Mac 5:42 water, he stationed the S of the people at
7:12 Then a group of S appeared in a body
2Mac 6:18 Eleazar, one of the S in high position, a
Mt 2:4 the chief priests and S of the people, he
5:20 exceeds that of the S and Pharisees, you will
7:29 one who had authority, and not as their S
9:3 behold, some of the S said to themselves, "This
12:38 Then some of the S and Pharisees said to
15:1 Pharisees and S came to Jesus from Jerusalem
16:21 and chief priests and S, and be killed, and
17:10 "Then why do the S say that first Elijah
20:18 the chief priests and S, and they will condemn
21:15 chief priests and the S saw the wonderful things
23:2 to his disciples, "The S and the Pharisees sit
23:13 "But woe to you, S and Pharisees, hypocrites!
23:14 Woe to you, S and Pharisees, hypocrites!
23:22 "Woe to you, S and Pharisees, hypocrites!
23:24 "Woe to you, S and Pharisees, hypocrites!
23:26 "Woe to you, S and Pharisees, hypocrites!
23:28 "Woe to you, S and Pharisees, hypocrites!
23:33 and wise men and S, some of whom you
26:57 high priest, where the S and the elders had
27:41 chief priests, with the S and elders, mocked him,
Mk 1:22 one who had authority, and not as the S
2:6 Now some of the S were sitting there, questioning
2:16 And the S of the Pharisees, when they saw
3:22 And the S who came down from Jerusalem said,
7:1 with some of the S, who had come from
7:5 the Pharisees and the S asked him, "Why do
8:31 chief priests and the S, and be killed, and
9:11 him, "Why do the S say that first Elijah
9:14 crowd about them, and S arguing with them.
10:33 chief priests and the S, and they will condemn
11:18 chief priests and the S heard it and sought
11:26 chief priests and the S and the elders came
12:28 And one of the S came up and heard
12:35 said, "How can the S say that the Christ
12:38 said, "Beware of the S, who like to go
14:1 chief priests and the S were seeking how to
14:43 chief priests and the S and the elders.
14:53 the elders and the S were assembled.
15:1 with the elders and S, and the whole council
15:30 one another with the S, saying, "He saved others;
Lk 5:21 And the S and the Pharisees began to question,
5:30 the Pharisees and their S murmured against his
6:7 And the S and the Pharisees watched him, to
9:22 and chief priests and S, and be killed, and
11:53 away from there, the S and the Pharisees began
15:2 Pharisees and the S murmured, saying, "This man
19:47 chief priests and the S and the principal men
20:1 chief priests and the S with the elders came
20:19 The S and the chief priests tried to lay
20:39 And some of the S answered, "Teacher, you have
20:46 disciples, "Beware of the S, who like to go
22:2 chief priests and the S were seeking how to
22:64 both chief priests and S; and they led him
23:10 chief priests and the S stood by, vehemently accusing
Jn 8:3 The S and the Pharisees brought a woman who
Acts 4:5 rulers and elders and S were gathered together in
6:12 the elders and the S, and they came upon
23:9 and some of the S of the Pharisees' party

SCRIPT (4)

Esth 1:22 province in its own S and to every people
3:12 province in its own S and every people in
8:9 province in its own S and to every people
8:9 the Jews in their S and their language.

SCRIPTURE (32)

Mk 12:10 you not read this S: 'The very stone which
Lk 4:21 to them, "Today this S has been fulfilled in
22:37 tell you that this S must be fulfilled in
Jn 2:22 and they believed the S and the word which
7:38 in me, as the S has said, 'Out of
7:42 Has not the S said that the Christ is
10:35 of God came (and S cannot be broken),
13:18 it is that the S may be fulfilled, 'He
17:12 of perdition, that the S might be fulfilled.
19:24 was to fulfill the S, "They parted my garments
19:28 said (to fulfill the S, "I thirst."
19:36 took place that the S might be fulfilled, "Not
19:37 And again another S says, "They shall look on
20:9 did not know the S, that he must rise
Acts 1:16 and said, "Brethren, the S had to be fulfilled,
8:32 the passage of the S which he was reading
8:35 and beginning with this S he told him the
Rom 4:3 For what does the S say?
9:17 For the S says to Pharaoh, "I have raised
10:11 The S says, "No one who believes in him
11:2 not know what the S says of Elijah, how
Gal 3:8 And the S, foreseeing that God would justify the
3:22 But the S consigned all things to sin, that
4:30 But what does the S say?
1Tim 4:13 the public reading of S, to preaching, to teaching.
5:18 and teaching; for the S says, "You shall not
2Tim 3:16 All S is inspired by God and profitable for
Jas 2:8 law, according to the S, "You shall love your
2:23 by works, and the S was fulfilled which says,
4:5 in vain that the S says, "He yearns jealously
1Pet 2:6 For it stands in S: "Behold, I am laying
2Pet 1:20 that no prophecy of S is a matter of

SCRIPTURES (19)

Mt 21:42 never read in the S: 'The very stone which
22:29 you know neither the S nor the power of
26:54 how then should the S be fulfilled, that it
26:56 taken place, that the S of the prophets might
Mk 12:24 you know neither the S nor the power of
14:49 But let the S be fulfilled."
Lk 24:27 them in all the S the things concerning himself.
24:32 the road, while he opened to us the S
24:45 minds to understand the S,
Jn 5:38 You search the S, because you think that in
Acts 17:2 with them from the S,
17:11 all eagerness, examining the S daily to see if
18:24 was an eloquent man, well versed in the S
18:28 public, showing by the S that the Christ was
Rom 1:2 prophets in the holy S,
15:4 the encouragement of the S we might have hope.
1Cor 15:3 in accordance with the S,
15:4 in accordance with the S,
2Pet 3:16 their own destruction, as they do the other S

SCROLL (42)

Ezra 6:2 province of Media, a S was found on which
Tob 7:14 Edna, and took a S and wrote out the
Is 34:4 away, and the skies roll up like a S
Jer 36:2 the LORD: "Take a S and write on it
36:4 Baruch wrote upon a S at the dictation of

36:6 the LORD from the S which you have written
36:8 about reading from the S the words of the
36:10 of Jeremiah from the S, in the house of
36:11 the LORD from the S,
36:13 when Baruch read the S in the hearing of
36:14 in your hand the S that you read in
36:14 of Neriah took the S in his hand and
36:18 while I wrote them with ink on the S
36:20 king, having put the S in the chamber of
36:21 Jehudi to get the S, and he took it
36:23 brazier, until the entire S was consumed in the
36:25 not to burn the S, he would not listen
36:27 king had burned the S with the words which
36:28 to Jeremiah: "Take another S and write on it
36:28 were in the first S, which Jehoiakim the king
36:29 You have burned this S, saying, "Why have you
36:32 Then Jeremiah took another S and gave it to
36:32 the words of the S which Jehoiakim king of
Ezek 2:9 and, lo, a written S was in it;
3:1 to you; eat this S, and go, speak to
3:2 he gave me the S to eat.
3:3 of man, eat this S that I give you
Zech 5:1 my eyes and saw, and behold, a flying S
5:2 "I see a flying S; its length is twenty
Rev 5:1 on the throne a S written within and on
5:2 worthy to open the S and break its seals?"
5:3 able to open the S or to look into
5:4 worthy to open the S or to into into
5:5 he can open the S and its seven seals."
5:7 went and took the S from the right hand
5:8 he had taken the S, the four living creatures
5:9 thou to take the S and to open its
6:14 sky vanished like a S that is rolled up,
10:2 He had a little S open in his hand.
10:8 saying, "Go, take the S which is open in
10:9 give me the little S; and he said to
10:10 I took the little S from the hand of

SCRUPLES

1Cor 10:29 should my liberty be determined by another man's S

SCRUPULOUS

Sir 19:22 a cleverness which is S but unjust, and there

SCULPTURED (2)

Judg 3:19 turned back at the S stones near Gilgal, and
3:26 and passed beyond the S stones, and escaped to

SCURVY

Deut 28:27 the ulcers and the S and the itch, of

SCYTHES

2Mac 13:2 elephants, and three hundred chariots armed with S

SCYTHIAN

Col 3:11 circumcised and uncircumcised, barbarian, S, slave,

SCYTHIANS

2Mac 4:47 uncondemned if they had pleaded even before S

SCYTHOPOLIS (3)

Jud 3:10 camped between Geba and S, and remained for a
2Mac 12:29 there, they hastened to S, which is seventy-five miles
12:30 which the people of S had shown them and

SE-IRAH

Judg 3:26 beyond the sculptured stones, and escaped to S

SE-ORIM

1Chr 24:8 Harim, the fourth to S,

SEA (427)

Gen 1:21 God created the great S monsters and every living
1:26 the fish of the S, and over the birds
1:28 the fish of the S and over the birds
9:2 the fish of the S; into your hand they
14:3 the Valley of Siddim (that is, the Salt S
32:12 the sand of the S, which cannot be numbered
41:49 the sand of the S, until he ceased to
49:13 the shore of the S; he shall become a
Ex 10:19 them into the Red S; not a single locust
13:18 the way of the wilderness toward the Red S
14:2 between Migdol and the S, in front of Baal-zephon;
14:2 you shall encamp over against it, by the S
14:9 them encamped at the S, by Pi-ha-hiroth, in front
14:16 your hand over the S and divide it, that
14:16 Israel may go on dry ground through the S
14:21 his hand over the S; and the LORD drove
14:21 the LORD drove the S back by a strong
14:21 night, and made the S dry land, and the
14:22 the midst of the S on dry ground, the
14:23 the midst of the S, all Pharaoh's horses, his
14:26 your hand over the S, that the water may
14:27 his hand over the S, and the sea returned
14:27 the sea, and the S returned to its wonted
14:27 routed the Egyptians in the midst of the S
14:28 followed them into the S; not so much as
14:29 dry ground through the S, the waters being a
15:1 and his rider he has thrown into the S
15:4 he cast into the S; and his picked officers
15:4 his picked officers are sunk in the Red S
15:8 the deeps congealed in the heart of the S
15:10 with thy wind, the S covered them; they sank
15:19 horsemen went into the S, the LORD brought back
15:19 the waters of the S upon them; but the
15:19 on dry ground in the midst of the S
15:21 and his rider he has thrown into the S
15:22 onward from the Red S, and they went into
20:11 heaven and earth, the S, and all that is
23:31 bounds from the Red S to the sea of
23:31 Red Sea to the S of the Philistines, and
Lev 11:16 the nighthawk, the S gull, the hawk according
Num 11:22 the fish of the S be gathered together for
11:31 brought quails from the S, and let them fall
13:29 Canaanites dwell by the S, and along the Jordan."
14:25 the wilderness by the way to the Red S
21:4 way to the Red S, to go around the
33:8 the midst of the S into the wilderness, and
33:10 out from Elim, and encamped by the Red S
33:11 out from the Red S, and encamped in the
34:3 end of the Salt S on the east;
34:5 Egypt, and its termination shall be at the S
34:6 shall have the Great S and its coast; this
34:7 boundary: from the Great S you shall mark out
34:11 the shoulder of the S of Chinnereth on the
34:12 and its end shall be at the Salt S
Deut 1:40 direction of the Red S
2:1 direction of the Red S, as the LORD told
3:17 as far as the S of the Arabah, the
3:17 the Arabah, the Salt S, under the slopes of
4:49 as far as the S of the Arabah, under
11:4 water of the Red S overflow them as they
11:24 the River, the river Euphrates, to the western S
14:15 ostrich, the nighthawk, the S gull, the hawk, after
30:13 is it beyond the S, that you should say,
30:13 will go over the S for us, and bring
34:2 far as the Western S,
Josh 1:4 Hittites to the Great S toward the going down
2:10 water of the Red S before you when you
3:16 flowing down toward the S of the Arabah, the
3:16 the Arabah, the Salt S, were wholly cut off;
4:23 did to the Red S, which he dried up
5:1 that were by the S, heard that the LORD
9:1 coast of the Great S toward Lebanon, the Hittites,
12:3 the Arabah to the S of Chinneroth eastward, and
12:3 of Beth-jeshimoth, to the S of the Arabah, the
12:3 the Arabah, the Salt S, southward to the foot
13:27 lower end of the S of Chinnereth, eastward beyond
15:2 end of the Salt S, from the bay that
15:4 Egypt, and comes to its end at the S
15:5 boundary is the Salt S, to the mouth of
15:5 the bay of the S at the mouth of
15:11 the boundary comes to an end at the S
15:12 boundary was the Great S with its coast-line.
15:46 from Ekron to the S, all that were by
15:47 Egypt, and the Great S with its coast-line.
16:3 then to Gezer, and it ends at the S
16:6 goes thence to the S; on the north is
16:8 to the brook Kanah, and ends at the S
17:9 and ends at the S;
17:10 being Manassehs, with the S forming its boundary;
18:19 bay of the Salt S, at the south end
19:29 it ends at the S; Mahalab, Achzib,
23:4 Jordan to the Great S in the west.
24:6 you came to the S; and the Egyptians pursued
24:6 fathers with chariots and horsemen to the Red S
24:7 Egyptians, and made the S come upon them and
Judg 5:17 the coast of the S, settling down by his
11:16 wilderness to the Red S and came to Kadesh.
2Sam 17:11 the sand by the S for multitude, and that
22:16 the channels of the S were seen, the foundations
1Kgs 4:20 the sand by the S; they ate and drank

S

5:9 it down to the S from Lebanon; and I
5:9 rafts to go by S to the place you
7:23 he made the molten S; it was round, ten
7:24 cubits, compassing the S round about; the gourds
7:25 three facing east; the S was set upon them,
7:39 and he set the S on the southeast corner
7:44 stands; and the one S, and the twelve oxen
7:44 one sea, and the twelve oxen underneath the S
9:26 shore of the Red S, in the land of
9:27 were familiar with the S, together with the servants
10:22 ships of Tarshish at S with the fleet of
18:43 his servant, "Go up now, look toward the S
18:44 a man's hand is rising out of the S
2Kgs 14:25 as far as the S of the Arabah, according
16:17 he took down the S from off the bronze
25:13 stands and the bronze S that were in the
25:16 two pillars, the one S, and the stands, which
1Chr 16:32 Let the S roar, and all that fills it,
18:8 Solomon made the bronze S and the pillars and
2Chr 2:16 you in rafts by S to Joppa, so that
4:2 he made the molten S; it was round, ten
4:3 thirty cubits, compassing the S round about; the
4:4 three facing east; the S was set upon them,
4:6 burnt offering, and the S was for the priests
4:10 and he set the S at the southeast corner
4:15 stands, and the one S, and the twelve oxen
8:17 the shore of the S, in the land of
8:18 servants familiar with the S, and they went to
20:2 Edom, from beyond the S; and, behold, they are
Ezra 3:7 from Lebanon to the S, to Joppa, according to
Neh 9:9 cry at the Red S,
9:11 thou didst divide the S before them, so that
9:11 the midst of the S on dry land; and
Jud 2:24 along the brook Abron, as far as the S
5:13 dried up the Red S before them,
Esth 10:1 the land and on the coastlands of the S
Job 6:3 the sand of the S; therefore my words have
7:12 Am I the S, or a sea monster, that
7:12 the sea, or a S monster, that thou settest
9:8 the waves of the S;
11:9 longer than the earth, and broader than the S
12:8 the fish of the S will declare to you.
26:12 power he stilled the S; by his understanding he
28:14 in me,' and the S says, 'It is not
36:30 about him, and covers the roots of the S
38:8 who shut in the S with doors, when it
38:16 the springs of the S, or walked in the
41:31 pot; he makes the S like a pot of
Ps 8:8 the fish of the S, whatever passes along the
8:8 sea, whatever passes along the paths of the S
18:15 the channels of the S were seen, and the
33:7 the waters of the S as in a bottle;
46:2 the heart of the S;
66:6 He turned the S into dry land; men passed
68:22 the depths of the S,
72:8 he have dominion from S to sea, and from
72:8 dominion from sea to S, and from the River
74:13 Thou didst divide the S by thy might; thou
77:19 way was through the S, thy path through the
78:13 He divided the S and let them pass through
78:53 not afraid; but the S overwhelmed their enemies.
80:11 its branches to the S, and its shoots to
89:9 the raging of the S; when its waves rise,
89:25 his hand on the S and his right hand
93:4 the waves of the S, the LORD on high
95:5 The S is his, for he made it; for
96:11 earth rejoice; let the S roar, and all that
98:7 Let the S roar, and all that fills it;
104:25 Yonder is the S, great and wide, which teems
106:7 rebelled against the Most High at the Red S
106:9 He rebuked the Red S, and it became dry;
106:22 of Ham, and terrible things by the Red S
107:23 went down to the S in ships, doing business
107:25 wind, which lifted up the waves of the S
107:29 the waves of the S were hushed.
114:3 The S looked and fled, Jordan turned back.
114:5 What ails you, O S, that you flee?
136:13 who divided the Red S in sunder, for his
136:15 host in the Red S, for his steadfast love
139:9 uttermost parts of the S,
146:6 heaven and earth, the S, and all that is
148:7 from the earth, you S monsters and all deeps,
Prov 8:29 he assigned to the S its limit, so that
23:34 the midst of the S, like one who lies
Eccl 1:7 streams run to the S, but the sea is
1:7 the sea, but the S is not full; to

S

Wis 5:22 the water of the S will rage against them,
10:18 them over the Red S, and led them through
10:19 cast them up from the depth of the S
14:3 a path in the S, and a safe way
14:4 a man lacks skill, he may put to S
19:7 out of the Red S, and a grassy plain
19:12 give them relief, quails came up from the S
Sir 1:2 The sand of the S, the drops of rain,
18:9 of water from the S and a grain of
24:6 the waves of the S, in the whole earth,
24:27 more abundant than the S, and her counsel deeper
24:29 became a river, and my river became a S
29:18 a wave of the S; it has driven men
40:11 what is from the waters returns to the S
43:24 Those who sail the S tell of its dangers,
43:25 of living things, and huge creatures of the S
44:22 them to inherit from S to sea and from
44:22 inherit from sea to S and from the River
50:3 a reservoir like the S in circumference.
Is 5:30 on that day, like the roaring of the S
9:1 the way of the S, the land beyond the
10:22 the sand of the S, only a remnant of
10:26 will be over the S, and he will lift
11:9 of the LORD as the waters cover the S
11:11 from Hamath, and from the coastlands of the S
11:15 the tongue of the S of Egypt; and will
16:8 its shoots spread abroad and passed over the S
17:12 peoples, they thunder like the thundering of the S
21:1 The oracle concerning the wilderness of the S
23:2 messengers passed over the S
23:4 O Sidon, for the S has spoken, the stronghold
23:4 the stronghold of the S, saying: "I have neither
23:11 his hand over the S, he has shaken the
24:15 the coastlands of the S, to the name of
27:1 will slay the dragon that is in the S
42:10 Let the S roar and all that fills it,
43:16 a way in the S, a path in the
48:18 the waves of the S;
50:2 I dry up the S, I make the rivers
51:10 didst dry up the S, the waters of the
51:10 the depths of the S a way for the
51:15 who stirs up the S so that its waves
57:20 are like the tossing S; for it cannot rest,
60:5 the abundance of the S shall be turned to
63:11 up out of the S the shepherds of his
Jer 5:22 the bound for the S, a perpetual barrier which
6:23 is like the roaring S; they ride upon horses,
25:22 the coastland across the S;
27:19 concerning the pillars, the S, the stands, and the
31:35 who stirs up the S so that its waves
33:22 the sands of the S cannot be measured, so
46:18 like Carmel by the S, shall one come.
48:32 branches passed over the S, reached as far as
49:21 their cry shall be heard at the Red S
49:23 are troubled like the S which cannot be quiet.
50:42 the roaring of the S; they ride upon horses,
51:36 will dry up her S and make her fountain
51:42 The S has come up on Babylon; she is
52:17 stands and the bronze S that were in the
52:20 two pillars, the one S, the twelve bronze bulls
52:20 which were under the S, and the stands, which
Lam 2:13 For vast as the S is your ruin; who
Bar 3:30 has gone over the S, and found her, and
Ezek 26:3 against you, as the S brings up its waves.
26:5 the midst of the S a place for the
26:16 the princes of the S will step down from
26:17 was mighty on the S, you and your inhabitants,
26:18 that are in the S are dismayed at your
27:3 the entrance to the S, merchant of the peoples
27:9 the ships of the S with their mariners were
27:29 the pilots of the S stand on the shore
27:32 destroyed like Tyre in the midst of the S
38:20 the fish of the S, and the birds of
39:11 Travelers east of the S; it will block the
47:8 stagnant waters of the S, the water will become
47:9 the waters of the S may become fresh; so
47:10 will stand beside the S; from Engedi to En-eglaim
47:10 many kinds, like the fish of the Great S
47:15 side, from the Great S by way of Hethlon
47:17 shall run from the S to Hazar-enon, which is
47:18 Israel; to the eastern S and as far as
47:19 along the Brook of Egypt to the Great S
47:20 west side, the Great S shall be the boundary
48:1 northern border, from the S by way of Hethlon
48:28 along the Brook of Egypt to the Great S
Dan 3:36 as the sand on the shore of the S

7:2 winds of heaven were stirring up the great S
7:3 up out of the S, different from one another.
11:45 palatial tents between the S and the glorious holy
Hos 1:10 the sand of the S, which can be neither
4:3 the fish of the S are taken away.
Joel 2:20 front into the eastern S, and his rear into
2:20 rear into the western S; the stench and foul
Amos 5:8 the waters of the S, and pours them out
6:12 Does one plow the S with oxen?
8:12 They shall wander from S to sea, and from
8:12 wander from sea to S, and from north to
9:3 the bottom of the S, there I will command
9:6 the waters of the S, and pours them out
Jon 1:4 great wind upon the S, and there was a
1:4 mighty tempest on the S, so that the ship
1:5 the ship into the S, to lighten it for
1:9 heaven, who made the S and the dry land."
1:11 to you, that the S may quiet down for
1:11 For the S grew more and more tempestuous.
1:12 throw me into the S; then the sea will
1:12 the sea; then the S will quiet down for
1:13 could not, for the S grew more and more
1:15 threw him into the S; and the sea ceased
1:15 the sea; and the S ceased from its raging.
Mic 7:12 to the River, from S to sea and from
7:12 River, from sea to S and from mountain to
7:19 all our sins into the depths of the S
Nah 1:4 He rebukes the S and makes it dry, he
3:8 her, her rampart a S, and water her wall?
Hab 1:14 the fish of the S, like crawling things that
2:14 of the LORD, as the waters cover the S
3:8 thy indignation against the S, when thou didst ride
3:15 Thou didst trample the S with thy horses, the
Zeph 1:3 of the air and the fish of the S
Hag 2:6 the earth and the S and the dry land;
Zech 9:4 her wealth into the S, and she shall be
9:10 dominion shall be from S to sea, and from
9:10 be from sea to S, and from the River
10:11 shall pass through the S of Egypt, and the
10:11 the waves of the S shall be smitten, and
14:8 them to the eastern S and half of them
14:8 them to the western S; it shall continue in
1Mac 4:9 saved at the Red S, when Pharaoh with his
4:23 cloth dyed blue and S purple, and great riches.
7:1 a city by the S, and there began to
8:23 of the Jews at S and on land for
8:32 and fight you on S and on land.'"
11:8 as Seleucia by the S, and he kept devising
13:29 could be seen by all who sail the S
14:5 opened a way to the isles of the S
14:34 which is by the S, and Gazara, which is
15:1 the islands of the S to Simon, the priest
15:11 which is by the S;
15:14 joined battle from the S; he pressed the city
15:14 hard from land and S, and permitted no one
2Mac 5:21 and walk on the S, because his mind was
9:8 the waves of the S, in his superhuman arrogance,
12:4 took them out to S and drowned them, not
Mt 4:13 in Caperna-um by the S, in the territory of
4:15 of Naphtali, toward the S, across the Jordan, Galilee
4:18 he walked by the S of Galilee, he saw
4:18 a net into the S; for they were fishermen.
8:24 great storm on the S, so that the boat
8:26 the winds and the S; and there was a
8:27 that even winds and S obey him?"
8:32 steep bank into the S, and perished in the
13:1 out of the house and sat beside the S
13:47 was thrown into the S and gathered fish of
14:25 night he came to them, walking on the S
14:26 him walking on the S, they were terrified, saying,
15:29 and passed along the S of Galilee.
17:26 them, go to the S and cast a hook,
18:6 to be drowned in the depth of the S
21:21 and cast into the S it will be done.
23:14 for you traverse S and land to make a
Mk 1:16 passing along by the S of Galilee, he saw
1:16 a net in the S; for they were fishermen.
2:13 out again beside the S; and all the crowd
3:7 his disciples to the S, and a great multitude
4:1 Again he began to teach beside the S
4:1 in it on the S; and the whole crowd
4:1 crowd was beside the S on the land.
4:39 and said to the S, "Peace!
4:41 that even wind and S obey him?"
5:1 other side of the S, to the country of
5:13 steep bank into the S, and were drowned in
5:13 into the sea, and were drowned in the S
5:21 gathered about him; and he was beside the S
6:47 was out on the S, and he was alone
6:48 night he came to them, walking on the S
6:49 him walking on the S they thought it was
7:30 through Sidon to the S of Galilee, through the
9:42 his neck and he were thrown into the S
11:23 and cast into the S and does not doubt
Lk 17:2 were cast into the S, than that he should
17:6 be planted in the S and it would obey
21:25 the roaring of the S and the waves,
Jn 6:1 other side of the S of Galilee, which is
6:1 Galilee, which is the S of Tiberi-as.
6:16 went down to the S,
6:17 and started across the S to Caperna-um.
6:18 The S rose because a strong wind was blowing.
6:19 Jesus walking on the S and drawing near to
6:22 other side of the S saw that there had
6:25 other side of the S, they said to him,
21:1 the disciples by the S of Tiberi-as; and he
21:7 was stripped for work, and sprang into the S
Acts 4:24 the earth and the S and everything in them,
7:36 and at the Red S, and in the wilderness
14:15 the earth and the S and all that is
17:14 his way to the S, but Silas and Timothy
27:2 Asia, we put to S, accompanied by Aristarchus, a
27:4 And putting to S from there we sailed under
27:5 had sailed across the S which is off Cilicia
27:12 advised to put to S from there, on the
27:27 were drifting across the S of Adria, about midnight
27:30 the boat into the S, under pretense of laying
27:38 the ship, throwing out the wheat into the S
27:40 left them in the S, at the same time
28:4 has escaped from the S, justice has not allowed
Rom 9:27 the sand of the S, only a remnant of
1Cor 10:1 all passed through the S,
10:2 cloud and in the S,
2Cor 11:25 have been adrift at S;
11:26 wilderness, danger at S, danger from false brethren;
Heb 11:29 people crossed the Red S as if on dry
Jas 1:6 a wave of the S that is driven and
3:7 bird, of reptile and S creature, can be tamed
Jude 1:13 wild waves of the S, casting up the foam
Rev 4:6 as it were a S of glass, like crystal.
5:13 earth and in the S, and all therein, saying,
7:1 blow on earth or S or against any tree.
7:2 to harm earth and S,
7:3 the earth or the S or the trees, till
8:8 was thrown into the S;
8:9 a third of the S became blood, a third
8:9 living creatures in the S died, and a third
10:2 right foot on the S, and his left foot
10:5 I saw standing on S and land lifted up
10:6 in it, and the S and what is in
10:8 is standing on the S and on the land."
12:12 you, O earth and S, for the devil has
12:17 And he stood on the sand of the S
13:1 rising out of the S, with ten horns and
14:7 heaven and earth, the S and the fountains of
15:2 appeared to be a S of glass mingled with
15:2 name, standing beside the S of glass with harps
16:3 his bowl into the S, and it became like
16:3 every living thing died that was in the S
18:17 trade is on the S, stood far-off
18:19 who had ships at S grew rich by her
18:21 threw it into the S, saying, "So shall Babylon
20:8 their number is like the sand of the S
20:13 And the S gave up the dead in it,
21:1 passed away, and the S was no more.

SEACOAST (11)

Deut 1:7 Negeb, and by the S, the land of the
Jud 1:7 who lived along the S,
2:28 who lived along the S, at Sidon and Tyre,
3:6 went down to the S with his army and
5:22 the men from the S and from Moab insisted
Ezek 25:16 the Cherethites, and destroy the rest of the S
Zeph 2:5 you inhabitants of the S, you nation of the
2:6 And you, O S, shall be pastures, meadows for
2:7 The S shall become the possession of the remnant
2Mac 8:11 the cities on the S, inviting them to buy
Lk 6:17 and Jerusalem and the S of Tyre and Sidon,

SEAFARING

Rev 18:17 And all shipmasters and S men, sailors and all

S

SEAL (33)

1Kgs 21:8 sealed them with his S, and she sent the
Neh 9:38 our priests set their S to it.
10:1 Those who set their S are Nehemiah the governor,
Esth 8:8 of the king, and S it with the king's
Job 38:14 like clay under the S, and it is dyed
41:15 of shields, shut up closely as with a S
Song 8:6 Set me as a S upon your heart, as
8:6 your heart, as a S upon your arm; for
Sir 22:25 my mouth, and a S of prudence upon my
32:5 A ruby S in a setting of gold is
32:6 A S of emerald in a rich setting of
42:6 an evil wife, a S is a good thing;
Is 8:16 Bind up the testimony, S the teaching among my
Dan 8:26 told is true; but S up the vision, for
9:24 righteousness, to S both vision and prophet,
12:4 up the words, and S the book, until the
14:11 shut the door and S it with your signet.
Jn 3:33 his testimony sets his S to this, that God
6:27 on him has God the Father set his S
Rom 4:11 as a sign or S of the righteousness which
1Cor 9:2 for you are the S of my apostleship in
2Cor 1:22 he has put his S upon us and given
2Tim 2:19 foundation stands, bearing this S: "The Lord knows
Rev 6:3 he opened the second S, I heard the second
6:5 he opened the third S, I heard the third
6:7 he opened the fourth S, I heard the voice
6:9 he opened the fifth S, I saw under the
6:12 he opened the sixth S, I looked, and behold,
7:2 the sun, with the S of the living God,
8:1 Lamb opened the seventh S, there was silence in
9:4 who have not the S of God upon their
10:4 voice from heaven saying, S up what the seven
22:10 to me, "Do not S up the words of

SEALED (27)

Deut 32:34 in store with me, S up in my treasuries?
1Kgs 21:8 in Ahab's name and S them with his seal,
Esth 3:12 of King Ahasuerus and S with the king's ring.
8:8 of the king and S with the king's ring
8:10 of King Ahasuerus and S with the king's ring,
Job 14:17 my transgression would be S up in a bag,
Song 4:12 sister, my bride, a garden locked, a fountain S
Wis 2:5 death, because it is S up and no one
Is 29:11 like the words of a book that is S
29:11 he says, "I cannot, for it is S
Jer 32:10 I signed the deed, S it, got witnesses, and
32:11 Then I took the S deed of purchase, containing
32:14 these deeds, both this S deed of purchase and
32:44 shall be signed and S and witnessed, in the
Dan 6:17 den, and the king S it with his own
12:9 are shut up and S until the time of
14:14 shut the door and S it with the king's
2Mac 2:5 of incense, and he S up the entrance.
Eph 1:13 believed in him, were S with the promised Holy
4:30 in whom you were S for the day of
Rev 5:1 and on the back, S with seven seals;
7:3 trees, till we have S the servants of our
7:4 the number of the S, a hundred and forty-four
7:4 hundred and forty-four thousand S, out of every tribe
7:5 of Israel, twelve thousand S out of the tribe
7:8 of Joseph, twelve thousand S out of the tribe
20:3 and shut it and S it over him, that

SEALING

Mt 27:66 the sepulchre secure by S the stone and setting

SEALS (11)

Tob 7:14 and they set their S to it.
9:5 money bags with their S intact and gave them
Job 9:7 does not rise; who S up the stars;
37:7 rain, 'Be strong.' He S up the hand of
Sir 38:27 cut the signets of S, each is diligent in
Dan 14:17 king said, "Are the S unbroken, Daniel?" He
Rev 5:1 back, sealed with seven S;
5:2 worthy to open the scroll and break its S
5:5 he can open the scroll and its seven S
5:9 and to open its S, for thou wast slain
6:1 one of the seven S, and I heard one

SEAM

Jn 19:23 the tunic was without S, woven from top to

SEAMEN

1Kgs 9:27 the fleet his servants, S who were familiar with

SEAMS

Ezek 27:9 in you, caulking your S; all the ships of

SEARCH (48)

Deut 4:29 find him, if you S after him with all
13:14 shall inquire and make S and ask diligently; and
Josh 2:2 come here tonight to S out the land."
2:3 they have come to S out all the land."
2:22 the pursuers had made S all along the way
Judg 6:29 after they had made S and inquired, they said,
1Sam 23:23 the land, I will S him out among all
2Sam 5:17 Philistines went up in S of David; but David
10:3 servants to you to S the city, and to
1Kgs 20:6 time, and they shall S your house and the
2Kgs 10:23 the worshipers of Baal, S, and see that there
1Chr 14:8 Philistines went up in S of David; and David
19:3 come to you to S and to overthrow and
26:31 year of David's reign S was made and men
Ezra 4:15 king, in order that S may be made in
4:19 made a decree, and S has been made, and
5:17 to the king, let S be made in the
6:1 made a decree, and S was made in Babylonia,
Jud 8:14 do you expect to S out God, who made
8:27 he did them, to S their hearts, nor has
Job 10:6 out my iniquity and S for my sin,
28:3 end to darkness, and S out to the farthest
Ps 64:6 Who can S out our crimes?
77:6 night; I meditate and S my spirit:
139:23 S me, O God, and know my heart!
Prov 2:4 it like silver and S for it as for
25:2 of kings is to S things out.
Eccl 1:13 to seek and to S out by wisdom all
7:25 to know and to S out and to seek
Wis 6:3 Most High, who will S out your works and
Sir 1:3 and wisdom—who can S them out?
6:27 S out and seek, and she will become known
18:3 works; and who can S out his mighty deeds?
51:14 her, and I will S for her to the
Jer 5:1 S her squares to see if you can find
17:10 "I the LORD S the mind and try the
Lam 1:11 people groan as they S for bread; they trade
Ezek 34:6 earth, with none to S or seek for them.
34:11 I, I myself will S for my sheep, and
39:14 end of seven months they will make their S
Amos 9:3 from there I will S out and take them;
Zeph 1:12 that time I will S Jerusalem with lamps, and
Mt 2:8 Bethlehem, saying, "Go and S diligently for the child,
2:13 Herod is about to S for the child, to
13:45 like a merchant in S of fine pearls,
18:11 mountains and go in S of the one that
Jn 5:38 You S the scriptures, because you think that in
7:52 S and you will see that no prophet is

SEARCHED (16)

Gen 31:35 So he S, but did not find the household
44:12 And he S, beginning with the eldest and ending
2Chr 22:9 He S for Ahaziah, and he was captured while
Tob 1:19 that I was being S for, to be put
Job 5:27 Lo, this we have S out; it is true.
28:27 he established it, and S it out.
29:16 the poor, and I S out the cause of
32:11 wise sayings, while you S out what to say.
Ps 139:1 O LORD, thou hast S me and known me!
Eccl 2:3 I S with my mind how to cheer my
Ezek 20:6 land that I had S out for them, a
34:8 my shepherds have not S for my sheep, but
1Mac 3:5 He S out and pursued the lawless; he burned
9:26 They sought and S for the friends of Judas,
2Tim 1:17 arrived in Rome he S for me eagerly and
1Pet 1:10 was to be yours S and inquired about this

SEARCHES (8)

1Chr 28:9 mind; for the LORD S all hearts, and understands
Job 13:9 with you when he S you out?
39:8 his pasture, and he S after every green thing.
Prov 11:27 comes to him who S for it.
Sir 42:18 He S out the abyss, and the hearts of
Rom 8:27 And he who S the hearts of men knows
1Cor 2:10 For the Spirit S everything, even the depths of
Rev 2:23 I am he who S mind and heart, and

SEARCHEST

Ps 139:3 Thou S out my path and my lying down,

SEARCHING (3)

Prov 20:27 lamp of the LORD, S all his innermost parts.

Wis 13:7 his works they keep S, and they trust in
Mk 1:37 him, "Every one is S for you."

SEARCHINGS (2)

Judg 5:15 Reuben there were great S of heart.
5:16 Reuben there were great S of heart.

SEARED

1Tim 4:2 liars whose consciences are S,

SEAS (29)

Gen 1:10 the waters that were gathered together he called S
1:22 the waters in the S, and let birds multiply
Lev 11:9 scales, whether in the S or in the rivers,
11:10 But anything in the S or the rivers that
Deut 33:19 the affluence of the S and the hidden treasures
Neh 9:6 is on it, the S and all that is
Jud 1:12 as far as the coasts of the two S
Ps 24:2 founded it upon the S, and established it upon
65:5 and of the farthest S;
65:7 the roaring of the S, the roaring of their
69:34 earth praise him, the S and everything that moves
78:27 the sand of the S;
135:6 on earth, in the S and all deeps.
Prov 30:19 ship on the high S, and the way of
Jer 15:8 the sand of the S; I have brought against
Ezek 26:17 have vanished from the S, O city renowned, that
27:4 the heart of the S; your builders made perfect
27:25 and heavily laden in the heart of the S
27:26 rowers have brought you out into the high S
27:26 has wrecked you in the heart of the S
27:27 the heart of the S on the day of
27:33 wares came from the S, you satisfied many peoples;
27:34 are wrecked by the S, in the depths of
28:2 the heart of the S yet you are but
28:8 of the slain in the heart of the S
32:2 a dragon in the S; you burst forth in
Dan 3:79 Bless the Lord, S and rivers, sing praise to
Jon 2:3 the heart of the S, and the flood was
1Mac 6:29 from other kingdoms and from islands of the S

SEASHORE (9)

Gen 22:17 and as the sand which is on the S
Ex 14:30 and Israel saw the Egyptians dead upon the S
Josh 11:4 that is upon the S, with very many horses
Judg 7:12 which is upon the S for multitude.
1Sam 13:5 the sand on the S in multitude; they came
1Kgs 4:29 the sand on the S,
Jer 47:7 Ashkelon and against the S he has appointed it."
1Mac 11:1 the sand by the S, and many ships; and
Heb 11:12 as the innumerable grains of sand by the S

SEASIDE (2)

Acts 10:6 Simon, a tanner, whose house is by the S
10:32 a tanner, by the S

SEASON (35)

Gen 17:21 to you at this S next year."
31:10 In the mating S of the flock I lifted
Lev 2:13 You shall S all your cereal offerings with salt;
26:4 your rains in their S, and the land shall
Num 13:20 the time was the S of the first-ripe grapes.
28:2 me in its due S
Deut 11:14 your land in its S, the early rain and
28:12 your land in its S and to bless all
2Kgs 4:16 he said, "At this S, when the time comes
Job 5:26 comes up to the threshing floor in its S
38:32 the Mazzaroth in their S, or can you guide
Ps 1:3 its fruit in its S, and its leaf does
104:27 thee, to give them their food in due S
145:15 and thou givest them their food in due S
Prov 15:23 and a word in S, how good it is!
Eccl 3:1 everything there is a S, and a time for
Sir 31:28 Wine drunk in S and temperately is rejoicing of
32:4 talk; do not display your cleverness out of S
39:34 for all things will prove good in their S
43:6 to serve in its S to make the times
Jer 5:24 the rain in its S, the autumn rain and
Ezek 34:26 the showers in their S; they shall be showers
Dan 7:12 were prolonged for a S and a time.
Hos 2:9 my wine in its S; and I will take
9:10 tree, in its first S, I saw your fathers.
Zech 10:1 the LORD in the S of the spring rain,
1Mac 4:54 At the very S and on the very day
4:59 every year at that S the days of dedication
Mt 21:34 When the S of fruit drew near, he sent
Mk 9:48 saltness, how will you S it?
11:13 it was not the S for figs.
1Cor 7:5 by agreement for a S, that you may devote
Gal 6:9 well-doing, for in due S we shall reap, if
2Tim 4:2 word, be urgent in S and out of season,
4:2 season and out of S, convince, rebuke, and exhort,

SEASONED (5)

Ex 30:35 as by the perfumer, S with salt, pure and
1Chr 12:33 Of Zebulun fifty thousand S troops, equipped for
12:36 Of Asher forty thousand S troops ready for battle.
28:1 men, and all the S warriors.
Col 4:6 speech always be gracious, S with salt, so that

SEASONS (15)

Gen 1:14 for signs and for S and for days and
Esth 9:31 observed at their appointed S, as Mordecai the Jew
Ps 104:19 moon to mark the S; the sun knows its
Wis 7:18 the changes of the S,
8:8 of the outcome of S and times.
Sir 33:8 he appointed the different S and feasts;
Bar 1:14 the days of the feasts and at appointed S
Ezek 46:11 feasts and the appointed S the cereal offering with
Dan 2:21 He changes times and S; he removes kings and
Zech 8:19 the house of Judah S of joy and gladness,
Mt 21:41 who will give him the fruits in their S
Acts 1:7 to know times or S which the Father has
14:17 heaven rains and fruitful S, satisfying your hearts
Gal 4:10 days, and months, and S, and years!
1Thes 5:1 the times and the S, brethren, you have no

SEAT (76)

Ex 25:17 shall make a mercy S of pure gold; two
25:18 them, on the two ends of the mercy S
25:19 piece with the mercy S shall you make the
25:20 above, overshadowing the mercy S with their wings,
25:20 another; toward the mercy S shall the faces of
25:21 shall put the mercy S on the top of
25:22 from above the mercy S, from between the two
26:34 shall put the mercy S upon the ark of
30:6 testimony, before the mercy S that is over the
31:7 testimony, and the mercy S that is thereon, and
35:12 its poles, the mercy S, and the veil of
37:6 he made a mercy S of pure gold; two
37:7 ends of the mercy S he made them,
37:8 piece with the mercy S he made the cherubim
37:9 above, overshadowing the mercy S with their wings,
37:9 another; toward the mercy S were the faces of
39:35 poles and the mercy S;
Lev 16:2 veil, before the mercy S which is upon the
16:2 will appear in the cloud upon the mercy S
16:13 may cover the mercy S which is upon the
16:14 front of the mercy S, and before the mercy
16:14 and before the mercy S he shall sprinkle the
16:15 it upon the mercy S and before the mercy
16:15 and before the mercy S;
Num 7:89 from above the mercy S that was upon the
21:15 that extends to the S of Ar, and leans
Judg 3:20 And he arose from his S
1Sam 1:9 was sitting on the S beside the doorpost of
2:8 princes and inherit a S of honor.
4:13 was sitting upon his S by the road watching,
4:18 over backward from his S by the side of
20:18 be missed, because your S will be empty.
20:25 king sat upon his S, as at other times,
20:25 other times, upon the S by the wall; Jonathan
2Sam 19:8 arose, and took his S in the gate.
1Kgs 2:19 throne, and had a S brought for the king's
10:19 each side of the S were arm rests and
2Kgs 11:19 And he took his S on the throne of
25:28 and gave him a S above the seats of
1Chr 28:11 room for the mercy S;
2Chr 9:18 each side of the S were arm rests and
19:8 They had their S at Jerusalem.
Esth 3:1 him and set his S above all the princes
Job 23:3 him, that I might come even to his S
29:7 when I prepared my S in the square,
Ps 1:1 nor sits in the S of scoffers;
7:7 over it take thy S on high.
Prov 9:14 house, she takes a S on the high places
Song 3:10 back of gold, its S of purple; it was
Sir 7:4 highest office, nor the S of honor from the
11:1 his head, and will S him among the great.
12:12 try to take your S of honor, and at
38:33 sit in the judge's S, nor do they understand
Jer 13:18 mother: "Take a lowly S, for your beautiful crown

S

S

2Chr 3:2 to build in the S month of the fourth
27:5 same amount in the S and the third years.
30:2 the passover in the S month--
30:13 unleavened bread in the S month, a very great
30:15 fourteenth day of the S month.
31:12 Shimei his brother as S;
34:22 in Jerusalem in the S Quarter) and spoke to
35:24 carried him in his S chariot and brought him
Ezra 3:8 Now in the S year of their coming to
3:8 at Jerusalem, in the S month, Zerubbabel the son
4:24 it ceased until the S year of the reign
Neh 8:13 On the S day the heads of fathers' houses
11:9 son of Hassenuah was S over the city.
11:17 prayer, and Bakbukiah, the S among his brethren;
Tob 1:7 ministered at Jerusalem; a S tenth I would sell,
1:22 Esarhaddon had appointed him S to himself.
Jud 2:4 general of his army, S only to himself, and
7:6 On the S day Holofernes led out all his
Esth 2:14 came back to the S harem in custody of
2:19 gathered together the S time, Mordecai was sitting
7:2 And on the S day, as they were drinking
9:29 authority, confirming this S letter about Purim.
11:2 In the S year of the reign of Artaxerxes
13:3 and has attained the S place in the kingdom,
13:6 affairs and is our S father, shall all, with
16:11 all as the person S to the royal throne.
Job 42:14 the name of the S Keziah; and the name
Ps 109:13 blotted out in the S generation!
Sir 23:23 of the Most High; S, she has committed an
50:21 down in worship a S time, to receive the
Is 11:11 his hand yet a S time to recover the
37:30 itself, and in the S year what springs of
Jer 1:13 came to me a S time, saying, "What do
13:3 came to me a S time,
33:1 came to Jeremiah a S time, while he was
52:22 And the S pillar had the like, with pomegranates.
52:24 priest, and Zephaniah the S priest, and the three
Ezek 4:6 shall lie down a S time, but on your
10:14 the cherub, and the S face was the face
43:22 And on the S day you shall offer a
Dan 2:1 In the S year of the reign of Nebuchadnezzar,
2:7 They answered a S time, "Let the king tell
7:5 behold, another beast, a S one, like a bear.
Jon 3:1 came to Jonah the S time, saying,
Zeph 1:10 a wail from the S Quarter, a loud crash
Hag 1:1 In the S year of Darius the
2:1 In the S year of Darius the king, in
2:10 ninth month, in the S year of Darius, the
2:20 the LORD came a S time to Haggai on
Zech 1:1 eighth month, in the S year of Darius, the
1:7 of Shebat, in the S year of Darius, the
4:12 And a S time I said to him, "What
6:2 had red horses, the S black horses,
11:14 Then I broke my S staff Union, annulling the
1Mac 9:1 land of Judah a S time, and with them
9:54 fifty-third year, in the S month, Alcimus gave orders
13:51 twenty-third day of the S month, in the one
2Mac 5:1 time Antiochus made his S invasion of Egypt.
7:7 they brought forward the S for their sport.
13:22 The king negotiated a S time with the people
14:8 of the king, and S because I have regard
Mt 21:30 he went to the S and said the same;
22:26 So too the S and third, down to the
22:39 And a S is like it, You shall love
26:42 Again, for the S time, he went away and
Mk 12:21 no children; and the S took her, and died,
12:31 all your strength.' The S is this, 'You shall
14:72 the cock crowed a S time.
Lk 12:38 he comes in the S watch, or in the
19:18 ten cities.' And the S came, saying, 'Lord, your
20:30 without children; and the S
Jn 3:4 Can he enter a S time into his mother's
4:54 This was now the S sign that Jesus did
9:24 So for the S time they called the man
21:16 A S time he said to him, "Simon, son
Acts 7:13 And at the S visit Joseph made himself known
10:15 to him again a S time, "What God has
11:9 the voice answered a S time from heaven, 'What
12:10 the first and the S guard, they came to
13:33 is written in the S psalm, 'Thou art my
28:13 up, and on the S day we came to
1Cor 12:28 the church first apostles, S prophets, third teachers,
15:47 man of dust; the S man is from heaven.
2Cor 13:2 when present on my S visit, that if I
Heb 8:7 there would have been no occasion for a S
9:3 Behind the S curtain stood a tent called the
9:7 duties; but into the S only the high priest
9:28 many, will appear a S time, not to deal
10:9 abolishes the first in order to establish the S
2Pet 3:1 This is now the S letter that I have
Rev 2:11 be hurt by the S death.'
4:7 like a lion, the S living creature like an
6:3 When he opened the S seal, I heard the
6:3 seal, I heard the S living creature say, "Come!"
8:8 The S angel blew his trumpet, and something like
11:14 The S woe has passed; behold, the third woe
14:8 Another angel, a S, followed, saying, "Fallen, fallen is
16:3 The S angel poured his bowl into the sea,
20:6 Over such the S death has no power, but
20:14 This is the S death, the lake of fire;
21:8 sulphur, which is the S death."
21:19 first was jasper, the S sapphire, the third agate,

SECRET (62)

Ex 7:11 the same by their S arts.
7:22 the same by their S arts; so Pharaoh's heart
8:7 the same by their S arts, and brought frogs
8:18 magicians tried by their S arts to bring forth
Deut 27:15 sets it up in S And all the people
27:24 slays his neighbor in S And all the people
29:29 at this day.' "The S things belong to the
Judg 3:19 said, "I have a S message for you, O
16:9 So the S of his strength was not known.
1Sam 19:2 morning, stay in a S place and hide yourself;
2Sam 15:10 Absalom sent S messengers throughout all the tribes
Tob 12:7 good to guard the S of a king, but
12:11 good to guard the S of a king, but
Jud 2:2 forth to them his S plan and recounted fully,
Job 13:10 rebuke you if in S you show partiality.
Ps 10:9 hapless, he lurks in S like a lion in
51:6 me wisdom in my S heart.
64:2 hide me from the S plots of the wicked,
81:7 answered you in the S place of thunder; I
90:8 iniquities before thee, our S sins in the light
139:15 was being made in S, intricately wrought in the
Prov 9:17 and bread eaten in S is pleasant."
21:14 A gift in S averts anger; and a bribe
25:9 do not disclose another's S;
Eccl 12:14 into judgment, with every S thing, whether good or
Wis 1:11 from slander; because no S word is without result,
2:22 did not know the S purposes of God, nor
7:21 learned both what is S and what is manifest,
14:15 on to his dependents S rites and initiations.
14:23 initiations, or celebrate S mysteries, or hold frenzied
17:3 thinking that in their S sins they were unobserved
18:9 For in S the holy children of good men
Sir 8:17 he will not be able to keep a S
8:18 is to be kept S, for you do not
Is 3:17 will lay bare their S parts.
45:3 and the hoards in S places, that you may
45:19 did not speak in S, in a land of
48:16 have not spoken in S, from the time it
65:4 spend the night in S places; who eat swine's
Jer 13:17 soul will weep in S for your pride; my
23:24 man hide himself in S places so that I
Ezek 28:3 wiser than Daniel; no S is hidden from you;
Dan 13:42 dost discern what is S, who art aware of
14:21 they showed him the S doors through which they
Amos 3:7 nothing, without revealing his S to his servants the
Hab 3:14 rejoicing as if to devour the poor in S
2Mac 1:16 Opening the S door in the ceiling, they threw
13:21 of the Jews, gave S information to the enemy;
Mt 6:4 alms may be in S; and your Father who
6:4 Father who sees in S will reward you.
6:6 Father who is in S; and your Father who
6:6 Father who sees in S will reward you.
6:18 Father who is in S; and your Father who
6:18 Father who sees in S will reward you.
Mk 4:11 has been given the S of the kingdom of
4:22 manifest; nor is anything S, except to come to
Lk 8:17 made manifest, nor anything S that shall not be
Jn 7:4 no man works in S if he seeks to
Rom 16:24 mystery which was kept S for long ages
1Cor 2:7 But we impart a S and hidden wisdom of
Eph 5:12 that they do in S;
Phil 4:12 I have learned the S of facing plenty and

SECRETARIES (3)

1Kgs 4:3 sons of Shisha were S; Jehoshaphat the son of
Esth 3:12 Then the king's S were summoned on the thirteenth
8:9 The king's S were summoned at that time, in

S

SECRETARY (30)

2Sam 8:17 priests; and Seraiah was S;
20:25 recorder; and Sheva was S; and Zadok and Abiathar
2Kgs 12:10 the chest, the king's S and the high priest
18:18 household, and Shebnah the S, and Joah the son
18:37 household, and Shebna the S, and Joah the son
19:2 household, and Shebna the S, and the senior priests,
22:3 son of Meshullam, the S, to the house of
22:8 said to Shaphan the S, "I have found the
22:9 And Shaphan the S came to the king, and
22:10 Then Shaphan the S told the king, "Hilkiah the
22:12 Micaiah, and Shaphan the S, and Asaiah the king's
25:19 the city; and the S of the commander of
1Chr 18:16 priests; and Shavsha was S;
2Chr 24:11 in it, the king's S and the officer of
26:11 made by Je-iel the S and Ma-aseiah the officer,
34:15 said to Shaphan the S, "I have found the
34:18 Then Shaphan the S told the king, "Hilkiah the
34:20 of Micah, Shaphan the S, and Asaiah the king's
Is 36:3 household, and Shebna the S, and Joah the son
36:22 household, and Shebna the S, and Joah the son
37:2 household, and Shebna the S, and the senior priests,
Jer 36:10 son of Shaphan the S, which was in the
36:12 king's house, into the S's chamber; and all the
36:12 sitting there: Elishama the S, Delaiah the son of
36:20 chamber of Elishama the S; and they reported all
36:21 chamber of Elishama the S; and Jehudi read it
36:26 to seize Baruch the S and Jeremiah the prophet,
37:15 house of Jonathan the S, for it had been
37:20 house of Jonathan the S, lest I die there."
52:25 the city; and the S of the commander of

SECRETLY (28)

Gen 31:27 Why did you flee S, and cheat me, and
Deut 13:6 own soul, entices you S, saying, 'Let us go
28:57 she will eat them S, for want of all
Josh 2:1 Nun sent two men S from Shittim as spies,
2Sam 12:12 For you did it S; but I will do
2Kgs 17:9 people of Israel did S against the LORD their
Tob 1:18 who came fleeing from Judea, I buried them S
Job 31:27 my heart has been S enticed, and my mouth
Ps 64:5 talk of laying snares S, thinking, "Who can see
101:5 who slanders his neighbor S I will destroy.
Sir 42:9 daughter keeps her father S wakeful, and worry over
Jer 37:17 The king questioned him S in his house, and
38:16 Then King Zedekiah swore S to Jeremiah, "As the
40:15 son of Kareah spoke S to Gedaliah at Mizpah,
Bar 6:10 and sometimes the priests S take gold and silver
1Mac 9:60 a large force, and S sent letters to all
10:79 Now Apollonius had S left a thousand cavalry behind
2Mac 1:19 of the altar and S hid it in the
6:11 observe the seventh day S, were betrayed to Philip
8:1 Maccabeus, and his companions S entered the
Mt 2:7 summoned the wise men S and ascertained from
Jn 18:20 all Jews come together; I have said nothing S
19:38 disciple of Jesus, but S, for fear of the
Acts 6:11 Then they S instigated men, who said, "We have
16:37 prison; and do they now cast us out S
Gal 2:4 because of false brethren S brought in, who slipped
2Pet 2:1 among you, who will S bring in destructive heresies,
Jude 1:4 For admission has been S gained by some who

SECRETS (18)

Job 11:6 would tell you the S of wisdom!
Ps 44:21 For he knows the S of the heart.
Prov 11:13 as a talebearer reveals S, but he who is
20:19 goes about gossiping reveals S; therefore do not
Wis 6:22 I will hide no S from you, but I
Sir 1:27 Lord will reveal your S and cast you down
4:18 and will reveal her S to him.
14:21 mind on her ways will also ponder her S
22:20 reviling, arrogance, disclosure of S, or a treacherous
27:16 Whoever betrays S destroys confidence, and he will
27:17 if you betray his S, do not run after
27:21 but whoever has betrayed S is without hope.
39:7 counsel and knowledge aright, and meditate on his S
41:23 and telling what you hear, and of revealing S
Mt 13:11 given to know the S of the kingdom of
Lk 8:10 given to know the S of the kingdom of
Rom 2:16 gospel, God judges the S of men by Christ
1Cor 14:25 account by all, the S of his heart are

SECT (3)

Acts 24:5 a ringleader of the S of the Nazarenes.
24:13 which they call a S, I worship the God
28:22 with regard to this S we know that everywhere

SECTION (10)

Neh 3:11 of Pahath-moab repaired another S and the Tower of
3:19 of Mizpah, repaired another S opposite the ascent to
3:20 of Zabbai repaired another S from the Angle to
3:21 of Hakkoz repaired another S from the door of
3:24 of Henadad repaired another S, from the house of
3:27 the Tekoites repaired another S opposite the great
3:30 Hanun the sixth son of Zalaph repaired another S
Ezek 45:3 shall measure off a S twenty-five thousand cubits
45:5 Another S, twenty-five thousand cubits long and ten
1Mac 12:37 and he repaired the S called Chaphenatha.

SECTIONS

Sir 9:7 a city, nor wander about in its deserted S

SECU

1Sam 19:22 well that is in S; and he asked, "Where

SECUNDUS

Acts 20:4 the Thessalonians, Aristarchus and S; and Gaius of

SECURE (34)

2Sam 22:34 feet, and set me S on the heights.
23:5 an everlasting covenant, ordered in all things and S
2Chr 11:17 the son of Solomon S, for they walked for
Ezra 9:8 to give us a S hold within his holy
Esth 13:7 leave our government completely S and untroubled
Job 11:15 blemish; you will be S, and will not fear.
12:6 who provoke God are S, who bring their god
21:23 wholly at ease and S,
Ps 16:9 and my soul rejoices; my body also dwells S
18:33 feet, and set me S on the heights.
40:2 my feet upon a rock, making my steps S
102:28 thy servants shall dwell S; their posterity shall be
Prov 1:33 to me will dwell S and will be at
11:15 for it, but he who hates suretyship is S
Sir 4:15 and whoever gives heed to her will dwell S
Is 32:18 a peaceful habitation, in S dwellings, and in quiet
47:10 You felt S in your wickedness, you said, "No
Bar 6:18 priests make their temples S with doors and locks
Ezek 27:24 with cords and made S; in these they traded
34:27 and they shall be S in their land; and
Amos 6:1 to those who feel S on the mountain of
Mic 5:4 And they shall dwell S, for now he shall
Zeph 2:15 exultant city that dwelt S, that said to herself,
1Mac 14:1 marched into Media to S help, so that he
2Mac 1:14 with his friends, to S most of its treasures
2:27 However, to S the gratitude of many we will
3:22 been entrusted safe and S for those who had
8:36 who had undertaken to S tribute for the Romans
Mt 27:64 sepulchre to be made S until the third day,
27:65 go, make it as S as you can."
27:66 and made the sepulchre S by sealing the stone
Acts 27:16 managed with difficulty to S the boat;
1Cor 7:35 good order and to S your undivided devotion to
9:15 I writing this to S any such provision.

SECURED (2)

2Mac 4:11 concessions to the Jews, S through John the father
4:24 air of authority, and S the high-priesthood for

SECURELY (19)

Lev 25:18 them; so you will dwell in the land S
25:19 will eat your fill, and dwell in it S
26:5 to the full, and dwell in your land S
Prov 3:23 walk on your way S and your foot will
10:9 walks in integrity walks S, but he who perverts
Is 47:8 of pleasures, who sit S, who say in your
Jer 23:6 Judah will be saved, and Israel will dwell S
33:16 Judah will be saved and Jerusalem will dwell S
49:31 at ease, that dwells S, says the LORD, that
Ezek 28:26 And they shall dwell S in it, and they
28:26 They shall dwell S, when I execute judgments upon
34:25 that they may dwell S in the wilderness and
34:28 them; they shall dwell S, and none shall make
38:8 nations and now dwell S, all of them.
38:11 quiet people who dwell S, all of them dwelling
38:14 people Israel are dwelling S, you will bestir yourself
39:6 on those who dwell S in the coastlands; and
39:26 me, when they dwell S in their land with
Acts 5:23 "We found the prison S locked and the sentries

SECURING

Heb 9:12 his own blood, thus S an eternal redemption.

SECURITY (14)
Lev 6:2 matter of deposit or S, or through robbery, or
Judg 18:7 how they dwelt in S, after the manner of
2Kgs 20:19 will be peace and S in my days?"
Job 24:23 He gives them S, and they are supported; and
Ps 37:3 you will dwell in the land, and enjoy S
122:7 within your walls, and S within your towers!"
Is 38:14 O Lord, I am oppressed; be thou my S
39:8 will be peace and S in my days."
Jer 33:6 and reveal to them abundance of prosperity and S
Zech 14:11 be no more curse; Jerusalem shall dwell in S
2Mac 4:21 government, and he took measures for his own S
9:21 thought for the general S of all.
Acts 17:9 when they had taken S from Jason and the
1Thes 5:3 When people say, "There is peace and S

SEDITION (3)
Ezra 4:15 and provinces, and that S was stirred up in
4:19 and that rebellion and S have been made in
2Mac 14:6 war and stirring up S, and will not let

SEDUCE
Dan 11:32 He shall S with flattery those who violate the

SEDUCED (2)
2Kgs 21:9 not listen, and Manasseh S them to do more
2Chr 33:9 Manasseh S Judah and the inhabitants of Jerusalem,

SEDUCES
Ex 22:16 "If a man S a virgin who is not

SEDUCTIVE
Prov 7:21 With much S speech she persuades him; with her

SEED (65)
Gen 1:11 forth vegetation, plants yielding S, and fruit trees
1:11 in which is their S, each according to its
1:12 forth vegetation, plants yielding S according to their
1:12 in which is their S, each according to its
1:29 you every plant yielding S which is upon the
1:29 and every tree with S in its fruit; you
3:15 woman, and between your S and her seed; he
3:15 your seed and her S; he shall bruise your
47:19 Pharaoh; and give us S, that we may live,
47:23 Now here is S for you, and you shall
47:24 be your own, as S for the field and
Ex 16:31 it was like coriander S, white, and the taste
Lev 11:37 carcass falls upon any S for sowing that is
11:38 is put on the S and any part of
19:19 with two kinds of S; nor shall there come
26:16 you shall sow your S in vain, for your
27:16 be according to the S for it; a sowing
27:30 land, whether of the S of the land or
Num 11:7 manna was like coriander S, and its appearance like
24:7 his buckets, and his S shall be in many
Deut 11:10 where you sowed your S and watered it with
14:22 the yield of your S, which comes forth from
22:9 with two kinds of S, lest the whole yield
28:38 You shall carry much S into the field, and
Judg 6:3 the Israelites put in S the Midianites and the
1Kgs 18:32 as great as would contain two measures of S
Ps 126:6 forth weeping, bearing the S for sowing, shall come
Eccl 11:6 the morning sow your S, and at evening withhold
Wis 7:2 with blood, from the S of a man and
14:6 to the world the S of a new generation.
Is 5:10 and a homer of S shall yield but an
6:13 The holy S is its stump.
30:23 give rain for the S with which you sow
55:10 forth and sprout, giving S to the sower and
Jer 2:21 planted you a choice vine, wholly of pure S
31:27 of Judah with the S of man and the
31:27 of man and the S of beast.
33:26 to rule over the S of Abraham, Isaac, and
35:7 you shall not sow S; you shall not plant
35:9 vineyard or field or S;
Ezek 17:5 he took of the S of the land and
17:13 took one of the S royal and made a
20:5 I swore to the S of the house of
Joel 1:16 The S shrivels under the clods, the storehouses are
Amos 9:13 him who sows the S; the mountains shall drip
Hag 2:19 laid, consider: Is the S yet in the barn?
Mt 13:24 man who sowed good S in his field;
13:27 you not sow good S in your field?
13:31 a grain of mustard S which a man took
13:37 who sows the good S is the Son of
13:38 world, and the good S means the sons of
17:20 a grain of mustard S, you will say to
Mk 4:4 as he sowed, some S fell along the path,
4:5 Other S fell on rocky ground, where it had
4:7 Other S fell among thorns and the thorns grew
4:26 a man should scatter S upon the ground,
4:27 and day, and the S should sprout and grow,
4:31 a grain of mustard S, which, when sown upon
Lk 8:5 out to sow his S; and as he sowed,
8:11 parable is this: The S is the word of
13:19 a grain of mustard S which a man took
17:6 a grain of mustard S, you could say to
1Cor 15:38 to each kind of S its own body.
2Cor 9:10 He who supplies S to the sower and bread
1Pet 1:23 anew, not of perishable S but of imperishable,

SEEDLINGS
Wis 4:3 none of their illegitimate S will strike a deep

SEEDS (8)
Num 6:4 grapevine, not even the S or the skins.
Mt 13:4 as he sowed, some S fell along the path,
13:5 Other S fell on rocky ground, where they had
13:7 Other S fell upon thorns, and the thorns grew
13:8 Other S fell on good soil and brought forth
13:32 the smallest of all S, but when it has
Mk 4:8 And other S fell into good soil and brought
4:31 smallest of all the S on earth;

SEEDTIME
Gen 8:22 While the earth remains, S and harvest, cold and

SEEK (270)
Gen 43:18 so that he may S occasion against us and
Lev 13:36 the priest need not S for the yellow hair;
19:31 or wizards; do not S them out, to be
Num 10:33 three days' journey, to S out a resting place
16:10 And would you S the priesthood also?
35:23 enemy, and did not S his harm;
Deut 1:33 in the way to S you out a place
4:29 from there you will S the LORD your God,
12:5 But you shall S the place which the LORD
23:6 You shall not S their peace or their prosperity
Ruth 3:1 daughter, should I not S a home for you,
1Sam 10:2 which you went to S are found, and now
10:14 And he said, "To S the asses; and when
16:16 are before you, to S out a man who
23:15 had come out to S his life.
23:25 his men went to S him.
24:2 Israel, and went to S David and his men
25:26 enemies and those who S to do evil to
25:29 pursue you and to S your life, the life
26:2 men of Israel, to S David in the wilderness
26:20 has come out to S my life, like one
28:7 said to his servants, S out for me a
2Sam 17:3 You S the life of only one man, and
20:19 faithful in Israel; you S to destroy a city
1Kgs 2:40 Gath to Achish, to S his slaves; Shimei went
18:10 has not sent to S you; and when they
19:10 am left; and they S my life, to take
19:14 am left; and they S my life, to take
2Kgs 2:16 let them go, and S your master; it may
6:19 will bring you to the man whom you S
1Chr 4:39 of the valley, to S pasture for their flocks,
10:14 guidance, and did not S guidance from the LORD.
16:10 hearts of those who S the LORD rejoice!
16:11 S the LORD and his strength, seek his presence
16:11 LORD and his strength, S his presence continually!
22:19 mind and heart to S the LORD your God.
28:8 our God, observe and S out all the commandments
28:9 If you S him, he will be found by
2Chr 7:14 themselves, and pray and S my face, and turn
11:16 set their hearts to S the LORD God of
12:14 set his heart to S the LORD.
14:4 and commanded Judah to S the LORD, the God
15:2 If you S him, he will be found by
15:12 into a covenant to S the LORD, the God
15:13 that whoever would not S the LORD, the God
16:12 disease he did not S the LORD, but sought
17:3 father; he did not S the Baals,
19:3 set your heart to S God."
20:3 and set himself to S the LORD, and proclaimed
20:4 And Judah assembled to S help from the LORD;
20:4 Judah they came to S the LORD.
26:5 He set himself to S God in the days
30:19 sets his heart to S God, the LORD the
34:3 boy, he began to S the God of David

S

Ezra 8:21 before our God, to S from him a straight
8:22 good upon all that S him, and the power
9:12 your sons, and never S their peace or prosperity,
Neh 2:10 one had come to S the welfare of the
Tob 4:18 S advice from every wise man, and do not
Esth 16:3 They not only S to injure our subjects, but
Job 3:4 May God above not S it, nor light shine
5:8 for me, I would S God, and to God
7:21 the earth; thou wilt S me, but I shall
8:5 If you will S God and make supplication to
10:6 years, that thou dost S out my iniquity and
20:10 His children will S the favor of the poor,
23:9 the left hand I S him, but I cannot
Ps 4:2 love vain words, and S after lies?
9:10 not forsaken those who S thee.
10:4 the wicked does not S him; all his thoughts
10:15 the wicked and evildoer; S out his wickedness till
14:2 that act wisely, that S after God.
17:7 savior of those who S refuge from their adversaries
22:26 be satisfied; those who S him shall praise the
24:6 generation of those who S him, who seek the
24:6 who seek him, who S the face of the
27:4 LORD, that will I S after; that I may
27:8 Thou hast said, S ye my face." My heart
27:8 says to thee, "Thy face, LORD, do I S
31:1 O LORD, do I S refuge; let me never
34:10 hunger; but those who S the LORD lack no
34:14 evil, and do good; S peace, and pursue it.
35:4 shame and dishonor who S after my life!
38:12 Those who S my life lay their snares, those
38:12 their snares, those who S my hurt speak of
40:14 and confusion altogether who S to snatch away my
40:16 But may all who S thee rejoice and be
53:2 that are wise, that S after God.
54:3 against me, ruthless men S my life; they do
56:5 All day long they S to injure my cause;
63:1 art my God, I S thee, my soul thirsts
63:9 But those who S to destroy my life shall
69:6 let not those who S thee be brought to
69:32 be glad; you who S God, let your hearts
70:2 shame and confusion who S my life!
70:4 May all who S thee rejoice and be glad
71:13 they be covered who S my hurt.
77:2 of my trouble I S the Lord; in the
83:16 shame, that they may S thy name, O LORD.
86:14 band of ruthless men S my life, and they
105:3 hearts of those who S the LORD rejoice!
105:4 S the LORD and his strength, seek his presence
105:4 LORD and his strength, S his presence continually!
119:2 keep his testimonies, who S him with their whole
119:10 my whole heart I S thee; let me not
119:155 for they do not S thy statutes.
119:176 like a lost sheep; S thy servant, for I
122:9 our God, I will S your good.
141:8 God; in thee I S refuge; leave me not
Prov 1:28 not answer; they will S me diligently but will
2:4 for understanding, if you S it like silver and
7:15 to meet you, to S you eagerly, and I
8:17 me, and those who S me diligently find me.
19:6 Many S the favor of a generous man, and
20:4 the autumn; he will S at harvest and have
23:35 I will S another drink."
28:5 justice, but those who S the LORD understand it
29:10 blameless, and the wicked S his life.
29:26 Many S the favor of a ruler, but from
Eccl 1:13 applied my mind to S and to search out
3:6 embracing; a time to S, and a time to
7:25 search out and to S wisdom and the sum
Song 3:2 the squares; I will S him whom my soul
6:1 turned, that we may S him with you?
Wis 1:1 Lord with uprightness, and S him with sincerity of
6:12 found by those who S her.
6:14 who rises early to S her will have no
Sir 2:16 fear the Lord will S his approval, and those
3:20 S not what is too difficult for you, nor
4:11 help to those who S her.
4:12 life, and those who S her early will be
6:27 Search out and S, and she will become known
7:4 Do not S from the Lord the highest office,
7:6 Do not S to become a judge, lest you
24:32 but for all who S instruction.
28:3 against another, and yet S for healing from the
32:14 who rise early to S him will find favor.
33:17 but for all who S instruction.
33:25 idle, and he will S liberty.
33:31 will you go to S him?
39:1 the Most High will S out the wisdom of
39:3 of parables; he will S out the hidden meanings
39:5 to rise early to S the Lord who made
40:26 is no need to S for help.
51:21 heart was stirred to S her, therefore I have
Is 1:17 learn to do good; S justice, correct oppression;
9:13 who smote them, nor S the LORD of hosts.
11:10 him shall the nations S, and his dwellings shall
30:2 of Pharaoh, and to S shelter in the shadow
34:16 S and read from the book of the LORD:
41:12 You shall S those who contend with you, but
41:17 the poor and needy S water, and there is
45:19 the offspring of Jacob, S me in chaos.' I
51:1 pursue deliverance, you who S the LORD; look to
55:6 S the LORD while he may be found, call
58:2 Yet they S me daily, and delight to know
58:3 of your fast you S your own pleasure, and
65:1 those who did not S me.
Jer 2:24 None who S her need weary themselves; in her
2:33 direct your course to S lovers!
4:30 lovers despise you; they S your life.
11:21 men of Anathoth, who S your life, and say,
19:7 hand of those who S their life.
19:9 enemies and those who S their life afflict them.'
21:7 hand of those who S their lives.
22:25 hand of those who S your life, into the
29:7 But S the welfare of the city where I
29:13 You will S me and find me; when you
29:13 find me; when you S me with all your
34:20 hand of those who S their lives.
34:21 hand of those who S their lives, into the
38:16 of these men who S your life."
44:30 hand of those who S his life, as I
45:5 And do you S great things for yourself?
45:5 S them not; for, behold, I am bringing evil
46:26 hand of those who S their life, into the
49:37 and before those who S their life; I will
50:4 come; and they shall S the LORD their God.
Bar 3:23 sons of Hagar, who S for understanding on the
4:28 with tenfold zeal to S him.
Ezek 7:25 anguish comes, they will S peace, but there shall
7:26 rumor follows rumor; they S a vision from the
34:6 none to search or S for them.
34:11 my sheep, and will S them out.
34:12 abroad, so will I S out my sheep; and
34:16 I will S the lost, and I will bring
Dan 2:18 and told them to S mercy of the God
3:41 we fear thee and S thy face.
Hos 2:7 them; and she shall S them, but shall not
3:5 Israel shall return and S the LORD their God,
5:6 they shall go to S the LORD, but they
5:15 acknowledge their guilt and S my face, and in
5:15 in their distress they S me, saying,
7:11 LORD their God, nor S him, for all this.
10:12 is the time to S the LORD, that he
Amos 5:4 the house of Israel: S me and live;
5:5 live; but do not S Bethel, and do not
5:6 S the LORD and live, lest he break out
5:14 S good, and not evil, that you may live;
8:12 to and fro, to S the word of the
Nah 3:7 whence shall I S comforters for her?
3:11 be dazed; you will S a refuge from the
Zeph 1:6 LORD, who do not S the LORD or inquire
2:3 S the LORD, all you humble of the land,
2:3 do his commands; S righteousness, S humility;
3:12 They shall S refuge in the name of the
Zech 8:21 the LORD, and to S the LORD of hosts;
8:22 nations shall come to S the LORD of hosts
11:16 for the perishing, or S the wandering, or heal
12:9 that day I will S to destroy all the
Mal 2:7 knowledge, and men should S instruction from his
3:1 the Lord whom you S will suddenly come to
1Mac 7:13 sons of Israel to S peace from them,
7:15 them, "We will not S to injure you or
15:19 that they should not S their harm or make
Mt 6:32 wear?' For the Gentiles S all these things; and
6:33 But S first his kingdom and his righteousness, and
7:7 will be given you; S, and you will find;
28:5 I know that you S Jesus who was crucified.
Mk 8:12 "Why does this generation S a sign?
16:6 not be amazed; you S Jesus of Nazareth, who
Lk 11:9 will be given you; S, and you will find;
12:29 And do not S what you are to eat
12:30 nations of the world S these things; and your
12:31 Instead, S his kingdom, and these things shall be
13:24 I tell you, will S to enter and will

S

	15:8	sweep the house and S diligently until she finds
	19:10	of man came to S and to save the
	24:5	them, "Why do you S the living among the
Jn	1:38	following, and said to them, "What do you S
	5:29	is just, because I S not my own will
	5:43	another and do not S the glory that comes
	6:26	say to you, you S me, not because you
	7:19	Why do you S to kill me?"
	7:25	the man whom they S to kill?
	7:34	sent me; you will S me and you will
	7:36	by saying, 'You will S me and you will
	8:21	away, and you will S me and die in
	8:37	of Abraham; yet you S to kill me, because
	8:40	did, but now you S to kill me, a
	8:50	Yet I do not S my own glory; there
	13:33	You will S me; and as I said to
	18:4	forward and said to them, "Whom do you S
	18:7	Again he asked them, "Whom do you S
	18:8	he; so, if you S me, let these men
	20:15	Whom do you S
Acts	15:17	rest of men may S the Lord, and all
	17:27	habitation, that they should S God, in the hope
	19:39	But if you S anything further, it shall be
	25:11	die, I do not S to escape death; but
Rom	2:7	by patience in well-doing S for glory and honor
	10:20	those who did not S me; I have shown
	11:3	am left, and they S my life."
1Cor	1:22	demand signs and Greeks S wisdom,
	7:18	Let him not S to remove the marks of
	7:18	Let him not S circumcision.
	7:27	Do not S to be free.
	7:27	Do not S marriage.
	10:24	Let no one S his own good, but the
2Cor	12:14	a burden, for I S not what is yours
Phil	4:17	Not that I S the gift; but I seek
	4:17	the gift; but I S the fruit which increases
Col	3:1	been raised with Christ, S the things that are
1Thes	2:6	witness; nor did we S glory from men, whether
	5:15	for evil, but always S to do good to
Heb	11:6	he rewards those who S him.
	13:14	lasting city, but we S the city which is
1Pet	3:11	do right; let him S peace and pursue it.
Rev	9:6	those days men will S death and will not

SEEKERS

Bar	3:23	the story-tellers and the S for understanding, have

SEEKING (46)

Gen	37:15	and the man asked him, "What are you S
	37:16	"I am S my brothers," he said, "tell me,
Ex	4:19	the men who were S your life are dead."
Judg	4:22	will show you the man whom you are S
	14:4	LORD; for he was S an occasion against the
	18:1	of the Danites was S for itself an inheritance
1Sam	27:1	Saul will despair of S me any longer within
2Sam	3:17	past you have been S David as king over
1Kgs	11:22	that you are now S to go to your
	20:7	how this man is S trouble; for he sent
2Kgs	5:7	see how he is S a quarrel with me."
1Chr	10:13	also consulted a medium, S guidance,
2Chr	31:21	law and the commandments, S his God, he did
Job	24:5	forth to their toil, S prey in the wilderness
Ps	104:21	roar for their prey, S their food from God.
Eccl	8:17	man may toil in S, he will not find
Wis	6:16	because she goes about S those worthy of her,
	8:18	words, I went about S how to get her
	13:6	they go astray while S God and desiring to
Is	58:13	your own ways, or S your own pleasure, or
Jer	38:4	this man is not S the welfare of this
Dan	9:3	to the Lord God, S him by prayer and
1Mac	2:29	Then many who were S righteousness and justice
	12:40	him, so he kept S to seize and kill
	16:22	out that they were S to destroy him.
Mt	12:43	passes through waterless places S rest, but he finds
Mk	8:11	to argue with him, S from him a sign
	14:1	and the scribes were S how to arrest him
Lk	2:45	they returned to Jerusalem, S him.
	11:24	passes through waterless places S rest; and finding
	13:6	vineyard; and he came S fruit on it and
	13:7	years I have come S fruit on this fig
	22:2	and the scribes were S how to put him
Jn	6:24	and went to Caperna-um, S Jesus.
	7:20	Who is S to kill you?"
	11:8	Jews were but now S to stone you, and
Acts	9:29	Hellenists; but they were S to kill him.
	13:8	his name) withstood them, S to turn away the
	13:11	and he went about S people to lead him
	17:5	the house of Jason, S to bring them out
	27:30	as the sailors were S to escape from the
Rom	10:3	comes from God, and S to establish their own,
1Cor	10:33	everything I do, not S my own advantage, but
Gal	1:10	Am I now S the favor of men, or
Heb	11:14	clear that they are S a homeland.
1Pet	5:8	like a roaring lion, S some one to devour.

SEEKS (41)

Deut	22:2	you until your brother S it; then you shall
1Sam	19:2	David, "Saul my father S to kill you; therefore
	20:1	your father, that he S my life?"
	22:23	not; for he that S my life seeks your
	22:23	that seeks my life S your life; with me
	23:10	surely heard that Saul S to come to Keilah,
	24:9	who say, 'Behold, David S your hurt?
2Sam	16:11	"Behold, my own son S my life; how much
Ps	37:32	watches the righteous, and S to slay him.
Prov	11:27	He who diligently S good seeks favor, but evil
	11:27	who diligently seeks good S favor, but evil comes
	14:6	A scoffer S wisdom in vain, but knowledge is
	15:14	who has understanding S knowledge, but the mouths
	17:9	who forgives an offense S love, but he who
	17:11	An evil man S only rebellion, and a cruel
	17:19	makes his door high S destruction.
	18:1	He who is estranged S pretexts to break out
	18:15	ear of the wise S knowledge.
	31:13	She S wool and flax, and works with willing
Eccl	3:15	has been; and God S what has been driven
Sir	27:1	a trifle, and whoever S to get rich will
	32:15	He who S the law will be filled with
Is	16:5	one who judges and S justice and is swift
	26:9	spirit within me earnestly S thee.
	40:20	will not rot; he S out a skilful craftsman
Jer	5:1	who does justice and S truth; that I may
Lam	3:25	to the soul that S him.
Ezek	34:12	As a shepherd S out his flock when some
2Mac	2:27	prepares a banquet and S the benefit of others.
Mt	7:8	receives, and he who S finds, and to him
	12:39	evil and adulterous generation S for a sign; but
	16:4	evil and adulterous generation S for a sign, but
Lk	11:10	receives, and he who S finds, and to him
	11:29	an evil generation; it S a sign, but no
	17:33	Whoever S to gain his life will lose it,
Jn	4:23	for such the Father S to worship him.
	7:4	in secret if he S to be known openly.
	7:18	on his own authority S his own glory; but
	7:18	glory; but he who S the glory of him
	8:50	there is One who S it and he will
Rom	3:11	one understands, no one S for God.

SEEM (15)

Gen	27:12	me, and I shall S to be mocking him,
Deut	15:18	It shall not S hard to you, when you
1Sam	18:23	David said, "Does it S to you a little
	24:4	him as it shall S good to you.'" Then
Ezra	5:17	finished.' Therefore, if it S good to the king,
Neh	9:32	not all the hardship S little to thee that
Tob	2:14	You S to know everything!"
Esth	8:5	and if the thing S right before the king,
Job	10:3	Does it S good to thee to oppress, to
Is	5:28	bent, their horses' hoofs S like flint, and their
Ezek	21:23	to them it will S like a false divination;
Hab	2:3	If it S slow, wait for it; it will
1Cor	12:22	of the body which S to be weaker are
2Cor	10:9	I would not S to be frightening you with
	13:7	right, though we may S to have failed.

SEEMED (25)

Gen	19:14	But he S to his sons-in-law to be jesting.
	29:20	for Rachel, and they S to him but a
	41:37	This proposal S good to Pharaoh and to all
Num	13:33	Nephilim); and we S to ourselves like grasshoppers,
	13:33	grasshoppers, and so we S to them."
Deut	1:23	shall come.' The thing S good to me, and
2Sam	13:2	a virgin, and it S impossible to Amnon to
2Chr	30:4	and the plan S right to the king
Ps	73:16	to understand this, it S to me a wearisome
Eccl	9:13	the sun, and it S great to me.
Wis	3:2	of the foolish they S to have died, and
Jer	18:4	another vessel, as it S good to the potter
Dan	4:2	It has S good to me to show the
	7:20	great things, and which S greater than its fellows.
1Mac	15:20	And it has S good to us to accept
2Mac	1:13	with a force that S irresistible, they were cut

S

Lk 1:3 of the word, it S good to me also,
24:11 apostles; but these words S to them an idle
Acts 15:22 Then it S good to the apostles and the
15:25 no instructions, it has S good to us, having
15:28 For it has S good to the Holy Spirit
Rev 6:6 and I heard what S to be a voice
13:3 One of its heads S to have a mortal
19:1 this I heard what S to be the loud
19:6 Then I heard what S to be the voice

SEEMLY (3)

Ps 147:1 is gracious, and a song of praise is S
Sir 14:3 Riches are not S for a stingy man; and
1Tim 2:9 modestly and sensibly in S apparel, not with braided

SEEMS (37)

Lev 14:35 tell the priest, 'There S to me to be
Josh 9:25 hand: do as it S good and right in
Judg 10:15 do to us whatever S good to thee; only
19:24 do with them what S good to you; but
1Sam 1:23 to her, "Do what S best to you, wait
3:18 let him do what S good to him."
11:10 do to us whatever S good to you."
14:36 they said, "Do whatever S good to you." But
14:40 to Saul, "Do what S good to you."
29:6 and to me it S right that you should
2Sam 10:12 the LORD do what S good to him."
15:26 do to me what S good to him."
18:4 said to them, "Whatever S best to you I
19:27 God; do therefore what S good to you.
19:37 do for him whatever S good to you."
19:38 do for him whatever S good to you; and
24:22 and offer up what S good to him; here
1Kgs 21:2 it; or, if it S good to you, I
1Chr 13:2 of Israel, "If it S good to you, and
19:13 the LORD do what S good to him."
21:23 the king do what S good to him; see,
Ezra 7:18 Whatever S good to you and your brethren to
Jud 3:4 in any way that S good to you."
Esth 3:11 with them as it S good to you."
Prov 14:12 is a way which S right to a man,
16:25 is a way which S right to a man,
18:17 states his case first S right, until the other
Sir 6:20 She S very harsh to the uninstructed; a weakling
Jer 26:14 Do with me as S good and right to
27:5 it to whomever it S right to me.
40:4 If it S good to you to come with
40:4 well; but if it S wrong to you to
Zech 11:12 to them, "If it S right to you, give
Acts 17:18 Others said, "He S to be a preacher of
25:27 For it S to me unreasonable, in sending a
1Cor 16:4 If it S advisable that I should go also,
Heb 12:11 moment all discipline S painful rather than pleasant;

SEER (23)

1Sam 9:9 us go to the S; for he who is
9:9 was formerly called a S
9:11 to them, "Is the S here?"
9:18 "Tell me where is the house of the S
9:19 Saul, "I am the S; go up before me
2Sam 24:11 the prophet Gad, David's S, saying,
2Kgs 17:13 every prophet and every S, saying, "Turn from your
1Chr 9:22 David and Samuel the S established them in their
21:9 spoke to Gad, David's S, saying,
25:5 of Heman the king's S, according to the promise
26:28 all that Samuel the S, and Saul the son
29:29 Chronicles of Samuel the S, and in the Chronicles
29:29 Chronicles of Gad the S,
2Chr 9:29 visions of Iddo the S concerning Jeroboam the son
12:15 of Shemaiah the prophet and of Iddo the S
16:7 that time Hanani the S came to Asa king
16:10 was angry with the S, and put him in
19:2 son of Hanani the S went out to meet
29:25 of Gad the king's S and of Nathan the
29:30 the words of David and of Asaph the S
35:15 and Jeduthun the king's S; and the gatekeepers were
Sir 46:15 his words he became known as a trustworthy S
Amos 7:12 said to Amos, "O S, go, flee away to

SEERS (5)

2Chr 33:18 the words of the S who spoke to him
33:19 they are written in the Chronicles of the S
Is 29:10 eyes, the prophets, and covered your heads, the S
30:10 who say to the S, "See not"; and to
Mic 3:7 black over them; the S shall be disgraced, and

SEES (68)

Gen 44:31 lad's life, when he S that the lad is
Ex 4:14 you, and when he S you he will be
12:23 Egyptians; and when he S the blood on the
Lev 20:17 of his mother, and S her nakedness, and she
20:17 her nakedness, and she S his nakedness, it is
Num 21:8 is bitten, when he S it, shall live."
24:4 words of God, who S the vision of the
24:16 the Most High, who S the vision of the
Deut 32:36 his servants, when he S that their power is
1Sam 16:7 him; for the LORD S not as man sees;
16:7 sees not as man S; man looks on the
2Kgs 2:19 pleasant, as my lord S; but the water is
Esth 16:4 of God, who always S everything.
Job 7:8 eye of him who S me will behold me
10:4 Dost thou see as man S
11:11 worthless men; when he S iniquity, will he not
28:10 rocks, and his eye S every precious thing.
28:24 of the earth, and S everything under the heavens.
34:21 a man, and he S all his steps.
42:5 but now my eye S thee;
Ps 33:13 down from heaven, he S all the sons of
37:13 the wicked, for he S that his day is
58:8 untimely birth that never S the sun.
58:10 will rejoice when he S the vengeance; he will
97:4 the world; the earth S and trembles.
112:8 be afraid, until he S his desire on his
112:10 The wicked man S it and is angry; he
Prov 22:3 A prudent man S danger and hides himself; but
27:12 A prudent man S danger and hides himself; but
Sir 15:18 mighty in power and S everything;
18:11 He S and recognizes that their end will be
23:18 says to himself, "Who S me?
23:18 me, and no one S me.
30:20 by the Lord; he S with his eyes and
Is 21:6 set a watchman, let him announce what he S
21:7 When he S riders, horsemen in pairs, riders on
28:4 summer: when a man S it, he eats it
29:15 and who say, "Who S us?
29:23 For when he S his children, the work of
42:20 He S many things, but does not observe them;
47:10 you said, "No one S me"; your wisdom and
Lam 3:50 heaven looks down and S;
Ezek 12:27 'The vision that he S is for many days
18:14 begets a son who S all the sins which
32:31 "When Pharaoh S them, he will comfort himself for
33:3 watchman; and if he S the sword coming upon
33:6 But if the watchman S the sword coming and
39:15 land and any one S a man's bone, then
Dan 13:20 are shut, no one S us, and we are
2Mac 12:22 them of him who S all things; and they
15:2 day which he who S all things has honored
Mt 6:4 and your Father who S in secret will reward
6:6 and your Father who S in secret will reward
6:18 and your Father who S in secret will reward
Jn 5:18 but only what he S the Father doing; for
6:40 that every one who S the Son and believes
9:21 but how he now S we do not know,
10:12 the sheep are not, S the wolf coming and
11:9 not stumble, because he S the light of this
12:45 And he who S me sees him who sent
12:45 he who sees me S him who sent me.
14:17 receive, because it neither S him nor knows him;
Rom 8:24 For who hopes for what he S
1Cor 4:7 For who S anything different in you?
8:10 For if any one S you, a man of
2Cor 12:6 of me than he S in me or hears
1Jn 3:17 the world's goods and S his brother in need,
5:16 If any one S his brother committing what is

SEEST (4)

Is 58:3 we fasted, and thou S it not?
Jer 12:3 LORD, knowest me; thou S me, and triest my
20:12 triest the righteous, who S the heart and the
32:24 pass, and behold, thou S it.

SEETHE

Ezek 24:5 it; boil its pieces, S also its bones in

SEGUB (3)

1Kgs 16:34 of his youngest son S, according to the word
1Chr 2:21 and she bore him S;
2:22 bore him Segub; and S was the father of

SEIGE

Sir 50:4 ruin, and fortified the city to withstand a S

SEINE (2)
Hab 1:15 gathers them in his S; so he rejoices and
1:16 burns incense to his S; for by them he

SEIR (39)
Gen 14:6 Horites in their Mount S as far as El-paran
32:3 in the land of S, the country of Edom,
33:14 children, until I come to my lord in S
33:16 Esau returned that day on his way to S
36:8 the hill country of S; Esau is Edom.
36:9 of the Edomites in the hill country of S
36:20 are the sons of S the Horite, the inhabitants
36:21 Horites, the sons of S in the land of
36:30 according to their clans in the land of S
Num 24:18 Edom shall be dispossessed, S also, his enemies, shall
Deut 1:2 the way of Mount S to Kadesh-barnea.
1:44 beat you down in S as far as Hormah.
2:1 and for many days we went about Mount S
2:4 Esau, who live in S; and they will be
2:5 I have given Mount S to Esau as a
2:8 Esau who live in S, away from the Arabah
2:12 Horites also lived in S formerly, but the sons
2:22 Esau, who live in S, when he destroyed the
2:29 Esau who live in S and the Moabites who
33:2 Sinai, and dawned from S upon us; he shone
Josh 11:17 Halak, that rises toward S, as far as Baal-gad
12:7 Halak, that rises toward S (and Joshua gave their
15:10 of Baalah to Mount S, passes along to the
24:4 the hill country of S to possess, but Jacob
Judg 5:4 didst go forth from S, when thou didst march
1Chr 1:38 The sons of S: Lotan, Shobal, Zibeon, Anah, Dishon,
4:42 Simeonites, went to Mount S, having as their leaders
2Chr 20:10 and Moab and Mount S, whom thou wouldest not
20:22 Ammon, Moab, and Mount S, who had come against
20:23 the inhabitants of Mount S, destroying them utterly,
20:23 of the inhabitants of S, they all helped to
25:11 of Salt and smote ten thousand men of S
25:14 of the men of S, and set them up
Sir 50:26 who live on Mount S, and the Philistines, and
Is 21:11 calling to me from S, "Watchman, what of the
Ezek 35:2 your face against Mount S, and prophesy against it,
35:3 am against you, Mount S, and I will stretch
35:7 I will make Mount S a waste and a
35:15 shall be desolate, Mount S, and all Edom, all

SEIZE (47)
Gen 43:18 slaves of us and S our asses."
Josh 8:7 from the ambush, and S the city; for the
Judg 7:24 against the Midianites and S the waters against
21:21 of the vineyards and S each man his wife
2Sam 2:21 to your left, and S one of the young
1Kgs 18:40 Elijah said to them, S the prophets of Baal;
22:26 king of Israel said, S Micaiah, and take him
2Kgs 6:13 I may send and S him." It was told
2Chr 18:25 king of Israel said, S Micaiah, and take him
Jud 2:10 You shall go and S all their territory for
4:7 Dothan, ordering them to S the passes up into
6:10 in his tent, to S Achior and take him
7:1 against Bethulia, and to S the passes up into
14:3 Then they will S their arms and go into
16:5 to the ground and S my children as prey,
Job 3:6 night--let thick darkness S it!
24:2 Men remove landmarks; they S flocks and pasture
36:17 wicked; judgment and justice S you.
Ps 10:9 lurks that he may S the poor, he seizes
71:11 forsaken him; pursue and S him, for there is
109:8 be few; may another S his goods!
109:11 May the creditor S all that he has; may
Is 5:29 roar; they growl and S their prey, they carry
10:6 to take spoil and S plunder, and to tread
13:8 Pangs and agony will S them; they will be
22:17 He will S firm hold on you,
Jer 20:5 shall plunder them, and S them, and carry them
36:26 son of Abdeel to S Baruch the secretary and
Ezek 23:25 They shall S your sons and your daughters, and
38:12 bars or gates'; to S spoil and carry off
38:13 'Have you come to S spoil?
38:13 cattle and goods, to S great spoil?'
Mic 2:2 They covet fields, and S them; and houses, and
Hab 1:6 of the earth, to S habitations not their own.
1Mac 4:18 fight them, and afterward S the plunder boldly."
6:56 he was trying to S control of the government.
7:29 enemy were ready to S Judas.
9:60 Judea, telling them to S Jonathan and his men;
12:40 he kept seeking to S and kill him, and
Mt 26:48 kiss is the man; S him."
26:55 and you did not S me.
Mk 3:21 they went out to S him, for people were
14:44 kiss is the man; S him and lead him
14:49 and you did not S me.
2Cor 11:32 Damascus in order to S me,
Heb 6:18 have strong encouragement to S the hope set before
Rev 3:11 that no one may S your crown.

SEIZED (86)
Gen 19:16 lingered; so the men S him and his wife
21:25 which Abimelech's servants had S,
34:2 land, saw her, he S her and lay with
Ex 15:14 they tremble; pangs have S on the inhabitants of
Judg 3:28 down after him, and S the fords of the
7:24 called out, and they S the waters as far
12:6 it right; then they S him and slew him
15:15 out his hand and S it, and with it
16:21 And the Philistines S him and gouged out his
19:25 So the man S his concubine, and put her
2Sam 1:9 me; for anguish has S me, and yet my
4:10 bringing good news, I S him and slew him
1Kgs 18:40 And they S them; and Elijah brought them down
2Kgs 14:14 And he S all the gold and silver, and
2Chr 25:24 And he S all the gold and silver, and
25:24 Obed-edom with them; he S also the treasuries of
Tob 6:3 So the young man S the fish and threw
Jud 2:25 He also S the territory of Cilicia, and killed
4:5 of Salem, and immediately S all the high hilltops
7:7 supplied their water, and S them and set guards
7:17 in the valley and S the water supply and
Esth 14:1 And Esther the queen, S with deathly anxiety, fled
Job 16:12 broke me asunder; he S me by the neck
20:19 the poor, he has S a house which he
Wis 17:17 wilderness, he was S, and endured the inescapable
Sir 23:21 where he least suspects it, he will be S
Is 21:3 with anguish; pangs have S me, like the pangs
33:14 are afraid; trembling has S the godless: "Who
Jer 37:13 Shelemiah, son of Hananiah, S Jeremiah the
37:14 listen to him, and S Jeremiah and brought him
38:23 hand, but shall be S by the king of
48:41 the cities shall be taken and the strongholds S
49:24 to flee, and panic S her; anguish and sorrows
50:43 hands fell helpless; anguish S him, pain as of
51:32 the fords have been S, the bulwarks are burned
51:41 is taken, the praise of the whole earth S
Ezek 23:10 uncovered her nakedness; they S her sons and her
Dan 13:40 So we S this woman and asked her who
14:21 was enraged, and he S the priests and their
Mic 4:9 perished, that pangs have S you like a woman
1Mac 1:32 women and children, and S the cattle.
2:10 palaces and has not S her spoils?
3:12 Then they S their spoils; and Judas took the
4:23 the camp, and they S much gold and silver,
5:28 the sword; then he S all its spoils and
6:12 I S all her vessels of silver and gold;
6:24 caught, and they have S our inheritances.
7:2 his fathers, the army S Antiochus and Lysias to
7:16 trusted him; but he S sixty of them and
7:19 And he sent and S many of the men
7:47 Then the Jews S the spoils and the plunder,
9:36 Medeba came out and S John and all that
9:61 And Jonathan's men S about fifty of the men
11:46 men of the city S the main streets of
11:48 to the city and S much spoil on that
12:48 closed the gates and S him, and all who
12:50 that Jonathan had been S and had perished along
14:3 army of Demetrius, and S him and took him
15:30 cities which you have S and the tribute money
15:33 taken foreign land nor S foreign property, but only
16:22 greatly shocked; and he S the men who came
2Mac 2:21 few in number they S the whole land and
9:5 ceased speaking he was S with a pain in
Mt 14:3 For Herod had S John and bound him and
22:6 business, while the rest S his servants, treated them
26:50 hands on Jesus and S him.
26:57 Then those who had S Jesus led him to
Mk 6:17 Herod had sent and S John, and bound him
14:46 hands on him and S him.
14:51 his body; and they S him,
Lk 5:26 And amazement S them all, and they glorified God
7:16 Fear S them all; and they glorified God, saying,
8:29 a time it had S him; he was kept
8:37 them; for they were S with great fear; so
22:52 Then they S him and led him away, bringing
23:25 led him away, they S one Simon of Cyrene,
Jn 18:12 officers of the Jews S Jesus and bound him.

S

Acts 6:12 came upon him and brought him
12:4 And when he had S him, he put him
16:19 gain was gone, they S Paul and Silas and
18:17 And they all S Sosthenes, the ruler of the
21:30 people ran together; they S Paul and dragged him
23:27 This man was S by the Jews, and was
24:6 the temple, but we S him.
26:21 this reason the Jews S me in the temple
Rev 20:2 And he S the dragon, that ancient serpent, who

SEIZES (13)

Ex 15:15 leaders of Moab, trembling S them; all the
Deut 22:25 betrothed, and the man S her and lies with
22:28 is not betrothed, and S her and lies with
25:11 out her hand and S him by the private
Job 18:9 A trap S him by the heel, a snare
18:20 his day, and horror S them of the east.
21:6 am dismayed, and shuddering S my flesh.
30:18 With violence it S my garment; it binds me
Ps 10:9 seize the poor, he S the poor when he
119:53 Hot indignation S me because of the wicked, who
Prov 7:13 She S him and kisses him, and with impudent
Mk 9:18 spirit; and wherever it S him, it dashes him
Lk 9:39 and behold, a spirit S him, and he suddenly

SEIZING

Mt 18:27 a hundred denarii; and S him by the throat

SELA (4)

Judg 1:36 ascent of Akrabbim, from S and upward.
2Kgs 14:7 of Salt and took S by storm, and called
Is 16:1 of the land, from S, by way of the
42:11 let the inhabitants of S sing for joy, let

SELAH (74)

Ps 3:2 in God. S But thou, O LORD, art a shield about
3:4 to the LORD, and he answers me from his holy hill. S
3:8 thy blessing be upon thy people. S
4:2 and seek after lies? S But know that the LORD has
4:4 on your beds, and be silent. S
7:5 lay my soul in the dust. S
9:16 Higgaion. S The wicked shall depart to Sheol, all the
9:20 nations know that they are but men. S
20:3 and regard with favor your burnt sacrifices. S
21:2 and hast not withheld the requestof his lips. S
24:6 of the God of Jacob. S
24:10 is the King of glory! S
32:4 was dried up as by the heat of summer. S
32:5 then thou didst forgive the guilt of my sin. S
32:7 thou dost encompass me with deliverance. S
39:5 to him; surely every man stands as a mere breath. S
39:11 every man is a mere breath. S
44:8 and we will gve thanks to thy name forever. S
46:3 though the mountains tremble with its tumult. S
46:7 the God of Jacob is our refuge. S
46:11 the God of Jacob is our refuge S
47:4 heritage for us, the pride of Jacob whom he loves. S
48:8 the city of our God, which God establishes forever. S
49:13 end of those who are pleased with their portion. S
49:15 from the power of Sheol, for he will receive me. S
50:6 for God himself is judge! S "Hear, O my people, and
52:3 more than speaking the truth. S You love all words
52:5 from the land of the living. S The righteous shall see
54:3 they do not set God before them. S Behold, God is
55:7 lodge in the wilderness, S
55:19 and do not fear God. S My companion stretched out
57:3 S God will send forth his steadfast love and
57:6 but they have fallen into it themselves. S
59:5 those who treacherously plot evil. S Each evening
59:13 to the ends of the earth. S Each evening they
60:4 to rally to it from the bow. S That thy beloved
61:4 under the shelter of thy wings! S For thou, O God
62:4 but inwardly they curse. S For God alone my soul
62:8 God is a refuge for us. S Men of low estate are
66:4 sing praises to thy name. S Come and see what God
66:7 the rebellious exalt themselves. S Bless our God, O
66:15 of bulls and goats. S Come and hear, all you who fear
67:1 to shine upon us, S
67:4 the nations upon earth. S Let the peoples praise thee
68:7 march through the wilderness, S
68:19 God is our salvation. S Our God is a God of
68:32 praises to the Lord, S
75:3 who keep steady its pillars. S I say to the boastful,
76:3 the sword, and the weapons of war. S Glorious art
76:9 all the oppressed of the earth. S Surely the wrath of
77:3 my spirit faints. S Thou dost hold my eyelids from
77:9 anger shut up his compassion? S And I say, " It is my
77:15 of Jacob and Joseph. S When the waters saw thee
81:7 at the waters of Meribah. S Hear, O my people,
82:2 show partiality to the wicked? S Give justice to the
83:8 of the children of Lot. S Do to them as thou didst to
84:4 ever singing thy praise. S Blessed ar the men whose
84:8 O God of Jacob! S Behold our shield,
85:2 pardon all their sin. S Thou didst withdraw all thy
87:3 O city of God. S Among those who know
87:6 as he registers the peoples. S This one was
88:7 and thou dost overwhelm me with all thy waves S
88:10 S Do the shades rise up to praise thee?
89:4 your throne for all generations. S Let the heavens
89:37 while the skies endure. S But now thou hast cast off
89:45 thou hast covered him with shame. S
89:48 Who can deliver his soul from the power of Sheol? S
140:3 S Guard me, O LORD, from the hands of the
140:5 by the wayside they have set snares for me. S
140:8 wicked; do not further his evil plot! S
143:6 like a parched land. S Make hast to answer me, O
Hab 3:3 and the earth was full of his praise. S
3:9 S Thou didst cleave the earth with rivers.
3:13 S Thou didst pierce with thy shafts the head of

SELDOM

Prov 25:17 Let your foot be S in your neighbor's house,

SELECT (4)

Gen 41:33 Now therefore let Pharaoh S a man discreet and
Ex 12:21 and said to them, S lambs for yourselves according
Num 35:11 Canaan, then you shall S cities to be cities
2Kgs 10:3 cities also, and weapons, S the best and fittest

SELECTED (3)

Ezra 10:16 Ezra the priest S men, heads of fathers' houses,
Sir 47:2 As the fat is S from the peace offering,
47:2 offering, so David was S from the sons of

SELED (2)

1Chr 2:30 The sons of Nadab: S and Appa-im; and Seled
2:30 Seled and Appa-im; and S died childless.

SELEUCIA (2)

1Mac 11:8 cities as far as S by the sea, and
Acts 13:4 they went down to S; and from there they

SELEUCUS (5)

1Mac 7:1 Demetrius the son of S set forth from Rome,
2Mac 3:3 presents, so that even S, the king of Asia,
4:7 When S died and Antiochus who was called
5:18 as Heliodorus was, whom S the king sent to
14:1 Demetrius, the son of S, had sailed into the

SELF (5)

Ex 32:13 swear by thine own S, and didst say to
Rom 6:6 know that our old S was crucified with him
7:22 God, in my inmost S,
2Tim 3:2 will be lovers of S, lovers of money, proud,
Philem 1:19 nothing of your owing me even your own S

SELF-ABASEMENT (2)

Col 2:18 disqualify you, insisting on S and worship of angels,
2:23 rigor of devotion and S and severity to the

SELF-CONCEIT

Gal 5:26 Let us have no S, no provoking of one

SELF-CONDEMNED

Tit 3:11 a person is perverted and sinful; he is S

SELF-CONTROL (10)

Prov 25:28 A man without S is like a city broken
Wis 8:7 virtues; for she teaches S and prudence, justice and
Acts 24:24 argued about justice and S and future judgment, Felix
1Cor 7:5 again, lest Satan tempt you through lack of S
7:9 if they cannot exercise S, they should marry.
9:25 Every athlete exercises S in all things.
Gal 5:23 goodness, faithfulness, gentleness, S; against such
2Tim 1:7 but a spirit of power and love and S
2Pet 1:6 knowledge with S, and S with steadfastness, and

SELF-CONTROLLED

Tit 1:7 himself, upright, holy, and S;

S

SELF-DENIAL
Sir 11:16 through his diligence and S, and this is the

SELF-INDULGENT
1Tim 5:6 whereas she who is S is dead even while

SELF-KINDLED
Wis 17:6 them except a dreadful, S fire, and in terror

SELF-RELIANT
Sir 40:18 is sweet for the S and the worker, but

SELFISH (4)
Sir 41:19 Be ashamed of S behavior at meals, of surliness
Lk 6:35 he is kind to the ungrateful and the S
Jas 3:14 have bitter jealousy and S ambition in your hearts,
3:16 For where jealousy and S ambition exist, there will

SELFISHNESS (3)
2Cor 12:20 quarreling, jealousy, anger, S, slander, gossip, conceit,
Gal 5:20 strife, jealousy, anger, S, dissension, party spirit,
Phil 2:3 Do nothing from S or conceit, but in humility

SELL (34)
Gen 25:31) Jacob said, "First S me your birthright."
37:27 Come, let us S him to the Ishmaelites, and
47:22 therefore they did not S their land.
Ex 21:8 have no right to S her to a foreign
21:35 dies, then they shall S the live ox and
Lev 25:14 And if you S to your neighbor or buy
25:15 for crops he shall S to you.
Deut 2:28 You shall S me food for money, that I
14:21 it, or you may S it to a foreigner;
21:14 but you shall not S her for money, you
Judg 4:9 for the LORD will S Sisera into the hand
2Kgs 4:7 and he said, "Go, S the oil and pay
Neh 5:8 nations; but you even S your brethren that they
10:31 the sabbath day to S, we will not buy
Tob 1:7 second tenth I would S, and I would go
Prov 23:23 truth, and do not S it; buy wisdom, instruction,
Bar 6:28 The priests S the sacrifices that are offered to
Ezek 30:12 the Nile, and will S the land into the
48:14 They shall not S or exchange any of it;
Joel 3:8 I will S your sons and your daughters into
3:8 Judah, and they will S them to the Sabeans,
Amos 2:6 punishment; because they S the righteous for silver,
8:5 over, that we may S grain?
8:6 pair of sandals, and S the refuse of the
Zech 11:5 unpunished; and those who S them say, 'Blessed be
1Mac 12:36 so that its garrison could neither buy nor S
13:49 to the country and back to buy and S
2Mac 5:24 grown men and to S the women and boys
Mt 19:21 would be perfect, go, S what you possess and
Mk 10:21 lack one thing; go, S what you have, and
Lk 12:33 S your possessions, and give alms; provide yourselves
18:22 S all that you have and distribute to the
22:36 who has no sword S his mantle and buy
Rev 13:17 one can buy or S unless he has the

SELLER (4)
Is 24:2 buyer, so with the S; as with the lender,
Ezek 7:12 buyer rejoice, nor the S mourn, for wrath is
7:13 For the S shall not return to what he
Acts 16:14 city of Thyatira, a S of purple goods, who

SELLERS
Neh 13:20 Then the merchants and S of all kinds of

SELLING (6)
Lev 25:16 crops that he is S to you.
Ruth 4:3 country of Moab, is S the parcel of land
Sir 27:2 is wedged in between S and buying.
37:11 with a buyer about S, with a grudging man
2Mac 8:10 two thousand talents, by S the captured Jews into
Jn 2:14 found those who were S oxen and sheep and

SELLS (11)
Ex 21:7 "When a man S his daughter as a slave,
21:16 a man, whether he S him or is found
22:1 and kills it or S it, he shall pay
Lev 25:25 brother becomes poor, and S part of his property,
25:29 "If a man S a dwelling house in a
25:39 poor beside you, and S himself to you, you
25:47 him becomes poor and S himself to the stranger
Deut 24:7 as a slave or S him, then that thief
Prov 11:26 head of him who S it.
31:24 makes linen garments and S them; she delivers
Mt 13:44 joy he goes and S all that he has

SELVES (2)
Acts 20:30 from among your own S will arise men speaking
1Thes 2:8 but also our own S, because you had become

SEMACHIAH
1Chr 26:7 whose brethren were able men, Elihu and S

SEMBLANCE (2)
Is 52:14 so marred, beyond human S, and his form beyond
Ezek 10:21 underneath their wings the S of human hands.

SEME-IN
Lk 3:26 Mattathias, the son of S, the son of Josech,

SEMEN (6)
Gen 38:9 wife he spilled the S on the ground, lest
Lev 15:16 has an emission of S, he shall bathe his
15:17 skin on which the S comes shall be washed
15:18 has an emission of S, both of them shall
15:32 has an emission of S, becoming unclean thereby;
22:4 had an emission of S,

SENAAH (2)
Ezra 2:35 The sons of S, three thousand six hundred and
Neh 7:38 The sons of S, three thousand nine hundred and

SENATE (11)
Jud 4:8 high priest and the S of the whole people
11:14 to bring back to them permission from the S
15:8 high priest, and the S of the people of
1Mac 8:15 built for themselves a S chamber, and every day
8:19 and they entered the S chamber and spoke as
12:3 Rome and entered the S chamber and said,
12:6 the high priest, the S of the nation, the
2Mac 1:10 in Judea and the S and Judas, To Aristobulus,
4:44 men sent by the S presented the case before
11:27 "King Antiochus to the S of the Jews and
Acts 5:21 council and all the S of Israel, and sent

SENATOR
2Mac 6:1 king sent an Athenian S to compel the Jews

SENATORS
1Mac 8:15 three hundred and twenty S constantly deliberate

SEND (281)
Gen 7:4 seven days I will S rain upon the earth
24:7 this land,' he will S his angel before you,
24:40 whom I walk, will S his angel with you
24:54 the morning, he said, S me back to my
27:45 him; then I will S, and fetch you from
30:25 Jacob said to Laban, S me away, that I
37:13 Come, I will S you to them." And he
38:17 He answered, "I will S you a kid from
38:17 a pledge, till you S it?"
42:4 But Jacob did not S Benjamin, Joseph's brother, with
42:16 S one of you, and let him bring your
43:4 you.' If you will S our brother with us,
43:5 if you will not S him, we will not
43:8 to Israel his father, S the lad with me,
43:14 man, that he may S back your other brother
Ex 3:10 Come, I will S you to Pharaoh that you
4:13 said, "Oh, my Lord, S, I pray, some other
5:22 Why didst thou ever S me?
6:1 strong hand he will S them out, yea, with
8:21 go, behold, I will S swarms of flies on
9:14 this time I will S all my plagues upon
9:19 Now therefore S, get your cattle and all that
12:33 with the people, to S them out of the
23:20 "Behold, I S an angel before you, to guard
23:27 I will S my terror before you, and will
23:28 And I will S hornets before you, which shall
33:2 it.' And I will S an angel before you,
33:12 know whom thou wilt S with me.
Lev 16:21 of the goat, and S him away into the
25:9 Then you shall S abroad the loud trumpet on
25:9 of atonement you shall S abroad the trumpet
26:25 your cities I will S pestilence among you, and
26:36 are left, I will S faintness into their hearts
Num 13:2 LORD said to Moses, S men to spy out
13:2 their fathers shall you S a man, every one
22:37 Balaam, "Did I not S to you to call
31:4 You shall S a thousand from each of the

S

Deut 1:22 and said, 'Let us S men before us, that
7:20 LORD your God will S hornets among them, until
19:12 of his city shall S and fetch him from
28:20 "The LORD will S upon you curses, confusion, and
28:48 whom the LORD will S against you, in hunger
32:24 pestilence; and I will S the teeth of beasts
Josh 1:16 do, and wherever you S us we will go.
18:4 tribe, and I will S them out that they
Judg 6:14 Midian; do not I S you?"
13:8 God whom thou didst S come again to us,
1Sam 5:11 the Philistines, and said, S away the ark of
6:2 with what we shall S it to its place."
6:3 They said, "If you S away the ark of
6:3 of Israel, do not S it empty, but by
6:8 Then S it off, and let it go its
9:16 this time I will S to you a man
9:26 "Up, that I may S you on your way."
11:3 respite that we may S messengers through all the
12:17 LORD, that he may S thunder and rain; and
16:1 and go; I will S you to Jesse the
16:11 Samuel said to Jesse, S and fetch him; for
16:19 to Jesse, and said, S me David your son,
20:12 shall I not then S and disclose it to
20:13 it to you, and S you away, that you
20:21 And behold, I will S the lad, saying, 'Go,
20:31 Therefore S and fetch him to me, for he
21:2 matter about which I S you, and with which
29:4 Philistines said to him, S the man back, that
2Sam 11:6 sent word to Joab, S me Uriah the Hittite."
13:9 And Amnon said, S out every one from me."
14:29 sent for Joab, to S him to the king;
14:32 here, that I may S you to the king,
15:36 by them you shall S to me everything you
17:16 Now therefore S quickly and tell David, 'Do not
18:3 is better that you S us help from the
1Kgs 8:44 whatever way thou shalt S them, and they pray
18:1 Ahab; and I will S rain upon the earth."
18:19 Now therefore S and gather all Israel to me
20:6 children"; nevertheless I will S my servants to you
2Kgs 2:16 And he said, "You shall not S
2:17 urged him till he was ashamed, he said, S
4:22 her husband, and said, S me one of the
5:5 now, and I will S a letter to the
6:13 is, that I may S and seize him." It
7:13 already perished; let us S and see."
9:17 "Take a horseman, and S to meet them, and
15:37 the LORD began to S Rezin the king of
17:27 king of Assyria commanded, S there one of the
1Chr 13:2 our God, let us S abroad to our brethren
2Chr 2:7 So now S me a man skilled to work
2:8 S me also cedar, cypress, and algum timber from
2:15 has spoken, let him S to his servants;
6:34 whatever way thou shalt S them, and they pray
7:13 devour the land, or S pestilence among my people,
28:11 Now hear me, and S back the captives from
Ezra 4:11 province Beyond the River, S greeting.
4:14 king's dishonor, therefore we S and inform the king,
5:17 And let the king S us his pleasure in
8:17 place Casiphia, namely, to S us ministers for the
Neh 2:5 your sight, that you S me to Judah, to
2:6 pleased the king to S me; and I set
8:10 drink sweet wine and S portions to him for
8:12 and drink and to S portions and to make
Tob 2:12 She used to S the product to the owners.
8:12 to his wife Edna, S one of the maids
10:7 Tobias said to Raguel, S me back, for my
10:8 me, and I will S messengers to your father,
10:9 Tobias replied, "No, S me back to my father."
Jud 6:3 He will S his forces and will destroy them
8:31 and the Lord will S us rain to fill
9:9 Behold their pride, and S thy wrath upon their
11:22 has done well to S you before the people,
16:14 Thou didst S forth thy Spirit, and it formed
Esth 9:19 day on which they S choice portions to one
Job 1:4 day; and they would S and invite their three
1:5 their course, Job would S and sanctify them, and
20:23 the full God will S his fierce anger into
21:11 They S forth their little ones like a flock,
38:35 Can you S forth lightnings, that they may go
Ps 20:2 May he S you help from the sanctuary, and
43:3 Oh S out thy light and thy truth; let
57:3 He will S from heaven and save me, he
57:3 [Selah] God will S forth his steadfast love and
144:6 lightning and scatter them, S out thy arrows and
Prov 10:26 sluggard to those who S him.
25:13 messenger to those who S him, he refreshes the

Wis 9:10 S her forth from the holy heavens, and from
9:10 throne of thy glory S her, that she may
11:15 worthless animals, thou didst S upon them a
11:17 lack the means to S upon them a multitude
12:8 but men, and didst S wasps as forerunners of
12:25 thoughtless children, thou didst S thy judgment to
Sir 29:9 his need do not S him away empty.
39:14 stream of water; S forth fragrance like frankincense,
45:9 bells round about, to S forth a sound as
Is 6:8 saying, "Whom shall I S, and who will go
6:8 S me."
10:6 a godless nation I S him, and against the
10:16 LORD of hosts, will S wasting sickness among his
19:20 of oppressors he will S them a savior, and
42:19 servant, or deaf as my messenger whom I S
43:14 your sake I will S to Babylon and break
48:20 of joy, proclaim it, S it forth to the
66:19 from them I will S survivors to the nations,
Jer 1:7 all to whom I S you you shall go,
2:10 Cyprus and see, or S to Kedar and examine
9:16 known; and I will S the sword after them,
9:17 mourning women to come; S for the skilful women
14:3 Her nobles S their servants for water; they come
14:14 name; I did not S them, nor did I
14:15 although I did not S them, and who say,
15:1 S them out of my sight, and let them
16:16 and afterwards I will S for many hunters, and
17:16 not pressed thee to S evil, nor have I
23:21 "I did not S the prophets, yet they ran;
23:32 when I did not S them or charge them;
24:10 And I will S sword, famine, and pestilence upon
25:9 words, behold, I will S for all the tribes
25:15 nations to whom I S you drink it.
26:5 the prophets whom I S to you urgently, though
27:3 S word to the king of Edom, the king
29:9 name; I did not S them, says the LORD.
29:31 LORD came to Jeremiah: S to all the exiles,
29:31 when I did not S him, and has made
37:20 you, and do not S me back to the
38:26 that he would not S me back to the
43:2 our God did not S you to say, 'Do
43:10 Israel: Behold, I will S and take Nebuchadrezzar the
48:12 LORD, when I shall S to him tilters who
49:37 I will S the sword after them, until I
51:2 Chaldea; and I will S to Babylon winnowers, and
Bar 1:10 they said: "Herewith we S you money; so buy
Ezek 2:3 "Son of man, I S you to the people
2:4 impudent and stubborn: I S you to them; and
5:17 I will S famine and wild beasts against you,
14:13 staff of bread and S famine upon it, and
14:19 Or if I S a pestilence into that land,
14:21 much more when I S upon Jerusalem my four
28:23 her; for I will S pestilence into her, and
32:18 multitude of Egypt, and S them down, her and
34:26 blessing; and I will S down the showers in
39:6 I will S fire on Magog and on those
Dan 11:20 place one who shall S an exactor of tribute
13:29 said before the people, S for Susanna, the daughter
Hos 8:14 cities; but I will S a fire upon his
Amos 1:4 So I will S a fire upon the house
1:7 So I will S a fire upon the wall
1:10 So I will S a fire upon the wall
1:12 So I will S a fire upon Teman, and
2:2 So I will S a fire upon Moab, and
2:5 So I will S a fire upon Judah, and
4:7 the harvest; I would S rain upon one city,
4:7 upon one city, and S no rain upon another
8:11 GOD, "when I will S a famine on the
Zech 5:4 I will S it forth, says the LORD of
Mal 2:2 hosts, then I will S the curse upon you
3:1 "Behold, I S my messenger to prepare the way
4:5 "Behold, I will S you Elijah the prophet before
1Mac 3:35 Jerusalem, Lysias was to S a force against them
7:7 Now then S a man whom you trust; let
11:43 will do well to S me men who will
12:10 we have undertaken to S to renew our brotherhood
12:18 And now please S us a reply to this."
13:16 S now a hundred talents of silver and two
13:18 "Because Simon did not S him the money and
13:21 the wilderness and to S them food.
16:18 king, asking him to S troops to aid him
2Mac 2:15 have need of them, S people to get them
3:37 would be suitable to S on another mission to
3:38 plotter against your government, S him there, for you
6:23 quickly, telling them to S him to Hades.
11:6 besought the Lord to S a good angel to

S

Prov 6:32 commits adultery has no S; he who does it
7:7 a young man without S,
9:4 him who is without S she says,
9:16 him who is without S she says,
10:13 is for the back of him who lacks S
10:21 feed many, but fools die for lack of S
11:12 belittles his neighbor lacks S, but a man of
12:8 according to his good S, but one of perverse
12:11 but he who follows worthless pursuits has no S
13:15 Good S wins favor, but the way of the
15:21 him who has no S, but a man of
17:18 A man without S gives a pledge, and becomes
19:11 Good S makes a man slow to anger, and
24:30 of a man without S;
Eccl 10:3 the road, he lacks S, and he says to
Sir 1:21 lips of many will tell of his good S
25:2 and an adulterous old man who lacks good S
25:9 who has gained good S, and he who speaks
29:14 who has lost his S of shame will fail
Jer 5:4 poor, they have no S; for they do not
Bar 6:42 this and abandon them, for they have no S
Hos 7:12 dove, silly and without S, calling to Egypt, going
1Cor 12:17 where would be the S of smell?

SENSELESS (8)

Deut 32:6 LORD, you foolish and S people?
Job 30:8 A S, a disreputable brood, they have been whipped
Sir 16:21 of understanding thinks; a S and misguided man
21:19 To a S man education is fetters on his
Jer 5:21 this, O foolish and S people, who have eyes,
Rom 1:21 their thinking and their S minds were darkened.
1Tim 6:9 a snare, into many S and hurtful desires that
2Tim 2:23 to do with stupid, S controversies; you know that

SENSES

2Mac 9:11 to come to his S under the scourge of

SENSIBLE (13)

Tob 6:12 The girl is also beautiful and S
Wis 6:24 the world, and a S king is the stability
Sir 19:26 his appearance, and a S man is known by
20:26 advance himself, and a S man will please great
21:7 from afar; but the S man, when he slips,
21:17 The utterance of a S man will be sought
21:21 To a S man education is like a golden
22:4 A S daughter obtains her husband, but one who
38:4 the earth, and a S man will not despise
1Cor 10:15 I speak as to S men; judge for yourselves
1Tim 3:2 one wife, temperate, S, dignified, hospitable, an apt
Tit 2:2 men be temperate, serious, S, sound in faith, in
2:5 and children, to be S, chaste, domestic, kind, and

SENSIBLY (2)

Sir 13:21 reproach him; he speaks S, and receives no attention.
1Tim 2:9 adorn themselves modestly and S in seemly apparel,

SENSUOUS

Col 2:18 without reason by his S mind,

SENT (797)

Gen 3:23 therefore the LORD God S him forth from the
8:7 he had made, and S forth a raven; and
8:8 Then he S forth a dove from him, to
8:10 days, and again he S forth the dove out
8:12 another seven days, and S forth the dove; and
19:13 and the LORD has S us to destroy it."
19:29 God remembered Abraham, and S Lot out of the
20:2 Abimelech king of Gerar S and took Sarah.
21:14 with the child, and S her away.
24:59 So they S away Rebekah their sister and her
25:6 was still living he S them away from his
26:27 hate me and have S me away from you?"
26:29 but good and have S you away in peace.
27:42 to Rebekah; so she S and called Jacob her
28:5 Thus Isaac S Jacob away; and he went to
28:6 had blessed Jacob and S him away to Paddan-aram
31:4 So Jacob S and called Rachel and Leah into
31:27 that I might have S you away with mirth
31:42 now you would have S me away empty-handed.
32:3 And Jacob S messengers before him to Esau his
32:5 maidservants; and I have S to tell my lord,
32:18 they are a present S to my lord Esau;
32:23 He took them and S them across the stream,
37:14 So he S him from the valley of Hebron,
37:32 the blood; and they S the long robe with
38:20 When Judah S the kid by his friend the
38:23 at; you see, I S this kid, and you
38:25 being brought out, she S word to her father-in-law,
41:8 was troubled; and he S and called for all
41:14 Then Pharaoh S and called Joseph, and they brought
44:3 light, the men were S awy with their asses.
45:5 me here; for God S me before you to
45:7 And God S me before you to preserve for
45:8 was not you who S me here, but God;
45:23 To his father he S as follows: ten asses
45:24 Then he S his brothers away, and as they
45:27 wagons which Joseph had S to carry him, the
46:5 wagons which Pharaoh had S to carry him.
46:28 He S Judah before him to Joseph, to appear
50:16 So they S a message to Joseph, saying, "Your
Ex 2:5 among the reeds and S her maid to fetch
3:12 you, that I have S you: when you have
3:13 of your fathers has S me to you,' and
3:14 Israel, 'I AM has S me to you.'"
3:15 God of Jacob, has S me to you: this
4:28 with which he had S him, and all the
7:16 God of the Hebrews, S me to you, saying,
9:7 And Pharaoh S, and behold, not one of the
9:23 heaven; and the LORD S thunder and hail, and
9:27 Then Pharaoh S, and called Moses and Aaron, and
18:2 wife, after he had S her away,
24:5 And he S young men of the people of
32:35 And the LORD S a plague upon the people,
Lev 16:10 that it may be S away into the wilderness
Num 13:3 So Moses S them from the wilderness of Paran,
13:16 the men whom Moses S to spy out the
13:17 Moses S them to spy out the land of
13:27 land to which you S us; it flows with
14:36 the men whom Moses S to spy out the
16:12 And Moses S to call Dathan and Abiram the
16:28 that the LORD has S me to do all
16:29 the LORD has not S me.
20:14 Moses S messengers from Kadesh to the king of
20:16 heard our voice, and S an angel and brought
21:6 Then the LORD S fiery serpents among the people,
21:21 Then Israel S messengers to Sihon king of the
21:32 And Moses S to spy out Jazer; and they
22:5 Moab at that time, S messengers to Balaam the
22:10 king of Moab, has S to me, saying,
22:15 Once again Balak S princes, more in number and
22:40 oxen and sheep, and S to Balaam and to
24:12 your messengers whom you S to me,
31:6 And Moses S them to the war, a thousand
32:8 your fathers, when I S them from Kadesh-barnea to
Deut 2:26 of you.' "So I S messengers from the wilderness
9:23 And when the LORD S you from Kadesh-barnea,
24:4 her former husband, who S her away, may not
34:11 wonders which the LORD S him to do in
Josh 2:1 the son of Nun S two men secretly from
2:3 the king of Jericho S to Rahab, saying, "Bring
2:21 Then she S them away, and they departed; and
6:17 live, because she hid the messengers that we S
6:25 the messengers whom Joshua S to spy out Jericho.
7:2 Joshua S men from Jericho to Ai, which is
7:22 So Joshua S messengers, and they ran to the
8:3 men of valor, and S them forth by night.
8:9 So Joshua S them forth; and they went to
10:3 Adoni-zedek king of Jerusalem S to Hoham king of
10:6 the men of Gibeon S to Joshua at the
11:1 heard of this, he S to Jobab king of
14:7 servant of the LORD S me from Kadesh-barnea to
14:11 the day that Moses S me; my strength now
22:6 Joshua blessed them, and S them away; and they
22:7 And when Joshua S them away to their homes
22:13 the people of Israel S to the Reubenites and
24:5 And I S Moses and Aaron, and I plagued
24:9 against Israel; and he S and invited Balaam the
24:12 And I S the hornet before you, which drove
24:28 So Joshua S the people away, every man to
Judg 1:23 the house of Joseph S to spy out Bethel.
3:15 The people of Israel S tribute by him to
3:18 presenting the tribute, he S away the people that
4:6 She S and summoned Barak the son of Abino-am
6:8 the Midianites, the LORD S a prophet to the
6:35 And he S messengers throughout all Manasseh; and
6:35 And he S messengers to Asher, Zebulun, and
7:8 their trumpets; and he S all the rest of
7:24 And Gideon S messengers throughout all the hill
9:23 And God S an evil spirit between Abimelech and
9:31 And he S messengers to Abimelech at Arumah,
11:12 Then Jephthah S messengers to the king of the
11:14 And Jephthah S messengers again to the king of

11:17 Israel then S messengers to the king of Edom,
11:17 And they S also to the king of Moab,
11:19 Israel then S messengers to Sihon king of the
11:28 of Jephthah which he S to him.
11:38 And he S her away for two months; and
16:18 all his mind, she S and called the lords
18:2 So the Danites S five able men from the
19:29 into twelve pieces, and S her throughout all the
20:6 her in pieces, and S her throughout all the
20:12 the tribes of Israel S men through all the
21:10 So the congregation S thither twelve thousand of
21:13 the whole congregation S word to the Benjaminites
1Sam 4:4 So the people S to Shiloh, and brought from
5:8 So they S and gathered together all the lords
5:10 So they S the ark of God to Ekron.
5:11 They S therefore and gathered together all the lords
6:21 So they S messengers to the inhabitants of
10:25 Then Samuel S all the people away, each one
11:7 them in pieces and S them throughout all the
12:8 LORD and the LORD S Moses and Aaron, who
12:11 thee.' And the LORD S Jerubbaal and Barak, and
12:18 LORD, and the LORD S thunder and rain that
13:2 of the people he S home, every man to
15:1 to Saul, "The LORD S me to anoint you
15:18 And the LORD S you on a mission, and
15:20 on which the LORD S me, I have brought
16:12 And he S, and brought him in.
16:19 Saul S messengers to Jesse, and said, "Send
16:20 and a kid, and S them by David his
16:22 And Saul S to Jesse, saying, "Let David remain
17:31 before Saul; and he S for him.
18:5 was successful wherever Saul S him; so that Saul
19:11 That night Saul S messengers to David's house to
19:14 And when Saul S messengers to take David, she
19:15 Then Saul S the messengers to see David, saying,
19:20 Then Saul S messengers to take David; and when
19:21 was told Saul, he S other messengers, and they
19:21 And Saul S messengers again the third time, and
20:22 for the LORD has S you away.
22:11 Then the king S to summon Ahimelech the priest,
25:5 So David S ten young men; and David said
25:14 Nabal's wife, "Behold, David S messengers out of the
25:25 the young men of my lord, whom you S
25:32 God of Israel, who S you this day to
25:39 Then David S and wooed Abigail, to make her
25:40 to her, "David has S us to you to
26:4 into the wilderness, David S out spies, and learned
30:26 came to Ziklag, he S part of the spoil
31:9 off his armor, and S messengers throughout the land
2Sam 2:5 David S messengers to the men of Jabesh-gilead,
3:12 And Abner S messengers to David at Hebron, saying,
3:14 Then David S messengers to Ish-bosheth Saul's son,
3:15 And Ish-bosheth S, and took her from her husband
3:21 So David S Abner away; and he went in
3:22 Hebron, for he had S him away, and he
3:24 it that you have S him away, so that
3:26 from David's presence, he S messengers after Abner,
5:11 Hiram king of Tyre S messengers to David, and
8:10 army of Hadadezer, Toi S his son Joram to
9:5 Then King David S and brought him from the
10:2 So David S by his servants to console him
10:3 think, because David has S comforters to you, that
10:3 Has not David S his servants to you to
10:4 at their hips, and S them away.
10:5 was told David, he S to meet them, for
10:6 to David, the Ammonites S and hired the Syrians
10:7 heard of it, he S Joab and all the
10:16 And Hadadezer S, and brought out the Syrians who
11:1 forth to battle, David S Joab, and his servants
11:3 And David S and inquired about the woman.
11:4 So David S messengers, and took her; and she
11:5 woman conceived; and she S and told David, "I
11:6 So David S word to Joab, "Send me Uriah
11:6 And Joab S Uriah to David.
11:14 letter to Joab, and S it by the hand
11:18 Then Joab S and told David all the news
11:22 all that Joab had S him to tell.
11:27 mourning was over, David S and brought her to
12:1 And the LORD S Nathan to David.
12:25 LORD loved him, and S a message by Nathan
12:27 And Joab S messengers to David, and said, "I
13:7 Then David S home to Tamar, saying, "Go to
14:2 And Joab S to Tekoa, and fetched from there
14:29 Then Absalom S for Joab, to send him to
14:29 And he S a second time, but Joab would
14:32 answered Joab, "Behold, I S word to you, 'Come
15:10 But Absalom S secret messengers throughout all the
15:12 offering the sacrifices, he S for Ahithophel the
18:2 And David S forth the army, one third under
18:29 Ahima-az answered, "When Joab S your servant, I
19:11 And King David S this message to Zadok and
19:14 man; so that they S word to the king,
22:15 And he S out arrows, and scattered them; lightning,
24:13 return to him who S me."
24:15 So the LORD S a pestilence upon Israel from
1Kgs 1:44 and the king has S with him Zadok the
1:53 So King Solomon S, and they brought him down
2:25 So King Solomon S Benaiah the son of Jehoiada;
2:29 Solomon S Benaiah the son of Jehoiada, saying, "Go,
2:36 Then the king S and summoned Shimei, and said
2:42 and returned, the king S and summoned Shimei, and
5:1 Hiram king of Tyre S his servants to Solomon,
5:2 And Solomon S word to Hiram,
5:8 And Hiram S to Solomon, saying, "I have heard
5:8 message which you have S to me; I am
5:14 And he S them to Lebanon, ten thousand a
7:13 And King Solomon S and brought Hiram from Tyre.
8:66 the eighth day he S the people away; and
9:14 Hiram had S to the king one hundred and
9:27 And Hiram S with the fleet his servants, seamen
12:3 And they S and called him; and Jeroboam and
12:18 King Rehoboam S Adoram, who was taskmaster
12:20 Jeroboam had returned, they S and called him to
15:18 servants; and King Asa S them to Ben-hadad the
15:20 to King Asa, and S the commanders of his
18:10 my lord has not S to seek you; and
18:20 So Ahab S to all the people of Israel,
19:2 Then Jezebel S a messenger to Elijah, saying, "So
20:2 And he S messengers into the city to Ahab
20:5 "Thus says Ben-hadad: 'I S to you, saying, "Deliver
20:7 seeking trouble; for he S to me for my
20:10 Ben-hadad S to him and said, "The gods do
20:17 And Ben-hadad S out scouts, and they reported to
21:8 his seal, and she S the letters to the
21:11 did as Jezebel had S word to them.
21:11 letters which she had S to them,
21:14 Then they S to Jezebel, saying, "Naboth has been
2Kgs 1:2 lay sick; so he S messengers, telling them, "Go,
1:6 to the king who S you, and say to
1:9 Then the king S to him a captain of
1:11 Again the king S to him another captain of
1:13 Again the king S the captain of a third
1:16 LORD, 'Because you have S messengers to inquire of
2:2 for the LORD has S me as far as
2:4 for the LORD has S me to Jericho." But
2:6 for the LORD has S me to the Jordan."
2:17 They S therefore fifty men; and for three days
3:7 And he went and S word to Jehoshaphat king
5:6 know that I have S to you Naaman my
5:8 rent his clothes, he S to the king, saying,
5:10 And Elisha S a messenger to him, saying, "Go
5:22 My master has S me to say, 'There have
5:24 the house; and he S the men away, and
6:9 the man of God S word to the king
6:10 the king of Israel S to the place of
6:14 So he S there horses and chariots and a
6:23 eaten and drunk, he S them away, and they
6:32 how this murderer has S to take off my
7:14 men, and the king S them after the army
8:9 king of Syria has S me to you, saying,
9:19 Then he S out a second horseman, who came
10:1 Jehu wrote letters, and S them to Samaria, to
10:5 elders and the guardians, S to Jehu, saying, "We
10:7 heads in baskets, and S them to him at
10:21 And Jehu S throughout all Israel; and all the
11:4 seventh year Jehoiada S and brought the captains
12:18 the king's house, and S these to Hazael king
14:8 Then Amaziah S messengers to Jehoash the son of
14:9 Jehoash king of Israel S word to Amaziah king
14:9 "A thistle on Lebanon S to a cedar on
14:19 But they S after him to Lachish, and slew
16:7 Ahaz S messengers to Tiglath-pileser king of Assyria,
16:8 the king's house, and S a present to the
16:10 And King Ahaz S to Uriah the priest a
16:11 that King Ahaz had S from Damascus, so Uriah
17:4 Hoshea; for he had S messengers to So, king
17:13 fathers, and which I S to you by my
17:25 LORD; therefore the LORD S lions among them,
17:26 land; therefore he has S lions among them, and
18:14 Hezekiah king of Judah S to the king of
18:17 the king of Assyria S the Tartan, the Rabsaris,
18:27 them, "Has my master S me to speak these

SENT

19:2 And he S Eliakim, who was over the household,
19:4 king of Assyria has S to mock the living
19:9 he S messengers again to Hezekiah, saying,
19:16 Sennacherib, which he has S to mock the living
19:20 the son of Amoz S to Hezekiah, saying, "Thus
20:12 Baladan, king of Babylon, S envoys with letters and
22:3 King Josiah, the king S Shaphan the son of
22:15 'Tell the man who S you to me,
22:18 king of Judah, who S you to inquire of
23:1 Then the king S, and all the elders of
23:16 the mount; and he S and took the bones
24:2 And the LORD S against him bands of the
24:2 of the Ammonites, and S them against Judah to
1Chr 6:15 exile when the LORD S Judah and Jerusalem into
8:8 Moab after he had S away Hushim and Baara
10:9 and his armor, and S messengers throughout the land
12:19 Philistines took counsel and S him away, saying, "At
14:1 Hiram king of Tyre S messengers to David, and
18:10 king of Zobah, he S his son Hadoram to
18:10 And he S all sorts of articles of gold,
19:2 So David S messengers to console him concerning
19:3 think, because David has S comforters to you, that
19:4 at their hips, and S them away;
19:5 concerning the men, he S to meet them, for
19:6 Hanun and the Ammonites S a thousand talents of
19:8 heard of it, he S Joab and all the
19:16 defeated by Israel, they S messengers and brought
21:12 return to him who S me."
21:14 So the LORD S a pestilence upon Israel; and
21:15 And God S the angel to Jerusalem to destroy
2Chr 2:3 And Solomon S word to Huram the king of
2:3 David my father and S him cedar to build
2:11 a letter which he S to Solomon, "Because the
2:13 "Now I have S a skilled man, endued with
7:10 the seventh month he S the people away to
8:18 And Huram S him by his servants ships and
10:3 And they S and called him; and Jeroboam and
10:18 King Rehoboam S Hadoram, who was taskmaster
13:13 Jeroboam had S an ambush around to come on
16:2 the king's house, and S them to Ben-hadad king
16:4 to King Asa, and S the commanders of his
17:7 of his reign he S his princes, Ben-hail, Obadiah,
24:19 Yet he S prophets among them to bring them
24:23 among the people, and S all their spoil to
25:13 the army whom Amaziah S back, not letting them
25:15 angry with Amaziah and S to him a prophet,
25:17 Judah took counsel and S to Joash the son
25:18 the king of Israel S word to Amaziah king
25:18 "A thistle on Lebanon S to a cedar on
25:27 But they S after him to Lachish, and slew
28:16 that time King Ahaz S to the king of
30:1 Hezekiah S to all Israel and Judah, and wrote
32:9 with all his forces, S his servants to Jerusalem
32:21 And the LORD S an angel, who cut off
32:31 Babylon, who had been S to him to inquire
34:8 and the house, he S Shaphan the son of
34:22 whom the king had S went to Huldah the
34:23 'Tell the man who S you to me,
34:26 king of Judah, who S you to inquire of
34:29 Then the king S and gathered together all the
35:21 But he S envoys to him, saying, "What have
36:10 the year King Nebuchadnezzar S and brought him to
36:15 God of their fathers, S persistently to them by
Ezra 4:11 the letter that they S -- "To Artaxerxes the
4:17 The king S an answer: "To Rehum the commander
4:18 the letter which you S to us has been
5:6 province Beyond the River S to Darius the king;
5:7 Darius the king; they S him a report, in
6:13 according to the word S by Darius the king,
7:14 For you are S by the king and his
8:16 Then I S for Eliezer, Ariel, Shemaiah, Elnathan,
8:17 men of insight, and S them to Iddo, the
Neh 2:9 Now the king had S with me officers of
6:2 Sanballat and Geshem S to me, saying, "Come
6:3 And I S messengers to them, saying, "I am
6:4 And they S to me four times in this
6:5 for the fifth time S his servant to me
6:8 Then I S to him, saying, "No such things
6:12 that God had not S him, but he had
6:17 the nobles of Judah S many letters to Tobiah,
6:19 And Tobiah S letters to make me afraid.
Tob 3:17 And Raphael was S to heal the two of
5:17 Tobit, "Why have you S our child away?
10:11 had blessed them he S them away, saying, "The
12:14 So now God S me to heal you and
12:20 ascending to him who S me.
Jud 1:7 king of the Assyrians S to all who lived
1:11 man, and they S back his messengers empty-handed
3:1 So they S messengers to sue for peace, and
4:4 So they S to every district of Samaria, and
7:18 opposite Dothan; and they S some of their men
7:33 women and children he S home.
8:10 after five days, she S her maid, who was
11:7 power endures, who had S you to direct every
11:14 They have S men to Jerusalem, because even the
11:16 them; and God has S me to accomplish with
11:19 me, and I was S to tell you."
12:6 watch she arose and S to Holofernes and said,
14:5 house of Israel and S him to us as
14:12 Assyrians saw them they S word to their
15:4 And Uzziah S men to Betomasthaim and Bebai and
Esth 1:22 as Memucan proposed; he S letters to all the
3:13 Letters were S by couriers to all the king's
4:4 distressed; she S garments to clothe Mordecai,
5:10 went home; and he S and fetched his friends
8:10 ring, and letters were S by mounted couriers riding
9:20 recorded these things, and S letters to all the
9:30 Letters were S to all the Jews, to the
16:17 in execution the letters S by Haman the son
Job 22:9 You have S widows away empty, and the arms
Ps 18:14 And he S out his arrows, and scattered them;
78:25 of the angels; he S them food in abundance.
78:45 He S among them swarms of flies, which devoured
80:11 with its branches; it S out its branches to
105:17 of bread, he had S a man ahead of
105:20 The king S and released him, the ruler of
105:26 He S Moses his servant, and Aaron whom he
105:28 He S darkness, and made the land dark; they
106:15 what they asked, but S a wasting disease among
107:20 from their distress; he S forth his word, and
111:9 He S redemption to his people; he has commanded
135:9 thy midst, O Egypt, S signs and wonders against
Prov 9:3 She has S out her maids to call from
17:11 cruel messenger will be S against him.
22:21 answer to those who S you?
Wis 9:17 hast given wisdom and S thy holy Spirit from
16:3 of the odious creatures S to them, while thy
16:18 not consume the creatures S against the ungodly, but
19:2 to depart and hastily S them forth, they would
Sir 15:9 it has not been S from the Lord.
28:23 It will be S out against them like a
34:6 Unless they are S from the Most High as
48:18 Sennacherib came up, and S the Rabshakeh; he
51:9 And I S up my supplication from the earth,
Is 9:8 The Lord has S a word against Jacob, and
16:1 They have S lambs to the ruler of the
20:1 commander-in-chief, who was S by Sargon the king
36:2 the king of Assyria S the Rabshakeh from Lachish
36:12 said, "Has my master S me to speak these
37:2 And he S Eliakim, who was over the household,
37:4 king of Assyria has S to mock the living
37:9 he heard it, he S messengers to Hezekiah, saying,
37:17 Sennacherib, which he has S to mock the living
37:21 the son of Amoz S to Hezekiah, saying, "Thus
39:1 Baladan, king of Babylon, S envoys with letters and
48:16 the Lord GOD has S me and his Spirit.
55:11 thing for which I S it.
57:9 multiplied your perfumes; you S your envoys far-off,
57:9 your envoys far-off, and S down even to Sheol.
61:1 the afflicted; he has S me to bind up
Jer 3:8 one, Israel, I had S her away with a
7:25 day, I have persistently S all my servants the
19:14 where the LORD had S him to prophesy, and
21:1 LORD, when King Zedekiah S to him Pashhur the
23:38 when I S to you, saying, "You shall not
24:5 Judah, whom I have S away from this place
25:4 although the LORD persistently S to you all his
25:17 to whom the Lord S me drink it:
26:12 people, saying, "The LORD S me to prophesy against
26:15 in truth the LORD S me to you to
26:22 Then King Jehoiakim S to Egypt certain men,
27:15 I have not S them, says the LORD, but
28:9 the LORD has truly S the prophet."
28:15 the LORD has not S you, and you have
29:1 which Jeremiah the prophet S from Jerusalem to
29:3 The letter was S by the hand of Elasah
29:3 Zedekiah king of Judah S to Babylon to
29:4 exiles whom I have S into exile from Jerusalem
29:7 city where I have S you into exile, and
29:14 place from which I S you into exile.
29:19 LORD, which I persistently S to you by my
29:20 you exiles whom I S away from Jerusalem to

	29:25	of Israel: You have S letters in your name
	29:28	For he has S to us in Babylon, saying,
	35:15	I have S to you all my servants the
	36:14	Then all the princes S Jehudi the son of
	36:21	Then the king S Jehudi to get the scroll,
	37:3	King Zedekiah S Jehucal the son of Shelemiah, and
	37:7	king of Judah who S you to me to
	37:17	many days, King Zedekiah S for him, and received
	38:14	King Zedekiah S for Jeremiah the prophet and
	39:14	the king of Babylon S and took Jeremiah from
	40:14	of the Ammonites has S Ishmael the son of
	42:9	Israel, to whom you S me to present your
	42:20	For you S me to the LORD your God,
	42:21	in anything that he S me to tell you.
	43:1	LORD their God had S him to them,
	44:4	Yet I persistently S to you all my servants
	49:14	a messenger has been S among the nations: "Gather
Lam	1:13	"From on high he S fire; into my bones
Bar	1:7	he could; and they S it to Jerusalem to
	1:21	the prophets whom he S to us, but we
	2:20	For thou hast S thy anger and thy wrath
	4:11	nurtured them, but I S them away with weeping
	4:23	For I S you out with sorrow and weeping,
	4:37	are coming, whom you S away; they are coming,
	6:1	a letter which Jeremiah S to those who were
	6:60	and stars, shining and S forth for service, are
	6:63	And the fire S from above to consume mountains
Ezek	3:5	For you are not S to a people of
	3:6	Surely, if I S you to such, they would
	13:6	the LORD has not S them, and yet they
	20:28	their offering; there they S up their soothing odors,
	23:16	doted upon them, and S messengers to them in
	23:40	They even S for men to come from far,
	23:40	whom a messenger was S, and lo, they came.
	39:28	their God because I S them into exile among
Dan	3:2	King Nebuchadnezzar S to assemble the satraps, the
	3:96	and Abednego, who has S his angel and delivered
	5:24	presence the hand was S, and this writing was
	6:22	My God S his angel and shut the lions'
	10:11	now I have been S to you." While he
	13:21	this was why you S your maids away."
	13:30	So they S for her.
	14:37	dinner which God has S you."
Hos	5:13	went to Assyria, and S to the great king.
Joel	2:25	great army, which I S among you.
Amos	4:10	"I S among you a pestilence after the manner
	7:10	the priest of Bethel S to Jeroboam king of
Obad	1:1	a messenger has been S among the nations: "Rise
Mic	6:4	of bondage; and I S before you Moses, Aaron,
Hag	1:12	LORD their God had S him; and the people
Zech	1:10	whom the LORD has S to patrol the earth.'
	2:8	hosts, after his glory S me to the nations
	2:9	LORD of hosts has S me.
	2:11	LORD of hosts has S me to you.
	4:9	LORD of hosts has S me to you.
	6:15	LORD of hosts has S me to you.
	7:2	people of Bethel had S Sharezer and Regem-melech
	7:12	LORD of hosts had S by his Spirit through
Mal	2:4	know that I have S this command to you,
1Mac	1:29	years later the king S to the cities of
	1:44	And the king S letters by messengers to Jerusalem
	3:27	greatly angered; and he S and gathered all the
	3:39	of the king, and S with them forty thousand
	5:10	stronghold of Dathema, and S to Judas and his
	5:38	Judas S men to spy out the camp, and
	5:48	And Judas S them this friendly message, "Let us
	6:12	and gold; and I S to destroy the inhabitants
	6:60	the commanders, and he S to the Jews an
	7:9	And he S him, and with him the ungodly
	7:10	of Judah; and he S messengers to Judas and
	7:19	And he S and seized many of the men
	7:26	Then the king S Nicanor, one of his honored
	7:27	large force, and treacherously S to Judas and his
	8:10	to them, and they S a general against the
	8:17	son of Eleazar, and S them to Rome to
	8:20	of the Jews have S us to you to
	8:22	on bronze tablets, and S to Jerusalem to remain
	9:1	fallen in battle, he S Bacchides and Alcimus into
	9:35	And Jonathan S his brother as leader of the
	9:60	large force, and secretly S letters to all his
	9:63	all his forces, and S orders to the men
	9:70	learned of this, he S ambassadors to him to
	10:3	Demetrius S Jonathan a letter in peaceable words
	10:15	promises which Demetrius had S to Jonathan, and
	10:17	wrote a letter and S it to him, in
	10:20	(and he S him a purple robe and a
	10:25	So he S a message to them in the
	10:51	Alexander S ambassadors to Ptolemy king of Egypt
	10:69	Then he S the following message to Jonathan the
	10:89	still more; and he S to him a golden
	11:9	He S envoys to Demetrius the king, saying, "Come,
	11:17	head of Alexander and S it to Ptolemy.
	11:41	Now Jonathan S to Demetrius the king the request
	11:42	And Demetrius S this message to Jonathan, "Not
	11:44	So Jonathan S three thousand stalwart men to him
	11:58	And he S him gold plate and a table
	11:62	rulers as hostages and S them to Jerusalem.
	12:1	he chose men and S them to Rome to
	12:2	He also S letters to the same effect to
	12:3	the Jewish nation have S us to renew the
	12:7	past a letter was S to Onias the high
	12:10	has passed since you S your letter to us.
	12:16	of Jason, and have S them to Rome to
	12:19	the letter which they S to Onias:
	12:26	He S spies to their camp, and they returned
	12:34	the stronghold to the men whom Demetrius had S
	12:46	as he said; he S away the troops, and
	12:49	Then Trypho S troops and cavalry into Galilee and
	13:11	He S Jonathan the son of Absalom to Joppa,
	13:14	with him, so he S envoys to him and
	13:17	to him, but he S to get the money
	13:19	So he S the sons and the hundred talents,
	13:25	And Simon S and took the bones of Jonathan
	13:34	also chose men and S them to Demetrius the
	13:35	Demetrius the king S him a favorable reply to
	13:37	palm branch which you S, and we are ready
	14:2	invaded his territory, he S one of his commanders
	14:20	letter which the Spartans S: "The rulers and the
	14:21	The envoys who were S to our people have
	14:23	And they have S a copy of this to
	14:24	After this Simon S Numenius to Rome with a
	15:1	of Demetrius the king, S a letter from the
	15:17	They had been S by Simon the high priest
	15:24	They also S a copy of these things to
	15:26	And Simon S to Antiochus two thousand picked men,
	15:28	He S to him Athenobius, one of his friends,
	16:18	about these things and S it to the king,
	16:19	He S other men to Gazara to do away
	16:19	away with John; he S letters to the captains
	16:20	and gifts; and he S other men to take
	16:21	and that "he has S men to kill you
2Mac	1:20	the king of Persia, S the descendants of the
	3:7	of his affairs, and S him with commands to
	4:19	present, the vile Jason S envoys, chosen as being
	4:21	son of Menestheus was S to Egypt for the
	4:23	of three years Jason S Menelaus, the brother of
	4:44	to Tyre, three men S by the senate presented
	5:18	whom Seleucus the king S to inspect the treasury.
	5:24	Jewish citizens, Antiochus S Apollonius, the captain
	6:1	after this, the king S an Athenian senator to
	8:9	king's chief friends, and S him, in command of
	8:11	And he immediately S to the cities on the
	11:13	So he S to them
	11:17	and Absalom, who were S by you, have delivered
	11:32	And I have also S Menelaus to encourage you.
	11:34	The Romans also S them a letter, which read
	12:21	approach of Judas, he S off the women and
	12:43	drachmas of silver, and S it to Jerusalem to
	13:20	Judas S in to the garrison whatever was necessary.
	14:12	governor of Judea, and S him off
	14:19	Therefore he S Posidonius and Theodotus and
	14:39	had for the Jews, S more than five hundred
	15:31	before the altar, he S for those who were
Mt	2:8	star appeared; and he S them to Bethlehem, saying,
	2:16	furious rage, and he S and killed all the
	10:5	These twelve Jesus S out, charging them, "Go
	10:40	me receives him who S me.
	11:2	of the Christ, he S word by his disciples
	14:10	to be given; he S and had John beheaded
	14:35	place recognized him, they S round to all that
	15:24	He answered, "I was S only to the lost
	20:2	denarius a day, he S them into his vineyard.
	21:1	of Olives, then Jesus S two disciples,
	21:34	fruit drew near, he S his servants to the
	21:36	Again he S other servants, more than the first;
	21:37	Afterward he S his son to them, saying, 'They
	22:3	for his son, and S his servants to call
	22:4	Again he S other servants, saying, 'Tell those who
	22:7	was angry, and he S his troops and destroyed
	22:16	And they S their disciples to him, along with
	23:36	stoning those who are S to you!
	27:19	judgment seat, his wife S word to him, "Have

S

Mk 1:43 sternly charged him, and S him away at once,
3:14 him, and to be S out to preach
3:31 and standing outside they S to him and called
6:17 For Herod had S and seized John, and bound
6:27 And immediately the king S a soldier of the
8:10 And he S them away; and immediately he got
8:26 And he S him away to his home, saying,
9:37 me but him who S me."
11:1 Mount of Olives, he S two of his disciples,
12:2 the time came, he S a servant to the
12:3 and beat him, and S him away empty-handed.
12:4 Again he S to them another servant, and they
12:5 And he S another, and him they killed; and
12:6 beloved son; finally he S him to them, saying,
12:13 And they S to him some of the Pharisees
14:13 And he S two of his disciples, and said
Lk 1:19 God; and I was S to speak to you,
1:26 the angel Gabriel was S from God to a
1:53 the rich he has S empty away.
4:18 He has S me to proclaim release to the
4:26 land; and Elijah was S to none of them
4:43 also; for I was S for this purpose."
7:3 heard of Jesus, he S to him elders of
7:6 the house, the centurion S friends to him, saying
7:10 those who had been S returned to the house,
7:19 two of his disciples, S them to the Lord,
7:20 "John the Baptist has S us to you, saying,
8:38 with him; but he S him away, saying,
9:2 cure diseases, and he S them out to preach
9:48 me receives him who S me; for he who
9:52 And he S messengers ahead of him, who went
10:1 appointed seventy others, and S them on ahead of
10:16 me rejects him who S me."
13:34 stoning those who are S to you!
14:17 for the banquet he S his servant to say
15:15 of that country, who S him into his fields
19:14 citizens hated him and S an embassy after him,
19:29 is called Olivet, he S two of the disciples,
19:32 So those who were S went away and found
20:10 the time came, he S a servant to the
20:10 tenants beat him, and S him away empty-handed.
20:11 And he S another servant; him also they beat
20:11 treated shamefully, and S him away empty-handed.
20:12 And he S yet a third; this one they
20:20 they watched him, and S spies, who pretended to
22:8 So Jesus S Peter and John, saying, "Go and
22:35 to them, "When I S you out with no
23:7 to Herod's jurisdiction, he S him over to Herod,
23:11 in gorgeous apparel, he S him back to Pilate.
23:15 did Herod, for he S him back to us.
Jn 1:6 There was a man S from God, whose name
1:19 John, when the Jews S priests and Levites from
1:22 answer for those who S us.
1:24 Now they had been S from the Pharisees.
1:33 him; but he who S me to baptize with
3:17 For God S the Son into the world, not
3:28 but I have been S before him.
3:34 he whom God has S utters the words of
4:34 will of him who S me, and to accomplish
4:38 and another reaps.' I S you to reap that
5:22 honor the Father who S him.
5:23 and believes him who S me, has eternal life;
5:29 will of him who S me.
5:32 You S to John, and he has borne witness
5:35 that the Father has S me.
5:36 And the Father who S me has himself borne
5:37 you do not believe him whom he has S
6:29 that you believe in him whom he has S
6:38 will of him who S me;
6:39 will of him who S me, that I should
6:44 unless the Father who S me draws him; and
6:57 As the living Father S me, and I live
7:16 mine, but his who S me;
7:18 glory of him who S him is true, and
7:28 own accord; he who S me is true, and
7:29 from him, and he S me."
7:32 chief priests and Pharisees S officers to arrest him.
7:33 go to him who S me;
8:16 I and he who S me.
8:18 and the Father who S me bears witness to
8:26 judge; but he who S me is true, and
8:29 And he who S me is with me; he
8:42 own accord, but he S me.
9:4 works of him who S me, while it is
9:7 (which means S
10:36 the Father consecrated and S into the world, 'You
11:3 So the sisters S to him, saying, "Lord, he
12:44 but in him who S me.
12:45 me sees him who S me.
12:49 authority; the Father who S me has himself given
13:16 is he who is S greater than he who
13:16 greater than he who S him.
13:20 me receives him who S me."
14:24 but the Father's who S me.
15:21 not know him who S me.
16:5 going to him who S me; yet none of
17:3 true God, and Jesus Christ whom thou hast S
17:18 world, so I have S them into the world.
17:21 believe that thou hast S me.
17:23 know that thou hast S me and hast loved
17:25 know that thou hast S me.
18:24 Annas then S him bound to Caiaphas the high
20:21 As the Father has S me, even so I
Acts 3:26 raised up his servant, S him to you first,
5:21 senate of Israel, and S to the prison to
7:12 grain in Egypt, he S forth our fathers the
7:14 And Joseph S and called to him Jacob his
7:35 and a judge?' God S as both ruler and
8:14 word of God, they S to them Peter and
9:17 which you came, has S me that you may
9:30 down to Caesarea, and S him off to Tarsus.
9:38 that Peter was there, S two men to him
10:8 everything to them, he S them to Joppa.
10:17 the men that were S by Cornelius, having made
10:20 hesitation; for I have S them."
10:29 So when I was S for, I came without
10:29 ask then why you S for me."
10:33 the seaside.' So I S to you at once,
10:36 the word which he S to Israel, preaching good
11:11 in which we were, S to me from Caesarea.
11:22 in Jerusalem, and they S Barnabas to Antioch.
12:11 that the Lord has S his angel and rescued
13:3 hands on them and S them off.
13:4 So, being S out by the Holy Spirit, they
13:15 rulers of the synagogue S to them, saying, "Brethren,
13:26 to us has been S the message of this
15:3 So, being S on their way by the church,
15:22 They S Judas called Barsabbas, and Silas, leading
15:27 We have therefore S Judas and Silas, who
15:30 So when they were S off, they went down
15:33 some time, they were S off in peace by
15:33 to those who had S them.
16:35 was day, the magistrates S the police, saying, "Let
16:36 saying, "The magistrates have S to let you go;
17:10 The brethren immediately S Paul and Silas away by
17:14 Then the brethren immediately S Paul off on his
19:22 And having S into Macedonia two of his helpers,
19:31 were friends of his, S to him and begged
20:1 the uproar ceased, Paul S for the disciples and
20:17 And from Miletus he S to Ephesus and called
21:25 have believed, we have S a letter with our
23:30 against the man, I S him to you at
24:23 a Jewess; and he S for Paul and heard
24:25 So he S for him often and conversed with
25:3 to have the man S to Jerusalem, planning an
28:28 of God has been S to the Gentiles; they
Rom 10:15 And how can men preach unless they are S
1Cor 4:17 Therefore I S to you Timothy, my beloved and
2Cor 12:17 of those whom I S to you?
12:18 Titus to go, and S the brother with him.
Gal 4:4 had fully come, God S forth his Son, born
4:6 are sons, God has S the Spirit of his
Eph 6:22 I have S him to you for this very
Phil 4:16 even in Thessalonica you S me help once and
4:18 Epaphroditus the gifts you S, a fragrant offering, a
Col 4:8 I have S him to you for this very
1Thes 3:2 Athens alone, and we S Timothy, our brother and
3:5 it no longer, I S that I might know
2Tim 4:12 Tychicus I have S to Ephesus.
Heb 1:14 not all ministering spirits S forth to serve, for
Jas 2:25 received the messengers and S them out another
1Pet 1:12 through the Holy Spirit S from heaven, things into
2:14 or to governors as S by him to punish
1Jn 4:9 among us, that God S his only Son into
4:10 he loved us and S his Son to be
4:14 that the Father has S his Son as the
Rev 5:6 seven spirits of God S out into all the
22:6 of the prophets, has S his angel to show
22:16 "I Jesus have S my angel to you with

SENTENCE (22)

1Sam 24:15 be judge, and give S between me and you,

2Kgs 25:6 at Riblah, who passed S upon him.
Ps 51:4 art justified in thy S and blameless in thy
Eccl 8:11 Because S against an evil deed is not executed
Sir 38:33 do they understand the S of judgment; they cannot
41:2 how welcome is your S to one who is
41:3 Do not fear the S of death; remember your
Jer 26:11 "This man deserves the S of death, because he
26:16 does not deserve the S of death, for he
39:5 Hamath; and he passed S upon him.
52:9 Hamath, and he passed S upon him.
Ezek 23:45 on them with the S of adulteresses, and with
23:45 adulteresses, and with the S of women that shed
Dan 2:9 there is but one S for you.
4:17 The S is by the decree of the watchers,
13:55 God has received the S from God and will
Lk 23:23 So Pilate gave S that their demand should be
23:39 are under the same S of condemnation?
Acts 25:15 about him, asking for S against him.
Rom 9:28 Lord will execute his S upon the earth with
13:9 summed up in this S, "You shall love your
2Cor 1:9 we had received the S of death; but that

SENTENCED (4)

Bar 6:18 as though he were S to death, so the
2Mac 4:47 against him, while he S to death those unfortunate
Mt 23:32 you to escape being S to hell?
1Cor 4:9 of all, like men S to death; because we

SENTRIES (3)

Acts 5:23 securely locked and the S standing at the doors,
12:6 with two chains, and S before the door were
12:19 him, he examined the S and ordered that they

SENTRY

Jer 37:13 the Benjamin Gate, a S there named Irijah the

SEPARATE (31)

Gen 1:6 waters, and let it S the waters from the
1:14 of the heavens to S the day from the
1:18 the night, and to S the light from the
13:9 S yourself from me.
49:26 of him who was S from his brothers.
Ex 26:24 rear; they shall be S beneath, but joined at
26:33 and the veil shall S for you the holy
36:29 And they were S beneath, but joined at the
Lev 15:31 the people of Israel S from their uncleanness, lest
Num 6:2 of a Nazirite, to S himself to the LORD,
6:3 the LORD, he shall S himself from wine and
6:12 that same day, and S himself to the LORD
8:14 "Thus you shall S the Levites from among the
16:21 Moses and to Aaron, S yourselves from among this
1Kgs 8:53 For thou didst S them from among all the
2Kgs 15:5 he dwelt in a S house.
2Chr 26:21 leper dwelt in a S house, for he was
Ezra 10:11 and do his will; S yourselves from the peoples
Wis 1:3 For perverse thoughts S men from God, and when
Sir 12:9 even his friend will S from him.
25:25 go as you direct, S her from yourself.
Is 56:3 "The LORD will surely S me from his people";
Dan 13:51 Daniel said to them, S them far from each
1Mac 12:36 and the city to S it from the city,
Mt 13:49 will come out and S the evil from the
25:32 nations, and he will S them one from another
Rom 8:35 Who shall S us from the love of Christ?
8:39 will be able to S us from the love
1Cor 7:10 the wife should not S from her husband
7:15 unbelieving partner desires to S, let it be so;
2Cor 6:17 from them, and be S from them, says the

SEPARATED (25)

Gen 1:4 was good; and God S the light from the
1:7 made the firmament and S the waters which were
13:11 journeyed east; thus they S from each other.
13:14 Abram, after Lot had S from him, "Lift up
30:40 And Jacob S the lambs, and set the faces
Lev 20:24 your God, who have S you from the peoples.
20:26 am holy, and have S you from the peoples,
Num 16:9 God of Israel has S you from the congregation
31:42 Israel's half, which Moses S from that of the
Deut 32:8 their inheritance, when he S the sons of men,
Judg 4:11 Heber the Kenite had S from the Kenites, the
2Kgs 2:11 and horses of fire S the two of them.
Ezra 6:21 had joined them and S himself from the pollutions
9:1 the Levites have not S themselves from the peoples
Neh 4:19 spread, and we are S on the wall, far
9:2 And the Israelites S themselves from all foreigners,
10:28 and all who have S themselves from the peoples
13:3 heard the law, they S from Israel all those
Job 41:17 another; they clasp each other and cannot be S
Dan 13:52 When they were S from each other, he summoned
1Mac 1:11 us, for since we S from them many evils
Acts 15:38 contention, so that they S from each other; Barnabas
Gal 2:12 he drew back and S himself, fearing the circumcision
Eph 2:12 were at that time S from Christ, alienated from
Heb 7:26 holy, blameless, unstained, S from sinners, exalted

SEPARATES (5)

Num 6:5 completed for which he S himself to the LORD,
6:6 the days that he S himself to the LORD
Prov 16:28 strife, and a whisperer S close friends.
Ezek 14:7 sojourn in Israel, who S himself from me, taking
Mt 25:32 another as a shepherd S the sheep from the

SEPARATION (11)

Num 6:4 the days of his S he shall eat nothing
6:5 of his vow of S no razor shall come
6:7 himself unclean; because his S to God is upon
6:8 the days of his S he is holy to
6:12 the days of his S, and bring a male
6:12 be void, because his S was defiled.
6:13 the time of his S has been completed: he
6:21 the law for his S as a Nazirite."
Is 59:2 iniquities have made a S between you and your
Ezek 42:20 broad, to make a S between the holy and
2Mac 14:3 in the times of S, realized that there was

SEPHAR

Gen 10:30 in the direction of S to the hill country

SEPHARAD

Obad 1:20 Jerusalem who are in S shall possess the cities

SEPHARVAIM (6)

2Kgs 17:24 Cuthah, Avva, Hamath, and S, and placed them in
17:31 fire to Adrammelech and Anammelech, the gods of S
18:34 are the gods of S, Hena, and Ivvah?
19:13 of the city of S, the king of Hena,
Is 36:19 Where are the gods of S
37:13 of the city of S, the king of Hena,

SEPHARVITES

2Kgs 17:31 and Tartak; and the S burned their children in

SEPULCHRE (7)

Gen 23:6 withhold from you his S, or hinder you from
Ps 5:9 throat is an open S, they flatter with their
Is 14:19 out, away from your S, like a loathed untimely
Mt 27:61 the other Mary were there, sitting opposite the S
27:64 again.' Therefore order the S to be made secure
27:66 went and made the S secure by sealing the
28:1 and the other Mary went to see the S

SEPULCHRES (5)

Gen 23:6 the choicest of our S; none of us will
Neh 2:3 place of my fathers' S, lies waste, and its
2:5 city of my fathers' S, that I may rebuild
3:16 a point opposite the S of David, to the
2Mac 12:39 their kinsmen in the S of their fathers.

SERAH (3)

Gen 46:17 Ishvah, Ishvi, Beriah, with S their sister.
Num 26:46 the name of the daughter of Asher was S
1Chr 7:30 Imnah, Ishvah, Ishvi, Beriah, and their sister S

SERAIAH (20)

2Sam 8:17 Abiathar were priests; and S was secretary;
2Kgs 25:18 of the guard took S the chief priest, and
25:23 son of Kareah, and S the son of Tanhumeth
1Chr 4:13 of Kenaz: Othni-el and S; and the sons of
4:14 father of Ophrah; and S was the father of
4:35 of Joshibiah, son of S, son of Asiel,
6:14 of Azariah, Azariah of S, Seraiah of Jehozadak;
6:14 Azariah, Azariah of Seraiah, S of Jehozadak;
Ezra 2:2 with Zerubbabel, Jeshua, Nehemiah, S, Re-el-aiah,
7:1 Ezra the son of S, son of Azariah, son
Neh 10:2 son of Hacaliah, Zedekiah, S, Azariah, Jeremiah,
11:11 son of Joiarib, Jachin, S the son of Hilkiah,
12:1 of Shealtiel, and Jeshua: S, Jeremiah, Ezra,
12:12 of fathers' houses: of S, Meraiah; of Jeremiah,
Jer 36:26 the king's son and S the son of Azriel
40:8 the son of Kareah, S the son of Tanhumeth,
51:59 Jeremiah the prophet commanded S the son of

	51:59	S was the quartermaster.
	51:61	And Jeremiah said to S: "When you come to
	52:24	of the guard took S the chief priest, and

SERAPHIM (2)

Is	6:2	Above him stood the S; each had six wings:
	6:6	flew one of the S to me, having in

SERED (2)

Gen	46:14	The sons of Zebulun: S, Elon, and Jahleel
Num	26:26	to their families: of S, the family of the

SEREDITES

Num	26:26	the family of the S; of Elon, the family

SERGIUS

Acts	13:7	was with the proconsul, S Paulus, a man of

SERIOUS (6)

Deut	15:21	blind, or has any S blemish whatever, you shall
2Mac	4:4	that the rivalry was S and that Apollonius, the
Acts	25:7	bringing against him many S charges which they
1Tim	3:8	Deacons likewise must be S, not double-tongued, not
	3:11	women likewise must be S, no slanderers, but
Tit	2:2	older men be temperate, S, sensible, sound in faith,

SERON (2)

1Mac	3:13	Now when S, the commander of the Syrian army,
	3:23	he rushed suddenly against S and his army, and

SERPENT (42)

Gen	3:1	Now the S was more subtle than any other
	3:2	woman said to the S, "We may eat of
	3:4	But the S said to the woman, "You will
	3:13	The woman said, "The S beguiled me, and I
	3:14	God said to the S, "Because you have done
	49:17	Dan shall be a S in the way, a
Ex	4:3	and it became a S; and Moses fled from
	7:9	down before Pharaoh, that it may become a S
	7:10	Pharaoh and his servants, and it became a S
	7:15	hand the rod which was turned into a S
Num	21:8	Moses, "Make a fiery S, and set it on
	21:9	Moses made a bronze S, and set it on
	21:9	pole; and if a S bit any man, he
	21:9	look at the bronze S and live.
1Kgs	1:9	and fatlings by the S's Stone, which is beside
2Kgs	18:4	in pieces the bronze S that Moses had made,
Job	26:13	were made fair; his hand pierced the fleeing S
Ps	58:4	the venom of a S, like the deaf adder
	91:13	young lion and the S you will trample under
Prov	23:32	it bites like a S, and stings like an
	30:19	the way of a S on a rock, the
Eccl	10:8	into it; and a S will bite him who
	10:11	If the S bites before it is charmed, there
Sir	12:13	charmer bitten by a S, or any who go
Is	14:29	broken, for from the S's root will come forth
	14:29	adder, and its fruit will be a flying S
	27:1	fleeing S, Leviathan the twisting S, and he will slay
	30:6	viper and the flying S, they carry their riches
	65:25	dust shall be the S's food.
Jer	46:22	a sound like a S gliding away; for her
Amos	5:19	the wall, and a S bit him.
	9:3	I will command the S, and it shall bite
Mic	7:17	the dust like a S, like the crawling things
Mt	7:10	asks for a fish, will give him a S
Lk	11:11	fish give him a S;
Jn	3:14	Moses lifted up the S in the wilderness, so
2Cor	11:3	afraid that as the S deceived Eve by his
Rev	12:9	thrown down, that ancient S, who is called the
	12:14	might fly from the S into the wilderness, to
	12:15	The S poured water like a river out of
	20:2	the dragon, that ancient S, who is the Devil

SERPENTS (17)

Ex	7:12	man cast down his rod, and they became S
Num	21:6	the LORD sent fiery S among the people, and
	21:7	he take away the S from us." So Moses
Deut	8:15	wilderness, with its fiery S and scorpions and thirsty
	32:33	is the poison of S, and the cruel venom
Ps	140:3	tongue sharp as a S, and under their lips
Wis	11:15	astray to worship irrational S and worthless animals,
	16:5	the bites of writhing S, thy wrath did not
	16:10	the teeth of venomous S, for thy mercy came
	17:9	and the hissing of S,
Jer	8:17	am sending among you S, adders which cannot be
Mt	10:16	so be wise as S and innocent as doves.
	23:32	You S, you brood of vipers, how are you
Mk	16:18	they will pick up S, and if they drink
Lk	10:19	authority to tread upon S and scorpions, and over
1Cor	10:9	and were destroyed by S;
Rev	9:19	their tails are like S, with heads, and by

SERUG (6)

Gen	11:20	became the father of S;
	11:21	after the birth of S two hundred and seven
	11:22	When S had lived thirty years, he became the
	11:23	father of Nahor; and S lived after the birth
1Chr	1:26	Eber, Peleg, Reu; S, Nahor, Terah;
Lk	3:35	Nahor, the son of S, the son of Reu,

SERVANT (501)

Gen	18:3	in your sight, do not pass by your S
	18:5	pass on—since you have come to your S
	18:7	gave it to the S, who hastened to prepare
	19:2	pray you, to your S's house and spend the
	19:19	my lords; behold, your S has found favor in
	24:2	Abraham said to his S, the oldest of his
	24:5	The S said to him, "Perhaps the woman may
	24:9	So the S put his hand under the thigh
	24:10	Then the S took ten of his master's camels
	24:14	hast appointed for thy S Isaac.
	24:17	Then the S ran to meet her, and said,
	24:34	So he said, "I am Abraham's S
	24:52	When Abraham's S heard their words, he bowed
	24:53	And the S brought forth jewelry of silver and
	24:59	her nurse, and Abraham's S and his men.
	24:61	the man; thus the S took Rebekah, and went
	24:65	and said to the S, "Who is the man
	24:65	The S said, "It is my master." So she
	24:66	And the S told Isaac all the things that
	26:24	your descendants for my S Abraham's sake."
	32:4	Esau: Thus says your S Jacob, 'I have sojourned
	32:10	hast shown to thy S, for with only my
	32:18	'They belong to your S Jacob; they are a
	32:20	shall say, 'Moreover your S Jacob is behind us.'"
	33:5	children whom God has graciously given your S
	33:14	pass on before his S, and I will lead
	39:17	story, saying, "The Hebrew S, whom you have
	39:19	is the way your S treated me," his anger
	41:12	there with us, a S of the captain of
	43:28	They said, "Your S our father is well, he
	44:18	my lord, let your S, I pray you, speak
	44:18	anger burn against your S; for you are like
	44:24	went back to your S my father we told
	44:27	with us.' Then your S my father said to
	44:30	I come to your S my father, and the
	44:31	gray hairs of your S our father with sorrow
	44:32	For your S became surety for the lad to
	44:33	Now therefore, let your S, I pray you, remain
Ex	4:10	hast spoken to thy S; but I am slow
	12:45	No sojourner or hired S may eat of it.
	14:31	LORD and in his S Moses.
	24:13	Moses rose with his S Joshua, and Moses went
	33:11	into the camp, his S Joshua the son of
Lev	19:13	wages of a hired S shall not remain with
	22:10	priest's or a hired S shall not eat of
	25:6	and for your hired S and the sojourner who
	25:40	you as a hired S and as a sojourner.
	25:50	be rated as the time of a hired S
	25:53	As a S hired year by year shall he
Num	11:11	LORD, "Why hast thou dealt ill with thy S
	12:7	Not so with my S Moses; he is entrusted
	12:8	to speak against my S Moses?"
	14:24	But my S Caleb, because he has a different
Deut	3:24	begun to show thy S thy greatness and thy
	5:15	that you were a S in the land of
	15:18	cost of a hired S he has served you
	24:14	not oppress a hired S who is poor and
	34:5	So Moses the S of the LORD died there
Josh	1:1	death of Moses the S of the LORD, the
	1:2	Moses' minister, "Moses my S is dead; now therefore
	1:7	law which Moses my S commanded you; turn not
	1:13	word which Moses the S of the LORD commanded
	1:15	land which Moses the S of the LORD gave
	5:14	to him, "What does my lord bid his S
	8:31	Israel, as Moses the S of the LORD had
	8:33	Ebal, as Moses the S of the LORD had
	9:24	God had commanded his S Moses to give you
	11:12	them, as Moses the S of the LORD had
	11:15	Moses his S, so Moses commanded Joshua,
	12:6	Moses, the S of the LORD, and the people
	12:6	them; and Moses the S of the LORD gave

13:8 eastward, as Moses the S of the LORD gave
14:7 old when Moses the S of the LORD sent
18:7 eastward, which Moses the S of the LORD gave
22:2 all that Moses the S of the LORD commanded
22:4 lies, which Moses the S of the LORD gave
22:5 law which Moses the S of the LORD commanded
24:29 son of Nun, the S of the LORD, died,
Judg 2:8 son of Nun, the S of the LORD, died
7:10 camp with Purah your S;
7:11 down with Purah his S to the outposts of
15:18 the hand of thy S; and shall I now
19:3 had with him his S and a couple of
19:9 his concubine and his S rose up to depart,
19:11 far spent, and the S said to his master,
19:13 he said to his S, "Come and let us
Ruth 2:5 Boaz said to his S who was in charge
2:6 And the S who was in charge of the
1Sam 2:13 offered sacrifice, the priest's S would come, while
2:15 was burned, the priest's S would come and say
3:9 'Speak, LORD, for thy S hears.'" So Samuel went
3:10 said, "Speak, for thy S hears."
9:5 Saul said to his S who was with him,
9:7 Saul said to his S, "But if we go,
9:8 The S answered Saul again, "Here, I have with
9:10 Saul said to his S, "Well said; come, let
9:22 took Saul and his S and brought them into
9:27 to Saul, "Tell the S to pass on before
10:14 him and to his S, "Where did you go?"
14:41 thou not answered thy S this day?
17:32 because of him; your S will go and fight
17:34 said to Saul, "Your S used to keep sheep
17:36 Your S has killed both lions and bears; and
17:58 the son of your S Jesse the Bethlehemite."
19:4 king sin against his S David; because he has
20:7 be well with your S; but if he is
20:8 deal kindly with your S, for you have brought
20:8 you have brought your S into a sacred covenant
22:8 has stirred up my S against me, to lie
22:15 impute anything to his S or to all the
22:15 my father; for your S has known nothing of
23:10 God of Israel, thy S has surely heard that
23:11 come down, as thy S has heard?
23:11 God of Israel, I beseech thee, tell thy S
25:27 this present which your S has brought to my
25:39 has kept back his S from evil; the LORD
25:41 your handmaid is a S to wash the feet
26:18 said, "Why does my lord pursue after his S
26:19 lord the king hear the words of his S
27:5 for why should your S dwell in the royal
27:12 he shall be my S always."
28:2 shall know what your S can do." And Achish
29:3 not this David, the S of Saul, king of
29:8 you found in your S from the day I
30:13 young man of Egypt, S to an Amalekite; and
2Sam 3:18 the hand of my S David I will save
7:5 "Go and tell my S David, 'Thus says the
7:8 shall say to my S David, 'Thus says the
7:19 spoken also of thy S's house for a great
7:20 For thou knowest thy S, O Lord GOD!
7:21 greatness, to make thy S know it.
7:25 spoken concerning thy S and concerning his house,
7:26 the house of thy S David will be established
7:27 this revelation to thy S, saying, 'I will build
7:27 a house'; therefore thy S has found courage to
7:28 good thing to thy S;
7:29 the house of thy S, that it may continue
7:29 the house of thy S be blessed for ever."
9:2 Now there was a S of the house of
9:2 And he said, "Your S is he."
9:6 And he answered, "Behold, your S
9:8 said, "What is your S, that you should look
9:9 king called Ziba, Saul's S, and said to him,
9:11 the king commands his S, so will your servant
9:11 servant, so will your S do." So Mephibosheth ate
11:21 you shall say, 'Your S Uriah the Hittite is
11:24 are dead; and your S Uriah the Hittite is
13:18 So his S put her out, and bolted the
13:24 and said, "Behold, your S has sheepshearers; pray let
13:24 the king and his servants go with your S
13:35 have come; as your S said, so it has
14:15 the king will perform the request of his S
14:16 hear, and deliver his S from the hand of
14:19 It was your S Joab who bade me; it
14:20 course of affairs your S Joab did this.
14:22 Joab said, "Today your S knows that I have
14:22 the king has granted the request of his S
15:2 when he said, "Your S is of such and
15:8 For your S vowed a vow while I dwelt
15:21 there also will your S be."
15:34 'I will be your S, O king; as I
15:34 have been your father's S in time past, so
15:34 I will be your S then you will defeat
16:1 the summit, Ziba the S of Mephibosheth met him,
18:29 "When Joab sent your S, I saw a great
19:17 And Ziba the S of the house of Saul,
19:19 or remember how your S did wrong on the
19:20 For your S knows that I have sinned; therefore,
19:26 lord, O king, my S deceived me; for your
19:26 deceived me; for your S said to him, 'Saddle
19:26 the king.' For your S is lame.
19:27 He has slandered your S to my lord the
19:28 but you set your S among those who eat
19:35 Can your S taste what he eats or what
19:35 Why then should your S be an added burden
19:36 Your S will go a little way over the
19:37 Pray let your S return, that I may die
19:37 But here is your S Chimham; let him go
24:10 the iniquity of thy S; for I have done
24:21 has my lord the king come to his S
1Kgs 1:19 army; but Solomon your S he has not invited.
1:26 Adonijah!' But me, your S, and Zadok the priest,
1:26 of Jehoiada, and your S Solomon, he has not
1:51 will not slay his S with the sword.'"
2:38 said, so will your S do." So Shimei dwelt
3:6 steadfast love to thy S David my father, because
3:7 thou hast made thy S king in place of
3:8 And thy S is in the midst of thy
3:9 Give thy S therefore an understanding mind to
8:24 hast kept with thy S David my father what
8:25 Israel, keep with thy S David my father what
8:26 hast spoken to thy S David my father.
8:28 the prayer of thy S and to his supplication,
8:28 the prayer which thy S prays before thee this
8:29 the prayer which thy S offers toward this place.
8:30 the supplication of thy S and of thy people
8:52 the supplication of thy S, and to the supplication
8:53 declare through Moses, thy S, when thou didst bring
8:56 good promise, which he uttered by Moses his S
8:59 the cause of his S, and the cause of
8:66 shown to David his S and to Israel his
11:11 from you and will give it to your S
11:13 sake of David my S and for the sake
11:26 Ephraimite of Zeredah, a S of Solomon, whose
11:32 the sake of my S David and for the
11:34 sake of David my S whom I chose, who
11:36 tribe, that David my S may always have a
11:38 commandments, as David my S did, I will be
12:7 you will be a S to this people today
14:8 not been like my S David, who kept my
14:18 he spoke by his S Ahijah the prophet.
15:29 he spoke by his S Ahijah the Shilonite;
16:9 But his S Zimri, commander of half his chariots,
18:9 you would give your S into the hand of
18:12 me, although I your S have revered the LORD
18:36 that I am thy S, and that I have
18:43 he said to his S, "Go up now, look
19:3 Judah, and left his S there.
20:9 first demanded of your S I will do; but
20:32 Israel and said, "Your S Ben-hadad says, 'Pray, let
20:39 king and said, "Your S went out into the
20:40 silver.' And as your S was busy here and
2Kgs 4:1 cried to Elisha, "Your S my husband is dead;
4:1 you know that your S feared the LORD, but
4:12 said to Gehazi his S, "Call this Shunammite." When
4:19 father said to his S, "Carry him to his
4:24 she said to her S, "Urge the beast on;
4:25 said to Gehazi his S, "Look, yonder is the
4:38 he said to his S, "Set on the great
4:43 But his S said, "How am I to set
5:6 to you Naaman my S, that you may cure
5:15 Israel; so accept now a present from your S
5:17 be given to your S two mules' burden of
5:17 earth; for henceforth your S will not offer burnt
5:18 the LORD pardon your S: when my master goes
5:18 the LORD pardon your S in this matter."
5:20 short distance, Gehazi, the S of Elisha the man
5:25 And he said, "Your S went nowhere."
6:15 When the S of the man of God rose
6:15 And the S said, "Alas, my master!
8:4 talking with Gehazi the S of the man of
8:13 said, "What is your S, who is but a
8:19 sake of David his S, since he promised to

S

9:36 he spoke by his S Elijah the Tishbite, 'In
10:10 he said by his S Elijah."
10:23 that there is no S of the LORD here
14:25 he spoke by his S Jonah the son of
16:7 saying, "I am your S and your son.
18:12 all that Moses the S of the LORD commanded;
19:34 the sake of my S David."
20:6 sake and for my S David's sake."
21:8 the law that my S Moses commanded them."
22:12 and Asaiah the king's S, saying,
24:1 and Jehoiakim became his S three years; then he
25:8 of the bodyguard, a S of the king of
1Chr 6:49 all that Moses the S of God had commanded.
16:13 offspring of Abraham his S, sons of Jacob, his
17:4 "Go and tell my S David, 'Thus says the
17:7 you say to my S David, 'Thus says the
17:17 also spoken of thy S's house for a great
17:18 can David say to thee for honoring thy S
17:18 For thou knowest thy S
17:19 For thy S's sake, O LORD, and according to
17:23 hast spoken concerning thy S and concerning his
17:24 the house of thy S David will be established
17:25 hast revealed to thy S that thou wilt build
17:25 for him; therefore thy S has found courage to
17:26 good thing to thy S;
17:27 the house of thy S, that it may continue
21:8 the iniquity of thy S; for I have done
2Chr 1:3 God, which Moses the S of the LORD had
6:15 hast kept with thy S David my father what
6:16 Israel, keep with thy S David my father what
6:17 hast spoken to thy S David.
6:19 the prayer of thy S and to his supplication,
6:19 the prayer which thy S prays before thee;
6:20 the prayer which thy S offers toward this place.
6:21 the supplications of thy S and of thy people
6:42 Remember thy steadfast love for David thy S
13:6 son of Nebat, a S of Solomon the son
24:6 levied by Moses, the S of the LORD, on
24:9 tax that Moses the S of God laid upon
32:16 GOD and against his S Hezekiah.
34:20 and Asaiah the king's S, saying,
Neh 1:6 the prayer of thy S which I now pray
1:7 thou didst command thy S Moses.
1:8 thou didst command thy S Moses, saying, 'If you
1:11 the prayer of thy S, and to the prayer
1:11 give success to thy S today, and grant him
2:5 king, and if your S has found favor in
2:10 Horonite and Tobiah the S, the Ammonite, heard this,
2:19 and Tobiah the S, the Ammonite, and Geshem
4:22 every man and his S pass the night within
6:5 fifth time sent his S to me with an
9:14 and statutes and a law by Moses thy S
10:29 given by Moses the S of God, and to
Tob 9:2 "Brother Azarias, take a S and two camels with
Jud 5:5 the mouth of your S, and I will tell
5:5 shall come from your S's mouth.
9:10 the prince with his S; crush their arrogance by
11:5 the words of your S, and let your maidservant
11:16 "Therefore, when I, your S, learned all this, I
11:17 For your S is religious, and serves the God
11:17 and every night your S will go out into
12:4 lives, my lord, your S will not use up
12:6 now command that your S be permitted to go
Esth 14:17 And thy S has not eaten at Haman's table,
14:18 Thy S has had no joy since the day
Job 1:8 "Have you considered my S Job, that there is
2:3 "Have you considered my S Job, that there is
19:16 I call to my S, but he gives me
41:4 take him for your S for ever?
42:7 is right, as my S Job has.
42:8 and go to my S Job, and offer up
42:8 burnt offering; and my S Job shall pray for
42:8 is right, as my S Job has."
Ps 19:11 by them is thy S warned; in keeping them
19:13 Keep back thy S also from presumptuous sins; let
27:9 Turn not thy S away in anger, thou who
31:16 face shine on thy S; save me in thy
35:27 LORD, who delights in the welfare of his S
69:17 thy face from thy S; for I am in
78:70 He chose David his S, and took him from
86:2 am godly; save thy S who trusts in thee.
86:4 the soul of thy S, for to thee, O
86:16 thy strength to thy S, and save the son
89:3 sworn to David my S:
89:20 have found David, my S; with my holy oil
89:39 the covenant with thy S; thou hast defiled his
89:50 O Lord, how thy S is scorned; how I
105:6 offspring of Abraham his S, sons of Jacob, his
105:26 He sent Moses his S, and Aaron whom he
105:42 he remembered his holy promise, and Abraham his S
109:28 to shame; may thy S be glad!
116:16 LORD, I am thy S; I am thy servant,
116:16 servant; I am thy S, the son of thy
119:17 Deal bountifully with thy S, that I may live
119:23 plotting against me, thy S will meditate on thy
119:38 Confirm to thy S thy promise, which is for
119:49 thy word to thy S, in which thou hast
119:65 dealt well with thy S, O LORD, according to
119:76 comfort me according to thy promise to thy S
119:84 How long must thy S endure?
119:122 Be surety for thy S for good; let not
119:124 Deal with thy S according to thy steadfast love,
119:125 I am thy S; give me understanding, that I
119:135 face shine upon thy S, and teach me thy
119:140 well tried, and thy S loves it.
119:176 lost sheep; seek thy S, for I do not
132:10 For thy S David's sake do not turn away
136:22 heritage to Israel his S, for his steadfast love
143:2 into judgment with thy S; for no man living
143:12 destroy all my adversaries, for I am thy S
144:10 givest victory to kings, who rescuest David thy S
Prov 11:29 the fool will be S to the wise.
14:35 A S who deals wisely has the king's favor,
29:19 By mere words a S is not disciplined, for
29:21 He who pampers his S from childhood, will in
30:10 Do not slander a S to his master, lest
Eccl 7:21 lest you hear your S cursing you;
Wis 10:16 the soul of a S of the Lord, and
18:21 to the disaster, showing that he was thy S
Sir 7:20 Do not abuse a S who performs his work
7:21 soul love an intelligent S; do not withhold from
10:24 service of a wise S, and a man of
23:10 One; for as a S who is continually examined
33:24 ass; bread and discipline and work for a S
33:26 and for a wicked S there are racks and
33:30 If you have a S, let him be as
33:31 If you have a S, treat him as a
37:11 work, with a lazy S about a big task--
42:5 of whipping a wicked S severely.
Is 20:3 LORD said, "As my S Isaiah has walked naked
22:20 I will call my S Eliakim the son of
37:35 the sake of my S David."
41:8 But you, Israel, my S, Jacob, whom I have
41:9 you, "You are my S, I have chosen you
42:1 Behold my S, whom I uphold, my chosen, in
42:19 is blind but my S, or deaf as my
42:19 or blind as the S of the LORD?
43:10 the LORD, "and my S whom I have chosen,
44:1 hear, O Jacob my S, Israel whom I have
44:2 not, O Jacob my S, Jeshurun whom I have
44:21 for you are my S; I formed you, you
44:21 you, you are my S; O Israel, you will
44:26 the word of his S, and performs the counsel
45:4 the sake of my S Jacob, and Israel my
48:20 LORD has redeemed his S Jacob!"
49:3 me, "You are my S, Israel, in whom I
49:5 womb to be his S, to bring Jacob back
49:6 you should be my S to raise up the
49:7 by the nations, the S of rulers: "Kings shall
50:10 the voice of his S, who walks in darkness
52:13 Behold, my S shall prosper, he shall be exalted
53:11 the righteous one, my S, make many to be
63:11 remembered the days of old, of Moses his S
Jer 2:14 Is he a homeborn S
25:9 king of Babylon, my S, and I will bring
27:6 king of Babylon, my S, and I have given
30:10 not, O Jacob my S, says the LORD, nor
33:21 covenant with David my S may be broken, so
33:22 descendants of David my S, and the Levitical priests
33:26 Jacob and David my S and will not choose
43:10 king of Babylon, my S, and he will set
46:27 not, O Jacob my S, nor be dismayed, O
46:28 not, O Jacob my S, says the LORD, for
Bar 1:20 declared through Moses his S at the time when
2:28 didst speak by thy S Moses on the day
3:36 her to Jacob his S and to Israel whom
Ezek 28:25 I gave to my S Jacob.
34:23 them one shepherd, my S David, and he shall
34:24 their God, and my S David shall be prince
37:24 "My S David shall be king over them; and
37:25 I gave to my S Jacob; they and their
37:25 ever; and David my S shall be their prince

S

Dan 3:35 sake of Isaac thy S and Israel thy holy
6:20 to Daniel, "O Daniel, S of the living God,
9:11 law of Moses the S of God have been
9:17 the prayer of thy S and to his supplications,
10:17 How can my lord's S talk with my lord?
Hag 2:23 you, O Zerubbabel my S, the son of Shealtiel,
Zech 3:8 I will bring my S the Branch.
Mal 1:6 his father, and a S his master.
4:4 the law of my S Moses, the statutes and
1Mac 4:30 the hand of thy S David, and didst give
Mt 8:6 and saying, "Lord, my S is lying paralyzed at
8:8 the word, and my S will be healed.
8:13 And the S was healed at that very moment.
10:24 his teacher, nor a S above his master;
10:25 his teacher, and the S like his master.
12:18 prophet Isaiah: "Behold, my S whom I have chosen,
18:25 So the S fell on his knees, imploring him,
18:26 the lord of that S released him and forgave
18:27 But that same S, as he went out, came
18:28 owe.' So his fellow S fell down and besought
18:31 summoned him and said to him, 'You wicked S
18:32 mercy on your fellow S, as I had mercy
20:26 you must be your S,
23:11 you shall be your S;
24:45 the faithful and wise S, whom his master has
24:46 Blessed is that S whom his master when he
24:48 But if that wicked S says to himself, 'My
24:50 the master of that S will come on a
25:21 done, good and faithful S; you have been faithful
25:23 done, good and faithful S; you have been faithful
25:26 his master answered him, 'You wicked and slothful S
25:30 And cast the worthless S into the outer darkness;
Mk 9:35 last of all and S of all."
10:43 you must be your S,
12:2 came, he sent a S to the tenants, to
12:4 sent to them another S, and they wounded him
Lk 1:54 He has helped his S Israel, in remembrance of
1:69 the house of his S David,
2:29 now lettest thou thy S depart in peace, according
7:7 word, and let my S be healed.
12:43 Blessed is that S whom his master when he
12:45 But if that S says to himself, 'My master
12:46 the master of that S will come on a
12:47 And that S who knew his master's will, but
14:17 banquet he sent his S to say to those
14:21 cannot come.' So the S came and reported this
14:21 anger said to his S, 'Go out quickly to
14:22 and lame.' And the S said, 'Sir, what you
14:23 master said to the S, 'Go out to the
16:13 No S can serve two masters; for either he
17:7 you, who has a S plowing or keeping sheep,
17:9 Does he thank the S because he did what
19:17 And he said to him, 'Well done, good S
19:22 you out of your own mouth, you wicked S
20:10 came, he sent a S to the tenants, that
20:11 And he sent another S; him also they beat
Jn 12:26 am, there shall my S be also; if any
13:16 say to you, a S is not greater than
15:15 you servants, for the S does not know what
15:20 said to you, 'A S is not greater than
Acts 3:13 our fathers, glorified his S Jesus, whom you
3:26 having raised up his S, sent him to you
4:25 our father David, thy S, didst say by the
4:27 together against thy holy S Jesus, whom thou didst
4:30 name of thy holy S Jesus."
Rom 1:1 Paul, a S of Jesus Christ, called
13:4 for he is God's S for your good.
13:4 vain; he is the S of God to execute
14:4 pass judgment on the S of another?
15:8 that Christ became a S to the circumcised to
Gal 1:10 should not be a S of Christ.
Phil 2:7 the form of a S, being born in the
Col 1:7 you learned it from Epaphras our beloved fellow S
4:7 faithful minister and fellow S in the Lord.
4:12 one of yourselves, a S of Christ Jesus, greets
1Thes 3:2 our brother and God's S in the gospel of
2Tim 2:24 And the Lord's S must not be quarrelsome but
Tit 1:1 Paul, a S of God and an
Heb 3:5 God's house as a S, to testify to the
Jas 1:1 James, a S of God and of
2Pet 1:1 Simeon Peter, a S and apostle of Jesus
Jude 1:1 Jude, a S of Jesus Christ and
Rev 1:1 his angel to his S John,
15:3 song of Moses, the S of God, and the
19:10 I am a fellow S with you and your
22:9 I am a fellow S with you and your

SERVANTS (489)

Gen 14:15 night, he and his S, and routed them and
20:8 and called all his S, and told them all
21:25 of water which Abimelech's S had seized,
26:15 wells which his father's S had dug in the
26:19 But when Isaac's S dug in the valley and
26:25 And there Isaac's S dug a well.
26:32 That same day Isaac's S came and told him
27:37 given to him for S, and with grain and
32:16 the hand of his S, every drove by itself,
32:16 and said to his S, "Pass on before me,
40:20 feast for all his S, and lifted up the
40:20 the head of the chief baker among his S
41:10 was angry with his S, and put me and
41:37 seemed good to Pharaoh and to all his S
41:38 Pharaoh said to his S, "Can we find such
42:10 buy food have your S come.
42:11 are honest men, your S are not spies."
42:13 they said, "We, your S, are twelve brothers, the
44:7 be it from your S that they should do
44:9 With whomever of your S it be found, let
44:16 the guilt of your S; behold, we are my
44:19 My lord asked his S, saying, 'Have you a
44:21 you said to your S, 'Bring him down to
44:23 you said to your S, 'Unless your youngest brother
44:31 will die; and your S will bring down the
45:16 pleased Pharaoh and his S well.
46:34 you shall say, 'Your S have been keepers of
47:3 said to Pharaoh, "Your S are shepherds, as our
47:4 no pasture for your S flocks, for the famine
47:4 pray you, let your S dwell in the land
50:2 Joseph commanded his S the physicians to embalm
50:7 went up all the S of Pharaoh, the elders
50:17 the transgression of the S of the God of
50:18 before him, and said, "Behold, we are your S
Ex 5:15 Pharaoh, "Why do you deal thus with your S
5:16 is given to your S, yet they say to
5:16 bricks!' And behold, your S are beaten; but the
5:21 of Pharaoh and his S, and have put a
7:10 before Pharaoh and his S, and it became a
7:20 the sight of his S, he lifted up the
8:3 the houses of your S and of your people,
8:4 and on your people and on all your S
8:9 you and for your S and for your people,
8:11 your houses and your S and your people; they
8:21 on you and your S and your people, and
8:24 Pharaoh and into his S houses, and in all
8:29 from Pharaoh, from his S, and from his people,
8:31 from Pharaoh, from his S, and from his people;
9:14 heart, and upon your S and your people, that
9:20 the LORD among the S of Pharaoh made his
9:30 for you and your S, I know that you
9:34 again, and hardened his heart, he and his S
10:1 the heart of his S, that I may show
10:6 houses of all your S and of all the
10:7 And Pharaoh's S said to him, "How long shall
11:3 the sight of Pharaoh's S and in the sight
11:8 And all these your S shall come down to
12:30 he, and all his S, and all the Egyptians;
14:5 of Pharaoh and his S was changed toward the
32:13 Isaac, and Israel, thy S, to whom thou didst
Lev 25:42 For they are my S, whom I brought forth
25:55 people of Israel are S, they are my servants
25:55 servants, they are my S whom I brought forth
Num 22:18 and said to the S of Balak, "Though Balak
22:22 ass, and his two S were with him.
31:49 said to Moses, "Your S have counted the men
32:4 for cattle; and your S have cattle."
32:5 be given to your S for a possession; do
32:25 said to Moses, "Your S will do as my
32:27 of Gilead; but your S will pass over, every
32:31 has said to your S, so we will do.
Deut 9:27 Remember thy S, Abraham, Isaac, and Jacob; do not
29:2 and to all his S and to all his
32:36 have compassion on his S, when he sees that
32:43 the blood of his S, and takes vengeance on
34:11 and to all his S and to all his
Josh 9:8 They said to Joshua, "We are your S
9:9 very far country your S have come, because of
9:11 them, "We are your S; come now, make a
9:24 was told to your S for a certainty that
10:6 your hand from your S; come up to us
Judg 3:24 he had gone, the S came; and when they
6:27 ten men of his S, and did as the
19:19 young man with your S; there is no lack
Ruth 2:21 keep close by my S, till they have finished

S

1Sam	8:14	and olive orchards and give them to his S
	8:15	give it to his officers and to his S
	9:3	"Take one of the S with you, and arise,
	12:19	Samuel, "Pray for your S to the LORD your
	16:15	And Saul's S said to him, "Behold now, an
	16:16	lord now command your S, who are before you,
	16:17	Saul said to his S, "Provide for me a
	17:8	and are you not S of Saul?
	17:9	we will be your S; but if I prevail
	17:9	you shall be our S and serve us."
	18:5	people and also in the sight of Saul's S
	18:22	And Saul commanded his S, "Speak to David in
	18:22	you, and all his S love you; now then
	18:23	And Saul's S spoke those words in the ears
	18:24	And the S of Saul told him, "Thus and
	18:26	And when his S told David these words, it
	18:30	success than all the S of Saul; so that
	19:1	and to all his S, that they should kill
	21:7	certain man of the S of Saul was there
	21:11	And the S of Achish said to him, "Is
	21:14	said Achish to his S, "Lo, you see the
	22:6	hand, and all his S were standing about him.
	22:7	Saul said to his S who stood about him,
	22:9	who stood by the S of Saul, "I saw
	22:14	who among all your S is so faithful as
	22:17	But the S of the king would not put
	25:8	at hand to your S and to your son
	25:10	And Nabal answered David's S, "Who is David?
	25:10	There are many S nowadays who are breaking away
	25:40	And when the S of David came to Abigail
	25:41	the feet of the S of my lord."
	28:7	Saul said to his S, "Seek out for me
	28:7	And his S said to him, "Behold, there is
	28:23	But his S, together with the woman, urged him;
	28:25	before Saul and his S; and they ate.
	29:10	the morning with the S of your lord who
2Sam	2:12	of Ner, and the S of Ish-bosheth the son
	2:13	of Zeruiah, and the S of David, went out
	2:15	and twelve of the S of David.
	2:17	were beaten before the S of David.
	2:30	missing of David's S nineteen men besides Asahel.
	2:31	But the S of David had slain of Benjamin
	3:22	Just then the S of David arrived with Joab
	3:38	king said to his S, "Do you not know
	6:20	the eyes of his S maids, as one of
	8:2	And the Moabites became S to David and brought
	8:6	and the Syrians became S to David and brought
	8:7	were carried by the S of Hadadezer, and brought
	8:14	put garrisons, and all the Edomites became David's S
	9:10	your sons and your S shall till the land
	9:10	Now Ziba had fifteen sons and twenty S
	9:12	dwelt in Ziba's house became Mephibosheth's S
	10:2	David sent by his S to console him concerning
	10:2	And David's S came into the land of the
	10:3	not David sent his S to you to search
	10:4	So Hanun took David's S, and shaved off half
	10:19	the kings who were S of Hadadezer saw that
	11:1	sent Joab, and his S with him, and all
	11:9	house with all the S of his lord, and
	11:11	lord Joab and the S of my lord are
	11:13	his couch with the S of his lord, but
	11:17	and some of the S of David among the
	11:24	archers shot at your S from the wall; some
	11:24	some of the king's S are dead; and your
	12:18	And the S of David feared to tell him
	12:19	David saw that his S were whispering together, David
	12:19	David said to his S, "Is the child dead?"
	12:21	Then his S said to him, "What is this
	13:24	the king and his S go with your servant."
	13:28	Absalom commanded his S, "Mark when Amnon's
	13:29	So the S of Absalom did to Amnon as
	13:31	earth; and all his S who were standing by
	13:36	also and all his S wept very bitterly.
	14:30	he said to his S, "See, Joab's field is
	14:30	So Absalom's S set the field on fire.
	14:31	him, "Why have your S set my field on
	15:14	said to all his S who were with him
	15:15	And the king's S said to the king, "Behold,
	15:15	the king, "Behold, your S are ready to do
	15:18	And all his S passed by him; and all
	16:6	and at all the S of King David; and
	16:11	and to all his S, "Behold, my own son
	17:20	When Absalom's S came to the woman at the
	18:7	defeated there by the S of David, and the
	18:9	chanced to meet the S of David.
	19:5	faces of all your S, who have this day
	19:6	today that commanders and S are nothing to you;
	19:7	speak kindly to your S; for I swear by
	19:14	the king, "Return, both you and all your S
	19:17	sons and his twenty S, rushed down to the
	20:6	Absalom; take your lord's S and pursue him, lest
	21:15	down together with his S, and they fought against
	21:22	of David and by the hand of his S
	24:20	the king and his S coming on toward him;
1Kgs	1:2	Therefore his S said to him, "Let a young
	1:27	have not told your S who should sit on
	1:33	"Take with you the S of your lord, and
	1:47	Moreover the king's S came to congratulate our lord
	3:15	offerings, and made a feast for all his S
	5:1	of Tyre sent his S to Solomon, when he
	5:6	for me; and my S will join your servants,
	5:6	servants will join your S, and I will pay
	5:6	pay you for your S such wages as you
	5:9	My S shall bring it down to the sea
	8:23	steadfast love to thy S who walk before thee
	8:32	act, and judge thy S, condemning the guilty by
	8:36	the sin of thy S, thy people Israel, when
	9:27	with the fleet his S, seamen who were familiar
	9:27	sea, together with the S of Solomon;
	10:5	attendance of his S, their clothing, his cupbearers,
	10:8	Happy are these your S, who continually stand
	10:13	went back to her own land, with her S
	11:17	Edomites of his father's S, Hadad being yet a
	12:7	they will be your S for ever."
	15:18	the hands of his S; and King Asa sent
	20:6	I will send my S to you tomorrow about
	20:6	the houses of your S, and lay hands on
	20:14	the LORD, By the S of the governors of
	20:15	Then he mustered the S of the governors of
	20:17	The S of the governors of the districts went
	20:19	of the city, the S of the governors of
	20:23	And the S of the king of Syria said
	20:31	And his S said to him, "Behold now, we
	22:3	Israel said to his S, "Do you know that
	22:49	to Jehoshaphat, "Let my S go with your servants
	22:49	servants go with your S in the ships," but
2Kgs	1:13	life of these fifty S of yours, be precious
	2:16	there are with your S fifty strong men; pray,
	3:11	the king of Israel's S answered, "Elisha the son
	4:22	me one of the S and one of the
	5:13	But his S came near and said to him,
	5:23	upon two of his S; and they carried them
	6:3	them said, "Be pleased to go with your S
	6:8	took counsel with his S, saying, "At such and
	6:11	and he called his S and said to them,
	6:12	And one of his S said, "None, my lord,
	7:12	and said to his S, "I will tell you
	7:13	And one of his S said, "Let some men
	9:7	the blood of my S the prophets, and the
	9:7	blood of all the S of the LORD.
	9:11	came out to the S of his master, they
	9:28	His S carried him in a chariot to Jerusalem,
	10:5	saying, "We are your S, and we will do
	12:20	His S arose and made a conspiracy, and slew
	12:21	son of Shomer, his S, who struck him down,
	14:5	hand he killed his S who had slain the
	17:13	to you by my S the prophets."
	17:23	spoken by all his S the prophets.
	18:24	least of my master's S, when you rely on
	18:26	"Pray, speak to your S in the Aramaic language,
	19:5	When the S of King Hezekiah came to Isaiah,
	19:6	heard, with which the S of the king of
	21:10	LORD said by his S the prophets,
	21:23	And the S of Amon conspired against him, and
	22:9	to the king, "Your S have emptied out the
	23:30	And his S carried him dead in a chariot
	24:2	he spoke by his S the prophets.
	24:10	At that time the S of Nebuchadnezzar king of
	24:11	the city, while his S were besieging it;
	24:12	his mother, and his S, and his princes, and
1Chr	9:2	Israel, the priests, the Levites, and the temple S
	18:2	and the Moabites became S to David and brought
	18:6	and the Syrians became S to David, and brought
	18:7	were carried by the S of Hadadezer, and brought
	18:13	in Edom; and all the Edomites became David's S
	19:2	And David's S came to Hanun in the land
	19:3	Have not his S come to you to search
	19:4	So Hanun took David's S, and shaved them, and
	19:19	And when the S of Hadadezer saw that they
	20:8	of David and by the hand of his S
	21:3	lord the king, all of them my lord's S
2Chr	2:8	I know that your S know how to cut

	2:8	And my S will be with your servants,
	2:8	will be with your S,
	2:10	will give for your S, the hewers who cut
	2:15	him send to his S;
	6:14	steadfast love to thy S who walk before thee
	6:23	act, and judge thy S, requiting the guilty by
	6:27	the sin of thy S, thy people Israel, when
	8:18	sent him by his S ships and servants familiar
	8:18	his servants ships and S familiar with the sea,
	8:18	Ophir together with the S of Solomon, and fetched
	9:4	the attendance of his S, and their clothing, his
	9:7	Happy are these your S, who continually stand
	9:10	Moreover the S of Huram and the servants of
	9:10	of Huram and the S of Solomon, who brought
	9:12	went back to her own land, with her S
	9:21	to Tarshish with the S of Huram; once every
	10:7	they will be your S for ever."
	12:8	Nevertheless they shall be S to him, that they
	24:25	him severely wounded, his S conspired against him
	25:3	hand he killed his S who had slain the
	32:9	his forces, sent his S to Jerusalem to Hezekiah
	32:16	And his S said still more against the Lord
	33:24	And his S conspired against him and killed him
	34:16	was committed to your S they are doing.
	35:23	king said to his S, "Take me away, for
	35:24	So his S took him out of the chariot
	36:20	sword, and they became S to him and to
Ezra	2:43	The temple S: the sons of Ziha, the sons
	2:55	The sons of Solomon's S: the sons of Sotai,
	2:58	All the temple S and the sons of Solomon's
	2:58	the sons of Solomon's S were three hundred and
	2:70	gatekeepers, and the temple S lived in their towns,
	4:11	Artaxerxes the king: Your S, the men of the
	5:11	us: 'We are the S of the God of
	7:7	the singers and gatekeepers, and the temple S
	7:24	the doorkeepers, the temple S, or other servants of
	7:24	temple servants, or other S of this house of
	8:17	his brethren the temple S at the place Casiphia,
	8:20	twenty of the temple S, whom David and his
	9:11	didst command by thy S the prophets, saying, 'The
Neh	1:6	people of Israel thy S, confessing the sins of
	1:10	there.' They are thy S and thy people, whom
	1:11	the prayer of thy S who delight to fear
	2:20	prosper, and we his S will arise and build;
	3:26	Parosh and the temple S living on Ophel repaired
	3:31	house of the temple S and of the merchants,
	4:16	on, half of my S worked on construction, and
	4:23	my brethren nor my S nor the men of
	5:10	my brethren and my S are lending them money
	5:15	Even their S lorded it over the people.
	5:16	land; and all my S were gathered there for
	7:46	The temple S: the sons of Ziha, the sons
	7:57	The sons of Solomon's S: the sons of Sotai,
	7:60	All the temple S and the sons of Solomon's
	7:60	the sons of Solomon's S were three hundred and
	7:73	the people, the temple S, and all Israel, lived
	9:10	Pharaoh and all his S and all the people
	10:28	the singers, the temple S, and all who have
	11:3	temple S, and the descendants of Solomon's S
	11:21	But the temple S lived on Ophel; and Ziha
	11:21	and Ziha and Gishpa were over the temple S
	13:19	set some of my S over the gates, that
Tob	8:18	Then he ordered his S to fill in the
Jud	3:2	said, "Behold, we the S of Nebuchadnezzar, the
	6:3	them--we the king's S will destroy them as
	6:6	the spear of my S shall pierce your sides,
	7:12	you; only let your S take possession of the
	7:16	Holofernes and all his S, and he gave orders
	10:20	companions and all his S came out and led
	10:23	of Holofernes and his S, they all marveled at
	11:4	as they do the S of my lord King
	11:20	Holofernes and all his S, and they marveled at
	12:5	Then the S of Holofernes brought her into the
Esth	1:3	all his princes and S, the army chiefs of
	2:2	Then the king's S who attended him said, "Let
	2:18	all his princes and S; it was Esther's banquet.
	3:2	And all the king's S who were at the
	3:3	Then the king's S who were at the king's
	4:11	saying, "All the king's S and the people of
	5:11	the princes and the S of the king.
	6:3	The king's S who attended him said, "Nothing has
	6:5	So the king's S told him, "Haman is there,"
	15:16	agitated, and all his S sought to comfort her.
Job	1:3	she-asses, and very many S; so that this man
	1:15	them, and slew the S with the edge of
	1:16	the sheep and the S, and consumed them; and
	1:17	them, and slew the S with the edge of
	4:18	Even in his S he puts no trust, and
Ps	34:22	the life of his S; none of those who
	69:35	of Judah; and his S shall dwell there and
	69:36	the children of his S shall inherit it, and
	79:2	the bodies of thy S to the birds of
	79:10	outpoured blood of thy S be known among the
	90:13	Have pity on thy S
	90:16	be manifest to thy S, and thy glorious power
	102:14	For thy S hold her stones dear, and have
	102:28	The children of thy S shall dwell secure; their
	105:25	hate his people, to deal craftily with his S
	113:1	Praise, O S of the LORD, praise the name
	119:91	stand this day; for all things are thy S
	123:2	as the eyes of S look to the hand
	134:1	the LORD, all you S of the LORD, who
	135:1	LORD, give praise, O S of the LORD,
	135:9	Pharaoh and all his S;
	135:14	vindicate his people, and have compassion on his S
Wis	6:4	Because as S of his kingdom you did not
	9:4	and do not reject me from among thy S
	12:7	worthy colony of the S of God.
	12:20	the enemies of thy S and those deserving of
Sir	4:30	your home, nor be a faultfinder with your S
	6:11	be bold with your S;
	36:17	the prayer of thy S, according to the blessing
Is	36:9	least of my master's S, when you rely on
	36:11	"Pray, speak to your S in Aramaic, for we
	37:5	When the S of King Hezekiah came to Isaiah,
	37:6	heard, with which the S of the king of
	37:24	By your S you have mocked the Lord, and
	54:17	the heritage of the S of the LORD and
	56:6	and to be his S, every one who keeps
	63:17	the sake of thy S, the tribes of thy
	65:8	will do for my S sake, and not destroy
	65:9	inherit it, and my S shall dwell there.
	65:13	Lord GOD: "Behold, my S shall eat, but you
	65:13	be hungry; behold, my S shall drink, but you
	65:13	be thirsty; behold, my S shall rejoice, but you
	65:14	to shame; behold, my S shall sing for gladness
	65:15	slay you; but his S he will call by
	66:14	LORD is with his S, and his indignation is
Jer	7:25	persistently sent all my S the prophets to them,
	14:3	Her nobles send their S for water; they come
	21:7	of Judah, and his S, and the people in
	22:2	David, you, and your S, and your people who
	22:4	horses, they, and their S, and their people.
	25:4	to you all his S the prophets,
	25:19	king of Egypt, his S, his princes, all his
	26:5	the words of my S the prophets whom I
	29:19	to you by my S the prophets, but you
	30:8	shall no more make S of them.
	35:15	to you all my S the prophets, sending them
	36:24	nor any of his S who heard all these
	36:31	his offspring and his S for their iniquity; I
	37:2	neither he nor his S nor the people of
	37:18	to you or your S or this people, that
	44:4	to you all my S the prophets, saying, Oh,
Bar	2:20	didst declare by thy S the prophets, saying:
	2:24	didst speak by thy S the prophets, that the
Ezek	38:17	former days by my S the prophets of Israel,
	46:17	to one of his S, it shall be his
Dan	1:12	and Azariah; "Test your S for ten days; let
	1:13	according to what you see deal with your S
	2:4	Tell your S the dream, and we will show
	2:7	the king tell his S the dream, and we
	3:33	disgrace have befallen thy S and worshipers.
	3:43	do harm to thy S be put to shame;
	3:46	Now the king's S who threw them in did
	3:86	Bless the Lord, you S of the Lord, sing
	3:94	"Shadrach, Meshach, and Abednego, S of the Most
	3:96	angel and delivered his S, who trusted in him,
	9:6	not listened to thy S the prophets, who spoke
	9:10	before us by his S the prophets.
	13:26	When the household S heard the shouting in the
	13:27	told their tale, the S were greatly ashamed, for
	14:14	Then Daniel ordered his S to bring ashes and
Amos	3:7	his secret to his S the prophets.
Zech	1:6	which I commanded my S the prophets, did they
1Mac	16:16	and his two sons and some of his S
2Mac	1:2	with Abraham and Isaac and Jacob, his faithful S
	7:6	said, ïAnd he will have compassion on his S
	7:33	he will again be reconciled with his own S
	8:29	merciful Lord to be wholly reconciled with his S
Mt	13:27	And the S of the householder came and said
	13:28	has done this.' The S said to him, 'Then

S

14:2 he said to his S, "This is John the
18:22 king who wished to settle accounts with his S
18:27 one of his fellow S who owed him a
18:30 When his fellow S saw what had taken place,
21:34 near, he sent his S to the tenants, to
21:35 the tenants took his S and beat one, killed
21:36 Again he sent other S, more than the first;
22:3 son, and sent his S to call those who
22:4 Again he sent other S, saying, 'Tell those who
22:6 the rest seized his S, treated them shamefully, and
22:8 he said to his S, 'The wedding is ready,
22:10 you find.' And those S went out into the
24:49 to beat his fellow S, and eats and drinks
25:14 a journey called his S and entrusted to them
25:19 the master of those S came and settled accounts
Mk 1:20 boat with the hired S, and followed him.
13:34 home and puts his S in charge, each with
Lk 12:37 Blessed are those S whom the master finds awake
12:38 third, and finds them so, blessed are those S
15:17 of my father's hired S have bread enough and
15:19 one of your hired S
15:22 father said to his S, 'Bring quickly the best
15:26 called one of the S and asked what this
17:10 say, 'We are unworthy S; we have only done
19:13 Calling ten of his S, he gave them ten
19:15 power, he commanded these S, to whom he had
Jn 2:5 mother said to the S, "Do whatever he tells
2:9 came from (though the S who had drawn the
4:51 was going down, his S met him and told
15:15 do I call you S, for the servant does
18:18 Now the S and officers had made a charcoal
18:26 One of the S of the high priest, a
18:36 of this world, my S would fight, that I
Acts 4:29 and grant to thy S to speak thy word
10:7 called two of his S and a devout soldier
16:17 crying, "These men are S of the Most High
1Cor 3:5 S through whom you believed, as the Lord assigned
4:1 should regard us, as S of Christ and stewards
2Cor 4:5 with ourselves as your S for Jesus' sake.
6:4 our ministry, but as S of God we commend
11:15 not strange if his S also disguise themselves as
11:15 also disguise themselves as S of righteousness.
11:23 Are they S of Christ?
Gal 5:13 but through love be S of one another.
Eph 6:6 as men-pleasers, but as S of Christ, doing the
Phil 1:1 Paul and Timothy, S of Christ Jesus, To
Heb 1:7 angels winds, and his S flames of fire."
1Pet 2:16 evil; but live as S of God.
2:18 S, be submissive to your masters with all respect,
Rev 1:1 to show to his S what must soon take
2:20 teaching and beguiling my S to practice immorality
6:11 number of their fellow S and their brethren should
7:3 we have sealed the S of our God upon
10:7 he announced to his S the prophets, should be
11:18 judged, for rewarding thy S, the prophets and saints,
19:2 has avenged on her the blood of his S
19:5 God, all you his S, you who fear him,
22:3 in it, and his S shall worship him;
22:6 angel to show his S what must soon take

S

SERVE (237)

Gen 6:21 up; and it shall S as food for you
15:14 the nation which they S, and afterward they shall
25:23 other, the elder shall S the younger."
27:29 Let peoples S you, and nations bow down to
27:40 live, and you shall S your brother; but when
29:15 kinsman, should you therefore S me for nothing?
29:18 he said, "I will S you seven years for
29:25 Did I not S with you for Rachel?
Ex 1:12 the people of Israel S with rigor,
1:13 work they made them S with rigor.
1:15 other Puah, "When you S as midwife to the
3:12 of Egypt, you shall S God upon this mountain."
4:23 go that he may S me"; if you refuse
7:16 go, that they may S me in the wilderness;
8:1 go, that they may S me.
8:20 go, that they may S me.
9:1 go, that they may S me.
9:13 go, that they may S me.
10:3 go, that they may S me.
10:7 go, that they may S the LORD their God;
10:8 said to them, "Go, S the LORD your God;
10:11 men among you, and S the LORD, for that
10:24 Moses, and said, "Go, S the LORD; your children
10:26 take of them to S the LORD our God,
10:26 with what we must S the LORD until we
12:31 of Israel; and go, S the LORD, as you
14:12 alone and let us S the Egyptians?
14:12 better for us to S the Egyptians than to
20:5 down to them or S them; for I the
21:2 Hebrew slave, he shall S six years, and in
21:6 awl; and he shall S him for life.
23:24 to their gods, nor S them, nor do according
23:25 You shall S the LORD your God, and I
23:33 me; for if you S their gods, it will
28:1 people of Israel, to S me as priests--Aaron
28:4 and his sons to S me as priests.
28:41 them, that they may S me as priests.
29:1 them, that they may S me as priests.
29:44 I will consecrate, to S me as priests.
30:30 them, that they may S me as priests.
39:41 of his sons to S as priests.
Lev 7:35 they were presented to S as priests of the
25:39 shall not make him S as a slave:
25:40 He shall S with you until the year of
Num 8:25 of the service and S no more,
10:10 peace offerings; they shall S you for remembrance
10:31 wilderness, and you will S as eyes for us.
18:7 that is within the veil; and you shall S
18:21 their service which they S, their service in the
Deut 4:19 and worship them and S them, things which the
4:28 And there you will S gods of wood and
5:9 down to them or S them; for I the
6:13 your God; you shall S him, and swear by
7:4 from following me, to S other gods; then the
7:16 them; neither shall you S their gods, for that
8:19 after other gods and S them and worship them,
10:12 to love him, to S the LORD your God
10:20 your God; you shall S him and cleave to
11:13 your God, and to S him with all your
11:16 you turn aside and S other gods and worship
12:30 'How did these nations S their gods?--that I
13:2 known, 'and let us S them,'
13:4 voice, and you shall S him and cleave to
13:6 'Let us go and S other gods,' which neither
13:13 'Let us go and S other gods,' which you
15:12 to you, he shall S you six years, and
20:11 for you and shall S you.
28:14 after other gods to S them.
28:36 and there you shall S other gods, of wood
28:47 "Because you did not S the LORD your God
28:48 things, therefore you shall S your enemies whom the
28:64 and there you shall S other gods, of wood
29:18 God to go and S the gods of those
30:17 worship other gods and S them,
31:20 to other gods and S them, and despise me
Josh 22:5 to him, and to S him with all your
23:7 swear by them, or S them, or bow down
23:16 you, and go and S other gods and bow
24:14 fear the LORD, and S him in sincerity and
24:14 and in Egypt, and S the LORD.
24:15 you be unwilling to S the LORD, choose this
24:15 day whom you will S, whether the gods your
24:15 my house, we will S the LORD."
24:16 forsake the LORD, to S other gods;
24:18 therefore we also will S the LORD, for he
24:19 the people, "You cannot S the LORD; for he
24:20 forsake the LORD and S foreign gods, then he
24:21 "Nay; but we will S the LORD."
24:22 chosen the LORD, to S him." And they said,
24:24 our God we will S, and his voice we
Judg 9:28 Shechem, that we should S him?
9:28 and Zebul his officer S the men of Hamor
9:28 Why then should we S him?
9:38 Abimelech, that we should S him?' Are not these
10:6 LORD, and did not S him.
1Sam 7:3 to the LORD, and S him only, and he
11:1 us, and we will S you."
12:10 enemies, and we will S thee.'
12:14 fear the LORD and S him and hearken to
12:20 following the LORD, but S the LORD with all
12:24 fear the LORD, and S him faithfully with all
17:9 be our servants and S us."
26:19 the LORD, saying, 'Go, S other gods.'
2Sam 16:19 And again, whom should I S
16:19 father, so I will S you."
1Kgs 9:6 you, but go and S other gods and worship
12:4 us, and we will S you."
12:7 this people today and S them, and speak good
2Kgs 3:14 hosts lives, whom I S, were it not that
5:16 LORD lives, whom I S, I will receive none."
10:18 little; but Jehu will S him much.

17:35 yourselves to them or S them or sacrifice to
18:7 Assyria, and would not S him.
25:24 in the land, and S the king of Babylon,
1Chr 28:9 of your father, and S him with a whole
2Chr 7:19 you, and go and S other gods and worship
10:4 us, and we will S you."
19:11 and the Levites will S you as officers.
30:8 sanctified for ever, and S the LORD your God,
33:16 he commanded Judah to S the LORD the God
34:33 who were in Israel S the LORD their God.
35:3 Now S the LORD your God and his people
Neh 9:35 They did not S thee in their kingdom, and
Tob 4:14 once; and if you S God you will receive
Jud 8:22 the Gentiles, wherever we S as slaves; and we
11:1 one who chose to S Nebuchadnezzar, the king of
11:7 not only do men S him because of you,
12:1 own food and to S her with his own
12:13 of the Assyrians who S in the house of
16:14 Let all thy creatures S thee, for thou didst
Esth 12:5 king ordered Mordecai to S in the court and
Job 21:15 Almighty, that we should S him?
36:11 If they hearken and S him, they complete their
39:9 wild ox willing to S you?
Ps 2:11 S the LORD with fear, with trembling
22:30 Posterity shall S him; men shall tell of the
72:11 before him, all nations S him!
100:2 S the LORD with gladness!
Wis 15:7 both the vessels that S clean uses and those
Sir 2:1 you come forward to S the Lord, prepare yourself
3:7 his mother; he will S his parents as his
4:14 Those who S her will minister to the Holy
8:8 and learn how to S great men.
39:4 He will S among great men and appear before
43:6 the moon also, to S in its season to
45:15 to the Lord and S as priest and bless
Is 14:3 you were made to S,
59:6 Their webs will not S as clothing; men will
60:12 kingdom that will not S you shall perish; those
Jer 2:20 said, 'I will not S Yea, upon every high
5:19 land, so you shall S strangers in a land
11:10 after other gods to S them; the house of
13:10 after other gods to S them and worship them,
15:14 I will make you S your enemies in a
16:13 and there you shall S other gods day and
17:4 I will make you S your enemies in a
22:13 who makes his neighbor S him for nothing, and
25:6 after other gods to S and worship them, or
25:11 and these nations shall S the king of Babylon
27:6 of the field to S him.
27:7 All the nations shall S him and his son
27:8 or kingdom will not S this Nebuchadnezzar king of
27:9 you, 'You shall not S the king of Babylon.'
27:11 king of Babylon and S him, I will leave
27:12 king of Babylon, and S him and his people,
27:13 nation which will not S the king of Babylon?
27:14 you, 'You shall not S the king of Babylon,'
27:17 not listen to them; S the king of Babylon
28:14 Babylon, and they shall S him, for I have
30:9 But they shall S the LORD their God and
35:15 after other gods to S them, and then you
40:9 not be afraid to S the Chaldeans.
40:9 in the land, and S the king of Babylon,
44:3 to burn incense and S other gods that they
Bar 1:12 son, and we shall S them many days and
2:21 Bend your shoulders and S the king of Babylon,
2:22 Lord and will not S the king of Babylon,
2:24 obey thy voice, to S the king of Babylon;
6:27 And those who S them are ashamed because
6:30 Women S meals for gods of silver and gold
6:39 mountain, and those who S them will be put
Ezek 20:39 the Lord GOD: Go S every one of you
20:40 all of them, shall S me in the land;
41:6 of the temple to S as supports for the
44:11 on the people, to S them.
44:13 near to me, to S me as priest, nor
Dan 1:4 learning, and competent to S in the king's palace,
3:12 you; they do not S your gods or worship
3:14 that you do not S my gods or worship
3:17 our God whom we S is able to deliver
3:18 that we will not S your gods or worship
3:96 their bodies rather than S and worship any god
6:16 your God, whom you S continually, deliver you!"
6:20 your God, whom you S continually, been able to
7:14 nations, and languages should S him; his dominion is
7:27 and all dominions shall S and obey them.'
Zeph 3:9 of the LORD and S him with one accord.

Mal 3:14 'It is vain to S God.
3:18 one who does not S him.
1Mac 6:23 We were happy to S your father, to live
2Mac 6:17 what we have said S as a reminder; we
Mt 4:10 Lord your God and him only shall you S
6:24 "No one can S two masters; for either he
6:24 You cannot S God and mammon.
20:28 be served but to S, and to give his
Mk 10:45 be served but to S, and to give his
Lk 1:74 of our enemies, might S him without fear,
4:8 Lord your God, and him only shall you S
10:40 has left me to S alone?
12:37 he will come and S them.
16:13 No servant can S two masters; for either he
16:13 You cannot S God and mammon."
17:8 and gird yourself and S me, till I eat
Acts 6:2 word of God to S tables.
7:7 the nation which they S said God, 'and after
26:16 to appoint you to S and bear witness to
Rom 1:9 my witness, whom I S with my spirit in
7:6 captive, so that we S not under the old
7:25 then, I of myself S the law of God
7:25 with my flesh I S the law of sin.
9:12 told, "The elder will S the younger."
12:11 aglow with the Spirit, S the Lord.
16:18 such persons do not S our Lord Christ, but
1Cor 9:13 temple, and those who S at the altar share
2Cor 11:8 them in order to S you.
1Thes 1:9 God from idols, to S a living and true
1Tim 3:10 themselves blameless let them S as deacons.
3:13 well; for those who S well as deacons gain
6:2 brethren; rather they must S all the better since
2Tim 1:3 thank God whom I S with a clear conscience,
Philem 1:13 order that he might S me on your behalf
Heb 1:14 spirits sent forth to S, for the sake of
8:5 They S a copy and shadow of the heavenly
9:14 from dead works to S the living God.
13:10 from which those who S the tent have no
Jude 1:7 indulged in unnatural lust, S as an example by
Rev 7:15 throne of God, and S him day and night

SERVED (87)

Gen 14:4 Twelve years they had S Ched-or-laomer, but in the
29:20 So Jacob S seven years for Rachel, and they
29:30 more than Leah, and S Laban for another seven
30:26 for whom I have S you, and let me
30:29 know how I have S you, and how your
31:6 know that I have S your father with all
31:41 in your house; I S you fourteen years for
43:31 and controlling himself he said, "Let food be S
43:32 They S him by himself, and them by themselves,
Num 3:4 So Eleazar and Ithamar S as priests in the
4:37 the Kohathites, all who S in the tent of
4:41 of Gershon, all who S in the tent of
Deut 12:2 whom you shall dispossess S their gods, upon the
15:18 hired servant he has S you six years.
17:3 and has gone and S other gods and worshiped
29:26 Egypt, and went and S other gods and worshiped
Josh 24:2 of Nahor; and they S other gods.
24:14 gods which your fathers S beyond the River, and
24:15 the gods your fathers S in the region beyond
24:31 And Israel S the LORD all the days of
Judg 2:7 And the people S the LORD all the days
2:11 of the LORD and S the Baals;
2:13 forsook the LORD, and S the Baals and the
3:6 their sons; and they S their gods.
3:8 the people of Israel S Cushan-rishathaim eight years.
3:14 the people of Israel S Eglon the king of
10:6 of the LORD, and S the Baals and the
10:10 our God and have S the Baals."
10:13 have forsaken me and S other gods; therefore I
10:16 from among them and S the LORD; and he
1Sam 2:22 with the women who S at the entrance to
7:4 the Ashtaroth, and they S the LORD only.
12:10 the LORD, and have S the Baals and the
2Sam 13:17 the young man who S him and said, "Put
16:19 As I have S your father, so I will
22:44 I had not known S me.
1Kgs 4:21 they brought tribute and S Solomon all the days
9:9 worshipped them and S them; therefore the LORD
16:31 Sidonians, and went and S Baal, and worshiped him.
22:53 He S Baal and worshiped him, and provoked the
2Kgs 10:18 said to them, "Ahab S Baal a little; but
17:12 to anger, and they S idols, of which the
17:16 host of heaven, and S Baal.
17:33 the LORD but also S their own gods, after

S

S

Ezra 6:18 their courses, for the S of God at Jerusalem,
7:19 given you for the S of the house of
Neh 10:32 a shekel for the S of the house of
12:9 Unno their brethren stood opposite them in the S
12:45 And they performed the S of their God and
12:45 their God and the S of purification, as did
13:14 the house of my God and for his S
Esth 8:10 used in the king's S, bred from the royal
8:14 used in the king's S, rode out in haste,
Job 7:1 not man a hard S upon earth, and are
14:14 the days of my S I would wait, till
Wis 15:7 each vessel for our S, he fashions out of
Sir 6:19 For in her S you will toil a little
10:24 will be at the S of a wise servant,
35:16 He whose S is pleasing to the Lord will
39:31 on earth for their S, and when their times
50:14 Finishing the S at the altars, and arranging the
50:19 the Lord was ended; so they completed his S
Is 14:3 turmoil and the hard S with which you were
Jer 34:14 him free from your S But your fathers did
52:18 used in the temple S;
Bar 6:60 and sent forth for S, are obedient.
Ezek 44:14 to do all its S and all that is
Hos 12:12 Aram, there Israel did S for a wife, and
1Mac 10:41 now on for the S of the temple.
11:58 plate and a table S, and granted him the
2Mac 3:3 expenses connected with the S of the sacrifices.
4:14 longer intent upon their S at the altar.
8:9 general and a man of experience in military S
Lk 1:23 when his time of S was ended, he went
Jn 16:2 think he is offering S to God.
Rom 12:7 to our faith; if S, in our serving; he
15:16 Gentiles in the priestly S of the gospel of
15:27 also to be of S to them in material
15:31 Judea, and that my S for Jerusalem may be
1Cor 9:13 employed in the temple S get their food from
12:5 there are varieties of S, but the same Lord;
16:15 devoted themselves to the S of the saints;
2Cor 8:23 fellow worker in your S; and as for our
9:12 the rendering of this S not only supplies the
9:13 the test of this S, you will glorify God
Eph 6:7 from the heart, rendering S with a good will
Phil 2:30 life to complete your S to me.
1Tim 1:12 appointing me to his S,
6:2 who benefit by their S are believers and beloved.
2Tim 1:18 well know all the S he rendered at Ephesus.
2:4 No soldier on S gets entangled in civilian pursuits,
Heb 2:17 high priest in the S of God, to make
10:11 stands daily at his S, offering repeatedly the same
1Pet 4:11 of God; whoever renders S, as one who renders
3Jn 1:5 when you render any S to the brethren, especially
1:6 send them on their journey as befits God's S
Rev 2:19 love and faith and S and patient endurance, and

SERVICES (2)

1Mac 10:42 the income of the S of the temple, this
2Mac 9:26 the public and private S rendered to you and

SERVING (22)

Gen 29:27 also in return for S me another seven years."
Ex 14:5 let Israel go from S us?"
Num 4:24 of the Gershonites, in S and bearing burdens:
4:49 to his task of S or carrying; thus they
Judg 2:19 going after other gods, S them and bowing down
3:7 LORD their God, and S the Baals and the
1Sam 8:8 day, forsaking me and S other gods, so they
2Chr 11:14 cast them out from S as priests of the
Esth 11:3 Susa, a great man, S in the court of
Wis 16:24 For creation, S thee who hast made it, exerts
Bar 1:21 own wicked heart by S other gods and doing
Ezek 27:7 Egypt was your sail, S as your ensign; blue
44:11 of the temple, and S in the temple; they
Lk 1:8 Now while he was S as priest before God
10:40 was distracted with much S; and she went to
Acts 20:19 set foot in Asia, S the Lord with all
Rom 12:7 if service, in our S; he who teaches, in
Col 3:23 task, work heartily, as S the Lord and not
3:24 your reward; you are S the Lord Christ.
2Tim 4:11 is very useful in S me.
Heb 6:10 for his sake in S the saints, as you
1Pet 1:12 them that they were S not themselves but you,

SERVINGS

Tob 7:8 flock and set large S of food before them.

SERVITUDE (3)

Neh 5:18 the governor, because the S was heavy upon this
Jer 28:14 an iron yoke of S to Nebuchadnezzar king of
Lam 1:3 of affliction and hard S; she dwells now among

SESSION

Jud 4:8 people of Israel, in S at Jerusalem, had given

SET (822)

Gen 1:17 And God S them in the firmament of the
6:16 a cubit above; and S the door of the
8:9 found no place to S her foot, and she
9:13 all future generations: I S my bow in the
12:5 in Haran; and they S forth to go to
12:20 concerning him; and they S him on the way,
18:8 he had prepared, and S it before them; and
18:16 Then the men S out from there, and they
18:16 went with them to S them on their way.
19:16 brought him forth and S him outside the city.
21:28 Abraham S seven ewe lambs of the flock apart.
21:29 lambs which you have S apart?"
24:33 Then food was S before him to eat; but
26:31 one another; and Isaac S them on their way,
28:11 stayed there that night, because the sun had S
28:12 there was a ladder S up on the earth,
28:18 under his head and S it up for a
28:22 stone, which I have S up for a pillar,
30:36 his sons; and he S a distance of three
30:38 He S the rods which he had peeled in
30:40 separated the lambs, and S the faces of the
31:17 So Jacob arose, and S his sons and his
31:21 crossed the Euphrates, and S his face toward the
31:37 S it here before my kinsmen and your kinsmen,
31:45 took a stone, and S it up as a
31:51 pillar, which I have S between you and me.
35:14 And Jacob S up a pillar in the place
35:20 is, Bethlehem), and Jacob S up a pillar upon
41:33 discreet and wise, and S him over the land
41:41 Joseph, "Behold, I have S you over all the
41:43 Thus he S him over all the land of
43:9 back to you and S him before you, then
44:21 me, that I may S my eyes upon him.'
46:5 Then Jacob S out from Beer-sheba; and the sons
47:7 Jacob his father, and S him before Pharaoh, and
Ex 1:10 Therefore they S taskmasters over them to afflict
4:20 and his sons and S them on an ass,
5:14 whom Pharaoh's taskmasters had S over them, were
8:22 that day I will S apart the land of
9:5 And the LORD S a time, saying, "Tomorrow the
13:12 to you, you shall S apart to the LORD
16:1 They S out from Elim, and all the congregation
19:2 And when they S out from Rephidim and came
19:7 of the people, and S before them all these
19:12 And you shall S bounds for the people round
19:23 didst charge us, saying, S bounds about the mountain,
21:1 ordinances which you shall S before them.
23:31 And I will S your bounds from the Red
25:30 And you shall S the bread of the Presence
25:37 the lamps shall be S up so as to
26:4 curtain in the first S; and likewise you shall
26:4 edge of the outmost curtain in the second S
26:5 is in the second S; the loops shall be
26:10 is outmost in one S, and fifty loops on
26:10 the curtain which is outmost in the second S
26:35 And you shall S the table outside the veil,
27:5 And you shall S it under the ledge of
27:20 a lamp may be S up to burn continually.
28:12 And you shall S the two stones upon the
28:17 And you shall S in it four rows of
28:20 jasper; they shall be S in gold filigree.
29:6 ephod; and you shall S the turban on his
32:22 people, that they are S on evil.
35:27 and stones to be S, for the ephod and
36:11 curtain of the first S; likewise he made them
36:11 curtain of the second S;
36:12 was in the second S; the loops were opposite
36:17 curtain of the one S, and fifty loops on
39:7 And he S them on the shoulder-pieces of the
39:10 And they S in it four rows of stones.
39:37 lamps with the lamps S and all its utensils,
Lev 8:9 And he S the turban upon his head, and
8:9 turban, in front, he S the golden plate, the
14:11 who cleanses him shall S the man who is
16:7 the two goats, and S them before the LORD
17:10 any blood, I will S my face against that
20:3 I myself will S my face against that man,

S

20:5 death, then I will S my face against that
20:6 after them, I will S my face against that
20:25 teems, which I have S apart for you to
24:6 And you shall S them in two rows, six
24:8 sabbath day Aaron shall S it in order before
26:1 and you shall not S up a figured stone
26:17 eat it; I will S my face against you,
Num 1:51 the tabernacle is to S out, the Levites shall
1:51 pitched, the Levites shall S it up.
2:9 They shall S out first on the march.
2:16 They shall S out second.
2:17 tent of meeting shall S out, with the camp
2:17 encamp, so shall they S out, each in position,
2:24 They shall S out third on the march.
2:31 They shall S out last, standard by standard."
2:34 standards, and so they S out, every one in
3:6 of Levi near, and S them before Aaron the
4:5 the camp is to S out, Aaron and his
5:16 bring her near, and S her before the LORD;
5:18 And the priest shall S the woman before the
5:30 wife; then he shall S the woman before the
8:2 to Aaron, When you S up the lamps, the
8:3 Aaron did so; he S up its lamps to
9:15 that the tabernacle was S up, the cloud covered
9:17 the people of Israel S out; and in the
9:18 the people of Israel S out, and at the
9:19 LORD, and did not S out.
9:20 of the LORD they S out.
9:21 in the morning, they S out, or if it
9:21 was taken up they S out.
9:22 camp and did not S out; but when it
9:22 was taken up they S out.
9:23 of the LORD they S out; they kept the
10:5 the east side shall S out.
10:6 the south side shall S out.
10:6 whenever they are to S out.
10:12 the people of Israel S out by stages from
10:13 They S out for the first time at the
10:14 the men of Judah S out first by their
10:17 who carried the tabernacle, S out.
10:18 the camp of Reuben S out by their companies;
10:21 Then the Kohathites S out, carrying the holy things,
10:21 and the tabernacle was S up before their arrival.
10:22 the men of Ephraim S out by their companies;
10:25 of all the camps, S out by their companies;
10:28 their hosts, when they S out.
10:33 So they S out from the mount of the
10:34 by day, whenever they S out from the camp.
10:35 And whenever the ark S out, Moses said, "Arise,
12:15 the people did not S out on the march
12:16 After that the people S out from Hazeroth, and
14:25 valleys, turn tomorrow and S out for the wilderness
21:4 From Mount Hor they S out by the way
21:8 a fiery serpent, and S it on a pole;
21:9 a bronze serpent, and S it on a pole;
21:10 the people of Israel S out, and encamped in
21:11 And they S out from Oboth, and encamped at
21:12 From there they S out, and encamped in the
21:13 From there they S out, and encamped on the
22:1 the people of Israel S out, and encamped in
24:1 look for omens, but S his face toward the
24:21 and your nest is S in the rock;
33:3 They S out from Rameses in the first month,
33:5 the people of Israel S out from Rameses, and
33:6 And they S out from Succoth, and encamped at
33:7 And they S out from Etham, and turned back
33:8 And they S out from before Hahiroth, and passed
33:9 And they S out from Marah, and came to
33:10 And they S out from Elim, and encamped by
33:11 And they S out from the Red Sea, and
33:12 And they S out from the wilderness of Sin,
33:13 And they S out from Dophkah, and encamped at
33:14 And they S out from Alush, and encamped at
33:15 And they S out from Rephidim, and encamped in
33:16 And they S out from the wilderness of Sinai,
33:17 And they S out from Kibroth-hattaavah, and
33:18 And they S out from Hazeroth, and encamped at
33:19 And they S out from Rithmah, and encamped at
33:20 And they S out from Rimmon-perez, and encamped
33:21 And they S out from Libnah, and encamped at
33:22 And they S out from Rissah, and encamped at
33:23 And they S out from Kehelathah, and encamped at
33:24 And they S out from Mount Shepher, and encamped
33:25 And they S out from Haradah, and encamped at
33:26 And they S out from Makheloth, and encamped at
33:27 And they S out from Tahath, and encamped at
33:28 And they S out from Terah, and encamped at
33:29 And they S out from Mithkah, and encamped at
33:30 And they S out from Hashmonah, and encamped at
33:31 And they S out from Moseroth, and encamped at
33:32 And they S out from Bene-jaakan, and encamped at
33:33 And they S out from Hor-haggidgad, and encamped
33:34 And they S out from Jotbathah, and encamped at
33:35 And they S out from Abronah, and encamped at
33:36 And they S out from Ezion-geber, and encamped in
33:37 And they S out from Kadesh, and encamped at
33:41 And they S out from Mount Hor, and encamped
33:42 And they S out from Zalmonah, and encamped at
33:43 And they S out from Punon, and encamped at
33:44 And they S out from Oboth, and encamped at
33:45 And they S out from Iyim, and encamped at
33:46 And they S out from Dibon-gad, and encamped at
33:47 they S out from Almon-diblathaim, and encamped in
33:48 And they S out from the mountains of Abarim,
Deut 1:8 Behold, I have S the land before you; go
1:15 and experienced men, and S them as heads over
1:19 "And we S out from Horeb, and went through
1:21 LORD your God has S the land before you;
4:8 this law which I S before you this day?
4:41 Then Moses S apart three cities in the east
4:44 the law which Moses S before the children of
7:7 people that the LORD S his love upon you
10:8 that time the LORD S apart the tribe of
10:15 it; yet the LORD S his heart in love
11:26 "Behold, I S before you this day a blessing
11:29 of it, you shall S the blessing on Mount
11:32 the ordinances which I S before you this day.
14:24 your God chooses, to S his name there,
16:22 And you shall not S up a pillar, which
17:14 then say, 'I will S a king over me,
17:15 me'; you may indeed S as king over you
17:15 your brethren you shall S as king over you;
19:2 their houses, you shall S apart three cities for
19:7 command you, You shall S apart three cities.
19:14 neighbor's landmark, which the men of old have S
21:8 thou hast redeemed, and S not the guilt of
26:4 from your hand, and S it down before the
26:10 me.' And you shall S it down before the
26:19 commandments, that he will S you high above all
27:2 gives you, you shall S up large stones, and
27:4 the Jordan, you shall S up these stones, concerning
28:1 LORD your God will S you high above all
28:36 your king whom you S over you, to a
28:56 would not venture to S the sole of her
30:1 curse, which I have S before you, and you
30:15 "See, I have S before you this day life
30:19 day, that I have S before you life and
31:10 seven years, at the S time of the year
Josh 3:1 morning Joshua rose and S out from Shittim, with
3:3 priests, then you shall S out from your place
3:14 So, when the people S out from their tents,
4:9 And Joshua S up twelve stones in the midst
4:20 of the Jordan, Joshua S up in Gilgal.
6:23 all her kindred, and S them outside the camp
6:26 youngest son shall he S up its gates."
8:8 the city, you shall S the city on fire,
8:12 five thousand men, and S them in ambush between
8:19 they made haste to S the city on fire.
9:12 on the day we S forth to come to
9:17 the people of Israel S out and reached their
10:18 of the cave, and S men by it to
10:27 hidden themselves, and they S great stones against
15:19 present; since you have S me in the land
16:9 the towns which were S apart for the Ephraimites
18:1 assembled at Shiloh, and S up the tent of
18:4 out that they may S out and go up
18:9 in the land and S down in a book
20:7 So they S apart Kedesh in Galilee in the
24:26 a great stone, and S it up there under
Judg 1:8 of the sword, and S the city on fire.
1:15 present; since you have S me in the land
5:14 From Ephraim they S out thither into the valley,
6:18 out my present, and S it before thee." And
7:5 dog laps, you shall S by himself; likewise every
7:19 when they had just S the watch; and they
7:22 hundred trumpets, the LORD S every man's sword
9:49 the stronghold, and they S the stronghold on fire
15:5 And when he had S fire to the torches,
18:11 with weapons of war, S forth from Zorah and
18:30 And the Danites S up the graven image for
18:31 So they S up Micah's graven image which he
20:29 So Israel S men in ambush round about Gibe-ah.

S

	20:30	the third day, and S themselves in array against
	20:33	of their place, and S themselves in array at
	20:36	ambush whom they had S against Gibe-ah.
	20:48	which they found they S on fire.
Ruth	1:7	So she S out from the place where she
	2:3	So she S forth and went and gleaned in
1Sam	2:8	on them he has S the world.
	4:15	and his eyes were S, so that he could
	5:2	house of Dagon and S it up beside Dagon.
	6:15	the golden figures, and S them upon the great
	6:18	stone, beside which they S down the ark of
	7:12	took a stone and S it up between Mizpah
	9:6	on which we have S out."
	9:20	days ago, do not S your mind on them,
	9:24	the upper portion and S them before Saul; and
	9:24	what was kept is S before you.
	10:19	but S a king over us.' Now therefore present
	12:13	behold, the LORD has S a king over you.
	15:12	Carmel, and behold, he S up a monument for
	18:5	him; so that Saul S him over the men
	28:22	your handmaid; let me S a morsel of bread
	29:11	So David S out with his men early in
	30:9	So David S out, and the six hundred men
2Sam	3:10	house of Saul, and S up the throne of
	4:5	Be-erothite, Rechab and Baanah, S out, and about
	6:17	of the LORD, and S it in its place,
	10:9	that the battle was S against him both in
	11:15	the letter he wrote, S Uriah in the forefront
	12:20	when he asked, they S food before him, and
	12:31	were in it, and S them to labor with
	14:17	lord the king will S me at rest'; for
	14:30	barley there; go and S it on fire." So
	14:30	So Absalom's servants S the field on fire.
	14:31	"Why have your servants S my field on fire?"
	15:24	of God; and they S down the ark of
	17:1	men, and I will S out and pursue David
	17:23	And he S his house in order, and hanged
	17:25	Now Absalom had S Amasa over the army instead
	18:1	were with him, and S over them commanders of
	18:18	lifetime had taken and S up for himself the
	19:28	the king; but you S your servant among those
	20:5	he delayed beyond the S time which had been
	22:34	like hinds' feet, and S me secure on the
	23:23	And David S him over his bodyguard.
1Kgs	5:5	son, whom I will S upon your throne in
	5:6	such wages as you S; for you know that
	6:19	of the house, to S there the ark of
	7:16	of molten bronze, to S upon the tops of
	7:21	He S up the pillars at the vestibule of
	7:21	of the temple; he S up the pillar on
	7:21	name Jachin; and he S up the pillar on
	7:25	east; the sea was S upon them, and all
	7:28	and the panels were S in the frames
	7:29	the panels that were S in the frames were
	7:39	And he S the stands, five on the south
	7:39	the house; and he S the sea on the
	8:12	said, "The LORD has S the sun in the
	9:6	statutes which I have S before you, but go
	10:9	delighted in you and S you on the throne
	11:18	They S out from Midian and came to Paran,
	12:29	And he S one in Bethel, and the other
	16:34	Abiram his first-born, and S up its gates at
	21:9	"Proclaim a fast, and S Naboth on high among
	21:10	among the people; and S two base fellows opposite
	21:12	proclaimed a fast, and S Naboth on high among
2Kgs	4:4	when one is full, S it aside."
	4:25	So she S out, and came to the man
	4:38	said to his servant, S on the great pot,
	4:43	"How am I to S this before a hundred
	4:44	So he S it before them.
	6:22	S bread and water before them, that they may
	8:12	of Israel; you will S on fire their fortresses,
	8:20	rule of Judah, and S up a king of
	9:21	Ahaziah king of Judah S out, each in his
	10:3	your master's sons and S him on his father's
	10:12	Then he S out and went to Samaria.
	11:15	the captains who were S over the army, "Bring
	12:9	lid of it, and S it beside the altar
	12:17	But when Hazael S his face to go up
	17:10	to fortified city; they S up for themselves pillars
	18:23	on your part to S riders upon them.
	19:9	Ethiopia, "Behold, he has S out to fight against
	20:1	"Thus says the LORD, S your house in order;
	21:7	he had made he S in the house of
1Chr	11:25	And David S him over his bodyguard.
	16:1	ark of God, and S it inside the tent
	18:3	as he went to S up his monument at
	19:10	that the battle was S against him both in
	19:17	And when David S the battle in array against
	20:3	were in it, and S them to labor with
	22:2	of Israel, and he S stonecutters to prepare dressed
	22:19	Now S your mind and heart to seek the
	23:13	Aaron was S apart to consecrate the most holy
	25:1	of the service also S apart for the service
2Chr	3:17	He S up the pillars in front of the
	4:4	east; the sea was S upon them, and all
	4:6	which to wash, and S five on the south
	4:7	lampstands as prescribed, and S them in the temple,
	4:10	with bronze; and he S the sea at the
	6:11	And there I have S the ark, in which
	6:13	cubits high, and had S it in the court;
	6:20	thou hast promised to S thy name, that thou
	7:19	commandments which I have S before you, and go
	9:8	delighted in you and S you on his throne
	11:16	And those who had S their hearts to seek
	12:14	for he did not S his heart to seek
	13:11	incense of sweet spices, S out the showbread on
	17:2	cities of Judah, and S garrisons in the land
	19:3	the land, and have S your heart to seek
	20:3	Then Jehoshaphat feared, and S himself to seek the
	20:22	and praise, the LORD S an ambush against the
	20:33	people had not yet S their hearts upon the
	21:8	rule of Judah, and S up a king of
	23:10	of God; and he S all the people as
	23:14	the captains who were S over the army, saying
	23:20	And they S the king upon the royal throne.
	24:8	made a chest, and S it outside the gate
	25:5	men of Judah, and S them by fathers' houses
	25:14	men of Seir, and S them up as his
	26:5	He S himself to seek God in the days
	30:14	They S to work and removed the altars that
	32:5	He S to work resolutely and built up all
	32:6	And he S combat commanders over the people, and
	33:7	he had made he S in the house of
	33:19	built high places and S up the Asherim and
	34:12	Over them were S Jahath and Obadiah the Levites,
	35:12	And they S aside the burnt offerings that they
Ezra	3:3	They S the altar in its place, for fear
	6:18	And they S the priests in their divisions and
	7:10	For Ezra had S his heart to study the
	8:20	and his officials had S apart to attend the
	8:24	Then I S apart twelve of the leading priests:
	9:9	us some reviving to S up the house of
Neh	2:6	send me; and I S him a time.
	3:1	They consecrated it and S its doors; they consecrated
	3:3	laid its beams and S its doors, its bolts,
	3:6	laid its beams and S its doors, its bolts,
	3:13	they rebuilt it and S its doors, its bolts,
	3:14	he rebuilt it and S its doors, its bolts,
	3:15	and covered it and S its doors, its bolts,
	4:9	to our God, and S a guard as a
	6:1	time I had not S up the doors in
	6:7	And you have also S up prophets to proclaim
	7:1	built and I had S up the doors, and
	9:35	land which thou didst S before them; and they
	9:37	kings whom thou hast S over us because of
	9:38	Levites, and our priests S their seal to it.
	10:1	Those who S their seal are Nehemiah the governor,
	12:47	the gatekeepers; and they S apart that which was
	12:47	Levites; and the Levites S apart that which was
	13:11	gathered them together and S them in their stations.
	13:19	And I S some of my servants over the
Tob	2:7	When the sun had S I went and dug
	7:8	from the flock and S large servings of food
	7:14	the contract; and they S their seals to it.
	14:10	deathtrap which Nadab had S for him; but Nadab
Jud	2:2	all his nobles and S forth to them his
	2:19	So he S out with his whole army, to
	5:1	the high hilltops and S up barricades in the
	5:11	advantage of them and S them to making bricks,
	6:16	the assembly; and they S Achior in the midst
	7:7	and seized them and S guards of soldiers over
	8:5	She S up a tent for herself on the
	8:24	therefore, brethren, let us S an example to our
	11:13	they had consecrated and S aside for the priests
	11:19	Jerusalem; and I will S your throne in the
	12:1	and ordered them to S a table for her
	14:2	of the city, and S a captain over them,
	16:7	nor did tall giants S upon him; but Judith
	16:23	She S her maid free.
Esth	2:17	virgins, so that he S the royal crown on
	3:1	and advanced him and S his seat above all

6:8 a royal crown is S;
8:2 And Esther S Mordecai over the house of Haman.
13:14 that I might not S the glory of man
16:5 of those who are S in places of authority
Job 7:17 and that thou dost S thy mind upon him,
11:13 "If you S your heart aright, you will stretch
14:13 wouldest appoint me a S time, and remember me!
16:12 me to pieces; he S me up as his
19:8 pass, and he has S darkness upon my paths.
30:1 would have disdained to S with the dogs of
33:5 me, if you can; S your words in order
36:16 cramping, and what was S on your table was
38:10 bounds for it, and S bars and doors,
Ps 2:2 kings of the earth S themselves, and the rulers
2:6 fury, saying, "I have S my king on Zion,
3:6 of people who have S themselves against me round
4:3 that the LORD has S apart the godly for
17:11 they surround me; they S their eyes to cast
18:33 like hinds' feet, and S me secure on the
19:4 In them he has S a tent for the
20:5 name of our God S up our banners!
21:3 goodly blessings; thou dost S a crown of fine
27:5 his tent, he will S me high upon a
31:8 the enemy; thou hast S my feet in a
40:2 the miry bog, and S my feet upon a
41:12 of my integrity, and S me in thy presence
44:2 but them thou didst S free;
54:3 life; they do not S God before them.
57:6 They S a net for my steps; my soul
60:4 Thou hast S up a banner for those who
62:3 How long will you S upon a man to
62:10 no confidence in extortion, S no vain hopes on
62:10 robbery; if riches increase, S not your heart on
69:18 to me, redeem me, S me free because of
69:29 thy salvation, O God, S me on high!
73:9 They S their mouths against the heavens, and their
73:18 Truly thou dost S them in slippery places; thou
74:4 thy holy place; they S up their own signs
74:7 They S thy sanctuary on fire; to the ground
75:2 At the S time which I appoint I will
78:7 so that they should S their hope in God,
86:14 and they do not S thee before them.
89:19 and say: "I have S the crown upon one
89:25 I will S his hand on the sea and
90:8 Thou hast S our iniquities before thee, our secret
101:3 house; I will not S before my eyes anything
102:20 of the prisoners, to S free those who were
104:5 Thou didst S the earth on its foundations, so
104:9 Thou didst S a bound which they should not
105:20 ruler of the peoples S him free;
118:5 LORD answered me and S me free.
119:30 way of faithfulness, I S thy ordinances before me.
122:5 thrones for judgment were S, the thrones of the
132:11 your body I will S on your throne.
137:6 if I do not S Jerusalem above my highest
140:5 the wayside they have S snares for me.
141:3 S a guard over my mouth, O LORD, keep
Prov 1:18 their own blood, they S an ambush for their
8:23 Ages ago I was S up, at the first,
9:1 her house, she has S up her seven pillars.
9:2 wine, she has also S her table.
19:18 hope; d o not S your heart on his
22:28 not the ancient landmark which your fathers have S
29:8 Scoffers S a city aflame, but wise men turn
Eccl 8:11 of men is fully S to do evil.
10:6 the ruler: folly is S in many high places,
Song 5:12 beside springs of water, bathed in milk, fitly S
5:14 arms are rounded gold, S with jewels.
5:15 legs are alabaster columns, S upon bases of gold.
6:12 was aware, my fancy S me in a chariot
8:6 S me as a seal upon your heart, as
Wis 6:11 Therefore S your desire on my words; long for
9:18 those on earth were S right, and men were
13:10 miserable, with their hopes S on dead things, are
16:14 the departed spirit, nor S free the imprisoned soul.
Sir 2:2 S your heart right and be steadfast, and do
5:1 Do not S your heart on your wealth, nor
17:7 He S his eye upon their hearts to show
22:16 Fences S on a high place will not stand
22:25 that a guard were S over my mouth, and
23:2 O that whips were S over my thoughts, and
31:16 human being what is S before you, and do
33:25 S your slave to work, and you will find
33:28 S him to work, as is fitting for him,
39:5 He will S his heart to rise early to
44:5 composed musical tunes, and S forth verses in
49:3 He S his heart upon the Lord; in the
49:6 a foreign nation, who S fire to the chosen
49:13 that had fallen, and S up the gates and
Is 7:6 it for ourselves, and S up the son of
14:1 choose Israel, and will S them in their own
14:13 of God I will S my throne on high;
17:10 plant pleasant plants and S out slips of an
21:6 said to me: "Go, S a watchman, let him
27:4 I would S out against them, I would burn
30:2 sin to sin; who S out to go down
36:8 on your part to S riders upon them.
37:9 of Ethiopia, "He has S out to fight against
38:1 "Thus says the LORD: S your house in order;
40:20 a skilful craftsman to S up an image that
41:19 the olive; I will S in the desert the
41:21 S forth your case, says the LORD; bring your
42:25 might of battle; it S him on fire round
43:26 let us argue together; S forth your case, that
44:7 let him declare and S it forth before me.
45:13 build my city and S my exiles free, not
46:7 they carry it, they S it in its place,
50:7 confounded; therefore I have S my face like a
50:11 kindle a fire, who S brands alight.
54:11 comforted, behold, I will S your stones in antimony,
57:7 lofty mountain you have S your bed, and thither
57:8 the doorpost you have S up your symbol; for,
62:6 O Jerusalem, I have S watchmen; all the day
65:5 me, for I am S apart from you." These
65:11 my holy mountain, who S a table for Fortune
66:19 glory, and I will S a sign among them.
Jer 1:10 See, I have S you this day over nations
1:15 and every one shall S his throne at the
3:19 thought how I would S you among my sons,
4:7 destroyer of nations has S out; he has gone
5:26 They S a trap; they catch men.
6:17 walk in it.' I S watchmen over you, saying,
6:23 they ride upon horses, S in array as a
7:30 the LORD; they have S their abominations in the
9:13 my law which I S before them, and have
10:20 tent again, and to S up my curtains.
11:13 the altars you have S up to shame, altars
11:16 great tempest he will S fire to it, and
12:3 for the slaughter, and S them apart for the
13:21 you say when they S as head over you
14:22 We S our hope on thee, for thou doest
17:12 A glorious throne S on high from the beginning
21:8 the LORD: Behold, I S before you the way
21:10 For I have S my face against this city
23:4 I will S shepherds over them who will care
24:6 I will S my eyes upon them for good,
26:4 law which I have S before you,
31:21 S up waymarks for yourself, make yourself
31:29 the children's teeth are S on edge.'
31:30 his teeth shall be S on edge.
32:29 city shall come and S this city on fire,
32:34 They S up their abominations in the house which
34:9 that every one should S free his Hebrew slaves,
34:10 that every one would S free his slave, male
34:10 again; they obeyed and S them free.
34:11 female slaves they had S free, and brought them
34:14 each of you must S free the fellow Hebrew
34:14 six years; you must S him free from your
34:16 slaves, whom you had S free according to their
35:5 Then I S before the Rechabites pitchers full of
37:12 of Pharaoh's army, Jeremiah S out from Jerusalem
41:10 took them captive and S out to cross over
42:15 of Israel: If you S your faces to enter
42:17 All the men who S their faces to go
43:3 son of Neriah has S you against us, to
43:10 servant, and he will S his throne above these
44:10 my statutes which I S before you and before
44:11 Israel: Behold, I will S my face against you
44:12 of Judah who have S their faces to come
49:38 them; and I will S my throne in Elam,
50:2 the nations and proclaim, S up a banner and
50:14 S yourselves in array against Babylon round about,
50:24 I S a snare for you and you were
51:12 S up a standard against the walls of Babylon;
51:12 make the watch strong; S up watchmen; prepare the
51:27 S up a standard on the earth, blow the
Lam 1:14 fastened together; they were S upon my neck; he
2:1 in his anger has S the daughter of Zion
2:4 with his right hand S like a foe; and
3:12 bent his bow and S me as a mark
Bar 1:18 the Lord which he S before us.
2:10 the Lord which he S before us.

	6:17	when they have been S up in the temples.
	6:34	They cannot S up a king or depose one.
	6:53	For they cannot S up a king over a
Ezek	2:2	entered into me and S me upon my feet;
	3:24	entered into me, and S me upon my feet;
	4:2	a mound against it; S camps also against it,
	4:3	and the city; and S your face toward it,
	4:7	And you shall S your face toward the siege
	5:5	is Jerusalem; I have S her in the center
	6:2	me: "Son of man, S your face toward the
	13:17	you, son of man, S your face against the
	14:3	into their hearts, and S the stumbling block of
	14:8	myself; and I will S my face against that
	15:7	And I will S my face against them; though
	15:7	the LORD, when I S my face against them.
	16:18	to cover them, and S my oil and my
	16:19	oil and honey--you S before them for a
	17:4	land of trade, and S it in a city
	17:5	He S it like a willow twig,
	17:22	the cedar, and will S it out; I will
	18:2	the children's teeth are S on edge?
	19:8	Then the nations S against him snares on every
	20:24	and their eyes were S on their fathers' idols.
	20:46	me: "Son of man, S your face toward the
	21:2	me: "Son of man, S your face toward Jerusalem
	21:22	with shouting, to S battering-rams against the gates,
	23:24	of peoples; they shall S themselves against you on
	24:3	says the Lord GOD: S on the pot, set
	24:3	Set on the pot, S it on, pour in
	24:8	take vengeance, I have S on the bare rock
	24:11	Then S it empty upon the coals, that it
	25:2	me: "Son of man, S your face toward the
	25:4	and they shall S their encampments among you
	26:8	the mainland; he will S up a siege wall
	28:21	me: "Son of man, S your face toward Sidon,
	29:2	me: "Son of man, S your face against Pharaoh
	30:8	LORD, when I have S fire to Egypt, and
	30:14	a desolation, and will S fire to Zoan, and
	30:16	And I will S fire to Egypt; Pelusium shall
	31:10	it towered high and S its top among the
	31:14	to lofty height or S their tops among the
	32:23	sword; whose graves are S in the uttermost parts
	33:31	but their heart is S on their gain.
	34:23	And I will S up over them one shepherd,
	35:2	me: "Son of man, S your face against Mount
	37:1	of the LORD, and S me down in the
	37:26	multiply them, and will S my sanctuary in the
	38:2	me: "Son of man, S your face toward Gog,
	39:14	They will S apart men to pass through the
	39:15	bone, then he shall S up a sign by
	39:21	"And I will S my glory among the nations;
	40:2	land of Israel, and S me down upon a
	40:4	with your ears, and S your mind upon all
	42:6	the upper chambers were S back from the ground
	44:8	things; but you have S foreigners to keep my
	45:1	a possession, you shall S apart for the LORD
	45:6	"Alongside the portion S apart as the holy district
	48:8	which you shall S apart, twenty-five thousand cubits
	48:9	portion which you shall S apart for the LORD
	48:20	portion which you shall S apart shall be twenty-five
Dan	2:44	God of heaven will S up a kingdom which
	3:1	He S it up on the plain of Dura,
	3:2	which King Nebuchadnezzar had S up.
	3:3	that King Nebuchadnezzar had S up; and they stood
	3:3	image that Nebuchadnezzar had S up.
	3:5	that King Nebuchadnezzar has S up;
	3:7	which King Nebuchadnezzar had S up.
	3:12	image which you have S up."
	3:14	image which I have S up?
	3:18	image which you have S up."
	3:96	trusted in him, and S at nought the king's
	6:1	It pleased Darius to S over the kingdom a
	6:3	the king planned to S him over the whole
	6:14	was much distressed, and S his mind to deliver
	8:18	he touched me and S me on my feet.
	9:10	his laws, which he S before us by his
	10:10	hand touched me and S me trembling on my
	10:12	first day that you S your mind to understand
	11:17	He shall S his face to come with the
	11:28	his heart shall be S against the holy covenant.
	11:31	And they shall S up the abomination that makes
	12:11	that makes desolate is S up, there shall be
	14:11	yourself, O king, shall S forth the food and
	14:14	gone out, the king S forth the food for
	14:36	by his hair and S him down in Babylon,
Hos	2:3	like a wilderness, and S her like a parched
	8:1	S the trumpet to your lips, for a vulture
	8:4	They S up princes, but without my knowledge.
Amos	9:4	them; and I will S my eyes upon them
Obad	1:4	though your nest is S among the stars, thence
	1:7	your trusted friends have S a trap under you--
Mic	2:12	of Israel; I will S them together like sheep
Nah	2:5	wall, the mantelet is S up.
Hab	2:9	for his house, to S his nest on high,
Zech	3:9	stone which I have S before Joshua, upon a
	5:11	is prepared, they will S the ephah down there
	6:8	the north country have S my Spirit at rest
	6:11	make a crown, and S it upon the head
	8:10	came in; for I S every man against his
	9:11	with you, I will S your captives free from
1Mac	6:17	king was dead, he S up Antiochus the king's
	6:51	He S up siege towers, engines of war to
	7:1	the son of Seleucus S forth from Rome, sailed
	9:67	from the city and S fire to the machines
	10:33	of my kingdom, I S free without payment; and
	10:50	strongly until the sun S, and Demetrius fell on
	10:57	So Ptolemy S out from Egypt, he and Cleopatra
	10:74	ten thousand men and S out from Jerusalem, and
	11:2	He S out for Syria with peaceable words, and
	11:22	he heard it he S out and came to
	11:48	They S fire to the city and seized much
	11:57	in the high-priesthood and S you over the four
	11:60	Then Jonathan S forth and traveled beyond the river
	11:66	of the city, and S a garrison over it.
	11:68	the plain; they had S an ambush against him
	12:27	So when the sun S, Jonathan commanded his men
	15:10	and seventy-fourth year Antiochus S out and invaded
2Mac	1:8	the lamps and we S out the loaves.
	1:15	temple of Nanea had S out the treasures and
	1:27	together our scattered people, S free those who are
	2:23	this, which has been S forth by Jason of
	3:8	Heliodorus at once S out on his journey, ostensibly
	3:14	So he S a day and went in to
	4:11	He S aside the existing royal concessions to the
	7:22	breath, nor I who S in order the elements
	8:6	without warning, he would S fire to towns and
	8:33	burned those who had S fire to the sacred
	10:3	and lighted lamps and S out the bread of
	10:19	them; and he himself S off for places where
	10:36	against the defenders and S fire to the towers;
	12:6	He S fire to the harbor by night, and
	12:9	Jamnia by night and S fire to the harbor
	12:20	his army in divisions, S men in command of
	13:26	their good will, and S out for Antioch.
	14:13	his men, and to S up Alcimus as high
	14:16	of the leader, they S out from there immediately
	14:21	And the leaders S a day on which to
	14:21	seats of honor were S in place;
Mt	4:5	the holy city, and S him on the pinnacle
	5:14	A city S on a hill cannot be hid.
	10:35	I have come to S a man against his
	21:33	planted a vineyard, and S a hedge around it,
	24:45	whom his master has S over his household, to
	24:47	to you, he will S him over all his
	25:21	a little, I will S you over much; enter
	25:23	a little, I will S you over much; enter
	27:9	a price had been S by some of the
Mk	6:41	to the disciples to S before the people; and
	8:6	to his disciples to S before the people; and
	8:6	the people; and they S them before the crowd.
	8:7	these also should be S before them.
	12:1	planted a vineyard, and S a hedge around it,
	13:14	see the desolating sacrilege S up where it ought
	14:16	And the disciples S out and went to the
Lk	2:34	"Behold, this child is S for the fall and
	4:9	him to Jerusalem, and S him on the pinnacle
	4:18	to the blind, to S at liberty those who
	7:8	I am a man S under authority, with soldiers
	8:22	So they S out,
	9:16	to the disciples to S before the crowd.
	9:51	be received up, he S his face to go
	9:53	because his face was S toward Jerusalem.
	10:8	you, eat what is S before you;
	10:34	and wine; then he S him on his own
	11:6	I have nothing to S before him';
	12:42	whom his master will S over his household, to
	12:44	to you, he will S him over all his
	19:35	on the colt they S Jesus upon it.
Jn	5:44	you, on whom you S your hope.
	6:27	has God the Father S his seal."
Acts	2:30	him that he would S one of his descendants
	4:7	And when they had S them in the midst,

4:26 kings of the earth S themselves in array, and
5:27 had brought them, they S them before the council.
6:6 These they S before the apostles, and they prayed
6:13 before the council, and S up false witnesses who
13:2 the Holy Spirit said, S apart for me Barnabas
13:13 Paul and his company S sail from Paphos, and
13:47 us, saying, 'I have S you to be a
15:16 ruins, and I will S it up,
16:34 into his house, and S food before them; and
17:5 they gathered a crowd, S the city in an
18:21 and he S sail from Ephesus.
20:3 he was about to S sail for Syria, he
20:13 to the ship, we S sail for Assos, intending
20:18 first day that I S foot in Asia,
21:1 parted from them and S sail, we came by
21:2 we went aboard, and S sail.
22:30 brought Paul down and S him before them.
26:32 man could have been S free if he had
27:21 and should not have S sail from Crete and
28:11 After three months we S sail in a ship
28:18 me, they wished to S me at liberty, because
Rom 1:1 to be an apostle, S apart for the gospel
6:18 committed, and, having been S free from sin, have
6:22 that you have been S free from sin and
8:2 in Christ Jesus has S me free from the
8:5 according to the flesh S their minds on the
8:5 according to the Spirit S their minds on the
8:6 To S the mind on the flesh is death,
8:6 is death, but to S the mind on the
8:7 the mind that is S on the flesh is
8:21 creation itself will be S free from its bondage
1Cor 10:27 go, eat whatever is S before you without raising
2Cor 1:10 on him we have S our hope that he
7:13 his mind has been S at rest by you
Gal 1:15 when he who had S me apart before I
4:2 trustees until the date S by the father.
5:1 For freedom Christ has S us free; stand fast
Eph 1:9 his purpose which he S forth in Christ
Phil 3:19 their shame, with minds S on earthly things.
Col 2:14 legal demands; this he S aside, nailing it to
3:2 S your minds on things that are above, not
1Tim 4:10 we have our hope S on the living God,
4:12 despise your youth, but S the believers an example
5:5 left all alone, has S her hope on God
6:17 be haughty, nor to S their hopes on uncertain
Heb 6:18 to seize the hope S before us.
7:18 a former commandment is S aside because of its
8:2 true tent which is S up not by man
12:1 the race that is S before us,
12:2 the joy that was S before him endured the
Jas 3:5 great a forest is S ablaze by a small
3:6 cycle of nature, and S on fire by hell.
1Pet 1:13 your minds, be sober, S your hope fully upon
3Jn 1:7 For they have S out for his sake and
Jude 1:19 It is these who S up divisions, worldly people,
Rev 3:8 Behold, I have S before you an open door,
10:2 And he S his right foot on the sea,

SETH (11)

Gen 4:25 and called his name S, for she said, "God
4:26 To S also a son was born, and he
5:3 own likeness, after his image, and named him S
5:4 became the father of S were eight hundred years;
5:6 When S had lived a hundred and five years,
5:7 S lived after the birth of Enosh eight hundred
5:8 all the days of S were nine hundred and
1Chr 1:1 Adam, S, Enosh;
1:1 Adam, Seth, Enosh; Adam, S, Enosh;
Sir 49:16 Shem and S were honored among men, and Adam
Lk 3:38 Enos, the son of S, the son of Adam,

SETHUR

Num 13:13 the tribe of Asher, S the son of Michael;

SETS (30)

Ex 30:8 it, and when Aaron S up the lamps in
Num 4:15 sanctuary, as the camp S out, after that the
Deut 24:15 he is poor, and S his heart upon it);
27:15 of a craftsman, and S it up in secret.'
32:22 and its increase, and S on fire the foundations
2Chr 30:19 pardon every one who S his heart to seek
Job 5:11 upon the fields; he S on high those who
34:24 mighty without investigation, and S others in their
36:7 upon the throne he S them for ever, and
Ps 36:4 on his bed; he S himself in a way
83:14 forest, as the flame S the mountains ablaze,
146:7 The LORD S the prisoners free;
Prov 17:24 A man of understanding S his face toward wisdom,
Wis 13:15 that befits it, and S it in the wall,
Sir 27:26 it, and he who S a snare will be
38:26 He S his heart on plowing furrows, and he
38:27 a great variety; he S his heart on painting
38:28 He S his heart on finishing his handiwork, and
38:30 with his feet; he S his heart to finish
Is 26:1 a strong city; he S up salvation as walls
30:29 heart, as when one S out to the sound
51:13 the oppressor, when he S himself to destroy?
Bar 6:27 If any one S one of them upright, it
Ezek 14:4 into his heart and S the stumbling block of
Dan 2:21 he removes kings and S up kings; he gives
4:17 whom he will, and S over it the lowliest
5:21 kingdom of men, and S over it whom he
Jn 3:33 who receives his testimony S his seal to this,
19:12 makes himself a king S himself against Caesar."
Heb 4:7 of disobedience, again he S a certain day, "Today,"

SETTEST (2)

Job 7:12 sea monster, that thou S a guard over me?
13:27 all my paths; thou S a bound to the

SETTING (31)

Ex 25:7 stones, and stones for S, for the ephod and
31:5 in cutting stones for S, and in carving wood,
35:9 stones and stones for S, for the ephod and
35:33 in cutting stones for S, and in carving wood,
Num 7:1 when Moses had finished S up the tabernacle, and
10:29 Moses' father-in-law, "We are S out for the place
Judg 18:5 on which we are S out will succeed."
1Sam 13:21 the axes and for S the goads.
1Kgs 15:4 a lamp in Jerusalem, S up his son after
1Chr 29:2 onyx and stones for S, antimony, colored stones, all
Jud 2:4 he had finished S forth his plan, Nebuchadnezzar
8:12 this day, and are S yourselves up in the
Ps 50:1 from the rising of the sun to its S
104:19 the seasons; the sun knows its time for S
113:3 the sun to its S the name of the
Prov 25:11 of gold in a S of silver.
Sir 32:5 ruby seal in a S of gold is a
32:6 emerald in a rich S of gold is the
45:11 like signets, in a S of gold, the work
Ezek 43:8 of their kings, by S their threshold by my
Amos 7:8 said, "Behold, I am S a plumb line in
Mal 1:11 the sun to its S my name is great
1Mac 13:29 he devised an elaborate S, erecting about them great
2Mac 5:6 imagining that he was S up trophies of victory
10:21 brethren for money by S their enemies free to
12:29 S out from there, they hastened to Scythopolis,
Mt 27:66 sealing the stone and S a guard.
Mk 10:17 And as he was S out on his journey,
Lk 4:40 when the sun was S, all those who had
Acts 16:11 S sail therefore from Troas, we made a direct
Jas 3:6 staining the whole body, S on fire the cycle

SETTINGS (10)

Ex 28:11 shall enclose them in S of gold filigree.
28:13 And you shall make S of gold filigree,
28:14 you shall attach the corded chains to the S
28:25 attach to the two S of filigree, and so
39:6 were prepared, enclosed in S of gold filigree and
39:13 they were enclosed in S of gold filigree.
39:16 and they made two S of gold filigree and
39:18 attached to the two S of filigree; thus they
2Chr 3:6 adorned the house with S of precious stones.
Ezek 28:13 in gold were your S and your engravings.

SETTLE (16)

Gen 47:6 Egypt is before you; S your father and your
Lev 26:32 that your enemies who S in it shall be
Num 33:53 of the land and S in it, for I
Deut 29:20 in this book would S upon him, and the
Ruth 3:18 not rest, but will S the matter today."
Esth 13:2 I have determined to S the lives of my
Sir 28:16 rest, nor will he S down in peace.
Is 7:19 will all come and S in the steep ravines,
23:7 feet carried her to S afar?
Ezek 32:4 of the air to S on you, and I
1Mac 3:36 them from the place, S aliens in all their
2Mac 4:31 king went hastily to S the trouble, leaving
11:14 and persuaded them to S everything on just terms,
Mt 18:22 king who wished to S accounts with his servants.
Lk 12:58 make an effort to S with him on the
21:14 S it therefore in your minds, not to meditate

SETTLED (41)

Gen	11:2	land of Shinar and S there.
	11:31	came to Haran, they S there.
	25:18	direction of Assyria; he S over against all his
	47:11	Then Joseph S his father and his brothers, and
Ex	10:14	land of Egypt, and S on the whole country
	24:16	glory of the LORD S on Mount Sinai, and
Num	9:17	place where the cloud S down, there the people
	10:12	Sinai; and the cloud S down in the wilderness
	21:25	these cities, and Israel S in all the cities
	32:40	of Manasseh, and he S in it.
Deut	2:12	from before them, and S in their stead; as
	2:21	they dispossessed them, and S in their stead;
	2:22	they dispossessed them, and S in their stead even
	2:23	Caphtor, destroyed them and S in their stead.)
	21:5	word every dispute and every assault shall be S
Josh	19:47	possession of it and S in it, calling Leshem,
	19:50	rebuilt the city, and S in it.
	21:43	possession of it, they S there.
	22:33	land where the Reubenites and the Gadites were S
Judg	1:16	and they went and S with the people.
2Sam	20:18	Abel'; and so they S a matter.
1Chr	4:41	to this day, and S in their place, because
2Chr	8:2	given to him, and S the people of Israel
	28:18	its villages; and they S there.
Ezra	4:10	noble Osnappar deported and S in the cities of
Neh	11:23	concerning them, and a S provision for the singers,
Tob	7:8	on the journey, and let the matter be S
Jud	5:9	There they S, and prospered, with much gold and
	5:19	sanctuary is, and have S in the hill country,
Ps	78:55	for a possession and S the tribes of Israel
Sir	22:15	A mind S on an intelligent thought is like
Jer	48:11	his youth and has S on his lees; he
	49:1	Gad, and his people S in its cities?
1Mac	2:1	moved from Jerusalem and S in Modein.
	13:48	it all uncleanness, and S in it men who
	14:34	He S Jews there, and provided in those cities
	14:37	He S Jews in it, and fortified it for
2Mac	13:23	observe all their rights, S with them and offered
	14:25	children; so he married, S down, and shared the
Mt	25:19	those servants came and S accounts with them.
Acts	19:39	further, it shall be S in the regular assembly.

SETTLEMENT

2Mac	4:6	again reach a peaceful S, and that Simon would

SETTLEMENTS (3)

1Chr	4:33	These were their S, and they kept a genealogical
	6:54	places according to their S within their borders: to
	7:28	Their possessions and S were Bethel and its towns,

SETTLING (3)

Judg	5:17	coast of the sea, S down by his landings.
Ps	65:10	waterest its furrows abundantly, S its ridges,
Nah	3:17	like clouds of locusts S on the fences in

SEVEN (444)

Gen	5:7	Enosh eight hundred and S years, and had other
	5:26	the birth of Lamech S hundred and eighty-two years,
	5:31	days of Lamech were S hundred and seventy-seven
	7:2	Take with you S pairs of all clean animals,
	7:3	and his mate; and S pairs of the birds
	7:4	For in S days I will send rain upon
	7:10	And after S days the waters of the flood
	8:10	He waited another S days, and again he sent
	8:12	Then he waited another S days, and sent forth
	11:21	Serug two hundred and S years, and had other
	21:28	Abraham set S ewe lambs of the flock apart.
	21:29	the meaning of these S ewe lambs which you
	21:30	He said, "These S ewe lambs you will take
	29:18	"I will serve you S years for your younger
	29:20	So Jacob served S years for Rachel, and they
	29:27	for serving me another S years."
	29:30	served Laban for another S years.
	31:23	and pursued him for S days and followed close
	33:3	himself to the ground S times, until he came
	41:2	out of the Nile S cows sleek and fat,
	41:3	And behold, S other cows, gaunt and thin, came
	41:4	cows ate up the S sleek and fat cows.
	41:5	second time; and behold, S ears of grain, plump
	41:6	behold, after them sprouted S ears, thin and blighted
	41:7	ears swallowed up the S plump and full ears.
	41:18	of the Nile; and S cows, fat and sleek,
	41:19	the reed grass; and S other cows came up
	41:20	ate up the first S fat cows,
	41:22	saw in my dream S ears growing on one
	41:23	full and good; and S ears, withered, thin, and
	41:24	ears swallowed up the S good ears.
	41:26	The S good cows are seven years, and the
	41:26	seven good cows are S years, and the seven
	41:26	seven years, and the S good ears are seven
	41:26	seven good ears are S years; the dream is
	41:27	The S lean and gaunt cows that came up
	41:27	up after them are S years, and the seven
	41:27	seven years, and the S empty ears blighted by
	41:27	east wind are also S years of famine.
	41:29	There will come S years of great plenty throughout
	41:30	them there will arise S years of famine, and
	41:34	of Egypt during the S plenteous years.
	41:36	the land against the S years of famine which
	41:47	During the S plenteous years the earth brought forth
	41:48	the food of the S years when there was
	41:53	The S years of plenty that prevailed in the
	41:54	an end; and the S years of famine began
	46:25	she bore to Jacob-- S persons in all).
	50:10	mourning for his father S days.
Ex	2:16	priest of Midian had S daughters; and they came
	7:25	S days passed after the LORD had struck the
	12:15	S days you shall eat unleavened bread; on the
	12:19	For S days no leaven shall be found in
	13:6	S days you shall eat unleavened bread, and on
	13:7	shall be eaten for S days; no leavened bread
	22:30	and with your sheep: S days it shall be
	23:15	eat unleavened bread for S days at the appointed
	25:37	you shall make the S lamps for it; and
	29:30	place shall wear them S days, when he comes
	29:35	have commanded you; through S days shall you
	29:37	S days you shall make atonement for the altar,
	34:18	S days you shall eat unleavened bread, as I
	37:23	And he made its S lamps and its snuffers
	38:24	was twenty-nine talents and S hundred and thirty
	38:25	talents and a thousand S hundred and seventy-five
	38:28	of the thousand S hundred and seventy-five shekels
Lev	4:6	part of the blood S times before the LORD
	4:17	blood and sprinkle it S times before the LORD
	8:11	it on the altar S times, and anointed the
	8:33	tent of meeting for S days, until the days
	8:33	for it will take S days to ordain you.
	8:35	day and night for S days, performing what the
	12:2	she shall be unclean S days; as at the
	13:4	the diseased person for S days;
	13:5	shall shut him up S days more;
	13:21	shall shut him up S days;
	13:26	shall shut him up S days,
	13:31	the itching disease for S days,
	13:33	the itching disease for S days more;
	13:50	has the disease for S days;
	13:54	shall shut it up S days more;
	14:7	he shall sprinkle it S times upon him who
	14:8	dwell outside his tent S days.
	14:16	oil with his finger S times before the LORD.
	14:27	in his left hand S times before the LORD;
	14:38	shut up the house S days.
	14:51	and sprinkle the house S times.
	15:13	shall count for himself S days for his cleansing,
	15:19	in her impurity for S days, and whoever touches
	15:24	he shall be unclean S days; and every bed
	15:28	shall count for herself S days, and after that
	16:14	blood with his finger S times.
	16:19	it with his finger S times, and cleanse it
	22:27	born, it shall remain S days with its mother;
	23:6	bread to the LORD; S days you shall eat
	23:8	fire to the LORD S days; on the seventh
	23:15	of the wave offering; S full weeks shall they
	23:18	present with the bread S lambs a year old
	23:34	seventh month and for S days is the feast
	23:36	S days you shall present offerings by fire to
	23:39	feast of the LORD S days; on the first
	23:40	the LORD your God S days.
	23:41	feast to the LORD S days in the year;
	23:42	dwell in booths for S days; all that are
	25:8	"And you shall count S weeks of years, seven
	25:8	seven weeks of years, S times seven years, so
	25:8	of years, seven times S years, so that the
	25:8	the time of the S weeks of years shall
Num	1:39	Dan was sixty-two thousand S hundred.
	2:26	numbered being sixty-two thousand S hundred.
	3:22	old and upward was S thousand five hundred.
	4:36	families was two thousand S hundred and fifty.
	8:2	up the lamps, the S lamps shall give light
	12:14	she not be shamed S days?
	12:14	up outside the camp S days, and after that

S

SEVEN

12:15 up outside the camp S days; and the people
13:22 (Hebron was built S years before Zoan in Egypt.)
16:49 plague were fourteen thousand S hundred, besides
19:4 the tent of meeting S times.
19:11 person shall be unclean S days;
19:14 tent, shall be unclean S days.
19:16 grave, shall be unclean S days.
23:1 "Build for me here S altars, and provide for
23:1 provide for me here S bulls and seven rams."
23:1 here seven bulls and S rams."
23:4 "I have prepared the S altars, and I have
23:14 of Pisgah, and built S altars, and offered a
23:29 "Build for me here S altars, and provide for
23:29 provide for me here S bulls and seven rams."
23:29 here seven bulls and S rams."
26:7 number was forty-three thousand S hundred and
26:34 number was fifty-two thousand S hundred.
26:51 hundred and one thousand S hundred and thirty.
28:11 young bulls, one ram, S male lambs a year
28:17 month is a feast; S days shall unleavened bread
28:19 bulls, one ram, and S male lambs a year
28:21 for each of the S lambs;
28:24 shall offer daily, for S days, the food of
28:27 young bulls, one ram, S male lambs a year
28:29 for each of the S lambs;
29:2 young bull, one ram, S male lambs a year
29:4 for each of the S lambs;
29:8 young bull, one ram, S male lambs a year
29:10 for each of the S lambs:
29:12 feast to the LORD S days;
29:32 "On the seventh day S bulls, two rams, fourteen
29:36 one bull, one ram, S male lambs a year
31:19 Encamp outside the camp S days; whoever of you
31:52 hundreds, was sixteen thousand S hundred and fifty

Deut 7:1 Hivites, and the Jebusites, S nations greater and
15:1 the end of every S years you shall grant
16:3 leavened bread with it; S days you shall eat
16:4 all your territory for S days; nor shall any
16:9 "You shall count S weeks; begin to count the
16:9 begin to count the S weeks from the time
16:13 the feast of booths S days, when you make
16:15 For S days you shall keep the feast to
28:7 and flee before you S ways.
28:25 against them, and flee S ways before them; and
31:10 the end of every S years, at the set

Josh 6:4 And S priests shall bear seven trumpets of rams'
6:4 seven priests shall bear S trumpets of rams' horns
6:4 march around the city S times, the priests blowing
6:6 the covenant, and let S priests bear seven trumpets
6:6 let seven priests bear S trumpets of rams' horns
6:8 commanded the people, the S priests bearing the
6:8 seven priests bearing the S trumpets of rams' horns
6:13 And the S priests bearing the seven trumpets of
6:13 seven priests bearing the S trumpets of rams' horns
6:15 in the same manner S times: it was only
6:15 marched around the city S times.
18:2 the people of Israel S tribes whose inheritance had
18:5 shall divide it into S portions, Judah continuing in
18:6 describe the land in S divisions and bring the
18:9 it by towns in S divisions; then they came

Judg 6:1 the hand of Midian S years.
6:25 bull, the second bull S years old, and pull
8:26 requested was one thousand S hundred shekels of
12:9 And he judged Israel S years.
14:12 it is, within the S days of the feast,
14:17 wept before him the S days that their feast
16:7 they bind me with S fresh bowstrings which have
16:8 the Philistines brought her S fresh bowstrings which
16:13 "If you weave the S locks of my head
16:14 slept, Delilah took the S locks of his head
16:19 him shave off the S locks of his head.
20:15 of Gibe-ah, who mustered S hundred picked men.
20:16 Among all these were S hundred picked men who

Ruth 4:15 more to you than S sons, has borne him."

1Sam 2:5 The barren has borne S, but she who has
6:1 country of the Philistines S months.
10:8 S days you shall wait, until I come to
11:3 to him, "Give us S days respite that we
13:8 He waited S days, the time appointed by Samuel;
16:10 And Jesse made S of his sons pass before
31:13 in Jabesh, and fasted S days.

2Sam 2:11 house of Judah was S years and six months.
5:5 he reigned over Judah S years and six months;
8:4 him a thousand and S hundred horsemen, and twenty
10:18 Syrians the men of S hundred chariots, and forty
21:6 territory of Israel, let S of his sons be
21:9 the LORD, and the S of them perished together.

1Kgs 2:11 forty years; he reigned S years in Hebron, and
6:6 and the third was S cubits broad; for around
6:38 He was S years in building it.
8:65 the LORD our God, S days.
11:3 He had S hundred wives, princesses, and three
16:15 of Judah, Zimri reigned S days in Tirzah.
18:43 he said, "Go again S times."
19:18 Yet I will leave S thousand in Israel, all
20:15 the people of Israel, S thousand.
20:29 encamped opposite one another S days.

2Kgs 3:9 a circuitous march of S days, there was no
3:26 he took with him S hundred swordsmen to break
4:35 him; the child sneezed S times, and the child
5:10 wash in the Jordan S times, and your flesh
5:14 down and dipped himself S times in the Jordan,
8:1 upon the land for S years."
8:2 land of the Philistines S years.
8:3 the end of the S years, when the woman
11:21 Jehoash was S years old when he began to
24:16 the men of valor, S thousand, and the craftsmen

1Chr 3:4 where he reigned for S years and six months.
3:24 Pelaiah, Akkub, Johanan, Delaiah, and Anani, S
5:13 Meshullam, Sheba, Jorai, Jacan, Zia, and Eber, S
5:18 in war, forty-four thousand S hundred and sixty,
9:13 fathers' houses, one thousand S hundred and sixty,
9:25 to come in every S days, from time to
10:12 in Jabesh, and fasted S days.
12:25 of valor for war, S thousand one hundred.
12:27 with him three thousand S hundred.
15:26 the LORD, they sacrificed S bulls and seven rams.
15:26 sacrificed seven bulls and S rams.
18:4 him a thousand chariots, S thousand horsemen, and
19:18 Syrians the men of S thousand chariots, and forty
26:30 his brethren, one thousand S hundred men of ability,
26:32 his brethren, two thousand S hundred men of ability,
29:4 gold of Ophir, and S thousand talents of refined
29:27 forty years; he reigned S years in Hebron, and

2Chr 7:8 held the feast for S days, and all Israel
7:9 dedication of the altar S days and the feast
7:9 days and the feast S days.
13:9 a young bull or S rams becomes a priest
15:11 which they had brought, S hundred oxen and seven
15:11 seven hundred oxen and S thousand sheep.
17:11 Arabs also brought him S thousand seven hundred
17:11 brought him seven thousand S hundred rams and
17:11 rams and S thousand seven hundred he-goats.
17:11 rams and seven thousand S hundred he-goats.
24:1 Joash was S years old when he began to
26:13 of three hundred and S thousand five hundred, who
29:21 And they brought S bulls, seven rams, seven lambs,
29:21 they brought seven bulls, S rams, seven lambs, and
29:21 seven bulls, seven rams, S lambs, and seven he-goats
29:21 rams, seven lambs, and S he-goats for a sin
30:21 feast of unleavened bread S days with great
30:22 of the festival for S days, sacrificing peace offerings
30:23 the feast for another S days; so they kept
30:23 kept it for another S days with gladness.
30:24 a thousand bulls and S thousand sheep for offerings,
35:17 feast of unleavened bread S days.

Ezra 2:5 The sons of Arah, S hundred and seventy-five.
2:9 The sons of Zaccai, S hundred and sixty.
2:25 Chephirah, and Be-eroth, S hundred and forty-three.
2:33 Lod, Hadid, and Ono, S hundred and twenty-five.
2:65 of whom there were S thousand three hundred and
2:66 Their horses were S hundred and thirty-six, their
2:67 asses were six thousand S hundred and twenty.
6:22 feast of unleavened bread S days with joy; for
7:14 the king and his S counselors to make inquiries

Neh 7:14 The sons of Zaccai, S hundred and sixty.
7:29 Kiriath-jearim, Chephirah, and Be-eroth, S hundred
7:37 Lod, Hadid, and Ono, S hundred and twenty-one.
7:67 of whom there were S thousand three hundred and
7:68 Their horses were S hundred and thirty-six, their
7:69 their asses six thousand S hundred and twenty.
8:18 They kept the feast S days; and on the

Tob 2:1 sacred festival of the S weeks, a good dinner
3:8 had been given to S husbands, and the evil
3:8 You already have had S and have had no
3:15 Already S husbands of mine are dead.
6:13 has been given to S husbands and that each
7:11 given my daughter to S husbands, and when each
11:19 marriage was celebrated for S days with great
12:15 Raphael, one of the S holy angels who present

Jud 16:24 Israel mourned for her S days.

Esth 1:5 a banquet lasting for S days, in the court

	1:10	Zethar and Carkas, the S eunuchs who served King
	1:14	Marsena, and Memucan, the S princes of Persia and
	2:9	of food, and with S chosen maids from the
Job	1:2	were born to him S sons and three daughters.
	1:3	He had S thousand sheep, three thousand camels,
	2:13	him on the ground S days and seven nights,
	2:13	ground seven days and S nights, and no one
	5:19	from six troubles; in S there shall no evil
	42:8	Now therefore take S bulls and seven rams, and
	42:8	take seven bulls and S rams, and go to
	42:13	He had also S sons and three daughters.
Ps	12:6	on the ground, purified S times.
	119:164	S times a day I praise thee for thy
Prov	6:16	which the LORD hates, S which are an abomination
	9:1	has set up her S pillars.
	24:16	a righteous man falls S times, and rises again;
	26:16	his own eyes than S men who can answer
	26:25	not, for there are S abominations in his heart;
Eccl	11:2	Give a portion to S, or even to eight,
Sir	20:11	but pays for it S times over.
	22:10	for the dead lasts S days, but for a
	37:14	him better informed than S watchmen sitting high on
	40:8	beast, and upon sinners S times more,
Is	4:1	And S women shall take hold of one man
	11:15	and smite it into S channels that men may
	30:26	as the light of S days, in the day
Jer	15:9	She who bore S has languished; she has swooned
	52:25	men of war, and S men of the king's
	52:30	captive of the Jews S hundred and forty-five persons;
Bar	6:3	long time, up to S generations; after that I
Ezek	3:15	there overwhelmed among them S days.
	3:16	at the end of S days, the word of
	39:9	fires of them for S years;
	39:12	For S months the house of Israel will be
	39:14	at the end of S months they will make
	40:22	toward the east; and S steps led up to
	40:26	And there were S steps leading up to it,
	41:3	sidewalls of the entrance, S cubits.
	43:25	For S days you shall provide daily a goat
	43:26	S days shall they make atonement for the altar
	44:26	shall count for himself S days, and then he
	45:21	the passover, and for S days unleavened bread shall
	45:23	And on the S days of the festival he
	45:23	offering to the LORD S young bulls and seven
	45:23	seven young bulls and S rams without blemish, on
	45:23	on each of the S days; and a he-goat
	45:25	month and for the S days of the feast,
Dan	3:19	ordered the furnace heated S times more than it
	4:16	to him; and let S times pass over him.
	4:23	of the field, till S times pass over him';
	4:25	dew of heaven, and S times shall pass over
	4:32	like an ox; and S times shall pass over
	9:25	prince, there shall be S weeks.
	14:32	There were S lions in the den, and every
Mic	5:5	will raise against him S shepherds and eight princes
Zech	3:9	a single stone with S facets, I will engrave
	4:2	top of it, and S lamps on it, with
	4:2	lamps on it, with S lips on each of
	4:10	"These S are the eyes of the LORD, which
1Mac	3:39	forty thousand infantry and S thousand cavalry to go
	13:28	He also erected S pyramids, opposite one another,
2Mac	7:1	It happened also that S brothers and their mother
	7:20	Though she saw her S sons perish within a
Mt	12:45	and brings with him S other spirits more evil
	15:34	They said, S, and a few small fish."
	15:36	ground, he took the S loaves and the fish,
	15:37	and they took up S baskets full of the
	16:10	Or the S loaves of the four thousand, and
	18:20	As many as S times?"
	18:21	not say to you S times, but seventy times
	18:21	say to you seven times, but seventy times S
	22:25	brother.' Now there were S brothers among us; the
	22:28	to which of the S will she be wife?
Mk	8:5	They said, S
	8:6	and he took the S loaves, and having given
	8:8	broken pieces left over, S baskets full.
	8:20	"And the S for the four thousand, how many
	8:20	And they said to him, S
	12:20	There were S brothers; the first took a wife,
	12:22	third likewise; and the S left no children.
	12:23	For the S had her as wife."
	16:9	he had cast out S demons.
Lk	2:36	lived with her husband S years from her virginity,
	8:2	called Magdalene, from whom S demons had gone
	11:26	he goes and brings S other spirits more evil
	17:4	he sins against you S times in the day,
	17:4	and turns to you S times, and says, 'I
	20:29	Now there were S brothers; the first took a
	20:31	her, and likewise all S left no children and
	20:33	For the S had her as wife."
	24:13	named Emmaus, about S miles from Jerusalem,
Acts	6:3	out from among you S men of good repute,
	13:19	when he had destroyed S nations in the land
	19:14	S sons of a Jewish high priest named Sceva
	20:6	where we stayed for S days.
	21:4	we stayed there for S days.
	21:8	was one of the S, and stayed with him.
	21:27	When the S days were almost completed, the Jews
	28:14	stay with them for S days.
Rom	11:4	have kept for myself S thousand men who have
Heb	11:30	had been encircled for S days.
2Pet	2:5	herald of righteousness, with S other persons, when
Rev	1:4	John to the S churches that are in Asia:
	1:4	come, and from the S spirits who are before
	1:11	send it to the S churches, to Ephesus and
	1:12	on turning I saw S golden lampstands,
	1:16	right hand he held S stars, from his mouth
	1:20	the mystery of the S stars which you saw
	1:20	right hand, and the S golden lampstands, the seven
	1:20	seven golden lampstands, the S stars are the angels
	1:20	the angels of the S churches and the seven
	1:20	seven churches and the S lampstands are the seven
	1:20	seven lampstands are the S churches.
	2:1	him who holds the S stars in his right
	2:1	who walks among the S golden lampstands.
	3:1	him who has the S spirits of God and
	3:1	of God and the S stars.
	4:5	before the throne burn S torches of fire, which
	4:5	fire, which are the S spirits of God;
	5:1	the back, sealed with S seals;
	5:5	the scroll and its S seals."
	5:6	had been slain, with S horns and with seven
	5:6	seven horns and with S eyes, which are the
	5:6	eyes, which are the S spirits of God sent
	6:1	opened one of the S seals, and I heard
	8:2	Then I saw the S angels who stand before
	8:2	stand before God, and S trumpets were given to
	8:6	Now the S angels who had the seven trumpets
	8:6	angels who had the S trumpets made ready to
	10:3	he called out, the S thunders sounded.
	10:4	And when the S thunders had sounded, I was
	10:4	"Seal up what the S thunders have said, and
	11:13	of the city fell; S thousand people were killed
	12:3	great red dragon, with S heads and ten horns,
	12:3	and ten horns, and S diadems upon his heads.
	13:1	with ten horns and S heads, with ten diadems
	15:1	heaven, great and wonderful, S angels with seven
	15:1	wonderful, seven angels with S plagues, which are
	15:6	the temple came the S angels with the seven
	15:6	seven angels with the S plagues, robed in pure
	15:7	creatures gave the S angels seven golden bowls
	15:7	gave the seven angels S golden bowls full of
	15:8	the temple until the S plagues of the seven
	15:8	seven plagues of the S angels were ended.
	16:1	the temple telling the S angels, "Go and pour
	16:1	on the earth the S bowls of the wrath
	17:1	Then one of the S angels who had the
	17:1	angels who had the S bowls came and said
	17:3	names, and it had S heads and ten horns.
	17:7	of the beast with S heads and ten horns
	17:9	mind with wisdom: the S heads are seven mountains
	17:9	the seven heads are S mountains on which the
	17:10	seated; they are also S kings, five of whom
	17:11	it belongs to the S, and it goes to
	21:9	came one of the S angels who had the
	21:9	angels who had the S bowls full of the
	21:9	bowls full of the S last plagues, and spoke

SEVENFOLD (11)

Gen	4:15	slays Cain, vengeance shall be taken on him S
	4:24	If Cain is avenged S, truly Lamech seventy-
Lev	26:18	will chastise you again S for your sins,
	26:21	more plagues upon you, S as many as your
	26:24	myself will smite you S for your sins.
	26:28	and chastise you myself S for your sins.
Ps	79:12	Return S into the bosom of our neighbors the
Prov	6:31	caught, he will pay S; he will give all
Sir	7:3	will not reap a S crop.
	35:11	one who repays, and he will repay you S
Is	30:26	the sun will be S, as the light of

SEVENTEEN (9)

Gen 37:2 Joseph, being S years old, was shepherding the flock
47:28 the land of Egypt S years; so the days
1Kgs 14:21 reign, and he reigned S years in Jerusalem, the
2Kgs 13:1 Samaria, and he reigned S years.
1Chr 7:11 fathers' houses, mighty warriors, S thousand and two
2Chr 12:13 reign, and he reigned S years in Jerusalem, the
Ezra 2:39 The sons of Harim, one thousand and S
Neh 7:42 The sons of Harim, a thousand and S
Jer 32:9 the money to him, S shekels of silver.

SEVENTEENTH (7)

Gen 7:11 second month, on the S day of the month,
8:4 seventh month, on the S day of the month,
1Kgs 22:51 in Samaria in the S year of Jehoshaphat king
2Kgs 16:1 In the S year of Pekah the son of
1Chr 24:15 sixteenth to Immer, the S to Hezir, the eighteenth
25:24 brethren, twelve; to the S, to Joshbekashah, his sons
Jud 1:13 In the S year he led his forces against

SEVENTH (122)

Gen 2:2 And on the S day God finished his work
2:2 he rested on the S day from all his
2:3 So God blessed the S day and hallowed it,
8:4 abated; and in the S month, on the seventeenth
Ex 12:15 first day until the S day, that person shall
12:16 assembly, and on the S day a holy assembly;
13:6 bread, and on the S day there shall be
16:26 it; but on the S day, which is a
16:27 On the S day some of the people went
16:29 his place on the S day."
16:30 people rested on the S day.
20:10 your work; but the S day is a sabbath
20:11 them, and rested the S day; therefore the LORD
21:2 years, and in the S he shall go out
23:11 its yield; but the S year you shall let
23:12 work, but on the S day you shall rest;
24:16 days; and on the S day he called to
31:15 be done, but the S day is a sabbath
31:17 earth, and on the S day he rested, and
34:21 work, but on the S day you shall rest;
35:2 done, but on the S day you shall have
Lev 13:5 examine him on the S day, and if in
13:6 him again on the S day, and if the
13:27 shall examine him the S day; if it is
13:32 days, and on the S day the priest shall
13:34 more; and on the S day the priest shall
13:51 the disease on the S day.
14:9 And on the S day he shall shave all
14:39 come again on the S day, and look; and
16:29 ever that in the S month, on the tenth
23:3 done; but on the S day is a sabbath
23:8 seven days; on the S day is a holy
23:16 the morrow after the S sabbath; then you shall
23:24 of Israel, In the S month, on the first
23:27 tenth day of this S month is the day
23:34 fifteenth day of this S month and for seven
23:39 fifteenth day of the S month, when you have
23:41 keep it in the S month.
25:4 fruits; but in the S year there shall be
25:9 tenth day of the S month; on the day
25:20 we eat in the S year, if we may
Num 6:9 his cleansing; on the S day he shall shave
7:48 On the S day Elishama the son of Ammihud,
19:12 day and on the S day, and so be
19:12 day and on the S day, he will not
19:19 day and on the S day; thus on the
19:19 day; thus on the S day he shall cleanse
28:25 And on the S day you shall have a
29:1 first day of the S month you shall have
29:7 tenth day of this S month you shall have
29:12 fifteenth day of the S month you shall have
29:32 "On the S day seven bulls, two rams, fourteen
31:19 day and on the S day.
31:24 your clothes on the S day, and you shall
Deut 5:14 your work; but the S day is a sabbath
15:9 and you say, 'The S year, the year of
15:12 years, and in the S year you shall let
16:8 bread; and on the S day there shall be
Josh 6:4 ark; and on the S day you shall march
6:15 On the S day they rose early at the
6:16 And at the S time, when the priests had
19:40 The S lot came out for the tribe of
Judg 14:17 lasted; and on the S day he told her,
14:18 to him on the S day before the sun
2Sam 12:18 On the S day the child died.
1Kgs 8:2 Ethanim, which is the S month.
18:44 And at the S time he said, "Behold, a
20:29 Then on the S day the battle was joined;
2Kgs 11:4 But in the S year Jehoiada sent and brought
12:1 In the S year of Jehu Jehoash began to
18:9 Hezekiah, which was the S year of Hoshea son
25:8 fifth month, on the S day of the month--
25:25 But in the S month, Ishmael the son of
1Chr 2:15 the sixth, David the S;
12:11 fifth, Attai sixth, Eliel S,
24:10 sixth to Mijamin, the S to Hakkoz, the eighth
25:14 his brethren, twelve; the S to Jesharelah, his sons
26:3 the fifth, Jehohanan the sixth, Eli-e-ho-enai the S
26:5 the sixth, Issachar the S, Pe-ullethai the eighth; for
27:10 S, for the seventh month, was Helez the Pelonite,
27:10 Seventh, for the S month, was Helez the Pelonite,
2Chr 5:3 which is in the S month.
7:10 twenty-third day of the S month he sent the
23:1 But in the S year Jehoiada took courage, and
31:7 finished them in the S month.
Ezra 3:1 When the S month came, and the sons of
3:6 first day of the S month they began to
7:7 to Jerusalem, in the S year of Artaxerxes the
7:8 which was in the S year of the king;
Neh 7:73 And when the S month had come, the children
8:2 first day of the S month.
8:14 the feast of the S month,
10:31 the crops of the S year and the exaction
Esth 1:10 On the S day, when the heart of the
2:16 of Tebeth, in the S year of his reign,
Jer 28:17 same year, in the S month, the prophet Hananiah
41:1 In the S month, Ishmael the son of Nethaniah,
52:28 away captive: in the S year, three thousand and
Bar 1:2 fifth year, on the S day of the month,
Ezek 20:1 In the S year, in the fifth month, on
30:20 first month, on the S day of the month,
45:20 the same on the S day of the month
45:25 In the S month, on the fifteenth day of
Dan 14:40 On the S day the king came to mourn
Hag 2:1 the king, in the S month, on the twenty-first
Zech 7:5 month and in the S, for these seventy years,
8:19 the fast of the S, and the fast of
1Mac 6:53 because it was the S year; those who found
10:21 holy garments in the S month of the one
2Mac 6:11 by, to observe the S day secretly, were betrayed
12:38 As the S day was coming on, they purified
15:4 us to observe the S day,"
Mt 22:26 too the second and third, down to the S
Jn 4:52 him, "Yesterday at the S hour the fever left
Heb 4:4 somewhere spoken of the S day in this way,
4:4 God rested on the S day from all his
Jude 1:14 Enoch in the S generation from Adam prophesied,
Rev 8:1 the Lamb opened the S seal, there was silence
10:7 be sounded by the S angel, the mystery of
11:15 Then the S angel blew his trumpet, and there
16:17 The S angel poured his bowl into the air,
21:20 the sixth carnelian, the S chrysolite, the eighth beryl,

SEVENTIETH

1Mac 13:41 the one hundred and S year the yoke of

SEVENTY (71)

Gen 5:12 When Kenan had lived S years, he became the
11:26 When Terah had lived S years, he became the
46:27 house of Jacob, that came into Egypt, were S
50:3 Egyptians wept for him S days.
Ex 1:4 offspring of Jacob were S persons; Joseph was
15:27 springs of water and S palm trees; and they
24:1 Nadab, and Abihu, and S of the elders of
24:9 Nadab, and Abihu, and S of the elders of
38:29 that was contributed was S talents, and two
Num 7:13 one silver basin of S shekels, according to the
7:19 one silver basin of S shekels, according to the
7:25 one silver basin of S shekels, according to the
7:31 one silver basin of S shekels, according to the
7:37 one silver basin of S shekels, according to the
7:43 one silver basin of S shekels, according to the
7:49 one silver basin of S shekels, according to the
7:55 one silver basin of S shekels, according to the
7:61 one silver basin of S shekels, according to the
7:67 one silver basin of S shekels, according to the
7:73 one silver basin of S shekels, according to the
7:79 one silver basin of S shekels, according to the
7:85 shekels and each basin S, all the silver of
11:16 Moses, "Gather for me S men of the elders
11:24 LORD; and he gathered S men of the elders

	11:25	put it upon the S elders; and when the
	33:9	springs of water and S palm trees, and they
Deut	10:22	went down to Egypt S persons; and now the
Judg	1:7	And Adoni-bezek said, S kings with their thumbs and
	8:30	Now Gideon had S sons, his own offspring, for
	9:2	for you, that all S of the sons of
	9:4	And they gave him S pieces of silver out
	9:5	the sons of Jerubbaal, S men, upon one stone;
	9:18	have slain his sons, S men on one stone,
	9:24	violence done to the S sons of Jerubbaal might
	9:56	father in killing his S brothers;
	12:14	grandsons, who rode on S asses; and he judged
1Sam	6:19	the LORD; he slew S men of them, and
2Sam	24:15	from Dan to Beer-sheba S thousand men.
1Kgs	5:15	Solomon also had S thousand burden-bearers and
2Kgs	10:1	Now Ahab had S sons in Samaria.
	10:6	Now the king's sons, S persons, were with the
	10:7	sons, and slew them, S persons, and put their
1Chr	21:5	Judah four hundred and S thousand who drew the
	21:14	Israel; and there fell S thousand men of Israel.
2Chr	2:2	And Solomon assigned S thousand men to bear
	2:18	S thousand of them he assigned to bear burdens,
	29:32	the assembly brought was S bulls, a hundred rams,
	36:21	kept sabbath, to fulfil S years.
Ezra	8:7	Athaliah, and with him S men.
	8:14	Zaccur, and with them S men.
Jud	1:2	he made the walls S cubits high and fifty
	1:4	its gates, which were S cubits high and forty
	7:2	was one hundred and S thousand infantry and twelve
Is	23:15	will be forgotten for S years, like the days
	23:15	At the end of S years, it will happen
	23:17	At the end of S years, the LORD will
Jer	25:11	the king of Babylon S years.
	25:12	Then after S years are completed, I will punish
	29:10	says the LORD: When S years are completed for
Ezek	8:11	And before them stood S men of the elders
	41:12	the west side was S cubits broad; and the
Dan	9:2	desolations of Jerusalem, namely, S years.
	9:24	S weeks of years are decreed concerning your
	14:10	Now there were S priests of Bel, besides their
Zech	1:12	hast had indignation these S years?'
	7:5	the seventh, for these S years, was it for
2Mac	10:20	towers, and on receiving S thousand drachmas let
Mt	18:21	you seven times, but S times seven.
Lk	10:1	this the Lord appointed S others, and sent them
	10:17	The S returned with joy, saying, "Lord, even the
Acts	23:23	two hundred soldiers with S horsemen and two

SEVENTY-FIRST

1Mac	13:51	the one hundred and S year, the Jews entered

SEVENTY-FIVE (10)

Gen	12:4	Abram was S years old when he departed from
	25:7	life, a hundred and S years.
Ex	38:25	thousand seven hundred and S shekels, by the shekel
	38:28	thousand seven hundred and S shekels he made
Num	31:32	was: six hundred and S thousand sheep,
	31:37	LORD's tribute of sheep was six hundred and S
Ezra	2:5	The sons of Arah, seven hundred and S
Esth	9:16	their enemies, and slew S thousand of those who
2Mac	12:29	to Scythopolis, which is S miles from Jerusalem.
Acts	7:14	and all his kindred, S souls;

SEVENTY-FOUR (4)

Num	1:27	tribe of Judah was S thousand six hundred.
	2:4	host as numbered being S thousand six hundred.
Ezra	2:40	Jeshua and Kadmi-el, of the sons of Hodaviah, S
Neh	7:43	namely of Kadmi-el of the sons of Hodevah, S

SEVENTY-FOURTH

1Mac	15:10	the one hundred and S year Antiochus set out

SEVENTY-SECOND (2)

1Mac	14:1	the one hundred and S year Demetrius the king
	14:27	the one hundred and S year, which is the

SEVENTY-SEVEN (3)

Gen	5:31	were seven hundred and S years; and he died.
Judg	8:14	and elders of Succoth, S men.
Ezra	8:35	all Israel, ninety-six rams, S lambs, and as a

SEVENTY-SEVENFOLD

Gen	4:24	If Cain is avenged sevenfold, truly Lamech S

SEVENTY-SEVENTH

1Mac	16:14	the one hundred and S year, in the eleventh

SEVENTY-SIX (2)

Num	26:22	according to their number, S thousand five hundred.
Acts	27:37	all two hundred and S persons in the ship.)

SEVENTY-THREE (4)

Num	3:43	were twenty-two thousand two hundred and S
	3:46	the two hundred and S of the first-born of
Ezra	2:36	of the house of Jeshua, nine hundred and S
Neh	7:39	namely the house of Jeshua, nine hundred and S

SEVENTY-TWO (7)

Num	31:33	and seventy-five thousand sheep, S thousand cattle,
	31:38	thousand, of which the LORD's tribute was S
Ezra	2:3	sons of Parosh, two thousand one hundred and S
	2:4	The sons of Shephatiah, three hundred and S
Neh	7:8	sons of Parosh, two thousand a hundred and S
	7:9	The sons of Shephatiah, three hundred and S
	11:19	watch at the gates, were a hundred and S

SEVER

Lev	5:8	neck, but shall not S it,

SEVERAL (7)

Josh	19:49	had finished distributing the S territories of the land
	21:33	The cities of the S families of the Gershonites
	21:40	the cities of the S Merarite families, that is,
2Chr	8:14	their divisions for the S gates; for so David
	31:19	were men in the S cities who were designated
Ezek	48:29	and these are their S portions, says the Lord
Acts	9:19	For S days he was with the disciples at

SEVERE (27)

Gen	12:10	for the famine was S in the land.
	41:56	for the famine was S in the land of
	41:57	because the famine was S over all the earth.
	43:1	Now the famine was S in the land.
	47:4	for the famine is S in the land of
	47:13	the famine was very S, so that the land
	47:20	because the famine was S upon them.
Ex	9:3	fall with a very S plague upon your cattle
Deut	28:59	offspring extraordinary afflictions, afflictions S and
1Kgs	17:17	his illness was so S that there was no
	18:2	Now the famine was S in Samaria.
2Kgs	25:3	the famine was so S in the city that
2Chr	16:12	and his disease became S; yet even in his
	21:15	yourself will have a S sickness with a disease
Prov	15:10	There is S discipline for him who forsakes the
Wis	6:5	terribly and swiftly, because S judgment falls on
Sir	5:14	the thief, and S condemnation to the double-tongued.
	31:2	prevents slumber, and a S illness carries off sleep.
Jer	52:6	the famine was so S in the city, that
Dan	2:15	"Why is the decree of the king so S
1Mac	1:30	city, dealt it a S blow, and destroyed many
2Mac	14:45	and his wounds were S he ran through the
Lk	12:47	will, shall receive a S beating.
	19:21	because you are a S man; you take up
	19:22	that I was a S man, taking up what
2Cor	8:2	Macedonia, for in a S test of affliction, their
	13:10	not have to be S in my use of

SEVERED (3)

Jud	13:8	all her might, and S it from his body.
	16:9	mind, and the sword S his neck.
Gal	5:4	You are S from Christ, you who would be

SEVERELY (5)

2Chr	24:25	him, leaving him S wounded, his servants conspired
Sir	30:14	rich man who is S afflicted in body.
	42:5	of children, and of whipping a wicked servant S
Mt	15:22	David; my daughter is S possessed by a demon."
2Cor	2:5	to put it too S -- to you all.

SEVERITY (3)

Rom	11:22	the kindness and the S of God: severity toward
	11:22	the severity of God: S toward those who have
Col	2:23	devotion and self-abasement and S to the body, but

SEW (2)

Eccl	3:7	and a time to S; a time to keep
Ezek	13:18	to the women who S magic bands upon all

SEWED (2)

Gen	3:7	were naked; and they S fig leaves together and
Job	16:15	I have S sackcloth upon my skin, and have

S

SEWS

Mk 2:21 No one S a piece of unshrunk cloth on

SEX (2)

Wis 14:26 pollution of souls, S perversion, disorder in marriage,
1Pet 3:7 woman as the weaker S, since you are joint

SHA-ALABBIN

Josh 19:42 included Zorah, Eshtaol, Ir-shemesh, S, Aijalon,

SHA-ALBIM (2)

Judg 1:35 in Aijalon, and in S, but the hand of
1Kgs 4:9 Ephraim; Ben-deker, in Makaz, S, Beth-shemesh,

SHA-ALBON (2)

2Sam 23:32 of Bahurim, Eliahba of S, the sons of Jashen,
1Chr 11:33 of Baharum, Eliahba of S,

SHA-ARAIM (2)

1Sam 17:52 on the way from S as far as Gath
1Chr 4:31 Hazar-susim, Beth-biri, and S. These were their

SHA-ASHGAZ

Esth 2:14 harem in custody of S the king's eunuch who

SHAALIM

1Sam 9:4 through the land of S, but they were not

SHAAPH (2)

1Chr 2:47 Regem, Jotham, Geshan, Pelet, Ephah, and S
2:49 She also bore S the father of Madmannah, Sheva

SHAARAIM

Josh 15:36 Jarmuth, Adullam, Socoh, Azekah, S, Adithaim,

SHABBETHAI (3)

Ezra 10:15 and Meshullum and S the Levite supported them.
Neh 8:7 Jamin, Akkub, S, Hodiah, Ma-aseiah, Kelita, Aza
11:16 son of Bunni; and S and Jozabad, of the

SHABBY

Jas 2:2 a poor man in S clothing also comes in,

SHADE (18)

Judg 9:15 take refuge in my S; but if not, let
Job 40:22 For his S the lotus trees cover him; the
Ps 80:10 were covered with its S, the mighty cedars with
121:5 the LORD is your S on your right hand.
Sir 34:16 hot wind and a S from noonday sun, a
Is 4:6 will be for a S by day from the
16:3 grant justice; make your S like night at the
25:4 the storm and a S from the heat; for
25:5 as heat by the S of a cloud, so
32:2 dry place, like the S of a great rock
Ezek 17:23 of beasts; in the S of its branches birds
31:3 fair branches and forest S, and of great height,
Dan 4:12 of the field found S under it, and the
4:21 of the field found S, and in whose branches
Hos 4:13 and terebinth, because their S is good.
Jon 4:5 under it in the S, till he should see
4:6 it might be a S over his head, to
Mk 4:32 of the air can make nests in its S

SHADED

Bar 5:8 every fragrant tree have S Israel at God's command.

SHADES (6)

Job 26:5 The S below tremble, the waters and their
Ps 88:10 Do the S rise up to praise thee?
Prov 2:18 her paths to the S;
Is 14:9 come, it rouses the S to greet you, all
26:14 not live; they are S, they will not arise;
26:19 the land of the S thou wilt let it

SHADOW (45)

Judg 9:36 him, "You see the S of the mountains as
2Kgs 20:9 has promised: shall the S go forward ten steps,
20:10 easy thing for the S to lengthen ten steps;
20:10 steps; rather let the S go back ten steps."
20:11 and he brought the S back ten steps, by
1Chr 29:15 earth are like a S, and there is no
Job 7:2 who longs for the S, and like a hireling
8:9 nothing, for our days on earth are a S
14:2 he flees like a S, and continues not.
17:7 grief, and all my members are like a S
Ps 17:8 hide me in the S of thy wings,
23:4 the valley of the S of death, I fear
36:7 take refuge in the S of thy wings.
39:6 [Selah] Surely man goes about as a S
57:1 takes refuge; in the S of thy wings I
63:7 help, and in the S of thy wings I
91:1 who abides in the S of the Almighty,
102:11 are like an evening S; I wither away like
109:23 am gone, like a S at evening; I am
144:4 a breath, his days are like a passing S
Eccl 6:12 his vain life, which he passes like a S
8:13 his days like a S, because he does not
Song 2:3 I sat in his S, and his fruit was
Wis 2:5 the passing of a S, and there is no
5:9 have vanished like a S, and like a rumor
Sir 34:2 who catches at a S and pursues the wind,
Is 30:2 seek shelter in the S of Egypt!
30:3 the shelter in the S of Egypt to your
34:15 her young in her S; yea, there shall the
38:8 I will make the S cast by the declining
49:2 sharp sword, in the S of his hand he
51:16 hid you in the S of my hand, stretching
Jer 48:45 "In the S of Heshbon fugitives stop without strength;
Lam 4:20 we said, "Under his S we shall live among
Ezek 31:6 young; and under its S dwelt all great nations.
31:12 will go from its S and leave it.
31:17 who dwelt under its S among the nations shall
Hos 14:7 and dwell beneath my S, they shall flourish as
Mt 4:16 in the region and S of death light has
Lk 1:79 darkness and in the S of death, to guide
Acts 5:15 by at least his S might fall on some
Col 2:17 These are only a S of what is to
Heb 8:5 serve a copy and S of the heavenly sanctuary;
10:1 law has but a S of the good things
Jas 1:16 is no variation or S due to change.

SHADOWS (3)

Song 2:17 day breathes and the S flee, turn, my beloved,
4:6 day breathes and the S flee, I will hie
Jer 6:4 day declines, for the S of evening lengthen!"

SHADRACH (15)

Dan 1:7 Hananiah he called S, Mishael he called Meshach,
2:49 king, and he appointed S, Meshach, and Abednego
3:12 the province of Babylon: S, Meshach, and Abednego.
3:13 furious rage commanded that S, Meshach, and
3:14 "Is it true, O S, Meshach, and Abednego, that
3:16 S, Meshach, and Abednego answered the king, "O,
3:19 face was changed against S, Meshach, and
3:20 his army to bind S, Meshach, and Abednego, and
3:22 men who took up S, Meshach, and Abednego.
3:23 And these three men, S, Meshach, and Abednego,
3:94 fiery furnace and said, S, Meshach, and Abednego,
3:94 Then S, Meshach, and Abednego came out from the
3:96 be the God of S, Meshach, and Abednego, who
3:97 against the God of S, Meshach, and Abednego shall
3:98 Then the king promoted S, Meshach, and Abednego

SHAFT (12)

Ex 25:31 The base and the S of the lampstand shall
37:17 The base and the S of the lampstand were
1Sam 17:7 And the S of his spear was like a
2Sam 5:8 get up the water S to attack the lame
21:19 Goliath the Gittite, the S of whose spear was
23:7 with iron and the S of a spear, and
1Chr 20:5 Goliath the Gittite, the S of whose spear was
Sir 38:25 who glories in the S of a goad, who
Rev 9:1 the key of the S of the bottomless pit;
9:2 pit; he opened the S of the bottomless pit,
9:2 pit, and from the S rose smoke like the
9:2 air were darkened with the smoke from the S

SHAFTS (4)

Job 28:4 They open S in a valley away from where
Ps 7:13 his deadly weapons, making his arrows fiery S
Wis 5:21 S of lightning will fly with true aim, and
Hab 3:14 didst pierce with thy S the head of his

SHAGEE

1Chr 11:34 Jonathan the son of S the Hararite,

SHAHARAIM

1Chr 8:8 And S had sons in the country of Moab

SHAHAZUMAH

Josh 19:22 boundary also touches Tabor, S, and Beth-shemesh,

SHAKE (31)

Judg 16:20 at other times, and S myself free." And he
Neh 5:13 said, "So may God S out every man from
Job 4:14 me, and trembling, which made all my bones S
15:33 He will S off his unripe grape, like the
16:4 together against you, and S my head at you.
Ps 46:2 change, though the mountains S in the heart of
Wis 4:19 to the ground, and S them from the foundations;
Sir 12:18 the heel; he will S his head, and clap
13:7 will forsake you, and S his head at you.
16:17 foundations of the earth S with trembling when he
22:2 picks it up will S it off his hand.
Is 7:2 trees of the forest S before the wind.
10:32 at Nob, he will S his fist at the
33:9 and Bashan and Carmel S off their leaves.
52:2 S yourself from the dust, arise, O captive Jerusalem;
Jer 23:9 me, all my bones S; I am like a
Ezek 26:10 you; your walls will S at the noise of
26:15 Will not the coastlands S at the sound of
29:7 all their loins to S;
Joel 3:16 from Jerusalem, and the heavens and the earth S
Amos 9:1 capitals until the thresholds S, and shatter them on
9:9 I will command, and S the house of Israel
Hag 2:6 little while, I will S the heavens and the
2:7 land; and I will S all nations, so that
2:21 I am about to S the heavens and the
Zech 2:9 eye: "Behold, I will S my hand over them,
Mt 10:14 listen to your words, S off the dust from
Mk 6:11 you, when you leave, S off the dust that
Lk 6:48 house, and could not S it, because it had
9:5 you leave that town S off the dust from
Heb 12:26 once more I will S not only the earth

SHAKEN (38)

1Kgs 14:15 as a reed is S in the water, and
Neh 5:13 So may he be S out and emptied." And
Jud 16:15 the mountains shall be S to their foundations with
Esth 15:13 and my heart was S with fear at your
Job 34:20 midnight the people are S and pass away, and
38:13 and the wicked be S out of it?
Ps 13:4 him"; lest my foes rejoice because I am S
62:6 my salvation, my fortress; I shall not be S
82:5 darkness; all the foundations of the earth are S
104:5 its foundations, so that it should never be S
109:23 at evening; I am S off like a locust.
Wis 4:4 insecurely they will be S by the wind, and
5:2 him, they will be S with dreadful fear, and
Sir 27:4 When a sieve is S, the refuse remains; so
28:14 Slander has S many, and scattered them from nation
29:18 were prosperous, and has S them like a wave
43:16 appearing the mountains are S; at his will the
48:19 Then their hearts were S and their hands trembled,
Is 13:13 the earth will be S out of its place,
23:11 the sea, he has S the kingdoms; the LORD
24:19 earth is rent asunder, the earth is violently S
Nah 3:12 with first-ripe figs—if S they fall into the
1Mac 6:8 heard this news, he was astounded and badly S
9:13 The earth was S by the noise of the
Mt 11:7 A reed S by the wind?
24:29 the heavens will be S;
Mk 13:25 and the powers in the heavens will be S
Lk 6:38 good measure, pressed down, S together, running
7:24 A reed S by the wind?
21:26 for the powers of the heavens will be S
Acts 2:25 I may not be S;
4:31 were gathered together was S; and they were all
16:26 of the prison were S; and immediately all the
2Thes 2:2 not to be quickly S in mind or excited,
Heb 12:27 removal of what is S, as of what has
12:27 that what cannot be S may remain.
12:28 kingdom that cannot be S, and thus let us
Rev 6:13 its winter fruit when S by a gale;

SHAKES (11)

Job 9:6 in his anger; who S the earth out of
Ps 29:8 voice of the LORD S the wilderness, the LORD
29:8 the wilderness, the LORD S the wilderness of
Sir 22:11 be soiled when he S himself off; avoid him
Is 19:16 the LORD of hosts S over them.
33:15 gain of oppressions, who S his hands, lest they
Jer 18:16 it is horrified and S his head.
Ezek 21:21 to use divination; he S the arrows, he consults
27:28 your pilots the countryside S,
Amos 9:9 the nations as one S with a sieve, but
Zeph 2:15 by her hisses and S his fist.

SHAKING

Ezek 38:19 shall be a great S in the land of

SHALISHAH

1Sam 9:4 through the land of S, but they did not

SHALLECHETH

1Chr 26:16 at the gate of S on the road that

SHALLOW

Jas 2:20 to be shown, you S man, that faith apart

SHALLUM (29)

2Kgs 15:10 S the son of Jabesh conspired against him, and
15:13 it came to pass.) S the son of Jabesh
15:14 and he struck down S the son of Jabesh
15:15 of the deeds of S, and the conspiracy which
22:14 prophetess, the wife of S the son of Tikvah,
1Chr 2:40 was the father of Sismai, and Sismai of S
2:41 S was the father of Jekamiah, and Jekamiah of
3:15 second Jehoiakim, the third Zedekiah, the fourth S
4:25 Jamin, Jarib, Zerah, Shaul; S was his son, Mibsam
6:12 of Zadok, Zadok of S,
6:13 Zadok, Zadok of Shallum, S of Hilkiah, Hilkiah of
7:13 Jahzi-el, Guni, Jezer, and S, the offspring of Bilhah.
9:17 The gatekeepers were: S, Akkub, Talmon, Ahiman,
9:17 Ahiman, and their kinsmen S being the chief),
9:19 S the son of Kore, son of Ebiasaph, son
9:31 Levites, the first-born of S the Korahite, was in
2Chr 28:12 Jehizkiah the son of S, and Amasa the son
34:22 prophetess, the wife of S the son of Tokhath,
Ezra 2:42 gatekeepers: the sons of S, the sons of Ater,
7:2 of Hilkiah, son of S, son of Zadok, son
10:24 Of the gatekeepers: S, Telem, and Uri.
10:42 Shelemiah, Shemariah, S, Amariah, and Joseph.
Neh 3:12 Next to him S the son of Hallohesh, ruler
3:15 And S the son of Colhozeh, ruler of the
7:45 gatekeepers: the sons of S, the sons of Ater,
Jer 22:11 says the LORD concerning S the son of Josiah,
32:7 Hanamel the son of S your uncle will come
35:4 Ma-aseiah the son of S, keeper of the threshold.
Bar 1:7 of Hilkiah, son of S, and to the priests,

SHALMAI

Neh 7:48 Hagaba, the sons of S,

SHALMAN

Hos 10:14 shall be destroyed, as S destroyed Beth-arbel on the

SHALMANESER (6)

2Kgs 17:3 Against him came up S king of Assyria; and
18:9 Elah, king of Israel, S king of Assyria came
Tob 1:2 in the days of S, king of the Assyrians,
1:13 in the sight of S, and I was his
1:15 But when S died, Sennacherib his son reigned in
1:16 In the days of S I performed many acts

SHALT (2)

1Kgs 8:44 by whatever way thou S send them, and they
2Chr 6:34 by whatever way thou S send them, and they

SHAMA

1Chr 11:44 Mithnite, Uzzia the Ashterathite, S and Je-iel the

SHAME (185)

Ex 32:25 break loose, to their S among their enemies),
1Sam 20:30 Jesse to your own S, and to the shame
20:30 shame, and to the S of your mother's nakedness?
2Sam 13:13 As for me, where could I carry my S
19:5 have today covered with S the faces of all
2Chr 30:15 Levites were put to S, so that they sanctified
32:21 So he returned with S of face to his
Ezra 9:7 plundering, and to utter S, as at this day.
Neh 1:3 in great trouble and S; the wall of Jerusalem
Jud 1:14 plundered its markets, and turned its beauty into S
5:21 shall be put to S before the whole world."
9:2 to put her to S, and polluted her womb
13:16 me, to defile and S me."
Job 8:22 will be clothed with S, and the tent of
11:3 mock, shall no one S you?
36:14 die in youth, and their life ends in S
Ps 4:2 O men, how long shall my honor suffer S
6:10 and be put to S in a moment.
25:2 not be put to S; let not my enemies
25:3 thee be put to S; let them be ashamed
25:20 not be put to S, for I take refuge

S

31:1 never be put to S; in thy righteousness deliver
31:17 not be put to S, O LORD, for I
31:17 wicked be put to S, let them go dumbfounded
35:4 them be put to S and dishonor who seek
35:26 them be put to S and confusion altogether who
35:26 them be clothed with S and dishonor who magnify
37:19 are not put to S in evil times, in
40:14 them be put to S and confusion altogether who
40:15 appalled because of their S who say to me,
44:15 is before me, and S has covered my face,
53:5 will be put to S, for God has rejected
57:3 he will put to S those who trample upon
69:6 thee be put to S through me, O Lord
69:7 have borne reproach, that S has covered my face.
69:19 my reproach, and my S and my dishonor; my
70:2 them be put to S and confusion who seek
70:3 appalled because of their S who say, "Aha, Aha!"
71:1 take refuge; let me never be put to S
71:13 accusers be put to S and consumed; with scorn
71:24 have been put to S and disgraced who sought
74:21 downtrodden be put to S; let the poor and
78:66 adversaries to rout; he put them to everlasting S
83:16 Fill their faces with S, that they may seek
83:17 them be put to S and dismayed for ever;
86:17 and be put to S because thou, LORD, hast
89:45 of his youth; thou hast covered him with S
97:7 images are put to S, who make their boast
109:28 assailants be put to S; may thy servant be
109:29 wrapped in their own S as in a mantle!
119:6 not be put to S, having my eyes fixed
119:31 O LORD; let me not be put to S
119:46 not be put to S;
119:78 godless be put to S, because they have subverted
119:80 statutes, that I may not be put to S
119:116 not be put to S in my hope!
127:5 not be put to S when he speaks with
129:5 Zion be put to S and turned backward!
132:18 I will clothe with S, but upon himself his
Prov 9:13 is noisy; she is wanton and knows no S
10:5 but a son who sleeps in harvest brings S
12:4 but she who brings S is like rottenness in
18:13 before he hears, it is his folly and S
19:26 a son who causes S and brings reproach.
25:8 the end, when your neighbor puts you to S
25:10 who hears you bring S upon you, and your
29:15 left to himself brings S to his mother.
Sir 2:10 trusted in the Lord and was put to S
4:20 and do not bring S on yourself.
4:21 For there is a S which brings sin, and
4:21 and there is a S which is glory and
5:14 with your tongue; for S comes to the thief,
6:1 a bad name incurs S and reproach: so fares
13:7 He will S you with his foods, until he
15:4 on her and will not be put to S
20:21 lose his life through S, or lose it because
20:22 A man may for S make promises to a
20:25 brings disgrace, and his S is ever with him.
24:21 not be put to S, and those who work
26:8 wife is drunken; she will not hide her S
29:14 lost his sense of S will fail him.
41:16 retain every kind of S, and not everything is
41:23 you will show proper S, and will find favor
42:11 and put you to S before the great multitude.
42:14 a woman who brings S and disgrace.
51:18 good; and I shall never be put to S
51:29 not be put to S when you praise him.
Is 3:24 robe, a girding of sackcloth; instead of beauty, S
20:4 buttocks uncovered, to the S of Egypt.
22:18 your splendid chariots, you S of your master's house.
30:3 Pharaoh turn to your S, and the shelter in
30:5 every one comes to S through a people that
30:5 help nor profit, but S and disgrace."
41:11 shall be put to S and confounded; those who
42:17 and utterly put to S, who trust in graven
44:9 nor know, that they may be put to S
44:11 shall be put to S, and the craftsmen are
44:11 shall be put to S together.
45:16 them are put to S and confounded, the makers
45:17 not be put to S or confounded to all
47:3 be uncovered, and your S shall be seen.
49:23 wait for me shall not be put to S
50:6 not my face from S and spitting.
50:7 not be put to S;
54:4 not be put to S; for you will forget
54:4 you will forget the S of your youth, and
61:7 Instead of your S you shall have a double
65:13 shall be put to S;
66:5 it is they who shall be put to S
Jer 2:36 shall be put to S by Egypt as you
2:36 you were put to S by Assyria.
3:25 lie down in our S, and let our dishonor
8:9 shall be put to S, they shall be dismayed
10:14 goldsmith is put to S by his idols; for
11:13 have set up to S, altars to burn incense
13:26 your face, and your S will be seen.
17:13 shall be put to S; those who turn away
17:18 those be put to S who persecute me, but
17:18 not be put to S; let them be dismayed,
20:18 toil and sorrow, and spend my days in S
23:40 everlasting reproach and perpetual S, which shall not
46:12 have heard of your S, and the earth is
46:24 shall be put to S, she shall be delivered
48:1 Kiriathaim is put to S, it is taken; the
48:1 fortress is put to S and broken down;
48:20 Moab is put to S, for it is broken;
48:39 How Moab has turned his back in S
50:2 Bel is put to S, Merodach is dismayed.
50:2 images are put to S, her idols are dismayed.'
51:17 goldsmith is put to S by his idols; for
51:47 shall be put to S, and all her slain
51:51 'We are put to S, for we have heard
Bar 6:39 those who serve them will be put to S
Ezek 7:18 and horror covers them; S is upon all faces,
16:36 Lord GOD, Because your S was laid bare and
16:63 again because of your S, when I forgive you
32:24 and they bear their S with those who go
32:25 and they bear their S with those who go
32:30 have gone down in S with the slain, for
32:30 sword, and bear their S with those who go
39:26 They shall forget their S, and all the treachery
44:13 they shall bear their S, because of the abominations
Dan 3:33 cannot open our mouths; S and disgrace have
3:40 there will be no S for those who trust
3:42 not put us to S, but deal with us
3:43 servants be put to S;
12:2 life, and some to S and everlasting contempt.
Hos 4:7 against me; I will change their glory into S
4:18 to harlotry; they love S more than their glory.
10:6 shall be put to S, and Israel shall be
Joel 2:26 my people shall never again be put to S
2:27 my people shall never again be put to S
Obad 1:10 to your brother Jacob, S shall cover you, and
Mic 1:11 Shaphir, in nakedness and S; the inhabitants of
3:7 the diviners put to S; they shall all cover
7:10 enemy will see, and S will cover her who
Nah 3:5 look on your nakedness and kingdoms on your S
Hab 2:10 You have devised S to your house by cutting
2:15 and makes them drunk, to gaze on their S
2:16 around to you, and S will come upon your
Zeph 3:5 does not fail; but the unjust knows no S
3:11 not be put to S because of the deeds
3:19 I will change their S into praise and renown
1Mac 1:28 all the house of Jacob was clothed with S
Mt 1:19 to put her to S, resolved to send her
Lk 13:17 adversaries were put to S; and all the people
14:9 you will begin with S to take the lowest
Rom 9:33 believes in him will not be put to S
10:11 who believes in him will be put to S
1Cor 1:27 in the world to S the wise, God chose
1:27 in the world to S the strong,
6:5 I say this to your S
15:34 I say this to your S
2Cor 7:14 was not put to S; but just as everything
10:8 destroying you, I shall not be put to S
11:21 To my S, I must say, we were too
Eph 5:12 For it is a S even to speak of
Phil 3:19 they glory in their S, with minds set on
Tit 2:8 may be put to S, having nothing evil to
Heb 12:2 the cross, despising the S, and is seated at
1Pet 2:6 believes in him will not be put to S
3:16 good behavior in Christ may be put to S
1Jn 2:28 shrink from him in S at his coming.
Jude 1:13 foam of their own S; wandering stars for whom
Rev 3:18 and to keep the S of your nakedness from

SHAMED (7)

Num 12:14 should she not be S seven days?
Jer 2:26 "As a thief is S when caught, so the
2:26 of Israel shall be S: they, their kings, their
9:19 We are utterly S, because we have left the
15:9 day; she has been S and disgraced.
20:11 They will be greatly S, for they will not

50:12 mother shall be utterly S, and she who bore

SHAMEFACED

Jud 1:11 they sent back his messengers empty-handed and S

SHAMEFUL (10)

Lev 20:17 nakedness, it is a S thing, and they shall
Deut 22:14 and charges her with S conduct, and brings an
22:17 lo, he has made S charges against her, saying,
Josh 7:15 he has done a S thing in Israel.'"
Wis 2:20 condemn him to a S death, for, according to
Jer 3:24 from our youth the S thing has devoured all
Dan 13:63 her kindred, because nothing S was found in her.
2Mac 9:2 inhabitants and beat a S retreat.
1Cor 14:35 For it is S for a woman to speak
1Pet 5:2 but willingly, not for S gain but eagerly,

SHAMEFULLY (10)

Prov 13:5 a wicked man acts S and disgracefully.
14:35 but his wrath falls on one who acts S
17:2 a son who acts S, and will share the
Sir 22:4 but one who acts S brings grief to her
Hos 2:5 the harlot; she that conceived them has acted S
Mt 22:6 his servants, treated them S, and killed them.
Mk 12:4 wounded him in the head, and treated him S
Lk 18:32 will be mocked and S treated and spit upon;
20:11 they beat and treated S, and sent him away
1Thes 2:2 already suffered and been S treated at Philippi, as

SHAMELESS (5)

Sir 23:6 surrender me to a S soul.
40:30 the mouth of the S begging is sweet, but
Bar 4:15 nation from afar, a S nation, of a strange
Zeph 2:1 and hold assembly, O S nation,
Rom 1:27 one another, men committing S acts with men and

SHAMELESSLY

2Sam 6:20 of the vulgar fellows S uncovers himself!"

SHAMELESSNESS

Sir 30:13 that you may not be offended by his S

SHAMES

Prov 28:7 a companion of gluttons S his father.

SHAMGAR (2)

Judg 3:31 After him was S the son of Anath, who
5:6 "In the days of S, son of Anath, in

SHAMHUTH

1Chr 27:8 the fifth month, was S, the Izrahite; in his

SHAMIR (4)

Josh 15:48 in the hill country, S, Jattir, Socoh,
Judg 10:1 and he lived at S in the hill country
10:2 Then he died, and was buried at S
1Chr 24:24 of Uzziel, Micah; of the sons of Micah, S

SHAMLAI

Ezra 2:46 Hagab, the sons of S, the sons of Hanan,

SHAMMA

1Chr 7:37 Imrah, Bezer, Hod, S, Shilshah, Ithran, and Be-era.

SHAMMAH (8)

Gen 36:13 of Reuel: Nahath, Zerah, S, and Mizzah.
36:17 the chiefs Nahath, Zerah, S, and Mizzah; these are
1Sam 16:9 Then Jesse made S pass by.
17:13 and next to him Abinadab, and the third S
2Sam 23:11 next to him was S, the son of Agee
23:25 of Dodo of Bethlehem, S of Harod, Elika of
23:33 sons of Jashen, Jonathan, S the Hararite, Ahiam the
1Chr 1:37 of Reuel: Nahath, Zerah, S, and Mizzah.

SHAMMAI (6)

1Chr 2:28 The sons of Onam: S and Jada.
2:28 The sons of S: Nadab and Abishur.
2:32 The sons of Jada, S's brother: Jether and Jonathan;
2:44 of Jorke-am; and Rekem was the father of S
2:45 The son of S: Maon; and Maon was the
4:17 conceived and bore Miriam, S, and Ishbah, the father

SHAMMOTH

1Chr 11:27 of Dodo of Bethlehem, S of Harod, Helez the

SHAMMUA (5)

Num 13:4 the tribe of Reuben, S the son of Zaccur;
2Sam 5:14 to him in Jerusalem: S, Shobab, Nathan, Solomon,
1Chr 14:4 he had in Jerusalem: S, Shobab, Nathan, Solomon,
Neh 11:17 Abda the son of S, son of Galal, son
12:18 Moadiah, Piltai; of Bilgah, S; of Shemaiah,

SHAMSHERAI

1Chr 8:26 S, Shehariah, Athaliah,

SHAPED (3)

Prov 8:25 the mountains had been S, before the hills, I
Hab 2:18 when its maker has S it, a metal image,
2Mac 7:23 of the world, who S the beginning of man

SHAPELY

Sir 9:8 your eyes from a S woman, and do not

SHAPES (3)

Wis 13:13 in his leisure, and S it with skill gained
Is 44:12 over the coals; he S it with hammers, and
44:13 with a compass; he S it into the figure

SHAPHAM

1Chr 5:12 Salecah: Joel the chief, S the second, Janai, and

SHAPHAN (30)

2Kgs 22:3 Josiah, the king sent S the son of Azaliah,
22:8 high priest said to S the secretary, "I have
22:8 gave the book to S, and he read it.
22:9 And S the secretary came to the king, and
22:10 Then S the secretary told the king, "Hilkiah the
22:10 And S read it before the king.
22:12 Ahikam the son of S, and Achbor the son
22:12 son of Micaiah, and S the secretary, and Asaiah
22:14 Ahikam, and Achbor, and S, and Asaiah went to
25:22 of Ahikam, son of S, governor.
2Chr 34:8 the house, he sent S the son of Azaliah,
34:15 Then Hilkiah said to S the secretary, "I have
34:15 the LORD"; and Hilkiah gave the book to S
34:16 S brought the book to the king, and further
34:18 Then S the secretary told the king, "Hilkiah the
34:18 And S read it before the king.
34:20 Ahikam the son of S, Abdon the son of
34:20 the son of Micah, S the secretary, and Asaiah
Jer 26:24 Ahikam the son of S was with Jeremiah so
29:3 Elasah the son of S and Gemariah the son
36:10 Gemariah the son of S the secretary, which was
36:11 of Gemariah, son of S, heard all the words
36:12 Gemariah the son of S, Zedekiah the son of
39:14 of Ahikam, son of S, that he should take
40:5 of Ahikam, son of S, whom the king of
40:9 of Ahikam, son of S, swore to them and
40:11 of Ahikam, son of S, as governor over them,
41:2 of Ahikam, son of S, with the sword, and
43:6 of Ahikam, son of S; also Jeremiah the prophet
Ezek 8:11 Ja-azaniah the son of S standing among them.

SHAPHAT (8)

Num 13:5 the tribe of Simeon, S the son of Hori;
1Kgs 19:16 Elisha the son of S of Abel-meholah you shall
19:19 Elisha the son of S, who was plowing, with
2Kgs 3:11 "Elisha the son of S is here, who poured
6:31 Elisha the son of S remains on his shoulders
1Chr 3:22 Igal, Bariah, Neariah, and S, six.
5:12 the second, Janai, and S in Bashan.
27:29 in the valleys was S the son of Adlai.

SHAPHIR

Mic 1:11 your way, inhabitants of S, in nakedness and shame;

SHAPING

Jer 18:11 LORD, Behold, I am S evil against you and

SHARAI

Ezra 10:40 Nathan, Adaiah, Machnadebai, Shashai, S,

SHARAR

2Sam 23:33 Ahiam the son of S the Hararite,

SHARE (50)

Gen 14:24 have eaten, and the S of the men who
14:24 me; let Aner, Eshcol, and Mamre take their S
1Sam 26:19 I should have no S in the heritage of
30:24 For as his S is who goes down into
30:24 battle, so shall his S be who stays by

30:24 the baggage; they shall S alike."
2Kgs 2:9 me inherit a double S of your spirit."
Job 17:5 friends to get a S of their property, the
39:17 and given her no S in understanding.
Prov 17:2 acts shamefully, and will S the inheritance as one
Eccl 9:6 more for ever any S in all that is
Wis 2:9 of us fail to S in our revelry, everywhere
18:9 that the saints would S alike the same things,
Sir 14:14 day; let not your S of desired good pass
22:21 affliction, that you may S with him in his
Is 58:7 Is it not to S your bread with the
2Mac 5:27 that they might not S in the defilement.
Lk 3:11 two coats, let him S with him who has
15:12 'Father, give me the S of property that falls
Acts 1:17 and was allotted his S in this ministry.
Rom 4:16 also to those who S the faith of Abraham,
11:17 in their place to S the richness of the
15:27 Gentiles have come to S in their spiritual blessings,
1Cor 4:8 so that we might S the rule with you!
9:10 in hope of a S in the crop.
9:12 If others S this rightful claim upon you, do
9:13 serve at the altar S in the sacrificial offerings?
9:23 gospel, that I may S in its blessings.
2Cor 1:5 For as we S abundantly in Christ's sufferings, so
1:5 so through Christ we S abundantly in comfort too.
1:7 know that as you S in our sufferings, you
1:7 sufferings, you will also S in our comfort.
Gal 6:6 is taught the word S all good things with
Phil 3:10 his resurrection, and may S his sufferings, becoming
4:14 kind of you to S my trouble.
Col 1:12 has qualified us to S in the inheritance of
1Thes 2:8 we were ready to S with you not only
2Tim 1:8 me his prisoner, but S in suffering for the
2:3 S in suffering as a good soldier of Christ
2:6 to have the first S of the crops.
Heb 2:14 Since therefore the children S in flesh and blood,
3:1 Therefore, holy brethren, who S in a heavenly call,
3:14 For we S in Christ, if only we hold
11:25 daughter, choosing rather to S ill-treatment with the
12:10 good, that we may S his holiness.
13:16 do good and to S what you have, for
1Pet 4:13 so far as you S Christ's sufferings, that you
Rev 1:9 John, your brother, who S with you in Jesus
18:4 her sins, lest you S in her plagues;
22:19 will take away his S in the tree of

SHARED (8)

1Kgs 2:26 father, and because you S in all the affliction
Prov 21:9 than in a house S with a contentious woman.
25:24 than in a house S with a contentious woman.
Wis 14:21 wood the name that ought not to be S
19:16 those who had already S the same rights.
2Mac 4:36 Onias, and the Greeks S their hatred of the
5:20 Therefore the place itself S in the misfortunes that
14:25 married, settled down, and S the common life.

SHARES (6)

2Sam 19:43 Judah, "We have ten S in the king, and
Prov 14:10 bitterness, and no stranger S its joy.
22:9 be blessed, for he S his bread with the
2Mac 8:30 also to the aged, S equal to their own.
2Jn 1:11 he who greets him S his wicked work.
Rev 20:6 holy is he who S in the first resurrection!

SHAREZER (3)

2Kgs 19:37 his god, Adrammelech and S, his sons, slew him
Is 37:38 his god, Adrammelech and S, his sons, slew him
Zech 7:2 of Bethel had sent S and Regem-melech and their

SHARING (3)

Wis 8:18 understanding, and renown in S her words, I went
Rom 5:2 in our hope of S the glory of God.
Philem 1:6 I pray that the S of your faith may

SHARON (7)

1Chr 5:16 the pasture lands of S to their limits.
27:29 herds that pastured in S was Shitrai the Sharonite;
Song 2:1 am a rose of S, a lily of the
Is 33:9 confounded and withers away; S is like a desert;
35:2 given to it, the majesty of Carmel and S
65:10 S shall become a pasture for flocks, and the
Acts 9:35 residents of Lydda and S saw him, and they

SHARONITE

1Chr 27:29 Sharon was Shitrai the S; over the herds in

SHARP (21)

Job 41:30 His underparts are like S potsherds; he spreads
Ps 45:5 Your arrows are S in the heart of the
52:2 tongue is like a S razor, you worker of
57:4 and arrows, their tongues S swords.
120:4 A warrior's S arrows, with glowing coals of the
140:3 They make their tongue S as a serpents, and
Prov 5:4 is bitter as wormwood, S as a two-edged sword.
25:18 a sword, or a S arrow.
Wis 18:16 stern warrior carrying the S sword of thy authentic
Is 5:28 broken; their arrows are S, all their bows bent,
41:15 a threshing sledge, new, S, and having teeth; you
49:2 my mouth like a S sword, in the shadow
Ezek 5:1 of man, take a S sword; use it as
2Mac 9:5 no relief and with S internal tortures--
Acts 15:38 And there arose a S contention, so that they
Rev 1:16 his mouth issued a S two-edged sword, and his
2:12 him who has the S two-edged sword.
14:14 his head, and a S sickle in his hand.
14:17 he too had a S sickle.
14:18 him who had the S sickle, "Put in your
19:15 his mouth issues a S sword with which to

SHARPEN (3)

1Sam 13:20 to the Philistines to S his plowshare, his mattock,
Wis 5:20 an invincible shield, and S stern wrath for a
Jer 51:11 S the arrows!

SHARPENED (3)

Ezek 21:9 sword, a sword is S and also polished,
21:10 sharpened and also polished, S for slaughter, polished
21:11 be handled; it is S and polished to be

SHARPENING

1Sam 13:21 of a shekel for S the axes and for

SHARPENS (3)

Job 16:9 at me; my adversary S his eyes against me.
Prov 27:17 Iron S iron, and one man sharpens another.
27:17 iron, and one man S another.

SHARPER

Heb 4:12 is living and active, S than any two-edged sword,

SHARPLY (2)

Ezek 21:16 Cut S to right and left where your edge
Tit 1:12 Therefore rebuke them S, that they may be sound

SHARUHEN

Josh 19:6 Beth-marcaboth, Hazar-susah, Beth-lebaoth, and S

SHASHAI

Ezra 10:40 Shelemiah, Nathan, Adaiah, Machnadebai, S, Sharai,

SHASHAK (2)

1Chr 8:14 of Gath); and Ahio, S, and Jeremoth.
8:25 Anthothijah, Iphdeiah, and Penuel were the sons of S

SHATTER (6)

Ps 48:7 east wind thou didst S the ships of Tarshish.
62:3 upon a man to S him, all of you,
68:21 But God will S the heads of his enemies,
110:5 right hand; he will S kings on the day
110:6 with corpses; he will S chiefs over the wide
Amos 9:1 the thresholds shake, and S them on the heads

SHATTERED (5)

Ex 9:25 of the field, and S every tree of the
Judg 5:26 crushed his head, she S and pierced his temple.
Ps 105:33 and fig trees, and S the trees of their
Is 21:9 her gods he has S to the ground."
Mal 1:4 Edom says, "We are S but we will rebuild

SHATTERER

Nah 2:1 The S has come up against you.

SHATTERING

Dan 12:7 and that when the S of the power of

SHATTERS (8)

Ex 15:6 right hand, O LORD, S the enemy.
Job 34:24 He S the mighty without investigation, and sets
Ps 46:9 breaks the bow, and S the spear, he burns
107:16 For he S the doors of bronze, and cuts
141:7 which one cleaves and S on the land, so
Dan 2:40 breaks to pieces and S all things; and like

2Mac	12:28	Sovereign who with power S the might of his
Lk	9:39	till he foams, and S him, and will hardly

SHAUL (9)

Gen	36:37	Samlah died, and S of Rehoboth on the Euphrates
	36:38	S died, and Baal-hanan the son of Achbor reigned
	46:10	Ohad, Jachin, Zohar, and S, the son of a
Ex	6:15	Ohad, Jachin, Zohar, and S, the son of a
Num	26:13	of the Zerahites; of S, the family of the
1Chr	1:48	When Samlah died, S of Rehoboth on the Euphrates
	1:49	When S died, Baal-hanan, the son of Achbor, reigned
	4:24	Nemuel, Jamin, Jarib, Zerah, S;
	6:24	Uzziah his son, and S his son.

SHAULITES

Num	26:13	the Zerahites; of Shaul, the family of the S

SHAVE (14)

Lev	13:33	skin, then he shall S himself, but the itch
	13:33	itch he shall not S; and the priest shall
	14:8	wash his clothes, and S off all his hair,
	14:9	seventh day he shall S all his hair off
	14:9	his head; he shall S off his beard and
	21:5	upon their heads, nor S off the edges of
Num	6:9	head, then he shall S his head on the
	6:9	seventh day he shall S it.
	6:18	And the Nazirite shall S his consecrated head at
Deut	21:12	house, and she shall S her head and pare
Judg	16:19	man, and had him S off the seven locks
Is	7:20	day the Lord will S with a razor which
Ezek	44:20	They shall not S their heads or let their
Acts	21:24	so that they may S their heads.

SHAVED (9)

Gen	41:14	and when he had S himself and changed his
Judg	16:17	If I be S, then my strength will leave
	16:22	began to grow again after it had been S
2Sam	10:4	took David's servants, and S off half the beard
1Chr	19:4	took David's servants, and S them, and cut off
Job	1:20	rent his robe, and S his head, and fell
Jer	41:5	Samaria, with their beards S and their clothes torn,
	48:37	"For every head is S and every beard cut
Bar	6:31	their heads and beards S, and their heads uncovered.

SHAVEH

Gen	14:17	at the Valley of S (that is, the King's

SHAVEH-KIRIATHAIM

Gen	14:5	Ham, the Emim in S,

SHAVEN (3)

Num	6:19	Nazirite, after he has S the hair of his
1Cor	11:5	is the same as if her head were S
	11:6	to be shorn or S, let her wear a

SHAVSHA

1Chr	18:16	Abiathar were priests; and S was secretary;

SHE-ARIAH (2)

1Chr	8:38	names: Azrikam, Bocheru, Ishmael, S, Obadiah, and
	9:44	Azrikam, Bocheru, Ishmael, S, Obadiah, and Hanan;

SHE-ASSES (6)

Gen	12:16	oxen, he-asses, menservants, maidservants, S, and
	32:15	and ten bulls, twenty S and ten he-asses.
	45:23	of Egypt, and ten S loaded with grain, bread,
1Chr	27:30	Ishmaelite; and over the S was Jehdeiah the
Job	1:3	oxen, and five hundred S, and very many servants;
	42:12	a thousand yoke of oxen, and a thousand S

SHE-BEAR

Prov	17:12	a man meet a S robbed of her cubs,

SHE-BEARS

2Kgs	2:24	And two S came out of the woods and

SHE-GOAT

Gen	15:9	three years old, a S three years old, a

SHE-GOATS (3)

Gen	30:35	spotted, and all the S that were speckled and
	31:38	your ewes and your S have not miscarried, and
	32:14	brother Esau, two hundred S and twenty he-goats,

SHEAF (7)

Gen	37:7	field, and lo, my S arose and stood upright;
	37:7	gathered round it, and bowed down to my S
Lev	23:10	you shall bring the S of the first fruits
	23:11	he shall wave the S before the LORD, that
	23:12	when you wave the S, you shall offer a
	23:15	that you brought the S of the wave offering;
Deut	24:19	and have forgotten a S in the field, you

SHEAL

Ezra	10:29	Meshullum, Malluch, Adaiah, Jashub, S, and

SHEALTIEL (13)

1Chr	3:17	of Jeconiah, the captive: S his son,
Ezra	3:2	Zerubbabel the son of S with his kinsmen, and
	3:8	Zerubbabel the son of S and Jeshua the son
	5:2	Zerubbabel the son of S and Jeshua the son
Neh	12:1	Zerubbabel the son of S, and Jeshua: Seraiah,
Hag	1:1	Zerubbabel the son of S, governor of Judah, and
	1:12	Zerubbabel the son of S, and Joshua the son
	1:14	Zerubbabel the son of S, governor of Judah, and
	2:2	Zerubbabel the son of S, governor of Judah, and
	2:23	servant, the son of S, says the LORD, and
Mt	1:12	was the father of S, and Shealtiel the father
	1:12	father of Shealtiel, and S the father of Zerubbabel,
Lk	3:27	Zerubbabel, the son of S, the son of Neri,

SHEAR (3)

Gen	31:19	Laban had gone to S his sheep, and Rachel
	38:13	up to Timnah to S his sheep,"
Deut	15:19	of your herd, nor S the firstling of your

SHEAR-JASHUB

Is	7:3	meet Ahaz, you and S your son, at the

SHEARER

Acts	8:32	a lamb before its S is dumb, so he

SHEARERS (3)

1Sam	25:7	hear that you have S; now your shepherds have
	25:11	have killed for my S, and give it to
Is	53:7	sheep that before its S is dumb, so he

SHEARING (2)

1Sam	25:2	He was S his sheep in Carmel.
	25:4	wilderness that Nabal was S his sheep.

SHEARINGS

Tob	1:6	produce and the first S, I would give these

SHEATH (9)

1Sam	17:51	it out of its S, and killed him, and
2Sam	20:8	a sword in its S fastened upon his loins,
1Chr	21:27	and he put his sword back into its S
Ezek	21:3	sword out of its S, and will cut off
	21:4	go out of its S against all flesh from
	21:5	sword out of its S; it shall not be
	21:30	Return it to its S
Hab	3:9	Thou didst strip the S from thy bow, and
Jn	18:11	your sword into its S; shall I not drink

SHEATHED

Ezek	21:5	it shall not be S again.

SHEAVES (12)

Gen	37:7	behold, we were binding S in the field, and
	37:7	upright; and behold, your S gathered round it, and
Ruth	2:7	and gather among the S after the reapers.' So
	2:15	glean even among the S, and do not reproach
Jud	8:3	men who were binding S in the field, he
Job	24:10	hungry, they carry the S;
Ps	126:6	of joy, bringing his S with him.
	129:7	or the binder of S his bosom,
Jer	9:22	the open field, like S after the reaper, and
Amos	2:13	a cart full of S presses down.
Mic	4:12	has gathered them as S to the threshing floor.
Zech	12:6	a flaming torch among S; and they shall devour

SHEBA (32)

Gen	10:7	The sons of Raamah: S and Dedan.
	10:28	Uzal, Diklah, Obal, Abima-el, S,
	25:3	was the father of S and Dedan.
Josh	19:2	for its inheritance Beer-sheba, S, Moladah,
2Sam	20:1	fellow, whose name was S, the son of Bichri,
	20:2	from David, and followed S the son of Bichri;
	20:6	said to Abishai, "Now S the son of Bichri
	20:7	from Jerusalem to pursue S the son of Bichri.
	20:10	Abishai his brother pursued S the son of Bichri.

20:13 after Joab to pursue S the son of Bichri.
20:14 And S passed through all the tribes of Israel
20:21 country of Ephraim, called S the son of Bichri,
20:22 off the head of S the son of Bichri,
1Kgs 10:1 when the queen of S heard of the fame
10:4 when the queen of S had seen all the
10:10 which the queen of S gave to King Solomon.
10:13 to the queen of S all that she desired,
1Chr 1:9 The sons of Raamah: S and Dedan.
1:22 Uzal, Diklah, Ebal, Abima-el, S,
1:32 The sons of Jokshan: S and Dedan.
5:13 fathers' houses: Michael, Meshullam, S, Jorai, Jacan,
2Chr 9:1 when the queen of S heard of the fame
9:3 when the queen of S had seen the wisdom
9:9 which the queen of S gave to King Solomon.
9:12 to the queen of S all that she desired,
Job 6:19 look, the travelers of S hope.
Ps 72:10 may the kings of S and Seba bring gifts!
72:15 live, may gold of S be given to him!
Is 60:6 Ephah; all those from S shall come.
Jer 6:20 come to me from S, or sweet cane from
Ezek 27:22 The traders of S and Raamah traded with you;
38:13 S and Dedan and the merchants of Tarshish and

SHEBANIAH (7)
1Chr 15:24 S, Joshaphat, Nethanel, Amasai, Zechariah, Benaiah,
Neh 9:4 stood Jeshua, Bani, Kadmi-el, S, Bunni, Sherebiah,
9:5 Sherebiah, Hodiah, S, and Pethahiah, said, "Stand
10:4 Pashhur, Amariah, Malchijah, Hattush, S, Malluch,
10:10 Kadmi-el; and their brethren, S, Hodiah, Kelita,
10:12 Rehob, Hashabiah, Zaccur, Sherebiah, S,
12:14 of Malluchi, Jonathan; of S, Joseph;

SHEBARIM
Josh 7:5 gate as far as S, and slew them at

SHEBAT (2)
Zech 1:7 is the month of S, in the second year
1Mac 16:14 the eleventh month, which is the month of S

SHEBER
1Chr 2:48 Maacah, Caleb's concubine, bore S and Tirhanah.

SHEBNA (7)
2Kgs 18:37 over the household, and S the secretary, and Joah
19:2 over the household, and S the secretary, and the
Is 22:15 to this steward, to S, who is over the
36:3 over the household, and S the secretary, and Joah
36:11 Then Eliakim, S, and Joah said to the Rabshakeh,
36:22 over the household, and S the secretary, and Joah
37:2 over the household, and S the secretary, and the

SHEBNAH (2)
2Kgs 18:18 over the household, and S the secretary, and Joah
18:26 son of Hilkiah, and S, and Joah, said to

SHEBUEL (3)
1Chr 23:16 The sons of Gershom: S the chief.
25:4 attaniah, Uzziel, S, and Jerimoth, Hananiah,
26:24 the Uzzielites-- and S the son of Gershom,

SHECANIAH (10)
1Chr 3:21 his son Arnan, his son Obadiah, his son S
3:22 The sons of S: Shemaiah.
24:11 Jeshua, the tenth to S,
2Chr 31:15 Jeshua, Shemaiah, Amariah, and S were faithfully
Ezra 8:3 sons of David, Hattush, of the sons of S
8:5 the sons of Zattu, S the son of Jahaziel,
10:2 And S the son of Jehiel, of the sons
Neh 3:29 Shemaiah the son of S, the keeper of the
6:18 was the son-in-law of S the son of Arah:
12:3 Amariah, Malluch, Hattush, S, Rehum, Meremoth,

SHECHEM (69)
Gen 12:6 to the place at S, to the oak of
33:18 to the city of S, which is in the
33:19 the sons of Hamor, S's father, he bought for
34:2 the land; and when S the son of Hamor
34:4 So S spoke to his father Hamor, saying, "Get
34:6 Hamor the father of S went out to Jacob
34:8 soul of my son S longs for your daughter;
34:11 S also said to her father and to her
34:13 sons of Jacob answered S and his father Hamor
34:18 Their words pleased Hamor and Hamor's son S
34:20 Hamor and his son S came to the gate
34:24 Hamor and his son S; and every male was
34:26 Hamor and his son S with the sword, and
34:26 took Dinah out of S's house, and went away.
35:4 hid them under the oak which was near S
37:12 brothers went to pasture their father's flock near S
37:13 "Are not your brothers pasturing the flock at S
37:14 the valley of Hebron, and he came to S
Num 26:31 the Asrielites; and of S, the family of the
Josh 17:2 families, Abi-ezer, Helek, Asriel, S, Hepher, and
17:7 which is east of S; then the boundary goes
20:7 country of Naphtali, and S in the hill country
21:21 To them were given S, the city of refuge
24:1 tribes of Israel to S, and summoned the elders,
24:25 and made statutes and ordinances for them at S
24:32 Egypt were buried at S, in the portion of
24:32 Hamor the father of S for a hundred pieces
Judg 8:31 concubine who was in S also bore him a
9:1 of Jerubbaal went to S to his mother's kinsmen
9:2 all the citizens of S, 'Which is better for
9:3 all the men of S; and their hearts inclined
9:6 all the citizens of S came together, and all
9:6 king, by the oak of the pillar at S
9:7 me, you men of S, that God may listen
9:18 over the citizens of S, because he is your
9:20 devour the citizens of S, and Beth-millo; and let
9:20 from the citizens of S, and from Beth-millo, and
9:23 and the men of S; and the men of
9:23 the men of S dealt treacherously with Abimelech;
9:24 upon the men of S, who strengthened his hands
9:25 And the men of S put men in ambush
9:26 of Ebed moved into S with his kinsmen; and
9:26 and the men of S put confidence in him.
9:28 who are we of S, that we should serve
9:28 serve the men of Hamor the father of S
9:31 kinsmen have come to S, and they are stirring
9:34 and laid wait against S in four companies.
9:39 of the men of S, and fought with Abimelech.
9:41 so that they could not live on at S
9:46 of the Tower of S heard of it, they
9:47 of the Tower of S were gathered together.
9:49 of the Tower of S also died, about a
9:57 of the men of S fall back upon their
21:19 up from Bethel to S, and south of Lebonah."
1Kgs 12:1 Rehoboam went to S, for all Israel had come
12:1 Israel had come to S to make him king.
12:25 Then Jeroboam built S in the hill country of
1Chr 6:67 the cities of refuge: S with its pasture lands
7:19 of Shemida were Ahian, S, Likhi, and Aniam.
7:28 Gezer and its towns, S and its towns, and
2Chr 10:1 Rehoboam went to S, for all Israel had come
10:1 Israel had come to S to make him king.
Ps 60:6 I will divide up S and portion out the
108:7 I will divide up S, and portion out the
Sir 50:26 Philistines, and the foolish people that dwell in S
Jer 41:5 eighty men arrived from S and Shiloh and Samaria,
Hos 6:9 on the way to S, yea, they commit villainy.
Acts 7:16 were carried back to S and laid in the
7:16 of silver from the sons of Hamor in S

SHECHEMITES (2)
Num 26:31 the family of the S;
Jud 5:16 the Jebusites and the S and all the Gergesites,

SHED (47)
Gen 9:6 shall his blood be S; for God made man
37:22 Reuben said to them, S no blood; cast him
Lev 17:4 that man; he has S blood; and that man
Num 35:33 the blood that is S in it, except by
35:33 blood of him who S it.
Deut 19:10 lest innocent blood be S in your land which
21:7 'Our hands did not S this blood, neither did
21:7 this blood, neither did our eyes see it S
1Sam 25:31 of conscience, for having S blood without cause or
2Sam 20:10 in the body, and S his bowels to the
1Kgs 2:5 blood which had been S in war, and putting
2:31 the blood which Joab S without cause.
2Kgs 21:16 Moreover Manasseh S very much innocent blood, till
24:4 blood that he had S; for he filled Jerusalem
1Chr 22:8 me, saying, 'You have S much blood and have
22:8 name, because you have S so much blood before
28:3 a warrior and have S blood.'
Ps 68:9 O God, thou didst S abroad; thou didst restore
119:136 My eyes S streams of tears, because men do
132:18 himself his crown will S its luster."
Prov 1:16 they make haste to S blood.
6:17 tongue, and hands that S innocent blood,
Sir 11:30 lies in wait to S blood.

S

34:22 his wages is to S blood.
Is 13:10 the moon will not S its light.
26:21 will disclose the blood S upon her, and will
59:7 they make haste to S innocent blood; their thoughts
Jer 7:6 or the widow, or S innocent blood in this
22:3 and the widow, nor S innocent blood in this
Lam 4:13 of her priests, who S in the midst of
Ezek 16:38 who break wedlock and S blood are judged, and
22:4 blood which you have S, and defiled by the
22:9 you who slander to S blood, and men in
22:12 men take bribes to S blood; you take interest
23:45 sentence of women that S blood; because they are
24:7 the blood she has S is still in the
24:8 the blood she has S, that it may not
33:25 to your idols, and S blood; shall you then
36:18 blood which they had S in the land, for
Joel 3:19 Judah, because they have S innocent blood in their
1Mac 1:37 of the sanctuary they S innocent blood; they even
2Mac 1:8 burned the gate and S innocent blood.
Mt 23:34 all the righteous blood S on earth, from the
Lk 11:50 of all the prophets, S from the foundation of
Acts 22:20 Stephen thy witness was S, I also was standing
Rom 3:15 feet are swift to S blood,
Rev 16:6 For men have S the blood of saints and

SHEDDER

Ezek 18:10 is a robber, a S of blood,

SHEDDING (7)

Esth 16:5 part responsible for the S of innocent blood, and
Jer 22:17 your dishonest gain, for S innocent blood, and for
Ezek 22:6 have been bent on S blood.
22:27 wolves tearing the prey, S blood, destroying lives to
Mt 23:29 part with them in S the blood of the
Heb 9:22 blood, and without the S of blood there is
12:4 to the point of S your blood.

SHEDEUR (5)

Num 1:5 Elizur the son of S;
2:10 Elizur the son of S,
7:30 Elizur the son of S, the leader of the
7:35 was the offering of Elizur the son of S
10:18 over their host was Elizur the son of S

SHEDS (6)

Gen 9:6 Whoever S the blood of man, by man shall
Sir 14:18 a spreading tree which S some and puts forth
28:11 fire, and urgent strife S blood.
31:13 Therefore it S tears from every face.
Ezek 22:3 GOD: A city that S blood in the midst
Rev 6:13 as the fig tree S its winter fruit when

SHEEP (204)

Gen 4:2 was a keeper of S, and Cain a tiller
12:16 Abram; and he had S, oxen, he-asses, menservants,
20:14 Then Abimelech took S and oxen, and male and
21:27 So Abraham took S and oxen and gave them
29:2 lo, three flocks of S lying beside it; for
29:3 well, and water the S, and put the stone
29:6 see, Rachel his daughter is coming with the S
29:7 gathered together; water the S, and go, pasture
29:8 mouth of the well; then we water the S
29:9 came with her father's S; for she kept them.
29:10 mother's brother, and the S of Laban his mother's
30:32 every speckled and spotted S and every black lamb,
31:19 gone to shear his S, and Rachel stole her
38:13 is going up to Timnah to shear his S
Ex 12:5 take it from the S or from the goats;
20:24 your peace offerings, your S and your oxen; in
22:1 an ox or a S, and kills it or
22:1 an ox, and four S for a sheep.
22:1 for an ox, and four sheep for a S
22:2 an ass or a S, he shall pay double.
22:9 ox, for ass, for S, for clothing, or for
22:10 an ox or a S or any beast to
22:30 oxen and with your S: seven days it shall
34:19 your male cattle, the firstlings of cow and S
Lev 1:10 the flock, from the S or goats, he shall
7:23 fat, of ox, or S, or goat.
22:19 the bulls or the S or the goats.
22:27 "When a bull or S or goat is born,
27:26 dedicate; whether ox or S, it is the LORDs.
Num 18:17 the firstling of a S, or the firstling of
22:40 Balak sacrificed oxen and S, and sent to Balaam
27:17 may not be as S which have no shepherd."
31:32 hundred and seventy-five thousand S,
31:36 thirty-seven thousand five hundred S,
31:37 the LORD's tribute of S was six hundred and
31:43 thirty-seven thousand five hundred S,
32:24 and folds for your S; and do what you
32:36 and Beth-haran, fortified cities, and folds for S
Deut 14:4 eat: the ox, the S, the goat,
14:26 you desire, oxen, or S, or wine or strong
17:1 an ox or a S in which is a
18:3 it be ox or S: they shall give to
18:4 the fleece of your S, you shall give him.
22:1 brother's ox or his S go astray, and withhold
28:31 restored to you; your S shall be given to
Josh 6:21 young and old, oxen, S, and asses, with the
7:24 oxen and asses and S, and his tent, and
Judg 6:4 in Israel, and no S or ox or ass.
1Sam 14:32 the spoil, and took S and oxen and calves,
14:34 his ox or his S, and slay them here,
15:3 and suckling, ox and S, camel and ass.'"
15:9 the best of the S and of the oxen
15:14 this bleating of the S in my ears, and
15:15 the best of the S and of the oxen,
15:21 took of the spoil, S and oxen, the best
16:11 the youngest, but behold, he is keeping the S
16:19 me David your son, who is with the S
17:15 to feed his father's S at Bethlehem.
17:20 morning, and left the S with a keeper, and
17:28 you left those few S in the wilderness?
17:34 servant used to keep S for his father; and
22:19 sucklings, oxen, asses and S, he put to the
25:2 he had three thousand S and a thousand goats.
25:2 He was shearing his S in Carmel.
25:4 in the wilderness that Nabal was shearing his S
25:16 the while we were with them keeping the S
25:18 of wine, and five S ready dressed, and five
27:9 but took away the S, the oxen, the asses,
2Sam 7:8 pasture, from following the S, that you should be
17:29 honey and curds and S and cheese from the
24:17 done wickedly; but these S, what have they done?
1Kgs 1:9 Adonijah sacrificed S, oxen, and fatlings by the
1:19 sacrificed oxen, fatlings, and S in abundance, and has
1:25 sacrificed oxen, fatlings, and S in abundance, and has
4:23 pasture-fed cattle, a hundred S, besides harts,
8:5 ark, sacrificing so many S and oxen that they
8:63 thousand oxen and a hundred and twenty thousand S
22:17 upon the mountains, as S that have no shepherd;
2Kgs 3:4 of Moab was a S breeder; and he had
5:26 olive orchards and vineyards, S and oxen,
1Chr 5:21 hundred and fifty thousand S, two thousand asses,
12:40 and oil, oxen and S, for there was joy
17:7 pasture, from following the S, that you should be
21:17 But these S, what have they done?
2Chr 5:6 ark, sacrificing so many S and oxen that they
7:5 thousand oxen and a hundred and twenty thousand S
14:15 cattle, and carried away S in abundance and camels.
15:11 brought, seven hundred oxen and seven thousand S
18:2 killed an abundance of S and oxen for him
18:16 upon the mountains, as S that have no shepherd;
29:33 were six hundred bulls and three thousand S
30:24 bulls and seven thousand S for offerings, and the
30:24 the assembly a thousand bulls and ten thousand S
31:6 tithe of cattle and S, and the dedicated things
Ezra 6:9 young bulls, rams, or S for burnt offerings to
Neh 3:1 and they built the S Gate.
3:32 the corner and the S Gate the goldsmiths and
5:18 ox and six choice S; fowls likewise were prepared
12:39 the Hundred, to the S Gate; and they came
Jud 2:17 for transport, and innumerable S and oxen and goats
8:26 he was keeping the S of Laban, his mother's
11:19 will lead them like S that have no shepherd,
Job 1:3 He had seven thousand S, three thousand camels,
1:16 and burned up the S and the servants, and
31:20 the fleece of my S;
42:12 he had fourteen thousand S, six thousand camels, a
Ps 8:7 under his feet, all S and oxen, and also
44:11 hast made us like S for slaughter, and hast
44:22 long, and accounted as S for the slaughter.
49:14 [Selah] Like S they are appointed for Sheol; Death
74:1 anger smoke against the S of thy pasture?
78:52 forth his people like S, and guided them in
95:7 his pasture, and the S of his hand.
100:3 his people, and the S of his pasture.
119:176 astray like a lost S; seek thy servant, for
144:13 of store; may our S bring forth thousands and
Is 7:21 young cow and two S;
7:25 let loose and where S tread.
13:14 hunted gazelle, or like S with none to gather

S

22:13 slaying oxen and killing S, eating flesh and drinking
43:23 not brought me your S for burnt offerings, or
53:6 All we like S have gone astray; we have
53:7 slaughter, and like a S that before its shearers
Jer 12:3 Pull them out like S for the slaughter, and
23:1 destroy and scatter the S of my pasture!" says
50:6 people have been lost S; their shepherds have led
50:17 "Israel is a hunted S driven away by lions.
Ezek 34:2 Should not shepherds feed the S
34:3 the fatlings; but you do not feed the S
34:6 My S were scattered, they wandered over all the
34:6 every high hill; my S were scattered over all
34:8 Lord GOD, because my S have become a prey,
34:8 a prey, and my S have become food for
34:8 not searched for my S, but the shepherds have
34:8 have not fed my S;
34:10 I will require my S at their hand, and
34:10 to their feeding the S; no longer shall the
34:10 I will rescue my S from their mouths, that
34:11 will search for my S, and will seek them
34:12 when some of his S have been scattered abroad,
34:12 I seek out my S; and I will rescue
34:15 the shepherd of my S, and I will make
34:17 Behold, I judge between S and sheep, rams and
34:17 judge between sheep and S, rams and he-goats.
34:19 And must my S eat what you have trodden
34:20 judge between the fat S and the lean sheep.
34:20 judge between the fat sheep and the lean S
34:22 I will judge between S and sheep.
34:22 prey; and I will judge between sheep and S
34:31 And you are my S, the sheep of my
34:31 are my sheep, the S of my pasture, and
45:15 ten baths); and one S from every flock of
Dan 14:3 fine flour and forty S and fifty gallons of
14:32 human bodies and two S; but these were not
Hos 12:12 a wife he herded S
Joel 1:17 even the flocks of S are dismayed.
Mic 2:12 set them together like S in a fold, like
5:8 among the flocks of S, which, when it goes
Zech 10:2 the people wander like S; they are afflicted for
11:7 be slain for those who trafficked in the S
11:7 And I tended the S
11:11 the traffickers in the S, who were watching me,
13:7 the shepherd, that the S may be scattered; I
Mt 7:15 come to you in S's clothing but inwardly are
9:36 harassed and helpless, like S without a shepherd.
10:6 rather to the lost S of the house of
10:16 send you out as S in the midst of
12:11 if he has one S and it falls into
12:12 much more value is a man than a S
15:24 only to the lost S of the house of
18:11 man has a hundred S, and one of them
25:32 a shepherd separates the S from the goats,
25:33 he will place the S at his right hand,
26:31 the shepherd, and the S of the flock will
Mk 6:34 because they were like S without a shepherd; and
14:27 the shepherd, and the S will be scattered.'
Lk 15:4 you, having a hundred S, if he has lost
15:6 I have found my S which was lost.'
17:7 servant plowing or keeping S, say to him when
Jn 2:14 were selling oxen and S and pigeons, and the
2:15 them all, with the S and oxen, out of
5:2 in Jerusalem by the S Gate a pool, in
10:2 by the door is the shepherd of the S
10:3 the gatekeeper opens; the S hear his voice, and
10:3 he calls his own S by name and leads
10:4 before them, and the S follow him, for they
10:7 to you, I am the door of the S
10:8 and robbers; but the S did not heed them.
10:11 good shepherd lays down his life for the S
10:12 shepherd, whose own the S are not, sees the
10:12 coming and leaves the S and flees; and the
10:13 is a hireling and cares nothing for the S
10:15 and I lay down my life for the S
10:16 And I have other S, that are not of
10:26 believe, because you do not belong to my S
10:27 My S hear my voice, and I know them,
21:16 He said to him, "Tend my S
21:17 Jesus said to him, "Feed my S
Acts 8:32 was this: "As a S led to the slaughter
Rom 8:36 we are regarded as S to be slaughtered."
Heb 11:37 about in skins of S and goats, destitute, afflicted,
13:20 great shepherd of the S, by the blood of
1Pet 2:25 you were straying like S, but have now returned
Rev 18:13 and wheat, cattle and S, horses and chariots, and

SHEEPFOLD (3)

Jer 49:19 Jordan against a strong S, I will suddenly make
50:44 Jordan against a strong S, I will suddenly make
Jn 10:1 does not enter the S by the door but

SHEEPFOLDS (9)

Gen 49:14 ass, crouching between the S;
Num 32:16 said, "We will build S here for our flocks,
Judg 5:16 you tarry among the S, to hear the piping
1Sam 24:3 he came to the S by the way, where
2Chr 32:28 and stalls for all kinds of cattle, and S
Jud 2:26 and burned their tents and plundered their S
3:3 herds, and all our S with their tents, lie
Ps 68:13 they stay among the S -- the wings of
78:70 took him from the S;

SHEEPSHEARERS (3)

Gen 38:12 to Timnah to his S, he and his friend
2Sam 13:23 full years Absalom had S at Baal-hazor, which is
13:24 "Behold, your servant has S; pray let the king

SHEER (4)

Sir 40:15 are unhealthy roots upon S rock.
48:17 it; he tunneled the S rock with iron and
Is 28:19 and it will be S terror to understand the
2Mac 6:29 were in their opinion S madness.

SHEERAH

1Chr 7:24 His daughter was S, who built both Lower and

SHEET (2)

Acts 10:11 descending, like a great S, let down by four
11:5 descending, like a great S, let down from heaven

SHEHARIAH

1Chr 8:26 Shamsherai, S, Athaliah,

SHEKEL (44)

Ex 30:13 give this: half a S according to the shekel
30:13 shekel according to the S of the sanctuary (the
30:13 of the sanctuary (the S is twenty gerahs), half
30:13 twenty gerahs), half a S as an offering to
30:24 hundred, according to the S of the sanctuary, and
38:24 thirty shekels, by the S of the sanctuary.
38:25 seventy-five shekels, by the S of the sanctuary:
38:26 (that is, half a S, by the shekel of
38:26 a shekel, by the S of the sanctuary), for
Lev 5:15 silver, according to the S of the sanctuary; it
27:3 silver, according to the S of the sanctuary.
27:25 be according to the S of the sanctuary: twenty
27:25 of the sanctuary: twenty gerahs shall make a S
Num 3:47 apiece; reckoning by the S of the sanctuary, the
3:47 of the sanctuary, the S of twenty gerahs, you
3:50 shekels, reckoned by the S of the sanctuary;
7:13 shekels, according to the S of the sanctuary, both
7:19 shekels, according to the S of the sanctuary, both
7:25 shekels, according to the S of the sanctuary, both
7:31 shekels, according to the S of the sanctuary, both
7:37 shekels, according to the S of the sanctuary, both
7:43 shekels, according to the S of the sanctuary, both
7:49 shekels, according to the S of the sanctuary, both
7:55 shekels, according to the S of the sanctuary, both
7:61 shekels, according to the S of the sanctuary, both
7:67 shekels, according to the S of the sanctuary, both
7:73 shekels, according to the S of the sanctuary, both
7:79 shekels, according to the S of the sanctuary, both
7:85 shekels according to the S of the sanctuary,
7:86 apiece according to the S of the sanctuary, all
18:16 silver, according to the S of the sanctuary, which
1Sam 9:8 fourth part of a S of silver, and I
13:21 a third of a S for sharpening the axes
2Kgs 7:1 be sold for a S, and two measures of
7:1 of barley for a S, at the gate of
7:16 was sold for a S, and two measures of
7:16 of barley for a S, according to the word
7:18 be sold for a S, and a measure of
7:18 fine meal for a S, about this time tomorrow
2Chr 3:9 the nails was one S to fifty shekels of
Neh 10:32 third part of a S for the service of
Ezek 45:12 The S shall be twenty gerahs; five shekels shall
Amos 8:5 ephah small and the S great, and deal deceitfully
Mt 17:26 you will find a S; take that and give

SHEKELS (100)

Gen 23:15 land worth four hundred S of silver, what is
23:16 the Hittites, four hundred S of silver, according to

24:22 arms weighing ten gold S,
37:28 the Ishmaelites for twenty S of silver; and they
45:22 he gave three hundred S of silver and five
Ex 21:32 to their master thirty S of silver, and the
30:23 liquid myrrh five hundred S, and of sweet-smelling
38:24 seven hundred and thirty S, by the shekel of
38:25 seven hundred and seventy-five S, by the shekel of
38:28 seven hundred and seventy-five S he made hooks for
38:29 thousand and four hundred S;
Lev 5:15 valued by you in S of silver, according to
27:3 old shall be fifty S of silver, according to
27:4 is a female, your valuation shall be thirty S
27:5 for a male twenty S, and for a female
27:5 male twenty shekels, and for a female ten S
27:6 for a male five S of silver, and for
27:6 valuation shall be three S of silver.
27:7 male shall be fifteen S, and for a female
27:7 be fifteen shekels, and for a female ten S
27:16 be valued at fifty S of silver.
Num 3:47 you shall take five S apiece; reckoning by the
3:50 three hundred and sixty-five S, reckoned by the
7:13 a hundred and thirty S, one silver basin of
7:13 silver basin of seventy S, according to the shekel
7:14 golden dish of ten S, full of incense;
7:19 a hundred and thirty S, one silver basin of
7:19 silver basin of seventy S, according to the shekel
7:20 golden dish of ten S, full of incense;
7:25 a hundred and thirty S, one silver basin of
7:25 silver basin of seventy S, according to the shekel
7:26 golden dish of ten S, full of incense;
7:31 a hundred and thirty S, one silver basin of
7:31 silver basin of seventy S, according to the shekel
7:32 golden dish of ten S, full of incense;
7:37 a hundred and thirty S, one silver basin of
7:37 silver basin of seventy S, according to the shekel
7:38 golden dish of ten S, full of incense;
7:43 a hundred and thirty S, one silver basin of
7:43 silver basin of seventy S, according to the shekel
7:44 golden dish of ten S, full of incense;
7:49 a hundred and thirty S, one silver basin of
7:49 silver basin of seventy S, according to the shekel
7:50 golden dish of ten S, full of incense;
7:55 a hundred and thirty S, one silver basin of
7:55 silver basin of seventy S, according to the shekel
7:56 golden dish of ten S, full of incense;
7:61 a hundred and thirty S, one silver basin of
7:61 silver basin of seventy S, according to the shekel
7:62 golden dish of ten S, full of incense;
7:67 a hundred and thirty S, one silver basin of
7:67 silver basin of seventy S, according to the shekel
7:68 golden dish of ten S, full of incense;
7:73 a hundred and thirty S, one silver basin of
7:73 silver basin of seventy S, according to the shekel
7:74 golden dish of ten S, full of incense;
7:79 a hundred and thirty S, one silver basin of
7:79 silver basin of seventy S, according to the shekel
7:80 golden dish of ten S, full of incense;
7:85 a hundred and thirty S and each basin seventy,
7:85 two thousand four hundred S according to the shekel
7:86 of incense, weighing ten S apiece according to the
7:86 a hundred and twenty S;
18:16 shall fix at five S in silver, according to
31:52 was sixteen thousand seven hundred and fifty S
Deut 22:19 fine him a hundred S of silver, and give
22:29 the young woman fifty S of silver, and she
Josh 7:21 Shinar, and two hundred S of silver, and a
7:21 of gold weighing fifty S, then I coveted them,
Judg 8:26 one thousand seven hundred S of gold; besides the
1Sam 17:5 coat was five thousand S of bronze.
17:7 head weighed six hundred S of iron; and his
2Sam 14:26 his head, two hundred S by the king's weight.
21:16 spear weighed three hundred S of bronze, and who
24:24 the oxen for fifty S of silver.
1Kgs 10:16 beaten gold; six hundred S of gold went into
10:29 Egypt for six hundred S of silver, and a
2Kgs 5:5 of silver, six thousand S of gold, and ten
6:25 was sold for eighty S of silver, and the
6:25 dove's dung for five S of silver.
15:20 the wealthy men, fifty S of silver from every
1Chr 21:25 paid Ornan six hundred S of gold by weight
2Chr 1:17 Egypt for six hundred S of silver, and a
3:9 one shekel to fifty S of gold.
9:15 beaten gold; six hundred S of beaten gold went
9:16 beaten gold; three hundred S of gold went into
Neh 5:15 and wine, besides forty S of silver.
Is 7:23 vines, worth a thousand S of silver, will become
Jer 32:9 money to him, seventeen S of silver.
Ezek 4:10 be by weight, twenty S a day; once a
45:12 be twenty gerahs; five S shall be five shekels,
45:12 shekels shall be five S, and ten shekels shall
45:12 five shekels, and ten S shall be ten shekels,
45:12 shekels shall be ten S, and your mina shall
45:12 ten shekels, and your mina shall be fifty S
Hos 3:2 bought her for fifteen S of silver and a
Zech 11:12 as my wages thirty S of silver.
11:13 I took the thirty S of silver and cast
1Mac 10:40 also grant fifteen thousand S of silver yearly out
10:42 Moreover, the five thousand S of silver which my

SHELAH (19)

Gen 10:24 became the father of S; and Shelah became the
10:24 father of Shelah; and S became the father of
11:12 became the father of S;
11:13 after the birth of S four hundred and three
11:14 When S had lived thirty years, he became the
11:15 father of Eber; and S lived after the birth
38:5 bore a son, and she called his name S
38:11 your father's house, till S my son grows up"—
38:14 for she saw that S was grown up, and
38:26 I did not give her to my son S
46:12 of Judah: Er, Onan, S, Perez, and Zerah (but
Num 26:20 their families were: of S, the family of the
1Chr 1:18 was the father of S; and Shelah was the
1:18 father of Shelah; and S was the father of
1:24 Shem, Arpachshad, S;
2:3 Judah: Er, Onan, and S; these three Bath-shua the
4:21 The sons of S the son of Judah: Er
Neh 3:15 of the Pool of S of the king's garden,
Lk 3:35 Eber, the son of S,

SHELANITES

Num 26:20 the family of the S; of Perez, the family

SHELEMIAH (10)

1Chr 26:14 The lot for the east fell to S
Ezra 10:39 sons of Binnui: Shimei, S, Nathan, Adaiah,
10:41 Machnadebai, Shashai, Sharai, Azarel, S,
Neh 3:30 Hananiah the son of S and Hanun the sixth
13:13 treasurers over the storehouses S the priest, Zadok
Jer 36:14 of Nethaniah, son of S, son of Cushi, to
36:26 son of Azriel and S the son of Abdeel
37:3 Jehucal the son of S, and Zephaniah the priest,
37:13 Irijah the son of S, son of Hananiah, seized
38:1 Jucal the son of S, and Pashhur the son

SHELEPH (2)

Gen 10:26 the father of Almodad, S, Hazarmaveth, Jerah,
1Chr 1:20 the father of Almodad, S, Hazarmaveth, Jerah,

SHELESH

1Chr 7:35 his brother: Zophah, Imna, S, and Amal.

SHELOMI

Num 34:27 of Asher a leader, Ahihud the son of S

SHELOMITH (5)

Lev 24:11 His mother's name was S, the daughter of Dibri,
1Chr 3:19 Meshullam and Hananiah, and S was their sister;
23:18 The sons of Izhar: S the chief.
2Chr 11:20 Absalom, who bore him Abijah, Attai, Ziza, and S
Ezra 8:10 the sons of Bani, S the son of Josiphiah,

SHELOMOTH (6)

1Chr 23:9 The sons of Shimei: S, Hazi-el, and Haran, three.
24:22 Of the Izharites, S; of the sons of Shelomoth,
24:22 of the sons of S, Jahath.
26:25 Joram, and his son Zichri, and his son S
26:26 This S and his brethren were in charge of
26:28 in the care of S and his brethren.

SHELTER (22)

Gen 19:8 have come under the S of my roof."
Ex 9:19 the field into safe S; for the hail shall
Tob 2:4 to a place of S until sunset.
Jud 6:13 they got under the S of the hill and
Job 24:8 and cling to the rock for want of S
Ps 27:5 hide me in his S in the day of
31:20 them safe under thy S from the strife of
55:8 to find me a S from the raging wind
61:4 be safe under the S of thy wings!
91:1 who dwells in the S of the Most High,
Wis 10:17 way, and became a S to them by day,

S

Sir 6:14 friend is a sturdy S: he that has found
14:26 his children under her S, and will camp under
29:22 poor man under the S of his roof than
34:16 and strong support, a S from the hot wind
Is 4:6 a refuge and a S from the storm and
25:4 in his distress, a S from the storm and
28:15 falsehood we have taken S;
28:17 refuge of lies, and waters will overwhelm the S
30:2 Pharaoh, and to seek S in the shadow of
30:3 your shame, and the S in the shadow of
Rev 7:15 upon the throne will S them with his presence.

SHELTERED (2)

Sir 2:13 Therefore it will not be S
14:27 boughs he will be S by her from the

SHELUMI-EL (5)

Num 1:6 of Shedeur; from Simeon, S the son of Zurishaddai;
2:12 people of Simeon being S the son of Zurishaddai,
7:36 On the fifth day S the son of Zurishaddai,
7:41 was the offering of S the son of Zurishaddai.
10:19 men of Simeon was S the son of Zurishaddai.

SHEM (19)

Gen 5:32 became the father of S, Ham, and Japheth.
6:10 Noah had three sons, S, Ham, and Japheth.
7:13 Noah and his sons, S and Ham and Japheth,
9:18 from the ark were S, Ham, and Japheth.
9:23 Then S and Japheth took a garment, laid it
9:26 LORD my God be S; and let Canaan be
9:27 in the tents of S; and let Canaan be
10:1 the sons of Noah, S, Ham, and Japheth; sons
10:21 To S also, the father of all the children
10:22 The sons of S: Elam, Asshur, Arpachshad, Lud, and
10:31 are the sons of S, by their families, their
11:10 These are the descendants of S
11:10 When S was a hundred years old, he became
11:11 after the flood; and S lived after the birth
1Chr 1:4 Enoch, Thuselah, Lamech, Noah, S, Ham, and
1:17 The sons of S: Elam, Asshur, Arpachshad, Lud, Aram,
1:24 S, Arpachshad, Shelah;
Sir 49:16 S and Seth were honored among men, and Adam
Lk 3:36 Arphaxad, the son of S, the son of Noah,

SHEMA (6)

Josh 15:26 (that is, Hazor), Amam, S, Moladah,
1Chr 2:43 The sons of Hebron: Korah, Tappuah, Rekem, and S
2:44 S was the father of Raham, the father of
5:8 of Azaz, son of S, son of Joel, who
8:13 towns, and Beriah and S (they were heads of
Neh 8:4 beside him stood Mattithiah, S, Anaiah, Uriah,

SHEMAAH

1Chr 12:3 Joash, both sons of S of Gibe-ah; also Jezi-el

SHEMAIAH (42)

1Kgs 12:22 of God came to S the man of God:
1Chr 3:22 The sons of Shecaniah: S
3:22 And the sons of S: Hattush, Igal, Bariah, Neariah,
4:37 of Shimri, son of S –
5:4 The sons of Joel: S his son, Gog his
9:14 Of the Levites: S the son of Hasshub, son
9:16 Obadiah the son of S, son of Galal, son
15:8 the sons of Eli-zaphan, S the chief, with two
15:11 Levites Uriel, Asaiah, Joel, S, Eliel, and Amminadab,
24:6 And the scribe S the son of Nethanel, a
26:4 And Obed-edom had sons: S the first-born,
26:6 Also to his son S were sons born who
26:7 The sons of S: Othni, Repha-el, Obed, and Elzabad,
2Chr 11:2 the LORD came to S the man of God:
12:5 Then S the prophet came to Rehoboam and to
12:7 the LORD came to S: "They have humbled
12:15 in the chronicles of S the prophet and of
17:8 them the Levites, S, Nethaniah, Zebadiah, Asahel,
29:14 the sons of Jeduthun, S and Uzziel.
31:15 Eden, Miniamin, Jeshua, S, Amariah, and Shecaniah
35:9 Conaniah also, and S and Nethanel his brothers, and
Ezra 8:13 being Eliphelet, Jeuel, and S, and with them sixty
8:16 sent for Eliezer, Ariel, S, Elnathan, Jarib, Elnathan,
10:21 of Harim: Ma-aseiah, Elijah, S, Jehiel, and Uzziah.
10:31 Harim: Eliezer, Isshijah, Malchijah, S, Shime-on,
Neh 3:29 After him S the son of Shecaniah, the keeper
6:10 into the house of S the son of Delaiah,
10:8 Abijah, Mijamin, Ma-aziah, Bilgai, S; these are the
11:15 And of the Levites: S the son of Hasshub,
12:6 Mijamin, Ma-adiah, Bilgah, S, Joiarib, Jedaiah,
12:18 of Bilgah, Shammua; of S, Jehonathan;
12:34 Ezra, Meshullam, Judah, Benjamin, S, and Jeremiah,
12:35 of Jonathan, son of S, son of Mattaniah, son
12:36 Asaph; and his kinsmen, S, Azarel, Milalai, Gilalai,
12:42 trumpets; and Ma-aseiah, S, Eleazar, Uzzi,
Tob 5:13 sons of the great S, when we went together
Jer 26:20 Uriah the son of S from Kiriath-jearim.
29:24 To S of Nehelam you shall say:
29:31 says the LORD concerning S of Nehelam: Because
29:31 Shemaiah of Nehelam: Because S has prophesied to
29:32 Behold, I will punish S of Nehelam and his
36:12 Delaiah the son of S, Elnathan the son of

SHEMARIAH (4)

1Chr 12:5 Gederah, Eluzai, Jerimoth, Bealiah, S, Shephatiah
2Chr 11:19 bore him sons, Jeush, S, and Zaham.
Ezra 10:32 Eliezer, Isshijah, Malchijah, Shemaiah, Shime-on,
10:41 Shashai, Sharai, Azarel, Shelemiah, S,

SHEMEBER

Gen 14:2 Shinab king of Admah, S king of Zeboiim, and

SHEMED

1Chr 8:12 Elpaal: Eber, Misham, and S, who built Ono and

SHEMER (4)

1Kgs 16:24 hill of Samaria from S for two talents of
16:24 after the name of S, the owner of the
1Chr 6:46 of Bani, son of S,
7:34 The sons of S his brother: Rohgah, Jehubbah, and

SHEMIDA (3)

Num 26:32 the Shechemites; and of S, the family of the
Josh 17:2 Shechem, Hepher, and S; these were the male
1Chr 7:19 The sons of S were Ahian, Shechem, Likhi, and

SHEMIDAITES

Num 26:32 the family of the S; and of Hepher, the

SHEMINITH

1Chr 15:21 were to lead with lyres according to the S

SHEMIRAMOTH (4)

1Chr 15:18 second order, Zechariah, Ja-aziel, S, Jehiel, Unni,
15:20 bronze cymbals; Zechariah, Azi-el, S, Jehiel, Unni,
16:5 him were Zechariah, Je-iel, S, Jehiel, Mattithiah, ,
2Chr 17:8 Shemaiah, Nethaniah, Zebadiah, Asahel, S,

SHEMUEL (2)

Num 34:20 the sons of Simeon, S the son of Ammihud.
1Chr 7:2 Jeri-el, Jahmai, Ibsam, and S, heads of their fathers'

SHENAZZAR

1Chr 3:18 his son, Malchiram, Pedaiah, S, Jekamiah, Hoshama,

SHEOL (65)

Gen 37:35 shall go down to S to my son, mourning."
42:38 bring down my gray hairs with sorrow to S
44:29 hairs in sorrow to S
44:31 of your servant our father with sorrow to S
Num 16:30 go down alive into S, then you shall know
16:33 went down alive into S; and the earth closed
Deut 32:22 to the depths of S, devours the earth and
1Sam 2:6 he brings down to S and raises up.
2Sam 22:6 me; the cords of S entangled me, the snares
1Kgs 2:6 head go down to S in peace.
2:9 bring his gray head down with blood to S
Job 7:9 who goes down to S does not come up;
11:8 Deeper than S –what can you know?
14:13 wouldest hide me in S, that thou wouldest conceal
17:13 If I look for S as my house, if
17:16 Will it go down to the bars of S
21:13 prosperity, and in peace they go down to S
24:19 snow waters; so does S those who have sinned.
26:6 S is naked before God, and Abaddon has no
Ps 6:5 remembrance of thee; in S who can give thee
9:17 wicked shall depart to S, all the nations that
16:10 give me up to S, or let thy godly
18:5 me; the cords of S entangled me, the snares
30:3 up my soul from S, restored me to life
31:17 put to shame, let them go dumbfounded to S
49:14 they are appointed for S; Death shall be their
49:14 form shall waste away; S shall be their home.
49:15 from the power of S, for he will receive
55:15 them go down to S alive; let them go
86:13 hast delivered my soul from the depths of S

S

88:3 of troubles, and my life draws near to S
89:48 can deliver his soul from the power of S
116:3 me; the pangs of S laid hold on me;
139:8 make my bed in S, thou art there!
141:7 their bones be strewn at the mouth of S
Prov 1:12 ambush the innocent; like S let us swallow them
5:5 follow the path to S;
7:27 is the way to S, going down to the
9:18 that her guests are in the depths of S
15:11 S and Abaddon lie open before the LORD, how
15:24 that he may avoid S beneath.
23:14 the rod you will save his life from S
27:20 S and Abaddon are never satisfied, and never
30:16 four never say, "Enough": S, the barren womb, the
Eccl 9:10 knowledge or wisdom in S, to which you are
Is 5:14 Therefore S has enlarged its appetite and opened its
7:11 it be deep as S or high as heaven."
14:9 comes up against us.' S beneath is stirred up
14:11 is brought down to S, the sound of your
14:15 are brought down to S, to the depths of
28:15 with death, and with S we have an agreement;
28:18 and your agreement with S will not stand; when
38:10 to the gates of S for the rest of
38:18 For S cannot thank thee, death cannot praise thee;
57:9 your envoys far-off, and sent down even to S
Ezek 31:15 it goes down to S I will make the
31:16 cast it down to S with those who go
31:17 shall go down to S with it, to those
32:21 of the midst of S: 'They have come down,
32:27 who went down to S with their weapons of
Hos 13:14 Shall I ransom them from the power of S
13:14 O S, where is your destruction?
Amos 9:2 "Though they dig into S, from there shall my
Jon 2:2 of the belly of S I cried, and thou
Hab 2:5 is as wide as S; like death he has

SHEPHAM (2)

Num 34:10 boundary from Hazar-enan to S;
34:11 shall go down from S to Riblah on the

SHEPHATIAH (13)

2Sam 3:4 Haggith; and the fifth, S the son of Abital;
1Chr 3:3 was Haggith; the fifth S, by Abital; the sixth
9:8 Meshullam the son of S, son of Reuel, son
12:5 Eluzai, Jerimoth, Bealiah, Shemariah, S the
27:16 officer; for the Simeonites, S the son of Maacah;
2Chr 21:2 Zechariah, Azariah, Michael, and S; all these were
Ezra 2:4 The sons of S, three hundred and seventy-two.
2:57 Giddel, the sons of S, the sons of Hattil,
8:8 Of the sons of S, Zebadiah the son of
Neh 7:9 The sons of S, three hundred and seventy-two.
7:59 Giddel, the sons of S, the sons of Hattil,
11:4 of Amariah, son of S, son of Mahalalel, of
Jer 38:1 Now S the son of Mattan, Gedaliah the son

SHEPHELAH (11)

1Kgs 10:27 cedar as plentiful as the sycamore of the S
1Chr 27:28 sycamore trees in the S was Baal-hanan the
2Chr 1:15 cedar as plentiful as the sycamore of the S
9:27 cedar as plentiful as the sycamore of the S
26:10 herds, both in the S and in the plain,
28:18 the cities in the S and the Negeb of
Jer 17:26 of Benjamin, from the S, from the hill country,
32:44 the cities of the S, and in the cities
33:13 the cities of the S, and in the cities
Obad 1:19 and those of the S the land of the
1Mac 12:38 built Adida in the S; he fortified it and

SHEPHER (2)

Num 33:23 set out from Kehelathah, and encamped at Mount S
33:24 set out from Mount S, and encamped at Haradah.

SHEPHERD (62)

Gen 46:34 of Goshen; for every S is an abomination to
49:24 the name of the S, the Rock of Israel),
Num 27:17 may not be as sheep which have no S
1Sam 17:40 put them in his S's bag or wallet; his
2Sam 5:2 you, 'You shall be S of my people Israel,
7:7 whom I commanded to S my people Israel, saying,
1Kgs 22:17 sheep that have no S; and the LORD said,
1Chr 11:2 you, 'You shall be S of my people Israel,
17:6 whom I commanded to S my people, saying, "Why
2Chr 18:16 sheep that have no S; and the LORD said,
Jud 11:19 sheep that have no S, and not a dog
Ps 23:1 The LORD is my S, I shall not want;
28:9 heritage; be thou their S, and carry them for
49:14 Death shall be their S; straight to the grave
78:71 him to be the S of Jacob his people,
80:1 Give ear, O S of Israel, thou who leadest
Eccl 12:11 the collected sayings which are given by one S
Wis 17:17 a farmer or a S or a workman who
Sir 18:12 them back, as a S his flock.
Is 38:12 from me like a S's tent; like a weaver
40:11 his flock like a S, he will gather the
44:28 Cyrus, 'He is my S, and he shall fulfil
Jer 22:22 The wind shall S all your shepherds, and your
31:10 keep him as a S keeps his flock.'
43:12 of Egypt, as a S cleans his cloak of
49:19 What S can stand before me?
50:44 What S can stand before me?
51:23 break in pieces the S and his flock; with
Ezek 34:5 because there was no S; and they became food
34:8 since there was no S; and because my shepherds
34:12 As a S seeks out his flock when some
34:15 myself will be the S of my sheep, and
34:23 up over them one S, my servant David, and
34:23 them: he shall feed them and be their S
37:24 over them; and they shall all have one S
Amos 3:12 the LORD: "As the S rescues from the mouth
Mic 7:14 S thy people with thy staff, the flock of
Zech 10:2 sheep; they are afflicted for want of a S
11:4 LORD my God: "Become S of the flock doomed
11:6 the hand of his S, and each into the
11:7 So I became the S of the flock doomed
11:9 So I said, "I will not be your S
11:15 "Take once more the implements of a worthless S
11:16 in the land a S who does not care
11:17 Woe to my worthless S, who deserts the flock!
13:7 O sword, against my S, against the man who
13:7 "Strike the S, that the sheep may be scattered;
Mt 9:36 were harassed and helpless, like sheep without a S
25:32 from another as a S separates the sheep from
26:31 'I will strike the S, and the sheep of
Mk 6:34 like sheep without a S; and he began to
14:27 'I will strike the S, and the sheep will
Jn 10:2 the door is the S of the sheep.
10:11 I am the good S
10:11 The good S lays down his life for the
10:12 hireling and not a S, whose own the sheep
10:14 I am the good S; I know my own
10:16 So there shall be one flock, one S
Heb 13:20 Lord Jesus, the great S of the sheep, by
1Pet 2:25 now returned to the S and Guardian of your
5:4 And when the chief S is manifested you will
Rev 7:17 throne will be their S, and he will guide

SHEPHERDING

Gen 37:2 seventeen years old, was S the flock with his

SHEPHERDS (49)

Gen 29:3 were gathered there, the S would roll the stone
46:32 and the men are S, for they have been
47:3 Pharaoh, "Your servants are S, as our fathers were."
Ex 2:17 The S came and drove them away; but Moses
2:19 the hand of the S, and even drew water
Num 14:33 your children shall be S in the wilderness forty
1Sam 25:7 have shearers; now your S have been with us,
2Kgs 10:12 at Beth-eked of the S,
Song 1:8 your kids beside the S tents.
Is 13:20 his tent there, no S will make their flocks
31:4 when a band of S is called forth against
56:11 The S also have no understanding; they have all
63:11 of the sea the S of his flock?
Jer 3:15 I will give you S after my own heart,
6:3 S with their flocks shall come against her; they
10:21 For the S are stupid, and do not inquire
12:10 Many S have destroyed my vineyard, they have
22:22 shall shepherd all your S, and your lovers shall
23:1 "Woe to the S who destroy and scatter the
23:2 of Israel, concerning the S who care for my
23:4 I will set S over them who will care
25:34 "Wail, you S, and cry, and roll in ashes,
25:35 will remain for the S, nor escape for the
25:36 the cry of the S, and the wail of
33:12 again be habitations of S resting their flocks.
50:6 been lost sheep; their S have led them astray,
Ezek 34:2 man, prophesy against the S of Israel, prophesy, and
34:2 them, even to the S, Thus says the Lord
34:2 the Lord GOD: Ho, S of Israel who have
34:2 Should not S feed the sheep?
34:7 "Therefore, you S, hear the word of the LORD:
34:8 shepherd; and because my S have not searched for

S

34:8 my sheep, but the S have fed themselves, and
34:9 my sheep; therefore, you S, hear the word of
34:10 I am against the S; and I will require
34:10 no longer shall the S feed themselves.
Amos 1:1 who was among the S of Tekoa, which he
1:2 the pastures of the S mourn, and the top
Mic 5:5 raise against him seven S and eight princes of
Nah 3:18 Your S are asleep, O king of Assyria; your
Zeph 2:6 be pastures, meadows for S and folds for flocks.
Zech 10:3 is hot against the S, and I will punish
11:3 the wail of the S, for their glory is
11:5 rich'; and their own S have no pity on
11:8 In one month I destroyed the three S
Lk 2:8 that region there were S out in the field,
2:15 them into heaven, the S said to one another,
2:18 wondered at what the S told them.
2:20 And the S returned, glorifying and praising God for

SHEPHI

1Chr 1:40 Shobal: Alian, Manahath, Ebal, S, and Onam.

SHEPHO

Gen 36:23 Shobal: Alvan, Manahath, Ebal, S, and Onam.

SHEPHUPHAM

Num 26:39 of the Ahiramites; of S, the family of the

SHEPHUPHAN

1Chr 8:5 Abishua, Naaman, Ahoah, Gera, S, and Huram.

SHERD

Is 30:14 its fragments not a S is found with which

SHEREBIAH (8)

Ezra 8:18 son of Israel, namely S with his sons and
8:24 of the leading priests: S, Hashabiah, and ten of
Neh 8:7 Also Jeshua, Bani, S, Jamin, Akkub, Shabbethai,
9:4 Bani, Kadmi-el, Shebaniah, Bunni, S, Bani, and
9:5 Jeshua, Kadmi-el, Bani, Hashabneiah, S, Hodiah,
10:12 Mica, Rehob, Hashabiah, Zaccur, S, Shebaniah,
12:8 Levites: Jeshua, Binnui, Kadmi-el, S, Judah, and
12:24 of the Levites: Hashabiah, S, and Jeshua the son

SHERESH

1Chr 7:16 of his brother was S; and his sons were

SHESH-BAZZAR (4)

Ezra 1:8 counted them out to S the prince of Judah.
1:11 All these did S bring up, when the exiles
5:14 one whose name was S, whom he had made
5:16 Then this S came and laid the foundations of

SHESHAI (3)

Num 13:22 to Hebron; and Ahiman, S, and Talmai, the
Josh 15:14 three sons of Anak, S and Ahiman and Talmai,
Judg 1:10 Kiriath-arba); and they defeated S and Ahiman and

SHESHAN (5)

1Chr 2:31 The sons of Ishi: S
2:31 The sons of S: Ahlai.
2:34 Now S had no sons, only daughters; but Sheshan
2:34 sons, only daughters; but S had an Egyptian slave,
2:35 So S gave his daughter in marriage to Jarha

SHETH

Num 24:17 Moab, and break down all the sons of S

SHETHAR

Esth 1:14 to him being Carshena, S, Admatha, Tarshish, Meres,

SHETHAR-BOZENAI (4)

Ezra 5:3 Beyond the River and S and their associates came
5:6 Beyond the River and S and his associates the
6:6 province Beyond the River, S, and your associates the
6:13 province Beyond the River, S, and their associates

SHEVA (2)

2Sam 20:25 was the recorder; and S was secretary; and Zadok
1Chr 2:49 the father of Madmannah, S the father of

SHIBAH

Gen 26:33 He called it S; therefore the name of the

SHIBBOLETH

Judg 12:6 they said to him, "Then say S

SHIELD (63)

Gen 15:1 Abram, I am your S; your reward shall be
Deut 33:29 by the LORD, the S of your help, and
Judg 5:8 Was S or spear to be seen among forty
2Sam 1:21 For there the S of the mighty was defiled,
1:21 mighty was defiled, the S of Saul, not anointed
22:3 I take refuge, my S and the horn of
22:31 true; he is a S for all those who
22:36 hast given me the S of thy salvation, and
1Kgs 10:16 six hundred shekels of gold went into each S
10:17 gold went into each S; and the king put
2Kgs 19:32 before it with a S or cast up a
1Chr 5:18 valiant men, who carried S and sword, and drew
12:8 warriors, expert with S and spear, whose faces
12:24 men of Judah bearing S and spear were six
12:34 thousand men armed with S and spear.
2Chr 9:15 hundred shekels of beaten gold went into each S
9:16 gold went into each S; and the king put
17:17 armed with bow and S,
25:5 fit for war, able to handle spear and S
Jud 9:7 soldiers; they trust in S and spear, in bow
Job 15:26 him with a thick-bossed S;
Ps 3:3 O LORD, art a S about me, my glory,
5:12 dost cover him with favor as with a S
7:10 My S is with God, who saves the upright
18:2 I take refuge, my S, and the horn of
18:30 true; he is a S for all those who
18:35 hast given me the S of thy salvation, and
28:7 my strength and my S; in him my heart
33:20 for the LORD; he is our help and S
35:2 Take hold of S and buckler, and rise for
59:11 power, and bring them down, O Lord, our S
76:3 the flashing arrows, the S, the sword, and the
84:9 [Selah] Behold our S, O God; look upon the
84:11 is a sun and S; he bestows favor and
89:18 For our S belongs to the LORD, our king
91:4 his faithfulness is a S and buckler.
115:9 He is their help and their S
115:10 He is their help and their S
115:11 He is their help and their S
119:114 hiding place and my S; I hope in thy
144:2 and my deliverer, my S and he in whom
Prov 2:7 upright; he is a S to those who walk
30:5 true; he is a S to those who take
Wis 5:16 his arm he will S them.
5:19 holiness as an invincible S,
18:21 he brought forward the S of his ministry, prayer
Sir 29:13 more than a mighty S and more than a
37:5 in the face of battle take up the S
Is 21:5 Arise, O princes, oil the S
22:6 with chariots and horsemen, and Kir uncovered the S
37:33 before it with a S, or cast up a
Jer 46:3 Judah: "Prepare buckler and S, and advance for
46:9 Put who handle the S, men of Lud, skilled
Ezek 23:24 every side with buckler, S, and helmet, and I
27:10 war; they hung the S and helmet in you;
38:4 them with buckler and S, wielding swords;
38:5 all of them with S and helmet;
Nah 2:3 ruined their branches.) The S of his mighty men
Zech 12:8 LORD will put a S about the inhabitants of
1Mac 14:24 with a large gold S weighing a thousand minas,
15:18 have brought a gold S weighing a thousand minas.
15:20 us to accept the S from them.
Eph 6:16 all these, taking the S of faith, with which

SHIELD-BEARER (2)

1Sam 17:7 of iron; and his S went before him.
17:41 to David, with his S in front of him.

SHIELDS (31)

2Sam 8:7 And David took the S of gold which were
1Kgs 10:16 made two hundred large S of beaten gold; six
10:17 he made three hundred S of beaten gold; three
14:26 took away all the S of gold which Solomon
14:27 made in their stead S of bronze, and committed
2Kgs 11:10 captains the spears and S that had been King
1Chr 18:7 And David took the S of gold which were
2Chr 9:15 made two hundred large S of beaten gold; six
9:16 he made three hundred S of beaten gold; three
11:12 And he put S and spears in all the
12:9 also took away the S of gold which Solomon
12:10 made in their stead S of bronze, and committed
14:8 from Benjamin, that carried S and drew bows; all
23:9 the large and small S that had been King
26:14 for all the army S, spears, helmets, coats of
32:5 also made weapons and S in abundance.

S

32:27 stones, for spices, for S, and for all kinds
Neh 4:16 half held the spears, S, bows, and coats of
Job 41:15 made of rows of S, shut up closely as
Ps 47:9 For the S of the earth belong to God;
Song 4:4 bucklers, all of them S of warriors.
Jer 51:11 Take up the S
Ezek 26:8 raise a roof of S against you.
27:11 towers; they hung their S upon your walls round
32:27 their heads, and whose S are upon their bones;
39:9 weapons and burn them, S and bucklers, bows and
1Mac 4:57 golden crowns and small S; they restored the gates
6:2 rich, containing golden S, breastplates, and weapons
6:39 sun shone upon the S of gold and brass,
2Mac 5:3 on that, brandishing of S, massing of spears, hurling
15:11 much with confidence in S and spears as with

SHIFTED

2Mac 4:10 office, he at once S his countrymen over to

SHIFTING

Col 1:23 stable and steadfast, not S from the hope of

SHIFTLESSNESS (2)

Tob 4:13 great confusion; and in S there is loss and
4:13 and great want, because S is the mother of

SHIGIONOTH

Hab 3:1 A prayer of Habakkuk the prophet, according to S

SHIHOR (3)

Josh 13:3 the Geshurites (from the S, which is east of
1Chr 13:5 all Israel from the S of Egypt to the
Is 23:3 was the grain of S, the harvest of the

SHIHOR-LIBNATH

Josh 19:26 it touches Carmel and S,

SHIKKERON

Josh 15:11 boundary bends round to S, and passes along to

SHILHI (2)

1Kgs 22:42 His mother's name was Azubah the daughter of S
2Chr 20:31 His mother's name was Azubah the daughter of S

SHILHIM

Josh 15:32 Ziklag, Madmannah, Sansannah, Lebaoth, S, Ain,

SHILLEM (2)

Gen 46:24 Jahzeel, Guni, Jezer, and S
Num 26:49 of the Jezerites; of S, the family of the

SHILLEMITES

Num 26:49 the Jezerites; of Shillem, the family of the S

SHILOAH

Is 8:6 refused the waters of S that flow gently, and

SHILOH (32)

Josh 18:1 of Israel assembled at S, and set up the
18:8 lots for you here before the LORD in S
18:9 in the camp at S,
18:10 lots for them in S before the LORD; and
19:51 distributed by lot at S before the LORD, at
21:2 said to them at S in the land of
22:9 people of Israel at S, which is in the
22:12 of Israel gathered at S, to make war against
Judg 18:31 long as the house of God was at S
21:12 to the camp at S, which is in the
21:19 of the LORD at S, which is north of
21:21 if the daughters of S come out to dance
21:21 from the daughters of S, and go to the
1Sam 1:3 LORD of hosts at S, where the two sons
1:9 eaten and drunk in S, Hannah rose.
1:24 of the LORD at S; and the child was
2:14 So they did at S to all the Israelites
3:21 LORD appeared again at S, for the LORD revealed
3:21 himself to Samuel at S by the word of
4:3 the LORD here from S, that he may come
4:4 the people sent to S, and brought from there
4:12 line, and came to S the same day, with
14:3 of the LORD in S, wearing an ephod.
1Kgs 2:27 had spoken concerning the house of Eli in S
14:2 Jeroboam, and go to S; behold, Ahijah the prophet
14:4 arose, and went to S, and came to the
Ps 78:60 forsook his dwelling at S, the tent where he
Jer 7:12 place that was in S, where I made my
7:14 and to your fathers, as I did to S
26:6 make this house like S, and I will make
26:9 house shall be like S, and this city shall
41:5 arrived from Shechem and S and Samaria, with

SHILONITE (6)

1Kgs 11:29 the prophet Ahijah the S found him on the
12:15 spoke by Ahijah the S to Jeroboam the son
15:29 his servant Ahijah the S;
2Chr 9:29 prophecy of Ahijah the S, and in the visions
10:15 spoke by Ahijah the S to Jeroboam the son
Neh 11:5 of Joiarib, son of Zechariah, son of the S

SHILONITES

1Chr 9:5 And of the S: Asaiah the first-born, and his

SHILSHAH

1Chr 7:37 Imrah, Bezer, Hod, Shamma, S, Ithran, and Be-era.

SHIME-ON

Ezra 10:31 Eliezer, Isshijah, Malchijah, Shemaiah, S,

SHIMEA (5)

1Chr 2:13 first-born, Abinadab the second, S the third,
3:5 him in Jerusalem: S, Shobab, Nathan and Solomon,
6:30 son, Uzzah his son, S his son, Haggiah his
6:39 of Berechiah, son of S,
20:7 Jonathan the son of S, David's brother, slew him.

SHIMEAH (3)

2Sam 13:3 Jonadab, the son of S, David's brother; and Jonadab
13:32 Jonadab the son of S, David's brother, said, "Let
1Chr 8:32 Zecher, and Mikloth (he was the father of S

SHIMEAM

1Chr 9:38 was the father of S; and these also dwelt

SHIMEATH (2)

2Kgs 12:21 Jozacar the son of S and Jehozabad the son
2Chr 24:26 Zabad the son of S the Ammonitess, and Jehozabad

SHIMEATHITES

1Chr 2:55 Jabez: the Tirathites, the S, and the Sucathites.

SHIMEI (46)

Ex 6:17 of Gershon: Libni and S, by their families.
Num 3:18 sons of Gershon by their families: Libni and S
2Sam 16:5 Saul, whose name was S, the son of Gera;
16:7 And S said as he cursed, "Begone, begone, you
16:13 on the road, while S went along on the
19:16 And S the son of Gera, the Benjaminite, from
19:18 And S the son of Gera fell down before
19:21 Zeruiah answered, "Shall not S be put to death
19:23 the king said to S, "You shall not die."
21:21 Jonathan the son of S, David's brother, slew him.
1Kgs 1:8 Nathan the prophet, and S, and Rei, and David's
2:8 is also with you S the son of Gera,
2:36 king sent and summoned S, and said to him,
2:38 And S said to the king, "What you say
2:38 So S dwelt in Jerusalem many days.
2:39 years that two of S's slaves ran away to
2:39 when it was told S, "Behold, your slaves are
2:40 S arose and saddled an ass, and went to
2:40 to seek his slaves; S went and brought his
2:41 Solomon was told that S had gone from Jerusalem
2:42 king sent and summoned S, and said to him,
2:44 king also said to S, "You know in your
4:18 of Paruah, in Issachar; S the son of Ela,
1Chr 3:19 of Pedaiah: Zerubbabel and S; and the sons of
4:26 son, Zaccur his son, S his son.
4:27 S had sixteen sons and six daughters; but his
5:4 son, Gog his son, S his son,
6:17 names of the sons of Gershom: Libni and S
6:29 Mahli, Libni his son, S his son, Uzzah his
6:42 of Zimmah, son of S,
8:21 Adaiah, Beraiah, and Shimrath were the sons of S
23:7 The sons of Gershom were Ladan and S
23:9 The sons of S: Shelomoth, Hazi-el, and Haran, three.
23:10 And the sons of S: Jahath, Zina, and Jeush,
23:10 These four were the sons of S
25:3 Zeri, Jeshaiah, S, Hashabiah, and Mattithiah, six,
25:17 twelve; the tenth to S, his sons and his
27:27 over the vineyards was S the Ramathite; and over
2Chr 29:14 of Heman, Jehuel and S; and of the sons
31:12 Conaniah the Levite, with S his brother as second;
31:13 overseers assisting Conaniah and S his brother, by

S

Ezra	10:23	Of the Levites: Jozabad, S, Kelaiah (that is, Kelita),
	10:33	Jeremai, Manasseh, and S. Of the sons of Bani:
	10:38	the sons of Binnui: S,
Esth	2:5	of Jair, son of S, son of Kish, a
	11:2	of Jair, son of S, son of Kish, of

SHIMEITES (2)

Num	3:21	the family of the S; these were the families
Zech	12:13	the family of the S by itself, and their

SHIMON

1Chr	4:20	The sons of S: Amnon, Rinnah, Ben-hanan, and Tilon.

SHIMRATH

1Chr	8:21	Eliel, Adaiah, Beraiah, and S were the sons of

SHIMRI (4)

1Chr	4:37	of Jedaiah, son of S, son of Shemaiah--
	11:45	Jedia-el the son of S, and Joha his brother,
	26:10	of Merari, had sons: S the chief (for though
2Chr	29:13	the sons of Eli-zaphan, S and Jeuel; and of

SHIMRITH

2Chr	24:26	Jehozabad the son of S the Moabitess.

SHIMRON (5)

Gen	46:13	The sons of Issachar: Tola, Puvah, Iob, and S
Num	26:24	of the Jashubites; of S, the family of the
Josh	11:1	to the king of S, and to the king
	19:15	Kattath, Nahalal, S, Idalah, and Bethlehem--twelve
1Chr	7:1	Tola, Puah, Jashub, and S, four.

SHIMRON-MERON

Josh	12:20	one; the king of S, one; the king of

SHIMRONITES

Num	26:24	the Jashubites; of Shimron, the family of the S

SHIMSHAI (4)

Ezra	4:8	Rehum the commander and S the scribe wrote a
	4:9	wrote Rehum the commander, S the scribe, and the
	4:17	Rehum the commander and S the scribe and the
	4:23	read before Rehum and S the scribe and their

SHINAB

Gen	14:2	Birsha king of Gomorrah, S king of Admah,

SHINAR (8)

Gen	10:10	Accad, all of them in the land of S
	11:2	in the land of S and settled there.
	14:1	of Amraphel king of S, Arioch king of Ellasar,
	14:9	Goiim, Amraphel king of S, and Arioch king of
Josh	7:21	a beautiful mantle from S, and two hundred shekels
Is	11:11	Ethiopia, from Elam, from S, from Hamath, and
Dan	1:2	to the land of S, to the house of
Zech	5:11	"To the land of S, to build a house

SHINE (32)

Num	6:25	make his face to S upon you, and be
Job	3:4	seek it, nor light S upon it.
	18:5	and the flame of his fire does not S
	22:28	you, and light will S on your ways.
	37:15	and causes the lightning of his cloud to S
Ps	31:16	Let thy face S on thy servant; save me
	67:1	make his face to S upon us, [Selah]
	80:1	enthroned upon the cherubim, S forth
	80:3	God; let thy face S, that we may be
	80:7	hosts; let thy face S, that we may be
	80:19	let thy face S, that we may be saved!
	94:1	thou God of vengeance, S forth!
	104:15	to make his face S, and bread to strengthen
	119:135	Make thy face S upon thy servant, and teach
Eccl	8:1	wisdom makes his face S, and the hardness of
Wis	3:7	their visitation they will S forth, and will run
	5:6	of righteousness did not S on us, and the
Sir	24:25	It makes instruction S forth like light, like the
	24:30	will again make instruction S forth like the dawn,
	24:30	I will make it S afar;
Is	60:1	Arise, S; for your light has come, and the
Bar	6:24	beauty--they will not S unless some one wipes
	6:67	among the nations, or S like the sun or
Dan	9:17	cause thy face to S upon thy sanctuary, which
	12:3	who are wise shall S like the brightness of
Zech	9:16	a crown they shall S on his land.
Mt	5:16	Let your light so S before men, that they
	13:43	Then the righteous will S like the sun in
2Cor	4:6	who said, "Let light S out of darkness," who
Phil	2:15	generation, among whom you S as lights in the
Rev	18:23	of a lamp shall S in thee no more;
	21:23	sun or moon to S upon it, for the

SHINED

Is	9:2	land of deep darkness, on them has light S

SHINES (4)

Ps	50:2	perfection of beauty, God S forth.
Prov	4:19	light of dawn, which S brighter and brighter until
Mt	24:27	from the east and S as far as the
Jn	1:5	The light S in the darkness, and the darkness

SHINING (19)

2Sam	23:4	light, like the sun S forth upon a cloudless
Job	41:32	him he leaves a S wake; one would think
Ps	148:3	praise him, all you S stars!
Wis	17:6	Nothing was S through to them except a dreadful,
Sir	26:17	Like the S lamp on the holy lampstand, so
	43:8	the hosts on high S forth in the firmament
	50:7	full; like the sun S upon the temple of
Is	4:5	and smoke and the S of a flaming fire
Bar	4:2	her; walk toward the S of her light.
	6:60	and moon and stars, S and sent forth for
Ezek	1:22	likeness of a firmament, S like crystal, spread out
Joel	2:10	moon are darkened, and the stars withdraw their S
	3:15	moon are darkened, and the stars withdraw their S
Jn	5:34	was a burning and S lamp, and you were
Acts	26:13	brighter than the sun, S round me and those
2Pet	1:19	as to a lamp S in a dark place,
1Jn	2:8	passing away and the true light is already S
Rev	1:16	was like the sun S in full strength.
	8:12	day was kept from S, and likewise a third

SHION

Josh	19:19	Jezreel, Chesulloth, Shunem, Haphara-im, S,

SHIP (31)

Prov	30:19	the way of a S on the high seas,
Wis	5:10	passes by; like a S that sails through the
	14:1	more fragile than the S which carries him.
Is	33:21	can go, nor stately S can pass.
Jon	1:3	Joppa and found a S going to Tarshish; so
	1:4	sea, so that the S threatened to break up.
	1:5	that were in the S into the sea, to
	1:5	inner part of the S and had lain down,
	1:13	hard to bring the S back to land, but
1Mac	15:37	Trypho embarked on a S and escaped to Orthosia.
Acts	20:13	going ahead to the S, we set sail for
	20:38	And they brought him to the S
	21:2	And having found a S crossing to Phoenicia, we
	21:3	Tyre; for there the S was to unload its
	21:6	went on board the S, and they returned home.
	27:2	And embarking in a S of Adramyttium, which was
	27:6	the centurion found a S of Alexandria sailing for
	27:10	the cargo and the S, but also of our
	27:11	the owner of the S than to what Paul
	27:15	land; and when the S was caught and could
	27:17	measures to undergird the S; then, fearing that they
	27:19	with their own hands the tackle of the S
	27:22	of life among you, but only of the S
	27:30	to escape from the S, and had lowered the
	27:31	men stay in the S, you cannot be saved."
	27:37	seventy-six persons in the S
	27:38	enough, they lightened the S, throwing out the wheat
	27:39	possible to bring the S ashore.
	27:44	rest on planks or on pieces of the S
	28:11	set sail in a S which had wintered in
	28:11	in the island, a S of Alexandria, with the

SHIPHI

1Chr	4:37	Ziza the son of S, son of Allon, son

SHIPHMITE

1Chr	27:27	vineyards for the wine cellars was Zabdi the S

SHIPHRAH

Ex	1:14	of whom was named S and the other Puah,

SHIPHTAN

Num	34:24	of Ephraim a leader, Kemuel the son of S

SHIPMASTERS

Rev	18:17	And all S and seafaring men, sailors and all

SHIPS (37)
Gen 49:13 become a haven for S, and his border shall
Num 24:24 But S shall come from Kittim and shall afflict
Deut 28:68 bring you back in S to Egypt, a journey
Judg 5:17 and Dan, why did he abide with the S
1Kgs 9:26 built a fleet of S at Ezion-geber, which is
10:22 had a fleet of S of Tarshish at sea
10:22 years the fleet of S of Tarshish used to
22:48 Jehoshaphat made S of Tarshish to go to Ophir
22:48 not go, for the S were wrecked at Ezion-geber.
22:49 my servants go with your servants in the S
2Chr 8:18 him by his servants S and servants familiar with
9:21 For the king's S went to Tarshish with the
9:21 every three years the S of Tarshish used to
20:36 joined him in building S to go to Tarshish,
20:36 and they built the S in Ezion-geber.
20:37 And the S were wrecked and were not able
Ps 48:7 thou didst shatter the S of Tarshish.
104:26 There go the S, and Leviathan which thou didst
107:23 to the sea in S, doing business on the
Prov 31:14 She is like the S of the merchant, she
Is 2:16 wall; against all the S of Tarshish, and against
23:1 Wail, O S of Tarshish, for Tyre is laid
23:14 Wail, O S of Tarshish, for your stronghold is
60:9 wait for me, the S of Tarshish first, to
Ezek 27:9 your seams; all the S of the sea with
27:25 The S of Tarshish traveled for you with your
27:29 and down from their S come all that handle
Dan 11:30 For S of Kittim shall come against him, and
11:40 horsemen, and with many S; and he shall come
1Mac 8:26 grain, arms, money, or S, as Rome has decided;
8:28 grain, arms, money, or S, as Rome has decided;
11:1 the seashore, and many S; and he tried to
13:29 suits of armor carved S, so that they could
15:14 the city, and the S joined battle from the
Jas 3:4 Look at the S also; though they are so
Rev 8:9 a third of the S were destroyed.
18:19 where all who had S at sea grew rich

SHIPWRECK
1Tim 1:19 certain persons have made S of their faith,

SHIPWRECKED
2Cor 11:25 times I have been S; a night and a

SHIRT
Lk 6:29 away your coat do not withhold even your S

SHISHA
1Kgs 4:3 Ahijah the sons of S were secretaries; Jehoshaphat

SHISHAK (7)
1Kgs 11:40 fled into Egypt, to S king of Egypt, and
14:25 year of King Rehoboam, S king of Egypt came
2Chr 12:2 unfaithful to the LORD, S king of Egypt came
12:5 at Jerusalem because of S, and said to them,
12:5 I have abandoned you to the hand of S
12:7 poured out upon Jerusalem by the hand of S
12:9 So S king of Egypt came up against Jerusalem;

SHITRAI
1Chr 27:29 pastured in Sharon was S the Sharonite; over the

SHITTIM (6)
Num 25:1 While Israel dwelt in S the people began to
Josh 2:1 two men secretly from S as spies, saying, "Go,
3:1 and set out from S, with all the people
Hos 5:2 deep the pit of S; but I will chastise
Joel 3:18 of the LORD and water the valley of S
Mic 6:5 and what happened from S to Gilgal, that you

SHIZA
1Chr 11:42 Adina the son of S the Reubenite, a leader

SHOA
Ezek 23:23 the Chaldeans, Pekod and S and Koa, and all

SHOAL (2)
Lk 5:6 they enclosed a great S of fish; and as
Acts 27:41 But striking a S they ran the vessel aground;

SHOBAB (4)
2Sam 5:14 him in Jerusalem: Shammua, S, Nathan, Solomon,
1Chr 2:18 were her sons: Jesher, S, and Ardon.
3:5 him in Jerusalem: Shimea, S, Nathan and Solomon,
14:4 had in Jerusalem: Shammua, S, Nathan, Solomon,

SHOBACH (2)
2Sam 10:16 came to Helam, with S the commander of the
10:18 thousand horsemen, and wounded S the commander

SHOBAI (2)
Ezra 2:42 and the sons of S, in all one hundred
Neh 7:45 Hatita, the sons of S, a hundred and thirty-eight.

SHOBAL (9)
Gen 36:20 of the land: Lotan, S, Zibeon, Anah,
36:23 are the sons of S: Alvan, Manahath, Ebal, Shepho,
36:29 Horites: the chiefs Lotan, S, Zibeon, Anah,
1Chr 1:38 sons of Seir: Lotan, S, Zibeon, Anah, Dishon, Ezer,
1:40 The sons of S: Alian, Manahath, Ebal, Shephi, and
2:50 first-born of Ephrathah: S the father of
2:52 S the father of Kiriath-jearim had other sons:
4:1 sons of Judah: Perez, Hezron, Carmi, Hur, and S
4:2 Re-aiah the son of S was the father of

SHOBEK
Neh 10:24 Hananiah, Hasshub, Hallohesh, Pilha, S,

SHOBI
2Sam 17:27 David came to Mahanaim, S the son of Nahash

SHOCK (2)
Job 5:26 old age, as a S of grain comes up
Ezek 26:9 He will direct the S of his battering-rams against

SHOCKED (2)
Jer 2:12 heavens, at this, be S, be utterly desolate, says
1Mac 16:22 this, he was greatly S; and he seized the

SHOCKS
Judg 15:5 and burned up the S and the standing grain,

SHOD (2)
Ezek 16:10 with embroidered cloth and S you with leather, I
Eph 6:15 of righteousness, and having S your feet with the

SHOE (2)
Ps 60:8 Edom I cast my S; over Philistia I shout
108:9 Edom I cast my S; over Philistia I shout

SHOES (10)
Ex 3:5 near; put off your S from your feet, for
Josh 5:15 Joshua, "Put off your S from your feet; for
9:13 and these garments and S of ours are worn-out
Sir 46:19 property, not so much as a pair of S
Is 20:2 and take off your S from your feet," and
Ezek 24:17 turban, and put your S on your feet; do
24:23 your heads and your S on your feet; you
Amos 2:6 for a pair of S –
Lk 15:22 on his hand, and S on his feet;
Acts 7:33 him, 'Take off the S from your feet, for

SHOHAM
1Chr 24:27 Merari: of Ja-aziah, Beno, S, Zaccur, and Ibri.

SHOMER (2)
2Kgs 12:21 Jehozabad the son of S, his servants, who struck
1Chr 7:32 the father of Japhlet, S, Hotham, and their sister

SHONE (18)
Ex 34:29 skin of his face S because he had been
34:30 skin of his face S, and they were afraid
34:35 skin of Moses' face S; and Moses would put
Deut 33:2 Seir upon us; he S forth from Mount Paran,
2Kgs 3:22 morning, and the sun S upon the water, the
Job 29:3 me; when his lamp S upon my head, and
31:26 the sun when it S, or the moon moving
Bar 3:34 in fear; the stars S in their watches, and
3:34 They S with gladness for him who made them.
Ezek 43:2 waters; and the earth S with his glory.
1Mac 6:39 When the sun S upon the shields of gold
2Mac 1:22 had been clouded over, S out, a great fire
1:32 light from the altar S back, it went out.
Mt 17:2 them, and his face S like the sun, and
Lk 2:9 glory of the Lord S around them, and they
Acts 12:7 appeared, and a light S in the cell; and
22:6 light from heaven suddenly S about me.
2Cor 4:6 who has S in our hearts to give the

SHOOK (12)
Neh 5:13 I also S out my lap and said, "So
Ps 77:18 lighted up the world; the earth trembled and S

Is	6:4	foundations of the thresholds S at the voice of
	7:2	heart of his people S as the trees of
	14:16	the earth tremble, who S kingdoms,
Hab	3:6	earth; he looked and S the nations; then the
1Mac	1:28	Even the land S for its inhabitants, and all
Mt	27:51	bottom; and the earth S, and the rocks were
Acts	13:51	But they S off the dust from their feet
	18:6	and reviled him, he S out his garments and
	28:5	He, however, S off the creature into the fire
Heb	12:26	His voice then S the earth; but now he

SHOOT (18)

1Sam	20:20	And I will S three arrows to the side
	20:36	lad, "Run and find the arrows which I S
2Sam	11:20	know that they would S from the wall?
2Kgs	9:27	pursued him, and said, S him also"; and they
	13:17	Then Elisha said, S; and he shot.
	19:32	into this city or S an arrow there, or
1Chr	12:2	were bowmen, and could S arrows and sling stones
2Chr	26:15	and the corners, to S arrows and great stones.
Ps	11:2	to the string, to S in the dark at
	64:7	But God will S his arrow at them; they
Sir	50:8	water, like a green S on Lebanon on a
Is	11:1	shall come forth a S from the stump of
	37:33	into this city, or S an arrow there, or
	60:21	land for ever, the S of my planting, the
Jer	50:14	that bend the bow; S at her, spare no
Ezek	36:8	mountains of Israel, shall S forth your branches, and
1Mac	6:51	and stones, machines to S arrows, and catapults.
Rom	11:17	you, a wild olive S, were grafted in their

SHOOTING (3)

Ps	64:4	bitter words like arrows, S from ambush at the
	64:4	ambush at the blameless, S at him suddenly and
Amos	7:1	the beginning of the S up of the latter

SHOOTS (13)

Job	8:16	the sun, and his S spread over his garden.
	14:7	again, and that its S will not cease.
	15:30	will dry up his S, and his blossom will
Ps	80:11	the sea, and its S to the River.
	128:3	will be like olive S around your table.
Song	4:13	Your S are an orchard of pomegranates with all
Sir	40:22	beauty, but the green S of grain more than
Is	16:8	to the desert; its S spread abroad and passed
	18:5	will cut off the S with pruning hooks, and
	27:6	blossom and put forth S, and fill the whole
	61:11	earth brings forth its S, and as a garden
Ezek	31:5	its branches long, from abundant water in its S
Hos	14:6	as the poplar; his S shall spread out; his

SHOPHACH (2)

1Chr	19:16	beyond the Euphrates, with S the commander of the
	19:18	soldiers, and killed also S the commander of their

SHORE (6)

Gen	49:13	shall dwell at the S of the sea; he
1Kgs	9:26	near Eloth on the S of the Red Sea,
2Chr	8:17	and Eloth on the S of the sea, in
Ezek	27:29	sea stand on the S
Dan	3:36	the sand on the S of the sea.
Mk	6:53	to land at Gennesaret, and moored to the S

SHORN (5)

2Kgs	19:26	ruins, while their inhabitants, S of strength, are
Song	4:2	like a flock of S ewes that have come
Is	15:2	baldness, every beard is S;
	37:27	ruins, while their inhabitants, S of strength, are
1Cor	11:6	a woman to be S or shaven, let her

SHORT (19)

Gen	44:4	had gone but a S distance from the city,
Lev	22:23	too long or too S you may present for
2Kgs	5:19	gone from him a S distance,
Job	20:5	of the wicked is S, and the joy of
Ps	89:45	Thou hast cut S the days of his youth;
Prov	10:27	but the years of the wicked will be S
Wis	2:1	unsoundly, saying to themselves, S and sorrowful is
	4:13	Being perfected in a S time, he fulfilled long
	15:8	made of earth a S time before and after
	16:3	after suffering want a S time, might partake of
Is	28:20	the bed is too S to stretch oneself on
2Mac	2:32	the preface while cutting S the history itself.
Acts	26:28	to Paul, "In a S time you think to
	26:29	And Paul said, "Whether S or long, I would
Rom	3:23	have sinned and fall S of the glory of
1Cor	7:29	time has grown very S; from now on, let
1Thes	2:17	you, brethren, for a S time, in person not
Heb	12:10	disciplined us for a S time at their pleasure,
Rev	12:12	wrath, because he knows that his time is S

SHORT-LIVED

Wis	9:5	who is weak and S, with little understanding of

SHORTEN

Sir	30:24	Jealousy and anger S life, and anxiety brings on

SHORTENED (9)

Num	11:23	LORD said to Moses, "Is the LORD's hand S
Job	18:7	His strong steps are S and his own schemes
Ps	102:23	in mid-course; he has S my days.
Is	50:2	Is my hand S, that it cannot redeem?
	59:1	LORD's hand is not S, that it cannot save,
Mt	24:22	days had not been S, no human being would
	24:22	sake of the elect those days will be S
Mk	13:20	the Lord had not S the days, no human
	13:20	whom he chose, he S the days.

SHORTLY (5)

Gen	41:32	God, and God will S bring it to pass.
Wis	14:20	worship the one whom S before they had honored
Jer	27:16	LORD's house will now S be brought back from
Acts	25:4	and that he himself intended to go there S
Phil	2:24	in the Lord that S I myself shall come

SHORTSIGHTED

2Pet	1:9	things is blind and S and has forgotten that

SHOT (14)

Gen	40:10	it budded, its blossoms S forth, and the clusters
	49:23	archers fiercely attacked him, S at him, and harassed
Ex	19:13	shall be stoned or S; whether beast or man,
1Sam	20:20	it, as though I S at a mark.
	20:36	the lad ran, he S an arrow beyond him.
	20:37	arrow which Jonathan had S, Jonathan called after
2Sam	11:24	Then the archers S at your servants from the
2Kgs	9:24	his full strength, and S Joram between the shoulders,
	9:27	him also"; and they S him in the chariot
	13:17	Then Elisha said, "Shoot"; and he S
2Chr	35:23	And the archers S King Josiah; and the king
Wis	5:12	when an arrow is S at a target, the
Ezek	17:7	roots toward him, and S forth its branches toward
1Mac	10:80	surrounded his army and S arrows at his men

SHOULDER (38)

Gen	21:14	putting it on her S, along with the child,
	24:15	came out with her water jar upon her S
	24:45	water jar on her S; and she went down
	24:46	her jar from her S, and said, 'Drink, and
	49:15	so he bowed his S to bear, and became
Num	6:19	priest shall take the S of the ram, when
	7:9	things which had to be carried on the S
	34:11	and reach to the S of the sea of
Deut	18:3	to the priest the S and the two cheeks
Josh	4:5	a stone upon his S, according to the number
	15:8	Hinnom at the southern S of the Jebusite (that
	15:10	along to the northern S of Mount Jearim (that
	15:11	goes out to the S of the hill north
	18:12	goes up to the S north of Jericho, then
	18:13	of Luz, to the S of Luz (the same
	18:16	Hinnom, south of the S of the Jebusites, and
	18:18	the north of the S of Beth-arabah it goes
	18:19	the north of the S of Beth-hoglah; and the
Judg	9:48	took it up and laid it on his S
Neh	9:29	and turned a stubborn S and stiffened their neck
Job	31:22	gate; then let my S blade fall from my
	31:22	blade fall from my S, and let my arm
	31:36	carry it on my S; I would bind it
Ps	81:6	known: "I relieved your S of the burden; your
Sir	6:25	Put your S under her and carry her, and
Is	9:4	the staff for his S, the rod of his
	9:6	will be upon his S, and his name will
	10:27	will depart from your S, and his yoke will
	11:14	swoop down upon the S of the Philistines in
	14:25	depart from them, and his burden from their S
	22:22	will place on his S the key of the
Ezek	12:6	the baggage upon your S, and carry it out
	12:7	my outfit upon my S in their sight.
	12:12	his baggage upon his S in the dark, and
	24:4	the thigh and the S; fill it with choice
	29:18	made bald and every S was rubbed bare; yet
	34:21	push with side and S, and thrust at all

S

Zech 7:11 and turned a stubborn S, and stopped their ears

SHOULDER-PIECES (8)

Ex 28:7 It shall have two S attached to its two
28:12 two stones upon the S of the ephod, as
28:25 in front to the S of the ephod.
28:27 part of the two S of the ephod, at
39:4 made for the ephod S, joined to it at
39:7 set them on the S of the ephod, to
39:18 in front to the S of the ephod.
39:20 part of the two S of the ephod, at

SHOULDERS (21)

Gen 9:23 it upon both their S, and walked backward and
Ex 12:34 being bound up in their mantles on their S
28:12 LORD upon his two S for remembrance.
Deut 33:12 day long, and makes his dwelling between his S
Judg 16:3 put them on his S and carried them to
1Sam 9:2 than he; from his S upward he was taller
10:23 the people from his S upward.
17:6 and a javelin of bronze slung between his S
2Kgs 6:31 Shaphat remains on his S today."
9:24 shot Joram between the S, so that the arrow
1Chr 15:15 of God upon their S with the poles, as
2Chr 35:3 you need no longer carry it upon your S
Sir 7:31 the gift of the S, the sacrifice of sanctification,
Is 46:7 lift it upon their S, they carry it, they
49:22 and your daughters shall be carried on their S
Bar 2:21 the Lord: Bend your S and serve the king
6:4 are carried on men's S and inspire fear in
6:26 are carried on men's S, revealing to mankind their
Ezek 29:7 and tore all their S; and when they leaned
Mt 23:4 lay them on men's S; but they themselves will
Lk 15:5 lays it on his S, rejoicing.

SHOULDST (8)

Num 11:12 them forth, that thou S say to me, 'Carry
Ps 44:19 thy way, that thou S have broken us in
130:3 If thou, O LORD, S mark iniquities, Lord, who
Wis 12:13 men, to whom thou S prove that thou hast
Jer 14:8 time of trouble, why S thou be like a
14:9 Why S thou be like a man confused, like
Jn 17:15 not pray that thou S take them out of
17:15 world, but that thou S keep them from the

SHOUT (49)

Num 23:21 with them, and the S of a king is
Josh 6:5 all the people shall S with a great shout;
6:5 shout with a great S; and the wall of
6:10 people, "You shall not S or let your voice
6:10 day I bid you S; then you shall shout."
6:10 day I bid you shout; then you shall S
6:16 said to the people, S; for the LORD has
6:20 people raised a great S, and the wall fell
Judg 7:18 all the camp, and S, 'For the LORD and
1Sam 4:5 Israel gave a mighty S, so that the earth
17:52 Judah rose with a S and pursued the Philistines
2Chr 13:15 Then the men of Judah raised the battle S
Ezra 3:11 shouted with a great S, when they praised the
3:13 sound of the joyful S from the sound of
3:13 shouted with a great S, and the sound was
Jud 14:9 people raised a great S and made a joyful
Job 30:5 from among men; they S after them as after
Ps 20:5 May we S for joy over your victory, and
32:11 rejoice, O righteous, and S for joy, all you
35:27 who desire my vindication S for joy and be
47:1 S to God with loud songs of joy!
47:5 gone up with a S, the LORD with the
60:8 shoe; over Philistia I S in triumph."
65:8 and the evening to S for joy.
65:13 themselves with grain, they S and sing together for
71:23 My lips will S for joy, when I sing
81:1 to God our strength; S for joy to the
89:15 who know the festal S, who walk, O LORD,
108:9 shoe; over Philistia I S in triumph."
132:9 and let thy saints S for joy.
132:16 and her saints will S for joy.
Is 12:6 S, and sing for joy, O inhabitant of Zion,
16:9 your harvest the battle S has fallen.
16:10 the presses; the vintage S is hushed.
24:14 of the LORD they S from the west.
42:11 for joy, let them S from the top of
44:23 LORD has done it; S, O depths of the
48:20 declare this with a S of joy, proclaim it,
Jer 4:16 a distant land; they S against the cities of
20:8 I cry out, I S, "Violence and destruction!" For
25:30 against his fold, and S, like those who tread
48:33 shouting is not the S of joy.
50:15 Raise a S against her round about, she has
51:14 they shall raise the S of victory over you.
Bar 6:32 They howl and S before their gods as some
Zeph 3:14 O daughter of Zion; S, O Israel!
Zech 9:9 S aloud, O daughter of Jerusalem!
1Mac 3:54 they sounded the trumpets and gave a loud S
Gal 4:27 bear; break forth and S, you who are not

SHOUTED (30)

Ex 32:17 the people as they S, he said to Moses,
Lev 9:24 people saw it, they S, and fell on their
Josh 6:20 So the people S, and the trumpets were blown.
Judg 18:23 And they S to the Danites, who turned round
1Sam 10:24 And all the people S, "Long live the king!"
17:8 He stood and S to the ranks of Israel,
2Chr 13:15 the men of Judah S, God defeated Jeroboam and
32:18 And they S it with a loud voice in
Ezra 3:11 And all the people S with a great shout,
3:12 being laid, though many S aloud for joy;
3:13 weeping, for the people S with a great shout,
Jud 14:16 wept and groaned and S, and rent his garments.
14:17 to the people and S,
16:11 Then my oppressed people S for joy; my weak
16:11 joy; my weak people S and the enemy trembled;
Esth 8:15 the city of Susa S and rejoiced.
Job 38:7 the sons of God S for joy?
Sir 50:16 the sons of Aaron S, they sounded the trumpets
Dan 13:24 and the two elders S against her.
13:60 Then all the assembly S loudly and blessed God,
14:18 at the table, and S in a loud voice,
14:37 Then Habakkuk S, "Daniel, Daniel!
14:41 And the king S with a loud voice, "Thou
Mt 21:9 and that followed him S, "Hosanna to the Son
27:23 But they S all the more, "Let him be
Mk 15:14 But they S all the more, "Crucify him."
Lk 23:20 release Jesus; but they S out, "Crucify, crucify him!"
Acts 12:22 And the people S, "The voice of a god,
21:34 Some in the crowd S one thing, some another;
22:24 find out why they S thus against him.

SHOUTING (23)

Ex 32:18 not the sound of S for victory, or the
Judg 15:14 Lehi, the Philistines came S to meet him; and
1Sam 4:6 the noise of the S, they said, "What does
4:6 "What does this great S in the camp of
17:20 to the battle line, S the war cry.
2Sam 6:15 of the LORD with S, and with the sound
1Chr 15:28 of the LORD with S, to the sound of
2Chr 15:14 loud voice, and with S, and with trumpets, and
Job 8:21 your mouth with laughter, and your lips with S
39:25 afar, the thunder of the captains, and the S
Ps 78:65 like a strong man S because of wine.
Eccl 9:17 are better than the S of a ruler among
Is 22:5 of walls and a S to the mountains.
31:4 not terrified by their S or daunted at their
43:14 the bars, and the S of the Chaldeans will
Jer 48:33 shouts of joy; the S is not the shout
Ezek 7:7 and not of joyful S upon the mountains.
21:22 up the voice with S, to set battering-rams against
Dan 13:26 household servants heard the S in the garden, they
Amos 1:14 devour her strongholds, with S in the day of
2:2 die amid uproar, amid S and the sound of
2Mac 15:29 Then there was S and tumult, and they blessed
Acts 25:24 at Jerusalem and here, S that he ought not

SHOUTINGS

Is 22:2 who are full of S, tumultuous city, exultant town?

SHOUTS (16)

Jud 14:19 their loud cries and S arose in the midst
Job 39:7 he hears not the S of the driver.
Ps 27:6 his tent sacrifices with S of joy; I will
33:3 song, play skilfully on the strings, with loud S
42:4 of God, with glad S and songs of thanksgiving,
126:2 and our tongue with S of joy; then they
126:5 in tears reap with S of joy!
126:6 shall come home with S of joy, bringing his
Prov 11:10 wicked perish there are S of gladness.
Is 16:10 songs are sung, no S are raised; no treader
42:13 he cries out, he S aloud, he shows himself
Jer 31:7 for Jacob, and raise S for the chief of
48:33 one treads them with S of joy; the shouting
Zech 4:7 the top stone amid S of 'Grace, grace to
1Mac 5:31 with trumpets and loud S,

2Mac 4:22 in with a blaze of torches and with S

SHOVEL

Is 30:24 has been winnowed with S and fork.

SHOVELS (9)

Ex 27:3 receive its ashes, and S and basins and forks
38:3 altar, the pots, the S, the basins, the forks,
Num 4:14 firepans, the forks, the S, and the basins, all
1Kgs 7:40 made the pots, the S, and the basins.
7:45 Now the pots, the S, and the basins, all
2Kgs 25:14 the pots, and the S, and the snuffers, and
2Chr 4:11 made the pots, the S, and the basins.
4:16 The pots, the S, the forks, and all the
Jer 52:18 the pots, and the S, and the snuffers, and

SHOW (204)

Gen 12:1 land that I will S you.
24:12 I pray thee, and S steadfast love to my
Ex 9:16 let you live, to S you my power, so
10:1 servants, that I may S these signs of mine
22:8 near to God, to S whether or not he
25:9 to all that I S you concerning the pattern
33:13 favor in thy sight, S me now thy ways,
33:18 said, "I pray thee, S me thy glory."
33:19 be gracious, and will S mercy on whom I
33:19 on whom I will S mercy.
Lev 10:3 has said, 'I will S myself holy among those
14:57 or a spot, to S when it is unclean
Num 16:5 morning the LORD will S who is his, and
Deut 1:33 fire by night, to S you by what way
3:24 hast only begun to S thy servant thy greatness
7:2 covenant with them, and S no mercy to them.
13:17 of his anger, and S you mercy, and have
16:19 justice; you shall not S partiality; and you shall
28:50 of the old or S favor to the young,
32:7 father, and he will S you; your elders, and
Judg 1:24 said to him, "Pray, S us the way into
4:22 "Come, and I will S you the man whom
6:17 favor with thee, then S me a sign that
8:35 and they did not S kindness to the family
1Sam 8:9 solemnly warn them, and S them the ways of
10:8 come to you and S you what you shall
14:8 men, and we will S ourselves to them.
14:12 us, and we will S you a thing." And
16:3 sacrifice, and I will S you what you shall
20:14 I am still alive, S me the loyal love
2Sam 2:6 Now may the LORD S steadfast love and faithfulness
9:1 Saul, that I may S him kindness for Jonathan's
9:3 Saul, that I may S the kindness of God
9:7 fear; for I will S you kindness for the
15:20 and may the LORD S steadfast love and faithfulness
22:26 the loyal thou dost S thyself loyal; with the
22:26 blameless man thou dost S thyself blameless;
22:27 the pure thou dost S thyself pure, and with
22:27 the crooked thou dost S thyself perverse.
1Kgs 2:2 Be strong, and S yourself a man,
18:1 third year, saying, "Go, S yourself to Ahab; and
18:2 So Elijah went to S himself to Ahab.
18:15 stand, I will surely S myself to him today."
2Kgs 6:11 them, "Will you not S me who of us
20:13 that Hezekiah did not S them.
20:15 that I did not S them."
2Chr 16:9 the whole earth, to S his might in behalf
Tob 8:17 S them mercy, O Lord; and bring their lives
13:5 and again he will S mercy, and will gather
13:6 my captivity, and I S his power and majesty
13:9 but again he will S mercy to the sons
Jud 10:13 report; and I will S him a way by
13:11 still with us, to S his power in Israel,
16:15 thou wilt continue to S mercy.
Esth 1:11 crown, in order to S the peoples and the
4:8 destruction, that he might S it to Esther and
Job 13:8 Will you S partiality toward him, will you plead
13:10 if in secret you S partiality.
15:17 "I will S you, hear me; and what I
24:25 me a liar, and S that there is nothing
32:21 I will not S partiality to any person or
36:2 little, and I will S you, for I have
Ps 16:11 Thou dost S me the path of life; in
17:7 Wondrously S thy steadfast love, O savior of those
18:25 the loyal thou dost S thyself loyal; with the
18:25 blameless man thou dost S thyself blameless;
18:26 the pure thou dost S thyself pure; and with
18:26 the crooked thou dost S thyself perverse.
50:23 way aright I will S the salvation of God!"
51:15 and my mouth shall S forth thy praise.
68:28 thy might, O God; S thy strength, O God,
82:2 you judge unjustly and S partiality to the wicked?
85:7 S us thy steadfast love, O LORD, and grant
86:17 S me a sign of thy favor, that those
91:16 will satisfy him, and S him my salvation.
92:15 sap and green, to S that the LORD is
106:2 of the LORD, or S forth all his praise?
109:16 did not remember to S kindness, but pursued the
Prov 22:21 admonition and knowledge, to S you what is right
28:21 To S partiality is not good; but for a
Eccl 3:18 is testing them to S them that they are
Wis 5:13 sign of virtue to S, but were consumed in
6:7 of any one, nor S deference to greatness; because
8:15 the people I shall S myself capable, and courageous
11:21 in thy power to S great strength, and who
12:17 For thou dost S thy strength when men doubt
16:2 this punishment thou didst S kindness to thy people,
Sir 3:13 is lacking in understanding, S forbearance; in all your
4:22 Do not S partiality, to your own harm, or
4:27 a foolish fellow, nor S partiality to a ruler.
7:24 chastity, and do not S yourself too indulgent with
17:7 upon their hearts to S them the majesty of
19:27 man's manner of walking, S what he is.
22:17 the heart makes it S feeling.
35:9 With every gift S a cheerful face, and dedicate
35:13 He will not S partiality in the case of
36:6 S signs anew, and work further wonders; make thy
41:16 Therefore S respect for my words: For it is
41:23 Then you will S proper shame, and will find
Is 27:11 that formed them will S them no favor.
30:18 he exalts himself to S mercy to you.
39:2 that Hezekiah did not S them.
39:4 that I did not S them."
43:9 can declare this, and S us the former things?
Jer 11:18 knew; then thou didst S me their evil deeds.
16:13 night, for I will S you no favor.'
18:17 I will S them my back, not my face,
42:3 LORD your God may S us the way we
Bar 5:3 God will S your splendor everywhere under heaven.
6:67 bless kings; they cannot S signs in the heavens
Ezek 9:5 spare, and you shall S no pity;
33:31 with their lips they S much love, but their
37:18 you, 'Will you not S us what you mean
38:23 So I will S my greatness and my holiness
39:13 the day that I S my glory, says the
40:4 all that I shall S you, for you were
40:4 order that I might S it to you; declare
44:23 and the common, and S them how to distinguish
Dan 2:4 dream, and we will S the interpretation."
2:6 But if you S the dream and its interpretation,
2:6 Therefore S me the dream and its interpretation."
2:7 dream, and we will S its interpretation."
2:9 know that you can S me its interpretation."
2:11 difficult, and none can S it to the king
2:16 time, that he might S to the king the
2:24 king, and I will S the king the interpretation."
2:27 magicians, or astrologers can S to the king the
4:2 good to me to S the signs and wonders
5:12 called, and he will S the interpretation."
5:15 but they could not S the interpretation of the
11:2 "And now I will S you the truth.
Mic 7:15 of Egypt I will S them marvelous things.
7:20 Thou wilt S faithfulness to Jacob and steadfast love
Zech 1:9 to me, 'I will S you what they are.'
7:9 hosts, Render true judgments, S kindness and mercy
Mal 1:8 pleased with you or S you favor?
1:9 your hand, will he S favor to any of
1Mac 2:50 Now, my children, S zeal for the law, and
7:33 him peaceably and to S him the burnt offering
11:33 the good will they S toward us.
2Mac 4:17 no light thing to S irreverence to the divine
6:27 life now, I will S myself worthy of my
7:37 appealing to God to S mercy soon to our
8:4 his name, and to S his hatred of evil.
12:36 upon the Lord to S himself their ally and
13:9 arrogance was coming to S the Jews things far
14:9 gracious kindness which you S to all.
15:2 savagely and barbarously, but S respect for the day
Mt 8:4 any one; but go, S yourself to the priest,
16:1 they asked him to S them a sign from
16:21 time Jesus began to S his disciples that he
22:19 S me the money for the tax." And they
24:24 prophets will arise and S great signs and wonders,
Mk 1:44 any one; but go, S yourself to the priest,
13:22 prophets will arise and S signs and wonders, to

14:15 disciples?' And he will S you a large upper
Lk 5:14 one; but "go and S yourself to the priest,
6:47 does them, I will S you what he is
17:14 to them, "Go and S yourselves to the priests."
20:21 and teach rightly, and S no partiality, but truly
20:24 and said to them, S me a coin.
22:12 disciples?' And he will S you a large upper
Jn 2:18 sign have you to S us for doing this?"
4:25 he comes, he will S us all things."
5:19 than these will he S him, that you may
7:4 you do these things, S yourself to the world."
12:33 He said this to S by what death he
14:8 said to him, "Lord, S us the Father, and
14:9 how can you say, S us the Father?
18:32 Jesus had spoken to S by what death he
21:19 (This he said to S by what death he
Acts 1:24 hearts of all men, S which one of these
2:19 And I will S wonders in the heaven above
7:3 land which I will S you.'
9:16 Israel; for I will S him how much he
Rom 2:15 They S that what the law requires is written
3:5 our wickedness serves to S the justice of God,
3:25 This was to S God's righteousness, because in his
9:22 if God, desiring to S his wrath and to
15:8 to the circumcised to S God's truthfulness, in order
1Cor 12:31 And I will S you a still more excellent
2Cor 3:3 all men; and you S that you are a
4:7 in earthen vessels, to S that the transcendent power
8:19 the Lord and to S our good will.
10:2 may not have to S boldness with such confidence
11:30 of the things that S my weakness.
Eph 2:7 coming ages he might S the immeasurable riches of
Tit 2:7 S yourself in all respects a model of good
2:7 and in your teaching S integrity, gravity,
2:10 to pilfer, but to S entire and true fidelity,
3:2 be gentle, and to S perfect courtesy toward all
Heb 6:11 one of you to S the same earnestness in
6:17 when God desired to S more convincingly to the
13:2 Do not neglect to S hospitality to strangers, for
Jas 2:1 My brethren, S no partiality as you hold the
2:9 But if you S partiality, you commit sin, and
2:18 S me your faith apart from your works, and
2:18 by my works will S you my faith.
3:13 good life let him S his works in the
Rev 1:1 God gave him to S to his servants what
4:1 hither, and I will S you what must take
17:1 me, "Come, I will S you the judgment of
21:9 saying, "Come, I will S you the Bride, the
22:6 sent his angel to S his servants what must

SHOWBREAD (7)

1Chr 9:32 had charge of the S, to prepare it every
23:29 assist also with the S, the flour for the
28:16 each table for the S, the silver for the
2Chr 2:4 continual offering of the S, and for burnt offerings
13:11 spices, set out the S on the table of
29:18 the table for the S and all its utensils.
Neh 10:33 our God: for the S, the continual cereal offering,

SHOWED (62)

Gen 39:21 was with Joseph and S him steadfast love, and
Ex 15:25 LORD; and the LORD S him a tree, and
Num 13:26 all the congregation, and S them the fruit of
20:13 the LORD, and he S himself holy among them.
Deut 6:22 hand; and the LORD S signs and wonders, great
34:1 And the LORD S him all the land, Gilead
Judg 1:25 And he S them the way into the city;
Ruth 2:18 into the city; she S her mother-in-law what she
1Sam 14:11 So both of them S themselves to the garrison
15:6 with them; for you S kindness to all the
19:7 called David, and Jonathan S him all these things.
2Sam 2:5 the LORD, because you S this loyalty to Saul
1Kgs 13:12 And his sons S him the way which the
16:27 the might that he S, are they not written
22:45 his might that he S, and how he warred,
2Kgs 6:6 When he S him the place, he cut off
11:4 the LORD, and he S them the king's son.
20:13 welcomed them, and he S them all his treasure
2Chr 30:22 all the Levites who S good skill in the
Jud 13:15 of the bag and S it to them, and
Esth 1:4 before him, while he S the riches of his
Job 42:11 his house; and they S him sympathy and comforted
Wis 10:10 on straight paths; she S him the kingdom of
10:14 who accused him she S to be false, and
Sir 16:9 He S no pity for a nation devoted to
17:6 knowledge and understanding, and S them good and
17:10 an eternal covenant, and S them his judgments.
45:3 for his people, and S him part of his
49:8 of glory which God S him above the chariot
Is 39:2 welcomed them; and he S them his treasure house,
40:14 taught him knowledge, and S him the way of
47:6 into your hand, you S them no mercy; on
Jer 24:1 to Babylon, the LORD S me this vision: Behold,
Ezek 11:25 that the LORD had S me.
20:11 them my statutes and S them my ordinances, by
35:11 and envy which you S because of your hatred
Dan 14:21 and children; and they S him the secret doors
Amos 7:1 Thus the Lord GOD S me: behold, he was
7:4 Thus the Lord GOD S me: behold, the Lord
7:7 He S me: behold, the Lord was standing beside
8:1 Thus the Lord GOD S me: behold, a basket
Mic 6:8 He has S you, O man, what is good;
Zech 1:20 Then the LORD S me four smiths.
3:1 Then he S me Joshua the high priest standing
1Mac 4:20 smoke that was seen S what had happened.
6:34 They S the elephants the juice of grapes and
11:4 he approached Azotus, they S him the temple of
2Mac 3:17 the man, which plainly S to those who looked
13:23 honored the sanctuary and S generosity to the holy
15:32 He S them the vile Nicanor's head and that
Mt 4:8 very high mountain, and S him all the kingdoms
Lk 4:5 took him up, and S him all the kingdoms
10:37 said, "The one who S mercy on him." And
20:37 are raised, even Moses S, in the passage about
24:40 had said this, he S them his hands and
Jn 20:20 had said this, he S them his hands and
Acts 28:2 And the natives S us unusual kindness, for they
Heb 6:10 the love which you S for his sake in
2Pet 1:14 our Lord Jesus Christ S me.
Rev 21:10 great, high mountain, and S me the holy city
22:1 Then he S me the river of the water
22:8 of the angel who S them to me;

SHOWER (3)

Job 37:6 earth'; and to the S and the rain, 'Be
Is 45:8 S, O heavens, from above, and let the skies
Lk 12:54 say at once, 'A S is coming'; and so

SHOWERED

2Mac 10:30 And they S arrows and thunderbolts upon the enemy,

SHOWERS (11)

Deut 32:2 grass, and as the S upon the herb.
Ps 65:10 ridges, softening it with S, and blessing its growth.
72:6 the mown grass, like S that water the earth!
Wis 16:22 and flashed in the S of rain;
Jer 3:3 Therefore the S have been withheld, and the spring
14:22 Or can the heavens give S
Ezek 34:26 will send down the S in their season; they
34:26 season; they shall be S of blessing.
Hos 6:3 to us as the S, as the spring rains
Mic 5:7 from the LORD, like S upon the grass, which
Zech 10:1 clouds, who gives men S of rain, to every

SHOWEST (2)

Ps 106:4 O LORD, when thou S favor to thy people;
Jer 32:18 hard for thee, who S steadfast love to thousands,

SHOWING (18)

Ex 20:6 who hate me, but S steadfast love to thousands
Deut 5:10 who hate me, but S steadfast love to thousands
2Sam 3:8 This day I keep S loyalty to the house
1Kgs 8:23 beneath, keeping covenant and S steadfast love to
2Chr 6:14 earth, keeping covenant and S steadfast love to thy
Tob 14:7 and righteousness will rejoice, S mercy to our
Wis 11:8 them abundant water unexpectedly, S by their thirst
14:4 way through the waves, S that thou canst save
18:21 end to the disaster, S that he was thy
Dan 4:27 and your iniquities by S mercy to the oppressed,
2Mac 4:49 Therefore even the Tyrians, S their hatred of the
10:12 took the lead in S justice to the Jews
Acts 9:39 beside him weeping, and S tunics and other
18:28 the Jews in public, S by the scriptures that
Rom 9:17 the very purpose of S my power in you,
12:10 outdo one another in S honor.
2Cor 10:2 as I count on S against some who suspect
Gal 6:12 to make a good S in the flesh that

SHOWN (60)

Gen 19:19 sight, and you have S me great kindness in
24:14 know that thou hast S steadfast love to my
32:10 faithfulness which thou hast S to thy servant, for

S

41:28 told Pharaoh, God has S to Pharaoh what he
41:39 Joseph, "Since God has S you all this, there
Ex 25:40 them, which is being S you on the mountain.
26:30 it which has been S you on the mountain.
27:8 as it has been S you on the mountain,
Lev 13:7 skin, after he has S himself to the priest
13:19 then it shall be S to the priest;
13:49 disease and shall be S to the priest.
Num 8:4 which the LORD had S Moses, so he made
Deut 4:35 To you it was S, that you might know
5:24 LORD our God has S us his glory and
Judg 13:23 at our hands, or S us all these things,
2Sam 7:19 to come, and hast S me future generations, O
1Kgs 3:6 Solomon said, "Thou hast S great and steadfast love
8:66 that the LORD had S to David his servant
2Kgs 8:10 but the LORD has S me that he shall
8:13 answered, "The LORD has S me that you are
1Chr 17:17 to come, and hast S me future generations, O
2Chr 1:8 to God, "Thou hast S great and steadfast love
7:10 that the LORD had S to David and to
24:22 Jehoiada, Zechariah's father, had S him, but killed
Ezra 9:8 moment favor has been S by the LORD our
Tob 3:15 command that respect be S to me and pity
Jud 8:29 your wisdom has been S, but from the beginning
Ps 31:21 for he has wondrously S his steadfast love to
48:3 her citadels God has S himself a sure defense.
78:11 miracles that he had S them.
111:6 He has S his people the power of his
Wis 3:14 special favor will be S him for his faithfulness,
16:4 these it was merely S how their enemies were
Sir 3:22 human understanding have been S you.
14:12 Hades has not been S to you.
Is 26:10 If favor is S to the wicked, he does
Jer 3:11 me, "Faithless Israel has S herself less guilty than
32:20 his doings; who hast S signs and wonders in
38:21 which the LORD has S to me:
Lam 4:16 more; no honor was S to the priests, no
5:12 hands; no respect is S to the elders.
Mal 2:9 my ways but have S partiality in your instruction."
1Mac 14:4 as was the honor S him, all his days.
2Mac 2:8 appear, as they were S in the case of
12:24 no consideration would be S them.
12:30 people of Scythopolis had S them and their kind
Lk 1:51 He has S strength with his arm, he has
1:58 that the Lord had S great mercy to her,
Jn 10:32 answered them, "I have S you many good works
Acts 10:28 nation; but God has S me that I should
20:35 all things I have S you that by so
Rom 1:19 them, because God has S it to them.
7:13 that sin might be S to be sin, and
10:20 seek me; I have S myself to those who
11:31 that by the mercy S to you they also
2Cor 8:1 God which has been S in the churches of
1Tim 5:10 has brought up children, S hospitality, washed the
Heb 8:5 the pattern which was S you on the mountain."
Jas 2:13 to one who has S no mercy; yet mercy
2:20 you want to be S, you shallow man, that

SHOWS (24)

Lev 13:49 skin, if the disease S greenish or reddish in
Num 23:3 me; and whatever he S me I will tell
2Sam 22:51 to his king, and S steadfast love to his
Tob 13:2 he afflicts, and he S mercy; he leads down
Job 34:19 nobles, 'Wicked man'; who S no partiality to princes,
Ps 18:50 to his king, and S steadfast love to his
59:17 fortress, the God who S me steadfast love.
Prov 3:34 to the humble he S favor.
Sir 26:9 A wife's harlotry S in her lustful eyes, and
29:1 He that S mercy will lend to his neighbor,
Is 5:16 and the Holy God S himself holy in righteousness.
42:13 he shouts aloud, he S himself mighty against his
Bar 6:59 be a king who S his courage, or a
Dan 5:7 reads this writing, and S me its interpretation, shall
Zeph 3:5 wrong; every morning he S forth his justice, each
1Mac 5:41 But if he S fear and camps on the
12:7 you are our brethren, as the appended copy S
2Mac 2:7 people together again and S his mercy.
10:38 blessed the Lord who S great kindness to Israel
Jn 5:19 loves the Son, and S him all that he
Acts 10:34 I perceive that God S no partiality,
Rom 2:11 For God S no partiality.
5:8 But God S his love for us in that
Gal 2:6 difference to me; God S no partiality)—those, I

SHRANK (2)

1Mac 3:6 Lawless men S back for fear of him; all
2Mac 14:18 battle for their country, S from deciding the issue

SHREWD (4)

1Chr 26:14 his son Zechariah, a S counselor, and his lot
Sir 37:19 A man may be S and the teacher of
Is 5:21 their own eyes, and S in their own sight!
Lk 16:8 this world are more S in dealing with their

SHREWDLY

Ex 1:9 Come, let us deal S with them, lest they

SHREWDNESS

Lk 16:8 dishonest steward for his S; for the sons of

SHRINE (2)

Judg 17:5 man Micah had a S, and he made an
Heb 6:19 enters into the inner S behind the curtain,

SHRINES (8)

2Kgs 17:29 put them in the S of the high places
17:32 for them in the S of the high places.
23:19 And all the S also of the high places
Jud 3:8 he demolished all their S and cut down their
Ezek 16:16 for yourself gaily decked S, and on them played
1Mac 1:47 and sacred precincts and S for idols, to sacrifice
Acts 17:24 does not live in S made by man,
19:24 silversmith, who made silver S of Artemis, brought

SHRINK (6)

Sir 7:35 Do not S from visiting a sick man, because
Nah 3:7 look on you will S from you and say,
Acts 20:20 how I did not S from declaring to you
20:27 for I did not S from declaring to you
Heb 10:39 not of those who S back and are destroyed,
1Jn 2:28 have confidence and not S from him in shame

SHRINKS

Heb 10:38 faith, and if he S back, my soul has

SHRIVELED (2)

Job 16:8 And he has S me up, which is a
Lam 4:8 streets; their skin has S upon their bones, it

SHRIVELS

Joel 1:16 The seed S under the clods, the storehouses are

SHROUD (4)

Mt 27:59 in a clean linen S,
Mk 15:45 he bought a linen S, and taking him down,
15:45 him in the linen S, and laid him in
Lk 23:52 it in a linen S, and laid him in

SHRUB

Jer 17:6 He is like a S in the desert, and

SHRUBS (2)

Mt 13:32 is the greatest of S and becomes a tree,
Mk 4:32 the greatest of all S, and puts forth large

SHUA (3)

Gen 38:2 Canaanite whose name was S; he married her and
38:12 the wife of Judah, S's daughter, died; and when
1Chr 7:32 father of Japhlet, Shomer, Hotham, and their sister S

SHUAH (2)

Gen 25:2 Zimran, Jokshan, Medan, Midian, Ishbak, and S
1Chr 1:32 Jokshan, Medan, Midian, Ishbak, and S

SHUAL (2)

1Sam 13:17 to the land of S,
1Chr 7:36 of Zophah: Suah, Harnepher, S, Beri, Imrah,

SHUBA-EL (3)

1Chr 24:20 the sons of Amram, S; of the sons of
24:20 of the sons of S, Jehdeiah.
25:20 twelve; to the thirteenth, S, his sons and his

SHUDDER (4)

Is 32:10 a year you will S, you complacent women; for
32:11 who are at ease, S, you complacent ones; strip,
Ezek 32:10 and their kings shall S because of you, when
Jas 2:19 Even the demons believe—and S

SHUDDERING

Job 21:6 I am dismayed, and S seizes my flesh.

SHUHAH
1Chr 4:11 Chelub, the brother of S, was the father of

SHUHAM
Num 26:42 to their families: of S, the family of the

SHUHAMITES (2)
Num 26:42 their families: of Shuham, the family of the S
26:43 the families of the S, according to their number,

SHUHITE (5)
Job 2:11 the Temanite, Bildad the S, and Zophar the
8:1 Then Bildad the S answered:
18:1 Then Bildad the S answered:
25:1 Then Bildad the S answered:
42:9 Temanite and Bildad the S and Zophar the

SHULAMMITE (2)
Song 6:13 Return, return, O S, return, return, that we may
6:13 you look upon the S, as upon a dance

SHUMATHITES
1Chr 2:53 Ithrites, the Puthites, the S, and the Mishra-ites;

SHUN (7)
Ps 88:8 caused my companions to S me; thou hast made
88:18 lover and friend to S me; my companions are
Sir 32:17 A sinful man will S reproof, and will find
1Cor 6:18 S immorality.
10:14 Therefore, my beloved, S the worship of idols.
1Tim 6:11 you, man of God, S all this; aim at
2Tim 2:22 So S youthful passions and aim at righteousness,

SHUNAMMITE (8)
1Kgs 1:3 and found Abishag the S, and brought her to
1:15 old, and Abishag the S was ministering to the
2:17 give me Abishag the S as my wife."
2:21 said, "Let Abishag the S be given to Adonijah
2:22 you ask Abishag the S for Adonijah?
2Kgs 4:12 he said to Gehazi his servant, "Call this S
4:25 "Look, yonder is the S;
4:36 Then he summoned Gehazi and said, "Call this S

SHUNEM (3)
Josh 19:18 territory included Jezreel, Chesulloth, S,
1Sam 28:4 came and encamped at S; and Saul gathered all
2Kgs 4:8 Elisha went on to S, where a wealthy woman

SHUNI (2)
Gen 46:16 of Gad: Ziphion, Haggi, S, Ezbon, Eri, Arodi, and
Num 26:15 of the Haggites; of S, the family of the

SHUNITES
Num 26:15 the family of the S;

SHUNS
Eccl 9:2 is as he who S an oath.

SHUPHAMITES
Num 26:39 the family of the S; of Hupham, the family

SHUPPIM (3)
1Chr 7:12 And S and Huppim were the sons of Ir,
7:15 Machir took a wife for Huppim and for S
26:16 For S and Hosah it came out for the

SHUR (6)
Gen 16:7 the wilderness, the spring on the way to S
20:1 dwelt between Kadesh and S; and he sojourned in
25:18 dwelt from Havilah to S, which is opposite Egypt
Ex 15:22 into the wilderness of S; they went three days
1Sam 15:7 Havilah as far as S, which is east of
27:8 old, as far as S, to the land of

SHUT (107)
Gen 7:16 him; and the LORD S him in.
19:6 door to the men, S the door after him,
19:10 house to them, and S the door.
Ex 14:3 land; the wilderness has S them in.'
Lev 13:4 white, the priest shall S up the diseased person
13:5 then the priest shall S him up seven days
13:11 unclean; he shall not S him up, for he
13:21 then the priest shall S him up seven days;
13:26 dim, the priest shall S him up seven days,
13:31 then the priest shall S up the person with
13:33 and the priest shall S up the person with
13:50 examine the disease, and S up that which has
13:54 disease, and he shall S it up seven days
14:38 of the house, and S up the house seven
14:46 house while it is S up shall be unclean
Num 12:14 Let her be S up outside the camp seven
12:15 So Miriam was S up outside the camp seven
Deut 11:17 against you, and he S up the heavens, so
15:7 harden your heart or S your hand against your
Josh 2:7 the pursuers had gone out, the gate was S
6:1 Now Jericho was S up from within and from
Judg 9:51 men and women, and S themselves in; and they
1Sam 6:10 to the cart, and S up their calves at
23:7 hand; for he has S himself in by entering
2Sam 20:3 So they were S up until the day of
1Kgs 8:35 "When heaven is S up and there is no
2Kgs 4:4 Then go in, and S the door upon yourself
4:5 went from him and S the door upon herself
4:21 man of God, and S the door upon him,
4:33 he went in and S the door upon the
6:32 when the messenger comes, S the door, and hold
17:4 the king of Assyria S him up, and bound
2Chr 6:26 "When heaven is S up and there is no
7:13 When I S up the heavens so that there
28:24 of God, and he S up the doors of
29:7 They also S the doors of the vestibule and
Neh 6:10 of Mehetabel, who was S up, he said, "Let
7:3 standing guard let them S and bar the doors.
13:19 the doors should be S and gave orders that
Tob 8:4 When the door was S and the two were
Jud 13:1 tent from outside and S out the attendants from
Job 3:10 because it did not S the doors of my
24:16 houses; by day they S themselves up; they do
38:8 "Or who S in the sea with doors, when
41:15 of rows of shields, S up closely as with
Ps 77:9 Has he in anger S up his compassion?" [Selah]
88:8 I am S in so that I cannot escape;
Eccl 12:4 on the street are S; when the sound of
Wis 17:2 prisoners of long night, S in under their roofs,
17:16 and thus was kept S up in a prison
Sir 48:3 of the Lord he S up the heavens, and
Is 6:10 their ears heavy, and S their eyes; lest they
22:22 open, and none shall S; and he shall shut,
22:22 shut; and he shall S, and none shall open.
24:10 down, every house is S up so that none
24:22 pit; they will be S up in a prison,
26:20 enter your chambers, and S your doors behind you;
44:18 discern; for he has S their eyes, so that
52:15 many nations; kings shall S their mouths because of
60:11 they shall not be S; that men may bring
66:9 cause to bring forth, S the womb?
Jer 13:19 of the Negeb are S up, with none to
20:9 were a burning fire S up in my bones,
32:2 Jeremiah the prophet was S up in the court
33:1 while he was still S up in the court
39:15 Jeremiah while he was S up in the court
Bar 6:18 as the gates are S on every side upon
Ezek 3:24 said to me, "Go, S yourself within your house.
44:1 the sanctuary, which faces east; and it was S
44:2 "This gate shall remain S; it shall not be
44:2 has entered by it; therefore it shall remain S
46:1 faces east shall be S on the six working
46:2 gate shall not be S until evening.
46:12 he has gone out the gate shall be S
Dan 6:22 sent his angel and S the lions' mouths, and
12:4 But you, Daniel, S up the words, and seal
12:9 for the words are S up and sealed until
13:17 oil and ointments, and S the garden doors so
13:18 did as she said, S the garden doors, and
13:20 the garden doors are S, no one sees us,
13:36 in with two maids, S the garden doors, and
14:11 place the wine, and S the door and seal
14:14 Then they went out, S the door and sealed
Mal 1:10 among you who would S the doors, that you
1Mac 5:5 They were S up by him in their towers;
5:26 of them have been S up in Bozrah and
5:27 "and some have been S up in the other
5:47 men of the city S them out and blocked
11:61 the men of Gaza S him out.
15:25 of war; and he S Trypho up and kept
Mt 6:6 into your room and S the door and pray
23:13 because you S the kingdom of heaven against men;
25:10 to the marriage feast; and the door was S
Lk 3:20 them all, that he S up John in prison.
4:25 when the heaven was S up three years and
11:7 the door is now S, and my children are
13:25 has risen up and S the door, you will

Jn 20:19 week, the doors being S where the disciples were,
20:26 The doors were S, but Jesus came and stood
Acts 21:30 the temple, and at once the gates were S
26:10 Jerusalem; I not only S up many of the
Gal 4:17 purpose; they want to S you out, that you
Rev 3:7 and no one shall S, who shuts and no
3:8 one is able to S; I know that you
11:6 They have power to S the sky, that no
20:3 into the pit, and S it and sealed it
21:25 gates shall never be S by day--and there

SHUTHELAH (4)

Num 26:35 to their families: of S, the family of the
26:36 are the sons of S: of Eran, the family
1Chr 7:20 The sons of Ephraim: S, and Bered his son,
7:21 son, Zabad his son, S his son, and Ezer

SHUTHELAHITES

Num 26:35 the family of the S; of Becher, the family

SHUTS (5)

Job 5:16 have hope, and injustice S her mouth.
12:14 can rebuild; if he S a man in, none
Is 33:15 hearing of bloodshed and S his eyes from looking
Lam 3:8 cry for help, he S out my prayer;
Rev 3:7 one shall shut, who S and no one opens.

SHUTTLE

Job 7:6 swifter than a weaver's S, and come to their

SIA

Neh 7:47 Keros, the sons of S, the sons of Padon,

SIAHA

Ezra 2:44 Keros, the sons of S, the sons of Padon,

SIBBECAI (4)

2Sam 21:18 Philistines at Gob; then S the Hushathite slew Saph,
1Chr 11:29 Tekoa, Abi-ezer of Anathoth, S the Hushathite, Ilai
20:4 Philistines at Gezer; then S the Hushathite slew
27:11 the eighth month, was S the Hushathite, of the

SIBBOLETH

Judg 12:6 and he said, S

SIBMAH (5)

Num 32:38 to be changed), and S; and they gave other
Josh 13:19 Mephaath, and Kiriathaim, and S, and Zereth-shahar
Is 16:8 and the vine of S; the lords of the
16:9 for the vine of S; I drench you with
Jer 48:32 Jazer I weep for you, O vine of S

SIBRAIM

Ezek 47:16 on to Zedad, Berothah, S (which lies on the

SICK (72)

Lev 15:33 for her who is S with her impurity; that
Deut 29:22 LORD has made it S --
1Sam 19:14 messengers to take David, she said, "He is S
30:13 behind because I fell S three days ago.
2Sam 12:15 Uriah's wife bore to David, and it became S
1Kgs 14:1 that time Abijah the son of Jeroboam fell S
14:5 of you concerning her son; for he is S
2Kgs 1:2 in Samaria, and lay S; so he sent messengers,
8:7 king of Syria was S; and when it was
8:29 son of Ahab in Jezreel, because he was S
13:14 when Elisha had fallen S with the illness of
20:1 those days Hezekiah became S and was at the
20:12 Hezekiah; for he heard that Hezekiah had been S
2Chr 22:6 son of Ahab in Jezreel, because he was S
32:24 those days Hezekiah became S and was at the
Neh 2:2 is your face sad, seeing you are not S
Ps 35:13 I, when they were S -- I wore sackcloth,
107:17 Some were S through their sinful ways, and because
Prov 13:12 deferred makes the heart S, but a desire fulfilled
Song 2:5 apples; for I am S with love.
5:8 tell him I am S with love.
Wis 17:8 and disorders of a S soul were sick themselves
17:8 a sick soul were S themselves with ridiculous fear.
Sir 7:35 shrink from visiting a S man, because for such
38:9 son, when you are S do not be negligent,
Is 1:5 The whole head is S, and the whole heart
10:18 be as when a S man wastes away.
33:24 will say, "I am S; the people who dwell
38:1 those days Hezekiah became S and was at the
38:9 after he had been S and had recovered from
39:1 that he had been S and had recovered.
Jer 8:18 healing, my heart is S within me.
Lam 5:17 our heart has become S, for these things our
Ezek 34:4 have not strengthened, the S you have not healed,
Dan 8:27 was overcome and lay S for some days; then
Hos 7:6 king the princes became S with the heat of
Mal 1:8 that are lame or S, is that no evil?
1:13 or is lame or S, and this you bring
1Mac 1:5 After this he fell S and perceived that he
6:8 his bed and became S from grief, because things
Mt 4:24 brought him all the S, those afflicted with various
8:14 saw his mother-in-law lying S with a fever;
8:16 with a word, and healed all who were S
9:12 need of a physician, but those who are S
10:8 at hand.' Heal the S, raise the dead, cleanse
14:14 he had compassion on them, and healed their S
14:35 him all that were S,
25:36 clothed me, I was S and you visited me,
25:39 did we see thee S or in prison and
25:43 did not clothe me, S and in prison and
25:44 stranger or naked or S or in prison, and
Mk 1:30 Now Simon's mother-in-law lay S with a fever, and
1:32 him all who were S or possessed with demons.
1:34 healed many who were S with various diseases, and
2:17 but those who are S; I came not to
6:5 hands upon a few S people and healed them.
6:13 oil many that were S and healed them.
6:55 and began to bring S people on their pallets
6:56 country, they laid the S in the market places,
16:18 their hands on the S, and they will recover."
Lk 4:40 had any that were S with various diseases brought
5:31 but those who are S;
7:2 to him, who was S and at the point
10:9 before you; heal the S in it and say
Jn 5:6 The S man answered him, "Sir, I have no
Acts 5:15 even carried out the S into the streets, and
5:16 around Jerusalem, bringing the S and those afflicted
9:37 those days she fell S and died; and when
19:12 his body to the S, and diseases left them
28:8 father of Publius lay S with fever and dysentery;
Jas 5:14 Is any among you S
5:15 faith will save the S man, and the Lord

SICKBED (2)

Ps 41:3 sustains him on his S; in his illness thou
Rev 2:22 throw her on a S, and those who commit

SICKLE (13)

Deut 16:9 you first put the S to the standing grain.
23:25 shall not put a S to your neighbor's standing
1Sam 13:20 his axe, or his S;
Jer 50:16 one who handles the S in time of harvest;
Joel 3:13 Put in the S, for the harvest is ripe.
Mk 4:29 he puts in the S, because the harvest has
Rev 14:14 head, and a sharp S in his hand.
14:15 cloud, "Put in your S, and reap, for the
14:16 the cloud swung his S on the earth, and
14:17 in heaven, and he too had a sharp S
14:18 who had the sharp S, "Put in your sickle,
14:18 sickle, "Put in your S, and gather the clusters
14:19 the angel swung his S on the earth and

SICKLY

Wis 6:23 in the company of S envy, for envy does

SICKNESS (19)

Ex 23:25 and I will take S away from the midst
Lev 20:18 a woman having her S, and uncovers her nakedness,
Deut 7:15 away from you all S; and none of the
28:61 Every S also, and every affliction which is not
1Kgs 8:37 cities; whatever plague, whatever S there is;
2Kgs 1:2 of Ekron, whether I shall recover from this S
8:8 through him, saying, 'Shall I recover from this S
8:9 to you, saying, 'Shall I recover from this S
2Chr 6:28 cities; whatever plague, whatever S there is;
21:15 will have a severe S with a disease of
Prov 18:14 man's spirit will endure S; but a broken spirit
Eccl 5:17 in much vexation and S and resentment?
Sir 30:17 a miserable life, and eternal rest than chronic S
31:22 be industrious, and no S will overtake you.
37:30 food; for overeating brings S, and gluttony leads to
Is 10:16 hosts, will send wasting S among his stout warriors,
38:9 had recovered from his S:
Jer 6:7 are heard within her; S and wounds are ever
Hos 5:13 When Ephraim saw his S, and Judah his wound,

SICKNESSES (2)

Deut	28:59	severe and lasting, and S grievous and lasting.
	29:22	that land and the S with which the LORD

SICYON

1Mac	15:23	to Myndos, and to S, and to Caria, and

SIDDIM (3)

Gen	14:3	in the Valley of S (that is, the Salt
	14:8	in the Valley of S
	14:10	Now the Valley of S was full of bitumen

SIDE (348)

Gen	6:16	the ark in its S; make it with lower,
	31:42	not been on my S, surely now you would
	38:16	her at the road S, and said, "Come, let
Ex	3:1	flock to the west S of the wilderness, and
	17:12	hands, one on one S, and the other on
	17:12	other on the other S; so his hands were
	25:12	rings on the one S of it, and two
	25:12	rings on the other S of it.
	25:32	lampstand out of one S of it and three
	25:32	out of the other S of it;
	26:13	cubit on the one S, and the cubit on
	26:13	cubit on the other S, of what remains in
	26:13	the tabernacle, on this S and that side, to
	26:13	this side and that S, to cover it.
	26:18	frames for the south S;
	26:20	and for the second S of the tabernacle, on
	26:20	tabernacle, on the north S twenty frames,
	26:26	frames of the one S of the tabernacle,
	26:27	frames of the other S of the tabernacle, and
	26:27	the frames of the S of the tabernacle at
	26:35	lampstand on the south S of the tabernacle opposite
	26:35	you shall put the table on the north S
	27:9	On the south S the court shall have hangings
	27:9	cubits long for one S;
	27:11	length on the north S there shall be hangings
	27:12	court on the west S there shall be hangings
	27:14	hangings for the one S of the gate shall
	27:15	On the other S the hangings shall be fifteen
	32:15	sides; on the one S and on the other
	32:26	camp, and said, "Who is on the LORD's S
	32:27	his sword on his S, and go to and
	36:23	frames for the south S;
	36:25	And for the second S of the tabernacle, on
	36:25	tabernacle, on the north S, he made twenty frames
	36:31	frames of the one S of the tabernacle,
	36:32	frames of the other S of the tabernacle, and
	37:3	rings on its one S and two rings on
	37:3	one side and two rings on its other S
	37:18	lampstand out of one S of it and three
	37:18	out of the other S of it;
	38:9	court; for the south S the hangings of the
	38:11	And for the north S a hundred cubits, their
	38:12	And for the west S were hangings of fifty
	38:14	The hangings for one S of the gate were
	38:15	so for the other S; on this hand and
Lev	1:11	it on the north S of the altar before
	1:15	drained out on the S of the altar;
	1:16	altar on the east S, in the place for
	5:9	sin offering on the S of the altar, while
Num	2:2	encamp facing the tent of meeting on every S
	2:3	encamp on the east S toward the sunrise shall
	2:10	"On the south S shall be the standard of
	2:18	"On the west S shall be the standard of
	2:25	"On the north S shall be the standard of
	3:29	encamp on the south S of the tabernacle,
	3:35	encamp on the north S of the tabernacle.
	10:5	are on the east S shall set out.
	10:6	are on the south S shall set out.
	11:31	day's journey on this S and a day's journey
	11:31	journey on the other S, round about the camp,
	21:13	encamped on the other S of the Arnon, which
	22:24	between the vineyards, with a wall on either S
	32:19	them on the other S of the Jordan and
	32:19	to us on this S of the Jordan to
	34:3	full extent), your south S shall be from the
	34:3	of Zin along the S of Edom, and your
	34:11	Riblah on the east S of Ain; and the
	35:5	city, for the east S two thousand cubits, and
	35:5	and for the south S two thousand cubits, and
	35:5	and for the west S two thousand cubits, and
	35:5	and for the north S two thousand cubits, the
Deut	4:49	Arabah on the east S of the Jordan as
	31:26	put it by the S of the ark of
Josh	8:11	encamped on the north S of Ai, with a
	8:22	Israel, some on this S, and some on that
	8:22	and some on that S; and Israel smote them,
	12:7	defeated on the west S of the Jordan, from
	15:5	boundary on the north S runs from the bay
	15:7	is on the south S of the valley; and
	15:46	that were by the S of Ashdod, with their
	17:5	is on the other S of the Jordan;
	17:9	goes on the north S of the brook and
	18:12	On the north S their boundary began at the
	18:14	on the western S southward from the mountain
	18:14	This forms the western S
	18:15	And the southern S begins at the outskirts of
	18:20	The Jordan forms its boundary on the eastern S
	21:44	them rest on every S just as he had
	22:4	you on the other S of the Jordan.
	22:11	the Jordan, on the S that belongs to the
	24:8	lived on the other S of the Jordan; they
Judg	7:18	trumpets also on every S of all the camp,
	8:34	their enemies on every S;
	11:18	arrived on the east S of the land of
	11:18	camped on the other S of the Arnon; but
1Sam	4:18	his seat by the S of the gate; and
	6:8	a box at its S the figures of gold,
	12:11	your enemies on every S; and you dwelt in
	14:1	go over to the Philistine garrison on yonder S
	14:4	crag on the one S and a rocky crag
	14:4	crag on the other S; the name of the
	14:40	shall be on one S, and I and Jonathan
	14:40	Jonathan my son will be on the other S
	14:47	his enemies on every S, against Moab, against the
	17:3	mountain on the one S, and Israel stood on
	17:3	mountain on the other S, with a valley between
	20:20	three arrows to the S of it, as though
	20:21	arrows are on this S of you, take them,'
	20:25	Abner sat by Saul's S, but David's place was
	23:26	Saul went on one S of the mountain, and
	23:26	men on the other S of the mountain; and
	26:13	over to the other S, and stood afar off
	31:7	were on the other S of the valley and
2Sam	2:13	one on the one S of the pool, and
	2:13	other on the other S of the pool.
	2:16	sword in his opponent's S; so they fell down
	13:34	Horonaim road by the S of the mountain.
	18:4	king stood at the S of the gate, while
1Kgs	2:22	brother, and on his S are Abiathar the priest
	4:12	far as the other S of Jokmeam;
	5:4	me rest on every S; there is neither adversary
	6:5	sanctuary; and he made S chambers all around.
	6:8	was on the south S of the house; and
	7:30	with wreaths at the S of each.
	7:39	five on the south S of the house, and
	7:39	five on the north S of the house; and
	7:49	five on the south S and five on the
	10:19	head, and on each S of the seat were
2Kgs	2:8	parted to the one S and to the other,
	2:14	parted to the one S and to the other;
	9:25	you and I rode S by side behind Ahab
	9:25	I rode side by S behind Ahab his father,
	9:32	the window, and said, "Who is on my S
	10:6	you are on my S, and if you are
	11:11	hand, from the south S of the house to
	11:11	house to the north S of the house, around
	12:9	altar on the right S as one entered the
	16:14	it on the north S of his altar.
1Chr	4:39	Gedor, to the east S of the valley, to
	5:9	of the desert this S of the Euphrates, because
	6:78	Jericho, on the east S of the Jordan, out
	9:18	hitherto in the king's gate on the east S
	22:18	has he not given you peace on every S
2Chr	4:6	five on the south S, and five on the
	4:6	the south side, and five on the north S
	4:7	five on the south S and five on the
	4:8	five on the south S and five on the
	9:18	throne, and on each S of the seat were
	14:7	and he has given us peace on every S
	23:10	hand, from the south S of the house to
	23:10	house to the north S of the house, around
	32:22	enemies; and he gave them rest on every S
	32:30	down to the west S of the city of
Neh	4:18	sword girded at his S while he built.
Job	1:10	house and all that he has, on every S
	18:11	frighten him on every S, and chase him at
	19:10	me down on every S, and I am gone,
	19:27	shall see on my S, and my eyes shall
Ps	12:8	On every S the wicked prowl, as vileness is

S

19:43 you in on every S,
Jn 6:1 went to the other S of the Sea of
6:22 remained on the other S of the sea saw
6:25 him on the other S of the sea, they
19:18 others, one on either S, and Jesus between them.
19:34 the soldiers pierced his S with a spear, and
20:20 this, he showed them his hands and his S
20:25 my hand in his S, I will not believe."
20:27 place it in my S; do not be faithless,
21:6 net on the right S of the boat, and
Acts 12:7 struck Peter on the S and woke him, saying,
Phil 1:27 with one mind striving S by side for the
1:27 mind striving side by S for the faith of
4:3 for they have labored S by side with me
4:3 have labored side by S with me in the
Rev 4:6 the throne, on each S of the throne, are
22:2 city; also, on either S of the river, the

SIDEBOARD

1Mac 15:32 of Simon, and the S with its gold and

SIDED (2)

1Mac 10:26 us, and have not S with our enemies, we
Acts 14:4 city were divided; some S with the Jews, and

SIDES (34)

Ex 25:14 the rings on the S of the ark, to
25:32 going out of its S, three branches of the
26:13 shall hang over the S of the tabernacle, on
27:7 be upon the two S of the altar, when
30:3 its top and its S round about and its
30:4 molding on two opposite S of it shall you
32:15 were written on both S; on the one side
37:5 the rings on the S of the ark, to
37:18 going out of its S, three branches of the
37:26 its top, and its S round about, and its
37:27 molding, on two opposite S of it, as holders
38:7 the rings on the S of the altar, to
Num 33:55 and thorns in your S, and they shall trouble
Josh 8:33 judges, stood on opposite S of the ark before
23:13 a scourge on your S, and thorns in your
1Kgs 4:24 had peace on all S round about him.
1Chr 9:24 were on the four S, east, west, north, and
Jud 6:6 servants shall pierce your S, and you shall fall
Sir 30:12 youth, and beat his S while he is young,
Jer 48:28 that nests in the S of the mouth of
52:23 ninety-six pomegranates on the S; all the
Ezek 1:8 wings on their four S they had human hands.
36:3 crushed you from all S, so that you became
37:21 gather them from all S, and bring them to
39:17 come, gather from all S to the sacrificial feast
42:20 He measured it on the four S
45:7 the land on both S of the holy district
47:12 the banks, on both S of the river, there
48:21 "What remains on both S of the holy portion
1Mac 4:34 Then both S attacked, and there fell of the
6:45 left, and they parted before him on both S
9:17 and many on both S were wounded and fell.
2Mac 13:5 it which on all S inclines precipitously into the
Heb 9:4 covenant covered on all S with gold, which contained

SIDEWALLS (4)

Ezek 40:48 fourteen cubits; and the S of the gate were
41:2 ten cubits; and the S of the entrance were
41:3 six cubits; and the S of the entrance, seven
41:26 either side, on the S of the vestibule.

SIDON (36)

Gen 10:15 became the father of S his first-born, and Heth,
10:19 the Canaanites extended from S, in the direction of
49:13 for ships, and his border shall be at S
Josh 11:8 far as Great S and Misrephoth-maim, and eastward
19:28 Kanah, as far as S the Great;
Judg 1:31 or the inhabitants of S, or of Ahlab, or
10:6 Syria, the gods of S, the gods of Moab,
18:28 it was far from S, and they had no
2Sam 24:6 they went around to S,
1Kgs 17:9 Zarephath, which belongs to S, and dwell there.
1Chr 1:13 was the father of S his first-born, and Heth,
Jud 2:28 along the seacoast, at S and Tyre, and those
Is 23:2 coast, O merchants of S; your messengers passed
23:4 Be ashamed, O S, for the sea has spoken,
23:12 oppressed virgin daughter of S; arise, pass over to
Jer 25:22 all the kings of S, and the kings of
27:3 and the king of S by the hand of
47:4 off from Tyre and S every helper that remains.
Ezek 27:8 The inhabitants of S and Arvad were your rowers;
28:21 set your face toward S, and prophesy against her
28:22 am against you, O S, and I will manifest
Joel 3:4 me, O Tyre and S, and all the regions
Zech 9:2 borders thereon, Tyre and S, though they are very
1Mac 5:15 Ptolemais and Tyre and S, and all Galilee of
Mt 11:21 done in Tyre and S, they would have repented
11:22 judgment for Tyre and S than for you.
15:21 and withdrew to the district of Tyre and S
Mk 3:8 from about Tyre and S a great multitude, hearing
7:23 went away to the region of Tyre and S
7:30 Tyre, and went through S to the Sea of
Lk 4:26 in the land of S, to a woman who
6:17 seacoast of Tyre and S, who came to hear
10:13 done in Tyre and S, they would have repented
10:14 judgment for Tyre and S than for you.
Acts 12:20 people of Tyre and S; and they came to
27:3 we put in at S; and Julius treated Paul

SIDONIAN

1Kgs 11:1 Moabite, Ammonite, Edomite, S, and Hittite women,

SIDONIANS (15)

Deut 3:9 to Mount Hermon (the S call Hermon Sirion, while
Josh 13:4 which belongs to the S, to Aphek, to the
13:6 from Lebanon to Misrephoth-maim, even all the S
Judg 3:3 the Canaanites, and the S, and the Hivites who
10:12 The S also, and the Amalekites, and the Maonites,
18:7 the manner of the S, quiet and unsuspecting, lacking
18:7 were far from the S and had no dealings
1Kgs 5:6 who knows how to cut timber like the S
11:5 the goddess of the S, and after Milcom the
11:33 the goddess of the S, Chemosh the god of
16:31 Ethbaal king of the S, and went and served
2Kgs 23:13 the abomination of the S, and for Chemosh the
1Chr 22:4 without number; for the S and Tyrians brought great
Ezra 3:7 and oil to the S and the Tyrians to
Ezek 32:30 them, and all the S, who have gone down

SIEGE (39)

Deut 28:53 given you, in the S and in the distress
28:55 left him, in the S and in the distress
28:57 all things, in the S and in the distress
Josh 10:31 to Lachish, and laid S to it, and assaulted
10:34 Eglon; and they laid S to it, and assaulted
1Kgs 15:27 all Israel were laying S to Gibbethon.
2Kgs 19:32 or cast up a S mound against it.
25:1 against Jerusalem, and laid S to it; and they
2Chr 32:10 relying, that you stand S in Jerusalem?
Is 21:2 up, O Elam, lay S, O Media; all the
37:33 or cast up a S mound against it.
Jer 6:6 trees; cast up a S mound against Jerusalem.
10:17 from the ground, O you who dwell under S
19:9 his neighbor in the S and in the distress,
32:24 Behold, the S mounds have come up to the
33:4 a defense against the S mounds and before the
52:4 Jerusalem, and they laid S to it and built
Ezek 4:2 it, and build a S wall against it, and
4:3 in a state of S, and press the siege
4:3 siege, and press the S against it.
4:7 your face toward the S of Jerusalem, with your
4:8 till you have completed the days of your S
5:2 the days of the S are completed; and a
17:17 are cast up and S walls built to cut
21:22 up mounds, to build S towers.
24:2 of Babylon has laid S to Jerusalem this very
26:8 will set up a S wall against you, and
Mic 5:1 about with a wall; S is laid against us;
Nah 3:14 Draw water for the S, strengthen your forts; go
Zech 12:2 Judah also in the S against Jerusalem.
1Mac 6:20 year; and he built S towers and other engines
6:21 garrison escaped from the S and some of the
6:49 there to withstand a S, since it was a
6:51 He set up S towers, engines of war to
11:22 not to continue the S, but to meet him
11:23 orders to continue the S; and he chose some
13:43 He made a S engine, brought it up to
13:44 The men in the S engine leaped out into
2Mac 10:18 equipped to withstand a S,

SIEGETOWERS

Is 23:13 They erected their S, they razed her palaces, they

SIEGEWORKS (8)

Deut 20:20 that you may build S against the city that
2Kgs 25:1 it; and they built S against it round about.

13:2 was evil in the S of the LORD, and
13:11 was evil in the S of the LORD; he
14:24 was evil in the S of the LORD; he
15:9 was evil in the S of the LORD, as
15:18 was evil in the S of the LORD; he
15:24 was evil in the S of the LORD; he
15:28 was evil in the S of the LORD; he
17:2 was evil in the S of the LORD, yet
17:17 do evil in the S of the LORD, provoking
17:18 them out of his S; none was left but
17:20 until he had cast them out of his S
17:23 Israel out of his S, as he had spoken
20:3 and have done what is good in thy S
21:2 was evil in the S of the LORD, according
21:6 much evil in the S of the LORD, provoking
21:15 is evil in my S and have provoked me
21:16 was evil in the S of the LORD.
21:20 was evil in the S of the LORD, as
23:27 also out of my S, as I have removed
23:32 was evil in the S of the LORD, according
23:37 was evil in the S of the LORD, according
24:3 them out of his S, for the sins of
24:9 was evil in the S of the LORD, according
24:19 was evil in the S of the LORD, according
1Chr 2:3 was wicked in the S of the LORD, and
28:8 Now therefore in the S of all Israel, the
29:25 great repute in the S of all Israel, and
2Chr 7:20 cast out of my S, and will make it
20:32 was right in the S of the LORD.
21:6 was evil in the S of the LORD.
22:4 was evil in the S of the LORD, as
29:6 was evil in the S of the LORD our
32:23 was exalted in the S of all nations from
33:2 was evil in the S of the LORD, according
33:6 much evil in the S of the LORD, provoking
33:22 was evil in the S of the LORD, as
36:5 was evil in the S of the LORD his
36:9 was evil in the S of the LORD.
36:12 was evil in the S of the LORD his
Neh 1:11 him mercy in the S of this man." Now
2:5 found favor in your S, that you send me
4:5 blotted out from thy S; for they have provoked
8:5 the book in the S of all the people,
Tob 1:13 good appearance in the S of Shalmaneser, and I
4:21 sin and do what is pleasing in his S
7:7 Tobit had lost his S, he was stricken with
11:6 And she caught S of him coming, and said
14:2 when he lost his S, and after eight years
Jud 5:12 so the Egyptians drove them out of their S
Esth 2:17 and favor in his S more than all the
5:2 found favor in his S and he held out
5:8 found favor in the S of the king, and
7:3 found favor in your S, O king, and if
8:5 found favor in his S, and if the thing
Job 15:15 not clean in his S;
18:3 Why are we stupid in your S
25:5 not clean in his S;
30:10 to spit at the S of me.
34:26 their wickedness in the S of men,
41:9 low even at the S of him.
Ps 10:5 high, out of his S; as for all his
18:24 to the cleanness of my hands in his S
19:14 be acceptable in thy S, O LORD, my rock
31:19 in thee, in the S of the sons of
31:22 my alarm, "I am driven far from thy S
39:5 and my lifetime is as nothing in thy S
44:16 and revilers, at the S of the enemy and
51:4 is evil in thy S, so that thou art
72:14 life; and precious is their blood in his S
78:12 In the S of their fathers he wrought marvels
90:4 thousand years in thy S are but as yesterday
98:2 his vindication in the S of the nations.
116:15 Precious in the S of the LORD is the
Prov 1:17 net spread in the S of any bird;
3:4 good repute in the S of God and man.
3:21 not escape from your S,
4:4 only one in the S of my mother,
4:22 not escape from your S; keep them within your
Eccl 6:9 Better is the S of the eyes than the
11:9 your heart and the S of your eyes.
Wis 2:15 our thoughts; the very S of him is a
3:4 For though in the S of men they were
7:9 little sand in her S, and silver will be
8:11 judgment, and in the S of rulers I shall
9:9 is pleasing in thy S and what is right
11:19 men, but the mere S of them could kill

19:17 also with loss of S -- just as were
19:18 clearly inferred from the S of what took place.
Sir 1:26 a hypocrite in men's S, and keep watch over
3:18 find favor in the S of the Lord.
8:16 as nothing in his S, and where no help
11:19 is easy in the S of the Lord to
11:24 is easy in the S of the Lord to
25:1 are beautiful in the S of the Lord and
45:1 found favor in the S of all flesh and
46:6 was fighting in the S of the Lord; for
Is 5:21 their own eyes, and shrewd in their own S
38:3 and have done what is good in thy S
Jer 7:15 you out of my S, as I cast out
7:30 done evil in my S, says the LORD; they
15:1 them out of my S, and let them go!
18:10 does evil in my S, not listening to my
18:23 iniquity, nor blot out their sin from thy S
19:10 the flask in the S of the men who
32:30 but evil in my S from their youth; the
32:31 remove it from my S
33:24 they are no longer a nation in their S
43:9 in Tahpanhes, in the S of the men of
52:2 was evil in the S of the LORD, according
Bar 1:12 them many days and find favor in their S
1:21 is evil in the S of the Lord our
2:14 us favor in the S of those who have
6:37 They cannot restore S to a blind man; they
Ezek 4:12 baking it in their S on human dung."
5:8 of you in the S of the nations.
5:14 you and in the S of all that pass
6:9 loathsome in their own S for the evils which
10:19 the earth in my S as they went forth,
12:3 by day in their S; you shall go like
12:3 from your place to another place in their S
12:4 by day in their S, as baggage for exile;
12:4 at evening in their S, as men do who
12:5 the wall in their S, and go out through
12:6 In their S you shall lift the baggage upon
12:7 carrying my outfit upon my shoulder in their S
16:41 upon you in the S of many women; I
20:9 be profaned in the S of the nations among
20:9 they dwelt, in whose S I made myself known
20:14 be profaned in the S of the nations, in
20:14 the nations, in whose S I had brought them
20:22 be profaned in the S of the nations, in
20:22 the nations, in whose S I had brought them
20:41 among you in the S of the nations.
22:16 through you in the S of the nations; and
28:18 the earth in the S of all who saw
28:25 in them in the S of the nations, then
36:34 it was in the S of all who passed
39:27 my holiness in the S of many nations.
43:11 it down in their S, so that they may
Dan 1:9 and compassion in the S of the chief of
3:40 sacrifice be in thy S this day, and may
13:23 to sin in the S of the Lord."
Hos 2:10 her lewdness in the S of her lovers, and
Amos 9:3 they hide from my S at the bottom of
Zeph 3:7 she will not lose S of all that I
Hag 2:3 it not in your S as nothing?
Zech 8:6 is marvelous in the S of the remnant of
8:6 be marvelous in my S, says the LORD of
Mal 2:17 is good in the S of the LORD, and
1Mac 2:23 came forward in the S of all to offer
3:18 few, for in the S of Heaven there is
Mt 11:5 the blind receive their S and the lame walk,
20:34 immediately they received their S and followed him.
Mk 10:51 said to him, "Master, let me receive my S
10:52 immediately he received his S and followed him on
Lk 4:18 captives and recovering of S to the blind, to
7:21 and on many that were blind he bestowed S
7:22 the blind receive their S, the lame walk, lepers
16:15 an abomination in the S of God.
18:41 He said, "Lord, let me receive my S
18:42 to him, "Receive your S; your faith has made
18:43 he received his S and followed him, glorifying
23:47 assembled to see the S, when they saw what
24:31 recognized him; and he vanished out of their S
Jn 9:11 so I went and washed and received my S
9:15 again asked him how he had received his S
9:18 and had received his S, until they called the
9:18 who had received his S,
Acts 1:9 and a cloud took him out of their S
4:19 is right in the S of God to listen
7:31 he wondered at the S; and as he drew
7:46 found favor in the S of God and asked

S

9:9 days he was without S, and neither ate nor
9:12 on him so that he might regain his S
9:17 you may regain your S and be filled with
9:18 fell from his eyes and he regained his S
10:33 here present in the S of God, to hear
19:19 burned them in the S of all; and they
21:3 we had come in S of Cyprus, leaving it
22:13 'Brother Saul, receive your S And in that very
22:13 hour I received my S and saw him.
Rom 3:20 be justified in his S by works of the
12:17 is noble in the S of all.
2Cor 2:17 by God, in the S of God we speak
4:2 man's conscience in the S of God.
5:7 Lord, for we walk by faith, not by S
7:12 to you in the S of God.
8:21 only in the Lord's S but also in the
8:21 but also in the S of men.
12:19 It is in the S of God that we
Gal 1:22 still not known by S to the churches of
1Tim 2:3 is acceptable in the S of God our Savior,
5:4 is acceptable in the S of God.
Heb 12:21 so terrifying was the S that Moses said, "I
13:21 is pleasing in his S, through Jesus Christ; to
1Pet 2:4 men but in God's S chosen and precious;
3:4 spirit, which in God's S is very precious.
Rev 3:2 works perfect in the S of my God.
11:12 And in the S of their foes they went
13:13 to earth in the S of men;

SIGHTS

Deut 28:67 shall fear, and the S which your eyes shall

SIGN (98)

Gen 9:12 said, "This is the S of the covenant which
9:13 it shall be a S of the covenant between
9:17 Noah, "This is the S of the covenant which
17:11 it shall be a S of the covenant between
Ex 3:12 this shall be the S for you, that I
4:8 "or heed the first S, they may believe the
4:8 the first sign, they may believe the latter S
8:23 By tomorrow shall this S be.'"
12:13 blood shall be a S for you, upon the
13:9 to you as a S on your hand and
31:13 for this is a S between me and you
31:17 It is a S for ever between me and
Num 16:38 they shall be a S to the people of
17:10 be kept as a S for the rebels, that
Deut 6:8 bind them as a S upon your hand, and
11:18 bind them as a S upon your hand, and
13:1 and gives you a S or a wonder,
13:2 a wonder, and the S or wonder which he
28:46 upon you as a S and a wonder, and
Josh 2:12 give me a sure S,
4:6 this may be a S among you, when your
Judg 6:17 then show me a S that it is thou
1Sam 2:34 Phinehas, shall be the S to you: both of
10:1 this shall be the S to you that the
14:10 this shall be the S to us."
1Kgs 13:3 And he gave a S the same day, saying,
13:3 saying, "This is the S that the LORD has
13:5 altar, according to the S which the man of
2Kgs 4:31 was no sound or S of life.
19:29 this shall be the S for you: this year
20:8 "What shall be the S that the LORD will
20:9 said, "This is the S to you from the
2Chr 32:24 and he answered him and gave him a S
32:31 to inquire about the S that had been done
Esth 14:16 that I abhor the S of my proud position,
Ps 86:17 Show me a S of thy favor, that those
Wis 5:11 wings, and afterward no S of its coming is
5:13 and we had no S of virtue to show,
Sir 43:6 make the times and to be an everlasting S
43:7 the moon comes the S for feast days, a
Is 7:11 to Ahaz, "Ask a S of the LORD your
7:14 Therefore the Lord himself will give you a S
19:20 It will be a S and a witness to
20:3 three years as a S and a portent against
37:30 this shall be the S for you: this year
38:7 "This is the S to you from the LORD,
38:22 said, "What is the S that I shall go
55:13 memorial, for an everlasting S which shall not be
66:19 I will set a S among them.
Jer 44:29 This shall be the S to you, says the
Ezek 4:3 This is a S for the house of Israel.
12:6 have made you a S for the house of
12:11 Say, 'I am a S for you: as I
14:8 will make him a S and a byword and
20:12 my sabbaths, as a S between me and them,
20:20 they may be a S between me and you,
24:24 be to you a S; according to all that
24:27 you will be a S to them; and they
39:15 shall set up a S by it, till the
Dan 6:8 establish the interdict and S the document, so that
6:12 Did you not S an interdict, that any man
2Mac 6:13 them immediately, is a S of great kindness.
15:35 a clear and conspicuous S to every one of
Mt 12:38 wish to see a S from you."
12:39 generation seeks for a S; but no sign shall
12:39 a sign; but no S shall be given to
12:39 to it except the S of the prophet Jonah.
16:1 to show them a S from heaven.
16:4 generation seeks for a S, but no sign shall
16:4 a sign, but no S shall be given to
16:4 to it except the S of Jonah." So he
24:3 what will be the S of your coming and
24:30 then will appear the S of the Son of
26:48 had given them a S, saying, "The one I
Mk 8:11 seeking from him a S from heaven, to test
8:12 and said, "Why does this generation seek a S
8:12 say to you, no S shall be given to
13:4 what will be the S when these things are
14:44 had given them a S, saying, "The one I
Lk 2:12 this will be a S for you: you will
2:34 Israel, and for a S that is spoken against
11:16 sought from him a S from heaven.
11:29 generation; it seeks a S, but no sign shall
11:29 a sign, but no S shall be given to
11:29 to it except the S of Jonah.
11:30 as Jonah became a S to the men of
21:7 what will be the S when this is about
23:8 hoping to see some S done by him.
Jn 2:18 said to him, "What S have you to show
4:54 was now the second S that Jesus did when
6:14 the people saw the S which he had done,
6:30 to him, "Then what S do you do, that
10:41 said, "John did no S, but everything that John
12:18 was that they heard he had done this S
Acts 4:16 For that a notable S has been performed through
4:22 man on whom this S of healing was performed
Rom 4:11 received circumcision as a S or seal of the
1Cor 14:22 Thus, tongues are a S not for believers but

SIGNAL (10)

Judg 20:38 Now the appointed S between the men of Israel
20:40 But when the S began to rise out of
Is 5:26 He will raise a S for a nation afar
13:2 bare hill raise a S, cry aloud to them;
18:3 the earth, when a S is raised on the
30:17 a mountain, like a S on a hill.
49:22 nations, and raise my S to the peoples; and
Jer 6:1 Tekoa, and raise a S on Beth-haccherem; for evil
Zech 10:8 "I will S for them and gather them in,
1Mac 4:40 ground, and sounded the S on the trumpets, and

SIGNATURE

Job 31:35 (Here is my S

SIGNED (7)

Jer 32:10 I S the deed, sealed it, got witnesses, and
32:12 of the witnesses who S the deed of purchase,
32:44 and deeds shall be S and sealed and witnessed,
Dan 6:9 Therefore King Darius S the document and interdict.
6:10 the document had been S, he went to his
6:13 the interdict you have S, but makes his petition
2Mac 11:17 you, have delivered your S communication and have

SIGNET (23)

Gen 38:18 She replied, "Your S and your cord, and your
38:25 whose these are, the S and the cord and
41:42 Then Pharaoh took his S ring from his hand
Ex 28:36 the engraving of a S, 'Holy to the LORD.'
35:22 brooches and earrings and S rings and armlets, all
39:6 the engravings of a S, according to the names
39:30 the engraving of a S, "Holy to the LORD."
Num 31:50 gold, armlets and bracelets, S rings, earrings, and
Tob 1:22 cupbearer, keeper of the S, and in charge of
Esth 3:10 the king took his S ring from his hand
8:2 king took off his S ring, which he had
Sir 17:17 almsgiving is like a S with the Lord, and
45:12 turban, inscribed like a S with "Holiness," a
49:11 He was like a S on the right hand,
Is 3:21 and the amulets; the S rings and nose rings;

S

Jer 22:24 of Judah, were the S ring on my right
Ezek 28:12 GOD: "You were the S of perfection, full of
Dan 6:17 it with his own S and with the signet
6:17 signet and with the S of his lords, that
14:11 shut the door and seal it with your S
14:14 it with the king's S, and departed.
Hag 2:23 make you like a S ring; for I have
1Mac 6:15 his robe and the S, that he might guide

SIGNETS (5)

Ex 28:11 As a jeweler engraves S, so shall you engrave
28:21 they shall be like S, each engraved with its
39:14 Israel; they were like S, each engraved with its
Sir 38:27 those who cut the S of seals, each is
45:11 precious stones engraved like S, in a setting of

SIGNPOST

Ezek 21:19 And make a S, make it at the head

SIGNS (87)

Gen 1:14 let them be for S and for seasons and
Ex 4:9 believe even these two S or heed your voice,
4:17 this rod, with which you shall do the S
4:28 him, and all the S which he had charged
4:30 Moses, and did the S in the sight of
7:3 though I multiply my S and wonders in the
10:1 I may show these S of mine among them,
10:2 the Egyptians and what S I have done among
Num 14:11 spite of all the S which I have wrought
14:22 my glory and my S which I wrought in
Deut 4:34 nation, by trials, by S, by wonders, and by
6:22 and the LORD showed S and wonders, great and
7:19 your eyes saw, the S, the wonders, the mighty
11:3 his outstretched arm, his S and his deeds which
26:8 with great terror, with S and wonders;
29:3 your eyes saw, the S, and those great wonders;
34:11 him for all the S and the wonders which
Josh 24:17 who did those great S in our sight, and
1Sam 10:7 Now when these S meet you, do whatever your
10:9 heart; and all these S came to pass that
Neh 9:10 and didst perform S and wonders against Pharaoh
Esth 10:9 God has done great S and wonders, which have
Ps 65:8 are afraid at thy S; thou makest the outgoings
74:4 set up their own S for signs.
74:4 place; they set up their own signs for S
74:9 do not see our S; there is no longer
78:43 when he wrought his S in Egypt, and his
105:27 They wrought his S among them, and miracles in
135:9 midst, O Egypt, sent S and wonders against Pharaoh
Wis 2:9 everywhere let us leave S of enjoyment, because this
8:8 she has foreknowledge of S and wonders and of
10:16 Lord, and withstood dread kings with wonders and S
19:13 the sinners without prior S in the violence of
Sir 36:6 Show S anew, and work further wonders; make thy
42:18 he looks into the S of the age.
45:3 his words he caused S to cease; the Lord
Is 8:18 has given me are S and portents in Israel
Jer 10:2 be dismayed at the S of the heavens because
32:20 doings; who hast shown S and wonders in the
32:21 land of Egypt with S and wonders, with a
Bar 2:11 mighty hand and with S and wonders and with
6:67 kings; they cannot show S in the heavens and
Dan 4:2 me to show the S and wonders that the
4:3 How great are his S, how mighty his wonders!
6:27 and rescues, he works S and wonders in heaven
Mt 16:3 you cannot interpret the S of the times.
24:24 arise and show great S and wonders, so as
Mk 13:22 will arise and show S and wonders, to lead
16:17 And these S will accompany those who believe: in
16:20 the message by the S that attended it.
Lk 1:22 temple; and he made S to them and remained
1:62 And they made S to his father, inquiring what
17:20 is not coming with S to be observed;
21:11 be terrors and great S from heaven.
21:25 "And there will be S in sun and moon
Jn 2:11 the first of his S, Jesus did at Cana
2:23 when they saw the S which he did;
3:2 one can do these S that you do, unless
4:48 him, "Unless you see S and wonders you will
6:2 because they saw the S which he did on
6:26 not because you saw S, but because you ate
7:31 will he do more S than this man has
9:16 a man who is a sinner do such S
11:47 For this man performs many S
12:37 had done so many S before them, yet they
20:30 Jesus did many other S in the presence of
Acts 2:19 the heaven above and S on the earth beneath,
2:22 works and wonders and S which God did through
2:43 and many wonders and S were done through the
4:30 hand to heal, and S and wonders are performed
5:12 Now many S and wonders were done among the
6:8 did great wonders and S among the people.
7:36 having performed wonders and S in Egypt and at
8:6 him and saw the S which he did.
8:13 And seeing S and great miracles performed, he was
14:3 of his grace, granting S and wonders to be
15:12 as they related what S and wonders God had
Rom 15:19 by the power of S and wonders, by the
1Cor 1:22 For Jews demand S and Greeks seek wisdom,
2Cor 12:12 The S of a true apostle were performed among
12:12 in all patience, with S and wonders and mighty
2Thes 2:9 power and with pretended S and wonders,
Heb 2:4 also bore witness by S and wonders and various
Rev 13:13 It works great S, even making fire come down
13:14 men; and by the S which it is allowed
16:14 are demonic spirits, performing S, who go abroad to
19:20 presence had worked the S by which he deceived

SIHON (36)

Num 21:21 Israel sent messengers to S king of the Amorites,
21:23 But S would not allow Israel to pass through
21:26 was the city of S the king of the
21:27 let the city of S be established.
21:28 forth from Heshbon, flame from the city of S
21:29 and his daughters captives, to an Amorite king, S
21:34 as you did to S king of the Amorites,
32:33 Joseph, the kingdom of S king of the Amorites
Deut 1:4 after he had defeated S the king of the
2:24 given into your hand S the Amorite, king of
2:26 wilderness of Kedemoth to S the king of Heshbon,
2:30 gives to us.' But S the king of Heshbon
2:31 have begun to give S and his land over
2:32 occupy his land.' Then S came out against us,
3:2 as you did to S the king of the
3:6 as we did to S the king of Heshbon,
4:46 in the land of S the king of the
29:7 came to this place, S the king of Heshbon
31:4 as he did to S and Og, the kings
Josh 2:10 beyond the Jordan, to S and Og, whom you
9:10 were beyond the Jordan, S the king of Heshbon,
12:2 all the Arabah eastward: S king of the Amorites
12:5 to the boundary of S king of Heshbon.
13:10 all the cities of S king of the Amorites,
13:21 all the kingdom of S king of the Amorites,
13:21 Reba, the princes of S, who dwelt in the
13:27 of the kingdom of S king of Heshbon, having
Judg 11:19 then sent messengers to S king of the Amorites,
11:20 to our country.' But S did not trust Israel
11:20 through his territory; so S gathered all his people
11:21 God of Israel, gave S and all his people
1Kgs 4:19 Gilead, the country of S king of the Amorites
Neh 9:22 of the land of S king of Heshbon and
Ps 135:11 and slew mighty kings, S, king of the Amorites,
136:19 love endures for ever; S, king of the Amorites,
Jer 48:45 from the house of S; it has destroyed the

SILAS (12)

Acts 15:22 Judas called Barsabbas, and S, leading men among
15:27 therefore sent Judas and S, who themselves will tell
15:32 And Judas and S, who were themselves prophets,
15:39 Cyprus, but Paul chose S and departed, being
16:19 they seized Paul and S and dragged them into
16:25 about midnight Paul and S were praying and singing
16:29 down before Paul and S,
17:4 and joined Paul and S; as did a great
17:10 immediately sent Paul and S away by night to
17:14 to the sea, but S and Timothy remained there.
17:15 receiving a command for S and Timothy to come
18:5 When S and Timothy arrived from Macedonia, Paul

SILENCE (33)

Gen 24:21 gazed at her in S to learn whether the
Deut 27:9 to all Israel, "Keep S and hear, O Israel:
Judg 3:19 And he commanded, S
Esth 4:14 For if you keep S at such a time
Job 4:16 my eyes; there was S, then I heard a
11:3 Should your babble S men, and when you mock,
13:13 "Let me have S, and I will speak, and
29:21 and waited, and kept S for my counsel.
31:34 so that I kept S, and did not go
41:12 "I will not keep S concerning his limbs, or
Ps 50:3 he does not keep S, before him is a

62:1 my soul waits in S; from him comes my
62:5 my soul waits in S, for my hope is
83:1 God, do not keep S; do not hold thy
94:17 would soon have dwelt in the land of S
115:17 LORD, nor do any that go down into S
Eccl 3:7 a time to keep S, and a time to
Wis 18:14 For while gentle S enveloped all things, and night
Sir 41:20 and giving, and of S, before those who greet
Is 41:1 Listen to me in S, O coastlands; let the
47:5 Sit in S, and go into darkness, O daughter
Jer 48:2 shall be brought to S; the sword shall pursue
Lam 2:10 on the ground in S; they have cast dust
3:28 him sit alone in S when he has laid
Amos 8:3 every place they shall be cast out in S
Hab 2:20 all the earth keep S before him.
Lk 9:36 And they kept S and told no one in
Acts 15:12 all the assembly kept S; and they listened to
1Cor 14:28 each of them keep S in church and speak
14:34 the women should keep S in the churches.
1Tim 2:11 a woman learn in S with all submissiveness.
1Pet 2:15 you should put to S the ignorance of foolish
Rev 8:1 seventh seal, there was S in heaven for about

SILENCED (4)

Mt 22:34 heard that he had S the Sadducees, they came
Acts 11:18 When they heard this they were S
2Cor 11:10 mine shall not be S in the regions of
Tit 1:10 party; they must be S, since they are upsetting

SILENT (53)

2Kgs 7:9 news; if we are S and wait until the
18:36 But the people were S and answered him not
Neh 5:8 They were S, and could not find a word
Job 6:24 and I will be S; make me understand how
13:5 that you would keep S, and it would be
13:19 then I would be S and die.
33:31 listen to me; be S, and I will speak.
33:33 listen to me; be S, and I will teach
Ps 4:4 your own hearts on your beds, and be S
28:1 lest, if thou be S to me, I become
30:12 my soul may praise thee and not be S
35:22 Thou hast seen, O LORD; be not S
39:2 I was dumb and S, I held my peace
50:21 and I have been S; you thought that I
109:1 Be not S, O God of my praise!
Prov 11:12 lacks sense, but a man of understanding remains S
17:28 a fool who keeps S is considered wise; when
Wis 8:12 When I am S they will wait for me,
Sir 13:22 man speaks all are S, and they extol to
20:1 a man who keeps S but is wise.
20:4 one who by keeping S is found wise, while
20:5 is one who keeps S because he has no
20:5 answer, while another keeps S because he knows
20:6 wise man will be S until the right moment,
26:14 A S wife is a gift of the Lord,
Is 36:21 But they were S and answered him not a
62:1 I will not keep S, and for Jerusalem's sake
62:6 and all the night they shall never be S
64:12 Wilt thou keep S, and afflict us sorely?
65:6 "I will not keep S, but I will repay,
Jer 4:19 wildly; I cannot keep S; for I hear the
Amos 5:13 is prudent will keep S in such a time;
Hab 1:13 faithless men, and art S when the wicked swallows
Zeph 1:7 Be S before the Lord GOD!
Zech 2:13 Be S, all flesh, before the LORD; for he
1Mac 11:5 throw blame on him; but the king kept S
Mt 20:31 telling them to be S; but they cried out
26:63 But Jesus was S
Mk 1:25 rebuked him, saying, "Be S, and come out of
3:4 But they were S
9:34 But they were S; for on the way they
10:48 telling him to be S; but he cried out
14:61 But he was S and made no answer.
Lk 1:20 behold, you will be S and unable to speak
4:35 rebuked him, saying, "Be S, and come out of
14:4 But they were S
18:39 telling him to be S; but he cried out
19:40 you, if these were S, the very stones would
20:26 said; but marveling at his answer they were S
Acts 12:17 his hand to be S, he described to them
18:9 and do not be S;
1Cor 14:30 to another sitting by, let the first be S
1Tim 2:12 have authority over men; she is to keep S

SILK (3)

Ezek 16:10 you in fine linen and covered you with S
16:13 of fine linen, and S, and embroidered cloth; you
Rev 18:12 pearls, fine linen, purple, S and scarlet, all kinds

SILLA

2Kgs 12:20 Millo, on the way that goes down to S

SILLY (3)

Hos 7:12 is like a dove, S and without sense, calling
Eph 5:4 be no filthiness, nor S talk, nor levity, which
1Tim 4:7 do with godless and S myths.

SILOAM (3)

Lk 13:4 whom the tower in S fell and killed them,
Jn 9:7 to him, "Go, wash in the pool of S
9:11 to me, 'Go to S and wash'; so I

SILVANUS (4)

2Cor 1:19 we preached among you, S and Timothy and I,
1Thes 1:1 Paul, S, and Timothy, to the
2Thes 1:1 Paul, S, and Timothy, to the
1Pet 5:12 By S, a faithful brother as I regard him,

SILVER (372)

Gen 13:2 rich in cattle, in S, and in gold.
20:16 a thousand pieces of S; it is your vindication
23:15 four hundred shekels of S, what is that between
23:16 out for Ephron the S which he had named
23:16 four hundred shekels of S, according to the weights
24:35 him flocks and herds, S and gold, menservants and
24:53 brought forth jewelry of S and of gold, and
37:28 for twenty shekels of S; and they took Joseph
44:2 put my cup, the S cup, in the mouth
44:4 have you stolen my S cup?
44:8 then should we steal S or gold from your
45:22 three hundred shekels of S and five festal garments.
Ex 3:22 her house, jewelry of S and of gold, and
11:2 her neighbor, jewelry of S and of gold."
12:35 the Egyptians jewelry of S and of gold, and
20:23 not make gods of S to be with me,
21:32 master thirty shekels of S, and the ox shall
25:3 receive from them: gold, S, and bronze,
26:19 and forty bases of S you shall make under
26:21 their forty bases of S, two bases under one
26:25 with their bases of S, sixteen bases; two bases
26:32 with hooks of gold, upon four bases of S
27:10 the pillars and their fillets shall be of S
27:11 the pillars and their fillets shall be of S
27:17 shall be filleted with S; their hooks shall be
27:17 hooks shall be of S, and their bases of
31:4 to work in gold, S, and bronze,
35:5 the LORD's offering: gold, S, and bronze;
35:24 make an offering of S or bronze brought it
35:32 work in gold and S and bronze,
36:24 made forty bases of S under the twenty frames,
36:26 their forty bases of S, two bases under one
36:30 with their bases of S: sixteen bases, under every
36:36 and he cast for them four bases of S
38:10 of the pillars and their fillets were of S
38:11 of the pillars and their fillets were of S
38:12 of the pillars and their fillets were of S
38:17 their fillets were of S; the overlaying of their
38:17 capitals was also of S, and all the pillars
38:17 the pillars of the court were filleted with S
38:19 bronze, their hooks of S, and the overlaying of
38:19 overlaying of their capitals and their fillets of S
38:25 And the S from those of the congregation who
38:27 The hundred talents of S were for casting the
Lev 5:15 you in shekels of S, according to the shekel
27:3 be fifty shekels of S, according to the shekel
27:6 male five shekels of S, and for a female
27:6 female your valuation shall be three shekels of S
27:16 barley shall be valued at fifty shekels of S
Num 7:13 his offering was one S plate whose weight was
7:13 and thirty shekels, one S basin of seventy shekels,
7:19 for his offering one S plate, whose weight was
7:19 and thirty shekels, one S basin of seventy shekels,
7:25 his offering was one S plate, whose weight was
7:25 and thirty shekels, one S basin of seventy shekels,
7:31 his offering was one S plate whose weight was
7:31 and thirty shekels, one S basin of seventy shekels,
7:37 his offering was one S plate, whose weight was
7:37 and thirty shekels, one S basin of seventy shekels,
7:43 his offering was one S plate, whose weight was
7:43 and thirty shekels, one S basin of seventy shekels,
7:49 his offering was one S plate, whose weight was
7:49 and thirty shekels, one S basin of seventy shekels,

7:55 his offering was one S plate, whose weight was
7:55 and thirty shekels, one S basin of seventy shekels,
7:61 his offering was one S plate, whose weight was
7:61 and thirty shekels, one S basin of seventy shekels,
7:67 his offering was one S plate, whose weight was
7:67 and thirty shekels, one S basin of seventy shekels,
7:73 his offering was one S plate, whose weight was
7:73 and thirty shekels, one S basin of seventy shekels,
7:79 his offering was one S plate, whose weight was
7:79 and thirty shekels, one S basin of seventy shekels,
7:84 leaders of Israel: twelve S plates, twelve silver
7:84 twelve silver plates, twelve S basins, twelve golden
7:85 twelve golden dishes, each S plate weighing a
7:85 basin seventy, all the S of the vessels two
10:2 to Moses, "Make two S trumpets; of hammered
18:16 at five shekels in S, according to the shekel
22:18 his house full of S and gold, I could
24:13 his house full of S and gold, I would
31:22 only the gold, the S, the bronze, the iron,
Deut 7:25 shall not covet the S or the gold that
8:13 flocks multiply, and your S and gold is multiplied,
17:17 greatly multiply for himself S and gold.
22:19 a hundred shekels of S, and give them to
22:29 woman fifty shekels of S, and she shall be
29:17 wood and stone, of S and gold, which were
Josh 6:19 But all S and gold, and vessels of bronze
6:24 within it; only the S and gold, and the
7:21 two hundred shekels of S, and a bar of
7:21 my tent, with the S underneath."
7:22 his tent with the S underneath.
7:24 of Zerah, and the S and the mantle and
22:8 very many cattle, with S, gold, bronze, and iron,
Judg 5:19 waters of Megiddo; they got no spoils of S
9:4 him seventy pieces of S out of the house
16:5 will each give you eleven hundred pieces of S
17:2 eleven hundred pieces of S which were taken from
17:2 my ears, behold, the S is with me; I
17:3 eleven hundred pieces of S to his mother; and
17:3 said, "I consecrate the S to the LORD from
17:4 two hundred pieces of S, and gave it to
17:10 you ten pieces of S a year, and a
1Sam 2:36 for a piece of S or a loaf of
9:8 of a shekel of S, and I will give
2Sam 8:10 with him articles of S, of gold, and of
8:11 LORD, together with the S and gold which he
18:11 you ten pieces of S and a girdle."
18:12 a thousand pieces of S, I would not put
21:4 not a matter of S or gold between us
24:24 floor and the oxen for fifty shekels of S
1Kgs 7:51 father had dedicated, the S, the gold, and the
10:21 gold; none were of S, it was not considered
10:22 to come bringing gold, S, ivory, apes, and peacocks.
10:25 his present, articles of S and gold, garments, myrrh,
10:27 And the king made S as common in Jerusalem
10:29 six hundred shekels of S, and a horse for
15:15 his own votive gifts, S, and gold, and vessels.
15:18 Asa took all the S and the gold that
15:19 you a present of S and gold; go, break
16:24 for two talents of S; and he fortified the
20:3 "Thus says Ben-hadad: 'Your S and your gold are
20:5 "Deliver to me your S and your gold, your
20:7 children, and for my S and my gold, and
20:39 pay a talent of S
2Kgs 5:5 him ten talents of S, six thousand shekels of
5:22 them a talent of S and two festal garments.'"
5:23 up two talents of S in two bags, with
6:25 for eighty shekels of S, and the fourth part
6:25 kab of dove's dung for five shekels of S
7:8 and they carried off S and gold and clothing,
12:13 the LORD basins of S, snuffers, bowls, trumpets, or
12:13 of gold, or of S, from the money that
14:14 all the gold and S, and all the vessels
15:19 a thousand talents of S, that he might help
15:20 men, fifty shekels of S from every man, to
16:8 Ahaz also took the S and gold that was
18:14 three hundred talents of S and thirty talents of
18:15 gave him all the S that was found in
20:13 his treasure house, the S, the gold, the spices,
23:33 a hundred talents of S and a talent of
23:35 And Jehoiakim gave the S and the gold to
23:35 He exacted the S and the gold of the
25:15 and what was of S, as silver.
25:15 as gold, and what was of silver, as S
1Chr 18:10 articles of gold, of S, and of bronze;
18:11 LORD, together with the S and gold which he
19:6 a thousand talents of S to hire chariots and
22:14 a million talents of S, and bronze and iron
22:16 skilled in working gold, S, bronze, and iron.
28:14 service, the weight of S vessels for each service,
28:15 lamps, the weight of S for a lampstand and
28:16 for the showbread, the S for the silver tables,
28:16 the silver for the S tables,
28:17 of each; for the S bowls and the weight
29:2 things of gold, the S for the things of
29:2 for the things of S, and the bronze for
29:3 own of gold and S, and because of my
29:4 thousand talents of refined S, for overlaying the
29:5 things of gold and S for the things of
29:5 of gold and silver for the things of S
29:7 ten thousand talents of S, eighteen thousand talents
2Chr 1:15 And the king made S and gold as common
1:17 six hundred shekels of S, and a horse for
2:7 to work in gold, S, bronze, and iron, and
2:14 to work in gold, S, bronze, iron, stone, and
5:1 dedicated, and stored the S, the gold, and all
9:14 land brought gold and S to Solomon.
9:20 were of pure gold; S was not considered as
9:21 to come bringing gold, S, ivory, apes, and peacocks.
9:24 his present, articles of S and of gold, garments,
9:27 And the king made S as common in Jerusalem
15:18 his own votive gifts, S, and gold, and vessels.
16:2 Then Asa took S and gold from the treasures
16:3 am sending to you S and gold; go, break
17:11 brought Jehoshaphat presents, and S for tribute; and
21:3 them great gifts, of S, gold, and valuable possessions,
24:14 dishes for incense, and vessels of gold and S
25:6 valor from Israel for a hundred talents of S
25:24 all the gold and S, and all the vessels
27:5 a hundred talents of S, and ten thousand cors
32:27 for himself treasuries for S, for gold, for precious
36:3 a hundred talents of S and a talent of
Ezra 1:4 of his place with S and gold, with goods
1:6 them with vessels of S, with gold, with goods,
1:9 a thousand basins of S, twenty-nine censers,
1:10 and ten bowls of S, and a thousand other
1:11 of gold and of S were five thousand four
2:69 five thousand minas of S, and one hundred priests'
5:14 And the gold and S vessels of the house
6:5 let the gold and S vessels of the house
7:15 also to convey the S and gold which the
7:16 Jerusalem, with all the S and gold which you
7:18 the rest of the S and gold, you may
7:22 a hundred talents of S, a hundred cors of
8:25 out to them the S and the gold and
8:26 and fifty talents of S, and silver vessels worth
8:26 talents of silver, and S vessels worth a hundred
8:28 are holy; and the S and the gold are
8:30 the weight of the S and the gold and
8:33 of our God, the S and the gold and
Neh 5:15 them food and wine, besides forty shekels of S
7:71 gold and two thousand two hundred minas of S
7:72 minas of S, and sixty-seven priests' garments.
Tob 1:14 left ten talents of S in trust with Gabael,
4:20 the ten talents of S which I left in
Jud 2:18 amount of gold and S from the royal palace.
5:9 with much gold and S and very many cattle.
8:7 left her gold and S, and men and women
10:22 of the tent, with S lamps carried before him.
12:1 her in where his S dishes were kept, and
15:11 Holofernes and all his S dishes and his beds
Esth 1:6 linen and purple to S rings and marble pillars,
1:6 couches of gold and S on a mosaic pavement
3:9 ten thousand talents of S into the hands of
Job 3:15 who had gold, who filled their houses with S
22:25 gold, and your precious S;
27:16 Though he heap up S like dust, and pile
27:17 wear it, and the innocent will divide the S
28:1 is a mine for S, and a place for
28:15 gotten for gold, and S cannot be weighed as
Ps 12:6 promises that are pure, S refined in a furnace
66:10 hast tried us as S is tried.
68:13 a dove covered with S, its pinions with green
105:37 led forth Israel with S and gold, and there
115:4 Their idols are S and gold, the work of
119:72 thousands of gold and S pieces.
135:15 of the nations are S and gold, the work
Prov 2:4 you seek it like S and search for it
3:14 better than gain from S and its profit better
8:10 my instruction instead of S, and knowledge rather
8:19 even fine gold, and my yield than choice S
10:20 the righteous is choice S; the mind of the
16:16 get understanding is to be chosen rather than S

S

17:3 The crucible is for S, and the furnace is
22:1 favor is better than S or gold.
25:4 the dross from the S, and the smith has
25:11 like apples of gold in a setting of S
27:21 The crucible is for S, and the furnace is
Eccl 2:8 also gathered for myself S and gold and the
12:6 the streets; before the S cord is snapped, or
Song 1:11 will make you ornaments of gold, studded with S
3:10 made its posts of S, its back of gold,
8:9 her a battlement of S; but if she is
8:11 bring for its fruit a thousand pieces of S
Wis 7:9 in her sight, and S will be accounted as
13:10 men's hands, gold and S fashioned with skill, and
15:9 workers in gold and S, and imitates workers in
Sir 26:18 on a base of S, so are beautiful feet
28:24 thorns, lock up your S and gold,
29:10 Lose your S for the sake of a brother
40:25 Gold and S make the foot stand sure, but
47:18 like tin and amassed S like lead.
51:28 a large sum of S, and you will gain
Is 1:22 Your S has become dross, your wine mixed with
2:7 land is filled with S and gold, and there
2:20 forth their idols of S and their idols of
7:23 a thousand shekels of S, will become briers and
13:17 have no regard for S and do not delight
31:7 away his idols of S and his idols of
39:2 his treasure house, the S, the gold, the spices,
40:19 and casts for it S chains.
46:6 purse, and weigh out S in the scales, hire
48:10 you, but not like S; I have tried you
60:9 sons from far, their S and gold with them,
60:17 iron I will bring S; instead of wood, bronze,
Jer 6:30 Refuse S they are called, for the LORD has
10:4 Men deck it with S and gold; they fasten
10:9 Beaten S is brought from Tarshish, and gold from
32:9 out the money to him, seventeen shekels of S
52:19 and what was of S, as silver.
52:19 as gold, and what was of silver, as S
Bar 1:8 land of Judah--the S vessels which Zedekiah the
3:17 and who hoard up S and gold, in which
3:18 who scheme to get S, and are anxious, whose
6:4 see gods made of S and gold and wood,
6:8 overlaid with gold and S; but they are false
6:10 secretly take gold and S from their gods and
6:11 men--these gods of S and gold and wood,
6:30 meals for gods of S and gold and wood;
6:39 overlaid with gold and S are like stones from
6:50 overlaid with gold and S, it will afterward be
6:55 overlaid with gold or S, their priests will flee
6:57 wood and overlaid with S and gold are not
6:58 of their gold and S and of the robes
6:70 their gods of wood, overlaid with gold and S
6:71 overlaid with gold and S, and like a thorn
Ezek 7:19 They cast their S into the streets, and their
7:19 an unclean thing; their S and gold are not
16:13 decked with gold and S; and your raiment was
16:17 gold and of my S, which I had given
22:18 me; all of them, S and bronze and tin
22:20 As men gather S and bronze and iron and
22:22 As S is melted in a furnace, so you
27:12 wealth of every kind; S, iron, tin, and lead
28:4 have gathered gold and S into your treasuries;
38:13 plunder, to carry away S and gold, to take
Dan 2:32 breast and arms of S, its belly and thighs
2:35 clay, the bronze, the S, and the gold, all
2:45 bronze, the clay, the S, and the gold.
5:2 of gold and of S which Nebuchadnezzar his father
5:3 in the golden and S vessels which had been
5:4 gods of gold and S, bronze, iron, wood, and
5:23 praised the gods of S and gold, of bronze,
11:8 their precious vessels of S and of gold; and
11:38 honor with gold and S, with precious stones and
11:43 of gold and of S, and all the precious
Hos 2:8 who lavished upon her S and gold which they
3:2 for fifteen shekels of S and a homer and
8:4 With their S and gold they made idols for
9:6 their precious things of S; thorns shall be in
13:2 skilfully made of their S, all of them the
Joel 3:5 you have taken my S and my gold, and
Amos 2:6 sell the righteous for S, and the needy for
8:6 buy the poor for S and the needy for
Nah 2:9 Plunder the S, plunder the gold!
Hab 2:19 overlaid with gold and S, and there is no
Zeph 1:11 all who weigh out S are cut off.
1:18 Neither their S nor their gold shall be able
Hag 2:8 The S is mine, and the gold is mine,
Zech 6:11 Take from them S and gold, and make a
9:3 rampart, and heaped up S like dust, and gold
11:12 weighed out as my wages thirty shekels of S
11:13 the thirty shekels of S and cast them into
13:9 them as one refines S, and test them as
14:14 shall be collected, gold, S, and garments in great
Mal 3:3 refiner and purifier of S, and he will purify
3:3 them like gold and S, till they present right
1Mac 1:23 He took the S and the gold, and the
2:18 will be honored with S and gold and many
3:41 to them, they took S and gold in immense
4:23 seized much gold and S, and cloth dyed blue
6:1 for its wealth in S and gold.
6:12 all her vessels of S and gold; and I
8:3 get control of the S and gold mines there,
10:40 fifteen thousand shekels of S yearly out of the
10:42 five thousand shekels of S which my officials have
10:60 them and their friends S and gold and many
11:24 king at Ptolemais, taking S and gold and clothing
13:16 a hundred talents of S and two of his
15:26 fight for him, and S and gold and much
15:31 five hundred talents of S, and for the destruction
15:32 with its gold and S plate, and his great
16:11 and he had much S and gold,
16:19 he might give them S and gold and gifts;
2Mac 2:2 seeing the gold and S statues and their adornment.
3:11 four hundred talents of S and two hundred of
4:8 and sixty talents of S and, from another source
4:19 to carry three hundred S drachmas for the sacrifice
4:24 outbidding Jason by three hundred talents of S
12:43 two thousand drachmas of S, and sent it to
Mt 10:9 Take no gold, nor S, nor copper in your
26:15 And they paid him thirty pieces of S
27:3 the thirty pieces of S to the chief priests
27:5 down the pieces of S in the temple, he
27:6 taking the pieces of S, said, "It is not
27:9 the thirty pieces of S, the price of him
Lk 15:8 what woman, having ten S coins, if she loses
Acts 3:6 said, "I have no S and gold, but I
7:16 for a sum of S from the sons of
8:20 said to him, "Your S perish with you, because
17:29 is like gold, or S, or stone, a representation
19:19 found it came to fifty thousand pieces of S
19:24 a silversmith, who made S shrines of Artemis,
20:33 I coveted no one's S or gold or apparel.
1Cor 3:12 foundation with gold, S, precious stones, wood, hay,
2Tim 2:20 vessels of gold and S but also of wood
Jas 5:3 Your gold and S have rusted, and their rust
1Pet 1:18 perishable things such as S or gold,
Rev 9:20 idols of gold and S and bronze and stone
18:12 more, cargo of gold, S, jewels and pearls, fine

SILVER-COVERED

Is 30:22 you will defile your S graven images and your

SILVERSMITH (2)

Judg 17:4 gave it to the S, who made it into
Acts 19:24 man named Demetrius, a S, who made silver shrines

SIMEON (53)

Gen 29:33 this son also"; and she called his name S
34:25 the sons of Jacob, S and Levi, Dinah's brothers,
34:30 Then Jacob said to S and Levi, "You have
35:23 Leah: Reuben (Jacob's first-born), S, Levi, Judah,
42:24 And he took S from them and bound him
42:36 is no more, and S is no more, and
43:23 Then he brought S out to them.
46:10 The sons of S: Jemuel, Jamin, Ohad, Jachin, Zohar,
48:5 mine, as Reuben and S are.
49:5 S and Levi are brothers; weapons of violence are
Ex 1:2 with his household: Reuben, S, Levi, and Judah,
6:15 The sons of S: Jemuel, Jamin, Ohad, Jachin, Zohar,
6:15 a Canaanite woman; these are the families of S
Num 1:6 son of Shedeur; from S, Shelumi-el the son of
1:22 Of the people of S, their generations, by their
1:23 of the tribe of S was fifty-nine thousand three
2:12 be the tribe of S, the leader of the
2:12 of the people of S being Shelumi-el the son
7:36 of the men of S:
10:19 of the men of S was Shelumi-el the son
13:5 from the tribe of S, Shaphat the son of
26:12 The sons of S according to their families: of
34:20 of the sons of S, Shemuel the son of
Deut 27:12 to bless the people: S, Levi, Judah, Issachar, Joseph,
Josh 19:1 lot came out for S, for the tribe of
19:1 for the tribe of S, according to its families;

S

	19:8	of the tribe of S according to its families.
	19:9	of the tribe of S formed part of the
	19:9	them, the tribe of S obtained an inheritance in
	21:4	the tribes of Judah, S, and Benjamin, thirteen cities.
	21:9	and the tribe of S they gave the following
Judg	1:3	And Judah said to S his brother, "Come up
	1:3	So S went with him.
	1:17	And Judah went with S his brother, and they
1Chr	2:1	sons of Israel: Reuben, S, Levi, Judah, Issachar,
	4:24	The sons of S: Nemuel, Jamin, Jarib, Zerah, Shaul;
	6:65	the tribes of Judah, S, and Benjamin these cities
2Chr	15:9	Ephraim, Manasseh, and S who were sojourning
	34:6	of Manasseh, Ephraim, and S, and as far as
Jud	6:15	of the tribe of S, and Chabris the son
	9:2	God of my father S, to whom thou gavest
Ezek	48:24	side to the west, S, one portion.
	48:25	Adjoining the territory of S, from the east side
	48:33	gates, the gate of S, the gate of Issachar,
1Mac	2:1	of John, son of S, a priest of the
	2:65	behold, I know that S your brother is wise
Lk	2:25	Jerusalem, whose name was S, and this man was
	2:34	said about him; and S blessed them and said
	3:30	Levi, the son of S, the son of Judah,
Acts	13:1	prophets and teachers, Barnabas, S who was called
	15:14	S has related how God first visited the Gentiles,
2Pet	1:1	S Peter, a servant and
Rev	7:7	of the tribe of S, twelve thousand of the

SIMEONITES (5)

Num	25:14	head of a fathers' house belonging to the S
	26:14	the families of the S, twenty-two thousand two
1Chr	4:42	hundred men of the S, went to Mount Seir,
	12:25	Of the S, mighty men of valor for war,
	27:16	chief officer; for the S, Shephatiah the son of

SIMILAR (4)

Jer	36:32	the fire; and many S words were added to
Ezek	42:11	of them; they were S to the chambers on
1Mac	5:14	Galilee and made a S report;
2Mac	2:3	And with other S words he exhorted them that

SIMON (154)

Sir	50:1	of his people was S the high priest, son
	50:20	Then S came down, and lifted up his hands
1Mac	2:3	sons, John surnamed Gaddi, S called Thassi,
	5:17	Then Judas said to S his brother, "Choose your
	5:20	men were assigned to S to go to Galilee,
	5:21	So S went to Galilee and fought many battles
	5:55	were in Gilead and S his brother was in
	9:19	Then Jonathan and S took Judas their brother and
	9:33	But Jonathan and S his brother and all who
	9:37	reported to Jonathan and S his brother, "The sons
	9:62	with his men, and S, withdrew to Bethbasi in
	9:65	But Jonathan left S his brother in the city,
	9:67	with his forces; and S and his men sallied
	10:74	out from Jerusalem, and S his brother met him
	10:82	Then S brought forward his force and engaged the
	11:59	S his brother he made governor from the Ladder
	11:64	but left his brother S in the country.
	11:65	S encamped before Bethzur and fought against it for
	12:33	S also went forth and marched through the country
	12:38	And S built Adida in the Shephelah; he fortified
	13:1	S heard that Trypho had assembled a large army
	13:13	And S encamped in Adida, facing the plain.
	13:14	Trypho learned that S had risen up in place
	13:17	S knew that they were speaking deceitfully to him,
	13:18	who might say, "Because S did not send him
	13:20	But S and his army kept marching along opposite
	13:25	And S sent and took the bones of Jonathan
	13:27	And S built a monument over the tomb of
	13:33	But S built up the strongholds of Judea and
	13:34	S also chose men and sent them to Demetrius
	13:36	follows, "King Demetrius to S, the high priest and
	13:42	the first year of S the great high priest
	13:43	In those days S encamped against Gazara and
	13:45	a loud voice, asking S to make peace with
	13:47	So S reached an agreement with them and stopped
	13:50	Then they cried to S to make peace with
	13:52	And S decreed that every year they should celebrate
	13:53	And S saw that John his son had reached
	14:4	The land had rest all the days of S
	14:17	When they heard that S his brother had become
	14:20	of the Spartans to S the high priest and
	14:23	copy of this to S the high priest."'
	14:24	After this S sent Numenius to Rome with a
	14:25	"How shall we thank S and his sons?
	14:27	the third year of S the great high priest,
	14:29	occurred in the country, S the son of Mattathias,
	14:32	on their sanctuary, then S rose up and fought
	14:35	"The people saw S's faithfulness and the glory which
	14:40	received the envoys of S with honor.
	14:41	their priests decided that S should be their leader
	14:46	people agreed to grant S the right to act
	14:47	So S accepted and agreed to be high priest,
	14:49	the treasury, so that S and his sons might
	15:1	of the sea to S, the priest and ethnarch
	15:2	follows: "King Antiochus to S the high priest and
	15:17	had been sent by S the high priest and
	15:21	hand them over to S the high priest, that
	15:24	of these things to S the high priest.
	15:26	And S sent to Antiochus two thousand picked men,
	15:27	formerly had made with S, and became estranged
	15:32	saw the splendor of S, and the sideboard with
	15:33	of the king, but S gave him this reply:
	15:36	and the splendor of S and all that he
	16:1	Gazara and reported to S his father what Cendebeus
	16:2	And S called in his two older sons Judas
	16:13	made treacherous plans against S and his sons, to
	16:14	Now S was visiting the cities of the country
	16:16	When S and his sons were drunk, Ptolemy and
	16:16	and rushed in against S in the banquet hall,
2Mac	3:4	But a man named S, of the tribe of
	3:11	an extent the impious S had misrepresented the
	4:1	The previously mentioned S, who had informed
	4:3	committed by one of S's approved agents,
	4:4	and Phoenicia, was intensifying the malice of S
	4:6	peaceful settlement, and that S would not stop his
	4:23	of the previously mentioned S, to carry the money
	8:22	his brothers also, S and Joseph and Jonathan,
	10:19	a siege, Maccabeus left S and Joseph, and also
	10:20	But the men with S, who were money-hungry, were
	14:17	S, the brother of Judas, had encountered Nicanor,
Mt	4:18	he saw two brothers, S who is called Peter
	10:2	apostles are these: first, S, who is called Peter,
	10:4	and Thaddaeus; S the Cananaean, and Judas
	13:55	James and Joseph and S and Judas?
	16:16	S Peter replied, "You are the Christ, the Son
	16:17	him, "Blessed are you, S Bar-Jona!
	17:24	to him first, saying, "What do you think, S
	26:6	in the house of S the leper,
	27:32	a man of Cyrene, S by name; this man
Mk	1:16	of Galilee, he saw S and Andrew the brother
	1:16	Andrew the brother of S casting a net in
	1:29	entered the house of S and Andrew, with James
	1:30	Now S's mother-in-law lay sick with a fever, and
	1:36	And S and those who were with him pursued
	3:16	to cast out demons: S whom he surnamed Peter;
	3:18	Alphaeus, and Thaddaeus, and S the Cananaean,
	6:3	Joses and Judas and S, and are not his
	14:3	in the house of S the leper, as he
	14:37	he said to Peter, S, are you asleep?
	15:21	they compelled a passer-by, S of Cyrene, who was
Lk	4:38	the synagogue, and entered S's house.
	4:38	Now S's mother-in-law was ill with a high fever,
	5:4	speaking, he said to S, "Put out into the
	5:5	And S answered, "Master, we toiled all night and
	5:8	But when S Peter saw it, he fell down
	5:10	John, sons of Zebedee, who were partners with S
	5:10	And Jesus said to S, "Do not be afraid;
	6:14	whom he named apostles; S, whom he named Peter,
	6:15	son of Alphaeus, and S who was called the
	7:40	answering said to him, S, I have something to
	7:43	S answered, "The one, I suppose, to whom he
	7:44	woman he said to S, "Do you see this
	22:31	S, Simon, behold, Satan demanded to have you, that
	22:31	"Simon, S, behold, Satan demanded to have you,
	23:25	away, they seized one S of Cyrene, who was
	24:34	Lord has risen indeed, and has appeared to S
Jn	1:40	followed him, was Andrew, S Peter's brother.
	1:41	first found his brother S, and said to him,
	1:42	said, "So you are S the son of John?
	6:8	of his disciples, Andrew, S Peter's brother, said to
	6:68	S Peter answered him, "Lord, to whom shall we
	6:71	Judas the son of S Iscariot, for he, one
	13:2	heart of Judas Iscariot, S's son, to betray him,
	13:6	He came to S Peter; and Peter said to
	13:9	S Peter said to him, "Lord, not my feet
	13:24	breast of Jesus; so S Peter beckoned to him
	13:26	Judas, the son of S Iscariot.
	13:36	S Peter said to him, "Lord, where are you
	18:10	Then S Peter, having a sword, drew it and
	18:15	S Peter followed Jesus, and so did another disciple.

18:25 Now S Peter was standing and warming himself.
20:2 ran, and went to S Peter and the other
20:6 Then S Peter came, following him, and went into
21:2 S Peter, Thomas called the Twin, Nathanael of Cana
21:3 S Peter said to them, "I am going fishing."
21:7 When S Peter heard that it was the Lord,
21:11 So S Peter went aboard and hauled the net
21:15 breakfast, Jesus said to S Peter, "Simon, son of
21:15 said to Simon Peter, S, son of John, do
21:16 he said to him, S, son of John, do
21:17 him the third time, S, son of John, do
Acts 1:13 son of Alphaeus and S the Zealot and Judas
8:9 was a man named S who had previously practiced
8:13 Even S himself believed, and after being baptized he
8:18 Now when S saw that the Spirit was given
8:24 And S answered, "Pray for me to the Lord,
9:43 many days with one S, a tanner.
10:5 Joppa, and bring one S who is called Peter;
10:6 he is lodging with S, a tanner, whose house
10:17 having made inquiry for S's house, stood before the
10:18 out to ask whether S who was called Peter
10:32 Joppa and ask for S who is called Peter;
10:32 in the house of S, a tanner, by the
11:13 to Joppa and bring S called Peter;

SIMONS

Lk 5:3 the boats, which was S, he asked him to

SIMPLE (18)

Job 5:2 vexation kills the fool, and jealousy slays the S
Ps 19:7 sure, making wise the S;
116:6 The LORD preserves the S; when I was brought
119:130 words gives light; it imparts understanding to the S
Prov 1:4 be given to the S, knowledge and discretion to
1:22 speaks: "How long, O S ones, will you love
1:22 long, O simple ones, will you love being S
1:32 For the S are killed by their turning away,
7:7 have seen among the S, I have perceived among
8:5 O S ones, learn prudence; O foolish men, pay
9:4 the town, "Whoever is S, let him turn in
9:16 their way, "Whoever is S, let him turn in
14:15 The S believes everything, but the prudent looks
14:18 The S acquire folly, but the prudent are crowned
19:25 a scoffer, and the S will learn prudence; reprove
21:11 scoffer is punished, the S becomes wise; when a
22:3 hides himself; but the S go on, and suffer
27:12 hides himself; but the S go on, and suffer

SIMPLE-MINDED

Rom 16:18 flattering words they deceive the hearts of the S

SIMPLENESS

Prov 9:6 Leave S, and live, and walk in the way

SIMPLICITY

2Sam 15:11 they went in their S, and knew nothing.

SIMPLY (3)

Wis 16:27 fire was melted when S warmed by a fleeting
1Mac 5:48 you harm; we will S pass by on foot."
Mt 5:37 what you say be S 'Yes' or 'No'; anything

SIN (510)

Gen 4:7 do not do well, S is couching at the
18:20 is great and their S is very grave,
20:9 brought on me and my kingdom a great S
31:36 What is my S, that you have hotly pursued
39:9 this great wickedness, and S against God?"
42:22 tell you not to S against the lad?
50:17 your brothers and their S, because they did evil
Ex 10:17 Now therefore, forgive my S, I pray you, only
16:1 to the wilderness of S, which is between Elim
17:1 from the wilderness of S by stages, according to
20:20 be before your eyes, that you may not S
23:33 lest they make you S against me; for if
29:14 camp; it is a S offering.
29:36 a bull as a S offering for atonement.
29:36 you shall offer a S offering for the altar,
30:10 the blood of the S offering of atonement he
32:21 have brought a great S upon them?"
32:30 to the people, "You have sinned a great S
32:30 LORD; perhaps I can make atonement for your S
32:31 have sinned a great S; they have made for
32:32 thou wilt forgive their S --and if not, blot
32:34 I will visit their S upon them."
34:7 iniquity and transgression and S, but who will by
34:9 our iniquity and our S, and take us for
Lev 4:3 him offer for the S which he has committed
4:3 the LORD for a S offering.
4:8 the bull of the S offering he shall take
4:13 of Israel commits a S unwittingly and the thing
4:14 are guilty; when the S which they have committed
4:14 young bull for a S offering and bring it
4:20 the bull of the S offering, so shall he
4:21 bull; it is the S offering for the assembly.
4:23 is guilty, if the S which he has committed
4:24 LORD; it is a S offering.
4:25 the blood of the S offering with his finger
4:26 for him for his S, and he shall be
4:28 is guilty, when the S which he has committed
4:28 without blemish, for his S which he has committed.
4:29 the head of the S offering, and kill the
4:29 offering, and kill the S offering in the place
4:32 his offering for a S offering, he shall bring
4:33 the head of the S offering, and kill it
4:33 kill it for a S offering in the place
4:34 the blood of the S offering with his finger
4:35 for him for the S which he has committed,
5:5 he shall confess the S he has committed,
5:6 the LORD for the S which he has committed,
5:6 a goat, for a S offering; and the priest
5:6 priest shall make atonement for him for his S
5:7 the LORD for the S which he has committed,
5:7 pigeons, one for a S offering and the other
5:8 the one for the S offering; he shall wring
5:9 the blood of the S offering on the side
5:9 altar; it is a S offering.
5:10 for him for the S which he has committed,
5:11 his offering for the S which he has committed,
5:11 fine flour for a S offering; he shall put
5:11 for it is a S offering.
5:12 LORD; it is a S offering.
5:13 for him for the S which he has committed
6:3 which men do and S therein,
6:17 most holy, like the S offering and the guilt
6:25 the law of the S offering.
6:25 is killed shall the S offering be killed before
6:26 who offers it for S shall eat it; in
6:30 But no S offering shall be eaten from which
7:7 offering is like the S offering, there is one
7:37 cereal offering, of the S offering, of the guilt
8:2 the bull of the S offering, and the two
8:14 the bull of the S offering; and Aaron and
8:14 the bull of the S offering.
9:2 bull calf for a S offering, and a ram
9:3 male goat for a S offering, and a calf
9:7 altar, and offer your S offering and your burnt
9:8 the calf of the S offering, which was for
9:10 the liver from the S offering he burned upon
9:15 the goat of the S offering which was for
9:15 and offered it for S, like the first sin
9:15 sin, like the first S offering.
9:22 down from offering the S offering and the burnt
10:16 the goat of the S offering, and behold, it
10:17 you not eaten the S offering in the place
10:19 they have offered their S offering and their burnt
10:19 I had eaten the S offering today, would it
12:6 a turtledove for a S offering,
12:8 the other for a S offering; and the priest
14:13 where they kill the S offering and the burnt
14:13 guilt offering, like the S offering, belongs to the
14:19 priest shall offer the S offering, to make atonement
14:22 one shall be a S offering and the other
14:31 afford, one for a S offering and the other
15:15 them, one for a S offering and the other
15:30 offer one for a S offering and the other
16:3 young bull for a S offering and a ram
16:5 male goats for a S offering, and one ram
16:6 the bull as a S offering for himself, and
16:9 offer it as a S offering;
16:11 the bull as a S offering for himself, and
16:11 the bull as a S offering for himself.
16:15 the goat of the S offering which is for
16:25 the fat of the S offering he shall burn
16:27 the bull for the S offering and the goat
16:27 the goat for the S offering, whose blood was
19:17 neighbor, lest you bear S because of him.
19:22 the LORD for his S which he has committed;
19:22 has committed; and the S which he has committed
20:20 they shall bear their S, they shall die childless.
22:9 charge, lest they bear S for it and die
23:19 male goat for a S offering, and two male

S

SIN

	24:15	Israel, Whoever curses his God shall bear his S
Num	5:7	he shall confess his S which he has committed;
	6:11	offer one for a S offering and the other
	6:14	without blemish as a S offering, and one ram
	6:16	LORD and offer his S offering and his burnt
	7:16	male goat for a S offering;
	7:22	male goat for a S offering;
	7:28	male goat for a S offering;
	7:34	male goat for a S offering;
	7:40	male goat for a S offering;
	7:46	male goat for a S offering;
	7:52	male goat for a S offering;
	7:58	male goat for a S offering;
	7:64	male goat for a S offering;
	7:70	male goat for a S offering;
	7:76	male goat for a S offering;
	7:82	male goat for a S offering;
	7:87	male goats for a S offering;
	8:8	young bull for a S offering.
	8:12	the one for a S offering and the other
	8:21	Levites purified themselves from S, and washed their
	9:13	its appointed time; that man shall bear his S
	15:24	male goat for a S offering.
	15:25	the LORD, and their S offering before the LORD,
	15:27	year old for a S offering.
	16:22	flesh, shall one man S, and wilt thou be
	18:9	of theirs and every S offering of theirs and
	18:22	meeting, lest they bear S and die.
	18:32	you shall bear no S by reason of it,
	19:9	the water for impurity, for the removal of S
	19:17	ashes of the burnt S offering, and running water
	27:3	died for his own S; and he had no
	28:15	male goat for a S offering to the LORD;
	28:22	male goat for a S offering, to make atonement
	29:5	male goat for a S offering, to make atonement
	29:11	male goat for a S offering, besides the sin
	29:11	sin offering, besides the S offering of atonement, and
	29:16	male goat for a S offering, besides the continual
	29:19	male goat for a S offering, besides the continual
	29:22	male goat for a S offering, besides the continual
	29:25	male goat for a S offering, besides the continual
	29:28	male goat for a S offering; besides the continual
	29:31	male goat for a S offering; besides the continual
	29:34	male goat for a S offering; besides the continual
	29:38	male goat for a S offering; besides the continual
	32:23	and be sure your S will find you out.
	33:11	Red Sea, and encamped in the wilderness of S
	33:12	from the wilderness of S, and encamped at Dophkah.
Deut	9:18	because of all the S which you had committed,
	9:27	their wickedness, or their S,
	15:9	you, and it be S in you.
	20:18	gods, and so to S against the LORD your
	23:21	and it would be S in you.
	23:22	it shall be no S in you.
	24:15	LORD, and it be S in you.
	24:16	shall be put to death for his own S
Josh	22:17	had enough of the S at Peor from which
1Sam	2:17	Thus the S of the young men was very
	12:23	me that I should S against the LORD by
	14:34	eat; and do not S against the LORD by
	14:38	and see how this S has arisen today.
	15:23	rebellion is as the S of divination, and stubbornness
	15:25	I pray, pardon my S, and return with me,
	19:4	"Let not the king S against his servant David;
	19:5	why then will you S against innocent blood by
	20:1	And what is my S before your father, that
2Sam	12:13	has put away your S; you shall not die.
1Kgs	8:34	heaven, and forgive the S of thy people Israel,
	8:35	and turn from their S, when thou dost afflict
	8:36	heaven, and forgive the S of thy servants, thy
	8:46	"If they S against thee--for there is no
	8:46	man who does not S --and thou art angry
	12:30	this thing became a S, for the people went
	13:34	And this thing became S to the house of
	14:16	he sinned and which he made Israel to S
	15:26	father, and in his S which he made Israel
	15:26	in his sin which he made Israel to S
	15:30	he made Israel to S, and because of the
	15:34	Jeroboam and in his S which he made Israel
	15:34	in his sin which he made Israel to S
	16:2	my people Israel to S, provoking me to anger
	16:13	they made Israel to S, provoking the LORD God
	16:19	Jeroboam, and for his S which he committed,
	16:19	his sin which he committed, making Israel to S
	16:26	he made Israel to S, provoking the LORD, the
	17:18	me to bring my S to remembrance, and to
	21:22	me, and because you have made Israel to S
	22:52	the son of Nebat, who made Israel to S
2Kgs	3:3	he clung to the S of Jeroboam the son
	3:3	he made Israel to S; he did not depart
	10:29	he made Israel to S, the golden calves that
	10:31	sins of Jeroboam, which he made Israel to S
	12:16	the money from the S offerings was not brought
	13:2	he made Israel to S; he did not depart
	13:6	he made Israel to S, but walked in them;
	13:11	he made Israel to S, but he walked in
	14:6	but every man shall die for his own S
	14:24	son of Nebat, which he made Israel to S
	15:9	son of Nebat, which he made Israel to S
	15:18	son of Nebat, which he made Israel to S
	15:24	son of Nebat, which he made Israel to S
	15:28	son of Nebat, which he made Israel to S
	17:21	following the LORD and made them commit great S
	21:11	made Judah also to S with his idols;
	21:16	to another, besides the S which he made Judah
	21:16	he made Judah to S so that they did
	21:17	he did, and the S that he committed, are
	23:15	who made Israel to S, that altar with the
2Chr	6:25	heaven, and forgive the S of thy people Israel,
	6:26	and turn from their S, when thou dost afflict
	6:27	heaven, and forgive the S of thy servants, thy
	6:36	"If they S against thee--for there is no
	6:36	man who does not S --and thou art angry
	7:14	and will forgive their S and heal their land.
	25:4	but every man shall die for his own S
	29:21	seven he-goats for a S offering for the kingdom
	29:23	the he-goats for the S offering were brought to
	29:24	them and made a S offering with their blood
	29:24	burnt offering and the S offering should be made
	33:19	entreaty, and all his S and his faithlessness, and
Ezra	6:17	lambs, and as a S offering for all Israel
	8:35	lambs, and as a S offering twelve he-goats; all
Neh	4:5	and let not their S be blotted out from
	6:13	in this way and S, and so they could
	10:33	holy things, and the S offerings to make atonement
	13:26	Solomon king of Israel S on account of such
	13:26	nevertheless foreign women made even him to S
Tob	3:14	am innocent of any S with man,
	4:5	son, and refuse to S or to transgress his
	4:21	and refrain from every S and do what is
	12:9	from death, and it will purge away every S
	12:10	but those who commit S are the enemies of
Jud	5:17	as they did not S against their God they
	5:20	this people and they S against their God and
	11:10	against them, unless they S against their God.
	11:11	upon them, for a S has overtaken them by
	13:16	committed no act of S with me, to defile
Job	1:22	this Job did not S or charge God with
	2:10	this Job did not S with his lips.
	7:20	If I S, what do I do to thee,
	10:6	and search for my S,
	10:14	If I S, thou dost mark me, and dost
	13:23	Make me know my transgression and my S
	14:16	keep watch over my S;
	31:30	not let my mouth S by asking for his
	34:37	adds rebellion to his S; he claps his hands
Ps	4:4	Be angry, but S not; commune with your own
	32:1	transgression is forgiven, whose S is covered.
	32:3	I declared not my S, my body wasted away
	32:5	[Selah] I acknowledged my S to thee, and I
	32:5	then thou didst forgive the guilt of my S
	38:3	no health in my bones because of my S
	38:18	confess my iniquity, I am sorry for my S
	39:1	that I may not S with my tongue; I
	39:11	man with rebukes for S, thou dost consume like
	40:6	Burnt offering and S offering thou hast not required.
	51:2	from my iniquity, and cleanse me from my S
	51:3	my transgressions, and my S is ever before me.
	51:5	in iniquity, and in S did my mother conceive
	59:3	For no transgression or S of mine, O LORD,
	59:12	For the S of their mouths, the words of
	85:2	of thy people; thou didst pardon all their S
	109:7	forth guilty; let his prayer be counted as S
	109:14	and let not the S of his mother be
	119:11	that I might not S against thee.
Prov	5:22	he is caught in the toils of his S
	10:16	to life, the gain of the wicked to S
	13:6	way is upright, but S overthrows the wicked.
	14:34	exalts a nation, but S is a reproach to
	16:10	his mouth does not S in judgment.
	20:9	my heart clean; I am pure from my S
	21:4	proud heart, the lamp of the wicked, are S

24:9 devising of folly is S, and the scoffer is
Eccl 5:6 mouth lead you into S, and do not say
Wis 1:4 soul, nor dwell in a body enslaved to S
10:13 did not desert him, but delivered him from S
12:2 the things wherein they S, that they may be
14:31 penalty for those who S, that always pursues the
15:2 For even if we S we are thine, knowing
15:2 but we will not S, because we know that
Sir 3:25 the sinner will heap S upon sin.
3:25 troubles, and the sinner will heap sin upon S
3:28 a blazing fire: so almsgiving atones for S
4:21 a shame which brings S, and there is a
5:5 atonement that you add S to sin.
5:5 confident of atonement that you add sin to S
7:8 Do not commit a S twice; even for one
7:36 of your life, and then you will never S
8:5 is turning away from S; remember that we all
10:13 beginning of pride is S, and the man who
13:23 they are free from S, and poverty is evil
14:1 his lips and need not suffer grief for S
15:20 he has not given any one permission to S
18:26 and in days of S he guards against wrongdoing.
19:8 it would be a S for you, do not
21:2 Flee from S as from a snake; for if
21:2 for if you approach S, it will bite you.
23:10 utters the Name will not be cleansed from S
23:11 if he offends, his S remains on him, and
24:21 those who work with my help will not S
25:23 From a woman S had its beginning, and because
26:19 back from righteousness to S – the Lord will
26:20 a tradesman will not be declared innocent of S
27:1 Many have committed S for a trifle, and whoever
27:2 fissure between stones, so S is wedged in between
27:10 for prey; so does S for the workers of
32:12 mind, but do not S through proud speech.
38:10 hands aright, and cleanse your heart from all S
42:1 partiality lead you to S:
46:7 restrained the people from S, and stilled their
47:23 who caused Israel to S and gave Ephraim a
Is 3:9 them; they proclaim their S like Sodom, they do
5:18 of falsehood, who draw S as with cart ropes,
6:7 taken away, and your S forgiven."
27:9 the removal of his S: when he makes all
30:1 that they may add S to sin;
30:1 may add sin to S;
53:10 himself an offering for S, he shall see his
53:12 yet he bore the S of many, and made
Jer 16:10 What is the S that we have committed against
16:18 their iniquity and their S, because they have polluted
17:1 "The S of Judah is written with a pen
17:3 the price of your S throughout all your territory.
18:23 nor blot out their S from thy sight.
31:30 die for his own S; each man who eats
31:34 I will remember their S no more."
32:35 should do this abomination, to cause Judah to S
33:8 the guilt of their S against me, and I
33:8 the guilt of their S and rebellion against me.
36:3 that I may forgive their iniquity and their S
50:20 shall be none; and S in Judah, and none
Bar 1:10 money burnt offerings and S offerings and incense,
Ezek 3:20 shall die for his S, and his righteous deeds
3:21 righteous man not to S, and he does not
3:21 and he does not S, he shall surely live,
18:24 is guilty and the S he has committed, he
33:14 he turns from his S and does what is
40:39 burnt offering and the S offering and the guilt
42:13 the cereal offering, the S offering, and the guilt
43:19 a bull for a S offering.
43:21 the bull of the S offering, and it shall
43:22 without blemish for a S offering; and the altar
43:25 a goat for a S offering; also a bull
44:27 he shall offer his S offering, says the Lord
44:29 the cereal offering, the S offering, and the guilt
45:17 he shall provide the S offerings, cereal offerings,
45:19 the blood of the S offering and put it
45:22 young bull for a S offering.
45:23 he-goat daily for a S offering.
45:25 the same provision for S offerings, burnt offerings,
46:20 guilt offering and the S offering, and where they
Dan 9:20 and praying, confessing my S and the sin of
9:20 my sin and the S of my people Israel,
9:24 put an end to S, and to atone for
13:23 hands, rather than to S in the sight of
Hos 4:8 They feed on the S of my people; they
10:8 places of Aven, the S of Israel, shall be
13:2 And now they S more and more, and make
13:12 is bound up, his S is kept in store.
Mic 1:5 And what is the S of the house of
1:13 were the beginning of S to the daughter of
3:8 to Jacob his transgression and to Israel his S
6:7 my body for the S of my soul?"
Zech 13:1 to cleanse them from S and uncleanness.
2Mac 2:11 were consumed because the S offering had not been
10:4 if they should ever S, they might be disciplined
12:42 prayer, beseeching that the S which had been
12:42 keep themselves free from S, for they had seen
12:42 happened because of the S of those who had
12:43 to provide for a S offering.
12:45 dead, that they might be delivered from their S
Mt 5:29 eye causes you to S, pluck it out and
5:30 hand causes you to S, cut it off and
12:31 I tell you, every S and blasphemy will be
13:41 kingdom all causes of S and all evildoers,
18:6 believe in me to S, it would be better
18:7 "Woe to the world for temptations to S
18:8 foot causes you to S, cut it off and
18:9 eye causes you to S, pluck it out and
18:20 often shall my brother S against me, and I
Mk 3:29 guilty of an eternal S –
9:42 believe in me to S, it would be better
9:43 hand causes you to S, cut it off; it
9:44 foot causes you to S, cut it off; it
9:45 eye causes you to S, pluck it out; it
Lk 17:1 his disciples, "Temptations to S are sure to come;
17:2 should cause one of these little ones to S
Jn 1:29 who takes away the S of the world!
5:13 S no more, that nothing worse befall you."
8:7 him who is without S among you be the
8:11 go, and do not S again."
8:21 and die in your S; where I am going,
8:34 every one who commits S is a slave to
8:34 one who commits sin is a slave to S
8:46 Which of you convicts me of S
9:34 were born in utter S, and would you teach
15:22 they would not have S; but now they have
15:22 but now they have no excuse for their S
15:24 they would not have S; but now they have
16:8 convince the world concerning S and righteousness
16:9 righteousness and judgment: concerning S, because
19:11 who delivered me to you has the greater S
Acts 7:60 do not hold this S against them." And when
Rom 3:9 under the power of S,
3:20 law, since through the law comes knowledge of S
4:8 against whom the Lord will not reckon his S
5:12 Therefore as S came into the world through one
5:12 man and death through S, and so death spread
5:13 all men sinned-- S indeed was in the
5:13 law was given, but S is not counted where
5:16 not like the effect of that one man's S
5:20 the trespass; but where S increased, grace abounded
5:21 more, so that, as S reigned in death, grace
6:1 we to continue in S that grace may abound?
6:2 we who died to S still live in it?
6:6 and we might no longer be enslaved to S
6:7 For he who has died is freed from S
6:10 died he died to S, once for all, but
6:11 consider yourselves dead to S and alive to God
6:12 Let not S therefore reign in your mortal bodies,
6:13 yield your members to S as instruments of
6:14 For S will have no dominion over you, since
6:15 Are we to S because we are not under
6:16 you obey, either of S, which leads to death,
6:17 were once slaves of S have become obedient from
6:18 been set free from S, have become slaves of
6:20 you were slaves of S, you were free in
6:22 been set free from S and have become slaves
6:23 For the wages of S is death, but the
7:7 That the law is S
7:7 for the law, I should not have known S
7:8 But S, finding opportunity in the commandment,
7:8 Apart from the law S lies dead.
7:9 when the commandment came, S revived and I died;
7:11 For S, finding opportunity in the commandment,
7:13 It was S, working death in me through what
7:13 good, in order that S might be shown to
7:13 be shown to be S, and through the commandment
7:14 is spiritual; but I am carnal, sold under S
7:17 that do it, but S which dwells within me.
7:20 that do it, but S which dwells within me.
7:23 to the law of S which dwells in my
7:25 with my flesh I serve the law of S
8:2 from the law of S and death.

S

8:3 sinful flesh and for S, he condemned sin in
8:3 for sin, he condemned S in the flesh,
8:10 are dead because of S, your spirits are alive
14:23 for whatever does not proceed from faith is S
1Cor 6:18 Every other S which a man commits is outside
7:28 marry, you do not S, and if a girl
7:28 and if a girl marries she does not S
7:36 he wishes: let them marry–it is no S
8:12 it is weak, you S against Christ.
15:34 your right mind, and S no more.
15:56 sting of death is S, and the power of
15:56 and the power of S is the law.
2Cor 5:21 made him to be S who knew no sin,
5:21 sin who knew no S, so that in him
11:7 Did I commit a S in abasing myself so
Gal 2:17 be sinners, is Christ then an agent of S
3:22 consigned all things to S, that what was promised
Eph 4:26 angry but do not S; do not let the
1Tim 5:20 those who persist in S, rebuke them in the
Heb 3:13 you may be hardened by the deceitfulness of S
4:15 has been tempted as we are, yet without S
9:26 age to put away S by the sacrifice of
9:28 not to deal with S but to save those
10:2 they would no longer have any consciousness of S
10:3 is a reminder of S year after year.
10:6 in burnt offerings and S offerings thou hast taken
10:8 burnt offerings and S offerings" (these are offered
10:18 these, there is no longer any offering for S
10:26 if we S deliberately after receiving the knowledge
11:25 God than to enjoy the fleeting pleasures of S
12:1 aside every weight, and S which clings so closely,
12:4 In your struggle against S you have not yet
13:11 as a sacrifice for S are burned outside the
Jas 1:14 conceived gives birth to S; and sin when it
1:14 birth to sin; and S when it is full-grown
2:9 show partiality, you commit S, and are convicted by
4:17 fails to do it, for him it is S
1Pet 2:22 He committed no S; no guile was found on
2:24 we might die to S and live to righteousness.
4:1 flesh has ceased from S,
2Pet 2:14 They have eyes full of adultery, insatiable for S
1Jn 1:7 of Jesus his Son cleanses us from all S
1:8 say we have no S, we deceive ourselves, and
2:1 that you may not S; but if any one
2:1 if any one does S, we have an advocate
3:4 Every one who commits S is guilty of lawlessness;
3:4 is guilty of lawlessness; S is lawlessness.
3:5 away sins, and in him there is no S
3:8 He who commits S is of the devil; for
3:9 born of God commits S; for God's nature abides
3:9 him, and he cannot S because he is born
5:16 is not a mortal S, he will ask, and
5:16 life for those whose S is not mortal.
5:16 There is S which is mortal; I do not
5:17 All wrongdoing is S, but there is sin which
5:17 sin, but there is S which is not mortal.
5:18 of God does not S, but He who was

SINAI (41)

Ex 16:1 is between Elim and S, on the fifteenth day
19:1 that day they came into the wilderness of S
19:2 into the wilderness of S, they encamped in the
19:11 come down upon Mount S in the sight of
19:18 And Mount S was wrapped in smoke, because the
19:20 came down upon Mount S, to the top of
19:23 come up to Mount S; for thou thyself didst
24:16 LORD settled on Mount S, and the cloud covered
31:18 with him upon Mount S, the two tables of
34:2 the morning to Mount S, and present yourself there
34:4 went up on Mount S, as the LORD had
34:29 came down from Mount S, with the two tables
34:32 the LORD had spoken with him in Mount S
Lev 7:38 commanded Moses on Mount S, on the day that
7:38 offerings to the LORD, in the wilderness of S
25:1 to Moses on Mount S,
26:46 of Israel on Mount S by Moses.
27:34 Moses for the people of Israel on Mount S
Num 1:1 in the wilderness of S, in the tent of
1:19 So he numbered them in the wilderness of S
3:1 when the LORD spoke with Moses on Mount S
3:4 in the wilderness of S; and they had no
3:14 in the wilderness of S,
9:1 in the wilderness of S, in the first month
9:5 in the wilderness of S; according to all that
10:12 from the wilderness of S; and the cloud settled
26:64 the people of Israel in the wilderness of S
28:6 was ordained at Mount S for a pleasing odor,
33:15 from Rephidim, and encamped in the wilderness of S
33:16 the wilderness of S, and encamped at Kibroth-
Deut 33:2 "The LORD came from S, and dawned from Seir
Judg 5:5 before the LORD, yon S before the LORD, the
Neh 9:13 come down upon Mount S, and speak with them
Jud 5:14 by the way of S and Kadesh-barnea, and drove
Ps 68:8 presence of God; yon S quaked at the presence
68:17 the Lord came from S into the holy place.
Sir 48:7 who heard rebuke at S and judgments of vengeance
Acts 7:30 the wilderness of Mount S, in a flame of
7:38 to him at Mount S, and with our fathers;
Gal 4:24 One is from Mount S, bearing children for slavery;
4:25 Now Hagar is Mount S in Arabia; she corresponds

SINCERE (8)

Esth 16:6 evil natures beguile the S good will of their
Wis 6:17 wisdom is the most S desire for instruction, and
Lk 20:20 who pretended to be S, that they might take
2Cor 11:3 led astray from a S and pure devotion to
1Tim 1:5 a good conscience and S faith.
2Tim 1:5 am reminded of your S faith, a faith that
1Pet 1:22 the truth for a S love of the brethren,
2Pet 3:1 I have aroused your S mind by way of

SINCERELY (2)

Job 33:3 heart, and what my lips know they speak S
Phil 1:17 out of partisanship, not S but thinking to afflict

SINCERITY (6)

Josh 24:14 and serve him in S and in faithfulness; put
Tob 8:7 sister of mine because of lust, but with S
Wis 1:1 and seek him with S of heart;
1Cor 5:8 the unleavened bread of S and truth.
2Cor 1:12 with holiness and godly S, not by earthly wisdom
2:17 but as men of S, as commissioned by God,

SINEW (3)

Gen 32:32 do not eat the S of the hip which
32:32 Jacob's thigh on the S of the hip.
Is 48:4 neck is an iron S and your forehead brass,

SINEWS (4)

Job 10:11 flesh, and knit me together with bones and S
40:17 like a cedar; the S of his thighs are
Ezek 37:6 And I will lay S upon you, and will
37:8 I looked, there were S on them, and flesh

SINFUL (26)

Num 32:14 stead, a brood of S men, to increase still
Deut 9:21 Then I took the S thing, the calf which
Ps 107:17 were sick through their S ways, and because of
Wis 3:13 not entered into a S union; she will have
Sir 10:22 proper to honor a S man.
15:7 not obtain her, and S men will not see
15:12 no need of a S man.
23:13 vulgarity, for it involves S speech.
27:13 fools is offensive, and their laughter is wantonly S
27:30 are abominations, and the S man will possess them.
28:9 kindle strife, and a S man will disturb friends
32:17 A S man will shun reproof, and will find
47:23 and gave Ephraim a S way.
Is 1:4 Ah, S nation, a people laden with iniquity, offspring
Ezek 23:49 the penalty for your S idolatry; and you shall
Amos 9:8 GOD are upon the S kingdom, and I will
1Mac 1:10 them came forth a S root, Antiochus Epiphanes, son
1:34 they stationed there a S people, lawless men.
Mk 8:38 in this adulterous and S generation, of him will
Lk 5:8 for I am a S man, O Lord."
24:7 into the hands of S men, and be crucified,
Rom 6:6 him so that the S body might be destroyed,
7:5 in the flesh, our S passions, aroused by the
7:13 the commandment might become S beyond measure.
8:3 in the likeness of S flesh and for sin,
Tit 3:11 person is perverted and S; he is self-condemned.

SINFULLY (2)

Is 31:7 which your hands have S made for you.
Dan 3:29 For we have S and lawlessly departed from thee,

SING (160)

Ex 15:1 LORD, saying, "I will S to the LORD, for
15:21 Miriam sang to them: S to the LORD, for
Num 21:17 "Spring up, O well!–S to it!–
Judg 5:3 the LORD I will S, I will make melody
1Sam 21:11 Did they not S to one another of him

S

29:5 David, of whom they S to one another in
2Sam 22:50 among the nations, and S praises to thy name.
1Chr 16:9 S to him, sing praises to him, tell of
16:9 Sing to him, S praises to him, tell of
16:23 S to the Lord, all the earth!
16:33 trees of the wood S for joy before the
2Chr 20:21 those who were to S to the LORD and
20:22 when they began to S and praise, the LORD
29:30 commanded the Levites to S praises to the LORD
Jud 16:2 my God with tambourines, S to my Lord with
16:13 I will S to my God a new song:
Esth 13:17 we may live and S praise to thy name,
Job 21:12 They S to the tambourine and the lyre, and
29:13 the widow's heart to S for joy.
Ps 5:11 rejoice, let them ever S for joy; and do
7:17 righteousness, and I will S praise to the name
9:2 in thee, I will S praise to thy name,
9:11 S praises to the LORD, who dwells in Zion!
13:6 I will S to the LORD, because he has
18:49 among the nations, and S praises to thy name.
21:13 We will S and praise thy power.
27:6 of joy; I will S and make melody to
30:4 S praises to the LORD, O you his saints,
33:3 S to him a new song, play skilfully on
47:6 S praises to God, sing praises!
47:6 Sing praises to God, S praises!
47:6 S praises to our King, sing praises!
47:6 praises to our King, S praises!
47:7 of all the earth; S praises with a psalm!
51:14 and my tongue will S aloud of thy deliverance.
57:7 I will S and make melody!
57:9 the peoples; I will S praises to thee among
59:9 my Strength, I will S praises to thee; for
59:16 But I will S of thy might; I will
59:16 thy might; I will S aloud of thy steadfast
59:17 my Strength, I will S praises to thee, for
61:8 So will I ever S praises to thy name,
63:7 of thy wings I S for joy.
65:13 grain, they shout and S together for joy.
66:2 God, all the earth; S the glory of his
66:4 earth worships thee; they S praises to thee, sing
66:4 sing praises to thee, S praises to thy name."
67:4 nations be glad and S for joy, for thou
68:4 S to God, sing praises to his name; lift
68:4 Sing to God, S praises to his name; lift
68:32 S to God, O kingdoms of the earth; sing
68:32 kingdoms of the earth; S praises to the Lord,
71:22 my God; I will S praises to thee with
71:23 for joy, when I S praises to thee; my
75:9 for ever, I will S praises to the God
81:1 S aloud to God our strength; shout for joy
84:2 my heart and flesh S for joy to the
89:1 I will S of thy steadfast love, O LORD,
92:1 to the LORD, to S praises to thy name,
92:4 of thy hands I S for joy.
95:1 O come, let us S to the LORD; let
96:1 O S to the LORD a new song; sing
96:1 LORD a new song; S to the LORD, all
96:2 S to the LORD, bless his name; tell of
96:12 trees of the wood S for joy
98:1 O S to the LORD a new song, for
98:4 into joyous song and S praises!
98:5 S praises to the LORD with the lyre, with
98:8 hands; let the hills S for joy together
101:1 I will S of loyalty and of justice; to
101:1 of justice; to thee, O LORD, I will S
104:12 have their habitation; they S among the branches.
104:33 I will S to the LORD as long as
104:33 I live; I will S praise to my God
105:2 S to him, sing praises to him, tell of
105:2 Sing to him, S praises to him, tell of
108:1 I will S and make melody!
108:3 the peoples; I will S praises to thee among
119:172 My tongue will S of thy word, for all
135:3 the LORD is good; S to his name, for
137:3 our tormentors, mirth, saying, S us one of the
137:4 How shall we S the LORD's song in a
138:1 before the gods I S thy praise;
138:5 mouth; and they shall S of the ways of
144:9 I will S a new song to thee, O
145:7 goodness, and shall S aloud of thy righteousness.
146:2 I live; I will S praises to my God
147:1 it is good to S praises to our God;
147:7 S to the LORD with thanksgiving; make melody to
149:1 S to the LORD a new song, his praise
149:5 in glory; let them S for joy on their
Sir 17:22 Who will S praises to the Most High in
39:14 Scatter the fragrance, and S a hymn of praise;
39:35 So now S praise with all your heart and
51:11 name continually, and will S praise with
Is 5:1 Let me S for my beloved a love song
12:5 S praises to the LORD, for he has done
12:6 Shout, and S for joy, O inhabitant of Zion,
23:16 Make sweet melody, S many songs, that you may
24:14 up their voices, they S for joy; over the
26:19 the dust, awake and S for joy!
27:2 day: "A pleasant vineyard, S of it!
35:6 tongue of the dumb S for joy.
38:20 me, and we will S to stringed instruments all
42:10 S to the LORD a new song, his praise
42:11 the inhabitants of Sela S for joy, let them
44:23 S, O heavens, for the LORD has done it;
49:13 S for joy, O heavens, and exult, O earth;
52:8 their voice, together they S for joy; for eye
54:1 S, O barren one, who did not bear; break
65:14 behold, my servants shall S for gladness of heart,
Jer 20:13 S to the LORD; praise the LORD!
31:7 thus says the LORD: S aloud with gladness for
31:12 They shall come and S aloud on the height
33:11 voices of those who S, as they bring thank
51:48 is in them, shall S for joy over Babylon;
Dan 3:58 works of the Lord, S praise to him and
3:59 the Lord, you heavens, S praise to him and
3:60 angels of the Lord, S praise to him and
3:61 waters above the heaven, S praise to him and
3:62 the Lord, all powers, S praise to him and
3:63 Lord, sun and moon, S praise to him and
3:64 Lord, stars of heaven, S praise to him and
3:65 all rain and dew, S praise to him and
3:66 the Lord, all winds, S praise to him and
3:67 Lord, fire and heat, S praise to him and
3:68 cold and summer heat, S praise to him and
3:69 Lord, dews and snows, S praise to him and
3:70 Lord, nights and days, S praise to him and
3:71 Lord, light and darkness, S praise to him and
3:72 Lord, ice and cold, S praise to him and
3:73 Lord, frosts and snows, S praise to him and
3:74 Lord, lightnings and clouds, S praise to him and
3:75 the Lord; let it S praise to him and
3:76 Lord, mountains and hills, S praise to him and
3:77 grow on the earth, S praise to him and
3:78 the Lord, you springs, S praise to him and
3:79 Lord, seas and rivers, S praise to him and
3:80 move in the waters, S praise to him and
3:81 birds of the air, S praise to him and
3:82 all beasts and cattle, S praise to him and
3:83 you sons of men, S praise to him and
3:84 the Lord, O Israel, S praise to him and
3:85 priests of the Lord, S praise to him and
3:86 servants of the Lord, S praise to him and
3:87 souls of the righteous, S praise to him and
3:88 and humble in heart, S praise to him and
3:89 Hananiah, Azariah, and Mishael, S praise to him and
3:91 the God of gods, S praise to him and
Amos 6:5 of the stall; who S idle songs to the
Zeph 3:14 S aloud, O daughter of Zion; shout, O Israel!
Zech 2:10 S and rejoice, O daughter of Zion; for lo,
Rom 15:9 among the Gentiles, and S to thy name";
1Cor 14:15 mind also; I will S with the spirit and
14:15 spirit and I will S with the mind also.
Col 3:16 in all wisdom, and S psalms and hymns and
Jas 5:13 Let him S praise.
Rev 4:8 they never cease to S, "Holy, holy, holy, is
14:3 their harps, and they S a new song before
15:3 And they S the song of Moses, the servant

SINGED

Dan 3:95 their heads was not S, their mantles were not

SINGER (2)

1Chr 6:33 the Kohathites: Heman the S the son of Joel,
Sir 9:4 associate with a woman S, lest you be caught

SINGERS (40)

Num 21:27 Therefore the ballad S say, "Come to Heshbon, let
1Kgs 10:12 and harps for the S; no such almug wood
1Chr 9:33 Now these are the S, the heads of fathers'
15:16 their brethren as the S who should play loudly
15:19 The S, Heman, Asaph, and Ethan, were to sound
15:27 the ark, and the S, and Chenaniah the leader
15:27 the music of the S; and David wore a
2Chr 5:12 and all the Levitical S, Asaph, Heman, and Jeduthun,

S

5:13 of the trumpeters and S to make themselves heard
9:11 and harps for the S; there never was seen
23:13 blowing trumpets, and the S with their musical
29:28 assembly worshiped, and the S sang, and the
35:15 The S, the sons of Asaph, were in their
Ezra 2:41 The S: the sons of Asaph, one hundred and
2:65 and they had two hundred male and female S
2:70 its vicinity; and the S, the gatekeepers, and the
7:7 priests and Levites, the S and gatekeepers, and the
7:24 priests, the Levites, the S, the doorkeepers, the
10:24 Of the S: Eliashib.
Neh 7:1 and the gatekeepers, the S, and the Levites had
7:44 The S: the sons of Asaph, a hundred and
7:67 two hundred and forty-five S, male and female.
7:73 Levites, the gatekeepers, the S, some of the people,
10:28 Levites, the gatekeepers, the S, the temple servants,
10:39 priests that minister, and the gatekeepers and the S
11:22 sons of Asaph, the S, over the work of
11:23 settled provision for the S, as every day required.
12:28 the sons of the S gathered together from the
12:29 and Azmaveth; for the S had built for themselves
12:42 And the S sang with Jezrahiah as their leader.
12:45 purification, as did the S and the gatekeepers,
12:46 a chief of the S, and there were songs
12:47 daily portions for the S and the gatekeepers; and
13:5 to the Levites, S, and gatekeepers, and the
13:10 the Levites and the S, who did the work,
Ps 68:25 the sanctuary-- the S in front, the minstrels
87:7 [Selah] S and dancers alike say, "All my springs
Eccl 2:8 and provinces; I got S, both men and women,
Sir 47:9 He placed S before the altar, to make sweet
50:18 And the S praised him with their voices in

SINGING (31)

Ex 32:18 but the sound of S that I hear."
1Sam 18:6 the cities of Israel, S and dancing, to meet
2Sam 19:35 to the voice of S men and singing women?
19:35 of singing men and S women?
1Chr 25:7 who were trained in S to the LORD, all
2Chr 23:18 with rejoicing and with S, according to the order
30:21 LORD day by day, S with all their might
35:25 Josiah; and all the S men and singing women
35:25 the singing men and S women have spoken of
Neh 12:27 with thanksgivings and with S, with cymbals, harps,
Ps 26:7 thy altar, O LORD, S aloud a song of
84:4 in thy house, ever S thy praise!
100:2 Come into his presence with S
105:43 his people with joy, his chosen ones with S
Song 2:12 earth, the time of S has come, and the
Wis 18:9 and already they were S the praises of the
Is 14:7 at rest and quiet; they break forth into S
24:9 they drink wine with S; strong drink is bitter
35:2 shall blossom abundantly, and rejoice with joy and S
35:10 come to Zion with S; everlasting joy shall be
44:23 earth; break forth into S, O mountains, O forest,
49:13 exult, O earth; break forth, O mountains, into S
51:11 come to Zion with S; everlasting joy shall be
52:9 Break forth together into S, you waste places of
54:1 bear; break forth into S and cry aloud, you
55:12 shall break forth into S, and all the trees
Dan 3:24 midst of the flames, S hymns to God and
Zeph 3:17 over you with loud S
Acts 16:25 Silas were praying and S hymns to God, and
Eph 5:19 hymns and spiritual songs, S and making melody to
Rev 4:10 crowns before the throne, S,

SINGLE (30)

Ex 10:19 Red Sea; not a S locust was left in
21:3 If he comes in S, he shall go out
21:3 he shall go out S; if he comes in
33:5 people; if for a S moment I should go
Num 13:23 a branch with a S cluster of grapes, and
Deut 19:15 "A S witness shall not prevail against a man
29:21 And the LORD would S him out from all
1Kgs 16:11 not leave him a S male of his kinsmen
2Kgs 18:24 can you repulse a S captain among the least
1Chr 12:38 Israel were of a S mind to make David
Jud 7:21 their fill for a S day, because it was
Wis 11:20 could fall at a S breath when pursued by
Is 36:9 can you repulse a S captain among the least
Ezek 4:9 put them into a S vessel, and make bread
Zech 3:9 before Joshua, upon a S stone with seven facets,
3:9 this land in a S day.
2Mac 2:23 to condense into a S book.
7:20 sons perish within a S day, she bore it
8:18 is able with a S nod to strike down
Mt 23:14 land to make a S proselyte, and when he
27:14 not even to a S charge; so that the
1Cor 7:8 for them to remain S as I do.
7:11 does, let her remain S or else be reconciled
10:8 thousand fell in a S day.
12:19 If all were a S organ, where would the
Heb 10:12 for all time a S sacrifice for sins, he
10:14 For by a S offering he has perfected for
12:16 his birthright for a S meal.
Rev 18:8 plagues come in a S day, pestilence and mourning
21:21 gates made of a S pearl, and the street

SINGLEHANDED

Jud 15:10 have done all this S; you have done great

SINGLENESS (3)

1Chr 12:33 to help David with S of purpose.
Eph 6:5 fear and trembling, in S of heart, as to
Col 3:22 as men-pleasers, but in S of heart, fearing the

SINGS (5)

Job 33:27 his salvation, and he S before men, and says:
Prov 25:20 He who S songs to a heavy heart is
29:6 but a righteous man S and rejoices.
Sir 17:23 is alive and well S the Lord's praises.
Ezek 33:32 them like one who S love songs with a

SINITES (2)

Gen 10:17 Hivites, the Arkites, the S,
1Chr 1:15 Hivites, the Arkites, the S,

SINK (9)

2Sam 22:40 didst make my assailants S under me.
Ps 18:39 didst make my assailants S under me.
69:2 I S in deep mire, where there is no
Jer 51:64 say, 'Thus shall Babylon S, to rise no more,
Ezek 27:27 is in your midst, S into the heart of
Amos 8:8 be tossed about and S again, like the Nile
Mt 14:30 afraid, and beginning to S he cried out, "Lord,
Lk 5:7 both the boats, so that they began to S
9:44 disciples, "Let these words S into your ears; for

SINKING

Ps 69:14 help rescue me from S in the mire; let

SINKS (5)

Ps 10:10 The hapless is crushed, S down, and falls by
Prov 2:18 God; for her house S down to death, and
Eccl 10:18 Through sloth the roof S in, and through indolence
Is 5:24 and as dry grass S down in the flame,
Amos 9:5 like the Nile, and S again, like the Nile

SINNED (116)

Gen 20:9 And how have I S against you, that you
Ex 9:27 to them, "I have S this time; the LORD
9:34 thunder had ceased, he S yet again, and hardened
10:16 and said, "I have S against the LORD your
32:30 the people, "You have S a great sin.
32:31 "Alas, this people have S a great sin; they
32:33 to Moses, "Whoever has S against me, him will
Lev 6:4 therein, when one has S and become guilty, he
Num 6:11 for him, because he S by reason of the
12:11 us because we have done foolishly and have S
14:40 which the LORD has promised; for we have S
16:38 these men who have S at the cost of
21:7 and said, "We have S, for we have spoken
22:34 the LORD, "I have S, for I did not
32:23 so, behold, you have S against the LORD; and
Deut 1:41 answered me, 'We have S against the LORD; we
9:16 and behold, you had S against the LORD your
Josh 7:11 Israel has S; they have transgressed my covenant
7:20 a truth I have S against the LORD God
Judg 10:10 LORD, saying, "We have S against thee, because we
10:15 the LORD, "We have S; do to us whatever
11:27 I therefore have not S against you, and you
1Sam 7:6 said there, "We have S against the LORD." And
12:10 and said, 'We have S, because we have forsaken
15:24 to Samuel, "I have S; for I have transgressed
15:30 he said, "I have S; yet honor me now
19:4 because he has not S against you, and because
24:11 I have not S against you, though you hunt
2Sam 12:13 to Nathan, "I have S against the LORD." And
19:20 knows that I have S; therefore, behold, I have
24:10 the LORD, "I have S greatly in what I
24:17 said, "Lo, I have S, and I have done
1Kgs 8:33 enemy because they have S against thee, if they

S

8:35 rain because they have S against thee, if they
8:47 captors, saying, 'We have S, and have acted
8:50 thy people who have S against thee, and all
14:16 of Jeroboam, which he S and which he made
15:30 of Jeroboam which he S and which he made
16:13 his son which they S, and which they made
18:9 said, "Wherein have I S, that you would give
2Kgs 17:7 people of Israel had S against the LORD their
1Chr 21:8 to God, "I have S greatly in that I
21:17 is I who have S and done very wickedly."
2Chr 6:24 enemy because they have S against thee, when they
6:26 rain because they have S against thee, if they
6:37 captivity, saying, 'We have S, and have acted
6:39 thy people who have S against thee.
Neh 1:6 Israel, which we have S against thee.
1:6 Yea, I and my father's house have S
9:29 thy commandments, but S against thy ordinances,
Esth 14:6 And now we have S before thee, and thou
Job 1:5 that my sons have S, and cursed God in
8:4 If your children have S against him, he has
24:19 snow waters; so does Sheol those who have S
33:27 men, and says: 'I S, and perverted what was
35:3 than if I had S
35:6 If you have S, what do you accomplish against
Ps 41:4 me, for I have S against thee!"
51:4 thee only, have I S, and done that which
78:17 Yet they S still more against him, rebelling against
78:32 all this they still S; despite his wonders they
106:6 and our fathers have S; we have committed iniquity,
Sir 5:4 Do not say, "I S, and what happened to
19:16 Who has never S with his tongue?
21:1 Have you S, my son?
49:4 and Josiah they all S greatly, for they forsook
Is 42:24 against whom we have S, in whose ways they
43:27 Your first father S, and your mediators transgressed
64:5 wast angry, and we S; in our sins we
Jer 2:35 saying, 'I have not S
3:25 us; for we have S against the LORD our
8:14 drink, because we have S against the LORD.
14:7 are many, we have S against thee.
14:20 fathers, for we have S against thee.
40:3 Because you S against the LORD, and did not
44:23 incense, and because you S against the LORD and
50:7 guilty, for they have S against the LORD, their
50:14 arrows, for she has S against the LORD.
Lam 1:8 Jerusalem S grievously, therefore she became filthy;
5:7 Our fathers S, and are no more; and we
5:16 our head; woe to us, for we have S
Bar 1:13 God, for we have S against the Lord our
1:17 fathers, because we have S before the Lord,
2:5 raised up, because we S against the Lord our
2:12 this day, we have S, we have been ungodly,
2:33 of their fathers, who S before the Lord.
3:2 mercy, for we have S before thee.
3:4 sons of those who S before thee, who did
3:7 of our fathers who S before thee.
Ezek 28:16 with violence, and you S; so I cast you
37:23 in which they have S, and will cleanse them;
45:20 any one who has S through error or ignorance;
Dan 3:29 from thee, and have S in all things and
9:5 his commandments, we have S and done wrong and
9:8 fathers, because we have S against thee.
9:11 us, because we have S against him.
9:15 this day, we have S, we have done wickedly.
Hos 4:7 increased, the more they S against me; I will
10:9 of Gibe-ah, you have S, O Israel; there they
Mic 7:9 LORD because I have S against him, until he
Zeph 1:17 blind, because they have S against the LORD; their
Mt 27:4 elders, saying, "I have S in betraying innocent blood."
Lk 15:18 him, "Father, I have S against heaven and before
15:21 him, 'Father, I have S against heaven and before
Jn 9:2 asked him, "Rabbi, who S, this man or his
9:3 not that this man S, or his parents, but
Rom 2:12 All who have S without the law will also
2:12 and all who have S under the law will
3:23 distinction; since all have S and fall short of
5:12 men because all men S –
2Cor 12:21 many of those who S before and have not
13:2 I warned those who S before and all the
Heb 3:17 not with those who S, whose bodies fell in
2Pet 2:4 the angels when they S, but cast them into
1Jn 1:10 say we have not S, we make him a
3:8 for the devil has S from the beginning.

SINNER (44)
Prov 11:31 earth, how much more the wicked and the S
13:22 children's children, but the S's wealth is laid up
14:21 his neighbor is a S, but happy is he
Eccl 2:26 joy; but to the S he gives the work
7:26 escapes her, but the S is taken by her.
8:12 Though a S does evil a hundred times and
9:2 man, so is the S; and he who swears
9:18 of war, but one S destroys much good.
Sir 1:22 sayings, but godliness is an abomination to a S
2:12 hands, and to the S who walks along two
3:25 by troubles, and the S will heap sin upon
5:9 every path: the double-tongued S does that.
6:1 shame and reproach: so fares the double-tongued S
8:10 the coals of a S, lest you be burned
9:11 the honors of a S, for you do not
11:19 the works of a S, but trust in the
11:30 burning coals, and a S lies in wait to
12:4 the godly man, but do not help the S
12:7 the good man, but do not help the S
12:14 who associates with a S and becomes involved in
13:16 No more has a S with a godly man.
15:9 the lips of a S, for it has not
16:13 The S will not escape with his plunder, and
21:6 the steps of the S, but he that fears
23:8 The S is overtaken through his lips, the reviler
25:18 wife's iniquity; may a S's lot befall her!
29:16 A S will overthrow the prosperity of his surety,
29:19 The S who has fallen into suretyship and pursues
33:14 of death; so the S is the opposite of
Is 65:20 years old, and the S a hundred years old
1Mac 2:48 they never let the S gain the upper hand.
2:62 the words of a S, for his splendor will
Lk 7:37 city, who was a S, when she learned that
7:39 who is touching him, for she is a S
15:7 in heaven over one S who repents than over
15:10 of God over one S who repents."
18:13 merciful to me a S
19:7 the guest of a man who is a S
Jn 9:16 man who is a S do such signs?" There
9:24 praise; we know that this man is a S
9:25 "Whether he is a S, I do not know;
Rom 3:7 why am I still being condemned as a S
Jas 5:20 whoever brings back a S from the error of
1Pet 4:18 will the impious and S appear?"

SINNERS (68)
Gen 13:13 Sodom were wicked, great S against the LORD.
1Sam 15:18 'Go, utterly destroy the S, the Amalekites, and fight
Tob 4:17 grave of the righteous, but give none to S
13:6 his power and majesty to a nation of S
13:6 Turn back, you S, and do right before him;
Ps 1:1 in the way of S, nor sits in the
1:5 in the judgment, nor S in the congregation of
25:8 LORD; therefore he instructs S in the way.
26:9 me not away with S, nor my life with
51:13 transgressors thy ways, and S will return to thee.
104:35 Let S be consumed from the earth, and let
Prov 1:10 My son, if S entice you, do not consent.
13:21 Misfortune pursues S, but prosperity rewards the
23:17 not your heart envy S, but continue in the
Wis 4:10 and while living among S he was taken up.
19:13 not come upon the S without prior signs in
Sir 5:6 are with him, and his anger rests on S
7:16 among the crowd of S; remember that wrath does
11:9 you, nor sit with S when they judge a
12:6 Most High also hates S and will inflict punishment
16:6 In an assembly of S a fire will be
19:19 is there prudence where S take counsel.
21:10 The way of S is smoothly paved with stones,
39:25 for good people, just as evil things for S
39:27 godly, just as they turn into evils for S
40:8 and beast, and upon S seven times more,
41:5 The children of S are abominable children, and they
41:6 of the children of S will perish, and on
41:11 the evil name of S will be blotted out.
Is 1:28 But rebels and S shall be destroyed together, and
13:9 and to destroy its S from it.
33:14 The S in Zion are afraid; trembling has seized
Amos 9:10 All the S of my people shall die by
1Mac 2:44 army, and struck down S in their anger and
2Mac 12:23 utmost vigor, putting the S to the sword, and
14:42 into the hands of S and suffer outrages unworthy
Mt 9:10 many tax collectors and S came and sat down
9:11 does your teacher eat with tax collectors and S
9:13 I came not to call the righteous, but S
11:19 of tax collectors and S Yet wisdom is justified
26:45 of man is betrayed into the hands of S

S

Mk 2:15 many tax collectors and S were sitting with Jesus
2:16 he was eating with S and tax collectors, said
2:16 "Why does he eat with tax collectors and S
2:17 I came not to call the righteous, but S
14:41 of man is betrayed into the hands of S
Lk 5:30 you eat and drink with tax collectors and S
5:32 call the righteous, but S to repentance."
6:32 For even S love those who love them.
6:33 For even S do the same.
6:34 Even S lend to sinners, to receive as much
6:34 Even sinners lend to S, to receive as much
7:34 of tax collectors and S
13:2 these Galileans were worse S than all the other
15:1 the tax collectors and S were all drawing near
15:2 saying, "This man receives S and eats with them."
Jn 9:31 does not listen to S, but if any one
Rom 5:8 while we were yet S Christ died for us.
5:19 disobedience many were made S, so by one man's
Gal 2:15 birth and not Gentile S,
2:17 were found to be S, is Christ then an
1Tim 1:9 for the ungodly and S, for the unholy and
1:15 Christ Jesus came into the world to save S
1:15 am the foremost of S;
Heb 7:26 blameless, unstained, separated from S, exalted
12:3 him who endured from S such hostility against
Jas 4:8 Cleanse your hands, you S, and purify your hearts,
Jude 1:15 harsh things which ungodly S have spoken against

SINNING (8)

Gen 20:6 who kept you from S against me; therefore I
1Sam 14:33 "Behold, the people are S against the LORD, by
Sir 18:20 on the point of S, turn back.
19:25 he is prevented from S, he will do evil
20:20 may be prevented from S by his poverty, so
Hos 8:11 has multiplied altars for S, they have become to
8:11 sinning, they have become to him altars for S
1Cor 8:12 Thus, S against your brethren and wounding their

SINS (244)

Lev 4:2 Israel, If any one S unwittingly in any of
4:3 the anointed priest who S, thus bringing guilt on
4:22 "When a ruler S, doing unwittingly any one of
4:27 of the common people S unwittingly in doing any
5:1 "If any one S in that he hears a
5:15 breach of faith and S unwittingly in any of
5:17 "If any one S, doing any of the things
6:2 Moses, "If any one S and commits a breach
16:16 their transgressions, all their S; and so he shall
16:21 their transgressions, all their S; and he shall put
16:30 you; from all your S you shall be clean
16:34 once in the year because of all their S
26:18 again sevenfold for your S,
26:21 plagues upon you, sevenfold as many as your S
26:24 I myself will smite you sevenfold for your S
26:28 fury, and chastise you myself sevenfold for your S
Num 5:6 commits any of the S that men commit by
15:27 "If one person S unwittingly, he shall offer a
15:28 an error, when he S unwittingly, to make atonement
16:26 lest you be swept away with all their S
Josh 24:19 he will not forgive your transgressions or your S
1Sam 2:25 If a man S against a man, God will
2:25 but if a man S against the LORD, who
12:19 added to all our S this evil, to ask
1Kgs 8:31 "If a man S against his neighbor and is
14:16 up because of the S of Jeroboam, which he
14:22 to jealousy with their S which they committed, more
15:3 walked in all the S which his father did
15:30 it was for the S of Jeroboam which he
16:2 to anger with their S,
16:13 prophet, for all the S of Baasha and the
16:13 of Baasha and the S of Elah his son
16:19 died, because of his S which he committed, doing
16:26 Nebat, and in the S which he made Israel
16:31 to walk in the S of Jeroboam the son
2Kgs 10:29 turn aside from the S of Jeroboam the son
10:31 not turn from the S of Jeroboam, which he
13:2 LORD, and followed the S of Jeroboam the son
13:6 not depart from the S of the house of
13:11 depart from all the S of Jeroboam the son
14:24 depart from all the S of Jeroboam the son
15:9 not depart from the S of Jeroboam the son
15:18 days from all the S of Jeroboam the son
15:24 turn away from the S of Jeroboam the son
15:28 not depart from the S of Jeroboam the son
17:22 walked in all the S which Jeroboam did; they
24:3 his sight, for the S of Manasseh, according to
2Chr 6:22 "If a man S against his neighbor and is
28:10 Have you not S of your own against the
28:13 addition to our present S and guilt.
Neh 1:6 thy servants, confessing the S of the people of
9:2 stood and confessed their S and the iniquities of
9:37 us because of our S; they have power also
Tob 3:3 punish me for my S and for my unwitting
3:5 from me for my S and those of my
Jud 7:29 us according to our S and the sins of
7:29 our sins and the S of our fathers.
11:17 will tell me when they have committed their S
Job 13:23 How many are my iniquities and my S
Ps 19:13 servant also from presumptuous S; let them not have
25:7 Remember not the S of my youth, or my
25:18 affliction and my trouble, and forgive all my S
51:9 thy face from my S, and blot out all
65:3 thee shall all flesh come on account of S
79:9 us, and forgive our S, for thy name's sake!
90:8 before thee, our secret S in the light of
103:10 us according to our S, nor requite us according
Eccl 7:20 man on earth who does good and never S
Wis 2:12 he reproaches us for S against the law, and
2:12 and accuses us of S against our training.
4:20 with dread when their S are reckoned up, and
11:16 punished by the very things by which he S
11:23 thou dost overlook men's S, that they may repent.
12:11 that thou didst leave them unpunished for their S
12:19 good hope, because thou givest repentance for S
15:13 others, knows that he S when he makes from
17:3 that in their secret S they were unobserved behind
Sir 2:11 and merciful; he forgives S and saves in time
3:3 his father atones for S,
3:14 forgotten, and against your S it will be credited
3:15 in fair weather, your S will melt away.
4:26 ashamed to confess your S, and do not try
5:6 great, he will forgive the multitude of my S
10:28 justify the man that S against himself?
12:14 with a sinner and becomes involved in his S
16:9 those destroyed in their S;
17:16 him, and all their S are before the Lord.
17:20 Lord and forsake your S; pray in his presence
19:4 lightminded, and one who S does wrong to himself.
21:1 so no more, but pray about your former S
23:2 not pass by my S;
23:3 be multiplied, and my S may not abound; then
23:11 he disregards it, he S doubly; if he has
23:12 the godly, and they will not wallow in S
23:16 sorts of men multiply S, and a third incurs
23:18 Most High will not take notice of my S
26:11 not wonder if she S against you.
28:1 the Lord, and he will firmly establish his S
28:2 done, and then your S will be pardoned when
28:4 like himself, and yet pray for his own S
28:5 maintains wrath, who will make expiation for his S
28:8 and you will lessen S; for a man given
34:19 is not propitiated for S by a multitude of
34:26 man fasts for his S, and goes again and
38:15 He who S before his Maker, may he fall
39:5 mouth in prayer and make supplication for his S
47:11 Lord took away his S, and exalted his power
47:24 Their S became exceedingly many, so as to remove
48:15 did not forsake their S, till they were carried
48:16 what was pleasing to God, but others multiplied S
Is 1:18 the LORD: though your S are like scarlet, they
38:17 hast cast all my S behind thy back.
40:2 from the LORD's hand double for all her S
43:24 burdened me with your S, you have wearied me
43:25 own sake, and I will not remember your S
44:22 a cloud, and your S like mist; return to
58:1 their transgression, to the house of Jacob their S
59:2 your God, and your S have hid his face
59:12 before thee, and our S testify against us; for
64:5 we sinned; in our S we have been a
Jer 5:25 these away, and your S have kept good from
14:10 he will remember their iniquity and punish their S
15:13 price, for all your S, throughout all your territory.
30:14 is great, because your S are flagrant.
30:15 is great, because your S are flagrant, I have
Lam 3:39 complain, a man, about the punishment of his S
4:13 This was for the S of her prophets and
4:22 Edom, he will punish, he will uncover your S
Bar 4:12 desolate because of the S of my children, because
6:2 Because of the S which you have committed before
Ezek 14:13 man, when a land S against me by acting
16:51 not committed half your S; you have committed
16:52 sisters; because of your S in which you acted

S

18:4 mine: the soul that S shall die.
18:14 who sees all the S which his father has
18:20 The soul that S shall die.
18:21 away from all his S which he has committed
21:24 all your doings your S appear--because you have
33:10 'Our transgressions and our S are upon us, and
33:12 able to live by his righteousness when he S
33:16 None of the S that he has committed shall
Dan 3:28 brought all this upon us because of our S
3:37 day in all the world because of our S
4:27 you; break off your S by practicing righteousness,
9:16 hill; because for our S, and for the iniquities
13:52 of wicked days, your S have now come home,
Hos 8:13 iniquity, and punish their S; they shall return to
9:9 will remember their iniquity, he will punish their S
Amos 5:12 how great are your S --you who afflict the
Mic 1:5 Jacob and for the S of the house of
6:13 smite you, making you desolate because of your S
7:19 wilt cast all our S into the depths of
2Mac 5:17 while because of the S of those who dwelt
5:18 were involved in many S, this man would have
6:14 full measure of their S; but he does not
6:15 us afterward when our S have reached their height.
7:18 account, because of our S against our own God.
7:32 For we are suffering because of our own S
13:8 he had committed many S against the altar whose
Mt 1:21 for he will save his people from their S
3:6 by him in the river Jordan, confessing their S
9:2 heart, my son; your S are forgiven."
9:5 easier, to say, 'Your S are forgiven,' or to
9:6 on earth to forgive S --he then said to
18:14 "If your brother S against you, go and tell
26:28 poured out for many for the forgiveness of S
Mk 1:4 a baptism of repentance for the forgiveness of S
1:5 by him in the river Jordan, confessing their S
2:5 paralytic, "My son, your S are forgiven."
2:7 Who can forgive S but God alone?"
2:9 to the paralytic, 'Your S are forgiven,' or to
2:10 on earth to forgive S --he said to the
3:28 say to you, all S will be forgiven the
Lk 1:77 the forgiveness of their S,
3:3 a baptism of repentance for the forgiveness of S
5:20 he said, "Man, your S are forgiven you."
5:21 Who can forgive S but God only?"
5:23 easier, to say, 'Your S are forgiven you,' or
5:24 on earth to forgive S --he said to the
7:47 I tell you, her S, which are many, are
7:48 said to her, "Your S are forgiven."
7:49 among themselves, "Who is this, who even forgives S
11:4 and forgive us our S, for we ourselves forgive
17:3 yourselves; if your brother S, rebuke him, and if
17:4 him; and if he S against you seven times
24:47 repentance and forgiveness of S should be preached
Jn 8:24 would die in your S, for you will die
8:24 will die in your S unless you believe that
20:23 If you forgive the S of any, they are
20:23 if you retain the S of any, they are
Acts 2:38 the forgiveness of your S; and you shall receive
3:19 turn again, that your S may be blotted out,
5:31 to give repentance to Israel and forgiveness of S
10:43 him receives forgiveness of S through his name."
13:38 this man forgiveness of S is proclaimed to you,
22:16 and wash away your S, calling on his name.'
26:18 may receive forgiveness of S and a place among
Rom 3:25 had passed over former S;
4:7 are forgiven, and whose S are covered;
5:14 even over those whose S were not like the
11:27 covenant with them when I take away their S
1Cor 6:18 but the immoral man S against his own body.
15:3 Christ died for our S in accordance with the
15:17 is futile and you are still in your S
Gal 1:4 gave himself for our S to deliver us from
Eph 2:1 through the trespasses and S
Col 1:14 in whom we have redemption, the forgiveness of S
1Thes 2:16 always to fill up the measure of their S
1Tim 5:22 participate in another man's S; keep yourself pure.
5:24 The S of some men are conspicuous, pointing to
5:24 to judgment, but the S of others appear later.
2Tim 3:6 weak women, burdened with S and swayed by
Heb 1:3 had made purification for S, he sat down at
2:17 make expiation for the S of the people.
5:1 to God, to offer gifts and sacrifices for S
5:3 sacrifice for his own S as well as for
7:27 first for his own S and then for those
8:12 I will remember their S no more."
9:22 shedding of blood there is no forgiveness of S
9:28 once to bear the S of many, will appear
10:4 blood of bulls and goats should take away S
10:11 the same sacrifices, which can never take away S
10:12 a single sacrifice for S, he sat down at
10:17 "I will remember their S and their misdeeds no
10:26 remains a sacrifice for S,
Jas 5:15 if he has committed S, he will be forgiven.
5:16 Therefore confess your S to one another, and pray
5:20 from death and will cover a multitude of S
1Pet 2:24 He himself bore our S in his body on
3:18 Christ also died for S once for all, the
4:8 one another, since love covers a multitude of S
2Pet 1:9 forgotten that he was cleansed from his old S
1Jn 1:9 If we confess our S, he is faithful and
1:9 and will forgive our S and cleanse us from
2:2 the expiation for our S, and not for ours
2:2 but also for the S of the whole world.
2:12 little children, because your S are forgiven for his
3:5 appeared to take away S, and in him there
3:6 who abides in him S; no one who sins
3:6 sins; no one who S has either seen him
4:10 his Son to be the expiation for our S
Rev 1:5 freed us from our S by his blood
18:4 take part in her S, lest you share in
18:5 her plagues; for her S are heaped high as

SIPHMOTH

1Sam 30:28 Jattir, in Aroer, in S, in Eshtemoa,

SIPPAI

1Chr 20:4 Sibbecai the Hushathite slew S, who was one of

SIR (16)

Judg 6:13 said to him, "Pray, S, if the LORD is
Dan 14:35 Habakkuk said, S, I have never seen Babylon, and
Mt 13:27 and said to him, S, did you not sow
21:30 he answered, 'I go, S but did not go.
27:63 before Pilate and said, S, we remember how that
Lk 13:8 him, 'Let it alone, S, this year also, till
14:22 And the servant said, S, what you commanded has
Jn 4:11 woman said to him, S, you have nothing to
4:15 woman said to him, S, give me this water,
4:19 woman said to him, S, I perceive that you
4:49 official said to him, S, come down before my
5:6 sick man answered him, S, I have no man
9:36 "And who is he, S, that I may believe
12:21 and said to him, S, we wish to see
20:15 she said to him, S, if you have carried
Rev 7:14 I said to him, S, you know." And he

SIRACH

Sir 50:27 Jesus the son of S, son of Eleazar, of

SIRAH

2Sam 3:26 from the cistern of S; but David did not

SIRION (4)

Deut 3:9 (the Sidonians call Hermon S, while the Amorites
4:48 as far as Mount S (that is, Hermon),
Ps 29:6 like a calf, and S like a young wild
Jer 18:14 the snow of Lebanon leave the crags of S

SIRS

Acts 27:10 Paul advised them, saying, S, I perceive that the

SISERA (21)

Judg 4:2 of his army was S, who dwelt in Harosheth-ha-goiim.
4:7 I will draw out S, the general of Jabin's
4:9 the LORD will sell S into the hand of
4:12 When S was told that Barak the son of
4:13 up to Mount Tabor, S called out all his
4:14 the LORD has given S into your hand.
4:15 And the LORD routed S and all his chariots
4:15 of the sword; and S alighted from his chariot
4:16 all the army of S fell by the edge
4:17 But S fled away on foot to the tent
4:18 came out to meet S, and said to him,
4:22 behold, as Barak pursued S, Jael went out to
4:22 tent; and there lay S dead, with the tent
5:20 the stars, from their courses they fought against S
5:26 workmen's mallet; she struck S a blow, she crushed
5:28 peered, the mother of S gazed through the lattice:
5:30 of dyed stuffs for S, spoil of dyed stuffs
1Sam 12:9 into the hand of S, commander of the army
Ezra 2:53 Barkos, the sons of S, the sons of Temah,
Neh 7:55 Barkos, the sons of S, the sons of Temah,

S

Ps 83:9 to Midian, as to S and Jabin at the

SISMAI (2)

1Chr 2:40 was the father of S, and Sismai of Shallum.
2:40 father of Sismai, and S of Shallum.

SISTER (118)

Gen 4:22 The S of Tubal-cain was Naamah.
12:13 Say you are my S, that it may go
12:19 say, 'She is my S so that I took
20:2 said of Sarah his wife, "She is my S
20:5 not himself say to me, 'She is my S
20:12 she is indeed my S, the daughter of my
24:30 the bracelets on his S's arms, and when he
24:30 words of Rebekah his S, "Thus the man spoke
24:59 sent away Rebekah their S and her nurse, and
24:60 said to her, "Our S, be the mother of
25:20 Aramean of Paddan-aram, the S of Laban the
26:7 said, "She is my S; for he feared to
26:9 how then could you say, 'She is my S
28:9 Ishmael Abraham's son, the S of Nebaioth.
29:13 tidings of Jacob his S's son, he ran to
30:1 children, she envied her S; and she said to
30:8 have wrestled with my S, and have prevailed"; so
34:13 he had defiled their S Dinah.
34:14 thing, to give our S to one who is
34:27 the city, because their S had been defiled;
34:31 "Should he treat our S as a harlot?"
36:3 Basemath, Ishmael's daughter, the S of Nebaioth.
36:22 and Heman; and Lotan's S was Timna.
46:17 Imnah, Ishvah, Ishvi, Beriah, with Serah their S
Ex 2:4 And his S stood at a distance, to know
2:7 Then his S said to Pharaoh's daughter, "Shall I
6:20 wife Jochebed his father's S and she bore him
6:23 of Amminadab and the S of Nahshon; and she
15:20 Miriam, the prophetess, the S of Aaron, took a
Lev 18:9 the nakedness of your S, the daughter of your
18:11 begotten by your father, since she is your S
18:12 nakedness of your father's S; she is your father's
18:13 nakedness of your mother's S, for she is your
18:18 rival wife to her S, uncovering her nakedness while
18:18 her nakedness while her S is yet alive.
20:17 a man takes his S, a daughter of his
20:17 he has uncovered his S's nakedness, he shall bear
20:19 nakedness of your mother's S or of your father's
20:19 or of your father's S, for that is to
21:3 brother, or his virgin S (who is near to
Num 6:7 nor for brother or S, if they die, shall
25:18 prince of Midian, their S, who was slain on
26:59 to Amram Aaron and Moses and Miriam their S
Deut 27:22 who lies with his S, whether the daughter of
Judg 15:2 Is not her younger S fairer than she?
2Sam 13:1 son, had a beautiful S, whose name was Tamar;
13:2 ill because of his S Tamar; for she was
13:4 to him, "I love Tamar, my brother Absalom's S
13:5 to him, 'Let my S Tamar come and give
13:6 king, "Pray let my S Tamar come and make
13:11 said to her, "Come, lie with me, my S
13:20 hold your peace, my S; he is your brother;
13:22 he had forced his S Tamar.
13:32 day he forced his S Tamar.
17:25 the daughter of Nahash, S of Zeruiah, Joab's mother.
1Kgs 11:19 him in marriage the S of his own wife,
11:19 his own wife, the S of Tahpenes the queen.
11:20 And the S of Tahpenes bore him Genubath his
2Kgs 11:2 daughter of King Joram, S of Ahaziah, took Joash
1Chr 1:39 and Homam; and Lotan's S was Timna.
3:9 sons of the concubines; and Tamar was their S
3:19 and Shelomith was their S;
4:3 the name of their S was Hazzelelponi,
4:19 wife of Hodiah, the S of Naham, were the
7:15 The name of his S was Maacah.
7:18 And his S Hammolecheth bore Ishhod, Abi-ezer, and
7:30 Ishvi, Beriah, and their S Serah.
7:32 Shomer, Hotham, and their S Shua.
2Chr 22:11 because she was a S of Ahaziah, hid him
Tob 5:20 "Do not worry, my S; he will return safe
7:16 and said to her, S, make up the other
8:4 the bed and said, S, get up, and let
8:7 am not taking this S of mine because of
Job 17:14 'My mother,' or 'My S
Prov 7:4 Say to wisdom, "You are my S
Song 4:9 ravished my heart, my S, my bride, you have
4:10 is your love, my S, my bride!
4:12 garden locked is my S, my bride, a garden
5:1 to my garden, my S, my bride, I gather
5:2 "Open to me, my S, my love, my dove,
8:8 We have a little S, and she has no
8:8 we do for our S, on the day when
Jer 3:7 return, and her false S Judah saw it.
3:8 divorce; yet her false S Judah did not fear,
3:10 all this her false S Judah did not return
22:18 my brother!' or 'Ah S They shall not lament
Ezek 16:45 and you are the S of your sisters, who
16:46 And your elder S is Samaria, who lived with
16:46 you; and your younger S, who lived to the
16:48 the Lord GOD, your S Sodom and her daughters
16:49 the guilt of your S Sodom: she and her
16:56 Was not your S Sodom a byword in your
22:11 in you defiles his S, his father's daughter.
23:4 the elder and Oholibah the name of her S
23:11 "Her S Oholibah saw this, yet she was more
23:11 harlotry, which was worse than that of her S
23:18 from her, as I had turned from her S
23:31 the way of your S; therefore I will give
23:32 "You shall drink your S's cup which is deep
23:33 the cup of your S Samaria;
44:25 for brother or unmarried S they may defile
Hos 2:1 and to your S, "She has obtained pity."
Mt 12:49 is my brother, and S, and mother."
Mk 3:35 is my brother, and S, and mother."
Lk 10:39 And she had a S called Mary, who sat
10:40 not care that my S has left me to
Jn 11:1 of Mary and her S Martha.
11:5 loved Martha and her S and Lazarus.
11:28 went and called her S Mary, saying quietly, "The
11:39 Martha, the S of the dead man, said to
19:25 mother, and his mother's S, Mary the wife of
Acts 23:16 the son of Paul's S heard of their ambush;
Rom 16:1 commend to you our S Phoebe, a deaconess of
16:15 Julia, Nereus and his S, and Olympas, and all
1Cor 7:15 case the brother or S is not bound.
Philem 1:2 worker and Apphia our S and Archippus our fellow
Jas 2:15 If a brother or S is ill-clad and in
2Jn 1:13 children of your elect S greet you.

SISTER-IN-LAW (2)

Ruth 1:15 she said, "See, your S has gone back to
1:15 people and to her gods; return after your S

SISTERS (18)

Josh 2:13 mother, my brothers and S, and all who belong
1Chr 2:16 the seventh; and their S were Zeruiah and Abigail.
Job 1:4 and invite their three S to eat and drink
42:11 all his brothers and S and all who had
Ezek 16:45 the sister of your S, who loathed their husbands
16:51 and have made your S appear righteous by all
16:52 judgment favorable to your S; because of your sins
16:52 you have made your S appear righteous.
16:55 As for your S, Sodom and her daughters shall
16:61 when I take your S, both your elder and
Mt 13:56 are not all his S with us?
19:29 houses or brothers or S or father or mother
Mk 6:3 and are not his S here with us?" And
10:29 house or brothers or S or mother or father
10:30 houses and brothers and S and mothers and children
Lk 14:26 children and brothers and S, yes, and even his
Jn 11:3 So the S sent to him, saying, "Lord, he
1Tim 5:2 mothers, younger women like S, in all purity.

SIT (132)

Gen 27:19 you told me; now S up and eat of
Ex 18:14 Why do you S alone, and all the people
Num 32:6 the war while you S here?
Deut 6:7 of them when you S in your house, and
23:13 weapons; and when you S down outside, you shall
Judg 4:5 She used to S under the palm of Deborah
5:10 tawny asses, you who S on rich carpets and
Ruth 4:1 said, "Turn aside, friend; S down here"; and he
4:2 the city, and said, S down here"; so they
1Sam 2:8 heap, to make them S with princes and inherit
16:11 for we will not S down till he comes
20:5 should not fail to S at table with the
1Kgs 1:13 me, and he shall S upon my throne"?
1:17 me, and he shall S upon my throne.'
1:20 tell them who shall S on the throne of
1:24 me, and he shall S upon my throne?
1:27 your servants who should S on the throne of
1:30 me, and he shall S upon my throne in
1:35 he shall come and S upon my throne; for
1:48 of my offspring to S on my throne this
3:6 him a son to S on his throne this

8:20 David my father, and S on the throne of
8:25 man before me to S upon the throne of
2Kgs 7:3 another, "Why do we S here till we die?
7:4 there; and if we S here, we die also.
10:30 the fourth generation shall S on the throne of
15:12 Jehu, "Your sons shall S upon the throne of
1Chr 28:5 Solomon my son to S upon the throne of
2Chr 6:10 David my father, and S on the throne of
6:16 man before me to S upon the throne of
Ps 26:4 I do not S with false men, nor do
26:5 and I will not S with the wicked.
50:20 You S and speak against your brother; you slander
69:12 talk of those who S in the gate, and
110:1 says to my lord: S at my right hand,
113:8 heap, to make them S with princes, with the
119:23 Even though princes S plotting against me, thy
132:12 also for ever shall S upon your throne."
139:2 Thou knowest when I S down and when I
143:3 he has made me S in darkness like those
Prov 3:24 If you S down, you will not be afraid;
23:1 When you S down to eat with a ruler,
Eccl 10:6 places, and the rich S in a low place.
Sir 11:5 kings have had to S on the ground, but
11:9 not concern you, nor S with sinners when they
12:12 do not have him S at your right, lest
23:14 and mother when you S among great men; lest
26:12 him, so will she S in front of every
38:33 They do not S in the judge's seat, nor
42:12 beauty, and do not S in the midst of
Is 3:26 mourn; ravaged, she shall S upon the ground.
14:13 on high; I will S on the mount of
16:5 and on it will S in faithfulness in the
42:7 the prison those who S in darkness.
47:1 Come down and S in the dust, O virgin
47:1 virgin daughter of Babylon; S on the ground without
47:5 S in silence, and go into darkness, O daughter
47:8 lover of pleasures, who S securely, who say in
47:8 me; I shall not S as a widow or
47:14 this, no fire to S before!
65:4 incense upon bricks; who S in tombs, and spend
Jer 8:14 Why do we S still?
13:13 land: the kings who S on David's throne, the
15:17 I did not S in the company of merrymakers,
16:8 house of feasting to S with them, to eat
17:25 this city kings who S on the throne of
22:2 King of Judah, who S on the throne of
22:4 this house kings who S on the throne of
33:17 lack a man to S on the throne of
36:15 they said to him, S down and read it."
36:30 shall have none to S upon the throne of
48:18 from your glory, and S on the parched ground,
Lam 2:10 the daughter of Zion S on the ground in
3:28 Let him S alone in silence when he has
Bar 6:31 their temples the priests S with their clothes rent,
6:43 with cords about them, S along the passageways,
Ezek 2:6 with you and you S upon scorpions; be not
26:16 with trembling; they will S upon the ground and
28:2 am a god, I S in the seat of
33:31 people come, and they S before you as my
44:3 Only the prince may S in it to eat
Dan 7:26 But the court shall S in judgment, and his
13:50 said to him, "Come, S among us and inform
Joel 3:12 for there I will S to judge all the
Mic 4:4 more; but they shall S every man under his
7:8 shall rise; when I S in darkness, the LORD
Zech 3:8 and your friends who S before you, for they
6:13 royal honor, and shall S and rule upon his
8:4 old women shall again S in the streets of
Mal 3:3 fullers' soap; he will S as a refiner and
Mt 8:11 east and west and S at table with Abraham,
14:19 ordered the crowds to S down on the grass;
15:35 commanding the crowd to S down on the ground,
19:28 Son of man shall S on his glorious throne,
19:28 followed me will also S on twelve thrones, judging
20:21 sons of mine may S, one at your right
20:23 my cup, but to S at my right hand
22:44 said to my Lord, S at my right hand,
23:2 scribes and the Pharisees S on Moses' seat;
25:31 him, then he will S on his glorious throne.
26:36 said to his disciples, S here, while I go
Mk 6:39 commanded them all to S down by companies upon
8:6 commanded the crowd to S down on the ground;
10:37 him, "Grant us to S, one at your right
10:40 be baptized; but to S at my right hand
12:36 said to my Lord, S at my right hand,
14:32 said to his disciples, S here, while I pray."
Lk 1:79 light to those who S in darkness and in
9:14 his disciples, "Make them S down in companies,
9:15 and made them all S down.
12:37 himself and have them S at table, and he
13:29 north and south, and S at table in the
14:8 marriage feast, do not S down in a place
14:10 are invited, go and S in the lowest place,
14:10 presence of all who S at table with you.
14:28 tower, does not first S down and count the
14:31 in war, will not S down first and take
16:6 'Take your bill, and S down quickly and write
17:7 'Come at once and S down at table'?
20:42 said to my Lord, S at my right hand,
22:30 in my kingdom, and S on thrones judging the
Jn 6:10 said, "Make the people S down." Now there was
9:8 man who used to S and beg?"
Acts 2:34 said to my Lord, S at my right hand,
8:31 to come up and S with him.
Eph 1:20 dead and made him S at his right hand
2:6 him, and made us S with him in the
Heb 1:13 has he ever said, S at my right hand,
Jas 2:3 or, S at my feet,"
Rev 3:21 will grant him to S with me on my
11:16 the twenty-four elders who S on their thrones before
18:7 says, 'A queen I S, I am no widow,

SITE (7)

1Chr 21:22 Ornan, "Give me the S of the threshing floor
21:25 hundred shekels of gold by weight for the S
Ezra 2:68 erect it on its S;
5:15 the house of God be rebuilt on its S
6:7 Jews rebuild this house of God on its S
Is 4:5 create over the whole S of Mount Zion and
Zech 14:10 remain aloft upon its S from the Gate of

SITES

2Chr 33:19 his faithlessness, and the S on which he built

SITHRI

Ex 6:22 And the sons of Uzziel: Mishael, Elzaphan, and S

SITNAH

Gen 26:21 over that also; so he called its name S

SITS (41)

Ex 11:5 first-born of Pharaoh who S upon his throne, even
Lev 15:4 everything on which he S shall be unclean.
15:6 And whoever S on anything on which he who
15:20 also upon which she S shall be unclean.
15:22 anything upon which she S shall wash his clothes,
15:23 anything upon which she S, when he touches it
15:26 everything on which she S shall be unclean, as
Deut 17:18 "And when he S on the throne of his
2Sam 6:2 LORD of hosts who S enthroned on the cherubim.
1Kgs 1:46 Solomon S upon the royal throne.
1Chr 13:6 of the LORD who S enthroned above the cherubim.
Esth 6:10 Mordecai the Jew who S at the king's gate.
Ps 1:1 way of sinners, nor S in the seat of
2:4 He who S in the heavens laughs; the LORD
9:7 But the LORD S enthroned for ever, he has
10:8 He S in ambush in the villages; in hiding
29:10 The LORD S enthroned over the flood; the LORD
29:10 the flood; the LORD S enthroned as king for
33:14 men; from where he S enthroned he looks forth
47:8 over the nations; God S on his holy throne.
99:1 He S enthroned upon the cherubim; let the earth
Prov 9:14 She S at the door of her house, she
20:8 A king who S on the throne of judgment
31:23 the gates, when he S among the elders of
Wis 9:4 me the wisdom that S by thy throne, and
Sir 33:6 under every one who S on him.
40:3 from the man who S on a splendid throne
Is 28:6 justice to him who S in judgment, and strength
30:7 called her "Rahab who S still."
40:22 It is he who S above the circle of
Jer 29:16 concerning the king who S on the throne of
Lam 1:1 How lonely S the city that was
Bar 6:71 on which every bird S; or like a dead
Mt 23:21 and by him who S upon it.
Lk 22:27 the greater, one who S at table, or one
22:27 not the one who S at table?
Rev 5:13 saying, "To him who S upon the throne and
7:10 to our God who S upon the throne, and
7:15 temple; and he who S upon the throne will
19:19 war against him who S upon the horse and
19:21 sword of him who S upon the horse, the

SITTEST

Dan 3:55 Blessed art thou, who S upon cherubim and lookest

SITTING (76)

Gen 19:1 evening; and Lot was S in the gate of
23:10 Now Ephron was S among the Hittites; and Ephron
Deut 11:19 them when you are S in your house, and
22:6 eggs and the mother S upon the young or
Judg 3:20 him, as he was S alone in his cool
Ruth 4:4 the presence of those S here, and in the
1Sam 1:9 Eli the priest was S on the seat beside
4:13 he arrived, Eli was S upon his seat by
22:6 Saul was S at Gibe-ah, under the tamarisk tree
24:3 and his men were S in the innermost parts
2Sam 18:24 Now David was S between the two gates; and
19:8 "Behold, the king is S in the gate"; and
1Kgs 13:14 God, and found him S under an oak; and
22:10 king of Judah were S on their thrones, arrayed
22:19 I saw the LORD S on his throne, and
2Kgs 1:9 to Elijah, who was S on the top of
4:38 of the prophets were S before him, he said
6:32 Elisha was S in his house, and the elders
6:32 and the elders were S with him.
18:27 not to the men S on the wall, who
19:27 "But I know your S down and your going
2Chr 18:9 king of Judah were S on their thrones, arrayed
18:9 robes; and they were S at the threshing floor
18:18 I saw the LORD S on his throne, and
Neh 2:6 to me (the queen S beside him), "How long
Esth 2:19 second time, Mordecai was S at the king's gate.
2:21 days, as Mordecai was S at the king's gate,
5:1 The king was S on his royal throne inside
5:13 see Mordecai the Jew S at the king's gate."
Wis 6:14 he will find her S at his gates.
Sir 1:6 greatly to be feared, S upon his throne.
37:14 informed than seven watchmen S high on a
38:28 too is the smith S by the anvil, intent
38:29 too is the potter S at his work and
Is 6:1 I saw the Lord S upon a throne, high
36:12 not to the men S on the wall, who
37:28 'I know your S down and your going out
Jer 22:30 offspring shall succeed in S on the throne of
32:12 the Jews who were S in the court of
36:12 all the princes were S there: Elishama the secretary,
36:22 and the king was S in the winter house
38:7 cistern--the king was S in the Benjamin Gate--
Lam 3:63 Behold their S and their rising; I am the
Ezek 8:1 the elders of Judah S before me, the hand
Zech 5:7 there was a woman S in the ephah!
Mt 9:9 a man called Matthew S at the tax office;
11:16 It is like children S in the market places
20:30 behold, two blind men S by the roadside, when
26:69 Now Peter was S outside in the courtyard.
27:19 Besides, while he was S on the judgment seat,
27:61 other Mary were there, S opposite the sepulchre.
Mk 2:6 of the scribes were S there, questioning in their
2:14 the son of Alphaeus S at the tax office,
2:15 collectors and sinners were S with Jesus and his
3:32 And a crowd was S about him; and they
5:15 and saw the demoniac S there, clothed and in
10:46 son of Timaeus, was S by the roadside.
14:54 priest; and he was S with the guards, and
16:5 saw a young man S on the right side,
Lk 2:46 him in the temple, S among the teachers, listening
5:17 teachers of the law S by, who had come
5:27 tax collector, named Levi, S at the tax office;
5:29 tax collectors and others S at table with them.
7:32 They are like children S in the market place
8:35 the demons had gone, S at the feet of
10:13 have repented long ago, S in sackcloth and ashes.
18:35 a blind man was S by the roadside begging
Jn 12:15 your king is coming, S on an ass's colt!"
20:12 two angels in white, S where the body of
Acts 2:2 it filled all the house where they were S
14:8 there was a man S, who could not use
20:9 man named Eutychus was S in the window.
23:3 Are you S to judge me according to the
26:30 and those who were S with them;
1Cor 14:30 is made to another S by, let the first
Rev 17:3 I saw a woman S on a scarlet beast

SITUATION (3)

2Kgs 2:19 to Elisha, "Behold, the S of this city is
Tob 7:10 me explain the true S to you.
2Mac 3:9 and he inquired whether this really was the S

SIVAN (2)

Esth 8:9 is the month of S, on the twenty-third day;
Bar 1:8 the tenth day of S, Baruch took the vessels

SIX (183)

Gen 7:6 Noah was S hundred years old when the flood
7:11 In the S hundredth year of Noah's life, in
8:13 In the S hundred and first year, in the
30:20 I have borne him S sons"; so she called
31:41 your two daughters, and S years for your flock,
Ex 12:37 Rameses to Succoth, about S hundred thousand men
14:7 with him, and took S hundred picked chariots and
16:26 S days you shall gather it; but on the
20:9 S days you shall labor, and do all your
20:11 your gates; for in S days the LORD made
21:2 slave, he shall serve S years, and in the
23:10 "For S years you shall sow your land and
23:12 S days you shall do your work, but on
24:16 the cloud covered it S days; and on the
25:32 and there shall be S branches going out of
25:33 branch--so for the S branches going out of
25:35 each pair of the S branches going out from
26:9 curtains by themselves, and S curtains by
26:22 westward you shall make S frames.
28:10 the sons of Israel, S of their names on
28:10 names of the remaining S on the other stone,
31:15 S days shall work be done, but the seventh
31:17 of Israel that in S days the LORD made
34:21 S days you shall work, but on the seventh
35:2 S days shall work be done, but on the
36:16 curtains by themselves, and S curtains by
36:27 tabernacle westward he made S frames.
37:18 And there were S branches going out of its
37:19 --so for the S branches going out of
37:21 each pair of the S branches going out of
38:26 old and upward, for S hundred and three thousand,
Lev 23:3 S days shall work be done; but on the
24:6 them in two rows, S in a row, upon
25:3 S years you shall sow your field, and six
25:3 sow your field, and S years you shall prune
Num 1:25 Gad was forty-five thousand S hundred and fifty.
1:27 Judah was seventy-four thousand S hundred.
1:46 their whole number was S hundred and three
2:4 numbered being seventy-four thousand S hundred.
2:15 numbered being forty-five thousand S hundred and
2:31 hundred and fifty-seven thousand S hundred.
2:32 by their companies were S hundred and three
3:28 there were eight thousand S hundred, attending to
3:34 old and upward was S thousand two hundred.
4:40 houses was two thousand S hundred and thirty.
7:3 offerings before the LORD, S covered wagons and
11:21 whom I am number S hundred thousand on foot;
26:41 number was forty-five thousand S hundred.
26:51 the people of Israel, S hundred and one thousand
31:32 of war took was: S hundred and seventy-five
31:37 tribute of sheep was S hundred and seventy-five.
35:6 Levites shall be the S cities of refuge, where
35:13 give shall be your S cities of refuge.
35:15 These S cities shall be for refuge for the
Deut 5:13 S days you shall labor, and do all your
15:12 he shall serve you S years, and in the
15:18 he has served you S years.
16:8 For S days you shall eat unleavened bread; and
Josh 6:3 shall you do for S days.
6:14 So they did for S days.
15:59 Beth-anoth, and Eltekon: S cities with their villages.
15:62 of Salt, and Engedi: S cities with their villages.
Judg 3:31 of Anath, who killed S hundred of the Philistines
12:7 Jephthah judged Israel S years.
18:11 And S hundred men of the tribe of Dan,
18:16 Now the S hundred men of the Danites, armed
18:17 the gate with the S hundred men armed with
20:47 But S hundred men turned and fled toward the
Ruth 3:15 and he measured out S measures of barley, and
3:17 for her, saying, "These S measures of barley he
1Sam 13:5 thirty thousand chariots, and S thousand horsemen,
13:15 present with him, about S hundred men.
14:2 with him were about S hundred men,
17:4 Gath, whose height was S cubits and a span.
17:7 his spear's head weighed S hundred shekels of iron;
23:13 men, who were about S hundred, arose and departed
27:2 over, he and the S hundred men who were
30:9 set out, and the S hundred men who were
2Sam 2:11 was seven years and S months.
5:5 Judah seven years and S months; and at Jerusalem
6:13 the LORD had gone S paces, he sacrificed an

15:18 Pelethites, and all the S hundred Gittites who had
21:20 great stature, who had S fingers on each hand,
21:20 on each hand, and S toes on each foot,
1Kgs 6:6 the middle one was S cubits broad, and the
10:14 in one year was S hundred and sixty-six talents
10:16 shields of beaten gold; S hundred shekels of gold
10:19 The throne had S steps, and at the back
10:20 a step on the S steps.
10:29 imported from Egypt for S hundred shekels of silver,
11:16 all Israel remained there S months, until he had
16:23 reigned for twelve years; S years he reigned in
2Kgs 5:5 ten talents of silver, S thousand shekels of gold,
11:3 he remained with her S years, hid in the
13:19 have struck five or S times; then you would
15:8 over Israel in Samaria S months.
1Chr 3:4 by his wife Eglah; S were born to him
3:4 for seven years and S months.
3:22 Hattush, Igal, Bariah, Neariah, and Shaphat, S
4:27 had sixteen sons and S daughters; but his brothers
7:2 David being twenty-two thousand S hundred.
8:38 Azel had S sons, and these are their names:
9:6 Jeuel and their kinsmen, S hundred and ninety.
9:44 Azel had S sons and these are their names:
12:24 shield and spear were S thousand eight hundred
12:26 the Levites four thousand S hundred.
12:35 Danites twenty-eight thousand S hundred men
20:6 great stature, who had S fingers on each hand,
20:6 on each hand, and S toes on each foot,
21:25 So David paid Ornan S hundred shekels of gold
23:4 house of the LORD, S thousand shall be officers
25:3 Shimei, Hashabiah, and Mattithiah, S, under the
26:17 the east there were S each day, on the
2Chr 1:17 chariot from Egypt for S hundred shekels of silver,
2:2 country, and three thousand S hundred to oversee
2:17 hundred and fifty-three thousand S hundred.
2:18 country, and three thousand S hundred as overseers
3:8 he overlaid it with S hundred talents of fine
9:13 in one year was S hundred and sixty-six talents
9:15 shields of beaten gold; S hundred shekels of beaten
9:18 The throne had S steps and a footstool of
9:19 a step on the S steps.
22:12 he remained with them S years, hid in the
26:12 valor was two thousand S hundred.
29:33 consecrated offerings were S hundred bulls and
35:8 passover offerings two thousand S hundred lambs
Ezra 2:10 The sons of Bani, S hundred and forty-two.
2:11 The sons of Bebai, S hundred and twenty-three.
2:13 The sons of Adonikam, S hundred and sixty-six.
2:26 of Ramah and Geba, S hundred and twenty-one.
2:35 of Senaah, three thousand S hundred and thirty.
2:60 the sons of Nekoda, S hundred and fifty-two.
2:67 and their asses were S thousand seven hundred and
8:26 out into their hand S hundred and fifty talents
Neh 5:18 was one ox and S choice sheep; fowls likewise
7:10 The sons of Arah, S hundred and fifty-two.
7:15 The sons of Binnui, S hundred and forty-eight.
7:16 The sons of Bebai, S hundred and twenty-eight.
7:18 The sons of Adonikam, S hundred and sixty-seven.
7:20 The sons of Adin, S hundred and fifty-five.
7:30 of Ramah and Geba, S hundred and twenty-one.
7:62 the sons of Nekoda, S hundred and forty-two.
7:69 thirty-five, and their asses S thousand seven hundred
Jud 1:2 three cubits thick and S cubits long; he made
Esth 2:12 period of their beautifying, S months with oil of
2:12 oil of myrrh and S months with spices and
Job 5:19 will deliver you from S troubles; in seven there
42:12 had fourteen thousand sheep, S thousand camels, a
Prov 6:16 There are S things which the LORD hates, seven
Sir 16:10 sins; nor for the S hundred thousand men on
46:8 were preserved out of S hundred thousand people on
Is 6:2 the seraphim; each had S wings: with two he
Jer 34:14 'At the end of S years each of you
34:14 and has served you S years; you must set
52:30 were four thousand and S hundred.
Ezek 9:2 And lo, S men came from the direction of
40:5 the man's hand was S long cubits, each being
40:12 the side rooms were S cubits on either side.
41:1 jambs; on each side S cubits was the breadth
41:3 breadth of the entrance, S cubits; and the sidewalls
41:5 wall of the temple, S cubits thick; and the
41:8 a full reed of S long cubits.
46:1 be shut on the S working days; but on
46:4 sabbath day shall be S lambs without blemish and
46:6 bull without blemish, and S lambs and a ram,
Dan 3:1 cubits and its breadth S cubits.
14:31 he was there for S days.
1Mac 6:42 to the battle, and S hundred men of the
2Mac 8:1 so they gathered about S thousand men.
8:16 together, to the number S thousand, and exhorted
10:31 were slaughtered, besides S hundred horsemen.
Mt 17:1 And after S days Jesus took with him Peter
Mk 9:2 And after S days Jesus took with him Peter
Lk 4:25 up three years and S months, when there came
13:14 the people, "There are S days on which work
Jn 2:6 Now S stone jars were standing there, for the
12:1 S days before the Passover, Jesus came to Bethany,
Acts 11:12 These S brethren also accompanied me, and we
18:11 stayed a year and S months, teaching the word
Jas 5:17 for three years and S months it did not
Rev 4:8 each of them with S wings, are full of
13:18 number, its number is S hundred and sixty-six.
14:20 bridle, for one thousand S hundred stadia.

SIXTEEN (22)

Gen 46:18 she bore to Jacob-- S persons).
Ex 26:25 their bases of silver, S bases; two bases under
36:30 their bases of silver: S bases, under every frame
Num 31:40 The persons were S thousand, of which the LORD's
31:46 five hundred asses, and S thousand persons--
31:52 commanders of hundreds, was S thousand seven
Josh 15:41 Beth-dagon, Naamah, and Makkedah: S cities with
19:22 ends at the Jordan-- S cities with their villages.
2Kgs 13:10 Samaria, and he reigned S years.
14:21 took Azariah, who was S years old, and made
15:2 He was S years old when he began to
15:33 reign, and he reigned S years in Jerusalem.
16:2 reign, and he reigned S years in Jerusalem.
1Chr 4:27 Shimei had S sons and six daughters; but his
24:4 they organized them under S heads of fathers'
2Chr 13:21 had twenty-two sons and S daughters.
26:1 took Uzziah, who was S years old, and made
26:3 Uzziah was S years old when he began to
27:1 reign, and he reigned S years in Jerusalem.
27:8 reign, and he reigned S years in Jerusalem.
28:1 reign, and he reigned S years in Jerusalem.
2Mac 11:11 thousand of them and S hundred horsemen, and

SIXTEENTH (3)

1Chr 24:14 fifteenth to Bilgah, the S to Immer,
25:23 brethren, twelve; to the S, to Hananiah, his sons
2Chr 29:17 LORD, and on the S day of the first

SIXTH (46)

Gen 1:31 there was morning, a S day.
30:19 she bore Jacob a S son.
Ex 16:5 On the S day, when they prepare what they
16:22 On the S day they gathered twice as much
16:29 sabbath, therefore on the S day he gives you
26:9 by themselves, and the S curtain you shall double
Lev 25:21 upon you in the S year, so that it
Num 7:42 On the S day Eliasaph the son of Deuel,
29:29 "On the S day eight bulls, two rams, fourteen
Josh 19:32 The S lot came out for the tribe of
2Sam 3:5 of Abital; and the S, Ithre-am, of Eglah, David's
2Kgs 18:10 In the S year of Hezekiah, which was the
1Chr 2:15 the fifth, Ozem the S, David the seventh;
3:3 Shephatiah, by Abital; the S Ithream, by his wife
12:11 fourth, Jeremiah fifth, Attai S, Eliel seventh,
24:9 fifth to Malchijah, the S to Mijamin,
25:13 his brethren, twelve; the S to Bukkiah, his sons
26:3 the fifth, Jehohanan the S, Eli-e-ho-enai the seventh.
26:5 fifth, Ammiel the S, Issachar the seventh, Pe-ullethai
27:9 S, for the sixth month, was Ira, the son
27:9 Sixth, for the S month, was Ira, the son
Ezra 6:15 of Adar, in the S year of the reign
Neh 3:30 Shelemiah and Hanun the S son of Zalaph repaired
Ezek 4:11 drink by measure, the S part of a hin;
8:1 In the S year, in the sixth month, on
8:1 sixth year, in the S month, on the fifth
45:13 you shall make: one S of an ephah from
45:13 of wheat, and one S of an ephah from
46:14 morning by morning, one S of an ephah, and
Hag 1:1 the king, in the S month, on the first
1:15 the month, in the S month.
2Mac 7:18 After him they brought forward the S
Mt 20:5 out again about the S hour and the ninth
27:45 Now from the S hour there was darkness over
Mk 15:32 And when the S hour had come, there was
Lk 1:26 In the S month the angel Gabriel was sent
1:36 and this is the S month with her who
23:43 was now about the S hour, and there was
Jn 4:6 It was about the S hour.

19:14 it was about the S hour.
Acts 10:9 to pray, about the S hour.
Rev 6:12 When he opened the S seal, I looked, and
9:13 Then the S angel blew his trumpet, and I
9:14 God, saying to the S angel who had the
16:12 The S angel poured his bowl on the great
21:20 the fifth onyx, the S carnelian, the seventh chrysolite,

SIXTIETH (2)
1Mac 10:1 the one hundred and S year Alexander Epiphanes,
10:21 the one hundred and S year, at the feast

SIXTY (43)
Gen 25:26 Isaac was S years old when she bore them.
Lev 27:3 years old up to S years old shall be
27:7 if the person is S years old and upward,
Num 7:88 twenty-four bulls, the rams S, the male goats sixty,
7:88 sixty, the male goats S, the male lambs a
7:88 goats sixty, the male lambs a year old S
26:27 according to their number, S thousand five hundred.
Deut 3:4 not take from them-- S cities, the whole region
Josh 13:30 which are in Bashan, S cities,
2Sam 2:31 Benjamin three hundred and S of Abner's men.
1Kgs 4:13 which is in Bashan, S great cities with walls
4:22 of fine flour, and S cors of meal,
6:2 for the LORD was S cubits long, twenty cubits
2Kgs 25:19 of the land; and S men of the people
1Chr 2:21 married when he was S years old; and she
2:23 Kenath and its villages, S towns.
5:18 thousand seven hundred and S, ready for service.
9:13 thousand seven hundred and S, very able men for
2Chr 3:3 the old standard, was S cubits, and the breadth
11:21 took eighteen wives and S concubines, and had
11:21 had twenty-eight sons and S daughters);
12:3 twelve hundred chariots and S thousand horsemen.
Ezra 2:9 The sons of Zaccai, seven hundred and S
2:64 thousand three hundred and S,
6:3 its height shall be S cubits and its breadth
6:3 cubits and its breadth S cubits,
8:10 him a hundred and S men.
8:13 Shemaiah, and with them S men.
Neh 7:14 The sons of Zaccai, seven hundred and S
7:66 thousand three hundred and S,
Jud 1:3 hundred cubits high and S cubits wide at the
Song 3:7 About it are S mighty men of the mighty
6:8 are S queens and eighty concubines, and maidens
Jer 52:25 of the land; and S men of the people
Dan 3:1 gold, whose height was S cubits and its breadth
1Mac 4:28 year he mustered S thousand picked infantrymen
7:16 him; but he seized S of them and killed
2Mac 4:8 interview three hundred and S talents of silver and,
Mt 13:8 some a hundredfold, some S, some thirty.
13:23 a hundredfold, in another S, and in another thirty."
1Tim 5:9 is not less than S years of age, having
Rev 11:3 two hundred and S days, clothed in sackcloth."
12:6 thousand two hundred and S days.

SIXTY-EIGHT (2)
1Chr 16:38 Obed-edom and his S brethren; while Obed-edom,
Neh 11:6 were four hundred and S valiant men.

SIXTY-FIFTH
1Mac 10:67 the one hundred and S year Demetrius the son

SIXTY-FIVE (5)
Gen 5:15 When Mahalalel had lived S years, he became the
5:21 When Enoch had lived S years, he became the
5:23 were three hundred and S years.
Num 3:50 thousand three hundred and S shekels, reckoned by
Is 7:8 (Within S years Ephraim will be broken to pieces

SIXTY-FOUR (2)
Num 26:25 according to their number, S thousand three hundred.
26:43 to their number, were S thousand four hundred.

SIXTY-NINE (2)
Gen 5:27 were nine hundred and S years; and he died.
Ezra 1:11 of silver were five thousand four hundred and S

SIXTY-NINTH
2Mac 1:7 the one hundred and S year, we Jews wrote

SIXTY-ONE (3)
Num 31:34 seventy-two thousand cattle, S thousand asses,
31:39 five hundred, of which the LORD's tribute was S
Ezra 2:69 treasury of the work S thousand darics of gold,

SIXTY-SECOND
1Mac 10:57 the one hundred and S year.

SIXTY-SEVEN (3)
Neh 7:18 The sons of Adonikam, six hundred and S
7:19 The sons of Bigvai, two thousand and S
7:72 minas of silver, and S priests' garments.

SIXTY-SEVENTH
1Mac 11:19 the one hundred and S year.

SIXTY-SIX (6)
Gen 46:26 Jacob's sons' wives, were S persons in all;
Lev 12:5 of her purifying for S days.
1Kgs 10:14 was six hundred and S talents of gold,
2Chr 9:13 was six hundred and S talents of gold,
Ezra 2:13 The sons of Adonikam, six hundred and S
Rev 13:18 human number, its number is six hundred and S

SIXTY-TWO (8)
Gen 5:18 lived a hundred and S years he became the
5:20 were nine hundred and S years; and he died.
Num 1:39 tribe of Dan was S thousand seven hundred.
2:26 host as numbered being S thousand seven hundred.
1Chr 26:8 qualified for the service; S of Obed-edom.
Dan 5:31 the kingdom, being about S years old.
9:25 Then for S weeks it shall be built again
9:26 And after the S weeks, an anointed one shall

SIXTYFOLD (2)
Mk 4:8 and yielding thirtyfold and S and a hundredfold."
4:20 bear fruit, thirtyfold and S and a hundredfold."

SIZE (15)
Josh 22:10 altar by the Jordan, an altar of great S
1Chr 23:29 with oil, and all measures of quantity or S
Ezek 40:10 were of the same S; and the jambs on
40:10 jambs on either side were of the same S
40:21 were of the same S as those of the
40:22 were of the same S as those of the
40:24 they had the same S as the others.
40:28 was of the same S as the others;
40:29 were of the same S as the others; and
40:32 was of the same S as the others.
40:33 were of the same S as the others; and
40:35 it had the same S as the others.
40:36 were of the same S as the others; and
46:22 thirty broad; the four were of the same S
1Mac 3:19 is not on the S of the army that

SKIES (14)
Deut 33:26 your help, and in his majesty through the S
Neh 1:9 be under the farthest S, I will gather them
Job 36:28 in rain which the S pour down, and drop
37:18 him, spread out the S, hard as a molten
37:21 is bright in the S, when the wind has
Ps 68:34 over Israel, and his power is in the S
77:17 poured out water; the S gave forth thunder; thy
78:23 Yet he commanded the S above, and opened the
89:6 For who in the S can be compared to
89:37 stand firm while the S endure.
Prov 8:28 he made firm the S above, when he established
Is 34:4 rot away, and the S roll up like a
45:8 above, and let the S rain down righteousness; let
Jer 51:9 and has been lifted up even to the S

SKIFFS
Job 9:26 They go by like S of reed, like an

SKILFUL (12)
Gen 25:27 up, Esau was a S hunter, a man of
1Sam 16:16 a man who is S in playing the lyre;
16:18 the Bethlehemite, who is S in playing, a man
1Chr 25:7 LORD, all who were S, was two hundred and
2Chr 26:15 made engines, invented by S men, to be on
34:12 Levites, all who were S with instruments of music,
Ps 78:72 and guided them with S hand.
Sir 38:31 hands, and each is S in his own work.
Is 3:3 the counselor and the S magician and the expert
40:20 he seeks out a S craftsman to set up
Jer 9:17 come; send for the S women to come;
Ezek 21:31 hands of brutal men, S to destroy.

SKILFULLY (16)
Ex 26:1 scarlet stuff; with cherubim S worked shall you
28:6 of fine twined linen, S worked.

28:8 And the S woven band upon it, to gird
28:27 its joining above the S woven band of the
28:28 may lie upon the S woven band of the
29:5 gird him with the S woven band of the
36:8 scarlet stuff, with cherubim S worked.
36:35 twined linen; with cherubim S worked he made it.
39:5 And the S woven band upon it, to gird
39:20 its joining above the S woven band of the
39:21 should lie upon the S woven band of the
Lev 8:7 girded him with the S woven band of the
Ps 33:3 a new song, play S on the strings, with
Wis 13:11 easy to handle and S strip off all its
14:19 to please his ruler, S forced the likeness to
Hos 13:2 themselves molten images, idols S made of their

SKILL (18)

1Kgs 7:14 of wisdom, understanding, and S, for making any
1Chr 28:21 willing man who has S for any kind of
2Chr 30:22 Levites who showed good S in the service of
Jud 11:8 of your wisdom and S, and it is reported
Prov 1:5 man of understanding acquire S,
Eccl 2:21 wisdom and knowledge and S must leave all to
4:4 all toil and all S in work come from
9:11 to the men of S; but time and chance
Wis 7:16 are all understanding and S in crafts.
13:10 silver fashioned with S, and likenesses of animals,
13:13 and shapes it with S gained in idleness; he
14:4 if a man lacks S, he may put to
Sir 9:17 be praised for the S of the craftsmen; so
26:13 her husband, and her S puts fat on his
38:3 The S of the physician lifts up his head,
38:6 And he gave S to men that he might
Is 25:11 pride together with the S of his hands.
Dan 1:17 gave them learning and S in all letters and

SKILLED (23)

Ex 26:31 fine twined linen; in S work shall it be
28:15 breastpiece of judgment, in S work; like the work
35:33 for work in every S craft.
35:35 sort of workman or S designer.
39:3 fine twined linen, in S design.
39:8 made the breastpiece, in S work, like the work
1Chr 22:15 of craftsmen without number, S in working
2Chr 2:7 send me a man S to work in gold,
2:7 to be with the S workers who are with
2:13 I have sent a S man, endued with understanding,
Ezra 7:6 He was a scribe S in the law of
Job 3:8 the day, who are S to rouse up Leviathan.
Wis 13:11 A S woodcutter may saw down a tree easy
Sir 18:28 who understand sayings become S themselves, and
37:20 A man S in words may be hated; he
Jer 4:22 They are S in doing evil, but how to
10:9 all the work of S men.
46:9 shield, men of Lud, S in handling the bow.
50:9 arrows are like a S warrior who does not
Ezek 27:8 Arvad were your rowers; S men of Zemer were
27:9 of Gebal and her S men were in you,
Amos 5:16 wailing those who are S in lamentation,
1Cor 3:10 to me, like a S master builder I laid

SKILLFUL (2)

Prov 22:29 you see a man S in his work?
Dan 1:4 without blemish, handsome and S in all wisdom,

SKIN (87)

Gen 21:14 took bread and a S of water, and gave
21:15 the water in the S was gone, she cast
21:19 went, and filled the S with water, and gave
Ex 29:14 the bull, and its S, and its dung, you
34:29 not know that the S of his face shone
34:30 saw Moses, behold, the S of his face shone,
34:35 of Moses, that the S of Moses' face shone;
Lev 4:11 But the S of the bull and all its
7:8 have for himself the S of the burnt offering
8:17 the bull, and its S, and its flesh, and
9:11 The flesh and the S he burned with fire
11:32 a garment or a S or a sack, any
13:2 man has on the S of his body a
13:2 leprous disease on the S of his body, then
13:3 diseased spot on the S of his body; and
13:3 be deeper than the S of his body, it
13:4 is white in the S of his body, and
13:4 no deeper than the S, and the hair in
13:5 not spread in the S, then the priest shall
13:6 not spread in the S, then the priest shall
13:7 eruption spreads in the S, after he has shown
13:8 has spread in the S, then the priest shall
13:10 white swelling in the S, which has turned the
13:11 chronic leprosy in the S of his body, and
13:12 breaks out in the S, so that the leprosy
13:12 leprosy covers all the S of the diseased person
13:18 there is in the S of one's body a
13:20 appears deeper than the S and its hair has
13:21 not deeper than the S, but is dim, then
13:22 it spreads in the S, then the priest shall
13:24 a burn on its S and the raw flesh
13:25 appears deeper than the S, then it is leprosy;
13:26 no deeper than the S, but is dim, the
13:27 is spreading in the S, then the priest shall
13:28 not spread in the S, but is dim, it
13:30 appears deeper than the S, and the hair in
13:31 no deeper than the S and there is no
13:32 no deeper than the S,
13:34 not spread in the S and it appears to
13:34 no deeper than the S, then the priest shall
13:35 itch spreads in the S after his cleansing,
13:36 has spread in the S, the priest need not
13:38 has spots on the S of the body, white
13:39 the spots on the S of the body are
13:39 broken out in the S; he is clean.
13:43 of leprosy in the S of the body,
13:48 wool, or in a S or in anything made
13:48 in anything made of S,
13:49 or woof or in S or in anything made
13:49 in anything made of S, it is a leprous
13:51 woof, or in the S, whatever be the use
13:51 the use of the S, the disease is a
13:52 linen, or anything of S, for it is a
13:53 or in anything of S,
13:56 the garment or the S or the warp or
13:57 or in anything of S, it is spreading; you
13:58 woof, or anything of S from which the disease
13:59 or in anything of S, to decide whether it
15:17 every garment and every S on which the semen
16:27 outside the camp; their S and their flesh and
Num 19:5 in his sight; her S, her flesh, and her
31:20 garment, every article of S, all work of goats'
Judg 4:19 So she opened a S of milk and gave
1Sam 1:24 of flour, and a S of wine; and she
10:3 and another carrying a S of wine.
16:20 with bread, and a S of wine and a
2Sam 16:1 summer fruits, and a S of wine.
Job 2:4 Satan answered the LORD, S for skin!
2:4 Then Satan answered the LORD, "Skin for S
7:5 worms and dirt; my S hardens, then breaks out
10:11 didst clothe me with S and flesh, and knit
16:15 sewed sackcloth upon my S, and have laid my
18:13 By disease his S is consumed, the first-born of
19:20 bones cleave to my S and to my flesh,
19:20 have escaped by the S of my teeth.
19:26 earth; and after my S has been thus destroyed,
30:30 My S turns black and falls from me, and
41:7 Can you fill his S with harpoons, or his
Jer 13:23 the Ethiopian change his S or the leopard his
Lam 3:4 my flesh and my S waste away, and broken
4:8 in the streets; their S has shriveled upon their
5:10 Our S is hot as an oven with the
Ezek 37:6 and cover you with S, and put breath in
37:8 come upon them, and S had covered them; but
Mic 3:2 evil, who tear the S from off my people,
3:3 people, and flay their S from off them, and
2Mac 7:7 They tore off the S of his head with

SKINS (19)

Gen 3:21 his wife garments of S, and clothed them.
27:16 younger son; and the S of the kids she
Ex 25:5 goats' hair, tanned rams' S, goatskins, acacia wood,
26:14 covering of tanned rams' S and goatskins.
35:7 goats' hair, tanned rams' S, and goatskins; acacia
35:23 hair or tanned rams' S or goatskins, brought them.
36:19 covering of tanned rams' S and goatskins.
39:34 covering of tanned rams' S and goatskins, and the
Num 6:4 the grapevine, not even the seeds or the S
1Sam 25:18 hundred loaves, and two S of wine, and five
Neh 5:18 and every ten days S of wine in abundance;
Mt 9:17 if it is, the S burst, and the wine
9:17 is spilled, and the S are destroyed; but new
Mk 2:22 wine will burst the S, and the wine is
2:22 and so are the S; but new wine is
2:22 the skins; but new wine is for fresh S
Lk 5:37 wine will burst the S and it will be
5:37 be spilled, and the S will be destroyed.

Heb 11:37 they went about in S of sheep and goats,

SKIP (2)

Ps 29:6 He makes Lebanon to S like a calf, and
114:6 O mountains, that you S like rams?

SKIPPED

Ps 114:4 The mountains S like rams, the hills like lambs.

SKIPS

Sir 36:26 a nimble robber that S from city to city?

SKIRT (9)

Ruth 3:9 spread your S over your maidservant,
1Sam 15:27 laid hold upon the S of his robe, and
24:4 stealthily cut off the S of Saul's robe.
24:5 smote him, because he had cut off Saul's S
24:11 my father, see the S of your robe in
24:11 I cut off the S of your robe, and
Ezek 16:8 and I spread my S over you, and covered
Hag 2:12 holy flesh in the S of his garment, and
2:12 and touches with his S bread, or pottage, or

SKIRTS (13)

Ex 28:33 On its S you shall make pomegranates of blue
28:33 scarlet stuff, around its S, with bells of gold
28:34 round about on the S of the robe.
39:24 On the S of the robe they made pomegranates
39:25 the pomegranates upon the S of the robe round
39:26 round about upon the S of the robe for
Job 38:13 take hold of the S of the earth, and
Jer 2:34 Also on your S is found the lifeblood of
13:22 your iniquity that your S are lifted up, and
13:26 will lift up your S over your face, and
Lam 1:9 uncleanness was in her S; she took no thought
Ezek 5:3 bind them in the S of your robe.
Nah 3:5 will lift up your S over your face; and

SKULL (6)

Judg 9:53 millstone upon Abimelech's head, and crushed his S
2Kgs 9:35 of her than the S and the feet and
Mt 27:33 the place of a S,
Mk 15:22 called Golgotha (which means the place of a S
Lk 23:32 which is called The S, there they crucified him,
Jn 19:17 the place of a S, which is called in

SKY (12)

Ps 85:11 ground, and righteousness will look down from the S
Prov 30:19 an eagle in the S, the way of a
Mt 16:2 fair weather; for the S is red.'
16:3 stormy today, for the S is red and threatening.'
16:3 the appearance of the S, but you cannot interpret
Lk 12:56 appearance of earth and S; but why do you
17:24 and lights up the S from one side to
Acts 19:35 of the sacred stone that fell from the S
Rev 6:13 the stars of the S fell to the earth
6:14 by a gale; the S vanished like a scroll
11:6 power to shut the S, that no rain may
20:11 his presence earth and S fled away, and no

SLACK (7)

Deut 7:10 he will not be S with him who hates
23:21 you shall not be S to pay it; for
Josh 18:3 long will you be S to go in and
Ezra 4:22 care not to be S in this matter; why
Prov 10:4 A S hand causes poverty, but the hand of
18:9 He who is S in his work is a
Sir 2:12 timid hearts and to S hands, and to the

SLACKED

Hab 1:4 So the law is S and justice never goes

SLACKEN

2Kgs 4:24 beast on; do not S the pace for me

SLACKNESS

Jer 48:10 of the LORD with S; and cursed is he

SLAIN (159)

Gen 4:23 I say: I have S a man for wounding
34:27 Jacob came upon the S, and plundered the city,
Num 14:16 them, therefore he has S them in the wilderness.'
19:16 touches one who is S with a sword, or
19:18 the bone, or the S, or the dead, or
22:33 now I would have S you and let her
23:24 the prey, and drinks the blood of the S
25:14 The name of the S man of Israel, who
25:14 of Israel, who was S with the Midianite woman,
25:15 Midianite woman who was S was Cozbi the
25:18 their sister, who was S on the day of
31:8 the rest of their S, Evi, Rekem, Zur, Hur,
31:19 whoever has touched any S, purify yourselves and
Deut 21:1 any one is found S, lying in the open
21:2 around him that is S;
21:3 is nearest to the S man shall take a
21:6 city nearest to the S man shall wash their
28:31 Your ox shall be S before your eyes, and
32:42 the blood of the S and the captives, from
Josh 11:6 over all of them, S, to Israel; you shall
13:22 with the sword among the rest of their S
Judg 9:18 this day, and have S his sons, seventy men
15:16 an ass have I S a thousand men."
16:24 our country, who has S many of us."
16:30 those whom he had S during his life.
20:45 Gidom, and two thousand men of them were S
1Sam 4:11 two sons of Eli, Hophni and Phinehas, were S
18:7 made merry, "Saul has S his thousands, and David
21:11 in dances, 'Saul has S his thousands, and David
29:5 in dances, 'Saul has S his thousands, and David
31:1 the Philistines, and fell S on Mount Gilboa.
31:8 came to strip the S, they found Saul and
2Sam 1:16 you, saying, 'I have S the LORD's anointed.'"
1:19 glory, O Israel, is S upon thy high places!
1:22 the blood of the S, from the fat of
1:25 "Jonathan lies S upon thy high places.
2:31 servants of David had S of Benjamin three hundred
3:29 spindle, or who is S by the sword, or
4:11 when wicked men have S a righteous man in
11:17 Uriah the Hittite was S also.
12:9 your wife, and have S him with the sword
13:30 to David, "Absalom has S all the king's sons,
23:10 men returned after him only to strip the S
1Kgs 9:16 with fire, and had S the Canaanites who dwelt
11:15 up to bury the S, he slew every male
13:26 has torn him and S him, according to the
19:1 and how he had S all the prophets with
19:10 down thy altars, and S thy prophets with the
19:14 down thy altars, and S thy prophets with the
2Kgs 3:23 surely fought together, and S one another.
11:2 were about to be S, and she put him
11:2 that he was not S;
11:8 and whoever approaches the ranks is to be S
11:15 "Let her not be S in the house of
11:16 to the king's house, and there she was S
11:20 after Athaliah had been S with the sword at
14:5 his servants who had S the king his father.
1Chr 5:22 For many fell S, because the war was of
10:1 the Philistines, and fell S on Mount Gilboa.
10:8 came to strip the S, they found Saul and
2Chr 13:17 slaughter; so there fell S of Israel five hundred
22:1 to the camp had S all the older sons.
22:11 were about to be S, and she put him
23:7 hand; and whoever enters the house shall be S
23:14 her is to be S with the sword." For
23:21 after Athaliah had been S with the sword.
25:3 his servants who had S the king his father.
28:9 hand, but you have S them in a rage
Tob 3:8 evil demon Asmodeus had S each of them before
Jud 9:3 their rulers to be S, and their bed, which
10:13 without losing one of his men, captured or S
Esth 7:4 be destroyed, to be S, and to be annihilated.
9:11 the number of those S in Susa the capital
9:12 capital the Jews have S five hundred men and
Job 39:30 blood; and where the S are, there is he."
Ps 44:22 thy sake we are S all the day long,
88:5 the dead, like the S that lie in the
Prov 7:26 low; yea, all her S are a mighty host.
22:13 I shall be S in the streets!"
Is 10:4 crouch among the prisoners or fall among the S
14:19 birth, clothed with the S, those pierced by the
14:20 your land, you have S your people.
22:2 Your S are not slain with the sword or
22:2 Your slain are not S with the sword or
26:21 upon her, and will no more cover her S
27:7 Or have they been S as their slayers were
27:7 have they been slain as their slayers were S
34:3 Their S shall be cast out, and the stench
66:16 all flesh; and those S by the LORD shall
Jer 9:1 and night for the S of the daughter of
14:18 the field, behold, those S by the sword!
18:21 pestilence, their youths be S by the sword in
25:33 "And those S by the LORD on that day

41:9 men whom he had S was the large cistern
41:9 the son of Nethaniah filled it with the S
41:16 Mizpah after he had S Gedaliah the son of
41:18 son of Nethaniah had S Gedaliah the son of
51:4 They shall fall down S in the land of
51:47 shame, and all her S shall fall in the
51:49 must fall for the S of Israel, as for
51:49 Babylon have fallen the S of all the earth.
Lam 2:4 foe; and he has S all the pride of
2:20 priest and prophet be S in the sanctuary of
2:21 thy anger thou hast S them, slaughtering without
Ezek 6:4 will cast down your S before your idols.
6:7 And the S shall fall in the midst of
6:13 the LORD, when their S lie among their idols
9:7 the house, and fill the courts with the S
11:6 You have multiplied your S in this city, and
11:6 city, and have filled its streets with the S
11:7 the Lord GOD: Your S whom you have laid
21:14 for those to be S; it is the sword
26:6 the mainland shall be S by the sword.
28:8 the death of the S in the heart of
28:23 her streets; and the S shall fall in the
30:4 in Ethiopia, when the S fall in Egypt, and
30:11 against Egypt, and fill the land with the S
31:17 to those who are S by the sword; yea,
31:18 with those who are S by the sword.
32:20 amid those who are S by the sword, and
32:21 lie still, the uncircumcised, S by the sword.'
32:22 her, all of them S, fallen by the sword;
32:23 grave; all of them S, fallen by the sword,
32:24 grave; all of them S, fallen by the sword,
32:25 a bed among the S with all her multitude,
32:25 all of them uncircumcised, S by the sword; for
32:25 to the Pit; they are placed among the S
32:26 all of them uncircumcised, S by the sword; for
32:28 with those who are S by the sword.
32:29 with those who are S by the sword; they
32:30 in shame with the S, for all the terror
32:30 with those who are S by the sword, and
32:31 and all his army, S by the sword, says
32:32 with those who are S by the sword, Pharaoh
35:8 your mountains with the S; on your hills and
35:8 all your ravines those S with the sword shall
37:9 and breathe upon these S, that they may live."
Dan 2:13 men were to be S, and they sought Daniel
5:30 That very night Belshazzar the Chaldean king was S
7:11 looked, the beast was S, and its body destroyed
11:26 be swept away, and many shall fall down S
14:28 has destroyed Bel, and S the dragon, and slaughtered
Hos 6:5 the prophets, I have S them by the words
Nah 3:3 glittering spear, hosts of S, heaps of corpses, dead
Zeph 2:12 O Ethiopians, shall be S by my sword.
Zech 11:7 flock doomed to be S for those who trafficked
1Mac 5:51 Then he passed through the city over the S
2Mac 5:14 as many were sold into slavery as were S
Acts 5:36 him; but he was S and all who followed
7:42 you offer to me S beasts and sacrifices, forty
Rev 5:6 though it had been S, with seven horns and
5:9 seals, for thou wast S and by thy blood
5:12 the Lamb who was S, to receive power and
6:9 those who had been S for the word of
13:8 book of life of the Lamb that was S
13:10 the sword, with the sword must he be S
13:15 worship the image of the beast to be S
18:24 all who have been S on earth."
19:21 And the rest were S by the sword of

SLAKING

Wis 11:4 of flinty rock, and S of thirst from hard

SLANDER (20)

Ps 15:3 heart; who does not S with his tongue, and
50:20 against your brother; you S your own mother's son.
Prov 10:18 and he who utters S is a fool.
30:10 Do not S a servant to his master, lest
Wis 1:11 keep your tongue from S; because no secret word
Sir 19:15 for often it is S; so do not believe
26:5 I am frightened: The S of a city, the
28:14 S has shaken many, and scattered them from nation
28:15 S has driven away courageous women, and deprived
28:16 Whoever pays heed to S will not find rest,
51:6 lying words-- the S of an unrighteous tongue
Ezek 22:9 men in you who S to shed blood, and
Mt 15:19 murder, adultery, fornication, theft, false witness, S
Mk 7:21 deceit, licentiousness, envy, S, pride, foolishness.
2Cor 12:20 jealousy, anger, selfishness, S, gossip, conceit, and
Eph 4:31 anger and clamor and S be put away from
Col 3:8 away: anger, wrath, malice, S, and foul talk from
1Tim 6:4 which produce envy, dissension, S, base suspicions,
1Pet 2:1 all guile and insincerity and envy and all S
Rev 2:9 are rich) and the S of those who say

SLANDERED (4)

2Sam 19:27 He has S your servant to my lord the
Ps 35:15 whom I knew not S me without ceasing;
2Mac 4:1 against his own country, S Onias, saying that it
1Cor 4:13 persecuted, we endure; when S, we try to conciliate;

SLANDERER (4)

Lev 19:16 and down as a S among your people, and
Ps 140:11 Let not the S be established in the land;
Sir 5:14 not be called a S, and do not lie
Jer 9:4 supplanter, and every neighbor goes about as a S

SLANDERERS (4)

Rom 1:30 malignity, they are gossips, S, haters of God, insolent,
1Tim 3:11 must be serious, no S, but temperate, faithful in
2Tim 3:3 unholy, inhuman, implacable, S, profligates, fierce,
Tit 2:3 behavior, not to be S or slaves to drink;

SLANDEROUS

Sir 51:2 the snare of a S tongue, from lips that

SLANDEROUSLY

Rom 3:8 come?--as some people S charge us with saying.

SLANDERS (3)

Ps 27:2 evildoers assail me, uttering S against me, my
101:5 Him who S his neighbor secretly I will destroy.
Jer 6:28 rebellious, going about with S; they are bronze and

SLAPPED

Mt 26:67 struck him; and some S him,

SLASHES

Job 16:13 He S open my kidneys, and does not spare;

SLAUGHTER (62)

Gen 43:16 into the house, and S an animal and make
Ex 29:16 ram, and you shall S the ram, and shall
Deut 12:15 "However, you may S and eat flesh within any
Josh 10:10 them with a great S at Gibeon, and chased
10:20 with a very great S, until they were wiped
Judg 11:33 as far as Abel-keramim, with a very great S
15:8 and thigh with great S; and he went down
1Sam 4:10 was a very great S, for there fell of
4:17 also been a great S among the people; your
6:19 had made a great S among the people.
14:14 him; and that first S, which Jonathan and his
14:30 found; for now the S among the Philistines has
17:57 David returned from the S of the Philistine, Abner
19:8 and made a great S among them, so that
23:5 and made a great S among them.
2Sam 1:1 had returned from the S of the Amalekites, David
17:9 'There has been a S among the people who
18:7 of David, and the S there was great on
1Kgs 11:24 marauding band, after the S by David; and they
20:21 chariots, and killed the Syrians with a great S
2Chr 13:17 them with a great S; so there fell slain
25:14 Amaziah came from the S of the Edomites, he
28:5 king of Israel, who defeated him with great S
Jud 2:11 hand them over to S and plunder throughout your
8:22 And the S of our brethren and the captivity
15:5 out-flanked them with great S, even beyond
15:7 they returned from the S, took possession of what
Ps 44:11 us like sheep for S, and hast scattered us
44:22 day long, and accounted as sheep for the S
Prov 7:22 ox goes to the S, or as a stag
24:11 hold back those who are stumbling to the S
Wis 12:5 unholy rites, their merciless S of children, and their
Is 13:18 Their bows will S the young men; they will
14:21 Prepare S for his sons because of the guilt
30:25 day of the great S, when the towers fall.
34:2 has doomed them, has given them over for S
34:6 in Bozrah, a great S in the land of
53:7 is led to the S, and like a sheep
65:12 bow down to the S; because, when I called,
Jer 7:32 but the valley of S: for they will bury
11:19 was like a gentle lamb led to the S
12:3 like sheep for the S, and set them apart
12:3 and set them apart for the day of S
19:6 the son of Hinnom, but the valley of S

S

25:34 the days of your S and dispersion have come,
48:15 have gone down to S, says the King, whose
50:27 her bulls, let them go down to the S
51:40 like lambs to the S, like rams and he-goats.
Ezek 9:2 with his weapon for S in his hand, and
21:10 also polished, sharpened for S, polished to flash like
21:14 sword for the great S, which encompasses them,
21:15 is made like lightning, it is polished for S
21:28 is drawn for the S, it is polished to
26:15 the wounded groan, when S is made in the
34:3 with the wool, you S the fatlings; but you
Hos 9:13 prey; Ephraim must lead forth his sons to S
Obad 1:9 from Mount Esau will be cut off by S
Zech 11:4 God: "Become shepherd of the flock doomed to S
2Mac 5:13 women, and children, and S of virgins and infants.
Acts 8:32 sheep led to the S or a lamb before
Heb 7:1 Abraham returning from the S of the kings and
Jas 5:5 have fattened your hearts in a day of S

SLAUGHTERED (13)

Num 11:22 flocks and herds be S for them, to suffice
19:3 outside the camp and S before him;
Prov 9:2 She has S her beasts, she has mixed her
Ezek 16:21 a matter that you S my children and delivered
23:39 For when they had S their children in sacrifice
40:39 offering and the guilt offering were to be S
40:41 tables, on which the sacrifices were to be S
40:42 which the burnt offerings and the sacrifices were S
Dan 14:28 slain the dragon, and S the priests."
2Mac 10:31 thousand five hundred were S, besides six hundred
12:16 will of God, and S untold numbers, so that
12:26 temple of Atargatis, and S twenty-five thousand
Rom 8:36 long; we are regarded as sheep to be S

SLAUGHTERING (5)

Josh 8:24 When Israel had finished S all the inhabitants of
2Kgs 3:24 and they went forward, S the Moabites as they
Esth 9:5 enemies with the sword, S, and destroying them, and
Lam 2:21 thou hast slain them, S without mercy.
2Mac 5:6 But Jason kept relentlessly S his fellow citizens, not

SLAUGHTERS

Is 66:3 "He who S an ox is like him who

SLAVE (91)

Gen 9:25 "Cursed be Canaan; a S of slaves shall he
9:26 God be Shem; and let Canaan be his S
9:27 tents of Shem; and let Canaan be his S
15:3 no offspring; and a S born in my house
21:10 Abraham, "Cast out this S woman with her son;
21:10 the son of this S woman shall not be
21:12 and because of your S woman; whatever Sarah says
21:13 the son of the S woman also, because he
44:10 found shall be my S, and the rest of
44:17 found shall be my S; but as for you,
44:33 the lad as a S to my lord; and
49:15 bear, and became a S at forced labor.
Ex 12:44 of it; but every S that is bought for
21:2 you buy a Hebrew S, he shall serve six
21:5 But if the S plainly says, 'I love my
21:7 his daughter as a S, she shall not go
21:20 a man strikes his S, male or female, with
21:20 a rod and the S dies under his hand,
21:21 But if the S survives a day or two,
21:21 be punished; for the S is his money.
21:26 the eye of his S, male or female, and
21:26 he shall let the S go free for the
21:27 the tooth of his S, male or female, he
21:27 he shall let the S go free for the
21:32 the ox gores a S, male or female, the
Lev 19:20 woman who is a S, betrothed to another man
22:11 a priest buys a S as his property for
22:11 property for money, the S may eat of it;
25:39 him serve as a S:
Deut 15:15 that you were a S in the land of
16:12 that you were a S in Egypt; and you
21:14 treat her as a S, since you have humiliated
23:15 to his master a S who has escaped from
24:7 treats him as a S or sells him, then
24:18 that you were a S in Egypt and the
24:22 that you were a S in the land of
1Chr 2:34 Sheshan had an Egyptian S, whose name was Jarha.
2:35 marriage to Jarha his S; and she bore him
Jud 4:10 hired laborer and purchased S—they all girded
9:10 lips strike down the S with the prince and
12:10 a banquet for his S only, and did not
Job 3:19 are there, and the S is free from his
7:2 Like a S who longs for the shadow, and
Ps 105:17 of them, Joseph, who was sold as a S
Prov 17:2 A S who deals wisely will rule over a
19:10 much less for a S to rule over princes.
22:7 the borrower is the S of the lender.
30:22 cannot bear up: a S when he becomes king,
Wis 9:5 For I am thy S and the son of
18:11 The S was punished with the same penalty as
Sir 33:25 Set your S to work, and you will find
Is 24:2 priest; as with the S, so with his master;
Jer 2:14 "Is Israel a S
27:7 nations and great kings shall make him their S
34:10 would set free his S, male or female, so
1Mac 2:11 away; no longer free, she has become a S
2Mac 8:35 alone like a runaway S across the country till
Mt 8:9 comes, and to my S, 'Do this,' and he
20:27 you must be your S;
26:51 sword, and struck the S of the high priest,
Mk 10:44 among you must be S of all.
14:47 sword, and struck the S of the high priest
Lk 7:2 a centurion had a S who was dear to
7:3 Jews, asking him to come and heal his S
7:8 comes; and to my S, 'Do this,' and he
7:10 house, they found the S well.
22:48 of them struck the S of the high priest
Jn 8:34 commits sin is a S to sin.
8:35 The S does not continue in the house for
18:10 struck the high priest's S and cut off his
18:10 The S's name was Malchus.
Acts 16:16 were met by a S girl who had a
1Cor 7:21 Were you a S when called?
7:22 the Lord as a S is a freedman of
7:22 when called is a S of Christ.
9:19 have made myself a S to all, that I
Gal 3:28 Greek, there is neither S nor free, there is
4:1 no better than a S, though he is the
4:7 are no longer a S but a son, and
4:22 sons, one by a S and one by a
4:23 the son of the S was born according to
4:30 "Cast out the S and her son; for the
4:30 the son of the S shall not inherit with
4:31 not children of the S but of the free
Eph 6:8 whether he is a S or free.
Col 3:11 uncircumcised, barbarian, Scythian, S, free man, but
Philem 1:16 no longer as a S but more than a
1:16 but more than a S, as a beloved brother,
Rev 6:15 strong, and every one, S and free, hid in
13:16 poor, both free and S, to be marked on
19:18 men, both free and S, both small and great."

SLAVERY (9)

Jud 8:23 For our S will not bring us into favor,
Esth 14:8 we are in bitter S, but they have covenanted
2Mac 5:14 many were sold into S as were slain.
8:10 thousand talents, by selling the captured Jews into S
Rom 8:15 receive the spirit of S to fall back into
Gal 4:24 Sinai, bearing children for S; she is Hagar.
4:25 for she is in S with her children.
5:1 do not submit again to a yoke of S
1Tim 6:1 under the yoke of S regard their masters as

SLAVES (92)

Gen 9:25 Canaan; a slave of S shall he be to
15:13 theirs, and will be S there, and they will
17:23 son and all the S born in his house
20:14 and male and female S, and gave them to
20:17 his wife and female S so that they bore
43:18 upon us, to make S of us and seize
44:9 die, and we also will be my lord's S
44:16 we are my lord's S, both we and he
47:19 our land will be S to Pharaoh; and give
47:21 the people, he made S of them from one
47:25 lord, we will be S to Pharaoh."
Ex 9:20 of Pharaoh made his S and his cattle flee
9:21 the LORD left his S and his cattle in
21:7 out as the male S do.
Lev 25:6 your male and female S and for your hired
25:42 of Egypt; they shall not be sold as S
25:44 your male and female S whom you may have:
25:44 buy male and female S from among the nations
25:46 ever; you may make S of them, but over
26:13 should not be their S; and I have broken
Deut 6:21 son, 'We were Pharaoh's S in Egypt; and the
28:68 as male and female S, but no man will
Josh 9:23 you shall always be S, hewers of wood and

16:10 day but have become S to do forced labor.
1Sam 4:9 Philistines, lest you become S to the Hebrews as
8:17 of your flocks, and you shall be his S
1Kgs 2:39 that two of Shimei's S ran away to Achish,
2:39 told Shimei, "Behold, your S are in Gath,"
2:40 Achish, to seek his S; Shimei went and brought
2:40 went and brought his S from Gath.
9:21 a forced levy of S, and so they are
9:22 Israel Solomon made no S; they were the soldiers,
2Kgs 4:1 to take my two children to be his S
2Chr 8:9 Israel Solomon made no S for his work; they
28:10 Judah and Jerusalem, male and female, as your S
Neh 5:5 our daughters to be S, and some of our
9:36 Behold, we are S this day; in the land
9:36 fruit and its good gifts, behold, we are S
Tob 10:10 of his property in S, cattle, and money.
Jud 3:4 their inhabitants are your S; come and deal with
5:11 humbled them and made S of them.
6:7 Now my S are going to take you back
6:10 Then Holofernes ordered his S, who waited on him
6:11 So the S took him and led him out
7:28 for we will be S, but our lives will
8:7 and men and women S, and cattle, and fields;
8:22 wherever we serve as S; and we shall be
9:3 thou didst strike down S along with princes, and
10:23 to him, and his S raised her up.
13:1 When evening came, his S quickly withdrew, and
14:13 our lord, for the S have been so bold
14:18 people and shouted, "The S have tricked us!
Esth 7:4 been sold merely as S, men and women, I
Eccl 2:7 bought male and female S, and had slaves who
2:7 female slaves, and had S who were born in
10:7 I have seen S on horses, and princes walking
10:7 on horses, and princes walking on foot like S
Wis 19:14 them, but these made S of guests who were
Is 14:2 as male and female S; they will take captive
Jer 25:14 great kings shall make S even of them; and
34:9 set free his Hebrew S, male and female, so
34:11 the male and female S they had set free,
34:11 set free, and brought them into subjection as S
34:16 his male and female S, whom you had set
34:16 you brought them into subjection to be your S
Lam 5:8 S rule over us; there is none to deliver
Bar 4:32 your children served as S; wretched will be the
1Mac 3:41 camp to get the sons of Israel for S
2Mac 1:27 free those who are S among the Gentiles, look
5:24 and to sell the women and boys as S
8:11 them to buy Jewish S and promising to hand
8:11 to hand over ninety S for a talent, not
8:25 those who had come to buy them as S
Rom 6:16 any one as obedient S, you are slaves of
6:16 obedient slaves, you are S of the one whom
6:17 you who were once S of sin have become
6:18 from sin, have become S of righteousness.
6:20 When you were S of sin, you were free
6:22 sin and have become S of God, the return
1Cor 7:23 price; do not become S of men.
12:13 body--Jews or Greeks, S or free--and all
2Cor 11:20 if a man makes S of you, or preys
Gal 4:3 were children, we were S to the elemental spirits
4:9 beggarly elemental spirits, whose S you want to be
Eph 6:5 S, be obedient to those who are your earthly
Col 3:22 S, obey in everything those who are your earthly
4:1 Masters, treat your S justly and fairly, knowing that
Tit 2:3 to be slanderers or S to drink; they are
2:9 Bid S to be submissive to their masters and
3:3 foolish, disobedient, led astray, S to various passions
2Pet 2:19 they themselves are S of corruption; for whatever
Rev 18:13 horses and chariots, and S, that is, human souls.

SLAY (91)

Gen 4:14 whoever finds me will S me."
18:25 such a thing, to S the righteous with the
20:4 said, "Lord, wilt thou S an innocent people?
22:10 took the knife to S his son.
32:11 lest he come and S us all, the mothers
37:26 is it if we S our brother and conceal
42:37 said to his father, S my two sons if
49:6 in their anger they S men, and in their
Ex 4:23 go, behold, I will S your first-born son.'"
12:23 will pass through to S the Egyptians; and when
12:23 enter your houses to S you.
23:7 charge, and do not S the innocent and righteous,
32:12 bring them forth, to S them in the mountains,
32:27 throughout the camp, and S every man his brother,
Lev 17:5 their sacrifices which they S in the open field,
17:5 tent of meeting, and S them as sacrifices of
17:7 they shall no more S their sacrifices for satyrs,
Num 25:5 "Every one of you S his men who have
Deut 9:28 brought them out to S them in the wilderness."
27:25 takes a bribe to S an innocent person.' And
Judg 8:19 alive, I would not S you."
8:20 his first-born, "Rise, and S them." But the youth
9:24 strengthened his hands to S his brothers.
1Sam 2:25 of the LORD to S them.
5:10 God of Israel to S us and our people."
5:11 that it may not S us and our people."
14:34 or his sheep, and S them here, and eat;
20:8 is guilt in me, S me yourself; for why
2Sam 1:9 'Stand beside me and S me; for anguish has
3:37 the king's will to S Abner the son of
14:11 the avenger of blood S no more, and my
21:2 Saul had sought to S them in his zeal
1Kgs 1:51 that he will not S his servant with the
3:26 and by no means S it." But the other
3:27 and by no means S it; she is its
19:17 of Hazael shall Jehu S; and him who escapes
19:17 escapes from the sword of Jehu shall Elisha S
2Kgs 6:21 "My father, shall I S them?
6:21 Shall I S them?"
6:22 answered, "You shall not S them.
6:22 Would you S those whom you have taken captive
8:12 fortresses, and you will S their young men with
10:25 officers, "Go in and S them; let not a
11:15 between the ranks; and S with the sword any
2Chr 22:11 that she did not S him;
23:14 priest said, "Do not S her in the house
Esth 3:13 provinces, to destroy, to S, and to annihilate all
8:11 lives, to destroy, to S, and to annihilate any
Job 13:15 Behold, he will S me; I have no hope;
Ps 34:21 Evil shall S the wicked; and those who hate
37:14 poor and needy, to S those who walk uprightly;
37:32 righteous, and seeks to S him.
59:11 S them not, lest my people forget; make them
94:6 They S the widow and the sojourner, and murder
139:19 O that thou wouldst S the wicked, O God,
Wis 11:7 for the decree to S the infants, thou gavest
Sir 47:5 his right hand to S a man mighty in
Is 11:4 his lips he shall S the wicked.
14:30 root with famine, and your remnant I will S
27:1 serpent, and he will S the dragon that is
57:5 every green tree; who S your children in the
65:15 the Lord GOD will S you; but his servants
Jer 5:6 from the forest shall S them, a wolf from
15:3 LORD: the sword to S, the dogs to tear,
18:23 all their plotting to S me.
20:4 to Babylon, and shall S them with the sword.
29:21 Babylon, and he shall S them before your eyes.
40:15 "Let me go and S Ishmael the son of
50:21 S, and utterly destroy after them, says the LORD,
50:27 S all her bulls, let them go down to
Ezek 9:6 shall show no pity; S old men outright, young
23:47 their swords; they shall S their sons and their
26:8 He will S with the sword your daughters on
26:11 your streets; he will S your people with the
28:9 presence of those who S you, though you are
44:11 the temple; they shall S the burnt offering and
Dan 2:13 and his companions, to S them.
2:14 had gone out to S the wise men of
14:26 me permission, I will S the dragon without sword
Hos 2:3 a parched land, and S her with thirst.
9:16 bring forth, I will S their beloved children.
Amos 2:3 its midst, and will S all its princes with
9:1 of them I will S with the sword; not
9:4 sword, and it shall S them; and I will
Zech 11:5 Those who buy them S them and go unpunished;
2Mac 5:12 they met and to S those who went into
5:24 and commanded him to S all the grown men
6:9 the sacrifices, and should S those who did not
Lk 19:27 bring them here and S them before me.'"
2Thes 2:8 the Lord Jesus will S him with the breath
Rev 6:4 so that men should S one another; and he

SLAYER (8)

Josh 20:5 not give up the S into his hand; because
20:6 the time: then the S may go again to
21:13 of refuge for the S, with its pasture lands,
21:21 of refuge for the S, with its pasture lands
21:27 of refuge for the S, and Beeshterah with its
21:32 of refuge for the S, Hammoth-dor with its pasture
21:38 of refuge for the S, Mahanaim with its pasture
Ezek 21:11 to be given into the hand of the S

SLAYERS

Is	27:7	been slain as their S were slain?

SLAYING (6)

Josh	10:20	of Israel had finished S them with a very
1Sam	18:6	David returned from S the Philistine, the women
1Kgs	17:20	whom I sojourn, by S her son?"
Is	22:13	behold, joy and gladness, S oxen and killing sheep,
Lam	3:43	anger and pursued us, S without pity;
Hab	1:17	his net, and mercilessly S nations for ever?

SLAYS (5)

Gen	4:15	If any one S Cain, vengeance shall be taken
Num	35:27	the avenger of blood S the manslayer, he shall
Deut	27:24	"'Cursed be he who S his neighbor in secret.'
Job	5:2	the fool, and jealousy S the simple.
Rev	13:10	goes; if any one S with the sword, with

SLEDGE (3)

Job	41:30	himself like a threshing S on the mire.
Is	28:27	threshed with a threshing S, nor is a cart
	41:15	of you a threshing S, new, sharp, and having

SLEDGES (3)

2Sam	24:22	offering, and the threshing S and the yokes of
1Chr	21:23	offerings, and the threshing S for the wood, and
Amos	1:3	threshed Gilead with threshing S of iron.

SLEEK (6)

Gen	41:2	the Nile seven cows S and fat, and they
	41:4	ate up the seven S and fat cows.
	41:18	seven cows, fat and S, came up out of
Deut	32:15	grew thick, you became S; then he forsook God
Ps	73:4	have no pangs; their bodies are sound and S
Jer	5:28	great and rich, they have grown fat and S

SLEEP (78)

Gen	2:21	God caused a deep S to fall upon the
	15:12	going down, a deep S fell on Abram; and
	28:11	head and lay down in that place to S
	28:16	Jacob awoke from his S and said, "Surely the
	31:40	by night, and my S fled from my eyes.
Ex	22:27	for his body; in what else shall he S
Deut	24:12	man, you shall not S in his pledge;
	24:13	pledge that he may S in his cloak and
	31:16	you are about to S with your fathers; then
Judg	16:14	he awoke from his S, and pulled away the
	16:19	She made him S upon her knees; and she
	16:20	he awoke from his S, and said, "I will
1Sam	9:25	upon the roof, and he lay down to S
	26:12	asleep, because a deep S from the LORD had
Tob	8:9	they both went to S for the night.
Esth	6:1	the king could not S; and he gave orders
Job	4:13	the night, when deep S falls on men,
	14:12	not awake, or be roused out of his S
	33:15	the night, when deep S falls upon men, while
Ps	3:5	I lie down and S; I wake again, for
	4:8	both lie down and S; for thou alone, O
	13:3	my eyes, lest I S the sleep of death;
	13:3	lest I sleep the S of death;
	76:5	spoil; they sank into S; all the men of
	78:65	Lord awoke as from S, like a strong man
	121:4	he who keeps Israel will neither slumber nor S
	127:2	anxious toil; for he gives to his beloved S
	132:4	I will not give S to my eyes or
Prov	3:24	you lie down, your S will be sweet.
	4:17	For they cannot S unless they have done wrong;
	4:17	they are robbed of S unless they have made
	6:4	Give your eyes no S and your eyelids no
	6:9	When will you arise from your S
	6:10	A little S, a little slumber, a little folding
	19:15	casts into a deep S, and an idle person
	20:13	Love not S, lest you come to poverty; open
	24:33	A little S, a little slumber, a little folding
Eccl	5:12	Sweet is the S of a laborer, whether he
	5:12	surfeit of the rich will not let him S
	8:16	night one's eyes see S;
Wis	17:14	all slept the same S,
Sir	31:1	away one's flesh, and anxiety about it removes S
	31:2	prevents slumber, and a severe illness carries off S
	31:20	Healthy S depends on moderate eating; he rises
	40:5	upon his bed, his S at night confuses his
	40:6	and afterward in his S, as though he were
	42:9	her robs him of S; when she is young,
	46:19	time of his eternal S, Samuel called men to
Is	29:10	a spirit of deep S, and has closed your
	38:15	All my S has fled because of the bitterness
Jer	31:26	and looked, and my S was pleasant to me.
	51:39	they swoon away and S a perpetual sleep and
	51:39	and sleep a perpetual S and not wake, says
	51:57	her warriors; they shall S a perpetual sleep and
	51:57	shall sleep a perpetual S and not wake, says
Ezek	34:25	in the wilderness and S in the woods.
Dan	2:1	was troubled, and his S left him.
	6:18	brought to him, and S fled from him.
	8:18	fell into a deep S with my face to
	10:9	face in a deep S with my face to
	12:2	many of those who S in the dust of
Zech	4:1	a man that is wakened out of his S
1Mac	6:10	and said to them, S departs from my eyes
2Mac	2:26	sweat and loss of S,
Mt	1:24	When Joseph woke from S, he did as the
Mk	4:27	the ground, and should S and rise night and
Lk	9:32	him were heavy with S, and when they wakened
	22:44	and he said to them, "Why do you S
Jn	11:11	but I go to awake him out of S
	11:13	they thought that he meant taking rest in S
Acts	20:9	sank into a deep S as Paul talked still
	20:9	and being overcome by S, he fell down from
Rom	13:11	full time now for you to wake from S
1Cor	15:51	We shall not all S, but we shall all
1Thes	5:6	then let us not S, as others do, but
	5:7	For those who S sleep at night, and those
	5:7	For those who sleep S at night, and those
	5:10	whether we wake or S we might live with

SLEEPER (3)

Sir	22:7	or who rouses a S from deep slumber.
Jon	1:6	said to him, "What do you mean, you S
Eph	5:14	is said, "Awake, O S, and arise from the

SLEEPEST

Ps	44:23	Why S thou, O Lord?

SLEEPING (14)

1Sam	26:7	and there lay Saul S within the encampment, with
Jud	14:14	supposed that he was S with Judith.
Mt	9:24	"Depart; for the girl is not dead but S
	13:25	but while men were S, his enemy came and
	26:40	disciples and found them S; and he said to
	26:43	came and found them S, for their eyes were
	26:45	them, "Are you still S and taking your rest?
Mk	5:39	The child is not dead but S
	14:37	came and found them S, and he said to
	14:40	came and found them S, for their eyes were
	14:41	them, "Are you still S and taking your rest?
Lk	8:52	not weep; for she is not dead but S
	22:43	disciples and found them S for sorrow,
Acts	12:6	him out, Peter was S between two soldiers, bound

SLEEPLESS

2Cor	11:27	hardship, through many a S night, in hunger and

SLEEPLESSNESS

Sir	31:20	The distress of S and of nausea and colic

SLEEPS (3)

1Kgs	1:21	my lord the king S with his fathers, that
Prov	10:5	but a son who S in harvest brings shame.
Is	5:27	stumbles, none slumbers or S, not a waistcloth is

SLEEVES (4)

Gen	37:3	and he made him a long robe with S
	37:23	the long robe with S that he wore;
	37:32	the long robe with S and brought it to
2Sam	13:18	a long robe with S; for thus were the

SLEPT (48)

Gen	2:21	man, and while he S took one of his
Judg	16:14	So while he S, Delilah took the seven locks
2Sam	4:6	she grew drowsy and S; so Rechab and Baanah
	11:9	But Uriah S at the door of the king's
1Kgs	2:10	Then David S with his fathers, and was buried
	3:20	me, while your maidservant S, and laid it in
	11:21	in Egypt that David S with his fathers and
	11:43	And Solomon S with his fathers, and was buried
	14:20	twenty-two years; and he S with his fathers, and
	14:31	And Rehoboam S with his fathers and was buried
	15:8	And Abijam S with his fathers; and they buried
	15:24	And Asa S with his fathers, and was buried
	16:6	And Baasha S with his fathers, and was buried
	16:28	And Omri S with his fathers, and was buried

S

19:5 he lay down and S under a broom tree;
22:40 So Ahab S with his fathers; and Ahaziah his
22:50 And Jehoshaphat S with his fathers, and was buried
2Kgs 8:24 So Joram S with his fathers, and was buried
10:35 So Jehu S with his fathers, and they buried
13:9 So Jehoahaz S with his fathers, and they buried
13:13 So Joash S with his fathers, and Jeroboam sat
14:16 And Jehoash S with his fathers, and was buried
14:22 Judah, after the king S with his fathers.
14:29 And Jeroboam S with his fathers, the kings of
15:7 And Azariah S with his fathers, and they buried
15:22 And Menahem S with his fathers, and Pekahiah his
15:38 Jotham S with his fathers, and was buried with
16:20 And Ahaz S with his fathers, and was buried
20:21 And Hezekiah S with his fathers; and Manasseh his
21:18 And Manasseh S with his fathers, and was buried
24:6 So Jehoiakim S with his fathers, and Jehoiachin his
2Chr 9:31 And Solomon S with his fathers, and was buried
12:16 And Rehoboam S with his fathers, and was buried
14:1 So Abijah S with his fathers, and they buried
16:13 And Asa S with his fathers, dying in the
21:1 Jehoshaphat S with his fathers, and was buried with
26:2 Judah, after the king S with his fathers.
26:23 And Uzziah S with his fathers, and they buried
27:9 And Jotham S with his fathers, and they buried
28:27 And Ahaz S with his fathers, and they buried
32:33 And Hezekiah S with his fathers, and they buried
33:20 So Manasseh S with his fathers, and they buried
Tob 2:9 I was defiled I S by the wall of
Jud 12:5 the tent, and she S until midnight.
Job 3:13 quiet; I should have S; then I should have
Song 5:2 I S, but my heart was awake.
Wis 17:14 powerless Hades, they all S the same sleep,
Mt 25:5 bridegroom was delayed, they all slumbered and S

SLEW (127)

Gen 4:25 of Abel, for Cain S him."
34:26 They S Hamor and his son Shechem with the
38:7 LORD; and the LORD S him.
38:10 the LORD, and he S him also.
Ex 12:27 in Egypt, when he S the Egyptians but spared
13:15 us go, the LORD S all the first-born in
Num 3:13 the day that I S all the first-born in
8:17 the day that I S all the first-born in
21:24 And Israel S him with the edge of the
21:35 So they S him, and his sons, and all
31:7 LORD commanded Moses, and S every male.
31:8 They S the kings of Midian with the rest
31:8 Midian; and they also S Balaam the son of
Josh 7:5 far as Shebarim, and S them at the descent.
10:10 panic before Israel, who S them with a great
Judg 8:17 tower of Penuel, and S the men of the
8:18 the men whom you S at Tabor?" They answered,
8:21 And Gideon arose and S Zebah and Zalmunna; and
9:5 house at Ophrah, and S his brothers the sons
9:24 Abimelech their brother, who S them, and upon the
9:43 rose against them and S them.
9:44 in the fields and S them.
12:6 they seized him and S him at the fords
15:15 and with it he S a thousand men.
16:30 the dead whom he S at his death were
1Sam 1:25 Then they S the bull, and they brought the
4:2 by the Philistines, who S about four thousand men
6:19 And he S some of the men of Beth-shemesh,
6:19 of the LORD; he S seventy men of them,
14:32 oxen and calves, and S them on the ground;
14:34 him that night, and S them there.
19:5 his hand and he S the Philistine, and the
31:2 sons; and the Philistines S Jonathan and Abinadab
2Sam 1:10 stood beside him, and S him, because I was
3:30 and Abishai his brother S Abner, because he had
4:7 they smote him, and S him, and beheaded him.
4:10 I seized him and S him at Ziklag, which
8:5 king of Zobah, David S twenty-two thousand men of
8:13 When he returned, he S eighteen thousand Edomites
10:18 before Israel; and David S of the Syrians the
14:7 his brother whom he S; and so they would
21:18 then Sibbecai the Hushathite S Saph, who was one
21:19 of Jaareoregim, the Bethlehemite, S Goliath the
21:21 of Shimei, David's brother, S him.
23:8 eight hundred whom he S at one time.
23:12 and defended it, and S the Philistines; and the
23:18 three hundred men and S them, and won a
23:20 also went down and S a lion in a
23:21 And he S an Egyptian, a handsome man.
23:21 the Egyptian's hand, and S him with his own
1Kgs 2:32 David, he attacked and S with the sword two
11:15 bury the slain, he S every male in Edom
19:21 yoke of oxen, and S them, and boiled their
2Kgs 10:7 the king's sons, and S them, seventy persons, and
10:9 against my master, and S him; but who struck
10:11 So Jehu S all that remained of the house
10:14 took them alive, and S them at the pit
10:17 came to Samaria, he S all that remained to
11:18 in pieces, and they S Mattan the priest of
12:20 made a conspiracy, and S Joash in the house
14:19 him to Lachish, and S him there.
15:14 Jabesh in Samaria and S him, and reigned in
15:25 of the Gileadites, and S him in Samaria, in
15:25 the king's house; he S him, and reigned in
15:30 struck him down, and S him, and reigned in
19:35 LORD went forth, and S a hundred and eighty-five
19:37 and Sharezer, his sons, S him with the sword,
21:24 people of the land S all those who had
23:20 And he S all the priests of the high
23:29 him; and Pharaoh Neco S him at Megiddo, when
25:7 They S the sons of Zedekiah before his eyes,
1Chr 2:3 the LORD, and he S him.
7:21 born in the land S, because they came down
10:2 sons; and the Philistines S Jonathan and Abinadab
10:14 Therefore the LORD S him, and turned the kingdom
11:11 three hundred whom he S at one time.
11:14 and defended it, and S the Philistines; and the
11:20 three hundred men and S them, and won a
11:22 also went down and S a lion in a
11:23 And he S an Egyptian, a man of great
11:23 the Egyptian's hand, and S him with his own
18:5 king of Zobah, David S twenty-two thousand men of
18:12 the son of Zeruiah, S eighteen thousand Edomites in
19:18 before Israel; and David S of the Syrians the
20:4 then Sibbecai the Hushathite S Sippai, who was one
20:5 the son of Jair S Lahmi the brother of
20:7 of Shimea, David's brother, S him.
2Chr 13:17 Abijah and his people S them with a great
21:4 and was established, he S all his brothers with
23:15 king's house, and they S her there.
23:17 in pieces, and they S Mattan the priest of
24:25 Jehoiada the priest, and S him on his bed.
25:27 him to Lachish, and S him there.
28:6 the son of Remaliah S a hundred and twenty
28:7 mighty man of Ephraim, S Ma-aseiah the king's son
33:25 people of the land S all those who had
36:17 of the Chaldeans, who S their young men with
Esth 9:6 capital itself the Jews S and destroyed five hundred
9:7 men, and also S Par-shan-datha and Dalphon and
9:15 of Adar and they S three hundred men in
9:16 from their enemies, and S seventy-five thousand of
Job 1:15 and took them, and S the servants with the
1:17 and took them, and S the servants with the
Ps 78:31 against them and he S the strongest of them,
78:34 When he S them, they sought for him; they
135:10 smote many nations and S mighty kings,
136:18 endures for ever; and S famous kings, for his
Wis 10:3 because in rage he S his brother.
Is 37:36 LORD went forth, and S a hundred and eighty-five
37:38 and Sharezer, his sons, S him with the sword,
Jer 26:23 to King Jehoiakim, who S him with the sword
39:6 The king of Babylon S the sons of Zedekiah
39:6 the king of Babylon S all the nobles of
41:3 Ishmael also S all the Jews who were with
41:7 the men with him S them, and cast them
52:10 The king of Babylon S the sons of Zedekiah
52:10 his eyes, and also S all the princes of
Ezek 23:10 daughters; and her they S with the sword; and
Dan 3:22 flame of the fire S those men who took
5:19 whom he would he S, and whom he would
Amos 4:10 manner of Egypt; I S your young men with
2Mac 8:24 as their ally, they S more than nine thousand
10:17 upon the wall, and S those whom they encountered,
10:22 Then he S these men who had turned traitor,
11:11 against the enemy, and S eleven thousand of them
13:15 pavilion at night and S as many as two
15:22 of Judea, and he S fully a hundred and

SLIGHT (3)

Sir 8:8 Do not S the discourse of the sages, but
Ezek 8:17 Is it too S a thing for the house
2Cor 4:17 For this S momentary affliction is preparing for us

SLIGHTED (2)

Jud 11:2 hill country had not S me, I would never
11:22 upon those who have S my lord.

SLIME (2)
Job 6:6 any taste in the S of the purslane?
Ps 58:8 snail which dissolves into S, like the untimely birth

SLING (9)
Judg 20:16 left-handed; every one could S a stone at a
1Sam 17:40 bag or wallet; his S was in his hand,
17:50 the Philistine with a S and with a stone,
25:29 your enemies he shall S out as from the
25:29 sling out as from the hollow of a S
1Chr 12:2 could shoot arrows and S stones with either the
Jud 9:7 spear, in bow and S, and know not that
Prov 26:8 the stone in the S is he who gives
Sir 47:4 a stone in the S and struck down the

SLINGERS (4)
2Kgs 3:25 in Kir-hareseth, and the S surrounded and conquered
Jud 6:12 hill, and all the S kept them from coming
Zech 9:15 and tread down the S; and they shall drink
1Mac 9:11 two companies, and the S and the archers went

SLINGING (2)
2Chr 26:14 helmets, coats of mail, bows, and stones for S
Jer 10:18 LORD: "Behold, I am S out the inhabitants of

SLINGSTONES
Job 41:28 him flee; for him S are turned to stubble.

SLIP (13)
Deut 32:35 when their foot shall S; for the day of
2Sam 22:37 my feet did not S;
2Kgs 9:15 then let no one S out of the city
Job 12:5 misfortune; it is ready for those whose feet S
Ps 18:36 steps under me, and my feet did not S
37:31 is in his heart; his steps do not S
66:9 the living, and has not let our feet S
Sir 3:23 and wrong opinion has caused their thoughts to S
19:16 person may make a S without intending it.
20:17 A S on the pavement is better than a
20:17 is better than a S of the tongue; so
25:8 has not made a S with his tongue, and
2Mac 10:20 let some of them S away.

SLIPPED (6)
2Sam 4:6 and Baanah his brother S in.
Ps 17:5 fast to thy paths, my feet have not S
73:2 had almost stumbled, my steps had well nigh S
1Mac 9:6 greatly frightened, and many S away from the camp,
9:7 that his army had S away and the battle
Gal 2:4 secretly brought in, who S in to spy out

SLIPPERY (3)
Ps 35:6 way be dark and S, with the angel of
73:18 dost set them in S places; thou dost make
Jer 23:12 be to them like S paths in the darkness,

SLIPS (8)
Deut 19:5 tree, and the head S from the handle and
Ps 38:16 me, who boast against me when my foot S
94:18 When I thought, "My foot S
Prov 25:19 like a bad tooth or a foot that S
Sir 13:21 If a rich man S, his helpers are many;
13:21 If a humble man S, they even reproach him;
21:7 sensible man, when he S, is aware of it.
Is 17:10 plants and set out S of an alien god,

SLOPE (2)
Gen 48:22 your brothers one mountain S which I took from
Num 21:15 the Arnon, and the S of the valleys that

SLOPES (8)
Deut 3:17 Salt Sea, under the S of Pisgah on the
4:49 the Arabah, under the S of Pisgah.
Josh 10:40 the lowland and the S, and all their kings;
12:3 the foot of the S of Pisgah;
12:8 the Arabah, in the S, in the wilderness, and
13:20 Beth-peor, and the S of Pisgah, and Beth-jeshimoth,
Song 4:1 goats, moving down the S of Gilead.
6:5 goats, moving down the S of Gilead.

SLOTH
Eccl 10:18 Through S the roof sinks in, and through indolence

SLOTHFUL (3)
Prov 12:24 will rule, while the S will be put to
12:27 A S man will not catch his prey, but
Mt 25:26 him, 'You wicked and S servant!

SLOTHFULNESS
Prov 19:15 S casts into a deep sleep, and an idle

SLOW (24)
Ex 4:10 servant; but I am S of speech and of
34:6 God merciful and gracious, S to anger, and
Num 14:18 saying, 'The LORD is S to anger, and abounding
Judg 18:9 Do not be S to go, and enter in
Neh 9:17 forgive, gracious and merciful, S to anger and
Tob 12:6 Do not be S to give him thanks.
Ps 86:15 God merciful and gracious, S to anger and abounding
103:8 is merciful and gracious, S to anger and abounding
145:8 is gracious and merciful, S to anger and abounding
Prov 14:29 He who is S to anger has great understanding,
15:18 but he who is S to anger quiets contention.
16:32 He who is S to anger is better than
19:11 sense makes a man S to anger, and it
Sir 5:4 for the Lord is S to anger.
6:21 he will not be S to cast her off.
11:12 is another who is S and needs help, who
Joel 2:13 is gracious and merciful, S to anger, and abounding
Jon 4:2 gracious God and merciful, S to anger, and
Nah 1:3 The LORD is S to anger and of great
Hab 2:3 If it seem S, wait for it; it will
Lk 24:25 "O foolish men, and S of heart to believe
Jas 1:18 be quick to hear, S to speak, slow to
1:18 hear, slow to speak, S to anger,
2Pet 3:9 The Lord is not S about his promise as

SLOWLY (2)
Gen 33:14 I will lead on S, according to the pace
Acts 27:7 We sailed S for a number of days, and

SLOWNESS
2Pet 3:9 promise as some count S, but is forbearing toward

SLUGGARD (14)
Prov 6:6 to the ant, O S; consider her ways, and
6:9 How long will you lie there, O S
10:26 eyes, so is the S to those who send
13:4 The soul of the S craves, and gets nothing,
15:19 The way of a S is overgrown with thorns,
19:24 The S buries his hand in the dish, and
20:4 The S does not plow in the autumn; he
21:25 The desire of the S kills him for his
22:13 The S says, "There is a lion outside!
24:30 the field of a S, by the vineyard of
26:13 The S says, "There is a lion in the
26:14 hinges, so does a S on his bed.
26:15 The S buries his hand in the dish; it
26:16 The S is wiser in his own eyes than

SLUGGISH (2)
Sir 4:29 in your speech, or S and remiss in your
Heb 6:12 you may not be S, but imitators of those

SLUMBER (11)
Job 33:15 upon men, while they S on their beds,
Ps 121:3 be moved, he who keeps you will not S
121:4 keeps Israel will neither S nor sleep.
132:4 to my eyes or S to my eyelids,
Prov 6:4 and your eyelids no S;
6:10 little sleep, a little S, a little folding of
24:33 little sleep, a little S, a little folding of
Sir 22:7 together, or who rouses a sleeper from deep S
31:2 Wakeful anxiety prevents S, and a severe illness
Is 56:10 they cannot bark; dreaming, lying down, loving to S
Nah 3:18 are asleep, O king of Assyria; your nobles S

SLUMBERED
Mt 25:5 was delayed, they all S and slept.

SLUMBERS
Is 5:27 weary, none stumbles, none S or sleeps, not a

SLUNG (2)
1Sam 17:6 a javelin of bronze S between his shoulders.
17:49 out a stone, and S it, and struck the

SMALL (97)
Gen 19:11 of the house, both S and great, so that
30:15 her, "Is it a S matter that you have
Ex 12:4 the household is too S for a lamb, then
18:22 to you, but any S matter they shall decide

S

18:26 to Moses, but any S matter they decided themselves.
30:36 some of it very S, and put part of
Lev 14:49 he shall take two S birds, with cedarwood and
16:12 of sweet incense beaten S; and he shall bring
Num 16:9 Levi: is it too S a thing for you
16:13 Is it a S thing that you have brought
26:54 inheritance, and to a S tribe you shall give
26:54 you shall give a S inheritance; every tribe shall
33:54 inheritance, and to a S tribe you shall give
33:54 you shall give a S inheritance; wherever the lot
Deut 1:17 you shall hear the S and the great alike;
9:21 it, grinding it very S, until it was as
25:13 two kinds of weights, a large and a S
25:14 two kinds of measures, a large and a S
1Sam 20:2 nothing either great or S without disclosing it to
30:2 were in it, both S and great; they killed
30:19 Nothing was missing, whether S or great, sons or
2Sam 7:19 yet this was a S thing in thy eyes,
1Kgs 2:20 said, "I have one S request to make of
8:64 the LORD was too S to receive the burnt
19:12 the fire a still S voice.
22:31 chariots, "Fight with neither S nor great, but only
2Kgs 2:23 on the way, some S boys came out of
4:10 Let us make a S roof chamber with walls,
6:1 your charge is too S for us.
23:2 all the people, both S and great; and he
25:26 all the people, both S and great, and the
1Chr 17:17 And this was a S thing in thy eyes,
25:8 lots for their duties, S and great, teacher and
26:13 lots by fathers' houses, S and great alike, for
2Chr 18:30 chariots, "Fight with neither S nor great, but only
23:9 and the large and S shields that had been
34:30 people both great and S; and he read in
36:18 of God, great and S, and the treasures of
Jud 13:4 and no one, either S or great, was left
13:13 all ran together, both S and great, for it
16:16 fragrant offering is a S thing, and all fat
Esth 1:5 capital, both great and S, a banquet lasting for
Job 3:19 The S and the great are there, and the
8:7 though your beginning was S, your latter days will
15:11 consolations of God too S for you, or the
26:14 his ways; and how S a whisper do we
40:4 "Behold, I am of S account; what shall I
Ps 104:25 innumerable, living things both S and great.
115:13 fear the LORD, both S and great.
119:141 I am S and despised, yet I do not
Prov 24:10 in the day of adversity, your strength is S
30:24 things on earth are S, but they are exceedingly
Wis 6:7 he himself made both S and great, and he
Sir 5:15 In great and S matters do not act amiss,
11:3 The bee is S among flying creatures, but her
19:1 rich; he who despises S things will fail little
Is 22:24 offspring and issue, every S vessel, from the cups
29:5 foes shall be like S dust, and the multitude
Jer 16:6 Both great and S shall die in this land;
30:19 make them honored, and they shall not be S
49:15 I will make you S among the nations, despised
52:19 temple service; also the S bowls, and the firepans,
Bar 1:4 of all the people, S and great, all who
2:29 surely turn into a S number among the nations,
Ezek 5:3 take from these a S number, and bind them
16:20 Were your harlotries so S a matter
29:15 will make them so S that they will never
46:22 of the court were S courts, forty cubits long
Dan 11:23 become strong with a S people.
Amos 7:2 He is so S
7:5 He is so S
8:5 may make the ephah S and the shekel great,
Obad 1:2 I will make you S among the nations, you
Zech 4:10 despised the day of S things shall rejoice, and
1Mac 3:16 meet him with a S company.
3:29 from the country were S because of the dissension
4:57 with golden crowns and S shields; they restored the
5:45 Israelites in Gilead, the S and the great, with
2Mac 10:24 from Asia in no S number.
14:8 is now in no S misfortune.
Mt 15:34 "Seven, and a few S fish."
Mk 8:7 they had a few S fish; and having blessed
Lk 12:26 able to do as S a thing as that,
19:3 crowd, because he was S of stature.
Acts 12:18 came, there was no S stir among the soldiers
15:2 and Barnabas had no S dissension and debate with
26:22 here testifying both to S and great, saying nothing
27:16 the lee of a S island called Cauda, we
27:20 a day, and no S tempest lay on us,
1Cor 4:3 it is a very S thing that I should
Jas 3:4 guided by a very S rudder wherever the will
3:5 set ablaze by a S fire!
Rev 11:18 fear thy name, both S and great, and for
13:16 it causes all, both S and great, both rich
19:5 you who fear him, S and great."
19:18 free and slave, both S and great."
20:12 the dead, great and S, standing before the throne,

SMALLER (3)

Num 26:56 according to lot between the larger and the S
35:8 many, and from the S tribes you shall take
Ezek 43:14 cubit; and from the S ledge to the larger

SMALLEST (4)

Wis 14:5 lives even to the S piece of wood, and
Is 60:22 a clan, and the S one a mighty nation;
Mt 13:32 field; it is the S of all seeds, but
Mk 4:31 the ground, is the S of all the seeds

SMART (3)

Tob 11:8 gall; and when they S he will rub them,
11:12 his eyes began to S he rubbed them,
Prov 11:15 for a stranger will S for it, but he

SMASHED (2)

Judg 7:19 blew the trumpets and S the jars that were
Is 30:14 potter's vessel which is S so ruthlessly that among

SMELL (11)

Gen 27:27 and he smelled the S of his garments, and
27:27 and said, "See, the S of my son is
27:27 son is as the S of a field which
Lev 26:31 and I will not S your pleasing odors.
Deut 4:28 that neither see, nor hear, nor eat, nor S
Tob 6:17 Then the demon will S it and flee away,
Ps 115:6 but do not hear; noses, but do not S
Sir 30:19 For it can neither eat nor S
Dan 3:95 not harmed, and no S of fire had come
Joel 2:20 the stench and foul S of him will rise,
1Cor 12:17 an ear, where would be the sense of S

SMELLED (3)

Gen 8:21 And when the LORD S the pleasing odor, the
27:27 kissed him; and he S the smell of his
Tob 8:3 And when the demon S the odor he fled

SMELLS

Job 39:25 he says 'Aha!' He S the battle from afar,

SMELT

Is 1:25 against you and will S away your dross as

SMELTED

Job 28:2 earth, and copper is S from the ore.

SMILE

Sir 13:6 deceive you, he will S at you and give

SMILED

Job 29:24 I S on them when they had no confidence;

SMILES (2)

Sir 13:11 talk, and while he S he will be examining
21:20 but a clever man S quietly.

SMITE (51)

Ex 3:20 out my hand and S Egypt with all the
12:12 night, and I will S all the first-born in
12:13 destroy you, when I S the land of Egypt.
Lev 26:24 and I myself will S you sevenfold for your
Num 25:17 "Harass the Midianites, and S them;
Deut 28:22 The LORD will S you with consumption, and with
28:27 The LORD will S you with the boils of
28:28 The LORD will S you with madness and blindness
28:35 The LORD will S you on the knees and
Josh 10:4 me, and let us S Gibeon; for it has
Judg 6:16 you, and you shall S the Midianites as one
20:31 times they began to S and kill some of
20:39 Benjamin had begun to S and kill about thirty
21:10 commanded them, "Go and S the inhabitants of
1Sam 15:3 Now go and S Amalek, and utterly destroy all
20:33 spear at him to S him; so Jonathan knew
26:10 lives, the LORD will S him; or his day
2Sam 2:22 me; why should I S you to the ground?
5:8 that day, "Whoever would S the Jebusites, let him
5:24 out before you to S the army of the

15:14 evil upon us, and S the city with the
1Kgs 14:15 henceforth the LORD will S Israel, as a reed
1Chr 11:6 David said, "Whoever shall S the Jebusites first shall
14:15 out before you to S the army of the
Jud 16:7 sons of the Titans S him, nor did tall
Ps 3:7 For thou dost S all my enemies on the
121:6 The sun shall not S you by day, nor
Is 3:17 feet; the Lord will S with a scab the
10:24 the Assyrians when they S with the rod and
11:4 earth; and he shall S the earth with the
11:15 his scorching wind, and S it into seven channels
19:22 And the LORD will S Egypt, smiting and healing,
49:10 wind nor sun shall S them, for he who
Jer 18:18 Come, let us S him with the tongue, and
21:6 And I will S the inhabitants of this city,
21:7 He shall S them with the edge of the
33:5 men whom I shall S in my anger and
43:11 He shall come and S the land of Egypt,
46:13 king of Babylon to S the land of Egypt:
Ezek 7:9 will know that I am the LORD, who S
9:5 city after him, and S; your eye shall not
21:12 S therefore upon your thigh.
32:15 fills it, when I S all who dwell in
Amos 3:15 I will S the winter house with the summer
9:1 altar, and he said: S the capitals until the
Mic 6:13 I have begun to S you, making you desolate
Zech 11:17 May the sword S his arm and his right
14:12 which the LORD will S all the peoples that
Mal 4:6 lest I come and S the land with a
Rev 11:6 into blood, and to S the earth with every
19:15 sword with which to S the nations, and he

SMITER

Lam 3:30 his cheek to the S, and be filled with

SMITERS

Is 50:6 my back to the S, and my cheeks to

SMITES (3)

Josh 15:16 Caleb said, "Whoever S Kiriath-sepher, and takes it,
Job 5:18 he binds up; he S, but his hands heal.
Is 30:31 the LORD, when he S with his rod.

SMITH (4)

1Sam 13:19 Now there was no S to be found throughout
Prov 25:4 the silver, and the S has material for a
Sir 38:28 So too is the S sitting by the anvil,
Is 54:16 I have created the S who blows the fire

SMITHS (5)

2Kgs 24:14 the craftsmen and the S; none remained, except the
24:16 the craftsmen and the S, one thousand, all of
Jer 24:1 the craftsmen, and the S, and had brought them
29:2 craftsmen, and the S had departed from Jerusalem.
Zech 1:20 Then the LORD showed me four S

SMITING (4)

2Sam 24:17 the angel who was S the people, and said,
1Kgs 20:37 the man struck him, S and wounding him.
Is 19:22 LORD will smite Egypt, S and healing, and they
Ezek 9:8 And while they were S, and I was left

SMITTEN (17)

Lev 26:17 and you shall be S before your enemies; those
Judg 20:39 said, "Surely they are S down before us, as
2Sam 12:9 You have S Uriah the Hittite with the sword,
2Kgs 14:10 You have indeed S Edom, and your heart has
2Chr 25:19 say, 'See, I have S Edom,' and your heart
26:20 because the LORD had S him.
Ps 69:26 him whom thou hast S, and him whom thou
102:4 My heart is S like grass, and withered; I
Is 1:5 will you still be S, that you continue to
27:7 Has he S them as he smote those who
53:4 we esteemed him stricken, S by God, and afflicted.
Jer 2:30 In vain have I S your children, they took
5:3 Thou hast S them, but they felt no anguish;
14:17 of my people is S with a great wound,
14:19 Why hast thou S us so that there is
Amos 6:11 great house shall be S into fragments, and the
Zech 10:11 the sea shall be S, and all the depths

SMOKE (59)

Gen 19:28 beheld, and lo, the S of the land went
19:28 went up like the S of a furnace.
Ex 19:18 Sinai was wrapped in S, because the LORD
19:18 in fire; and the S of it went up
19:18 went up like the S of a kiln, and
Deut 29:20 and his jealousy would S against that man, and
Josh 8:20 looked back, behold, the S of the city went
8:21 city, and that the S of the city went
Judg 20:38 a great cloud of S rise up out of
20:40 in a column of S, the Benjaminites looked behind
20:40 city went up in S to heaven.
2Sam 22:9 S went up from his nostrils, and devouring fire
Tob 6:7 one, you make a S from these before the
6:16 of the fish so as to make a S
8:2 of the fish upon them and made a S
Job 41:20 his nostrils comes forth S, as from a boiling
Ps 18:8 S went up from his nostrils, and devouring fire
37:20 pastures, they vanish—like S they vanish away.
66:15 of fatlings, with the S of the sacrifice of
68:2 As S is driven away, so drive them away;
74:1 Why does thy anger S against the sheep of
102:3 days pass away like S, and my bones burn
104:32 it trembles, who touches the mountains and they S
119:83 a wineskin in the S, yet I have not
144:5 Touch the mountains that they S
Prov 10:26 to the teeth, and S to the eyes, so
Song 3:6 like a column of S, perfumed with myrrh and
Wis 2:2 in our nostrils is S, and reason is a
5:14 it is dispersed like S before the wind, and
11:18 a thick pall of S, or flash terrible sparks
Sir 22:22 The vapor and S of the furnace precede the
Is 4:5 cloud by day, and S and the shining of
6:4 who called, and the house was filled with S
9:18 and they roll upward in a column of S
14:31 For S comes out of the north, and there
30:27 and in thick rising S; his lips are full
34:10 not be quenched; its S shall go up for
51:6 heavens will vanish like S, the earth will wear
65:5 These are a S in my nostrils, a fire
Bar 6:21 been blackened by the S of the temple.
Ezek 8:11 his hand, and the S of the cloud of
Hos 13:3 threshing floor or like S from a window.
Joel 2:30 the earth, blood and fire and columns of S.
Nah 2:13 burn your chariots in S, and the sword shall
1Mac 4:20 the camp, for the S that was seen showed
2Mac 7:5 The S from the pan spread widely, but the
Acts 2:19 fire, and vapor of S;
Rev 8:4 the throne; and the S of the incense rose
9:2 from the shaft rose S like the smoke of
9:2 rose smoke like the S of a great furnace,
9:2 were darkened with the S from the shaft.
9:3 Then from the S came locusts on the earth,
9:17 heads, and fire and S and sulphur issued from
9:18 by the fire and S and sulphur issuing from
14:11 And the S of their torment goes up for
15:8 temple was filled with S from the glory of
18:9 when they see the S of her burning;
18:18 as they saw the S of her burning, "What
19:3 The S from her goes up for ever and

SMOKING (3)

Gen 15:17 was dark, behold, a S fire pot and a
Ex 20:18 trumpet and the mountain S, the people were afraid
Wis 10:7 a continually S wasteland, plants bearing fruit

SMOLDERING (2)

Is 7:4 because of these two S stumps of firebrands, at
Mt 12:20 reed or quench a S wick, till he brings

SMOLDERS

Hos 7:7 all night their anger S; in the morning it

SMOOTH (15)

Gen 27:11 and I am a S man.
27:16 hands and upon the S part of his neck;
1Sam 17:40 hand, and chose five S stones from the brook,
Prov 2:16 the adventuress with her S words,
6:24 evil woman, from the S tongue of the adventuress.
7:5 the adventuress with her S words.
7:21 persuades him; with her S talk she compels him.
26:23 an earthen vessel are S lips with an evil
Sir 32:21 be overconfident on a S way,
Is 18:2 a nation, tall and S, to a people feared
18:7 a people tall and S, from a people feared
26:7 level; thou dost make S the path of the
30:10 right; speak to us S things, prophesy illusions,
57:6 Among the S stones of the valley is your
Lk 3:5 ways shall be made S;

SMOOTHED

Bar 6:8 Their tongues are S by the craftsman, and they

SMOOTHER (2)

Ps 55:21 His speech was S than butter, yet war was
Prov 5:3 and her speech is S than oil;

SMOOTHLY (3)

Prov 23:31 it sparkles in the cup and goes down S
Song 7:9 wine that goes down S, gliding over lips and
Sir 21:10 way of sinners is S paved with stones, but

SMOOTHS

Is 41:7 goldsmith, and he who S with the hammer him

SMOTE (93)

Ex 12:29 At midnight the LORD S all the first-born in
Num 11:33 people, and the LORD S the people with a
32:4 land which the LORD S before the congregation of
Deut 3:3 his people; and we S him until no survivor
Josh 8:21 they turned back and S the men of Ai.
8:22 that side; and Israel S them, until there was
8:24 returned to Ai, and S it with the edge
10:10 ascent of Beth-horon, and S them as far as
10:26 And afterward Joshua S them and put them to
10:28 on that day, and S it and its king
10:30 of Israel; and he S it with the edge
10:32 the second day, and S it with the edge
10:33 help Lachish; and Joshua S him and his people,
10:35 on that day, and S it with the edge
10:37 and took it, and S it with the edge
10:39 its towns; and they S them with the edge
11:8 hand of Israel, who S them and chased them
11:8 of Mizpeh; and they S them, until they left
11:10 and took Hazor, and S its king with the
11:12 kings, Joshua took, and S them with the edge
11:14 but every man they S with the edge of
11:17 all their kings, and S them, and put them
Judg 1:8 and took it, and S it with the edge
1:25 the city; and they S the city with the
11:33 And he S them from Aroer to the neighborhood
12:4 the men of Gilead S Ephraim, because they said,
15:8 And he S them hip and thigh with great
18:27 quiet and unsuspecting, and S them with the edge
20:37 ambush moved out and S all the city with
20:48 against the Benjaminites, and S them with the edge
1Sam 4:8 are the gods who S the Egyptians with every
7:11 pursued the Philistines, and S them, as far as
14:48 he did valiantly, and S the Amalekites, and delivered
17:35 went after him and S him and delivered it
17:35 by his beard, and S him and killed him.
24:5 And afterward David's heart S him, because he had
25:38 days later the LORD S Nabal; and he died.
27:9 And David S the land, and left neither man
30:17 And David S them from twilight until the evening
2Sam 1:15 And he S him so that he died.
2:23 turn aside; therefore Abner S him in the belly
3:27 privately, and there he S him in the belly,
4:7 in his bedchamber, they S him, and slew him,
5:25 LORD commanded him, and S the Philistines from
6:7 against Uzzah; and God S him there because he
23:20 of great deeds; he S two ariels of Moab.
24:10 But David's heart S him after he had numbered
1Kgs 20:29 the people of Israel S of the Syrians a
2Kgs 8:21 and his chariot commanders S the Edomites who
15:5 And the LORD S the king, so that he
18:8 He S the Philistines as far as Gaza and
25:21 the king of Babylon S them, and put them
1Chr 11:22 of great deeds; he S two ariels of Moab.
13:10 against Uzzah; and he S him because he put
14:16 commanded him, and they S the Philistine army
20:1 And Joab S Rabbah, and overthrew it.
21:7 this thing, and he S Israel.
2Chr 13:20 Abijah; and the LORD S him, and he died.
14:14 And they S all the cities round about Gerar,
14:15 And they S the tents of those who had
21:9 rose by night and S the Edomites who had
21:18 all this the LORD S him in his bowels
25:11 Valley of Salt and S ten thousand men of
Esth 9:5 So the Jews S all their enemies with the
Job 26:12 by his understanding he S Rahab.
Ps 78:20 He S the rock so that water gushed out
78:51 He S all the first-born in Egypt, the first
105:33 He S their vines and fig trees, and shattered
105:36 He S all the first-born in their land, the
135:8 He it was who S the first-born of Egypt,
135:10 all his servants; who S many nations and slew
136:10 ever; to him who S the first-born of Egypt,
136:17 ever; to him who S great kings, for his
Sir 48:21 The Lord S the camp of the Assyrians, and
Is 5:25 hand against them and S them, and the mountains
9:13 turn to him who S them, nor seek the
10:20 lean upon him that S them, but will lean
10:26 scourge, as when he S Midian at the rock
14:6 scepter of rulers, that S the peoples in wrath
14:29 that the rod which S you is broken, for
27:7 smitten them as he S those who smote them?
27:7 he smote those who S them?
57:17 I was angry, I S him, I hid my
60:10 in my wrath I S you, but in my
Jer 31:19 I was instructed, I S upon my thigh; I
47:1 the Philistines, before Pharaoh S Gaza.
49:28 of Hazor which Nebuchadrezzar king of Babylon S
52:27 the king of Babylon S them, and put them
Ezek 9:7 they went forth, and S in the city.
Dan 2:34 human hand, and it S the image on its
Amos 4:9 "I S you with blight and mildew; I laid
Hag 2:17 I S you and all the products of your
Acts 12:23 angel of the Lord S him, because he did

SMYRNA (2)

Rev 1:11 to Ephesus and to S and to Pergamum and
2:8 of the church in S write: 'The words of

SNAIL

Ps 58:8 them be like the S which dissolves into slime,

SNAKE (3)

Sir 12:13 Who will pity a S charmer bitten by a
21:2 sin as from a S; for if you approach
25:14 venom worse than a S's venom, and no wrath

SNAPPED (3)

Judg 16:9 But he S the bowstrings, as a string of
16:12 But he S the ropes off his arms like
Eccl 12:6 the silver cord is S, or the golden bowl

SNAPS

Judg 16:9 a string of tow S when it touches the

SNARE (49)

Ex 10:7 this man be a S to us?
23:33 will surely be a S to you."
34:12 lest it become a S in the midst of
Deut 7:16 that would be a S to you.
Josh 23:13 they shall be a S and a trap for
Judg 2:3 gods shall be a S to you."
8:27 and it became a S to Gideon and to
1Sam 18:21 she may be a S for him, and that
28:9 are you laying a S for my life to
Job 18:9 by the heel, a S lays hold of him.
40:24 with hooks, or pierce his nose with a S
Ps 69:22 before them become a S; let their sacrificial feasts
91:3 deliver you from the S of the fowler and
106:36 idols, which became a S to them.
119:110 wicked have laid a S for me, but I
124:7 a bird from the S of the fowlers; the
124:7 of the fowlers; the S is broken, and we
Prov 7:23 bird rushes into a S; he does not know
18:7 his lips are a S to himself.
20:25 It is a S for a man to say
21:6 fleeting vapor and a S of death.
22:25 learn his ways and entangle yourself in a S
29:25 of man lays a S, but he who trusts
Eccl 9:12 are caught in a S, so the sons of
Wis 14:11 of men and a S to the feet of
Sir 27:20 and has escaped like a gazelle from a S
27:26 he who sets a S will be caught in
27:29 be caught in a S, and pain will consume
51:2 destruction and from the S of a slanderous tongue,
Is 8:14 a trap and a S to the inhabitants of
24:17 the pit, and the S are upon you, O
24:18 of the pit shall be caught in the S
29:21 offender, and lay a S for him who reproves
Jer 48:43 Terror, pit, and S are before you, O inhabitant
48:44 of the pit shall be caught in the S
50:24 I set a S for you and you were
Ezek 12:13 be taken in my S; and I will bring
17:20 be taken in my S, and I will bring
Hos 5:1 you have been a S at Mizpah, and a
9:8 God, yet a fowler's S is on all his
Amos 3:5 bird fall in a S on the earth, when

3:5 Does a S spring up from the ground, when
1Mac 1:35 they stored them there, and became a great S
5:4 a trap and a S to the people and
Lk 21:34 you suddenly like a S;
Rom 11:9 their table become a S and a trap, a
1Tim 3:7 into reproach and the S of the devil.
6:9 into temptation, into a S, into many senseless and
2Tim 2:26 may escape from the S of the devil, after

SNARED (5)
Ps 9:16 judgment; the wicked are S in the work of
Prov 6:2 stranger; if you are S in the utterance of
Eccl 9:12 sons of men are S at an evil time,
Is 8:15 broken; they shall be S and taken."
28:13 and be broken, and S, and taken.

SNARES (16)
2Sam 22:6 Sheol entangled me, the S of death confronted me.
Job 22:10 Therefore S are round about you, and sudden terror
Ps 18:5 Sheol entangled me, the S of death confronted me.
38:12 my life lay their S, those who seek my
64:5 they talk of laying S secretly, thinking, "Who can
116:3 The S of death encompassed me; the pangs of
140:5 wayside they have set S for me.
141:9 me, and from the S of evildoers!
Prov 13:14 one may avoid the S of death.
14:27 one may avoid the S of death.
22:5 Thorns and S are in the way of the
Eccl 7:26 woman whose heart is S and nets, and whose
Sir 9:3 a loose woman, lest you fall into her S
9:13 in the midst of S, and that you are
Jer 18:22 take me, and laid S for my feet.
Ezek 19:8 nations set against him S on every side; they

SNARLING
Ps 59:7 with their mouths, and S with their lips--

SNATCH (7)
Job 24:9 (There are those who S the fatherless child from
24:19 Drought and heat S away the snow waters; so
Ps 40:14 altogether who seek to S away my life; let
52:5 for ever; he will S and tear you from
Is 9:20 They S on the right, but are still hungry,
Jn 10:28 and no one shall S them out of my
10:29 one is able to S them out of the

SNATCHED (4)
2Sam 23:21 with a staff, and S the spear out of
1Chr 11:23 with a staff, and S the spear out of
Job 22:16 They were S away before their time; their
Sir 19:3 reckless soul will be S away.

SNATCHES (3)
Job 9:12 Behold, he S away; who can hinder him?
Mt 13:19 evil one comes and S away what is sown
Jn 10:12 flees; and the wolf S them and scatters them.

SNATCHING
Jude 1:23 doubt; save some, by S them out of the

SNEEZED
2Kgs 4:35 upon him; the child S seven times, and the

SNEEZINGS
Job 41:18 His S flash forth light, and his eyes are

SNIFF
Mal 1:13 you say, and you S at me, says the

SNIFFING
Jer 2:24 wilderness, in her heat S the wind!

SNORTING (2)
Job 39:20 His majestic S is terrible.
Jer 8:16 "The S of their horses is heard from Dan;

SNOUT
Prov 11:22 ring in a swine's S is a beautiful woman

SNOW (29)
Ex 4:6 behold, his hand was leprous, as white as S
Num 12:10 tent, behold, Miriam was leprous, as white as S
2Sam 23:20 on a day when S had fallen.
2Kgs 5:27 from his presence a leper, as white as S
1Chr 11:22 on a day when S had fallen.
Job 6:16 ice, and where the S hides itself.
9:30 I wash myself with S, and cleanse my hands
24:19 heat snatch away the S waters; so does Sheol
37:6 For to the S he says, 'Fall on the
38:22 the storehouses of the S, or have you seen
Ps 51:7 wash me, and I shall be whiter than S
68:14 Almighty scattered kings there, S fell on Zalmon.
147:16 He gives S like wool; he scatters hoarfrost like
148:8 deeps, fire and hail, S and frost, stormy wind
Prov 25:13 Like the cold of S in the time of
26:1 Like S in summer or rain in harvest, so
31:21 is not afraid of S for her household, for
Wis 16:22 S and ice withstood fire without melting, so that
Sir 43:13 he sends the driving S and speeds the lightnings
43:17 He scatters the S like birds flying down, and
Is 1:18 be as white as S; though they are red
55:10 the rain and the S come down from heaven,
Jer 18:14 Does the S of Lebanon leave the crags of
Lam 4:7 princes were purer than S, whiter than milk; their
Dan 7:9 raiment was white as S, and the hair of
1Mac 13:22 night a very heavy S fell, and he did
13:22 and he did not go because of the S
Mt 28:3 was like lightning, and his raiment white as S
Rev 1:14 white wool, white as S; his eyes were like

SNOWS (2)
Dan 3:69 the Lord, dews and S, sing praise to him
3:73 the Lord, frosts and S, sing praise to him

SNUFFERS (8)
Ex 25:38 Its S and their trays shall be of pure
37:23 seven lamps and its S and its trays of
Num 4:9 with its lamps, its S, its trays, and all
1Kgs 7:50 of gold; the cups, S, basins, dishes for incense,
2Kgs 12:13 LORD basins of silver, S, bowls, trumpets, or any
25:14 the shovels, and the S, and the dishes for
2Chr 4:22 of purest gold; the S, basins, dishes for incense,
Jer 52:18 the shovels, and the S, and the basins, and

SO-CALLED (3)
1Chr 4:14 father of Ge-harashim, S because they were
1Cor 8:5 although there may be S gods in heaven or
2Thes 2:4 exalts himself against every S god or object of

SOAK
Ps 109:18 his coat, may it S into his body like

SOAKED
Is 34:7 Their land shall be S with blood, and their

SOAP (2)
Jer 2:22 lye and use much S, the stain of your
Mal 3:2 fire and like fullers' S;

SOAR
Obad 1:4 Though you S aloft like the eagle, though your

SOARS
Job 39:26 wisdom that the hawk S, and spreads his wings

SOBER (8)
Acts 26:25 I am speaking the S truth.
Rom 12:3 but to think with S judgment, each according to
1Thes 5:6 do, but let us keep awake and be S
5:8 day, let us be S, and put on the
Tit 2:12 passions, and to live S, upright, and godly lives
1Pet 1:13 up your minds, be S, set your hope fully
4:7 therefore keep sane and S for your prayers.
5:8 Be S, be watchful.

SOCKET
Job 31:22 and let my arm be broken from its S

SOCKETS (4)
Ex 38:12 pillars ten, and their S ten; the hooks of
1Kgs 7:50 pure gold; and the S of gold, for the
2Chr 4:22 pure gold; and the S of the temple, for
Zech 14:12 shall rot in their S, and their tongues shall

SOCO (3)
1Chr 4:18 Heber the father of S, and Jekuthiel the father
2Chr 11:7 Bethlehem, Etam, Tekoa, Bethzur, S, Adullam,
28:18 taken Beth-shemesh, Aijalon, Gederoth, S with its

SOCOH (5)
Josh 15:35 Tappuah, Enam, Jarmuth, Adullam, S, Azekah,
15:48 hill country, Shamir, Jattir, S,

S

1Sam 17:1 they were gathered at S, which belongs to Judah,
17:1 Judah, and encamped between S and Azekah, in
1Kgs 4:10 Arubboth (to him belonged S and all the land

SODI

Num 13:10 Gaddiel the son of S;

SODOM (48)

Gen 10:19 in the direction of S, Gomorrah, Admah, and
13:10 before the LORD destroyed S and Gomorrah.
13:12 valley and moved his tent as far as S
13:13 Now the men of S were wicked, great sinners
14:2 with Bera king of S, Birsha king of Gomorrah,
14:8 Then the king of S, the king of Gomorrah,
14:10 as the kings of S and Gomorrah fled, some
14:11 all the goods of S and Gomorrah, and all
14:12 brother, who dwelt in S, and his goods, and
14:17 him, the king of S went out to meet
14:21 And the king of S said to Abram, "Give
14:22 to the king of S, "I have sworn to
18:16 and they looked toward S; and Abraham went with
18:20 "Because the outcry against S and Gomorrah is
18:22 there, and went toward S; but Abraham still stood
18:26 "If I find at S fifty righteous in the
19:1 two angels came to S in the evening; and
19:1 and Lot was sitting in the gate of S
19:4 city, the men of S, both young and old,
19:24 the LORD rained on S and Gomorrah brimstone and
19:28 he looked down toward S and Gomorrah and toward
Deut 29:23 overthrow like that of S and Gomorrah, Admah and
32:32 from the vine of S, and from the fields
Is 1:9 should have been like S, and become like Gomorrah.
1:10 the word of the LORD, you rulers of S
3:9 proclaim their sin like S, they do not hide
13:19 Chaldeans, will be like S and Gomorrah when God
Jer 23:14 them have become like S to me, and its
49:18 As when S and Gomorrah and their neighbor cities
50:40 As when God overthrew S and Gomorrah and their
Lam 4:6 than the punishment of S, which was overthrown in
Ezek 16:46 south of you, is S with her daughters.
16:48 Lord GOD, your sister S and her daughters have
16:49 guilt of your sister S: she and her daughters
16:53 both the fortunes of S and her daughters, and
16:55 As for your sisters, S and her daughters shall
16:56 Was not your sister S a byword in your
Amos 4:11 as when God overthrew S and Gomorrah, and you
Zeph 2:9 "Moab shall become like S, and the Ammonites like
Mt 10:15 for the land of S and Gomorrah than for
11:23 had been done in S, it would have remained
11:24 for the land of S than for you."
Lk 10:12 on that day for S than for that town.
17:29 Lot went out from S fire and sulphur rained
Rom 9:29 would have fared like S and been made like
2Pet 2:6 turning the cities of S and Gomorrah to ashes
Jude 1:7 great day; just as S and Gomorrah and the
Rev 11:8 which is allegorically called S and Egypt, where

SODOMITES

1Tim 1:10 manslayers, immoral persons, S, kidnapers, liars,

SOFT (8)

Jud 12:15 her before Holofernes the S fleeces which she had
Job 41:3 he speak to you S words?
Prov 15:1 A S answer turns away wrath, but a harsh
25:15 be persuaded, and a S tongue will break a
Wis 15:7 a potter kneads the S earth and laboriously molds
Mt 11:8 a man clothed in S raiment?
11:8 Behold, those who wear S raiment are in kings'
Lk 7:25 A man clothed in S clothing?

SOFTENED

Is 1:6 or bound up, or S with oil.

SOFTENING

Ps 65:10 abundantly, settling its ridges, S it with showers, and

SOFTER

Ps 55:21 heart; his words were S than oil, yet they

SOFTLY (2)

Judg 4:21 her hand, and went S to him and drove
Ruth 3:7 Then she came S, and uncovered his feet, and

SOIL (27)

Gen 9:20 Noah was the first tiller of the S
1Chr 27:26 field for tilling the S was Ezri the son
2Chr 26:10 in the fertile lands, for he loved the S
Job 14:19 torrents wash away the S of the earth; so
Song 5:3 feet, how could I S them?
Sir 20:27 Whoever cultivates the S will heap up his harvest,
Is 32:13 fruitful vine, for the S of my people growing
34:7 with blood, and their S made rich with fat.
34:9 into pitch, and her S into brimstone; her land
Ezek 17:5 planted it in fertile S; he placed it beside
17:8 transplanted it to good S by abundant waters, that
26:4 I will scrape her S from her, and make
26:12 stones and timber and S they will cast into
Joel 1:10 O tillers of the S, wail, O vinedressers, for
Mic 5:5 and treads upon our S, that we will raise
Zech 13:5 a tiller of the S; for the land has
Mal 3:11 the fruits of your S; and your vine in
Mt 13:5 they had not much S, and immediately they sprang
13:5 had no depth of S,
13:8 seeds fell on good S and brought forth grain,
13:23 was sown on good S, this is he who
Mk 4:5 it had not much S, and immediately it sprang
4:5 had no depth of S;
4:8 seeds fell into good S and brought forth grain,
4:20 sown upon the good S are the ones who
Lk 8:8 some fell into good S and grew, and yielded
8:15 that in the good S, they are those who,

SOILED (2)

Sir 22:11 you will not be S when he shakes himself
Rev 3:4 people who have not S their garments; and they

SOJOURN (27)

Gen 12:10 down to Egypt to S there, for the famine
19:9 "This fellow came to S, and he would play
26:3 S in this land, and I will be with
47:4 "We have come to S in the land; for
Ex 12:48 when a stranger shall S with you and would
Lev 17:8 of the strangers that S among them, who offers
17:10 of the strangers that S among them eats any
17:13 of the strangers that S among them, who takes
20:2 of the strangers that S in Israel, who gives
25:45 among the strangers who S with you and their
Judg 17:9 I am going to S where I may find
Ruth 1:1 in Judah went to S in the country of
1Kgs 17:20 widow with whom I S, by slaying her son?"
2Kgs 8:1 with your household, and S wherever you can; for
Ps 5:4 wickedness; evil may not S with thee.
15:1 O LORD, who shall S in thy tent?
120:5 is me, that I S in Meshech, that I
Wis 19:10 the events of their S, how instead of producing
Sir 38:32 and men can neither S nor live there.
Is 16:4 the outcasts of Moab S among you; be a
52:4 first into Egypt to S there, and the Assyrian
Jer 35:7 the land where you S
49:18 there, no man shall S in her.
49:33 there, no man shall S in her."
50:40 son of man shall S in her.
Ezek 14:7 of the strangers that S in Israel, who separates
20:38 the land where they S, but they shall not

SOJOURNED (10)

Gen 20:1 and Shur; and he S in Gerar.
21:23 me and with the land where you have S
21:34 And Abraham S many days in the land of
32:4 servant Jacob, 'I have S with Laban, and stayed
35:27 (that is, Hebron), where Abraham and Isaac had S
Deut 26:5 down into Egypt and S there, few in number;
Judg 17:7 a Levite; and he S there.
2Kgs 8:2 with her household and S in the land of
Ps 105:23 came to Egypt; Jacob S in the land of
Heb 11:9 By faith he S in the land of promise,

SOJOURNER (48)

Gen 23:4 a stranger and a S among you; give me
Ex 2:22 "I have been a S in a foreign land."
12:19 whether he is a S or a native of
12:45 No S or hired servant may eat of it.
18:3 "I have been a S in a foreign land"),
20:10 your cattle, or the S who is within your
Lev 17:15 a native or a S, shall wash his clothes,
19:10 poor and for the S: I am the LORD
22:10 A S of the priest's or a hired servant
24:16 shall stone him; the S as well as the
24:22 one law for the S and for the native;
25:6 hired servant and the S who lives with you;
25:35 a stranger and a S he shall live with
25:40 you as a hired servant and as a S

S

25:47 "If a stranger or S with you becomes rich,
25:47 to the stranger or S with you, or to
Num 9:14 statute, both for the S and for the native."
15:15 are, so shall the S be before the LORD.
15:30 is native or a S, reviles the LORD, and
35:15 stranger and for the S among them, that any
Deut 5:14 your cattle, or the S who is within your
10:18 widow, and loves the S, giving him food and
10:19 Love the S therefore; for you were sojourners in
14:29 with you, and the S, the fatherless, and the
16:11 within your towns, the S, the fatherless, and the
16:14 maidservant, the Levite, the S, the fatherless, and
23:7 because you were a S in his land.
24:17 justice due to the S or to the fatherless,
24:19 shall be for the S, the fatherless, and the
24:20 shall be for the S, the fatherless, and the
24:21 shall be for the S, the fatherless, and the
26:11 the Levite, and the S who is among you.
26:12 to the Levite, the S, the fatherless, and the
26:13 to the Levite, the S, the fatherless, and the
27:19 justice due to the S, the fatherless, and the
28:43 The S who is among you shall mount above
29:11 your wives, and the S who is in your
31:12 little ones, and the S within your towns, that
Josh 8:33 And all Israel, S as well as homeborn, with
2Sam 1:13 the son of a S, an Amalekite."
Job 31:32 with his meat?' (the S has not lodged in
Ps 39:12 thy passing guest, a S, like all my fathers.
94:6 the widow and the S, and murder the fatherless;
119:19 I am a S on earth; hide not thy
Ezek 22:7 contempt in you; the S suffers extortion in your
22:29 have extorted from the S without redress.
Zech 7:10 widow, the fatherless, the S, or the poor; and
Mal 3:5 who thrust aside the S, and do not fear

SOJOURNERS (15)

Gen 15:13 your descendants will be S in a land that
Ex 6:4 Canaan, the land in which they dwelt as S
Lev 22:18 Israel or of the S in Israel presents his
25:23 you are strangers and S with me.
Deut 10:19 therefore; for you were S in the land of
24:14 or one of the S who are in your
Josh 8:35 little ones, and the S who lived among them.
2Sam 4:3 Gittaim, and have been S there to this day).
1Chr 16:19 of little account, and S in it,
29:15 strangers before thee, and S, as all our fathers
2Chr 30:25 of Israel, and the S who came out of
30:25 of Israel, and the S who dwelt in Judah,
Ps 105:12 of little account, and S in it,
146:9 LORD watches over the S, he upholds the widow
Eph 2:19 no longer strangers and S, but you are fellow

SOJOURNING (7)

Gen 47:9 the years of my S are a hundred and
47:9 of my fathers in the days of their S
Num 15:14 if a stranger is S with you, or any
Josh 20:9 and for the stranger S among them, that any
Judg 19:1 a certain Levite was S in the remote parts
19:16 Ephraim, and he was S in Gibe-ah; the men
2Chr 15:9 and Simeon who were S with them, for great

SOJOURNINGS (4)

Gen 17:8 the land of your S, all the land of
28:4 the land of your S which God gave to
36:7 the land of their S could not support them
37:1 land of his father's S, in the land of

SOJOURNS (14)

Ex 3:22 and of her who S in her house, jewelry
12:49 for the stranger who S among you."
Lev 16:29 or the stranger who S among you;
17:12 shall any stranger who S among you eat blood.
18:26 or the stranger who S among you
19:33 "When a stranger S with you in your land,
19:34 The stranger who S with you shall be to
Num 9:14 And if a stranger S among you, and will
15:15 for the stranger who S with you, a perpetual
15:16 for the stranger who S with you."
15:26 and the stranger who S among them, because the
15:29 for the stranger who S among them.
19:10 to the stranger who S among them, a perpetual
Ezra 1:4 in whatever place he S, be assisted by the

SOLACE

Job 16:5 my mouth, and the S of my lips would

SOLD (87)

Gen 25:33 swore to him, and S his birthright to Jacob.
31:15 For he has S us, and he has been
37:28 of the pit, and S him to the Ishmaelites
37:36 Meanwhile the Midianites had S him in Egypt to
41:56 all the storehouses, and S to the Egyptians, for
42:6 he it was who S to all the people
45:4 brother, Joseph, whom you S into Egypt.
45:5 with yourselves, because you S me here; for God
47:20 for all the Egyptians S their fields, because the
Ex 22:1 then he shall be S for his theft.
Lev 25:23 land shall not be S in perpetuity, for the
25:25 shall come and redeem what his brother has S
25:27 the years since he S it and pay back
25:27 man to whom he S it; and he shall
25:28 himself, then what he S shall remain in the
25:33 the house that was S in a city of
25:34 cities may not be S; for that is their
25:42 they shall not be S as slaves.
25:48 then after he is S he may be redeemed;
25:50 the year when he S himself to him until
27:20 or if he has S the field to another
27:27 redeemed, it shall be S at your valuation.
27:28 inherited field, shall be S or redeemed; every
Deut 15:12 a Hebrew woman, is S to you, he shall
32:30 unless their Rock had S them, and the LORD
Judg 2:14 plundered them; and he S them into the power
3:8 against Israel, and he S them into the hand
4:2 And the LORD S them into the hand of
10:7 against Israel, and he S them into the hand
1Sam 12:9 their God; and he S them into the hand
1Kgs 21:20 you, because you have S yourself to do what
21:25 (There was none who S himself to do what
2Kgs 6:25 an ass's head was S for eighty shekels of
7:1 fine meal shall be S for a shekel, and
7:16 of fine meal was S for a shekel, and
7:18 of barley shall be S for a shekel, and
17:17 divination and sorcery, and S themselves to do evil
Neh 5:8 brethren who have been S to the nations; but
5:8 that they may be S to us!" They were
13:15 the day when they S food.
13:16 kinds of wares and S them on the sabbath
Jud 7:26 help us; God has S us into their hands,
Esth 7:4 For we are S, I and my people, to
7:4 If we had been S merely as slaves, men
Ps 44:12 Thou hast S thy people for a trifle, demanding
105:17 them, Joseph, who was S as a slave.
Wis 10:13 a righteous man was S, wisdom did not desert
Is 50:1 to whom I have S you?
50:1 iniquities you were S, and for your transgressions
52:3 the LORD: "You were S for nothing, and you
Jer 34:14 Hebrew who has been S to you and has
Bar 4:6 destruction that you were S to the nations, but
Ezek 7:13 to what he has S, while they live.
Joel 3:3 a harlot, and have S a girl for wine,
3:6 You have S the people of Judah and Jerusalem
3:7 to which you have S them, and I will
1Mac 1:15 with the Gentiles and S themselves to do evil.
2Mac 4:32 it happened, he had S to Tyre and the
5:14 and as many were S into slavery as were
8:14 Others S all their remaining property, and at the
8:14 those who had been S by the ungodly Nicanor
10:21 these men of having S their brethren for money
Mt 10:29 Are not two sparrows S for a penny?
13:46 great value, went and S all that he had
18:24 ordered him to be S, with his wife and
21:12 drove out all who S and bought in the
21:12 seats of those who S pigeons.
26:9 ointment might have been S for a large sum,
Mk 11:15 drive out those who S and those who bought
11:15 seats of those who S pigeons;
14:5 ointment might have been S for more than three
Lk 12:6 Are not five sparrows S for two pennies?
17:28 drank, they bought, they S, they planted, they built,
19:45 drive out those who S,
Jn 2:16 he told those who S the pigeons, "Take these
12:5 was this ointment not S for three hundred denarii
Acts 2:45 in common; and they S their possessions and goods
4:34 of lands or houses S them, and brought the
4:34 proceeds of what was S
4:37 a native of Cyprus, S a field which belonged
5:1 with his wife Sapphira S a piece of property,
5:4 And after it was S, was it not at
5:8 "Tell me whether you S the land for so
7:9 patriarchs, jealous of Joseph, S him into Egypt; but
Rom 7:14 but I am carnal, S under sin.

1Cor 10:25 Eat whatever is S in the meat market without
Heb 12:16 irreligious like Esau, who S his birthright for a

SOLDERING

Is 41:7 anvil, saying of the S, "It is good"; and

SOLDIER (13)

2Sam 20:8 Joab was wearing a S's garment, and over it
1Kgs 20:39 battle; and behold, a S turned and brought a
Jud 15:3 one that was a S, rushed out upon them.
Is 3:2 mighty man and the S, the judge and the
Mk 6:27 the king sent a S of the guard and
Jn 19:23 parts, one for each S; also his tunic.
Acts 10:7 servants and a devout S from among those that
28:16 by himself, with the S that guarded him.
1Cor 9:7 Who serves as a S at his own expense?
Phil 2:25 fellow worker and fellow S, and your messenger and
2Tim 2:3 suffering as a good S of Christ Jesus.
2:4 No S on service gets entangled in civilian pursuits,
Philem 1:2 and Archippus our fellow S, and the church in

SOLDIERS (62)

1Sam 4:10 for there fell of Israel thirty thousand foot S
2Sam 8:4 and twenty thousand foot S; and David hamstrung all
10:6 Zobah, twenty thousand foot S, and the king of
1Kgs 9:22 slaves; they were the S, they were his officials,
20:29 a hundred thousand foot S in one day.
1Chr 18:4 and twenty thousand foot S; and David hamstrung all
19:18 and forty thousand foot S, and killed also Shophach
2Chr 8:9 his work; they were S, and his officers, the
17:13 He had S, mighty men of valor, in Jerusalem.
26:11 had an army of S, fit for war, in
Ezra 8:22 for a band of S and horsemen to protect
Jud 2:5 twenty thousand foot S and twelve thousand cavalry.
7:2 baggage and the foot S handling it, a very
7:7 and set guards of S over them, and then
9:7 strength of their foot S; they trust in shield
Jer 38:4 the hands of the S who are left in
39:4 Judah and all the S saw them, they fled,
41:3 Mizpah, and the Chaldean S who happened to be
41:16 son of Ahikam-- S, women, children, and eunuchs,
46:21 Even her hired S in her midst are like
49:26 squares, and all her S shall be destroyed in
50:30 squares, and all her S shall be destroyed on
51:32 with fire, and the S are in panic.
Ezek 26:7 and with horsemen and a host of many S
Joel 2:7 warriors they charge, like S they scale the wall.
Nah 2:3 men is red, his S are clothed in scarlet.
1Mac 6:30 thousand foot S, twenty thousand horsemen, and
6:48 The S of the king's army went up to
9:4 twenty thousand foot S and two thousand cavalry.
12:49 and the Great Plain to destroy all Jonathan's S
16:6 he saw that the S were afraid to cross
2Mac 5:12 And he commanded his S to cut down relentlessly
14:39 more than five hundred S to arrest him;
Mt 8:9 man under authority, with S under me; and I
27:27 Then the S of the governor took Jesus into
27:65 have a guard of S; go, make it as
28:12 of money to the S
Mk 15:16 And the S led him away inside the palace
Lk 3:14 S also asked him, "And we, what shall we
7:8 set under authority, with S under me: and I
23:11 And Herod with his S treated him with contempt
23:35 The S also mocked him, coming up and offering
Jn 18:3 procuring a band of S and some officers from
18:12 So the band of S and their captain and
19:2 And the S plaited a crown of thorns, and
19:23 When the S had crucified Jesus they took his
19:25 So the S did this.
19:32 So the S came and broke the legs of
19:34 But one of the S pierced his side with
Acts 12:4 to four squads of S to guard him, intending
12:6 was sleeping between two S, bound with two chains,
12:18 small stir among the S over what had become
21:32 He at once took S and centurions, and ran
21:32 the tribune and the S, they stopped beating Paul.
21:35 actually carried by the S because of the violence
23:10 by them, commanded the S to go down and
23:23 get ready two hundred S with seventy horsemen and
23:27 upon them with the S and rescued him, having
23:31 So the S, according to their instructions, took Paul
27:31 the centurion and the S, "Unless these men stay
27:32 Then the S cut away the ropes of the
27:42 The S plan was to kill the prisoners, lest

SOLE (12)

Deut 2:5 much as for the S of the foot to
11:24 place on which the S of your foot treads
28:35 be healed, from the S of your foot to
28:56 venture to set the S of her foot upon
28:65 no rest for the S of your foot; but
Josh 1:3 Every place that the S of your foot will
2Sam 14:25 as Absalom; from the S of his foot to
2Kgs 19:24 dried up with the S of my foot all
Job 2:7 loathsome sores from the S of his foot to
Is 1:6 From the S of the foot even to the
37:25 dried up with the S of my foot all
Ezek 1:7 feet were like the S of a calf's foot;

SOLEMN (25)

Ex 16:23 is a day of S rest, a holy sabbath
31:15 is a sabbath of S rest, holy to the
35:2 a holy sabbath of S rest to the LORD;
Lev 16:31 is a sabbath of S rest to you, and
23:3 is a sabbath of S rest, a holy convocation;
23:24 observe a day of S rest, a memorial proclaimed
23:32 you a sabbath of S rest, and you shall
23:36 LORD; it is a S assembly; you shall do
23:39 day shall be a S rest, and on the
23:39 day shall be a S rest.
25:4 be a sabbath of S rest for the land,
25:5 be a year of S rest for the land.
Num 29:35 you shall have a S assembly: you shall do
Deut 16:8 there shall be a S assembly to the LORD
2Kgs 10:20 Jehu ordered, "Sanctify a S assembly for Baal." So
2Chr 7:9 day they held a S assembly; for they had
Neh 8:18 day there was a S assembly, according to the
Ps 68:24 Thy S processions are seen, O God, the processions
Is 1:13 cannot endure iniquity and S assembly.
Ezek 21:23 divination; they have sworn S oaths; but he brings
Joel 1:13 a fast, call a S assembly.
2:15 a fast; call a S assembly;
Amos 5:21 no delight in your S assemblies.
2Mac 10:16 after making S supplication and beseeching God
12:25 he had confirmed his S promise to restore them

SOLEMNLY (7)

Gen 43:3 to him, "The man S warned us, saying, 'You
Ex 13:19 him; for Joseph had S sworn the people of
Deut 8:19 and worship them, I S warn you this day
1Sam 8:9 voice; only, you shall S warn them, and show
1Kgs 2:42 by the LORD, and S admonish you, saying, 'Know
Jer 11:7 For I S warned your fathers when I brought
1Thes 4:6 these things, as we S forewarned you.

SOLES (8)

Josh 3:13 And when the S of the feet of the
4:18 the Jordan, and the S of the priests' feet
1Kgs 5:3 put them under the S of his feet.
Esth 13:13 willing to kiss the S of his feet, to
Job 13:27 a bound to the S of my feet.
Ezek 1:7 were straight, and the S of their feet were
43:7 the place of the S of my feet, where
Mal 4:3 be ashes under the S of your feet, on

SOLICITED

Ezek 16:34 in your harlotries: none S you to play the

SOLID (3)

1Cor 3:2 you with milk, not S food; for you were
Heb 5:12 You need milk, not S food;
5:14 But S food is for the mature, for those

SOLITARY (2)

Lev 16:22 upon him to a S land; and he shall
Is 27:10 the fortified city is S, a habitation deserted and

SOLOMON (307)

2Sam 5:14 Jerusalem: Shammua, Shobab, Nathan, S,
12:24 bore a son, and he called his name S
1Kgs 1:10 the mighty men or S his brother.
1:11 Bathsheba the mother of S, "Have you not heard
1:12 own life and the life of your son S
1:13 to your maidservant, saying, S your son shall reign
1:17 LORD your God, saying, S your son shall reign
1:19 of the army; but S your servant he has
1:21 I and my son S will be counted offenders."
1:26 Jehoiada, and your servant S, he has not invited.
1:30 God of Israel, saying, S your son shall reign
1:33 your lord, and cause S my son to ride
1:34 say, 'Long live King S

S

SOLOMON

1:37 may he be with S, and make his throne
1:38 went down and caused S to ride on King
1:39 horn of oil from the tent, and anointed S
1:39 and all the people said, "Long live King S
1:43 King David has made S king;
1:46 S sits upon the royal throne.
1:47 make the name of S more famous than yours,
1:50 And Adonijah feared S; and he arose, and went,
1:51 And it was told S, "Behold, Adonijah fears King
1:51 "Behold, Adonijah fears King S; for, lo, he has
1:51 altar, saying, 'Let King S swear to me first
1:52 And S said, "If he prove to be a
1:53 So King S sent, and they brought him down
1:53 did obeisance to King S; and Solomon said to
1:53 to King Solomon; and S said to him, "Go
2:1 drew near, he charged S his son, saying,
2:12 So S sat upon the throne of David his
2:13 of Haggith came to Bathsheba the mother of S
2:17 said, "Pray ask King S --he will not refuse
2:19 Bathsheba went to King S, to speak to him
2:22 King S answered his mother, "And why do you
2:23 Then King S swore by the LORD, saying, "God
2:25 So King S sent Benaiah the son of Jehoiada;
2:27 So S expelled Abiathar from being priest to the
2:29 it was told King S, "Joab has fled to
2:29 S sent Benaiah the son of Jehoiada, saying, "Go,
2:41 And when S was told that Shimei had gone
2:45 But King S shall be blessed, and the throne
2:46 the kingdom was established in the hand of S
3:1 S made a marriage alliance with Pharaoh king of
3:3 S loved the LORD, walking in the statutes of
3:4 the great high place; S used to offer a
3:5 the LORD appeared to S in a dream by
3:6 And S said, "Thou hast shown great and steadfast
3:10 pleased the Lord that S had asked this.
3:15 And S awoke, and behold, it was a dream.
4:1 King S was king over all Israel,
4:7 S had twelve officers over all Israel, who provided
4:11 Taphath the daughter of S as his wife);
4:15 Basemath the daughter of S as his wife);
4:21 S ruled over all the kingdoms from the Euphrates
4:21 brought tribute and served S all the days of
4:22 S's provision for one day was thirty cors of
4:25 under his fig tree, all the days of S
4:26 S also had forty thousand stalls of horses for
4:27 supplied provisions for King S, and for all who
4:27 who came to King S's table, each one in
4:29 And God gave S wisdom and understanding beyond
4:30 the seashore, so that S's wisdom surpassed the
4:34 hear the wisdom of S, and from all the
5:1 sent his servants to S, when he heard that
5:2 And S sent word to Hiram,
5:7 heard the words of S, he rejoiced greatly, and
5:8 And Hiram sent to S, saying, "I have heard
5:10 So Hiram supplied S with all the timber of
5:11 that he desired, while S gave Hiram twenty thousand
5:11 S gave this to Hiram year by year.
5:12 And the LORD gave S wisdom, as he promised
5:12 peace between Hiram and S; and the two of
5:13 King S raised a levy of forced labor out
5:15 S also had seventy thousand burden-bearers and
5:16 the hill country, besides S's three thousand three
5:18 So S's builders and Hiram's builders and the men
6:1 the fourth year of S's reign over Israel, in
6:2 The house which King S built for the LORD
6:11 the LORD came to S,
6:14 So S built the house, and finished it.
6:21 And S overlaid the inside of the house with
7:1 S was building his own house thirteen years, and
7:8 S also made a house like this hall for
7:13 And King S sent and brought Hiram from Tyre.
7:14 He came to King S, and did all his
7:40 he did for King S on the house of
7:45 Hiram made for King S, were of burnished bronze.
7:47 And S left all the vessels unweighed, because there
7:48 So S made all the vessels that were in
7:51 the work that King S did on the house
7:51 And S brought in the things which David his
8:1 Then S assembled the elders of Israel and all
8:1 of Israel, before King S in Jerusalem, to bring
8:2 Israel assembled to King S at the feast in
8:5 And King S and all the congregation of Israel,
8:12 Then S said, "The LORD has set the sun
8:22 Then S stood before the altar of the LORD
8:54 Now as S finished offering all this prayer and
8:63 S offered as peace offerings to the LORD
8:65 So S held the feast at that time, and
9:1 When S had finished building the house of the
9:1 house and all that S desired to build,
9:2 the LORD appeared to S a second time, as
9:10 twenty years, in which S had built the two
9:11 of Tyre had supplied S with cedar and cypress
9:11 as he desired, King S gave to Hiram twenty
9:12 see the cities which S had given him, they
9:15 forced labor which King S levied to build the
9:16 dowry to his daughter, S's wife;
9:17 daughter, Solomon's wife; so S rebuilt Gezer) and
9:19 all the store-cities that S had, and the cities
9:19 his horsemen, and whatever S desired to build in
9:21 to destroy utterly--these S made a forced levy
9:22 the people of Israel S made no slaves; they
9:23 officers who were over S's work: five hundred and
9:24 her own house which S had built for her;
9:25 Three times a year S used to offer up
9:26 King S built a fleet of ships at Ezion-geber,
9:27 with the servants of S;
9:28 twenty talents; and they brought it to King S
10:1 of the fame of S concerning the name of
10:2 when she came to S, she told him all
10:3 And S answered all her questions; there was nothing
10:4 all the wisdom of S, the house that he
10:10 which the queen of Sheba gave to King S
10:13 And King S gave to the queen of Sheba
10:13 was given her by the bounty of King S
10:14 gold that came to S in one year was
10:16 King S made two hundred large shields of beaten
10:21 All King S's drinking vessels were of gold, and
10:21 not considered as anything in the days of S
10:23 Thus King S excelled all the kings of the
10:24 sought the presence of S to hear his wisdom,
10:26 And S gathered together chariots and horsemen; he
10:28 And S's import of horses was from Egypt and
11:1 King S loved many foreign women: the daughter
11:2 heart after their gods"; S clung to these in
11:4 For when S was old his wives turned away
11:5 For S went after Ashtoreth the goddess of the
11:6 So S did what was evil in the sight
11:7 Then S built a high place for Chemosh the
11:9 LORD was angry with S, because his heart had
11:11 the LORD said to S, "Since this has been
11:14 up an adversary against S, Hadad the Edomite; he
11:25 all the days of S, doing mischief as Hadad
11:26 Zeredah, a servant of S, whose mother's name was
11:27 S built the Millo, and closed up the breach
11:28 very able, and when S saw that the young
11:31 from the hand of S, and will give you
11:40 S sought therefore to kill Jeroboam; but Jeroboam
11:40 and was in Egypt until the death of S
11:41 of the acts of S, and all that he
11:41 written in the book of the acts of S
11:42 And the time that S reigned in Jerusalem over
11:43 And S slept with his fathers, and was buried
12:2 had fled from King S, then Jeroboam returned from
12:6 who had stood before S his father while he
12:21 restore the kingdom to Rehoboam the son of S
12:23 Rehoboam the son of S, king of Judah, and
14:21 Rehoboam the son of S reigned in Judah.
14:26 shields of gold which S had made;
2Kgs 21:7 to David and to S his son, "In this
23:13 mount of corruption, which S the king of Israel
24:13 of the LORD, which S king of Israel had
25:16 and the stands, which S had made for the
1Chr 3:5 Shimea, Shobab, Nathan and S, four by Bath-shua,
3:10 The descendants of S: Rehoboam, Abijah his son, Asa
6:10 in the house that S built in Jerusalem).
6:32 tent of meeting, until S had built the house
14:4 Jerusalem: Shammua, Shobab, Nathan, S,
18:8 much bronze; with it S made the bronze sea
22:5 For David said, S my son is young and
22:6 Then he called for S his son, and charged
22:7 David said to S, "My son, I had it
22:9 his name shall be S, and I will give
22:17 of Israel to help S his son, saying,
23:1 of days, he made S his son king over
28:5 sons) he has chosen S my son to sit
28:6 to me, 'It is S your son who shall
28:9 "And you, S my son, know the God of
28:11 Then David gave S his son the plan of
28:20 Then David said to S his son, "Be strong
29:1 to all the assembly, S my son, whom alone
29:19 Grant to S my son that with a whole
29:22 And they made S the son of David king

29:23 Then S sat on the throne of the LORD
29:24 of King David, pledged their allegiance to King S
29:25 And the LORD gave S great repute in the
29:28 riches, and honor; and S his son reigned in
2Chr 1:1 S the son of David
1:2 S spoke to all Israel, to the commanders of
1:3 And S, and all the assembly with him, went
1:5 And S and the assembly sought the LORD.
1:6 And S went up there to the bronze altar
1:7 night God appeared to S, and said to him,
1:8 And S said to God, "Thou hast shown great
1:11 God answered S, "Because this was in your heart,
1:13 So S came from the high place at Gibeon,
1:14 S gathered together chariots and horsemen; he had
1:16 And S's import of horses was from Egypt and
2:1 Now S purposed to build a temple for the
2:2 And S assigned seventy thousand men to bear
2:3 And S sent word to Huram the king of
2:11 which he sent to S, "Because the LORD loves
2:17 Then S took a census of all the aliens
3:1 Then S began to build the house of the
3:3 These are S's measurements for building the house
4:11 he did for King S on the house of
4:16 burnished bronze for King S for the house of
4:18 S made all these things in great quantities, so
4:19 So S made all the things that were in
5:1 all the work that S did for the house
5:1 And S brought in the things which David his
5:2 Then S assembled the elders of Israel and all
5:6 And King S and all the congregation of Israel,
6:1 Then S said, "The LORD has said that he
6:12 Then S stood before the altar of the LORD
6:13 S had made a bronze platform five cubits long,
7:1 When S had ended his prayer, fire came down
7:5 King S offered as a sacrifice twenty-two thousand
7:7 And S consecrated the middle of the court that
7:7 because the bronze altar S had made could not
7:8 At that time S held the feast for seven
7:10 to David and to S and to Israel his
7:11 Thus S finished the house of the LORD and
7:11 king's house; all that S had planned to do
7:12 the LORD appeared to S in the night and
8:1 twenty years, in which S had built the house
8:2 and his own house, S rebuilt the cities which
8:3 And S went to Hamath-zobah, and took it.
8:6 all the store-cities that S had, and all the
8:6 his horsemen, and whatever S desired to build in
8:8 had not destroyed--these S made a forced levy
8:9 the people of Israel S made no slaves for
8:10 chief officers of King S, two hundred and fifty,
8:11 S brought Pharaoh's daughter up from the city of
8:12 Then S offered up burnt offerings to the LORD
8:16 all the work of S from the day the
8:17 Then S went to Ezion-geber and Eloth on the
8:18 with the servants of S, and fetched from there
8:18 talents of gold and brought it to King S
9:1 of the fame of S she came to Jerusalem
9:1 When she came to S, she told him all
9:2 And S answered all her questions; there was nothing
9:2 was nothing hidden from S which he could not
9:3 seen the wisdom of S, the house that he
9:9 which the queen of Sheba gave to King S
9:10 and the servants of S, who brought gold from
9:12 And King S gave to the queen of Sheba
9:13 gold that came to S in one year was
9:14 of the land brought gold and silver to S
9:15 King S made two hundred large shields of beaten
9:20 All King S's drinking vessels were of gold, and
9:20 not considered as anything in the days of S
9:22 Thus King S excelled all the kings of the
9:23 sought the presence of S to hear his wisdom,
9:25 And S had four thousand stalls for horses and
9:28 horses were imported for S from Egypt and from
9:29 of the acts of S, from first to last,
9:30 S reigned in Jerusalem over all Israel forty years.
9:31 And S slept with his fathers, and was buried
10:2 had fled from King S, then Jeroboam returned from
10:6 who had stood before S his father while he
11:3 Rehoboam the son of S king of Judah, and
11:17 Rehoboam the son of S secure, for they walked
11:17 three years in the way of David and S
12:9 shields of gold which S had made;
13:6 Nebat, a servant of S the son of David,
13:7 Rehoboam the son of S, when Rehoboam was young
30:26 since the time of S the son of David
33:7 to David and to S his son, "In this
35:3 in the house which S the son of David,
35:4 and the directions of S his son.
Ezra 2:55 The sons of S's servants: the sons of Sotai,
2:58 and the sons of S's servants were three hundred
Neh 7:57 The sons of S's servants: the sons of Sotai,
7:60 and the sons of S's servants were three hundred
11:3 and the descendants of S's servants.
12:45 to the command of David and his son S
13:26 Did not S king of Israel sin on account
Prov 1:1 The proverbs of S, son of David, king
10:1 The proverbs of S
25:1 also are proverbs of S which the men of
Song 1:5 the tents of Kedar, like the curtains of S
3:7 Behold, it is the litter of S
3:9 King S made himself a palanquin from the wood
3:11 Zion, and behold King S, with the crown with
8:11 S had a vineyard at Baal-hamon; he let out
8:12 for myself; you, O S, may have the thousand,
Sir 47:13 amply because of him; S reigned in days of
47:23 S rested with his fathers, and left behind him
Jer 52:20 and the stands, which S the king had made
2Mac 2:8 of Moses, and as S asked that the place
2:9 being possessed of wisdom S offered sacrifice for the
2:10 the sacrifices, so also S prayed, and the fire
2:12 Likewise S also kept the eight days.
Mt 1:6 was the father of S by the wife of
1:7 wife of Uriah, and S the father of Rehoboam,
6:29 I tell you, even S in all his glory
12:42 hear the wisdom of S, and behold, something greater
12:42 behold, something greater than S is here.
Lk 11:31 hear the wisdom of S, and behold, something greater
11:31 behold, something greater than S is here.
12:27 I tell you, even S in all his glory
Jn 10:23 walking in the temple, in the portico of S
Acts 5:12 were all together in S's Portico.
7:47 But it was S who built a house for

SOLOMONS (2)

Song 1:1 The Song of Songs, which is S
Acts 3:11 in the portico called S, astounded.

SOLSTICES

Wis 7:18 the alternations of the S and the changes of

SOLUTIONS

Wis 8:8 of speech and the S of riddles; she has

SOLVE (3)

Ps 49:4 a proverb; I will S my riddle to the
Dan 5:12 dreams, explain riddles, and S problems were found
5:16 can give interpretations and S problems.

SOME (474)

Gen 3:6 and she also gave S to her husband, and
14:10 Sodom and Gomorrah fled, S fell into them, and
25:30 Jacob, "Let me eat S of that red pottage,
30:14 "Give me, I pray, S of your son's mandrakes."
33:15 me leave with you S of the men who
35:16 they were still S distance from Ephrath, Rachel
40:1 S time after this, the butler of the king
40:4 and they continued for S time in custody.
43:11 then do this: take S of the choice fruits
48:7 when there was still S distance to go to
Ex 4:9 voice, you shall take S water from the Nile
4:13 Lord, send, I pray, S other person."
10:10 Look, you have S evil purpose in mind.
12:7 Then they shall take S of the blood, and
16:17 did so; they gathered, S more, some less.
16:17 they gathered, some more, S less.
16:20 not listen to Moses; S left part of it
16:27 On the seventh day S of the people went
17:5 people, taking with you S of the elders of
30:36 and you shall beat S of it very small,
Lev 4:5 anointed priest shall take S of the blood of
4:7 the priest shall put S of the blood on
4:16 anointed priest shall bring S of the blood of
4:18 And he shall put S of the blood on
4:25 the priest shall take S of the blood of
4:30 the priest shall take S of its blood with
4:34 the priest shall take S of the blood of
5:9 and he shall sprinkle S of the blood of
8:11 And he sprinkled S of it on the altar
8:12 And he poured S of the anointing oil on
8:23 killed it, and took S of its blood and
8:24 brought, and Moses put S of the blood on
8:30 Then Moses took S of the anointing oil and

14:14 The priest shall take S of the blood of
14:15 the priest shall take S of the log of
14:16 left hand, and sprinkle S oil with his finger
14:17 And S of the oil that remains in his
14:25 the priest shall take S of the blood of
14:26 the priest shall pour S of the oil into
14:27 with his right finger S of the oil that
14:28 the priest shall put S of the oil that
14:35 to me to be S sort of disease in
16:14 and he shall take S of the blood of
16:18 it, and shall take S of the blood of
16:19 And he shall sprinkle S of the blood upon
Num 5:17 earthen vessel, and take S of the dust that
5:20 have defiled yourself, and S man other than your
11:1 among them, and consumed S outlying parts of the
11:17 and I will take S of the spirit which
11:25 to him, and took S of the spirit that
13:20 good courage, and bring S of the fruit of
13:23 them; they brought also S pomegranates and figs.
19:4 the priest shall take S of her blood with
19:4 his finger, and sprinkle S of her blood toward
19:17 unclean they shall take S ashes of the burnt
21:1 against Israel, and took S of them captive.
27:20 shall invest him with S of your authority, that
Deut 1:25 took in their hands S of the fruit of
13:7 your fathers have known, S of the gods of
24:1 because he has found S indecency in her, and
26:2 it, you shall take S of the first of
Josh 7:1 tribe of Judah, took S of the devoted things;
7:11 them; they have taken S of the devoted things;
8:22 the midst of Israel, S on this side, and
8:22 on this side, and S on that side; and
9:23 you are cursed, and S of you shall always
11:22 and in Ashdod, did S remain.
Judg 14:9 and mother, and gave S to them, and they
19:2 Judah, and was there S four months.
20:31 to smite and kill S of the people, in
Ruth 2:14 "Come here, and eat S bread, and dip your
2:14 satisfied, and she had S left over.
2:16 And also pull out S from the bundles for
1Sam 6:19 And he slew S of the men of Beth-shemesh,
7:2 a long time passed, S twenty years, and all
8:12 commanders of fifties, and S to plow his ground
10:27 But S worthless fellows said, "How can this man
17:18 brothers fare, and bring S token from them."
24:10 in the cave; and S bade me kill you,
2Sam 3:17 of Israel, saying, "For S time past you have
9:3 "Is there not still S one of the house
10:9 the rear, he chose S of the picked men
11:17 fought with Joab; and S of the servants of
11:24 servants from the wall; S of the king's servants
12:18 He may do himself S harm."
17:9 the pits, or in S other place.
17:9 And when S of the people fall at the
17:12 come upon him in S place where he is
23:15 said longingly, "O that S one would give me
1Kgs 14:3 with you ten loaves, S cakes, and a jar
18:5 alive, and not lose S of the animals."
2Kgs 2:7 went, and stood at S distance from them, as
2:16 and cast him upon S mountain or into some
2:16 some mountain or into S valley." And he said,
2:23 up on the way, S small boys came out
4:8 urged him to eat S food.
4:43 shall eat and have S left.'"
4:44 they ate, and had S left, according to the
5:13 commanded you to do S great thing, would you
5:21 And when Naaman saw S one running after him,
7:13 his servants said, "Let S men take five of
9:33 threw her down; and S of her blood spattered
17:25 among them, which killed S of them.
20:18 And S of your own sons, who are born
25:12 of the guard left S of the poorest of
1Chr 4:42 And S of them, five hundred men of the
6:66 And S of the families of the sons of
9:3 And S of the people of Judah, Benjamin, Ephraim,
9:28 S of them had charge of the utensils of
9:32 Also S of their kinsmen of the Kohathites had
11:17 said longingly, "O that S one would give me
12:16 And S of the men of Benjamin and Judah
12:19 S of the men of Manasseh deserted to David
19:10 the rear, he chose S of the picked men
2Chr 11:23 dealt wisely, and distributed S of his sons through
12:7 I will grant them S deliverance, and my wrath
16:10 Asa inflicted cruelties upon S of the people at
17:11 S of the Philistines brought Jehoshaphat presents,
18:2 After S years he went down to Ahab in
19:3 Nevertheless S good is found in you, for you
20:1 Ammonites, and with them S of the Me-unites, came
20:2 S men came and told Jehoshaphat, "A great
21:4 the sword, and also S of the princes of
32:21 house of his god, S of his own sons
34:13 kind of service; and S of the Levites were
Ezra 2:68 S of the heads of families, when they came
2:70 priests, the Levites, and S of the people lived
7:7 of Artaxerxes the king, S of the people of
7:7 people of Israel, and S of the priests and
9:2 For they have taken S of their daughters to
9:9 Persia, to grant us S reviving to set up
Neh 2:10 displeased them greatly that S one had come to
5:5 to be slaves, and S of our daughters have
7:70 Now S of the heads of fathers' houses gave
7:71 And S of the heads of fathers' houses gave
7:73 the gatekeepers, the singers, S of the people, the
11:25 villages, with their fields, S of the people of
13:6 And after S time I asked leave of the
13:19 And I set S of my servants over the
13:25 cursed them and beat S of them and pulled
Tob 5:8 father, "I have found S one to go with
6:16 and lay upon them S of the heart and
Jud 7:18 Dothan; and they sent S of their men toward
10:15 once to his tent; S of us will escort
12:1 table for her with S of his own food
15:12 and blessed her, and S of them performed a
Ps 4:6 that we might see S good!
20:7 S boast of chariots, and some of horses; but
20:7 boast of chariots, and S of horses; but we
107:4 S wandered in desert wastes, finding no way to
107:10 S sat in darkness and in gloom, prisoners in
107:17 S were sick through their sinful ways, and because
107:23 S went down to the sea in ships, doing
Prov 4:17 unless they have made S one stumble.
Eccl 10:20 carry your voice, or S winged creature tell the
Wis 13:14 or makes it like S worthless animal, giving it
19:15 so, but punishment of S sort will come upon
Sir 8:6 he is old, for S of us are growing
10:17 He has removed S of them and destroyed them,
14:18 spreading tree which sheds S and puts forth others,
19:9 not disclose it; for S one has heard you
22:24 from him; but if S harm should happen to
33:9 different seasons and feasts; S of them he exalted
33:9 exalted and hallowed, and S of them he made
33:12 appointed their different ways; S of them he blessed
33:12 blessed and exalted, and S of them he made
33:12 near to himself; but S of them he cursed
37:1 am a friend"; but S friends are friends only
37:4 S companions rejoice in the happiness of a friend,
37:5 S companions help a friend for their stomach's sake,
37:7 counselor praises counsel, but S give counsel in their
41:21 kinsman; of taking away S one's portion or gift,
44:9 There are S of them who have left a
44:10 And there are S who have no memorial, who
48:16 S of them did what was pleasing to God,
Is 39:7 And S of your own sons, who are born
66:21 And S of them also I will take for
Jer 19:1 earthen flask, and take S of the elders of
19:1 of the people and S of the senior priests,
39:10 the land of Judah S of the poor people
44:14 shall not return, except S fugitives."
52:15 guard carried away captive S of the poorest of
52:16 of the guard left S of the poorest of
Bar 6:11 themselves, and even give S of it to the
6:24 will not shine unless S one wipes off the
6:28 likewise their wives preserve S with salt, but give
6:32 before their gods as S do at a funeral
6:33 The priests take S of the clothing of their
Ezek 5:4 again you shall take S, and cast them into
6:8 "Yet I will leave S of you alive.
6:8 have among the nations S who escape the sword,
10:7 the cherubim, and took S of it, and put
16:16 You took S of your garments, and made for
34:12 out his flock when S of his sheep have
43:20 And you shall take S of its blood, and
45:19 The priest shall take S of the blood of
Dan 1:2 into his hand, with S of the vessels of
1:3 chief eunuch, to bring S of the people of
2:41 a divided kingdom; but S of the firmness of
8:10 host of heaven; and S of the host of
8:27 and lay sick for S days; then I rose
11:6 After S years they shall make an alliance, and
11:8 of gold; and for S years he shall refrain
11:13 the former; and after S years he shall come
11:33 captivity and plunder, for S days.

11:35 them with flattery; and S of those who are
12:2 the earth shall awake, S to everlasting life, and
12:2 to everlasting life, and S to shame and everlasting
Amos 2:11 And I raised up S of your sons for
2:11 sons for prophets, and S of your young men
4:11 "I overthrew S of you, as when God overthrew
1Mac 1:13 proposal pleased them, and S of the people eagerly
5:27 and large-- "and S have been shut up
5:67 On that day S priests, who wished to do
6:5 Then S one came to him in Persia and
6:21 But S of the garrison escaped from the siege
6:21 from the siege and S of the ungodly Israelites
6:40 the high hills, and S troops were on the
7:19 deserted to him, and S of the people, and
7:33 S of the priests came out of the sanctuary,
7:33 of the sanctuary, and S of the elders of
8:7 give hostages and surrender S of their best,
10:14 Only in Bethzur did S remain who had forsaken
10:37 Let S of them be stationed in the great
10:37 the king, and let S of them be put
11:23 siege; and he chose S of the elders of
11:23 elders of Israel and S of the priests, and
16:16 his two sons and S of his servants.
16:21 But S one ran ahead and reported to John
2Mac 1:19 of that time took S of the fire of
1:22 this was done and S time had passed and
2:1 being deported to take S of the fire, as
2:6 S of those who followed him came up to
3:10 explained that there were S deposits belonging to
3:11 and orphans, and also S money of Hyrcanus, son
3:19 S of the maidens who were kept indoors ran
3:19 to the gates, and S to the walls, while
3:31 Quickly S of Heliodorus' friends asked Onias to call
3:32 get the notion that S foul play had been
3:38 is about the place S power of God.
4:32 a suitable opportunity, stole S of the gold vessels
4:41 aware of Lysimachus' attack, S picked up stones,
4:41 some picked up stones, S blocks of wood, and
4:42 of them, and killed S, and put them all
8:25 After pursuing them for S distance, they were
8:28 the sabbath they gave S of the spoils to
8:30 and got possession of S exceedingly high strongholds,
8:33 sacred gates, Callisthenes and S others, who had fled
10:20 money-hungry, were bribed by S of those who were
10:20 seventy thousand drachmas let S of them slip away.
11:36 have considered them, send S one promptly, so that
11:37 make haste and send S men, so that we
12:2 But S of the governors in various places, Timothy
12:3 And S men of Joppa did so ungodly a
12:24 and the brothers of S and no consideration would
14:4 palm, and besides these S of the customary olive
Mt 8:30 swine was feeding at S distance from them.
9:3 And behold, S of the scribes said to themselves,
12:38 Then S of the scribes and Pharisees said to
13:4 And as he sowed, S seeds fell along the
13:8 and brought forth grain, S a hundredfold, some sixty,
13:8 grain, some a hundredfold, S sixty, some thirty.
13:8 a hundredfold, some sixty, S thirty.
16:14 And they said, S say John the Baptist, others
16:28 to you, there are S standing here who will
23:33 wise men and scribes, S of whom you will
23:33 kill and crucify, and S you will scourge in
25:8 the wise, 'Give us S of your oil, for
26:67 and struck him; and S slapped him,
27:9 had been set by S of the sons of
27:47 And S of the bystanders hearing it said, "This
28:11 they were going, behold, S of the guard went
28:17 they worshipped him; but S doubted.
Mk 2:1 returned to Caperna-um after S days, it was
2:6 Now S of the scribes were sitting there, questioning
4:4 And as he sowed, S seed fell along the
5:35 from the ruler's house S who said, "Your daughter
6:14 S said, "John the baptizer has been raised from
7:1 together to him, with S of the scribes, who
7:2 Jerusalem, they saw that S of his disciples ate
8:3 on the way; and S of them have come
8:22 And S people brought to him a blind man,
9:1 to you, there are S standing here who will
12:2 to get from them S of the fruit of
12:5 so with many others, S they beat and some
12:5 some they beat and S they killed.
12:13 they sent to him S of the Pharisees and
12:13 of the Pharisees and S of the Herodi-ans, to
14:4 But there were S who said to themselves indignantly,
14:57 And S stood up and bore false witness against
14:65 And S began to spit on him, and to
15:34 And S of the bystanders hearing it said, "Behold,
Lk 1:3 all things closely for S time past, to write
6:1 disciples plucked and ate S heads of grain, rubbing
6:2 But S of the Pharisees said, "Why are you
8:2 with him, and also S women who had been
8:5 and as he sowed, S fell along the path,
8:6 And S fell on the rock; and as it
8:7 And S fell among thorns; and the thorns grew
8:8 And S fell into good soil and grew, and
8:46 But Jesus said, S one touched me; for I
9:7 it was said by S that John had been
9:8 from the dead, by S that Elijah had appeared,
9:27 you truly, there are S standing here who will
11:15 But S of them said, "He casts out demons
11:49 them prophets and apostles, S of whom they will
13:1 There were S present at that very time who
13:23 And S one said to him, "Lord, will those
13:30 And behold, S are last who will be first,
13:30 will be first, and S are first who will
13:31 At that very hour S Pharisees came, and said
16:30 father Abraham; but if S one goes to them
16:31 they be convinced if S one should rise from
18:9 told this parable to S who trusted in themselves
19:39 And S of the Pharisees in the multitude said
20:10 they should give him S of the fruit of
20:27 There came to him S Sadducees, those who say
20:39 And S of the scribes answered, "Teacher, you have
21:5 And as S spoke of the temple, how it
21:16 kinsmen and friends, and S of you they will
22:56 And a little later S one else saw him
23:8 was hoping to see S sign done by him.
23:9 he questioned him at S length; but he made
24:22 Moreover, S women of our company amazed us.
24:24 S of those who were with us went to
Jn 2:8 to them, "Now draw S out, and take it
6:64 But there are S of you that do not
7:12 While S said, "He is a good man," others
7:25 S of the people of Jerusalem therefore said, "Is
7:40 they heard these words, S of the people said,
7:41 But S said, "Is the Christ to come from
7:44 S of them wanted to arrest him, but no
8:6 that they might have S charge to bring against
9:9 S said, "It is he"; others said, "No, but
9:16 S of the Pharisees said, "This man is not
9:40 S of the Pharisees near him heard this, and
11:37 But S of them said, "Could not he who
11:46 believed in him; but S of them went to
12:20 at the feast were S Greeks.
13:29 S thought that, because Judas had the money box,
16:17 S of his disciples said to one another, "What
18:3 band of soldiers and S officers from the chief
21:6 side of the boat, and you will find S
21:10 said to them, "Bring S of the fish that
Acts 5:2 knowledge he kept back S of the proceeds, and
5:15 shadow might fall on S of them.
5:25 And S one came and told them, "The men
5:37 census and drew away S of the people after
6:9 Then S of those who belonged to the synagogue
8:31 "How can I, unless S one guides me?" And
8:34 about himself or about S one else?"
8:36 road they came to S water, and the eunuch
10:23 off with them, and S of the brethren from
10:48 him to remain for S days.
11:20 But there were S of them, men of Cyprus
12:1 laid violent hands upon S who belonged to the
14:4 the city were divided; S sided with the Jews,
14:4 with the Jews, and S with the apostles.
15:1 But S men came down from Judea and were
15:2 Paul and Barnabas and S of the others were
15:5 But S believers who belonged to the party of
15:24 we have heard that S persons from us have
15:33 after they had spent S time, they were sent
15:35 And after S days Paul said to Barnabas, "Come,
16:12 remained in this city S days;
17:4 And S of them were persuaded, and joined Paul
17:5 were jealous, and taking S wicked fellows of the
17:6 they dragged Jason and S of the brethren before
17:18 S also of the Epicurean and Stoic philosophers met
17:18 And S said, "What would this babbler say?" Others
17:20 For you bring S strange things to our ears;
17:28 our being'; as even S of your poets have
17:32 resurrection of the dead, S mocked; but others said,
17:34 But S men joined him and believed, among them
18:23 After spending S time there he departed and went
19:1 There he found S disciples.
19:9 of God; but when S were stubborn and disbelieved,

	19:13	Then S of the itinerant Jewish exorcists undertook
	19:31	would not let him; S of the Asi-archs also,
	19:32	Now S cried one thing, some another; for the
	19:32	some cried one thing, S another; for the assembly
	19:33	S of the crowd prompted Alexander, whom the Jews
	21:10	we were staying for S days, a prophet named
	21:16	And S of the disciples from Caesarea went with
	21:34	S in the crowd shouted one thing, some another;
	21:34	crowd shouted one thing, S another; and as he
	23:9	great clamor arose; and S of the scribes of
	24:1	Ananias came down with S elders and a spokesman,
	24:16	Now after S years I came to bring to
	24:17	But S Jews from Asia–
	24:22	custody but should have S liberty, and that none
	24:23	After S days Felix came with his wife Drusilla,
	25:13	Now when S days had passed, Agrippa the king
	27:1	they delivered Paul and S other prisoners to a
	27:26	have to run on S island."
	27:33	them all to take S food, saying, "Today is
	27:34	urge you to take S food; it will give
	27:36	were encouraged and ate S food themselves.
	28:24	And S were convinced by what he said, while
Rom	1:11	may impart to you S spiritual gift to strengthen
	1:13	that I may reap S harvest among you as
	3:3	What if S were unfaithful?
	3:8	good may come?--as S people slanderously charge
	11:14	jealous, and thus save S of them.
	11:17	But if S of the branches were broken off,
	15:15	But on S points I have written to you
	15:26	been pleased to make S contribution for the poor
1Cor	4:18	S are arrogant, as though I were not coming
	6:11	And such were S of you.
	8:7	But S, through being hitherto accustomed to idols,
	9:7	a flock without getting S of the milk?
	9:22	men, that I might by all means save S
	10:7	not be idolaters as S of them were; as
	10:8	indulge in immorality as S of them did, and
	10:9	to the test, as S of them did and
	10:10	serpents; nor grumble, as S of them did and
	10:28	(But if S one says to you, "This has
	11:30	weak and ill, and S have died.
	14:5	speaks in tongues, unless S one interprets, so that
	14:6	unless I bring you S revelation or knowledge or
	15:6	are still alive, though S have fallen asleep.
	15:12	the dead, how can S of you say that
	15:34	For S have no knowledge of God.
	15:35	But S one will ask, "How are the dead
	15:37	of wheat or of S other grain.
	16:7	I hope to spend S time with you, if
2Cor	2:5	to me, but in S measure--not to put
	3:1	do we need, as S do, letters of recommendation
	7:14	have expressed to him S pride in you, I
	9:4	would be; lest if S Macedonians come with me
	10:2	count on showing against S who suspect us of
	10:12	or compare ourselves with S of those who commend
	11:4	For if S one comes and preaches another Jesus
Gal	1:7	gospel, but there are S who trouble you and
Eph	4:11	gifts were that S should be apostles, S prophets, S
	4:11	prophets, some evangelists, S pastors and teachers,
Phil	1:15	S indeed preach Christ from envy and rivalry, but
2Thes	3:11	For we hear that S of you are living
1Tim	4:1	that in later times S will depart from the
	4:8	bodily training is of S value, godliness is of
	5:4	own family and make S return to their parents;
	5:15	For S have already strayed after Satan.
	5:24	The sins of S men are conspicuous, pointing to
	6:10	through this craving that S have wandered away
	6:21	for by professing it S have missed the mark
2Tim	2:18	They are upsetting the faith of S
	2:20	wood and earthenware, and S for noble use, some
	2:20	some for noble use, S for ignoble.
Philem	1:20	Yes, brother, I want S benefit from you in
Heb	3:4	house is built by S one, but the builder
	4:6	therefore it remains for S to enter it, and
	5:12	be teachers, you need S one to teach you
	10:25	is the habit of S, but encouraging one another,
	11:35	S were tortured, refusing to accept release, that they
	13:2	to strangers, for thereby S have entertained angels
Jas	2:18	But S one will say, "You have faith and
	5:19	from the truth and S one brings him back,
1Pet	3:1	your husbands, so that S, though they do not
	5:8	a roaring lion, seeking S one to devour.
2Pet	3:9	about his promise as S count slowness, but is
	3:16	There are S things in them hard to understand,
2Jn	1:4	rejoiced greatly to find S of your children following
3Jn	1:3	I greatly rejoiced when S of the brethren arrived
Jude	1:4	been secretly gained by S who long ago were
	1:22	And convince S, who doubt;
	1:23	some, who doubt; save S, by snatching them out
	1:23	of the fire; on S have mercy with fear,
Rev	2:10	is about to throw S of you into prison,
	2:14	against you: you have S there who hold the
	2:15	So you also have S who hold the teaching
	2:17	conquers I will give S of the hidden manna,
	2:24	have not learned what S call the deep things

SOMEBODY (2)

Acts	5:36	himself out to be S, and a number of
	8:9	that he himself was S great.

SOMEHOW (5)

Acts	27:12	on the chance that S they could reach Phoenix,
Rom	1:10	my prayers, asking that S by God's will I
1Cor	8:9	this liberty of yours S become a stumbling block
Gal	2:2	among the Gentiles, lest S I should be running
1Thes	3:5	faith, for fear that S the tempter had tempted

SOMETHING (56)

Num	16:30	if the LORD creates S new, and the ground
Judg	14:14	of the eater came S to eat.
	14:14	of the strong came S sweet." And they could
1Sam	20:26	day; for he thought, S has befallen him; he
1Kgs	2:14	he said, "I have S to say to you."
	14:13	him there is found S pleasing to the LORD,
2Kgs	5:20	after him, and get S from him."
Jud	11:6	maidservant, God will accomplish S through you, and
Job	36:2	for I have yet S to say on God's
Ps	17:14	enough; may they leave S over to their babes.
Wis	2:16	considered by him as S base, and he avoids
Sir	13:5	If you own S, he will live with you;
	34:4	And from S false what will be true?
Ezek	1:13	living creatures there was S that looked like burning
	10:1	there appeared above them S like a sapphire, in
	41:21	the holy place was S resembling
Joel	3:4	Are you paying me back for S
Mic	3:5	when they have S to eat, but declare war
2Mac	3:21	There was S pitiable in the prostration of the
Mt	5:23	that your brother has S against you,
	12:6	I tell you, S greater than the temple is
	12:41	of Jonah, and behold, S greater than Jonah is
	12:42	of Solomon, and behold, S greater than Solomon is
	14:16	away; you give them S to eat."
	20:20	and kneeling before him she asked him for S
Mk	5:43	them to give her S to eat.
	6:36	about and buy themselves S to eat."
	6:37	them, "You give them S to eat." And they
Lk	7:40	him, "Simon, I have S to say to you."
	8:55	and he directed that S should be given her
	9:13	them, "You give them S to eat." They said,
	11:31	of Solomon, and behold, S greater than Solomon is
	11:32	of Jonah, and behold, S greater than Jonah is
	11:54	him, to catch at S he might say.
Jn	13:29	that he should give S to the poor.
Acts	3:5	them, expecting to receive S from them.
	9:18	And immediately S like scales fell from his eyes
	10:10	became hungry and desired S to eat; but while
	10:11	the heaven opened, and S descending, like a great
	11:5	I saw a vision, S descending, like a great
	17:21	except telling or hearing S new.
	21:37	tribune, "May I say S to you?" And he
	23:17	tribune; for he has S to tell him."
	23:18	you, as he has S to say to you."
	25:26	him, I may have S to write.
Rom	2:28	nor is true circumcision S external and physical.
	4:2	by works, he has S to boast about, but
1Cor	8:2	imagines that he knows S, he does not yet
	16:2	you is to put S aside and store it
Gal	2:6	were reputed to be S (what they were makes
	6:3	one thinks he is S, when he is nothing,
Heb	8:3	priest also to have S to offer.
	11:40	since God had foreseen S better for us, that
1Pet	4:12	prove you, as though S strange were happening to
3Jn	1:9	I have written S to the church; but Diotrephes,
Rev	8:8	blew his trumpet, and S like a great mountain,

SOMETIME

Jer	28:12	S after the prophet Hananiah had broken the

SOMETIMES (7)

Num	9:20	S the cloud was a few days over the
	9:21	And S the cloud remained from evening until
Eccl	2:21	under the sun, because S a man who has

S

Sir 37:14 For a man's soul S keeps him better informed
Bar 6:10 who loves ornaments; and S the priests secretly take
Heb 10:33 struggle with sufferings, S being publicly exposed to
10:33 abuse and affliction, and S being partners with those

SOMEWHAT

Acts 23:20 were going to inquire S more closely about him.

SOMEWHERE (2)

Heb 2:6 It has been testified S, "What is man that
4:4 For he has S spoken of the seventh day

SON (2,528)

Gen 4:17 the name of his S, Enoch.
4:25 and she bore a S and called his name
4:26 To Seth also a S was born, and he
5:3 the father of a S in his own likeness,
5:28 the father of a S,
9:24 knew what his youngest S had done to him,
11:31 Terah took Abram his S and Lot the son
11:31 son and Lot the S of Haran, his grandson,
11:31 Sarai his daughter-in-law, his S Abram's wife, and
12:5 and Lot his brother's S, and all their possessions
14:12 also took Lot, the S of Abram's brother, who
15:4 your heir; your own S shall be your heir."
16:11 and shall bear a S; you shall call his
16:15 Hagar bore Abram a S; and Abram called the
16:15 the name of his S, whom Hagar bore, Ishmael.
17:16 will give you a S by her; I will
17:19 shall bear you a S, and you shall call
17:23 Abraham took Ishmael his S and all the slaves
17:25 And Ishmael his S was thirteen years old when
17:26 day Abraham and his S Ishmael were circumcised;
18:10 spring, and Sarah your wife shall have a S
18:14 in the spring, and Sarah shall have a S
19:37 The first-born bore a S, and called his name
19:38 younger also bore a S, and called his name
21:2 and bore Abraham a S in his old age
21:3 the name of his S who was born to
21:4 And Abraham circumcised his S Isaac when he was
21:5 years old when his S Isaac was born to
21:7 have borne him a S in his old age."
21:9 But Sarah saw the S of Hagar the Egyptian,
21:9 Abraham, playing with her S Isaac.
21:10 slave woman with her S; for the son of
21:10 her son; for the S of this slave woman
21:10 be heir with my S Isaac."
21:11 very displeasing to Abraham on account of his S
21:13 a nation of the S of the slave woman
22:2 He said, "Take your S, your only son Isaac,
22:2 your son, your only S Isaac, whom you love,
22:3 with him, and his S Isaac; and he cut
22:6 it on Isaac his S; and he took in
22:7 And he said, "Here am I, my S
22:8 himself the lamb for a burnt offering, my S
22:9 and bound Isaac his S, and laid him on
22:10 hand, and took the knife to slay his S
22:12 have not withheld your S, your only son, from
22:12 your son, your only S, from me."
22:13 up as a burnt offering instead of his S
22:16 have not withheld your S, your only son,
22:16 your son, your only S,
23:8 for me Ephron the S of Zohar,
24:3 a wife for my S from the daughters of
24:4 a wife for my S Isaac."
24:5 I then take your S back to the land
24:6 do not take my S back there.
24:7 a wife for my S from there.
24:8 must not take my S back there."
24:15 born to Bethuel the S of Milcah, the wife
24:24 daughter of Bethuel the S of Milcah, whom she
24:36 master's wife bore a S to my master when
24:37 a wife for my S from the daughters of
24:38 a wife for my S
24:40 a wife for my S from my kindred and
24:44 appointed for my master's S
24:47 daughter of Bethuel, Nahor's S, whom Milcah bore
24:48 the daughter of my master's kinsman for his S
24:51 wife of your master's S, as the LORD has
25:6 them away from his S Isaac, eastward to the
25:9 field of Ephron the S of Zohar the Hittite,
25:11 the death of Abraham God blessed Isaac his S
25:12 descendants of Ishmael, Abraham's S, whom Hagar
25:19 of Isaac, Abraham's S: Abraham was the father
27:1 called Esau his older S, and said to him,
27:1 said to him, "My S; and he answered, "Here
27:5 Isaac spoke to his S Esau.
27:6 Rebekah said to her S Jacob, "I heard your
27:8 die.' Now therefore, my S, obey my word as
27:13 be your curse, my S; only obey my word,
27:15 of Esau her older S, which were with her
27:15 on Jacob her younger S;
27:17 the hand of her S Jacob.
27:18 said, "Here I am; who are you, my S
27:20 Isaac said to his S, "How is it that
27:20 that you have found it so quickly, my S
27:21 may feel you, my S, to know whether you
27:21 you are really my S Esau or not."
27:24 "Are you really my S Esau?" He answered, "I
27:25 may eat of my S's game and bless you."
27:26 to him, "Come near and kiss me, my S
27:27 the smell of my S is as the smell
27:31 and eat of his S's game, that you may
27:32 answered, "I am your S, your first-born, Esau."
27:37 What then can I do for you, my S
27:42 of Esau her older S were told to Rebekah;
27:42 called Jacob her younger S, and said to him,
27:43 Now therefore, my S, obey my voice; arise, flee
28:5 Paddan-aram to Laban, the S of Bethuel the
28:9 daughter of Ishmael Abraham's S, the sister of
29:5 you know Laban the S of Nahor?" They said,
29:12 that he was Rebekah's S; and she ran and
29:13 of Jacob his sister's S, he ran to meet
29:32 conceived and bore a S, and she called his
29:33 again and bore a S, and said, "Because the
29:33 has given me this S also"; and she called
29:34 conceived and bore a S, and said, "Now this
29:35 again and bore a S, and said, "This time
30:5 And Bilhah conceived and bore Jacob a S
30:6 and given me a S; therefore she called his
30:7 Bilhah conceived again and bore Jacob a second S
30:10 Then Leah's maid Zilpah bore Jacob a S
30:12 Leah's maid Zilpah bore Jacob a second S
30:14 pray, some of your S's mandrakes."
30:15 you take away my S's mandrakes also?" Rachel said,
30:15 you tonight for your S's mandrakes."
30:16 hired you with my S's mandrakes." So he lay
30:17 and she conceived and bore Jacob a fifth S
30:19 conceived again, and she bore Jacob a sixth S
30:23 conceived and bore a S, and said, "God has
30:24 saying, "May the LORD add to me another S
34:2 and when Shechem the S of Hamor the Hivite,
34:8 "The soul of my S Shechem longs for your
34:18 pleased Hamor and Hamor's S Shechem.
34:20 So Hamor and his S Shechem came to the
34:24 to Hamor and his S Shechem; and every male
34:26 slew Hamor and his S Shechem with the sword,
35:17 "Fear not; for now you will have another S
36:2 daughter of Anah the S of Zibeon the Hivite,
36:10 Esau's sons: Eliphaz the S of Adah the wife
36:10 of Esau, Reuel the S of Basemath the wife
36:12 concubine of Eliphaz, Esau's S; she bore Amalek to
36:14 daughter of Anah the S of Zibeon, Esau's wife:
36:17 sons of Reuel, Esau's S: the chiefs Nahath, Zerah,
36:32 Bela the S of Beor reigned in Edom, the
36:33 died, and Jobab the S of Zerah of Bozrah
36:35 died, and Hadad the S of Bedad, who defeated
36:38 died, and Baal-hanan the S of Achbor reigned in
36:39 Baal-hanan the S of Achbor died, and Hadar reigned
37:3 because he was the S of his old age;
37:32 whether it is your S's robe or not."
37:33 said, "It is my S's robe; a wild beast
37:34 and mourned for his S many days.
37:35 to Sheol to my S, mourning." Thus his father
38:3 conceived and bore a S, and he called his
38:4 conceived and bore a S, and she called his
38:5 again she bore a S, and she called his
38:11 house, till Shelah my S grows up"—for he
38:26 give her to my S Shelah." And he did
42:38 But he said, "My S shall not go down
43:29 brother Benjamin, his mother's S, and said, "Is this
43:29 God be gracious to you, my S
45:9 him, 'Thus says your S Joseph, God has made
45:28 is enough; Joseph my S is still alive; I
46:10 Zohar, and Shaul, the S of a Canaanitish woman.
47:29 die, he called his S Joseph and said to
48:2 told to Jacob, "Your S Joseph has come to
48:19 said, "I know, my S, I know; he also
49:9 from the prey, my S, you have gone up.
50:23 also of Machir the S of Manasseh were born
Ex 1:15 if it is a S, you shall kill him;
1:21 all his people, "Every S that is born to

2:2 conceived and bore a S; and when she saw
2:10 and he became her S; and she named him
2:22 She bore a S, and he called his name
4:22 Israel is my first-born S,
4:23 to you, "Let my S go that he may
4:23 him go, behold, I will slay your first-born S
4:25 and cut off her S's foreskin, and touched Moses'
6:15 Zohar, and Shaul, the S of a Canaanite woman;
6:25 Eleazar, Aaron's S, took to wife one of the
10:2 the hearing of your S and of your son's
10:2 son and of your S's son how I have
10:2 and of your son's S how I have made
13:8 you shall tell your S on that day, 'It
13:14 time to come your S asks you, 'What does
20:10 work, you, or your S, or your daughter, your
21:9 designates her for his S, he shall deal with
21:31 it gores a man's S or daughter, he shall
23:12 have rest, and the S of your bondmaid, and
29:30 The S who is priest in his place shall
31:2 by name Bezalel the S of Uri, son of
31:2 the son of Uri, S of Hur, of the
31:6 with him Oholiab, the S of Ahisamach, of the
32:29 the cost of his S and of his brother,
33:11 his servant Joshua the S of Nun, a young
35:30 by name Bezalel the S of Uri, son of
35:30 the son of Uri, S of Hur, of the
35:34 him and Oholiab the S of Ahisamach of the
38:21 direction of Ithamar the S of Aaron the priest.
38:22 Bezalel the S of Uri, son of Hur, of
38:22 the son of Uri, S of Hur, of the
38:23 him was Oholiab the S of Ahisamach, of the
Lev 12:6 completed, whether for a S or for a daughter,
18:10 the nakedness of your S's daughter or of your
18:15 daughter-in-law; she is your S's wife, you shall not
18:17 shall not take her S's daughter or her daughter's
21:2 mother, his father, his S, his daughter, his brother,
24:10 Now an Israelite woman's S, whose father was an
24:10 and the Israelite woman's S and a man of
24:11 and the Israelite woman's S blasphemed the Name,
Num 1:5 From Reuben, Elizur the S of Shedeur;
1:6 from Simeon, Shelumi-el the S of Zurishaddai;
1:7 from Judah, Nahshon the S of Amminadab;
1:8 from Issachar, Nethanel the S of Zuar;
1:9 from Zebulun, Eliab the S of Helon;
1:10 from Ephraim, Elishama the S of Ammihud, and
1:10 from Manasseh, Gamaliel the S of Pedahzur;
1:11 from Benjamin, Abidan the S of Gideoni;
1:12 from Dan, Ahiezer the S of Ammishaddai;
1:13 from Asher, Pagiel the S of Ochran;
1:14 from Gad, Eliasaph the S of Deuel;
1:15 from Naphtali, Ahira the S of Enan."
2:3 Judah being Nahshon the S of Amminadab,
2:5 Issachar being Nethanel the S of Zuar,
2:7 Zebulun being Eliab the S of Helon,
2:10 Reuben being Elizur the S of Shedeur,
2:12 Simeon being Shelumi-el the S of Zurishaddai,
2:14 Gad being Eliasaph the S of Reuel,
2:18 Ephraim being Elishama the S of Ammihud,
2:20 Manasseh being Gamaliel the S of Pedahzur,
2:22 Benjamin being Abidan the S of Gideoni,
2:25 Dan being Ahiezer the S of Ammishaddai,
2:27 Asher being Pagiel the S of Ochran,
2:29 Naphtali being Ahira the S of Enan,
3:24 west, with Eliasaph, the S of Lael as head
3:30 tabernacle, with Eli-zaphan the S of Uzziel as head
3:32 And Eleazar the S of Aaron the priest was
3:35 Merari was Zuriel the S of Abihail; they were
4:16 "And Eleazar the S of Aaron the priest shall
4:28 oversight of Ithamar the S of Aaron the priest.
4:33 hand of Ithamar the S of Aaron the priest."
7:8 direction of Ithamar the S of Aaron the priest.
7:12 day was Nahshon the S of Amminadab, of the
7:17 offering of Nahshon the S of Amminadab.
7:18 second day Nethanel the S of Zuar, the leader
7:23 offering of Nethanel the S of Zuar.
7:24 third day Eliab the S of Helon, the leader
7:29 offering of Eliab the S of Helon.
7:30 fourth day Elizur the S of Shedeur, the leader
7:35 offering of Elizur the S of Shedeur.
7:36 fifth day Shelumi-el the S of Zurishaddai, the leader
7:41 offering of Shelumi-el the S of Zurishaddai.
7:42 sixth day Eliasaph the S of Deuel, the leader
7:47 offering of Eliasaph the S of Deuel.
7:48 seventh day Elishama the S of Ammihud, the leader
7:53 offering of Elishama the S of Ammihud.
7:54 eighth day Gamaliel the S of Pedahzur, the leader
7:59 offering of Gamaliel the S of Pedahzur.
7:60 ninth day Abidan the S of Gideoni, the leader
7:65 offering of Abidan the S of Gideoni.
7:66 tenth day Ahiezer the S of Ammishaddai, the leader
7:71 offering of Ahiezer the S of Ammishaddai.
7:72 eleventh day Pagiel the S of Ochran, the leader
7:77 offering of Pagiel the S of Ochran.
7:78 twelfth day Ahira the S of Enan, the leader
7:83 offering of Ahira the S of Enan.
10:14 host was Nahshon the S of Amminadab.
10:15 Issachar was Nethanel the S of Zuar.
10:16 Zebulun was Eliab the S of Helon.
10:18 host was Elizur the S of Shedeur.
10:19 Simeon was Shelumi-el the S of Zurishaddai.
10:20 Gad was Eliasaph the S of Deuel.
10:22 host was Elishama the S of Ammihud.
10:23 Manasseh was Gamaliel the S of Pedahzur.
10:24 Benjamin was Abidan the S of Gideoni.
10:25 host was Ahiezer the S of Ammishaddai.
10:26 Asher was Pagiel the S of Ochran.
10:27 Naphtali was Ahira the S of Enan.
10:29 said to Hobab the S of Reuel the Midianite,
11:28 And Joshua the S of Nun, the minister of
13:4 of Reuben, Shammua the S of Zaccur;
13:5 of Simeon, Shaphat the S of Hori;
13:6 of Judah, Caleb the S of Jephunneh;
13:7 of Issachar, Igal the S of Joseph;
13:8 of Ephraim, Hoshea the S of Nun;
13:9 of Benjamin, Palti the S of Raphu;
13:10 of Zebulun, Gaddiel the S of Sodi;
13:11 of Manasseh), Gaddi the S of Susi;
13:12 of Dan, Ammiel the S of Gemalli;
13:13 of Asher, Sethur the S of Michael;
13:14 of Naphtali, Nahbi the S of Vophsi;
13:15 of Gad, Geuel the S of Machi.
13:16 Moses called Hoshea the S of Nun Joshua.
14:6 And Joshua the S of Nun and Caleb the
14:6 Nun and Caleb the S of Jephunneh, who were
14:30 dwell, except Caleb the S of Jephunneh and Joshua
14:30 Jephunneh and Joshua the S of Nun.
14:38 But Joshua the S of Nun and Caleb the
14:38 Nun and Caleb the S of Jephunneh remained alive,
16:1 Now Korah the S of Izhar, son of Kohath,
16:1 the son of Izhar, S of Kohath, son of
16:1 Izhar, son of Kohath, S of Levi, and Dathan
16:1 Eliab, and On the S of Peleth, sons of
16:37 Moses, "Tell Eleazar the S of Aaron the priest
20:25 Aaron and Eleazar his S, and bring them up
20:26 them upon Eleazar his S; and Aaron shall be
20:28 them upon Eleazar his S; and Aaron died there
22:2 And Balak the S of Zippor saw all that
22:4 So Balak the S of Zippor, who was king
22:5 messengers to Balaam the S of Beor at Pethor,
22:10 to God, "Balak the S of Zippor, king of
22:16 "Thus says Balak the S of Zippor: 'Let nothing
23:18 hearken to me, O S of Zippor:
23:19 should lie, or a S of man, that he
24:3 oracle of Balaam the S of Beor, the oracle
24:15 oracle of Balaam the S of Beor, the oracle
25:7 When Phinehas the S of Eleazar, son of Aaron
25:7 the son of Eleazar, S of Aaron the priest,
25:11 to Moses, "Phinehas the S of Eleazar, son of
25:11 the son of Eleazar, S of Aaron the priest,
25:14 woman, was Zimri the S of Salu, head of
26:1 and to Eleazar the S of Aaron, the priest,
26:33 Now Zelophehad the S of Hepher had no sons,
26:65 them, except Caleb the S of Jephunneh and Joshua
26:65 Jephunneh and Joshua the S of Nun.
27:1 daughters of Zelophehad the S of Hepher, son of
27:1 the son of Hepher, S of Gilead, son of
27:1 Hepher, son of Gilead, S of Machir, son of
27:1 Gilead, son of Machir, S of Manasseh, from the
27:1 families of Manasseh the S of Joseph.
27:4 away from his family, because he had no S
27:8 dies, and has no S, then you shall cause
27:18 Moses, "Take Joshua the S of Nun, a man
31:6 together with Phinehas the S of Eleazar the priest,
31:8 also slew Balaam the S of Beor with the
32:12 none except Caleb the S of Jephunneh the Kenizzite
32:12 Kenizzite and Joshua the S of Nun, for they
32:28 and to Joshua the S of Nun, and to
32:33 half-tribe of Manasseh the S of Joseph, the kingdom
32:39 sons of Machir the S of Manasseh went to
32:40 Gilead to Machir the S of Manasseh, and he
32:41 And Jair the S of Manasseh went and took
34:17 priest and Joshua the S of Nun.

34:19 of Judah, Caleb the S of Jephunneh.
34:20 of Simeon, Shemuel the S of Ammihud.
34:21 of Benjamin, Elidad the S of Chislon.
34:22 a leader, Bukki the S of Jogli.
34:23 a leader, Hanniel the S of Ephod.
34:24 a leader, Kemuel the S of Shiphtan.
34:25 a leader, Eli-zaphan the S of Parnach.
34:26 a leader, Paltiel the S of Azzan.
34:27 a leader, Ahihud the S of Shelomi.
34:28 a leader, Pedahel the S of Ammihud.
36:1 sons of Gilead the S of Machir, son of
36:1 the son of Machir, S of Manasseh, of the
36:12 sons of Manasseh the S of Joseph, and their
Deut 1:31 a man bears his S, in all the way
1:36 fathers, except Caleb the S of Jephunneh; he shall
1:38 in there; Joshua the S of Nun, who stands
5:14 work, you, or your S, or your daughter, or
6:2 God, you and your S and your son's son,
6:2 your son and your S's son, by keeping all
6:2 son and your son's S, by keeping all his
6:20 "When your S asks you in time to come,
6:21 shall say to your S, 'We were Pharaoh's slaves
8:5 a man disciplines his S, the LORD your God
10:6 was buried; and his S Eleazar ministered as priest
11:6 the sons of Eliab, S of Reuben; how the
12:18 choose, you and your S and your daughter, your
13:6 "If your brother, the S of your mother, or
13:6 your mother, or your S, or your daughter, or
16:11 God, you and your S and your daughter, your
16:14 feast, you and your S and your daughter, your
18:10 one who burns his S or his daughter as
21:15 and if the first-born S is hers that is
21:16 may not treat the S of the loved as
21:16 in preference to the S of the disliked, who
21:17 acknowledge the first-born, the S of the disliked, by
21:18 a stubborn and rebellious S, who will not obey
21:20 his city, 'This our S is stubborn and rebellious,
23:4 against you Balaam the S of Beor from Pethor
25:5 dies and has no S, the wife of the
25:6 And the first S whom she bears shall succeed
28:56 her bosom, to her S and to her daughter,
31:23 LORD commissioned Joshua the S of Nun and said,
32:44 he and Joshua the S of Nun.
34:9 And Joshua the S of Nun was full of
Josh 1:1 said to Joshua the S of Nun, Moses' minister,
2:1 And Joshua the S of Nun sent two men
2:23 came to Joshua the S of Nun; and they
6:6 So Joshua the S of Nun called the priests
6:26 cost of his youngest S shall he set up
7:1 things; for Achan the S of Carmi, son of
7:1 the son of Carmi, S of Zabdi, son of
7:1 Carmi, son of Zabdi, S of Zerah, of the
7:18 man, and Achan the S of Carmi, son of
7:18 the son of Carmi, S of Zabdi, son of
7:18 Carmi, son of Zabdi, S of Zerah, of the
7:19 said to Achan, "My S, give glory to the
7:24 him took Achan the S of Zerah, and the
13:22 Balaam also, the S of Beor, the soothsayer, the
13:31 people of Machir the S of Manasseh for the
14:1 priest, and Joshua the S of Nun, and the
14:6 Gilgal; and Caleb the S of Jephunneh the Kenizzite
14:13 Hebron to Caleb the S of Jephunneh for an
14:14 inheritance of Caleb the S of Jephunneh the
15:6 stone of Bohan the S of Reuben;
15:8 the valley of the S of Hinnom at the
15:13 gave to Caleb the S of Jephunneh a portion
15:17 And Othni-el the S of Kenaz, the brother of
17:2 descendants of Manasseh the S of Joseph, by their
17:3 Now Zelophehad the S of Hepher, son of Gilead,
17:3 the son of Hepher, S of Gilead, son of
17:3 Hepher, son of Gilead, S of Machir, son of
17:3 Gilead, son of Machir, S of Manasseh, had no
17:4 priest and Joshua the S of Nun and the
18:16 the valley of the S of Hinnom, which is
18:17 Stone of Bohan the S of Reuben;
19:49 them to Joshua the S of Nun.
19:51 priest and Joshua the S of Nun and the
21:1 and to Joshua the S of Nun and to
21:12 given to Caleb the S of Jephunneh as his
22:13 of Gilead, Phinehas the S of Eleazar the priest,
22:20 Did not Achan the S of Zerah break faith
22:31 And Phinehas the S of Eleazar the priest said
22:32 Then Phinehas the S of Eleazar the priest, and
24:9 Then Balak the S of Zippor, king of Moab,
24:9 and invited Balaam the S of Beor to curse
24:29 these things Joshua the S of Nun, the servant
24:33 And Eleazar the S of Aaron died; and they
24:33 town of Phinehas his S, which had been given
Judg 1:13 And Othni-el the S of Kenaz, Caleb's younger brother,
2:8 And Joshua the S of Nun, the servant of
3:9 delivered them, Othni-el the S of Kenaz, Caleb's
3:11 Then Othni-el the S of Kenaz died.
3:15 a deliverer, Ehud, the S of Gera, the Benjaminite,
3:31 him was Shamgar the S of Anath, who killed
4:6 and summoned Barak the S of Abino-am from
4:12 told that Barak the S of Abino-am had gone
5:1 Deborah and Barak the S of Abino-am on that
5:6 the days of Shamgar, S of Anath, in the
5:12 away your captives, O S of Abino-am.
6:11 the Abiezrite, as his S Gideon was beating out
6:29 they said, "Gideon the S of Joash has done
6:30 Joash, "Bring out your S, that he may die,
7:14 sword of Gideon the S of Joash, a man
8:13 Then Gideon the S of Joash returned from the
8:22 us, you and your S and your grandson also;
8:23 over you, and my S will not rule over
8:29 Jerubbaal the S of Joash went and dwelt in
8:31 also bore him a S, and he called his
8:32 And Gideon the S of Joash died in a
9:1 Now Abimelech the S of Jerubbaal went to
9:5 but Jotham the youngest S of Jerubbaal was left,
9:18 have made Abimelech, the S of his maidservant, king
9:26 And Gaal the S of Ebed moved into Shechem
9:28 And Gaal the S of Ebed said, "Who is
9:28 Did not the S of Jerubbaal and Zebul his
9:30 words of Gaal the S of Ebed, his anger
9:31 saying, "Behold, Gaal the S of Ebed and his
9:35 And Gaal the S of Ebed went out and
9:57 curse of Jotham the S of Jerubbaal.
10:1 deliver Israel Tola the S of Puah, son of
10:1 the son of Puah, S of Dodo, a man
11:1 but he was the S of a harlot.
11:2 for you are the S of another woman."
11:25 better than Balak the S of Zippor, king of
11:34 her he had neither S nor daughter.
12:13 After him Abdon the S of Hillel the Pirathonite
12:15 Then Abdon the S of Hillel the Pirathonite died,
13:3 children; but you shall conceive and bear a S
13:5 for lo, you shall conceive and bear a S
13:7 conceive and bear a S; so then drink no
13:24 the woman bore a S, and called his name
17:2 said, "Blessed be my S by the LORD."
17:3 my hand for my S, to make a graven
18:30 themselves; and Jonathan the S of Gershom, son of
18:30 the son of Gershom, S of Moses, and his
20:28 days, and Phinehas the S of Eleazar, son of
20:28 the son of Eleazar, S of Aaron, ministered before
Ruth 4:13 LORD gave her conception, and she bore a S
4:17 a name, saying, "A S has been born to
1Sam 1:1 name was Elkanah the S of Jeroham, son of
1:1 the son of Jeroham, S of Elihu, son of
1:1 Jeroham, son of Elihu, S of Tohu, son of
1:1 Elihu, son of Tohu, S of Zuph, an Ephraimite.
1:11 to thy maidservant a S, then I will give
1:20 conceived and bore a S, and she called his
1:23 remained and nursed her S, until she weaned him.
3:6 did not call, my S; lie down again."
3:16 But Eli called Samuel and said, "Samuel, my S
4:16 And he said, "How did it go, my S
4:20 her, "Fear not, for you have borne a S
7:1 and they consecrated his S, Eleazar, to have charge
8:2 name of his first-born S was Joel, and the
9:1 name was Kish, the S of Abiel, son of
9:1 the son of Abiel, S of Zeror, son of
9:1 Abiel, son of Zeror, S of Becorath, son of
9:1 Zeror, son of Becorath, S of Aphiah, a Benjaminite,
9:2 and he had a S whose name was Saul,
9:3 said to Saul his S, "Take one of the
10:2 I do about my S
10:11 has come over the S of Kish?
10:21 man, and Saul the S of Kish was taken
13:16 Saul, and Jonathan his S, and the people who
13:22 Saul and Jonathan his S had them.
14:1 One day Jonathan the S of Saul said to
14:3 men, and Ahijah the S of Ahitub, Ichabod's brother,
14:3 of Ahitub, Ichabod's brother, S of Phinehas, son of
14:3 brother, son of Phinehas, S of Eli, the priest
14:39 be in Jonathan my S, he shall surely die."
14:40 I and Jonathan my S will be on the
14:41 or in Jonathan my S, O LORD, God of
14:42 between me and my S Jonathan." And Jonathan was
14:50 army was Abner the S of Ner, Saul's uncle;

S

14:51 of Abner was the S of Abiel.
16:18 I have seen a S of Jesse the Bethlehemite,
16:19 "Send me David your S, who is with the
16:20 them by David his S to Saul.
17:12 Now David was the S of an Ephrathite of
17:17 said to David his S, "Take for your brothers
17:55 the army, "Abner, whose S is this youth?" And
17:56 king said, "Inquire whose S the stripling is."
17:58 said to him, "Whose S are you, young man?"
17:58 answered, "I am the S of your servant Jesse
19:1 spoke to Jonathan his S and to all his
19:1 But Jonathan, Saul's S, delighted much in David.
20:27 said to Jonathan his S, "Why has not the
20:27 "Why has not the S of Jesse come to
20:30 said to him, "You S of a perverse, rebellious
20:30 you have chosen the S of Jesse to your
20:31 as long as the S of Jesse lives upon
22:7 you Benjaminites; will the S of Jesse give every
22:8 to me when my S makes a league with
22:8 a league with the S of Jesse, none of
22:8 to me that my S has stirred up my
22:9 Saul, "I saw the S of Jesse coming to
22:9 Nob, to Ahimelech the S of Ahitub,
22:11 Ahimelech the priest, the S of Ahitub, and all
22:12 Saul said, "Hear now, S of Ahitub." And he
22:13 me, you and the S of Jesse, in that
22:20 sons of Ahimelech the S of Ahitub, named Abiathar,
23:6 When Abiathar the S of Ahimelech fled to David
23:16 And Jonathan, Saul's S, rose, and went to David
24:16 this your voice, my S David?" And Saul lifted
25:8 servants and to your S David.'"
25:10 Who is the S of Jesse?
25:44 wife, to Palti the S of Laish, who was
26:5 lay, with Abner the S of Ner, the commander
26:6 Joab's brother Abishai the S of Zeruiah, "Who will
26:14 and to Abner the S of Ner, saying, "Will
26:17 this your voice, my S David?" And David said,
26:21 done wrong; return, my S David, for I will
26:25 "Blessed be you, my S David!
27:2 him, to Achish the S of Maoch, king of
30:7 Abiathar the priest, the S of Ahimelech, "Bring me
2Sam 1:4 and Saul and his S Jonathan are also dead."
1:5 that Saul and his S Jonathan are dead?"
1:12 and for Jonathan his S and for the people
1:13 answered, "I am the S of a sojourner, an
1:17 Saul and Jonathan his S,
2:8 Now Abner the S of Ner, commander of Saul's
2:8 had taken Ish-bosheth the S of Saul, and brought
2:10 Ish-bosheth, Saul's S, was forty years old when he
2:12 Abner the S of Ner, and the servants of
2:12 servants of Ish-bosheth the S of Saul, went out
2:13 And Joab the S of Zeruiah, and the servants
2:15 Benjamin and Ish-bosheth the S of Saul, and twelve
3:3 the third, Absalom the S of Maacah the daughter
3:4 the fourth, Adonijah the S of Haggith; and the
3:4 the fifth, Shephatiah the S of Abital;
3:14 messengers to Ish-bosheth Saul's S, saying, "Give me
3:15 her husband Paltiel the S of Laish.
3:23 told Joab, "Abner the S of Ner came to
3:25 know that Abner the S of Ner came to
3:28 blood of Abner the S of Ner.
3:37 to slay Abner the S of Ner.
4:1 When Ish-bosheth, Saul's S, heard that Abner had
4:2 Now Saul's S had two men who were captains
4:4 Jonathan, the S of Saul, had a son who
4:4 of Saul, had a S who was crippled in
4:8 head of Ish-bosheth, the S of Saul, your enemy,
7:14 be his father, and he shall be my S
8:3 also defeated Hadadezer the S of Rehob, king of
8:10 Hadadezer, Toi sent his S Joram to King David,
8:12 spoil of Hadadezer the S of Rehob, king of
8:16 And Joab the S of Zeruiah was over the
8:16 and Jehoshaphat the S of Ahilud was recorder;
8:17 recorder; and Zadok the S of Ahitub and Ahimelech
8:17 and Ahimelech the S of Abiathar were priests;
8:18 secretary; and Benaiah the S of Jehoiada was over
9:3 "There is still a S of Jonathan; he is
9:4 house of Machir the S of Ammiel, at Lo-debar."
9:5 house of Machir the S of Ammiel, at Lo-debar.
9:6 And Mephibosheth the S of Jonathan, son of Saul,
9:6 the son of Jonathan, S of Saul, came to
9:9 his house I have given to your master's S
9:10 produce, that your master's S may have bread to
9:10 but Mephibosheth your master's S shall always eat
9:12 Mephibosheth had a young S, whose name was
10:1 died, and Hanun his S reigned in his stead.
10:2 loyally with Hanun the S of Nahash, as his
11:21 Who killed Abimelech the S of Jerubbesheth?
11:27 she became his wife, and bore him a S
12:24 and she bore a S, and he called his
13:1 Now Absalom, David's S, had a beautiful sister,
13:1 a time Amnon, David's S, loved her.
13:3 name was Jonadab, the S of Shimeah, David's
13:4 said to him, "O S of the king, why
13:25 to Absalom, "No, my S, let us not all
13:32 But Jonadab the S of Shimeah, David's brother, said,
13:37 went to Talmai the S of Ammihud, king of
13:37 David mourned for his S day after day.
14:1 Now Joab the S of Zeruiah perceived that the
14:11 no more, and my S be not destroyed." He
14:11 one hair of your S shall fall to the
14:16 destroy me and my S together from the heritage
15:27 two sons, Ahima-az your S, and Jonathan the son
15:27 son, and Jonathan the S of Abiathar.
15:36 Ahima-az, Zadok's S, and Jonathan, Abiathar's son;
15:36 son, and Jonathan, Abiathar's S; and by them you
16:3 the king said, "And where is your master's S
16:5 name was Shimei, the S of Gera; and as
16:8 the hand of your S Absalom.
16:9 Then Abishai the S of Zeruiah said to the
16:11 servants, "Behold, my own S seeks my life; how
16:19 Should it not be his S
17:25 Amasa was the S of a man named Ithra
17:27 to Mahanaim, Shobi the S of Nahash from Rabbah
17:27 and Machir the S of Ammiel from Lo-debar,
18:2 command of Abishai the S of Zeruiah, Joab's brother,
18:12 hand against the king's S; for in our hearing
18:18 said, "I have no S to keep my name
18:19 Then said Ahima-az the S of Zadok, "Let me
18:20 tidings, because the king's S is dead."
18:22 Then Ahima-az the S of Zadok said again to
18:22 will you run, my S, seeing that you will
18:27 running of Ahima-az the S of Zadok." And the
18:33 he said, "O my S Absalom, my son, my
18:33 my son Absalom, my S, my son Absalom!
18:33 Absalom, my son, my S Absalom!
18:33 you, O Absalom, my S, my son!"
18:33 instead of you, O Absalom, my son, my S
19:2 that day, "The king is grieving for his S
19:4 loud voice, "O my S Absalom, O Absalom, my
19:4 Absalom, O Absalom, my S, my son!"
19:4 my son Absalom, O Absalom, my son, my S
19:16 And Shimei the S of Gera, the Benjaminite, from
19:18 And Shimei the S of Gera fell down before
19:21 Abishai the S of Zeruiah answered, "Shall not
19:24 And Mephibosheth the S of Saul came down to
20:1 name was Sheba, the S of Bichri, a Benjaminite;
20:1 no inheritance in the S of Jesse; every man
20:2 and followed Sheba the S of Bichri; but the
20:6 Abishai, "Now Sheba the S of Bichri will do
20:7 to pursue Sheba the S of Bichri.
20:10 brother pursued Sheba the S of Bichri.
20:13 to pursue Sheba the S of Bichri.
20:21 Ephraim, called Sheba the S of Bichri, has lifted
20:22 head of Sheba the S of Bichri, and threw
20:23 Israel; and Benaiah the S of Jehoiada was in
20:24 labor; and Jehoshaphat the S of Ahilud was the
21:7 spared Mephibosheth, the S of Saul's son Jonathan,
21:7 the son of Saul's S Jonathan, because of the
21:7 David and Jonathan the S of Saul.
21:8 bore to Adriel the S of Barzillai the Meholathite;
21:12 the bones of his S Jonathan from the men
21:13 the bones of his S Jonathan; and they gathered
21:14 of Saul and his S Jonathan in the land
21:17 But Abishai the S of Zeruiah came to his
21:19 Gob; and Elhanan the S of Jaareoregim, the
21:21 taunted Israel, Jonathan the S of Shimei, David's
23:1 oracle of David, the S of Jesse, the oracle
23:9 men was Eleazar the S of Dodo, son of
23:9 the son of Dodo, S of Ahohi.
23:11 him was Shammah, the S of Agee the Hararite.
23:18 brother of Joab, the S of Zeruiah, was chief
23:20 And Benaiah the S of Jehoiada was a valiant
23:22 things did Benaiah the S of Jehoiada, and won
23:24 the thirty; Elhanan the S of Dodo of Bethlehem,
23:26 the Paltite, Ira the S of Ikkesh of Tekoa,
23:29 of Netophah, Heleb the S of Baanah of Netophah,
23:29 of Netophah, Ittai the S of Ribai of Gibe-ah
23:33 the Hararite, Ahiam the S of Sharar the Hararite,
23:34 the Hararite, Eliphelet the S of Ahasbai of Maacah,
23:34 of Maacah, Eliam the S of Ahithophel of Gilo,
23:36 the Arbite, Igal the S of Nathan of Zobah,

23:37 armor-bearer of Joab the S of Zeruiah,
1Kgs 1:5 Now Adonijah the S of Haggith exalted himself,
1:7 conferred with Joab the S of Zeruiah and with
1:8 priest, and Benaiah the S of Jehoiada, and Nathan
1:11 heard that Adonijah the S of Haggith has become
1:12 the life of your S Solomon.
1:13 maidservant, saying, "Solomon your S shall reign
1:17 God, saying, 'Solomon your S shall reign after me,
1:21 that I and my S Solomon will be counted
1:26 priest, and Benaiah the S of Jehoiada, and your
1:30 Israel, saying, 'Solomon your S shall reign after me,
1:32 prophet, and Benaiah the S of Jehoiada." So they
1:33 and cause Solomon my S to ride on my
1:36 And Benaiah the S of Jehoiada answered the king,
1:38 prophet, and Benaiah the S of Jehoiada, and the
1:42 speaking, behold, Jonathan the S of Abiathar the
1:44 prophet, and Benaiah the S of Jehoiada, and the
2:1 he charged Solomon his S, saying,
2:5 also what Joab the S of Zeruiah did to
2:5 of Israel, Abner the S of Ner, and Amasa
2:5 Ner, and Amasa the S of Jether, whom he
2:8 with you Shimei the S of Gera, the Benjaminite
2:13 Then Adonijah the S of Haggith came to Bathsheba
2:22 priest and Joab the S of Zeruiah."
2:25 Solomon sent Benaiah the S of Jehoiada; and he
2:29 sent Benaiah the S of Jehoiada, saying, "Go,
2:32 than himself, Abner the S of Ner, commander of
2:32 Israel, and Amasa the S of Jether, commander of
2:34 Then Benaiah the S of Jehoiada went up, and
2:35 king put Benaiah the S of Jehoiada over the
2:39 ran away to Achish, S of Maacah, king of
2:46 king commanded Benaiah the S of Jehoiada; and he
3:6 hast given him a S to sit on his
3:19 And this woman's S died in the night, because
3:20 midnight, and took my S from beside me, while
3:20 and laid her dead S in my bosom.
3:23 says, 'This is my S that is alive, and
3:23 is alive, and your S is dead'; and the
3:23 says, 'No; but your S is dead, and my
3:23 is dead, and my S is the living one.'"
3:26 Then the woman whose S was alive said to
3:26 heart yearned for her S, "Oh, my lord, give
4:2 high officials: Azariah the S of Zadok was the
4:3 Jehoshaphat the S of Ahilud was recorder;
4:4 was recorder; Benaiah the S of Jehoiada was in
4:5 were priests; Azariah the S of Nathan was over
4:5 the officers; Zabud the S of Nathan was priest
4:6 palace; and Adoniram the S of Abda was in
4:12 his wife); Baana the S of Ahilud, in Taanach,
4:13 villages of Jair the S of Manasseh, which are
4:14 bronze bars); Ahinadab the S of Iddo, in Mahanaim;
4:16 his wife); Baana the S of Hushai, in Asher
4:17 Bealoth; Jehoshaphat the S of Paruah, in Issachar;
4:18 in Issachar; Shimei the S of Ela, in Benjamin;
4:19 in Benjamin; Geber the S of Uri, in the
5:5 David my father, 'Your S, whom I will set
5:7 to David a wise S to be over this
7:14 He was the S of a widow of the
8:19 the house, but your S who shall be born
11:12 tear it out of the hand of your S
11:13 one tribe to your S, for the sake of
11:20 bore him Genubath his S, whom Tahpenes weaned in
11:23 to him, Rezon the S of Eliada, who had
11:26 Jeroboam the S of Nebat, an Ephraimite of Zeredah,
11:35 kingdom out of his S's hand, and will give
11:36 Yet to his S I will give one tribe,
11:43 father; and Rehoboam his S reigned in his stead.
12:2 And when Jeroboam the S of Nebat heard of
12:15 Shilonite to Jeroboam the S of Nebat.
12:16 no inheritance in the S of Jesse.
12:21 kingdom to Rehoboam the S of Solomon.
12:23 "Say to Rehoboam the S of Solomon, king of
13:2 the LORD: 'Behold, a S shall be born to
14:1 that time Abijah the S of Jeroboam fell sick.
14:5 of you concerning her S; for he is sick.
14:20 fathers, and Nadab his S reigned in his stead.
14:21 Now Rehoboam the S of Solomon reigned in Judah.
14:31 And Abijam his S reigned in his stead.
15:1 of King Jeroboam the S of Nebat, Abijam began
15:4 Jerusalem, setting up his S after him, and
15:8 And Asa his S reigned in his stead.
15:18 them to Ben-hadad the S of Tabrimmon, the son
15:18 son of Tabrimmon, the S of Hezi-on, king of
15:24 father; and Jehoshaphat his S reigned in his stead.
15:25 Nadab the S of Jeroboam began to reign over
15:27 Baasha the S of Ahijah, of the house of
15:33 of Judah, Baasha the S of Ahijah began to
16:1 came to Jehu the S of Hanani against Baasha,
16:3 house of Jeroboam the S of Nebat.
16:6 Tirzah; and Elah his S reigned in his stead.
16:7 the prophet Jehu the S of Hanani against Baasha
16:8 of Judah, Elah the S of Baasha began to
16:13 sins of Elah his S which they sinned, and
16:21 people followed Tibni the S of Ginath, to make
16:22 who followed Tibni the S of Ginath; so Tibni
16:26 way of Jeroboam the S of Nebat, and in
16:28 Samaria; and Ahab his S reigned in his stead.
16:29 of Judah, Ahab the S of Omri began to
16:29 Israel, and Ahab the S of Omri reigned over
16:30 And Ahab the S of Omri did evil in
16:31 sins of Jeroboam the S of Nebat, he took
16:34 cost of his youngest S Segub, according to the
16:34 spoke by Joshua the S of Nun.
17:12 for myself and my S, that we may eat
17:13 me, and afterward make for yourself and your S
17:17 After this the S of the woman, the mistress
17:18 remembrance, and to cause the death of my S
17:19 And he said to her, "Give me your S
17:20 widow with whom I sojourn, by slaying her S
17:23 Elijah said, "See, your S lives."
19:16 Syria; and Jehu the S of Nimshi you shall
19:16 Israel; and Elisha the S of Shaphat of Abel-meholah
19:19 and found Elisha the S of Shaphat, who was
21:22 house of Jeroboam the S of Nebat, and like
21:22 house of Baasha the S of Ahijah, for the
21:29 days; but in his S's days I will bring
22:8 the LORD, Micaiah the S of Imlah; but I
22:9 "Bring quickly Micaiah the S of Imlah."
22:11 And Zedekiah the S of Chenaanah made for himself
22:24 Then Zedekiah the S of Chenaanah came near and
22:26 to Joash the king's S;
22:40 fathers; and Ahaziah his S reigned in his stead.
22:41 Jehoshaphat the S of Asa began to reign over
22:49 Then Ahaziah the S of Ahab said to Jehoshaphat,
22:50 father; and Jehoram his S reigned in his stead.
22:51 Ahaziah the S of Ahab began to reign over
22:52 way of Jeroboam the S of Nebat, who made
2Kgs 1:17 year of Jehoram the S of Jehoshaphat, king of
1:17 king of Judah, because Ahaziah had no S
3:1 of Judah, Jehoram the S of Ahab became king
3:3 sin of Jeroboam the S of Nebat, which he
3:11 servants answered, "Elisha the S of Shaphat is here,
3:27 he took his eldest S who was to reign
4:6 she said to her S, "Bring me another vessel."
4:14 "Well, she has no S, and her husband is
4:16 the time comes round, you shall embrace a S
4:17 and she bore a S about that time the
4:28 said, "Did I ask my lord for a S
4:36 came to him, he said, "Take up your S
4:37 she took up her S and went out.
6:28 to me, 'Give your S, that we may eat
6:28 we will eat my S tomorrow.'
6:29 So we boiled my S, and ate him.
6:29 to her, 'Give your S, that we may eat
6:29 may eat him'; but she has hidden her S
6:31 head of Elisha the S of Shaphat remains on
8:1 to the woman whose S he had restored to
8:5 behold, the woman whose S he had restored to
8:5 and here is her S whom Elisha restored to
8:9 him, he said, "Your S Ben-hadad king of Syria
8:16 year of Joram the S of Ahab, king of
8:16 of Israel, Jehoram the S of Jehoshaphat, king of
8:24 David; and Ahaziah his S reigned in his stead.
8:25 year of Joram the S of Ahab, king of
8:25 of Israel, Ahaziah the S of Jehoram, king of
8:28 went with Joram the S of Ahab to make
8:29 And Ahaziah the S of Jehoram king of Judah
8:29 to see Joram the S of Ahab in Jezreel,
9:2 there for Jehu the S of Jehoshaphat, son of
9:2 the son of Jehoshaphat, S of Nimshi; and go
9:9 house of Jeroboam the S of Nebat, and like
9:9 house of Baasha the S of Ahijah.
9:14 Thus Jehu the S of Jehoshaphat the son of
9:14 son of Jehoshaphat the S of Nimshi conspired
9:20 driving of Jehu the S of Nimshi; for he
9:29 year of Joram the S of Ahab, Ahaziah began
10:15 he met Jehonadab the S of Rechab coming to
10:23 Baal with Jehonadab the S of Rechab; and he
10:29 sins of Jeroboam the S of Nebat, which he
10:35 And Jehoahaz his S reigned in his stead.
11:1 Ahaziah saw that her S was dead, she arose
11:2 Ahaziah, took Joash the S of Ahaziah, and stole

11:4 the LORD, and he showed them the king's S
11:12 brought out the king's S, and put the crown
12:21 It was Jozacar the S of Shimeath and Jehozabad
12:21 and Jehozabad the S of Shomer, his servants,
12:21 David, and Amaziah his S reigned in his stead.
13:1 year of Joash the S of Ahaziah, king of
13:1 of Judah, Jehoahaz the S of Jehu began to
13:2 sins of Jeroboam the S of Nebat, which he
13:3 hand of Ben-hadad the S of Hazael.
13:9 Samaria; and Joash his S reigned in his stead.
13:10 of Judah Jehoash the S of Jehoahaz began to
13:11 sins of Jeroboam the S of Nebat, which he
13:24 Syria died, Ben-hadad his S became king in his
13:25 Then Jehoash the S of Jehoahaz took again from
13:25 again from Ben-hadad the S of Hazael the cities
14:1 year of Joash the S of Joahaz, king of
14:1 of Israel, Amaziah the S of Joash, king of
14:8 messengers to Jehoash the S of Jehoahaz, son of
14:8 the son of Jehoahaz, S of Jehu, king of
14:9 your daughter to my S for a wife'; and
14:13 king of Judah, the S of Jehoash, son of
14:13 the son of Jehoash, S of Ahaziah, at Beth-shemesh,
14:16 Israel; and Jeroboam his S reigned in his stead.
14:17 Amaziah the S of Joash, king of Judah, lived
14:17 the death of Jehoash S of Jehoahaz, king of
14:23 year of Amaziah the S of Joash, king of
14:23 of Judah, Jeroboam the S of Joash, king of
14:24 sins of Jeroboam the S of Nebat, which he
14:25 his servant Jonah the S of Amittai, the prophet,
14:27 hand of Jeroboam the S of Joash.
14:29 Israel, and Zechariah his S reigned in his stead.
15:1 of Israel Azariah the S of Amaziah, king of
15:5 And Jotham the king's S was over the household,
15:7 David, and Jotham his S reigned in his stead.
15:8 of Judah Zechariah the S of Jeroboam reigned over
15:9 sins of Jeroboam the S of Nebat, which he
15:10 Shallum the S of Jabesh conspired against him, and
15:13 to pass.) Shallum the S of Jabesh began to
15:14 Then Menahem the S of Gadi came up from
15:14 struck down Shallum the S of Jabesh in Samaria
15:17 of Judah Menahem the S of Gadi began to
15:18 sins of Jeroboam the S of Nebat, which he
15:22 fathers, and Pekahiah his S reigned in his stead.
15:23 of Judah Pekahiah the S of Menahem began to
15:24 sins of Jeroboam the S of Nebat, which he
15:25 And Pekah the S of Remaliah, his captain, conspired
15:27 of Judah Pekah the S of Remaliah began to
15:28 sins of Jeroboam the S of Nebat, which he
15:30 Then Hoshea the S of Elah made a conspiracy
15:30 conspiracy against Pekah the S of Remaliah, and
15:30 year of Jotham the S of Uzziah.
15:32 year of Pekah the S of Remaliah, king of
15:32 of Israel, Jotham the S of Uzziah, king of
15:37 Syria and Pekah the S of Remaliah against Judah.
15:38 father; and Ahaz his S reigned in his stead.
16:1 year of Pekah the S of Remaliah, Ahaz the
16:1 of Remaliah, Ahaz the S of Jotham, king of
16:3 He even burned his S as an offering, according
16:5 Syria and Pekah the S of Remaliah, king of
16:7 Assyria, saying, "I am your servant and your S
16:20 David; and Hezekiah his S reigned in his stead.
17:1 of Judah Hoshea the S of Elah began to
17:21 they made Jeroboam the S of Nebat king.
18:1 third year of Hoshea S of Elah, king of
18:1 of Israel, Hezekiah the S of Ahaz, king of
18:9 seventh year of Hoshea S of Elah, king of
18:18 to them Eliakim the S of Hilkiah, who was
18:18 secretary, and Joah the S of Asaph, the recorder.
18:26 Then Eliakim the S of Hilkiah, and Shebnah, and
18:37 Then Eliakim the S of Hilkiah, who was over
18:37 secretary, and Joah the S of Asaph, the recorder,
19:2 the prophet Isaiah the S of Amoz.
19:20 Then Isaiah the S of Amoz sent to Hezekiah,
19:37 And Esarhaddon his S reigned in his stead.
20:1 Isaiah the prophet the S of Amoz came to
20:12 that time Merodach-baladan the S of Baladan, king
20:21 fathers; and Manasseh his S reigned in his stead.
21:6 And he burned his S as an offering, and
21:7 and to Solomon his S, "In this house, and
21:18 Uzza; and Amon his S reigned in his stead.
21:24 land made Josiah his S king in his stead.
21:26 Uzza; and Josiah his S reigned in his stead.
22:3 king sent Shaphan the S of Azaliah, son of
22:3 the son of Azaliah, S of Meshullam, the secretary,
22:12 priest, and Ahikam the S of Shaphan, and Achbor
22:12 Shaphan, and Achbor the S of Micaiah, and Shaphan
22:14 wife of Shallum the S of Tikvah, son of
22:14 the son of Tikvah, S of Harhas, keeper of
23:10 one might burn his S or his daughter as
23:15 erected by Jeroboam the S of Nebat, who made
23:30 land took Jehoahaz the S of Josiah, and anointed
23:34 Neco made Eliakim the S of Josiah king in
24:6 fathers, and Jehoiachin his S reigned in his stead.
25:22 he appointed Gedaliah the S of Ahikam, son of
25:22 the son of Ahikam, S of Shaphan, governor.
25:23 Mizpah, namely, Ishmael the S of Nethaniah, and
25:23 Nethaniah, and Johanan the S of Kareah, and
25:23 Kareah, and Seraiah the S of Tanhumeth the
25:23 and Ja-azaniah the S of the Ma-acathite.
25:25 seventh month, Ishmael the S of Nethaniah, son of
25:25 the son of Nethaniah, S of Elishama, of the
1Chr 1:43 the Israelites: Bela the S of Beor, the name
1:44 Bela died, Jobab the S of Zerah of Bozrah
1:46 Husham died, Hadad the S of Bedad, who defeated
1:49 Shaul died, Baal-hanan, the S of Achbor, reigned in
2:8 devoted thing; and Ethan's S was Azariah.
2:18 Caleb the S of Hezron had children by his
2:45 The S of Shammai: Maon; and Maon was the
3:10 Solomon: Rehoboam, Abijah his S, Asa his son,
3:10 his son, Asa his S, Jehoshaphat his son,
3:10 his son, Jehoshaphat his S,
3:11 his son, Joram his S, Ahaziah his son, Joash
3:11 his son, Ahaziah his S, Joash his son,
3:11 his son, Joash his S,
3:12 his son, Amaziah his S, Azariah his son, Jotham
3:12 his son, Azariah his S, Jotham his son,
3:12 his son, Jotham his S,
3:13 his son, Ahaz his S, Hezekiah his son, Manasseh
3:13 his son, Hezekiah his S, Manasseh his son,
3:13 his son, Manasseh his S,
3:14 his son, Amon his S, Josiah his son.
3:14 Manasseh his son, Amon his son, Josiah his S
3:16 of Jehoiakim: Jeconiah his S, Zedekiah his son;
3:16 his son, Zedekiah his S;
3:17 the captive: Shealtiel his S,
3:21 Pelatiah and Jeshaiah, his S Rephaiah, his son
3:21 his son Rephaiah, his S Arnan, his son Obadiah,
3:21 his son Arnan, his S Obadiah, his son Shecaniah.
3:21 his son Obadiah, his S Shecaniah.
4:2 Re-aiah the S of Shobal was the father of
4:8 families of Aharhel the S of Harum.
4:15 sons of Caleb the S of Jephunneh: Iru, Elah,
4:21 sons of Shelah the S of Judah: Er the
4:25 Shaul; Shallum was his S, Mibsam his son, Mishma
4:25 his son, Mibsam his S, Mishma his son.
4:25 was his son, Mibsam his son, Mishma his S
4:26 of Mishma: Hammu-el his S, Zaccur his son, Shimei
4:26 his son, Zaccur his S, Shimei his son.
4:26 Hammu-el his son, Zaccur his son, Shimei his S
4:34 Meshobab, Jamlech, Joshah the S of Amaziah,
4:35 Amaziah, Joel, Jehu the S of Joshibiah, son of
4:35 the son of Joshibiah, S of Seraiah, son of
4:35 Joshibiah, son of Seraiah, S of Asiel,
4:37 Jesimiel, Benaiah, Ziza the S of Shiphi, son of
4:37 the son of Shiphi, S of Allon, son of
4:37 Shiphi, son of Allon, S of Jedaiah, son of
4:37 Allon, son of Jedaiah, S of Shimri, son of
4:37 Jedaiah, son of Shimri, S of Shemaiah–
5:1 sons of Joseph the S of Israel, so that
5:4 of Joel: Shemaiah his S, Gog his son, Shimei
5:4 his son, Gog his S, Shimei his son,
5:4 his son, Shimei his S,
5:5 his son, Micah his S, Re-aiah his son, Baal
5:5 his son, Re-aiah his S, Baal his son,
5:5 his son, Baal his S,
5:6 his son, Be-erah his S, whom Tilgath-pilneser king of
5:8 Zechariah, and Bela the S of Azaz, son of
5:8 the son of Azaz, S of Shema, son of
5:8 Azaz, son of Shema, S of Joel, who dwelt
5:14 sons of Abihail the S of Huri, son of
5:14 the son of Huri, S of Jaroah, son of
5:14 Huri, son of Jaroah, S of Gilead, son of
5:14 Jaroah, son of Gilead, S of Michael, son of
5:14 Gilead, son of Michael, S of Jeshishai, son of
5:14 Michael, son of Jeshishai, S of Jahdo, son of
5:14 Jeshishai, son of Jahdo, S of Buz;
5:15 of Buz; Ahi the S of Abdi-el, son of
5:15 the son of Abdi-el, S of Guni, was chief
6:20 Of Gershom: Libni his S, Jahath his son, Zimmah
6:20 his son, Jahath his S, Zimmah his son,
6:20 his son, Zimmah his S,
6:21 his son, Joah his S, Iddo his son, Zerah

6:21 his son, Iddo his S, Zerah his son, Je-atherai
6:21 his son, Zerah his S, Je-atherai his son.
6:21 Iddo his son, Zerah his son, Je-atherai his S
6:22 of Kohath: Amminadab his S, Korah his son, Assir
6:22 his son, Korah his S, Assir his son,
6:22 his son, Assir his S,
6:23 his son, Elkanah his S, Ebiasaph his son, Assir
6:23 his son, Ebiasaph his S, Assir his son,
6:23 his son, Assir his S,
6:24 his son, Tahath his S, Uriel his son, Uzziah
6:24 his son, Uriel his S, Uzziah his son, and
6:24 his son, Uzziah his S, and Shaul his son.
6:24 his son, Uzziah his son, and Shaul his S
6:26 and Ahimoth, Elkanah his S, Zophai his son, Nahath
6:26 his son, Zophai his S, Nahath his son,
6:26 his son, Nahath his S,
6:27 his son, Eliab his S, Jeroham his son, Elkanah
6:27 his son, Jeroham his S, Elkanah his son.
6:27 Eliab his son, Jeroham his son, Elkanah his S
6:29 Merari: Mahli, Libni his S, Shimei his son, Uzzah
6:29 his son, Shimei his S, Uzzah his son,
6:29 his son, Uzzah his S,
6:30 his son, Shimea his S, Haggiah his son, and
6:30 his son, Haggiah his S, and Asaiah his son.
6:30 his son, Haggiah his son, and Asaiah his S
6:33 Heman the singer the S of Joel, son of
6:33 the son of Joel, S of Samuel,
6:34 Joel, son of Samuel, S of Elkanah, son of
6:34 Samuel, son of Elkanah, S of Jeroham, son of
6:34 Elkanah, son of Jeroham, S of Eliel, son of
6:34 Jeroham, son of Eliel, S of Toah,
6:35 Eliel, son of Toah, S of Zuph, son of
6:35 Toah, son of Zuph, S of Elkanah, son of
6:35 Zuph, son of Elkanah, S of Mahath, son of
6:35 Elkanah, son of Mahath, S of Amasai,
6:36 Mahath, son of Amasai, S of Elkanah, son of
6:36 Amasai, son of Elkanah, S of Joel, son of
6:36 Elkanah, son of Joel, S of Azariah, son of
6:36 Joel, son of Azariah, S of Zephaniah,
6:37 Azariah, son of Zephaniah, S of Tahath, son of
6:37 Zephaniah, son of Tahath, S of Assir, son of
6:37 Tahath, son of Assir, S of Ebiasaph, son of
6:37 Assir, son of Ebiasaph, S of Korah,
6:38 Ebiasaph, son of Korah, S of Izhar, son of
6:38 Korah, son of Izhar, S of Kohath, son of
6:38 Izhar, son of Kohath, S of Levi, son of
6:38 Kohath, son of Levi, S of Israel;
6:39 hand, namely, Asaph the S of Berechiah, son of
6:39 the son of Berechiah, S of Shimea,
6:40 Berechiah, son of Shimea, S of Michael, son of
6:40 Shimea, son of Michael, S of Ba-aseiah, son of
6:40 Michael, son of Ba-aseiah, S of Malchijah,
6:41 Ba-aseiah, son of Malchijah, S of Ethni, son of
6:41 Malchijah, son of Ethni, S of Zerah, son of
6:41 Ethni, son of Zerah, S of Adaiah,
6:42 Zerah, son of Adaiah, S of Ethan, son of
6:42 Adaiah, son of Ethan, S of Zimmah, son of
6:42 Ethan, son of Zimmah, S of Shimei,
6:43 Zimmah, son of Shimei, S of Jahath, son of
6:43 Shimei, son of Jahath, S of Gershom, son of
6:43 Jahath, son of Gershom, S of Levi.
6:44 of Merari: Ethan the S of Kishi, son of
6:44 the son of Kishi, S of Abdi, son of
6:44 Kishi, son of Abdi, S of Malluch,
6:45 Abdi, son of Malluch, S of Hashabiah, son of
6:45 Malluch, son of Hashabiah, S of Amaziah, son of
6:45 Hashabiah, son of Amaziah, S of Hilkiah,
6:46 Amaziah, son of Hilkiah, S of Amzi, son of
6:46 Hilkiah, son of Amzi, S of Bani, son of
6:46 Amzi, son of Bani, S of Shemer,
6:47 Bani, son of Shemer, S of Mahli, son of
6:47 Shemer, son of Mahli, S of Mushi, son of
6:47 Mahli, son of Mushi, S of Merari, son of
6:47 Mushi, son of Merari, S of Levi;
6:50 of Aaron: Eleazar his S, Phinehas his son, Abishua
6:50 his son, Phinehas his S, Abishua his son,
6:50 his son, Abishua his S,
6:51 his son, Bukki his S, Uzzi his son, Zerahiah
6:51 his son, Uzzi his S, Zerahiah his son,
6:51 his son, Zerahiah his S,
6:52 his son, Meraioth his S, Amariah his son, Ahitub
6:52 his son, Amariah his S, Ahitub his son,
6:52 his son, Ahitub his S,
6:53 his son, Zadok his S, Ahima-az his son.
6:53 Ahitub his son, Zadok his son, Ahima-az his S
6:56 gave to Caleb the S of Jephunneh.

7:16 of Machir bore a S, and she called his
7:17 sons of Gilead the S of Machir, son of
7:17 the son of Machir, S of Manasseh.
7:20 Shuthelah, and Bered his S, Tahath his son, Ele-adah
7:20 his son, Tahath his S, Ele-adah his son, Tahath
7:20 his son, Ele-adah his S, Tahath his son,
7:20 his son, Tahath his S,
7:21 his son, Zabad his S, Shuthelah his son, and
7:21 his son, Shuthelah his S, and Ezer and Ele-ad,
7:23 conceived and bore a S; and he called his
7:25 Rephah was his S, Resheph his son, Telah his
7:25 his son, Resheph his S, Telah his son, Tahan
7:25 his son, Telah his S, Tahan his son,
7:25 his son, Tahan his S,
7:26 his son, Ladan his S, Ammihud his son, Elishama
7:26 his son, Ammihud his S, Elishama his son,
7:26 his son, Elishama his S,
7:27 his son, Nun his S, Joshua his son.
7:27 Elishama his son, Nun his son, Joshua his S
7:29 sons of Joseph the S of Israel.
8:30 His first-born S: Abdon, then Zur, Kish, Baal, Nadab,
8:34 and Eshbaal; and the S of Jonathan was Merib-baal;
8:37 Bine-a; Raphah was his S, Ele-asah his son, Azel
8:37 his son, Ele-asah his S, Azel his son.
8:37 was his son, Ele-asah his son, Azel his S
9:4 in Jerusalem: Uthai the S of Ammihud, son of
9:4 the son of Ammihud, S of Omri, son of
9:4 Ammihud, son of Omri, S of Imri, son of
9:4 Omri, son of Imri, S of Bani, from the
9:4 sons of Perez the S of Judah.
9:7 the Benjaminites: Sallu the S of Meshullam, son of
9:7 the son of Meshullam, S of Hodaviah, son of
9:7 Meshullam, son of Hodaviah, S of Hassenuah,
9:8 of Hassenuah, Ibneiah the S of Jeroham, Elah the
9:8 of Jeroham, Elah the S of Uzzi, son of
9:8 the son of Uzzi, S of Michri, and Meshullam
9:8 Michri, and Meshullam the S of Shephatiah, son of
9:8 the son of Shephatiah, S of Reuel, son of
9:8 Shephatiah, son of Reuel, S of Ibnijah;
9:11 Jachin, and Azariah the S of Hilkiah, son of
9:11 the son of Hilkiah, S of Meshullam, son of
9:11 Hilkiah, son of Meshullam, S of Zadok, son of
9:11 Meshullam, son of Zadok, S of Meraioth, son of
9:11 Zadok, son of Meraioth, S of Ahitub, the chief
9:12 God; and Adaiah the S of Jeroham, son of
9:12 the son of Jeroham, S of Pashhur, son of
9:12 Jeroham, son of Pashhur, S of Malchijah, and Maasai
9:12 Malchijah, and Maasai the S of Adi-el, son of
9:12 the son of Adi-el, S of Jahzerah, son of
9:12 Adi-el, son of Jahzerah, S of Meshullam, son of
9:12 Jahzerah, son of Meshullam, S of Meshillemith, son
9:12 Meshullam, son of Meshillemith, S of Immer;
9:14 the Levites: Shemaiah the S of Hasshub, son of
9:14 the son of Hasshub, S of Azrikam, son of
9:14 Hasshub, son of Azrikam, S of Hashabiah, of the
9:15 Galal, and Mattaniah the S of Mica, son of
9:15 the son of Mica, S of Zichri, son of
9:15 Mica, son of Zichri, S of Asaph;
9:16 Asaph; and Obadiah the S of Shemaiah, son of
9:16 the son of Shemaiah, S of Galal, son of
9:16 Shemaiah, son of Galal, S of Jeduthun, and
9:16 Jeduthun, and Berechiah the S of Asa, son of
9:16 the son of Asa, S of Elkanah, who dwelt
9:19 Shallum the S of Kore, son of Ebiasaph, son
9:19 the son of Kore, S of Ebiasaph, son of
9:19 Kore, son of Ebiasaph, S of Korah, and his
9:20 And Phinehas the S of Eleazar was the ruler
9:21 Zechariah the S of Meshelemiah was gatekeeper at
9:36 Maacah, and his first-born S Abdon, then Zur, Kish,
9:40 and Eshbaal; and the S of Jonathan was Merib-baal;
9:43 and Rephaiah was his S, Ele-asah his son, Azel
9:43 his son, Ele-asah his S, Azel his son.
9:43 was his son, Ele-asah his son, Azel his S
10:14 over to David the S of Jesse.
11:6 And Joab the S of Zeruiah went up first,
11:12 men was Eleazar the S of Dodo, the Ahohite.
11:22 And Benaiah the S of Jehoiada was a valiant
11:24 things did Benaiah the S of Jehoiada, and won
11:26 of Joab, Elhanan the S of Dodo of Bethlehem,
11:28 the Pelonite, Ira the S of Ikkesh of Tekoa,
11:30 of Netophah, Heled the S of Baanah of Netophah,
11:31 of Netophah, Ithai the S of Ribai of Gibe-ah
11:34 the Gizonite, Jonathan the S of Shagee the Hararite,
11:35 the Hararite, Ahiam the S of Sachar the Hararite,
11:35 the Hararite, Eliphal the S of Ur,
11:37 of Carmel, Naarai the S of Ezbai,

11:38 of Nathan, Mibhar the S of Hagri,
11:39 armor-bearer of Joab the S of Zeruiah,
11:41 the Hittite, Zabad the S of Ahlai,
11:42 of Ahlai, Adina the S of Shiza the Reubenite,
11:43 with him, Hanan the S of Maacah, and Joshaphat
11:45 the Aroerite, Jedia-el the S of Shimri, and Joha
12:1 because of Saul the S of Kish; and they
12:18 and with you, O S of Jesse!
15:17 Levites appointed Heman the S of Joel; and of
15:17 his brethren Asaph the S of Berechiah; and of
15:17 their brethren, Ethan the S of Kushaiah;
16:38 brethren; while Obed-edom, the S of Jeduthun, and
17:13 he shall be my S; I will not take
18:10 Zobah, he sent his S Hadoram to King David,
18:12 And Abishai, the S of Zeruiah, slew eighteen
18:15 And Joab the S of Zeruiah was over the
18:15 army; and Jehoshaphat the S of Ahilud was
18:16 recorder; and Zadok the S of Ahitub and Ahimelech
18:16 Ahitub and Ahimelech the S of Abiathar were
18:17 secretary; and Benaiah the S of Jehoiada was over
19:1 Ammonites died, and his S reigned in his stead.
19:2 loyally with Hanun the S of Nahash, for his
20:5 Philistines; and Elhanan the S of Jair slew Lahmi
20:7 taunted Israel, Jonathan the S of Shimea, David's
22:5 David said, "Solomon my S is young and
22:6 called for Solomon his S, and charged him to
22:7 said to Solomon, "My S, I had it in
22:9 Behold, a S shall be born to you; he
22:10 He shall be my S, and I will be
22:11 for ever.' Now, my S, the LORD be with
22:17 to help Solomon his S, saying,
23:1 he made Solomon his S king over Israel.
24:6 the scribe Shemaiah the S of Nethanel, a Levite,
24:6 priest, and Ahimelech the S of Abiathar, and the
26:1 the Korahites, Meshelemiah the S of Kore, of the
26:6 Also to his S Shemaiah were sons born who
26:14 lots also for his S Zechariah, a shrewd counselor,
26:24 and Shebuel the S of Gershom, son of
26:24 the son of Gershom, S of Moses, was chief
26:25 from Eliezer were his S Rehabiah, and his son
26:25 son Rehabiah, and his S Jeshaiah, and his son
26:25 son Jeshaiah, and his S Joram, and his son
26:25 son Joram, and his S Zichri, and his son
26:25 son Zichri, and his S Shelomoth.
26:28 seer, and Saul the S of Kish, and Abner
26:28 Kish, and Abner the S of Ner, and Joab
26:28 Ner, and Joab the S of Zeruiah had dedicated—
27:2 twenty-four thousand: Jashobeam the S of Zabdiel
27:5 month, was Benaiah, the S of Jehoiada the priest,
27:6 the thirty; Ammizabad his S was in charge of
27:7 fourth month, and his S Zebadiah after him; in
27:9 month, was Ira, the S of Ikkesh the Tekoite;
27:16 the Reubenites Eliezer the S of Zichri was chief
27:16 the Simeonites, Shephatiah the S of Maacah;
27:17 for Levi, Hashabiah the S of Kemuel; for Aaron,
27:18 for Issachar, Omri the S of Michael;
27:19 for Zebulun, Ishmaiah the S of Obadiah; for
27:19 for Naphtali, Jeremoth the S of Azriel;
27:20 the Ephraimites, Hoshea the S of Azaziah; for the
27:20 of Manasseh, Joel the S of Pedaiah;
27:21 in Gilead, Iddo the S of Zechariah; for Benjamin,
27:21 for Benjamin, Jaasiel the S of Abner;
27:22 for Dan, Azarel the S of Jeroham.
27:24 Joab the S of Zeruiah began to number, but
27:25 treasuries was Azmaveth the S of Adi-el; and over
27:25 towers, was Jonathan the S of Uzziah;
27:26 soil was Ezri the S of Chelub;
27:29 valleys was Shaphat the S of Adlai.
27:32 he and Jehiel the S of Hachmoni attended the
27:34 succeeded by Jehoiada the S of Benaiah, and
28:5 has chosen Solomon my S to sit upon the
28:6 'It is Solomon your S who shall build my
28:6 him to be my S, and I will be
28:9 "And you, Solomon my S, know the God of
28:11 David gave Solomon his S the plan of the
28:20 said to Solomon his S, "Be strong and of
29:1 the assembly, "Solomon my S, whom alone God has
29:19 Grant to Solomon my S that with a whole
29:22 they made Solomon the S of David king the
29:26 Thus David the S of Jesse reigned over all
29:28 honor; and Solomon his S reigned in his stead.
2Chr 1:1 Solomon the S of David established himself
1:5 altar that Bezalel the S of Uri, son of
1:5 the son of Uri, S of Hur, had made,
2:12 King David a wise S, endued with discretion and
2:14 with understanding, Huram-abi, the S of a woman of
6:9 the house, but your S who shall be born
9:29 seer concerning Jeroboam the S of Nebat?
9:31 father; and Rehoboam his S reigned in his stead.
10:2 And when Jeroboam the S of Nebat heard of
10:15 Shilonite to Jeroboam the S of Nebat.
10:16 no inheritance in the S of Jesse.
11:3 "Say to Rehoboam the S of Solomon king of
11:17 they made Rehoboam the S of Solomon secure, for
11:18 daughter of Jerimoth the S of David, and of
11:18 daughter of Eliab the S of Jesse;
11:22 Rehoboam appointed Abijah the S of Maacah as
12:16 David; and Abijah his S reigned in his stead.
13:6 Yet Jeroboam the S of Nebat, a servant of
13:6 servant of Solomon the S of David, rose up
13:7 and defied Rehoboam the S of Solomon, when
14:1 David; and Asa his S reigned in his stead.
15:1 came upon Azariah the S of Oded,
15:8 prophecy of Azariah the S of Oded, he took
17:1 Jehoshaphat his S reigned in his stead, and
17:16 to him Amasiah the S of Zichri, a volunteer
18:7 the LORD, Micaiah the S of Imlah; but I
18:8 "Bring quickly Micaiah the S of Imlah."
18:10 And Zedekiah the S of Chenaanah made for himself
18:23 Then Zedekiah the S of Chenaanah came near and
18:25 to Joash the king's S;
19:2 But Jehu the S of Hanani the seer went
19:11 LORD; and Zebadiah the S of Ishmael, the governor
20:14 came upon Jahaziel the S of Zechariah, son of
20:14 the son of Zechariah, S of Benaiah, son of
20:14 Zechariah, son of Benaiah, S of Je-iel, son of
20:14 Benaiah, son of Je-iel, S of Mattaniah, a Levite
20:34 chronicles of Jehu the S of Hanani, which are
20:37 Then Eliezer the S of Do-davahu of Mareshah
21:1 David; and Jehoram his S reigned in his stead.
21:17 wives, so that no S was left to him
21:17 was left to him except Jehoahaz, his youngest S
22:1 made Ahaziah his youngest S king in his stead;
22:1 So Ahaziah the S of Jehoram king of Judah
22:5 went with Jehoram the S of Ahab king of
22:6 And Ahaziah the S of Jehoram king of Judah
22:6 to see Joram the S of Ahab in Jezreel,
22:7 to meet Jehu the S of Nimshi, whom the
22:10 Ahaziah saw that her S was dead, she arose
22:11 king, took Joash the S of Ahaziah, and stole
23:1 of hundreds, Azariah the S of Jeroham, Ishmael the
23:1 of Jeroham, Ishmael the S of Jehohanan, Azariah
23:1 of Jehohanan, Azariah the S of Obed, Ma-aseiah the
23:1 of Obed, Ma-aseiah the S of Adaiah, and Elishaphat
23:1 Adaiah, and Elishaphat the S of Zichri.
23:3 And Jehoiada said to them, "Behold, the king's S
23:11 brought out the king's S, and put the crown
24:20 possession of Zechariah the S of Jehoiada the priest;
24:22 Zechariah's father, had shown him, but killed his S
24:25 the blood of the S of Jehoiada the priest,
24:26 him were Zabad the S of Shimeath the Ammonitess,
24:26 Ammonitess, and Jehozabad the S of Shimrith the
24:27 And Amaziah his S reigned in his stead.
25:17 sent to Joash the S of Jehoahaz, son of
25:17 the son of Jehoahaz, S of Jehu, king of
25:18 your daughter to my S for a wife'; and
25:23 king of Judah, the S of Joash, son of
25:23 the son of Joash, S of Ahaziah, at Beth-shemesh,
25:25 Amaziah the S of Joash king of Judah lived
25:25 death of Joash the S of Jehoahaz, king of
26:21 And Jotham his S was over the king's household,
26:22 Isaiah the prophet the S of Amoz wrote.
26:23 And Jotham his S reigned in his stead.
27:9 David; and Ahaz his S reigned in his stead.
28:3 the valley of the S of Hinnom, and burned
28:6 For Pekah the S of Remaliah slew a hundred
28:7 slew Ma-aseiah the king's S and Azrikam the
28:12 of Ephraim, Azariah the S of Johanan, Berechiah the
28:12 of Johanan, Berechiah the S of Meshillemoth,
28:12 of Meshillemoth, Jehizkiah the S of Shallum, and
28:12 Shallum, and Amasa the S of Hadlai, stood up
28:27 And Hezekiah his S reigned in his stead.
29:12 Levites arose, Mahath the S of Amasai, and Joel
29:12 Amasai, and Joel the S of Azariah, of the
29:12 of Merari, Kish the S of Abdi, and Azariah
29:12 Abdi, and Azariah the S of Jehallelel; and of
29:12 the Gershonites, Joah the S of Zimmah, and Eden
29:12 Zimmah, and Eden the S of Joah;
30:26 time of Solomon the S of David king of
31:14 And Kore the S of Imnah the Levite, keeper
32:20 Isaiah the prophet, the S of Amoz, prayed because
32:32 Isaiah the prophet the S of Amoz, in the

32:33 And Manasseh his S reigned in his stead.
33:6 the valley of the S of Hinnom, and practiced
33:7 and to Solomon his S, "In this house, and
33:20 house; and Amon his S reigned in his stead.
33:25 land made Josiah his S king in his stead.
34:8 he sent Shaphan the S of Azaliah, and Ma-aseiah
34:8 city, and Joah the S of Joahaz, the recorder,
34:20 commanded Hilkiah, Ahikam the S of Shaphan,
34:20 of Shaphan, Abdon the S of Micah, Shaphan the
34:22 wife of Shallum the S of Tokhath, son of
34:22 the son of Tokhath, S of Hasrah, keeper of
35:3 house which Solomon the S of David, king of
35:4 of Israel and the directions of Solomon his S
36:1 land took Jehoahaz the S of Josiah and made
36:8 Judah; and Jehoiachin his S reigned in his stead.
Ezra 3:2 Then arose Jeshua the S of Jozadak, with his
3:2 priests, and Zerubbabel the S of Shealtiel with his
3:8 month, Zerubbabel the S of Shealtiel and Jeshua
3:8 Shealtiel and Jeshua the S of Jozadak made a
5:1 Haggai and Zechariah the S of Iddo, prophesied to
5:2 Then Zerubbabel the S of Shealtiel and Jeshua the
5:2 Shealtiel and Jeshua the S of Jozadak arose and
6:14 prophet and Zechariah the S of Iddo.
7:1 of Persia, Ezra the S of Seraiah, son of
7:1 the son of Seraiah, S of Azariah, son of
7:1 Seraiah, son of Azariah, S of Hilkiah,
7:2 Azariah, son of Hilkiah, S of Shallum, son of
7:2 Hilkiah, son of Shallum, S of Zadok, son of
7:2 Shallum, son of Zadok, S of Ahitub,
7:3 Zadok, son of Ahitub, S of Amariah, son of
7:3 Ahitub, son of Amariah, S of Azariah, son of
7:3 Amariah, son of Azariah, S of Meraioth,
7:4 Azariah, son of Meraioth, S of Zerahiah, son of
7:4 Meraioth, son of Zerahiah, S of Uzzi, son of
7:4 Zerahiah, son of Uzzi, S of Bukki,
7:5 Uzzi, son of Bukki, S of Abishua, son of
7:5 Bukki, son of Abishua, S of Phinehas, son of
7:5 Abishua, son of Phinehas, S of Eleazar, son of
7:5 Phinehas, son of Eleazar, S of Aaron the chief
8:4 of Pahath-moab, Eli-e-ho-enai the S of Zerahiah,
8:5 of Zattu, Shecaniah the S of Jahaziel, and with
8:6 of Adin, Ebed the S of Jonathan, and with
8:7 of Elam, Jeshaiah the S of Athaliah, and with
8:8 of Shephatiah, Zebadiah the S of Michael, and with
8:9 of Joab, Obadiah the S of Jehiel, and with
8:10 of Bani, Shelomith the S of Josiphiah, and with
8:11 of Bebai, Zechariah, the S of Bebai, and with
8:12 of Azgad, Johanan the S of Hakkatan, and with
8:18 sons of Mahli the S of Levi, son of
8:18 the son of Levi, S of Israel, namely Sherebiah
8:33 of Meremoth the priest, S of Uriah, and with
8:33 him was Eleazar the S of Phinehas, and with
8:33 the Levites, Jozabad the S of Jeshua and No-adiah
8:33 Jeshua and No-adiah the S of Binnui.
10:2 And Shecaniah the S of Jehiel, of the sons
10:6 chamber of Jehohanan the S of Eliashib, where he
10:15 Only Jonathan the S of Asahel and Jahzeiah the
10:15 Asahel and Jahzeiah the S of Tikvah opposed this,
10:18 sons of Jeshua the S of Jozadak and his
Neh 1:1 words of Nehemiah the S of Hacaliah.
3:2 to them Zaccur the S of Imri built.
3:4 to them Meremoth the S of Uriah, son of
3:4 the son of Uriah, S of Hakkoz repaired.
3:4 to them Meshullam the S of Berechiah, son of
3:4 the son of Berechiah, S of Meshezabel repaired.
3:4 to them Zadok the S of Baana repaired.
3:6 And Joiada the S of Paseah and Meshullam the
3:6 Paseah and Meshullam the S of Besodeiah repaired
3:8 to them Uzziel the S of Harhaiah, goldsmiths, .
3:9 to them Rephaiah the S of Hur, ruler of
3:10 to them Jedaiah the S of Harumaph repaired
3:10 to him Hattush the S of Hashabneiah repaired.
3:11 Malchijah the S of Harim and Hasshub the son
3:11 Harim and Hasshub the S of Pahath-moab repaired
3:12 to him Shallum the S of Hallohesh, ruler of
3:14 Malchijah the S of Rechab, ruler of the district
3:15 And Shallum the S of Colhozeh, ruler of the
3:16 After him Nehemiah the S of Azbuk, ruler of
3:17 Levites repaired: Rehum the S of Bani; next to
3:18 brethren repaired: Bavvai the S of Henadad, ruler of
3:19 to him Ezer the S of Jeshua, ruler of
3:20 After him Baruch the S of Zabbai repaired another
3:21 After him Meremoth the S of Uriah, son of
3:21 the son of Uriah, S of Hakkoz repaired another
3:23 After them Azariah the S of Ma-aseiah, son of
3:23 the son of Ma-aseiah, S of Ananiah repaired beside
3:24 After him Binnui the S of Henadad repaired another
3:25 Palal the S of Uzai repaired opposite the Angle
3:25 After him Pedaiah the S of Parosh
3:29 After them Zadok the S of Immer repaired opposite
3:29 After him Shemaiah the S of Shecaniah, the keeper
3:30 After him Hananiah the S of Shelemiah and Hanun
3:30 and Hanun the sixth S of Zalaph repaired another
3:30 After him Meshullam the S of Berechiah repaired
6:10 house of Shemaiah the S of Delaiah, son of
6:10 the son of Delaiah, S of Mehetabel, who was
6:18 son-in-law of Shecaniah the S of Arah: and his
6:18 of Arah: and his S Jehohanan had taken the
6:18 daughter of Meshullam the S of Berechiah as his
8:17 days of Jeshua the S of Nun to that
10:1 Nehemiah the governor, the S of Hacaliah, Zedekiah,
10:9 the Levites: Jeshua the S of Azaniah, Binnui of
10:38 And the priest, the S of Aaron, shall be
11:4 of Judah: Athaiah the S of Uzziah, son of
11:4 the son of Uzziah, S of Zechariah, son of
11:4 Uzziah, son of Zechariah, S of Amariah, son of
11:4 Zechariah, son of Amariah, S of Shephatiah, son of
11:4 Amariah, son of Shephatiah, S of Mahalalel, of the
11:5 Perez; and Ma-aseiah the S of Baruch, son of
11:5 the son of Baruch, S of Colhozeh, son of
11:5 Baruch, son of Colhozeh, S of Hazaiah, son of
11:5 Colhozeh, son of Hazaiah, S of Adaiah, son of
11:5 Hazaiah, son of Adaiah, S of Joiarib, son of
11:5 Adaiah, son of Joiarib, S of Zechariah, son of
11:5 Joiarib, son of Zechariah, S of the Shilonite.
11:7 of Benjamin: Sallu the S of Meshullam, son of
11:7 the son of Meshullam, S of Joed, son of
11:7 Meshullam, son of Joed, S of Pedaiah, son of
11:7 Joed, son of Pedaiah, S of Kolaiah, son of
11:7 Pedaiah, son of Kolaiah, S of Ma-aseiah, son of
11:7 Kolaiah, son of Ma-aseiah, S of Ithi-el, son of
11:7 Ma-aseiah, son of Ithi-el, S of Jeshaiah.
11:9 Joel the S of Zichri was their overseer; and
11:9 overseer; and Judah the S of Hassenuah was second
11:10 the priests: Jedaiah the S of Joiarib, Jachin,
11:11 Joiarib, Jachin, Seraiah the S of Hilkiah, son of
11:11 the son of Hilkiah, S of Meshullam, son of
11:11 Hilkiah, son of Meshullam, S of Zadok, son of
11:11 Meshullam, son of Zadok, S of Meraioth, son of
11:11 Zadok, son of Meraioth, S of Ahitub, ruler of
11:12 twenty-two; and Adaiah the S of Jeroham, son of
11:12 the son of Jeroham, S of Pelaliah, son of
11:12 Jeroham, son of Pelaliah, S of Amzi, son of
11:12 Pelaliah, son of Amzi, S of Zechariah, son of
11:12 Amzi, son of Zechariah, S of Pashhur, son of
11:12 Zechariah, son of Pashhur, S of Malchijah,
11:13 forty-two; and Amashsai, the S of Azarel, son of
11:13 the son of Azarel, S of Ahzai, son of
11:13 Azarel, son of Ahzai, S of Meshillemoth, son of
11:13 Ahzai, son of Meshillemoth, S of Immer,
11:14 overseer was Zabdiel the S of Haggedolim.
11:15 the Levites: Shemaiah the S of Hasshub, son of
11:15 the son of Hasshub, S of Azrikam, son of
11:15 Hasshub, son of Azrikam, S of Hashabiah, son of
11:15 Azrikam, son of Hashabiah, S of Bunni;
11:17 God; and Mattaniah the S of Mica, son of
11:17 the son of Mica, S of Zabdi, son of
11:17 Mica, son of Zabdi, S of Asaph, who was
11:17 brethren; and Abda the S of Shammua, son of
11:17 the son of Shammua, S of Galal, son of
11:17 Shammua, son of Galal, S of Jeduthun.
11:22 Jerusalem was Uzzi the S of Bani, son of
11:22 the son of Bani, S of Hashabiah, son of
11:22 Bani, son of Hashabiah, S of Mattaniah, son of
11:22 Hashabiah, son of Mattaniah, S of Mica, of the
11:24 And Pethahiah the S of Meshezabel, of the sons
11:24 sons of Zerah the S of Judah, was at
12:1 up with Zerubbabel the S of Shealtiel, and Jeshua:
12:23 days of Johanan the S of Eliashib.
12:24 Sherebiah, and Jeshua the S of Kadmi-el, with their
12:26 days of Joiakim the S of Jeshua son of
12:26 the son of Jeshua S of Jozadak, and in
12:35 with trumpets: Zechariah the S of Jonathan, son of
12:35 the son of Jonathan, S of Shemaiah, son of
12:35 Jonathan, son of Shemaiah, S of Mattaniah, son of
12:35 Shemaiah, son of Mattaniah, S of Micaiah, son of
12:35 Mattaniah, son of Micaiah, S of Zaccur, son of
12:35 Micaiah, son of Zaccur, S of Asaph;
12:45 of David and his S Solomon.
13:13 their assistant Hanan the S of Zaccur, son of
13:13 the son of Zaccur, S of Mattaniah, for they
13:28 sons of Jehoiada, the S of Eliashib the high

Tob	1:1	acts of Tobit the S of Tobiel, son of
	1:1	the son of Tobiel, S of Ananiel, son of
	1:1	Tobiel, son of Ananiel, S of Aduel, son of
	1:1	Ananiel, son of Aduel, S of Gabael, of the
	1:15	Shalmaneser died, Sennacherib his S reigned in his
	1:20	wife Anna and my S Tobias.
	1:21	Then Esarhaddon, his S, reigned in his place; and
	1:21	he appointed Ahikar, the S of my brother Anael,
	2:1	wife Anna and my S Tobias were restored to
	2:2	I said to my S, "Go and bring whatever
	3:9	we never see a S or daughter of yours!"
	3:15	near kinsman or kinsman's S for whom I should
	3:17	marriage to Tobias the S of Tobit, and to
	4:2	I not call my S Tobias so that I
	4:3	him and said, "My S, when I die, bury
	4:4	Remember, my S, that she faced many dangers for
	4:5	all your days, my S, and refuse to sin
	4:12	"Beware, my S, of all immorality.
	4:12	Remember, my S, that Noah, Abraham, Isaac, and
	4:13	So now, my S, love your brethren, and in
	4:14	"Watch yourself, my S, in everything you do, and
	4:19	"So, my S, remember my commands, and do not
	4:20	trust with Gabael the S of Gabrias at Rages
	4:21	not be afraid, my S, because we have become
	5:11	whom you will pay to go with your S
	5:12	"I am Azarias the S of the great Ananias,
	5:14	day, and expenses for yourself as for my S
	5:16	So his S made the preparations for the journey.
	6:14	I am the only S my father has, and
	6:14	they have no other S to bury them."
	7:7	blessed him and exclaimed, S of that good and
	10:7	stopped mourning for her S Tobias, until the fourteen
	11:5	sat looking intently down the road for her S
	11:6	his father, "Behold, your S is coming, and so
	11:9	them, and embraced her S, and said to him,
	11:10	But his S ran to him
	11:14	Then he saw his S and embraced him, and
	11:15	here I see my S Tobias!" And his son
	11:15	And his S went in rejoicing, and he reported
	12:1	Tobit then called his S Tobias and said to
	12:1	said to him, "My S, see to the wages
	14:3	old he called his S and grandsons, and said
	14:3	said to him, "My S, take your sons; behold,
	14:4	Go to Media, my S, for I fully believe
	14:8	"So now, my S, leave Nineveh, because what the
	14:10	See, my S, what Nadab did to Ahikar who
Jud	6:15	days were Uzziah the S of Micah, of the
	6:15	Simeon, and Chabris the S of Gothoniel, and
	6:15	Gothoniel, and Charmis the S of Melchiel.
	8:1	daughter of Merari the S of Ox, son of
	8:1	the son of Ox, S of Joseph, son of
	8:1	Ox, son of Joseph, S of Oziel, son of
	8:1	Joseph, son of Oziel, S of Elkiah, son of
	8:1	Oziel, son of Elkiah, S of Ananias, son of
	8:1	Elkiah, son of Ananias, S of Gideon, son of
	8:1	Ananias, son of Gideon, S of Raphaim, son of
	8:1	Gideon, son of Raphaim, S of Ahitub, son of
	8:1	Raphaim, son of Ahitub, S of Elijah, son of
	8:1	Ahitub, son of Elijah, S of Hilkiah, son of
	8:1	Elijah, son of Hilkiah, S of Eliab, son of
	8:1	Hilkiah, son of Eliab, S of Nathanael, son of
	8:1	Eliab, son of Nathanael, S of Salamiel, son of
	8:1	Nathanael, son of Salamiel, S of Sarasadai, son of
	8:1	Salamiel, son of Sarasadai, S of Israel.
Esth	2:5	name was Mordecai, the S of Jair, son of
	2:5	the son of Jair, S of Shimei, son of
	2:5	Jair, son of Shimei, S of Kish, a Benjaminite,
	3:1	Haman the Agagite, the S of Hammedatha, and
	3:10	the Agagite, the S of Hammedatha, the enemy
	8:5	Haman the Agagite, the S of Hammedatha, which he
	9:10	sons of Haman the S of Hammedatha, the enemy
	9:24	Haman the Agagite, the S of Hammedatha, the
	11:1	Levite, and Ptolemy his S brought to Egypt the
	11:1	translated by Lysimachus the S of Ptolemy, one of
	11:2	of Nisan, Mordecai the S of Jair, son of
	11:2	the son of Jair, S of Shimei, son of
	11:2	Jair, son of Shimei, S of Kish, of the
	12:6	But Haman, the S of Hammedatha, a Bougaean, was
	16:10	Haman, the S of Hammedatha, a Macedonian
	16:17	sent by Haman the S of Hammedatha,
Job	25:6	a maggot, and the S of man, who is
	32:2	Then Elihu the S of Barachel the Buzite, of
	32:6	And Elihu the S of Barachel the Buzite answered:
	35:8	and your righteousness a S of man.
Ps	2:7	me, "You are my S, today I have begotten
	8:4	of him, and the S of man that thou
	50:20	your brother; you slander your own mother's S
	72:1	O God, and thy righteousness to the royal S
	72:20	prayers of David, the S of Jesse, are ended.
	80:17	thy right hand, the S of man whom thou
	86:16	servant, and save the S of thy handmaid.
	116:16	am thy servant, the S of thy handmaid.
	144:3	regard him, or the S of man that thou
	146:3	in princes, in a S of man, in whom
Prov	1:1	The proverbs of Solomon, S of David, king of
	1:8	and Violence Hear, my S, your father's instruction,
	1:10	My S, if sinners entice you, do not consent.
	1:15	one purse"– my S, do not walk in
	2:1	My S, if you receive my words and treasure
	3:1	My S, do not forget my teaching, but let
	3:11	My S, do not despise the LORD's discipline or
	3:12	as a father the S in whom he delights.
	3:21	My S, keep sound wisdom and discretion; let them
	4:4	When I was a S with my father, tender,
	4:11	and Evil Hear, my S, and accept my words,
	4:21	My S, be attentive to my words; incline your
	5:1	My S, be attentive to my wisdom, incline your
	5:20	you be infatuated, my S, with a loose woman
	6:1	My S, if you have become surety for your
	6:3	then do this, my S, and save yourself, for
	6:20	My S, keep your father's commandment, and forsake
	7:1	My S, keep my words and treasure up my
	10:1	A wise S makes a glad father, but a
	10:1	father, but a foolish S is a sorrow to
	10:5	A S who gathers in summer is prudent, but
	10:5	is prudent, but a S who sleeps in harvest
	13:1	A wise S hears his father's instruction, but a
	13:24	the rod hates his S, but he who loves
	15:20	A wise S makes a glad father, but a
	17:2	will rule over a S who acts shamefully, and
	17:21	A stupid S is a grief to a father;
	17:25	A foolish S is a grief to his father
	19:13	A foolish S is ruin to his father, and
	19:18	Discipline your S while there is hope; d o
	19:26	his mother is a S who causes shame and
	19:27	Cease, my S, to hear instruction only to stray
	23:15	My S, if your heart is wise, my heart
	23:19	Hear, my S, and be wise, and direct your
	23:24	who begets a wise S will be glad in
	23:26	My S, give me your heart, and let your
	24:13	My S, eat honey, for it is good, and
	24:21	My S, fear the LORD and the king, and
	27:11	Be wise, my S, and make my heart glad,
	28:7	law is a wise S, but a companion of
	29:17	Discipline your S, and he will give you rest;
	30:1	The words of Agur S of Jakeh of Massa.
	30:4	and what is his S's name?
	31:2	Massa, which his mother taught him: What, my S
	31:2	What, S of my womb?
	31:2	What, S of my vows?
Eccl	1:1	of the Preacher, the S of David, king in
	4:8	has no one, either S or brother, yet there
	5:14	is father of a S, but he has nothing
	10:17	your king is the S of free men, and
	12:12	My S, beware of anything beyond these.
Wis	2:18	righteous man is God's S, he will help him,
	9:5	thy slave and the S of thy maidservant, a
	18:13	they acknowledged thy people to be God's S
Sir	2:1	My S, if you come forward to serve the
	3:12	O S, help your father in his old age,
	3:17	My S, perform your tasks in meekness; then you
	4:1	My S, deprive not the poor of his living,
	4:10	then be like a S of the Most High,
	6:18	My S, from your youth up choose instruction, and
	6:23	Listen, my S, and accept my judgment; do not
	6:32	you are willing, my S, you will be taught,
	7:3	My S, do not sow the furrows of injustice,
	10:27	My S, glorify yourself with humility, and ascribe to
	11:10	My S, do not busy yourself with many matters;
	14:11	My S, treat yourself well, according to your means,
	16:22	Listen to me, my S, and acquire knowledge, and
	17:25	in men, since a S of man is not
	18:14	My S, do not mix reproach with your good
	21:1	Have you sinned, my S
	22:3	father of an undisciplined S, and the birth of
	30:1	He who loves his S will whip him often,
	30:2	He who disciplines his S will profit by him,
	30:3	He who teaches his S will make his enemies
	30:7	He who spoils his S will bind up his
	30:8	be stubborn, and a S unrestrained turns out to
	30:13	Discipline your S and take pains with him, that
	31:22	Listen to me, my S, and do not disregard

33:19 To S or wife, to brother or friend, do
34:20 one who kills a S before his father's eyes
36:12 Israel, whom thou hast likened to a first-born S
37:27 My S, test your soul while you live; see
38:9 My S, when you are sick do not be
38:16 My S, let your tears fall for the dead,
40:28 My S, do not lead the life of a
45:23 Phinehas the S of Eleazar is the third in
45:25 established with David, the S of Jesse, of the
45:25 the king is from S to son only; so
45:25 is from son to S only; so the heritage
46:1 Joshua the S of Nun was mighty in war,
46:7 he and Caleb the S of Jephunneh: they withstood
47:12 rose up a wise S who fared amply because
47:23 Also Jeroboam the S of Nebat, who caused Israel
48:10 the father to the S, and to restore the
49:12 so was Jeshua the S of Jozadak; in their
50:1 Simon the high priest, S of Onias, who in
50:27 this book, Jesus the S of Sirach, son of
50:27 the son of Sirach, S of Eleazar, of Jerusalem,
Is 1:1 vision of Isaiah the S of Amoz, which he
2:1 word which Isaiah the S of Amoz saw concerning
7:1 days of Ahaz the S of Jotham, son of
7:1 the son of Jotham, S of Uzziah, king of
7:1 Syria and Pekah the S of Remaliah the king
7:3 you and Shear-jashub your S, at the end of
7:4 and Syria and the S of Remaliah.
7:5 with Ephraim and the S of Remaliah, has devised
7:6 and set up the S of Tabeel as king
7:9 of Samaria is the S of Remaliah.
7:14 conceive and bear a S, and shall call his
8:2 priest and Zechariah the S of Jeberechiah, to attest
8:3 the prophetess, and she conceived and bore a S
8:6 before Rezin and the S of Remaliah;
9:6 born, to us a S is given; and the
13:1 Babylon which Isaiah the S of Amoz saw.
14:12 heaven, O Day Star, S of Dawn!
19:11 Pharaoh, "I am a S of the wise, a
19:11 of the wise, a S of ancient kings"?
20:2 spoken by Isaiah the S of Amoz, saying, "Go,
22:20 my servant Eliakim the S of Hilkiah,
36:3 to him Eliakim the S of Hilkiah, who was
36:3 secretary, and Joah the S of Asaph, the recorder.
36:22 Then Eliakim the S of Hilkiah, who was over
36:22 secretary, and Joah the S of Asaph, the recorder,
37:2 the prophet Isaiah the S of Amoz.
37:21 Then Isaiah the S of Amoz sent to Hezekiah,
37:38 And Esarhaddon his S reigned in his stead.
38:1 Isaiah the prophet the S of Amoz came to
39:1 that time Merodach-baladan the S of Baladan, king
49:15 no compassion on the S of her womb?
51:12 who dies, of the S of man who is
56:2 does this, and the S of man who holds
66:7 came upon her she was delivered of a S
Jer 1:1 words of Jeremiah, the S of Hilkiah, of the
1:2 days of Josiah the S of Amon, king of
1:3 days of Jehoiakim the S of Josiah, king of
1:3 year of Zedekiah, the S of Josiah, king of
6:26 as for an only S, most bitter lamentation; for
7:31 the valley of the S of Hinnom, to burn
7:32 the valley of the S of Hinnom, but the
15:4 of what Manasseh the S of Hezekiah, king of
19:2 the valley of the S of Hinnom at the
19:6 the valley of the S of Hinnom, but the
20:1 Pashhur the priest, the S of Immer, who was
20:15 to my father, "A S is born to you,"
21:1 to him Pashhur the S of Malchiah and Zephaniah
21:1 Zephaniah the priest, the S of Ma-aseiah, saying,
22:11 LORD concerning Shallum the S of Josiah, king of
22:18 LORD concerning Jehoiakim the S of Josiah, king of
22:24 LORD, though Coniah the S of Jehoiakim, king of
24:1 from Jerusalem Jeconiah the S of Jehoiakim, king of
25:1 year of Jehoiakim the S of Josiah, king of
25:3 year of Josiah the S of Amon, king of
26:1 reign of Jehoiakim the S of Josiah, king of
26:20 LORD, Uriah the S of Shemaiah from Kiriath-
26:22 certain men, Elnathan the S of Achbor and others
26:24 hand of Ahikam the S of Shaphan was with
27:1 reign of Zedekiah the S of Josiah, king of
27:7 serve him and his S and his grandson, until
27:20 to Babylon Jeconiah the S of Jehoiakim, king of
28:1 fourth year, Hananiah the S of Azzur, the prophet
28:4 this place Jeconiah the S of Jehoiakim, king of
29:3 hand of Elasah the S of Shaphan and Gemariah
29:3 Shaphan and Gemariah the S of Hilkiah, whom
29:21 Israel, concerning Ahab the S of Kolaiah and
29:21 Kolaiah and Zedekiah the S of Ma-aseiah, who are
29:25 and to Zephaniah the S of Ma-aseiah the priest,
31:20 disgrace of my youth.' Is Ephraim my dear S
32:7 me: Behold, Hanamel the S of Shallum your uncle
32:12 purchase to Baruch the S of Neriah son of
32:12 the son of Neriah S of Mahseiah, in the
32:16 purchase to Baruch the S of Neriah, I prayed
32:35 the valley of the S of Hinnom, to offer
33:21 shall not have a S to reign on his
35:1 days of Jehoiakim the S of Josiah, king of
35:3 I took Ja-azaniah the S of Jeremiah, son of
35:3 the son of Jeremiah, S of Habazziniah, and his
35:4 sons of Hanan the S of Igdaliah, the man
35:4 chamber of Ma-aseiah the S of Shallum, keeper of
35:6 wine, for Jonadab the S of Rechab, our father,
35:8 voice of Jonadab the S of Rechab, our father,
35:14 command which Jonadab the S of Rechab gave to
35:16 sons of Jonadab the S of Rechab have kept
35:19 of Israel: Jonadab the S of Rechab shall never
36:1 year of Jehoiakim the S of Josiah, king of
36:4 Jeremiah called Baruch the S of Neriah, and Baruch
36:8 And Baruch the S of Neriah did all that
36:9 year of Jehoiakim the S of Josiah, king of
36:10 chamber of Gemariah the S of Shaphan the
36:11 When Micaiah the S of Gemariah, son of Shaphan,
36:11 the son of Gemariah, S of Shaphan, heard all
36:12 the secretary, Delaiah the S of Shemaiah, Elnathan
36:12 of Shemaiah, Elnathan the S of Achbor, Gemariah
36:12 of Achbor, Gemariah the S of Shaphan, Zedekiah the
36:12 of Shaphan, Zedekiah the S of Hananiah, and all
36:14 princes sent Jehudi the S of Nethaniah, son of
36:14 the son of Nethaniah, S of Shelemiah, son of
36:14 Nethaniah, son of Shelemiah, S of Cushi, to say
36:14 So Baruch the S of Neriah took the scroll
36:26 commanded Jerahmeel the king's S and Seraiah the
36:26 son and Seraiah the S of Azriel and Shelemiah
36:26 Azriel and Shelemiah the S of Abdeel to seize
36:32 Baruch the scribe, the S of Neriah, who wrote
37:1 the S of Josiah, whom Nebuchadrezzar king of
37:1 instead of Coniah the S of Jehoiakim.
37:3 Zedekiah sent Jehucal the S of Shelemiah, and
37:3 Zephaniah the priest, the S of Ma-aseiah, to
37:13 there named Irijah the S of Shelemiah, son of
37:13 son of Shelemiah, S of Hananiah, seized Jeremiah
38:1 Now Shephatiah the S of Mattan, Gedaliah the son
38:1 of Mattan, Gedaliah the S of Pashhur, Jucal the
38:1 of Pashhur, Jucal the S of Shelemiah, and Pashhur
38:1 Shelemiah, and Pashhur the S of Malchiah heard
38:6 of Malchiah, the king's S, which was in the
39:14 him to Gedaliah the S of Ahikam, son of
39:14 the son of Ahikam, S of Shaphan, that he
40:5 return to Gedaliah the S of Ahikam, son of
40:5 the son of Ahikam, S of Shaphan, whom the
40:6 went to Gedaliah the S of Ahikam, at Mizpah,
40:7 had appointed Gedaliah the S of Ahikam governor in
40:8 at Mizpah--Ishmael the S of Nethaniah, Johanan the
40:8 of Nethaniah, Johanan the S of Kareah, Seraiah the
40:8 of Kareah, Seraiah the S of Tanhumeth, the sons
40:8 the Netophathite, Jezaniah the S of the Ma-acathite,
40:9 Gedaliah the S of Ahikam, son of Shaphan, swore
40:9 the son of Ahikam, S of Shaphan, swore to
40:11 had appointed Gedaliah the S of Ahikam, son of
40:11 the son of Ahikam, S of Shaphan, as governor
40:13 Now Johanan the S of Kareah and all the
40:14 has sent Ishmael the S of Nethaniah to take
40:14 But Gedaliah the S of Ahikam would not believe
40:15 Then Johanan the S of Kareah spoke secretly to
40:15 and slay Ishmael the S of Nethaniah, and no
40:16 But Gedaliah the S of Ahikam said to Johanan
40:16 said to Johanan the S of Kareah, "You shall
41:1 seventh month, Ishmael the S of Nethaniah, son of
41:1 the son of Nethaniah, S of Elishama, of the
41:1 men to Gedaliah the S of Ahikam, at Mizpah.
41:2 at Mizpah, Ishmael the S of Nethaniah and the
41:2 struck down Gedaliah the S of Ahikam, son of
41:2 the son of Ahikam, S of Shaphan, with the
41:6 And Ishmael the S of Nethaniah came out from
41:6 in to Gedaliah the S of Ahikam."
41:7 the city, Ishmael the S of Nethaniah and the
41:9 of Israel; Ishmael the S of Nethaniah filled it
41:10 committed to Gedaliah the S of Ahikam.
41:10 Ishmael the S of Nethaniah took them captive and
41:11 But when Johanan the S of Kareah and all
41:11 evil which Ishmael the S of Nethaniah had done,
41:12 fight against Ishmael the S of Nethaniah.
41:13 Ishmael saw Johanan the S of Kareah and all

SON

41:14 went to Johanan the S of Kareah.
41:15 But Ishmael the S of Nethaniah escaped from
41:16 Then Johanan the S of Kareah and all the
41:16 people whom Ishmael the S of Nethaniah had
41:16 slain Gedaliah the S of Ahikam--soldiers, women,
41:18 them, because Ishmael the S of Nethaniah had slain
41:18 had slain Gedaliah the S of Ahikam, whom the
42:1 forces, and Johanan the S of Kareah and Azariah
42:1 Kareah and Azariah the S of Hoshaiah, and all
42:8 he summoned Johanan the S of Kareah and all
43:2 to them, Azariah the S of Hoshaiah and Johanan
43:2 Hoshaiah and Johanan the S of Kareah and all
43:3 there'; but Baruch the S of Neriah has set
43:4 So Johanan the S of Kareah and all the
43:5 But Johanan the S of Kareah and all the
43:6 left with Gedaliah the S of Ahikam, son of
43:6 the son of Ahikam, S of Shaphan; also Jeremiah
43:6 prophet and Baruch the S of Neriah.
45:1 spoke to Baruch the S of Neriah, when he
45:1 year of Jehoiakim the S of Josiah, king of
46:2 year of Jehoiakim the S of Josiah, king of
50:40 dwell there, and no S of man shall sojourn
51:43 and through which no S of man passes.
51:59 prophet commanded Seraiah the S of Neriah, son of
51:59 the son of Neriah, S of Mahseiah, when he
Bar 1:1 book which Baruch the S of Neraiah, son of
1:1 the son of Neraiah, S of Mahseiah, son of
1:1 Neraiah, son of Mahseiah, S of Zedekiah, son of
1:1 Mahseiah, son of Zedekiah, S of Hasadiah, son of
1:1 Zedekiah, son of Hasadiah, S of Hilkiah, wrote in
1:3 hearing of Jeconiah the S of Jehoiakim, king of
1:7 the high priest, the S of Hilkiah, son of
1:7 the son of Hilkiah, S of Shallum, and to
1:8 vessels which Zedekiah the S of Josiah, king of
1:11 life of Belshazzar his S, that their days on
1:12 protection of Belshazzar his S, and we shall serve
2:3 the flesh of his S and another the flesh
Ezek 1:3 Ezekiel the priest, the S of Buzi, in the
2:1 he said to me, S of man, stand upon
2:3 he said to me, S of man, I send
2:6 And you, S of man, be not afraid of
2:8 "But you, S of man, hear what I say
3:1 he said to me, S of man, eat what
3:3 he said to me, S of man, eat this
3:4 he said to me, S of man, go, get
3:10 he said to me, S of man, all my
3:17 LORD came to me: S of man, I have
3:25 And you, O S of man, behold, cords will
4:1 "And you, O S of man, take a brick
4:16 he said to me, S of man, behold, I
5:1 "And you, O S of man, take a sharp
6:2 LORD came to me: S of man, set your
7:2 me: "And you, O S of man, thus says
8:5 he said to me, S of man, lift up
8:6 he said to me, S of man, do you
8:8 said he to me, S of man, dig in
8:11 Israel, with Ja-azaniah the S of Shaphan standing
8:12 he said to me, S of man, have you
8:15 you seen this, O S of man?
8:17 you seen this, O S of man?
11:1 among them Ja-azaniah the S of Azzur, and Pelatiah
11:1 Azzur, and Pelatiah the S of Benaiah, princes of
11:2 he said to me, S of man, these are
11:4 against them, prophesy, O S of man."
11:13 prophesying, that Pelatiah the S of Benaiah died.
11:15 LORD came to me: S of man, your brethren,
12:2 LORD came to me: S of man, you dwell
12:3 Therefore, S of man, prepare for yourself an exile's
12:9 LORD came to me: S of man, has not
12:18 LORD came to me: S of man, eat your
12:22 LORD came to me: S of man, what is
12:27 LORD came to me: S of man, behold, they
13:2 LORD came to me: S of man, prophesy against
13:17 "And you, S of man, set your face against
14:3 LORD came to me: S of man, these men
14:13 LORD came to me: S of man, when a
14:20 they would deliver neither S nor daughter; they
15:2 LORD came to me: S of man, how does
16:2 LORD came to me: S of man, make known
17:2 LORD came to me: S of man, propound a
18:4 the soul of the S is mine: the soul
18:10 "If he begets a S who is a robber,
18:14 this man begets a S who sees all the
18:19 'Why should not the S suffer for the iniquity
18:19 the father?' When the S has done what is
18:20 The S shall not suffer for the iniquity of
18:20 the iniquity of the S; the righteousness of the
20:3 LORD came to me: S of man, speak to
20:4 Will you judge them, S of man, will you
20:27 "Therefore, S of man, speak to the house of
20:46 LORD came to me: S of man, set your
21:2 LORD came to me: S of man, set your
21:6 Sigh therefore, S of man; sigh with breaking heart
21:9 LORD came to me: S of man, prophesy and
21:10 despised the rod, my S, with everything of wood.
21:12 Cry and wail, S of man, for it is
21:14 "Prophesy therefore, S of man; clap your hands and
21:19 came to me again: S of man, mark two
21:28 "And you, S of man, prophesy, and say, Thus
22:2 me, saying, "And you, S of man, will you
22:18 LORD came to me: S of man, the house
22:24 LORD came to me: S of man, say to
23:2 LORD came to me: S of man, there were
23:36 LORD said to me: S of man, will you
24:2 LORD came to me: S of man, write down
24:16 LORD came to me: S of man, behold, I
24:25 Lord GOD.' "And you, S of man, on the
25:2 LORD came to me: S of man, set your
26:2 LORD came to me: S of man, because Tyre
27:2 to me: "Now you, S of man, raise a
28:2 LORD came to me: S of man, say to
28:12 LORD came to me: S of man, raise a
28:21 LORD came to me: S of man, set your
29:2 LORD came to me: S of man, set your
29:18 LORD came to me: S of man, Nebuchadrezzar king
30:2 LORD came to me: S of man, prophesy, and
30:21 LORD came to me: S of man, I have
31:2 LORD came to me: S of man, say to
32:2 LORD came to me: S of man, raise a
32:18 LORD came to me: S of man, wail over
33:2 LORD came to me: S of man, speak to
33:7 "So you, S of man, I have made a
33:10 "And you, S of man, say to the house
33:12 And you, S of man, say to your people,
33:24 LORD came to me: S of man, the inhabitants
33:30 "As for you, S of man, your people who
34:2 LORD came to me: S of man, prophesy against
35:2 LORD came to me: S of man, set your
36:1 "And you, S of man, prophesy to the mountains
36:17 LORD came to me: S of man, when the
37:3 he said to me, S of man, can these
37:9 to the breath, prophesy, S of man, and say
37:11 he said to me, S of man, these bones
37:16 LORD came to me: S of man, take a
38:2 LORD came to me: S of man, set your
38:14 seize great spoil?' "Therefore, S of man, prophesy,
39:1 "And you, S of man, prophesy against Gog, and
39:17 "As for you, S of man, thus says the
40:4 man said to me, S of man, look with
43:7 he said to me, S of man, this is
43:10 "And you, S of man, describe to the house
43:18 he said to me, S of man, thus says
44:5 LORD said to me, S of man, mark well,
44:25 father or mother, for S or daughter, for brother
47:6 he said to me, S of man, have you
Dan 3:93 fourth is like a S of the gods."
5:22 And you his S, Belshazzar, have not humbled your
7:13 came one like a S of man, and he
8:17 to me, "Understand, O S of man, that the
9:1 year of Darius the S of Ahasuerus, by birth
Hos 1:1 came to Hosea the S of Be-eri, in the
1:1 days of Jeroboam the S of Joash, king of
1:3 Diblaim, and she conceived and bore him a S
1:8 weaned Not pitied, she conceived and bore a S
11:1 him, and out of Egypt I called my S
13:13 he is an unwise S; for now he does
Joel 1:1 came to Joel, the S of Pethuel:
Amos 1:1 days of Jeroboam the S of Joash, king of
7:14 prophet, nor a prophet's S; but I am a
8:10 mourning for an only S, and the end of
Jon 1:1 came to Jonah the S of Amittai, saying,
Mic 6:5 and what Balaam the S of Beor answered him,
7:6 your bosom; for the S treats the father with
Zeph 1:1 came to Zephaniah the S of Cushi, son of
1:1 the son of Cushi, S of Gedaliah, son of
1:1 Cushi, son of Gedaliah, S of Amariah, son of
1:1 Gedaliah, son of Amariah, S of Hezekiah, in the
1:1 days of Josiah the S of Amon, king of
Hag 1:1 prophet to Zerubbabel the S of Shealtiel, governor
1:1 and to Joshua the S of Jehozadak, the high
1:12 Then Zerubbabel the S of Shealtiel, and Joshua the
1:12 Shealtiel, and Joshua the S of Jehozadak, the high

S

	1:14	spirit of Zerubbabel the S of Shealtiel, governor of
	1:14	spirit of Joshua the S of Jehozadak, the high
	2:2	now to Zerubbabel the S of Shealtiel, governor of
	2:2	and to Joshua the S of Jehozadak, the high
	2:4	take courage, O Joshua, S of Jehozadak, the high
	2:23	Zerubbabel my servant, the S of Shealtiel, says the
Zech	1:1	came to Zechariah the S of Berechiah, son of
	1:1	the son of Berechiah, S of Iddo, the prophet,
	1:7	came to Zechariah the S of Berechiah, son of
	1:7	the son of Berechiah, S of Iddo, the prophet;
	6:10	house of Josiah, the S of Zephaniah.
	6:11	head of Joshua, the S of Jehozadak, the high
	6:14	Jedaiah, and Josiah the S of Zephaniah.
Mal	1:6	"A S honors his father, and a servant his
	3:17	a man spares his S who serves him.
1Mac	1:1	After Alexander S of Philip, the Macedonian,
	1:10	sinful root, Antiochus Epiphanes, S of Antiochus the
	2:1	those days Mattathias the S of John, son of
	2:1	the son of John, S of Simeon, a priest
	2:26	did against Zimri the S of Salu.
	3:1	Then Judas his S, who was called Maccabeus, took
	3:33	care of Antiochus his S until he returned.
	3:38	Lysias chose Ptolemy the S of Dorymenes, and
	4:30	hands of Jonathan, the S of Saul, and of
	5:18	he left Joseph, the S of Zechariah, and Azariah,
	5:56	before Ptolemais, Joseph, the S of Zechariah, and
	6:2	there by Alexander, the S of Philip, the Macedonian
	6:15	might guide Antiochus his S and bring him up
	6:17	up Antiochus the king's S to reign.
	6:55	bring up Antiochus his S to be king,
	7:1	fifty-first year Demetrius the S of Seleucus set forth
	8:17	Judas chose Eupolemus the S of John, son of
	8:17	the son of John, S of Accos, and Jason
	8:17	Accos, and Jason the S of Eleazar, and sent
	10:1	Alexander Epiphanes, the S of Antiochus, landed and
	10:67	sixty-fifth year Demetrius the S of Demetrius came
	11:39	up Antiochus, the young S of Alexander,
	11:70	left except Mattathias the S of Absalom and Judas
	11:70	Absalom and Judas the S of Chalphi, commanders of
	12:16	chosen Numenius the S of Antiochus and Antipater
	12:16	Antiochus and Antipater the S of Jason, and have
	13:11	He sent Jonathan the S of Absalom to Joppa,
	13:53	saw that John his S had reached manhood, so
	14:22	follows, 'Numenius the S of Antiochus and Antipater
	14:22	Antiochus and Antipater the S of Jason, envoys of
	14:29	the country, Simon the S of Mattathias, a priest
	15:1	Antiochus, the S of Demetrius the king, sent a
	16:11	Now Ptolemy the S of Abubus had been appointed
	16:15	The S of Abubus received them treacherously in the
2Mac	2:20	Antiochus Epiphanes and his S Eupator,
	3:11	some money of Hyrcanus, S of Tobias, a man
	4:4	that Apollonius, the S of Menestheus and governor
	4:21	When Apollonius the S of Menestheus was sent to
	4:45	substantial bribe to Ptolemy S of Dorymenes to win
	7:26	on his part, she undertook to persuade her S
	7:27	the cruel tyrant: "My S, have pity on me.
	8:9	promptly appointed Nicanor the S of Patroclus, one
	9:25	I have appointed my S Antiochus to be king,
	9:26	will, each of you, toward me and my S
	9:29	home; then, fearing the S of Antiochus, he betook
	10:10	Eupator, who was the S of that ungodly man,
	12:2	Timothy and Apollonius the S of Gennaeus, as well
	14:1	men that Demetrius, the S of Seleucus, had sailed
Mt	1:1	of Jesus Christ, the S of David, the son
	1:1	son of David, the S of Abraham.
	1:20	a dream, saying, "Joseph, S of David, do not
	1:21	she will bear a S, and you shall call
	1:23	conceive and bear a S, and his name shall
	1:25	she had borne a S; and he called his
	2:15	prophet, "Out of Egypt have I called my S
	3:17	"This is my beloved S, with whom I am
	4:3	"If you are the S of God, command these
	4:6	"If you are the S of God, throw yourself
	4:21	other brothers, James the S of Zebedee and John
	7:9	of you, if his S asks him for bread,
	8:20	have nests; but the S of man has nowhere
	8:29	do with us, O S of God?
	9:2	paralytic, "Take heart, my S; your sins are forgiven."
	9:6	may know that the S of man has authority
	9:27	"Have mercy on us, S of David."
	10:2	his brother; James the S of Zebedee, and John
	10:3	tax collector; James the S of Alphaeus, and
	10:23	of Israel, before the S of man comes.
	10:37	and he who loves S or daughter more than
	11:19	has a demon'; the S of man came eating
	11:27	no one knows the S except the Father, and

	11:27	the Father except the S and any one to
	11:27	one to whom the S chooses to reveal him.
	12:8	For the S of man is lord of the
	12:23	"Can this be the S of David?"
	12:32	a word against the S of man will be
	12:40	whale, so will the S of man be three
	13:37	good seed is the S of man;
	13:41	The S of man will send his angels, and
	13:55	Is not this the carpenter's S
	14:33	"Truly you are the S of God."
	15:22	on me, O Lord, S of David; my daughter
	16:13	men say that the S of man is?"
	16:16	are the Christ, the S of the living God."
	16:27	For the S of man is to come with
	16:28	before they see the S of man coming in
	17:5	"This is my beloved S, with whom I am
	17:9	the vision, until the S of man is raised
	17:12	So also the S of man will suffer at
	17:15	have mercy on my S, for he is an
	17:21	said to them, "The S of man is to
	19:28	new world, when the S of man shall sit
	20:18	to Jerusalem; and the S of man will be
	20:28	slave; even as the S of man came not
	20:30	"Have mercy on us, S of David!"
	20:31	have mercy on us, S of David!"
	21:9	shouted, "Hosanna to the S of David!
	21:15	temple, "Hosanna to the S of David!" they were
	21:28	the first and said, S, go and work in
	21:37	Afterward he sent his S to them, saying, 'They
	21:37	'They will respect my S
	21:38	the tenants saw the S, they said to themselves,
	22:2	marriage feast for his S,
	22:42	Whose S is he?" They said to him, "The
	22:42	said to him, "The S of David."
	22:45	thus calls him Lord, how is he his S
	23:34	blood of Zechariah the S of Barachiah, whom you
	24:27	the coming of the S of man.
	24:30	the sign of the S of man in heaven,
	24:30	they will see the S of man coming on
	24:36	of heaven, nor the S, but the Father only.
	24:37	the coming of the S of man.
	24:39	the coming of the S of man.
	24:44	be ready; for the S of man is coming
	25:31	their teeth.' "When the S of man comes in
	26:2	is coming, and the S of man will be
	26:24	The S of man goes as it is written
	26:24	man by whom the S of man is betrayed!
	26:45	at hand, and the S of man is betrayed
	26:63	are the Christ, the S of God."
	26:64	you will see the S of man seated at
	27:40	If you are the S of God, come down
	27:43	said, 'I am the S of God.'"
	27:54	"Truly this was the S of God!"
	28:19	Father and of the S and of the Holy
Mk	1:1	of Jesus Christ, the S of God.
	1:11	"Thou art my beloved S; with thee I am
	1:19	he saw James the S of Zebedee and John
	2:5	to the paralytic, "My S, your sins are forgiven."
	2:10	may know that the S of man has authority
	2:14	he saw Levi the S of Alphaeus sitting at
	2:28	the sabbath; so the S of man is lord
	3:11	out, "You are the S of God."
	3:17	surnamed Peter; James the S of Zebedee and John
	3:18	Thomas, and James the S of Alphaeus, and
	5:7	do with me, Jesus, S of the Most High
	6:3	this the carpenter, the S of Mary and brother
	8:31	teach them that the S of man must suffer
	8:38	of him will the S of man also be
	9:7	"This is my beloved S; listen to him."
	9:9	had seen, until the S of man should have
	9:12	it written of the S of man, that he
	9:17	"Teacher, I brought my S to you, for he
	9:31	saying to them, "The S of man will be
	10:33	to Jerusalem; and the S of man will be
	10:45	For the S of man also came not to
	10:46	a blind beggar, the S of Timaeus, was sitting
	10:47	out and say, "Jesus, S of David, have mercy
	10:48	out all the more, S of David, have mercy
	12:6	one other, a beloved S; finally he sent him
	12:6	'They will respect my S
	12:35	the Christ is the S of David?
	12:37	calls him Lord; so how is he his S
	13:26	they will see the S of man coming in
	13:32	in heaven, nor the S, but only the Father.
	14:21	For the S of man goes as it is
	14:21	man by whom the S of man is betrayed!

	14:41	hour has come; the S of man is betrayed
	14:61	you the Christ, the S of the Blessed?"
	14:62	you will see the S of man seated at
	15:38	this man was the S of God!"
Lk	1:13	will bear you a S, and you shall call
	1:31	womb and bear a S, and you shall call
	1:32	will be called the S of the Most High;
	1:35	be called holy, the S of God.
	1:36	has also conceived a S; and this is the
	1:57	be delivered, and she gave birth to a S
	2:7	birth to her first-born S and wrapped him in
	2:48	mother said to him, S, why have you treated
	3:2	came to John the S of Zechariah in the
	3:22	"Thou art my beloved S; with thee I am
	3:23	of age, being the S (as was supposed) of
	3:23	supposed) of Joseph, the S of Heli,
	3:24	son of Heli, the S of Matthat, the son
	3:24	son of Matthat, the S of Levi, the son
	3:24	son of Levi, the S of Melchi, the son
	3:24	son of Melchi, the S of Janna-i, the son
	3:24	son of Janna-i, the S of Joseph,
	3:25	son of Joseph, the S of Mattathias, the son
	3:25	son of Mattathias, the S of Amos, the son
	3:25	son of Amos, the S of Nah, the son
	3:25	son of Nah, the S of Esli, the son
	3:25	son of Esli, the S of Naggai,
	3:26	son of Naggai, the S of Maath, the son
	3:26	son of Maath, the S of Mattathias, the son
	3:26	son of Mattathias, the S of Seme-in, the son
	3:26	son of Seme-in, the S of Josech, the son
	3:26	son of Josech, the S of Joda,
	3:27	son of Joda, the S of Jo-anan, the son
	3:27	son of Jo-anan, the S of Rhesa, the son
	3:27	son of Rhesa, the S of Zerubbabel, the son
	3:27	son of Zerubbabel, the S of Shealtiel, the son
	3:27	son of Shealtiel, the S of Neri,
	3:28	son of Neri, the S of Melchi, the son
	3:28	son of Melchi, the S of Addi, the son
	3:28	son of Addi, the S of Cosam, the son
	3:28	son of Cosam, the S of Elmadam, the son
	3:28	son of Elmadam, the S of Er,
	3:29	son of Er, the S of Joshua, the son
	3:29	son of Joshua, the S of Eliezer, the son
	3:29	son of Eliezer, the S of Jorim, the son
	3:29	son of Jorim, the S of Matthat, the son
	3:29	son of Matthat, the S of Levi,
	3:30	son of Levi, the S of Simeon, the son
	3:30	son of Simeon, the S of Judah, the son
	3:30	son of Judah, the S of Joseph, the son
	3:30	son of Joseph, the S of Jonam, the son
	3:30	son of Jonam, the S of Eliakim,
	3:31	son of Eliakim, the S of Mele-a, the son
	3:31	son of Mele-a, the S of Menna, the son
	3:31	son of Menna, the S of Mattatha, the son
	3:31	son of Mattatha, the S of Nathan, the son
	3:31	son of Nathan, the S of David,
	3:32	son of David, the S of Jesse, the son
	3:32	son of Jesse, the S of Obed, the son
	3:32	son of Obed, the S of Boaz, the son
	3:32	son of Boaz, the S of Sala, the son
	3:32	son of Sala, the S of Nahshon,
	3:33	son of Nahshon, the S of Amminadab, the son
	3:33	son of Amminadab, the S of Admin, the son
	3:33	son of Admin, the S of Arni, the son
	3:33	son of Arni, the S of Hezron, the son
	3:33	son of Hezron, the S of Perez, the son
	3:33	son of Perez, the S of Judah,
	3:34	son of Judah, the S of Jacob, the son
	3:34	son of Jacob, the S of Isaac, the son
	3:34	son of Isaac, the S of Abraham, the son
	3:34	son of Abraham, the S of Terah, the son
	3:34	son of Terah, the S of Nahor,
	3:35	son of Nahor, the S of Serug, the son
	3:35	son of Serug, the S of Reu, the son
	3:35	son of Reu, the S of Peleg, the son
	3:35	son of Peleg, the S of Eber, the son
	3:35	son of Eber, the S of Shelah,
	3:36	son of Shelah, the S of Ca-inan, the son
	3:36	son of Ca-inan, the S of Arphaxad, the son
	3:36	son of Arphaxad, the S of Shem, the son
	3:36	son of Shem, the S of Noah, the son
	3:36	son of Noah, the S of Lamech,
	3:37	son of Lamech, the S of Methuselah, the son
	3:37	son of Methuselah, the S of Enoch, the son
	3:37	son of Enoch, the S of Jared, the son
	3:37	son of Jared, the S of Mahalale-el, the son

	3:37	son of Mahalale-el, the S of Ca-inan,
	3:38	son of Ca-inan, the S of Enos, the son
	3:38	son of Enos, the S of Seth, the son
	3:38	son of Seth, the S of Adam, the son
	3:38	son of Adam, the S of God.
	4:3	"If you are the S of God, command this
	4:9	"If you are the S of God, throw yourself
	4:22	mouth; and they said, "Is not this Joseph's S
	4:41	crying, "You are the S of God!" But he
	5:24	may know that the S of man has authority
	6:5	said to them, "The S of man is lord
	6:15	Thomas, and James the S of Alphaeus, and Simon
	6:16	Zealot, and Judas the S of James, and Judas
	6:22	on account of the S of man!
	7:12	carried out, the only S of his mother, and
	7:34	has a demon.' The S of man has come
	8:28	do with me, Jesus, S of the Most High
	9:22	no one, saying, "The S of man must suffer
	9:26	of him will the S of man be ashamed
	9:35	saying, "This is my S, my Chosen; listen to
	9:38	to look upon my S, for he is my
	9:41	Bring your S here."
	9:44	your ears; for the S of man is to
	9:58	have nests; but the S of man has nowhere
	10:6	house!' And if a S of peace is there,
	10:22	one knows who the S is except the Father,
	10:22	Father is except the S and any one to
	10:22	one to whom the S chooses to reveal him."
	11:11	among you, if his S asks for a fish,
	11:30	Nineveh, so will the S of man be to
	12:8	me before men, the S of man also will
	12:10	a word against the S of man will be
	12:40	be ready; for the S of man is coming
	12:53	be divided, father against S and son against father,
	12:53	father against son and S against father, mother
	15:13	days later, the younger S gathered all he had
	15:19	to be called your S; treat me as one
	15:21	And the S said to him, 'Father, I have
	15:21	to be called your S
	15:24	merry; for this my S was dead, and is
	15:25	"Now his elder S was in the field; and
	15:30	But when this S of yours came, who has
	15:31	he said to him, S, you are always with
	16:25	flame.' But Abraham said, S, remember that you in
	17:22	the days of the S of man, and you
	17:24	other, so will the S of man be in
	17:26	the days of the S of man.
	17:30	the day when the S of man is revealed.
	18:8	Nevertheless, when the S of man comes, will he
	18:31	is written of the S of man by the
	18:38	And he cried, "Jesus, S of David, have mercy
	18:39	out all the more, S of David, have mercy
	19:9	he also is a S of Abraham.
	19:10	For the S of man came to seek and
	20:13	will send my beloved S; it may be they
	20:41	can they say that the Christ is David's S
	20:44	calls him Lord; so how is he his S
	21:27	they will see the S of man coming in
	21:36	to stand before the S of man."
	22:22	For the S of man goes as it has
	22:46	would you betray the S of man with a
	22:67	from now on the S of man shall be
	22:68	said, "Are you the S of God, then?" And
	24:7	in Galilee, that the S of man must be
Jn	1:14	as of the only S from the Father.
	1:18	seen God; the only S, who is in the
	1:34	that this is the S of God."
	1:42	you are Simon the S of John?
	1:45	Jesus of Nazareth, the S of Joseph."
	1:49	"Rabbi, you are the S of God!
	1:51	and descending upon the S of man."
	3:13	descended from heaven, the S of man.
	3:14	wilderness, so must the S of man be lifted
	3:16	he gave his only S, that whoever believes in
	3:17	For God sent the S into the world, not
	3:18	name of the only S of God.
	3:35	the Father loves the S, and has given all
	3:36	who believes in the S has eternal life; he
	3:36	does not obey the S shall not see life,
	4:5	Jacob gave to his S Joseph.
	4:46	was an official whose S was ill.
	4:47	down and heal his S, for he was at
	4:50	to him, "Go; your S will live." The man
	4:51	told him that his S was living.
	4:53	said to him, "Your S will live"; and he
	5:18	say to you, the S can do nothing of

S

5:18 he does, that the S does likewise.
5:19 the Father loves the S, and shows him all
5:20 life, so also the S gives life to whom
5:21 all judgment to the S,
5:22 all may honor the S, even as they honor
5:22 does not honor the S does not honor the
5:24 the voice of the S of God, and those
5:25 he has granted the S also to have life
5:26 because he is the S of man.
6:27 eternal life, which the S of man will give
6:40 one who sees the S and believes in him
6:42 not this Jesus, the S of Joseph, whose father
6:53 the flesh of the S of man and drink
6:62 were to see the S of man ascending where
6:71 spoke of Judas the S of Simon Iscariot, for
8:28 have lifted up the S of man, then you
8:35 house for ever; the S continues for ever.
8:36 So if the S makes you free, you will
9:19 them, "Is this your S, who you say was
9:20 that this is our S, and that he was
9:35 you believe in the S of man?"
10:36 said, 'I am the S of God?
11:4 God, so that the S of God may be
11:27 are the Christ, the S of God, he who
12:23 has come for the S of man to be
12:34 you say that the S of man must be
12:34 Who is this S of man?"
13:2 of Judas Iscariot, Simon's S, to betray him,
13:26 it to Judas, the S of Simon Iscariot.
13:31 said, "Now is the S of man glorified, and
14:13 be glorified in the S;
17:1 has come; glorify thy S that the Son may
17:1 thy Son that the S may glorify thee,
17:12 is lost but the S of perdition, that the
19:7 has made himself the S of God."
19:26 he said to his mother, "Woman, behold, your S
20:31 is the Christ, the S of God, and that
21:15 to Simon Peter, "Simon, S of John, do you
21:16 said to him, "Simon, S of John, do you
21:17 the third time, "Simon, S of John, do you
Acts 1:13 and Matthew, James the S of Alphaeus and Simon
1:13 Zealot and Judas the S of James.
4:36 Barnabas (which means, S of encouragement),
7:21 him and brought him up as her own S
7:56 heavens opened, and the S of man standing at
9:20 saying, "He is the S of God."
13:10 him and said, "You S of the devil, you
13:21 gave them Saul the S of Kish, a man
13:22 found in David the S of Jesse a man
13:33 psalm, 'Thou art my S, today I have begotten
16:1 there, named Timothy, the S of a Jewish woman
20:4 Sopater of Beroea, the S of Pyrrhus, accompanied
23:6 am a Pharisee, a S of Pharisees; with respect
23:16 Now the S of Paul's sister heard of their
Rom 1:3 the gospel concerning his S, who was descended
1:4 the flesh and designated S of God in power
1:9 the gospel of his S, that without ceasing I
5:10 the death of his S, much more, now that
8:3 do: sending his own S in the likeness of
8:29 the image of his S, in order that he
8:32 not spare his own S but gave him up
9:9 I will return and Sarah shall have a S
1Cor 1:9 the fellowship of his S, Jesus Christ our Lord.
15:28 to him, then the S himself will also be
2Cor 1:19 For the S of God, Jesus Christ, whom we
Gal 1:16 pleased to reveal his S to me, in order
2:20 by faith in the S of God, who loved
4:4 God sent forth his S, born of woman, born
4:6 the Spirit of his S into our hearts, crying,
4:7 a slave but a S, and if a son
4:7 son, and if a S then an heir.
4:23 But the S of the slave was born according
4:23 to the flesh, the S of the free woman
4:30 the slave and her S; for the son of
4:30 her son; for the S of the slave shall
4:30 not inherit with the S of the free woman."
Eph 4:13 the knowledge of the S of God, to mature
Phil 2:22 know, how as a S with a father he
Col 1:13 kingdom of his beloved S,
1Thes 1:10 to wait for his S from heaven, whom he
2Thes 2:3 lawlessness is revealed, the S of perdition,
1Tim 1:18 to you, Timothy, my S, in accordance with the
2Tim 2:1 You then, my S, be strong in the grace
Heb 1:2 to us by a S, whom he appointed the
1:5 say, "Thou art my S, today I have begotten
1:5 father, and he shall be to me a S
1:8 But of the S he says, "Thy throne, O
2:6 of him, or the S of man, that thou
3:6 Christ was faithful over God's house as a S
4:14 the heavens, Jesus, the S of God, let us
5:5 him, "Thou art my S, today I have begotten
5:8 Although he was a S, he learned obedience through
6:6 since they crucify the S of God on their
7:3 life, but resembling the S of God he continues
7:28 the law, appoints a S who has been made
10:29 who has spurned the S of God, and profaned
11:17 offer up his only S,
11:24 to be called the S of Pharaoh's daughter,
12:5 as sons?—"My S, do not regard lightly
12:6 loves, and chastises every S whom he receives."
12:7 as sons; for what S is there whom his
Jas 2:21 when he offered his S Isaac upon the altar?
1Pet 5:13 and so does my S Mark.
2Pet 1:17 "This is my beloved S, with whom I am
2:15 way of Balaam, the S of Beor, who loved
1Jn 1:3 Father and with his S Jesus Christ.
1:7 blood of Jesus his S cleanses us from all
2:22 antichrist, he who denies the Father and the S
2:23 one who denies the S has the Father.
2:23 He who confesses the S has the Father also.
2:24 will abide in the S and in the Father.
3:8 The reason the S of God appeared was to
3:23 the name of his S Jesus Christ and love
4:9 God sent his only S into the world, so
4:10 us and sent his S to be the expiation
4:14 Father has sent his S as the Savior of
4:15 that Jesus is the S of God, God abides
5:5 that Jesus is the S of God?
5:9 God that he has borne witness to his S
5:10 who believes in the S of God has the
5:10 the testimony that God has borne to his S
5:11 eternal life, and this life is in his S
5:12 He who has the S has life; he who
5:12 who has not the S of God has not
5:13 the name of the S of God, that you
5:20 we know that the S of God has come
5:20 is true, in his S Jesus Christ.
2Jn 1:3 Jesus Christ the Father's S, in truth and love.
1:9 the doctrine has both the Father and the S
Rev 1:13 lampstands one like a S of man, clothed with
2:18 'The words of the S of God, who has
14:14 cloud one like a S of man, with a
21:7 be his God and he shall be my S

SON-IN-LAW (14)

Judg 15:6 they said, "Samson, the S of the Timnite, because
19:5 father said to his S, "Strengthen your heart with
1Sam 18:18 that I should be S to the king?"
18:21 a second time, "You shall now be my S
18:22 servants love you; now then become the king's S
18:23 to become the king's S, seeing that I am
18:26 it pleased David well to be the king's S
18:27 the king, that he might become the king's S
22:14 who is the king's S, and captain over your
2Kgs 8:27 done, for he was S to the house of
Neh 6:18 because he was the S of Shecaniah the son
13:28 high priest, was the S of Sanballat the Horonite;
1Mac 10:54 I will become your S, and will make gifts
16:12 gold, for he was S of the high priest.

SONG (57)

Ex 15:1 of Israel sang this S to the LORD, saying,
15:2 my strength and my S, and he has become
Num 21:17 Then Israel sang this S: "Spring up, O well!—
Deut 31:19 Now therefore write this S, and teach it to
31:19 their mouths, that this S may be a witness
31:21 come upon them, this S shall confront them as
31:22 So Moses wrote this S the same day, and
31:30 the words of this S until they were finished,
32:44 the words of this S in the hearing of
Judg 5:12 Awake, awake, utter a S
2Sam 22:1 the words of this S on the day when
1Chr 6:31 of the service of S in the house of
6:32 They ministered with S before the tabernacle of the
13:8 all their might, with S and lyres and harps
16:42 cymbals for the music and instruments for sacred S
2Chr 5:13 LORD), and when the S was raised, with trumpets
29:27 burnt offering began, the S to the LORD began
Jud 16:1 people loudly sang this S of praise.
16:2 Judith said, Begin a S to my God with
16:13 my God a new S: O Lord, thou are
Job 30:9 I have become their S, I am a byword

S

36:19 These are the S of Esau (that is, Edom),
36:20 These are the S of Seir the Horite, the
36:21 of the Horites, the S of Seir in the
36:22 The S of Lotan were Hori and Heman; and
36:23 These are the S of Shobal: Alvan, Manahath, Ebal,
36:24 These are the S of Zibeon: Aiah and Anah;
36:26 These are the S of Dishon: Hemdan, Eshban, Ithran,
36:27 These are the S of Ezer: Bilhan, Zaavan, and
36:28 These are the S of Dishan: Uz and Aran.
37:2 a lad with the S of Bilhah and Zilpah,
37:35 All his S and all his daughters rose up
41:50 Joseph had two S, whom Asenath, the daughter
42:1 he said to his S, "Why do you look
42:5 Thus the S of Israel came to buy among
42:11 We are all S of one man, we are
42:13 are twelve brothers, the S of one man in
42:32 we are twelve brothers, S of our father; one
42:37 father, "Slay my two S if I do not
44:27 wife bore me two S;
45:21 The S of Israel did so; and Joseph gave
46:5 from Beer-sheba; and the S of Israel carried Jacob
46:7 offspring with him, his S, and his sons' sons
46:7 his sons, and his S sons with him, his
46:7 sons, and his sons' S with him, his daughters,
46:7 his daughters, and his S daughters; all his offspring
46:8 Israel, who came into Egypt, Jacob and his S
46:9 Jacob's first-born, and the S of Reuben: Hanoch,
46:10 The S of Simeon: Jemuel, Jamin, Ohad, Jachin,
46:11 The S of Levi: Gershon, Kohath, and Merari.
46:12 The S of Judah: Er, Onan, Shelah, Perez, and
46:12 of Canaan); and the S of Perez were Hezron
46:13 The S of Issachar: Tola, Puvah, Iob, and Shimron.
46:14 The S of Zebulun: Sered, Elon, and Jahleel
46:15 Jahleel (these are the S of Leah, whom she
46:15 daughter Dinah; altogether his S and his daughters
46:16 The S of Gad: Ziphion, Haggi, Shuni, Ezbon, Eri,
46:17 The S of Asher: Imnah, Ishvah, Ishvi, Beriah, with
46:17 And the S of Beriah: Heber and Malchi-el
46:18 Malchi-el (these are the S of Zilpah, whom Laban
46:19 The S of Rachel, Jacob's wife: Joseph and Benjamin.
46:21 And the S of Benjamin: Bela, Becher, Ashbel, Gera,
46:22 Ard (these are the S of Rachel, who were
46:23 The S of Dan: Hushim.
46:24 The S of Naphtali: Jahzeel, Guni, Jezer, and Shillem
46:25 Shillem (these are the S of Bilhah, whom Laban
46:26 offspring, not including Jacob's S wives, were
46:27 in all; and the S of Joseph, who were
48:1 with him his two S, Manasseh and Ephraim.
48:5 And now your two S, who were born to
48:8 When Israel saw Joseph's S, he said, "Who are
48:9 father, "They are my S, whom God has given
49:1 Then Jacob called his S, and said, "Gather yourselves
49:2 Assemble and hear, O S of Jacob, and hearken
49:8 your enemies; your father's S shall bow down before
49:33 Jacob finished charging his S, he drew up his
50:12 Thus his S did for him as he had
50:13 commanded them; for his S carried him to the
50:25 an oath of the S of Israel, saying, "God
Ex 1:1 the names of the S of Israel who came
3:10 forth my people, the S of Israel, out of
3:11 Pharaoh, and bring the S of Israel out of
3:22 put them on your S and on your daughters;
4:20 his wife and his S and set them on
6:14 their fathers' houses: the S of Reuben, the first-born
6:15 The S of Simeon: Jemuel, Jamin, Ohad, Jachin,
6:16 the names of the S of Levi according to
6:17 The S of Gershon: Libni and Shimei, by their
6:18 The S of Kohath: Amram, Izhar, Hebron, and Uzziel,
6:19 The S of Merari: Mahli and Mushi.
6:21 The S of Izhar: Korah, Nepheg, and Zichri.
6:22 And the S of Uzziel: Mishael, Elzaphan, and Sithri.
6:24 The S of Korah: Assir, Elkanah, and Abiasaph; these
7:4 hosts, my people the S of Israel, out of
10:9 will go with our S and daughters and with
12:24 you and for your S for ever.
13:13 of man among your S you shall redeem.
13:15 the first-born of my S I redeem.'
18:3 away, and her two S, of whom the name
18:5 father-in-law, came with his S and his wife to
18:6 wife and her two S with her,"
21:4 and she bears him S or daughters, the wife
22:29 "The first-born of your S you shall give to
27:21 testimony, Aaron and his S shall tend it from
28:1 your brother, and his S with him, from among
28:1 priests--Aaron and Aaron's S, Nadab and Abihu,
28:4 your brother and his S to serve me as
28:9 the names of the S of Israel,
28:11 the names of the S of Israel; you shall
28:12 of remembrance for the S of Israel; and Aaron
28:21 the names of the S of Israel; they shall
28:29 the names of the S of Israel in the
28:40 "And for Aaron's S you shall make coats and
28:41 brother, and upon his S with him, and shall
28:43 Aaron, and upon his S, when they go into
29:4 bring Aaron and his S to the door of
29:8 you shall bring his S, and put coats on
29:9 Thus you shall ordain Aaron and his S
29:10 Aaron and his S shall lay their hands upon
29:15 and Aaron and his S shall lay their hands
29:19 and Aaron and his S shall lay their hands
29:20 right ears of his S, and upon the thumbs
29:21 garments, and upon his S and his sons' garments
29:21 his sons and his S garments with him; and
29:21 be holy, and his S and his sons' garments
29:21 his sons and his S garments with him.
29:24 the hands of his S, and wave them for
29:27 since it is for Aaron and for his S
29:28 for Aaron and his S as a perpetual due
29:29 shall be for his S after him, to be
29:32 and Aaron and his S shall eat the flesh
29:35 Aaron and to his S, according to all that
29:44 Aaron also and his S I will consecrate, to
30:19 which Aaron and his S shall wash their hands
30:30 anoint Aaron and his S, and consecrate them, that
31:10 the garments of his S, for their service as
32:2 of your wives, your S, and your daughters, and
32:26 And all the S of Levi gathered themselves together
32:28 And the S of Levi did according to the
34:16 their daughters for your S, and their daughters play
34:16 gods and make your S play the harlot after
34:20 the first-born of your S you shall redeem.
35:19 the garments of his S, for their service as
39:6 the names of the S of Israel.
39:7 of remembrance for the S of Israel; as the
39:14 the names of the S of Israel; they were
39:27 for Aaron and his S,
39:41 the garments of his S to serve as priests.
Lev 1:5 the LORD; and Aaron's S the priests shall present
1:7 into pieces; and the S of Aaron the priest
1:8 the fire; and Aaron's S the priests shall lay
1:11 the LORD, and Aaron's S the priests shall throw
2:2 bring it to Aaron's S the priests.
2:3 for Aaron and his S; it is a most
2:10 for Aaron and his S; it is a most
3:2 of meeting; and Aaron's S the priests shall throw
3:5 Then Aaron's S shall burn it on the altar
3:8 of meeting; and Aaron's S shall throw its blood
3:13 of meeting; and the S of Aaron shall throw
6:9 "Command Aaron and his S, saying, This is the
6:14 The S of Aaron shall offer it before the
6:16 it Aaron and his S shall eat; it shall
6:20 which Aaron and his S shall offer to the
6:22 priest from among Aaron's S, who is anointed to
6:25 to Aaron and his S, This is the law
7:10 be for all the S of Aaron, one as
7:31 the breast shall be for Aaron and his S
7:33 offerings; he among the S of Aaron who offers
7:34 priest and to his S, as a perpetual due
7:35 Aaron and of his S from the offerings made
8:2 "Take Aaron and his S with him, and the
8:6 brought Aaron and his S, and washed them with
8:13 And Moses brought Aaron's S, and clothed them with
8:14 and Aaron and his S laid their hands upon
8:18 and Aaron and his S laid their hands on
8:22 and Aaron and his S laid their hands on
8:24 And Aaron's S were brought, and Moses put some
8:27 the hands of his S, and waved them as
8:30 and also upon his S and his sons' garments;
8:30 his sons and his S garments; so he consecrated
8:30 his garments, and his S and his sons' garments
8:30 his sons and his S garments with him.
8:31 to Aaron and his S, "Boil the flesh at
8:31 saying, 'Aaron and his S shall eat it';
8:36 And Aaron and his S did all the things
9:1 called Aaron and his S and the elders of
9:9 And the S of Aaron presented the blood to
9:12 burnt offering; and Aaron's S delivered to him the
9:18 the people; and Aaron's S delivered to him the
10:1 Nadab and Abihu, the S of Aaron, each took
10:4 Mishael and Elzaphan, the S of Uzziel the uncle
10:6 Eleazar and Ithamar, his S, "Do not let the
10:9 drink, you nor your S with you, when you

10:12 Eleazar and Ithamar, his S who were left, "Take
10:13 your due and your S due, from the offerings
10:14 place, you and your S and your daughters with
10:14 your due and your S due, from the sacrifices
10:15 be yours, and your S with you, as a
10:16 Eleazar and Ithamar, the S of Aaron who were
13:2 to one of his S the priests,
16:1 death of the two S of Aaron, when they
17:2 to Aaron and his S, and to all the
19:18 any grudge against the S of your own people,
21:1 to the priests, the S of Aaron, and say
21:24 Aaron and to his S and to all the
22:2 "Tell Aaron and his S to keep away from
22:18 to Aaron and his S and all the people
24:9 for Aaron and his S, and they shall eat
25:46 bequeath them to your S after you, to inherit
26:29 the flesh of your S, and you shall eat
Num 1:10 of Helon; from the S of Joseph, from Ephraim,
3:2 the names of the S of Aaron: Nadab the
3:3 the names of the S of Aaron, the anointed
3:9 to Aaron and his S; they are wholly given
3:10 appoint Aaron and his S, and they shall attend
3:15 of Sinai, "Number the S of Levi, by fathers'
3:17 And these were the S of Levi by their
3:18 the names of the S of Gershon by their
3:19 And the S of Kohath by their families: Amram,
3:20 And the S of Merari by their families: Mahli
3:25 the charge of the S of Gershon in the
3:29 The families of the S of Kohath were to
3:36 appointed charge of the S of Merari was to
3:38 and Aaron and his S, having charge of the
3:48 of them is redeemed to Aaron and his S
3:51 to Aaron and his S, according to the word
4:2 a census of the S of Kohath from among
4:2 Kohath from among the S of Levi, by their
4:4 the service of the S of Kohath in the
4:5 out, Aaron and his S shall go in and
4:15 when Aaron and his S have finished covering the
4:15 out, after that the S of Kohath shall come
4:15 of meeting which the S of Kohath are to
4:19 things: Aaron and his S shall go in and
4:22 a census of the S of Gershon also, by
4:27 the service of the S of the Gershonites shall
4:27 of Aaron and his S, in all that they
4:28 the families of the S of the Gershonites in
4:29 "As for the S of Merari, you shall number
4:33 the families of the S of Merari, the whole
4:34 the congregation numbered the S of the Kohathites,
4:38 The number of the S of Gershon, by their
4:41 the families of the S of Gershon, all who
4:42 the families of the S of Merari, by their
4:45 the families of the S of Merari, whom Moses
6:23 to Aaron and his S, Thus you shall bless
7:7 he gave to the S of Gershon, according to
7:8 he gave to the S of Merari, according to
7:9 But to the S of Kohath he gave none,
8:13 attend Aaron and his S, and shall offer them
8:19 to Aaron and his S from among the people
8:22 upon Aaron and his S; as the LORD had
10:8 And the S of Aaron, the priests, shall blow
10:17 was taken down, the S of Gershon and the
10:17 of Gershon and the S of Merari, who carried
13:33 saw the Nephilim (the S of Anak, who come
16:1 Dathan and Abiram the S of Eliab, and On
16:1 the son of Peleth, S of Reuben,
16:7 have gone too far, S of Levi!"
16:8 Korah, "Hear now, you S of Levi:
16:10 all your brethren the S of Levi with you?
16:12 Dathan and Abiram the S of Eliab; and they
16:27 with their wives, their S, and their little ones.
18:1 Aaron, "You and your S and your fathers' house
18:1 and you and your S with you shall bear
18:2 while you and your S with you are before
18:7 And you and your S with you shall attend
18:8 portion, and to your S as a perpetual due.
18:9 be most holy to you and to your S
18:11 you, and to your S and daughters with you,
18:19 you, and to your S and daughters with you,
21:29 He has made his S fugitives, and his daughters
21:35 slew him, and his S, and all his people,
24:17 break down all the S of Sheth.
26:5 first-born of Israel; the S of Reuben: of Hanoch,
26:8 And the S of Pallu: Eliab.
26:9 The S of Eliab: Nemuel, Dathan, and Abiram.
26:11 Notwithstanding, the S of Korah did not die.
26:12 The S of Simeon according to their families: of
26:15 The S of Gad according to their families: of
26:18 the families of the S of Gad according to
26:19 The S of Judah were Er and Onan; and
26:20 And the S of Judah according to their families
26:21 And the S of Perez were: of Hezron, the
26:23 The S of Issachar according to their families: of
26:26 The S of Zebulun, according to their families: of
26:28 The S of Joseph according to their families:
26:29 The S of Manasseh: of Machir, the family of
26:30 These are the S of Gilead: of Iezer, the
26:33 of Hepher had no S, but daughters: and the
26:35 These are the S of Ephraim according to their
26:36 And these are the S of Shuthelah: of Eran,
26:37 the families of the S of Ephraim according to
26:37 These are the S of Joseph according to their
26:38 The S of Benjamin according to their families: of
26:40 And the S of Bela were Ard and Naaman:
26:41 These are the S of Benjamin according to their
26:42 These are the S of Dan according to their
26:44 The S of Asher according to their families: of
26:45 Of the S of Beriah: of Heber, the family
26:47 the families of the S of Asher according to
26:48 The S of Naphtali according to their families: of
27:3 for his own sin; and he had no S
32:1 Now the S of Reuben and the sons of
32:1 of Reuben and the S of Gad had a
32:2 So the S of Gad and the sons of
32:2 of Gad and the S of Reuben came and
32:6 Moses said to the S of Gad and to
32:6 Gad and to the S of Reuben, "Shall your
32:25 And the S of Gad and the sons of
32:25 of Gad and the S of Reuben said to
32:29 to them, "If the S of Gad and the
32:29 of Gad and the S of Reuben, every man
32:31 And the S of Gad and the sons of
32:31 of Gad and the S of Reuben answered, "As
32:33 to them, to the S of Gad and to
32:33 Gad and to the S of Reuben and to
32:34 And the S of Gad built Dibon, Ataroth, Aroer,
32:37 And the S of Reuben built Heshbon, Elealeh,
32:39 And the S of Machir the son of Manasseh
34:14 the tribe of the S of Reuben by fathers'
34:14 the tribe of the S of Gad by their
34:20 the tribe of the S of Simeon, Shemuel the
34:22 the tribe of the S of Dan a leader,
34:23 Of the S of Joseph: of the tribe of
34:23 the tribe of the S of Manasseh a leader,
34:24 the tribe of the S of Ephraim a leader,
34:25 the tribe of the S of Zebulun a leader,
34:26 the tribe of the S of Issachar a leader,
34:27 the tribe of the S of Asher a leader,
34:28 the tribe of the S of Naphtali a leader,
36:1 the families of the S of Gilead the son
36:1 fathers' houses of the S of Joseph, came near
36:3 to any of the S of the other tribes
36:5 "The tribe of the S of Joseph is right.
36:11 Zelophehad, were married to S of their father's
36:12 the families of the S of Manasseh the son
Deut 1:28 we have seen the S of the Anakim there."'
2:4 of your brethren the S of Esau, who live
2:8 from our brethren the S of Esau who live
2:9 given Ar to the S of Lot for a
2:12 Seir formerly, but the S of Esau dispossessed them,
2:19 the frontier of the S of Ammon, do not
2:19 the land of the S of Ammon as a
2:19 given it to the S of Lot for a
2:22 he did for the S of Esau, who live
2:29 on foot, as the S of Esau who live
2:33 defeated him and his S and all his people.
2:37 the land of the S of Ammon you did
7:3 your daughters to their S or taking their daughters
7:3 their sons or taking their daughters for your S
7:4 would turn away your S from following me, to
9:2 great and tall, the S of the Anakim, whom
9:2 can stand before the S of Anak?'
11:6 Dathan and Abiram the S of Eliab, son of
12:12 God, you and your S and your daughters, your
12:31 they even burn their S and their daughters in
14:1 "You are the S of the LORD your God;
18:5 LORD, him and his S for ever.
21:5 And the priests the S of Levi shall come
21:16 an inheritance to his S, he may not treat
23:17 cult prostitute of the S of Israel.
28:32 Your S and your daughters shall be given to
28:41 You shall beget S and daughters, but they shall
28:53 the flesh of your S and daughters, whom the

S

31:9 to the priests the S of Levi, who carried
32:8 when he separated the S of men, he fixed
32:8 the number of the S of God.
32:19 the provocation of his S and his daughters.
33:24 he said, "Blessed above S be Asher; let him
Josh 4:12 The S of Reuben and the sons of Gad
4:12 of Reuben and the S of Gad and the
7:24 of gold, and his S and daughters, and his
15:14 from there the three S of Anak, Sheshai and
17:3 of Manasseh, had no S, but only daughters; and
17:6 Manasseh received an inheritance along with his S
17:8 Manasseh belonged to the S of Ephraim.
17:12 Yet the S of Manasseh could not take possession
24:32 Jacob bought from the S of Hamor the father
Judg 1:20 from it the three S of Anak.
3:6 they gave to their S; and they served their
8:18 them; they resembled the S of a king."
8:19 were my brothers, the S of my mother; as
8:30 Now Gideon had seventy S, his own offspring, for
9:2 all seventy of the S of Jerubbaal rule over
9:5 slew his brothers the S of Jerubbaal, seventy men,
9:18 and have slain his S, seventy men on one
9:24 done to the seventy S of Jerubbaal might come
10:4 And he had thirty S who rode on thirty
11:2 wife also bore him S; and when his wife's
11:2 and when his wife's S grew up, they thrust
12:9 He had thirty S; and thirty daughters he gave
12:9 daughters he brought in from outside for his S
12:14 He had forty S and thirty grandsons, who rode
17:5 installed one of his S, who became his priest.
17:11 man became to him like one of his S
18:30 of Moses, and his S were priests to the
Ruth 1:1 Moab, he and his wife and his two S
1:2 names of his two S were Mahlon and Chilion;
1:3 died, and she was left with her two S
1:5 bereft of her two S and her husband.
1:11 Have I yet S in my womb that they
1:12 night and should bear S,
4:15 to you than seven S, has borne him."
1Sam 1:3 Shiloh, where the two S of Eli, Hophni and
1:4 and to all her S and daughters;
1:8 Am I not more to you than ten S
2:12 Now the S of Eli were worthless men; they
2:21 conceived and bore three S and two daughters.
2:22 heard all that his S were doing to all
2:24 No, my S; it is no good report that
2:29 commanded, and honor your S above me by fattening
2:34 shall befall your two S, Hophni and Phinehas, shall
3:13 he knew, because his S were blaspheming God, and
4:4 cherubim; and the two S of Eli, Hophni and
4:11 captured; and the two S of Eli, Hophni and
4:17 the people; your two S also, Hophni and Phinehas,
8:1 old, he made his S judges over Israel.
8:3 Yet his S did not walk in his ways,
8:5 are old and your S do not walk in
8:11 he will take your S and appoint them to
12:2 gray, and behold, my S are with you; and
14:49 Now the S of Saul were Jonathan, Ishvi, and
16:1 have provided for myself a king among his S
16:5 consecrated Jesse and his S, and invited them to
16:10 made seven of his S pass before Samuel.
16:11 Jesse, "Are all your S here?" And he said,
17:12 Bethlehem in Judah, named Jesse, who had eight S
17:13 The three eldest S of Jesse had followed Saul
17:13 names of his three S who went to the
22:20 But one of the S of Ahimelech the son
28:19 tomorrow you and your S shall be with me;
30:3 and their wives and S and daughters taken captive.
30:6 soul, each for his S and daughters.
30:19 whether small or great, S or daughters, spoil or
31:2 overtook Saul and his S; and the Philistines slew
31:2 Abinadab and Malchishua, the S of Saul.
31:6 died, and his three S, and his armor-bearer, and
31:7 that Saul and his S were dead, they forsook
31:8 Saul and his three S fallen on Mount Gilboa.
31:12 the bodies of his S from the wall of
2Sam 2:18 And the three S of Zeruiah were there, Joab,
3:2 And S were born to David at Hebron: his
3:39 king; these men the S of Zeruiah are too
4:2 of the other Rechab, S of Rimmon a man
4:5 Now the S of Rimmon the Be-erothite, Rechab and
4:9 his brother, the S of Rimmon the Be-erothite,
5:13 from Hebron; and more S and daughters were born
6:3 Uzzah and Ahio, the S of Abinadab, were driving
7:14 the stripes of the S of men;
8:18 the Pelethites; and David's S were priests.
9:10 And you and your S and your servants shall
9:10 Now Ziba had fifteen S and twenty servants.
9:11 at David's table, like one of the king's S
13:23 near Ephraim, and Absalom invited all the king's S
13:27 and all the king's S go with him.
13:29 Then all the king's S arose, and each mounted
13:30 slain all the king's S, and not one of
13:32 young men the king's S, for Amnon alone is
13:33 that all the king's S are dead; for Amnon
13:35 king, "Behold, the king's S have come; as your
13:36 speaking, behold, the king's S came, and lifted up
14:6 your handmaid had two S, and they quarreled with
14:27 born to Absalom three S, and one daughter whose
15:27 Abiathar, with your two S, Ahima-az your son, and
15:36 Behold, their two S are with them there, Ahima-az,
16:10 do with you, you S of Zeruiah?
19:5 the lives of your S and your daughters, and
19:17 Saul, with his fifteen S and his twenty servants,
19:22 do with you, you S of Zeruiah, that you
21:6 let seven of his S be given to us,
21:8 king took the two S of Rizpah the daughter
21:8 Mephibosheth; and the five S of Merab the daughter
23:32 Eliahba of Sha-albon, the S of Jashen, Jonathan,
1Kgs 1:9 his brothers, the king's S, and all the royal
1:19 has invited all the S of the king, Abiathar
1:25 invited all the king's S, Joab the commander of
2:4 me, saying, 'If your S take heed to their
2:7 deal loyally with the S of Barzillai the Gileadite,
4:3 Elihoreph and Ahijah the S of Shisha were
4:31 Calcol, and Darda, the S of Mahol; and his
8:25 Israel, if only your S take heed to their
11:20 Pharaoh's house among the S of Pharaoh.
13:11 And his S came and told him all that
13:12 And his S showed him the way which the
13:13 he said to his S, "Saddle the ass for
13:27 he said to his S, "Saddle the ass for
13:31 he said to his S, "When I die, bury
18:31 the tribes of the S of Jacob, to whom
20:35 certain man of the S of the prophets said
2Kgs 2:3 And the S of the prophets who were in
2:5 The S of the prophets who were at Jericho
2:7 Fifty men of the S of the prophets also
2:15 Now when the S of the prophets who were
4:1 of one of the S of the prophets cried
4:4 upon yourself and your S, and pour into all
4:5 upon herself and her S; and as she poured
4:7 and you and your S can live on the
4:38 And as the S of the prophets were sitting
4:38 boil pottage for the S of the prophets."
5:22 young men of the S of the prophets; pray,
6:1 Now the S of the prophets said to Elisha,
8:19 him and to his S for ever.
9:1 called one of the S of the prophets and
9:26 the blood of his S --says the LORD--I
10:1 Now Ahab had seventy S in Samaria.
10:1 the guardians of the S of Ahab, saying,
10:2 you, seeing your master's S are with you, and
10:3 fittest of your master's S and set him on
10:6 heads of your master's S, and come to me
10:6 Now the king's S, seventy persons, were with the
10:7 they took the king's S, and slew them, seventy
10:8 "They have brought the heads of the king's S
10:13 royal princes and the S of the queen mother."
10:30 in my heart, your S of the fourth generation
11:2 from among the king's S who were about to
15:12 gave to Jehu, "Your S shall sit upon the
17:17 And they burned their S and their daughters as
19:37 Adrammelech and Sharezer, his S, slew him with the
20:18 some of your own S, who are born to
23:10 the valley of the S of Hinnom, that no
25:7 They slew the S of Zedekiah before his eyes,
1Chr 1:5 The S of Japheth: Gomer, Magog, Madai, Javan,
1:6 The S of Gomer: Ashkenaz, Diphath, and Togarmah.
1:7 The S of Javan: Elishah, Tarshish, Kittim, and
1:8 The S of Ham: Cush, Egypt, Put, and Canaan.
1:9 The S of Cush: Seba, Havilah, Sabta, Raama, and
1:9 The S of Raamah: Sheba and Dedan.
1:17 The S of Shem: Elam, Asshur, Arpachshad, Lud,
1:19 Eber were born two S: the name of the
1:23 all these were the S of Joktan.
1:28 The S of Abraham: Isaac and Ishmael.
1:31 These are the S of Ishmael.
1:32 The S of Keturah, Abraham's concubine: she bore
1:32 The S of Jokshan: Sheba and Dedan.
1:33 The S of Midian: Ephah, Epher, Hanoch, Abida, and
1:34 The S of Isaac: Esau and Israel.

S

1:35 The S of Esau: Eliphaz, Reuel, Jeush, Jalam, and
1:36 The S of Eliphaz: Teman, Omar, Zephi, Gatam,
1:37 The S of Reuel: Nahath, Zerah, Shammah, and
1:38 The S of Seir: Lotan, Shobal, Zibeon, Anah, Dishon,
1:39 The S of Lotan: Hori and Homam; and Lotan's
1:40 The S of Shobal: Alian, Manahath, Ebal, Shephi, and
1:40 The S of Zibeon: Aiah and Anah.
1:41 The S of Anah: Dishon.
1:41 The S of Dishon: Hamran, Eshban, Ithran, and
1:42 The S of Ezer: Bilhan, Zaavan, and Jaakan.
1:42 The S of Dishan: Uz and Aran.
2:1 These are the S of Israel: Reuben, Simeon, Levi,
2:3 The S of Judah: Er, Onan, and Shelah; these
2:4 Judah had five S in all.
2:5 The S of Perez: Hezron and Hamul.
2:6 The S of Zerah: Zimri, Ethan, Heman, Calcol, and
2:7 The S of Carmi: Achar, the troubler of Israel,
2:9 The S of Hezron, that were born to him:
2:10 Nahshon, prince of the S of Judah.
2:16 The S of Zeruiah: Abishai, Joab, and Asahel, three.
2:18 and these were her S: Jesher, Shobab, and Ardon.
2:25 The S of Jerahmeel, the first-born of Hezron: Ram,
2:27 The S of Ram, the first-born of Jerahmeel: Maaz,
2:28 The S of Onam: Shammai and Jada.
2:28 The S of Shammai: Nadab and Abishur.
2:30 The S of Nadab: Seled and Appa-im; and Seled
2:31 The S of Appa-im: Ishi.
2:31 The S of Ishi: Sheshan.
2:31 The S of Sheshan: Ahlai.
2:32 S of Jada, Shammai's brother: Jether and Jonathan;
2:33 The S of Jonathan: Peleth and Zaza.
2:34 Now Sheshan had no S, only daughters; but Sheshan
2:42 The S of Caleb the brother of Jerahmeel: Mareshah
2:42 The S of Mareshah: Hebron.
2:43 The S of Hebron: Korah, Tappuah, Rekem, and
2:47 The S of Jahdai: Regem, Jotham, Geshan, Pelet,
2:50 The S of Hur the first-born of Ephrathah: Shobal
2:52 of Kiriath-jearim had other S: Haroeh, half of the
2:54 The S of Salma: Bethlehem, the Netophathites,
3:1 These are the S of David that were born
3:9 All these were David's S, besides the sons of
3:9 David's sons, besides the S of the concubines; and
3:15 The S of Josiah: Johanan the first-born, the second
3:17 his son; and the S of Jeconiah, the captive:
3:19 and Nedabiah; and the S of Pedaiah: Zerubbabel
3:19 and Shimei; and the S of Zerubbabel: Meshullam
3:21 The S of Hananiah: Pelatiah and Jeshaiah, his son
3:22 The S of Shecaniah: Shemaiah.
3:22 And the S of Shemaiah: Hattush, Igal, Bariah,
3:23 The S of Neariah: Eli-o-enai, Hizkiah, and Azrikam,
3:24 S of Eli-o-enai: Hodaviah, Eliashib, Pelaiah, Akkub,
4:1 The S of Judah: Perez, Hezron, Carmi, Hur, and
4:3 These were the S of Etam: Jezreel, Ishma, and
4:4 These were the S of Hur, the first-born of
4:6 These were the S of Naarah.
4:7 The S of Helah: Zereth, Izhar, and Ethnan.
4:13 The S of Kenaz: Othni-el and Seraiah; and the
4:13 and Seraiah; and the S of Othni-el: Hathath and
4:15 The S of Caleb the son of Jephunneh: Iru,
4:15 and Naam; and the S of Elah: Kenaz.
4:16 The S of Jehallelel: Ziph, Ziphah, Tiri-a, and Asarel.
4:17 The S of Ezrah: Jether, Mered, Epher, and Jalon.
4:17 These are the S of Bithi-ah, the daughter of
4:19 The S of the wife of Hodiah, the sister
4:20 The S of Shimon: Amnon, Rinnah, Ben-hanan, and
4:20 The S of Ishi: Zoheth and Ben-zoheth.
4:21 The S of Shelah the son of Judah: Er
4:24 The S of Simeon: Nemuel, Jamin, Jarib, Zerah,
4:26 The S of Mishma: Hammu-el his son, Zaccur his
4:27 Shimei had sixteen S and six daughters; but his
4:42 Rephaiah, and Uzziel, the S of Ishi;
5:1 The S of Reuben the first-born of Israel (for
5:1 was given to the S of Joseph the son
5:3 belonged to Joseph), the S of Reuben, the first-born
5:4 The S of Joel: Shemaiah his son, Gog his
5:11 The S of Gad dwelt over against them in
5:14 These were the S of Abihail the son of
6:1 The S of Levi: Gershom, Kohath, and Merari.
6:2 The S of Kohath: Amram, Izhar, Hebron, and Uzziel.
6:3 The S of Aaron: Nadab, Abihu, Eleazar, and Ithamar.
6:16 The S of Levi: Gershom, Kohath, and Merari.
6:17 the names of the S of Gershom: Libni and
6:18 The S of Kohath: Amram, Izhar, Hebron, and Uzziel.
6:19 The S of Merari: Mahli and Mushi.
6:22 The S of Kohath: Amminadab his son, Korah his
6:25 The S of Elkanah: Amasai and Ahimoth,
6:28 The S of Samuel: Joel his first-born, the second
6:29 The S of Merari: Mahli, Libni his son, Shimei
6:33 These are the men who served and their S
6:33 Of the S of the Kohathites: Heman the singer
6:44 were their brethren the S of Merari: Ethan the
6:49 But Aaron and his S made offerings upon the
6:50 These are the S of Aaron: Eleazar his son,
6:54 their borders: to the S of Aaron of the
6:57 To the S of Aaron they gave the cities
6:66 the families of the S of Kohath had cities
7:1 The S of Issachar: Tola, Puah, Jashub, and Shimron,
7:2 The S of Tola: Uzzi, Rephaiah, Jeri-el, Jahmai,
7:3 The S of Uzzi: Izrahiah.
7:3 And the S of Izrahiah: Michael, Obadiah, Joel, and
7:4 thirty-six thousand, for they had many wives and S
7:6 The S of Benjamin: Bela, Becher, and Jedia-el,
7:7 The S of Bela: Ezbon, Uzzi, Uzziel, Jerimoth, and
7:8 The S of Becher: Zemirah, Joash, Eliezer, Eli-o-enai,
7:8 All these were the S of Becher;
7:10 The S of Jedia-el: Bilhan.
7:10 And the S of Bilhan: Jeush, Benjamin, Ehud,
7:11 All these were the S of Jedia-el according to
7:12 and Huppim were the S of Ir, Hushim the
7:12 of Ir, Hushim the S of Aher.
7:13 The S of Naphtali: Jahzi-el, Guni, Jezer, and
7:14 The S of Manasseh: Asriel, whom his Aramean
7:16 was Sheresh; and his S were Ulam and Rakem.
7:17 The S of Ulam: Bedan.
7:17 These were the S of Gilead the son of
7:19 The S of Shemida were Ahian, Shechem, Likhi, and
7:20 The S of Ephraim: Shuthelah, and Bered his son,
7:29 In these dwelt the S of Joseph the son
7:30 The S of Asher: Imnah, Ishvah, Ishvi, Beriah, and
7:31 The S of Beriah: Heber and Malchi-el, who was
7:33 The S of Japhlet: Pasach, Bimhal, and Ashvath.
7:33 These are the S of Japhlet.
7:34 The S of Shemer his brother: Rohgah, Jehubbah,
7:35 The S of Helem his brother: Zophah, Imna, Shelesh,
7:36 The S of Zophah: Suah, Harnepher, Shual, Beri,
7:38 The S of Jether: Jephunneh, Pispa, and Ara.
7:39 The S of Ulla: Arah, Hanniel, and Rizia.
8:3 And Bela had S: Addar, Gera, Abihud,
8:6 These are the S of Ehud (they were heads
8:8 And Shaharaim had S in the country of Moab
8:9 He had S by Hodesh his wife: Jobab, Zibi-a,
8:10 These were his S, heads of fathers' houses.
8:11 He also had S by Hushim: Abitub and Elpaal.
8:12 The S of Elpaal: Eber, Misham, and Shemed, who
8:16 Ishpah, and Joha were S of Beriah.
8:18 and Jobab were the S of Elpaal.
8:21 and Shimrath were the S of Shimei.
8:25 and Penuel were the S of Shashak.
8:27 and Zichri were the S of Jeroham.
8:35 The S of Micah: Pithon, Melech, Tarea, and Ahaz.
8:38 Azel had six S, and these are their names:
8:38 All these were the S of Azel.
8:39 The S of Eshek his brother: Ulam his first-born,
8:40 The S of Ulam were men who were mighty
8:40 bowmen, having many S and grandsons, one hundred
9:4 of Bani, from the S of Perez the son
9:5 of the Shilonites: Asaiah the first-born, and his S
9:6 Of the S of Zerah: Jeuel and their kinsmen,
9:14 of Hashabiah, of the S of Merari;
9:23 So they and their S were in charge of
9:30 Others, of the S of the priests, prepared the
9:41 The S of Micah: Pithon, Melech, Tahre-a, and Ahaz;
9:44 Azel had six S and these are their names:
9:44 Hanan; these were the S of Azel.
10:2 overtook Saul and his S; and the Philistines slew
10:2 Abinadab and Malchishua, the S of Saul.
10:6 he and his three S and all his house
10:7 that Saul and his S were dead, they forsook
10:8 found Saul and his S fallen on Mount Gilboa.
10:12 the bodies of his S, and brought them to
11:44 Shama and Je-iel the S of Hotham the Aroerite,
11:46 Jeribai, and Joshaviah, the S of Elna-am, and Ithmah
12:3 Ahiezer, then Joash, both S of Shemaah of Gibe-ah;
12:3 Jezi-el and Pelet the S of Azmaveth; Beracah, Jehu
12:7 Joelah and Zebadiah, the S of Jeroham of Gedor.
14:3 and David begot more S and daughters.
15:4 David gathered together the S of Aaron and the
15:5 the Levites: of the S of Kohath, Uriel the
15:6 his brethren; of the S of Merari, Asaiah the
15:7 his brethren; of the S of Gershom, Joel the
15:8 his brethren; of the S of Eli-zaphan, Shemaiah the
15:9 his brethren; of the S of Hebron, Eliel the

15:10 his brethren; of the S of Uzziel, Amminadab the
15:17 Berechiah; and of the S of Merari, their brethren,
16:13 of Abraham his servant, S of Jacob, his chosen
16:42 The S of Jeduthun were appointed to the gate.
17:11 one of your own S, and I will establish
18:17 the Pelethites; and David's S were the chief officials
21:20 angel, and his four S who were with him
23:6 divisions corresponding to the S of Levi: Gershom,
23:7 The S of Gershom were Ladan and Shimei.
23:8 The S of Ladan: Jehiel the chief, and Zetham,
23:9 The S of Shimei: Shelomoth, Hazi-el, and Haran,
23:10 And the S of Shimei: Jahath, Zina, and Jeush,
23:10 These four were the S of Shimei.
23:11 Beriah had not many S, therefore they became a
23:12 The S of Kohath: Amram, Izhar, Hebron, and Uzziel,
23:13 The S of Amram: Aaron and Moses.
23:13 that he and his S for ever should burn
23:14 But the S of Moses the man of God
23:15 The S of Moses: Gershom and Eliezer.
23:16 The S of Gershom: Shebuel the chief.
23:17 The S of Eliezer: Rehabiah the chief; Eliezer had
23:17 Eliezer had no other S, but the sons of
23:17 other sons, but the S of Rehabiah were very
23:18 The S of Izhar: Shelomith the chief.
23:19 The S of Hebron: Jeriah the chief, Amariah the
23:20 The S of Uzziel: Micah the chief and Isshiah
23:21 The S of Merari: Mahli and Mushi.
23:21 The S of Mahli: Eleazar and Kish.
23:22 Eleazar died having no S, but only daughters; their
23:22 daughters; their kinsmen, the S of Kish, married
23:23 The S of Mushi: Mahli, Eder, and Jeremoth, three.
23:24 These were the S of Levi by their fathers'
23:28 be to assist the S of Aaron for the
23:32 and shall attend the S of Aaron, their brethren,
24:1 The divisions of the S of Aaron were these.
24:1 The S of Aaron: Nadab, Abihu, Eleazar, and Ithamar.
24:3 of Zadok of the S of Eleazar, and Ahimelech
24:3 and Ahimelech of the S of Ithamar, David organized
24:4 were found among the S of Eleazar than among
24:4 Eleazar than among the S of Ithamar, they
24:4 fathers' houses of the S of Eleazar, and eight
24:4 and eight of the S of Ithamar.
24:5 God among both the S of Eleazar and the
24:5 of Eleazar and the S of Ithamar.
24:20 the rest of the S of Levi: of the
24:20 of Levi: of the S of Amram, Shuba-el; of
24:20 Amram, Shuba-el; of the S of Shuba-el, Jehdeiah.
24:21 Of Rehabiah: of the S of Rehabiah, Isshiah the
24:22 Izharites, Shelomoth; of the S of Shelomoth, Jahath.
24:23 The S of Hebron: Jeriah the chief, Amariah the
24:24 The S of Uzziel, Micah; of the sons of
24:24 Uzziel, Micah; of the S of Micah, Shamir.
24:25 Micah, Isshiah; of the S of Isshiah, Zechariah.
24:26 The S of Merari: Mahli and Mushi.
24:26 The S of Ja-aziah: Beno.
24:27 The S of Merari: of Ja-aziah, Beno, Shoham, Zaccur,
24:28 Of Mahli: Eleazar, who had no S
24:29 Of Kish, the S of Kish: Jerahmeel.
24:30 The S of Mushi: Mahli, Eder, and Jerimoth.
24:30 These were the S of the Levites according to
24:31 as their brethren the S of Aaron, in the
25:1 service certain of the S of Asaph, and of
25:2 duties was: Of the S of Asaph: Zaccur, Joseph,
25:2 Joseph, Nethaniah, and Asharelah, S of Asaph, under
25:3 Of Jeduthun, the S of Jeduthun: Gedaliah, Zeri, ,
25:4 Of Heman, the S of Heman: Bukkiah, Mattaniah,
25:5 All these were the S of Heman the king's
25:5 had given Heman fourteen S and three daughters.
25:9 his brethren and his S, twelve;
25:10 third to Zaccur, his S and his brethren, twelve;
25:11 fourth to Izri, his S and his brethren, twelve;
25:12 fifth to Nethaniah, his S and his brethren, twelve;
25:13 sixth to Bukkiah, his S and his brethren, twelve;
25:14 seventh to Jesharelah, his S and his brethren, twelve;
25:15 eighth to Jeshaiah, his S and his brethren, twelve;
25:16 ninth to Mattaniah, his S and his brethren, twelve;
25:17 tenth to Shimei, his S and his brethren, twelve;
25:18 eleventh to Azarel, his S and his brethren, twelve;
25:19 twelfth to Hashabiah, his S and his brethren, twelve;
25:20 the thirteenth, Shuba-el, his S and his brethren,
25:21 the fourteenth, Mattithiah, his S and his brethren,
25:22 fifteenth, to Jeremoth, his S and his brethren, twelve;
25:23 sixteenth, to Hananiah, his S and his brethren,
25:24 seventeenth, to Joshbekashah, his S and his brethren,
25:25 eighteenth, to Hanani, his S and his brethren, twelve;
25:26 nineteenth, to Mallothi, his S and his brethren,
25:27 twentieth, to Eliathah, his S and his brethren, twelve;
25:28 twenty-first, to Hothir, his S and his brethren, twelve;
25:29 twenty-second, to Giddalti, his S and his brethren,
25:30 twenty-third, to Mahazi-oth, his S and his brethren,
25:31 twenty-fourth, to Romamti-ezer, his S and his
26:1 of Kore, of the S of Asaph.
26:2 had S: Zechariah the first-born, Jedia-el the
26:4 And Obed-edom had S: Shemaiah the first-born,
26:6 his son Shemaiah were S born who were rulers
26:7 The S of Shemaiah: Othni, Repha-el, Obed, and
26:8 these were of the S of Obed-edom with their
26:8 of Obed-edom with their S and brethren, able men
26:9 And Meshelemiah had S and brethren, able men,
26:10 And Hosah, of the S of Merari, had sons:
26:10 sons of Merari, had S: Shimri the chief (for
26:11 the fourth: all the S and brethren of Hosah
26:15 south, and to his S was allotted the storehouse.
26:19 the Korahites and the S of Merari.
26:21 The S of Ladan, the sons of the Gershonites
26:21 sons of Ladan, the S of the Gershonites belonging
26:22 The S of Jehieli, Zetham and Joel his brother,
26:29 Izharites, Chenaniah and his S were appointed to
27:10 the Pelonite, of the S of Ephraim; in his
27:14 of Pirathon, of the S of Ephraim; in his
27:32 Jehiel the son of Hachmoni attended the king's S
28:1 the king and his S, together with the palace
28:4 and among my father's S he took pleasure in
28:5 And of all my S (for the LORD has
28:5 has given me many S he has chosen Solomon
29:24 and also all the S of King David, pledged
2Chr 5:12 Heman, and Jeduthun, their S and kinsmen, arrayed
6:16 Israel, if only your S take heed to their
11:14 because Jeroboam and his S cast them out from
11:19 and she bore him S, Jeush, Shemariah, and Zaham.
11:21 concubines, and had twenty-eight S and sixty
11:23 distributed some of his S through all the districts
13:5 to David and his S by a covenant of
13:8 the hand of the S of David, because you
13:9 of the LORD, the S of Aaron, and the
13:10 the LORD who are S of Aaron, and Levites
13:12 O S of Israel, do not fight against the
13:21 wives, and had twenty-two S and sixteen daughters.
20:14 a Levite of the S of Asaph, in the
21:2 He had brothers, the S of Jehoshaphat: Azariah, ,
21:2 all these were the S of Jehoshaphat king of
21:7 him and to his S for ever.
21:17 house, and also his S and his wives, so
22:1 to the camp had slain all the older S
22:8 of Judah and the S of Ahaziah's brothers, who
22:11 from among the king's S who were about to
23:3 LORD spoke concerning the S of David.
23:11 and Jehoiada and his S anointed him, and they
24:3 wives, and he had S and daughters.
24:7 For the S of Athaliah, that wicked woman, had
24:27 Accounts of his S, and of the many oracles
26:18 for the priests the S of Aaron, who are
28:3 Hinnom, and burned his S as an offering, according
28:8 of their kinsfolk, women, S, and daughters; they also
29:9 the sword and our S and our daughters and
29:11 My S, do not now be negligent, for the
29:12 of Azariah, of the S of the Kohathites; and
29:12 Kohathites; and of the S of Merari, Kish the
29:13 Joah; and of the S of Eli-zaphan, Shimri and
29:13 Jeuel; and of the S of Asaph, Zechariah and
29:14 Mattaniah; and of the S of Heman, Jehuel and
29:14 Shimei; and of the S of Jeduthun, Shemaiah and
29:21 commanded the priests the S of Aaron to offer
31:18 children, their wives, their S, and their daughters, the
31:19 And for the S of Aaron, the priests, who
32:21 some of his own S struck him down there
32:33 the tombs of the S of David; and all
33:6 And he burned his S as an offering in
34:12 the Levites, of the S of Merari, and Zechariah
34:12 and Meshullam, of the S of the Kohathites, to
35:14 because the priests the S of Aaron were busied
35:14 for the priests the S of Aaron.
35:15 The singers, the S of Asaph, were in their
36:20 him and to his S until the establishment of
Ezra 2:3 people of Israel: the S of Parosh, two thousand
2:4 The S of Shephatiah, three hundred and seventy-two.
2:5 The S of Arah, seven hundred and seventy-five.
2:6 The S of Pahath-moab, namely the sons of Jeshua
2:6 of Pahath-moab, namely the S of Jeshua and Joab,
2:7 The S of Elam, one thousand two hundred and
2:8 The S of Zattu, nine hundred and forty-five.
2:9 The S of Zaccai, seven hundred and sixty.

S

2:10 The S of Bani, six hundred and forty-two.
2:11 The S of Bebai, six hundred and twenty-three.
2:12 The S of Azgad, one thousand two hundred and
2:13 The S of Adonikam, six hundred and sixty-six.
2:14 The S of Bigvai, two thousand and fifty-six.
2:15 The S of Adin, four hundred and fifty-four.
2:16 The S of Ater, namely of Hezekiah, ninety-eight.
2:17 The S of Bezai, three hundred and twenty-three.
2:18 The S of Jorah, one hundred and twelve.
2:19 The S of Hashum, two hundred and twenty-three.
2:20 The S of Gibbar, ninety-five.
2:21 The S of Bethlehem, one hundred and twenty-three.
2:24 The S of Azmaveth, forty-two.
2:25 The S of Kiriatharim, Chephirah, and Be-eroth,
2:26 The S of Ramah and Geba, six hundred and
2:29 The S of Nebo, fifty-two.
2:30 The S of Magbish, one hundred and fifty-six.
2:31 The S of the other Elam, one thousand two
2:32 The S of Harim, three hundred and twenty.
2:33 The S of Lod, Hadid, and Ono, seven hundred
2:34 The S of Jericho, three hundred and forty-five.
2:35 The S of Senaah, three thousand six hundred and
2:36 The priests: the S of Jedaiah, of the house
2:37 The S of Immer, one thousand and fifty-two.
2:38 The S of Pashhur, one thousand two hundred and
2:39 The S of Harim, one thousand and seventeen.
2:40 The Levites: the S of Jeshua and Kadmi-el, of
2:40 and Kadmi-el, of the S of Hodaviah, seventy-four.
2:41 The singers: the S of Asaph, one hundred and
2:42 The S of the gatekeepers: the sons of Shallum,
2:42 of the gatekeepers: the S of Shallum, the sons
2:42 sons of Shallum, the S of Ater, the sons
2:42 sons of Ater, the S of Talmon, the sons
2:42 sons of Talmon, the S of Akkub, the sons
2:42 sons of Akkub, the S of Hatita, and the
2:42 of Hatita, and the S of Shobai, in all
2:43 The temple servants: the S of Ziha, the sons
2:43 sons of Ziha, the S of Hasupha, the sons
2:43 sons of Hasupha, the S of Tabbaoth,
2:44 sons of Tabbaoth, the S of Keros, the sons
2:44 sons of Keros, the S of Siaha, the sons
2:44 sons of Siaha, the S of Padon,
2:45 sons of Padon, the S of Lebanah, the sons
2:45 sons of Lebanah, the S of Hagabah, the sons
2:45 sons of Hagabah, the S of Akkub,
2:46 sons of Akkub, the S of Hagab, the sons
2:46 sons of Hagab, the S of Shamlai, the sons
2:46 sons of Shamlai, the S of Hanan,
2:47 sons of Hanan, the S of Giddel, the sons
2:47 sons of Giddel, the S of Gahar, the sons
2:47 sons of Gahar, the S of Re-aiah,
2:48 sons of Re-aiah, the S of Rezin, the sons
2:48 sons of Rezin, the S of Nekoda, the sons
2:48 sons of Nekoda, the S of Gazzam,
2:49 sons of Gazzam, the S of Uzza, the sons
2:49 sons of Uzza, the S of Paseah, the sons
2:49 sons of Paseah, the S of Besai,
2:50 sons of Besai, the S of Asnah, the sons
2:50 sons of Asnah, the S of Me-unim, the sons
2:50 sons of Me-unim, the S of Nephisim,
2:51 sons of Nephisim, the S of Bakbuk, the sons
2:51 sons of Bakbuk, the S of Hakupha, the sons
2:51 sons of Hakupha, the S of Harhur,
2:52 sons of Harhur, the S of Bazluth, the sons
2:52 sons of Bazluth, the S of Mehida, the sons
2:52 sons of Mehida, the S of Harsha,
2:53 sons of Harsha, the S of Barkos, the sons
2:53 sons of Barkos, the S of Sisera, the sons
2:53 sons of Sisera, the S of Temah,
2:54 sons of Temah, the S of Neziah, and the
2:54 of Neziah, and the S of Hatipha.
2:55 The S of Solomon's servants: the sons of Sotai,
2:55 of Solomon's servants: the S of Sotai, the sons
2:55 sons of Sotai, the S of Hassophereth, the sons
2:55 sons of Hassophereth, the S of Peruda,
2:56 sons of Peruda, the S of Jaalah, the sons
2:56 sons of Jaalah, the S of Darkon, the sons
2:56 sons of Darkon, the S of Giddel,
2:57 sons of Giddel, the S of Shephatiah, the sons
2:57 sons of Shephatiah, the S of Hattil, the sons
2:57 sons of Hattil, the S of Pochereth-hazzebaim, and
2:57 of Pochereth-hazzebaim, and the S of Ami.
2:58 temple servants and the S of Solomon's servants
2:60 belonged to Israel: the S of Delaiah, the sons
2:60 sons of Delaiah, the S of Tobiah, and the
2:60 of Tobiah, and the S of Nekoda, six hundred
2:61 Also, of the S of the priests: the sons
2:61 of the priests: the S of Habaiah, the sons
2:61 sons of Habaiah, the S of Hakkoz, and the
2:61 of Hakkoz, and the S of Barzillai (who had
3:1 month came, and the S of Israel were in
3:9 And Jeshua with his S and his kinsmen, and
3:9 and Kadmi-el and his S, the sons of Judah,
3:9 and his sons, the S of Judah, together took
3:9 God, along with the S of Henadad and the
3:9 and the Levites, their S and kinsmen.
3:10 and the Levites, the S of Asaph, with cymbals,
6:10 for the life of the king and his S
7:23 against the realm of the king and his S
8:2 the king: Of the S of Phinehas, Gershom.
8:2 Of the S of Ithamar, Daniel.
8:2 Of the S of David, Hattush,
8:3 David, Hattush, of the S of Shecaniah.
8:3 Of the S of Parosh, Zechariah, with whom were
8:4 Of the S of Pahath-moab, Eli-e-ho-enai the son of
8:5 Of the S of Zattu, Shecaniah the son of
8:6 Of the S of Adin, Ebed the son of
8:7 Of the S of Elam, Jeshaiah the son of
8:8 Of the S of Shephatiah, Zebadiah the son of
8:9 Of the S of Joab, Obadiah the son of
8:10 Of the S of Bani, Shelomith the son of
8:11 Of the S of Bebai, Zechariah, the son of
8:12 Of the S of Azgad, Johanan the son of
8:13 Of the S of Adonikam, those who came later,
8:14 Of the S of Bigvai, Uthai and Zaccur, and
8:15 there none of the S of Levi.
8:18 of discretion, of the S of Mahli the son
8:18 namely Sherebiah with his S and kinsmen, eighteen;
8:19 him Jeshaiah of the S of Merari, with his
8:19 his kinsmen and their S, twenty;
9:2 themselves and for their S; so that the holy
9:12 daughters to their S, neither take their daughters
9:12 their daughters for your S, and never seek their
10:2 of Jehiel, of the S of Elam, addressed Ezra:
10:18 Of the S of the priests who had married
10:18 and Gedaliah, of the S of Jeshua the son
10:20 Of the S of Immer: Hanani and Zebadiah.
10:21 Of the S of Harim: Ma-aseiah, Elijah, Shemaiah, ,
10:22 Of the S of Pashhur: Eli-o-enai, Ma-aseiah, Ishmael,
10:25 of Israel: of the S of Parosh: Ramiah, Izziah,
10:26 Of the S of Elam: Mattaniah, Zechariah, Jehiel,
10:27 Of the S of Zattu: Eli-o-enai, Eliashib, Mattaniah,
10:28 Of the S of Bebai were Jehohanan, Hananiah,
10:29 Of the S of Bani were Meshullum, Malluch, Adaiah,
10:30 Of the S of Pahath-moab: Adna, Chelal, Benaiah,
10:31 Of the S of Harim: Eliezer, Isshijah, Malchijah,
10:33 Of the S of Hashum: Mattenai, Mattattah, Zabad,
10:34 Of the S of Bani: Ma-adai, Amram, Uel,
10:38 Of the S of Binnui: Shimei,
10:43 Of the S of Nebo: Je-iel, Mattithiah, Zabad, Zebina,
Neh 3:3 And the S of Hassenaah built the Fish Gate;
4:14 for your brethren, your S, your daughters, your wives,
5:2 who said, "With our S and our daughters, we
5:5 we are forcing our S and our daughters to
7:8 people of Israel: the S of Parosh, two thousand
7:9 The S of Shephatiah, three hundred and seventy-two.
7:10 The S of Arah, six hundred and fifty-two.
7:11 The S of Pahath-moab, namely the sons of Jeshua
7:11 of Pahath-moab, namely the S of Jeshua and Joab,
7:12 The S of Elam, a thousand two hundred and
7:13 The S of Zattu, eight hundred and forty-five.
7:14 The S of Zaccai, seven hundred and sixty.
7:15 The S of Binnui, six hundred and forty-eight.
7:16 The S of Bebai, six hundred and twenty-eight.
7:17 The S of Azgad, two thousand three hundred and
7:18 The S of Adonikam, six hundred and sixty-seven.
7:19 The S of Bigvai, two thousand and sixty-seven.
7:20 The S of Adin, six hundred and fifty-five.
7:21 The S of Ater, namely of Hezekiah, ninety-eight.
7:22 The S of Hashum, three hundred and twenty-eight.
7:23 The S of Bezai, three hundred and twenty-four.
7:24 The S of Hariph, a hundred and twelve.
7:25 The S of Gibeon, ninety-five.
7:34 The S of the other Elam, a thousand two
7:35 The S of Harim, three hundred and twenty.
7:36 The S of Jericho, three hundred and forty-five.
7:37 The S of Lod, Hadid, and Ono, seven hundred
7:38 The S of Senaah, three thousand nine hundred and
7:39 The priests: the S of Jedaiah, namely the house
7:40 The S of Immer, a thousand and fifty-two.
7:41 The S of Pashhur, a thousand two hundred and
7:42 The S of Harim, a thousand and seventeen.

7:43 The Levites: the S of Jeshua, namely of Kadmi-el
7:43 of Kadmi-el of the S of Hodevah, seventy-four.
7:44 The singers: the S of Asaph, a hundred and
7:45 The gatekeepers: the S of Shallum, the sons of
7:45 sons of Shallum, the S of Ater, the sons
7:45 sons of Ater, the S of Talmon, the sons
7:45 sons of Talmon, the S of Akkub, the sons
7:45 sons of Akkub, the S of Hatita, the sons
7:45 sons of Hatita, the S of Shobai, a hundred
7:46 The temple servants: the S of Ziha, the sons
7:46 sons of Ziha, the S of Hasupha, the sons
7:46 sons of Hasupha, the S of Tabbaoth,
7:47 sons of Tabbaoth, the S of Keros, the sons
7:47 sons of Keros, the S of Sia, the sons
7:47 sons of Sia, the S of Padon,
7:48 sons of Padon, the S of Lebana, the sons
7:48 sons of Lebana, the S of Hagaba, the sons
7:48 sons of Hagaba, the S of Shalmai,
7:49 sons of Shalmai, the S of Hanan, the sons
7:49 sons of Hanan, the S of Giddel, the sons
7:49 sons of Giddel, the S of Gahar,
7:50 sons of Gahar, the S of Re-aiah, the sons
7:50 sons of Re-aiah, the S of Rezin, the sons
7:50 sons of Rezin, the S of Nekoda,
7:51 sons of Nekoda, the S of Gazzam, the sons
7:51 sons of Gazzam, the S of Uzza, the sons
7:51 sons of Uzza, the S of Paseah,
7:52 sons of Paseah, the S of Besai, the sons
7:52 sons of Besai, the S of Me-unim, the sons
7:52 sons of Me-unim, the S of Nephushesim,
7:53 sons of Nephushesim, the S of Bakbuk, the sons
7:53 sons of Bakbuk, the S of Hakupha, the sons
7:53 sons of Hakupha, the S of Harhur,
7:54 sons of Harhur, the S of Bazlith, the sons
7:54 sons of Bazlith, the S of Mehida, the sons
7:54 sons of Mehida, the S of Harsha,
7:55 sons of Harsha, the S of Barkos, the sons
7:55 sons of Barkos, the S of Sisera, the sons
7:55 sons of Sisera, the S of Temah,
7:56 sons of Temah, the S of Neziah, the sons
7:56 sons of Neziah, the S of Hatipha.
7:57 The S of Solomon's servants: the sons of Sotai,
7:57 of Solomon's servants: the S of Sotai, the sons
7:57 sons of Sotai, the S of Sophereth, the sons
7:57 sons of Sophereth, the S of Perida,
7:58 sons of Perida, the S of Jaala, the sons
7:58 sons of Jaala, the S of Darkon, the sons
7:58 sons of Darkon, the S of Giddel,
7:59 sons of Giddel, the S of Shephatiah, the sons
7:59 sons of Shephatiah, the S of Hattil, the sons
7:59 sons of Hattil, the S of Pochereth-hazzebaim, the
7:59 sons of Pochereth-hazzebaim, the S of Amon.
7:60 temple servants and the S of Solomon's servants
7:62 belonged to Israel: the S of Delaiah, the sons
7:62 sons of Delaiah, the S of Tobiah, the sons
7:62 sons of Tobiah, the S of Nekoda, six hundred
7:63 of the priests: the S of Hobaiah, the sons
7:63 sons of Hobaiah, the S of Hakkoz, the sons
7:63 sons of Hakkoz, the S of Barzillai (who had
10:9 Azaniah, Binnui of the S of Henadad, Kadmi-el;
10:28 God, their wives, their S, their daughters, all who
10:30 their daughters for our S;
10:36 the first-born of our S and of our cattle,
10:39 of Israel and the S of Levi shall bring
11:4 lived certain of the S of Judah and of
11:4 Judah and of the S of Benjamin.
11:4 Of the S of Judah: Athaiah the son of
11:4 of Mahalalel, of the S of Perez;
11:6 All the S of Perez who lived in Jerusalem
11:7 And these are the S of Benjamin: Sallu the
11:22 of Mica, of the S of Asaph, the singers,
11:24 of Meshezabel, of the S of Zerah the son
12:23 The S of Levi, heads of fathers' houses, were
12:28 And the S of the singers gathered together from
12:35 certain of the priests' S with trumpets: Zechariah
12:47 which was for the S of Aaron.
13:25 your daughters to their S, or take their daughters
13:25 their daughters for your S or for yourselves.
13:28 And one of the S of Jehoiada, the son

Tob 1:6 to the priests, the S of Aaron, at the
1:7 a tenth to the S of Levi who ministered
1:21 before two of Sennacherib's S killed him, and they
4:12 for we are the S of the prophets.
4:13 your brethren and the S and daughters of your
5:13 Ananias and Jathan, the S of the great Shemaiah,
7:3 "We belong to the S of Naphtali, who are
13:3 before the nations, O S of Israel; for he
13:9 the deeds of your S, but again he will
13:9 show mercy to the S of the righteous.
13:13 be glad for the S of the righteous; for
14:3 "My son, take your S; behold, I have grown
14:12 his wife and his S to Ecbatana, to Raguel

Jud 7:18 And the S of Esau and the sons of
7:18 of Esau and the S of Ammon went up
8:12 of God among the S of men?
9:4 divided among thy beloved S, who were zealous for
16:7 men, nor did the S of the Titans smite
16:12 The S of maidservants have pierced them through;

Esth 5:11 the number of his S, all the promotions with
9:10 and Vaizatha, the ten S of Haman the son
9:12 and also the ten S of Haman.
9:13 And let the ten S of Haman be hanged
9:14 Susa, and the ten S of Haman were hanged.
9:25 that he and his S should be hanged on
16:16 righteous laws and are S of the Most High,

Job 1:2 born to him seven S and three daughters.
1:4 His S used to go and hold a feast
1:5 may be that my S have sinned, and cursed
1:6 a day when the S of God came to
1:13 a day when his S and daughters were eating
1:18 another, and said, "Your S and daughters were eating
2:1 a day when the S of God came to
5:4 His S are far from safety, they are crushed
14:21 His S come to honor, and he does not
19:17 wife, loathsome to the S of my own mother.
21:19 their iniquity for their S Let him recompense it
38:7 together, and all the S of God shouted for
41:34 king over all the S of pride."
42:13 He had also seven S and three daughters.
42:16 years, and saw his S, and his sons' sons,
42:16 his sons, and his S sons, four generations.
42:16 sons, and his sons' S, four generations.

Ps 12:1 vanished from among the S of men.
12:8 is exalted among the S of men.
21:10 children from among the S of men.
22:23 all you S of Jacob, glorify him, and stand
22:23 of him, all you S of Israel!
31:19 the sight of the S of men!
33:13 he sees all the S of men;
34:11 Come, O S, listen to me, I will teach
45:2 the fairest of the S of men; grace is
45:16 fathers shall be your S; you will make them
53:2 from heaven upon the S of men to see
57:4 that greedily devour the S of men; their teeth
58:1 Do you judge the S of men uprightly?
69:8 to my brethren, an alien to my mother's S
77:15 redeem thy people, the S of Jacob and Joseph.
82:6 say, "You are gods, S of the Most High,
89:47 hast created all the S of men!
105:6 of Abraham his servant, S of Jacob, his chosen
106:37 They sacrificed their S and their daughters to the
106:38 the blood of their S and daughters, whom they
107:8 wonderful works to the S of men!
107:15 wonderful works to the S of men!
107:21 wonderful works to the S of men!
107:31 wonderful works to the S of men!
115:16 has given to the S of men.
127:3 Lo, S are a heritage from the LORD, the
127:4 a warrior are the S of one's youth.
132:11 back: "One of the S of your body I
132:12 If your S keep my covenant and my testimonies
132:12 shall teach them, their S also for ever shall
144:12 May our S in their youth be like plants
145:12 make known to the S of men thy mighty
147:13 gates; he blesses your S within you.
149:2 his Maker, let the S of Zion rejoice in

Prov 4:2 of Wisdom Hear, O S, a father's instruction, and
5:7 And now, O S, listen to me, and do
7:24 And now, O S, listen to me, and be
8:4 cry is to the S of men.
8:31 and delighting in the S of men.
8:32 And now, my S, listen to me: happy are
17:6 and the glory of S is their fathers.
20:7 blessed are his S after him!

Eccl 1:13 has given to the S of men to be
2:3 was good for the S of men to do
3:10 has given to the S of men to be
3:18 with regard to the S of men that God
3:19 the fate of the S of men and the
8:11 the heart of the S of men is fully
9:12 a snare, so the S of men are snared

Song 1:6 My mother's S were angry with me, they made

13:17 the money and the S, lest he arouse great
13:18 the money and the S, he perished."
13:19 So he sent the S and the hundred talents,
14:25 said, "How shall we thank Simon and his S
14:29 a priest of the S of Joarib, and his
14:49 that Simon and his S might have them.
16:2 in his two older S Judas and John, and
16:13 against Simon and his S, to do away with
16:14 Mattathias and Judas his S, in the one hundred
16:16 When Simon and his S were drunk, Ptolemy and
16:16 him and his two S and some of his
2Mac 7:20 she saw her seven S perish within a single
7:41 Last of all, the mother died, after her S
Mt 5:9 they shall be called S of God.
5:45 that you may be S of your Father who
8:12 of heaven, while the S of the kingdom will
12:27 by whom do your S cast them out?
13:38 good seed means the S of the kingdom; the
13:38 the weeds are the S of the evil one,
17:24 From their S or from others?"
17:25 to him, "Then the S are free.
20:20 the mother of the S of Zebedee came up
20:20 to him, with her S, and kneeling before him
20:21 "Command that these two S of mine may sit,
21:28 A man had two S; and he went to
23:30 yourselves, that you are S of those who murdered
26:37 Peter and the two S of Zebedee, he began
27:9 by some of the S of Israel,
27:56 the mother of the S of Zebedee.
Mk 3:17 surnamed Bo-anerges, that is, S of thunder;
3:28 will be forgiven the S of men, and whatever
10:35 James and John, the S of Zebedee, came forward
Lk 1:16 turn many of the S of Israel to the
5:10 were James and John, S of Zebedee, who were
6:35 and you will be S of the Most High;
11:19 by whom do your S cast them out?
15:11 man who had two S;
16:8 his shrewdness; for the S of this world are
16:8 own generation than the S of light.
20:34 said to them, "The S of this age marry
20:36 to angels and are S of God, being sons
20:36 sons of God, being S of the resurrection.
Jn 4:12 it himself, and his S, and his cattle?"
12:36 that you may become S of light." When Jesus
21:2 Cana in Galilee, the S of Zebedee, and two
Acts 2:17 all flesh, and your S and your daughters shall
3:25 You are the S of the prophets and of
7:16 of silver from the S of Hamor in Shechem.
7:23 visit his brethren, the S of Israel.
7:29 Midian, where he became the father of two S
9:15 and kings and the S of Israel;
13:26 worthy to untie.' "Brethren, S of the family of
19:14 Seven S of a Jewish high priest named Sceva
Rom 8:14 Spirit of God are S of God.
8:19 the revealing of the S of God;
8:23 wait for adoption as S, the redemption of our
9:27 the number of the S of Israel be as
2Cor 6:18 you shall be my S and daughters, says the
Gal 3:7 faith who are the S of Abraham.
3:26 Jesus you are all S of God, through faith.
4:5 law, so that we might receive adoption as S
4:6 And because you are S, God has sent the
4:22 that Abraham had two S, one by a slave
Eph 1:5 love to be his S through Jesus Christ, according
2:2 at work in the S of disobedience.
3:5 made known to the S of men in other
5:6 God comes upon the S of disobedience.
1Thes 5:5 For you are all S of light and sons
5:5 sons of light and S of the day; we
Heb 2:10 exist, in bringing many S to glory, should make
11:21 blessed each of the S of Joseph, bowing in
12:5 which addresses you as S – "My son, do
12:7 is treating you as S; for what son is
12:8 , then you are illegitimate children and not S
Rev 2:14 stumbling block before the S of Israel, that they
7:4 every tribe of the S of Israel,
21:12 twelve tribes of the S of Israel were inscribed;

SONS-IN-LAW (3)

Gen 19:12 S, sons, daughters, or any one you have in
19:14 and said to his S, who were to marry
19:14 he seemed to his S to be jesting.

SONSHIP (2)

Rom 8:15 fear, but you have received the spirit of S
9:4 to them belong the S, the glory, the covenants,

SOON (100)

Gen 27:30 As S as Isaac had finished blessing Jacob, when
39:18 insult me; but as S as I lifted up
40:10 were three branches; as S as it budded, its
44:3 As S as the morning was light, the men
Ex 2:18 you have come so S today?"
9:29 said to him, "As S as I have gone
32:19 And as S as he came near the camp
Deut 4:26 day, that you will S utterly perish from the
Josh 2:7 the fords; and as S as the pursuers had
2:11 And as S as we heard it, our hearts
6:5 the ram's horn, as S as you hear the
6:20 As S as the people heard the sound of
8:19 their place, and as S as he had stretched
Judg 2:17 down to them; they S turned aside from the
8:33 As S as Gideon died, the people of Israel
9:33 in the morning, as S as the sun is
1Sam 1:22 to her husband, "As S as the child is
9:13 As S as you enter the city, you will
13:10 As S as he had finished offering the burnt
20:41 And as S as the lad had gone, David
29:10 morning, and depart as S as you have light."
2Sam 13:36 And as S as he had finished speaking, behold,
15:10 of Israel, saying, "As S as you hear the
22:45 cringing to me; as S as they heard of
1Kgs 15:29 And as S as he was king, he killed
16:11 began to reign, as S as he had seated
18:12 is here.'" And as S as I have gone
20:36 the LORD, behold, as S as you have gone
20:36 And as S as he had departed from him,
21:15 As S as Jezebel heard that Naboth had been
21:16 And as S as Ahab heard that Naboth was
2Kgs 6:20 As S as they entered Samaria, Elisha said, "O
10:2 saying, "Now then, as S as this letter comes
10:25 So as S as he had made an end
13:21 of Elisha; and as S as the man touched
14:5 And as S as the royal power was firmly
2Chr 25:3 And as S as the royal power was firmly
31:5 As S as the command was spread abroad, the
Tob 6:12 her father, and as S as we return from
Jud 14:2 And as S as morning comes and the sun
14:11 As S as it was dawn they hung the
16:18 As S as the people were purified, they offered
Job 32:22 else would my Maker S put an end to
Ps 18:44 As S as they heard of me they obeyed
37:2 For they will S fade like the grass, and
48:5 As S as they saw it, they were astounded,
81:14 I would S subdue their enemies, and turn my
90:10 and trouble; they are S gone, and we fly
94:17 help, my soul would S have dwelt in the
106:13 But they S forgot his works; they did not
Wis 5:13 So we also, as S as we were born,
6:15 on her account will S be free from care,
Sir 6:19 a little while, and S you will eat of
30:24 life, and anxiety brings on old age too S
Is 28:4 eats it up as S as it is in
56:1 and do righteousness, for S my salvation will come,
66:8 For as S as Zion was in labor she
Bar 4:22 of the mercy which S will come to you
4:24 your capture, so they S will see your salvation
4:25 you, but you will S see their destruction and
Ezek 7:8 Now I will S pour out my wrath upon
36:8 Israel; for they will S come home.
Dan 3:7 Therefore, as S as all the peoples heard the
14:18 As S as the doors were opened, the king
Hos 8:10 the nations, I will S gather them up.
1Mac 11:22 was angry, and as S as he heard it
2Mac 1:15 closed the temple as S as he entered it.
2:18 God that he will S have mercy upon us
5:18 his rash act as S as he came forward,
7:37 God to show mercy S to our nation and
8:5 As S as Maccabeus got his army organized, the
9:5 As S as he ceased speaking he was seized
11:1 Very S after this, Lysias, the king's guardian and
11:36 to the king, as S as you have considered
Mt 24:32 learn its lesson: as S as its branch becomes
Mk 9:39 name will be able S after to speak evil
13:28 learn its lesson: as S as its branch becomes
15:1 And as S as it was morning the chief
Lk 7:11 S afterward he went to a city called Nain,
8:1 S afterward he went on through cities and villages,
21:30 all the trees; as S as they come out
Acts 17:15 come to him as S as possible, they departed.
27:14 But S a tempestuous wind, called the northeaster,
Rom 16:20 God of peace will S crush Satan under your
1Cor 4:19 will come to you S, if the Lord wills,

Phil 2:19 send Timothy to you S, so that I may
2:23 send him just as S as I see how
1Tim 3:14 to come to you S, but I am writing
2Tim 4:9 Do your best to come to me S
Heb 13:23 whom I shall see you if he comes S
2Pet 1:14 my body will be S, as our Lord Jesus
3Jn 1:14 hope to see you S, and we will talk
Rev 1:1 his servants what must S take place; and he
2:16 will come to you S and war against them
3:11 I am coming S; hold fast what you have,
11:14 the third woe is S to come.
22:6 his servants what must S take place.
22:7 And behold, I am coming S
22:12 "Behold, I am coming S, bringing my recompense, to
22:20 to these things says, "Surely I am coming S

SOONER (3)
Ps 58:9 S than your pots can feel the heat of
Wis 13:9 they fail to find S the Lord of these
Heb 13:19 that I may be restored to you the S

SOOT
Lam 4:8 visage is blacker than S, they are not recognized

SOOTHING (2)
Esth 15:8 he comforted her with S words, and said to
Ezek 20:28 they sent up their S odors, and there they

SOOTHSAYER (2)
Deut 18:10 who practices divination, a S, or an augur, or
Josh 13:22 son of Beor, the S, the people of Israel

SOOTHSAYERS (4)
Deut 18:14 dispossess, give heed to S and to diviners; but
Is 2:6 the east and of S like the Philistines, and
Jer 27:9 diviners, your dreamers, your S, or your sorcerers,
Mic 5:12 shall have no more S;

SOOTHSAYING (3)
2Kgs 21:6 an offering, and practiced S and augury, and dealt
2Chr 33:6 of Hinnom, and practiced S and augury and sorcery,
Acts 16:16 divination and brought her owners much gain by S

SOPATER
Acts 20:4 S of Beroea, the son of Pyrrhus, accompanied him;

SOPHERETH
Neh 7:57 Sotai, the sons of S, the sons of Perida,

SORCERER
Deut 18:10 an augur, or a S,

SORCERERS (7)
Ex 7:11 wise men and the S; and they also, the
Is 19:3 the idols and the S, and the mediums and
Jer 27:9 your soothsayers, or your S, who are saying to
Dan 2:2 magicians, the enchanters, the S, and the Chaldeans
Mal 3:5 swift witness against the S, against the adulterers,
Rev 21:8 as for murderers, fornicators, S, idolaters, and all
22:15 are the dogs and S and fornicators and murderers

SORCERESS (2)
Ex 22:18 shall not permit a S to live.
Is 57:3 hither, sons of the S, offspring of the adulterer

SORCERIES (5)
2Kgs 9:22 the harlotries and the S of your mother Jezebel
Is 47:9 spite of your many S and the great power
47:12 enchantments and your many S, with which you have
Mic 5:12 I will cut off S from your hand, and
Rev 9:21 their murders or their S or their immorality or

SORCERY (5)
2Kgs 17:17 and used divination and S, and sold themselves to
2Chr 33:6 soothsaying and augury and S, and dealt with
Wis 12:4 practices, their works of S and unholy rites,
Gal 5:20 impurity, licentiousness, idolatry, S, enmity,
Rev 18:23 earth, and all nations were deceived by thy S

SORE (5)
Gen 34:25 day, when they were S, two of the sons
Judg 2:15 and they were in S straits.
Ps 71:20 made me see many S troubles wilt revive me
Eccl 6:2 vanity; it is a S affliction.
Ezek 14:21 upon Jerusalem my four S acts of judgment, sword,

SOREK
Judg 16:4 in the valley of S, whose name was Delilah.

SORELY (11)
Gen 49:23 him, and harassed him S;
Judg 10:9 so that Israel was S distressed.
1Sam 1:6 used to provoke her S, to irritate her, because
1:15 I am a woman S troubled; I have drunk
Ps 6:3 My soul also is S troubled.
6:10 shall be ashamed and S troubled; they shall turn
118:18 LORD has chastened me S, but he has not
119:107 I am S afflicted; give me life, O LORD,
129:1 S have they afflicted me from my youth," let
129:2 Israel now say-- S have they afflicted me
Is 64:12 Wilt thou keep silent, and afflict us S

SORES (8)
Ex 9:9 boils breaking out in S on man and beast
9:10 boils breaking out in S on man and beast.
Job 2:7 afflicted Job with loathsome S from the sole of
Is 1:6 it, but bruises and S and bleeding wounds; they
Lk 16:20 named Lazarus, full of S,
16:21 table; moreover the dogs came and licked his S
Rev 16:2 and foul and evil S came upon the men
16:11 for their pain and S, and did not repent

SORREL
Zech 1:8 behind him were red, S, and white horses.

SORROW (55)
Gen 42:38 my gray hairs with S to Sheol."
44:29 my gray hairs in S to Sheol.'
44:31 servant our father with S to Sheol.
48:7 Paddan, Rachel to my S died in the land
2Chr 6:29 affliction, and his own S and stretching out his
Tob 2:5 I washed myself and ate my food in S
3:6 and great is the S within me.
3:10 old age down in S to the grave."
6:14 to the grave in S on my account.
7:18 in place of this S of yours.
Esth 9:22 turned for them from S into gladness and from
Ps 13:2 my soul, and have S in my heart all
31:10 life is spent with S, and my years with
88:9 I cannot escape; my eye grows dim through S
107:39 through oppression, trouble, and S,
119:28 soul melts away for S; strengthen me according to
Prov 10:1 foolish son is a S to his mother.
10:22 and he adds no S with it.
15:13 cheerful countenance, but by S of heart the spirit
23:29 Who has S
Eccl 1:18 and he who increases knowledge increases S
7:3 S is better than laughter, for by sadness of
Sir 26:6 grief of heart and S when a wife is
30:10 him, lest you have S with him, and in
30:12 you, and you have S of soul from him.
30:21 give yourself over to S, and do not afflict
30:23 your heart, and remove S far from you, for
30:23 far from you, for S has destroyed many, and
37:12 soul, and who will S with you if you
38:17 to avoid criticism; then be comforted for your S
38:18 For S results in death, and sorrow of heart
38:18 results in death, and S of heart saps one's
38:19 In calamity S continues, and the life of the
38:20 give your heart to S; drive it away, remembering
Is 35:10 joy and gladness, and S and sighing shall flee
51:11 joy and gladness, and S and sighing shall flee
Jer 20:18 to see toil and S, and spend my days
31:13 will comfort them, and give them gladness for S
45:3 the LORD has added S to my pain; I
Lam 1:12 if there is any S like my sorrow which
1:12 any sorrow like my S which was brought upon
Bar 4:9 God has brought great S upon me;
4:11 but I sent them away with weeping and S
4:23 sent you out with S and weeping, but God
5:1 the garment of your S and affliction, O Jerusalem,
Ezek 23:33 much; you will be filled with drunkenness and S
Lk 22:43 found them sleeping for S,
Jn 16:6 these things to you, S has filled your hearts.
16:20 be sorrowful, but your S will turn into joy.
16:21 in travail she has S, because her hour has
16:22 So you have S now, but I will see
Rom 9:2 that I have great S and unceasing anguish in
2Cor 2:7 him, or he may be overwhelmed by excessive S
Phil 2:27 lest I should have S upon sorrow.
2:27 me also, lest I should have sorrow upon S

SORROWFUL (11)
Gen 50:10 a very great and S lamentation; and he made
Wis 2:1 to themselves, "Short and S is our life, and
Mt 19:22 this he went away S; for he had great
26:22 And they were very S, and began to say
26:37 he began to be S and troubled.
26:38 "My soul is very S, even to death; remain
Mk 10:22 and he went away S; for he had great
14:19 They began to be S, and to say to
14:34 "My soul is very S, even to death; remain
Jn 16:20 rejoice; you will be S, but your sorrow will
2Cor 6:10 yet not killed; as S, yet always rejoicing; as

SORROWING
Acts 20:38 Paul and kissed him, S most of all because

SORROWS (4)
Ps 16:4 another god multiply their S; their libations of blood
Is 53:3 men; a man of S, and acquainted with grief;
53:4 griefs and carried our S; yet we esteemed him
Jer 49:24 seized her; anguish and S have taken hold of

SORRY (7)
Gen 6:6 And the LORD was S that he had made
6:7 air, for I am S that I have made
1Sam 22:8 none of you is S for me or discloses
Ps 38:18 my iniquity, I am S for my sin.
Mt 14:9 And the king was S; but because of his
Mk 6:26 the king was exceedingly S; but because of his
2Cor 7:8 if I made you S with my letter, I

SORT (28)
Gen 6:19 bring two of every S into the ark, to
6:20 kind, two of every S shall come in to
6:21 take with you every S of food that is
7:14 according to its kind, every bird of every S
Ex 35:35 ability to do every S of work done by
35:35 a weaver--by any S of workman or skilled
36:4 who were doing every S of task on the
Lev 5:3 human uncleanness, of whatever S the uncleanness
5:4 to do good, any S of rash oath that
14:35 me to be some S of disease in my
Deut 24:10 a loan of any S, you shall not go
1Sam 4:8 the Egyptians with every S of plague in the
2Chr 15:6 troubled them with every S of distress.
Wis 19:15 but punishment of some S will come upon the
Sir 47:25 they sought out every S of wickedness, till vengeance
Ezek 17:23 branches birds of every S will nest.
23:42 men of the common S drunkards were brought from
39:4 of prey of every S and to the wild
39:17 the birds of every S and to all beasts
2Mac 3:37 king asked Heliodorus what S of person would be
5:10 no funeral of any S and no place in
15:11 relating a dream, a S of vision, which was
Mt 8:27 men marveled, saying, "What S of man is this,
Lk 1:29 in her mind what S of greeting this might
7:39 known who and what S of woman this is
1Cor 3:13 fire will test what S of work each one
Heb 4:11 fall by the same S of disobedience.
2Pet 3:11 to be dissolved, what S of persons ought you

SORTED
Mt 13:48 and sat down and S the good into vessels

SORTS (11)
Gen 24:10 and departed, taking all S of choice gifts from
40:17 basket there were all S of baked food for
Ex 35:22 rings and armlets, all S of gold objects, every
2Kgs 17:32 from among themselves all S of people as priests
1Chr 18:10 And he sent all S of articles of gold,
29:2 antimony, colored stones, all S of precious stones,
2Chr 2:14 and to do all S of engraving and execute
Sir 23:16 Two S of men multiply sins, and a third
2Mac 5:3 flash of golden trappings, and armor of all S
7:31 who have contrived all S of evil against the
12:13 and inhabited by all S of Gentiles.

SOSIPATER (3)
2Mac 12:19 Dositheus and S, who were captains under
12:24 hands of Dositheus and S and their men.
Rom 16:21 Lucius and Jason and S, my kinsmen.

SOSTHENES (2)
Acts 18:17 And they all seized S, the ruler of the
1Cor 1:1 Jesus, and our brother S,

SOSTRATUS (2)
2Mac 4:28 When S the captain of the citadel kept requesting
4:29 in the high-priesthood, while S left Crates, the

SOTAI (2)
Ezra 2:55 servants: the sons of S, the sons of Hassophereth,
Neh 7:57 servants: the sons of S, the sons of Sophereth,

SOUGHT (119)
Gen 43:30 his brother, and he S a place to weep.
Ex 2:15 heard of it, he S to kill Moses.
4:24 LORD met him and S to kill him.
33:7 And every one who S the LORD would go
Deut 13:10 with stones, because he S to draw you away
1Sam 10:21 But when they S him, he could not be
13:14 continue; the LORD has S out a man after
14:4 pass, by which Jonathan S to go over to
19:10 And Saul S to pin David to the wall
23:14 And Saul S him every day, but God did
27:4 fled to Gath, he S for him no more.
2Sam 4:8 Saul, your enemy, who S your life; the LORD
17:20 And when they had S and could not find
21:1 after year; and David S the face of the
21:2 spare them, Saul had S to slay them in
1Kgs 1:2 a young maiden be S for my lord the
1:3 So they S for a beautiful maiden throughout all
10:24 And the whole earth S the presence of Solomon
11:40 Solomon S therefore to kill Jeroboam; but Jeroboam
2Kgs 2:17 for three days they S him but did not
2Chr 1:5 Solomon and the assembly S the LORD.
9:23 kings of the earth S the presence of Solomon
14:7 ours, because we have S the LORD our God;
14:7 our God; we have S him, and he has
15:4 God of Israel, and S him, he was found
15:15 their heart, and had S him with their whole
16:12 seek the LORD, but S help from physicians.
17:4 seek the Baals, but S the God of his
22:9 grandson of Jehoshaphat, who S the LORD with all
25:20 enemies, because they had S the gods of Edom.
26:5 as long as he S the LORD, God made
Ezra 2:62 These S their registration among those enrolled in
Neh 7:64 These S their registration among those enrolled in
12:27 wall of Jerusalem they S the Levites in all
Tob 1:18 When the bodies were S by the king, they
Esth 2:2 beautiful young virgins be S out for the king.
2:21 threshold, became angry and S to lay hands on
3:6 people of Mordecai, Haman S to destroy all the
6:2 threshold, and who had S to lay hands upon
9:2 hands on such as S their hurt.
10:3 his brethren, for he S the welfare of his
11:12 on his mind and S all day to understand
12:6 the king, and he S to injure Mordecai and
15:16 and all his servants S to comfort her.
Ps 34:4 I S the LORD, and he answered me, and
37:36 no more; though I S him, he could not
52:7 of his riches, and S refuge in his wealth!"
71:24 shame and disgraced who S to do me hurt.
78:34 he slew them, they S for him; they repented
78:34 him; they repented and S God earnestly.
119:45 liberty, for I have S thy precepts.
119:94 me; for I have S thy precepts.
Eccl 7:28 which my mind has S repeatedly, but I have
7:29 upright, but they have S out many devices.
12:10 The Preacher S to find pleasing words, and uprightly
Song 3:1 bed by night I S him whom my soul
3:1 my soul loves; I S him, but found him
3:2 I S him, but found him not.
5:6 I S him, but found him not; I called
Wis 8:2 I loved her and S her from my youth,
Sir 21:17 sensible man will be S in the assembly, and
24:7 Among all these I S a resting place; I
24:7 a resting place; I S in whose territory I
38:33 Yet they are not S out for the council
39:17 all things will be S after.
47:25 For they S out every sort of wickedness, till
51:3 hand of those who S my life, from the
51:13 on my travels, I S wisdom openly in my
Is 26:16 LORD, in distress they S thee, they poured out
62:12 you shall be called S out, a city not
65:1 was ready to be S by those who did
65:10 my people who have S me.
Jer 8:2 and which they have S and worshiped; and they
26:21 his words, the king S to put him to
31:2 the wilderness; when Israel S for rest,
44:30 was his enemy and S his life."
50:20 LORD, iniquity shall be S in Israel, and there

Lam 1:19 the city, while they S food to revive their
Ezek 22:30 And I S for a man among them who
26:21 more; though you be S for, you will never
34:4 lost you have not S, and with force and
Dan 2:13 be slain, and they S Daniel and his companions,
4:36 counselors and my lords S me, and I was
6:4 presidents and the satraps S to find a ground
8:15 seen the vision, I S to understand it; and
Hos 12:4 prevailed, he wept and S his favor.
Obad 1:6 been pillaged, his treasures S out!
1Mac 9:26 They S and searched for the friends of Judas,
14:4 He S the good of his nation; his rule
14:14 of his people; he S out the law, and
14:35 He S in every way to exalt his people.
2Mac 13:21 the enemy; he was S for, caught, and put
14:32 man was whom he S,
Mt 2:20 Israel, for those who S the child's life are
26:16 from that moment he S an opportunity to betray
26:59 the whole council S false testimony against Jesus
Mk 11:18 scribes heard it and S a way to destroy
14:11 And he S an opportunity to betray him.
14:55 and the whole council S testimony against Jesus to
Lk 2:44 day's journey, and they S him among their kinsfolk
2:49 is it that you S me?
4:42 And the people S him and came to him,
5:18 was paralyzed, and they S to bring him in
6:19 And all the crowd S to touch him, for
9:9 And he S to see him.
11:16 others, to test him, S from him a sign
19:3 And he S to see who Jesus was, but
19:47 men of the people S to destroy him;
22:6 So he agreed, and S an opportunity to betray
Jn 5:17 was why the Jews S all the more to
7:1 Judea, because the Jews S to kill him.
7:30 So they S to arrest him; but no one
19:12 Upon this Pilate S to release him, but the
Acts 12:19 And when Herod had S for him and could
13:7 Barnabas and Saul and S to hear the word
16:10 the vision, immediately we S to go on into
21:4 And having S out the disciples, we stayed there
Rom 11:7 Israel failed to obtain what it S
Heb 12:17 to repent, though he S it with tears.

SOUL (277)

Gen 34:3 And his S was drawn to Dinah the daughter
34:8 with them, saying, "The S of my son Shechem
35:18 And as her S was departing (for she died),
42:21 the distress of his S, when he besought us
49:6 O my S, come not into their council; O
Ex 31:14 work on it, that S shall be cut off
Lev 26:11 among you, and my S shall not abhor you.
26:15 statutes, and if your S abhors my ordinances, so
26:30 your idols; and my S will abhor you.
26:43 my ordinances, and their S abhorred my statutes.
Deut 4:9 heed, and keep your S diligently, lest you forget
4:29 with all your heart and with all your S
6:5 and with all your S, and with all your
10:12 and with all your S,
11:13 and with all your S,
11:18 heart and in your S; and you shall bind
13:3 with all your heart and with all your S
13:6 is as your own S, entices you secretly, saying,
26:16 with all your heart and with all your S
28:65 eyes, and a languishing S;
30:2 and with all your S;
30:6 and with all your S, that you may live.
30:10 with all your heart and with all your S
Josh 22:5 with all your heart and with all your S
Judg 5:21 March on, my S, with might!
16:16 and urged him, his S was vexed to death.
1Sam 1:15 been pouring out my S before the LORD.
17:55 Abner said, "As your S lives, O king, I
18:1 speaking to Saul, the S of Jonathan was knit
18:1 was knit to the S of David, and Jonathan
18:1 David, and Jonathan loved him as his own S
18:3 David, because he loved him as his own S
20:3 lives and as your S lives, there is but
20:17 he loved him as he loved his own S
25:26 lives, and as your S lives, seeing the LORD
30:6 people were bitter in S, each for his sons
2Sam 5:8 and the blind, who are hated by David's S
11:11 live, and as your S lives, I will not
1Kgs 1:29 who has redeemed my S out of every adversity,
2:4 and with all their S, there shall not fail
11:37 over all that your S desires, and you shall
17:21 God, let this child's S come into him again."
17:22 of Elijah; and the S of the child came
2Kgs 23:3 heart and all his S, to perform the words
23:25 and with all his S and with all his
2Chr 15:12 and with all their S;
34:31 heart and all his S, to perform the words
Tob 13:6 and with all your S, to do what is
13:7 exalt my God; my S exalts the King of
13:15 Let my S praise God the great King.
Jud 11:7 to direct every living S, not only do men
12:4 Judith replied, "As your S lives, my lord, your
Job 3:20 to the bitter in S,
7:11 I will complain in the bitterness of my S
10:1 I will speak in the bitterness of my S
21:25 dies in bitterness of S, never having tasted of
24:12 dying groan, and the S of the wounded cries
27:2 who has made my S bitter;
30:16 "And now my S is poured out within me;
30:25 Was not my S grieved for the poor?
33:18 he keeps back his S from the Pit, his
33:22 His S draws near the Pit, and his life
33:28 He has redeemed my S from going down into
33:30 to bring back his S from the Pit, that
Ps 6:3 My S also is sorely troubled.
7:5 ground, and lay my S in the dust.
11:5 the wicked, and his S hates him that loves
13:2 bear pain in my S, and have sorrow in
16:9 is glad, and my S rejoices; my body also
19:7 is perfect, reviving the S; the testimony of the
22:20 Deliver my S from the sword, my life from
22:21 the lion, my afflicted S from the horns of
23:3 leads me beside still waters; he restores my S
24:4 not lift up his S to what is false,
25:1 To thee, O LORD, I lift up my S
30:3 hast brought up my S from Sheol, restored me
30:12 with gladness, that my S may praise thee and
31:9 wasted from grief, my S and my body also.
33:19 he may deliver their S from death, and keep
33:20 Our S waits for the LORD; he is our
34:2 My S makes its boast in the LORD; let
35:3 Say to my S, "I am your deliverance!"
35:9 Then my S shall rejoice in the LORD, exulting
35:12 evil for good; my S is forlorn.
42:1 streams, so longs my S for thee, O God.
42:2 My S thirsts for God, for the living God.
42:4 I pour out my S: how I went with
42:5 cast down, O my S, and why are you
42:6 My S is cast down within me, therefore I
42:11 cast down, O my S, and why are you
43:5 cast down, O my S, and why are you
44:25 For our S is bowed down to the dust;
49:15 God will ransom my S from the power of
55:18 He will deliver my S in safety from the
56:13 thou hast delivered my S from death, yea, my
57:1 for in thee my S takes refuge; in the
57:6 for my steps; my S was bowed down.
57:8 Awake, my S
62:1 For God alone my S waits in silence; from
62:5 For God alone my S waits in silence, for
63:1 I seek thee, my S thirsts for thee; my
63:5 My S is feasted as with marrow and fat,
63:8 My S clings to thee; thy right hand upholds
69:10 When I humbled my S with fasting, it became
71:23 praises to thee; my S also, which thou hast
73:21 When my S was embittered, when I was pricked
74:19 Do not deliver the S of thy dove to
77:2 out without wearying; my S refuses to be comforted.
84:2 My S longs, yea, faints for the courts of
86:4 Gladden the S of thy servant, for to thee,
86:4 thee, O Lord, do I lift up my S
86:13 thou hast delivered my S from the depths of
88:3 For my S is full of troubles, and my
89:48 Who can deliver his S from the power of
94:17 been my help, my S would soon have dwelt
94:19 my heart are many, thy consolations cheer my S
103:1 the LORD, O my S; and all that is
103:2 the LORD, O my S, and forget not all
103:22 Bless the LORD, O my S
104:1 Bless the LORD, O my S
104:35 Bless the LORD, O my S
107:5 hungry and thirsty, their S fainted within them.
108:1 Awake, my S
116:7 Return, O my S, to your rest; for the
116:8 thou hast delivered my S from death, my eyes
119:20 My S is consumed with longing for thy ordinances
119:25 My S cleaves to the dust; revive me according
119:28 My S melts away for sorrow; strengthen me

S

119:81 My S languishes for thy salvation; I hope in
119:129 are wonderful; therefore my S keeps them.
119:167 My S keeps thy testimonies; I love them exceedingly.
123:4 Too long our S has been sated with the
130:5 for the LORD, my S waits, and in his
130:6 word I hope; my S waits for the LORD
131:2 calmed and quieted my S, like a child quieted
131:2 like a child that is quieted is my S
138:3 me, my strength of S thou didst increase.
143:6 hands to thee; my S thirsts for thee like
143:8 go, for to thee I lift up my S
146:1 Praise the LORD, O my S
Prov 2:10 be pleasant to your S;
3:22 be life for your S and adornment for your
13:4 The S of the sluggard craves, and gets nothing,
13:4 gets nothing, while the S of the diligent is
13:19 is sweet to the S; but to turn away
16:24 honeycomb, sweetness to the S and health to the
21:10 The S of the wicked desires evil; his neighbor
23:16 My S will rejoice when your lips speak what
24:12 keeps watch over your S know it, and will
24:14 is such to your S; if you find it,
25:25 water to a thirsty S, so is good news
27:9 heart glad, but the S is torn by trouble.
Song 1:7 me, you whom my S loves, where you pasture
3:1 sought him whom my S loves; I sought him,
3:2 seek him whom my S loves." I sought him,
3:3 seen him whom my S loves?"
3:4 found him whom my S loves.
5:6 My S failed me when he spoke.
Wis 1:4 not enter a deceitful S, nor dwell in a
1:11 without result, and a lying mouth destroys the S
4:11 evil change his understanding or guile deceive his S
4:14 long years; for his S was pleasing to the
8:19 endowed, and a good S fell to my lot;
9:3 judgment in uprightness of S,
9:15 body weighs down the S, and this earthy tent
10:7 salt standing as a monument to an unbelieving S
10:16 She entered the S of a servant of the
15:8 required to return the S that was lent him.
15:11 him with an active S and breathed into him
16:14 the departed spirit, nor set free the imprisoned S
17:8 disorders of a sick S were sick themselves with
Sir 4:6 if in bitterness of S he calls down a
6:2 exalt yourself through your S's counsel, lest your soul
6:2 soul's counsel, lest your S be torn in pieces
6:4 An evil S will destroy him who has it,
6:26 her with all your S, and keep her ways
7:11 who is bitter in S, for there is One
7:21 Let your S love an intelligent servant; do not
7:29 With all your S fear the Lord, and honor
14:9 with a portion, and mean injustice withers the S
16:15 for what is my S in the boundless creation?
18:30 If you allow your S to take pleasure in
19:3 him, and the reckless S will be snatched away.
21:27 man curses his adversary, he curses his own S
21:28 whisperer defiles his own S and is hated in
23:6 and do not surrender me to a shameless S
23:16 The S heated like a burning fire will not
25:1 My S takes pleasure in three things, and they
25:2 My S hates three kinds of men, and I
26:14 there is nothing so precious as a disciplined S
26:15 balance can weigh the value of a chaste S
30:12 you have sorrow of S from him.
30:23 Delight your S and comfort your heart, and remove
31:28 temperately is rejoicing of heart and gladness of S
31:29 excess is bitterness of S, with provocation and
33:31 for as your own S you will need him.
34:15 Blessed is the S of the man who fears
34:17 He lifts up the S and gives light to
37:12 of the commandments, whose S is in accord with
37:12 in accord with your S, and who will sorrow
37:14 For a man's S sometimes keeps him better informed
37:27 My son, test your S while you live; see
45:23 ready goodness of his S, and made atonement for
47:15 Your S covered the earth, and you filled it
50:25 With two nations my S is vexed, and the
51:6 My S drew near to death, and my life
51:19 My S grappled with wisdom, and in my conduct
51:20 I directed my S to her, and through purification
51:29 May your S rejoice in his mercy, and may
Is 1:14 your appointed feasts my S hates; they have become
10:18 LORD will destroy, both S and body, and it
15:4 Moab cry aloud; his S trembles.
16:11 Therefore my S moans like a lyre for Moab,
26:8 thy memorial name is the desire of our S
26:9 My S yearns for thee in the night, my
38:15 has fled because of the bitterness of my S
42:1 chosen, in whom my S delights; I have put
53:11 the travail of his S and be satisfied; by
53:12 he poured out his S to death, and was
55:3 me; hear, that your S may live; and I
61:10 in the LORD, my S shall exult in my
66:3 own ways, and their S delights in their abominations;
Jer 12:7 the beloved of my S into the hands of
13:17 will not listen, my S will weep in secret
14:19 Does thy S loathe Zion?
31:14 I will feast the S of the priests with
31:25 will satisfy the weary S, and every languishing soul
31:25 soul, and every languishing S I will replenish."
32:41 faithfulness, with all my heart and all my S
Lam 1:20 am in distress, my S is in tumult, my
2:11 spent with weeping; my S is in tumult; my
3:17 cower in ashes; my S is bereft of peace,
3:20 My S continually thinks of it and is bowed
3:24 says my S, "therefore I will hope in him."
3:25 for him, to the S that seeks him.
Bar 3:1 God of Israel, the S in anguish and the
Ezek 18:4 souls are mine; the S of the father as
18:4 as well as the S of the son is
18:4 son is mine: the S that sins shall die.
18:20 The S that sins shall die.
24:21 the desire of your S; and your sons and
27:31 you in bitterness of S, with bitter mourning.
Jon 2:7 When my S fainted within me, I remembered the
Mic 6:7 of my body for the sin of my S
7:1 first-ripe fig which my S desires.
7:3 evil desire of his S; thus they weave it
Hab 2:4 Behold, he whose S is not upright in him
2Mac 3:16 in his color disclosed the anguish of his S
6:30 beating, but in my S I am glad to
15:30 ever in body and S the defender of his
Mt 10:28 but cannot kill the S; rather fear him who
10:28 who can destroy both S and body in hell.
12:18 beloved with whom my S is well pleased.
22:37 and with all your S, and with all your
26:38 said to them, "My S is very sorrowful, even
Mk 12:30 and with all your S, and with all your
14:34 said to them, "My S is very sorrowful, even
Lk 1:46 And Mary said, "My S magnifies the Lord,
2:35 pierce through your own S also), that thoughts out
10:27 and with all your S, and with all your
12:19 will say to my S, Soul, you have ample
12:19 say to my soul, S, you have ample goods
12:20 This night your S is required of you; and
Jn 12:27 "Now is my S troubled.
Acts 2:27 wilt not abandon my S to Hades, nor let
2:43 fear came upon every S; and many wonders and
3:23 shall be that every S that does not listen
4:32 of one heart and S, and no one said
1Thes 5:23 may your spirit and S and body be kept
Heb 4:12 to the division of S and spirit, of joints
6:19 steadfast anchor of the S, a hope that enters
10:38 he shrinks back, my S has no pleasure in
Jas 5:20 way will save his S from death and will
1Pet 2:11 of the flesh that wage war against your S
2Pet 2:8 vexed in his righteous S day after day with
3Jn 1:2 I know that it is well with your S
Rev 18:14 fruit for which thy S longed has gone from

SOULS (39)

Lev 17:11 make atonement for your S; for it is the
Josh 23:14 in your hearts and S, all of you, that
Wis 2:22 the prize for blameless S;
3:1 But the S of the righteous are in the
3:13 union; she will have fruit when God examines S
7:27 she passes into holy S and makes them friends
14:11 became traps for the S of men and a
14:26 of favors, pollution of S, sex perversion, disorder in
17:1 describe; therefore unintructed S have gone astray.
17:15 were paralyzed by their S surrender, for sudden and
Sir 21:2 teeth, and destroy the S of men.
51:24 and why are your S very thirsty?
51:26 yoke, and let your S receive instruction; it is
Jer 6:16 walk in it, and find rest for your S
38:16 lives, who made our S, I will not put
Ezek 13:18 persons of every stature, in the hunt for S
13:18 Will you hunt down S belonging to my people,
13:18 people, and keep other S alive for your profit?
13:20 which you hunt the S, and I will tear
13:20 I will let the S that you hunt go
18:4 Behold, all S are mine; the soul of the

Dan 3:87 the Lord, spirits and S of the righteous, sing
2Mac 15:17 awaking manliness in the S of the young, they
Mt 11:29 heart, and you will find rest for your S
Acts 2:41 there were added that day about three thousand S
7:14 all his kindred, seventy-five S;
14:22 Antioch, strengthening the S of the disciples,
2Cor 12:15 most gladly spend and be spent for your S
Heb 10:39 of those who have faith and keep their S
13:17 keeping watch over your S, as men who will
Jas 1:20 implanted word, which is able to save your S
1Pet 1:9 your faith you obtain the salvation of your S
1:22 Having purified your S by your obedience to the
2:25 returned to the Shepherd and Guardian of your S
4:19 right and entrust their S to a faithful Creator.
2Pet 2:14 They entice unsteady S
Rev 6:9 under the altar the S of those who had
18:13 horses and chariots, and slaves, that is, human S
20:4 Also I saw the S of those who had

SOUND (154)

Gen 3:8 And they heard the S of the LORD God
3:10 said, "I heard the S of thee in the
Ex 19:19 And as the S of the trumpet grew louder
20:18 the lightnings and the S of the trumpet and
28:35 he ministers, and its S shall be heard when
32:18 "It is not the S of shouting for victory,
32:18 for victory, or the S of the cry of
32:18 of defeat, but the S of singing that I
Lev 26:36 of their enemies; the S of a driven leaf
Num 10:7 but you shall not S an alarm.
10:9 you, then you shall S an alarm with the
Deut 4:12 fire; you heard the S of words, but saw
Josh 6:5 as you hear the S of the trumpet, then
6:20 the people heard the S of the trumpet, the
Judg 5:11 To the S of musicians at the watering places,
1Sam 4:14 When Eli heard the S of the outcry, he
2Sam 5:24 when you hear the S of marching in the
6:15 shouting, and with the S of the horn.
15:10 as you hear the S of the trumpet, then
1Kgs 1:41 when Joab heard the S of the trumpet, he
14:6 when Ahijah heard the S of her feet, as
18:41 for there is a S of the rushing of
2Kgs 4:31 but there was no S or sign of life.
6:32 Is not the S of his master's feet behind
7:6 the Syrians hear the S of chariots, and of
7:6 and of horses, the S of a great army,
1Chr 14:15 when you hear the S of marching in the
15:19 and Ethan, were to S bronze cymbals;
15:28 with shouting, to the S of the horn, trumpets,
16:5 lyres; Asaph was to S the cymbals,
2Chr 13:12 their battle trumpets to S the call to battle
Ezra 3:13 could not distinguish the S of the joyful shout
3:13 joyful shout from the S of the people's weeping,
3:13 great shout, and the S was heard afar.
Neh 4:20 where you hear the S of the trumpet, rally
Tob 5:15 your wages if you both return safe and S
5:20 will return safe and S, and your eyes will
5:21 successful, and he will come back safe and S
Esth 13:3 excels among us in S judgment, and is distinguished
Job 21:12 and rejoice to the S of the pipe.
26:3 wisdom, and plentifully declared S knowledge!
33:8 I have heard the S of your words.
39:24 stand still at the S of the trumpet.
Ps 5:2 Hearken to the S of my cry, my King
6:8 LORD has heard the S of my weeping.
47:5 the LORD with the S of a trumpet.
66:8 O peoples, let the S of his praise be
73:4 pangs; their bodies are S and sleek.
81:2 Raise a song, S the timbrel, the sweet lyre
98:5 the lyre and the S of melody!
98:6 With trumpets and the S of the horn make
104:7 they fled; at the S of thy thunder they
115:7 do not make a S in their throat.
150:3 Praise him with trumpet S; praise him with lute
Prov 2:7 understanding; he stores up S wisdom for the
3:21 My son, keep S wisdom and discretion; let them
8:14 I have counsel and S wisdom, I have insight,
18:1 break out against all S judgment.
Eccl 12:4 are shut; when the S of the grinding is
Wis 1:10 all things, and the S of murmurings does not
7:3 earth, and my first S was a cry, like
17:18 wind, or a melodious S of birds in wide-spreading
17:19 leaping animals, or the S of the most savage
Sir 38:28 his ear to the S of the hammer, and
45:9 to send forth a S as he walked, to
46:17 heard with a mighty S;

Is 14:11 down to Sheol, the S of your harps; maggots
24:18 who flees at the S of the terror shall
30:19 to you at the S of your cry; when
30:29 sets out to the S of the flute to
30:32 will be to the S of timbrels and lyres;
65:19 heard in it the S of weeping and the
Jer 4:19 for I hear the S of the trumpet, the
4:21 standard, and hear the S of the trumpet?
6:17 'Give heed to the S of the trumpet!' But
6:23 have no mercy, the S of them is like
8:16 from Dan; at the S of the neighing of
9:19 For a S of wailing is heard from Zion:
42:14 war, or hear the S of the trumpet, or
46:22 "She makes a S like a serpent gliding away;
49:21 At the S of their fall the earth shall
49:21 earth shall tremble; the S of their cry shall
50:42 The S of them is like the roaring of
50:46 At the S of the capture of Babylon the
Ezek 1:24 went, I heard the S of their wings like
1:24 their wings like the S of many waters, like
1:24 of the Almighty, a S of tumult like the
1:24 of tumult like the S of a host; when
3:12 heard behind me the S of a great earthquake;
3:13 earthquake; it was the S of the wings of
3:13 one another, and the S of the wheels beside
10:5 And the S of the wings of the cherubim
19:7 in it at the S of his roaring.
23:42 The S of a carefree multitude was with her;
26:13 your songs, and the S of your lyres shall
26:15 coastlands shake at the S of your fall, when
27:28 At the S of the cry of your pilots
31:16 nations quake at the S of its fall, when
33:4 one who hears the S of the trumpet does
33:5 He heard the S of the trumpet, and did
43:2 the east; and the S of his coming was
43:2 coming was like the S of many waters; and
Dan 3:5 when you hear the S of the horn, pipe,
3:7 the peoples heard the S of the horn, pipe,
3:10 man who hears the S of the horn, pipe,
3:15 when you hear the S of the horn, pipe,
7:11 then because of the S of the great words
10:6 burnished bronze, and the S of his words like
10:9 Then I heard the S of his words; and
10:9 when I heard the S of his words, I
14:36 den, with the rushing S of the wind itself.
Hos 5:8 S the alarm at Beth-aven; tremble, O Benjamin!
Joel 2:1 the trumpet in Zion; S the alarm on my
Amos 2:2 amid shouting and the S of the trumpet;
6:5 idle songs to the S of the harp, and
Mic 6:9 city--and it is S wisdom to fear thy
Hab 3:16 lips quiver at the S; rottenness enters into my
Zeph 1:14 and hastening fast; the S of the day of
Zech 9:14 the Lord GOD will S the trumpet, and march
11:16 maimed, or nourish the S, but devours the flesh
1Mac 9:12 phalanx advanced to the S of the trumpets; and
Mt 6:2 when you give alms, S no trumpet before you,
6:22 if your eye is S, your whole body will
6:23 your eye is not S, your whole body will
7:17 So, every S tree bears good fruit, but the
7:18 A S tree cannot bear evil fruit, nor can
Lk 11:34 when your eye is S, your whole body is
11:34 when it is not S, your body is full
15:27 received him safe and S
Jn 3:8 and you hear the S of it, but you
Acts 2:2 And suddenly a S came from heaven like the
2:6 And at this S the multitude came together, and
1Cor 14:8 bugle gives an indistinct S, who will get ready
15:52 For the trumpet will S, and the dead will
1Thes 4:16 call, and with the S of the trumpet of
5:23 and body be kept S and blameless at the
1Tim 1:10 else is contrary to S doctrine,
6:3 not agree with the S words of our Lord
2Tim 1:13 the pattern of the S words which you have
4:3 people will not endure S teaching, but having itching
Tit 1:8 to give instruction in S doctrine and also to
1:12 that they may be S in the faith,
2:1 you, teach what befits S doctrine.
2:2 be temperate, serious, sensible, S in faith, in love,
2:8 show integrity, gravity, and S speech that cannot be
Heb 12:19 a tempest, and the S of a trumpet, and
Rev 1:15 voice was like the S of many waters;
14:2 from heaven like the S of many waters and
14:2 waters and like the S of loud thunder; the
14:2 heard was like the S of harpers playing on
18:22 no more; and the S of harpers and minstrels,
18:22 no more; and the S of the millstone shall

19:6 great multitude, like the S of many waters and
19:6 waters and like the S of mighty thunderpeals, crying,

SOUNDED (20)

Judg 3:27 When he arrived, he S the trumpet in the
6:34 of Gideon; and he S the trumpet, and the
1Sam 20:12 When I have S my father, about this time
2Chr 7:6 opposite them the priests S trumpets; and all Israel
29:28 sang, and the trumpeters S; all this continued until
Neh 4:18 The man who S the trumpet was beside me.
Sir 50:16 of Aaron shouted, they S the trumpets of hammered
Ezek 3:13 wheels beside them, that S like a great earthquake.
19:4 The nations S an alarm against him; he was
1Mac 3:54 Then they S the trumpets and gave a loud
4:40 on the ground, and S the signal on the
5:33 in three companies, who S their trumpets and cried
6:33 ready for battle and S their trumpets.
16:8 And they S the trumpets, and Cendebeus and his
Acts 27:28 So they S and found twenty fathoms; a little
27:28 little farther on they S again and found fifteen
1Thes 1:8 word of the Lord S forth from you in
Rev 10:3 roaring; when he called out, the seven thunders S
10:4 the seven thunders had S, I was about to
10:7 trumpet call to be S by the seventh angel,

SOUNDING (2)

Ps 150:5 Praise him with S cymbals; praise him with loud
1Mac 7:45 as they followed kept S the battle call on

SOUNDNESS (4)

Ps 38:3 There is no S in my flesh because of
38:7 and there is no S in my flesh.
Sir 30:15 Health and S are better than all gold, and
Is 1:6 head, there is no S in it, but bruises

SOUNDS (5)

Ex 19:13 live.' When the trumpet S a long blast, they
1Chr 15:16 and cymbals, to raise S of joy.
Job 15:21 Terrifying S are in his ears; in prosperity the
39:25 When the trumpet S, he says 'Aha!' He smells
Wis 17:4 from fear, but terrifying S rang out around them,

SOUR (3)

Jer 31:29 'The fathers have eaten S grapes, and the children's
31:30 each man who eats S grapes, his teeth shall
Ezek 18:2 'The fathers have eaten S grapes, and the children's

SOURCE (4)

Wis 12:16 thy strength is the S of righteousness, and thy
2Mac 4:8 silver and, from another S of revenue, eighty talents.
1Cor 1:30 He is the S of your life in Christ
Heb 5:9 perfect he became the S of eternal salvation to

SOURCES

Is 7:18 which is at the S of the streams of

SOUTH (121)

Gen 28:14 north and to the S; and by you and
Ex 26:18 twenty frames for the S side;
26:35 the lampstand on the S side of the tabernacle
27:9 On the S side the court shall have hangings
36:23 twenty frames for the S side;
38:9 the court; for the S side the hangings of
Num 2:10 "On the S side shall be the standard of
3:29 to encamp on the S side of the tabernacle,
10:6 that are on the S side shall set out.
34:3 its full extent), your S side shall be from
34:4 your boundary shall turn S of the ascent of
34:4 its end shall be S of Kadesh-barnea; then it
35:5 cubits, and for the S side two thousand cubits,
Deut 33:23 of the LORD, possess the lake and the S
Josh 11:2 and in the Arabah S of Chinneroth, and in
13:4 the Avvim, in the S, all the land of
15:1 to the wilderness of Zin at the farthest S
15:2 And their S boundary ran from the end of
15:3 Zin, and goes up S of Kadesh-barnea, along by
15:4 This shall be your S boundary.
15:7 which is on the S side of the valley;
15:21 Judah in the extreme S, toward the boundary of
17:9 cities here, to the S of the brook, among
17:10 the land to the S being Ephraim's and that
18:5 his territory on the S, and the house of
18:13 the mountain that lies S of Lower Beth-horon.
18:14 that lies to the S, opposite Beth-horon, and it
18:16 the valley of Hinnom, S of the shoulder of
18:19 Salt Sea, at the S end of the Jordan:
19:34 touching Zebulun at the S, and Asher on the
Judg 21:19 Bethel to Shechem, and S of Lebonah."
1Sam 14:5 the other on the S in front of Geba.
23:19 of Hachilah, which is S of Jeshimon?
23:24 the Arabah to the S of Jeshimon.
1Kgs 6:8 story was on the S side of the house;
7:21 the pillar on the S and called its name
7:25 facing west, three facing S, and three facing east;
7:39 stands, five on the S side of the house,
7:49 gold, five on the S side and five on
2Kgs 11:11 his hand, from the S side of the house
23:13 of Jerusalem, to the S of the mount of
1Chr 9:24 east, west, north, and S;
26:15 came out for the S, and to his sons
26:17 each day, on the S four each day, as
2Chr 3:17 temple, one on the S, the other on the
3:17 north; that on the S he called Jachin, and
4:4 facing west, three facing S, and three facing east;
4:6 set five on the S side, and five on
4:7 temple, five on the S side and five on
4:8 temple, five on the S side and five on
23:10 his hand, from the S side of the house
Tob 1:2 which is to the S of Kedesh Naphtali in
Jud 2:23 lived along the desert, S of the country of
7:18 their men toward the S and the east, toward
Job 9:9 the chambers of the S;
37:17 still because of the S wind?
39:26 hawk soars, and spreads his wings toward the S
Ps 78:26 he led out the S wind;
89:12 The north and the S, thou hast created them;
107:3 the west, from the north and from the S
Eccl 1:6 wind blows to the S, and goes round to
11:3 tree falls to the S or to the north,
Song 4:16 wind, and come, O S wind!
Sir 43:16 at his will the S wind blows.
Is 43:6 up, and to the S, Do not withhold; bring
Ezek 10:3 were standing on the S side of the house,
16:46 who lived to the S of you, is Sodom
20:46 your face toward the S, preach against the south,
20:46 south, preach against the S, and prophesy against the
20:47 and all faces from S to north shall be
21:4 against all flesh from S to north;
40:24 led me toward the S, and behold, there was
40:24 a gate on the S; and he measured its
40:27 a gate on the S of the inner court;
40:27 to gate toward the S, a hundred cubits.
40:28 inner court by the S gate, and he measured
40:28 and he measured the S gate; it was of
40:44 the north gate facing S, the other at the
40:44 the side of the S gate facing north.
40:45 This chamber which faces S is for the priests
41:11 another door toward the S; and the breadth of
42:10 On the S also, opposite the yard and opposite
42:12 And below the S chambers was an entrance on
42:13 chambers and the S chambers opposite the yard
42:18 turned and measured the S side, five hundred cubits
46:9 go out by the S gate; and he who
46:9 who enters by the S gate shall go out
47:1 down from below the S end of the threshold
47:1 threshold of the temple, S of the altar.
47:2 coming out on the S side.
47:19 "On the S side, it shall run from Tamar
47:19 This shall be the S side.
48:16 five hundred cubits, the S side four thousand five
48:17 fifty cubits, on the S two hundred and fifty,
48:28 of Gad to the S, the boundary shall run
48:33 On the S side, which is to be four
Dan 8:9 exceedingly great toward the S, toward the east, and
11:5 the king of the S shall be strong, but
11:6 the king of the S shall come to the
11:9 the king of the S but shall return into
11:11 the king of the S, moved with anger, shall
11:14 the king of the S; and the men of
11:15 the forces of the S shall not stand, or
11:25 the king of the S with a great army;
11:25 the king of the S shall wage war with
11:29 and come into the S; but it shall not
11:40 the king of the S shall attack him; but
Zech 6:6 ones go toward the S country."
7:7 about her, and the S and the lowland were
9:14 and march forth in the whirlwinds of the S
14:10 from Geba to Rimmon S of Jerusalem.
1Mac 3:57 and encamped to the S of Emmaus.
5:65 sons of Esau in the land to the S
Mt 12:42 The queen of the S will arise at the
Lk 11:31 The queen of the S will arise at the

S

12:55 when you see the S wind blowing, you say,
13:29 and from north and S, and sit at table
Acts 8:26 and go toward the S to the road that
27:13 And when the S wind blew gently, supposing that
28:13 after one day a S wind sprang up, and
Rev 21:13 three gates, on the S three gates, and on

SOUTHEAST (3)
1Kgs 7:39 the sea on the S corner of the house.
2Chr 4:10 the sea at the S corner of the house.
Acts 27:12 Crete, looking northeast and S, and winter there.

SOUTHERN (6)
Num 34:3 of Edom, and your S boundary shall be from
Josh 15:8 of Hinnom at the S shoulder of the Jebusite
18:15 And the S side begins at the outskirts of
18:19 Jordan: this is the S border.
Jud 2:25 and came to the S borders of Japheth, fronting
Ezek 48:10 in length on the S side, with the sanctuary

SOUTHWARD (11)
Gen 13:14 are, northward and S and eastward and westward;
Deut 3:27 westward and northward and S and eastward, and
Josh 12:3 Arabah, the Salt Sea, S to the foot of
15:1 to their families reached S to the boundary of
15:2 the bay that faces S;
15:3 southward; it goes out S of the ascent of
17:7 the boundary goes along S to the inhabitants of
18:13 the boundary passes along S in the direction of
18:14 on the western side S from the mountain that
Dan 8:4 westward and northward and S; no beast could stand
Zech 14:4 shall withdraw northward, and the other half S

SOVEREIGN (14)
Jud 2:13 transgress any of your S's commands, but be sure
Wis 12:18 Thou who art S in strength dost judge with
2Mac 3:24 then and there the S of spirits and of
3:28 they recognized clearly the S power of God.
12:15 calling upon the great S of the world, who
12:28 Jews called upon the S who with power shatters
15:3 if there were a S in heaven who had
15:4 living Lord himself, the S in heaven, who ordered
15:5 "And I am a S also, on earth, and
15:23 So now, O S of the heavens, send a
15:29 and they blessed the S Lord in the language
Acts 4:24 to God and said, S Lord, who didst make
1Tim 6:15 the blessed and only S, the King of kings
Rev 6:10 a loud voice, "O S Lord, holy and true,

SOVEREIGNS
Esth 16:6 natures beguile the sincere good will of their S

SOVEREIGNTY (5)
Wis 6:3 the Lord, and your S from the Most High,
12:16 of righteousness, and thy S over all causes thee
Sir 10:8 S passes from nation to nation on account of
47:21 folly, so that the S was divided and a
Dan 2:44 destroyed, nor shall its S be left to another

SOW (43)
Gen 47:23 you, and you shall S the land.
Ex 23:10 six years you shall S your land and gather
23:16 labor, of what you S in the field.
Lev 19:19 kind; you shall not S your field with two
25:3 Six years you shall S your field, and six
25:4 LORD; you shall not S your field or prune
25:11 it you shall neither S, nor reap what grows
25:20 if we may not S or gather in our
25:22 When you S in the eighth year, you will
26:16 And you shall S your seed in vain, for
Deut 22:9 "You shall not S your vineyard with two kinds
2Kgs 19:29 in the third year S, and reap, and plant
Job 4:8 who plow iniquity and S trouble reap the same.
31:8 hands; then let me S, and another eat; and
Ps 107:37 to live in; they S fields, and plant vineyards,
126:5 May those who S in tears reap with shouts
Eccl 11:4 the wind will not S; and he who regards
11:6 In the morning S your seed, and at evening
Sir 7:3 My son, do not S the furrows of injustice,
Is 17:11 the morning that you S; yet the harvest will
28:25 he not scatter dill, S cummin, and put in
30:23 seed with which you S the ground, and grain,
32:20 Happy are you who S beside all waters, who
37:30 in the third year S and reap, and plant
Jer 4:3 your fallow ground, and S not among thorns.
31:27 LORD, when I will S the house of Israel
35:7 house; you shall not S seed; you shall not
Hos 2:23 Jezreel; and I will S him for myself in
8:7 For they S the wind, and they shall reap
10:12 S for yourselves righteousness, reap the fruit of
Mic 6:15 You shall S, but not reap; you shall tread
Mt 6:26 the air: they neither S nor reap nor gather
13:3 in parables, saying: "A sower went out to S
13:27 'Sir, did you not S good seed in your
25:24 where you did not S, and gathering where you
Mk 4:3 A sower went out to S
Lk 8:5 sower went out to S his seed; and as
12:24 the ravens: they neither S nor reap, they have
19:21 what you did not S
19:22 lay down and reaping what I did not S
1Cor 15:36 What you S does not come to life unless
15:37 And what you S is not the body which
2Pet 2:22 own vomit, and the S is washed only to

SOWED (12)
Gen 26:12 And Isaac S in that land, and reaped in
Deut 11:10 have come, where you S your seed and watered
Judg 9:45 razed the city and S it with salt.
Mt 13:4 And as he S, some seeds fell along the
13:24 to a man who S good seed in his
13:25 his enemy came and S weeds among the wheat,
13:31 a man took and S in his field;
13:39 and the enemy who S them is the devil;
25:26 where I have not S, and gather where I
Mk 4:4 And as he S, some seed fell along the
Lk 8:5 seed; and as he S, some fell along the
13:19 a man took and S in his garden; and

SOWER (9)
Is 55:10 giving seed to the S and bread to the
Jer 50:16 off from Babylon the S, and the one who
Mt 13:3 in parables, saying: "A S went out to sow.
13:18 "Hear then the parable of the S
Mk 4:3 A S went out to sow.
4:14 The S sows the word.
Lk 8:5 in a parable: "A S went out to sow
Jn 4:36 eternal life, so that S and reaper may rejoice
2Cor 9:10 supplies seed to the S and bread for food

SOWING (7)
Lev 11:37 upon any seed for S that is to be
26:5 to the time for S; and you shall eat
27:16 seed for it; a S of a homer of
Ps 126:6 bearing the seed for S, shall come home with
Prov 6:14 heart devises evil, continually S discord;
Is 28:24 he who plows for S plow continually?
Zech 8:12 there shall be a S of peace; the vine

SOWN (29)
Lev 11:37 that is to be S, it is clean;
Deut 21:4 is neither plowed nor S, and shall break the
22:9 crop which you have S and the yield of
Esth 16:11 and was continually bowed S to by all as
Is 19:7 and all that is S by the Nile will
40:24 are they planted, scarcely S, scarcely has their stem
61:11 garden causes what is S in it to spring
Jer 2:2 me in the wilderness, in a land not S
12:13 They have S wheat and have reaped thorns, they
Ezek 36:9 shall be tilled and S;
Hag 1:6 You have S much, and harvested little; you eat,
Mt 13:19 snatches away what is S in his heart; this
13:19 this is what was S along the path.
13:20 As for what was S on rocky ground, this
13:22 As for what was S among thorns, this is
13:23 As for what was S on good soil, this
Mk 4:15 where the word is S; when they hear, Satan
4:15 the word which is S in them.
4:16 manner are the ones S upon rocky ground, who,
4:18 others are the ones S among thorns; they are
4:20 But those that were S upon the good soil
4:31 mustard seed, which, when S upon the ground, is
4:32 yet when it is S it grows up and
1Cor 9:11 If we have S spiritual good among you, is
15:42 What is S is perishable, what is raised is
15:43 It is S in dishonor, it is raised in
15:43 It is S in weakness, it is raised in
15:44 It is S a physical body, it is raised
Jas 3:18 harvest of righteousness is S in peace by those

SOWS (13)
Prov 6:19 and a man who S discord among brothers.
11:18 wages, but one who S righteousness gets a sure

	22:8	He who S injustice will reap calamity, and the
Sir	6:19	one who plows and S, and wait for her
Amos	9:13	of grapes him who S the seed; the mountains
Mt	13:37	He answered, "He who S the good seed is
Mk	4:14	The sower S the word.
Jn	4:37	saying holds true, 'One S and another reaps.'
2Cor	9:6	is this: he who S sparingly will also reap
	9:6	sparingly, and he who S bountifully will also reap
Gal	6:7	for whatever a man S, that he will also
	6:8	For he who S to his own flesh will
	6:8	corruption; but he who S to the Spirit will

SPACE (11)

Gen	32:16	me, and put a S between drove and drove."
Ex	25:37	give light upon the S in front of it.
Josh	3:4	there shall be a S between you and it,
1Sam	26:13	mountain, with a great S between them;
1Kgs	7:36	trees, according to the S of each, with wreaths
Neh	4:13	lowest parts of the S behind the wall, in
Ezek	40:7	reed broad; and the S between the side rooms,
	41:17	were covered), to the S above the door, even
	45:2	cubits for an open S around it.
2Mac	14:44	quickly drew back, a S opened and he fell
	14:44	he fell in the middle of the empty S

SPACIOUS (3)

Ps	66:12	us forth to a S place.
Jer	22:14	a great house with S upper rooms,' and cuts
Dan	13:4	rich, and had a S garden adjoining his house;

SPAIN (3)

1Mac	8:3	in the land of S to get control of
Rom	15:24	as I go to S, and to be sped
	15:28	way of you to S;

SPAN (10)

Ex	28:16	square and double, a S its length and a
	28:16	its length and a S its breadth.
	39:9	was made double, a S its length and a
	39:9	its length and a S its breadth when doubled.
1Sam	17:4	Gath, whose height was six cubits and a S
Ps	90:10	strength fourscore; yet their S is but toil and
Is	40:12	the heavens with a S, enclosed the dust of
Ezek	43:13	a rim of one S around its edge.
Mt	6:27	one cubit to his S of life?
Lk	12:25	a cubit to his S of life?

SPARE (49)

Gen	18:24	the place and not S it for the fifty
	18:26	the city, I will S the whole place for
Deut	13:8	him, nor shall you S him, nor shall you
Josh	22:22	faith toward the LORD, S us not today
1Sam	15:3	they have; do not S them, but kill both
2Sam	21:2	Israel had sworn to S them, Saul had sought
1Kgs	20:31	Israel; perhaps he will S your life."
2Kgs	7:4	the Syrians; if they S our lives we shall
Neh	13:22	O my God, and S me according to the
Jud	2:11	your eye shall not S and you shall hand
	13:20	because you did not S your own life when
Esth	13:15	King, God of Abraham, S thy people; for the
Job	2:6	in your power; only S his life."
	16:13	kidneys, and does not S; he pours out my
Ps	59:5	punish all the nations; S none of those who
	78:50	anger; he did not S them from death, but
	119:88	In thy steadfast love S my life, that I
Prov	6:34	and he will not S when he takes revenge.
Wis	2:10	man; let us not S the widow nor regard
	12:8	even these thou didst S, since they were but
	12:16	all causes thee to S all.
Sir	16:8	He did not S the neighbors of Lot, whom
	23:2	That they may not S me in my errors,
Is	31:5	deliver it, he will S and rescue it.
	47:3	vengeance, and I will S no man.
	58:1	"Cry aloud, S not, lift up your voice like
Jer	13:14	will not pity or S or have compassion, that
	21:7	not pity them, or S them, or have compassion.'
	50:14	bow; shoot at her, S no arrows, for she
	51:3	S not her young men; utterly destroy all her
Ezek	5:11	my eye will not S, and I will have
	7:4	my eye will not S you, nor will I
	7:9	my eye will not S, nor will I have
	8:18	my eye will not S, nor will I have
	9:5	your eye shall not S, and you shall show
	9:10	my eye will not S, nor will I have
	24:14	back, I will not S, I will not repent;
Joel	2:17	LORD, weep and say, S thy people, O LORD,
Mal	3:17	act, and I will S them as a man
1Mac	13:5	it from me to S my life in any
Lk	15:17	bread enough and to S, but I perish here
Rom	8:32	He who did not S his own Son but
	11:21	if God did not S the natural branches, neither
	11:21	branches, neither will he S you.
1Cor	7:28	troubles, and I would S you that.
2Cor	1:23	me—it was to S you that I refrained
	13:2	again I will not S them—
2Pet	2:4	if God did not S the angels when they
	2:5	if he did not S the ancient world, but

SPARED (17)

Gen	12:13	my life may be S on your account."
Ex	12:27	slew the Egyptians but S our houses.'" And the
1Sam	2:33	my altar shall be S to weep out his
	15:9	Saul and the people S Agag, and the best
	15:15	Amalekites; for the people S the best of the
	24:10	kill you, but I S you.
2Sam	8:2	to death, and one full line to be S
	21:7	But the king S Mephibosheth, the son of Saul's
2Kgs	5:20	"See, my master has S this Naaman the Syrian,
	10:14	forty-two persons, and he S none of them.
Jud	7:28	our lives will be S, and we shall not
	11:9	the men of Bethulia S him and he told
Job	21:30	the wicked man is S in the day of
Jer	38:17	your life shall be S, and this city shall
	38:20	well with you, and your life shall be S
Ezek	20:17	Nevertheless my eye S them, and I did not
Hos	10:11	to thresh, and I S her fair neck; but

SPARES (3)

Prov	13:24	He who S the rod hates his son, but
Is	9:19	the fire; no man S his brother.
Mal	3:17	them as a man S his son who serves

SPAREST

Wis	11:26	Thou S all things, for they are thine, O

SPARING (2)

Prov	25:27	much honey, so be S of complimentary words.
Acts	20:29	in among you, not S the flock;

SPARINGLY (2)

2Cor	9:6	this: he who sows S will also reap sparingly,
	9:6	sparingly will also reap S, and he who sows

SPARK (4)

Wis	2:2	and reason is a S kindled by the beating
Sir	11:30	From a S of fire come many burning coals,
	28:12	you blow on a S, it will glow; if
Is	1:31	and his work a S, and both of them

SPARKLED

Ezek	1:7	calf's foot; and they S like burnished bronze.

SPARKLES

Prov	23:31	is red, when it S in the cup and

SPARKLING (2)

Sir	42:22	his works, and how S they are to see!
Ezek	10:9	the wheels was like S chrysolite.

SPARKS (4)

Job	5:7	to trouble as the S fly upward.
	41:19	mouth go flaming torches; S of fire leap forth.
Wis	3:7	and will run like S through the stubble.
	11:18	smoke, or flash terrible S from their eyes;

SPARROW (2)

Ps	84:3	Even the S finds a home, and the swallow
Prov	26:2	Like a S in its flitting, like a swallow

SPARROWS (5)

Tob	2:10	know that there were S on the wall and
Mt	10:29	Are not two S sold for a penny?
	10:31	therefore; you are of more value than many S
Lk	12:6	Are not five S sold for two pennies?
	12:7	not; you are of more value than many S

SPARTA

1Mac	14:16	as far away as S, that Jonathan had died,

SPARTANS (9)

1Mac	12:2	same effect to the S and to other places.
	12:5	Jonathan wrote to the S:

S

12:6 to their brethren the S, greeting.
12:20 "Arius, king of the S, to Onias the high
12:21 in writing concerning the S and the Jews that
14:20 the letter which the S sent: "The rulers and
14:20 the city of the S to Simon the high
14:23 the people of the S may have a record
15:23 Sampsames, and to the S, and to Delos, and

SPAT (5)

Mt 26:67 Then they S in his face, and struck him;
27:30 And they S upon him, and took the reed
Mk 7:32 his ears, and he S and touched his tongue;
15:19 with a reed, and S upon him, and they
Jn 9:6 he said this, he S on the ground and

SPATTERED

2Kgs 9:33 some of her blood S on the wall and

SPEAK (391)

Gen 18:27 taken upon myself to S to the Lord, I
18:30 not the Lord be angry, and I will S
18:31 taken upon myself to S to the Lord.
18:32 angry, and I will S again but this once.
24:33 He said, S on."
24:50 the LORD; we cannot S to you bad or
27:6 "I heard your father S to your brother Esau,
31:29 'Take heed that you S to Jacob neither good
34:6 out to Jacob to S with him.
37:4 him, and could not S peaceably to him.
44:7 "Why does my lord S such words as these?
44:16 What shall we S
44:18 servant, I pray you, S a word in my
50:4 favor in your eyes, S, I pray you, in
Ex 4:12 your mouth and teach you what you shall S
4:14 know that he can S well; and behold, he
4:15 And you shall S to him and put the
4:16 He shall S for you to the people; and
5:23 came to Pharaoh to S in thy name, he
7:2 You shall S all that I command you; and
11:2 S now in the hearing of the people, that
19:6 words which you shall S to the children of
19:9 may hear when I S with you, and may
20:19 said to Moses, "You S to us, and we
20:19 but let not God S to us, lest we
25:2 LORD said to Moses, S to the people of
25:22 the testimony, I will S with you of all
28:3 And you shall S to all who have ability,
29:42 meet with you, to S there to you.
33:9 and the LORD would S with Moses.
33:11 the LORD used to S to Moses face to
34:34 before the LORD to S with him, he took
34:35 he went in to S with him.
Lev 1:2 tent of meeting, saying, S to the people of
5:1 matter, yet does not S, he shall bear his
21:1 LORD said to Moses, S to the priests, the
Num 7:89 tent of meeting to S with the LORD, he
12:6 in a vision, I S with him in a
12:8 With him I S mouth to mouth, clearly, and
12:8 you not afraid to S against my servant Moses?"
15:38 LORD said to Moses, S to the people of
17:2 LORD said to Moses, S to the people of
22:35 word which I bid you, that shall you S
22:38 power at all to S anything?
22:38 God puts in my mouth, that must I S
23:5 said, "Return to Balak, and thus you shall S
23:12 not take heed to S what the LORD puts
23:16 said, "Return to Balak, and thus shall you S
24:13 will; what the LORD speaks, that will I S
Deut 3:26 'Let it suffice you; S no more to me
5:1 the ordinances which I S in your hearing this
5:24 this day seen God S with man and man
5:27 God will say; and S to us all that
5:27 LORD our God will S to you; and we
18:18 mouth, and he shall S to them all that
18:19 words which he shall S in my name, I
18:20 prophet who presumes to S a word in my
18:20 not commanded him to S, or who speaks in
20:2 shall come forward and S to the people,
20:5 Then the officers shall S to the people, saying,
20:8 And the officers shall S further to the people,
25:8 shall call him, and S to him: and if
31:1 So Moses continued to S these words to all
31:28 officers, that I may S these words in their
32:1 heavens, and I will S; and let the earth
Judg 6:39 against me, let me S but this once; pray,
19:3 went after her, to S kindly to her and
19:30 until this day; consider it, take counsel, and S
1Sam 3:9 you, you shall say, S, LORD, for thy servant
3:10 And Samuel said, S, for thy servant hears."
18:22 Saul commanded his servants, S to David in private
18:24 Saul told him, "Thus and so did David S
19:3 are, and I will S to my father about
25:17 ill-natured that one cannot S to him."
25:24 pray let your handmaid S in your ears, and
2Sam 3:27 of the gate to S with him privately, and
7:7 of Israel, did I S a word with any
13:13 therefore, I pray you, S to the king; for
14:3 to the king, and S thus to him." So
14:12 "Pray let your handmaid S a word to my
14:12 He said, S
14:15 handmaid thought, 'I will S to the king; it
14:18 the woman said, "Let my lord the king S
17:6 If not, you S
19:7 arise, go out and S kindly to your servants;
19:29 said to him, "Why S any more of your
19:43 not the first to S of bringing back our
20:16 here, that I may S to you.'"
1Kgs 2:18 "Very well; I will S for you to the
2:19 to King Solomon, to S to him on behalf
8:24 him; yea, thou didst S with thy mouth, and
12:7 and serve them, and S good words to them
12:10 him, "Thus shall you S to this people who
22:13 one of them, and S favorably."
22:14 the LORD says to me, that I will S
22:16 adjure you that you S to me nothing but
22:24 go from me to S to you?"
2Kgs 6:12 the words that you S in your bedchamber."
18:26 to the Rabshakeh, "Pray, S to your servants in
18:26 understand it; do not S to us in the
18:27 master sent me to S these words to your
19:10 saying, "Thus shall you S to Hezekiah king of
1Chr 17:6 all Israel, did I S a word with any
2Chr 6:15 him; yea, thou didst S with thy mouth, and
10:7 and please them, and S good words to them,
10:10 him, "Thus shall you S to the people who
18:12 one of them, and S favorably."
18:13 lives, what my God says, that I will S
18:15 adjure you that you S to me nothing but
18:23 go from me to S to you?"
32:17 of Israel and to S against him, saying, "Like
Neh 9:13 upon Mount Sinai, and S with them from heaven
13:24 and they could not S the language of Judah,
Tob 6:12 I will S to her father, and as soon
7:8 to Raphael, "Brother Azarias, S of those things
13:8 Let all men S, and give him thanks in
Jud 11:5 and let your maidservant S in your presence, and
16:14 thee, for thou didst S, and they were made.
Esth 1:22 his own house and S according to the language
4:8 Beseech the Lord and S to the king concerning
6:4 the king's palace to S to the king about
15:12 embraced her, and said, S to me."
Job 2:10 said to her, "You S as one of the
2:10 speak as one of the foolish women would S
7:11 my mouth; I will S in the anguish of
9:35 Then I would S without fear of him, for
10:1 my complaint; I will S in the bitterness of
11:5 oh, that God would S, and open his lips
13:3 But I would S to the Almighty, and I
13:7 Will you S falsely for God, and speak deceitfully
13:7 falsely for God, and S deceitfully for him?
13:13 silence, and I will S, and let come on
13:22 answer; or let me S, and do thou reply
16:4 I also could S as you do, if you
16:6 "If I S, my pain is not assuaged, and
18:2 Consider, and then we will S
21:3 me, and I will S, and after I have
27:4 my lips will not S falsehood, and my tongue
29:22 spoke they did not S again, and my word
32:4 Elihu had waited to S to Job because they
32:7 I said, 'Let days S, and many years teach
32:16 because they do not S, because they stand there,
32:20 I must S, that I may find relief; I
33:3 my lips know they S sincerely.
33:31 listen to me; be silent, and I will S
33:32 to say, answer me; S, for I desire to
37:20 Shall it be told him that I would S
41:3 Will he S to you soft words?
42:4 'Hear, and I will S; I will question you,
Ps 2:5 Then he will S to them in his wrath,
5:6 Thou destroyest those who S lies; the LORD abhors
12:2 with flattering lips and a double heart they S
17:10 with their mouths they S arrogantly.

28:3 workers of evil, who S peace with their neighbors,
31:18 lips be dumb, which S insolently against the
35:20 For they do not S peace, but against those
38:12 who seek my hurt S of ruin, and meditate
49:3 My mouth shall S wisdom; the meditation of my
50:7 people, and I will S, O Israel, I will
50:20 You sit and S against your brother; you slander
71:10 For my enemies S concerning me, those who watch
73:8 They scoff and S with malice; loftily they threaten
73:15 had said, "I will S thus," I would have
75:5 horn on high, or S with insolent neck."
77:4 closing; I am so troubled that I cannot S
85:8 God the LORD will S, for he will speak
85:8 speak, for he will S peace to his people,
89:19 Of old thou didst S in a vision to
109:20 LORD, of those who S evil against my life!
115:5 mouths, but do not S; eyes, but do not
119:46 I will also S of thy testimonies before kings,
120:7 peace; but when I S, they are for war!
135:16 have mouths, but they S not, they have eyes,
144:8 of aliens, whose mouths S lies, and whose right
144:11 of aliens, whose mouths S lies, and whose right
145:11 They shall S of the glory of thy kingdom,
145:21 My mouth will S the praise of the LORD,
Prov 8:6 Hear, for I will S noble things, and from
23:9 Do not S in the hearing of a fool,
23:16 rejoice when your lips S what is right.
Eccl 3:7 and a time to S;
Wis 5:3 They will S to one another in repentance, and
7:15 God grant that I S with judgment and have
8:12 me, and when I S they will give heed;
8:12 heed; and when I S at greater length they
10:21 the tongues of babes S clearly.
Sir 4:25 Never S against the truth, but be mindful of
12:16 An enemy will S sweetly with his lips, but
13:6 He will S to you kindly and say, "What
18:18 Before you S, learn, and before you fall ill,
20:5 another keeps silent because he knows when to S
20:7 usurps the right to S will be hated.
20:15 who eat my bread S unkindly."
21:25 lips of strangers will S of these things, but
31:31 him in his merrymaking; S no word of reproach
32:3 S, you who are older, for it is fitting
32:7 S, young man, if there is need of you,
32:8 S concisely, say much in few words; be as
34:9 with much experience will S with understanding.
43:27 Though we S much we cannot reach the end,
Is 3:7 that day he will S out, saying: "I will
8:10 will come to nought; S a word, but it
8:20 this word which they S there is no dawn.
14:10 All of them will S and say to you:
19:18 land of Egypt which S the language of Canaan
28:11 tongue the LORD will S to this people,
29:4 the earth you shall S, from low in the
30:10 us what is right; S to us smooth things,
32:4 of the stammerers will S readily and distinctly.
36:11 to the Rabshakeh, "Pray, S to your servants in
36:11 understand it; do not S to us in the
36:12 master sent me to S these words to your
37:10 saying, "Thus shall you S to Hezekiah king of
40:2 S tenderly to Jerusalem, and cry to her that
40:27 say, O Jacob, and S, O Israel, "My way
41:1 approach, then let them S; let us together draw
45:19 I did not S in secret, in a land
45:19 chaos.' I the LORD S the truth, I declare
52:6 it is I who S; here am I."
59:4 on empty pleas, they S lies, they conceive mischief
61:6 the LORD, men shall S of you as the
Jer 1:6 not know how to S, for I am only
1:7 go, and whatever I command you you shall S
4:12 it is I who S in judgment upon them."
5:5 the great, and will S to them; for they
6:10 To whom shall I S and give warning, that
7:22 Egypt, I did not S to your fathers or
7:27 "So you shall S all these words to them,
9:5 taught their tongue to S lies; they commit iniquity
9:22 S, "Thus says the LORD: 'The dead bodies of
10:5 field, and they cannot S; they have to be
11:2 of this covenant, and S to the men of
12:6 them not, though they S fair words to you."
13:12 "You shall S to them this word: 'Thus says
14:14 I command them or S to them.
18:20 stood before thee to S good for them, to
20:8 For whenever I S, I cry out, I shout,
20:9 not mention him, or S any more in his
22:1 king of Judah, and S there this word,
23:16 with vain hopes; they S visions of their own
23:21 ran; I did not S to them, yet they
23:28 who has my word S my word faithfully.
26:2 the LORD's house, and S to all the cities
26:2 I command you to S to them; do not
26:8 had commanded him to S to all the people,
26:15 me to you to S all these words in
28:7 this word which I S in your hearing and
31:20 as often as I S against him, I do
32:4 of Babylon, and shall S with him face to
32:24 What thou didst S has come to pass, and
34:2 of Israel: Go and S to Zedekiah king of
34:3 eye to eye and S with him face to
35:2 of the Rechabites, and S with them, and bring
Bar 2:24 words, which thou didst S by thy servants the
2:28 compassion, as thou didst S by thy servant Moses
6:8 and silver; but they are false and cannot S
6:41 dumb man, who cannot S, they bring him and
6:41 that the man may S, as though Bel were
Ezek 2:1 feet, and I will S with you."
2:7 And you shall S my words to them, whether
3:1 this scroll, and go, S to the house of
3:4 house of Israel, and S with my words to
3:10 words that I shall S to you receive in
3:18 him no warning, nor S to warn the wicked
3:22 and there I will S with you."
3:27 But when I S with you, I will open
12:25 I the LORD will S the word which I
12:25 word which I will S, and it will be
12:25 rebellious house, I will S the word and perform
12:28 the word which I S will be performed, says
14:4 Therefore S to them, and say to them, Thus
14:9 prophet be deceived and S a word, I, the
17:2 propound a riddle, and S an allegory to the
20:3 me: "Son of man, S to the elders of
20:27 "Therefore, son of man, S to the house of
24:27 fugitive, and you shall S and be no longer
29:3 and against all Egypt; S, and say, Thus says
32:21 The mighty chiefs shall S of them, with their
33:2 me: "Son of man, S to your people and
33:8 and you do not S to warn the wicked
36:5 the Lord GOD: I S in my hot jealousy
36:6 Lord GOD: Behold, I S in my jealous wrath,
39:17 says the Lord GOD: S to the birds of
Dan 2:9 You have agreed to S lying and corrupt words
7:25 He shall S words against the Most High, and
10:11 the words that I S to you, and stand
10:19 said, "Let my lord S, for you have strengthened
11:27 on mischief; they shall S lies at the same
11:36 every god, and shall S astonishing things against the
Hos 2:14 into the wilderness, and S tenderly to her.
7:14 redeem them, but they S lies against me.
Mic 6:12 of violence; your inhabitants S lies, and their tongue
Hag 2:2 by Haggai the prophet, S now to Zerubbabel the
2:21 day of the month, S to Zerubbabel, governor of
Zech 8:16 that you shall do: S the truth to one
13:3 not live, for you S lies in the name
1Mac 10:47 been the first to S peaceable words to them,
Mt 10:19 how you are to S or what you are
10:20 is not you who S, but the Spirit of
11:7 away, Jesus began to S to the crowds concerning
12:34 how can you S good, when you are evil?
12:46 stood outside, asking to S to him.
13:10 him, "Why do you S to them in parables?"
13:13 This is why I S to them in parables,
16:11 that I did not S about bread?
Mk 1:34 permit the demons to S, because they knew him.
2:7 "Why does this man S thus?
4:34 it; he did not S to them without a
7:36 even makes the deaf hear and the dumb S
9:39 able soon after to S evil of me.
12:1 And he began to S to them in parables.
13:11 is not you who S, but the Holy Spirit.
14:71 do not know this man of whom you S
16:17 out demons; they will S in new tongues;
Lk 1:19 I was sent to S to you, and to
1:20 silent and unable to S until the day that
1:22 out, he could not S to them, and they
4:41 not allow them to S, because they knew that
6:26 you, when all men S well of you, for
7:15 the dead man sat up, and began to S
7:24 gone, he began to S to the crowds concerning
11:53 to provoke him to S of many things,
20:21 we know that you S and teach rightly, and
Jn 1:40 two who heard John S, and followed him, was
3:11 say to you, we S of what we know,

S

	4:26	to her, "I who S to you am he."
	8:28	my own authority but S thus as the Father
	8:38	I S of what I have seen with my
	9:21	of age, he will S for himself."
	12:49	me commandment what to say and what to S
	14:10	you I do not S on my own authority;
	16:13	for he will not S on his own authority,
	16:13	he hears he will S, and he will declare
	16:25	I shall no longer S to you in figures
	17:13	and these things I S in the world, that
	19:10	him, "You will not S to me?
Acts	2:4	Spirit and began to S in other tongues, as
	4:17	us warn them to S no more to any
	4:18	charged them not to S or teach at all
	4:20	for we cannot but S of what we have
	4:29	to thy servants to S thy word with all
	5:20	in the temple and S to the people all
	5:40	charged them not to S in the name of
	6:11	have heard him S blasphemous words against Moses
	6:13	man never ceases to S words against this holy
	11:15	As I began to S, the Holy Spirit fell
	16:6	the Holy Spirit to S the word in Asia.
	18:9	not be afraid, but S and do not be
	18:26	He began to S boldly in the synagogue; but
	21:39	beg you, let me S to the people."
	23:5	written, 'You shall not S evil of a ruler
	24:9	motioned to him to S, Paul replied: "Realizing that
	24:23	Paul and heard him S upon faith in Christ
	26:1	"You have permission to S for yourself." Then Paul
	26:26	and to him I S freely; for I am
	28:20	to see you and S with you, since it
Rom	3:5	(I S in a human way.)
	15:18	will not venture to S of anything except what
1Cor	9:10	Does he not S entirely for our sake?
	10:15	I S as to sensible men; judge for yourselves
	12:30	Do all S with tongues?
	13:1	If I S in the tongues of men and
	14:5	want you all to S in tongues, but even
	14:18	thank God that I S in tongues more than
	14:19	church I would rather S five words with my
	14:21	of foreigners will I S to this people, and
	14:23	church assembles and all S in tongues, and outsiders
	14:27	If any S in a tongue, let there be
	14:28	silence in church and S to himself and to
	14:29	two or three prophets S, and let the others
	14:34	are not permitted to S, but should be subordinate,
	14:35	for a woman to S in church.
2Cor	2:17	sight of God we S in Christ.
	4:13	believe, and so we S,
	6:13	In return—I S as to children—widen your
Eph	4:25	falsehood, let every one S the truth with his
	5:12	a shame even to S of the things that
	6:20	may declare it boldly, as I ought to S
Phil	1:14	much more bold to S the word of God
Col	4:4	may make it clear, as I ought to S
1Thes	2:4	the gospel, so we S, not to please men,
Tit	3:2	any honest work, to S evil of no one,
Heb	4:8	rest, God would not S later of another day.
	6:9	Though we S thus, yet in your case, beloved,
	9:5	things we cannot now S in detail.
	11:14	For people who S thus make it clear that
Jas	1:18	to hear, slow to S, slow to anger,
	2:12	So S and so act as those who are
	4:11	Do not S evil against one another, brethren.
1Pet	2:12	that in case they S against you as wrongdoers,
Rev	13:15	the beast should even S, and to cause those

SPEAKER (4)

Sir	11:8	heard, nor interrupt a S in the midst of
Acts	14:12	he was the chief S, they called Hermes.
1Cor	14:11	a foreigner to the S and the speaker a
	14:11	the speaker and the S a foreigner to me.

SPEAKERS

1Cor	12:28	healers, helpers, administrators, S in various kinds of

SPEAKEST

Judg	6:17	it is thou who S with me.

SPEAKING (119)

Gen	18:33	when he had finished S to Abraham; and Abraham
	24:15	Before he had done S, behold, Rebekah, who was
	24:45	"Before I had done S in my heart, behold,
	29:9	While he was still S with them, Rachel came
Ex	31:18	made an end of S with him upon Mount
	34:33	when Moses had finished S with them, he put
Num	7:89	he heard the voice S to him from above
	16:31	And as he finished S all these words, the
Deut	4:33	voice of a god S out of the midst
	5:26	of the living God S out of the midst
	11:2	(since I am not S to your children who
	20:9	made an end of S to the people, then
	32:45	when Moses had finished S all these words to
Judg	15:17	When he had finished S, he threw away the
1Sam	1:13	Hannah was S in her heart; only her lips
	1:16	along I have been S out of my great
	18:1	When he had finished S to Saul, the soul
	24:16	When David had finished S these words to Saul,
2Sam	13:36	as he had finished S, behold, the king's sons
1Kgs	1:14	while you are still S with the king, I
	1:22	While she was still S with the king, Nathan
	1:42	While he was still S, behold, Jonathan the son
2Kgs	6:33	while he was still S with them, the king
2Chr	25:16	But as he was S the king said to
Jud	14:8	the moment of her S to them.
Esth	15:15	But as she was S, she fell fainting.
Job	1:16	While he was yet S, there came another, and
	1:17	While he was yet S, there came another, and
	1:18	While he was yet S, there came another, and
	4:2	Yet who can keep from S
Ps	34:13	and your lips from S deceit.
	52:3	and lying more than S the truth.
	58:3	err from their birth, S lies.
	109:2	are opened against me, S against me with lying
Sir	4:23	Do not refrain from S at the crucial time,
	5:13	and dishonor come from S, and a man's tongue
	29:5	lower his voice in S of his neighbor's money;
	32:9	and when another is S, do not babble.
Is	58:9	of the finger, and S wickedness,
	59:13	our God, S oppression and revolt, conceiving
	65:24	while they are yet S I will hear.
Jer	26:7	the people heard Jeremiah S these words in the
	26:8	when Jeremiah had finished S all that the LORD
	38:4	all the people, by S such words to them.
	38:27	So they left off S with him, for the
	40:16	thing, for you are S falsely of Ishmael."
	43:1	When Jeremiah finished S to all the people all
Ezek	1:28	face, and I heard the voice of one S
	2:2	and I heard him S to me.
	43:6	me, I heard one S to me out of
Dan	7:8	man, and a mouth S great things.
	7:11	of the great words which the horn was S
	8:13	heard a holy one S; and another holy one
	8:18	As he was S to me, I fell into
	9:20	While I was S and praying, confessing my sin
	9:21	God; while I was S in prayer, the man
	10:11	While he was S this word to me, I
1Mac	2:23	When he had finished S these words, a Jew
	3:23	When he finished S, he rushed suddenly against
	13:17	knew that they were S deceitfully to him, but
2Mac	7:30	While she was still S, the young man said,
	9:5	soon as he ceased S he was seized with
Mt	9:18	While he was thus S to them, behold, a
	10:20	Spirit of your Father S through you.
	12:46	While he was still S to the people, behold,
	15:31	they saw the dumb S, the maimed whole, the
	17:5	He was still S, when lo, a bright cloud
	17:13	understood that he was S to them of John
	21:45	perceived that he was S about them.
	26:47	While he was still S, Judas came, one of
Mk	5:35	While he was still S, there came from the
	14:43	while he was still S, Judas came, one of
Lk	5:4	when he had ceased S, he said to Simon,
	8:49	While he was still S, a man from the
	11:37	While he was S, a Pharisee asked him to
	22:45	While he was still S, there came a crowd,
	22:58	while he was still S, the cock crowed.
Jn	7:17	or whether I am S on my own authority.
	7:26	And here he is, S openly, and they say
	13:18	I am not S of you all; I know
	16:29	"Ah, now you are S plainly, not in any
Acts	1:3	during forty days, and S of the kingdom of
	2:6	each one heard them S in his own language.
	2:7	all these who are S Galileans?
	4:1	And as they were S to the people, the
	10:46	For they heard them S in tongues and extolling
	11:19	and Cyprus and Antioch, S the word to none
	14:3	for a long time, S boldly for the Lord,
	14:9	He listened to Paul S; and Paul, looking intently
	15:13	After they finished S, James replied, "Brethren,
	19:9	were stubborn and disbelieved, S evil of the Way
	20:30	selves will arise men S perverse things, to draw

S

22:9 the one who was S to me.
26:25 Festus, but I am S the sober truth.
Rom 6:19 I am S in human terms, because of your
7:1 brethren—for I am S to those who know
9:1 I am S the truth in Christ, I am
11:13 Now I am S to you Gentiles.
1Cor 12:3 understand that no one S by the Spirit of
14:6 I come to you S in tongues, how shall
14:9 For you will be S into the air.
14:39 and do not forbid S in tongues;
15:32 I gain if, humanly S, I fought with beasts
2Cor 11:6 I am unskilled in S, I am not in
11:21 boast of—I am S as a fool—I
12:6 for I shall be S the truth.
12:19 that we have been S in Christ, and all
13:3 proof that Christ is S in me.
Eph 4:15 Rather, S the truth in love, we are to
1Thes 2:16 by hindering us from S to the Gentiles that
Heb 2:5 the world to come, of which we are S
8:13 In S of a new covenant he treats the
11:4 died, but through his faith he is still S
11:19 the dead; hence, figuratively S, he did receive him
12:25 that you do not refuse him who is S
1Pet 3:10 and his lips from S guile;
2Pet 3:16 the wisdom given him, S of this as he
Rev 1:12 the voice that was S to me, and on
4:1 which I had heard S to me like a

SPEAKS (60)

Gen 45:12 is my mouth that S to you.
Ex 33:11 face, as a man S to his friend.
Num 22:8 you, as the LORD S to me"; so the
24:13 will; what the LORD S, that will I speak?
Deut 18:20 to speak, or who S in the name of
18:22 when a prophet S in the name of
2Sam 23:2 Spirit of the LORD S by me, his word
Job 33:2 open my mouth; the tongue in my mouth S
33:14 For God S in one way, and in two,
34:35 me will say: 'Job S without knowledge, his words
Ps 15:2 what is right, and S truth from his heart;
36:1 Transgression S to the wicked deep in his heart;
37:30 wisdom, and his tongue S justice.
50:1 One, God the LORD, S and summons the earth
127:5 to shame when he S with his enemies in
Prov 1:21 the city gates she S:
12:17 He who S the truth gives honest evidence, but
16:13 he loves him who S what is right.
20:19 associate with one who S foolishly.
26:25 his heart; when he S graciously, believe him not,
Song 2:10 My beloved S and says to me: "Arise, my
Sir 13:21 helpers are many; he S unseemly words, and they
13:21 even reproach him; he S sensibly, and receives no
13:22 When the rich man S all are silent, and
13:22 When the poor man S they say, "Who is
20:26 He who S wisely will advance himself, and a
25:9 sense, and he who S to attentive listeners.
Is 9:17 evildoer, and every mouth S folly.
32:6 For the fool S folly, and his mind plots
33:15 who walks righteously and S uprightly, who despises
Jer 9:5 neighbor, and no one S the truth; they have
9:8 a deadly arrow; it S deceitfully; with his mouth
9:8 with his mouth each S peaceably to his neighbor,
10:1 word which the LORD S to you, O house
Ezek 10:5 like the voice of God Almighty when he S
Dan 3:97 nation, or language that S anything against the God
Amos 5:10 they abhor him who S the truth.
Mt 12:32 be forgiven; but whoever S against the Holy Spirit
12:34 of the abundance of the heart the mouth S
15:4 mother,' and, 'He who S evil of father or
Mk 7:10 mother'; and, 'He who S evil of father or
Lk 5:21 "Who is this that S blasphemies?
6:45 of the abundance of the heart his mouth S
12:10 And every one who S a word against the
Jn 3:31 of the earth he S; he who comes from
7:18 He who S on his own authority seeks his
8:44 When he lies, he S according to his own
9:37 it is he who S to you."
13:24 "Tell us who it is of whom he S
Rom 3:19 the law says it S to those who are
1Cor 14:2 For one who S in a tongue speaks not
14:2 speaks in a tongue S not to men but
14:3 hand, he who prophesies S to men for their
14:4 He who S in a tongue edifies himself, but
14:5 greater than he who S in tongues, unless some
14:13 Therefore, he who S in a tongue should pray
Heb 12:24 the sprinkled blood that S more graciously than the

Jas 4:11 He that S evil against a brother or judges
4:11 or judges his brother, S evil against the law
1Pet 4:11 God's varied grace: whoever S, as one who utters

SPEAR (56)

Num 25:7 congregation, and took a S in his hand
Judg 5:8 Was shield or S to be seen among forty
1Sam 13:22 was neither sword nor S found in the hand
17:7 the shaft of his S was like a weaver's
17:7 weaver's beam, and his S's head weighed six hundred
17:45 sword and with a S and with a javelin;
17:47 not with sword and S; for the battle is
18:10 Saul had his S in his hand;
18:11 and Saul cast the S, for he thought, "I
19:9 his house with his S in his hand; and
19:10 the wall with the S; but he eluded Saul,
19:10 that he struck the S into the wall.
20:33 But Saul cast his S at him to smite
21:8 you not here a S or a sword at
22:6 the height, with his S in his hand, and
26:7 the encampment, with his S stuck in the ground
26:8 one stroke of the S, and I will not
26:11 but take now the S that is at his
26:12 So David took the S and the jar of
26:16 see where the king's S is, and the jar
26:22 answer, "Here is the S, O king!
2Sam 1:6 Saul leaning upon his S; and lo, the chariots
2:23 the butt of his S, so that the spear
2:23 spear, so that the S came out at his
21:16 the giants, whose S weighed three hundred shekels
21:19 the shaft of whose S was like a weaver's
23:7 the shaft of a S, and they are utterly
23:8 three; he wielded his S against eight hundred whom
23:18 And he wielded his S against three hundred men
23:21 The Egyptian had a S in his hand; but
23:21 staff, and snatched the S out of the Egyptian's
23:21 Egyptian's hand, and slew him with his own S
1Chr 11:11 three; he wielded his S against three hundred whom
11:20 And he wielded his S against three hundred men
11:23 in his hand a S like a weaver's beam;
11:23 staff, and snatched the S out of the Egyptian's
11:23 Egyptian's hand, and slew him with his own S
12:8 expert with shield and S, whose faces were like
12:24 Judah bearing shield and S were six thousand eight
12:34 thirty-seven thousand men armed with shield and S
20:5 the shaft of whose S was like a weaver's
2Chr 25:5 war, able to handle S and shield.
Jud 6:6 my army and the S of my servants shall
9:7 trust in shield and S, in bow and sling,
11:2 never have lifted my S against them; but they
Esth 16:24 destroyed in wrath with S and fire.
Job 39:23 the quiver, the flashing S and the javelin.
41:26 not avail; nor the S, the dart, or the
Ps 35:3 Draw the S and javelin against my pursuers!
46:9 bow, and shatters the S, he burns the chariots
Sir 29:13 more than a heavy S, it will fight on
Jer 6:23 hold on bow and S, they are cruel and
50:42 hold of bow and S; they are cruel, and
Nah 3:3 flashing sword and glittering S, hosts of slain, heaps
Hab 3:11 they sped, at the flash of thy glittering S
Jn 19:34 his side with a S, and at once there

SPEARMEN

Acts 23:23 horsemen and two hundred S to go as far

SPEARS (20)

1Sam 13:19 make themselves swords or S;
2Kgs 11:10 to the captains the S and shields that had
2Chr 11:12 he put shields and S in all the cities,
14:8 armed with bucklers and S, and two hundred and
23:9 to the captains the S and the large and
26:14 all the army shields, S, helmets, coats of mail,
Neh 4:13 with their swords, their S, and their bows.
4:16 and half held the S, shields, bows, and coats
4:21 of them held the S from the break of
Jud 1:15 him down with hunting S; and he utterly destroyed
7:10 not rely on their S but on the height
Job 41:7 skin with harpoons, or his head with fishing S
Ps 57:4 men; their teeth are S and arrows, their tongues
Is 2:4 into plowshares, and their S into pruning hooks;
Jer 46:4 your helmets, polish your S, put on your coats
Ezek 39:9 and arrows, handpikes and S, and they will make
Joel 3:10 your pruning hooks into S; let the weak say,
Mic 4:3 plowshares, and their S into pruning hooks; nation
2Mac 5:3 of shields, massing of S, hurling of missiles, the
15:11 confidence in shields and S as with the inspiration

SPECIAL (8)
Lev 27:2 a man makes a S vow of persons to
Num 6:2 a woman makes a S vow, the vow of
Wis 3:14 against the Lord; for S favor will be shown
Ezek 27:15 coastlands were your own S markets, they brought
48:12 to them as a S portion from the holy
Mal 3:17 LORD of hosts, my S possession on the day
1Mac 6:37 upon each beast by S harness, and upon each
1Cor 7:7 each has his own S gift from God, one

SPECIALLY
2Mac 2:8 the place should be S consecrated."

SPECIES
Sir 13:15 living beings associate by S, and a man clings

SPECIFICATIONS
1Kgs 6:38 all its parts, and according to all its S

SPECK (7)
Wis 11:22 thee is like a S that tips the scales,
Mt 7:3 do you see the S that is in your
7:4 'Let me take the S out of your eye,'
7:5 clearly to take the S out of your brother's
Lk 6:41 do you see the S that is in your
6:42 me take out the S that is in your
6:42 to take out the S that is in your

SPECKLED (6)
Gen 30:32 removing from it every S and spotted sheep and
30:32 and the spotted and S among the goats; and
30:33 one that is not S and spotted among the
30:35 the she-goats that were S and spotted, every one
30:39 flocks brought forth striped, S, and spotted.
Jer 12:9 to me like a S bird of prey?

SPECTACLE (2)
Sir 43:1 of heaven in a S of glory.
1Cor 4:9 we have become a S to the world, to

SPECTERS (2)
Wis 17:3 were scattered, terribly alarmed, and appalled by S
17:15 were driven by monstrous S, and now were

SPECULATIONS
1Tim 1:4 genealogies which promote S rather than the divine

SPED (2)
Hab 3:11 thine arrows as they S, at the flash of
Rom 15:24 Spain, and to be S on my journey there

SPEECH (64)
Gen 11:7 that they may not understand one another's S
Ex 4:10 I am slow of S and of tongue."
Num 12:8 and not in dark S; and he beholds the
Deut 32:2 as the rain, my S distil as the dew,
1Sam 16:18 of war, prudent in S, and a man of
Jud 11:21 either for beauty of face or wisdom of S
11:23 appearance, but wise in S; and if you do
Esth 14:13 Put eloquent S in my mouth before the lion,
Job 6:26 reprove words, when the S of a despairing man
12:20 He deprives of S those who are trusted, and
33:1 "But now, hear my S, O Job, and listen
Ps 19:2 to day pours forth S, and night to night
19:3 There is no S, nor are there words; their
55:21 His S was smoother than butter, yet war was
Prov 2:12 from men of perverted S,
4:25 away from you crooked S, and put devious talk
5:3 drip honey, and her S is smoother than oil;
6:12 goes about with crooked S,
7:21 With much seductive S she persuades him; with her
8:13 of evil and perverted S I hate.
16:21 discernment, and pleasant S increases
16:23 the wise makes his S judicious, and adds
16:27 plots evil, and his S is like a scorching
17:7 Fine S is not becoming to a fool; still
17:7 still less is false S to a prince.
19:1 who is perverse in S, and is a fool.
22:11 of heart, and whose S is gracious, will have
Song 5:16 His S is most sweet, and he is altogether
Wis 8:8 she understands turns of S and the solutions of
Sir 4:24 wisdom is known through S, and education through
4:29 be reckless in your S, or sluggish and remiss
5:10 understanding, and let your S be consistent.
9:18 who is reckless in S will be hated.
21:7 who is mighty in S is known from afar;
21:16 be found in the S of the intelligent.
23:7 children, to instruction concerning S; the one who
23:13 mouth to lewd vulgarity, for it involves sinful S
25:24 and no boldness of S in an evil wife.
27:23 he will twist his S and with your own
32:12 in mind, but do not sin through proud S
36:23 and humility mark her S, her husband is not
Is 3:8 has fallen; because their S and their deeds are
28:23 and hear my voice; hearken, and hear my S
29:4 a ghost, and your S shall whisper out of
32:9 voice; you complacent daughters, give ear to my S
33:19 people of an obscure S which you cannot
Ezek 3:5 a people of foreign S and a hard language,
3:6 many peoples of foreign S and a hard language,
Zeph 3:9 I will change the S of the peoples to
3:9 peoples to a pure S, that all of them
1Mac 4:19 Judas was finishing this S, a detachment appeared,
6:60 The S pleased the king and the commanders, and
Mk 7:31 an impediment in his S; and they besought him
Acts 20:7 and he prolonged his S until midnight.
1Cor 1:5 in him with all S and all knowledge—
2:4 and trembling; and my S and my message were
14:9 in a tongue utter S that is not intelligible,
2Cor 6:7 Spirit, genuine love, truthful S, and the power of
10:10 is weak, and his S of no account."
Col 2:4 that no one may delude you with beguiling S
4:6 Let your S always be gracious, seasoned with salt,
1Tim 4:12 believers an example in S and conduct, in love,
Tit 2:8 integrity, gravity, and sound S that cannot be
1Jn 3:18 love in word or S but in deed and

SPEECHES
Job 32:14 and I will not answer him with your S

SPEECHLESS (4)
Wis 4:19 he will dash them S to the ground, and
2Mac 3:29 While he lay prostrate, S because of the divine
Mt 22:12 here without a wedding garment?' And he was S
Acts 9:7 traveling with him stood S, hearing the voice but

SPEED (7)
Is 5:19 make haste, let him S his work that we
30:16 We will S upon horses," therefore you shall speed
30:16 therefore you shall S away; and, "We will ride
1Cor 16:6 so that you may S me on my journey,
16:11 S him on his way in peace, that he
2Thes 3:1 of the Lord may S on and triumph, as
Tit 3:13 Do your best to S Zenas the lawyer and

SPEEDILY (14)
Esth 16:18 over all things, has S inflicted on him the
Ps 31:2 Incline thy ear to me, rescue me S
79:8 let thy compassion come S to meet us, for
102:2 to me; answer me S in the day when
140:11 land; let evil hunt down the violent man S
Eccl 8:11 deed is not executed S, the heart of the
Sir 20:17 so the downfall of the wicked will occur S
21:5 the ears of God, and his judgment comes S
Is 5:26 earth; and lo, swiftly, S it comes!
51:5 My deliverance draws near S, my salvation has gone
51:14 is bowed down shall S be released; he shall
58:8 healing shall spring up S; your righteousness shall go
Joel 3:4 your deed upon your own head swiftly and S
Lk 18:8 I tell you, he will vindicate them S

SPEEDS (2)
Sir 32:10 Lightning S before the thunder, and approval
43:13 the driving snow and S the lightnings of his

SPEEDY
Wis 14:14 world, and therefore their S end has been planned.

SPELT (3)
Ex 9:32 the wheat and the S were not ruined, for
Is 28:25 its proper place, and S as the border?
Ezek 4:9 and lentils, millet and S, and put them into

SPEND (36)
Gen 19:2 your servant's house and S the night, and wash
19:2 said, "No; we will S the night in the
Deut 14:26 your God chooses, and S the money for whatever
32:23 upon them; I will S my arrows upon them;
Judg 19:6 man, "Be pleased to S the night, and let
19:10 the man would not S the night; he rose
19:11 of the Jebusites, and S the night in it."
19:13 of these places, and S the night at Gibe-ah

S

	19:15	to go in and S the night at Gibe-ah.
	19:15	into his house to S the night.
	19:20	wants; only, do not S the night in the
	20:4	and my concubine, to S the night.
2Sam	17:8	war; he will not S the night with the
Tob	1:7	I would go and S the proceeds each year
	10:7	sworn that he should S there.
Job	21:13	They S their days in prosperity, and in peace
	39:9	Will he S the night at your crib?
Is	55:2	Why do you S your money for that which
	65:4	sit in tombs, and S the night in secret
Jer	20:18	toil and sorrow, and S my days in shame?
Bar	6:10	from their gods and S it upon themselves,
Ezek	5:13	"Thus shall my anger S itself, and I will
	5:13	my jealousy, when I S my fury upon them.
	6:12	Thus I will S my fury upon them.
	7:8	wrath upon you, and S my anger against you,
	13:15	Thus will I S my wrath upon the wall,
	20:8	wrath upon them and S my anger against them
	20:21	wrath upon them and S my anger against them
Lk	10:35	and whatever more you S, I will repay you
Acts	20:16	might not have to S time in Asia; for
1Cor	16:6	with you or even S the winter, so that
	16:7	passing; I hope to S some time with you,
2Cor	12:15	I will most gladly S and be spent for
Tit	3:12	I have decided to S the winter there.
Jas	4:3	you ask wrongly, to S it on your passions.
	4:13	such a town and S a year there and

SPENDING

Acts	18:23	After S some time there he departed and went

SPENT (32)

Gen	24:54	and drank, and they S the night there.
	47:15	the money was all S in the land of
	47:18	our money is all S; and the herds of
Lev	26:20	your strength shall be S in vain, for your
Josh	6:11	into the camp, and S the night in the
	8:9	of Ai; but Joshua S that night among the
	8:13	But Joshua S that night in the valley.
Judg	19:11	the day was far S, and the servant said
1Kgs	17:14	meal shall not be S, and the cruse of
	17:16	of meal was not S, neither did the cruse
Ezra	10:6	of Eliashib, where he S the night, neither eating
Ps	31:10	For my life is S with sorrow, and my
	38:8	I am utterly S and crushed; I groan because
	39:10	from me; I am S by the blows of
	71:9	age; forsake me not when my strength is S
Eccl	2:11	the toil I had S in doing it, and
	5:17	for the wind, and S all his days in
Is	49:4	in vain, I have S my strength for nothing
Lam	2:11	My eyes are S with weeping; my soul is
Dan	6:18	to his palace, and S the night fasting; no
	14:3	and every day they S on it twelve bushels
1Mac	11:6	greeted one another and S the night there.
	14:32	He S great sums of his own money; he
Mk	5:26	many physicians, and had S all that she had,
Lk	8:43	twelve years and had S all her living upon
	15:14	And when he had S everything, a great famine
	24:29	toward evening and the day is now far S
Acts	15:33	And after they had S some time, they were
	17:21	foreigners who lived there S their time in nothing
	20:3	There he S three months, and when a plot
	26:4	life from my youth, S from the beginning among
2Cor	12:15	gladly spend and be S for your souls.

SPEW

Rev	3:16	nor hot, I will S you out of my

SPEWED

Wis	19:10	of fish the river S out vast numbers of

SPICE (3)

Song	4:10	and the fragrance of your oils than any S
	5:1	my myrrh with my S, I eat my honeycomb
Rev	18:13	marble, cinnamon, S, incense, myrrh, frankincense,

SPICED

Song	8:2	I would give you S wine to drink, the

SPICES (35)

Ex	25:6	oil for the lamps, S for the anointing oil
	30:23	Moses, "Take the finest S: of liquid myrrh five
	30:34	to Moses, "Take sweet S, stacte, and onycha, and
	30:34	and galbanum, sweet S with pure frankincense (of
	35:8	oil for the light, S for the anointing oil
	35:28	for the breastpiece, and S and oil for the
1Kgs	10:2	retinue, with camels bearing S, and very much gold,
	10:10	very great quantity of S, and precious stones; never
	10:10	such an abundance of S as these which the
	10:25	and gold, garments, myrrh, S, horses, and mules, so
2Kgs	20:13	silver, the gold, the S, the precious oil, his
1Chr	9:29	the wine, the oil, the incense, and the S
	9:30	the mixing of the S,
2Chr	2:4	of incense of sweet S before him, and for
	9:1	retinue and camels bearing S and very much gold
	9:9	very great quantity of S, and precious stones: there
	9:9	stones: there were no S such as those which
	9:24	of gold, garments, myrrh, S, horses, and mules, so
	13:11	and incense of sweet S, set out the showbread
	16:14	with various kinds of S prepared by the perfumer's
	32:27	for precious stones, for S, for shields, and for
Esth	2:12	and six months with S and ointments for women—
Song	4:14	aloes, with all chief S —
	5:13	are like beds of S, yielding fragrance.
	6:2	to the beds of S, to pasture his flock
	8:14	or a young stag upon the mountains of S
Sir	24:15	forth the aroma of S, and like choice myrrh
Is	39:2	silver, the gold, the S, the precious oil, his
Jer	34:5	And as S were burned for your fathers, the
	34:5	so men shall burn S for you and lament
Ezek	27:22	of all kinds of S, and all precious stones,
Mk	16:1	James, and Salome, bought S, so that they might
Lk	23:55	they returned, and prepared S and ointments.
	24:1	the tomb, taking the S which they had prepared.
Jn	19:40	linen cloths with the S, as is the burial

SPIDER (3)

Job	8:14	his trust is a S's web.
	27:18	builds is like a S's web, like a booth
Is	59:5	eggs, they weave the S's web; he who eats

SPIED (8)

Num	13:21	they went up and S out the land from
	13:32	land which they had S out, saying, "The land,
	14:6	among those who had S out the land, rent
	14:34	days in which you S out the land, forty
Deut	1:24	Valley of Eshcol and S it out.
Josh	6:22	two men who had S out the land, "Go
	7:2	men went up and S out Ai.
2Kgs	9:17	in Jezreel, and he S the company of Jehu

SPIES (15)

Gen	42:9	to them, "You are S, you have come to
	42:11	we are honest men, your servants are not S
	42:14	is as I said to you, you are S
	42:16	by the life of Pharaoh, surely you are S
	42:30	took us to be S of the land.
	42:31	men, we are not S;
	42:34	that you are not S but honest men, and
Josh	2:1	secretly from Shittim as S, saying, "Go, view the
	6:23	men who had been S went in, and brought
Judg	1:24	formerly Luz.) And the S saw a man coming
1Sam	26:4	wilderness, David sent out S, and learned of a
Job	39:29	Thence he S out the prey; his eyes behold
1Mac	12:26	He sent S to their camp, and they returned
Lk	20:20	watched him, and sent S, who pretended to be
Heb	11:31	because she had given friendly welcome to the S

SPILLED (3)

Gen	38:9	his brother's wife he S the semen on the
Mt	9:17	and the wine is S, and the skins are
Lk	5:37	and it will be S, and the skins will

SPILT

2Sam	14:14	we are like water S on the ground, which

SPIN (2)

Mt	6:28	they neither toil nor S;
Lk	12:27	they neither toil nor S; yet I tell you,

SPINDLE (2)

2Sam	3:29	or who holds a S, or who is slain
Prov	31:19	to the distaff, and her hands hold the S

SPIRIT (601)

Gen	1:2	the deep; and the S of God was moving
	6:3	the LORD said, "My S shall not abide in
	41:8	in the morning his S was troubled; and he
	41:38	in whom is the S of God?"

45:27 to carry him, the S of their father Jacob
49:6 their council; O my S, be not joined to
Ex 6:9 because of their broken S and their cruel bondage.
31:3 filled him with the S of God, with ability
35:21 and every one whose S moved him, and brought
35:31 filled him with the S of God, with ability,
Num 5:14 act; and if the S of jealousy comes upon
5:14 herself; or if the S of jealousy comes upon
5:30 herself, or when the S of jealousy comes upon
11:17 take some of the S which is upon you
11:25 took some of the S that was upon him
11:25 elders; and when the S rested upon them, they
11:26 named Medad, and the S rested upon them; they
11:29 LORD would put his S upon them!"
14:24 he has a different S and has followed me
24:2 And the S of God came upon him,
27:18 in whom is the S, and lay your hand
Deut 2:30 your God hardened his S and made his heart
34:9 was full of the S of wisdom, for Moses
Josh 5:1 was no longer any S in them, because of
Judg 3:10 The S of the LORD came upon him, and
6:34 But the S of the LORD took possession of
9:23 God sent an evil S between Abimelech and the
11:29 Then the S of the LORD came upon Jephthah,
13:25 And the S of the LORD began to stir
14:6 against him; and the S of the LORD came
14:19 And the S of the LORD came mightily upon
15:14 meet him; and the S of the LORD came
15:19 when he drank, his S returned, and he revived.
1Sam 10:6 Then the S of the LORD will come mightily
10:10 met him; and the S of God came mightily
11:6 And the S of God came mightily upon Saul
16:13 his brothers; and the S of the LORD came
16:14 Now the S of the LORD departed from Saul,
16:14 Saul, and an evil S from the LORD tormented
16:15 "Behold now, an evil S from God is tormenting
16:16 and when the evil S from God is upon
16:23 And whenever the evil S from God was upon
16:23 well, and the evil S departed from him.
18:10 the morrow an evil S from God rushed upon
19:9 Then an evil S from the LORD came upon
19:20 head over them, the S of God came upon
19:23 in Ramah; and the S of God came upon
28:8 for me by a S, and bring up for
30:12 he had eaten, his S revived; for he had
2Sam 13:39 And the S of the king longed to go
23:2 psalmist of Israel: "The S of the LORD speaks
1Kgs 10:5 there was no more S in her.
18:12 gone from you, the S of the LORD will
21:5 him, "Why is your S so vexed that you
22:21 Then a S came forward and stood before the
22:22 will be a lying S in the mouth of
22:23 has put a lying S in the mouth of
22:24 said, "How did the S of the LORD go
2Kgs 2:9 let me inherit a double share of your S
2:15 them, they said, "The S of Elijah rests on
2:16 may be that the S of the LORD has
5:26 go with you in S when the man turned
19:7 I will put a S in him, so that
1Chr 5:26 Israel stirred up the S of Pul king of
5:26 king of Assyria, the S of Tilgath-pilneser king of
12:18 Then the S came upon Amasai, chief of the
2Chr 9:4 there was no more S in her.
15:1 The S of God came upon Azariah the son
18:20 Then a S came forward and stood before the
18:21 will be a lying S in the mouth of
18:22 has put a lying S in the mouth of
18:23 "Which way did the S of the LORD go
20:14 And the S of the LORD came upon Jahaziel
24:20 Then the S of God took possession of Zechariah
36:22 LORD stirred up the S of Cyrus king of
Ezra 1:1 LORD stirred up the S of Cyrus king of
1:5 Levites, every one whose S God had stirred to
Neh 9:20 Thou gavest thy good S to instruct them, and
9:30 warn them by thy S through thy prophets; yet
Tob 3:6 thy pleasure; command my S to be taken up,
6:7 a demon or evil S gives trouble to any
Jud 14:6 his face and his S failed him.
16:14 didst send forth thy S, and it formed them;
Esth 15:8 Then God changed the S of the king to
Job 4:15 A S glided past my face; the hair of
6:4 are in me; my S drinks their poison; the
7:11 the anguish of my S; I will complain in
10:12 steadfast love; and thy care has preserved my S
15:13 that you turn your S against God, and let
17:1 My S is broken, my days are extinct, the
20:3 of my understanding a S answers me.
26:4 uttered words, and whose S has come forth from
27:3 in me, and the S of God is in
32:8 But it is the S in a man, the
32:18 full of words, the S within me constrains me.
33:4 The S of God has made me, and the
34:14 should take back his S to himself, and gather
Ps 31:5 hand I commit my S; thou hast redeemed me,
32:2 iniquity, and in whose S there is no deceit.
34:18 to the brokenhearted, and saves the crushed in S
51:10 a new and right S within me.
51:11 take not thy holy S from me.
51:12 thy salvation, and uphold me with a willing S
51:17 God is a broken S; a broken and contrite
76:12 who cuts off the S of princes, who is
77:3 I meditate, and my S faints.
77:6 meditate and search my S:
78:8 was not steadfast, whose S was not faithful to
104:30 thou sendest forth thy S, they are created; and
106:33 for they made his S bitter, and he spoke
139:7 Whither shall I go from thy S
142:3 When my S is faint, thou knowest my way!
143:4 Therefore my S faints within me; my heart within
143:7 My S fails!
143:10 Let thy good S lead me on a level
Prov 11:13 who is trustworthy in S keeps a thing hidden.
15:4 of life, but perverseness in it breaks the S
15:13 sorrow of heart the S is broken.
16:2 his own eyes, but the LORD weighs the S
16:18 destruction, and a haughty S before a fall.
16:19 be of a lowly S with the poor than
16:32 he who rules his S than he who takes
17:22 medicine, but a downcast S dries up the bones.
17:27 who has a cool S is a man of
18:14 A man's S will endure sickness; but a broken
18:14 sickness; but a broken S who can bear?
20:27 The S of man is the lamp of the
25:13 him, he refreshes the S of his masters.
29:23 who is lowly in S will obtain honor.
Eccl 3:21 Who knows whether the S of man goes upward
3:21 goes upward and the S of the beast goes
7:8 and the patient in S is better than the
7:8 in spirit is better than the proud in S
8:8 power to retain the S, or authority over the
11:5 not know how the S comes to the bones
12:7 it was, and the S returns to God who
Wis 1:5 a holy and disciplined S will flee from deceit,
1:6 wisdom is a kindly S and will not free
1:7 Because the S of the Lord has filled the
2:3 to ashes, and the S will dissolve like empty
5:3 and in anguish of S they will groan, and
7:7 upon God, and the S of wisdom came to
7:22 her there is a S that is intelligent, holy,
9:17 and sent thy holy S from on high?
12:1 For thy immortal S is in all things.
15:11 active soul and breathed into him a living S
15:16 them, and one whose S is borrowed formed them;
16:14 bring back the departed S, nor set free the
Sir 34:13 The S of those who fear the Lord will
38:23 for him when his S is departed.
39:6 be filled with the S of understanding; he will
48:12 was filled with his S; in all his days
48:24 By the S of might he saw the last
Is 4:4 its midst by a S of judgment and by
4:4 judgment and by a S of burning.
11:2 And the S of the LORD shall rest upon
11:2 rest upon him, the S of wisdom and understanding,
11:2 wisdom and understanding, the S of counsel and
11:2 counsel and might, the S of knowledge and the
19:3 against kingdom; and the S of the Egyptians within
19:14 mingled within her a S of confusion; and they
26:9 in the night, my S within me earnestly seeks
28:6 his people; and a S of justice to him
29:10 out upon you a S of deep sleep, and
29:24 those who err in S will come to understanding,
30:1 but not of my S, that they may add
31:3 God; and their horses are flesh, and not S
32:15 of flocks; until the S is poured upon us
34:16 has commanded, and his S has gathered them.
37:7 I will put a S in him, so that
38:16 in all these is the life of my S
40:13 Who has directed the S of the LORD, or
42:1 I have put my S upon him, he will
42:5 people upon it and S to those who walk
44:3 I will pour my S upon your descendants, and
48:16 the Lord GOD has sent me and his S

54:6 forsaken and grieved in S, like a wife of
57:15 a contrite and humble S, to revive the spirit
57:15 spirit, to revive the S of the humble, and
57:16 from me proceeds the S, and I have made
59:21 says the LORD: my S which is upon you,
61:1 The S of the Lord GOD is upon me,
61:3 instead of a faint S; that they may be
63:10 and grieved his holy S; therefore he turned to
63:11 of them his holy S,
63:14 into the valley, the S of the LORD gave
65:14 of heart, and shall wail for anguish of S
66:2 humble and contrite in S, and trembles at my
Jer 51:1 will stir up the S of a destroyer against
51:11 has stirred up the S of the kings of
Bar 2:17 are in Hades, whose S has been taken from
3:1 anguish and the wearied S cry out to thee.
Ezek 1:12 straight forward; wherever the S would go, they
1:20 Wherever the S would go, they went, and the
1:20 with them; for the S of the living creatures
1:21 with them; for the S of the living creatures
2:2 spoke to me, the S entered into me and
3:12 Then the S lifted me up, and as the
3:14 The S lifted me up and took me away,
3:14 the heat of my S, the hand of the
3:24 But the S entered into me, and set me
8:3 my head; and the S lifted me up between
10:17 with them; for the S of the living creatures
11:1 The S lifted me up, and brought me to
11:5 And the S of the LORD fell upon me,
11:19 and put a new S within them; I will
11:24 And the S lifted me up and brought me
11:24 the vision by the S of God into Chaldea,
13:3 who follow their own S, and have seen nothing!
18:31 get yourselves a new heart and a new S
21:7 will be feeble, every S will faint and all
36:26 you, and a new S I will put within
36:27 I will put my S within you, and cause
37:1 me out by the S of the LORD, and
37:14 I will put my S within you, and you
39:29 I pour out my S upon the house of
43:5 gate facing east, the S lifted me up, and
Dan 2:1 had dreams; and his S was troubled, and his
2:3 a dream, and my S is troubled to know
3:39 heart and a humble S may we be accepted,
4:8 in whom is the S of the holy gods
4:9 I know that the S of the holy gods
4:18 are able, for the S of the holy gods
5:11 in whom is the S of the holy gods.
5:12 astrologers, because an excellent S, knowledge, and
5:14 of you that the S of the holy gods
5:20 lifted up and his S was hardened so that
6:3 satraps, because an excellent S was in him; and
7:15 for me, Daniel, my S within me was anxious
13:45 God aroused the holy S of a young lad
Hos 4:12 For a S of harlotry has led them astray,
5:4 For the S of harlotry is within them, and
9:7 the man of the S is mad, because of
Joel 2:28 will pour out my S on all flesh; your
2:29 in those days, I will pour out my S
Mic 2:7 Is the S of the LORD impatient?
3:8 with power, with the S of the LORD, and
Hag 1:14 LORD stirred up the S of Zerubbabel the son
1:14 of Judah, and the S of Joshua the son
1:14 high priest, and the S of all the remnant
2:5 My S abides among you; fear not.
Zech 4:6 power, but by my S, says the LORD of
6:8 country have set my S at rest in the
7:12 had sent by his S through the former prophets.
12:1 earth and formed the S of man within him:
12:10 inhabitants of Jerusalem a S of compassion and
13:2 from the land the prophets and the unclean S
Mal 2:15 sustained for us the S of life?
1Mac 9:7 he was crushed in S, for he had no
10:74 words of Apollonius, his S was aroused.
13:7 The S of the people was rekindled when they
2Mac 1:3 will with a strong heart and a willing S
5:17 Antiochus was elated in S, and did not perceive
7:12 at the young man's S, for he regarded his
7:21 Filled with a noble S, she fired her woman's
9:11 was that, broken in S, he began to lose
14:46 Lord of life and S to give them back
Mt 1:18 child of the Holy S;
1:20 is of the Holy S;
3:11 you with the Holy S and with fire.
3:16 and he saw the S of God descending like
4:1 led up by the S into the wilderness to
5:3 are the poor in S, for theirs is the
10:20 who speak, but the S of your Father speaking
12:18 I will put my S upon him, and he
12:28 it is by the S of God that I
12:31 the blasphemy against the S will not be forgiven.
12:32 speaks against the Holy S will not be forgiven,
12:43 "When the unclean S has gone out of a
22:43 David, inspired by the S, calls him Lord, saying,
26:41 enter into temptation; the S indeed is willing, but
27:50 with a loud voice and yielded up his S
28:19 and of the Holy S,
Mk 1:8 but he will baptize you with the Holy S
1:10 heavens opened and the S descending upon him like
1:12 The S immediately drove him out into the
1:23 man with an unclean S;
1:26 And the unclean S, convulsing him and crying with
2:8 Jesus, perceiving in his S that they thus questioned
3:29 blasphemes against the Holy S never has forgiveness,
3:30 for they had said, "He has an unclean S
5:2 man with an unclean S,
5:8 him, "Come out of the man, you unclean S
7:24 possessed by an unclean S, heard of him, and
8:12 sighed deeply in his S, and said, "Why does
9:17 he has a dumb S;
9:20 him; and when the S saw him, immediately it
9:25 he rebuked the unclean S, saying to it, "You
9:25 "You dumb and deaf S, I command you, come
12:36 inspired by the Holy S, declared, 'The Lord said
13:11 is not you who speak, but the Holy S
14:38 enter into temptation; the S indeed is willing, but
Lk 1:15 filled with the Holy S, even from his mother's
1:17 before him in the S and power of Elijah,
1:35 to her, "The Holy S will come upon you,
1:41 filled with the Holy S
1:47 the Lord, and my S rejoices in God my
1:67 filled with the Holy S, and prophesied, saying,
1:80 and became strong in S, and he was in
2:25 Israel, and the Holy S was upon him.
2:26 him by the Holy S that he should not
2:27 And inspired by the S he came into the
3:16 you with the Holy S and with fire.
3:22 opened, and the Holy S descended upon him in
4:1 full of the Holy S, returned from the Jordan,
4:1 was led by the S
4:14 the power of the S into Galilee, and a
4:18 it was written, "The S of the Lord is
4:33 man who had the S of an unclean demon;
8:29 had commanded the unclean S to come out of
8:55 And her S returned, and she got up at
9:39 child; and behold, a S seizes him, and he
9:42 Jesus rebuked the unclean S, and healed the boy,
10:21 rejoiced in the Holy S and said, "I thank
11:13 Father give the Holy S to those who ask
11:24 "When the unclean S has gone out of a
12:10 blasphemes against the Holy S will not be forgiven.
12:12 say; for the Holy S will teach you in
13:11 who had had a S of infirmity for eighteen
23:45 said, "Father, into thy hands I commit my S
24:37 and frightened, and supposed that they saw a S
24:39 and see; for a S has not flesh and
Jn 1:32 witness, "I saw the S descend as a dove
1:33 whom you see the S descend and remain, this
1:33 baptizes with the Holy S
3:5 of water and the S, he cannot enter the
3:6 is born of the S is spirit.
3:6 that which is born of the Spirit is S
3:8 with every one who is born of the S
3:34 that he gives the S;
4:23 worship the Father in S and truth, for such
4:24 God is S, and those who worship him must
4:24 him must worship in S and truth."
6:63 It is the S that gives life, the flesh
6:63 spoken to you are S and life.
7:39 he said about the S, which those who believed
7:39 for as yet the S had not been given,
11:33 was deeply moved in S and troubled;
13:21 he was troubled in S, and testified, "Truly, truly,
14:17 for ever, even the S of truth, whom the
14:26 the Counselor, the Holy S, whom the Father will
15:26 the Father, even the S of truth, who proceeds
16:13 When the S of truth comes, he will guide
19:30 he bowed his head and gave up his S
20:22 them, and said to them, "Receive the Holy S
Acts 1:2 commandment through the Holy S to the apostles
1:5 days you shall be baptized with the Holy S
1:8 power when the Holy S has come upon you;

S

1:16 fulfilled, which the Holy S spoke beforehand by the
2:4 filled with the Holy S and began to speak
2:4 other tongues, as the S gave them utterance.
2:17 will pour out my S upon all flesh, and
2:18 will pour out my S; and they shall prophesy.
2:33 promise of the Holy S, he has poured out
2:38 you shall receive the gift of the Holy S
4:8 filled with the Holy S, said to them, "Rulers
4:25 say by the Holy S, 'Why did the Gentiles
4:31 filled with the Holy S and spoke the word
5:3 lie to the Holy S and to keep back
5:9 together to tempt the S of the Lord?
5:32 so is the Holy S whom God has given
6:3 repute, full of the S and of wisdom, whom
6:5 and of the Holy S, and Philip, and Prochorus,
6:10 the wisdom and the S with which he spoke.
7:51 heart and ears, you always resist the Holy S
7:55 full of the Holy S, gazed into heaven and
7:59 Stephen, he prayed, "Lord Jesus, receive my S
8:15 might receive the Holy S;
8:17 hands on them and they received the Holy S
8:18 Simon saw that the S was given through the
8:19 I lay my hands may receive the Holy S
8:29 And the S said to Philip, "Go up and
8:38 of the water, the S of the Lord caught
9:17 your sight and be filled with the Holy S
9:31 comfort of the Holy S it was multiplied.
10:19 pondering the vision, the S said to him, "Behold,
10:38 Nazareth with the Holy S and with power; how
10:44 saying this, the Holy S fell on all who
10:45 gift of the Holy S had been poured out
10:47 have received the Holy S just as we have?"
11:12 And the S told me to go with them,
11:15 to speak, the Holy S fell on them just
11:16 baptized with the Holy S
11:24 full of the Holy S and of faith.
11:28 and foretold by the S that there would be
13:2 and fasting, the Holy S said, "Set apart for
13:4 out by the Holy S, they went down to
13:9 filled with the Holy S, looked intently at him
13:52 were filled with joy and with the Holy S
15:8 giving them the Holy S just as he did
15:28 good to the Holy S and to us to
16:6 forbidden by the Holy S to speak the word
16:7 into Bithynia, but the S of Jesus did not
16:16 girl who had a S of divination and brought
16:18 and said to the S, "I charge you in
17:16 them at Athens, his S was provoked within him
18:25 and being fervent in S, he spoke and taught
19:2 you receive the Holy S when you believed?" And
19:2 never even heard that there is a Holy S
19:6 upon them, the Holy S came on them; and
19:15 But the evil S answered them, "Jesus I know,
19:16 in whom the evil S was leaped on them,
19:21 Paul resolved in the S to pass through Macedonia
20:22 Jerusalem, bound in the S, not knowing what shall
20:23 except that the Holy S testifies to me in
20:28 in which the Holy S has made you overseers,
21:4 Through the S they told Paul not to go
21:11 "Thus says the Holy S, 'So shall the Jews
23:8 resurrection, nor angel, nor S; but the Pharisees
23:9 What if a S or an angel spoke to
28:25 one statement: "The Holy S was right in saying
Rom 1:4 power according to the S of holiness by his
1:9 I serve with my S in the gospel of
5:5 hearts through the Holy S which has been given
7:6 code but in the new life of the S
8:2 the law of the S of life in Christ
8:4 according to the flesh but according to the S
8:5 live according to the S set their minds on
8:5 set their minds on the things of the S
8:6 the mind on the S is life and peace.
8:9 you are in the S, if in fact the
8:9 if in fact the S of God dwells in
8:9 does not have the S of Christ does not
8:11 If the S of him who raised Jesus from
8:11 bodies also through his S which dwells in you.
8:13 but if by the S you put to death
8:14 are led by the S of God are sons
8:15 did not receive the S of slavery to fall
8:15 you have received the S of sonship.
8:16 it is the S himself bearing witness with our
8:16 bearing witness with our S that we are children
8:23 first fruits of the S, groan inwardly as we
8:26 Likewise the S helps us in our weakness; for
8:26 we ought, but the S himself intercedes for us
8:27 the mind of the S, because the Spirit intercedes
8:27 the Spirit, because the S intercedes for the saints
9:1 witness in the Holy S,
11:8 "God gave them a S of stupor, eyes that
12:11 be aglow with the S, serve the Lord.
14:17 joy in the Holy S;
15:13 power of the Holy S you may abound in
15:16 Gentiles may be acceptable, sanctified by the Holy S
15:19 power of the Holy S, so that from Jerusalem
15:30 the love of the S, to strive together with
1Cor 2:4 in demonstration of the S and of power,
2:10 God has revealed to us through the S
2:10 For the S searches everything, even the depths of
2:11 man's thoughts except the S of the man which
2:11 of God except the S of God.
2:12 have received not the S of the world, but
2:12 the world, but the S which is from God,
2:13 but taught by the S, interpreting spiritual truths to
2:13 spiritual truths to those who possess the S
2:14 the gifts of the S of God, for they
3:16 temple and that God's S dwells in you?
4:21 with love in a S of gentleness?
5:3 I am present in S, and as if present,
5:4 are assembled, and my S is present, with the
5:5 the flesh, that his S may be saved in
6:11 Christ and in the S of our God.
6:17 the Lord becomes one S with him.
6:19 temple of the Holy S within you, which you
7:34 holy in body and S; but the married woman
7:40 that I have the S of God.
12:3 one speaking by the S of God ever says
12:3 except by the Holy S
12:4 gifts, but the same S;
12:7 the manifestation of the S for the common good.
12:8 is given through the S the utterance of wisdom,
12:8 according to the same S,
12:9 faith by the same S, to another gifts of
12:9 healing by the one S,
12:11 one and the same S, who apportions to each
12:13 For by one S we were all baptized into
12:13 and all were made to drink of one S
14:2 understands him, but he utters mysteries in the S
14:12 for manifestations of the S, strive to excel in
14:14 in a tongue, my S prays but my mind
14:15 will pray with the S and I will pray
14:15 will sing with the S and I will sing
14:16 you bless with the S, how can any one
15:45 living being"; the last Adam became a life-giving S
16:18 for they refreshed my S as well as yours.
2Cor 1:22 and given us his S in our hearts as
3:3 ink but with the S of the living God,
3:6 code but in the S; for the written code
3:6 code kills, but the S gives life.
3:8 the dispensation of the S be attended with greater
3:17 the Lord is the S, and where the Spirit
3:17 Spirit, and where the S of the Lord is,
3:18 this comes from the Lord who is the S
4:13 we have the same S of faith as he
5:5 has given us the S as a guarantee.
6:6 forbearance, kindness, the Holy S, genuine love,
7:1 defilement of body and S, and make holiness perfect
11:4 you receive a different S from the one you
12:18 Did we not act in the same S
13:14 fellowship of the Holy S be with you all.
Gal 3:2 Did you receive the S by works of the
3:3 Having begun with the S, are you now ending
3:5 he who supplies the S to you and works
3:14 the promise of the S through faith.
4:6 God has sent the S of his Son into
4:29 born according to the S, so it is now.
5:5 For through the S, by faith, we wait for
5:16 say, walk by the S, and do not gratify
5:17 flesh are against the S, and the desires of
5:17 the desires of the S are against the flesh;
5:18 are led by the S you are not under
5:20 anger, selfishness, dissension, party S,
5:22 the fruit of the S is love, joy, peace,
5:25 we live by the S, let us also walk
5:25 the Spirit, let us also walk by the S
6:1 restore him in a S of gentleness.
6:8 who sows to the S will from the Spirit
6:8 Spirit will from the S reap eternal life.
6:18 Christ be with your S, brethren.
Eph 1:13 with the promised Holy S,
1:17 may give you a S of wisdom and of
2:2 of the air, the S that is now at

S

2:18 have access in one S to the Father.
2:22 for a dwelling place of God in the S
3:5 and prophets by the S;
3:16 with might through his S in the inner man,
4:3 the unity of the S in the bond of
4:4 one body and one S, just as you were
4:23 be renewed in the S of your minds,
4:30 not grieve the Holy S of God, in whom
5:18 be filled with the S,
6:17 the sword of the S, which is the word
6:18 all times in the S, with all prayer and
Phil 1:19 the help of the S of Jesus Christ this
1:27 stand firm in one S, with one mind striving
2:1 participation in the S, any affection and sympathy,
3:3 who worship God in S, and glory in Christ
4:23 of the Lord Jesus Christ be with your S
Col 1:8 made known to us your love in the S
2:5 am with you in S, rejoicing to see your
1Thes 1:5 and in the Holy S and with full conviction.
1:6 inspired by the Holy S;
4:8 who gives his Holy S to you.
5:19 Do not quench the S,
5:23 wholly; and may your S and soul and body
2Thes 2:2 or excited, either by S or by word, or
2:13 through sanctification by the S and belief in the
1Tim 3:16 flesh, vindicated in the S, seen by angels, preached
4:1 Now the S expressly says that in later times
2Tim 1:7 not give us a S of timidity but a
1:7 of timidity but a S of power and love
1:14 you by the Holy S who dwells within us.
4:22 The Lord be with your S
Tit 3:5 renewal in the Holy S,
Philem 1:25 of the Lord Jesus Christ be with your S
Heb 2:4 gifts of the Holy S distributed according to his
3:7 Therefore, as the Holy S says, "Today, when you
4:12 division of soul and S, of joints and marrow,
6:4 partakers of the Holy S,
9:8 By this the Holy S indicates that the way
9:14 the eternal S offered himself without blemish
10:15 And the Holy S also bears witness to us;
10:29 sanctified, and outraged the S of grace?
Jas 2:26 body apart from the S is dead, so faith
4:5 yearns jealously over the S which he has made
1Pet 1:2 and sanctified by the S for obedience to Jesus
1:11 was indicated by the S of Christ within them
1:12 you through the Holy S sent from heaven, things
3:4 a gentle and quiet S, which in God's sight
3:8 you, have unity of S, sympathy, love of the
3:18 made alive in the S;
4:6 might live in the S like God.
4:14 are blessed, because the S of glory and of
2Pet 1:21 moved by the Holy S spoke from God.
1Jn 3:24 in us, by the S which he has given
4:1 do not believe every S, but test the spirits
4:2 this you know the S of God: every spirit
4:2 Spirit of God: every S which confesses that Jesus
4:3 of God, and every S which does not confess
4:3 This is the S of antichrist, of which you
4:6 this we know the S of truth and the
4:6 of truth and the S of error.
4:13 because he has given us of his own S
5:7 And the S is the witness, because the Spirit
5:7 the witness, because the S is the truth.
5:8 are three witnesses, the S, the water, and the
Jude 1:19 set up divisions, worldly people, devoid of the S
1:20 pray in the Holy S;
Rev 1:10 I was in the S on the Lord's day,
2:7 him hear what the S says to the churches.
2:11 him hear what the S says to the churches.
2:17 him hear what the S says to the churches.
2:29 him hear what the S says to the churches.'
3:6 him hear what the S says to the churches.'
3:13 him hear what the S says to the churches.'
3:22 him hear what the S says to the churches.'"
4:2 I was in the S, and lo, a throne
14:13 says the S, "that they may rest from their
17:3 me away in the S into a wilderness, and
18:2 haunt of every foul S, a haunt of every
19:10 of Jesus is the S of prophecy.
21:10 And in the S he carried me away to
22:17 The S and the Bride say, "Come." And let

SPIRITS (43)

Num 16:22 the God of the S of all flesh, shall
27:16 the God of the S of all flesh, appoint
Wis 7:20 beasts, the powers of S and the reasonings of
7:23 and penetrating through all S that are intelligent and
Dan 3:87 Bless the Lord, S and souls of the righteous,
2Mac 3:24 there the Sovereign of S and of all authority
Mt 8:16 he cast out the S with a word, and
10:1 them authority over unclean S, to cast them out,
12:45 with him seven other S more evil than himself,
Mk 1:27 commands even the unclean S, and they obey him."
3:11 And whenever the unclean S beheld him, they fell
5:13 And the unclean S came out, and entered the
6:7 two, and gave them authority over the unclean S
Lk 4:36 he commands the unclean S, and they come out."
6:18 were troubled with unclean S were cured.
7:21 and plagues and evil S, and on many that
8:2 been healed of evil S and infirmities: Mary, called
10:20 in this, that the S are subject to you;
11:26 and brings seven other S more evil than himself,
Acts 5:16 those afflicted with unclean S, and they were all
8:7 For unclean S came out of many who were
19:12 them and the evil S came out of them.
19:13 those who had evil S, saying, "I adjure you
Rom 8:10 because of sin, your S are alive because of
1Cor 12:10 ability to distinguish between S, to another various
14:32 be encouraged; and the S of prophets are subject
Gal 4:3 slaves to the elemental S of the universe.
4:9 weak and beggarly elemental S, whose slaves you
Col 2:8 according to the elemental S of the universe, and
2:20 died to the elemental S of the universe, why
1Tim 4:1 giving heed to deceitful S and doctrines of demons,
Heb 1:14 they not all ministering S sent forth to serve,
12:9 to the Father of S and live?
12:23 all, and to the S of just men made
1Pet 3:19 and preached to the S in prison,
1Jn 4:1 spirit, but test the S to see whether they
Rev 1:4 and from the seven S who are before his
3:1 who has the seven S of God and the
4:5 which are the seven S of God;
5:6 which are the seven S of God sent out
16:13 false prophet, three foul S like frogs;
16:14 for they are demonic S, performing signs, who go
22:6 the God of the S of the prophets, has

SPIRITUAL (26)

Rom 1:11 impart to you some S gift to strengthen you,
2:29 matter of the heart, S and not literal.
7:14 that the law is S; but I am carnal,
12:1 God, which is your S worship.
15:27 to share in their S blessings, they ought also
1Cor 1:7 not lacking in any S gift, as you wait
2:13 by the Spirit, interpreting S truths to those who
2:15 The S man judges all things, but is himself
3:1 not address you as S men, but as men
9:11 If we have sown S good among you, is
12:1 Now concerning S gifts, brethren, I do not want
14:1 and earnestly desire the S gifts, especially that you
14:37 is a prophet, or S, he should acknowledge that
15:44 it is raised a S body.
15:44 there is also a S body.
15:46 it is not the S which is first but
15:46 is first but the physical, and then the S
Gal 6:1 trespass, you who are S should restore him in
Eph 1:3 in Christ with every S blessing in the heavenly
5:19 psalms and hymns and S songs, singing and making
6:12 present darkness, against the S hosts of wickedness
Col 1:9 his will in all S wisdom and understanding,
3:16 psalms and hymns and S songs with thankfulness in
1Pet 2:2 long for the pure S milk, that by it
2:5 yourselves built into a S house, to be a
2:5 priesthood, to offer S sacrifices acceptable to God

SPIRITUALLY

1Cor 2:14 them because they are S discerned.

SPIT (9)

Num 12:14 her father had but S in her face, should
Deut 25:9 off his foot, and S in his face; and
Job 17:6 peoples, and I am one before whom men S
30:10 do not hesitate to S at the sight of
Sir 28:12 will glow; if you S on it, it will
Mk 8:23 and when he had S on his eyes and
10:34 will mock him, and S upon him, and scourge
14:65 And some began to S on him, and to
Lk 18:32 and shamefully treated and S upon;

SPITE (13)

Lev 26:18 And if in S of this you will not
26:27 "And if in S of this you will not

Num 14:11 believe in me, in S of all the signs
Deut 1:32 this place.' Yet in S of this word you
Ezra 10:2 hope for Israel in S of this.
Jud 8:25 In S of everything let us give thanks to
Job 23:2 hand is heavy in S of my groaning.
34:6 away my right; in S of my right I
Ps 78:32 In S of all this they still sinned; despite
Is 16:14 brought into contempt, in S of all his great
47:9 in full measure, in S of your many sorceries
Jer 2:34 Yet in S of all these things
2Mac 4:34 right hand, and in S of his suspicion persuaded

SPITS

Lev 15:8 who has the discharge S on one who is

SPITTING (2)

Is 50:6 I hid not my face from shame and S
2Mac 6:19 of his own accord, S out the flesh,

SPITTLE (3)

1Sam 21:13 gate, and let his S run down his beard.
Job 7:19 nor let me alone till I swallow my S
Jn 9:6 made clay of the S and anointed the man's

SPLENDID (8)

Esth 14:2 she took off her S apparel and put on
15:1 and arrayed herself in S attire.
Sir 40:3 who sits on a S throne to the one
45:7 He blessed him with S vestments, and put a
Is 22:18 there shall be your S chariots, you shame of
2Mac 8:35 account, took off his S uniform and made his
12:45 was looking to the S reward that is laid
14:33 will build here a S temple to Dionysus."

SPLENDIDLY

2Mac 3:26 strong, gloriously beautiful and S dressed, who stood

SPLENDOR (40)

Gen 45:13 father of all my S in Egypt, and of
Tob 14:5 of their captivity, and will rebuild Jerusalem in S
Esth 1:4 royal glory and the S and pomp of his
5:11 recounted to them the S of his riches, the
14:15 that I hate the S of the wicked and
15:7 his face, flushed with S, he looked at her
Job 31:26 the moon moving in S,
37:22 the north comes golden S; God is clothed with
40:10 majesty and dignity; clothe yourself with glory and S
Ps 21:5 great through thy help; S and majesty thou dost
145:5 On the glorious S of thy majesty, and on
145:12 deeds, and the glorious S of thy kingdom.
Sir 50:13 of Aaron in their S with the Lord's offering
Is 13:19 glory of kingdoms, the S and pride of the
Lam 2:1 heaven to earth the S of Israel; he has
Bar 4:24 glory and with the S of the Everlasting.
5:3 God will show your S everywhere under heaven.
Ezek 16:14 was perfect through the S which I had bestowed
27:10 shield and helmet in you; they gave you S
28:7 the beauty of your wisdom and defile your S
28:17 corrupted your wisdom for the sake of your S
Dan 4:36 kingdom, my majesty and S returned to me.
Hag 2:7 fill this house with S, says the LORD of
2:9 The latter S of this house shall be greater
1Mac 2:62 a sinner, for his S will turn into dung
15:32 when he saw the S of Simon, and the
15:36 these words and the S of Simon and all
2Cor 3:7 stone, came with such S that the Israelites could
3:8 dispensation of the Spirit be attended with greater S
3:9 For if there was S in the dispensation of
3:9 dispensation of righteousness must far exceed it in S
3:10 case, what once had S has come to have
3:10 come to have no S at all, because of
3:10 all, because of the S that surpasses it.
3:11 faded away came with S, what is permanent must
3:11 splendor, what is permanent must have much more S
3:13 might not see the end of the fading S
Eph 5:27 church to himself in S, without spot or wrinkle
Rev 18:1 and the earth was made bright with his S
18:14 thy dainties and thy S are lost to thee,

SPLENDORS

Sir 42:21 He has ordained the S of his wisdom, and

SPLINTERED

Joel 1:7 waste my vines, and S my fig trees; it

SPLIT (7)

Num 16:31 the ground under them S asunder;
Judg 15:19 And God S open the hollow place that is
1Sam 6:14 was there; and they S up the wood of
1Kgs 1:40 that the earth was S by their noise.
Zech 14:4 of Olives shall be S in two from east
Mt 27:51 and the rocks were S;
Rev 16:19 The great city was S into three parts, and

SPLITS

Eccl 10:9 them; and he who S logs is endangered by

SPOIL (84)

Gen 49:27 devouring the prey, and at even dividing the S
Ex 15:9 I will divide the S, my desire shall have
Num 31:11 and took all the S and all the booty,
31:12 the booty and the S to Moses, and to
31:32 booty remaining of the S that the men of
Deut 2:35 cattle we took as S for ourselves, with the
3:7 the cattle and the S of the cities we
13:16 shall gather all its S into the midst of
13:16 city and all its S with fire, as a
20:14 the city, all its S, you shall take as
20:14 you shall enjoy the S of your enemies, which
Josh 7:21 I saw among the S a beautiful mantle from
8:2 its king; only its S and its cattle you
8:27 the cattle and the S of that city Israel
11:14 And all the S of these cities and the
22:8 much clothing; divide the S of your enemies with
Judg 5:30 finding and dividing the S —A maiden or two
5:30 two for every man; S of dyed stuffs for
5:30 dyed stuffs for Sisera, S of dyed stuffs embroidered,
5:30 for my neck as S
8:24 every man of you the earrings of his S
8:25 man cast in it the earrings of his S
14:19 town, and took their S and gave the festal
1Sam 14:30 freely today of the S of their enemies which
14:32 people flew upon the S, and took sheep and
15:19 you swoop on the S, and do what was
15:21 people took of the S, sheep and oxen, the
30:16 of all the great S they had taken from
30:19 great, sons or daughters, S or anything that had
30:20 cattle before him, and said, "This is David's S
30:22 them any of the S which we have recovered,
30:26 sent part of the S to his friends, the
30:26 for you from the S of the enemies of
2Sam 2:21 one of the young men, and take his S
3:22 a raid, bringing much S with them.
8:12 Amalek, and from the S of Hadadezer the son
12:30 he brought forth the S of the city, a
2Kgs 3:23 Now then, Moab, to the S
21:14 a prey and a S to all their enemies,
1Chr 20:2 he brought forth the S of the city, a
26:27 From S won in battles they dedicated gifts for
2Chr 15:11 that day, from the S which they had brought,
20:25 came to take the S from them, they found
20:25 days in taking the S, it was so much.
24:23 and sent all their S to the king of
25:13 three thousand people in them, and took much S
28:8 they also took much S from them and brought
28:8 them and brought the S to Samaria.
28:14 the captives and the S before the princes and
28:15 captives, and with the S they clothed all that
Ps 44:10 from the foe; and our enemies have gotten S
68:12 at home divide the S,
76:5 were stripped of their S; they sank into sleep;
119:162 at thy word like one who finds great S
Prov 1:13 fill our houses with S;
16:19 than to divide the S with the proud.
Song 2:15 the little foxes, that S the vineyards, for our
Is 3:14 devoured the vineyard, the S of the poor is
8:4 of Damascus and the S of Samaria will be
9:3 harvest, as men rejoice when they divide the S
10:2 widows may be their S, and that they may
10:6 command him, to take S and seize plunder, and
33:4 nations are scattered; and S is gathered as the
33:23 Then prey and S in abundance will be divided;
42:22 none to rescue, a S with none to say,
53:12 he shall divide the S with the strong; because
Jer 13:9 Even so will I S the pride of Judah
15:13 I will give as S, without price, for all
17:3 I will give for S as the price of
30:16 you shall become a S, and all who prey
49:32 shall become booty, their herds of cattle a S
Ezek 7:21 the earth for a S; and they shall profane
23:46 make them an object of terror and a S

25:7 hand you over as S to the nations; and
26:5 she shall become a S to the nations;
26:12 They will make a S of your riches and
38:12 or gates'; to seize S and carry off plunder;
38:13 say to you, 'Have you come to seize S
38:13 goods, to seize great S
Dan 11:24 scattering among them plunder, S, and goods.
Zech 14:1 is coming, when the S taken from you will
1Mac 11:48 city and seized much S on that day, and
11:51 and they returned to Jerusalem with much S
Lk 11:22 armor in which he trusted, and divides his S

SPOILED (2)

Jer 13:7 behold, the waistcloth was S; it was good for
18:4 making of clay was S in the potter's hand,

SPOILER

Is 42:24 up Jacob to the S, and Israel to the

SPOILERS

2Kgs 17:20 into the hand of S, until he had cast

SPOILS (12)

Judg 5:19 Megiddo; they got no S of silver.
Sir 30:7 He who S his son will bind up his
1Mac 1:35 food, and collecting the S of Jerusalem they stored
2:10 inherited her palaces and has not seized her S
3:12 Then they seized their S; and Judas took the
5:28 he seized all its S and burned it with
6:6 arms, supplies, and abundant S which they had taken
7:47 the Jews seized the S and the plunder, and
2Mac 8:27 stripped them of their S, they kept the sabbath,
8:28 gave some of the S to those who had
8:31 the rest of the S to Jerusalem.
Heb 7:4 the patriarch gave him a tithe of the S

SPOKE (270)

Gen 16:13 of the LORD who S to her, "Thou art
18:29 Again he S to him, and said, "Suppose forty
24:7 my birth, and who S to me and swore
24:30 sister, "Thus the man S to me," he went
27:5 was listening when Isaac S to his son Esau.
31:29 God of your father S to me last night,
34:3 loved the maiden and S tenderly to her.
34:4 So Shechem S to his father Hamor, saying, "Get
34:8 But Hamor S with them, saying, "The soul of
34:20 of their city and S to the men of
39:10 And although she S to Joseph day after day,
39:19 words which his wife S to him, "This is
42:7 them like strangers and S roughly to them.
42:24 returned to them and S to them.
42:30 lord of the land, S roughly to us, and
43:19 of Joseph's house, and S with him at the
43:27 father well, the old man of whom you S
43:29 brother, of whom you S to me?
44:6 he overtook them, he S to them these words.
46:2 And God S to Israel in visions of the
50:4 him were past, Joseph S to the household of
50:17 Joseph wept when they S to him.
Ex 4:30 And Aaron S all the words which the LORD
6:9 Moses S thus to the people of Israel; but
6:13 But the LORD S to Moses and Aaron, and
6:27 It was they who S to Pharaoh king of
6:28 day when the LORD S to Moses in the
7:7 years old, when they S to Pharaoh.
16:10 And as Aaron S to the whole congregation of
19:19 louder and louder, Moses S, and God answered him
20:1 And God S all these words, saying,
Lev 1:1 LORD called Moses, and S to him from the
10:8 And the LORD S to Aaron, saying,
16:1 The LORD S to Moses, after the death of
21:24 So Moses S to Aaron and to his sons
24:23 So Moses S to the people of Israel; and
Num 1:1 The LORD S to Moses in the
3:1 time when the LORD S with Moses on Mount
7:89 two cherubim; and it S to him.
9:1 And the LORD S to Moses in the wilderness
11:25 in the cloud and S to him, and took
12:1 Miriam and Aaron S against Moses because of the
17:6 Moses S to the people of Israel; and all
21:5 And the people S against God and against Moses,
26:3 and Eleazar the priest S with them in the
36:1 Joseph, came near and S before Moses and before
Deut 1:1 the words that Moses S to all Israel beyond
1:3 the eleventh month, Moses S to the people of
1:43 your enemies.' So I S to you, and you
4:12 Then the LORD S to you out of the
4:15 day that the LORD S to you at Horeb
4:45 the ordinances, which Moses S to the children of
5:4 The LORD S with you face to face at
5:22 "These words the LORD S to all your assembly
5:28 your words, when you S to me; and the
31:30 Then Moses S the words of this song until
Josh 10:12 Then S Joshua to the LORD in the day
14:10 time that the LORD S this word to Moses,
14:12 of which the LORD S on that day; for
17:14 the tribe of Joseph S to Joshua, saying, "Why
20:2 refuge, of which I S to you through Moses,
22:30 Gadites and the Manassites S, it pleased them well.
22:33 Israel blessed God and S no more of making
24:27 the LORD which he S to us; therefore it
Judg 2:4 angel of the LORD S these words to all
8:8 up to Penuel, and S to them in the
9:3 And his mother's kinsmen S all these words on
9:37 Gaal S again and said, "Look, men are coming
11:11 over them; and Jephthah S all his words before
13:11 you the man who S to this woman?" And
17:2 a curse, and also S it in my ears,
1Sam 9:17 man of whom I S to you!
17:23 of the Philistines, and S the same words as
17:28 brother heard when he S to the men; and
17:30 him toward another, and S in the same way;
17:31 the words which David S were heard, they repeated
18:23 And Saul's servants S those words in the ears
19:1 And Saul S to Jonathan his son and to
19:4 And Jonathan S well of David to Saul his
28:17 to you as he S by me; for the
30:6 distressed; for the people S of stoning him, because
2Sam 3:19 Abner also S to Benjamin; and then Abner went
7:17 all this vision, Nathan S to David.
12:18 was yet alive, we S to him, and he
13:22 But Absalom S to Amnon neither good nor bad;
22:1 And David S to the LORD the words of
24:17 Then David S to the LORD when he saw
1Kgs 2:4 his word which he S concerning me, saying, 'If
3:22 Thus they S before the king.
4:33 He S of trees, from the cedar that is
4:33 of the wall; he S also of beasts, and
6:12 with you, which I S to David your father.
12:14 had given him, he S to them according to
12:15 word, which the LORD S by Ahijah the Shilonite
13:18 are, and an angel S to me by the
13:26 word which the LORD S to him."
14:18 the LORD, which he S by his servant Ahijah
15:29 the LORD which he S by his servant Ahijah
16:12 the LORD, which he S against Baasha by Jehu
16:34 the LORD, which he S by Joshua the son
17:16 the LORD which he S by Elijah.
21:6 to her, "Because I S to Naboth the Jezreelite,
2Kgs 2:22 this day, according to the word which Elisha S
5:4 lord, "Thus and so S the maiden from the
9:12 "Thus and so he S to me, saying, 'Thus
9:36 the LORD, which he S by his servant Elijah
10:10 LORD, which the LORD S concerning the house of
10:17 the LORD which he S to Elijah.
14:25 of Israel, which he S by his servant Jonah
22:19 you heard how I S against this place, and
24:2 the LORD which he S by his servants the
25:28 from prison; and he S kindly to him, and
1Chr 17:15 all this vision, Nathan S to David.
21:9 And the LORD S to Gad, David's seer, saying,
2Chr 1:2 Solomon S to all Israel, to the commanders of
10:14 old men, King Rehoboam S to them according to
10:15 his word, which he S by Ahijah the Shilonite
23:3 reign, as the LORD S concerning the sons of
30:22 And Hezekiah S encouragingly to all the Levites
32:6 of the city and S encouragingly to them, saying,
32:19 And they S of the God of Jerusalem as
32:19 of Jerusalem as they S of the gods of
33:10 The LORD S to Manasseh and to his people,
33:18 of the seers who S to him in the
34:22 the Second Quarter) and S to her to that
36:12 Jeremiah the prophet, who S from the mouth of
Ezra 5:3 came to them and S to them thus, "Who
5:9 asked those elders and S to them thus, 'Who
Neh 6:19 Also they S of his good deeds in my
13:24 half of their children S the language of Ashdod,
Jud 8:8 No one S ill of her, for she feared
10:9 things about which you S with me." So they
Esth 3:4 And when they S to him day after day
4:8 next to the king, S against us for our
4:10 Then Esther S to Hathach and gave him a

	8:3	Then Esther S again to the king; she fell
	10:3	of his people and S peace to all his
Job	2:13	nights, and no one S a word to him,
	29:22	After I S they did not speak again, and
Ps	33:9	For he S, and it came to be; he
	39:3	fire burned; then I S with my tongue:
	78:19	They S against God, saying, "Can God spread a
	99:7	He S to them in the pillar of cloud;
	105:31	He S, and there came swarms of flies, and
	105:34	He S, and the locusts came, and young locusts
	106:33	spirit bitter, and he S words that were rash.
Song	5:6	My soul failed me when he S
Is	7:10	Again the LORD S to Ahaz,
	8:5	The LORD S to me again:
	8:11	For the LORD S thus to me with his
	16:13	word which the LORD S concerning Moab in the
	65:12	not answer, when I S, you did not listen,
	66:4	one answered, when I S they did not listen;
Jer	7:13	LORD, and when I S to you persistently you
	22:21	I S to you in your prosperity, but you
	25:2	which Jeremiah the prophet S to all the people
	26:12	Then Jeremiah S to all the princes and all
	26:17	the land arose and S to all the assembled
	27:12	king of Judah I S in like manner: "Bring
	27:16	Then I S to the priests and to all
	28:1	the prophet from Gibeon, S to me in the
	28:5	the prophet Jeremiah S to Hananiah the prophet
	28:11	And Hananiah S in the presence of all the
	30:4	words which the LORD S concerning Israel and
	34:6	Then Jeremiah the prophet S all these words to
	36:2	from the day I S to you, from the
	37:2	the LORD which he S through Jeremiah the prophet.
	40:15	the son of Kareah S secretly to Gedaliah at
	45:1	that Jeremiah the prophet S to Baruch the son
	46:13	word which the LORD S to Jeremiah the prophet
	48:27	thieves, that whenever you S of him you wagged
	50:1	which the LORD S concerning Babylon, concerning
	51:12	and done what he S concerning the inhabitants of
	52:32	of prison; and he S kindly to him, and
Bar	2:1	his word, which he S against us, and against
Ezek	2:2	And when he S to me, the Spirit entered
	3:24	my feet; and he S with me and said
	24:18	So I S to the people in the morning,
	38:17	he of whom I S in former days by
Dan	1:19	And the king S with them, and among them
	7:20	and a mouth that S great things, and which
	8:13	to the one that S, "For how long is
	9:6	servants the prophets, who S in thy name to
	9:12	his words, which he S against us and against
	10:16	my lips; then I opened my mouth and S
	10:19	And when he S to me, I was strengthened
Hos	1:2	When the LORD first S through Hosea, the LORD
	12:4	Bethel, and there God S with him –
	12:10	I S to the prophets; it was I who
	13:1	When Ephraim S, men trembled; he was exalted in
Jon	2:10	And the LORD S to the fish, and it
Hag	1:13	messenger of the LORD, S to the people with
Mal	3:16	who feared the LORD S with one another; the
1Mac	1:24	deeds of murder, and S with great arrogance.
	1:30	Deceitfully he S peaceable words to them, and they
	2:17	Then the king's officers S to Mattathias as follows:
	7:15	And he S peaceable words to them and swore
	7:34	and defiled them and S arrogantly,
	7:41	messengers from the king S blasphemy, thy angel
	8:19	the senate chamber and S as follows:
2Mac	7:27	close to him, she S in their native tongue
	15:12	gentle manner, one who S fittingly and had been
	15:14	And Onias S, saying, "This is a man who
Mt	9:33	out, the dumb man S; and the crowds marveled,
	12:22	that the dumb man S and saw.
	14:27	But immediately he S to them, saying, "Take heart,
	17:24	he came home, Jesus S to him first, saying,
	22:1	And again Jesus S to them in parables, saying,
Mk	4:33	many such parables he S the word to them,
	6:50	But immediately he S to them and said, "Take
	7:34	was released, and he S plainly.
Lk	1:55	his mercy, as he S to our fathers, to
	1:64	tongue loosed, and he S, blessing God.
	1:70	servant David, as he S by the mouth of
	2:38	thanks to God, and S of him to all
	2:50	the saying which he S to them.
	4:22	And all S well of him, and wondered at
	9:11	he welcomed them and S to them of the
	9:31	appeared in glory and S of his departure, which
	11:14	out, the dumb man S, and the people marveled.
	14:3	And Jesus S to the lawyers and Pharisees, saying,
	21:5	And as some S of the temple, how it
	22:63	And they S many other words against him, reviling
	24:44	my words which I S to you, while I
Jn	2:21	But he S of the temple of his body.
	4:50	the word that Jesus S to him and went
	6:71	He S of Judas the son of Simon Iscariot,
	7:13	the Jews no one S openly of him.
	7:46	answered, "No man ever S like this man!"
	8:12	Again Jesus S to them, saying, "I am the
	8:20	These words he S in the treasury, as he
	8:27	not understand that he S to them of the
	8:30	As he S thus, many believed in him.
	11:11	Thus he S, and then he said to them,
	12:41	saw his glory and S of him.
	13:22	looked at one another, uncertain of whom he S
	18:16	priest, went out and S to the maid who
Acts	1:16	which the Holy Spirit S beforehand by the mouth
	2:31	throne, he foresaw and S of the resurrection of
	3:21	establishing all that God S by the mouth of
	4:31	the Holy Spirit and S the word of God
	6:10	the wisdom and the Spirit with which he S
	7:6	And God S to this effect, that his posterity
	7:38	with the angel who S to him at Mount
	7:44	even as he who S to Moses directed him
	9:27	seen the Lord, who S to him, and how
	9:29	And he S and disputed against the Hellenists; but
	10:7	When the angel who S to him had departed,
	11:20	on coming to Antioch S to the Greeks also,
	13:34	return to corruption, he S in this way, 'I
	13:43	Paul and Barnabas, who S to them and urged
	13:46	And Paul and Barnabas S out boldly, saying, "It
	14:1	Jewish synagogue, and so S that a great company
	16:13	we sat down and S to the women who
	16:32	And they S the word of the Lord to
	18:25	fervent in spirit, he S and taught accurately the
	19:6	on them; and they S with tongues and prophesied.
	19:8	and for three months S boldly, arguing and pleading
	21:40	a great hush, he S to them in the
	23:9	spirit or an angel S to him?"
1Cor	13:11	was a child, I S like a child, I
2Cor	4:13	had who wrote, "I believed, and so I S
Heb	1:1	and various ways God S of old to our
	13:7	your leaders, those who S to you the word
Jas	5:10	take the prophets who S in the name of
2Pet	1:21	by the Holy Spirit S from God.
	2:16	transgression; a dumb ass S with human voice and
Rev	10:8	had heard from heaven S to me again, saying,
	13:11	a lamb and it S like a dragon.
	21:9	seven last plagues, and S to me, saying, "Come,

SPOKEN (225)

Gen	19:21	not overthrow the city of which you have S
	21:2	of which God had S to him.
	24:51	of your master's son, as the LORD has S
	28:15	of which I have S to you."
	35:13	place where he had S with him.
	35:14	place where he had S with him, a pillar
	35:15	place where God had S with him, Bethel.
Ex	4:10	or since thou hast S to thy servant; but
	4:30	which the LORD had S to Moses, and did
	9:12	as the LORD had S to Moses.
	9:35	as the LORD had S through Moses.
	19:8	that the LORD has S we will do." And
	24:3	which the LORD has S we will do."
	24:7	that the LORD has S we will do, and
	32:34	of which I have S to you; behold, my
	33:17	thing that you have S I will do; for
	34:32	that the LORD had S with him in Mount
Lev	10:11	which the LORD has S to them by Moses."
Num	12:2	"Has the LORD indeed S only through Moses?
	12:2	Has he not S through us also?" And the
	14:35	I, the LORD, have S; surely this will I
	15:22	which the LORD has S to Moses,
	21:7	sinned, for we have S against the LORD and
	23:17	Balak said to him, "What has the LORD S
	23:19	Or has he S, and will he not fulfil
Deut	1:14	thing that you have S is good for us
	5:28	people, which they have S to you; they have
	5:28	they have rightly said all that they have S
	9:10	which the LORD had S with you on the
	10:4	which the LORD had S to you on the
	18:17	'They have rightly said all that they have S
	18:21	the LORD has not S –
	18:22	the LORD has not S; the prophet has spoken
	18:22	spoken; the prophet has S it presumptuously, you
	26:19	to the LORD your God, as he has S

31:3 over at your head, as the LORD has S
Josh 11:23 that the LORD had S to Moses; and Joshua
Ruth 2:13 comforted me and S kindly to your maidservant,
4:1 of whom Boaz had S, came by.
1Sam 3:12 all that I have S concerning his house, from
9:21 Why then have you S to me in this
10:16 of which Samuel had S, he did not tell
20:23 you and I have S, behold, the LORD is
25:30 good that he has S concerning you, and has
2Sam 2:27 if you had not S, surely the men would
6:22 of whom you have S, by them I shall
7:19 Lord GOD; thou hast S also of thy servant's
7:25 word which thou hast S concerning thy servant and
7:25 do as thou hast S;
7:29 O Lord GOD, hast S, and with thy blessing
17:6 him, "Thus has Ahithophel S; shall we do as
23:3 God of Israel has S, the Rock of Israel
1Kgs 2:27 LORD which he had S concerning the house of
8:26 confirmed, which thou hast S to thy servant David
13:3 that the LORD has S: 'Behold, the altar shall
13:11 also which he had S to the king, they
14:11 for the LORD has S it.'"
18:24 And all the people answered, "It is well S
22:23 prophets; the LORD has S evil concerning you."
22:28 the LORD has not S by me." And he
22:38 the word of the LORD which he had S
2Kgs 1:17 the word of the LORD which Elijah had S
4:13 you have a word S on your behalf to
17:23 sight, as he had S by all his servants
19:21 that the LORD has S concerning him: "She despises
20:19 LORD which you have S is good." For he
1Chr 17:17 God; thou hast also S of thy servant's house
17:23 word which thou hast S concerning thy servant and
17:23 do as thou hast S;
21:19 word, which he had S in the name of
22:11 God, as he has S concerning you.
2Chr 2:15 which my lord has S, let him send to
6:17 confirmed, which thou hast S to thy servant David.
18:22 prophets; the LORD has S evil concerning you."
18:27 the LORD has not S by me." And he
35:25 and singing women have S of Josiah in their
Neh 2:18 which the king had S to me.
Jud 2:12 kingdom, what I have S my hand will execute.
6:4 For he has S; none of his words shall
6:9 I have S and none of my words shall
8:9 heard the wicked words S by the people against
8:28 have said has been S out of a true
Job 21:3 and after I have S, mock on.
33:8 "Surely, you have S in my hearing, and I
40:5 I have S once, and I will not answer;
42:7 After the LORD had S these words to Job,
42:7 for you have not S of me what is
42:8 for you have not S of me what is
Ps 40:10 my heart, I have S of thy faithfulness and
60:6 God has S in his sanctuary: "With exultation I
62:11 Once God has S; twice have I heard this:
87:3 Glorious things are S of you, O city of
Prov 25:11 A word fitly S is like apples of gold
Song 8:8 day when she is S for?
Sir 36:15 and fulfil the prophecies S in thy name.
Is 1:2 for the LORD has S: "Sons have I reared
1:20 sword; for the mouth of the LORD has S
20:2 time the LORD had S by Isaiah the son
21:17 for the LORD, the God of Israel, has S
22:25 will be cut off, for the LORD has S
23:4 for the sea has S, the stronghold of the
24:3 for the LORD has S this word.
25:8 from all the earth; for the LORD has S
37:22 that the LORD has S concerning him: 'She despises
38:15 For he has S to me, and he himself
39:8 LORD which you have S is good." For he
40:5 together, for the mouth of the LORD has S
46:11 I have S, and I will bring it to
48:15 I, even I, have S and called him, I
48:16 beginning I have not S in secret, from the
58:14 father, for the mouth of the LORD has S
59:3 iniquity; your lips have S lies, your tongue mutters
Jer 3:5 end?' Behold, you have S, but you have done
4:28 black; for I have S, I have purposed; I
5:12 They have S falsely of the LORD, and have
5:14 hosts: "Because they have S this word, behold, I
8:6 but they have not S aright; no man repents
9:12 mouth of the LORD S, that he may declare
13:15 ear; be not proud, for the LORD has S
18:8 concerning which I have S, turns from its evil,
23:35 'What has the LORD S
23:37 'What has the LORD S
25:3 me, and I have S persistently to you, but
26:16 death, for he has S to us in the
27:13 as the LORD has S concerning any nation which
29:23 wives, and they have S in my name lying
30:2 words that I have S to you.
34:5 lord!'" For I have S the word, says the
35:14 I have S to you persistently, but you have
35:17 them; because I have S to them and they
36:2 words that I have S to you against Israel
36:4 LORD which he had S to him.
38:25 hear that I have S with you and come
44:16 word which you have S to us in the
48:8 plain shall be destroyed, as the LORD has S
Ezek 5:13 I, the LORD, have S in my jealousy, when
5:15 I, the LORD, have S –
5:17 I, the LORD, have S
13:6 They have S falsehood and divined a lie; they
13:7 said, 'Says the LORD,' although I have not S
17:21 you shall know that I, the LORD, have S
17:24 I the LORD have S, and I will do
21:17 will satisfy my fury; I the LORD have S
21:32 no more remembered; for I the LORD have S
22:14 I the LORD have S, and I will do
22:28 the Lord GOD,' when the LORD has not S
23:34 breasts; for I have S, says the Lord GOD.
24:14 I the LORD have S; it shall come to
26:5 nets; for I have S, says the Lord GOD;
26:14 I the LORD have S, says the Lord GOD.
28:10 foreigners; for I have S, says the Lord GOD."
30:12 the hand of foreigners; I, the LORD, have S
34:24 be prince among them; I, the LORD, have S
36:36 I, the LORD, have S, and I will do
37:14 I, the LORD, have S, and I have done
39:5 field; for I have S, says the Lord GOD.
39:8 That is the day of which I have S
Dan 4:31 to you it is S: The kingdom has departed
10:15 When he had S to me according to these
Joel 3:8 to a nation far-off; for the LORD has S
Amos 3:1 that the LORD has S against you, O people
3:8 The Lord GOD has S; who can but prophesy?"
Obad 1:18 the house of Esau; for the LORD has S
Mic 4:4 the mouth of the LORD of hosts has S
Mal 3:13 say, 'How have we S against thee?'
1Mac 7:42 that Nicanor has S wickedly against the sanctuary,
2Mac 4:48 so those who had S for the city and
Mt 1:22 what the Lord had S by the prophet:
2:15 what the Lord had S by the prophet, "Out
2:17 was fulfilled what was S by the prophet Jeremiah:
2:23 Nazareth, that what was S by the prophets might
3:3 is he who was S of by the prophet
4:14 Naphtali, that what was S by the prophet Isaiah
8:17 to fulfil what was S by the prophet Isaiah,
12:17 to fulfil what was S by the prophet Isaiah:
13:35 to fulfil what was S by the prophet: "I
21:4 to fulfil what was S by the prophet, saying,
24:15 see the desolating sacrilege S of by the prophet
27:9 fulfilled what had been S by the prophet Jeremiah,
Mk 16:19 Jesus, after he had S to them, was taken
Lk 1:45 fulfilment of what was S to her from the
2:34 a sign that is S against
9:36 when the voice had S, Jesus was found alone.
20:39 answered, "Teacher, you have S well."
24:25 heart to believe all that the prophets have S
Jn 2:22 the scripture and the word which Jesus had S
6:63 words that I have S to you are spirit
9:29 know that God has S to Moses, but as
11:13 Now Jesus had S of his death, but they
12:29 said, "An angel has S to him."
12:38 was that the word S by the prophet Isaiah
12:48 word that I have S will be his judge
12:49 For I have not S on my own authority;
13:21 When Jesus had thus S, he was troubled in
14:25 "These things I have S to you, while I
15:3 word which I have S to you.
15:11 These things I have S to you, that my
15:22 had not come and S to them, they would
17:1 When Jesus had S these words, he lifted up
18:1 When Jesus had S these words, he went forth
18:9 word which he had S, "Of those whom thou
18:20 answered him, "I have S openly to the world;
18:23 him, "If I have S wrongly, bear witness to
18:23 but if I have S rightly, why do you
18:32 word which Jesus had S to show by what
Acts 2:16 this is what was S by the prophet Joel:
3:24 the prophets who have S, from Samuel and those

8:25 they had testified and S the word of the
10:22 man, who is well S of by the whole
13:45 and contradicted what was S by Paul, and reviled
13:46 of God should be S first to you.
14:25 And when they had S the word in Perga,
16:2 He was well S of by the brethren at
20:36 And when he had S thus, he knelt down
20:38 the word he had S, that they should see
22:12 to the law, well S of by all the
28:21 here has reported or S any evil about you.
28:22 that everywhere it is S against."
Rom 14:16 let your good be S of as evil.
Heb 1:2 last days he has S to us by a
3:5 that were to be S later,
4:4 For he has somewhere S of the seventh day
7:13 whom these things are S belonged to another tribe,
12:19 no further messages be S to them.
Jude 1:15 which ungodly sinners have S against him."

SPOKES (3)

1Kgs 7:33 axles, their rims, their S, and their hubs, were
Ezek 1:18 rims and they had S; and their rims were
10:12 their rims, and their S, and the wheels were

SPOKESMAN (3)

2Mac 7:2 them, acting as their S, said, "What do you
7:4 the tongue of their S be cut out and
Acts 24:1 some elders and a S, one Tertullus.

SPONGE (3)

Mt 27:48 ran and took a S, filled it with vinegar,
Mk 15:35 ran and, filling a S full of vinegar, put
Jn 19:29 so they put a S full of the vinegar

SPORT (17)

Ex 10:2 how I have made S of the Egyptians and
Num 22:29 "Because you have made S of me.
Judg 16:25 that he may make S for us." So they
16:25 prison, and he made S before them.
16:27 and women, who looked on while Samson made S
1Sam 6:6 After he had made S of them, did not
31:4 me through, and make S of me." But his
1Chr 10:4 uncircumcised come and make S of me." But his
Job 30:1 "But now they make S of me, men who
Ps 104:26 thou didst form to S in it.
Prov 10:23 It is like S to a fool to do
Is 57:4 Of whom are you making S
Bar 3:17 earth; those who have S with the birds of
Hab 1:10 kings they scoff, and of rulers they make S
1Mac 9:26 on them and made S of them.
2Mac 7:7 way, they brought forward the second for their S
7:10 him, the third was the victim of their S

SPOT (20)

Lev 13:2 an eruption or a S, and it turns into
13:3 shall examine the diseased S on the skin of
13:3 hair in the diseased S has turned white and
13:4 But if the S is white in the skin
13:6 and if the diseased S is dim and the
13:19 swelling or a reddish-white S, then it shall be
13:23 But if the S remains in one place and
13:24 the burn becomes a S, reddish-white or white,
13:25 the hair in the S has turned white and
13:26 the hair in the S is not white and
13:28 But if the S remains in one place and
13:42 forehead a reddish-white diseased S, it is leprosy
13:55 And if the diseased S has not changed color,
13:55 fire, whether the leprous S is on the back
13:56 he shall tear the S out of the garment
14:56 an eruption or a S,
Job 31:7 eyes, and if any S has cleaved to my
Eph 5:27 himself in splendor, without S or wrinkle or any
1Pet 1:19 like that of a lamb without blemish or S
2Pet 3:14 found by him without S or blemish, and at

SPOTLESS (2)

Wis 7:26 of eternal light, a S mirror of the working
Rev 14:5 mouth no lie was found, for they are S

SPOTS (5)

Lev 13:38 or a woman has S on the skin of
13:38 of the body, white S,
13:39 examination, and if the S on the skin of
14:37 with greenish or reddish S, and if it appears
Jer 13:23 Ethiopian change his skin or the leopard his S

SPOTTED (11)

Gen 30:32 it every speckled and S sheep and every black
30:32 black lamb, and the S and speckled among the
30:33 is not speckled and S among the goats and
30:35 that were striped and S, and all the she-goats
30:35 that were speckled and S, every one that had
30:39 so the flocks brought forth striped, speckled, and S
31:8 If he said, 'The S shall be your wages,'
31:8 all the flock bore S; and if he said,
31:10 the flock were striped, S, and mottled.
31:12 the flock are striped, S, and mottled; for I
Jude 1:23 hating even the garment S by the flesh.

SPRANG (10)

Judg 6:21 unleavened cakes; and there S up fire from the
Tob 2:4 I tasted anything I S up and removed the
7:6 Then Raguel S up and kissed him and wept.
Esth 15:8 and in alarm he S from his throne and
Mt 13:5 soil, and immediately they S up, since they had
Mk 4:5 soil, and immediately it S up, since it had
10:50 off his mantle he S up and came to
Jn 21:7 stripped for work, and S into the sea.
Acts 14:10 And he S up and walked.
28:13 day a south wind S up, and on the

SPREAD (144)

Gen 10:5 From these the coastland peoples S
10:18 families of the Canaanites S abroad.
10:32 from these the nations S abroad on the earth
28:14 earth, and you shall S abroad to the west
41:56 when the famine had S over all the land,
Ex 1:11 and the more they S abroad.
25:20 The cherubim shall S out their wings above,
29:2 oil, and unleavened wafers S with oil.
37:9 cherubim S out their wings above, overshadowing
Lev 2:4 oil, or unleavened wafers S with oil.
7:12 with oil, unleavened wafers S with oil, and cakes
13:5 the disease has not S in the skin, then
13:6 the disease has not S in the skin, then
13:8 if the eruption has S in the skin, then
13:23 place and does not S, it is the scar
13:28 place and does not S in the skin, but
13:32 the itch has not S, and there is in
13:34 the itch has not S in the skin and
13:36 if the itch has S in the skin, the
13:51 If the disease has S in the garment, in
13:53 the disease has not S in the garment in
13:55 the disease has not S, it is unclean; you
14:39 if the disease has S in the walls of
14:44 if the disease has S in the house, it
14:48 the disease has not S in the house after
Num 4:6 covering of goatskin, and S over that a cloth
4:7 the Presence they shall S a cloth of blue,
4:8 it; then they shall S over them a cloth
4:11 golden altar they shall S a cloth of blue,
4:13 from the altar, and S a purple cloth over
4:14 altar; and they shall S upon it a covering
6:15 oil, and unleavened wafers S with oil, and their
11:32 ten homers; and they S them out for themselves
21:30 laid waste until fire S to Medeba."
Deut 22:17 virginity.' And they shall S the garment before the
Judg 8:25 And they S a garment, and every man cast
Ruth 3:9 am Ruth, your maidservant; S your skirt over your
1Sam 4:2 and when the battle S, Israel was defeated by
9:25 city, a bed was S for Saul upon the
30:16 down, behold, they were S abroad over all the
2Sam 5:18 Philistines had come and S out in the valley
5:22 up yet again, and S out in the valley
17:19 the woman took and S a covering over the
18:8 The battle S over the face of all the
21:10 Aiah took sackcloth, and S it for herself on
1Kgs 6:27 of the cherubim were S out so that a
6:32 them with gold, and S gold upon the cherubim
8:7 For the cherubim S out their wings over the
8:22 assembly of Israel, and S forth his hands toward
2Kgs 8:15 it in water and S it over his face,
19:14 of the LORD, and S it before the LORD.
1Chr 28:18 of the cherubim that S their wings and covered
2Chr 5:8 For the cherubim S out their wings over the
6:12 assembly of Israel, and S forth his hands.
6:13 assembly of Israel, and S forth his hands toward
26:8 Uzziah, and his fame S even to the border
26:15 And his fame S far, for he was marvelously
31:5 as the command was S abroad, the people of
Ezra 9:5 upon my knees and S out my hands to
Neh 4:19 is great and widely S, and we are separated

S

Jud 4:11 on their heads and S out their sackcloth before
5:10 When a famine S over Canaan they went down
7:3 the spring, and they S out in breadth over
7:18 tents and supply trains S out in great number,
12:15 her maid went and S on the ground for
16:25 no one ever again S terror among the people
Esth 9:4 house, and his fame S throughout all the provinces;
Job 8:16 sun, and his shoots S over his garden.
17:13 my house, if I S my couch in darkness,
29:19 the sand, my roots S out to the waters,
37:18 Can you, like him, S out the skies, hard
Ps 44:20 of our God, or S forth our hands to
78:19 God, saying, "Can God S a table in the
88:9 thee, O LORD; I S out my hands to
105:39 He S a cloud for a covering, and fire
136:6 ever; to him who S out the earth upon
140:5 with cords they have S a net, by the
Prov 1:17 vain is a net S in the sight of
15:7 lips of the wise S knowledge; not so the
Wis 17:21 alone heavy night was S, an image of the
18:10 for their children was S abroad.
Sir 24:15 like choice myrrh I S a pleasant odor, like
24:16 Like a terebinth I S out my branches, and
51:19 I was strict; I S out my hands to
Is 1:15 When you S forth your hands, I will hide
16:8 the desert; its shoots S abroad and passed over
19:8 they will languish who S nets upon the water.
21:5 prepare the table, they S the rugs, they eat,
25:7 the veil that is S over all nations.
25:11 And he will S out his hands in the
33:23 or keep the sail S out.
37:14 of the LORD, and S it before the LORD.
42:5 stretched them out, who S forth the earth and
44:24 the heavens alone, who S out the earth—
48:13 and my right hand S out the heavens; when
54:3 For you will S abroad to the right and
58:5 a rush, and to S sackcloth and ashes under
65:2 I S out my hands all the day to
Jer 8:2 and they shall be S before the sun and
10:20 is no one to S my tent again, and
43:10 hid, and he will S his royal canopy over
48:40 like an eagle, and S his wings against Moab;
49:22 like an eagle, and S his wings against Bozrah,
Lam 1:13 made it descend; he S a net for my
Ezek 1:11 And their wings were S out above; each creature
1:22 firmament, shining like crystal, S out above their
2:10 in it; and he S it before me; and
12:13 And I will S my net over him, and
16:8 for love; and I S my skirt over you,
17:20 I will S my net over him, and he
19:8 on every side; they S their net over him;
23:41 couch, with a table S before it on which
32:23 by the sword, who S terror in the land
32:24 the nether world, who S terror in the land
32:25 terror of them was S in the land of
32:26 the sword; for they S terror in the land
32:32 For he S terror in the land of the
Hos 5:1 Mizpah, and a net S upon Tabor.
7:13 they go, I will S over them my net;
14:6 poplar; his shoots shall S out; his beauty shall
Joel 2:2 Like blackness there is S upon the mountains a
Zech 2:6 LORD; for I have S you abroad as the
Mal 2:3 rebuke your offspring, and S dung upon your faces,
1Mac 6:40 the king's army was S out on the high
11:47 about him and then S out through the city;
14:10 defense, till his renown S to the ends of
2Mac 4:39 report of them had S abroad, the populace gathered
7:5 smoke from the pan S widely, but the brothers
8:7 talk of his valor S everywhere.
Mt 4:24 So his fame S throughout all Syria, and they
9:31 they went away and S his fame through all
21:8 Most of the crowd S their garments on the
21:8 from the trees and S them on the road.
28:15 this story has been S among the Jews to
Mk 1:28 at once his fame S everywhere throughout all the
1:45 about it, and to S the news, so that
11:8 And many S their garments on the road, and
11:8 the road, and others S leafy branches which they
Lk 7:17 this report concerning him S through the whole of
19:36 he rode along, they S their garments on the
Jn 21:23 The saying S abroad among the brethren that this
Acts 4:17 order that it may S no further among the
13:49 word of the Lord S throughout all the region.
Rom 5:12 sin, and so death S to all men because

SPREADING (12)

Lev 13:27 day; if it is S in the skin, then
13:57 of skin, it is S; you shall burn with
Deut 32:11 flutters over its young, S out its wings, catching
1Sam 2:24 people of the LORD S abroad.
Job 36:29 any one understand the S of the clouds, the
Sir 14:18 flourishing leaves on a S tree which sheds some
48:20 Lord who is merciful, S forth their hands toward
Is 18:5 pruning hooks, and the S branches he will hew
Ezek 17:6 and became a low S vine, and its branches
26:5 a place for the S of nets; for I
26:14 a place for the S of nets; you shall
47:10 a place for the S of nets; its fish

SPREADS (13)

Lev 13:7 But if the eruption S in the skin, after
13:22 days; and if it S in the skin, then
13:35 But if the itch S in the skin after
Job 26:9 of the moon, and S over it his cloud.
39:26 the hawk soars, and S his wings toward the
41:30 like sharp potsherds; he S himself like a threshing
Prov 7:16 couch with coverings, colored S of Egyptian linen;
16:28 A perverse man S strife, and a whisperer separates
29:5 who flatters his neighbor S a net for his
Is 25:11 it as a swimmer S his hands out to
40:22 like a curtain, and S them like a tent
Nah 3:16 The locust S its wings and flies away.
2Cor 2:14 triumph, and through us S the fragrance of the

SPRIG

Ezek 17:22 myself will take a S from the lofty top

SPRING (62)

Gen 16:7 found her by a S of water in the
16:7 in the wilderness, the S on the way to
18:10 to you in the S, and Sarah your wife
18:14 to you, in the S, and Sarah shall have
24:13 am standing by the S of water, and the
24:16 went down to the S, and filled her jar,
24:29 Laban ran out to the man, to the S
24:30 he was standing by the camels at the S
24:42 came today to the S, and said, 'O LORD,
24:43 am standing by the S of water; let the
24:45 went down to the S, and drew.
35:11 you, and kings shall S from you.
49:22 fruitful bough by a S; his branches run over
Lev 11:36 Nevertheless a S or a cistern holding water shall
Num 21:17 Israel sang this song: S up, O well!—Sing
Josh 15:9 the mountain to the S of the Waters of
18:15 to Ephron, to the S of the Waters of
Judg 7:1 and encamped beside the S of Harod; and the
2Sam 11:1 In the S of the year, the time when
1Kgs 20:22 do; for in the S the king of Syria
20:26 In the S Ben-hadad mustered the Syrians, and went
2Kgs 2:21 he went to the S of water and threw
3:25 covered; they stopped every S of water, and felled
4:17 that time the following S, as Elisha had said
13:20 the land in the S of the year.
1Chr 20:1 In the S of the year, the time when
2Chr 36:10 In the S of the year King Nebuchadnezzar sent
Jud 7:3 near Bethulia, beside the S, and they spread out
7:12 take possession of the S of water that flows
12:7 and bathed at the S in the camp.
12:8 came up from the S she prayed the Lord
Esth 10:6 The tiny S which became a river, and there
11:10 though from a tiny S there came a great
Job 8:19 way; and out of the earth others will S
29:23 mouths as for the S rain.
Ps 85:11 Faithfulness will S up from the ground, and
114:8 the flint into a S of water.
Prov 16:15 clouds that bring the S rain.
25:26 Like a muddied S or a polluted fountain is
Wis 2:7 let no flower of S pass by us.
Sir 21:13 a flood, and his counsel like a flowing S
50:8 like lilies by a S of water, like a
Is 42:9 now declare; before they S forth I tell you
44:4 They shall S up like grass amid waters, like
45:8 it cause righteousness to S up also; I the
58:8 your healing shall S up speedily; your righteousness
58:11 watered garden, like a S of water, whose waters
61:11 sown in it to S up, so the Lord
61:11 righteousness and praise to S forth before all the
Jer 3:3 been withheld, and the S rain has not come;
5:24 autumn rain and the S rain, and keeps for
33:15 a righteous Branch to S forth for David; and
Ezek 29:21 cause a horn to S forth to the house

S

Hos 6:3 the showers, as the S rains that water the
13:15 shall dry up, his S shall be parched; it
Amos 3:5 Does a snare S up from the ground, when
Zech 10:1 the season of the S rain, from the LORD
2Mac 14:30 this austerity did not S from the best motives.
Jn 4:14 become in him a S of water welling up
1Thes 2:3 our appeal does not S from error or uncleanness,
Heb 12:15 S up and cause trouble, and by it the
Jas 3:11 Does a S pour forth from the same opening

SPRINGING

Gen 26:19 there a well of S water,

SPRINGS (38)

Gen 36:24 who found the hot S in the wilderness, as
Ex 15:27 where there were twelve S of water and seventy
Num 33:9 Elim there were twelve S of water and seventy
Deut 8:7 water, of fountains and S, flowing forth in valleys
Josh 15:19 Negeb, give me also S of water." And Caleb
15:19 gave her the upper S and the lower springs.
15:19 gave her the upper springs and the lower S
Judg 1:15 Negeb, give me also S of water." And Caleb
1:15 gave her the upper S and the lower springs.
1:15 gave her the upper springs and the lower S
1Kgs 18:5 land to all the S of water and to
2Kgs 3:19 and stop up all S of water, and ruin
19:29 the second year what S of the same; then
2Chr 32:3 the water of the S that were outside the
32:4 they stopped all the S and the brook that
Jud 6:11 and came to the S below Bethulia.
7:7 city, and visited the S that supplied their water,
7:17 water supply and the S of the Israelites.
Job 38:16 you entered into the S of the sea, or
Ps 74:15 Thou didst cleave open S and brooks; thou didst
84:6 it a place of S; the early rain also
87:7 alike say, "All my S are in you."
104:10 Thou makest S gush forth in the valleys; they
107:33 rivers into a desert, S of water into thirsty
107:35 a parched land into S of water.
Prov 4:24 from it flow the S of life.
5:16 Should your S be scattered abroad, streams of water
8:24 when there were no S abounding with water.
Song 5:12 are like doves beside S of water, bathed in
Is 35:7 and the thirsty ground S of water; the haunt
37:30 the second year what S of the same; then
41:18 and the dry land S of water.
43:19 new thing; now it S forth, do you not
49:10 lead them, and by S of water will guide
Dan 3:78 Bless the Lord, you S, sing praise to him
Hos 10:4 covenants; so judgment S up like poisonous weeds
2Pet 2:17 These are waterless S and mists driven by a
Rev 7:17 will guide them to S of living water; and

SPRINKLE (20)

Ex 29:21 the anointing oil, and S it upon Aaron and
Lev 4:6 in the blood and S part of the blood
4:17 in the blood and S it seven times before
5:9 it, and he shall S some of the blood
14:7 water; and he shall S it seven times upon
14:16 his left hand, and S some oil with his
14:27 left hand; and shall S with his right finger
14:51 the running water, and S the house seven times.
16:14 of the bull, and S it with his finger
16:14 mercy seat he shall S the blood with his
16:19 And he shall S some of the blood upon
17:6 and the priest shall S the blood on the
Num 8:7 them, to cleanse them: S the water of expiation
18:17 You shall S their blood upon the altar, and
19:4 with his finger, and S some of her blood
19:18 in the water, and S it upon the tent,
19:19 the clean person shall S upon the unclean on
Ezek 36:25 I will S clean water upon you, and you
43:24 and the priests shall S salt upon them and
2Mac 1:21 ordered the priests to S the liquid on the

SPRINKLED (19)

Lev 6:27 of its blood is S on a garment, you
6:27 on which it was S in a holy place.
8:11 And he S some of it on the altar
8:30 on the altar, and S it upon Aaron and
2Chr 30:16 of God; the priests S the blood which they
35:11 lamb, and the priests S the blood which they
Tob 11:11 his father, and he S the gall upon his
Job 2:12 rent their robes and S dust upon their heads
Is 63:3 wrath; their lifeblood is S upon my garments, and
Hos 7:10 not; gray hairs are S upon him, and he
1Mac 3:47 put on sackcloth and S ashes on their heads,
4:39 great lamentation, and S themselves with ashes.
2Mac 10:25 Maccabeus and his men S dust upon their heads
14:15 of the Gentiles, they S dust upon their heads
Heb 9:19 wool and hyssop, and S both the book itself
9:21 the same way he S with the blood both
10:22 faith, with our hearts S clean from an evil
11:28 kept the Passover and S the blood, so that
12:24 covenant, and to the S blood that speaks more

SPRINKLES

Num 19:21 He who S the water for impurity shall wash

SPRINKLING (3)

Lev 16:15 blood of the bull, S it upon the mercy
Heb 9:13 For if the S of defiled persons with the
1Pet 1:2 Jesus Christ and for S with his blood: May

SPROUT (10)

Num 17:5 whom I choose shall S; thus I will make
Deut 29:23 where no grass can S, an overthrow like that
2Sam 23:4 that makes grass to S from the earth.
Job 5:6 dust, nor does trouble S from the ground;
14:7 down, that it will S again, and that its
Ps 92:7 that, though the wicked S like grass and all
132:17 make a horn to S for David; I have
Is 45:8 open, that salvation may S forth, and let it
55:10 it bring forth and S, giving seed to the
Mk 4:27 and the seed should S and grow, he knows

SPROUTED (4)

Gen 41:6 And behold, after them S seven ears, thin and
41:23 by the east wind, S after them,
Num 17:8 house of Levi had S and put forth buds,
Ezek 17:6 willow twig, and it S and became a low

SPROUTING

Ezek 17:9 that all its fresh S leaves wither?

SPRUNG (3)

Gen 2:5 the field had yet S up–for the LORD
Tob 8:6 From them the race of mankind has S
1Mac 4:38 courts they saw bushes S up as in a

SPUN (3)

Ex 35:25 women who had ability S with their hands, and
35:25 brought what they had S in blue and purple
35:26 were moved with ability S the goats' hair.

SPURN (5)

Lev 26:15 these commandments, if you S my statutes, and if
26:44 enemies, I will not S them, neither will I
Ps 77:7 spirit: "Will the Lord S for ever, and never
119:118 Thou dost S all who go astray from thy
Jer 14:21 Do not S us, for thy name's sake; do

SPURNED (7)

Lev 26:43 their iniquity, because they S my ordinances, and
Deut 32:19 LORD saw it, and S them, because of the
Ps 107:11 words of God, and S the counsel of the
Lam 2:6 his fierce indignation has S king and priest.
Hos 8:3 Israel has S the good; the enemy shall pursue
8:5 I have S your calf, O Samaria.
Heb 10:29 the man who has S the Son of God,

SPURNS (3)

Deut 22:13 to her, and then S her,
22:16 to wife, and he S her;
Ps 36:4 is not good; he S not evil.

SPY (20)

Num 13:2 Moses, "Send men to S out the land of
13:16 whom Moses sent to S out the land.
13:17 Moses sent them to S out the land of
13:32 we have gone, to S it out, is a
14:7 we passed through to S it out, is an
14:36 whom Moses sent to S out the land, and
14:38 men who went to S out the land.
21:32 And Moses sent to S out Jazer; and they
Josh 6:25 whom Joshua sent to S out Jericho.
7:2 them, "Go up and S out the land." And
14:7 me from Kadesh-barnea to S out the land; and
Judg 1:23 of Joseph sent to S out Bethel.
18:2 and from Eshtaol, to S out the land and
18:14 who had gone to S out the country of
18:17 who had gone to S out the land went

S

STAGGER (9)
Job 12:25 and he makes them S like a drunken man.
Is 19:14 they have made Egypt S in all her doings
28:7 reel with wine and S with strong drink; the
28:7 confused with wine, they S with strong drink; they
29:9 but not with wine; S, but not with strong
Jer 25:16 They shall drink and S and be crazed because
Lam 5:13 the mill; and boys S under loads of wood.
Obad 1:16 they shall drink, and S, and shall be as
Hab 2:16 Drink, yourself, and S

STAGGERED
Ps 107:27 plight; they reeled and S like drunken men, and

STAGGERING (2)
Is 51:17 have drunk to the dregs the bowl of S
51:22 hand the cup of S; the bowl of my

STAGGERS (2)
Is 19:14 as a drunken man S in his vomit.
24:20 The earth S like a drunken man, it sways

STAGNANT
Ezek 47:8 when it enters the S waters of the sea,

STAIN (4)
Tob 3:15 that I did not S my name or the
Sir 33:22 you do; bring no S upon your honor.
47:20 You put S upon your honor, and defiled your
Jer 2:22 use much soap, the S of your guilt is

STAINED (3)
Jud 9:3 had practiced, to be S with blood, and thou
Wis 15:4 of painters, a figure S with varied colors,
Is 63:3 garments, and I have S all my raiment.

STAINING
Jas 3:6 world among our members, S the whole body, setting

STAIRS (4)
1Kgs 6:8 one went up by S to the middle story,
Neh 3:15 as far as the S that go down from
9:4 Upon the S of the Levites stood Jeshua, Bani,
12:37 before them by the S of the city of

STAIRWAY (4)
Ezek 40:31 its jambs, and its S had eight steps.
40:34 either side; and its S had eight steps.
40:37 either side; and its S had eight steps.
41:7 of the temple a S led upward, and thus

STAKE (2)
Job 6:29 Turn now, my vindication is at S
Sir 27:2 As a S is driven firmly into a fissure

STAKES (2)
Is 33:20 an immovable tent, whose S will never be plucked
54:2 not back, lengthen your cords and strengthen your S

STALK (2)
Gen 41:5 grain, plump and good, were growing on one S
41:22 ears growing on one S, full and good;

STALKS (3)
Josh 2:6 hid them with the S of flax which she
Ps 91:6 nor the pestilence that S in darkness, nor the
Prov 6:26 bread, but an adulteress S a man's very life.

STALL (2)
Amos 6:4 the midst of the S;
Mal 4:2 shall go forth leaping like calves from the S

STALLION
Sir 33:6 A S is like a mocking friend; he neighs

STALLIONS (4)
Jer 5:8 They were well-fed lusty S, each neighing for his
8:16 the neighing of their S the whole land quakes.
47:3 the hoofs of his S, at the rushing of
50:11 grass, and neigh like S,

STALLS (4)
1Kgs 4:26 also had forty thousand S of horses for his
2Chr 9:25 Solomon had four thousand S for horses and
32:28 wine, and oil; and S for all kinds of
Hab 3:17 no herd in the S,

STALWART (2)
1Mac 11:44 Jonathan sent three thousand S men to him at
2Mac 12:27 S young men took their stand before the walls

STAMMERERS
Is 32:4 the tongue of the S will speak readily and

STAMMERING
Is 33:19 which you cannot comprehend, S in a tongue which

STAMP (2)
Ezek 6:11 "Clap your hands, and S your foot, and say,
Heb 1:3 and bears the very S of his nature, upholding

STAMPED (4)
2Sam 22:43 I crushed them and S them down like the
Ezek 25:6 clapped your hands and S your feet and rejoiced
Dan 7:7 broke in pieces, and S the residue with its
7:19 broke in pieces, and S the residue with its

STAMPING
Jer 47:3 the noise of the S of the hoofs of

STAND (286)
Gen 19:9 But they said, S back!" And they said, "This
24:31 LORD; why do you S outside?
Ex 8:21 flies, and also the ground on which they S
9:11 the magicians could not S before Moses because of
9:13 in the morning and S before Pharaoh, and say
14:13 the people, "Fear not, S firm, and see the
17:6 Behold, I will S before you there on the
17:9 Amalek; tomorrow I will S on the top of
18:14 and all the people S about you from morning
19:17 and they took their S at the foot of
33:9 cloud would descend and S at the door of
33:21 me where you shall S upon the rock;
Lev 19:16 and you shall not S forth against the life
26:37 have no power to S before your enemies.
27:14 as the priest values it, so it shall S
27:17 of jubilee, it shall S at your full valuation;
Num 11:16 let them take their S there with you.
16:9 the LORD, and to S before the congregation to
22:22 the LORD took his S in the way as
22:34 know that thou didst S in the road against
23:3 Balaam said to Balak, S beside your burnt offering,
23:15 Balaam said to Balak, S here beside your burnt
27:19 him; cause him to S before Eleazar the priest
27:21 And he shall S before Eleazar the priest, who
27:22 and caused him to S before Eleazar the priest
30:4 all her vows shall S, and every pledge by
30:4 pledge by which she has bound herself shall S
30:5 has bound herself, shall S; and the LORD will
30:7 then her vows shall S, and her pledges by
30:7 pledges by which she has bound herself shall S
30:9 has bound herself, shall S against her.
30:11 all her vows shall S, and every pledge by
30:11 every pledge by which she bound herself shall S
30:12 of herself, shall not S: her husband has made
31:23 lead, everything that can S the fire, you shall
31:23 impurity; and whatever cannot S the fire, you shall
Deut 5:31 But you, S here by me, and I will
7:24 shall be able to S against you, until you
9:2 it said, 'Who can S before the sons of
10:8 of the LORD, to S before the LORD to
11:25 shall be able to S against you; the LORD
18:5 all your tribes, to S and minister in the
18:7 all his fellow-Levites who S to minister there before
24:11 You shall S outside, and the man to whom
27:12 the Jordan, these shall S upon Mount Gerizim to
27:13 And these shall S upon Mount Ebal for the
29:10 "You S this day all of you before the
Josh 1:5 shall be able to S before you all the
3:8 the Jordan, you shall S still in the Jordan.'"
3:13 down from above shall S in one heap."
5:15 the place where you S is holy." And Joshua
7:12 people of Israel cannot S before their enemies; they
7:13 O Israel; you cannot S before your enemies, until
10:8 a man of them S before you."
10:12 sight of Israel, "Sun, S thou still at Gibeon,
20:4 these cities and shall S at the entrance of
Judg 4:20 he said to her, S at the door of
16:25 They made him S between the pillars;
1Sam 6:20 "Who is able to S before the LORD, this
12:7 Now therefore S still, that I may plead with
12:16 Now therefore S still and see this great thing,
14:9 you,' then we will S still in our place,

S

	17:16	forward and took his S, morning and evening.
	19:3	will go out and S beside my father in
2Sam	1:9	he said to me, S beside me and slay
	2:25	band, and took their S on the top of
	15:2	to rise early and S beside the way of
	18:30	said, "Turn aside, and S here." So he turned
	20:11	Joab's men took his S by Amasa, and said,
	23:5	does not my house S so with God?
	23:12	But he took his S in the midst of
1Kgs	7:27	stands of bronze; each S was four cubits long,
	7:30	Moreover each S had four bronze wheels and axles
	7:34	four corners of each S; the supports were of
	7:35	the top of the S there was a round
	7:35	the top of the S its stays and its
	8:11	the priests could not S to minister because of
	10:8	your servants, who continually S before you and hear
	17:1	lives, before whom I S, there shall be neither
	18:15	lives, before whom I S, I will surely show
	19:11	said, "Go forth, and S upon the mount before
2Kgs	5:11	out to me, and S, and call on the
	10:4	two kings could not S before him; how then
	10:4	not stand before him; how then can we S
1Chr	11:14	But he took his S in the midst of
	23:30	And they shall S every morning, thanking and
2Chr	5:14	the priests could not S to minister because of
	9:7	your servants, who continually S before you and hear
	20:9	or famine, we will S before this house, and
	20:17	battle; take your position, S still, and see the
	29:11	has chosen you to S in his presence, to
	32:10	you relying, that you S siege in Jerusalem?
	34:32	Jerusalem and in Benjamin S to it.
	35:5	And S in the holy place according to the
Ezra	9:15	guilt, for none can S before thee because of
	10:13	heavy rain; we cannot S in the open.
	10:14	Let our officials S for the whole assembly; let
Neh	9:5	Shebaniah, and Pethahiah, said, S up and bless the
Jud	8:33	S at the city gate tonight, and I will
	10:16	And when you S before him, do not be
	13:3	told her maid to S outside the bedchamber and
Esth	9:2	one could make a S against them, for the
	16:3	in their inability to S prosperity they even undertake
Job	8:15	but it does not S; he lays hold of
	19:25	at last he will S upon the earth;
	30:20	not answer me; I S, and thou dost not
	30:28	by the sun; I S up in the assembly,
	32:16	not speak, because they S there, and answer no
	33:5	your words in order before me; take your S
	39:24	the ground; he cannot S still at the sound
	40:12	low; and tread down the wicked where they S
	41:10	is he that can S before me?
Ps	1:5	the wicked will not S in the judgment, nor
	5:5	The boastful may not S before thy eyes; thou
	10:1	[Selah] Why dost thou S afar off, O LORD?
	20:8	we shall rise and S upright.
	22:23	Jacob, glorify him, and S in awe of him,
	24:3	And who shall S in his holy place?
	33:8	inhabitants of the world S in awe of him!
	38:11	My friends and companions S aloof from my plague,
	38:11	plague, and my kinsmen S afar off.
	76:7	Who can S before thee when once thy anger
	78:13	and made the waters S like a heap.
	89:28	and my covenant will S firm for him.
	89:37	for ever; it shall S firm while the skies
	89:43	hast not made him S in battle.
	119:91	By thy appointment they S this day; for all
	130:3	O LORD, shouldst mark iniquities, Lord, who could S
	134:1	of the LORD, who S by night in the
	135:2	the LORD, you that S in the house of
	147:17	like morsels; who can S before his cold?
Prov	8:2	paths she takes her S;
	12:7	more, but the house of the righteous will S
	22:29	he will S before kings; he will not stand
	22:29	kings; he will not S before obscure men.
	25:6	the king's presence or S in the place of
	27:4	overwhelming; but who can S before jealousy?
Eccl	4:15	youth, who was to S in his place;
Wis	5:1	the righteous man will S with great confidence in
	6:7	of all will not S in awe of any
Sir	6:8	convenience, but will not S by you in your
	6:10	companion, but will not S by you in your
	6:34	S in the assembly of the elders.
	11:18	S by your covenant and attend to it, and
	12:15	falter, he will not S by you.
	22:16	high place will not S firm against the wind;
	22:16	fool's purpose will not S firm against any fear.
	22:21	him in his prosperity; S by him in time
	27:14	swearing makes one's hair S on end, and their
	37:9	and then S aloof to see what will happen
	40:12	but good faith will S for ever.
	40:25	silver make the foot S sure, but good counsel
	42:17	that the universe may S firm in his glory.
	43:10	the Holy One they S as ordered, they never
	44:13	Their descendants S by the covenants; their children
	47:13	prepare a sanctuary to S for ever.
Is	7:7	GOD: It shall not S, and it shall not
	8:10	but it will not S, for God is with
	11:10	root of Jesse shall S as an ensign to
	14:24	purposed, so shall it S,
	21:8	"Upon a watchtower I S, O Lord, continually by
	22:7	the horsemen took their S at the gates.
	28:18	Sheol will not S; when the overwhelming scourge
	29:23	of Jacob, and will S in awe of the
	40:8	of our God will S for ever.
	44:11	all assemble, let them S forth, they shall be
	46:10	saying, 'My counsel shall S, and I will accomplish
	47:12	S fast in your enchantments and your many
	47:13	many counsels; let them S forth and save you,
	48:13	call to them, they S forth together.
	50:8	Let us S up together.
	51:17	Rouse yourself, rouse yourself, S up, O Jerusalem,
	61:5	Aliens shall S and feed your flocks, foreigners shall
Jer	6:16	Thus says the LORD: S by the roads, and
	7:2	Jeremiah from the LORD: S in the gate of
	7:10	and then come and S before me in this
	14:6	The wild asses S on the bare heights, they
	15:19	you, and you shall S before me.
	17:19	to me: "Go and S in the Benjamin Gate,
	26:2	"Thus says the LORD: S in the court of
	30:18	and the palace shall S where it used to
	35:19	lack a man to S before me."
	40:10	dwell at Mizpah, to S for you before the
	44:28	know whose word will S, mine or theirs.
	44:29	my words will surely S against you for evil:
	46:14	Memphis and Tahpanhes; Say, S ready and be
	46:15	Why did not your bull S
	46:21	together, they did not S; for the day of
	48:19	S by the way and watch, O inhabitant of
	49:19	What shepherd can S before me?
	50:44	What shepherd can S before me?
	51:3	and let him not S up in his coat
	51:29	LORD's purposes against Babylon S, to make the
	51:50	from the sword, go, S not still!
Bar	5:5	Arise, O Jerusalem, S upon the height and look
	6:27	gods are made to S, lest they fall to
Ezek	2:1	me, "Son of man, S upon your feet, and
	13:5	Israel, that it might S in battle in the
	17:14	his covenant it might S
	22:30	up the wall and S in the breach before
	27:29	pilots of the sea S on the shore
	46:2	and shall take his S by the post of
	47:10	Fishermen will S beside the sea; from Engedi to
Dan	1:5	time they were to S before the king.
	2:44	end, and it shall S for ever;
	7:4	ground and made to S upon two feet like
	8:4	southward; no beast could S before him, and there
	8:7	had no power to S before him, but he
	10:11	speak to you, and S upright, for now I
	11:15	the south shall not S, or even his picked
	11:15	troops, for there shall be no strength to S
	11:16	will, and none shall S before him; and he
	11:16	him; and he shall S in the glorious land,
	11:17	but it shall not S or be to his
	11:25	but he shall not S, for plots shall be
	11:32	know their God shall S firm and take action.
	12:13	shall rest, and shall S in your allotted place
	13:48	Taking his S in the midst of them, he
Amos	2:15	the bow shall not S, and he who is
	7:2	How can Jacob S
	7:5	How can Jacob S
Mic	5:4	And he shall S and feed his flock in
Nah	1:6	Who can S before his indignation?
Hab	2:1	I will take my S to watch, and station
Zech	4:14	the two anointed who S by the Lord of
	14:4	day his feet shall S on the Mount of
Mal	3:2	coming, and who can S when he appears?
1Mac	4:18	But S now against our enemies and fight them,
	5:44	was conquered; they could S before Judas no longer.
	9:11	camp and took its S for the encounter.
	10:72	you that you cannot S before us, for your
2Mac	12:27	young men took their S before the walls and
	13:12	and ordered them to S ready.
Mt	5:15	bushel, but on a S, and it gives light

S

6:5 for they love to S and pray in the
12:25 divided against itself will S;
12:26 divided against himself; how then will his kingdom S
20:6 them, 'Why do you S here idle all day?'
Mk 3:24 is divided against itself, that kingdom cannot S
3:25 itself, that house will not be able to S
3:26 is divided, he cannot S, but is coming to
4:21 or under a bed, and not on a S
11:25 And whenever you S praying, forgive, if you have
13:9 synagogues; and you will S before governors and
Lk 1:19 "I am Gabriel, who S in the presence of
6:8 withered hand, "Come and S here." And he rose
8:16 puts it on a S, that those who enter
11:18 is divided against himself, how will his kingdom S
11:33 bushel, but on a S, that those who enter
13:25 you will begin to S outside and to knock
21:36 take place, and to S before the Son of
Acts 1:11 Galilee, why do you S looking into heaven?
5:20 and said, "Go and S in the temple and
10:26 lifted him up, saying, S up; I too am
14:10 in a loud voice, S upright on your feet."
26:6 And now I S here on trial for hope
26:16 But rise and S upon your feet; for I
26:22 God, and so I S here testifying both to
27:24 afraid, Paul; you must S before Caesar; and lo,
Rom 5:2 grace in which we S, and we rejoice in
11:20 their unbelief, but you S fast only through faith.
11:20 not become proud, but S in awe.
14:4 for the Master is able to make him S
14:10 For we shall all S before the judgment seat
1Cor 15:1 received, in which you S,
16:13 Be watchful, S firm in your faith, be courageous,
2Cor 1:24 your joy, for you S firm in your faith.
Gal 5:1 has set us free; S fast therefore, and do
Eph 6:11 may be able to S against the wiles of
6:13 the evil day, and having done all, to S
6:14 S therefore, having girded your loins with truth, and
Phil 1:27 of you that you S firm in one spirit,
4:1 my joy and crown, S firm thus in the
Col 2:18 of angels, taking his S on visions, puffed up
4:12 prayers, that you may S mature and fully assured
1Thes 3:8 we live, if you S fast in the Lord.
2Thes 2:15 So then, brethren, S firm and hold to the
1Tim 5:20 that the rest may S in fear.
Jas 2:3 to the poor man, S there," or, "Sit at
1Pet 5:12 true grace of God; S fast in it.
Rev 3:20 Behold, I S at the door and knock; if
6:17 come, and who can S before it?"
8:2 the seven angels who S before God, and seven
11:4 the two lampstands which S before the Lord of
18:10 her burning; they will S far-off, in fear of
18:15 wealth from her, will S far-off, in fear of

STANDARD (22)

Num 1:52 man by his own S;
2:2 each by his own S, with the ensigns of
2:3 shall be of the S of the camp of
2:10 side shall be the S of the camp of
2:17 out, each in position, S by standard.
2:17 they set out, each in position, standard by S
2:18 side shall be the S of the camp of
2:25 side shall be the S of the camp of
2:31 shall set out last, S by standard."
2:31 They shall set out last, standard by S
10:14 The S of the camp of the men of
10:18 And the S of the camp of Reuben set
10:22 And the S of the camp of the men
10:25 Then the S of the camp of the men
2Chr 3:3 cubits of the old S, was sixty cubits, and
Is 31:9 his officers desert the S in panic," says the
Jer 4:6 fortified cities!' Raise a S toward Zion, flee for
4:21 must I see the S, and hear the sound
51:12 Set up a S against the walls of Babylon;
51:27 "Set up a S on the earth, blow the
Ezek 45:11 homer shall be the S measure.
Rom 6:17 the heart to the S of teaching to which

STANDARDS (2)

Num 2:34 they encamped by their S, and so they set
1Cor 1:26 wise according to worldly S, not many were

STANDING (130)

Gen 24:13 Behold, I am S by the spring of water,
24:30 and behold, he was S by the camels at
24:43 go, behold, I am S by the spring of
41:1 dreamed that he was S by the Nile,
41:17 my dream I was S on the banks of
Ex 3:5 on which you are S is holy ground."
22:6 stacked grain or the S grain or the field
33:10 the pillar of cloud S at the door of
Num 22:23 angel of the LORD S in the road, with
22:31 angel of the LORD S in the way, with
23:6 princes of Moab were S beside his burnt offering.
23:17 and, lo, he was S beside his burnt offering,
Deut 16:9 the sickle to the S grain.
23:25 go into your neighbor's S grain, you may pluck
23:25 sickle to your neighbor's S grain.
Judg 15:5 foxes go into the S grain of the Philistines,
15:5 the shocks and the S grain, as well as
1Sam 1:26 the woman who was S here in your presence,
19:20 prophets prophesying, and Samuel S as head over
22:6 all his servants were S about him.
2Sam 13:31 his servants who were S by rent their garments.
1Kgs 10:19 rests and two lions S beside the arm rests,
13:1 Jeroboam was S by the altar to burn incense.
13:25 road, and the lion S by the body.
13:28 ass and the lion S beside the body.
22:19 the host of heaven S beside him on his
2Kgs 2:7 as they both were S by the Jordan.
9:17 Now the watchman was S on the tower in
11:14 there was the king S by the pillar, according
1Chr 21:15 of the LORD was S by the threshing floor
21:16 angel of the LORD S between earth and heaven,
2Chr 9:18 rests and two lions S beside the arm rests,
18:18 the host of heaven S on his right hand
23:13 there was the king S by his pillar at
Neh 7:3 while they are still S guard let them shut
12:25 Akkub were gatekeepers S guard at the storehouses
Jud 5:22 this, all the men S around the tent began
10:6 Bethulia, and found Uzziah S there with the elders
13:4 Then Judith, S beside his bed, said in her
Esth 5:2 king saw Queen Esther S in the court, she
6:5 him, "Haman is there, S in the court." And
7:9 saved the king, is S in Haman's house, fifty
Ps 122:2 Our feet have been S within your gates, O
Prov 12:9 a man of humble S who works for himself
Wis 4:4 boughs for a while, S insecurely they will be
10:7 a pillar of salt S as a monument to
18:16 and touched heaven while S on the earth.
Sir 8:14 the decision will favor him because of his S
Is 6:13 oak, whose stump remains S when it is felled."
17:5 when the reaper gathers S grain and his arm
27:9 pieces, no Asherim or incense altars will remain S
Jer 28:5 the people who were S in the house of
Ezek 8:11 the son of Shaphan S among them.
10:3 Now the cherubim were S on the south side
40:3 hand; and he was S in the gateway.
43:6 While the man was S beside me, I heard
Dan 8:3 and behold, a ram S on the bank of
8:6 which I had seen S on the bank of
10:4 month, as I was S on the bank of
Hos 8:7 The S grain has no heads, it shall yield
Amos 7:7 behold, the Lord was S beside a wall built
9:1 I saw the LORD S beside the altar, and
Mic 1:11 away from you its S place.
Zech 1:8 He was S among the myrtle trees in the
1:10 the man who was S among the myrtle trees
1:11 the LORD who was S among the myrtle trees,
3:1 Joshua the high priest S before the angel of
3:1 the LORD, and Satan S at his right hand
3:3 Now Joshua was S before the angel, clothed with
3:4 to those who were S before him, "Remove the
3:5 of the LORD was S by.
3:7 among those who are S here.
2Mac 14:45 through the crowd; and S upon a steep rock,
Mt 16:28 you, there are some S here who will not
20:3 hour he saw others S idle in the market
20:6 out and found others S; and he said to
24:15 by the prophet Daniel, S in the holy place
Mk 3:31 his brethren came; and S outside they sent to
9:1 you, there are some S here who will not
Lk 1:11 angel of the Lord S on the right side
5:1 of God, he was S by the lake of
7:38 flask of ointment, and S behind him at his
8:20 and your brrethren are S outside, desiring to see
9:27 truly, there are some S here who will not
18:13 But the tax collector, S far-off, would not even
Jn 1:35 day again John was S with two of his
2:6 six stone jars were S there, for the Jewish
8:9 alone with the woman S before him.
11:42 account of the people S by, that they may
12:29 The crowd S by heard it and said that

S

18:5 who betrayed him, was S with them.
18:18 and they were S and warming themselves; Peter
18:18 also was with them, S and warming himself.
18:22 one of the officers S by struck Jesus with
18:25 Now Simon Peter was S and warming himself.
19:25 But S by the cross of Jesus were his
19:26 disciple whom he loved S near, he said to
20:14 round and saw Jesus S, but she did not
Acts 2:14 But Peter, S with the eleven, lifted up his
4:10 him this man is S before you well.
4:14 that had been healed S beside them, they had
5:23 locked and the sentries S at the doors, but
5:25 put in prison are S in the temple and
7:33 place where you are S is holy ground.
7:55 of God, and Jesus S at the right hand
7:56 the Son of man S at the right hand
11:13 had seen the angel S in his house and
12:14 told that Peter was S at the gate.
13:50 devout women of high S and the leading men
16:9 man of Macedonia was S beseeching him and saying,
17:12 Greek women of high S as well as men.
17:22 So Paul, S in the middle of the Are-opagus,
21:40 given him leave, Paul, S on the steps, motioned
22:13 came to me, and S by me said to
22:20 shed, I also was S by and approving, and
22:25 the centurion who was S by, "Is it lawful
24:20 I cried out while S among them, 'With respect
25:10 Paul said, "I am S before Caesar's tribunal, where
1Tim 3:13 deacons gain a good S for themselves and also
Heb 9:8 outer tent is still S
Jas 5:9 behold, the Judge is S at the doors.
2Pet 1:1 a faith of equal S with ours in the
Rev 5:6 I saw a Lamb S, as though it had
7:1 I saw four angels S at the four corners
7:9 and peoples and tongues, S before the throne and
10:5 angel whom I saw S on sea and land
10:8 the angel who is S on the sea and
15:2 number of its name, S beside the sea of
19:17 I saw an angel S in the sun, and
20:12 dead, great and small, S before the throne, and

STANDS (56)

Gen 47:26 of Egypt, and it S to this day, that
Num 14:14 face, and thy cloud S over them and thou
35:12 not die until he S before the congregation for
Deut 1:38 son of Nun, who S before you, he shall
17:12 obeying the priest who S to minister there before
29:15 as with him who S here with us this
Josh 8:29 heap of stones, which S there to this day.
22:19 the LORD's tabernacle S, and take for yourselves
22:29 LORD our God that S before his tabernacle!"
Judg 6:24 this day it still S at Ophrah, which belongs
1Kgs 7:27 also made the ten S of bronze; each stand
7:28 the construction of the S: they had panels, and
7:32 one piece with the S; and the height of
7:34 the supports were of one piece with the S
7:37 he made the ten S; all of them were
7:38 was a laver for each of the ten S
7:39 And he set the S, five on the south
7:43 the pillars; the ten S, and the ten lavers
7:43 ten lavers upon the S;
2Kgs 16:17 the frames of the S, and removed the laver
25:13 the LORD, and the S and the bronze sea
25:16 one sea, and the S, which Solomon had made
1Chr 16:30 earth; yea, the world S firm, never to be
2Chr 4:14 He made the S also, and the lavers upon
4:14 the lavers upon the S,
Esth 13:5 people, and it alone, S constantly in opposition to
Ps 1:1 of the wicked, nor S in the way of
26:12 My foot S on level ground; in the great
33:11 counsel of the LORD S for ever, the thoughts
39:5 Surely every man S as a mere breath!
45:9 at your right hand S the queen in gold
87:1 On the holy mount S the city he founded;
94:16 Who S up for me against evildoers?
109:31 For he S at the right hand of the
119:90 the earth, and it S fast.
119:161 cause, but my heart S in awe of thy
Prov 12:12 root of the righteous S firm.
Song 2:9 Behold, there he S behind our wall, gazing in
Sir 21:22 a man of experience S respectfully before it.
Is 3:13 place to contend, he S to judge his people.
32:8 devises noble things, and by noble things he S
46:7 its place, and it S there; it cannot move
59:14 turned back, and righteousness S afar off; for truth
Jer 27:19 pillars, the sea, the S, and the rest of
52:17 the LORD, and the S and the bronze sea
52:20 the sea, and the S, which Solomon the king
Ezek 21:21 the king of Babylon S at the parting of
Dan 6:12 king answered, "The thing S fast, according to the
Zech 13:7 against the man who S next to me," says
Jn 1:26 water; but among you S one whom you do
3:29 of the bridegroom, who S and hears him, rejoices
Rom 14:4 own master that he S or falls.
1Cor 10:12 who thinks that he S take heed lest he
2Tim 2:19 But God's firm foundation S, bearing this seal: "The
Heb 10:11 And every priest S daily at his service, offering
1Pet 2:6 For it S in scripture: "Behold, I am laying

STANK

Ex 8:14 gathered them together in heaps, and the land S

STAR (16)

Num 24:17 but not nigh: a S shall come forth out
Sir 50:6 Like the morning S among the clouds, like the
Is 14:12 from heaven, O Day S, son of Dawn!
Mt 2:2 we have seen his S in the East, and
2:7 them what time the S appeared;
2:9 way; and lo, the S which they had seen
2:10 When they saw the S, they rejoiced exceedingly with
Acts 7:43 of Moloch, and the S of the god Rephan,
1Cor 15:41 of the stars; for S differs from star in
15:41 for star differs from S in glory.
2Pet 1:19 dawns and the morning S rises in your hearts.
Rev 2:28 Father; and I will give him the morning S
8:10 trumpet, and a great S fell from heaven, blazing
8:11 The name of the S is Wormwood.
9:1 and I saw a S fallen from heaven to
22:16 and the offspring of David, the bright morning S

STAR-GOD

Amos 5:26 king, and Kaiwan your S, your images, which you

STARE (3)

Ps 22:17 my bones– they S and gloat over me;
Is 14:16 who see you will S at you, and ponder
Acts 3:12 or why do you S at us, as though

STARED (2)

2Kgs 8:11 fixed his gaze and S at him, until he
Acts 10:4 And he S at him in terror, and said,

STARRY

Wis 10:17 by day, and a S flame through the night.

STARS (62)

Gen 1:16 night; he made the S also.
15:5 heaven, and number the S, if you are able
22:17 your descendants as the S of heaven and as
26:4 your descendants as the S of heaven, and will
37:9 the moon, and eleven S were bowing down to
Ex 32:13 your descendants as the S of heaven, and all
Deut 1:10 this day as the S of heaven for multitude.
4:19 the moon and the S, all the host of
10:22 made you as the S of heaven for multitude.
28:62 you were as the S of heaven for multitude,
Judg 5:20 From heaven fought the S, from their courses they
1Chr 27:23 as many as the S of heaven.
Neh 4:21 of dawn till the S came out.
9:23 their descendants as the S of heaven, and thou
Job 3:9 Let the S of its dawn be dark; let
9:7 who seals up the S;
22:12 See the highest S, how lofty they are!
25:5 not bright and the S are not clean in
38:7 cornerstone, when the morning S sang together, and
Ps 8:3 the moon and the S which thou hast established;
136:9 ever; the moon and S to rule over the
147:4 the number of the S, he gives to all
148:3 sun and moon, praise him, all you shining S
Eccl 12:2 the moon and the S are darkened and the
Wis 7:19 the constellations of the S,
7:29 the sun, and excels every constellation of the S
13:2 the circle of the S, or turbulent water, of
17:5 brilliant flames of the S avail to illumine that
Sir 43:9 The glory of the S is the beauty of
44:22 his posterity like the S, and cause them to
Is 13:10 For the S of the heavens and their constellations
14:13 to heaven; above the S of God I will
47:13 who gaze at the S, who at the new
Jer 31:35 the moon and the S for light by night,
Bar 3:34 him in fear; the S shone in their watches,
6:60 sun and moon and S, shining and sent forth

Ezek 32:7 heavens, and make their S dark; I will cover
Dan 3:36 as many as the S of heaven and as
3:64 Bless the Lord, S of heaven, sing praise to
8:10 the host of the S it cast down to
12:3 to righteousness, like the S for ever and ever.
Joel 2:10 are darkened, and the S withdraw their shining.
3:15 are darkened, and the S withdraw their shining.
Obad 1:4 is set among the S, thence I will bring
Nah 3:16 merchants more than the S of the heavens.
2Mac 9:10 he could touch the S of heaven.
Mt 24:29 its light, and the S will fall from heaven,
Mk 13:25 its light, and the S will be falling from
Lk 21:25 sun and moon and S, and upon the earth
Acts 27:20 when neither sun nor S appeared for many a
1Cor 15:41 another glory of the S; for star differs from
Heb 11:12 as many as the S of heaven and as
Jude 1:13 their own shame; wandering S for whom the nether
Rev 1:16 hand he held seven S, from his mouth issued
1:20 mystery of the seven S which you saw in
1:20 golden lampstands, the seven S are the angels of
2:1 who holds the seven S in his right hand,
3:1 the seven spirits of God and the seven S
6:13 like blood, and the S of the sky fell
8:12 a third of the S, so that a third
12:1 a crown of twelve S;
12:4 a third of the S of heaven, and cast

START

1Sam 29:10 came with you; and S early in the morning,

STARTED (6)

Josh 18:8 So the men S on their way; and Joshua
Ruth 1:6 Then she S with her daughters-in-law to return from
Tob 11:10 Tobit S toward the door, and stumbled.
1Mac 9:60 He S to come with a large force, and
Lk 23:18 prison for an insurrection S in the city, and
Jn 6:17 into a boat, and S across the sea to

STARTING (2)

Num 33:2 Moses wrote down their S places, stage by stage,
33:2 stages according to their S places.

STARTLE

Is 52:15 so shall he S many nations; kings shall

STARTLED (2)

Ruth 3:8 midnight the man was S, and turned over, and
Lk 24:37 But they were S and frightened, and supposed that

STARTS

Prov 26:27 back upon him who S it rolling.

STATE (10)

Ezek 4:3 it be in a S of siege, and press
Dan 8:14 the sanctuary shall be restored to its rightful S
2Mac 4:30 While such was the S of affairs, it happened
Mt 12:45 there; and the last S of that man becomes
Lk 11:26 there; and the last S of that man becomes
Acts 23:30 his accusers also to S before you what they
1Cor 7:20 should remain in the S in which he was
7:24 So, brethren, in whatever S each was called, there
Phil 4:11 have learned, in whatever S I am, to be
2Pet 2:20 and overpowered, the last S has become worse for

STATED

2Mac 3:9 had been made and S why he had come,

STATELY (6)

Prov 30:29 Three things are S in their tread; four are
30:29 their tread; four are S in their stride:
Song 7:7 You are S as a palm tree, and your
Sir 26:17 beautiful face on a S figure.
Is 33:21 oars can go, nor S ship can pass.
Ezek 23:41 you sat upon a S couch, with a table

STATEMENT (2)

Acts 28:25 Paul had made one S: "The Holy Spirit was
2Cor 4:2 but by the open S of the truth we

STATES

Prov 18:17 He who S his case first seems right, until

STATING (3)

1Mac 12:7 was king among you, S that you are our
2Mac 9:13 have mercy on him, S
14:27 man, wrote to Nicanor, S that he was displeased

STATION (4)

Neh 7:3 Jerusalem, each to his S and each opposite his
Is 22:19 and you will be cast down from your S
Hab 2:1 stand to watch, and S myself on the tower,
1Mac 10:32 priest, that he may S in it men of

STATIONED (24)

Josh 8:13 So they S the forces, the main encampment which
1Kgs 10:26 thousand horsemen, whom he S in the chariot cities
2Kgs 10:24 Now Jehu had S eighty men outside, and said,
1Chr 9:18 (Shallum being the chief), S hitherto in the king's
2Chr 1:14 thousand horsemen, whom he S in the chariot cities
9:25 thousand horsemen, whom he S in the chariot cities
23:19 He S the gatekeepers at the gates of the
29:25 And he S the Levites in the house of
Neh 4:13 in open places, I S the people according to
Jud 3:6 with his army and S garrisons in the hilltop
Is 21:8 my post I am S whole nights.
1Mac 1:34 And they S there a sinful people, lawless men.
4:61 And he S a garrison there to hold it.
5:42 stream of water, he S the scribes of the
6:35 with each elephant they S a thousand men armed
6:38 of the horsemen were S on either side, on
6:50 king took Bethzur and S a guard there to
10:37 some of them be S in the great strongholds
11:3 entered the cities he S forces as a garrison
12:27 for battle, and he S outposts around the camp.
12:34 And he S a garrison there to guard it.
15:41 built up Kedron and S there horsemen and troops,
2Mac 15:20 battle, the elephants strategically S and the cavalry
15:31 his countrymen together and S the priests before the

STATIONS (2)

Neh 13:11 gathered them together and set them in their S
Jer 46:4 Take your S with your helmets, polish your spears,

STATUES

2Mac 2:2 the gold and silver S and their adornment.

STATURE (12)

Num 13:32 we saw in it are men of great S
1Sam 2:26 to grow both in S and in favor with
16:7 the height of his S, because I have rejected
2Sam 21:20 a man of great S, who had six fingers
1Chr 11:23 a man of great S, five cubits tall.
20:6 a man of great S, who had six fingers
Is 45:14 the Sabeans, men of S, shall come over to
Bar 3:26 of old, great in S, expert in war.
Ezek 13:18 of persons of every S, in the hunt for
Lk 2:52 in wisdom and in S, and in favor with
19:3 of the crowd, because he was small of S
Eph 4:13 the measure of the S of the fulness of

STATUTE (35)

Gen 47:26 Joseph made it a S concerning the land of
Ex 15:25 made for them a S and an ordinance and
27:21 It shall be a S for ever to be
28:43 shall be a perpetual S for him and for
29:9 the priesthood shall be theirs by a perpetual S
30:21 it shall be a S for ever to them,
Lev 3:17 shall be a perpetual S throughout your generations,
10:9 it shall be a S for ever throughout your
16:29 it shall be a S to you for ever
16:31 yourselves; it is a S for ever.
16:34 shall be an everlasting S for you, that atonement
17:7 This shall be a S for ever to them
23:14 God: it is a S for ever throughout your
23:21 work: it is a S for ever in all
23:31 work: it is a S for ever throughout your
23:41 year; it is a S for ever throughout your
24:3 it shall be a S for ever throughout your
Num 9:12 according to all the S for the passover they
9:14 LORD, according to the S of the passover and
9:14 you shall have one S, both for the sojourner
10:8 you for a perpetual S throughout your generations.
15:15 there shall be one S for you and for
15:15 with you, a perpetual S throughout your generations;
18:23 shall be a perpetual S throughout your generations;
19:2 Aaron, "This is the S of the law which
19:10 stranger who sojourns among them, a perpetual S
19:21 shall be a perpetual S for them.
27:11 people of Israel a S and ordinance, as the
31:21 battle: "This is the S of the law which
35:29 shall be for a S and ordinance to you
1Sam 30:25 he made it a S and an ordinance for
1Chr 16:17 he confirmed as a S to Jacob, as an

S

Ps 81:4 For it is a S for Israel, an ordinance
94:20 be allied with thee, who frame mischief by S
105:10 to Jacob as a S, to Israel as an

STATUTES (143)

Gen 26:5 charge, my commandments, my S, and my laws."
Ex 15:26 and keep all his S, I will put none
18:16 make them know the S of God and his
18:20 shall teach them the S and the decisions, and
Lev 10:11 of Israel all the S which the LORD has
18:3 You shall not walk in their S
18:4 ordinances and keep my S and walk in them.
18:5 shall therefore keep my S and my ordinances, by
18:26 you shall keep my S and my ordinances and
19:19 "You shall keep my S
19:37 shall observe all my S and all my ordinances,
20:8 Keep my S, and do them; I am the
20:22 therefore keep all my S and all my ordinances,
25:18 you shall do my S, and keep my ordinances
26:3 you walk in my S and observe my commandments
26:15 if you spurn my S, and if your soul
26:43 my ordinances, and their soul abhorred my S
26:46 These are the S and ordinances and laws which
Num 9:3 according to all its S and all its ordinances
30:16 are the S which the LORD commanded Moses,
Deut 4:1 give heed to the S and the ordinances which
4:5 I have taught you S and ordinances, as the
4:6 they hear all these S, will say, 'Surely this
4:8 is there, that has S and ordinances so righteous
4:14 time to teach you S and ordinances, that you
4:40 you shall keep his S and his commandments, which
4:45 are the testimonies, the S, and the ordinances, which
5:1 "Hear, O Israel, the S and the ordinances which
5:31 the commandment and the S and the ordinances
6:1 is the commandment, the S and the ordinances
6:2 by keeping all his S and his commandments, which
6:17 his testimonies, and his S, which he has commanded
6:20 the testimonies and the S and the ordinances which
6:24 to do all these S, to fear the LORD
7:11 the commandment, and the S, and the ordinances,
8:11 his ordinances and his S, which I command you
10:13 keep the commandments and S of the LORD, which
11:1 keep his charge, his S, his ordinances, and his
11:32 to do all the S and the ordinances which
12:1 "These are the S and ordinances which you shall
16:12 and you shall be careful to observe these S
17:19 this law and these S, and doing them;
26:16 you to do these S and ordinances; you shall
26:17 ways, and keep his S and his commandments and
27:10 his commandments and his S, which I command you
28:15 his commandments and his S which I command you
28:45 commandments and his S which he commanded you.
30:10 his commandments and his S which are written in
30:16 his commandments and his S and his ordinances,
Josh 24:25 that day, and made S and ordinances for them
2Sam 22:23 me, and from his S I did not turn
1Kgs 2:3 keeping his S, his commandments, his ordinances,
3:3 LORD, walking in the S of David his father;
3:14 my ways, keeping my S and my commandments, as
6:12 will walk in my S and obey my ordinances
8:58 keep his commandments, his S, and his ordinances,
8:61 God, walking in his S and keeping his
9:4 you, and keeping my S and my ordinances,
9:6 my commandments and my S which I have set
11:11 my covenant and my S which I have commanded
11:33 sight and keeping my S and my ordinances, as
11:34 my commandments and my S;
11:38 eyes by keeping my S and my commandments, as
2Kgs 17:13 my commandments and my S, in accordance with all
17:15 They despised his S, and his covenant that he
17:34 do not follow the S or the ordinances or
17:37 And the S and the ordinances and the law
23:3 his testimonies and his S, with all his heart
1Chr 22:13 careful to observe the S and the ordinances which
29:19 thy testimonies, and thy S, performing all, and that
2Chr 7:17 you and keeping my S and my ordinances,
7:19 aside and forsake my S and my commandments
19:10 bloodshed, law or commandment, S or ordinances,
33:8 all the law, the S, and the ordinances given
34:31 his testimonies and his S, with all his heart
Ezra 7:10 and to teach his S and ordinances in Israel.
7:11 the LORD and his S for Israel:
Neh 1:7 kept the commandments, the S, and the ordinances
9:13 and true laws, good S and commandments,
9:14 command them commandments and S and a law by
10:29 LORD our Lord and his ordinances and his S

Ps 18:22 before me, and his S I did not put
50:16 you to recite my S, or take my covenant
89:31 if they violate my S and do not keep
99:7 his testimonies, and the S that he gave them.
105:45 they should keep his S, and observe his laws.
119:5 my ways may be steadfast in keeping thy S
119:8 I will observe thy S; O forsake me not
119:12 Blessed be thou, O LORD; teach me thy S
119:16 will delight in thy S; I will not forget
119:23 against me, thy servant will meditate on thy S
119:26 ways, thou didst answer me; teach me thy S
119:33 the way of thy S; and I will keep
119:48 I love, and I will meditate on thy S
119:54 Thy S have been my songs in the house
119:64 full of thy steadfast love; teach me thy S
119:68 art good and doest good; teach me thy S
119:71 I was afflicted, that I might learn thy S
119:80 be blameless in thy S, that I may not
119:83 the smoke, yet I have not forgotten thy S
119:112 heart to perform thy S for ever, to the
119:117 have regard for thy S continually!
119:118 go astray from thy S; yea, their cunning is
119:124 to thy steadfast love, and teach me thy S
119:135 shine upon thy servant, and teach me thy S
119:145 I will keep thy S
119:155 the wicked, for they do not seek thy S
119:171 forth praise that thou dost teach me thy S
147:19 word to Jacob, his S and ordinances to Israel.
Sir 6:37 Reflect on the S of the Lord, and meditate
45:17 gave him authority and S and judgments, to teach
Is 24:5 laws, violated the S, broken the everlasting covenant.
Jer 44:10 my law and my S which I set before
44:23 law and in his S and in his testimonies,
Bar 1:18 to walk in the S of the Lord which
2:10 to walk in the S of the Lord which
4:13 no regard for his S; they did not walk
Ezek 5:6 nations, and against my S more than the countries
5:6 rejecting my ordinances and not walking in my S
5:7 not walked in my S or kept my ordinances,
11:12 not walked in my S, nor executed my ordinances,
11:20 may walk in my S and keep my ordinances
18:9 man, walks in my S, and is careful to
18:17 and walks in my S; he shall not die
18:19 to observe all my S, he shall surely live.
18:21 and keeps all my S and does what is
20:11 I gave them my S and showed them my
20:13 not walk in my S but rejected my ordinances,
20:16 not walk in my S, and profaned my sabbaths;
20:18 not walk in the S of your fathers, nor
20:19 God; walk in my S, and be careful to
20:21 not walk in my S, and were not careful
20:24 but had rejected my S and profaned my sabbaths,
20:25 Moreover I gave them S that were not good
33:15 and walks in the S of life, committing no
36:27 to walk in my S and be careful to
37:24 my ordinances and be careful to observe my S
44:24 my laws and my S in all my appointed
Amos 2:4 have not kept his S, but their lies have
Mic 6:16 you have kept the S of Omri, and all
Zech 1:6 my words and my S, which I commanded my
Mal 3:7 turned aside from my S and have not kept
4:4 my servant Moses, the S and ordinances that I

STAVES

Num 21:18 people delved, with the scepter and with their S

STAY (59)

Gen 22:5 to his young men, S here with the ass;
27:44 brother in Haran, and S with him a while,
29:19 to any other man; S with me."
Ex 9:28 go, and you shall S no longer."
Josh 10:19 them; but do not S there yourselves, pursue your
Judg 6:18 he said, "I will S till you return."
17:10 Micah said to him, S with me, and be
19:4 girl's father, made him S, and he remained with
1Sam 19:2 yourself in the morning, S in a secret place
20:38 lad, "Hurry, make haste, S not." So Jonathan's lad
22:3 father and my mother S with you, till I
22:23 S with me, fear not; for he that seeks
2Sam 15:19 Go back, and S with the king; for you
19:7 not a man will S with you this night;
22:19 of my calamity; but the LORD was my S
24:16 "It is enough; now S your hand." And the
2Kgs 14:10 with your glory, and S at home; for why
15:20 back, and did not S there in the land.
1Chr 21:15 "It is enough; now S your hand." And the

S

2Chr 25:19 But now S at home; why should you provoke
Tob 6:10 "Brother, today we shall S with Raguel.
10:8 father-in-law said to him, S with me, and I
Job 24:13 ways, and do not S in its paths.
Ps 18:18 of my calamity; but the LORD was my S
37:24 the LORD is the S of his hand.
68:13 the spoil, though they S among the sheepfolds–
Prov 7:11 her feet do not S at home;
Sir 7:2 S away from wrong, and it will turn away
12:15 He will S with you for a time, but
20:2 to reprove than to S angry!
27:12 but among thoughtful people S on.
29:27 brother has come to S with me; I need
37:12 But S constantly with a godly man whom you
Is 3:1 Jerusalem and from Judah S and staff, the whole
3:1 and staff, the whole S of bread, and the
3:1 bread, and the whole S of water;
48:2 the holy city, and S themselves on the God
Jer 4:6 Zion, flee for safety, S not, for I bring
37:9 "The Chaldeans will surely S away from us," for
37:9 for they will not S away.
Lam 4:15 the nations, "They shall S with us no longer."
Dan 4:35 earth; and none can S his hand or say
1Mac 12:45 a few men to S with you, and come
Mt 10:11 worthy in it, and S with him until you
Mk 6:10 you enter a house, S there until you leave
Lk 9:4 whatever house you enter, S there, and from there
19:5 down; for I must S at your house today."
24:29 they constrained him, saying, S with us, for it
24:29 he went in to S with them.
24:49 Father upon you; but S in the city, until
Jn 4:40 they asked him to S with them; and he
Acts 13:17 people great during their S in the land of
16:15 to the Lord, come to my house and S
18:20 they asked him to S for a longer period,
27:31 soldiers, "Unless these men S in the ship, you
28:14 and were invited to S with them for seven
28:16 Paul was allowed to S by himself, with the
1Cor 16:6 and perhaps I will S with you or even
16:8 But I will S in Ephesus until Pentecost,

STAYED (49)

Gen 28:11 a certain place, and S there that night, because
29:14 And he S with him a month.
32:4 sojourned with Laban, and S until now;
45:1 So no one S with him when Joseph made
Ex 2:15 fled from Pharaoh, and S in the land of
Num 20:1 month, and the people S in Kadesh; and Miriam
22:8 the princes of Moab S with Balaam.
25:8 Thus the plague was S from the people of
Deut 1:6 in Horeb, 'You have S long enough at this
10:10 said to him.) "I S on the mountain, as
Josh 10:13 still, and the moon S, until the nation took
10:13 The sun S in the midst of heaven, and
Judg 5:17 Gilead S beyond the Jordan; and Dan, why did
15:8 he went down and S in the cleft of
1Sam 13:16 were present with them, S in Geba of Benjamin;
22:4 of Moab, and they S with him all the
30:9 brook Besor, where those S who were left behind.
30:10 hundred men; two hundred S behind, who were too
2Sam 19:32 with food while he S at Mahanaim; for he
Tob 5:6 way, and I have S with our brother Gabael."
9:5 made the journey and S over night with Gabael.
Jud 12:9 she returned clean and S in the tent until
14:17 tent where Judith had S, and when he did
Esth 7:7 palace garden; but Haman S to beg his life
Job 38:11 farther, and here shall your proud waves be S
Ps 106:30 stood up and interposed, and the plague was S
Is 26:3 peace, whose mind is S on thee, because he
Jer 41:17 And they went and S at Geruth Chimham near
1Mac 3:13 of faithful men who S with him and went
11:40 for him; and he S there many days.
2Mac 14:23 Nicanor S on in Jerusalem and did nothing out
Lk 2:43 returning, the boy Jesus S behind in Jerusalem.
Jn 1:39 was staying; and they S with him that day,
2:12 disciples; and there they S for a few days.
4:40 with them; and he S there two days.
11:6 he was ill, he S two days longer in
11:54 Ephraim; and there he S with the disciples.
Acts 9:43 And he S in Joppa for many days with
18:3 the same trade he S with them, and they
18:11 And he S a year and six months, teaching
18:18 After this Paul S many days longer, and then
19:22 and Erastus, he himself S in Asia for a
20:6 at Troas, where we S for seven days.
21:4 out the disciples, we S there for seven days.
21:7 greeted the brethren and S with them for one
21:8 of the seven, and S with him.
25:6 When he had S among them not more than
25:14 And as they S there many days, Festus laid
28:12 in at Syracuse, we S there for three days.

STAYING (6)

1Sam 14:2 Saul was S in the outskirts of Gibe-ah under
Jn 1:38 (which means Teacher), "where are you S
1:39 saw where he was S; and they stayed with
Acts 1:4 And while S with them he charged them not
1:13 room, where they were S, Peter and John and
21:10 While we were S for some days, a prophet

STAYS (7)

1Sam 30:24 his share be who S by the baggage; they
1Kgs 7:35 of the stand its S and its panels were
7:36 the surfaces of its S and on its panels,
Ps 127:1 the city, the watchman S awake in vain.
Wis 5:14 of a guest who S but a day.
Jer 21:9 He who S in this city shall die by
38:2 the LORD, He who S in this city shall

STEAD (82)

Gen 36:33 son of Zerah of Bozrah reigned in his S
36:34 the land of the Temanites reigned in his S
36:35 Moab, reigned in his S, the name of his
36:36 died, and Samlah of Masrekah reigned in his S
36:37 of Rehoboth on the Euphrates reigned in his S
36:38 Baal-hanan the son of Achbor reigned in his S
36:39 Hadar reigned in his S, the name of his
Num 32:14 risen in your fathers' S, a brood of sinful
Deut 2:12 and settled in their S; as Israel did to
2:21 and settled in their S;
2:22 and settled in their S even to this day.
2:23 and settled in their S
10:6 his son Eleazar ministered as priest in his S
Josh 5:7 raised up in their S, that Joshua circumcised; for
2Sam 10:1 died, and Hanun his son reigned in his S
1Kgs 1:30 my throne in my S; even so will I
1:35 be king in my S; and I have appointed
11:43 father; and Rehoboam his son reigned in his S
14:20 fathers, and Nadab his son reigned in his S
14:27 Rehoboam made in their S shields of bronze, and
14:31 And Abijam his son reigned in his S
15:8 And Asa his son reigned in his S
15:24 father; and Jehoshaphat his son reigned in his S
15:28 Asa king of Judah, and reigned in his S
16:6 Tirzah; and Elah his son reigned in his S
16:10 Asa king of Judah, and reigned in his S
16:28 Samaria; and Ahab his son reigned in his S
22:40 fathers; and Ahaziah his son reigned in his S
22:50 father; and Jehoram his son reigned in his S
2Kgs 1:17 became king in his S in the second year
3:27 to reign in his S, and offered him for
8:15 And Hazael became king in his S
8:24 David; and Ahaziah his son reigned in his S
10:35 And Jehoahaz his son reigned in his S
12:21 David, and Amaziah his son reigned in his S
13:9 Samaria; and Joash his son reigned in his S
13:24 died, Ben-hadad his son became king in his S
14:16 Israel; and Jeroboam his son reigned in his S
14:29 Israel, and Zechariah his son reigned in his S
15:7 David, and Jotham his son reigned in his S
15:10 Ibleam, and killed him, and reigned in his S
15:14 Samaria and slew him, and reigned in his S
15:22 fathers, and Pekahiah his son reigned in his S
15:25 house; he slew him, and reigned in his S
15:30 and reigned in his S, in the twentieth year
15:38 father; and Ahaz his son reigned in his S
16:20 David; and Hezekiah his son reigned in his S
19:37 And Esarhaddon his son reigned in his S
20:21 fathers; and Manasseh his son reigned in his S
21:18 Uzza; and Amon his son reigned in his S
21:24 land made Josiah his son king in his S
21:26 Uzza; and Josiah his son reigned in his S
23:30 him, and made him king in his father's S
24:6 fathers, and Jehoiachin his son reigned in his S
24:17 uncle, king in his S, and changed his name
1Chr 1:44 son of Zerah of Bozrah reigned in his S
1:45 the land of the Temanites reigned in his S
1:46 Moab, reigned in his S; and the name of
1:47 Hadad died, Samlah of Masrekah reigned in his S
1:48 of Rehoboth on the Euphrates reigned in his S
1:49 Baal-hanan, the son of Achbor, reigned in his S
1:50 Hadad reigned in his S; and the name of

S

19:1 Ammonites died, and his son reigned in his S
29:28 honor; and Solomon his son reigned in his S
2Chr 1:8 father, and hast made me king in his S
9:31 father; and Rehoboam his son reigned in his S
12:10 Rehoboam made in their S shields of bronze, and
12:16 David; and Abijah his son reigned in his S
14:1 David; and Asa his son reigned in his S
17:1 son reigned in his S, and strengthened himself
21:1 David; and Jehoram his son reigned in his S
22:1 son king in his S; for the band of
24:27 And Amaziah his son reigned in his S
26:23 And Jotham his son reigned in his S
27:9 David; and Ahaz his son reigned in his S
28:27 And Hezekiah his son reigned in his S
32:33 And Manasseh his son reigned in his S
33:20 house; and Amon his son reigned in his S
33:25 land made Josiah his son king in his S
36:1 king in his father's S in Jerusalem.
36:8 Judah; and Jehoiachin his son reigned in his S
Is 37:38 And Esarhaddon his son reigned in his S

STEADFAST (198)

Gen 24:12 pray thee, and show S love to my master
24:14 that thou hast shown S love to my master."
24:27 has not forsaken his S love and his faithfulness
32:10 least of all the S love and all the
39:21 Joseph and showed him S love, and gave him
Ex 15:13 hast led in thy S love the people whom
20:6 hate me, but showing S love to thousands of
34:6 anger, and abounding in S love and faithfulness,
34:7 faithfulness, keeping S love for thousands, forgiving
Num 14:18 anger, and abounding in S love, forgiving iniquity and
14:19 the greatness of thy S love, and according as
Deut 5:10 hate me, but showing S love to thousands of
7:9 who keeps covenant and S love with those who
7:12 the covenant and the S love which he swore
Josh 23:6 Therefore be very S to keep and do all
2Sam 2:6 may the LORD show S love and faithfulness to
7:15 will not take my S love from him, as
15:20 may the LORD show S love and faithfulness to
22:51 his king, and shows S love to his anointed,
1Kgs 3:6 hast shown great and S love to thy servant
3:6 him this great and S love, and hast given
8:23 keeping covenant and showing S love to thy servants
1Chr 16:34 is good; for his S love endures for ever!
16:41 the LORD, for his S love endures for ever.
17:13 will not take my S love from him, as
2Chr 1:8 hast shown great and S love to David my
5:13 is good, for his S love endures for ever,"
6:14 keeping covenant and showing S love to thy servants
6:42 Remember thy S love for David thy servant."
7:3 is good, for his S love endures for ever,"
7:6 the LORD--for his S love endures for ever--
20:21 the LORD, for his S love endures for ever."
Ezra 3:11 is good, for his S love endures for ever
7:28 extended to me his S love before the king
9:9 extended to us his S love before the kings
Neh 1:5 who keeps covenant and S love with those who
9:17 anger and abounding in S love, and didst not
9:32 who keepest covenant and S love, let not all
13:22 the greatness of thy S love.
Esth 13:3 unchanging good will and S fidelity, and has attained
Job 10:12 granted me life and S love; and thy care
Ps 5:7 the abundance of thy S love will enter thy
6:4 the sake of thy S love.
13:5 have trusted in thy S love; my heart shall
17:7 Wondrously show thy S love, O savior of those
18:50 his king, and shows S love to his anointed,
21:7 LORD; and through the S love of the Most
25:6 LORD, and of thy S love, for they have
25:7 transgressions; according to thy S love remember
25:10 of the LORD are S love and faithfulness, for
26:3 For thy S love is before my eyes, and
31:7 be glad for thy S love, because thou hast
31:16 save me in thy S love!
31:21 has wondrously shown his S love to me when
32:10 of the wicked; but S love surrounds him who
33:5 is full of the S love of the LORD.
33:18 who hope in his S love,
33:22 Let thy S love, O LORD, be upon us,
36:5 Thy S love, O LORD, extends to the heavens,
36:7 How precious is thy S love, O God!
36:10 O continue thy S love to those who know
40:10 have not concealed thy S love and thy faithfulness
40:11 from me, let thy S love and thy faithfulness
42:8 the LORD commands his S love; and at night
44:26 the sake of thy S love!
48:9 have thought on thy S love, O God, in
51:1 God, according to thy S love; according to thy
52:8 I trust in the S love of God for
57:3 will send forth his S love and his faithfulness!
57:7 [Selah] My heart is S, O God, my heart
57:7 heart is steadfast, O God, my heart is S
57:10 For thy S love is great to the heavens,
59:10 My God in his S love will meet me;
59:16 sing aloud of thy S love in the morning.
59:17 God who shows me S love.
61:7 ever before God; bid S love and faithfulness watch
62:12 thee, O Lord, belongs S love.
63:3 Because thy S love is better than life, my
66:20 prayer or removed his S love from me!
69:13 the abundance of thy S love answer me.
69:16 O LORD, for thy S love is good; according
77:8 Has his S love for ever ceased?
78:8 whose heart was not S, whose spirit was not
78:37 Their heart was not S toward him; they were
85:7 Show us thy S love, O LORD, and grant
85:10 S love and faithfulness will meet; righteousness and
86:5 and forgiving, abounding in S love to all who
86:13 For great is thy S love toward me; thou
86:15 anger and abounding in S love and faithfulness.
88:11 [Selah] Is thy S love declared in the grave,
89:1 will sing of thy S love, O LORD, for
89:2 For thy S love was established for ever, thy
89:14 foundation of thy throne; S love and faithfulness go
89:24 My faithfulness and my S love shall be with
89:28 My S love I will keep for him for
89:33 remove from him my S love, or be false
89:49 Lord, where is thy S love of old, which
90:14 the morning with thy S love, that we may
92:2 High; to declare thy S love in the morning,
94:18 thy S love, O LORD, held me up.
98:3 He has remembered his S love and faithfulness to
100:5 LORD is good; his S love endures for ever,
103:4 who crowns you with S love and mercy,
103:8 anger and abounding in S love.
103:11 so great is his S love toward those who
103:17 But the S love of the LORD is from
106:1 is good; for his S love endures for ever!
106:7 the abundance of thy S love, but rebelled against
106:45 the abundance of his S love.
107:1 is good; for his S love endures for ever!
107:8 the LORD for his S love, for his wonderful
107:15 the LORD for his S love, for his wonderful
107:21 the LORD for his S love, for his wonderful
107:31 the LORD for his S love, for his wonderful
107:43 let men consider the S love of the LORD.
108:1 My heart is S, O God, my heart is
108:1 heart is steadfast, O God, my heart is S
108:4 For thy S love is great above the heavens,
109:21 name's sake; because thy S love is good, deliver
109:26 me according to thy S love!
115:1 the sake of thy S love and thy faithfulness!
117:2 For great is his S love toward us; and
118:1 he is good; his S love endures for ever!
118:2 Let Israel say, "His S love endures for ever."
118:3 of Aaron say, "His S love endures for ever."
118:4 the LORD say, "His S love endures for ever."
118:29 is good; for his S love endures for ever!
119:5 my ways may be S in keeping thy statutes!
119:41 Let thy S love come to me, O LORD,
119:64 is full of thy S love; teach me thy
119:76 Let thy S love be ready to comfort me
119:88 In thy S love spare my life, that I
119:124 servant according to thy S love, and teach me
119:149 my voice in thy S love; O LORD, in
119:159 life according to thy S love.
130:7 the LORD there is S love, and with him
136:1 is good, for his S love endures for ever.
136:2 of gods, for his S love endures for ever.
136:3 of lords, for his S love endures for ever;
136:4 great wonders, for his S love endures for ever;
136:5 the heavens, for his S love endures for ever;
136:6 the waters, for his S love endures for ever;
136:7 great lights, for his S love endures for ever;
136:8 the day, for his S love endures for ever;
136:9 the night, for his S love endures for ever;
136:10 of Egypt, for his S love endures for ever;
136:11 among them, for his S love endures for ever;
136:12 outstretched arm, for his S love endures for ever;
136:13 in sunder, for his S love endures for ever;
136:14 of it, for his S love endures for ever;

136:15 Red Sea, for his S love endures for ever;
136:16 the wilderness, for his S love endures for ever;
136:17 great kings, for his S love endures for ever;
136:18 famous kings, for his S love endures for ever;
136:19 the Amorites, for his S love endures for ever;
136:20 of Bashan, for his S love endures for ever;
136:21 a heritage, for his S love endures for ever;
136:22 his servant, for his S love endures for ever.
136:23 low estate, for his S love endures for ever;
136:24 our foes, for his S love endures for ever;
136:25 all flesh, for his S love endures for ever.
136:26 of heaven, for his S love endures for ever.
138:2 thy name for thy S love and thy faithfulness;
138:8 purpose for me; thy S love, O LORD, endures
143:8 the morning of thy S love, for in thee
143:12 And in thy S love cut off my enemies,
145:8 anger and abounding in S love.
147:11 who hope in his S love.
Prov 11:19 He who is S in righteousness will live, but
Wis 7:23 keen, irresistible, beneficent, humane, S, sure, free
Sir 2:2 heart right and be S, and do not be
5:10 Be S in your understanding, and let your speech
26:18 beautiful feet with a S heart.
27:3 a man is not S and zealous in the
Is 16:5 will be established in S love and on it
54:10 be removed, but my S love shall not depart
55:3 an everlasting covenant, my S, sure love for David.
63:7 I will recount the S love of the LORD,
63:7 the abundance of his S love.
Jer 9:24 LORD who practice S love, justice, and righteousness
16:5 says the LORD, my S love and mercy.
32:18 for thee, who showest S love to thousands, but
33:11 is good, for his S love endures for ever!'
Lam 3:22 I have hope: The S love of the LORD
3:32 the abundance of his S love;
Dan 9:4 who keepest covenant and S love with those who
Hos 2:19 and in justice, in S love, and in mercy.
6:6 For I desire S love and not sacrifice, the
10:12 reap the fruit of S love; break up your
Joel 2:13 anger, and abounding in S love, and repents of
Jon 4:2 anger, and abounding in S love, and repentest of
Mic 7:18 because he delights in S love.
7:20 faithfulness to Jacob and S love to Abraham, as
Acts 11:23 to the Lord with S purpose;
1Cor 15:58 beloved brethren, be S, immovable, always
Col 1:23 the faith, stable and S, not shifting from the
Heb 6:19 as a sure and S anchor of the soul,
Jas 5:11 Behold, we call those happy who were S

STEADFASTLY (2)

2Sam 20:2 Judah followed their king S from the Jordan to
Col 4:2 Continue S in prayer, being watchful in it with

STEADFASTNESS (13)

Rom 15:4 our instruction, that by S and by the encouragement
15:5 May the God of S and encouragement grant you
1Thes 1:3 labor of love and S of hope in our
2Thes 1:4 of God for your S and faith in all
3:5 God and to the S of Christ.
1Tim 6:11 righteousness, godliness, faith, love, S, gentleness.
2Tim 3:10 patience, my love, my S,
Tit 2:2 sensible, sound in faith, in love, and in S
Jas 1:3 know that the testing of your faith produces S
1:4 And let S have its full effect, that you
5:11 have heard of the S of Job, and you
2Pet 1:6 and self-control with S, and steadfastness with
1:6 self-control with steadfastness, and S with godliness,

STEADIED

Sir 13:20 man totters, he is S by friends, but when

STEADILY (2)

2Chr 17:12 And Jehoshaphat grew S greater.
1Mac 6:40 plain, and they advanced S and in good order.

STEADY (5)

Ex 17:12 so his hands were S until the going down
Ps 75:3 is I who keep S its pillars.
112:8 His heart is S, he will not be afraid,
119:133 Keep S my steps according to thy promise, and
2Tim 4:5 for you, always be S, endure suffering, do the

STEAL (21)

Gen 31:30 but why did you S my gods?"
44:8 how then should we S silver or gold from
Ex 20:15 "You shall not S
Lev 19:11 "You shall not S, nor deal falsely, nor lie
Deut 5:19 "'Neither shall you S
2Sam 19:3 that day as people S in who are ashamed
Ps 69:4 What I did not S must I now restore?
Prov 30:9 I be poor, and S, and profane the name
Jer 7:9 Will you S, murder, commit adultery, swear falsely,
23:30 says the LORD, who S my words from one
Obad 1:5 destroyed!--would they not S only enough for
Mt 6:19 thieves break in and S,
6:20 and where thieves do not break in and S
19:18 adultery, You shall not S, You shall not bear
27:64 his disciples go and S him away, and tell
Mk 10:19 commit adultery, Do not S, Do not bear false
Lk 18:20 not kill, Do not S, Do not bear false
Jn 10:10 thief comes only to S and kill and destroy;
Rom 2:21 While you preach against stealing, do you S
13:9 kill, You shall not S, You shall not covet,"
Eph 4:28 the thief no longer S, but rather let him

STEALING (3)

Deut 24:7 a man is found S one of his brethren,
Hos 4:2 swearing, lying, killing, S, and committing adultery;
Rom 2:21 While you preach against S, do you steal?

STEALS (4)

Ex 21:16 "Whoever S a man, whether he sells him or
22:1 "If a man S an ox or a sheep,
Prov 6:30 a thief if he S to satisfy his appetite
Zech 5:3 for every one who S shall be cut off

STEALTH (2)

Mt 26:4 to arrest Jesus by S and kill him.
Mk 14:1 to arrest him by S, and kill him;

STEALTHILY (3)

1Sam 24:4 Then David arose and S cut off the skirt
Job 4:12 was brought to me S, my ear received the
Ps 10:8 His eyes S watch for the hapless,

STEED

Zech 10:3 them like his proud S in battle.

STEEDS (5)

Judg 5:22 horses' hoofs with the galloping, galloping of his S
1Kgs 4:28 the horses and swift S they brought to the
Is 30:16 speed away; and, "We will ride upon swift S
Mic 1:13 Harness the S to the chariots, inhabitants of Lachish;
Zech 6:7 When the S came out, they were impatient to

STEEL

Sir 31:26 prove the temper of S, so wine tests hearts

STEEP (6)

Is 7:19 and settle in the S ravines, and in the
Mic 1:4 waters poured down a S place.
2Mac 14:45 and standing upon a S rock,
Mt 8:32 herd rushed down the S bank into the sea,
Mk 5:13 thousand, rushed down the S bank into the sea,
Lk 8:33 herd rushed down the S bank into the lake

STEERING

Wis 10:4 wisdom again saved it, S the righteous man by

STEERS (2)

Wis 14:3 providence, O Father, that S its course, because thou
Is 34:7 with them, and young S with the mighty bulls.

STEM (5)

Is 40:24 sown, scarcely has their S taken root in the
Ezek 19:11 Its strongest S became a ruler's scepter; it towered
19:12 stripped off, its strong S was withered; the fire
19:14 gone out from its S, has consumed its branches
19:14 in it no strong S, no scepter for a

STENCH (6)

Is 34:3 cast out, and the S of their corpses shall
Joel 2:20 the western sea; the S and foul smell of
Amos 4:10 and I made the S of your camp go
2Mac 9:9 and because of his S the whole army felt
9:10 Because of his intolerable S no one was able
9:12 not endure his own S, he uttered these words:

STEP (8)

1Sam 20:3 there is but a S between me and death."
1Kgs 10:20 each end of a S on the six steps.
2Chr 9:19 each end of a S on the six steps.

Job 31:7 my integrity!) if my S has turned aside from
Prov 4:13 When you walk, your S will not be hampered;
Wis 13:18 that cannot take a S;
Is 41:2 from the east whom victory meets at every S
Ezek 26:16 of the sea will S down from their thrones,

STEPHANAS (3)
1Cor 1:16 (I did baptize also the household of S
16:15 that the household of S were the first converts
16:17 at the coming of S and Fortunatus and Achaicus,

STEPHEN (8)
Acts 6:5 multitude, and they chose S, a man full of
6:8 And S, full of grace and power, did great
6:9 from Cilicia and Asia, arose and disputed with S
7:2 And S said: "Brethren and fathers, hear me.
7:59 as they were stoning S, he prayed, "Lord Jesus,
8:2 Devout men buried S, and made great lamentation
11:19 persecution that arose over S traveled as far as
22:20 when the blood of S thy witness was shed,

STEPPE (2)
1Chr 6:78 Reuben: Bezer in the S with its pasture lands,
Job 39:6 I have given the S for his home, and

STEPPED
Lk 8:27 And as he S out on land, there met

STEPS (59)
Ex 20:26 not go up by S to my altar, that
Deut 33:3 they followed in thy S, receiving direction from thee,
2Sam 22:37 wide place for my S under me, and my
1Kgs 10:19 The throne had six S, and at the back
10:20 each end of a step on the six S
2Kgs 9:13 him on the bare S, and they blew the
20:9 shadow go forward ten S, or go back ten
20:9 go forward ten steps, or go back ten S
20:10 shadow to lengthen ten S; rather let the shadow
20:10 steps; rather let the shadow go back ten S
20:11 the shadow back ten S, by which the sun
2Chr 9:11 of the algum wood S for the house of
9:18 The throne had six S and a footstool of
9:19 each end of a step on the six S
Job 14:16 thou wouldest number my S, thou wouldest not keep
18:7 His strong S are shortened and his own schemes
23:11 held fast to his S; I have kept his
29:6 about me; when my S were washed with milk,
31:4 he see my ways, and number all my S
31:37 account of all my S; like a prince I
34:21 of a man, and he sees all his S
Ps 17:5 My S have held fast to thy paths, my
18:36 wide place for my S under me, and my
37:23 The S of a man are from the LORD,
37:31 in his heart; his S do not slip.
40:2 a rock, making my S secure.
44:18 back, nor have our S departed from thy way,
56:6 band themselves together, they lurk, they watch my S
57:6 a net for my S; my soul was bowed
73:2 had almost stumbled, my S had well nigh slipped.
74:3 Direct thy S to the perpetual ruins; the enemy
119:128 Therefore I direct my S by all thy precepts;
119:133 Keep steady my S according to thy promise, and
Prov 5:5 down to death; her S follow the path to
16:9 plans his way, but the LORD directs his S
20:24 A man's S are ordered by the LORD; how
Eccl 5:1 Guard your S when you go to the house
Sir 21:6 reproof walks in the S of the sinner, but
51:15 straight path; from my youth I followed her S
Is 26:6 of the poor, the S of the needy."
38:8 on the dial of Ahaz turn back ten S
38:8 the dial the ten S by which it had
Jer 10:23 not in man who walks to direct his S
Lam 4:18 Men dogged our S so that we could not
Ezek 40:6 east, going up its S, and measured the threshold
40:22 the east; and seven S led up to it;
40:26 And there were seven S leading up to it,
40:31 on its jambs, and its stairway had eight S
40:34 on either side; and its stairway had eight S
40:37 on either side; and its stairway had eight S
40:49 twelve cubits; and ten S led up to it;
43:17 The S of the altar shall face east."
Hab 3:16 into my bones, my S totter beneath me.
2Mac 10:26 Falling upon the S before the altar, they besought
Jn 5:6 I am going another S down before me."
Acts 21:35 he came to the S, he was actually carried
21:40 Paul, standing on the S, motioned with his hand

2Cor 12:18 Did we not take the same S
1Pet 2:21 an example, that you should follow in his S

STERN (9)
Deut 28:50 understand, a nation of S countenance, who shall not
Wis 5:20 invincible shield, and sharpen S wrath for a sword,
11:10 the ungodly as a S king does in condemnation.
12:9 wild beasts or thy S word.
18:15 that was doomed, a S warrior
Is 21:2 A S vision is told to me; the plunderer
Mk 4:38 he was in the S, asleep on the cushion;
Acts 27:29 four anchors from the S, and prayed for day
27:41 remained immovable, and the S was broken up by

STERNLY (2)
Mt 9:30 And Jesus S charged them, "See that no one
Mk 1:43 And he S charged him, and sent him away

STEWARD (19)
Gen 43:16 he said to the S of his house, "Bring
43:19 went up to the S of Joseph's house, and
44:1 Then he commanded the S of his house, "Fill
44:4 Joseph said to his S, "Up, follow after the
Jud 14:13 and said to the S in charge of all
Is 22:15 "Come, go to this S, to Shebna, who is
Dan 1:11 Daniel said to the S whom the chief of
1:16 So the S took away their rich food and
Mt 20:8 vineyard said to his S, 'Call the laborers and
Lk 8:3 wife of Chuza, Herod's S, and Susanna, and many
12:42 the faithful and wise S, whom his master will
16:1 man who had a S, and charges were brought
16:2 can no longer be S
16:3 be steward.' And the S said to himself, 'What
16:8 commended the dishonest S for his shrewdness;
Jn 2:8 take it to the S of the feast." So
2:9 When the S of the feast tasted the water
2:9 the water knew), the S of the feast called
Tit 1:6 a bishop, as God's S, must be blameless; he

STEWARDS (5)
1Chr 27:31 All these were S of King David's property.
28:1 commanders of hundreds, the S of all the property
1Cor 4:1 servants of Christ and S of the mysteries of
4:2 it is required of S that they be found
1Pet 4:10 one another, as good S of God's varied grace:

STEWARDSHIP (4)
Lk 16:2 the account of your S, for you can no
16:3 master is taking the S away from me?
16:4 put out of the S
Eph 3:2 have heard of the S of God's grace that

STICK (15)
Deut 23:13 you shall have a S with your weapons; and
2Kgs 6:6 he cut off a S, and threw it in
Job 33:21 which were not seen S out.
Wis 13:13 useful for nothing, a S crooked and full of
Sir 33:24 Fodder and a S and burdens for an ass;
Is 28:27 beaten out with a S, and cummin with a
Ezek 29:4 fish of your streams S to your scales; and
29:4 of your streams which S to your scales.
37:16 of man, take a S and write on it,
37:16 him'; then take another S and write upon it,
37:16 it, 'For Joseph (the S of Ephraim) and all
37:17 them together into one S, that they may become
37:19 about to take the S of Joseph (which is
37:19 join with it the S of Judah, and make
37:19 and make them one S, that they may be

STICKS (8)
Num 15:32 found a man gathering S on the sabbath day.
15:33 who found him gathering S brought him to Moses
1Sam 17:43 a dog, that you come to me with S
1Kgs 17:10 widow was there gathering S; and he called to
17:12 gathering a couple of S, that I may go
Prov 18:24 is a friend who S closer than a brother.
Ezek 37:20 When the S on which you write are in
Acts 28:3 gathered a bundle of S and put them on

STIFF
Job 40:17 He makes his tail S like a cedar; the

STIFF-NECKED (8)
Ex 32:9 behold, it is a S people;
33:3 for you are a S people."
33:5 Israel, 'You are a S people; if for a

34:9 although it is a S people; and pardon our
2Chr 30:8 Do not now be S as your fathers were,
Sir 16:11 there is only one S person, it will be
Bar 2:30 for they are a S people.
Acts 7:51 these things?' "You S people, uncircumcised in heart

STIFFENED (7)

2Chr 36:13 swear by God; he S his neck and hardened
Neh 9:16 fathers acted presumptuously and S their neck and
9:17 among them; but they S their neck and appointed
9:29 a stubborn shoulder and S their neck and would
Jer 7:26 incline their ear, but S their neck.
17:23 incline their ear, but S their neck, that they
19:15 it, because they have S their neck, refusing to

STIFFENS

Prov 29:1 is often reproved, yet S his neck will suddenly

STILL (236)

Gen 8:9 for the waters were S on the face of
12:9 And Abram journeyed on, S going toward the Negeb.
18:22 Sodom; but Abraham S stood before the LORD.
25:6 and while he was S living he sent them
29:7 said, "Behold, it is S high day, it is
29:9 While he was S speaking with them, Rachel came
35:16 and when they were S some distance from Ephrath,
41:21 them, for they were S as gaunt as at
43:7 saying, 'Is your father S alive?
43:27 Is he S alive?"
43:28 is well, he is S alive." And they bowed
44:14 Joseph's house, he was S there; and they fell
45:3 Joseph; is my father S alive?" But his brothers
45:26 told him, "Joseph is S alive, and he is
45:28 Joseph my son is S alive; I will go
46:30 know that you are S alive."
48:7 way, when there was S some distance to go
Ex 4:18 see whether they are S alive." And Jethro said
7:13 S Pharaoh's heart was hardened, and he would not
9:2 let them go and S hold them,
9:17 You are S exalting yourself against my people, and
14:14 for you, and you have only to be S
15:16 arm, they are as S as a stone, till
36:3 They S kept bringing him freewill offerings every
Lev 25:51 If there are S many years, according to them
Num 9:10 a journey, he shall S keep the passover to
19:13 unclean; his uncleanness is S on him.
32:14 sinful men, to increase S more the fierce anger
Deut 4:33 you have heard, and S live?
5:24 with man and man S live.
5:26 we have, and has S lived?
Josh 3:8 Jordan, you shall stand S in the Jordan.'"
9:12 our bread; it was S warm when we took
10:12 Israel, "Sun, stand thou S at Gibeon, and thou
10:13 And the sun stood S, and the moon stayed,
14:11 I am S as strong to this day as
Judg 3:25 loss; but when he S did not open the
5:17 Asher sat S at the coast of the sea,
5:27 he fell, he lay S at her feet; at
6:24 To this day it S stands at Ophrah, which
7:4 Gideon, "The people are S too many; take them
8:20 afraid, because he was S a youth.
1Sam 12:7 Now therefore stand S, that I may plead with
12:16 Now therefore stand S and see this great thing,
12:25 But if you S do wickedly, you shall be
13:7 Saul was S at Gilgal, and all the people
14:9 then we will stand S in our place, and
18:29 loved him, Saul was S more afraid of David.
20:14 If I am S alive, show me the loyal
2Sam 1:9 and yet my life S lingers.'
2:23 place where Asahel had fallen and died, stood S
9:1 David said, "Is there S any one left of
9:3 said, "Is there not S some one of the
9:3 the king, "There is S a son of Jonathan;
12:22 "While the child was S alive, I fasted and
14:32 would be better for me to be there S
18:14 Absalom, while he was S alive in the oak.
18:30 So he turned aside, and stood S
19:34 many years have I S to live, that I
19:35 Can I S listen to the voice of singing
24:3 my lord the king S see it; but why
1Kgs 1:14 Then while you are S speaking with the king,
1:22 While she was S speaking with the king, Nathan
1:42 While he was S speaking, behold, Jonathan the son
12:2 it (for he was S in Egypt, whither he
19:12 after the fire a S small voice.
20:32 he said, "Does he S live?
22:43 away, and the people S sacrificed and burned incense
2Kgs 2:11 And as they S went on and talked, behold,
6:33 And while he was S speaking with them, the
14:4 removed; the people S sacrificed and burned incense
15:4 taken away; the people S sacrificed and burned
15:35 not removed; the people S sacrificed and burned
17:29 But every nation S made gods of its own,
23:26 S the LORD did not turn from the fierceness
2Chr 14:7 bars; the land is S ours, because we have
20:17 take your position, stand S, and see the victory
27:2 But the people S followed corrupt practices.
32:16 And his servants said S more against the Lord
33:17 Nevertheless the people S sacrificed at the high
Neh 7:3 and while they are S standing guard let them
Tob 1:4 Israel, while I was S a young man, the
10:6 said to her, "Be S and stop worrying; he
10:7 she answered him, "Be S and stop deceiving me;
Jud 13:11 God, our God, is S with us, to show
Job 2:3 He S holds fast his integrity, although you moved
2:9 to him, "Do you S hold fast your integrity?
4:16 It stood S, but I could not discern its
30:27 turmoil, and is never S; days of affliction come
37:17 when the earth is S because of the south
39:24 ground; he cannot stand S at the sound of
Ps 8:2 of thy foes, to S the enemy and the
23:2 He leads me beside S waters;
37:7 Be S before the LORD, and wait patiently for
46:10 "Be S, and know that I am God.
65:7 with might; who dost S the roaring of the
69:26 hast wounded, they afflict S more.
71:17 taught me, and I S proclaim thy wondrous deeds.
76:8 earth feared and was S,
78:17 Yet they sinned S more against him, rebelling
78:30 while the food was S in their mouths,
78:32 of all this they S sinned; despite his wonders
83:1 thy peace or be S, O God!
92:14 They S bring forth fruit in old age, they
107:29 made the storm be S, and the waves of
139:18 I awake, I am S with thee.
Prov 9:9 and he will be S wiser; teach a righteous
17:7 becoming to a fool; S less is false speech
Eccl 2:3 with wine—my mind S guiding me with wisdom—
4:2 the living who are S alive;
Wis 10:7 of their wickedness S remains: a continually smoking
16:17 things, the fire had S greater effect, for the
17:21 to receive them; but S heavier than darkness were
19:3 For while they were S busy at mourning, and
19:4 punishment which their torments S lacked,
19:10 For they S recalled the events of their sojourn,
Sir 33:20 While you are S alive and have breath in
41:1 in everything, and who S has the vigor to
51:13 While I was S young, before I went on
Is 1:5 Why will you S be smitten, that you continue
5:25 turned away and his hand is stretched out S
9:12 turned away and his hand is stretched out S
9:17 turned away and his hand is stretched out S
9:20 the right, but are S hungry, and they devour
9:21 turned away and his hand is stretched out S
10:4 turned away and his hand is stretched out S
23:2 Be S, O inhabitants of the coast, O merchants
30:7 therefore I have called her "Rahab who sits S
42:14 peace, I have kept S and restrained myself; now
Jer 2:9 "Therefore I S contend with you, says the LORD,
2:22 of your guilt is S before me, says the
8:14 Why do we sit S
31:20 I speak against him, I do remember him S
33:1 time, while he was S shut up in the
37:4 Now Jeremiah was S going in and out among
47:6 Put yourself into your scabbard, rest and be S
51:50 have escaped from the sword, go, stand not S
Ezek 1:24 host; when they stood S, they let down their
1:25 heads; when they stood S, they let down their
8:6 But you will see S greater abominations."
8:13 me, "You will see S greater abominations which they
8:15 You will see S greater abominations than these."
10:17 When they stood S, these stood still, and when
10:17 stood still, these stood S, and when they mounted
16:28 harlot with them, and S you were not satisfied.
24:7 she has shed is S in the midst of
28:9 Will you S say, 'I am a god,' in
32:21 come down, they lie S, the uncircumcised, slain by
Dan 4:31 While the words were S in the king's mouth,
4:36 in my kingdom, and S more greatness was added
Hos 11:12 deceit; but Judah is S known by God, and
Amos 6:10 the house, "Is there S any one with you?"
Hab 2:3 For S the vision awaits its time; it hastens

S

	3:11	sun and moon stood S in their habitation at
Hag	2:19	and the olive tree S yield nothing?
Zech	12:6	about, while Jerusalem shall S be inhabited in its
	14:12	rot while they are S on their feet, their
1Mac	1:6	them while he was S alive.
	4:4	while the division was S absent from the camp.
	5:14	While the letter was S being read, behold, other
	6:27	them, they will do S greater things, and you
	6:55	whom King Antiochus while S living had appointed
	10:27	And now continue S to keep faith with us,
	10:88	things, he honored Jonathan S more;
	12:36	the walls of Jerusalem S higher, and to erect
2Mac	7:5	him to the fire, S breathing, and to fry
	7:24	The youngest brother being S alive, Antiochus not
	7:30	While she was S speaking, the young man said,
	9:9	and while he was S living in anguish and
	11:8	while they were S near Jerusalem, a horseman
	14:11	Judas, quickly inflamed Demetrius S more.
	14:45	S alive and aflame with anger, he rose, and
Mt	12:46	While he was S speaking to the people, behold,
	15:16	said, "Are you also S without understanding?
	17:5	He was S speaking, when lo, a bright cloud
	19:20	observed; what do I S lack?"
	26:45	to them, "Are you S sleeping and taking your
	26:47	While he was S speaking, Judas came, one of
	26:65	Why do we S need witnesses?
	27:63	said, while he was S alive, 'After three days
Mk	4:24	measure you get, and S more will be given
	4:39	Be S
	5:35	While he was S speaking, there came from the
	12:6	He had S one other, a beloved son; finally
	14:41	to them, "Are you S sleeping and taking your
	14:43	immediately, while he was S speaking, Judas came,
	14:63	said, "Why do we S need witnesses?
Lk	7:14	and touched the bier, and the bearers stood S
	8:49	While he was S speaking, a man from the
	14:22	has been done, and S there is room.'
	18:22	him, "One thing you S lack.
	22:45	While he was S speaking, there came a crowd,
	22:57	about an hour S another insisted, saying, "Certainly
	22:58	immediately, while he was S speaking, the cock
	24:6	you, while he was S in Galilee,
	24:17	And they stood S, looking sad.
	24:41	And while they S disbelieved for joy, and wondered,
	24:44	you, while I was S with you, that everything
Jn	5:16	"My Father is working S, and I am working."
	11:30	the village, but was S in the place where
	14:25	you, while I am S with you.
	20:1	early, while it was S dark, and saw that
Acts	9:1	But Saul, S breathing threats and murder against
	10:44	While Peter was S saying this, the Holy Spirit
	20:9	sleep as Paul talked S longer; and being overcome
Rom	3:7	glory, why am I S being condemned as a
	4:11	faith while he was S uncircumcised.
	5:6	While we were S weak, at the right time
	6:2	who died to sin S live in it?
	9:19	then, "Why does he S find fault?
1Cor	3:3	ready, for you are S of the flesh.
	9:12	you, do not we S more?
	12:31	will show you a S more excellent way.
	15:6	most of whom are S alive, though some have
	15:17	futile and you are S in your sins.
2Cor	1:12	in the world, and S more toward you, with
	5:4	For while we are S in this tent, we
	7:7	so that I rejoiced S more.
	7:13	own comfort we rejoiced S more at the joy
Gal	1:10	If I were S pleasing men, I should not
	1:22	And I was S not known by sight to
	5:11	But if I, brethren, S preach circumcision, why am
	5:11	circumcision, why am I S persecuted?
Col	2:20	live as if you S belonged to the world?
2Thes	2:5	that when I was S with you I told
Heb	6:10	the saints, as you S do.
	7:10	Abraham, for he was S in the loins of
	9:8	the outer tent is S standing
	11:4	his faith he is S speaking.
1Jn	2:9	and hates his brother is in the darkness S
Rev	3:4	Yet you have S a few names in Sardis,
	9:12	behold, two woes are S to come.
	22:11	Let the evildoer S do evil, and the filthy
	22:11	evil, and the filthy S be filthy, and the
	22:11	filthy, and the righteous S do right, and the
	22:11	right, and the holy S be holy."

STILLED (7)

Neh	8:11	So the Levites S all the people, saying, "Be
Job	26:12	By his power he S the sea; by his
Sir	43:23	By his counsel he S the great deep and
	46:7	people from sin, and S their wicked murmuring.
Is	24:8	of the timbrels is S, the noise of the
	24:8	has ceased, the mirth of the lyre is S
	25:5	cloud, so the song of the ruthless is S

STILLEST

Ps	89:9	its waves rise, thou S them.

STILLING

Jer	51:55	laying Babylon waste, and S her mighty voice.

STING (2)

1Cor	15:55	O death, where is thy S
	15:56	The S of death is sin, and the power

STINGS (3)

Prov	23:32	like a serpent, and S like an adder.
Rev	9:5	a scorpion, when it S a man.
	9:10	tails like scorpions, and S, and their power of

STINGY (3)

Prov	23:6	a man who is S; do not desire his
Sir	14:3	not seemly for a S man; and of what
	14:10	A S man's eye begrudges bread, and it is

STINK

Is	50:2	a desert; their fish S for lack of water,

STINT

Sir	35:8	generously, and do not S the first fruits of

STIR (19)

Deut	32:21	So I will S them to jealousy with those
Judg	13:25	the LORD began to S him in Mahaneh-dan, between
Job	41:10	that he dares to S him up.
Ps	78:38	often, and did not S up all his wrath.
	80:2	S up thy might, and come to save us!
	140:2	in their heart, and S up wars continually.
Song	2:7	the field, that you S not up nor awaken
	3:5	the field, that you S not up nor awaken
	8:4	of Jerusalem, that you S not up nor awaken
Is	19:2	And I will S up Egyptians against Egyptians, and
Jer	51:1	LORD: "Behold, I will S up the spirit of
Dan	11:2	his riches, he shall S up all against the
	11:25	And he shall S up his power and his
Hos	7:5	whose baker ceases to S the fire, from the
Joel	3:7	But now I will S them up from the
	3:9	the nations: Prepare war, S up the mighty men.
Acts	12:18	there was no small S among the soldiers over
	19:23	there arose no little S concerning the Way.
Heb	10:24	us consider how to S up one another to

STIRRED (30)

Ex	35:21	every one whose heart S him, and every one
	36:2	every one whose heart S him up to come
Deut	32:16	They S him to jealousy with strange gods; with
	32:21	They have S me to jealousy with what is
Ruth	1:19	the whole town was S because of them; and
1Sam	22:8	that my son has S up my servant against
	26:19	the LORD who has S you up against me,
1Chr	5:26	the God of Israel S up the spirit of
2Chr	21:16	And the LORD S up against Jehoram the anger
	36:22	be accomplished, the LORD S up the spirit of
Ezra	1:1	be accomplished, the LORD S up the spirit of
	1:5	whose spirit God had S to go up to
	4:15	and that sedition was S up in it from
Wis	11:6	of an ever-flowing river, S up and defiled with
Sir	51:21	My heart was S to seek her, therefore I
Is	14:9	us.' Sheol beneath is S up to meet you
	41:2	Who S up one from the east whom victory
	41:25	I S up one from the north, and he
Jer	51:11	The LORD has S up the spirit of the
Hag	1:14	And the LORD S up the spirit of Zerubbabel
1Mac	2:24	be burned with zeal and his heart was S
	3:49	the tithes, and they S up the Nazirites who
Mt	21:10	all the city was S, saying, "Who is this?"
Mk	15:11	But the chief priests S up the crowd to
Acts	6:12	And they S up the people and the elders
	13:50	of the city, and S up persecution against Paul
	14:2	But the unbelieving Jews S up the Gentiles and
	21:27	him in the temple, S up all the crowd,
	21:38	Egyptian, then, who recently S up a revolt and
2Cor	9:2	and your zeal has S up most of them.

S

STIRRING (10)

Judg 9:31 Shechem, and they are S up the city against
Is 13:17 Behold, I am S up the Medes against them,
Jer 6:22 a great nation is S from the farthest parts
25:32 a great tempest is S from the farthest parts
50:9 For behold, I am S up and bringing against
50:41 and many kings are S from the farthest parts
Dan 7:2 winds of heaven were S up the great sea.
2Mac 14:6 keeping up war and S up sedition, and will
Acts 17:13 they came there too, S up and inciting the
24:11 with any one or S up a crowd, either

STIRS (14)

Deut 32:11 Like an eagle that S up its nest, that
Job 17:8 this, and the innocent S himself up against the
Prov 10:12 Hatred S up strife, but love covers all offenses.
15:1 but a harsh word S up anger.
15:18 A hot-tempered man S up strife, but he who
28:25 A greedy man S up strife, but he who
29:22 A man of wrath S up strife, and a
Is 9:11 adversaries against them, and S up their enemies.
42:13 man of war he S up his fury; he
51:15 LORD your God, who S up the sea so
54:15 If any one S up strife, it is not
54:15 not from me; whoever S up strife with you
Jer 31:35 light by night, who S up the sea so
Lk 23:5 were urgent, saying, "He S up the people, teaching

STOCK (4)

Tob 5:13 My brother, you come of good S
Ps 80:15 for this vine, the S which thy right hand
Sir 47:22 Jacob, and to David a root of his S
Ezek 44:22 a virgin of the S of the house of

STOCKS (7)

2Chr 16:10 put him in the S, in prison, for he
Job 13:27 my feet in the S, and watchest all my
33:11 my feet in the S, and watches all my
Jer 20:2 put him in the S that were in the
20:3 released Jeremiah from the S, Jeremiah said to him,
29:26 put him in the S and collar.
Acts 16:24 inner prison and fastened their feet in the S

STOIC

Acts 17:18 of the Epicurean and S philosophers met him.

STOLE (7)

Gen 31:19 his sheep, and Rachel S her father's household gods.
2Sam 15:6 for judgment; so Absalom S the hearts of the
19:3 And the people S into the city that day
2Kgs 11:2 son of Ahaziah, and S him away from among
2Chr 22:11 son of Ahaziah, and S him away from among
2Mac 4:32 obtained a suitable opportunity, S some of the gold
Mt 28:13 came by night and S him away while we

STOLEN (16)

Gen 30:33 lambs, if found with me, shall be counted S
31:32 know that Rachel had S them.
31:39 you required it, whether S by day or stolen
31:39 stolen by day or S by night.
40:15 For I was indeed S out of the land
44:4 Why have you S my silver cup?
Ex 22:2 If the S beast is found alive in his
22:7 keep, and it is S out of the man's
22:12 But if it is S from him, he shall
Josh 7:11 devoted things; they have S, and lied, and put
2Sam 19:41 the men of Judah S you away, and brought
21:12 of Jabesh-gilead, who had S them from the public
Tob 2:13 It is not S, is it?
2:13 it is not right to eat what is S
Prov 9:17 without sense she says, S water is sweet, and
2Mac 4:39 many of the gold vessels had already been S

STOMACH (13)

Deut 18:3 the shoulder and the two cheeks and the S
Job 20:14 is turned in his S; it is the gall
Sir 36:18 The S will take any food, yet one food
37:5 a friend for their S's sake, and in the
40:30 sweet, but in his S a fire is kindled.
Ezek 3:3 you and fill your S with it." Then I
Mt 15:17 mouth passes into the S, and so passes on?
Mk 7:18 his heart but his S, and so passes on?"
1Cor 6:13 is meant for the S and the stomach for
6:13 the stomach and the S for food"--and God
1Tim 5:23 the sake of your S and your frequent ailments.
Rev 10:9 be bitter to your S, but sweet as honey
10:10 had eaten it my S was made bitter.

STOMACHS

Ezek 7:19 hunger or fill their S with it.

STONE (196)

Gen 2:12 good; bdellium and onyx S are there.
11:3 they had brick for S, and bitumen for mortar.
28:18 and he took the S which he had put
28:22 my God, and this S, which I have set
29:2 The S on the well's mouth was large,
29:3 shepherds would roll the S from the mouth of
29:3 sheep, and put the S back in its place
29:8 gathered together, and the S is rolled from the
29:10 up and rolled the S from the well's mouth,
31:45 So Jacob took a S, and set it up
35:14 him, a pillar of S; and he poured out
Ex 7:19 in vessels of wood and in vessels of S
8:26 eyes, will they not S us?
15:5 they went down into the depths like a S
15:16 as still as a S, till thy people, O
17:4 are almost ready to S me."
17:12 so they took a S and put it under
20:25 me an altar of S, you shall not build
21:18 the other with a S or with his fist
24:10 a pavement of sapphire S, like the very heaven
24:12 you the tables of S, with the law and
28:10 names on the one S, and the names of
28:10 six on the other S, in the order of
31:18 the testimony, tables of S, written with the finger
34:1 "Cut two tables of S like the first; and
34:4 cut two tables of S like the first; and
34:4 and took in his hand two tables of S
Lev 20:2 of the land shall S him with stones.
24:14 let all the congregation S him.
24:16 all the congregation shall S him; the sojourner as
26:1 set up a figured S in your land, to
Num 14:10 the congregation said to S them with stones.
15:35 all the congregation shall S him with stones outside
35:17 him down with a S in the hand, by
35:23 wait, or used a S, by which a man
Deut 4:13 and he wrote them upon two tables of S
4:28 gods of wood and S, the work of men's
5:22 upon two tables of S, and gave them to
9:9 receive the tables of S, the tables of the
9:10 the two tables of S written with the finger
9:11 the two tables of S, the tables of the
10:1 'Hew two tables of S like the first, and
10:3 hewed two tables of S like the first, and
13:10 You shall S him to death with stones, because
17:5 thing, and you shall S that man or woman
21:21 of the city shall S him to death with
22:21 of her city shall S her to death with
22:24 city, and you shall S them to death with
28:36 you shall serve other gods, of wood and S
28:64 gods, of wood and S, which neither you nor
29:17 idols of wood and S, of silver and gold,
Josh 4:5 each of you a S upon his shoulder, according
15:6 goes up to the S of Bohan the son
18:17 goes down to the S of Bohan the son
24:26 he took a great S, and set it up
24:27 the people, "Behold, this S shall be a witness
Judg 9:5 seventy men, upon one S; but Jotham the youngest
9:18 seventy men on one S, and have made Abimelech,
20:16 one could sling a S at a hair, and
1Sam 6:14 A great S was there; and they split up
6:15 them upon the great S; and the men of
6:18 The great S, beside which they set down the
7:12 Then Samuel took a S and set it up
14:33 treacherously; roll a great S to me here.
17:49 and took out a S, and slung it, and
17:49 on his forehead; the S sank into his forehead,
17:50 sling and with a S, and struck the Philistine,
20:19 and remain beside yonder S heap.
20:41 rose from beside the S heap and fell on
25:37 died within him, and he became as a S
2Sam 12:30 it was a precious S; and it was placed
20:8 were at the great S which is in Gibeon,
1Kgs 1:9 fatlings by the Serpent's S, which is beside En-rogel,
5:15 eighty thousand hewers of S in the hill country,
5:18 the timber and the S to build the house.
6:7 built, it was with S prepared at the quarry;
6:18 all was cedar, no S was seen.
6:36 three courses of hewn S and one course of
7:12 three courses of hewn S round about, and a
8:9 the two tables of S which Moses put there

S

10:27 common in Jerusalem as S, and he made cedar
21:10 take him out, and S him to death."
2Kgs 3:25 every man threw a S, until it was covered;
12:12 buy timber and quarried S for making repairs on
16:17 it, and put it upon a pediment of S
19:18 hands, wood and S; therefore they were destroyed.
22:6 buying timber and quarried S to repair the house.
1Chr 20:2 it was a precious S; and it was placed
22:14 of it; timber and S too I have provided.
2Chr 1:15 common in Jerusalem as S, and he made cedar
2:14 gold, silver, bronze, iron, S, and wood, and in
9:27 common in Jerusalem as S, and cedar as plentiful
34:11 builders to buy quarried S, and timber for binders
Neh 4:3 will break down their S wall!"
9:11 the depths, as a S into mighty waters.
Job 38:30 waters become hard like S, and the face of
41:24 is hard as a S, hard as the nether
Ps 91:12 up, lest you dash your foot against a S
118:22 The S which the builders rejected has become the
Prov 17:8 is like a magic S in the eyes of
24:31 with nettles, and its S wall was broken down.
26:8 one who binds the S in the sling is
26:27 into it, and a S will come back upon
27:3 S is heavy, and sand is weighty, but a
Wis 11:4 flinty rock, and slaking of thirst from hard S
13:10 animals, or a useless S, the work of an
14:21 bestowed on objects of S or wood the name
Sir 6:21 like a heavy testing S, and he will not
22:1 compared to a filthy S, and every one hisses
22:18 One who throws a S at birds scares them
27:25 Whoever throws a S straight up throws it on
29:10 it rust under a S and be lost.
47:4 his hand with a S in the sling and
Is 8:14 a sanctuary, and a S of offense, and a
28:16 for a foundation a S, a tested stone, a
28:16 a stone, a tested S, a precious cornerstone, of
37:19 \ hands, wood and S; therefore they were destroyed.
Jer 2:27 father,' and to a S, 'You gave me birth.'
3:9 land, committing adultery with S and tree.
51:26 No S shall be taken from you for a
51:26 a corner and no S for a foundation, but
51:63 this book, bind a S to it, and cast
Ezek 16:40 you, and they shall S you and cut you
20:32 and worship wood and S
23:47 And the host shall S them and dispatch them
28:13 God; every precious S was your covering, carnelian,
36:26 flesh the heart of S and give you a
40:42 four tables of hewn S for the burnt offering,
Dan 2:34 As you looked, a S was cut out by
2:35 But the S that struck the image became a
2:45 you saw that a S was cut from a
5:4 of gold and silver, bronze, iron, wood, and S
5:23 bronze, iron, wood, and S, which do not see
6:17 And a S was brought and laid upon the
Hos 12:11 also shall be like S heaps on the furrows
Amos 5:11 built houses of hewn S, but you shall not
Hab 2:11 For the S will cry out from the wall,
2:19 Awake; to a dumb S, Arise!
Hag 2:15 Before a S was placed upon a stone in
2:15 was placed upon a S in the temple of
Zech 3:9 For behold, upon the S which I have set
3:9 Joshua, upon a single S with seven facets, I
4:7 bring forward the top S amid shouts of 'Grace,
12:3 make Jerusalem a heavy S for all the peoples;
1Mac 2:36 them or hurl a S at them or block
10:73 where there is no S or pebble, or place
13:27 be seen, with polished S at the front and
Mt 4:6 up, lest you strike your foot against a S
7:9 asks him for bread, will give him a S
21:42 scriptures: 'The very S which the builders rejected
21:44 who falls on this S will be broken to
24:2 be left here one S upon another, that will
27:60 he rolled a great S to the door of
27:66 secure by sealing the S and setting a guard.
28:2 and rolled back the S, and sat upon it.
Mk 12:10 scripture: 'The very S which the builders rejected
13:2 be left here one S upon another, that will
15:45 and he rolled a S against the door of
16:3 will roll away the S for us from the
16:4 they saw that the S was rolled back; --
Lk 4:3 of God, command this S to become bread."
4:11 up, lest you strike your foot against a S
19:44 will not leave one S upon another in you;
20:6 all the people will S us; for they are
20:17 is written: 'The very S which the builders rejected
20:18 who falls on that S will be broken to
21:6 be left here one S upon another that will
22:41 from them about a S's throw, and knelt down
24:2 And they found the S rolled away from the
Jn 2:6 Now six S jars were standing there, for the
8:5 Moses commanded us to S such.
8:7 first to throw a S at her."
10:31 up stones again to S him.
10:32 of these do you S me?"
10:33 good work that we S you but for blasphemy;
11:8 but now seeking to S you, and are you
11:38 a cave, and a S lay upon it.
11:39 Jesus said, "Take away the S
11:41 So they took away the S
20:1 and saw that the S had been taken away
Acts 4:11 This is the S which was rejected by you
14:5 molest them and to S them,
17:29 gold, or silver, or S, a representation by the
19:35 and of the sacred S that fell from the
Rom 9:32 stumbled over the stumbling S,
9:33 laying in Zion a S that will make men
2Cor 3:3 not on tablets of S but on tablets of
3:7 carved in letters on S, came with such splendor
1Pet 2:4 him, to that living S, rejected by men but
2:6 laying in Zion a S, a cornerstone chosen and
2:7 not believe, "The very S which the builders rejected
2:8 and "A S that will make men stumble, a
Rev 2:17 give him a white S, with a new name
2:17 name written on the S which no one knows
9:20 silver and bronze and S and wood, which cannot
18:21 angel took up a S like a great millstone

STONECUTTERS (3)

2Kgs 12:12 the masons and the S, as well as to
1Chr 22:2 Israel, and he set S to prepare dressed stones
22:15 abundance of workmen: S, masons, carpenters, and

STONED (22)

Ex 19:13 but he shall be S or shot; whether beast
21:28 the ox shall be S, and its flesh shall
21:29 the ox shall be S, and its owner also
21:32 shekels of silver, and the ox shall be S
Lev 20:27 death; they shall be S with stones, their blood
24:23 of the camp, and S him with stones.
Num 15:36 outside the camp, and S him to death with
Josh 7:25 And all Israel S him with stones; they burned
7:25 them with fire, and S them with stones.
1Kgs 12:18 labor, and all Israel S him to death with
21:13 outside the city, and S him to death with
21:14 saying, "Naboth has been S; he is dead."
21:15 that Naboth had been S and was dead, Jezebel
2Chr 10:18 the people of Israel S him to death with
24:21 of the king they S him with stones in
Mt 21:35 one, killed another, and S another.
Acts 5:26 were afraid of being S by the people.
7:58 of the city and S him; and the witnesses
14:19 persuaded the people, they S Paul and dragged him
2Cor 11:25 have been beaten with rods; once I was S
Heb 11:37 They were S, they were sawn in two, they
12:20 a beast touches the mountain, it shall be S

STONEHEAP

Job 8:17 roots twine about the S; he lives among the

STONES (172)

Gen 28:11 Taking one of the S of the place, he
31:46 And Jacob said to his kinsmen, "Gather S
31:46 and they took S, and made a heap; and
Ex 20:25 build it of hewn S; for if you wield
25:7 the fragrant incense, onyx S, and stones for setting,
25:7 incense, onyx stones, and S for setting, for the
28:9 shall take two onyx S, and engrave on them
28:11 you engrave the two S with the names of
28:12 shall set the two S upon the shoulder-pieces of
28:12 of the ephod, as S of remembrance for the
28:17 you shall set in it four rows of S
28:21 There shall be twelve S with their names according
31:5 and bronze, in cutting S for setting, and in
35:9 fragrant incense, and onyx S and stones for setting,
35:9 and onyx stones and S for setting, for the
35:27 the leaders brought onyx S and stones to be
35:27 brought onyx stones and S to be set, for
35:33 and bronze, in cutting S for setting, and in
39:6 The onyx S were prepared, enclosed in settings of
39:7 the ephod, to be S of remembrance for the
39:10 And they set in it four rows of S
39:14 There were twelve S with their names according to

Lev 14:40 they take out the S in which is the
14:42 they shall take other S and put them in
14:42 the place of those S, and he shall take
14:43 has taken out the S and scraped the house
14:45 down the house, its S and timber and all
20:2 people of the land shall stone him with S
20:27 shall be stoned with S, their blood shall be
24:23 out of the camp, and stoned him with S
Num 14:10 all the congregation said to stone them with S
15:35 shall stone him with S outside the camp."
15:36 him to death with S, as the LORD commanded
33:52 destroy all their figured S, and destroy all their
Deut 8:9 nothing, a land whose S are iron, and out
13:10 him to death with S, because he sought to
17:5 stone that man or woman to death with S
21:21 him to death with S; so you shall purge
22:21 her to death with S, because she has wrought
22:24 them to death with S, the young woman because
27:2 shall set up large S, and plaster them with
27:4 shall set up these S, concerning which I command
27:5 God, an altar of S; you shall lift up
27:6 your God of unhewn S; and you shall offer
27:8 shall write upon the S all the words of
Josh 4:3 command them, 'Take twelve S from here out of
4:6 come, 'What do those S mean to you?'
4:7 So these S shall be to the people of
4:8 and took up twelve S out of the midst
4:9 Joshua set up twelve S in the midst of
4:20 And those twelve S, which they took out of
4:21 come, 'What do these S mean?'
7:25 Israel stoned him with S; they burned them with
7:25 burned them with fire, and stoned them with S
7:26 a great heap of S that remains to this
8:29 a great heap of S, which stands there to
8:31 "an altar of unhewn S, upon which no man
8:32 he wrote upon the S a copy of the
10:11 LORD threw down great S from heaven upon them
10:18 Joshua said, "Roll great S against the mouth of
10:27 and they set great S against the mouth of
Judg 3:19 back at the sculptured S near Gilgal, and said,
3:26 beyond the sculptured S, and escaped to Se-irah.
6:26 the stronghold here, with S laid in due order;
1Sam 17:40 and chose five smooth S from the brook, and
2Sam 16:6 And he threw S at David, and at all
16:13 he went, and threw S at him and flung
18:17 very great heap of S; and all Israel fled
1Kgs 5:17 quarried out great, costly S in order to lay
5:17 lay the foundation of the house with dressed S
7:9 were made of costly S, hewn according to measure,
7:10 foundation was of costly S, huge stones, stones of
7:10 of costly stones, huge S, stones of eight and
7:10 costly stones, huge stones, S of eight and ten
7:11 were costly S, hewn according to measurement,
10:2 much gold, and precious S; and when she came
10:10 of spices, and precious S; never again came such
10:11 very great amount of almug wood and precious S
12:18 and all Israel stoned him to death with S
15:22 they carried away the S of Ramah and its
18:31 down; Elijah took twelve S, according to the number
18:32 name"; and with the S he built an altar
18:38 the wood, and the S, and the dust, and
19:6 cake baked on hot S and a jar of
21:13 the city, and stoned him to death with S
2Kgs 3:19 and ruin every good piece of land with S
3:25 trees; till only its S were left in Kir-hareseth,
23:15 broke in pieces its S, crushing them to dust;
1Chr 12:2 shoot arrows and sling S with either the right
22:2 stonecutters to prepare dressed S for building the
29:2 of onyx and S for setting, antimony, colored
29:2 for setting, antimony, colored S, all sorts of precious
29:2 all sorts of precious S, and marble.
29:8 And whoever had precious S gave them to the
2Chr 3:6 He adorned the house with settings of precious S
9:1 bearing spices and very much gold and precious S
9:9 of spices, and precious S: there were no spices
9:10 gold from Ophir, brought algum wood and precious S
10:18 people of Israel stoned him to death with S
16:6 they carried away the S of Ramah and its
24:21 they stoned him with S in the court of
26:14 of mail, bows, and S for slinging.
26:15 and the corners, to shoot arrows and great S
32:27 for gold, for precious S, for spices, for shields,
Ezra 5:8 being built with huge S, and timber is laid
6:4 three courses of great S and one course of
Neh 4:2 Will they revive the S out of the heaps
Tob 13:16 her walls with precious S, and her towers and
13:17 beryl and ruby and S of Ophir;
Jud 1:2 about Ecbatana with hewn S three cubits thick and
6:12 coming up by casting S at them.
10:21 with purple and gold and emeralds and precious S
Esth 1:6 of porphyry, marble, mother-of-pearl and precious S
15:6 his majesty, all covered with gold and precious S
Job 5:23 in league with the S of the field, and
6:12 strength the strength of S, or is my flesh
14:19 waters wear away the S; the torrents wash away
22:24 of Ophir among the S of the torrent-bed,
28:6 Its S are the place of sapphires, and it
Ps 102:14 thy servants hold her S dear, and have pity
Prov 20:15 and abundance of costly S; but the lips of
Eccl 3:5 time to cast away S, and a time to
3:5 a time to gather S together; a time to
10:9 He who quarries S is hurt by them; and
Wis 18:24 the four rows of S, and thy majesty on
Sir 21:8 like one who gathers S for his burial mound.
21:10 is smoothly paved with S, but at its end
27:2 into a fissure between S, so sin is wedged
45:11 a craftsman; with precious S engraved like signets,
50:9 all kinds of precious S;
Is 5:2 and cleared it of S, and planted it with
9:10 will build with dressed S; the sycamores have been
14:19 go down to the S of the Pit, like
27:9 he makes all the S of the altars like
54:11 I will set your S in antimony, and lay
54:12 of carbuncles, and all your wall of precious S
57:6 Among the smooth S of the valley is your
60:17 wood, bronze, instead of S, iron.
62:10 highway, clear it of S, lift up an ensign
Jer 43:9 in your hands large S, and hide them in
43:10 his throne above these S which I have hid,
Lam 3:9 my ways with hewn S, he has made my
3:53 the pit and cast S on me;
4:1 The holy S lie scattered at the head of
Bar 6:39 and silver are like S from the mountain, and
Ezek 26:12 your pleasant houses; your S and timber and soil
27:22 spices, and all precious S, and gold.
28:14 the midst of the S of fire you walked.
28:16 the midst of the S of fire.
Dan 11:38 and silver, with precious S and costly gifts.
Mic 1:6 will pour down her S into the valley, and
Zech 5:4 his house and consume it, both timber and S
1Mac 4:43 and removed the defiled S to an unclean place.
4:46 altar, and stored the S in a convenient place
4:47 Then they took unhewn S, as the law directs,
5:47 them out and blocked up the gates with S
6:51 to throw fire and S, machines to shoot arrows,
10:11 Mount Zion with squared S, for better fortification;
2Mac 1:16 the ceiling, they threw S and struck down the
1:31 that was left should be poured upon large S
4:41 attack, some picked up S, some blocks of wood,
Mt 3:9 is able from these S to raise up children
4:3 of God, command these S to become loaves of
Mk 5:5 was always crying out, and bruising himself with S
13:1 "Look, Teacher, what wonderful S and what
Lk 3:8 is able from these S to raise up children
19:40 were silent, the very S would cry out."
21:5 was adorned with noble S and offerings, he said,
Jn 8:59 So they took up S to throw at him;
10:31 The Jews took up S again to stone him.
1Cor 3:12 with gold, silver, precious S, wood, hay, straw—
1Pet 2:5 precious; and like living S be yourselves built into

STONING (4)

1Sam 30:6 the people spoke of S him, because all the
Mt 23:36 killing the prophets and S those who are sent
Lk 13:34 killing the prophets and S those who are sent
Acts 7:59 And as they were S Stephen, he prayed, "Lord

STONY (2)

Sir 32:20 do not stumble over S ground.
Ezek 11:19 I will take the S heart out of their

STOOD (272)

Gen 18:2 and behold, three men S in front of him.
18:8 before them; and he S by them under the
18:22 Sodom; but Abraham still S before the LORD.
19:27 place where he had S before the LORD;
28:13 And behold, the LORD S above it and said,
37:7 my sheaf arose and S upright; and behold, your
41:3 Nile after them, and S by the other cows
43:15 down to Egypt, and S before Joseph.
45:1 before all those who S by him; and he
Ex 2:4 And his sister S at a distance, to know

	2:17	them away; but Moses S up and helped them,
	9:10	from the kiln, and S before Pharaoh, and Moses
	14:19	from before them and S behind them,
	15:8	piled up, the floods S up in a heap;
	18:13	people, and the people S about Moses from morning
	20:18	and trembled; and they S afar off,
	20:21	And the people S afar off, while Moses drew
	32:26	their enemies), then Moses S in the gate of
	33:8	up, and every man S at his tent door,
	34:5	in the cloud and S with him there, and
Lev	9:5	congregation drew near and S before the LORD.
Num	12:5	pillar of cloud, and S at the door of
	16:18	upon them, and they S at the entrance of
	16:27	Abiram came out and S at the door of
	16:48	And he S between the dead and the living;
	22:24	angel of the LORD S in a narrow path
	22:26	LORD went ahead, and S in a narrow place,
	27:2	And they S before Moses, and before Eleazar the
Deut	4:10	the day that you S before the LORD your
	4:11	you came near and S at the foot of
	5:5	the fire, while I S between the LORD and
	31:15	the pillar of cloud S by the door of
Josh	3:16	coming down from above S and rose up in
	3:17	covenant of the LORD S on dry ground in
	4:3	where the priests' feet S, and carry them over
	4:9	of the covenant had S; and they are there
	4:10	who bore the ark S in the midst of
	4:14	all Israel; and they S in awe of him,
	4:14	him, as they had S in awe of Moses,
	5:13	and behold, a man S before him with his
	8:33	officers and their judges, S on opposite sides of
	10:13	And the sun S still, and the moon stayed,
	11:13	of the cities that S on mounds did Israel
	20:6	city until he has S before the congregation for
	20:9	of blood, till he S before the congregation.
Judg	7:21	They S every man in his place round about
	9:7	Jotham, he went and S on the top of
	9:35	Ebed went out and S in the entrance of
	9:44	him rushed forward and S at the entrance of
	18:16	their weapons of war, S by the entrance of
	18:17	image, while the priest S by the entrance of
1Sam	3:10	the LORD came and S forth, calling as at
	10:23	there; and when he S among the people, he
	17:3	And the Philistines S on the mountain on the
	17:3	one side, and Israel S on the mountain on
	17:8	He S and shouted to the ranks of Israel,
	17:26	to the men who S by him, "What shall
	17:51	Then David ran and S over the Philistine, and
	18:15	had great success, he S in awe of him.
	22:7	to his servants who S about him, "Hear now,
	22:9	Doeg the Edomite, who S by the servants of
	22:17	to the guard who S about him, "Turn and
	26:13	the other side, and S afar off on the
2Sam	1:10	still lingers.' So I S beside him, and slew
	2:23	had fallen and died, S still.
	12:17	elders of his house S beside him, to raise
	18:4	So the king S at the side of the
	18:13	you yourself would have S aloof."
	18:30	he turned aside, and S still.
	20:15	the city, and it S against the rampart; and
1Kgs	1:28	the king's presence, and S before the king.
	3:15	came to Jerusalem, and S before the ark of
	3:16	to the king, and S before him.
	3:28	had rendered; and they S in awe of the
	7:25	It S upon twelve oxen, three facing north, three
	8:14	of Israel, while all the assembly of Israel S
	8:22	Then Solomon S before the altar of the LORD
	8:55	toward heaven; and he S, and blessed all the
	10:20	rests, while twelve lions S there, one on each
	12:6	old men, who had S before Solomon his father
	12:8	up with him and S before him.
	13:24	road, and the ass S beside it; the lion
	13:24	it; the lion also S beside the body.
	19:13	and went out and S at the entrance of
	22:21	spirit came forward and S before the LORD, saying,
2Kgs	2:7	prophets also went, and S at some distance from
	2:13	and went back and S on the bank of
	4:12	had called her, she S before him.
	4:15	had called her, she S in the doorway.
	5:15	and he came and S before him; and he
	5:25	He went in, and S before his master, and
	8:9	When he came and S before him, he said,
	10:9	he went out, he S, and said to all
	11:11	LORD; and the guards S, every man with his
	13:21	Elisha, he revived, and S on his feet.
	18:17	arrived, they came and S by the conduit of
	18:28	Then the Rabshakeh S and called out in a
	23:3	And the king S by the pillar and made
1Chr	6:39	his brother Asaph, who S on his right hand,
	21:1	Satan S up against Israel, and incited David to
2Chr	3:13	twenty cubits; the cherubim S on their feet, facing
	4:4	It S upon twelve oxen, three facing north, three
	5:12	cymbals, harps, and lyres, S east of the altar
	6:3	of Israel, while all the assembly of Israel S
	6:12	Then Solomon S before the altar of the LORD
	6:13	the court; and he S upon it.
	7:6	The priests S at their posts; the Levites also,
	7:6	them the priests sounded trumpets; and all Israel S
	9:19	rests, while twelve lions S there, one on each
	10:6	old men, who had S before Solomon his father
	10:8	up with him and S before him.
	13:4	Then Abijah S up on Mount Zemaraim which is
	18:20	spirit came forward and S before the LORD, saying,
	20:5	And Jehoshaphat S in the assembly of Judah and
	20:13	the men of Judah S before the LORD, with
	20:19	Kohathites and the Korahites, S up to praise the
	20:20	they went out, Jehoshaphat S and said, "Hear me,
	24:20	the priest; and he S above the people, and
	28:12	the son of Hadlai, S up against those who
	29:26	The Levites S with the instruments of David, and
	34:4	the incense altars which S above them; and he
	34:31	And the king S in his place and made
	35:10	prepared for, the priests S in their place, and
Ezra	10:10	And Ezra the priest S up and said to
Neh	4:16	mail; and the leaders S behind all the house
	8:4	And Ezra the scribe S on a wooden pulpit
	8:4	and beside him S Mattithiah, Shema, Anaiah, Uriah,
	8:5	and when he opened it all the people S
	9:2	from all foreigners, and S and confessed their sins
	9:3	And they S up in their place and read
	9:4	stairs of the Levites S Jeshua, Bani, Kadmi-el,
	12:9	and Unno their brethren S opposite them in the
	12:40	those who gave thanks S in the house of
Tob	12:21	Then they S up; but they saw him no
Jud	4:14	all the priests who S before the Lord and
	8:3	For as he S overseeing the men who were
	10:18	and they came and S around her as she
Esth	5:1	her royal robes and S in the inner court
	8:5	and Esther rose and S before the king.
	15:6	all the doors, she S before the king.
Job	4:15	hair of my flesh S up.
	4:16	It S still, but I could not discern its
	29:8	the aged rose and S;
	31:34	my bosom, because I S in great fear of
Ps	33:9	he commanded, and it S forth.
	104:6	a garment; the waters S above the mountains.
	106:23	Moses, his chosen one, S in the breach before
	106:30	Then Phinehas S up and interposed, and the plague
Wis	10:11	oppressors were covetous, she S by him and made
	18:16	thy authentic command, and S and filled all things
	19:7	emerging where water had S before, an unhindered
Sir	39:17	his word the waters S in a heap, and
	45:23	of the Lord, and S fast, when the people
	46:3	Who before him ever S so firm?
	50:12	the priests, as he S by the hearth of
	51:2	Before those who S by thou wast my helper
Is	6:2	Above him S the seraphim; each had six wings:
	36:2	And he S by the conduit of the upper
	36:13	Then the Rabshakeh S and called out in a
Jer	15:1	"Though Moses and Samuel S before me, yet my
	18:20	Remember how I S before thee to speak good
	19:14	to prophesy, and he S in the court of
	23:18	who among them has S in the council of
	23:22	But if they had S in my council, then
	36:21	all the princes who S beside the king.
	44:15	all the women who S by, a great assembly,
Ezek	1:21	went; and when those S, these stood; and when
	1:21	when those stood, these S; and when those rose
	1:24	a host; when they S still, they let down
	1:25	their heads; when they S still, they let down
	3:23	glory of the LORD S there, like the glory
	8:11	And before them S seventy men of the elders
	9:2	they went in and S beside the bronze altar.
	10:6	he went in and S beside a wheel.
	10:17	When they S still, these stood still, and when
	10:17	they stood still, these S still, and when they
	10:18	of the house, and S over the cherubim.
	10:19	beside them; and they S at the door of
	11:23	of the city, and S upon the mountain which
	17:6	toward him, and its roots remained where it S
	37:10	and they lived, and S upon their feet, an
Dan	1:19	and Azariah; therefore they S before the king.

2:2 they came in and S before the king.
2:31 and of exceeding brightness, S before you, and its
3:3 set up; and they S before the image that
3:25 Then Azariah S and offered this prayer; in the
7:10 thousand times ten thousand S before him; the court
7:16 one of those who S there and asked him
8:15 it; and behold, there S before me one having
8:17 came near where I S; and when he came,
10:11 word to me, I S up trembling.
10:16 said to him who S before me, "O my
11:1 Darius the Mede, I S up to confirm and
12:5 and behold, two others S, one on this bank
13:34 Then the two elders S up in the midst
Obad 1:11 the day that you S aloof, on the day
1:14 You should not have S at the parting of
Hab 3:6 He S and measured the earth; he looked and
3:11 The sun and moon S still in their habitation
Mal 2:5 he feared me, he S in awe of my
1Mac 1:62 But many in Israel S firm and were resolved
7:36 priests went in and S before the altar and
10:81 But his men S fast, as Jonathan commanded, and
14:26 of his father have S firm; they have fought
2Mac 3:26 and splendidly dressed, who S on each side of
3:33 same clothing, and they S and said, "Be very
Mt 12:46 mother and his brethren S outside, asking to speak
13:2 and the whole crowd S on the beach.
26:62 And the high priest S up and said, "Have
27:11 Now Jesus S before the governor; and the governor
Mk 11:5 And those who S there said to them, "What
14:47 one of those who S by drew his sword,
14:57 And some S up and bore false witness against
14:60 And the high priest S up in the midst,
15:38 when the centurion, who S facing him, saw that
Lk 4:16 And he S up to read;
4:39 And he S over her and rebuked the fever,
6:8 And he rose and S there.
6:17 down with them and S on a level place,
7:14 bier, and the bearers S still.
9:32 the two men who S with him.
10:25 And behold, a lawyer S up to put him
17:12 by ten lepers, who S at a distance
18:11 The Pharisee S and prayed thus with himself, 'God,
19:8 And Zacchaeus S and said to the Lord, "Behold,
19:24 said to those who S by, 'Take the pound
23:10 priests and the scribes S by, vehemently accusing
23:34 And the people S by, watching; but the rulers
23:48 followed him from Galilee S at a distance and
24:4 this, behold, two men S by them in dazzling
24:17 And they S still, looking sad.
24:36 saying this, Jesus himself S among them, and said
Jn 7:37 the great day, Jesus S up and proclaimed, "If
8:7 to ask him, he S up and said to
11:56 one another as they S in the temple, "What
18:16 with Jesus, while Peter S outside at the door.
19:29 bowl full of vinegar S there; so they put
20:11 But Mary S weeping outside the tomb, and as
20:19 Jews, Jesus came and S among them and said
20:26 but Jesus came and S among them, and said,
21:4 day was breaking, Jesus S on the beach; yet
Acts 1:10 went, behold, two men S by them in white
1:15 In those days Peter S up among the brethren
3:8 And leaping up he S and walked and entered
5:34 by all the people, S up and ordered the
9:7 traveling with him S speechless, hearing the voice
9:39 All the widows S beside him weeping, and showing
10:17 inquiry for Simon's house, S before the gate
10:30 and behold, a man S before me in bright
11:28 of them named Agabus S up and foretold by
13:16 So Paul S up, and motioning with his hand
23:2 Ananias commanded those who S by him to strike
23:4 Those who S by said, "Would you revile God's
23:9 of the Pharisees' party S up and contended, "We
23:11 following night the Lord S by him and said,
24:19 they found when I S before the council,
25:7 gone down from Jerusalem S about him, bringing
25:18 When the accusers S up, they brought no charge
27:23 this very night there S by me an angel
Gal 2:11 his face, because he S condemned.
Col 2:14 canceled the bond which S against us with its
2Tim 4:17 But the Lord S by me and gave me
Heb 9:3 Behind the second curtain S a tent called the
Jas 1:11 for when he has S the test he will
Rev 4:2 and lo, a throne S in heaven, with one
7:11 And all the angels S round the throne and
8:3 another angel came and S at the altar with
11:11 entered them, and they S up on their feet,
12:4 And the dragon S before the woman who was
12:17 And he S on the sand of the sea.
14:1 lo, on Mount Zion S the Lamb, and with
18:17 is on the sea, S far-off

STOOL (4)

Lk 20:43 make thy enemies a S for thy feet.'
Acts 2:35 make thy enemies a S for thy feet.'
Heb 1:13 make thy enemies a S for thy feet"?
10:13 should be made a S for his feet.

STOOP (2)

Is 46:2 They S, they bow down together, they cannot save
Mk 1:7 am not worthy to S down and untie.

STOOPED (2)

Gen 49:9 He S down, he couched as a lion, and
Jn 20:11 as she wept she S to look into the

STOOPING (2)

Lk 24:12 ran to the tomb; S and looking in, he
Jn 20:5 the tomb first; and S to look in, he

STOOPS

Is 46:1 Bel bows down, Nebo S, their idols are on

STOP (28)

Gen 19:17 not look back or S anywhere in the valley;
1Sam 9:27 he has passed on S here yourself for a
15:16 Then Samuel said to Saul, S
1Kgs 18:44 down, lest the rain S you.'"
2Kgs 3:19 every good tree, and S up all springs of
2Chr 25:16 S! Why should you be put to death?" So the prophet
32:3 his mighty men to S the water of the
Ezra 5:5 and they did not S them till a report
Neh 4:11 and kill them and S the work."
6:3 Why should the work S while I leave it
Tob 10:6 her, "Be still and S worrying; he is well."
10:7 him, "Be still and S deceiving me; my child
Jud 4:7 it was easy to S any who tried to
Esth 14:9 destroy thy inheritance, to S the mouths of those
Job 37:14 "Hear this, O Job; S and consider the wondrous
Sir 4:26 do not try to S the current of a
27:14 quarrels make a man S his ears.
31:17 Be the first to S eating, for the sake
Jer 48:45 shadow of Heshbon fugitives S without strength; for
Ezek 16:41 I will make you S playing the harlot, and
26:13 And I will S the music of your songs,
34:10 hand, and put a S to their feeding the
1Mac 6:27 not be able to S them."
11:50 and make the Jews S fighting against us and
2Mac 4:6 that Simon would not S his folly.
9:7 not in any way S his insolence, but was
Acts 8:37 commanded the chariot to S, and they both went
13:10 villainy, will you not S making crooked the straight

STOPPED (33)

Gen 26:15 (Now the Philistines had S and filled with earth
26:18 for the Philistines had S them after the death
Lev 15:3 or his body is S from discharge, it is
Num 16:48 dead and the living; and the plague was S
16:50 the tent of meeting, when the plague was S
Josh 3:13 the Jordan shall be S from flowing, and the
1Sam 6:14 Joshua of Beth-shemesh, and S there.
2Sam 2:28 and all the men S, and pursued Israel no
20:12 came by, seeing him, S; and when the man
20:12 that all the people S, he carried Amasa out
1Kgs 15:21 heard of it, he S building Ramah, and he
2Kgs 3:25 it was covered; they S every spring of water,
4:6 Then the oil S flowing.
13:18 with them"; and he struck three times, and S
2Chr 16:5 heard of it, he S building Ramah, and let
25:16 So the prophet S, but said, "I know that
32:4 were gathered, and they S all the springs and
Ezra 4:24 which is in Jerusalem S; and it ceased until
Tob 5:21 So she S weeping.
10:7 the nights she never S mourning for her son
Ps 63:11 glory; for the mouths of liars will be S
Ezek 31:15 many waters shall be S; I will clothe Lebanon
Zech 7:11 a stubborn shoulder, and S their ears that they
14:5 my mountains shall be S up, for the valley
1Mac 9:55 hindered; his mouth was S and he was paralyzed,
13:47 agreement with them and S fighting against them.
Mt 20:32 And Jesus S and called them, saying, "What do
Mk 10:49 And Jesus S and said, "Call him." And they
Lk 18:40 And Jesus S, and commanded him to be brought

S

Acts 7:57 a loud voice and S their ears and rushed
21:32 and the soldiers, they S beating Paul.
Rom 3:19 every mouth may be S, and the whole world
Heb 11:33 justice, received promises, S the mouths of lions,

STOPPING

2Mac 9:4 charioteer to drive without S until he completed the

STOPS (5)

Ps 58:4 the deaf adder that S its ear,
107:42 glad; and all wickedness S its mouth.
Sir 18:6 beginning, and when he S, he will be at
Is 33:15 hold a bribe, who S his ears from hearing
3Jn 1:10 the brethren, and also S those who want to

STORAGE

1Mac 6:53 had no food in S, because it was the

STORE (14)

Gen 6:21 that is eaten, and S it up; and it
Lev 26:10 you shall eat old S long kept, and you
Deut 32:34 this laid up in S with me, sealed up
2Chr 31:10 we have this great S left."
Ps 144:13 providing all manner of S; may our sheep bring
Wis 6:8 strict inquiry is in S for the mighty.
Sir 29:12 S up almsgiving in your treasury, and it will
Jer 40:10 fruits and oil, and S them in your vessels,
Hos 13:12 is bound up, his sin is kept in S
Amos 3:10 the LORD, "those who S up violence and robbery
1Mac 9:35 friends, for permission to S with them the great
Lk 12:17 I have nowhere to S my crops?'
12:18 and there I will S all my grain and
1Cor 16:2 put something aside and S it up, as he

STORE-CITIES (6)

Ex 1:10 they built for Pharaoh S, Pithom and Raamses.
1Kgs 9:19 Judah, and all the S that Solomon had, and
2Chr 8:4 wilderness and all the S which he built in
8:6 Baalath, and all the S that Solomon had, and
16:4 Abel-maim, and all the S of Naphtali.
17:12 in Judah fortresses and S,

STORED (18)

Gen 41:48 land of Egypt, and S up food in the
41:48 in the cities; he S up in every city
41:49 And Joseph S up grain in great abundance, like
1Kgs 7:51 and the vessels, and S them in the treasuries
2Kgs 20:17 which your fathers have S up till this day,
2Chr 5:1 father had dedicated, and S the silver, the gold,
Ezra 6:1 house of the archives where the documents were S
Jud 4:5 villages on them and S up food in preparation
Ps 17:14 with what thou hast S up for them; may
Is 23:18 it will not be S or hoarded, but her
39:6 which your fathers have S up till this day,
1Mac 1:35 strengthened their position; they S up arms and food,
1:35 spoils of Jerusalem they S them there, and became
4:46 down the altar, and S the stones in a
13:33 and bolts, and he S food in the strongholds.
14:33 the enemy had been S, and he placed there
2Mac 8:31 of the enemy, they S them all carefully in
2Pet 3:7 now exist have been S up for fire, being

STOREHOUSE (6)

1Chr 26:15 south, and to his sons was allotted the S
26:17 and two at the S;
Neh 10:38 of our God, to the chambers, to the S
Jer 38:11 a wardrobe of the S, and took from there
Mal 3:10 full tithes into the S, that there may be
Lk 12:24 reap, they have neither S nor barn, and yet

STOREHOUSES (19)

Gen 41:56 Joseph opened all the S, and sold to the
2Kgs 20:13 was found in his S; there was nothing in
20:15 is nothing in my S that I did not
2Chr 32:28 kinds of costly vessels; S also for the yield
Neh 12:25 standing guard at the S of the gates.
13:12 of the grain, wine, and oil into the S
13:13 as treasurers over the S Shelemiah the priest, Zadok
Job 38:22 "Have you entered the S of the snow, or
38:22 have you seen the S of the hail,
Ps 33:7 in a bottle; he put the deeps in S
135:7 rain and brings forth the wind from his S
Sir 1:15 desirable goods, and their S with her produce.
43:14 Therefore the S are opened, and the clouds fly
Is 39:2 whole armory, all that was found in his S
39:4 is nothing in my S that I did not
Jer 10:13 and he brings forth the wind from his S
51:16 and he brings forth the wind from his S
Bar 3:15 And who has entered her S
Joel 1:16 under the clods, the S are desolate; the granaries

STORES (13)

1Chr 22:3 David also provided great S of iron for nails
27:28 Gederite; and over the S of oil was Joash.
2Chr 11:11 commanders in them, and S of food, oil, and
17:13 and he had great S in the cities of
Neh 12:44 the chambers for the S, the contributions, the first
Job 21:19 You say, 'God S up their iniquity for their
Prov 2:7 and understanding; he S up sound wisdom for
Sir 41:12 than a thousand great S of gold.
Is 10:28 Migron, at Michmash he S his baggage;
Jer 41:8 us, for we have S of wheat, barley, oil,
1Mac 6:53 the Gentiles had consumed the last of the S
9:52 he put troops and S of food.
2Mac 12:27 vigorous defense; and great S of war engines and

STORIES (3)

Ezek 41:6 chambers were in three S, one over another, thirty
42:3 outer court, was gallery against gallery in three S
42:6 they were in three S, and they had no

STORING

Rom 2:5 impenitent heart you are S up wrath for yourself

STORK (5)

Lev 11:19 the carrion vulture, the S, the heron according to
Deut 14:18 and the cormorant, the S, the heron, after their
Ps 104:17 build their nests; the S has her home in
Jer 8:7 Even the S in the heavens knows her times;
Zech 5:9 the wings of a S, and they lifted up

STORM (27)

2Kgs 14:7 and took Sela by S, and called it Joktheel,
Job 21:18 like chaff that the S carries away?
30:22 tossest me about in the roar of the S
Ps 107:29 distress; he made the S be still, and the
Prov 1:27 strikes you like a S, and your calamity comes
Wis 5:14 driven away by a S; it is dispersed like
Sir 33:2 about it is like a boat in a S
49:9 remembered his enemies with S, and did good to
Is 4:6 a shelter from the S and rain.
10:3 of punishment, in the S which will come from
17:13 before the wind and whirling dust before the S
25:4 a shelter from the S and a shade from
25:4 ruthless is like a S against a wall,
28:2 and strong; like a S of hail, a destroying
28:2 destroying tempest, like a S of mighty, overflowing
Jer 23:19 Behold, the S of the LORD!
30:23 Behold the S of the LORD!
Ezek 38:9 coming on like a S, you will be like
Hos 10:15 In the S the king of Israel shall be
Nah 1:3 is in whirlwind and S, and the clouds are
Zech 10:1 LORD who makes the S clouds, who gives men
2Mac 5:11 he left Egypt and took the city by S
10:24 He came on, intending to take Judea by S
Mt 8:24 there arose a great S on the sea, so
Mk 4:37 And a great S of wind arose, and the
Lk 8:23 And a S of wind came down on the
2Pet 2:17 mists driven by a S; for them the nether

STORM-TOSSED (2)

Is 54:11 "O afflicted one, S, and not comforted, behold, I
Acts 27:18 As we were violently S, they began next day

STORMED

2Mac 10:35 of the blasphemies, bravely S the wall and with

STORMS (2)

Ps 57:1 take refuge, till the S of destruction pass by.
Wis 16:16 and hail and relentless S, and utterly consumed by

STORMWIND

Is 66:15 his chariots like the S, to render his anger

STORMY (6)

Ps 107:25 commanded, and raised the S wind, which lifted up
148:8 hail, snow and frost, S wind fulfilling his command!
Ezek 1:4 I looked, behold, a S wind came out of
13:11 will fall, and a S wind break out;
13:13 I will make a S wind break out in
Mt 16:3 morning, 'It will be S today, for the sky

STORY (24)
Gen 39:17 told him the same S, saying, "The Hebrew servant,
1Kgs 6:6 The lowest S was five cubits broad, the middle
6:8 entrance for the lowest S was on the south
6:8 stairs to the middle S, and from the middle
6:8 and from the middle S to the third.
6:10 the whole house, each S five cubits high, and
2Chr 13:22 are written in the S of the prophet Iddo.
Sir 20:18 man is like a S told at the wrong
22:8 He who tells a S to a fool tells
35:14 nor the widow when she pours out her S
Ezek 41:6 three stories, one over another, thirty in each S
41:7 as they rose from S to S, corresponding to
41:7 of the offset from S to S round about
41:7 the lowest S to the top S through the middle story.
2Mac 2:19 The S of Judas Maccabeus and his brothers, and
6:17 reminder; we must go on briefly with the S
15:37 So I too will here end my S
15:39 the style of the S delights the ears of
Mt 28:15 were directed; and this S has been spread among
Acts 20:9 down from the third S and was taken up

STORY-TELLERS
Bar 3:23 Merran and Teman, the S and the seekers for

STOUT (3)
Is 10:16 wasting sickness among his S warriors, and under his
Amos 2:16 and he who is S of heart among the
Mal 3:13 "Your words have been S against me, says the

STOUTHEARTED (2)
Ps 76:5 The S were stripped of their spoil; they sank
1Mac 9:14 right; then all the S men went with him,

STOVE
Lev 11:35 unclean; whether oven or S, it shall be broken

STRAGGLER
Is 14:31 and there is no S in his ranks."

STRAIGHT (47)
Josh 6:5 go up every man S before him."
6:20 the city, every man S before him, and they
1Sam 6:12 And the cows went S in the direction of
Ezra 8:21 seek from him a S way for ourselves, our
Neh 12:37 Gate they went up S before them by the
Tob 4:19 ways may be made S and that all your
Jud 10:11 The women went S on through the valley; and
13:20 ruin, walking in the S path before our God."
Ps 5:8 enemies; make thy way S before me.
49:14 shall be their shepherd; S to the grave they
107:7 led them by a S way, till they reached
Prov 3:6 and he will make S your paths.
4:26 and your gaze be S before you.
8:9 They are all S to him who understands and
9:15 by, who are going S on their way,
11:5 blameless keeps his way S, but the wicked falls
29:27 he whose way is S is an abomination to
Eccl 1:15 crooked cannot be made S, and what is lacking
7:13 God; who can make S what he has made
Wis 10:10 she guided him on S paths; she showed him
Sir 2:6 you; make your ways S, and hope in him.
4:18 Then she will come S back to him and
27:25 Whoever throws a stone S up throws it on
39:24 holy his ways are S, just as they are
51:15 foot entered upon the S path; from my youth
Is 40:3 of the LORD, make S in the desert a
45:13 and I will make S all his ways; he
Jer 31:9 of water, in a S path in which they
31:39 shall go out farther, S to the hill Gareb,
49:5 driven out, every man S before him, with none
Ezek 1:7 Their legs were S, and the soles of their
1:9 they went every one S forward, without turning as
1:12 And each went S forward; wherever the spirit would
1:23 wings were stretched out S, one toward another; and
10:22 They went every one S forward.
46:9 each shall go out S ahead.
Amos 4:3 the breaches, every one S before her; and you
Mt 3:3 the way of the Lord, make his paths S
Mk 1:3 Lord, make his paths S —"
Lk 3:4 the way of the Lord, make his paths S
3:5 crooked shall be made S, and the rough ways
13:13 immediately she was made S, and she praised God.
Jn 1:23 in the wilderness, 'Make S the way of the
Acts 9:11 to the street called S, and inquire in the
13:10 stop making crooked the S paths of the Lord?
21:1 we came by a S course to Cos, and
Heb 12:13 weak knees, and make S paths for your feet,

STRAIGHTEN (2)
Bar 6:27 tipped over, it cannot S itself; but gifts are
Lk 13:11 and could not fully S herself.

STRAIGHTFORWARD
Gal 2:14 that they were not S about the truth of

STRAIN
Eccl 2:22 all the toil and S with which he toils

STRAINING (2)
Mt 23:23 You blind guides, S out a gnat and swallowing
Phil 3:13 what lies behind and S forward to what lies

STRAITS (3)
Judg 2:15 sworn to them; and they were in sore S
1Sam 13:6 that they were in S (for the people were
Job 20:22 he will be in S; all the force of

STRANGE (27)
Deut 31:16 the harlot after the S gods of the land,
32:16 to jealousy with S gods; with abominable practices
Esth 13:5 men, perversely following a S manner of life and
Ps 44:20 our hands to a S god,
81:9 There shall be no S god among you; you
114:1 from a people of S language,
Prov 23:33 Your eyes will see S things, and your mind
Wis 2:15 unlike that of others, and his ways are S
14:23 hold frenzied revels with S customs,
19:5 themselves might meet a S death.
Sir 43:25 for in it are S and marvelous works, all
Is 28:11 but by men of S lips and with an
28:21 do his deed-- S is his deed!
43:12 when there was no S god among you; and
Bar 4:15 shameless nation, of a S language, who had no
Hos 8:12 be regarded as a S thing.
1Mac 1:38 of strangers; she became S to her offspring, and
1:44 them to follow customs S to the land,
6:13 deep grief in a S land."
2Mac 9:6 others with many and S inflictions.
9:28 the mountains in a S land.
Lk 5:26 saying, "We have seen S things today."
Acts 17:20 For you bring some S things to our ears;
1Cor 14:21 written, "By men of S tongues and by the
2Cor 11:15 So it is not S if his servants also
Heb 13:9 away by diverse and S teachings; for it is
1Pet 4:12 you, as though something S were happening to you.

STRANGER (48)
Gen 23:4 Hittites, "I am a S and a sojourner among
Ex 12:48 And when a S shall sojourn with you and
12:49 native and for the S who sojourns among you."
22:21 shall not wrong a S or oppress him, for
23:9 shall not oppress a S; you know the heart
23:9 the heart of a S, for you were strangers
Lev 16:29 the native or the S who sojourns among you;
17:12 blood, neither shall any S who sojourns among you
18:26 the native or the S who sojourns among you
19:33 "When a S sojourns with you in your land,
19:34 The S who sojourns with you shall be to
23:22 poor and for the S: I am the LORD
25:35 maintain him; as a S and a sojourner he
25:47 "If a S or sojourner with you becomes rich,
25:47 sells himself to the S or sojourner with you,
25:47 a member of the S's family,
Num 9:14 And if a S sojourns among you, and will
15:14 And if a S is sojourning with you, or
15:15 you and for the S who sojourns with you,
15:16 you and for the S who sojourns with you."
15:26 be forgiven, and the S who sojourns among them,
15:29 Israel, and for the S who sojourns among them.
19:10 Israel, and to the S who sojourns among them,
35:15 Israel, and for the S and for the sojourner
Deut 25:5 the family to a S; her husband's brother shall
Josh 20:9 Israel, and for the S sojourning among them, that
Job 15:19 was given, and no S passed among them).
19:15 count me as a S; I have become an
Ps 69:8 I have become a S to my brethren, an
Prov 6:1 your pledge for a S;
11:15 gives surety for a S will smart for it,
14:10 own bitterness, and no S shares its joy.
20:16 given surety for a S, and hold him in
27:2 your own mouth; a S, and not your own

27:13 given surety for a S, and hold him in
Eccl 6:2 enjoy them, but a S enjoys them; this is
Sir 8:18 the presence of a S do nothing that is
11:32 Receive a S into your home and he will
23:22 her husband and provides an heir by a S
29:24 where you are a S you may not open
29:26 bitter words: "Come here, S, prepare the table, and
29:27 "Give place, S, to an honored person; my brother
Jer 14:8 thou be like a S in the land, like
Mt 25:35 drink, I was a S and you welcomed me,
25:38 we see thee a S and welcome thee, or
25:43 drink, I was a S and you did not
25:44 or thirsty or a S or naked or sick
Jn 10:5 A S they will not follow, but they will

STRANGERS (37)

Gen 42:7 he treated them like S and spoke roughly to
Ex 22:21 him, for you were S in the land of
23:9 stranger, for you were S in the land of
Lev 17:8 Israel, or of the S that sojourn among them,
17:10 Israel or of the S that sojourn among them
17:13 Israel, or of the S that sojourn among them,
19:34 yourself; for you were S in the land of
20:2 Israel, or of the S that sojourn in Israel,
25:23 mine; for you are S and sojourners with me.
25:45 buy from among the S who sojourn with you
1Chr 29:15 For we are S before thee, and sojourners, as
Jud 9:2 take revenge on the S who had loosed the
Ps 109:11 that he has; may S plunder the fruits of
Prov 5:10 to the merciless; lest S take their fill of
5:17 alone, and not for S with you.
Wis 19:13 for they practiced a more bitter hatred of S
19:14 had refused to receive S when they came to
Sir 21:25 The lips of S will speak of these things,
Jer 2:25 for I have loved S, and after them I
3:13 scattered your favors among S under every green
5:19 so you shall serve S in a land that
30:8 burst their bonds, and S shall no more make
Lam 5:2 been turned over to S, our homes to aliens.
Ezek 14:7 Israel, or of the S that sojourn in Israel,
16:32 Adulterous wife, who receives S instead of her
28:7 behold, I will bring S upon you, the most
Joel 3:17 shall be holy and S shall never again pass
Obad 1:11 on the day that S carried off his wealth,
1Mac 1:38 became a dwelling of S; she became strange to
2Mac 6:2 Zeus the Friend of S, as did the people
Mt 27:7 potter's field, to bury S in.
Jn 10:5 for they do not know the voice of S
Eph 2:12 commonwealth of Israel, and S to the covenants of
2:19 you are no longer S and sojourners, but you
Heb 11:13 acknowledged that they were S and exiles on the
13:2 to show hospitality to S, for thereby some have
3Jn 1:5 the brethren, especially to S,

STRANGLE

Tob 3:8 not know that you S your husbands?

STRANGLED (5)

Tob 2:3 our people has been S and thrown into the
Nah 2:12 for his whelps and S prey for his lionesses;
Acts 15:20 and from what is S and from blood.
15:29 and from what is S and from unchastity.
21:25 and from what is S and from unchastity."

STRANGLING

Job 7:15 that I would choose S and death rather than

STRATAGEM

2Mac 14:29 for an opportunity to accomplish this by a S

STRATEGIC (2)

2Mac 8:6 He captured S positions and put to flight not
8:31 them all carefully in S places, and carried the

STRATEGICALLY

2Mac 15:20 for battle, the elephants S stationed and the cavalry

STRATEGY (4)

2Kgs 18:20 that mere words are S and power for war?
Jud 11:8 thoroughly informed and marvelous in military S
Is 36:5 that mere words are S and power for war?
2Mac 13:18 of the Jews, tried S in attacking their positions.

STRAW (19)

Gen 24:25 added, "We have both S and provender enough, and
24:32 camels, and gave him S and provender for the
Ex 5:7 longer give the people S to make bricks, as
5:7 them go and gather S for themselves.
5:10 "Thus says Pharaoh, 'I will not give you S
5:11 Go yourselves, get your S wherever you can find
5:12 the land of Egypt, to gather stubble for S
5:13 work, your daily task, as when there was S
5:16 No S is given to your servants, yet they
5:18 and work; for no S shall be given you,
Judg 19:19 We have S and provender for our asses, with
1Kgs 4:28 Barley also and S for the horses and swift
Job 21:18 That they are like S before the wind, and
41:27 He counts iron as S, and bronze as rotten
Is 11:7 the lion shall eat S like the ox.
25:10 in his place, as S is trodden down in
65:25 the lion shall eat S like the ox; and
Jer 23:28 What has S in common with wheat?
1Cor 3:12 precious stones, wood, hay, S –

STRAY (3)

Ps 119:110 but I do not S from thy precepts.
Prov 7:25 her ways, do not S into her paths;
19:27 hear instruction only to S from the words of

STRAYED (7)

Wis 5:6 it was we who S from the way of
Is 16:8 reached to Jazer and S to the desert; its
Bar 3:21 Their sons have S far from her way.
Ezek 34:4 not bound up, the S you have not brought
34:16 will bring back the S, and I will bind
Hos 7:14 them, for they have S from me!
1Tim 5:15 For some have already S after Satan.

STRAYING

1Pet 2:25 For you were S like sheep, but have now

STRAYS (2)

Prov 27:8 Like a bird that S from its nest, is
27:8 is a man who S from his home.

STREAKS

Gen 30:37 plane, and peeled white S in them, exposing the

STREAM (26)

Gen 32:23 sent them across the S, and likewise everything that
Prov 18:4 waters; the fountain of wisdom is a gushing S
21:1 king's heart is a S of water in the
Sir 39:13 rose growing by a S of water;
Is 30:28 is like an overflowing S that reaches up to
30:33 the LORD, like a S of brimstone, kindles it.
59:19 come like a rushing S, which the wind of
66:12 nations like an overflowing S; and you shall suck,
Jer 17:8 its roots by the S, and does not fear
Lam 2:18 Let tears S down like a torrent day and
Dan 7:10 A S of fire issued and came forth from
12:5 this bank of the S and one on that
12:5 stream and one on that bank of the S
12:6 the waters of the S, "How long shall it
12:7 the waters of the S, raised his right hand
Joel 3:18 milk, and all the S beds of Judah shall
Amos 5:24 waters, and righteousness like an ever-flowing S
1Mac 5:37 opposite Raphon, on the other side of the S
5:39 are encamped across the S, ready to come and
5:40 drew near to the S of water, Timothy said
5:42 When Judas approached the S of water, he stationed
5:42 the people at the S and gave them this
16:5 meet them; and a S lay between them.
16:6 afraid to cross the S, so he crossed over
Lk 6:48 a flood arose, the S broke against that house,
6:49 foundation; against which the S broke, and

STREAM-BED (2)

2Kgs 3:16 will make this dry S full of pools.'
3:17 or rain, but that S shall be filled with

STREAMED

Dan 3:47 And the flame S out above the furnace forty-nine

STREAMS (32)

2Kgs 19:24 my foot all the S of Egypt.'
Job 20:17 upon the rivers, the S flowing with honey and
28:11 He binds up the S so that they do
29:6 poured out for me S of oil!
Ps 1:3 a tree planted by S of water, that yields
42:1 hart longs for flowing S, so longs my soul
46:4 is a river whose S make glad the city
74:15 springs and brooks; thou didst dry up ever-flowing S

78:16 He made S come out of the rock, and
78:20 water gushed out and S overflowed.
78:44 so that they could not drink of their S
119:136 My eyes shed S of tears, because men do
Prov 5:16 springs be scattered abroad, S of water in the
Eccl 1:7 All S run to the sea, but the sea
1:7 the place where the S flow, there they flow
Song 4:15 living water, and flowing S from Lebanon.
Is 7:18 the sources of the S of Egypt, and for
32:2 from the tempest, like S of water in a
33:21 of broad rivers and S, where no galley with
34:9 And the S of Edom shall be turned into
35:6 in the wilderness, and S in the desert;
37:25 my foot all the S of Egypt.
44:3 the thirsty land, and S on the dry ground;
44:4 like grass amid waters, like willows by flowing S
Jer 18:14 the mountain waters run dry, the cold flowing S
Ezek 29:3 the midst of his S, that says, 'My Nile
29:4 the fish of your S stick to your scales;
29:4 the midst of your S, with all the fish
29:4 the fish of your S which stick to your
29:5 the fish of your S; you shall fall upon
29:10 you, and against your S, and I will make
31:4 planting, sending forth its S to all the trees

STREET (28)

Gen 19:2 "No; we will spend the night in the S
Josh 2:19 your house into the S, his blood shall be
1Sam 9:26 both he and Samuel went out into the S
Job 18:17 earth, and he has no name in the S
31:32 not lodged in the S; I have opened my
Ps 31:11 see me in the S flee from me.
Prov 1:20 cries aloud in the S; in the markets she
7:8 sense, passing along the S near her corner, taking
7:12 home; now in the S, now in the market,
Eccl 12:4 the doors on the S are shut; when the
Is 42:2 it heard in the S;
51:20 the head of every S like an antelope in
51:23 ground and like the S for them to pass
Jer 6:11 the children in the S, and upon the gatherings
37:21 daily from the bakers' S, until all the bread
Lam 1:20 In the S the sword bereaves; in the house
2:19 faint for hunger at the head of every S
4:1 stones lie scattered at the head of every S
Ezek 16:25 the head of every S you built your lofty
16:31 the head of every S, and making your lofty
Nah 3:10 the head of every S; for her honored men
Mt 6:5 synagogues and at the S corners, that they may
Mk 11:4 out in the open S; and they untied it.
Acts 9:11 and go to the S called Straight, and inquire
12:10 passed on through one S; and immediately the angel
Rev 11:8 will lie in the S of the great city
21:21 single pearl, and the S of the city was
22:2 the middle of the S of the city; also,

STREETS (65)

2Sam 1:20 it not in the S of Ashkelon; lest the
22:43 stamped them down like the mire of the S
Tob 13:17 The S of Jerusalem will be paved with beryl
Jud 7:14 strewn about in the S where they live.
7:23 fell down in the S of the city and
Ps 18:42 cast them out like the mire of the S
144:14 there be no cry of distress in our S
Prov 5:16 be scattered abroad, streams of water in the S
22:13 I shall be slain in the S
26:13 There is a lion in the S
Eccl 12:5 mourners go about the S;
Song 3:2 the city, in the S and in the squares;
Sir 9:7 look around in the S of a city, nor
23:21 be punished in the S of the city, and
49:6 sanctuary, and made her S desolate, according to the
Is 5:25 were as refuse in the midst of the S
10:6 tread them down like the mire of the S
15:3 is shorn; in the S they gird on sackcloth;
24:11 an outcry in the S for lack of wine;
58:12 breach, the restorer of S to dwell in.
Jer 5:1 and fro through the S of Jerusalem, look and
7:17 Judah and in the S of Jerusalem?
7:34 Judah and from the S of Jerusalem the voice
9:21 the children from the S and the young men
11:6 Judah, and in the S of Jerusalem: Hear the
11:13 as many as the S of Jerusalem are the
14:16 cast out in the S of Jerusalem, victims of
33:10 of Judah and the S of Jerusalem that are
44:6 Judah and in the S of Jerusalem; and they
44:9 Judah and in the S of Jerusalem?
44:17 Judah and in the S of Jerusalem; for then
44:21 Judah and in the S of Jerusalem, you and
51:4 land of the Chaldeans, and wounded in her S
Lam 2:11 babes faint in the S of the city.
2:12 wounded men in the S of the city, as
2:21 the dust of the S lie the young and
4:5 dainties perish in the S; those who were brought
4:8 not recognized in the S; their skin has shriveled
4:14 wandered, blind, through the S, so defiled with blood
4:18 not walk in our S; our end drew near;
Ezek 7:19 their silver into the S, and their gold is
11:6 and have filled its S with the slain.
26:11 will trample all your S; he will slay your
28:23 and blood into her S; and the slain shall
Amos 5:16 and in all the S they shall say, Alas!
Mic 7:10 be trodden down like the mire of the S
Nah 2:4 chariots rage in the S, they rush to and
Zeph 3:6 have laid waste their S so that none walks
Zech 8:4 again sit in the S of Jerusalem, each with
8:5 And the S of the city shall be full
8:5 full of boys and girls playing in its S
9:3 dust, and gold like the dirt of the S
10:5 the mud of the S; they shall fight because
1Mac 1:55 the doors of the houses and in the S
2:9 been killed in her S, her youths by the
11:46 city seized the main S of the city and
14:9 men sat in the S; they all talked together
2Mac 3:19 with sackcloth under their breasts, thronged the S
Mt 6:2 synagogues and in the S, that they may be
12:19 his voice in the S;
22:10 went out into the S and gathered all whom
Lk 10:10 you, go into its S and say,
13:26 you taught in our S
14:21 out quickly to the S and lanes of the
Acts 5:15 the sick into the S, and laid them on

STRENGTH (217)

Gen 4:12 yield to you its S; you shall be a
31:6 father with all my S;
48:2 then Israel summoned his S, and sat up in
49:3 first fruits of my S, pre-eminent in pride and
Ex 13:3 of bondage, for by S of hand the LORD
13:14 say to him, 'By S of hand the LORD
15:2 The LORD is my S and my song, and
15:13 guided them by thy S to thy holy abode.
Lev 26:20 like brass; and your S shall be spent in
Num 11:6 garlic; but now our S is dried up, and
Deut 21:17 first issue of his S; the right of the
33:25 days, so shall your S be.
Josh 14:11 Moses sent me; my S now is as my
14:11 now is as my S was then, for war,
Judg 8:21 for as the man is, so is his S
16:5 see wherein his great S lies, and by what
16:6 me wherein your great S lies, and how you
16:9 the secret of his S was not known.
16:15 me wherein your great S lies."
16:17 be shaved, then my S will leave me, and
16:19 torment him, and his S left him.
1Sam 2:1 in the LORD; my S is exalted in the
2:4 mighty are broken, but the feeble gird on S
2:10 earth; he will give S to his king, and
2:31 will cut off your S and the strength of
2:31 your strength and the S of your father's house,
28:20 and there was no S in him, for he
28:22 that you may have S when you go on
30:4 they had no more S to weep.
2Sam 22:40 didst gird me with S for the battle; thou
1Kgs 19:8 and went in the S of that food forty
2Kgs 9:24 bow with his full S, and shot Joram between
19:3 and there is no S to bring them forth.
19:26 their inhabitants, shorn of S, are dismayed and
1Chr 16:11 the LORD and his S, seek his presence continually!
16:27 majesty are before him; S and joy are in
16:28 the peoples, ascribe to the LORD glory and S
29:12 great and to give S to all.
Neh 4:10 But Judah said, "The S of the burden-bearers is
8:10 for the joy of the LORD is your S
Jud 2:5 men confident in their S, to the number of
5:3 does their power or S consist?
5:23 a people with no S or power for making
7:23 gates; there was no S left in them any
9:7 they glory in the S of their foot soldiers;
9:8 Break their S by thy might, and bring down
9:9 me, a widow, the S to do what I
9:11 might upon men of S; for thou art God
11:22 the people, to lend S to our hands and

S

13:7 and said, "Give me S this day, O Lord
13:11 in Israel, and his S against our enemies, even
16:13 and glorious, wonderful in S, invincible.
Job 6:11 What is my S, that I should wait?
6:12 Is my S the strength of stones, or is
6:12 Is my strength the S of stones, or is
9:4 heart, and mighty in S --who has hardened
9:19 is a contest of S, behold him!
12:16 With him are S and wisdom; the deceived and
16:15 and have laid my S in the dust.
18:12 His S is hunger-bitten, and calamity is ready for
26:2 you have saved the arm that has no S
30:2 I gain from the S of their hands, men
36:5 he is mighty in S of understanding.
36:19 from distress, or all the force of your S
39:11 on him because his S is great, and will
39:19 Do you clothe his neck with S
39:21 and exults in his S; he goes out to
40:16 Behold, his S in his loins, and his power
41:12 limbs, or his mighty S, or his goodly frame.
41:22 In his neck abides S, and terror dances before
Ps 18:1 I love thee, O LORD, my S
18:32 who girded me with S, and made my way
18:39 didst gird me with S for the battle; thou
21:1 In thy S the king rejoices, O LORD; and
21:13 Be exalted, O LORD, in thy S
22:15 within my breast; my S is dried up like
28:7 The LORD is my S and my shield; in
28:8 The LORD is the S of his people, he
29:1 heavenly beings, ascribe to the LORD glory and S
29:11 May the LORD give S to his people!
31:10 years with sighing; my S fails because of my
32:4 heavy upon me; my S was dried up as
33:16 a warrior is not delivered by his great S
38:10 My heart throbs, my S fails me; and the
46:1 is our refuge and S, a very present help
59:9 O my S, I will sing praises to thee;
59:17 O my S, I will sing praises to thee,
65:6 seas; who by thy S hast established the mountains,
68:28 O God; show thy S, O God, thou who
68:35 he gives power and S to his people.
71:9 me not when my S is spent.
73:26 but God is the S of my heart and
78:51 first issue of their S in the tents of
81:1 aloud to God our S; shout for joy to
84:5 are the men whose S is in thee, in
84:7 They go from S to strength; the God of
84:7 go from strength to S; the God of gods
86:16 on me; give thy S to thy servant, and
88:4 man who has no S,
89:17 the glory of their S; by thy favor our
90:10 even by reason of S fourscore; yet their span
93:1 the LORD is robed, he is girded with S
96:6 majesty are before him; S and beauty are in
96:7 the peoples, ascribe to the LORD glory and S
102:23 He has broken my S in mid-course; he has
105:4 the LORD and his S, seek his presence continually!
105:36 their land, the first issue of all their S
118:14 The LORD is my S and my song; he
138:3 didst answer me, my S of soul thou didst
147:10 is not in the S of the horse, nor
Prov 5:10 their fill of your S, and your labors go
8:14 and sound wisdom, I have insight, I have S
14:4 crops come by the S of the ox.
20:29 young men is their S, but the beauty of
24:5 than he who has S;
24:10 day of adversity, your S is small.
31:3 Give not your S to women, your ways to
31:17 girds her loins with S and makes her arms
31:25 S and dignity are her clothing, and she laughs
Eccl 7:19 Wisdom gives S to the wise man more than
10:10 must put forth more S; but wisdom helps one
10:17 the proper time, for S, and not for drunkenness!
Wis 10:2 transgression, and gave him S to rule all things.
11:21 power to show great S, and who can withstand
12:16 For thy S is the source of righteousness, and
12:17 thou dost show thy S when men doubt the
12:18 who art sovereign in S dost judge with mildness,
13:19 his hands he asks S of a thing whose
13:19 strength of a thing whose hands have no S
16:16 were scourged by the S of thy arm, pursued
18:22 the wrath not by S of body, and not
Sir 3:13 forbearance; in all your S do not despise him.
5:2 follow your inclination and S, walking according to
9:2 woman so that she gains mastery over your S
11:12 needs help, who lacks S and abounds in poverty;
13:2 a weight beyond your S, nor associate with a
17:3 He endowed them with S like his own, and
19:25 if by lack of S he is prevented from
28:10 in proportion to the S of the man will
31:30 his injury, reducing his S and adding wounds.
38:18 in death, and sorrow of heart saps one's S
39:28 will pour out their S and calm the anger
40:26 Riches and S lift up the heart, but the
41:2 and is failing in S, very old and distracted
43:28 Where shall we find S to praise him?
43:30 put forth all your S, and do not grow
46:9 the Lord gave Caleb S, which remained with him
47:5 and he gave him S in his right hand
Is 10:13 he says: "By the S of my hand I
12:2 LORD GOD is my S and my song, and
28:6 sits in judgment, and S to those who turn
30:15 in quietness and in trust shall be your S
37:3 and there is no S to bring them forth.
37:27 their inhabitants, shorn of S, are dismayed and
40:9 up your voice with S, O Jerusalem, herald of
40:29 to him who has no might he increases S
40:31 LORD shall renew their S, they shall mount up
41:1 the peoples renew their S; let them approach, then
44:12 becomes hungry and his S fails, he drinks no
45:24 me, are righteousness and S; to him shall come
49:4 I have spent my S for nothing and vanity;
49:5 God has become my S --
51:9 Awake, awake, put on S, O arm of the
52:1 awake, put on your S, O Zion; put on
57:10 new life for your S, and so you were
63:1 his apparel, marching in the greatness of his S
Jer 16:19 O LORD, my S and my stronghold, my refuge
48:45 Heshbon fugitives stop without S; for a fire has
51:30 in their strongholds; their S has failed, they have
Lam 1:6 pasture; they fled without S before the pursuer.
1:11 trade their treasures for food to revive their S
1:14 neck; he caused my S to fail; the Lord
1:19 city, while they sought food to revive their S
Bar 1:12 Lord will give us S, and he will give
3:14 wisdom, where there is S, where there is,
Dan 2:23 given me wisdom and S, and hast now made
3:44 dominion, and let their S be broken.
10:8 great vision, and no S was left in me;
10:8 was fearfully changed, and I retained no S
10:16 have come upon me, and I retain no S
10:17 For now no S remains in me, and no
11:6 shall not retain the S of her arm, and
11:15 there shall be no S to stand.
11:17 to come with the S of his whole kingdom,
Hos 7:10 Aliens devour his S, and he knows it not;
Amos 2:14 shall not retain his S, nor shall the mighty
6:13 not by our own S taken Karnaim for ourselves?"
Mic 5:4 his flock in the S of the LORD, in
Nah 2:1 the road; gird your loins; collect all your S
3:9 Ethiopia was her S, Egypt too, and that without
Hab 3:19 the Lord, is my S; he makes my feet
Hag 2:22 about to destroy the S of the kingdoms of
Zech 12:5 inhabitants of Jerusalem have S through the LORD
1Mac 2:61 who put their trust in him will lack S
3:19 in battle depends, but S comes from Heaven.
3:35 out and destroy the S of Israel and the
4:32 the boldness of their S; let them tremble in
9:14 that Bacchides and the S of his army were
10:71 and let us match S with each other there,
2Mac 10:34 within, relying on the S of the place, blasphemed
12:14 within, relying on the S of the walls and
12:35 him off by main S, wishing to take the
Mk 5:4 no one had the S to subdue him.
12:30 and with all your S
12:33 and with all the S, and to love one's
Lk 1:51 He has shown S with his arm, he has
10:27 and with all your S, and with all your
21:36 that you may have S to escape all these
Acts 9:22 all the more in S, and confounded the Jews
27:34 it will give you S, since not a hair
1Cor 10:13 be tempted beyond your S, but with the temptation
Eph 6:10 Lord and in the S of his might.
1Tim 1:12 who has given me S for this, Christ Jesus
2Tim 4:17 me and gave me S to proclaim the message
Heb 11:34 of the sword, won S out of weakness, became
1Pet 4:11 renders it by the S which God supplies; in
Rev 1:16 face was like the sun shining in full S

STRENGTHEN (31)

Deut 3:28 Joshua, and encourage and S him; for he shall
Judg 16:28 I pray thee, and S me, I pray thee,

19:5 said to his son-in-law, S your heart with a
19:8 the girl's father said, S your heart, and tarry
2Sam 11:25 one and now another; S your attack upon the
1Kgs 20:22 said to him, "Come, S yourself, and consider well
Neh 6:9 But now, O God, S thou my hands.
Job 16:5 I could S you with my mouth, and the
Ps 10:17 the meek; thou wilt S their heart, thou wilt
89:21 my arm also shall S him.
104:15 shine, and bread to S man's heart.
119:28 melts away for sorrow; S me according to thy
Is 35:3 S the weak hands, and make firm the feeble
41:10 your God; I will S you, I will help
54:2 lengthen your cords and S your stakes.
Jer 23:14 walk in lies; they S the hands of evildoers,
Ezek 30:24 And I will S the arms of the king
30:25 I will S the arms of the king of
34:16 crippled, and I will S the weak, and the
Dan 11:1 up to confirm and S him.
Nah 3:14 water for the siege, S your forts; go into
Zech 10:6 "I will S the house of Judah, and I
1Mac 6:18 to harm them and S the Gentiles.
10:23 with the Jews to S himself.
Lk 22:32 you have turned again, S your brethren."
Rom 1:11 some spiritual gift to S you,
16:24 who is able to S you according to my
2Thes 3:3 is faithful; he will S you and guard you
Heb 12:12 your drooping hands and S your weak knees,
1Pet 5:10 himself restore, establish, and S you.
Rev 3:2 Awake, and S what remains and is on the

STRENGTHENED (30)

Judg 3:12 LORD; and the LORD S Eglon the king of
7:11 your hands shall be S to go down against
9:24 men of Shechem, who S his hands to slay
1Sam 23:16 David at Horesh, and S his hand in God.
30:6 But David S himself in the LORD his God.
2Sam 16:21 of all who are with you will be S
2Chr 11:17 They S the kingdom of Judah, and for three
17:1 in his stead, and S himself against Israel.
24:13 its proper condition and S it.
32:5 another wall; and he S the Millo in the
Neh 2:18 So they S their hands for the good work.
Job 4:3 many, and you have S the weak hands.
Sir 45:8 with superb perfection, and S him with the symbols
49:3 of wicked men he S godliness.
Ezek 34:4 weak you have not S, the sick you have
Dan 10:18 man touched me and S me.
10:19 to me, I was S and said, "Let my
10:19 speak, for you have S me."
Hos 7:16 Although I trained and S their arms, yet they
1Mac 1:34 These S their position;
13:48 He also S its fortifications and built in it
13:52 He S the fortifications of the temple hill alongside
14:14 He S all the humble of his people; he
2Mac 11:9 merciful God, and were S in heart, ready to
Acts 9:19 and was baptized, and took food and was S
15:32 with many words and S them.
16:5 So the churches were S in the faith, and
Eph 3:16 grant you to be S with might through his
Col 1:11 May you be S with all power, according to
Heb 13:9 that the heart be S by grace, not by

STRENGTHENING (4)

2Chr 28:20 afflicted him instead of S him.
Acts 14:22 Iconium and to Antioch, S the souls of the
15:40 through Syria and Cilicia, S the churches.
18:23 of Galatia and Phrygia, S all the disciples.

STRENGTHENS (4)

Ps 147:13 For he S the bars of your gates; he
Sir 3:9 For a father's blessing S the houses of the
29:1 neighbor, and he that S him with his hand
Phil 4:13 things in him who S me.

STRESS

2Tim 3:1 the last days there will come times of S

STRETCH (43)

Ex 3:20 So I will S out my hand and smite
7:5 the LORD, when I S forth my hand upon
7:19 'Take your rod and S out your hand over
8:5 Moses, "Say to Aaron, S out your hand with
8:16 Moses, "Say to Aaron, S out your rod and
9:22 LORD said to Moses, S forth your hand toward
9:29 the city, I will S out my hands to
10:12 LORD said to Moses, S out your hand over
10:21 LORD said to Moses, S out your hand toward
14:16 up your rod, and S out your hand over
14:26 LORD said to Moses, S out your hand over
15:12 Thou didst S out thy right hand, the earth
Num 24:6 Like valleys that S afar, like gardens beside a
Josh 8:18 LORD said to Joshua, S out the javelin that
2Kgs 21:13 And I will S over Jerusalem the measuring line
Job 11:13 heart aright, you will S out your hands toward
30:24 a heap of ruins S out his hand, and
Ps 68:31 let Ethiopia hasten to S out her hands to
138:7 my life; thou dost S out thy hand against
143:6 I S out my hands to thee; my soul
144:7 S forth thy hand from on high, rescue me
Sir 7:32 S forth your hand to the poor, so that
15:16 you fire and water: S out your hand for
Is 28:20 is too short to S oneself on it, and
34:11 He shall S the line of confusion over it,
Jer 6:12 together; for I will S out my hand against
51:25 whole earth; I will S out my hand against
Ezek 6:14 And I will S out my hand against them,
14:9 prophet, and I will S out my hand against
14:13 acting faithlessly, and I S out my hand against
25:13 Lord GOD, I will S out my hand against
25:16 GOD, Behold, I will S out my hand against
30:25 of Babylon, he shall S it out against the
35:3 Seir, and I will S out my hand against
Dan 11:42 He shall S out his hand against the countries,
Amos 6:4 beds of ivory, and S themselves upon their couches,
6:7 revelry of those who S themselves shall pass away."
Zeph 1:4 "I will S out my hand against Judah, and
2:13 And he will S out his hand against the
Mt 12:13 said to the man, S out your hand." And
Mk 3:5 said to the man, S out your hand." He
Lk 6:10 and said to him, S out your hand." And
Jn 21:18 are old, you will S out your hands, and

STRETCHED (71)

Gen 48:14 And Israel S out his right hand and laid
Ex 8:6 So Aaron S out his hand over the waters
8:17 they did so; Aaron S out his hand with
9:23 Then Moses S forth his rod toward heaven; and
9:33 city from Pharaoh, and S out his hands to
10:13 So Moses S forth his rod over the land
10:22 So Moses S out his hand toward heaven, and
14:21 Then Moses S out his hand over the sea;
14:27 So Moses S forth his hand over the sea,
Josh 8:18 And Joshua S out the javelin that was in
8:19 soon as he had S out his hand, they
8:26 hand, with which he S out the javelin, until
2Sam 24:16 And when the angel S forth his hand toward
1Kgs 13:4 altar at Bethel, Jeroboam S out his hand from
13:4 his hand, which he S out against him, dried
17:21 Then he S himself upon the child three times,
2Kgs 4:34 hands; and as he S himself upon him, the
4:35 and went up, and S himself upon him; the
1Chr 21:16 hand a drawn sword S out over Jerusalem.
Jud 13:2 tent, with Holofernes S out on his bed,
Job 9:8 the stars; who alone S out the heavens, and
15:25 Because he has S forth his hand against God,
38:5 Or who S the line upon it?
Ps 55:20 [Selah] My companion S out his hand against his
77:2 night my hand is S out without wearying; my
104:2 a garment, who hast S out the heavens like
Prov 1:24 refused to listen, have S out my hand and
Sir 43:12 the Most High have S it out.
46:2 lifted his hands and S out his sword against
Is 5:25 his people, and he S out his hand against
5:25 and his hand is S out still.
9:12 and his hand is S out still.
9:17 and his hand is S out still.
9:21 and his hand is S out still.
10:4 and his hand is S out still.
14:26 the hand that is S out over all the
14:27 His hand is S out, and who will turn
23:11 He has S out his hand over the sea,
42:5 created the heavens and S them out, who spread
44:24 made all things, who S out the heavens alone,
45:12 was my hands that S out the heavens, and
51:13 LORD, your Maker, who S out the heavens and
54:2 of your habitations be S out; hold not back,
Jer 10:12 and by his understanding S out the heavens.
15:6 backward; so I have S out my hand against
51:15 and by his understanding S out the heavens.
Lam 1:10 The enemy has S out his hands over all
Ezek 1:23 firmament their wings were S out straight, one
2:9 behold, a hand was S out to me, and,

10:7 And a cherub S forth his hand from between
16:27 Behold, therefore, I S out my hand against you,
25:7 therefore, behold, I have S out my hand against
Hos 7:6 heat of wine; he S out his hand with
Zech 1:16 measuring line shall be S out over Jerusalem.
12:1 says the LORD, who S out the heavens and
1Mac 6:25 us alone have they S out their hands, but
7:47 which he so arrogantly S out, and brought them
9:47 battle began, and Jonathan S out his hand to
2Mac 7:10 his tongue and courageously S forth his hands,
14:33 whom he sought, he S out his right hand
14:34 Then the priests S forth their hands toward heaven
15:15 Jeremiah S out his right hand and gave to
15:21 savagery of the elephants, S out his hands toward
15:32 which had been boastfully S out against the holy
Mt 8:3 And he S out his hand and touched him,
12:13 And the man S it out, and it was
26:51 who were with Jesus S out his hand and
Mk 1:41 Moved with pity, he S out his hand and
3:5 He S it out, and his hand was restored.
Lk 5:13 And he S out his hand, and touched him,
Acts 26:1 Then Paul S out his hand and made his

STRETCHER
2Mac 3:27 put him on a S

STRETCHES (6)
Job 26:7 He S out the north over the void, and
Is 31:3 When the LORD S out his hand, the helper
33:17 behold a land that S afar.
40:22 are like grasshoppers; who S out the heavens like
44:13 The carpenter S a line, he marks it out
Lam 1:17 Zion S out her hands, but there is none

STRETCHEST
Acts 4:30 all boldness, while thou S out thy hand to

STRETCHING (5)
1Kgs 8:38 his own heart and S out his hands toward
2Chr 6:29 his own sorrow and S out his hands toward
Is 51:16 shadow of my hand, S out the heavens and
Jer 4:31 Zion gasping for breath, S out her hands, "Woe
Mt 12:48 And S out his hand toward his disciples, he

STREW (2)
Jud 7:26 into their hands, to S us on the ground
Ezek 32:5 I will S your flesh upon the mountains, and

STREWED
2Chr 34:4 dust of them and S it over the graves

STREWN (2)
Jud 7:14 them they will be S about in the streets
Ps 141:7 shall their bones be S at the mouth of

STRICKEN (13)
1Sam 5:12 did not die were S with tumors, and the
Tob 7:7 his sight, he was S with grief and wept.
Ps 73:5 are; they are not S like other men.
73:14 long I have been S, and chastened every morning.
109:22 and my heart is S within me.
Wis 19:17 They were S also with loss of sight--
Is 16:7 Mourn, utterly S, for the raisin-cakes of Kir-hareseth.
53:4 yet we esteemed him S, smitten by God, and
53:8 land of the living, S for the transgression of
Lam 4:9 hunger, who pined away, S by want of the
Hos 6:1 heal us; he has S, and he will bind
9:16 Ephraim is S, their root is dried up, they
1Mac 9:55 that time Alcimus was S and his work was

STRICT (6)
Wis 6:8 But a S inquiry is in store for the
Sir 26:10 Keep S watch over a headstrong daughter, lest, when
42:11 Keep S watch over a headstrong daughter, lest she
51:19 my conduct I was S; I spread out my
Dan 3:22 the king's order was S and the furnace very
Acts 22:3 educated according to the S manner of the law

STRICTEST
Acts 26:5 that according to the S party of our religion

STRICTLY (7)
1Sam 14:28 people said, "Your father S charged the people with
Ezra 7:26 king, let judgment be S executed upon him, whether
Mt 16:20 Then he S charged the disciples to tell no
Mk 3:12 And he S ordered them not to make him
5:43 And he S charged them that no one should
Acts 5:28 questioned them, saying, "We S charged you not to
23:14 and said, "We have S bound ourselves by an

STRICTNESS (2)
Wis 12:21 their wickedness, with what S thou hast judged thy
Jas 3:1 we who teach shall be judged with greater S

STRIDE
Prov 30:29 are stately in their S:

STRIDING
Prov 30:31 he-goat, and a king S before his people.

STRIFE (41)
Gen 13:7 together, and there was S between the herdsmen of
13:8 "Let there be no S between you and me,
Num 27:14 of Zin during the S of the congregation, to
Deut 1:12 the weight and burden of you and your S
2Sam 19:9 the people were at S throughout all the tribes
22:44 didst deliver me from S with the peoples; thou
Job 33:19 bed, and with continual S in his bones;
Ps 18:43 didst deliver me from S with the peoples; thou
31:20 thy shelter from the S of tongues.
55:9 I see violence and S in the city.
Prov 10:12 Hatred stirs up S, but love covers all offenses.
13:10 insolence the heedless make S, but with those who
15:18 hot-tempered man stirs up S, but he who is
16:28 A perverse man spreads S, and a whisperer
17:1 quiet than a house full of feasting with S
17:14 The beginning of S is like letting out water;
17:19 who loves transgression loves S; he who makes his
18:6 A fool's lips bring S, and his mouth invites
20:3 to keep aloof from S; but every fool will
22:10 out a scoffer, and S will go out, and
23:29 Who has S
26:21 fire, so is a quarrelsome man for kindling S
28:25 greedy man stirs up S, but he who trusts
29:22 of wrath stirs up S, and a man given
30:33 nose produces blood, and pressing anger produces S
Wis 14:22 they live in great S due to ignorance, and
Sir 27:15 The S of the proud leads to bloodshed, and
28:8 Refrain from S, and you will lessen sins; for
28:8 to anger will kindle S,
28:10 to the obstinacy of S will be the burning;
28:11 kindles fire, and urgent S sheds blood.
31:26 tests hearts in the S of the proud.
40:5 unrest, and fear of death, and fury and S
40:9 and bloodshed and S and sword, calamities, famine
Is 54:15 any one stirs up S, it is not from
54:15 me; whoever stirs up S with you shall fall
Jer 15:10 me, a man of S and contention to the
Hab 1:3 violence are before me; S and contention arise.
Rom 1:29 Full of envy, murder, S, deceit, malignity, they are
1Cor 3:3 there is jealousy and S among you, are you
Gal 5:20 idolatry, sorcery, enmity, S, jealousy, anger, selfi

STRIKE (56)
Ex 2:13 wrong, "Why do you S your fellow?"
7:17 LORD: behold, I will S the water that is
8:16 out your rod and S the dust of the
17:6 Horeb; and you shall S the rock, and water
Num 14:12 I will S them with the pestilence and disinherit
1Sam 17:46 hand, and I will S you down, and cut
26:8 and I will not S him twice."
2Sam 13:28 I say to you, S Amnon,' then kill him.
17:2 I will S down the king only,
18:11 then did you not S him there to the
1Kgs 2:29 of Jehoiada, saying, "Go, S him down."
2:31 as he has said, S him down and bury
20:35 command of the LORD, S me, I pray." But
20:35 the man refused to S him.
20:37 another man, and said, S me, I pray." And
2Kgs 6:18 the LORD, and said, S this people, I pray
9:7 And you shall S down the house of Ahab
13:18 the king of Israel, S the ground with them";
13:19 but now you will S down Syria only three
Jud 9:3 blood, and thou didst S down slaves along with
9:10 deceit of my lips S down the slave with
13:18 has guided you to S the head of the
Job 15:29 endure, nor will he S root in the earth;
20:24 a bronze arrow will S him through.
36:32 and commands it to S the mark.
Ps 10:18 of the earth may S terror no more.
89:23 foes before him and S down those who hate
141:5 Let a good man S or rebuke me in

S

Prov 19:25 S a scoffer, and the simple will learn prudence;
Wis 4:3 their illegitimate seedlings will S a deep root or
Sir 8:16 at hand, he will S you down.
13:2 The pot will S against it, and will itself
Is 2:6 the Philistines, and they S hands with foreigners.
Ezek 5:2 you shall take and S with the sword round
22:13 "Behold, therefore, I S my hands together at the
39:3 Israel; then I will S your bow from your
Hos 14:5 the lily, he shall S root as the poplar;
Mic 5:1 with a rod they S upon the cheek the
Zech 12:4 the LORD, I will S every horse with panic,
12:4 my eyes, when I S every horse of the
13:7 S the shepherd, that the sheep may be scattered;
1Mac 4:33 S them down with the sword of those who
9:47 out his hand to S Bacchides, but he eluded
2Mac 8:18 a single nod to S down those who are
15:16 with which you will S down your adversaries."
Mt 4:6 you up, lest you S your foot against a
26:31 is written, 'I will S the shepherd, and the
Mk 14:27 is written, 'I will S the shepherd, and the
14:65 his face, and to S him, saying to him,
Lk 4:11 you up, lest you S your foot against a
22:47 said, "Lord, shall we S with the sword?"
Jn 18:23 rightly, why do you S me?"
Acts 23:2 stood by him to S him on the mouth.
23:3 to him, "God shall S you, you whitewashed wall!
Rev 2:23 doings; and I will S her children dead.
7:16 the sun shall not S them, nor any scorching

STRIKES (15)

Ex 21:12 "Whoever S a man so that he dies shall
21:15 "Whoever S his father or his mother shall be
21:18 men quarrel and one S the other with a
21:20 "When a man S his slave, male or female,
21:26 "When a man S the eye of his slave,
Deut 19:5 from the handle and S his neighbor so that
Job 34:26 He S them for their wickedness in the sight
Prov 1:26 will mock when panic S you,
1:27 strikes you, when panic S you like a storm,
Is 41:7 the hammer him who S the anvil, saying of
Ezek 17:10 when the east wind S it—wither away on
2Mac 3:39 it aid, and he S and destroys those who
Mt 5:39 But if any one S you on the right
Lk 6:29 To him who S you on the cheek, offer
2Cor 11:20 puts on airs, or S you in the face.

STRIKING (6)

Gen 4:23 a young man for S me.
2Sam 20:10 to the ground, without S a second blow; and
Sir 16:5 has heard things more S than these.
2Mac 10:3 altar of sacrifice; then, S fire out of flint,
Acts 7:24 and avenged him by S the Egyptian.
27:41 But S a shoal they ran the vessel aground;

STRING (4)

Judg 16:9 the bowstrings, as a S of tow snaps when
Ps 11:2 their arrow to the S, to shoot in the
Ezek 16:4 were born your navel S was not cut, nor
Hab 3:9 thy bow, and put the arrows to the S

STRINGED (4)

Ps 45:8 From ivory palaces S instruments make you glad;
Is 38:20 we will sing to S instruments all the days
Hab 3:19 To the choirmaster: with S instruments.
1Mac 13:51 harps and cymbals and S instruments, and with

STRINGS (4)

Ps 33:2 melody to him with the harp of ten S
33:3 play skilfully on the S, with loud shouts.
150:4 dance; praise him with S and pipe!
Song 1:10 ornaments, your neck with S of jewels.

STRIP (21)

Lev 19:10 And you shall not S your vineyard bare, neither
Num 20:26 to Mount Hor; and S Aaron of his garments,
1Sam 31:8 the Philistines came to S the slain, they found
2Sam 23:10 after him only to S the slain.
1Chr 10:8 the Philistines came to S the slain, they found
Job 41:13 Who can S off his outer garment?
Wis 13:11 to handle and skilfully S off all its bark,
Is 32:11 you complacent ones; S, and make yourselves bare,
47:2 put off your veil, S off your robe, uncover
Jer 5:10 not a full end; S away her branches, for
Lam 4:21 shall become drunk and S yourself bare.
Bar 6:58 Strong men will S them of their gold and
Ezek 16:39 lofty places; they shall S you of your clothes
23:26 They shall also S you of your clothes and
26:16 remove their robes, and S off their embroidered
Dan 4:14 cut off its branches, S off its leaves and
Hos 2:3 her breasts; lest I S her naked and make
13:15 be parched; it shall S his treasury of every
Mic 2:8 as an enemy; you S the robe from the
Hab 3:9 Thou didst S the sheath from thy bow, and
Zech 9:4 lo, the Lord will S her of her possessions

STRIPE (3)

Ex 21:25 burn, wound for wound, S for stripe.
21:25 burn for burn, wound for wound, stripe for S
Jud 9:13 be their wound and S, for they have planned

STRIPED (7)

Gen 30:35 the he-goats that were S and spotted, and all
30:39 the flocks brought forth S, speckled, and spotted.
30:40 the flocks toward the S and all the black
31:8 if he said, 'The S shall be your wages,'
31:8 be your wages,' then all the flock bore S
31:10 upon the flock were S, spotted, and mottled.
31:12 upon the flock are S, spotted, and mottled; for

STRIPES (5)

Deut 25:2 with a number of S in proportion to his
25:3 Forty S may be given him, but not more;
25:3 beat him with more S than these, your brother
2Sam 7:14 of men, with the S of the sons of
Is 53:5 whole, and with his S we are healed.

STRIPLING

1Sam 17:56 "Inquire whose son the S is."

STRIPPED (30)

Gen 37:23 to his brothers, they S him of his robe,
Ex 33:6 the people of Israel S themselves of their ornaments,
Num 20:28 And Moses S Aaron of his garments, and put
1Sam 18:4 And Jonathan S himself of the robe that was
19:24 And he too S off his clothes, and he
31:9 off his head, and S off his armor, and
2Kgs 18:16 At that time Hezekiah S the gold from the
1Chr 10:9 And they S him and took his head and
Job 12:17 He leads counselors away S, and judges he makes
12:19 He leads priests away S, and overthrows the mighty.
19:9 He has S from me my glory, and taken
22:6 brothers for nothing, and S the naked of their
Ps 76:5 The stouthearted were S of their spoil; they sank
Jer 49:10 But I have S Esau bare, I have uncovered
Ezek 12:19 their land will be S of all it contains,
19:12 up; its fruit was S off, its strong stem
32:15 when the land is S of all that fills
Joel 1:7 fig trees; it has S off their bark and
Mic 1:8 wail; I will go S and naked; I will
Nah 2:2 Israel, for plunderers have S them and ruined their
2:7 dismay; its mistress is S, she is carried off,
1Mac 1:22 of the temple; he S it all off.
2Mac 4:38 with anger, he immediately S off the purple robe
8:27 of the enemy and S them of their spoils,
11:12 of them got away S and wounded, and Lysias
Mt 27:28 And they S him and put a scarlet robe
27:31 had mocked him, they S him of the robe,
Mk 15:20 had mocked him, they S him of the purple
Lk 10:30 fell among robbers, who S him and beat him,
Jn 21:7 clothes, for he was S for work, and sprang

STRIPS (2)

Ps 29:9 oaks to whirl, and S the forests bare; and
Is 27:10 he lies down, and S its branches.

STRIVE (14)

Ex 21:22 "When men S together, and hurt a woman with
Deut 33:8 with whom thou didst S at the waters of
Judg 11:25 Did he ever S against Israel, or did he
Prov 28:4 who keep the law S against them.
Sir 4:28 S even to death for the truth and the
Is 41:11 and confounded; those who S against you shall be
2Mac 2:31 should be allowed to S for brevity of expression
Lk 13:24 he said to them, S to enter by the
Rom 15:30 of the Spirit, to S together with me in
1Cor 14:12 manifestations of the Spirit, S to excel in building
Col 2:1 know how greatly I S for you, and for
1Tim 4:10 end we toil and S, because we have our
Heb 4:11 Let us therefore S to enter that rest, that
12:14 S for peace with all men, and for the

STRIVEN

Gen 32:28 Israel, for you have S with God and with

STRIVES

Is 45:9 "Woe to him who S with his Maker, an

STRIVING (11)

Eccl 1:14 is vanity and a S after wind.
1:17 also is but a S after wind.
2:11 was vanity and a S after wind, and there
2:17 is vanity and a S after wind.
2:26 is vanity and a S after wind.
4:4 is vanity and a S after wind.
4:6 of toil and a S after wind.
4:16 is vanity and a S after wind.
6:9 is vanity and a S after wind.
Phil 1:27 spirit, with one mind S side by side for
Col 1:29 For this I toil, S with all the energy

STROKE (4)

1Sam 26:8 the earth with one S of the spear, and
Ps 39:10 Remove thy S from me; I am spent by
Is 30:32 And every S of the staff of punishment which
Ezek 24:16 from you at a S; yet you shall not

STROKES

Prov 20:30 wound cleanse away evil; S make clean the

STRONG (250)

Gen 49:14 Issachar is a S ass, crouching between the
Ex 1:6 multiplied and grew exceedingly S; so that the land
1:19 midwives; and the people multiplied and grew very S
6:1 Pharaoh; for with a S hand he will send
6:1 out, yea, with a S hand he will drive
10:19 LORD turned a very S west wind, which lifted
13:9 mouth; for with a S hand the LORD has
13:16 eyes; for by a S hand the LORD brought
14:21 sea back by a S east wind all night,
Lev 10:9 "Drink no wine nor S drink, you nor your
Num 6:3 himself from wine and S drink; he shall drink
6:3 made from wine or S drink, and shall not
11:4 among them had a S craving; and the people
13:18 dwell in it are S or weak, whether they
13:28 in the land are S, and the cities are
20:20 men, and with a S force.
28:7 a drink offering of S drink to the LORD.
Deut 11:8 that you may be S, and go in and
14:26 sheep, or wine or S drink, whatever your appetite
29:6 not drunk wine or S drink; that you may
31:6 Be S and of good courage, do not fear
31:7 of all Israel, "Be S and of good courage;
31:23 Nun and said, "Be S and of good courage;
Josh 1:6 Be S and of good courage; for you shall
1:7 Only be S and very courageous, being careful to
1:9 Be S and of good courage; be not frightened,
1:18 Only be S and of good courage."
10:25 afraid or dismayed; be S and of good courage;
14:11 I am still as S to this day as
17:13 people of Israel grew S, they put the Canaanites
17:18 have chariots of iron, and though they are S
23:9 before you great and S nations; and as for
Judg 1:28 When Israel grew S, they put the Canaanites to
3:29 of the Moabites, all S, able-bodied men; not a
9:51 But there was a S tower within the city,
13:4 drink no wine or S drink, and eat nothing
13:7 drink no wine or S drink, and eat nothing
13:14 her drink wine or S drink, or eat any
14:14 Out of the S came something sweet." And they
18:26 that they were too S for him, he turned
1Sam 1:15 drunk neither wine nor S drink, but I have
14:52 when Saul saw any S man, or any valiant
2Sam 2:7 let your hands be S, and be valiant; for
3:6 Abner was making himself S in the house of
10:11 the Syrians are too S for me, then you
10:11 the Ammonites are too S for you, then I
15:12 And the conspiracy grew S, and the people with
22:18 delivered me from my S enemy, from those who
22:33 This God is my S refuge, and has made
1Kgs 2:2 Be S, and show yourself a man,
19:11 and a great and S wind rent the mountains,
2Kgs 2:16 with your servants fifty S men; pray, let them
24:16 thousand, all of them S and fit for war.
1Chr 5:2 birthright; though Judah became S among his
11:10 men, who gave him S support in his kingdom,
19:12 the Syrians are too S for me, then you
19:12 the Ammonites are too S for you, then I
22:13 Be S, and of good courage.
28:10 for the sanctuary; be S, and do it."
28:20 Solomon his son, "Be S and of good courage,
2Chr 11:11 He made the fortresses S, and put commanders in
11:12 in all the cities, and made them very S
12:1 was established and was S, he forsook the law
25:8 way you will be S for war, God will
26:8 the border of Egypt, for he became very S
26:15 for he was marvelously helped, till he was S
26:16 But when he was S he grew proud, to
32:7 to them, saying, "Be S and of good courage.
Ezra 9:12 that you may be S, and eat the good
10:4 are with you; be S and do it."
Neh 1:10 power and by thy S hand.
Job 4:11 The S lion perishes for lack of prey, and
12:21 on princes, and looses the belt of the S
18:7 His S steps are shortened and his own schemes
37:6 and the rain, 'Be S
39:4 Their young ones become S, they grow up in
Ps 18:17 delivered me from my S enemy, and from those
19:5 chamber, and like a S man runs its course
22:12 Many bulls encompass me, S bulls of Bashan
24:8 The LORD, S and mighty, the LORD, mighty in
27:14 for the LORD; be S, and let your heart
30:7 established me as a S mountain; thou didst hide
31:2 refuge for me, a S fortress to save me!
31:24 Be S, and let your heart take courage, all
35:10 him who is too S for him, the weak
61:3 art my refuge, a S tower against the enemy.
71:3 rock of refuge, a S fortress, to save me,
71:7 but thou art my S refuge.
78:65 from sleep, like a S man shouting because of
80:17 whom thou hast made S for thyself!
83:8 them; they are the S arm of the children
89:13 hast a mighty arm; S is thy hand, high
136:12 for ever; with a S hand and an outstretched
140:7 LORD, my Lord, my S deliverer, thou hast covered
142:6 for they are too S for me!
Prov 10:15 man's wealth is his S city; the poverty of
12:12 The S tower of the wicked comes to ruin,
14:26 the LORD one has S confidence, and his children
18:10 the LORD is a S tower; the righteous man
18:11 man's wealth is his S city, and like a
18:19 helped is like a S city, but quarreling is
20:1 Wine is a mocker, S drink a brawler; and
21:14 bribe in the bosom, S wrath.
23:11 for their Redeemer is S; he will plead their
24:5 is mightier than a S man, and a man
30:25 are a people not S, yet they provide their
31:4 for rulers to desire S drink;
31:6 Give S drink to him who is perishing, and
31:17 her loins with strength and makes her arms S
Eccl 9:11 the battle to the S, nor bread to the
12:3 house tremble, and the S men are bent, and
Song 8:6 arm; for love is S as death, jealousy is
Wis 10:5 God, and kept him S in the face of
14:16 the ungodly custom, grown S with time, was kept
Sir 6:29 become for you a S protection, and her collar
28:14 to nation, and destroyed S cities, and overturned the
30:14 who is well and S in constitution than a
34:16 a mighty protection and S support, a shelter from
50:29 them, he will be S for all things, for
Is 1:31 And the S shall become tow, and his work
5:11 they may run after S drink, who tarry late
5:22 valiant men in mixing S drink,
8:11 to me with his S hand upon me, and
17:9 In that day their S cities will be like
22:17 away violently, O you S man.
24:9 drink wine with singing; S drink is bitter to
25:3 Therefore S peoples will glorify thee; cities of
26:1 Judah: "We have a S city; he sets up
27:1 hard and great and S sword will punish Leviathan
28:2 who is mighty and S; like a storm of
28:7 wine and stagger with S drink; the priest and
28:7 the prophet reel with S drink, they are confused
28:7 wine, they stagger with S drink; they err in
28:22 your bonds be made S; for I have heard
29:9 stagger, but not with S drink!
31:1 because they are very S, but do not look
35:4 a fearful heart, "Be S, fear not!
40:26 and because he is S in power not one
44:12 forges it with his S arm; he becomes hungry
44:14 and lets it grow S among the trees of
53:12 the spoil with the S; because he poured out
56:12 us fill ourselves with S drink; and tomorrow will
58:11 and make your bones S; and you shall be

Jer 9:3 not truth has grown S in the land; for
21:5 with outstretched hand and S arm, in anger, and
31:11 him from hands too S for him.
32:21 and wonders, with a S hand and outstretched arm,
49:19 the Jordan against a S sheepfold, I will suddenly
50:34 Their Redeemer is S; the LORD of hosts is
50:44 the Jordan against a S sheepfold, I will suddenly
51:12 Babylon; make the watch S; set up watchmen;
51:53 she should fortify her S height, yet destroyers would
Bar 6:36 from death or rescue the weak from the S
6:58 S men will strip them of their gold and
Ezek 3:14 of the LORD being S upon me;
17:9 will not take a S arm or many people
19:12 was stripped off, its S stem was withered; the
19:14 remains in it no S stem, no scepter for
22:14 can your hands be S, in the days that
30:21 that it may become S to wield the sword.
30:22 his arms, both the S arm and the one
34:16 the fat and the S I will watch over;
Dan 2:40 be a fourth kingdom, S as iron, because iron
2:42 kingdom shall be partly S and partly brittle.
4:11 tree grew and became S, and its top reached
4:20 which grew and became S, so that its top
4:22 you, O king, who have grown and become S
7:7 and dreadful and exceedingly S; and it had great
8:8 but when he was S, the great horn was
9:27 he shall make a S covenant with many for
10:19 be with you; be S and of good courage."
11:2 when he has become S through his riches, he
11:5 the south shall be S, but one of his
11:23 and he shall become S with a small people.
13:39 for he was too S for us, and he
Amos 2:9 and who was as S as the oaks; I
2:14 the swift, and the S shall not retain his
5:9 flash forth against the S, so that destruction comes
Mic 2:11 you of wine and S drink," he would be
4:3 and shall decide for S nations afar off; and
4:7 were cast off, a S nation; and the LORD
Nah 1:12 LORD, "Though they be S and many, they will
Zech 8:9 "Let your hands be S, you who in these
8:13 Fear not, but let your hands be S
8:22 going.' Many peoples and S nations shall come to
10:12 I will make them S in the LORD and
1Mac 1:4 He gathered a very S army and ruled over
1:17 invaded Egypt with a S force, with chariots and
1:20 to Jerusalem with a S force.
1:33 David with a great S wall and strong towers,
1:33 great strong wall and S towers, and it became
2:49 reproach have now become S; it is a time
2:64 be courageous and grow S in the law, for
3:15 And again a S army of ungodly men went
3:17 against so great and S a multitude?
3:27 his kingdom, a very S army.
4:7 camp of the Gentiles, S and fortified, with cavalry
4:30 that the army was S, he prayed, saying, "Blessed
4:60 with high walls and S towers round about, to
5:6 where he found a S band and many people
5:26 all these cities were S and large--
5:46 a large and very S city on the road,
6:6 gone first with a S force, but had turned
6:6 the Jews had grown S from the arms, supplies,
6:37 elephants were wooden towers, S and covered; they
6:41 trembled, for the army was very large and S
6:57 we are fighting is S, and the affairs of
6:62 and saw what a S fortress the place was,
7:25 with him had grown S, and realized that he
8:1 they were very S and were well-disposed toward
8:2 came to them, and that they were very S
9:50 to Jerusalem and built S cities in Judea: the
11:15 met him with a S force, and put him
2Mac 1:3 his will with a S heart and a willing
1:24 who art awe-inspiring and S and just and merciful,
3:26 appeared to him, remarkably S, gloriously beautiful
10:18 refuge in two very S towers well equipped to
12:18 had left a very S garrison.
12:35 horseback and was a S man, caught hold of
13:19 advanced against Bethzur, a S fortress of the Jews,
14:1 of Tripolis with a S army and a fleet,
Mt 12:29 can one enter a S man's house and plunder
12:29 he first binds the S man?
Mk 3:27 one can enter a S man's house and plunder
3:27 he first binds the S man; then indeed he
Lk 1:15 drink no wine nor S drink, and he will
1:80 child grew and became S in spirit, and he
2:40 child grew and became S, filled with wisdom; and
11:21 When a S man, fully armed, guards his own
16:3 I am not S enough to dig, and I
Jn 6:18 sea rose because a S wind was blowing.
Acts 3:7 and immediately his feet and ankles were made S
3:16 has made this man S whom you see and
Rom 4:20 God, but he grew S in his faith as
15:1 We who are S ought to bear with the
1Cor 1:27 world to shame the S,
4:10 We are weak, but you are S
7:36 if his passions are S, and it has to
16:13 stand firm in your faith, be courageous, be S
2Cor 10:10 letters are weighty and S, but his bodily presence
12:10 for when I am weak, then I am S
13:9 glad when we are weak and you are S
Eph 6:10 Finally, be S in the Lord and in the
2Thes 2:11 sends upon them a S delusion, to make them
2Tim 2:1 then, my son, be S in the grace that
Heb 6:18 for refuge might have S encouragement to seize the
Jas 3:4 and are driven by S winds, they are guided
1Jn 2:14 men, because you are S, and the word of
Rev 5:2 and I saw a S angel proclaiming with a
6:15 the rich and the S, and every one, slave

STRONGER (22)

Gen 25:23 the one shall be S than the other, the
30:41 Whenever the S of the flock were breeding Jacob
30:42 were Labans, and the S Jacobs.
Num 13:31 people; for they are S than we."
Judg 14:18 What is S than a lion?" And he said
2Sam 1:23 than eagles, they were S than lions.
3:1 David; and David grew S and stronger, while the
3:1 David grew stronger and S, while the house of
13:14 to her; and being S than she, he forced
1Kgs 20:23 and so they were S than we; but let
20:23 surely we shall be S than they.
20:25 surely we shall be S than they." And he
Job 17:9 has clean hands grows S and stronger.
17:9 he that has clean hands grows stronger and S
Ps 105:24 fruitful, and made them S than their foes.
Eccl 6:10 to dispute with one S than he.
Sir 8:12 a man who is S than you; but if
Jer 20:7 was deceived; thou art S than I, and thou
Dan 11:5 his princes shall be S than he and his
Lk 11:22 peace; but when one S than he assails him
1Cor 1:25 weakness of God is S than men.
10:22 Are we S than he?

STRONGEST (3)

Ps 78:31 and he slew the S of them, and laid
Ezek 19:11 Its S stem became a ruler's scepter; it towered
Dan 11:39 shall deal with the S fortresses by the help

STRONGHOLD (47)

Judg 6:26 the top of the S here, with stones laid
9:46 it, they entered the S of the house of
9:49 put it against the S, and they set the
9:49 and they set the S on fire over them,
1Sam 22:4 all the time that David was in the S
22:5 not remain in the S; depart, and go into
24:22 David and his men went up to the S
2Sam 5:7 Nevertheless David took the S of Zion, that is,
5:9 David dwelt in the S, and called it the
5:17 heard of it and went down to the S
22:3 of my salvation, my S and my refuge, my
23:14 was then in the S; and the garrison of
1Chr 11:5 Nevertheless David took the S of Zion, that is,
11:7 David dwelt in the S; therefore it was called
11:16 was then in the S; and the garrison of
12:8 to David at the S in the wilderness mighty
12:16 Judah came to the S to David.
Ps 9:9 The LORD is a S for the oppressed, a
9:9 for the oppressed, a S in times of trouble.
18:2 shield, and the horn of my salvation, my S
27:1 The LORD is the S of my life; of
94:22 LORD has become my S, and my God the
144:2 and my fortress, my S and my deliverer, my
Prov 10:29 The LORD is a S to him whose way
21:22 and brings down the S in which they trust.
Is 23:4 sea has spoken, the S of the sea, saying:
23:14 of Tarshish, for your S is laid waste.
25:4 thou hast been a S to the poor, a
25:4 to the poor, a S to the needy in
29:7 against her and her S and distress her, shall
Jer 16:19 my strength and my S, my refuge in the
Ezek 24:25 take from them their S, their joy and glory,
30:15 wrath upon Pelusium, the S of Egypt, and cut
Joel 3:16 to his people, a S to the people of

S

Nah 1:7 LORD is good, a S in the day of
Zech 9:12 Return to your S, O prisoners of hope; today
1Mac 4:61 people might have a S that faced Idumea.
5:9 they fled to the S of Dathema,
5:11 come and capture the S to which we have
5:29 the way to the S of Dathema.
5:30 war to capture the S, and attacking the Jews
6:61 On these conditions the Jews evacuated the S
12:34 to hand over the S to the men whom
16:8 wounded and fell; the rest fled into the S
16:15 treacherously in the little S called Dok, which he
2Mac 10:32 himself fled to a S called Gazara, especially well
12:19 had left in the S, more than ten thousand

STRONGHOLDS (56)

Num 13:19 in are camps or S,
Judg 6:2 in the mountains, and the caves and the S
1Sam 23:14 David remained in the S in the wilderness, in
23:19 among us in the S at Horesh, on the
23:29 and dwelt in the S of Engedi.
Ps 89:40 thou hast laid his S in ruins.
Is 23:11 given command concerning Canaan to destroy its S
34:13 shall grow over its S, nettles and thistles in
Jer 48:7 you trusted in your S and your treasures, you
48:18 come up against you; he has destroyed your S
48:41 be taken and the S seized.
49:27 it shall devour the S of Ben-hadad."
51:30 they remain in their S; their strength has failed,
Lam 2:2 has broken down the S of the daughter of
2:5 laid in ruins its S; and he has multiplied
Ezek 19:7 And he ravaged their S, and laid waste their
33:27 those who are in S and in caves shall
Dan 11:24 shall devise plans against S, but only for a
Hos 8:14 upon his cities, and it shall devour his S
Amos 1:4 it shall devour the S of Ben-hadad.
1:7 wall of Gaza, and it shall devour her S
1:10 wall of Tyre, and it shall devour her S
1:12 it shall devour the S of Bozrah."
1:14 it shall devour her S, with shouting in the
2:2 it shall devour the S of Kerioth, and Moab
2:5 it shall devour the S of Jerusalem."
3:9 Proclaim to the S in Assyria, and to the
3:9 Assyria, and to the S in the land of
3:10 who store up violence and robbery in their S
3:11 from you, and your S shall be plundered."
6:8 Jacob, and hate his S; and I will deliver
Mic 5:11 throw down all your S;
7:17 trembling out of their S, they shall turn in
1Mac 1:2 fought many battles, conquered S, and put to death
5:27 ready to attack the S tomorrow and take and
5:65 and tore down its S and burned its towers
8:10 land, tore down their S, and enslaved them to
10:12 who were in the S that Bacchides had built
10:37 stationed in the great S of the king, and
11:18 his troops in the S were killed by the
11:18 strongholds were killed by the inhabitants of the S
11:41 the troops in the S; for they kept fighting
12:33 country as far as Askalon and the neighboring S
12:35 with them to build S in Judea,
12:45 well as the other S and the remaining troops
13:33 Simon built up the S of Judea and walled
13:33 and bolts, and he stored food in the S
13:38 valid, and let the S that you have built
14:42 the weapons and the S, and that he should
15:7 have prepared and the S which you have built
2Mac 8:30 of some exceedingly high S, and they divided very
10:15 had control of important S, were harassing the Jews;
10:16 side, rushed to the S of the Idumeans.
10:23 destroyed more than twenty thousand in the two S
11:6 Lysias was besieging the S, they and all the
2Cor 10:4 not worldly but have divine power to destroy S

STRONGLY (6)

Gen 19:3 But he urged them S; so they turned aside
Sir 48:22 Lord, and he held S to the ways of
1Mac 10:50 He pressed the battle S until the sun set,
2Mac 12:13 certain city which was S fortified with earthworks
1Cor 16:12 our brother Apollos, I S urged him to visit
2Tim 4:15 him yourself, for he S opposed our message.

STROVE (5)

Jer 50:24 and caught, because you S against the LORD.
Hos 12:3 in his manhood he S with God.
12:4 He S with the angel and prevailed, he wept
1Mac 7:21 Alcimus S for the high-priesthood,
2Mac 2:21 heaven to those who S zealously on behalf of

STRUCK (97)

Gen 19:11 And they S with blindness the men who were
Ex 7:20 up the rod and S the water that was
7:25 after the LORD had S the Nile.
8:17 with his rod, and S the dust of the
9:15 forth my hand and S you and your people
9:25 The hail S down everything that was in the
9:25 beast; and the hail S down every plant of
17:5 rod with which you S the Nile, and go.
21:19 his staff, he that S him shall be clear;
22:3 breaking in, and is S so that he dies,
Num 14:42 up lest you be S down before your enemies,
20:11 up his hand and S the rock with his
22:23 the field; and Balaam S the ass, to turn
22:25 the wall; so he S her again.
22:27 was kindled, and he S the ass with his
22:28 you, that you have S me these three times?"
22:32 him, "Why have you S your ass these three
24:10 against Balaam, and he S his hands together; and
33:4 whom the LORD had S down among them; upon
35:16 "But if he S him down with an instrument
35:17 And if he S him down with a stone
35:18 Or if he S him down with a weapon
35:21 died, or in enmity S him down with his
35:21 died, then he who S the blow shall be
Judg 5:26 the workmen's mallet; she S Sisera a blow, she
7:13 to the tent, and S it so that it
1Sam 6:9 not his hand that S us, it happened to
14:31 They S down the Philistines that day from Michmash
17:49 and slung it, and S the Philistine on his
17:50 with a stone, and S the Philistine, and killed
19:10 Saul, so that he S the spear into the
2Sam 11:15 that he may be S down, and die."
12:15 And the LORD S the child that Uriah's wife
14:6 part them, and one S the other and killed
14:7 up the man who S his brother, that we
18:15 armor-bearers, surrounded Absalom and S him, and
20:10 Joab's hand; so Joab S him with it in
23:10 He rose and S down the Philistines until his
1Kgs 2:25 of Jehoiada; and he S him down, and he
2:34 Jehoiada went up, and S him down and killed
2:46 he went out and S him down, and he
15:27 against him; and Baasha S him down at Gibbethon,
16:10 Zimri came in and S him down and killed
20:37 And the man S him, smiting and wounding him.
22:24 Chenaanah came near and S Micaiah on the cheek,
22:34 at a venture, and S the king of Israel
2Kgs 2:8 rolled it up, and S the water, and the
2:14 fallen from him, and S the water, saying, "Where
2:14 And when he had S the water, the water
6:18 So he S them with blindness in accordance with
10:9 slew him; but who S down all these?
12:21 Shomer, his servants, who S him down, so that
13:18 with them"; and he S three times, and stopped.
13:19 said, "You should have S five or six times;
13:19 then you would have S down Syria until you
15:10 conspired against him, and S him down at Ibleam,
15:14 to Samaria, and he S down Shallum the son
15:30 son of Remaliah, and S him down, and slew
2Chr 18:23 Chenaanah came near and S Micaiah on the cheek,
18:33 at a venture, and S the king of Israel
32:21 of his own sons S him down there with
Jud 1:15 mountains of Ragae and S him down with hunting
13:8 And she S his neck twice with all her
13:15 The Lord has S him down by the hand
Job 1:19 across the wilderness, and S the four corners of
16:10 their mouth, they have S me insolently upon the
Prov 23:35 "They S me," you will say, "but I was
Sir 47:4 in the sling and S down the boasting of
Is 16:8 of the nations have S down its branches, which
Jer 41:2 him rose up and S down Gedaliah the son
Dan 2:35 But the stone that S the image became a
8:7 enraged against him and S the ram and broke
1Mac 2:44 organized an army, and S down sinners in their
5:7 crushed before him; he S them down.
5:65 He S Hebron and its villages and tore down
7:41 angel went forth and S down one hundred and
9:66 He S down Odomera and his brothers and the
2Mac 1:16 they threw stones and S down the leader and
3:25 furiously at Heliodorus and S at him with its
9:5 the God of Israel, S him an incurable and
15:24 thy holy people be S down." With these words
Mt 26:51 drew his sword, and S the slave of the
26:67 in his face, and S him; and some slapped
26:68 Who is it that S you?"
27:30 took the reed and S him on the head.

Mk 14:47 drew his sword, and S the slave of the
15:19 And they S his head with a reed, and
Lk 22:48 And one of them S the slave of the
22:62 Who is it that S you?"
Jn 18:10 sword, drew it and S the high priest's slave
18:22 the officers standing by S Jesus with his hand,
19:3 and S him with their hands.
Acts 12:7 the cell; and he S Peter on the side
23:3 to the law you order me to be S
27:14 wind, called the northeaster, S down from the land;
2Cor 4:9 persecuted, but not forsaken; S down, but not
Rev 8:12 of the sun was S, and a third of

STRUCTURE (8)
1Kgs 6:5 He also built a S against the wall of
6:10 He built the S against the whole house, each
Ezra 5:3 to build this house and to finish this S
5:9 and to finish this S
Ps 144:12 pillars cut for the S of a palace;
Wis 7:17 exists, to know the S of the world and
Ezek 40:2 on which was a S like a city opposite
Eph 2:21 in whom the whole S is joined together and

STRUCTURES
1Mac 10:44 rebuilding and restoring the S of the sanctuary be

STRUGGLE (3)
2Mac 14:43 the heat of the S he did not hit
Heb 10:32 you endured a hard S with sufferings,
12:4 In your S against sin you have not yet

STRUGGLED
Gen 25:22 The children S together within her; and she said,

STRUGGLES
2Mac 15:9 them also of the S they had won, he

STRUGGLING
Ex 2:13 behold, two Hebrews were S together; and he said

STRUNG
Ps 7:12 he has bent and S his bow;

STRUTS
Ps 73:9 heavens, and their tongue S through the earth.

STRUTTING
Prov 30:31 back before any; the S cock, the he-goat, and

STUBBLE (14)
Ex 5:12 of Egypt, to gather S for straw.
15:7 sendest forth thy fury, it consumes them like S
Job 41:28 him flee; for him slingstones are turned to S
41:29 Clubs are counted as S; he laughs at the
Wis 3:7 forth, and will run like sparks through the S
Is 5:24 of fire devours the S, and as dry grass
33:11 chaff, you bring forth S; your breath is a
40:24 wither, and the tempest carries them off like S
41:2 his sword, like driven S with his bow.
47:14 Behold, they are like S, the fire consumes them;
Joel 2:5 of fire devouring the S, like a powerful army
Obad 1:18 the house of Esau S; they shall burn them
Nah 1:10 Like entangled thorns they are consumed, like dry S
Mal 4:1 all evildoers will be S; the day that comes

STUBBORN (24)
Deut 9:6 for you are a S people.
9:13 behold, it is a S people;
10:16 foreskin of your heart, and be no longer S
21:18 a man has a S and rebellious son, who
21:20 'This our son is S and rebellious, he will
31:27 know how rebellious and S you are; behold, while
Judg 2:19 their practices or their S ways.
2Kgs 17:14 not listen, but were S, as their fathers had
Neh 9:29 live, and turned a S shoulder and stiffened their
Ps 78:8 like their fathers, a S and rebellious generation, a
81:12 them over to their S hearts, to follow their
Sir 3:24 A S mind will be afflicted at the end,
3:25 A S mind will be burdened by troubles, and
30:8 turns out to be S, and a son unrestrained
30:12 young, lest he become S and disobey you, and
Is 46:12 "Hearken to me, you S of heart, you who
Jer 5:23 this people has a S and rebellious heart; they
16:12 of you follows his S evil will, refusing to
Ezek 2:4 also are impudent and S: I send you to
3:7 forehead and of a S heart.
Hos 4:16 Like a S heifer, Israel is stubborn; can the
4:16 stubborn heifer, Israel is S; can the LORD now
Zech 7:11 hearken, and turned a S shoulder, and stopped their
Acts 19:9 but when some were S and disbelieved, speaking evil

STUBBORNLY (7)
Ex 13:15 For when Pharaoh S refused to let us go,
Job 15:26 to the Almighty, running S against him with a
Jer 3:17 they shall no more S follow their own evil
6:28 They are all S rebellious, going about with slanders;
9:14 with it, but have S followed their own hearts
13:10 hear my words, who S follow their own heart
23:17 to every one who S follows his own heart,

STUBBORNNESS (8)
Deut 9:27 do not regard the S of this people, or
29:19 I walk in the S of my heart.' This
1Sam 15:23 sin of divination, and S is as iniquity and
Sir 16:10 men on foot, who rebelliously assembled in their S
Jer 7:24 own counsels and the S of their evil hearts,
11:8 one walked in the S of his evil heart.
18:12 act according to the S of his evil heart.'
Bar 2:33 will turn from their S and their wicked deeds;

STUCCO
Sir 22:15 thought is like the S decoration on the wall

STUCK (3)
1Sam 26:7 encampment, with his spear S in the ground at
Sir 19:12 Like an arrow S in the flesh of the
Acts 27:41 vessel aground; the bow S and remained immovable,

STUD
Esth 8:10 in the king's service, bred from the royal S

STUDDED
Song 1:11 you ornaments of gold, S with silver.

STUDIED (2)
Ps 111:2 works of the LORD, S by all who have
Jn 7:15 this man has learning, when he has never S

STUDY (4)
Ezra 7:10 set his heart to S the law of the
Neh 8:13 scribe in order to S the words of the
Eccl 12:12 no end, and much S is a weariness of
Sir 39:1 devotes himself to the S of the law of

STUDYING
Eccl 12:9 knowledge, weighing and S and arranging proverbs

STUFF (37)
Ex 25:4 and purple and scarlet S and fine twined linen,
26:1 and purple and scarlet S; with cherubim skilfully
26:31 and purple and scarlet S and fine twined linen;
26:36 and purple and scarlet S and fine twined linen,
27:16 and purple and scarlet S and fine twined linen,
28:5 and purple and scarlet S, and fine twined linen.
28:6 and purple and scarlet S, and of fine twined
28:8 and purple and scarlet S, and fine twined linen.
28:15 and purple and scarlet S, and fine twined linen
28:33 and purple and scarlet S, around its skirts, with
35:6 and purple and scarlet S and fine twined linen;
35:23 or purple or scarlet S or fine linen or
35:25 and purple and scarlet S and fine twined linen;
35:35 and purple and scarlet S and fine twined linen,
36:7 from bringing; for the S they had was sufficient
36:8 purple and scarlet S, with cherubim skilfully worked.
36:35 and purple and scarlet S and fine twined linen;
36:37 and purple and scarlet S and fine twined linen,
38:18 and purple and scarlet S and fine twined linen;
38:23 and purple and scarlet S and fine twined linen.
39:1 and purple and scarlet S they made finely wrought
39:2 and purple and scarlet S, and fine twined linen.
39:3 purple and the scarlet S, and into the fine
39:5 and purple and scarlet S, and fine twined linen;
39:8 and purple and scarlet S, and fine twined linen.
39:24 and purple and scarlet S and fine twined linen.
39:29 purple and scarlet S, embroidered with needlework;
Lev 14:4 and cedarwood and scarlet S and hyssop;
14:6 cedarwood and the scarlet S and the hyssop, and
14:49 with cedarwood and scarlet S and hyssop,
14:51 hyssop and the scarlet S, along with the living
14:52 and hyssop and scarlet S;
19:19 garment of cloth made of two kinds of S
Num 19:6 and hyssop and scarlet S, and cast them into

S

Deut 22:11 not wear a mingled S, wool and linen together.
Josh 7:11 and lied, and put them among their own S
Ezek 27:24 in carpets of colored S, bound with cords and

STUFFS (2)

Judg 5:30 man; spoil of dyed S for Sisera, spoil of
5:30 Sisera, spoil of dyed S embroidered, two pieces of

STUMBLE (36)

Lev 26:37 They shall S over one another, as if to
Ps 27:2 and foes, they shall S and fall.
119:165 who love thy law; nothing can make them S
Prov 3:23 your way securely and your foot will not S
4:13 hampered; and if you run, you will not S
4:17 of sleep unless they have made some one S
4:20 darkness; they do not know over what they S
Sir 9:5 a virgin, lest you S and incur penalties for
13:22 And should he S, they even push him down.
32:15 but the hypocrite will S at it.
32:20 hazards, and do not S over stony ground.
Is 8:15 And many shall S thereon; they shall fall and
28:7 err in vision, they S in giving judgment.
31:3 hand, the helper will S, and he who is
59:10 have no eyes; we S at noon as in
63:13 a horse in the desert, they did not S
Jer 6:21 against which they shall S; fathers and sons together,
13:16 darkness, before your feet S on the twilight
20:11 therefore my persecutors will S, they will not
31:9 which they shall not S; for I am a
50:32 The proud one shall S and fall, with none
Ezek 36:15 cause your nation to S, says the Lord GOD."
Dan 11:19 land; but he shall S and fall, and shall
Hos 4:5 You shall S by day, the prophet also shall
4:5 the prophet also shall S with you by night;
5:5 his face; Ephraim shall S in his guilt; Judah
5:5 guilt; Judah also shall S with them.
14:9 in them, but transgressors S in them.
Nah 2:5 officers are summoned, they S as they go, they
3:3 bodies without end--they S over the bodies!
Mal 2:8 have caused many to S by your instruction; you
Jn 11:9 day, he does not S, because he sees the
Rom 9:33 that will make men S, a rock that will
14:21 wine or do anything that makes your brother S
1Pet 2:8 that will make men S, a rock that will
2:8 them fall"; for they S because they disobey the

STUMBLED (14)

2Sam 6:6 and took hold of it, for the oxen S
1Chr 13:9 hand to hold the ark, for the oxen S
Tob 11:10 Tobit started toward the door, and S
Ps 9:3 enemies turned back, they S and perished before
73:2 my feet had almost S, my steps had well
105:37 and there was none among his tribes who S
Is 3:8 For Jerusalem has S, and Judah has fallen; because
Jer 18:15 false gods; they have S in their ways, in
46:6 river Euphrates they have S and fallen.
46:12 cry; for warrior has S against warrior; they have
46:16 Your multitude S and fell, and they said one
Hos 14:1 God, for you have S because of your iniquity.
Rom 9:32 They have S over the stumbling stone,
11:11 I ask, have they S so as to fall?

STUMBLES (3)

Prov 24:17 be glad when he S;
Is 5:27 None is weary, none S, none slumbers or sleeps,
Jn 11:10 in the night, he S, because the light is

STUMBLING (24)

Lev 19:14 deaf or put a S block before the blind,
Job 4:4 upheld him who was S, and you have made
18:12 is hunger-bitten, and calamity is ready for his S
Ps 35:15 But at my S they gathered in glee, they
116:8 tears, my feet from S;
Prov 24:11 back those who are S to the slaughter.
Sir 31:7 It is a S block to those who are
31:29 excess is bitterness of soul, with provocation and S
34:16 sun, a guard against S and a defense against
Is 8:14 and a rock of S to both houses of
Jer 6:21 lay before this people S blocks against which they
Ezek 3:20 and I lay a S block before him, he
7:19 For it was the S block of their iniquity.
14:3 hearts, and set the S block of their iniquity
14:4 heart and sets the S block of his iniquity
14:7 heart and putting the S block of his iniquity
44:12 idols and became a S block of iniquity to
Rom 9:32 have stumbled over the S stone,
14:13 never to put a S block or hindrance in
1Cor 1:23 preach Christ crucified, a S block to Jews and
8:9 yours somehow become a S block to the weak.
Gal 5:11 In that case the S block of the cross
1Jn 2:10 and in it there is no cause for S
Rev 2:14 Balak to put a S block before the sons

STUMP (7)

Job 14:8 the earth, and its S die in the ground,
Is 6:13 or an oak, whose S remains standing when it
6:13 The holy seed is its S
11:1 a shoot from the S of Jesse, and a
Dan 4:15 But leave the S of its roots in the
4:23 it, but leave the S of its roots in
4:26 commanded to leave the S of the roots of

STUMPS

Is 7:4 of these two smoldering S of firebrands, at the

STUNG

Sir 12:12 my words, and be S by what I have

STUNNED (2)

Ps 76:6 God of Jacob, both rider and horse lay S
Lam 1:13 he has left me S, faint all the day

STUPEFY

Is 29:9 S yourselves and be in a stupor, blind yourselves

STUPID (19)

Job 11:12 But a S man will get understanding, when a
18:3 Why are we S in your sight?
Ps 49:10 the fool and the S alike must perish and
73:22 in heart, I was S and ignorant, I was
92:6 man cannot know, the S cannot understand this:
Prov 12:1 loves knowledge, but he who hates reproof is S
17:21 A S son is a grief to a father;
30:2 Surely I am too S to be a man.
Sir 22:13 to bear than a S man.
27:12 Among S people watch for a chance to leave,
42:8 ashamed to instruct the S or foolish or the
Is 19:11 counselors of Pharaoh give S counsel.
Jer 4:22 me not; they are S children, they have no
10:8 They are both S and foolish; the instruction of
10:14 Every man is S and without knowledge; every
10:21 For the shepherds are S, and do not inquire
51:17 man is S and without knowledge; every goldsmith
2Tim 2:23 nothing to do with S, senseless controversies; you
Tit 3:9 avoid S controversies, genealogies, dissensions, and

STUPOR (3)

Jud 13:15 canopy beneath which he lay in his drunken S
Is 29:9 and be in a S, blind yourselves and be
Rom 11:8 them a spirit of S, eyes that should not

STURDY

Sir 6:14 faithful friend is a S shelter: he that has

STYLE

2Mac 15:39 enjoyment, so also the S of the story delights

SUAH

1Chr 7:36 The sons of Zophah: S, Harnepher, Shual, Beri,

SUBDUE (14)

Gen 1:28 fill the earth and S it; and have dominion
Deut 9:3 will destroy them and S them before you; so
Judg 16:5 may bind him to S him; and we will
16:6 bound, that one could S you."
1Chr 17:10 Israel; and I will S all your enemies.
Neh 9:24 land, and thou didst S before them the inhabitants
Ps 74:8 themselves, "We will utterly S them"; they burned
81:14 I would soon S their enemies, and turn my
Sir 12:5 means of it he S you; for you will
Is 25:5 Thou dost S the noise of the aliens; as
45:1 I have grasped, to S nations before him and
1Mac 4:28 five thousand cavalry to S them.
Mk 5:4 had the strength to S him.
1Cor 9:27 pommel my body and S it, lest after preaching

SUBDUED (21)

Gen 14:5 with him came and S the Rephaim in Ashteroth-
14:7 (that is, Kadesh), and S all the country of
Num 32:22 and the land is S before the LORD; then
32:29 the land shall be S before you, then you
Josh 18:1 there; the land lay S before them.

Judg 3:30 So Moab was S that day under the hand
4:23 on that day God S Jabin the king of
8:28 So Midian was S before the people of Israel,
11:33 So the Ammonites were S before the people of
1Sam 7:13 So the Philistines were S and did not again
2Sam 8:1 defeated the Philistines and S them, and David took
8:11 all the nations he S,
1Chr 18:1 defeated the Philistines and S them, and he took
20:4 descendants of the giants; and the Philistines were S
22:18 and the land is S before the LORD and
2Chr 13:18 men of Israel were S at that time, and
Ps 18:47 gave me vengeance and S peoples under me;
47:3 He S peoples under us, and nations under our
Wis 18:22 by his word he S the punisher, appealing to
1Mac 8:4 They also S the kings who came against them
8:12 They have S kings far and near, and as

SUBDUES

Ps 144:2 I take refuge, who S the peoples under him.

SUBDUING

1Mac 1:20 After S Egypt, Antiochus returned in the one

SUBJECT (26)

Judg 1:30 among them, and became S to forced labor.
1:33 and of Beth-anath became S to forced labor for
1:35 them, and they became S to forced labor.
1Sam 2:27 they were in Egypt S to the house of
2Sam 10:19 with Israel, and became S to them.
1Chr 19:19 with David, and became S to him.
Wis 8:14 and nations will be S to me;
Sir 4:27 Do not S yourself to a foolish fellow, nor
2Mac 9:12 is right to be S to God, and no
Lk 10:17 even the demons are S to us in your
10:20 that the spirits are S to you; but rejoice
Rom 13:1 Let every person be S to the governing authorities.
13:5 Therefore one must be S, not only to avoid
1Cor 14:32 spirits of prophets are S to prophets.
16:16 urge you to be S to such men and
Eph 5:21 Be S to one another out of reverence for
5:22 Wives, be S to your husbands, as to the
5:24 As the church is S to Christ, so let
5:24 let wives also be S in everything to their
Phil 3:21 enables him even to S all things to himself.
Col 3:18 Wives, be S to your husbands, as is fitting
Heb 2:15 fear of death were S to lifelong bondage.
12:9 not much more be S to the Father of
1Pet 2:13 Be S for the Lord's sake to every human
3:22 angels, authorities, and powers S to him.
5:5 that are younger be S to the elders.

SUBJECTED (5)

Rom 8:20 for the creation was S to futility, not of
8:20 will of him who S it in hope;
1Cor 15:28 When all things are S to him, then the
15:28 himself will also be S to him who put
Heb 2:5 to angels that God S the world to come,

SUBJECTION (11)

Ps 106:42 they were brought into S under their power.
Sir 47:19 and through your body you were brought into S
48:12 any ruler, and no one brought him into S
Jer 34:11 and brought them into S as slaves.
34:16 you brought them into S to be your slaves.
Bar 2:4 he gave them into S to all the kingdoms
1Cor 15:27 put all things in S under his feet." But
15:27 things are put in S under him," it is
Heb 2:8 honor, putting everything in S under his feet." Now
2:8 in putting everything in S to him, he left
2:8 yet see everything in S to him.

SUBJECTS (3)

Esth 13:2 the lives of my S in lasting tranquillity and,
16:3 seek to injure our S, but in their inability
2Mac 11:23 we desire that the S of the kingdom be

SUBJUGATE

2Chr 28:10 now you intend to S the people of Judah

SUBMISSION

Gal 2:5 we did not yield S even for a moment,

SUBMISSIVE (7)

1Tim 3:4 well, keeping his children S and respectful in every
Tit 2:5 chaste, domestic, kind, and S to their husbands, that
2:9 Bid slaves to be S to their masters and
3:1 Remind them to be S to rulers and authorities,
1Pet 2:18 Servants, be S to your masters with all respect,
3:1 Likewise you wives, be S to your husbands, so
3:5 adorn themselves and were S to their husbands,

SUBMISSIVENESS

1Tim 2:11 Let a woman learn in silence with all S

SUBMIT (8)

Gen 16:9 to your mistress, and S to her."
Rom 8:7 God; it does not S to God's law, indeed
10:3 own, they did not S to God's righteousness.
2Cor 11:4 one you accepted, you S to it readily enough.
Gal 5:1 therefore, and do not S again to a yoke
Col 2:20 Why do you S to regulations,
Heb 13:17 Obey your leaders and S to them; for they
Jas 4:7 S yourselves therefore to God.

SUBORDINATE

1Cor 14:34 speak, but should be S, as even the law

SUBSEQUENT

1Pet 1:11 of Christ and the S glory.

SUBSIDED (3)

Gen 8:1 earth, and the waters S;
8:8 if the waters had S from the face of
8:11 that the waters had S from the earth.

SUBSTANCE (7)

Deut 33:11 Bless, O LORD, his S, and accept the work
Josh 14:4 their pasture lands for their cattle and their S
Ps 139:16 eyes beheld my unformed S; in thy book were
Prov 3:9 the LORD with your S and with the first
29:3 one who keeps company with harlots squanders his S
Dan 11:28 his land with great S, but his heart shall
Col 2:17 to come; but the S belongs to Christ.

SUBSTANTIAL

2Mac 4:45 as beaten, promised a S bribe to Ptolemy son

SUBSTITUTE

Lev 27:10 He shall not S anything for it or exchange

SUBTLE (3)

Gen 3:1 the serpent was more S than any other wild
Wis 7:22 intelligent, holy, unique, manifold, S, mobile, clear,
7:23 spirits that are intelligent and pure and most S

SUBTLETIES

Sir 39:2 men and penetrate the S of parables;

SUBURBS (2)

1Mac 11:4 and Azotus and its S destroyed, and the corpses
11:61 it and burned its S with fire and plundered

SUBVERT

Lam 3:36 the Most High, to S a man in his

SUBVERTED

Ps 119:78 shame, because they have S me with guile; as

SUBVERTS (2)

Ex 23:8 blinds the officials, and S the cause of those
Deut 16:19 of the wise and S the cause of the

SUCATHITES

1Chr 2:55 at Jabez: the Tirathites, the Shimeathites, and the S

SUCCEED (24)

Lev 6:22 who is anointed to S him, shall offer it
Num 14:41 command of the LORD, for that will not S
Deut 25:6 whom she bears shall S to the name of
Judg 18:5 journey on which we are setting out will S
1Sam 26:25 many things and will S in them." So David
1Kgs 22:22 him, and you shall S; go forth and do
1Chr 22:11 so that you may S in building the house
2Chr 13:12 the God of your fathers; for you cannot S
18:21 him, and you shall S; go forth and do
20:20 be established; believe his prophets, and you will S
Ps 21:11 you, if they devise mischief, they will not S
Prov 15:22 plans go wrong, but with many advisers they S
Eccl 10:10 forth more strength; but wisdom helps one to S
Sir 48:8 retribution, and prophets to S you.
Is 47:12 may be able to S, perhaps you may inspire
Jer 20:11 will be greatly shamed, for they will not S

S

22:30 man who shall not S in his days; for
22:30 of his offspring shall S in sitting on the
32:5 you fight against the Chaldeans, you shall not S
Ezek 17:15 Will he S
Dan 8:24 fearful destruction, and shall S in what he does,
2Mac 15:5 Nevertheless, he did not S in carrying out his
Rom 1:10 may now at last S in coming to you.
9:31 on law did not S in fulfilling that law.

SUCCEEDED (8)
1Chr 27:34 Ahithophel was S by Jehoiada the son of Benaiah,
Job 9:4 himself against him, and S —
Wis 7:30 superior, for it is S by the night, but
1Mac 1:1 and the Medes, he S him as king.
2Mac 4:7 who was called Epiphanes S to the kingdom, Jason
8:35 reached Antioch, having S chiefly in the destruction
10:11 This man, when he S to the kingdom, appointed
Acts 24:26 had elapsed, Felix was S by Porcius Festus; and

SUCCEEDS
Prov 30:23 a maid when she S her mistress.

SUCCESS (21)
Gen 24:12 master Abraham, grant me S today, I pray thee,
27:20 "Because the LORD your God granted me S
Josh 1:7 you may have good S wherever you go.
1:8 way prosperous, and then you shall have good S
1Sam 18:14 And David had S in all his undertakings; for
18:15 that he had great S, he stood in awe
18:30 out David had more S than all the servants
Neh 1:11 thy name; and give S to thy servant today,
Tob 5:16 the journey, and good S to you both." So
11:1 God because he had made his journey a S
Job 5:12 the crafty, so that their hands achieve no S
Ps 118:25 O LORD, we beseech thee, give us S
Wis 13:19 money-making and work and S with his hands he
Sir 10:5 The S of a man is in the hands
11:15 godly, and what he approves will have lasting S
38:13 is a time when S lies in the hands
38:14 he should grant them S in diagnosis and in
2Mac 5:6 citizens, not realizing that S at the cost of
10:7 him who had given S to the purifying of
10:23 Having S at arms in everything he undertook, he
10:28 having as pledge of S and victory not only

SUCCESSES
2Mac 8:8 ahead with more frequent S, he wrote to Ptolemy,

SUCCESSFUL (3)
Gen 39:2 and he became a S man; and he was
1Sam 18:5 went out and was S wherever Saul sent him;
Tob 5:21 his journey will be S, and he will come

SUCCESSFULLY
2Chr 7:11 his own house he S accomplished.

SUCCESSOR (3)
Sir 46:1 war, and was the S of Moses in prophesying.
2Mac 9:23 upper country, appointed his S,
14:26 conspirator against the kingdom, Judas, to be his S

SUCCOTH (18)
Gen 33:17 But Jacob journeyed to S, and built himself a
33:17 therefore the name of the place is called S
Ex 12:37 journeyed from Rameses to S, about six hundred
13:20 they moved on from S, and encamped at Etham,
Num 33:5 Israel set out from Rameses, and encamped at S
33:6 they set out from S, and encamped at Etham,
Josh 13:27 valley Beth-haram, Beth-nimrah, S, and Zaphon, the
Judg 8:5 to the men of S, "Pray, give loaves of
8:6 And the officials of S said, "Are Zebah and
8:8 as the men of S had answered.
8:14 a young man of S, and questioned him; and
8:14 officials and elders of S, seventy-seven men.
8:15 to the men of S, and said, "Behold Zebah
8:16 briers and with them taught the men of S
1Kgs 7:46 the clay ground between S and Zarethan.
2Chr 4:17 the clay ground between S and Zeredah.
Ps 60:6 up Shechem and portion out the Vale of S
108:7 up Shechem, and portion out the Vale of S

SUCCOTH-BENOTH
2Kgs 17:30 men of Babylon made S, the men of Cuth

SUCH (239)
Gen 6:2 they took to wife S of them as they
18:25 from thee to do S a thing, to slay
27:4 for me savory food, S as I love, and
27:9 food for your father, S as he loves;
27:14 mother prepared savory food, S as his father loved.
27:46 of the Hittite women S as these, one of
30:32 among the goats; and S shall be my wages.
33:10 face of God, with S favor have you received
34:7 with Jacob's daughter, for S a thing ought not
41:19 very gaunt and thin, S as I had never
41:38 servants, "Can we find S a man as this,
44:7 does my lord speak S words as these?
44:7 that they should do S a thing!
44:15 you not know that S a man as I
Ex 9:18 heavy hail to fall, S as never has been
9:24 hail, very heavy hail, S as had never been
10:14 whole country of Egypt, S a dense swarm of
11:6 the land of Egypt, S as there has never
18:21 from all the people, S as fear God, men
18:21 a bribe; and place S men over the people
23:13 other gods, nor let S be heard out of
34:10 I will do marvels, S as have not been
Lev 7:14 And of S he shall offer one cake from
10:1 fire before the LORD, S as he had not
10:19 the LORD; and yet S things as these have
11:34 be drunk from every S vessel shall be unclean.
14:22 or two young pigeons, S as he can afford;
14:30 turtledoves or young pigeons S as he can afford,
15:10 and he who carries S a thing shall wash
22:6 person who touches any S shall be unclean until
22:7 the holy things, because S are his food.
22:25 of your God any S animals gotten from a
27:9 it is an animal S as men offer as
27:9 the LORD, all of S that any man gives
27:11 is an unclean animal S as is not offered
Deut 3:24 earth who can do S works and mighty acts
4:32 to the other, whether S a great thing as
5:29 Oh that they had S a mind as this
13:11 never again do any S wickedness as this among
13:14 true and certain that S an abominable thing has
17:4 true and certain that S an abominable thing has
19:20 never again commit any S evil among you.
25:16 For all who do S things, all who act
33:17 ends of the earth; S are the ten thousands
33:17 thousands of Ephraim, and S are the thousands of
Josh 16:8 S is the inheritance of the tribe of the
Judg 3:2 might teach war to S at least as had
13:23 now announced to us S things as these."
18:23 that you come with S a company?"
19:30 who saw it said, S a thing has never
1Sam 2:23 "Why do you do S things?
21:2 the young men for S and such a place.
21:2 men for such and S a place.
27:11 S was his custom all the while he dwelt
2Sam 9:8 upon a dead dog S as I?"
13:12 not force me; for S a thing is not
14:13 then have you planned S a thing against the
15:2 "Your servant is of S and such a tribe
15:2 is of such and S a tribe in Israel,"
19:36 king recompense me with S a reward?
1Kgs 2:7 your table; for with S loyalty they met me
5:6 you for your servants S wages as you set;
10:10 stones; never again came S an abundance of spices
10:12 for the singers; no S almug wood has come
2Kgs 6:8 his servants, saying, "At S and such a place
6:8 saying, "At such and S a place shall be
7:19 windows in heaven, could S a thing be?" And
18:21 S is Pharaoh king of Egypt to all who
21:12 upon Jerusalem and Judah S evil that the ears
23:22 For no S passover had been kept since the
1Chr 29:18 fathers, keep for ever S purposes and thoughts in
29:25 and bestowed upon him S royal majesty as had
2Chr 1:12 riches, possessions, and honor, S as none of the
9:9 there were no spices S as those which the
35:18 of Israel had kept S a passover as was
Ezra 7:25 Beyond the River, all S as know the laws
7:27 our fathers, who put S a thing as this
9:13 and hast given us S a remnant as this,
Neh 4:17 burdens were laden in S a way that each
6:8 to him, saying, "No S things as you say
6:11 But I said, "Should S a man as I
6:11 And what man S as I could go into
13:26 sin on account of S women?
Jud 11:21 said, "There is not S a woman from one
12:12 disgrace if we let S a woman go without
Esth 4:14 you keep silence at S a time as this,
4:14 to the kingdom for S a time as this?"

9:2 to lay hands on S as sought their hurt.
Job 6:21 S you have now become to me; you see
8:13 S are the paths of all who forget God;
12:3 Who does not know S things as these?
14:3 open thy eyes upon S a one and bring
15:13 against God, and let S words go out of
16:2 "I have heard many S things; miserable comforters
18:21 Surely S are the dwellings of the ungodly, such
18:21 dwellings of the ungodly, S is the place of
23:14 for me; and many S things are in his
Ps 24:6 S is the generation of those who seek him,
53:5 great terror, in terror S as has not been!
139:6 S knowledge is too wonderful for me; it is
144:15 the people to whom S blessings fall!
Prov 1:19 S are the ways of all who get gain
24:14 Know that wisdom is S to your soul; if
29:7 man does not understand S knowledge.
Eccl 8:10 where they had done S things.
Wis 4:15 not understand, nor take S a thing to heart,
11:18 full of rage, or S as breathe out fiery
12:19 Through S works thou has taught thy people that
12:20 thou didst punish with S great care and indulgence
14:22 ignorance, and they call S great evils peace.
15:6 things and fit for S objects of hope are
16:1 deservedly punished through S creatures, and were
16:9 to be punished by S things;
Sir 6:8 a friend who is S at his own convenience,
7:35 sick man, because for S deeds you will be
16:5 Many S things my eye has seen, and my
19:11 With S a word a fool will suffer pangs
20:14 he asks it back; S a one is a
25:19 of the aged-- S is a garrulous wife
29:7 Because of S wickedness, therefore, many have
34:8 Without S deceptions the law will be fulfilled, and
45:13 time there never were S beautiful things.
Is 7:17 upon your father's house S days as have not
36:6 S is Pharaoh king of Egypt to all who
47:15 S to you are those with whom you have
58:5 Is S the fast that I choose, a day
66:8 Who has heard S a thing?
66:8 Who has seen S things?
Jer 2:10 if there has been S a thing.
5:9 myself on a nation S as this?
5:29 myself on a nation S as this?"
9:9 myself on a nation S as this?
16:20 S are no gods!"
19:3 Behold, I am bringing S evil upon this place
38:4 the people, by speaking S words to them.
52:3 LORD things came to S a pass in Jerusalem
Ezek 1:11 S were their faces.
1:28 S was the appearance of the likeness of the
3:6 I sent you to S, they would listen to
17:15 man escape who does S things?
41:25 cherubim and palm trees, S as were carved on
Dan 2:10 powerful king has asked S a thing of any
3:40 thousands of fat lambs; S may our sacrifice be
12:1 a time of trouble, S as never has been
13:48 he said, "Are you S fools, you sons of
Joel 1:2 Has S a thing happened in your days, or
Amos 5:13 will keep silent in S a time; for it
Mic 2:6 should not preach of S things; disgrace will not
Mal 1:9 With S a gift from your hand, will he
1Mac 1:51 In S words he wrote to his whole kingdom.
3:30 he might not have S funds as he had
4:6 have armor and swords S as they desired.
9:10 from us to do S a thing as to
9:27 great distress in Israel, S as had not been
10:16 "Shall we find another S man?
10:73 withstand my cavalry and S an army in the
10:89 him a golden buckle, S as it is the
15:8 royal treasury and any S future debts shall be
2Mac 1:19 cistern, where they took S precautions that the place
2:29 suitable for its adornment, S in my judgment is
3:11 To S an extent the impious Simon had
4:3 his hatred progressed to S a degree that even
4:13 There was S an extreme of Hellenization and
4:30 While S was the state of affairs, it happened
6:12 to be depressed by S calamities, but to recognize
6:24 S pretense is not worthy of our time of
8:7 nights most advantageous for S attacks.
9:28 the more intense suffering, S as he had inflicted
10:4 never again fall into S misfortunes, but that, if
10:9 S then was the end of Antiochus, who was
13:7 By S a fate it came about that Menelaus
Mt 8:10 Israel have I found S faith.
9:8 God, who had given S authority to men.
11:26 babes; yea, Father, for S was thy gracious will.
18:5 "Whoever receives one S child in my name receives
19:10 said to him, "If S is the case of
19:14 hinder them; for to S belongs the kingdom of
24:21 will be great tribulation, S as has not been
Mk 4:33 With many S parables he spoke the word to
7:13 And many S things you do."
9:37 them, "Whoever receives one S child in my name
10:14 hinder them; for to S belongs the kingdom of
13:19 days there will be S tribulation as has not
Lk 7:9 Israel have I found S faith."
9:9 about whom I hear S things?" And he sought
10:21 babes; yea, Father, for S was thy gracious will.
18:16 hinder them; for to S belongs the kingdom of
Jn 4:23 spirit and truth, for S the Father seeks to
6:58 down from heaven, not S as the fathers ate
8:5 in the law Moses commanded us to stone S
9:16 is a sinner do S signs?" There was a
Acts 22:22 and said, "Away with S a fellow from the
25:18 in his case of S evils as I supposed;
26:29 this day might become S as I am--except
Rom 1:32 that those who do S things deserve to die,
2:2 upon those who do S things.
2:3 judge those who do S things and yet do
15:5 you to live in S harmony with one another,
16:18 For S persons do not serve our Lord Christ,
1Cor 5:4 man who has done S a thing.
5:11 even to eat with S a one.
6:4 If then you have S cases, why do you
6:11 And S were some of you.
7:15 it be so; in S a case the brother
9:15 this to secure any S provision.
14:7 If even lifeless instruments, S as the flute or
16:16 to be subject to S men and to every
16:18 Give recognition to S men.
2Cor 2:6 For S a one this punishment by the majority
3:4 S is the confidence that we have through Christ
3:7 on stone, came with S splendor that the Israelites
3:12 Since we have S a hope, we are very
10:2 to show boldness with S confidence as I count
10:11 Let S people understand that what we say by
11:13 For S men are false apostles, deceitful workmen,
Gal 5:21 that those who do S things shall not inherit
5:23 gentleness, self-control; against S there is no law.
Eph 4:29 your mouths, but only S as is good for
5:27 or wrinkle or any S thing, that she might
Phil 2:29 all joy; and honor S men,
2Thes 3:12 Now S persons we command and exhort in the
2Tim 2:16 Avoid S godless chatter, for it will lead people
3:5 Avoid S people.
Tit 3:11 with him, knowing that S a person is perverted
Heb 2:3 escape if we neglect S a great salvation?
7:26 that we should have S a high priest, holy,
8:1 is this: we have S a high priest, one
12:3 who endured from sinners S hostility against himself,
13:16 what you have, for S sacrifices are pleasing to
Jas 3:15 This wisdom is not S as comes down from
4:13 we will go into S and such a town
4:13 go into such and S a town and spend
4:16 All S boasting is evil.
1Pet 1:18 not with perishable things S as silver or gold,
2Jn 1:7 Christ in the flesh; S a one is the
3Jn 1:8 we ought to support S men, that we may
Jude 1:15 they have committed in S an ungodly way, and
Rev 16:18 and a great earthquake S as had never been
20:6 Over S the second death has no power, but

SUCK (14)

Gen 33:13 flocks and herds giving S are a care to
Deut 32:13 and he made him S honey out of the
33:19 right sacrifices; for they S the affluence of the
Job 3:12 Or why the breasts, that I should S
20:16 He will S the poison of asps; the tongue
39:30 His young ones S up blood; and where the
Is 60:16 You shall S the milk of nations, you shall
60:16 of nations, you shall S the breast of kings;
66:11 her; that you may S and be satisfied with
66:12 stream; and you shall S, you shall be carried
Mt 24:19 for those who give S in those days!
Mk 13:17 for those who give S in those days!
Lk 21:23 for those who give S in those days!
23:28 breasts that never gave S

SUCKED

Lk 11:27 that bore you, and the breasts that you S

SUCKING (6)
Num 11:12 a nurse carries the S child, to the land
Deut 32:25 man and virgin, the S child with the man
1Sam 7:9 So Samuel took a S lamb and offered it
Sir 46:16 offered in sacrifice a S lamb.
Is 11:8 The S child shall play over the hole of
49:15 a woman forget her S child, that she should

SUCKLE (2)
Gen 21:7 Abraham that Sarah would S children?
Lam 4:3 give the breast and S their young, but the

SUCKLING
1Sam 15:3 and woman, infant and S, ox and sheep, camel

SUCKLINGS (2)
1Sam 22:19 and women, children and S, oxen, asses and sheep,
Mt 21:16 mouth of babes and S thou hast brought perfect

SUD
Bar 1:4 all who dwelt in Babylon by the river S

SUDDEN (9)
Lev 26:16 will appoint over you S terror, consumption, and
Job 9:23 When disaster brings S death, he mocks at the
22:10 round about you, and S terror overwhelms you;
Prov 3:25 not be afraid of S panic, or of the
Wis 17:15 their souls' surrender, for S and unexpected fear
Zeph 1:18 for a full, yea, S end he will make
2Mac 14:17 checked because of the S consternation created by
14:22 key places to prevent S treachery on the part
1Thes 5:3 then S destruction will come upon them as travail

SUDDENLY (45)
Num 6:9 any man dies very S beside him, and he
12:4 And S the LORD said to Moses and to
35:22 if he stabbed him S without enmity, or hurled
Josh 10:9 Joshua came upon them S, having marched up all
11:7 So Joshua came S upon them with all his
2Chr 29:36 for the people; for the thing came about S
Job 5:3 fool taking root, but S I cursed his dwelling.
Ps 64:4 blameless, shooting at him S and without fear.
64:7 his arrow at them; they will be wounded S
Prov 6:15 will come upon him S; in a moment he
23:5 it is gone; for S it takes to itself
24:22 from them will rise S, and who knows the
29:1 stiffens his neck will S be broken beyond healing.
Eccl 9:12 evil time, when it S falls upon them.
Wis 14:15 child, who had been S taken from him; and
Sir 5:7 day to day; for S the wrath of the
11:19 Lord to enrich a poor man quickly and S
Is 29:5 And in an instant, S,
30:13 collapse, whose crash comes S, in an instant;
47:11 shall come on you S, of which you know
48:3 made them known; then S I did them and
Jer 4:20 S my tents are destroyed, my curtains in a
6:26 most bitter lamentation; for S the destroyer will
15:8 have made anguish and terror fall upon them S
18:22 thou bringest the marauder S upon them!
49:19 strong sheepfold, I will S make them run away
50:44 strong sheepfold, I will S make them run away
51:8 S Babylon has fallen and been broken; wail for
Hab 2:7 Will not your debtors S arise, and those awake
Mal 3:1 whom you seek will S come to his temple;
1Mac 1:30 believed him; but he S fell upon the city,
3:23 finished speaking, he rushed S against Seron and his
4:2 the camp of the Jews and attack them S
2Mac 3:27 When he S fell to the ground and deep
5:5 a thousand men and S made an assault upon
Mk 9:8 And S looking around they no longer saw any
13:36 lest he come S and find you asleep.
Lk 2:13 And S there was with the angel a multitude
9:39 seizes him, and he S cries out; it convulses
21:34 day come upon you S like a snare;
Acts 2:2 And S a sound came from heaven like the
9:3 he approached Damascus, and S a light from heaven
16:26 listening to them, and S there was a great
22:6 great light from heaven S shone about me.
28:6 to swell up or S fall down dead; but

SUE (3)
Jud 3:1 they sent messengers to S for peace, and said,
Ps 45:12 people of Tyre will S your favor with gifts,
Mt 5:40 if any one would S you and take your

SUFFER (64)
Num 14:33 forty years, and shall S for your faithlessness, until
Neh 2:17 we may no longer S disgrace."
9:27 enemies, who made them S; and in the time
Job 24:11 the wine presses, but S thirst.
Ps 4:2 long shall my honor S shame?
9:13 Behold what I S from those who hate me,
34:10 The young lions S want and hunger; but those
60:3 hast made thy people S hard things; thou hast
88:15 my youth up, I S thy terrors; I am
Prov 13:20 companion of fools will S harm.
19:15 an idle person will S hunger.
22:3 simple go on, and S for it.
27:12 simple go on, and S for it.
Wis 4:19 barren, and they will S anguish, and the memory
14:29 oaths and expect to S no harm.
Sir 14:1 lips and need not S grief for sin.
19:11 word a fool will S pangs like a woman
28:1 takes vengeance will S vengeance from the Lord,
32:24 the Lord will not S loss.
41:7 ungodly father, for they S reproach because of him.
Is 24:6 earth, and its inhabitants S for their guilt; therefore
Jer 13:22 lifted up, and you S violence.
Lam 1:5 LORD has made her S for the multitude of
Ezek 18:19 should not the son S for the iniquity of
18:20 The son shall not S for the iniquity of
18:20 father, nor the father S for the iniquity of
34:29 land, and no longer S the reproach of the
36:7 about you shall themselves S reproach.
36:30 you may never again S the disgrace of famine
Dan 6:2 that the king might S no loss.
2Mac 6:30 I am glad to S these things because I
14:42 hands of sinners and S outrages unworthy of his
Mt 16:21 go to Jerusalem and S many things from the
17:12 Son of man will S at their hands."
Mk 8:31 Son of man must S many things, and be
9:12 man, that he should S many things and be
Lk 9:22 Son of man must S many things, and be
17:25 But first he must S many things and be
22:15 with you before I S;
24:26 that the Christ should S these things and enter
24:46 that the Christ should S and on the third
Acts 3:18 that his Christ should S, he thus fulfilled.
5:41 were counted worthy to S dishonor for the name.
9:16 how much he must S for the sake of
17:3 for the Christ to S and to rise from
26:23 that the Christ must S, and that, by being
Rom 8:17 with Christ, provided we S with him in order
1Cor 3:15 burned up, he will S loss, though he himself
6:7 Why not rather S wrong?
12:26 one member suffers, all S together; if one member
2Cor 1:6 you patiently endure the same sufferings that we S
2:3 came I might not S pain from those who
Phil 1:29 in him but also S for his sake,
1Thes 3:4 that we were to S affliction; just as it
2Thes 1:9 They shall S the punishment of eternal destruction
2Tim 1:12 teacher, and therefore I S as I do.
Heb 9:26 would have had to S repeatedly since the foundation
1Pet 1:6 you may have to S various trials,
2:20 you do right and S for it you take
3:14 even if you do S for righteousness' sake, you
3:17 it is better to S for doing right, if
4:15 let none of you S as a murderer, or
4:19 Therefore let those who S according to God's will
Rev 2:10 Do not fear what you are about to S

SUFFERED (33)
1Sam 25:15 to us, and we S no harm, and we
Jud 8:19 plundered, and so they S a great catastrophe before
Ps 107:17 because of their iniquities S affliction;
116:3 hold on me; I S distress and anguish.
Wis 18:1 happy for not having S,
18:11 and the common man S the same loss as
18:19 they might not perish without knowing why they S
19:13 thunder, for they justly S because of their wicked
Ezek 36:6 wrath, because you have S the reproach of the
1Mac 5:61 Thus the people S a great rout because, thinking
2Mac 4:48 the holy vessels quickly S the unjust penalty.
9:21 region of Persia I S an annoying illness, and
Mt 9:20 a woman who had S from a hemorrhage for
11:12 kingdom of heaven has S violence, and men of
27:19 man, for I have S much over him today
Mk 5:26 years, and who had S much under many physicians,
Lk 13:2 other Galileans, because they S thus?
Acts 28:5 into the fire and S no harm.
2Cor 7:9 grief, so that you S no loss through us.

7:12 of the one who S the wrong, but in
Phil 3:8 his sake I have S the loss of all
1Thes 2:2 we had already S and been shamefully treated
2:14 in Judea; for you S the same things from
Heb 2:18 because he himself has S and been tempted, he
5:8 obedience through what he S;
11:26 He considered abuse S for the Christ greater wealth
11:36 Others S mocking and scourging, and even chains
13:12 So Jesus also S outside the gate in order
1Pet 2:21 called, because Christ also S for you, leaving you
2:23 in return; when he S, he did not threaten;
4:1 Since therefore Christ S in the flesh, arm yourselves
4:1 thought, for whoever has S in the flesh has
5:10 And after you have S a little while, the

SUFFERING (26)

Neh 9:27 the time of their S they cried to thee
Job 2:13 they saw that his S was very great.
9:28 afraid of all my S, for I know thou
Ps 144:14 be heavy with young, S no mischance or failure
Wis 12:27 For when in their S they became incensed at
16:3 while thy people, after S want a short time,
Sir 38:16 as one who is S grievously begin the lament.
Lam 1:18 peoples, and behold my S; my maidens and my
2Mac 7:18 For we are S these things on our own
7:32 For we are S because of our own sins.
7:36 after enduring a brief S have drunk of everflowing
9:28 endured the more intense S, such as he had
Rom 5:3 our sufferings, knowing that S produces endurance,
Eph 3:13 over what I am S for you, which is
2Thes 1:5 for which you are S --
2Tim 1:8 prisoner, but share in S for the gospel in
2:3 Share in S as a good soldier of Christ
2:9 for which I am S and wearing fetters like
4:5 always be steady, endure S, do the work of
Heb 2:9 honor because of the S of death, so that
2:10 the pioneer of their salvation perfect through S
Jas 5:10 As an example of S and patience, brethren, take
5:13 Is any one among you S
1Pet 2:19 he endures pain while S unjustly.
5:9 the same experience of S is required of your
2Pet 2:13 same destruction with them, S wrong for their

SUFFERINGS (17)

Ex 3:7 taskmasters; I know their S,
Wis 19:16 celebrations, afflicted with terrible S those who had
2Mac 6:30 I am enduring terrible S in my body under
7:12 for he regarded his S as nothing.
9:18 But when his S did not in any way
Rom 5:3 we rejoice in our S, knowing that suffering produces
8:18 I consider that the S of this present time
2Cor 1:5 share abundantly in Christ's S, so through Christ we
1:6 patiently endure the same S that we suffer.
1:7 you share in our S, you will also share
Phil 3:10 and may share his S, becoming like him in
Col 1:24 I rejoice in my S for your sake, and
2Tim 3:11 steadfastness, my persecutions, my S, what befell me
Heb 10:32 a hard struggle with S,
1Pet 1:11 them when predicting the S of Christ and the
4:13 as you share Christ's S, that you may also
5:1 a witness of the S of Christ as well

SUFFERS (9)

Lev 22:4 is a leper or S a discharge may eat
Prov 11:24 should give, and only S want.
13:25 belly of the wicked S want.
Sir 13:3 reproaches; a poor man S wrong, and he must
Lam 1:4 away, and she herself S bitterly.
Ezek 22:7 in you; the sojourner S extortion in your midst;
Mt 17:15 an epileptic and he S terribly; for often he
1Cor 12:26 If one member S, all suffer together; if one
1Pet 4:16 mischief-maker; yet if one S as a Christian, let

SUFFICE (8)

Num 11:22 slaughtered for them, to S them?
11:22 together for them, to S them?"
Deut 3:26 to me, 'Let it S you; speak no more
Judg 21:14 but they did not S for them.
1Kgs 20:10 dust of Samaria shall S for handfuls for all
Ps 49:8 costly, and can never S,
Is 40:16 Lebanon would not S for fuel, nor are its
1Pet 4:3 time that is past S for doing what the

SUFFICIENCY

Job 20:22 the fulness of his S he will be in

SUFFICIENT (10)

Ex 36:7 stuff they had was S to do all the
Lev 25:26 becomes prosperous and finds S means to redeem it,
25:28 if he has not S means to get it
Deut 15:8 him, and lend him S for his need, whatever
2Chr 30:3 not sanctified themselves in S number, nor had the
Wis 18:12 the living were not S even to bury them,
2Mac 10:19 his men, a force S to besiege them; and
Mt 6:34 day's own trouble be S for the day.
2Cor 2:16 Who is S for these things?
12:9 me, "My grace is S for you, for my

SUGGEST

Tob 6:10 I will S that she be given to you

SUGGESTION

2Mac 6:8 At the S of Ptolemy a decree was issued

SUIT (10)

Ex 23:2 bear witness in a S, turning aside after a
23:3 be partial to a poor man in his S
23:6 the justice due to your poor in his S
Judg 17:10 a year, and a S of apparel, and your
2Sam 15:2 any man had a S to come before the
15:4 every man with a S or cause might come
Job 34:33 then make requital to S you, because you reject
Wis 16:21 it, was changed to S every one's liking.
Is 59:4 No one enters S justly, no one goes to
2Tim 4:3 for themselves teachers to S their own likings,

SUITABLE (5)

Gen 49:28 each with the blessing S to him.
2Mac 2:29 consider only what is S for its adornment, such
3:37 of person would be S to send on another
4:32 he had obtained a S opportunity, stole some of
Acts 27:12 the harbor was not S to winter in, the

SUITED

Wis 16:20 providing every pleasure and S to every taste.

SUITS (3)

Dan 13:6 and all who had S at law came to
1Mac 13:29 the columns he put S of armor for a
13:29 memorial, and beside the S of armor carved ships,

SUKKI-IM

2Chr 12:3 him from Egypt—Libyans, S, and Ethiopians.

SULLEN (2)

1Kgs 20:43 his house resentful and S, and came to Samaria.
21:4 his house vexed and S because of what Naboth

SULPHUR (8)

Lk 17:29 from Sodom fire and S rained from heaven and
Rev 9:17 of sapphire and of S, and the heads of
9:17 fire and smoke and S issued from their mouths.
9:18 fire and smoke and S issuing from their mouths.
14:10 tormented with fire and S in the presence of
19:20 into the lake of fire that burns with S
20:10 lake of fire and S where the beast and
21:8 burns with fire and S, which is the second

SULTRY

Jon 4:8 rose, God appointed a S east wind, and the

SUM (15)

Ex 38:21 This is the S of the things for the
2Sam 24:9 And Joab gave the S of the numbering of
1Chr 21:5 And Joab gave the S of the numbering of
Esth 4:7 him, and the exact S of money that Haman
Ps 119:160 The S of thy word is truth; and every
139:17 How vast is the S of them!
Eccl 7:25 seek wisdom and the S of things, and to
7:27 another to find the S,
Sir 43:27 the end, and the S of our words is:
51:28 instruction with a large S of silver, and you
Dan 7:1 dream, and told the S of the matter.
Mt 26:9 sold for a large S, and given to the
28:12 counsel, they gave a S of money to the
Acts 7:16 had bought for a S of silver from the
22:28 answered, "I bought this citizenship for a large S

SUMMARY

2Mac 10:10 will give a brief S of the principal calamities

SUMMED

Rom 13:9 any other commandment, are S up in this sentence,

SUMMER (26)

Gen 8:22 harvest, cold and heat, S and winter, day and
2Sam 16:1 raisins, a hundred of S fruits, and a skin
16:2 on, the bread and S fruit for the young
Ps 32:4 was dried up as by the heat of S
74:17 earth; thou hast made S and winter.
Prov 6:8 prepares her food in S, and gathers her sustenance
10:5 son who gathers in S is prudent, but a
26:1 Like snow in S or rain in harvest, so
30:25 their food in the S;
Sir 50:8 on Lebanon on a S day;
Is 18:6 birds of prey will S upon them, and all
28:4 first-ripe fig before the S: when a man sees
Jer 8:20 harvest is past, the S is ended, and we
40:10 you, gather wine and S fruits and oil, and
40:12 they gathered wine and S fruits in great abundance.
48:32 as Jazer, upon your S fruits and your vintage
Dan 2:35 the chaff of the S threshing floors; and the
3:68 Lord, winter cold and S heat, sing praise to
Amos 3:15 winter house with the S house; and the houses
8:1 behold, a basket of S fruit.
8:2 said, "A basket of S fruit." Then the LORD
Mic 7:1 become as when the S fruit has been gathered,
Zech 14:8 it shall continue in S as in winter.
Mt 24:32 leaves, you know that S is near.
Mk 13:28 leaves, you know that S is near.
Lk 21:30 and know that the S is already near.

SUMMIT (3)

2Sam 15:32 David came to the S, where God was worshiped,
16:1 a little beyond the S, Ziba the servant of
Jer 22:6 to me, as the S of Lebanon, yet surely

SUMMON (14)

1Sam 22:11 the king sent to S Ahimelech the priest, the
2Sam 20:5 So Amasa went to S Judah; but he delayed
1Kgs 22:13 messenger who went to S Micaiah said to him,
2Chr 18:12 messenger who went to S Micaiah said to him,
Jud 8:10 all she possessed, to S Chabris and Charmis, the
Job 9:19 of justice, who can S him?
Ps 68:28 S thy might, O God; show thy strength, O
Jer 49:19 Who will S me?
50:29 S archers against Babylon, all those who bend the
50:44 Who will S me?
51:27 for war against her, S against her the kingdoms,
Ezek 36:29 uncleannesses; and I will S the grain and make
38:21 I will S every kind of terror against Gog,
Acts 24:24 an opportunity I will S you."

SUMMONED (45)

Gen 48:2 to you"; then Israel S his strength, and sat
Ex 7:11 Then Pharaoh S the wise men and the sorcerers;
12:31 And he S Moses and Aaron by night, and
Deut 5:1 And Moses S all Israel, and said to them,
29:2 And Moses S all Israel and said to them:
31:7 Then Moses S Joshua, and said to him in
Josh 9:22 Joshua S them, and he said to them, "Why
10:24 out to Joshua, Joshua S all the men of
22:1 Then Joshua S the Reubenites, and the Gadites, and
23:2 advanced in years, Joshua S all Israel, their elders
24:1 Israel to Shechem, and S the elders, the heads,
Judg 4:6 She sent and S Barak the son of Abino-am
4:10 And Barak S Zebulun and Naphtali to Kedesh; and
1Sam 15:4 So Saul S the people, and numbered them in
23:8 And Saul S all the people to war, to
28:15 dreams; therefore I have S you to tell me
2Sam 14:33 told him; and he S Absalom.
1Kgs 2:36 the king sent and S Shimei, and said to
2:42 the king sent and S Shimei, and said to
22:9 the king of Israel S an officer and said,
2Kgs 4:36 Then he S Gehazi and said, "Call this Shunammite."
12:7 Therefore King Jehoash S Jehoiada the priest and
1Chr 15:11 Then David S the priests Zadok and Abiathar, and
2Chr 18:8 the king of Israel S an officer and said,
24:6 So the king S Jehoiada the chief, and said
Jud 14:6 So they S Achior from the house of Uzziah.
Esth 2:14 her and she was S by name.
3:12 the king's secretaries were S on the thirteenth day
8:9 The king's secretaries were S at that time, in
Job 9:16 If I S him and he answered me, I
Ps 105:16 When he S a famine on the land, and
Wis 1:16 their words and deeds S death; considering him a
Is 13:3 my consecrated ones, have S my mighty men to
Jer 42:8 Then he S Johanan the son of Kareah and
Lam 1:15 midst of me; he S an assembly against me
Dan 2:2 and the Chaldeans be S, to tell the king
13:52 from each other, he S one of them and
Nah 2:5 The officers are S, they stumble as they go,
1Mac 1:6 So he S his most honored officers, who had
2Mac 4:28 two of them were S by the king on
8:1 entered the villages and S their kinsmen and enlisted
Mt 2:7 Then Herod S the wise men secretly and ascertained
18:31 Then his lord S him and said to him,
Acts 6:2 And the twelve S the body of the disciples
13:7 man of intelligence, who S Barnabas and Saul and

SUMMONING (4)

Num 10:2 shall use them for S the congregation, and for
Jer 25:29 unpunished, for I am S a sword against all
Mk 15:43 were already dead; and S the centurion, he asked
Lk 16:5 of the stewardship.' So, S his master's debtors one

SUMMONS

Ps 50:1 the LORD, speaks and S the earth from the

SUMPTUOUS

Sir 29:22 of his roof than S food in another man's

SUMPTUOUSLY

Lk 16:19 linen and who feasted S every day.

SUMS (3)

1Mac 14:32 He spent great S of his own money; he
2Mac 3:6 was full of untold S of money, so that
Mk 12:41 Many rich people put in large S

SUN (187)

Gen 15:12 As the S was going down, a deep sleep
15:17 When the S had gone down and it was
19:23 The S had risen on the earth when Lot
28:11 that night, because the S had set.
32:31 The S rose upon him as he passed Penuel,
37:9 dream; and behold, the S, the moon, and eleven
Ex 16:21 eat; but when the S grew hot, it melted.
17:12 were steady until the going down of the S
22:4 him; but if the S has risen upon him,
22:26 to him before the S goes down;
Lev 22:7 When the S is down he shall be clean;
Num 25:4 hang them in the S before the LORD, that
Deut 4:19 when you see the S and the moon and
11:30 going down of the S, in the land of
16:6 going down of the S, at the time you
17:3 worshiped them, or the S or the moon or
23:11 water, and when the S is down, he may
24:13 his pledge; when the S goes down, you shall
24:15 earns it, before the S goes down (for he
33:14 choicest fruits of the S, and the rich yield
Josh 1:4 going down of the S shall be your territory.
8:29 going down of the S Joshua commanded, and they
10:12 the sight of Israel, S, stand thou still at
10:13 And the S stood still, and the moon stayed,
10:13 The S stayed in the midst of heaven, and
10:27 going down of the S, Joshua commanded, and they
Judg 5:31 friends be like the S as he rises in
9:33 as soon as the S is up, rise early
14:18 seventh day before the S went down, "What is
19:14 their way; and the S went down on them
1Sam 11:9 by the time the S is hot, you shall
2Sam 2:24 Abner; and as the S was going down they
3:35 anything else till the S goes down!"
12:11 with your wives in the sight of this S
12:12 this thing before all Israel, and before the S
23:4 morning light, like the S shining forth upon a
1Kgs 8:12 LORD has set the S in the heavens, but
2Kgs 3:22 the morning, and the S shone upon the water,
20:11 steps, by which the S had declined on the
23:5 to Baal, to the S, and the moon, and
23:11 had dedicated to the S, at the entrance to
23:11 the chariots of the S with fire.
Neh 7:3 be opened until the S is hot; and while
Tob 2:7 When the S had set I went and dug
Jud 14:2 morning comes and the S rises, let every valiant
Esth 10:6 was light and the S and abundant water
11:11 light came, and the S rose, and the lowly
Job 8:16 He thrives before the S, and his shoots spread
9:7 tremble; who commands the S, and it does not
30:28 but not by the S; I stand up in
31:26 have looked at the S when it shone, or
Ps 19:4 a tent for the S,

50:1 the rising of the S to its setting.
58:8 like the untimely birth that never sees the S
72:5 he live while the S endures, and as long
72:17 ever, his fame continue as long as the S
74:16 night; thou hast established the luminaries and the S
84:11 LORD God is a S and shield; he bestows
89:36 as long as the S before me.
104:19 mark the seasons; the S knows its time for
104:22 When the S rises, they get them away and
113:3 the rising of the S to its setting the
121:6 The S shall not smite you by day, nor
136:8 endures for ever; the S to rule over the
148:3 Praise him, S and moon, praise him, all you
Eccl 1:3 the toil at which he toils under the S
1:5 The S rises and the sun goes down, and
1:5 sun rises and the S goes down, and hastens
1:9 done; and there is nothing new under the S
1:14 is done under the S; and behold, all is
2:11 there was nothing to be gained under the S
2:17 is done under the S was grievous to me;
2:18 had toiled under the S, seeing that I must
2:19 I toiled and used my wisdom under the S
2:20 my labors under the S,
2:22 and strain with which he toils beneath the S
3:16 I saw under the S that in the place
4:1 all the oppressions that are practiced under the S
4:3 the evil deeds that are done under the S
4:7 saw vanity under the S:
4:15 move about under the S, as well as that
5:13 have seen under the S: riches were kept by
5:18 one toils under the S the few days of
6:1 have seen under the S, and it lies heavy
6:5 has not seen the S or known anything; yet
6:12 man what will be after him under the S
7:11 inheritance, an advantage to those who see the S
8:9 is done under the S, while man lords it
8:15 good thing under the S but to eat and
8:15 of life which God gives him under the S
8:17 out the work that is done under the S
9:3 is done under the S, that one fate comes
9:6 share in all that is done under the S
9:9 given you under the S, because that is your
9:9 your toil at which you toil under the S
9:11 saw that under the S the race is not
9:13 of wisdom under the S, and it seemed great
10:5 have seen under the S, as it were an
11:7 is pleasant for the eyes to behold the S
12:2 in them"; before the S and the light and
Song 1:6 am swarthy, because the S has scorched me.
6:10 moon, bright as the S, terrible as an army
Wis 2:4 the rays of the S and overcome by its
5:6 on us, and the S did not rise upon
7:29 beautiful than the S, and excels every constellation
16:27 fleeting ray of the S,
16:28 must rise before the S to give thee thanks,
18:3 and a harmless S for their glorious wandering.
Sir 17:15 works are as the S before him, and his
17:26 What is brighter than the S
23:19 times brighter than the S; they look upon all
26:16 Like the S rising in the heights of the
33:7 the daylight in the year is from the S
34:16 a shade from noonday S, a guard against stumbling
42:16 The S looks down on everything with its light,
43:2 The S, when it appears, making proclamation as it
43:4 burning heat, but the S burns the mountains three
46:4 Was not the S held back by his hand?
48:23 In his days the S went backward, and he
50:7 is full; like the S shining upon the temple
Is 13:10 give their light; the S will be dark at
19:18 these will be called the City of the S
24:23 be confounded, and the S ashamed; for the LORD
30:26 the light of the S, and the light of
30:26 the light of the S will be sevenfold, as
38:8 cast by the declining S on the dial of
38:8 So the S turned back on the dial the
41:25 the rising of the S, and he shall call
45:6 the rising of the S and from the west,
49:10 neither scorching wind nor S shall smite them, for
59:19 the rising of the S; for he will come
60:19 The S shall be no more your light by
60:20 Your S shall no more go down, nor your
Jer 8:2 be spread before the S and the moon and
15:9 has swooned away; her S went down while it
31:35 LORD, who gives the S for light by day
Bar 6:60 For S and moon and stars, shining and sent
6:67 or shine like the S or give light like
Ezek 8:16 the east, worshiping the S toward the east.
32:7 I will cover the S with a cloud, and
Dan 3:63 Bless the Lord, S and moon, sing praise to
6:14 he labored till the S went down to rescue
Joel 2:10 The S and the moon are darkened, and the
2:31 The S shall be turned to darkness, and the
3:15 The S and the moon are darkened, and the
Amos 8:9 "I will make the S go down at noon,
Jon 4:8 When the S rose, God appointed a sultry east
4:8 east wind, and the S beat upon the head
Mic 3:6 The S shall go down upon the prophets, and
Nah 3:17 of cold--when the S rises, they fly away;
Hab 3:11 The S and moon stood still in their habitation
Mal 1:11 the rising of the S to its setting my
4:2 fear my name the S of righteousness shall rise,
1Mac 6:39 When the S shone upon the shields of gold
10:50 battle strongly until the S set, and Demetrius fell
12:27 So when the S set, Jonathan commanded his men
2Mac 1:22 had passed and the S, which had been clouded
Mt 5:45 for he makes his S rise on the evil
13:6 soil, but when the S rose they were scorched;
13:43 will shine like the S in the kingdom of
17:2 face shone like the S, and his garments became
24:29 of those days the S will be darkened, and
Mk 4:6 soil; and when the S rose it was scorched,
13:24 after that tribulation, the S will be darkened, and
16:2 the tomb when the S had risen.
Lk 4:40 Now when the S was setting, all those who
21:25 will be signs in S and moon and stars,
23:44 ninth hour, while the S's light failed; and the
Acts 2:20 vapor of smoke; the S shall be turned into
13:11 unable to see the S for a time." Immediately
26:13 heaven, brighter than the S, shining round me and
27:20 And when neither S nor stars appeared for many
1Cor 15:41 one glory of the S, and another glory of
Eph 4:26 do not let the S go down on your
Jas 1:10 For the S rises with its scorching heat and
Rev 1:16 face was like the S shining in full strength.
6:12 earthquake; and the S became black as sackcloth,
7:2 the rising of the S, with the seal of
7:16 thirst any more; the S shall not strike them,
8:12 a third of the S was struck, and a
9:2 great furnace, and the S and the air were
10:1 face was like the S, and his legs like
12:1 woman clothed with the S, with the moon under
16:8 his bowl on the S, and it was allowed
19:17 angel standing in the S, and with a loud
21:23 has no need of S or moon to shine
22:5 light of lamp or S, for the Lord God

SUNDER (2)

Job 8:14 His confidence breaks in S, and his trust is
Ps 136:13 the Red Sea in S, for his steadfast love

SUNDOWN

Mk 1:32 That evening, at S, they brought to him all

SUNG (7)

1Chr 16:7 appointed that thanksgiving be S to the LORD by
Job 36:24 to extol his work, of which men have S
Is 16:10 vineyards no songs are S, no shouts are raised;
26:1 this song will be S in the land of
Dan 3:57 heaven and to be S and glorified for ever.
Mt 26:30 And when they had S a hymn, they went
Mk 14:26 And when they had S a hymn, they went

SUNK (7)

Ex 15:4 his picked officers are S in the Red Sea.
Job 38:6 what were its bases S, or who laid its
Ps 9:15 The nations have S in the pit which they
38:2 For thy arrows have S into me, and thy
Jer 38:22 that your feet are S in the mire, they
Lam 2:9 Her gates have S into the ground; he has
Ezek 27:34 all your crew have S with you.

SUNRISE (7)

Num 2:3 east side toward the S shall be of the
3:38 of meeting toward the S, were Moses and Aaron
21:11 the wilderness which is opposite Moab, toward the S
34:15 the Jordan at Jericho eastward, toward the S
Josh 1:15 LORD gave you beyond the Jordan toward the S
19:12 direction eastward toward the S to the boundary of
19:13 the east toward the S to Gath-hepher, to Eth-kazin,

SUNRISING (2)

Josh 12:1 the Jordan toward the S, from the valley of

13:5 all Lebanon, toward the S, from Baal-gad below

SUNSET (3)
1Kgs 22:36 And about S a cry went through the army,
2Chr 18:34 until evening; then at S he died.
Tob 2:4 the body to a place of shelter until S

SUNSHINE
Is 18:4 like clear heat in S, like a cloud of

SUPERB (2)
Sir 45:8 He clothed him with S perfection, and strengthened him
50:11 and clothed himself with S perfection and went up

SUPERFLUOUS (2)
2Mac 12:44 it would have been S and foolish to pray
2Cor 9:1 Now it is S for me to write to

SUPERHUMAN
2Mac 9:8 the sea, in his S arrogance, and imagining that

SUPERIOR (4)
Wis 7:29 is found to be S,
Sir 25:10 there is no one S to him who fears
Heb 1:4 having become as much S to angels as the
7:7 dispute that the inferior is blessed by the S

SUPERLATIVE (2)
2Cor 11:5 least inferior to these S apostles.
12:11 all inferior to these S apostles, even though I

SUPERNATURAL (3)
1Cor 10:3 all ate the same S food
10:4 all drank the same S drink.
10:4 they drank from the S Rock which followed them,

SUPERSTITION
Acts 25:19 him about their own S and about one Jesus,

SUPH
Deut 1:1 the Arabah over against S, between Paran and

SUPHAH
Num 21:14 the LORD, "Waheb in S, and the valleys of

SUPPER (10)
Lk 17:8 say to him, 'Prepare S for me, and gird
22:20 likewise the cup after S, saying, "This cup which
Jn 12:2 they made him a S; Martha served, and Lazarus
13:2 And during S, when the devil had already put
13:4 to God, rose from S, laid aside his garments,
21:20 his breast at the S and had said, "Lord,
1Cor 11:20 is not the Lord's S that you eat.
11:25 also the cup, after S, saying, "This cup is
Rev 19:9 invited to the marriage S of the Lamb." And
19:17 gather for the great S of God,

SUPPLANTED (2)
Gen 27:36 For he has S me these two times.
2Mac 4:26 his own brother was S by another man, was

SUPPLANTER
Jer 9:4 every brother is a S, and every neighbor goes

SUPPLANTING
2Mac 4:26 So Jason, who after S his own brother was

SUPPLEMENT
2Pet 1:5 make every effort to S your faith with virtue,

SUPPLIANT
Sir 4:4 not reject an afflicted S, nor turn your face

SUPPLIANTS
Zeph 3:10 rivers of Ethiopia my S, the daughter of my

SUPPLICATION (50)
1Kgs 8:28 servant and to his S, O LORD my God,
8:30 hearken thou to the S of thy servant and
8:33 and pray and make S to thee in this
8:38 is; whatever prayer, whatever S is made by any
8:45 their prayer and their S, and maintain their cause.
8:47 and repent, and make S to thee in the
8:49 their prayer and their S, and maintain their cause
8:52 be open to the S of thy servant, and
8:52 servant, and to the S of thy people Israel,
8:54 all this prayer and S to the LORD, he
8:59 wherewith I have made S before the LORD, be
9:3 your prayer and your S, which you have made
2Chr 6:19 servant and to his S, O LORD my God,
6:24 and pray and make S to thee in this
6:29 is; whatever prayer, whatever S is made by any
6:35 their prayer and their S, and maintain their cause.
6:37 and repent, and make S to thee in the
33:13 entreaty and heard his S and brought him again
Esth 4:8 the king to make S to him and entreat
Job 8:5 seek God and make S to the Almighty,
Ps 6:9 LORD has heard my S; the LORD accepts my
28:2 the voice of my S, as I cry to
30:8 the LORD I made S:
55:1 O God; and hide not thyself from my S
86:6 to my prayer; hearken to my cry of S
102:17 of the destitute, and will not despise their S
119:170 Let my S come before thee; deliver me according
142:1 my voice I make S to the LORD,
Sir 35:14 will not ignore the S of the fatherless, nor
39:5 him, and will make S before the Most High;
39:5 in prayer and make S for his sins.
51:9 I sent up my S from the earth, and
Is 45:14 They will make S to you, saying: 'God is
Jer 36:7 may be that their S will come before the
42:2 the prophet, "Let our S come before you, and
42:9 me to present your S before him:
Bar 2:14 our prayer and our S, and for thy own
4:20 the sackcloth of my S; I will cry to
Dan 6:11 Daniel making petition and S before his God.
9:20 Israel, and presenting my S before the LORD my
Zech 12:10 spirit of compassion and S, so that, when they
1Mac 7:37 for thy people a house of prayer and S
2Mac 3:18 to make a general S because the holy place
8:29 this, they made common S and besought the merciful
9:18 the following letter, in the form of a S
10:16 men, after making solemn S and beseeching God to
10:25 loins with sackcloth, in S to God.
Eph 6:18 times in the Spirit, with all prayer and S
6:18 with all perseverance, making S for all the saints,
Phil 4:6 everything by prayer and S with thanksgiving let

SUPPLICATIONS (19)
2Sam 21:14 after that God heeded S for the land.
24:25 So the LORD heeded S for the land, and
2Chr 6:21 hearken thou to the S of thy servant and
6:39 their prayer and their S, and maintain their cause
Job 41:3 Will he make many S to you?
Ps 28:6 for he has heard the voice of my S
31:22 thou didst hear my S, when I cried to
116:1 because he has heard my voice and my S
130:2 ears be attentive to the voice of my S
140:6 the voice of my S, O LORD!
143:1 my prayer, O LORD; give ear to my S
Is 19:22 he will heed their S and heal them.
Dan 9:3 him by prayer and S with fasting and sackcloth
9:17 servant and to his S, and for thy own
9:18 do not present our S before thee on the
9:23 the beginning of your S a word went forth,
1Tim 2:1 I urge that S, prayers, intercessions, and
5:5 God and continues in S and prayers night and
Heb 5:7 offered up prayers and S, with loud cries and

SUPPLIED (11)
Gen 47:17 the asses: and he S them with food in
Num 4:9 with which it is S:
1Kgs 4:27 And those officers S provisions for King Solomon,
5:10 So Hiram S Solomon with all the timber of
9:11 king of Tyre had S Solomon with cedar and
Jud 7:7 visited the springs that S their water, and seized
Prov 13:4 while the soul of the diligent is richly S
Sir 1:8 his gift, and he S her to those who
1Mac 14:10 He S the cities with food, and furnished them
2Cor 11:9 for my needs were S by the brethren who
Eph 4:16 with which it is S, when each part is

SUPPLIES (7)
Jud 3:10 to assemble all the S for his army.
Dan 11:13 come on with a great army and abundant S
1Mac 6:6 strong from the arms, S, and abundant spoils which
2Cor 9:10 He who S seed to the sower and bread
9:12 this service not only S the wants of the
Gal 3:5 Does he who S the Spirit to you and
1Pet 4:11 the strength which God S; in order that in

SUPPLY (17)
Jud 7:17 and seized the water S and the springs of
7:18 and their tents and S trains spread out in
11:12 Since their food S is exhausted and their water
12:3 to her, "If your S runs out, where can
Wis 16:20 their toil thou didst S them from heaven with
Sir 1:23 and the Lord will S it for you.
39:33 good, and he will S every need in its
Is 23:18 but her merchandise will S abundant food and fine
1Mac 6:57 grow weaker, our food S is scant, the place
8:26 shall not give or S grain, arms, money, or
2Mac 12:14 walls and on their S of provisions, behaved most
15:21 him and the varied S of arms and the
2Cor 8:14 the present time should S their want, so that
8:14 that their abundance may S your want, that there
9:10 bread for food will S and multiply your resources
Phil 4:19 And my God will S every need of yours
1Thes 3:10 face to face and S what is lacking in

SUPPORT (13)
Gen 13:6 the land could not S both of them dwelling
36:7 their sojournings could not S them because of their
1Chr 11:10 who gave him strong S in his kingdom, together
Tob 8:6 him Eve his wife as a helper and S
Ps 20:2 sanctuary, and give you S from Zion!
Sir 3:29 the moment of his falling he will find S
34:15 And who is his S
34:16 mighty protection and strong S, a shelter from the
36:24 helper fit for him and a pillar of S
Ezek 30:6 the LORD: Those who S Egypt shall fall, and
Rom 11:18 is not you that S the root, but the
2Cor 11:8 other churches by accepting S from them in order
3Jn 1:8 So we ought to S such men, that we

SUPPORTED (7)
1Kgs 2:28 --for Joab had S Adonijah although he had
2:28 although he had not S Absalom--Joab fled
Ezra 10:15 and Shabbethai the Levite S them.
Job 24:23 security, and they are S; and his eyes are
Ps 18:35 and thy right hand S me, and thy help
Ezek 41:6 they should not be S by the wall of
1Mac 2:17 in this city, and S by sons and brothers.

SUPPORTERS
1Mac 11:39 Now Trypho had formerly been one of Alexander's S

SUPPORTING
1Kgs 6:6 in order that the S beams should not be

SUPPORTS (9)
1Kgs 7:30 the four corners were S for a laver.
7:30 The S were cast, with wreaths at the side
7:34 There were four S at the four corners of
7:34 of each stand; the S were of one piece
10:12 of the almug wood S for the house of
Sir 25:21 disgrace when a wife S her husband.
Ezek 41:6 temple to serve as S for the side chambers,
1Mac 2:27 for the law and S the covenant come out
Rom 11:18 but the root that S you.

SUPPOSE (19)
Gen 18:24 S there are fifty righteous within the city; wilt
18:28 S five of the fifty righteous are lacking?
18:29 to him, and said, S forty are found there."
18:30 S thirty are found there." He answered, "I will
18:31 S twenty are found there." He answered, "For the
18:32 S ten are found there." He answered, "For the
2Sam 13:32 "Let not my lord S that they have killed
13:33 to heart as to S that all the king's
2Chr 25:8 But if you S that in this way you
Tob 6:17 with you, and I S that you will have
Esth 16:4 nothing of goodness they S that they will escape
2Mac 6:24 of the young should S that Eleazar in his
Lk 7:43 answered, "The one, I S, to whom he forgave
Jn 21:25 to be written, I S that the world itself
Acts 2:15 not drunk, as you S, since it is only
13:25 said, 'What do you S that I am?
Rom 2:3 Do you S, O man, that when you judge
Jas 1:7 that person must not S that a double-minded man,
4:5 Or do you S it is in vain that

SUPPOSED (13)
Jud 14:14 the tent, for he S that he was sleeping
Wis 13:2 his works; but they S that either fire or
17:2 For when lawless men S that they held the
Dan 13:5 were judges, who were S to govern the people."
1Mac 6:43 the others, and he S that the king was
Mk 10:42 that those who are S to rule over the
Lk 3:23 the son (as was S of Joseph, the son
19:11 Jerusalem, and because they S that the kingdom of
24:37 startled and frightened, and S that they saw a
Acts 7:25 He S that his brethren understood that God was
16:13 the riverside, where we S there was a place
21:29 the city, and they S that Paul had brought
25:18 such evils as I S;

SUPPOSING (6)
Lk 2:44 not know it, but S him to be in
Jn 11:31 out, they followed her, S that she was going
20:15 S him to be the gardener, she said to
Acts 14:19 out of the city, S that he was dead.
16:27 about to kill himself, S that the prisoners had
27:13 south wind blew gently, S that they had obtained

SUPPRESS
Rom 1:18 who by their wickedness S the truth.

SUPREME (4)
Prov 4:1 The S Guidance of Wisdom
Eccl 8:4 of the king is S, and who may say
2Mac 3:36 the deeds of the S God, which he had
1Pet 2:13 to the emperor as S,

SUR (2)
2Kgs 11:6 being at the gate S and a third at
Jud 2:28 those who lived in S and Ocina and all

SURE (60)
Lev 25:30 city shall be made S in perpetuity to him
Num 32:23 the LORD; and be S your sin will find
Deut 12:23 Only be S that you do not eat the
Josh 2:12 and give me a S sign,
1Sam 2:35 will build him a S house, and he shall
23:22 Go, make yet more S; know and see the
23:23 back to me with S information.
25:28 make my lord a S house, because my lord
2Sam 1:10 him, because I was S that he could not
7:16 kingdom shall be made S for ever before me;
1Kgs 11:38 will build you a S house, as I built
Jud 2:13 sovereign's commands, but be S to carry them out
Ps 19:7 of the LORD is S, making wise the simple;
48:3 has shown himself a S defense.
93:5 Thy decrees are very S; holiness befits thy house,
119:86 All thy commandments are S; they persecute me
132:11 swore to David a S oath from which he
Prov 4:27 your feet, then all your ways will be S
11:18 sows righteousness gets a S reward.
Wis 7:23 beneficent, humane, steadfast, S, free from anxiety,
18:6 they might rejoice in S knowledge of the oaths
Sir 40:25 make the foot stand S, but good counsel is
Is 22:23 a peg in a S place, and he will
22:25 was fastened in a S place will give way;
25:1 wonderful things, plans formed of old, faithful and S
28:16 precious cornerstone, of a S foundation: 'He who
33:16 will be given him, his water will be S
55:3 everlasting covenant, my steadfast, S love for David.
Jer 38:15 will you not be S to put me to
Dan 2:5 word from me is S: if you do not
2:8 word from me is S
2:45 The dream is certain, and its interpretation S
4:26 your kingdom shall be S for you from the
Hos 5:9 the tribes of Israel I declare what is S
6:3 his going forth is S as the dawn; he
2Mac 9:27 For I am S that he will follow my
Lk 17:1 "Temptations to sin are S to come; but woe
Acts 12:11 said, "Now I am S that the Lord has
13:34 you the holy and S blessings of David.'
Rom 2:19 and if you are S that you are a
8:38 For I am S that neither death, nor life,
2Cor 1:15 Because I was S of this, I wanted to
2:3 rejoice, for I felt S of all of you,
Eph 5:5 Be S of this, that no fornicator or impure
Phil 1:6 And I am S that he who began a
1Tim 1:15 The saying is S and worthy of full acceptance,
3:1 The saying is S: If any one aspires to
4:9 The saying is S and worthy of full acceptance.
2Tim 1:5 and now, I am S, dwells in you.
1:12 believed, and I am S that he is able
2:11 The saying is S: If we have died with
Tit 1:8 hold firm to the S word as taught, so
3:8 The saying is S
Heb 6:9 case, beloved, we feel S of better things that

S

6:19 have this as a S and steadfast anchor of
13:18 us, for we are S that we have a
2Pet 1:19 And we have the prophetic word made more S
1Jn 2:3 this we may be S that we know him,
2:5 this we may be S that we are in
2:29 righteous, you may be S that every one who

SURELY (174)

Gen 9:5 your lifeblood I will S require a reckoning; of
18:10 LORD said, "I will S return to you in
20:7 know that you shall S die, you, and all
28:16 his sleep and said, S the LORD is in
29:14 Laban said to him, S you are my bone
29:32 looked upon my affliction; S now my husband will
31:42 been on my side, S now you would have
42:16 the life of Pharaoh, S you are spies."
44:28 me, and I said, S he has been torn
Ex 2:14 was afraid, and thought, S the thing is known."
4:25 with it, and said, S you are a bridegroom
22:23 to me, I will S hear their cry;
23:33 their gods, it will S be a snare to
Num 14:35 the LORD, have spoken; S this will I do
22:17 me; for I will S do you great honor,
22:33 turned aside from me, S just now I would
32:11 and he swore, saying, S none of the men
Deut 4:6 these statutes, will say, S this great nation is
8:19 day that you shall S perish.
12:2 You shall S destroy all the places where the
13:15 among you, you shall S put the inhabitants of
23:21 LORD your God will S require it of you,
31:18 us?' And I will S hide my face in
31:29 my death you will S act corruptly, and turn
Josh 14:9 on that day, saying, S the land on which
Judg 4:9 she said, "I will S go with you; nevertheless,
11:10 between us; we will S do as you say."
13:22 his wife, "We shall S die, for we have
20:39 of Israel; they said, S they are smitten down
1Sam 14:39 my son, he shall S die." But there was
14:44 more also; you shall S die, Jonathan."
15:32 Agag said, S the bitterness of death is past."
16:6 on Eliab and thought, S the LORD's anointed is
17:25 S he has come up to defy Israel; and
20:26 he is not clean, S he is not clean."
20:31 me, for he shall S die."
22:16 king said, "You shall S die, Ahimelech, you and
22:22 there, that he would S tell Saul.
23:10 Israel, thy servant has S heard that Saul seeks
24:20 know that you shall S be king, and that
25:21 Now David had said, S in vain have I
25:34 For as S as the LORD the God of
28:9 woman said to him, S you know what Saul
30:8 "Pursue; for you shall S overtake and shall surely
30:8 surely overtake and shall S rescue."
2Sam 2:27 you had not spoken, S the men would have
14:19 answered and said, "As S as you live, my
1Kgs 11:2 they with you, for S they will turn away
11:11 commanded you, I will S tear the kingdom from
13:32 cities of Samaria, shall S come to pass."
18:15 I stand, I will S show myself to him
20:23 in the plain, and S we shall be stronger
20:25 in the plain, and S we shall be stronger
22:32 they said, "It is S the king of Israel."
2Kgs 1:4 gone, but you shall S die."' So Elijah went.
1:6 have gone, but shall S die."'
1:16 gone, but you shall S die."'
3:23 blood; the kings have S fought together, and slain
5:11 thought that he would S come out to me,
9:26 oracle against him: 'As S as I saw yesterday
18:30 saying, The LORD will S deliver us, and this
24:3 S this came upon Judah at the command of
Tob 14:8 prophet Jonah said will S happen.
Jud 1:12 kingdom that he would S take revenge on the
10:19 S not a man of them had better be
12:14 S whatever pleases him I will do at once,
Esth 6:13 against him but will S fall before him."
Job 5:2 S vexation kills the fool, and jealousy slays the
8:6 are pure and upright, S then he will rouse
11:15 S then you will lift up your face without
13:10 He will S rebuke you if in secret you
16:7 S now God has worn me out; he has
17:2 S there are mockers about me, and my eye
18:21 S such are the dwellings of the ungodly, such
22:2 S he who is wise is profitable to himself.
22:20 them to scorn, saying, S our adversaries are cut
28:1 S there is a mine for silver, and a
31:36 S I would carry it on my shoulder; I
33:8 S, you have spoken in my hearing, and I
35:13 S God does not hear an empty cry, nor
38:5 Who determined its measurements-- S you know!
Ps 23:6 S goodness and mercy shall follow me all the
39:5 S every man stands as a mere breath!
39:6 [Selah] S man goes about as a shadow!
39:6 S for nought are they in turmoil; man heaps
39:11 is dear to him; S every man is a
58:11 Men will say, S there is a reward for
58:11 reward for the righteous; S there is a God
76:10 [Selah] S the wrath of men shall praise thee;
85:9 S his salvation is at hand for those who
140:13 S the righteous shall give thanks to thy name;
Prov 21:5 of the diligent lead S to abundance, but every
23:18 S there is a future, and your hope will
30:2 to Ithi-el and Ucal: S I am too stupid
30:4 S you know!
Eccl 4:16 S this also is vanity and a striving after
7:7 S oppression makes the wise man foolish, and a
7:20 S there is not a righteous man on earth
Sir 5:3 for the Lord will S punish you.
14:17 old is, "You must S die!"
48:11 for we also shall S live.
Is 5:9 sworn in my hearing: S many houses shall be
7:9 you will not believe, S you shall not be
8:20 S for this word which they speak there is
22:14 himself in my ears: S this iniquity will not
30:19 He will S be gracious to you at the
36:15 saying, "The LORD will S deliver us; this city
40:7 LORD blows upon it; S the people is grass.
49:4 nothing and vanity; yet S my right is with
49:19 S your waste and your desolate places and your
49:19 your devastated land-- S now you will be
49:25 S, thus says the LORD: "Even the captives of
53:4 S he has borne our griefs and carried our
56:3 say, "The LORD will S separate me from his
63:8 For he said, S they are my people, sons
Jer 2:35 say, 'I am innocent; S his anger has turned
3:20 S, as a faithless wife leaves her husband, so
4:10 said, "Ah, Lord GOD, S thou hast utterly deceived
22:6 summit of Lebanon, yet S I will make you
23:39 therefore, behold, I will S lift you up and
31:20 for him; I will S have mercy on him,
32:4 the Chaldeans, but shall S be given into the
34:3 his hand, but shall S be captured and delivered
37:9 saying, "The Chaldeans will S stay away from us,"
38:3 LORD, This city shall S be given into the
39:18 For I will S save you, and you shall
44:25 hands, saying, 'We will S perform our vows that
44:29 that my words will S stand against you for
49:20 shall be dragged away; S their fold shall be
50:34 He will S plead their cause, that he may
50:45 land of the Chaldeans: S the little ones of
50:45 shall be dragged away; S their fold shall be
51:14 has sworn by himself: S I will fill you
51:56 of recompense, he will S requite.
52:3 S because of the anger of the LORD things
Lam 3:3 darkness without any light; S against me he turns
Bar 2:29 very great multitude will S turn into a small
Ezek 3:6 S, if I sent you to such, they would
3:18 the wicked, 'You shall S die,' and you give
3:21 not sin, he shall S live, because he took
5:11 says the Lord GOD, S, because you have defiled
17:16 says the Lord GOD, S in the place where
17:19 GOD: As I live, S my oath which he
18:9 is righteous, he shall S live, says the Lord
18:13 abominable things; he shall S die; his blood shall
18:17 father's iniquity; he shall S live.
18:19 my statutes, he shall S live.
18:21 and right, he shall S live; he shall not
18:28 had committed, he shall S live, he shall not
20:33 says the Lord GOD, S with a mighty hand
31:11 the nations; he shall S deal with it as
33:8 wicked man, you shall S die, and you do
33:13 righteous that he shall S live, yet if he
33:14 the wicked, 'You shall S die,' yet if he
33:15 no iniquity; he shall S live, he shall not
33:16 and right, he shall S live.
33:24 many; the land is S given us to possess.'
33:27 GOD: As I live, S those who are in
Hos 12:11 in Gilead they shall S come to nought; if
Amos 3:7 S the Lord GOD does nothing, without revealing his
5:5 Beer-sheba; for Gilgal shall S go into exile, and
7:17 land, and Israel shall S go into exile away
8:7 the pride of Jacob: S I will never forget
Mic 2:12 I will S gather all of you, O Jacob,

Hab 2:3 for it; it will S come, it will not
Zeph 3:7 I said, S she will fear me, she will
1Mac 5:40 him, for he will S defeat us.
Mt 15:4 or mother, let him S die.'
Mk 7:10 or mother, let him S die';
Acts 7:34 I have S seen the ill-treatment of my people
2Cor 1:18 As S as God is faithful, our word to
Heb 2:16 For S it is not with angels that he
6:14 swore by himself, saying, S I will bless you
Rev 22:20 to these things says, S I am coming soon."

SURETY (20)

Gen 15:13 Abram, "Know of a S that your descendants will
43:9 I will be S for him; of my hand
44:32 For your servant became S for the lad to
Job 17:3 there that will give S for me?
Ps 119:122 Be S for thy servant for good; let not
Prov 6:1 if you have become S for your neighbor, have
11:15 He who gives S for a stranger will smart
17:18 a pledge, and becomes S in the presence of
20:16 when he has given S for a stranger, and
20:16 pledge when he gives S for foreigners.
22:26 give pledges, who become S for debts.
27:13 when he has given S for a stranger, and
27:13 pledge when he gives S for foreigners.
Sir 8:13 Do not give S beyond your means, but if
8:13 but if you give S, be concerned as one
29:14 good man will be S for his neighbor, but
29:15 the kindness of your S, for he has given
29:16 the prosperity of his S,
29:18 Being S has ruined many men who were prosperous,
Heb 7:22 This makes Jesus the S of a better covenant.

SURETYSHIP (2)

Prov 11:15 but he who hates S is secure.
Sir 29:19 who has fallen into S and pursues gain will

SURF

Acts 27:41 and the stern was broken up by the S

SURFACE (11)

Lev 14:37 be deeper than the S,
Wis 13:14 paint and coloring its S red and covering every
Sir 16:28 beings he covered its S, and to it they
Is 24:1 he will twist its S and scatter its inhabitants.
28:25 he has leveled its S, does he not scatter
Jer 8:2 as dung on the S of the ground.
16:4 as dung on the S of the ground.
25:33 be dung on the S of the ground.
Amos 5:8 them out upon the S of the earth, the
9:6 them out upon the S of the earth–
9:8 destroy it from the S of the ground; except

SURFACES

1Kgs 7:36 And on the S of its stays and on

SURFEIT (2)

Eccl 5:12 or much; but the S of the rich will
Ezek 16:49 her daughters had pride, S of food, and prosperous

SURGE (2)

Jer 46:7 rising like the Nile, like rivers whose waters S
46:8 rises like the Nile, like rivers whose waters S

SURGING (2)

1Sam 14:16 behold, the multitude was S hither and thither.
Hab 3:15 with thy horses, the S of mighty waters.

SURLINESS

Sir 41:19 behavior at meals, of S in receiving and giving,

SURNAME (2)

Is 44:5 hand, 'The LORDs,' and S himself by the name
45:4 by your name, I S you, though you do

SURNAMED (5)

1Mac 2:2 had five sons, John S Gaddi,
Mk 3:16 demons: Simon whom he S Peter;
3:17 of James, whom he S Bo-anerges, that is, sons
Acts 1:23 called Barsabbas, who was S Justus, and Matthias.
4:36 Thus Joseph who was S by the apostles Barnabas

SURPASS (7)

1Kgs 10:7 your wisdom and prosperity S the report which I
2Chr 9:6 not told me; you S the report which I
Prov 31:29 done excellently, but you S them all."
Sir 18:16 does not a word S a good gift?
43:30 can; for he will S even that.
Ezek 15:2 wood of the vine S any wood, the vine
32:19 Pit: 'Whom do you S in beauty?

SURPASSED (2)

1Kgs 4:30 so that Solomon's wisdom S the wisdom of all
Eccl 2:9 I became great and S all who were before

SURPASSES (4)

Sir 25:11 fear of the Lord S everything; to whom shall
36:22 gladdens the countenance, and S every human
2Cor 3:10 of the splendor that S it.
Eph 3:19 love of Christ which S knowledge, that you may

SURPASSING (4)

Eccl 1:16 have acquired great wisdom, S all who were over
2Mac 4:13 ways because of the S wickedness of Jason, who
2Cor 9:14 you, because of the S grace of God in
Phil 3:8 loss because of the S worth of knowing Christ

SURPLUS

Tob 4:16 Give all your S to charity, and do not

SURPRISE (2)

1Mac 12:33 and took it by S,
1Thes 5:4 for that day to S you like a thief.

SURPRISED (2)

1Pet 4:4 They are S that you do not now join
4:12 Beloved, do not be S at the fiery ordeal

SURRENDER (16)

1Sam 23:11 the men of Keilah S me into his hand?
23:12 the men of Keilah S me and my men
23:12 LORD said, "They will S you."
23:20 part shall be to S him into the king's
Jud 7:27 call them in and S the whole city to
8:9 them under oath to S the city to the
8:11 and you, promising to S the city to our
8:33 you have promised to S the city to our
Esth 14:11 O Lord, do not S thy scepter to what
Wis 17:12 fear is nothing but S of the helps that
17:15 paralyzed by their souls' S, for sudden and
Sir 23:6 me, and do not S me to a shameless
Jer 38:17 Israel, If you will S to the princes of
38:18 if you do not S to the princes of
38:21 if you refuse to S, this is the vision
1Mac 8:7 and give hostages and S some of their best

SURRENDERED

Jer 50:15 round about, she has S; her bulwarks have fallen,

SURRENDERS

Jer 21:9 who goes out and S to the Chaldeans who

SURROUND (16)

Josh 7:9 of it, and will S us, and cut off
2Kgs 11:8 of the LORD, shall S the king, each with
2Chr 14:7 build these cities, and S them with walls and
23:7 The Levites shall S the king, each with his
Job 16:13 his target, his archers S me.
40:22 willows of the brook S him.
Ps 17:9 my deadly enemies who S me.
17:11 me down; now they S me; they set their
22:12 strong bulls of Bashan S me;
88:17 They S me like a flood all day long;
140:9 [Selah] Those who S me lift up their head,
142:7 The righteous will S me; for thou wilt deal
Amos 3:11 GOD: "An adversary shall S the land, and bring
Hab 1:4 For the wicked S the righteous, so justice goes
Lk 8:45 said, "Master, the multitudes S you and press upon
19:43 bank about you and S you, and hem you

SURROUNDED (27)

Gen 19:4 to the last man, S the house;
Judg 16:2 and they S the place and lay in wait
2Sam 18:15 young men, Joab's armor-bearers, S Absalom and,
1Kgs 5:3 with which his enemies S him, until the LORD
2Kgs 3:25 Kir-hareseth, and the slingers S and conquered it.
6:14 came by night, and S the city.
8:21 the Edomites who had S him; but his army
2Chr 21:9 the Edomites who had S him and his chariot
Jud 2:26 He S all the Midianites, and burned their tents
4:12 They even S the altar with sackcloth and cried
7:19 all their enemies had S them and there was

S

7:20 infantry, chariots, and cavalry, S them for thirty-four
Ps 118:10 All nations S me; in the name of the
118:11 They S me, surrounded me on every side; in
118:11 They surrounded me, S me on every side; in
118:12 They S me like bees, they blazed like a
Wis 19:17 righteous man-- when, S by yawning darkness, each
Sir 50:12 on Lebanon; and they S him like the trunks
51:7 They S me on every side, and there was
1Mac 6:7 and that they had S the sanctuary with high
10:80 behind him, for they S his army and shot
13:43 encamped against Gazara and S it with troops.
15:14 He S the city, and the ships joined battle
2Mac 14:41 Being S, Razis fell upon his own sword,
Lk 21:20 when you see Jerusalem S by armies, then know
Heb 12:1 Therefore, since we are S by so great a
Rev 20:9 the broad earth and S the camp of the

SURROUNDING (16)
1Chr 6:55 of Judah and its S pasture lands,
28:12 the LORD, all the S chambers, the treasuries of
Jud 1:9 in Samaria and its S towns, and beyond the
Bar 2:4 desolation among all the S peoples, where the Lord
1Mac 1:31 its houses and its S walls.
1:54 built altars in the S cities of Judah,
7:24 out into all the S parts of Judea, and
10:84 burned Azotus and the S towns and plundered them;
2Mac 10:30 S Maccabeus and protecting him with their own
Mk 1:28 everywhere throughout all the S region of Galilee.
Lk 4:14 out through all the S country.
4:37 every place in the S region.
7:17 Judea and all the S country.
8:37 the people of the S country of the Gerasenes
Acts 14:6 Lycaonia, and to the S country;
Jude 1:7 and Gomorrah and the S cities, which likewise acted

SURROUNDS (3)
Ps 32:10 wicked; but steadfast love S him who trusts in
49:5 iniquity of my persecutors S me,
Sir 23:18 Darkness S me, and the walls hide me, and

SURVIVAL
Sir 16:3 not trust in their S, and do not rely

SURVIVE (6)
Job 27:15 Those who S him the pestilence buries, and their
Sir 23:27 Those who S her will recognize that nothing is
Is 16:14 multitude, and those who S will be very few
Jer 21:7 in this city who S the pestilence, sword, and
44:14 Egypt shall escape or S or return to the
Ezek 5:10 any of you who S I will scatter to

SURVIVED (5)
Josh 8:22 was left none that S or escaped.
1Sam 11:11 day; and those who S were scattered, so that
Neh 1:2 concerning the Jews that S, who had escaped exile,
Jer 31:2 LORD: "The people who S the sword found grace
Lam 2:22 LORD none escaped or S; those whom I dandled

SURVIVES (4)
Ex 21:21 But if the slave S a day or two,
Sir 36:9 Let him who S be consumed in the fiery
Zech 14:16 Then every one that S of all the nations
1Cor 3:14 built on the foundation S, he will receive a

SURVIVING (2)
2Kgs 19:30 And the S remnant of the house of Judah
Is 37:31 And the S remnant of the house of Judah

SURVIVOR (6)
Num 21:35 there was not one S left to him; and
Deut 3:3 smote him until no S was left to him.
Ezra 1:4 Jerusalem; and let each S, in whatever place he
Job 18:19 his people, and no S where he used to
Jer 42:17 have no remnant or S from the evil which
Obad 1:18 there shall be no S to the house of

SURVIVORS (20)
Gen 45:7 earth, and to keep alive for you many S
Num 24:19 be exercised, and the S of cities be destroyed!"
Judg 21:17 an inheritance for the S of Benjamin, that a
2Kgs 19:31 and out of Mount Zion a band of S
Neh 1:3 said to me, "The S there in the province
Is 1:9 left us a few S, we should have been
4:2 and glory of the S of Israel.
10:20 of Israel and the S of the house of
37:32 and out of Mount Zion a band of S

45:20 draw near together, you S of the nations!
66:19 them I will send S to the nations, to
Ezek 7:16 And if any S escape, they will be on
14:22 left in it any S to lead out sons
17:21 the sword, and the S shall be scattered to
23:25 your ears, and your S shall fall by the
23:25 your daughters, and your S shall be devoured by
Joel 2:32 said, and among the S shall be those whom
Obad 1:14 have delivered up his S in the day of
Zeph 2:9 plunder them, and the S of my nation shall
1Mac 2:44 in their wrath; the S fled to the Gentiles

SUSA (24)
Ezra 4:9 Babylonians, the men of S, that is, the Elamites,
Neh 1:1 as I was in S the capital,
Esth 1:2 his royal throne in S the capital,
1:5 the people present in S the capital, both great
2:3 to the harem in S the capital, under custody
2:5 was a Jew in S the capital whose name
2:8 maidens were gathered in S the capital in custody
3:15 decree was issued in S the capital.
3:15 but the city of S was perplexed.
4:8 written decree issued in S for their destruction, that
4:16 to be found in S, and hold a fast
8:14 decree was issued in S the capital.
8:15 while the city of S shouted and rejoiced.
9:6 In S the capital itself the Jews slew and
9:11 of those slain in S the capital was reported
9:12 to Queen Esther, "In S the capital the Jews
9:13 Jews who are in S be allowed tomorrow also
9:14 decree was issued in S, and the ten sons
9:15 Jews who were in S gathered also on the
9:15 three hundred men in S; but they laid no
9:18 Jews who were in S gathered on the thirteenth
11:3 in the city of S, a great man, serving
16:18 at the gate of S, with all his household.
Dan 8:2 saw, I was in S the capital, which is

SUSANNA (11)
Dan 13:2 took a wife named S, the daughter of Hilkiah,
13:7 people departed at noon, S would go into her
13:22 S sighed deeply, and said, "I am hemmed in
13:24 Then S cried out with a loud voice, and
13:27 nothing like this had ever been said about S
13:28 wicked plot to have S put to death.
13:29 the people, "Send for S, the daughter of Hilkiah,
13:31 Now S was a woman of great refinement, and
13:42 Then S cried out with a loud voice, and
13:63 God for their daughter S, and so did Joakim
Lk 8:3 Chuza, Herod's steward, and S, and many others,

SUSI
Num 13:11 Gaddi the son of S;

SUSPECT
2Cor 10:2 showing against some who S us of acting in

SUSPECTED (2)
2Mac 12:4 to live peaceably and S nothing, the men of
Acts 27:27 about midnight the sailors S that they were nearing

SUSPECTS
Sir 23:21 and where he least S it, he will be

SUSPENSE (2)
Jn 10:24 him, "How long will you keep us in S
Acts 27:33 you have continued in S and without food, having

SUSPICION
2Mac 4:34 in spite of his S persuaded Onias to come

SUSPICIONS
1Tim 6:4 envy, dissension, slander, base S,

SUSPICIOUS
2Mac 7:24 contempt, and he was S of her reproachful tone.

SUSPICIOUSLY
Sir 37:10 who looks at you S; hide your counsel from

SUSTAIN (5)
Neh 9:21 Forty years didst thou S them in the wilderness,
Ps 55:22 LORD, and he will S you; he will never
Song 2:5 S me with raisins, refresh me with apples; for
Is 50:4 may know how to S with a word him
1Cor 1:8 Jesus Christ; who will S you to the end,

S

SUSTAINED (4)
Gen 27:37 and wine I have S him.
Deut 19:15 or of three witnesses, shall a charge be S
Mal 2:15 one God made and S for us the spirit
2Cor 13:1 Any charge must be S by the evidence of

SUSTAINS (2)
Ps 3:5 again, for the LORD S me.
41:3 The LORD S him on his sickbed; in his

SUSTENANCE (3)
Judg 6:4 Gaza, and leave no S in Israel, and no
Prov 6:8 summer, and gathers her S in harvest.
Wis 16:21 thy S manifested thy sweetness toward thy children;

SWADDLING (4)
Job 38:9 and thick darkness its S band,
Wis 7:4 nursed with care in S cloths.
Lk 2:7 and wrapped him in S cloths, and laid him
2:12 a babe wrapped in S cloths and lying in

SWALLOW (14)
Num 16:34 said, "Lest the earth S us up!"
2Sam 20:19 Israel; why will you S up the heritage of
20:20 it, that I should S up or destroy!
Job 7:19 me alone till I S my spittle?
20:18 toil, and will not S it down; from the
Ps 21:9 The LORD will S them up in his wrath;
69:15 me, or the deep S me up, or the
84:3 a home, and the S a nest for herself,
Prov 1:12 like Sheol let us S them alive and whole,
26:2 its flitting, like a S in its flying, a
Is 25:8 He will S up death for ever, and the
38:14 Like a S or a crane I clamor, I
Jer 8:7 times; and the turtledove, S, and crane keep the
Jon 1:17 a great fish to S up Jonah; and Jonah

SWALLOWED (21)
Gen 41:7 And the thin ears S up the seven plump
41:24 and the thin ears S up the seven good
Ex 7:12 But Aaron's rod S up their rods.
15:12 right hand, the earth S them.
Num 16:32 opened its mouth and S them up, with their
26:10 opened its mouth and S them up together with
Deut 11:6 opened its mouth and S them up, with their
2Sam 17:16 are with him be S up.'"
Tob 6:2 river and would have S the young man;
Job 37:20 that he would be S up?
Ps 35:25 not say, "We have S him up."
106:17 the earth opened and S up Dathan, and covered
124:3 then they would have S us up alive, when
Is 9:16 led by them are S up.
49:19 inhabitants, and those who S you up will be
Jer 51:34 empty vessel, he has S me like a monster;
51:44 take out of his mouth what he has S
Hos 8:8 Israel is S up; already they are among the
1Cor 15:54 is written: "Death is S up in victory."
2Cor 5:4 is mortal may be S up by life.
Rev 12:16 opened its mouth and S the river which the

SWALLOWING
Mt 23:23 out a gnat and S a camel!

SWALLOWS (5)
Num 16:30 opens its mouth, and S them up, with all
Job 20:15 He S down riches and vomits them up again;
39:24 fierceness and rage he S the ground; he cannot
Bar 6:22 Bats, S, and birds light on their bodies and
Hab 1:13 silent when the wicked S up the man more

SWAM
1Mac 9:48 into the Jordan and S across to the other

SWAMP
Is 35:7 jackals shall become a S, the grass shall become

SWAMPED
Mt 8:24 the boat was being S by the waves; but

SWAMPS
Ezek 47:11 But its S and marshes will not become fresh;

SWARM (9)
Gen 1:21 with which the waters S, according to their kinds,
7:21 all swarming creatures that S upon the earth, and
Ex 8:3 frogs; the Nile shall S with frogs which shall
10:14 Egypt, such a dense S of locusts as had
Lev 11:29 the swarming things that S upon the earth: the
11:31 you among all that S; whoever touches them when
11:42 the swarming things that S upon the earth, you
Judg 14:8 behold, there was a S of bees in the
Jud 2:20 mixed crowd like a S of locusts, like the

SWARMED (2)
Ps 105:30 Their land S with frogs, even in the chambers
2Mac 9:9 the ungodly man's body S with worms, and while

SWARMING (11)
Gen 7:21 birds, cattle, beasts, all S creatures that swarm upon
Lev 5:2 a carcass of unclean S things, and it is
11:10 and scales, of the S creatures in the waters
11:29 to you among the S things that swarm upon
11:41 "Every S thing that swarms upon the earth is
11:42 many feet, all the S things that swarm upon
11:43 yourselves abominable with any S thing that swarms;
11:44 defile yourselves with any S thing that crawls upon
Joel 1:4 cutting locust left, the S locust has eaten.
1:4 What the S locust left, the hopping locust has
2:25 the years which the S locust has eaten, the

SWARMS (13)
Gen 1:20 the waters bring forth S of living creatures, and
Ex 8:21 behold, I will send S of flies on you
8:21 shall be filled with S of flies, and also
8:22 dwell, so that no S of flies shall be
8:24 so; there came great S of flies into the
8:29 the LORD that the S of flies may depart
8:31 asked, and removed the S of flies from Pharaoh,
Lev 11:41 "Every swarming thing that S upon the earth is
11:43 any swarming thing that S; and you shall not
11:46 and every creature that S upon the earth,
Ps 78:45 He sent among them S of flies, which devoured
105:31 spoke, and there came S of flies, and gnats
Ezek 47:9 every living creature which S will live, and there

SWARTHY
Song 1:6 me because I am S, because the sun has

SWATHED (2)
Ezek 16:4 rubbed with salt, nor S with bands.
16:10 you with leather, I S you in fine linen

SWAY (3)
Judg 9:9 honored, and go to S over the trees?'
9:11 fruit, and go to S over the trees?'
9:13 men, and go to S over the trees?'

SWAYED (2)
2Sam 19:14 And he S the heart of all the men
2Tim 3:6 burdened with sins and S by various impulses,

SWAYS
Is 24:20 a drunken man, it S like a hut; its

SWEAR (63)
Gen 21:23 you do; now therefore S to me here by
21:24 And Abraham said, "I will S
24:3 I will make you S by the LORD, the
24:37 My master made me S, saying, 'You shall not
25:33 Jacob said, S to me first." So he swore
47:31 And he said, S to me"; and he swore
50:5 My father made me S, saying, 'I am about
50:6 and bury your father, as he made you S
Ex 32:13 to whom thou didst S by thine own self,
Lev 5:4 rash oath that men S, and it is hidden
19:12 And you shall not S by my name falsely,
Num 11:12 land which thou didst S to give their fathers?'
Deut 6:13 shall serve him, and S by his name.
10:20 to him, and by his name you shall S
26:15 us, as thou didst S to our fathers, a
32:40 hand to heaven, and S, As I live for
Josh 2:12 Now then, S to me by the LORD that
2:17 oath of yours which you have made us S
2:20 to your oath which you have made us S
23:7 of their gods, or S by them, or serve
Judg 15:7 what you do, I S I will be avenged
15:12 Samson said to them, S to me that you
1Sam 3:14 Therefore I S to the house of Eli that
20:17 And Jonathan made David S again by his love
24:21 S to me therefore by the LORD that you
30:15 And he said, S to me by God, that
2Sam 19:7 your servants; for I S by the LORD, if

S

1Kgs	1:13	my lord the king, S to your maidservant, saying,
	1:51	saying, 'Let King Solomon S to me first that
	2:42	I not make you S by the LORD, and
2Chr	36:13	who had made him S by God; he stiffened
Ps	24:4	false, and does not S deceitfully.
	63:11	in God; all who S by him shall glory;
	89:49	thy faithfulness thou didst S to David?
Wis	14:29	in lifeless idols they S wicked oaths and expect
	14:31	things by which men S, but the just penalty
Is	19:18	language of Canaan and S allegiance to the LORD
	45:23	bow, every tongue shall S
	48:1	loins of Judah; who S by the name of
	65:16	in the land shall S by the God of
Jer	4:2	waver, and if you S, 'As the LORD lives,'
	5:2	yet they S falsely.
	7:9	murder, commit adultery, S falsely, burn incense to
	12:16	of my people, to S by my name, 'As
	12:16	taught my people to S by Baal, then they
	22:5	heed these words, I S by myself, says the
	32:22	land, which thou didst S to their fathers to
Ezek	36:7	the Lord GOD: I S that the nations that
Dan	12:7	and I heard him S by him who lives
Hos	4:15	up to Beth-aven, and S not, "As the LORD
Amos	8:14	Those who S by Ashimah of Samaria, and say,
Zeph	1:5	who bow down and S to the LORD and
	1:5	the LORD and yet S by Milcom;
Mal	3:5	adulterers, against those who S falsely, against those
Mt	5:33	old, 'You shall not S falsely, but shall perform
	5:34	to you, Do not S at all, either by
	5:36	And do not S by your head, for you
	26:74	on himself and to S, "I do not know
Mk	14:71	on himself and to S, "I do not know
Heb	3:18	to whom did he S that they should never
	6:13	greater by whom to S, he swore by himself,
	6:16	Men indeed S by a greater than themselves, and
Jas	5:12	my brethren, do not S, either by heaven or

SWEARING (3)

Lev	6:3	and lied about it, S falsely—in any of
Sir	27:14	of men given to S makes one's hair stand
Hos	4:2	the land; there is S, lying, killing, stealing, and

SWEARS (19)

Num	30:2	to the LORD, or S an oath to bind
1Kgs	8:31	oath, and comes and S his oath before thine
2Chr	6:22	oath, and comes and S his oath before thy
Ps	15:4	fear the LORD; who S to his own hurt
Eccl	9:2	sinner; and he who S is as he who
Sir	23:10	the man who always S and utters the Name
	23:11	A man who S many oaths will be filled
Zech	5:3	and every one who S falsely shall be cut
	5:4	house of him who S falsely by my name;
Mt	23:15	say, 'If any one S by the temple, it
	23:15	but if any one S by the gold of
	23:17	say, 'If any one S by the altar, it
	23:17	but if any one S by the gift that
	23:19	So he who S by the altar, swears by
	23:19	swears by the altar, S by it and by
	23:20	it; and he who S by the temple, swears
	23:20	swears by the temple, S by it and by
	23:21	it; and he who S by heaven, swears by
	23:21	who swears by heaven, S by the throne of

SWEAT (3)

Gen	3:19	In the S of your face you shall eat
Ezek	44:18	shall not gird themselves with anything that causes S
2Mac	2:26	matter but calls for S and loss of sleep,

SWEEP (18)

1Kgs	16:3	behold, I will utterly S away Baasha and his
	21:21	you; I will utterly S you away, and will
Ps	26:9	S me not away with sinners, nor my life
	58:9	or ablaze, may he S them away!
	69:15	Let not the flood S over me, or the
	90:5	Thou dost S men away; they are like a
Prov	21:7	of the wicked will S them away, because they
Is	7:20	feet, and it will S away the beard also.
	8:8	banks; and it will S on into Judah, it
	14:23	water, and I will S it with the broom
	21:1	whirlwinds in the Negeb S on, it comes from
	28:17	plummet; and hail will S away the refuge of
Hab	1:11	Then they S by like the wind and go
Zeph	1:2	"I will utterly S away everything from the face
	1:3	"I will S away man and beast; I will
	1:3	and beast; I will S away the birds of
Lk	15:8	light a lamp and S the house and seek
Rev	12:15	after the woman, to S her away with the

SWEEPING

Deut	29:19	would lead to the S away of moist and

SWEEPS (2)

Job	27:21	he is gone; it S him out of his
Ps	69:2	waters, and the flood S over me.

SWEET (46)

Ex	15:25	it into the water, and the water became S
	30:34	said to Moses, "Take S spices, stacte, and onycha,
	30:34	and galbanum, S spices with pure frankincense
Lev	16:12	and two handfuls of S incense beaten small; and
Judg	14:14	Out of the strong came something S
2Sam	23:1	God of Jacob, the S psalmist of Israel:
2Chr	2:4	burning of incense of S spices before him, and
	13:11	offerings and incense of S spices, set out the
Neh	8:10	the fat and drink S wine and send portions
Job	20:12	"Though wickedness is S in his mouth, though he
	21:33	of the valley are S to him; all men
Ps	55:14	We used to hold S converse together; within God's
	81:2	sound the timbrel, the S lyre with the harp.
	119:103	How S are thy words to my taste, sweeter
Prov	3:24	when you lie down, your sleep will be S
	9:17	says, Stolen water is S, and bread eaten in
	13:19	A desire fulfilled is S to the soul; but
	20:17	gained by deceit is S to a man, but
	24:13	of the honeycomb are S to your taste.
	27:7	to one who is hungry everything bitter is S
Eccl	5:12	S is the sleep of a laborer, whether he
	11:7	Light is S, and it is pleasant for the
Song	2:3	and his fruit was S to my taste.
	2:14	for your voice is S, and your face is
	4:10	How S is your love, my sister, my bride!
	5:16	His speech is most S, and he is altogether
Sir	11:3	is the best of S things.
	23:17	fornicator all bread tastes S; he will never cease
	38:5	Was not water made S with a tree in
	40:18	Life is S for the self-reliant and the worker,
	40:30	the shameless begging is S, but in his stomach
	47:9	the altar, to make S melody with their voices.
	49:1	the perfumer; it is S as honey to every
	50:18	with their voices in S and full-toned melody.
Is	5:20	who put bitter for S and sweet for bitter!
	5:20	bitter for sweet and S for bitter!
	23:16	Make S melody, sing many songs, that you may
	43:24	have not bought me S cane with money, or
Jer	6:20	me from Sheba, or S cane from a distant
Ezek	3:3	in my mouth as S as honey.
Joel	1:5	wine, because of the S wine, for it is
	3:18	the mountains shall drip S wine, and the hills
Amos	9:13	the mountains shall drip S wine, and all the
2Mac	15:39	mixed with water is S and delicious and enhances
Rev	10:9	to your stomach, but S as honey in your
	10:10	ate it; it was S as honey in my

SWEET-SMELLING (2)

Ex	30:23	hundred shekels, and of S cinnamon half as much,
Sir	38:11	Offer a S sacrifice, and a memorial portion of

SWEETER (6)

Judg	14:18	went down, "What is S than honey?
Ps	19:10	even much fine gold; S also than honey and
	119:103	words to my taste, S than honey to my
Sir	23:27	the Lord, and nothing S than to heed the
	24:19	remembrance of me is S than honey, and my
	24:19	honey, and my inheritance S than the honeycomb.

SWEETLY

Sir	12:16	An enemy will speak S with his lips, but

SWEETNESS (4)

Judg	9:11	'Shall I leave my S and my good fruit,
Prov	16:24	are like a honeycomb, S to the soul and
Wis	16:21	thy sustenance manifested thy S toward thy children;
Sir	27:23	his mouth is all S, and he admires your

SWELL (7)

Num	5:21	away and your body S;
	5:22	and make your body S and your thigh fall
	5:27	and her body shall S, and her thigh shall
Deut	8:4	your foot did not S, these forty years.
Neh	9:21	not wear out and their feet did not S
Ps	73:7	Their eyes S out with fatness, their hearts overflow
Acts	28:6	waited, expecting him to S up or suddenly fall

S

SWELLING (7)
Lev 13:2 of his body a S or an eruption or
13:10 there is a white S in the skin, which
13:10 raw flesh in the S,
13:19 there comes a white S or a reddish-white spot,
13:28 dim, it is a S from the burn, and
13:43 and if the diseased S is reddish-white on his
14:56 house, and for a S or an eruption or

SWEPT (19)
Num 16:26 theirs, lest you be S away with all their
Judg 5:21 The torrent Kishon S them away, the onrushing
1Sam 12:25 wickedly, you shall be S away, both you and
Job 15:30 his blossom will be S away by the wind.
Ps 73:19 destroyed in a moment, S away utterly by terrors!
88:16 Thy wrath has S over me; thy dread assaults
124:4 the flood would have S us away, the torrent
Prov 13:23 food, but it is S away through injustice.
Is 44:22 I have S away your transgressions like a cloud,
Jer 12:4 and the birds are S away, because men said,
Dan 11:22 Armies shall be utterly S away before him and
11:26 his army shall be S away, and many shall
Hab 3:10 writhed; the raging waters S on; the deep gave
2Mac 5:16 his polluted hands, and S away with profane hands
12:22 in flight and were S on, this way and
Mt 12:44 he finds it empty, S, and put in order.
24:39 the flood came and S them all away, so
Lk 11:25 comes he finds it S and put in order.
Rev 12:4 His tail S down a third of the stars

SWERVE (3)
Ps 119:157 but I do not S from thy testimonies.
Prov 4:28 Do not S to the right or to the
Joel 2:7 way, they do not S from their paths.

SWERVED
2Tim 2:18 and Philetus, who have S from the truth by

SWERVING
1Tim 1:6 Certain persons by S from these have wandered

SWIFT (24)
Deut 28:49 of the earth, as S as the eagle flies,
2Sam 2:18 Now Asahel was as S of foot as a
1Kgs 4:28 for the horses and S steeds they brought to
1Chr 12:8 lions, and who were S as gazelles upon the
Esth 8:10 mounted couriers riding on S horses that were used
8:14 couriers, mounted on their S horses that were used
Job 39:5 the bonds of the S ass,
Eccl 9:11 is not to the S, nor the battle to
Wis 13:2 fire or wind or S air, or the circle
18:14 and night in its S course was now half
Is 16:5 seeks justice and is S to do righteousness."
18:2 Go, you S messengers, to a nation, tall and
19:1 is riding on a S cloud and comes to
30:16 "We will ride upon S steeds," therefore your
30:16 therefore your pursuers shall be S
Jer 46:6 The S cannot flee away, nor the warrior escape;
Ezek 30:9 "On that day S messengers shall go forth from
Dan 9:21 came to me in S flight at the time
Amos 2:14 shall perish from the S, and the strong shall
2:15 and he who is S of foot shall not
Hab 1:8 fly like an eagle S to devour.
Mal 3:5 I will be a S witness against the sorcerers,
Rom 3:15 "Their feet are S to shed blood,
2Pet 2:1 them, bringing upon themselves S destruction.

SWIFTER (6)
2Sam 1:23 not divided; they were S than eagles, they were
Job 7:6 My days are S than a weaver's shuttle, and
9:25 "My days are S than a runner; they flee
Jer 4:13 whirlwind; his horses are S than eagles– woe
Lam 4:19 Our pursuers were S than the vultures in the
Hab 1:8 Their horses are S than leopards, more fierce than

SWIFTLY (10)
Deut 32:35 calamity is at hand, and their doom comes S
Job 24:18 "You say, "They are S carried away upon the
Ps 18:10 and flew; he came S upon the wings of
147:15 his command to the earth; his word runs S
Wis 6:5 upon you terribly and S, because severe judgment
Sir 18:25 and all things move S before the Lord.
Is 5:26 the earth; and lo, S, speedily it comes!
Jer 48:40 "Behold, one shall fly S like an eagle, and
49:22 mount up and fly S like an eagle, and
Joel 3:4 upon your own head S and speedily.

SWIM (5)
Wis 19:19 creatures, and creatures that S moved over to the
Is 25:11 his hands out to S; but the LORD will
Ezek 47:5 was deep enough to S in, a river that
Acts 27:42 prisoners, lest any should S away and escape;
27:43 ordered those who could S to throw themselves

SWIMMER
Is 25:11 of it as a S spreads his hands out

SWINE (21)
Lev 11:7 And the S, because it parts the hoof and
Deut 14:8 And the S, because it parts the hoof but
Prov 11:22 gold ring in a S's snout is a beautiful
Is 65:4 secret places; who eat S's flesh, and broth of
66:3 like him who offers S's blood; he who makes
66:17 in the midst, eating S's flesh and the abomination
1Mac 1:47 for idols, to sacrifice S and unclean animals,
2Mac 6:18 his mouth to eat S's flesh.
7:1 to partake of unlawful S's flesh.
Mt 7:6 throw your pearls before S, lest they trample them
8:30 a herd of many S was feeding at some
8:31 out, send us away into the herd of S
8:32 and went into the S; and behold, the whole
Mk 5:11 a great herd of S was feeding there on
5:12 "Send us to the S, let us enter them."
5:13 out, and entered the S; and the herd, numbering
5:16 had happened to the demoniac and to the S
Lk 8:32 a large herd of S was feeding there on
8:33 man and entered the S, and the herd rushed
15:15 who sent him into his fields to feed S
15:16 the pods that the S ate; and no one

SWING
Job 28:4 afar from men, they S to and fro.

SWINGING
Ezek 41:24 two leaves apiece, two S leaves for each door.

SWINGS
Deut 19:5 wood, and his hand S the axe to cut

SWIRLS
Hos 13:3 like the chaff that S from the threshing floor

SWOLLEN
2Tim 3:4 of good, treacherous, reckless, S with conceit, lovers

SWOON
Jer 51:39 them drunk, till they S away and sleep a

SWOONED
Jer 15:9 has languished; she has S away; her sun went

SWOOP (2)
1Sam 15:19 Why did you S on the spoil, and do
Is 11:14 But they shall S down upon the shoulder of

SWOOPING
Job 9:26 reed, like an eagle S on the prey.

SWORD (460)
Gen 3:24 cherubim, and a flaming S which turned every way,
27:40 By your S you shall live, and you shall
31:26 carried away my daughters like captives of the S
34:26 son Shechem with the S, and took Dinah out
48:22 the Amorites with my S and with my bow."
Ex 5:3 fall upon us with pestilence or with the S
5:21 and have put a S in their hand to
15:9 I will draw my S, my hand shall destroy
17:13 and his people with the edge of the S
18:4 delivered me from the S of Pharaoh").
22:24 kill you with the S, and your wives shall
32:27 'Put every man his S on his side, and
Lev 26:6 the land, and the S shall not go through
26:7 and they shall fall before you by the S
26:8 your enemies shall fall before you by the S
26:25 I will bring a S upon you, that shall
26:33 I will unsheathe the S after you; and your
26:36 one flees from the S, and they shall fall
26:37 if to escape a S, though none pursues; and
Num 14:3 us into this land, to fall by the S
14:43 shall fall by the S; because you have turned
19:16 is slain with a S, or a dead body,
20:18 come out with the S against you."
21:24 the edge of the S, and took possession of

S

22:23 road, with a drawn S in his hand; and
22:29 wish I had a S in my hand, for
22:31 way, with his drawn S in his hand; and
31:8 slew Balaam the son of Beor with the S
Deut 13:15 that city to the S, destroying it utterly, all
13:15 and its cattle, with the edge of the S
20:13 its males to the S,
32:25 In the open the S shall bereave, and in
32:41 I whet my glittering S, and my hand takes
32:42 with blood, and my S shall devour flesh--with
33:29 your help, and the S of your triumph!
Josh 5:13 him with his drawn S in his hand; and
6:21 sheep, and asses, with the edge of the S
8:24 the edge of the S, all Israel returned to
8:24 and smote it with the edge of the S
10:11 than the men of Israel killed with the S
10:28 the edge of the S; he utterly destroyed every
10:30 the edge of the S, and every person in
10:32 the edge of the S, and every person in
10:35 the edge of the S; and every person in
10:37 the edge of the S, and its king and
10:39 the edge of the S, and utterly destroyed every
11:10 its king with the S; for Hazor formerly was
11:11 they put to the S all who were in
11:12 the edge of the S, utterly destroying them, as
11:14 the edge of the S, until they had destroyed
13:22 Israel killed with the S among the rest of
19:47 putting it to the S they took possession of
24:12 was not by your S or by your bow.
Judg 1:8 the edge of the S, and set the city
1:25 the edge of the S, but they let the
3:16 made for himself a S with two edges, a
3:21 left hand, took the S from his right thigh,
3:22 did not draw the S out of his belly;
4:15 the edge of the S; and Sisera alighted from
4:16 the edge of the S; not a man was
7:14 no other than the S of Gideon the son
7:20 and they cried, "A S for the LORD and
7:22 LORD set every man's S against his fellow and
8:10 hundred and twenty thousand men who drew the S
8:20 did not draw his S; for he was afraid,
9:54 to him, "Draw your S and kill me, lest
18:27 the edge of the S, and burned the city
20:2 hundred thousand men on foot that drew the S
20:15 men that drew the S, besides the inhabitants of
20:17 thousand men that drew S; all these were men
20:25 Israel; all these were men who drew the S
20:35 day; all these were men who drew the S
20:37 all the city with the edge of the S
20:46 men that drew the S, all of them men
20:48 the edge of the S, men and beasts and
21:10 the edge of the S; also the women and
1Sam 2:33 shall die by the S of men.
13:22 battle there was neither S nor spear found in
14:20 and behold, every man's S was against his fellow,
15:8 all the people with the edge of the S
15:33 Samuel said, "As your S has made women childless,
17:39 And David girded his S over his armor, and
17:45 to me with a S and with a spear
17:47 LORD saves not with S and spear; for the
17:50 him; there was no S in the hand of
17:51 Philistine, and took his S and drew it out
18:4 armor, and even his S and his bow and
21:8 a spear or a S at hand?
21:8 have brought neither my S nor my weapons with
21:9 the priest said, "The S of Goliath the Philistine,
22:10 and gave him the S of Goliath the Philistine."
22:13 him bread and a S, and have inquired of
22:19 he put to the S; both men and women,
22:19 oxen, asses and sheep, he put to the S
25:13 to his men, "Every man gird on his S
25:13 them girded on his S; David also girded on
25:13 also girded on his S; and about four hundred
31:4 his armor-bearer, "Draw your S, and thrust me
31:4 Saul took his own S, and fell upon it.
31:5 also fell upon his S, and died with him.
2Sam 1:12 of Israel, because they had fallen by the S
1:22 not back, and the S of Saul returned not
2:16 head, and thrust his S in his opponent's side;
2:26 to Joab, "Shall the S devour for ever?
3:29 is slain by the S, or who lacks bread!"
11:25 trouble you, for the S devours now one and
12:9 the Hittite with the S, and have taken his
12:9 slain him with the S of the Ammonites.
12:10 Now therefore the S shall never depart from your
15:14 smite the city with the edge of the S
18:8 forest devoured more people that day than the S
20:8 a girdle with a S in its sheath fastened
20:10 did not observe the S which was in Joab's
21:16 girded with a new S, thought to kill David.
23:10 hand cleaved to the S; and the LORD wrought
24:9 men who drew the S, and the men of
1Kgs 1:51 he will not slay his servant with the S
2:8 to death with the S
2:32 and slew with the S two men more righteous
3:24 And the king said, "Bring me a S
3:24 So a S was brought before the king.
19:1 he had slain all the prophets with the S
19:10 thy prophets with the S; and I, even I
19:14 thy prophets with the S; and I, even I
19:17 who escapes from the S of Hazael shall Jehu
19:17 who escapes from the S of Jehu shall Elisha
2Kgs 6:22 taken captive with your S and with your bow?
8:12 young men with the S, and dash in pieces
10:25 put them to the S, the guard and the
11:15 and slay with the S any one who follows
11:20 been slain with the S at the king's house.
19:7 to fall by the S in his own land.'"
19:37 slew him with the S, and escaped into the
1Chr 5:18 who carried shield and S, and drew the bow,
10:4 his armor-bearer, "Draw your S, and thrust me
10:4 Saul took his own S, and fell upon it.
10:5 also fell upon his S, and died.
21:5 men who drew the S, and in Judah four
21:5 four hundred and seventy thousand who drew the S
21:12 your foes, while the S of your enemies overtakes
21:12 three days of the S of the LORD, pestilence
21:16 his hand a drawn S stretched out over Jerusalem.
21:27 and he put his S back into its sheath.
21:30 was afraid of the S of the angel of
2Chr 20:9 comes upon us, the S, judgment, or pestilence, or
21:4 his brothers with the S, and also some of
23:14 follows her is to be slain with the S
23:21 quiet, after Athaliah had been slain with the S
29:9 have fallen by the S and our sons and
32:21 own sons struck him down there with the S
36:17 young men with the S in the house of
36:20 had escaped from the S, and they became servants
Ezra 9:7 the lands, to the S, to captivity, to plundering,
Neh 4:18 the builders had his S girded at his side
Jud 1:12 kill them by the S, and also all the
2:27 their young men with the edge of the S
6:6 Then the S of my army and the spear
7:14 famine, and before the S reaches them they will
8:19 handed over to the S, and to be plundered,
9:2 whom thou gavest a S to take revenge on
9:8 down the horn of thy altar with the S
11:10 punished, nor can the S prevail against them, unless
13:6 and took down his S that hung there.
16:5 young men with the S, and dash my infants
16:9 his mind, and the S severed his neck.
Esth 9:5 their enemies with the S, slaughtering, and
13:6 utterly destroyed by the S of their enemies, without
Job 1:15 the edge of the S; and I alone have
1:17 the edge of the S; and I alone have
5:20 and in war from the power of the S
15:22 of darkness, and he is destined for the S
19:29 be afraid of the S, for wrath brings the
19:29 the punishment of the S, that you may know
27:14 it is for the S; and his offspring have
33:18 the Pit, his life from perishing by the S
36:12 they perish by the S, and die without knowledge.
39:22 dismayed; he does not turn back from the S
40:19 let him who made him bring near his S
41:26 Though the S reaches him, it does not avail;
Ps 7:12 God will whet his S; he has bent and
17:13 the wicked by thy S,
22:20 my soul from the S, my life from the
37:14 The wicked draw the S and bend their bows,
37:15 who walk uprightly; their S shall enter their own
44:3 not by their own S did they win the
44:6 trust, nor can my S save me.
45:3 Gird your S upon your thigh, O mighty one,
63:10 the power of the S, they shall be prey
76:3 arrows, the shield, the S, and the weapons of
78:62 people over to the S, and vented his wrath
78:64 priests fell by the S, and their widows made
89:43 the edge of his S, and thou hast not
144:11 me from the cruel S, and deliver me from
Prov 5:4 is bitter as wormwood, sharp as a two-edged S
12:18 rash words are like S thrusts, but the tongue
25:18 war club, or a S, or a sharp arrow.

Song 3:8 war, each with his S at his thigh, against
Wis 5:20 stern wrath for a S, and creation will join
18:16 warrior carrying the sharp S of thy authentic
Sir 21:3 is like a two-edged S; there is no healing
22:19 you have drawn your S against a friend, do
26:19 the Lord will prepare him for the S
28:18 the edge of the S, but not so many
39:30 and vipers, and the S that punishes the ungodly
40:9 bloodshed and strife and S, calamities, famine and
46:2 and stretched out his S against the cities!
Is 1:20 be devoured by the S; for the mouth of
2:4 shall not lift up S against nation, neither shall
3:25 shall fall by the S and your mighty men
13:15 and whoever is caught will fall by the S
14:19 those pierced by the S, who go down to
21:15 swords, from the drawn S, from the bent bow,
22:2 not slain with the S or dead in battle.
27:1 and great and strong S will punish Leviathan the
31:8 shall fall by a S, not of man; and
31:8 of man; and a S, not of man, shall
31:8 shall flee from the S, and his young men
34:5 For my S has drunk its fill in the
34:6 The LORD has a S; it is sated with
37:7 him fall by the S in his own land.'"
37:38 slew him with the S, and escaped into the
41:2 like dust with his S, like driven stubble with
49:2 mouth like a sharp S, in the shadow of
51:19 destruction, famine and S; who will comfort you?
65:12 destine you to the S, and all of you
66:16 judgment, and by his S, upon all flesh; and
Jer 2:30 no correction; your own S devoured your prophets
4:10 with you'; whereas the S has reached their very
5:12 nor shall we see S or famine.
5:17 which you trust they shall destroy with the S
6:25 the enemy has a S, terror is on every
9:16 I will send the S after them, until I
11:22 shall die by the S; their sons and their
12:12 have come; for the S of the LORD devours
14:12 consume them by the S, by famine, and by
14:13 shall not see the S, nor shall you have
14:15 them, and who say, S and famine shall not
14:15 on this land: By S and famine those prophets
14:16 victims of famine and S, with none to bury
14:18 into the field, behold, those slain by the S
15:2 who are for the S, to the sword; those
15:2 the sword, to the S; those who are for
15:3 says the LORD: the S to slay, the dogs
15:9 will give to the S before their enemies, says
16:4 shall perish by the S and by famine, and
18:21 the power of the S, let their wives become
18:21 be slain by the S in battle.
19:7 to fall by the S before their enemies, and
20:4 shall fall by the S of their enemies while
20:4 to Babylon, and shall slay them with the S
21:7 who survive the pestilence, S, and famine, into the
21:7 the edge of the S; he shall not pity
21:9 shall die by the S, by famine, and by
24:10 And I will send S, famine, and pestilence upon
25:16 crazed because of the S which I am sending
25:27 more, because of the S which I am sending
25:29 I am summoning a S against all the inhabitants
25:31 will put to the S, says the LORD.'
25:38 waste because of the S of the oppressor, and
26:23 slew him with the S and cast his dead
27:8 that nation with the S, with famine, and with
27:13 people die by the S, by famine, and by
29:17 am sending on them S, famine, and pestilence, and
29:18 will pursue them with S, famine, and pestilence, and
31:2 people who survived the S found grace in the
32:24 it, and because of S and famine and pestilence
32:36 king of Babylon by S, by famine, and by
33:4 mounds and before the S:
34:4 concerning you: 'You shall not die by the S
34:17 you liberty to the S, to pestilence, and to
38:2 shall die by the S, by famine, and by
39:18 not fall by the S; but you shall have
41:2 of Shaphan, with the S, and killed him, whom
42:16 live there, then the S which you fear shall
42:17 shall die by the S, by famine, and by
42:22 shall die by the S, by famine, and by
43:11 captivity, and to the S those who are doomed
43:11 the sword those who are doomed to the S
44:12 shall fall; by the S and by famine they
44:12 shall die by the S and by famine; and
44:13 punished Jerusalem, with the S, with famine, and
44:18 been consumed by the S and by famine."
44:27 be consumed by the S and by famine, until
44:28 those who escape the S shall return from the
46:10 The S shall devour and be sated, and drink
46:14 be prepared, for the S shall devour round about
46:16 birth, because of the S of the oppressor.'
47:6 Ah, S of the LORD!
48:2 brought to silence; the S shall pursue you.
48:10 who keeps back his S from bloodshed.
49:37 I will send the S after them, until I
50:16 harvest; because of the S of the oppressor, every
50:35 "A S upon the Chaldeans, says the LORD, and
50:36 A S upon the diviners, that they may become
50:36 A S upon her warriors, that they may be
50:37 A S upon her horses and upon her chariots,
50:37 A S upon all her treasures, that they may
51:50 have escaped from the S, go, stand not still!
Lam 1:20 In the street the S bereaves; in the house
2:21 have fallen by the S; in the day of
4:9 the victims of the S than the victims of
5:9 lives, because of the S in the wilderness.
Bar 2:25 misery, by famine and S and pestilence.
Ezek 5:1 man, take a sharp S; use it as a
5:2 and strike with the S round about the city;
5:2 I will unsheathe the S after them.
5:12 shall fall by the S round about you; and
5:12 and will unsheathe the S after them.
5:17 I will bring the S upon you.
6:3 I, will bring a S upon you, and I
6:8 some who escape the S, and when you are
6:11 shall fall by the S, by famine, and by
6:12 shall fall by the S; and he that is
7:15 The S is without, pestilence and famine are within;
7:15 field dies by the S; and him that is
11:8 You have feared the S; and I will bring
11:8 I will bring the S upon you, says the
11:10 shall fall by the S; I will judge you
12:14 I will unsheathe the S after them.
12:16 them escape from the S, from famine and pestilence,
14:17 if I bring a S upon that land, and
14:17 and say, Let a S go through the land;
14:21 sore acts of judgment, S, famine, evil beasts, and
17:21 shall fall by the S, and the survivors shall
21:3 will draw forth my S out of its sheath,
21:4 and wicked, therefore my S shall go out of
21:5 LORD have drawn my S out of its sheath;
21:9 the Lord, Say: A S, a sword is sharpened
21:9 Say: A sword, a S is sharpened and also
21:11 So the S is given to be polished, that
21:12 delivered over to the S with my people.
21:14 hands and let the S come down twice, yea
21:14 twice, yea thrice, the S for those to be
21:14 slain; it is the S for the great slaughter,
21:15 have given the glittering S; ah!
21:19 two ways for the S of the king of
21:20 a way for the S to come to Rabbah
21:28 their reproach; say, A S, a sword is drawn
21:28 say, A sword, a S is drawn for the
23:10 they slew with the S; and she became a
23:25 ears, and your survivors shall fall by the S
24:21 whom you left behind shall fall by the S
25:13 even to Dedan they shall fall by the S
26:6 on the mainland shall be slain by the S
26:8 will slay with the S your daughters on the
26:11 your people with the S; and your mighty pillars
28:23 of her, by the S that is against her
29:8 I will bring a S upon you, and will
30:4 A S shall come upon Egypt, and anguish shall
30:5 in league, shall fall with them by the S
30:6 within her by the S, says the Lord GOD.
30:17 shall fall by the S; and the women shall
30:21 that it may become strong to wield the S
30:22 I will make the S fall from his hand.
30:24 Babylon, and put my S in his hand; but
30:25 When I put my S into the hand of
31:17 are slain by the S; yea, those who dwelt
31:18 uncircumcised, with those who are slain by the S
32:10 when I brandish my S before them; they shall
32:11 the Lord GOD: The S of the king of
32:20 are slain by the S, and with her shall
32:21 uncircumcised, slain by the S
32:22 slain, fallen by the S;
32:23 slain, fallen by the S, who spread terror in
32:24 slain, fallen by the S, who went down uncircumcised
32:25 uncircumcised, slain by the S; for terror of them
32:26 uncircumcised, slain by the S; for they spread terror
32:28 uncircumcised, with those who are slain by the S

S

32:29 are slain by the S; they lie with the
32:30 are slain by the S, and bear their shame
32:31 army, slain by the S, says the Lord GOD.
32:32 are slain by the S, Pharaoh and all his
33:2 If I bring the S upon a land, and
33:3 if he sees the S coming upon the land
33:4 take warning, and the S comes and takes him
33:6 the watchman sees the S coming and does not
33:6 not warned, and the S comes, and takes any
33:26 You resort to the S, you commit abominations and
33:27 shall fall by the S; and him that is
35:5 the power of the S at the time of
35:8 those slain with the S shall fall.
38:21 Lord GOD; every man's S will be against his
39:23 their adversaries, and they all fell by the S
Dan 11:33 they shall fall by S and flame, by captivity
13:59 is waiting with his S to saw you in
14:26 slay the dragon without S or club." The king
Hos 1:7 by bow, nor by S, nor by war, nor
2:18 abolish the bow, the S, and war from the
7:17 shall fall by the S because of the insolence
11:6 The S shall rage against their cities, consume the
13:16 shall fall by the S, their little ones shall
Amos 1:11 his brother with the S, and cast off all
4:10 young men with the S; I carried away your
7:9 rise against the house of Jeroboam with the S
7:11 shall die by the S, and Israel must go
7:17 shall fall by the S, and your land shall
9:1 will slay with the S; not one of them
9:4 I will command the S, and it shall slay
9:10 shall die by the S, who say, 'Evil shall
Mic 4:3 shall not lift up S against nation, neither shall
5:6 of Assyria with the S, and the land of
5:6 Nimrod with the drawn S; and they shall deliver
6:14 what you save I will give to the S
Nah 2:13 in smoke, and the S shall devour your young
3:3 Horsemen charging, flashing S and glittering spear,
3:15 fire devour you, the S will cut you off.
Zeph 2:12 also, O Ethiopians, shall be slain by my S
Hag 2:22 every one by the S of his fellow.
Zech 9:13 O Greece, and wield you like a warrior's S
11:17 May the S smite his arm and his right
13:7 "Awake, O S, against my shepherd, against the man
1Mac 2:9 her youths by the S of the foe.
3:3 and waged battles, protecting the host by his S
3:12 and Judas took the S of Apollonius, and used
4:15 all those in the rear fell by the S
4:33 them down with the S of those who love
5:28 the edge of the S; then he seized all
5:51 the edge of the S, and razed and plundered
7:38 them fall by the S; remember their blasphemies, and
7:46 all fell by the S; not even one of
8:23 for ever, and may S and enemy be far
9:73 Thus the S ceased from Israel.
10:85 who fell by the S, with those burned alive,
12:48 had entered with him they killed with the S
2Mac 5:26 He put to the S all those who came
12:23 the sinners to the S, and destroyed as many
14:41 fell upon his own S,
15:15 to Judas a golden S, and as he gave
15:16 thus: "Take this holy S, a gift from God,
Mt 10:34 have not come to bring peace, but a S
26:51 hand and drew his S, and struck the slave
26:52 to him, "Put your S back into its place;
26:52 all who take the S will perish by the
26:52 who take the sword will perish by the S
Mk 14:47 stood by drew his S, and struck the slave
Lk 2:35 spoken against (and a S will pierce through your
21:24 the edge of the S, and be led captive
22:36 him who has no S sell his mantle and
22:47 they said, "Lord, shall we strike with the S
Jn 18:10 Simon Peter, having a S, drew it and struck
18:11 to Peter, "Put your S into its sheath; shall
Acts 12:2 of John with the S;
16:27 open, he drew his S and was about to
Rom 8:35 persecution, or famine, or nakedness, or peril, or S
13:4 does not bear the S in vain; he is
Eph 6:17 of salvation, and the S of the Spirit, which
Heb 4:12 sharper than any two-edged S, piercing to the
11:34 the edge of the S, won strength out of
11:37 were killed with the S; they went about in
Rev 1:16 issued a sharp two-edged S, and his face was
2:12 words of him who has the sharp two-edged S
2:16 against them with the S of my mouth.
6:4 one another; and he was given a great S
6:8 earth, to kill with S and with famine and
13:10 one slays with the S, with the sword must
13:10 the sword, with the S must he be slain.
13:14 was wounded by the S and yet lived;
19:15 mouth issues a sharp S with which to smite
19:21 were slain by the S of him who sits
19:21 upon the horse, the S that issues from his

SWORDS (31)

Gen 34:25 Dinah's brothers, took their S and came upon the
49:5 Levi are brothers; weapons of violence are their S
1Sam 13:19 the Hebrews make themselves S or spears";
1Kgs 18:28 after their custom with S and lances, until the
Neh 4:13 their families, with their S, their spears, and their
Ps 55:21 were softer than oil, yet they were drawn S
57:4 teeth are spears and arrows, their tongues sharp S
64:3 whet their tongues like S, who aim bitter words
149:6 their throats and two-edged S in their hands,
Prov 30:14 those whose teeth are S, whose teeth are knives,
Song 3:8 Israel, all girt with S and expert in war,
Is 2:4 they shall beat their S into plowshares, and their
21:15 have fled from the S, from the drawn sword,
Ezek 16:40 you and cut you to pieces with their S
23:47 dispatch them with their S; they shall slay their
28:7 they shall draw their S against the beauty of
30:11 they shall draw their S against Egypt, and fill
32:12 to fall by the S of mighty ones, all
32:27 weapons of war, whose S were laid under their
38:4 buckler and shield, wielding S;
Joel 3:10 Beat your plowshares into S, and your pruning hooks
Mic 4:3 they shall beat their S into plowshares, and their
1Mac 4:6 not have armor and S such as they desired.
2Mac 5:2 with lances and drawn S –
12:22 men and pierced by the points of their S
Mt 26:47 a great crowd with S and clubs, from the
26:55 against a robber, with S and clubs to capture
Mk 14:43 him a crowd with S and clubs, from the
14:48 against a robber, with S and clubs to capture
Lk 22:38 And they said, "Look, Lord, here are two S
22:50 against a robber, with S and clubs?

SWORDSMEN

2Kgs 3:26 with him seven hundred S to break through, opposite

SWORE (91)

Gen 21:31 there both of them S an oath.
24:7 spoke to me and S to me, 'To your
24:9 Abraham his master, and S to him concerning this
25:33 So he S to him, and sold his birthright
26:3 the oath which I S to Abraham your father.
31:53 So Jacob S by the Fear of his father
47:31 to me"; and he S to him.
50:24 the land which he S to Abraham, to Isaac,
Ex 6:8 the land which I S to give to Abraham,
13:5 the Jebusites, which he S to your fathers to
13:11 the Canaanites, as he S to you and your
33:1 land of which I S to Abraham, Isaac, and
Num 14:16 the land which he S to give to them,
14:23 the land which I S to give to their
14:30 the land where I S that I would make
32:10 that day, and he S, saying,
32:11 the land which I S to give to Abraham,
Deut 1:8 land which the LORD S to your fathers, to
1:34 was angered, and he S,
1:35 good land which I S to give to your
4:21 your account, and he S that I should not
4:31 your fathers which he S to them.
6:10 the land which he S to your fathers, to
6:18 land which the LORD S to give to your
6:23 the land which he S to give to our
7:8 the oath which he S to your fathers, that
7:12 steadfast love which he S to your fathers to
7:13 the land which he S to your fathers to
8:1 land which the LORD S to give to your
8:18 his covenant which he S to your fathers, as
9:5 word which the LORD S to your fathers, to
10:11 the land, which I S to their fathers to
11:9 land which the LORD S to your fathers to
11:21 land which the LORD S to your fathers to
13:17 multiply you, as he S to your fathers,
26:3 land which the LORD S to our fathers to
28:11 land which the LORD S to your fathers to
29:13 you, and as he S to your fathers, to
30:20 land which the LORD S to your fathers, to
31:20 and honey, which I S to give to their
31:21 the land that I S to give."
31:23 the land which I S to give them: I

34:4 land of which I S to Abraham, to Isaac,
Josh 1:6 the land which I S to their fathers to
5:6 to them the LORD S that he would not
6:22 to her, as you S to her."
9:15 leaders of the congregation S to them.
9:20 the oath which we S to them."
14:9 And Moses S on that day, saying, 'Surely the
21:43 the land which he S to give to their
Judg 2:1 the land which I S to give to your
1Sam 19:6 voice of Jonathan; Saul S, "As the LORD lives,
24:22 And David S this to Saul.
28:10 But Saul S to her by the LORD, "As
2Sam 3:35 yet day; but David S, saying, "God do so
1Kgs 1:17 him, "My lord, you S to your maidservant by
1:29 And the king S, saying, "As the LORD lives,
1:30 every adversity, as I S to you by the
2:8 at the Jordan, I S to him by the
2:23 Then King Solomon S by the LORD, saying, "God
2Kgs 25:24 And Gedaliah S to them and their men, saying,
Jud 1:12 this whole region, and S by his throne and
Ps 95:11 Therefore I S in my anger that they should
106:26 raised his hand and S to them that he
132:2 he endured; how he S to the LORD and
132:11 The LORD S to David a sure oath from
Wis 14:30 in deceit they S unrighteously through contempt for
Is 54:9 to me: as I S that the waters of
Jer 11:5 the oath which I S to your fathers, to
38:16 Then King Zedekiah S secretly to Jeremiah, "As the
40:9 Ahikam, son of Shaphan, S to them and their
Bar 2:34 the land which I S to give to their
Ezek 20:5 I chose Israel, I S to the seed of
20:5 land of Egypt, I S to them, saying, I
20:6 On that day I S to them that I
20:15 Moreover I S to them in the wilderness that
20:23 Moreover I S to them in the wilderness that
20:28 the land which I S to give them, then
20:42 the country which I S to give to your
47:14 divide it equally; I S to give it to
1Mac 7:15 words to them and S this oath to them,
7:18 violated the agreement and the oath which they S
7:35 and in anger he S this oath, "Unless Judas
9:71 he said; and he S to Jonathan that he
2Mac 13:23 the Jews, yielded and S to observe all their
14:33 toward the sanctuary, and S this oath: "If you
Lk 1:73 the oath which he S to our father Abraham,
Heb 3:11 my ways.' As I S in my wrath, 'They
4:3 has said, "As I S in my wrath, 'They
6:13 whom to swear, he S by himself,
Rev 10:6 hand to heaven and S by him who lives

SWORN (54)

Gen 14:22 of Sodom, "I have S to the LORD God
22:16 "By myself I have S, says the LORD, because
Ex 13:19 for Joseph had solemnly S the people of Israel,
Lev 6:5 about which he has S falsely; he shall restore
Deut 2:14 as the LORD had S to them.
19:8 border, as he has S to your fathers, and
28:9 himself, as he has S to you, if you
29:12 may enter into the S covenant of the LORD
29:14 that I make this S covenant,
29:19 the words of this S covenant, blesses himself in
31:7 which the LORD has S to their fathers to
Josh 5:6 which the LORD had S to their fathers to
9:18 of the congregation had S to them by the
9:19 the congregation, "We have S to them by the
21:44 just as he had S to their fathers; not
Judg 2:15 as the LORD had S to them; and they
21:1 men of Israel had S at Mizpah, "No one
21:7 left, since we have S by the LORD that
21:18 people of Israel had S, "Cursed be he who
1Sam 20:42 forasmuch as we have S both of us in
2Sam 3:9 what the LORD has S to him,
21:2 people of Israel had S to spare them, Saul
1Chr 16:16 made with Abraham, his S promise to Isaac,
2Chr 15:15 oath; for they had S with all their heart,
Neh 9:15 land which thou hadst S to give them.
Tob 9:3 For Raguel has S that I should not leave;
10:7 expired which Raguel had S that he should spend
Jud 8:11 right; you have even S and pronounced this oath
Ps 89:3 chosen one, I have S to David my servant:
89:35 for all I have S by my holiness; I
105:9 made with Abraham, his S promise to Isaac,
110:4 The LORD has S and will not change his
119:106 I have S an oath and confirmed it, to
Sir 23:11 doubly; if he has S needlessly, he will not
Is 5:9 LORD of hosts has S in my hearing: "Surely
14:24 LORD of hosts has S: "As I have planned,
45:23 By myself I have S, from my mouth has
54:9 earth, so I have S that I will not
62:8 The LORD has S by his right hand and
Jer 5:7 forsaken me, and have S by those who are
44:26 Egypt: Behold, I have S by my great name,
49:13 For I have S by myself, says the LORD,
51:14 LORD of hosts has S by himself: Surely I
Ezek 21:23 false divination; they have S solemn oaths; but he
44:12 Israel, therefore I have S concerning them, says the
Amos 4:2 The Lord GOD has S by his holiness that,
6:8 The Lord GOD has S by himself (says the
8:7 The LORD has S by the pride of Jacob:
Mic 7:20 Abraham, as thou hast S to our fathers from
1Mac 6:62 the oath he had S and gave orders to
2Mac 4:34 to treachery offered him S pledges and gave him
Mt 5:33 Lord what you have S
Acts 2:30 knowing that God had S with an oath to
Heb 7:21 oath, "The Lord has S and will not change

SWUNG (3)

Ezek 26:2 is broken, it has S open to me; I
Rev 14:16 sat upon the cloud S his sickle on the
14:19 So the angel S his sickle on the earth

SYCAMINE

Lk 17:6 could say to this S tree, 'Be rooted up,

SYCAMORE (6)

1Kgs 10:27 as plentiful as the S of the Shephelah.
1Chr 27:28 Over the olive and S trees in the Shephelah
2Chr 1:15 as plentiful as the S of the Shephelah.
9:27 as plentiful as the S of the Shephelah.
Amos 7:14 and a dresser of S trees,
Lk 19:4 climbed up into a S tree to see him,

SYCAMORES (2)

Ps 78:47 with hail, and their S with frost.
Is 9:10 with dressed stones; the S have been cut down,

SYCHAR

Jn 4:5 city of Samaria, called S, near the field that

SYENE (3)

Is 49:12 the west, and these from the land of S
Ezek 29:10 desolation, from Migdol to S, as far as the
30:6 down; from Migdol to S they shall fall within

SYMBOL

Is 57:8 have set up your S; for, deserting me, you

SYMBOLIC

Heb 9:9 still standing (which is S for the present age).

SYMBOLS

Sir 45:8 strengthened him with the S of authority, the linen

SYMPATHIZE

Heb 4:15 who is unable to S with our weaknesses, but

SYMPATHY (3)

Job 42:11 and they showed him S and comforted him for
Phil 2:1 Spirit, any affection and S,
1Pet 3:8 have unity of spirit, S, love of the brethren,

SYNAGOGUE (40)

Mt 12:9 he went on from there, and entered their S
13:54 taught them in their S, so that they were
Mk 1:21 sabbath he entered the S and taught.
1:23 there was in their S a man with an
1:29 immediately he left the S, and entered the house
3:1 Again he entered the S, and a man was
5:22 the rulers of the S, Jairus by name; and
5:36 the ruler of the S, "Do not fear, only
5:38 the ruler of the S, he saw a tumult,
6:2 to teach in the S; and many who heard
Lk 4:16 he went to the S, as his custom was,
4:20 of all in the S were fixed on him.
4:28 this, all in the S were filled with wrath.
4:33 And in the S there was a man who
4:38 arose and left the S, and entered Simon's house.
6:6 when he entered the S and taught, a man
7:5 loves our nation, and he built us our S
8:41 a ruler of the S; and falling at Jesus'
13:14 the ruler of the S, indignant because Jesus had
Jn 6:59 he said in the S, as he taught at

S

	9:22	he was to be put out of the S
	12:42	put out of the S:
Acts	6:9	who belonged to the S of the Freedmen (as
	13:14	they went into the S and sat down.
	13:15	the rulers of the S sent to them, saying,
	13:43	the meeting of the S broke up, many Jews
	14:1	together into the Jewish S, and so spoke that
	17:1	where there was a S of the Jews.
	17:10	when they arrived they went into the Jewish S
	17:17	he argued in the S with the Jews and
	18:4	he argued in the S every sabbath, and persuaded
	18:7	God; his house was next door to the S
	18:8	the ruler of the S, believed in the Lord,
	18:17	the ruler of the S, and beat him in
	18:19	himself went into the S and argued with the
	18:26	speak boldly in the S; but when Priscilla and
	19:8	And he entered the S and for three months
	22:19	know that in every S I imprisoned and beat
Rev	2:9	not, but are a S of Satan.
	3:9	make those of the S of Satan who say

SYNAGOGUES (25)

Mt	4:23	Galilee, teaching in their S and preaching the gospel
	6:2	hypocrites do in the S and in the streets,
	6:5	and pray in the S and at the street
	9:35	villages, teaching in their S and preaching the gospel
	10:17	flog you in their S,
	23:6	best seats in the S,
	23:33	will scourge in your S and persecute from town
Mk	1:39	Galilee, preaching in their S and casting out demons.
	12:39	best seats in the S and the places of
	13:9	will be beaten in S; and you will stand
Lk	4:15	he taught in their S, being glorified by all.
	4:44	was preaching in the S of Judea.
	11:43	best seat in the S and salutations in the
	12:11	bring you before the S and the rulers and
	13:10	in one of the S on the sabbath.
	20:46	best seats in the S and the places of
	21:12	you up to the S and prisons, and you
Jn	16:2	you out of the S; indeed, the hour is
	18:20	have always taught in S and in the temple,
Acts	9:2	for letters to the S at Damascus, so that
	9:20	And in the S immediately he proclaimed Jesus,
	13:5	of God in the S of the Jews.
	15:21	for he is read every sabbath in the S
	24:11	temple or in the S, or in the city.
	26:11	often in all the S and tried to make

SYNTYCHE

Phil	4:2	Eu-odia and I entreat S to agree in the

SYRACUSE

Acts	28:12	Putting in at S, we stayed there for three

SYRIA (68)

Judg	10:6	Ashtaroth, the gods of S, the gods of Sidon,
1Kgs	10:29	kings of the Hittites and the kings of S
	11:25	did; and he abhorred Israel, and reigned over S
	15:18	of Hezi-on, king of S, who dwelt in Damascus,
	19:15	to be king over S;
	20:1	Ben-hadad the king of S gathered all his army
	20:20	but Ben-hadad king of S escaped on a horse
	20:22	spring the king of S will come up against
	20:23	of the king of S said to him, "Their
	22:1	For three years S and Israel continued without war.
	22:3	out of the hand of the king of S
	22:31	Now the king of S had commanded the thirty-two
2Kgs	5:1	of the king of S, was a great man
	5:1	by him the LORD had given victory to S
	5:5	And the king of S said, "Go now, and
	6:8	when the king of S was warring against Israel,
	6:11	of the king of S was greatly troubled because
	6:24	Afterward Ben-hadad king of S mustered his entire
	8:7	Ben-hadad the king of S was sick; and when
	8:9	son Ben-hadad king of S has sent me to
	8:13	me that you are to be king over S
	8:28	against Hazael king of S at Ramoth-gilead, where
	8:29	Ramah, when he fought against Hazael king of S
	9:14	against Hazael king of S;
	9:15	with Hazael king of S So Jehu said, "If
	12:17	time Hazael king of S went up and fought
	12:18	house, and sent these to Hazael king of S
	13:3	of Hazael king of S and into the hand
	13:4	how the king of S oppressed them.
	13:7	for the king of S had destroyed them and
	13:17	arrow of victory, the arrow of victory over S
	13:19	would have struck down S until you had made
	13:19	you will strike down S only three times."
	13:22	Now Hazael king of S oppressed Israel all the
	13:24	When Hazael king of S died, Ben-hadad his son
	15:37	Rezin the king of S and Pekah the son
	16:5	Then Rezin king of S and Pekah the son
	16:7	of the king of S and from the hand
1Chr	18:6	David put garrisons in S of Damascus; and the
2Chr	1:17	kings of the Hittites and the kings of S
	16:2	to Ben-hadad king of S, who dwelt in Damascus,
	16:7	on the king of S, and did not rely
	16:7	of the king of S has escaped you.
	18:30	Now the king of S had commanded the captains
	22:5	against Hazael king of S at Ramoth-gilead.
	22:6	Ramah, when he fought against Hazael king of S
	28:5	of the king of S, who defeated him and
	28:23	of the kings of S helped them, I will
Jud	1:12	Cilicia and Damascus and S, that he would kill
	8:26	Jacob in Mesopotamia in S, while he was keeping
Is	7:1	Rezin the king of S and Pekah the son
	7:2	of David was told, S is in league with
	7:4	anger of Rezin and S and the son of
	7:5	Because S, with Ephraim and the son of Remaliah,
	7:8	For the head of S is Damascus, and the
	17:3	and the remnant of S will be like the
Amos	1:5	and the people of S shall go into exile
1Mac	3:41	And forces from S and the land of the
	11:2	He set out for S with peaceable words, and
	11:60	all the army of S gathered to him as
Mt	4:24	fame spread throughout all S, and they brought him
Lk	2:2	first enrollment, when Quirinius was governor of S
Acts	15:23	Gentiles in Antioch and S and Cilicia, greeting.
	15:40	And he went through S and Cilicia, strengthening the
	18:18	brethren and sailed for S, and with him Priscilla
	20:3	to set sail for S, he determined to return
	21:3	left we sailed to S, and landed at Tyre;
Gal	1:21	into the regions of S and Cilicia.

SYRIAN (5)

2Kgs	5:20	spared this Naaman the S, in not accepting from
1Mac	3:13	the commander of the S army, heard that Judas
	7:39	in Beth-horon, and the S army joined him.
2Mac	15:36	called Adar in the S language -- the
Lk	4:27	of them was cleansed, but only Naaman the S

SYRIANS (64)

2Sam	8:5	And when the S of Damascus came to help
	8:5	David slew twenty-two thousand men of the S
	8:6	of Damascus; and the S became servants to David
	10:6	sent and hired the S of Beth-rehob, and the
	10:6	of Beth-rehob, and the S of Zobah, twenty thousand
	10:8	the gate; and the S of Zobah and of
	10:9	arrayed them against the S;
	10:11	he said, "If the S are too strong for
	10:13	to battle against the S; and they fled before
	10:14	Ammonites saw that the S fled, they likewise fled
	10:15	But when the S saw that they had been
	10:16	and brought out the S who were beyond the
	10:17	the S arrayed themselves against David, and fought
	10:18	And the S fled before Israel; and David slew
	10:18	David slew of the S the men of seven
	10:19	So the S feared to help the Ammonites any
1Kgs	20:20	killed his man; the S fled and Israel pursued
	20:21	chariots, and killed the S with a great slaughter.
	20:26	spring Ben-hadad mustered the S, and went up to
	20:27	of goats, but the S filled the country.
	20:28	the LORD, 'Because the S have said, "The LORD
	20:29	Israel smote of the S a hundred thousand foot
	22:11	you shall push the S until they are destroyed."'
	22:35	his chariot facing the S, until at evening he
2Kgs	5:2	Now the S on one of their raids had
	6:9	this place, for the S are going down there."
	6:18	And when the S came down against him, Elisha
	6:23	And the S came no more on raids into
	7:4	the camp of the S; if they spare our
	7:5	the camp of the S; but when they came
	7:5	the camp of the S, behold, there was no
	7:6	the army of the S hear the sound of
	7:10	the camp of the S, and behold, there was
	7:12	tell you what the S have prepared against us.
	7:14	the army of the S, saying, "Go and see."
	7:15	and equipment which the S had thrown away in
	7:16	went out, and plundered the camp of the S
	8:28	at Ramoth-gilead, where the S wounded Joram.
	8:29	the wounds which the S had given him at
	9:15	the wounds which the S had given him, when

13:5 the hand of the S; and the people of
13:17 you shall fight the S in Aphek until you
24:2 and bands of the S, and bands of the
1Chr 18:5 And when the S of Damascus came to help
18:5 David slew twenty-two thousand men of the S
18:6 of Damascus; and the S became servants to David,
19:10 arrayed them against the S;
19:12 he said, "If the S are too strong for
19:14 drew near before the S for battle; and they
19:15 Ammonites saw that the S fled, they likewise fled
19:16 But when the S saw that they had been
19:16 and brought out the S who were beyond the
19:17 in array against the S, they fought with him.
19:18 And the S fled before Israel; and David slew
19:18 David slew of the S the men of seven
19:19 So the S were not willing to help the
2Chr 18:10 you shall push the S until they are destroyed.'"
18:34 his chariot facing the S until evening; then at
22:5 And the S wounded Joram,
24:23 the army of the S came up against Joash.
24:24 the army of the S had come with few
Is 9:12 The S on the east and the Philistines on
Jer 35:11 the army of the S So we are living
Amos 9:7 from Caphtor and the S from Kir?

SYROPHOENICIAN

Mk 7:25 was a Greek, a S by birth.

SYRTIS

Acts 27:17 should run on the S, they lowered the gear,

T

TAANACH (7)

Josh 12:21 one; the king of T, one; the king of
17:11 and the inhabitants of T and its villages, and
21:25 the half-tribe of Manasseh, T with its pasture lands,
Judg 1:27 and its villages, or T and its villages, or
5:19 kings of Canaan, at T, by the waters of
1Kgs 4:12 son of Ahilud, in T, Megiddo, and all Beth-shean
1Chr 7:29 Beth-shean and its towns, T and its towns, Megiddo

TAANATH-SHILOH

Josh 16:6 boundary turns round toward T, and passes along

TABBAOTH (2)

Ezra 2:43 Hasupha, the sons of T,
Neh 7:46 Hasupha, the sons of T,

TABBATH

Judg 7:22 as far as the border of Abel-meholah, by T

TABEEL (2)

Ezra 4:7 Bishlam and Mithredath and T and the rest of
Is 7:6 up the son of T as king in the

TABERAH (2)

Num 11:3 that place was called T, because the fire of
Deut 9:22 "At T also, and at Massah, and at Kibroth-hattaavah,

TABERNACLE (94)

Ex 25:9 the pattern of the T, and of all its
26:1 you shall make the T with ten curtains of
26:6 the clasps, that the T may be one whole.
26:7 a tent over the T; eleven curtains shall you
26:12 remains, shall hang over the back of the T
26:13 the sides of the T, on this side and
26:15 upright frames for the T of acacia wood.
26:17 you do for all the frames of the T
26:18 the frames for the T: twenty frames for the
26:20 second side of the T, on the north side
26:22 the rear of the T westward you shall make
26:23 for corners of the T in the rear;
26:26 one side of the T,
26:27 other side of the T, and five bars for
26:27 the side of the T at the rear westward.
26:30 you shall erect the T according to the plan
26:35 south side of the T opposite the table; and
27:9 "You shall make the court of the T
27:19 the utensils of the T for every use, and
35:10 LORD has commanded: the T,
35:15 the door of the T;
35:18 the pegs of the T and the pegs of
36:8 the workmen made the T with ten curtains; they
36:13 with clasps; so the T was one whole.
36:14 a tent over the T; he made eleven curtains.
36:20 upright frames for the T of acacia wood.
36:22 did this for all the frames of the T
36:23 The frames for the T he made thus: twenty
36:25 second side of the T, on the north side,
36:27 the rear of the T westward he made six
36:28 for corners of the T in the rear.
36:31 one side of the T,
36:32 other side of the T, and five bars for
36:32 the frames of the T at the rear westward.
38:20 the pegs for the T and for the court
38:21 the things for the T, the tabernacle of the
38:21 for the tabernacle, the T of the testimony, as
38:31 the pegs of the T, and all the pegs
39:32 the work of the T of the tent of
39:33 And they brought the T to Moses, the tent
39:40 the service of the T, for the tent of
Lev 8:10 oil, and anointed the T and all that was
15:31 uncleanness by defiling my T that is in their
17:4 the LORD before the T of the LORD, bloodguilt
Num 1:50 the Levites over the T of the testimony, and
1:50 are to carry the T and all its furnishings,
1:50 shall tend it, and shall encamp around the T
1:51 When the T is to set out, the Levites
1:51 down; and when the T is to be pitched,
1:53 shall encamp around the T of the testimony, that
1:53 keep charge of the T of the testimony."
3:7 they minister at the T;
3:8 people of Israel as they minister at the T
3:23 to encamp behind the T on the west,
3:25 was to be the T, the tent with its
3:26 which is around the T and the altar, and
3:29 south side of the T,
3:35 to encamp on the north side of the T
3:36 the frames of the T, the bars, the pillars,
3:38 to encamp before the T on the east, before
4:16 oversight of all the T and all that is
4:25 the curtains of the T, and the tent of
4:26 which is around the T and the altar, and
4:31 the frames of the T, with its bars, pillars,
5:17 the floor of the T and put it into
7:1 finished setting up the T, and had anointed and
7:3 one an ox; they offered them before the T
9:15 the day that the T was set up, the
9:15 the cloud covered the T, the tent of the
9:15 it was over the T like the appearance of
9:18 cloud rested over the T, they remained in camp.
9:19 cloud continued over the T many days, the people
9:20 few days over the T, and according to the
9:22 cloud continued over the T, abiding there, the people
10:11 up from over the T of the testimony,
10:17 And when the T was taken down, the sons
10:17 Merari, who carried the T, set out.
10:21 holy things, and the T was set up before
16:9 do service in the T of the LORD, and
17:13 comes near to the T of the LORD, shall
19:13 cleanse himself, defiles the T of the LORD, and
31:30 have charge of the T of the LORD."
31:47 had charge of the T of the LORD; as
Josh 22:19 land where the LORD's T stands, and take for
22:29 the LORD our God that stands before his T
1Chr 6:32 with song before the T of the tent of
6:48 the service of the T of the house of
16:39 the priests before the T of the LORD in
21:29 For the T of the LORD, which Moses had
23:26 need to carry the T or any of the
2Chr 1:5 was there before the T of the LORD.
Jud 9:8 and to pollute the T where thy glorious name
Sir 24:10 In the holy T I ministered before him, and
24:15 and like the fragrance of frankincense in the T

TABERNACLES (3)

2Chr 8:13 the feast of weeks, and the feast of T
1Mac 10:21 at the feast of T, and he recruited troops
Jn 7:2 the Jews' feast of T was at hand.

TABITHA (2)

Acts 9:36 Joppa a disciple named T, which means Dorcas.
9:40 the body he said, T, rise." And she opened

TABLE (105)

Gen 43:34 to them from Joseph's T, but Benjamin's portion was
Ex 25:23 you shall make a T of acacia wood; two
25:27 as holders for the poles to carry the T
25:28 with gold, and the T shall be carried with

25:30 the Presence on the T before me always.
26:35 you shall set the T outside the veil, and
26:35 the tabernacle opposite the T; and you shall put
26:35 you shall put the T on the north side.
30:27 the testimony, and the T and all its utensils,
31:8 of the tent, the T and its utensils, and
35:13 of the screen; the T with its poles and
37:10 He also made the T of acacia wood; two
37:14 as holders for the poles to carry the T
37:15 wood to carry the T, and overlaid them with
37:16 to be upon the T, its plates and dishes
39:36 the mercy seat; the T with all its utensils,
Lev 24:6 a row, upon the T of pure gold.
Num 3:31 be the ark, the T, the lampstand, the altars,
4:7 And over the T of the bread of the
Judg 1:7 up scraps under my T; as I have done,
1Sam 20:5 fail to sit at T with the king; but
20:29 reason he has not come to the king's T
20:34 Jonathan rose from the T in fierce anger and
2Sam 9:7 shall eat at my T always."
9:10 your master's son shall always eat at my T
9:11 Mephibosheth ate at David's T, like one of the
9:13 Jerusalem; for he ate always at the king's T
19:28 your servant among those who eat at your T
1Kgs 2:7 who eat at your T; for with such loyalty
4:27 came to King Solomon's T, each one in his
7:48 golden altar, the golden T for the bread of
10:5 the food of his T, the seating of his
13:20 they sat at the T, the word of the
18:19 hundred prophets of Asherah, who eat at Jezebel's T
2Kgs 4:10 him a bed, a T, a chair, and a
25:29 regularly at the king's T;
1Chr 28:16 of gold for each T for the showbread, the
2Chr 9:4 the food of his T, the seating of his
13:11 the showbread on the T of pure gold, and
29:18 its utensils, and the T for the showbread and
Neh 5:17 there were at my T a hundred and fifty
Jud 12:1 them to set a T for her with some
Esth 14:17 not eaten at Haman's T, and I have not
Job 36:16 was set on your T was full of fatness.
Ps 23:5 Thou preparest a T before me in the presence
69:22 Let their own T before them become a snare;
78:19 "Can God spread a T in the wilderness?
128:3 children will be like olive shoots around your T
Prov 9:2 mixed her wine, she has also set her T
Sir 6:10 friend who is a T companion, but will not
14:10 begrudges bread, and it is lacking at his T
29:26 here, stranger, prepare the T, and if you have
31:12 you seated at the T of a great man?
40:29 man looks to the T of another, his existence
Is 21:5 They prepare the T, they spread the rugs, they
65:11 mountain, who set a T for Fortune and fill
Jer 52:33 regularly at the king's T;
Ezek 23:41 stately couch, with a T spread before it on
39:20 be filled at my T with horses and riders,
41:22 me, "This is the T which is before the
44:16 they shall approach my T, to minister to me,
Dan 11:27 lies at the same T, but to no avail;
14:13 unconcerned, for beneath the T they had made a
14:18 king looked at the T, and shouted in a
14:21 to enter and devour what was on the T
Mal 1:7 thinking that the LORD's T may be despised.
1:12 say that the LORD's T is polluted, and the
1Mac 1:22 He took also the T for the bread of
4:49 of incense, and the T into the temple.
4:51 the bread on the T and hung up the
11:58 gold plate and a T service, and granted him
Mt 8:11 west and sit at T with Abraham, Isaac, and
9:10 as he sat at T in the house, behold,
15:27 eat the crumbs that fall from their masters' T
26:7 it on his head, as he sat at T
26:20 evening, he sat at T with the twelve disciples;
Mk 2:15 as he sat at T in his house, many
7:27 the dogs under the T eat the children's crumbs."
14:3 as he sat at T, a woman came with
14:18 as they were at T eating, Jesus said, "Truly,
16:14 as they sat at T; and he upbraided them
Lk 5:29 and others sitting at T with them.
7:36 the Pharisee's house, and took his place at T
7:37 that he was at T in the Pharisee's house,
7:49 those who were at T with him began to
11:37 him; so he went in and sat at T
12:37 have them sit at T, and he will come
13:29 south, and sit at T in the kingdom of
14:10 all who sit at T with you.
14:15 those who sat at T with him heard this,
16:21 from the rich man's T; moreover the dogs came
17:7 field, 'Come at once and sit down at T
22:14 came, he sat at T, and the apostles with
22:21 who betrays me is with me on the T
22:27 one who sits at T, or one who serves?
22:27 Is it not the one who sits at T
22:30 and drink at my T in my kingdom, and
24:30 When he was at T with them, he took
Jn 12:2 one of those at T with him.
13:28 no one at the T knew why he said
Rom 11:9 David says, "Let their T become a snare and
1Cor 8:10 man of knowledge, at T in an idol's temple,
10:21 cannot partake of the T of the Lord and
10:21 the Lord and the T of demons.
Heb 9:2 the lampstand and the T and the bread of

TABLELAND (8)

Deut 3:10 the cities of the T and all Gilead and
4:43 the wilderness on the T for the Reubenites, and
Josh 13:9 valley, and all the T of Medeba as far
13:16 valley, and all the T by Medeba;
13:17 that are in the T; Dibon, and Bamoth-baal, and
13:21 the cities of the T, and all the kingdom
20:8 the wilderness on the T, from the tribe of
Jer 48:21 has come upon the T, upon Holon, and Jahzah,

TABLES (50)

Ex 24:12 will give you the T of stone, with the
31:18 Mount Sinai, the two T of the testimony, tables
31:18 tables of the testimony, T of stone, written with
32:15 mountain with the two T of the testimony in
32:15 testimony in his hands, T that were written on
32:16 And the T were the work of God, and
32:16 was the writing of God, graven upon the T
32:19 and he threw the T out of his hands
34:1 to Moses, "Cut two T of stone like the
34:1 will write upon the T the words that were
34:1 were on the first T, which you broke.
34:4 So Moses cut two T of stone like the
34:4 in his hand two T of stone.
34:28 he wrote upon the T the words of the
34:29 Sinai, with the two T of the testimony in
Deut 4:13 wrote them upon two T of stone.
5:22 wrote them upon two T of stone, and gave
9:9 mountain to receive the T of stone, the tables
9:9 tables of stone, the T of the covenant which
9:10 gave me the two T of stone written with
9:11 gave me the two T of stone, the tables
9:11 tables of stone, the T of the covenant.
9:15 fire; and the two T of the covenant were
9:17 hold of the two T, and cast them out
10:1 to me, 'Hew two T of stone like the
10:2 will write on the T the words that were
10:2 were on the first T which you broke, and
10:3 wood, and hewed two T of stone like the
10:3 mountain with the two T in my hand.
10:4 he wrote on the T, as at the first
10:5 mountain, and put the T in the ark which
1Kgs 8:9 ark except the two T of stone which Moses
1Chr 28:16 silver for the silver T,
2Chr 4:8 He also made ten T, and placed them in
4:19 the golden altar, the T for the bread of
5:10 ark except the two T which Moses put there
Is 28:8 For all T are full of vomit, no place
Ezek 40:39 the gate were two T on either side, on
40:40 north gate were two T; and on the other
40:40 of the vestibule of the gate were two T
40:41 Four T were on the inside, and four tables
40:41 the inside, and four T on the outside of
40:41 of the gate, eight T, on which the sacrifices
40:42 there were also four T of hewn stone for
40:43 And on the T the flesh of the offering
Mt 21:12 and he overturned the T of the money-changers and
Mk 11:15 and he overturned the T of the money-changers and
Jn 2:15 coins of the money-changers and overturned their T
Acts 6:2 up preaching the word of God to serve T
Heb 9:4 that budded, and the T of the covenant;

TABLET (6)

Prov 3:3 write them on the T of your heart.
7:3 write them on the T of your heart.
Is 8:1 me, "Take a large T and write upon it
30:8 before them on a T, and inscribe it in
Jer 17:1 is engraved on the T of their heart, and
Lk 1:63 asked for a writing T, and wrote, "His name

TABLETS (7)

Hab 2:2 make it plain upon T, so he may run
1Mac 8:22 in reply, on bronze T, and sent to Jerusalem
14:18 to him on bronze T to renew with him
14:27 a record on bronze T and put it upon
14:48 this decree upon bronze T, to put them up
2Cor 3:3 living God, not on T of stone but on
3:3 of stone but on T of human hearts.

TABOR (10)

Josh 19:22 boundary also touches T, Shahazumah, and
Judg 4:6 your men at Mount T, taking ten thousand from
4:12 gone up to Mount T,
4:14 went down from Mount T with ten thousand men
8:18 "Where are the men whom you slew at T
1Sam 10:3 to the oak of T; three men going up
1Chr 6:77 with its pasture lands, T with its pasture lands,
Ps 89:12 thou hast created them; T and Hermon joyously
Jer 46:18 LORD of hosts, like T among the mountains, and
Hos 5:1 snare at Mizpah, and a net spread upon T

TABRIMMON

1Kgs 15:18 Ben-hadad the son of T, the son of Hezi-on,

TACKLE (2)

Is 33:23 Your T hangs loose; it cannot hold the mast
Acts 27:19 their own hands the T of the ship.

TADMOR

2Chr 8:4 He built T in the wilderness and all the

TAH-CHEMONITE

2Sam 23:8 David had: Josheb-basshebeth a T; he was chief of

TAHAN (2)

Num 26:35 of the Becherites; of T, the family of the
1Chr 7:25 son, Telah his son, T his son,

TAHANITES

Num 26:35 the Becherites; of Tahan, the family of the T

TAHASH

Gen 22:24 Reumah, bore Tebah, Gaham, T, and Maacah.

TAHATH (6)

Num 33:26 they set out from Makheloth, and encamped at T
33:27 they set out from T, and encamped at Terah.
1Chr 6:24 son, Assir his son, T his son, Uriel his
6:37 of Zephaniah, son of T, son of Assir, son
7:20 and Bered his son, T his son, Ele-adah his
7:20 son, Ele-adah his son, T his son,

TAHPANHES (7)

Jud 1:9 river of Egypt, and T and Raamses and the
Jer 2:16 men of Memphis and T have broken the crown
43:7 And they arrived at T
43:8 came to Jeremiah in T:
43:9 to Pharaoh's palace in T, in the sight of
44:1 Egypt, at Migdol, at T, at Memphis, and in
46:14 proclaim in Memphis and T; Say, 'Stand ready and

TAHPENES (3)

1Kgs 11:19 wife, the sister of T the queen.
11:20 And the sister of T bore him Genubath his
11:20 Genubath his son, whom T weaned in Pharaoh's

TAHRE-A

1Chr 9:41 of Micah: Pithon, Melech, T, and Ahaz;

TAIL (15)

Ex 4:4 take it by the T -- so he put
29:22 ram, and the fat T, and the fat that
Lev 3:9 its fat, the fat T entire, taking it away
7:3 be offered, the fat T, the fat that covers
8:25 fat, and the fat T, and all the fat
9:19 the ram, the fat T, and that which covers
Deut 28:13 head, and not the T; and you shall tend
28:44 be the head, and you shall be the T
Judg 15:4 and he turned them T to tail, and put
15:4 turned them tail to T, and put a torch
Job 40:17 He makes his T stiff like a cedar; the
Is 9:14 from Israel head and T, palm branch and reed
9:15 teaches lies is the T;
19:15 Egypt which head or T, palm branch or reed,
Rev 12:4 His T swept down a third of the stars

TAILS (5)

Judg 15:4 and put a torch between each pair of T
Rev 9:10 They have T like scorpions, and stings, and their
9:10 hurting men for five months lies in their T
9:19 mouths and in their T; their tails are like
9:19 in their tails; their T are like serpents, with

TAKE (996)

Gen 3:22 forth his hand and T also of the tree
6:21 Also T with you every sort of food that
7:2 T with you seven pairs of all clean animals,
12:19 here is your wife, T her, and be gone."
13:9 If you T the left hand, then I will
13:9 right; or if you T the right hand, then
14:21 me the persons, but T the goods for yourself."
14:23 that I would not T a thread or a
14:24 Abram rich.' I will T nothing but what the
14:24 Aner, Eshcol, and Mamre T their share."
19:15 urged Lot, saying, "Arise, T your wife and your
21:30 ewe lambs you will T from my hand, that
22:2 He said, T your son, your only son Isaac,
24:3 that you will not T a wife for my
24:4 to my kindred, and T a wife for my
24:5 land; must I then T your son back to
24:6 that you do not T my son back there.
24:7 you, and you shall T a wife for my
24:8 only you must not T my son back there."
24:37 saying, 'You shall not T a wife for my
24:38 to my kindred, and T a wife for my
24:40 way; and you shall T a wife for my
24:48 the right way to T the daughter of my
24:51 Rebekah is before you, T her and go, and
27:3 Now then, T your weapons, your quiver and your
28:2 your mother's father; and T as wife from there
28:4 you, that you may T possession of the land
28:6 away to Paddan-aram to T a wife from there,
30:15 you T away my son's mandrakes also?" Rachel
31:24 and said to him, T heed that you say
31:29 me last night, saying, T heed that you speak
31:31 thought that you would T your daughters from me
31:32 that is yours, and T it." Now Jacob did
31:50 daughters, or if you T wives besides my daughters,
34:9 daughters to us, and T our daughters for yourselves.
34:16 you, and we will T your daughters to ourselves,
34:17 circumcised, then we will T our daughter, and we
34:21 for them; let us T their daughters in marriage,
37:21 saying, "Let us not T his life."
41:34 over the land, and T the fifth part of
42:33 brothers with me, and T grain for the famine
42:36 and now you would T Benjamin; all this has
43:11 so, then do this: T some of the choice
43:12 T double the money with you; carry back with
43:13 T also your brother, and arise, go again to
44:29 If you T this one also from me, and
45:18 land of Canaan; and T your father and your
45:19 them also, 'Do this: T wagons from the land
Ex 2:9 daughter said to her, T this child away, and
4:4 out your hand, and T it by the tail"--
4:9 your voice, you shall T some water from the
4:9 water which you shall T from the Nile will
4:17 And you shall T in your hand this rod,
5:4 Aaron, why do you T the people away from
6:7 judgment, and I will T you for my people,
7:9 shall say to Aaron, T your rod and cast
7:15 the river's brink, and T in your hand the
7:19 Moses, "Say to Aaron, T your rod and stretch
8:8 "Entreat the LORD to T away the frogs from
9:8 to Moses and Aaron, T handfuls of ashes from
10:26 behind, for we must T of them to serve
10:28 "Get away from me; T heed to yourself; never
12:3 this month they shall T every man a lamb
12:4 to his house shall T according to the number
12:5 year old; you shall T it from the sheep
12:7 Then they shall T some of the blood, and
12:22 T a bunch of hyssop and dip it in
12:32 T your flocks and your herds, as you have
16:16 can eat; you shall T an omer apiece, according
16:33 Moses said to Aaron, T a jar, and put
17:5 elders of Israel; and T in your hand the
19:12 people round about, saying, T heed that you do
20:7 "You shall not T the name of the LORD
21:14 him treacherously, you shall T him from my altar,
22:26 If ever you T your neighbor's garment in pledge,
23:8 And you shall T no bribe, for a bribe
23:13 T heed to all that I have said to
23:25 water; and I will T sickness away from the

T

25:2 of Israel, that they T for me an offering;
28:9 And you shall T two onyx stones, and engrave
28:38 forehead, and Aaron shall T upon himself any guilt
29:1 T one young bull and two rams without blemish,
29:5 And you shall T the garments, and put on
29:7 And you shall T the anointing oil, and pour
29:12 of meeting, and shall T part of the blood
29:13 And you shall T all the fat that covers
29:15 "Then you shall T one of the rams, and
29:16 the ram, and shall T its blood and throw
29:19 "You shall T the other ram; and Aaron and
29:20 kill the ram, and T part of its blood
29:21 Then you shall T part of the blood that
29:22 "You shall also T the fat of the ram,
29:25 Then you shall T them from their hands, and
29:26 "And you shall T the breast of the ram
29:31 "You shall T the ram of ordination, and boil
30:12 to Moses, "When you T the census of the
30:16 And you shall T the atonement money from the
30:23 LORD said to Moses, T the finest spices: of
30:34 LORD said to Moses, T sweet spices, stacte, and
32:2 Aaron said to them, T off the rings of
32:24 any who have gold T it off'; so they
33:7 Now Moses used to T the tent and pitch
33:23 by; then I will T away my hand, and
34:9 and our sin, and T us for thy inheritance."
34:12 T heed to yourself, lest you make a covenant
34:16 his sacrifice, and you T of their daughters for
35:5 T from among you an offering to the LORD;
Lev 1:16 altar; and he shall T away its crop with
2:2 And he shall T from it a handful of
2:9 And the priest shall T from the cereal offering
3:4 liver which he shall T away with the kidneys.
3:10 liver which he shall T away with the kidneys.
3:15 liver which he shall T away with the kidneys.
4:5 the anointed priest shall T some of the blood
4:8 sin offering he shall T from it, the fat
4:9 liver which he shall T away with the kidneys
4:19 its fat he shall T from it and burn
4:25 Then the priest shall T some of the blood
4:30 And the priest shall T some of its blood
4:34 Then the priest shall T some of the blood
5:12 and the priest shall T a handful of it
6:10 body, and he shall T up the ashes to
6:15 And one shall T from it a handful of
7:4 liver which he shall T away with the kidneys;
8:2 LORD said to Moses, T Aaron and his sons
8:33 completed, for it will T seven days to ordain
9:2 he said to Aaron, T a bull calf for
9:3 the people of Israel, T a male goat for
10:12 sons who were left, T the cereal offering that
12:8 lamb, then she shall T two turtledoves or two
14:4 shall command them to T for him who is
14:6 He shall T the living bird with the cedarwood
14:10 eighth day he shall T two male lambs without
14:12 And the priest shall T one of the male
14:14 The priest shall T some of the blood of
14:15 Then the priest shall T some of the log
14:21 much, then he shall T one male lamb for
14:24 and the priest shall T the lamb of the
14:25 and the priest shall T some of the blood
14:40 shall command that they T out the stones in
14:42 city; then they shall T other stones and put
14:42 stones, and he shall T other plaster and plaster
14:49 the house he shall T two small birds, with
14:51 running water, and shall T the cedarwood and the
15:14 eighth day he shall T two turtledoves or two
15:29 eighth day she shall T two turtledoves or two
16:5 And he shall T from the congregation of the
16:7 Then he shall T the two goats, and set
16:12 And he shall T a censer full of coals
16:14 die; and he shall T some of the blood
16:18 for it, and shall T some of the blood
18:17 and you shall not T her son's daughter or
18:18 And you shall not T a woman as a
19:18 You shall not T vengeance or bear any grudge
21:13 And he shall T a wife in her virginity.
21:14 marry; but he shall T to wife a virgin
22:5 from whom he may T uncleanness, whatever his
23:40 And you shall T on the first day the
24:5 "And you shall T fine flour, and bake twelve
25:36 T no interest from him or increase, but fear
Num 1:2 land of Egypt, saying, T a census of all
1:49 and you shall not T a census of them
1:51 out, the Levites shall T it down; and when
3:41 And you shall T the Levites for me–I

3:45 LORD said to Moses, T the Levites instead of
3:47 male Levites, you shall T five shekels apiece;
3:47 twenty gerahs, you shall T them,
4:2 to Moses and Aaron, T a census of the
4:5 shall go in and T down the veil of
4:9 And they shall T a cloth of blue, and
4:12 poles; and they shall T all the vessels of
4:13 And they shall T away the ashes from the
4:22 LORD said to Moses, T a census of the
5:17 and the priest shall T holy water in an
5:17 an earthen vessel, and T some of the dust
5:19 priest shall make her T an oath, saying, 'If
5:21 priest make the woman T the oath of the
5:25 And the priest shall T the cereal offering of
5:26 and the priest shall T a handful of the
6:18 of meeting, and shall T the hair from his
6:19 And the priest shall T the shoulder of the
8:6 LORD said to Moses, T the Levites from among
8:8 Then let them T a young bull and its
8:8 oil, and you shall T another young bull for
11:16 meeting, and let them T their stand there with
11:17 there; and I will T some of the spirit
16:6 Do this: T censers, Korah and all his company;
16:17 every one of you T his censer, and put
16:37 Aaron the priest to T up the censers out
16:46 Moses said to Aaron, T your censer, and put
18:26 the Levites, 'When you T from the people of
19:4 Eleazar the priest shall T some of her blood
19:6 and the priest shall T cedarwood and hyssop and
19:17 the unclean they shall T some ashes of the
19:18 a clean person shall T hyssop, and dip it
20:8 LORD said to Moses, T the rod, and assemble
20:25 T Aaron and Eleazar his son, and bring them
21:7 the LORD, that he T away the serpents from
23:12 answered, "Must I not T heed to speak what
23:27 "Come now, I will T you to another place;
24:22 How long shall Asshur T you away captive?"
25:4 LORD said to Moses, T all the chiefs of
26:2 of Aaron, the priest, T a census of all
26:4 Jordan at Jericho, saying, T a census of the
27:18 LORD said to Moses, T Joshua the son of
28:2 pleasing odor, you shall T heed to offer to
31:26 LORD said to Moses, T the count of the
31:29 and of the flocks; T it from their half,
31:30 Israel's half you shall T one drawn out of
32:5 a possession; do not T us across the Jordan."
32:17 ones, but we will T up arms, ready to
32:20 this, if you will T up arms to go
33:53 places; and you shall T possession of the land
34:18 You shall T one leader of every tribe, to
35:8 larger tribes you shall T many, and from the
35:8 smaller tribes you shall T few; each, in proportion
Deut 1:7 this mountain; turn and T your journey, and go
1:8 you; go in and T possession of the land
1:21 before you; go up, T possession, as the LORD,
2:4 So T good heed;
2:24 their stead.) 'Rise up, T your journey, and go
2:24 his land; begin to T possession, and contend with
2:31 to you; begin to T possession, that you may
3:4 which we did not T from them--sixty cities,
4:1 and go in and T possession of the land
4:2 I command you, nor T from it; that you
4:5 you are entering to T possession of it.
4:9 "Only T heed, and keep your soul diligently, lest
4:15 "Therefore T good heed to yourselves.
4:22 shall go over and T possession of that good
4:23 T heed to yourselves, lest you forget the covenant
4:34 attempted to go and T a nation for himself
5:11 "'You shall not T the name of the LORD
6:12 and are full, then T heed lest you forget
6:18 may go in and T possession of the good
7:1 you are entering to T possession of it, and
7:15 And the LORD will T away from you all
7:25 is on them, or T it for yourselves, lest
8:11 T heed lest you forget the LORD your God,
9:23 saying, 'Go up and T possession of the land
11:8 and go in and T possession of the land
11:10 you are entering to T possession of it is
11:16 T heed lest your heart be deceived, and you
11:29 you are entering to T possession of it, you
11:31 to go in to T possession of the land
12:13 T heed that you do not offer your burnt
12:19 T heed that you do not forsake the Levite
12:26 votive offerings, you shall T, and you shall go
12:30 dwell in their land, T heed that you be
12:32 add to it or T from it.

15:9 T heed lest there be a base thought in
15:17 you, then you shall T an awl, and thrust
16:19 and you shall not T a bribe, for a
20:7 battle and another man T her.'
20:14 its spoil, you shall T as booty for yourselves;
20:19 it in order to T it, you shall not
21:3 the slain man shall T a heifer which has
21:10 your hands, and you T them captive,
21:11 for her and would T her for yourself as
21:19 and his mother shall T hold of him and
22:1 from them; you shall T them back to your
22:6 eggs, you shall not T the mother with the
22:7 the young you may T to yourself; that it
22:15 and her mother shall T and bring out the
22:18 of that city shall T the man and whip
22:30 "A man shall not T his father's wife, nor
23:20 you are entering to T possession of it.
24:4 her away, may not T her again to be
24:6 "No man shall T a mill or an upper
24:8 T heed, in an attack of leprosy, to be
24:17 to the fatherless, or T a widow's garment in
25:5 in to her, and T her as his wife,
25:7 does not wish to T his brother's wife, then
25:8 do not wish to T her,'
26:2 in it, you shall T some of the first
26:4 Then the priest shall T the basket from your
28:21 you are entering to T possession of it.
28:63 so the LORD will T delight in bringing ruin
28:63 you are entering to T possession of it.
30:9 the LORD will again T delight in prospering you,
30:16 you are entering to T possession of it.
31:26 covenant of the LORD, T this book of the
32:41 on judgment, I will T vengeance on my adversaries,
Josh 1:11 to go in to T possession of the land
1:15 you, and they also T possession of the land
3:6 said to the priests, T up the ark of
3:12 Now therefore T twelve men from the tribes of
4:2 LORD said to Joshua, T twelve men from the
4:3 man, and command them, T twelve stones from here
4:5 of the Jordan, and T up each of you
6:6 and said to them, T up the ark of
6:18 have devoted them you T any of the devoted
7:13 your enemies, until you T away the devoted things
8:1 fear or be dismayed; T all the fighting men
8:2 its cattle you shall T as booty for yourselves;
9:11 country said to us, T provisions in your hand
17:12 of Manasseh could not T possession of those cities;
18:3 to go in and T possession of the land,
20:4 city; then they shall T him into the city,
22:5 T good care to observe the commandment and the
22:19 LORD's tabernacle stands, and T for yourselves a
22:23 may the LORD himself T vengeance.
23:11 T good heed to yourselves, therefore, to love the
Judg 2:6 to his inheritance to T possession of the land.
2:22 Israel, whether they will T care to walk in
6:20 God said to him, T the meat and the
6:25 LORD said to him, T your father's bull, the
6:26 in due order; then T the second bull, and
7:4 are still too many; T them down to the
9:15 you, then come and T refuge in my shade;
11:15 Jephthah: Israel did not T away the land of
11:23 and are you to T possession of them?
11:35 LORD, and I cannot T back my vow."
14:3 you must go to T a wife from the
14:8 while he returned to T her; and he turned
15:2 Pray T her instead."
18:24 And he said, "You T my gods which I
19:30 this day; consider it, T counsel, and speak."
20:10 lot, and we will T ten men of a
21:22 because we did not T for each man of
Ruth 2:10 eyes, that you should T notice of me, when
2:12 you have come to T refuge!"
4:6 T my right of redemption yourself, for I cannot
1Sam 2:14 up the priest would T for himself.
2:16 fat first, and then T as much as you
2:16 if not, I will T it by force."
2:19 a little robe and T it to him each
4:9 T courage, and acquit yourselves like men, O
6:7 Now then, T and prepare a new cart and
6:7 to the cart, but T their calves home, away
6:8 And T the ark of the LORD and place
6:21 Come down and T it up to you."
8:11 over you: he will T your sons and appoint
8:13 He will T your daughters to be perfumers and
8:14 He will T the best of your fields and
8:15 He will T the tenth of your grain and
8:16 He will T your menservants and maidservants, and
8:17 He will T the tenth of your flocks, and
9:3 to Saul his son, T one of the servants
16:2 And the LORD said, T a heifer with you,
17:17 to David his son, T for your brothers an
17:18 to your brothers; also T these ten cheeses to
19:2 to kill you; therefore T heed to yourself in
19:14 Saul sent messengers to T David, she said, "He
19:20 Saul sent messengers to T David; and when they
20:16 may the LORD T vengeance on David's enemies."
20:21 this side of you, T them,' then you are
21:9 ephod; if you will T that, take it, for
21:9 you will take that, T it, for there is
23:23 See therefore, and T note of all the lurking
24:11 hunt my life to T it.
25:11 Shall I T my bread and my water and
25:40 us to you to T you to him as
26:11 the LORD's anointed; but T now the spear that
30:15 to him, "Will you T me down to this
30:15 master, and I will T you down to this
2Sam 2:21 the young men, and T his spoil." But Asahel
6:10 was not willing to T the ark of the
7:15 but I will not T my steadfast love from
12:4 he was unwilling to T one of his own
12:11 house; and I will T your wives before your
12:28 against the city, and T it; lest I take
12:28 take it; lest I T the city, and it
13:20 your brother; do not T this to heart." So
13:33 lord the king so T it to heart as
14:14 but God will not T away the life of
15:5 out his hand, and T hold of him, and
15:20 Go back, and T your brethren with you; and
16:9 me go over and T off his head."
19:30 king, "Oh, let him T it all, since my
20:6 more harm than Absalom; T your lord's servants and
22:3 rock, in whom I T refuge, my shield and
22:31 for all those who T refuge in him.
24:10 LORD, I pray thee, T away the iniquity of
24:22 my lord the king T and offer up what
1Kgs 1:33 king said to them, T with you the servants
2:4 saying, 'If your sons T heed to their way,
2:31 bury him; and thus T away from me and
8:25 if only your sons T heed to their way,
8:31 and is made to T an oath, and comes
11:31 he said to Jeroboam, T for yourself ten pieces;
11:34 Nevertheless I will not T the whole kingdom out
11:35 statutes; but I will T the kingdom out of
11:37 And I will T you, and you shall reign
14:3 T with you ten loaves, some cakes, and a
18:10 not here,' he would T an oath of the
19:4 enough; now, O LORD, T away my life; for
19:10 seek my life, to T it away."
19:14 seek my life, to T it away."
20:6 whatever pleases them, and T it away.'"
20:12 said to his men, T your positions." And they
20:18 come out for peace, T them alive; or if
20:18 come out for war, T them alive."
20:41 he made haste to T the bandage away from
21:10 and the king.' Then T him out, and stone
21:15 said to Ahab, "Arise, T possession of the vineyard
21:16 Naboth the Jezreelite, to T possession of it.
21:18 he has gone to T possession.
22:3 quiet and do not T it out of the
22:26 said, "Seize Micaiah, and T him back to Amon
2Kgs 2:1 LORD was about to T Elijah up to heaven
2:3 today the LORD will T away your master from
2:5 today the LORD will T away your master from
4:1 creditor has come to T my two children to
4:29 up your loins, and T my staff in your
4:36 to him, he said, T up your son."
5:16 he urged him to T it, but he refused.
6:7 And he said, T it up." So he reached
6:32 murderer has sent to T off my head?
7:12 the city, we shall T them alive and get
7:13 said, "Let some men T five of the remaining
8:8 king said to Hazael, T a present with you
9:1 up your loins, and T this flask of oil
9:3 Then T the flask of oil, and pour it
9:17 And Joram said, T a horseman, and send to
9:25 to Bidkar his aide, T him up, and cast
9:26 of ground.' Now therefore T him up and cast
10:6 ready to obey me, T the heads of your
10:14 He said, T them alive." And they took them
12:5 LORD, let the priests T, each from his acquaintance;
12:7 therefore T no more money from your acquaintances,
12:8 agreed that they should T no more money from

13:15 Elisha said to him, T a bow and arrows";
13:18 And he said, T the arrows"; and he took
18:32 until I come and T you away to a
19:30 of Judah shall again T root downward, and bear
20:7 And let them T and lay it on the
1Chr 13:13 So David did not T the ark home into
17:13 son; I will not T my steadfast love from
21:8 now, I pray thee, T away the iniquity of
21:11 "Thus says the LORD, T which you will:
21:23 Ornan said to David, T it; and let my
21:24 price; I will not T for the LORD what
28:10 T heed now, for the LORD has chosen you
2Chr 2:16 so that you may T it up to Jerusalem."
6:16 if only your sons T heed to their way,
6:22 and is made to T an oath, and comes
15:7 But you, T courage!
18:25 said, "Seize Micaiah, and T him back to Amon
19:7 LORD be upon you; T heed what you do,
20:17 fight in this battle; T your position, stand still,
20:25 his people came to T the spoil from them,
24:11 empty the chest and T it and return it
32:18 order that they might T the city.
35:23 said to his servants, T me away, for I
36:6 him in fetters to T him to Babylon.
Ezra 4:22 And T care not to be slack in this
5:15 he said to him, T these vessels, go and
9:11 you are entering, to T possession of it, is
9:12 to their sons, neither T their daughters for your
10:5 Levites and all Israel T oath that they would
Neh 6:7 come, and let us T counsel together."
10:30 of the land or T their daughters for our
13:25 and I made them T oath in the name
13:25 to their sons, or T their daughters for your
Tob 3:15 pleasing to thee to T my life, command that
4:12 First of all T a wife from among the
4:13 people by refusing to T a wife for yourself
6:4 open the fish and T the heart and liver
6:15 father commanded you to T a wife from among
6:16 bridal chamber, you shall T live ashes of incense
7:10 is your right to T my child.
7:12 So Raguel said, T her right now, in accordance
7:13 saying, "Here she is; T her according to the
7:13 law of Moses, and T her with you to
7:16 the other room, and T her into it."
8:21 that then he should T half of Raguel's property
9:2 to him, "Brother Azarias, T a servant and two
11:4 And T the gall of the fish with you."
12:5 and said to him, T half of all that
14:3 to him, "My son, T your sons; behold, I
Jud 1:12 that he would surely T revenge on the whole
2:5 you leave my presence, T with you men confident
2:13 And you-- T care not to transgress any of
6:5 this day until I T revenge on this race
6:7 slaves are going to T you back into the
6:10 to seize Achior and T him to Bethulia and
7:12 only let your servants T possession of the spring
8:30 promised, and made us T an oath which we
8:35 go before you, to T revenge upon our enemies."
9:2 gavest a sword to T revenge on the strangers
11:1 Holofernes said to her, T courage, woman, and do
14:1 me, my brethren, and T this head and hang
14:2 let every valiant man T his weapons and go
16:5 children as prey, and T my virgins as booty.
16:17 The Lord Almighty will T vengeance on them in
Esth 2:13 whatever she desired to T with her from the
4:4 so that he might T off his sackcloth, but
6:10 to Haman, "Make haste, T the robes and the
14:5 thou, O Lord, didst T Israel out of all
15:9 T courage;
16:4 They not only T away thankfulness from among men,
16:8 the future we will T care to render our
Job 7:21 pardon my transgression and T away my iniquity?
8:20 a blameless man, nor T the hand of evildoers.
9:34 Let him T his rod away from me, and
11:18 will be protected and T your rest in safety.
13:14 I will T my flesh in my teeth, and
23:10 the way that I T; when he has tried
24:3 of the fatherless; they T the widow's ox for
24:9 from the breast, and T in pledge the infant
27:10 Will he T delight in the Almighty?
33:5 in order before me; T your stand.
34:9 nothing that he should T delight in God.'
34:14 If he should T back his spirit to himself,
36:21 T heed, do not turn to iniquity, for this
38:13 place, that it might T hold of the skirts
38:20 darkness, that you may T it to its territory
40:24 Can one T him with hooks, or pierce his
41:4 covenant with you to T him for your servant
42:8 Now therefore T seven bulls and seven rams, and
Ps 2:2 themselves, and the rulers T counsel together, against
2:12 Blessed are all who T refuge in him.
5:11 But let all who T refuge in thee rejoice,
7:1 in thee do I T refuge; save me from
7:7 thee; and over it T thy seat on high.
10:14 vexation, that thou mayest T it into thy hands;
11:1 In the LORD I T refuge; how can you
15:5 interest, and does not T a bribe against the
16:1 for in thee I T refuge.
16:4 not pour out or T their names upon my
18:2 rock, in whom I T refuge, my shield, and
18:30 for all those who T refuge in him.
25:20 to shame, for I T refuge in thee.
27:10 but the LORD will T me up.
27:14 and let your heart T courage; yea, wait for
28:3 T me not off with the wicked, with those
31:4 me and guide me, T me out of the
31:13 as they plot to T my life.
31:19 wrought for those who T refuge in thee, in
31:24 and let your heart T courage, all you who
34:22 none of those who T refuge in him will
35:2 T hold of shield and buckler, and rise for
36:7 The children of men T refuge in the shadow
37:4 T delight in the LORD, and he will give
37:40 saves them, because they T refuge in him.
43:2 God in whom I T refuge; why hast thou
50:16 recite my statutes, or T my covenant on your
51:11 from thy presence, and T not thy holy Spirit
57:1 thy wings I will T refuge, till the storms
62:4 They T pleasure in falsehood.
64:10 in the LORD, and T refuge in him!
71:1 O LORD, do I T refuge; let me never
83:12 who said, "Let us T possession for ourselves of
86:16 Turn to me and T pity on me; give
102:24 I say, T me not hence in the midst
118:8 It is better to T refuge in the LORD
118:9 It is better to T refuge in the LORD
119:22 wander from thy commandments; T away from me
119:43 And T not the word of truth utterly out
119:52 from of old, I T comfort, O LORD.
139:9 If I T the wings of the morning and
144:2 he in whom I T refuge, who subdues the
Prov 4:27 T heed to the path of your feet, then
5:6 Sheol; she does not T heed to the path
5:10 the merciless; lest strangers T their fill of your
7:18 Come, let us T our fill of love till
8:10 T my instruction instead of silver, and knowledge
13:10 but with those who T advice is wisdom.
20:16 T a man's garment when he has given surety
25:4 T away the dross from the silver, and the
25:5 material for a vessel; T away the wicked from
27:13 T a man's garment when he has given surety
30:5 shield to those who T refuge in him.
30:28 the lizard you can T in your hands, yet
Eccl 3:13 eat and drink and T pleasure in all his
4:13 who will no longer T advice,
5:15 he came, and shall T nothing for his toil,
7:18 good that you should T hold of this, and
Wis 2:7 Let us T our fill of costly wine and
4:3 a deep root or T a firm hold.
4:15 did not understand, nor T such a thing to
5:17 The Lord will T his zeal as his whole
5:19 a helmet; he will T holiness as an invincible
8:2 and I desired to T her for my bride,
8:9 Therefore I determined to T her to live with
13:18 a thing that cannot T a step;
14:19 forced the likeness to T more beautiful form,
18:5 thou didst in punishment T away a multitude of
Sir 12:12 he overthrow you and T your place; do not
12:12 lest he try to T your seat of honor,
13:8 T care not to be led astray, and not
14:16 Give, and T, and beguile yourself, because in Hades
18:18 before you fall ill, T care of your health.
18:30 allow your soul to T pleasure in base desire,
19:17 of the Most High T its course.
19:19 there prudence where sinners T counsel.
23:18 Most High will not T notice of my sins."
23:25 Her children will not T root, and her branches
29:20 to your ability, but T heed to yourself lest
30:13 Discipline your son and T pains with him, that
32:1 as one of them; T good care of them
32:2 have fulfilled your duties, T your place, that you
33:20 not let any one T your place.

	34:22	To T away a neighbor's living is to murder
	36:18	The stomach will T any food, yet one food
	37:5	the face of battle T up the shield.
	37:8	for he will T thought for himself–
	42:7	you give out or T in.
	46:1	of God's elect, to T vengeance on the enemies
	47:4	kill a giant, and T away reproach from the
Is	3:18	day the Lord will T away the finery of
	4:1	And seven women shall T hold of one man
	4:1	called by your name; T away our reproach."
	7:4	and say to him, T heed, be quiet, do
	8:1	LORD said to me, T a large tablet and
	8:10	T counsel together, but it will come to nought;
	10:6	I command him, to T spoil and seize plunder,
	14:2	And the peoples will T them and bring them
	14:2	female slaves; they will T captive those who were
	14:4	to serve, you will T up this taunt against
	20:2	from your loins and T off your shoes from
	23:16	song of the harlot: T a harp, go about
	25:8	his people he will T away from all the
	27:6	to come Jacob shall T root, Israel shall blossom
	28:19	passes through it will T you; for morning by
	30:2	for my counsel, to T refuge in the protection
	30:14	found with which to T fire from the hearth,
	33:23	even the lame will T the prey.
	36:17	until I come and T you away to a
	37:31	of Judah shall again T root downward, and bear
	38:21	had said, "Let them T a cake of figs,
	41:6	says to his brother, T courage!"
	42:25	but he did not T it to heart.
	45:21	your case; let them T counsel together!
	47:2	T the millstones and grind meal, put off your
	47:3	I will T vengeance, and I will spare no
	51:18	there is none to T her by the hand
	57:13	off, a breath will T them away.
	58:9	"If you T away from the midst of you
	58:14	idly; then you shall T delight in the LORD,
	62:6	the LORD in remembrance, T no rest,
	64:6	iniquities, like the wind, T us away.
	64:7	that bestirs himself to T hold of thee; for
	66:21	them also I will T for priests and for
Jer	3:14	your master; I will T you, one from a
	5:1	of Jerusalem, look and T note!
	5:3	but they refused to T correction.
	6:10	object of scorn, they T no pleasure in it.
	9:10	T up weeping and wailing for the mountains, and
	12:2	plantest them, and they T root; they grow and
	13:4	me a second time, T the waistcloth which you
	13:6	to the Euphrates, and T from there the waistcloth
	13:18	and the queen mother: T a lowly seat, for
	13:21	Will not pangs T hold of you, like those
	15:15	and visit me, and T vengeance for me on
	15:15	In thy forbearance T me not away; know that
	16:2	me: "You shall not T a wife, nor shall
	17:21	Thus says the LORD: T heed for the sake
	18:22	dug a pit to T me, and laid snares
	19:1	potter's earthen flask, and T some of the elders
	20:10	can overcome him, and T our revenge on him."
	25:15	Israel, said to me: T from my hand this
	27:20	of Babylon did not T away, when he took
	29:6	T wives and have sons and daughters; take wives
	29:6	have sons and daughters; T wives for your sons,
	30:3	fathers, and they shall T possession of it."
	32:3	Babylon, and he shall T it;
	32:5	eye; and he shall T Zedekiah to Babylon, and
	32:14	the God of Israel: T these deeds, both this
	32:24	to the city to T it, and because of
	32:28	Babylon, and he shall T it.
	34:22	fight against it, and T it, and burn it
	36:2	Jeremiah from the LORD: T a scroll and write
	36:14	to say to Baruch, T in your hand the
	36:28	LORD came to Jeremiah: T another scroll and write
	37:8	this city; they shall T it and burn it
	38:10	commanded Ebed-melech, the Ethiopian, T three
	39:7	him in fetters to T him to Babylon.
	39:12	of the guard, saying, T him, look after him
	39:14	Shaphan, that he should T him home.
	40:14	son of Nethaniah to T your life?" But Gedaliah
	40:15	Why should he T your life, so that all
	43:3	may kill us or T us into exile in
	43:9	to Jeremiah in Tahpanhes: T in your hands large
	43:10	I will send and T Nebuchadrezzar the king of
	44:12	I will T the remnant of Judah who have
	46:4	T your stations with your helmets, polish your spears,
	46:11	up to Gilead, and T balm, O virgin daughter
	50:15	vengeance of the LORD: T vengeance on her, do
	51:8	T balm for her pain; perhaps she may be
	51:11	T up the shields!
	51:36	plead your cause and T vengeance for you.
	51:44	Bel in Babylon, and T out of his mouth
Bar	4:2	Turn, O Jacob, and T her; walk toward the
	4:5	T courage, my people, O memorial of Israel!
	4:21	T courage, my children, cry to God, and he
	4:27	T courage, my children, and cry to God, for
	4:30	T courage, O Jerusalem, for he who named you
	4:34	And I will T away her pride in her
	5:1	T off the garment of your sorrow and affliction,
	6:5	So T care not to become at all like
	6:9	People T gold and make crowns for the heads
	6:10	sometimes the priests secretly T gold and silver from
	6:33	The priests T some of the clothing of their
	6:38	They cannot T pity on a widow or do
Ezek	4:1	O son of man, T a brick and lay
	4:3	And T an iron plate, and place it as
	4:9	"And you, T wheat and barley, beans and lentils,
	5:1	O son of man, T a sharp sword; use
	5:1	and your beard; then T balances for weighing, and
	5:2	third part you shall T and strike with the
	5:3	And you shall T from these a small number,
	5:4	these again you shall T some, and cast them
	7:24	of the nations to T possession of their houses;
	10:6	man clothed in linen, T fire from between the
	11:19	within them; I will T the stony heart out
	15:3	Do men T a peg from it to hang
	16:39	of your clothes and T your fair jewels, and
	16:61	be ashamed when I T your sisters, both your
	17:9	It will not T a strong arm or many
	17:22	GOD: "I myself will T a sprig from the
	18:8	lend at interest or T any increase, withholds his
	19:1	And you, T up a lamentation for the princes
	21:26	Remove the turban, and T off the crown; things
	22:12	In you men T bribes to shed blood; you
	22:12	to shed blood; you T interest and increase and
	23:26	of your clothes and T away your fine jewels.
	23:29	you in hatred, and T away all the fruit
	23:48	that all women may T warning and not commit
	24:5	T the choicest one of the flock, pile the
	24:6	T out of it piece after piece, without making
	24:8	rouse my wrath, to T vengeance, I have set
	24:16	I am about to T the delight of your
	24:25	the day when I T from them their stronghold,
	33:2	people of the land T a man from among
	33:4	the trumpet does not T warning, and the sword
	33:5	trumpet, and did not T warning; his blood shall
	35:10	mine, and we will T possession of them,–although
	36:24	For I will T you from the nations, and
	36:26	you; and I will T out of your flesh
	37:16	me: "Son of man, T a stick and write
	37:16	associated with him'; then T another stick and write
	37:19	I am about to T the stick of Joseph
	37:21	GOD: Behold, I will T the people of Israel
	38:13	silver and gold, to T away cattle and goods,
	39:10	will not need to T wood out of the
	43:20	And you shall T some of its blood, and
	43:21	You shall also T the bull of the sin
	45:18	the month, you shall T a young bull without
	45:19	The priest shall T some of the blood of
	46:2	from without, and shall T his stand by the
	46:18	The prince shall not T any of the inheritance
Dan	11:15	throw up siegeworks, and T a well-fortified city.
	11:18	the coastlands, and shall T many of them; but
	11:30	and be enraged and T action against the holy
	11:31	and fortress, and shall T away the continual burnt
	11:32	shall stand firm and T action.
	14:33	into the field to T it to the reapers.
	14:34	Lord said to Habakkuk, T the dinner which you
	14:37	T the dinner which God has sent you."
Hos	1:2	said to Hosea, "Go, T to yourself a wife
	2:9	Therefore I will T back my grain in its
	2:9	season; and I will T away my wool and
	4:11	Wine and new wine T away the understanding.
	14:2	T with you words and return to the LORD;
	14:2	LORD; say to him, T away all iniquity; accept
Amos	4:2	you, when they shall T you away with hooks,
	5:1	this word which I T up over you in
	5:11	upon the poor and T from him exactions of
	5:12	afflict the righteous, who T a bribe, and turn
	5:21	your feasts, and I T no delight in your
	5:23	T away from me the noise of your songs;
	5:26	You shall T up Sakkuth your king, and Kaiwan
	5:27	yourselves; therefore I will T you into exile beyond
	6:10	who burns him, shall T him up to bring

	9:2	there shall my hand T them; though they climb
	9:3	will search out and T them; and though they
Jon	1:12	He said to them, T me up and throw
	4:3	Therefore now, O LORD, T my life from me,
Mic	1:11	wailing of Beth-ezel shall T away from you its
	2:2	them; and houses, and T them away; they oppress
	2:4	that day they shall T up a taunt song
	2:9	their young children you T away my glory for
Nah	1:7	he knows those who T refuge in him.
	1:9	end; he will not T vengeance twice on his
	3:14	clay, tread the mortar, T hold of the brick
Hab	1:10	heap up earth and T it.
	2:1	I will T my stand to watch, and station
	2:6	Shall not all these T up their taunt against
Hag	1:8	house, that I may T pleasure in it and
	2:4	Yet now T courage, O Zerubbabel, says the LORD;
	2:4	Zerubbabel, says the LORD; T courage, O Joshua,
	2:4	Jehozadak, the high priest; T courage, all you people
	2:23	of hosts, I will T you, O Zerubbabel my
Zech	6:10	LORD came to me: T from the exiles Heldai,
	6:11	T from them silver and gold, and make a
	8:23	of every tongue shall T hold of the robe
	9:7	I will T away its blood from its mouth,
	11:15	LORD said to me, T once more the implements
	14:21	sacrifice may come and T of them and boil
Mal	2:15	So T heed to yourselves, and let none be
	2:16	So T heed to yourselves and do not be
1Mac	3:15	to help him, to T vengeance on the sons
	3:33	Lysias was also to T care of Antiochus his
	3:50	Where shall we T them?
	5:19	gave them this command, T charge of this people,
	5:27	the strongholds tomorrow and T and destroy all these
	6:3	came and tried to T the city and plunder
	6:26	citadel in Jerusalem to T it; they have fortified
	7:9	he commanded him to T vengeance on the sons
	7:38	T vengeance on this man and on his army,
	9:30	chosen you today to T his place as our
	10:20	"and you are to T our side and keep
	10:62	king gave orders to T off Jonathan's garments and
	11:37	Now therefore T care to make a copy of
	14:2	of his commanders to T him alive.
	14:42	and that he should T charge of the sanctuary
	14:42	and that he should T charge of the sanctuary,
	15:40	and invade Judea and T the people captive and
	16:3	T my place and my brother's, and go out
	16:20	sent other men to T possession of Jerusalem and
2Mac	2:1	were being deported to T some of the fire,
	2:30	every side and to T trouble with details,
	4:14	sacrifices, they hastened to T part in the unlawful
	6:15	that he may not T vengeance on us afterward
	7:5	king ordered them to T him to the fire,
	7:24	and that he would T him for his friend
	9:21	deemed it necessary to T thought for the general
	10:24	came on, intending to T Judea by storm.
	11:7	was the first to T up arms, and he
	12:35	main strength, wishing to T the accursed man alive,
	12:39	his men went to T up the bodies of
	13:4	he ordered them to T him to Beroea and
	14:9	this matter, deign to T thought for our country
	15:5	I command you to T up arms and finish
	15:16	he addressed him thus: T this holy sword, a
Mt	1:20	do not fear to T Mary your wife, for
	2:13	dream and said, "Rise, T the child and his
	2:20	in Egypt, saying, "Rise, T the child and his
	5:40	would sue you and T your coat, let him
	7:4	your brother, 'Let me T the speck out of
	7:5	You hypocrite, first T the log out of your
	7:5	will see clearly to T the speck out of
	9:2	said to the paralytic, T heart, my son; your
	9:6	to the paralytic--"Rise, T up your bed and
	9:22	seeing her he said, T heart, daughter; your faith
	10:9	T no gold, nor silver, nor copper in your
	10:38	he who does not T his cross and follow
	11:12	and men of violence T it by force.
	11:29	T my yoke upon you, and learn from me;
	14:27	spoke to them, saying, T heart, it is I;
	15:26	is not fair to T the children's bread and
	16:6	Jesus said to them, T heed and beware of
	16:24	him deny himself and T up his cross and
	17:24	kings of the earth T toll or tribute?
	17:26	cast a hook, and T the first fish that
	17:26	will find a shekel; T that and give it
	18:15	he does not listen, T one or two others
	20:14	T what belongs to you, and go; I choose
	24:4	And Jesus answered them, T heed that no one
	24:6	alarmed; for this must T place, but the end
	24:17	not go down to T what is in his
	24:18	not turn back to T his mantle.
	24:34	till all these things T place.
	25:28	So T the talent from him, and give it
	26:26	the disciples and said, T, eat; this is my
	26:52	place; for all who T the sword will perish
Mk	2:9	or to say,' Rise, T up your pallet and
	2:11	say to you, rise, T up your pallet and
	4:24	he said to them, T heed what you hear;
	6:8	He charged them to T nothing for their journey
	6:50	to them and said, T heart, it is I;
	7:26	is not right to T the children's bread and
	8:15	he cautioned them, saying, T heed, beware of the
	8:19	broken pieces did you T up?" They said to
	8:20	broken pieces did you T up?" And they said
	8:34	him deny himself and T up his cross and
	10:49	man, saying to him, T heart; rise, he is
	12:19	child, the man must T the wife, and raise
	13:5	to say to them, T heed that no one
	13:7	be alarmed; this must T place, but the end
	13:9	"But T heed to yourselves; for they will deliver
	13:15	enter his house, to T anything away;
	13:16	not turn back to T his mantle.
	13:23	But T heed; I have told you all things
	13:30	before all these things T place.
	13:33	T heed, watch and pray; for you do not
	14:22	to them, and said, T; this is my body."
	15:23	but he did not T it.
	15:24	lots for them, to decide what each should T
	15:35	Elijah will come to T him down."
Lk	1:25	looked on me, to T away my reproach among
	5:24	say to you, rise, T up your bed and
	6:42	brother, 'Brother, let me T out the speck that
	6:42	You hypocrite, first T the log out of your
	6:42	will see clearly to T out the speck that
	8:18	T heed then how you hear; for to him
	9:3	he said to them, T nothing for your journey,
	9:23	him deny himself and T up his cross daily
	10:35	to the innkeeper, saying, T care of him; and
	12:15	he said to them, T heed, and beware of
	12:19	up for many years; T your ease, eat, drink,
	14:9	begin with shame to T the lowest place.
	14:31	sit down first and T counsel whether he is
	16:6	he said to him, T your bill, and sit
	16:7	He said to him, T your bill, and write
	17:3	T heed to yourselves; if your brother sins, rebuke
	17:31	not come down to T them away; and likewise
	19:21	a severe man; you T up what you did
	19:24	those who stood by, T the pound from him,
	20:20	sincere, that they might T hold of what he
	20:28	children, the man must T the wife and raise
	21:7	this is about to T place?"
	21:8	And he said, T heed that you are not
	21:9	for this must first T place, but the end
	21:28	these things begin to T place, look up and
	21:34	"But T heed to yourselves lest your hearts be
	21:36	these things that will T place, and to stand
	22:17	given thanks he said, T this, and divide it
	22:36	who has a purse T it, and likewise a
Jn	2:8	draw some out, and T it to the steward
	2:16	who sold the pigeons, T these things away; you
	5:7	said to him, "Rise, T up your pallet, and
	5:10	me said to me, T up your pallet, and
	5:11	who said to you, T up your pallet, and
	6:15	about to come and T him by force to
	6:21	they were glad to T him into the boat,
	6:61	to them, "Do you T offense at this?
	10:17	life, that I may T it again.
	10:18	I have power to T it again; this charge
	11:39	Jesus said, T away the stone." Martha, the sister
	12:6	box he used to T what was put into
	13:19	that when it does T place you may believe
	14:3	come again and will T you to myself, that
	14:29	that when it does T place, you may believe.
	16:14	me, for he will T what is mine and
	16:15	said that he will T what is mine and
	16:22	and no one will T your joy from you.
	17:15	pray that thou shouldst T them out of the
	18:31	Pilate said to them, T him yourselves and judge
	19:6	Pilate said to them, T him yourselves and crucify
	19:38	Pilate that he might T away the body of
	20:15	him, and I will T him away."
Acts	1:20	'His office let another T
	1:25	thou hast chosen to T the place in this
	4:28	plan had predestined to T place.
	5:35	them, "Men of Israel, T care what you do

7:33 Lord said to him, T off the shoes from
15:14 visited the Gentiles, to T out of them a
15:36 And Barnabas wanted to T with them John called
15:37 thought best not to T with them one who
16:37 them come themselves and T us out."
20:13 for Assos, intending to T Paul aboard there; for
20:28 T heed to yourselves and to all the flock,
21:24 are under a vow; T these men and purify
22:5 journeyed to Damascus to T those also who were
23:10 to go down and T him by force from
23:11 by him and said, T courage, for as you
23:17 the centurions and said, T this young man to
24:15 So I always T pains to have a clear
27:22 I now bid you T heart; for there will
27:25 sail with you.' So T heart, men, for I
27:33 urged them all to T some food, saying, "Today
27:34 I urge you to T some food; it will
Rom 11:27 with them when I T away their sins."
12:17 evil for evil, but T thought for what is
16:17 to you, brethren, to T note of those who
1Cor 3:10 Let each man T care how he builds upon
6:15 Shall I therefore T the members of Christ and
8:9 Only T care lest this liberty of yours somehow
10:12 thinks that he stands T heed lest he fall.
2Cor 10:5 knowledge of God, and T every thought captive to
12:17 Did I T advantage of you through any of
12:18 Did Titus T advantage of you?
12:18 Did we not T the same steps?
Gal 5:10 Lord that you will T no other view than
5:15 and devour one another T heed that you are
Eph 5:11 T no part in the unfruitful works of darkness,
6:13 Therefore T the whole armor of God, that you
6:17 And T the helmet of salvation, and the sword
1Thes 4:4 you know how to T a wife for himself
1Tim 4:16 T heed to yourself and to your teaching; hold
6:7 world, and we cannot T anything out of the
6:12 fight of the faith; T hold of the eternal
6:19 so that they may T hold of the life
Heb 3:12 T care, brethren, lest there be in any of
5:4 And one does not T the honor upon himself,
7:5 in the law to T tithes from the people,
10:4 bulls and goats should T away sins.
10:11 sacrifices, which can never T away sins.
Jas 5:10 suffering and patience, brethren, T the prophets who
1Pet 2:20 beaten for it you T it patiently?
2:20 suffer for it you T it patiently, you have
1Jn 3:5 that he appeared to T away sins, and in
Rev 1:1 servants what must soon T place; and he made
1:19 and what is to T place hereafter.
4:1 show you what must T place after this."
5:9 "Worthy art thou to T the scroll and to
6:4 rider was permitted to T peace from the earth,
10:8 me again, saying, "Go, T the scroll which is
10:9 he said to me, T it and eat; it
18:4 my people, lest you T part in her sins,
22:6 servants what must soon T place.
22:17 let him who desires T the water of life
22:19 this prophecy, God will T away his share in

TAKEN (333)

Gen 2:22 the LORD God had T from the man he
2:23 Woman, because she was T out of Man."
3:19 of it you were T; you are dust, and
3:23 to till the ground from which he was T
4:15 Cain, vengeance shall be T on him sevenfold." And
12:15 And the woman was T into Pharaoh's house.
14:14 his kinsman had been T captive, he led forth
18:27 answered, "Behold, I have T upon myself to speak
18:31 said, "Behold, I have T upon myself to speak
20:3 woman whom you have T; for she is a
25:26 and his hand had T hold of Esau's heel;
27:35 guile, and he has T away your blessing."
27:36 behold, now he has T away my blessing." Then
30:15 matter that you have T away my husband?
30:23 and said, "God has T away my reproach";
31:1 were saying, "Jacob has T all that was our
31:9 Thus God has T away the cattle of your
31:16 property which God has T away from our father
31:34 Now Rachel had T the household gods and put
39:1 Now Joseph was T down to Egypt, and Potiphar,
43:34 Portions were T to them from Joseph's table, but
Ex 14:11 Egypt that you have T us away to die
18:2 Moses' father-in-law, had T Zipporah, Moses' wife,
25:15 they shall not be T from it.
Lev 4:10 (just as these are T from the ox of
7:34 is offered I have T from the people of
14:43 house, after he has T out the stones and
Num 3:12 Moses, "Behold, I have T the Levites from among
5:13 since she was not T in the act;
8:16 of Israel, I have T them for myself.
8:18 myself, and I have T the Levites instead of
9:17 whenever the cloud was T up from over the
9:21 when the cloud was T up in the morning,
9:21 when the cloud was T up they set out.
9:22 but when it was T up they set out.
10:11 month, the cloud was T up from over the
10:17 when the tabernacle was T down, the sons of
16:15 I have not T one ass from them, and
18:6 And behold, I have T your brethren the Levites
19:3 and she shall be T outside the camp and
21:26 king of Moab and T all his land out
27:4 of our father be T away from his family,
31:26 the booty that was T, both of man and
31:53 men of war had T booty, every man for
36:3 their inheritance will be T from the inheritance of
36:3 so it will be T away from the lot
36:4 their inheritance will be T from the inheritance of
Deut 4:20 But the LORD has T you, and brought you
20:7 wife and has not T her?
24:5 be happy with his wife whom he has T
26:1 an inheritance, and have T possession of it, and
28:31 ass shall be violently T away before your face,
Josh 2:4 But the woman had T the two men and
7:11 commanded them; they have T some of the devoted
7:15 And he who is T with the devoted things
7:16 tribe of Judah was T;
7:17 of the Zerahites was T; and he brought near
7:17 man, and Zabdi was T;
7:18 of Zerah, of the tribe of Judah, was T
8:8 And when you have T the city, you shall
8:21 that the ambush had T the city, and that
10:1 heard how Joshua had T Ai, and had utterly
21:43 their fathers; and having T possession of it, they
Judg 14:9 them that he had T the honey from the
15:6 Timnite, because he has T his wife and given
17:2 of silver which were T from you, about which
20:12 is this that has T place among you?
21:5 For they had T a great oath concerning him
1Sam 7:14 the Philistines had T from Israel were restored
10:20 tribe of Benjamin was T by lot.
10:21 of the Matrites was T by lot; finally he
10:21 son of Kish was T by lot.
12:3 Whose ox have I T
12:3 Or whose ass have I T
12:3 whose hand have I T a bribe to blind
12:4 or oppressed us or T anything from any man's
14:41 Jonathan and Saul were T, but the people escaped.
14:42 And Jonathan was T
14:47 When Saul had T the kingship over Israel, he
21:6 the day it is T away.
28:21 to you; I have T my life in my
30:2 it with fire, and T captive the women and
30:3 and sons and daughters T captive.
30:5 wives also had been T captive, Ahino-am of Jezreel,
30:16 And when he had T him down, behold, they
30:16 great spoil they had T from the land of
30:18 that the Amalekites had T; and David rescued his
30:19 anything that had been T; David brought back all.
2Sam 2:8 of Saul's army, had T Ish-bosheth the son of
12:9 the sword, and have T his wife to be
12:10 despised me, and have T the wife of Uriah
12:27 Rabbah; moreover, I have T the city of waters.
18:18 in his lifetime had T and set up for
20:13 When he was T out of the highway, all
23:6 for they cannot be T with the hand;
1Kgs 4:15 in Naphtali (he had T Basemath the daughter of
7:8 daughter whom he had T in marriage.
15:14 high places were not T away.
16:18 that the city was T, he went into the
21:19 you killed, and also T possession?"' And you shall
22:43 high places were not T away, and the people
2Kgs 2:9 you, before I am T from you." And Elisha
2:10 as I am being T from you, it shall
4:13 her, See, you have T all this trouble for
6:22 those whom you have T captive with your sword
12:3 high places were not T away; the people continued
13:25 cities which he had T from Jehoahaz his father
15:4 high places were not T away; the people still
18:10 year of Hoshea king of Israel, Samaria was T
20:18 to you, shall be T away; and they shall
24:7 king of Babylon had T all that belonged to
25:21 So Judah was T into exile out of its

T

1Chr 9:1 And Judah was T into exile in Babylon because
9:28 were brought in and T out.
2Chr 2:17 David his father had T; and there were found
15:8 cities which he had T in the hill country
15:17 high places were not T out of Israel.
17:2 cities of Ephraim which Asa his father had T
20:21 And when he had T counsel with the people,
20:33 places, however, were not T away; the people had
28:11 kinsfolk whom you have T, for the fierce wrath
28:18 Judah, and had T Beth-shemesh, Aijalon, Gederoth,
30:2 assembly in Jerusalem had T counsel to keep the
32:12 not this same Hezekiah T away his high places
Ezra 2:61 of Barzillai (who had T a wife from the
5:14 God, which Nebuchadnezzar had T out of the temple
9:2 For they have T some of their daughters to
10:14 our cities who have T foreign wives come at
Neh 6:18 his son Jehohanan had T the daughter of Meshullam
7:63 of Barzillai (who had T a wife of the
Tob 1:2 of the Assyrians, was T into captivity from Thisbe,
3:6 my spirit to be T up, that I may
3:15 me and pity be T upon me, and that
Jud 6:9 they will not be T, do not look downcast!
6:17 told them what had T place at the council
8:27 hearts, nor has he T revenge upon us; but
15:4 to tell what had T place and to urge
Esth 2:8 Hegai, Esther also was T into the king's palace
2:16 And when Esther was T to King Ahasuerus into
8:2 ring, which he had T from Haman, and gave
Job 1:21 and the LORD has T away; blessed be the
19:9 me my glory, and T the crown from my
27:2 God lives, who has T away my right, and
28:2 Iron is T out of the earth, and copper
30:16 days of affliction have T hold of me.
34:5 innocent, and God has T away my right;
34:20 and the mighty are T away by no human
Ps 31:7 my affliction, thou hast T heed of my adversities,
82:1 God has T his place in the divine council;
102:10 anger; for thou hast T me up and thrown
Prov 11:6 but the treacherous are T captive by their lust.
22:27 should your bed be T from under you?
24:11 those who are being T away to death; hold
Eccl 3:14 to it, nor anything T from it; God has
5:8 justice and right violently T away, do not be
7:26 but the sinner is T by her.
9:12 Like fish which are T in an evil net,
Wis 4:10 among sinners he was T up.
14:15 who had been suddenly T from him; and he
15:8 from which he was T, when he is required
Sir 3:26 plant of wickedness has T root in him.
31:7 every fool will be T captive by it.
42:21 can be added or T away, and he needs
44:17 the Lord, and was T up; he was an
44:18 of wrath he was T in exchange; therefore a
44:21 Most High, and was T into covenant with him;
46:19 anointed: "I have not T any one's property, not
48:9 You who were T up by a whirlwind of
49:14 earth, for he was T up from the earth.
Is 3:13 The LORD has T his place to contend, he
6:6 coal which he had T with tongs from the
6:7 lips; your guilt is T away, and your sin
8:15 and be broken; they shall be snared and T
16:10 joy and gladness are T away from the fruitful
22:8 He has T away the covering of Judah.
28:9 from the milk, those T from the breast?
28:13 fall backward, and be broken, and snared, and T
28:15 in falsehood we have T shelter";
39:7 to you, shall be T away; and they shall
40:24 scarcely has their stem T root in the earth,
42:6 in righteousness, I have T you by the hand
49:24 Can the prey be T from the mighty, or
49:25 the mighty shall be T, and the prey of
51:22 people: "Behold, I have T from your hand the
52:5 that my people are T away for nothing?
53:8 and judgment he was T away; and as for
57:1 heart; devout men are T away, while no one
57:1 the righteous man is T away from calamity,
Jer 6:11 and wife shall be T, the old folk and
6:24 fall helpless; anguish has T hold of us, pain
8:9 shall be dismayed and T; lo, they have rejected
8:21 mourn, and dismay has T hold on me.
13:17 LORD's flock has been T captive.
13:19 them; all Judah is T into exile, wholly taken
13:19 taken into exile, wholly T into exile.
16:5 them; for I have T away my peace from
24:1 king of Babylon had T into exile from Jerusalem
29:1 people, whom Nebuchadnezzar had T into exile from
38:3 army of the king of Babylon and be T
38:28 the guard until the day that Jerusalem was T
39:3 When Jerusalem was T, all the princes of the
39:5 and when they had T him, they brought him
40:7 who had not been T into exile to Babylon,
40:10 and dwell in your cities that you have T
48:1 to shame, it is T; the fortress is put
48:7 you also shall be T; and Chemosh shall go
48:33 and joy have been T away from the fruitful
48:41 the cities shall be T and the strongholds seized.
48:46 your sons have been T captive, and your daughters
49:24 anguish and sorrows have T hold of her, as
49:29 their flocks shall be T, their curtains and all
50:2 and say: 'Babylon is T, Bel is put to
50:9 themselves against her; from there she shall be T
50:24 you and you were T, O Babylon, and you
51:26 No stone shall be T from you for a
51:31 that his city is T on every side;
51:41 "How Babylon is T, the praise of the whole
51:56 Babylon; her warriors are T, their bows are broken
Lam 3:58 not fear!' "Thou hast T up my cause, O
4:20 the LORD's anointed, was T in their pits, he
Bar 2:17 whose spirit has been T from their bodies, will
3:29 up into heaven, and T her, and brought her
4:20 I have T off the robe of peace and
4:26 rough roads; they were T away like a flock
6:1 who were to be T to Babylon as captives
6:2 God, you will be T to Babylon as captives
Ezek 12:13 and he shall be T in my snare; and
14:3 man, these men have T their idols into their
15:3 Is wood T from it to make anything?
17:13 the land he had T away,
17:20 and he shall be T in my snare, and
19:4 against him; he was T in their pit; and
19:8 over him; he was T in their pit.
21:24 remembrance, you shall be T in them.
22:25 human lives; they have T treasure and precious
33:5 But if he had T warning, he would have
33:6 them; that man is T away in his iniquity,
33:15 back what he has T by robbery, and walks
Dan 5:2 Nebuchadnezzar his father had T out of the temple
5:3 vessels which had been T out of the temple,
5:20 and his glory was T from him;
6:23 commanded that Daniel be T up out of the
6:23 So Daniel was T up out of the den,
7:12 beasts, their dominion was T away, but their lives
7:26 his dominion shall be T away, to be consumed
8:11 continual burnt offering was T away from him, and
11:12 when the multitude is T, his heart shall be
12:11 continual burnt offering is T away, and the
Hos 4:3 of the sea are T away.
13:11 anger, and I have T them away in my
Joel 3:5 For you have T my silver and my gold,
Amos 2:8 every altar upon garments T in pledge; and in
3:4 den, if he has T nothing?
3:5 ground, when it has T nothing?
6:13 by our own strength T Karnaim for ourselves?"
Zeph 3:15 The LORD has T away the judgments against you,
Zech 3:4 said, "Behold, I have T your iniquity away from
14:1 coming, when the spoil T from you will be
14:2 the city shall be T and the houses plundered
Mal 1:13 bring what has been T by violence or is
1Mac 2:11 her adornment has been T away; no longer free,
2:58 for the law was T up into heaven.
3:45 Joy was T from Jacob; the flute and the
6:6 spoils which they had T from the armies they
9:72 whom he had formerly T from the land of
10:33 one of the Jews T as a captive from
10:52 my kingdom and have T my seat on the
10:53 us, and we have T our seat on the
10:84 and those who had T refuge in it he
15:29 land, and you have T possession of many places
15:33 reply: "We have neither T foreign land nor seized
15:33 time had been unjustly T by our enemies.
2Mac 5:5 the city was being T, Menelaus took refuge in
6:7 birthday, the Jews were T, under bitter constraint, to
7:27 your life, and have T care of you.
12:6 massacred those who had T refuge there.
14:2 a fleet, and had T possession of the country,
Mt 9:15 when the bridegroom is T away from them, and
13:12 he has will be T away.
18:30 servants saw what had T place, they were greatly
18:30 lord all that had T place.
21:21 to this mountain, 'Be T up and cast into
21:43 of God will be T away from you and
23:29 we would not have T part with them in

24:40 the field; one is T and one is left.
24:41 the mill; one is T and one is left.
25:29 he has will be T away.
26:56 But all this has T place, that the scriptures
28:11 priests all that had T place.
28:12 with the elders and T counsel, they gave a
Mk 2:20 when the bridegroom is T away from them, and
4:25 he has will be T away."
6:46 And after he had T leave of them, he
11:23 to this mountain, 'Be T up and cast into
16:19 spoken to them, was T up into heaven, and
Lk 5:9 fish which they had T;
5:35 when the bridegroom is T away from them, and
8:18 he has will be T away."
10:42 which shall not be T away from her."
11:52 for you have T away the key of knowledge;
17:34 bed; one will be T and the other left.
17:35 together; one will be T and the other left."
19:26 he has will be T away.
21:32 away till all has T place.
23:46 centurion saw what had T place, he praised God,
23:47 they saw what had T place, returned home beating
Jn 2:20 then said, "It has T forty-six years to build
13:12 washed their feet, and T his garments, and resumed
19:31 that they might be T away.
20:1 the stone had been T away from the tomb.
20:2 to them, "They have T the Lord out of
20:13 them, "Because they have T away my Lord, and
Acts 1:2 day when he was T up, after he had
1:11 This Jesus, who was T up from you into
1:22 day when he was T up from us--one
8:33 For his life is T up from the earth."
10:16 and the thing was T up at once to
17:9 And when they had T security from Jason and
20:9 third story and was T up dead.
27:33 and without food, having T nothing.
28:9 And when this had T place, the rest of
2Cor 3:14 through Christ is it T away.
7:2 no one, we have T advantage of no one.
Col 4:9 of everything that has T place here.
1Tim 3:16 on in the world, T up in glory.
Heb 10:6 sin offerings thou hast T no pleasure.
10:8 hast neither desired nor T pleasure in sacrifices and
11:5 By faith Enoch was T up so that he
11:5 found, because God had T him.
11:5 Now before he was T he was attested as
Rev 5:8 And when he had T the scroll, the four
11:17 wast, that thou hast T thy great power and
13:10 one is to be T captive, to captivity he

TAKES (85)

Ex 20:7 hold him guiltless who T his name in vain.
21:10 If he T another wife to himself, he shall
Lev 17:13 sojourn among them, who T in hunting any beast
20:14 If a man T a wife and her mother
20:17 "If a man T his sister, a daughter of
20:21 If a man T his brother's wife, it is
Num 6:21 for the Nazirite who T a vow.
6:21 the vow which he T, so shall he do
Deut 5:11 hold him guiltless who T his name in vain.
10:17 is not partial and T no bribe.
22:13 "If any man T a wife, and goes in
24:1 "When a man T a wife and marries her,
27:25 "'Cursed be he who T a bribe to slay
32:41 sword, and my hand T hold on judgment, I
32:43 of his servants, and T vengeance on his adversaries,
Josh 7:14 tribe which the LORD T shall come near by
7:14 family which the LORD T shall come near by
7:14 household which the LORD T shall come near man
15:16 "Whoever smites Kiriath-sepher, and T it, to him will
Judg 1:12 who attacks Kiriath-sepher and T it, I will give
19:18 my home; and nobody T me into his house.
1Sam 17:26 kills this Philistine, and T away the reproach from
Job 5:5 hungry eat, and he T it even out of
5:13 He T the wise in their own craftiness; and
12:20 who are trusted, and T away the discernment of
12:24 He T away understanding from the chiefs of the
27:8 him off, when God T away his life?
30:17 pain that gnaws me T no rest.
Ps 15:3 to his friend, nor T up a reproach against
34:8 is the man who T refuge in him!
40:17 needy; but the Lord T thought for me.
57:1 in thee my soul T refuge; in the shadow
137:9 shall he be who T your little ones and
142:4 there is none who T notice of me; no
147:11 man; but the LORD T pleasure in those who
149:4 For the LORD T pleasure in his people; he
Prov 1:19 gain by violence; it T away the life of
6:34 not spare when he T revenge.
8:2 in the paths she T her stand;
9:14 of her house, she T a seat on the
11:30 of life, but lawlessness T away lives.
16:32 spirit than he who T a city.
18:2 A fool T no pleasure in understanding, but only
23:5 gone; for suddenly it T to itself wings, flying
25:20 is like one who T off a garment on
26:17 is like one who T a passing dog by
Eccl 8:14 is a vanity which T place on earth, that
Wis 5:15 Lord; the Most High T care of them.
6:7 and great, and he T thought for all alike.
13:13 full of knots, he T and carves with care
13:16 So he T thought for it, that it may
Sir 25:1 My soul T pleasure in three things, and they
25:17 Her husband T his meals among the neighbors, and
28:1 He that T vengeance will suffer vengeance from the
35:18 the nations; till he T away the multitude of
38:7 them he heals and T away pain;
Is 3:6 When a man T hold of his brother in
40:15 the scales; behold, he T up the isles like
44:15 for a man; he T a part of it
57:13 But he who T refuge in me shall possess
65:16 truth, and he who T an oath in the
Jer 4:29 and archer every city T to flight; they enter
Ezek 14:4 house of Israel who T his idols into his
18:13 lends at interest, and T increase; shall he then
18:17 his hand from iniquity, T no interest or increase,
33:4 the sword comes and T him away, his blood
33:6 the sword comes, and T any one of them;
Nah 1:2 and wrathful; the LORD T vengeance on his
1Mac 10:43 And whoever T refuge at the temple in Jerusalem,
Mt 11:6 blessed is he who T no offense at me."
Mk 4:15 Satan immediately comes and T away the word
Lk 6:29 and from him who T away your coat do
6:30 and of him who T away your goods do
7:23 blessed is he who T no offense at me."
8:12 the devil comes and T away the word from
11:22 and overcomes him, he T away his armor in
Jn 1:29 Lamb of God, who T away the sin of
10:18 No one T it from me, but I lay
13:19 this now, before it T place, that when it
14:29 told you before it T place, so that when
15:2 bears no fruit, he T away, and every branch
2Cor 11:20 preys upon you, or T advantage of you, or
2Thes 2:4 worship, so that he T his seat in the
Heb 9:17 For a will T effect only at death, since
Rev 22:19 and if any one T away from the words

TAKEST (2)

Ps 104:29 are dismayed; when thou T away their breath, they
Is 58:3 humbled ourselves, and thou T no knowledge of it?'

TAKING (66)

Gen 24:10 master's camels and departed, T all sorts of choice
28:11 T one of the stones of the place, he
38:19 and went away, and T off her veil she
Ex 17:5 on before the people, T with you some of
Lev 3:9 the fat tail entire, T it away close by
Num 3:40 month old and upward, T their number by names.
Deut 7:3 to their sons or T their daughters for your
24:6 for he would be T a life in pledge.
Judg 4:6 men at Mount Tabor, T ten thousand from the
18:27 And T what Micah had made, and the priest
1Sam 25:26 from bloodguilt, and from T vengeance with your
25:31 or for my lord T vengeance himself.
2Sam 4:5 Ish-bosheth, as he was T his noonday rest.
2Kgs 5:5 So he went, T with him ten talents of
2Chr 19:7 God, or partiality, or T bribes."
20:25 were three days in T the spoil, it was
Neh 13:6 While this was T place I was not in
Tob 1:6 T the first fruits and the tithes of my
7:13 his daughter Sarah, and T her by the hand
8:7 Lord, I am not T this sister of mine
Job 5:3 have seen the fool T root, but suddenly I
Prov 7:8 street near her corner, T the road to her
Sir 26:7 ox yoke which chafes; T hold of her is
41:21 of a kinsman; of T away some one's portion
Is 3:1 LORD of hosts, is T away from Jerusalem and
Ezek 14:7 separates himself from me, T his idols into his
25:12 has grievously offended in T vengeance upon them,
Dan 13:48 T his stand in the midst of them, he
Zech 5:10 me, "Where are they T the ephah?"
1Mac 1:24 T them all, he departed to his own land.

11:24 the king at Ptolemais, T silver and gold and
2Mac 1:11 thank him greatly for T our side against the
4:34 Menelaus, T Andronicus aside, urged him to kill
4:46 Therefore Ptolemy, T the king aside into a colonnade
12:43 well and honorably, T account of the resurrection.
Mt 14:19 on the grass; and T the five loaves and
26:37 And T with him Peter and the two sons
26:45 you still sleeping and T your rest?
27:6 But the chief priests, T the pieces of silver,
Mk 5:41 T her by the hand he said to her,
6:41 And T the five loaves and the two fish
7:32 And T him aside from the multitude privately, he
9:36 midst of them; and T him in his arms,
10:32 And T the twelve again, he began to tell
13:29 you see these things T place, you know that
14:41 you still sleeping and T your rest?
15:45 a linen shroud, and T him down, wrapped him
Lk 8:54 But T her by the hand he called, saying,
9:16 And T the five loaves and the two fish
16:3 since my master is T the stewardship away from
18:31 And T the twelve, he said to them, "Behold,
19:22 was a severe man, T up what I did
21:31 you see these things T place, you know that
24:1 went to the tomb, T the spices which they
Jn 11:13 thought that he meant T rest in sleep.
Acts 17:5 Jews were jealous, and T some wicked fellows of
18:21 he declined; but on T leave of them he
19:9 he withdrew from them, T the disciples with him,
2Cor 8:4 for the favor of T part in the relief
Gal 2:1 to Jerusalem with Barnabas, T Titus along with me.
Eph 6:16 peace; besides all these, T the shield of faith,
Phil 2:7 grasped, but emptied himself, T the form of a
Col 2:18 and worship of angels, T his stand on visions,
1Thes 2:7 you, like a nurse T care of her children.
Heb 9:7 year, and not without T blood which he offers
9:12 into the Holy Place, T not the blood of

TALE (3)

Sir 22:6 in mourning is a T told at the wrong
Dan 13:27 the elders told their T, the servants were greatly
Lk 24:11 to them an idle T, and they did not

TALEBEARER

Prov 11:13 goes about as a T reveals secrets, but he

TALENT (14)

Ex 25:39 Of a T of pure gold shall it be
37:24 its utensils of a T of pure gold.
38:27 the hundred talents, a T for a base.
2Sam 12:30 of it was a T of gold, and in
1Kgs 20:39 you shall pay a T of silver.'
2Kgs 5:22 pray, give them a T of silver and two
23:33 of silver and a T of gold.
1Chr 20:2 that it weighed a T of gold, and in
2Chr 36:3 of silver and a T of gold.
2Mac 8:11 ninety slaves for a T, not expecting the judgment
Mt 25:18 had received the one T went and dug in
25:24 received the one T came forward, saying, 'Master,
25:25 went and hid your T in the ground.
25:28 So take the T from him, and give it

TALENTS (67)

Ex 38:24 the offering, was twenty-nine T and seven hundred
38:25 numbered was a hundred T and a thousand seven
38:27 The hundred T of silver were for casting the
38:27 bases for the hundred T, a talent for a
38:29 was contributed was seventy T, and two thousand and
1Kgs 9:14 one hundred and twenty T of gold.
9:28 four hundred and twenty T; and they brought it
10:10 a hundred and twenty T of gold, and a
10:14 six hundred and sixty-six T of gold,
16:24 from Shemer for two T of silver; and he
2Kgs 5:5 taking with him ten T of silver, six thousand
5:23 And Naaman said, "Be pleased to accept two T
5:23 and tied up two T of silver in two
15:19 gave Pul a thousand T of silver, that he
18:14 of Judah three hundred T of silver and thirty
18:14 of silver and thirty T of gold.
23:33 tribute of a hundred T of silver and a
1Chr 19:6 Ammonites sent a thousand T of silver to hire
22:14 LORD a hundred thousand T of gold, a million
22:14 of gold, a million T of silver, and bronze
29:4 my God: three thousand T of gold, of the
29:4 Ophir, and seven thousand T of refined silver, for
29:7 of God five thousand T and ten thousand darics
29:7 of gold, ten thousand T of silver, eighteen thousand
29:7 of silver, eighteen thousand T of bronze, and a
29:7 and a hundred thousand T of iron.
2Chr 3:8 it with six hundred T of fine gold.
8:18 four hundred and fifty T of gold and brought
9:9 a hundred and twenty T of gold, and a
9:13 six hundred and sixty-six T of gold,
25:6 Israel for a hundred T of silver.
25:9 do about the hundred T which I have given
27:5 that year a hundred T of silver, and ten
36:3 tribute of a hundred T of silver and a
Ezra 7:22 up to a hundred T of silver, a hundred
8:26 six hundred and fifty T of silver, and silver
8:26 vessels worth a hundred T, and a hundred talents
8:26 talents, and a hundred T of gold,
Tob 1:14 Media I left ten T of silver in trust
4:20 you about the ten T of silver which I
Esth 3:9 will pay ten thousand T of silver into the
1Mac 11:28 from tribute, and promised him three hundred T
13:16 Send now a hundred T of silver and two
13:19 sons and the hundred T, but Trypho broke his
15:31 for them five hundred T of silver, and for
15:31 the cities, five hundred T more.
15:35 for them we will give you a hundred T
2Mac 3:11 in all four hundred T of silver and two
4:8 three hundred and sixty T of silver and, from
4:8 silver and, from another source of revenue, eighty T
4:24 Jason by three hundred T of silver.
5:21 carried off eighteen hundred T from the temple, and
8:10 the Romans, two thousand T, by selling the captured
Mt 18:23 owed him ten thousand T;
25:15 one he gave five T, to another two, to
25:16 had received the five T went at once and
25:16 and he made five T more.
25:17 who had the two T made two talents more.
25:17 two talents made two T more.
25:20 had received the five T came forward, bringing five
25:20 came forward, bringing five T more, saying, 'Master,
25:20 delivered to me five T; here I have made
25:20 I have made five T more.'
25:22 who had the two T came forward, saying, 'Master,
25:22 delivered to me two T; here I have made
25:22 I have made two T more.'
25:28 give it to him who has the ten T

TALITHA

Mk 5:41 he said to her, T cumi"; which means, "Little

TALK (43)

Num 11:17 will come down and T with you there; and
Deut 6:7 your children, and shall T of them when you
1Sam 2:3 T no more so very proudly, let not arrogance
2Kgs 9:11 to them, "You know the fellow and his T
Jud 2:1 first month, there was T in the palace of
Job 11:2 a man full of T be vindicated?
15:3 he argue in unprofitable T, or in words with
19:18 when I rise they T against me.
35:16 his mouth in empty T, he multiplies words without
Ps 64:5 their evil purpose; they T of laying snares secretly,
69:12 I am the T of those who sit in
71:24 And my tongue will T of thy righteous help
Prov 4:25 speech, and put devious T far from you.
6:22 you awake, they will T with you.
7:21 him; with her smooth T she compels him.
14:3 The T of a fool is a rod for
14:23 is profit, but mere T tends only to want.
24:2 violence, and their lips T of mischief.
Eccl 10:13 the end of his T is wicked madness.
Sir 13:11 test you through much T, and while he smiles
21:18 and the knowledge of the ignorant is unexamined T
22:11 Do not T much with a foolish man, and
27:11 The T of the godly man is always wise,
27:13 The T of fools is offensive, and their laughter
27:14 The T of men given to swearing makes one's
32:4 do not pour out T; do not display your
38:25 their work, and whose T is about bulls?
Ezek 33:30 man, your people who T together about you by
36:3 and you became the T and evil gossip of
Dan 10:17 can my lord's servant T with my lord?
2Mac 8:7 And T of his valor spread everywhere.
Mt 22:15 took counsel how to entangle him in his T
Mk 1:45 out and began to T freely about it, and
12:13 of the Herodi-ans, to entrap him in his T
Jn 14:30 I will no longer T much with you, for
1Cor 4:19 find out not the T of these arrogant people
4:20 does not consist in T but in power.
Eph 4:29 Let no evil T come out of your mouths,

5:4 no filthiness, nor silly T, nor levity, which are
Col 3:8 malice, slander, and foul T from your mouth.
2Tim 2:17 more ungodliness, and their T will eat its way
2Jn 1:12 to see you and T with you face to
3Jn 1:14 soon, and we will T together face to face.

TALKATIVE

Sir 20:4 wise, while another is detested for being too T

TALKED (29)

Gen 45:15 after that his brothers T with him.
Ex 20:22 yourselves that I have T with you from heaven.
34:31 to him, and Moses T with them.
Judg 14:7 he went down and T with the woman; and
1Sam 17:23 As he T with them, behold, the champion, the
2Kgs 2:11 still went on and T, behold, a chariot of
22:14 Second Quarter); and they T with her.
Tob 7:8 those things which you T about on the journey,
Jer 29:32 LORD, for he has T rebellion against the LORD.'"
Zech 1:9 lord?' The angel who T with me said to
1:13 to the angel who T with me.
1:14 So the angel who T with me said to
1:19 to the angel who T with me, "What are
2:3 behold, the angel who T with me came forward,
4:1 And the angel who T with me came again,
4:4 to the angel who T with me, "What are
4:5 Then the angel who T with me answered me,
5:5 Then the angel who T with me came forward
5:10 to the angel who T with me, "Where are
6:4 to the angel who T with me, "What are
1Mac 3:26 king, and the Gentiles T of the battles of
14:9 the streets; they all T together of good things;
Lk 1:65 all these things were T about through all the
9:30 And behold, two men T with him, Moses and
24:32 within us while he T to us on the
Acts 10:27 And as he T with him, he went in
20:7 to break bread, Paul T with them, intending to
20:9 deep sleep as Paul T still longer; and being
Rev 21:15 And he who T to me had a measuring

TALKERS

Tit 1:9 insubordinate men, empty T and deceivers, especially

TALKING (15)

Gen 17:22 When he had finished T with him, God went
Ex 34:29 because he had been T with God.
Deut 11:19 them to your children, T of them when you
1Sam 14:19 And while Saul was T to the priest, the
2Kgs 8:4 Now the king was T with Gehazi the servant
Esth 6:14 While they were yet T with him, the king's
Job 29:9 the princes refrained from T, and laid their hand
Is 58:13 your own pleasure, or T idly;
Mt 17:3 them Moses and Elijah, T with him.
Mk 9:4 Moses; and they were T to Jesus.
Lk 24:14 miles from Jerusalem, and T with each other about
24:15 While they were T and discussing together, Jesus
Jn 4:27 marveled that he was T with a woman, but
4:27 or, "Why are you T with her?"
2Cor 11:23 better one--I am T like a madman--with

TALL (12)

Deut 2:10 great and many, and T as the Anakim;
2:21 great and many, and T as the Anakim; but
9:2 a people great and T, the sons of the
1Chr 11:23 Egyptian, a man of great stature, five cubits T
Jud 16:7 smite him, nor did T giants set upon him;
Sir 24:13 I grew T like a cedar in Lebanon, and
24:14 I grew T like a palm tree in En-ge'di,
24:14 field, and like a plane tree I grew T
Is 18:2 messengers, to a nation, T and smooth, to a
18:7 hosts from a people T and smooth, from a
Ezek 16:7 grew up and became T and arrived at full
31:4 deep made it grow T, making its rivers flow

TALLER (4)

Deut 1:28 people are greater and T than we; the cities
1Sam 9:2 shoulders upward he was T than any of the
10:23 the people, he was T than any of the
1Mac 6:43 It was T than all the others, and he

TALLEST (2)

2Kgs 19:23 Lebanon; I felled its T cedars, its choicest cypresses;
Is 37:24 Lebanon; I felled its T cedars, its choicest cypresses;

TALMAI (6)

Num 13:22 and Ahiman, Sheshai, and T, the descendants of
Anak,
Josh 15:14 Sheshai and Ahiman and T, the descendants of Anak.
Judg 1:10 and they defeated Sheshai and Ahiman and T
2Sam 3:3 Maacah the daughter of T king of Geshur;
13:37 fled, and went to T the son of Ammihud,
1Chr 3:2 Maacah, the daughter of T, king of Geshur; the

TALMON (5)

1Chr 9:17 gatekeepers were: Shallum, Akkub, T, Ahiman, and
Ezra 2:42 Ater, the sons of T, the sons of Akkub,
Neh 7:45 Ater, the sons of T, the sons of Akkub,
11:19 The gatekeepers, Akkub, T and their brethren, who
12:25 Bakbukiah, Obadiah, Meshullam, T, and Akkub were

TAMAR (27)

Gen 38:6 for Er his first-born, and her name was T
38:11 Then Judah said to T his daughter-in-law, "Remain a
38:11 So T went and dwelt in her father's house.
38:13 And when T was told, "Your father-in-law is going
38:24 Judah was told, T your daughter-in-law has played
Ruth 4:12 house of Perez, whom T bore to Judah, because
2Sam 13:1 sister, whose name was T; and after a time
13:2 because of his sister T; for she was a
13:4 to him, "I love T, my brother Absalom's sister."
13:5 him, 'Let my sister T come and give me
13:6 "Pray let my sister T come and make a
13:7 David sent home to T, saying, "Go to your
13:8 So T went to her brother Amnon's house, where
13:10 Then Amnon said to T, "Bring the food into
13:10 And T took the cakes she had made, and
13:19 And T put ashes on her head, and rent
13:20 So T dwelt, a desolate woman, in her brother
13:22 hated Amnon, because he had forced his sister T
13:32 determined from the day he forced his sister T
14:27 daughter whose name was T; she was a beautiful
1Kgs 9:18 Beth-horon and Baalath and T in the wilderness, in
1Chr 2:4 daughter-in-law T also bore him Perez and Zerah.
3:9 of the concubines; and T was their sister.
Ezek 47:18 to the eastern sea and as far as T
47:19 it shall run from T as far as the
48:28 boundary shall run from T to the waters of
Mt 1:3 Perez and Zerah by T, and Perez the father

TAMARISK (3)

Gen 21:33 Abraham planted a T tree in Beer-sheba, and called
1Sam 22:6 at Gibe-ah, under the T tree on the height,
31:13 buried them under the T tree in Jabesh, and

TAMBOURINE (3)

Gen 31:27 mirth and songs, with T and lyre?
1Sam 10:5 high place with harp, T, flute, and lyre before
Job 21:12 They sing to the T and the lyre, and

TAMBOURINES (5)

2Sam 6:5 lyres and harps and T and castanets and cymbals.
1Chr 13:8 lyres and harps and T and cymbals and trumpets.
Jud 3:7 about welcomed him with garlands and dances and T
16:2 to my God with T, sing to my Lord
1Mac 9:39 to meet them with T and musicians and many

TAME

Jas 3:8 no human being can T the tongue--a restless

TAMED (2)

Jas 3:7 sea creature, can be T and has been tamed
3:7 tamed and has been T by humankind,

TAMMUZ

Ezek 8:14 LORD; and behold, there sat women weeping for T

TAMPER

2Cor 4:2 practice cunning or to T with God's word, but

TANGLED

Esth 14:2 she covered with her T hair.

TANHUMETH (2)

2Kgs 25:23 the son of T the Netophathite, and Ja-azaniah
Jer 40:8 Seraiah the son of T, the sons of Ephai

TANIS

Jud 1:10 of Goshen, even beyond T and Memphis, and all

TANNED (6)

Ex 25:5 linen, goats' hair, T rams' skins, goatskins, acacia
26:14 tent a covering of T rams' skins and goatskins.

35:7 twined linen; goats' hair, T rams' skins, and goatskins;
35:23 or goats' hair or T rams' skins or goatskins,
36:19 tent a covering of T rams' skins and goatskins.
39:34 bases; the covering of T rams' skins and goatskins,

TANNER (3)
Acts 9:43 Joppa for many days with one Simon, a T
10:6 lodging with Simon, a T, whose house is by
10:32 house of Simon, a T, by the seaside.'

TAPHATH
1Kgs 4:11 all Naphath-dor (he had T the daughter of Solomon

TAPPUAH (7)
Josh 12:17 one; the king of T, one; the king of
15:34 Zorah, Ashnah, Zanoah, En-gannim, T, Enam,
16:8 From T the boundary goes westward to the brook
17:8 The land of T belonged to Manasseh, but the
17:8 but the town of T on the boundary of
2Kgs 15:16 that time Menahem sacked T and all who were
1Chr 2:43 sons of Hebron: Korah, T, Rekem, and Shema.

TARALAH
Josh 18:27 Chephirah, Mozah, Rekem, Irpeel, T,

TAREA
1Chr 8:35 of Micah: Pithon, Melech, T, and Ahaz.

TARGET (3)
Job 16:12 me up as his T,
Wis 5:12 is shot at a T, the air, thus divided,
5:21 will leap to the T as from a well-drawn

TARNISHED
Sir 12:11 you will know that it was not hopelessly T

TARRIED (2)
Gen 31:54 they ate bread and T all night on the
2Kgs 2:18 to him, while he T at Jericho, and he

TARRY (21)
Gen 45:9 to me, do not T;
Ex 12:39 Egypt and could not T, neither had they prepared
24:14 said to the elders, T here for us, until
Num 22:19 Pray, now, T here this night also, that I
Judg 5:16 Why did you T among the sheepfolds, to hear
5:28 Why T the hoofbeats of his chariots?'
19:8 "Strengthen your heart, and T until the day
19:9 waned toward evening; pray T all night.
2Kgs 2:2 Elijah said to Elisha, T here, I pray you;
2:4 said to him, "Elisha, T here, I pray you;
2:6 Elijah said to him, T here, I pray you;
9:3 Then open the door and flee; do not T
Ps 30:5 Weeping may T for the night, but joy comes
40:17 my deliverer; do not T, O my God!
70:5 help and my deliverer; O LORD, do not T
Prov 23:30 Those who T long over wine, those who go
Is 5:11 after strong drink, who T late into the evening
46:13 my salvation will not T; I will put salvation
Jer 14:8 who turns aside to T for a night?
Mic 5:7 upon the grass, which T not for men nor
Heb 10:37 come and shall not T;

TARSHISH (28)
Gen 10:4 sons of Javan: Elishah, T, Kittim, and Dodanim.
1Kgs 10:22 fleet of ships of T at sea with the
10:22 fleet of ships of T used to come bringing
22:48 Jehoshaphat made ships of T to go to Ophir
1Chr 1:7 sons of Javan: Elishah, T, Kittim, and Rodanim.
7:10 Benjamin, Ehud, Chenaanah, Zethan, T, and
2Chr 9:21 king's ships went to T with the servants of
9:21 years the ships of T used to come bringing
20:36 ships to go to T, and they built the
20:37 wrecked and were not able to go to T
Esth 1:14 Carshena, Shethar, Admatha, T, Meres, Marsena, and
Ps 48:7 east wind thou didst shatter the ships of T
72:10 May the kings of T and of the isles
Is 2:16 all the ships of T, and against all the
23:1 Wail, O ships of T, for Tyre is laid
23:6 Pass over to T, wail, O inhabitants of the
23:10 Nile, O daughter of T; there is no restraint
23:14 Wail, O ships of T, for your stronghold is
60:9 me, the ships of T first, to bring your
66:19 to the nations, to T, Put, and Lud, who
Jer 10:9 silver is brought from T, and gold from Uphaz.
Ezek 27:12 T trafficked with you because of your great wealth
27:25 The ships of T traveled for you with your
38:13 and the merchants of T and all its villages
Jon 1:3 rose to flee to T from the presence of
1:3 a ship going to T; so he paid the
1:3 go with them to T, away from the presence
4:2 haste to flee to T; for I knew that

TARSUS (7)
2Mac 3:5 went to Apollonius of T, who at that time
4:30 that the people of T and of Mallus revolted
Acts 9:11 for a man of T named Saul; for behold,
9:30 down to Caesarea, and sent him off to T
11:25 So Barnabas went to T to look for Saul;
21:39 am a Jew, from T in Cilicia, a citizen
22:3 a Jew, born at T in Cilicia, but brought

TARTAK
2Kgs 17:31 made Nibhaz and T; and the Sepharvites burned

TARTAN
2Kgs 18:17 of Assyria sent the T, the Rabsaris, and the

TASK (12)
Ex 5:13 your work, your daily T, as when there was
5:14 not done all your T of making bricks today,
36:4 doing every sort of T on the sanctuary came,
36:4 came, each from the T that he was doing,
Num 4:19 them each to his T and to his burden,
4:49 appointed, each to his T of serving or carrying;
Ezra 10:4 for it is your T, and we are with
Ps 73:16 to me a wearisome T,
Sir 7:25 in marriage; you will have finished a great T
37:11 servant about a big T -- pay no attention
Col 3:23 Whatever your T, work heartily, as serving the Lord
1Tim 3:1 the office of bishop, he desires a noble T

TASKMASTER (3)
1Kgs 12:18 sent Adoram, who was T over the forced labor,
2Chr 10:18 sent Hadoram, who was T over the forced labor,
Job 3:18 together; they hear not the voice of the T

TASKMASTERS (7)
Ex 1:10 Therefore they set T over them to afflict them
3:7 cry because of their T; I know their sufferings,
5:6 day Pharaoh commanded the T of the people and
5:10 So the T and the foremen of the people
5:13 The T were urgent, saying, "Complete your work,
5:14 of Israel, whom Pharaoh's T had set over them,
Is 60:17 overseers peace and your T righteousness.

TASKS (4)
Prov 31:15 for her household and T for her maidens.
Sir 3:17 My son, perform your T in meekness; then you
3:22 what is beyond your T, for matters too great
1Mac 14:42 appoint men over its T and over the country

TASSEL (2)
Num 15:38 to put upon the T of each corner a
15:39 be to you a T to look upon and

TASSELS (2)
Num 15:38 bid them to make T on the corners of
Deut 22:12 "You shall make yourself T on the four corners

TASTE (26)
Ex 16:31 seed, white, and the T of it was like
Num 11:8 of it; and the T of it was like
11:8 it was like the T of cakes baked with
2Sam 3:35 more also, if I T bread or anything else
19:35 Can your servant T what he eats or what
Job 6:6 or is there any T in the slime of
6:30 Cannot my T discern calamity?
Ps 34:8 O T and see that the LORD is good!
119:103 thy words to my T, sweeter than honey to
Prov 24:13 drippings of the honeycomb are sweet to your T
Song 2:3 shadow, and his fruit was sweet to my T
Wis 16:20 eat, providing every pleasure and suited to every T
Jer 48:11 into exile; so his T remains in him, and
Jon 3:7 beast, herd nor flock, T anything; let them not
2Mac 6:20 is not right to T, even for the natural
13:18 king, having had a T of the daring of
Mt 5:13 salt has lost its T, how shall its saltness
16:28 here who will not T death before they see
Mk 9:1 here who will not T death before they see
Lk 9:27 here who will not T death before they see
14:24 who were invited shall T my banquet.'"

	14:34	salt has lost its T, how shall its saltness
Jn	8:52	word, he will never T death.'
Acts	23:14	by an oath to T no food till we
Col	2:21	not handle, Do not T, Do not touch"
Heb	2:9	of God he might T death for every one.

TASTED (11)

1Sam	14:24	none of the people T food.
	14:29	become bright, because I T a little of this
	14:43	Jonathan told him, "I T a little honey with
Tob	2:4	So before I T anything I sprang up and
Job	21:25	of soul, never having T of good.
Dan	5:2	Belshazzar, when he T the wine, commanded that
Mt	27:34	gall; but when he T it, he would not
Jn	2:9	steward of the feast T the water now become
Heb	6:4	been enlightened, who have T the heavenly gift, and
	6:5	Holy Spirit, and have T the goodness of the
1Pet	2:3	salvation; for you have T the kindness of the

TASTELESS

Job	6:6	Can that which is T be eaten without salt,

TASTES (4)

Job	12:11	words as the palate T food?
	34:3	words as the palate T food.
Sir	23:17	a fornicator all bread T sweet; he will never
	36:19	As the palate T the kinds of game, so

TATTENAI (4)

Ezra	5:3	At the same time T the governor of the
	5:6	of the letter which T the governor of the
	6:6	"Now therefore, T, governor of the province Beyond
	6:13	by Darius the king, T, the governor of the

TATTOO

Lev	19:28	of the dead or T any marks upon you:

TAUGHT (76)

Deut	4:5	Behold, I have T you statutes and ordinances, as
	13:5	death, because he has T rebellion against the LORD
	31:22	the same day, and T it to the people
Judg	8:16	briers and with them T the men of Succoth.
2Sam	1:18	said it should be T to the people of
2Kgs	17:28	dwelt in Bethel, and T them how they should
2Chr	17:9	And they T in Judah, having the book of
	17:9	cities of Judah and T among the people.
	35:3	to the Levites who T all Israel and who
Neh	8:9	and the Levites who T the people said to
Ps	71:17	my youth thou hast T me, and I still
	119:102	ordinances, for thou hast T me.
Prov	4:5	of my mother, he T me, and said to
	4:12	I have T you the way of wisdom; I
	31:1	Massa, which his mother T him:
Eccl	12:9	the Preacher also T the people knowledge, weighing
Wis	6:10	those who have been T them will find a
	7:22	fashioner of all things, T me.
	9:18	right, and men were T what pleases thee, and
	12:19	such works thou has T thy people that the
Sir	6:32	son, you will be T, and if you apply
	21:12	not clever cannot be T, but there is a
Is	40:14	his enlightenment, and who T him the path of
	40:14	path of justice, and T him knowledge, and showed
	50:4	of those who are T, that I may know
	50:4	my ear to hear as those who are T
	54:13	your sons shall be T by the LORD, and
Jer	2:33	wicked women you have T your ways.
	9:5	the truth; they have T their tongue to speak
	9:14	Baals, as their fathers T them.
	12:16	lives,' even as they T my people to swear
	13:21	whom you yourself have T to be friends to
	32:33	and though I have T them persistently they have
Ezek	22:26	common, neither have they T the difference between
Dan	13:3	were righteous, and had T their daughter according
Hos	11:3	it was I who T Ephraim to walk, I
Mt	5:2	opened his mouth and T them, saying:
	7:29	his teaching, for he T them as one who
	13:54	his own country he T them in their synagogue,
Mk	1:21	on the sabbath he entered the synagogue and T
	1:22	his teaching, for he T them as one who
	2:13	about him, and he T them.
	4:2	And he T them many things in parables, and
	6:30	told him all that they had done and T
	10:1	his custom was, he T them.
	11:17	And he T, and said to them, "Is it
	12:35	And as Jesus T in the temple, he said,
Lk	4:15	And he T in their synagogues, being glorified by
	5:3	he sat down and T the people from the
	6:6	entered the synagogue and T, a man was there
	6:40	when he is fully T will be like his
	11:1	to pray, as John T his disciples."
	13:26	your presence, and you T in our streets.'
Jn	6:45	they shall all be T by God.' Every one
	6:59	the synagogue, as he T at Caperna-um.
	7:14	feast Jesus went up into the temple and T
	7:28	Jesus proclaimed, as he T in the temple, "You
	8:2	he sat down and T them.
	8:20	the treasury, as he T in the temple; but
	8:28	thus as the Father T me.
	18:20	world; I have always T in synagogues and in
Acts	5:21	this, they entered the temple at daybreak and T
	11:26	with the church, and T a large company of
	18:25	spirit, he spoke and T accurately the things
Rom	16:17	which you have been T; avoid them.
1Cor	2:13	this in words not T by human wisdom but
	2:13	by human wisdom but T by the Spirit, interpreting
Gal	1:12	man, nor was I T it, but it came
	6:6	Let him who is T the word share all
Eph	4:21	about him and were T in him, as the
Col	2:7	just as you were T, abounding in thanksgiving.
1Thes	4:9	you yourselves have been T by God to love
2Thes	2:15	traditions which you were T by us, either by
Tit	1:8	the sure word as T, so that he may
1Jn	2:27	just as it has T you, abide in him.
Rev	2:14	teaching of Balaam, who T Balak to put a

TAUNT (17)

Neh	4:4	despised; turn back their T upon their own heads,
	6:13	name, in order to T me.
Ps	42:10	my body, my adversaries T me, while they say
	44:13	hast made us the T of our neighbors, the
	79:4	We have become a T to our neighbors, mocked
	89:51	with which thy enemies T, O LORD, with which
	102:8	the day my enemies T me, those who deride
	119:42	answer for those who T me, for I trust
Is	14:4	will take up this T against the king of
Jer	24:9	reproach, a byword, a T, and a curse in
	42:18	an execration, a horror, a curse, and a T
	44:8	a curse and a T among all the nations
	44:12	an execration, a horror, a curse, and a T
	49:13	become a horror, a T, a waste, and a
Ezek	5:15	a reproach and a T, a warning and a
Mic	2:4	shall take up a T song against you, and
Hab	2:6	these take up their T against him, in scoffing

TAUNTED (5)

Judg	8:15	Zalmunna, about whom you T me, saying, 'Are Zebah
2Sam	21:21	And when he T Israel, Jonathan the son of
1Chr	20:7	And when he T Israel, Jonathan the son of
Ps	79:12	with which they have T thee, O Lord!
Zeph	2:8	Ammonites, how they have T my people and made

TAUNTERS

Ps	44:16	the words of the T and revilers, at the

TAUNTS (5)

Neh	5:9	God to prevent the T of the nations our
Ps	55:12	not an enemy who T me-- then I
	79:12	of our neighbors the T with which they have
Lam	3:61	"Thou hast heard their T, O LORD, all their
Zeph	2:8	"I have heard the T of Moab and the

TAVERNS

Acts	28:15	of Appius and Three T to meet us.

TAWNY

Judg	5:10	you who ride on T asses, you who sit

TAX (37)

2Chr	24:6	Judah and Jerusalem the T levied by Moses, the
	24:9	for the LORD the T that Moses the servant
	24:10	rejoiced and brought their T and dropped it into
Neh	5:4	money for the king's T upon our fields and
1Mac	10:29	of tribute and salt T and crown levies,
	10:31	and her revenues, be holy and free from T
	13:39	and cancel the crown T which you owe; and
	13:39	owe; and whatever other T has been collected in
	15:5	to you all the T remissions that the kings
Mt	5:46	Do not even the T collectors do the same?
	9:9	Matthew sitting at the T office; and he said
	9:10	house, behold, many T collectors and sinners came
	9:11	your teacher eat with T collectors and sinners?"
	10:3	Thomas and Matthew the T collector; James the son

T

11:19 drunkard, a friend of T collectors and sinners!' Yet
17:23 collectors of the half-shekel T went up to Peter
17:23 and said, "Does not your teacher pay the T
18:16 a Gentile and a T collector.
21:31 say to you, the T collectors and the harlots
21:32 believe him, but the T collectors and the harlots
22:19 Show me the money for the T
Mk 2:14 Alphaeus sitting at the T office, and he said
2:15 in his house, many T collectors and sinners were
2:16 eating with sinners and T collectors, said to his
2:16 does he eat with T collectors and sinners?"
Lk 3:12 T collectors also came to be baptized, and said
5:27 out, and saw a T collector, named Levi, sitting
5:27 Levi, sitting at the T office; and he said
5:29 a large company of T collectors and others sitting
5:30 eat and drink with T collectors and sinners?"
7:29 the people and the T collectors justified God, having
7:34 drunkard, a friend of T collectors and sinners!'
15:1 Now the T collectors and sinners were all drawing
18:10 and the other a T collector.
18:11 or even like this T collector.
18:13 I get.' But the T collector, standing far-off, would
19:2 he was a chief T collector, and rich.

TAXED

2Kgs 23:35 to Pharaoh, but he T the land to give

TAXES (10)

Esth 2:18 granted a remission of T to the provinces, and
1Mac 10:33 officials cancel also the T on their cattle.
11:34 release from the royal T which the king formerly
11:35 the tithes, and the T due to us, and
11:35 pits and the crown T due to us --
Mt 22:17 it lawful to pay T to Caesar, or not?"
Mk 12:14 it lawful to pay T to Caesar, or not?
Rom 13:6 reason you also pay T, for the authorities are
13:7 of them their dues, T to whom taxes are
13:7 dues, taxes to whom T are due, revenue to

TEACH (107)

Ex 4:12 with your mouth and T you what you shall
4:15 his mouth, and will T you what you shall
18:20 God; and you shall T them the statutes and
35:34 has inspired him to T, both him and Oholiab
Lev 10:11 and you are to T the people of Israel
Deut 4:1 the ordinances which I T you, and do them;
4:10 and that they may T their children so.'
4:14 at that time to T you statutes and ordinances,
5:31 ordinances which you shall T them, that they may
6:1 God commanded me to T you, that you may
6:7 heart; and you shall T them diligently to your
11:19 And you shall T them to your children, talking
20:18 that they may not T you to do according
31:19 write this song, and T it to the people
33:10 They shall T Jacob thy ordinances, and Israel thy
Judg 3:2 war, that he might T war to such at
13:8 again to us, and T us what we are
1Kgs 8:36 Israel, when thou dost T them the good way
2Kgs 17:27 and dwell there, and T them the law of
2Chr 6:27 Israel, when thou dost T them the good way
17:7 Nethanel, and Micaiah, to T in the cities of
Ezra 7:10 do it, and to T his statutes and ordinances
7:25 those who do not know them, you shall T
Job 6:24 T me, and I will be silent; make me
8:10 Will they not T you, and tell you, and
12:7 beasts, and they will T you; the birds of
12:8 earth, and they will T you; and the fish
21:22 Will any T God knowledge, seeing that he judges
27:11 I will T you concerning the hand of God;
32:7 speak, and many years T wisdom.'
33:33 silent, and I will T you wisdom."
34:32 not offend any more; T me what I do
37:19 T us what we shall say to him; we
Ps 25:4 thy ways, O LORD; T me thy paths.
25:5 in thy truth, and T me, for thou art
27:11 T me thy way, O LORD; and lead me
32:8 will instruct you and T you the way you
34:11 to me, I will T you the fear of
45:4 let your right hand T you dread deeds!
51:6 the inward being; therefore T me wisdom in my
51:13 Then I will T transgressors thy ways, and sinners
78:5 commanded our fathers to T to their children;
86:11 T me thy way, O LORD, that I may
90:12 So T us to number our days that we
94:12 and whom thou dost T out of thy law
105:22 his pleasure, and to T his elders wisdom.
119:12 be thou, O LORD; T me thy statutes!
119:26 thou didst answer me; T me thy statutes!
119:29 from me; and graciously T me thy law!
119:33 T me, O LORD, the way of thy statutes;
119:64 of thy steadfast love; T me thy statutes!
119:66 T me good judgment and knowledge, for I believe
119:68 good and doest good; T me thy statutes.
119:108 praise, O LORD, and T me thy ordinances.
119:124 thy steadfast love, and T me thy statutes.
119:135 upon thy servant, and T me thy statutes.
119:171 praise that thou dost T me thy statutes.
132:12 testimonies which I shall T them, their sons also
143:8 T me the way I should go, for to
143:10 T me to do thy will, for thou art
Prov 9:9 will be still wiser; T a righteous man and
Sir 9:1 bosom, and do not T her an evil lesson
45:5 life and knowledge, to T Jacob the covenant, and
45:17 statutes and judgments, to T Jacob the testimonies,
Is 2:3 Jacob; that he may T us his ways and
28:9 "Whom will he T knowledge, and to whom will
Jer 9:20 word of his mouth; T to your daughters a
31:34 longer shall each man T his neighbor and each
Ezek 44:23 They shall T my people the difference between the
Dan 1:4 king's palace, and to T them the letters and
Mic 3:11 a bribe, its priests T for hire, its prophets
4:2 Jacob; that he may T us his ways and
Mt 11:1 on from there to T and preach in their
22:16 you are true, and T the way of God
Mk 4:1 Again he began to T beside the sea.
6:2 sabbath he began to T in the synagogue; and
6:34 and he began to T them many things.
8:31 And he began to T them that the Son
12:14 of men, but truly T the way of God.
Lk 11:1 said to him, "Lord, T us to pray, as
12:12 the Holy Spirit will T you in that very
20:21 that you speak and T rightly, and show no
20:21 no partiality, but truly T the way of God.
Jn 7:35 among the Greeks and T the Greeks?
9:34 sin, and would you T us?" And they cast
14:26 my name, he will T you all things, and
Acts 1:1 began to do and T,
4:18 not to speak or T at all in the
5:28 charged you not to T in this name, yet
21:21 about you that you T all the Jews who
Rom 2:21 you then who T others, will you not
2:21 others, will you not T yourself?
1Cor 4:17 in Christ, as I T them everywhere in every
11:14 Does not nature itself T you that for a
Col 3:16 dwell in you richly, T and admonish one another
1Tim 1:3 certain persons not to T any different doctrine,
2:12 permit no woman to T or to have authority
4:11 Command and T these things.
6:2 T and urge these duties.
2Tim 2:2 will be able to T others also.
Tit 1:10 base gain what they have no right to T
2:1 But as for you, T what befits sound doctrine.
2:3 drink; they are to T what is good,
Heb 5:12 need some one to T you again the first
8:11 And they shall not T every one his fellow
Jas 3:1 know that we who T shall be judged with
1Jn 2:27 that any one should T you; as his anointing

TEACHER (61)

1Chr 25:8 duties, small and great, T and pupil alike.
Job 36:22 power; who is a T like him?
Sir 37:19 be shrewd and the T of many, and yet
Is 30:20 of affliction, yet your T will not hide himself
30:20 any more, but your eyes shall see your T
Hab 2:18 a metal image, a T of lies?
2Mac 1:10 of the anointed priests, T of Ptolemy the king,
Mt 8:19 and said to him, T, I will follow you
9:11 disciples, "Why does your T eat with tax collectors
10:24 is not above his T, nor a servant above
10:25 to be like his T, and the servant like
12:38 Pharisees said to him, T, we wish to see
17:23 said, "Does not your T pay the tax?"
19:16 up to him, saying, T, what good deed must
22:16 with the Herodi-ans, saying, T, we know that you
22:24 him a question, saying, T, Moses said, 'If a
22:36 T, which is the great commandment in the law?"
23:8 for you have one T, and you are all
26:18 say to him, 'The T says, My time is
Mk 4:38 and said to him, T, do you not care
5:35 Why trouble the T any further?"
9:17 the crowd answered him, T, I brought my son
9:38 John said to him, T, we saw a man

10:17 and asked him, "Good T, what must I do
10:20 he said to him, T, all these I have
10:35 and said to him, T, we want you to
12:14 and said to him, T, we know that you
12:19 him a question, saying, T, Moses wrote for us
12:32 him, "You are right, T; you have truly said
13:1 said to him, "Look, T, what wonderful stones and
14:14 to the householder, 'The T says, Where is my
Lk 3:12 and said to him, T, what shall we do?"
6:40 is not above his T, but every one when
6:40 he is fully taught will be like his T
7:40 And he answered, "What is it, T
8:49 do not trouble the T any more."
9:38 from the crowd cried, T, I beg you to
10:25 to the test, saying, T, what shall I do
11:45 the lawyers answered him, T, in saying this you
12:13 multitude said to him, T, bid my brother divide
18:18 ruler asked him, "Good T, what shall I do
19:39 multitude said to him, T, rebuke your disciples."
20:21 They asked him, T, we know that you speak
20:28 him a question, saying, T, Moses wrote for us
20:39 of the scribes answered, T, you have spoken well."
21:7 And they asked him, T, when will this be,
22:11 tell the householder, 'The T says to you, Where
Jn 1:38 (which means T, "where are you staying?"
3:2 that you are a T come from God; for
3:10 him, "Are you a T of Israel, and yet
8:4 they said to him, T, this woman has been
11:28 Mary, saying quietly, "The T is here and is
13:13 You call me T and Lord; and you are
13:14 then, your Lord and T, have washed your feet,
20:16 (which means T
Acts 5:34 council named Gamali-el, a T of the law, held
Rom 2:20 of the foolish, a T of children, having in
1Tim 2:7 am not lying), a T of the Gentiles in
3:2 dignified, hospitable, an apt T,
2Tim 1:11 preacher and apostle and T,
2:24 every one, an apt T, forbearing,

TEACHERS (13)

Ps 119:99 understanding than all my T, for thy testimonies are
Prov 5:13 the voice of my T or incline my ear
Lk 2:46 temple, sitting among the T, listening to them and
5:17 there were Pharisees and T of the law sitting
Acts 13:1 there were prophets and T, Barnabas, Simeon who
1Cor 12:28 apostles, second prophets, third T, then workers of
12:29 Are all T
Eph 4:11 evangelists, some pastors and T,
1Tim 1:7 discussion, desiring to be T of the law, without
2Tim 4:3 will accumulate for themselves T to suit their own
Heb 5:12 you ought to be T, you need some one
Jas 3:1 many of you become T, my brethren, for you
2Pet 2:1 there will be false T among you, who will

TEACHES (18)

Job 15:5 For your iniquity T your mouth, and you choose
35:11 in the night, who T us more than the
Ps 25:9 what is right, and T the humble his way.
94:10 He who T men knowledge,
Wis 8:7 are virtues; for she T self-control and prudence,
Sir 18:12 rebukes and trains and T them, and turns them
22:7 He who T a fool is like one who
30:3 He who T his son will make his enemies
33:27 be idle, for idleness T much evil.
Is 9:15 and the prophet who T lies is the tail;
28:26 instructed aright; his God T him.
48:17 LORD your God, who T you to profit, who
Mt 5:19 of these commandments and T men so, shall be
5:19 who does them and T them shall be called
Rom 12:7 our serving; he who T, in his teaching;
Gal 6:6 word share all good things with him who T
1Tim 6:3 If any one T otherwise and does not agree
1Jn 2:27 you; as his anointing T you about everything, and

TEACHING (78)

Deut 32:2 May my T drop as the rain, my speech
2Chr 15:3 God, and without a T priest, and without law;
Ps 78:1 my people, to my T; incline your ears to
Prov 1:8 reject not your mother's T;
3:1 do not forget my T, but let your heart
4:3 give you good precepts: do not forsake my T
6:20 commandment, and forsake not your mother's T
6:23 a lamp and the T a light, and the
13:14 The T of the wise is a fountain of
31:26 with wisdom, and the T of kindness is on
Sir 24:31 will again pour out T like prophecy, and leave
39:8 reveal instruction in his T, and will glory in
Is 1:10 Give ear to the T of our God, you
8:16 the testimony, seal the T among my disciples.
8:20 To the T and to the testimony!
Mt 4:23 went about all Galilee, T in their synagogues and
7:28 were astonished at his T,
9:35 the cities and villages, T in their synagogues and
15:9 do they worship me, T as doctrines the precepts
16:12 bread, but of the T of the Pharisees and
21:23 him as he was T, and said, "By what
22:33 crowd heard it, they were astonished at his T
26:55 sat in the temple T, and you did not
28:20 of the Holy Spirit, T them to observe all
Mk 1:22 were astonished at his T, for he taught them
1:27 A new T
4:2 parables, and in his T he said to them:
6:6 And he went about among the villages T
7:7 do they worship me, T as doctrines the precepts
9:31 it; for he was T his disciples, saying to
11:18 because all the multitude was astonished at his T
12:38 And in his T he said, "Beware of the
14:49 you in the temple T, and you did not
Lk 4:31 And he was T them on the sabbath;
4:32 were astonished at his T, for his word was
5:17 days, as he was T, there were Pharisees and
10:39 at the Lord's feet and listened to his T
13:10 Now he was T in one of the synagogues
13:22 and villages, T, and journeying toward Jerusalem.
19:47 And he was T daily in the temple.
20:1 day, as he was T the people in the
21:37 every day he was T in the temple, but
23:5 stirs up the people, T throughout all Judea, from
Jn 7:16 Jesus answered them, "My T is not mine, but
7:17 shall know whether the T is from God or
18:19 then questioned Jesus about his disciples and his T
Acts 2:42 themselves to the apostles' T and fellowship, to the
4:2 annoyed because they were T the people and
5:25 in the temple and T the people."
5:28 filled Jerusalem with your T and you intend to
5:42 they did not cease T and preaching Jesus as
13:12 was astonished at the T of the Lord.
15:1 from Judea and were T the brethren, "Unless you
15:34 Barnabas remained in Antioch, T and preaching the
17:19 know what this new T is which you present?
18:11 year and six months, T the word of God
20:20 that was profitable, and T you in public and
21:28 the man who is T men everywhere against the
28:30 kingdom of God and T about the Lord Jesus
Rom 6:17 to the standard of T to which you were
12:7 who teaches, in his T;
1Cor 14:6 you some revelation or knowledge or prophecy or T
Col 1:28 warning every man and T every man in all
1Tim 4:13 the public reading of scripture, to preaching, to T
4:16 yourself and to your T; hold to that, for
5:17 labor in preaching and T;
6:1 of God and the T may not be defamed.
6:3 Jesus Christ and the T which accords with godliness,
2Tim 3:10 you have observed my T, my conduct, my aim
3:16 God and profitable for T, for reproof, for correction,
4:2 and exhort, be unfailing in patience and in T
4:3 will not endure sound T, but having itching ears
Tit 1:10 upsetting whole families by T for base gain what
2:7 deeds, and in your T show integrity, gravity,
Rev 2:14 there who hold the T of Balaam, who taught
2:15 some who hold the T of the Nicolaitans.
2:20 a prophetess and is T and beguiling my servants
2:24 do not hold this T, who have not learned

TEACHINGS (2)

Prov 7:2 and live, keep my T as the apple of
Heb 13:9 by diverse and strange T; for it is well

TEAM

Jer 51:23 the farmer and his T; with you I break

TEAR (32)

Ex 34:13 You shall T down their altars, and break their
Lev 1:17 for ashes; he shall T it by its wings,
13:56 is washed, he shall T the spot out of
Deut 12:3 green tree; you shall T down their altars, and
1Kgs 11:11 you, I will surely T the kingdom from you
11:12 days, but I will T it out of the
11:13 However I will not T away all the kingdom;
11:31 I am about to T the kingdom from the
Job 18:4 You who T yourself in your anger, shall the
Ps 17:12 a lion eager to T, as a young lion

T

	52:5	he will snatch and T you from your tent;
	58:6	teeth in their mouths; T out the fangs of
Jer	15:3	slay, the dogs to T, and the birds of
	22:24	hand, yet I would T you off
	24:6	them up, and not T them down; I will
Ezek	13:20	souls, and I will T them from your arms;
	13:21	veils also I will T off, and deliver my
	23:34	out your hair, and T your breasts; for I
Hos	13:8	her cubs, I will T open their breast, and
Mic	3:2	love the evil, who T the skin from off
Mal	1:4	build, but I will T down, till they are
1Mac	4:45	thought it best to T it down, lest it
	6:62	and gave orders to T down the wall all
	9:54	Alcimus gave orders to T down the wall of
	9:55	he only began to T it down, for at
2Mac	14:33	to the ground and T down the altar, and
Mt	9:16	garment, and a worse T is made.
Mk	2:21	old, and a worse T is made.
Lk	5:36	he does, he will T the new, and the
Jn	19:24	another, "Let us not T it, but cast lots
Rev	7:17	will wipe away every T from their eyes."
	21:4	will wipe away every T from their eyes, and

TEARING (4)

Ezek	22:25	like a roaring lion T the prey; they have
	22:27	her are like wolves T the prey, shedding blood,
Zech	11:16	of the fat ones, T off even their hoofs.
2Cor	13:10	up and not for T down.

TEARS (55)

Deut	33:20	like a lion, he T the arm, and the
Judg	14:6	lion asunder as one T a kid; and he
2Kgs	20:5	I have seen your T; behold, I will heal
Tob	7:17	her daughter in her T, and said to her,
Esth	8:3	and besought him with T to avert the evil
Job	12:14	If he T down, none can rebuild; if he
	16:20	my eye pours out T to God,
Ps	6:6	flood my bed with T; I drench my couch
	39:12	my cry; hold not thy peace at my T
	42:3	My T have been my food day and night,
	56:8	tossings; put thou my T in thy bottle!
	80:5	with the bread of T, and given them tears
	80:5	tears, and given them T to drink in full
	102:9	like bread, and mingle T with my drink,
	116:8	death, my eyes from T, my feet from stumbling;
	119:136	eyes shed streams of T, because men do not
	126:5	those who sow in T reap with shouts of
Prov	14:1	with her own hands T it down.
	15:25	The LORD T down the house of the proud,
Eccl	4:1	And behold, the T of the oppressed, and they
Sir	22:17	an eye will make T fall, and one who
	31:13	Therefore it sheds T from every face.
	34:23	one builds and another T down, what do they
	35:15	Do not the T of the widow run down
	38:16	My son, let your T fall for the dead,
Is	15:3	the squares every one wails and melts in T
	16:9	drench you with my T, O Heshbon and Ele-aleh;
	22:4	let me weep bitter T; do not labor to
	25:8	GOD will wipe away T from all faces, and
	38:5	I have seen your T; behold, I will add
Jer	9:1	eyes a fountain of T, that I might weep
	9:18	may run down with T, and our eyelids gush
	13:17	and run down with T, because the LORD's flock
	14:17	eyes run down with T night and day, and
	31:16	and your eyes from T; for your work shall
Lam	1:2	bitterly in the night, T on her cheeks; among
	1:16	my eyes flow with T; for a comforter is
	2:18	Let T stream down like a torrent day and
	3:48	flow with rivers of T because of the destruction
Ezek	24:16	weep nor shall your T run down.
Mic	5:8	through, treads down and T in pieces, and there
Mal	2:13	the LORD's altar with T, with weeping and groaning
2Mac	11:6	people, with lamentations and T, besought the Lord
Mt	9:16	garment, for the patch T away from the garment,
Mk	2:21	he does, the patch T away from it, the
Lk	5:36	parable also: "No one T a piece from a
	7:38	his feet with her T, and wiped them with
	7:44	my feet with her T and wiped them with
Acts	20:19	all humility and with T and with trials which
	20:31	night or day to admonish every one with T
2Cor	2:4	heart and with many T, not to cause you
Phil	3:18	tell you even with T, live as enemies of
2Tim	1:4	As I remember your T, I long night and
Heb	5:7	with loud cries and T, to him who was
	12:17	chance to repent, though he sought it with T

TEBAH

Gen	22:24	name was Reumah, bore T, Gaham, Tahash, and

TEBALIAH

1Chr	26:11	chief), Hilkiah the second, T the third, Zechariah the

TEBETH

Esth	2:16	is the month of T, in the seventh year

TEEMS (2)

Lev	20:25	with which the ground T, which I have set
Ps	104:25	great and wide, which T with things innumerable,

TEETH (52)

Gen	49:12	with wine, and his T white with milk.
Num	11:33	was yet between their T, before it was consumed,
Deut	32:24	I will send the T of beasts against them,
Job	4:10	the fierce lion, the T of the young lions,
	13:14	my flesh in my T, and put my life
	16:9	he has gnashed his T at me; my adversary
	19:20	I have escaped by the skin of my T
	29:17	and made him drop his prey from his T
	41:14	Round about his T is terror.
Ps	3:7	thou dost break the T of the wicked.
	35:16	more and more, gnashing at me with their T
	37:12	righteous, and gnashes his T at him;
	57:4	sons of men; their T are spears and arrows,
	58:6	O God, break the T in their mouths; tear
	112:10	angry; he gnashes his T and melts away; the
	124:6	has not given us as prey to their T
Prov	10:26	Like vinegar to the T, and smoke to the
	30:14	There are those whose T are swords, whose teeth
	30:14	teeth are swords, whose T are knives, to devour
Song	4:2	Your T are like a flock of shorn ewes
	6:6	Your T are like a flock of ewes, that
	7:9	that goes down smoothly, gliding over lips and T
Wis	16:10	conquered even by the T of venomous serpents, for
Sir	21:2	Its T are lion's teeth, and destroy the souls
	21:2	Its teeth are lion's T, and destroy the souls
	30:10	and in the end you will gnash your T
	39:30	created for vengeance; the T of wild beasts, and
	51:3	from the gnashings of T about to devour me,
Is	41:15	new, sharp, and having T; you shall thresh the
Jer	31:29	grapes, and the children's T are set on edge.'
	31:30	eats sour grapes, his T shall be set on
Lam	2:16	hiss, they gnash their T, they cry: "We have
	3:16	He has made my T grind on gravel, and
Ezek	18:2	grapes, and the children's T are set on edge?
Dan	7:5	its mouth between its T; and it was told,
	7:7	it had great iron T; it devoured and broke
	7:19	exceedingly terrible, with its T of iron and claws
Joel	1:6	and without number; its T are lions' teeth, and
	1:6	its teeth are lions' T, and it has the
Amos	4:6	gave you cleanness of T in all your cities,
Zech	9:7	abominations from between its T; it too shall be
Mt	8:12	darkness; there men will weep and gnash their T
	13:42	fire; there men will weep and gnash their T
	13:50	fire; there men will weep and gnash their T
	22:13	weep and gnash their T
	24:51	hypocrites; there men will weep and gnash their T
	25:30	weep and gnash their T
Mk	9:18	foams and grinds his T and becomes rigid; and
Lk	13:28	weep and gnash your T, when you see Abraham
Acts	7:54	and they ground their T against him.
Rev	9:8	women's hair, and their T like lions' teeth;
	9:8	their teeth like lions' T;

TEHAPHNEHES

Ezek	30:18	At T the day shall be dark, when I

TEHINNAH

1Chr	4:12	of Bethrapha, Paseah, and T the father of Irnahash.

TEKEL (2)

Dan	5:25	was inscribed: MENE, MENE, T, and PARSIN.
	5:27	it to an end; T, you have been weighed

TEKOA (12)

2Sam	14:2	And Joab sent to T, and fetched from there
	14:4	When the woman of T came to the king,
	14:9	And the woman of T said to the king,
	23:26	son of Ikkesh of T,
1Chr	2:24	and she bore him Ashhur, the father of T
	4:5	Ashhur, the father of T, had two wives, Helah
	11:28	son of Ikkesh of T, Abi-ezer of Anathoth,
2Chr	11:6	He built Bethlehem, Etam, T,

T

	20:20	into the wilderness of T; and as they went
Jer	6:1	Blow the trumpet in T, and raise a signal
Amos	1:1	among the shepherds of T, which he saw concerning
1Mac	9:33	into the wilderness of T and camped by the

TEKOITE

1Chr	27:9	son of Ikkesh the T; in his division were

TEKOITES (2)

Neh	3:5	next to them the T repaired; but their nobles
	3:27	After him the T repaired another section opposite

TEL-ABIB

Ezek	3:15	to the exiles at T, who dwelt by the

TEL-ASSAR (2)

2Kgs	19:12	and the people of Eden who were in T
Is	37:12	and the people of Eden who were in T

TEL-HARSHA (2)

Ezra	2:59	came up from Tel-melah, T, Cherub, Addan, and
Neh	7:61	up from Tel-melah, T, Cherub, Addon, and Immer,

TEL-MELAH (2)

Ezra	2:59	who came up from T, Tel-harsha, Cherub, Addan, and
Neh	7:61	who came up from T, Tel-harsha, Cherub, Addon, and

TELAH

1Chr	7:25	son, Resheph his son, T his son, Tahan his

TELAIM

1Sam	15:4	and numbered them in T, two hundred thousand men

TELEM (2)

Josh	15:24	Kedesh, Hazor, Ithnan, Ziph, T, Bealoth,
Ezra	10:24	Of the gatekeepers: Shallum, T, and Uri.

TELL (365)

Gen	12:18	Why did you not T me that she was
	21:26	thing; you did not T me, and I have
	22:2	of which I shall T you."
	24:23	gold shekels, and said, T me whose daughter you
	24:49	truly with my master, T me; and if not,
	24:49	me; and if not, T me; that I may
	26:2	of which I shall T you.
	29:15	T me, what shall your wages be?"
	31:20	that he did not T him that he intended
	31:27	me, and did not T me, so that I
	32:5	I have sent to T my lord, in order
	32:29	Then Jacob asked him, T me, I pray, your
	37:16	he said, T me, I pray you, where they
	40:8	T them to me, I pray you."
	42:22	them, "Did I not T you not to sin
	43:6	so ill as to T the man that you
	45:13	You must T my father of all my splendor
	46:31	will go up and T Pharaoh, and will say
	49:1	together, that I may T you what shall befall
Ex	6:11	to Moses, "Go in, T Pharaoh king of Egypt
	6:29	"I am the LORD; T Pharaoh king of Egypt
	7:2	Aaron your brother shall T Pharaoh to let the
	10:2	and that you may T in the hearing of
	12:3	T all the congregation of Israel that on the
	13:8	And you shall T your son on that day,
	14:2	LORD said to Moses, T the people of Israel
	14:15	T the people of Israel to go forward.
	19:3	house of Jacob, and T the people of Israel:
Lev	14:35	house shall come and T the priest, 'There seems
	16:2	LORD said to Moses, T Aaron your brother not
	22:2	LORD said to Moses, T Aaron and his sons
Num	14:14	them, and they will T the inhabitants of this
	16:37	LORD said to Moses, T Eleazar the son of
	19:2	the LORD has commanded: T the people of Israel
	20:8	Aaron your brother, and T the rock before their
	23:3	shows me I will T you." And he went
	23:26	Balak, "Did I not T you, 'All that the
	24:12	Balak, "Did I not T your messengers whom you
Deut	5:31	me, and I will T you all the commandment
	32:7	elders, and they will T you.
Josh	2:14	If you do not T this business of ours,
	2:20	But if you T this business of ours, then
	4:7	you?' Then you shall T them that the waters
	4:10	LORD commanded Joshua to T the people, according
	7:19	praise to him; and T me now what you
Judg	5:10	T of it, you who ride on tawny asses,
	13:6	and he did not T me his name;
	14:6	But he did not T his father or his
	14:9	But he did not T them that he had
	14:12	you; if you can T me what it is,
	14:13	but if you cannot T me what it is,
	14:14	not in three days T what the riddle was.
	14:15	"Entice your husband to T us what the riddle
	14:16	mother, and shall I T you?"
	16:6	said to Samson, "Please T me wherein your great
	16:10	told me lies; please T me how you might
	16:13	and told me lies; T me how you might
	20:3	people of Israel said, T us, how was this
Ruth	3:4	down; and he will T you what to do."
	4:4	I thought I would T you of it, and
	4:4	if you will not, T me, that I may
1Sam	3:13	And I T him that I am about to
	3:15	Samuel was afraid to T the vision to Eli.
	6:2	T us with what we shall send it to
	9:6	there; perhaps he can T us about the journey
	9:8	man of God, to T us our way."
	9:18	the gate, and said, T me where is the
	9:19	you go and will T you all that is
	9:27	Samuel said to Saul, T the servant to pass
	10:15	Saul's uncle said, "Pray, T me what Samuel said
	10:16	spoken, he did not T him anything.
	14:1	But he did not T his father.
	14:43	Saul said to Jonathan, T me what you have
	15:16	I will T you what the LORD said to
	17:55	"As your soul lives, O king, I cannot T
	19:3	learn anything I will T you."
	20:9	you, would I not T you?"
	20:10	to Jonathan, "Who will T me if your father
	22:22	that he would surely T Saul.
	23:11	Israel, I beseech thee, T thy servant." And the
	25:8	men, and they will T you.
	25:19	But she did not T her husband Nabal.
	27:11	thinking, "Lest they should T about us, and say,
	28:15	have summoned you to T me what I shall
2Sam	1:4	T me." And he answered, "The people have fled
	1:20	T it not in Gath, publish it not in
	3:19	then Abner went to T David at Hebron all
	7:5	to Nathan, "Go and T my servant David, 'Thus
	11:22	David all that Joab had sent him to T
	12:18	of David feared to T him that the child
	13:4	Will you not T me?" Amnon said to him,
	15:35	from the king's house, T it to Zadok and
	17:16	therefore send quickly and T David, 'Do not lodge
	17:17	used to go and T them, and they would
	17:17	they would go and T King David; for they
	18:21	to the Cushite, "Go, T the king what you
	20:16	T Joab, 'Come here, that I may speak to
1Kgs	1:20	are upon you, to T them who shall sit
	14:3	to him; he will T you what shall happen
	14:7	Go, T Jeroboam, 'Thus says the LORD, the God
	18:8	Go, T your lord, 'Behold, Elijah is here.'"
	18:11	now you say, 'Go, T your lord, "Behold, Elijah
	18:12	when I come and T Ahab and he cannot
	18:14	now you say, 'Go, T your lord, "Behold, Elijah
	20:9	the messengers of Ben-hadad, T my lord the king,
	20:11	king of Israel answered, T him, 'Let not him
	22:18	Jehoshaphat, "Did I not T you that he would
2Kgs	4:2	T me; what have you in the house?" And
	4:24	for me unless I T you."
	7:9	let us go and T the king's household."
	7:12	his servants, "I will T you what the Syrians
	8:4	man of God, saying, T me all the great
	9:12	"That is not true; T us now." And he
	9:15	city to go and T the news in Jezreel."
	22:15	the God of Israel: T the man who sent
1Chr	16:9	sing praises to him, T of all his wonderful
	16:23	T of his salvation from day to day.
	17:4	to Nathan, "Go and T my servant David, 'Thus
2Chr	18:17	Jehoshaphat, "Did I not T you that he would
	34:23	the God of Israel: T the man who sent
Neh	9:15	thirst, and thou didst T them to go in
Tob	5:7	me, and I shall T my father."
	5:10	T me.
	5:14	But T me, what wages am I to pay
Jud	2:7	T them to prepare earth and water, for I
	5:3	and said to them, T me, you Canaanites, what
	5:5	servant, and I will T you the truth about
	6:2	have done today and T us not to make
	8:34	for I will not T you until I have
	10:16	in your heart, but T him just what you
	11:3	And now T me why you have fled from
	11:5	presence, and I will T nothing false to my
	11:17	God and he will T me when they have
	11:18	I will come and T you, and then you

11:19 I was sent to T you."
14:8 Now T me what you have done during these
15:4 frontiers of Israel, to T what had taken place
Esth 5:14 and in the morning T the king to have
Job 1:15 alone have escaped to T you."
1:16 alone have escaped to T you."
1:17 alone have escaped to T you."
1:19 alone have escaped to T you."
8:10 not teach you, and T you, and utter words
11:6 and that he would T you the secrets of
12:7 air, and they will T you;
38:4 T me, if you have understanding.
Ps 2:7 I will T of the decree of the LORD:
9:1 whole heart; I will T of all thy wonderful
9:11 T among the peoples his deeds!
22:22 I will T of thy name to my brethren;
22:30 serve him; men shall T of the Lord to
30:9 Will it T of thy faithfulness?
35:28 Then my tongue shall T of thy righteousness and
40:5 I to proclaim and T of them, they would
48:13 citadels; that you may T the next generation
50:12 hungry, I would not T you; for the world
64:9 will fear; they will T what God has wrought,
66:16 God, and I will T what he has done
71:15 My mouth will T of thy righteous acts, of
73:28 refuge, that I may T of all thy works.
78:4 from their children, but T to the coming generation
78:6 unborn, and arise and T them to their children,
96:2 LORD, bless his name; T of his salvation from
105:2 sing praises to him, T of all his wonderful
107:22 sacrifices of thanksgiving, and T of his deeds in
142:2 complaint before him, I T my trouble before him.
145:11 of thy kingdom, and T of thy power,
Eccl 6:12 For who can T man what will be after
8:7 be, for who can T him how it will
10:14 be, and who can T him what will be
10:20 or some winged creature T the matter.
Song 1:7 T me, you whom my soul loves, where you
5:8 my beloved, that you T him I am sick
Wis 6:22 I will T you what wisdom is and how
Sir 1:21 lips of many will T of his good sense.
20:19 for he does not T it at its proper
25:7 a tenth I shall T with my tongue: a
37:9 lot against you and T you, "Your way is
43:24 who sail the sea T of its dangers, and
Is 3:10 T the righteous that it shall be well with
5:5 And now I will T you what I will
19:12 Let them T you and make known what the
41:22 them bring them, and T us what is to
41:22 T us the former things, what they are, that
41:23 T us what is to come hereafter, that we
42:9 they spring forth I T you of them."
44:7 Let them T us what is yet to be.
57:12 I will T of your righteousness and your doings,
Jer 16:10 "And when you T this people all these words,
19:2 the words that I T you.
23:27 their dreams which they T one another, even as
23:28 who has a dream T the dream, but let
23:32 the LORD, and who T them and lead my
28:13 came to Jeremiah: "Go, T Hananiah, 'Thus says the
33:3 answer you, and will T you great and hidden
36:17 Then they asked Baruch, T us, how did you
38:15 to Zedekiah, "If I T you, will you not
38:25 and say to you, T us what you said
42:4 answers you I will T you; I will keep
42:21 he sent me to T you.
48:20 T it by the Arnon, that Moab is laid
51:31 to meet another, to T the king of Babylon
Ezek 12:23 T them therefore, 'Thus says the Lord GOD: I
17:12 T them, Behold, the king of Babylon came to
24:19 me, "Will you not T us what these things
44:5 all that I shall T you concerning all the
Dan 2:2 Chaldeans be summoned, to T the king his dreams.
2:4 T your servants the dream, and we will show
2:7 time, "Let the king T his servants the dream,
2:9 Therefore T me the dream, and I shall know
2:36 dream; now we will T the king its interpretation.
4:9 dream which I saw; T me its interpretation.
9:23 I have come to T it to you, for
10:21 But I will T you what is inscribed in
13:10 but they did not T each other of their
13:40 but she would not T us.
13:54 you really saw her, T me this: Under what
13:58 Now then, T me: Under what tree did you
14:8 "If you do not T me who is eating
Joel 1:3 T your children of it, and let your children
1:3 and let your children T their children, and their
Jon 1:8 they said to him, T us, on whose account
3:2 the message that I T you."
Mic 1:10 T it not in Gath, weep not at all;
Zech 10:2 see lies; the dreamers T false dreams, and give
1Mac 4:46 come a prophet to T what to do with
10:72 Men will T you that you cannot stand before
2Mac 10:10 Now we will T what took place under Antiochus
Mt 2:13 remain there till I T you; for Herod is
3:9 our father'; for I T you, God is able
5:20 For I T you, unless your righteousness exceeds that
6:25 "Therefore I T you, do not be anxious about
6:29 nor spin; yet I T you, even Solomon in
8:11 I T you, many will come from east and
10:27 What I T you in the dark, utter in
11:4 answered them, "Go and T John what you hear
11:9 Yes, I T you, and more than a prophet.
11:22 But I T you, it shall be more tolerable
11:24 But I T you that it shall be more
12:6 I T you, something greater than the temple is
12:31 Therefore I T you, every sin and blasphemy will
12:36 I T you, on the day of judgment men
13:30 harvest time I will T the reapers, Gather the
16:12 that he did not T them to beware of
16:18 And I T you, you are Peter, and on
16:20 charged the disciples to T no one that he
17:9 mountain, Jesus commanded them, T no one the
17:12 all things; but I T you that Elijah has
18:10 little ones; for I T you that in heaven
18:14 against you, go and T him his fault, between
18:16 to listen to them, T it to the church;
19:24 Again I T you, it is easier for a
21:5 by the prophet, saying, T the daughter of Zion,
21:24 question; and if you T me the answer, then
21:24 then I also will T you by what authority
21:27 them, "Neither will I T you by what authority
21:43 Therefore I T you, the kingdom of God will
22:4 sent other servants, saying, T those who are invited,
22:17 T us, then, what you think.
23:3 and observe whatever they T you, but not what
23:38 For I T you, you will not see me
24:3 to him privately, saying, T us, when will this
26:29 I T you I shall not drink again of
26:63 by the living God, T us if you are
26:64 But I T you, hereafter you will see the
27:64 steal him away, and T the people, 'He has
28:7 Then go quickly and T his disciples that he
28:8 joy, and ran to T his disciples.
28:10 be afraid; go and T my brethren to go
28:13 the soldiers and said, T people, 'His disciples came
Mk 5:19 to your friends, and T them how much the
7:35 he charged them to T no one; but the
8:30 he charged them to T no one about him.
9:9 he charged them to T no one what they
9:13 But I T you that Elijah has come, and
10:32 again, he began to T them what was to
11:24 Therefore I T you, whatever you ask in prayer,
11:28 me, and I will T you by what authority
11:32 them, "Neither will I T you by what authority
13:4 Andrew asked him privately, T us, when will this
16:7 But go, T his disciples and Peter that he
Lk 3:8 our father'; for I T you, God is able
4:25 But in truth, I T you, there were many
5:14 he charged him to T no one; but "go
6:46 not do what I T you?
7:9 that followed him, "I T you, not even in
7:22 answered them, "Go and T John what you have
7:26 Yes, I T you, and more than a prophet.
7:28 way before thee.' I T you, among those born
7:47 Therefore I T you, her sins, which are many,
8:56 he charged them to T no one what had
9:21 and commanded them to T this to no one,
9:27 But I T you truly, there are some standing
10:12 has come near.' I T you, it shall be
10:24 For I T you that many prophets and kings
10:40 T her then to help me."
11:8 I T you, though he will not get up
11:9 And I T you, Ask, and it will be
11:51 Yes, I T you, it shall be required of
12:4 "I T you, my friends, do not fear those
12:5 into hell; yes, I T you, fear him!
12:8 "And I T you, every one who acknowledges me
12:22 his disciples, "Therefore I T you, do not be
12:27 nor spin; yet I T you, even Solomon in
12:51 No, I T you, but rather division;
12:59 I T you, you will never get out till

13:3 I T you, No; but unless you repent you
13:5 I T you, No; but unless you repent you
13:24 door; for many, I T you, will seek to
13:27 he will say, 'I T you, I do not
13:32 to them, "Go and T that fox, 'Behold, I
13:35 And I T you, you will not see me
14:24 For I T you, none of those men who
15:7 lost.' Just so, I T you, there will be
15:10 lost.' Just so, I T you, there is joy
16:9 And I T you, make friends for yourselves by
17:34 I T you, in that night there will be
18:8 I T you, he will vindicate them speedily.
18:14 me a sinner!' I T you, this man went
19:11 things, he proceeded to T a parable, because he
19:26 has ten pounds!') 'I T you, that to every
19:40 He answered, "I T you, if these were silent,
20:2 and said to him, T us by what authority
20:3 you a question; now T me,
20:8 them, "Neither will I T you by what authority
20:9 And he began to T the people this parable:
21:3 he said, "Truly I T you, this poor widow
22:11 which he enters, and T the householder, 'The Teacher
22:16 I suffer; for I T you I shall not
22:18 among yourselves; for I T you that from now
22:34 He said, "I T you, Peter, the cock will
22:37 For I T you that this scripture must be
22:65 you are the Christ, T us." But he said
22:65 to them, "If I T you, you will not
Jn 3:12 you believe if I T you heavenly things?
4:35 I T you, lift up your eyes, and see
8:45 But, because I T the truth, you do not
8:46 If I T the truth, why do you not
10:24 you are the Christ, T us plainly."
11:40 her, "Did I not T you that if you
13:19 heel against me.' I T you this now, before
13:24 to him and said, T us who it is
16:7 Nevertheless I T you the truth: it is to
16:25 you in figures but T you plainly of the
20:15 have carried him away, T me where you have
Acts 5:8 Peter said to her, T me whether you sold
5:38 the present case I T you, keep away from
12:17 And he said, T this to James and to
15:27 Silas, who themselves will T you the same things
21:23 Do therefore what we T you.
22:27 and said to him, T me, are you a
23:17 he has something to T him."
23:19 that you have to T me?"
23:22 young man, charging him, T no one that you
Rom 15:8 For I T you that Christ became a servant
1Cor 15:50 I T you this, brethren: flesh and blood cannot
15:51 I T you a mystery.
Gal 4:21 T me, you who desire to be under law,
Eph 6:21 in the Lord will T you everything.
Phil 1:22 Yet which I shall choose I cannot T
3:18 told you and now T you even with tears,
Col 4:7 Tychicus will T you all about my affairs; he
4:9 They will T you of everything that has taken
Heb 11:32 would fail me to T of Gideon, Barak, Samson,
Rev 17:7 I will T you the mystery of the woman,

TELLING (26)

Judg 7:13 behold, a man was T a dream to his
7:15 When Gideon heard the T of the dream and
2Sam 11:19 "When you have finished T all the news about
2Kgs 1:2 so he sent messengers, T them, "Go, inquire of
8:5 And while he was T the king how Elisha
Ezra 8:17 at the place Casiphia, T them what to say
Esth 1:18 queen's behavior will be T it to all the
Ps 19:1 The heavens are T the glory of God; and
26:7 song of thanksgiving, and T all thy wondrous deeds.
Sir 41:23 gift; of repeating and T what you hear, and
Jer 43:2 to Jeremiah, "You are T a lie.
Dan 14:12 Daniel will, who is T lies about us."
1Mac 9:60 his allies in Judea, T them to seize Jonathan
2Mac 6:23 he declared himself quickly, T them to send him
Mt 20:31 The crowd rebuked them, T them to be silent;
Mk 10:48 And many rebuked him, T him to be silent;
Lk 12:41 said, "Lord, are you T this parable for us
18:39 in front rebuked him, T him to be silent;
Jn 13:29 money box, Jesus was T him, "Buy what we
Acts 2:11 Arabians, we hear them T in our own tongues
17:21 time in nothing except T or hearing something new.
19:4 the baptism of repentance, T the people to believe
21:21 Gentiles to forsake Moses, T them not to circumcise
Gal 4:16 become your enemy by T you the truth?
1Tim 2:7 and apostle (I am T the truth, I am

Rev 16:1 voice from the temple T the seven angels, "Go

TELLS (13)

Gen 21:12 you, do as she T you, for through Isaac
Deut 13:2 or wonder which he T you comes to pass,
2Kgs 6:12 who is in Israel, T the king of Israel
2Chr 32:11 by thirst, when he T you, "The LORD our
Ps 41:6 he goes out, he T it abroad.
Sir 22:8 He who T a story to a fool tells
22:8 story to a fool T it to a drowsy
Jer 39:12 with him as he T you."
Mt 15:5 say, 'If any one T his father or his
Mk 7:11 say, 'If a man T his father or his
Jn 2:5 servants, "Do whatever he T you."
19:35 he knows that he T the truth—that you
Acts 3:22 him in whatever he T you.

TEMA (5)

Gen 25:15 Dumah, Massa, Hadad, T, Jetur, Naphish, and
1Chr 1:30 Mishma, Dumah, Massa, Hadad, T,
Job 6:19 The caravans of T look, the travelers of Sheba
Is 21:14 with bread, O inhabitants of the land of T
Jer 25:23 across the sea; Dedan, T, Buz, and all who

TEMAH (2)

Ezra 2:53 Sisera, the sons of T,
Neh 7:55 Sisera, the sons of T,

TEMAN (13)

Gen 36:11 sons of Eliphaz were T, Omar, Zepho, Gatam, and
36:15 of Esau: the chiefs T, Omar, Zepho, Kenaz,
36:42 Oholibamah, Elah, Pinon, Kenaz, T, Mibzar,
1Chr 1:36 The sons of Eliphaz: T, Omar, Zephi, Gatam, Kenaz,
1:53 Oholibamah, Elah, Pinon, Kenaz, T, Mibzar,
Jer 49:7 LORD of hosts: "Is wisdom no more in T
49:20 against the inhabitants of T: Even the little ones
Bar 3:22 Canaan, nor seen in T;
3:23 merchants of Merran and T, the story-tellers and the
Ezek 25:13 make it desolate; from T even to Dedan they
Amos 1:12 send a fire upon T, and it shall devour
Obad 1:9 shall be dismayed, O T, so that every man
Hab 3:3 God came from T, and the Holy One from

TEMANITE (6)

Job 2:11 own place, Eliphaz the T, Bildad the Shuhite, and
4:1 Then Eliphaz the T answered:
15:1 Then Eliphaz the T answered:
22:1 Then Eliphaz the T answered:
42:7 said to Eliphaz the T: "My wrath is kindled
42:9 So Eliphaz the T and Bildad the Shuhite and

TEMANITES (2)

Gen 36:34 the land of the T reigned in his stead.
1Chr 1:45 the land of the T reigned in his stead.

TEMENI

1Chr 4:6 bore him Ahuzzam, Hepher, T, and Ha-ahashtari.

TEMPER (4)

Prov 14:17 A man of quick T acts foolishly, but a
14:29 who has a hasty T exalts folly.
Sir 31:26 and water prove the T of steel, so wine
2Mac 4:25 but having the hot T of a cruel tyrant

TEMPERATE (3)

1Tim 3:2 husband of one wife, T, sensible, dignified, hospitable,
3:11 serious, no slanderers, but T, faithful in all things.
Tit 2:2 the older men be T, serious, sensible, sound in

TEMPERATELY

Sir 31:28 drunk in season and T is rejoicing of heart

TEMPERS

Wis 7:20 of animals and the T of wild beasts, the

TEMPEST (23)

Job 9:17 crushes me with a T, and multiplies my wounds
Ps 50:3 a devouring fire, round about him a mighty T
55:8 me a shelter from the raging wind and T
83:15 pursue them with thy T and terrify them with
Prov 10:25 When the T passes, the wicked is no more,
Wis 5:23 them, and like a T it will winnow them
Sir 16:19 Like a T which no man can see, so
43:17 earth; so do the T from the north and
Is 28:2 of hail, a destroying T, like a storm of
29:6 noise, with whirlwind and T, and the flame of

30:30 with a cloudburst and T and hailstones.
32:2 a covert from the T, like streams of water
40:24 they wither, and the T carries them off like
41:16 them away, and the T shall scatter them.
Jer 11:16 roar of a great T he will set fire
23:19 gone forth, a whirling T; it will burst upon
25:32 nation, and a great T is stirring from the
30:23 gone forth, a whirling T; it will burst upon
Amos 1:14 of battle, with a T in the day of
Jon 1:4 there was a mighty T on the sea, so
1:12 me that this great T has come upon you."
Acts 27:20 day, and no small T lay on us, all
Heb 12:18 and gloom, and a T,

TEMPESTUOUS (3)

Jon 1:11 For the sea grew more and more T
1:13 grew more and more T against them.
Acts 27:14 But soon a T wind, called the northeaster, struck

TEMPLE (342)

Judg 4:21 the peg into his T, till it went down
4:22 Sisera dead, with the tent peg in his T
5:26 crushed his head, she shattered and pierced his T
1Sam 1:9 the doorpost of the T of the LORD.
3:3 lying down within the T of the LORD, where
31:10 his armor in the T of Ashtaroth; and they
2Sam 22:7 From his T he heard my voice, and my
1Kgs 6:7 was heard in the T, while it was being
7:21 the vestibule of the T; he set up the
7:50 for the doors of the nave of the T
2Kgs 18:16 the doors of the T of the LORD, and
23:4 bring out of the T of the LORD all
24:13 of gold in the T of the LORD, which
25:14 bronze used in the T service,
1Chr 9:2 the Levites, and the T servants.
9:33 the chambers of the T free from other service,
10:10 his armor in the T of their gods, and
10:10 his head in the T of Dagon.
28:11 the vestibule of the T, and of its houses,
2Chr 2:1 purposed to build a T for the name of
2:12 who will build a T for the LORD, and
3:17 in front of the T, one on the south,
4:7 set them in the T, five on the south
4:8 placed them in the T, five on the south
4:22 the sockets of the T, for the inner doors
4:22 the nave of the T were of gold.
7:1 and the glory of the LORD filled the T
7:3 the LORD upon the T, they bowed down with
26:16 God, and entered the T of the LORD to
27:2 did not invade the T of the LORD.
29:16 they found in the T of the LORD into
35:20 Josiah had prepared the T, Neco king of Egypt
Ezra 2:43 The T servants: the sons of Ziha, the sons
2:58 All the T servants and the sons of Solomon's
2:70 the gatekeepers, and the T servants lived in their
3:6 the foundation of the T of the LORD was
3:10 the foundation of the T of the LORD, the
4:1 exiles were building a T to the LORD, the
5:14 taken out of the T that was in Jerusalem
5:14 and brought into the T of Babylon, these Cyrus
5:14 took out of the T of Babylon, and they
5:15 put them in the T which is in Jerusalem,
6:5 took out of the T that is in Jerusalem
6:5 brought back to the T which is in Jerusalem,
7:7 and gatekeepers, and the T servants.
7:24 singers, the doorkeepers, the T servants, or other
8:17 and his brethren the T servants at the place
8:20 and twenty of the T servants, whom David and
Neh 2:8 the fortress of the T, and for the wall
3:26 of Parosh and the T servants living on Ophel
3:31 the house of the T servants and of the
6:10 of God, within the T, and let us close
6:10 the doors of the T; for they are coming
6:11 could go into the T and live?
7:46 The T servants: the sons of Ziha, the sons
7:60 All the T servants and the sons of Solomon's
7:73 of the people, the T servants, and all Israel,
10:28 gatekeepers, the singers, the T servants, and all who
11:3 the Levites, the T servants, and the descendants
11:21 But the T servants lived on Ophel; and Ziha
11:21 Gishpa were over the T servants.
Tob 1:4 sacrifice and where the T of the dwelling of
Jud 4:2 Jerusalem and for the T of the Lord their
4:3 the altar and the T had been consecrated after
4:11 prostrated themselves before the T and put ashes on
5:18 a foreign country; the T of their God was

8:24 the sanctuary and the T and the altar rest
Ps 5:7 worship toward thy holy T in the fear of
11:4 is in his holy T, the LORD's throne is
18:6 From his T he heard my voice, and my
27:4 of the LORD, and to inquire in his T
29:9 bare; and in his T all cry, "Glory!"
48:9 love, O God, in the midst of thy T
65:4 with the goodness of thy house, thy holy T
68:29 Because of thy T at Jerusalem kings bear gifts
79:1 have defiled thy holy T; they have laid Jerusalem
138:2 down toward thy holy T and give thanks to
Wis 3:14 great delight in the T of the Lord.
9:8 command to build a T on thy holy mountain,
Sir 36:14 wondrous deeds, and thy T with thy glory.
45:9 ringing heard in the T as a reminder to
49:12 house and raised a T holy to the Lord,
50:1 the house, and in his time fortified the T
50:2 retaining walls for the T enclosure.
50:7 sun shining upon the T of the Most High,
51:14 Before the T I asked for her, and I
Is 6:1 and lifted up; and his train filled the T
44:28 built,' and of the T, 'Your foundation shall be
66:6 A voice from the T
Jer 7:4 words: 'This is the T of the LORD, the
7:4 of the LORD, the T of the LORD, the
7:4 of the LORD, the T of the LORD.'
24:1 figs placed before the T of the LORD.
38:14 third entrance of the T of the LORD.
41:5 to present at the T of the LORD.
50:28 of the LORD our God, vengeance for his T
51:11 vengeance of the LORD, the vengeance for his T
52:18 bronze used in the T service;
Bar 1:8 carried away from the T, to return them to
6:13 the dust from the T, which is thick upon
6:20 a beam of the T, but men say their
6:21 have been blackened by the smoke of the T
6:55 breaks out in a T of wooden gods overlaid
Ezek 8:16 the door of the T of the LORD, between
8:16 their backs to the T of the LORD, and
40:5 the outside of the T area, and the length
40:45 have charge of the T,
40:47 and the altar was in front of the T
40:48 the vestibule of the T and measured the jambs
41:5 the wall of the T, six cubits thick; and
41:5 the side chambers, four cubits, round about the T
41:6 the wall of the T to serve as supports
41:6 not be supported by the wall of the T
41:7 story round about the T; on the side of
41:7 the side of the T a stairway led upward,
41:8 saw also that the T had a raised platform
41:9 the platform of the T and the
41:10 cubits round about the T on every side.
41:12 that was facing the T yard on the west
41:13 Then he measured the T, a hundred cubits long;
41:14 east front of the T and the yard, a
41:15 The nave of the T and the inner room
41:16 against the threshold the T was paneled with wood
41:19 carved on the whole T round about;
42:1 which were opposite the T yard and opposite the
42:8 while those opposite the T were a hundred cubits
42:15 the interior of the T, he led me
42:15 east, and measured the T area round about.
43:4 the LORD entered the T by the gate facing
43:5 behold, the glory of the LORD filled the T
43:6 me out of the T;
43:10 house of Israel the T and its appearance and
43:11 have done, portray the T, its arrangement, its exits
43:12 the law of the T: the whole territory round
43:12 Behold, this is the law of the T
43:21 place belonging to the T, outside the sacred area.
44:4 the front of the T; and I looked, and
44:4 the LORD filled the T of the LORD; and
44:5 the ordinances of the T of the LORD and
44:5 be admitted to the T and all those who
44:11 the gates of the T, and serving in the
44:11 and serving in the T; they shall slay the
44:14 keep charge of the T, to do all its
45:5 who minister at the T, as their possession for
45:19 the doorposts of the T, the four corners of
45:20 ignorance; so you shall make atonement for the T
46:24 who minister at the T shall boil the sacrifices
47:1 the door of the T; and behold, water was
47:1 the threshold of the T toward the east (for
47:1 the east (for the T faced east); and the
47:1 the threshold of the T, south of the altar.
48:21 the sanctuary of the T in its midst,

Dan 3:54 art thou in the T of thy holy glory
5:2 taken out of the T in Jerusalem be brought,
5:3 taken out of the T, the house of God
11:31 appear and profane the T and fortress, and shall
14:10 with Daniel into the T of Bel.
14:14 them throughout the whole T in the presence of
14:22 over to Daniel, who destroyed it and its T
Amos 7:13 and it is a T of the kingdom."
8:3 The songs of the T shall become wailings in
Jon 2:4 look upon thy holy T
2:7 my prayer came to thee, into thy holy T
Mic 1:2 witness against you, the Lord from his holy T
Hab 2:20 is in his holy T; let all the earth
Hag 2:15 a stone in the T of the LORD,
2:18 foundation of the LORD's T was laid, consider:
Zech 6:12 he shall build the T of the LORD.
6:13 who shall build the T of the LORD, and
6:14 shall be in the T of the LORD as
6:15 help to build the T of the LORD; and
8:9 was laid, that the T might be built.
Mal 3:1 suddenly come to his T; the messenger of the
1Mac 1:22 the front of the T; he stripped it all
2:8 Her T has become like a man without honor;
4:46 convenient place on the T hill until there should
4:48 the interior of the T, and consecrated the courts.
4:49 altar of incense, and the table into the T
4:50 the lampstand, and these gave light in the T
4:57 the front of the T with golden crowns and
6:2 Its T was very rich, containing golden shields,
7:36 the altar and the T, and they wept and
10:41 from now on for the service of the T
10:42 the services of the T, this too is canceled,
10:43 takes refuge at the T in Jerusalem, or in
10:83 and entered Beth-dagon, the T of their idol, for
10:84 plundered them; and the T of Dagon, and those
11:4 they showed him the T of Dagon burned down,
13:52 the fortifications of the T hill alongside the citadel,
15:9 your nation and the T, so that your glory
16:20 of Jerusalem and the T hill.
2Mac 1:13 to pieces in the T of Nanea by a
1:15 the priests of the T of Nanea had set
1:15 precinct, they closed the T as soon as he
1:18 the purification of the T, we thought it necessary
1:18 Nehemiah, who built the T and the altar, offered
2:9 sacrifice for the dedication and completion of the T
2:19 purification of the great T, and the dedication of
2:22 hordes, and recovered the T famous throughout the
3:2 place and glorified the T with the finest presents,
3:4 made captain of the T, had a disagreement with
3:12 and inviolability of the T which is honored throughout
3:30 And the T, which a little while before was
4:32 gold vessels of the T and gave them to
4:42 to flight; and the T robber himself they killed
5:15 enter the most holy T in all the world,
5:21 hundred talents from the T, and hurried away to
6:2 also to pollute the T in Jerusalem and call
6:2 and call it the T of Olympian Zeus, and
6:2 one in Gerizim the T of Zeus the Friend
6:4 For the T was filled with debauchery and reveling
8:2 have pity on the T which had been profaned
10:1 them on, recovered the T and the city;
11:3 levy tribute on the T as he did on
11:25 decision is that their T be restored to them
12:26 against Carnaim and the T of Atargatis, and
13:10 country and the holy T,
13:14 death for the laws, T, city, country, and,
14:4 some of the customary olive branches from the T
14:13 up Alcimus as high priest of the greatest T
14:31 the great and holy T while the priests were
14:33 build here a splendid T to Dionysus."
14:35 that there be a T for thy habitation among
15:17 the sanctuary and the T were in danger.
Mt 4:5 the pinnacle of the T,
12:5 the priests in the T profane the sabbath, and
12:6 something greater than the T is here.
21:12 And Jesus entered the T of God and drove
21:12 and bought in the T, and he overturned the
21:14 to him in the T, and he healed them.
21:15 crying out in the T, "Hosanna to the Son
21:23 when he entered the T, the chief priests and
23:15 one swears by the T, it is nothing; but
23:15 the gold of the T, he is bound by
23:16 the gold or the T that has made the
23:20 who swears by the T, swears by it and
24:1 Jesus left the T and was going away, when
24:1 point out to him the buildings of the T
26:55 I sat in the T teaching, and you did
26:61 able to destroy the T of God, and to
27:5 of silver in the T, he departed; and he
27:40 who would destroy the T and build it in
27:51 the curtain of the T was torn in two,
Mk 11:11 and went into the T; and when he had
11:15 And he entered the T and began to drive
11:15 who bought in the T, and he overturned the
11:16 allow any one to carry anything through the T
11:26 was walking in the T, the chief priests and
12:35 Jesus taught in the T, he said, "How can
13:1 came out of the T, one of his disciples
13:3 of Olives opposite the T, Peter and James and
14:49 with you in the T teaching, and you did
14:58 'I will destroy this T that is made with
15:28 who would destroy the T and build it in
15:37 the curtain of the T was torn in two,
Lk 1:9 lot to enter the T of the Lord and
1:21 and they wondered at his delay in the T
1:22 a vision in the T; and he made signs
2:27 he came into the T; and when the parents
2:37 not depart from the T, worshiping with fasting and
2:46 found him in the T, sitting among the teachers,
4:9 the pinnacle of the T, and said to him,
18:10 went up into the T to pray, one a
19:45 And he entered the T and began to drive
19:47 And he was teaching daily in the T
20:1 the people in the T and preaching the gospel,
21:5 some spoke of the T, how it was adorned
21:37 was teaching in the T, but at night he
21:38 to him in the T to hear him.
22:50 and officers of the T and elders, who had
22:51 after day in the T, you did not lay
23:44 the curtain of the T was torn in two.
24:53 were continually in the T blessing God.
Jn 2:14 In the T he found those who were selling
2:15 oxen, out of the T; and he poured out
2:19 answered them, "Destroy this T, and in three days
2:20 years to build this T, and will you raise
2:21 he spoke of the T of his body.
5:13 found him in the T, and said to him,
7:14 went up into the T and taught.
7:28 he taught in the T, "You know me, and
8:2 came again to the T; all the people came
8:20 he taught in the T; but no one arrested
8:59 Jesus hid himself, and went out of the T
10:23 was walking in the T, in the portico of
11:56 they stood in the T, "What do you think?
18:20 synagogues and in the T, where all Jews come
Acts 2:46 by day, attending the T together and breaking bread
3:1 going up to the T at the hour of
3:2 that gate of the T which is called Beautiful
3:2 to ask alms of those who entered the T
3:3 to go into the T, he asked for alms.
3:8 walked and entered the T with them, walking and
3:10 Beautiful Gate of the T; and they were filled
4:1 the captain of the T and the Sadducees came
5:20 and stand in the T and speak to the
5:21 this, they entered the T at daybreak and taught.
5:24 the captain of the T and the chief priests
5:25 are standing in the T and teaching the people."
5:42 every day in the T and at home they
14:13 priest of Zeus, whose T was in front of
19:27 but also that the T of the great goddess
19:35 of the Ephesians is T keeper of the great
21:26 and went into the T, to give notice when
21:27 seen him in the T, stirred up all the
21:28 brought Greeks into the T, and he has defiled
21:29 supposed that Paul had brought him into the T
21:30 him out of the T, and at once the
22:17 was praying in the T, I fell into a
24:6 tried to profane the T, but we seized him.
24:11 crowd, either in the T or in the synagogues,
24:17 me purified in the T, without any crowd or
25:8 Jews, nor against the T, nor against Caesar have
26:21 seized me in the T and tried to kill
1Cor 3:16 that you are God's T and that God's Spirit
3:17 any one destroys God's T, God will destroy him.
3:17 For God's T is holy, and that temple you
3:17 is holy, and that T you are.
6:19 your body is a T of the Holy Spirit
8:10 table in an idol's T, might he not be
9:13 are employed in the T service get their food
9:13 their food from the T, and those who serve
2Cor 6:16 What agreement has the T of God with idols?
6:16 For we are the T of the living God;

Eph 2:21 grows into a holy T in the Lord;
2Thes 2:4 his seat in the T of God, proclaiming himself
Rev 3:12 a pillar in the T of my God; never
7:15 and night within his T; and he who sits
11:1 "Rise and measure the T of God and the
11:2 the court outside the T; leave that out, for
11:19 Then God's T in heaven was opened, and the
11:19 was seen within his T; and there were flashes
14:15 came out of the T, calling with a loud
14:17 came out of the T in heaven, and he
15:5 I looked, and the T of the tent of
15:6 and out of the T came the seven angels
15:8 and ever; and the T was filled with smoke
15:8 one could enter the T until the seven plagues
16:1 loud voice from the T telling the seven angels,
16:17 came out of the T, from the throne, saying,
21:22 And I saw no T in the city, for
21:22 the city, for its T is the Lord God

TEMPLES (11)

Lev 13:41 from his forehead and T, he has baldness of
19:27 the hair on your T or mar the edges
Jud 4:1 and destroyed all their T;
Jer 43:12 a fire in the T of the gods of
43:13 of Egypt; and the T of the gods of
Bar 6:17 when they have been set up in the T
6:18 the priests make their T secure with doors and
6:31 wood; and in their T the priests sit with
Joel 3:5 and have carried my rich treasures into your T
2Mac 9:2 attempted to rob the T and control the city.
Rom 2:22 You who abhor idols, do you rob T

TEMPORARILY

2Mac 14:17 Nicanor, but had been T checked because of the

TEMPT (4)

Mt 4:7 written, 'You shall not T the Lord your God.'"
Lk 4:12 said, 'You shall not T the Lord your God.'"
Acts 5:9 have agreed together to T the Spirit of the
1Cor 7:5 together again, lest Satan T you through lack of

TEMPTATION (14)

Sir 2:1 forward to serve the Lord, prepare yourself for T
Mt 6:13 lead us not into T, But deliver us from
18:7 man by whom the T comes!
26:41 may not enter into T; the spirit indeed is
Mk 14:38 may not enter into T; the spirit indeed is
Lk 4:13 devil had ended every T, he departed from him
8:13 and in time of T fall away.
11:4 indebted to us; and lead us not into T
22:40 them, "Pray that you may not enter into T
22:44 and pray that you may not enter into T
1Cor 7:2 But because of the T to immorality, each man
10:13 No T has overtaken you that is not common
10:13 strength, but with the T will also provide the
1Tim 6:9 be rich fall into T, into a snare, into

TEMPTATIONS (3)

Mt 18:7 to the world for T to sin!
18:7 it is necessary that T come, but woe to
Lk 17:1 said to his disciples, T to sin are sure

TEMPTED (13)

Mt 4:1 the wilderness to be T by the devil.
Mk 1:13 the wilderness forty days, T by Satan; and he
Lk 4:2 days in the wilderness, T by the devil.
1Cor 10:13 not let you be T beyond your strength, but
Gal 6:1 Look to yourself, lest you too be T
1Thes 3:5 somehow the tempter had T you and that our
Heb 2:18 has suffered and been T, he is able to
2:18 he is able to help those who are T
4:15 every respect has been T as we are, yet
Jas 1:12 say when he is T, "I am tempted by
1:12 is tempted, "I am T by God"; for God
1:12 for God cannot be T with evil and he
1:13 but each person is T when he is lured

TEMPTER (2)

Mt 4:3 And the T came and said to him, "If
1Thes 3:5 fear that somehow the T had tempted you and

TEMPTS (2)

Sir 18:22 like a man who T the Lord.
Jas 1:12 evil and he himself T no one;

TEN (234)

Gen 5:14 were nine hundred and T years; and he died.
16:3 after Abram had dwelt T years in the land
18:32 Suppose T are found there." He answered, "For the
18:32 "For the sake of T I will not destroy
24:10 Then the servant took T of his master's camels
24:22 for her arms weighing T gold shekels,
24:55 a while, at least T days; after that she
24:60 mother of thousands of T thousands; and may your
31:7 and changed my wages T times, but God did
31:41 have changed my wages T times.
32:15 colts, forty cows and T bulls, twenty she-asses and
32:15 bulls, twenty she-asses and T he-asses.
42:3 So T of Joseph's brothers went down to buy
45:23 he sent as follows: T asses loaded with the
45:23 things of Egypt, and T she-asses loaded with grain,
50:22 lived a hundred and T years.
50:26 being a hundred and T years old; and they
Ex 26:1 make the tabernacle with T curtains of fine twined
26:16 T cubits shall be the length of a frame,
27:12 for fifty cubits, with T pillars and ten bases.
27:12 with ten pillars and T bases.
34:28 of the covenant, the T commandments.
36:8 made the tabernacle with T curtains; they were
36:21 T cubits was the length of a frame, and
38:12 fifty cubits, their pillars T, and their sockets ten;
38:12 ten, and their sockets T; the hooks of the
Lev 26:8 of you shall chase T thousand; and your enemies
26:26 your staff of bread, T women shall bake your
27:5 and for a female T shekels.
27:7 and for a female T shekels.
Num 7:14 one golden dish of T shekels, full of incense;
7:20 one golden dish of T shekels, full of incense;
7:26 one golden dish of T shekels, full of incense;
7:32 one golden dish of T shekels, full of incense;
7:38 one golden dish of T shekels, full of incense;
7:44 one golden dish of T shekels, full of incense;
7:50 one golden dish of T shekels, full of incense;
7:56 one golden dish of T shekels, full of incense;
7:62 one golden dish of T shekels, full of incense;
7:68 one golden dish of T shekels, full of incense;
7:74 one golden dish of T shekels, full of incense;
7:80 one golden dish of T shekels, full of incense;
7:86 full of incense, weighing T shekels apiece according
10:36 O LORD, to the T thousand thousands of Israel."
11:19 or five days, or T days, or twenty days,
11:32 gathered least gathered T homers; and they spread
14:22 to the proof these T times and have not
29:23 "On the fourth day T bulls, two rams, fourteen
Deut 4:13 perform, that is, the T commandments; and he wrote
10:4 first writing, the T commandments which the LORD
32:30 thousand, and two put T thousand to flight, unless
33:2 he came from the T thousands of holy ones,
33:17 earth; such are the T thousands of Ephraim, and
Josh 15:57 Gibe-ah, and Timnah: T cities with their villages.
17:5 there fell to Manasseh T portions, besides the land
21:5 the half-tribe of Manasseh, T cities.
21:26 of the Kohathites were T in all with their
22:14 priest, and with him T chiefs, one from each
24:29 being a hundred and T years old.
Judg 1:4 hand; and they defeated T thousand of them at
2:8 of one hundred and T years.
3:29 at that time about T thousand of the Moabites,
4:6 at Mount Tabor, taking T thousand from the tribe
4:10 Naphtali to Kedesh; and T thousand men went up
4:14 from Mount Tabor with T thousand men following
6:27 So Gideon took T men of his servants, and
12:11 and he judged Israel T years.
17:10 I will give you T pieces of silver a
20:10 and we will take T men of a hundred
20:10 and a thousand of T thousand, to bring provisions
20:34 there came against Gibe-ah T thousand picked men
Ruth 1:4 They lived there about T years;
4:2 And he took T men of the elders of
1Sam 1:8 more to you than T sons?"
15:4 men on foot, and T thousand men of Judah.
17:17 parched grain, and these T loaves, and carry them
17:18 brothers; also take these T cheeses to the
18:7 thousands, and David his T thousands."
18:8 have ascribed to David T thousands, and to me
21:11 thousands, and David his T thousands'?"
25:5 So David sent T young men; and David said
25:38 And about T days later the LORD smote Nabal;
29:5 thousands, and David his T thousands'?"
2Sam 15:16 And the king left T concubines to keep the
18:3 But you are worth T thousand of us; therefore

18:11 glad to give you T pieces of silver and
18:15 And T young men, Joab's armor-bearers, surrounded
19:43 of Judah, "We have T shares in the king,
20:3 the king took the T concubines whom he had
1Kgs 4:23 sixty cors of meal, T fat oxen, and twenty
5:14 sent them to Lebanon, T thousand a month in
6:3 of the house, and T cubits deep in front
6:23 cherubim of olivewood, each T cubits high.
6:24 the cherub; it was T cubits from the tip
6:25 other cherub also measured T cubits; both cherubim
6:26 of one cherub was T cubits, and so was
7:10 stones of eight and T cubits.
7:23 sea; it was round, T cubits from brim to
7:27 He also made the T stands of bronze; each
7:37 manner he made the T stands; all of them
7:38 And he made T lavers of bronze; each laver
7:38 for each of the T stands.
7:43 upon the pillars; the T stands, and the ten
7:43 ten stands, and the T lavers upon the stands;
11:31 Jeroboam, "Take for yourself T pieces; for thus says
11:31 and will give you T tribes
11:35 give it to you, T tribes.
14:3 Take with you T loaves, some cakes, and a
2Kgs 5:5 went, taking with him T talents of silver, six
5:5 shekels of gold, and T festal garments.
13:7 than fifty horsemen and T chariots and ten thousand
13:7 and ten chariots and T thousand footmen; for the
14:7 He killed T thousand Edomites in the Valley of
15:17 Israel, and he reigned T years in Samaria.
20:9 the shadow go forward T steps, or go back
20:9 steps, or go back T steps?"
20:10 the shadow to lengthen T steps; rather let the
20:10 the shadow go back T steps."
20:11 brought the shadow back T steps, by which the
24:14 mighty men of valor, T thousand captives, and all
25:25 royal family, came with T men, and attacked and
1Chr 6:61 the half of Manasseh, T cities.
29:7 five thousand talents and T thousand darics of gold,
29:7 thousand darics of gold, T thousand talents of silver,
2Chr 4:1 twenty cubits wide, and T cubits high.
4:2 sea; it was round, T cubits from brim to
4:6 He also made T lavers in which to wash,
4:7 And he made T golden lampstands as prescribed, and
4:8 He also made T tables, and placed them in
14:1 land had rest for T years.
25:11 of Salt and smote T thousand men of Seir.
25:12 of Judah captured another T thousand alive, and took
27:5 talents of silver, and T thousand cors of wheat
27:5 cors of wheat and T thousand of barley.
30:24 a thousand bulls and T thousand sheep.
36:9 reigned three months and T days in Jerusalem.
Ezra 1:10 thousand four hundred and T bowls of silver, and
8:12 him a hundred and T men.
8:24 priests: Sherebiah, Hashabiah, and T of their
Neh 4:12 they said to us T times, "From all the
5:18 for me, and every T days skins of wine
11:1 bring one out of T to live in Jerusalem
Tob 1:14 in Media I left T talents of silver in
4:20 to you about the T talents of silver which
Esth 3:9 and I will pay T thousand talents of silver
9:10 Aridai and Vaizatha, the T sons of Haman the
9:12 men and also the T sons of Haman.
9:13 And let the T sons of Haman be hanged
9:14 in Susa, and the T sons of Haman were
Job 19:3 These T times you have cast reproach upon me;
Ps 3:6 am not afraid of T thousands of people who
33:2 with the harp of T strings!
68:17 With mighty chariotry, twice T thousand, thousands
90:10 life are threescore and T, or even by reason
91:7 fall at your side, T thousand at your right
144:13 bring forth thousands and T thousands in our fields;
Eccl 7:19 wise man more than T rulers that are in
Song 5:10 and ruddy, distinguished among T thousand.
Wis 7:2 within the period of T months, compacted with blood,
12:22 thou scourgest our enemies T thousand times more,
Sir 23:19 of the Lord are T thousand times brighter than
41:4 Whether life is for T or a hundred or
47:6 glorified him for his T thousands, and praised him
Is 5:10 For T acres of vineyard shall yield but one
38:8 of Ahaz turn back T steps." So the sun
38:8 on the dial the T steps by which it
Jer 41:1 the king, came with T men to Gedaliah the
41:2 of Nethaniah and the T men with him rose
41:8 But there were T men among them who said
42:7 At the end of T days the word of
Ezek 40:11 opening of the gateway, T cubits; and the breadth
40:49 breadth twelve cubits; and T steps led up to
41:2 of the entrance was T cubits; and the sidewalls
42:4 was a passage inward, T cubits wide and a
45:3 thousand cubits long and T thousand broad, in which
45:5 thousand cubits long and T thousand cubits broad,
45:12 be five shekels, and T shekels shall be ten
45:12 ten shekels shall be T shekels, and your mina
45:14 like the homer, contains T baths);
48:10 on the northern side, T thousand cubits in breadth
48:10 on the western side, T thousand in breadth on
48:13 cubits in length and T thousand in breadth.
48:18 holy portion shall be T thousand cubits to the
48:18 to the east, and T thousand to the west,
Dan 1:12 "Test your servants for T days; let us be
1:14 and tested them for T days.
1:15 At the end of T days it was seen
1:20 them, he found them T times better than all
7:7 it; and it had T horns.
7:10 thousands served him, and T thousand times ten
7:10 and ten thousand times T thousand stood before him;
7:20 feet; and concerning the T horns that were on
7:24 As for the T horns, out of this kingdom
7:24 out of this kingdom T kings shall arise, and
Hos 8:12 him my laws by T thousands, they would be
Amos 5:3 a hundred shall have T left to the house
6:9 And if T men remain in one house, they
Mic 6:7 thousands of rams, with T thousands of rivers of
Hag 2:16 measures, there were but T; when one came to
Zech 5:2 cubits, and its breadth T cubits."
8:23 hosts: In those days T men from the nations
1Mac 4:29 Judas met them with T thousand men.
10:74 He chose T thousand men and set out from
2Mac 11:4 was elated with his T thousands of infantry, and
12:19 the stronghold, more than T thousand men.
13:2 of one hundred and T thousand infantry, five
Mt 18:23 him who owed him T thousand talents;
20:24 And when the T heard it, they were indignant
25:1 shall be compared to T maidens who took their
25:28 him who has the T talents.
Mk 10:41 And when the T heard it, they began to
Lk 14:31 he is able with T thousand to meet him
15:8 "Or what woman, having T silver coins, if she
17:12 he was met by T lepers, who stood at
17:17 said Jesus, "Were not T cleansed?
19:13 Calling T of his servants, he gave them ten
19:13 servants, he gave them T pounds, and said to
19:16 your pound has made T pounds more.'
19:17 shall have authority over T cities.'
19:24 him who has the T pounds.'
19:25 him, 'Lord, he has T pounds!')
Acts 25:6 more than eight or T days, he went down
1Cor 14:19 to instruct others, than T thousand words in a
Rev 2:10 be tested, and for T days you will have
9:16 of cavalry was twice T thousand times ten thousand;
9:16 twice ten thousand times T thousand; I heard their
12:3 with seven heads and T horns, and seven diadems
13:1 of the sea, with T horns and seven heads,
13:1 and seven heads, with T diadems upon its horns
17:3 had seven heads and T horns.
17:7 with seven heads and T horns that carries her.
17:12 And the T horns that you saw are ten
17:12 that you saw are T kings who have not
17:16 And the T horns that you saw, they and

TEN-STRINGED

Ps 144:9 O God; upon a T harp I will play

TENANTS (15)

Mt 21:33 let it out to T, and went into another
21:34 his servants to the T, to get his fruit;
21:35 his fruit; and the T took his servants and
21:38 son.' But when the T saw the son, they
21:40 vineyard comes, what will he do to those T
21:41 the vineyard to other T who will give him
Mk 12:1 let it out to T, and went into another
12:2 a servant to the T, to get from them
12:7 my son.' But those T said to one another,
12:9 come and destroy the T, and give the vineyard
Lk 20:9 let it out to T, and went into another
20:10 a servant to the T, that they should give
20:10 the vineyard; but the T beat him, and sent
20:14 him.' But when the T saw him, they said
20:16 come and destroy those T, and give the vineyard

TEND (5)

Ex 27:21 and his sons shall T it from evening to

Num 1:50 furnishings, and they shall T it, and shall encamp
Deut 28:13 tail; and you shall T upward only, and not
Jn 21:16 He said to him, T my sheep."
1Pet 5:2 T the flock of God that is your charge,

TENDED (2)

Ps 78:72 With upright heart he T them, and guided them
Zech 11:7 And I T the sheep.

TENDER (20)

Gen 18:7 and took a calf, T and good, and gave
Deut 28:54 who is the most T and delicately bred among
28:56 The most T and delicately bred woman among you,
28:56 is so delicate and T, will grudge to the
32:2 gentle rain upon the T grass, and as the
2Kgs 19:26 the field, and like T grass, like grass on
Prov 4:4 son with my father, T, the only one in
Sir 43:21 wilderness, and withers the T grass like fire.
Is 37:27 the field and like T grass, like grass on
47:1 no more be called T and delicate.
Lam 2:20 the children of their T care?
Bar 4:26 My T sons have traveled rough roads; they were
Ezek 17:22 its young twigs a T one, and I myself
Dan 4:15 and bronze, amid the T grass of the field.
4:23 and bronze, in the T grass of the field;
Hos 11:8 recoils within me, my compassion grows warm and T
Mt 24:32 as its branch becomes T and puts forth its
Mk 13:28 as its branch becomes T and puts forth its
Lk 1:78 their sins, through the T mercy of our God,
1Pet 3:8 of the brethren, a T heart and a humble

TENDERHEARTED

Eph 4:32 kind to one another, T, forgiving one another, as

TENDERLY (3)

Gen 34:3 the maiden and spoke T to her.
Is 40:2 Speak T to Jerusalem, and cry to her that
Hos 2:14 the wilderness, and speak T to her.

TENDING (2)

Ps 78:71 from the sheepfolds; from T the ewes that had
Sir 43:4 A man T a furnace works in burning heat,

TENDS (4)

Ps 37:8 Fret not yourself; it T only to evil.
Prov 14:23 profit, but mere talk T only to want.
27:18 He who T a fig tree will eat its
1Cor 9:7 Who T a flock without getting some of the

TENFOLD

Bar 4:28 from God, return with T zeal to seek him.

TENONS (6)

Ex 26:17 There shall be two T in each frame, for
26:19 frame for its two T, and two bases under
26:19 frame for its two T;
36:22 Each frame had two T, for fitting together; he
36:24 frame for its two T, and two bases under
36:24 two bases under another frame for its two T

TENS (7)

Ex 18:21 of thousands, of hundreds, of fifties, and of T
18:25 of thousands, of hundreds, of fifties, and of T
Deut 1:15 of fifties, commanders of T, and officers, throughout
Dan 3:39 and bulls, and with T of thousands of fat
11:12 he shall cast down T of thousands, but he
11:41 And T of thousands shall fall, but these shall
1Mac 3:55 charge of thousands and hundreds and fifties and T

TENT (315)

Gen 9:21 and became drunk, and lay uncovered in his T
12:8 Bethel, and pitched his T, with Bethel on the
13:3 the place where his T had been at the
13:12 valley and moved his T as far as Sodom.
13:18 So Abram moved his T, and came and dwelt
18:1 the door of his T in the heat of
18:2 he ran from the T door to meet them,
18:6 Abraham hastened into the T to Sarah, and said,
18:9 And he said, "She is in the T
18:10 was listening at the T door behind him.
24:67 brought her into the T, and took Rebekah, and
26:25 LORD, and pitched his T there.
31:25 Jacob had pitched his T in the hill country,
31:33 Laban went into Jacob's T, and into Leah's tent,
31:33 tent, and into Leah's T, and into the tent
31:33 tent, and into the T of the two maidservants,
31:33 went out of Leah's T, and entered Rachels.
31:34 felt all about the T, but did not find
33:19 of land on which he had pitched his T
35:21 on, and pitched his T beyond the tower of
Ex 16:16 persons whom each of you has in his T
18:7 other of their welfare, and went into the T
26:7 goats' hair for a T over the tabernacle; eleven
26:9 shall double over at the front of the T
26:11 loops, and couple the T together that it may
26:12 the curtains of the T, the half curtain that
26:13 the curtains of the T shall hang over the
26:14 shall make for the T a covering of tanned
26:36 the door of the T, of blue and purple
27:21 In the T of meeting, outside the veil which
28:43 they go into the T of meeting, or when
29:4 the door of the T of meeting, and wash
29:10 the bull before the T of meeting.
29:11 the door of the T of meeting,
29:30 he comes into the T of meeting to minister
29:32 the door of the T of meeting.
29:42 the door of the T of meeting before the
29:44 I will consecrate the T of meeting and the
30:16 the service of the T of meeting; that it
30:18 put it between the T of meeting and the
30:20 they go into the T of meeting, or when
30:26 anoint with it the T of meeting and the
30:36 the testimony in the T of meeting where I
31:7 have commanded you: the T of meeting, and the
31:7 the furnishings of the T,
33:7 used to take the T and pitch it outside
33:7 he called it the T of meeting.
33:7 go out to the T of meeting, which was
33:8 went out to the T, all the people rose
33:8 man stood at his T door, and looked after
33:8 after Moses, until he had gone into the T
33:9 When Moses entered the T, the pillar of cloud
33:9 the door of the T, and the LORD would
33:10 the door of the T, all the people would
33:10 every man at his T door.
33:11 a young man, did not depart from the T
35:11 commanded: the tabernacle, its T and its covering, its
35:21 be used for the T of meeting, and for
36:14 goats' hair for a T over the tabernacle; he
36:18 bronze to couple the T together that it might
36:19 he made for the T a covering of tanned
36:37 the door of the T, of blue and purple
38:8 the door of the T of meeting.
38:30 the door of the T of meeting, the bronze
39:32 the tabernacle of the T of meeting was finished;
39:33 tabernacle to Moses, the T and all its utensils,
39:38 the door of the T;
39:40 the tabernacle, for the T of meeting;
Lev 1:1 to him from the T of meeting, saying,
1:3 the door of the T of meeting, that he
1:5 the door of the T of meeting.
3:2 the door of the T of meeting; and Aaron's
3:8 killing it before the T of meeting; and Aaron's
3:13 kill it before the T of meeting; and the
4:4 the door of the T of meeting before the
4:5 bring it to the T of meeting;
4:7 which is in the T of meeting, and the
4:7 the door of the T of meeting.
4:14 bring it before the T of meeting;
4:16 the bull to the T of meeting,
4:18 which is in the T of meeting before the
4:18 the door of the T of meeting.
6:16 the court of the T of meeting they shall
6:26 the court of the T of meeting.
6:30 is brought into the T of meeting to make
8:3 the door of the T of meeting."
8:4 the door of the T of meeting.
8:31 the door of the T of meeting, and there
8:33 the door of the T of meeting for seven
8:35 the door of the T of meeting you shall
9:5 Moses commanded before the T of meeting; and all
9:23 Aaron went into the T of meeting; and when
10:7 the door of the T of meeting, lest you
10:9 you go into the T of meeting, lest you
12:6 the door of the T of meeting a lamb
14:8 shall dwell outside his T seven days.
14:11 the door of the T of meeting.
14:23 the door of the T of meeting, before the
15:14 the door of the T of meeting, and give
15:29 the door of the T of meeting.
16:7 the door of the T of meeting;
16:16 shall do for the T of meeting, which abides

16:17 no man in the T of meeting when he
16:20 holy place and the T of meeting and the
16:23 shall come into the T of meeting, and shall
16:33 make atonement for the T of meeting and for
17:4 the door of the T of meeting, to offer
17:5 the door of the T of meeting, and slay
17:6 the door of the T of meeting, and burn
17:9 the door of the T of meeting, to sacrifice
19:21 the door of the T of meeting, a ram
24:3 the testimony, in the T of meeting, Aaron shall
Num 1:1 of Sinai, in the T of meeting, on the
2:2 shall encamp facing the T of meeting on every
2:17 "Then the T of meeting shall set out, with
3:7 whole congregation before the T of meeting, as they
3:8 the furnishings of the T of meeting, and attend
3:25 of Gershon in the T of meeting was to
3:25 be the tabernacle, the T with its covering, the
3:25 the door of the T of meeting,
3:38 the east, before the T of meeting toward the
4:3 the work in the T of meeting.
4:4 of Kohath in the T of meeting: the most
4:15 the things of the T of meeting which the
4:23 the work in the T of meeting.
4:25 the tabernacle, and the T of meeting with its
4:25 the door of the T of meeting,
4:28 the Gershonites in the T of meeting, and their
4:30 the work of the T of meeting.
4:31 their service in the T of meeting: the frames
4:33 their service in the T of meeting, under the
4:35 for work in the T of meeting;
4:37 who served in the T of meeting, whom Moses
4:39 for work in the T of meeting--
4:41 who served in the T of meeting, whom Moses
4:43 for work in the T of meeting--
4:47 bearing burdens in the T of meeting,
6:10 the door of the T of meeting,
6:13 the door of the T of meeting,
6:18 the door of the T of meeting, and shall
7:5 the service of the T of meeting, and give
7:89 Moses went into the T of meeting to speak
8:9 the Levites before the T of meeting, and assemble
8:15 do service at the T of meeting, when you
8:19 of Israel at the T of meeting, and to
8:22 their service in the T of meeting in attendance
8:24 the service of the T of meeting;
8:26 their brethren in the T of meeting, to keep
9:15 covered the tabernacle, the T of the testimony; and
9:17 up from over the T, after that the people
10:3 the entrance of the T of meeting.
11:10 the door of his T; and the anger of
11:16 bring them to the T of meeting, and let
11:24 the people, and placed them round about the T
11:26 gone out to the T, and so they prophesied
12:4 you three, to the T of meeting." And the
12:5 the door of the T, and called Aaron and
12:10 from over the T, behold, Miriam was leprous,
14:10 LORD appeared at the T of meeting to all
16:18 the entrance of the T of meeting with Moses
16:19 the entrance of the T of meeting.
16:42 they turned toward the T of meeting; and behold,
16:43 the front of the T of meeting,
16:50 the entrance of the T of meeting, when the
17:4 deposit them in the T of meeting before the
17:7 the LORD in the T of the testimony.
17:8 Moses went into the T of the testimony; and
18:2 you are before the T of the testimony.
18:3 all duties of the T; but shall not come
18:4 and attend to the T of meeting, for all
18:4 the service of the T; and no one else
18:6 the service of the T of meeting.
18:21 their service in the T of meeting.
18:22 not come near the T of meeting, lest they
18:23 the service of the T of meeting, and they
18:31 your service in the T of meeting.
19:4 the front of the T of meeting seven times.
19:14 man dies in a T: every one who comes
19:14 who comes into the T, and every one who
19:14 who is in the T, shall be unclean seven
19:18 sprinkle it upon the T, and upon all the
20:6 the door of the T of meeting, and fell
25:6 the door of the T of meeting.
27:2 the door of the T of meeting, saying,
31:54 brought it into the T of meeting, as a
Deut 31:14 present yourselves in the T of meeting, that I
31:14 presented themselves in the T of meeting.
31:15 LORD appeared in the T in a pillar of
31:15 of cloud stood by the door of the T
Josh 7:21 the earth inside my T, with the silver underneath."
7:22 they ran to the T; and behold, it was
7:22 was hidden in his T with the silver underneath.
7:23 them out of the T and brought them to
7:24 and sheep, and his T, and all that he
18:1 and set up the T of meeting there; the
19:51 the door of the T of meeting.
Judg 4:11 and had pitched his T as far away as
4:17 on foot to the T of Jael, the wife
4:18 to her into the T, and she covered him
4:20 the door of the T, and if any man
4:21 of Heber took a T peg, and took a
4:22 went in to her T; and there lay Sisera
4:22 Sisera dead, with the T peg in his temple.
5:26 her hand to the T peg and her right
7:8 every man to his T, but retained the three
7:13 and came to the T, and struck it so
7:13 down, so that the T lay flat."
20:8 us go to his T, and none of us
1Sam 2:22 the entrance to the T of meeting.
13:2 people he sent home, every man to his T
17:54 Jerusalem; but he put his armor in his T
2Sam 6:17 its place, inside the T which David had pitched
7:2 but the ark of God dwells in a T
7:6 moving about in a T for my dwelling.
16:22 So they pitched a T for Absalom upon the
1Kgs 1:39 of oil from the T, and anointed Solomon.
2:28 Joab fled to the T of the LORD and
2:29 has fled to the T of the LORD, and
2:30 Benaiah came to the T of the LORD, and
8:4 of the LORD, the T of meeting, and all
8:4 that were in the T; the priests and the
2Kgs 7:8 they went into a T, and ate and drank,
7:8 back, and entered another T, and carried off things
1Chr 6:32 the tabernacle of the T of meeting, until Solomon
9:19 the thresholds of the T, as their fathers had
9:21 the entrance of the T of meeting.
9:23 the house of the T, as guards.
15:1 God, and pitched a T for it.
16:1 set it inside the T which David had pitched
17:1 the covenant of the LORD is under a T
17:5 I have gone from T to tent and from
17:5 gone from tent to T and from dwelling to
23:32 keep charge of the T of meeting and the
2Chr 1:3 at Gibeon; for the T of meeting of God,
1:4 he had pitched a T for it in Jerusalem.)
1:6 which was at the T of meeting, and offered
1:13 Gibeon, from before the T of meeting, to Jerusalem.
5:5 up the ark, the T of meeting, and all
5:5 that were in the T; the priests and the
24:6 of Israel for the T of testimony?"
Tob 13:10 the ages, that his T may be raised for
Jud 5:22 around the T began to complain; Holofernes'
6:10 on him in his T, to seize Achior and
8:5 She set up a T for herself on the
8:36 they returned from the T and went to their
10:15 at once to his T; some of us will
10:17 brought them to the T of Holofernes.
10:18 arrival was reported from T to tent, and they
10:18 reported from tent to T, and they came and
10:18 she waited outside the T of Holofernes while they
10:20 servants came out and led her into the T
10:22 the front of the T, with silver lamps carried
12:5 brought her into the T, and she slept until
12:9 and stayed in the T until she ate her
13:1 and Bagoas closed the T from outside and shut
13:2 left alone in the T, with Holofernes stretched
14:3 will rush into the T of Holofernes, and will
14:7 are you in every T of Judah!
14:13 they came to Holofernes' T and said to the
14:14 the door of the T, for he supposed that
14:17 he went to the T where Judith had stayed,
15:11 They gave Judith the T of Holofernes and all
Job 5:24 shall know that your T is safe, and you
8:22 with shame, and the T of the wicked will
18:6 is dark in his T, and his lamp above
18:14 is torn from the T in which he trusted,
18:15 In his T dwells that which is none of
19:12 against me, and encamp round about my T
20:26 is left in his T will be consumed.
21:28 Where is the T in which the wicked dwelt?'
29:4 God was upon my T;
31:31 the men of my T have not said, 'Who
Ps 15:1 O LORD, who shall sojourn in thy T
19:4 he has set a T for the sun,

T

27:5 the cover of his T, he will set me
27:6 will offer in his T sacrifices with shouts of
52:5 tear you from your T; he will uproot you
61:4 me dwell in thy T for ever!
78:60 dwelling at Shiloh, the T where he dwelt among
78:67 He rejected the T of Joseph, he did not
91:10 shall befall you, no scourge come near your T
104:2 the heavens like a T,
Prov 14:11 be destroyed, but the T of the upright will
Wis 9:8 copy of the holy T which thou didst prepare
9:15 soul, and this earthy T burdens the thoughtful mind.
Sir 14:24 will also fasten his T peg to her walls;
14:25 he will pitch his T near her, and will
24:8 who created me assigned a place for my T
Is 13:20 Arab will pitch his T there, no shepherds will
16:5 in faithfulness in the T of David one who
33:20 quiet habitation, an immovable T, whose stakes will
38:12 me like a shepherd's T; like a weaver I
40:22 spreads them like a T to dwell in;
54:2 the place of your T, and let the curtains
Jer 10:20 My T is destroyed, and all my cords are
10:20 one to spread my T again, and to set
37:10 every man in his T, they would rise up
Lam 2:4 our eyes in the T of the daughter of
Zech 10:4 out of them the T peg, out of them
2Mac 2:4 oracle, ordered that the T and the ark should
2:5 he brought there the T and the ark and
Acts 7:43 you took up the T of Moloch, and the
7:44 "Our fathers had the T of witness in the
2Cor 5:1 that if the earthly T we live in is
5:4 are still in this T, we sigh with anxiety;
Heb 8:2 sanctuary and the true T which is set up
8:5 about to erect the T, he was instructed by
9:2 For a T was prepared, the outer one, in
9:3 second curtain stood a T called the Holy of
9:6 continually into the outer T, performing their ritual
9:8 long as the outer T is still standing
9:11 greater and more perfect T (not made with hands,
9:21 the blood both the T and all the vessels
13:10 those who serve the T have no right to
Rev 15:5 the temple of the T of witness in heaven

TENT-CORD

Job 4:21 If their T is plucked up within them, do

TENT-DWELLING

Judg 5:24 Heber the Kenite, of T women most blessed.

TENTH (65)

Gen 8:5 to abate until the T month; in the tenth
8:5 tenth month; in the T month, on the first
14:20 Abram gave him a T of everything.
28:22 I will give the T to thee."
Ex 12:3 Israel that on the T day of this month
16:36 (An omer is the T part of an ephah.)
29:40 the first lamb a T measure of fine flour
Lev 5:11 he has committed, a T of an ephah of
6:20 he is anointed: a T of an ephah of
14:21 for him, and a T of an ephah of
16:29 seventh month, on the T day of the month,
23:27 to Moses, "On the T day of this seventh
25:9 loud trumpet on the T day of the seventh
27:32 herds and flocks, every T animal of all that
Num 5:15 required of her, a T of an ephah of
7:66 On the T day Ahiezer the son of Ammishaddai,
15:4 cereal offering of a T of an ephah of
28:5 the evening; also a T of an ephah of
28:13 one ram; and a T of fine flour mixed
28:21 for a ram; a T shall you offer for
28:29 for one ram, a T for each of the
29:4 the ram, and one T for each of the
29:7 "On the T day of this seventh month you
29:10 the one ram, a T for each of the
29:15 two rams, and a T for each of the
Deut 23:2 LORD; even to the T generation none of his
23:3 LORD; even to the T generation none belonging to
Josh 4:19 the Jordan on the T day of the first
1Sam 8:15 He will take the T of your grain and
8:17 He will take the T of your flocks, and
2Kgs 25:1 his reign, in the T month, on the tenth
25:1 tenth month, on the T day of the month,
1Chr 12:13 eighth, Elzabad ninth, Jeremiah T, Machbannai
24:11 ninth to Jeshua, the T to Shecaniah,
25:17 his brethren, twelve; the T to Shimei, his sons
27:13 T, for the tenth month, was Maharai of Netophah,
27:13 Tenth, for the T month, was Maharai of Netophah,
Ezra 10:16 first day of the T month they sat down
Tob 1:7 I would give a T to the sons of
1:7 at Jerusalem; a second T I would sell, and
1:8 at Jerusalem; the third T I would give to
Esth 2:16 royal palace in the T month, which is the
Sir 25:7 my heart, and a T I shall tell with
Is 6:13 And though a T remain in it, it will
Jer 32:1 the LORD in the T year of Zedekiah king
39:1 of Judah, in the T month, Nebuchadrezzar king of
52:4 his reign, in the T month, on the tenth
52:4 tenth month, on the T day of the month,
52:12 fifth month, on the T day of the month—
Bar 1:8 same time, on the T day of Sivan, Baruch
Ezek 20:1 fifth month, on the T day of the month,
24:1 ninth year, in the T month, on the tenth
24:1 tenth month, on the T day of the month,
29:1 In the T year, in the tenth month, on
29:1 tenth year, in the T month, on the twelfth
33:21 our exile, in the T month, on the fifth
40:1 the year, on the T day of the month,
45:11 the bath containing one T of a homer, and
45:11 and the ephah one T of a homer; the
45:14 portion of oil, one T of a bath from
Zech 8:19 the fast of the T, shall be to the
Jn 1:39 it was about the T hour.
Heb 7:2 him Abraham apportioned a T part of everything.
Rev 11:13 great earthquake, and a T of the city fell;
21:20 the ninth topaz, the T chrysoprase, the eleventh

TENTHS (20)

Lev 14:10 cereal offering of three T of an ephah of
23:13 it shall be two T of an ephah of
23:17 waved, made of two T of an ephah; they
24:5 cakes of it; two T of an ephah shall
Num 15:6 a cereal offering two T of an ephah of
15:9 cereal offering of three T of an ephah of
28:9 without blemish, and two T of an ephah of
28:12 without blemish; also three T of an ephah of
28:12 each bull; and two T of fine flour for
28:20 mixed with oil; three T of an ephah shall
28:20 a bull, and two T for a ram;
28:28 mixed with oil, three T of an ephah for
28:28 for each bull, two T for one ram,
29:3 mixed with oil, three T of an ephah for
29:3 for the bull, two T for the ram,
29:9 mixed with oil, three T of an ephah for
29:9 for the bull, two T for the one ram,
29:14 mixed with oil, three T of an ephah for
29:14 the thirteen bulls, two T for each of the
Neh 11:1 holy city, while nine T remained in the other

TENTMAKERS

Acts 18:3 and they worked, for by trade they were T

TENTS (60)

Gen 4:20 those who dwell in T and have cattle.
9:27 him dwell in the T of Shem; and let
13:5 flocks and herds and T,
25:27 while Jacob was a quiet man, dwelling in T
Num 1:52 Israel shall pitch their T by their companies, every
16:26 pray you, from the T of these wicked men,
16:27 the door of their T, together with their wives,
24:5 how fair are your T, O Jacob, your encampments,
Deut 1:27 you murmured in your T, and said, 'Because the
1:33 place to pitch your T, in fire by night,
5:30 Go and say to them, "Return to your T
11:6 with their households, their T, and every living thing
16:7 morning you shall turn and go to your T
33:18 in your going out; and Issachar, in your T
Josh 3:14 set out from their T, to pass over the
Judg 6:5 their cattle and their T, coming like locusts for
2Sam 20:1 every man to his T, O Israel!"
1Kgs 12:16 To your T, O Israel!
12:16 So Israel departed to their T
2Kgs 7:7 twilight and forsook their T, their horses, and their
7:10 asses tied, and the T as they were."
1Chr 4:41 Judah, and destroyed their T and the Me-unim who
5:10 they dwelt in their T throughout all the region
2Chr 10:16 of you to your T, O Israel!
10:16 So all Israel departed to their T
14:15 And they smote the T of those who had
Jud 2:26 Midianites, and burned their T and plundered their
3:3 our sheepfolds with their T, lie before you; do
7:18 the land, and their T and supply trains spread
15:1 the men in the T heard it, they were
Job 11:14 away, and let not wickedness dwell in your T

12:6 The T of robbers are at peace, and those
15:34 and fire consumes the T of bribery.
22:23 unrighteousness far from your T,
Ps 69:25 a desolation, let no one dwell in their T
78:51 their strength in the T of Ham.
78:55 and settled the tribes of Israel in their T
83:6 a covenant– the T of Edom and the
84:10 than dwell in the T of wickedness.
106:25 They murmured in their T, and did not obey
118:15 of victory in the T of the righteous: "The
120:5 I dwell among the T of Kedar!
Song 1:5 of Jerusalem, like the T of Kedar, like the
1:8 flock, and pasture your kids beside the shepherds' T
Wis 11:2 wilderness, and pitched their T in untrodden places.
Jer 4:20 Suddenly my T are destroyed, my curtains in a
6:3 they shall pitch their T around her, they shall
30:18 the fortunes of the T of Jacob, and have
35:7 you shall live in T all your days, that
35:10 we have lived in T, and have obeyed and
49:29 Their T and their flocks shall be taken, their
Dan 11:45 shall pitch his palatial T between the sea and
Hos 9:6 things of silver; thorns shall be in their T
12:9 make you dwell in T, as in the days
Hab 3:7 I saw the T of Cushan in affliction; the
Zech 12:7 give victory to the T of Judah first, that
Mal 2:12 cut off from the T of Jacob, for the
1Mac 9:66 brothers and the sons of Phasiron in their T
2Mac 12:12 after receiving his pledges they departed to their T
Heb 11:9 foreign land, living in T with Isaac and Jacob,

TEPHON

1Mac 9:50 Timnath, and Pharathon, and T, with high walls and

TERAH (14)

Gen 11:24 became the father of T;
11:25 after the birth of T a hundred and nineteen
11:26 When T had lived seventy years, he became the
11:27 Now these are the descendants of T
11:27 T was the father of Abram, Nahor, and Haran;
11:28 died before his father T in the land of
11:31 T took Abram his son and Lot the son
11:32 The days of T were two hundred and five
11:32 and five years; and T died in Haran.
Num 33:27 they set out from Tahath, and encamped at T
33:28 they set out from T, and encamped at Mithkah.
Josh 24:2 old beyond the Euphrates, T, the father of Abraham
1Chr 1:26 Peleg, Reu; Serug, Nahor, T;
Lk 3:34 Abraham, the son of T, the son of Nahor,

TERAPHIM (9)

Judg 17:5 made an ephod and T, and installed one of
18:14 there are an ephod, T, a graven image, and
18:17 image, the ephod, the T, and the molten image,
18:18 image, the ephod, the T, and the molten image,
18:20 the ephod, and the T, and the graven image,
2Kgs 23:24 the wizards and the T and the idols and
Ezek 21:21 arrows, he consults the T, he looks at the
Hos 3:4 prince, without sacrifice or pillar, without ephod or T
Zech 10:2 For the T utter nonsense, and the diviners see

TEREBINTH (3)

Sir 24:16 Like a T I spread out my branches, and
Is 6:13 burned again, like a T or an oak, whose
Hos 4:13 under oak, poplar, and T, because their shade is

TERESH (2)

Esth 2:21 king's gate, Bigthan and T, two of the king's
6:2 told about Bigthana and T, two of the king's

TERM

Esth 9:26 days Purim, after the T Pur.

TERMED (2)

Is 62:4 shall no more be T Forsaken, and your land
62:4 shall no more be T Desolate; but you shall

TERMINATION

Num 34:5 of Egypt, and its T shall be at the

TERMS (18)

Deut 20:10 fight against it, offer T of peace to it.
1Kgs 20:34 said, "I will let you go on these T
Tob 5:15 So they agreed to these T
Jer 32:11 of purchase, containing the T and conditions, and the
34:18 did not keep the T of the covenant which
Dan 11:17 and he shall bring T of peace and perform
1Mac 6:58 let us come to T with these men, and
7:12 before Alcimus and Bacchides to ask for just T
8:29 Thus on these T the Romans make a treaty
8:30 If after these T are in effect both parties
11:66 him to grant them T of peace, and he
2Mac 11:14 settle everything on just T, promising that he would
13:25 so angry that they wanted to annul its T
14:20 When the T had been fully considered, and the
Lk 14:32 an embassy and asks T of peace.
Rom 6:19 am speaking in human T, because of your natural
1Cor 15:1 you, brethren, in what T I preached to you
2Cor 11:12 work on the same T as we do.

TERRESTRIAL (2)

1Cor 15:40 bodies and there are T bodies; but the glory
15:40 the glory of the T is another.

TERRIBLE (50)

Ex 15:11 thee, majestic in holiness, T in glorious deeds, doing
34:10 for it is a T thing that I will
Deut 1:19 all that great and T wilderness which you saw,
7:21 you, a great and T God.
8:15 through the great and T wilderness, with its fiery
10:17 the mighty, and the T God, who is not
10:21 you these great and T things which your eyes
34:12 all the great and T deeds which Moses wrought
Judg 13:6 angel of God, very T; I did not ask
2Sam 7:23 for them great and T things, by driving out
1Chr 17:21 name for great and T things, in driving out
Neh 1:5 heaven, the great and T God who keeps covenant
4:14 who is great and T, and fight for your
9:32 great and mighty and T God, who keepest covenant
Job 37:22 God is clothed with T majesty.
39:20 His majestic snorting is T
Ps 47:2 the Most High, is T, a great king over
66:3 Say to God, "How T are thy deeds!
66:5 has done: he is T in his deeds among
68:35 T is God in his sanctuary, the God of
76:7 But thou, T art thou!
76:12 of princes, who is T to the kings of
89:7 holy ones, great and T above all that are
99:3 praise thy great and T name!
106:22 land of Ham, and T things by the Red
111:9 Holy and T is his name!
145:6 the might of thy T acts, and I will
Song 6:4 love, comely as Jerusalem, T as an army with
6:10 bright as the sun, T as an army with
Wis 11:18 of smoke, or flash T sparks from their eyes;
16:5 For when the T rage of wild beasts came
19:16 festal celebrations, afflicted with T sufferings those
Sir 43:29 T is the Lord and very great, and marvelous
Is 21:1 the desert, from a T land.
64:3 When thou didst T things which we looked not
Lam 1:9 therefore her fall is T, she has no comforter.
Ezek 28:7 upon you, the most T of the nations; and
30:11 with him, the most T of the nations, shall
31:12 Foreigners, the most T of the nations, will cut
32:12 all of them most T among the nations.
Dan 7:7 behold, a fourth beast, T and dreadful and
7:19 all the rest, exceedingly T, with its teeth of
9:4 Lord, the great and T God, who keepest covenant
Joel 2:11 is great and very T; who can endure it?
2:31 before the great and T day of the LORD
Hab 1:7 Dread and T are they; their justice and dignity
Zeph 2:11 The LORD will be T against them; yea, he
Mal 4:5 before the great and T day of the LORD
2Mac 6:30 death, I am enduring T sufferings in my body
Mt 8:6 paralyzed at home, in T distress."

TERRIBLY (6)

Esth 11:6 forward, both ready to fight, and they roared T
Wis 6:5 will come upon you T and swiftly, because severe
17:3 forgetfulness, they were scattered, T alarmed, and
2Mac 10:34 of the place, blasphemed T and hurled out wicked
Mt 17:15 epileptic and he suffers T; for often he falls
Mk 9:26 out and convulsing him T, it came out, and

TERRIFIED (15)

1Sam 5:6 of Ashdod, and he T and afflicted them with
28:21 saw that he was T, she said to him,
Jud 4:2 were therefore very greatly T at his approach, and
7:4 numbers they were greatly T, and every one said
Job 23:15 Therefore I am T at his presence; when I
23:16 faint; the Almighty has T me;
31:34 the contempt of families T me, so that I
Is 31:4 against him is not T by their shouting or

T

	41:23	do harm, that we may be dismayed and T
	44:11	forth, they shall be T, they shall be put
1Mac	12:28	were afraid and were T at heart; so they
Mt	14:26	the sea, they were T, saying, "It is a
Mk	6:50	out; for they all saw him, and were T
Lk	21:9	tumults, do not be T; for this must first
Rev	11:13	and the rest were T and gave glory to

TERRIFIES

Job	33:16	ears of men, and T them with warnings,

TERRIFY (18)

2Chr	32:18	wall, to frighten and T them, in order that
Job	3:5	blackness of the day T it.
	7:14	me with dreams and T me with visions,
	9:34	not dread of him T me.
	13:11	Will not his majesty T you, and the dread
	13:21	not dread of thee T me.
	15:24	hand; distress and anguish T him; they prevail against
	33:7	fear of me need T you; my pressure will
Ps	2:5	in his wrath, and T them in his fury,
	83:15	with thy tempest and T them with thy hurricane!
Is	2:19	when he rises to T the earth.
	2:21	when he rises to T the earth.
	7:6	up against Judah and T it, and let us
Jer	49:37	I will T Elam before their enemies, and before
Ezek	30:9	forth from me to T the unsuspecting Ethiopians; and
Hab	2:17	of the beasts will T you, for the blood
Zech	1:21	these have come to T them, to cast down
1Pet	3:6	right and let nothing T you.

TERRIFYING (5)

Esth	15:6	And he was most T
Job	15:21	T sounds are in his ears; in prosperity the
Wis	17:4	them from fear, but T sounds rang out around
Is	10:33	lop the boughs with T power; the great in
Heb	12:21	Indeed, so T was the sight that Moses said,

TERRITORIES (2)

Num	32:33	its cities with their T, the cities of the
Josh	19:49	finished distributing the several T of the land as

TERRITORY (100)

Gen	10:19	And the T of the Canaanites extended from Sidon,
	10:30	The T in which they lived extended from Mesha
	20:1	Abraham journeyed toward the T of the Negeb, and
Ex	13:7	shall be seen with you in all your T
Num	20:16	Kadesh, a city on the edge of your T
	20:17	the left, until we have passed through your T
	20:21	Israel passage through his T; so Israel turned away
	21:22	King's Highway, until we have passed through your T
	21:23	would not allow Israel to pass through his T
	33:44	at Iye-abarim, in the T of Moab.
Deut	2:4	to pass through the T of your brethren the
	3:12	and the Gadites the T beginning at Aroer, which
	3:16	Gadites I gave the T from Gilead as far
	11:24	shall be yours; your T shall be from the
	12:20	your God enlarges your T, as he has promised
	16:4	you in all your T for seven days; nor
	28:40	trees throughout all your T, but you shall not
Josh	1:4	going down of the sun shall be your T
	13:16	So their T was from Aroer, which is on
	13:25	Their T was Jazer, and all the cities of
	13:26	from Mahanaim to the T of Debir,
	16:2	along to Ataroth, the T of the Archites;
	16:3	down westward to the T of the Japhletites, as
	16:3	as far as the T of Lower Beth-horon, then
	16:5	The T of the Ephraimites by their families was
	17:7	The T of Manasseh reached from Asher to Mich-
	18:5	Judah continuing in his T on the south, and
	18:5	of Joseph in their T on the north.
	18:11	came up, and the T allotted to it fell
	19:9	formed part of the T of Judah; because the
	19:10	And the T of its inheritance reached as far
	19:18	Its T included Jezreel, Chesulloth, Shunem,
	19:25	Its T included Helkath, Hali, Beten, Achshaph,
	19:41	And the T of its inheritance included Zorah, Eshtaol,
	19:46	and Rakkon with the T over against Joppa.
	19:47	When the T of the Danites was lost to
Judg	1:3	with me into the T allotted to me, that
	1:3	with you into the T allotted to you." So
	1:18	took Gaza with its T, and Ashkelon with its
	1:18	and Ashkelon with its T, and Ekron with its
	1:18	Ashkelon with its territory, and Ekron with its T
	11:18	did not enter the T of Moab, for the
	11:20	to pass through his T; so Sihon gathered all
	11:22	possession of all the T of the Amorites from
	19:29	her throughout all the T of Israel.
1Sam	5:6	afflicted them with tumors, both Ashdod and its T
	7:13	not again enter the T of Israel.
	7:14	and Israel rescued their T from the hand of
	10:2	Rachel's tomb in the T of Benjamin at Zelzah,
	11:3	messengers through all the T of Israel.
	11:7	them throughout all the T of Israel by the
2Sam	21:5	place in all the T of Israel,
1Kgs	1:3	maiden throughout all the T of Israel, and found
2Kgs	9:10	eat Jezebel in the T of Jezreel, and none
	9:36	the Tishbite, 'In the T of Jezreel the dogs
	9:37	the field in the T of Jezreel, so that
	10:32	defeated them throughout the T of Israel:
	15:16	in it and its T from Tirzah on; because
	18:8	as Gaza and its T, from watchtower to fortified
1Chr	6:66	had cities of their T out of the tribe
	21:12	destroying throughout all the T of Israel.' Now decide
2Chr	26:6	built cities in the T of Ashdod and elsewhere
	34:33	abominations from all the T that belonged to the
Jud	1:12	revenge on the whole T of Cilicia and Damascus
	2:10	and seize all their T for me in advance.
	2:25	He also seized the T of Cilicia, and killed
	16:5	would burn up my T, and kill my young
Job	38:20	take it to its T and that you may
Sir	24:7	I sought in whose T I might lodge.
Jer	15:13	price, for all your sins, throughout all your T
	17:3	the price of your sin throughout all your T
Bar	3:24	And how vast the T that he possesses!
Ezek	43:12	the temple: the whole T round about upon the
	48:2	Adjoining the T of Dan, from the east side
	48:3	Adjoining the T of Asher, from the east side
	48:4	Adjoining the T of Naphtali, from the east side
	48:5	Adjoining the T of Manasseh, from the east side
	48:6	Adjoining the T of Ephraim, from the east side
	48:7	Adjoining the T of Reuben, from the east side
	48:8	"Adjoining the T of Judah, from the east side
	48:12	holy place, adjoining the T of the Levites.
	48:13	And alongside the T of the priests, the Levites
	48:22	shall lie between the T of Judah and the
	48:22	of Judah and the T of Benjamin.
	48:24	Adjoining the T of Benjamin, from the east side
	48:25	Adjoining the T of Simeon, from the east side
	48:26	Adjoining the T of Issachar, from the east side
	48:27	Adjoining the T of Zebulun, from the east side
	48:28	And adjoining the T of Gad to the south,
Amos	6:2	Or is their T greater than your territory,
	6:2	territory greater than your T,
Zeph	2:8	taunted my people and made boasts against their T
1Mac	3:36	aliens in all their T, and distribute their land.
	3:42	and that the forces were encamped in their T
	5:9	who lived in their T, and planned to destroy
	9:72	own land, and came no more into their T
	11:34	their possession both the T of Judea and the
	14:2	Demetrius had invaded his T, he sent one of
	15:29	You have devastated their T, you have done great
Mt	4:13	the sea, in the T of Zebulun and Naphtali,

TERROR (72)

Gen	35:5	as they journeyed, a T from God fell upon
Ex	15:16	T and dread fall upon them; because of the
	23:27	I will send my T before you, and will
Lev	26:16	appoint over you sudden T, consumption, and fever
Deut	26:8	outstretched arm, with great T, with signs and
	32:25	the chambers shall be T, destroying both young man
Jud	2:28	So fear and T of him fell upon all
	16:25	one ever again spread T among the people of
Esth	7:6	Then Haman was in T before the king and
Job	22:10	about you, and sudden T overwhelms you;
	31:23	For I was in T of calamity from God,
	41:14	Round about his teeth is T
	41:22	neck abides strength, and T dances before him.
Ps	10:18	the earth may strike T no more.
	14:5	shall be in great T, for God is with
	31:13	whispering of many-- T on every side!--
	53:5	they are, in great T, in terror such as
	53:5	in great terror, in T such as has not
	55:15	them go away in T into their graves.
	78:33	vanish like a breath, and their years in T
	91:5	will not fear the T of the night, nor
Wis	17:6	self-kindled fire, and in T they deemed the things
	17:19	hollow of the mountains, it paralyzed them with T
Sir	21:4	T and violence will lay waste riches; thus the
Is	2:10	dust from before the T of the LORD, and
	2:19	ground, from before the T of the LORD, and
	2:21	cliffs, from before the T of the LORD, and

17:14 At evening time, behold, T
19:17 Judah will become a T to the Egyptians; every
24:17 T, and the pit, and the snare are upon
24:18 the sound of the T shall fall into the
28:19 it will be sheer T to understand the message.
31:9 shall pass away in T, and his officers desert
33:18 will muse on the T: "Where is he who
47:12 be able to succeed, perhaps you may inspire T
54:14 not fear; and from T, for it shall not
Jer 6:25 enemy has a sword, T is on every side.
8:15 came, for a time of healing, but behold, T
14:19 came; for a time of healing, but behold, T
15:8 have made anguish and T fall upon them suddenly.
17:17 Be not a T to me; thou art my
20:3 your name Pashhur, but T on every side.
20:4 will make you a T to yourself and to
20:10 T is on every side!
29:18 be a curse, a T, a hissing, and a
30:5 cry of panic, of T, and no peace.
32:21 arm, and with great T;
46:5 they look not back--T on every side!
48:43 T, pit, and snare are before you, O inhabitant
48:44 who flees from the T shall fall into the
49:5 Behold, I will bring T upon you, says the
49:29 shall cry to them: T on every side!'
Ezek 7:27 the people of the land are palsied by T
23:46 them an object of T and a spoil.
26:17 inhabitants, who imposed your T on all the mainland!
32:23 the sword, who spread T in the land of
32:24 nether world, who spread T in the land of
32:25 by the sword; for T of them was spread
32:26 sword; for they spread T in the land of
32:27 their bones; for the T of the mighty men
32:30 slain, for all the T which they caused by
32:32 For he spread T in the land of the
38:21 summon every kind of T against Gog, says the
Hab 1:9 all come for violence; T of them goes before
1Mac 3:25 to be feared, and T fell upon the Gentiles
2Mac 3:17 For T and bodily trembling had come over the
3:24 the power of God, and became faint with T
12:22 Judas' first division appeared, T and fear came over
13:16 filled the camp with T and confusion and withdrew
15:23 good angel to carry T and trembling before us.
Acts 10:4 stared at him in T, and said, "What is
Rom 13:3 rulers are not a T to good conduct, but

TERROR-STRICKEN
Is 30:31 The Assyrians will be T at the voice of

TERRORS (14)
Deut 4:34 arm, and by great T, according to all that
Job 6:4 drinks their poison; the T of God are arrayed
18:11 T frighten him on every side, and chase him
18:14 trusted, and is brought to the king of T
20:25 out of his gall; T come upon him.
24:17 are friends with the T of deep darkness.
27:20 T overtake him like a flood; in the night
30:15 T are turned upon me; my honor is pursued
Ps 55:4 anguish within me, the T of death have fallen
73:19 destroyed in a moment, swept away utterly by T
88:15 up, I suffer thy T; I am helpless.
Eccl 12:5 what is high, and T are in the way;
Lam 2:22 an appointed feast my T on every side; and
Lk 21:11 and there will be T and great signs from

TERTIUS
Rom 16:22 I T, the writer of this letter, greet you

TERTULLUS (2)
Acts 24:1 down with some elders and a spokesman, one T
24:2 when he was called, T began to accuse him,

TEST (56)
Deut 6:16 your God to the T, as you tested him
8:16 might humble you and T you, to do you
33:8 one, whom thou didst T at Massah, with whom
Judg 2:22 by them I may T Israel, whether they will
3:1 the LORD left, to T Israel by them, that
7:4 water and I will T them for you there;
1Kgs 10:1 LORD, she came to T him with hard questions.
2Chr 9:1 came to Jerusalem to T him with hard questions,
Jud 8:12 put God to the T this day, and are
8:13 Lord Almighty to the T --but you will never
8:25 putting us to the T as he did our
Job 7:18 him every morning, and T him every moment?
Ps 11:4 eyes behold, his eyelids T, the children of men.
26:2 LORD, and try me; T my heart and my
106:14 put God to the T in the desert;
Eccl 2:1 I will make a T of pleasure; enjoy yourself."
Wis 1:2 put him to the T, and manifests himself to
2:17 true, and let us T what will happen at
2:19 Let us T him with insult and torture, that
11:10 For thou didst T them as a father does
18:25 feared; for merely to T the wrath was enough.
Sir 4:17 him, and she will T him with her ordinances.
13:11 words; for he will T you through much talk,
27:5 potter's vessels; so the T of a man is
27:7 for this is the T of men.
37:27 My son, T your soul while you live; see
Is 7:12 I will not put the LORD to the T
Jer 9:7 will refine them and T them, for what else
Lam 3:40 Let us T and examine our ways, and return
Dan 1:12 Hananiah, Mishael, and Azariah; T your servants for
Zech 13:9 one refines silver, and T them as gold is
Mal 3:10 put me to the T, says the LORD of
3:15 put God to the T they escape.'"
Mt 16:1 Sadducees came, and to T him they asked him
22:18 put me to the T, you hypocrites?
22:35 him a question, to T him.
Mk 8:11 sign from heaven, to T him.
10:2 and in order to T him asked, "Is it
12:15 said to them, "Why put me to the T
Lk 10:25 put him to the T, saying, "Teacher, what shall
11:16 demons"; while others, to T him, sought from him
Jn 6:6 This he said to T him, for he himself
8:6 This they said to T him, that they might
1Cor 3:13 and the fire will T what sort of work
10:9 the Lord to the T, as some of them
2Cor 2:9 wrote, that I might T you and know whether
8:2 for in a severe T of affliction, their abundance
9:13 Under the T of this service, you will glorify
13:5 T yourselves.
13:5 you?--unless indeed you fail to meet the T
13:7 to have met the T, but that you may
Gal 6:4 But let each one T his own work, and
1Thes 5:21 not despise prophesying, but T everything; hold fast
Heb 3:9 put me to the T and saw my works
Jas 1:11 he has stood the T he will receive the
1Jn 4:1 believe every spirit, but T the spirits to see

TESTED (31)
Gen 22:1 After these things God T Abraham, and said to
42:15 this you shall be T: by the life of
42:16 your words may be T, whether there is truth
Deut 6:16 the test, as you T him at Massah.
Judg 7:3 And Gideon T them; twenty-two thousand returned,
Jud 8:26 Abraham, and how he T Isaac, and what happened
Ps 66:10 thou, O God, hast T us; thou hast tried
78:18 They T God in their heart by demanding the
78:41 They T him again and again, and provoked the
78:56 Yet they T and rebelled against the Most High
81:7 place of thunder; I T you at the waters
95:9 wilderness, when your fathers T me, and put me
105:19 word of the LORD T him.
Eccl 7:23 All this I have T by wisdom; I said,
Wis 1:3 when his power is T, it convicts the foolish;
3:5 great good, because God T them and found them
6:6 in mercy, but mighty men will be mightily T
Sir 2:5 For gold is T in the fire, and acceptable
31:10 Who has been T by it and been found
44:21 and when he was T he was found faithful.
Is 28:16 foundation a stone, a T stone, a precious cornerstone,
Dan 1:14 in this matter, and T them for ten days.
Zech 13:9 refines silver, and test them as gold is T
1Mac 2:52 Abraham found faithful when T, and it was reckoned
Mt 19:3 up to him and T him by asking, "Is
2Cor 8:22 whom we have often T and found earnest in
1Tim 3:10 let them also be T first; then if they
Heb 11:17 Abraham, when he was T, offered up Isaac, and
1Pet 1:7 which though perishable is T by fire, may redound
Rev 2:2 evil men but have T those who call themselves
2:10 that you may be T, and for ten days

TESTER
Jer 6:27 you an assayer and T among my people, that

TESTEST
Ps 17:3 by night, if thou T me, thou wilt find

TESTICLES (3)
Lev 21:20 or scabs or crushed T;
22:24 animal which has its T bruised or crushed or

Deut 23:1 "He whose T are crushed or whose male member

TESTIFIED (14)

2Sam 1:16 your own mouth has T against you, saying, 'I
2Chr 24:19 to the LORD; these T against them, but they
1Mac 2:56 Caleb, because he T in the assembly, received an
Jn 4:44 For Jesus himself T that a prophet has no
13:21 troubled in spirit, and T, "Truly, truly, I say
Acts 2:40 And he T with many other words and exhorted
8:25 Now when they had T and spoken the word
13:22 king; of whom he T and said, 'I have
23:11 for as you have T about me at Jerusalem,
1Cor 15:15 misrepresenting God, because we T of God that he
Heb 2:6 It has been T somewhere, "What is man that
7:8 of whom it is T that he lives.
3Jn 1:3 the brethren arrived and T to the truth of
1:6 to strangers, who have T to your love before

TESTIFIES (4)

Job 16:8 up against me, it T to my face.
Hos 5:5 The pride of Israel T to his face; Ephraim
Acts 20:23 that the Holy Spirit T to me in every
Rev 22:20 He who T to these things says, "Surely I

TESTIFY (27)

Lev 5:1 a public adjuration to T and though he is
Deut 21:7 valley; and they shall T, 'Our hands did not
1Sam 12:3 Here I am; T against me before the LORD
12:3 T against me and I will restore it to
Job 15:6 I; your own lips T against you.
Ps 50:7 O Israel, I will T against you.
Is 59:12 thee, and our sins T against us; for our
Jer 14:7 "Though our iniquities T against us, act, O LORD,
Dan 13:21 you refuse, we will T against you that a
13:40 These things we T
Amos 3:13 "Hear, and T against the house of Jacob," says
1Mac 2:37 innocence; heaven and earth T for us that you
Mt 26:62 it that these men T against you?"
27:13 how many things they T against you?"
Mk 14:60 it that these men T against you?"
Jn 7:7 hates me because I T of it that its
Acts 10:42 the people, and to T that he is the
20:24 the Lord Jesus, to T to the gospel of
20:26 Therefore I T to you this day that I
26:5 they are willing to T, that according to the
2Cor 8:3 means, as I can T, and beyond their means,
Gal 5:3 I T again to every man who receives circumcision
Eph 4:17 this I affirm and T in the Lord, that
Heb 3:5 as a servant, to T to the things that
1Jn 1:2 we saw it, and T to it, and proclaim
4:14 we have seen and T that the Father has
3Jn 1:12 the truth itself; I T to him too, and

TESTIFYING (5)

Acts 18:5 was occupied with preaching, T to the Jews that
20:21 from house to house, T both to Jews and
26:22 so I stand here T both to small and
28:23 from morning till evening, T to the kingdom of
2Tim 1:8 be ashamed then of T to our Lord, nor

TESTIMONIES (36)

Deut 4:45 Israel; these are the T, the statutes, and the
6:17 your God, and his T, and his statutes, which
6:20 the meaning of the T and the statutes and
1Kgs 2:3 his ordinances, and his T, as it is written
2Kgs 23:3 his commandments and his T and his statutes, with
1Chr 29:19 keep thy commandments, thy T, and thy statutes,
2Chr 34:31 his commandments and his T and his statutes, with
Ps 25:10 for those who keep his covenant and his T
78:56 did not observe his T,
99:7 cloud; they kept his T, and the statutes that
119:2 those who keep his T, who seek him with
119:14 the way of thy T I delight as much
119:22 scorn and contempt, for I have kept thy T
119:24 Thy T are my delight, they are my counselors.
119:31 I cleave to thy T, O LORD; let me
119:36 my heart to thy T, and not to gain!
119:46 also speak of thy T before kings, and shall
119:59 my feet to thy T;
119:79 turn to me, that they may know thy T
119:88 I may keep the T of thy mouth.
119:95 wait to destroy me; but I consider thy T
119:99 my teachers, for thy T are my meditation.
119:111 Thy T are my heritage for ever; yea, they
119:119 dost count as dross; therefore I love thy T
119:125 give me understanding, that I may know thy T
119:129 Thy T are wonderful; therefore my soul keeps them.
119:138 Thou hast appointed thy T in righteousness and in
119:144 Thy T are righteous for ever; give me understanding
119:146 thee; save me, that I may observe thy T
119:152 I known from thy T that thou hast founded
119:157 adversaries, but I do not swerve from thy T
119:167 My soul keeps thy T; I love them exceedingly.
119:168 keep thy precepts and T, for all my ways
132:12 my covenant and my T which I shall teach
Sir 45:17 to teach Jacob the T, and to enlighten Israel
Jer 44:23 statutes and in his T, that this evil has

TESTIMONY (97)

Ex 16:34 placed it before the T, to be kept.
25:16 into the ark the T which I shall give
25:21 you shall put the T that I shall give
25:22 the ark of the T, I will speak with
26:33 the ark of the T in thither within the
26:34 the ark of the T in the most holy
27:21 which is before the T, Aaron and his sons
30:6 the ark of the T, before the mercy seat
30:6 that is over the T, where I will meet
30:26 the ark of the T,
30:36 of it before the T in the tent of
31:7 the ark of the T, and the mercy seat
31:18 two tables of the T, tables of stone, written
32:15 two tables of the T in his hands, tables
34:29 two tables of the T in his hand as
38:21 the tabernacle of the T, as they were counted
39:35 the ark of the T with its poles and
Lev 16:13 which is upon the T, lest he die;
24:3 the veil of the T, in the tent of
Num 1:50 the tabernacle of the T, and over all its
1:53 the tabernacle of the T, that there may be
1:53 shall keep charge of the tabernacle of the T
4:5 the ark of the T with it;
7:89 the ark of the T, from between the two
9:15 the tent of the T; and at evening it
10:11 the tabernacle of the T,
17:4 of meeting before the T, where I meet with
17:7 before the LORD in the tent of the T
17:8 the tent of the T; and behold, the rod
17:10 of Aaron before the T, to be kept as
18:2 with you are before the tent of the T
35:30 to death on the T of one witness.
Josh 4:16 the ark of the T to come up out
2Kgs 11:12 and gave him the T; and they proclaimed him
2Chr 23:11 and gave him the T; and they proclaimed him
24:6 the congregation of Israel for the tent of T
Job 21:29 you not accept their T
Ps 19:7 reviving the soul; the T of the LORD is
78:5 He established a T in Jacob, and appointed a
Wis 17:11 condemned by its own T; distressed by conscience, it
Sir 31:23 with food, and their T to his excellence is
31:24 with food, and their T to his niggardliness is
Is 8:16 Bind up the T, seal the teaching among my
8:20 To the teaching and to the T
2Mac 3:36 And he bore T to all men of the
Mt 10:18 my sake, to bear T before them and the
24:14 whole world, as a T to all nations; and
26:59 whole council sought false T against Jesus that they
Mk 6:11 your feet for a T against them."
13:9 my sake, to bear T before them.
14:55 the whole council sought T against Jesus to put
14:59 even so did their T agree.
Lk 9:5 your feet as a T against them."
21:13 will be a time for you to bear T
22:69 they said, "What further T do we need?
Jn 1:7 He came for T, to bear witness to the
1:19 And this is the T of John, when the
3:11 have seen; but you do not receive our T
3:32 no one receives his T;
3:33 he who receives his T sets his seal to
4:39 because of the woman's T, "He told me all
5:30 witness to myself, my T is not true;
5:31 I know that the T which he bears to
5:33 Not that the T which I receive is from
5:35 But the T which I have is greater than
8:13 witness to yourself; your T is not true."
8:14 witness to myself, my T is true, for I
8:17 is written that the T of two men is
19:35 has borne witness—his T is true, and he
21:24 we know that his T is true.
Acts 4:33 the apostles gave their T to the resurrection of
22:18 will not accept your T about me.'
1Cor 1:6 even as the T to Christ was confirmed

2:1 proclaiming to you the T of God in lofty
2Cor 1:12 boast is this, the T of our conscience that
2Thes 1:10 have believed, because our T to you was believed.
1Tim 2:6 ransom for all, the T to which was borne
6:13 Jesus who in his T before Pontius Pilate made
Tit 1:12 This T is true.
Heb 10:28 without mercy at the T of two or three
1Jn 5:9 If we receive the T of men, the testimony
5:9 testimony of men, the T of God is greater;
5:9 for this is the T of God that he
5:10 of God has the T in himself.
5:10 not believed in the T that God has borne
5:11 And this is the T, that God gave us
3Jn 1:12 Demetrius has T from every one, and from the
1:12 and you know my T is true.
Rev 1:2 God and to the T of Jesus Christ, even
1:9 of God and the T of Jesus.
11:7 they have finished their T, the beast that ascends
12:11 the word of their T, for they loved not
12:17 of God and bear T to Jesus.
19:10 brethren who hold the T of Jesus.
19:10 For the T of Jesus is the spirit of
20:4 been beheaded for their T to Jesus and for
22:16 to you with this T for the churches.

TESTING (9)

Deut 8:2 he might humble you, T you to know what
13:3 LORD your God is T you, to know whether
Judg 3:4 They were for the T of Israel, to know
Eccl 3:18 men that God is T them to show them
Sir 6:7 friend, gain him through T, and do not trust
6:21 down like a heavy T stone, and he will
Ezek 21:13 will not be a T—what could it do
Heb 3:8 on the day of T in the wilderness,
Jas 1:3 you know that the T of your faith produces

TESTS (6)

Job 34:3 know; for the ear T words as the palate
Ps 11:5 The LORD T the righteous and the wicked, and
Sir 27:5 The kiln T the potter's vessels; so the test
31:26 of steel, so wine T hearts in the strife
39:4 foreign nations, for he T the good and the
1Thes 2:4 to please God who T our hearts.

TETRARCH (7)

Mt 14:1 that time Herod the T heard about the fame
Lk 3:1 Judea, and Herod being T of Galilee, and his
3:1 and his brother Philip T of the region of
3:1 and Trachonitis, and Lysani-as T of Abilene,
3:19 But Herod the T, who had been reproved by
9:7 Now Herod the T heard of all that was
Acts 13:1 court of Herod the T, and Saul.

TETTER

Lev 13:39 dull white, it is T that has broken out

THADDAEUS (2)

Mt 10:3 son of Alphaeus, and T;
Mk 3:18 son of Alphaeus, and T, and Simon the Cananaean,

THANK (32)

Lev 7:12 shall offer with the T offering unleavened cakes
1Chr 16:4 LORD, to invoke, to T, and to praise the
29:13 And now we T thee, our God, and praise
2Chr 29:31 near, bring sacrifices and T offerings to the house
29:31 assembly brought sacrifices and T offerings; and all
Ps 35:18 Then I will T thee in the great congregation;
52:9 I will T thee for ever, because thou hast
56:12 God; I will render T offerings to thee.
107:8 Let them T the LORD for his steadfast love,
107:15 Let them T the LORD for his steadfast love,
107:21 Let them T the LORD for his steadfast love,
107:31 Let them T the LORD for his steadfast love,
118:21 I T thee that thou hast answered me and
Sir 35:2 gives alms sacrifices a T offering.
Is 38:18 For Sheol cannot T thee, death cannot praise thee;
Jer 17:26 and frankincense, and bringing T offerings to the
33:11 sing, as they bring T offerings to the house
1Mac 14:25 said, "How shall we T Simon and his sons?
2Mac 1:11 of grave dangers we T him greatly for taking
Mt 11:25 time Jesus declared, "I T thee, Father, Lord of
Lk 10:21 Spirit and said, "I T thee, Father, Lord of
17:9 Does he T the servant because he did what
18:11 with himself, 'God, I T thee that I am
Jn 11:41 and said, "Father, I T thee that thou hast
Rom 1:8 First, I T my God through Jesus Christ for
1Cor 14:18 I T God that I speak in tongues more
Phil 1:3 I T my God in all my remembrance of
Col 1:3 We always T God, the Father of our Lord
1Thes 2:13 And we also T God constantly for this, that
1Tim 1:12 I T him who has given me strength for
2Tim 1:3 I T God whom I serve with a clear
Philem 1:4 I T my God always when I remember you

THANKED (4)

Sir 12:1 and you will be T for your good deeds.
29:25 provide drink without being T, and besides this you
2Mac 12:31 times of misfortune, they T them and exhorted them
Acts 28:15 On seeing them Paul T God and took courage.

THANKFUL (4)

Wis 18:2 having suffered, and were T that thy holy ones,
1Cor 1:14 I am T that I baptized none of you
Phil 1:5 my prayer with joy, T for your partnership in
Col 3:15 And be T

THANKFULNESS (3)

Esth 16:4 not only take away T from among men, but,
1Cor 10:30 If I partake with T, why am I denounced
Col 3:16 and spiritual songs with T in your hearts to

THANKING

1Chr 23:30 shall stand every morning, T and praising the LORD,

THANKS (114)

1Chr 16:8 O give T to the LORD, call on his
16:34 O give T to the LORD, for he is
16:35 that we may give T to thy holy name,
16:41 expressly named to give T to the LORD, for
2Chr 7:3 and worshiped and gave T to the LORD, saying,
7:6 had made for giving T to the LORD—for
20:21 army, and say, "Give T to the LORD, for
30:22 peace offerings and giving T to the LORD the
31:2 LORD and to give T and praise.
Ezra 3:11 responsively, praising and giving T to the LORD, "For
Neh 12:24 praise and to give T, according to the commandment
12:31 companies which gave T and went in procession.
12:38 of those who gave T went to the left,
12:40 of those who gave T stood in the house
Tob 11:17 And Tobit gave T before them that God had
12:6 "Praise God and give T to him; exalt him
12:6 exalt him and give T to him in the
12:6 Do not be slow to give him T
12:20 And now give T to God, for I am
13:6 do with you; give T to him with your
13:6 I give him T in the land of my
13:8 speak, and give him T in Jerusalem.
13:10 Give T worthily to the Lord, and praise the
14:7 his people will give T to God, and the
Jud 8:25 everything let us give T to the Lord our
Ps 7:17 to the LORD the T due to his righteousness,
9:1 I will give T to the LORD with my
28:7 my song I give T to him.
30:4 his saints, and give T to his holy name.
30:12 God, I will give T to thee for ever.
44:8 and we will give T to thy name for
54:6 thee; I will give T to thy name, O
57:9 I will give T to thee, O Lord, among
75:1 We give T to thee, O God; we give
75:1 O God; we give T; we call on thy
79:13 thy pasture, will give T to thee for ever;
86:12 I give T to thee, O Lord my God,
92:1 is good to give T to the LORD, to
97:12 you righteous, and give T to his holy name!
100:4 Give T to him, bless his name!
105:1 O give T to the LORD, call on his
106:1 O give T to the LORD, for he is
106:47 that we may give T to thy holy name
107:1 O give T to the LORD, for he is
108:3 I will give T to thee, O LORD, among
109:30 I will give great T to the LORD; I
111:1 I will give T to the LORD with my
118:1 O give T to the LORD, for he is
118:19 through them and give T to the LORD.
118:28 and I will give T to thee; thou art
118:29 O give T to the LORD, for he is
122:4 for Israel, to give T to the name of
136:1 O give T to the LORD, for he is
136:2 O give T to the God of gods, for
136:3 O give T to the Lord of lords, for
136:26 O give T to the God of heaven, for
138:1 I give thee T, O LORD, with my whole

138:2 holy temple and give T to thy name for
140:13 the righteous shall give T to thy name; the
142:7 that I may give T to thy name!
145:10 thy works shall give T to thee, O LORD,
Wis 16:28 sun to give thee T, and must pray to
Sir 17:22 as do those who are alive and give T
39:6 of wisdom and give T to the Lord in
39:15 his name and give T to him with praise,
47:8 he did he gave T to the Holy One,
51:1 I will give T to thee, O Lord and
51:1 I give T to thy name,
51:12 Therefore I will give T to thee and praise
Is 12:1 day: "I will give T to thee, O LORD,
12:4 in that day: "Give T to the LORD, call
38:19 living, the living, he T thee, as I do
Jer 33:11 of the LORD: 'Give T to the LORD of
Dan 2:23 my fathers, I give T and praise, for thou
3:90 Give T to the Lord, for he is good,
3:91 to him and give T to him, for his
6:10 and prayed and gave T before his God, as
2Mac 8:27 giving great praise and T to the Lord, who
Mt 15:36 fish, and having given T he broke them and
26:27 when he had given T he gave it to
Mk 8:6 loaves, and having given T he broke them and
14:23 when he had given T he gave it to
Lk 2:38 very hour she gave T to God, and spoke
17:16 on his face at Jesus' feet, giving him T
22:17 when he had given T he said, "Take this,
22:19 when he had given T he broke it and
Jn 6:11 when he had given T, he distributed them to
6:23 ate the bread after the Lord had given T
Acts 27:35 took bread, and giving T to God in the
Rom 1:21 as God or give T to him, but they
6:17 But T be to God, that you who were
7:25 T be to God through Jesus Christ our Lord!
14:6 Lord, since he gives T to God; while he
14:6 the Lord and gives T to God.
16:4 of the Gentiles give T;
1Cor 1:4 I give T to God always for you because
10:30 denounced because of that for which I give T
11:24 when he had given T, he broke it, and
14:17 For you may give T well enough, but the
15:57 But T be to God, who gives us the
2Cor 1:11 that many will give T on our behalf for
2:14 But T be to God, who in Christ always
8:16 But T be to God who puts the same
9:15 T be to God for his inexpressible gift!
Eph 1:16 not cease to give T for you, remembering you
5:20 and for everything giving T in the name of
Col 1:12 patience with joy, giving T to the Father, who
3:17 the Lord Jesus, giving T to God the Father
1Thes 1:2 We give T to God always for you all,
5:18 pray constantly, give T in all circumstances; for
2Thes 1:3 are bound to give T to God always for
2:13 are bound to give T to God always for
Rev 4:9 glory and honor and T to him who is
11:17 God, saying, "We give T to thee, Lord God

THANKSGIVING (41)

Lev 7:12 offers it for a T, then he shall offer
7:13 his peace offerings for T he shall bring his
7:15 his peace offerings for T shall be eaten on
22:29 sacrifice a sacrifice of T to the LORD, you
1Chr 16:7 David first appointed that T be sung to the
25:3 with the lyre in T and praise to the
2Chr 5:13 unison in praise and T to the LORD), and
33:16 peace offerings and of T; and he commanded Judah
Neh 11:17 leader to begin the T in prayer, and Bakbukiah,
12:8 brethren was in charge of the songs of T
12:46 songs of praise and T to God.
Jud 16:1 Then Judith began this T before all Israel, and
Ps 26:7 aloud a song of T, and telling all thy
42:4 shouts and songs of T, a multitude keeping festival.
50:14 God a sacrifice of T, and pay your vows
50:23 He who brings T as his sacrifice honors me;
69:30 with a song; I will magnify him with T
95:2 into his presence with T; let us make a
100:4 Enter his gates with T, and his courts with
107:22 them offer sacrifices of T, and tell of his
116:17 thee the sacrifice of T and call on the
147:7 to the LORD with T; make melody to our
Sir 17:23 who does not exist, T has ceased; he who
39:15 you shall say in T:
51:11 thy name continually, and will sing praise with T
Is 51:3 be found in her, T and the voice of
Jer 30:19 shall come songs of T, and the voices of

Amos 4:5 offer a sacrifice of T of that which is
Jon 2:9 with the voice of T will sacrifice to thee;
2Mac 10:7 they offered hymns of T to him who had
1Cor 14:16 to your T when he does not know what
2Cor 4:15 people it may increase T, to the glory of
9:11 through us will produce T to God;
Eph 5:4 are not fitting; but instead let there be T
Phil 4:6 prayer and supplication with T let your requests be
Col 2:7 faith, just as you were taught, abounding in T
4:2 watchful in it with T;
1Thes 3:9 For what T can we render to God for
1Tim 4:3 to be received with T by those who believe
4:4 it is received with T;
Rev 7:12 glory and wisdom and T and honor and power

THANKSGIVINGS (4)

Neh 12:27 dedication with gladness, with T and with singing,
2Mac 10:38 things, with hymns and T they blessed the Lord
2Cor 9:12 also overflows in many T to God.
1Tim 2:1 supplications, prayers, intercessions, and T be made

THARRA

Esth 12:1 courtyard with Gabatha and T, the two eunuchs of

THASSI

1Mac 2:3 surnamed Gaddi, Simon called T,

THEATER (2)

Acts 19:29 rushed together into the T, dragging with them Gaius
19:31 and begged him not to venture into the T

THEBES (5)

Jer 46:25 punishment upon Amon of T, and Pharaoh, and Egypt
Ezek 30:14 Zoan, and will execute acts of judgment upon T
30:15 of Egypt, and cut off the multitude of T
30:16 be in great agony; T shall be breached, and
Nah 3:8 Are you better than T that sat by the

THEBEZ (3)

Judg 9:50 Then Abimelech went to T, and encamped against
9:50 Thebez, and encamped against T, and took it.
2Sam 11:21 from the wall, so that he died at T

THEE (581)

Gen 3:10 heard the sound of T in the garden, and
18:25 Far be it from T to do such a
18:25 Far be that from T
24:12 success today, I pray T, and show steadfast love
28:22 givest me I will give the tenth to T
32:11 Deliver me, I pray T, from the hand of
Ex 15:11 "Who is like T, O LORD, among the gods?
15:11 Who is like T, majestic in holiness, terrible in
32:32 blot me, I pray T, out of thy book
33:13 Now therefore, I pray T, if I have found
33:13 that I may know T and find favor in
33:18 Moses said, "I pray T, show me thy glory."
34:9 the Lord, I pray T, go in the midst
Num 10:35 let them that hate T flee before thee."
10:35 and let them that hate thee flee before T
12:13 the LORD, "Heal her, O God, I beseech T
14:17 And now, I pray T, let the power of
14:19 this people, I pray T, according to the greatness
Deut 33:3 steps, receiving direction from T,
33:10 shall put incense before T, and whole burnt offering
Judg 6:17 have found favor with T, then show me a
6:18 from here, I pray T, until I come to
6:18 until I come to T, and bring out my
6:18 bring out my present, and set it before T
10:10 "We have sinned against T, because we have
10:15 whatever seems good to T; only deliver us, we
10:15 deliver us, we pray T, this day."
13:8 "O, LORD, I pray T, let the man of
16:28 remember me, I pray T, and strengthen me, I
16:28 strengthen me, I pray T, only this once, O
18:5 of God, we pray T, that we may know
1Sam 2:2 there is none besides T; there is no rock
12:10 and we will serve T
23:11 of Israel, I beseech T, tell thy servant." And
2Sam 7:20 And what more can David say to T
7:22 there is none like T, and there is no
7:22 is no God besides T, according to all that
7:26 of thy servant David will be established before T
7:27 has found courage to pray this prayer to T
7:29 therefore may it please T to bless the house
7:29 continue for ever before T; for thou, O Lord
15:31 "O LORD, I pray T, turn the counsel of

22:30 Yea, by T I can crush a troop, and
22:50 this I will extol T, O LORD, among the
24:10 O LORD, I pray T, take away the iniquity
24:17 thy hand, I pray T, be against me and
1Kgs 3:6 he walked before T in faithfulness, in righteousness,
3:6 uprightness of heart toward T; and thou hast kept
8:13 I have built T an exalted house, a place
8:13 house, a place for T to dwell in for
8:23 is no God like T, in heaven above or
8:23 servants who walk before T with all their heart;
8:27 highest heaven cannot contain T; how much less this
8:28 thy servant prays before T this day;
8:33 they have sinned against T, if they turn again
8:33 they turn again to T, and acknowledge thy name,
8:33 and make supplication to T in this house;
8:35 they have sinned against T, if they pray toward
8:40 that they may fear T all the days that
8:43 the foreigner calls to T; in order that all
8:43 thy name and fear T, as do thy people
8:46 "If they sin against T --for there is no
8:47 and make supplication to T in the land of
8:48 captive, and pray to T toward their land, which
8:50 have sinned against T, and all their transgressions
8:50 they have committed against T; and grant them
8:52 giving ear to them whenever they call to T
2Kgs 6:17 "O LORD, I pray T, open his eyes that
6:18 this people, I pray T, with blindness." So he
19:19 save us, I beseech T, from his hand, that
20:3 O LORD, I beseech T, how I have walked
20:3 I have walked before T in faithfulness and with
1Chr 17:18 can David say to T for honoring thy servant?
17:20 There is none like T, O LORD, and there
17:20 is no God besides T, according to all that
17:24 of thy servant David will be established before T
17:25 thy servant has found courage to pray before T
17:27 therefore may it please T to bless the house
17:27 continue for ever before T; for what thou, O
21:8 But now, I pray T, take away the iniquity
21:17 thy hand, I pray T, O LORD my God,
29:12 and honor come from T, and thou rulest over
29:13 And now we thank T, our God, and praise
29:14 all things come from T, and of thy own
29:14 thee, and of thy own have we given T
29:15 we are strangers before T, and sojourners, as all
29:16 have provided for building T a house for thy
29:17 are present here, offering freely and joyously to T
29:18 of thy people, and direct their hearts toward T
2Chr 6:2 I have built T an exalted house, a place
6:2 house, a place for T to dwell in for
6:14 is no God like T, in heaven or on
6:14 servants who walk before T with all their heart;
6:18 highest heaven cannot contain T; how much less this
6:19 thy servant prays before T;
6:24 they have sinned against T, when they turn again
6:24 and make supplication to T in this house,
6:26 they have sinned against T, if they pray toward
6:31 that they may fear T and walk in thy
6:33 the foreigner calls to T; in order that all
6:33 thy name and fear T, as do thy people
6:34 and they pray to T toward this city which
6:36 "If they sin against T --for there is no
6:37 and make supplication to T in the land of
6:39 and forgive thy people who have sinned against T
14:11 there is none like T to help, between the
14:11 for we rely on T, and in thy name
14:11 art our God; let not man prevail against T
20:6 might, so that none is able to withstand T
20:8 it, and have built T in it a sanctuary
20:9 this house, and before T, for thy name is
20:9 house, and cry to T in our affliction, and
20:12 what to do, but our eyes are upon T
Ezra 9:6 lift my face to T, my God, for our
9:15 Behold, we are before T in our guilt, for
9:15 none can stand before T because of this."
Neh 1:6 I now pray before T day and night for
1:6 people of Israel, which we have sinned against T
1:7 acted very corruptly against T, and have not kept
4:5 for they have provoked T to anger before the
9:6 of them; and the host of heaven worships T
9:8 his heart faithful before T, and didst make with
9:10 and thou didst get T a name, as it
9:26 disobedient and rebelled against T and cast thy law
9:26 turn them back to T, and they committed great
9:27 suffering they cried to T and thou didst hear
9:28 did evil again before T, and thou didst abandon
9:28 turned and cried to T thou didst hear from
9:32 hardship seem little to T that has come upon
9:35 They did not serve T in their kingdom, and
Tob 3:3 and those which my fathers committed before T
3:5 For we did not walk in truth before T
3:11 all thy works praise T for ever.
3:12 have turned my eyes and my face toward T
3:15 be not pleasing to T to take my life,
8:5 Let the heavens and all thy creatures bless T
8:15 all thy creatures bless T; let all thy angels
8:15 thy chosen people bless T for ever.
Jud 6:19 the faces of those who are consecrated to T
9:4 who were zealous for T, and abhorred the pollution
9:4 blood, and called on T for help--O God,
16:14 all thy creatures serve T, for thou didst speak,
16:15 to those who fear T thou wilt continue to
16:16 for burnt offerings to T is a very little
Esth 13:9 one who can oppose T if it is thy
13:11 one who can resist T, who art the Lord.
13:14 any one but to T, who art my Lord;
13:17 not destroy the mouth of those who praise T
14:3 have no helper but T,
14:6 we have sinned before T, and thou hast given
14:9 of those who praise T and to quench thy
14:14 have no helper but T, O Lord.
14:18 until now, except in T, O Lord God of
Job 1:11 and he will curse T to thy face."
2:5 and he will curse T to thy face."
7:20 do I do to T, thou watcher of men?
7:20 Why have I become a burden to T
10:3 it seem good to T to oppress, to despise
13:21 let not dread of T terrify me.
14:3 a one and bring him into judgment with T
14:5 his months is with T, and thou hast appointed
14:15 and I would answer T; thou wouldest long for
30:20 I cry to T and thou dost not answer
40:4 am of small account; what shall I answer T
42:5 I had heard of T by the hearing of
42:5 now my eye sees T;
Ps 5:2 my God, for to T do I pray.
5:3 prepare a sacrifice for T, and watch.
5:4 delights in wickedness; evil may not sojourn with T
5:7 toward thy holy temple in the fear of T
5:10 cast them out, for they have rebelled against T
5:11 who take refuge in T rejoice, let them ever
5:11 those who love thy name may exult in T
6:5 is no remembrance of T; in Sheol who can
6:5 Sheol who can give T praise?
7:1 LORD my God, in T do I take refuge;
7:7 peoples be gathered about T; and over it take
9:2 glad and exult in T, I will sing praise
9:3 turned back, they stumbled and perished before T
9:10 put their trust in T, for thou, O LORD,
9:10 O LORD, hast not forsaken those who seek T
9:19 man prevail; let the nations be judged before T
10:14 hapless commits himself to T; thou hast been the
16:1 O God, for in T I take refuge.
16:2 my Lord; I have no good apart from T
17:2 From T let my vindication come!
17:6 I call upon T, for thou wilt answer me,
18:1 I love T, O LORD, my strength.
18:29 Yea, by T I can crush a troop; and
18:49 this I will extol T, O LORD, among the
21:4 He asked life of T; thou gavest it to
22:4 In T our fathers trusted; they trusted, and thou
22:5 To T they cried, and were saved; in thee
22:5 and were saved; in T they trusted, and were
22:10 Upon T was I cast from my birth, and
22:22 congregation I will praise T:
22:25 From T comes my praise in the great congregation;
25:1 [Selah] To T, O LORD, I lift up my
25:2 O my God, in T I trust, let me
25:3 none that wait for T be put to shame;
25:5 of my salvation; for T I wait all the
25:20 put to shame, for I take refuge in T
25:21 and uprightness preserve me, for I wait for T
26:3 my eyes, and I walk in faithfulness to T
27:8 My heart says to T, "Thy face, LORD, do
28:1 To T, O LORD, I call; my rock, be
28:2 as I cry to T for help, as I
30:1 I will extol T, O LORD, for thou hast
30:2 God, I cried to T for help, and thou
30:8 To T, O LORD, I cried; and to the
30:9 Will the dust praise T
30:12 my soul may praise T and not be silent.
30:12 will give thanks to T for ever.
31:1 In T, O LORD, do I seek refuge; let

31:14 But I trust in T, O LORD, I say,
31:17 for I call on T; let the wicked be
31:19 for those who fear T, and wrought for those
31:19 who take refuge in T, in the sight of
31:22 when I cried to T for help.
32:5 acknowledged my sin to T, and I did not
32:6 godly offer prayer to T; at a time of
33:22 be upon us, even as we hope in T
35:10 LORD, who is like T, thou who deliverest the
35:18 Then I will thank T in the great congregation;
35:18 congregation; in the mighty throng I will praise T
36:9 For with T is the fountain of life; in
36:10 to those who know T, and thy salvation to
38:9 longing is known to T, my sighing is not
38:9 to thee, my sighing is not hidden from T
38:15 But for T, O LORD, do I wait; it
39:7 My hope is in T
40:5 thy thoughts toward us; none can compare with T
40:16 may all who seek T rejoice and be glad
40:16 and be glad in T; may those who love
41:4 me; heal me, for I have sinned against T
42:1 longs my soul for T, O God.
42:6 me, therefore I remember T from the land of
43:4 and I will praise T with the lyre, O
44:5 Through T we push down our foes; through thy
44:17 we have not forgotten T, or been false to
51:4 Against T, thee only, have I sinned, and done
51:4 Against thee, T only, have I sinned, and done
51:13 transgressors thy ways, and sinners will return to T
52:9 I will thank T for ever, because thou hast
54:6 I will sacrifice to T; I will give thanks
55:23 But I will trust in T
56:3 I am afraid, I put my trust in T
56:12 My vows to T I must perform, O God;
56:12 O God; I will render thank offerings to T
57:1 to me, for in T my soul takes refuge;
57:9 will give thanks to T, O Lord, among the
57:9 will sing praises to T among the nations.
59:9 will sing praises to T; for thou, O God,
59:17 will sing praises to T, for thou, O God,
60:4 for those who fear T, to rally to it
61:2 earth I call to T, when my heart is
62:12 God; and that to T, O Lord, belongs steadfast
63:1 my God, I seek T, my soul thirsts for
63:1 my soul thirsts for T; my flesh faints for
63:1 my flesh faints for T, as in a dry
63:2 I have looked upon T in the sanctuary, beholding
63:3 is better than life, my lips will praise T
63:4 So I will bless T as long as I
63:5 and my mouth praises T with joyful lips,
63:6 when I think of T upon my bed, and
63:6 bed, and meditate on T in the watches of
63:8 My soul clings to T; thy right hand upholds
65:1 Praise is due to T, O God, in Zion;
65:1 in Zion; and to T shall vows be performed,
65:2 To T shall all flesh come
66:3 is thy power that thy enemies cringe before T
66:4 All the earth worships T; they sing praises to
66:4 they sing praises to T, sing praises to thy
66:13 offerings; I will pay T my vows,
66:15 I will offer to T burnt offerings of fatlings,
67:3 Let the peoples praise T, O God; let all
67:3 thee, O God; let all the peoples praise T
67:5 Let the peoples praise T, O God; let all
67:5 thee, O God; let all the peoples praise T
68:29 thy temple at Jerusalem kings bear gifts to T
69:5 wrongs I have done are not hidden from T
69:6 those who hope in T be put to shame
69:6 not those who seek T be brought to dishonor
69:9 of those who insult T have fallen on me.
69:13 my prayer is to T, O LORD.
69:19 my dishonor; my foes are all known to T
69:27 upon punishment; may they have no acquittal from T
70:4 May all who seek T rejoice and be glad
70:4 who seek thee rejoice and be glad in T
71:1 In T, O LORD, do I take refuge; let
71:6 Upon T I have leaned from my birth; thou
71:6 My praise is continually of T
71:14 continually, and will praise T yet more and more.
71:19 done great things, O God, who is like T
71:22 I will also praise T with the harp for
71:22 will sing praises to T with the lyre, O
71:23 I sing praises to T; my soul also, which
73:22 and ignorant, I was like a beast toward T
73:23 I am continually with T; thou dost hold my
73:25 Whom have I in heaven but T
73:25 is nothing upon earth that I desire besides T
73:27 who are far from T shall perish; thou dost
73:27 an end to those who are false to T
74:22 the impious scoff at T all the day!
75:1 We give thanks to T, O God; we give
76:7 Who can stand before T when once thy anger
76:10 of men shall praise T; the residue of wrath
76:10 the residue of wrath thou wilt gird upon T
77:16 When the waters saw T, O God, when the
77:16 when the waters saw T, they were afraid, yea,
79:6 that do not know T, and on the kingdoms
79:11 the prisoners come before T; according to thy great
79:12 which they have taunted T, O Lord!
79:13 will give thanks to T for ever; from generation
80:18 never turn back from T; give us life, and
82:8 the earth; for to T belong all the nations!
83:2 tumult; those who hate T have raised their heads.
83:5 with one accord; against T they make a covenant–
84:5 whose strength is in T, in whose heart are
84:12 hosts, blessed is the man who trusts in T
85:6 us again, that thy people may rejoice in T
86:2 am godly; save thy servant who trusts in T
86:3 O Lord, for to T do I cry all
86:4 thy servant, for to T, O Lord, do I
86:5 in steadfast love to all who call on T
86:7 trouble I call on T, for thou dost answer
86:8 There is none like T among the gods, O
86:9 and bow down before T, O Lord, and shall
86:12 I give thanks to T, O Lord my God,
86:14 they do not set T before them.
88:1 day; I cry out in the night before T
88:2 my prayer come before T, incline thy ear to
88:9 day I call upon T, O LORD; I spread
88:9 O LORD; I spread out my hands to T
88:10 Do the shades rise up to praise T
88:13 O LORD, cry to T; in the morning my
88:13 thee; in the morning my prayer comes before T
89:8 art, O LORD, with thy faithfulness round about T
89:14 throne; steadfast love and faithfulness go before T
90:8 set our iniquities before T, our secret sins in
90:11 and thy wrath according to the fear of T
94:20 rulers be allied with T, who frame mischief by
101:1 and of justice; to T, O LORD, I will
102:1 prayer, O LORD; let my cry come to T
102:28 secure; their posterity shall be established before T
104:27 These all look to T, to give them their
108:3 will give thanks to T, O LORD, among the
108:3 will sing praises to T among the nations.
116:4 "O LORD, I beseech T, save my life!"
116:17 I will offer to T the sacrifice of thanksgiving
118:21 I thank T that thou hast answered me and
118:25 Save us, we beseech T, O LORD!
118:25 O LORD, we beseech T, give us success!
118:28 will give thanks to T; thou art my God,
118:28 thee; thou art my God, I will extol T
119:7 I will praise T with an upright heart, when
119:10 whole heart I seek T; let me not wander
119:11 my heart, that I might not sin against T
119:38 thy promise, which is for those who fear T
119:62 I rise to praise T, because of thy righteous
119:63 of all who fear T, of those who keep
119:74 Those who fear T shall see me and rejoice,
119:79 Let those who fear T turn to me, that
119:120 trembles for fear of T, and I am afraid
119:146 I cry to T; save me, that I may
119:164 a day I praise T for thy righteous ordinances.
119:168 and testimonies, for all my ways are before T
119:169 my cry come before T, O LORD; give me
119:170 my supplication come before T; deliver me according
119:175 that I may praise T, and let thy ordinances
123:1 To T I lift up my eyes, O thou
130:1 depths I cry to T, O LORD!
130:4 there is forgiveness with T, that thou mayest be
138:1 I give T thanks, O LORD, with my whole
138:4 the earth shall praise T, O LORD, for they
139:12 is not dark to T, the night is bright
139:12 the day; for darkness is as light with T
139:14 I praise T, for thou art fearful and wonderful.
139:15 was not hidden from T, when I was being
139:18 When I awake, I am still with T
139:20 men who maliciously defy T, who lift themselves up
139:20 lift themselves up against T for evil!
139:21 hate them that hate T, O LORD?
139:21 I not loathe them that rise up against T
141:1 I call upon T, O LORD; make haste to
141:1 ear to my voice, when I call to T

141:2 counted as incense before T, and the lifting up
141:8 my eyes are toward T, O LORD God; in
141:8 O LORD God; in T I seek refuge; leave
142:5 I cry to T, O LORD; I say, Thou
143:2 servant; for no man living is righteous before T
143:6 out my hands to T; my soul thirsts for
143:6 my soul thirsts for T like a parched land.
143:8 steadfast love, for in T I put my trust.
143:8 should go, for to T I lift up my
143:9 I have fled to T for refuge!
144:9 a new song to T, O God; upon a
144:9 I will play to T,
145:1 I will extol T, my God and King, and
145:2 day I will bless T, and praise thy name
145:10 shall give thanks to T, O LORD, and all
145:10 O LORD, and all thy saints shall bless T
145:15 of all look to T, and thou givest them
Prov 30:7 things I ask of T; deny them not to
30:9 be full, and deny T, and say, "Who is
Wis 9:6 wisdom that comes from T he will be regarded
9:9 With T is wisdom, who knows thy works and
9:10 that I may learn what is pleasing to T
9:18 were taught what pleases T, and were saved by
11:4 thirsted they called upon T, and water was given
11:22 the whole world before T is like a speck
11:25 not called forth by T have been preserved?
12:2 put their trust in T, O Lord.
12:7 precious of all to T might receive a worthy
12:12 Who will accuse T for the destruction of nations
12:12 who will come before T to plead as an
12:13 there any god besides T, whose care is for
12:14 king or monarch confront T about those whom thou
12:16 sovereignty over all causes T to spare all.
15:3 For to know T is complete righteousness, and to
16:7 he saw, but by T, the Savior of all.
16:16 ungodly, refusing to know T, were scourged by the
16:24 For creation, serving T who hast made it, exerts
16:24 relaxes on behalf of those who trust in T
16:26 that thy word preserves those who trust in T
16:28 the sun to give T thanks, and must pray
16:28 and must pray to T at the dawning of
19:9 leaped like lambs, praising T, O Lord, who didst
Sir 36:2 cause the fear of T to fall upon all
36:5 and let them know T, as we have known
36:5 is not God but T, O Lord.
36:16 those who wait for T, and let thy prophets
51:1 will give thanks to T, O Lord and King,
51:1 King, and will praise T as God my Savior.
51:8 those who wait for T and dost save them
51:12 will give thanks to T and praise thee, and
51:12 to thee and praise T, and I will bless
Is 9:3 joy; they rejoice before T as with joy at
12:1 will give thanks to T, O LORD, for though
25:1 God; I will exalt T, I will praise thy
25:3 strong peoples will glorify T; cities of ruthless nations
25:3 glorify thee; cities of ruthless nations will fear T
26:3 mind is stayed on T, because he trusts in
26:3 is stayed on thee, because he trusts in T
26:8 LORD, we wait for T; thy memorial name is
26:9 My soul yearns for T in the night, my
26:9 the night, my spirit within me earnestly seeks T
26:13 God, other lords besides T have ruled over us,
26:16 in distress they sought T, they poured out a
26:17 were we because of T, O LORD;
33:2 LORD, be gracious to us; we wait for T
38:3 O LORD, I beseech T, how I have walked
38:3 I have walked before T in faithfulness and with
38:18 For Sheol cannot thank T, death cannot praise thee;
38:18 thee, death cannot praise T; those who go down
38:19 the living, he thanks T, as I do this
59:12 transgressions are multiplied before T, and our sins
63:17 so that we fear T not?
64:4 seen a God besides T, who works for those
64:5 righteousness, those that remember T in thy ways.
64:7 to take hold of T; for thou hast hid
64:11 where our fathers praised T, has been burned by
Jer 2:31 are free, we will come no more to T
3:22 "Behold, we come to T; for thou art the
10:6 There is none like T, O LORD; thou art
10:7 Who would not fear T, O King of the
10:7 in all their kingdoms there is none like T
10:25 the nations that know T not, and upon the
11:20 upon them, for to T have I committed my
12:1 when I complain to T; yet I would plead
12:1 thee; yet I would plead my case before T
12:3 thou seest me, and triest my mind toward T
14:7 our backslidings are many, we have sinned against T
14:20 of our fathers, for we have sinned against T
14:22 set our hope on T, for thou doest all
15:11 I have not entreated T for their good, if
15:11 have not pleaded with T on behalf of the
16:19 day of trouble, to T shall the nations come
17:13 Israel, all who forsake T shall be put to
17:13 who turn away from T shall be written in
17:16 I have not pressed T to send evil, nor
18:20 how I stood before T to speak good for
18:23 them be overthrown before T; deal with them in
20:12 upon them, for to T have I committed my
32:17 is too hard for T,
32:20 mankind, and hast made T a name, as at
Lam 1:22 their evil-doing come before T; and deal with them
3:57 when I called on T; thou didst say, 'Do
Bar 2:11 arm, and hast made T a name, as at
2:18 hungers, will ascribe to T glory and righteousness, O
2:19 that we bring before T our prayer for mercy,
3:1 anguish and the wearied spirit cry out to T
3:2 and have mercy, for we have sinned before T
3:4 those who sinned before T, who did not heed
3:6 Lord our God, and T, O Lord, will we
3:7 put the fear of T in our hearts in
3:7 and we will praise T in our exile, for
3:7 the iniquity of our fathers who sinned before T
Dan 2:23 To T, O God of my fathers, I give
2:23 what we asked of T, for thou hast made
3:29 and lawlessly departed from T, and have sinned in
3:38 make an offering before T or to find mercy.
3:40 may we wholly follow T, for there will be
3:40 be no shame for those who trust in T
3:41 our heart we follow T, we fear thee and
3:41 follow thee, we fear T and seek thy face.
9:7 To T, O Lord, belongs righteousness, but to us
9:7 the treachery which they have committed against T
9:8 to our fathers, because we have sinned against T
9:15 hand, and hast made T a name, as at
9:18 present our supplications before T on the ground of
14:38 God, and hast not forsaken those who love T
14:41 of Daniel, and there is no other besides T
Hos 8:2 me they cry, My God, we Israel know T
14:3 In T the orphan finds mercy."
Joel 1:18 Unto T, O LORD, I cry.
1:19 wild beasts cry to T because the water brooks
Amos 7:2 I said, "O Lord GOD, forgive, I beseech T
7:5 I said, "O Lord GOD, cease, I beseech T
Jon 1:14 the LORD, "We beseech T, O LORD, let us
1:14 thou, O LORD, hast done as it pleased T
2:7 my prayer came to T, into thy holy temple.
2:9 thanksgiving will sacrifice to T; what I have vowed
4:2 and said, "I pray T, LORD, is not this
4:3 from me, I beseech T, for it is better
Mic 7:17 our God, and they shall fear because of T
7:18 is a God like T, pardoning iniquity and passing
Hab 1:2 Or cry to T "Violence!" and thou wilt not
3:2 heard the report of T, and thy work, O
3:10 The mountains saw T, and writhed; the raging waters
Mal 3:8 'How are we robbing T In your tithes and
3:13 have we spoken against T
1Mac 4:33 of those who love T, and let all who
4:33 know thy name praise T with hymns."
Mt 11:10 prepare thy way before T
11:25 Jesus declared, "I thank T, Father, Lord of heaven
25:37 when did we see T hungry and feed thee,
25:37 thee hungry and feed T, or thirsty and give
25:37 or thirsty and give T drink?
25:38 when did we see T a stranger and welcome
25:38 a stranger and welcome T, or naked and clothe
25:38 stranger and welcome thee, or naked and clothe T
25:39 when did we see T sick or in prison
25:39 in prison and visit T
25:44 when did we see T hungry or thirsty or
25:44 did not minister to T
Mk 1:11 my beloved Son; with T I am well pleased."
14:36 things are possible to T; remove this cup from
Lk 3:22 my beloved Son; with T I am well pleased."
7:27 prepare thy way before T
10:21 and said, "I thank T, Father, Lord of heaven
18:11 himself, 'God, I thank T that I am not
Jn 11:41 said, "Father, I thank T that thou hast heard
17:1 the Son may glorify T,
17:3 life, that they know T the only true God,
17:4 I glorified T on earth, having accomplished the work
17:5 which I had with T before the world was
17:7 given me is from T;

17:8 that I came from T; and they have believed
17:11 in the world, and I am coming to T
17:13 I am coming to T; and these things I
17:21 me, and I in T, that they also may
17:25 world has not known T, but I have known
17:25 but I have known T; and these know that
Acts 13:33 today I have begotten T
22:19 I imprisoned and beat those who believed in T
Rom 15:3 of those who reproached T fell on me."
15:9 "Therefore I will praise T among the Gentiles, and
Heb 1:5 "Thou art my Son, today I have begotten T
1:9 thy God, has anointed T with the oil of
2:12 the midst of the congregation I will praise T
5:5 today I have begotten T;
Rev 11:17 "We give thanks to T, Lord God Almighty, who
15:4 shall come and worship T, for thy judgments have
18:14 longed has gone from T, and all thy dainties
18:14 splendor are lost to T, never to be found
18:22 shall be heard in T no more; and a
18:22 shall be found in T no more; and the
18:22 shall be heard in T no more;
18:23 lamp shall shine in T no more; and the
18:23 shall be heard in T no more; for thy

THEFT (5)

Ex 22:1 nothing, then he shall be sold for his T
Wis 14:25 and murder, T and deceit, corruption, faithlessness,
Sir 41:19 or friend; and of T, in the place where
Mt 15:19 murder, adultery, fornication, T, false witness, slander.
Mk 7:20 come evil thoughts, fornication, T, murder, adultery,

THEFTS

Rev 9:21 or their sorceries or their immorality or their T

THEIRS (19)

Gen 15:13 land that is not T, and will be slaves
43:34 was five times as much as any of T
Ex 29:9 the priesthood shall be T by a perpetual statute.
Num 8:11 that it may be T to do the service
16:26 and touch nothing of T, lest you be swept
18:9 fire; every offering of T, every cereal offering of
18:9 every cereal offering of T and every sin offering
18:9 every sin offering of T and every guilt offering
18:9 every guilt offering of T, which they render to
35:3 The cities shall be T to dwell in, and
1Chr 6:54 families of Kohathites, for T was the lot,
Jer 44:28 shall know whose word will stand, mine or T
Ezek 44:29 and every devoted thing in Israel shall be T
Hos 9:15 Every evil of T is in Gilgal; there I
1Mac 6:52 of war to match T, and fought for many
2Mac 13:22 gave pledges, received T, withdrew, attacked Judas
Mt 5:3 poor in spirit, for T is the kingdom of
5:10 for righteousness' sake, for T is the kingdom of
Heb 1:4 name he has obtained is more excellent than T

THEME

Ps 45:1 overflows with a goodly T; I address my verses

THEMSELVES (352)

Gen 3:7 leaves together and made T aprons.
3:8 and his wife hid T from the presence of
12:3 all the families of the earth shall bless T
18:18 the earth shall bless T by him?
19:11 so that they wearied T groping for the door.
22:18 of the earth bless T, because you have obeyed
26:4 the earth shall bless T:
28:14 shall all the families of the earth bless T
34:30 and if they gather T against me and attack
41:40 my people shall order T as you command; only
42:6 brothers came, and bowed T before him with their
43:32 himself, and them by T, and the Egyptians who
43:32 ate with him by T, because the Egyptians might
Ex 5:7 heretofore; let them go and gather straw for T
12:39 had they prepared for T any provisions.
18:22 matter they shall decide T; so it will be
18:26 to Moses, but any small matter they decided T
19:22 to the LORD consecrate T, lest the LORD break
26:9 couple five curtains by T, and six curtains by
26:9 and six curtains by T, and the sixth curtain
28:43 they bring guilt upon T and die.
32:1 mountain, the people gathered T together to Aaron,
32:7 of Egypt, have corrupted T;
32:8 they have made for T a molten calf, and
32:26 sons of Levi gathered T together to him.
32:31 they have made for T gods of gold.
33:6 people of Israel stripped T of their ornaments, from
36:16 coupled five curtains by T, and six curtains by
36:16 five curtains by themselves, and six curtains by T
Lev 15:18 of them shall bathe T in water, and be
18:24 out before you defiled T;
Num 1:18 together, who registered T by families, by fathers'
8:7 their body, and wash their clothes and cleanse T
8:21 And the Levites purified T from sin, and washed
10:3 the congregation shall gather T to you at the
10:4 of Israel, shall gather T to you.
11:32 spread them out for T all around the camp.
16:3 men; and they assembled T together against Moses
20:2 and they assembled T together against Moses and
25:5 men who have yoked T to Baal of Peor."
27:3 of those who gathered T together against the LORD
Deut 7:20 are left and hide T from you are destroyed.
9:12 them; they have made T a molten image.'
31:14 Joshua went and presented T in the tent of
32:31 Rock, even our enemies T being judges.
Josh 10:16 kings fled, and hid T in the cave at
10:27 where they had hidden T, and they set great
22:9 which they had possessed T by command of the
24:1 Israel; and they presented T before God.
Judg 3:6 took their daughters to T for wives, and their
5:2 that the people offered T willingly, bless the LORD!
5:9 of Israel who offered T willingly among the people.
6:2 of Israel made for T the dens which are
7:2 hand, lest Israel vaunt T against me, saying, 'My
9:51 and women, and shut T in; and they went
18:30 the graven image for T; and Jonathan the son
20:2 tribes of Israel, presented T in the assembly of
20:30 third day, and set T in array against Gibe-ah,
20:33 their place, and set T in array at Baal-tamar;
1Sam 2:5 were full have hired T out for bread, but
13:6 hard-pressed), the people hid T in caves and in
13:19 "Lest the Hebrews make T swords or spears";
14:11 both of them showed T to the garrison of
14:11 out of the holes where they have hid T
14:22 Israel who had hid T in the hill country
21:4 young men have kept T from women."
2Sam 2:25 the Benjaminites gathered T together behind Abner,
10:8 and Maacah, were by T in the open country.
10:15 by Israel, they gathered T together.
10:17 And the Syrians arrayed T against David, and fought
1Kgs 14:23 they also built for T high places, and pillars,
18:23 choose one bull for T, and cut it in
18:28 cried aloud, and cut T after their custom with
22:38 and the harlots washed T in it, according to
2Kgs 7:12 the camp to hide T in the open country,
17:9 They built for T high places at all their
17:10 they set up for T pillars and Asherim on
17:16 God, and made for T molten images of two
17:17 and sorcery, and sold T to do evil in
17:32 and appointed from among T all sorts of people
1Chr 15:14 and the Levites sanctified T to bring up the
19:6 that they had made T odious to David, Hanun
19:9 had come were by T in the open country.
21:20 his four sons who were with him hid T
2Chr 5:11 were present had sanctified T, without regard to their
5:13 and singers to make T heard in unison in
7:14 by my name humble T, and pray and seek
12:6 and the king humbled T and said, "The LORD
12:7 saw that they humbled T, the word of the
12:7 Shemaiah: "They have humbled T; I will not destroy
20:25 which they took for T until they could carry
29:15 their brethren, and sanctified T, and went in as
29:29 present with him bowed T and worshiped.
29:34 other priests had sanctified T their brethren the
29:34 upright in heart than the priests in sanctifying T
30:3 priests had not sanctified T in sufficient number, nor
30:11 and of Zebulun humbled T and came to Jerusalem.
30:15 so that they sanctified T, and brought burnt offerings
30:17 who had not sanctified T; therefore the Levites had
30:18 Zebulun, had not cleansed T, yet they ate the
30:24 And the priests sanctified T in great numbers.
31:4 that they might give T to the law of
31:18 were faithful in keeping T holy.
35:14 afterward they prepared for T and for the priests,
35:14 the Levites prepared for T and for the priests
Ezra 6:20 the Levites had purified T together; all of them
6:20 fellow priests, and for T;
9:1 Levites have not separated T from the peoples of
9:2 to be wives for T and for their sons;
10:19 They pledged T to put away their wives, and
Neh 8:16 and made booths for T, each on his roof,
9:2 And the Israelites separated T from all foreigners,
9:18 they had made for T a molten calf and

T

9:25 became fat, and delighted T in thy great goodness.
10:28 all who have separated T from the peoples of
12:29 singers had built for T villages around Jerusalem.
12:30 and the Levites purified T; and they purified the
13:22 that they should purify T and come and guard
Jud 2:10 They will yield T to you, and you shall
4:9 fervor, and they humbled T with much fasting.
4:10 slave--they all girded T with sackcloth.
4:11 living at Jerusalem, prostrated T before the temple
9:6 thou didst will presented T and said, 'Lo, we
11:2 them; but they have brought all this on T
15:13 her; and they crowned T with olive wreaths, she
Esth 8:13 that day to avenge T upon their enemies.
8:17 of the country declared T Jews, for the fear
9:27 and took it upon T and their descendants and
9:31 had laid down for T and for their descendants,
14:11 turn their plan against T, and make an example
16:20 day they may defend T against those who attach
Job 1:6 God came to present T before the LORD, and
2:1 God came to present T before the LORD, and
3:14 who rebuilt ruins for T,
16:10 the cheek, they mass T together against me.
21:19 him recompense it to T, that they may know
24:4 road; the poor of the earth all hide T
24:16 by day they shut T up; they do not
30:4 bushes, and to warm T the roots of the
34:22 gloom or deep darkness where evildoers may hide T
41:25 are afraid; at the crashing they are beside T
Ps 2:2 of the earth set T, and the rulers take
3:6 people who have set T against me round about.
35:25 them not say to T, "Aha, we have our
35:26 and dishonor who magnify T against me!
37:11 the land, and delight T in abundant prosperity.
56:6 They band T together, they lurk, they watch my
57:6 my way, but they have fallen into it T
59:3 life; fierce men band T against me.
65:12 drip, the hills gird T with joy,
65:13 joy, the meadows clothe T with flocks, the valleys
65:13 flocks, the valleys deck T with grain, they shout
66:7 the nations-- let not the rebellious exalt T
72:17 May men bless T by him, all nations call
74:8 They said to T, "We will utterly subdue them";
80:6 of our neighbors; and our enemies laugh among T
106:28 Then they attached T to the Baal of Peor,
110:3 Your people will offer T freely on the day
139:20 defy thee, who lift T up against thee for
Prov 28:12 glory; but when the wicked rise, men hide T
28:28 wicked rise, men hide T, but when they perish,
Eccl 3:12 be happy and enjoy T as long as they
11:3 of rain, they empty T on the earth; and
Wis 2:1 unsoundly, saying to T, "Short and sorrowful is
11:5 enemies were punished, they T received benefit in
14:30 of God in devoting T to idols, and because
17:2 in their power they T lay as captives of
17:8 sick soul were sick T with ridiculous fear.
17:21 but still heavier than darkness were they to T
19:2 actions, that, though they T had permitted thy people
19:5 incredible journey, but they T might meet a strange
Sir 2:17 hearts, and will humble T before him.
8:9 the aged, for they T learned from their fathers;
18:28 understand sayings become skilled T, and pour forth
Is 2:20 which they made for T to worship, to the
3:9 For they have brought evil upon T
46:2 save the burden, but T go into captivity.
47:14 them; they cannot deliver T from the power of
48:2 For they call T after the holy city, and
48:2 holy city, and stay T on the God of
49:7 and they shall prostrate T; because of the LORD,
56:6 the foreigners who join T to the LORD, to
59:6 men will not cover T with what they make.
66:17 who sanctify and purify T to go into the
Jer 2:13 hewed out cisterns for T, broken cisterns, that can
2:24 seek her need weary T; in her month they
4:2 then nations shall bless T in him, and in
7:19 Is it not T, to their own confusion?
12:13 thorns, they have tired T out but profit nothing.
30:21 shall be one of T, their ruler shall come
44:10 They have not humbled T even to this day,
49:9 night, would they not destroy only enough for T
50:9 and they shall array T against her; from there
51:58 and the nations weary T only for fire."
Bar 2:30 they will come to T,
6:8 the craftsman, and they T are overlaid with gold
6:10 and spend it upon T,
6:12 wood, which cannot save T from rust and corrosion.
6:19 than they light for T, though their gods can

6:40 Besides, even the Chaldeans T dishonor them;
6:42 Yet they T cannot perceive this and abandon them,
6:46 not live very long T; how then can the
6:48 where they can hide T and their gods.
6:49 for they cannot save T from war or calamity?
6:57 not able to save T from thieves and robbers.
6:58 and they will not be able to help T
6:68 for they can flee to cover and help T
6:72 and they will finally T be consumed, and be
Ezek 7:18 They gird T with sackcloth, and horror covers them;
14:11 from me, nor defile T any more with all
23:24 peoples; they shall set T against you on every
26:16 garments; they will clothe T with trembling; they will
27:31 in ashes; they make T bald for you, and
27:31 for you, and gird T with sackcloth, and they
34:8 the shepherds have fed T, and have not fed
34:10 the sheep; no longer shall the shepherds feed T
36:5 gave my land to T as a possession with
36:7 round about you shall T suffer reproach.
37:23 They shall not defile T any more with their
44:18 they shall not gird T with anything that causes
44:25 They shall not defile T by going near to
44:25 for brother or unmarried sister they may defile T
Dan 10:7 fell upon them, and they fled to hide T
11:14 own people shall lift T up in order to
11:34 And many shall join T to them with flattery;
12:10 Many shall purify T, and make themselves white, and
12:10 purify themselves, and make T white, and be refined;
13:16 elders, who had hid T and were watching her.
Hos 1:11 they shall appoint for T one head; and they
4:14 adultery; for the men T go aside with harlots,
4:18 of drunkards, they give T to harlotry; they love
7:15 and wine they gash T, they rebel against me.
9:9 They have deeply corrupted T as in the days
9:10 to Baal-peor, and consecrated T to Baal, and became
13:2 more, and make for T molten images, idols skilfully
Joel 3:12 Let the nations bestir T, and come up to
Amos 2:8 is profaned; they lay T down beside every altar
6:4 of ivory, and stretch T upon their couches, and
6:5 like David invent for T instruments of music;
6:6 in bowls, and anoint T with the finest oils,
6:7 of those who stretch T shall pass away."
9:3 Though they hide T on the top of Carmel,
Obad 1:5 destroyed!--would they not steal only enough for T
Hab 1:7 are they; their justice and dignity proceed from T
2:13 fire, and nations weary T for nought?
Zeph 1:8 and all who array T in foreign attire.
Zech 2:11 many nations shall join T to the LORD in
6:5 of heaven, after presenting T before the LORD of
12:3 peoples; all who lift it shall grievously hurt T
12:5 Judah shall say to T, 'The inhabitants of Jerusalem
12:12 and their wives by T; the family of the
12:12 and their wives by T;
12:13 and their wives by T; the family of the
12:13 and their wives by T;
12:14 left, each by itself, and their wives by T
14:18 go up and present T, then upon them shall
1Mac 1:15 the Gentiles and sold T to do evil.
1:48 were to make T abominable by everything unclean
4:39 great lamentation, and sprinkled T with ashes.
6:38 the enemy while being T protected by the phalanxes.
8:15 they have built for T a senate chamber, and
8:18 alliance, and to free T from the yoke; for
11:68 the mountains, but they T met him face to
14:29 and his brothers, exposed T to danger and resisted
14:36 Jerusalem, who had built T a citadel from which
2Mac 3:2 about that the kings T honored the place and
3:15 The priests prostrated T before the altar in their
6:11 kept them from defending T, in view of their
8:28 distributed the rest among T and their children.
11:11 They hurled T like lions against the enemy, and
12:38 coming on, they purified T according to the custom,
12:42 the people to keep T free from sin, for
14:14 calamities of the Jews would mean prosperity for T
14:21 set a day on which to meet by T
Mt 9:3 the scribes said to T, "This man is blaspheming."
14:15 go into the villages and buy food for T
16:7 they discussed it among T, saying, "We brought no
19:12 eunuchs who have made T eunuchs for the sake
21:38 son, they said to T, 'This is the heir;
23:4 men's shoulders; but they T will not move them
Mk 1:27 that they questioned among T, saying, "What is this?
2:8 they thus questioned within T, said to them, "Why
4:17 have no root in T, but endure for a
6:32 in the boat to a lonely place by T
6:36 round about and buy T something to eat."

7:4 eat unless they purify T; and there are many
9:2 high mountain apart by T; and he was transfigured
9:10 kept the matter to T, questioning what the rising
14:4 some who said to T indignantly, "Why was the
16:14 appeared to the eleven T as they sat at
Lk 7:30 purpose of God for T, not having been baptized
7:49 began to say among T, "Who is this, who
18:9 some who trusted in T that they were righteous
20:14 him, they said to T, 'This is the heir;
24:12 the linen clothes by T; and he went home
Jn 6:24 nor his disciples, they T got into the boats
6:52 Jews then disputed among T, saying, "How can this
11:55 country to Jerusalem before the Passover, to purify T
14:11 believe me for the sake of the works T
17:13 that they may have my joy fulfilled in T
18:18 were standing and warming T; Peter also was with
18:28 They T did not enter the praetorium, so that
Acts 1:14 with one accord devoted T to prayer, together with
2:42 And they devoted T to the apostles' teaching and
4:26 of the earth set T in array, and the
15:27 Judas and Silas, who T will tell you the
15:32 Silas, who were T prophets, exhorted the brethren
16:37 let them come T and take us out."
22:19 I said, 'Lord, they T know that in every
23:12 a plot and bound T by an oath neither
23:21 for him, having bound T by an oath neither
24:14 in God which these T accept, that there will
24:19 else let these men T say what wrongdoing they
27:36 they all were encouraged and ate some food T
27:43 could swim to throw T overboard first and make
28:25 as they disagreed among T, they departed, after Paul
Rom 1:24 of their bodies among T,
2:14 are a law to T, even though they do
1Cor 16:15 and they have devoted T to the service of
2Cor 5:12 answer those who pride T on a man's position
5:15 live no longer for T but for him who
8:5 but first they gave T to the Lord and
10:12 ourselves with some of those who commend T
10:12 But when they measure T by one another, and
10:12 one another, and compare T with one another, they
11:13 deceitful workmen, disguising T as apostles of Christ.
11:15 servants also disguise T as servants of righteousness.
Gal 5:12 I wish those who unsettle you would mutilate T
6:13 receive circumcision do not T keep the law, but
Eph 4:19 callous and have given T up to licentiousness, greedy
1Thes 1:9 For they T report concerning us what a welcome
1Tim 1:4 doctrine, nor to occupy T with myths and endless
2:9 that women should adorn T modestly and sensibly in
3:10 then if they prove T blameless let them serve
3:13 a good standing for T and also great confidence
6:19 thus laying up for T a good foundation for
2Tim 4:3 they will accumulate for T teachers to suit their
Tit 1:11 One of T, a prophet of their own, said,
2:6 Likewise urge the younger men to control T
3:8 be careful to apply T to good deeds; these
3:14 people learn to apply T to good deeds, so
Heb 6:16 by a greater than T, and in all their
9:23 but the heavenly things T with better sacrifices than
1Pet 1:12 they were serving not T but you, in the
3:5 God used to adorn T and were submissive to
2Pet 2:1 bought them, bringing upon T swift destruction.
2:19 them freedom, but they T are slaves of corruption;
Jude 1:11 of Cain, and abandon T for the sake of
1:12 carouse together, looking after T; waterless clouds,
Rev 2:2 tested those who call T apostles but are not,
6:11 be killed as they T had been.
14:4 who have not defiled T with women, for they

THENCE (14)

Gen 12:8 T he removed to the mountain on the east
Deut 5:15 God brought you out T with a mighty hand
Josh 16:6 and the boundary goes T to the sea; on
18:17 on to En-shemesh, and T goes to Geliloth, which
19:12 the boundary of Chisloth-tabor; T it goes to,
2Kgs 2:25 to Mount Carmel, and T he returned to Samaria.
17:27 whom you carried away T; and let him go
Neh 1:9 I will gather them T and bring them to
Job 39:29 T he spies out the prey; his eyes behold
Is 52:11 Depart, depart, go out T, touch no unclean thing;
Ezek 47:19 the waters of Meribath-kadesh, T along the Brook of
48:28 the waters of Meribath-kadesh, T along the Brook of
Amos 6:2 Calneh, and see; and T go to Hamath the
Obad 1:4 set among the stars, T I will bring you

THEODOTUS

2Mac 14:19 he sent Posidonius and T and Mattathias to give

THEOPHILUS (2)

Lk 1:3 for you, most excellent T,
Acts 1:1 the first book, O T, I have dealt with

THEREBY (9)

Lev 6:7 one may do and T become guilty."
15:32 of semen, becoming unclean T;
22:9 for it and die T when they profane it:
Deut 32:47 is your life, and T you shall live long
Job 22:21 and be at peace; T good will come to
Mal 3:10 in my house; and T put me to the
1Cor 4:4 but I am not T acquitted.
Eph 2:16 body through the cross, T bringing the hostility to
Heb 13:2 hospitality to strangers, for T some have entertained

THEREIN (15)

Lev 6:3 men do and sin T,
Num 16:46 censer, and put fire T from off the altar,
Josh 24:13 built, and you dwell T; you eat the fruit
Ps 24:1 and those who dwell T;
35:8 them; let them fall T to ruin!
69:34 praise him, the seas and everything that moves T
Sir 51:17 I made progress T; to him who gives wisdom
Is 35:8 pass over it, and fools shall not err T
Nah 1:5 before him, the world and all that dwell T
Hab 2:8 the earth, to cities and all who dwell T
2:17 the earth, to cities and all who dwell T
2Mac 11:17 and have asked about the matters indicated T
Rev 1:3 keep what is written T; for the time is
5:13 the sea, and all T, saying, "To him who
12:12 Rejoice then, O heaven and you that dwell T

THEREOF

Ps 24:1 LORD's and the fulness T, the world and those

THEREON (6)

Ex 30:9 offer no unholy incense T, nor burnt offering, nor
30:9 cereal offering; and you shall pour no libation T
31:7 mercy seat that is T, and all the furnishings
Is 8:15 And many shall stumble T; they shall fall and
Zech 9:2 Hamath also, which borders T, Tyre and Sidon,
Mt 21:7 put their garments on them, and he sat T

THEREUPON

Jer 31:26 T I awoke and looked, and my sleep was

THEREWITH

Lev 8:7 band of the ephod, binding it to him T

THESSALONIANS (3)

Acts 20:4 him; and of the T, Aristarchus and Secundus; and
1Thes 1:1 the Church of the T in God the Father
2Thes 1:1 the Church of the T in God our father

THESSALONICA (6)

Acts 17:1 Apollonia, they came to T, where there was a
17:11 noble than those in T, for they received the
17:13 when the Jews of T learned that the word
27:2 accompanied by Aristarchus, a Macedonian from T
Phil 4:16 only; for even in T you sent me help
2Tim 4:10 me and gone to T; Crescens has gone to

THEUDAS

Acts 5:36 For before these days T arose, giving himself out

THICK (37)

Ex 10:22 heaven, and there was T darkness in all the
19:9 to you in a T cloud, that the people
19:16 and lightnings, and a T cloud upon the mountain,
20:21 drew near to the T darkness where God was.
Deut 5:22 the cloud, and the T darkness, with a loud
32:15 waxed fat, you grew T, you became sleek; then
2Sam 18:9 mule went under the T branches of a great
22:10 heavens, and came down; T darkness was under his
22:12 around him his canopy, T clouds, a gathering of
1Kgs 8:12 he would dwell in T darkness.
2Chr 6:1 he would dwell in T darkness.
Jud 1:2 hewn stones three cubits T and six cubits long;
Job 3:6 That night—let T darkness seize it!
22:14 T clouds enwrap him, so that he does not
23:17 in by darkness, and T darkness covers my face.
26:8 the waters in his T clouds, and the cloud
37:11 He loads the T cloud with moisture; the clouds
38:9 clouds its garment, and T darkness its swaddling
Ps 18:9 heavens, and came down; T darkness was under his
18:11 around him, his canopy T clouds dark with water.

T

97:2 Clouds and T darkness are round about him;
Wis 11:18 or belch forth a T pall of smoke, or
Sir 45:5 led him into the T darkness, and gave him
Is 8:22 will be thrust into T darkness.
30:27 his anger, and in T rising smoke; his lips
60:2 cover the earth, and T darkness the peoples; but
Jer 2:31 or a land of T darkness?
Bar 6:13 the temple, which is T upon them.
Ezek 19:11 towered aloft among the T boughs; it was seen
24:12 have wearied myself; its T rust does not go
34:12 day of clouds and T darkness.
41:5 the temple, six cubits T; and the breadth of
41:12 building was five cubits T round about, and its
Joel 2:2 day of clouds and T darkness!
Zeph 1:15 day of clouds and T darkness,
Zech 11:2 of Bashan, for the T forest has been felled!
2Mac 1:20 not found fire but T liquid, he ordered them

THICK-BOSSED
Job 15:26 against him with a T shield;

THICKENING
Zeph 1:12 the men who are T upon their lees, those

THICKER (2)
1Kgs 12:10 'My little finger is T than my father's loins.
2Chr 10:10 'My little finger is T than my father's loins.

THICKET (4)
Gen 22:13 ram, caught in a T by his horns; and
Jer 4:7 gone up from his T, a destroyer of nations
1Mac 4:38 up as in a T, or as on one
9:45 that, with marsh and T; there is no place

THICKETS (4)
Is 9:18 thorns; it kindles the T of the forest, and
10:34 will cut down the T of the forest with
21:13 In the T in Arabia you will lodge, O
Jer 4:29 to flight; they enter T; they climb among rocks;

THICKNESS (6)
1Kgs 7:15 was hollow, and its T was four fingers; the
7:26 Its T was a handbreadth; and its brim was
2Chr 4:5 Its T was a handbreadth; and its brim was
Jer 52:21 twelve cubits, and its T was four fingers, and
Ezek 40:5 so he measured the T of the wall, one
41:9 The T of the outer wall of the side

THIEF (28)
Ex 22:3 "If a T is found breaking in, and is
22:7 house, then, if the T is found, he shall
22:8 If the T is not found, the owner of
Deut 24:7 sells him, then that T shall die; so you
Job 24:14 and in the night he is as a T
30:5 men; they shout after them as after a T
Ps 50:18 If you see a T, you are a friend
Prov 6:30 not men despise a T if he steals to
29:24 The partner of a T hates his own life;
Sir 5:14 shame comes to the T, and severe condemnation to
20:24 A T is preferable to a habitual liar, but
Jer 2:26 will go.' "As a T is shamed when caught,
Hos 7:2 they deal falsely, the T breaks in, and the
Joel 2:9 houses, they enter through the windows like a T
Zech 5:4 the house of the T, and the house of
Mt 24:43 of the night the T was coming, he would
Lk 12:33 not fail, where no T approaches and no moth
12:39 at what hour the T was coming, he would
Jn 10:1 that man is a T and a robber;
10:10 The T comes only to steal and kill and
12:6 because he was a T, and as he had
Eph 4:28 Let the T no longer steal, but rather let
1Thes 5:2 will come like a T in the night.
5:4 for that day to surprise you like a T
1Pet 4:15 a murderer, or a T, or a wrongdoer, or
2Pet 3:10 will come like a T, and then the heavens
Rev 3:3 will come like a T, and you will not
16:15 ("Lo, I am coming like a T

THIEVES (9)
Is 1:23 Your princes are rebels and companions of T
Jer 48:27 Was he found among T, that whenever you spoke
49:9 If T came by night, would they not destroy
Bar 6:57 to save themselves from T and robbers.
Obad 1:5 If T came to you, if plunderers by night--
Mt 6:19 rust consume and where T break in and steal,
6:20 rust consumes and where T do not break in
Jn 10:8 came before me are T and robbers; but the
1Cor 6:10 adulterers, nor homosexuals, nor T, nor the greedy,

THIGH (35)
Gen 24:2 your hand under my T,
24:9 his hand under the T of Abraham his master,
32:25 the hollow of his T; and Jacob's thigh was
32:25 his thigh; and Jacob's T was put out of
32:31 as he passed Penuel, limping because of his T
32:32 the hollow of the T, because he touched the
32:32 the hollow of Jacob's T on the sinew of
47:29 your hand under my T, and promise to deal
Ex 29:22 them, and the right T (for it is a
29:27 wave offering, and the T of the priests' portion,
Lev 7:32 And the right T you shall give to the
7:33 shall have the right T for a portion.
7:34 is waved and the T that is offered I
8:25 fat, and the right T;
8:26 and on the right T;
9:21 breasts and the right T Aaron waved for a
10:14 is waved and the T that is offered you
10:15 The T that is offered and the breast that
Num 5:21 the LORD makes your T fall away and your
5:22 body swell and your T fall away.' And the
5:27 shall swell, and her T shall fall away, and
6:20 is waved and the T that is offered; and
18:18 and as the right T are yours.
Judg 3:16 it on his right T under his clothes.
3:21 sword from his right T, and thrust it into
15:8 smote them hip and T with great slaughter; and
Jud 9:2 her, and uncovered her T to put her to
Ps 45:3 your sword upon your T, O mighty one, in
Song 3:8 his sword at his T, against alarms by night.
Sir 19:12 the flesh of the T, so is a word
Jer 31:19 I smote upon my T; I was ashamed, and
Ezek 21:12 Smite therefore upon your T
24:4 the good pieces, the T and the shoulder; fill
Hab 3:13 laying him bare from T to neck.
Rev 19:16 robe and on his T he has a name

THIGHS (4)
Ex 28:42 the loins to the T they shall reach;
Job 40:17 the sinews of his T are knit together.
Song 7:1 Your rounded T are like jewels, the work of
Dan 2:32 silver, its belly and T of bronze,

THIN (9)
Gen 41:3 other cows, gaunt and T, came up out of
41:4 And the gaunt and T cows ate up the
41:6 them sprouted seven ears, T and blighted by the
41:7 And the T ears swallowed up the seven plump
41:19 and very gaunt and T, such as I had
41:20 And the T and gaunt cows ate up the
41:23 and seven ears, withered, T, and blighted by the
41:24 after them, and the T ears swallowed up the
Lev 13:30 it is yellow and T, then the priest shall

THINE (28)
Ex 32:13 thou didst swear by T own self, and didst
Deut 3:24 can do such works and mighty acts as T
Judg 5:31 spoil?' "So perish all T enemies, O LORD!
1Kgs 8:31 swears his oath before T altar in this house,
1Chr 29:11 T, O LORD, is the greatness, and the power,
29:11 in the earth is T; thine is the kingdom,
29:11 the earth is thine; T is the kingdom, O
Esth 13:15 inheritance that has been T from the beginning.
Job 42:2 that no purpose of T can be thwarted.
Ps 71:16 will praise thy righteousness, T alone.
74:16 T is the day, thine also the night; thou
74:16 Thine is the day, T also the night; thou
84:9 upon the face of T anointed!
86:8 O Lord, nor are there any works like T
89:11 The heavens are T, the earth also is thine;
89:11 the earth also is T; the world and all
119:94 I am T, save me; for I have sought
Wis 11:26 things, for they are T, O Lord who lovest
15:2 we sin we are T, knowing thy power; but
15:2 sin, because we know that we are accounted T
Jer 18:23 in the time of T anger.
Lam 3:56 plea, 'Do not close T ear to my cry
Hab 3:11 at the light of T arrows as they sped,
Lk 22:42 not my will, but T, be done."
Jn 17:6 out of the world; T they were, and thou
17:9 me, for they are T;
17:10 thine; all mine are T, and thine are mine,
17:10 mine are thine, and T are mine, and I

THING (255)

Gen 1:26 and over every creeping T that creeps upon the
1:28 and over every living T that moves upon the
6:19 And of every living T of all flesh, you
6:20 kinds, of every creeping T of the ground according
7:4 nights; and every living T that I have made
7:14 kinds, and every creeping T that creeps on the
7:23 blotted out every living T that was upon the
8:17 with you every living T that is with you
8:17 animals and every creeping T that creeps on the
8:19 every beast, every creeping T, and every bird,
9:3 Every moving T that lives shall be food for
18:25 to do such a T, to slay the righteous
20:10 were you thinking of, that you did this T
21:11 And the T was very displeasing to Abraham on
21:26 who has done this T; you did not tell
24:50 Bethuel answered, "The T comes from the LORD;
32:19 shall say the same T to Esau when you
34:7 daughter, for such a T ought not to be
34:14 "We cannot do this T, to give our sister
34:19 delay to do the T, because he had delight
41:32 dream means that the T is fixed by God,
44:7 your servants that they should do such a T
Ex 2:14 and thought, "Surely the T is known."
9:5 LORD will do this T in the land."
9:6 the LORD did this T; all the cattle of
10:15 left; not a green T remained, neither tree nor
16:14 wilderness a fine, flake-like T, fine as hoarfrost on
18:18 yourselves out, for the T is too heavy for
22:9 any kind of lost T, of which one says,
33:17 to Moses, "This very T that you have spoken
34:10 it is a terrible T that I will do
35:4 Israel, "This is the T which the LORD has
Lev 4:13 sin unwittingly and the T is hidden from the
5:2 one touches an unclean T, whether the carcass of
5:16 amiss in the holy T, and shall add a
6:4 him, or the lost T which he found,
6:17 fire; it is a T most holy, like the
7:19 that touches any unclean T shall not be eaten;
7:21 one touches an unclean T, whether the uncleanness
8:5 congregation, "This is the T which the LORD has
9:6 said, "This is the T which the LORD commanded
10:17 since it is a T most holy and has
11:41 "Every swarming T that swarms upon the earth is
11:43 abominable with any swarming T that swarms; and
11:44 yourselves with any swarming T that crawls upon the
12:4 not touch any hallowed T, nor come into the
13:54 that they wash the T in which is the
13:55 shall examine the diseased T after it has been
15:10 who carries such a T shall wash his clothes,
17:2 Israel, This is the T which the LORD has
19:8 has profaned a holy T of the LORD; and
20:17 it is a shameful T, and they shall be
22:5 whoever touches a creeping T by which he may
22:10 "An outsider shall not eat of a holy T
22:10 eat of a holy T;
22:14 eats of a holy T unwittingly, he shall add
22:14 and give the holy T to the priest.
27:23 day as a holy T to the LORD.
27:28 "But no devoted T that a man devotes to
27:28 or redeemed; every devoted T is most holy to
Num 16:9 it too small a T for you that the
16:13 Is it a small T that you have brought
18:14 Every devoted T in Israel shall be yours.
Deut 1:14 you answered me, 'The T that you have spoken
1:23 we shall come.' The T seemed good to me,
4:32 whether such a great T as this has ever
7:26 not bring an abominable T into your house, and
7:26 and abhor it; for it is an accursed T
9:21 I took the sinful T, the calf which you
11:6 tents, and every living T that followed them, in
12:31 God; for every abominable T which the LORD hates
13:14 that such an abominable T has been done among
14:3 "You shall not eat any abominable T
17:4 that such an abominable T has been done in
17:5 has done this evil T, and you shall stone
22:3 do with any lost T of your brothers, which
22:20 But if the T is true, that the tokens
23:9 then you shall keep yourself from every evil T
27:15 to the LORD, a T made by the hands
Josh 6:18 camp of Israel a T for destruction, and bring
7:12 they have become a T for destruction.
7:15 has done a shameful T in Israel.'"
9:24 our lives because of you, and did this T
23:14 you, that not one T has failed of all
Judg 6:29 said to one another, "Who has done this T
6:29 "Gideon the son of Joash has done this T
11:37 her father, "Let this T be done for me;
13:14 or eat any unclean T; all that I commanded
19:23 into my house, do not do this vile T
19:24 this man do not do so vile a T
19:30 it said, "Such a T has never happened or
1Sam 3:11 about to do a T in Israel, at which
8:6 But the T displeased Samuel when they said, "Give
12:16 and see this great T, which the LORD will
14:12 to us, and we will show you a T
18:20 told Saul, and the T pleased him.
18:23 to you a little T to become the king's
24:6 I should do this T to my lord, the
26:16 This T that you have done is not good.
28:10 no punishment shall come upon you for this T
28:18 LORD has done this T to you this day.
2Sam 2:6 good to you because you have done this T
3:13 with you; but one T I require of you;
7:19 this was a small T in thy eyes, O
7:28 hast promised this good T to thy servant;
11:11 your soul lives, I will not do this T
11:27 But the T that David had done displeased the
12:6 because he did this T, and because he had
12:12 I will do this T before all Israel, and
12:21 him, "What is this T that you have done?
13:12 me; for such a T is not done in
14:13 you planned such a T against the people of
24:3 does my lord the king delight in this T
1Kgs 1:27 Has this T been brought about by my lord
11:10 commanded him concerning this T, that he should not
12:24 his home, for this T is from me.'" So
12:30 And this T became a sin, for the people
13:33 After this T Jeroboam did not turn from his
13:34 And this T became sin to the house of
16:31 had been a light T for him to walk
20:9 will do; but this T I cannot do.'" And
22:20 And one said one T, and another said another.
2Kgs 2:10 have asked a hard T; yet, if you see
3:18 This is a light T in the sight of
5:13 to do some great T, would you not have
6:11 troubled because of this T; and he called his
7:2 in heaven, could this T be?" But he said,
7:19 heaven, could such a T be?" And he had
8:13 a dog, that he should do this great T
11:5 them, "This is the T that you shall do:
20:9 LORD will do the T that he has promised:
20:10 "It is an easy T for the shadow to
1Chr 2:7 matter of the devoted T;
13:4 do so, for the T was right in the
17:17 this was a small T in thy eyes, O
17:26 hast promised this good T to thy servant;
21:7 was displeased with this T, and he smote Israel.
21:8 sinned greatly in that I have done this T
2Chr 11:4 his home, for this T is from me.'" So
18:19 And one said one T, and another said another.
23:4 This is the T that you shall do: of
29:36 the people; for the T came about suddenly.
Ezra 7:27 who put such a T as this into the
Neh 2:19 said, "What is this T that you are doing?
5:9 So I said, "The T that you are doing
13:17 "What is this evil T which you are doing,
Jud 8:32 about to do a T which will go down
13:3 had said the same T to Bagoas.
16:16 offering is a small T, and all fat for
16:16 is a very little T, but he who fears
Esth 8:5 sight, and if the T seem right before the
13:10 earth and every wonderful T under heaven,
Job 3:25 For the T that I fear comes upon me,
12:10 life of every living T and the breath of
13:28 away like a rotten T, like a garment that
14:4 can bring a clean T out of an unclean?
28:10 the rocks, and his eye sees every precious T
28:11 not trickle, and the T that is hid he
39:8 his pasture, and he searches after every green T
Ps 27:4 One T have I asked of the LORD, that
34:10 those who seek the LORD lack no good T
41:8 They say, "A deadly T has fastened upon him;
84:11 No good T does the LORD withhold from those
88:8 hast made me a T of horror to them.
145:16 hand, thou satisfiest the desire of every living T
Prov 11:13 in spirit keeps a T hidden.
18:22 wife finds a good T, and obtains favor from
Eccl 1:10 Is there a T of which it is said,
7:8 the end of a T than its beginning; and
7:27 the Preacher, adding one T to another to find
8:1 And who knows the interpretation of a T

8:15 man has no good T under the sun but
12:14 judgment, with every secret T, whether good or evil.
Wis 4:15 nor take such a T to heart, that God's
13:17 he is not ashamed to address a lifeless T
13:18 he appeals to a T that is weak; for
13:18 he prays to a T that is dead; for
13:18 aid he entreats a T that is utterly inexperienced;
13:18 a prosperous journey, a T that cannot take a
13:19 asks strength of a T whose hands have no
14:8 work, and the perishable T was named a god.
17:11 wickedness is a cowardly T, condemned by its own
Sir 25:4 What an attractive T is judgment in gray-haired men,
31:13 Remember that a greedy eye is a bad T
34:4 From an unclean T what will be made clean?
42:6 seal is a good T; and where there are
Is 29:16 the clay; that the T made should say of
29:16 make me"; or the T formed say of him
38:7 LORD will do this T that he has promised:
43:19 am doing a new T; now it springs forth,
49:6 is too light a T that you should be
52:11 thence, touch no unclean T; go out from the
55:11 and prosper in the T for which I sent
66:8 Who has heard such a T
Jer 2:10 care; see if there has been such a T
3:24 our youth the shameful T has devoured all for
5:30 An appalling and horrible T has happened in the
18:13 The virgin Israel has done a very horrible T
18:16 land a horror, a T to be hissed at
19:8 city a horror, a T to be hissed at;
23:13 I saw an unsavory T: they prophesied by Baal
23:14 have seen a horrible T: they commit adultery and
31:22 has created a new T on the earth: a
40:3 obey his voice, this T has come upon you.
40:16 shall not do this T, for you are speaking
42:3 should go, and the T that we should do."
44:4 not do this abominable T that I hate!'
Lam 1:17 has become a filthy T among them.
Ezek 7:19 is like an unclean T; their silver and gold
7:20 make it an unclean T to them.
8:17 it too slight a T for the house of
28:16 you as a profane T from the mountain of
44:29 offering; and every devoted T in Israel shall be
Dan 2:10 has asked such a T of any magician or
2:11 The T that the king asks is difficult, and
6:12 The king answered, "The T stands fast, according to
13:22 if I do this T, it is death for
Hos 4:12 people inquire of a T of wood, and their
6:10 have seen a horrible T; Ephraim's harlotry is there,
8:12 thousands, they would be regarded as a strange T
9:10 became detestable like the T they loved.
10:6 Yea, the T itself shall be carried to Assyria,
13:15 it shall strip his treasury of every precious T
Joel 1:2 Has such a T happened in your days, or
Mic 1:14 shall be a deceitful T to the kings of
Nah 2:9 end of treasure, or wealth of every precious T
Hab 2:19 says to a wooden T, Awake; to a dumb
1Mac 9:10 to do such a T as to flee from
15:22 consul wrote the same T to Demetrius the king
2Mac 4:17 it is no light T to show irreverence to
Mt 26:10 has done a beautiful T to me.
Mk 10:21 him, "You lack one T; go, sell what you
14:6 has done a beautiful T to me.
16:18 they drink any deadly T, it will not hurt
Lk 2:15 Bethlehem and see this T that has happened, which
10:42 about many things; one T is needful.
12:26 do as small a T as that, why are
18:22 said to him, "One T you still lack.
Jn 9:25 do not know; one T I know, that though
Acts 10:16 three times, and the T was taken up at
19:32 Now some cried one T, some another; for the
21:34 the crowd shouted one T, some another; and as
24:20 council, except this one T which I cried out
Rom 7:15 I do the very T I hate.
13:6 are ministers of God, attending to this very T
1Cor 4:3 is a very small T that I should be
5:4 on the man who has done such a T
2Cor 5:5 us for this very T is God, who has
Gal 2:10 the poor, which very T I was eager to
Eph 5:27 wrinkle or any such T, that she might be
Phil 2:6 equality with God a T to be grasped,
3:13 my own; but one T I do, forgetting what
Heb 10:31 It is a fearful T to fall into the
3Jn 1:5 it is a loyal T you do when you
Rev 16:3 man, and every living T died that was in

THINGS (799)

Gen 1:24 kinds: cattle and creeping T and beasts of the
6:7 and beast and creeping T and birds of the
7:23 and animals and creeping T and birds of the
15:1 After these T the word of the LORD came
20:8 told them all these T; and the men were
20:9 have done to me T that ought not to
22:1 After these T God tested Abraham, and said to
22:20 Now after these T it was told Abraham, "Behold,
24:1 and the LORD had blessed Abraham in all T
24:28 ran and told her mother's household about these T
24:66 told Isaac all the T that he had done.
29:13 told Laban all these T,
38:23 "Let her keep the T as her own, lest
45:23 loaded with the good T of Egypt, and ten
Ex 21:11 not do these three T for her, she shall
29:33 They shall eat those T with which atonement was
35:1 them, "These are the T which the LORD has
38:21 the sum of the T for the tabernacle, the
Lev 2:8 is made of these T to the LORD; and
4:2 in any of the T which the LORD has
4:13 any one of the T which the LORD has
4:22 one of all the T which the LORD his
4:27 any one of the T which the LORD has
5:2 carcass of unclean swarming T, and it is hidden
5:13 any one of these T, and he shall be
5:15 any of the holy T of the LORD, he
5:17 doing any of the T which the LORD has
6:3 any of all the T which men do and
6:7 for any of the T which one may do
8:36 sons did all the T which the LORD commanded
10:19 LORD; and yet such T as these have befallen
11:2 These are the living T which you may eat
11:29 you among the swarming T that swarm upon the
11:42 feet, all the swarming T that swarm upon the
14:11 be cleansed and these T before the LORD, at
15:27 And whoever touches these T shall be unclean, and
18:24 by any of these T, for by all these
20:23 they did all these T, and therefore I abhorred
21:22 and of the holy T,
22:2 away from the holy T of the people of
22:3 generations approaches the holy T, which the people
22:4 eat of the holy T until he is clean.
22:6 eat of the holy T unless he has bathed
22:7 eat of the holy T, because such are his
22:12 not eat of the offering of the holy T
22:15 not profane the holy T of the people of
22:16 by eating their holy T: for I am the
Num 4:4 in the tent of meeting: the most holy T
4:15 not touch the holy T, lest they die.
4:15 These are the T of the tent of meeting
4:19 to the most holy T: Aaron and his sons
4:20 look upon the holy T even for a moment,
5:9 offering, all the holy T of the people of
5:10 and every man's holy T shall be his; whatever
7:9 care of the holy T which had to be
10:21 out, carrying the holy T, and the tabernacle was
15:13 native shall do these T in this way, in
18:8 me, all the consecrated T of the people of
18:9 of the most holy T, reserved from the fire;
18:32 not profane the holy T of the people of
35:29 "And these T shall be for a statute and
Deut 1:18 that time all the T that you should do.
4:9 lest you forget the T which your eyes have
4:19 them and serve them, T which the LORD your
4:30 tribulation, and all these T come upon you in
6:11 full of all good T, which you did not
10:21 these great and terrible T which your eyes have
12:26 But the holy T which are due from you,
13:17 None of the devoted T shall cleave to your
14:20 All clean winged T you may eat.
18:12 For whoever does these T is an abomination to
22:5 for whoever does these T is an abomination to
25:16 all who do such T, all who act dishonestly,
28:47 the abundance of all T,
28:48 in want of all T; and he will put
28:57 for want of all T, in the siege and
29:17 have seen their detestable T, their idols of wood
29:29 this day.' "The secret T belong to the LORD
29:29 our God; but the T that are revealed belong
30:1 "And when all these T come upon you, the
32:24 with venom of crawling T of the dust.
Josh 1:17 obeyed Moses in all T, so we will obey
6:18 keep yourselves from the T devoted to destruction,
6:18 any of the devoted T and make the camp
7:1 regard to the devoted T; for Achan the son

T

7:1 some of the devoted T; and the anger of
7:11 some of the devoted T; they have stolen, and
7:12 you destroy the devoted T from among you.
7:13 Israel, "There are devoted T in the midst of
7:13 take away the devoted T from among you."
7:15 taken with the devoted T shall be burned with
22:20 matter of the devoted T, and wrath fell upon
23:14 of all the good T which the LORD your
23:15 as all the good T which the LORD your
23:15 you all the evil T, until he have destroyed
24:29 After these T Joshua the son of Nun, the
Judg 13:23 shown us all these T, or now announced to
13:23 announced to us such T as these."
1Sam 2:23 said to them, "Why do you do such T
5:7 of Ashdod saw how T were, they said, "The
12:21 turn aside after vain T which cannot profit or
12:24 for consider what great T he has done for
15:21 the best of the T devoted to destruction, to
17:22 And David left the T in charge of the
19:7 called David, and Jonathan showed him all these T
25:37 wife told him these T, and his heart died
26:25 You will do many T and will succeed in
2Sam 7:23 them great and terrible T, by driving out before
13:21 heard of all these T, he was very angry.
14:20 God to know all T that are on the
23:5 covenant, ordered in all T and secure.
23:17 These T did the three mighty men.
23:22 These T did Benaiah the son of Jehoiada, and
24:12 says the LORD, Three T I offer you; choose
1Kgs 7:51 Solomon brought in the T which David his father
18:36 have done all these T at thy word.
2Kgs 1:7 came to meet you and told you these T
7:8 tent, and carried off T from it, and went
8:4 me all the great T that Elisha has done."
12:4 money of the holy T which is brought into
14:3 he did in all T as Joash his father
17:9 the LORD their God T that were not right.
17:11 And they did wicked T, provoking the LORD to
21:11 abominations, and has done T more wicked than all
23:16 man of God proclaimed, who had predicted these T
23:17 Judah and predicted these T which you have done
1Chr 11:19 These T did the three mighty men.
11:24 These T did Benaiah the son of Jehoiada, and
17:19 this greatness, in making known all these great T
17:21 for great and terrible T, in driving out nations
21:10 says the LORD, Three T I offer you; choose
23:13 consecrate the most holy T, that he and his
23:26 or any of the T for its service"—
29:2 the gold for the T of gold, the silver
29:2 the silver for the T of silver, and the
29:2 the bronze for the T of bronze, the iron
29:2 the iron for the T of iron, and wood
29:2 and wood for the T of wood, besides great
29:5 craftsmen, gold for the T of gold and silver
29:5 and silver for the T of silver.
29:14 For all T come from thee, and of thy
29:17 freely offered all these T, and now I have
2Chr 4:18 Solomon made all these T in great quantities, so
4:19 Solomon made all the T that were in the
5:1 Solomon brought in the T which David his father
20:25 goods, clothing, and precious T, which they took for
24:7 used all the dedicated T of the house of
31:6 sheep, and the dedicated T which had been
31:12 in the contributions, the tithes and the dedicated T
32:1 After these T and these acts of faithfulness
32:23 to Jerusalem and precious T to Hezekiah king of
Ezra 9:1 After these T had been done, the officials
Neh 4:2 Will they restore T
6:8 him, saying, "No such T as you say have
6:14 God, according to these T that they did, and
9:25 full of all good T, cisterns hewn out, vineyards,
10:33 appointed feasts, the holy T, and the sin offerings
Tob 3:10 When she heard these T she was deeply grieved,
4:19 himself gives all good T, and according to his
6:17 When Tobias heard these T, he fell in love
7:8 Azarias, speak of those T which you talked about
10:8 will inform him how T are with you."
11:15 his father the great T that had happened to
Jud 7:29 do this day the T which we have described!"
8:1 Judith heard about these T: she was the daughter
8:14 who made all these T, and find out his
9:5 thou hast done these T and those that went
9:5 thou hast designed the T that are now, and
9:5 Yea, the T thou didst intend came to pass,
9:6 to pass, and the T thou didst will presented
9:13 they have planned cruel T against thy covenant, and
10:9 out and accomplish the T about which you spoke
11:9 "Now as for the T Achior said in your
11:13 as to touch these T with their hands.
11:16 to accomplish with you T that will astonish the
12:2 be provided from the T I have brought with
12:4 not use up the T I have with me
15:8 to witness the good T which the Lord had
15:11 carts and piled the T on them.
Esth 2:1 After these T, when the anger of King Ahasuerus
3:1 After these T King Ahasuerus promoted Haman the
9:20 And Mordecai recorded these T, and sent letters to
10:4 And Mordecai said, "These T have come from God.
12:4 permanent record of these T, and Mordecai wrote an
12:5 in the court and rewarded him for these T
13:9 who rulest over all T, for the universe is
13:12 Thou knowest all T; thou knowest, O Lord, that
13:14 will not do these T in pride.
14:15 hast knowledge of all T; and thou knowest that
16:18 himself who did these T has been hanged at
16:18 who rules over all T, has speedily inflicted on
16:21 who rules over all T, has made this day
Job 5:9 who does great T and unsearchable, marvelous
5:9 and unsearchable, marvelous T without number:
8:2 will you say these T, and the words of
9:10 south; who does great T beyond understanding, and
9:10 beyond understanding, and marvelous T without
10:13 Yet these T thou didst hide in thy heart;
11:7 find out the deep T of God?
12:3 does not know such T as these?
13:20 Only grant two T to me, then I will
13:26 For thou writest bitter T against me, and makest
16:2 have heard many such T; miserable comforters are
22:18 their houses with good T – but the counsel
23:14 me; and many such T are in his mind.
33:29 God does all these T, twice, three times, with
37:5 voice; he does great T which we cannot comprehend.
42:2 thou canst do all T, and that no purpose
42:3 I did not understand, T too wonderful for me,
Ps 8:6 thou hast put all T under his feet,
15:5 He who does these T shall never be moved.
35:11 they ask me of T that I know not.
42:4 These T I remember, as I pour out my
50:21 These T you have done and I have been
60:3 thy people suffer hard T; thou hast given us
71:19 who hast done great T, O God, who is
72:18 the God of Israel, who alone does wondrous T
78:3 sayings from of old, T that we have heard
86:10 great and doest wondrous T, thou alone art God.
87:3 Glorious T are spoken of you, O city of
98:1 a new song, for he has done marvelous T
104:25 wide, which teems with T innumerable, living things
104:25 things innumerable, living T both small and great.
104:28 openest thy hand, they are filled with good T
106:21 who had done great T in Egypt,
106:22 of Ham, and terrible T by the Red Sea.
107:9 thirsty, and the hungry he fills with good T
107:43 give heed to these T; let men consider the
119:18 I may behold wondrous T out of thy law.
119:91 this day; for all T are thy servants.
126:2 LORD has done great T for them."
126:3 LORD has done great T for us; we are
131:1 not occupy myself with T too great and too
140:2 men, who plan evil T in their heart, and
148:10 and all cattle, creeping T and flying birds!
Prov 6:16 There are six T which the LORD hates, seven
8:6 I will speak noble T, and from my lips
15:28 the mouth of the wicked pours out evil T
16:30 his eyes plans perverse T, he who compresses his
23:33 eyes will see strange T, and your mind utter
23:33 see strange things, and your mind utter perverse T
25:2 of God to conceal T, but the glory of
25:2 kings is to search T out.
30:7 Two T I ask of thee; deny them not
30:15 Three T are never satisfied; four never say,
30:18 Three T are too wonderful for me; four I
30:21 Under three T the earth trembles; under four it
30:24 Four T on earth are small, but they are
30:29 Three T are stately in their tread; four are
Eccl 1:8 All T are full of weariness; a man cannot
1:11 no remembrance of former T, nor will there be
1:11 any remembrance of later T yet to happen among
6:3 not enjoy life's good T, and also has no
7:21 heed to all the T that men say, lest
7:25 and the sum of T, and to know the
8:10 in the city where they had done such T
11:9 that for all these T God will bring you

Wis 1:7 that which holds all T together knows what is
1:8 one who utters unrighteous T will escape notice, and
1:10 jealous ear hears all T, and the sound of
1:14 For he created all T that they might exist,
2:6 us enjoy the good T that exist, and make
3:14 has not devised wicked T against the Lord; for
5:9 "All those T have vanished like a shadow, and
6:10 holy who observe holy T in holiness, and those
7:11 All good T came to me along with her,
7:22 the fashioner of all T, taught me.
7:24 of her pureness she pervades and penetrates all T
7:27 she can do all T, and while remaining in
7:27 herself, she renews all T; in every generation she
8:1 and she orders all T well.
8:5 what is richer than wisdom who effects all T
8:8 experience, she knows the T of old, and infers
8:8 old, and infers the T to come; she understands
8:17 When I considered these T inwardly, and thought
9:1 who hast made all T by thy word,
9:11 knows and understands all T, and she will guide
10:2 transgression, and gave him strength to rule all T
11:5 For through the very T by which their enemies
11:16 punished by the very T by which he sins.
11:20 thou hast arranged all T by measure and number
11:23 thou canst do all T, and thou dost overlook
11:24 For thou lovest all T that exist, and hast
11:24 for none of the T which thou hast made,
11:26 Thou sparest all T, for they are thine, O
12:1 For thy immortal spirit is in all T
12:2 warn them of the T wherein they sin, that
12:15 righteous and rulest all T righteously, deeming it
13:1 unable from the good T that are seen to
13:3 the beauty of these T men assumed them to
13:5 and beauty of created T comes a corresponding
13:7 they see, because the T that are seen are
13:9 fail to find sooner the Lord of these T
13:10 hopes set on dead T, are the men who
14:31 the power of the T by which men swear,
15:1 patient, and ruling all T in mercy.
15:6 Lovers of evil T and fit for such objects
16:9 be punished by such T;
16:17 water, which quenches all T, the fire had still
16:20 Instead of these T thou didst give thy people
17:6 terror they deemed the T which they saw to
18:9 share alike the same T, both blessings and dangers;
18:14 gentle silence enveloped all T, and night in its
18:16 stood and filled all T with death, and touched
Sir 1:4 was created before all T, and prudent understanding
2:9 Lord, hope for good T, for everlasting joy and
7:31 sanctification, and the first fruits of the holy T
10:11 he will inherit creeping T, and wild beasts, and
11:3 but her product is the best of sweet T
11:14 Good T and bad, life and death, poverty and
16:5 Many such T my eye has seen, and my
16:5 my ear has heard T more striking than these.
16:27 it with his good T;
17:2 them authority over the T upon the earth.
17:25 For all T cannot be in men, since a
18:25 conditions change, and all T move swiftly before the
19:1 he who despises small T will fail little by
21:25 will speak of these T, but the words of
24:8 the Creator of all T gave me a commandment,
25:1 takes pleasure in three T, and they are beautiful
26:5 Of three T my heart is afraid, and of
26:19 At two T my heart is grieved, and because
27:24 I have hated many T, but none to be
29:28 These T are hard to bear for a man
30:18 Good T poured out upon a mouth that is
31:9 he has done wonderful T among his people.
32:13 And for these T bless him who made you
34:9 educated man knows many T, and one with much
34:10 is inexperienced knows few T, but he that has
34:11 I have seen many T in my travels, and
34:26 and does the same T, who will listen to
35:5 empty-handed, for all these T are to be done
39:16 say in thanksgiving: "All T are the works of
39:17 in God's time all T will be sought after.
39:25 From the beginning good T were created for good
39:25 people, just as evil T for sinners.
39:34 for all T will prove good in their season.
40:11 All T that are from the earth turn back
42:1 Of the following T do not be ashamed, and
42:6 are many hands, lock T up.
42:19 be, and he reveals the tracks of hidden T
42:23 All these T live and remain for ever for
42:24 All T are twofold, one opposite the other, and
42:25 One confirms the good T of the other, and
43:22 mist quickly heals all T; when the dew appears,
43:25 all kinds of living T, and huge creatures of
43:26 by his word all T hold together.
43:32 Many T greater than these lie hidden, for we
43:33 Lord has made all T, and to the godly
45:13 Before his time there never were such beautiful T
48:24 he saw the last T, and comforted those who
48:25 time, and the hidden T before they came to
50:22 every way does great T; who exalts our days
50:28 concerns himself with these T, and he who lays
50:29 be strong for all T, for the light of
51:24 are lacking in these T, and why are your
51:25 and said, Get these T for yourselves without money.
Is 25:1 thou hast done wonderful T, plans formed of old,
25:6 a feast of fat T, a feast of wine
25:6 the lees, of fat T full of marrow, of
29:14 again do marvelous T with this people, wonderful
29:16 You turn T upside down!
30:10 speak to us smooth T, prophesy illusions,
30:22 scatter them as unclean T; you will say to
32:8 is noble devises noble T, and by noble things
32:8 things, and by noble T he stands.
38:16 O Lord, by these T men live, and in
41:22 Tell us the former T, what they are, that
41:22 declare to us the T to come.
42:9 Behold, the former T have come to pass, and
42:9 to pass, and new T I now declare; before
42:16 These are the T I will do, and I
42:20 He sees many T, but does not observe them;
43:9 can declare this, and show us the former T
43:18 "Remember not the former T, nor consider the
43:18 things, nor consider the T of old.
44:7 from of old the T to come?
44:9 are nothing, and the T they delight in do
44:21 Remember these T, O Jacob, and Israel, for you
44:24 LORD, who made all T, who stretched out the
45:7 I am the LORD, who do all these T
46:1 beasts and cattle; these T you carry are loaded
46:9 transgressors, remember the former T of old; for I
46:10 and from ancient times T not yet done, saying,
47:7 did not lay these T to heart or remember
47:9 of children": These two T shall come to you
48:3 "The former T I declared of old, they went
48:6 make you hear new T, hidden things which you
48:6 hear new things, hidden T which you have not
48:14 Who among them has declared these T
51:19 These two T have befallen you— who will
56:4 sabbaths, who choose the T that please me and
57:6 Shall I be appeased for these T
58:11 your desire with good T, and make your bones
64:3 When thou didst terrible T which we looked not
64:12 restrain thyself at these T, O LORD?
65:4 and broth of abominable T is in their vessels;
65:17 earth; and the former T shall not be remembered
66:2 All these T my hand has made, and so
66:2 and so all these T are mine, says the
66:8 Who has seen such T
Jer 2:7 land to enjoy its fruits and its good T
2:8 Baal, and went after T that do not profit.
2:34 spite of all these T
5:9 Shall I not punish them for these T
5:19 God done all these T to us?' you shall
5:29 Shall I not punish them for these T
7:13 have done all these T, says the LORD, and
9:9 Shall I not punish them for these T
9:24 earth; for in these T I delight, says the
10:16 one who formed all T, and Israel is the
13:22 heart, 'Why have these T come upon me?' it
14:22 hope on thee, for thou doest all these T
16:19 nought but lies, worthless T in which there is
17:9 is deceitful above all T, and desperately corrupt; who
20:1 of the LORD, heard Jeremiah prophesying these T
26:10 of Judah heard these T, they came up from
30:15 I have done these T to you.
33:3 you great and hidden T which you have not
45:5 do you seek great T for yourself?
48:44 I will bring these T upon Moab in the
51:19 one who formed all T, and Israel is the
52:3 anger of the LORD T came to such a
52:20 bronze of all these T was beyond weight.
Lam 1:7 bitterness all the precious T that were hers from
1:10 over all her precious T; yea, she has seen
1:16 "For these T I weep; my eyes flow with
5:17 become sick, for these T our eyes have grown
Bar 3:32 he who knows all T knows her, he found

T

6:29 you know by these T that they are not
6:39 These T that are made of wood and overlaid
6:46 how then can the T that are made by
Ezek 5:11 with all your detestable T and with all your
7:20 images and their detestable T of it; therefore I
8:10 all kinds of creeping T, and loathsome beasts, and
11:5 for I know the T that come into your
11:18 it all its detestable T and all its abominations.
11:21 after their detestable T and their abominations,
11:25 the exiles all the T that the LORD had
16:5 do any of these T to you out of
16:30 you did all these T, the deeds of a
16:43 me with all these T; therefore, behold, I will
16:50 haughty, and did abominable T before me; therefore
17:12 not know what these T mean?
17:15 Can a man escape who does such T
17:18 yet did all these T, he shall not escape.
18:13 done all these abominable T; he shall surely die;
18:24 does the same abominable T that the wicked man
20:7 Cast away the detestable T your eyes feast on,
20:8 cast away the detestable T their eyes feasted on,
20:30 your fathers and go astray after their detestable T
21:26 take off the crown; T shall not remain as
22:8 have despised my holy T, and profaned my sabbaths.
22:25 taken treasure and precious T; they have made many
22:26 have profaned my holy T; they have made no
24:19 tell us what these T mean for us, that
37:23 idols and their detestable T, or with any of
38:20 field, and all creeping T that creep on the
44:8 charge of my holy T; but you have set
44:13 any of my sacred T and the things that
44:13 sacred things and the T that are most sacred;
Dan 2:22 reveals deep and mysterious T; he knows what is
2:40 pieces and shatters all T; and like iron which
3:29 have sinned in all T and have not obeyed
3:77 Bless the Lord, all T that grow on the
7:8 of a man, and a mouth speaking great T
7:16 made known to me the interpretation of the T
7:20 mouth that spoke great T, and which seemed greater
11:36 and shall speak astonishing T against the God of
11:43 and all the precious T of Egypt; and the
12:7 an end all these T would be accomplished.
12:8 lord, what shall be the issue of these T
13:40 These T we testify."
13:42 art aware of all T before they come to
13:43 done none of the T that they have wickedly
Hos 2:18 air, and the creeping T of the ground; and
9:6 shall possess their precious T of silver; thorns shall
14:9 let him understand these T; whoever is discerning, let
Joel 2:20 him will rise, for he has done great T
2:21 and rejoice, for the LORD has done great T
Mic 2:6 not preach of such T; disgrace will not overtake
7:15 land of Egypt I will show them marvelous T
7:17 serpent, like the crawling T of the earth; they
Hab 1:14 the sea, like crawling T that have no ruler.
Zech 4:10 the day of small T shall rejoice, and shall
8:12 remnant of this people to possess all these T
8:16 These are the T that you shall do: Speak
8:17 oath, for all these T I hate, says the
1Mac 4:27 perplexed and discouraged, for T had not happened
5:37 After these T Timothy gathered another army and
6:8 sick from grief, because T had not turned out
6:27 will do still greater T, and you will not
6:59 that they became angry and did all these T
9:37 After these T it was reported to Jonathan and
9:44 our lives, for today T are not as they
10:22 Demetrius heard of these T he was grieved and
10:88 king heard of these T, he honored Jonathan still
11:29 Jonathan about all these T; its contents were as
11:42 will I do these T for you and your
12:9 no need of these T, since we have as
13:3 yourselves know what great T I and my brothers
14:9 talked together of good T; and the youths donned
14:25 the people heard these T they said, "How shall
14:35 had done all these T and because of the
14:36 And in his days T prospered in his hands,
14:38 "In view of these T King Demetrius confirmed him
15:24 a copy of these T to Simon the high
16:2 until this day, and T have prospered in our
16:18 a report about these T and sent it to
2Mac 1:24 God, Creator of all T, who art awe-inspiring and
2:8 Lord will disclose these T, and the glory of
2:13 The same T are reported in the records and
6:4 and besides brought in T for sacrifice that were
6:20 the courage to refuse T that it is not
6:30 glad to suffer these T because I fear him."

7:18 we are suffering these T on our own account,
7:18 Therefore astounding T have happened.
7:23 the origin of all T, will in his mercy
7:28 make them out of T that existed.
10:38 accomplished these T, with hymns and thanksgivings
12:14 at them and even blaspheming and saying unholy T
12:22 him who sees all T; and they rushed off
12:41 Judge, who reveals the T that are hidden;
13:9 to show the Jews T far worse than those
15:2 he who sees all T has honored and hallowed
Mt 6:32 Gentiles seek all these T; and your heavenly Father
6:33 righteousness, and all these T shall be yours as
7:11 in heaven give good T to those who ask
11:25 thou hast hidden these T from the wise and
11:27 All T have been delivered to me by my
13:3 he told them many T in parables, saying: "A
16:21 Jerusalem and suffer many T from the elders and
17:11 is to restore all T;
19:26 but with God all T are possible."
21:15 scribes saw the wonderful T that he did, and
21:23 are you doing these T, and who gave you
21:24 tell you by what authority I do these T
21:27 tell you by what authority I do these T
22:21 therefore to Caesar the T that are Caesars, and
22:21 and to God the T that are Gods."
24:33 you see all these T, you know that he
24:34 away till all these T take place.
27:13 not hear how many T they testify against you?"
Mk 4:2 he taught them many T in parables, and in
4:19 the desire for other T, enter in and choke
6:34 shepherd; and he began to teach them many T
7:13 And many such T you do."
7:15 defile him; but the T which come out of
7:22 All these evil T come from within, and they
7:36 "He has done all T well; he even makes
8:31 man must suffer many T, and be rejected by
9:12 first to restore all T; and how is it
9:12 he should suffer many T and be treated with
9:23 All T are possible to him who believes."
10:27 with God; for all T are possible with God."
11:27 are you doing these T, or who gave you
11:28 tell you by what authority I do these T
11:32 tell you by what authority I do these T
12:17 "Render to Caesar the T that are Caesars, and
12:17 and to God the T that are Gods." And
13:4 the sign when these T are all to be
13:23 have told you all T beforehand.
13:29 when you see these T taking place, you know
13:30 away before all these T take place.
14:36 said, "Abba, Father, all T are possible to thee;
15:3 And the chief priests accused him of many T
Lk 1:1 a narrative of the T which have been accomplished
1:3 also, having followed all T closely for some time
1:4 the truth concerning the T of which you have
1:20 the day that these T come to pass, because
1:49 mighty has done great T for me, and holy
1:53 the hungry with good T, and the rich he
1:65 And all these T were talked about through all
2:19 Mary kept all these T, pondering them in her
2:51 mother kept all these T in her heart.
3:19 for all the evil T that Herod had done,
5:26 "We have seen strange T today."
7:18 disciples of John told him of all these T
9:9 who is this about whom I hear such T
9:22 man must suffer many T, and be rejected by
10:21 thou hast hidden these T from the wise and
10:22 All T have been delivered to me by my
10:41 and troubled about many T;
11:41 give for alms those T which are within; and
11:53 to speak of many T,
12:20 of you; and the T you have prepared, whose
12:30 the world seek these T; and your Father knows
12:31 his kingdom, and these T shall be yours as
13:17 at all the glorious T that were done by
16:25 lifetime received your good T, and Lazarus in like
16:25 in like manner evil T; but now he is
17:25 he must suffer many T and be rejected by
18:34 understood none of these T; this saying was hid
19:11 As they heard these T, he proceeded to tell
19:42 today you knew the T that make for peace!
20:2 authority you do these T, or who it is
20:8 tell you by what authority I do these T
20:25 render to Caesar the T that are Caesars, and
20:25 and to God the T that are Gods."
21:6 said, "As for these T which you see, the
21:28 Now when these T begin to take place, look

T

	21:31	when you see these T taking place, you know
	21:36	to escape all these T that will take place,
	23:48	Galilee stood at a distance and saw these T
	24:14	other about all these T that had happened.
	24:18	does not know the T that have happened there
	24:19	And he said to them, "What T
	24:26	Christ should suffer these T and enter into his
	24:27	all the scriptures the T concerning himself.
	24:48	You are witnesses of these T
Jn	1:3	beginning with God; all T were made through him,
	1:50	You shall see greater T than these."
	2:16	the pigeons, "Take these T away; you shall not
	3:12	have told you earthly T and you do not
	3:12	can you believe if I tell you heavenly T
	3:35	and has given all T into his hand.
	4:25	when he comes, he will show us all T
	7:4	If you do these T, show yourself to the
	13:3	Father had given all T into his hands, and
	13:17	If you know these T, blessed are you if
	14:25	"These T I have spoken to you, while I
	14:26	will teach you all T, and bring to your
	15:11	These T I have spoken to you, that my
	16:4	I have said these T to you, that when
	16:4	did not say these T to you from the
	16:6	I have said these T to you, sorrow has
	16:12	"I have yet many T to say to you,
	16:13	declare to you the T that are to come.
	16:30	that you know all T, and need none to
	17:13	to thee; and these T I speak in the
	19:36	For these T took place that the scripture might
	20:18	he had said these T to her.
	21:24	bearing witness to these T, and who has written
	21:24	who has written these T; and we know that
	21:25	are also many other T which Jesus did; were
Acts	2:44	together and had all T in common;
	4:25	the Gentiles rage, and the peoples imagine vain T
	4:32	that any of the T which he possessed was
	5:11	church, and upon all who heard of these T
	5:32	are witnesses to these T, and so is the
	7:50	hand make all these T
	7:54	when they heard these T they were enraged, and
	13:42	people begged that these T might be told them
	14:15	turn from these vain T to a living God
	15:18	who has made these T known from of old.'
	15:27	tell you the same T by word of mouth.
	15:28	burden than these necessary T:
	17:11	to see if these T were so.
	17:20	you bring some strange T to our ears; we
	17:20	know therefore what these T mean."
	18:15	I refuse to be a judge of these T
	18:25	and taught accurately the T concerning Jesus, though
	19:36	Seeing then that these T cannot be contradicted, you
	20:30	arise men speaking perverse T, to draw away the
	20:35	In all T I have shown you that by
	21:19	one by one the T that God had done
	26:9	ought to do many T in opposing the name
	26:16	bear witness to the T in which you have
	26:26	king knows about these T, and to him I
	26:26	that none of these T has escaped his notice,
Rom	1:20	clearly perceived in the T that have been made.
	1:32	those who do such T deserve to die, they
	2:1	you, the judge, are doing the very same T
	2:2	God rightly falls upon those who do such T
	2:3	those who do such T and yet do them
	4:17	calls into existence the T that do not exist.
	6:21	you get from the T of which you are
	6:21	The end of those T is death.
	8:5	their minds on the T of the flesh, but
	8:5	their minds on the T of the Spirit.
	8:32	also give us all T with him?
	8:37	No, in all these T we are more than
	8:38	angels, nor principalities, nor T present, nor things to
	8:38	nor things present, nor T to come, nor powers,
	11:36	and through him and to him are all T
1Cor	1:28	in the world, even T that are not, to
	1:28	to bring to nothing T that are,
	2:15	spiritual man judges all T, but is himself to
	3:21	For all T are yours,
	4:5	bring to light the T now hidden in darkness
	4:13	refuse of the world, the offscouring of all T
	6:12	"All T are lawful for me," but not all
	6:12	but not all T are helpful.
	6:12	"All T are lawful for me," but I will
	8:6	from whom are all T and for whom we
	8:6	through whom are all T and through whom we
	9:22	I have become all T to all men, that
	9:25	Every athlete exercises self-control in all T
	10:6	Now these T are warnings for us, not to
	10:11	Now these T happened to them as a warning,
	10:23	"All T are lawful," but not all things are
	10:23	but not all T are helpful.
	10:23	"All T are lawful," but not all things build
	10:23	but not all T build up.
	11:12	And all T are from God.)
	11:34	About the other T I will give directions when
	13:7	Love bears all T, believes all things, hopes all
	13:7	all things, believes all T, hopes all things, endures
	13:7	all things, hopes all T, endures all things.
	13:7	believes all things, hopes all things, endures all T
	14:26	Let all T be done for edification.
	14:40	in tongues; but all T should be done decently
	15:27	God has put all T in subjection under his
	15:27	when it says, "All T are put in subjection
	15:27	excepted who put all T under him.
	15:28	When all T are subjected to him, then the
	15:28	him who put all T under him, that God
2Cor	2:16	Who is sufficient for these T
	4:18	look not to the T that are seen but
	4:18	seen but to the T that are unseen; for
	4:18	are unseen; for the T that are seen are
	4:18	are transient, but the T that are unseen are
	11:6	have made this plain to you in all T
	11:18	many boast of worldly T, I too will boast.)
	11:28	And, apart from other T, there is the daily
	11:30	will boast of the T that show my weakness.
	12:4	and he heard T that cannot be told,
Gal	2:18	build up again those T which I tore down,
	3:4	you experience so many T in vain?--if it
	3:10	not abide by all T written in the book
	3:22	the scripture consigned all T to sin, that what
	5:21	those who do such T shall not inherit the
	6:6	word share all good T with him who teaches.
Eph	1:10	time, to unite all T in him, things in
	1:10	all things in him, T in heaven and things
	1:10	things in heaven and T on earth.
	1:11	him who accomplishes all T according to the counsel
	1:22	he has put all T under his feet and
	1:22	the head over all T for the church,
	3:9	God who created all T;
	4:10	he might fill all T
	5:6	is because of these T that the wrath of
	5:12	to speak of the T that they do in
Phil	2:14	Do all T without grumbling or questioning,
	3:1	To write the same T to you is not
	3:8	the loss of all T, and count them as
	3:19	in their shame, with minds set on earthly T
	3:21	even to subject all T to himself.
	4:8	is anything worthy of praise, think about these T
	4:13	I can do all T in him who strengthens
Col	1:16	for in him all T were created, in heaven
	1:16	principalities or authorities--all T were created
	1:17	He is before all T, and in him all
	1:17	and in him all T hold together.
	1:20	reconcile to himself all T, whether on earth or
	2:22	(referring to T which all perish as they are
	3:1	with Christ, seek the T that are above, where
	3:2	Set your minds on T that are above, not
	3:2	are above, not on T that are on earth.
1Thes	2:14	you suffered the same T from your own countrymen
	4:6	avenger in all these T, as we solemnly forewarned
2Thes	3:4	and will do the T which we command.
1Tim	1:7	are saying or the T about which they make
	3:11	serious, no slanderers, but temperate, faithful in all T
	4:11	Command and teach these T
	6:13	gives life to all T, and of Christ Jesus
Tit	1:14	To the pure all T are pure, but to
	2:15	Declare these T; exhort and reprove with all
	3:8	to insist on these T, so that those who
Heb	1:2	the heir of all T, through whom also he
	2:10	and by whom all T exist, in bringing many
	3:4	the builder of all T is God.)
	3:5	to testify to the T that were to be
	6:9	feel sure of better T that belong to salvation.
	6:18	that through two unchangeable T, in which it is
	7:13	one of whom these T are spoken belonged to
	9:5	Of these T we cannot now speak in detail.
	9:11	priest of the good T that have come, then
	9:23	copies of the heavenly T to be purified with
	9:23	but the heavenly T themselves with better sacrifices
	10:1	shadow of the good T to come instead of
	11:1	is the assurance of T hoped for, the conviction
	11:1	for, the conviction of T not seen.

11:3 was made out of T which do not appear.
13:18 clear conscience, desiring to act honorably in all T
Jas 2:16 without giving them the T needed for the body,
3:5 is a little member and boasts of great T
1Pet 1:12 but you, in the T which have now been
1:12 Spirit sent from heaven, T into which angels long
1:18 fathers, not with perishable T such as silver or
4:7 The end of all T is at hand; therefore
2Pet 1:3 granted to us all T that pertain to life
1:8 For if these T are yours and abound, they
1:9 For whoever lacks these T is blind and shortsighted
1:12 remind you of these T, though you know them
1:15 be able at any time to recall these T
3:4 fathers fell asleep, all T have continued as they
3:11 Since all these T are thus to be dissolved,
3:16 There are some T in them hard to understand,
1Jn 2:15 the world or the T in the world.
Jude 1:10 understand, and by those T that they know by
1:15 of all the harsh T which ungodly sinners have
Rev 2:14 I have a few T against you: you have
2:24 some call the deep T of Satan, to you
4:11 thou didst create all T, and by thy will
21:4 more, for the former T have passed away."
21:5 "Behold, I make all T new." Also he said,
22:8 John am he who heard and saw these T
22:20 who testifies to these T says, "Surely I am

THINK (76)

Num 36:6 them marry whom they T best; only, they shall
2Sam 10:3 their lord, "Do you T, because David has sent
18:27 the watchman said, "I T the running of the
2Kgs 18:20 Do you T that mere words are strategy and
1Chr 19:3 to Hanun, "Do you T, because David has sent
2Chr 13:8 "And now you T to withstand the kingdom of
Esth 4:13 return answer to Esther, T not that in the
Job 4:7 T now, who that was innocent ever perished?
6:26 Do you T that you can reprove words, when
21:6 When I T of it I am dismayed, and
35:2 Elihu said: "Do you T this to be just?
41:8 Lay hands on him; T of the battle; you
41:32 shining wake; one would T the deep to be
Ps 59:7 they T, "will hear us?"
63:6 joyful lips, when I T of thee upon my
77:3 I T of God, and I moan; I meditate,
119:52 When I T of thy ordinances from of old,
119:59 When I T of thy ways, I turn my
144:3 man that thou dost T of him?
Wis 1:1 rulers of the earth, T of the Lord with
Sir 15:8 and liars will never T of her.
18:23 T of his wrath on the day of death,
18:24 the time of plenty T of the time of
18:24 the days of wealth T of poverty and need.
Is 10:7 mind does not so T; but it is in
36:5 Do you T that mere words are strategy and
Jer 22:15 Do you T you are a king because you
23:27 their own heart, who T to make my people
40:4 you; go wherever you T it good and right
40:5 or go wherever you T it right to go."
Bar 6:40 then must any one T that they are gods,
6:44 then must any one T that they are gods,
6:56 any one admit or T that they are gods?
6:64 Therefore one must not T that they are gods
Ezek 11:5 the LORD: So you T, O house of Israel;
Dan 7:25 Most High, and shall T to change the times
14:6 him, "Do you not T that Bel is a
2Mac 7:16 But do not T that God has forsaken our
7:19 But do not T that you will go unpunished
9:12 and no mortal should T that he is equal
Mt 5:17 T not that I have come to abolish the
6:7 Gentiles do; for they T that they will be
9:4 said, "Why do you T evil in your hearts?
10:34 "Do not T that I have come to bring
17:24 saying, "What do you T, Simon?
18:11 What do you T
21:28 "What do you T
22:17 Tell us, then, what you T
22:42 saying, "What do you T of the Christ?
26:53 Do you T that I cannot appeal to my
Lk 10:36 these three, do you T, proved neighbor to the
12:51 Do you T that I have come to give
13:2 answered them, "Do you T that these Galileans were
13:4 killed them, do you T that they were worse
Jn 5:38 the scriptures, because you T that in them you
5:44 Do not T that I shall accuse you to
11:56 they stood in the temple, "What do you T
16:2 whoever kills you will T he is offering service
Acts 17:29 we ought not to T that the Deity is
26:2 made his defense: "I T myself fortunate that it
26:28 a short time you T to make me a
Rom 12:3 among you not to T of himself more highly
12:3 than he ought to T, but to think with
12:3 to think, but to T with sober judgment, each
1Cor 4:9 For I T that God has exhibited us apostles
7:26 I T that in view of the present distress
7:40 And I T that I have the Spirit of
12:23 the body which we T less honorable we invest
2Cor 11:5 I T that I am not in the least
11:16 repeat, let no one T me foolish; but even
12:6 that no one may T more of me than
Eph 3:20 that we ask or T,
Phil 4:8 anything worthy of praise, T about these things.
2Tim 2:7 T over what I say, for the Lord will
Heb 10:29 worse punishment do you T will be deserved by
2Pet 1:13 I T it right, as long as I am

THINKING (28)

Gen 20:10 Abraham, "What were you T of, that you did
26:7 T, "lest the men of the place should kill
32:8 camels, into two companies, T, "If Esau comes to
1Sam 27:11 bring tidings to Gath, T, "Lest they should tell
27:12 And Achish trusted David, T, "He has made himself
2Sam 5:6 will ward you off"—T, "David cannot come in
2Kgs 7:12 in the open country, T, 'When they come out
2Chr 32:1 against the fortified cities, T to win them for
Neh 6:9 wanted to frighten us, T, "Their hands will drop
Jud 8:14 what a man is T; how do you expect
Ps 64:5 of laying snares secretly, T, "Who can see us?
Wis 12:10 that their way of T would never change.
17:3 For T that in their secret sins they were
Sir 13:25 face, but to devise proverbs requires painful T
17:5 he gave them ears and a mind for T
Mal 1:7 we polluted it?' By T that the LORD's table
1Mac 5:61 a great rout because, T to do a brave
2Mac 4:32 But Menelaus, T he had obtained a suitable
5:21 hurried away to Antioch, T in his arrogance that
9:8 who had just been T that he could command
12:12 Judas, T that they might really be useful in
14:14 flocked to join Nicanor, T that the misfortunes and
Rom 1:21 became futile in their T and their senseless minds
1Cor 14:20 be children in your T; be babes in evil,
14:20 in evil, but in T be mature.
2Cor 12:19 Have you been T all along that we have
Phil 1:17 partisanship, not sincerely but T to afflict me in
Heb 11:15 If they had been T of that land from

THINKS (15)

1Sam 20:3 your eyes; and he T, 'Let not Jonathan know
Ps 10:6 He T in his heart, "I shall not be
10:11 He T in his heart, "God has forgotten, he
Sir 16:21 one devoid of understanding T; a senseless and
16:21 senseless and misguided man T foolishly.
Lam 3:20 My soul continually T of it and is bowed
Lk 8:18 not, even what he T that he has will
Rom 14:14 for any one who T it unclean.
1Cor 3:18 any one among you T that he is wise
7:36 If any one T that he is not behaving
10:12 let any one who T that he stands take
14:37 If any one T that he is a prophet,
Gal 6:3 For if any one T he is something, when
Phil 3:4 If any other man T he has reason for
Jas 1:25 If any one T he is religious, and does

THIRD (195)

Gen 1:13 there was morning, a T day.
2:14 the name of the T river is Tigris, which
6:16 with lower, second, and T decks.
22:4 On the T day Abraham lifted up his eyes
31:22 told Laban on the T day that Jacob had
32:19 the second and the T and all who followed
34:25 On the T day, when they were sore, two
40:20 On the T day, which was Pharaoh's birthday, he
42:18 On the T day Joseph said to them, "Do
50:23 Ephraim's children of the T generation; the children
Ex 19:1 On the T new moon after the people of
19:11 be ready by the T day; for on the
19:11 day; for on the T day the LORD will
19:15 "Be ready by the T day; do not go
19:16 the morning of the T day there were thunders
20:5 the children to the T and the fourth generation
28:19 a diamond; and the T row a jacinth, an
34:7 children's children, to the T and the fourth
39:12 a diamond; and the T row, a jacinth, an

T

T

12:4 tail swept down a T of the stars of
14:9 And another angel, a T, followed them, saying with
16:4 The T angel poured his bowl into the rivers
21:19 the second sapphire, the T agate, the fourth emerald,

THIRDS

Zech 13:8 says the LORD, two T shall be cut off

THIRST (37)

Ex 17:3 us and our children and our cattle with T
Deut 28:48 you, in hunger and T, in nakedness, and in
Judg 15:18 I now die of T, and fall into the
2Chr 32:11 by famine and by T, when he tells you,
Neh 9:15 the rock for their T, and thou didst tell
9:20 their mouth, and gavest them water for their T
Jud 7:13 So T will destroy them, and they will give
7:23 young men fainted from T and fell down in
7:26 ground before them with T and utter destruction.
Job 24:11 oil; they tread the wine presses, but suffer T
Ps 69:21 food, and for my T they gave me vinegar
104:11 of the field; the wild asses quench their T
Wis 11:4 rock, and slaking of T from hard stone.
11:8 unexpectedly, showing by their T at that time how
11:14 at him, for their T was not like that
Sir 12:16 finds an opportunity his T for blood will be
24:20 who drink me will T for more.
Is 5:13 of hunger, and their multitude is parched with T
29:8 awakes faint, with his T not quenched, so shall
41:17 tongue is parched with T, I the LORD will
49:10 shall not hunger or T, neither scorching wind nor
50:2 stink for lack of water, and die of T
Jer 2:25 feet from going unshod and your throat from T
Lam 4:4 of its mouth for T; the children beg for
Hos 2:3 like a parched land, and slay her with T
Amos 8:11 of bread, nor a T for water, but of
8:13 virgins and the young men shall faint for T
Mt 5:6 those who hunger and T for righteousness, for they
Jn 4:13 of this water will T again,
4:14 give him will never T; the water that I
4:15 that I may not T, nor come here to
6:35 and he who believes in me shall never T
7:37 proclaimed, "If any one T, let him come to
19:28 now finished, said (to fulfill the scripture), "I T
1Cor 4:11 hour we hunger and T, we are ill-clad and
2Cor 11:27 night, in hunger and T, often without food, in
Rev 7:16 hunger no more, neither T any more; the sun

THIRSTED (3)

Ex 17:3 But the people T there for water, and the
Wis 11:4 When they T they called upon thee, and water
Is 48:21 They T not when he led them through the

THIRSTS (4)

Ps 42:2 My soul T for God, for the living God.
63:1 seek thee, my soul T for thee; my flesh
143:6 to thee; my soul T for thee like a
Is 55:1 "Ho, every one who T, come to the waters;

THIRSTY (29)

Deut 8:15 serpents and scorpions and T ground where there
Judg 4:19 a little water to drink; for I am T
15:18 And he was very T, and he called on
Ruth 2:9 And when you are T, go to the vessels
2Sam 17:29 hungry and weary and T in the wilderness."
Jud 8:30 the people were very T, and they compelled us
Job 5:5 of thorns; and the T pant after his wealth.
Ps 107:5 dwell in; hungry and T, their soul fainted within
107:9 satisfies him who is T, and the hungry he
107:33 springs of water into T ground,
Prov 25:21 and if he is T, give him water to
25:25 cold water to a T soul, so is good
30:16 womb, the earth ever T for water, and the
Sir 26:12 As a T wayfarer opens his mouth and drinks
51:24 these things, and why are your souls very T
Is 21:14 To the T bring water, meet the fugitive with
29:8 or as when a T man dreams he is
32:6 and to deprive the T of drink.
35:7 a pool, and the T ground springs of water;
44:3 pour water on the T land, and streams on
65:13 but you shall be T; behold, my servants shall
Ezek 19:13 in a dry and T land.
Mt 25:35 me food, I was T and you gave me
25:37 and feed thee, or T and give thee drink?
25:42 no food, I was T and you gave me
25:44 see thee hungry or T or a stranger or
Rom 12:20 him; if he is T, give him drink; for

T

Rev 21:6 To the T I will give from the fountain
22:17 let him who is T come, let him who

THIRTEEN (13)

Gen 17:25 Ishmael his son was T years old when he
Num 29:13 odor to the LORD, T young bulls, two rams,
29:14 for each of the T bulls, two tenths for
Josh 19:6 Beth-lebaoth, and Sharuhen-- T cities with their
21:4 Judah, Simeon, and Benjamin, T cities.
21:6 of Manasseh in Bashan, T cities.
21:19 priests, were in all T cities with their pasture
21:33 Gershonites were in all T cities with their pasture
1Kgs 7:1 building his own house T years, and he finished
1Chr 6:60 All their cities throughout their families were T
6:62 their families were allotted T cities out of the
26:11 all the sons and brethren of Hosah were T
Ezek 40:11 breadth of the gateway, T cubits.

THIRTEENTH (15)

Gen 14:4 Ched-or-laomer, but in the T year they rebelled.
1Chr 24:13 twelfth to Jakim, the T to Huppah, the fourteenth
25:20 brethren, twelve; to the T, Shuba-el, his sons and
Esth 3:12 were summoned on the T day of the first
3:13 in one day, the T day of the twelfth
8:12 King Ahasuerus, on the T day of the twelfth
9:1 of Adar, on the T day of the same,
9:17 This was on the T day of the month
9:18 Susa gathered on the T day and on the
16:20 so that on the T day of the twelfth
Jer 1:2 of Judah, in the T year of his reign.
25:3 twenty-three years, from the T year of Josiah the
1Mac 7:43 in battle on the T day of the month
7:49 each year on the T day of Adar.
2Mac 15:36 but to celebrate the T day of the twelfth

THIRTIETH (2)

Ezek 1:1 In the T year, in the fourth
2Mac 11:30 go home by the T day of Xanthicus will

THIRTY (123)

Gen 5:3 lived a hundred and T years, he became the
5:5 were nine hundred and T years; and he died.
5:16 Jared eight hundred and T years, and had other
6:15 cubits, and its height T cubits.
11:14 When Shelah had lived T years, he became the
11:17 Peleg four hundred and T years, and had other
11:18 When Peleg had lived T years, he became the
11:22 When Serug had lived T years, he became the
18:30 Suppose T are found there." He answered, "I will
18:30 it, if I find T there."
32:15 ewes and twenty rams, T milch camels and their
41:46 Joseph was T years old when he entered the
47:9 are a hundred and T years; few and evil
Ex 12:40 was four hundred and T years.
12:41 of four hundred and T years, on that very
21:32 give to their master T shekels of silver, and
26:8 each curtain shall be T cubits, and the breadth
36:15 of each curtain was T cubits, and the breadth
38:24 and seven hundred and T shekels, by the shekel
Lev 27:4 your valuation shall be T shekels.
Num 4:3 their fathers' houses, from T years old up to
4:23 their fathers' houses; from T years old up to
4:30 their fathers' houses; from T years old up to
4:35 their fathers' houses, from T years old up to
4:39 their fathers' houses, from T years old up to
4:40 fathers' houses was two thousand six hundred and T
4:43 their fathers' houses, from T years old up to
4:47 their fathers' houses, from T years old up to
7:13 was a hundred and T shekels, one silver basin
7:19 was a hundred and T shekels, one silver basin
7:25 was a hundred and T shekels, one silver basin
7:31 was a hundred and T shekels, one silver basin
7:37 was a hundred and T shekels, one silver basin
7:43 was a hundred and T shekels, one silver basin
7:49 was a hundred and T shekels, one silver basin
7:55 was a hundred and T shekels, one silver basin
7:61 was a hundred and T shekels, one silver basin
7:67 was a hundred and T shekels, one silver basin
7:73 was a hundred and T shekels, one silver basin
7:79 was a hundred and T shekels, one silver basin
7:85 weighing a hundred and T shekels and each basin
20:29 Israel wept for Aaron T days.
26:7 was forty-three thousand seven hundred and T
26:51 six hundred and one thousand seven hundred and T
31:39 The asses were T thousand five hundred, of which
31:45 thirty-six thousand cattle, and T thousand five

Deut 34:8 the plains of Moab T days; then the days
Josh 8:3 Ai; and Joshua chose T thousand mighty men of
Judg 10:4 And he had T sons who rode on thirty
10:4 sons who rode on T asses; and they had
10:4 asses; and they had T cities, called Havvoth-jair to
12:9 He had T sons; and thirty daughters he gave
12:9 had thirty sons; and T daughters he gave in
12:9 outside his clan, and T daughters he brought in
12:14 had forty sons and T grandsons, who rode on
14:11 saw him, they brought T companions to be with
14:12 I will give you T linen garments and thirty
14:12 thirty linen garments and T festal garments;
14:13 you shall give me T linen garments and thirty
14:13 thirty linen garments and T festal garments." And
14:19 to Ashkelon and killed T men of the town,
20:31 the open country, about T men of Israel.
20:39 smite and kill about T men of Israel; they
1Sam 4:10 there fell of Israel T thousand foot soldiers.
9:22 invited, who were about T persons.
11:8 the men of Judah T thousand.
13:5 to fight with Israel, T thousand chariots, and six
2Sam 5:4 David was T years old when he began to
6:1 chosen men of Israel, T thousand.
23:13 And three of the T chief men went down,
23:18 the son of Zeruiah, was chief of the T
23:19 renowned of the T, and became their commander;
23:23 was renowned among the T, but he did not
23:24 was one of the T; Elhanan the son of
1Kgs 4:22 for one day was T cors of fine flour,
5:13 and the levy numbered T thousand men.
6:2 twenty cubits wide, and T cubits high.
7:2 cubits, and its height T cubits, and it was
7:6 cubits, and its breadth T cubits; there was a
7:23 and a line of T cubits measured its circumference.
7:24 brim were gourds, for T cubits, compassing the sea
2Kgs 18:14 talents of silver and T talents of gold.
1Chr 11:15 Three of the T chief men went down to
11:20 the brother of Joab, was chief of the T
11:21 renowned of the T, and became their commander;
11:25 was renowned among the T, but he did not
11:42 of the Reubenites, and T with him,
12:4 mighty man among the T and a leader over
12:4 a leader over the T; Jeremiah, Jahaziel, Johanan,
12:18 Amasai, chief of the T, and he said, "We
15:7 with a hundred and T of his brethren;
23:3 The Levites, T years old and upward, were
27:6 mighty man of the T and in command of
27:6 in command of the T; Ammizabad his son was
2Chr 4:2 and a line of T cubits measured its circumference.
4:3 figures of gourds, for T cubits, compassing the sea
24:15 was a hundred and T years old at his
35:7 to the number of T thousand, and three thousand
Ezra 1:10 of silver, twenty-nine censers, T bowls of gold, two
2:35 sons of Senaah, three thousand six hundred and T
Neh 7:38 sons of Senaah, three thousand nine hundred and T
7:70 basins, five hundred and T priests' garments.
Jud 15:11 plundered the camp for T days.
Esth 4:11 to the king these T days."
Prov 22:20 not written for you T sayings of admonition and
Ezek 40:17 round about the court; T chambers fronted on the
41:6 stories, one over another, T in each story.
46:22 forty cubits long and T broad; the four were
Dan 6:7 god or man for T days, except to you,
6:12 god or man within T days except to you,
Zech 11:12 out as my wages T shekels of silver.
11:13 So I took the T shekels of silver and
1Mac 10:36 to the number of T thousand men, and let
2Mac 12:9 was seen in Jerusalem, T miles distant.
12:23 destroyed as many as T thousand men.
Mt 13:8 forth grain, some a hundredfold, some sixty, some T
13:23 a hundredfold, in another sixty, and in another T
26:15 And they paid him T pieces of silver.
27:3 and brought back the T pieces of silver to
27:9 "And they took the T pieces of silver, the
Lk 3:23 his ministry, was about T years of age, being
Jn 2:6 each holding twenty or T gallons.
Gal 3:17 came four hundred and T years afterward, does not

THIRTY-EIGHT (4)

Deut 2:14 the brook Zered was T years, until the entire
1Chr 23:3 and the total was T thousand men.
Neh 7:45 Hatita, the sons of Shobai, a hundred and T
Jn 5:4 had been ill for T years.

THIRTY-EIGHTH (2)

1Kgs 16:29 In the T year of Asa king of Judah,
2Kgs 15:8 In the T year of Azariah king of Judah

THIRTY-FIFTH

2Chr 15:19 more war until the T year of the reign

THIRTY-FIRST

1Kgs 16:23 In the T year of Asa king of Judah,

THIRTY-FIVE (10)

Gen 11:12 When Arpachshad had lived T years, he became the
Num 1:37 tribe of Benjamin was T thousand four hundred.
2:23 host as numbered being T thousand four hundred.
1Kgs 22:42 Jehoshaphat was T years old when he began to
2Chr 3:15 he made two pillars T cubits high, with a
20:31 He was T years old when he began to
Ezra 2:67 were four hundred and T, and their asses were
Neh 7:69 camels four hundred and T, and their asses six
Dan 12:12 thousand three hundred and T days.
2Mac 15:27 low no less than T thousand men, and were

THIRTY-FOUR (3)

Gen 11:16 When Eber had lived T years, he became the
1Chr 7:7 enrollment by genealogies was twenty-two thousand
Jud 7:20 cavalry, surrounded them for T days, until all the

THIRTY-NINE

Ezra 2:42 sons of Shobai, in all one hundred and T

THIRTY-NINTH (3)

2Kgs 15:13 to reign in the T year of Uzziah king
15:17 In the T year of Azariah king of Judah
2Chr 16:12 In the T year of his reign Asa was

THIRTY-ONE (3)

Josh 12:24 Tirzah, one: in all, T kings.
2Kgs 22:1 reign, and he reigned T years in Jerusalem.
2Chr 34:1 reign, and he reigned T years in Jerusalem.

THIRTY-SECOND (2)

Neh 5:14 twentieth year to the T year of Artaxerxes the
13:6 Jerusalem, for in the T year of Artaxerxes king

THIRTY-SEVEN (9)

Gen 25:17 Ishmael, a hundred and T years; he breathed his
Ex 6:16 being a hundred and T years.
6:20 being one hundred and T years.
Num 31:36 number three hundred and T thousand five hundred
31:43 was three hundred and T thousand five hundred
2Sam 23:39 Ithrite, Uriah the Hittite: T in all.
1Chr 12:34 commanders with whom were T thousand men
Ezra 2:65 thousand three hundred and T; and they had two
Neh 7:67 thousand three hundred and T; and they had two

THIRTY-SEVENTH (4)

2Kgs 13:10 In the T year of Joash king of Judah
25:27 And in the T year of the exile of
Jer 52:31 And in the T year of the captivity of
1Mac 1:10 the one hundred and T year of the kingdom

THIRTY-SIX (6)

Num 31:38 The cattle were T thousand, of which the LORD's
31:44 thousand five hundred sheep, T thousand cattle,
Josh 7:5 of Ai killed about T men of them, and
1Chr 7:4 the army for war, T thousand, for they had
Ezra 2:66 were seven hundred and T, their mules were two
Neh 7:68 were seven hundred and T, their mules two hundred

THIRTY-SIXTH

2Chr 16:1 In the T year of the reign of Asa,

THIRTY-THREE (7)

Gen 46:15 altogether his sons and his daughters numbered T
Ex 6:18 being a hundred and T years.
Lev 12:4 she shall continue for T days in the blood
2Sam 5:5 all Israel and Judah T years.
1Kgs 2:11 years in Hebron, and T years in Jerusalem.
1Chr 3:4 And he reigned T years in Jerusalem.
29:27 years in Hebron, and T years in Jerusalem.

THIRTY-TWO (16)

Gen 11:20 When Reu had lived T years, he became the
Num 1:35 tribe of Manasseh was T thousand two hundred.
2:21 host as numbered being T thousand two hundred.
26:37 according to their number, T thousand five hundred.
31:35 sixty-one thousand asses, and T thousand persons in
31:40 the LORD's tribute was T persons.

T

1Kgs 20:1 all his army together; T kings were with him,
20:15 were two hundred and T; and after them he
20:16 booths, he and the T kings who helped him.
22:31 Syria had commanded the T captains of his chariots,
2Kgs 8:17 He was T years old when he became king,
1Chr 19:7 They hired T thousand chariots and the king of
2Chr 21:5 Jehoram was T years old when he became king,
21:20 He was T years old when he began to
Jer 52:29 Jerusalem eight hundred and T persons;
1Mac 6:30 thousand horsemen, and T elephants accustomed to

THIRTYFOLD (2)

Mk 4:8 and increasing and yielding T and sixtyfold and a
4:20 it and bear fruit, T and sixtyfold and a

THISBE

Tob 1:2 taken into captivity from T, which is to the

THISTLE (5)

2Kgs 14:9 king of Judah, "A T on Lebanon sent to
14:9 of Lebanon passed by and trampled down the T
2Chr 25:18 king of Judah, "A T on Lebanon sent to
25:18 of Lebanon passed by and trampled down the T
Hos 10:8 Thorn and T shall grow up on their altars;

THISTLES (4)

Gen 3:18 your life; thorns and T it shall bring forth
Is 34:13 its strongholds, nettles and T in its fortresses.
Mt 7:16 Are grapes gathered from thorns, or figs from T
Heb 6:8 it bears thorns and T, it is worthless and

THITHER (12)

Ex 26:33 of the testimony in T within the veil; and
Deut 12:5 make his habitation there; T you shall go,
12:6 you shall go, and T you shall bring your
12:11 his name dwell there, T you shall bring all
Judg 5:14 Ephraim they set out T into the valley, following
18:15 And they turned aside T, and came to the
21:10 So the congregation sent T twelve thousand of their
1Sam 14:16 and behold, the multitude was surging hither and T
Neh 13:9 and I brought back T the vessels of the
Job 6:20 were confident; they come T and are confounded.
Is 55:10 heaven, and return not T but water the earth,
57:7 set your bed, and T you went up to

THOMAS (11)

Mt 10:3 Philip and Bartholomew; T and Matthew the tax
Mk 3:18 Bartholomew, and Matthew, and T, and James the
Lk 6:15 and Matthew, and T, and James the son
Jn 11:16 T, called the Twin, said to his fellow disciples,
14:5 T said to him, "Lord, we do not know
20:24 Now T, one of the twelve, called the Twin,
20:26 in the house, and T was with them.
20:27 Then he said to T, "Put your finger here,
20:28 T answered him, "My Lord and my God!"
21:2 Simon Peter, T called the Twin, Nathanael of Cana
Acts 1:13 Andrew, Philip and T, Bartholomew and Matthew,

THONG (4)

Sir 33:26 Yoke and T will bow the neck, and for
Mk 1:7 mightier than I, the T of whose sandals I
Lk 3:16 I is coming, the T of whose sandals I
Jn 1:27 comes after me, the T of whose sandal I

THONGS (3)

Is 58:6 wickedness, to undo the T of the yoke, to
Jer 27:2 to me: "Make yourself T and yoke-bars, and put
Acts 22:25 him up with the T, Paul said to the

THORN (8)

Prov 26:9 Like a T that goes up into the hand
Sir 24:15 Like cassia and camel's T I gave forth the
Is 55:13 Instead of the T shall come up the cypress;
Bar 6:71 silver, and like a T bush in a garden,
Ezek 28:24 to prick or a T to hurt them among
Hos 10:8 T and thistle shall grow up on their altars;
Mic 7:4 upright of them a T hedge.
2Cor 12:7 abundance of revelations, a T was given me in

THORNBUSHES

Is 7:19 and on all the T, and on all the

THORNS (49)

Gen 3:18 days of your life; T and thistles it shall
Ex 22:6 out and catches in T so that the stacked
Num 33:55 in your eyes and T in your sides, and
Josh 23:13 on your sides, and T in your eyes, till
Judg 8:7 your flesh with the T of the wilderness and
8:16 city and he took T of the wilderness and
2Sam 23:6 men are all like T that are thrown away;
Job 5:5 it even out of T; and the thirsty pant
31:40 of its owners; let T grow instead of wheat,
Ps 58:9 feel the heat of T, whether green or ablaze,
118:12 like a fire of T; in the name of
Prov 15:19 sluggard is overgrown with T, but the path of
22:5 T and snares are in the way of the
24:31 was all overgrown with T; the ground was covered
Eccl 7:6 as the crackling of T under a pot, so
Sir 28:24 in your property with T, lock up your silver
43:19 salt, and when it freezes, it becomes pointed T
Is 5:6 hoed, and briers and T shall grow up; I
7:23 thousand shekels of silver, will become briers and T
7:24 will be briers and T;
7:25 fear of briers and T; but they will become
9:18 it consumes briers and T; it kindles the thickets
10:17 burn and devour his T and briers in one
27:4 Would that I had T and briers to battle!
32:13 people growing up in T and briers; yea, for
33:12 burned to lime, like T cut down, that are
34:13 T shall grow over its strongholds, nettles and thistles
Jer 4:3 up your fallow ground, and sow not among T
12:13 wheat and have reaped T, they have tired themselves
Ezek 2:6 words, though briers and T are with you and
Hos 2:6 up her way with T; and I will build
9:6 precious things of silver; T shall be in their
Nah 1:10 Like entangled T they are consumed, like dry
Mt 7:16 Are grapes gathered from T, or figs from thistles?
13:7 Other seeds fell upon T, and the thorns grew
13:7 upon thorns, and the T grew up and choked
13:22 what was sown among T, this is he who
27:29 plaiting a crown of T they put it on
Mk 4:7 Other seed fell among T and the thorns grew
4:7 among thorns and the T grew up and choked
4:18 the ones sown among T; they are those who
15:17 plaiting a crown of T they put it on
Lk 6:44 are not gathered from T, nor are grapes picked
8:7 And some fell among T; and the thorns grew
8:7 among thorns; and the T grew with it and
8:14 what fell among the T, they are those who
Jn 19:2 plaited a crown of T, and put it on
19:5 wearing the crown of T and the purple robe.
Heb 6:8 But if it bears T and thistles, it is

THOROUGHFARES

Mt 22:9 Go therefore to the T, and invite to the

THOROUGHLY (6)

Gen 11:3 "Come, let us make bricks, and burn them T
Ex 21:19 and shall have him T healed.
Jud 11:8 in the whole kingdom, T informed and marvelous in
Ps 51:2 Wash me T from my iniquity, and cleanse me
Jer 6:9 LORD of hosts: "Glean T as a vine the
2Mac 3:38 will get him back T scourged, if he escapes

THOU (1,225)

Gen 3:12 said, "The woman whom T gavest to be with
4:14 Behold, T hast driven me this day away from
15:2 Lord GOD, what wilt T give me, for I
15:3 And Abram said, "Behold, T hast given me no
16:13 who spoke to her, T art a God of
18:23 near, and said, "Wilt T indeed destroy the righteous
18:24 within the city; wilt T then destroy the place
18:28 Wilt T destroy the whole city for lack of
20:4 he said, "Lord, wilt T slay an innocent people?
24:14 be the one whom T hast appointed for thy
24:14 I shall know that T hast shown steadfast love
24:42 master Abraham, if now T wilt prosper the way
28:22 and of all that T givest me I will
32:10 all the faithfulness which T hast shown to thy
32:12 But T didst say, 'I will do you good,
Ex 4:10 either heretofore or since T hast spoken to thy
5:22 "O LORD, why hast T done evil to this
5:22 Why didst T ever send me?
5:23 to this people, and T hast not delivered thy
15:7 greatness of thy majesty T overthrowest thy
15:7 overthrowest thy adversaries; T sendest forth thy
15:10 hand shall destroy them.' T didst blow with thy
15:12 T didst stretch out thy right hand, the earth
15:13 T hast led in thy steadfast love the people
15:13 love the people whom T hast redeemed, thou hast
15:13 whom thou hast redeemed, T hast guided them by
15:16 people pass by whom T hast purchased.

	15:17	T wilt bring them in, and plant them on
	15:17	place, O LORD, which T hast made for thy
	19:23	to Mount Sinai; for T thyself didst charge us,
	32:11	against thy people, whom T hast brought forth out
	32:13	thy servants, to whom T didst swear by thine
	32:32	But now, if T wilt forgive their sin--and
	32:32	of thy book which T hast written."
	33:12	to the LORD, "See, T sayest to me, 'Bring
	33:12	up this people'; but T hast not let me
	33:12	let me know whom T wilt send with me.
	33:12	Yet T hast said, 'I know you by name,
Num	11:11	the LORD, "Why hast T dealt ill with thy
	11:11	in thy sight, that T dost lay the burden
	11:12	bring them forth, that T shouldst say to me,
	11:12	to the land which T didst swear to give
	11:15	If T wilt deal thus with me, kill me
	11:21	thousand on foot; and T hast said, 'I will
	14:13	hear of it, for T didst bring up this
	14:14	They have heard that T, O LORD, art in
	14:14	of this people; for T, O LORD, art seen
	14:14	stands over them and T goest before them, in
	14:15	Now if T dost kill this people as one
	14:17	LORD be great as T hast promised, saying,
	14:19	love, and according as T hast forgiven this people,
	16:22	man sin, and wilt T be angry with all
	21:2	LORD, and said, "If T wilt indeed give this
	22:34	did not know that T didst stand in the
Deut	3:24	saying, 'O Lord GOD, T hast only begun to
	9:26	and thy heritage, whom T hast redeemed through thy
	9:26	through thy greatness, whom T hast brought out of
	9:28	the land from which T didst bring us say,
	9:29	and thy heritage, whom T didst bring out by
	21:8	thy people Israel, whom T hast redeemed, and set
	26:10	of the ground, which T, O LORD, hast given
	26:13	thy commandment which T hast commanded me; I
	26:14	according to all that T hast commanded me.
	26:15	and the ground which T hast given us, as
	26:15	hast given us, as T didst swear to our
	33:8	thy godly one, whom T didst test at Massah,
	33:8	at Massah, with whom T didst strive at the
Josh	7:7	Lord GOD, why hast T brought this people over
	7:9	earth; and what wilt T do for thy great
	10:12	of Israel, "Sun, stand T still at Gibeon, and
	10:12	still at Gibeon, and T Moon in the valley
Judg	5:4	"LORD, when T didst go forth from Seir, when
	5:4	forth from Seir, when T didst march from the
	6:17	sign that it is T who speakest with me.
	6:36	said to God, "If T wilt deliver Israel by
	6:36	by my hand, as T hast said,
	6:37	I shall know that T wilt deliver Israel by
	6:37	by my hand, as T hast said."
	11:30	LORD, and said, "If T wilt give the Ammonites
	13:8	man of God whom T didst send come again
	15:18	the LORD and said, T hast granted this great
1Sam	1:11	LORD of hosts, if T wilt indeed look on
	14:37	Wilt T give them into the hand of Israel?"
	14:41	of Israel, why hast T not answered thy servant
2Sam	5:19	Wilt T give them into my hand?" And the
	7:18	is my house, that T hast brought me thus
	7:19	eyes, O Lord GOD; T hast spoken also of
	7:20	For T knowest thy servant, O Lord GOD!
	7:21	to thy own heart, T hast wrought all this
	7:22	Therefore T art great, O LORD God; for there
	7:24	And T didst establish for thyself thy people Israel
	7:24	people for ever; and T, O LORD, didst become
	7:25	ever the word which T hast spoken concerning thy
	7:25	house, and do as T hast spoken;
	7:27	For T, O LORD of hosts, the God of
	7:28	now, O Lord GOD, T art God, and thy
	7:28	words are true, and T hast promised this good
	7:29	ever before thee; for T, O Lord GOD, hast
	22:3	my refuge, my savior; T savest me from violence.
	22:26	"With the loyal T dost show thyself loyal; with
	22:26	with the blameless man T dost show thyself
	22:27	blameless; with the pure T dost show thyself pure,
	22:27	and with the crooked T dost show thyself perverse.
	22:28	T dost deliver a humble people, but thy eyes
	22:29	Yea, T art my lamp, O LORD, and my
	22:36	T hast given me the shield of thy salvation,
	22:37	T didst give a wide place for my steps
	22:40	For T didst gird me with strength for the
	22:40	strength for the battle; T didst make my assailants
	22:41	T didst make my enemies turn their backs to
	22:44	T didst deliver me from strife with the peoples;
	22:44	strife with the peoples; T didst keep me as
	22:49	out from my enemies; T didst exalt me above
	22:49	me above my adversaries, T didst deliver me from
1Kgs	3:6	And Solomon said, T hast shown great and steadfast
	3:6	heart toward thee; and T hast kept for him
	3:7	O LORD my God, T hast made thy servant
	3:8	of thy people whom T hast chosen, a great
	8:24	David my father what T didst declare to him;
	8:24	declare to him; yea, T didst speak with thy
	8:25	David my father what T hast promised him, saying,
	8:26	word be confirmed, which T hast spoken to thy
	8:29	the place of which T hast said, 'My name
	8:29	shall be there,' that T mayest hearken to the
	8:30	And hearken T to the supplication of thy servant
	8:30	this place; yea, hear T in heaven thy dwelling
	8:30	dwelling place; and when T hearest, forgive.
	8:32	this house, then hear T in heaven, and act,
	8:34	this house; then hear T in heaven, and forgive
	8:34	to the land which T gavest to their fathers.
	8:35	from their sin, when T dost afflict them,
	8:36	afflict them, then hear T in heaven, and forgive
	8:36	thy people Israel, when T dost teach them the
	8:36	upon thy land, which T hast given to thy
	8:39	this house; then hear T in heaven thy dwelling
	8:39	to each whose heart T knowest, according to all
	8:39	all his ways (for T, thou only, knowest the
	8:39	his ways (for thou, T only, knowest the hearts
	8:40	in the land which T gavest to our fathers.
	8:43	toward this house, hear T in heaven thy dwelling
	8:44	enemy, by whatever way T shalt send them, and
	8:44	toward the city which T hast chosen and the
	8:45	thy name, then hear T in heaven their prayer
	8:46	does not sin--and T art angry with them,
	8:48	toward their land, which T gavest to their fathers,
	8:48	fathers, the city which T hast chosen, and the
	8:49	thy name; then hear T in heaven thy dwelling
	8:51	and thy heritage, which T didst bring out of
	8:53	For T didst separate them from among all the
	8:53	be thy heritage, as T didst declare through Moses,
	8:53	Moses, thy servant, when T didst bring our fathers
	17:20	LORD my God, hast T brought calamity even upon
	18:36	known this day that T art God in Israel,
	18:37	people may know that T, O LORD, art God,
	18:37	art God, and that T hast turned their hearts
2Kgs	19:15	enthroned above the cherubim, T art the God, thou
	19:15	thou art the God, T alone, of all the
	19:15	kingdoms of the earth; T hast made heaven and
	19:19	earth may know that T, O LORD, art God
1Chr	4:10	Israel, saying, "Oh that T wouldst bless me and
	4:10	with me, and that T wouldst keep me from
	14:10	Wilt T give them into my hand?" And the
	17:16	is my house, that T hast brought me thus
	17:17	thy eyes, O God; T hast also spoken of
	17:18	For T knowest thy servant.
	17:19	to thy own heart, T hast wrought all this
	17:21	before thy people whom T didst redeem from Egypt?
	17:22	And T didst make thy people Israel to be
	17:22	people for ever; and T, O LORD, didst become
	17:23	let the word which T hast spoken concerning thy
	17:23	ever, and do as T hast spoken;
	17:25	For T, my God, hast revealed to thy servant
	17:25	to thy servant that T wilt build a house
	17:26	And now, O LORD, T art God, and thou
	17:26	thou art God, and T hast promised this good
	17:27	before thee; for what T, O LORD, hast blessed
	29:10	David said: "Blessed art T, O LORD, the God
	29:11	kingdom, O LORD, and T art exalted as head
	29:12	come from thee, and T rulest over all.
	29:17	know, my God, that T triest the heart, and
2Chr	1:8	Solomon said to God, T hast shown great and
	1:9	be now fulfilled, for T hast made me king
	6:15	David my father what T didst declare to him;
	6:15	declare to him; yea, T didst speak with thy
	6:16	David my father what T hast promised him, saying,
	6:17	word be confirmed, which T hast spoken to thy
	6:20	house, the place where T hast promised to set
	6:20	set thy name, that T mayest hearken to the
	6:21	And hearken T to the supplications of thy servant
	6:21	this place; yea, hear T from heaven thy dwelling
	6:21	dwelling place; and when T hearest, forgive.
	6:23	this house, then hear T from heaven, and act,
	6:25	this house, then hear T from heaven, and forgive
	6:25	to the land which T gavest to them and
	6:26	from their sin, when T dost afflict them,
	6:27	afflict them, then hear T in heaven, and forgive
	6:27	thy people Israel, when T dost teach them the
	6:27	upon thy land, which T hast given to thy
	6:30	this house; then hear T from heaven thy dwelling

T

6:30 to each whose heart T knowest, according to all
6:30 all his ways (for T, thou only, knowest the
6:30 his ways (for thou, T only, knowest the hearts
6:31 in the land which T gavest to our fathers.
6:33 toward this house, hear T from heaven thy dwelling
6:34 enemies, by whatever way T shalt send them, and
6:34 toward this city which T hast chosen and the
6:35 thy name, then hear T from heaven their prayer
6:36 does not sin--and T art angry with them,
6:38 toward their land, which T gavest to their fathers,
6:38 fathers, the city which T hast chosen, and the
6:39 thy name, then hear T from heaven thy dwelling
6:41 to thy resting place, T and the ark of
14:11 O LORD, T art our God; let not man
20:6 of our fathers, art T not God in heaven?
20:6 Dost T not rule over all the kingdoms of
20:7 Didst T not, O our God, drive out the
20:9 in our affliction, and T wilt hear and save.'
20:10 and Mount Seir, whom T wouldest not let Israel
20:11 of thy possession, which T hast given us to
20:12 O our God, wilt T not execute judgment upon
Ezra 9:11 forsaken thy commandments, which T didst
9:13 great guilt, seeing that T, our God, hast punished
9:14 Wouldst T not be angry with us till thou
9:14 angry with us till T wouldst consume us, so
9:15 the God of Israel, T art just, for we
Neh 1:7 the ordinances which T didst command thy servant
1:8 Remember the word which T didst command thy
1:10 and thy people, whom T hast redeemed by thy
6:9 now, O God, strengthen T my hands.
9:6 And Ezra said: T art the LORD, thou alone;
9:6 "Thou art the LORD, T alone; thou hast made
9:6 the LORD, thou alone; T hast made heaven, the
9:6 is in them; and T preservest all of them;
9:7 T art the LORD, the God who didst choose
9:8 the name Abraham; and T didst find his heart
9:8 and the Girgashite; and T hast fulfilled thy promise,
9:8 fulfilled thy promise, for T art righteous.
9:9 "And T didst see the affliction of our fathers
9:10 of his land, for T knewest that they acted
9:10 against our fathers; and T didst get thee a
9:11 And T didst divide the sea before them, so
9:11 on dry land; and T didst cast their pursuers
9:12 a pillar of cloud T didst lead them in
9:13 T didst come down upon Mount Sinai, and speak
9:14 statutes and commandments, and T didst make
9:15 T didst give them bread from heaven for their
9:15 for their thirst, and T didst tell them to
9:15 possess the land which T hadst sworn to give
9:17 of the wonders which T didst perform among them;
9:17 But T art a God ready to forgive, gracious
9:19 committed great blasphemies, T in thy great mercies
9:20 T gavest thy good Spirit to instruct them, and
9:21 Forty years didst T sustain them in the wilderness,
9:22 And T didst give them kingdoms and peoples, and
9:23 T didst multiply their descendants as the stars of
9:23 stars of heaven, and T didst bring them into
9:23 into the land which T hadst told their fathers
9:24 possessed the land, and T didst subdue before them
9:27 Therefore T didst give them into the hand of
9:27 cried to thee and T didst hear them from
9:27 to thy great mercies T didst give them saviors
9:28 again before thee, and T didst abandon them to
9:28 and cried to thee T didst hear from heaven,
9:28 heaven, and many times T didst deliver them
9:29 And T didst warn them in order to turn
9:30 Many years T didst bear with them, and didst
9:30 Therefore T didst give them into the hand of
9:31 in thy great mercies T didst not make an
9:31 or forsake them; for T art a gracious and
9:33 Yet T hast been just in all that has
9:33 come upon us, for T hast dealt faithfully and
9:34 and thy warnings which T didst give them.
9:35 thy great goodness which T gavest them, and in
9:35 and rich land which T didst set before them;
9:36 in the land that T gavest to our fathers
9:37 to the kings whom T hast set over us
Tob 3:2 anguish, saying, "Righteous art T, O Lord; all thy
3:2 mercy and truth, and T dost render true and
3:4 disobeyed thy commandments, and T gavest us over
3:4 plunder, captivity, and death; T madest us a byword
3:11 and said, "Blessed art T, O Lord my God,
3:14 T knowest, O Lord, that I am innocent of
8:5 to pray, "Blessed art T, O God of our
8:6 T madest Adam and gavest him Eve his wife
8:6 T didst say, 'It is not good that the
8:15 and said, "Blessed art T, O God, with every
8:16 Blessed art T, because thou hast made me glad.
8:16 Blessed art thou, because T hast made me glad.
8:16 as I expected; but T hast treated us according
8:17 Blessed art T, because thou hast had compassion on
8:17 Blessed art thou, because T hast had compassion on
11:14 and said, "Blessed art T, O God, and blessed
11:15 For T hast afflicted me, but thou hast had
11:15 hast afflicted me, but T hast had mercy upon
Jud 9:2 father Simeon, to whom T gavest a sword to
9:2 to disgrace her; for T hast said, 'It shall
9:3 So T gavest up their rulers to be slain,
9:3 stained with blood, and T didst strike down slaves
9:4 on their thrones; and T gavest their wives for
9:5 "For T hast done these things and those that
9:5 and those that followed; T hast designed the things
9:5 Yea, the things T didst intend came to pass,
9:6 pass, and the things T didst will presented themselves
9:7 and know not that T art the Lord who
9:11 men of strength; for T art God of the
9:14 know and understand that T art God, the God
9:14 people of Israel but T alone!"
13:17 one accord, "Blessed art T, our God, who hast
16:13 new song: O Lord, T are great and glorious,
16:14 creatures serve thee, for T didst speak, and they
16:14 T didst send forth thy Spirit, and it formed
16:15 those who fear thee T wilt continue to show
Esth 13:10 For T hast made heaven and earth and every
13:11 thing under heaven, and T art Lord of all,
13:12 T knowest all things; thou knowest, O Lord, that
13:12 Thou knowest all things; T knowest, O Lord, that
13:16 neglect thy portion, which T didst redeem for thyself
14:3 said: "O my Lord, T only art our King;
14:5 of my family that T, O Lord, didst take
14:5 everlasting inheritance, and that T didst do for them
14:5 for them all that T didst promise.
14:6 sinned before thee, and T hast given us into
14:7 T art righteous, O Lord!
14:15 T hast knowledge of all things; and thou knowest
14:15 of all things; and T knowest that I hate
14:16 T knowest my necessity _ that I abhor the
Job 1:10 Hast T not put a hedge about him and
1:10 T hast blessed the work of his hands, and
7:12 a sea monster, that T settest a guard over
7:14 ease my complaint,' then T dost scare me with
7:17 What is man, that T dost make so much
7:17 of him, and that T dost set thy mind
7:19 How long wilt T not look away from me,
7:20 I do to thee, T watcher of men?
7:20 Why hast T made me thy mark?
7:21 Why dost T not pardon my transgression and take
7:21 lie in the earth; T wilt seek me, but
9:12 who will say to him, 'What doest T
9:28 suffering, for I know T wilt not hold me
9:31 hands with lye, yet T wilt plunge me into
10:2 let me know why T dost contend against me.
10:4 Hast T eyes of flesh?
10:4 Dost T see as man sees?
10:6 as man's years, that T dost seek out my
10:7 for my sin, although T knowest that I am
10:8 made me; and now T dost turn about and
10:9 Remember that T hast made me of clay; and
10:9 of clay; and wilt T turn me to dust
10:10 Didst T not pour me out like milk and
10:11 T didst clothe me with skin and flesh, and
10:12 T hast granted me life and steadfast love; and
10:13 Yet these things T didst hide in thy heart;
10:14 If I sin, T dost mark me, and dost
10:16 I lift myself up, T dost hunt me like
10:17 work wonders against me; T dost renew thy
10:17 thy vexation toward me; T dost bring fresh hosts
10:18 "Why didst T bring me forth from the womb?
13:22 me speak, and do T reply to me.
13:24 Why dost T hide thy face, and count me
13:25 Wilt T frighten a driven leaf and pursue dry
13:26 For T writest bitter things against me, and makest
13:27 T puttest my feet in the stocks, and watchest
13:27 watchest all my paths; T settest a bound to
14:3 And dost T open thy eyes upon such a
14:5 is with thee, and T hast appointed his bounds
14:13 Oh that T wouldest hide me in Sheol, that
14:13 me in Sheol, that T wouldest conceal me until
14:13 wrath be past, that T wouldest appoint me a
14:15 T wouldest call, and I would answer thee; thou
14:15 I would answer thee; T wouldest long for the
14:16 For then T wouldest number my steps, thou wouldest

14:16 wouldest number my steps, T wouldest not keep
14:17 in a bag, and T wouldest cover over my
14:19 of the earth; so T destroyest the hope of
14:20 T prevailest for ever against him, and he passes;
14:20 him, and he passes; T changest his countenance, and
17:4 Since T hast closed their minds to understanding,
17:4 minds to understanding, therefore T wilt not let them
30:20 cry to thee and T dost not answer me;
30:20 me; I stand, and T dost not heed me.
30:21 T hast turned cruel to me; with the might
30:21 might of thy hand T dost persecute me.
30:22 T liftest me up on the wind, thou makest
30:22 up on the wind, T makest me ride on
30:22 ride on it, and T tossest me about in
30:23 Yea, I know that T wilt bring me to
36:23 or who can say, T hast done wrong?
42:2 LORD: "I know that T canst do all things,
Ps 3:3 [Selah] But T, O LORD, art a shield about
3:7 For T dost smite all my enemies on the
3:7 enemies on the cheek, T dost break the teeth
4:1 T hast given me room when I was in
4:7 T hast put more joy in my heart than
4:8 down and sleep; for T alone, O LORD, makest
5:3 LORD, in the morning T dost hear my voice;
5:4 For T art not a God who delights in
5:5 stand before thy eyes; T hatest all evildoers.
5:6 T destroyest those who speak lies; the LORD abhors
5:11 for joy; and do T defend them, that those
5:12 For T dost bless the righteous, O LORD; thou
5:12 the righteous, O LORD; T dost cover him with
6:3 But T, O LORD--how long?
7:6 awake, O my God; T hast appointed a judgment.
7:9 an end, but establish T the righteous, thou who
7:9 establish thou the righteous, T who triest the minds
7:9 the minds and hearts, T righteous God.
8:1 T whose glory above the heavens is chanted
8:2 of babes and infants, T hast founded a bulwark
8:3 and the stars which T hast established;
8:4 what is man that T art mindful of him,
8:4 son of man that T dost care for him?
8:5 Yet T hast made him little less than God,
8:6 T hast given him dominion over the works of
8:6 works of thy hands; T hast put all things
9:4 For T hast maintained my just cause; thou hast
9:4 maintained my just cause; T hast sat on the
9:5 T hast rebuked the nations, thou hast destroyed the
9:5 rebuked the nations, T hast destroyed the wicked;
9:5 hast destroyed the wicked; T hast blotted out their
9:6 everlasting ruins; their cities T hast rooted out; the
9:10 trust in thee, for T, O LORD, hast not
9:13 who hate me, O T who liftest me up
10:1 [Selah] Why dost T stand afar off, O LORD?
10:1 Why dost T hide thyself in times of trouble?
10:13 say in his heart, T wilt not call to
10:14 T dost see; yea, thou dost note trouble and
10:14 Thou dost see; yea, T dost note trouble and
10:14 trouble and vexation, that T mayest take it into
10:14 commits himself to thee; T hast been the helper
10:15 Break T the arm of the wicked and evildoer;
10:15 out his wickedness till T find none.
10:17 O LORD, T wilt hear the desire of the
10:17 desire of the meek; T wilt strengthen their heart,
10:17 wilt strengthen their heart, T wilt incline thy ear
12:7 Do T, O LORD, protect us, guard us ever
13:1 Wilt T forget me for ever?
13:1 How long wilt T hide thy face from me?
16:2 say to the LORD, T art my Lord; I
16:5 portion and my cup; T holdest my lot.
16:10 For T dost not give me up to Sheol,
16:11 T dost show me the path of life; in
17:3 If T triest my heart, if thou visitest me
17:3 triest my heart, if T visitest me by night,
17:3 me by night, if T testest me, thou wilt
17:3 if thou testest me, T wilt find no wickedness
17:6 call upon thee, for T wilt answer me, O
17:14 be filled with what T hast stored up for
18:25 With the loyal T dost show thyself loyal; with
18:25 the blameless man T dost show thyself blameless;
18:26 blameless; with the pure T dost show thyself pure;
18:26 and with the crooked T dost show thyself perverse.
18:27 For T dost deliver a humble people; but the
18:27 but the haughty eyes T dost bring down.
18:28 Yea, T dost light my lamp; the LORD my
18:35 T hast given me the shield of thy salvation,
18:36 T didst give a wide place for my steps
18:39 For T didst gird me with strength for the
18:39 strength for the battle; T didst make my assailants
18:40 T didst make my enemies turn their backs to
18:43 T didst deliver me from strife with the peoples;
18:43 strife with the peoples; T didst make me the
18:48 from my enemies; yea, T didst exalt me above
18:48 me above my adversaries; T didst deliver me from
19:12 Clear T me from hidden faults.
21:2 T hast given him his heart's desire, and hast
21:3 [Selah] For T dost meet him with goodly blessings;
21:3 him with goodly blessings; T dost set a crown
21:4 asked life of thee; T gavest it to him,
21:5 help; splendor and majesty T dost bestow upon him.
21:6 Yea, T dost make him most blessed for ever;
21:6 most blessed for ever; T dost make him glad
22:1 my God, why hast T forsaken me?
22:1 Why art T so far from helping me, from
22:2 cry by day, but T dost not answer; and
22:3 Yet T art holy, enthroned on the praises of
22:4 trusted; they trusted, and T didst deliver them.
22:9 Yet T art he who took me from the
22:9 me from the womb; T didst keep me safe
22:10 my mother bore me T hast been my God.
22:15 cleaves to my jaws; T dost lay me in
22:19 But T, O LORD, be not far-off!
22:19 O T my help, hasten to my aid!
23:4 fear no evil; for T art with me; thy
23:5 T preparest a table before me in the presence
23:5 presence of my enemies; T anointest my head with
25:5 and teach me, for T art the God of
25:16 Turn T to me, and be gracious to me;
27:8 T hast said, "Seek ye my face." My heart
27:9 servant away in anger, T who hast been my
28:1 to me, lest, if T be silent to me,
28:9 bless thy heritage; be T their shepherd, and carry
30:1 thee, O LORD, for T hast drawn me up,
30:2 thee for help, and T hast healed me.
30:3 O LORD, T hast brought up my soul from
30:7 thy favor, O LORD, T hadst established me as
30:7 as a strong mountain; T didst hide thy face,
30:10 O LORD, be T my helper!"
30:11 T hast turned for me my mourning into dancing;
30:11 m mourning into dancing; T hast loosed my sackcloth
31:2 Be T a rock of refuge for me, a
31:3 Yea, T art my rock and my fortress; for
31:4 hidden for me, for T art my refuge.
31:5 I commit my spirit; T hast redeemed me, O
31:6 T hatest those who pay regard to vain idols;
31:7 thy steadfast love, because T hast seen my affliction,
31:7 hast seen my affliction, T hast taken heed of
31:8 hand of the enemy; T hast set my feet
31:14 O LORD, I say, T art my God."
31:19 is thy goodness, which T hast laid up for
31:20 covert of thy presence T hidest them from the
31:20 the plots of men; T holdest them safe under
31:22 But T didst hear my supplications, when I cried
32:5 to the LORD"; then T didst forgive the guilt
32:7 T art a hiding place for me, thou preservest
32:7 hiding place for me, T preservest me from trouble;
32:7 preservest me from trouble; T dost encompass me
35:10 who is like thee, T who deliverest the weak
35:17 long, O LORD, wilt T look on?
35:22 T hast seen, O LORD; be not silent!
36:6 deep; man and beast T savest, O LORD.
36:8 of thy house, and T givest them drink from
38:15 I wait; it is T, O LORD my God,
39:5 Behold, T hast made my days a few handbreadths,
39:9 mouth; for it is T who hast done it.
39:11 When T dost chasten man with rebukes for sin,
39:11 with rebukes for sin, T dost consume like a
40:5 T hast multiplied, O LORD my God, thy wondrous
40:6 Sacrifice and offering T dost not desire; but thou
40:6 dost not desire; but T hast given me an
40:6 offering and sin offering T hast not required.
40:9 restrained my lips, as T knowest, O LORD.
40:11 Do not T, O LORD, withhold thy mercy from
40:17 T art my help and my deliverer; do not
41:2 blessed in the land; T dost not give him
41:3 sickbed; in his illness T healest all his infirmities.
41:10 But do T, O LORD, be gracious to me,
41:11 this I know that T art pleased with me,
41:12 But T hast upheld me because of my integrity,
42:9 my rock: "Why hast T forgotten me?
43:2 For T art the God in whom I take
43:2 take refuge; why hast T cast me off?
44:1 told us, what deeds T didst perform in their
44:2 the days of old: T with thy own hand

44:2 the nations, but them T didst plant; thou didst
44:2 them thou didst plant; T didst afflict the peoples,
44:2 the peoples, but them T didst set free;
44:3 of thy countenance; for T didst delight in them.
44:4 T art my King and my God, who ordainest
44:7 But T hast saved us from our foes, and
44:9 [Selah] Yet T hast cast us off and abased
44:10 T hast made us turn back from the foe;
44:11 T hast made us like sheep for slaughter, and
44:12 T hast sold thy people for a trifle, demanding
44:13 T hast made us the taunt of our neighbors,
44:14 T hast made us a byword among the nations,
44:19 from thy way, that T shouldst have broken us
44:23 Why sleepest T, O Lord?
44:24 Why dost T hide thy face?
44:24 Why dost T forget our affliction and oppression?
48:7 By the east wind T didst shatter the ships
51:4 thy sight, so that T art justified in thy
51:6 Behold, T desirest truth in the inward being;
51:8 let the bones which T hast broken rejoice.
51:14 from bloodguiltiness, O God, T God of my salvation,
51:15 O Lord, open T my lips, and my mouth
51:16 For T hast no delight in sacrifice; were I
51:16 give a burnt offering, T wouldst not be pleased.
51:17 contrite heart, O God, T wilt not despise.
51:19 of Jerusalem, then wilt T delight in right sacrifices,
52:9 thee for ever, because T hast done it.
54:7 For T hast delivered me from every trouble, and
55:23 But T, O God, wilt cast them down into
56:8 T hast kept count of my tossings; put thou
56:8 of my tossings; put T my tears in thy
56:13 For T hast delivered my soul from death, yea,
59:5 T, LORD God of hosts, art God of Israel.
59:8 But T, O LORD, dost laugh at them; thou
59:8 dost laugh at them; T dost hold all the
59:9 praises to thee; for T, O God, art my
59:16 For T hast been to me a fortress and
59:17 praises to thee, for T, O God, art my
60:1 O God, T hast rejected us, broken our defenses;
60:1 us, broken our defenses; T hast been angry; oh,
60:2 T hast made the land to quake, thou hast
60:2 the land to quake, T hast rent it open;
60:3 T hast made thy people suffer hard things; thou
60:3 people suffer hard things; T hast given us wine
60:4 T hast set up a banner for those who
60:10 Hast T not rejected us, O God?
60:10 T dost not go forth, O God, with our
61:2 Lead T me to the rock that is higher
61:3 higher than I; for T art my refuge, a
61:5 [Selah] For T, O God, hast heard my vows,
61:5 hast heard my vows, T hast given me the
62:12 For T dost requite a man according to his
63:1 O God, T art my God, I seek thee,
63:7 of the night; for T hast been my help,
65:2 vows be performed, O T who hearest prayer!
65:3 transgressions prevail over us, T dost forgive them.
65:4 Blessed is he whom T dost choose and bring
65:5 By dread deeds T dost answer us with deliverance,
65:8 afraid at thy signs; T makest the outgoings of
65:9 T visitest the earth and waterest it, thou greatly
65:9 earth and waterest it, T greatly enrichest it; the
65:9 is full of water; T providest their grain, for
65:9 their grain, for so T hast prepared it.
65:10 T waterest its furrows abundantly, settling its ridges,
65:11 T crownest the year with thy bounty; the tracks
66:10 For T, O God, hast tested us; thou hast
66:10 God, hast tested us; T hast tried us as
66:11 T didst bring us into the net; thou didst
66:11 us into the net; T didst lay affliction on
66:12 affliction on our loins; T didst let men ride
66:12 and through water; yet T hast brought us forth
67:4 sing for joy, for T dost judge the peoples
68:7 O God, when T didst go forth before thy
68:7 before thy people, when T didst march through the
68:9 in abundance, O God, T didst shed abroad; thou
68:9 thou didst shed abroad; T didst restore thy heritage
68:10 thy goodness, O God, T didst provide for the
68:18 T didst ascend the high mount, leading captives in
68:28 thy strength, O God, T who hast wrought for
69:5 O God, T knowest my folly; the wrongs I
69:19 T knowest my reproach, and my shame and my
69:26 they persecute him whom T hast smitten, and him
69:26 smitten, and him whom T hast wounded, they afflict
70:5 T art my help and my deliverer; O LORD,
71:3 Be T to me a rock of refuge, a
71:3 to save me, for T art my rock and
71:5 For T, O Lord, art my hope, my trust,
71:6 leaned from my birth; T art he who took
71:7 portent to many; but T art my strong refuge.
71:17 God, from my youth T hast taught me, and
71:19 T who hast done great things, O God, who
71:20 T who hast made me see many sore troubles
71:20 depths of the earth T wilt bring me up
71:21 T wilt increase my honor, and comfort me again.
71:23 my soul also, which T hast rescued.
73:18 Truly T dost set them in slippery places; thou
73:18 them in slippery places; T dost make them fall
73:23 am continually with thee; T dost hold my right
73:24 T dost guide me with thy counsel, and afterward
73:24 thy counsel, and afterward T wilt receive me to
73:27 from thee shall perish; T dost put an end
74:1 O God, why dost T cast us off for
74:2 Remember thy congregation, which T hast gotten of
74:2 gotten of old, which T hast redeemed to be
74:2 Remember Mount Zion, where T hast dwelt.
74:11 Why dost T hold back thy hand, why dost
74:11 thy hand, why dost T keep thy right hand
74:13 T didst divide the sea by thy might; thou
74:13 sea by thy might; T didst break the heads
74:14 T didst crush the heads of Leviathan, thou didst
74:14 the heads of Leviathan, T didst give him as
74:15 T didst cleave open springs and brooks; thou didst
74:15 open springs and brooks; T didst dry up ever-flowing
74:16 also the night; T hast established the luminaries
74:17 T hast fixed all the bounds of the earth;
74:17 bounds of the earth; T hast made summer and
76:4 [Selah] Glorious art T, more majestic than the
76:7 But T, terrible art thou!
76:7 But thou, terrible art T
76:8 From the heavens T didst utter judgment; the earth
76:10 the residue of wrath T wilt gird upon thee.
77:4 [Selah] T dost hold my eyelids from closing; I
77:14 T art the God who workest wonders, who hast
77:15 T didst with thy arm redeem thy people, the
77:20 T didst lead thy people like a flock by
79:5 Wilt T be angry for ever?
80:1 O Shepherd of Israel, T who leadest Joseph like
80:1 T who art enthroned upon the cherubim, shine forth
80:4 hosts, how long wilt T be angry with thy
80:5 T hast fed them with the bread of tears,
80:6 T dost make us the scorn of our neighbors;
80:8 T didst bring a vine out of Egypt; thou
80:8 vine out of Egypt; T didst drive out the
80:9 T didst clear the ground for it; it took
80:12 Why then hast T broken down its walls, so
80:17 son of man whom T hast made strong for
83:9 Do to them as T didst to Midian, as
83:15 mountains ablaze, so do T pursue them with thy
83:18 Let them know that T alone, whose name is
85:1 LORD, T wast favorable to thy land; thou didst
85:1 favorable to thy land; T didst restore the fortunes
85:2 T didst forgive the iniquity of thy people; thou
85:2 iniquity of thy people; T didst pardon all their
85:3 [Selah] T didst withdraw all thy wrath; thou didst
85:3 withdraw all thy wrath; T didst turn from thy
85:5 Wilt T be angry with us for ever?
85:5 Wilt T prolong thy anger to all generations?
85:6 Wilt T not revive us again, that thy people
86:2 T art my God;
86:5 For T, O Lord, art good and forgiving, abounding
86:7 call on thee, for T dost answer me.
86:9 All the nations T hast made shall come and
86:10 For T art great and doest wondrous things, thou
86:10 and doest wondrous things, T alone art God.
86:13 steadfast love toward me; T hast delivered my soul
86:15 But T, O Lord, art a God merciful and
86:17 put to shame because T, LORD, hast helped me
88:5 grave, like those whom T dost remember no more,
88:6 T hast put me in the depths of the
88:7 heavy upon me, and T dost overwhelm me with
88:8 [Selah] T hast caused my companions to shun me;
88:8 companions to shun me; T hast made me a
88:10 Dost T work wonders for the dead?
88:14 O LORD, why dost T cast me off?
88:14 Why dost T hide thy face from me?
88:18 T hast caused lover and friend to shun me;
89:3 T hast said, "I have made a covenant with
89:8 who is mighty as T art, O LORD, with
89:9 T dost rule the raging of the sea; when
89:9 when its waves rise, T stillest them.
89:10 T didst crush Rahab like a carcass, thou didst
89:10 Rahab like a carcass, T didst scatter thy enemies

T

89:11 that is in it, T hast founded them.
89:12 north and the south, T hast created them; Tabor
89:13 T hast a mighty arm; strong is thy hand,
89:17 For T art the glory of their strength; by
89:19 Of old T didst speak in a vision to
89:26 shall cry to me, T art my Father, my
89:38 [Selah] But now T hast cast off and rejected,
89:38 cast off and rejected, T art full of wrath
89:39 T hast renounced the covenant with thy servant; thou
89:39 covenant with thy servant; T hast defiled his crown
89:40 T hast breached all his walls; thou hast laid
89:40 breached all his walls; T hast laid his strongholds
89:42 T hast exalted the right hand of his foes;
89:42 hand of his foes; T hast made all his
89:43 Yea, T hast turned back the edge of his
89:43 of his sword, and T hast not made him
89:44 T hast removed the scepter from his hand, and
89:45 T hast cut short the days of his youth;
89:45 days of his youth; T hast covered him with
89:46 Wilt T hide thyself for ever?
89:47 is, for what vanity T hast created all the
89:49 which by thy faithfulness T didst swear to David?
90:1 LORD, T hast been our dwelling place in all
90:2 brought forth, or ever T hadst formed the earth
90:2 from everlasting to everlasting T art God.
90:3 T turnest man back to the dust, and sayest,
90:5 T dost sweep men away; they are like a
90:8 T hast set our iniquities before thee, our secret
90:15 as many days as T hast afflicted us, and
90:17 upon us, and establish T the work of our
90:17 of our hands establish T it.
92:4 For T, O LORD, hast made me glad by
92:8 destruction for ever, but T, O LORD, art on
92:10 But T hast exalted my horn like that of
92:10 of the wild ox; T hast poured over me
93:2 established from of old; T art from everlasting.
94:1 O LORD, T God of vengeance, thou God of
94:1 thou God of vengeance, T God of vengeance, shine
94:12 is the man whom T dost chasten, O LORD,
94:12 O LORD, and whom T dost teach out of
97:9 For T, O LORD, art most high over all
97:9 over all the earth; T art exalted far above
99:4 King, lover of justice, T hast established equity; thou
99:4 thou hast established equity; T hast executed justice
99:8 O LORD our God, T didst answer them; thou
99:8 thou didst answer them; T wast a forgiving God
101:2 Oh when wilt T come to me?
102:10 indignation and anger; for T hast taken me up
102:12 But T, O LORD, art enthroned for ever; thy
102:13 T wilt arise and have pity on Zion; it
102:24 midst of my days, T whose years endure throughout
102:25 Of old T didst lay the foundation of the
102:26 They will perish, but T dost endure; they will
102:26 T changest them like raiment, and they pass away;
102:27 they pass away; but T art the same, and
104:1 O LORD my God, T art very great!
104:1 T art clothed with honor and majesty,
104:5 T didst set the earth on its foundations, so
104:6 T didst cover it with the deep as with
104:8 to the place which T didst appoint for them.
104:9 T didst set a bound which they should not
104:10 T makest springs gush forth in the valleys; they
104:13 From thy lofty abode T waterest the mountains; the
104:14 T dost cause the grass to grow for the
104:19 T hast made the moon to mark the seasons;
104:20 T makest darkness, and it is night, when all
104:24 In wisdom hast T made them all; the earth
104:26 ships, and Leviathan which T didst form to sport
104:28 When T givest to them, they gather it up;
104:28 gather it up; when T openest thy hand, they
104:29 When T hidest thy face, they are dismayed; when
104:29 they are dismayed; when T takest away their breath,
104:30 When T sendest forth thy Spirit, they are created;
104:30 they are created; and T renewest the face of
106:4 me, O LORD, when T showest favor to thy
106:4 people; help me when T deliverest them;
108:11 Hast T not rejected us, O God?
108:11 T dost not go forth, O God, with our
109:21 But T, O GOD my Lord, deal on my
109:27 this is thy hand; T, O LORD, hast done
109:28 them curse, but do T bless!
116:8 For T hast delivered my soul from death, my
116:16 T hast loosed my bonds.
118:21 I thank thee that T hast answered me and
118:28 T art my God, and I will give thanks
118:28 give thanks to thee; T art my God, I
119:4 T hast commanded thy precepts to be kept diligently.
119:12 Blessed be T, O LORD; teach me thy statutes!
119:21 T dost rebuke the insolent, accursed ones, who
119:26 told of my ways, T didst answer me; teach
119:32 commandments when T enlargest my understanding!
119:49 thy servant, in which T hast made me hope.
119:65 T hast dealt well with thy servant, O LORD,
119:68 T art good and doest good; teach me thy
119:75 and that in faithfulness T hast afflicted me.
119:82 I ask, "When wilt T comfort me?"
119:84 When wilt T judge those who persecute me?
119:90 endures to all generations; T hast established the
119:93 precepts; for by them T hast given me life.
119:102 from thy ordinances, for T hast taught me.
119:114 T art my hiding place and my shield; I
119:118 T dost spurn all who go astray from thy
119:119 wicked of the earth T dost count as dross;
119:137 Righteous art T, O LORD, and right are thy
119:138 T hast appointed thy testimonies in righteousness
119:151 But T art near, O LORD, and all thy
119:152 from thy testimonies that T hast founded them for
119:171 pour forth praise that T dost teach me thy
123:1 up my eyes, O T who art enthroned in
130:3 If T, O LORD, shouldst mark iniquities, Lord, who
130:4 forgiveness with thee, that T mayest be feared.
132:8 to thy resting place, T and the ark of
138:2 and thy faithfulness; for T hast exalted above
138:3 the day I called, T didst answer me, my
138:3 my strength of soul T didst increase.
138:7 the midst of trouble, T dost preserve my life;
138:7 dost preserve my life; T dost stretch out thy
139:1 O LORD, T hast searched me and known me!
139:2 T knowest when I sit down and when I
139:2 when I rise up; T discernest my thoughts from
139:3 T searchest out my path and my lying down,
139:4 tongue, lo, O LORD, T knowest it altogether.
139:5 T dost beset me behind and before, and layest
139:8 I ascend to heaven, T art there!
139:8 my bed in Sheol, T art there!
139:13 For T didst form my inward parts, thou didst
139:13 form my inward parts, T didst knit me together
139:14 I praise thee, for T art fearful and wonderful.
139:14 T knowest me right well;
139:19 O that T wouldst slay the wicked, O God,
140:6 say to the LORD, T art my God; give
140:7 Lord, my strong deliverer, T hast covered my head
142:3 my spirit is faint, T knowest my way!
142:5 O LORD; I say, T art my refuge, my
142:7 will surround me; for T wilt deal bountifully with
143:5 meditate on all that T hast done; I muse
143:10 do thy will, for T art my God!
144:3 what is man that T dost regard him, or
144:3 son of man that T dost think of him?
145:15 look to thee, and T givest them their food
145:16 T openest thy hand, thou satisfiest the desire of
145:16 Thou openest thy hand, T satisfiest the desire of
Wis 9:2 dominion over the creatures T hast made,
9:7 T hast chosen me to be king of thy
9:8 T hast given command to build a temple on
9:8 the holy tent which T didst prepare from the
9:9 and was present when T didst make the world,
9:17 learned thy counsel, unless T hast given wisdom and
11:7 to slay the infants, T gavest them abundant water
11:8 at that time how T didst punish their enemies.
11:10 For T didst test them as a father does
11:10 does in warning, but T didst examine the ungodly
11:15 serpents and worthless animals, T didst send upon
11:20 But T hast arranged all things by measure and
11:23 But T art merciful to all, for thou canst
11:23 merciful to all, for T canst do all things,
11:23 do all things, and T dost overlook men's sins,
11:24 For T lovest all things that exist, and hast
11:24 of the things which T hast made, for thou
11:24 thou hast made, for T wouldst not have made
11:24 have made anything if T hadst hated it.
11:25 anything have endured if T hadst not willed it?
11:26 T sparest all things, for they are thine, O
12:2 Therefore T dost correct little by little those who
12:4 in thy holy land T didst hate for their
12:6 who murder helpless lives, T didst will to destroy
12:8 But even these T didst spare, since they were
12:9 little by little, though T wast not unable to
12:10 them little by little T gavest them a chance
12:10 chance to repent, though T wast not unaware that
12:11 of any one that T didst leave them unpunished
12:12 will say, "What hast T done?" Or will resist

12:12 destruction of nations which T didst make?
12:13 all men, to whom T shouldst prove that thou
12:13 thou shouldst prove that T hast not judged unjustly;
12:14 thee about those whom T hast punished.
12:15 T art righteous and rulest all things righteously,
12:17 For T dost show thy strength when men doubt
12:18 T who art sovereign in strength dost judge with
12:18 and with great forbearance T dost govern us; for
12:18 dost govern us; for T hast power to act
12:18 power to act whenever T dost choose.
12:19 Through such works T has taught thy people that
12:19 must be kind, and T hast filled thy sons
12:19 with good hope, because T givest repentance for sins.
12:20 For if T didst punish with such great care
12:21 wickedness, with what strictness T hast judged thy
12:21 sons, to whose fathers T gavest oaths and covenants
12:22 So while chastening us T scourgest our enemies ten
12:23 of life lived unrighteously T didst torment through
12:25 as to thoughtless children, T didst send thy judgment
14:3 steers its course, because T hast given it a
14:4 the waves, showing that T canst save from every
15:1 But T, our God, art kind and true, patient,
16:2 Instead of this punishment T didst show kindness to
16:2 to thy people, and T didst prepare quails to
16:8 And by this also T didst convince our enemies
16:8 enemies that it is T who deliverest from every
16:13 For T hast power over life and death; thou
16:13 over life and death; T dost lead men down
16:20 Instead of these things T didst give thy people
16:20 and without their toil T didst supply them from
16:26 that thy sons, whom T didst love, O Lord,
18:3 Therefore T didst provide a flaming pillar of fire
18:5 been exposed and rescued, T didst in punishment
18:5 of their children; and T didst destroy them all
18:8 same means by which T didst punish our enemies
18:8 didst punish our enemies T didst call us to
19:22 in everything, O Lord, T hast exalted and glorified
19:22 glorified thy people; and T hast not neglected to
Sir 36:4 As in us T hast been sanctified before them,
36:4 so in them be T magnified before us;
36:12 name, upon Israel, whom T hast likened to a
36:15 witness to those whom T didst create in the
36:17 earth will know that T art the Lord, the
51:2 to thy name, for T hast been my protector
51:2 those who stood by T wast my helper
51:8 from of old, that T dost deliver those who
51:12 prayer was heard, for T didst save me from
Is 2:6 For T hast rejected thy people, the house of
9:3 T hast multiplied the nation, thou hast increased its
9:3 hast multiplied the nation, T hast increased its joy;
9:4 rod of his oppressor, T hast broken as on
12:1 O LORD, for though T wast angry with me,
12:1 anger turned away, and T didst comfort me.
25:1 O LORD, T art my God; I will exalt
25:1 praise thy name; for T hast done wonderful things,
25:2 For T hast made the city a heap, the
25:4 For T hast been a stronghold to the poor,
25:5 T dost subdue the noise of the aliens; as
26:3 T dost keep him in perfect peace, whose mind
26:7 the righteous is level; T dost make smooth the
26:12 O LORD, T wilt ordain peace for us, thou
26:12 ordain peace for us, T hast wrought for us
26:14 arise; to that end T hast visited them with
26:15 But T hast increased the nation, O LORD, thou
26:15 the nation, O LORD, T hast increased the nation;
26:15 hast increased the nation; T art glorified; thou hast
26:15 nation; thou art glorified; T hast enlarged all the
26:19 land of the shades T wilt let it fall.
27:8 by measure, by exile T didst contend with them;
37:16 enthroned above the cherubim, T art the God, thou
37:16 thou art the God, T alone, of all the
37:16 kingdoms of the earth; T hast made heaven and
37:20 earth may know that T alone art the LORD."
38:12 from day to night T dost bring me to
38:13 from day to night T dost bring me to
38:14 I am oppressed; be T my security!
38:17 had great bitterness; but T hast held back my
38:17 pit of destruction, for T hast cast all my
44:17 says, "Deliver me, for T art my god!"
45:15 Truly, T art a God who hidest thyself, O
51:9 Was it not T that didst cut Rahab in
51:10 Was it not T that didst dry up the
58:3 have we fasted, and T seest it not?
58:3 we humbled ourselves, and T takest no knowledge of
63:14 So T didst lead thy people, to make for
63:16 For T art our Father, though Abraham does not
63:16 does not acknowledge us; T, O LORD, art our
63:17 O LORD, why dost T make us err from
63:19 like those over whom T hast never ruled, like
64:1 O that T wouldst rend the heavens and come
64:3 When T didst terrible things which we looked not
64:3 we looked not for, T camest down, the mountains
64:5 T meetest him that joyfully works righteousness,
64:5 Behold, T wast angry, and we sinned; in our
64:7 hold of thee; for T hast hid thy face
64:8 Yet, O LORD, T art our Father; we are
64:8 are the clay, and T art our potter; we
64:12 Wilt T restrain thyself at these things, O LORD?
64:12 Wilt T keep silent, and afflict us sorely?
Jer 3:4 to me, 'My father, T art the friend of
3:22 come to thee; for T art the LORD our
4:10 "Ah, Lord GOD, surely T hast utterly deceived this
5:3 T hast smitten them, but they felt no anguish;
5:3 they felt no anguish; T hast consumed them, but
10:6 like thee, O LORD; T art great, and thy
10:24 in thy anger, lest T bring me to nothing.
11:18 and I knew; then T didst show me their
12:1 Righteous art T, O LORD, when I complain to
12:2 T plantest them, and they take root; they grow
12:2 and bring forth fruit; T art near in their
12:3 But T, O LORD, knowest me; thou seest me,
12:3 O LORD, knowest me; T seest me, and triest
14:8 O T hope of Israel, its savior in time
14:8 of trouble, why shouldst T be like a stranger
14:9 Why shouldst T be like a man confused, like
14:9 Yet T, O LORD, art in the midst of
14:19 Hast T utterly rejected Judah?
14:19 Why hast T smitten us so that there is
14:22 Art T not he, O LORD our God?
14:22 hope on thee, for T doest all these things.
15:15 O LORD, T knowest; remember me and visit me,
15:17 was upon me, for T hadst filled me with
15:18 Wilt T be to me like a deceitful brook,
17:14 shall be saved; for T art my praise.
17:16 the day of disaster, T knowest; that which came
17:17 a terror to me; T art my refuge in
18:22 from their houses, when T bringest the marauder
18:23 Yet, T, O LORD, knowest all their plotting to
20:7 O LORD, T hast deceived me, and I was
20:7 and I was deceived; T art stronger than I,
20:7 stronger than I, and T hast prevailed.
31:18 have heard Ephraim bemoaning, T hast chastened
31:18 may be restored, for T art the LORD my
32:17 It is T who hast made the heavens and
32:21 T didst bring thy people Israel out of the
32:22 with great terror; and T gavest them this land,
32:22 them this land, which T didst swear to their
32:23 did nothing of all T didst command them to
32:23 Therefore T hast made all this evil come upon
32:24 What T didst speak has come to pass, and
32:24 to pass, and behold, T seest it.
32:25 Yet T, O Lord GOD, hast said to me,
51:62 and say, 'O LORD, T hast said concerning this
51:62 concerning this place that T wilt cut it off,
Lam 1:10 her sanctuary, those whom T didst forbid to enter
1:21 they are glad that T hast done it.
1:21 Bring T the day thou hast announced, and let
1:21 Bring thou the day T hast announced, and let
1:22 deal with them as T hast dealt with me
2:20 With whom hast T dealt thus?
2:21 day of thy anger T hast slain them, slaughtering
2:22 T didst invite as to the day of an
3:42 transgressed and rebelled, and T hast not forgiven.
3:43 T hast wrapped thyself with anger and pursued us,
3:44 us, slaying without pity; T hast wrapped thyself with
3:45 T hast made us offscouring and refuse among the
3:56 depths of the pit; T didst hear my plea,
3:57 my cry for help!' T didst come near when
3:57 I called on thee; T didst say, 'Do not
3:58 say, 'Do not fear!' T hast taken up my
3:58 my cause, O Lord, T hast redeemed my life.
3:59 T hast seen the wrong done to me, O
3:59 me, O LORD; judge T my cause.
3:60 T hast seen all their vengeance, all their devices
3:61 T hast heard their taunts, O LORD, all their
3:64 T wilt requite them, O LORD, according to the
3:65 T wilt give them dullness of heart; thy curse
3:66 T wilt pursue them in anger and destroy them
5:19 But T, O LORD, dost reign for ever; thy
5:20 Why dost T forget us for ever, why dost
5:20 for ever, why dost T so long forsake us?
5:22 Or hast T utterly rejected us?

5:22 Art T exceedingly angry with us?
Bar 2:13 among the nations where T hast scattered us.
2:15 earth may know that T art the Lord our
2:20 For T hast sent thy anger and thy wrath
2:20 wrath upon us, as T didst declare by thy
2:24 king of Babylon; and T hast confirmed thy words,
2:24 confirmed thy words, which T didst speak by thy
2:26 called by thy name T hast made as it
2:27 "'Yet T hast dealt with us, O Lord our
2:28 thy great compassion, as T didst speak by thy
2:28 on the day when T didst command him to
3:3 For T art enthroned for ever, and we are
3:6 For T art the Lord our God, and thee,
3:7 For T hast put the fear of thee in
3:8 in our exile where T hast scattered us, to
6:6 your heart, "It is T, O Lord, whom we
Ezek 9:8 wilt T destroy all that remains of Israel in
9:11 "I have done as T didst command me."
11:13 wilt T make a full end of the remnant
37:3 answered, "O Lord GOD, T knowest."
Dan 2:23 thanks and praise, for T hast given me wisdom
2:23 asked of thee, for T hast made known to
3:26 and said: "Blessed art T, O Lord, God of
3:27 For T art just in all that thou hast
3:27 just in all that T hast done to us,
3:28 T hast executed true judgments in all that thou
3:28 judgments in all that T hast brought upon us
3:28 in truth and justice T hast brought all this
3:30 or done them, as T hast commanded us that
3:31 So all that T hast brought upon us, and
3:31 us, and all that T hast done to us,
3:31 hast done to us, T hast done in true
3:32 T hast given us into the hands of lawless
3:36 holy one, to whom T didst promise to make
3:45 Let them know that T art the Lord, the
3:52 furnace, saying: "Blessed art T, O Lord, God of
3:54 for ever; Blessed art T in the temple of
3:55 Blessed art T, who sittest upon cherubim and lookest
3:56 Blessed art T upon the throne of thy kingdom
3:57 Blessed art T in the firmament of heaven and
4:35 his hand or say to him, "What doest T
9:7 the lands to which T hast driven them, because
13:43 they come to be, T knowest that these men
14:38 And Daniel said, T hast remembered me, O God,
14:41 with a loud voice, T art great, O Lord
Hos 2:23 and he shall say T art my God.'"
9:14 O LORD--what wilt T give?
Jon 1:14 us innocent blood; for T, O LORD, hast done
2:2 Sheol I cried, and T didst hear my voice.
2:3 For T didst cast me into the deep, into
2:6 me for ever; yet T didst bring up my
4:2 for I knew that T art a gracious God
Mic 7:19 T wilt cast all our sins into the depths
7:20 T wilt show faithfulness to Jacob and steadfast love
7:20 love to Abraham, as T hast sworn to our
Hab 1:2 cry for help, and T wilt not hear?
1:2 and T wilt not save?
1:3 Why dost T make me see wrongs and look
1:12 Art T not from everlasting, O LORD my God,
1:12 O LORD, T hast ordained them as a judgment;
1:12 as a judgment; and T, O Rock, hast established
1:13 T who art of purer eyes than to behold
1:13 on wrong, why dost T look on faithless men,
1:14 For T makest men like the fish of the
3:8 against the sea, when T didst ride upon thy
3:9 T didst strip the sheath from thy bow, and
3:9 Selah T didst cleave the earth with rivers.
3:12 T didst bestride the earth in fury, thou didst
3:12 the earth in fury, T didst trample the nations
3:13 T wentest forth for the salvation of thy people,
3:13 T didst crush the head of the wicked, laying
3:14 Selah T didst pierce with thy shafts the head
3:15 T didst trample the sea with thy horses, the
Zech 1:12 hosts, how long wilt T have no mercy on
1:12 of Judah, against which T hast had indignation these
Mal 1:2 you say, "How hast T loved us?" "Is not
1Mac 3:52 us to destroy us; T knowest what they plot
3:53 to withstand them, if T dost not help us?"
4:30 prayed, saying, "Blessed art T, O Savior of Israel,
4:31 So do T hem in this army by the
7:37 they wept and said, T didst choose this house
2Mac 1:27 the Gentiles know that T art our God.
14:35 hast need of nothing, T wast pleased that there
15:22 these words: "O Lord, T didst send thy angel
Mt 11:25 heaven and earth, that T hast hidden these things
21:16 babes and sucklings T hast brought perfect praise'?"
26:39 I will, but as T wilt."
27:46 my God, why hast T forsaken me?"
Mk 1:11 voice came from heaven, T art my beloved Son;
14:36 I will, but what T wilt."
15:33 my God, why hast T forsaken me?"
Lk 2:29 said, "Lord, now lettest T thy servant depart in
2:31 seen thy salvation which T hast prepared in the
3:22 voice came from heaven, T art my beloved Son;
10:21 heaven and earth, that T hast hidden these things
22:42 and prayed, "Father, if T art willing, remove this
Jn 11:41 I thank thee that T hast heard me.
11:42 I knew that T hearest me always, but I
11:42 they may believe that T didst send me."
17:2 may glorify thee, since T hast given him power
17:2 life to all whom T hast given him.
17:3 and Jesus Christ whom T hast sent.
17:4 accomplished the work which T gavest me to do;
17:5 and now, Father, glorify T me in thy own
17:6 to the men whom T gavest me out of
17:6 thine they were, and T gavest them to me,
17:7 know that everything that T hast given me is
17:8 them the words which T gavest me, and they
17:8 they have believed that T didst send me.
17:9 but for those whom T hast given me, for
17:11 in thy name, which T hast given me, that
17:12 in thy name, which T hast given me; I
17:15 do not pray that T shouldst take them out
17:15 the world, but that T shouldst keep them from
17:18 As T didst send me into the world, so
17:21 be one; even as T, Father, art in me,
17:21 world may believe that T hast sent me.
17:22 The glory which T hast given me I have
17:23 I in them and T in me, that they
17:23 world may know that T hast sent me and
17:23 loved them even as T hast loved me.
17:24 that they also, whom T hast given me, may
17:24 behold my glory which T hast given me in
17:25 and these know that T hast sent me.
17:26 the love with which T hast loved me may
18:9 spoken, "Of those whom T gavest me I lost
Acts 1:24 one of these two T hast chosen
2:27 For T wilt not abandon my soul to Hades,
2:28 T hast made known to me the ways of
2:28 the ways of life; T wilt make me full
4:27 holy servant Jesus, whom T didst anoint, both Herod
4:30 with all boldness, while T stretchest out thy hand
13:33 in the second psalm, T art my Son, today
13:35 also in another psalm, T wilt not let thy
Rom 3:4 it is written, "That T mayest be justified in
3:4 words, and prevail when T art judged."
Heb 1:5 did God ever say, T art my Son, today
1:9 T hast loved righteousness and hated lawlessness;
1:10 And, T, Lord, didst found the earth in the
1:11 they will perish, but T remainest; they will all
1:12 garment, like a mantle T wilt roll them up,
1:12 But T art the same, and thy years will
2:6 "What is man that T art mindful of him,
2:6 son of man, that T carest for him?
2:7 T didst make him for a little while lower
2:7 lower than the angels, T hast crowned him with
5:5 who said to him, T art my Son, today
5:6 also in another place, T art a priest for
7:17 is witnessed of him, T art a priest for
7:21 not change his mind, T art a priest for
10:5 said, "Sacrifices and offerings T hast not desired, but
10:5 but a body hast T prepared for me;
10:6 offerings and sin offerings T hast taken no pleasure.
10:8 When he said above, T hast neither desired nor
Rev 4:11 throne, singing, "Worthy art T, our Lord and God,
4:11 honor and power, for T didst create all things,
5:9 song, saying, "Worthy art T to take the scroll
5:9 open its seals, for T wast slain and by
6:10 true, how long before T wilt judge and avenge
11:17 and who wast, that T hast taken thy great
15:4 For T alone art holy.
16:5 water say, "Just art T in these thy judgments,
16:5 in these thy judgments, T who art and wast,
16:6 saints and prophets, and T hast given them blood
18:10 T great city, thou mighty city, Babylon!
18:10 thou great city, T mighty city, Babylon!

THOUGH (289)

Ex 7:3 harden Pharaoh's heart, and T I multiply my signs
Lev 5:1 adjuration to testify and T he is a witness,
5:17 not to be done, T he does not know
13:55 has not changed color, T the disease has not

T

	26:37	to escape a sword, T none pursues; and you
Num	5:13	and she is undetected T she has defiled herself,
	5:14	jealous of his wife, T she has not defiled
	5:20	you have gone astray, T you are under your
	5:29	jealousy, when a wife, T under her husband's
	18:27	reckoned to you as T it were the grain
	22:18	the servants of Balak, T Balak were to give
	35:23	so that he died, T he was not his
Deut	15:22	may eat it, as T it were a gazelle
	19:6	and wound him mortally, T the man did not
	21:18	of his mother, and, T they chastise him, will
	22:24	not cry for help T she was in the
	22:27	the open country, and T the betrothed young woman
	29:19	'I shall be safe, T I walk in the
Josh	5:5	T all the people who came out had been
	17:18	shall be yours, for T it is a forest,
	17:18	drive out the Canaanites, T they have chariots of
	17:18	chariots of iron, and T they are strong."
Ruth	2:13	kindly to your maidservant, T I am not one
1Sam	14:39	lives who saves Israel, T it be in Jonathan
	15:17	And Samuel said, T you are little in your
	20:20	side of it, as T I shot at a
	24:11	not sinned against you, T you hunt my life
2Sam	3:39	am this day weak, T anointed king; these men
2Kgs	3:2	sight of the LORD, T not like his father
	25:4	by the king's garden, T the Chaldeans were around
1Chr	5:2	according to the birthright; T Judah became strong
	26:10	Shimri the chief (for T he was not the
2Chr	24:24	T the army of the Syrians had come with
	30:19	of his fathers, even T not according to the
Ezra	2:59	Cherub, Addan, and Immer, T they could not prove
	3:12	this house being laid, T many shouted aloud for
Neh	1:9	commandments and do them, T your dispersed be
Tob	14:5	the house of God, T it will not be
Esth	4:16	go to the king, T it is against the
	11:10	from their cry, as T from a tiny spring
Job	8:7	And T your beginning was small, your latter days
	9:15	T I am innocent, I cannot answer him; I
	9:20	T I am innocent, my own mouth would condemn
	9:20	mouth would condemn me; T I am blameless, he
	10:19	me, and were as T I had not been,
	14:8	T its root grow old in the earth, and
	20:6	T his height mount up to the heavens, and
	20:12	T wickedness is sweet in his mouth, though he
	20:12	sweet in his mouth, T he hides it under
	20:13	it under his tongue, T he is loath to
	27:16	T he heap up silver like dust, and pile
	33:14	way, and in two, T man does not perceive
	34:6	my wound is incurable, T I am without transgression.'
	39:16	they were not hers; T her labor be in
	40:23	frightened; he is confident T Jordan rushes against
	41:26	T the sword reaches him, it does not avail;
Ps	23:4	Even T I walk through the valley of the
	27:3	T a host encamp against me, my heart shall
	27:3	heart shall not fear; T war arise against me,
	35:14	on my bosom, as T I grieved for my
	37:10	will be no more; T you look well at
	37:24	whose way he delights; T he fall, he shall
	37:36	he was no more; T I sought him, he
	44:17	has come upon us, T we have not forgotten
	46:2	we will not fear T the earth should change,
	46:2	the earth should change, T the mountains shake in
	46:3	heart of the sea; T its waters roar and
	46:3	waters roar and foam, T the mountains tremble with
	49:11	places to all generations, T they named lands their
	49:18	T, while he lives, he counts himself happy, and
	49:18	counts himself happy, and T a man gets praise
	68:13	home divide the spoil, T they stay among the
	92:7	cannot understand this: that, T the wicked sprout like
	95:9	me to the proof, T they had seen my
	119:23	Even T princes sit plotting against me, thy servant
	119:61	T the cords of the wicked ensnare me, I
	138:6	For T the LORD is high, he regards the
	138:7	T I walk in the midst of trouble, thou
Prov	6:35	compensation, nor be appeased T you multiply gifts.
	26:26	abominations in his heart; T his hatred be covered
	29:19	is not disciplined, for T he understands, he will
Eccl	4:12	And T a man might prevail against one who
	4:14	longer take advice, even T he had gone from
	6:6	Even T he should live a thousand years twice
	8:12	T a sinner does evil a hundred times and
	8:17	find it out; even T a wise man claims
	9:16	is better than might, T the poor man's wisdom
	10:14	A fool multiplies words, T no man knows what
Wis	2:2	we shall be as T we had never been;
	3:4	For T in the sight of men they were
	4:7	But the righteous man, T he die early, will
	7:27	T she is but one, she can do all
	8:10	presence of the elders, T I am young.
	11:9	when they were tried, T they were being disciplined
	11:14	For T they had mockingly rejected him who long
	12:9	them little by little, T thou wast not unable
	12:10	a chance to repent, T thou wast not unaware
	14:11	the heathen idols, because, T part of what God
	14:17	the absent one as T present.
	15:15	heathen idols were gods, T these have neither the
	17:10	even at the air, T it nowhere could be
	18:2	that thy holy ones, T previously wronged, were doing
	18:13	For T they had disbelieved everything because of
	19:2	future actions, that, T they themselves had permitted
Sir	40:6	in his sleep, as T he were on watch,
	42:10	she prove unfaithful, or, T married, lest she be
	43:27	T we speak much we cannot reach the end,
	44:10	who have perished as T they had not lived;
	44:10	they have become as T they had not been
Is	1:15	eyes from you; even T you make many prayers,
	1:18	together, says the LORD: T your sins are like
	1:18	as white as snow; T they are red like
	6:13	And T a tenth remain in it, it will
	10:22	For T your people Israel be as the sand
	12:1	thee, O LORD, for T thou wast angry with
	17:10	of your refuge; therefore, T you plant pleasant plants
	17:11	of an alien god, T you make them grow
	22:3	were found were captured, T they had fled far
	30:4	For T his officials are at Zoan and his
	30:20	And T the Lord give you the bread of
	45:4	name, I surname you, T you do not know
	45:5	God; I gird you, T you do not know
	63:16	thou art our Father, T Abraham does not know
Jer	2:11	changed its gods, even T they are no gods?
	2:22	T you wash yourself with lye and use much
	5:2	T they say, "As the LORD lives," yet they
	5:22	which it cannot pass; T the waves toss, they
	5:22	toss, they cannot prevail, T they roar, they cannot
	11:11	which they cannot escape; T they cry to me,
	12:6	you; believe them not, T they speak fair words
	14:7	T our iniquities testify against us, act, O LORD,
	14:12	T they fast, I will not hear their cry,
	14:12	hear their cry, and T they offer burnt offering
	15:1	LORD said to me, T Moses and Samuel stood
	22:24	live, says the LORD, T Coniah the son of
	26:5	send to you urgently, T you have not heeded,
	31:32	covenant which they broke, T I was their husband,
	32:5	him, says the LORD; T you fight against the
	32:25	money and get witnesses"—T the city is given
	32:33	not their face; and T I have taught them
	32:35	and daughters to Molech, T I did not command
	46:23	forest, says the LORD, T it is impenetrable, because
	49:16	T you make your nest as high as the
	50:11	T you rejoice, though you exult, O plunderers of
	50:11	"Though you rejoice, T you exult, O plunderers of
	50:11	plunderers of my heritage, T you are wanton as
	51:53	T Babylon should mount up to heaven, and though
	51:53	up to heaven, and T she should fortify her
Lam	3:8	heavy chains on me; T I call and cry
	3:32	off for ever, but, T he cause grief, he
Bar	6:14	god holds a scepter, T unable to destroy any
	6:18	offended a king, as T he were sentenced to
	6:19	they light for themselves, T their gods can see
	6:41	man may speak, as T Bel were able to
Ezek	2:6	afraid of their words, T briers and thorns are
	8:18	I have pity; and T they cry in my
	11:16	says the Lord GOD: T I removed them far-off
	11:16	among the nations, and T I scattered them among
	12:3	Perhaps they will understand, T they are a rebellious
	14:18	it man and beast; T these three men were
	15:7	my face against them; T they escape from the
	26:21	shall be no more; T you be sought for,
	28:2	man, and no god, T you consider yourself as
	28:9	those who slay you, T you are but a
	33:13	T I say to the righteous that he shall
	33:14	Again, T I say to the wicked, 'You shall
Dan	3:39	we be accepted, as T it were with burnt
	5:22	not humbled your heart, T you knew all this,
	11:33	shall make many understand, T they shall fall by
	13:53	the guilty go free, T the Lord said, 'Do
Hos	3:1	the people of Israel, T they turn to other
	4:15	T you play the harlot, O Israel, let not
	8:10	T they hire allies among the nations, I will
	9:16	Even T they bring forth, I will slay their
	13:15	T he may flourish as the reed plant, the
Amos	5:22	Even T you offer me your burnt offerings and

THOUGHTFUL (3)

THOUGHTLESS (3)

THOUGHTS (62)

T

2Mac 2:2 led astray in their T upon seeing the gold
Mt 9:4 But Jesus, knowing their T, said, "Why do you
12:25 Knowing their T, he said to them, "Every kingdom
15:19 the heart come evil T, murder, adultery, fornication,
Mk 7:20 of man, come evil T, fornication, theft, murder,
Lk 2:35 own soul also), that T out of many hearts
6:8 But he knew their T, and he said to
11:17 But he, knowing their T, said to them, "Every
Rom 2:15 and their conflicting T accuse or perhaps excuse
1Cor 2:11 person knows a man's T except the spirit of
2:11 no one comprehends the T of God except the
3:20 Lord knows that the T of the wise are
2Cor 11:3 by his cunning, your T will be led astray
Heb 4:12 marrow, and discerning the T and intentions of the
Jas 2:4 among yourselves, and become judges with evil T

THOUSAND (596)

Gen 20:16 given your brother a T pieces of silver; it
Ex 12:37 Succoth, about six hundred T men on foot, besides
32:28 that day about three T men.
38:25 talents and a T seven hundred and seventy-five
38:26 six hundred and three T, five hundred and fifty
38:28 And of the T seven hundred and seventy-five shekels
38:29 seventy talents, and two T and four hundred shekels;
Lev 26:8 you shall chase ten T; and your enemies shall
Num 1:21 of Reuben was forty-six T five hundred.
1:23 of Simeon was fifty-nine T three hundred.
1:25 of Gad was forty-five T six hundred and fifty.
1:27 of Judah was seventy-four T six hundred.
1:29 of Issachar was fifty-four T four hundred.
1:31 of Zebulun was fifty-seven T four hundred.
1:33 of Ephraim was forty T five hundred.
1:35 of Manasseh was thirty-two T two hundred.
1:37 of Benjamin was thirty-five T four hundred.
1:39 of Dan was sixty-two T seven hundred.
1:41 of Asher was forty-one T five hundred.
1:43 of Naphtali was fifty-three T four hundred.
1:46 six hundred and three T five hundred and fifty.
2:4 as numbered being seventy-four T six hundred.
2:6 as numbered being fifty-four T four hundred.
2:8 as numbered being fifty-seven T four hundred.
2:9 a hundred and eighty-six T four hundred.
2:11 as numbered being forty-six T five hundred.
2:13 as numbered being fifty-nine T three hundred.
2:15 as numbered being forty-five T six hundred and fifty.
2:16 a hundred and fifty-one T four hundred and fifty.
2:19 as numbered being forty T five hundred.
2:21 as numbered being thirty-two T two hundred.
2:23 as numbered being thirty-five T four hundred.
2:24 a hundred and eight T one hundred.
2:26 as numbered being sixty-two T seven hundred.
2:28 as numbered being forty-one T five hundred.
2:30 as numbered being fifty-three T four hundred.
2:31 a hundred and fifty-seven T six hundred.
2:32 six hundred and three T five hundred and fifty.
3:22 and upward was seven T five hundred.
3:28 upward, there were eight T six hundred, attending to
3:34 and upward was six T two hundred.
3:39 from a month old and upward, were twenty-two T
3:43 as numbered were twenty-two T two hundred and
3:50 took the money, one T three hundred and sixty-five
4:36 by families was two T seven hundred and fifty.
4:40 fathers' houses was two T six hundred and thirty.
4:44 by families was three T two hundred.
4:48 of them were eight T five hundred and eighty.
7:85 of the vessels two T four hundred shekels according
10:36 LORD, to the ten T thousands of Israel."
11:21 am number six hundred T on foot; and thou
16:49 the plague were fourteen T seven hundred, besides
25:9 those that died by the plague were twenty-four T
26:7 their number was forty-three T seven hundred and
26:14 of the Simeonites, twenty-two T two hundred.
26:18 to their number, forty T five hundred.
26:22 to their number, seventy-six T five hundred.
26:25 to their number, sixty-four T three hundred.
26:27 to their number, sixty T five hundred.
26:34 their number was fifty-two T seven hundred.
26:37 to their number, thirty-two T five hundred.
26:41 their number was forty-five T six hundred.
26:43 their number, were sixty-four T four hundred.
26:47 to their number, fifty-three T four hundred.
26:50 their number was forty-five T four hundred.
26:51 six hundred and one T seven hundred and thirty.
26:62 of them were twenty-three T, every male from a
31:4 You shall send a T from each of the
31:5 thousands of Israel, a T from each tribe, twelve
31:5 from each tribe, twelve T armed for war.
31:6 to the war, a T from each tribe, together
31:32 six hundred and seventy-five T sheep,
31:33 seventy-five thousand sheep, seventy-two T cattle,
31:34 seventy-two thousand cattle, sixty-one T asses,
31:35 thousand asses, and thirty-two T persons in all,
31:36 three hundred and thirty-seven T five hundred sheep,
31:38 The cattle were thirty-six T, of which the LORD's
31:39 The asses were thirty T five hundred, of which
31:40 The persons were sixteen T, of which the LORD's
31:43 three hundred and thirty-seven T five hundred sheep,
31:44 five hundred sheep, thirty-six T cattle,
31:45 thousand cattle, and thirty T five hundred asses,
31:46 hundred asses, and sixteen T persons--
31:52 of hundreds, was sixteen T seven hundred and fifty
35:4 the city outward a T cubits all round.
35:5 the east side two T cubits, and for the
35:5 the south side two T cubits, and for the
35:5 the west side two T cubits, and for the
35:5 the north side two T cubits, the city being
Deut 1:11 fathers, make you a T times as many as
7:9 his commandments, to a T generations,
32:30 should one chase a T, and two put ten
32:30 and two put ten T to flight, unless their
Josh 3:4 distance of about two T cubits; do not come
4:13 bidden them; about forty T ready armed for war
7:3 about two or three T men go up and
7:4 So about three T went up there from the
8:3 and Joshua chose thirty T mighty men of valor,
8:12 he took about five T men, and set them
8:25 and women, were twelve T, all the people of
23:10 puts to flight a T, since it is the
Judg 1:4 and they defeated ten T of them at Bezek.
3:29 that time about ten T of the Moabites, all
4:6 Mount Tabor, taking ten T from the tribe of
4:10 to Kedesh; and ten T men went up at
4:14 Mount Tabor with ten T men following him.
5:8 be seen among forty T in Israel?
7:3 Gideon tested them; twenty-two T returned, and en
7:3 thousand returned, and en T remained.
8:10 their army, about fifteen T men, all who were
8:10 a hundred and twenty T men who drew the
8:26 he requested was one T seven hundred shekels of
9:49 also died, about a T men and women.
12:6 at that time forty-two T of the Ephraimites.
15:11 Then three T men of Judah went down to
15:15 it he slew a T men.
15:16 have I slain a T men."
16:27 there were about three T men and women, who
20:2 of God, four hundred T men on foot that
20:10 a hundred of a T, and a thousand of
20:10 a thousand, and a T of ten thousand, to
20:10 a thousand of ten T, to bring provisions for
20:15 on that day twenty-six T men that drew the
20:17 Benjamin, mustered four hundred T men that drew
20:21 on that day twenty-two T men of the Israelites.
20:25 to the ground eighteen T men of the people
20:34 came against Gibe-ah ten T picked men out of
20:35 of Israel destroyed twenty-five T one hundred men of
20:44 Eighteen T men of Benjamin fell, all of them
20:45 rock of Rimmon; five T men of them were
20:45 to Gidom, and two T men of them were
20:46 of Benjamin were twenty-five T men that drew the
21:10 congregation sent thither twelve T of their bravest
1Sam 4:2 who slew about four T men on the field
4:10 fell of Israel thirty T foot soldiers.
11:8 Israel were three hundred T, and the men of
11:8 hundred thousand, and the men of Judah thirty T
13:2 Saul chose three T men of Israel; two thousand
13:2 men of Israel; two T were with Saul in
13:2 of Bethel, and a T were with Jonathan in
13:5 fight with Israel, thirty T chariots, and six thousand
13:5 thousand chariots, and six T horsemen, and troops
15:4 in Telaim, two hundred T men on foot, and
15:4 on foot, and ten T men of Judah.
17:5 the coat was five T shekels of bronze.
17:18 these ten cheeses to the commander of their T
18:13 a commander of a T; and he went out
24:2 Then Saul took three T chosen men out of
25:2 rich; he had three T sheep and a thousand
25:2 thousand sheep and a T goats.
26:2 of Ziph, with three T chosen men of Israel,
2Sam 6:1 gathered all the chosen men of Israel, thirty T
8:4 took from him a T and seven hundred horsemen,
8:4 horsemen, and twenty T foot soldiers; and David
8:5 Zobah, David slew twenty-two T men of the Syrians.

8:13 returned, he slew eighteen T Edomites in the Valley
10:6 Syrians of Zobah, twenty T foot soldiers, and the
10:6 of Maacah with a T men, and the men
10:6 men of Tob, twelve T men.
10:18 chariots, and forty T horsemen, and wounded
17:1 "Let me choose twelve T men, and I will
18:3 you are worth ten T of us; therefore it
18:7 on that day, twenty T men.
18:12 the weight of a T pieces of silver, I
19:17 with him were a T men from Benjamin.
24:9 there were eight hundred T valiant men who drew
24:9 and the men of Judah were five hundred T
24:15 Dan to Beer-sheba seventy T men.
1Kgs 3:4 used to offer a T burnt offerings upon that
4:26 Solomon also had forty T stalls of horses for
4:26 his chariots, and twelve T horsemen.
4:32 He also uttered three T proverbs; and his songs
4:32 his songs were a T and five.
5:11 Solomon gave Hiram twenty T cors of wheat as
5:11 his household, and twenty T cors of beaten oil.
5:13 the levy numbered thirty T men.
5:14 them to Lebanon, ten T a month in relays;
5:15 Solomon also had seventy T burden-bearers and
5:15 thousand burden-bearers and eighty T hewers of
5:16 besides Solomon's three T three hundred chief
7:26 lily; it held two T baths.
8:63 to the LORD twenty-two T oxen and a hundred
8:63 a hundred and twenty T sheep.
10:26 hundred chariots and twelve T horsemen, whom he
12:21 a hundred and eighty T chosen warriors, to fight
19:18 I will leave seven T in Israel, all the
20:15 he mustered all the people of Israel, seven T
20:29 the Syrians a hundred T foot soldiers in one
20:30 wall fell upon twenty-seven T men that were left.
2Kgs 3:4 of Israel a hundred T lambs, and the wool
3:4 wool of a hundred T rams.
5:5 talents of silver, six T shekels of gold, and
13:7 ten chariots and ten T footmen; for the king
14:7 He killed ten T Edomites in the Valley of
15:19 Menahem gave Pul a T talents of silver, that
18:23 will give you two T horses, if you are
19:35 a hundred and eighty-five T in the camp of
24:14 men of valor, ten T captives, and all the
24:16 men of valor, seven T, and the craftsmen and
24:16 and the smiths, one T, all of them strong
1Chr 5:18 expert in war, forty-four T seven hundred and sixty,
5:21 off their livestock: fifty T of their camels, two
5:21 two hundred and fifty T sheep, two thousand asses,
5:21 fifty thousand sheep, two T asses, and a hundred
5:21 asses, and a hundred T men alive.
7:2 of David being twenty-two T six hundred.
7:4 army for war, thirty-six T, for they had many
7:5 were in all eighty-seven T mighty warriors, enrolled
7:7 by genealogies was twenty-two T and thirty-four.
7:9 mighty warriors, was twenty T two hundred.
7:11 mighty warriors, seventeen T and two hundred, ready
7:40 in war, was twenty-six T men.
9:13 their fathers' houses, one T seven hundred and sixty,
12:14 over a hundred and the greater over a T
12:24 and spear were six T eight hundred armed troops.
12:25 valor for war, seven T one hundred.
12:26 Of the Levites four T six hundred.
12:27 and with him three T seven hundred.
12:29 kinsmen of Saul, three T, of whom the majority
12:30 Of the Ephraimites twenty T eight hundred, mighty
12:31 half-tribe of Manasseh eighteen T, who were
12:33 Of Zebulun fifty T seasoned troops, equipped for
12:34 Of Naphtali a T commanders with whom were thirty-
12:34 with whom were thirty-seven T men armed with
12:35 Of the Danites twenty-eight T six hundred men
12:36 Of Asher forty T seasoned troops ready for battle.
12:37 one hundred and twenty T men armed with all
16:15 he commanded, for a T generations,
18:4 took from him a T chariots, seven thousand
18:4 a thousand chariots, seven T horsemen, and twenty
18:4 horsemen, and twenty T foot soldiers; and David
18:5 Zobah, David slew twenty-two T men of the Syrians.
18:12 of Zeruiah, slew eighteen T Edomites in the Valley
19:6 the Ammonites sent a T talents of silver to
19:7 They hired thirty-two T chariots and the king of
19:18 the men of seven T chariots, and forty thousand
19:18 thousand chariots, and forty T foot soldiers, and killed
21:5 one million one hundred T men who drew the
21:5 four hundred and seventy T who drew the sword.
21:14 and there fell seventy T men of Israel.
22:14 the LORD a hundred T talents of gold, a
23:3 the total was thirty-eight T men.
23:4 "Twenty-four T of these," David said, "shall have
23:4 of the LORD, six T shall be officers and
23:5 officers and judges, four T gatekeepers, and four
23:5 thousand gatekeepers, and four T shall offer praises
26:30 and his brethren, one T seven hundred men of
26:32 and his brethren, two T seven hundred men of
27:1 each division numbering twenty-four T:
27:2 the first month; in his division were twenty-four T
27:4 the second month; in his division were twenty-four T
27:5 priest, as chief; in his division were twenty-four T
27:7 after him; in his division were twenty-four T
27:8 the Izrahite; in his division were twenty-four T
27:9 Ikkesh the Tekoite; in his division were twenty-four T
27:10 sons of Ephraim; in his division were twenty-four T
27:11 of the Zerahites; in his division were twenty-four T
27:12 a Benjaminite; in his division were twenty-four T
27:13 of the Zerahites; in his division were twenty-four T
27:14 sons of Ephraim; in his division were twenty-four T
27:15 of Othni-el; in his division were twenty-four T
29:4 of my God: three T talents of gold, of
29:4 of Ophir, and seven T talents of refined silver,
29:7 house of God five T talents and ten thousand
29:7 thousand talents and ten T darics of gold, ten
29:7 darics of gold, ten T talents of silver, eighteen
29:7 talents of silver, eighteen T talents of bronze, and
29:7 bronze, and a hundred T talents of iron.
29:21 to the LORD, a T bulls, a thousand rams,
29:21 a thousand bulls, a T rams, and a thousand
29:21 thousand rams, and a T lambs, with their drink
2Chr 1:6 meeting, and offered a T burnt offerings upon it.
1:14 hundred chariots and twelve T horsemen, whom he
2:2 And Solomon assigned seventy T men to bear
2:2 bear burdens and eighty T to quarry in the
2:2 hill country, and three T six hundred to oversee
2:10 who cut timber, twenty T cors of crushed wheat,
2:10 of crushed wheat, twenty T cors of barley, twenty
2:10 cors of barley, twenty T baths of wine, and
2:10 of wine, and twenty T baths of oil."
2:17 a hundred and fifty-three T six hundred.
2:18 Seventy T of them he assigned to bear burdens,
2:18 to bear burdens, eighty T to quarry in the
2:18 hill country, and three T six hundred as overseers
4:5 it held over three T baths.
7:5 as a sacrifice twenty-two T oxen and a hundred
7:5 a hundred and twenty T sheep.
9:25 And Solomon had four T stalls for horses and
9:25 chariots, and twelve T horsemen, whom he stationed
11:1 a hundred and eighty T chosen warriors, to fight
12:3 hundred chariots and sixty T horsemen.
13:3 of war, four hundred T picked men; and Jeroboam
13:3 him with eight hundred T picked mighty warriors.
13:17 of Israel five hundred T picked men.
14:8 army of three hundred T from Judah, armed with
14:8 two hundred and eighty T men from Benjamin, that
15:11 hundred oxen and seven T sheep.
17:11 also brought him seven T seven hundred rams and
17:11 hundred rams and seven T seven hundred he-goats.
17:14 commander, with three hundred T mighty men of
17:15 two hundred and eighty T,
17:16 LORD, with two hundred T mighty men of valor.
17:17 valor, with two hundred T men armed with bow
17:18 a hundred and eighty T armed for war.
25:5 they were three hundred T picked men, fit for
25:6 hired also a hundred T mighty men of valor
25:11 Salt and smote ten T men of Seir.
25:12 Judah captured another ten T alive, and took them
25:13 Beth-horon, and killed three T people in them, and
26:12 of valor was two T six hundred.
26:13 three hundred and seven T five hundred, who could
27:5 of silver, and ten T cors of wheat and
27:5 of wheat and ten T of barley.
28:6 a hundred and twenty T in Judah in one
28:8 took captive two hundred T of their kinsfolk, women,
29:33 hundred bulls and three T sheep.
30:24 gave the assembly a T bulls and seven thousand
30:24 thousand bulls and seven T sheep for offerings, and
30:24 gave the assembly a T bulls and ten thousand
30:24 thousand bulls and ten T sheep.
35:7 the number of thirty T, and three thousand bulls;
35:7 thirty thousand, and three T bulls; these were from
35:8 the passover offerings two T six hundred lambs and
35:9 the passover offerings five T lambs and kids and
Ezra 1:9 number of them: a T basins of gold, a
1:9 basins of gold, a T basins of silver, twenty-nine
1:10 bowls of gold, two T four hundred and ten

1:10 of silver, and a T other vessels;
1:11 of silver were five T four hundred and sixty-nine.
2:3 sons of Parosh, two T one hundred and seventy-two.
2:6 Jeshua and Joab, two T eight hundred and twelve.
2:7 sons of Elam, one T two hundred and fifty-four.
2:12 sons of Azgad, one T two hundred and twenty-two.
2:14 sons of Bigvai, two T and fifty-six.
2:31 the other Elam, one T two hundred and fifty-four.
2:35 sons of Senaah, three T six hundred and thirty.
2:37 sons of Immer, one T and fifty-two.
2:38 sons of Pashhur, one T two hundred and forty-seven.
2:39 sons of Harim, one T and seventeen.
2:64 assembly together was forty-two T three hundred
2:65 whom there were seven T three hundred and thirty-
2:67 their asses were six T seven hundred and twenty.
2:69 of the work sixty-one T darics of gold, five
2:69 darics of gold, five T minas of silver, and
8:27 of gold worth a T darics, and two vessels
Neh 3:13 bars, and repaired a T cubits of the wall,
7:8 sons of Parosh, two T a hundred and seventy-two.
7:11 Jeshua and Joab, two T eight hundred and eighteen.
7:12 sons of Elam, a T two hundred and fifty-four.
7:17 sons of Azgad, two T three hundred and twenty-two.
7:19 sons of Bigvai, two T and sixty-seven.
7:34 the other Elam, a T two hundred and fifty-four.
7:38 sons of Senaah, three T nine hundred and thirty.
7:40 sons of Immer, a T and fifty-two.
7:41 sons of Pashhur, a T two hundred and forty-seven.
7:42 sons of Harim, a T and seventeen.
7:66 assembly together was forty-two T three hundred
7:67 whom there were seven T three hundred and thirty-
7:69 and their asses six T seven hundred and twenty.
7:70 to the treasury a T darics of gold, fifty
7:71 of the work twenty T darics of gold and
7:71 of gold and two T two hundred minas of
7:72 people gave was twenty T darics of gold, two
7:72 darics of gold, two T minas of silver, and
Jud 2:5 one hundred and twenty T foot soldiers and twelve
2:5 foot soldiers and twelve T cavalry.
2:15 one hundred and twenty T of them, together with
2:15 them, together with twelve T archers on horseback,
7:2 one hundred and seventy T infantry and twelve
7:2 thousand infantry and twelve T cavalry, together with
7:17 forward, together with five T Assyrians, and they
Esth 3:9 I will pay ten T talents of silver into
9:16 enemies, and slew seventy-five T of those who hated
Job 1:3 He had seven T sheep, three thousand camels, five
1:3 thousand sheep, three T camels, five hundred yoke
9:3 him once in a T times.
33:23 mediator, one of the T, to declare to man
42:12 and he had fourteen T sheep, six thousand camels,
42:12 fourteen thousand sheep, six T camels, a thousand
42:12 six thousand camels, a T yoke of oxen, and
42:12 of oxen, and a T she-asses.
Ps 50:10 the cattle on a T hills.
68:17 chariotry, twice ten T, thousands upon thousands, the
84:10 is better than a T elsewhere.
90:4 For a T years in thy sight are but
91:7 A T may fall at your side, ten thousand
91:7 at your side, ten T at your right hand;
105:8 he commanded, for a T generations,
Eccl 6:6 he should live a T years twice told, yet
7:28 One man among a T I found, but a
Song 4:4 arsenal, whereon hang a T bucklers, all of them
5:10 is all radiant and ruddy, distinguished among ten T
8:11 for its fruit a T pieces of silver.
8:12 Solomon, may have the T, and the keepers of
Wis 12:22 scourgest our enemies ten T times more, so that
Sir 6:6 but let your advisers be one in a T
16:3 is better than a T, and to die childless
16:10 for the six hundred T men on foot, who
23:19 the Lord are ten T times brighter than the
39:11 name greater than a T, and if he goes
41:4 a hundred or a T years, there is no
41:12 you longer than a T great stores of gold.
46:8 out of six hundred T people on foot, to
Is 7:23 used to be a T vines, worth a thousand
7:23 thousand vines, worth a T shekels of silver, will
30:17 A T shall flee at the threat of one,
36:8 will give you two T horses, if you are
37:36 a hundred and eighty-five T in the camp of
Jer 52:28 the seventh year, three T and twenty-three Jews;
52:30 the persons were four T and six hundred.
Ezek 45:1 a holy district, twenty-five T cubits long and twenty
45:1 cubits long and twenty T cubits broad; it shall
45:3 off a section twenty-five T cubits long and ten
45:3 cubits long and ten T broad, in which shall
45:5 Another section, twenty-five T cubits long and ten
45:5 cubits long and ten T cubits broad, shall be
45:6 city an area five T cubits broad, and twenty-five
45:6 cubits broad, and twenty-five T cubits long; it shall
47:3 the man measured a T cubits, and then led
47:4 Again he measured a T, and led me through
47:4 Again he measured a T, and led me through
47:5 Again he measured a T, and it was a
48:8 shall set apart, twenty-five T cubits in breadth, and
48:9 LORD shall be twenty-five T cubits in length, and
48:9 in length, and twenty T in breadth.
48:10 an allotment measuring twenty-five T cubits on the
48:10 the northern side, ten T cubits in breadth on
48:10 the western side, ten T in breadth on the
48:10 eastern side, and twenty-five T in length on the
48:13 have an allotment twenty-five T cubits in length and
48:13 in length and ten T in breadth.
48:13 length shall be twenty-five T cubits and the breadth
48:13 twenty-five thousand cubits and the breadth twenty T
48:15 "The remainder, five T cubits in breadth and twenty-
48:15 in breadth and twenty-five T in length, shall be
48:16 the north side four T five hundred cubits, the
48:16 the south side four T five hundred, the east
48:16 the east side four T five hundred, and the
48:16 the west side four T and five hundred.
48:18 portion shall be ten T cubits to the east,
48:18 the east, and ten T to the west, and
48:20 apart shall be twenty-five T cubits square, that is,
48:21 Extending from the twenty-five T cubits of the holy
48:21 westward from the twenty-five T cubits to the west
48:30 is to be four T five hundred cubits by
48:32 is to be four T five hundred cubits, three
48:33 is to be four T five hundred cubits by
48:34 is to be four T five hundred cubits, three
48:35 city shall be eighteen T cubits.
Dan 5:1 great feast for a T of his lords, and
5:1 lords, and drank wine in front of the T
7:10 from before him; a T thousands served him, and
7:10 served him, and ten T times ten thousand stood
7:10 ten thousand times ten T stood before him; the
8:14 to him, "For two T and three hundred evenings
12:11 there shall be a T two hundred and ninety
12:12 and comes to the T three hundred and thirty-five
Amos 5:3 that went forth a T shall have a hundred
Jon 4:11 a hundred and twenty T persons who do not
1 Mac 2:38 the number of a T persons.
3:39 sent with them forty T infantry and seven thousand
3:39 thousand infantry and seven T cavalry to go into
4:1 Now Gorgias took five T infantry and a thousand
4:1 thousand infantry and a T picked cavalry, and this
4:6 the plain with three T men, but they did
4:15 and Jamnia; and three T of them fell.
4:28 year he mustered sixty T picked infantrymen and five
4:28 picked infantrymen and five T cavalry to subdue
4:29 met them with ten T men.
4:34 army of Lysias five T men; they fell in
5:13 have destroyed about a T men there."
5:20 Then three T men were assigned to Simon to
5:20 to Galilee, and eight T to Judas for Gilead.
5:22 as many as three T of the Gentiles fell,
5:34 As many as eight T of them fell that
5:60 as many as two T of the people of
6:30 forces was a hundred T foot soldiers, twenty
6:30 thousand foot soldiers, twenty T horsemen, and
6:35 elephant they stationed a T men armed with coats
7:40 in Adasa with three T men.
7:41 one hundred and eighty-five T of the Assyrians.
9:4 to Berea with twenty T foot soldiers and two
9:4 foot soldiers and two T cavalry.
9:5 with him were three T picked men.
9:49 And about one T of Bacchides' men fell that
10:36 the number of thirty T men, and let the
10:40 I also grant fifteen T shekels of silver yearly
10:42 Moreover, the five T shekels of silver which my
10:74 He chose ten T men and set out from
10:77 it, he mustered three T cavalry and a large
10:79 had secretly left a T cavalry behind them.
10:85 alive, came to eight T men.
11:44 So Jonathan sent three T stalwart men to him
11:45 a hundred and twenty T, and they wanted to
11:47 many as a hundred T men.
11:74 As many as three T of the foreigners fell
12:41 meet him with forty T picked fighting men, and
12:47 kept with himself three T men, two thousand of
12:47 three thousand men, two T of whom he left

12:47 in Galilee, while a T accompanied him.
14:24 gold shield weighing a T minas, to confirm the
15:13 a hundred and twenty T warriors and eight thousand
15:13 thousand warriors and eight T cavalry.
15:18 gold shield weighing a T minas.
15:26 sent to Antiochus two T picked men, to fight
16:4 of the country twenty T warriors and horsemen, and
16:10 fire, and about two T of them fell.
2Mac 4:40 Lysimachus armed about three T men and launched
5:5 no less than a T men and suddenly made
5:14 of three days eighty T were destroyed, forty thousand
5:14 thousand were destroyed, forty T in hand-to-hand
5:24 an army of twenty-two T, and commanded him to
8:1 they gathered about six T men.
8:9 no fewer than twenty T Gentiles of all nations,
8:10 to the Romans, two T talents, by selling the
8:16 to the number six T, and exhorted them not
8:19 one hundred and eighty-five T perished,
8:20 in Babylonia, when eight T in all went into
8:20 the affair, with four T Macedonians; and when the
8:20 were hard-pressed, the eight T, by the help that
8:20 one hundred and twenty T and took much booty.
8:24 slew more than nine T of the enemy, and
8:30 killed more than twenty T of them and got
8:34 who had brought the T merchants to buy the
10:17 they encountered, killing no fewer than twenty T
10:18 no less than nine T took refuge in two
10:20 and on receiving seventy T drachmas let some of
10:23 destroyed more than twenty T in the two strongholds.
10:31 Twenty T five hundred were slaughtered, besides six
11:2 happened, gathered about eighty T men and all his
11:11 enemy, and slew eleven T of them and sixteen
12:10 not less than five T Arabs with five hundred
12:19 stronghold, more than ten T men.
12:20 a hundred and twenty T infantry and two thousand
12:20 thousand infantry and two T five hundred cavalry.
12:23 as many as thirty T men.
12:26 Atargatis, and slaughtered twenty-five T people.
12:28 as many as twenty-five T of those who were
12:33 came out with three T infantry and four hundred
12:43 the amount of two T drachmas of silver, and
13:2 one hundred and ten T infantry, five thousand three
13:2 ten thousand infantry, five T three hundred cavalry,
13:15 as many as two T men in the camp.
15:22 a hundred and eighty-five T in the camp of
15:27 no less than thirty-five T men, and were greatly
Mt 14:21 ate were about five T men, besides women and
15:38 who ate were four T men, besides women and
16:9 loaves of the five T, and how many baskets
16:10 loaves of the four T, and how many baskets
18:23 who owed him ten T talents;
Mk 5:13 herd, numbering about two T, rushed down the steep
6:44 the loaves were five T men.
8:9 there were about four T people.
8:19 loaves for the five T, how many baskets full
8:20 seven for the four T, how many baskets full
Lk 9:14 there were about five T men.
14:31 is able with ten T to meet him who
14:31 meet him who comes against him with twenty T
Jn 6:10 the men sat down, in number about five T
Acts 2:41 that day about three T souls.
4:4 number of the men came to about five T
19:19 it came to fifty T pieces of silver.
21:38 and led the four T men of the Assassins
Rom 11:4 kept for myself seven T men who have not
1Cor 10:8 them did, and twenty-three T fell in a single
14:19 instruct others, than ten T words in a tongue.
2Pet 3:8 day is as a T years, and a thousand
3:8 thousand years, and a T years as one day.
Rev 7:4 a hundred and forty-four T sealed, out of every
7:5 sons of Israel, twelve T sealed out of the
7:5 tribe of Judah, twelve T of the tribe of
7:5 tribe of Reuben, twelve T of the tribe of
7:6 tribe of Gad, twelve T of the tribe of
7:6 tribe of Asher, twelve T of the tribe of
7:6 tribe of Naphtali, twelve T of the tribe of
7:7 tribe of Manasseh, twelve T of the tribe of
7:7 tribe of Simeon, twelve T of the tribe of
7:7 tribe of Levi, twelve T of the tribe of
7:8 tribe of Issachar, twelve T of the tribe of
7:8 tribe of Zebulun, twelve T of the tribe of
7:8 tribe of Joseph, twelve T sealed out of the
9:16 cavalry was twice ten T times ten thousand; I
9:16 ten thousand times ten T; I heard their number.
11:3 to prophesy for one T two hundred and sixty
11:13 the city fell; seven T people were killed in
12:6 be nourished for one T two hundred and sixty
14:1 a hundred and forty-four T who had his name
14:3 hundred and forty-four T who had been redeemed
14:20 horse's bridle, for one T six hundred stadia.
20:2 bound him for a T years,
20:3 no more, till the T years were ended.
20:4 reigned with Christ a T years.
20:5 to life until the T years were ended.
20:6 reign with him a T years.
20:7 And when the T years are ended, Satan will
21:16 with his rod, twelve T stadia; its length and

THOUSANDS (65)

Gen 24:60 be the mother of T of ten thousands; and
24:60 of thousands of ten T; and may your descendants
Ex 18:21 people as rulers of T, of hundreds, of fifties,
18:25 the people, rulers of T, of hundreds, of fifties,
20:6 showing steadfast love to T of those who love
34:7 love for T, forgiving iniquity and transgression
Num 10:36 to the ten thousand T of Israel."
31:5 provided, out of the T of Israel, a thousand
31:14 army, the commanders of T and the commanders of
31:48 who were over the T of the army, the
31:48 army, the captains of T and the captains of
31:52 from the commanders of T and the commanders of
31:54 from the commanders of T and of hundreds, and
Deut 1:15 over you, commanders of T, commanders of
5:10 showing steadfast love to T of those who love
33:2 came from the ten T of holy ones, with
33:17 such are the ten T of Ephraim, and such
33:17 and such are the T of Manasseh."
1Sam 8:12 for himself commanders of T and commanders of
10:19 the LORD by your tribes and by your T
18:7 "Saul has slain his T, and David his ten
18:7 has slain his thousands, and David his ten T
18:8 ascribed to David ten T, and to me they
18:8 me they have ascribed T; and what more can
21:11 'Saul has slain his T, and David his ten
21:11 has slain his thousands, and David his ten T
22:7 you all commanders of T and commanders of
23:23 out among all the T of Judah."
29:2 by hundreds and by T, and David and his
29:5 'Saul has slain his T, and David his ten
29:5 has slain his thousands, and David his ten T
2Sam 18:1 over them commanders of T and commanders of
18:4 the army marched out by hundreds and by T
1Chr 12:20 and Zillethai, chiefs of T in Manasseh.
13:1 with the commanders of T and of hundreds, with
15:25 and the commanders of T, went to bring up
26:26 the officers of the T and the hundreds, and
27:1 houses, the commanders of T and hundreds, and their
28:1 king, the commanders of T, the commanders of
29:6 tribes, the commanders of T and of hundreds, and
2Chr 1:2 to the commanders of T and of hundreds, to
17:14 Judah, the commanders of T: Adnah the commander,
25:5 houses under commanders of T and of hundreds for
Ps 3:6 not afraid of ten T of people who have
68:17 chariotry, twice ten thousand, T upon thousands, the
68:17 ten thousand, thousands upon T, the Lord came from
119:72 better to me than T of gold and silver
144:13 our sheep bring forth T and ten thousands in
144:13 forth thousands and ten T in our fields;
Sir 47:6 him for his ten T, and praised him for
Jer 32:18 showest steadfast love to T, but dost requite the
Dan 3:39 and with tens of T of fat lambs;
7:10 before him; a thousand T served him, and ten
11:12 cast down tens of T, but he shall not
11:41 And tens of T shall fall, but these shall
Hos 8:12 my laws by ten T, they would be regarded
Mic 6:7 LORD be pleased with T of rams, with ten
6:7 of rams, with ten T of rivers of oil?
1Mac 3:55 people, in charge of T and hundreds and fifties
2Mac 11:4 elated with his ten T of infantry, and his
11:4 of infantry, and his T of cavalry, and his
Lk 12:1 meantime, when so many T of the multitude had
Acts 21:20 see, brother, how many T there are among the
Rev 5:11 myriads of myriads and T of thousands,
5:11 myriads and thousands of T,

THRACIAN

2Mac 12:35 when one of the T horsemen bore down upon

THREAD (6)

Gen 14:23 would not take a T or a sandal-thong or
38:28 his hand a scarlet T, saying, "This came out
38:30 out with the scarlet T upon his hand; and

T

17:13 The T eldest sons of Jesse had followed Saul
17:13 the names of his T sons who went to
17:14 was the youngest; the T eldest followed Saul,
20:20 And I will shoot T arrows to the side
20:41 the ground, and bowed T times; and they kissed
24:2 Then Saul took T thousand chosen men out of
25:2 very rich; he had T thousand sheep and a
26:2 wilderness of Ziph, with T thousand chosen men of
30:12 or drunk water for T days and three nights.
30:12 for three days and T nights.
30:13 because I fell sick T days ago.
31:6 Saul died, and his T sons, and his armor-bearer,
31:8 found Saul and his T sons fallen on Mount
2Sam 2:18 And the T sons of Zeruiah were there, Joab,
2:31 had slain of Benjamin T hundred and sixty of
6:11 of Obed-edom the Gittite T months; and the LORD
13:38 Geshur, and was there T years.
14:27 were born to Absalom T sons, and one daughter
18:14 And he took T darts in his hand, and
20:4 together to me within T days, and be here
21:1 days of David for T years, year after year;
21:16 giants, whose spear weighed T hundred shekels of
23:8 was chief of the T; he wielded his spear
23:9 to him among the T mighty men was Eleazar
23:13 And T of the thirty chief men went down,
23:16 Then the T mighty men broke through the camp
23:17 These things did the T mighty men.
23:18 wielded his spear against T hundred men and slew
23:18 slew them, and won a name beside the T
23:19 commander; but he did not attain to the T
23:22 a name beside the T mighty men.
23:23 thirty, but he did not attain to the T
24:12 'Thus says the LORD, T things I offer you;
24:13 said to him, "Shall T years of famine come
24:13 Or will you flee T months before your foes
24:13 Or shall there be T days' pestilence in your
1Kgs 2:39 at the end of T years that two of
4:32 He also uttered T thousand proverbs; and his songs
5:16 country, besides Solomon's T thousand three hundred
5:16 Solomon's three thousand T hundred chief officers
6:36 the inner court with T courses of hewn stone
7:2 it was built upon T rows of cedar pillars,
7:4 were window frames in T rows, and window opposite
7:4 window opposite window in T tiers.
7:5 was opposite window in T tiers.
7:12 The great court had T courses of hewn stone
7:25 stood upon twelve oxen, T facing north, three facing
7:25 oxen, three facing north, T facing west, three facing
7:25 north, three facing west, T facing south, and three
7:25 three facing south, and T facing east; the sea
7:27 four cubits wide, and T cubits high.
9:25 T times a year Solomon used to offer up
10:17 And he made T hundred shields of beaten gold;
10:17 shields of beaten gold; T minas of gold went
10:22 Once every T years the fleet of ships of
11:3 wives, princesses, and T hundred concubines; and his
12:5 to them, "Depart for T days, then come again
15:2 He reigned for T years in Jerusalem.
17:21 himself upon the child T times, and cried to
22:1 For T years Syria and Israel continued without war.
2Kgs 2:17 fifty men; and for T days they sought him
3:10 LORD has called these T kings to give them
3:13 who has called these T kings to give them
9:32 Two or T eunuchs looked out at him.
13:18 them"; and he struck T times, and stopped.
13:19 strike down Syria only T times."
13:25 T times Joash defeated him and recovered the cities
17:5 to Samaria, and for T years he besieged it.
18:10 at the end of T years he took it.
18:14 Hezekiah king of Judah T hundred talents of silver
23:31 reign, and he reigned T months in Jerusalem.
24:1 Jehoiakim became his servant T years; then he
24:8 king, and he reigned T months in Jerusalem.
25:17 of the capital was T cubits; a network and
25:18 second priest, and the T keepers of the threshold;
1Chr 2:3 Onan, and Shelah; these T Bath-shua the Canaanitess
2:16 The sons of Zeruiah: Abishai, Joab, and Asahel, T
3:23 sons of Neariah: Eli-o-enai, Hizkiah, and Azrikam, T
7:6 The sons of Benjamin: Bela, Becher, and Jedia-el, T
10:6 died; he and his T sons and all his
11:11 was chief of the T; he wielded his spear
11:11 wielded his spear against T hundred whom he slew
11:12 to him among the T mighty men was Eleazar
11:15 T of the thirty chief men went down to
11:18 Then the T mighty men broke through the camp
11:19 These things did the T mighty men.
11:20 wielded his spear against T hundred men and slew
11:20 slew them, and won a name beside the T
11:21 commander; but he did not attain to the T
11:24 a name beside the T mighty men.
11:25 thirty, but he did not attain to the T
12:27 Aaron, and with him T thousand seven hundred.
12:29 the kinsmen of Saul, T thousand, of whom the
12:39 there with David for T days, eating and drinking,
13:14 Obed-edom in his house T months; and the LORD
21:10 'Thus says the LORD, T things I offer you;
21:12 which you will: either T years of famine; or
21:12 years of famine; or T months of devastation by
21:12 overtakes you; or else T days of the sword
23:8 Ladan: Jehiel the chief, and Zetham, and Joel, T
23:9 sons of Shimei: Shelomoth, Hazi-el, and Haran, T
23:23 The sons of Mushi: Mahli, Eder, and Jeremoth, T
25:5 Heman fourteen sons and T daughters.
29:4 house of my God: T thousand talents of gold,
2Chr 2:2 the hill country, and T thousand six hundred to
2:18 the hill country, and T thousand six hundred as
4:4 stood upon twelve oxen, T facing north, three facing
4:4 oxen, three facing north, T facing west, three facing
4:4 north, three facing west, T facing south, and three
4:4 three facing south, and T facing east; the sea
4:5 lily; it held over T thousand baths.
6:13 five cubits wide, and T cubits high, and had
8:13 new moons, and the T annual feasts--the feast
9:16 And he made T hundred shields of beaten gold;
9:16 shields of beaten gold; T hundred shekels of gold
9:21 of Huram; once every T years the ships of
10:5 to me again in T days." So the people
11:17 of Judah, and for T years they made Rehoboam
11:17 for they walked for T years in the way
13:2 He reigned for T years in Jerusalem.
14:8 had an army of T hundred thousand from Judah,
14:9 a million men and T hundred chariots, and came
17:14 the commander, with T hundred thousand mighty
20:25 They were T days in taking the spoil, it
25:5 found that they were T hundred thousand picked
25:13 to Beth-horon, and killed T thousand people in them,
26:13 was an army of T hundred and seven thousand
29:33 six hundred bulls and T thousand sheep.
31:16 by genealogy, males from T years old and upwards,
35:7 of thirty thousand, and T thousand bulls; these were
35:8 lambs and kids and T hundred bulls.
36:2 reign; and he reigned T months in Jerusalem.
36:9 reign, and he reigned T months and ten days
Ezra 2:4 The sons of Shephatiah, T hundred and seventy-two.
2:17 The sons of Bezai, T hundred and twenty-three.
2:32 The sons of Harim, T hundred and twenty.
2:34 The sons of Jericho, T hundred and forty-five.
2:35 The sons of Senaah, T thousand six hundred and
2:58 Solomon's servants were T hundred and ninety-two.
2:64 together was forty-two thousand T hundred and sixty,
2:65 were seven thousand T hundred and thirty-seven; and
6:4 breadth sixty cubits, with T courses of great stones
8:5 Jahaziel, and with him T hundred men.
8:15 and there we encamped T days.
8:32 and there we remained T days.
10:8 did not come within T days, by order of
10:9 at Jerusalem within the T days; it was the
Neh 2:11 Jerusalem and was there T days.
7:9 The sons of Shephatiah, T hundred and seventy-two.
7:17 of Azgad, two thousand T hundred and twenty-two.
7:22 The sons of Hashum, T hundred and twenty-eight.
7:23 The sons of Bezai, T hundred and twenty-four.
7:35 The sons of Harim, T hundred and twenty.
7:36 The sons of Jericho, T hundred and forty-five.
7:38 The sons of Senaah, T thousand nine hundred and
7:60 Solomon's servants were T hundred and ninety-two.
7:66 together was forty-two thousand T hundred and sixty,
7:67 were seven thousand T hundred and thirty-seven; and
Jud 1:2 Ecbatana with hewn stones T cubits thick and six
2:21 They marched for T days from Nineveh to the
8:4 as a widow for T years and four months.
12:7 in the camp for T days, and went out
16:20 the sanctuary for T months, and Judith remained
Esth 4:16 eat nor drink for T days, night or day.
9:15 Adar and they slew T hundred men in Susa;
Job 1:2 him seven sons and T daughters.
1:3 had seven thousand sheep, T thousand camels, five
1:4 send and invite their T sisters to eat and
1:17 said, "The Chaldeans formed T companies, and made
2:11 Now when Job's T friends heard of all this
32:1 So these T men ceased to answer Job, because
32:3 angry also at Job's T friends because they had

T

32:5 the mouth of these T men, he became angry.
33:29 all these things, twice, T times, with a man,
42:13 also seven sons and T daughters.
Prov 30:15 T things are never satisfied; four never say,
30:18 T things are too wonderful for me; four I
30:21 Under T things the earth trembles; under four it
30:29 T things are stately in their tread; four are
Sir 13:7 drained you two or T times; and finally he
25:1 soul takes pleasure in T things, and they are
25:2 My soul hates T kinds of men, and I
26:5 Of T things my heart is afraid, and of
43:4 sun burns the mountains T times as much; it
48:3 the heavens, and also T times brought down fire.
Is 16:14 the LORD says, "In T years, like the years
17:6 beaten– two or T berries in the top
20:3 naked and barefoot for T years as a sign
Jer 36:23 As Jehudi read T or four columns, the king
38:10 Ebed-melech, the Ethiopian, "Take T men with you
52:24 second priest, and the T keepers of the threshold;
52:28 the seventh year, T thousand and twenty-three Jews;
Ezek 4:5 a number of days, T hundred and ninety days,
4:9 lie upon your side, T hundred and ninety days,
14:14 beast, even if these T men, Noah, Daniel, and
14:16 beasts; even if these T men were in it,
14:18 and beast; though these T men were in it,
40:10 And there were T side rooms on either side
40:10 the east gate; the T were of the same
40:21 Its side rooms, T on either side, and its
40:48 of the gate were T cubits on either side.
41:6 side chambers were in T stories, one over another,
41:16 and round about all T had windows with recessed
41:22 an altar of wood, T cubits high, two cubits
42:3 gallery against gallery in T stories.
42:6 For they were in T stories, and they had
48:31 hundred cubits by measure, T gates, the gate of
48:32 thousand five hundred cubits, T gates, the gate of
48:33 hundred cubits by measure, T gates, the gate of
48:34 thousand five hundred cubits, T gates, the gate of
Dan 1:5 to be educated for T years, and at the
3:23 these T men, Shadrach, Meshach, and Abednego, fell
3:51 Then the T, as with one mouth, praised and
3:92 "Did we not cast T men bound into the
6:2 kingdom; and over them T presidents, of whom
6:10 down upon his knees T times a day and
6:13 but makes his petition T times a day."
7:5 one side; it had T ribs in its mouth
7:8 little one, before which T of the first horns
7:20 up and before which T of them fell, the
7:24 and shall put down T kings.
8:14 "For two thousand and T hundred evenings and
10:2 Daniel, was mourning for T weeks.
10:3 all, for the full T weeks.
11:2 Behold, T more kings shall arise in Persia; and
12:12 comes to the thousand T hundred and thirty-five
Amos 1:3 says the LORD: "For T transgressions of Damascus,
1:6 says the LORD: "For T transgressions of Gaza, and
1:9 says the LORD: "For T transgressions of Tyre, and
1:11 says the LORD: "For T transgressions of Edom, and
1:13 says the LORD: "For T transgressions of the
2:1 says the LORD: "For T transgressions of Moab, and
2:4 says the LORD: "For T transgressions of Judah, and
2:6 says the LORD: "For T transgressions of Israel, and
4:4 morning, your tithes every T days;
4:7 when there were yet T months to the harvest;
4:8 withered; so two or T cities wandered to one
Jon 1:17 belly of the fish T days and three nights.
1:17 fish three days and T nights.
3:3 an exceedingly great city, T days' journey in breadth.
Zech 11:8 month I destroyed the T shepherds.
1Mac 4:6 in the plain with T thousand men, but they
4:15 Azotus and Jamnia; and T thousand of them fell.
5:20 Then T thousand men were assigned to Simon to
5:22 and as many as T thousand of the Gentiles
5:24 the Jordan and went T days' journey into the
5:33 up behind them in T companies, who sounded their
7:40 encamped in Adasa with T thousand men.
8:15 chamber, and every day T hundred and twenty
9:5 and with him were T thousand picked men.
10:30 Judah or from the T districts added to it
10:34 appointed days, and the T days before a feast
10:34 a feast and the T after a feast –
10:38 "As for the T districts that have been added
10:77 of it, he mustered T thousand cavalry and a
11:18 But King Ptolemy died T days later, and his
11:28 free Judea and the T districts of Samaria from
11:28 tribute, and promised him T hundred talents.
11:34 of Judea and the T districts of Aphairema and
11:44 So Jonathan sent T thousand stalwart men to him
11:74 As many as T thousand of the foreigners fell
12:47 He kept with himself T thousand men, two thousand
2Mac 4:8 king at an interview T hundred and sixty talents
4:19 from Jerusalem, to carry T hundred silver drachmas
4:23 After a period of T years Jason sent Menelaus,
4:24 himself, outbidding Jason by T hundred talents of
4:40 anger, Lysimachus armed about T thousand men and
4:44 king came to Tyre, T men sent by the
5:14 Within the total of T days eighty thousand were
7:27 and nursed you for T years, and have reared
12:33 he came out with T thousand infantry and four
13:2 thousand infantry, five thousand T hundred cavalry,
13:2 twenty-two elephants, and T hundred chariots armed
13:12 and lying prostrate for T days without ceasing, Judas
14:1 T years later, word came to Judas and his
Mt 12:40 For as Jonah was T days and three nights
12:40 was three days and T nights in the belly
12:40 Son of man be T days and three nights
12:40 be three days and T nights in the heart
13:33 took and hid in T measures of flour, till
15:32 been with me now T days, and have nothing
17:4 wish, I will make T booths here, one for
18:15 evidence of two or T witnesses.
18:19 For where two or T are gathered in my
26:34 you will deny me T times."
26:61 to build it in T days.'"
26:75 you will deny me T times." And he went
27:40 and build it in T days, save yourself!
27:63 was still alive, 'After T days I will rise
Mk 8:2 been with me now T days, and have nothing
8:31 be killed, and after T days rise again.
9:5 here; let us make T booths, one for you
9:31 he is killed, after T days he will rise."
10:34 kill him; and after T days he will rise."
14:5 sold for more than T hundred denarii, and given
14:30 you will deny me T times."
14:58 with hands, and in T days I will build
14:72 you will deny me T times." And he broke
15:28 and build it in T days,
Lk 1:56 remained with her about T months, and returned to
2:46 After T days they found him in the temple,
4:25 heaven was shut up T years and six months,
9:33 here; let us make T booths, one for you
10:36 back.' Which of these T, do you think, proved
11:5 him, 'Friend, lend me T loaves;
12:52 will be five divided, T against two and two
12:52 two and two against T;
13:7 the vinedresser, 'Lo, these T years I have come
13:21 took and hid in T measures of flour, till
22:34 this day, until you T times deny that you
22:59 you will deny me T times."
Jn 2:19 this temple, and in T days I will raise
2:20 raise it up in T days?"
6:19 they had rowed about T or four miles, they
12:5 ointment not sold for T hundred denarii and given
13:38 you have denied me T times.
Acts 2:41 added that day about T thousand souls.
5:7 an interval of about T hours his wife came
7:20 was brought up for T months in his father's
9:9 And for T days he was without sight, and
10:16 This happened T times, and the thing was taken
10:19 said to him, "Behold, T men are looking for
11:10 call common.' This happened T times, and all was
11:11 At that very moment T men arrived at the
17:2 his custom, and for T weeks he argued with
19:8 synagogue and for T months spoke boldly, arguing
20:3 There he spent T months, and when a plot
20:31 alert, remembering that for T years I did not
25:1 into his province, after T days he went up
28:7 entertained us hospitably for T days.
28:11 After T months we set sail in a ship
28:12 we stayed there for T days.
28:15 Forum of Appius and T Taverns to meet us.
28:17 After T days he called together the local leaders
1Cor 13:13 hope, love abide, these T; but the greatest of
14:27 two or at most T, and each in turn;
14:29 Let two or T prophets speak, and let the
2Cor 11:25 T times I have been beaten with rods; once
11:25 T times I have been shipwrecked; a night and
12:8 T times I besought the Lord about this, that
13:1 evidence of two or T witnesses.
Gal 1:18 Then after T years I went up to Jerusalem
1Tim 5:19 evidence of two or T witnesses.
Heb 10:28 testimony of two or T witnesses.

T

7:44 Nicanor had fallen, they T down their arms and
11:11 He T blame on Alexander because he coveted his
11:51 And they T down their arms and made peace.
2Mac 1:16 in the ceiling, they T stones and struck down
1:16 off their heads and T them to the people
4:41 were lying about, and T them in wild confusion
14:43 the wall, and manfully T himself down into the
Mt 13:48 good into vessels but T away the bad.
Mk 11:7 colt to Jesus, and T their garments on it;
Acts 16:23 blows upon them, they T them into prison, charging
22:23 waved their garments and T dust into the air,
Rev 8:5 from the altar and T it on the earth;
14:19 of the earth, and T it into the great
18:19 And they T dust on their heads, as they
18:21 a great millstone and T it into the sea,
20:3 a thousand years, and T him into the pit,

THRICE

Ezek 21:14 come down twice, yea T, the sword for those

THRICE-ACCURSED (3)

Esth 16:15 to annihilation by this T man, are not evildoers
2Mac 8:34 The T Nicanor, who had brought the thousand
15:3 the T wretch asked if there were a sovereign

THRILL

Is 60:5 radiant, your heart shall T and rejoice; because the

THRILLED

Song 5:4 and my heart was T within me.

THRIVE (3)

Jer 12:1 Why do all who are treacherous T
Ezek 17:9 Say, Thus says the Lord GOD: Will it T
17:10 Behold, when it is transplanted, will it T

THRIVES

Job 8:16 He T before the sun, and his shoots spread

THROAT (7)

Ps 5:9 heart is destruction, their T is an open sepulchre,
69:3 with my crying; my T is parched.
115:7 they do not make a sound in their T
Prov 23:2 a knife to your T if you are a
Jer 2:25 going unshod and your T from thirst.
Mt 18:27 seizing him by the T he said, 'Pay what
Rom 3:13 "Their T is an open grave, they use their

THROATS

Ps 149:6 God be in their T and two-edged swords in

THROBS

Ps 38:10 My heart T, my strength fails me; and the

THRONE (193)

Gen 41:40 only as regards the T will I be greater
Ex 11:5 who sits upon his T, even to the first-born
12:29 who sat on his T to the first-born of
Deut 17:18 he sits on the T of his kingdom, he
2Sam 3:10 and set up the T of David over Israel
7:13 I will establish the T of his kingdom for
7:16 ever before me; your T shall be established for
14:9 the king and his T be guiltless."
1Kgs 1:13 after me, and he shall sit upon my T
1:17 shall sit upon my T
1:20 shall sit on the T of my lord the
1:24 after me, and he shall sit upon my T
1:27 should sit on the T of my lord the
1:30 shall sit upon my T in my stead'; even
1:35 and sit upon my T; for he shall be
1:37 Solomon, and make his T greater than the throne
1:37 throne greater than the T of my lord King
1:46 Solomon sits upon the royal T
1:47 yours, and make his T greater than your throne.'
1:47 throne greater than your T And the king bowed
1:48 to sit on my T this day, my own
2:4 a man on the T of Israel.'
2:12 Solomon sat upon the T of David his father;
2:19 he sat on his T, and had a seat
2:24 placed me on the T of David my father,
2:33 house, and to his T, there shall be peace
2:45 be blessed, and the T of David shall be
3:6 to sit on his T this day.
5:5 will set upon your T in your place, shall
7:7 the Hall of the T where he was to
8:20 and sit on the T of Israel, as the
8:25 to sit upon the T of Israel, if only
9:5 will establish your royal T over Israel for ever,
9:5 a man upon the T of Israel.'
10:9 set you on the T of Israel!
10:18 made a great ivory T, and overlaid it with
10:19 The T had six steps, and at the back
10:19 the back of the T was a calf's head,
16:11 seated himself on his T, he killed all the
22:19 LORD sitting on his T, and all the host
2Kgs 10:3 him on his father's T, and fight for your
10:30 shall sit on the T of Israel."
11:19 his seat on the T of the kings.
13:13 Jeroboam sat upon his T; and Joash was buried
15:12 shall sit upon the T of Israel to the
1Chr 17:12 I will establish his T for ever.
17:14 for ever and his T shall be established for
22:10 will establish his royal T in Israel for ever.'
28:5 to sit upon the T of the kingdom of
29:23 Solomon sat on the T of the LORD as
2Chr 6:10 and sit on the T of Israel, as the
6:16 to sit upon the T of Israel, if only
7:18 will establish your royal T, as I covenanted with
9:8 set you on his T as king for the
9:17 made a great ivory T, and overlaid it with
9:18 The T had six steps and a footstool of
9:18 were attached to the T, and on each side
18:18 LORD sitting on his T, and all the host
21:4 Jehoram had ascended the T of his father and
23:20 And they set the king upon the royal T
Jud 1:12 and swore by his T and kingdom that he
11:19 I will set your T in the midst of
Esth 1:2 sat on his royal T in Susa the capital,
5:1 sitting on his royal T inside the palace opposite
15:6 seated on his royal T, clothed in the full
15:8 he sprang from his T and took her in
16:11 all as the person second to the royal T
Job 36:7 with kings upon the T he sets them for
Ps 9:4 hast sat on the T giving righteous judgment.
9:7 he has established his T for judgment;
11:4 holy temple, the LORD's T is in heaven; his
45:6 Your divine T endures for ever and ever.
47:8 over the nations; God sits on his holy T
89:4 ever, and build your T for all generations.'" [Selah]
89:14 the foundation of thy T; steadfast love and
89:29 for ever and his T as the days of
89:36 endure for ever, his T as long as the
89:44 hand, and cast his T to the ground.
93:2 never be moved; thy T is established from of
97:2 righteousness and justice are the foundation of his T
103:19 LORD has established his T in the heavens, and
132:11 of your body I will set on your T
132:12 sons also for ever shall sit upon your T
Prov 16:12 do evil, for the T is established by righteousness.
20:8 who sits on the T of judgment winnows all
20:28 the king, and his T is upheld by righteousness.
25:5 the king, and his T will be established in
29:14 poor with equity his T will be established for
Eccl 4:14 from prison to the T or in his own
Wis 9:4 that sits by thy T, and do not reject
9:10 heavens, and from the T of thy glory send
9:12 be worthy of the T of my father.
18:15 heaven, from the royal T, into the midst of
Sir 1:6 wise, greatly to be feared, sitting upon his T
24:4 high places, and my T was in a pillar
40:3 sits on a splendid T to the one who
47:11 of kings and a T of glory in Israel.
Is 6:1 Lord sitting upon a T, high and lifted up;
9:7 no end, upon the T of David, and over
14:13 I will set my T on high; I will
16:5 the land, then a T will be established in
22:23 he will become a T of honor to his
47:1 the ground without a T, O daughter of the
66:1 LORD: "Heaven is my T and the earth is
Jer 1:15 one shall set his T at the entrance of
3:17 shall be called the T of the LORD, and
13:13 who sit on David's T, the priests, the prophets,
14:21 not dishonor thy glorious T; remember and do not
17:12 A glorious T set on high from the beginning
17:25 who sit on the T of David, riding in
22:2 who sit on the T of David, you, and
22:4 who sit on the T of David, riding in
22:30 in sitting on the T of David, and ruling
29:16 who sits on the T of David, and concerning
33:17 to sit on the T of the house of
33:21 to reign on his T, and my covenant with
36:30 to sit upon the T of David, and his

43:10 he will set his T above these stones which
49:38 I will set my T in Elam, and destroy
Lam 5:19 reign for ever; thy T endures to all generations.
Bar 5:6 you, carried in glory, as on a royal T
Ezek 1:26 the likeness of a T, in appearance like sapphire;
1:26 the likeness of a T was a likeness as
10:1 something like a sapphire, in form resembling a T
43:7 the place of my T and the place of
Dan 3:56 art thou upon the T of thy kingdom and
5:20 deposed from his kingly T, and his glory was
7:9 like pure wool; his T was fiery flames, its
Jon 3:6 he arose from his T, removed his robe, and
Hag 2:22 and to overthrow the T of kingdoms; I am
Zech 6:13 honor, and shall sit and rule upon his T
6:13 a priest by his T, and peaceful understanding shall
1Mac 2:57 was merciful, inherited the T of the kingdom for
7:4 his seat upon the T of his kingdom.
10:52 my seat on the T of my fathers, and
10:53 our seat on the T of his kingdom—
10:55 your seat on the T of their kingdom.
11:52 king sat on the T of his kingdom, and
Mt 5:34 for it is the T of God,
19:28 sit on his glorious T, you who have followed
23:21 heaven, swears by the T of God and by
25:31 him, then he will sit on his glorious T
Lk 1:32 give to him the T of his father David,
Acts 2:30 his descendants upon his T,
7:49 says, 'Heaven is my T, and earth my footstool.
12:21 his seat upon the T, and made an oration
Heb 1:8 Son he says, "Thy T, O God, is for
4:16 draw near to the T of grace, that we
8:1 right hand of the T of the Majesty in
12:2 right hand of the T of God.
Rev 1:4 who are before his T,
2:13 you dwell, where Satan's T is; you hold fast
3:21 with me on my T, as I myself conquered
3:21 and sat down with my Father on his T
4:2 Spirit, and lo, a T stood in heaven, with
4:2 stood in heaven, with one seated on the T
4:3 carnelian, and round the T was a rainbow that
4:4 Round the T were twenty-four thrones, and seated on
4:5 From the T issue flashes of lightning, and voices
4:5 thunder, and before the T burn seven torches of
4:6 God; and before the T there is as it
4:6 And round the T, on each side of the
4:6 each side of the T, are four living creatures,
4:9 is seated on the T, who lives for ever
4:10 is seated on the T and worship him who
4:10 their crowns before the T, singing,
5:1 was seated on the T a scroll written within
5:6 And between the T and the four living creatures
5:7 hand of him who was seated on the T
5:11 I heard around the T and the living creatures
5:13 who sits upon the T and to the Lamb
6:16 is seated on the T, and from the wrath
7:9 tongues, standing before the T and before the Lamb,
7:10 who sits upon the T, and to the Lamb!"
7:11 angels stood round the T and round the elders
7:11 their faces before the T and worshiped God,
7:15 are they before the T of God, and serve
7:15 who sits upon the T will shelter them with
7:17 the midst of the T will be their shepherd,
8:3 golden altar before the T;
12:5 God and to his T,
13:2 his power and his T and great authority.
14:3 new song before the T and before the four
16:10 his bowl on the T of the beast, and
16:17 the temple, from the T, saying, "It is done!"
19:4 is seated on the T, saying, "Amen.
19:5 And from the T came a voice crying, "Praise
20:11 saw a great white T and him who sat
20:12 small, standing before the T, and books were opened.
21:3 loud voice from the T saying, "Behold, the dwelling
21:5 who sat upon the T said, "Behold, I make
22:1 crystal, flowing from the T of God and of
22:3 anything accursed, but the T of God and of

THRONES (21)

1Kgs 22:10 were sitting on their T, arrayed in their robes,
2Chr 18:9 were sitting on their T, arrayed in their robes;
Jud 9:3 and princes on their T;
Ps 122:5 There T for judgment were set, the thrones of
122:5 judgment were set, the T of the house of
Wis 5:23 evil-doing will overturn the T of rulers.
6:21 if you delight in T and scepters, O monarchs
7:8 her to scepters and T, and I accounted wealth
Sir 10:14 has cast down the T of rulers, and has
Is 10:13 I have brought down those who sat on T
14:9 it raises from their T all who were kings
Ezek 26:16 step down from their T, and remove their robes,
Dan 7:9 As I looked, T were placed and one that
Mt 19:28 also sit on twelve T, judging the twelve tribes
Lk 1:52 the mighty from their T, and exalted those of
22:30 kingdom, and sit on T judging the twelve tribes
Col 1:16 invisible, whether T or dominions or principalities
Rev 4:4 the throne were twenty-four T, and seated on the
4:4 and seated on the T were twenty-four elders, clad
11:16 who sit on their T before God fell on
20:4 Then I saw T, and seated on them were

THRONG (9)

Ps 35:18 congregation; in the mighty T I will praise thee.
42:4 I went with the T, and led them in
68:27 of Judah in their T, the princes of Zebulun,
109:30 will praise him in the midst of the T
Is 5:14 multitude go down, her T and he who exults
Mt 14:14 he saw a great T; and he had compassion
15:31 them, so that the T wondered, when they saw
Mk 6:34 he saw a great T, and he had compassion
12:37 And the great T heard him gladly.

THRONGED (2)

2Mac 3:19 sackcloth under their breasts, T the streets.
Mk 5:24 crowd followed him and T about him.

THROW (53)

Gen 37:20 us kill him and T him into one of
Ex 9:8 kiln, and let Moses T them toward heaven in
23:27 before you, and will T into confusion all the
29:16 take its blood and T it against the altar
29:20 their right feet, and T the rest of the
Lev 1:5 present the blood, and T the blood round about
1:11 sons the priests shall T its blood against the
3:2 sons the priests shall T the blood against the
3:8 and Aaron's sons shall T its blood against the
3:13 sons of Aaron shall T its blood against the
14:40 is the disease and T them into an unclean
Deut 7:23 over to you, and T them into great confusion,
2Sam 17:2 weary and discouraged, and T him into a panic;
20:15 battering the wall, to T it down.
2Kgs 9:33 He said, T her down." So they threw her
16:15 their drink offering; and T upon it all the
Job 18:7 and his own schemes T him down.
Prov 1:14 our houses with spoil; T in your lot among
Sir 12:16 he will plan to T you into a pit;
Is 22:18 round and round, and T you like a ball
Jer 36:23 with a penknife and T them into the fire
Ezek 16:39 lovers, and they shall T down your vaulted chamber
26:8 wall against you, and T up a mound against
32:3 Lord GOD: I will T my net over you
Dan 11:15 north shall come and T up siegeworks, and take
Jon 1:12 "Take me up and T me into the sea;
Mic 5:11 of your land and T down all your strongholds;
Nah 3:6 I will T filth at you and treat you
1Mac 6:51 engines of war to T fire and stones, machines
11:5 Jonathan had done, to T blame on him; but
2Mac 9:15 but had planned to T out with their children
Mt 4:6 the Son of God, T yourself down; for it
5:29 pluck it out and T it away; it is
5:30 cut it off and T it away; it is
7:6 holy; and do not T your pearls before swine,
13:42 and all evildoers, and T them into the furnace
13:50 from the righteous, and T them into the furnace
15:26 the children's bread and T it to the dogs."
18:8 cut it off and T it away; it is
18:9 pluck it out and T it away; it is
Mk 7:26 the children's bread and T it to the dogs."
Lk 4:9 the Son of God, T yourself down from here;
4:29 built, that they might T him down headlong.
14:35 for the dunghill; men T it away.
22:41 them about a stone's T, and knelt down and
Jn 8:7 be the first to T a stone at her."
8:59 took up stones to T at him; but Jesus
Acts 27:18 began next day to T the cargo overboard;
27:43 who could swim to T themselves overboard first and
Heb 10:35 Therefore do not T away your confidence, which has
Rev 2:10 devil is about to T some of you into
2:22 Behold, I will T her on a sickbed, and
2:22 with her I will T into great tribulation, unless

THROWING (6)

Ezek 43:18 upon it and for T blood against it,

1Mac 15:25 besieged Dor anew, continually T his forces against it
Mt 27:5 And T down the pieces of silver in the
Mk 10:50 And T off his mantle he sprang up and
Lk 19:35 it to Jesus, and T their garments on the
Acts 27:38 they lightened the ship, T out the wheat into

THROWN (58)

Ex 15:1 his rider he has T into the sea.
15:21 his rider he has T into the sea."
Lev 7:2 its blood shall be T on the altar round
Num 19:13 for impurity was not T upon him, he shall
19:20 impurity has not been T upon him, he is
2Sam 20:21 his head shall be T to you over the
23:6 like thorns that are T away; for they cannot
1Kgs 13:24 And his body was T in the road, and
13:25 and saw the body T in the road, and
13:28 and found his body T in the road, and
18:30 LORD that had been T down;
19:10 have forsaken thy covenant, T down thy altars, and
19:14 have forsaken thy covenant, T down thy altars, and
2Kgs 7:15 which the Syrians had T away in their haste.
2Chr 29:22 and their blood was T against the altar; and
29:22 and their blood was T against the altar.
Tob 1:17 my people dead and T out behind the wall
2:3 has been strangled and T into the market place."
Jud 14:15 bedchamber and found him T down on the platform
Ps 102:10 taken me up and T me away.
Wis 17:19 beasts, or an echo T back from a hollow
Jer 50:15 fallen, her walls are T down.
Ezek 38:20 the mountains shall be T down, and the cliffs
Joel 1:7 off their bark and T it down; their branches
2Mac 10:30 and blinded, they were T into disorder and cut
Mt 3:10 is cut down and T into the fire.
5:13 anything except to be T out and trodden under
5:29 your whole body be T into hell.
6:30 alive and tomorrow is T into the oven, will
7:19 is cut down and T into the fire.
8:12 the kingdom will be T into the outer darkness;
13:47 a net which was T into the sea and
18:8 two feet to be T into the eternal fire.
18:9 two eyes to be T into the hell of
24:2 that will not be T down."
Mk 9:42 neck and he were T into the sea.
9:44 two feet to be T into hell.
9:45 two eyes to be T into hell,
13:2 that will not be T down."
Lk 3:9 is cut down and T into the fire."
4:35 when the demon had T him down in the
12:28 today and tomorrow is T into the oven, how
21:6 that will not be T down."
23:18 man who had been T into prison for an
23:24 man who had been T into prison for insurrection
Jn 15:6 the branches are gathered, T into the fire and
Acts 16:37 Roman citizens, and have T us into prison; and
Rev 8:8 burning with fire, was T into the sea;
12:9 the great dragon was T down, that ancient serpent,
12:9 whole world—he was T down to the earth,
12:9 and his angels were T down with him.
12:10 our brethren has been T down, who accuses them
12:13 that he had been T down to the earth,
18:21 the great city be T down with violence, and
19:20 These two were T alive into the lake of
20:10 had deceived them was T into the lake of
20:14 Death and Hades were T into the lake of
20:15 of life, he was T into the lake of

T

THROWS (6)

Lev 7:14 to the priest who T the blood of the
Prov 14:16 evil, but a fool T off restraint and is
26:18 Like a madman who T firebrands, arrows, and death,
Sir 22:18 One who T a stone at birds scares them
27:25 Whoever T a stone straight up throws it on
27:25 a stone straight up T it on his own

THRUST (36)

Ex 12:39 leavened, because they were T out of Egypt and
Deut 9:4 LORD your God has T them out before you,
15:17 take an awl, and T it through his ear
33:27 And he T out the enemy before you, and
Judg 3:21 his right thigh, and T it into his belly;
9:54 And his young man T him through, and he
11:2 sons grew up, they T Jephthah out, and said
1Sam 2:14 hand, and he would T it into the pan,
31:4 "Draw your sword, and T me through with it,
31:4 these uncircumcised come and T me through, and
2Sam 2:16 by the head, and T his sword in his
18:14 in his hand, and T them into the heart
22:39 I consumed them; I T them through, so that
2Kgs 4:27 And Gehazi came to T her away.
1Chr 10:4 "Draw your sword, and T me through with it,
2Chr 26:20 And they T him out quickly, and he himself
Job 18:18 He is T from light into darkness, and driven
24:4 They T the poor off the road; the poor
Ps 18:38 I T them through, so that they were not
36:12 lie prostrate, they are T down, unable to rise.
62:4 They only plan to T him down from his
Is 8:22 and they will be T into thick darkness.
13:15 is found will be T through, and whoever is
22:19 I will T you from your office, and you
Jer 46:15 Because the LORD T him down.
Ezek 26:20 you, then I will T you down with those
28:8 They shall T you down into the Pit, and
34:21 side and shoulder, and T at all the weak
Zech 5:8 And he T her back into the ephah, and
5:8 into the ephah, and T down the leaden weight
Mal 3:5 orphan, against those who T aside the sojourner, and
Lk 13:28 God and you yourselves T out.
Acts 7:27 was wronging his neighbor T him aside, saying, 'Who
7:39 to obey him, but T him aside, and in
7:45 the nations which God T out before our fathers.
13:46 Since you T it from you, and judge yourselves

THRUSTING (2)

Deut 6:19 to your fathers by T out all your enemies
Ezek 46:18 inheritance of the people, T them out of their

THRUSTS

Prov 12:18 words are like sword T, but the tongue of

THUMB (5)

Lev 8:23 ear and on the T of his right hand
14:14 cleansed, and on the T of his right hand,
14:17 cleansed, and on the T of his right hand,
14:25 cleansed, and on the T of his right hand,
14:28 cleansed, and on the T of his right hand,

THUMBS (4)

Ex 29:20 sons, and upon the T of their right hands,
Lev 8:24 ears and on the T of their right hands
Judg 1:6 and cut off his T and his great toes.
1:7 "Seventy kings with their T and their great toes

THUMMIM (7)

Ex 28:30 the Urim and the T, and they shall be
Lev 8:8 the breastpiece he put the Urim and the T
Deut 33:8 "Give to Levi thy T, and thy Urim to
1Sam 14:41 this guilt is in thy people Israel, give T
Ezra 2:63 should be a priest to consult Urim and T
Neh 7:65 priest with Urim and T should arise.
Sir 45:10 of judgment, Urim and T;

THUNDER (34)

Ex 9:23 and the LORD sent T and hail, and fire
9:28 been enough of this T and hail; I will
9:29 to the LORD; the T will cease, and there
9:33 the LORD; and the T and the hail ceased,
9:34 the hail and the T had ceased, he sinned
19:19 louder, Moses spoke, and God answered him in T
1Sam 2:10 against them he will T in heaven.
12:17 that he may send T and rain; and you
12:18 and the LORD sent T and rain that day;
Job 26:14 But the T of his power who can understand?"
28:26 the lightning of the T;
37:2 Hearken to the T of his voice and the
39:25 battle from afar, the T of the captains, and
40:9 God, and can you T with a voice like
Ps 42:7 to deep at the T of thy cataracts; all
77:17 the skies gave forth T; thy arrows flashed on
77:18 The crash of thy T was in the whirlwind;
81:7 the secret place of T; I tested you at
104:7 the sound of thy T they took to flight.
Wis 19:13 in the violence of T, for they justly suffered
Sir 32:10 Lightning speeds before the T, and approval precedes
40:13 a loud clap of T in a rain.
43:17 The voice of his T rebukes the earth; so
Is 17:12 Ah, the T of many peoples, they thunder like
17:12 of many peoples, they T like the thundering of
29:6 LORD of hosts with T and with earthquake and
Ezek 1:24 many waters, like the T of the Almighty, a
Mk 3:17 that is, sons of T;
Rev 4:5 voices and peals of T, and before the throne
6:1 with a voice of T, "Come!"

8:5 there were peals of T, voices, flashes of lightning,
11:19 lightning, voices, peals of T, an earthquake, and heavy
14:2 the sound of loud T; the voice I heard
16:18 lightning, voices, peals of T, and a great earthquake

THUNDERBOLT

Job 38:25 a way for the T,

THUNDERBOLTS (2)

Ps 78:48 cattle to the hail, and their flocks to T
2Mac 10:30 they showered arrows and T upon the enemy, so

THUNDERED (5)

1Sam 7:10 Israel; but the LORD T with a mighty voice
2Sam 22:14 The LORD T from heaven, and the Most High
Ps 18:13 The LORD also T in the heavens, and the
Sir 46:17 Then the Lord T from heaven, and made his
Jn 12:29 by heard it and said that it had T

THUNDERING

Is 17:12 they thunder like the T of the sea!

THUNDERINGS (2)

Ex 20:18 the people perceived the T and the lightnings and
Job 36:29 of the clouds, the T of his pavilion?

THUNDEROUS

Is 33:3 At the T noise peoples flee, at the lifting

THUNDERPEALS

Rev 19:6 the sound of mighty T, crying, "Hallelujah!

THUNDERS (9)

Ex 19:16 third day there were T and lightnings, and a
Esth 11:5 Behold, noise and confusion, T and earthquake,
Job 37:4 his voice roars; he T with his majestic voice
37:5 God T wondrously with his voice; he does great
Ps 29:3 the God of glory T, the LORD, upon many
93:4 Mightier than the T of many waters, mightier than
Rev 10:3 called out, the seven T sounded.
10:4 And when the seven T had sounded, I was
10:4 up what the seven T have said, and do

THUSELAH

1Chr 1:3 Kenan, Mahalalel, Jared, Enoch, T, Lamech,

THWART

1Cor 1:19 and the cleverness of the clever I will T

THWARTED

Job 42:2 and that no purpose of thine can be T

THWARTS

Prov 10:3 go hungry, but he T the craving of the

THY (1,554)

Gen 4:14 the ground; and from T face I shall be
17:18 Ishmael might live in T sight!"
24:14 thou hast appointed for T servant Isaac.
32:10 thou hast shown to T servant, for with only
49:18 I wait for T salvation, O LORD.
Ex 4:10 thou hast spoken to T servant; but I am
5:23 Pharaoh to speak in T name, he has done
5:23 thou hast not delivered T people at all."
15:6 T right hand, O LORD, glorious in power, thy
15:6 LORD, glorious in power, T right hand, O LORD,
15:7 In the greatness of T majesty thou overthrowest thy
15:7 majesty thou overthrowest T adversaries; thou
15:7 adversaries; thou sendest forth T fury, it consumes
15:8 At the blast of T nostrils the waters piled
15:10 Thou didst blow with T wind, the sea covered
15:12 Thou didst stretch out T right hand, the earth
15:13 "Thou hast led in T steadfast love the people
15:13 hast guided them by T strength to thy holy
15:13 by thy strength to T holy abode.
15:16 of the greatness of T arm, they are as
15:16 as a stone, till T people, O LORD, pass
15:17 and plant them on T own mountain, the place,
15:17 thou hast made for T abode, the sanctuary, O
15:17 sanctuary, O LORD, which T hands have established.
32:11 "O LORD, why does T wrath burn hot against
32:11 wrath burn hot against T people, whom thou hast
32:12 Turn from T fierce wrath, and repent of this
32:12 of this evil against T people.
32:13 Abraham, Isaac, and Israel, T servants, to whom thou
32:32 pray thee, out of T book which thou hast
33:13 have found favor in T sight, show me now
33:13 sight, show me now T ways, that I may
33:13 and find favor in T sight.
33:13 that this nation is T people."
33:15 said to him, "If T presence will not go
33:16 have found favor in T sight, I and thy
33:16 thy sight, I and T people?
33:16 Is it not in T going with us, so
33:16 are distinct, I and T people, from all other
33:18 pray thee, show me T glory."
34:9 have found favor in T sight, O Lord, let
34:9 and take us for T inheritance."
Num 10:35 O LORD, and let T enemies be scattered; and
11:11 thou dealt ill with T servant?
11:11 not found favor in T sight, that thou dost
11:15 I find favor in T sight, that I may
14:13 up this people in T might from among them,
14:14 face to face, and T cloud stands over them
14:15 nations who have heard T fame will say,
14:19 to the greatness of T steadfast love, and according
22:34 it is evil in T sight, I will go
Deut 3:24 only begun to show T servant thy greatness and
3:24 to show thy servant T greatness and thy mighty
3:24 servant thy greatness and T mighty hand; for what
9:26 Lord GOD, destroy not T people and thy heritage,
9:26 not thy people and T heritage, whom thou hast
9:26 thou hast redeemed through T greatness, whom thou
9:27 Remember T servants, Abraham, Isaac, and Jacob;
9:29 For they are T people and thy heritage, whom
9:29 are thy people and T heritage, whom thou didst
9:29 didst bring out by T great power and by
9:29 great power and by T outstretched arm.'
21:8 Forgive, O LORD, T people Israel, whom thou hast
21:8 in the midst of T people Israel; but let
26:13 widow, according to all T commandment which thou
26:13 transgressed any of T commandments, neither have I
26:15 Look down from T holy habitation, from heaven, and
26:15 from heaven, and bless T people Israel and the
33:3 so they followed in T steps, receiving direction from
33:7 With T hands contend for him, and be a
33:8 said, "Give to Levi T Thummim, and thy Urim
33:8 Levi thy Thummim, and T Urim to thy godly
33:8 and thy Urim to T godly one, whom thou
33:9 For they observed T word, and kept thy covenant.
33:9 thy word, and kept T covenant.
33:10 They shall teach Jacob T ordinances, and Israel thy
33:10 thy ordinances, and Israel T law; they shall put
33:10 whole burnt offering upon T altar.
Josh 7:9 wilt thou do for T great name?"
Judg 5:31 But T friends be like the sun as he
6:39 to God, "Let not T anger burn against me,
15:18 by the hand of T servant; and shall I
1Sam 1:11 on the affliction of T maidservant, and remember
1:11 me, and not forget T maidservant, but wilt give
1:11 but wilt give to T maidservant a son, then
2:1 because I rejoice in T salvation.
3:9 say, 'Speak, LORD, for T servant hears.'" So Samuel
3:10 Samuel said, "Speak, for T servant hears."
14:41 hast thou not answered T servant this day?
14:41 this guilt is in T people Israel, give Thummim."
23:10 the God of Israel, T servant has surely heard
23:11 Saul come down, as T servant has heard?
23:11 I beseech thee, tell T servant." And the LORD
2Sam 1:19 He said: T glory, O Israel, is slain upon
1:19 Israel, is slain upon T high places!
1:25 "Jonathan lies slain upon T high places.
7:19 a small thing in T eyes, O Lord GOD;
7:19 hast spoken also of T servant's house for a
7:20 For thou knowest T servant, O Lord GOD!
7:21 Because of T promise, and according to thy own
7:21 promise, and according to T own heart, thou hast
7:21 this greatness, to make T servant know it.
7:23 on earth is like T people Israel, whom God
7:24 didst establish for thyself T people Israel to be
7:24 people Israel to be T people for ever; and
7:25 hast spoken concerning T servant and concerning his
7:26 thou hast spoken; and T name will be magnified
7:26 and the house of T servant David will be
7:27 made this revelation to T servant, saying, 'I will
7:27 you a house'; therefore T servant has found courage
7:28 thou art God, and T words are true, and
7:28 this good thing to T servant;
7:29 bless the house of T servant, that it may
7:29 hast spoken, and with T blessing shall the house
7:29 shall the house of T servant be blessed for
22:28 a humble people, but T eyes are upon the

22:36 me the shield of T salvation, and thy help
22:36 of thy salvation, and T help made me great.
22:50 and sing praises to T name.
24:10 away the iniquity of T servant; for I have
24:17 Let T hand, I pray thee, be against me
1Kgs 3:6 and steadfast love to T servant David my father,
3:7 God, thou hast made T servant king in place
3:8 And T servant is in the midst of thy
3:8 in the midst of T people whom thou hast
3:9 Give T servant therefore an understanding mind to
govern
3:9 understanding mind to govern T people, that I may
3:9 able to govern this T great people?"
8:23 showing steadfast love to T servants who walk before
8:24 who hast kept with T servant David my father
8:24 thou didst speak with T mouth, and with thy
8:24 thy mouth, and with T hand hast fulfilled it
8:25 of Israel, keep with T servant David my father
8:26 God of Israel, let T word be confirmed, which
8:26 thou hast spoken to T servant David my father.
8:28 to the prayer of T servant and to his
8:28 to the prayer which T servant prays before thee
8:29 thee this day; that T eyes may be open
8:29 to the prayer which T servant offers toward this
8:30 to the supplication of T servant and of thy
8:30 thy servant and of T people Israel, when they
8:30 hear thou in heaven T dwelling place; and when
8:32 and act, and judge T servants, condemning the guilty
8:33 "When T people Israel are defeated before the
8:33 to thee, and acknowledge T name, and pray and
8:34 forgive the sin of T people Israel, and bring
8:35 this place, and acknowledge T name, and turn from
8:36 forgive the sin of T servants, thy people Israel,
8:36 sin of thy servants, T people Israel, when thou
8:36 and grant rain upon T land, which thou hast
8:36 thou hast given to T people as an inheritance.
8:38 man or by all T people Israel, each knowing
8:39 hear thou in heaven T dwelling place, and forgive,
8:41 who is not of T people Israel, comes from
8:41 a far country for T name's sake
8:42 they shall hear of T great name, and thy
8:42 thy great name, and T mighty hand, and of
8:42 mighty hand, and of T outstretched arm), when he
8:43 hear thou in heaven T dwelling place, and do
8:43 the earth may know T name and fear thee,
8:43 fear thee, as do T people Israel, and that
8:43 built is called by T name.
8:44 "If T people go out to battle against their
8:44 I have built for T name,
8:48 I have built for T name;
8:49 hear thou in heaven T dwelling place their prayer
8:50 their cause and forgive T people who have sinned
8:51 them (for they are T people, and thy heritage,
8:51 are thy people, and T heritage, which thou didst
8:52 Let T eyes be open to the supplication of
8:52 to the supplication of T servant, and to the
8:52 to the supplication of T people Israel, giving ear
8:53 the earth, to be T heritage, as thou didst
8:53 didst declare through Moses, T servant, when thou
18:36 and that I am T servant, and that I
18:36 all these things at T word.
19:10 of Israel have forsaken T covenant, thrown down thy
19:10 thy covenant, thrown down T altars, and slain thy
19:10 thy altars, and slain T prophets with the sword;
19:14 of Israel have forsaken T covenant, thrown down thy
19:14 thy covenant, thrown down T altars, and slain thy
19:14 thy altars, and slain T prophets with the sword;
2Kgs 19:16 Incline T ear, O LORD, and hear; open thy
19:16 LORD, and hear; open T eyes, O LORD, and
20:3 what is good in T sight." And Hezekiah wept
1Chr 4:10 my border, and that T hand might be with
16:35 may give thanks to T holy name, and glory
16:35 name, and glory in T praise.
17:17 a small thing in T eyes, O God; thou
17:17 hast also spoken of T servant's house for a
17:18 to thee for honoring T servant?
17:18 For thou knowest T servant.
17:19 For T servant's sake, O LORD, and according to
17:19 LORD, and according to T own heart, thou hast
17:21 on earth is like T people Israel, whom God
17:21 driving out nations before T people whom thou didst
17:22 And thou didst make T people Israel to be
17:22 people Israel to be T people for ever; and
17:23 thou hast spoken concerning T servant and
17:24 thou hast spoken; and T name will be established
17:24 and the house of T servant David will be
17:25 God, hast revealed to T servant that thou wilt
17:25 house for him; therefore T servant has found courage
17:26 this good thing to T servant;
17:27 bless the house of T servant, that it may
21:8 away the iniquity of T servant; for I have
21:17 Let T hand, I pray thee, O LORD my
21:17 the plague be upon T people."
29:12 In T hand are power and might; and in
29:12 and might; and in T hand it is to
29:13 our God, and praise T glorious name.
29:14 from thee, and of T own have we given
29:16 thee a house for T holy name comes from
29:16 holy name comes from T hand and is all
29:16 hand and is all T own.
29:17 now I have seen T people, who are present
29:18 in the hearts of T people, and direct their
29:19 heart he may keep T commandments, thy
29:19 may keep thy commandments, T testimonies, and thy
29:19 commandments, thy testimonies, and T statutes,
2Chr 1:9 O LORD God, let T promise to David my
1:10 who can rule this T people, that is so
6:14 showing steadfast love to T servants who walk before
6:15 who hast kept with T servant David my father
6:15 thou didst speak with T mouth, and with thy
6:15 thy mouth, and with T hand hast fulfilled it
6:16 of Israel, keep with T servant David my father
6:17 God of Israel, let T word be confirmed, which
6:17 thou hast spoken to T servant David.
6:19 to the prayer of T servant and to his
6:19 to the prayer which T servant prays before thee;
6:20 prays before thee; that T eyes may be open
6:20 hast promised to set T name, that thou mayest
6:20 to the prayer which T servant offers toward this
6:21 to the supplications of T servant and of thy
6:21 thy servant and of T people Israel, when they
6:21 hear thou from heaven T dwelling place; and when
6:22 swears his oath before T altar in this house,
6:23 and act, and judge T servants, requiting the guilty
6:24 "If T people Israel are defeated before the enemy
6:24 turn again and acknowledge T name, and pray and
6:25 forgive the sin of T people Israel, and bring
6:26 this place, and acknowledge T name, and turn from
6:27 forgive the sin of T servants, thy people Israel,
6:27 sin of thy servants, T people Israel, when thou
6:27 and grant rain upon T land, which thou hast
6:27 thou hast given to T people as an inheritance.
6:29 man or by all T people Israel, each knowing
6:30 hear thou from heaven T dwelling place, and forgive,
6:31 thee and walk in T ways all the days
6:32 who is not of T people Israel, comes from
6:32 for the sake of T great name, and thy
6:32 thy great name, and T mighty hand, and thy
6:32 thy mighty hand, and T outstretched arm, when he
6:33 hear thou from heaven T dwelling place, and do
6:33 the earth may know T name and fear thee,
6:33 fear thee, as do T people Israel, and that
6:33 built is called by T name.
6:34 "If T people go out to battle against their
6:34 I have built for T name,
6:38 I have built for T name,
6:39 hear thou from heaven T dwelling place their prayer
6:39 their cause and forgive T people who have sinned
6:40 O my God, let T eyes be open and
6:40 eyes be open and T ears attentive to a
6:41 God, and go to T resting place, thou and
6:41 and the ark of T might.
6:41 Let T priests, O LORD God, be clothed with
6:41 with salvation, and let T saints rejoice in thy
6:41 thy saints rejoice in T goodness.
6:42 away the face of T anointed one!
6:42 Remember T steadfast love for David thy servant."
6:42 steadfast love for David T servant."
14:11 on thee, and in T name we have come
20:6 In T hand are power and might, so that
20:7 of this land before T people Israel, and give
20:7 the descendants of Abraham T friend?
20:8 it a sanctuary for T name, saying,
20:9 and before thee, for T name is in this
20:11 drive us out of T possession, which thou hast
Ezra 9:10 For we have forsaken T commandments,
9:11 thou didst command by T servants the prophets,
9:14 we break T commandments again and intermarry
Neh 1:6 keep his commandments; let T ear be attentive, and
1:6 ear be attentive, and T eyes open, to hear
1:6 hear the prayer of T servant which I now
1:6 the people of Israel T servants, confessing the sins

T

19:13 Keep back T servant also from presumptuous sins; let
19:14 heart be acceptable in T sight, O LORD, my
21:1 In T strength the king rejoices, O LORD; and
21:1 O LORD; and in T help how greatly he
21:5 glory is great through T help; splendor and majesty
21:6 with the joy of T presence.
21:13 exalted, O LORD, in T strength!
21:13 will sing and praise T power.
22:22 I will tell of T name to my brethren;
23:4 thou art with me; T rod and thy staff,
23:4 me; thy rod and T staff, they comfort me.
25:4 Make me to know T ways, O LORD; teach
25:4 O LORD; teach me T paths.
25:5 Lead me in T truth, and teach me, for
25:6 Be mindful of T mercy, O LORD, and of
25:6 O LORD, and of T steadfast love, for they
25:7 my transgressions; according to T steadfast love
25:7 love remember me, for T goodness' sake, O LORD!
25:11 For T name's sake, O LORD, pardon my guilt,
26:3 For T steadfast love is before my eyes, and
26:6 innocence, and go about T altar, O LORD,
26:7 thanksgiving, and telling all T wondrous deeds.
26:8 love the habitation of T house, and the place
26:8 and the place where T glory dwells.
27:8 heart says to thee, T face, LORD, do I
27:9 Hide not T face from me.
27:9 Turn not T servant away in anger, thou who
27:11 Teach me T way, O LORD; and lead me
28:2 up my hands toward T most holy sanctuary.
28:9 O save T people, and bless thy heritage; be
28:9 thy people, and bless T heritage; be thou their
30:7 By T favor, O LORD, thou hadst established me
30:7 mountain; thou didst hide T face, I was dismayed.
30:9 Will it tell of T faithfulness?
31:1 put to shame; in T righteousness deliver me!
31:2 Incline T ear to me, rescue me speedily!
31:3 and my fortress; for T name's sake lead me
31:5 Into T hand I commit my spirit; thou hast
31:7 and be glad for T steadfast love, because thou
31:15 My times are in T hand; deliver me from
31:16 Let T face shine on thy servant; save me
31:16 thy face shine on T servant; save me in
31:16 servant; save me in T steadfast love!
31:19 O how abundant is T goodness, which thou hast
31:20 In the covert of T presence thou hidest them
31:20 holdest them safe under T shelter from the strife
31:22 am driven far from T sight." But thou didst
32:4 For day and night T hand was heavy upon
33:22 Let T steadfast love, O LORD, be upon us,
35:24 my God, according to T righteousness; and let them
35:28 tongue shall tell of T righteousness and of thy
35:28 thy righteousness and of T praise all the day
36:5 T steadfast love, O LORD, extends to the heavens,
36:5 extends to the heavens, T faithfulness to the clouds.
36:6 T righteousness is like the mountains of God, thy
36:6 the mountains of God, T judgments are like the
36:7 How precious is T steadfast love, O God!
36:7 in the shadow of T wings.
36:8 on the abundance of T house, and thou givest
36:8 from the river of T delights.
36:9 fountain of life; in T light do we see
36:10 O continue T steadfast love to those who know
36:10 who know thee, and T salvation to the upright
38:1 rebuke me not in T anger, nor chasten me
38:1 nor chasten me in T wrath!
38:2 For T arrows have sunk into me, and thy
38:2 sunk into me, and T hand has come down
38:3 my flesh because of T indignation; there is no
39:5 is as nothing in T sight.
39:10 Remove T stroke from me; I am spent by
39:10 by the blows of T hand.
39:12 my cry; hold not T peace at my tears!
39:12 For I am T passing guest, a sojourner, like
40:5 O LORD my God, T wondrous deeds and thy
40:5 thy wondrous deeds and T thoughts toward us; none
40:8 I delight to do T will, O my God;
40:8 will, O my God; T law is within my
40:10 I have not hid T saving help within my
40:10 I have spoken of T faithfulness and thy salvation;
40:10 of thy faithfulness and T salvation; I have not
40:10 I have not concealed T steadfast love and thy
40:10 thy steadfast love and T faithfulness from the great
40:11 thou, O LORD, withhold T mercy from me, let
40:11 mercy from me, let T steadfast love and thy
40:11 steadfast love and T faithfulness ever preserve me!
40:16 those who love T salvation say continually, "Great

41:12 and set me in T presence for ever.
42:7 at the thunder of T cataracts; all thy waves
42:7 of thy cataracts; all T waves and thy billows
42:7 all thy waves and T billows have gone over
43:3 Oh send out T light and thy truth; let
43:3 out thy light and T truth; let them lead
43:3 them bring me to T holy hill and to
43:3 holy hill and to T dwelling!
44:2 of old: thou with T own hand didst drive
44:3 give them victory; but T right hand, and thy
44:3 thy right hand, and T arm, and the light
44:3 and the light of T countenance; for thou didst
44:5 down our foes; through T name we tread down
44:8 will give thanks to T name for ever.
44:12 Thou hast sold T people for a trifle, demanding
44:17 or been false to T covenant.
44:18 our steps departed from T way,
44:22 Nay, for T sake we are slain all the
44:24 Why dost thou hide T face?
44:26 for the sake of T steadfast love!
48:9 We have thought on T steadfast love, O God,
48:9 in the midst of T temple.
48:10 As T name, O God, so thy praise reaches
48:10 name, O God, so T praise reaches to the
48:10 T right hand is filled with victory;
48:11 Judah rejoice because of T judgments!
51:1 O God, according to T steadfast love; according to
51:1 steadfast love; according to T abundant mercy blot
51:4 which is evil in T sight, so that thou
51:4 thou art justified in T sentence and blameless in
51:4 sentence and blameless in T judgment.
51:9 Hide T face from my sins, and blot out
51:11 me not away from T presence, and take not
51:11 presence, and take not T holy Spirit from me.
51:12 me the joy of T salvation, and uphold me
51:13 I will teach transgressors T ways, and sinners will
51:14 will sing aloud of T deliverance.
51:15 mouth shall show forth T praise.
51:18 good to Zion in T good pleasure; rebuild the
51:19 will be offered on T altar.
52:9 I will proclaim T name, for it is good,
54:1 me, O God, by T name, and vindicate me
54:1 and vindicate me by T might.
54:5 enemies with evil; in T faithfulness put an end
54:6 will give thanks to T name, O LORD, for
56:8 thou my tears in T bottle!
56:8 Are they not in T book?
57:1 in the shadow of T wings I will take
57:5 Let T glory be over all the earth!
57:10 For T steadfast love is great to the heavens,
57:10 great to the heavens, T faithfulness to the clouds.
57:11 Let T glory be over all the earth!
59:11 make them totter by T power, and bring them
59:16 I will sing of T might; I will sing
59:16 will sing aloud of T steadfast love in the
60:3 Thou hast made T people suffer hard things; thou
60:5 [Selah] That T beloved may be delivered, give
60:5 delivered, give victory by T right hand and answer
61:4 Let me dwell in T tent for ever!
61:4 under the shelter of T wings!
61:5 of those who fear T name.
61:8 ever sing praises to T name, as I pay
63:2 in the sanctuary, beholding T power and glory.
63:3 Because T steadfast love is better than life, my
63:4 hands and call on T name.
63:7 in the shadow of T wings I sing for
63:8 soul clings to thee; T right hand upholds me.
65:4 near, to dwell in T courts!
65:4 with the goodness of T house, thy holy temple!
65:4 goodness of thy house, T holy temple!
65:6 farthest seas; who by T strength hast established the
65:8 bounds are afraid at T signs; thou makest the
65:11 crownest the year with T bounty; the tracks of
65:11 bounty; the tracks of T chariot drip with fatness.
66:3 God, "How terrible are T deeds!
66:3 So great is T power that thy enemies cringe
66:3 is thy power that T enemies cringe before thee.
66:4 thee, sing praises to T name." [Selah]
66:13 I will come into T house with burnt offerings;
67:2 upon us, [Selah] that T way may be known
67:2 be known upon earth, T saving power among all
68:7 didst go forth before T people, when thou didst
68:9 abroad; thou didst restore T heritage as it
68:10 heritage as it languished; T flock found a dwelling
68:10 dwelling in it; in T goodness, O God, thou
68:18 mount, leading captives in T train, and receiving gifts

68:24 T solemn processions are seen, O God, the
68:28 Summon T might, O God; show thy strength, O
68:28 might, O God; show T strength, O God, thou
68:29 Because of T temple at Jerusalem kings bear gifts
69:7 For it is for T sake that I have
69:9 For zeal for T house has consumed me, and
69:13 in the abundance of T steadfast love answer me.
69:13 With T faithful help
69:16 me, O LORD, for T steadfast love is good;
69:16 is good; according to T abundant mercy, turn to
69:17 Hide not T face from thy servant; for I
69:17 not thy face from T servant; for I am
69:24 Pour out T indignation upon them, and let thy
69:24 upon them, and let T burning anger overtake them.
69:29 and in pain; let T salvation, O God, set
70:4 May those who love T salvation say evermore, "God
71:2 In T righteousness deliver me and rescue me; incline
71:2 and rescue me; incline T ear to me, and
71:8 mouth is filled with T praise, and with thy
71:8 thy praise, and with T glory all the day.
71:15 mouth will tell of T righteous acts, of thy
71:15 thy righteous acts, of T deeds of salvation all
71:16 come, I will praise T righteousness, thine alone.
71:17 and I still proclaim T wondrous deeds.
71:18 me, till I proclaim T might to all the
71:18 T power
71:19 Thy power and T righteousness, O God, reach the
71:22 with the harp for T faithfulness, O my God;
71:24 tongue will talk of T righteous help all the
72:1 Give the king T justice, O God, and thy
72:1 justice, O God, and T righteousness to the royal
72:2 May he judge T people with righteousness, and thy
72:2 people with righteousness, and T poor with justice!
73:15 to the generation of T children.
73:24 dost guide me with T counsel, and afterward thou
73:28 may tell of all T works.
74:1 Why does T anger smoke against the sheep of
74:1 against the sheep of T pasture?
74:2 Remember T congregation, which thou hast gotten
74:2 be the tribe of T heritage!
74:3 Direct T steps to the perpetual ruins; the enemy
74:4 T foes have roared in the midst of thy
74:4 in the midst of T holy place; they set
74:7 They set T sanctuary on fire; to the ground
74:7 the dwelling place of T name.
74:10 the enemy to revile T name for ever?
74:11 dost thou hold back T hand, why dost thou
74:11 why dost thou keep T right hand in thy
74:11 thy right hand in T bosom?
74:13 divide the sea by T might; thou didst break
74:18 an impious people reviles T name.
74:19 deliver the soul of T dove to the wild
74:19 forget the life of T poor for ever.
74:20 Have regard for T covenant; for the dark places
74:21 poor and needy praise T name.
74:22 Arise, O God, plead T cause; remember how the
74:23 forget the clamor of T foes, the uproar of
74:23 foes, the uproar of T adversaries which goes up
75:1 thanks; we call on T name and recount thy
75:1 thy name and recount T wondrous deeds.
76:6 At T rebuke, O God of Jacob, both rider
76:7 before thee when once T anger is roused?
77:11 yea, I will remember T wonders of old.
77:12 will meditate on all T work, and muse on
77:12 work, and muse on T mighty deeds.
77:13 T way, O God, is holy.
77:14 wonders, who hast manifested T might among the
77:15 Thou didst with T arm redeem thy people, the
77:15 with thy arm redeem T people, the sons of
77:17 skies gave forth thunder; T arrows flashed on every
77:18 The crash of T thunder was in the whirlwind;
77:18 was in the whirlwind; T lightnings lighted up the
77:19 T way was through the sea, thy path through
77:19 was through the sea, T path through the great
77:19 the great waters; yet T footprints were unseen.
77:20 Thou didst lead T people like a flock by
79:1 heathen have come into T inheritance; they have
79:1 inheritance; they have defiled T holy temple; they
79:2 given the bodies of T servants to the birds
79:2 food, the flesh of T saints to the beasts
79:5 Will T jealous wrath burn like fire?
79:6 Pour out T anger on the nations that do
79:6 do not call on T name!
79:8 of our forefathers; let T compassion come speedily to
79:9 for the glory of T name; deliver us, and
79:9 forgive our sins, for T name's sake!
79:10 the outpoured blood of T servants be known among
79:11 before thee; according to T great power preserve
79:13 Then we T people, the flock of thy pasture,
79:13 people, the flock of T pasture, will give thanks
79:13 generation we will recount T praise.
80:2 Stir up T might, and come to save us!
80:3 us, O God; let T face shine, that we
80:4 thou be angry with T people's prayers?
80:7 God of hosts; let T face shine, that we
80:15 vine, the stock which T right hand planted.
80:16 at the rebuke of T countenance!
80:17 But let T hand be upon the man of
80:17 upon the man of T right hand, the son
80:18 we will call on T name!
80:19 let T face shine, that we may be saved!
83:1 silence; do not hold T peace or be still,
83:2 For lo, T enemies are in tumult; those who
83:3 lay crafty plans against T people; they consult
83:3 they consult together against T protected ones.
83:15 thou pursue them with T tempest and terrify them
83:15 and terrify them with T hurricane!
83:16 that they may seek T name, O LORD.
84:1 How lovely is T dwelling place, O LORD of
84:3 lay her young, at T altars, O LORD of
84:4 those who dwell in T house, ever singing thy
84:4 thy house, ever singing T praise!
84:10 For a day in T courts is better than
85:1 thou wast favorable to T land; thou didst restore
85:2 forgive the iniquity of T people; thou didst pardon
85:3 Thou didst withdraw all T wrath; thou didst turn
85:3 thou didst turn from T hot anger.
85:4 salvation, and put away T indignation toward us!
85:5 Wilt thou prolong T anger to all generations?
85:6 revive us again, that T people may rejoice in
85:7 Show us T steadfast love, O LORD, and grant
85:7 LORD, and grant us T salvation.
86:1 Incline T ear, O LORD, and answer me, for
86:2 I am godly; save T servant who trusts in
86:4 Gladden the soul of T servant, for to thee,
86:9 Lord, and shall glorify T name.
86:11 Teach me T way, O LORD, that I may
86:11 I may walk in T truth; unite my heart
86:11 my heart to fear T name.
86:12 and I will glorify T name for ever.
86:13 For great is T steadfast love toward me; thou
86:16 pity on me; give T strength to thy servant,
86:16 give thy strength to T servant, and save the
86:16 save the son of T handmaid.
86:17 me a sign of T favor, that those who
88:2 come before thee, incline T ear to my cry!
88:5 are cut off from T hand.
88:7 T wrath lies heavy upon me, and thou dost
88:7 overwhelm me with all T waves.
88:11 [Selah] Is T steadfast love declared in the grave,
88:11 in the grave, or T faithfulness in Abaddon?
88:12 Are T wonders known in the darkness, or thy
88:12 in the darkness, or T saving help in the
88:14 Why dost thou hide T face from me?
88:15 youth up, I suffer T terrors; I am helpless.
88:16 T wrath has swept over me; thy dread assaults
88:16 has swept over me; T dread assaults destroy me.
89:1 I will sing of T steadfast love, O LORD,
89:1 mouth I will proclaim T faithfulness to all
89:2 For T steadfast love was established for ever, thy
89:2 was established for ever, T faithfulness is firm as
89:5 Let the heavens praise T wonders, O LORD, thy
89:5 thy wonders, O LORD, T faithfulness in the assembly
89:8 art, O LORD, with T faithfulness round about thee?
89:10 carcass, thou didst scatter T enemies with thy mighty
89:10 scatter thy enemies with T mighty arm.
89:12 and Hermon joyously praise T name.
89:13 mighty arm; strong is T hand, high thy right
89:13 is thy hand, high T right hand.
89:14 are the foundation of T throne; steadfast love and
89:15 in the light of T countenance,
89:16 countenance, who exult in T name all the day,
89:16 the day, and extol T righteousness.
89:17 of their strength; by T favor our horn is
89:19 in a vision to T faithful one, and say:
89:38 full of wrath against T anointed.
89:39 renounced the covenant with T servant; thou hast
89:46 How long will T wrath burn like fire?
89:49 [Selah] Lord, where is T steadfast love of old,
89:49 of old, which by T faithfulness thou didst swear
89:50 Remember, O Lord, how T servant is scorned; how
89:51 the peoples, with which T enemies taunt, O LORD,

THY

119:78 I will meditate on T precepts.
119:79 that they may know T testimonies.
119:80 heart be blameless in T statutes, that I may
119:81 My soul languishes for T salvation; I hope in
119:81 salvation; I hope in T word.
119:82 fail with watching for T promise; I ask, "When
119:83 I have not forgotten T statutes.
119:84 How long must T servant endure?
119:85 do not conform to T law.
119:86 All T commandments are sure; they persecute me
119:87 I have not forsaken T precepts.
119:88 In T steadfast love spare my life, that I
119:88 keep the testimonies of T mouth.
119:89 For ever, O LORD, T word is firmly fixed
119:90 T faithfulness endures to all generations; thou hast
119:91 By T appointment they stand this day; for all
119:91 for all things are T servants.
119:92 If T law had not been my delight, I
119:93 I will never forget T precepts; for by them
119:94 for I have sought T precepts.
119:95 me; but I consider T testimonies.
119:96 to all perfection, but T commandment is exceedingly.
119:97 Oh, how I love T law!
119:98 T commandment makes me wiser than my enemies,
119:99 all my teachers, for T testimonies are my meditation.
119:100 aged, for I keep T precepts.
119:101 in order to keep T word.
119:102 not turn aside from T ordinances, for thou hast
119:103 How sweet are T words to my taste, sweeter
119:104 Through T precepts I get understanding; therefore I
119:105 T word is a lamp to my feet and
119:106 confirmed it, to observe T righteous ordinances.
119:107 O LORD, according to T word!
119:108 LORD, and teach me T ordinances.
119:109 I do not forget T law.
119:110 do not stray from T precepts.
119:111 T testimonies are my heritage for ever; yea, they
119:112 my heart to perform T statutes for ever, to
119:113 men, but I love T law.
119:114 shield; I hope in T word.
119:116 Uphold me according to T promise, that I may
119:117 and have regard for T statutes continually!
119:118 who go astray from T statutes; yea, their cunning
119:119 dross; therefore I love T testimonies.
119:120 I am afraid of T judgments.
119:122 Be surety for T servant for good; let not
119:123 fail with watching for T salvation, and for the
119:123 for the fulfilment of T righteous promise.
119:124 Deal with T servant according to thy steadfast love,
119:124 thy servant according to T steadfast love, and teach
119:124 love, and teach me T statutes.
119:125 I am T servant; give me understanding, that I
119:125 that I may know T testimonies!
119:126 LORD to act, for T law has been broken.
119:127 Therefore I love T commandments above gold, above
119:128 my steps by all T precepts; I hate every
119:129 T testimonies are wonderful; therefore my soul
119:130 The unfolding of T words gives light; it imparts
119:131 because I long for T commandments.
119:132 to me, as is T wont toward those who
119:132 toward those who love T name.
119:133 my steps according to T promise, and let no
119:134 that I may keep T precepts.
119:135 Make T face shine upon thy servant, and teach
119:135 thy face shine upon T servant, and teach me
119:135 servant, and teach me T statutes.
119:136 men do not keep T law.
119:137 LORD, and right are T judgments.
119:138 Thou hast appointed T testimonies in righteousness
119:139 because my foes forget T words.
119:140 T promise is well tried, and thy servant loves
119:140 is well tried, and T servant loves it.
119:141 I do not forget T precepts.
119:142 T righteousness is righteous for ever, and thy law
119:142 righteous for ever, and T law is true.
119:143 come upon me, but T commandments are my delight.
119:144 T testimonies are righteous for ever; give me
119:145 I will keep T statutes.
119:146 that I may observe T testimonies.
119:147 help; I hope in T words.
119:148 I may meditate upon T promise.
119:149 Hear my voice in T steadfast love; O LORD,
119:149 love; O LORD, in T justice preserve my life.
119:150 they are far from T law.
119:151 O LORD, and all T commandments are true.
119:152 have I known from T testimonies that thou hast
119:153 I do not forget T law.
119:154 me life according to T promise!
119:155 they do not seek T statutes.
119:156 Great is T mercy, O LORD; give me life
119:156 me life according to T justice.
119:157 do not swerve from T testimonies.
119:158 they do not keep T commands.
119:159 Consider how I love T precepts!
119:159 my life according to T steadfast love.
119:160 The sum of T word is truth; and every
119:160 and every one of T righteous ordinances endures for
119:161 stands in awe of T words.
119:162 I rejoice at T word like one who finds
119:163 falsehood, but I love T law.
119:164 I praise thee for T righteous ordinances.
119:165 have those who love T law; nothing can make
119:166 I hope for T salvation, O LORD, and I
119:166 LORD, and I do T commandments.
119:167 My soul keeps T testimonies; I love them
119:168 I keep T precepts and testimonies, for all my
119:169 me understanding according to T word!
119:170 deliver me according to T word.
119:171 thou dost teach me T statutes.
119:172 tongue will sing of T word, for all thy
119:172 thy word, for all T commandments are right.
119:173 Let T hand be ready to help me, for
119:173 for I have chosen T precepts.
119:174 I long for T salvation, O LORD, and thy
119:174 salvation, O LORD, and T law is my delight.
119:175 praise thee, and let T ordinances help me.
119:176 a lost sheep; seek T servant, for I do
119:176 I do not forget T commandments.
130:2 Let T ears be attentive to the voice of
132:8 LORD, and go to T resting place, thou and
132:8 and the ark of T might.
132:9 Let T priests be clothed with righteousness, and let
132:9 with righteousness, and let T saints shout for joy.
132:10 For T servant David's sake do not turn away
132:10 away the face of T anointed one.
135:9 of beast; who in T midst, O Egypt, sent
135:13 T name, O LORD, endures for ever, thy renown,
135:13 LORD, endures for ever, T renown, O LORD,
138:1 the gods I sing T praise;
138:2 I bow down toward T holy temple and give
138:2 and give thanks to T name for thy steadfast
138:2 to thy name for T steadfast love and thy
138:2 thy steadfast love and T faithfulness; for thou hast
138:2 hast exalted above everything T name and thy word.
138:2 everything thy name and T word.
138:4 heard the words of T mouth;
138:7 thou dost stretch out T hand against the wrath
138:7 of my enemies, and T right hand delivers me.
138:8 his purpose for me; T steadfast love, O LORD,
138:8 forsake the work of T hands.
139:5 and before, and layest T hand upon me.
139:7 shall I go from T Spirit?
139:7 shall I flee from T presence?
139:10 the sea, even there T hand shall lead me,
139:10 shall lead me, and T right hand shall hold
139:14 Wonderful are T works!
139:16 T eyes beheld my unformed substance; in thy book
139:16 my unformed substance; in T book were written,
139:17 precious to me are T thoughts, O God!
140:13 shall give thanks to T name; the upright shall
140:13 upright shall dwell in T presence.
142:7 may give thanks to T name!
143:1 In T faithfulness answer me, in thy righteousness!
143:1 faithfulness answer me, in T righteousness!
143:2 not into judgment with T servant; for no man
143:5 I muse on what T hands have wrought.
143:7 Hide not T face from me, lest I be
143:8 in the morning of T steadfast love, for in
143:10 Teach me to do T will, for thou art
143:10 Let T good spirit lead me on a level
143:11 For T name's sake, O LORD, preserve my life!
143:11 In T righteousness bring me out of trouble!
143:12 And in T steadfast love cut off my enemies,
143:12 adversaries, for I am T servant.
144:5 Bow T heavens, O LORD, and come down!
144:6 scatter them, send out T arrows and rout them!
144:7 Stretch forth T hand from on high, rescue me
144:10 kings, who rescuest David T servant.
145:1 and King, and bless T name for ever and
145:2 bless thee, and praise T name for ever and
145:4 One generation shall laud T works to another, and
145:4 another, and shall declare T mighty acts.

	145:5	the glorious splendor of T majesty, and on thy
	145:5	thy majesty, and on T wondrous works, I will
	145:6	proclaim the might of T terrible acts, and I
	145:6	and I will declare T greatness.
	145:7	forth the fame of T abundant goodness, and shall
	145:7	shall sing aloud of T righteousness.
	145:10	All T works shall give thanks to thee, O
	145:10	O LORD, and all T saints shall bless thee!
	145:11	of the glory of T kingdom, and tell of
	145:11	kingdom, and tell of T power,
	145:12	the sons of men T mighty deeds, and the
	145:12	the glorious splendor of T kingdom.
	145:13	T kingdom is an everlasting kingdom, and thy
	145:13	everlasting kingdom, and T dominion endures
	145:16	Thou openest T hand, thou satisfiest the desire of
	146:10	will reign for ever, T God, O Zion, to
Wis	9:1	made all things by T word,
	9:2	thy word, and by T wisdom hast formed man,
	9:4	wisdom that sits by T throne, and do not
	9:4	reject me from among T servants.
	9:5	For I am T slave and the son of
	9:5	and the son of T maidservant, a man who
	9:7	to be king of T people and to be
	9:7	to be judge over T sons and daughters.
	9:8	build a temple on T holy mountain, and an
	9:8	in the city of T habitation, a copy of
	9:9	is wisdom, who knows T works and was present
	9:9	what is pleasing in T sight and what is
	9:9	is right according to T commandments.
	9:10	from the throne of T glory send her, that
	9:12	and I shall judge T people justly, and shall
	9:17	Who has learned T counsel, unless thou hast given
	9:17	given wisdom and sent T holy Spirit from on
	10:20	hymns, O Lord, to T holy name, and praised
	10:20	praised with one accord T defending hand,
	11:17	For T all-powerful hand, which created the world out
	11:20	by the breath of T power.
	11:21	it is always in T power to show great
	11:21	withstand the might of T arm?
	12:1	For T immortal spirit is in all things.
	12:3	dwelt of old in T holy land
	12:8	wasps as forerunners of T army, to destroy them
	12:9	dread wild beasts or T stern word.
	12:12	Or will resist T judgment?
	12:15	deeming it alien to T power to condemn him
	12:16	For T strength is the source of righteousness, and
	12:16	source of righteousness, and T sovereignty over all
	12:17	For thou dost show T strength when men doubt
	12:17	doubt the completeness of T power, and dost rebuke
	12:19	works thou has taught T people that the righteous
	12:19	and thou hast filled T sons with good hope,
	12:20	indulgence the enemies of T servants and those
	12:21	strictness thou hast judged T sons, to whose fathers
	12:22	we may meditate upon T goodness when we judge,
	12:25	children, thou didst send T judgment to mock them.
	14:3	it; but it is T providence, O Father, that
	14:5	It is T will that works of thy wisdom
	14:5	will that works of T wisdom should not be
	14:6	raft, and guided by T hand left to the
	15:2	we are thine, knowing T power; but we will
	15:3	righteousness, and to know T power is the root
	15:14	the enemies who oppressed T people.
	15:18	The enemies of T people worship even the most
	16:2	didst show kindness to T people, and thou didst
	16:3	sent to them, while T people, after suffering want
	16:5	wild beasts came upon T people and they were
	16:5	bites of writhing serpents, T wrath did not continue
	16:6	to remind them of T law's command.
	16:10	by such things; but T sons were not conquered
	16:10	of venomous serpents, for T mercy came to their
	16:11	To remind them of T oracles they were bitten,
	16:11	and become unresponsive to T kindness.
	16:12	them, but it was T word, O Lord, which
	16:15	To escape from T hand is impossible;
	16:16	by the strength of T arm, pursued by unusual
	16:20	things thou didst give T people food of angels,
	16:21	For T sustenance manifested T sweetness toward T
	16:25	all forms, it served T all-nourishing bounty, according
	16:26	had need, so that T sons, whom thou didst
	16:26	feeds man, but that T word preserves those who
	17:1	Great are T judgments and hard to describe;
	18:1	But for T holy ones there was very great
	18:2	and were thankful that T holy ones, though previously
	18:3	as a guide for T people's unknown journey, and
	18:4	those who had kept T sons imprisoned, through
	18:5	kill the babes of T holy ones, and one
	18:7	enemies were expected by T people.
	18:13	destroyed, they acknowledged T people to be God's
	18:15	was now half gone, T all-powerful word leaped from
	18:16	the sharp sword of T authentic command, and stood
	18:21	showing that he was T servant.
	18:24	rows of stones, and T majesty on the diadem
	19:2	they themselves had permitted T people to depart
	19:5	still lacked, and that T people might experience an
	19:6	anew, complying with T commands, that thy children
	19:6	with thy commands, that T children might be kept
	19:8	where those protected by T hand passed through as
	19:22	hast exalted and glorified T people; and thou hast
Sir	36:3	Lift up T hand against foreign nations and let
	36:3	and let them see T might.
	36:6	work further wonders; make T hand and thy right
	36:6	make thy hand and T right arm glorious.
	36:7	Rouse T anger and pour out thy wrath; destroy
	36:7	anger and pour out T wrath; destroy the adversary
	36:8	and let people recount T mighty deeds.
	36:9	may those who harm T people meet destruction.
	36:12	the people called by T name, upon Israel, whom
	36:13	on the city of T sanctuary, Jerusalem, the place
	36:13	Jerusalem, the place of T rest.
	36:14	with the celebration of T wondrous deeds, and thy
	36:14	thy wondrous deeds, and T temple with thy glory.
	36:14	and thy temple with T glory.
	36:15	the prophecies spoken in T name.
	36:16	for thee, and let T prophets be found trustworthy.
	36:17	to the prayer of T servants, according to the
	36:17	blessing of Aaron for T people, and all who
	51:1	I give thanks to T name,
	51:3	in the greatness of T mercy and of thy
	51:3	thy mercy and of T name, from the gnashings
	51:8	Then I remembered T mercy, O Lord, and thy
	51:8	mercy, O Lord, and T work from of old,
	51:11	I will praise T name continually, and will sing
Is	2:6	For thou hast rejected T people, the house of
	12:1	wast angry with me, T anger turned away, and
	25:1	thee, I will praise T name; for thou hast
	26:8	In the path of T judgments, O LORD, we
	26:8	we wait for thee; T memorial name is the
	26:9	For when T judgments are in the earth, the
	26:11	O LORD, T hand is lifted up, but they
	26:11	Let them see T zeal for thy people, and
	26:11	see thy zeal for T people, and be ashamed.
	26:11	Let the fire for T adversaries consume them.
	26:13	ruled over us, but T name alone we acknowledge.
	26:16	out a prayer when T chastening was upon them.
	26:19	T dead shall live, their bodies shall rise.
	26:19	For T dew is a dew of light, and
	37:17	Incline T ear, O LORD, and hear; open thy
	37:17	LORD, and hear; open T eyes, O LORD, and
	38:3	what is good in T sight." And Hezekiah wept
	38:17	all my sins behind T back.
	38:18	pit cannot hope for T faithfulness.
	38:19	known to the children T faithfulness.
	63:2	Why is T apparel red, and thy garments like
	63:2	thy apparel red, and T garments like his that
	63:14	So thou didst lead T people, to make for
	63:15	heaven and see, from T holy and glorious habitation.
	63:15	Where are T zeal and thy might?
	63:15	are thy zeal and T might?
	63:15	The yearning of T heart and thy compassion are
	63:15	of thy heart and T compassion are withheld from
	63:16	from of old is T name.
	63:17	make us err from T ways and harden our
	63:17	for the sake of T servants, the tribes of
	63:17	servants, the tribes of T heritage.
	63:18	T holy people possessed thy sanctuary a little while;
	63:18	Thy holy people possessed T sanctuary a little while;
	63:19	are not called by T name.
	64:1	mountains might quake at T presence—
	64:2	boil— to make T name known to thy
	64:2	thy name known to T adversaries, and that the
	64:2	nations might tremble at T presence!
	64:3	the mountains quaked at T presence.
	64:5	that remember thee in T ways.
	64:7	one that calls upon T name, that bestirs himself
	64:7	for thou hast hid T face from us, and
	64:8	all the work of T hand.
	64:9	consider, we are all T people.
	64:10	T holy cities have become a wilderness, Zion has
Jer	5:3	O LORD, do not T eyes look for truth?
	10:6	thou art great, and T name is great in
	10:7	For this is T due; for among all the
	10:24	just measure; not in T anger, lest thou bring

T

10:25 Pour out T wrath upon the nations that know
10:25 that call not on T name; for they have
11:20 mind, let me see T vengeance upon them, for
14:7 act, O LORD, for T name's sake; for our
14:9 we are called by T name; leave us not."
14:19 Does T soul loathe Zion?
14:21 not spurn us, for T name's sake; do not
14:21 sake; do not dishonor T glorious throne; remember
14:21 and do not break T covenant with us.
15:15 In T forbearance take me not away; know that
15:15 away; know that for T sake I bear reproach.
15:16 T words were found, and I ate them, and
15:16 I ate them, and T words became to me
15:16 I am called by T name, O LORD, God
15:17 I sat alone, because T hand was upon me,
17:16 my lips was before T face.
18:20 them, to turn away T wrath from them.
18:23 out their sin from T sight.
20:12 mind, let me see T vengeance upon them, for
32:17 and the earth by T great power and by
32:17 great power and by T outstretched arm!
32:21 Thou didst bring T people Israel out of the
32:23 they did not obey T voice or walk in
32:23 voice or walk in T law; they did nothing
Lam 1:10 didst forbid to enter T congregation.
2:21 in the day of T anger thou hast slain
3:23 every morning; great is T faithfulness.
3:55 lost.' "I called on T name, O LORD, from
3:65 them dullness of heart; T curse will be on
3:66 destroy them from under T heavens, O LORD."
5:19 dost reign for ever; T throne endures to all
Bar 2:11 Israel, who didst bring T people out of the
2:12 our God, against all T ordinances.
2:13 Let T anger turn away from us, for we
2:14 our supplication, and for T own sake deliver us,
2:15 descendants are called by T name.
2:16 Lord, look down from T holy habitation, and consider
2:16 Incline T ear, O Lord, and hear;
2:17 Lord, and hear; open T eyes, O Lord, and
2:20 For thou hast sent T anger and thy wrath
2:20 sent thy anger and T wrath upon us, as
2:20 thou didst declare by T servants the prophets, saying:
2:24 we did not obey T voice, to serve the
2:24 and thou hast confirmed T words, which thou didst
2:24 thou didst speak by T servants the prophets, that
2:26 which is called by T name thou hast made
2:27 our God, in all T kindness and in all
2:27 kindness and in all T great compassion,
2:28 thou didst speak by T servant Moses on the
2:28 command him to write T law in the presence
3:5 in this crisis remember T power and thy name.
3:5 remember thy power and T name.
3:7 we should call upon T name; and we will
Ezek 9:8 in the outpouring of T wrath upon Jerusalem?"
Dan 3:26 worthy of praise; and T name is glorified for
3:27 to us, and all T works are true and
3:27 works are true and T ways right, and all
3:27 ways right, and all T judgments are truth.
3:29 and have not obeyed T commandments;
3:33 disgrace have befallen T servants and worshipers.
3:34 For T name's sake do not give us up
3:34 and do not break T covenant,
3:35 and do not withdraw T mercy from us, for
3:35 the sake of Abraham T beloved and for the
3:35 the sake of Isaac T servant and Israel thy
3:35 thy servant and Israel T holy one,
3:40 our sacrifice be in T sight this day, and
3:41 fear thee and seek T face.
3:42 deal with us in T forbearance and in thy
3:42 thy forbearance and in T abundant mercy.
3:43 us in accordance with T marvelous works, and give
3:43 and give glory to T name, O Lord!
3:43 who do harm to T servants be put to
3:53 ever; And blessed is T glorious, holy name and
3:54 in the temple of T holy glory and to
3:56 upon the throne of T kingdom and to be
9:5 rebelled, turning aside from T commandments and
9:6 have not listened to T servants the prophets, who
9:6 prophets, who spoke in T name to our kings,
9:11 All Israel has transgressed T law and turned aside,
9:11 aside, refusing to obey T voice.
9:13 and giving heed to T truth.
9:15 God, who didst bring T people out of the
9:16 Lord, according to all T righteous acts, let thy
9:16 thy righteous acts, let T anger and thy wrath
9:16 let thy anger and T wrath turn away from
9:16 wrath turn away from T city Jerusalem, thy holy
9:16 from thy city Jerusalem, T holy hill; because for
9:16 our fathers, Jerusalem and T people have become a
9:17 to the prayer of T servant and to his
9:17 his supplications, and for T own sake, O Lord,
9:17 sake, O Lord, cause T face to shine upon
9:17 face to shine upon T sanctuary, which is desolate.
9:18 O my God, incline T ear and hear; open
9:18 ear and hear; open T eyes and behold our
9:18 which is called by T name; for we do
9:18 on the ground of T great mercy.
9:19 act; delay not, for T own sake, O my
9:19 O my God, because T city and thy people
9:19 because thy city and T people are called by
9:19 people are called by T name."
Joel 2:17 weep and say, "Spare T people, O LORD, and
2:17 LORD, and make not T heritage a reproach, a
3:11 Bring down T warriors, O LORD.
Amos 8:14 Samaria, and say, 'As T god lives, O Dan,'
Jon 2:3 round about me; all T waves and thy billows
2:3 all thy waves and T billows passed over me.
2:4 am cast out from T presence; how shall I
2:4 I again look upon T holy temple?'
2:7 came to thee, into T holy temple.
Mic 6:9 sound wisdom to fear T name: "Hear, O tribe
7:14 Shepherd T people with thy staff, the flock of
7:14 Shepherd thy people with T staff, the flock of
7:14 staff, the flock of T inheritance, who dwell alone
Hab 3:2 report of thee, and T work, O LORD, do
3:8 Was T wrath against the rivers, O LORD?
3:8 Was T anger against the rivers, or thy indignation
3:8 against the rivers, or T indignation against the sea,
3:8 thou didst ride upon T horses, upon thy chariot
3:8 upon thy horses, upon T chariot of victory?
3:9 strip the sheath from T bow, and put the
3:11 at the flash of T glittering spear.
3:13 for the salvation of T people, for the salvation
3:13 for the salvation of T anointed.
3:14 Thou didst pierce with T shafts the head of
3:15 trample the sea with T horses, the surging of
Mal 1:6 'How have we despised T name?'
1Mac 3:51 T sanctuary is trampled down and profaned, and thy
3:51 and profaned, and T priests mourn in humiliation.
4:30 by the hand of T servant David, and didst
4:31 by the hand of T people Israel, and let
4:33 let all who know T name praise thee with
7:17 written, "The flesh of T saints and their blood
7:37 to be called by T name, and to be
7:37 and to be for T people a house of
7:41 the king spoke blasphemy, T angel went forth and
2Mac 1:26 on behalf of all T people Israel and preserve
1:26 people Israel and preserve T portion and make it
1:29 Plant T people in thy holy place, as Moses
1:29 Plant thy people in T holy place, as Moses
14:35 be a temple for T habitation among us;
15:22 Lord, thou didst send T angel in the time
15:24 By the might of T arm may these blasphemers
15:24 blasphemers who come against T holy people be
Mt 6:9 in heaven, Hallowed be T name.
6:10 T kingdom come.
6:10 T will be done, On earth as it is
11:10 send my messenger before T face, who shall prepare
11:10 face, who shall prepare T way before thee.'
11:26 Father, for such was T gracious will.
22:44 hand, till I put T enemies under thy feet?
22:44 put thy enemies under T feet?
26:42 unless I drink it, T will be done."
Mk 1:2 send my messenger before T face, who shall prepare
1:2 face, who shall prepare T way;
12:36 hand, till I put T enemies under thy feet.'
12:36 put thy enemies under T feet.'
Lk 2:29 "Lord, now lettest thou T servant depart in peace,
2:29 in peace, according to T word;
2:30 mine eyes have seen T salvation
2:32 and for glory to T people Israel."
7:27 send my messenger before T face, who shall prepare
7:27 face, who shall prepare T way before thee.'
10:21 Father, for such was T gracious will.
11:2 say: "Father, hallowed be T name.
11:2 T kingdom come.
20:43 hand, till I make T enemies a stool for
20:43 enemies a stool for T feet.'
23:45 voice, said, "Father, into T hands I commit my
Jn 2:17 was written, "Zeal for T house will consume me."
12:28 Father, glorify T name." Then a voice came from
17:1 hour has come; glorify T Son that the Son

17:5 glorify thou me in T own presence with the
17:6 "I have manifested T name to the men whom
17:6 and they have kept T word
17:11 Father, keep them in T name, which thou hast
17:12 I kept them in T name, which thou hast
17:14 I have given them T word; and the world
17:17 them in the truth; T word is truth.
17:24 hast given me in T love for me before
17:26 made known to them T name, and I will
Acts 2:27 to Hades, nor let T Holy One see corruption.
2:28 full of gladness with T presence.'
2:35 hand, till I make T enemies a stool for
2:35 enemies a stool for T feet.'
4:25 of our father David, T servant, didst say by
4:27 were gathered together against T holy servant Jesus,
4:28 Israel, to do whatever T hand and thy plan
4:28 whatever thy hand and T plan had predestined to
4:29 threats, and grant to T servants to speak thy
4:29 thy servants to speak T word with all boldness,
4:30 while thou stretchest out T hand to heal, and
4:30 through the name of T holy servant Jesus."
9:13 he has done to T saints at Jerusalem;
9:14 all who call upon T name."
13:35 'Thou wilt not let T Holy One see corruption.'
22:20 the blood of Stephen T witness was shed, I
Rom 3:4 mayest be justified in T words, and prevail when
8:36 it is written, "For T sake we are being
11:3 "Lord, they have killed T prophets, they have
11:3 prophets, they have demolished T altars, and I alone
15:9 Gentiles, and sing to T name";
1Cor 15:55 "O death, where is T victory?
15:55 O death, where is T sting?"
Heb 1:8 the Son he says, T throne, O God, is
1:8 is the scepter of T kingdom.
1:9 lawlessness; therefore God, T God, has anointed thee
1:9 oil of gladness beyond T comrades."
1:10 are the work of T hands;
1:12 art the same, and T years will never end."
1:13 hand, till I make T enemies a stool for
1:13 enemies a stool for T feet"?
2:12 saying, "I will proclaim T name to my brethren,
10:7 have come to do T will, O God,' as
10:9 have come to do T will." He abolishes the
Rev 4:11 all things, and by T will they existed and
5:9 wast slain and by T blood didst ransom men
11:17 that thou hast taken T great power and begun
11:18 The nations raged, but T wrath came, and the
11:18 be judged, for rewarding T servants, the prophets and
11:18 and those who fear T name, both small and
15:3 "Great and wonderful are T deeds, O Lord God
15:3 Just and true are T ways, O King of
15:4 not fear and glorify T name, O Lord?
15:4 worship thee, for T judgments have been revealed."
16:5 art thou in these T judgments, thou who art
16:7 true and just are T judgments!"
18:10 In one hour has T judgment come."
18:14 "The fruit for which T soul longed has gone
18:14 from thee, and all T dainties and thy splendor
18:14 all thy dainties and T splendor are lost to
18:23 thee no more; for T merchants were the great
18:23 nations were deceived by T sorcery.

THYATIRA (4)

Acts 16:14 from the city of T, a seller of purple
Rev 1:11 to Pergamum and to T and to Sardis and
2:18 of the church in T write: 'The words of
2:24 rest of you in T, who do not hold

THYSELF (31)

Ex 19:23 Mount Sinai; for thou T didst charge us, saying,
2Sam 7:24 thou didst establish for T thy people Israel to
22:26 loyal thou dost show T loyal; with the blameless
22:26 man thou dost show T blameless;
22:27 pure thou dost show T pure, and with the
22:27 crooked thou dost show T perverse.
1Chr 17:21 his people, making for T a name for great
Esth 13:16 thou didst redeem for T out of the land
14:12 Remember, O Lord; make T known in this time
Job 17:3 pledge for me with T; who is there that
Ps 7:6 in thy anger, lift T up against the fury
10:1 Why dost thou hide T in times of trouble?
18:25 loyal thou dost show T loyal; with the blameless
18:25 man thou dost show T blameless;
18:26 pure thou dost show T pure; and with the
18:26 crooked thou dost show T perverse.
35:23 Bestir T, and awake for my right, for my
44:23 Rouse T
55:1 God; and hide not T from my supplication!
59:4 Rouse T, come to my help, and see!
80:17 of man whom thou hast made strong for T
89:46 Wilt thou hide T for ever?
104:2 and majesty, who coverest T with light as with
Wis 18:8 didst call us to T and glorify us.
Is 33:3 the lifting up of T nations are scattered;
45:15 a God who hidest T, O God of Israel,
63:14 people, to make for T a glorious name.
64:12 Wilt thou restrain T at these things, O LORD?
Lam 3:43 "Thou hast wrapped T with anger and pursued us,
3:44 pity; thou hast wrapped T with a cloud so
5:21 Restore us to T, O LORD, that we may

TIARA (2)

Jud 10:3 and put on a T, and arrayed herself in
16:8 her hair with a T and put on a

TIBERI-AS (3)

Jn 6:1 Sea of Galilee, which is the Sea of T
6:23 However, boats from T came near the place where
21:1 by the Sea of T; and he revealed himself

TIBERI-US

Lk 3:1 of the reign of T Caesar, Pontius Pilate being

TIBHATH

1Chr 18:8 And from T and from Cun, cities of Hadadezer,

TIBNI (3)

1Kgs 16:21 of the people followed T the son of Ginath,
16:22 the people who followed T the son of Ginath;
16:22 son of Ginath; so T died, and Omri became

TIDAL (2)

Gen 14:1 king of Elam, and T king of Goiim,
14:9 Ched-or-laomer king of Elam, T king of Goiim,

TIDINGS (32)

Gen 29:13 When Laban heard the T of Jacob his sister's
Ex 33:4 people heard these evil T, they mourned; and no
1Sam 4:17 He who brought the T answered and said, "Israel
4:19 when she heard the T that the ark of
11:5 they told him the T of the men of
27:11 woman alive, to bring T to Gath, thinking, "Lest
2Sam 13:30 were on the way, T came to David, "Absalom
18:19 me run, and carry T to the king that
18:20 are not to carry T today; you may carry
18:20 today; you may carry T another day, but today
18:20 you shall carry no T, because the king's son
18:22 that you will have no reward for the T
18:25 is alone, there are T in his mouth." And
18:26 The king said, "He also brings T
18:27 is a good man, and comes with good T
18:31 the Cushite said, "Good T for my lord the
1Kgs 14:6 am charged with heavy T for you.
Ps 68:11 those who bore the T:
112:7 not afraid of evil T; his heart is firm,
Is 40:9 Zion, herald of good T; lift up your voice
40:9 Jerusalem, herald of good T, lift it up, fear
41:27 I give to Jerusalem a herald of good T
52:7 him who brings good T, who publishes peace, who
52:7 peace, who brings good T of good, who publishes
61:1 me to bring good T to the afflicted; he
Jer 49:14 I have heard T from the LORD, and a
49:23 they have heard evil T; they melt in fear,
Ezek 21:7 you sigh?' you shall say, 'Because of the T
Dan 11:44 But T from the east and the north shall
Obad 1:1 Edom: We have heard T from the LORD, and
Jon 3:6 Then T reached the king of Nineveh, and he
Nah 1:15 him who brings good T, who proclaims peace!

TIE

Prov 6:21 upon your heart always; T them about your neck.

TIED (11)

Ex 39:31 And they T to it a lace of blue,
2Kgs 5:23 he urged him, and T up two talents of
7:10 nothing but the horses T, and the asses tied,
7:10 tied, and the asses T, and the tents as
12:10 and they counted and T up in bags the
Mt 21:2 will find an ass T, and a colt with
Mk 11:2 will find a colt T, on which no one
11:4 and found a colt T at the door out
Lk 19:30 will find a colt T, on which no one

Acts 22:25 But when they had T him up with the
27:40 loosening the ropes that T the rudders; then hoisting

TIERS (2)

1Kgs 7:4 three rows, and window opposite window in three T
7:5 frames, and window was opposite window in three T

TIGHT (2)

Judg 16:13 web and make it T with the pin, then
16:14 And she made them T with the pin, and

TIGLATH-PILESER (3)

2Kgs 15:29 Pekah king of Israel T king of Assyria came
16:7 Ahaz sent messengers to T king of Assyria, saying,
16:10 to Damascus to meet T king of Assyria, he

TIGRIS (5)

Gen 2:14 the third river is T, which flows east of
Tob 6:1 at evening to the T river and camped there.
Jud 1:6 the Euphrates and the T and the Hydaspes and
Sir 24:23 Pishon, and like the T at the time of
Dan 10:4 river, that is, the T,

TIKVAH (2)

2Kgs 22:14 Shallum the son of T, son of Harhas, keeper
Ezra 10:15 Jahzeiah the son of T opposed this, and Meshullum

TILES

Lk 5:19 his bed through the T into the midst before

TILGATH-PILNESER (3)

1Chr 5:6 Be-erah his son, whom T king of Assyria carried
5:26 Assyria, the spirit of T king of Assyria, and
2Chr 28:20 So T king of Assyria came against him, and

TILL (172)

Gen 2:5 was no man to T the ground;
2:15 garden of Eden to T it and keep it.
3:19 you shall eat bread T you return to the
3:23 garden of Eden, to T the ground from which
4:12 When you T the ground, it shall no longer
19:22 I can do nothing T you arrive there." Therefore
38:11 in your father's house, T Shelah my son grows
38:17 give me a pledge, T you send it?"
Ex 15:16 still as a stone, T thy people, O LORD,
15:16 O LORD, pass by, T the people pass by
16:19 leave any of it T the morning."
16:20 left part of it T the morning, and it
16:23 by to be kept T the morning.'"
16:24 they laid it by T the morning, as Moses
16:35 the manna forty years, T they came to a
16:35 they ate the manna, T they came to the
18:13 about Moses from morning T evening.
18:14 about you from morning T evening?"
Lev 24:12 put him in custody, T the will of the
Num 12:15 out on the march T Miriam was brought in
23:24 does not lie down T it devours the prey,
Deut 28:45 you and overtake you, T you are destroyed, because
Josh 5:6 years in the wilderness, T all the nation, the
5:8 places in the camp T they were healed.
8:6 come out after us, T we have drawn them
20:9 the avenger of blood, T he stood before the
23:13 thorns in your eyes, T you perish from off
Judg 3:25 And they waited T they were utterly at a
4:21 peg into his temple, T it went down into
6:18 said, "I will stay T you return."
16:2 saying, "Let us wait T the light of the
16:3 But Samson lay T midnight, and at midnight he
19:7 his father-in-law urged him, T he lodged there again.
19:26 where her master was, T it was light.
21:2 Bethel, and sat there T evening before God, and
Ruth 1:13 would you therefore wait T they were grown?
2:21 close by my servants, T they have finished all
1Sam 9:13 people will not eat T he comes, since he
16:11 will not sit down T he comes here."
20:5 myself in the field T the third day at
22:3 mother stay with you, T I know what God
2Sam 3:35 bread or anything else T the sun goes down!"
9:10 and your servants shall T the land for him,
2Kgs 2:8 and to the other, T the two of them
2:17 when they urged him T he was ashamed, he
3:20 the direction of Edom, T the country was filled
3:24 and attacked the Moabites, T they fled before them;
3:25 all the good trees; T only its stones were
4:20 sat on her lap T noon, and then he
7:3 do we sit here T we die?
8:15 it over his face, T he died.
10:17 to Ahab in Samaria, T he had wiped them
20:17 fathers have stored up T this day, shall be
21:16 very much innocent blood, T he had filled Jerusalem
25:2 the city was besieged T the eleventh year of
2Chr 26:15 he was marvelously helped, T he was strong.
36:16 scoffing at his prophets, T the wrath of the
36:16 rose against his people, T there was no remedy.
Ezra 5:5 did not stop them T a report should reach
9:14 be angry with us T thou wouldst consume us,
10:14 judges of every city, T the fierce wrath of
Neh 4:11 not know or see T we come into the
4:21 the break of dawn T the stars came out.
Tob 4:14 Do not hold over T the next day the
Jud 2:8 plundered by my troops, T their wounded shall fill
2:10 hold them for me T the day of their
11:19 the middle of Judea, T you come to Jerusalem;
Esth 3:7 it month after month T the twelfth month, which
Job 7:4 am full of tossing T the dawn.
7:19 nor let me alone T I swallow my spittle?
14:12 and rises not again; T the heavens are no
14:14 service I would wait, T my release should come.
27:5 that you are right; T I die I will
Ps 10:15 seek out his wickedness T thou find none.
18:37 did not turn back T they were consumed.
40:12 iniquities have overtaken me, T I cannot see; they
57:1 I will take refuge, T the storms of destruction
59:13 in wrath, consume them T they are no more,
71:18 do not forsake me, T I proclaim thy might
72:7 flourish, and peace abound, T the moon be no
107:7 by a straight way, T they reached a city
110:1 at my right hand, T I make your enemies
123:2 the LORD our God, T he have mercy upon
Prov 7:18 our fill of love T morning; let us delight
7:23 stag is caught fast T an arrow pierces its
Eccl 2:3 lay hold on folly, T I might see what
Sir 35:18 be patient with them, T he crushes the loins
35:18 vengeance on the nations; T he takes away the
35:19 scepters of the unrighteous; T he repays the man
35:19 according to their devices; T he judges the case
40:1 from their mother's womb T the day they return
47:25 every sort of wickedness, T vengeance came upon
48:15 not forsake their sins, T they were carried away
50:19 him who is merciful, T the order of worship
Is 5:11 late into the evening T wine inflames them!
22:14 not be forgiven you T you die," says the
30:17 five you shall flee, T you are left like
30:24 and the asses that T the ground will eat
39:6 fathers have stored up T this day, shall be
42:4 fail or be discouraged T he has established justice
Jer 27:11 its own land, to T it and dwell there,
47:6 How long T you are quiet?
51:39 and make them drunk, T they swoon away and
52:5 the city was besieged T the eleventh year of
52:11 put him in prison T the day of his
Ezek 4:8 side to the other, T you have completed the
4:14 from my youth up T now I have never
24:13 be cleansed any more T I have satisfied my
28:15 day you were created, T iniquity was found in
34:21 weak with your horns, T you have scattered them
39:15 a sign by it, T the buriers have buried
39:19 you shall eat fat T you are filled, and
39:19 filled, and drink blood T you are drunk, at
48:19 tribes of Israel, shall T it.
Dan 2:9 corrupt words before me T the times change.
4:23 beasts of the field, T seven times pass over
4:25 shall pass over you, T you know that the
4:33 the dew of heaven T his hair grew as
6:14 Daniel; and he labored T the sun went down
11:36 He shall prosper T the indignation is accomplished;
12:1 there was a nation T that time; but at
12:6 long shall it be T the end of these
12:13 But go your way T the end; and you
Hos 8:5 long will it be T they are pure
9:12 I will bereave them T none is left.
Jon 4:5 it in the shade, T he should see what
Zeph 2:5 I will destroy you T no inhabitant is left.
3:3 wolves that leave nothing T the morning.
Zech 10:10 Gilead and to Lebanon, T there is no room
Mal 1:4 I will tear down, T they are called the
3:3 like gold and silver, T they present right offerings
1Mac 5:53 people all the way T he came to the
9:13 battle raged from morning T evening.
10:80 men from early morning T late afternoon.
14:10 the means of defense, T his renown spread to
2Mac 8:35 slave across the country T he reached Antioch, having

T

Mt 2:9 East went before them, T it came to rest
2:13 Egypt, and remain there T I tell you; for
5:18 I say to you, T heaven and earth pass
5:26 will never get out T you have paid the
12:20 quench a smoldering wick, T he brings justice to
13:33 three measures of flour, T it was all leavened."
18:29 put him in prison T he should pay the
18:33 him to the jailers, T he should pay all
22:44 at my right hand, T I put thy enemies
24:34 will not pass away T all these things take
Mk 12:36 at my right hand, T I put thy enemies
Lk 1:80 was in the wilderness T the day of his
2:37 and as a widow T she was eighty-four.
9:39 out; it convulses him T he foams, and shatters
12:59 will never get out T you have paid the
13:8 sir, this year also, T I dig about it
13:21 three measures of flour, T it was all leavened."
17:8 yourself and serve me, T I eat and drink;
19:13 them, 'Trade with these T I come.'
20:43 at my right hand, T I make thy enemies
21:32 will not pass away T all has taken place.
Jn 13:38 cock will not crow, T you have denied me
Acts 2:35 at my right hand, T I make thy enemies
7:18 and multiplied in Egypt T there arose over Egypt
8:39 to all the towns T he came to Caesarea.
21:5 us on our way T we were outside the
23:12 to eat nor drink T they had killed Paul.
23:14 to taste no food T we have killed Paul.
23:21 to eat nor drink T they have killed him;
28:23 to them from morning T evening, testifying to the
Gal 3:19 because of transgressions, T the offspring should
1Tim 4:13 T I come, attend to the public reading of
Heb 1:13 at my right hand, T I make thy enemies
Rev 7:3 sea or the trees, T we have sealed the
16:21 on men from heaven, T men cursed God for
20:3 the nations no more, T the thousand years were

TILLED (3)
Ezek 36:9 and you shall be T and sown;
36:34 was desolate shall be T, instead of being the
1Mac 14:8 They T their land in peace; the ground gave

TILLER (3)
Gen 4:2 sheep, and Cain a T of the ground.
9:20 Noah was the first T of the soil.
Zech 13:5 prophet, I am a T of the soil; for

TILLERS
Joel 1:10 Be confounded, O T of the soil, wail, O

TILLING
1Chr 27:26 of the field for T the soil was Ezri

TILLS (2)
Prov 12:11 He who T his land will have plenty of
28:19 He who T his land will have plenty of

TILON
1Chr 4:20 sons of Shimon: Amnon, Rinnah, Ben-hanan, and T

TILT (2)
Job 38:37 Or who can T the waterskins of the heavens,
Jer 48:12 him tilters who will T him, and empty his

TILTERS
Jer 48:12 shall send to him T who will tilt him,

TIMAEUS
Mk 10:46 beggar, the son of T, was sitting by the

TIMBER (22)
Lev 14:45 house, its stones and T and all the plaster
1Kgs 5:6 knows how to cut T like the Sidonians."
5:8 desire in the matter of cedar and cypress T
5:10 Solomon with all the T of cedar and cypress
5:18 hewing and prepared the T and the stone to
9:11 with cedar and cypress T and gold, as much
15:22 of Ramah and its T, with which Baasha had
2Kgs 12:12 well as to buy T and quarried stone for
22:6 well as for buying T and quarried stone to
1Chr 22:14 so much of it; T and stone too I
2Chr 2:8 cedar, cypress, and algum T from Lebanon, for I
2:8 know how to cut T in Lebanon.
2:9 your servants, to prepare T for me in abundance,
2:10 the hewers who cut T, twenty thousand cors of
2:16 we will cut whatever T you need from Lebanon,
16:6 of Ramah and its T, with which Baasha had
34:11 buy quarried stone, and T for binders and beams
Ezra 5:8 with huge stones, and T is laid in the
6:4 and one course of T; let the cost be
Neh 2:8 he may give me T to make beams for
Ezek 26:12 houses; your stones and T and soil they will
Zech 5:4 and consume it, both T and stones."

TIMBERS (2)
1Kgs 6:10 to the house with T of cedar.
1Chr 22:4 beyond weighing, and cedar T without number; for

TIMBREL (5)
Ex 15:20 of Aaron, took a T in her hand; and
Ps 81:2 a song, sound the T, the sweet lyre with
149:3 melody to him with T and lyre!
150:4 Praise him with T and dance; praise him with
Is 5:12 have lyre and harp, T and flute and wine

TIMBRELS (7)
Ex 15:20 out after her with T and dancing.
Judg 11:34 to meet him with T and with dances; she
1Sam 18:6 meet King Saul, with T, with songs of joy,
Ps 68:25 between them maidens playing T:
Is 24:8 The mirth of the T is stilled, the noise
30:32 to the sound of T and lyres; battling with
Jer 31:4 shall adorn yourself with T, and shall go forth

TIME (705)
Gen 4:3 In the course of T Cain brought to the
4:26 At that T men began to call upon the
12:6 At that T the Canaanites were in the land.
13:7 At that T the Canaanites and the Perizzites dwelt
18:14 At the appointed T I will return to you,
21:2 old age at the T of which God had
21:22 At that T Abimelech and Phicol the commander of
22:15 to Abraham a second T from heaven,
24:11 of water at the T of evening, the time
24:11 time of evening, the T when women go out
26:8 been there a long T, Abimelech king of the
29:7 day, it is not T for the animals to
29:21 to her, for my T is completed."
29:34 and said, "Now this T my husband will be
29:35 son, and said, "This T I will praise the
38:1 It happened at that T that Judah went down
38:12 In course of T the wife of Judah, Shua's
38:27 When the T of her delivery came, there were
39:5 From the T that he made him overseer in
39:7 And after a T his master's wife cast her
40:1 Some T after this, the butler of the king
40:4 they continued for some T in custody.
41:5 and dreamed a second T; and behold, seven ears
43:18 our sacks the first T, that we are brought
43:20 came down the first T to buy food;
47:29 And when the T drew near that Israel must
Ex 8:32 hardened his heart this T also, and did not
9:5 the LORD set a T, saying, "Tomorrow the LORD
9:14 For this T I will send all my plagues
9:18 Behold, tomorrow about this T I will cause very
9:27 "I have sinned this T; the LORD is in
12:40 The T that the people of Israel dwelt in
13:10 ordinance at its appointed T from year to year.
13:14 And when in T to come your son asks
21:19 the loss of his T, and shall have him
23:15 days at the appointed T in the month of
34:18 commanded you, at the T appointed in the month
34:21 shall rest; in plowing T and in harvest you
Lev 12:2 days; as at the T of her menstruation, she
13:58 be washed a second T, and be clean."
15:25 days, not at the T of her impurity, or
15:25 a discharge beyond the T of her impurity, all
23:4 shall proclaim at the T appointed for them.
23:27 be for you a T of holy convocation, and
25:8 years, so that the T of the seven weeks
25:32 their possession, the Levites may redeem at any T
25:50 number of years; the T he was with his
25:50 be rated as the T of a hired servant.
26:5 shall last to the T of vintage, and the
26:5 shall last to the T for sowing; and you
Num 3:1 and Moses at the T when the LORD spoke
6:5 his head; until the T is completed for which
6:12 offering; but the former T shall be void, because
6:13 the Nazirite, when the T of his separation has
9:2 of Israel keep the passover at its appointed T
9:3 it at its appointed T; according to all its
9:7 offering at its appointed T among the people of

T

T

6:5 Sanballat for the fifth T sent his servant to
9:27 suffer; and in the T of their suffering they
9:32 thy people, since the T of the kings of
13:6 And after some T I asked leave of the
13:21 From that T on they did not come on
Tob 10:7 At that T Tobias said to Raguel, "Send me
14:4 in Media there will be peace for a T
14:4 down and will be in ruins for a T
Jud 4:1 By this T the people of Israel living in
4:6 in Jerusalem at the T, wrote to the people
5:7 At one T they lived in Mesopotamia, because they
5:8 to Mesopotamia, and lived there for a long T
5:16 all the Gergesites, and lived there a long T
7:31 more days; by that T the Lord our God
8:1 At that T Judith heard about these things: she
8:15 protect us within any T he pleases, or even
8:29 is not the first T your wisdom has been
9:1 and at the very T when that evening's incense
13:5 For now is the T to help thy inheritance,
16:21 was honored in her T throughout the whole country.
16:25 or for a long T after her death.
Esth 2:19 gathered together the second T, Mordecai was sitting
4:14 silence at such a T as this, relief and
4:14 kingdom for such a T as this?"
8:9 were summoned at that T, in the third month,
9:27 written and at the T appointed every year,
14:12 thyself known in this T of our affliction, and
16:20 attach them at the T of their affliction.
16:24 most hateful for all T to beasts and birds."
Job 6:17 In T of heat they disappear; when it is
14:13 appoint me a set T, and remember me!
15:32 in full before his T, and his branch will
22:16 snatched away before their T; their foundation was
34:23 has not appointed a T for any man to
38:23 have reserved for the T of trouble, for the
39:2 do you know the T when they bring forth,
Ps 32:6 to thee; at a T of distress, in the
37:39 their refuge in the T of trouble.
69:13 At an acceptable T, O God, in the abundance
71:9 me off in the T of old age; forsake
75:2 At the set T which I appoint I will
77:8 Are his promises at an end for all T
102:13 Zion; it is the T to favor her; the
102:13 favor her; the appointed T has come.
104:19 the sun knows its T for setting.
113:2 the LORD from this T forth and for evermore!
115:18 the LORD from this T forth and for evermore.
119:126 It is T for the LORD to act, for
121:8 coming in from this T forth and for evermore.
125:2 his people, from this T forth and for evermore.
131:3 the LORD from this T forth and for evermore.
Prov 7:9 the evening, at the T of night and darkness.
25:13 of snow in the T of harvest is a
25:19 a faithless man in T of trouble is like
31:25 she laughs at the T to come.
Eccl 3:1 a season, and a T for every matter under
3:2 matter under heaven: a T to be born, and
3:2 be born, and a T to die; a time
3:2 time to die; a T to plant, and a
3:2 to plant, and a T to pluck up what
3:3 what is planted; a T to kill, and a
3:3 to kill, and a T to heal; a time
3:3 time to heal; a T to break down, and
3:3 break down, and a T to build up;
3:4 to build up; a T to weep, and a
3:4 to weep, and a T to laugh; a time
3:4 time to laugh; a T to mourn, and a
3:4 to mourn, and a T to dance;
3:5 time to dance; a T to cast away stones,
3:5 away stones, and a T to gather stones together;
3:5 gather stones together; a T to embrace, and a
3:5 to embrace, and a T to refrain from embracing;
3:6 refrain from embracing; a T to seek, and a
3:6 to seek, and a T to lose; a time
3:6 time to lose; a T to keep, and a
3:6 to keep, and a T to cast away;
3:7 to cast away; a T to rend, and a
3:7 to rend, and a T to sew; a time
3:7 time to sew; a T to keep silence, and
3:7 keep silence, and a T to speak;
3:8 time to speak; a T to love, and a
3:8 to love, and a T to hate; a time
3:8 time to hate; a T for war, and a
3:8 for war, and a T for peace.
3:11 everything beautiful in its T; also he has put
3:17 he has appointed a T for every matter, and
7:17 a fool; why should you die before your T
8:5 man will know the T and way.
8:6 every matter has its T and way, although man's
9:11 men of skill; but T and chance happen to
9:12 For man does not know his T
9:12 snared at an evil T, when it suddenly falls
10:17 feast at the proper T, for strength, and not
Song 2:12 on the earth, the T of singing has come,
Wis 2:4 will be forgotten in T and no one will
2:5 For our allotted T is the passing of a
3:7 In the T of their visitation they will shine
4:2 gone; and throughout all T it marches crowned in
4:8 honored for length of T, nor measured by number
4:13 perfected in a short T, he fulfilled long years;
11:8 their thirst at that T how thou didst punish
12:20 of death, granting them T and opportunity to give
14:16 custom, grown strong with T, was kept as a
15:8 of earth a short T before and after a
16:3 suffering want a short T, might partake of delicacies.
16:18 At one T the flame was restrained, so that
16:19 God; and at another T even in the midst
16:25 Therefore at that T also, changed into all forms,
Sir 2:2 not be hasty in T of calamity.
2:11 sins and saves in T of affliction.
4:20 Observe the right T, and beware of evil; and
4:23 speaking at the crucial T, and do not hide
4:31 withdrawn when it is T to repay.
5:7 forth, and at the T of punishment you will
8:9 give an answer in T of need.
10:4 will raise up the right man for the T
10:25 glorify yourself at a T when you are in
11:17 not know how much T will pass until he
12:15 with you for a T, but if you falter,
17:2 few days, a limited T, but granted them authority
18:24 In the T of plenty think of the time
18:24 plenty think of the T of hunger; in the
19:9 you, and when the T comes he will hate
20:18 told at the wrong T, which is continually on
20:19 he does not tell it at its proper T
22:6 told at the wrong T, but chastising and discipline
22:21 stand by him in T of affliction, that you
24:23 the Tigris at the T of the first fruits.
24:24 the Euphrates, and like the Jordan at harvest T
24:25 the Gihon at the T of vintage.
29:2 your neighbor in the T of his need; and
29:5 money; but at the T for repayment he will
29:5 of unconcern, and will find fault with the T
32:11 Leave in good T and do not be the
33:23 At the T when you end the days of
35:20 of rain in the T of drought.
36:8 remember the appointed T, and let people recount
37:4 a friend, but in T of trouble are against
38:13 There is a T when success lies in the
39:16 whatever he commands will be done in his T
39:17 for in God's T all things will be sought
39:28 scourge heavily; in the T of consummation they will
40:24 help are for a T of trouble, but almsgiving
44:18 and righteous; in the T of wrath he was
45:13 Before his T there never were such beautiful things.
46:19 Before the T of his eternal sleep, Samuel called
48:10 ready at the appointed T, it is written, to
48:25 to the end of T, and the hidden things
50:1 house, and in his T fortified the temple.
50:21 in worship a second T, to receive the blessing
51:10 of affliction, at the T when there is no
51:30 work before the appointed T, and in God's time
51:30 time, and in God's T he will give you
Is 9:1 In the former T he brought into contempt the
9:1 but in the latter T he will make glorious
9:7 righteousness from this T forth and for evermore.
11:11 hand yet a second T to recover the remnant
13:22 the pleasant palaces; its T is close at hand
17:14 At evening T, behold, terror!
18:7 At that T gifts will be brought to the
20:2 it,-- at that T the LORD had spoken
26:17 she is near her T, so were we because
30:8 may be for the T to come as a
33:2 our salvation in the T of trouble.
39:1 At that T Merodach-baladan the son of Baladan, king
42:14 For a long T I have held my peace,
42:23 and listen for the T to come?
48:6 From this T forth I make you hear new
48:16 in secret, from the T it came to be
49:8 the LORD: "In a T of favor I have
49:20 children born in the T of your bereavement will
57:11 even for a long T, and so you do

	59:21	the LORD, from this T forth and for evermore."
	60:22	the LORD; in its T I will hasten it.
	64:5	have been a long T, and shall we be
Jer	1:13	to me a second T, saying, "What do you
	2:27	But in the T of their trouble they say,
	2:28	save you, in your T of trouble; for as
	3:17	At that T Jerusalem shall be called the throne
	4:11	At that T it will be said to this
	6:15	who fall; at the T that I punish them,
	8:1	"At that T, says the LORD, the bones of
	8:7	and crane keep the T of their coming; but
	8:15	good came, for a T of healing, but behold,
	10:15	of delusion; at the T of their punishment they
	10:18	the land at this T, and I will bring
	11:12	save them in the T of their trouble.
	11:14	to me in the T of their trouble.
	13:3	to me a second T,
	14:8	Israel, its savior in T of trouble, why shouldst
	14:19	good came; for a T of healing, but behold,
	15:11	the enemy in the T of trouble and in
	15:11	trouble and in the T of distress!
	18:7	If at any T I declare concerning a nation
	18:9	And if at any T I declare concerning a
	18:23	with them in the T of thine anger.
	27:7	his grandson, until the T of his own land
	30:7	it; it is a T of distress for Jacob;
	31:1	"At that T, says the LORD, I will be
	32:2	At that T the army of the king of
	32:14	vessel, that they may last for a long T
	33:1	to Jeremiah a second T, while he was still
	33:15	days and at that T I will cause a
	33:20	come at their appointed T,
	39:10	gave them vineyards and fields at the same T
	46:21	come upon them, the T of their punishment.
	49:8	Esau upon him, the T when I punish him.
	50:4	days and in that T, says the LORD, the
	50:16	handles the sickle in T of harvest; because of
	50:20	days and in that T, says the LORD, iniquity
	50:27	day has come, the T of their punishment.
	50:31	day has come, the T when I will punish
	51:6	for this is the T of the LORD's vengeance,
	51:18	of delusion; at the T of their punishment they
	51:33	threshing floor at the T when it is trodden;
	51:33	little while and the T of her harvest will
Bar	1:2	the month, at the T when the Chaldeans took
	1:8	At the same T, on the tenth day of
	1:20	his servant at the T when he brought our
	3:14	may at the same T discern where there is
	3:32	the earth for all T filled it with four-footed
	4:35	and for a long T she will be inhabited
	6:3	years, for a long T, up to seven generations;
Ezek	4:6	lie down a second T, but on your right
	7:7	of the land; the T has come, the day
	7:12	The T has come, the day draws near.
	11:3	city; who say, 'The T is not near to
	16:47	within a very little T you were more corrupt
	18:6	a woman in her T of impurity,
	21:25	day has come, the T of your final punishment,
	21:29	day has come, the T of their final punishment.
	22:3	of her, that her T may come, and that
	22:4	day near, the appointed T of your years has
	30:3	day of clouds, a T of doom for the
	33:22	my mouth by the T the man came to
	35:5	the sword at the T of their calamity, at
	35:5	their calamity, at the T of their final punishment;
Dan	1:5	the end of that T they were to stand
	1:18	the end of the T, when the king had
	2:7	They answered a second T, "Let the king tell
	2:8	are trying to gain T, because you see that
	2:16	to appoint him a T, that he might show
	3:8	Therefore at that T certain Chaldeans came forward
	3:38	And at this T there is no prince, or
	4:26	for you from the T that you know that
	4:36	At the same T my reason returned to me;
	7:12	lives were prolonged for a season and a T
	7:22	Most High, and the T came when the saints
	7:25	his hand for a T, two times, and half
	7:25	for a time, two times, and half a T
	8:17	vision is for the T of the end."
	8:19	pertains to the appointed T of the end.
	9:21	swift flight at the T of the evening sacrifice.
	9:25	with squares and moat, but in a troubled T
	11:23	And from the T that an alliance is made
	11:24	devise plans against strongholds, but only for a T
	11:27	to be at the T appointed.
	11:29	"At the T appointed he shall return and come
	11:29	shall not be this T as it was before.
	11:35	them white, until the T of the end, for
	11:35	is yet for the T appointed.
	11:40	"At the T of the end the king of
	12:1	"At that T shall arise Michael, the great prince
	12:1	there shall be a T of trouble, such as
	12:1	a nation till that T; but at that time
	12:1	time; but at that T your people shall be
	12:4	the book, until the T of the end.
	12:7	would be for a T, two times, and half
	12:7	times, and half a T; and that when the
	12:9	and sealed until the T of the end.
	12:11	And from the T that the continual burnt offering
	13:14	they arranged for a T when they could find
Hos	2:9	my grain in its T, and my wine in
	2:15	youth, as at the T when she came out
	10:12	for it is the T to seek the LORD,
Joel	3:1	days and at that T, when I restore the
Amos	5:13	silent in such a T; for it is an
	5:13	such a time; for it is an evil T
Jon	3:1	to Jonah the second T, saying,
Mic	2:3	walk haughtily, for it will be an evil T
	3:4	from them at that T, because they have made
	4:7	Mount Zion from this T forth and for evermore.
	5:3	them up until the T when she who is
Hab	2:3	the vision awaits its T; it hastens to the
Zeph	1:12	At that T I will search Jerusalem with lamps,
	3:9	"Yea, at that T I will change the speech
	3:19	Behold, at that T I will deal with all
Hag	1:2	This people say the T has not yet come
	1:4	prophet, "Is it a T for you yourselves to
	2:20	LORD came a second T to Haggai on the
Zech	4:12	And a second T I said to him, "What
	14:7	night, for at evening T there shall be light.
1Mac	2:25	At the same T he killed the king's officer
	2:49	strong; it is a T of ruin and furious
	2:53	Joseph in the T of his distress kept the
	4:60	At that T they fortified Mount Zion with high
	7:35	into my hands this T, then if I return
	9:1	of Judah a second T, and with them the
	9:7	for he had no T to assemble them.
	9:10	If our T has come, let us die bravely
	9:27	not been since the T that prophets ceased to
	9:31	And Jonathan at that T accepted the leadership and
	9:55	down, for at that T Alcimus was stricken and
	9:56	Alcimus died at that T in great agony.
	10:30	and Galilee, from this day and for all T
	10:77	At the same T he advanced into the plain,
	11:14	in Cilicia at that T, because the people of
	11:36	be canceled from this T forth for ever.
	12:1	Jonathan saw that the T was favorable for him,
	12:7	Already in T past a letter was sent to
	12:10	from you, for considerable T has passed since you
	13:5	my life in any T of distress, for I
	15:8	canceled for you from henceforth and for all T
	15:33	fathers, which at one T had been unjustly taken
	16:9	At that T Judas the brother of John was
	16:24	his high-priesthood, from the T that he became high
2Mac	1:5	not forsake you in T of evil.
	1:19	pious priests of that T took some of the
	1:22	was done and some T had passed and the
	3:5	Tarsus, who at that T was governor of Coelesyria
	5:1	About this T Antiochus made his second invasion of
	6:24	not worthy of our T of life," he said,
	8:14	and at the same T besought the Lord to
	8:19	their ancestors; both the T of Sennacherib, when one
	8:20	thousand perished, and the T of the battle with
	9:1	About that T, as it happened, Antiochus had retreated
	12:36	fighting for a long T and were weary, Judas
	12:39	day, as by that T it had become necessary,
	13:9	those that had been done in his father's T
	13:22	king negotiated a second T with the people in
	15:10	orders, at the same T pointing out the perfidy
	15:22	thy angel in the T of Hezekiah king of
	15:37	And from that T the city has been in
Mt	1:11	his brothers, at the T of the deportation to
	2:7	ascertained from them what T the star appeared;
	2:16	under, according to the T which he had ascertained
	4:17	From that T Jesus began to preach, saying, "Repent,
	8:29	you come here to torment us before the T
	11:25	At that T Jesus declared, "I thank thee, Father,
	12:1	At that T Jesus went through the grainfields on
	13:30	harvest; and at harvest T I will tell the
	14:1	At that T Herod the tetrarch heard about the
	14:24	the boat by this T was many furlongs distant
	16:21	From that T Jesus began to show his disciples

18:1 At that T the disciples came to Jesus, saying,
24:45 to give them their food at the proper T
25:19 Now after a long T the master of those
26:18 'The Teacher says, My T is at hand; I
26:42 Again, for the second T, he went away and
26:44 prayed for the third T, saying the same words.
Mk 1:15 God, and saying, "The T is fulfilled, and the
10:30 hundredfold now in this T, houses and brothers and
12:2 When the T came, he sent a servant to
13:33 not know when the T will come.
14:41 he came the third T, and said to them,
14:72 And immediately the cock crowed a second T
Lk 1:3 things closely for some T past, to write an
1:20 my words, which will be fulfilled in their T
1:23 And when his T of service was ended, he
1:57 Now the T came for Elizabeth to be delivered,
2:6 they were there, the T came for her to
2:22 And when the T came for their purification according
4:5 in a moment of T,
4:13 he departed from him until an opportune T
4:27 in Israel in the T of the prophet Elisha;
7:45 kiss, but from the T I came in she
8:13 a while and in T of temptation fall away.
8:27 demons; for a long T he had worn no
8:29 (For many a T it had seized him; he
12:42 them their portion of food at the proper T
12:56 you not know how to interpret the present T
13:1 present at that very T who told him of
14:17 many; and at the T for the banquet he
18:30 manifold more in this T, and in the age
19:44 did not know the T of your visitation."
20:10 When the T came, he sent a servant to
21:8 am he!' and, 'The T is at hand!' Do
21:13 This will be a T for you to bear
23:7 Herod, who was himself in Jerusalem at that T
23:21 A third T he said to them, "Why, what
Jn 3:4 he enter a second T into his mother's womb
5:5 lying there a long T, he said to him,
7:6 said to them, "My T has not yet come,
7:6 yet come, but your T is always here.
7:8 this feast, for my T has not yet fully
9:24 So for the second T they called the man
11:39 him, "Lord, by this T there will be an
21:14 was now the third T that Jesus was revealed
21:16 A second T he said to him, "Simon, son
21:17 to him the third T, "Simon, son of John,
21:17 to him the third T, "Do you love me?"
Acts 1:6 will you at this T restore the kingdom to
1:21 us during all the T that the Lord Jesus
3:21 must receive until the T for establishing all that
7:12 Egypt, he sent forth our fathers the first T
7:17 "But as the T of the promise drew near,
7:20 At this T Moses was born, and was beautiful
8:11 because for a long T he had amazed them
10:15 him again a second T, "What God has cleansed,
11:9 voice answered a second T from heaven, 'What God
11:26 were for the first T called Christians.
12:1 About that T Herod the king laid violent hands
13:11 and unable to see the sun for a T
14:3 remained for a long T, speaking boldly for the
14:28 they remained no little T with the disciples.
15:33 they had spent some T, they were sent off
17:21 lived there spent their T in nothing except telling
18:23 After spending some T there he departed and went
19:23 About that T there arose no little stir concerning
20:16 not have to spend T in Asia; for he
20:18 among you all the T from the first day
24:25 At the same T he hoped that money would
26:5 known for a long T, if they are willing
26:28 Paul, "In a short T you think to make
27:9 As much T had been lost, and the voyage
27:40 sea, at the same T loosening the ropes that
28:6 had waited a long T and saw no misfortune
Rom 3:26 prove at the present T that he himself is
5:6 weak, at the right T Christ died for the
8:18 sufferings of this present T are not worth comparing
9:9 promise said, "About this T I will return and
11:5 too at the present T there is a remnant,
13:11 how it is full T now for you to
1Cor 4:5 pronounce judgment before the T, before the Lord
7:18 any one at the T of his call already
7:18 any one at the T of his call uncircumcised?
7:29 mean, brethren, the appointed T has grown very
15:6 hundred brethren at one T, most of whom are
16:7 hope to spend some T with you, if the
2Cor 6:2 says, "At the acceptable T I have listened to
6:2 now is the acceptable T; behold, now is the
8:14 abundance at the present T should supply their want,
12:14 Here for the third T I am ready to
13:1 This is the third T I am coming to
Gal 4:4 But when the T had fully come, God sent
4:29 But as at that T he who was born
Eph 1:10 for the fullness of T, to unite all things
2:11 remember that at one T you Gentiles in the
2:12 you were at that T separated from Christ, alienated
5:16 the most of the T, because the days are
Col 4:5 wisely toward outsiders, making the most of the T
1Thes 2:17 brethren, for a short T, in person not in
2Thes 2:6 so that he may be revealed in his T
1Tim 2:6 testimony to which was borne at the proper T
6:15 manifest at the proper T by the blessed and
2Tim 4:3 For the T is coming when people will not
4:6 of being sacrificed; the T of my departure has
Tit 1:3 and at the proper T manifested in his word
Philem 1:22 At the same T, prepare a guest room for
Heb 4:16 grace to help in T of need.
5:12 For though by this T you ought to be
7:25 is able for all T to save those who
9:10 body imposed until the T of reformation.
9:28 will appear a second T, not to deal with
10:12 had offered for all T a single sacrifice for
10:14 has perfected for all T those who are sanctified.
11:32 For T would fail me to tell of Gideon,
12:10 us for a short T at their pleasure, but
Jas 4:14 appears for a little T and then vanishes.
1Pet 1:5 salvation ready to be revealed in the last T
1:11 inquired what person or T was indicated by the
1:17 with fear throughout the T of your exile.
4:2 the rest of the T in the flesh no
4:3 Let the T that is past suffice for doing
4:17 For the T has come for judgment to begin
5:6 God, that in due T he may exalt you.
2Pet 1:15 be able at any T to recall these things.
Jude 1:18 you, "In the last T there will be scoffers,
1:25 and authority, before all T and now and for
Rev 1:3 written therein; for the T is near.
2:21 I gave her T to repent, but she refuses
11:18 wrath came, and the T for the dead to
12:12 he knows that his T is short!"
12:14 be nourished for a T, and times, and half
12:14 for a time, and times, and half a T
22:10 this book, for the T is near.

TIMELY

Sir 20:1 reproof which is not T; and there is a

TIMES (171)

Gen 27:36 For he has supplanted me these two T
31:7 changed my wages ten T, but God did not
31:41 flock, and you have changed my wages ten T
33:3 to the ground seven T, until he came near
43:34 Benjamin's portion was five T as much as any
Ex 18:22 the people at all T; every great matter they
18:26 the people at all T; hard cases they brought
23:14 "Three T in the year you shall keep a
23:17 Three T in the year shall all your males
34:23 Three T in the year shall all your males
34:24 LORD your God three T in the year.
Lev 4:6 of the blood seven T before the LORD in
4:17 and sprinkle it seven T before the LORD in
8:11 on the altar seven T, and anointed the altar
14:7 shall sprinkle it seven T upon him who is
14:16 with his finger seven T before the LORD.
14:27 his left hand seven T before the LORD;
14:51 the running water, and sprinkle the house seven T
16:2 to come at all T into the holy place
16:14 shall sprinkle the blood with his finger seven T
16:19 with his finger seven T, and cleanse it and
23:37 you shall proclaim as T of holy convocation, for
25:8 weeks of years, seven T seven years, so that
Num 14:22 the proof these ten T and have not hearkened
19:4 the front of the tent of meeting seven T
22:28 you, that you have struck me these three T
22:32 "Why have you struck your ass these three T
22:33 me, and turned aside before me these three T
24:1 go, as at other T, to look for omens,
24:10 and behold, you have blessed them these three T
Deut 1:11 make you a thousand T as many as you
16:16 "Three T a year all your males shall appear
Josh 6:4 around the city seven T, the priests blowing the
6:15 the same manner seven T: it was only on
6:15 day that they marched around the city seven T

20:5 enmity against him in T past.
Judg 16:15 mocked me these three T, and you have not
16:20 out as at other T, and shake myself free."
20:30 themselves in array against Gibe-ah, as at other T
20:31 and as at other T they began to smite
Ruth 4:7 custom in former T in Israel concerning redeeming
1Sam 3:10 calling as at other T, "Samuel!
20:25 seat, as at other T, upon the seat by
20:41 ground, and bowed three T; and they kissed one
2Sam 5:2 In T past, when Saul was king over us,
24:3 the people a hundred T as many as they
1Kgs 9:25 Three T a year Solomon used to offer up
17:21 upon the child three T, and cried to the
18:43 And he said, "Go again seven T
22:16 to him, "How many T shall I adjure you
2Kgs 4:35 the child sneezed seven T, and the child opened
5:10 in the Jordan seven T, and your flesh shall
5:14 and dipped himself seven T in the Jordan, according
13:18 and he struck three T, and stopped.
13:19 struck five or six T; then you would have
13:19 now you will strike down Syria only three T
13:25 Three T Joash defeated him and recovered the cities
1Chr 11:2 In T past, even when Saul was king, it
12:32 had understanding of the T, to know what Israel
21:3 his people a hundred T as many as they
2Chr 15:5 In those T there was no peace to him
18:15 to him, "How many T shall I adjure you
Ezra 10:14 wives come at appointed T, and with them the
Neh 4:12 said to us ten T, "From all the places
6:4 sent to me four T in this way and
9:28 from heaven, and many T thou didst deliver them
10:34 our fathers' houses, at T appointed, year by year,
13:31 wood offering, at appointed T, and for the first
Tob 14:5 former one until the T of the age are
Esth 1:13 men who knew the T – for this was
Job 9:3 could not answer him once in a thousand T
19:3 These ten T you have cast reproach upon me;
24:1 "Why are not T of judgment kept by the
27:10 Will he call upon God at all T
33:29 these things, twice, three T, with a man,
Ps 9:9 oppressed, a stronghold in T of trouble.
10:1 thou hide thyself in T of trouble?
10:5 ways prosper at all T; thy judgments are on
12:6 in a furnace on the ground, purified seven T
31:15 My T are in thy hand; deliver me from
34:1 the LORD at all T; his praise shall continually
37:19 to shame in evil T, in the days of
49:5 should I fear in T of trouble, when the
62:8 in him at all T, O people; pour out
106:3 who observe justice, who do righteousness at all T
106:43 Many T he delivered them, but they were rebellious
119:20 consumed with longing for thy ordinances at all T
119:164 Seven T a day I praise thee for thy
Prov 5:19 fill you at all T with delight, be infatuated
17:17 friend loves at all T, and a brother is
24:16 righteous man falls seven T, and rises again; but
Eccl 7:22 heart knows that many T you have yourself cursed
8:12 does evil a hundred T and prolongs his life,
Wis 7:18 end and middle of T, the alternations of the
8:8 wonders and of the outcome of seasons and T
12:22 our enemies ten thousand T more, so that we
19:22 help them at all T and in all places.
Sir 6:37 and meditate at all T on his commandments.
13:7 you two or three T; and finally he will
20:11 pays for it seven T over.
22:6 but chastising and discipline are wisdom at all T
23:19 Lord are ten thousand T brighter than the sun;
26:4 glad, and at all T his face is cheerful.
39:31 service, and when their T come they will not
40:8 and upon sinners seven T more,
43:4 burns the mountains three T as much; it breathes
43:6 season to make the T and to be an
44:8 their generations, and were the glory of their T
47:10 feasts, and arranged their T throughout the year,
48:3 heavens, and also three T brought down fire.
Is 33:6 the stability of your T, abundance of salvation,
46:10 beginning and from ancient T things not yet done,
Jer 8:7 the heavens knows her T; and the turtledove, swallow,
28:8 and me from ancient T prophesied war, famine, and
Ezek 12:27 and he prophesies of T far-off.'
36:11 as in your former T, and will do more
Dan 1:20 he found them ten T better than all the
2:9 before me till the T change.
2:21 He changes T and seasons; he removes kings and
3:19 the furnace heated seven T more than it was
4:16 him; and let seven T pass over him.
4:23 the field, till seven T pass over him';
4:25 of heaven, and seven T shall pass over you,
4:32 an ox; and seven T shall pass over you,
6:10 upon his knees three T a day and prayed
6:13 makes his petition three T a day."
7:10 him, and ten thousand T ten thousand stood before
7:25 think to change the T and the law; and
7:25 for a time, two T, and half a time.
11:7 "In those T a branch from her roots shall
11:14 "In those T many shall rise against the king
12:7 for a time, two T, and half a time;
1Mac 16:2 hands so that we have delivered Israel many T
2Mac 8:19 told them of the T when help came to
9:16 all of them, many T over; and the expenses
12:30 treatment of them in T of misfortune,
14:3 defiled himself in the T of separation, realized that
14:38 For in former T, when there was no mingling
15:8 in mind the former T when help had come
Mt 16:3 but you cannot interpret the signs of the T
18:20 As many as seven T
18:21 say to you seven T, but seventy times seven.
18:21 seven times, but seventy T seven.
26:34 the cock crows, you will deny me three T
26:75 the cock crows, you will deny me three T
Mk 14:30 cock crows twice, you will deny me three T
14:72 cock crows twice, you will deny me three T
Lk 17:4 sins against you seven T in the day, and
17:4 turns to you seven T, and says, 'I repent,'
21:24 the Gentiles, until the T of the Gentiles are
21:36 But watch at all T, praying that you may
22:34 day, until you three T deny that you know
22:59 cock crows today, you will deny me three T
Jn 13:38 not crow, till you have denied me three T
Acts 1:7 for you to know T or seasons which the
3:19 be blotted out, that T of refreshing may come
10:16 This happened three T, and the thing was taken
11:10 common.' This happened three T, and all was drawn
17:30 The T of ignorance God overlooked, but now he
2Cor 11:24 Five T I have received at the hands of
11:25 Three T I have been beaten with rods; once
11:25 Three T I have been shipwrecked; a night and
12:8 Three T I besought the Lord about this, that
Eph 6:18 Pray at all T in the Spirit, with all
1Thes 5:1 But as to the T and the seasons, brethren,
2Thes 3:16 you peace at all T in all ways.
1Tim 4:1 says that in later T some will depart from
2Tim 3:1 days there will come T of stress.
1Pet 1:20 the end of the T for your sake.
Rev 9:16 was twice ten thousand T ten thousand; I heard
12:14 for a time, and T, and half a time.

TIMID (4)

Job 32:6 aged; therefore I was T and afraid to declare
Sir 2:12 Woe to T hearts and to slack hands, and
22:16 the wind; so a T heart with a fool's
34:14 Lord will not be T, nor play the coward,

TIMIDITY

2Tim 1:7 us a spirit of T but a spirit of

TIMNA (6)

Gen 36:12 T was a concubine of Eliphaz, Esau's son; she
36:22 were Hori and Heman; and Lotan's sister was T
36:40 their names: the chiefs T, Alvah, Jetheth,
1Chr 1:36 Omar, Zephi, Gatam, Kenaz, T, and Amalek.
1:39 Lotan: Hori and Homam; and Lotan's sister was T
1:51 of Edom were: chiefs T, Aliah, Jetheth,

TIMNAH (12)

Gen 38:12 he went up to T to his sheepshearers, he
38:13 is going up to T to shear his sheep,"
38:14 on the road to T; for she saw that
Josh 15:10 and passes along by T;
15:57 Zanoah, Kain, Gibe-ah, and T: ten cities with their
19:43 Sha-alabbin, Aijalon, Ithlah, Elon, T, Ekron,
Judg 14:1 Samson went down to T, and at Timnah he
14:1 to Timnah, and at T he saw one of
14:2 of the Philistines at T; now get her for
14:5 father and mother to T, and he came to
14:5 Timnah, and he came to the vineyards of T
2Chr 28:18 Soco with its villages, T with its villages, and

TIMNATH

1Mac 9:50 Beth-horon, and Bethel, and T, and Pharathon, and

TIMNATH-HERES
Judg 2:9 of his inheritance in T, in the hill country

TIMNATH-SERAH (2)
Josh 19:50 city which he asked, T in the hill country
24:30 his own inheritance at T, which is in the

TIMNITE
Judg 15:6 the son-in-law of the T, because he has taken

TIMON
Acts 6:5 Prochorus, and Nicanor, and T, and Parmenas, and

TIMOTHY (44)
1Mac 5:6 and many people with T as their leader.
5:11 we have fled, and T is leading their forces.
5:34 when the army of T realized that it was
5:37 After these things T gathered another army and
5:40 the stream of water, T said to the officers
2Mac 8:30 with the forces of T and Bacchides they killed
8:32 killed the commander of T's forces, a most unholy
9:3 had happened to Nicanor and the forces of T
10:24 Now T, who had been defeated by the Jews
10:32 T himself fled to a stronghold called Gazara,
10:37 They killed T, who was hidden in a cistern,
12:2 governors in various places, T and Apollonius the son
12:10 on their march against T, not less than five
12:18 They did not find T in that region, for
12:19 and destroyed those whom T had left in the
12:20 divisions, and hastened after T, who had with him
12:21 When T learned of the approach of Judas, he
12:24 T himself fell into the hands of Dositheus and
Acts 16:1 disciple was there, named T, the son of a
16:3 Paul wanted T to accompany him; and he took
17:14 sea, but Silas and T remained there.
17:15 command for Silas and T to come to him
18:5 When Silas and T arrived from Macedonia, Paul was
19:22 two of his helpers, T and Erastus, he himself
20:4 Gaius of Derbe, and T; and the Asians, Tychicus
Rom 16:21 T, my fellow worker, greets you; so do Lucius
1Cor 4:17 I sent to you T, my beloved and faithful
16:10 When T comes, see that you put him at
2Cor 1:1 will of God, and T our brother.
1:19 among you, Silvanus and T and I, was not
Phil 1:1 Paul and T, servants of Christ Jesus,
2:19 Lord Jesus to send T to you soon, so
2:22 But T's worth you know, how as a son
Col 1:1 will of God, and T our brother,
1Thes 1:1 Paul, Silvanus, and T, to the Church of
3:2 alone, and we sent T, our brother and God's
3:6 But now that T has come to us from
2Thes 1:1 Paul, Silvanus, and T, to the Church of
1Tim 1:2 Jesus our hope, To T, my true child in
1:18 I commit to you, T, my son, in accordance
6:20 O T, guard what has been entrusted to you.
2Tim 1:2 in Christ Jesus, To T, my beloved child: Grace,
Philem 1:1 for Christ Jesus, and T our brother, To Philemon
Heb 13:23 understand that our brother T has been released,

TIN (5)
Num 31:22 bronze, the iron, the T, and the lead,
Sir 47:18 you gathered gold like T and amassed silver like
Ezek 22:18 silver and bronze and T and iron and lead
22:20 iron and lead and T into a furnace, to
27:12 every kind; silver, iron, T, and lead they exchanged

TINGLE (3)
1Sam 3:11 ears of every one that hears it will T
2Kgs 21:12 of every one who hears of it will T
Jer 19:3 of every one who hears of it will T

TINKLING
Is 3:16 along as they go, T with their feet;

TINY (2)
Esth 10:6 The T spring which became a river, and there
11:10 as though from a T spring there came a

TIP (11)
Ex 29:20 put it upon the T of the right ear
Lev 8:23 put it on the T of Aaron's right ear
14:14 put it on the T of the right ear
14:17 shall put on the T of the right ear
14:25 put it on the T of the right ear
14:28 his hand on the T of the right ear
Judg 6:21 LORD reached out the T of the staff that
1Sam 14:27 he put forth the T of the staff that
14:43 little honey with the T of the staff that
1Kgs 6:24 ten cubits from the T of one wing to
6:24 one wing to the T of the other.

TIPHSAH
1Kgs 4:24 of the Euphrates from T to Gaza, over all

TIPPED
Bar 6:27 and if it is T over, it cannot straighten

TIPS (4)
Ex 29:20 Aaron and upon the T of the right ears
Lev 8:24 the blood on the T of their right ears
Wis 11:22 like a speck that T the scales, and like
Sir 1:19 for a man's anger T the scale to his

TIRAS (2)
Gen 10:2 Gomer, Magog, Madai, Javan, Tubal, Meshech, and T
1Chr 1:5 Gomer, Magog, Madai, Javan, Tubal, Meshech, and T

TIRATHITES
1Chr 2:55 dwelt at Jabez: the T, the Shimeathites, and the

TIRED (2)
Jer 12:13 reaped thorns, they have T themselves out but profit
1Mac 10:81 commanded, and the enemy's horses grew T

TIRHAKAH (2)
2Kgs 19:9 king heard concerning T king of Ethiopia, "Behold,
Is 37:9 the king heard concerning T king of Ethiopia, "He

TIRHANAH
1Chr 2:48 Maacah, Caleb's concubine, bore Sheber and T

TIRI-A
1Chr 4:16 of Jehallelel: Ziph, Ziphah, T, and Asarel.

TIRZAH (18)
Num 26:33 were Mahlah, Noah, Hoglah, Milcah, and T
27:1 were: Mahlah, Noah, Hoglah, Milcah, and T
36:11 commanded Moses; for Mahlah, T, Hoglah, Milcah,
Josh 12:24 one; the king of T, one: in all, thirty-one
17:3 his daughters: Mahlah, Noah, Hoglah, Milcah, and T
1Kgs 14:17 Jeroboam's wife arose, and departed, and came to T
15:21 he stopped building Ramah, and he dwelt in T
15:33 over all Israel at T, and reigned twenty-four years.
16:6 and was buried at T; and Elah his son
16:8 reign over Israel in T, and reigned two years.
16:9 When he was at T, drinking himself drunk in
16:9 over the household in T,
16:15 king of Judah, Zimri reigned seven days in T
16:17 and all Israel with him, and they besieged T
16:23 for twelve years; six years he reigned in T
2Kgs 15:14 Gadi came up from T and came to Samaria,
15:16 and its territory from T on; because they did
Song 6:4 You are beautiful as T, my love, comely as

TISHBE
1Kgs 17:1 Elijah the Tishbite, of T in Gilead, said to

TISHBITE (6)
1Kgs 17:1 Now Elijah the T, of Tishbe in Gilead, said
21:17 came to Elijah the T, saying,
21:28 came to Elijah the T, saying,
2Kgs 1:3 said to Elijah the T, "Arise, go up to
1:8 And he said, "It is Elijah the T
9:36 his servant Elijah the T, 'In the territory of

TITANS
Jud 16:7 the sons of the T smite him, nor did

TITHE (23)
Lev 27:30 "All the T of the land, whether of the
27:31 redeem any of his T, he shall add a
27:32 And all the T of herds and flocks, every
Num 18:21 I have given every T in Israel for an
18:24 For the T of the people of Israel, which
18:26 people of Israel the T which I have given
18:26 to the LORD, a T of the tithe.
18:26 it to the LORD, a tithe of the T
Deut 12:17 within your towns the T of your grain or
14:22 "You shall T all the yield of your seed,
14:23 you shall eat the T of your grain, of
14:24 able to bring the T, when the LORD your
14:28 bring forth all the T of your produce in

	26:12	finished paying all the T of your produce in
	26:14	not eaten of the T while I was mourning,
2Chr	31:5	brought in abundantly the T of everything.
	31:6	also brought in the T of cattle and sheep,
Neh	10:38	shall bring up the T of the tithes to
	13:12	all Judah brought the T of the grain, wine,
Sir	35:9	face, and dedicate your T with gladness.
Mt	23:22	for you T mint and dill and cummin, and
Lk	11:42	for you T mint and rue and every herb,
Heb	7:4	patriarch gave him a T of the spoils.

TITHES (25)

Num	18:28	LORD from all your T, which you receive from
Deut	12:6	and your sacrifices, your T and the offering that
	12:11	and your sacrifices, your T and the offering that
2Chr	31:12	in the contributions, the T and the dedicated things.
Neh	10:37	to the Levites the T from our ground, for
	10:37	Levites who collect the T in all our rural
	10:38	the Levites receive the T; and the Levites shall
	10:38	the tithe of the T to the house of
	12:44	first fruits, and the T, to gather into them
	13:5	the vessels, and the T of grain, wine, and
Tob	1:6	first fruits and the T of my produce and
	5:13	our flocks and the T of our produce.
Jud	11:13	the grain and the T of the wine and
Amos	4:4	sacrifices every morning, your T every three days;
Mal	3:8	robbing thee?' In your T and offerings.
	3:10	Bring the full T into the storehouse, that there
1Mac	3:49	first fruits and the T, and they stirred up
	10:31	and her environs, her T and her revenues, be
	11:35	to us of the T, and the taxes due
Lk	18:12	a week, I give T of all that I
Heb	7:5	the law to take T from the people, that
	7:6	genealogy received T from Abraham and blessed
	7:8	Here T are received by mortal men; there, by
	7:9	himself, who receives T, paid tithes through Abraham,
	7:9	who receives tithes, paid T through Abraham,

TITHING

Deut	26:12	is the year of T, giving it to the

TITIUS

Acts	18:7	of a man named T Justus, a worshiper of

TITLE (2)

Jn	19:19	Pilate also wrote a T and put it on
	19:20	the Jews read this T, for the place where

TITUS (14)

2Mac	11:34	thus: "Quintus Memmius and T Manius, envoys of the
2Cor	2:13	not find my brother T there.
	7:6	by the coming of T,
	7:13	at the joy of T, because his mind has
	7:14	so our boasting before T has proved true.
	8:6	Accordingly we have urged T that as he had
	8:16	earnest care for you into the heart of T
	8:23	As for T, he is my partner and fellow
	12:18	I urged T to go, and sent the brother
	12:18	Did T take advantage of you?
Gal	2:1	Jerusalem with Barnabas, taking T along with me.
	2:3	But even T, who was with me, was not
2Tim	4:10	has gone to Galatia, T to Dalmatia.
Tit	1:3	God our Savior; To T, my true child in

TIZITE

1Chr	11:45	Joha his brother, the T,

TOAH

1Chr	6:34	of Eliel, son of T,

TOB (5)

Judg	11:3	in the land of T; and worthless fellows collected
	11:5	from the land of T;
2Sam	10:6	and the men of T, twelve thousand men.
	10:8	and the men of T and Maacah, were by
1Mac	5:13	in the land of T have been killed; the

TOBADONIJAH

2Chr	17:8	Jehonathan, Adonijah, Tobijah, and T; and with these

TOBIAH (16)

Ezra	2:60	Delaiah, the sons of T, and the sons of
Neh	2:10	Sanballat the Horonite and T the servant, the
	2:19	Sanballat the Horonite and T the servant, the
	4:3	T the Ammonite was by him, and he said,
	4:7	But when Sanballat and T and the Arabs and
	6:1	reported to Sanballat and T and to Geshem the
	6:12	prophecy against me because T and Sanballat had
	6:14	Remember T and Sanballat, O my God, according to
	6:17	sent many letters to T, and Tobiah's letters came
	6:17	letters to Tobiah, and T's letters came to them.
	6:19	And T sent letters to make me afraid.
	7:62	Delaiah, the sons of T, the sons of Nekoda,
	13:4	who was connected with T,
	13:5	with Tobiah, prepared for T a large chamber where
	13:7	Eliashib had done for T, preparing for him a
	13:8	the household furniture of T out of the chamber.

TOBIAS (37)

Tob	1:9	and by her I became the father of T
	1:20	me except my wife Anna and my son T
	2:1	Anna and my son T were restored to me,
	3:17	Raguel in marriage to T the son of Tobit,
	3:17	the evil demon, because T was entitled to possess
	4:2	not call my son T so that I may
	5:1	Then T answered him, "Father, I will do everything
	5:5	was an angel, but T did not know it.
	5:5	T said to him, "Can you go with me
	5:7	Then T said to him, "Wait for me, and
	5:9	So T invited him in; he entered and they
	5:16	Then he said to T, "Get ready for the
	6:17	When T heard these things, he fell in love
	7:5	And T said, "He is my father."
	7:8	Then T said to Raphael, "Brother Azarias, speak of
	7:9	And Raguel said to T, "Eat, drink, and be
	7:11	And T said, "I will eat nothing here until
	7:13	he gave her to T to be his wife,
	8:1	finished eating, they escorted T in to her.
	8:4	the two were alone, T got up from the
	8:5	And T began to pray, "Blessed art thou, O
	8:20	declared by oath to T that he should not
	9:1	Then T called Raphael and said to him,
	9:6	And Gabael blessed T and his wife.
	10:7	mourning for her son T, until the fourteen days
	10:7	At that time T said to Raguel, "Send me
	10:9	T replied, "No, send me back to my father."
	10:12	And Edna said to T, "The Lord of heaven
	11:1	After this T went on his way, praising God
	11:2	Then Raphael said to T, "Are you not aware,
	11:7	Raphael said, "I know, T, that your father will
	11:15	mercy upon me; here I see my son T
	11:19	Nadab came, and T marriage was celebrated for
	12:1	then called his son T and said to him,
	14:11	fifty-eight years old; and T gave him a magnificent
	14:12	Then T returned with his wife and his sons
2Mac	3:11	of Hyrcanus, son of T, a man of very

TOBIEL

Tob	1:1	Tobit the son of T, son of Ananiel, son

TOBIJAH (3)

2Chr	17:8	Shemiramoth, Jehonathan, Adonijah, T, and Tobado
Zech	6:10	from the exiles Heldai, T, and Jedaiah, who have
	6:14	a reminder to Heldai, T, Jedaiah, and Josiah the

TOBIT (25)

Tob	1:1	of the acts of T the son of Tobiel,
	1:3	I, T, walked in the ways of truth and
	3:17	the white films of T's eyes; to give Sarah
	3:17	Tobias the son of T, and to bind Asmodeus
	3:17	At that very moment T returned and entered his
	4:1	On that day T remembered the money which he
	5:3	Then T gave him the receipt, and said to
	5:10	Then T said to him, "My brother, to what
	5:11	And T said to him, "I should like to
	5:13	Then T said to him, "You are welcome, my
	5:17	weep, and said to T, "Why have you sent
	5:20	And T said to her, "Do not worry, my
	7:2	"How much the young man resembles my cousin T
	7:4	said to them, "Do you know our brother T
	7:7	When he heard that T had lost his sight,
	10:1	Now his father T was counting each day, and
	10:6	But T said to her, "Be still and stop
	11:10	T started toward the door, and stumbled.
	11:16	Then T went out to meet his daughter-in-law at
	11:17	And T gave thanks before them that God had
	11:17	When T came near to Sarah his daughter-in-law, he
	12:1	T then called his son Tobias and said to
	13:1	Then T wrote a prayer of rejoicing, and said:
	14:1	Here T ended his words of praise.
	14:13	inherited their property and that of his father T

T

TOCHEN
1Chr 4:32 were Etam, Ain, Rimmon, T, and Ashan, five cities,

TODAY (129)
Gen 21:26 and I have not heard of it until T
24:12 Abraham, grant me success T, I pray thee, and
24:42 my oath.' "I came T to the spring, and
30:32 through all your flock T, removing from it every
31:48 heap is a witness between you and me T
40:7 his master's house, "Why are your faces downcast T
41:9 butler said to Pharaoh, "I remember my faults T
50:20 people should be kept alive, as they are T
Ex 2:18 is it that you have come so soon T
5:14 task of making bricks T, as hitherto?"
14:13 will work for you T; for the Egyptians whom
14:13 Egyptians whom you see T, you shall never see
16:25 Moses said, "Eat it T, for today is a
16:25 "Eat it today, for T is a sabbath to
16:25 sabbath to the LORD; T you will not find
19:10 people and consecrate them T and tomorrow, and let
32:29 And Moses said, T you have ordained yourselves for
Lev 8:34 As has been done T, the LORD has commanded
9:4 mixed with oil; for T the LORD will appear
10:19 said to Moses, "Behold, T they have offered their
10:19 eaten the sin offering T, would it have been
Deut 15:15 God redeemed you; therefore I command you this T
31:27 yet alive with you, T you have been rebellious
Josh 7:25 The LORD brings trouble on you T
22:18 rebel against the LORD T he will be angry
22:22 LORD, spare us not T
22:31 Gadites and the Manassites, T we know that the
Judg 21:3 that there should be T one tribe lacking in
Ruth 2:19 mother-in-law said to her, "Where did you glean T
2:19 with whom I worked T is Boaz."
3:18 will not rest, but will settle the matter T
1Sam 4:3 put us to rout T before the Philistines?
4:16 from the battle; I fled from the battle T
9:12 people have a sacrifice T on the high place.
9:19 the high place, for T you shall eat with
10:2 you depart from me T you will meet two
11:13 death this day, for T the LORD has wrought
12:17 Is it not wheat harvest T
14:30 people had eaten freely T of the spoil of
14:38 know and see how this sin has arisen T
20:27 Jesse come to the meal, either yesterday or T
21:5 journey; how much more T will their vessels be
22:15 Is T the first time that I have inquired
24:10 the LORD gave you T into my hand in
26:23 you into my hand T, and I would not
27:10 asked, "Against whom have you made a raid T
2Sam 3:8 yet you charge me T with a fault concerning
6:20 of Israel honored himself T, uncovering himself today
6:20 himself today, uncovering himself T before the eyes
11:12 to Uriah, "Remain here T also, and tomorrow I
14:22 king; and Joab said, T your servant knows that
15:20 yesterday, and shall I T make you wander about
16:3 Jerusalem; for he said, T the house of Israel
16:12 me with good for this cursing of me T
18:20 not to carry tidings T; you may carry tidings
18:20 tidings another day, but T you shall carry no
19:5 and said, "You have T covered with shame the
19:6 have made it clear T that commanders and servants
19:6 nothing to you; for T I perceive that if
19:6 of us were dead T, then you would be
1Kgs 12:7 servant to this people T and serve them, and
14:14 who shall cut off the house of Jeroboam T
18:15 stand, I will surely show myself to him T
2Kgs 2:3 "Do you know that T the LORD will take
2:5 "Do you know that T the LORD will take
4:23 he said, "Why will you go to him T
6:28 we may eat him T, and we will eat
6:31 the son of Shaphat remains on his shoulders T
1Chr 28:7 ordinances, as he is T
29:5 offer willingly, consecrating himself T to the LORD?"
Neh 1:11 success to thy servant T, and grant him mercy
Tob 6:10 the young man, "Brother, T we shall stay with
Jud 6:2 as you have done T and tell us not
8:11 said to the people T is not right; you
8:29 T is not the first time your wisdom has
12:13 with us, and become T like one of the
12:18 means more to me T than in all the
Job 23:2 Then Job answered: T also my complaint is
Ps 2:7 "You are my son, T I have begotten you.
95:7 O that T you would hearken to his voice!
Prov 7:14 to offer sacrifices, and T I have paid my
22:19 them known to you T, even to you.
Sir 10:10 physician; the king of T will die tomorrow.
20:14 mouth like a herald; T he lends and tomorrow
38:22 it was mine, and T it is yours."
Is 48:7 not long ago; before T you have never heard
Jer 36:2 to you, from the days of Josiah until T
40:4 behold, I release you T from the chains on
Bar 1:19 land of Egypt until T, we have been disobedient
2:26 made as it is T, because of the wickedness
3:8 Behold, we are T in our exile where thou
Zech 9:12 O prisoners of hope; T I declare that I
1Mac 2:63 T he will be exalted, but tomorrow he will
3:17 we are faint, for we have eaten nothing T
4:10 our fathers and crush this army before us T
5:32 of his forces, "Fight T for your brethren!"
6:26 And behold, T they have encamped against the
7:42 this army before us T; let the rest learn
9:30 we have chosen you T to take his place
9:44 for our lives, for T things are not as
10:20 we have appointed you T to be the high
Mt 6:30 of the field, which T is alive and tomorrow
16:3 'It will be stormy T, for the sky is
21:28 work in the vineyard T
27:19 suffered much over him T in a dream."
Lk 4:21 to say to them, T this scripture has been
5:26 with awe, saying, "We have seen strange things T
12:28 alive in the field T and tomorrow is thrown
13:32 demons and perform cures T and tomorrow, and the
13:33 go on my way T and tomorrow and the
19:5 down; for I must stay at your house T
19:9 Jesus said to him, T salvation has come to
19:42 saying, "Would that even T you knew the things
22:59 "Before the cock crows T, you will deny me
23:42 I say to you, T you will be with
Acts 4:9 we are being examined T concerning a good deed
13:33 'Thou art my Son, T I have begotten thee.'
19:40 being charged with rioting T, there being no cause
26:2 to make my defense T against all the accusations
27:33 take some food, saying, T is the fourteenth day
Heb 1:5 "Thou art my Son, T I have begotten thee"?
3:7 the Holy Spirit says, T, when you hear his
3:13 every day, as long as it is called T
3:15 while it is said, T, when you hear his
4:7 of disobedience, again he sets a certain day, T
4:7 the words already quoted, T, when you hear his
5:5 "Thou art my Son, T I have begotten thee";
13:8 the same yesterday and T and for ever.
Jas 4:13 now, you who say, T or tomorrow we will

TOE (5)
Lev 8:23 and on the great T of his right foot.
14:14 and on the great T of his right foot.
14:17 and on the great T of his right foot,
14:25 and on the great T of his right foot.
14:28 hand, and the great T of his right foot,

TOES (8)
Ex 29:20 and upon the great T of their right feet,
Lev 8:24 and on the great T of their right feet;
Judg 1:6 and cut off his thumbs and his great T
1:7 thumbs and their great T cut off used to
2Sam 21:20 each hand, and six T on each foot, twenty-four
1Chr 20:6 each hand, and six T on each foot, twenty-four
Dan 2:41 saw the feet and T partly of potter's clay
2:42 And as the T of the feet were partly

TOGARMAH (2)
Gen 10:3 The sons of Gomer: Ashkenaz, Riphath, and T
1Chr 1:6 The sons of Gomer: Ashkenaz, Diphath, and T

TOGETHER (391)
Gen 1:9 the heavens be gathered T into one place, and
1:10 waters that were gathered T he called Seas.
3:7 they sewed fig leaves T and made themselves aprons.
11:31 and they went forth T from Ur of the
13:6 both of them dwelling T; for their possessions were
13:6 they could not dwell T,
22:6 So they went both of them T
22:8 So they went both of them T
22:19 they arose and went T to Beer-sheba; and Abraham
25:22 The children struggled T within her; and she said,
29:7 animals to be gathered T; water the sheep, and
29:8 the flocks are gathered T, and the stone is
29:22 So Laban gathered T all the men of the
36:7 for them to dwell T; the land of their
42:17 he put them all T in prison for three
46:15 to Jacob in Paddan-aram, T with his daughter Dinah;

49:1 and said, "Gather yourselves T, that I may tell
Ex 2:13 two Hebrews were struggling T; and he said to
3:16 the elders of Israel T, and say to them,
4:29 Aaron went and gathered T all the elders of
8:14 And they gathered them T in heaps, and the
19:8 all the people answered T and said, "All that
21:22 "When men strive T, and hurt a woman with
26:11 and couple the tent T that it may be
26:17 each frame, for fitting T; so shall you do
28:7 its two edges, that it may be joined T
32:1 the people gathered themselves T to Aaron, and said
32:26 of Levi gathered themselves T to him.
36:18 to couple the tent T that it might be
36:22 two tenons, for fitting T; he did this for
Num 1:18 assembled the whole congregation T, who registered
6:20 portion for the priest, T with the breast that
10:7 is to be gathered T, you shall blow, but
11:22 the sea be gathered T for them, to suffice
14:35 congregation that are gathered T against me: in this
16:3 and they assembled themselves T against Moses and
16:11 your company have gathered T; what is Aaron that
16:27 door of their tents, T with their wives, their
20:2 and they assembled themselves T against Moses and
20:10 Aaron gathered the assembly T before the rock, and
21:16 Moses, "Gather the people T, and I will give
21:23 gathered all his men T, and went out against
24:10 he struck his hands T; and Balak said to
26:10 and swallowed them up T with Korah, when that
27:3 those who gathered themselves T against the LORD
31:6 thousand from each tribe, T with Phinehas the son
Deut 4:49 Sirion (that is, Hermon), T with all the Arabah
22:10 not plow with an ox and an ass T
22:11 not wear a mingled stuff, wool and linen T
25:5 "If brothers dwell T, and one of them dies
33:5 people were gathered, all the tribes of Israel T
Josh 8:16 the city were called T to pursue them, and
9:2 of this, they gathered T with one accord to
11:5 and came and encamped T at the waters of
16:9 Ephraimites by their families, T with the towns
19:8 cities with their villages; T with all the villages
Judg 6:33 of the East came T, and crossing the Jordan
9:6 citizens of Shechem came T, and all Beth-millo, and
9:47 people of the Tower of Shechem were gathered T
10:17 people of Israel came T, and they encamped at
11:20 gathered all his people T, and encamped at Jahaz,
19:6 and ate and drank T; and the girl's father
20:14 And the Benjaminites came T out of the cities
Ruth 4:11 Rachel and Leah, who T built up the house
1Sam 5:8 they sent and gathered T all the lords of
5:11 sent therefore and gathered T all the lords of
8:4 elders of Israel gathered T and came to Samuel
10:17 Samuel called the people T to the LORD at
11:11 so that no two of them were left T
17:10 give me a man, that we may fight T
28:23 But his servants, T with the woman, urged him;
31:6 and all his men, on the same day T
2Sam 2:16 in his opponent's side; so they fell down T
2:25 Benjaminites gathered themselves T behind Abner,
2:30 gathered all the people T, there were missing of
8:11 dedicated to the LORD, T with the silver and
10:15 been defeated by Israel, they gathered themselves T
10:17 he gathered all Israel T, and crossed the Jordan,
12:19 his servants were whispering T, David perceived that
12:28 rest of the people T, and encamp against the
12:29 gathered all the people T and went to Rabbah,
14:16 me and my son T from the heritage of
20:4 the men of Judah T to me within three
21:9 the LORD, and the seven of them perished T
21:15 and David went down T with his servants, and
23:11 The Philistines gathered T at Lehi, where there was
1Kgs 9:27 familiar with the sea, T with the servants of
10:26 And Solomon gathered T chariots and horsemen; he
11:17 Hadad fled to Egypt, T with certain Edomites of
18:20 and gathered the prophets T at Mount Carmel.
20:1 gathered all his army T; thirty-two kings were with
22:6 Israel gathered the prophets T, about four hundred
2Kgs 3:23 kings have surely fought T, and slain one another.
8:6 all that was hers, T with all the produce
10:5 was over the city, T with the elders and
25:11 the king of Babylon, T with the rest of
1Chr 10:6 his three sons and all his house died T
11:1 Then all Israel gathered T to David at Hebron,
11:10 support in his kingdom, T with all Israel, to
13:2 that they may come T to us.
15:4 And David gathered T the sons of Aaron and
18:11 dedicated to the LORD, T with the silver and
19:17 he gathered all Israel T, and crossed the Jordan,
22:2 David commanded to gather T the aliens who were
28:1 king and his sons, T with the palace officials,
2Chr 1:14 Solomon gathered T chariots and horsemen; he had
3:11 wings of the cherubim T extended twenty cubits: one
8:18 they went to Ophir T with the servants of
18:5 Israel gathered the prophets T, four hundred men,
21:3 gold, and valuable possessions, T with fortified cities
28:24 And Ahaz gathered T the vessels of the house
30:13 And many people came T in Jerusalem to keep
30:23 the whole assembly agreed T to keep the feast
32:6 people, and gathered them T to him in the
34:29 king sent and gathered T all the elders of
Ezra 2:64 The whole assembly T was forty-two thousand three
3:8 Jozadak made a beginning, T with the rest of
3:9 the sons of Judah, T took the oversight of
6:20 Levites had purified themselves T; all of them were
Neh 4:6 the wall was joined T to half its height.
4:8 and they all plotted T to come and fight
6:2 and let us meet T in one of the
6:7 So now come, and let us take counsel T
6:10 said, "Let us meet T in the house of
7:66 The whole assembly T was forty-two thousand three
8:13 and the Levites, came T to Ezra the scribe
12:28 of the singers gathered T from the circuit round
13:11 And I gathered them T and set them in
Tob 5:13 Shemaiah, when we went T to Jerusalem to worship
8:7 and may grow old T with her."
13:13 they will be gathered T, and will praise the
Jud 2:2 He called T all his officers and all his
2:14 his master, and called T all the commanders, ,
2:15 twenty thousand of them, T with twelve thousand
4:3 Judea were newly gathered T, and the sacred vessels
5:2 So he called T all the princes of Moab
6:16 They called T all the elders of the city,
7:2 and twelve thousand cavalry, T with the baggage and
7:17 the Ammonites moved forward, T with five thousand
13:10 of them went out T, as they were accustomed
13:12 city gate and called T the elders of the
13:13 They all ran T, both small and great, for
Esth 2:19 virgins were gathered T the second time, Mordecai
5:12 am invited by her T with the king.
16:13 partner of our kingdom, T with their whole nation.
Job 2:11 They made an appointment T to come to condole
3:18 prisoners are at ease T; they hear not the
9:32 answer him, that we should come to trial T
10:11 flesh, and knit me T with bones and sinews.
16:4 I could join words T against you, and shake
16:10 cheek, they mass themselves T against me.
17:16 Shall we descend T into the dust?"
19:12 His troops come on T; they have cast up
30:7 bushes they bray; under the nettles they huddle T
31:38 its furrows have wept T;
34:15 all flesh would perish T, and man would return
38:7 the morning stars sang T, and all the sons
38:38 into a mass and the clods cleave fast T
40:13 all in the dust T; bind their faces in
40:17 cedar; the sinews of his thighs are knit T
41:23 of his flesh cleave T, firmly cast upon him
Ps 2:2 the rulers take counsel T, against the LORD and
31:13 as they scheme T against me, as they
34:3 with me, and let us exalt his name T
35:15 in glee, they gathered T against me; cripples whom
41:7 who hate me whisper T about me; they imagine
48:4 For lo, the kings assembled, they came on T
49:2 world, both low and high, rich and poor T
55:14 to hold sweet converse T; within God's house we
56:6 They band themselves T, they lurk, they watch my
62:9 go up; they are T lighter than a breath.
65:13 they shout and sing T for joy.
71:10 for my life consult T,
83:3 thy people; they consult T against thy protected ones.
88:17 all day long; they close in upon me T
94:21 They band T against the life of the righteous,
98:8 hills sing for joy T
102:22 praise, when peoples gather T, and kingdoms, to
122:3 which is bound firmly T,
139:13 thou didst knit me T in my mother's womb.
141:10 Let the wicked T fall into their own nets,
148:12 Young men and maidens T, old men and children!
Prov 22:2 and the poor meet T; the LORD is the
29:13 and the oppressor meet T; the LORD gives light
Eccl 3:5 time to gather stones T; a time to embrace,
4:11 Again, if two lie T, they are warm; but
Wis 1:7 which holds all things T knows what is said;
5:12 air, thus divided, comes T at once, so that

T

14:10 done will be punished T with him who did
18:5 didst destroy them all T by a mighty flood.
18:12 kin; and they all T, by the one form
Sir 21:9 is like tow gathered T, and their end is
22:7 one who glues potsherds T, or who rouses a
33:4 will be heard; bind T your instruction, and make
43:26 way, and by his word all things hold T
50:17 Then all the people T made haste and fell
Is 1:18 now, let us reason T, says the LORD: though
1:28 sinners shall be destroyed T, and those who forsake
1:31 of them shall burn T, with none to quench
8:10 Take counsel T, but it will come to nought;
9:21 Ephraim Manasseh, and T they are against Judah.
11:6 lion and the fatling T, and a little child
11:7 young shall lie down T; and the lion shall
11:14 in the west, and T they shall plunder the
13:4 Hark, an uproar of kingdoms, of nations gathering T
22:3 your rulers have fled T, without the bow they
24:4 withers; the heavens languish T with the earth.
24:22 They will be gathered T as prisoners in a
25:11 lay low his pride T with the skill of
27:4 out against them, I would burn them up T
31:3 helped will fall, and they will all perish T
40:5 flesh shall see it T, for the mouth of
41:1 them speak; let us T draw near for judgment.
41:19 plane and the pine T;
41:20 may consider and understand T, that the hand of
43:9 all the nations gather T, and let the peoples
43:26 remembrance, let us argue T; set forth your case,
44:11 be terrified, they shall be put to shame T
45:16 confounded, the makers of idols go in confusion T
45:20 and come, draw near T, you survivors of the
45:21 and present your case; let them take counsel T
46:2 stoop, they bow down T, they cannot save the
48:13 when I call to them, they stand forth T
50:8 Let us stand up T
52:8 lift up their voice, T they sing for joy;
52:9 Break forth T into singing, you waste places of
60:4 see; they all gather T, they come to you;
65:7 and their fathers' iniquities T, says the LORD;
65:25 the lamb shall feed T, the lion shall eat
66:17 come to an end T, says the LORD.
Jer 3:18 house of Israel, and T they shall come from
6:12 their fields and wives T; for I will stretch
6:21 stumble; fathers and sons T, neighbor and friend shall
8:14 Gather T, let us go into the fortified cities
13:14 another, fathers and sons T, says the LORD.
21:4 I will bring them T into the midst of
24:1 Jehoiakim, king of Judah, T with the princes of
31:8 who is in travail, T; a great company, they
31:24 cities shall dwell there T, and the farmers and
41:1 As they ate bread T there at Mizpah,
46:12 has stumbled against warrior; they have both fallen T
46:21 have turned and fled T, they did not stand;
49:14 nations: "Gather yourselves T and come against her,
50:4 of Judah shall come T, weeping as they come;
51:38 "They shall roar T like lions; they shall growl
52:15 the king of Babylon, T with the rest of
Lam 1:14 hand they were fastened T; they were set upon
2:8 caused rampart and wall to lament, they languish T
Bar 6:48 them, the priests consult T as to where they
Ezek 22:13 I strike my hands T at the dishonest gain
33:30 your people who talk T about you by the
37:7 and the bones came T, bone to its bone.
37:17 him'; and join them T into one stick, that
46:5 as he is able, T with a hin of
46:7 as he is able, T with a hin of
46:11 is able to give, T with a hin of
48:20 is, the holy portion T with the property of
Dan 2:35 and the gold, all T were broken in pieces,
2:43 they will not hold T, just as iron does
3:95 the king's counselors gathered T and saw that the
5:6 his limbs gave way, and his knees knocked T
8:12 given over to it T with the continual burnt
13:14 And then T they arranged for a time when
14:27 hair, and boiled them T and made cakes, which
Hos 1:11 Israel shall be gathered T, and they shall appoint
6:9 the priests are banded T; they murder on the
Amos 1:15 shall go into exile, he and his princes T
3:3 "Do two walk T, unless they have made an
Mic 2:12 I will set them T like sheep in a
7:3 desire of his soul; thus they weave it T
Zeph 2:1 Come T and hold assembly, O shameless nation,
Zech 10:5 T they shall be like mighty men in battle,
12:3 the earth will come T against it.
1Mac 3:10 But Apollonius gathered T Gentiles and a large force
5:9 Gentiles in Gilead gathered T against the Israelites
5:10 around us have gathered T against us to destroy
5:15 against them had gathered T men of Ptolemais and
5:44 sacred precincts with fire, T with all who were
5:45 Then Judas gathered T all the Israelites in Gilead,
6:20 They gathered T and besieged the citadel in the
10:61 Israel, lawless men, gathered T against him to accuse
12:37 So they gathered T to build up the city;
13:2 and gathering the people T
13:6 the nations have gathered T out of hatred to
14:9 streets; they all talked T of good things; and
2Mac 1:14 came to the place T with his friends, to
1:27 Gather T our scattered people, set free those who
2:7 God gathers his people T again and shows his
3:19 were kept indoors ran T to the gates, and
6:11 and were all burned T, because their piety kept
8:16 Maccabeus gathered his men T, to the number six
11:7 Then they eagerly rushed off T
11:9 And they all T praised the merciful God, and
15:31 had called his countrymen T and stationed the priests
Mt 1:18 Joseph, before they came T she was found to
13:30 Let both grow T until the harvest; and at
19:6 therefore God has joined T, let not man put
22:34 that he had silenced the Sadducees, they came T
22:41 the Pharisees were gathered T, Jesus asked them a
23:36 have gathered your children T as a hen gathers
24:28 body is, there the eagles will be gathered T
26:4 Caiaphas, and took counsel T in order to arrest
Mk 1:33 whole city was gathered T about the door.
2:2 And many were gathered T, so that there was
3:20 and the crowd came T again, so that they
7:1 when the Pharisees gathered T to him, with some
9:25 a crowd came running T, he rebuked the unclean
10:9 therefore God has joined T, let not man put
15:16 praetorium); and they called T the whole battalion.
Lk 6:38 measure, pressed down, shaken T, running over, will
8:4 a great crowd came T and people from town
9:1 he called the twelve T and gave them power
12:1 the multitude had gathered T that they trod upon
13:34 have gathered your children T as a hen gathers
15:6 comes home, he calls T his friends and his
15:9 found it, she calls T her friends and neighbors,
17:35 be two women grinding T; one will be taken
17:36 body is, there the eagles will be gathered T
22:53 courtyard and sat down T, Peter sat among them.
22:64 of the people gathered T, both chief priests and
23:13 Pilate then called T the chief priests and the
23:17 they all cried out T, "Away with this man,
24:15 were talking and discussing T, Jesus himself drew
24:33 found the eleven gathered T and those who were
Jn 4:36 life, so that sower and reaper may rejoice T
18:20 where all Jews come T; I have said nothing
21:2 Zebedee, and two others of his disciples were T
Acts 1:6 when they had come T, they asked him, "Lord,
1:14 devoted themselves to prayer, T with the women and
2:1 come, they were all T in one place.
2:6 the multitude came T, and they were bewildered,
2:44 all who believed were T and had all things
2:46 day, attending the temple T and breaking bread in
3:11 all the people ran T to them in the
4:5 and scribes were gathered T in Jerusalem,
4:24 they lifted their voices T to God and said,
4:26 the rulers were gathered T, against the Lord and
4:27 city there were gathered T against thy holy servant
4:31 which they were gathered T was shaken; and they
5:9 that you have agreed T to tempt the Spirit
5:12 And they were all T in Solomon's Portico.
5:21 with him and called T the council and all
7:57 their ears and rushed T upon him.
10:24 them and had called T his kinsmen and close
12:12 where many were gathered T and were praying.
13:44 the whole city gathered T to hear the word
14:1 Iconium they entered T into the Jewish synagogue,
14:27 they gathered the church T and declared all that
15:6 the elders were gathered T to consider this matter.
15:30 the congregation T, they delivered the letter.
16:13 and spoke to the women who had come T
18:8 believed in the Lord, T with all his household;
19:19 arts brought their books T and burned them in
19:25 These he gathered T, with the workmen of like
19:29 confusion; and they rushed T into the theater,
19:32 them did not know why they had come T
20:7 when we were gathered T to break bread, Paul
21:30 and the people ran T; they seized Paul and
25:17 When therefore they came T here, I made no
28:17 three days he called T the local leaders of

Rom	3:12	All have turned aside, T they have gone wrong;
	8:22	been groaning in travail T until now;
	15:6	with Christ Jesus, that T you may with one
	15:30	the Spirit, to strive T with me in your
1Cor	1:2	called to be saints T with all those who
	7:5	prayer; but then come T again, lest Satan tempt
	11:17	because when you come T it is not for
	11:20	When you meet T, it is not the Lord's
	11:33	brethren, when you come T to eat, wait for
	11:34	home—lest you come T to be condemned.
	12:26	member suffers, all suffer T; if one member is
	12:26	together; if one member is honored, all rejoice T
	14:26	When you come T, each one has a hymn,
	16:19	Aquila and Prisca, T with the church in their
2Cor	6:1	Working T with him, then, we entreat you not
	7:3	our hearts, to die T and to live together.
	7:3	our hearts, to die together and to live T
Eph	2:5	trespasses, made us alive T with Christ (by grace
	2:21	whole structure is joined T and grows into a
	4:16	body, joined and knit T by every joint with
Phil	4:3	me in the gospel T with Clement and the
Col	1:17	all things, and in him all things hold T
	2:2	as they are knit T in love, to have
	2:13	flesh, God made alive T with him, having forgiven
	2:19	body, nourished and knit T through its joints and
	3:14	love, which binds everything T in perfect harmony.
1Thes	4:17	shall be caught up T with them in the
Heb	10:25	not neglecting to meet T, as is the habit
3Jn	1:14	and we will talk T face to face.
Jude	1:12	as they boldly carouse T, looking after themselves;
Rev	17:12	kings for one hour, T with the beast.

TOHU

1Sam	1:1	of Elihu, son of T, son of Zuph, an

TOI (3)

2Sam	8:9	When T king of Hamath heard that David had
	8:10	whole army of Hadadezer, T sent his son Joram
	8:10	for Hadadezer had often been at war with T

TOIL (59)

Gen	3:17	because of you; in T you shall eat of
	5:29	work and from the T of our hands."
Deut	26:7	saw our affliction, our T, and our oppression;
Josh	7:3	make the whole people T up there, for they
2Sam	12:31	axes, and made them T at the brickkilns; and
Job	20:18	the fruit of his T, and will not swallow
	24:5	go forth to their T, seeking prey in the
Ps	90:10	their span is but T and trouble; they are
	105:44	fruit of the peoples' T,
	109:11	has; may strangers plunder the fruits of his T
	127:2	the bread of anxious T; for he gives to
Prov	14:23	In all T there is profit, but mere talk
	23:4	Do not T to acquire wealth; be wise enough
Eccl	1:3	gain by all the T at which he toils
	2:10	pleasure in all my T, and this was my
	2:10	and this was my reward for all my T
	2:11	had done and the T I had spent in
	2:18	I hated all my T in which I had
	2:20	despair over all the T of my labors under
	2:21	man who did not T for it.
	2:22	man from all the T and strain with which
	2:24	eat and drink, and find enjoyment in his T
	3:9	What gain has the worker from his T
	3:13	and drink and take pleasure in all his T
	4:4	I saw that all T and all skill in
	4:6	two hands full of T and a striving after
	4:8	end to all his T, and his eyes are
	4:9	because they have a good reward for their T
	5:15	take nothing for his T, which he may carry
	5:18	enjoyment in all the T with which one toils
	5:19	find enjoyment in his T --this is the gift
	6:7	All the T of man is for his mouth,
	8:15	with him in his T through the days of
	8:17	However much man may T in seeking, he will
	9:9	life and in your T at which you toil
	9:9	toil at which you T under the sun.
	10:15	The T of a fool wearies him, so that
Wis	9:10	be with me and T, and that I may
	10:10	his labors, and increased the fruit of his T
	15:4	us, nor the fruitless T of painters, a figure
	15:8	With misspent T, he forms a futile god from
	16:20	angels, and without their T thou didst supply them
Sir	6:19	her service you will T a little while, and
	11:19	and keep at your T; for it is easy
	14:15	what you acquired by T to be divided by
	28:15	and deprived them of the fruit of their T
	34:23	another tears down, what do they gain but T
Jer	20:18	the womb to see T and sorrow, and spend
Hag	2:17	the products of your T with blight and mildew
2Mac	2:26	who have undertaken the T of abbreviating, it is
	2:27	gladly endure the uncomfortable T,
Mt	6:28	they grow; they neither T nor spin;
Lk	12:27	they grow; they neither T nor spin; yet I
2Cor	11:27	from false brethren; in T and hardship, through many
Col	1:29	For this I T, striving with all the energy
1Thes	2:9	remember our labor and T, brethren; we worked
2Thes	3:8	without paying, but with T and labor we worked
1Tim	4:10	to this end we T and strive, because we
Rev	2:2	know your works, your T and your patient endurance,

TOILED (6)

Eccl	2:18	in which I had T under the sun, seeing
	2:19	all for which I T and used my wisdom
	2:21	a man who has T with wisdom and knowledge
	5:16	has he that he T for the wind,
Wis	17:17	or a workman who T in the wilderness, he
Lk	5:5	Simon answered, "Master, we T all night and took

TOILING (2)

Eccl	4:8	"For whom am I T and depriving myself of
Acts	20:35	you that by so T one must help the

TOILS (7)

Prov	5:22	is caught in the T of his sin.
Eccl	1:3	toil at which he T under the sun?
	2:22	strain with which he T beneath the sun?
	5:18	toil with which one T under the sun the
Sir	11:11	man who works, and T, and presses on, but
	31:3	The rich man T as his wealth accumulates, and
	31:4	The poor man T as his livelihood diminishes, and

TOILSOME

Sir	7:15	Do not hate T labor, or farm work, which

TOKEN (2)

1Sam	17:18	fare, and bring some T from them."
Wis	16:6	warning, and received a T of deliverance to remind

TOKENS (6)

Deut	22:14	find in her the T of virginity,'
	22:15	and bring out the T of her virginity to
	22:17	in your daughter the T of virginity." And yet
	22:17	yet these are the T of my daughter's virginity.'
	22:20	is true, that the T of virginity were not
2Mac	12:40	dead they found sacred T of the idols of

TOKHATH

2Chr	34:22	Shallum the son of T, son of Hasrah, keeper

TOLA (6)

Gen	46:13	The sons of Issachar: T, Puvah, Iob, and Shimron.
Num	26:23	to their families: of T, the family of the
Judg	10:1	arose to deliver Israel T the son of Puah,
1Chr	7:1	The sons of Issachar: T, Puah, Jashub, and Shimron,
	7:2	The sons of T: Uzzi, Rephaiah, Jeri-el, Jahmai,
	7:2	fathers' houses, namely of T, mighty warriors of their

TOLAD

1Chr	4:29	Moladah, Hazar-shual, Bilhah, Ezem, T,

TOLAITES

Num	26:23	the family of the T; of Puvah, the family

TOLD (365)

Gen	3:11	He said, "Who T you that you were naked?
	9:22	of his father, and T his two brothers outside.
	12:4	as the LORD had T him; and Lot went
	14:13	had escaped came, and T Abram the Hebrew, who
	20:8	all his servants, and T them all these things;
	22:3	of which God had T him.
	22:9	of which God had T him, Abraham built an
	22:20	these things it was T Abraham, "Behold, Milcah also
	24:28	the maiden ran and T her mother's household about
	24:33	eat until I have T my errand." He said,
	24:66	And the servant T Isaac all the things that
	26:32	Isaac's servants came and T him about the well
	27:19	have done as you T me; now sit up
	27:42	her older son were T to Rebekah; so she
	29:12	And Jacob T Rachel that he was her father's
	29:12	and she ran and T her father.
	29:13	Jacob T Laban all these things,

31:22 When it was T Laban on the third day
37:5 dream, and when he T it to his brothers
37:9 dreamed another dream, and T it to his brothers,
37:10 But when he T it to his father and
38:13 And when Tamar was T, "Your father-in-law is going
38:24 later Judah was T, "Tamar your daughter-in-law has
39:17 came home, and she T him the same story,
40:9 So the chief butler T his dream to Joseph,
41:8 wise men; and Pharaoh T them his dream, but
41:12 guard; and when we T him, he interpreted our
41:24 And I T it to the magicians, but there
41:28 It is as I T Pharaoh, God has shown
42:29 land of Canaan, they T him all that had
43:7 another brother?' What we T him was in answer
44:2 he did as Joseph T him.
44:24 servant my father we T him the words of
45:26 And they T him, "Joseph is still alive, and
45:27 But when they T him all the words of
47:1 Joseph went in and T Pharaoh, "My father and
48:1 After this Joseph was T, "Behold, your father is
48:2 And it was T to Jacob, "Your son Joseph
Ex 4:28 And Moses T Aaron all the words of the
12:35 also done as Moses T them, for they had
14:5 king of Egypt was T that the people had
16:22 the congregation came and T Moses,
17:10 Joshua did as Moses T him, and fought with
18:6 And when one T Moses, "Lo, your father-in-law
18:8 Then Moses T his father-in-law all that the LORD
19:9 Then Moses T the words of the people to
19:25 to the people and T them.
24:3 Moses came and T the people all the words
34:34 he came out, and T the people of Israel
Num 9:4 So Moses T the people of Israel that they
11:24 Moses went out and T the people the words
11:27 young man ran and T Moses, "Eldad and Medad
13:27 And they T him, "We came to the land
14:39 And Moses T these words to all the people
29:40 And Moses T the people of Israel everything just
Deut 1:21 of your fathers, has T you; do not fear
2:1 Sea, as the LORD T me; and for many
17:4 forbidden, and it is T you and you hear
Josh 2:2 And it was T the king of Jericho, "Behold,
2:23 of Nun; and they T him all that had
4:8 Israel, as the LORD T Joshua; and they carried
9:24 Joshua, "Because it was T to your servants for
10:17 And it was T Joshua, "The five kings have
Judg 4:12 When Sisera was T that Barak the son of
6:27 as the LORD had T him; but because he
9:7 When it was T to Jotham, he went and
9:25 way; and it was T Abimelech.
9:42 And Abimelech was T
9:47 Abimelech was T that all the people of the
13:6 the woman came and T her husband, "A man
13:10 ran in haste and T her husband, "Behold, the
14:2 he came up, and T his father and mother,
14:16 and you have not T me what it is."
14:16 "Behold, I have not T my father nor my
14:17 the seventh day he T her, because she pressed
14:17 Then she T the riddle to her countrymen.
14:19 to those who had T the riddle.
16:2 The Gazites were T, "Samson has come here," and
16:10 have mocked me, and T me lies; please tell
16:13 have mocked me, and T me lies; tell me
16:15 and you have not T me wherein your great
16:17 And he T her all his mind, and said
16:18 saw that he had T her all his mind,
16:18 once, for he has T me all his mind."
Ruth 2:11 husband has been fully T me, and how you
2:19 So she T her mother-in-law with whom she had
3:6 as her mother-in-law had T her.
3:16 Then she T her all that the man had
1Sam 3:17 was it that he T you?
3:17 of all that he T you."
3:18 So Samuel T him everything and hid nothing from
4:13 into the city and T the news, all the
4:14 hastened and came and T Eli.
8:10 So Samuel T all the words of the LORD
9:17 saw Saul, the LORD T him, "Here is the
10:16 to his uncle, "He T us plainly that the
10:25 Then Samuel T the people the rights and duties
11:5 So they T him the tidings of the men
11:9 the messengers came and T the men of Jabesh,
14:33 Then they T Saul, "Behold, the people are sinning
14:43 And Jonathan T him, "I tasted a little honey
15:12 morning; and it was T Samuel, "Saul came to
18:20 loved David; and they T Saul, and the thing
18:24 the servants of Saul T him, "Thus and so
18:26 And when his servants T David these words, it
19:2 And Jonathan T David, "Saul my father seeks to
19:11 But Michal, David's wife, T him, "If you do
19:18 Samuel at Ramah, and T him all that Saul
19:19 And it was T Saul, "Behold, David is at
19:21 When it was T Saul, he sent other messengers,
22:21 And Abiathar T David that Saul had killed the
23:1 Now they T David, "Behold, the Philistines are
23:7 Now it was T Saul that David had come
23:13 When Saul was T that David had escaped from
23:22 there; for it is T me that he is
23:25 And David was T; therefore he went down to
24:1 the Philistines, he was T, "Behold, David is in
25:12 and came back and T him all this.
25:14 of the young men T Abigail, Nabal's wife, "Behold,
25:36 very drunk; so she T him nothing at all
25:37 of Nabal, his wife T him these things, and
27:4 And when it was T Saul that David had
2Sam 1:5 the young man who T him, "How do you
1:6 the young man who T him said, "By chance
1:13 the young man who T him, "Where do you
2:4 When they T David, "It was the men of
3:23 him came, it was T Joab, "Abner the son
4:10 every adversity, when one T me, 'Behold, Saul is
6:12 And it was T King David, "The LORD has
10:5 When it was T David, he sent to meet
10:17 And when it was T David, he gathered all
11:5 and she sent and T David, "I am with
11:10 When they T David, "Uriah did not go down
11:18 Then Joab sent and T David all the news
11:22 went, and came and T David all that Joab
14:33 to the king, and T him; and he summoned
15:31 And it was T David, "Ahithophel is among the
17:18 lad saw them, and T Absalom; so both of
17:21 well, and went and T King David.
18:10 man saw it, and T Joab, "Behold, I saw
18:11 to the man who T him, "What, you saw
18:25 watchman called out and T the king.
19:1 It was T Joab, "Behold, the king is weeping
19:8 the people were all T, "Behold, the king is
21:11 When David was T what Rizpah the daughter of
24:13 came to David and T him, and said to
1Kgs 1:23 And they T the king, "Here is Nathan the
1:27 and you have not T your servants who should
1:51 And it was T Solomon, "Behold, Adonijah fears King
2:29 And when it was T King Solomon, "Joab has
2:39 And when it was T Shimei, "Behold, your slaves
2:41 And when Solomon was T that Shimei had gone
10:2 came to Solomon, she T him all that was
10:7 the half was not T me; your wisdom and
13:11 his sons came and T him all that the
13:11 to the king, they T to their father.
13:25 And they came and T it in the city
18:13 Has it not been T my lord what I
18:16 to meet Ahab, and T him; and Ahab went
19:1 Ahab T Jezebel all that Elijah had done, and
2Kgs 1:7 to meet you and T you these things?"
4:7 She came and T the man of God, and
4:27 me, and has not T me."
4:31 to meet him, and T him, "The child has
5:4 Naaman went in and T his lord, "Thus and
6:10 the man of God T him.
6:13 It was T him, "Behold, he is in Dothan."
7:10 of the city, and T them, "We came to
7:11 out, and it was T within the king's household.
7:15 the messengers returned, and T the king.
8:6 asked the woman, she T him.
8:7 and when it was T him, "The man of
8:14 And he answered, "He T me that you would
9:36 they came back and T him, he said, "This
10:8 the messenger came and T him, "They have brought
17:26 king of Assyria was T, "The nations which you
18:37 their clothes rent, and T him the words of
22:10 Then Shaphan the secretary T the king, "Hilkiah the
23:17 men of the city T him, "It is the
1Chr 19:5 When David was T concerning the men, he sent
19:17 And when it was T David, he gathered all
2Chr 9:1 came to Solomon, she T him all that was
9:6 your wisdom was not T me; you surpass the
20:2 Some men came and T Jehoshaphat, "A great
34:18 Then Shaphan the secretary T the king, "Hilkiah the
Ezra 2:63 as unclean; the governor T them that they were
8:22 way; since we had T the king, "The hand
Neh 2:12 with me; and I T no one what my
2:16 I had not yet T the Jews, the priests,

T

2:18 And I T them of the hand of my
7:65 as unclean; the governor T them that they were
8:1 Water Gate; and they T Ezra the scribe to
9:23 land which thou hadst T their fathers to enter
Tob 2:14 not believe her, and T her to return it
6:5 did as the angel T him; and they roasted
8:14 she came out and T them that he was
Jud 3:5 came to Holofernes and T him all this.
6:17 He answered and T them what had taken place
10:18 of Holofernes while they T him about her.
10:22 When they T him of her he came forward
11:9 spared him and he T them all he had
11:19 For this has been T me, by my foreknowledge;
13:3 Now Judith had T her maid to stand outside
15:5 came, for they were T what had happened in
Esth 2:22 of Mordecai, and he T it to Queen Esther,
2:22 Queen Esther, and Esther T the king in the
3:4 listen to them, they T Haman, in order to
3:4 avail; for he had T them that he was
4:4 her eunuchs came and T her, the queen was
4:7 king's gate, and Mordecai T him all that had
4:9 And Hathach went and T Esther what Mordecai had
4:12 And they T Mordecai what Esther had said.
4:13 Then Mordecai T them to return answer to Esther,
4:15 Then Esther T them to reply to Mordecai,
6:2 written how Mordecai had T about Bigthana and
6:5 So the king's servants T him, "Haman is there,
6:13 And Haman T his wife Zeresh and all his
8:1 king, for Esther had T what he was to
Job 15:18 (what wise men have T, and their fathers have
37:20 Shall it be T him that I would speak?
42:9 what the LORD had T them; and the LORD
Ps 40:9 I have T the glad news of deliverance in
44:1 God, our fathers have T us, what deeds thou
78:3 that our fathers have T us.
119:26 When I T of my ways, thou didst answer
Prov 25:7 is better to be T, "Come up here," than
Eccl 6:6 a thousand years twice T, yet enjoy no good—
Sir 20:18 is like a story T at the wrong time,
22:6 mourning is a tale T at the wrong time,
Is 7:2 house of David was T, "Syria is in league
21:2 A stern vision is T to me; the plunderer
36:22 their clothes rent, and T him the words of
40:21 Has it not been T you from the beginning?
44:8 afraid; have I not T you from of old
45:21 Who T this long ago?
52:15 which has not been T them they shall see,
Jer 36:13 And Micaiah T them all the words that he
Ezek 11:25 And I T the exiles all the things that
Dan 2:18 Azariah, his companions, and T them to seek mercy
4:7 came in; and I T them the dream, but
4:8 gods—and I T him the dream, saying,
7:1 down the dream, and T the sum of the
7:5 teeth; and it was T, 'Arise, devour much flesh.'
7:16 So he T me, and made known to me
8:26 mornings which has been T is true; but seal
13:27 And when the elders T their tale, the servants
Jon 1:10 LORD, because he had T them.
Hab 1:5 your days that you would not believe if T
1Mac 5:25 met them peaceably and T them all that had
8:2 Men T him of their wars and of the
10:15 to Jonathan, and men T him of the battles
11:5 They also T the king what Jonathan had done,
11:40 Demetrius had done and T of the hatred which
14:21 to our people have T us about your glory
2Mac 2:1 fire, as has been T,
3:7 met the king, he T him of the money
3:9 of the city, he T about the disclosure that
8:12 invasion; and when he T his companions of the
8:19 Moreover, he T them of the times when help
14:26 He T him that Nicanor was disloyal to the
15:38 If it is well T and to the point,
Mt 2:5 They T him, "In Bethlehem of Judea; for so
8:33 into the city they T everything, and what had
12:47 to the man who T him, "Who is my
13:3 And he T them many things in parables, saying:
13:33 He T them another parable.
14:12 and they went and T Jesus.
16:24 Then Jesus T his disciples, "If any man would
24:25 Lo, I have T you beforehand.
26:13 has done will be T in memory of her."
28:7 Lo, I have T you."
28:11 into the city and T the chief priests all
Mk 1:30 fever, and immediately they T him of her.
3:9 And he T his disciples to have a boat
5:14 The herdsmen fled, and T it in the city
5:16 who had seen it T what had happened to
5:33 down before him, and T him the whole truth.
5:43 should know this, and T them to give her
6:30 returned to Jesus, and T him all that they
8:28 And they T him, "John the Baptist; and others
11:6 And they T them what Jesus had said; and
12:12 perceived that he had T the parable against them;
13:23 take heed; I have T you all things beforehand.
14:9 has done will be T in memory of her."
14:16 it as he had T them; and they prepared
16:7 see him, as he T you."
16:10 She went and T those who had been with
16:13 they went back and T the rest, but they
Lk 2:17 saying which had been T them concerning this child;
2:18 at what the shepherds T them.
2:20 as it had been T them.
5:36 He T them a parable also: "No one tears
6:39 He also T them a parable: "Can a blind
7:18 The disciples of John T him of all these
8:20 And he was T, "Your mother and your brrethren
8:34 happened, they fled, and T it in the city
8:36 who had seen it T them how he who
9:10 their return the apostles T him what they had
9:36 they kept silence and T no one in those
12:16 And he T them a parable, saying, "The land
13:1 that very time who T him of the Galileans
13:6 And he T this parable: "A man had a
14:7 Now he T a parable to those who were
15:3 So he T them this parable:
18:1 And he T them a parable, to the effect
18:9 He also T this parable to some who trusted
18:37 They T him, "Jesus of Nazareth is passing by."
19:32 it as he had T them.
20:19 perceived that he had T this parable against them.
21:29 And he T them a parable: "Look at the
22:13 it as he had T them; and they prepared
24:6 "Remember how he T you, while he was still
24:9 from the tomb they T all this to the
24:10 women with them who T this to the apostles;
24:35 Then they T what had happened on the road,
Jn 2:16 And he T those who sold the pigeons, "Take
3:12 If I have T you earthly things and you
4:29 see a man who T me all that I
4:39 the woman's testimony, "He T me all that I
4:51 servants met him and T him that his son
5:14 man went away and T the Jews that it
6:12 eaten their fill, he T his disciples, "Gather up
6:65 "This is why I T you that no one
8:24 I T you that you would die in your
8:25 "Even what I have T you from the beginning.
8:40 a man who has T you the truth which
9:27 answered them, "I have T you already, and you
10:25 Jesus answered them, "I T you, and you do
11:14 Then Jesus T them plainly, "Lazarus is dead;
11:46 to the Pharisees and T them what Jesus had
12:22 Philip went and T Andrew; Andrew went with Philip
12:22 with Philip and they T Jesus.
14:2 so, would I have T you that I go
14:29 And now I have T you before it takes
16:4 may remember that I T you of them.
18:8 Jesus answered, "I T you that I am he;
18:38 the Jews again, and T them, "I find no
20:18 the Lord"; and she T them that he had
20:25 So the other disciples T him, "We have seen
Acts 5:25 some one came and T them, "The men whom
8:35 with this scripture he T him the good news
9:6 and you will be T what you are to
11:12 And the Spirit T me to go with them,
11:13 And he T us how he had seen the
12:14 but ran in and T that Peter was standing
13:42 these things might be T them the next sabbath.
21:4 Through the Spirit they T Paul not to go
21:21 and they have been T about you that you
21:24 what they have been T about you but that
22:10 there you will be T all that is appointed
23:16 entered the barracks and T Paul.
27:25 it will be exactly as I have been T
Rom 4:18 as he had been T, "So shall your descendants
9:12 his call, she was T, "The elder will serve
15:21 who have never been T of him, and they
2Cor 7:7 in you, as he T us of your longing,
12:4 things that cannot be T, which man may not
Phil 3:18 whom I have often T you and now tell
1Thes 3:4 were with you, we T you beforehand that we
2Thes 2:5 still with you I T you this?
Rev 6:11 a white robe and T to rest a little

T

9:4 the earth; they were T not to harm the
10:9 to the angel and T him to give me
10:11 And I was T, "You must again prophesy about
11:1 staff, and I was T: "Rise and measure the

TOLERABLE (5)

Mt 10:15 it shall be more T on the day of
11:22 it shall be more T on the day of
11:24 it shall be more T on the day of
Lk 10:12 it shall be more T on that day for
10:14 it shall be more T in the judgment for

TOLERATE (2)

Esth 3:8 the king's profit to T them.
Rev 2:20 against you, that you T the woman Jezebel, who

TOLL (4)

Ezra 4:13 pay tribute, custom, or T, and the royal revenue
4:20 whom tribute, custom, and T were paid.
7:24 impose tribute, custom, or T upon any one of
Mt 17:24 of the earth take T or tribute?

TOMB (62)

Gen 35:20 the pillar of Rachel's T, which is there to
50:5 to die: in my T which I hewed out
Judg 8:32 was buried in the T of Joash his father,
16:31 and Eshtaol in the T of Manoah his father.
1Sam 10:2 two men by Rachel's T in the territory of
2Sam 2:32 buried him in the T of his father, which
4:12 buried it in the T of Abner at Hebron.
17:23 was buried in the T of his father.
21:14 in Zela, in the T of Kish his father;
1Kgs 13:22 not come to the T of your fathers.'"
2Kgs 9:28 buried him in his T with his fathers in
21:26 was buried in his T in the garden of
23:17 him, "It is the T of the man of
23:30 to Jerusalem, and buried him in his own T
2Chr 16:14 buried him in the T which he had hewn
Job 21:32 to the grave, watch is kept over his T
Is 14:18 each in his own T;
22:16 have hewn here a T for yourself, you who
22:16 you who hew a T on the height, and
Jer 5:16 is like an open T, they are all mighty
1Mac 2:70 was buried in the T of his fathers at
9:19 buried him in the T of their fathers at
13:27 a monument over the T of his father and
13:30 This is the T which he built in Modein;
2Mac 5:10 no place in the T of his fathers.
Mt 27:60 in his own new T, which he had hewn
27:60 the door of the T, and departed.
28:8 departed quickly from the T with fear and great
Mk 6:29 took his body, and laid it in a T
15:45 laid him in a T which had been hewn
15:45 rolled a stone against the door of the T
16:2 they went to the T when the sun had
16:3 stone for us from the door of the T
16:5 And entering the T, they saw a young man
16:8 and fled from the T; for trembling and astonishment
Lk 23:52 him in a rock-hewn T, where no one had
23:54 followed, and saw the T, and how his body
24:1 they went to the T, taking the spices which
24:2 rolled away from the T,
24:9 and returning from the T they told all this
24:12 and ran to the T; stooping and looking in,
24:22 They were at the T early in the morning
24:24 us went to the T, and found it just
Jn 11:17 already been in the T four days.
11:31 was going to the T to weep there.
11:38 again, came to the T; it was a cave,
12:17 Lazarus out of the T and raised him from
19:41 the garden a new T where no one had
19:42 of Preparation, as the T was close at hand,
20:1 Magdalene came to the T early, while it was
20:1 the stone had been taken away from the T
20:2 Lord out of the T, and we do not
20:3 the other disciple, and they went toward the T
20:4 Peter and reached the T first;
20:6 and went into the T; he saw the linen
20:8 disciple, who reached the T first, also went in,
20:11 stood weeping outside the T, and as she wept
20:11 to look into the T;
Acts 2:29 was buried, and his T is with us to
7:16 and laid in the T that Abraham had bought
13:29 from the tree, and laid him in a T
Rev 11:9 be placed in a T,

TOMBS (22)

1Sam 13:6 in rocks and in T and in cisterns,
2Kgs 23:16 turned, he saw the T there on the mount;
23:16 bones out of the T, and burned them upon
2Chr 21:20 but not in the T of the kings.
24:25 bury him in the T of the kings.
28:27 bring him into the T of the kings of
32:33 the ascent of the T of the sons of
35:24 was buried in the T of his fathers.
Is 65:4 bricks; who sit in T, and spend the night
Jer 8:1 brought out of their T;
Mt 8:28 coming out of the T, so fierce that no
23:26 whitewashed T, which outwardly appear beautiful,
23:28 for you build the T of the prophets and
27:52 rocks were split; the T also were opened, and
27:53 coming out of the T after his resurrection they
Mk 5:2 him out of the T a man with an
5:3 who lived among the T; and no one could
5:5 and day among the T and on the mountains
Lk 8:27 lived not in a house but among the T
11:47 for you build the T of the prophets whom
11:48 for they killed them, and you build their T
Jn 5:27 who are in the T will hear his voice

TOMORROW (60)

Ex 8:10 And he said, T
8:23 By T shall this sign be.'"
8:29 and from his people, T; only let not Pharaoh
9:5 set a time, saying, T the LORD will do
9:18 Behold, T about this time I will cause very
10:4 my people go, behold, T I will bring locusts
16:23 the LORD has commanded: T is a day of
17:9 out, fight with Amalek; T I will stand on
19:10 consecrate them today and T, and let them wash
32:5 made proclamation and said, T shall be a feast
Num 11:18 'Consecrate yourselves for T, and you shall eat
14:25 in the valleys, turn T and set out for
16:7 them before the LORD T, and the man whom
16:16 and they, and Aaron, T;
Josh 3:5 people, "Sanctify yourselves; for T the LORD will do
7:13 say, 'Sanctify yourselves for T; for thus says the
11:6 afraid of them, for T at this time I
22:18 be angry with the whole congregation of Israel T
Judg 19:9 heart be merry; and T you shall arise early
20:28 said, "Go up; for T I will give them
1Sam 9:16 had revealed to Samuel: T about this time I
11:9 the men of Jabesh-gilead: T, by the time the
11:10 men of Jabesh said, T we will give ourselves
19:11 save your life tonight, T you will be killed."
20:5 said to Jonathan, "Behold, T is the new moon,
20:12 father, about this time T, or the third day,
20:18 Jonathan said to him, T is the new moon;
28:19 of the Philistines; and T you and your sons
2Sam 11:12 here today also, and T I will let you
1Kgs 19:2 life of one of them by this time T
20:6 my servants to you T about this time, and
2Kgs 6:28 will eat my son T
7:1 thus says the LORD, T about this time a
7:18 shekel, about this time T in the gate of
10:6 to me at Jezreel T at this time." Now
2Chr 20:16 T go down against them; behold, they will come
20:17 and be not dismayed; T go out against them,
Esth 5:8 king and Haman come T to the dinner which
5:8 prepare for them, and T I will do as
5:12 And T also I am invited by her together
9:13 in Susa be allowed T also to do according
Prov 3:28 "Go, and come again, T I will give it"—
27:1 Do not boast about T, for you do not
Sir 10:10 the physician; the king of today will die T
20:14 today he lends and T he asks it back;
Is 22:13 eat and drink, for T we die."
56:12 with strong drink; and T will be like this
1Mac 2:63 will be exalted, but T he will not be
5:27 to attack the strongholds T and take and destroy
Mt 6:30 today is alive and T is thrown into the
6:34 not be anxious about T, for tomorrow will be
6:34 anxious about tomorrow, for T will be anxious for
Lk 12:28 the field today and T is thrown into the
13:32 perform cures today and T, and the third day
13:33 my way today and T and the day following;
Acts 23:20 down to the council T, as though they were
25:22 hear the man myself." "T," said he, you shall
1Cor 15:32 eat and drink, for T we die."
Jas 4:13 who say, "Today or T we will go into
4:14 get gain"; whereas you do not know about T

T

TONE (3)

Dan	6:20	cried out in a T of anguish and said
2Mac	7:24	contempt, and he was suspicious of her reproachful T
Gal	4:20	and to change my T, for I am perplexed

TONGS (3)

1Kgs	7:49	the lamps, and the T, of gold;
2Chr	4:21	the lamps, and the T, of purest gold;
Is	6:6	he had taken with T from the altar.

TONGUE (132)

Ex	4:10	but I am slow of speech and of T
Josh	10:21	a man moved his T against any of the
Judg	7:5	the water with his T, as a dog laps,
2Sam	23:2	speaks by me, his word is upon my T
Job	5:21	the scourge of the T, and shall not fear
	6:30	Is there any wrong on my T
	15:5	and you choose the T of the crafty.
	20:12	hides it under his T,
	20:16	poison of asps; the T of a viper will
	27:4	speak falsehood, and my T will not utter deceit.
	29:10	was hushed, and their T cleaved to the roof
	33:2	open my mouth; the T in my mouth speaks.
	41:1	or press down his T with a cord?
Ps	5:9	is an open sepulchre, they flatter with their T
	10:7	and oppression; under his T are mischief and iniquity.
	12:3	all flattering lips, the T that makes great boasts,
	12:4	who say, "With our T we will prevail, our
	15:3	not slander with his T, and does no evil
	22:15	a potsherd, and my T cleaves to my jaws;
	34:13	Keep your T from evil, and your lips from
	35:28	Then my T shall tell of thy righteousness and
	37:30	utters wisdom, and his T speaks justice.
	39:1	not sin with my T; I will bridle my
	39:3	I spoke with my T:
	45:1	to the king; my T is like the pen
	50:19	for evil, and your T frames deceit.
	51:14	my salvation, and my T will sing aloud of
	52:2	Your T is like a sharp razor, you worker
	52:4	You love all words that devour, O deceitful T
	64:8	Because of their T he will bring them to
	66:17	to him, and he was extolled with my T
	71:24	And my T will talk of thy righteous help
	73:9	the heavens, and their T struts through the earth.
	119:172	My T will sing of thy word, for all
	120:2	O LORD, from lying lips, from a deceitful T
	120:3	more shall be done to you, you deceitful T
	126:2	with laughter, and our T with shouts of joy;
	137:6	Let my T cleave to the roof of my
	139:4	word is on my T, lo, O LORD, thou
	140:3	They make their T sharp as a serpents, and
Prov	6:17	haughty eyes, a lying T, and hands that shed
	6:24	woman, from the smooth T of the adventuress.
	10:20	The T of the righteous is choice silver; the
	10:31	wisdom, but the perverse T will be cut off.
	12:18	sword thrusts, but the T of the wise brings
	12:19	ever, but a lying T is but for a
	15:2	The T of the wise dispenses knowledge, but the
	15:4	A gentle T is a tree of life, but
	16:1	the answer of the T is from the LORD.
	17:4	and a liar gives heed to a mischievous T
	17:20	one with a perverse T falls into calamity.
	18:21	the power of the T, and those who love
	21:6	treasures by a lying T is a fleeting vapor
	21:23	his mouth and his T keeps himself out of
	25:15	persuaded, and a soft T will break a bone.
	25:23	rain; and a backbiting T, angry looks.
	26:28	A lying T hates its victims, and a flattering
	28:23	more favor than he who flatters with his T
	31:26	and the teaching of kindness is on her T
Song	4:11	milk are under your T; the scent of your
Wis	1:6	of his heart, and a hearer of his T
	1:11	murmuring, and keep your T from slander; because
Sir	4:24	speech, and education through the words of the T
	5:13	speaking, and a man's T is his downfall.
	5:14	in ambush with your T; for shame comes to
	6:5	friends, and a gracious T multiplies courtesies.
	17:5	He made for them T and eyes; he gave
	19:16	Who has never sinned with his T
	20:17	a slip of the T; so the downfall of
	22:25	falling, so that my T may not destroy me!
	25:7	shall tell with my T: a man rejoicing in
	25:8	a slip with his T, and he who has
	28:17	a blow of the T crushes the bones.
	28:18	so many as have fallen because of the T
	28:26	you err with your T, lest you fall before
	32:8	as one who knows and yet holds his T
	37:18	and it is the T that continually rules them.
	51:2	snare of a slanderous T, from lips that utter
	51:5	Hades, from an unclean T and lying words–
	51:6	slander of an unrighteous T to the king.
	51:22	Lord gave me a T as my reward, and
Is	5:24	Therefore, as the T of fire devours the stubble,
	11:15	will utterly destroy the T of the sea of
	28:11	and with an alien T the LORD will speak
	30:27	of indignation, and his T is like a devouring
	32:4	good judgment, and the T of the stammerers will
	33:19	comprehend, stammering in a T which you cannot
	35:6	a hart, and the T of the dumb sing
	41:17	is none, and their T is parched with thirst,
	45:23	knee shall bow, every T shall swear.'
	50:4	has given me the T of those who are
	54:17	you shall confute every T that rises against you
	57:4	open your mouth wide and put out your T
	59:3	have spoken lies, your T mutters wickedness.
Jer	9:3	They bend their T like a bow; falsehood and
	9:5	they have taught their T to speak lies; they
	9:8	Their T is a deadly arrow; it speaks deceitfully;
	18:18	smite him with the T, and let us not
Lam	4:4	The T of the nursling cleaves to the roof
Ezek	3:26	I will make your T cleave to the roof
Hos	7:17	the sword because of the insolence of their T
Mic	6:12	speak lies, and their T is deceitful in their
Zeph	3:13	there be found in their mouth a deceitful T
Zech	8:23	the nations of every T shall take hold of
2Mac	7:4	he commanded that the T of their spokesman be
	7:10	quickly put out his T and courageously stretched
	7:27	spoke in their native T as follows, deriding the
	15:33	he cut out the T of the ungodly Nicanor
Mk	7:32	spat and touched his T;
	7:34	ears were opened, his T was released, and he
Lk	1:64	was opened and his T loosed, and he spoke,
	16:24	water and cool my T; for I am in
Acts	2:26	was glad, and my T rejoiced; moreover my flesh
Rom	14:11	to me, and every T shall give praise to
1Cor	14:2	who speaks in a T speaks not to men
	14:4	who speaks in a T edifies himself, but he
	14:9	if you in a T utter speech that is
	14:13	who speaks in a T should pray for the
	14:14	I pray in a T, my spirit prays but
	14:19	instruct others, than ten thousand words in a T
	14:26	lesson, a revelation, a T, or an interpretation.
	14:27	any speak in a T, let there be only
Phil	2:11	the earth, and every T confess that Jesus Christ
Jas	1:25	does not bridle his T but deceives his heart,
	3:5	So the T is a little member and boasts
	3:6	And the T is a fire.
	3:6	The T is an unrighteous world among our members,
	3:8	being can tame the T –a restless evil, full
1Pet	3:10	let him keep his T from evil and his
Rev	5:9	from every tribe and T and people and nation,
	13:7	tribe and people and T and nation,
	14:6	nation and tribe and T and people;

TONGUE-LASHING

Sir	26:6	a rival, and a T makes it known to

TONGUES (39)

Jud	3:8	only, and all their T and tribes should call
Ps	31:20	safe under thy shelter from the strife of T
	55:9	O Lord, confuse their T; for I see violence
	57:4	spears and arrows, their T sharp swords.
	64:3	evildoers, who whet their T like swords, who aim
	68:23	in blood, that the T of your dogs may
	78:36	their mouths; they lied to him with their T
	109:2	opened against me, speaking against me with lying T
Wis	10:21	dumb, and made the T of babes speak clearly.
Is	66:18	gather all nations and T; and they shall come
Jer	23:31	LORD, who use their T and say, 'Says the
Bar	6:8	Their T are smoothed by the craftsman, and they
Zech	14:12	their sockets, and their T shall rot in their
Mk	16:17	will speak in new T;
Acts	2:3	there appeared to them T as of fire, distributed
	2:4	to speak in other T, as the Spirit gave
	2:11	telling in our own T the mighty works of
	10:46	heard them speaking in T and extolling God.
	19:6	and they spoke with T and prophesied.
Rom	3:13	grave, they use their T to deceive." "The venom
1Cor	12:10	another various kinds of T, to another the
	12:10	kinds of tongues, to another the interpretation of T
	12:28	administrators, speakers in various kinds of T
	12:30	Do all speak with T

T

13:1 I speak in the T of men and of
13:8 pass away; as for T, they will cease; as
14:5 all to speak in T, but even more to
14:5 he who speaks in T, unless some one interprets,
14:6 to you speaking in T, how shall I benefit
14:18 that I speak in T more than you all;
14:21 "By men of strange T and by the lips
14:22 Thus, T are a sign not for believers but
14:23 and all speak in T, and outsiders or unbelievers
14:39 not forbid speaking in T;
Rev 7:9 tribes and peoples and T, standing before the throne
10:11 peoples and nations and T and kings."
11:9 peoples and tribes and T and nations gaze at
16:10 darkness; men gnawed their T in anguish
17:15 seated, are peoples and multitudes and nations and T

TONIGHT (11)

Gen 19:5 "Where are the men who came to you T
19:34 make him drink wine T also; then you go
30:15 may lie with you T for your son's mandrakes."
Josh 2:2 Israel have come here T to search out the
4:3 them down in the place where you lodge T
Ruth 3:2 he is winnowing barley T at the threshing floor.
1Sam 19:11 not save your life T, tomorrow you will be
2Sam 17:1 and I will set out and pursue David T
17:16 David, 'Do not lodge T at the fords of
Jud 8:33 at the city gate T, and I will go
11:4 courage; you will live, T and from now on.

TONSURES

Lev 21:5 They shall not make T upon their heads, nor

TOOK (854)

Gen 2:15 The LORD God T the man and put him
2:21 and while he slept T one of his ribs
3:6 make one wise, she T of its fruit and
4:19 And Lamech T two wives; the name of the
5:24 was not, for God T him.
6:2 were fair; and they T to wife such of
8:9 forth his hand and T her and brought her
8:20 to the LORD, and T of every clean animal
9:23 Then Shem and Japheth T a garment, laid it
11:29 And Abram and Nahor T wives; the name of
11:31 Terah T Abram his son and Lot the son
12:5 And Abram T Sarai his wife, and Lot his
12:19 sister,' so that I T her for my wife?
14:11 So the enemy T all the goods of Sodom
14:12 their way; they also T Lot, the son of
16:3 Canaan, Sarai, Abram's wife, T Hagar the Egyptian,
17:23 Then Abraham T Ishmael his son and all the
18:7 to the herd, and T a calf, tender and
18:8 Then he T curds, and milk, and the calf
20:2 of Gerar sent and T Sarah.
20:14 Then Abimelech T sheep and oxen, and male and
21:14 in the morning, and T bread and a skin
21:21 Paran; and his mother T a wife for him
21:27 So Abraham T sheep and oxen and gave them
22:3 saddled his ass, and T two of his young
22:6 And Abraham T the wood of the burnt offering,
22:6 his son; and he T in his hand the
22:10 forth his hand, and T the knife to slay
22:13 and Abraham went and T the ram, and offered
24:7 God of heaven, who T me from my father's
24:10 Then the servant T ten of his master's camels
24:22 done drinking, the man T a gold ring weighing
24:61 man; thus the servant T Rebekah, and went his
24:65 So she T her veil and covered herself.
24:67 into the tent, and T Rebekah, and she became
25:1 Abraham T another wife, whose name was Keturah.
25:20 years old when he T to wife Rebekah, the
26:31 they rose early and T oath with one another;
26:34 forty years old, he T to wife Judith the
27:14 So he went and T them and brought them
27:15 Then Rebekah T the best garments of Esau her
27:36 He T away my birthright; and behold, now he
28:9 went to Ishmael and T to wife, besides the
28:18 the morning, and he T the stone which he
29:23 in the evening he T his daughter Leah and
30:9 ceased bearing children, she T her maid Zilpah and
30:37 Then Jacob T fresh rods of poplar and almond
31:23 Jacob had fled, he T his kinsmen with him
31:45 So Jacob T a stone, and set it up
31:46 and they T stones, and made a heap; and
32:13 there that night, and T from what he had
32:22 night he arose and T his two wives, his
32:23 He T them and sent them across the stream,
33:11 urged him, and he T it.
34:25 and Levi, Dinah's brothers, T their swords and came
34:26 with the sword, and T Dinah out of Shechem's
34:28 had been defiled; they T their flocks and their
36:2 Esau T his wives from the Canaanites: Adah the
36:6 Then Esau T his wives, his sons, his daughters,
37:24 he wore; and they T him and cast him
37:28 of silver; and they T Joseph to Egypt.
37:31 Then they T Joseph's robe, and killed a goat,
38:6 And Judah T a wife for Er his first-born,
38:28 hand; and the midwife T and bound on his
39:20 And Joseph's master T him and put him into
40:11 my hand; and I T the grapes and pressed
41:42 Then Pharaoh T his signet ring from his hand
42:24 And he T Simeon from them and bound him
42:30 roughly to us, and T us to be spies
43:15 So the men T the present, and they took
43:15 the present, and they T double the money with
46:1 So Israel T his journey with all that he
46:6 They also T their cattle and their goods, which
47:2 among his brothers he T five men and presented
48:1 is ill"; so he T with him his two
48:13 And Joseph T them both, Ephraim in his right
48:17 displeased him; and he T his father's hand, to
48:22 mountain slope which I T from the hand of
50:25 Then Joseph T an oath of the sons of
Ex 2:1 of Levi went and T to wife a daughter
2:3 him no longer she T for him a basket
2:6 She T pity on him and said, "This is
2:9 So the woman T the child and nursed him.
4:6 bosom; and when he T it out, behold, his
4:7 bosom; and when he T it out, behold, it
4:20 So Moses T his wife and his sons and
4:20 in his hand Moses T the rod of God.
4:25 Then Zipporah T a flint and cut off her
6:20 Amram T to wife Jochebed his father's sister and
6:23 Aaron T to wife Elisheba, the daughter of
6:25 Eleazar, Aaron's son, T to wife one of the
9:10 So they T ashes from the kiln, and stood
12:34 So the people T their dough before it was
13:19 And Moses T the bones of Joseph with him;
14:6 ready his chariot and T his army with him,
14:7 army with him, and T six hundred picked chariots
15:20 the sister of Aaron, T a timbrel in her
17:12 grew weary; so they T a stone and put
19:17 meet God; and they T their stand at the
24:6 And Moses T half of the blood and put
24:7 Then he T the book of the covenant, and
24:8 And Moses T the blood and threw it upon
32:3 So all the people T off the rings of
32:20 And he T the calf which they had made,
34:4 had commanded him, and T in his hand two
34:34 speak with him, he T the veil off, until
Lev 6:4 shall restore what he T by robbery, or what
8:10 Then Moses T the anointing oil, and anointed the
8:15 Moses killed it, and T the blood, and with
8:16 And he T all the fat that was on
8:23 Moses killed it, and T some of its blood
8:25 Then he T the fat, and the fat tail,
8:26 before the LORD he T one unleavened cake, and
8:28 Then Moses T them from their hands, and burned
8:29 And Moses T the breast, and waved it for
8:30 Then Moses T some of the anointing oil and
9:15 the people's offering, and T the goat of the
10:1 sons of Aaron, each T his censer, and put
Num 1:17 Moses and Aaron T these men who have been
3:49 So Moses T the redemption money from those who
3:50 people of Israel he T the money, one thousand
7:6 So Moses T the wagons and the oxen, and
11:25 spoke to him, and T some of the spirit
16:2 Peleth, sons of Reuben, T men; and they rose
16:18 So every man T his censer, and they put
16:39 So Eleazar the priest T the bronze censers, which
16:47 So Aaron T it as Moses said, and ran
17:9 looked, and each man T his rod.
20:9 And Moses T the rod from before the LORD,
21:1 fought against Israel, and T some of them captive.
21:24 of the sword, and T possession of his land
21:25 And Israel T all these cities, and Israel settled
21:32 out Jazer; and they T its villages, and dispossessed
22:22 angel of the LORD T his stand in the
22:41 on the morrow Balak T Balaam and brought him
23:7 And Balaam T up his discourse, and said, "From
23:11 I T you to curse my enemies, and behold,
23:14 And he T him to the field of Zophim,
23:18 And Balaam T up his discourse, and said, "Rise,

23:28 So Balak T Balaam to the top of Peor,
24:3 upon him, and he T up his discourse, and
24:15 And he T up his discourse, and said, "The
24:20 looked on Amalek, and T up his discourse, and
24:21 on the Kenite, and T up his discourse, and
24:23 And he T up his discourse, and said, "Alas,
25:7 left the congregation, and T a spear in his
27:22 LORD commanded him; he T Joshua and caused him
31:9 the people of Israel T captive the women of
31:9 little ones; and they T as booty all their
31:11 burned with fire, and T all the spoil and
31:32 the men of war T was: six hundred and
31:47 of Israel's half Moses T one of every fifty,
32:39 went to Gilead and T it, and dispossessed the
32:41 of Manasseh went and T their villages, and called
32:42 And Nobah went and T Kenath and its villages,
Deut 1:15 to do.' So I T the heads of your
1:23 to me, and I T twelve men of you,
1:25 And they T in their hands some of the
2:35 only the cattle we T as spoil for ourselves,
3:4 And we T all his cities at that time—
3:7 of the cities we T as our booty.
3:8 So we T the land at that time out
3:12) "When we T possession of this land at
3:14 Jair the Manassite T all the region of Argob,
4:47 And they T possession of his land and the
9:17 So I T hold of the two tables, and
9:21 Then I T the sinful thing, the calf which
22:14 upon her, saying, 'I T this woman, and when
24:3 latter husband dies, who T her to be his
28:63 And as the LORD T delight in doing you
29:8 we defeated them; we T their land, and gave
30:9 prospering you, as he T delight in your fathers,
32:37 rock in which they T refuge,
Josh 3:6 And they T up the ark of the covenant,
4:8 as Joshua commanded, and T up twelve stones out
4:20 twelve stones, which they T out of the Jordan,
6:12 morning, and the priests T up the ark of
6:20 before him, and they T the city.
7:1 the tribe of Judah, T some of the devoted
7:21 I coveted them, and T them; and behold, they
7:23 And they T them out of the tent and
7:24 all Israel with him T Achan the son of
8:12 And he T about five thousand men, and set
8:19 entered the city and T it; and they made
8:23 king of Ai they T alive, and brought him
8:27 of that city Israel T as their booty, according
8:29 Joshua commanded, and they T his body down from
9:4 made ready provisions, and T worn-out sacks upon
9:12 still warm when we T it from our houses
10:13 stayed, until the nation T vengeance on their
10:27 Joshua commanded, and they T them down from the
10:28 And Joshua T Makkedah on that day, and smote
10:32 of Israel, and he T it on the second
10:35 assaulted it; and they T it on that day,
10:37 they assaulted it, and T it, and smote it
10:39 assaulted it, and he T it with its king
10:42 And Joshua T all these kings and their land
11:10 at that time, and T Hazor, and smote its
11:12 all their kings, Joshua T, and smote them with
11:14 the people of Israel T for their booty; but
11:16 So Joshua T all that land, the hill country
11:17 And he T all their kings, and smote them,
11:19 inhabitants of Gibeon; they T all in battle.
11:23 So Joshua T the whole land, according to all
12:1 of Israel defeated, and T possession of their land
15:17 the brother of Caleb, T it; and he gave
19:47 to the sword they T possession of it and
24:3 Then I T your father Abraham from beyond the
24:8 your hand, and you T possession of their land,
24:26 of God; and he T a great stone, and
Judg 1:8 fought against Jerusalem, and T it, and smote it
1:13 Kenaz, Caleb's younger brother, T it; and he gave
1:18 Judah also T Gaza with its territory, and Ashkelon
1:19 with Judah, and he T possession of the hill
3:6 the Jebusites; and they T their daughters to
3:13 defeated Israel; and they T possession of the city
3:21 with his left hand, T the sword from his
3:25 the roof chamber, they T the key and opened
4:21 the wife of Heber T a tent peg, and
4:21 a tent peg, and T a hammer in her
5:2 day: "That the leaders T the lead in Israel,
6:27 So Gideon T ten men of his servants, and
6:34 Spirit of the LORD T possession of Gideon; and
7:8 So he T the jars of the people from
7:25 And they T the two princes of Midian, Oreb
8:12 he pursued them and T the two kings of
8:16 And he T the elders of the city and
8:16 the city and he T thorns of the wilderness
8:21 and Zalmunna; and he T the crescents that were
9:43 He T his men and divided them into three
9:45 all that day; he T the city, and killed
9:48 with him; and Abimelech T an axe in his
9:48 bundle of brushwood, and T it up and laid
9:50 encamped against Thebez, and T it.
11:13 on coming from Egypt T away my land, from
11:21 defeated them; so Israel T possession of all the
11:22 And they T possession of all the territory of
12:3 not deliver me, I T my life in my
12:5 And the Gileadites T the fords of the Jordan
13:19 So Manoah T the kid with the cereal offering,
14:19 of the town, and T their spoil and gave
15:4 three hundred foxes, and T torches; and he turned
16:3 midnight he arose and T hold of the doors
16:12 So Delilah T new ropes and bound him with
16:14 while he slept, Delilah T the seven locks of
16:31 family came down and T him and brought him
17:2 is with me; I T it." And his mother
17:4 his mother, his mother T two hundred pieces of
18:17 up, and entered and T the graven image, the
18:18 into Micah's house and T the graven image, the
18:20 heart was glad; he T the ephod, and the
19:1 country of Ephraim, who T to himself a concubine
19:15 city; for no man T them into his house
19:29 entered his house, he T a knife, and laying
20:6 And I T my concubine and cut her in
20:22 the men of Israel, T courage, and again formed
21:23 Benjaminites did so, and T their wives, according to
Ruth 1:4 These T Moabite wives; the name of the one
2:18 And she T it up and went into the
2:19 be the man who T notice of you." So
4:2 And he T ten men of the elders of
4:13 So Boaz T Ruth and she became his wife;
4:16 Then Naomi T the child and laid him in
1Sam 1:13 not heard; therefore Eli T her to be a
1:24 had weaned him, she T him up with her,
5:2 Ashdod; then the Philistines T the ark of God
5:3 So they T Dagon and put him back in
6:10 men did so, and T two milch cows and
6:15 And the Levites T down the ark of the
7:1 of Kiriath-jearim came and T up the ark of
7:9 So Samuel T a sucking lamb and offered it
7:12 Then Samuel T a stone and set it up
8:3 aside after gain; they T bribes and perverted justice.
9:22 Then Samuel T Saul and his servant and brought
9:24 So the cook T up the leg and the
10:1 Then Samuel T a vial of oil and poured
11:7 He T a yoke of oxen, and cut them
14:32 upon the spoil, and T sheep and oxen and
15:8 And he T Agag the king of the Amalekites
15:21 But the people T of the spoil, sheep and
16:13 Then Samuel T the horn of oil, and anointed
16:20 And Jesse T an ass laden with bread, and
16:23 was upon Saul, David T the lyre and played
17:16 Philistine came forward and T his stand, morning
17:20 with a keeper, and T the provisions, and went,
17:34 or a bear, and T a lamb from the
17:40 Then he T his staff in his hand, and
17:49 in his bag and T out a stone, and
17:51 over the Philistine, and T his sword and drew
17:54 And David T the head of the Philistine and
17:57 of the Philistine, Abner T him, and brought him
18:2 And Saul T him that day, and would not
19:5 to you; for he T his life in his
19:13 Michal T an image and laid it on the
21:12 And David T these words to heart, and was
24:2 Then Saul T three thousand chosen men out of
25:18 Abigail made haste, and T two hundred loaves, and
25:43 David also T Ahino-am of Jezreel; and both of
26:12 So David T the spear and the jar of
27:9 nor woman alive, but T away the sheep, the
28:24 killed it, and she T flour, and kneaded it
31:4 Therefore Saul T his own sword, and fell upon
31:12 went all night, and T the body of Saul
31:13 And they T their bones and buried them under
2Sam 1:10 had fallen; and I T the crown which was
1:11 Then David T hold of his clothes, and rent
2:25 became one band, and T their stand on the
2:32 And they T up Asahel, and buried him in
3:15 And Ish-bosheth sent, and T her from her husband
3:27 returned to Hebron, Joab T him aside into the
3:36 And all the people T notice of it, and

T

4:4 Jezreel; and his nurse T him up, and fled;
4:7 They T his head, and went by the way
4:12 But they T the head of Ish-bosheth, and buried
5:7 Nevertheless David T the stronghold of Zion, that is,
5:13 David T more concubines and wives from Jerusalem,
6:6 ark of God and T hold of it, for
6:10 of David; but David T it aside to the
7:8 LORD of hosts, I T you from the pasture,
7:15 from him, as I T it from Saul, whom
8:1 subdued them, and David T Metheg-ammah out of
8:4 And David T from him a thousand and seven
8:7 And David T the shields of gold which were
8:8 of Hadadezer, King David T very much bronze.
10:4 So Hanun T David's servants, and shaved off half
11:4 David sent messengers, and T her; and she came
12:4 to him, but he T the poor man's lamb,
12:26 of the Ammonites, and T the royal city.
12:29 fought against it and T it.
12:30 And he T the crown of their king from
13:8 And she T dough, and kneaded it, and made
13:9 And she T the pan and emptied it out
13:10 And Tamar T the cakes she had made, and
13:11 him to eat, he T hold of her, and
17:19 And the woman T and spread a covering over
18:14 And he T three darts in his hand, and
18:17 And they T Absalom, and threw him into a
19:8 the king arose, and T his seat in the
20:3 Jerusalem; and the king T the ten concubines whom
20:9 And Joab T Amasa by the beard with his
20:11 one of Joab's men T his stand by Amasa,
21:8 The king T the two sons of Rizpah the
21:10 the daughter of Aiah T sackcloth, and spread it
21:12 done, David went and T the bones of Saul
22:17 from on high, he T me, he drew me
23:12 But he T his stand in the midst of
23:16 by the gate, and T and brought it to
1Kgs 1:39 There Zadok the priest T the horn of oil
3:1 king of Egypt; he T Pharaoh's daughter, and brought
3:20 arose at midnight, and T my son from beside
8:3 came, and the priests T up the ark.
11:18 came to Paran, and T men with them from
12:6 Then King Rehoboam T counsel with the old men,
12:8 men gave him, and T counsel with the young
12:28 So the king T counsel, and made two calves
13:29 And the prophet T up the body of the
14:26 up against Jerusalem; he T away the treasures of
14:26 the king's house; he T away everything.
14:26 He also T away all the shields of gold
15:18 Then Asa T all the silver and the gold
16:31 son of Nebat, he T for wife Jezebel the
17:19 And he T him from her bosom, and carried
17:23 And Elijah T the child, and brought him down
18:4 of the LORD, Obadiah T a hundred prophets and
18:26 And they T the bull which was given them,
18:31 been thrown down; Elijah T twelve stones, according
19:21 from following him, and T the yoke of oxen,
20:12 And they T their positions against the city.
20:33 omen, and they quickly T it up from him
20:34 cities which my father T from your father I
21:13 So they T him outside the city, and stoned
2Kgs 2:8 Then Elijah T his mantle, and rolled it up,
2:12 Then he T hold of his own clothes and
2:13 And he T up the mantle of Elijah that
2:14 Then he T the mantle of Elijah that had
3:26 going against him, he T with him seven hundred
3:27 Then he T his eldest son who was to
4:37 the ground; then she T up her son and
5:24 to the hill, he T them from their hand,
6:7 out his hand and T it.
6:8 warring against Israel, he T counsel with his
7:14 So they T two mounted men, and the king
8:9 to meet him, and T a present with him,
8:15 on the morrow he T the coverlet and dipped
9:13 every man of them T his garment, and put
10:7 came to them, they T the king's sons, and
10:14 And they T them alive, and slew them at
10:15 And Jehu T him up with him into the
11:2 Joram, sister of Ahaziah, T Joash the son of
11:19 And he T the captains, the Carites, the guards,
11:19 And he T his seat on the throne of
12:9 Then Jehoiada the priest T a chest, and bored
12:17 fought against Gath, and T it.
12:18 Jehoash king of Judah T all the votive gifts
13:15 and arrows"; so he T a bow and arrows.
13:18 the arrows"; and he T them.
13:25 the son of Jehoahaz T again from Ben-hadad the
14:7 Valley of Salt and T Sela by storm, and
14:21 the people of Judah T Azariah, who was sixteen
16:8 Ahaz also T the silver and gold that was
16:9 up against Damascus, and T it, carrying its people
16:17 from them, and he T down the sea from
17:24 of Israel; and they T possession of Samaria, and
18:10 of three years he T it.
18:13 cities of Judah and T them.
23:16 and he sent and T the bones out of
23:30 people of the land T Jehoahaz the son of
23:34 But he T Jehoahaz away; and he came to
24:12 The king of Babylon T him prisoner in the
24:15 of the land, he T into captivity from Jerusalem
25:7 him in fetters, and T him to Babylon.
25:14 And they T away the pots, and the shovels,
25:15 captain of the guard T away as gold, and
25:18 captain of the guard T Seraiah the chief priest,
25:19 from the city he T an officer who had
25:20 captain of the guard T them, and brought them
1Chr 2:23 But Geshur and Aram T from them Havvoth-jair,
7:15 And Machir T a wife for Huppim and for
10:4 Therefore Saul T his own sword, and fell upon
10:9 they stripped him and T his head and his
10:12 valiant men arose, and T away the body of
11:5 Nevertheless David T the stronghold of Zion, that is,
11:14 But he T his stand in the midst of
11:18 by the gate, and T and brought it to
12:19 rulers of the Philistines T counsel and sent him
13:13 city of David, but T it aside to the
14:3 And David T more wives in Jerusalem, and David
17:7 LORD of hosts, I T you from the pasture,
17:13 from him, as I T it from him who
18:1 subdued them, and he T Gath and its villages
18:4 And David T from him a thousand chariots, seven
18:7 And David T the shields of gold which were
18:8 cities of Hadadezer, David T very much bronze; with
19:4 So Hanun T David's servants, and shaved them, and
20:2 And David T the crown of their king from
28:4 my father's sons he T pleasure in me to
2Chr 2:17 Then Solomon T a census of all the aliens
5:4 came, and the Levites T up the ark.
8:3 went to Hamath-zobah, and T it.
10:6 Then King Rehoboam T counsel with the old men,
10:8 men gave him, and T counsel with the young
11:18 Rehoboam T as wife Mahalath the daughter of
11:20 After her he T Maacah the daughter of Absalom,
11:21 wives and concubines (he T eighteen wives and sixty
12:4 And he T the fortified cities of Judah and
12:9 up against Jerusalem; he T away the treasures of
12:9 the king's house; he T away everything.
12:9 He also T away the shields of gold which
13:19 Abijah pursued Jeroboam, and T cities from him,
13:21 And he T fourteen wives, and had twenty-two sons
14:3 He T away the foreign altars and the high
14:5 He also T out of all the cities of
15:8 son of Oded, he T courage, and put away
15:14 They T oath to the LORD with a loud
16:2 Then Asa T silver and gold from the treasures
16:6 Then King Asa T all Judah, and they carried
17:6 LORD; and furthermore he T the high places and
20:25 precious things, which they T for themselves until
22:11 daughter of the king, T Joash the son of
23:1 the seventh year Jehoiada T courage, and entered
23:20 And he T the captains, the nobles, the governors
24:20 the Spirit of God T possession of Zechariah the
25:11 But Amaziah T courage, and led out his people,
25:12 ten thousand alive, and T them to the top
25:13 people in them, and T much spoil.
25:17 Amaziah king of Judah T counsel and sent to
26:1 the people of Judah T Uzziah, who was sixteen
28:5 who defeated him and T captive a great number
28:8 The men of Israel T captive two hundred thousand
28:8 and daughters; they also T much spoil from them
28:15 by name rose and T the captives, and with
28:21 For Ahaz T from the house of the LORD
29:16 LORD; and the Levites T it and carried it
30:14 for burning incense they T away and threw into
30:16 They T their accustomed posts according to the law
32:8 And the people T confidence from the words of
33:11 king of Assyria, who T Manasseh with hooks and
33:15 And he T away the foreign gods and the
34:33 And Josiah T away all the abominations from all
35:24 So his servants T him out of the chariot
36:1 people of the land T Jehoahaz the son of
36:4 to Jehoiakim; but Neco T Jehoahaz his brother and
36:20 He T into exile in Babylon those who had

Ezra 3:9 sons of Judah, together T the oversight of the
5:14 these Cyrus the king T out of the temple
6:5 of God, which Nebuchadnezzar T out of the temple
7:28 I T courage, for the hand of the LORD
8:30 priests and the Levites T over the weight of
10:5 So they T the oath.
Neh 2:1 was before him, I T up the wine and
4:23 me, none of us T off our clothes; each
5:7 I T counsel with myself, and I brought charges
5:12 called the priests, and T an oath of them
5:15 upon the people, and T from them food and
9:22 every corner; so they T possession of the land
9:25 a rich land, and T possession of houses full
Tob 2:10 Ahikar, however, T care of me until he went
4:12 fathers of old, all T wives from among their
7:14 his wife Edna, and T a scroll and wrote
7:17 as he said, and T her there; and the
8:2 of Raphael, and he T the live ashes of
11:11 ran to him and T hold of his father,
Jud 1:14 Thus he T possession of his cities, and came
2:22 From there Holofernes T his whole army, his
3:6 the hilltop cities and T picked men from them
5:11 hostile to them; he T advantage of them and
5:15 over the Jordan they T possession of all the
6:11 So the slaves T him and led him out
6:21 And Uzziah T him from the assembly to his
7:5 Then each man T up his weapons, and when
8:3 the burning heat, and T to his bed and
10:3 had been wearing, and T off her widow's garments,
10:12 patrol met her and T her into custody, and
12:19 Then she T and ate and drank before him
13:6 above Holofernes' head, and T down his sword that
13:7 to his bed and T hold of the hair
13:15 Then she T the head out of the bag
14:11 wall, and every man T his weapons, and they
15:3 hills around Bethulia also T to flight.
15:7 returned from the slaughter, T possession of what
15:11 his furniture; and she T them and loaded her
15:12 for her; and she T branches in her hands
16:8 For she T off her widow's mourning to exalt
16:19 the canopy which she T for herself from his
Esth 3:10 So the king T his signet ring from his
6:11 So Haman T the robes and the horse, and
8:2 her; and the king T off his signet ring,
9:27 the Jews ordained and T it upon themselves and
12:1 Now Mordecai T his rest in the courtyard with
14:2 to the Lord; she T off her splendid apparel
15:1 ended her prayer, she T off the garments in
15:2 God and Savior, she T her two maids with
15:8 from his throne and T her in his arms
Job 1:15 fell upon them and T them, and slew the
1:17 upon the camels and T them, and slew the
2:8 And he T a potsherd with which to scrape
27:1 And Job again T up his discourse, and said:
29:1 And Job again T up his discourse, and said:
Ps 18:16 from on high, he T me, he drew me
22:9 thou art he who T me from the womb;
48:5 were in panic, they T to flight;
48:6 took to flight; trembling T hold of them there,
71:6 thou art he who T me from my mother's
78:70 David his servant, and T him from the sheepfolds;
80:9 ground for it; it T deep root and filled
104:7 of thy thunder they T to flight.
105:44 the nations; and they T possession of the fruit
Prov 7:20 a long journey; he T a bag of money
Song 5:7 they wounded me, they T away my mantle, those
Wis 4:14 the Lord, therefore he T him quickly from the
5:7 We T our fill of the paths of lawlessness
14:6 hope of the world T refuge on a raft,
16:21 of the one who T it, was changed to
19:18 the sight of what T place.
Sir 24:12 So I T root in an honored people, in
47:11 The Lord T away his sins, and exalted his
49:2 converting the people, and T away the abominations
Is 20:1 fought against it and T it,—
22:7 chariots, and the horsemen T their stand at the
36:1 cities of Judah and T them.
41:9 friend; you whom I T from the ends of
Jer 2:30 smitten your children, they T no correction; your own
13:7 and dug, and I T the waistcloth from the
25:17 So I T the cup from the LORD's hand,
26:10 of the LORD and T their seat in the
27:20 take away, when he T into exile from Jerusalem
28:3 Nebuchadnezzar king of Babylon T away from this
28:10 Then the prophet Hananiah T the yoke-bars from the
31:32 their fathers when I T them by the hand
32:11 Then I T the sealed deed of purchase, containing
32:23 and they entered and T possession of it.
34:11 they turned around and T back the male and
34:16 when each of you T back his male and
35:3 So I T Ja-azaniah the son of Jeremiah, son
36:14 the son of Neriah T the scroll in his
36:21 the scroll, and he T it from the chamber
36:32 Then Jeremiah T another scroll and gave it to
38:6 So they T Jeremiah and cast him into the
38:11 So Ebed-melech T the men with him and went
38:11 of the storehouse, and T from there old rags
39:14 of Babylon sent and T Jeremiah from the court
40:1 from Ramah, when he T him bound in chains
40:2 captain of the guard T Jeremiah and said to
41:10 Then Ishmael T captive all the rest of the
41:10 the son of Nethaniah T them captive and set
41:12 Nethaniah had done, they T all their men and
41:16 the forces with him T all the rest of
43:5 commanders of the forces T all the remnant of
50:33 with them; all who T them captive have held
52:11 the king of Babylon T him to Babylon, and
52:18 And they T away the pots, and the shovels,
52:19 captain of the guard T away as gold, and
52:24 captain of the guard T Seraiah the chief priest,
52:25 from the city he T an officer who had
52:26 captain of the guard T them, and brought them
Lam 1:9 in her skirts; she T no thought of her
Bar 1:2 time when the Chaldeans T Jerusalem and burned it
1:8 day of Sivan, Baruch T the vessels of the
Ezek 3:14 lifted me up and T me away, and I
3:21 surely live, because he T warning; and you will
8:3 of a hand, and T me by a lock
10:7 between the cherubim, and T some of it, and
10:7 clothed in linen, who T it and went out.
16:16 You T some of your garments, and made for
16:17 You also T your fair jewels of my gold
16:18 the harlot; and you T your embroidered garments to
16:20 And you T your sons and your daughters, whom
16:37 lovers, with whom you T pleasure, all those you
17:3 came to Lebanon and T the top of the
17:5 Then he T of the seed of the land
17:12 came to Jerusalem, and T her king and her
17:13 And he T one of the seed royal and
19:5 hope was lost, she T another of her whelps
23:13 was defiled; they both T the same way.
25:15 Philistines acted revengefully and T vengeance with
27:5 trees from Senir; they T a cedar from Lebanon
42:5 narrower, for the galleries T more away from them
Dan 1:16 So the steward T away their rich food and
3:22 slew those men who T up Shadrach, Meshach, and
7:9 was ancient of days T his seat; his raiment
13:2 And he T a wife named Susanna, the daughter
14:27 Then Daniel T pitch, fat, and hair, and boiled
14:36 angel of the Lord T him by the crown
Hos 1:3 So he went and T Gomer the daughter of
11:3 Ephraim to walk, I T them up in my
12:3 In the womb he T his brother by the
Amos 7:15 trees, and the LORD T me from following the
Jon 1:15 So they T up Jonah and threw him into
Zech 11:7 And I T two staffs; one I named Grace,
11:10 And I T my staff Grace, and I broke
11:13 So I T the thirty shekels of silver and
1Mac 1:21 entered the sanctuary and T the golden altar, the
1:22 He T also the table for the bread of
1:23 He T the silver and the gold, and the
1:23 the costly vessels; he T also the hidden treasures
1:27 Every bridegroom T up the lament; she who sat
1:32 And they T captive the women and children, and
3:1 who was called Maccabeus, T command in his place.
3:12 their spoils; and Judas T the sword of Apollonius,
3:37 Then the king T the remaining half of his
3:41 said to them, they T silver and gold in
4:1 Now Gorgias T five thousand infantry and a thousand
4:47 Then they T unhewn stones, as the law directs,
5:8 He also T Jazer and its villages; then he
5:23 Then he T the Jews of Galilee and Arbatta,
5:28 to Bozrah; and he T the city, and killed
5:35 fought against it and T it; and he killed
5:36 he marched on and T Chaspho, Maked, and Bosor,
5:44 But he T the city and burned the sacred
6:8 He T to his bed and became sick from
6:33 the king rose and T his army by a
6:36 These T their position beforehand wherever the
6:50 So the king T Bethzur and stationed a guard
6:63 fought against him, and T the city by force.
7:4 killed them, and Demetrius T his seat upon the

7:24 parts of Judea, and T vengeance on the men
8:7 crushed by them; they T him alive and decreed
8:8 These they T from him and gave to Eumenes
8:10 fell, and the Romans T captive their wives and
9:2 in Arbela, and they T it and killed many
9:11 from the camp and T its stand for the
9:19 Then Jonathan and Simon T Judas their brother and
9:26 to Bacchides, and he T vengeance on them and
9:31 accepted the leadership and T the place of Judas
9:40 the mountain; and they T all their goods.
9:53 And he T the sons of the leading men
10:55 of your fathers and T your seat on the
11:12 So he T his daughter away from him and
11:62 peace with them, and T the sons of their
11:66 removed them from there, T possession of the city,
12:33 aside to Joppa and T it by surprise,
13:25 And Simon sent and T the bones of Jonathan
14:3 and seized him and T him to Arsaces, who
14:5 all his honors he T Joppa for a harbor,
16:16 his men rose up, T their weapons, and rushed
2Mac 1:19 priests of that time T some of the fire
1:19 dry cistern, where they T such precautions that the
3:27 over him, his men T him up and put
4:21 his government, and he T measures for his own
4:41 of wood, and others T handfuls of the ashes
5:5 Antiochus was dead, Jason T no less than a
5:5 was being taken, Menelaus T refuge in the citadel.
5:11 reached the king, he T it to mean that
5:11 he left Egypt and T the city by storm.
5:16 He T the holy vessels with his polluted hands,
6:21 of that unlawful sacrifice T the man aside, because
8:20 with the Galatians that T place in Babylonia, when
8:20 and twenty thousand and T much booty.
8:35 of the least account, T off his splendid uniform
9:29 one of his courtiers, T his body home; then,
10:5 purification of the sanctuary T place, that is, on
10:10 we will tell what T place under Antiochus Eupator,
10:12 who was called Macron, T the lead in showing
10:13 due his office, he T poison and ended his
10:18 less than nine thousand T refuge in two very
10:27 from their prayer they T up their arms and
11:4 He T no account whatever of the power of
12:4 the men of Joppa T them out to sea
12:16 They T the city by the will of God,
12:27 Stalwart young men T their stand before the walls
12:43 He also T up a collection, man by man,
13:26 Lysias T the public platform, made the best possible
14:26 for one another, he T the covenant that had
14:46 tore out his entrails, T them with both hands
Mt 1:18 birth of Jesus Christ T place in this way.
1:22 All this T place to fulfil what the Lord
1:24 Lord commanded him; he T his wife,
2:14 And he rose and T the child and his
2:21 And he rose and T the child and his
4:5 Then the devil T him to the holy city,
4:8 Again, the devil T him to a very high
8:17 the prophet Isaiah, "He T our infirmities and bore
9:25 he went in and T her by the hand,
12:14 Pharisees went out and T counsel against him, how
13:31 seed which a man T and sowed in his
13:33 leaven which a woman T and hid in three
13:57 And they T offense at him.
14:12 his disciples came and T the body and buried
14:20 And they T up twelve baskets full of the
15:36 on the ground, he T the seven loaves and
15:37 were satisfied; and they T up seven baskets full
16:22 And Peter T him and began to rebuke him,
17:1 after six days Jesus T with him Peter and
20:17 up to Jerusalem, he T the twelve disciples aside,
21:4 This T place to fulfil what was spoken by
21:35 fruit; and the tenants T his servants and beat
21:39 his inheritance.' And they T him and cast him
22:15 the Pharisees went and T counsel how to entangle
25:1 to ten maidens who T their lamps and went
25:3 For when the foolish T their lamps, they took
25:3 took their lamps, they T no oil with them;
25:4 them; but the wise T flasks of oil with
26:4 was called Caiaphas, and T counsel together in order
26:26 they were eating, Jesus T bread, and blessed, and
26:27 And he T a cup, and when he had
27:1 elders of the people T counsel against Jesus to
27:7 So they T counsel, and bought with them the
27:9 Jeremiah, saying, "And they T the thirty pieces of
27:24 riot was beginning, he T water and washed his
27:27 soldiers of the governor T Jesus into the praetorium,
27:30 spat upon him, and T the reed and struck
27:48 at once ran and T a sponge, filled it
27:54 the earthquake and what T place, they were filled
27:59 And Joseph T the body, and wrapped it in
28:9 they came up and T hold of his feet
28:15 So they T the money and did as they
Mk 1:31 And he came and T her by the hand
2:12 he rose, and immediately T up the pallet and
4:36 leaving the crowd, they T him with them in
5:40 them all outside, and T the child's father and
6:3 And they T offense at him.
6:29 it, they came and T his body, and laid
6:43 And they T up twelve baskets full of broken
8:6 the ground; and he T the seven loaves, and
8:8 were satisfied; and they T up the broken pieces
8:23 And he T the blind man by the hand,
8:32 And Peter T him, and began to rebuke him.
9:2 after six days Jesus T with him Peter and
9:27 But Jesus T him by the hand and lifted
9:36 And he T a child, and put him in
10:16 And he T them in his arms and blessed
12:3 And they T him and beat him, and sent
12:8 be ours.' And they T him and killed him,
12:20 seven brothers; the first T a wife, and when
12:21 children; and the second T her, and died, leaving
14:22 they were eating, he T bread, and blessed, and
14:23 And he T a cup, and when he had
14:33 And he T with him Peter and James and
15:42 the kingdom of God, T courage and went to
Lk 2:28 of the law, he T him up in his
4:5 And the devil T him up, and showed him
4:9 And he T him to Jerusalem, and set him
5:5 toiled all night and T nothing!
5:25 rose before them, and T up that on which
6:4 house of God, and T and ate the bread
7:36 the Pharisee's house, and T his place at table.
9:10 And he T them and withdrew apart to a
9:17 And they T up what was left over, twelve
9:28 after these sayings he T with him Peter and
9:47 of their hearts, he T a child and put
10:34 to an inn, and T care of him.
10:35 the next day he T out two denarii and
13:19 seed which a man T and sowed in his
13:21 leaven which a woman T and hid in three
14:4 Then he T him and healed him, and let
15:13 all he had and T his journey into a
20:29 seven brothers; the first T a wife, and died
20:31 second and the third T her, and likewise all
22:17 And he T a cup, and when he had
22:19 And he T bread, and when he had given
23:52 Then he T it down and wrapped it in
24:30 table with them, he T the bread and blessed,
24:43 broiled fish, and he T it and ate before
Jn 1:28 This T place in Bethany beyond the Jordan, where
2:8 So they T it.
5:8 was healed, and he T up his pallet and
6:11 Jesus then T the loaves, and when he had
8:59 So they T up stones to throw at him;
10:31 The Jews T up stones again to stone him.
11:41 So they T away the stone.
11:53 that day on they T counsel how to put
12:3 Mary T a pound of costly ointment of pure
12:13 So they T branches of palm trees and went
19:1 Then Pilate T Jesus and scourged him.
19:17 So they T Jesus, and he went out, bearing
19:23 had crucified Jesus they T his garments and made
19:27 that hour the disciple T her to his own
19:36 For these things T place that the scripture might
19:38 So he came and T away his body.
19:40 They T the body of Jesus, and bound it
21:13 Jesus came and T the bread and gave it
Acts 1:9 up, and a cloud T him out of their
3:7 And he T him by the right hand and
5:40 So they T his advice, and when they had
7:43 And you T up the tent of Moloch, and
9:19 and was baptized, and T food and was strengthened.
9:25 him; but his disciples T him by night and
9:27 But Barnabas T him, and brought him to the
9:39 he had come, they T him to the upper
11:28 the world; and this T place in the days
12:21 on his royal robes, T his seat upon the
13:29 written of him, they T him down from the
15:38 from each other; Barnabas T Mark with him and
16:3 accompany him; and he T him and circumcised him
16:33 And he T them the same hour of the
16:39 And they T them out and asked them to
17:19 And they T hold of him and brought him

18:18 days longer, and then T leave of the brethren
18:26 Aquila heard him, they T him and expounded to
20:1 and having exhorted them T leave of them and
20:12 And they T the lad away alive, and were
20:14 us at Assos, we T him on board and
21:11 coming to us he T Paul's girdle and bound
21:26 Then Paul T the men, and the next day
21:32 He at once T soldiers and centurions, and ran
23:18 So he T him and brought him to the
23:19 The tribune T him by the hand, and going
23:31 according to their instructions, T Paul and brought
25:6 the next day he T his seat on the
25:17 on the next day T my seat on the
27:17 hoisting it up, they T measures to undergird the
27:35 had said this, he T bread, and giving thanks
28:15 Paul thanked God and T courage.
1Cor 11:23 when he was betrayed T bread,
2Cor 2:13 So I T leave of them and went on
2Tim 4:16 first defense no one T my part; all deserted
Heb 7:21 who formerly became priests T their office without
8:9 the day when I T them by the hand
9:19 all the people, he T the blood of calves
11:7 events as yet unseen, T heed and constructed an
Rev 5:7 and he went and T the scroll from the
8:5 Then the angel T the censer and filled it
10:10 And I T the little scroll from the hand
18:21 Then a mighty angel T up a stone like

TOOL (5)
Ex 20:25 if you wield your T upon it you profane
32:4 it with a graving T, and made a molten
Deut 27:5 lift up no iron T upon them.
Josh 8:31 has lifted an iron T; and they offered on
1Kgs 6:7 nor axe nor any T of iron was heard

TOOTH (11)
Ex 21:24 life, eye for eye, T for tooth, hand for
21:24 for eye, tooth for T, hand for hand, foot
21:27 he knocks out the T of his slave, male
21:27 go free for the T's sake.
Lev 24:20 fracture, eye for eye, T for tooth; as he
24:20 for eye, tooth for T; as he has disfigured
Deut 19:21 life, eye for eye, T for tooth, hand for
19:21 for eye, tooth for T, hand for hand, foot
Prov 25:19 is like a bad T or a foot that
Mt 5:38 an eye and a T for a tooth.'
5:38 a tooth for a T

TOP (63)
Gen 11:4 a tower with its T in the heavens, and
28:12 the earth, and the T of it reached to
28:18 poured oil on the T of it.
Ex 17:9 will stand on the T of the hill with
17:10 went up to the T of the hill.
19:20 Mount Sinai, to the T of the mountain; and
19:20 called Moses to the T of the mountain, and
24:17 devouring fire on the T of the mountain in
25:21 mercy seat on the T of the ark; and
26:24 but joined at the T, at the first ring;
30:3 with pure gold, its T and its sides round
34:2 to me on the T of the mountain.
36:29 but joined at the T, at the first ring;
37:26 with pure gold, its T, and its sides round
Num 4:25 goatskin that is on T of it, and the
20:28 died there on the T of the mountain.
21:20 of Moab by the T of Pisgah which looks
23:9 For from the T of the mountains I see
23:14 of Zophim, to the T of Pisgah, and built
23:28 took Balaam to the T of Peor, that overlooks
Deut 3:27 Go up to the T of Pisgah, and lift
34:1 Mount Nebo, to the T of Pisgah, which is
Josh 15:8 goes up to the T of the mountain that
15:9 boundary extends from the T of the mountain to
Judg 6:26 your God on the T of the stronghold here,
9:7 and stood on the T of Mount Gerizim, and
16:3 carried them to the T of the hill that
1Sam 26:13 afar off on the T of the mountain, with
2Sam 2:25 their stand on the T of a hill.
1Kgs 7:18 that was upon the T of the pillar; and
7:35 And on the T of the stand there was
7:35 high; and on the T of the stand its
18:42 went up to the T of Carmel; and he
2Kgs 1:9 was sitting on the T of a hill, and
2Chr 3:15 five cubits on the T of each.
4:12 two capitals on the T of the pillars; and
4:12 that were on the T of the pillars;
25:12 took them to the T of a rock and
25:12 them down from the T of the rock; and
Jud 6:12 the city to the T of the hill, and
9:13 house, and against the T of Zion, and against
Esth 5:2 approached and touched the T of the scepter.
Prov 1:21 her voice; on the T of the walls she
23:34 who lies on the T of a mast.
Is 17:6 three berries in the T of the highest bough,
30:17 a flagstaff on the T of a mountain, like
42:11 them shout from the T of the mountains.
Ezek 17:3 Lebanon and took the T of the cedar;
17:22 sprig from the lofty T of the cedar, and
31:3 of great height, its T among the clouds.
31:10 high and set its T among the clouds, and
41:7 lowest story to the T story through the middle
43:12 round about upon the T of the mountain shall
Dan 4:11 became strong, and its T reached to heaven, and
4:20 strong, so that its T reached to heaven, and
Amos 1:2 shepherds mourn, and the T of Carmel withers."
9:3 hide themselves on the T of Carmel, from there
Zech 4:2 a bowl on the T of it, and seven
4:2 which are on the T of it.
4:7 shall bring forward the T stone amid shouts of
Mt 27:51 torn in two, from T to bottom; and the
Mk 15:37 torn in two, from T to bottom.
Jn 19:23 without seam, woven from T to bottom;

TOPAZ (5)
Ex 28:17 A row of sardius, T, and carbuncle shall be
39:10 A row of sardius, T, and carbuncle was the
Job 28:19 The T of Ethiopia cannot compare with it, nor
Ezek 28:13 was your covering, carnelian, T, and jasper, chrysolite,
Rev 21:20 eighth beryl, the ninth T, the tenth chrysoprase, the

TOPHEL
Deut 1:1 Suph, between Paran and T, Laban, Hazeroth, and

TOPHETH (9)
2Kgs 23:10 And he defiled T, which is in the valley
Jer 7:31 the high place of T, which is in the
7:32 no more be called T, or the valley of
7:32 they will bury in T, because there is no
19:6 no more be called T, or the valley of
19:11 Men shall bury in T because there will be
19:12 and to its inhabitants, making this city like T
19:13 gods--shall be defiled like the place of T
19:14 Then Jeremiah came from T, where the LORD had

TOPMOST (2)
Ezek 17:4 he broke off the T of its young twigs
17:22 break off from the T of its young twigs

TOPS (19)
Gen 8:5 of the month, the T of the mountains were
Judg 9:25 him on the mountain T, and they robbed all
9:36 "Look, men are coming down from the mountain T
2Sam 5:24 of marching in the T of the balsam trees,
1Kgs 7:16 to set upon the T of the pillars; the
7:17 the capitals upon the T of the pillars; a
7:19 that were upon the T of the pillars in
7:22 And upon the T of the pillars was lily-work.
7:41 that were on the T of the pillars, and
7:41 that were on the T of the pillars;
1Chr 14:15 of marching in the T of the balsam trees,
2Chr 3:16 put them on the T of the pillars; and
Jud 7:10 easy to reach the T of their mountains.
7:13 go up to the T of the nearby mountains
Ps 72:16 the land; on the T of the mountains may
Ezek 6:13 on all the mountain T, under every green tree,
31:14 height or set their T among the clouds, and
Hos 4:13 They sacrifice on the T of the mountains, and
Joel 2:5 they leap on the T of the mountains, like

TORCH (6)
Gen 15:17 pot and a flaming T passed between these pieces.
Judg 15:4 tail, and put a T between each pair of
Sir 48:1 a fire, and his word burned like a T
Is 62:1 as brightness, and her salvation as a burning T
Zech 12:6 wood, like a flaming T among sheaves; and they
Rev 8:10 heaven, blazing like a T, and it fell on

TORCHES (12)
Judg 7:16 and empty jars, with T inside the jars.
7:20 their left hands the T, and in their right
15:4 hundred foxes, and took T; and he turned them
15:5 set fire to the T, he let the foxes

Job 41:19 his mouth go flaming T; sparks of fire leap
Ezek 1:13 coals of fire, like T moving to and fro
Dan 10:6 his eyes like flaming T, his arms and legs
Nah 2:4 squares; they gleam like T, they dart like lightning.
1Mac 6:39 were ablaze with them and gleamed like flaming T
2Mac 4:22 with a blaze of T and with shouts.
Jn 18:3 there with lanterns and T and weapons.
Rev 4:5 the throne burn seven T of fire, which are

TORE (30)

Judg 14:6 upon him, and he T the lion asunder as
1Sam 15:27 upon the skirt of his robe, and it T
1Kgs 11:30 was on him, and T it into twelve pieces.
14:8 my people Israel, and T the kingdom away from
2Kgs 2:24 of the woods and T forty-two of the boys.
11:18 house of Baal, and T it down; his altars
2Chr 23:17 house of Baal, and T it down; his altars
Lam 3:11 off my way and T me to pieces; he
Ezek 29:7 hand, you broke, and T all their shoulders; and
Amos 1:11 pity, and his anger T perpetually, and he kept
Nah 2:12 The lion T enough for his whelps and strangled
1Mac 1:31 it with fire, and T down its houses and
1:56 which they found they T to pieces and burned
2:25 to sacrifice, and he T down the altar.
2:45 friends went about and T down the altars;
4:45 So they T down the altar,
5:65 and its villages and T down its strongholds and
5:68 of the Philistines; he T down their altars, and
8:10 them, conquered the land, T down their strongholds,
9:54 He T down the work of the prophets!
2Mac 4:38 purple robe from Andronicus, T off his garments, and
7:7 They T off the skin of his head with
10:2 the city; and they T down the altars which
14:46 drained from him, he T out his entrails, took
Mt 26:65 Then the high priest T his robes, and said,
Mk 14:63 And the high priest T his garments, and said,
Lk 9:42 was coming, the demon T him and convulsed him.
Acts 14:14 heard of it, they T their garments and rushed
16:22 them; and the magistrates T the garments off them
Gal 2:18 those things which I T down, then I prove

TORMENT (17)

Judg 16:19 Then she began to T him, and his strength
Job 19:2 "How long will you T me, and break me
Wis 3:1 of God, and no T will ever touch them.
12:23 lived unrighteously thou didst T through their own
17:13 being weak, prefers ignorance of what causes the T
Sir 4:17 upon him, and will T him by her discipline
Is 50:11 from my hand: you shall lie down in T
Mt 8:29 you come here to T us before the time?"
Mk 5:7 by God, do not T me."
Lk 8:28 beseech you, do not T me."
16:23 in Hades, being in T, he lifted up his
16:28 into this place of T
Rev 11:10 prophets had been a T to those who dwell
14:11 the smoke of their T goes up for ever
18:7 a like measure of T and mourning.
18:10 in fear of her T, and say, "Alas!
18:15 in fear of her T, weeping and mourning aloud,

TORMENTED (7)

1Sam 16:14 spirit from the LORD T him.
2Sam 13:2 And Amnon was so T that he made himself
Wis 11:9 how the ungodly were T when judged in wrath.
16:1 such creatures, and were T by a multitude of
16:4 was merely shown how their enemies were being T
Rev 14:10 and he shall be T with fire and sulphur
20:10 and they will be T day and night for

TORMENTING

1Sam 16:15 spirit from God is T you.

TORMENTORS (2)

Ps 137:3 us songs, and our T, mirth, saying, "Sing us
Is 51:23 the hand of your T, who have said to

TORMENTS

Wis 19:4 the punishment which their T still lacked,

TORN (42)

Gen 31:39 That which was T by wild beasts I did
37:33 Joseph is without doubt T to pieces."
44:28 Surely he has been T to pieces; and I
Ex 22:13 If it is T by beasts, let him bring
22:13 shall not make restitution for what has been T
22:31 any flesh that is T by beasts in the
28:32 in a garment, that it may not be T
39:23 around the opening, that it might not be T
Lev 7:24 of one that is T by beasts, may be
13:45 the disease shall wear T clothes and let the
17:15 itself or what is T by beasts, whether he
22:8 of itself or is T by beasts he shall
22:24 bruised or crushed or T or cut, you shall
Josh 9:4 and wineskins, worn-out and T and mended,
1Sam 15:28 him, "The LORD has T the kingdom of Israel
28:17 for the LORD has T the kingdom out of
1Kgs 13:3 the altar shall be T down, and the ashes
13:5 The altar also was T down, and the ashes
13:26 the lion, which has T him and slain him,
13:28 eaten the body or T the ass.
2Kgs 17:21 When he had T Israel from the house of
Job 16:9 He has T me in his wrath, and hated
18:14 He is T from the tent in which he
Prov 27:9 but the soul is T by trouble.
Sir 6:2 lest your soul be T in pieces like a
22:14 building will not be T loose by an earthquake;
Jer 5:6 of them shall be T in pieces; because their
33:4 of Judah which were T down to make a
41:5 shaved and their clothes T, and their bodies gashed,
Ezek 4:14 of itself or was T by beasts, nor has
30:4 and her foundations are T down.
44:31 beast, that has died of itself or is T
Dan 2:5 interpretation, you shall be T limb from limb, and
3:97 and Abednego shall be T limb from limb, and
Hos 6:1 LORD; for he has T, that he may heal
Nah 2:12 and his dens with T flesh.
1Mac 6:7 down; that they had T down the abomination which
Mt 27:51 of the temple was T in two, from top
Mk 15:37 of the temple was T in two, from top
Lk 23:44 of the temple was T in two.
Jn 21:11 there were so many, the net was not T
Acts 23:10 that Paul would be T in pieces by them,

TORRENT (7)

Judg 5:21 The T Kishon swept them away, the onrushing
5:21 them away, the onrushing T, the torrent Kishon.
5:21 the onrushing torrent, the T Kishon.
Ps 124:4 swept us away, the T would have gone over
Sir 40:13 dry up like a T, and crash like a
Jer 47:2 shall become an overflowing T; they shall overflow
Lam 2:18 stream down like a T day and night!

TORRENT-BED (2)

Job 6:15 are treacherous as a T, as freshets that pass
22:24 the stones of the T,

TORRENTIAL

Ezek 38:22 that are with him, T rains and hailstones, fire

TORRENTS (5)

2Sam 22:5 death encompassed me, the T of perdition assailed
Job 14:19 away the stones; the T wash away the soil
30:6 the gullies of the T they must dwell, in
38:25 a channel for the T of rain, and a
Ps 18:4 death encompassed me, the T of perdition assailed

TORTUOUS

Sir 4:17 walk with him on T paths, she will bring

TORTURE (9)

Wis 2:19 him with insult and T, that we may find
Sir 23:10 is continually examined under T will not lack bruises,
2Mac 7:1 by the king, under T with whips and cords,
7:17 his mighty power will T you and your descendants!"
8:17 holy place, and the T of the derided city,
9:7 so hard as to T every limb of his
Rev 9:5 they were allowed to T them for five months,
9:5 kill them, and their T was like the torture
9:5 torture was like the T of a scorpion, when

TORTURED (6)

2Mac 7:13 died, they maltreated and T the fourth in the
8:28 those who had been T and to the widows
8:30 those who had been T and to the orphans
9:6 justly, for he had T the bowels of others
9:11 God, for he was T with pain every moment.
Heb 11:35 Some were T, refusing to accept release, that they

TORTURES (4)

Sir 33:26 for a wicked servant there are racks and T
2Mac 7:8 he in turn underwent T as the first brother
7:42 about the eating of sacrifices and the extreme T

9:5 and with sharp internal T –

TOSS (2)
Is 57:20 rest, and its waters T up mire and dirt.
Jer 5:22 pass; though the waves T, they cannot prevail, though

TOSSED (3)
Amos 8:8 the Nile, and be T about and sink again,
Eph 4:14 no longer be children, T to and fro and
Jas 1:6 that is driven and T by the wind.

TOSSEST
Job 30:22 on it, and thou T me about in the

TOSSING (2)
Job 7:4 I am full of T till the dawn.
Is 57:20 wicked are like the T sea; for it cannot

TOSSINGS
Ps 56:8 kept count of my T; put thou my tears

TOTAL (2)
1Chr 23:3 were numbered, and the T was thirty-eight thousand
2Mac 5:14 Within the T of three days eighty thousand were

TOTALED
2Mac 3:11 position, and that it T in all four hundred

TOTTER (3)
Ps 46:6 nations rage, the kingdoms T; he utters his voice,
59:11 people forget; make them T by thy power, and
Hab 3:16 my bones, my steps T beneath me.

TOTTERING
Ps 62:3 a leaning wall, a T fence?

TOTTERS (3)
Ps 60:2 rent it open; repair its breaches, for it T
75:3 When the earth T, and all its inhabitants, it
Sir 13:20 When a rich man T, he is steadied by

TOU (2)
1Chr 18:9 When T king of Hamath heard that David had
18:10 for Hadadezer had often been at war with T

TOUBIANI
2Mac 12:17 to Charax, to the Jews who are called T

TOUCH (45)
Gen 3:3 garden, neither shall you T it, lest you die.'"
20:6 did not let you T her.
Ex 12:22 in the basin, and T the lintel and the
19:12 into the mountain or T the border of it;
19:13 death; no hand shall T him, but he shall
Lev 11:8 carcasses you shall not T; they are unclean to
12:4 purifying; she shall not T any hallowed thing, nor
Num 4:15 but they must not T the holy things, lest
16:26 these wicked men, and T nothing of theirs, lest
Deut 14:8 not eat, and their carcasses you shall not T
Josh 9:19 now we may not T them.
1Sam 1:11 and no razor shall T his head."
2Sam 14:10 and he shall never T you again."
1Chr 16:22 on their account, saying, T not my anointed ones,
Jud 11:13 so much as to T these things with their
Job 1:11 thy hand now, and T all that he has,
2:5 thy hand now, and T his bone and his
5:19 there shall no evil T you.
6:7 My appetite refuses to T them; they are as
Ps 105:15 on their account, saying, T not my anointed ones,
144:5 T the mountains that they smoke!
Wis 3:1 no torment will ever T them.
Is 52:11 depart, go out thence, T no unclean thing; go
Jer 12:14 my evil neighbors who T the heritage which I
Lam 4:14 blood that none could T their garments.
4:15 T not!" So they became fugitives and wanderers;
Ezek 9:6 children and women, but T no one upon whom
Dan 3:50 the fire did not T them at all or
Zech 14:5 of the mountains shall T the side of it;
2Mac 9:10 thought that he could T the stars of heaven.
Mt 9:21 herself, "If I only T his garment, I shall
14:36 that they might only T the fringe of his
Mk 3:10 pressed upon him to T him.
5:28 she said, "If I T even his garments, I
6:56 him that they might T even the fringe of
8:22 and begged him to T him.
10:13 him, that he might T them; and the disciples
Lk 6:19 the crowd sought to T him, for power came
11:46 you yourselves do not T the burdens with one
18:15 him that he might T them; and when the
1Cor 7:1 a man not to T a woman.
2Cor 6:17 says the Lord, and T nothing unclean; then I
Col 2:21 "Do not handle, Do not taste, Do not T
Heb 11:28 the first-born might not T them.
1Jn 5:18 evil one does not T him.

TOUCHED (56)
Gen 26:29 as we have not T you and have done
32:25 prevail against Jacob, he T the hollow of his
32:32 the thigh, because he T the hollow of Jacob's
Ex 4:25 her son's foreskin, and T Moses' feet with it,
Num 19:18 and upon him who T the bone, or the
31:19 person, and whoever has T any slain, purify
Judg 6:21 in his hand, and T the meat and the
1Sam 10:26 went men of valor whose hearts God had T
1Kgs 6:27 a wing of one T the one wall, and
6:27 of the other cherub T the other wall; their
6:27 wall; their other wings T each other in the
19:5 and behold, an angel T him, and said to
19:7 a second time, and T him, and said, "Arise
2Kgs 13:21 soon as the man T the bones of Elisha,
2Chr 3:11 one, of five cubits, T the wall of the
3:11 wing, of five cubits, T the wing of the
3:12 wing, of five cubits, T the wall of the
Esth 5:2 Then Esther approached and T the top of the
15:11 the golden scepter and T it to her neck;
Job 19:21 hand of God has T me!
Wis 18:16 things with death, and T heaven while standing on
18:20 The experience of death T also the righteous, and
Is 6:7 And he T my mouth, and said: "Behold, this
6:7 said: "Behold, this has T your lips; your guilt
Jer 1:9 forth his hand and T my mouth; and the
Bar 6:29 to them may be T by women in menstruation
Ezek 1:9 wings thus: their wings T one another; they went
1:11 wings, each of which T the wing of another,
3:13 living creatures as they T one another, and the
Dan 8:18 the ground; but he T me and set me
10:10 And behold, a hand T me and set me
10:16 the sons of men T my lips; then I
10:18 appearance of a man T me and strengthened me.
Mt 8:3 out his hand and T him, saying, "I will;
8:15 with a fever; he T her hand, and the
9:20 up behind him and T the fringe of his
9:29 Then he T their eyes, saying, "According to your
14:36 and as many as T it were made well.
17:7 But Jesus came and T them, saying, "Rise, and
20:34 And Jesus in pity T their eyes, and immediately
Mk 1:41 out his hand and T him, and said to
5:27 in the crowd and T his garment.
5:30 crowd, and said, "Who T my garments?"
5:31 you say, 'Who T me?'"
6:56 and as many as T it were made well.
7:32 and he spat and T his tongue;
Lk 5:13 out his hand, and T him, saying, "I will;
7:14 And he came and T the bier, and the
8:44 up behind him, and T the fringe of his
8:45 "Who was it that T me?" When all denied
8:46 Jesus said, "Some one T me; for I perceive
8:47 people why she had T him, and how she
22:49 And he T his ear and healed him.
Acts 20:15 the next day we T at Samos; and the
Heb 12:18 to what may be T, a blazing fire, and
1Jn 1:1 have looked upon and T with our hands, concerning

TOUCHES (53)
Gen 26:11 the people, saying, "Whoever T this man or his
Ex 19:12 border of it; whoever T the mountain shall be
29:37 be most holy; whatever T the altar shall become
30:29 be most holy; whatever T them will become holy.
Lev 5:2 Or if any one T an unclean thing, whether
5:3 Or if he T human uncleanness, of whatever sort
6:18 offerings by fire; whoever T them shall become holy."
6:27 Whatever T its flesh shall be holy; and when
7:19 "Flesh that T any unclean thing shall not be
7:21 And if any one T an unclean thing, whether
11:24 shall become unclean; whoever T their carcass shall
11:26 you; every one who T them shall be unclean.
11:27 unclean to you; whoever T their carcass shall be
11:31 all that swarm; whoever T them when they are
11:36 be clean; but whatever T their carcass shall be
11:39 eat dies, he who T its carcass shall be
15:5 And any one who T his bed shall wash
15:7 And whoever T the body of him who has

T

15:10 And whoever T anything that was under him shall
15:11 that has the discharge T without having rinsed his
15:12 who has the discharge T shall be broken; and
15:19 seven days, and whoever T her shall be unclean
15:21 And whoever T her bed shall wash his clothes,
15:22 And whoever T anything upon which she sits shall
15:23 she sits, when he T it he shall be
15:27 And whoever T these things shall be unclean, and
22:4 Whoever T anything that is unclean through contact
22:5 of semen, and whoever T a creeping thing by
22:6 the person who T any such shall be
Num 19:11 "He who T the dead body of any person
19:13 Whoever T a dead person, the body of any
19:16 in the open field T one who is slain
19:21 clothes; and he who T the water for impurity
19:22 whatever the unclean person T shall be unclean; and
19:22 and any one who T it shall be unclean
Josh 16:7 and to Naarah, and T Jericho, ending at the
19:11 on to Mareal, and T Dabbesheth, then the brook
19:22 the boundary also T Tabor, Shahazumah,
19:26 on the west it T Carmel and Shihor-libnath,
19:27 goes to Beth-dagon, and T Zebulun and the valley
Judg 16:9 tow snaps when it T the fire.
2Sam 23:7 but the man who T them arms himself with
Job 4:5 you are impatient; it T you, and you are
Ps 104:32 and it trembles, who T the mountains and they
Prov 6:29 neighbor's wife; none who T her will go unpunished.
Sir 13:1 Whoever T pitch will be defiled, and whoever
34:25 a dead body, and T it again, what has
Amos 9:5 of hosts, he who T the earth and it
Hag 2:12 of his garment, and T with his skirt bread,
2:13 with a dead body T any of these, does
Zech 2:8 you, for he who T you touches the apple
2:8 he who touches you T the apple of his
Heb 12:20 "If even a beast T the mountain, it shall

TOUCHING (7)

Num 9:6 who were unclean through T the dead body of
9:7 "We are unclean through T the dead body of
9:10 descendants is unclean through T a dead body, or
Josh 19:34 from there to Hukkok, T Zebulun at the south,
Sir 34:25 a man washes after T a dead body, and
Dan 8:5 the whole earth, without T the ground; and the
Lk 7:39 this is who is T him, for she is

TOUR

2Mac 3:8 ostensibly to make a T of inspection of the

TOW (4)

Judg 16:9 as a string of T snaps when it touches
Sir 21:9 the wicked is like T gathered together, and their
Is 1:31 the strong shall become T, and his work a
Dan 3:46 fires with naphtha, pitch, T, and brush.

TOWEL (2)

Jn 13:4 aside his garments, and girded himself with a T
13:5 wipe them with the T with which he was

TOWER (40)

Gen 11:4 a city, and a T with its top in
11:5 the city and the T, which the sons of
35:21 his tent beyond the T of Eder.
Judg 8:9 again in peace, I will break down this T
8:17 he broke down the T of Penuel, and slew
9:46 the people of the T of Shechem heard of
9:47 the people of the T of Shechem were gathered
9:49 the people of the T of Shechem also died,
9:51 there was a strong T within the city, and
9:51 and they went to the roof of the T
9:52 Abimelech came to the T, and fought against it,
9:52 the door of the T to burn it with
2Kgs 9:17 was standing on the T in Jezreel, and he
Neh 3:1 as far as the T of the Hundred, as
3:1 as far as the T of Hananel.
3:11 another section and the T of the Ovens.
3:25 the Angle and the T projecting from the upper
3:26 Water Gate on the east and the projecting T
3:27 opposite the great projecting T as far as the
12:38 the wall, above the T of the Ovens, to
12:39 Fish Gate and the T of Hananel and the
12:39 of Hananel and the T of the Hundred, to
Ps 61:3 my refuge, a strong T against the enemy.
Prov 12:12 The strong T of the wicked comes to ruin,
18:10 LORD is a strong T; the righteous man runs
Song 4:4 neck is like the T of David, built for
7:4 Your neck is like an ivory T
7:4 nose is like a T of Lebanon, overlooking Damascus.
Is 2:15 hills; against every high T, and against every fortified
Jer 31:38 the LORD from the T of Hananel to the
Mic 4:8 And you, O T of the flock, hill of
Hab 2:1 station myself on the T, and look forth to
Zech 14:10 Gate, and from the T of Hananel to the
1Mac 13:43 to the city, and battered and captured one T
2Mac 13:5 For there is a T in that place, fifty
14:41 about to capture the T and were forcing the
Mt 21:33 it, and built a T, and let it out
Mk 12:1 press, and built a T, and let it out
Lk 13:4 eighteen upon whom the T in Siloam fell and
14:28 desiring to build a T, does not first sit

TOWERED (3)

Ezek 19:11 a ruler's scepter; it T aloft among the thick
31:5 So it T high above all the trees of
31:10 Lord GOD: Because it T high and set its

TOWERING (2)

Ps 37:35 wicked man overbearing, and T like a cedar of
Sir 50:10 and like a cypress T in the clouds.

TOWERS (37)

1Chr 27:25 villages and in the T, was Jonathan the son
2Chr 14:7 them with walls and T, gates and bars; the
26:9 Moreover Uzziah built T in Jerusalem at the Corner
26:10 And he built T in the wilderness, and hewed
26:15 to be on the T and the corners, to
27:4 Judah, and forts and T on the wooded hills.
32:5 broken down, and raised T upon it, and outside
Tob 13:16 precious stones, and her T and battlements with pure
Jud 1:3 the gates he built T a hundred cubits high
1:14 to Ecbatana, captured its T, plundered its markets,
7:5 kindled fires on their T they remained on guard
7:33 on the walls and T of their city.
Ps 48:12 about her, number her T,
122:7 be within your walls, and security within your T
Song 8:10 my breasts were like T; then I was in
Is 13:22 will cry in its T, and jackals in the
29:3 will besiege you with T and I will raise
30:25 great slaughter, when the T fall.
33:18 Where is he who counted the T
Ezek 21:22 gates, to cast up mounds, to build siege T
26:4 and break down her T; and I will scrape
26:9 with his axes he will break down your T
27:11 Gamad were in your T; they hung their shields
1Mac 1:33 strong wall and strong T, and it became their
4:60 high walls and strong T round about, to keep
5:5 by him in their T; and he encamped against
5:5 burned with fire their T and all who were
5:65 strongholds and burned its T round about.
6:20 and he built siege T and other engines of
6:37 the elephants were wooden T, strong and covered;
6:51 He set up siege T, engines of war to
13:33 all around, with high T and great walls and
16:10 also fled into the T that were in the
2Mac 10:18 in two very strong T well equipped to withstand
10:20 who were in the T, and on receiving seventy
10:22 turned traitor, and immediately captured the two T
10:36 set fire to the T; they kindled fires and

TOWN (40)

Josh 17:8 to Manasseh, but the T of Tappuah on the
20:6 again to his own T and his own home,
20:6 own home, to the T from which he fled.'"
24:33 him at Gibe-ah, the T of Phinehas his son,
Judg 6:27 the men of the T to do it by
6:28 the men of the T rose early in the
6:30 the men of the T said to Joash, "Bring
14:19 thirty men of the T, and took their spoil
17:8 man departed from the T of Bethlehem in Judah,
Ruth 1:19 to Bethlehem, the whole T was stirred because of
1Sam 23:7 in by entering a T that has gates and
Ezra 2:1 to Jerusalem and Judah, each to his own T
Neh 7:6 returned to Jerusalem and Judah, each to his T
Job 24:20 The squares of the T forget them; their name
Prov 8:3 in front of the T, at the entrance of
9:3 highest places in the T,
9:14 high places of the T,
Is 22:2 who are full of shoutings, tumultuous city, exultant T
Hab 2:12 him who builds a T with blood, and founds
Mt 10:5 Gentiles, and enter no T of the Samaritans,
10:11 And whatever T or village you enter, find out
10:14 your feet as you leave that house or T
10:15 land of Sodom and Gomorrah than for that T

10:23 persecute you in one T, flee to the next;
23:33 synagogues and persecute from T to town,
23:33 persecute from town to T,
Mk 1:45 longer openly enter a T, but was out in
Lk 8:4 together and people from T after town came to
8:4 people from town after T came to him, he
9:5 when you leave that T shake off the dust
10:1 by two, into every T and place where he
10:8 Whenever you enter a T and they receive you,
10:10 whenever you enter a T and they do not
10:11 the dust of your T that clings to our
10:12 on that day for Sodom than for that T
23:49 Joseph from the Jewish T of Arimathea.
Jn 11:54 the wilderness, to a T called Ephraim; and there
Acts 19:35 And when the T clerk had quieted the crowd,
Tit 1:4 appoint elders in every T as I directed you,
Jas 4:13 such and such a T and spend a year

TOWNS (77)

Deut 12:12 that is within your T, since he has no
12:15 within any of your T, as much as you
12:17 not eat within your T the tithe of your
12:18 who is within your T; and you shall rejoice
12:21 may eat within your T as much as you
14:21 who is within your T, that he may eat
14:27 who is within your T, for he has no
14:28 it up within your T;
14:29 who are within your T, shall come and eat
15:7 in any of your T within your land which
15:22 eat it within your T; the unclean and the
16:5 within any of your T which the LORD your
16:11 who is within your T, the sojourner, the fatherless,
16:14 fatherless, and the widow who are within your T
16:18 officers in all your T which the LORD your
17:2 within any of your T which the LORD your
17:8 any case within your T which is too difficult
18:6 from any of your T out of all Israel,
23:16 within one of your T, where it pleases him
24:14 your land within your T;
26:12 may eat within your T and be filled,
28:52 you in all your T, until your high and
28:52 you in all your T throughout all your land,
28:55 your enemy shall distress you in all your T
28:57 which your enemy shall distress you in your T
31:12 the sojourner within your T, that they may hear
Josh 10:37 its king and its T, and every person in
10:39 king and all its T; and they smote them
13:30 Bashan, and all the T of Jair, which are
15:45 Ekron, with its T and its villages;
15:47 Ashdod, its T and its villages; Gaza, its towns
15:47 its villages; Gaza, its T and its villages; to
16:9 families, together with the T which were set apart
16:9 the Manassites, all those T with their villages.
18:9 description of it by T in seven divisions; then
Judg 20:48 And all the T which they found they set
21:23 inheritance, and rebuilt the T, and dwelt in them.
1Sam 27:5 one of the country T, that I may dwell
2Sam 2:3 they dwelt in the T of Hebron.
2Kgs 17:9 places at all their T, from watchtower to fortified
1Chr 2:23 them Havvoth-jair, Kenath and its villages, sixty T
5:16 Bashan and in its T, and in all the
7:28 were Bethel and its T, and eastward Naaran, and
7:28 westward Gezer and its T, Shechem and its towns,
7:28 towns, Shechem and its T, and Ayyah and its
7:28 and Ayyah and its T;
7:29 Manassites, Beth-shean and its T, Taanach and its
7:29 towns, Taanach and its T, Megiddo and its towns,
7:29 towns, Megiddo and its T, Dor and its towns.
7:29 towns, Megiddo and its towns, Dor and its T
8:12 and Lod with its T,
Ezra 2:70 servants lived in their T, and all Israel in
2:70 in their towns, and all Israel in their T
3:1 Israel were in the T, the people gathered as
Neh 7:73 temple servants, and all Israel, lived in their T
7:73 come, the children of Israel were in their T
8:15 proclaim in all their T and in Jerusalem, "Go
10:37 who collect the tithes in all our rural T
11:1 city, while nine tenths remained in the other T
11:3 Jerusalem; but in the T of Judah every one
11:3 his property in their T: Israel, the priests, the
11:20 were in all the T of Judah, every one
12:44 the fields of the T; for Judah rejoiced over
Jud 1:9 Samaria and its surrounding T, and beyond the
15:7 and the villages and T in the hill country
Esth 9:19 live in the open T, hold the fourteenth day
Jer 19:15 and upon all its T all the evil that
Lam 5:11 Zion, virgins in the T of Judah.
1Mac 10:84 Azotus and the surrounding T and plundered them;
2Mac 8:6 would set fire to T and villages.
Mt 10:23 gone through all the T of Israel, before the
14:13 it, they followed him on foot from the T
Mk 1:38 on to the next T, that I may preach
6:33 foot from all the T, and got there ahead
Lk 13:22 on his way through T and villages, teaching, and
Acts 5:16 also gathered from the T around Jerusalem, bringing
8:39 gospel to all the T till he came to

TOWNSMEN

Ruth 3:11 for all my fellow T know that you are

TQHE

Prov 8:13 The fear of T LORD is hatred of evil.

TRACE (5)

Wis 5:10 it has passed no T can be found, nor
6:22 you, but I will T her course from the
Sir 18:5 is it possible to T the wonders of the
Ezek 21:27 not be even a T of it until he
Dan 2:35 so that not a T of them could be

TRACED

Wis 9:16 labor; but who has T out what is in

TRACES

Wis 2:4 pass away like the T of a cloud, and

TRACHONITIS

Lk 3:1 region of Ituraea and T, and Lysani-as tetrarch of

TRACK (2)

Ps 17:11 They T me down; now they surround me; they
Wis 5:10 can be found, nor T of its keel in

TRACKED

Hos 6:8 a city of evildoers, T with blood.

TRACKLESS (2)

Ps 107:40 makes them wander in T wastes;
Wis 5:7 and we journeyed through T deserts, but the way

TRACKS (4)

Ps 65:11 with thy bounty; the T of thy chariot drip
Song 1:8 women, follow in the T of the flock, and
Sir 42:19 and he reveals the T of hidden things.
Jer 2:23 young camel interlacing her T,

TRADE (17)

Gen 34:10 to you; dwell and T in it, and get
34:21 in the land and T in it, for behold,
42:34 brother, and you shall T in the land.'"
Sir 38:34 their prayer is in the practice of their T
Jer 14:18 and priest ply their T through the land, and
Lam 1:11 search for bread; they T their treasures for food
Ezek 17:4 to a land of T, and set it in
28:5 your great wisdom in T you have increased your
28:16 the abundance of your T you were filled with
28:18 of your T you profaned your sanctuaries;
Lk 19:13 and said to them, T with these till I
Jn 2:16 not make my Father's house a house of T
Acts 18:3 was of the same T he stayed with them,
18:3 they worked, for by T they were tentmakers.
19:27 not only that this T of ours may come
Jas 4:13 a year there and T and get gain";
Rev 18:17 sailors and all whose T is on the sea,

TRADED (9)

Ezek 27:13 Tubal, and Meshech T with you; they exchanged
27:15 The men of Rhodes T with you; many coastlands
27:17 the land of Israel T with you; they exchanged
27:20 Dedan T with you in saddlecloths for riding.
27:22 of Sheba and Raamah T with you; they exchanged
27:23 Eden, Asshur, and Chilmad T with you.
27:24 These T with you in choice garments, in clothes
27:24 secure; in these they T with you.
Mt 25:16 went at once and T with them; and he

TRADER (2)

Hos 12:7 A T, in whose hands are false balances, he
Zech 14:21 no longer be a T in the house of

TRADERS (11)

Gen 37:28 Then Midianite T passed by; and they drew Joseph

T

1Kgs 10:15 which came from the T and from the traffic
10:28 Kue, and the king's T received them from Kue
10:29 so through the king's T they were exported to
2Chr 1:16 Kue, and the king's T received them from Kue
9:14 besides that which the T and merchants brought; and
Job 41:6 Will T bargain over him?
Is 23:8 merchants were princes, whose T were the honored
Ezek 27:22 The T of Sheba and Raamah traded with you;
Zeph 1:11 For all the T are no more; all who
1Mac 3:41 When the T of the region heard what was

TRADESMAN
Sir 26:20 from wrongdoing, and a T will not be declared

TRADING (3)
Job 20:18 the profit of his T he will get no
Ezek 16:29 harlotry also with the T land of Chaldea; and
Lk 19:15 he might know what they had gained by T

TRADITION (10)
Mt 15:2 your disciples transgress the T of the elders?
15:3 commandment of God for the sake of your T
15:6 the sake of your T, you have made void
Mk 7:3 their hands, observing the T of the elders;
7:5 live according to the T of the elders, but
7:8 and hold fast the T of men."
7:9 commandment of God, in order to keep your T
7:13 of God through your T which you hand on.
Col 2:8 deceit, according to human T, according to the
2Thes 3:6 in accord with the T that you received from

TRADITIONS (4)
Mk 7:4 there are many other T which they observe, the
1Cor 11:2 everything and maintain the T even as I have
Gal 1:14 was I for the T of my fathers.
2Thes 2:15 and hold to the T which you were taught

TRAFFIC
1Kgs 10:15 traders and from the T of the merchants, and

TRAFFICKED (6)
Is 47:15 have labored, who have T with you from your
Ezek 27:12 "Tarshish T with you because of your great wealth
27:16 Edom T with you because of your abundant goods;
27:18 Damascus T with you for your abundant goods,
27:21 goats; in these they T with you.
Zech 11:7 slain for those who T in the sheep.

TRAFFICKERS
Zech 11:11 that day, and the T in the sheep, who

TRAIN (8)
Esth 15:4 on one, while the other followed carrying her T
Ps 45:14 with her virgin companions, her escort, in her T
68:18 leading captives in thy T, and receiving gifts among
Prov 22:6 T up a child in the way he should
Is 6:1 lifted up; and his T filled the temple.
Dan 11:43 Libyans and the Ethiopians shall follow in his T
1Tim 4:7 T yourself in godliness;
Tit 2:4 is good, and so T the young women to

TRAINED (12)
Gen 14:14 he led forth his T men, born in his
1Chr 25:7 their brethren, who were T in singing to the
2Chr 2:7 crimson, and blue fabrics, T also in engraving, to
2:14 He is T to work in gold, silver, bronze,
Hos 7:16 Although I T and strengthened their arms, yet they
10:11 Ephraim was a T heifer that loved to thresh,
1Mac 4:7 and these men were T in war.
2Mac 15:12 fittingly and had been T from childhood in all
Mt 13:52 scribe who has been T for the kingdom of
Heb 5:14 who have their faculties T by practice to distinguish
12:11 those who have been T by it.
2Pet 2:14 They have hearts T in greed.

TRAINING (5)
Wis 2:12 law, and accuses us of sins against our T
1Tim 1:4 rather than the divine T that is in faith;
4:8 godliness; for while bodily T is of some value,
2Tim 3:16 for correction, and for T in righteousness,
Tit 2:12 salvation of all men, T us to renounce irreligion

TRAINS (5)
2Sam 22:35 He T my hands for war, so that my
Jud 7:18 their tents and supply T spread out in great
Ps 18:34 He T my hands for war, so that my
144:1 LORD, my rock, who T my hands for war,
Sir 18:12 He rebukes and T and teaches them, and turns

TRAITOR (4)
2Mac 5:15 who had become a T both to the laws
10:13 heard himself called a T at every turn, because
10:22 men who had turned T, and immediately captured
Lk 6:16 of James, and Judas Iscariot, who became a T

TRAMPING
Is 9:5 every boot of the T warrior in battle tumult

TRAMPLE (18)
Job 39:15 the wild beast may T them.
Ps 7:5 me, and let him T my life to the
56:1 O God, for men T upon me; all day
56:2 oppress me; my enemies T upon me all day
57:3 to shame those who T upon me.
68:30 T under foot those who lust after tribute; scatter
91:13 the serpent you will T under foot.
Is 14:25 and upon my mountains T him under foot; and
41:25 my name; he shall T on rulers as on
Ezek 26:11 his horses he will T all your streets; he
Dan 7:23 the whole earth, and T it down, and break
Amos 2:7 shoes-- they that T the head of the
5:11 Therefore because you T upon the poor and take
8:4 Hear this, you who T upon the needy, and
Hab 3:12 in fury, thou didst T the nations in anger.
3:15 Thou didst T the sea with thy horses, the
Mt 7:6 before swine, lest they T them under foot and
Rev 11:2 nations, and they will T over the holy city

TRAMPLED (12)
2Kgs 9:33 the horses, and they T on her.
14:9 Lebanon passed by and T down the thistle.
2Chr 25:18 Lebanon passed by and T down the thistle.
Job 9:8 out the heavens, and T the waves of the
Is 5:5 and it shall be T down.
63:3 in my anger and T them in my wrath;
Jer 12:10 my vineyard, they have T down my portion, they
Dan 8:7 to the ground and T upon him; and there
8:10 to the ground, and T upon them.
8:13 and host to be T under foot?"
1Mac 3:45 The sanctuary was T down, and the sons of
3:51 Thy sanctuary is T down and profaned, and thy

TRAMPLES (3)
Is 16:4 ceased, and he who T under foot has vanished
26:6 The foot T it, the feet of the poor,
41:2 him, so that he T kings under foot; he

TRAMPLING (4)
Is 1:12 requires of you this T of my courts?
22:5 day of tumult and T and confusion in the
Zech 10:5 mighty men in battle, T the foe in the
1Mac 4:60 Gentiles from coming and T them down as they

TRANCE (3)
Acts 10:10 he fell into a T
11:5 praying; and in a T I saw a vision,
22:17 I fell into a T

TRANQUIL
Prov 14:30 A T mind gives life to the flesh, but

TRANQUILLITY (3)
Esth 13:2 my subjects in lasting T and, in order to
Dan 4:27 there may perhaps be a lengthening of your T
2Mac 14:6 sedition, and will not let the kingdom attain T

TRANSACTION
Ruth 4:7 exchanging: to confirm a T, the one drew off

TRANSCENDENT
2Cor 4:7 to show that the T power belongs to God

TRANSFER (2)
2Sam 3:10 sworn to him, to T the kingdom from the
Esth 16:14 us undefended and would T the kingdom of the

TRANSFERRED (3)
Num 36:7 Israel shall not be T from one tribe to
36:9 no inheritance shall be T from one tribe to
Col 1:13 dominion of darkness and T us to the kingdom

T

T

TRANSIENT
2Cor 4:18 that are seen are T, but the things that

TRANSLATED (2)
Ezra 4:7 Persia; the letter was written in Aramaic and T
Esth 11:1 genuine and had been T by Lysimachus the son

TRANSLATION
Heb 7:2 He is first, by T of his name, king

TRANSPARENT
Rev 21:21 city was pure gold, T as glass.

TRANSPLANTED (4)
Ezek 17:8 it was planted he T it to good soil
17:10 Behold, when it is T, will it thrive?
19:10 vine in a vineyard T by the water, fruitful
19:13 Now it is T in the wilderness, in a

TRANSPORT
Jud 2:17 asses and mules for T, and innumerable sheep and

TRANSPORTED
2Mac 9:4 T with rage, he conceived the idea of turning

TRAP (15)
Josh 23:13 a snare and a T for you, a scourge
Tob 14:10 Nadab fell into the T and perished.
Job 18:9 A T seizes him by the heel, a snare
18:10 in the ground, a T for him in the
Ps 69:22 a snare; let their sacrificial feasts be a T
140:5 men have hidden a T for me, and with
141:9 Keep me from the T which they have laid
142:3 they have hidden a T for me.
Wis 14:21 this became a hidden T for mankind, because men,
Is 8:14 houses of Israel, a T and a snare to
Jer 5:26 They set a T; they catch men.
Amos 3:5 when there is no T for it?
Obad 1:7 friends have set a T under you-- there
1Mac 5:4 Baean, who were a T and a snare to
Rom 11:9 a snare and a T, a pitfall and a

TRAPPED (2)
Ps 59:12 lips, let them be T in their pride.
Is 42:22 are all of them T in holes and hidden

TRAPPINGS
2Mac 5:3 the flash of golden T, and armor of all

TRAPS
Wis 14:11 an abomination, and became T for the souls of

TRAVAIL (26)
Ps 48:6 them there, anguish as of a woman in T
Song 8:5 your mother was in T with you, there she
8:5 you, there she who bore you was in T
Sir 34:5 like a woman in T the mind has fancies.
48:19 and they were in anguish, like women in T
Is 13:8 will be in anguish like a woman in T
21:3 of a woman in T; I am bowed down
42:14 like a woman in T, I will gasp and
45:10 to a woman, 'With what are you in T
53:11 the fruit of the T of his soul and
54:1 cry aloud, you who have not been in T
Jer 4:31 of a woman in T, anguish as of one
6:24 of us, pain as of a woman in T
13:21 of you, like those of a woman in T
22:23 upon you, pain as of a woman in T
31:8 her who is in T, together; a great company,
49:24 hold of her, as of a woman in T
50:43 seized him, pain as of a woman in T
Mic 4:9 pangs have seized you like a woman in T
4:10 like a woman in T; for now you shall
5:3 she who is in T has brought forth; then
Jn 16:21 a woman is in T she has sorrow, because
Rom 8:22 has been groaning in T together until now;
Gal 4:19 I am again in T until Christ be formed
4:27 who are not in T; for the children of
1Thes 5:3 come upon them as T comes upon a woman

TRAVAILED (2)
Gen 35:16 distance from Ephrath, Rachel T, and she had hard
Is 23:4 saying: "I have neither T nor given birth, I

TRAVEL (8)
Ex 13:21 light, that they might T by day and by
Esth 13:2 peaceable and open to T throughout all its extent,
Job 21:29 not asked those who T the roads, and do
Wis 6:23 truth; neither will I T in the company of
Sir 8:15 Do not T on the road with a foolhardy
39:4 before rulers; he will T through the lands of
Acts 19:29 Macedonians who were Paul's companions in T
2Cor 8:19 by the churches to T with us in this

TRAVELED (5)
Sir 34:10 but he that has T acquires much cleverness.
Bar 4:26 My tender sons have T rough roads; they were
Ezek 27:25 The ships of Tarshish T for you with your
1Mac 11:60 Jonathan set forth and T beyond the river and
Acts 11:19 that arose over Stephen T as far as Phoenicia

TRAVELER
2Sam 12:4 Now there came a T to the rich man,

TRAVELERS (5)
Judg 5:6 Jael, caravans ceased and T kept to the byways.
Job 6:19 of Tema look, the T of Sheba hope.
28:4 they are forgotten by T, they hang afar from
Ezek 39:11 the Valley of the T east of the sea;
39:11 it will block the T, for there Gog and

TRAVELING (2)
Sir 42:3 a partner or with T companions, and of dividing
Acts 9:7 The men who were T with him stood speechless,

TRAVELS (2)
Sir 34:11 many things in my T, and I understand more
51:13 I went on my T, I sought wisdom openly

TRAVERSE
Mt 23:14 for you T sea and land to make a

TRAVERSED
Wis 5:11 its rushing flight, is T by the movement of

TRAYS (3)
Ex 25:38 Its snuffers and their T shall be of pure
37:23 its snuffers and its T of pure gold.
Num 4:9 lamps, its snuffers, its T, and all the vessels

TREACHEROUS (20)
Job 6:15 My brethren are T as a torrent-bed, as freshets
Ps 25:3 shame; let them be ashamed who are wantonly T
Prov 2:22 the land, and the T will be rooted out
11:3 the crookedness of the T destroys them.
11:6 delivers them, but the T are taken captive by
12:5 are just; the counsels of the wicked are T
13:2 the desire of the T is for violence.
Sir 22:20 of secrets, or a T blow-- in these
27:25 own head; and a T blow opens up wounds.
Is 24:16 For the T deal treacherously, the treacherous deal
24:16 deal treacherously, the T deal very treacherously."
33:1 not been destroyed; you T one, with whom none
Jer 9:2 adulterers, a company of T men.
12:1 do all who are T thrive?
Hos 7:17 they are like a T bow, their princes shall
Hab 2:5 Moreover, wine is T; the arrogant man shall not
1Mac 7:10 brothers with peaceable but T words.
7:30 come to him with T intent, and he was
16:13 the country, and made T plans against Simon and
2Tim 3:4 fierce, haters of good, T, reckless, swollen with

TREACHEROUSLY (22)
Ex 21:14 another to kill him T, you shall take him
Num 31:16 of Balaam, to act T against the LORD in
Judg 9:23 men of Shechem dealt T with Abimelech;
1Sam 14:33 said, "You have dealt T; roll a great stone
2Sam 18:13 if I had dealt T against his life (and
Neh 13:27 great evil and act T against our God by
Ps 59:5 none of those who T plot evil.
78:57 turned away and acted T like their fathers; they
Wis 14:24 pure, but they either T kill one another, or
Is 24:16 For the treacherous deal T, the treacherous deal very
24:16 deal treacherously, the treacherous deal very T
33:1 you treacherous one, with whom none has dealt T
33:1 an end of dealing T, you will be dealt
33:1 of dealing treacherously, you will be dealt with T
48:8 you would deal very T, and that from birth
Jer 12:6 even they have dealt T with you; they are
Lam 1:2 her friends have dealt T with her, they have
Ezek 20:27 blasphemed me, by dealing T with me.
39:23 because they dealt so T with me that I

1Mac 7:27 a large force, and T sent to Judas and
13:31 Trypho dealt T with the young king Antiochus; he
16:15 of Abubus received them T in the little stronghold

TREACHERY (17)

Lev 26:40 their fathers in their T which they committed against
Josh 22:16 LORD, 'What is this T which you have committed
22:31 have not committed this T against the LORD; now
2Kgs 9:23 fled, saying to Ahaziah, T, O Ahaziah!"
17:4 king of Assyria found T in Hoshea; for he
Ps 38:12 of ruin, and meditate T all the day long.
52:2 is like a sharp razor, you worker of T
55:23 men of blood and T shall not live out
Jer 5:27 houses are full of T; therefore they have become
Ezek 18:24 be remembered; for the T of which he is
39:26 shame, and all the T they have practiced against
Dan 9:7 them, because of the T which they have committed
Hos 7:4 the king glad, and the princes by their T
1Mac 9:61 were leaders in this T, and killed them.
16:17 an act of great T and returned evil for
2Mac 4:34 Onias, and resorting to T offered him sworn pledges
14:22 places to prevent sudden T on the part of

TREAD (29)

Deut 2:5 of the foot to T on, because I have
11:25 land that you shall T, as he promised you.
33:29 you; and you shall T upon their high places."
Josh 1:3 of your foot will T upon I have given
1Sam 5:5 of Dagon do not T on the threshold of
Job 24:11 they make oil; they T the wine presses, but
40:12 bring him low; and T down the wicked where
Ps 44:5 through thy name we T down our assailants.
60:12 is he who will T down our foes.
91:13 You will T on the lion and the adder,
108:13 is he who will T down our foes.
Prov 30:29 are stately in their T; four are stately in
Is 7:25 where cattle are let loose and where sheep T
10:6 seize plunder, and to T them down like the
Jer 25:30 shout, like those who T grapes, against all the
Bar 4:13 of God's commandments, nor T the paths of discipline
4:25 their destruction and will T upon their necks.
Ezek 34:18 pasture, that you must T down with your feet
Joel 3:13 Go in, T, for the wine press is full.
Mic 1:3 will come down and T upon the high places
6:15 not reap; you shall T olives, but not anoint
6:15 with oil; you shall T grapes, but not drink
7:19 upon us, he will T our iniquities under foot.
Nah 3:14 go into the clay, T the mortar, take hold
Hab 3:19 feet, he makes me T upon my high places.
Zech 9:15 they shall devour and T down the slingers; and
Mal 4:3 And you shall T down the wicked, for they
Lk 10:19 given you authority to T upon serpents and scorpions,
Rev 19:15 of iron; he will T the wine press of

TREADER (3)

Job 24:18 in the land; no T turns toward their vineyards.
Is 16:10 shouts are raised; no T treads out wine in
Amos 9:13 the reaper and the T of grapes him who

TREADING (3)

Neh 13:15 saw in Judah men T wine presses on the
1Cor 9:9 ox when it is T out the grain." Is
1Tim 5:18 ox when it is T out the grain," and,

TREADS (10)

Deut 11:24 sole of your foot T shall be yours; your
25:4 an ox when it T out the grain.
Is 16:10 are raised; no treader T out wine in the
41:25 mortar, as the potter T clay.
63:2 garments like his that T in the wine press?
Jer 48:33 wine presses; no one T them with shouts of
Amos 4:13 the morning darkness, and T on the heights of
Mic 5:5 into our land and T upon our soil, that
5:6 into our land and T within our border.
5:8 when it goes through, T down and tears in

TREASON (6)

1Sam 24:11 is no wrong or T in my hands.
2Kgs 11:14 And Athaliah rent her clothes, and cried, T! T!"
2Chr 23:13 And Athaliah rent her clothes, and cried, "T, T!"
Ezek 17:20 him there for the T he has committed against

TREASURE (38)

Gen 43:23 father must have put T in your sacks for
2Kgs 20:13 showed them all his T house, the silver, the
1Chr 29:3 house, I have a T of my own of
Tob 4:9 laying up a good T for yourself against the
12:8 give alms than to T up gold.
Prov 2:1 receive my words and T up my commandments with
7:1 keep my words and T up my commandments with
15:6 righteous there is much T, but trouble befalls the
15:16 the LORD than great T and trouble with it.
21:20 Precious T remains in a wise man's dwelling, but
Eccl 2:8 and gold and the T of kings and provinces;
Wis 7:14 it is an unfailing T for men; those who
Sir 3:4 his mother is like one who lays up T
6:14 he that has found one has found a T
20:29 Hidden wisdom and unseen T, what advantage is
29:11 Lay up your T according to the commandments of
40:18 but he who finds T is better off than
41:14 hidden wisdom and unseen T, what advantage is
Is 33:6 knowledge; the fear of the LORD is his T
39:2 he showed them his T house, the silver, the
Ezek 22:25 lives; they have taken T and precious things; they
Nah 2:9 is no end of T, or wealth of every
Mt 6:21 For where your T is, there will your heart
12:35 out of his good T brings forth good, and
12:35 out of his evil T brings forth evil.
13:44 of heaven is like T hidden in a field,
13:52 brings out of his T what is new and
19:21 and you will have T in heaven; and come,
Mk 10:21 and you will have T in heaven; and come,
Lk 6:45 out of the good T of his heart produces
6:45 out of his evil T produces evil; for out
12:21 he who lays up T for himself, and is
12:33 grow old, with a T in the heavens that
12:34 For where your T is, there will your heart
18:22 and you will have T in heaven; and come,
Acts 8:27 charge of all her T, had come to Jerusalem
2Cor 4:7 But we have this T in earthen vessels, to
Jas 5:3 You have laid up T for the last days.

TREASURED

Job 23:12 his lips; I have T in my bosom the

TREASURER (2)

Ezra 1:8 charge of Mithredath the T, who counted them out
Rom 16:23 Erastus, the city T, and our brother Quartus, greet

TREASURERS (4)

Ezra 7:21 decree to all the T in the province Beyond
Neh 13:13 And I appointed as T over the storehouses Shelemiah
Dan 3:2 governors, the counselors, the T, the justices, the
3:3 governors, the counselors, the T, the justices, the

TREASURES (44)

Deut 33:19 seas and the hidden T of the sand."
1Kgs 14:26 he took away the T of the house of
14:26 the LORD and the T of the king's house;
15:18 were left in the T of the house of
15:18 the LORD and the T of the king's house,
2Kgs 16:8 LORD and in the T of the king's house,
24:13 carried off all the T of the house of
24:13 the LORD, and the T of the king's house,
1Chr 9:26 the chambers and the T of the house of
2Chr 12:9 he took away the T of the house of
12:9 the LORD and the T of the king's house;
16:2 and gold from the T of the house of
36:18 and small, and the T of the house of
36:18 the LORD, and the T of the king and
Job 3:21 more than for hid T;
20:26 laid up for his T; a fire not blown
Prov 2:4 it as for hidden T;
10:2 T gained by wickedness do not profit, but
21:6 The getting of T by a lying tongue is
Is 2:7 no end to their T; their land is filled
10:13 and have plundered their T; like a bull I
30:6 of asses, and their T on the humps of
45:3 will give you the T of darkness and the
Jer 15:13 "Your wealth and your T I will give as
17:3 wealth and all your T I will give for
20:5 belongings, and all the T of the kings of
48:7 your strongholds and your T, you also shall be
49:4 who trusted in her T, saying, 'Who will come
50:37 sword upon all her T, that they may be
51:13 many waters, rich in T, your end has come,
Lam 1:11 bread; they trade their T for food to revive
Dan 11:43 become ruler of the T of gold and of
Joel 3:5 have carried my rich T into your temples.
Obad 1:6 has been pillaged, his T sought out!
Mic 6:10 Can I forget the T of wickedness in the
Hag 2:7 nations, so that the T of all nations shall

T

1Mac	1:23	took also the hidden T which he found.
2Mac	1:14	secure most of its T as a dowry.
	1:15	had set out the T and Antiochus had come
Mt	2:11	Then, opening their T, they offered him gifts, gold
	6:19	lay up for yourselves T on earth, where moth
	6:20	lay up for yourselves T in heaven, where neither
Col	2:3	are hid all the T of wisdom and knowledge.
Heb	11:26	greater wealth than the T of Egypt, for he

TREASURIES (24)

Deut	32:34	in store with me, sealed up in my T
1Kgs	7:51	stored them in the T of the house of
2Kgs	12:18	was found in the T of the house of
	14:14	LORD and in the T of the king's house,
	18:15	LORD, and in the T of the king's house.
1Chr	26:20	had charge of the T of the house of
	26:20	of God and the T of the dedicated gifts.
	26:22	in charge of the T of the house of
	26:24	Moses, was chief officer in charge of the T
	26:26	charge of all the T of the dedicated gifts
	27:25	Over the king's T was Azmaveth the son of
	27:25	Adi-el; and over the T in the country, in
	28:11	of its houses, its T, its upper rooms, and
	28:12	the surrounding chambers, the T of the house of
	28:12	of God, and the T for dedicated gifts;
2Chr	5:1	the vessels in the T of the house of
	8:15	Levites concerning any matter and concerning the T
	25:24	he seized also the T of the king's house,
	32:27	he made for himself T for silver, for gold,
Esth	3:9	that they may put it into the king's T
	4:7	pay into the king's T for the destruction of
Prov	8:21	wealth those who love me, and filling their T
Sir	1:22	In the T of wisdom are wise sayings, but
Ezek	28:4	and silver into your T;

TREASURY (31)

Deut	28:12	to you his good T the heavens, to give
Josh	6:19	shall go into the T of the LORD."
	6:24	they put into the T of the house of
1Chr	29:8	gave them to the T of the house of
Ezra	2:69	they gave to the T of the work sixty-one
	6:4	let the cost be paid from the royal T
	7:20	you may provide it out of the king's T
Neh	7:70	governor gave to the T a thousand darics of
	7:71	houses gave into the T of the work twenty
Sir	29:12	up almsgiving in your T, and it will rescue
Dan	1:2	the vessels in the T of his god.
Hos	13:15	it shall strip his T of every precious thing.
Zech	11:13	LORD said to me, "Cast it into the T
	11:13	cast them into the T in the house of
1Mac	3:29	the money in the T was exhausted, and that
	13:15	brother owed the royal T, in connection with the
	14:49	of them in the T, so that Simon and
	15:8	owe to the royal T and any such future
2Mac	3:6	to him that the T in Jerusalem was full
	3:13	in any case be confiscated for the king's T
	3:24	he arrived at the T with his bodyguard, then
	3:28	just entered the aforesaid T with a great retinue
	3:40	episode of Heliodorus and the protection of the T
	4:42	temple robber himself they killed close by the T
	5:18	whom Seleucus the king sent to inspect the T
Mt	27:6	put them into the T, since they are blood
Mk	12:41	sat down opposite the T, and watched the multitude
	12:41	and watched the multitude putting money into the T
	12:43	than all those who are contributing to the T
Lk	21:1	their gifts into the T;
Jn	8:20	he spoke in the T, as he taught in

TREAT (17)

Gen	34:31	they said, "Should he T our sister as a
	43:6	said, "Why did you T me so ill as
Deut	21:14	money, you shall not T her as a slave,
	21:16	sons, he may not T the son of the
Jud	10:16	said, and he will T you well."
	11:4	you, but all will T you well, as they
Sir	13:11	Do not try to T him as an equal,
	14:11	My son, T yourself well, according to your means,
	33:31	you have a servant, T him as a brother,
Jer	24:8	eaten, so will I T Zedekiah the king of
Hos	11:8	How can I T you like Zeboiim!
Nah	3:6	filth at you and T you with contempt, and
1Mac	13:46	they said, "Do not T us according to our
2Mac	9:27	my policy and will T you with moderation and
Lk	15:19	be called your son; T me as one of
Col	4:1	Masters, T your slaves justly and fairly, knowing that
1Tim	5:1	you would a father; T younger men like brothers,

TREATED (25)

Gen	39:19	the way your servant T me," his anger was
	42:7	knew them, but he T them like strangers and
Deut	26:6	And the Egyptians T us harshly, and afflicted us,
1Sam	2:17	LORD; for the men T the offering of the
Tob	8:16	expected; but thou hast T us according to thy
Sir	26:19	intelligent men who are T contemptuously; a man
Ezek	22:7	Father and mother are T with contempt in you;
	28:24	their neighbors who have T them with contempt.
	28:26	their neighbors who have T them with contempt.
1Mac	11:26	against him, the king T him as his predecessors
	11:26	as his predecessors had T him; he exalted him
2Mac	6:22	from death, and be T kindly on account of
	7:24	that he was being T with contempt, and he
Mt	22:6	rest seized his servants, T them shamefully, and killed
Mk	9:12	many things and be T with contempt?
	12:4	in the head, and T him shamefully.
Lk	2:48	"Son, why have you T us so?
	18:32	be mocked and shamefully T and spit upon;
	20:11	also they beat and T shamefully, and sent him
	23:11	Herod with his soldiers T him with contempt and
Acts	27:3	at Sidon; and Julius T Paul kindly, and gave
1Cor	12:23	our unpresentable parts are T with greater modesty,
2Cor	6:8	We are T as impostors, and yet are true;
1Thes	2:2	suffered and been shamefully T at Philippi, as you
Heb	10:33	and sometimes being partners with those so T

TREATING

Heb	12:7	God is T you as sons; for what son

TREATMENT (2)

2Mac	2:31	for brevity of expression and to forego exhaustive T
	12:30	them and their kind T of them in times

TREATS (3)

Deut	24:7	Israel, and if he T him as a slave
Mic	7:6	bosom; for the son T the father with contempt,
Heb	8:13	a new covenant he T the first as obsolete.

TREATY (5)

1Sam	11:1	to Nahash, "Make a T with us, and we
	11:2	I will make a T with you, that I
1Kgs	5:12	Solomon; and the two of them made a T
1Mac	8:29	the Romans make a T with the Jewish people.
2Mac	13:25	were indignant over the T; in fact they were

TREE (182)

Gen	1:29	the earth, and every T with seed in its
	2:9	made to grow every T that is pleasant to
	2:9	good for food, the T of life also in
	2:9	the garden, and the T of the knowledge of
	2:16	freely eat of every T of the garden;
	2:17	garden; but of the T of the knowledge of
	3:1	not eat of any T of the garden'?"
	3:3	the fruit of the T which is in the
	3:6	woman saw that the T was good for food,
	3:6	eyes, and that the T was to be desired
	3:11	you eaten of the T of which I commanded
	3:12	me fruit of the T, and I ate."
	3:17	have eaten of the T of which I commanded
	3:22	take also of the T of life, and eat,
	3:24	the way to the T of life.
	18:4	rest yourselves under the T,
	18:8	by them under the T while they ate.
	21:33	Abraham planted a tamarisk T in Beer-sheba, and
	40:19	hang you on a T; and the birds will
Ex	9:25	field, and shattered every T of the field.
	10:5	they shall eat every T of yours which grows
	10:15	green thing remained, neither T nor plant of the
	15:25	LORD showed him a T, and he threw it
Deut	12:2	and under every green T;
	16:21	shall not plant any T as an Asherah beside
	19:5	to cut down a T, and the head slips
	21:22	hang him on a T,
	21:23	all night upon the T, but you shall bury
	22:6	bird's nest, in any T or on the ground,
Josh	8:29	of Ai on a T until evening; and at
	8:29	body down from the T, and cast it at
Judg	9:8	said to the olive T, 'Reign over us.'
	9:9	us.' But the olive T said to them, 'Shall
	9:10	said to the fig T, 'Come you, and reign
	9:11	us.' But the fig T said to them, 'Shall
1Sam	14:2	Gibe-ah under the pomegranate T which is at
	22:6	Gibe-ah, under the tamarisk T on the height, with
	31:13	them under the tamarisk T in Jabesh, and fasted
1Kgs	4:25	and under his fig T, all the days of

	14:23	and under every green T;
	19:4	down under a broom T; and he asked that
	19:5	slept under a broom T; and behold, an angel
2Kgs	3:19	shall fell every good T, and stop up all
	16:4	and on the hills, and under every green T
	17:10	and under every green T;
	18:31	of his own fig T, and every one of
2Chr	28:4	and on the hills, and under every green T
Neh	10:35	all fruit of every T, year by year, to
	10:37	the fruit of every T, the wine and the
Job	14:7	is hope for a T, if it be cut
	15:33	and cast off his blossom, like the olive T
	19:10	my hope has he pulled up like a T
	24:20	is broken like a T
Ps	1:3	He is like a T planted by streams of
	52:8	like a green olive T in the house of
	92:12	flourish like the palm T, and grow like a
	120:4	sharp arrows, with glowing coals of the broom T
Prov	3:18	She is a T of life to those who
	11:30	the righteous is a T of life, but lawlessness
	13:12	desire fulfilled is a T of life.
	15:4	gentle tongue is a T of life, but perverseness
	27:18	who tends a fig T will eat its fruit,
Eccl	11:3	earth; and if a T falls to the south
	11:3	the place where the T falls, there it will
	12:5	the way; the almond T blossoms, the grasshopper
Song	2:3	As an apple T among the trees of the
	2:13	The fig T puts forth its figs, and the
	7:7	stately as a palm T, and your breasts are
	7:8	will climb the palm T and lay hold of
	8:5	Under the apple T I awakened you.
Wis	13:11	may saw down a T easy to handle and
Sir	6:3	fruit, and will be left like a withered T
	14:18	leaves on a spreading T which sheds some and
	24:14	tall like a palm T in En-ge'di, and like
	24:14	like a beautiful olive T in the field, and
	24:14	and like a plane T I grew tall.
	27:6	the cultivation of a T; so the expression of
	38:5	made sweet with a T in order that his
	50:10	stones; like an olive T putting forth its fruit,
Is	17:6	as when an olive T is beaten-- two
	17:6	branches of a fruit T, says the LORD God
	24:13	as when an olive T is beaten, as at
	34:4	the vine, like leaves falling from the fig T
	36:16	of his own fig T, and every one of
	44:14	he chooses a holm T or an oak and
	44:23	O forest, and every T in it!
	56:3	the eunuch say, "Behold, I am a dry T
	57:5	oaks, under every green T; who slay your children
	65:22	the days of a T shall the days of
Jer	2:20	and under every green T you bowed down as
	2:27	who say to a T, 'You are my father,'
	3:6	and under every green T, and there played the
	3:9	the land, committing adultery with stone and T
	3:13	strangers under every green T, and that you have
	8:13	figs on the fig T; even the leaves are
	10:3	A T from the forest is cut down, and
	11:16	you, 'A green olive T, fair with goodly fruit';
	11:19	"Let us destroy the T with its fruit, let
	17:2	Asherim, beside every green T, and on the high
	17:8	He is like a T planted by water, that
Bar	5:8	woods and every fragrant T have shaded Israel at
Ezek	6:13	tops, under every green T, and under every leafy
	17:24	bring low the high T, and make high the
	17:24	make high the low T, dry up the green
	17:24	dry up the green T, and make the dry
	17:24	and make the dry T flourish.
	20:28	hill or any leafy T, there they offered their
	20:47	shall devour every green T in you and every
	20:47	you and every dry T; the blazing flame shall
	31:8	with its branches; no T in the garden of
	36:30	the fruit of the T and the increase of
	41:18	palm trees, a palm T between cherub and cherub.
	41:19	man toward the palm T on the one side,
	41:19	lion toward the palm T on the other side.
Dan	4:10	saw, and behold, a T in the midst of
	4:11	The T grew and became strong, and its top
	4:14	thus, 'Hew down the T and cut off its
	4:20	The T you saw, which grew and became strong,
	4:23	saying, 'Hew down the T and destroy it, but
	4:26	the roots of the T, your kingdom shall be
	13:54	me this: Under what T did you see them
	13:54	He answered, "Under a mastic T
	13:58	tell me: Under what T did you catch them
Hos	9:10	fruit on the fig T, in its first season,
Joel	1:11	vine withers, the fig T languishes.
	2:22	wilderness are green; the T bears its fruit, the
	2:22	its fruit, the fig T and vine give their
Mic	4:4	and under his fig T, and none shall make
Hab	3:17	Though the fig T do not blossom, nor fruit
Hag	2:19	the vine, the fig T, the pomegranate, and the
	2:19	pomegranate, and the olive T still yield nothing?
Zech	3:10	neighbor under his vine and under his fig T
1Mac	14:12	vine and his fig T, and there was none
Mt	3:10	of the trees; every T therefore that does not
	7:17	So, every sound T bears good fruit, but the
	7:17	fruit, but the bad T bears evil fruit.
	7:18	A sound T cannot bear evil fruit, nor can
	7:18	nor can a bad T bear good fruit.
	7:19	Every T that does not bear good fruit is
	12:33	"Either make the T good, and its fruit good;
	12:33	good; or make the T bad, and its fruit
	12:33	fruit bad; for the T is known by its
	13:32	shrubs and becomes a T, so that the birds
	21:19	And seeing a fig T by the wayside he
	21:19	And the fig T withered at once.
	21:20	"How did the fig T wither at once?"
	21:21	done to the fig T, but even if you
	24:32	"From the fig T learn its lesson: as soon
Mk	11:13	the distance a fig T in leaf, he went
	11:20	they saw the fig T withered away to its
	11:21	The fig T which you cursed has withered."
	13:28	"From the fig T learn its lesson: as soon
Lk	3:9	of the trees; every T therefore that does not
	6:43	"For no good T bears bad fruit, nor again
	6:43	again does a bad T bear good fruit;
	6:44	good fruit; for each T is known by its
	13:6	man had a fig T planted in his vineyard;
	13:7	fruit on this fig T, and I find none.
	13:19	grew and became a T, and the birds of
	17:6	say to this sycamine T, 'Be rooted up, and
	19:4	up into a sycamore T to see him, for
	21:29	"Look at the fig T, and all the trees;
Jn	1:48	were under the fig T, I saw you."
	1:50	you under the fig T, do you believe?
Acts	5:30	whom you killed by hanging him on a T
	10:39	hanging him on a T;
	13:29	him down from the T, and laid him in
Rom	11:17	richness of the olive T,
	11:24	nature a wild olive T, and grafted, contrary to
	11:24	into a cultivated olive T, how much more will
	11:24	branches be grafted back into their own olive T
Gal	3:13	who hangs on a T --
Jas	3:12	Can a fig T, my brethren, yield olives, or
1Pet	2:24	his body on the T, that we might die
Rev	2:7	to eat of the T of life, which is
	6:13	earth as the fig T sheds its winter fruit
	7:1	blow on earth or sea or against any T
	9:4	green growth or any T, but only those of
	22:2	of the river, the T of life with its
	22:2	the leaves of the T were for the healing
	22:14	the right to the T of life and that
	22:19	his share in the T of life and in

TREES (136)

Gen	1:11	yielding seed, and fruit T bearing fruit in which
	1:12	their own kinds, and T bearing fruit in which
	3:2	the fruit of the T of the garden;
	3:8	LORD God among the T of the garden.
	23:17	it and all the T that were in the
Ex	10:15	the fruit of the T which the hail had
	15:27	water and seventy palm T; and they encamped there
Lev	19:23	plant all kinds of T for food, then you
	23:40	the fruit of goodly T, branches of palm trees,
	23:40	trees, branches of palm T, and boughs of leafy
	23:40	and boughs of leafy T, and willows of the
	26:4	its increase, and the T of the field shall
	26:20	its increase, and the T of the land shall
	27:30	the fruit of the T, is the LORDs; it
Num	24:6	has planted, like cedar T beside the waters.
	33:9	water and seventy palm T, and they encamped there.
Deut	6:11	and vineyards and olive T, which you did not
	8:8	of vines and fig T and pomegranates, a land
	8:8	a land of olive T and honey,
	20:19	shall not destroy its T by wielding an axe
	20:19	Are the T in the field men that they
	20:20	Only the T which you know are not trees
	20:20	you know are not T for food you may
	24:20	you beat your olive T, you shall not go
	28:40	You shall have olive T throughout all your territory,
	28:42	All your T and the fruit of your ground
	34:3	the city of palm T, as far as Zoar.

Josh	10:26	to death, and he hung them on five T
	10:26	they hung upon the T until evening;
	10:27	them down from the T, and threw them into
Judg	9:8	The T once went forth to anoint a king
	9:9	to sway over the T
	9:10	the trees?' And the T said to the fig
	9:11	to sway over the T
	9:12	the trees?' And the T said to the vine,
	9:13	to sway over the T
	9:14	trees?' Then all the T said to the bramble,
	9:15	bramble said to the T, 'If in good faith
2Sam	5:11	to David, and cedar T, also carpenters and masons
	5:23	rear, and come upon them opposite the balsam T
	5:24	tops of the balsam T, then bestir yourself; for
1Kgs	4:33	He spoke of T, from the cedar that is
	6:29	of cherubim and palm T and open flowers, in
	6:32	carvings of cherubim, palm T, and open flowers; he
	6:32	gold upon the cherubim and upon the palm T
	6:35	carved cherubim and palm T and open flowers; and
	7:36	cherubim, lions, and palm T, according to the space
2Kgs	3:25	felled all the good T; till only its stones
	6:4	they came to the Jordan, they cut down T
	18:32	a land of olive T and honey, that you
1Chr	14:1	to David, and cedar T, also masons and carpenters
	14:14	around and come upon them opposite the balsam T
	14:15	tops of the balsam T, then go out to
	16:33	Then shall the T of the wood sing for
	27:28	the olive and sycamore T in the Shephelah was
2Chr	28:15	their kinsfolk at Jericho, the city of palm T
Ezra	3:7	Tyrians to bring cedar T from Lebanon to the
Neh	8:15	palm, and other leafy T to make booths, as
	9:25	olive orchards and fruit T in abundance; so they
Job	40:22	his shade the lotus T cover him; the willows
Ps	96:12	Then shall all the T of the wood sing
	104:16	The T of the LORD are watered abundantly, the
	104:17	the stork has her home in the fir T
	105:33	their vines and fig T, and shattered the trees
	105:33	trees, and shattered the T of their country.
	148:9	and all hills, fruit T and all cedars!
Eccl	2:5	and planted in them all kinds of fruit T
	2:6	from which to water the forest of growing T
Song	2:3	apple tree among the T of the wood, so
	4:14	and cinnamon, with all T of frankincense, myrrh and
Sir	50:12	the trunks of palm T,
Is	7:2	people shook as the T of the forest shake
	10:19	The remnant of the T of his forest will
	10:34	Lebanon with its majestic T will fall.
	44:14	grow strong among the T of the forest; he
	55:12	singing, and all the T of the field shall
Jer	5:17	vines and your fig T; your fortified cities in
	6:6	hosts: "Hew down her T; cast up a siege
	7:20	and beast, upon the T of the field and
	46:22	against her with axes, like those who fell T
Ezek	15:2	which is among the T of the forest?
	15:6	the vine among the T of the forest, which
	17:24	And all the T of the field shall know
	27:5	your planks of fir T from Senir; they took
	31:4	streams to all the T of the forest.
	31:5	high above all the T of the forest; its
	31:8	it, nor the fir T equal its boughs; the
	31:8	its boughs; the plane T were as nothing compared
	31:9	branches, and all the T of Eden envied it,
	31:14	in order that no T by the waters may
	31:14	clouds, and that no T that drink water may
	31:15	it, and all the T of the field shall
	31:16	Pit; and all the T of Eden, the choice
	31:18	in greatness among the T of Eden?
	31:18	brought down with the T of Eden to the
	34:27	And the T of the field shall yield their
	40:16	about inside, and on the jambs were palm T
	40:22	vestibule, and its palm T were of the same
	40:26	and it had palm T on its jambs, one
	40:31	outer court, and palm T were on its jambs,
	40:34	and it had palm T on its jambs, one
	40:37	and it had palm T on its jambs, one
	41:18	of cherubim and palm T, a palm tree between
	41:20	door cherubim and palm T were carved on the
	41:25	carved cherubim and palm T, such as were carved
	41:26	recessed windows and palm T on either side, on
	47:7	the river very many T on the one side
	47:12	grow all kinds of T for food.
Hos	2:12	vines and her fig T, of which she said,
Joel	1:7	and splintered my fig T; it has stripped off
	1:11	and apple, all the T of the field are
	1:18	has burned all the T of the field.
Amos	4:9	your vineyards; your fig T and your olive trees
	4:9	trees and your olive T the locust devoured; yet
	7:14	a dresser of sycamore T,
Nah	3:12	fortresses are like fig T with first-ripe figs--if
Zech	1:8	standing among the myrtle T in the glen; and
	1:10	standing among the myrtle T answered, 'These are
	1:11	standing among the myrtle T, 'We have patrolled the
	4:3	there are two olive T by it, one on
	4:11	are these two olive T on the right and
	4:12	branches of the olive T, which are beside the
	11:2	fallen, for the glorious T are ruined!
1Mac	10:30	the fruit of the T that I should receive,
	11:34	of the land and the fruit of the T
	14:8	its increase, and the T of the plains their
Mt	3:10	the root of the T; every tree therefore that
	21:8	cut branches from the T and spread them on
Mk	8:24	but they look like T, walking."
Lk	3:9	the root of the T; every tree therefore that
	21:29	tree, and all the T;
Jn	12:13	took branches of palm T and went out to
Jude	1:12	along by winds; fruitless T in late autumn, twice
Rev	7:3	the sea or the T, till we have sealed
	8:7	a third of the T were burnt up, and
	11:4	are the two olive T and the two lampstands

TRELLIS

Ps	74:5	they hacked the wooden T with axes.

TREMBLE (43)

Ex	15:14	peoples have heard, they T; pangs have seized on
Deut	2:25	of you and shall T and be in anguish
	20:3	do not fear, or T, or be in dread
1Chr	16:30	LORD in holy array; T before him, all the
Ezra	10:3	and of those who T at the commandment of
Job	9:6	place, and its pillars T;
	26:5	The shades below T, the waters and their inhabitants.
	26:11	The pillars of heaven T, and are astounded at
Ps	46:3	foam, though the mountains T with its tumult.
	69:23	and make their loins T continually.
	96:9	LORD in holy array; T before him, all the
	99:1	The LORD reigns; let the peoples T
	114:7	T, O earth, at the presence of the LORD,
Eccl	12:3	keepers of the house T, and the strong men
Sir	16:16	and the earth, will T at his visitation.
	48:12	days he did not T before any ruler, and
Is	13:13	will make the heavens T, and the earth will
	14:16	who made the earth T, who shook kingdoms,
	19:1	idols of Egypt will T at his presence, and
	19:16	be like women, and T with fear before the
	24:18	are opened, and the foundations of the earth T
	32:11	T, you women who are at ease, shudder, you
	41:5	ends of the earth T; they have drawn near
	64:2	that the nations might T at thy presence!
	66:5	the LORD, you who T at his word: "Your
Jer	5:22	LORD; Do you not T before me?
	33:9	they shall fear and T because of all the
	49:21	fall the earth shall T; the sound of their
	50:46	Babylon the earth shall T, and her cry shall
Ezek	26:16	upon the ground and T every moment, and be
	26:18	Now the isles T on the day of your
	32:10	before them; they shall T every moment, every one
Dan	6:26	my royal dominion men T and fear before the
Hos	5:8	the alarm at Beth-aven; T, O Benjamin!
	10:5	The inhabitants of Samaria T for the calf of
Joel	2:1	inhabitants of the land T, for the day of
	2:10	The earth quakes before them, the heavens T
Amos	8:8	Shall not the land T on this account, and
Nah	2:10	Hearts faint and knees T, anguish is on all
Hab	2:7	arise, and those awake who will make you T
	3:7	the curtains of the land of Midian did T
1Mac	4:32	their strength; let them T in their destruction.
Heb	12:21	that Moses said, "I T with fear."

TREMBLED (22)

Gen	27:33	Then Isaac T violently, and said, "Who was it
Ex	19:16	all the people who were in the camp T
	20:18	people were afraid and T; and they stood afar
Judg	5:4	of Edom, the earth T, and the heavens dropped,
1Sam	4:13	watching, for his heart T for the ark of
	14:15	and even the raiders T; the earth quaked; and
	28:5	afraid, and his heart T greatly.
2Sam	22:8	foundations of the heavens T and quaked, because he
1Kgs	1:49	the guests of Adonijah T, and rose, and each
Ezra	9:4	Then all who T at the words of the
Jud	16:10	The Persians T at her boldness, the Medes were
	16:11	shouted and the enemy T; they lifted up their
Esth	5:9	he neither rose nor T before him, he was

Ps 18:7 also of the mountains T and quaked, because he
77:16 saw thee, they were afraid, yea, the deep T
77:18 the world; the earth T and shook.
Sir 48:19 shaken and their hands T, and they were in
Dan 5:19 peoples, nations, and languages T and feared before
Hos 13:1 When Ephraim spoke, men T; he was exalted in
1Mac 6:41 clanking of their arms, T, for the army was
Mt 28:4 of him the guards T and became like dead
Acts 7:32 of Jacob.' And Moses T and did not dare

TREMBLES (10)

Job 37:1 this also my heart T, and leaps out of
Ps 97:4 lightnings lighten the world; the earth sees and T
104:32 the earth and it T, who touches the mountains
119:120 My flesh T for fear of thee, and I
Prov 30:21 three things the earth T; under four it cannot
Is 10:29 for the night; Ramah T, Gibe-ah of Saul has
15:4 armed men of Moab cry aloud; his soul T
66:2 contrite in spirit, and T at my word.
Jer 51:29 The land T and writhes in pain, for the
Hab 3:16 hear, and my body T, my lips quiver at

TREMBLING (38)

Gen 42:28 them, and they turned T to one another, saying,
Ex 15:15 the leaders of Moab, T seizes them; all the
Deut 28:65 give you there a T heart, and failing eyes,
Judg 7:3 'Whoever is fearful and T, let him return home.'"
1Sam 13:7 at Gilgal, and all the people followed him T
16:4 came to meet him T, and said, "Do you
21:1 came to meet David T, and said to him,
2Sam 22:46 lost heart, and came T out of their fastnesses.
Ezra 10:9 the house of God, T because of this matter
Jud 15:2 Fear and T came over them, so that they
Job 4:14 came upon me, and T, which made all my
Ps 2:11 LORD with fear, with T
18:45 lost heart, and came T out of their fastnesses.
48:6 they took to flight; T took hold of them
55:5 Fear and T come upon me, and horror overwhelms
Wis 17:10 serpents, they perished in T fear, refusing to look
Sir 16:17 the earth shake with T when he looks upon
Is 21:4 longed for has been turned for me into T
33:14 in Zion are afraid; T has seized the godless:
Ezek 12:18 and drink water with T and with fearfulness;
26:16 will clothe themselves with T; they will sit upon
Dan 10:7 vision, but a great T fell upon them, and
10:10 me and set me T on my hands and
10:11 speaking this word to me, I stood up T
Hos 11:10 his sons shall come T from the west;
11:11 west; they shall come T like birds from Egypt,
Mic 7:17 earth; they shall come T out of their strongholds,
1Mac 13:2 that the people were T and fearful.
2Mac 3:17 For terror and bodily T had come over the
15:23 to carry terror and T before us.
Mk 5:33 came in fear and T and fell down before
16:8 from the tomb; for T and astonishment had come
Lk 8:47 not hidden, she came T, and falling down before
Acts 16:29 and rushed in, and T with fear he fell
1Cor 2:3 in much fear and T;
2Cor 7:15 and the fear and T with which you received
Eph 6:5 masters, with fear and T, in singleness of heart,
Phil 2:12 salvation with fear and T;

TREMENDOUS

2Mac 10:24 Jews before, gathered a T force of mercenaries and

TRENCH (3)

1Kgs 18:32 And he made a T about the altar, as
18:35 altar, and filled the T also with water.
18:38 licked up the water that was in the T

TRESPASS (11)

1Sam 25:28 Pray forgive the T of your handmaid; for the
Wis 12:2 by little those who T, and dost remind and
Rom 5:15 But the free gift is not like the T
5:15 died through one man's T, much more have the
5:16 the judgment following one T brought condemnation,
5:17 because of one man's T, death reigned through that
5:18 Then as one man's T led to condemnation for
5:20 in, to increase the T; but where sin increased,
11:11 But through their T salvation has come to the
11:12 Now if their T means riches for the world,
Gal 6:1 is overtaken in any T, you who are spiritual

TRESPASSED

Ezra 10:10 to them, "You have T and married foreign women,

TRESPASSES (12)

Mt 6:14 you forgive men their T, your heavenly Father also
6:15 not forgive men their T, neither will your Father
6:15 their trespasses, neither will your Father forgive your
T
Mk 11:25 who is in heaven may forgive you your T
Rom 4:25 to death for our T and raised for our
5:16 free gift following many T brings justification.
2Cor 5:19 himself, not counting their T against them, and
Eph 1:7 the forgiveness of our T, according to the riches
2:1 were dead through the T and sins
2:5 were dead through our T, made us alive together
Col 2:13 who were dead in T and the uncircumcision of
2:13 forgiven us all our T,

TRESSES

Song 7:5 purple; a king is held captive in the T

TRIAL (15)

Judg 6:39 pray, let me make T only this once with
Job 9:32 we should come to T together.
Ps 37:33 him be condemned when he is brought to T
109:6 against him; let an accuser bring him to T
Wis 2:19 he is, and make T of his forbearance.
Sir 33:1 the Lord, but in T he will deliver him
Mk 13:11 they bring you to T and deliver you up,
Acts 15:10 why do you make T of God by putting
23:6 the resurrection of the dead I am on T
24:20 dead I am on T before you this day.'"
26:6 I stand here on T for hope in the
Gal 4:14 my condition was a T to you, you did
Jas 1:11 the man who endures T, for when he has
2Pet 2:9 rescue the godly from T, and to keep the
Rev 3:10 from the hour of T which is coming on

TRIALS (7)

Deut 4:34 of another nation, by T, by signs, by wonders,
7:19 all Egypt, the great T which your eyes saw,
29:3 his land, the great T which your eyes saw,
Lk 22:28 with me in my T;
Acts 20:19 with tears and with T which befell me through
Jas 1:2 when you meet various T,
1Pet 1:6 have to suffer various T,

TRIBAL (5)

Josh 11:23 Israel according to their T allotments.
22:14 from each of the T families of Israel, every
Ezek 45:7 to one of the T portions, and extending from
48:8 to one of the T portions, from the east
48:21 border, parallel to the T portions, it shall belong

TRIBE (248)

Ex 31:2 of Hur, of the T of Judah:
31:6 of Ahisamach, of the T of Dan; and I
35:30 of Hur, of the T of Judah;
35:34 of Ahisamach of the T of Dan.
38:22 of Hur, of the T of Judah, made all
38:23 of Ahisamach, of the T of Dan, a craftsman
Lev 24:11 of Dibri, of the T of Dan.
Num 1:4 a man from each T, each man being the
1:21 the number of the T of Reuben was forty-six
1:23 the number of the T of Simeon was fifty-nine
1:25 the number of the T of Gad was forty-five
1:27 the number of the T of Judah was seventy-four
1:29 the number of the T of Issachar was fifty-four
1:31 the number of the T of Zebulun was fifty-seven
1:33 the number of the T of Ephraim was forty
1:35 the number of the T of Manasseh was thirty-two
1:37 the number of the T of Benjamin was thirty-five
1:39 the number of the T of Dan was sixty-two
1:41 the number of the T of Asher was forty-one
1:43 the number of the T of Naphtali was fifty-three
1:47 numbered by their ancestral T along with them.
1:49 to Moses, "Only the T of Levi you shall
2:5 him shall be the T of Issachar, the leader
2:7 Then the T of Zebulun, the leader of the
2:12 him shall be the T of Simeon, the leader
2:14 Then the T of Gad, the leader of the
2:20 him shall be the T of Manasseh, the leader
2:22 Then the T of Benjamin, the leader of the
2:27 him shall be the T of Asher, the leader
2:29 Then the T of Naphtali, the leader of the
3:6 to Moses, "Bring the T of Levi near, and
4:18 Aaron, "Let not the T of the families of
7:12 of Amminadab, of the T of Judah;
10:15 the host of the T of the men of

10:16 the host of the T of the men of
10:19 the host of the T of the men of
10:20 the host of the T of the men of
10:23 the host of the T of the men of
10:24 the host of the T of the men of
10:26 the host of the T of the men of
10:27 the host of the T of the men of
13:2 of Israel; from each T of their fathers shall
13:4 their names: From the T of Reuben, Shammua the
13:5 of Zaccur; from the T of Simeon, Shaphat the
13:6 of Hori; from the T of Judah, Caleb the
13:7 of Jephunneh; from the T of Issachar, Igal the
13:8 of Joseph; from the T of Ephraim, Hoshea the
13:9 of Nun; from the T of Benjamin, Palti the
13:10 of Raphu; from the T of Zebulun, Gaddiel the
13:11 of Sodi; from the T of Joseph (that is
13:11 (that is from the T of Manasseh), Gaddi the
13:12 of Susi; from the T of Dan, Ammiel the
13:13 of Gemalli; from the T of Asher, Sethur the
13:14 of Michael; from the T of Naphtali, Nahbi the
13:15 of Vophsi; from the T of Gad, Geuel the
18:2 your brethren also, the T of Levi, the tribe
18:2 tribe of Levi, the T of your father, that
24:2 and saw Israel encamping T by tribe.
24:2 his eyes, and saw Israel encamping tribe by T
26:54 To a large T you shall give a large
26:54 and to a small T you shall give a
26:54 a small inheritance; every T shall be given its
31:5 a thousand from each T, twelve thousand armed for
31:6 a thousand from each T, together with Phinehas the
33:54 families; to a large T you shall give a
33:54 and to a small T you shall give a
34:14 the half-tribe; for the T of the sons of
34:14 fathers' houses and the T of the sons of
34:18 one leader of every T, to divide the land
34:19 the men: Of the T of Judah, Caleb the
34:20 Of the T of the sons of Simeon, Shemuel
34:21 Of the T of Benjamin, Elidad the son of
34:22 Of the T of the sons of Dan a
34:23 of Joseph: of the T of the sons of
34:24 And of the T of the sons of Ephraim
34:25 Of the T of the sons of Zebulun a
34:26 Of the T of the sons of Issachar a
34:27 And of the T of the sons of Asher
34:28 Of the T of the sons of Naphtali a
36:3 the inheritance of the T to which they belong;
36:4 the inheritance of the T to which they belong;
36:4 the inheritance of the T of our fathers."
36:5 the LORD, saying, "The T of the sons of
36:6 the family of the T of their father.
36:7 be transferred from one T to another; for every
36:7 the inheritance of the T of his fathers.
36:8 an inheritance in any T of the people of
36:8 the family of the T of her father, so
36:9 be transferred from one T to another; for each
36:12 inheritance remained in the T of the family of
Deut 1:23 one man for each T;
10:8 LORD set apart the T of Levi to carry
18:1 that is, all the T of Levi, shall have
29:18 woman or family or T, whose heart turns away
Josh 3:12 of Israel, from each T a man.
4:2 the people, from each T a man,
4:4 a man from each T;
7:1 of Zerah, of the T of Judah, took some
7:14 your tribes; and the T which the LORD takes
7:16 and brought Israel near T by tribe, and the
7:16 Israel near tribe by T, and the tribe of
7:16 by tribe, and the T of Judah was taken;
7:18 of Zerah, of the T of Judah, was taken.
13:7 tribes and half the T of Manasseh."
13:8 other half of the T of Manasseh the Reubenites
13:14 To the T of Levi alone Moses gave no
13:15 an inheritance to the T of the Reubenites according
13:24 inheritance also to the T of the Gadites, according
13:33 But to the T of Levi Moses gave no
15:1 The lot for the T of the people of
15:20 the inheritance of the T of the people of
15:21 cities belonging to the T of the people of
16:8 the inheritance of the T of the Ephraimites by
17:1 was made to the T of Manasseh, for he
17:2 the rest of the T of Manasseh, by their
17:14 And the T of Joseph spoke to Joshua, saying,
17:16 The T of Joseph said, "The hill country is
18:4 three men from each T, and I will send
18:7 Reuben and half the T of Manasseh have received
18:11 The lot of the T of Benjamin according to
18:11 it fell between the T of Judah and the
18:11 of Judah and the T of Joseph.
18:14 city belonging to the T of Judah.
18:20 the inheritance of the T of Benjamin, according to
18:21 the cities of the T of Benjamin according to
18:28 the inheritance of the T of Benjamin according to
19:1 for Simeon, for the T of Simeon, according to
19:1 the inheritance of the T of Judah.
19:8 the inheritance of the T of Simeon according to
19:9 The inheritance of the T of Simeon formed part
19:9 the portion of the T of Judah was too
19:9 large for them, the T of Simeon obtained an
19:10 came up for the T of Zebulun, according to
19:16 the inheritance of the T of Zebulun, according to
19:17 for Issachar, for the T of Issachar, according to
19:23 the inheritance of the T of Issachar, according to
19:24 came out for the T of Asher according to
19:31 the inheritance of the T of Asher according to
19:32 came out for the T of Naphtali, for the
19:32 of Naphtali, for the T of Naphtali, according to
19:39 the inheritance of the T of Naphtali according to
19:40 came out for the T of Dan, according to
19:48 the inheritance of the T of Dan, according to
20:8 the tableland, from the T of Reuben, and Ramoth
20:8 in Gilead, from the T of Gad, and Golan
20:8 in Bashan, from the T of Manasseh.
21:5 the families of the T of Ephraim, from the
21:5 of Ephraim, from the T of Dan and the
21:6 the families of the T of Issachar, from the
21:6 of Issachar, from the T of Asher, from the
21:6 of Asher, from the T of Naphtali, and from
21:7 families received from the T of Reuben, the tribe
21:7 tribe of Reuben, the T of Gad, and the
21:7 of Gad, and the T of Zebulun, twelve cities.
21:9 Out of the T of Judah and the tribe
21:9 of Judah and the T of Simeon they gave
21:17 then out of the T of Benjamin, Gibeon with
21:20 were out of the T of Ephraim.
21:23 and out of the T of Dan, Elteke with
21:28 and out of the T of Issachar, Kishion with
21:30 and out of the T of Asher, Mishal with
21:32 and out of the T of Naphtali, Kedesh in
21:34 given out of the T of Zebulun, Jokne-am with
21:36 and out of the T of Reuben, Bezer with
21:38 and out of the T of Gad, Ramoth in
22:7 one half of the T of Manasseh Moses had
Judg 4:6 ten thousand from the T of Naphtali and the
4:6 of Naphtali and the T of Zebulun.
13:2 of Zorah, of the T of the Danites, whose
18:1 in those days the T of the Danites was
18:2 whole number of their T, from Zorah and from
18:11 hundred men of the T of Dan, armed with
18:19 be priest to a T and family in Israel?"
18:30 were priests to the T of the Danites until
20:12 men through all the T of Benjamin, saying, "What
21:3 should be today one T lacking in Israel?"
21:6 brother, and said, "One T is cut off from
21:17 of Benjamin, that a T be not blotted out
21:24 every man to his T and family, and they
1Sam 9:21 the families of the T of Benjamin?
10:20 Israel near, and the T of Benjamin was taken
10:21 He brought the T of Benjamin near by its
2Sam 15:2 such and such a T in Israel,"
1Kgs 7:14 a widow of the T of Naphtali, and his
11:13 I will give one T to your son, for
11:32 he shall have one T, for the sake of
11:36 I will give one T, that David my servant
12:20 of David, but the T of Judah only.
12:21 of Judah, and the T of Benjamin, a hundred
2Kgs 17:18 was left but the T of Judah only.
1Chr 6:60 lands; and from the T of Benjamin, Geba with
6:61 the family of the T, out of the half-tribe,
6:66 territory out of the T of Ephraim.
6:72 and out of the T of Issachar: Kedesh with
6:74 lands; out of the T of Asher: Mashal with
6:76 and out of the T of Naphtali: Kedesh in
6:77 allotted out of the T of Zebulun: Rimmono with
6:78 Jordan, out of the T of Reuben: Bezer in
6:80 and out of the T of Gad: Ramoth in
23:14 were named among the T of Levi.
Tob 1:1 of Asiel and the T of Naphtali,
1:4 young man, the whole T of Naphtali my forefather
4:12 not of your father's T; for we are the
5:8 may learn to what T he belongs, and whether
5:10 "My brother, to what T and family do you
5:11 you looking for a T and a family or

5:13 tried to learn your T and family.
Jud 6:15 of Micah, of the T of Simeon, and Chabris
8:2 who belonged to her T and family, had died
8:18 has there been any T or family or people
9:14 whole nation and every T to know and understand
Esth 11:2 of Kish, of the T of Benjamin, had a
14:5 have heard in the T of my family that
Ps 74:2 redeemed to be the T of thy heritage!
78:67 did not choose the T of Ephraim;
78:68 but he chose the T of Judah, Mount Zion,
Sir 16:4 people, but through a T of lawless men it
45:6 like him, of the T of Levi.
45:25 of Jesse, of the T of Judah: the heritage
Jer 10:16 and Israel is the T of his inheritance; the
51:19 and Israel is the T of his inheritance; the
Ezek 47:23 In whatever T the alien resides, there you shall
Dan 1:6 and Azariah of the T of Judah.
Mic 6:9 thy name: "Hear, O T and assembly of the
2Mac 3:4 named Simon, of the T of Benjamin, who had
Lk 2:36 of Phanu-el, of the T of Asher; she was
Acts 13:21 a man of the T of Benjamin, for forty
Rom 11:1 a member of the T of Benjamin.
Phil 3:5 of Israel, of the T of Benjamin, a Hebrew
Heb 7:13 spoken belonged to another T, from which no one
7:14 in connection with that T Moses said nothing about
Rev 5:5 the Lion of the T of Judah, the Root
5:9 for God from every T and tongue and people
7:4 sealed, out of every T of the sons of
7:5 sealed out of the T of Judah, twelve thousand
7:5 twelve thousand of the T of Reuben, twelve thousand
7:5 twelve thousand of the T of Gad,
7:6 twelve thousand of the T of Asher, twelve thousand
7:6 twelve thousand of the T of Naphtali, twelve
7:6 twelve thousand of the T of Manasseh,
7:7 twelve thousand of the T of Simeon, twelve thousand
7:7 twelve thousand of the T of Levi, twelve thousand
7:7 twelve thousand of the T of Issachar,
7:8 twelve thousand of the T of Zebulun, twelve thousand
7:8 twelve thousand of the T of Joseph, twelve thousand
7:8 sealed out of the T of Benjamin.
13:7 given it over every T and people and tongue
14:6 to every nation and T and tongue and people;

TRIBES (127)

Gen 25:16 encampments, twelve princes according to their T
49:16 as one of the T of Israel.
49:28 these are the twelve T of Israel; and this
Ex 24:4 according to the twelve T of Israel.
28:21 each engraved with its name, for the twelve T
39:14 each engraved with its name, for the twelve T
Num 1:16 leaders of their ancestral T, the heads of the
7:2 the leaders of the T, who were over those
10:4 the heads of the T of Israel, shall gather
26:55 the names of the T of their fathers they
30:1 the heads of the T of the people of
31:4 from each of the T of Israel to the
32:28 fathers' houses of the T of the people of
33:54 his; according to the T of your fathers you
34:13 give to the nine T and to the half-tribe;
34:15 of Manasseh; the two T and the half-tribe have
35:8 Israel, from the larger T you shall take many,
35:8 and from the smaller T you shall take few;
36:3 sons of the other T of the people of
36:9 for each of the T of the people of
Deut 1:13 men, according to your T, and I will appoint
1:15 the heads of your T, wise and experienced men,
1:15 commanders of tens, and officers, throughout your T
5:23 the heads of your T, and your elders;
12:5 out of all your T to put his name
12:14 in one of your T, there you shall offer
16:18 you, according to your T; and they shall judge
18:5 out of all your T, to stand and minister
29:10 the heads of your T, your elders, and your
29:21 out from all the T of Israel for calamity,
31:28 the elders of your T, and your officers, that
33:5 were gathered, all the T of Israel together.
Josh 3:12 twelve men from the T of Israel, from each
4:5 the number of the T of the people of
4:8 the number of the T of the people of
7:14 brought near by your T; and the tribe which
12:7 their land to the T of Israel as a
13:7 inheritance to the nine T and half the tribe
14:1 fathers' houses of the T of the people of
14:2 had commanded Moses for the nine and one-half T
14:3 the two and one-half T beyond the Jordan; but
14:4 of Joseph were two T, Manasseh and Ephraim; and
18:2 people of Israel seven T whose inheritance had not
19:51 fathers' houses of the T of the people of
21:1 fathers' houses of the T of the people of
21:4 by lot from the T of Judah, Simeon, and
21:16 out of these two T;
23:4 an inheritance for your T those nations that remain,
24:1 Joshua gathered all the T of Israel to Shechem,
Judg 18:1 no inheritance among the T of Israel had fallen
20:2 people, of all the T of Israel, presented themselves
20:10 hundred throughout all the T of Israel, and a
20:12 And the T of Israel sent men through all
21:5 "Which of all the T of Israel did not
21:8 is there of the T of Israel that did
21:15 a breach in the T of Israel.
1Sam 2:28 out of all the T of Israel to be
9:21 the least of the T of Israel?
10:19 the LORD by your T and by your thousands."
10:20 Samuel brought all the T of Israel near, and
15:17 the head of the T of Israel?
2Sam 5:1 Then all the T of Israel came to David
15:10 messengers throughout all the T of Israel, saying,
19:9 strife throughout all the T of Israel, saying, "The
20:14 passed through all the T of Israel to Abel
24:2 "Go through all the T of Israel, from Dan
1Kgs 8:1 the heads of the T, the leaders of the
8:16 city in all the T of Israel in which
11:31 will give you ten T
11:32 out of all the T of Israel),
11:35 hand, and will give it to you, ten T
14:21 out of all the T of Israel, to put
18:31 the number of the T of the sons of
2Kgs 21:7 out of all the T of Israel, I will
1Chr 6:62 cities out of the T of Issachar, Asher, Naphtali,
6:63 cities out of the T of Reuben, Gad, and
6:65 lot out of the T of Judah, Simeon, and
27:16 Over the T of Israel, for the Reubenites Eliezer
27:22 the leaders of the T of Israel.
28:1 the officials of the T, the officers of the
29:6 the leaders of the T, the commanders of thousands
2Chr 5:2 the heads of the T, the leaders of the
6:5 city in all the T of Israel in which
11:16 them from all the T of Israel to Jerusalem
12:13 out of all the T of Israel to put
33:7 out of all the T of Israel, I will
Ezra 6:17 the number of the T of Israel.
Tob 1:4 from among all the T of Israel, where all
1:4 Israel, where all the T should sacrifice and where
1:5 All the T that joined in apostasy used to
Jud 3:8 all their tongues and T should call upon him
Ps 78:55 possession and settled the T of Israel in their
105:37 was none among his T who stumbled.
122:4 together, to which the T go up, the tribes
122:4 tribes go up, the T of the LORD, as
Sir 36:11 Gather all the T of Jacob, and give them
44:24 his portions, and distributed them among twelve T
45:11 the number of the T of Israel;
48:10 and to restore the T of Jacob.
Is 19:13 the cornerstones of her T have led Egypt astray.
49:6 to raise up the T of Jacob and to
63:17 of thy servants, the T of thy heritage.
Jer 1:15 am calling all the T of the kingdoms of
25:9 send for all the T of the north, says
25:24 kings of the mixed T that dwell in the
Ezek 20:32 the nations, like the T of the countries, and
37:19 of Ephraim) and the T of Israel associated with
45:8 of Israel have the land according to their T
47:13 inheritance among the twelve T of Israel.
47:21 you according to the T of Israel.
47:22 an inheritance among the T of Israel.
48:1 the names of the T: Beginning at the northern
48:19 city, from all the T of Israel, shall till
48:23 the rest of the T: from the east side
48:29 an inheritance among the T of Israel, and these
48:31 being named after the T of Israel.
Hos 5:9 of punishment; among the T of Israel I declare
Zech 9:1 even as all the T of Israel;
Mt 19:28 thrones, judging the twelve T of Israel.
24:30 and then all the T of the earth will
Lk 22:30 thrones judging the twelve T of Israel.
Acts 26:7 to which our twelve T hope to attain, as
Jas 1:1 Christ, to the twelve T in the dispersion: Greeting.
Rev 1:7 pierced him; and all T of the earth will
7:9 every nation, from all T and peoples and tongues,
11:9 from the peoples and T and tongues and nations
21:12 names of the twelve T of the sons of

T

TRIGON (4)
Dan 3:5 the horn, pipe, lyre, T, harp, bagpipe, and every
3:7 the horn, pipe, lyre, T, harp, bagpipe, and every
3:10 the horn, pipe, lyre, T, harp, bagpipe, and every
3:15 the horn, pipe, lyre, T, harp, bagpipe, and every

TRIM
Ezek 44:20 long; they shall only T the hair of their

TRIMMED (2)
2Sam 19:24 dressed his feet, nor T his beard, nor washed
Mt 25:7 those maidens rose and T their lamps.

TRIP (2)
Ps 140:4 who have planned to T up my feet.
Sir 12:17 help you, he will T you by the heel;

TRIPOLIS
2Mac 14:1 into the harbor of T with a strong army

TRIPPED
Sir 23:8 and the arrogant are T by them.

TRIREMES
2Mac 4:20 carriers it was applied to the construction of T

TRIUMPH (17)
Deut 33:29 of your help, and the sword of your T
1Kgs 22:12 up to Ramoth-gilead and T; the LORD will give
22:15 him, "Go up and T; the LORD will give
2Chr 18:11 up to Ramoth-gilead and T; the LORD will give
18:14 answered, "Go up and T; they will be given
Job 17:4 to understanding, therefore thou wilt not let them T
Ps 54:7 eye has looked in T on my enemies.
59:10 let me look in T on my enemies.
60:8 cast my shoe; over Philistia I shout in T
108:9 cast my shoe; over Philistia I shout in T
118:7 I shall look in T on those who hate
Prov 28:12 When the righteous T, there is great glory; but
Wis 4:2 it marches crowned in T, victor in the contest
Is 45:25 offspring of Israel shall T and glory."
2Mac 13:16 camp with terror and confusion and withdrew in T
2Cor 2:14 always leads us in T, and through us spreads
2Thes 3:1 may speed on and T, as it did among

TRIUMPHANT (2)
Deut 32:27 say, "Our hand is T, the LORD has not
Zech 9:9 king comes to you; T and victorious is he,

TRIUMPHANTLY
Num 33:3 of Israel went out T in the sight of

TRIUMPHED (4)
Ex 15:1 LORD, for he has T gloriously; the horse and
15:21 LORD, for he has T gloriously; the horse and
Ps 41:11 my enemy has not T over me.
Lam 1:9 LORD, behold my affliction, for the enemy has T

TRIUMPHING
Col 2:15 public example of them, T over them in him.

TRIUMPHS (5)
Judg 5:11 there they repeat the T of the LORD, the
5:11 of the LORD, the T of his peasantry in
2Sam 22:51 Great T he gives to his king, and shows
Ps 18:50 Great T he gives to his king, and shows
Jas 2:13 no mercy; yet mercy T over judgment.

TRIVIAL
1Cor 6:2 you incompetent to try T cases?

TROAS (6)
Acts 16:8 so, passing by Mysia, they went down to T
16:11 Setting sail therefore from T, we made a direct
20:5 waiting for us at T,
20:6 came to them at T, where we stayed for
2Cor 2:12 When I came to T to preach the gospel
2Tim 4:13 left with Carpus at T, also the books, and

TROD (9)
Judg 9:27 from their vineyards and T them, and held festival,
20:43 they pursued them and T them down from Nohah
2Kgs 7:17 gate; and the people T upon him in the
7:20 him, for the people T upon him in the
Job 22:15 to the old way which wicked men have T
Is 41:3 on safely, by paths his feet have not T
63:3 was with me; I T them in my anger
63:6 I T down the peoples in my anger, I
Lk 12:1 gathered together that they T upon one another, he

TRODDEN (18)
Deut 1:36 upon which he has T, because he has wholly
Josh 14:9 which your foot has T shall be an inheritance
Job 28:8 proud beasts have not T it; the lion has
Ps 58:7 grass let them be T down and wither.
Is 14:19 like a dead body T under foot.
25:10 and Moab shall be T down in his place,
25:10 place, as straw is T down in a dung-pit.
28:3 of Ephraim will be T under foot;
63:3 "I have T the wine press alone, and from
63:18 while; our adversaries have T it down.
Jer 51:33 time when it is T; yet a little while
Lam 1:15 men; the Lord has T as in a wine
Ezek 34:19 eat what you have T with your feet, and
Mic 7:10 now she will be T down like the mire
Mt 5:13 be thrown out and T under foot by men.
Lk 8:5 the path, and was T under foot, and the
21:24 and Jerusalem will be T down by the Gentiles,
Rev 14:20 the wine press was T outside the city, and

TROOP (3)
2Sam 22:30 I can crush a T, and by my God
Ps 18:29 I can crush a T; and by my God
1Mac 10:77 he had a large T of cavalry and put

TROOPED
Jer 5:7 they committed adultery and T to the houses of

TROOPS (62)
Josh 11:4 out, with all their T, a great host, in
Judg 4:7 his chariots and his T; and I will give
1Sam 4:3 And when the T came to the camp, the
13:5 six thousand horsemen, and T like the sand on
2Sam 18:16 the trumpet, and the T came back from pursuing
1Kgs 16:15 Now the T were encamped against Gibbethon, which
16:16 the Philistines, and the T who were encamped heard
1Chr 12:18 received them, and made them officers of his T
12:23 divisions of the armed T, who came to David
12:24 and spear were six thousand eight hundred armed T
12:33 Zebulun fifty thousand seasoned T, equipped for
12:36 Asher forty thousand seasoned T ready for battle.
2Chr 13:13 from behind; thus his T were in front of
Jud 1:16 a vast body of T; and there he and
2:7 be plundered by my T,
2:15 and mustered the picked T by divisions as his
2:19 and horsemen and picked T of infantry.
Job 19:12 His T come on together; they have cast up
29:25 a king among his T, like one who comforts
Jer 50:37 upon all the foreign T in her midst, that
Ezek 12:14 helpers and all his T; and I will unsheathe
17:21 the pick of his T shall fall by the
Dan 11:15 or even his picked T, for there shall be
Nah 3:13 Behold, your T are women in your midst.
1Mac 2:31 officers, and to the T in Jerusalem the city
3:34 Lysias half of his T and the elephants, and
3:37 remaining half of his T and departed from Antioch
4:31 be ashamed of their T and their cavalry.
4:35 the rout of his T and observed the boldness
6:33 to Beth-zechariah, and his T made ready for battle
6:40 high hills, and some T were on the plain,
9:52 in them he put T and stores of food.
10:6 him authority to recruit T, to equip them with
10:8 the king had given him authority to recruit T
10:21 tabernacles, and he recruited T and equipped them
11:18 days later, and his T in the strongholds were
11:38 he dismissed all his T, each man to his
11:38 place, except the foreign T which he had recruited
11:38 So all the T who had served his fathers
11:39 that all the T were murmuring against Demetrius.
11:40 the hatred which the T of Demetrius had for
11:41 that he remove the T of the citadel from
11:41 from Jerusalem, and the T in the strongholds; for
11:43 me, for all my T have revolted."
11:55 All the T that Demetrius had cast off gathered
12:43 his friends and his T to obey him as
12:45 strongholds and the remaining T and all the officials,
12:46 he sent away the T, and they returned to
12:49 Then Trypho sent T and cavalry into Galilee and
13:43 encamped against Gazara and surrounded it with T
15:3 a host of mercenary T and have equipped warships,
15:10 All the T rallied to him, so that there
15:12 upon him, and his T had deserted him.

T

15:38 country, and gave him T of infantry and cavalry.
15:41 stationed there horsemen and T, so that they might
16:18 asking him to send T to aid him and
2Mac 4:29 left Crates, the commander of the Cyprian T
5:3 and drawn swords– T of horsemen drawn up,
5:5 When the T upon the wall had been forced
14:41 When the T were about to capture the tower
Mt 22:7 and he sent his T and destroyed those murderers
Rev 9:16 The number of the T of cavalry was twice

TROPHIES

2Mac 5:6 he was setting up T of victory over enemies

TROPHIMUS (3)

Acts 20:4 Derbe, and Timothy; and the Asians, Tychicus and T
21:29 they had previously seen T the Ephesian with him
2Tim 4:20 Erastus remained at Corinth; T I left ill at

TROTH

Ezek 16:8 yea, I plighted my T to you and entered

TROUBLE (118)

Gen 34:30 Levi, "You have brought T on me by making
Num 23:21 nor has he seen T in Israel.
33:55 sides, and they shall T you in the land
Josh 6:18 for destruction, and bring T upon it.
7:25 "Why did you bring T on us?
7:25 The LORD brings T on you today." And all
Judg 11:7 come to me now when you are in T
11:35 the cause of great T to me; for I
2Sam 11:25 not let this matter T you, for the sword
14:5 the king said to her, "What is your T
20:6 he get himself fortified cities, and cause us T
1Kgs 20:7 this man is seeking T; for he sent to
2Kgs 4:13 have taken all this T for us; what is
6:28 And the king asked her, "What is your T
6:33 him and said, "This T is from the LORD!
14:10 why should you provoke T so that you fall,
2Chr 25:19 why should you provoke T so that you fall,
Neh 1:3 exile are in great T and shame; the wall
2:17 them, "You see the T we are in, how
Tob 6:7 or evil spirit gives T to any one, you
Job 3:10 mother's womb, nor hide T from my eyes.
3:26 have no rest; but T comes."
4:8 plow iniquity and sow T reap the same.
5:6 the dust, nor does T sprout from the ground;
5:7 man is born to T as the sparks fly
14:1 woman is of few days, and full of T
27:9 hear his cry, when T comes upon him?
38:23 for the time of T, for the day of
Ps 9:9 for the oppressed, a stronghold in times of T
10:1 Why dost thou hide thyself in times of T
10:14 yea, thou dost note T and vexation, that thou
20:1 The LORD answer you in the day of T
22:11 far from me, for T is near and there
25:18 my affliction and my T, and forgive all my
27:5 in the day of T; he will conceal me
32:7 thou preservest me from T; thou dost encompass me
37:39 he is their refuge in the time of T
41:1 in the day of T;
46:1 refuge and strength, a very present help in T
49:5 fear in times of T, when the iniquity of
50:15 in the day of T; I will deliver you,
54:7 delivered me from every T, and my eye has
55:2 and answer me; I am overcome by my T
55:3 For they bring T upon me, and in anger
55:10 walls; and mischief and T are within it,
66:14 and my mouth promised when I was in T
73:5 They are not in T as other men are;
77:2 the day of my T I seek the Lord;
86:7 the day of my T I call on thee,
90:10 is but toil and T; they are soon gone,
91:15 be with him in T, I will rescue him
94:13 respite from days of T, until a pit is
107:2 he has redeemed from T
107:6 the LORD in their T, and he delivered them
107:13 the LORD in their T, and he delivered them
107:19 the LORD in their T, and he delivered them
107:28 the LORD in their T, and he delivered them
107:39 brought low through oppression, T, and sorrow,
119:143 T and anguish have come upon me, but thy
138:7 in the midst of T, thou dost preserve my
142:2 him, I tell my T before him.
143:11 In thy righteousness bring me out of T
Prov 10:10 winks the eye causes T, but he who boldly
11:8 righteous is delivered from T, and the wicked gets
12:13 of his lips, but the righteous escapes from T
12:21 the righteous, but the wicked are filled with T
13:17 messenger plunges men into T, but a faithful envoy
15:6 is much treasure, but T befalls the income of
15:16 than great treasure and T with it.
15:27 for unjust gain makes T for his household, but
16:4 purpose, even the wicked for the day of T
21:23 mouth and his tongue keeps himself out of T
25:19 man in time of T is like a bad
27:9 heart glad, but the soul is torn by T
Eccl 8:6 and way, although man's T lies heavy upon him.
Sir 6:8 not stand by you in your day of T
6:10 not stand by you in your day of T
22:11 from him to escape T, and you will not
29:4 a windfall, and cause T to those who help
37:4 but in time of T are against him.
40:5 anger and envy and T and unrest, and fear
40:24 for a time of T, but almsgiving rescues better
Is 30:6 Through a land of T and anguish, from where
33:2 every morning, our salvation in the time of T
46:7 does not answer or save him from his T
Jer 2:27 the time of their T they say, 'Arise and
2:28 in your time of T; for as many as
11:12 cannot save them in the time of their T
11:14 call to me in the time of their T
14:8 savior in time of T, why shouldst thou be
15:11 in the time of T and in the time
16:19 in the day of T, to thee shall the
51:2 her from every side on the day of T
Lam 1:21 have heard of my T; they are glad that
Ezek 32:2 forth in your rivers, T the waters with your
32:9 "I will T the hearts of many peoples, when
32:13 foot of man shall T them any more, nor
32:13 the hoofs of beasts T them.
Dan 3:50 all or hurt or T them.
12:1 be a time of T, such as never has
Nah 1:7 in the day of T; he knows those who
Hab 1:3 thou make me see wrongs and look upon T
3:16 for the day of T to come upon people
2Mac 2:30 side and to take T with details,
4:31 hastily to settle the T, leaving Andronicus, a man
13:4 blame for all the T, he ordered them to
Mt 6:34 Let the day's own T be sufficient for the
26:10 them, "Why do you T the woman?
28:14 will satisfy him and keep you out of T
Mk 5:35 Why T the Teacher any further?"
14:6 alone; why do you T her?
Lk 7:6 him, "Lord, do not T yourself, for I am
8:49 is dead; do not T the Teacher any more."
Acts 15:19 that we should not T those of the Gentiles
Gal 1:7 there are some who T you and want to
6:17 Henceforth let no man T me; for I bear
Phil 4:14 it was kind of you to share my T
Heb 12:15 spring up and cause T, and by it the

TROUBLED (41)

Gen 40:6 in the morning and saw them, they were T
41:8 morning his spirit was T; and he sent and
1Sam 1:15 am a woman sorely T; I have drunk neither
14:29 said, "My father has T the land; see how
1Kgs 18:18 answered, "I have not T Israel; but you have,
2Kgs 6:11 of Syria was greatly T because of this thing;
2Chr 15:6 against city, for God T them with every sort
Tob 6:7 person will never be T again.
Esth 11:9 whole righteous nation was T; they feared the evils
Ps 6:2 O LORD, heal me, for my bones are T
6:3 My soul also is sorely T
6:10 be ashamed and sorely T; they shall turn back,
77:4 closing; I am so T that I cannot speak.
Wis 16:6 the end; they were T for a little while
18:17 in dreadful dreams greatly T them, and unexpected
Sir 30:7 his feelings will be T at every cry.
40:6 on watch, he is T by the visions of
Jer 49:23 in fear, they are T like the sea which
Dan 2:1 and his spirit was T, and his sleep left
2:3 and my spirit is T to know the dream."
9:25 moat, but in a T time.
1Mac 3:5 he burned those who T his people.
2Mac 8:32 one who had greatly T the Jews.
9:24 realm would not be T, for they would know
14:28 to Nicanor, he was T and grieved that he
Mt 2:3 heard this, he was T, and all Jerusalem with
26:37 of Zebedee, he began to be sorrowful and T
Mk 14:33 John, and began to be greatly distressed and T
Lk 1:12 And Zechariah was T when he saw him, and
1:29 But she was greatly T at the saying, and

6:18 and those who were T with unclean spirits were
10:41 you are anxious and T about many things;
24:38 them, "Why are you T, and why do questionings
Jn 5:6 when the water is T, and while I am
11:33 moved in spirit and T;
12:27 "Now is my soul T
13:21 thus spoken, he was T in spirit, and testified,
14:1 not your hearts be T; believe in God, believe
14:27 not your hearts be T, neither let them be
Acts 15:24 persons from us have T you with words, unsettling
1Pet 3:14 of them, nor be T,

TROUBLER (2)

1Kgs 18:17 "Is it you, you T of Israel?"
1Chr 2:7 of Carmi: Achar, the T of Israel, who transgressed

TROUBLES (19)

Gen 21:17 said to her, "What T you, Hagar?
Deut 31:17 and many evils and T will come upon them,
31:21 when many evils and T have come upon them,
Job 5:19 deliver you from six T; in seven there shall
Ps 25:17 Relieve the T of my heart, and bring me
25:22 Redeem Israel, O God, out of all his T
34:6 him, and saved him out of all his T
34:17 hears, and delivers them out of all their T
71:20 me see many sore T wilt revive me again;
88:3 soul is full of T, and my life draws
Prov 11:29 He who T his household will inherit wind, and
Wis 10:9 Wisdom rescued from T those who served her.
Sir 3:25 will be burdened by T, and the sinner will
4:3 not add to the T of an angry mind,
Is 65:16 truth; because the former T are forgotten and are
1Mac 2:43 fugitives to escape their T joined them and
10:15 done, and of the T that they had endured.
15:12 for he knew that T had converged upon him,
1Cor 7:28 marry will have worldly T, and I would spare

TROUBLING (3)

Job 3:17 the wicked cease from T, and there the weary
1Mac 7:22 and all who were T their people joined him.
Gal 5:10 and he who is T you will bear his

TROUGH

Gen 24:20 her jar into the T and ran again to

TROUGHS (2)

Gen 30:38 that is, the watering T, where the flocks came
Ex 2:16 water, and filled the T to water their father's

TRUE (132)

Num 11:23 my word will come T for you or not."
Deut 13:14 behold, if it be T and certain that such
17:4 and if it is T and certain that such
18:22 to pass or come T, that is a word
22:20 if the thing is T, that the tokens of
Josh 2:4 them; and she said, T, men came to me,
Judg 13:12 when your words come T, what is to be
13:17 when your words come T, we may honor you?"
Ruth 3:12 And now it is T that I am a
1Sam 9:6 held in honor; all that he says comes T
2Sam 7:28 and thy words are T, and thou hast promised
20:21 That is not T
22:31 of the LORD proves T; he is a shield
1Kgs 8:61 heart therefore be wholly T to the LORD our
10:6 king, "The report was T which I heard in
11:4 heart was not wholly T to the LORD his
15:3 heart was not wholly T to the LORD his
15:14 of Asa was wholly T to the LORD all
2Kgs 9:12 said, "That is not T; tell us now." And
10:15 him, "Is your heart T to my heart as
2Chr 9:5 king, "The report was T which I heard in
15:3 Israel was without the T God, and without a
Neh 9:13 them right ordinances and T laws, good statutes and
Tob 3:2 and thou dost render T and righteous judgment for
3:5 thy many judgments are T in exacting penalty from
4:6 you do what is T, your ways will prosper
7:10 let me explain the T situation to you.
13:6 to do what is T before him, then he
Jud 8:28 spoken out of a T heart, and there is
10:13 to give him a T report; and I will
11:10 mind, for it is T: our nation cannot be
Job 5:27 Lo, this we have searched out; it is T
19:4 even if it be T that I have erred,
Ps 18:30 of the LORD proves T; he is a shield
19:9 of the LORD are T, and righteous altogether.
78:37 him; they were not T to his covenant.
119:142 is righteous for ever, and thy law is T
119:151 near, O LORD, and all thy commandments are T
141:6 learn that the word of the LORD is T
Prov 22:21 what is right and T, that you may give
22:21 you may give a T answer to those who
30:5 word of God proves T; he is a shield
Wis 1:6 inmost feelings, and a T observer of his heart,
2:17 if his words are T, and let us test
5:21 lightning will fly with T aim, and will leap
12:27 and recognized as the T God him whom they
15:1 God, art kind and T, patient, and ruling all
Sir 28:6 and death, and be T to the commandments.
32:16 the Lord will form T judgments, and like a
34:4 And from something false what will be T
Is 43:9 and let them hear and say, It is T
Jer 10:10 the LORD is the T God; he is the
28:6 you have prophesied come T, and bring back to
42:5 the LORD be a T and faithful witness against
50:7 against the LORD, their T habitation, the LORD, the
Ezek 18:8 hand from iniquity, executes T justice between man
Dan 3:14 to them, "Is it T, O Shadrach, Meshach, and
3:27 all thy works are T and thy ways right,
3:28 Thou hast executed T judgments in all that thou
3:31 thou hast done in T judgment.
3:92 They answered the king, T, O king."
8:26 has been told is T; but seal up the
10:1 And the word was T, and it was a
Jon 2:8 vain idols forsake their T loyalty.
Zech 7:9 LORD of hosts, Render T judgments, show kindness
8:16 gates judgments that are T and make for peace,
Mal 2:6 T instruction was in his mouth, and no wrong
Mt 22:16 know that you are T, and teach the way
Mk 12:14 know that you are T, and care for no
Lk 16:11 entrust to you the T riches?
Jn 1:9 The T light that enlightens every man was coming
3:21 who does what is T comes to the light,
3:33 sets his seal to this, that God is T
4:23 now is, when the T worshipers will worship the
4:37 here the saying holds T, 'One sows and another
5:30 my testimony is not T;
5:31 the testimony which he bears to me is T
6:32 Father gives you the T bread from heaven.
7:18 who sent him is T, and in him there
7:28 who sent me is T, and him you do
8:13 bearing witness to yourself; your testimony is not T
8:14 myself, my testimony is T, for I know whence
8:16 judge, my judgment is T, for it is not
8:17 of two men is T;
8:26 who sent me is T, and I declare to
10:41 everything that John said about this man was T
15:1 "I am the T vine, and my Father is
17:3 know thee the only T God, and Jesus Christ
19:35 witness—his testimony is T, and he knows that
21:24 things; and we know that his testimony is T
Rom 2:28 one outwardly, nor is T circumcision something
3:4 Let God be T though every man be false,
11:20 That is T
1Cor 15:15 raise if it is T that the dead are
2Cor 6:8 impostors, and yet are T;
7:14 said to you was T, so our boasting before
7:14 true, so our boasting before Titus has proved T
12:12 The signs of a T apostle were performed among
Eph 4:24 likeness of God in T righteousness and holiness.
5:9 good and right and T,
Phil 3:3 For we are the T circumcision, who worship God
3:16 Only let us hold T to what we have
4:3 I ask you also, T yokefellow, help these women,
4:8 brethren, whatever is T, whatever is honorable,
1Thes 1:9 serve a living and T God,
1Tim 1:2 hope, To Timothy, my T child in the faith:
Tit 1:3 Savior; To Titus, my T child in a common
1:12 This testimony is T
2:10 to show entire and T fidelity, so that in
Heb 8:2 the sanctuary and the T tent which is set
9:24 a copy of the T one, but into heaven
10:1 come instead of the T form of these realities,
10:22 draw near with a T heart in full assurance
1Pet 5:12 that this is the T grace of God; stand
2Pet 2:22 them according to the T proverb, The dog turns
1Jn 2:8 new commandment, which is T in him and in
2:8 passing away and the T light is already shining.
2:27 about everything, and is T, and is no lie,
5:20 know him who is T; and we are in
5:20 in him who is T, in his Son Jesus
5:20 This is the T God and eternal life.
3Jn 1:12 him too, and you know my testimony is T

Rev 3:7 the holy one, the T one, who has the
3:14 Amen, the faithful and T witness, the beginning of
6:10 Sovereign Lord, holy and T, how long before thou
15:3 Just and T are thy ways, O King of
16:7 Lord God the Almighty, T and just are thy
19:2 for his judgments are T and just; he has
19:9 to me, "These are T words of God."
19:11 is called Faithful and T, and in righteousness he
21:5 "Write this, for these words are trustworthy and T
22:6 said to me, "These words are trustworthy and T

TRULY (138)

Gen 4:24 Cain is avenged sevenfold, T Lamech seventy-
24:49 will deal loyally and T with my master, tell
33:10 from my hand; for T to see your face
47:29 to deal loyally and T with me.
Num 14:21 to your word; but T, as I live, and
Josh 2:24 they said to Joshua, T the LORD has given
1Sam 20:3 he be grieved.' But T, as the LORD lives
25:34 come to meet me, T by morning there had
Job 9:2 Then Job answered: T I know that it
36:4 For T my words are not false; one who
Ps 49:7 T no man can ransom himself, or give to
66:19 But T God has listened; he has given heed
73:1 T God is good to the upright, to those
73:18 T thou dost set them in slippery places; thou
Song 1:16 are beautiful, my beloved, T lovely.
Sir 42:8 Then you will be T instructed, and will be
Is 45:15 T, thou art a God who hidest thyself, O
Jer 3:23 T the hills are a delusion, the orgies on
3:23 T in the LORD our God is the salvation
7:5 LORD.' "For if you T amend your ways and
7:5 your doings, if you T execute justice one with
10:19 But I said, T this is an affliction, and
28:9 that the LORD has T sent the prophet."
Dan 2:47 king said to Daniel, T, your God is God
Mt 5:18 For T, I say to you, till heaven and
5:26 be put in prison; T, I say to you,
6:2 T, I say to you, they have received their
6:5 T, I say to you, they have received their
6:16 T, I say to you, they have received their
8:10 those who followed him, T, I say to you,
10:15 T, I say to you, it shall be more
10:23 to the next; for T, I say to you,
10:42 he is a disciple, T, I say to you,
11:11 thy way before thee.' T, I say to you,
13:17 T, I say to you, many prophets and righteous
14:33 boat worshiped him, saying, T you are the Son
16:28 T, I say to you, there are some standing
17:20 For T, I say to you, if you have
18:3 of them, and said, T, I say to you,
18:12 if he finds it, T, I say to you,
18:17 T, I say to you, whatever you bind on
19:23 said to his disciples, T, I say to you,
19:28 Jesus said to them, T, I say to you,
21:21 And Jesus answered them, T, I say to you,
21:31 Jesus said to them, T, I say to you,
23:35 T, I say to you, all this will come
24:2 T, I say to you, there will not be
24:34 T, I say to you, this generation will not
24:47 T, I say to you, he will set him
25:12 us.' But he replied, T, I say to you,
25:40 King will answer them, T, I say to you,
25:45 he will answer them, T, I say to you,
26:13 T, I say to you, wherever this gospel is
26:21 were eating, he said, T, I say to you,
26:34 Jesus said to him, T, I say to you,
27:54 with awe, and said, T this was the Son
Mk 3:28 T, I say to you, all sins will be
8:12 T, I say to you, no sign shall be
9:1 he said to them, T, I say to you,
9:41 For T, I say to you, whoever gives you
10:15 T, I say to you, whoever does not receive
10:29 Jesus said, T, I say to you, there is
11:23 T, I say to you, whoever says to this
12:14 position of men, but T teach the way of
12:32 right, Teacher; you have T said that he is
12:43 and said to them, T, I say to you,
13:30 T, I say to you, this generation will not
14:9 And T, I say to you, wherever the gospel
14:18 table eating, Jesus said, T, I say to you,
14:25 T, I say to you, I shall not drink
14:30 Jesus said to him, T, I say to you,
15:38 his last, he said, T this man was the
Lk 4:24 And he said, T, I say to you, no
9:27 But I tell you T, there are some standing
12:37 awake when he comes; T, I say to you,
12:44 T, I say to you, he will set him
18:17 T, I say to you, whoever does not receive
18:29 he said to them, T, I say to you,
20:21 show no partiality, but T teach the way of
21:3 And he said, T I tell you, this poor
21:32 T, I say to you, this generation will not
23:42 he said to him, T, I say to you,
Jn 1:51 he said to him, T, truly, I say to
1:51 said to him, "Truly, T, I say to you,
3:3 Jesus answered him, T, truly, I say to you,
3:3 Jesus answered him, "Truly, T, I say to you,
3:5 Jesus answered, T, truly, I say to you, unless
3:5 Jesus answered, "Truly, T, I say to you, unless
3:11 T, truly, I say to you, we speak of
3:11 Truly, T, I say to you, we speak of
4:18 have is not your husband; this you said T
5:18 Jesus said to them, T, truly, I say to
5:18 said to them, "Truly, T, I say to you,
5:23 T, truly, I say to you, he who hears
5:23 Truly, T, I say to you, he who hears
5:24 T, truly, I say to you, the hour is
5:24 "Truly, T, I say to you, the hour is
6:26 Jesus answered them, T, truly, I say to you,
6:26 Jesus answered them, "Truly, T, I say to you,
6:32 then said to them, T, truly, I say to
6:32 said to them, "Truly, T, I say to you,
6:47 T, truly, I say to you, he who believes
6:47 Truly, T, I say to you, he who believes
6:53 Jesus said to them, T, truly, I say to
6:53 said to them, "Truly, T, I say to you,
8:31 my word, you are T my disciples,
8:34 Jesus answered them, T, truly, I say to you,
8:34 Jesus answered them, "Truly, T, I say to you,
8:51 T, truly, I say to you, if any one
8:51 Truly, T, I say to you, if any one
8:58 Jesus said to them, T, truly, I say to
8:58 said to them, "Truly, T, I say to you,
10:1 T, truly, I say to you, he who does
10:1 "Truly, T, I say to you, he who does
10:7 again said to them, T, truly, I say to
10:7 said to them, "Truly, T, I say to you,
12:24 T, truly, I say to you, unless a grain
12:24 Truly, T, I say to you, unless a grain
13:16 T, truly, I say to you, a servant is
13:16 Truly, T, I say to you, a servant is
13:20 T, truly, I say to you, he who receives
13:20 Truly, T, I say to you, he who receives
13:21 in spirit, and testified, T, truly, I say to
13:21 spirit, and testified, "Truly, T, I say to you,
13:38 T, truly, I say to you, the cock will
13:38 Truly, T, I say to you, the cock will
14:12 T, truly, I say to you, he who believes
14:12 "Truly, T, I say to you, he who believes
16:20 T, truly, I say to you, you will weep
16:20 Truly, T, I say to you, you will weep
16:23 T, truly, I say to you, if you ask
16:23 Truly, T, I say to you, if you ask
21:18 T, truly, I say to you, when you were
21:18 Truly, T, I say to you, when you were
Acts 4:27 his Anointed– for T in this city there
10:34 his mouth and said: T I perceive that God
1Cor 11:31 if we judged ourselves T, we should not be
1Jn 2:5 his word, in him T love for God is

TRUMPET (68)

Ex 19:13 not live.' When the T sounds a long blast,
19:16 and a very loud T blast, so that all
19:19 the sound of the T grew louder and louder,
20:18 the sound of the T and the mountain smoking,
Lev 25:9 send abroad the loud T on the tenth day
25:9 shall send abroad the T throughout all your land.
Josh 6:5 the sound of the T, then all the people
6:20 the sound of the T, the people raised a
Judg 3:27 arrived, he sounded the T in the hill country
6:34 and he sounded the T, and the Abiezrites were
7:18 When I blow the T, I and all who
1Sam 13:3 And Saul blew the T throughout all the land,
2Sam 2:28 So Joab blew the T; and all the men
15:10 the sound of the T, then say, 'Absalom is
18:16 Then Joab blew the T, and the troops came
20:1 and he blew the T, and said, "We have
20:22 So he blew the T, and they dispersed from
1Kgs 1:34 Israel; then blow the T, and say, 'Long live
1:39 Then they blew the T; and all the people
1:41 the sound of the T, he said, "What does

T

2Kgs 9:13 and they blew the T, and proclaimed, "Jehu is
Neh 4:18 man who sounded the T was beside me.
4:20 the sound of the T, rally to us there.
Job 39:24 cannot stand still at the sound of the T
39:25 When the T sounds, he says 'Aha!' He smells
Ps 47:5 shout, the LORD with the sound of a T
81:3 Blow the T at the new moon, at the
150:3 Praise him with T sound; praise him with lute
Is 18:3 When a T is blown, hear!
27:13 that day a great T will be blown, and
58:1 your voice like a T; declare to my people
Jer 4:5 and say, "Blow the T through the land; cry
4:19 the sound of the T, the alarm of war.
4:21 the standard, and hear the sound of the T
6:1 Blow the T in Tekoa, and raise a signal
6:17 the sound of the T But they said, 'We
42:14 the sound of the T, or be hungry for
51:27 the earth, blow the T among the nations; prepare
Ezek 7:14 "They have blown the T and made all ready;
33:3 land and blows the T and warns the people;
33:4 the sound of the T does not take warning,
33:5 the sound of the T, and did not take
33:6 does not blow the T, so that the people
Hos 5:8 horn in Gibe-ah, the T in Ramah.
8:1 Set the T to your lips, for a vulture
Joel 2:1 Blow the T in Zion; sound the alarm on
2:15 Blow the T in Zion; sanctify a fast; call
Amos 2:2 the sound of the T;
3:6 Is a T blown in a city, and the
Zeph 1:16 darkness, a day of T blast and battle cry
Zech 9:14 GOD will sound the T, and march forth in
Mt 6:2 give alms, sound no T before you, as the
24:31 angels with a loud T call, and they will
1Cor 15:52 the twinkling of an eye, at the last T
15:52 For the T will sound, and the dead will
1Thes 4:16 the sound of the T of God.
Heb 12:19 the sound of a T, and a voice whose
Rev 1:10 loud voice like a T
4:1 to me like a T, said, "Come up hither,
8:7 first angel blew his T, and there followed hail
8:8 second angel blew his T, and something like a
8:10 third angel blew his T, and a great star
8:12 fourth angel blew his T, and a third of
9:1 fifth angel blew his T, and I saw a
9:13 sixth angel blew his T, and I heard a
9:14 angel who had the T, "Release the four angels
10:7 the days of the T call to be sounded
11:15 seventh angel blew his T, and there were loud

TRUMPETERS (6)

2Kgs 11:14 the captains and the T beside the king, and
2Chr 5:12 twenty priests who were T;
5:13 the duty of the T and singers to make
23:13 the captains and the T beside the king, and
29:28 singers sang, and the T sounded; all this continued
Rev 18:22 of flute players and T, shall be heard in

TRUMPETS (62)

Lev 23:24 proclaimed with blast of T, a holy convocation.
Num 10:2 Moses, "Make two silver T; of hammered work you
10:8 sons of Aaron, the priests, shall blow the T
10:8 The T shall be to you for a perpetual
10:9 an alarm with the T, that you may be
10:10 you shall blow the T over your burnt offerings
29:1 you to blow the T,
31:6 the sanctuary and the T for the alarm in
Josh 6:4 priests shall bear seven T of rams' horns before
6:4 the city seven times, the priests blowing the T
6:6 seven priests bear seven T of rams' horns before
6:8 priests bearing the seven T of rams' horns before
6:8 went forward, blowing the T, with the ark of
6:9 priests who blew the T, and the rear guard
6:9 the ark, while the T blew continually.
6:13 priests bearing the seven T of rams' horns before
6:13 passed on, blowing the T continually; and the armed
6:13 the LORD, while the T blew continually.
6:16 priests had blown the T, Joshua said to the
6:20 people shouted, and the T were blown.
Judg 7:8 their hands, and their T; and he sent all
7:16 three companies, and put T into the hands of
7:18 me, then blow the T also on every side
7:19 and they blew the T and smashed the jars
7:20 three companies blew the T and broke the jars,
7:20 their right hands the T to blow; and they
7:22 blew the three hundred T, the LORD set every
2Kgs 11:14 the people of the land rejoicing and blowing T
12:13 of silver, snuffers, bowls, T, or any vessels of
1Chr 13:8 lyres and harps and tambourines and cymbals and T
15:24 priests, should blow the T before the ark of
15:28 sound of the horn, T, and cymbals, and made
16:6 priests were to blow T continually, before the ark
16:42 Heman and Jeduthun had T and cymbals for the
2Chr 5:13 song was raised, with T and cymbals and other
7:6 them the priests sounded T; and all Israel stood.
13:12 priests with their battle T to sound the call
13:14 to the LORD, and the priests blew the T
15:14 with shouting, and with T, and with horns.
20:28 harps and lyres and T, to the house of
23:13 land rejoicing and blowing T, and the singers with
29:26 instruments of David, and the priests with the T
29:27 also, and the T, accompanied by the instruments
Ezra 3:10 vestments came forward with T, and the Levites, the
Neh 12:35 the priests' sons with T: Zechariah the son of
12:41 Zechariah, and Hananiah, with T;
Ps 98:6 With T and the sound of the horn make
Sir 50:16 shouted, they sounded the T of hammered work, they
1Mac 3:54 Then they sounded the T and gave a loud
4:13 with Judas blew their T
4:40 the signal on the T, and cried out to
5:31 up to Heaven with T and loud shouts,
5:33 companies, who sounded their T and cried aloud in
6:33 troops made ready for battle and sounded their T
7:45 followed kept sounding the battle call on the T
9:12 the sound of the T; and the men with
9:12 and the men with Judas also blew their T
16:8 And they sounded the T, and Cendebeus and his
2Mac 15:25 his men advanced with T and battle songs;
Rev 8:2 before God, and seven T were given to them.
8:6 who had the seven T made ready to blow
8:13 blasts of the other T which the three angels

TRUNK

1Sam 5:4 the threshold; only the T of Dagon was left

TRUNKS

Sir 50:12 surrounded him like the T of palm trees,

TRUST (102)

Ex 22:9 "For every breach of T, whether it is for
Judg 11:20 But Sihon did not T Israel to pass through
1Chr 9:22 the seer established them in their office of T
Tob 1:14 talents of silver in T with Gabael, the brother
4:1 he had left in T with Gabael at Rages
4:20 which I left in T with Gabael the son
Jud 9:7 their foot soldiers; they T in shield and spear,
Job 4:18 servants he puts no T, and his angels he
8:14 in sunder, and his T is a spider's web.
15:15 Behold, God puts no T in his holy ones,
15:31 Let him not T in emptiness, deceiving himself; for
31:24 have made gold my T, or called fine gold
Ps 4:5 sacrifices, and put your T in the LORD.
9:10 thy name put their T in thee, for thou,
25:2 God, in thee I T, let me not be
31:6 vain idols; but I T in the LORD.
31:14 But I T in thee, O LORD, I say,
33:21 in him, because we T in his holy name.
37:3 T in the LORD, and do good; so you
37:5 way to the LORD; T in him, and he
40:3 fear, and put their T in the LORD.
40:4 makes the LORD his T, who does not turn
44:6 my bow do I T, nor can my sword
49:6 surrounds me, men who T in their wealth and
52:8 I T in the steadfast love of God for
55:23 But I will T in thee.
56:3 afraid, I put my T in thee.
56:4 praise, in God I T without a fear.
56:11 praise, in God I T without a fear.
62:8 T in him at all times, O people; pour
71:5 art my hope, my T, O LORD, from my
78:22 God, and did not T his saving power.
91:2 and my fortress; my God, in whom I T
115:8 so are all who T in them.
115:9 O Israel, T in the LORD!
115:10 of Aaron, put your T in the LORD!
115:11 who fear the LORD, T in the LORD!
119:42 taunt me, for I T in thy word.
125:1 Those who T in the LORD are like Mount
143:8 steadfast love, for in thee I put my T
146:3 Put not your T in princes, in a son
Prov 3:5 T in the LORD with all your heart, and
21:22 and brings down the stronghold in which they T
22:19 That your T may be in the LORD, I

T

	25:19	T in a faithless man in time of trouble
Wis	3:9	Those who T in him will understand truth, and
	12:2	wickedness and put their T in thee, O Lord.
	13:7	keep searching, and they T in what they see,
	14:5	without effect; therefore men T their lives even to
	14:29	perjury; for because they T in lifeless idols they
	16:24	behalf of those who T in thee.
	16:26	word preserves those who T in thee.
Sir	2:6	T in him, and he will help you; make
	2:8	who fear the Lord, T in him, and your
	2:13	to the faint heart, for it has no T
	6:7	testing, and do not T him hastily.
	7:26	out; but do not T yourself to one whom
	11:19	of a sinner, but T in the Lord and
	12:10	Never T your enemy, for like the rusting of
	13:11	as an equal, nor T his abundance of words;
	16:3	Do not T in their survival, and do not
	22:21	Gain the T of your neighbor in his poverty,
	33:3	man of understanding will T in the law; for
	35:12	it; and do not T to an unrighteous sacrifice;
	36:26	For who will T a nimble robber that skips
	36:26	So who will T a man that has no
Is	12:2	my salvation; I will T, and will not be
	26:4	T in the LORD for ever, for the LORD
	30:12	despise this word, and T in oppression and
	30:15	in quietness and in T shall be your strength."
	31:1	rely on horses, who T in chariots because they
	32:17	of righteousness, quietness and T for ever.
	42:17	put to shame, who T in graven images, who
Jer	2:37	those in whom you T, and you will not
	5:17	cities in which you T they shall destroy with
	7:4	Do not T in these deceptive words: 'This is
	7:8	"Behold, you T in deceptive words to no avail.
	7:14	and in which you T, and to the place
	9:4	neighbor, and put no T in any brother; for
	17:7	in the LORD, whose T is the LORD.
	28:15	have made this people T in a lie.
	29:31	and has made you T in a lie,
	39:18	you have put your T in me, says the
	46:25	Pharaoh and those who T in him.
	49:11	and let your widows T in me."
Bar	3:17	gold, in which men T, and there is no
Dan	3:40	shame for those who T in thee.
Mic	7:5	Put no T in a neighbor, have no confidence
Zeph	3:2	She does not T in the LORD, she does
1Mac	2:61	none who put their T in him will lack
	7:7	a man whom you T; let him go and
	8:16	They T one man each year to rule over
	10:37	put in positions of T in the kingdom.
2Mac	7:40	integrity, putting his whole T in the Lord.
	8:18	"For they T to arms and acts of daring,"
	8:18	he said, "but we T in the Almighty God,
	15:7	did not cease to T with all confidence that
Mk	10:23	be for those who T in riches to enter
	10:24	is for those who T in riches to enter
Jn	2:24	but Jesus did not T himself to them,
Phil	2:24	with me; and I T in the Lord that
Heb	2:13	"I will put my T in him." And again,

TRUSTED (33)

Deut	28:52	walls, in which you T, come down throughout all
Judg	20:36	to Benjamin, because they T to the men in
1Sam	27:12	And Achish T David, thinking, "He has made himself
2Kgs	18:5	He T in the LORD the God of Israel;
1Chr	5:20	their entreaty because they T in him.
Job	12:20	speech those who are T, and takes away the
	18:14	tent in which he T, and is brought to
Ps	13:5	But I have T in thy steadfast love; my
	22:4	In thee our fathers T; they trusted, and thou
	22:4	our fathers trusted; they T, and thou didst deliver
	22:5	saved; in thee they T, and were not disappointed.
	26:1	integrity, and I have T in the LORD without
	41:9	friend in whom I T, who ate of my
	52:7	God his refuge, but T in the abundance of
Wis	18:6	sure knowledge of the oaths in which they T
Sir	1:13	and among their descendants she will be T
	2:10	and see: who ever T in the Lord and
Jer	13:25	have forgotten me and T in lies.
	38:22	and were saying, 'Your T friends have deceived you
	48:7	For, because you T in your strongholds and your
	49:4	O faithless daughter, who T in her treasures, saying,
Ezek	16:15	"But you T in your beauty, and played the
Dan	3:96	delivered his servants, who T in him, and set
	6:23	him, because he had T in his God.
	13:35	heaven, for her heart T in the Lord.
Hos	10:13	Because you have T in your chariots and in
Obad	1:7	prevailed against you; your T friends have set a
1Mac	7:16	So they T him; but he seized sixty of
	12:46	Jonathan T him and did as he said; he
2Mac	3:12	those people who had T in the holiness of
Lk	11:22	armor in which he T, and divides his spoil.
	18:9	parable to some who T in themselves that they
1Pet	2:23	not threaten; but he T to him who judges

TRUSTEES

Gal	4:2	is under guardians and T until the date set

TRUSTING

Ps	112:7	his heart is firm, T in the LORD.

TRUSTINGLY (2)

Prov	3:29	your neighbor who dwells T beside you.
Mic	2:8	those who pass by T with no thought of

TRUSTS (23)

Ps	21:7	For the king T in the LORD; and through
	28:7	in him my heart T; so I am helped,
	32:10	love surrounds him who T in the LORD.
	84:12	is the man who T in thee!
	86:2	save thy servant who T in thee.
	135:18	yea, every one who T in them!
Prov	11:28	He who T in his riches will wither, but
	16:20	happy is he who T in the LORD.
	28:25	strife, but he who T in the LORD will
	28:26	He who T in his own mind is a
	29:25	snare, but he who T in the LORD is
	31:11	heart of her husband T in her, and he
Sir	4:17	her discipline until she T him, and she will
	19:4	One who T others too quickly is lightminded, and
	32:24	commandments, and he who T the Lord will not
Is	26:3	on thee, because he T in thee.
	50:10	has no light, yet T in the name of
Jer	17:5	is the man who T in man and makes
	17:7	is the man who T in the LORD, whose
Ezek	33:13	live, yet if he T in his righteousness and
Hab	2:18	For the workman T in his own creation when
Mt	27:43	He T in God; let God deliver him now,
Rom	4:5	does not work but T him who justifies the

TRUSTWORTHY (13)

Ex	18:21	God, men who are T and who hate a
Ps	111:7	all his precepts are T,
Prov	11:13	but he who is T in spirit keeps a
Sir	31:23	food, and their testimony to his excellence is T
	36:16	for thee, and let thy prophets be found T
	37:22	his understanding may be T on his lips.
	37:23	and the fruits of his understanding will be T
	46:15	became known as a T seer.
1Mac	14:41	for ever, until a T prophet should arise,
1Cor	4:2	is required of stewards that they be found T
	7:25	as one who by the Lord's mercy is T
Rev	21:5	for these words are T and true."
	22:6	me, "These words are T and true.

TRUTH (168)

Gen	42:16	tested, whether there is T in you; or else,
	42:21	to one another, "In T we are guilty concerning
Josh	7:20	answered Joshua, "Of a T I have sinned against
1Sam	21:5	the priest, "Of a T women have been kept
1Kgs	17:24	word of the LORD in your mouth is T
	22:16	me nothing but the T in the name of
2Kgs	19:17	Of a T, O LORD, the kings of Assyria
2Chr	18:15	me nothing but the T in the name of
Tob	1:3	in the ways of T and righteousness all the
	3:2	ways are mercy and T, and thou dost render
	3:5	did not walk in T before thee.
	14:6	the Lord God in T, and will bury their
	14:7	the Lord God in T and righteousness will rejoice,
Jud	5:5	will tell you the T about this people that
Esth	9:30	words of peace and T,
Job	6:13	In T I have no help in me, and
	34:12	Of a T, God will not do wickedly, and
Ps	5:9	For there is no T in their mouth; their
	15:2	is right, and speaks T from his heart;
	25:5	Lead me in thy T, and teach me, for
	43:3	thy light and thy T; let them lead me,
	45:4	for the cause of T and to defend the
	51:6	Behold, thou desirest T in the inward being;
	52:3	than good, and lying more than speaking the T
	86:11	may walk in thy T; unite my heart to
	96:13	world with righteousness, and the peoples with his T
	119:43	not the word of T utterly out of my

119:160 of thy word is T; and every one of
145:18 him, to all who call upon him in T
Prov 8:7 my mouth will utter T; wickedness is an abomination
12:17 He who speaks the T gives honest evidence, but
23:23 Buy T, and do not sell it; buy wisdom,
Eccl 12:10 pleasing words, and uprightly he wrote words of T
Wis 3:9 in him will understand T, and the faithful will
5:6 from the way of T, and the light of
6:22 not pass by the T;
Sir 4:25 Never speak against the T, but be mindful of
4:28 to death for the T and the Lord God
12:12 you will realize the T of my words, and
27:9 with their kind; so T returns to those who
37:15 High that he may direct your way in T
41:19 Be ashamed before the T of God and his
Is 10:20 the LORD, the Holy One of Israel, in T
37:18 Of a T, O LORD, the kings of Assyria
45:19 the LORD speak the T, I declare what is
48:1 Israel, but not in T or right.
59:14 stands afar off; for T has fallen in the
59:15 T is lacking, and he who departs from evil
65:16 by the God of T, and he who takes
65:16 by the God of T; because the former troubles
Jer 4:2 the LORD lives,' in T, in justice, and in
5:1 does justice and seeks T; that I may pardon
5:3 O LORD, do not thy eyes look for T
7:28 did not accept discipline; T has perished; it is
9:3 bow; falsehood and not T has grown strong in
9:5 no one speaks the T; they have taught their
26:15 its inhabitants, for in T the LORD sent me
Dan 3:27 thy ways right, and all thy judgments are T
3:28 our fathers, for in T and justice thou hast
7:16 and asked him the T concerning all this.
7:19 desired to know the T concerning the fourth beast,
8:12 offering through transgression; and T was cast down
9:13 from our iniquities and giving heed to thy T
10:21 in the book of T: there is none who
11:2 "And now I will show you the T
Amos 5:10 gate, and they abhor him who speaks the T
Zech 8:16 shall do: Speak the T to one another, render
8:19 cheerful feasts; therefore love T and peace.
1Mac 7:18 said, "There is no T or justice in them,
2Mac 7:6 over us and in T has compassion on us,
Mk 5:33 down before him, and told him the whole T
Lk 1:4 you may know the T concerning the things of
4:25 But in T, I tell you, there were many
Jn 1:14 full of grace and T; we have beheld his
1:17 Moses; grace and T came through Jesus Christ.
4:23 Father in spirit and T, for such the Father
4:24 who worship him must worship in spirit and T
5:32 John, and he has borne witness to the T
8:32 you will know the T, and the truth will
8:32 the truth, and the T will make you free."
8:40 has told you the T which I heard from
8:44 to do with the T, because there is no
8:44 because there is no T in him.
8:45 because I tell the T, you do not believe
8:46 If I tell the T, why do you not
14:6 the way, and the T, and the life; no
14:17 even the Spirit of T, whom the world cannot
15:26 even the Spirit of T, who proceeds from the
16:7 I tell you the T: it is to your
16:13 When the Spirit of T comes, he will guide
16:13 you into all the T; for he will not
17:8 them and know in T that I came from
17:17 Sanctify them in the T; thy word is truth.
17:17 Sanctify them in the truth; thy word is T
17:19 myself, that they also may be consecrated in T
18:37 into the world, to bear witness to the T
18:37 who is of the T hears my voice."
18:38 Pilate said to him, "What is T
19:35 that he tells the T —that you also may
Acts 26:25 excellent Festus, but I am speaking the sober T
Rom 1:18 of men who by their wickedness suppress the T
1:25 because they exchanged the T about God for a
2:8 do not obey the T, but obey wickedness, there
2:20 embodiment of knowledge and T —
9:1 I am speaking the T in Christ, I am
1Cor 5:8 but with the unleavened bread of sincerity and T
2Cor 4:2 open statement of the T we would commend
11:10 As the T of Christ is in me, this
12:6 a fool, for I shall be speaking the T
13:8 do anything against the T, but only for the
13:8 anything against the truth, but only for the T
Gal 2:5 a moment, that the T of the gospel might
2:14 not straightforward about the T of the gospel, I
4:16 then become your enemy by telling you the T
5:7 running well; who hindered you from obeying the T
Eph 1:13 heard the word of T, the gospel of your
4:15 Rather, speaking the T in love, we are to
4:21 in him, as the T is in Jesus.
4:25 every one speak the T with his neighbor, for
6:14 girded your loins with T, and having put on
Phil 1:18 in pretense or in T, Christ is proclaimed; and
Col 1:5 the word of the T, the gospel
1:6 grace of God in T,
2Thes 2:10 refused to love the T and so be saved.
2:12 did not believe the T but had pleasure in
2:13 sanctification by the Spirit and belief in the T
1Tim 2:4 and to come to the knowledge of the T
2:7 (I am telling the T, I am not lying),
2:7 a teacher of the Gentiles in faith and T
3:15 living God, the pillar and bulwark of the T
4:3 thanksgiving by those who believe and know the T
6:5 and bereft of the T, imagining that godliness is
2Tim 1:14 Christ Jesus; guard the T that has been entrusted
2:15 to be ashamed, rightly handling the word of T
2:18 have swerved from the T by holding that the
2:25 come to know the T,
3:7 can never arrive at a knowledge of the T
3:8 men also oppose the T, men of corrupt mind
4:4 from listening to the T and wander into myths.
Tit 1:1 knowledge of the T which accords with godliness,
1:13 or to commands of men who reject the T
Heb 10:26 the knowledge of the T, there no longer remains
Jas 1:17 by the word of T that we should be
3:14 do not boast and be false to the T
5:19 you wanders from the T and some one brings
1Pet 1:22 your obedience to the T for a sincere love
2Pet 1:12 are established in the T that you have.
2:2 them the way of T will be reviled.
1Jn 1:6 live according to the T;
1:8 deceive ourselves, and the T is not in us.
2:4 a liar, and the T is not in him;
2:21 do not know the T, but because you know
2:21 and know that no lie is of the T
3:18 word or speech but in deed and in T
3:19 we are of the T, and reassure our hearts
4:6 know the spirit of T and the spirit of
5:7 is the witness, because the Spirit is the T
2Jn 1:1 I love in the T, and not only I
1:1 all who know the T,
1:2 truth, because of the T which abides in us
1:3 the Father's Son, in T and love.
1:4 your children following the T, just as we have
3Jn 1:1 the beloved Gaius, whom I love in the T
1:3 and testified to the T of your life, as
1:3 your life, as indeed you do follow the T
1:4 this, to hear that my children follow the T
1:8 that we may be fellow workers in the T
1:12 one, and from the T itself; I testify to

TRUTHFUL (4)

Prov 12:19 T lips endure for ever, but a lying tongue
14:25 A T witness saves lives, but one who utters
Sir 34:8 is made perfect in T lips.
2Cor 6:7 Holy Spirit, genuine love, T speech, and the power

TRUTHFULLY

Mt 22:16 the way of God T, and care for no

TRUTHFULNESS (2)

Rom 3:7 through my falsehood God's T abounds to his glory,
15:8 circumcised to show God's T, in order to confirm

TRUTHS

1Cor 2:13 the Spirit, interpreting spiritual T to those who

TRY (17)

2Chr 32:31 himself, in order to T him and to know
Jud 8:16 Do not T to bind the purposes of the
8:34 Only, do not T to find out what I
Job 12:11 Does not the ear T words as the palate
Ps 26:2 me, O LORD, and T me; test my heart
139:23 T me and know my thoughts!
Prov 23:30 those who go to T mixed wine.
Sir 4:26 sins, and do not T to stop the current
12:12 your right, lest he T to take your seat
13:11 Do not T to treat him as an equal,
Jer 17:10 search the mind and T the heart, to give
1Mac 9:71 that he would not T to harm him as
1Cor 4:13 endure; when slandered, we T to conciliate; we have

6:2 are you incompetent to T trivial cases?
10:33 God, just as I T to please all men
Eph 5:10 right and true), and T to learn what is
Rev 3:10 the whole world, to T those who dwell upon

TRYING (6)

Dan 2:8 certainty that you are T to gain time, because
1Mac 6:18 They were T in every way to harm them
6:56 and that he was T to seize control of
Acts 21:31 And as they were T to kill him, word
28:23 kingdom of God and T to convince them about
Gal 1:10 Or am I T to please men?

TRYPHAENA

Rom 16:12 workers in the Lord, T and Tryphosa.

TRYPHO (21)

1Mac 11:39 Now T had formerly been one of Alexander's
11:54 After this T returned, and with him the young
11:56 And T captured the elephants and gained control of
12:39 Then T attempted to become king in Asia and
12:42 When T saw that he had come with a
12:49 Then T sent troops and cavalry into Galilee and
13:1 Simon heard that T had assembled a large army
13:12 Then T departed from Ptolemais with a large army
13:14 T learned that Simon had risen up in place
13:19 the hundred talents, but T broke his word and
13:20 After this T came to invade the country and
13:21 kept sending envoys to T urging him to come
13:22 So T got all his cavalry ready to go,
13:24 Then T turned back and departed to his own
13:31 T dealt treacherously with the young king Antiochus;
13:34 country, for all that T did was to plunder.
14:1 help, so that he could make war against T
15:10 to him, so that there were few with T
15:25 war; and he shut T up and kept him
15:37 Now T embarked on a ship and escaped to
15:39 war on the people; but the king pursued T

TRYPHOSA

Rom 16:12 Greet those workers in the Lord, Tryphaena and T

TUBAL (8)

Gen 10:2 Gomer, Magog, Madai, Javan, T, Meshech, and Tiras.
1Chr 1:5 Gomer, Magog, Madai, Javan, T, Meshech, and Tiras.
Is 66:19 draw the bow, to T and Javan, to the
Ezek 27:13 Javan, T, and Meshech traded with you; they
32:26 "Meshech and T are there, and all their multitude,
38:2 prince of Meshech and T, and prophesy against him
38:3 prince of Meshech and T;
39:1 prince of Meshech and T;

TUBAL-CAIN (2)

Gen 4:22 Zillah bore T; he was the forger of all
4:22 The sister of T was Naamah.

TUBES

Job 40:18 His bones are T of bronze, his limbs like

TUMBLE

Ezek 38:20 and every wall shall T to the ground.

TUMBLED (2)

Judg 7:13 cake of barley bread T into the camp of
Jud 13:9 Then she T his body off the bed and

TUMORS (7)

1Sam 5:6 and afflicted them with T, both Ashdod and its
5:9 and old, so that T broke out upon them.
5:12 die were stricken with T, and the cry of
6:4 They answered, "Five golden T and five golden mice,
6:5 make images of your T and images of your
6:11 the golden mice and the images of their T
6:17 These are the golden T, which the Philistines

TUMULT (30)

1Sam 14:19 to the priest, the T in the camp of
2Sam 18:29 I saw a great T, but I do not
Esth 11:5 thunders and earthquake, T upon the earth!
11:8 distress, affliction and great T upon the earth!
Job 39:7 He scorns the T of the city; he hears
Ps 38:8 groan because of the T of my heart.
46:3 and foam, though the mountains tremble with its T
65:7 of their waves, the T of the peoples;
83:2 thy enemies are in T; those who hate thee
Wis 14:25 and deceit, corruption, faithlessness, T, perjury,
Is 9:5 tramping warrior in battle T and every garment
13:4 Hark, a T on the mountains as of a
22:5 has a day of T and trampling and confusion
Jer 10:13 voice there is a T of waters in the
48:45 of Moab, the crown of the sons of T
51:16 voice there is a T of waters in the
Lam 1:20 my soul is in T, my heart is wrung
2:11 my soul is in T; my heart is poured
Ezek 1:24 Almighty, a sound of T like the sound of
7:7 near, a day of T, and not of joyful
22:5 will mock you, you infamous one, full of T
Hos 10:14 your warriors, therefore the T of war shall arise
1Mac 13:44 city, and a great T arose in the city.
2Mac 15:29 there was shouting and T, and they blessed the
Mt 9:23 the crowd making a T,
26:5 lest there be a T among the people."
Mk 5:38 synagogue, he saw a T, and people weeping and
5:39 do you make a T and weep?
14:2 lest there be a T of the people."
Acts 24:17 purified in the temple, without any crowd or T

TUMULTS (3)

Amos 3:9 and see the great T within her, and the
Lk 21:9 hear of wars and T, do not be terrified;
2Cor 6:5 calamities, beatings, imprisonments, T, labors, watch

TUMULTUOUS (3)

Is 22:2 are full of shoutings, T city, exultant town?
Jer 51:42 is covered with its T waves.
1Mac 9:39 looked, and saw a T procession with much baggage;

TUNES

Sir 44:5 those who composed musical T, and set forth verses

TUNIC (4)

Job 30:18 binds me about like the collar of my T
2Mac 12:40 Then under the T of every one of the
Jn 19:23 four parts, one for each soldier; also his T
19:23 But the T was without seam, woven from top

TUNICS (6)

Jud 14:19 this, they rent their T and were greatly dismayed,
Dan 3:21 in their mantles, their T, their hats, and their
Mt 10:10 your journey, nor two T, nor sandals, nor a
Mk 6:9 to wear sandals and not put on two T
Lk 9:3 bread, nor money; and do not have two T
Acts 9:39 him weeping, and showing T and other garments

TUNNELED

Sir 48:17 midst of it; he T the sheer rock with

TURBAN (17)

Ex 28:4 of checker work, a T, and a girdle; they
28:37 fasten it on the T by a lace of
28:37 it shall be on the front of the T
28:39 you shall make a T of fine linen, and
29:6 you shall set the T on his head, and
29:6 head, and put the holy crown upon the T
39:28 his sons, and the T of fine linen, and
39:31 fasten it on the T above; as the LORD
Lev 8:9 And he set the T upon his head, and
8:9 head, and on the T, in front, he set
16:4 and wear the linen T; these are the holy
Job 29:14 my justice was like a robe and a T
Sir 45:12 gold crown upon his T, inscribed like a signet
Ezek 21:26 Lord GOD: Remove the T, and take off the
24:17 Bind on your T, and put your shoes on
Zech 3:5 them put a clean T on his head." So
3:5 they put a clean T on his head and

TURBANS (5)

Jud 4:15 With ashes upon their T, they cried out to
Is 3:23 the linen garments, the T, and the veils.
Ezek 23:15 their loins, with flowing T on their heads, all
24:23 Your T shall be on your heads and your
44:18 They shall have linen T upon their heads, and

TURBULENT (3)

Job 40:23 if the river is T he is not frightened;
Wis 13:2 of the stars, or T water, of the luminaries
Ezek 5:7 Because you are more T than the nations that

TURMOIL (3)

Job 30:27 My heart is in T, and is never still;
Ps 39:6 nought are they in T; man heaps up, and
Is 14:3 from your pain and T and the hard service

TURN (338)

Gen 19:2 and said, "My lords, T aside, I pray you,
24:49 me; that I may T to the right hand
Ex 3:3 Moses said, "I will T aside and see this
14:2 people of Israel to T back and encam in
23:27 make all your enemies T their backs to you.
32:12 T from thy fierce wrath, and repent of this
Lev 19:4 Do not T to idols or make for yourselves
19:31 "Do not T to mediums or wizards; do not
Num 14:25 dwell in the valleys, T tomorrow and set out
20:17 Highway, we will not T aside to the right
21:22 land; we will not T aside into field or
22:23 struck the ass, to T her into the road.
22:26 was no way to T either to the right
25:4 of the LORD may T away from Israel."
32:15 For if you T away from following him, he
34:4 and your boundary shall T south of the ascent
34:5 and the boundary shall T from Azmon to the
Deut 1:7 enough at this mountain; T and take your journey,
1:40 But as for you, T, and journey into the
2:3 mountain country long enough; T northward.
2:27 the road, I will T aside neither to the
5:32 you; you shall not T aside to the right
7:4 For they would T away your sons from following
11:16 be deceived, and you T aside and serve other
11:28 LORD your God, but T aside from the way
13:17 that the LORD may T from the fierceness of
14:25 there, then you shall T it into money, and
16:7 the morning you shall T and go to your
17:11 do; you shall not T aside from the verdict
17:17 himself, lest his heart T away; nor shall he
17:20 that he may not T aside from the commandment,
23:13 hole with it, and T back and cover up
23:14 indecent among you, and T away from you.
28:14 if you do not T aside from any of
30:10 the law, if you T to the LORD your
31:20 grown fat, they will T to other gods and
31:29 surely act corruptly, and T aside from the way
Josh 1:7 my servant commanded you; T not from it to
7:12 before their enemies; they T their backs before their
22:4 he promised them; therefore T and go to your
22:18 LORD, that you must T away this day from
22:23 building an altar to T away from following the
22:29 against the LORD, and T away this day from
23:12 For if you T back, and join the remnant
24:20 gods, then he will T and do you harm,
Judg 4:18 and said to him, T aside, my lord, turn
4:18 "Turn aside, my lord, T aside to me; have
19:11 "Come now, let us T aside to this city
19:12 him, "We will not T aside into the city
20:39 men of Israel should T in battle.
Ruth 1:11 But Naomi said, T back, my daughters, why will
1:12 T back, my daughters, go your way, for I
4:1 So Boaz said, T aside, friend; sit down here";
1Sam 6:3 his hand does not T away from you."
12:20 evil, yet do not T aside from following the
12:21 heart; and do not T aside after vain things
22:17 who stood about him, T and kill the priests
22:18 said to Doeg, "You T and fall upon the
2Sam 2:21 Abner said to him, T aside to your right
2:21 But Asahel would not T aside from following him.
2:22 said again to Asahel, T aside from following me;
2:23 But he refused to T aside; therefore Abner smote
2:26 you bid your people T from the pursuit of
14:19 the king, one cannot T to the right hand
15:31 LORD, I pray thee, T the counsel of Ahithophel
18:30 And the king said, T aside, and stand here."
22:23 statutes I did not T aside.
22:38 them, and did not T back until they were
22:41 didst make my enemies T their backs to me,
1Kgs 2:3 do and wherever you T;
8:33 against thee, if they T again to thee, and
8:35 acknowledge thy name, and T from their sin, when
9:6 Israel.' But if you T aside from following me,
11:2 for surely they will T away your heart after
12:15 for it was a T of affairs brought about
12:26 "Now the kingdom will T back to the house
12:27 of this people will T again to their lord,
13:33 thing Jeroboam did not T from his evil way,
15:5 LORD, and did not T aside from anything that
17:3 "Depart from here and T eastward, and hide yourself
22:34 driver of his chariot, T about, and carry me
22:43 father; he did not T aside from it, doing
2Kgs 4:8 that way, he would T in there to eat
9:18 T round and ride behind me." And the watchman
9:19 T round and ride behind me."
10:29 But Jehu did not T aside from the sins
10:31 heart; he did not T from the sins of
15:24 LORD; he did not T away from the sins
17:13 and every seer, saying, T from your evil ways
19:25 pass, that you should T fortified cities into heaps
19:28 mouth, and I will T you back on the
20:5 LORD came to him: T back, and say to
22:2 and he did not T aside to the right
23:26 the LORD did not T from the fierceness of
1Chr 12:23 David in Hebron, to T the kingdom of Saul
2Chr 6:24 against thee, when they T again and acknowledge thy
6:26 acknowledge thy name, and T from their sin, when
6:42 LORD God, do not T away the face of
7:14 seek my face, and T from their wicked ways,
7:19 Israel.' "But if you T aside and forsake my
8:15 And they did not T aside from what the
10:15 for it was a T of affairs brought about
18:33 driver of his chariot, T about, and carry me
20:32 father and did not T aside from it; he
29:10 his fierce anger may T away from us.
30:6 Israel, that he may T again to the remnant
30:8 his fierce anger may T away from you.
30:9 merciful, and will not T away his face from
34:2 and he did not T aside to the right
34:33 days they did not T away from following the
35:22 Nevertheless Josiah would not T away from him, but
Neh 4:4 for we are despised; T back their taunt upon
9:26 them in order to T them back to thee,
9:29 them in order to T them back to thy
9:35 and they did not T from their wicked works.
Tob 3:6 eternal abode; do not T thy face away from
4:7 Do not T your face away from any poor
13:6 If you T to him with all your heart
13:6 him, then he will T to you and will
13:6 T back, you sinners, and do right before him;
14:6 all the Gentiles will T to fear the Lord
Jud 8:23 Lord our God will T it to dishonor.
Esth 2:12 Now when the T came for each maiden to
2:15 When the T came for Esther the daughter of
13:17 mercy upon thy inheritance; T our mourning into
14:11 at our downfall; but T their plan against themselves,
14:13 before the lion, and T his heart to hate
Job 5:1 To which of the holy ones will you T
6:18 The caravans T aside from their course; they go
6:29 T, I pray, let no wrong be done.
6:29 T now, my vindication is at stake.
9:13 "God will not T back his anger; beneath him
10:8 and now thou dost T about and destroy me.
10:9 clay; and wilt thou T me to dust again?
15:13 eyes flash, that you T your spirit against God,
23:9 cannot behold him; I T to the right hand,
23:13 unchangeable and who can T him?
33:17 warnings, that he may T man aside from his
36:18 greatness of the ransom T you aside.
36:21 Take heed, do not T to iniquity, for this
37:12 They T round and round by his guidance, to
39:22 dismayed; he does not T back from the sword.
Ps 6:4 T, O LORD, save my life; deliver me for
6:10 sorely troubled; they shall T back, and be put
18:37 them; and did not T back till they were
18:40 didst make my enemies T their backs to me,
22:27 earth shall remember and T to the LORD; and
25:16 T thou to me, and be gracious to me;
27:9 T not thy servant away in anger, thou who
40:4 trust, who does not T to the proud, to
44:10 Thou hast made us T back from the foe;
69:16 to thy abundant mercy, T to me.
73:10 Therefore the people T and praise them; and find
80:14 T again, O God of hosts!
80:18 Then we will never T back from thee; give
81:14 subdue their enemies, and T my hand against their
85:3 thy wrath; thou didst T from thy hot anger.
85:8 saints, to those who T to him in their
86:16 T to me and take pity on me; give
90:3 the dust, and sayest, T back, O children of
106:23 breach before him, to T away his wrath from
114:5 O Jordan, that you T back?
119:37 T my eyes from looking at vanities; and give
119:39 T away the reproach which I dread; for thy
119:51 but I do not T away from thy law.
119:59 of thy ways, I T my feet to thy
119:79 those who fear thee T to me, that they
119:102 I do not T aside from thy ordinances, for
119:132 T to me and be gracious to me, as
125:5 But those who T aside upon their crooked ways
132:10 David's sake do not T away the face of

132:11 which he will not T back: "One of the
Prov 3:7 fear the LORD, and T away from evil.
4:6 forget, and do not T away from the words
4:16 not go on it; T away from it and
4:28 or to the left; T your foot away from
7:25 Let not your heart T aside to her ways,
9:4 is simple, let him T in here!" To him
9:16 is simple, let him T in here!" And to
13:19 the soul; but to T away from evil is
24:18 and be displeased, and T away his anger from
29:8 aflame, but wise men T away wrath.
30:30 beasts and does not T back before any;
Eccl 3:20 the dust, and all T to dust again.
Song 2:17 and the shadows flee, T, my beloved, be like
6:5 T away your eyes from me, for they disturb
Wis 2:3 extinguished, the body will T to ashes, and the
Sir 2:7 for his mercy; and T not aside, lest you
4:4 an afflicted suppliant, nor T your face away from
5:7 Do not delay to T to the Lord, nor
6:12 brought low he will T against you, and will
7:2 wrong, and it will T away from you.
9:8 T away your eyes from a shapely woman, and
9:9 wine; lest your heart T aside to her, and
17:20 T to the Lord and forsake your sins; pray
17:21 the Most High and T away from iniquity, and
17:24 forgiveness for those who T to him!
18:20 the point of sinning, T back.
29:2 his need; and in T, repay your neighbor promptly.
39:27 godly, just as they T into evils for sinners.
40:11 are from the earth T back to the earth,
46:11 and who did not T away from the Lord--
48:10 out in fury, to T the heart of the
Is 1:25 I will T my hand against you and will
2:22 T away from man in whose nostrils is breath,
6:10 with their hearts, and T and be healed."
8:21 and their God, and T their faces upward;
9:13 The people did not T to him who smote
10:2 keep writing oppression, to T aside the needy from
13:14 them, every man will T to his own people,
14:27 out, and who will T it back?
28:6 strength to those who T back the battle at
29:16 You T things upside down!
29:21 with an empty plea T aside him who is
30:3 the protection of Pharaoh T to your shame, and
30:11 illusions, leave the way, T aside from the path,
30:21 when you T to the right or when you
30:21 right or when you T to the left.
31:6 T to him from whom you have deeply revolted,
37:29 mouth, and I will T you back on the
38:8 the dial of Ahaz T back ten steps." So
42:15 their herbage; I will T the rivers into islands,
42:16 I will T the darkness before them into light,
45:22 T to me and be saved, all the ends
58:13 "If you T back your foot from the sabbath,
59:20 those in Jacob who T from transgression, says the
Jer 3:19 Father, and would not T from following me.
4:28 relented nor will I T back."
15:1 my heart would not T toward this people.
15:5 Who will T aside to ask about your welfare?
15:7 people; they did not T from their ways.
15:19 They shall T to you, but you shall not
15:19 but you shall not T to them.
17:13 to shame; those who T away from thee shall
18:20 good for them, to T away thy wrath from
21:4 Israel: Behold, I will T back the weapons of
23:20 the LORD will not T back until he has
25:5 servants the prophets, saying, T now, every one of
26:3 listen, and every one T from his evil way,
30:24 the LORD will not T back until he has
31:13 I will T their mourning into joy, I will
31:39 Gareb, and shall then T to Goah.
32:40 that I will not T away from doing good
32:40 that they may not T from me.
35:15 sending them persistently, saying, T now every one of
36:3 that every one may T from his evil way,
36:7 that every one will T from his evil way,
38:22 in the mire, they T away from you.'
44:5 incline their ear, to T from their wickedness and
49:8 Flee, T back, dwell in the depths, O inhabitants
50:16 oppressor, every one shall T to his own people,
Lam 3:35 of the earth, to T aside the right of
Bar 2:13 Let thy anger T away from us, for we
2:29 great multitude will surely T into a small number
2:33 my name, and will T from their stubbornness and
4:2 T, O Jacob, and take her; walk toward the
Ezek 3:19 and he does not T from his wickedness, or
4:8 so that you cannot T from one side to
6:9 blinded their eyes which T wantonly after their idols;
7:13 multitude; it shall not T back; and because of
7:22 I will T my face from them, that they
10:16 the wheels did not T from beside them.
13:22 that he should not T from his wicked way
14:6 Lord GOD: Repent and T away from your idols;
14:6 from your idols; and T away your faces from
18:23 rather that he should T from his way and
18:30 Repent and T from all your transgressions, lest
18:32 the Lord GOD; so T, and live."
29:16 their iniquity, when they T to them for aid.
33:8 warn the wicked to T from his way, that
33:9 warn the wicked to T from his way, and
33:9 and he does not T from his way; he
33:11 but that the wicked T from his way and
33:11 his way and live; T back, turn back from
33:11 and live; turn back, T back from your evil
36:9 you, and I will T to you, and you
38:4 Tubal; and I will T you about, and put
39:2 Tubal; and I will T you about and drive
Dan 9:16 anger and thy wrath T away from thy city
11:18 Afterward he shall T his face to the coastlands,
11:18 insolence; indeed he shall T his insolence back upon
11:19 Then he shall T his face back toward the
11:30 and withdraw, and shall T back and be enraged
11:30 He shall T back and give heed to those
12:3 firmament; and those who T many to righteousness,
Hos 3:1 of Israel, though they T to other gods and
7:17 They T to Baal; they are like a treacherous
12:14 upon him, and will T back upon him his
Joel 2:14 whether he will not T and repent, and leave
Amos 1:8 from Ashkelon; I will T my hand against Ekron;
2:7 of the earth, and T aside the way of
5:7 Bethel, O you who T justice to wormwood, and
5:12 take a bribe, and T aside the needy in
8:10 I will T your feasts into mourning, and all
Jon 3:8 yea, let every one T from his evil way
3:9 may yet repent and T from his fierce anger,
Mic 7:17 their strongholds, they shall T in dread to the
Zech 13:7 be scattered; I will T my hand against the
Mal 4:6 And he will T the hearts of fathers to
1Mac 2:62 for his splendor will T into dung and worms.
9:45 marsh and thicket; there is no place to T
12:45 the officials, and will T round and go home.
16:18 aid him and to T over to him the
2Mac 7:8 Therefore he in T underwent tortures as the first
7:24 enviable if he would T from the ways of
10:13 a traitor at every T, because he had abandoned
10:14 mercenaries, and at every T kept on warring against
Mt 5:39 on the right cheek, T to him the other
7:6 them under foot and T to attack you.
13:15 with their heart, and T for me to heal
18:3 to you, unless you T and become like children,
24:18 in the field not T back to take his
Mk 4:12 lest they should T again, and be forgiven."
13:16 in the field not T back to take his
Lk 1:16 And he will T many of the sons of
1:17 power of Elijah, to T the hearts of the
16:2 T in the account of your stewardship, for you
17:31 in the field not T back.
Jn 12:40 with their heart, and T for me to heal
16:20 but your sorrow will T into joy.
Acts 3:19 Repent therefore, and T again, that your sins may
7:45 Our fathers in T brought it in with Joshua
13:8 withstood them, seeking to T away the proconsul
13:46 eternal life, behold, we T to the Gentiles.
14:15 news, that you should T from these vain things
15:19 of the Gentiles who T to God,
26:18 eyes, that they may T from darkness to light
26:20 they should repent and T to God and perform
28:27 with their heart, and T for me to heal
1Cor 14:27 three, and each in T; and let one interpret.
2Cor 2:7 so you should rather T to forgive and comfort
7:5 were afflicted at every T –fighting without and fear
Gal 4:9 God, how can you T back again to the
Phil 1:19 Jesus Christ this will T out for my deliverance,
2Tim 4:4 own likings, and will T away from listening to
1Pet 3:11 speaking guile; let him T away from evil and
2Pet 2:21 after knowing it to T back from the holy
Rev 11:6 over the waters to T them into blood, and

TURNED (307)

Gen 3:24 a flaming sword which T every way, to guard
9:23 father; their faces were T away, and they did
14:7 the wilderness; then they T back and came to

T

18:22 So the men T from there, and went toward
19:3 them strongly; so they T aside to him and
30:30 and the LORD has blessed you wherever I T
38:1 from his brothers, and T in to a certain
42:24 Then he T away from them and wept; and
42:28 failed them, and they T trembling to one another,
Ex 3:4 LORD saw that he T aside to see, God
5:22 Then Moses T again to the LORD and said,
7:15 the rod which was T into a serpent.
7:17 and it shall be T to blood,
7:20 was in the Nile T to blood.
7:23 Pharaoh T and went into his house, and he
10:6 Then he T and went out from Pharaoh.
10:19 And the LORD T a very strong west wind,
32:8 corrupted themselves; they have T aside quickly out
32:15 And Moses T, and went down from the mountain
33:11 When Moses T again into the camp, his servant
Lev 13:3 the diseased spot has T white and the disease
13:4 in it has not T white, the priest shall
13:10 the skin, which has T the hair white, and
13:13 disease; it has all T white, and he is
13:17 if the disease has T white, then the priest
13:20 and its hair has T white, then the priest
13:25 in the spot has T white and it appears
26:23 discipline you are not T to me, but walk
Num 5:19 if you have not T aside to uncleanness, while
12:10 And Aaron T towards Miriam, and behold, she was
14:43 sword; because you have T back from following the
16:42 and against Aaron, they T toward the tent of
20:21 his territory; so Israel T away from him.
21:33 Then they T and went up by the way
22:23 hand; and the ass T aside out of the
22:33 ass saw me, and T aside before me these
22:33 If she had not T aside from me, surely
25:11 Aaron the priest, has T back my wrath from
33:7 out from Etham, and T back to Pi-hahiroth, which
Deut 1:24 each tribe; and they T and went up into
2:1 "Then we T, and journeyed into the wilderness in
2:8 "And we T and went in the direction of
3:1 "Then we T and went up the way to
9:12 acted corruptly; they have T aside quickly out of
9:15 than they.' So I T and came down from
9:16 molten calf; you had T aside quickly from the
10:5 Then I T and came down from the mountain,
23:5 the LORD your God T the curse into a
31:18 done, because they have T to other gods.
Josh 7:8 say, when Israel has T their backs before their
7:26 day; then the LORD T from his burning anger.
8:20 fled to the wilderness T back upon the pursuers.
8:21 went up, then they T back and smote the
10:38 Joshua, with all Israel, T back to Debir and
11:10 And Joshua T back at that time, and took
Judg 2:17 to them; they soon T aside from the way
2:19 the judge died, they T back and behaved worse
3:19 But he himself T back at the sculptured stones
4:18 So he T aside to her into the tent,
6:14 And the LORD T to him and said, "Go
7:13 that it fell, and T it upside down, so
8:33 the people of Israel T again and played the
11:8 is why we have T to you now, that
14:8 take her; and he T aside to see the
15:4 took torches; and he T them tail to tail,
18:3 young Levite; and they T aside and said to
18:15 And they T aside thither, and came to the
18:21 So they T and departed, putting the little ones
18:23 to the Danites, who T round and said to
18:26 strong for him, he T and went back to
19:15 to Benjamin, and they T aside there, to go
20:41 the men of Israel T, and the men of
20:42 Therefore they T their backs before the men of
20:45 And they T and fled toward the wilderness to
20:47 But six hundred men T and fled toward the
20:48 the men of Israel T back against the Benjaminites,
Ruth 3:8 man was startled, and T over, and behold, a
4:1 down here"; and he T aside and sat down.
1Sam 6:12 as they went; they T neither to the right
8:3 in his ways, but T aside after gain; they
10:6 with them and be T into another man.
10:9 When he T his back to leave Samuel, God
13:17 three companies; one company T toward Ophrah, to
13:18 of Shual, another company T toward Beth-horon, and
13:18 Beth-horon, and another company T toward the
14:21 camp, even they also T to be with the
14:47 the Philistines; wherever he T he put them to
15:11 king; for he has T back from following me,
15:12 monument for himself and T, and passed on, and
15:27 As Samuel T to go away, Saul laid hold
15:31 So Samuel T back after Saul; and Saul worshiped
17:30 And he T away from him toward another, and
22:18 And Doeg the Edomite T and fell upon the
25:12 So David's young men T away, and came back
28:15 me, and God has T away from me and
28:16 since the LORD has T from you and become
2Sam 1:22 the bow of Jonathan T not back, and the
2:19 as he went he T neither to the right
18:30 So he T aside, and stood still.
19:2 victory that day was T into mourning for all
1Kgs 2:15 however the kingdom has T about and become my
10:13 So she T and went back to her own
11:3 concubines; and his wives T away his heart.
11:4 was old his wives T away his heart after
11:9 because his heart had T away from the LORD,
18:37 and that thou hast T their hearts back."
20:39 and behold, a soldier T and brought a man
21:4 on his bed, and T away his face, and
22:32 So they T to fight against him; and Jehoshaphat
22:33 king of Israel, they T back from pursuing him.
2Kgs 2:24 And he T around, and when he saw them,
4:11 came there, and he T into the chamber and
5:12 So he T and went away in a rage.
5:26 spirit when the man T from his chariot to
13:23 on them, and he T toward them, because of
15:20 the king of Assyria T back, and did not
20:2 Then Hezekiah T his face to the wall, and
23:16 And as Josiah T, he saw the tombs there
23:25 king like him, who T to the LORD with
24:1 three years; then he T and rebelled against him.
1Chr 10:14 LORD slew him, and T the kingdom over to
21:20 was threshing wheat; he T and saw the angel,
2Chr 9:12 So she T and went back to her own
12:12 wrath of the LORD T from him, so as
15:4 in their distress they T to the LORD, the
18:31 So they T to fight against him; and Jehoshaphat
18:32 king of Israel, they T back from pursuing him.
25:27 the time when he T away from the LORD
29:6 forsaken him, and have T away their faces from
29:6 of the LORD, and T their backs.
Ezra 6:22 them joyful, and had T the heart of the
Neh 2:15 the wall; and I T back and entered by
9:28 them; yet when they T and cried to thee
9:29 man shall live, and T a stubborn shoulder and
13:2 yet our God T the curse into a
Tob 2:6 "Your feasts shall be T into mourning, and all
3:12 O Lord, I have T my eyes and my
4:7 God will not be T away from you.
Jud 1:14 plundered its markets, and T its beauty into shame.
16:11 and the enemy were T back.
Esth 9:22 month that had been T for them from sorrow
15:7 the queen faltered, and T pale and faint, and
Job 1:1 who feared God, and T away from evil.
19:19 whom I loved have T against me.
20:14 yet his food is T in his stomach; it
23:11 way and have not T aside.
28:5 but underneath it is T up as by fire.
30:15 Terrors are T upon me; my honor is pursued
30:21 Thou hast T cruel to me; with the might
30:31 My lyre is T to mourning, and my pipe
31:7 if my step has T aside from the way,
34:27 of men, because they T aside from following him,
41:28 for him slingstones are T to stubble.
Ps 9:3 When my enemies T back, they stumbled and
30:11 Thou hast T for me my mourning into dancing;
35:4 Let them be T back and confounded who devise
40:14 life; let them be T back and brought to
44:18 Our heart has not T back, nor have our
56:9 my enemies will be T back in the day
66:6 He T the sea into dry land; men passed
70:2 Let them be T back and brought to dishonor
78:9 armed with the bow, T back on the day
78:44 He T their rivers to blood, so that they
78:57 observe his testimonies, but T away and acted
89:43 Yea, thou hast T back the edge of his
105:25 He T their hearts to hate his people, to
105:29 He T their waters into blood, and caused their
114:3 looked and fled, Jordan T back.
129:5 put to shame and T backward!
Eccl 2:12 So I T to consider wisdom and madness and
2:20 So I T about and gave my heart up
7:25 I T my mind to know and to search
Song 5:6 but my beloved had T and gone.
6:1 Whither has your beloved T, that we may seek
Wis 16:7 For he who T toward it was saved, not

Sir 17:1 out of earth, and T him back to it
33:12 brought low, and he T them out of their
45:23 fast, when the people T away, in the ready
Is 5:25 his anger is not T away and his hand
9:12 his anger is not T away and his hand
9:17 his anger is not T away and his hand
9:21 his anger is not T away and his hand
10:4 his anger is not T away and his hand
12:1 with me, thy anger T away, and thou didst
21:4 longed for has been T for me into trembling.
29:17 until Lebanon shall be T into a fruitful field,
34:9 of Edom shall be T into pitch, and her
38:2 Then Hezekiah T his face to the wall, and
38:8 So the sun T back on the dial the
42:17 They shall be T back and utterly put to
43:14 the Chaldeans will be T to lamentations.
50:5 was not rebellious, I T not backward.
53:6 gone astray; we have T every one to his
56:11 understanding; they have all T to their own way,
59:14 Justice is T back, and righteousness stands afar off;
60:5 the sea shall be T to you, the wealth
63:10 holy Spirit; therefore he T to be their enemy,
Jer 2:21 How then have you T degenerate and become a
2:27 birth.' For they have T their back to me,
2:35 surely his anger has T from me.' Behold, I
4:8 the LORD has not T back from us."
5:23 rebellious heart; they have T aside and gone away.
5:25 harvest.' Your iniquities have T these away, and your
6:12 Their houses shall be T over to others, their
8:5 then has this people T away in perpetual backsliding?
11:10 They have T back to the iniquities of their
23:22 and they would have T them from their evil
30:6 Why has every face T pale?
31:19 For after I had T away I repented; and
32:33 They have T to me their back and not
34:11 But afterward they T around and took back the
34:16 name; but then you T around and profaned my
36:16 all the words, they T one to another in
41:14 away captive from Mizpah T about and came back,
46:5 are dismayed and have T backward.
46:21 calves; yea, they have T and fled together, they
48:39 How Moab has T his back in shame!
49:24 has become feeble, she T to flee, and panic
50:5 to Zion, with faces T toward it, saying, 'Come,
Lam 1:13 for my feet; he T me back; he has
5:2 Our inheritance has been T over to strangers, our
5:15 our dancing has been T to mourning.
Bar 1:13 his wrath have not T away from us.
4:12 my children, because they T away from the law
4:34 her insolence will be T to grief.
Ezek 17:6 vine, and its branches T toward him, and its
18:28 Because he considered and T away from all the
23:17 polluted by them, she T from them in disgust.
23:18 flaunted her nakedness, I T in disgust from her,
23:18 her, as I had T from her sister.
23:22 lovers from whom you T in disgust, and I
23:28 those from whom you T in disgust;
28:18 consumed you, and I T you to ashes upon
42:17 Then he T and measured the north side, five
42:18 Then he T and measured the south side, five
42:19 Then he T to the west side and measured,
Dan 9:3 Then I T my face to the Lord God,
9:11 transgressed thy law and T aside, refusing to obey
10:15 to these words, I T my face toward the
13:9 perverted their minds and T away their eyes from
13:47 All the people T to him, and said, "What
Hos 7:9 with the peoples; Ephraim is a cake not T
14:4 for my anger has T from them.
Joel 2:31 The sun shall be T to darkness, and the
Amos 6:12 But you have T justice into poison and the
Jon 3:10 they did, how they T from their evil way,
Zeph 1:6 Milcom; those who have T back from following the
Zech 7:11 refused to hearken, and T a stubborn shoulder, and
14:10 whole land shall be T into a plain from
Mal 2:6 and uprightness, and he T many from iniquity.
2:8 But you have T aside from the way; you
3:7 your fathers you have T aside from my statutes
1Mac 1:18 in battle, and Ptolemy T and fled before him,
1:39 desert; her feasts were T into mourning, her sabbaths
1:40 glory; her exaltation was T into mourning.
3:8 the land; thus he T away wrath from Israel.
3:34 And he T over to Lysias half of his
4:16 Judas and his force T back from pursuing them,
4:27 intended, nor had they T out as the king
5:28 and his army quickly T back by the wilderness
5:35 Next he T aside to Alema, and fought against
5:68 But Judas T aside to Azotus in the land
6:6 strong force, but had T and fled before the
6:8 because things had not T out for him as
6:47 of the forces, they T away in flight.
9:16 wing was crushed, they T and followed close behind
9:41 Thus the wedding was T into mourning and the
9:72 of Judah; then he T and departed to his
11:72 Then he T back to the battle against the
12:31 So Jonathan T aside against the Arabs who are
12:33 He T aside to Joppa and took it by
12:51 for their lives, they T back.
13:24 Then Trypho T back and departed to his own
2Mac 5:18 have been scourged and T back from his rash
8:5 of the Lord had T to mercy.
10:22 these men who had T traitor, and immediately
12:42 are hidden; and they T to prayer, beseeching that
13:19 of the Jews, was T back, attacked again, and
13:26 king's attack and withdrawal T out.
15:37 then, is how matters T out with Nicanor.
Mt 9:22 Jesus T, and seeing her he said, "Take heart,
16:23 But he T and said to Peter, "Get behind
Mk 5:30 forth from him, immediately T about in the crowd,
Lk 7:9 marveled at him, and T and said to the
9:55 But he T and rebuked them.
14:25 accompanied him; and he T and said to them,
17:15 that he was healed, T back, praising God with
22:32 when you have T again, strengthen your brethren."
22:59 And the Lord T and looked at Peter.
Jn 1:38 Jesus T, and saw them following, and said to
20:14 Saying this, she T round and saw Jesus standing,
20:16 She T and said to him in Hebrew, "Rab-boni!"
21:20 Peter T and saw following them the disciple whom
Acts 1:25 apostleship from which Judas T aside, to go to
2:20 the sun shall be T into darkness and the
7:39 in their hearts they T to Egypt,
7:42 But God T and gave them over to worship
9:35 saw him, and they T to the Lord.
11:21 great number that believed T to the Lord.
16:18 Paul was annoyed, and T and said to the
17:6 "These men who have T the world upside down
19:26 Paul has persuaded and T away a considerable
Rom 3:12 All have T aside, together they have gone wrong;
1Thes 1:9 you, and how you T to God from idols,
2Tim 1:15 who are in Asia T away from me, and
Jas 4:9 Let your laughter be T to mourning and your
Rev 1:12 Then I T to see the voice that was

TURNEST

Ps 90:3 Thou T man back to the dust, and sayest,

TURNING (36)

Ex 23:2 witness in a suit, T aside after a multitude,
Josh 15:7 Achor, and so northward, T toward Gilgal, which is
18:14 goes in another direction, T on the western side
22:16 God of Israel in T away this day from
23:6 the law of Moses, T aside from it neither
2Kgs 21:13 dish, wiping it and T it upside down.
2Chr 36:13 hardened his heart against T to the LORD, the
Prov 1:32 are killed by their T away, and the complacence
Sir 8:5 a man who is T away from sin; remember
11:29 he lies in wait, T good into evil, and
33:5 his thoughts like a T axle.
38:29 at his work and T the wheel with his
Is 59:13 denying the LORD, and T away from following our
Jer 50:6 have led them astray, T them away on the
Bar 2:8 of the Lord by T away, each of us,
Ezek 1:9 one straight forward, without T as they went.
1:12 go, they went, without T as they went.
1:17 their four directions without T as they went.
10:11 their four directions without T as they went, but
10:11 the others followed without T as they went.
Dan 9:5 and rebelled, T aside from thy commandments
9:13 the LORD our God, T from our iniquities and
13:14 But T back, they met again; and when each
Hos 11:7 people are bent on T away from me; so
1Mac 2:22 the king's words by T aside from our religion
2Mac 9:4 conceived the idea of T upon the Jews the
Mk 8:33 But T and seeing his disciples, he rebuked Peter,
Lk 7:44 Then T toward the woman he said to Simon,
10:23 Then T to the disciples he said privately, "Blessed
23:27 But Jesus T to them said, "Daughters of Jerusalem,
Acts 3:26 to bless you in T every one of you
9:40 down and prayed; then T to the body he
26:24 your great learning is T you mad."
Gal 1:6 grace of Christ and T to a different gospel—
2Pet 2:6 the ungodly; if by T the cities of Sodom

Rev 1:12 to me, and on T I saw seven golden

TURNS (66)

Gen 27:44 until your brother's fury T away;
27:45 until your brother's anger T away, and he forgets
Lev 13:2 a spot, and it T into a leprous disease
13:16 if the raw flesh T again and is changed
20:6 "If a person T to mediums and wizards, playing
Deut 29:18 or tribe, whose heart T away this day from
30:17 But if your heart T away, and you will
Josh 15:3 Hezron, up to Addar, T about to Karka,
16:6 the east the boundary T round toward Taanath-shiloh,
19:14 the north the boundary T about to Hannathon, and
19:27 and Shihor-libnath, then it T eastward, it goes to
19:29 Great; then the boundary T to Ramah, reaching to
19:29 Tyre; then the boundary T to Hosah, and it
19:34 Jordan; then the boundary T westward to Aznoth-
Ruth 3:18 learn how the matter T out, for the man
Jud 8:11 enemies unless the Lord T and helps us within
Job 1:8 who fears God and T away from evil?"
2:3 who fears God and T away from evil?
24:18 the land; no treader T toward their vineyards.
30:30 My skin T black and falls from me, and
Ps 107:33 He T rivers into a desert, springs of water
107:35 He T a desert into pools of water, a
114:8 God of Jacob, who T the rock into a
Prov 12:26 A righteous man T away from evil, but the
14:16 man is cautious and T away from evil, but
15:1 A soft answer T away wrath, but a harsh
16:17 highway of the upright T aside from evil; he
17:8 gives it; wherever he T he prospers.
21:1 of the LORD; he T it wherever he will.
26:14 As a door T on its hinges, so does
28:9 If one T away his ear from hearing the
Wis 2:5 up and no one T back.
8:8 to come; she understands T of speech and the
Sir 18:12 and teaches them, and T them back, as a
18:23 of vengeance when he T away his face.
26:19 a man who T back from righteousness to
30:1 at the way he T out.
30:8 horse that is untamed T out to be stubborn,
30:8 and a son unrestrained T out to be wilful.
37:2 a companion and friend T to enmity?
37:18 changes of heart four T of fortune appear, good
39:23 wrath, just as he T fresh water into salt.
Is 44:25 fools of diviners; who T wise men back, and
Jer 8:4 If one T away, does he not return?
8:6 I done?' Every one T to his own course,
13:16 look for light he T it into gloom and
14:8 like a wayfarer who T aside to tarry for
17:5 his arm, whose heart T away from the LORD.
18:8 which I have spoken, T from its evil, I
23:14 so that no one T from his wickedness; all
Lam 1:8 she herself groans, and T her face away.
3:3 surely against me he T his hand again and
Ezek 3:20 if a righteous man T from his righteousness and
18:21 if a wicked man T away from all his
18:24 when a righteous man T away from his righteousness
18:26 When a righteous man T away from his
18:27 when a wicked man T away from the wickedness
33:12 by it when he T from his wickedness; and
33:14 die,' yet if he T from his sin and
33:18 When the righteous T from his righteousness, and
33:19 And when the wicked T from his wickedness, and
Amos 5:8 Pleiades and Orion, and T deep darkness into the
Nah 2:8 they cry; but none T back.
Lk 17:4 in the day, and T to you seven times,
2Cor 3:16 but when a man T to the Lord the
2Pet 2:22 true proverb, The dog T back to his own

TURTLEDOVE (4)

Gen 15:9 three years old, a T, and a young pigeon."
Lev 12:6 young pigeon or a T for a sin offering,
Song 2:12 the voice of the T is heard in our
Jer 8:7 her times; and the T, swallow, and crane keep

TURTLEDOVES (10)

Lev 1:14 bring his offering of T or of young pigeons.
5:7 he has committed, two T or two young pigeons,
5:11 he cannot afford two T or two young pigeons,
12:8 she shall take two T or two young pigeons,
14:22 of oil; also two T or two young pigeons,
14:30 shall offer, of the T or young pigeons such
15:14 he shall take two T or two young pigeons,
15:29 she shall take two T or two young pigeons,
Num 6:10 he shall bring two T or two young pigeons

Lk 2:24 Lord, "a pair of T, or two young pigeons."

TUSKS

Ezek 27:15 you in payment ivory T and ebony.

TWELFTH (27)

Num 7:78 On the T day Ahira the son of Enan,
1Kgs 19:19 oxen before him, and he was with the T
2Kgs 8:25 In the T year of Joram the son of
17:1 In the T year of Ahaz king of Judah
25:27 of Judah, in the T month, on the twenty-seventh
1Chr 24:12 eleventh to Eliashib, the T to Jakim,
25:19 his brethren, twelve; the T to Hashabiah, his sons
27:15 T, for the T month, was Heldai the Netophathite,
2Chr 34:3 father; and in the T year he began to
Ezra 8:31 river Ahava on the T day of the first
Jud 1:1 In the T year of the reign
Esth 3:7 of Nisan, in the T year of King Ahasuerus,
3:7 after month till the T month, which is the
3:13 thirteenth day of the T month, which is the
8:12 thirteenth day of the T month, which is the
9:1 Now in the T month, which is the month
13:6 fourteenth day of the T month, Adar, of this
16:20 thirteenth day of the T month, Adar, on that
Jer 52:31 of Judah, in the T month, on the twenty-fifth
Ezek 29:1 tenth month, on the T day of the month,
32:1 In the T year, in the twelfth month, on
32:1 twelfth year, in the T month, on the first
32:17 In the T year, in the first month, on
33:21 In the T year of our exile, in the
2Mac 15:36 thirteenth day of the T month – which
Rev 21:20 the eleventh jacinth, the T amethyst.

TWELVE (194)

Gen 5:8 were nine hundred and T years; and he died.
14:4 T years they had served Ched-or-laomer, but in the
17:20 be the father of T princes, and I will
25:16 and by their encampments, T princes according to
35:22 Now the sons of Jacob were T
42:13 "We, your servants, are T brothers, the sons of
42:32 not spies; we are T brothers, sons of our
49:28 All these are the T tribes of Israel; and
Ex 15:27 Elim, where there were T springs of water and
24:4 of the mountain, and T pillars, according to the
24:4 pillars, according to the T tribes of Israel.
28:21 There shall be T stones with their names according
28:21 its name, for the T tribes.
39:14 There were T stones with their names according to
39:14 its name, for the T tribes.
Lev 24:5 fine flour, and bake T cakes of it; two
Num 1:44 the leaders of Israel, T men, each representing his
7:3 six covered wagons and T oxen, a wagon for
7:84 the leaders of Israel: T silver plates, twelve silver
7:84 Israel: twelve silver plates, T silver basins, twelve
7:84 plates, twelve silver basins, T golden dishes,
7:86 of the sanctuary, the T golden dishes, full of
7:87 for the burnt offering T bulls, twelve rams, twelve
7:87 burnt offering twelve bulls, T rams, twelve male
7:87 twelve bulls, twelve rams, T male lambs a year
7:87 their cereal offering; and T male goats for a
17:2 to their fathers' houses, T rods.
17:6 to their fathers' houses, T rods; and the rod
29:17 "On the second day T young bulls, two rams,
31:5 thousand from each tribe, T thousand armed for war.
33:9 at Elim there were T springs of water and
Deut 1:23 me, and I took T men of you, one
Josh 3:12 Now therefore take T men from the tribes of
4:2 said to Joshua, "Take T men from the people,
4:3 and command them, 'Take T stones from here out
4:4 Then Joshua called the T men from the people
4:8 commanded, and took up T stones out of the
4:9 And Joshua set up T stones in the midst
4:20 And those T stones, which they took out of
8:25 men and women, were T thousand, all the people
18:24 Ophrah, Chephar-ammoni, Ophni, Geba– T cities with
19:15 Shimron, Idalah, and Bethlehem– T cities with their
21:7 the tribe of Zebulun, T cities.
21:40 them were in all T cities.
Judg 19:29 limb by limb, into T pieces, and sent her
21:10 the congregation sent thither T thousand of their
2Sam 2:15 over by number, T for Benjamin and Ish-bosheth
2:15 son of Saul, and T of the servants of
10:6 the men of Tob, T thousand men.
17:1 Absalom, "Let me choose T thousand men, and I
1Kgs 4:7 Solomon had T officers over all Israel, who provided
4:26 for his chariots, and T thousand horsemen.

T

	7:15	and a line of T cubits measured its circumference;
	7:25	It stood upon T oxen, three facing north, three
	7:44	one sea, and the T oxen underneath the sea.
	10:20	the arm rests, while T lions stood there, one
	10:26	hundred chariots and T thousand horsemen, whom
	11:30	and tore it into T pieces.
	16:23	Israel, and reigned for T years; six years he
	18:31	thrown down; Elijah took T stones, according to the
	19:19	who was plowing, with T yoke of oxen before
2Kgs	3:1	Samaria, and he reigned T years.
	21:1	Manasseh was T years old when he began to
1Chr	6:63	their families were allotted T cities out of the
	9:22	at the thresholds, were two hundred and T
	15:10	with a hundred and T of his brethren.
	25:9	brethren and his sons, T;
	25:10	sons and his brethren, T;
	25:11	sons and his brethren, T;
	25:12	sons and his brethren, T;
	25:13	sons and his brethren, T;
	25:14	sons and his brethren, T;
	25:15	sons and his brethren, T;
	25:16	sons and his brethren, T;
	25:17	sons and his brethren, T;
	25:18	sons and his brethren, T;
	25:19	sons and his brethren, T;
	25:20	sons and his brethren, T;
	25:21	sons and his brethren, T;
	25:22	sons and his brethren, T;
	25:23	sons and his brethren, T;
	25:24	sons and his brethren, T;
	25:25	sons and his brethren, T;
	25:26	sons and his brethren, T;
	25:27	sons and his brethren, T;
	25:28	sons and his brethren, T;
	25:29	sons and his brethren, T;
	25:30	sons and his brethren, T;
	25:31	to Romamti-ezer, his sons and his brethren, T
2Chr	1:14	fourteen hundred chariots and T thousand horsemen,
	4:4	It stood upon T oxen, three facing north, three
	4:15	one sea, and the T oxen underneath it.
	9:19	the arm rests, while T lions stood there, one
	9:25	horses and chariots, and T thousand horsemen, whom
	12:3	up against Jerusalem with T hundred chariots and
	33:1	Manasseh was T years old when he began to
Ezra	2:6	Jeshua and Joab, two thousand eight hundred and T
	2:18	The sons of Jorah, one hundred and T
	6:17	offering for all Israel T he-goats, according to the
	8:24	Then I set apart T of the leading priests:
	8:35	the God of Israel, T bulls for all Israel,
	8:35	as a sin offering T he-goats; all this was
Neh	5:14	of Artaxerxes the king, T years, neither I nor
	7:24	The sons of Hariph, a hundred and T
Jud	2:5	thousand foot soldiers and T thousand cavalry.
	2:15	together with T thousand archers on horseback,
	7:2	seventy thousand infantry and T thousand cavalry,
Esth	2:12	King Ahasuerus, after being T months under the
Sir	44:24	and distributed them among T tribes.
	49:10	the bones of the T prophets revive from where
Jer	52:20	the one sea, the T bronze bulls which were
	52:21	cubits, its circumference was T cubits, and its
Ezek	40:49	cubits, and the breadth T cubits; and ten steps
	43:16	hearth shall be square, T cubits long by twelve
	43:16	twelve cubits long by T broad.
	47:13	for inheritance among the T tribes of Israel.
Dan	4:29	At the end of T months he was walking
	14:3	they spent on it T bushels of fine flour
1Mac	1:7	after Alexander had reigned T years, he died.
Mt	9:20	from a hemorrhage for T years came up behind
	10:1	called to him his T disciples and gave them
	10:2	The names of the T apostles are these: first,
	10:5	These T Jesus sent out, charging them, "Go nowhere
	11:1	had finished instructing his T disciples, he went on
	14:20	And they took up T baskets full of the
	19:28	will also sit on T thrones, judging the twelve
	19:28	twelve thrones, judging the T tribes of Israel.
	20:17	Jerusalem, he took the T disciples aside, and on
	26:14	Then one of the T, who was called Judas
	26:20	at table with the T disciples;
	26:47	came, one of the T, and with him a
	26:53	send me more than T legions of angels?
Mk	3:14	And he appointed T, to be with him, and
	4:10	about him with the T asked him concerning the
	5:25	flow of blood for T years,
	5:42	and walked (she was T years of age), and
	6:7	called to him the T, and began to send
	6:43	And they took up T baskets full of broken
	8:19	They said to him, T
	9:35	down and called the T; and he said to
	10:32	And taking the T again, he began to tell
	11:11	late, he went out to Bethany with the T
	14:10	was one of the T, went to the chief
	14:17	when it was evening he came with the T
	14:20	is one of the T, one who is dipping
	14:43	came, one of the T, and with him a
Lk	2:42	And when he was T years old, they went
	6:13	and chose from them T, whom he named apostles;
	8:1	And the T were with him,
	8:42	an only daughter, about T years of age, and
	8:43	flow of blood for T years and had spent
	9:1	And he called the T together and gave them
	9:12	wear away; and the T came and said to
	9:17	what was left over, T baskets of broken pieces.
	18:31	And taking the T, he said to them, "Behold,
	22:3	the number of the T;
	22:30	on thrones judging the T tribes of Israel.
	22:45	Judas, one of the T, was leading them.
Jn	6:13	them up and filled T baskets with fragments from
	6:67	Jesus said to the T, "Do you also wish
	6:70	not choose you, the T, and one of you
	6:71	he, one of the T, was to betray him.
	11:9	answered, "Are there not T hours in the day?
	20:24	Thomas, one of the T, called the Twin, was
Acts	6:2	And the T summoned the body of the disciples
	7:8	and Jacob of the T patriarchs.
	19:7	There were about T of them in all.
	24:10	is not more than T days since I went
	26:7	fathers, to which our T tribes hope to attain,
1Cor	15:5	that he appeared to Cephas, then to the T
Jas	1:1	Jesus Christ, to the T tribes in the dispersion:
Rev	7:5	the sons of Israel, T thousand sealed out of
	7:5	the tribe of Judah, T thousand of the tribe
	7:5	the tribe of Reuben, T thousand of the tribe
	7:6	the tribe of Gad, T thousand of the tribe
	7:6	the tribe of Asher, T thousand of the tribe
	7:6	the tribe of Naphtali, T thousand of the tribe
	7:7	the tribe of Manasseh, T thousand of the tribe
	7:7	the tribe of Simeon, T thousand of the tribe
	7:7	the tribe of Levi, T thousand of the tribe
	7:8	the tribe of Issachar, T thousand of the tribe
	7:8	the tribe of Zebulun, T thousand of the tribe
	7:8	the tribe of Joseph, T thousand sealed out of
	12:1	head a crown of T stars;
	21:12	great, high wall, with T gates, and at the
	21:12	and at the gates T angels, and on the
	21:12	the names of the T tribes of the sons
	21:14	of the city had T foundations, and on them
	21:14	and on them the T names of the twelve
	21:14	twelve names of the T apostles of the Lamb.
	21:16	city with his rod, T thousand stadia; its length
	21:21	And the T gates were twelve pearls, each of
	21:21	the twelve gates were T pearls, each of the
	22:2	of life with its T kinds of fruit, yielding

TWENTIETH (9)

Num	10:11	second month, on the T day of the month,
1Kgs	15:9	In the T year of Jeroboam king of Israel
2Kgs	15:30	his stead, in the T year of Jotham the
1Chr	24:16	nineteenth to Pethahiah, the T to Jehezkel,
	25:27	brethren, twelve; to the T, to Eliathah, his sons
Ezra	10:9	ninth month, on the T day of the month.
Neh	1:1	of Chislev, in the T year, as I was
	2:1	of Nisan, in the T year of King Artaxerxes,
	5:14	of Judah, from the T year to the thirty-second

TWENTY (169)

Gen	6:3	be a hundred and T years."
	18:31	Suppose T are found there." He answered, "For the
	18:31	"For the sake of T I will not destroy
	31:38	These T years I have been with you; your
	31:41	These T years I have been in your house;
	32:14	hundred she-goats and T he-goats, two hundred ewes
	32:14	two hundred ewes and T rams,
	32:15	cows and ten bulls, T she-asses and ten he-asses.
	37:28	to the Ishmaelites for T shekels of silver; and
Ex	26:18	frames for the tabernacle: T frames for the south
	26:19	shall make under the T frames, two bases under
	26:20	on the north side T frames,
	27:10	their pillars shall be T and their bases twenty,
	27:10	twenty and their bases T, of bronze, but the
	27:11	cubits long, their pillars T and their bases twenty,
	27:11	twenty and their bases T, of bronze, but the
	27:16	shall be a screen T cubits long, of blue

T

TWENTY-EIGHT (13)

TWENTY-FIFTH (8)

1Mac 1:59 And on the T day of the month they
4:52 the morning on the T day of the ninth
4:59 days, beginning with the T day of the month
2Mac 1:18 Since on the T day of Chislev we shall
10:5 that is, on the T day of the same

TWENTY-FIRST (4)

Ex 12:18 and so until the T day of the month
1Chr 24:17 twentieth to Jehezkel, the T to Jachin, the
25:28 brethren, twelve; to the T, to Hothir, his sons
Hag 2:1 seventh month, on the T day of the month,

TWENTY-FIVE (39)

Num 8:24 to the Levites: from T years old and upward
Judg 20:35 men of Israel destroyed T thousand one hundred
20:46 day of Benjamin were T thousand men that drew
1Kgs 22:42 reign, and he reigned T years in Jerusalem.
2Kgs 14:2 He was T years old when he began to
15:33 He was T years old when he began to
18:2 He was T years old when he began to
23:36 Jehoiakim was T years old when he began to
2Chr 20:31 reign, and he reigned T years in Jerusalem.
25:1 Amaziah was T years old when he began to
27:1 Jotham was T years old when he began to
27:8 He was T years old when he began to
29:1 reign when he was T years old, and he
36:5 Jehoiakim was T years old when he began to
Ezra 2:33 of Lod, Hadid, and Ono, seven hundred and T
Ezek 8:16 the altar, were about T men, with their backs
11:1 the gateway there were T men; and I saw
40:21 cubits, and its breadth T cubits.
40:25 cubits, and its breadth T cubits.
40:29 cubits, and its breadth T cubits.
40:30 were vestibules round about, T cubits long and five
40:33 cubits, and its breadth T cubits.
40:36 cubits, and its breadth T cubits.
45:1 as a holy district, T thousand cubits long and
45:3 measure off a section T thousand cubits long and
45:5 Another section, T thousand cubits long and ten
45:6 thousand cubits broad, and T thousand cubits long; it
48:8 you shall set apart, T thousand cubits in breadth,
48:9 the LORD shall be T thousand cubits in length,
48:10 have an allotment measuring T thousand cubits on
48:10 the eastern side, and T thousand in length on
48:13 shall have an allotment T thousand cubits in length
48:13 whole length shall be T thousand cubits and the
48:15 cubits in breadth and T thousand in length, shall
48:20 set apart shall be T thousand cubits square, that
48:21 Extending from the T thousand cubits of the holy
48:21 and westward from the T thousand cubits to the
2Mac 12:26 of Atargatis, and slaughtered T thousand people.
12:28 killed as many as T thousand of those who

TWENTY-FOUR (26)

Num 7:88 sacrifice of peace offerings T bulls, the rams sixty,
25:9 by the plague were T thousand.
2Sam 21:20 toes on each foot, T in number; and he
1Kgs 15:33 at Tirzah, and reigned T years.
1Chr 20:6 toes on each foot, T in number; and he
23:4 T thousand of these," David said, "shall have charge
27:1 year, each division numbering T thousand:
27:2 in his division were T thousand.
27:4 in his division were T thousand.
27:5 in his division were T thousand.
27:7 in his division were T thousand.
27:8 in his division were T thousand.
27:9 in his division were T thousand.
27:10 in his division were T thousand.
27:11 in his division were T thousand.
27:12 in his division were T thousand.
27:13 in his division were T thousand.
27:14 in his division were T thousand.
27:15 in his division were T thousand.
Neh 7:23 The sons of Bezai, three hundred and T
Rev 4:4 Round the throne were T thrones, and seated on
4:4 on the thrones were T elders, clad in white
4:10 ever and ever, the T elders fall down before
5:8 living creatures and the T elders fell down before
11:16 And the T elders who sit on their thrones
19:4 And the T elders and the four living creatures

TWENTY-FOURTH (10)

1Chr 24:18 twenty-third to Delaiah, the T to Ma-aziah.
25:31 brethren, twelve; to the T, to Romamti-ezer, his sons
Neh 9:1 Now on the T day of this month the
Dan 10:4 On the T day of the first month, as

Hag 1:15 their God, on the T day of the month,
2:10 On the T day of the ninth month, in
2:18 day onward, from the T day of the ninth
2:20 to Haggai on the T day of the month,
Zech 1:7 On the T day of the eleventh month which
2Mac 11:21 one hundred and forty-eighth year, Dioscorinthius T

TWENTY-NINE (8)

Gen 11:24 When Nahor had lived T years, he became the
Ex 38:24 from the offering, was T talents and seven hundred
Josh 15:32 and Rimmon: in all, T cities, with their villages.
2Kgs 14:2 reign, and he reigned T years in Jerusalem.
18:2 reign, and he reigned T years in Jerusalem.
2Chr 25:1 reign, and he reigned T years in Jerusalem.
29:1 old, and he reigned T years in Jerusalem.
Ezra 1:9 thousand basins of silver, T censers,

TWENTY-ONE (7)

2Kgs 24:18 Zedekiah was T years old when he became king,
2Chr 36:11 Zedekiah was T years old when he began to
Ezra 2:26 sons of Ramah and Geba, six hundred and T
Neh 7:30 men of Ramah and Geba, six hundred and T
7:37 of Lod, Hadid, and Ono, seven hundred and T
Jer 52:1 Zedekiah was T years old when he became king;
Dan 10:13 of Persia withstood me T days; but Michael, one

TWENTY-SECOND (3)

1Chr 24:17 twenty-first to Jachin, the T to Gamul,
25:29 brethren, twelve; to the T, to Giddalti, his sons
Jud 2:1 eighteenth year, on the T day of the first

TWENTY-SEVEN (8)

Gen 23:1 lived a hundred and T years; these were the
1Kgs 20:30 the wall fell upon T thousand men that were
Tob 14:14 of a hundred and T years.
Esth 1:1 over one hundred and T provinces,
8:9 Ethiopia, a hundred and T provinces, to every
9:30 to the hundred and T provinces of the kingdom
13:1 of the hundred and T provinces from India to
16:1 Ethiopia, one hundred and T satrapies, and to those

TWENTY-SEVENTH (6)

Gen 8:14 second month, on the T day of the month,
1Kgs 16:10 killed him, in the T year of Asa king
16:15 In the T year of Asa king of Judah,
2Kgs 15:1 In the T year of Jeroboam king of Israel
25:27 twelfth month, on the T day of the month,
Ezek 29:17 In the T year, in the first month, on

TWENTY-SIX (2)

Judg 20:15 cities on that day T thousand men that drew
1Chr 7:40 service in war, was T thousand men.

TWENTY-SIXTH

1Kgs 16:8 In the T year of Asa king of Judah,

TWENTY-THIRD (8)

2Kgs 12:6 But by the T year of King Jehoash the
13:1 In the T year of Joash the son of
1Chr 24:18 twenty-second to Gamul, the T to Delaiah, the
25:30 brethren, twelve; to the T, to Mahazi-oth, his sons
2Chr 7:10 On the T day of the seventh month he
Esth 8:9 of Sivan, on the T day; and an edict
Jer 52:30 thirty-two persons; in the T year of Nebuchadrezzar,
1Mac 13:51 On the T day of the second month, in

TWENTY-THREE (15)

Num 26:62 numbered of them were T thousand, every male
33:39 was a hundred and T years old when he
Judg 10:2 And he judged Israel T years.
2Kgs 23:31 Jehoahaz was T years old when he began to
1Chr 2:22 of Jair, who had T cities in the land
2Chr 36:2 Jehoahaz was T years old when he began to
Ezra 2:11 The sons of Bebai, six hundred and T
2:17 The sons of Bezai, three hundred and T
2:19 The sons of Hashum, two hundred and T
2:21 The sons of Bethlehem, one hundred and T
2:28 men of Bethel and Ai, two hundred and T
Neh 7:32 men of Bethel and Ai, a hundred and T
Jer 25:3 inhabitants of Jerusalem: "For T years, from the
52:28 year, three thousand and T Jews;
1Cor 10:8 of them did, and T thousand fell in a

TWENTY-TWO (27)

Num 3:39 old and upward, were T thousand.
3:43 upward as numbered were T thousand two hundred

26:14 families of the Simeonites, T thousand two hundred.
Josh 19:30 Ummah, Aphek and Rehob-- T cities with their
Judg 7:3 And Gideon tested them; T thousand returned, and
10:3 Gileadite, who judged Israel T years.
20:21 ground on that day T thousand men of the
2Sam 8:5 of Zobah, David slew T thousand men of the
1Kgs 8:63 offerings to the LORD T thousand oxen and a
14:20 that Jeroboam reigned was T years; and he slept
16:29 over Israel in Samaria T years.
2Kgs 8:26 Ahaziah was T years old when he began to
21:19 Amon was T years old when he began to
1Chr 7:2 days of David being T thousand six hundred.
7:7 enrollment by genealogies was T thousand and
12:28 mighty in valor, and T commanders from his own
18:5 of Zobah, David slew T thousand men of the
2Chr 7:5 offered as a sacrifice T thousand oxen and a
13:21 fourteen wives, and had T sons and sixteen
33:21 Amon was T years old when he began to
Ezra 2:12 sons of Azgad, one thousand two hundred and T
2:27 The men of Michmas, one hundred and T
Neh 7:17 sons of Azgad, two thousand three hundred and T
7:31 The men of Michmas, a hundred and T
11:12 house, eight hundred and T; and Adaiah the son
2Mac 5:24 with an army of T thousand, and commanded him
13:2 thousand three hundred cavalry, T elephants, and

TWICE (30)

Gen 43:10 had not delayed, we would now have returned T
Ex 16:5 in, it will be T as much as they
16:22 sixth day they gathered T as much bread, two
Num 20:11 rock with his rod T; and water came forth
1Sam 18:11 But David evaded him T
26:8 the spear, and I will not strike him T
1Kgs 11:9 had appeared to him T,
2Kgs 6:10 he saved himself there more than once or T
Neh 13:20 kinds of wares lodged outside Jerusalem once or T
Jud 13:8 she struck his neck T with all her might,
Job 33:29 does all these things, T, three times, with a
40:5 I will not answer; T, but I will proceed
42:10 the LORD gave Job T as much as he
Ps 62:11 Once God has spoken; T have I heard this:
68:17 With mighty chariotry, T ten thousand, thousands
Eccl 6:6 live a thousand years T told, yet enjoy no
Sir 7:8 not commit a sin T; even for one you
12:5 for you will receive T as much evil for
32:7 but no more than T, and only if asked.
45:14 shall be wholly burned T every day continually.
Ezek 21:14 the sword come down T, yea thrice, the sword
Nah 1:9 will not take vengeance T on his foes.
1Mac 10:72 for your fathers were T put to flight in
Mt 23:14 proselyte, you make him T as much a child
Mk 14:30 before the cock crows T, you will deny me
14:72 "Before the cock crows T, you will deny me
Lk 18:12 I fast T a week, I give tithes of
Tit 3:10 admonishing him once or T, have nothing more to
Jude 1:12 trees in late autumn, T dead, uprooted;
Rev 9:16 troops of cavalry was T ten thousand times ten

TWIG

Ezek 17:5 it like a willow T,

TWIGS (2)

Ezek 17:4 topmost of its young T and carried it to
17:22 topmost of its young T a tender one, and

TWILIGHT (9)

Ex 16:12 say to them, 'At T you shall eat flesh,
1Sam 30:17 David smote them from T until the evening of
2Kgs 7:5 So they arose at T to go to the
7:7 fled away in the T and forsook their tents,
Job 24:15 also waits for the T, saying, 'No eye will
Prov 7:9 her house in the T, in the evening, at
Is 21:4 has appalled me; the T I longed for has
59:10 noon as in the T, among those in full
Jer 13:16 feet stumble on the T mountains, and while you

TWIN (4)

Jn 11:16 Thomas, called the T, said to his fellow disciples,
20:24 the twelve, called the T, was not with them
21:2 Peter, Thomas called the T, Nathanael of Cana in
Acts 28:11 of Alexandria, with the T Brothers as figurehead.

TWINE

Job 8:17 His roots T about the stoneheap; he lives among

TWINED (28)

Ex 25:4 scarlet stuff and fine T linen, goats' hair,
26:1 ten curtains of fine T linen and blue and
26:31 scarlet stuff and fine T linen; in skilled work
26:36 scarlet stuff and fine T linen, embroidered with
27:9 have hangings of fine T linen a hundred cubits
27:16 scarlet stuff and fine T linen, embroidered with
27:18 with hangings of fine T linen and bases of
28:5 scarlet stuff, and fine T linen.
28:6 stuff, and of fine T linen, skilfully worked.
28:8 scarlet stuff, and fine T linen.
28:15 scarlet stuff, and fine T linen shall you make
35:6 scarlet stuff and fine T linen; goats' hair,
35:25 scarlet stuff and fine T linen;
35:35 scarlet stuff and fine T linen, or by a
36:8 were made of fine T linen and blue and
36:35 scarlet stuff and fine T linen; with cherubim skilfully
36:37 stuff and fine T linen, embroidered with needlework;
38:9 court were of fine T linen, a hundred cubits;
38:16 court were of fine T linen.
38:18 scarlet stuff and fine T linen; it was twenty
38:23 scarlet stuff and fine T linen.
39:2 scarlet stuff, and fine T linen.
39:3 and into the fine T linen, in skilled design.
39:5 scarlet stuff, and fine T linen; as the LORD
39:8 scarlet stuff, and fine T linen.
39:24 scarlet stuff and fine T linen.
39:28 linen breeches of fine T linen,
39:29 the girdle of fine T linen and of blue

TWINKLING

1Cor 15:52 a moment, in the T of an eye, at

TWINS (6)

Gen 25:24 fulfilled, behold, there were T in her womb.
38:27 delivery came, there were T in her womb.
Song 4:2 all of which bear T, and not one among
4:5 are like two fawns, T of a gazelle, that
6:6 all of them bear T, not one among them
7:3 are like two fawns, T of a gazelle.

TWIST (3)

Sir 27:23 but later he will T his speech and with
Is 24:1 desolate, and he will T its surface and scatter
2Pet 3:16 the ignorant and unstable T to their own destruction,

TWISTED (6)

Ex 28:14 chains of pure gold, T like cords; and you
28:22 make for the breastpiece T chains like cords, of
39:15 made on the breastpiece T chains like cords, of
Ps 78:57 like their fathers; they T like a deceitful bow.
Prov 8:8 righteous; there is nothing T or crooked in them.
Sir 45:11 Urim and Thummim; with T scarlet, the work of

TWISTING

Is 27:1 fleeing serpent, Leviathan the T serpent, and he will

TWO (831)

Gen 1:16 And God made the T great lights, the greater
4:19 And Lamech took T wives; the name of the
6:19 flesh, you shall bring T of every sort into
6:20 according to its kind, T of every sort shall
7:9 creeps on the ground, T and two, male and
7:9 the ground, two and T, male and female, went
7:15 the ark with Noah, T and two of all
7:15 with Noah, two and T of all flesh in
9:22 father, and told his T brothers outside.
10:25 To Eber were born T sons: the name of
11:10 the father of Arpachshad T years after the flood;
11:19 the birth of Reu T hundred and nine years,
11:21 the birth of Serug T hundred and seven years,
11:23 the birth of Nahor T hundred years, and had
11:32 days of Terah were T hundred and five years;
15:10 these, cut them in T, and laid each half
15:10 but he did not cut the birds in T
19:1 The T angels came to Sodom in the evening;
19:8 Behold, I have T daughters who have not known
19:15 your wife and your T daughters who are here,
19:16 his wife and his T daughters by the hand,
19:30 the hills with his T daughters, for he was
19:30 a cave with his T daughters.
21:27 to Abimelech, and the T men made a covenant.
22:3 his ass, and took T of his young men
24:22 weighing a half-shekel, and T bracelets for her arms
25:23 LORD said to her, T nations are in your
25:23 in your womb, and T peoples, born of you,

T

27:9 flock, and fetch me T good kids, that I
27:36 has supplanted me these T times.
29:16 Now Laban had T daughters; the name of the
31:33 the tent of the T maidservants, but he did
31:37 your kinsmen, that they may decide between us T
31:41 fourteen years for your T daughters, and six years
32:7 herds and camels, into T companies,
32:10 now I have become T companies.
32:14 for his brother Esau, T hundred she-goats and twenty
32:14 she-goats and twenty he-goats, T hundred ewes and
32:22 arose and took his T wives, his two maids,
32:22 his two wives, his T maids, and his eleven
33:1 and Rachel and the T maids.
34:25 when they were sore, T of the sons of
40:2 was angry with his T officers, the chief butler
41:1 After T whole years, Pharaoh dreamed that he was
41:50 famine came, Joseph had T sons, whom Asenath, the
42:37 his father, "Slay my T sons if I do
44:27 my wife bore me T sons;
45:6 in the land these T years; and there are
46:27 him in Egypt, were T; all the persons of
48:1 took with him his T sons, Manasseh and Ephraim.
48:5 possession.' And now your T sons, who were born
Ex 2:13 the next day, behold, T Hebrews were struggling
4:9 not believe even these T signs or heed your
12:7 put it on the T doorposts and the lintel
12:22 the lintel and the T doorposts with the blood
12:23 lintel and on the T doorposts, the LORD will
16:22 twice as much bread, T omers apiece; and when
16:29 gives you bread for T days; remain every man
18:3 her away, and her T sons, of whom the
18:6 your wife and her T sons with her,"
21:21 survives a day or T, he is not to
25:10 ark of acacia wood; T cubits and a half
25:12 on its four feet, T rings on the one
25:12 side of it, and T rings on the other
25:17 seat of pure gold; T cubits and a half
25:18 And you shall make T cherubim of gold; of
25:18 make them, on the T ends of the mercy
25:19 the cherubim on its T ends.
25:22 seat, from between the T cherubim that are upon
25:23 table of acacia wood; T cubits shall be its
26:17 There shall be T tenons in each frame, for
26:19 under the twenty frames, T bases under one frame
26:19 one frame for its T tenons, and two bases
26:19 its two tenons, and T bases under another frame
26:19 another frame for its T tenons;
26:21 forty bases of silver, T bases under one frame,
26:21 under one frame, and T bases under another frame;
26:23 And you shall make T frames for corners of
26:24 they shall form the T corners.
26:25 of silver, sixteen bases; T bases under one frame,
26:25 under one frame, and T bases under another frame.
27:7 shall be upon the T sides of the altar,
28:7 It shall have T shoulder-pieces attached to its two
28:7 shoulder-pieces attached to its T edges, that it may
28:9 And you shall take T onyx stones, and engrave
28:11 shall you engrave the T stones with the names
28:12 you shall set the T stones upon the shoulder-pieces
28:12 the LORD upon his T shoulders for remembrance.
28:14 of gold filigree, and T chains of pure gold,
28:23 make for the breastpiece T rings of gold, and
28:23 gold, and put the T rings on the two
28:23 two rings on the T edges of the breastpiece.
28:24 you shall put the T cords of gold in
28:24 of gold in the T rings at the edges
28:25 of the breastpiece; the T ends of the two
28:25 two ends of the T cords you shall attach
28:25 shall attach to the T settings of filigree, and
28:26 And you shall make T rings of gold, and
28:26 put them at the T ends of the breastpiece,
28:27 And you shall make T rings of gold, and
28:27 lower part of the T shoulder-pieces of the ephod,
29:1 one young bull and T rams without blemish,
29:3 the bull and the T rams.
29:13 the liver, and the T kidneys with the fat
29:22 the liver, and the T kidneys with the fat
29:38 offer upon the altar: T lambs a year old
30:2 shall be square, and T cubits shall be its
30:4 And T golden rings shall you make for it;
30:4 under its molding on T opposite sides of it
30:23 as much, that is, T hundred and fifty, and
30:23 and of aromatic cane T hundred and fifty,
31:18 upon Mount Sinai, the T tables of the testimony,
32:15 the mountain with the T tables of the testimony
34:1 said to Moses, "Cut T tables of stone like
34:4 So Moses cut T tables of stone like the
34:4 took in his hand T tables of stone.
34:29 Mount Sinai, with the T tables of the testimony
36:22 Each frame had T tenons, for fitting together; he
36:24 under the twenty frames, T bases under one frame
36:24 one frame for its T tenons, and two bases
36:24 its two tenons, and T bases under another frame
36:24 another frame for its T tenons.
36:26 forty bases of silver, T bases under one frame
36:26 under one frame and T bases under another frame.
36:28 And he made T frames for corners of the
36:29 first ring; he made T of them thus, for
36:29 them thus, for the T corners.
36:30 bases, under every frame T bases.
37:1 ark of acacia wood; T cubits and a half
37:3 for its four corners, T rings on its one
37:3 its one side and T rings on its other
37:6 seat of pure gold; T cubits and a half
37:7 And he made T cherubim of hammered gold; on
37:7 hammered gold; on the T ends of the mercy
37:8 the cherubim on its T ends.
37:10 table of acacia wood; T cubits was its length,
37:25 it was square, and T cubits was its height;
37:27 about it, and made T rings of gold on
37:27 under its molding, on T opposite sides of it,
38:29 was seventy talents, and T thousand and four hundred
39:4 to it at its T edges.
39:16 gold; and they made T settings of gold filigree
39:16 of gold filigree and T gold rings, and put
39:16 rings, and put the T rings on the two
39:16 two rings on the T edges of the breastpiece;
39:17 and they put the T cords of gold in
39:17 of gold in the T rings at the edges
39:18 T ends of the two cords they had attached
39:18 Two ends of the T cords they had attached
39:18 had attached to the T settings of filigree; thus
39:19 Then they made T rings of gold, and put
39:19 put them at the T ends of the breastpiece,
39:20 And they made T rings of gold, and attached
39:20 lower part of the T shoulder-pieces of the ephod,
Lev 3:4 the entrails, and the T kidneys with the fat
3:10 the entrails, and the T kidneys with the fat
3:15 the entrails, and the T kidneys with the fat
4:9 the entrails, and the T kidneys with the fat
5:7 which he has committed, T turtledoves or two young
5:7 committed, two turtledoves or T young pigeons, one
5:11 if he cannot afford T turtledoves or two young
5:11 afford two turtledoves or T young pigeons, then he
7:4 covers the entrails, the T kidneys with the fat
8:2 sin offering, and the T rams, and the basket
8:16 the liver, and the T kidneys with their fat,
8:25 the liver, and the T kidneys with their fat,
12:5 she shall be unclean T weeks, as in her
12:8 then she shall take T turtledoves or two young
12:8 take two turtledoves or T young pigeons, one for
14:4 is to be cleansed T living clean birds and
14:10 day he shall take T male lambs without blemish,
14:22 log of oil; also T turtledoves or two young
14:22 also two turtledoves or T young pigeons, such as
14:49 house he shall take T small birds, with cedarwood
15:14 day he shall take T turtledoves or two young
15:14 take two turtledoves or T young pigeons, and come
15:29 day she shall take T turtledoves or two young
15:29 take two turtledoves or T young pigeons, and bring
16:1 the death of the T sons of Aaron, when
16:5 the people of Israel T male goats for a
16:7 he shall take the T goats, and set them
16:8 cast lots upon the T goats, one lot for
16:12 before the LORD, and T handfuls of sweet incense
19:19 sow your field with T kinds of seed; nor
19:19 of cloth made of T kinds of stuff.
23:13 with it shall be T tenths of an ephah
23:17 bring from your dwellings T loaves of bread to
23:17 be waved, made of T tenths of an ephah;
23:18 one young bull, and T rams; they shall be
23:19 a sin offering, and T male lambs a year
23:20 the LORD, with the T lambs; they shall be
24:5 twelve cakes of it; T tenths of an ephah
24:6 shall set them in T rows, six in a
Num 1:35 Manasseh was thirty-two thousand T hundred.
2:21 numbered being thirty-two thousand T hundred.
3:34 upward was six thousand T hundred.
3:43 numbered were twenty-two thousand T hundred and
3:46 the redemption of the T hundred and seventy-three
4:36 number by families was T thousand seven hundred
4:40 their fathers' houses was T thousand six hundred and

4:44 families was three thousand T hundred.
6:10 day he shall bring T turtledoves or two young
6:10 bring two turtledoves or T young pigeons to the
7:3 a wagon for every T of the leaders, and
7:7 T wagons and four oxen he gave to the
7:17 sacrifice of peace offerings, T oxen, five rams, five
7:23 sacrifice of peace offerings, T oxen, five rams, five
7:29 sacrifice of peace offerings, T oxen, five rams, five
7:35 sacrifice of peace offerings, T oxen, five rams, five
7:41 sacrifice of peace offerings, T oxen, five rams, five
7:47 sacrifice of peace offerings, T oxen, five rams, five
7:53 sacrifice of peace offerings, T oxen, five rams, five
7:59 sacrifice of peace offerings, T oxen, five rams, five
7:65 sacrifice of peace offerings, T oxen, five rams, five
7:71 sacrifice of peace offerings, T oxen, five rams, five
7:77 sacrifice of peace offerings, T oxen, five rams, five
7:83 sacrifice of peace offerings, T oxen, five rams, five
7:85 silver of the vessels T thousand four hundred shekels
7:89 testimony, from between the T cherubim; and it
9:22 Whether it was T days, or a month, or
10:2 said to Moses, "Make T silver trumpets; of
11:19 eat one day, or T days, or five days,
11:26 Now T men remained in the camp, one named
11:31 the camp, and about T cubits above the face
13:23 on a pole between T of them; they brought
15:6 for a cereal offering T tenths of an ephah
16:2 the people of Israel, T hundred and fifty leaders
16:17 the LORD his censer, T hundred and fifty censers;
16:35 LORD, and consumed the T hundred and fifty men
22:22 the ass, and his T servants were with him.
26:10 when the fire devoured T hundred and fifty men;
26:14 the Simeonites, twenty-two thousand T hundred.
28:3 offer to the LORD: T male lambs a year
28:9 "On the sabbath day T male lambs a year
28:9 old without blemish, and T tenths of an ephah
28:11 offering to the LORD: T young bulls, one ram,
28:12 for each bull; and T tenths of fine flour
28:19 offering to the LORD: T young bulls, one ram,
28:20 for a bull, and T tenths for a ram;
28:27 odor to the LORD; T young bulls, one ram,
28:28 ephah for each bull, T tenths for one ram,
29:3 ephah for the bull, T tenths for the ram,
29:9 ephah for the bull, T tenths for the one
29:13 LORD, thirteen young bulls, T rams, fourteen male
29:14 of the thirteen bulls, T tenths for each of
29:14 for each of the T rams,
29:17 day twelve young bulls, T rams, fourteen male lambs
29:20 third day eleven bulls, T rams, fourteen male lambs
29:23 fourth day ten bulls, T rams, fourteen male lambs
29:26 fifth day nine bulls, T rams, fourteen male lambs
29:29 sixth day eight bulls, T rams, fourteen male lambs
29:32 seventh day seven bulls, T rams, fourteen male lambs
31:27 divide the booty into T parts, between the warriors
34:15 half-tribe of Manasseh; the T tribes and the
35:5 for the east side T thousand cubits, and for
35:5 for the south side T thousand cubits, and for
35:5 for the west side T thousand cubits, and for
35:5 for the north side T thousand cubits, the city
Deut 3:8 the hand of the T kings of the Amorites
3:21 has done to these T kings; so will the
4:13 he wrote them upon T tables of stone.
4:47 king of Bashan, the T kings of the Amorites,
5:22 he wrote them upon T tables of stone, and
9:10 LORD gave me the T tables of stone written
9:11 LORD gave me the T tables of stone, the
9:15 with fire; and the T tables of the covenant
9:15 covenant were in my T hands.
9:17 took hold of the T tables, and cast them
9:17 them out of my T hands, and broke them
10:1 said to me, 'Hew T tables of stone like
10:3 acacia wood, and hewed T tables of stone like
10:3 the mountain with the T tables in my hand.
14:6 the hoof cloven in T, and chews the cud,
17:6 On the evidence of T witnesses or of three
18:3 the shoulder and the T cheeks and the stomach.
19:15 on the evidence of T witnesses, or of three
21:15 "If a man has T wives, the one loved
22:9 sow your vineyard with T kinds of seed, lest
25:13 have in your bag T kinds of weights, a
25:14 have in your house T kinds of measures, a
32:30 chase a thousand, and T put ten thousand to
Josh 2:1 son of Nun sent T men secretly from Shittim
2:4 woman had taken the T men and hidden them;
2:10 you did to the T kings of the Amorites
2:23 Then the T men came down again from the
3:4 a distance of about T thousand cubits; do not
6:22 Joshua said to the T men who had spied
7:3 up, but let about T or three thousand men
7:21 mantle from Shinar, and T hundred shekels of silver,
9:10 he did to the T kings of the Amorites
14:3 an inheritance to the T and one-half tribes beyond
14:4 of Joseph were T tribes, Manasseh and Ephraim;
15:60 is, Kiriath-jearim), and Rabbah: T cities with their
21:16 cities out of these T tribes;
21:25 with its pasture lands-- T cities.
21:27 with its pasture lands-- T cities;
24:12 out before you, the T kings of the Amorites;
Judg 3:16 himself a sword with T edges, a cubit in
5:30 spoil?--A maiden or T for every man; spoil
5:30 of dyed stuffs embroidered, T pieces of dyed work
7:25 And they took the T princes of Midian, Oreb
8:12 them and took the T kings of Midian, Zebah
9:44 the city, while the T companies rushed upon all
11:37 me; let me alone T months, that I may
11:38 sent her away for T months; and she departed,
11:39 at the end of T months, she returned to
15:13 they bound him with T new ropes, and brought
16:3 the city and the T posts, and pulled them
16:28 for one of my T eyes."
16:29 And Samson grasped the T middle pillars upon which
17:4 mother, his mother took T hundred pieces of silver,
19:6 So the T men sat and ate and drank
20:45 hard to Gidom, and T thousand men of them
Ruth 1:1 his wife and his T sons.
1:2 the names of his T sons were Mahlon and
1:3 was left with her T sons.
1:5 was bereft of her T sons and her husband.
1:7 she was, with her T daughters-in-law, and they went
1:8 Naomi said to her T daughters-in-law, "Go, return
1:19 So the T of them went on until they
1Sam 1:2 He had T wives; the name of the one
1:3 at Shiloh, where the T sons of Eli, Hophni
2:21 bore three sons and T daughters.
2:34 which shall befall your T sons, Hophni and Phinehas,
3:11 Israel, at which the T ears of every one
4:4 the cherubim; and the T sons of Eli, Hophni
4:11 was captured; and the T sons of Eli, Hophni
4:17 among the people; your T sons also, Hophni and
6:7 a new cart and T milch cows upon which
6:10 did so, and took T milch cows and yoked
10:2 today you will meet T men by Rachel's tomb
10:4 you and give you T loaves of bread, which
11:11 scattered, so that no T of them were left
13:1 and T years over Israel.
13:2 thousand men of Israel; T thousand were with Saul
14:49 the names of his T daughters were these: the
15:4 numbered them in Telaim, T hundred thousand men
18:27 his men, and killed T hundred of the Philistines;
23:18 And the T of them made a covenant before
25:13 up after David, while T hundred remained with the
25:18 made haste, and took T hundred loaves, and two
25:18 two hundred loaves, and T skins of wine, and
25:18 clusters of raisins, and T hundred cakes of figs,
27:3 and David with his T wives, Ahino-am of Jezreel,
28:8 and went, he and T men with him; and
30:5 David's T wives also had been taken captive,
30:10 and four hundred men; T hundred stayed behind, who
30:12 cake of figs and T clusters of raisins.
30:18 and David rescued his T wives.
30:21 David came to the T hundred men, who had
2Sam 1:1 the Amalekites, David remained T days in Ziklag;
2:2 up there, and his T wives also, Ahino-am of
2:10 Israel, and he reigned T years.
4:2 Now Saul's son had T men who were captains
8:2 down on the ground; T lines he measured to
12:1 to him, "There were T men in a certain
13:23 After T full years Absalom had sheepshearers at
14:6 And your handmaid had T sons, and they quarreled
14:26 hair of his head, T hundred shekels by the
14:28 So Absalom dwelt T full years in Jerusalem, without
15:11 With Absalom went T hundred men from Jerusalem
15:27 and Abiathar, with your T sons, Ahima-az your son,
15:36 Behold, their T sons are with them there, Ahima-az,
16:1 of asses saddled, bearing T hundred loaves of bread,
18:24 was sitting between the T gates; and the watchman
21:8 The king took the T sons of Rizpah the
23:20 great deeds; he smote T ariels of Moab.
1Kgs 2:5 he dealt with the T commanders of the armies
2:32 slew with the sword T men more righteous and
2:39 of three years that T of Shimei's slaves ran
3:16 Then T harlots came to the king, and stood
3:18 the house, only we T were in the house.

3:25 the living child in T, and give half to
5:12 and Solomon; and the T of them made a
5:14 month in Lebanon and T months at home; Adoniram
6:23 inner sanctuary he made T cherubim of olivewood,
6:32 He covered the T doors of olivewood with carvings
6:34 of a square, and T doors of cypress wood;
6:34 of cypress wood; the T leaves of the one
6:34 were folding, and the T leaves of the other
7:15 He cast T pillars of bronze.
7:16 He also made T capitals of molten bronze, to
7:17 Then he made T nets of checker work with
7:18 he made pomegranates; in T rows round about upon
7:20 capitals were upon the T pillars and also above
7:20 the network; there were T hundred pomegranates, in
7:20 two hundred pomegranates, in T rows round about;
7:24 the gourds were in T rows, cast with it
7:26 a lily; it held T thousand baths.
7:41 of the LORD: the T pillars, the two bowls
7:41 the two pillars, the T bowls of the capitals
7:41 the pillars, and the T networks to cover the
7:41 networks to cover the T bowls of the capitals
7:42 hundred pomegranates for the T networks, two rows
7:42 for the two networks, T rows of pomegranates for
7:42 network, to cover the T bowls of the capitals
8:9 the ark except the T tables of stone which
9:10 Solomon had built the T houses, the house of
10:16 King Solomon made T hundred large shields of
10:19 were arm rests and T lions standing beside the
11:29 new garment; and the T of them were alone
12:28 took counsel, and made T calves of gold.
15:25 he reigned over Israel T years.
16:8 in Tirzah, and reigned T years.
16:21 Israel were divided into T parts; half of the
16:24 Samaria from Shemer for T talents of silver; and
18:21 you go limping with T different opinions?
18:23 Let T bulls be given to us; and let
18:32 great as would contain T measures of seed.
20:15 districts, and they were T hundred and thirty-two;
20:27 encamped before them like T little flocks of goats,
21:10 the people; and set T base fellows opposite him,
21:13 And the T base fellows came in and sat
22:51 Judah, and he reigned T years over Israel.
2Kgs 1:14 heaven, and consumed the T former captains of fifty
2:6 So the T of them went on.
2:8 the other, till the T of them could go
2:11 of fire separated the T of them.
2:12 and rent them in T pieces.
2:24 And T she-bears came out of the woods and
4:1 come to take my T children to be his
4:33 the door upon the T of them, and prayed
5:17 given to your servant T mules' burden of earth;
5:22 hill country of Ephraim T young men of the
5:22 talent of silver and T festal garments.'"
5:23 "Be pleased to accept T talents." And he urged
5:23 him, and tied up T talents of silver in
5:23 talents of silver in T bags, with two festal
5:23 in two bags, with T festal garments, and laid
5:23 and laid them upon T of his servants; and
7:1 for a shekel, and T measures of barley for
7:14 So they took T mounted men, and the king
7:16 for a shekel, and T measures of barley for
7:18 said to the king, T measures of barley shall
9:32 T or three eunuchs looked out at him.
10:4 and said, "Behold, the T kings could not stand
10:8 said, "Lay them in T heaps at the entrance
11:7 the palace; and the T divisions of you, which
15:23 Samaria, and he reigned T years.
17:16 themselves molten images of T calves; and they
18:23 I will give you T thousand horses, if you
21:5 of heaven in the T courts of the house
21:19 reign, and he reigned T years in Jerusalem.
23:12 had made in the T courts of the house
25:4 the gate between the T walls, by the king's
25:16 As for the T pillars, the one sea, and
1Chr 1:19 To Eber were born T sons: the name of
4:5 father of Tekoa, had T wives, Helah and Naarah;
5:21 thousand of their camels, T hundred and fifty
5:21 and fifty thousand sheep, T thousand asses, and a
7:9 warriors, was twenty thousand T hundred.
7:11 seventeen thousand and T hundred, ready for service
9:22 at the thresholds, were T hundred and twelve.
11:22 great deeds; he smote T ariels of Moab.
12:32 Israel ought to do, T hundred chiefs, and all
15:6 Asaiah the chief, with T hundred and twenty of
15:8 Shemaiah the chief, with T hundred of his brethren;
25:7 who were skilful, was T hundred and eighty-eight.
26:17 day, as well as T and two at the
26:17 well as two and T at the storehouse;
26:18 at the road and T at the parbar.
26:32 him and his brethren, T thousand seven hundred men
2Chr 3:10 holy place he made T cherubim of wood and
3:15 the house he made T pillars thirty-five cubits high,
4:3 the gourds were in T rows, cast with it
4:12 house of God: the T pillars, the bowls, and
4:12 the bowls, and the T capitals on the top
4:12 the pillars; and the T networks to cover the
4:12 networks to cover the T bowls of the capitals
4:13 hundred pomegranates for the T networks, two rows
4:13 for the two networks, T rows of pomegranates for
4:13 network, to cover the T bowls of the capitals
5:10 the ark except the T tables which Moses put
8:10 officers of King Solomon, T hundred and fifty, who
9:15 King Solomon made T hundred large shields of
9:18 were arm rests and T lions standing beside the
14:8 bucklers and spears, and T hundred and eighty
17:15 Jehohanan the commander, with T hundred and
17:16 of the LORD, with T hundred thousand mighty men
17:17 man of valor, with T hundred thousand men armed
21:19 at the end of T years, his bowels came
24:3 Jehoiada got for him T wives, and he had
26:12 men of valor was T thousand six hundred.
28:8 of Israel took captive T hundred thousand of their
29:32 a hundred rams, and T hundred lambs; all these
33:5 of heaven in the T courts of the house
33:21 reign, and he reigned T years in Jerusalem.
35:8 the passover offerings T thousand six hundred lambs
Ezra 1:10 thirty bowls of gold, T thousand four hundred and
2:3 the sons of Parosh, T thousand one hundred and
2:6 of Jeshua and Joab, T thousand eight hundred and
2:7 of Elam, one thousand T hundred and fifty-four.
2:12 of Azgad, one thousand T hundred and twenty-two.
2:14 The sons of Bigvai, T thousand and fifty-six.
2:19 The sons of Hashum, T hundred and twenty-three.
2:28 of Bethel and Ai, T hundred and twenty-three.
2:31 other Elam, one thousand T hundred and fifty-four.
2:38 of Pashhur, one thousand T hundred and forty-seven.
2:65 and they had T hundred male and female
2:66 thirty-six, their mules were T hundred and forty-five,
6:17 God one hundred bulls, T hundred rams, four hundred
8:4 Zerahiah, and with him T hundred men.
8:9 Jehiel, and with him T hundred and eighteen men.
8:20 their sons, twenty; besides T hundred and twenty of
8:27 a thousand darics, and T vessels of fine bright
10:13 one day or for T; for we have greatly
Neh 7:8 the sons of Parosh, T thousand a hundred and
7:11 of Jeshua and Joab, T thousand eight hundred and
7:12 of Elam, a thousand T hundred and fifty-four.
7:17 The sons of Azgad, T thousand three hundred and
7:19 The sons of Bigvai, T thousand and sixty-seven.
7:34 other Elam, a thousand T hundred and fifty-four.
7:41 of Pashhur, a thousand T hundred and forty-seven.
7:67 and they had T hundred and forty-five singers,
7:68 and thirty-six, their mules T hundred and forty-five,
7:71 darics of gold and T thousand two hundred minas
7:71 gold and two thousand T hundred minas of silver.
7:72 thousand darics of gold, T thousand minas of silver,
11:13 heads of fathers' houses, T hundred and forty-two;
11:18 the holy city were T hundred and eighty-four.
12:31 the wall, and appointed T great companies which
Tob 1:21 days passed before T of Sennacherib's sons killed
3:17 sent to heal the T of them: to scale
8:4 was shut and the T were alone, Tobias got
8:17 hast had compassion on T only children.
9:2 take a servant and T camels with you and
12:5 of all that you T have brought back."
12:6 the angel called the T of them privately and
Jud 1:12 the coasts of the T seas.
4:7 only wide enough for T men at the most.
13:10 Then the T of them went out together, as
Esth 2:21 gate, Bigthan and Teresh, T of the king's eunuchs,
6:2 about Bigthana and Teresh, T of the king's eunuchs,
9:27 they would keep these T days according to what
10:7 The T dragons are Haman and myself.
10:10 this purpose he made T lots, one for the
10:11 And these T lots came to the hour and
11:6 And behold, T great dragons came forward, both
12:1 Gabatha and Tharra, the T eunuchs of the king
12:3 the king examined the T eunuchs, and when they
12:6 people because of the T eunuchs of the king.
15:2 Savior, she took her T maids with her,
Job 13:20 Only grant T things to me, then I will
33:14 one way, and in T, though man does not

42:7 you and against your T friends; for you have
Ps 107:16 bronze, and cuts in T the bars of iron.
Prov 30:7 T things I ask of thee; deny them not
30:15 The leech has T daughters; "Give, give," they cry.
Eccl 4:6 handful of quietness than T hands full of toil
4:9 T are better than one, because they have a
4:11 Again, if T lie together, they are warm; but
4:12 one who is alone, T will withstand him.
Song 4:5 Your T breasts are like two fawns, twins of
4:5 two breasts are like T fawns, twins of a
6:13 upon a dance before T armies?
7:3 Your T breasts are like two fawns, twins of
7:3 two breasts are like T fawns, twins of a
8:12 keepers of the fruit T hundred.
Wis 14:30 will overtake them on T counts: because they
Sir 2:12 sinner who walks along T ways!
13:7 he has drained you T or three times; and
23:16 T sorts of men multiply sins, and a third
26:19 At T things my heart is grieved, and because
38:17 for one day, or T, to avoid criticism; then
46:4 did not one day become as long as T
46:8 And these T alone were preserved out of six
50:25 With T nations my soul is vexed, and the
Is 6:2 had six wings: with T he covered his face,
6:2 his face, and with T he covered his feet,
6:2 his feet, and with T he flew.
7:4 because of these T smoldering stumps of firebrands,
7:16 the land before whose T kings you are in
7:21 a young cow and T sheep;
17:6 tree is beaten-- T or three berries in
22:11 a reservoir between the T walls for the water
36:8 I will give you T thousand horses, if you
47:9 loss of children": These T things shall come to
51:19 These T things have befallen you-- who will
Jer 2:13 my people have committed T evils: they have
3:14 from a city and T from a family, and
24:1 me this vision: Behold, T baskets of figs placed
28:3 Within T years I will bring back to this
28:11 all the nations within T years." But Jeremiah the
33:24 LORD has rejected the T families which he chose?
34:18 which they cut in T and passed between its
39:4 the gate between the T walls; and they went
52:7 a gate between the T walls, by the king's
52:20 As for the T pillars, the one sea, the
Bar 6:55 will be burnt in T like beams.
Ezek 1:11 above; each creature had T wings, each of which
1:11 wing of another, while T covered their bodies.
1:23 and each creature had T wings covering its body.
21:19 "Son of man, mark T ways for the sword
21:21 the head of the T ways, to use divination;
23:2 of man, there were T women, the daughters of
35:10 "Because you said, 'These T nations and these two
35:10 two nations and these T countries shall be mine,
37:22 shall be no longer T nations, and no longer
37:22 no longer divided into T kingdoms.
40:9 cubits; and its jambs, T cubits; and the vestibule
40:39 of the gate were T tables on either side,
40:40 the north gate were T tables; and on the
40:40 of the gate were T tables.
40:44 and behold, there were T chambers in the inner
41:3 jambs of the entrance, T cubits; and the breadth
41:18 Every cherub had T faces:
41:22 wood, three cubits high, T cubits long, and two
41:22 two cubits long, and T cubits broad; its corners,
41:24 The doors had T leaves apiece, two swinging leaves
41:24 had two leaves apiece, T swinging leaves for each
43:14 to the lower ledge, T cubits, with a breadth
45:15 from every flock of T hundred, from the families
47:13 Joseph shall have T portions.
48:17 land: on the north T hundred and fifty cubits,
48:17 cubits, on the south T hundred and fifty, on
48:17 fifty, on the east T hundred and fifty, and
48:17 and on the west T hundred and fifty.
Dan 7:4 made to stand upon T feet like a man;
7:25 hand for a time, T times, and half a
8:3 It had T horns; and both horns were high,
8:6 the ram with the T horns, which I had
8:7 ram and broke his T horns; and the ram
8:14 said to him, "For T thousand and three hundred
8:20 you saw with the T horns, these are the
11:27 And as for the T kings, their minds shall
12:5 Daniel looked, and behold, T others stood, one on
12:7 be for a time, T times, and half a
12:11 shall be a thousand T hundred and ninety days.
13:5 In that year T elders from the people were
13:8 The T elders used to see her every day,
13:15 as before with only T maids, and wished to
13:16 was there except the T elders, who had hid
13:19 had gone out, the T elders rose and ran
13:24 loud voice, and the T elders shouted against her.
13:28 her husband Joakim, the T elders came, full of
13:34 Then the T elders stood up in the midst
13:36 woman came in with T maids, shut the garden
13:55 from God and will immediately cut you in T
13:59 to saw you in T, that he may destroy
13:61 they rose against the T elders, for out of
14:32 they had been given T human bodies and two
14:32 two human bodies and T sheep; but these were
Hos 6:2 After T days he will revive us; on the
Amos 1:1 Joash, king of Israel, T years before the earthquake.
3:3 "Do T walk together, unless they have made an
3:12 mouth of the lion T legs, or a piece
4:8 not rain withered; so T or three cities wandered
Zech 4:3 And there are T olive trees by it, one
4:11 him, "What are these T olive trees on the
4:12 him, "What are these T branches of the olive
4:12 which are beside the T golden pipes from which
4:14 said, "These are the T anointed who stand by
5:9 and saw, and behold, T women coming forward!
6:1 came out from between T mountains; and the
11:7 And I took T staffs; one I named Grace,
13:8 land, says the LORD, T thirds shall be cut
14:4 shall be split in T from east to west
1Mac 1:29 T years later the king sent to the cities
5:60 Judea; as many as T thousand of the people
6:38 either side, on the T flanks of the army,
9:4 thousand foot soldiers and T thousand cavalry.
9:11 was divided into T companies, and the slingers
9:12 Flanked by the T companies, the phalanx advanced
9:57 Judah had rest for T years.
10:49 The T kings met in battle, and the army
10:60 Ptolemais and met the T kings; he gave them
11:13 Thus he put T crowns upon his head, the
12:47 himself three thousand men, T thousand of whom he
13:16 talents of silver and T of his sons as
15:26 Simon sent to Antiochus T thousand picked men, to
16:2 Simon called in his T older sons Judas and
16:10 with fire, and about T thousand of them fell.
16:16 killed him and his T sons and some of
2Mac 3:11 talents of silver and T hundred of gold.
3:26 T young men also appeared to him, remarkably
4:28 was his responsibility, the T of them were summoned
6:10 For example, T women were brought in for having
8:10 due to the Romans, T thousand talents, by selling
10:3 after a lapse of T years, and they burned
10:18 thousand took refuge in T very strong towers well
10:22 and immediately captured the T towers.
10:23 twenty thousand in the T strongholds.
10:28 dawn was breaking, the T armies joined battle, the
12:4 them, not less than T hundred.
12:20 infantry and T thousand five hundred cavalry.
12:43 to the amount of T thousand drachmas of silver,
13:15 slew as many as T thousand men in the
Mt 2:16 that region who were T years old or under,
4:18 of Galilee, he saw T brothers, Simon who is
4:21 from there he saw T other brothers, James the
5:41 mile, go with him T miles.
6:24 "No one can serve T masters; for either he
8:28 country of the Gadarenes, T demoniacs met him,
9:27 passed on from there, T blind men followed him,
10:10 for your journey, nor T tunics, nor sandals, nor
10:29 Are not T sparrows sold for a penny?
14:17 five loaves here and T fish."
14:19 five loaves and the T fish he looked up
18:8 or lame than with T hands or two feet
18:8 with two hands or T feet to be thrown
18:9 one eye than with T eyes to be thrown
18:15 listen, take one or T others along with you,
18:15 by the evidence of T or three witnesses.
18:18 say to you, if T of you agree on
18:19 For where T or three are gathered in my
19:5 his wife, and the T shall become one'?
19:6 they are no longer T but one.
20:21 him, "Command that these T sons of mine may
20:24 were indignant at the T brothers.
20:30 And behold, T blind men sitting by the roadside,
21:1 Olives, then Jesus sent T disciples,
21:28 A man had T sons; and he went to
21:31 Which of the T did the will of his
22:40 On these T commandments depend all the law and
24:40 Then T men will be in the field; one
24:41 T women will be grinding at the mill; one

T

25:15 five talents, to another T, to another one, to
25:17 he who had the T talents made two talents
25:17 the two talents made T talents more.
25:22 also who had the T talents came forward, saying,
25:22 you delivered to me T talents; here I have
25:22 here I have made T talents more.'
26:2 "You know that after T days the Passover is
26:37 him Peter and the T sons of Zebedee, he
26:60 At last T came forward
27:21 them, "Which of the T do you want me
27:38 Then T robbers were crucified with him, one on
27:51 temple was torn in T, from top to bottom;
Mk 5:13 the herd, numbering about T thousand, rushed down
6:7 to send them out T by two, and gave
6:7 them out two by T, and gave them authority
6:9 and not put on T tunics.
6:37 we go and buy T hundred denarii worth of
6:38 they said, "Five, and T fish."
6:41 five loaves and the T fish he looked up
6:41 and he divided the T fish among them all.
9:43 life maimed than with T hands to go to
9:44 life lame than with T feet to be thrown
9:45 one eye than with T eyes to be thrown
10:8 his wife, and the T shall become one.' So
10:8 they are no longer T but one.
11:1 of Olives, he sent T of his disciples,
12:42 came, and put in T copper coins, which make
14:1 It was now T days before the Passover and
14:13 And he sent T of his disciples, and said
15:27 with him they crucified T robbers, one on his
15:37 temple was torn in T, from top to bottom.
16:12 in another form to T of them, as they
Lk 2:24 pair of turtledoves, or T young pigeons."
3:11 them, "He who has T coats, let him share
5:2 And he saw T boats by the lake; but
7:19 John, calling to him T of his disciples, sent
7:41 "A certain creditor had T debtors; one owed five
9:3 and do not have T tunics.
9:13 than five loaves and T fish--unless we are
9:16 five loaves and the T fish he looked up
9:30 And behold, T men talked with him, Moses and
9:32 his glory and the T men who stood with
10:1 on ahead of him, T by two, into every
10:1 of him, two by T, into every town and
10:35 day he took out T denarii and gave them
12:6 five sparrows sold for T pennies?
12:52 five divided, three against T and two against three;
12:52 three against two and T against three;
15:11 a man who had T sons;
16:13 No servant can serve T masters; for either he
17:34 night there will be T in one bed; one
17:35 There will be T women grinding together; one will
18:10 righteous and despised others: T men went up into
19:29 called Olivet, he sent T of the disciples,
21:2 poor widow put in T copper coins.
22:38 "Look, Lord, here are T swords." And he said
23:31 T others also, who were criminals, were led away
23:44 the curtain of the temple was torn in T
24:4 perplexed about this, behold, T men stood by them
24:13 That very day T of them were going to
Jn 1:35 John was standing with T of his disciples;
1:37 The T disciples heard him say this, and they
1:40 One of the T who heard John speak, and
4:40 and he stayed there T days.
4:43 After the T days he departed to Galilee.
6:7 Philip answered him, T hundred denarii would not
6:9 five barley loaves and T fish; but what are
8:17 that the testimony of T men is true;
11:6 was ill, he stayed T days longer in the
11:18 was near Jerusalem, about T miles off,
19:18 him, and with him T others, one on either
20:12 tomb; and she saw T angels in white, sitting
21:2 sons of Zebedee, and T others of his disciples
Acts 1:10 as he went, behold, T men stood by them
1:23 And they put forward T, Joseph called Barsabbas,
1:24 which one of these T thou hast chosen
7:29 became the father of T sons.
9:38 Peter was there, sent T men to him entreating
10:7 had departed, he called T of his servants and
12:6 Peter was sleeping between T soldiers, bound with
12:6 two soldiers, bound with T chains, and sentries before
19:10 This continued for T years, so that all the
19:22 having sent into Macedonia T of his helpers, Timothy
19:34 a Jew, for about T hours they all with
21:33 to be bound with T chains.
23:23 Then he called T of the centurions and said,
23:23 the night get ready T hundred soldiers with seventy
23:23 with seventy horsemen and T hundred spearmen to
24:26 But when T years had elapsed, Felix was succeeded
27:37 (We were in all T hundred and seventy-six persons
28:29 And he lived there T whole years at his
1Cor 6:16 it is written, "The T shall become one."
14:27 let there be only T or at most three,
14:29 Let T or three prophets speak, and let the
2Cor 13:1 by the evidence of T or three witnesses.
Gal 4:22 written that Abraham had T sons, one by a
4:24 allegory: these women are T covenants.
Eph 2:15 in place of the T, so making peace,
5:31 his wife, and the T shall become one flesh."
Phil 1:23 I am hard-pressed between the T
1Tim 5:19 on the evidence of T or three witnesses.
2Tim 3:9 was that of those T men.
Heb 6:18 oath, so that through T unchangeable things, in which
10:28 at the testimony of T or three witnesses.
11:37 they were sawn in T, they were killed with
Rev 9:12 woe has passed; behold, T woes are still to
11:3 I will grant my T witnesses power to prophesy
11:3 prophesy for one thousand T hundred and sixty days,
11:4 These are the T olive trees and the two
11:4 olive trees and the T lampstands which stand before
11:10 exchange presents, because these T prophets had
12:6 nourished for one thousand T hundred and sixty days.
12:14 woman was given the T wings of the great
13:11 the earth; it had T horns like a lamb
19:20 These T were thrown alive into the lake of

TWO-EDGED (6)

Ps 149:6 in their throats and T swords in their hands,
Prov 5:4 wormwood, sharp as a T sword.
Sir 21:3 lawlessness is like a T sword; there is no
Heb 4:12 active, sharper than any T sword, piercing to the
Rev 1:16 mouth issued a sharp T sword, and his face
2:12 who has the sharp T sword.

TWOFOLD (2)

Wis 11:12 equally distressed, for a T grief possessed them, and
Sir 42:24 All things are T, one opposite the other, and

TYCHICUS (5)

Acts 20:4 Timothy; and the Asians, T and Trophimus.
Eph 6:21 what I am doing, T the beloved brother and
Col 4:7 T will tell you all about my affairs; he
2Tim 4:12 T I have sent to Ephesus.
Tit 3:12 I send Artemas or T to you, do your

TYPE

Rom 5:14 Adam, who was a T of the one who

TYRANNUS

Acts 19:9 him, and argued daily in the hall of T

TYRANT (4)

Is 49:24 the captives of a T be rescued?
49:25 the prey of the T be rescued, for I
2Mac 4:25 temper of a cruel T and the rage of
7:27 follows, deriding the cruel T: "My son, have pity

TYRE (64)

Josh 19:29 the fortified city of T; then the boundary turns
2Sam 5:11 And Hiram king of T sent messengers to David,
24:7 to the fortress of T and to all the
1Kgs 5:1 Now Hiram king of T sent his servants to
7:13 And King Solomon sent and brought Hiram from T
7:14 was a man of T, a worker in bronze;
9:11 and Hiram king of T had supplied Solomon with
9:12 when Hiram came from T to see the cities
1Chr 14:1 And Hiram king of T sent messengers to David,
2Chr 2:3 Huram the king of T: "As you dealt with
2:11 Huram the king of T answered in a letter
2:14 Dan, and his father was a man of T
Neh 13:16 Men of T also, who lived in the city,
Jud 2:28 seacoast, at Sidon and T, and those who lived
Ps 45:12 him; the people of T will sue your favor
83:7 with the inhabitants of T;
87:4 Babylon; behold, Philistia and T, with Ethiopia--
Sir 46:18 of the people of T and all the rulers
Is 23:1 The oracle concerning T
23:1 ships of Tarshish, for T is laid waste, without
23:5 will be in anguish over the report about T
23:8 has purposed this against T, the bestower of crowns,
23:13 They destined T for wild beasts.
23:15 In that day T will be forgotten for seventy

23:15 it will happen to T as in the song
23:17 the LORD will visit T, and she will return
Jer 25:22 all the kings of T, all the kings of
27:3 Ammon, the king of T, and the king of
47:4 to cut off from T and Sidon every helper
Ezek 26:2 "Son of man, because T said concerning Jerusalem,
26:3 am against you, O T, and will bring up
26:4 destroy the walls of T, and break down her
26:7 I will bring upon T from the north Nebuchadrezzar
26:15 the Lord GOD to T: Will not the coastlands
27:2 raise a lamentation over T,
27:3 Tyre, and say to T, who dwells at the
27:3 the Lord GOD: "O T, you have said, 'I
27:32 was ever destroyed like T in the midst of
28:2 to the prince of T, Thus says the Lord
28:12 over the king of T, and say to him,
29:18 army labor hard against T; every head was made
29:18 army got anything from T to pay for the
Joel 3:4 you to me, O T and Sidon, and all
Amos 1:9 "For three transgressions of T, and for four, I
1:10 upon the wall of T, and it shall devour
Zech 9:2 also, which borders thereon, T and Sidon, though
9:3 T has built herself a rampart, and heaped up
1Mac 5:15 men of Ptolemais and T and Sidon, and all
11:59 from the Ladder of T to the borders of
2Mac 4:18 were being held at T and the king was
4:32 he had sold to T and the neighboring cities.
4:44 the king came to T, three men sent by
Mt 11:21 had been done in T and Sidon, they would
11:22 day of judgment for T and Sidon than for
15:21 to the district of T and Sidon.
Mk 3:8 Jordan and from about T and Sidon a great
7:23 to the region of T and Sidon.
7:30 from the region of T, and went through Sidon
Lk 6:17 and the seacoast of T and Sidon, who came
10:13 had been done in T and Sidon, they would
10:14 in the judgment for T and Sidon than for
Acts 12:20 with the people of T and Sidon; and they
21:3 Syria, and landed at T; for there the ship
21:7 finished the voyage from T, we arrived at Ptolemais;

TYRIANS (3)
1Chr 22:4 for the Sidonians and T brought great quantities of
Ezra 3:7 the Sidonians and the T to bring cedar trees
2Mac 4:49 Therefore even the T, showing their hatred of the

U

UCAL
Prov 30:1 Ithi-el, to Ithi-el and U:

UEL
Ezra 10:34 of Bani: Ma-adai, Amram, U,

UGLY
Sir 20:23 A lie is an U blot on a man;

ULAI (2)
Dan 8:2 the vision, and I was at the river U
8:16 the banks of the U, and it called, "Gabriel,

ULAM (4)
1Chr 7:16 and his sons were U and Rakem.
7:17 The sons of U: Bedan.
8:39 of Eshek his brother: U his first-born, Jeush the
8:40 The sons of U were men who were mighty

ULCERS
Deut 28:27 Egypt, and with the U and the scurvy and

ULLA
1Chr 7:39 The sons of U: Arah, Hanniel, and Rizia.

UMMAH
Josh 19:30 the sea; Mahalab, Achzib, U, Aphek and Rehob--

UMPIRE
Job 9:33 There is no U between us, who might lay

UNABLE (16)
1Kgs 9:21 people of Israel were U to destroy utterly--these
Esth 16:12 But, U to restrain his arrogance, he undertook to
Ps 36:12 they are thrust down, U to rise.
76:5 men of war were U to use their hands.
Wis 12:9 though thou wast not U to give the ungodly
13:1 nature; and they were U from the good things
Sir 7:6 judge, lest you be U to remove iniquity, lest
Bar 6:14 holds a scepter, though U to destroy any one
Ezek 3:26 shall be dumb and U to reprove them; for
1Mac 9:60 men; but they were U to do it, because
2Mac 3:28 bodyguard but was now U to help himself; and
10:13 U to command the respect due his office, he
Lk 1:20 will be silent and U to speak until the
Acts 13:11 shall be blind and U to see the sun
Heb 3:19 see that they were U to enter because of
4:15 high priest who is U to sympathize with our

UNANSWERED
Job 11:2 multitude of words go U, and a man full

UNAPPROACHABLE
1Tim 6:16 immortality and dwells in U light, whom no man

UNAWARE
Wis 12:10 though thou wast not U that their origin was

UNAWARES (3)
Gen 34:25 came upon the city U, and killed all the
Ps 35:8 Let ruin come upon them U
Heb 13:2 for thereby some have entertained angels U

UNBEARABLY
2Cor 1:8 we were so utterly, U crushed that we despaired

UNBELIEF (8)
Mt 13:58 do many mighty works there, because of their U
Mk 6:6 And he marveled because of their U
9:24 cried out and said, "I believe; help my U
16:14 upbraided them for their U and hardness of heart,
Rom 11:20 off because of their U, but you stand fast
11:23 not persist in their U, will be grafted in,
1Tim 1:13 had acted ignorantly in U,
Heb 3:19 that they were unable to enter because of U

UNBELIEVABLE
Jud 13:13 great, for it was U that she had returned;

UNBELIEVER (5)
1Cor 7:12 wife who is an U, and she consents to
7:13 husband who is an U, and he consents to
14:24 all prophesy, and an U or outsider enters, he
2Cor 6:15 what has a believer in common with an U
1Tim 5:8 disowned the faith and is worse than an U

UNBELIEVERS (8)
Rom 15:31 be delivered from the U in Judea, and that
1Cor 6:6 goes to law against brother, and that before U
10:27 If one of the U invites you to dinner
14:22 for believers but for U, while prophecy is not
14:22 prophecy is not for U but for believers.
14:23 tongues, and outsiders or U enter, will they not
2Cor 4:4 the minds of the U, to keep them from
6:14 Do not be mismated with U

UNBELIEVING (7)
Wis 10:7 a monument to an U soul.
Acts 14:2 But the U Jews stirred up the Gentiles and
1Cor 7:14 For the U husband is consecrated through his wife,
7:14 his wife, and the U wife is consecrated through
7:15 But if the U partner desires to separate, let
Tit 1:14 to the corrupt and U nothing is pure; their
Heb 3:12 of you an evil, U heart, leading you to

UNBIND (2)
Num 5:18 before the LORD, and U the hair of the
Jn 11:44 Jesus said to them, U him, and let him

UNBLAMABLE
1Thes 3:13 may establish your hearts U in holiness before our

UNBORN (4)
Tob 4:4 many dangers for you while you were yet U
Ps 22:31 to a people yet U, that he has wrought
78:6 them, the children yet U, and arise and tell
102:18 that a people yet U may praise the LORD:

UNBOUND
Acts 22:30 Jews accused him, he U him, and commanded the

UNBROKEN (3)

Dan 14:17 said, "Are the seals U, Daniel?" He answered, "They
14:17 He answered, "They are U, O king."
2Mac 3:1 city was inhabited in U peace and the laws

UNBURIED

2Mac 5:10 out many to lie U had no one to

UNCEASING (4)

Is 14:6 peoples in wrath with U blows, that ruled the
Jer 15:18 Why is my pain U, my wound incurable, refusing
Nah 3:19 has not come your U evil?
Rom 9:2 have great sorrow and U anguish in my heart.

UNCERTAIN (3)

2Mac 7:34 and puffed up by U hopes, when you raise
Jn 13:22 looked at one another, U of whom he spoke.
1Tim 6:17 set their hopes on U riches but on God

UNCERTAINTY

Jas 3:17 and good fruits, without U or insincerity.

UNCHANGEABLE (3)

Job 23:13 But he is U and who can turn him?
Heb 6:17 of the promise the U character of his purpose,
6:18 so that through two U things, in which it

UNCHANGING

Esth 13:3 is distinguished for his U good will and steadfast

UNCHASTITY (6)

Mt 5:32 on the ground of U, makes her an adulteress;
19:9 his wife, except for U, and marries another, commits
Acts 15:20 of idols and from U and from what is
15:29 blood and from what is strangled and from U
21:25 blood and from what is strangled and from U
1Thes 4:3 that you abstain from U;

UNCIRCUMCISED (45)

Gen 17:14 Any U male who is not circumcised in the
34:14 to one who is U, for that would be
Ex 6:12 am a man of U lips?"
6:30 "Behold, I am of U lips; how then shall
12:48 But no U person shall eat of it.
Lev 26:41 enemies; if then their U heart is humbled and
Josh 5:7 circumcised; for they were U, because they had not
Judg 14:3 a wife from the U Philistines?" But Samson said
15:18 thirst, and fall into the hands of the U
1Sam 14:6 the garrison of these U; it may be that
17:26 For who is this U Philistine, that he should
17:36 and bears; and this U Philistine shall be like
31:4 with it, lest these U come and thrust me
2Sam 1:20 the daughters of the U exult.
1Chr 10:4 with it, lest these U come and make sport
Esth 14:15 the bed of the U and of any alien.
Is 52:1 come into you the U and the unclean.
Jer 9:25 are circumcised but yet U –
9:26 all these nations are U, and all the house
9:26 house of Israel is U in heart."
Ezek 28:10 the death of the U by the hand of
31:18 shall lie among the U, with those who are
32:19 be laid with the U
32:21 they lie still, the U, slain by the sword.'
32:24 sword, who went down U into the nether world,
32:25 her, all of them U, slain by the sword;
32:26 them, all of them U, slain by the sword;
32:28 and lie among the U, with those who are
32:29 they lie with the U, with those who go
32:30 their might; they lie U with those who are
32:32 be laid among the U, with those who are
44:7 in admitting foreigners, U in heart and flesh,
44:9 Lord GOD: No foreigner, U in heart and flesh,
1Mac 1:48 and unclean animals, and to leave their sons U
2:46 forcibly circumcised all the U boys that they found
Acts 7:51 things?' "You stiff-necked people, U in heart and
11:3 did you go to U men and eat with
Rom 2:26 a man who is U keeps the precepts of
2:27 those who are physically U but keep the law
3:30 their faith and the U through their faith.
4:9 only upon the circumcised, or also upon the U
4:11 he had by faith while he was still U
1Cor 7:18 any one at the time of his call U
Gal 2:7 the gospel to the U, just as Peter had
Col 3:11 and Jew, circumcised and U, barbarian, Scythian,

UNCIRCUMCISION (7)

Rom 2:25 if you break the law, your circumcision becomes U
2:26 law, will not his U be regarded as circumcision?
1Cor 7:19 for anything nor U, but keeping the commandments
Gal 5:6 Jesus neither circumcision nor U is of any avail,
6:15 counts for anything, nor U, but a new creation.
Eph 2:11 the flesh, called the U by what is called
Col 2:13 in trespasses and the U of your flesh, God

UNCLE (13)

Lev 10:4 sons of Uzziel the U of Aaron, and said
20:20 man lies with his U's wife, he has uncovered
20:20 he has uncovered his U's nakedness; they shall bear
25:49 redeem him, or his U, or his cousin may
1Sam 10:14 Saul's U said to him and to his servant,
10:15 And Saul's U said, "Pray, tell me what Samuel
10:16 Saul said to his U, "He told us plainly
14:50 son of Ner, Saul's U;
2Kgs 24:17 Babylon made Mattaniah, Jehoiachin's U, king in his
1Chr 27:32 Jonathan, David's U, was a counselor, being a man
Esth 2:7 the daughter of his U, for she had neither
2:15 daughter of Abihail the U of Mordecai, who had
Jer 32:7 son of Shallum your U will come to you

UNCLEAN (212)

Lev 5:2 any one touches an U thing, whether the carcass
5:2 the carcass of an U beast or a carcass
5:2 or a carcass of U cattle or a carcass
5:2 or a carcass of U swarming things, and it
5:2 and he has become U, he shall be guilty.
5:3 with which one becomes U, and it is hidden
7:19 "Flesh that touches any U thing shall not be
7:21 any one touches an U thing, whether the uncleanness
7:21 of man or an U beast or any unclean
7:21 unclean beast or any U abomination, and then eats
10:10 common, and between the U and the clean;
11:4 part the hoof, is U to you.
11:5 part the hoof, is U to you.
11:6 part the hoof, is U to you.
11:7 chew the cud, is U to you.
11:8 not touch; they are U to you.
11:24 you shall become U; whoever touches their carcass
11:24 their carcass shall be U until the evening,
11:25 his clothes and be U until the evening.
11:26 chew the cud is U to you; every one
11:26 you; every one who touches them shall be U
11:27 on all fours, are U to you; whoever touches
11:27 their carcass shall be U until the evening,
11:28 his clothes and be U until the evening; they
11:28 the evening; they are U to you.
11:29 "And these are U to you among the swarming
11:31 These are U to you among all that swarm;
11:31 are dead shall be U until the evening.
11:32 are dead shall be U, whether it is an
11:32 and it shall be U until the evening; then
11:33 in it shall be U, and you shall break
11:34 may come, shall be U; and all drink which
11:34 be drunk from every such vessel shall be U
11:35 carcass falls shall be U; whether oven or stove,
11:35 in pieces; they are U, and shall be unclean
11:35 unclean, and shall be U to you.
11:36 clean; but whatever touches their carcass shall be U
11:38 on it, it is U to you.
11:39 its carcass shall be U until the evening,
11:40 his clothes and be U until the evening; he
11:40 his clothes and be U until the evening.
11:43 not defile yourselves with them, lest you become U
11:47 a distinction between the U and the clean and
12:2 then she shall be U seven days; as at
12:2 the time of her menstruation, she shall be U
12:5 then she shall be U two weeks, as in
13:3 priest has examined him he shall pronounce him U
13:8 priest shall pronounce him U; it is leprosy.
13:11 priest shall pronounce him U; he shall not shut
13:11 shall not shut him up, for he is U
13:14 raw flesh appears on him, he shall be U
13:15 flesh, and pronounce him U; raw flesh is unclean,
13:15 unclean; raw flesh is U, for it is leprosy.
13:20 priest shall pronounce him U; it is the disease
13:22 priest shall pronounce him U; it is diseased.
13:25 priest shall pronounce him U; it is a leprous
13:27 priest shall pronounce him U; it is a leprous
13:30 priest shall pronounce him U; it is an itch,
13:36 not seek for the yellow hair; he is U
13:44 leprous man, he is U; the priest must pronounce
13:44 priest must pronounce him U; his disease is on

UNCLEANNESS (31)

U

Ezra 9:11 filled it from end to end with their U
Lam 1:9 Her U was in her skirts; she took no
Ezek 36:17 me was like the U of a woman in
39:24 them according to their U and their transgressions,
Mic 2:10 to rest; because of U that destroys with a
Zech 13:1 of Jerusalem to cleanse them from sin and U
1Mac 13:48 out of it all U, and settled in it
14:7 and he removed its U from it; and there
Mt 23:26 are full of dead men's bones and all U
Eph 4:19 to licentiousness, greedy to practice every kind of U
1Thes 2:3 spring from error or U, nor is it made
4:7 not called us for U, but in holiness.

UNCLEANNESSES (5)
Lev 16:16 place, because of the U of the people of
16:16 abides with them in the midst of their U
16:19 hallow it from the U of the people of
Ezek 36:25 clean from all your U, and from all your
36:29 you from all your U; and I will summon

UNCLOTHED
2Cor 5:4 that we would be U, but that we would

UNCOMFORTABLE
2Mac 2:27 will gladly endure the U toil,

UNCONCERN
Sir 29:5 pay in words of U, and will find fault

UNCONCERNED
Dan 14:13 They were U, for beneath the table they had

UNCONDEMNED (3)
2Mac 4:47 would have been freed U if they had pleaded
Acts 16:37 have beaten us publicly, U, men who are Roman
22:25 a man who is a Roman citizen, and U

UNCOUNTED
Wis 7:11 and in her hands U wealth.

UNCOVER (25)
Lev 18:6 kin to him to U nakedness.
18:7 You shall not U the nakedness of your father,
18:7 mother, you shall not U her nakedness.
18:8 You shall not U the nakedness of your father's
18:9 You shall not U the nakedness of your sister,
18:10 You shall not U the nakedness of your son's
18:11 You shall not U the nakedness of your father's
18:12 You shall not U the nakedness of your father's
18:13 You shall not U the nakedness of your mother's
18:14 You shall not U the nakedness of your father's
18:15 You shall not U the nakedness of your daughter-in-
18:15 wife, you shall not U her nakedness.
18:16 You shall not U the nakedness of your brother's
18:17 You shall not U the nakedness of a woman
18:17 her daughter's daughter to U her nakedness; they
18:19 approach a woman to U her nakedness while she
20:19 You shall not U the nakedness of your mother's
Deut 22:30 wife, nor shall he U her who is his
Ruth 3:4 lies; then, go and U his feet and lie
Is 47:2 strip off your robe, U your legs, pass through
Lam 4:22 will punish, he will U your sins.
Ezek 16:37 every side, and will U your nakedness to them,
22:10 In you men U their fathers' nakedness; in you
Hos 2:10 Now I will U her lewdness in the sight
Mic 1:6 into the valley, and U her foundations.

UNCOVERED (25)
Gen 9:21 became drunk, and lay U in his tent.
Lev 20:11 his father's wife has U his father's nakedness; both
20:17 their people; he has U his sister's nakedness, he
20:18 fountain, and she has U the fountain of her
20:20 uncle's wife, he has U his uncle's nakedness; they
20:21 is impurity; he has U his brother's nakedness, they
Num 24:4 but having his eyes U:
24:16 but having his eyes U:
Deut 27:20 wife, because he has U her who is his
Ruth 3:7 she came softly, and U his feet, and lay
Tob 2:9 wall of the courtyard, and my face was U
Jud 9:1 on her head, and U the sackcloth she was
9:2 to defile her, and U her thigh to put
Is 20:4 and barefoot, with buttocks U, to the shame of
22:6 and horsemen, and Kir U the shield.
47:3 Your nakedness shall be U, and your shame shall
57:8 deserting me, you have U your bed, you have
Jer 49:10 Esau bare, I have U his hiding places, and
Bar 6:31 their heads and beards shaved, and their heads U
Ezek 16:36 bare and your nakedness U in your harlotries with
16:57 day of your pride, before your wickedness was U
21:24 that your transgressions are U, so that in all
23:10 These U her nakedness; they seized her sons and
23:29 and the nakedness of your harlotry shall be U
1Cor 11:13 woman to pray to God with her head U

UNCOVERING (2)
Lev 18:18 wife to her sister, U her nakedness while her
2Sam 6:20 Israel honored himself today, U himself today before

UNCOVERS (3)
Lev 20:18 having her sickness, and U her nakedness, he has
2Sam 6:20 the vulgar fellows shamelessly U himself!"
Job 12:22 He U the deeps out of darkness, and brings

UNDEFENDED
Esth 16:14 he would find us U and would transfer the

UNDEFILED (8)
Wis 3:13 barren woman who is U, who has not entered
4:2 victor in the contest for prizes that are U
8:20 good, I entered an U body.
2Mac 14:36 of all holiness, keep U for ever this house
15:34 is he who has kept his own place U
Heb 13:4 the marriage bed be U; for God will judge
Jas 1:26 that is pure and U before God and the
1Pet 1:4 inheritance which is imperishable, U, and unfading,

UNDERGIRD
Acts 27:17 they took measures to U the ship; then, fearing

UNDERGOING
Jude 1:7 as an example by U a punishment of eternal

UNDERHANDED
2Cor 4:2 We have renounced disgraceful, U ways; we refuse

UNDERMINE
2Cor 11:12 do, in order to U the claim of those

UNDERNEATH (12)
Deut 33:27 your dwelling place, and U are the everlasting arms.
Josh 7:21 the earth inside my tent, with the silver U
7:22 was hidden in his tent with the silver U
1Kgs 7:32 the four wheels were U the panels; the axles
7:44 and the twelve oxen U the sea.
8:6 the most holy place, U the wings of the
2Chr 4:15 and the twelve oxen U it.
5:7 the most holy place, U the wings of the
Job 28:5 it comes bread; but U it is turned up
Ezek 10:2 among the whirling wheels U the cherubim; fill your
10:20 creatures that I saw U the God of Israel
10:21 each four wings, and U their wings the semblance

UNDERPARTS
Job 41:30 His U are like sharp potsherds; he spreads himself

UNDERSTAND (130)
Gen 11:7 that they may not U one another's speech."
Ex 10:7 do you not yet U that Egypt is ruined?"
Deut 28:49 language you do not U,
29:4 you a mind to U, or eyes to see,
32:29 were wise, they would U this, they would discern
1Sam 28:1 Achish said to David, U that you and your
2Kgs 18:26 Aramaic language, for we U it; do not speak
Neh 8:3 and those who could U; and the ears of
8:7 helped the people to U the law, while the
Jud 9:14 tribe to know and U that thou art God,
Esth 11:12 sought all day to U it in every detail.
13:5 We U that this people, and it alone, stands
Job 6:24 be silent; make me U how I have erred.
15:9 What do you U that is not clear to
23:5 would answer me, and U what he would say
26:14 But the thunder of his power who can U
32:8 the breath of the Almighty, that makes him U
32:9 nor the aged that U what is right.
36:29 Can any one U the spreading of the clouds,
42:3 what I did not U, things too wonderful for
Ps 73:16 I thought how to U this, it seemed to
92:6 know, the stupid cannot U this:
94:8 U, O dullest of the people!
119:27 Make me U the way of thy precepts, and
119:100 I U more than the aged, for I keep
Prov 1:2 know wisdom and instruction, U words of insight,

1:6 understanding acquire skill, to U a proverb and a
2:5 treasures; then you will U the fear of the
2:9 Then you will U righteousness and justice and equity,
20:24 how then can man U his way?
28:5 Evil men do not U justice, but those who
28:5 who seek the LORD U it completely.
29:7 wicked man does not U such knowledge.
30:18 four I do not U:
Wis 3:9 trust in him will U truth, and the faithful
4:15 saw and did not U, nor take such a
4:17 man, and will not U what the Lord purposed
6:1 therefore, O kings, and U; learn, O judges of
9:9 the world, and who U what is pleasing in
Sir 18:28 Those who U sayings become skilled themselves, and
34:11 my travels, and I U more than I can
38:33 seat, nor do they U the sentence of judgment;
Is 1:3 Israel does not know, my people does not U
6:9 hear, but do not U; see and see, but
6:10 with their ears, and U with their hearts, and
28:19 be sheer terror to U the message.
33:19 stammering in a tongue which you cannot U
36:11 in Aramaic, for we U it; do not speak
41:20 know, may consider and U together, that the hand
42:25 but he did not U; it burned him, but
43:10 and believe me and U that I am He.
44:18 see, and their minds, so that they cannot U
52:15 that which they have not heard they shall U
Jer 5:15 know, nor can you U what they say.
9:12 wise that he can U this?
17:9 desperately corrupt; who can U it?
23:20 latter days you will U it clearly.
30:24 latter days you will U this.
Bar 6:41 may speak, as though Bel were able to U
Ezek 3:6 and a hard language, whose words you cannot U
12:3 Perhaps they will U, though they are a rebellious
Dan 8:15 vision, I sought to U it; and behold, there
8:16 "Gabriel, make this man U the vision."
8:17 he said to me, U, O son of man,
8:27 vision and did not U it.
9:23 consider the word and U the vision.
9:25 Know therefore and U that from the going forth
10:12 set your mind to U and humbled yourself before
10:14 came to make you U what is to befall
11:33 wise shall make many U, though they shall fall
12:8 I heard, but I did not U
12:10 of the wicked shall U; but those who are
12:10 shall understand; but those who are wise shall U
Hos 14:9 is wise, let him U these things; whoever is
Mic 4:12 LORD, they do not U his plan, that he
2Mac 9:25 Moreover, I U how the princes along the borders
Mt 13:13 hearing they do not hear, nor do they U
13:14 indeed hear but never U, and you shall indeed
13:15 with their ears, and U with their heart, and
13:19 kingdom and does not U it, the evil one
15:10 to them, "Hear and U:
24:15 place (let the reader U,
Mk 4:12 indeed hear but not U; lest they should turn
4:13 them, "Do you not U this parable?
4:13 How then will you U all the parables?
6:52 for they did not U about the loaves, but
7:14 all of you, and U:
8:17 Do you not yet perceive or U
8:21 he said to them, "Do you not yet U
9:32 But they did not U the saying, and they
13:14 be (let the reader U, then let those who
14:68 "I neither know nor U what you mean." And
Lk 2:50 And they did not U the saying which he
8:10 may not see, and hearing they may not U
9:45 But they did not U this saying, and it
24:45 opened their minds to U the scriptures,
Jn 3:10 yet you do not U this?
8:27 They did not U that he spoke to them
8:43 Why do you not U what I say?
10:6 but they did not U what he was saying
10:38 you may know and U that the Father is
11:50 all; you do not U that it is expedient
12:16 His disciples did not U this at first; but
13:7 do not know now, but afterward you will U
Acts 7:25 deliverance by his hand, but they did not U
8:30 and asked, "Do you U what you are reading?"
13:27 not recognize him nor U the utterances of the
28:26 indeed hear but never U, and you shall indeed
28:27 with their ears, and U with their heart, and
Rom 7:15 I do not U my own actions.
10:19 Again I ask, did Israel not U
11:25 I want you to U this mystery, brethren: a
15:21 him, and they shall U who have never heard
1Cor 2:12 God, that we might U the gifts bestowed on
2:14 is not able to U them because they are
11:3 I want you to U that the head of
12:3 I want you to U that no one speaking
13:2 have prophetic powers, and U all mysteries and all
13:12 part; then I shall U fully, even as I
2Cor 1:13 you can read and U; I hope you will
1:13 I hope you will U fully,
10:11 Let such people U that what we say by
Eph 5:17 not be foolish, but U what the will of
2Tim 3:1 But U this, that in the last days there
Heb 11:3 By faith we U that the world was created
13:23 You should U that our brother Timothy has been
2Pet 1:20 of all you must U this, that no prophecy
3:3 of all you must U this, that scoffers will
3:16 in them hard to U, which the ignorant and
Jude 1:10 whatever they do not U, and by those things

UNDERSTANDING (177)

Deut 1:13 Choose wise, U, and experienced men, according to
4:6 your wisdom and your U in the sight of
4:6 is a wise and U people.'
32:28 and there is no U in them.
1Sam 25:3 woman was of good U and beautiful, but the
1Kgs 3:9 thy servant therefore an U mind to govern thy
3:11 have asked for yourself U to discern what is
4:29 gave Solomon wisdom and U beyond measure, and
7:14 was full of wisdom, U, and skill, for making
1Chr 12:32 Issachar men who had U of the times, to
22:12 grant you discretion and U, that when he gives
27:32 being a man of U and a scribe; he
2Chr 2:12 endued with discretion and U, who will build a
2:13 skilled man, endued with U, Huram-abi,
Neh 8:2 who could hear with U, on the first day
10:28 who have knowledge and U,
Tob 4:19 of the nations has U; but the Lord himself
Jud 8:29 have recognized your U, for your heart's disposition
Job 8:10 tell you, and utter words out of their U
9:10 does great things beyond U, and marvelous things
11:6 For he is manifold in U
11:12 stupid man will get U, when a wild ass's
12:3 But I have U as well as you; I
12:12 with the aged, and U in length of days.
12:13 are wisdom and might; he has counsel and U
12:24 He takes away U from the chiefs of the
17:4 closed their minds to U, therefore thou wilt not
20:3 and out of my U a spirit answers me.
26:12 the sea; by his U he smote Rahab.
28:12 And where is the place of U
28:20 And where is the place of U
28:28 is wisdom; and to depart from evil is U
34:10 me, you men of U, far be it from
34:16 "If you have U, hear this; listen to what
34:34 Men of U will say to me, and the
36:5 despise any; he is mighty in strength of U
38:4 Tell me, if you have U
38:36 the clouds, or given U to the mists?
39:17 forget wisdom, and given her no share in U
Ps 32:9 or a mule, without U, which must be curbed
49:3 wisdom; the meditation of my heart shall be U
53:4 who work evil no U, who eat up my
82:5 have neither knowledge nor U, they walk about in
111:10 of wisdom; a good U have all those who
119:32 of thy commandments when thou enlargest my U
119:34 Give me U, that I may keep thy law
119:73 fashioned me; give me U that I may learn
119:99 I have more U than all my teachers, for
119:104 thy precepts I get U; therefore I hate every
119:125 thy servant; give me U, that I may know
119:130 gives light; it imparts U to the simple.
119:144 for ever; give me U that I may live.
119:169 O LORD; give me U according to thy word!
136:5 to him who by U made the heavens, for
147:5 abundant in power; his U is beyond measure.
Prov 1:5 and the man of U acquire skill,
2:2 inclining your heart to U;
2:3 raise your voice for U,
2:6 mouth come knowledge and U;
2:11 will watch over you; U will guard you;
3:13 the man who gets U,
3:19 founded the earth; by U he established the heavens;
4:6 my commandments, and live; "Get Wisdom, get U
5:1 your ear to my U;
8:1 wisdom call, does not U raise her voice?
10:13 of him who has U wisdom is found, but

10:23 wise conduct is pleasure to a man of U
11:12 but a man of U remains silent.
14:6 but knowledge is easy for a man of U
14:29 to anger has great U, but he who has
14:33 of a man of U, but it is not
15:14 of him who has U seeks knowledge, but the
15:21 but a man of U walks aright.
15:32 himself, but he who heeds admonition gains U
16:16 than gold; to get U is to be chosen
17:10 into a man of U than a hundred blows
17:24 A man of U sets his face toward wisdom,
17:27 has a cool spirit is a man of U
18:2 takes no pleasure in U, but only in expressing
19:8 himself; he who keeps U will prosper.
19:25 reprove a man of U, and he will gain
20:5 but a man of U will draw it out.
21:16 from the way of U will rest in the
21:30 No wisdom, no U, no counsel, can avail against
23:23 do not sell it; buy wisdom, instruction, and U
24:3 is built, and by U it is established;
28:2 but with men of U and knowledge its stability
28:11 poor man who has U will find him out.
28:16 A ruler who lacks U is a cruel oppressor;
30:2 I have not the U of a man.
Wis 3:15 and the root of U does not fail.
4:9 number of years; but U is gray hair for
4:11 lest evil change his U or guile deceive his
6:15 on her is perfect U, and he who is
7:7 Therefore I prayed, and U was given me; I
7:16 hand, as are all U and skill in crafts.
8:6 And if U is effective, who more than she
8:18 experience of her company, U, and renown in sharing
9:5 and short-lived, with little U of judgment and laws;
Sir 1:4 all things, and prudent U from eternity.
3:13 he is lacking in U, show forbearance; in all
3:22 too great for human U have been shown you.
5:10 Be steadfast in your U, and let your speech
5:12 If you have U, answer your neighbor; but if
7:25 But give her to a man of U
8:9 them you will gain U and learn how to
9:15 be with men of U, and let all your
10:1 the rule of an U man will be well-ordered.
10:3 will grow through the U of its rulers.
10:24 and a man of U will not grumble.
15:3 with the bread of U, and give him the
16:4 through one man of U a city will be
16:21 what one devoid of U thinks; a senseless and
17:6 them with knowledge and U, and showed them good
21:15 When a man of U hears a wise saying,
24:24 makes them full of U, like the Euphrates, and
25:5 in the aged, and U and counsel in honorable
33:3 A man of U will trust in the law;
34:1 A man of no U has vain and false
34:9 and one with much experience will speak with U
37:22 the fruits of his U may be trustworthy on
37:23 the fruits of his U will be trustworthy.
39:6 with the spirit of U; he will pour forth
39:9 Many will praise his U, and it will never
44:3 giving counsel by their U, and proclaiming
44:4 their deliberations and in U of learning for the
47:14 You overflowed like a river with U
47:23 folly and lacking in U, Rehoboam, whose policy
50:27 Instruction in U and knowledge I have written in
51:20 I gained U with her from the first, therefore
Is 10:13 wisdom, for I have U; I have removed the
11:2 spirit of wisdom and U, the spirit of counsel
29:16 of him who formed it, "He has no U
29:24 spirit will come to U, and those who murmur
40:14 him knowledge, and showed him the way of U
40:28 or grow weary, his U is unsearchable.
56:11 shepherds also have no U; they have all turned
Jer 3:15 heart, who will feed you with knowledge and U
4:22 not; they are stupid children, they have no U
10:12 wisdom, and by his U stretched out the heavens.
51:15 wisdom, and by his U stretched out the heavens.
Bar 3:14 strength, where there is U, that you may at
3:23 Hagar, who seek for U on the earth, the
3:23 and the seekers for U, have not learned the
3:32 things knows her, he found her by his U
Ezek 28:4 your wisdom and your U you have gotten wealth
Dan 1:4 endowed with knowledge, U learning, and competent
1:17 wisdom; and Daniel had U in all visions and
1:20 matter of wisdom and U concerning which the king
2:21 to those who have U;
5:11 your father light and U and wisdom, like the
5:12 excellent spirit, knowledge, and U to interpret
5:14 and that light and U and excellent wisdom are
9:22 now come out to give you wisdom and U
10:1 the word and had U of the vision.
Hos 4:11 Wine and new wine take away the U
4:14 and a people without U shall come to ruin.
Obad 1:7 there is no U of it.
1:8 out of Edom, and U out of Mount Esau?
Zech 6:13 his throne, and peaceful U shall be between them
Mt 11:25 from the wise and U and revealed them to
15:16 And he said, "Are you also still without U
Mk 7:17 said to them, "Then are you also without U
12:33 and with all the U, and with all the
Lk 2:47 were amazed at his U and his answers.
10:21 from the wise and U and revealed them to
2Cor 10:12 themselves with one another, they are without U
Eph 4:18 are darkened in their U, alienated from the life
Phil 4:7 God, which passes all U, will keep your hearts
Col 1:9 all spiritual wisdom and U,
2:2 the riches of assured U and the knowledge of
1Tim 1:7 of the law, without U either what they are
1:9 one uses it lawfully, U this, that the law
2Tim 2:7 Lord will grant you U in everything.
Jas 3:13 Who is wise and U among you?
1Jn 5:20 and has given us U, to know him who
Rev 13:18 let him who has U reckon the number of

UNDERSTANDS (12)

1Chr 28:9 searches all hearts, and U every plan and thought.
Job 28:23 with our ears.' "God U the way to it,
Prov 8:9 straight to him who U and right to those
29:19 disciplined, for though he U, he will not give
Wis 8:8 things to come; she U turns of speech and
9:11 For she knows and U all things, and she
Is 57:1 devout men are taken away, while no one U
Jer 9:24 in this, that he U and knows me, that
Dan 8:23 bold countenance, one who U riddles, shall arise.
Mt 13:23 hears the word and U it; he indeed bears
Rom 3:11 not one; no one U, no one seeks for
1Cor 14:2 God; for no one U him, but he utters

UNDERSTOOD (19)

Gen 42:23 not know that Joseph U them, for there was
2Sam 3:37 people and all Israel U that day that it
1Chr 15:22 the music, for he U it.
Neh 6:12 And I U, and saw that God had not
8:8 so that the people U the reading.
8:12 rejoicing, because they had U the words that were
Job 13:1 ear has heard and U it.
Is 40:21 Have you not U from the foundations of the
Bar 3:20 way to knowledge, nor U her paths, nor laid
Dan 10:1 And he U the word and had understanding of
Mt 13:51 "Have you U all this?" They said to him,
16:12 Then they U that he did not tell them
17:13 Then the disciples U that he was speaking to
Lk 18:34 But they U none of these things; this saying
Acts 7:25 supposed that his brethren U that God was giving
1Cor 2:8 rulers of this age U this; for if they
13:12 understand fully, even as I have been fully U
2Cor 1:14 fully, as you have U in part, that you
Col 1:6 day you heard and U the grace of God

UNDERTAKE (7)

Deut 12:7 in all that you U, in which the LORD
12:18 the LORD your God in all that you U
15:10 all your work and in all that you U
23:20 in all that you U in the land which
28:8 in all that you U; and he will bless
28:20 in all that you U to do, until you
Esth 16:3 stand prosperity they even U to scheme against their

UNDERTAKEN (5)

1Mac 4:51 Thus they finished all the work they had U
12:10 our hands, we have U to send to renew
2Mac 2:26 For us who have U the toil of abbreviating,
8:36 Thus he who had U to secure tribute for
Lk 1:1 Inasmuch as many have U to compile a narrative

UNDERTAKES

2Mac 2:29 while the one who U its painting and decoration

UNDERTAKING (3)

Jud 13:5 to carry out my U for the destruction of
Sir 37:16 of every work, and counsel precedes every U
Acts 5:38 this plan or this U is of men, it

UNDERTAKINGS

1Sam 18:14 success in all his U; for the LORD was

UNDERTOOK (7)

Deut 1:5 land of Moab, Moses U to explain this law,
2Chr 31:21 every work that he U in the service of
Esth 9:23 So the Jews U to do as they had
16:12 restrain his arrogance, he U to deprive us of
2Mac 7:26 on his part, she U to persuade her son.
10:23 arms in everything he U, he destroyed more than
Acts 19:13 the itinerant Jewish exorcists U to pronounce the

UNDERWENT

2Mac 7:8 Therefore he in turn U tortures as the first

UNDETECTED

Num 5:13 husband, and she is U though she has defiled

UNDID

Jud 16:7 the daughter of Merari U him with the beauty

UNDISCIPLINED (2)

Sir 10:3 An U king will ruin his people, but a
22:3 the father of an U son, and the birth

UNDISTURBED

2Mac 11:23 of the kingdom be U in caring for their

UNDIVIDED

1Cor 7:35 and to secure your U devotion to the Lord.

UNDO

Is 58:6 bonds of wickedness, to U the thongs of the

UNDOING (2)

2Chr 22:4 his father they were his counselors, to his U
Dan 11:26 food shall be his U; his army shall be

UNDONE (7)

Num 17:12 we perish, we are U, we are all undone.
17:12 we perish, we are undone, we are all U
21:29 You are U, O people of Chemosh!
Josh 11:15 did; he left nothing U of all that the
Is 15:1 a night Moab is U; because Kir is laid
15:1 is laid waste in a night Moab is U
Jer 48:46 people of Chemosh is U; for your sons have

UNDRESSED (2)

Lev 25:5 the grapes of your U vine you shall not
25:11 the grapes from the U vines.

UNDYING

Eph 6:24 who love our Lord Jesus Christ with love U

UNEDUCATED

Acts 4:13 perceived that they were U, common men, they

UNERRING

Wis 7:17 he who gave me U knowledge of what exists,

UNEVEN

Is 40:4 be made low; the U ground shall become level,

UNEXAMINED

Sir 21:18 of the ignorant is U talk.

UNEXPECTED (5)

Wis 5:2 be amazed at his U salvation.
17:15 surrender, for sudden and U fear overwhelmed them.
18:17 greatly troubled them, and U fears assailed them;
2Mac 9:24 so that, if anything U happened or any unwelcome
Lk 12:40 is coming at an U hour."

UNEXPECTEDLY

Wis 11:7 gavest them abundant water U,

UNFADING (3)

Wis 6:12 Wisdom is radiant and U, and she is easily
1Pet 1:4 is imperishable, undefiled, and U, kept in heaven for
5:4 you will obtain the U crown of glory.

UNFAILING (4)

Wis 7:14 for it is an U treasure for men; those
8:18 labors of her hands, U wealth, and in the
2Tim 4:2 rebuke, and exhort, be U in patience and in
1Pet 4:8 Above all hold U your love for one another,

UNFAITHFUL (9)

1Chr 10:13 his unfaithfulness; he was U to the LORD in
2Chr 12:2 because they had been U to the LORD, Shishak
29:6 our fathers have been U and have done what
36:14 were exceedingly U, following all the abominations
Neh 1:8 saying, 'If you are U, I will scatter you
Sir 42:10 husband, lest she prove U, or, though married, lest
Lk 12:46 will punish him, and put him with the U
Rom 3:3 What if some were U
Jas 4:4 U creatures!

UNFAITHFULLY (2)

Num 5:12 goes astray and acts U against him,
5:27 herself and has acted U against her husband, the

UNFAITHFULNESS (5)

1Chr 9:1 taken into exile in Babylon because of their U
10:13 Saul died for his U; he was unfaithful to
2Chr 21:11 inhabitants of Jerusalem into U, and made Judah go
21:13 inhabitants of Jerusalem into U, as the house of
21:13 Ahab led Israel into U, and also you have

UNFASTENED

Acts 16:26 doors were opened and every one's fetters were U

UNFIT (3)

2Mac 6:4 besides brought in things for sacrifice that were U
1Cor 15:9 least of the apostles, U to be called an
Tit 1:15 they are detestable, disobedient, U for any good

UNFOLDING

Ps 119:130 The U of thy words gives light; it imparts

UNFORGOTTEN

Deut 31:21 (for it will live U in the mouths of

UNFORMED

Ps 139:16 Thy eyes beheld my U substance; in thy book

UNFORTUNATE

2Mac 4:47 sentenced to death those U men, who would have

UNFRUITFUL (7)

2Kgs 2:19 the water is bad, and the land is U
Mt 13:22 in riches choke the word, and it proves U
Mk 4:19 in and choke the word, and it proves U
1Cor 14:14 tongue, my spirit prays but my mind is U
Eph 5:11 no part in the U works of darkness, but
Tit 3:14 cases of urgent need, and not to be U
2Pet 1:8 from being ineffective or U in the knowledge of

UNGIRD

Is 45:1 nations before him and U the loins of kings,

UNGIRDED

Gen 24:32 the house; and Laban U the camels, and gave

UNGODLINESS (7)

Wis 14:9 ungodly man and his U,
Is 32:6 plots iniquity: to practice U, to utter error concerning
Jer 23:15 the prophets of Jerusalem U has gone forth into
Rom 1:18 from heaven against all U and wickedness of men
11:26 Zion, he will banish U from Jacob";
2Tim 2:16 into more and more U,
Jude 1:15 all their deeds of U which they have committed

UNGODLY (65)

Job 16:11 me up to the U, and casts me into
18:21 the dwellings of the U, such is the place
Ps 43:1 my cause against an U people; from deceitful and
53:5 the bones of the U; they will be put
Wis 1:9 the counsels of an U man, and a report
1:16 But U men by their words and deeds summoned
3:10 But the U will be punished as their reasoning
4:3 prolific brood of the U will be of no
4:16 died will condemn the U who are living, and
5:14 the hope of the U man is like chaff
10:6 righteous man when the U were perishing; he
10:20 the righteous plundered the U; they sang hymns, O
11:9 learned how the U were tormented when judged
11:10 thou didst examine the U as a stern king
12:9 unable to give the U into the hands of
14:9 to God are the U man and his ungodliness,
14:16 Then the U custom, grown strong with time, was
16:16 is impossible; for the U, refusing to know thee,
16:18 creatures sent against the U, but that seeing this

U

19:1 But the U were assailed to the end by
Sir 7:17 the punishment of the U is fire and worms.
9:12 in what pleases the U; remember that they will
12:5 not give to the U; hold back his bread,
12:6 hates sinners and will inflict punishment on the U
13:23 poverty is evil in the opinion of the U
15:20 any one to be U, and he has not
16:1 children, nor rejoice in U sons.
16:3 better than to have U children.
21:27 When an U man curses his adversary, he curses
22:10 a fool or an U man it lasts all
34:19 the offerings of the U; and he is not
39:30 sword that punishes the U with destruction;
40:15 The children of the U will not put forth
41:5 children, and they frequent the haunts of the U
41:7 Children will blame an U father, for they suffer
41:8 Woe to you, U men, who have forsaken the
41:10 to dust; so the U go from curse to
42:2 judgment to acquit the U;
Jer 23:11 prophet and priest are U; even in my house
Bar 2:12 sinned, we have been U, we have done wrong,
1Mac 3:8 Judah; he destroyed the U out of the land;
3:15 a strong army of U men went up with
6:21 and some of the U Israelites joined them.
7:5 all the lawless and U men of Israel; they
7:9 and with him the U Alcimus, whom he made
9:25 And Bacchides chose the U and put them in
9:73 and he destroyed the U out of Israel.
2Mac 4:13 of Jason, who was U and no high priest,
8:2 had been profaned by U men,
8:14 been sold by the U Nicanor before he ever
9:9 And so the U man's body swarmed with worms,
10:10 the son of that U man, and will give
12:3 of Joppa did so U a deed as this:
15:33 the tongue of the U Nicanor and said that
Rom 4:5 him who justifies the U, his faith is reckoned
5:6 at the right time Christ died for the U
1Tim 1:9 and disobedient, for the U and sinners, for the
2Pet 2:5 the world of the U;
2:6 who were to be U;
3:7 judgment and destruction of U men.
Jude 1:4 designated for this condemnation, U persons who
1:15 to convict all the U of all their deeds
1:15 committed in such an U way, and of all
1:15 the harsh things which U sinners have spoken against
1:18 scoffers, following their own U passions."

UNGRACIOUS (2)
Sir 18:17 A fool is U and abusive, and the gift
20:18 An U man is like a story told at

UNGRATEFUL (3)
Wis 16:29 the hope of an U man will melt like
Lk 6:35 is kind to the U and the selfish.
2Tim 3:2 disobedient to their parents, U, unholy,

UNGRUDGINGLY
1Pet 4:9 Practice hospitality U to one another.

UNHALLOWED (2)
Ezek 21:25 And you, O U wicked one, prince of Israel,
21:29 the necks of the U wicked, whose day has

UNHAPPY (2)
Eccl 1:13 heaven; it is an U business that God has
4:8 is vanity and an U business.

U

UNHARMED (2)
Wis 19:6 thy commands, that thy children might be kept U
2Mac 12:25 promise to restore them U, they let him go,

UNHEALTHY
Sir 40:15 many branches; they are U roots upon sheer rock.

UNHEARD
Wis 1:10 and the sound of murmurings does not go U

UNHEWN (3)
Deut 27:6 LORD your God of U stones; and you shall
Josh 8:31 Moses, "an altar of U stones, upon which no
1Mac 4:47 Then they took U stones, as the law directs,

UNHINDERED (3)
Wis 17:20 and was engaged in U work,
19:7 had stood before, an U way out of the
Acts 28:30 about the Lord Jesus Christ quite openly and U

UNHOLY (10)
Ex 30:9 You shall offer no U incense thereon, nor burnt
Lev 10:1 on it, and offered U fire before the LORD,
Num 3:4 LORD when they offered U fire before the LORD
26:61 died when they offered U fire before the LORD.
Wis 12:4 works of sorcery and U rites,
2Mac 7:34 But you, U wretch, you most defiled of all
8:32 Timothy's forces, a most U man, and one who
12:14 even blaspheming and saying U things.
1Tim 1:9 and sinners, for the U and profane, for murderers
2Tim 3:2 to their parents, ungrateful, U,

UNIFORM
2Mac 8:35 took off his splendid U and made his way

UNIFYING
Esth 13:4 kings, so that the U of the kingdom which

UNINFORMED
1Cor 12:1 brethren, I do not want you to be U

UNINHABITED (8)
Jud 5:19 settled in the hill country, because it was U
Wis 11:2 They journeyed through an U wilderness, and
Jer 6:8 you a desolation, an U land."
17:6 the wilderness, in an U salt land.
22:6 you a desert, an U city.
Ezek 29:11 it; it shall be U forty years.
Zech 9:5 Gaza; Ashkelon shall be U;
1Mac 3:45 Jerusalem was U like a wilderness; not one of

UNINSTRUCTED
Sir 6:20 very harsh to the U; a weakling will not

UNINTELLIGENT
Sir 22:11 do not visit an U man; guard yourself from

UNINTENTIONALLY (3)
Deut 4:42 who kills his neighbor U, without being at enmity
19:4 one kills his neighbor U without having been at
Sir 14:7 good, he does it U, and betrays his baseness

UNINTRUCTED
Wis 17:1 hard to describe; therefore U souls have gone astray.

UNION (4)
Wis 3:13 entered into a sinful U; she will have fruit
3:16 offspring of an unlawful U will perish.
Zech 11:7 one I named Grace, the other I named U
11:14 broke my second staff U, annulling the brotherhood

UNIONS
Wis 4:6 children born of unlawful U are witnesses of evil

UNIQUE
Wis 7:22 that is intelligent, holy, U, manifold, subtle, mobile,

UNISON (2)
2Chr 5:13 make themselves heard in U in praise and
Jud 4:12 and cried out in U, praying earnestly to the

UNITE (2)
Ps 86:11 walk in thy truth; U my heart to fear
Eph 1:10 fullness of time, to U all things in him,

UNITED (7)
Judg 20:11 gathered against the city, U as one man.
1Mac 2:42 Then there U with them a company of Hasideans,
Acts 18:12 the Jews made a U attack upon Paul and
Rom 6:5 if we have been U with him in a
6:5 we shall certainly be U with him in a
1Cor 1:10 but that you be U in the same mind
6:17 But he who is U to the Lord becomes

UNITS
1Chr 7:4 their fathers' houses, were U of the army for

UNITY (4)
Ps 133:1 and pleasant it is when brothers dwell in U
Eph 4:3 eager to maintain the U of the Spirit in
4:13 all attain to the U of the faith and
1Pet 3:8 all of you, have U of spirit, sympathy, love

UNIVERSE (10)
Esth 13:9 all things, for the U is in thy power
Wis 16:17 greater effect, for the U defends the righteous.

Sir	18:1	ever created the whole U;
	23:20	Before the U was created, it was known to
	42:17	has established that the U may stand firm in
2Mac	7:9	the King of the U will raise us up
Gal	4:3	were slaves to the elemental spirits of the U
Col	2:8	elemental spirits of the U, and not according to
	2:20	elemental spirits of the U, why do you live
Heb	1:3	his nature, upholding the U by his word of

UNJUST (21)

Ps	43:1	people; from deceitful and U men deliver me!
	71:4	the grasp of the U and cruel man.
Prov	15:27	who is greedy for U gain makes trouble for
	28:16	but he who hates U gain will prolong his
	29:27	An U man is an abomination to the righteous,
Sir	19:22	which is scrupulous but U, and there are people
	40:13	The wealth of the U will dry up like
	41:18	or the people; of U dealing, before your partner
Jer	6:13	one is greedy for U gain; and from prophet
	8:10	one is greedy for U gain; from prophet to
Dan	3:32	rebels, and to an U king, the most wicked
	13:53	in the past, pronouncing U judgments, condemning
Zeph	3:5	not fail; but the U knows no shame.
2Mac	4:35	and displeased at the U murder of the man.
	4:40	men and launched an U attack, under the leadership
	4:48	vessels quickly suffered the U penalty.
Mt	5:45	sends rain on the just and on the U
Lk	18:11	like other men, extortioners, U, adulterers, or even
Acts	24:14	a resurrection of both the just and the U
Rom	3:5	That God is U to inflict wrath on us?
Heb	6:10	God is not so U as to overlook your

UNJUSTLY (5)

Ps	82:2	long will you judge U and show partiality to
Wis	12:13	thou hast not judged U;
1Mac	2:37	testify for us that you are killing us U
	15:33	one time had been U taken by our enemies.
1Pet	2:19	mindful of God, he endures pain while suffering U

UNKINDLY

Sir	20:15	good deeds; those who eat my bread speak U

UNKNOWN (8)

Gen	41:31	the plenty will be U in the land by
Wis	11:18	lions, or newly created U beasts full of rage,
	18:3	guide for thy people's U journey, and a harmless
2Mac	1:19	that the place was U to any one.
	2:7	"The place shall be U until God gathers his
Acts	17:23	this inscription, 'To an U god.' What therefore you
	17:23	therefore you worship as U, this I proclaim to
2Cor	6:9	yet are true; as U, and yet well-known; as

UNLAWFUL (6)

Wis	3:16	the offspring of an U union will perish.
	4:6	For children born of U unions are witnesses of
2Mac	4:14	take part in the U proceedings in the wrestling
	6:21	in charge of that U sacrifice took the man
	7:1	cords, to partake of U swine's flesh.
Acts	10:28	"You yourselves know how U it is for a

UNLEAVENED (62)

Gen	19:3	a feast, and baked U bread, and they ate.
Ex	12:8	that night, roasted; with U bread and bitter herbs
	12:15	days you shall eat U bread; on the first
	12:17	observe the feast of U bread, for on this
	12:18	evening, you shall eat U bread, and so until
	12:20	dwellings you shall eat U bread."
	12:39	And they baked U cakes of the dough which
	13:6	days you shall eat U bread, and on the
	13:7	U bread shall be eaten for seven days; no
	23:15	keep the feast of U bread; as I commanded
	23:15	you, you shall eat U bread for seven days
	29:2	rams without blemish, and U bread, unleavened
	29:2	and unleavened bread, U cakes mixed with oil,
	29:2	mixed with oil, and U wafers spread with oil.
	29:23	of the basket of U bread that is before
	34:18	he feast of U bread you shall keep.
	34:18	days you shall eat U bread, as I commanded
Lev	2:4	offering, it shall be U cakes of fine flour
	2:4	mixed with oil, or U wafers spread with oil.
	2:5	be of fine flour U, mixed with oil;
	6:16	it shall be eaten U in a holy place;
	7:12	with the thank offering U cakes mixed with oil,
	7:12	cakes mixed with oil, U wafers spread with oil,
	8:2	and the basket of U bread;
	8:26	of the basket of U bread which was before
	8:26	LORD he took one U cake, and one cake
	10:12	LORD, and eat it U beside the altar, for
	23:6	is the feast of U bread to the LORD;
	23:6	days you shall eat U bread.
Num	6:15	and a basket of U bread, cakes of fine
	6:15	mixed with oil, and U wafers spread with oil,
	6:17	with the basket of U bread; the priest shall
	6:19	is boiled, and one U cake out of the
	6:19	the basket, and one U wafer, and shall put
	9:11	shall eat it with U bread and bitter herbs.
	28:17	feast; seven days shall U bread be eaten.
Deut	16:3	shall eat it with U bread, the bread of
	16:8	days you shall eat U bread; and on the
	16:16	at the feast of U bread, at the feast
Josh	5:11	produce of the land, U cakes and parched grain.
Judg	6:19	prepared a kid, and U cakes from an ephah
	6:20	the meat and the U cakes, and put them
	6:21	the meat and the U cakes; and there sprang
	6:21	the flesh and the U cakes; and the angel
1Sam	28:24	kneaded it and baked U bread of it,
2Kgs	23:9	Jerusalem, but they ate U bread among their
1Chr	23:29	offering, the wafers of U bread, the baked offering,
2Chr	8:13	feasts--the feast of U bread, the feast of
	30:13	keep the feast of U bread in the second
	30:21	kept the feast of U bread seven days with
	35:17	and the feast of U bread seven days.
Ezra	6:22	kept the feast of U bread seven days with
Ezek	45:21	and for seven days U bread shall be eaten.
Mt	26:17	the first day of U Bread the disciples came
Mk	14:1	and the feast of U Bread.
	14:12	the first day of U Bread, when they sacrificed
Lk	22:1	Now the feast of U Bread drew near, which
	22:7	came the day of U Bread, on which the
Acts	12:3	during the days of U Bread.
	20:6	after the days of U Bread, and in five
1Cor	5:7	be a new lump, as you really are U
	5:8	evil, but with the U bread of sincerity and

UNLESS (69)

Gen	32:26	not let you go, U you bless me."
	42:15	go from this place U your youngest brother comes
	43:3	not see my face, U your brother is with
	43:5	not see my face, U your brother is with
	44:23	said to your servants, U your youngest brother comes
	44:26	see the man's face U our youngest brother is
Ex	3:19	not let you go U compelled by a mighty
Lev	22:6	of the holy things U he has bathed his
Deut	32:30	ten thousand to flight, U their Rock had sold
Josh	7:12	with you no more, U you destroy the devoted
1Sam	25:34	me from hurting you, U you had made haste
2Sam	3:13	not see my face, U you first bring Michal,
2Kgs	4:24	the pace for me U I tell you."
Jud	8:11	city to our enemies U the Lord turns and
	11:10	sword prevail against them, U they sin against their
Esth	2:14	to the king again, U the king delighted in
Ps	127:1	U the LORD builds the house, those who build
	127:1	U the LORD watches over the city, the watchman
Prov	4:17	For they cannot sleep U they have done wrong;
	4:17	are robbed of sleep U they have made some
Wis	8:21	would not possess wisdom U God gave her to
	9:17	has learned thy counsel, U thou hast given wisdom
Sir	16:2	not rejoice in them, U the fear of the
	19:8	not report it, and U it would be a
	34:6	U they are sent from the Most High as
Lam	3:37	it came to pass, U the Lord has ordained
Bar	6:24	they will not shine U some one wipes off
Dan	6:5	complaint against this Daniel U we find it in
Amos	3:3	"Do two walk together, U they have made an
	3:6	evil befall a city, U the LORD has done
1Mac	6:27	sanctuary and Bethzur; and U you quickly prevent,
	7:35	he swore this oath, U Judas and his army
Mt	5:20	For I tell you, U your righteousness exceeds that
	12:29	and plunder his goods, U he first binds the
	18:3	I say to you, U you turn and become
	26:42	if this cannot pass U I drink it, thy
Mk	3:27	and plunder his goods, U he first binds the
	7:3	Jews, do not eat U they wash their hands,
	7:4	they do not eat U they purify themselves; and
Lk	9:13	loaves and two fish-- U we are to go
	13:3	tell you, No; but U you repent you will
	13:5	tell you, No; but U you repent you will
Jn	3:2	signs that you do, U God is with him."
	3:3	I say to you, U one is born anew,
	3:5	I say to you, U one is born of
	4:48	therefore said to him, U you see signs and
	6:44	can come to me U the Father who sent

6:53 I say to you, U you eat the flesh
6:65 can come to me U it is granted him
8:24 die in your sins U you believe that I
12:24 I say to you, U a grain of wheat
15:4 bear fruit by itself, U it abides in the
15:4 vine, neither can you, U you abide in me.
19:11 no power over me U it had been given
20:25 he said to them, U I see in his
Acts 8:31 said, "How can I, U some one guides me?"
15:1 teaching the brethren, U you are circumcised
27:31 centurion and the soldiers, U these men stay in
Rom 10:15 how can men preach U they are sent?
1Cor 14:5 who speaks in tongues, U some one interprets, so
14:6 shall I benefit you U I bring you some
15:2 you hold it fast-- U you believed in vain.
15:36 not come to life U it dies.
2Cor 13:5 Christ is in you?-- U indeed you fail to
2Thes 2:3 day will not come, U the rebellion comes first,
2Tim 2:5 athlete is not crowned U he competes according to
Rev 2:5 lampstand from its place, U you repent.
2:22 throw into great tribulation, U they repent of her
13:17 can buy or sell U he has the mark,

UNLIFTED
2Cor 3:14 same veil remains U, because only through Christ

UNLIKE
Wis 2:15 manner of life is U that of others, and

UNLOAD
Acts 21:3 the ship was to U its cargo.

UNLOVED
Prov 30:23 filled with food; an U woman when she gets

UNMARRIED (6)
Ezek 44:25 daughter, for brother or U sister they may defile
Acts 21:9 And he had four U daughters, who prophesied.
1Cor 7:8 To the U and the widows I say that
7:25 Now concerning the U, I have no command of
7:32 The U man is anxious about the affairs of
7:34 And the U woman or girl is anxious about

UNMERCIFUL
Sir 35:18 the loins of the U and repays vengeance on

UNMINDFUL (2)
Deut 32:18 You were U of the Rock that begot you,
Sir 37:6 heart, and be not U of him in your

UNMIXED
Rev 14:10 of God's wrath, poured U into the cup of

UNMOVED
Gen 49:24 yet his bow remained U, his arms were made

UNNATURAL (2)
Rom 1:26 exchanged natural relations for U,
Jude 1:7 immorally and indulged in U lust, serve as an

UNNI (2)
1Chr 15:18 Zechariah, Ja-aziel, Shemiramoth, Jehiel, U, Eliab,
15:20 Zechariah, Azi-el, Shemiramoth, Jehiel, U, Eliab,

UNNO
Neh 12:9 And Bakbukiah and U their brethren stood opposite

UNNOTICED
Wis 10:8 folly, so that their failures could never go U

UNOBSERVED (2)
Wis 17:3 secret sins they were U behind a dark curtain
2Mac 15:36 let this day go U, but to celebrate the

UNPLEASANT
Eccl 8:3 when the matter is U, for he does whatever

UNPOLLUTED
Wis 7:22 subtle, mobile, clear, U, distinct, invulnerable,

UNPRESENTABLE
1Cor 12:23 greater honor, and our U parts are treated with

UNPROFITABLE (4)
Job 15:3 Should he argue in U talk, or in words
Wis 3:11 vain, their labors are U, and their works are
Sir 37:19 many, and yet be U to himself.
Tit 3:9 law, for they are U and futile.

UNPUNISHED (19)
Prov 6:29 neighbor's wife; none who touches her will go U
11:21 man will not go U, but those who are
16:5 the LORD; be assured, he will not go U
17:5 who is glad at calamity will not go U
19:5 witness will not go U, and he who utters
19:9 witness will not go U, and he who utters
28:20 who hastens to be rich will not go U
Wis 12:11 thou didst leave them U for their sins.
Sir 7:8 twice; even for one you will not go U
11:10 you will not go U, and if you pursue
16:11 it will be a wonder if he remains U
Jer 25:29 called by my name, and shall you go U
25:29 You shall not go U, for I am summoning
30:11 and I will by no means leave you U
46:28 and I will by no means leave you U
49:12 the cup must drink it, will you go U
49:12 You shall not go U, but you must drink.
Zech 11:5 slay them and go U; and those who sell
2Mac 7:19 that you will go U for having tried to

UNQUENCHABLE (3)
Mt 3:12 he will burn with U fire."
Mk 9:43 to hell, to the U fire.
Lk 3:17 he will burn with U fire."

UNREASONABLE (2)
2Mac 4:36 with regard to the U murder of Onias, and
Acts 25:27 it seems to me U, in sending a prisoner,

UNRELENTING
Is 14:6 nations in anger with U persecution.

UNRESPONSIVE
Wis 16:11 deep forgetfulness and become U to thy kindness.

UNREST (2)
Sir 40:5 envy and trouble and U, and fear of death,
Jer 50:34 to the earth, but U to the inhabitants of

UNRESTRAINED
Sir 30:8 stubborn, and a son U turns out to be

UNRIGHTEOUS (24)
Job 27:7 that rises up against me be as the U
29:17 the fangs of the U, and made him drop
31:3 not calamity befall the U, and disaster the workers
Wis 1:8 no one who utters U things will escape notice,
3:19 the end of an U generation is grievous.
4:16 old age of the U man.
10:3 But when an U man departed from her in
12:12 as an advocate for U men?
14:31 sin, that always pursues the transgression of the U
16:19 the crops of the U land.
16:24 itself to punish the U, and in kindness relaxes
Sir 1:19 U anger cannot be justified, for a man's anger
35:12 not trust to an U sacrifice; for the Lord
35:18 the scepters of the U;
51:6 the slander of an U tongue to the king.
Is 55:7 his way, and the U man his thoughts; let
Lk 16:9 yourselves by means of U mammon, so that when
16:11 been faithful in the U mammon, who will entrust
18:6 said, "Hear what the U judge says.
1Cor 6:1 to law before the U instead of the saints?
6:9 not know that the U will not inherit the
Jas 3:6 The tongue is an U world among our members,
1Pet 3:18 the righteous for the U, that he might bring
2Pet 2:9 and to keep the U under punishment until the

UNRIGHTEOUSLY (3)
Wis 12:23 folly of life lived U thou didst torment through
14:28 prophesy lies, or live U, or readily commit perjury;
14:30 deceit they swore U through contempt for holiness.

UNRIGHTEOUSNESS (9)
Job 22:23 yourself, if you remove U far from your tents,
Ps 92:15 and there is no U in him.
Wis 1:5 and will be ashamed at the approach of U
Sir 17:12 And he said to them, "Beware of all U
35:3 Lord, and to forsake U is atonement.
Jer 22:13 builds his house by U, and his upper rooms
Ezek 28:18 your iniquities, in the U of your trade you
2Thes 2:12 not believe the truth but had pleasure in U

1Jn 1:9 forgive our sins and cleanse us from all U

UNRIPE

Job 15:33 will shake off his U grape, like the vine,

UNSAFE

Tob 1:15 him the highways were U, so that I could

UNSATISFIED

Is 32:6 craving of the hungry U, and to deprive the

UNSAVORY

Jer 23:13 Samaria I saw an U thing: they prophesied by

UNSEARCHABLE (7)

Job 5:9 does great things and U, marvelous things without
36:26 him not; the number of his years is U
Ps 145:3 greatly to be praised, and his greatness is U
Prov 25:3 for depth, so the mind of kings is U
Is 40:28 not faint or grow weary, his understanding is U
Rom 11:33 How U are his judgments and how inscrutable his
Eph 3:8 to the Gentiles the U riches of Christ,

UNSEEMLY

Sir 13:21 are many; he speaks U words, and they justify

UNSEEN (9)

Ps 77:19 through the great waters; yet thy footprints were U
Wis 17:6 be worse than that U appearance.
17:19 hurled down, or the U running of leaping animals,
Sir 20:29 Hidden wisdom and U treasure, what advantage is
41:14 peace; hidden wisdom and U treasure, what
2Mac 9:5 him an incurable and U blow.
2Cor 4:18 the things that are U; for the things that
4:18 the things that are U are eternal.
Heb 11:7 concerning events as yet U, took heed and

UNSETTLE

Gal 5:12 I wish those who U you would mutilate themselves!

UNSETTLING

Acts 15:24 troubled you with words, U your minds, although we

UNSHAKEN

2Cor 1:7 hope for you is U; for we know that

UNSHEATHE (4)

Lev 26:33 nations, and I will U the sword after you;
Ezek 5:2 wind, and I will U the sword after them.
5:12 the winds and will U the sword after them.
12:14 troops; and I will U the sword after them.

UNSHOD

Jer 2:25 your feet from going U and your throat from

UNSHRUNK (2)

Mt 9:16 puts a piece of U cloth on an old
Mk 2:21 sews a piece of U cloth on an old

UNSKILLED (2)

2Cor 11:6 Even if I am U in speaking, I am
Heb 5:13 lives on milk is U in the word of

UNSOLD

Acts 5:4 While it remained U, did it not remain your

UNSOUNDLY

Wis 2:1 For they reasoned U, saying to themselves, "Short

UNSOWN

Deut 29:23 and a burnt-out waste, U, and growing nothing,

UNSPARING

Job 6:10 even exult in pain U; for I have not

UNSPIRITUAL (2)

1Cor 2:14 The U man does not receive the gifts of
Jas 3:15 above, but is earthly, U, devilish.

UNSTABLE (3)

Gen 49:4 U as water, you shall not have pre-eminence because
Jas 1:7 that a double-minded man, U in all his ways,
2Pet 3:16 which the ignorant and U twist to their own

UNSTAINED (3)

1Tim 6:14 to keep the commandment U and free from
Heb 7:26 high priest, holy, blameless, U, separated from
Jas 1:26 and to keep oneself U from the world.

UNSTEADY

2Pet 2:14 They entice U souls.

UNSTOPPED

Is 35:5 ears of the deaf U;

UNSUSPECTING (4)

Judg 18:7 the Sidonians, quiet and U, lacking nothing that is
18:10 will come to an U people.
18:27 a people quiet and U, and smote them with
Ezek 30:9 me to terrify the U Ethiopians; and anguish shall

UNTAMED

Sir 30:8 A horse that is U turns out to be

UNTAUGHT

Sir 51:23 me, you who are U, and lodge in my

UNTIE (8)

Mt 21:2 a colt with her; U them and bring them
Mk 1:7 I am not worthy to stoop down and U
11:2 one has ever sat; U it and bring it.
Lk 3:16 am not worthy to U; he will baptize you
13:15 you on the sabbath U his ox or his
19:30 has ever yet sat; U it and bring it
Jn 1:27 of whose sandal I am not worthy to U
Acts 13:25 am not worthy to U

UNTIED (2)

Jud 6:14 found him; and they U him and brought him
Mk 11:4 open street; and they U it.

UNTIMELY (6)

Job 3:16 not as a hidden U birth, as infants that
Ps 58:8 into slime, like the U birth that never sees
Eccl 6:3 I say that an U birth is better off
Wis 14:15 with grief at an U bereavement, made an image
Is 14:19 sepulchre, like a loathed U birth, clothed with the
1Cor 15:8 all, as to one U born, he appeared also

UNTO (8)

Job 31:12 a fire which consumes U Abaddon, and it would
Joel 1:18 U thee, O LORD, I cry.
Jn 11:4 "This illness is not U death; it is for
Acts 11:18 God has granted repentance U life."
Phil 2:8 himself and became obedient U death, even death on
Jude 1:21 our Lord Jesus Christ U eternal life.
Rev 2:10 Be faithful U death, and I will give you
12:11 not their lives even U death.

UNTOLD (2)

2Mac 3:6 Jerusalem was full of U sums of money, so
12:16 of God, and slaughtered U numbers, so that the

UNTRAINED

Jer 31:18 was chastened, like an U calf; bring me back

UNTRODDEN

Wis 11:2 pitched their tents in U places.

UNTROUBLED

Esth 13:7 government completely secure and U hereafter."

UNTRUE

Ps 73:15 I would have been U to the generation of

UNTYING (4)

Mk 11:5 "What are you doing, U the colt?"
Lk 19:31 you, 'Why are you U it?' you shall say
19:33 And as they were U the colt, its owners
19:33 them, "Why are you U the colt?"

UNUSUAL (2)

Wis 16:16 thy arm, pursued by U rains and hail and
Acts 28:2 the natives showed us U kindness, for they kindled

UNUTTERABLE

1Pet 1:8 him and rejoice with U and exalted joy.

UNVEILED (3)

Dan 13:32 ordered her to be U, that they might feed
1Cor 11:5 prophesies with her head U dishonors her head—it
2Cor 3:18 And we all, with U face, beholding the glory

U

UNWALLED (3)
Deut 3:5 bars, besides very many U villages.
1Sam 6:18 both fortified cities and U villages.
Ezek 38:11 against the land of U villages; I will fall

UNWASHED (2)
Mt 15:20 but to eat with U hands does not defile
Mk 7:2 his disciples ate with hands defiled, that is, U

UNWEIGHED
1Kgs 7:47 left all the vessels U, because there were so

UNWELCOME
2Mac 9:24 unexpected happened or any U news came, the

UNWILLING (6)
Deut 10:10 also; the LORD was U to destroy you.
Josh 24:15 And if you be U to serve the LORD,
2Sam 12:4 man, and he was U to take one of
1Mac 12:14 We were U to annoy you and our other
Mt 1:19 a just man and U to put her to
15:32 eat; and I am U to send them away

UNWISE (2)
Hos 13:13 but he is an U son; for now he
Eph 5:15 you walk, not as U men but as wise,

UNWISELY
1Mac 5:67 in battle, for they went out to battle U

UNWITTING (2)
Tob 3:3 sins and for my U offences and those which
Jud 5:20 if there is any U error in this people

UNWITTINGLY (13)
Lev 4:2 If any one sins U in any of the
4:13 Israel commits a sin U and the thing is
4:22 a ruler sins, doing U any one of all
4:27 the common people sins U in doing any one
5:15 of faith and sins U in any of the
5:18 error which he committed U, and he shall be
22:14 of a holy thing U, he shall add the
Num 15:24 if it was done U without the knowledge of
15:27 "If one person sins U, he shall offer a
15:28 error, when he sins U, to make atonement for
15:29 him who does anything U, for him who is
Josh 20:3 person without intent or U may flee there; they
20:5 he killed his neighbor U, having had no enmity

UNWORTHILY
Esth 16:7 those who exercise authority U, can be seen not

UNWORTHY (6)
Sir 10:19 What race is U of honor?
10:19 What race is U of honor?
2Mac 14:42 sinners and suffer outrages U of his noble birth.
Lk 17:10 you, say, 'We are U servants; we have only
Acts 13:46 you, and judge yourselves U of eternal life, behold,
1Cor 11:27 the Lord in an U manner will be guilty

UPBRAID (2)
Sir 41:22 and do not U after making a gift;
Mt 11:20 Then he began to U the cities where most

UPBRAIDED (3)
Gen 31:36 Jacob became angry, and U Laban; Jacob said to
Judg 8:1 And they U him violently.
Mk 16:14 at table; and he U them for their unbelief

UPBRAIDS
Sir 20:14 He gives little and U much, he opens his

UPBUILDING (3)
Rom 14:19 pursue what makes for peace and for mutual U
1Cor 14:3 to men for their U and encouragement and
2Cor 12:19 and all for your U, beloved.

UPBUILDS
Eph 4:16 makes bodily growth and U itself in love.

UPHAZ (2)
Jer 10:9 silver is brought from Tarshish, and gold from U
Dan 10:5 linen, whose loins were girded with gold of U

UPHELD (6)
Job 4:4 Your words have U him who was stumbling, and
Ps 41:12 But thou hast U me because of my integrity,
Prov 20:28 and his throne is U by righteousness.
Is 59:16 victory, and his righteousness U him.
63:5 victory, and my wrath U me.
Rom 14:4 And he will be U, for the Master is

UPHOLD (8)
Ps 51:12 of thy salvation, and U me with a willing
119:116 U me according to thy promise, that I may
Is 9:7 establish it, and to U it with justice and
41:10 help you, I will U you with my victorious
42:1 my servant, whom I U, my chosen, in whom
63:5 was no one to U; so my own arm
Jer 30:13 There is none to U your cause, no medicine
Rom 3:31 On the contrary, we U the law.

UPHOLDER (2)
Jud 9:11 helper of the oppressed, U of the weak, protector
Ps 54:4 the Lord is the U of my life.

UPHOLDING
Heb 1:3 stamp of his nature, U the universe by his

UPHOLDS (5)
Ps 37:17 broken; but the LORD U the righteous.
63:8 thee; thy right hand U me.
145:14 The LORD U all who are falling, and raises
146:9 over the sojourners, he U the widow and the
2Mac 14:15 for ever and always U his own heritage by

UPLIFTED (2)
Job 38:15 is withheld, and their U arm is broken.
Acts 13:17 of Egypt, and with U arm he led them

UPPER (51)
Lev 13:45 he shall cover his U lip and cry, 'Unclean,
Deut 24:6 a mill or an U millstone in pledge; for
Josh 15:19 Caleb gave her the U springs and the lower
16:5 Ataroth-addar as far as U Beth-horon,
Judg 1:15 Caleb gave her the U springs and the lower
9:53 woman threw an U millstone upon Abimelech's head,
1Sam 9:24 the leg and the U portion and set them
2Sam 11:21 a woman cast an U millstone upon him from
1Kgs 17:19 him up into the U chamber, where he lodged,
17:23 him down from the U chamber into the house,
2Kgs 1:2 the lattice in his U chamber in Samaria, and
15:35 He built the U gate of the house of
18:17 the conduit of the U pool, which is on
23:12 the roof of the U chamber of Ahaz, which
1Chr 7:24 built both Lower and U Beth-horon, and
28:11 houses, its treasuries, its U rooms, and its inner
2Chr 3:9 And he overlaid the U chambers with gold.
8:5 He also built U Beth-horon and Lower Beth-horon,
23:20 LORD, marching through the U gate to the king's
27:3 He built the U gate of the house of
32:30 same Hezekiah closed the U outlet of the waters
Neh 3:25 tower projecting from the U house of the king
3:31 Gate, and to the U chamber of the corner.
3:32 And between the U chamber of the corner and
Tob 3:17 came down from her U room.
Jud 1:8 Carmel and Gilead, and U Galilee and the great
2:21 to the north of U Cilicia.
Ps 74:5 At the U entrance they hacked the wooden trellis
Is 7:3 the conduit of the U pool on the highway
36:2 the conduit of the U pool on the highway
Jer 20:2 that were in the U Benjamin Gate of the
22:13 by unrighteousness, and his U rooms by injustice;
22:14 great house with spacious U rooms,' and cuts out
36:10 which was in the U court, at the entry
Ezek 9:2 the direction of the U gate, which faces north,
42:5 the U chambers were narrower, for the galleries
42:6 outer court; hence the U chambers were set back
Dan 6:10 windows in his U chamber open toward Jerusalem;
Amos 9:6 Egypt; who builds his U chambers in the heavens,
1Mac 2:48 the sinner gain the U hand.
3:37 and went through the U provinces.
6:1 was going through the U provinces when he heard
2Mac 9:23 made expeditions into the U country, appointed his
9:25 hastened off to the U provinces; and I have
Mk 14:15 show you a large U room furnished and ready;
Lk 22:12 show you a large U room furnished; there make
Acts 1:13 went up to the U room, where they were
9:37 laid her in an U room.
9:39 took him to the U room.
19:1 Paul passed through the U country and came to
20:8 many lights in the U chamber where we were

UPPERMOST

Gen 40:17 head, and in the U basket there were all

UPRIGHT (63)

Gen 37:7 sheaf arose and stood U; and behold, your sheaves
Ex 26:15 "And you shall make U frames for the tabernacle
36:20 Then he made the U frames for the tabernacle
2Chr 19:11 courageously, and may the LORD be with the U
29:34 the Levites were more U in heart than the
Job 1:1 man was blameless and U, one who feared God,
1:8 earth, a blameless and U man, who fears God
2:3 earth, a blameless and U man, who fears God
4:7 Or where were the U cut off?
8:6 you are pure and U, surely then he will
17:8 U men are appalled at this, and the innocent
23:7 There an U man could reason with him, and
Ps 7:10 God, who saves the U in heart.
11:2 the dark at the U in heart;
11:7 loves righteous deeds; the U shall behold his face.
20:8 and fall; but we shall rise and stand U
25:8 Good and U is the LORD; therefore he instructs
32:11 for joy, all you U in heart!
33:1 Praise befits the U
33:4 of the LORD is U; and all his work
36:10 thy salvation to the U of heart!
37:37 man, and behold the U, for there is posterity
64:10 Let all the U in heart glory!
73:1 is good to the U, to those who are
78:72 With U heart he tended them, and guided them
92:15 that the LORD is U; he is my rock,
94:15 righteous, and all the U in heart will follow
97:11 and joy for the U in heart.
107:42 The U see it and are glad; and all
111:1 the company of the U, in the congregation.
112:2 the generation of the U will be blessed.
112:4 the darkness for the U; the LORD is gracious,
119:7 praise thee with an U heart, when I learn
125:4 to those who are U in their hearts!
140:13 to thy name; the U shall dwell in thy
Prov 2:7 sound wisdom for the U; he is a shield
2:21 For the U will inhabit the land, and men
3:32 the LORD, but the U are in his confidence.
10:29 him whose way is U, but destruction to evildoers.
11:3 The integrity of the U guides them, but the
11:6 The righteousness of the U delivers them, but the
11:11 the blessing of the U a city is exalted,
12:6 the mouth of the U delivers men.
13:6 him whose way is U, but sin overthrows the
14:9 the wicked, but the U enjoy his favor.
14:11 the tent of the U will flourish.
15:8 the prayer of the U is his delight.
15:19 the path of the U is a level highway.
16:17 The highway of the U turns aside from evil;
21:18 for the righteous, and the faithless for the U
21:29 bold face, but an U man considers his ways.
28:10 He who misleads the U into an evil way
Eccl 7:29 that God made man U, but they have sought
Bar 6:27 sets one of them U, it cannot move itself;
Dan 10:11 to you, and stand U, for now I have
Hos 14:9 are right, and the U walk in them, but
Mic 7:2 and there is none U among men; they all
7:4 a brier, the most U of them a thorn
Hab 2:4 whose soul is not U in him shall fail,
Acts 10:22 "Cornelius, a centurion, an U and God-fearing man,
14:10 a loud voice, "Stand U on your feet." And
Tit 1:7 master of himself, U, holy, and self-controlled;
2:12 and to live sober, U, and godly lives in

UPRIGHTLY (8)

Tob 4:5 Live U all the days of your life, and
4:7 to all who live U, and do not let
Ps 37:14 slay those who walk U;
58:1 Do you judge the sons of men U
84:11 does the LORD withhold from those who walk U
Eccl 12:10 find pleasing words, and U he wrote words of
Is 33:15 walks righteously and speaks U, who despises the
Mic 2:7 my words do good to him who walks U

UPRIGHTNESS (18)

Deut 9:5 your righteousness or the U of your heart are
1Kgs 3:6 in righteousness, and in U of heart toward thee;
9:4 integrity of heart and U, doing according to all
1Chr 29:17 and hast pleasure in U; in the uprightness of
29:17 in uprightness; in the U of my heart I
Job 33:3 My words declare the U of my heart, and
Ps 25:21 May integrity and U preserve me, for I wait
111:8 and ever, to be performed with faithfulness and U
Prov 2:13 forsake the paths of U to walk in the
4:12 I have led you in the paths of U
14:2 He who walks in U fears the LORD, but
Wis 1:1 of the Lord with U, and seek him with
9:3 and pronounce judgment in U of soul,
Is 26:10 in the land of U he deals perversely and
57:2 rest in their beds who walk in their U
59:14 the public squares, and U cannot enter.
Jer 4:2 in justice, and in U, then nations shall bless
Mal 2:6 me in peace and U, and he turned many

UPROAR (10)

1Sam 4:14 of the outcry, he said, "What is this U
1Kgs 1:41 said, "What does this U in the city mean?"
1:45 rejoicing, so that the city is in an U
Ps 74:23 of thy foes, the U of thy adversaries which
Is 13:4 Hark, an U of kingdoms, of nations gathering
66:6 "Hark, an U from the city!
Amos 2:2 Moab shall die amid U, amid shouting and the
Acts 17:5 the city in an U, and attacked the house
20:1 After the U ceased, Paul sent for the disciples
21:34 facts because of the U, he ordered him to

UPROOT (2)

Ps 52:5 your tent; he will U you from the land
Jer 24:6 plant them, and not U them.

UPROOTED (5)

Deut 29:28 book; and the LORD U them from their land
Wis 4:4 the violence of the winds they will be U
Jer 31:40 It shall not be U or overthrown any more
Zeph 2:4 driven out at noon, and Ekron shall be U
Jude 1:12 late autumn, twice dead, U;

UPROOTS

Sir 3:9 but a mother's curse U their foundations.

UPSET

Sir 11:32 home and he will U you with commotion, and

UPSETTING (2)

2Tim 2:18 They are U the faith of some.
Tit 1:10 silenced, since they are U whole families by teaching

UPSIDE (4)

Judg 7:13 fell, and turned it U down, so that the
2Kgs 21:13 it and turning it U down.
Is 29:16 You turn things U down!
Acts 17:6 have turned the world U down have come here

UPSURGING

2Sam 1:21 rain upon you, nor U of the deep!

UPWARD (53)

Ex 30:14 twenty years old and U, shall give the LORD's
38:26 twenty years old and U, for six hundred and
Lev 27:7 sixty years old and U, then your valuation for
Num 1:3 twenty years old and U, all in Israel who
1:18 twenty years old and U, head by head,
1:20 twenty years old and U, all who were able
1:22 twenty years old and U, all who were able
1:24 twenty years old and U, all who were able
1:26 twenty years old and U, every man able to
1:28 twenty years old and U, every man able to
1:30 twenty years old and U, every man able to
1:32 twenty years old and U, every man able to
1:34 twenty years old and U, every man able to
1:36 twenty years old and U, every man able to
1:38 twenty years old and U, every man able to
1:40 twenty years old and U, every man able to
1:42 twenty years old and U, every man able to
1:45 twenty years old and U, every man able to
3:15 a month old and U you shall number."
3:22 a month old and U was seven thousand five
3:28 a month old and U, there were eight thousand
3:34 a month old and U was six thousand two
3:39 a month old and U, were twenty-two thousand.
3:40 a month old and U, taking their number by
3:43 a month old and U as numbered were twenty-two
8:24 twenty-five years old and U they shall go in
14:29 twenty years old and U, who have murmured against
26:2 twenty years old and U, by their fathers' houses,
26:4 of the people, from twenty years old and U
26:62 a month old and U; for they were not
32:11 twenty years old and U, shall see the land

Deut	28:13	and you shall tend U only, and not downward;
Judg	1:36	from the ascent of Akrabbim, from Sela and U
1Sam	9:2	he; from his shoulders U he was taller than
	10:23	than any of the people from his shoulders U
1Kgs	7:31	a crown which projected U one cubit; its opening
2Kgs	19:30	downward, and bear fruit U;
1Chr	23:3	thirty years old and U, were numbered, and the
	23:24	twenty years old and U who were to do
	23:27	twenty years old and U —
2Chr	25:5	twenty years old and U, and found that they
Ezra	3:8	twenty years old and U, to have the oversight
Job	5:7	is born to trouble as the sparks fly U
Prov	15:24	wise man's path leads U to life, that he
Eccl	3:21	spirit of man goes U and the spirit of
Is	8:21	and turn their faces U;
	9:18	forest, and they roll U in a column of
	37:31	downward, and bear fruit U;
	38:14	My eyes are weary with looking U
Ezek	1:27	And U from what had the appearance of his
	41:7	temple a stairway led U, and thus one went
	43:15	the altar hearth projecting U, four horns, one cubit
Phil	3:14	the prize of the U call of God in

UPWARDS (2)

2Chr	31:16	three years old and U, all who entered the
	31:17	twenty years old and U was according to their

UR (5)

Gen	11:28	of his birth, in U of the Chaldeans.
	11:31	went forth together from U of the Chaldeans to
	15:7	who brought you from U of the Chaldeans, to
1Chr	11:35	Eliphal the son of U,
Neh	9:7	him forth out of U of the Chaldeans and

URBANUS

Rom	16:9	Greet U, our fellow worker in Christ, and my

URGE (12)

2Kgs	4:24	said to her servant, U the beast on; do
Jud	15:4	taken place and to U all to rush out
2Mac	6:12	Now I U those who read this book not
	9:26	I therefore U and beseech you to remember the
Acts	27:34	Therefore I U you to take some food; it
1Cor	4:16	I U you, then, be imitators of me.
	16:16	of the saints; I U you to be subject
2Cor	9:5	thought it necessary to U the brethren to go
1Tim	2:1	then, I U that supplications, prayers, intercessions,
	6:2	Teach and U these duties.
Tit	2:6	Likewise U the younger men to control themselves.
Heb	13:19	I U you the more earnestly to do this

URGED (29)

Gen	19:3	But he U them strongly; so they turned aside
	19:15	morning dawned, the angels U Lot, saying, "Arise,
	33:11	Thus he U him, and he took it.
Josh	15:18	came to him, she U him to ask her
Judg	1:14	came to him, she U him to ask her
	16:16	day after day, and U him, his soul was
	19:7	to go, his father-in-law U him, till he lodged
1Sam	28:23	together with the woman, U him; and he hearkened
2Kgs	2:17	But when they U him till he was ashamed,
	4:8	wealthy woman lived, who U him to eat some
	5:16	And he U him to take it, but he
	5:23	And he U him, and tied up two talents
Esth	8:14	rode out in haste, U by the king's command;
Jer	36:25	and Delaiah and Gemariah U the king not to
1Mac	11:40	of Alexander, and insistently U him to hand Antiochus
2Mac	4:34	Menelaus, taking Andronicus aside, U him to kill
	6:21	with him, and privately U him to bring meat
	7:25	mother to him and U her to advise the
	11:7	up arms, and he U the others to risk
	11:15	the common good, agreed to all that Lysias U
	13:3	and with utter hypocrisy U Antiochus on, not for
	14:25	And he U him to marry and have children;
Acts	13:43	spoke to them and U them to continue in
	25:2	against Paul; and they U him,
	27:33	about to dawn, Paul U them all to take
1Cor	16:12	brother Apollos, I strongly U him to visit you
2Cor	8:6	Accordingly we have U Titus that as he had
	12:18	I U Titus to go, and sent the brother
1Tim	1:3	As I U you when I was going to

URGENT (7)

Ex	5:13	The taskmasters were U, saying, "Complete your
	12:33	And the Egyptians were U with the people, to
Sir	28:11	quarrel kindles fire, and U strife sheds blood.
Lk	23:5	But they were U, saying, "He stirs up the
	23:22	But they were U, demanding with loud cries that
2Tim	4:2	preach the word, be U in season and out
Tit	3:14	to help cases of U need, and not to

URGENTLY (3)

Jer	26:5	I send to you U, though you have not
1Mac	6:57	of the kingdom press U upon us.
2Mac	10:19	where he was more U needed.

URGES

Prov	16:26	for him; his mouth U him on.

URGING (2)

1Mac	13:21	sending envoys to Trypho U him to come to
2Mac	7:26	After much U on his part, she undertook to

URI (8)

Ex	31:2	Bezalel the son of U, son of Hur, of
	35:30	Bezalel the son of U, son of Hur, of
	38:22	Bezalel the son of U, son of Hur, of
1Kgs	4:19	Geber the son of U, in the land of
1Chr	2:20	was the father of U, and Uri was the
	2:20	father of Uri, and U was the father of
2Chr	1:5	Bezalel the son of U, son of Hur, had
Ezra	10:24	Of the gatekeepers: Shallum, Telem, and U

URIAH (40)

2Sam	11:3	Eliam, the wife of U the Hittite?"
	11:6	to Joab, "Send me U the Hittite." And Joab
	11:6	And Joab sent U to David.
	11:7	When U came to him, David asked how Joab
	11:8	Then David said to U, "Go down to your
	11:8	And U went out of the king's house, and
	11:9	But U slept at the door of the king's
	11:10	When they told David, U did not go down
	11:10	David said to U, "Have you not come from
	11:11	U said to David, "The ark and Israel and
	11:12	Then David said to U, "Remain here today also,
	11:12	So U remained in Jerusalem that day, and the
	11:14	Joab, and sent it by the hand of U
	11:15	letter he wrote, "Set U in the forefront of
	11:16	the city, he assigned U to the place where
	11:17	U the Hittite was slain also.
	11:21	shall say, 'Your servant U the Hittite is dead
	11:24	dead; and your servant U the Hittite is dead
	11:26	When the wife of U heard that Uriah her
	11:26	of Uriah heard that U her husband was dead,
	12:9	You have smitten U the Hittite with the sword,
	12:10	taken the wife of U the Hittite to be
	12:15	struck the child that U's wife bore to David,
	23:39	Ithrite, Gareb the Ithrite, U the Hittite: thirty-seven
1Kgs	15:5	in the matter of U the Hittite.
2Kgs	16:10	King Ahaz sent to U the priest a model
	16:11	And U the priest built the altar; in accordance
	16:11	sent from Damascus, so U the priest made it,
	16:15	King Ahaz commanded U the priest, saying, "Upon
	16:16	U the priest did all this, as King Ahaz
1Chr	11:41	Ithrite, Gareb the Ithrite, U the Hittite, Zabad the
Ezra	8:33	the priest, son of U, and with him was
Neh	3:4	Meremoth the son of U, son of Hakkoz repaired.
	3:21	Meremoth the son of U, son of Hakkoz repaired
	8:4	stood Mattithiah, Shema, Anaiah, U, Hilkiah, and
Is	8:2	I got reliable witnesses, U the priest and Zechariah
Jer	26:20	name of the LORD, U the son of Shemaiah
	26:21	to death; but when U heard of it, he
	26:23	him, and they fetched U from Egypt and brought
Mt	1:6	by the wife of U,

URIEL (4)

1Chr	6:24	son, Tahath his son, U his son, Uzziah his
	15:5	the sons of Kohath, U the chief, with a
	15:11	Abiathar, and the Levites U, Asaiah, Joel, Shemaiah,
2Chr	13:2	Micaiah the daughter of U of Gibe-ah.

URIM (10)

Ex	28:30	you shall put the U and the Thummim, and
Lev	8:8	breastpiece he put the U and the Thummim.
Num	27:21	the judgment of the U before the LORD; at
Deut	33:8	thy Thummim, and thy U to thy godly one,
1Sam	14:41	God of Israel, give U; but if this guilt
	28:6	by dreams, or by U, or by prophets.
Ezra	2:63	a priest to consult U and Thummim.
Neh	7:65	until a priest with U and Thummim should arise.
Sir	33:3	as dependable as an inquiry by means of U
	45:10	the oracle of judgment, U and Thummim;

URINE (2)
2Kgs 18:27 their own dung and to drink their own U
Is 36:12 eat their own dung and drink their own U

URN
Heb 9:4 which contained a golden U holding the manna, and

USE (57)
Gen 25:32 to die; of what U is a birthright to
Ex 27:19 the tabernacle for every U, and all its pegs
30:38 any like it to U as perfume shall be
35:24 acacia wood of any U in the work, brought
Lev 7:24 put to any other U, but on no account
13:51 skin, whatever be the U of the skin, the
Num 10:2 them; and you shall U them for summoning the
Deut 28:30 and you shall not U the fruit of it.
1Chr 28:15 lamps, according to the U of each lampstand in
Tob 6:6 "Brother Azarias, of what U is the liver and
Jud 11:12 and have determined to U all that God by
12:4 your servant will not U up the things I
12:15 Bagoas for her daily U, so that she might
Job 32:21 to any person or U flattery toward any man.
Ps 76:5 war were unable to U their hands.
102:8 those who deride me U my name for a
Prov 18:23 The poor U entreaties, but the rich answer roughly.
Eccl 2:2 and of pleasure, "What U is it?"
Wis 2:6 that exist, and make U of the creation to
4:3 will be of no U, and none of their
15:7 which shall be the U of each of these
15:15 these have neither the U of their eyes to
15:15 feet are of no U for walking.
Sir 13:4 you can be of U to him, but if
14:3 man; and of what U is property to an
18:7 man, and of what U is he?
23:15 A man accustomed to U insulting words will never
26:10 she finds liberty, she U it to her hurt.
30:19 Of what U to an idol is an offering
39:21 for everything has been created for its U
Jer 2:22 yourself with lye and U much soap, the stain
23:31 says the LORD, who U their tongues and say,
31:23 "Once more they shall U these words in the
Bar 6:28 to these gods and U the money; and likewise
Ezek 5:1 take a sharp sword; U it as a barber's
12:23 they shall no more U it as a proverb
16:44 who uses proverbs will U this proverb about you,
21:21 the two ways, to U divination; he shakes the
48:15 shall be for ordinary U for the city, for
1Mac 11:20 engines of war to U against it.
2Mac 4:19 thought best not to U it for sacrifice, because
6:21 proper for him to U, and pretend that he
Mk 4:30 what parable shall we U for it?
Lk 13:7 down; why should it U up the ground?'
Acts 14:8 sitting, who could not U his feet; he was
Rom 3:13 an open grave, they U their tongues to deceive."
9:21 one vessel for beauty and another for menial U
12:6 to us, let us U them: if prophecy, in
1Cor 9:12 we have not made U of this right, but
9:15 I have made no U of any of these
9:18 charge, not making full U of my right in
2Cor 13:10 be severe in my U of the authority which
Gal 5:13 brethren; only do not U your freedom as an
1Tim 5:23 drink only water, but U a little wine for
2Tim 2:20 and some for noble U, some for ignoble.
2:21 a vessel for noble U, consecrated and useful to
2Jn 1:12 I would rather not U paper and ink, but

USED (72)
Ex 33:7 Now Moses U to take the tent and pitch
33:11 Thus the LORD U to speak to Moses face
35:21 LORD's offering to be U for the tent of
38:24 the gold that was U for the work, in
Lev 11:32 any vessel that is U for any purpose; it
Num 4:12 the service which are U in the sanctuary, and
4:14 the altar, which are U for the service there,
7:5 that they may be U in doing the service
35:23 lying in wait, or U a stone, by which
Judg 1:7 great toes cut off U to pick up scraps
4:5 She U to sit under the palm of Deborah
14:10 so the young men U to do.
16:11 that have not been U, then I shall become
1Sam 1:3 Now this man U to go up year by
1:6 And her rival U to provoke her sorely, to
1:7 of the LORD, she U to provoke her.
2:19 And his mother U to make for him a
17:34 to Saul, "Your servant U to keep sheep for
17:39 for he was not U to them.
17:39 for I am not U to them." And David
2Sam 12:3 with his children; it U to eat of his
14:26 of every year he U to cut it; when
15:2 And Absalom U to rise early and stand beside
17:17 at En-rogel; a maidservant U to go and tell
1Kgs 3:4 great high place; Solomon U to offer a thousand
9:25 times a year Solomon U to offer up burnt
10:22 of ships of Tarshish U to come bringing gold,
2Kgs 6:10 Thus he U to warn him, so that he
13:20 Now bands of Moabites U to invade the land
17:17 daughters as offerings, and U divination and sorcery,
25:14 the vessels of bronze U in the temple service,
2Chr 4:6 rinse off what was U for the burnt offering,
9:21 the ships of Tarshish U to come bringing gold,
24:7 God; and had also U all the dedicated things
Tob 1:5 that joined in apostasy U to sacrifice to the
1:14 So I U to go into Media, and once
2:12 She U to send the product to the owners.
5:13 For I U to know Ananias and Jathan, the
Jud 10:3 gayest apparel, which she U to wear while her
Esth 8:10 swift horses that were U in the king's service,
8:14 swift horses that were U in the king's service,
Job 1:4 His sons U to go and hold a feast
18:19 no survivor where he U to live.
Ps 55:14 We U to hold sweet converse together; within God's
Eccl 2:19 which I toiled and U my wisdom under the
8:10 the wicked buried; they U to go in and
Is 7:23 every place where there U to be a thousand
7:25 all the hills which U to be hoed with
Jer 2:24 tracks, a wild ass U to the wilderness, in
29:22 this curse shall be U by all the exiles
30:18 shall stand where it U to be.
46:11 In vain you have U many medicines; there is
52:18 the vessels of bronze U in the temple service;
Ezek 7:20 Their beautiful ornament they U for vainglory, and
15:5 was whole, it was U for nothing; how much
15:5 can it ever be U for anything!
18:3 shall no more be U by you in Israel.
Dan 13:4 house; and the Jews U to come to him
13:8 The two elders U to see her every day,
14:13 entrance, through which they U to go in regularly
Hos 2:8 and gold which they U for Baal.
1Mac 3:12 sword of Apollonius, and U it in battle the
3:30 the gifts which he U to give more lavishly
14:36 citadel from which they U to sally forth and
Mk 15:6 at the feast he U to release for them
Jn 9:8 this the man who U to sit and beg?"
10:6 This figure Jesus U with them, but they did
12:6 the money box he U to take what was
Col 2:22 perish as they are U, according to human precepts
1Thes 2:5 For we never U either words of flattery, as
Heb 9:21 and all the vessels U in worship.
1Pet 3:5 who hoped in God U to adorn themselves and

USEFUL (9)
Tob 4:18 do not despise any U counsel.
Wis 13:11 workmanship make a U vessel that serves life's
13:13 piece from among them, U for nothing, a stick
Ezek 15:4 is charred, is it U for anything?
2Mac 12:12 they might really be U in many ways, agreed
2Tim 2:21 noble use, consecrated and U to the master of
4:11 for he is very U in serving me.
Philem 1:11 now he is indeed U to you and to
Heb 6:7 and brings forth vegetation U to those for whose

USELESS (10)
Prov 26:7 man's legs, which hang U, is a proverb in
Wis 1:11 Beware then of U murmuring, and keep your tongue
2:11 for what is weak proves itself to be U
3:11 their labors are unprofitable, and their works are U
4:5 their fruit will be U, not ripe enough to
13:10 of animals, or a U stone, the work of
Sir 16:1 desire a multitude of U children, nor rejoice in
Bar 6:17 as one's dish is U when it is broken,
Hos 8:8 the nations as a U vessel.
Philem 1:11 (Formerly he was U to you, but now he

USELESSNESS
Heb 7:18 of its weakness and U

USES (5)
Wis 15:7 vessels that serve clean U and those for contrary
15:7 and those for contrary U, making all in like
Sir 20:7 Whoever U too many words will be loathed, and
Ezek 16:44 Behold, every one who U proverbs will use this
1Tim 1:8 good, if any one U it lawfully,

U

U

20:17 breathes, but you shall U destroy them, the Hittites
Josh 2:10 and Og, whom you U destroyed.
6:21 Then they U destroyed all in the city, both
8:26 javelin, until he had U destroyed all the inhabitants
10:1 taken Ai, and had U destroyed it, doing to
10:28 of the sword; he U destroyed every person in
10:35 person in it he U destroyed that day, as
10:37 done to Eglon, and U destroyed it with every
10:39 of the sword, and U destroyed every person in
10:40 none remaining, but U destroyed all that breathed,
11:11 who were in it, U destroying them; there was
11:12 edge of the sword, U destroying them, as Moses
11:20 that they should be U destroyed, and should receive
11:21 country of Israel; Joshua U destroyed them with
17:13 labor, and did not U drive them out.
Judg 1:17 who inhabited Zephath, and U destroyed it.
1:28 labor, but did not U drive them out.
3:25 waited till they were U at a loss; but
15:2 really thought that you U hated her; so I
21:11 a male you shall U destroy."
1Sam 15:3 and smite Amalek, and U destroy all that they
15:8 the Amalekites alive, and U destroyed all the people
15:9 good, and would not U destroy them; all that
15:9 despised and worthless they U destroyed.
15:15 the rest we have U destroyed."
15:18 mission, and said, 'Go, U destroy the sinners, the
15:20 Amalek, and I have U destroyed the Amalekites.
27:12 "He has made himself U abhorred by his people
2Sam 12:14 this deed you have U scorned the LORD, the
17:10 of a lion, will U melt with fear; for
23:7 spear, and they are U consumed with fire."
1Kgs 9:21 were unable to destroy U –these Solomon made a
14:10 in Israel, and will U consume the house of
16:3 sins, behold, I will U sweep away Baasha and
21:21 upon you; I will U sweep you away, and
2Kgs 19:11 Assyria have done to all lands, destroying them U
2Chr 20:23 Mount Seir, destroying them U, and when they had
32:14 nations which my fathers U destroyed was able to
Jud 1:15 hunting spears; and he U destroyed him, to this
5:18 for them, they were U defeated in many battles
6:4 withstand us, but will U perish.
7:31 his mercy, for he will not forsake us U
Esth 13:6 wives and children, be U destroyed by the sword
14:2 and dung, and she U humbled her body, and
Ps 38:6 my foolishness, I am U bowed down and prostrate;
38:8 I am U spent and crushed; I groan because
73:19 a moment, swept away U by terrors!
74:8 themselves, "We will U subdue them"; they burned
78:59 of wrath, and he U rejected Israel.
119:8 will observe thy statutes; O forsake me not U
119:43 the word of truth U out of my mouth,
119:51 Godless men U deride me, but I do not
Song 8:7 house, it would be U scorned.
Wis 4:19 they will be left U dry and barren, and
13:18 a thing that is U inexperienced; for a prosperous
16:16 and relentless storms, and U consumed by fire.
Sir 10:13 extraordinary afflictions, and destroyed them U
40:14 glad; likewise transgressors will U fail.
Is 1:4 of Israel, they are U estranged.
2:18 And the idols shall U pass away.
6:11 and the land is U desolate,
11:15 And the LORD will U destroy the tongue of
16:7 Mourn, U stricken, for the raisin-cakes of
19:11 princes of Zoan are U foolish; the wise counselors
24:3 The earth shall be U laid waste and utterly
24:3 utterly laid waste and U despoiled; for the LORD
24:19 The earth is U broken, the earth is rent
32:19 And the forest will U go down, and the
32:19 the city will be U laid low.
37:11 Assyria have done to all lands, destroying them U
42:17 be turned back and U put to shame, who
60:12 those nations shall be U laid waste.
Jer 2:12 this, be shocked, be U desolate, says the LORD,
4:10 GOD, surely thou hast U deceived this people and
5:11 of Judah have been U faithless to me, says
9:19 We are U shamed, because we have left the
12:17 listen, then I will U pluck it up and
14:19 Hast thou U rejected Judah?
24:10 until they shall be U destroyed from the land
25:9 round about; I will U destroy them, and make
50:12 your mother shall be U shamed, and she who
50:21 Slay, and U destroy after them, says the LORD,
50:26 grain, and destroy her U; let nothing be left
51:3 not her young men; U destroy all her host.
Lam 5:22 Or hast thou U rejected us?
Ezek 17:10 Will it not U wither when the east wind
Dan 3:34 not give us up U, and do not break
11:22 Armies shall be U swept away before him and
11:44 fury to exterminate and U destroy many.
Hos 10:15 of Israel shall be U cut off.
Amos 9:8 that I will not U destroy the house of
Obad 1:2 nations, you shall be U despised.
Mic 2:4 and say, "We are U ruined; he changes the
Nah 1:15 against you, he is U cut off.
Zeph 1:2 "I will U sweep away everything from the face
Zech 11:17 withered, his right eye U blinded!"
2Mac 3:12 said that it was U impossible that wrong should
6:3 Harsh and U grievous was the onslaught of evil.
7:5 When he was U helpless, the king ordered them
Mk 6:51 And they were U astounded,
2Cor 1:8 for we were so U, unbearably crushed that we

UTTERMOST (7)

Deut 30:4 outcasts are in the U parts of heaven, from
Ps 139:9 and dwell in the U parts of the sea,
Ezek 32:23 are set in the U parts of the Pit,
38:6 hordes; Beth-togarmah from the U parts of the north
38:15 place out of the U parts of the north,
39:2 you up from the U parts of the north,
Acts 13:47 bring salvation to the U parts of the earth.'"

UTTERS (22)

Lev 5:4 Or if any one U with his lips a
Ps 12:2 Every one U lies to his neighbor; with flattering
37:30 mouth of the righteous U wisdom, and his tongue
41:6 to see me, he U empty words, while his
46:6 the kingdoms totter; he U his voice, the earth
101:7 house; no man who U lies shall continue in
Prov 10:18 lips, and he who U slander is a fool.
12:17 but a false witness U deceit.
14:25 lives, but one who U lies is a betrayer.
19:5 unpunished, and he who U lies will not escape.
19:9 unpunished, and he who U lies will perish.
Wis 1:8 therefore no one who U unrighteous things will
Sir 23:10 who always swears and U the Name will not
Jer 10:13 When he U his voice there is a tumult
51:16 When he U his voice there is a tumult
Joel 2:11 The LORD U his voice before his army, for
3:16 roars from Zion, and U his voice from Jerusalem,
Amos 1:2 roars from Zion, and U his voice from Jerusalem;
Mic 7:3 and the great man U the evil desire of
Jn 3:34 whom God has sent U the words of God,
1Cor 14:2 understands him, but he U mysteries in the Spirit.
1Pet 4:11 speaks, as one who U oracles of God; whoever

UZ (8)

Gen 10:23 The sons of Aram: U, Hul, Gether, and Mash.
22:21 to your brother Nahor: U the first-born, Buz his
36:28 the sons of Dishan: U and Aran.
1Chr 1:17 Asshur, Arpachshad, Lud, Aram, U, Hul, Gether, and
1:42 The sons of Dishan: U and Aran.
Job 1:1 in the land of U, whose name was Job;
Jer 25:20 of the land of U and all the kings
Lam 4:21 in the land of U; but to you also

UZAI

Neh 3:25 Palal the son of U repaired opposite the Angle

UZAL (3)

Gen 10:27 Sheleph, Hazarmaveth, Jerah, Hadoram, U, Diklah,
1Chr 1:21 Sheleph, Hazarmaveth, Jerah, Hadoram, U, Diklah,
Ezek 27:19 wool, and wine from U they exchanged for your

UZZA (5)

2Kgs 21:18 in the garden of U; and Amon his son
21:26 in the garden of U; and Josiah his son
1Chr 8:7 was the father of U and Ahihud.
Ezra 2:49 Gazzam, the sons of U, the sons of Paseah,
Neh 7:51 Gazzam, the sons of U, the sons of Paseah,

UZZAH (9)

2Sam 6:3 on the hill; and U and Ahio, the sons
6:6 threshing floor of Nacon, U put out his hand
6:7 LORD was kindled against U; and God smote him
6:8 had broken forth upon U; and that place is
1Chr 6:29 son, Shimei his son, U his son,
13:7 house of Abinadab, and U and Ahio were driving
13:9 threshing floor of Chidon, U put out his hand
13:10 LORD was kindled against U; and he smote him
13:11 had broken forth upon U; and that place is

UZZEN-SHEERAH

1Chr 7:24 who built both Lower and Upper Beth-horon, and U

UZZI (11)

1Chr 6:5 of Bukki, Bukki of U,
6:6 Bukki, Bukki of Uzzi, U of Zerahiah, Zerahiah of
6:51 son, Bukki his son, U his son, Zerahiah his
7:2 The sons of Tola: U, Rephaiah, Jeri-el, Jahmai,
7:3 The sons of U: Izrahiah.
7:7 sons of Bela: Ezbon, U, Uzziel, Jerimoth, and Iri,
9:8 Elah the son of U, son of Michri, and
Ezra 7:4 of Zerahiah, son of U, son of Bukki,
Neh 11:22 Levites in Jerusalem was U the son of Bani,
12:19 Joiarib, Mattenai; of Jedaiah, U;
12:42 Ma-aseiah, Shemaiah, Eleazar, U, Jehohanan,

UZZIA

1Chr 11:44 and Joshaphat the Mithnite, U the Ashterathite,

UZZIAH (41)

2Kgs 15:13 the thirty-ninth year of U king of Judah, and
15:30 the twentieth year of Jotham the son of U
15:32 Jotham the son of U, king of Judah, began
15:34 all that his father U had done.
1Chr 6:24 son, Uriel his son, U his son, and Shaul
27:25 Jonathan the son of U;
2Chr 26:1 people of Judah took U, who was sixteen years
26:3 U was sixteen years old when he began to
26:8 Ammonites paid tribute to U, and his fame spread
26:9 Moreover U built towers in Jerusalem at the Corner
26:11 Moreover U had an army of soldiers, fit for
26:14 And U prepared for all the army shields, spears,
26:18 and they withstood King U, and said to him,
26:18 is not for you, U, to burn incense to
26:19 Then U was angry.
26:21 And King U was a leper to the day
26:22 of the acts of U, from first to last,
26:23 And U slept with his fathers, and they buried
27:2 all that his father U had done--only he
Ezra 10:21 Harim: Ma-aseiah, Elijah, Shemaiah, Jehiel, and U
Neh 11:4 Athaiah the son of U, son of Zechariah, son
Jud 6:15 in those days were U the son of Micah,
6:16 all their people, and U asked him what had
6:21 And U took him from the assembly to his
7:24 the children, gathered about U and the rulers of
7:31 And U said to them, "Have courage, my brothers!
8:9 she heard all that U said to them, and
8:28 Then U said to her, "All that you have
8:35 U and the rulers said to her, "Go in
10:6 of Bethulia, and found U standing there with the
13:18 And U said to her, "O daughter, you are
14:6 So they summoned Achior from the house of U
15:4 And U sent men to Betomasthaim and Bebai and
Is 1:1 in the days of U, Jotham, Ahaz, and Hezekiah,
6:1 the year that King U died I saw the
7:1 of Jotham, son of U, king of Judah, Rezin
Hos 1:1 in the days of U, Jotham, Ahaz, and Hezekiah,
Amos 1:1 in the days of U king of Judah and
Zech 14:5 in the days of U king of Judah.
Mt 1:8 Joram the father of U,
1:9 father of Uzziah, and U the father of Jotham,

UZZIEL (16)

Ex 6:18 Amram, Izhar, Hebron, and U, the years of the
6:22 And the sons of U: Mishael, Elzaphan, and Sithri.
Lev 10:4 Elzaphan, the sons of U the uncle of Aaron,
Num 3:19 by their families: Amram, Izhar, Hebron, and U
3:30 Eli-zaphan the son of U as head of the
1Chr 4:42 Pelatiah, Neariah, Rephaiah, and U, the sons of Ishi;
6:2 The sons of Kohath: Amram, Izhar, Hebron, and U
6:18 The sons of Kohath: Amram, Izhar, Hebron, and U
7:7 of Bela: Ezbon, Uzzi, U, Jerimoth, and Iri, five,
15:10 of the sons of U, Amminadab the chief, with
23:12 Amram, Izhar, Hebron, and U, four.
23:20 The sons of U: Micah the chief and Isshiah
24:24 The sons of U, Micah; of the sons of
25:4 of Heman: Bukkiah, Mattaniah, U, Shebuel, and
2Chr 29:14 and of the sons of Jeduthun, Shemaiah and U
Neh 3:8 Next to them U the son of Harhaiah, goldsmiths,

UZZIELITES (2)

Num 3:27 the family of the U; these are the families
1Chr 26:23 the Hebronites, and the U –

U

V

V

VACILLATING

2Cor 1:17 Was I V when I wanted to do this?

VAGABOND

Prov 6:11 upon you like a V, and want like an

VAIN (76)

Ex 20:7 LORD your God in V; for the LORD will
20:7 hold him guiltless who takes his name in V
Lev 26:16 sow your seed in V, for your enemies shall
26:20 shall be spent in V, for your land shall
Deut 5:11 LORD your God in V: for the LORD will
5:11 hold him guiltless who takes his name in V
1Sam 12:21 not turn aside after V things which cannot profit
12:21 which cannot profit or save, for they are V
17:39 and he tried in V to go, for he
25:21 had said, "Surely in V have I guarded all
Jud 6:4 spoken; none of his words shall be in V
Esth 14:10 for the praise of V idols, and to magnify
Job 9:29 be condemned; why then do I labor in V
27:12 yourselves; why then have you become altogether V
39:16 her labor be in V, yet she has no
Ps 2:1 the nations conspire, and the peoples plot in V
4:2 long will you love V words, and seek after
31:6 who pay regard to V idols; but I trust
33:17 war horse is a V hope for victory, and
60:11 against the foe, for V is the help of
62:10 in extortion, set no V hopes on robbery; if
73:13 All in V have I kept my heart clean
108:12 against the foe, for V is the help of
116:11 "Men are all a V hope."
119:118 from thy statutes; yea, their cunning is in V
127:1 the house, those who build it labor in V
127:1 over the city, the watchman stays awake in V
127:2 It is in V that you rise up early
Prov 1:17 For in V is a net spread in the
14:6 scoffer seeks wisdom in V, but knowledge is easy
31:30 deceitful, and beauty is V, but a woman who
Eccl 6:12 few days of his V life, which he passes
7:15 In my V life I have seen everything; there
9:9 the days of your V life which he has
Wis 3:11 Their hope is V, their labors are unprofitable, and
Sir 34:1 of no understanding has V and false hopes, and
Is 1:13 Bring no more V offerings; incense is an abomination
49:4 "I have labored in V, I have spent my
65:23 shall not labor in V, or bear children for
Jer 2:30 In V have I smitten your children, they took
4:30 In V you beautify yourself.
6:29 by the fire; in V the refining goes on,
18:12 your doings.' "But they say, 'That is in V
23:16 you, filling you with V hopes; they speak visions
46:11 In V you have used many medicines; there is
Ezek 6:10 have not said in V that I would do
24:12 In V I have wearied myself; its thick rust
Jon 2:8 who pay regard to V idols forsake their true
Mal 1:10 might not kindle fire upon my altar in V
3:14 have said, 'It is V to serve God.
1Mac 9:68 his plan and his expedition had been in V
2Mac 7:18 die, he said, "Do not deceive yourself in V
7:34 not be elated in V and puffed up by
Mt 15:9 far from me; in V do they worship me,
Mk 7:7 far from me; in V do they worship me,
Acts 4:25 and the peoples imagine V things?
14:15 should turn from these V things to a living
Rom 13:4 bear the sword in V; he is the servant
1Cor 15:2 you hold it fast--unless you believed in V
15:10 and his grace toward me was not in V
15:14 our preaching is in V and your faith is
15:14 is in vain and your faith is in V
15:58 in the Lord your labor is not in V
2Cor 6:1 not to accept the grace of God in V
9:3 you may not prove V in this case, so
Gal 2:2 I should be running or had run in V
3:4 so many things in V --if it really is
3:4 things in vain?--if it really is in V
4:11 am afraid I have labored over you in V
Phil 2:16 did not run in V or labor in vain.
2:16 did not run in vain or labor in V
1Thes 2:1 you was not in V;
3:5 you and that our labor would be in V
1Tim 1:6 have wandered away into V discussion,
Jas 1:25 but deceives his heart, this man's religion is V
4:5 suppose it is in V that the scripture says,

VAINGLORY
Ezek 7:20 ornament they used for V, and they made their

VAINLY
Lam 4:17 eyes failed, ever watching V for help; in our

VAIZATHA
Esth 9:9 Arisai and Aridai and V,

VALE (2)
Ps 60:6 and portion out the V of Succoth.
108:7 and portion out the V of Succoth.

VALIANT (20)
1Sam 14:52 strong man, or any V man, he attached him
18:17 a wife; only be V for me and fight
31:12 to Saul, all the V men arose, and went
2Sam 2:7 be strong, and be V; for Saul your lord
11:16 he knew there were V men.
13:28 Be courageous and be V
17:10 Absalom.' Then even the V man, whose heart is
17:10 are with him are V men.
23:20 of Jehoiada was a V man of Kabzeel, a
24:9 were eight hundred thousand V men who drew the
1Chr 5:18 half-tribe of Manasseh had V men, who carried
10:12 to Saul, all the V men arose, and took
11:22 of Jehoiada was a V man of Kabzeel, a
2Chr 13:3 having an army of V men of war, four
Neh 11:6 four hundred and sixty-eight V men.
Jud 14:2 sun rises, let every V man take his weapons
Sir 31:25 not aim to be V over wine, for wine
Is 5:22 at drinking wine, and V men in mixing strong
33:7 Behold, the V ones cry without; the envoys of
1Mac 3:58 And Judas said, "Gird yourselves and be V

VALIANTLY (6)
Num 24:18 enemies, shall be dispossessed, while Israel does V
1Sam 14:48 And he did V, and smote the Amalekites, and
Ps 60:12 God we shall do V; it is he who
108:13 God we shall do V; it is he who
118:15 of the LORD does V,
118:16 exalted, the right hand of the LORD does V

VALID (3)
1Mac 8:30 or deletion that they may make shall be V
13:38 made to you remain V, and let the strongholds
Heb 2:2 declared by angels was V and every transgression or

VALLEY (168)
Gen 13:10 saw that the Jordan V was well watered everywhere
13:11 himself all the Jordan V, and Lot journeyed east;
13:12 the cities of the V and moved his tent
14:3 joined forces in the V of Siddim (that is,
14:8 joined battle in the V of Siddim
14:10 Now the V of Siddim was full of bitumen
14:17 meet him at the V of Shaveh (that is,
14:17 the Valley of Shaveh (that is, the King's V
19:17 stop anywhere in the V; flee to the hills,
19:25 cities, and all the V, and all the inhabitants
19:28 the land of the V, and beheld, and lo,
19:29 the cities of the V, God remembered Abraham, and
26:17 and encamped in the V of Gerar and dwelt
26:19 servants dug in the V and found there a
37:14 sent him from the V of Hebron, and he
Num 13:23 they came to the V of Eshcol, and cut
13:24 place was called the V of Eshcol, because of
21:12 and encamped in the V of Zered.
21:20 from Bamoth to the V lying in the region
32:9 went up to the V of Eshcol, and saw
Deut 1:24 and came to the V of Eshcol and spied
2:24 and go over the V of the Arnon; behold,
2:36 the edge of the V of the Arnon, and
2:36 that is in the V, as far as Gilead,
3:8 the Jordan, from the V of the Arnon to
3:12 the edge of the V of the Arnon, and
3:16 as far as the V of the Arnon, with
3:16 the middle of the V as a boundary, as
3:29 we remained in the V opposite Beth-peor.
4:46 the Jordan in the V opposite Beth-peor, in the
4:48 the edge of the V of the Arnon, as
21:4 heifer down to a V with running water, which
21:4 shall break the heifer's neck there in the V
21:6 was broken in the V;
34:3 Plain, that is, the V of Jericho the city
34:6 buried him in the V in the land of
Josh 7:24 them up to the V of Achor.
7:26 place is called the V of Achor.
8:13 But Joshua spent that night in the V
10:12 thou Moon in the V of Aijalon."
11:8 as far as the V of Mizpeh; and they
11:17 as Baal-gad in the V of Lebanon below Mount
12:1 the sunrising, from the V of the Arnon to
12:2 the edge of the V of the Arnon, and
12:2 the middle of the V as far as the
12:7 from Baal-gad in the V of Lebanon to Mount
13:9 the edge of the V of the Arnon, and
13:9 the middle of the V, and all the tableland
13:16 the edge of the V of the Arnon, and
13:16 the middle of the V, and all the tableland
13:19 the hill of the V,
13:27 Debir, and in the V Beth-haram, Beth-nimrah,
15:7 to Debir from the V of Achor, and so
15:7 south side of the V; and the boundary passes
15:8 goes up by the V of the son of
15:8 lies over against the V of Hinnom, on the
15:8 northern end of the V of Rephaim;
17:16 and those in the V of Jezreel."
18:16 mountain that overlooks the V of the son of
18:16 north end of the V of Rephaim; and it
18:16 then goes down the V of Hinnom, south of
19:14 it ends at the V of Iphtahel;
19:27 touches Zebulun and the V of Iphtahel northward to
Judg 5:14 out thither into the V, following you, Benjamin, with
5:15 to Barak; into the V they rushed forth at
6:33 they encamped in the V of Jezreel.
7:1 them, by the hill of Moreh, in the V
7:8 camp of Midian was below him in the V
7:12 East lay along the V like locusts for multitude;
16:4 a woman in the V of Sorek, whose name
18:28 It was in the V which belongs to Beth-rehob.
1Sam 6:13 wheat harvest in the V; and when they lifted
13:18 looks down upon the V of Zeboim toward the
15:5 of Amalek, and lay in wait in the V
17:2 and encamped in the V of Elah, and drew
17:3 other side, with a V between them.
17:19 Israel, were in the V of Elah, fighting with
21:9 you killed in the V of Elah, behold, it
31:7 other side of the V and those beyond the
2Sam 5:18 spread out in the V of Rephaim.
5:22 spread out in the V of Rephaim.
8:13 thousand Edomites in the V of Salt.
17:13 drag it into the V, until not even a
18:18 is in the King's V, for he said, "I
23:13 was encamped in the V of Rephaim.
24:5 the middle of the V, toward Gad and on
2Kgs 2:16 cast him upon some mountain or into some V
10:33 which is by the V of the Arnon, that
14:7 thousand Edomites in the V of Salt and took
23:10 which is in the V of the sons of
1Chr 4:39 east side of the V, to seek pasture for
10:7 who were in the V saw that the army
11:15 was encamped in the V of Rephaim.
14:9 a raid in the V of Rephaim.
14:13 Philistines yet again made a raid in the V
18:12 thousand Edomites in the V of Salt.
2Chr 14:10 of battle in the V of Zephathah at Mareshah.
20:16 the end of the V, east of the wilderness
20:26 they assembled in the V of Beracah, for there
20:26 has been called the V of Beracah to this
25:11 and went to the V of Salt and smote
26:9 Gate and at the V Gate and at the
28:3 burned incense in the V of the son of
30:14 they took away and threw into the Kidron V
33:6 an offering in the V of the son of
33:14 of Gihon, in the V, and for the entrance
Neh 2:13 by night by the V Gate to the Jackal's
2:15 the night by the V and inspected the wall;
2:15 and entered by the V Gate, and so returned.
3:13 of Zanoah repaired the V Gate; they rebuilt it
11:30 from Beer-sheba to the V of Hinnom.
11:35 Lod, and Ono, the V of craftsmen.
Jud 4:4 and Aesora and the V of Salem,
7:3 They encamped in the V near Bethulia, beside the
7:17 they encamped in the V and seized the water
10:10 and passed through the V and they could no
10:11 straight on through the V; and an Assyrian patrol
11:17 go out into the V, and I will pray
12:7 each night to the V of Bethulia, and bathed
13:10 and circled around the V and went up the
Job 21:33 The clods of the V are sweet to him;
28:4 open shafts in a V away from where men
39:21 He paws in the V, and exults in his

Ps	23:4	I walk through the V of the shadow of
	84:6	they go through the V of Baca they make
Prov	30:17	the ravens of the V and eaten by the
Song	6:11	the blossoms of the V, to see whether the
Is	17:5	of grain in the V of Rephaim.
	22:1	The oracle concerning the V of vision.
	22:5	and confusion in the V of vision, a battering
	28:1	head of the rich V of those overcome with
	28:4	head of the rich V, will be like a
	28:21	wroth as in the V of Gibeon; to do
	40:4	Every V shall be lifted up, and every mountain
	57:6	smooth stones of the V is your portion; they,
	63:14	go down into the V, the Spirit of the
	65:10	for flocks, and the V of Achor a place
Jer	2:23	your way in the V; know what you have
	7:31	which is in the V of the son of
	7:32	called Topheth, or the V of the son of
	7:32	of Hinnom, but the V of Slaughter: for they
	19:2	go out to the V of the son of
	19:6	called Topheth, or the V of the son of
	19:6	of Hinnom, but the V of Slaughter.
	21:13	O inhabitant of the V, O rock of the
	31:40	The whole V of the dead bodies and the
	32:35	of Baal in the V of the son of
	48:8	city shall escape; the V shall perish, and the
Ezek	37:1	the midst of the V; it was full of
	37:2	very many upon the V; and lo, they were
	39:11	burial in Israel, the V of the Travelers east
	39:11	will be called the V of Hamon-gog.
	39:15	buried it in the V of Hamon-gog.
Hos	1:5	of Israel in the V of Jezreel."
	2:15	vineyards, and make the V of Achor a door
Joel	3:2	them down to the V of Jehoshaphat, and I
	3:12	come up to the V of Jehoshaphat; for there
	3:14	Multitudes, multitudes, in the V of decision!
	3:14	is near in the V of decision.
	3:18	LORD and water the V of Shittim.
Amos	1:5	the inhabitants from the V of Aven, and him
Mic	1:6	her stones into the V, and uncover her foundations.
Zech	14:4	by a very wide V; so that one half
	14:5	And the V of my mountains shall be stopped
	14:5	stopped up, for the V of the mountains shall
1Mac	12:37	the wall on the V to the east had
Lk	3:5	Every V shall be filled, and every mountain and
Jn	18:1	disciples across the Kidron V, where there was a

VALLEYS (31)

Num	14:25	Canaanites dwell in the V, turn tomorrow and set
	21:14	in Suphah, and the V of the Arnon,
	21:15	the slope of the V that extends to the
	24:6	Like V that stretch afar, like gardens beside a
Deut	8:7	springs, flowing forth in V and hills,
	11:11	land of hills and V, which drinks water by
1Kgs	18:5	and to all the V; perhaps we may find
	20:28	but he is not a god of the V
1Chr	12:15	all those in the V, to the east and
	27:29	the herds in the V was Shaphat the son
Jud	2:8	wounded shall fill their V, and every brook and
	7:4	high mountains nor the V nor the hills will
	16:4	multitude blocked up the V, their cavalry covered the
Job	39:10	will he harrow the V after you?
Ps	65:13	themselves with flocks, the V deck themselves with
	104:8	The mountains rose, the V sank down to the
	104:10	gush forth in the V; they flow between the
Song	2:1	a rose of Sharon, a lily of the V
Is	22:7	Your choicest V were full of chariots, and the
	41:18	the midst of the V; I will make the
	57:5	your children in the V, under the clefts of
Jer	49:4	you boast of your V, O faithless daughter, who
Bar	5:7	made low and the V filled up, to make
Ezek	6:3	the ravines and the V: Behold, I, even I,
	7:16	like doves of the V, all of them moaning,
	31:12	and in all the V its branches will fall,
	32:5	mountains, and fill the V with your carcass.
	35:8	hills and in your V and in all your
	36:4	the ravines and the V, the desolate wastes and
	36:6	to the ravines and V, Thus says the Lord
Mic	1:4	under him and the V will be cleft, like

VALOR (31)

Deut	3:18	all your men of V shall pass over armed
Josh	1:14	all the men of V among you shall pass
	6:2	Jericho, with its king and mighty men of V
	8:3	thousand mighty men of V, and sent them forth
	10:7	with him, and all the mighty men of V
Judg	6:12	LORD is with you, you mighty man of V
	20:44	of Benjamin fell, all of them men of V
	20:46	drew the sword, all of them men of V
1Sam	10:26	him went men of V whose hearts God had
	16:18	playing, a man of V, a man of war,
2Kgs	5:1	a mighty man of V, but he was a
	24:14	the mighty men of V, ten thousand captives, and
	24:16	all the men of V, seven thousand, and the
1Chr	12:21	all mighty men of V, and were commanders in
	12:25	Simeonites, mighty men of V for war, seven thousand
	12:28	young man mighty in V, and twenty-two commanders
	12:30	hundred, mighty men of V, famous men in their
2Chr	14:8	drew bows; all these were mighty men of V
	17:13	soldiers, mighty men of V, in Jerusalem.
	17:14	thousand mighty men of V,
	17:16	LORD, with two hundred thousand mighty men of V
	17:17	a mighty man of V, with two hundred thousand
	25:6	thousand mighty men of V from Israel for a
	26:12	of mighty men of V was two thousand six
	26:17	who were men of V;
	28:6	of them men of V, because they had forsaken
Neh	11:14	mighty men of V, a hundred and twenty-eight;
2Mac	8:7	And talk of his V spread everywhere.
	10:28	victory not only their V but their reliance upon
	14:18	Nicanor, hearing of the V of Judas and his
	15:17	so effective in arousing V and awaking manliness in

VALUABLE

2Chr	21:3	silver, gold, and V possessions, together with fortified

VALUATION (19)

Lev	27:2	the LORD at your V,
	27:3	your valuation, then your V of a male from
	27:4	is a female, your V shall be thirty shekels.
	27:5	twenty years old, your V shall be for a
	27:6	five years old, your V shall be for a
	27:6	for a female your V shall be three shekels
	27:7	and upward, then your V for a male shall
	27:8	poor to pay your V, then he shall bring
	27:13	it, he shall add a fifth to the V
	27:15	a fifth of the V in money to it,
	27:16	by inheritance, then your V shall be according to
	27:17	stand at your full V;
	27:18	and a deduction shall be made from your V
	27:19	a fifth of the V in money to it,
	27:23	priest shall compute the V for it up to
	27:23	the amount of the V on that day as
	27:25	Every V shall be according to the shekel of
	27:27	it back at your V, and add a fifth
	27:27	not redeemed, it shall be sold at your V

VALUE (23)

Lev	22:14	the fifth of its V to it, and give
	27:8	and the priest shall V him; according to the
	27:8	vowed the priest shall V him.
	27:12	and the priest shall V it as either good
	27:12	as you, the priest, V it, so it shall
	27:14	LORD, the priest shall V it as either good
1Kgs	21:2	will give you its V in money."
Prov	3:12	Wisdom's V
Sir	26:15	balance can weigh the V of a chaste soul.
2Mac	4:15	and putting the highest V upon Greek forms of
Mt	6:26	you not of more V than they?
	10:31	you are of more V than many sparrows.
	12:12	Of how much more V is a man than
	13:46	one pearl of great V, went and sold all
Lk	12:7	you are of more V than many sparrows.
	12:24	Of how much more V are you than the
Acts	19:19	and they counted the V of them and found
	20:24	my life of any V nor as precious to
Rom	2:25	Circumcision indeed is of V if you obey the
	3:1	Or what is the V of circumcision?
Col	2:23	they are of no V in checking the indulgence
1Tim	4:8	training is of some V, godliness is of value
	4:8	value, godliness is of V in every way, as

VALUED (7)

Lev	5:15	out of the flock, V by you in shekels
	5:18	out of the flock, V by you at the
	6:6	out of the flock, V by you at the
	27:16	of barley shall be V at fifty shekels of
Job	28:16	It cannot be V in the gold of Ophir,
	28:19	nor can it be V in pure gold.
Wis	18:12	instant their most V children had been destroyed.

VALUES

Lev	27:14	bad; as the priest V it, so it shall

V

VANIAH
Ezra 10:36 Benaiah, Bedeiah, Cheluhi, V, Meremoth, Eliashib,

VANISH (8)
Job 6:17 it is hot, they V from their place.
Ps 37:20 of the pastures, they V --like smoke they vanish
37:20 vanish--like smoke they V away.
58:7 Let them V like water that runs away; like
78:33 he made their days V like a breath, and
Sir 45:26 their prosperity may not V, and that their glory
Is 51:6 for the heavens will V like smoke, the earth
Heb 8:13 old is ready to V away.

VANISHED (12)
Judg 6:21 angel of the LORD V from his sight.
Ps 9:6 The enemy have V in everlasting ruins; their cities
12:1 for the faithful have V from among the sons
Wis 5:9 "All those things have V like a shadow, and
Sir 21:18 a house that has V, so is wisdom to
Is 16:4 tramples under foot has V from the land,
Jer 49:7 Has their wisdom V
Bar 3:19 They have V and gone down to Hades, and
Ezek 26:17 you, 'How you have V from the seas, O
2Mac 3:34 Having said this they V
Lk 24:31 recognized him; and he V out of their sight.
Rev 6:14 a gale; the sky V like a scroll that

VANISHES (2)
Job 7:9 the cloud fades and V, so he who goes
Jas 4:14 that appears for a little time and then V

VANITIES (4)
Ps 119:37 eyes from looking at V; and give me life
Eccl 1:2 Vanity of V, says the Preacher, vanity of vanities!
1:2 Vanity of vanities, says the Preacher, vanity of V
12:8 Vanity of V, says the Preacher; all is vanity.

VANITY (35)
Ps 89:47 life is, for what V thou hast created all
Eccl 1:2 V of vanities, says the Preacher, vanity of vanities!
1:2 vanities, says the Preacher, V of vanities!
1:2 All is V
1:14 and behold, all is V and a striving after
2:1 But behold, this also was V
2:11 and behold, all was V and a striving after
2:15 I said to myself that this also is V
2:17 me; for all is V and a striving after
2:19 This also is V
2:21 This also is V and a great evil.
2:23 This also is V
2:26 This also is V and a striving after wind.
3:19 no advantage over the beasts; for all is V
4:4 This also is V and a striving after wind.
4:7 Again, I saw V under the sun:
4:8 This also is V and an unhappy business.
4:16 Surely this also is V and a striving after
5:10 who loves wealth, with gain: this also is V
6:2 enjoys them; this is V; it is a sore
6:4 For it comes into V and goes into darkness,
6:9 desire; this also is V and a striving after
6:11 more words, the more V, and what is man
7:6 the laughter of the fools; this also is V
8:10 This also is V
8:14 There is a V which takes place on earth,
8:14 I said that this also is V
9:1 Everything before them is V,
11:8 All that comes is V
11:10 for youth and the dawn of life are V
12:8 V of vanities, says the Preacher; all is vanity.
12:8 Vanity of vanities, says the Preacher; all is V
Wis 14:14 For through the V of men they entered the
Is 49:4 strength for nothing and V; yet surely my right
Hos 5:11 judgment, because he was determined to go after V

VANQUISH
Job 32:13 found wisdom; God may V him, not man.'

VAPOR (3)
Prov 21:6 tongue is a fleeting V and a snare of
Sir 22:22 The V and smoke of the furnace precede the
Acts 2:19 blood, and fire, and V of smoke;

VAPORS
Sir 43:4 it breathes out fiery V, and with bright beams

VARIANCE
Wis 18:2 for having been at V with them.

VARIATION
Jas 1:16 whom there is no V or shadow due to

VARIED (3)
Wis 15:4 a figure stained with V colors,
2Mac 15:21 before him and the V supply of arms and
1Pet 4:10 good stewards of God's V grace:

VARIETIES (4)
Wis 7:20 reasonings of men, the V of plants and the
1Cor 12:4 Now there are V of gifts, but the same
12:5 Spirit; and there are V of service, but the
12:6 Lord; and there are V of working, but it

VARIETY
Sir 38:27 in making a great V; he sets his heart

VARIOUS (18)
2Chr 16:14 had been filled with V kinds of spices prepared
Jud 7:33 the people to their V posts, and they went
2Mac 12:2 of the governors in V places, Timothy and Apollonius
Mt 4:24 those afflicted with V diseases and pains, demoniacs,
24:7 famines and earthquakes in V places:
Mk 1:34 who were sick with V diseases, and cast out
13:8 will be earthquakes in V places, there will be
Lk 4:40 that were sick with V diseases brought them to
21:11 and in V places famines and pestilences;
1Cor 12:10 between spirits, to another V kinds of tongues, to
12:28 administrators, speakers in V kinds of tongues.
2Tim 3:6 sins and swayed by V impulses,
Tit 3:3 led astray, slaves to V passions and pleasures, passing
Heb 1:1 In many and V ways God spoke of
2:4 signs and wonders and V miracles and by gifts
9:10 food and drink and V ablutions, regulations for the
Jas 1:2 brethren, when you meet V trials,
1Pet 1:6 may have to suffer V trials,

VARY
Wis 19:18 a harp the notes V the nature of the

VASHTI (10)
Esth 1:9 Queen V also gave a banquet for the women
1:11 chamberlains, to bring Queen V before the king with
1:12 But Queen V refused to come at the king's
1:15 be done to Queen V, because she has not
1:16 the king has Queen V done wrong, but also
1:17 'King Ahasuerus commanded Queen V to be brought
1:19 not be altered, that V is to come no
2:1 had abated, he remembered V and what she had
2:4 who pleases the king be queen instead of V
2:17 her head and made her queen instead of V

VASSAL (2)
2Kgs 17:3 and Hoshea became his V, and paid him tribute.
Lam 1:1 a princess among the cities has become a V

VAST (11)
Jud 1:16 his combined forces, a V body of troops; and
2:17 He collected a V number of camels and asses
5:24 be devoured by your V army."
7:4 the Israelites saw their V numbers they were greatly
7:18 and they formed a V multitude.
15:7 for there was a V quantity of it.
Esth 1:20 throughout all his kingdom, V as it is, all
Ps 139:17 How V is the sum of them!
Wis 19:10 the river spewed out V numbers of frogs.
Lam 2:13 For V as the sea is your ruin; who
Bar 3:24 And how V the territory that he possesses!

VAT
Is 5:2 hewed out a wine V in it; and he

VATS (3)
Prov 3:10 with plenty, and your V will be bursting with
Joel 2:24 full of grain, the V shall overflow with wine
3:13 The V overflow, for their wickedness is great.

VAULT (3)
Job 22:14 he walks on the V of heaven.'
Sir 24:5 the circuit of the V of heaven and have
Amos 9:6 heavens, and founds his V upon the earth; who

VAULTED (3)
Ezek 16:24 you built yourself a V chamber, and made yourself
16:31 brazen harlot; building your V chamber at the head
16:39 shall throw down your V chamber and break down

VAUNT (2)
Judg 7:2 their hand, lest Israel V themselves against me,
Is 10:15 Shall the axe V itself over him who hews

VEGETABLE
1Kgs 21:2 have it for a V garden, because it is

VEGETABLES (4)
Deut 11:10 like a garden of V;
Dan 1:12 let us be given V to eat and water
1:16 wine they were to drink, and gave them V
Rom 14:2 eat anything, while the weak man eats only V

VEGETATION (5)
Gen 1:11 the earth put forth V, plants yielding seed, and
1:12 The earth brought forth V, plants yielding seed
Ps 105:35 which devoured all the V in their land, and
Zech 10:1 to every one the V in the field.
Heb 6:7 it, and brings forth V useful to those for

VEHEMENT
Song 8:6 of fire, a most V flame.

VEHEMENTLY (2)
Mk 14:31 But he said V, "If I must die with
Lk 23:10 the scribes stood by, V accusing him.

VEIL (39)
Gen 24:65 So she took her V and covered herself.
38:14 and put on a V, wrapping herself up, and
38:19 and taking off her V she put on the
Ex 26:31 you shall make a V of blue and purple
26:33 you shall hang the V from the clasps, and
26:33 in thither within the V; and the veil shall
26:33 the veil; and the V shall separate for you
26:35 the table outside the V, and the lampstand on
27:21 of meeting, outside the V which is before the
30:6 put it before the V that is by the
34:33 them, he put a V on his face;
34:34 him, he took the V off, until he came
34:35 Moses would put the V upon his face again,
35:12 mercy seat, and the V of the screen;
36:35 And he made the V of blue and purple
38:27 the bases of the V; a hundred bases for
39:34 and goatskins, and the V of the screen;
Lev 4:6 in front of the V of the sanctuary.
4:17 times before the LORD in front of the V
16:2 holy place within the V, before the mercy seat
16:12 bring it within the V
16:15 its blood within the V, and do with its
21:23 not come near the V or approach the altar,
24:3 Outside the V of the testimony, in the tent
Num 4:5 and take down the V of the screen, and
18:7 that is within the V; and you shall serve.
2Chr 3:14 And he made the V of blue and purple
Song 4:1 Your eyes are doves behind your V
4:3 are like halves of a pomegranate behind your V
6:7 are like halves of a pomegranate behind your V
Is 25:7 over all peoples, the V that is spread over
47:2 meal, put off your V, strip off your robe,
1Cor 11:6 a woman will not V herself, then she should
11:6 be shorn or shaven, let her wear a V
11:10 ought to have a V on her head, because
2Cor 3:13 Moses, who put a V over his face so
3:14 old covenant, that same V remains unlifted, because
3:15 Moses is read a V lies over their minds;
3:16 to the Lord the V is removed.

VEILED (4)
Dan 13:32 As she was V, the wicked men ordered her
Hab 3:4 hand; and there he V his power.
2Cor 4:3 if our gospel is V, it is veiled only
4:3 is veiled, it is V only to those who

VEILS (3)
Is 3:23 gauze, the linen garments, the turbans, and the V
Ezek 13:18 all wrists, and make V for the heads of
13:21 Your V also I will tear off, and deliver

VENGEANCE (70)
Gen 4:15 any one slays Cain, V shall be taken on
Lev 19:18 You shall not take V or bear any grudge
26:25 you, that shall execute V for the covenant; and
Num 31:3 to execute the LORD's V on Midian.
Deut 32:35 V is mine, and recompense, for the time when
32:41 judgment, I will take V on my adversaries, and
32:43 his servants, and takes V on his adversaries, and
Josh 10:13 until the nation took V on their enemies.
22:23 offerings on it, may the LORD himself take V
1Sam 20:16 may the LORD take V on David's enemies."
25:26 bloodguilt, and from taking V with your own hand,
25:31 for my lord taking V himself.
2Sam 22:48 God who gave me V and brought down peoples
Jud 16:17 Lord Almighty will take V on them in the
Ps 18:47 God who gave me V and subdued peoples under
58:10 when he sees the V; he will bathe his
94:1 LORD, thou God of V, thou God of vengeance,
94:1 vengeance, thou God of V, shine forth!
149:7 their hands, to wreak V on the nations and
Sir 18:23 of the moment of V when he turns away
25:13 And any V, but not the vengeance of enemies!
25:13 vengeance, but not the V of enemies!
27:28 the proud man, but V lies in wait for
28:1 He that takes V will suffer vengeance from the
28:1 takes vengeance will suffer V from the Lord, and
35:18 the unmerciful and repays V on the nations; till
39:28 have been created for V, and in their anger
39:29 have been created for V;
46:1 God's elect, to take V on the enemies that
47:25 sort of wickedness, till V came upon them.
48:7 Sinai and judgments of V at Horeb;
Is 34:8 has a day of V, a year of recompense
35:4 God will come with V, with the recompense of
47:3 I will take V, and I will spare no
59:17 put on garments of V for clothing, and wrapped
61:2 and the day of V of our God; to
63:4 For the day of V was in my heart,
Jer 11:20 let me see thy V upon them, for to
15:15 visit me, and take V for me on my
20:12 let me see thy V upon them, for to
46:10 hosts, a day of V, to avenge himself on
50:15 For this is the V of the LORD: take
50:15 of the LORD: take V on her, do to
50:28 declare in Zion the V of the LORD our
50:28 the LORD our God, V for his temple.
51:6 time of the LORD's V, the requital he is
51:11 for that is the V of the LORD, the
51:11 of the LORD, the V for his temple.
51:36 your cause and take V for you.
Lam 3:60 hast seen all their V, all their devices against
Ezek 24:8 my wrath, to take V, I have set on
25:12 grievously offended in taking V upon them,
25:14 I will lay my V upon Edom by the
25:14 they shall know my V, says the Lord GOD.
25:15 acted revengefully and took V with malice of heart
25:17 I will execute great V upon them with wrathful
25:17 when I lay my V upon them."
Mic 5:15 wrath I will execute V upon the nations that
Nah 1:2 wrathful; the LORD takes V on his adversaries and
1:9 he will not take V twice on his foes.
1Mac 3:15 help him, to take V on the sons of
7:9 commanded him to take V on the sons of
7:24 of Judea, and took V on the men who
7:38 Take V on this man and on his army,
9:26 Bacchides, and he took V on them and made
2Mac 6:15 he may not take V on us afterward when
Lk 21:22 these are days of V, to fulfil all that
Rom 12:19 for it is written, V is mine, I will
2Thes 1:8 in flaming fire, inflicting V upon those who do
Heb 10:30 know him who said, V is mine, I will

VENOM (7)
Deut 32:24 beasts against them, with V of crawling things of
32:33 serpents, and the cruel V of asps.
Ps 58:4 They have V like the venom of a serpent,
58:4 have venom like the V of a serpent, like
Sir 25:14 There is no V worse than a snake's venom,
25:14 worse than a snake's V, and no wrath worse
Rom 3:13 "The V of asps is under their lips."

VENOMOUS
Wis 16:10 by the teeth of V serpents, for thy mercy

VENT (6)
Job 32:19 wine that has no V; like new wineskins, it
Prov 29:11 A fool gives full V to his anger, but
Is 1:24 Israel: "Ah, I will V my wrath on my

Lam 4:11 The LORD gave full V to his wrath, he
Ezek 5:13 itself, and I will V my fury upon them
1Mac 2:24 He gave V to righteous anger; he ran and

VENTED
Ps 78:62 to the sword, and V his wrath on his

VENTURE (7)
Deut 28:56 you, who would not V to set the sole
1Kgs 22:34 his bow at a V, and struck the king
2Chr 18:33 his bow at a V, and struck the king
Eccl 5:14 lost in a bad V; and he is father
Acts 19:31 begged him not to V into the theater.
Rom 15:18 For I will not V to speak of anything
2Cor 10:12 Not that we V to class or compare ourselves

VENTURES
Job 4:2 Temanite answered: "If one V a word with you,

VERDICT (2)
Deut 17:11 turn aside from the V which they declare to
Sir 19:22 are people who distort kindness to gain a V

VERDURE
Is 15:6 new growth fails, the V is no more.

VERIFIED
Gen 42:20 your words will be V, and you shall not

VERMILION (2)
Jer 22:14 paneling it with cedar, and painting it with V
Ezek 23:14 the Chaldeans portrayed in V,

VERMIN
Jer 43:12 cleans his cloak of V; and he shall go

VERSED (2)
Esth 1:13 toward all who were V in law and judgment,
Acts 18:24 an eloquent man, well V in the scriptures.

VERSES (2)
Ps 45:1 theme; I address my V to the king; my
Sir 44:5 tunes, and set forth V in writing;

VESSEL (43)
Lev 6:28 And the earthen V in which it is boiled
6:28 boiled in a bronze V, that shall be scoured,
11:32 or a sack, any V that is used for
11:33 falls into any earthen V, all that is in
11:34 drunk from every such V shall be unclean.
14:5 birds in an earthen V over running water.
14:50 birds in an earthen V over running water,
15:12 And the earthen V which he who has the
15:12 be broken; and every V of wood shall be
Num 5:17 water in an earthen V, and take some of
19:15 And every open V, which has no cover fastened
19:17 be added in a V;
Deut 23:24 but you shall not put any in your V
1Kgs 17:10 little water in a V, that I may drink."
2Kgs 4:6 she said to her son, "Bring me another V
Ps 2:9 and dash them in pieces like a potter's V
31:12 is dead; I have become like a broken V
Prov 25:4 has material for a V;
26:23 glaze covering an earthen V are smooth lips with
Wis 13:11 workmanship make a useful V that serves life's
14:2 gain that planned that V, and wisdom was the
15:7 and laboriously molds each V for our service, he
Sir 50:9 the censer, like a V of hammered gold adorned
Is 22:24 and issue, every small V, from the cups to
30:14 that of a potter's V which is smashed so
45:9 his Maker, an earthen V with the potter!
66:20 offering in a clean V to the house of
Jer 18:4 And the V he was making of clay was
18:4 reworked it into another V, as it seemed good
19:11 one breaks a potter's V, so that it can
22:28 despised, broken pot, a V no one cares for?
32:14 them in an earthenware V, that they may last
48:11 not been emptied from V to vessel, nor has
48:11 emptied from vessel to V, nor has he gone
48:38 broken Moab like a V for which no one
51:34 made me an empty V, he has swallowed me
Ezek 4:9 them into a single V, and make bread of
15:3 it to hang any V on?
Hos 8:8 they are among the nations as a useless V
Lk 8:16 covers it with a V, or puts it under
Acts 27:41 shoal they ran the V aground; the bow stuck
Rom 9:21 the same lump one V for beauty and another
2Tim 2:21 he will be a V for noble use, consecrated

VESSELS (118)
Ex 7:19 of Egypt, both in V of wood and in
7:19 of wood and in V of stone.'"
37:16 And he made the V of pure gold which
Num 3:31 lampstand, the altars, the V of the sanctuary with
4:9 trays, and all the V for oil with which
4:12 shall take all the V of the service which
4:16 is in it, of the sanctuary and its V
7:85 the silver of the V two thousand four hundred
18:3 come near to the V of the sanctuary or
31:6 the priest, with the V of the sanctuary and
Josh 6:19 silver and gold, and V of bronze and iron,
6:24 and gold, and the V of bronze and of
Ruth 2:9 thirsty, go to the V and drink what the
1Sam 21:5 on an expedition; the V of the young men
21:5 more today will their V be holy?"
2Sam 17:28 basins, and earthen V, wheat, barley, meal, parched
1Kgs 7:45 the basins, all these V in the house of
7:47 Solomon left all the V unweighed, because there
7:48 Solomon made all the V that were in the
7:51 the gold, and the V, and stored them in
8:4 and all the holy V that were in the
10:21 All King Solomon's drinking V were of gold, and
10:21 gold, and all the V of the House of
15:15 his own votive gifts, silver, and gold, and V
2Kgs 4:3 said, "Go outside, borrow V of all your neighbors,
4:3 all your neighbors, empty V and not too few.
4:4 pour into all these V; and when one is
4:5 poured they brought the V to her.
4:6 When the V were full, she said to her
12:13 bowls, trumpets, or any V of gold, or of
14:14 silver, and all the V that were found in
23:4 the LORD all the V made for Baal, for
24:13 in pieces all the V of gold in the
25:14 incense and all the V of bronze used in
25:16 bronze of all these V was beyond weight.
1Chr 18:8 the pillars and the V of bronze.
22:19 LORD and the holy V of God may be
28:13 LORD; for all the V for the service in
28:14 gold for all golden V for each service, the
28:14 the weight of silver V for each service,
2Chr 5:1 gold, and all the V in the treasuries of
5:5 and all the holy V that were in the
9:20 All King Solomon's drinking V were of gold, and
9:20 gold, and all the V of the House of
15:18 his own votive gifts, silver, and gold, and V
24:14 dishes for incense, and V of gold and silver.
25:24 silver, and all the V that were found in
28:24 Ahaz gathered together the V of the house of
28:24 cut in pieces the V of the house of
32:27 all kinds of costly V;
36:7 carried part of the V of the house of
36:10 Babylon, with the precious V of the house of
36:18 And all the V of the house of God,
36:19 palaces with fire, and destroyed all its precious V
Ezra 1:6 them aided them with V of silver, with gold,
1:7 also brought out the V of the house of
1:10 and a thousand other V;
1:11 other vessels; all the V of gold and of
5:14 the gold and silver V of the house of
5:15 to him, "Take these V, go and put them
6:5 the gold and silver V of the house of
7:19 The V that have been given you for the
8:25 the gold and the V, the offering for the
8:26 of silver, and silver V worth a hundred talents,
8:27 thousand darics, and two V of fine bright bronze
8:28 the LORD, and the V are holy; and the
8:30 the gold and the V, to bring them to
8:33 the gold and the V were weighed into the
Neh 10:39 chambers, where are the V of the sanctuary, and
13:5 offering, the frankincense, the V, and the tithes of
13:9 brought back thither the V of the house of
Jud 4:3 together, and the sacred V and the altar and
7:20 days, until all the V of water belonging to
10:5 wrapped up all her V and gave them to
16:19 to God all the V of Holofernes, which the
Wis 15:7 same clay both the V that serve clean uses
15:13 from earthy matter fragile V and graven images.
Sir 27:5 kiln tests the potter's V; so the test of
Is 18:2 by the Nile, in V of papyrus upon the
52:11 you who bear the V of the LORD.
65:4 things is in their V;
Jer 14:3 they return with their V empty; they are ashamed

V

	27:16	you, saying, 'Behold, the V of the LORD's house
	27:18	of hosts, that the V which are left in
	27:19	the rest of the V which are left in
	27:21	of Israel, concerning the V which are left in
	28:3	this place all the V of the LORD's house,
	28:6	place from Babylon the V of the house of
	40:10	store them in your V, and dwell in your
	48:12	him, and empty his V, and break his jars
	52:18	incense, and all the V of bronze used in
Bar	1:8	Sivan, Baruch took the V of the house of
	1:8	of Judah--the silver V which Zedekiah the son
Ezek	27:13	persons of men and V of bronze for your
Dan	1:2	with some of the V of the house of
	1:2	god, and placed the V in the treasury of
	5:2	wine, commanded that the V of gold and of
	5:3	the golden and silver V which had been taken
	5:23	of heaven; and the V of his house have
	11:8	and with their precious V of silver and of
1Mac	1:23	gold, and the costly V; he took also the
	2:9	without honor; her glorious V have been carried into
	4:49	They made new holy V, and brought the lampstand,
	6:12	I seized all her V of silver and gold;
	14:15	and added to the V of the sanctuary.
2Mac	4:32	some of the gold V of the temple and
	4:32	them to Andronicus; other V, as it happened, he
	4:39	many of the gold V had already been stolen.
	4:48	villages and the holy V quickly suffered the unjust
	5:16	He took the holy V with his polluted hands,
	9:16	offerings; and the holy V he would give back,
Mt	13:48	sorted the good into V but threw away the
Mk	7:4	cups and pots and V of bronze.
Rom	9:22	with much patience the V of wrath made for
	9:23	his glory for the V of mercy, which he
2Cor	4:7	this treasure in earthen V, to show that the
2Tim	2:20	there are not only V of gold and silver
Heb	9:21	tent and all the V used in worship.

VESTIBULE (46)

Judg	3:23	went out into the V, and closed the doors
1Kgs	6:3	The V in front of the nave of the
	7:12	the LORD, and the V of the house.
	7:19	the pillars in the V were of lily-work, four
	7:21	the pillars at the V of the temple; he
1Chr	28:11	the plan of the V of the temple, and
2Chr	3:4	The V in front of the nave of the
	8:12	had built before the V,
	15:8	in front of the V of the house of
	29:7	the doors of the V and put out the
	29:17	they came to the V of the LORD; then
Ezek	40:7	the gate by the V of the gate at
	40:8	Then he measured the V of the gateway, eight
	40:9	two cubits; and the V of the gate was
	40:14	He measured also the V, twenty cubits; and round
	40:14	and round about the V of the gateway was
	40:15	end of the inner V of the gate was
	40:16	rooms, and likewise the V had windows round about
	40:21	its jambs and its V were of the same
	40:22	And its windows, its V, and its palm trees
	40:22	to it; and its V was on the inside.
	40:24	its jambs and its V; they had the same
	40:25	it and in its V, like the windows of
	40:26	to it, and its V was on the inside;
	40:29	its jambs, and its V were of the same
	40:29	it and in its V; its length was fifty
	40:31	Its V faced the outer court, and palm trees
	40:33	its jambs, and its V were of the same
	40:33	it and in its V; its length was fifty
	40:34	Its V faced the outer court, and it had
	40:36	its jambs, and its V were of the same
	40:37	Its V faced the outer court, and it had
	40:38	its door in the V of the gate, where
	40:39	And in the V of the gate were two
	40:40	the outside of the V at the entrance of
	40:40	other side of the V of the gate were
	40:48	brought me to the V of the temple and
	40:48	the jambs of the V, five cubits on either
	40:49	The length of the V was twenty cubits, and
	41:15	room and the outer V
	41:25	in front of the V outside.
	41:26	on either side, on the sidewalls of the V
	44:3	by way of the V of the gate, and
	46:2	shall enter by the V of the gate from
	46:8	go in by the V of the gate, and
Joel	2:17	Between the V and the altar let the priests,

VESTIBULES

Ezek	40:30	And there were V round about, twenty-five cubits

VESTMENTS (4)

2Kgs	10:22	wardrobe, "Bring out the V for all the worshipers
	10:22	he brought out the V for them.
Ezra	3:10	the priests in their V came forward with trumpets,
Sir	45:7	blessed him with splendid V, and put a glorious

VESTURE

Gen	49:11	in wine and his V in the blood of

VEXATION (10)

1Sam	1:16	been speaking out of my great anxiety and V
Job	5:2	Surely V kills the fool, and jealousy slays the
	6:2	answered: "O that my V were weighed, and all
	10:17	me, and increase thy V toward me; thou dost
Ps	10:14	dost note trouble and V, that thou mayest take
Prov	12:16	The V of a fool is known at once,
Eccl	1:18	much wisdom is much V, and he who increases
	2:23	his work is a V; even in the night
	5:17	and grief, in much V and sickness and resentment?
	11:10	Remove V from your mind, and put away pain

VEXED (6)

Judg	16:16	him, his soul was V to death.
1Kgs	21:4	went into his house V and sullen because of
	21:5	is your spirit so V that you eat no
Sir	50:25	nations my soul is V, and the third is
2Mac	11:1	of the government, being V at what had happened,
2Pet	2:8	among them, he was V in his righteous soul

VIAL

1Sam	10:1	Then Samuel took a V of oil and poured

VICINITY

Ezra	2:70	in Jerusalem and its V; and the singers, the

VICIOUS

Acts	18:14	matter of wrongdoing or V crime, I should have

VICTIM (2)

Prov	7:26	paths; for many a V has she laid low;
2Mac	7:10	the third was the V of their sport.

VICTIMS (5)

2Chr	35:11	received from them while the Levites flayed the V
Prov	26:28	lying tongue hates its V, and a flattering mouth
Jer	14:16	the streets of Jerusalem, V of famine and sword,
Lam	4:9	Happier were the V of the sword than the
	4:9	the sword than the V of hunger, who pined

VICTOR

Wis	4:2	marches crowned in triumph, V in the contest for

VICTORIES (2)

Ps	20:6	holy heaven with mighty V by his right hand.
	44:4	my God, who ordainest V for Jacob.

VICTORIOUS (3)

Judg	11:31	me, when I return V from the Ammonites, shall
Is	41:10	uphold you with my V right hand.
Zech	9:9	to you; triumphant and V is he, humble and

VICTORIOUSLY

Ps	45:4	your majesty ride forth V for the cause of

VICTORY (55)

Ex	32:18	sound of shouting for V, or the sound of
Deut	20:4	to give you the V
1Sam	14:45	has wrought this great V in Israel?
	19:5	LORD wrought a great V for all Israel.
2Sam	8:6	And the LORD gave V to David wherever he
	8:14	And the LORD gave V to David wherever he
	19:2	So the V that day was turned into mourning
	23:10	LORD wrought a great V that day; and the
	23:12	the Philistines; and the LORD wrought a great V
2Kgs	5:1	the LORD had given V to Syria.
	13:17	"The LORD's arrow of V, the arrow of victory
	13:17	victory, the arrow of V over Syria!
1Chr	11:14	and the LORD saved them by a great V
	18:6	And the LORD gave V to David wherever he
	18:13	And the LORD gave V to David wherever he
	29:11	the glory, and the V, and the majesty; for
2Chr	20:17	still, and see the V of the LORD on
Job	40:14	that your own right hand can give you V

1Kgs 4:13 Ramoth-gilead (he had the V of Jair the son
1Chr 2:23 Havvoth-jair, Kenath and its V, sixty towns.
4:32 And their V were Etam, Ain, Rimmon, Tochen, and
4:33 along with all their V which were round about
6:56 the city and its V they gave to Caleb
9:16 who dwelt in the V of the Netophathites.
9:22 They were enrolled by genealogies in their V
9:25 who were in their V were obliged to come
18:1 took Gath and its V out of the hand
27:25 the cities, in the V and in the towers,
2Chr 13:19 him, Bethel with its V and Jeshanah with its
13:19 and Jeshanah with its V and Ephron with its
13:19 Jeshanah with its villages and Ephron with its V
28:18 Gederoth, Soco with its V, Timnah with its villages,
28:18 villages, Timnah with its V, and Gimzo with its
28:18 and Gimzo with its V; and they settled there.
Neh 6:2 in one of the V in the plain of
11:25 And as for the V, with their fields, some
11:25 in Kiriath-arba and its V, and in Dibon and
11:25 in Dibon and its V, and in Jekabzeel and
11:25 in Jekabzeel and its V,
11:27 in Beer-sheba and its V,
11:28 in Meconah and its V,
11:30 Zanoah, Adullam, and their V, Lachish and its fields,
11:30 Lachish and its fields, and Azekah and its V
11:31 Aija, Bethel and its V,
12:28 Jerusalem and from the V of the Netophathites;
12:29 had built for themselves V around Jerusalem.
Jud 4:5 hilltops and fortified the V on them and stored
15:7 what remained, and the V and towns in the
Esth 9:19 the Jews of the V, who live in the
Ps 10:8 in ambush in the V; in hiding places he
Song 7:11 and lodge in the V;
Is 42:11 up their voice, the V that Kedar inhabits; let
Jer 49:2 desolate mound, and its V shall be burned with
Ezek 38:11 the land of unwalled V; I will fall upon
38:13 Tarshish and all its V will say to you,
Zech 2:4 shall be inhabited as V without walls, because of
1Mac 5:8 took Jazer and its V; then he returned to
5:65 struck Hebron and its V and tore down its
7:46 out of all the V of Judea round about,
2Mac 4:48 the city and the V and the holy vessels
8:1 secretly entered the V and summoned their kinsmen
8:6 warning, he would set fire to towns and V
Mt 9:35 all the cities and V, teaching in their synagogues
14:15 to go into the V and buy food for
Mk 6:6 went about among the V teaching.
6:36 into the country and V round about and buy
6:56 wherever he came, in V, cities, or country, they
8:27 his disciples, to the V of Caesarea Philippi; and
Lk 8:1 on through cities and V, preaching and bringing the
9:6 and went through the V, preaching the gospel and
9:12 to go into the V and country round about,
13:22 way through towns and V, teaching, and journeying
Acts 8:25 the gospel to many V of the Samaritans.

VILLAINY (3)

Hos 6:9 on the way to Shechem, yea, they commit V
Nah 1:11 who plotted evil against the LORD, and counseled V
Acts 13:10 of all deceit and V, will you not stop

VINDICATE (13)

Deut 32:36 For the LORD will V his people and have
Ps 26:1 V me, O LORD, for I have walked in
35:24 V me, O LORD, my God, according to thy
43:1 V me, O God, and defend my cause against
54:1 by thy name, and V me by thy might.
135:14 For the LORD will V his people, and have
Ezek 36:23 And I will V the holiness of my great
36:23 when through you I V my holiness before their
38:16 you, O Gog, I V my holiness before their
Lk 18:3 to him and saying, V me against my adversary.'
18:5 bothers me, I will V her, or she will
18:7 And will not God V his elect, who cry
18:8 tell you, he will V them speedily.

VINDICATED (5)

Esth 10:12 remembered his people and V his inheritance.
Job 11:2 unanswered, and a man full of talk be V
13:18 my case; I know that I shall be V
Ezek 39:27 and through them have V my holiness in the
1Tim 3:16 manifested in the flesh, V in the Spirit, seen

VINDICATES

Is 50:8 to shame; he who V me is near.

VINDICATING (2)

1Kgs 8:32 his own head, and V the righteous by rewarding
2Chr 6:23 his own head, and V the righteous by rewarding

VINDICATION (14)

Gen 20:16 silver; it is your V in the eyes of
Job 6:29 Turn now, my V is at stake.
Ps 17:2 From thee let my V come!
24:5 from the LORD, and V from the God of
35:27 those who desire my V shout for joy and
37:6 will bring forth your V as the light, and
98:2 he has revealed his V in the sight of
103:6 The LORD works V and justice for all who
Is 54:17 the LORD and their V from me, says the
62:1 not rest, until her V goes forth as brightness,
62:2 nations shall see your V, and all the kings
63:1 "It is I, announcing V, mighty to save."
Jer 51:10 has brought forth our V; come, let us declare
Joel 2:23 early rain for your V, he has poured down

VINE (56)

Gen 40:9 dream there was a V before me,
40:10 me, and on the V there were three branches;
49:11 his foal to the V and his ass's colt
49:11 colt to the choice V, he washes his garments
Lev 25:5 grapes of your undressed V you shall not gather;
Deut 32:32 For their V comes from the vine of Sodom,
32:32 vine comes from the V of Sodom, and from
Judg 9:12 trees said to the V, 'Come you, and reign
9:13 over us.' But the V said to them, 'Shall
13:14 that comes from the V, neither let her drink
1Kgs 4:25 every man under his V and under his fig
2Kgs 4:39 and found a wild V and gathered from it
18:31 eat of his own V, and every one of
Job 15:33 unripe grape, like the V, and cast off his
Ps 80:8 Thou didst bring a V out of Egypt; thou
80:14 have regard for this V,
128:3 be like a fruitful V within your house; your
Song 7:8 like clusters of the V, and the scent of
Sir 24:17 Like a V I caused loveliness to bud, and
Is 16:8 Heshbon languish, and the V of Sibmah; the lords
16:9 of Jazer for the V of Sibmah; I drench
24:7 wine mourns, the V languishes, all the merry-hearted
32:12 fields, for the fruitful V,
34:4 leaves fall from the V, like leaves falling from
36:16 eat of his own V, and every one of
Jer 2:21 planted you a choice V, wholly of pure seed.
2:21 have you turned degenerate and become a wild V
6:9 "Glean thoroughly as a V the remnant of Israel;
8:13 no grapes on the V, nor figs on the
48:32 weep for you, O V of Sibmah!
Ezek 15:2 the wood of the V surpass any wood, the
15:2 surpass any wood, the V branch which is among
15:6 the wood of the V among the trees of
17:6 became a low spreading V, and its branches turned
17:6 So it became a V, and brought forth branches
17:7 plumage; and behold, this V bent its roots toward
17:8 branches, and bear fruit, and become a noble V
19:10 mother was like a V in a vineyard transplanted
19:12 But the V was plucked up in fury, cast
Hos 10:1 Israel is a luxuriant V that yields its fruit.
14:7 shall blossom as the V, their fragrance shall be
Joel 1:11 The V withers, the fig tree languishes.
2:22 the fig tree and V give their full yield.
Mic 4:4 every man under his V and under his fig
Hag 2:19 Do the V, the fig tree, the pomegranate, and
Zech 3:10 his neighbor under his V and under his fig
8:12 sowing of peace; the V shall yield its fruit,
Mal 3:11 your soil; and your V in the field shall
1Mac 14:12 man sat under his V and his fig tree,
Mt 26:29 this fruit of the V until that day when
Mk 14:25 the fruit of the V until that day when
Lk 22:18 the fruit of the V until the kingdom of
Jn 15:1 "I am the true V, and my Father is
15:4 it abides in the V, neither can you, unless
15:5 I am the V, you are the branches.
Rev 14:18 the clusters of the V of the earth, for

VINE-ROWS

Jer 5:10 "Go up through her V and destroy, but make

VINEDRESSER (2)

Lk 13:7 he said to the V, 'Lo, these three years
Jn 15:1 the true vine, and my Father is the V

VINEDRESSERS (5)
2Kgs 25:12 the land to be V and plowmen.
2Chr 26:10 he had farmers and V in the hills and
Is 61:5 be your plowmen and V;
Jer 52:16 the land to be V and plowmen.
Joel 1:10 the soil, wail, O V, for the wheat and

VINEGAR (10)
Num 6:3 he shall drink no V made from wine or
Ps 69:21 thirst they gave me V to drink.
Prov 10:26 Like V to the teeth, and smoke to the
25:20 cold day, and like V on a wound.
Mt 27:48 sponge, filled it with V, and put it on
Mk 15:35 a sponge full of V, put it on a
Lk 23:35 up and offering him V,
Jn 19:29 A bowl full of V stood there; so they
19:29 sponge full of the V on hyssop and held
19:30 Jesus had received the V, he said, "It is

VINES (14)
Lev 25:11 itself, nor gather the grapes from the undressed V
Num 20:5 grain, or figs, or V, or pomegranates; and there
Deut 8:8 wheat and barley, of V and fig trees and
Ps 78:47 He destroyed their V with hail, and their sycamores
105:33 He smote their V and fig trees, and shattered
Song 2:13 its figs, and the V are in blossom; they
6:11 to see whether the V had budded, whether the
7:12 and see whether the V have budded, whether the
Is 5:2 planted it with choice V; he built a watchtower
7:23 to be a thousand V, worth a thousand shekels
Jer 5:17 shall eat up your V and your fig trees;
Hos 2:12 will lay waste her V and her fig trees,
Joel 1:7 has laid waste my V, and splintered my fig
Hab 3:17 fruit be on the V, the produce of the

VINEYARD (70)
Gen 9:20 He planted a V;
Ex 22:5 causes a field or V to be grazed over,
22:5 in his own field and in his own V
23:11 do likewise with your V, and with your olive
Lev 19:10 shall not strip your V bare, neither shall you
19:10 fallen grapes of your V; you shall leave them
25:3 you shall prune your V, and gather in its
25:4 shall not sow your field or prune your V
Num 20:17 pass through field or V, neither will we drink
21:22 aside into field or V; we will not drink
Deut 20:6 that has planted a V and has not enjoyed
22:9 shall not sow your V with two kinds of
22:9 you have sown and the yield of the V
23:24 go into your neighbor's V, you may eat your
24:21 the grapes of your V, you shall not glean
28:30 you shall plant a V, and you shall not
1Kgs 21:1 the Jezreelite had a V in Jezreel, beside the
21:2 Naboth, "Give me your V, that I may have
21:2 give you a better V for it; or, if
21:6 him, 'Give me your V for money; or else,
21:6 will give you another V for it'; and he
21:6 he answered, 'I will not give you my V
21:7 will give you the V of Naboth the Jezreelite."
21:15 take possession of the V of Naboth the Jezreelite,
21:16 go down to the V of Naboth the Jezreelite,
21:18 he is in the V of Naboth, where he
Job 24:6 and they glean the V of the wicked man.
Prov 24:30 a sluggard, by the V of a man without
31:16 the fruit of her hands she plants a V
Song 1:6 vineyards; but, my own V I have not kept!
8:11 Solomon had a V at Baal-hamon; he let out
8:11 he let out the V to keepers; each one
8:12 My V, my very own, is for myself; you,
Is 1:8 a booth in a V, like a lodge in
3:14 who have devoured the V, the spoil of the
5:1 love song concerning his V: My beloved had a
5:1 My beloved had a V on a very fertile
5:3 judge, I pray you, between me and my V
5:4 to do for my V, that I have not
5:5 tell you what I will do to my V
5:7 For the V of the LORD of hosts is
5:10 For ten acres of V shall yield but one
27:2 that day: "A pleasant V, sing of it!
Jer 12:10 shepherds have destroyed my V, they have trampled
35:7 plant or have a V; but you shall live
35:9 We have no V or field or seed;
Ezek 19:10 a vine in a V transplanted by the water,
Mt 20:1 in the morning to hire laborers for his V
20:2 denarius a day, he sent them into his V
20:4 'You go into the V too, and whatever is
20:7 'You go into the V too.'
20:8 the owner of the V said to his steward,
21:28 and work in the V today.'
21:33 householder who planted a V, and set a hedge
21:39 him out of the V, and killed him.
21:40 the owner of the V comes, what will he
21:41 and let out the V to other tenants who
Mk 12:1 "A man planted a V, and set a hedge
12:2 from them some of the fruit of the V
12:8 killed him, and cast him out of the V
12:9 the owner of the V do?
12:9 tenants, and give the V to others.
Lk 13:6 tree planted in his V; and he came seeking
20:9 "A man planted a V, and let it out
20:10 the fruit of the V; but the tenants beat
20:13 the owner of the V said, 'What shall I
20:15 him out of the V and killed him.
20:15 the owner of the V do to them?
20:16 tenants, and give the V to others." When they
1Cor 9:7 Who plants a V without eating any of its

VINEYARDS (46)
Num 16:14 honey, nor given us inheritance of fields and V
22:24 narrow path between the V, with a wall on
Deut 6:11 did not hew, and V and olive trees, which
28:39 You shall plant V and dress them, but you
Josh 24:13 eat the fruit of V and oliveyards which you
Judg 9:27 the grapes from their V and trod them, and
14:5 he came to the V of Timnah.
21:20 in wait in the V,
21:21 come out of the V and seize each man
1Sam 8:14 of your fields and V and olive orchards and
8:15 grain and of your V and give it to
22:7 of you fields and V, will he make you
2Kgs 5:26 garments, olive orchards and V, sheep and oxen,
18:32 land of bread and V, a land of olive
19:29 and reap, and plant V, and eat their fruit.
1Chr 27:27 Chelub; and over the V was Shimei the Ramathite;
27:27 the produce of the V for the wine cellars
Neh 5:3 mortgaging our fields, our V, and our houses to
5:4 the king's tax upon our fields and our V
5:5 for other men have our fields and our V
5:11 day their fields, their V, their olive orchards, and
9:25 things, cisterns hewn out, V, olive orchards and fruit
Job 24:18 in the land; no treader turns toward their V
Ps 107:37 sow fields, and plant V, and get a fruitful
Eccl 2:4 built houses and planted V for myself;
Song 1:6 me keeper of the V; but, my own vineyard
1:14 henna blossoms in the V of Engedi.
2:15 foxes, that spoil the V, for our vineyards are
2:15 the vineyards, for our V are in blossom."
7:12 out early to the V, and see whether the
Is 16:10 field; and in the V no songs are sung,
36:17 grain and wine, a land of bread and V
37:30 and reap, and plant V, and eat their fruit.
65:21 them; they shall plant V and eat their fruit.
Jer 31:5 Again you shall plant V upon the mountains of
32:15 Houses and fields and V shall again be bought
39:10 nothing, and gave them V and fields at the
Ezek 28:26 it, and they shall build houses and plant V
Hos 2:15 will give her her V, and make the Valley
Amos 4:9 your gardens and your V; your fig trees and
5:11 you have planted pleasant V, but you shall not
5:17 lamentation, and in all V there shall be wailing,
9:14 them; they shall plant V and drink their wine,
Mic 1:6 a place for planting V; and I will pour
Zeph 1:13 them; though they plant V, they shall not drink
1Mac 3:56 betrothed, or were planting V, or were fainthearted,

VINTAGE (10)
Lev 26:5 to the time of V, and the vintage shall
26:5 of vintage, and the V shall last to the
Judg 8:2 Ephraim better than the V of Abi-ezer?
Sir 24:25 light, like the Gihon at the time of V
Is 16:10 in the presses; the V shout is hushed.
24:13 the gleaning when the V is done.
32:10 complacent women; for the V will fail, the fruit
Jer 48:32 summer fruits and your V the destroyer has fallen.
Mic 7:1 gathered, as when the V has been gleaned: there
Rev 14:19 earth and gathered the V of the earth, and

VIOLATE (5)
Job 37:23 and justice, and abundant righteousness he will not V
Ps 89:31 my ordinances, if they V my statutes and do
89:34 I will not V my covenant, or alter the
Sir 20:3 a eunuch's desire to V a maiden is a

Dan 11:32 with flattery those who V the covenant; but the

VIOLATED (7)

Deut 22:24 the man because he V his neighbor's wife; so
22:29 wife, because he has V her; he may not
Ps 55:20 against his friends, he V his covenant.
Is 24:5 have transgressed the laws, V the statutes, broken
1Mac 7:18 them, for they have V the agreement and the
1Tim 5:12 incur condemnation for having V their first pledge.
Heb 10:28 A man who has V the law of Moses

VIOLATION

2Mac 15:10 the Gentiles and their V of oaths.

VIOLENCE (79)

Gen 6:11 God's sight, and the earth was filled with V
6:13 earth is filled with V through them; behold, I
49:5 are brothers; weapons of V are their swords.
Judg 9:24 with Abimelech; that the V done to the seventy
2Sam 22:3 my refuge, my savior; thou savest me from V
22:49 adversaries, thou didst deliver me from men of V
Esth 13:7 day go down in V to Hades, and leave
Job 16:17 although there is no V in my hands, and
19:7 Behold, I cry out, V but I am not
30:18 With V it seizes my garment; it binds me
Ps 7:16 his own pate his V descends.
11:5 wicked, and his soul hates him that loves V
18:48 adversaries; thou didst deliver me from men of V
27:12 have risen against me, and they breathe out V
55:9 tongues; for I see V and strife in the
58:2 your hands deal out V on earth.
72:14 From oppression and V he redeems their life; and
73:6 pride is their necklace; V covers them as a
74:20 the land are full of the habitations of V
Prov 1:7 Path of Greed and V
1:19 who get gain by V; it takes away the
3:31 envy a man of V and do not choose
4:18 bread of wickedness and drink the wine of V
10:6 righteous, but the mouth of the wicked conceals V
10:11 life, but the mouth of the wicked conceals V
13:2 but the desire of the treacherous is for V
16:29 A man of V entices his neighbor and leads
19:26 He who does V to his father and chases
21:7 The V of the wicked will sweep them away,
24:2 for their minds devise V, and their lips talk
24:15 the righteous; do not V to his home;
26:6 fool cuts off his own feet and drinks V
Wis 4:4 wind, and by the V of the winds they
19:13 prior signs in the V of thunder, for they
Sir 20:3 maiden is a man who executes judgments by V
21:4 Terror and V will lay waste riches; thus the
Is 28:2 he will cast down to the earth with V
53:9 he had done no V, and there was no
59:6 iniquity, and deeds of V are in their hands.
60:18 V shall no more be heard in your land,
Jer 6:7 keeps fresh her wickedness; V and destruction are
13:22 your skirts are lifted up, and you suffer V
20:8 cry out, I shout, V and destruction!" For the
22:3 do no wrong or V to the alien, the
22:17 innocent blood, and for practicing oppression and V
51:35 The V done to me and to my kinsmen
51:46 in another year, and V is in the land,
Ezek 7:11 V has grown up into a rod of wickedness;
7:23 city is full of V,
8:17 fill the land with V, and provoke me further
12:19 on account of the V of all those who
22:26 Her priests have done V to my law and
28:16 you were filled with V, and you sinned; so
45:9 Put away V and oppression, and execute justice and
Dan 11:14 and the men of V among your own people
Hos 12:1 they multiply falsehood and V; they make a bargain
Joel 3:19 desolate wilderness, for the V done to the people
Amos 3:10 "those who store up V and robbery in their
6:3 evil day, and bring near the seat of V
Obad 1:10 For the V done to your brother Jacob, shame
Jon 3:8 way and from the V which is in his
Mic 6:12 men are full of V; your inhabitants speak lies,
Hab 1:2 Or cry to thee V
1:3 Destruction and V are before me; strife and
1:9 They all come for V; terror of them goes
2:8 blood of men and V to the earth, to
2:17 The V done to Lebanon will overwhelm you; the
2:17 blood of men and V to the earth, to
Zeph 1:9 their master's house with V and fraud."
3:4 is sacred, they do V to the law.
Mal 1:13 has been taken by V or is lame or
2:16 covering one's garment with V, says the LORD of
1Mac 1:58 They kept using V against Israel, against those found
Mt 11:12 of heaven has suffered V, and men of violence
11:12 violence, and men of V take it by force.
Lk 3:14 "Rob no one by V or by false accusation,
Acts 5:26 brought them, but without V, for they were afraid
21:35 soldiers because of the V of the crowd;
Rev 18:21 be thrown down with V, and shall be found

VIOLENT (12)

2Sam 7:10 disturbed no more; and V men shall afflict them
1Chr 17:9 disturbed no more; and V men shall waste them
Ps 17:4 lips I have avoided the ways of the V
25:19 foes, and with what V hatred they hate me.
140:1 men; preserve me from V men,
140:4 wicked; preserve me from V men, who have planned
140:11 evil hunt down the V man speedily!
Prov 11:16 woman gets honor, and V men get riches.
Acts 12:1 Herod the king laid V hands upon some who
23:10 when the dissension became V, the tribune, afraid
1Tim 3:3 teacher, no drunkard, not V but gentle, not
Tit 1:6 or a drunkard or V or greedy for gain,

VIOLENTLY (10)

Gen 27:33 Then Isaac trembled V, and said, "Who was it
Deut 28:31 your ass shall be V taken away before your
Judg 8:1 And they upbraided him V
Eccl 5:8 and justice and right V taken away, do not
Wis 17:18 or the rhythm of V rushing water,
Is 22:17 will hurl you away V, O you strong man.
24:19 asunder, the earth is V shaken.
Lk 16:16 God is preached, and every one enters it V
Acts 27:18 As we were V storm-tossed, they began next day
Gal 1:13 the church of God V and tried to destroy

VIOLET

Jer 10:9 goldsmith; their clothing is V and purple; they are

VIPER (5)

Gen 49:17 in the way, a V by the path, that
Job 20:16 the tongue of a V will kill him.
Is 30:6 and the lion, the V and the flying serpent,
59:5 which is crushed a V is hatched.
Acts 28:3 the fire, when a V came out because of

VIPERS (6)

Ps 140:3 and under their lips is the poison of V
Sir 39:30 beasts, and scorpions and V, and the sword that
Mt 3:7 baptism, he said to them, "You brood of V
12:34 You brood of V
23:32 serpents, you brood of V, how are you to
Lk 3:7 to be baptized by him, "You brood of V

VIRGIN (37)

Gen 24:16 to look upon, a V, whom no man had
Ex 22:16 a man seduces a V who is not betrothed,
Lev 21:3 his brother, or his V sister (who is near
21:14 take to wife a V of his own people,
Deut 22:19 evil name upon a V of Israel; and she
22:23 there is a betrothed V, and a man meets
22:28 a man meets a V who is not betrothed,
32:25 both young man and V, the sucking child with
Judg 19:24 Behold, here are my V daughter and his concubine;
2Sam 13:2 for she was a V, and it seemed impossible
13:18 for thus were the V daughters of the king
2Kgs 19:21 she scorns you--the V daughter of Zion; she
2Chr 36:17 on young man or V, old man or aged;
Jud 9:2 the girdle of a V to defile her, and
Job 31:1 eyes; how then could I look upon a V
Ps 45:14 the king, with her V companions, her escort, in
Sir 9:5 look intently at a V, lest you stumble and
42:10 be hated; while a V, lest she be defiled
Is 23:12 more exult, O oppressed V daughter of Sidon; arise,
37:22 scorns you-- the V daughter of Zion; she
47:1 in the dust, O V daughter of Babylon; sit
62:5 young man marries a V, so shall your sons
Jer 14:17 not cease, for the V daughter of my people
18:13 The V Israel has done a very horrible thing.
31:4 shall be built, O V Israel!
31:21 Return, O V Israel, return to these your cities.
46:11 and take balm, O V daughter of Egypt!
Lam 1:15 a wine press the V daughter of Judah.
2:13 may comfort you, O V daughter of Zion?
Ezek 23:3 were pressed and their V bosoms handled.
23:8 her and handled her V bosom and poured out
44:22 woman, but only a V of the stock of

Joel 1:8 Lament like a V girded with sackcloth for the
Amos 5:2 to rise, is the V Israel; forsaken on her
Mt 1:23 the prophet: "Behold, a V shall conceive and bear
Lk 1:27 named Nazareth, to a V betrothed to a man
1:27 of David; and the V's name was Mary.

VIRGINITY (9)

Lev 21:13 And he shall take a wife in her V
Deut 22:14 her the tokens of V
22:15 the tokens of her V to the elders of
22:17 not find in your daughter the tokens of V
22:17 tokens of my daughter's V And they shall spread
22:20 that the tokens of V were not found in
Judg 11:37 mountains, and bewail my V, I and my companions."
11:38 companions, and bewailed her V upon the mountains.
Lk 2:36 seven years from her V,

VIRGINS (11)

Ex 22:17 pay money equivalent to the marriage present for V
Judg 21:12 Jabesh-gilead four hundred young V who had not
Jud 16:5 prey, and take my V as booty.
Esth 2:2 said, "Let beautiful young V be sought out for
2:3 all the beautiful young V to the harem in
2:17 more than all the V, so that he set
2:19 When the V were gathered together the second time,
Is 23:4 have neither reared young men nor brought up V
Lam 5:11 are ravished in Zion, V in the towns of
Amos 8:13 that day the fair V and the young men
2Mac 5:13 children, and slaughter of V and infants.

VIRTUE (8)

Wis 4:1 this is childlessness with V, for in the memory
4:1 in the memory of V is immortality, because it
5:13 had no sign of V to show, but were
2Tim 1:9 holy calling, not in V of our works but
1:9 our works but in V of his own purpose
Tit 3:5 in righteousness, but in V of his own mercy,
2Pet 1:5 supplement your faith with V, and virtue with
1:5 faith with virtue, and V with knowledge,

VIRTUES (2)

Wis 7:20 of plants and the V of roots;
8:7 righteousness, her labors are V; for she teaches

VISAGE

Lam 4:8 Now their V is blacker than soot, they are

VISIBLE (6)

Wis 14:17 away, and made a V image of the king
Dan 4:11 heaven, and it was V to the end of
4:20 heaven, and it was V to the end of
Eph 5:13 the light it becomes V, for anything that becomes
5:13 for anything that becomes V is light.
Col 1:16 heaven and on earth, V and invisible, whether

VISION (82)

Gen 15:1 to Abram in a V, "Fear not, Abram, I
Num 12:6 to him in a V, I speak with him
24:4 God, who sees the V of the Almighty, falling
24:16 High, who sees the V of the Almighty, falling
1Sam 3:1 rare in those days; there was no frequent V
3:15 afraid to tell the V to Eli.
2Sam 7:17 accordance with all this V, Nathan spoke to David.
1Chr 17:15 accordance with all this V, Nathan spoke to David.
2Chr 32:32 are written in the V of Isaiah the prophet
Tob 12:19 eat or drink, but you were seeing a V
Job 20:8 chased away like a V of the night.
33:15 a dream, in a V of the night, when
Ps 89:19 didst speak in a V to thy faithful one,
Sir 34:3 The V of dreams is this against that, the
48:22 commanded, who was great and faithful in his V
49:8 Ezekiel who saw the V of glory which God
Is 1:1 The V of Isaiah the son
21:2 A stern V is told to me; the plunderer
22:1 The oracle concerning the valley of V
22:5 in the valley of V, a battering down of
28:7 drink; they err in V, they stumble in giving
29:7 like a dream, a V of the night.
29:11 And the V of all this has become to
Jer 14:14 to you a lying V, worthless divination, and the
24:1 LORD showed me this V: Behold, two baskets of
38:21 surrender, this is the V which the LORD has
Lam 2:9 her prophets obtain no V from the LORD.
Ezek 7:26 rumor; they seek a V from the prophet, but
8:4 was there, like the V that I saw in
11:24 brought me in the V by the Spirit of
11:24 Then the V that I had seen went up
12:22 grow long, and every V comes to nought?
12:23 are at hand, and the fulfilment of every V
12:24 no more any false V or flattering divination within
12:27 of Israel say, 'The V that he sees is
13:7 not seen a delusive V, and uttered a lying
43:3 And the V I saw was like the vision
43:3 saw was like the V which I had seen
43:3 city, and like the V which I had seen
Dan 2:19 to Daniel in a V of the night.
7:2 "I saw in my V by night, and behold,
8:1 of King Belshazzar a V appeared to me, Daniel,
8:2 I saw in the V; and when I saw,
8:2 I saw in the V, and I was at
8:13 how long is the V concerning the continual burnt
8:15 Daniel, had seen the V, I sought to understand
8:16 it called, "Gabriel, make this man understand the V
8:17 of man, that the V is for the time
8:26 The V of the evenings and the mornings which
8:26 but seal up the V, for it pertains to
8:27 was appalled by the V and did not understand
9:21 had seen in the V at the first, came
9:23 therefore consider the word and understand the V
9:24 righteousness, to seal both V and prophet, and to
10:1 understood the word and had understanding of the V
10:7 Daniel, alone saw the V, for the men who
10:7 did not see the V, but a great trembling
10:8 and saw this great V, and no strength was
10:14 For the V is for days yet to come."
10:16 by reason of the V pains have come upon
11:14 order to fulfil the V; but they shall fail.
Obad 1:1 The V of Obadiah.
Mic 3:6 night to you, without V, and darkness to you,
Nah 1:1 The book of the V of Nah of Elkosh.
Hab 2:2 answered me: "Write the V; make it plain upon
2:3 For still the V awaits its time; it hastens
Zech 13:4 be ashamed of his V when he prophesies; he
2Mac 15:11 dream, a sort of V, which was worthy of
Mt 17:9 "Tell no one the V, until the Son of
Lk 1:22 he had seen a V in the temple; and
24:23 had even seen a V of angels, who said
Acts 9:10 to him in a V, "Ananias." And he said,
10:3 saw clearly in a V an angel of God
10:17 as to what the V which he had seen
10:19 Peter was pondering the V, the Spirit said to
11:5 trance I saw a V, something descending, like a
12:9 was real, but thought he was seeing a V
16:9 And a V appeared to Paul in the night:
16:10 he had seen the V, immediately we sought to
18:9 one night in a V, "Do not be afraid,
26:19 disobedient to the heavenly V,
Rev 9:17 the horses in my V: the riders wore breastplates

VISIONS (29)

Gen 46:2 spoke to Israel in V of the night, and
2Chr 9:29 Shilonite, and in the V of Iddo the seer
Job 4:13 Amid thoughts from V of the night, when deep
7:14 and terrify me with V,
Sir 40:6 is troubled by the V of his mind like
Jer 23:16 vain hopes; they speak V of their own minds,
Lam 2:14 you false and deceptive V; they have not exposed
Ezek 1:1 opened, and I saw V of God.
8:3 and brought me in V of God to Jerusalem,
13:9 prophets who see delusive V and who give lying
13:16 concerning Jerusalem and saw V of peace for her,
13:23 no more see delusive V nor practice divination; I
21:29 see for you false V, while they divine lies
22:28 with whitewash, seeing false V and divining lies for
40:2 brought me in the V of God into the
Dan 1:17 had understanding in all V and dreams.
2:28 Your dream and the V of your head as
4:5 the fancies and the V of my head alarmed
4:10 The V of my head as I lay in
4:13 "I saw in the V of my head as
7:1 had a dream and V of his head as
7:7 saw in the night V, and behold, a fourth
7:13 saw in the night V, and behold, with the
7:15 was anxious and the V of my head alarmed
Hos 12:10 was I who multiplied V, and through the prophets
Joel 2:28 dream dreams, and your young men shall see V
Acts 2:17 young men shall see V, and your old men
2Cor 12:1 will go on to V and revelations of the
Col 2:18 taking his stand on V, puffed up without reason

VISIT (33)

Gen 34:1 Jacob, went out to V the women of the

V

V

15:24 because I feared the people and obeyed their V
19:6 Saul hearkened to the V of Jonathan; Saul swore,
24:16 said, "Is this your V, my son David?" And
24:16 Saul lifted up his V and wept.
25:35 have hearkened to your V, and I have granted
26:17 Saul recognized David's V, and said, "Is this your
26:17 said, "Is this your V, my son David?" And
26:17 said, "It is my V, my lord, O king."
28:12 out with a loud V; and the woman said
28:18 did not obey the V of the LORD, and
2Sam 3:32 king lifted up his V and wept at the
13:36 and lifted up their V and wept; and the
19:4 cried with a loud V, "O my son Absalom,
19:35 still listen to the V of singing men and
22:7 temple he heard my V, and my cry came
22:14 from heaven, and the Most High uttered his V
1Kgs 8:55 Israel with a loud V, saying,
17:22 LORD hearkened to the V of Elijah; and the
18:26 But there was no V, and no one answered.
18:29 but there was no V; no one answered, no
19:12 fire; and after the fire a still small V
19:13 behold, there came a V to him, and said,
20:25 he hearkened to their V, and did so.
20:36 have not obeyed the V of the LORD, behold,
2Kgs 18:12 did not obey the V of the LORD their
18:28 out in a loud V in the language of
19:22 have you raised your V and haughtily lifted your
2Chr 15:14 LORD with a loud V, and with shouting, and
20:19 the God of Israel, with a very loud V
30:27 the people, and their V was heard, and their
32:18 it with a loud V in the language of
Ezra 3:12 wept with a loud V when they saw the
10:12 answered with a loud V, "It is so; we
Neh 9:4 cried with a loud V to the LORD their
Tob 13:6 you; give thanks to him with your full V
Jud 7:24 out with a loud V, and said before all
7:30 out to the Lord God with a loud V
8:17 he will hear our V, if it pleases him.
9:1 Lord with a loud V, and said,
13:12 her city heard her V, they hurried down to
13:14 them with a loud V, "Praise God, O praise
14:16 out with a loud V and wept and groaned
16:14 them; there is none that can resist thy V
Esth 14:19 over all, hear the V of the despairing, and
Job 3:18 they hear not the V of the taskmaster.
4:10 of the lion, the V of the fierce lion,
4:16 then I heard a V:
9:16 not believe that he was listening to my V
29:10 on their mouth; the V of the nobles was
30:31 my pipe to the V of those who weep.
37:2 the thunder of his V and the rumbling that
37:4 After it his V roars; he thunders with his
37:4 thunders with his majestic V and he does not
37:4 the lightnings when his V is heard.
37:5 thunders wondrously with his V; he does great things
38:34 you lift up your V to the clouds, that
40:9 you thunder with a V like his?
Ps 5:3 thou dost hear my V; in the morning I
18:6 temple he heard my V, and my cry to
18:13 Most High uttered his V, hailstones and coals of
19:3 are there words; their V is not heard;
19:4 not heard; yet their V goes out through all
28:2 Hear the V of my supplication, as I cry
28:6 he has heard the V of my supplications.
29:3 The V of the LORD is upon the waters;
29:4 The V of the LORD is powerful, the voice
29:4 LORD is powerful, the V of the LORD is
29:5 The V of the LORD breaks the cedars, the
29:7 The V of the LORD flashes forth flames of
29:8 The V of the LORD shakes the wilderness, the
29:9 The V of the LORD makes the oaks to
46:6 totter; he utters his V, the earth melts.
55:17 complaint and moan, and he will hear my V
58:5 does not hear the V of charmers or of
64:1 Hear my V, O God, in my complaint; preserve
66:19 given heed to the V of my prayer.
68:33 he sends forth his V, his mighty voice.
68:33 lo, he sends forth his voice, his mighty V
81:5 I hear a V I had not known:
81:11 not listen to my V; Israel would have none
93:3 have lifted up their V, the floods lift up
95:7 O that today you would hearken to his V
103:20 word, hearkening to the V of his word!
106:25 did not obey the V of the LORD.
116:1 he has heard my V and my supplications.
119:149 Hear my V in thy steadfast love; O LORD,
130:2 Lord, hear my V
130:2 be attentive to the V of my supplications!
140:6 give ear to the V of my supplications, O
141:1 Give ear to my V, when I call to
142:1 I cry with my V to the LORD, with
142:1 the LORD, with my V I make supplication to
Prov 1:20 markets she raises her V;
2:3 insight and raise your V for understanding,
5:13 not listen to the V of my teachers or
8:1 not wisdom call, does not understanding raise her V
27:14 neighbor with a loud V, rising early in the
Eccl 5:3 business, and a fool's V with many words.
5:6 be angry at your V, and destroy the work
10:20 air will carry your V, or some winged creature
12:4 rises up at the V of a bird, and
Song 2:8 The V of my beloved!
2:12 has come, and the V of the turtledove is
2:14 let me hear your V, for your voice is
2:14 your voice, for your V is sweet, and your
8:13 are listening for your V; let me hear it.
Sir 6:5 A pleasant V multiplies friends, and a gracious
17:11 and their ears heard the glory of his V
21:20 A fool raises his V when he laughs, but
29:5 and will lower his V in speaking of his
34:24 another curses, to whose V will the Lord listen?
39:35 all your heart and V, and bless the name
40:21 melody, but a pleasant V is better than both.
43:17 The V of his thunder rebukes the earth; so
45:5 made him hear his V, and led him into
46:17 heaven, and made his V heard with a mighty
46:20 and lifted up his V out of the earth
Is 6:4 thresholds shook at the V of him who called,
6:8 And I heard the V of the Lord saying,
15:4 Ele-aleh cry out, their V is heard as far
28:23 ear, and hear my V; hearken, and hear my
29:4 words shall come; your V shall come from the
29:4 the ground like the V of a ghost, and
30:30 will cause his majestic V to be heard and
30:31 be terror-stricken at the V of the LORD, when
32:9 at ease, hear my V; you complacent daughters, give
36:13 out in a loud V in the language of
37:23 have you raised your V and haughtily lifted your
40:3 A V cries: "In the wilderness prepare the way
40:6 A V says, "Cry!" And I said, "What shall
40:9 tidings; lift up your V with strength, O Jerusalem,
42:2 or lift up his V, or make it heard
42:11 cities lift up their V, the villages that Kedar
50:10 LORD and obeys the V of his servant, who
51:3 her, thanksgiving and the V of song.
52:8 watchmen lift up their V, together they sing for
58:1 not, lift up your V like a trumpet; declare
58:4 will not make your V to be heard on
66:6 A V from the temple!
66:6 The V of the LORD, rendering recompense to his
Jer 3:13 have not obeyed my V, says the LORD.
3:21 A V on the bare heights is heard, the
3:25 have not obeyed the V of the LORD our
4:15 For a V declares from Dan and proclaims evil
7:23 gave them, 'Obey my V, and I will be
7:28 did not obey the V of the LORD their
7:34 streets of Jerusalem the V of mirth and the
7:34 of mirth and the V of gladness, the voice
7:34 voice of gladness, the V of the bridegroom and
7:34 the bridegroom and the V of the bride; for
9:13 have not obeyed my V, or walked in accord
10:13 When he utters his V there is a tumult
11:4 saying, Listen to my V, and do all that
11:7 persistently, even to this day, saying, Obey my V
12:8 has lifted up her V against me; therefore I
16:9 in your days, the V of mirth and the
16:9 of mirth and the V of gladness, the voice
16:9 voice of gladness, the V of the bridegroom and
16:9 the bridegroom and the V of the bride.
18:10 not listening to my V, then I will repent
22:20 and lift up your V in Bashan; cry from
22:21 your youth, that you have not obeyed my V
25:10 banish from them the V of mirth and the
25:10 of mirth and the V of gladness, the voice
25:10 voice of gladness, the V of the bridegroom and
25:10 the bridegroom and the V of the bride, the
25:30 holy habitation utter his V; he will roar mightily
26:13 doings, and obey the V of the LORD your
31:15 says the LORD: "A V is heard in Ramah,
31:16 the LORD: "Keep your V from weeping, and your
32:23 did not obey thy V or walk in thy
33:11 be heard again the V of mirth and the

V

V

	21:3	I heard a loud V from the throne saying,

VOICES (23)

Judg	2:4	people lifted up their V and wept.
	21:2	they lifted up their V and wept bitterly.
Ruth	1:9	they lifted up their V and wept.
	1:14	they lifted up their V and wept again; and
1Sam	30:4	with him raised their V and wept, until they
Jud	16:11	they lifted up their V, and the enemy were
Job	2:12	and they raised their V and wept; and they
Wis	18:1	Their enemies heard their V but did not see
Sir	47:9	the altar, to make sweet melody with their V
	50:18	praised him with their V in sweet and full-toned
Is	24:14	They lift up their V, they sing for joy;
Jer	30:19	of thanksgiving, and the V of those who make
	33:11	of the bride, the V of those who sing,
Lk	17:13	and lifted up their V and said, "Jesus, Master,
	23:22	And their V prevailed.
Acts	4:24	it, they lifted their V together to God and
	14:11	they lifted up their V, saying in Lycaonian, "The
	22:22	they lifted up their V and said, "Away with
Rev	4:5	flashes of lightning, and V and peals of thunder,
	8:5	were peals of thunder, V, flashes of lightning, and
	11:15	and there were loud V in heaven, saying, "The
	11:19	were flashes of lightning, V, peals of thunder, an
	16:18	were flashes of lightning, V, peals of thunder, and

VOID (16)

Gen	1:2	was without form and V, and darkness was upon
Num	6:12	former time shall be V, because his separation was
	30:8	then he shall make V her vow which was
	30:12	makes them null and V on the day that
	30:12	husband has made them V, and the LORD will
	30:13	husband may establish, or her husband may make V
	30:15	makes them null and V after he has heard
Deut	32:28	they are a nation V of counsel, and there
Job	26:7	the north over the V, and hangs the earth
Jer	4:23	it was waste and V; and to the heavens,
	19:7	place I will make V the plans of Judah
Mt	15:6	tradition, you have made V the word of God.
Mk	7:13	or mother, thus making V the word of God
Lk	16:17	for one dot of the law to become V
Rom	4:14	heirs, faith is null and the promise is V
Gal	3:17	by God, so as to make the promise V

VOLUMES

2Mac	2:23	of Cyrene in five V, we shall attempt to

VOLUNTARILY

Deut	23:23	lips, for you have V vowed to the LORD

VOLUNTEER

2Chr	17:16	son of Zichri, a V for the service of

VOMIT (10)

Lev	18:28	defiled); lest the land V you out, when you
	20:22	to dwell may not V you out.
Prov	23:8	You will V up the morsels which you have
	25:16	sated with it and V it.
	26:11	that returns to his V is a fool that
Is	19:14	doings as a drunken man staggers in his V
	28:8	tables are full of V, no place is without
Jer	25:27	Drink, be drunk and V, fall and rise no
	48:26	shall wallow in his V, and he too shall
2Pet	2:22	back to his own V, and the sow is

VOMITED (3)

Lev	18:25	iniquity, and the land V out its inhabitants.
	18:28	defile it, as it V out the nation that
Jon	2:10	the fish, and it V out Jonah upon the

VOMITS

Job	20:15	swallows down riches and V them up again; God

VOPHSI

Num	13:14	Nahbi the son of V;

VOTE (4)

2Mac	10:8	by public ordinance and V that the whole nation
	12:4	was done by public V of the city.
	15:36	all decreed by public V never to let this
Acts	26:10	death I cast my V against them.

VOTIVE (17)

Lev	7:16	his offering is a V offering or a freewill
	22:23	offering; but for a V offering it cannot be
	23:38	and besides all your V offerings, and besides all
Num	29:39	in addition to your V offerings and your freewill
Deut	12:6	you present, your V offerings, your freewill offerings,
	12:11	present, and all your V offerings which you vow
	12:17	or any of your V offerings which you vow,
	12:26	from you, and your V offerings, you shall take,
1Kgs	15:15	of the LORD the V gifts of his father
	15:15	father and his own V gifts, silver, and gold,
2Kgs	12:18	Judah took all the V gifts that Jehoshaphat and
	12:18	dedicated, and his own V gifts, and all the
2Chr	15:18	house of God the V gifts of his father
	15:18	father and his own V gifts, silver, and gold,
Jud	16:19	she gave as a V offering to the Lord.
2Mac	2:13	letters of kings about V offerings.
	5:16	with profane hands the V offerings which other kings

VOUCHES

Job	16:19	heaven, and he that V for me is on

VOW (43)

Gen	28:20	Then Jacob made a V, saying, "If God will
	31:13	pillar and made a V to me.
Lev	22:18	in payment of a V or as a freewill
	22:21	LORD, to fulfil a V or as a freewill
	27:2	man makes a special V of persons to the
Num	6:2	woman makes a special V, the vow of a
	6:2	a special vow, the V of a Nazirite, to
	6:5	the days of his V of separation no razor
	6:21	the law for the Nazirite who takes a V
	6:21	be according to his V as a Nazirite, apart
	6:21	in accordance with the V which he takes, so
	15:3	sacrifice, to fulfil a V or as a freewill
	15:8	sacrifice, to fulfil a V, or for peace offerings
	21:2	And Israel vowed a V to the LORD, and
	30:2	a man vows a V to the LORD, or
	30:3	a woman vows a V to the LORD, and
	30:4	father hears of her V and of her pledge
	30:5	hears of it, no V of hers, no pledge
	30:8	shall make void her V which was on her,
	30:9	But any V of a widow or of a
	30:13	Any V and any binding oath to afflict herself,
Deut	12:11	votive offerings which you V to the LORD.
	12:17	offerings which you V, or your freewill offerings,
	23:18	in payment for any V; for both of these
	23:21	"When you make a V to the LORD your
Judg	11:30	And Jephthah made a V to the LORD, and
	11:35	the LORD, and I cannot take back my V
	11:39	her according to his V which he had made.
1Sam	1:11	And she vowed a V and said, "O LORD
	1:21	LORD the yearly sacrifice, and to pay his V
2Sam	15:7	go and pay my V, which I have vowed
	15:8	your servant vowed a V while I dwelt at
Eccl	5:4	When you V a vow to God, do not
	5:4	When you vow a V to God, do not
	5:4	Pay what you V
	5:5	that you should not V than that you should
	5:5	than that you should V and not pay.
Sir	18:21	you from paying a V promptly, and do not
	18:22	Before making a V, prepare yourself; and do not
Bar	6:35	if one makes a V to them and does
2Mac	9:13	abominable fellow made a V to the Lord, who
Acts	18:18	he cut his hair, for he had a V
	21:23	who are under a V;

VOWED (13)

Lev	27:8	ability of him who V the priest shall value
Num	21:2	And Israel V a vow to the LORD, and
	30:10	And if she V in her husband's house, or
Deut	23:23	for you have voluntarily V to the LORD your
1Sam	1:11	And she V a vow and said, "O LORD
2Sam	15:7	vow, which I have V to the LORD, in
	15:8	For your servant V a vow while I dwelt
Ezra	7:16	people and the priests, V willingly for the house
Ps	132:2	to the LORD and V to the Mighty One
Jer	44:17	everything that we have V, burn incense to the
Jon	2:9	thee; what I have V I will pay.
1Mac	5:5	he encamped against them, V their complete
Mk	6:23	And he V to her, "Whatever you ask me,

VOWING

Deut	23:22	if you refrain from V, it shall be no

VOWS (33)

Num	30:2	When a man V a vow to the LORD,
	30:3	Or when a woman V a vow to the
	30:4	her; then all her V shall stand, and every

V

30:6 husband, while under her V or any thoughtless
30:7 he hears; then her V shall stand, and her
30:11 her; then all her V shall stand, and every
30:12 her lips concerning her V, or concerning her pledge
30:14 he establishes all her V, or all her pledges,
Jud 4:14 burnt offerings and the V and freewill offerings of
Job 22:27 will hear you; and you will pay your V
Ps 22:25 the great congregation; my V I will pay before
50:14 thanksgiving, and pay your V to the Most High;
56:12 My V to thee I must perform, O God;
61:5 God, hast heard my V, thou hast given me
61:8 as I pay my V day after day.
65:1 and to thee shall V be performed,
66:13 will pay thee my V,
76:11 Make your V to the LORD your God, and
116:14 I will pay my V to the LORD in
116:18 I will pay my V to the LORD in
Prov 7:14 I have paid my V;
20:25 and to reflect only after making his V
31:2 What, son of my V
Sir 23:18 who breaks his marriage V says to himself, "Who
Is 19:21 and they will make V to the LORD and
Jer 11:15 Can V and sacrificial flesh avert your doom?
44:25 will surely perform our V that we have made,
44:25 her.' Then confirm your V and perform your vows!
44:25 her.' Then confirm your vows and perform your V
Jon 1:16 offered a sacrifice to the LORD and made V
Nah 1:15 O Judah, fulfil your V, for never again shall
Mal 1:14 in his flock, and V it, and yet sacrifices
2Mac 3:35 and made very great V to the Savior of

VOYAGE (5)
Wis 14:1 sail and about to V over raging waves calls
Acts 16:11 we made a direct V to Samothrace, and the
21:7 we had finished the V from Tyre, we arrived
27:9 been lost, and the V was already dangerous because
27:10 I perceive that the V will be with injury

VULGAR
2Sam 6:20 as one of the V fellows shamelessly uncovers

VULGARITY
Sir 23:13 your mouth to lewd V, for it involves sinful

VULTURE (7)
Lev 11:13 abomination: the eagle, the V, the osprey,
11:18 the pelican, the carrion V,
Deut 14:12 eat: the eagle, the V, the osprey,
14:17 the pelican, the carrion V and the cormorant,
Ps 102:6 I am like a V of the wilderness, like
Hos 8:1 your lips, for a V is over the house
Zeph 2:14 of the field; the V and the hedgehog shall

VULTURES (2)
Prov 30:17 ravens of the valley and eaten by the V
Lam 4:19 were swifter than the V in the heavens; they

W

WAFER (3)
Ex 29:23 with oil, and one W, out of the basket
Lev 8:26 with oil, and one W, and placed them on
Num 6:19 basket, and one unleavened W, and shall put them

WAFERS (6)
Ex 16:31 of it was like W made with honey.
29:2 with oil, and unleavened W spread with oil.
Lev 2:4 with oil, or unleavened W spread with oil.
7:12 mixed with oil, unleavened W spread with oil, and
Num 6:15 with oil, and unleavened W spread with oil, and
1Chr 23:29 the cereal offering, the W of unleavened bread, the

WAFTED
Song 4:16 let its fragrance be W abroad.

WAG (4)
Ps 22:7 mouths at me, they W their heads;
64:8 who see them will W their heads.
109:25 they see me, they W their heads.
Lam 2:15 you; they hiss and W their heads at the

WAGE (15)
2Kgs 16:5 Israel, came up to W war on Jerusalem, and
Ps 55:18 the battle that I W, for many are arrayed
Prov 10:16 The W of the righteous leads to life, the
20:18 counsel; by wise guidance W war.
24:6 wise guidance you can W your war, and in
Is 7:1 up to Jerusalem to W war against it, but
Dan 11:10 "His sons shall W war and assemble a multitude
11:25 of the south shall W war with an exceedingly
Zech 8:10 days there was no W for man or any
8:10 for man or any W for beast, neither was
14:12 all the peoples that W war against Jerusalem: their
1Mac 12:24 force than before, to W war against him.
1Tim 1:18 by them you may W the good warfare,
Jas 4:2 so you fight and W war.
1Pet 2:11 of the flesh that W war against your soul.

WAGED (4)
1Chr 22:8 much blood and have W great wars; you shall
Sir 46:3 For he W the wars of the Lord.
1Mac 3:3 armor of war and W battles, protecting the host
12:13 round about us have W war against us.

WAGER (2)
2Kgs 18:23 Come now, make a W with my master the
Is 36:8 Come now, make a W with my master the

WAGES (40)
Gen 29:15 me, what shall your W be?"
30:28 of you; name your W, and I will give
30:32 among the goats; and such shall be my W
30:33 to look into my W with you.
31:7 me and changed my W ten times, but God
31:8 spotted shall be your W then all the flock
31:8 striped shall be your W then all the flock
31:41 you have changed my W ten times.
Ex 2:9 for me, and I will give you your W
Lev 19:13 The W of a hired servant shall not remain
Deut 23:18 a harlot, or the W of a dog, into
1Kgs 5:6 for your servants such W as you set; for
Tob 2:12 when they paid her W, they also gave her
2:14 me as a gift in addition to my W
4:14 the next day the W of any man who
5:3 I will pay him W as long as I
5:14 But tell me, what W am I to pay
5:15 will add to your W if you both return
12:1 son, see to the W of the man who
Job 7:2 who looks for his W,
Prov 11:18 wicked man earns deceptive W, but one who sows
Wis 2:22 nor hope for the W of holiness, nor discern
Sir 34:22 an employee of his W is to shed blood.
Jer 22:13 not give him his W;
Ezek 29:19 it shall be the W for his army.
Hag 1:6 and he who earns W earns wages to put
1:6 who earns wages earns W to put them into
Zech 11:12 you, give me my W; but if not, keep
11:12 weighed out as my W thirty shekels of silver.
Mal 3:5 the hireling in his W, the widow and the
1Mac 14:32 men of his nation's forces and paid them W
Mt 20:8 and pay them their W, beginning with the last,
Lk 3:14 by false accusation, and be content with your W
10:7 the laborer deserves his W; do not go from
Jn 4:36 He who reaps receives W, and gathers fruit for
Rom 4:4 one who works, his W are not reckoned as
6:23 For the W of sin is death, but the
1Cor 3:8 each shall receive his W according to his labor.
1Tim 5:18 and, "The laborer deserves his W
Jas 5:4 Behold, the W of the laborers who mowed your

WAGGED
Jer 48:27 spoke of him you W your head?

WAGGING (2)
Mt 27:39 passed by derided him, W their heads
Mk 15:28 passed by derided him, W their heads, and saying,

WAGON
Num 7:3 and twelve oxen, a W for every two of

WAGONS (10)
Gen 45:19 also, 'Do this: take W from the land of
45:21 and Joseph gave them W, according to the command
45:27 when he saw the W which Joseph had sent
46:5 their wives, in the W which Pharaoh had sent
Num 7:3 the LORD, six covered W and twelve oxen, a
7:6 So Moses took the W and the oxen, and
7:7 Two W and four oxen he gave to the
7:8 their service; and four W and eight oxen he
Ezek 23:24 north with chariots and W and a host of

26:10 of the horsemen and W and chariots, when he

WAGS (2)
2Kgs 19:21 daughter of Zion; she W her head behind you–
Is 37:22 daughter of Zion; she W her head behind you–

WAHEB
Num 21:14 Wars of the LORD, W in Suphah, and the

WAIL (36)
Is 13:6 W, for the day of the LORD is near;
14:31 W, O gate; cry, O city; melt in fear,
16:7 Therefore let Moab W, let every one wail for
16:7 wail, let every one W for Moab.
23:1 W, O ships of Tarshish, for Tyre is laid
23:6 Pass over to Tarshish, W, O inhabitants of the
23:14 W, O ships of Tarshish, for your stronghold is
52:5 Their rulers W, says the LORD, and continually all
65:14 of heart, and shall W for anguish of spirit.
Jer 4:8 with sackcloth, lament and W; for the fierce anger
25:34 W, you shepherds, and cry, and roll in ashes,
25:36 the shepherds, and the W of the lords of
47:2 out, and every inhabitant of the land shall W
48:20 for it is broken; W and cry!
48:31 Therefore I W for Moab; I cry out for
48:39 How they W
49:3 W, O Heshbon, for Ai is laid waste!
51:8 fallen and been broken; W for her!
Ezek 21:12 Cry and W, son of man, for it is
27:30 on the shore and W aloud over you, and
30:2 says the Lord GOD: W, 'Alas for the day!'
32:18 me: "Son of man, W over the multitude of
Hos 7:15 the heart, but they W upon their beds; for
10:5 its idolatrous priests shall W over it, over its
Joel 1:5 drunkards, and weep; and W, all you drinkers of
1:10 tillers of the soil, W, O vinedressers, for the
1:12 and lament, O priests, W, O ministers of the
Mic 1:8 I will lament and W; I will go stripped
2:4 song against you, and W with bitter lamentation, and
Zeph 1:10 the Fish Gate, a W from the Second Quarter,
1:11 W, O inhabitants of the Mortar!
Zech 11:2 W, O cypress, for the cedar has fallen, for
11:2 W, oaks of Bashan, for the thick forest has
11:3 Hark, the W of the shepherds, for their glory
Rev 1:7 of the earth will W on account of him.
18:9 her, will weep and W over her when they

WAILED (2)
Mt 11:17 did not dance; we W, and you did not
Lk 7:32 did not dance; we W, and you did not

WAILING (14)
Esth 4:1 midst of the city, W with a loud and
Sir 38:17 be bitter and your W fervent; observe the mourning
Is 15:8 land of Moab; the W reaches to Eglaim, the
15:8 reaches to Eglaim, the W reaches to Beer-elim.
Jer 9:10 "Take up weeping and W for the mountains, and
9:18 haste and raise a W over us, that our
9:19 For a sound of W is heard from Zion:
Ezek 27:32 In their W they raise a lamentation for you,
Amos 5:16 squares there shall be W; and in all the
5:16 to mourning and to W those who are skilled
5:17 vineyards there shall be W, for I will pass
Mic 1:11 not come forth; the W of Beth-ezel shall take
Mt 2:18 heard in Ramah, W and loud lamentation, Rachel
Mk 5:38 and people weeping and W loudly.

WAILINGS
Amos 8:3 the temple shall become W in that day," says

WAILS (2)
Is 15:2 to weep; over Nebo and over Medeba Moab W
15:3 the squares every one W and melts in tears.

WAIST (3)
Is 11:5 the girdle of his W, and faithfulness the girdle
Mt 3:4 leather girdle around his W; and his food was
Mk 1:6 leather girdle around his W, and ate locusts and

WAISTCLOTH (10)
Job 12:18 kings, and binds a W on their loins.
Is 5:27 or sleeps, not a W is loose, not a
Jer 13:1 and buy a linen W, and put it on
13:2 So I bought a W according to the word
13:4 second time, "Take the W which you have bought,
13:6 take from there the W which I commanded you
13:7 and I took the W from the place where
13:7 And behold, the W was spoiled; it was good
13:10 shall be like this W, which is good for
13:11 For as the W clings to the loins of

WAIT (116)
Gen 49:18 I W for thy salvation, O LORD.
Ex 7:15 out to the water; W for him by the
8:20 in the morning and W for Pharaoh, as he
21:13 did not lie in W for him, but God
24:12 on the mountain, and W there; and I will
Num 9:8 Moses said to them, W, that I may hear
35:20 at him, lying in W, so that he died,
35:22 him without lying in W,
Deut 19:11 neighbor, and lies in W for him, and attacks
Judg 9:32 you, and lie in W in the fields.
9:34 by night, and laid W against Shechem in four
9:43 three companies, and laid W in the fields; and
16:2 place and lay in W for him all night
16:2 night, saying, "Let us W till the light of
16:9 had men lying in W in an inner chamber.
16:12 the men lying in W were in an inner
21:20 "Go and lie in W in the vineyards,
Ruth 1:13 sons, would you therefore W till they were grown?
3:18 She replied, W, my daughter, until you learn how
1Sam 1:23 seems best to you, W until you have weaned
10:8 Seven days you shall W, until I come to
14:9 they say to us, W until we come to
15:5 Amalek, and lay in W in the valley.
22:8 me, to lie in W, as at this day."
22:13 me, to lie in W, as at this day?"
2Sam 15:28 See, I will W at the fords of the
1Kgs 1:2 king, and let her W upon the king, and
2Kgs 6:33 Why should I W for the LORD any longer?"
7:9 we are silent and W until the morning light,
Tob 2:2 Lord, and I will W for you."
5:7 Tobias said to him, W for me, and I
Jud 8:17 Therefore, while we W for his deliverance, let us
13:3 the bedchamber and to W for her to come
15:2 that they did not W for one another, but
Job 6:11 What is my strength, that I should W
14:14 my service I would W, till my release should
31:9 I have lain in W at my neighbor's door;
32:16 And shall I W, because they do not speak,
38:40 dens, or lie in W in their covert?
Ps 25:3 Yea, let none that W for thee be put
25:5 salvation; for thee I W all the day long.
25:21 preserve me, for I W for thee.
27:14 W for the LORD; be strong, and let your
27:14 heart take courage; yea, W for the LORD!
31:24 courage, all you who W for the LORD!
37:7 before the LORD, and W patiently for him; fret
37:9 off; but those who W for the LORD shall
37:34 W for the LORD, and keep to his way,
38:15 O LORD, do I W; it is thou, O
39:7 "And now, Lord, for what do I W
59:3 lo, they lie in W for my life; fierce
106:13 works; they did not W for his counsel.
119:95 The wicked lie in W to destroy me; but
130:5 I W for the LORD, my soul waits, and
Prov 1:11 let us lie in W for blood, let us
1:18 these men lie in W for their own blood,
7:12 market, and at every corner she lies in W
12:6 the wicked lie in W for blood, but the
20:22 "I will repay evil"; W for the LORD, and
23:28 She lies in W like a robber and increases
24:15 Lie not in W as a wicked man against
Wis 2:12 "Let us lie in W for the righteous man,
8:12 am silent they will W for me, and when
10:12 those who lay in W for him; in his
Sir 2:7 who fear the Lord, W for his mercy; and
6:19 plows and sows, and W for her good harvest.
11:29 for he lies in W, turning good into evil,
11:30 a sinner lies in W to shed blood.
14:22 hunter, and lie in W on her paths.
18:21 promptly, and do not W until death to be
27:10 A lion lies in W for prey; so does
27:28 but vengeance lies in W for him like a
28:26 lest you fall before him who lies in W
29:8 do not make him W for your alms.
36:16 Reward those who W for thee, and let thy
51:8 dost deliver those who W for thee and dost
Is 8:17 I will W for the LORD, who is hiding
26:8 judgments, O LORD, we W for thee; thy memorial
30:18 are all those who W for him.
33:2 gracious to us; we W for thee.

40:31 exhausted; but they who W for the LORD shall
42:4 earth; and the coastlands W for his law.
49:23 the LORD; those who W for me shall not
51:5 the peoples; the coastlands W for me, and for
60:9 For the coastlands shall W for me, the ships
64:4 works for those who W for him.
Jer 5:26 my people; they lurk like fowlers lying in W
Lam 3:10 a bear lying in W, like a lion in
3:25 good to those who W for him, to the
3:26 good that one should W quietly for the salvation
4:19 mountains, they lay in W for us in the
Hos 6:9 As robbers lie in W for a man, so
12:6 love and justice, and W continually for your God."
Mic 1:12 inhabitants of Maroth W anxiously for good, because
5:7 not for men nor W for the sons of
7:2 they all lie in W for blood, and each
7:7 the LORD, I will W for the God of
Hab 2:3 If it seem slow, W for it; it will
3:16 I will quietly W for the day of trouble
Zeph 3:8 "Therefore W for me," says the LORD, "for the
1Mac 5:3 they kept lying in W for Israel.
Mt 27:49 But the others said, W, let us see whether
Mk 15:35 him to drink, saying, W, let us see whether
Lk 11:54 many things, lying in W for him, to catch
Acts 1:4 from Jerusalem, but to W for the promise of
22:16 And now why do you W
Rom 8:23 groan inwardly as we W for adoption as sons,
8:25 do not see, we W for it with patience.
1Cor 1:7 spiritual gift, as you W for the revealing of
11:33 come together to eat, W for one another--
Gal 5:5 Spirit, by faith, we W for the hope of
1Thes 1:10 true God, and to W for his Son from
Heb 10:13 of God, then to W until his enemies should
2Pet 3:13 to his promise we W for new heavens and
3:14 Therefore, beloved, since you W for these, be zealous
Jude 1:21 the love of God; W for the mercy of

WAITED (24)

Gen 8:10 He W another seven days, and again he sent
8:12 Then he W another seven days, and sent forth
40:4 with them, and he W on them; and they
Judg 3:25 And they W till they were utterly at a
1Sam 13:8 He W seven days, the time appointed by Samuel;
25:9 in the name of David; and then they W
1Kgs 20:38 the prophet departed, and W for the king by
2Kgs 5:2 of Israel, and she W on Naaman's wife.
Jud 6:10 ordered his slaves, who W on him in his
10:18 around her as she W outside the tent of
Job 29:21 listened to me, and W, and kept silence for
29:23 They W for me as for the rain; and
30:26 came; and when I W for light, darkness came.
32:4 Now Elihu had W to speak to Job because
32:11 my opinion.' "Behold, I W for your words, I
Ps 40:1 I W patiently for the LORD; he inclined to
56:6 As they have W for my life,
Is 25:9 our God; we have W for him, that he
25:9 the LORD; we have W for him; let us
2Mac 5:25 be peaceably disposed and W until the holy sabbath
Acts 10:7 from among those that W on him,
28:6 They W, expecting him to swell up or suddenly
28:6 but when they had W a long time and
1Pet 3:20 obey, when God's patience W in the days of

WAITING (18)

Ex 5:20 and Aaron, who were W for them, as they
2Sam 17:17 Jonathan and Ahima-az were W at En-rogel; a
Jud 12:16 for he had been W for an opportunity to
Job 35:14 him, and you are W for him!
Ps 69:3 eyes grow dim with W for my God.
Prov 8:34 daily at my gates, W beside my doors.
Sir 4:1 his living, and do not keep needy eyes W
Dan 13:59 angel of God is W with his sword to
2Mac 7:30 said, "What are you W for?
9:25 watching for opportunities and W to see what will
Lk 1:21 And the people were W for Zechariah, and they
8:40 for they were all W for him.
12:36 like men who are W for their master to
Acts 17:16 Now while Paul was W for them at Athens,
20:5 went on and were W for us at Troas,
23:21 now they are ready, W for the promise from
Heb 9:28 those who are eagerly W for him.
2Pet 3:12 of holiness and godliness, W for and hastening the

WAITS (11)

Job 24:15 of the adulterer also W for the twilight, saying,
Ps 33:20 Our soul W for the LORD; he is our
62:1 God alone my soul W in silence; from him
62:5 God alone my soul W in silence, for my
130:5 the LORD, my soul W, and in his word
130:6 I hope; my soul W for the LORD more
Is 30:18 Therefore the LORD W to be gracious to you;
Dan 12:12 Blessed is he who W and comes to the
2Mac 6:14 other nations the Lord W patiently to punish them
Rom 8:19 For the creation W with eager longing for the
Jas 5:7 Behold, the farmer W for the precious fruit of

WAKE (7)

Jud 14:13 all his personal affairs, W up our lord, for
Job 41:32 he leaves a shining W; one would think the
Ps 3:5 down and sleep; I W again, for the LORD
Jer 51:39 perpetual sleep and not W, says the LORD.
51:57 perpetual sleep and not W, says the King, whose
Rom 13:11 now for you to W from sleep.
1Thes 5:10 so that whether we W or sleep we might

WAKED

Zech 4:1 me came again, and W me, like a man

WAKEFUL (2)

Sir 31:2 W anxiety prevents slumber, and a severe illness
42:9 keeps her father secretly W, and worry over her

WAKEFULNESS

Sir 31:1 W over wealth wastes away one's flesh, and anxiety

WAKENED (2)

Zech 4:1 a man that is W out of his sleep.
Lk 9:32 sleep, and when they W they saw his glory

WAKENS (2)

Is 50:4 Morning by morning he W, he wakens my ear
50:4 morning he wakens, he W my ear to hear

WAKES

Sir 40:7 of his rescue he W up, and wonders that

WALK (173)

Gen 13:17 Arise, W through the length and the breadth of
17:1 "I am God Almighty; W before me, and be
24:40 LORD, before whom I W, will send his angel
Ex 16:4 them, whether they will W in my law or
18:20 in which they must W and what they must
Lev 18:3 You shall not W in their statutes.
18:4 keep my statutes and W in them.
20:23 And you shall not W in the customs of
26:3 "If you W in my statutes and observe my
26:12 And I will W among you, and will be
26:13 yoke and made you W erect.
26:21 "Then if you W contrary to me, and will
26:23 turned to me, but W contrary to me,
26:24 then I also will W contrary to you, and
26:27 hearken to me, but W contrary to me,
26:28 me, then I will W contrary to you in
Deut 5:33 You shall W in all the way which the
6:7 house, and when you W by the way, and
10:12 LORD your God, to W in all his ways,
13:4 You shall W after the LORD your God and
13:5 which the LORD your God commanded you to W
26:17 and that you will W in his ways, and
28:9 LORD your God, and W in his ways.
29:19 be safe, though I W in the stubbornness of
Josh 22:5 your God, and to W in all his ways,
Judg 2:22 will take care to W in the way of
5:10 carpets and you who W by the way.
1Sam 8:3 his sons did not W in his ways, but
8:5 your sons do not W in your ways; now
1Kgs 2:4 to their way, to W before me in faithfulness
3:14 And if you will W in my ways, keeping
6:12 building, if you will W in my statutes and
6:12 all my commandments and W in them, then I
8:23 to thy servants who W before thee with all
8:25 to their way, to W before me as you
8:36 in which they should W; and grant rain upon
8:58 hearts to him, to W in all his ways,
9:4 you, if you will W before me, as David
11:38 command you, and will W in my ways, and
16:31 thing for him to W in the sins of
2Kgs 10:31 was not careful to W in the law of
21:22 fathers, and did not W in the way of
23:3 before the LORD, to W after the LORD and
2Chr 6:14 to thy servants who W before thee with all
6:16 to their way, to W in my law as

6:27 in which they should W; and grant rain upon
6:31 may fear thee and W in thy ways all
7:17 for you, if you W before me, as David
34:31 before the LORD, to W after the LORD and
Neh 5:9 Ought you not to W in the fear of
10:29 and an oath to W in God's law which
Tob 3:5 For we did not W in truth before thee.
4:5 life, and do not W in the ways of
Ps 23:4 Even though I W through the valley of the
26:3 my eyes, and I W in faithfulness to thee.
26:11 as for me, I W in my integrity; redeem
37:14 to slay those who W uprightly;
48:12 W about Zion, go round about her, number her
56:13 falling, that I may W before God in the
78:10 covenant, but refused to W according to his law.
81:13 me, that Israel would W in my ways!
82:5 knowledge nor understanding, they W about in
84:11 withhold from those who W uprightly.
86:11 LORD, that I may W in thy truth; unite
89:15 the festal shout, who W, O LORD, in the
89:30 law and do not W according to my ordinances,
101:2 I will W with integrity of heart within my
115:7 feet, but do not W; and they do not
116:9 feet from stumbling; I W before the LORD in
119:1 way is blameless, who W in the law of
119:3 do no wrong, but W in his ways!
119:45 ever; and I shall W at liberty, for I
138:7 Though I W in the midst of trouble, thou
142:3 the path where I W they have hidden a
Prov 1:15 my son, do not W in the way with
2:7 shield to those who W in integrity,
2:13 paths of uprightness to W in the ways of
2:20 So you will W in the way of good
3:23 Then you will W on your way securely and
4:13 When you W, your step will not be hampered;
4:15 wicked, and do not W in the way of
6:22 When you W, they will lead you; when you
6:28 Or can one W upon hot coals and his
8:20 I W in the way of righteousness, in the
9:6 simpleness, and live, and W in the way of
Eccl 11:9 days of your youth; W in the ways of
Wis 6:4 keep the law, nor W according to the purpose
Sir 4:17 at first she will W with him on tortuous
Is 2:3 and that we may W in his paths." For
2:5 Jacob, come, let us W in the light of
3:16 Zion are haughty and W with outstretched necks,
8:11 warned me not to W in the way of
30:21 "This is the way, W in it," when you
35:9 but the redeemed shall W there.
40:31 be weary, they shall W and not faint.
42:5 spirit to those who W in it:
42:24 ways they would not W, and whose law they
43:2 overwhelm you; when you W through fire you shall
50:11 W by the light of your fire, and by
57:2 in their beds who W in their uprightness.
59:9 for brightness, but we W in gloom.
65:2 a rebellious people, who W in a way that
Jer 6:16 good way is; and W in it, and find
6:16 said, 'We will not W in it.'
6:25 into the field, nor W on the road; for
7:23 be my people; and W in all the way
10:5 they have to be carried, for they cannot W
23:14 they commit adultery and W in lies; they strengthen
26:4 listen to me, to W in my law which
31:9 I will make them W by brooks of water,
32:23 obey thy voice or W in thy law; they
44:23 of the LORD or W in his law and
Lam 4:18 that we could not W in our streets; our
Bar 1:18 Lord our God, to W in the statutes of
2:10 obeyed his voice, to W in the statutes of
4:2 Jacob, and take her; W toward the shining of
4:13 statutes; they did not W in the ways of
5:7 so that Israel may W safely in the glory
Ezek 11:20 flesh, that they may W in my statutes and
16:47 were not content to W in their ways, or
20:13 wilderness; they did not W in my statutes but
20:16 ordinances and did not W in my statutes, and
20:18 the wilderness, Do not W in the statutes of
20:19 LORD am your God; W in my statutes, and
20:21 me; they did not W in my statutes, and
36:12 I will let men W upon you, even my
36:27 and cause you to W in my statutes and
Dan 4:37 just; and those who W in pride he is
13:7 Susanna would go into her husband's garden to W
Hos 11:3 who taught Ephraim to W, I took them up
14:9 right, and the upright W in them, but transgressors
Amos 3:3 "Do two W together, unless they have made an
Mic 2:3 and you shall not W haughtily, for it will
4:2 ways and we may W in his paths." For
4:5 For all the peoples W each in the name
4:5 god, but we will W in the name of
6:8 love kindness, and to W humbly with your God?
Zeph 1:17 so that they shall W like the blind, because
Zech 3:7 hosts: If you will W in my ways and
2Mac 5:21 on the land and W on the sea, because
6:7 they were compelled to W in the procession in
Mt 9:5 sins are forgiven,' or to say, 'Rise and W
11:5 sight and the lame W, lepers are cleansed and
Mk 2:9 to say,' Rise, take up your pallet and W
Lk 5:23 are forgiven you,' or to say, 'Rise and W
7:22 their sight, the lame W, lepers are cleansed, and
11:44 not seen, and men W over them without knowing
24:17 you are holding with each other as you W
Jn 5:7 to him, "Rise, take up your pallet, and W
5:10 said to me, 'Take up your pallet, and W
5:11 said to you, 'Take up your pallet, and W
8:12 follows me will not W in darkness, but will
12:35 W while you have the light, lest the darkness
Acts 3:6 in the name of Jesus Christ of Nazareth, W
3:12 own power or piety we had made him W
14:16 all the nations to W in their own ways;
Rom 6:4 Father, we too might W in newness of life.
8:4 fulfilled in us, who W not according to the
2Cor 5:7 the Lord, for we W by faith, not by
Gal 5:16 But I say, W by the Spirit, and do
5:25 Spirit, let us also W by the Spirit.
6:16 be upon all who W by this rule, upon
Eph 2:10 beforehand, that we should W in them.
5:2 And W in love, as Christ loved us and
5:8 light in the Lord; W as children of light
5:15 carefully then how you W, not as unwise men
1Jn 1:6 with him while we W in darkness, we lie
1:7 truth; but if we W in the light, as
2:6 in him ought to W in the same way
Jude 1:11 For they W in the way of Cain, and
Rev 3:4 garments; and they shall W with me in white,
9:20 see or hear or W;
21:24 light shall the nations W; and the kings of

WALKED (87)

Gen 5:22 Enoch W with God after the birth of Methuselah
5:24 Enoch W with God; and he was not, for
6:9 in his generation; Noah W with God.
9:23 both their shoulders, and W backward and covered
48:15 fathers Abraham and Isaac W, the God who has
Ex 2:5 river, and her maidens W beside the river; she
14:29 the people of Israel W on dry ground through
15:19 the people of Israel W on dry ground in
Lev 26:41 me, so that I W contrary to them and
Josh 5:6 the people of Israel W forty years in the
14:10 to Moses, while Israel W in the wilderness; and
Judg 2:17 which their fathers had W, who had obeyed the
1Sam 12:2 you; and I have W before you from my
1Kgs 3:6 my father, because he W before thee in faithfulness,
3:14 as your father David W, then I will lengthen
8:25 me as you have W before me.'
9:4 as David your father W, with integrity of heart
11:33 Ammonites, and has not W in my ways, doing
15:3 And he W in all the sins which his
15:26 of the LORD, and W in the way of
15:34 of the LORD, and W in the way of
16:2 Israel, and you have W in the way of
16:26 For he W in all the way of Jeroboam
22:43 He W in all the way of Asa his
22:52 of the LORD, and W in the way of
2Kgs 4:35 got up again, and W once to and fro
8:18 And he W in the way of the kings
8:27 He also W in the way of the house
13:6 Israel to sin, but W in them; and the
13:11 to sin, but he W in them.
16:3 had done, but he W in the way of
17:8 feared other gods and W in the customs of
17:19 LORD their God, but W in the customs which
17:22 The people of Israel W in all the sins
20:3 thee, how I have W before thee in faithfulness
21:21 He W in all the way in which his
21:21 in which his father W, and served the idols
22:2 of the LORD, and W in all the way
2Chr 6:16 law as you have W before me.'
7:17 as David your father W, doing according to all
11:17 Solomon secure, for they W for three years in
17:3 with Jehoshaphat, because he W in the earlier ways

W

	17:4	of his father and W in his commandments, and
	20:32	He W in the way of Asa his father
	21:6	And he W in the way of the kings
	21:12	'Because you have not W in the ways of
	21:13	of Judah, but have W in the way of
	22:3	He also W in the ways of the house
	28:2	his father David, but W in the ways of
	34:2	of the LORD, and W in the ways of
Tob	1:3	I, Tobit, W in the ways of truth and
Esth	2:11	And every day Mordecai W in front of the
Job	29:3	by his light I W through darkness;
	31:5	"If I have W with falsehood, and my foot
	38:16	of the sea, or W in the recesses of
Ps	26:1	LORD, for I have W in my integrity, and
	55:14	within God's house we W in fellowship.
Wis	19:21	of perishable creatures that W among them, nor did
Sir	24:5	of heaven and have W in the depths of
	45:9	a sound as he W, to make their ringing
Is	9:2	The people who W in darkness have seen a
	20:3	my servant Isaiah has W naked and barefoot for
	38:3	thee, how I have W before thee in faithfulness
Jer	7:24	incline their ear, but W in their own counsels
	9:13	obeyed my voice, or W in accord with it,
	11:8	ear, but every one W in the stubbornness of
	44:10	have they feared, nor W in my law and
Bar	3:13	If you had W in the way of God,
Ezek	5:7	you, and have not W in my statutes or
	11:12	for you have not W in my statutes, nor
	28:14	the midst of the stones of fire you W
Dan	3:24	And they W about in the midst of the
Amos	2:4	have led them astray, after which their fathers W
Mic	6:16	Ahab; and you have W in their counsels; that
Mal	2:6	He W with me in peace and uprightness, and
Mt	4:18	As he W by the Sea of Galilee, he
	14:29	of the boat and W on the water and
Mk	5:42	girl got up and W (she was twelve years
Jn	1:36	at Jesus as he W, and said, "Behold, the
	5:8	healed, and he took up his pallet and W
	21:18	you girded yourself and W where you would; but
Acts	3:8	up he stood and W and entered the temple
	14:8	was a cripple from birth, who had never W
	14:10	And he sprang up and W
Eph	2:2	in which you once W, following the course of
Col	3:7	In these you once W, when you lived in
1Jn	2:6	walk in the same way in which he W

WALKING (45)

Gen	3:8	of the LORD God W in the garden in
	24:65	is the man yonder, W in the field to
Lev	26:40	me, and also in W contrary to me,
Deut	8:6	LORD your God, by W in his ways and
	11:19	and when you are W by the way, and
	11:22	the LORD your God, W in all his ways,
	19:9	your God and by W ever in his ways--
	30:16	LORD your God, by W in his ways, and
2Sam	11:2	his couch and was W upon the roof of
1Kgs	2:3	the LORD your God, W in his ways and
	3:3	Solomon loved the LORD, W in the statutes of
	8:61	the LORD our God, W in his statutes and
	16:19	sight of the LORD, W in the way of
Jud	13:20	have avenged our ruin, W in the straight path
Job	1:7	the earth, and from W up and down on
	2:2	the earth, and from W up and down on
Eccl	10:7	on horses, and princes W on foot like slaves.
Wis	15:15	and their feet are of no use for W
Sir	5:2	inclination and strength, W according to the desires
	9:13	Know that you are W in the midst of
	13:13	watchful, for you are W about with your own
	19:27	a man's manner of W, show what he is.
Is	20:2	he had done so, W naked and barefoot--
Ezek	5:6	my ordinances and not W in my statutes.
Dan	3:93	see four men loose, W in the midst of
	4:29	twelve months he was W on the roof of
	13:8	day, going in and W about, and they began
	13:36	said, "As we were W in the garden alone,
Mal	3:14	his charge or of W as in mourning before
Mt	14:25	he came to them, W on the sea.
	14:26	the disciples saw him W on the sea, they
	15:31	maimed whole, the lame W, and the blind seeing;
Mk	6:48	he came to them, W on the sea.
	6:49	when they saw him W on the sea they
	8:24	"I see men; but they look like trees, W
	10:32	Jerusalem, and Jesus was W ahead of them; and
	11:26	And as he was W in the temple, the
	16:12	them, as they were W into the country.
Lk	1:6	righteous before God, W in all the commandments
Jn	6:19	miles, they saw Jesus W on the sea and
	10:23	winter, and Jesus was W in the temple, in
Acts	3:8	the temple with them, W and leaping and praising
	3:9	the people saw him W and praising God,
	9:31	was built up; and W in the fear of
Rom	14:15	you are no longer W in love.

WALKS (38)

Ex	21:19	man rises again and W abroad with his staff,
Deut	23:14	the LORD your God W in the midst of
1Sam	12:2	now, behold, the king W before you; and I
Job	18:8	own feet, and he W on a pitfall.
	22:14	not see, and he W on the vault of
	34:8	company with evildoers and W with wicked men?
Ps	1:1	is the man who W not in the counsel
	15:2	He who W blamelessly, and does what is right,
	68:21	crown of him who W in his guilty ways.
	101:6	with me; he who W in the way that
	128:1	fears the LORD, who W in his ways!
Prov	10:9	He who W in integrity walks securely, but he
	10:9	who walks in integrity W securely, but he who
	13:20	He who W with wise men becomes wise, but
	14:2	He who W in uprightness fears the LORD, but
	15:21	a man of understanding W aright.
	19:1	a poor man who W in his integrity than
	20:7	A righteous man who W in his integrity--
	28:6	a poor man who W in his integrity than
	28:18	He who W in integrity will be delivered, but
	28:26	fool; but he who W in wisdom will be
Eccl	2:14	head, but the fool W in darkness; and yet
	10:3	Even when the fool W on the road, he
Sir	2:12	to the sinner who W along two ways!
	21:6	Whoever hates reproof W in the steps of the
Is	33:15	He who W righteously and speaks uprightly, who
	50:10	of his servant, who W in darkness and has
Jer	10:23	not in man who W to direct his steps.
Ezek	18:9	between man and man, W in my statutes, and
	18:17	observes my ordinances, and W in my statutes; he
	33:15	taken by robbery, and W in the statutes of
Mic	2:7	good to him who W uprightly?
Zeph	3:6	streets so that none W in them; their cities
Jn	11:9	If any one W in the day, he does
	11:10	But if any one W in the night, he
	12:35	overtake you; he who W in the darkness does
1Jn	2:11	in the darkness and W in the darkness, and
Rev	2:1	his right hand, who W among the seven golden

WALL (181)

Gen	49:22	by a spring; his branches run over the W
Ex	14:22	the waters being a W to them on their
	14:29	the waters being a W to them on their
Lev	25:31	villages which have no W around them shall be
Num	22:24	the vineyards, with a W on either side.
	22:25	she pushed against the W, and pressed Balaam's foot
	22:25	Balaam's foot against the W; so he struck her
	35:4	shall reach from the W of the city outward
Josh	2:15	built into the city W, so that she dwelt
	2:15	city wall, so that she dwelt in the W
	6:5	great shout; and the W of the city will
	6:20	great shout, and the W fell down flat, so
1Sam	18:11	he thought, "I will pin David to the W
	19:10	pin David to the W with the spear; but
	19:10	so that he struck the spear into the W
	20:25	the seat by the W; Jonathan sat opposite, and
	25:16	them; they were a W to us both by
	31:10	his body to the W of Beth-shan.
	31:12	his sons from the W of Beth-shan; and they
2Sam	11:20	not know that they would shoot from the W
	11:21	upon him from the W, so that he died
	11:21	go so near the W then you shall say,
	11:24	your servants from the W; some of the king's
	18:24	the gate by the W, and when he lifted
	20:15	they were battering the W, to throw it down.
	20:21	head shall be thrown to you over the W
	22:30	by my God I can leap over a W
1Kgs	3:1	the LORD and the W around Jerusalem.
	4:33	grows out of the W; he spoke also of
	6:5	a structure against the W of the house, running
	6:6	made offsets on the W in order that the
	6:27	one touched the one W, and a wing of
	6:27	cherub touched the other W; their other wings
	9:15	the Millo and the W of Jerusalem and Hazor
	20:30	of Aphek; and the W fell upon twenty-seven thousand
2Kgs	3:27	offered him for a burnt offering upon the W
	6:26	passing by upon the W, a woman cried out
	6:30	passing by upon the W --and the people looked,

W

9:33 blood spattered on the W and on the horses,
14:13 and broke down the W of Jerusalem for four
18:26 hearing of the people who are on the W
18:27 men sitting on the W, who are doomed with
20:2 his face to the W, and prayed to the
2Chr 3:11 five cubits, touched the W of the house, and
3:12 five cubits, touched the W of the house, and
25:23 and broke down the W of Jerusalem for four
26:6 and broke down the W of Gath and the
26:6 of Gath and the W of Jabneh and the
26:6 of Jabneh and the W of Ashdod; and he
27:3 much building on the W of Ophel.
32:5 built up all the W that was broken down,
32:5 it he built another W; and he strengthened the
32:18 who were upon the W, to frighten and terrify
33:14 he built an outer W for the city of
36:19 and broke down the W of Jerusalem, and burned
Neh 1:3 trouble and shame; the W of Jerusalem is broken
2:8 temple, and for the W of the city, and
2:15 valley and inspected the W; and I turned back
2:17 let us build the W of Jerusalem, that we
3:8 they restored Jerusalem as far as the Broad W
3:13 thousand cubits of the W, as far as the
3:15 and he built the W of the Pool of
3:27 as far as the W of Ophel.
4:1 we were building the W, he was angry and
4:3 on it he will break down their stone W
4:6 So we built the W; and all the wall
4:6 wall; and all the W was joined together to
4:10 we are not able to work on the W
4:13 the space behind the W, in open places, I
4:15 all returned to the W, each to his work.
4:17 house of Judah, who were building on the W
4:19 are separated on the W, far from one another.
5:16 the work on this W, and acquired no land;
6:1 I had built the W and that there was
6:6 you are building the W; and you wish to
6:15 So the W was finished on the twenty-fifth day
7:1 Now when the W had been built and I
12:27 the dedication of the W of Jerusalem they sought
12:30 purified the people and the gates and the W
12:31 of Judah upon the W, and appointed two great
12:31 the right upon the W to the Dung Gate;
12:37 the ascent of the W, above the house of
12:38 the people, upon the W, above the Tower of
12:38 Ovens, to the Broad W,
13:21 to them, "Why do you lodge before the W
Tob 1:17 thrown out behind the W of Nineveh, I would
2:9 I slept by the W of the courtyard, and
2:10 were sparrows on the W and their fresh droppings
Jud 14:1 and hang it upon the parapet of your W
14:11 of Holofernes on the W, and every man took
Ps 18:29 by my God I can leap over a W
62:3 you, like a leaning W, a tottering fence?
Prov 18:11 and like a high W protecting him.
24:31 nettles, and its stone W was broken down.
Eccl 10:8 serpent will bite him who breaks through a W
Song 2:9 he stands behind our W, gazing in at the
8:9 If she is a W, we will build upon
8:10 I was a W, and my breasts were like
Wis 13:15 sets it in the W, and fastens it there
Sir 22:15 stucco decoration on the W of a colonnade.
Is 2:15 and against every fortified W;
5:5 will break down its W, and it shall be
22:10 you broke down the houses to fortify the W
25:4 a storm against a W,
30:13 break in a high W, bulging out, and about
36:11 hearing of the people who are on the W
36:12 men sitting on the W, who are doomed with
38:2 his face to the W, and prayed to the
54:12 carbuncles, and all your W of precious stones.
59:10 We grope for the W like the blind, we
Jer 15:20 this people a fortified W of bronze; they will
49:27 a fire in the W of Damascus, and it
51:44 flow to him; the W of Babylon has fallen.
51:58 of hosts: The broad W of Babylon shall be
Lam 2:8 lay in ruins the W of the daughter of
2:8 he caused rampart and W to lament, they languish
Ezek 4:2 and build a siege W against it, and cast
4:3 it as an iron W between you and the
8:7 looked, behold, there was a hole in the W
8:8 man, dig in the W; and when I dug
8:8 I dug in the W, lo, there was a
8:10 there, portrayed upon the W round about, were all
12:5 Dig through the W in their sight, and go
12:7 I dug through the W with my own hands;
12:12 shall dig through the W and go out through
13:5 or built up a W for the house of
13:10 the people build a W, these prophets daub it
13:12 out; and when the W falls, will it not
13:14 will break down the W that you have daubed
13:15 my wrath upon the W, and upon those who
13:15 say to you, The W is no more, nor
22:30 should build up the W and stand in the
23:14 men portrayed upon the W, the images of the
26:8 set up a siege W against you, and throw
38:20 shall fall, and every W shall tumble to the
40:5 behold, there was a W all around the outside
40:5 the thickness of the W, one reed; and the
41:5 Then he measured the W of the temple, six
41:6 offsets all around the W of the temple to
41:6 be supported by the W of the temple.
41:9 thickness of the outer W of the side chambers
41:12 cubits broad; and the W of the building was
41:20 cherubim and palm trees were carved on the W
42:7 And there was a W outside parallel to the
42:10 court, where the outside W begins.
42:12 the passage, and opposite them was a dividing W
42:20 It had a W around it, five hundred cubits
43:8 doorposts, with only a W between me and them.
Dan 5:5 the plaster of the W of the king's palace,
Hos 2:6 I will build a W against her, so that
Joel 2:7 warriors they charge, like soldiers they scale the W
Amos 1:7 a fire upon the W of Gaza, and it
1:10 a fire upon the W of Tyre, and it
1:14 a fire in the W of Rabbah, and it
5:19 his hand against the W, and a serpent bit
7:7 was standing beside a W built with a plumb
Mic 5:1 walled about with a W; siege is laid against
Nah 2:5 they hasten to the W, the mantelet is set
3:8 her, her rampart a sea, and water her W
Hab 2:11 cry out from the W, and the beam from
Zech 2:5 be to her a W of fire round about,
1Mac 1:33 with a great strong W and strong towers, and
6:62 to tear down the W all around.
9:54 to tear down the W of the inner court
12:37 city; part of the W on the valley to
13:45 went up on the W with their clothes rent,
2Mac 1:15 few men inside the W of the sacred precinct,
5:5 the troops upon the W had been forced back
6:10 breasts, then hurled them down headlong from the W
10:17 who fought upon the W, and slew those whom
10:35 blasphemies, bravely stormed the W and with savage
14:43 ran up on the W, and manfully threw himself
Acts 9:25 him down over the W, lowering him in a
23:3 to him, "God shall strike you, you whitewashed W
2Cor 11:33 a window in the W, and escaped his hands.
Eph 2:14 broken down the dividing W of hostility,
Rev 21:12 had a great, high W, with twelve gates, and
21:14 And the W of the city had twelve foundations,
21:17 He also measured its W, a hundred and forty-four
21:18 The W was built of jasper, while the city
21:19 The foundations of the W of the city were

WALLED (6)

Lev 25:29 dwelling house in a W city, he may redeem
25:30 that is in the W city shall be made
Job 19:8 He has W up my way, so that I
Lam 3:7 He has W me about so that I cannot
Mic 5:1 Now you are W about with a wall; siege
1Mac 13:33 strongholds of Judea and W them all around, with

WALLET

1Sam 17:40 his shepherd's bag or W; his sling was in

WALLOW (4)

Sir 23:12 and they will not W in sins.
Jer 48:26 so that Moab shall W in his vomit, and
Ezek 27:30 on their heads and W in ashes;
2Pet 2:22 is washed only to W in the mire.

WALLOWING

2Sam 20:12 And Amasa lay W in his blood in the

WALLS (98)

Lev 14:37 disease is in the W of the house with
14:39 has spread in the W of the house,
Deut 3:5 cities fortified with high W, gates, and bars, besides
28:52 your high and fortified W, in which you trusted,
1Kgs 4:13 sixty great cities with W and bronze bars);
6:5 house, running round the W of the house, both
6:6 be inserted into the W of the house.

6:15 He lined the W of the house on the
6:29 He carved all the W of the house round
2Kgs 4:10 small roof chamber with W, and put there for
25:4 gate between the two W, by the king's garden,
25:10 guard, broke down the W around Jerusalem.
1Chr 29:4 silver, for overlaying the W of the house,
2Chr 3:7 beams, its thresholds, its W, and its doors; and
3:7 its doors; and he carved cherubim on the W
8:5 Beth-horon, fortified cities with W, gates, and bars,
14:7 and surround them with W and towers, gates and
Ezra 4:12 are finishing the W and repairing the foundations.
4:13 is rebuilt and the W finished, they will not
4:16 is rebuilt and its W finished, you will then
5:8 is laid in the W; this work goes on
Neh 2:13 and I inspected the W of Jerusalem which were
4:7 the repairing of the W of Jerusalem was going
Tob 13:16 sapphires and emeralds, her W with precious stones,
Jud 1:2 the king who built W about Ecbatana with hewn
1:2 long; he made the W seventy cubits high and
7:33 went up on the W and towers of their
Ps 51:18 good pleasure; rebuild the W of Jerusalem,
55:10 around it on its W; and mischief and trouble
80:12 thou broken down its W, so that all who
89:40 hast breached all his W; thou hast laid his
122:7 Peace be within your W, and security within your
Prov 1:21 the top of the W she cries out; at
25:28 like a city broken into and left without W
Song 5:7 took away my mantle, those watchmen of the W
Sir 14:24 tent peg to her W;
23:18 surrounds me, and the W hide me, and no
49:13 raised for us the W that had fallen, and
50:2 for the high double W, the high retaining walls
50:2 walls, the high retaining W for the temple enclosure.
Is 22:5 a battering down of W and a shouting to
22:11 reservoir between the two W for the water of
25:12 high fortifications of his W he will bring down,
26:1 sets up salvation as W and bulwarks.
49:16 of my hands; your W are continually before me.
56:5 house and within my W a monument and a
60:10 shall build up your W, and their kings shall
60:18 you shall call your W Salvation, and your gates
62:6 Upon your W, O Jerusalem, I have set watchmen;
Jer 1:15 Jerusalem, against all its W round about, and against
1:18 iron pillar, and bronze W, against the whole land,
4:19 Oh, the W of my heart!
21:4 besieging you outside the W; and I will bring
39:4 gate between the two W; and they went toward
39:8 and broke down the W of Jerusalem.
50:15 bulwarks have fallen, her W are thrown down.
51:12 a standard against the W of Babylon; make the
52:7 gate between the two W, by the king's garden,
52:14 broke down all the W round about Jerusalem.
Lam 2:7 of the enemy the W of her palaces; a
Ezek 17:17 cast up and siege W built to cut off
26:4 They shall destroy the W of Tyre, and break
26:9 his battering-rams against your W, and with his axes
26:10 will cover you; your W will shake at the
26:12 will break down your W and destroy your pleasant
27:11 Helech were upon your W round about, and men
27:11 their shields upon your W round about; they made
30:16 be breached, and its W broken down.
33:30 about you by the W and at the doors
38:11 of them dwelling without W, and having no bars
41:13 the building with its W, a hundred cubits long;
41:15 the west and its W on either side, a
41:17 And on all the W round about in the
41:22 its base, and its W were of wood.
41:25 were carved on the W; and there was a
Joel 2:9 they run upon the W; they climb up into
Mic 7:11 A day for the building of your W
Zech 2:4 inhabited as villages without W, because of the
1Mac 1:31 and tore down its houses and its surrounding W
4:60 Mount Zion with high W and strong towers round
6:7 the sanctuary with high W as before, and also
9:50 and Tephon, with high W and gates and bars.
10:11 work to build the W and encircle Mount Zion
10:45 cost of rebuilding the W of Jerusalem and fortifying
10:45 cost of rebuilding the W in Judea, also be
12:36 Judea, to build the W of Jerusalem still higher,
13:10 hastened to complete the W of Jerusalem, and he
13:33 high towers and great W and gates and bolts,
14:37 city, and built the W of Jerusalem higher.
16:23 the building of the W which he built, and
2Mac 3:19 and some to the W, while others peered out
11:9 the wildest beasts or W of iron.
12:13 fortified with earthworks and W, and inhabited by all
12:14 the strength of the W and on their supply
12:15 the days of Joshua, rushed furiously upon the W
12:27 their stand before the W and made a vigorous
Heb 11:30 By faith the W of Jericho fell down after
Rev 21:15 to measure the city and its gates and W

WANDER (22)

Gen 20:13 God caused me to W from my father's house,
Num 32:13 and he made them W in the wilderness forty
Judg 11:37 I may go and W on the mountains, and
2Sam 15:20 I today make you W about with us, seeing
2Kgs 21:8 feet of Israel to W any more out of
Job 12:24 earth, and makes them W in a pathless waste.
38:41 cry to God, and W about for lack of
Ps 55:7 rest; yea, I would W afar, I would lodge
107:40 princes and makes them W in trackless wastes;
109:10 May his children W about and beg; may they
119:10 thee; let me not W from thy commandments!
119:21 accursed ones, who W from thy commandments;
Prov 5:6 of life; her ways W, and she does not
Sir 9:7 of a city, nor W about in its deserted
36:25 wife, a man will W about and sigh.
Is 47:15 from your youth; they W about each in his
Jer 14:10 "They have loved to W thus, they have not
31:24 farmers and those who W with their flocks.
49:30 on every side!' Flee, W far away, dwell in
Amos 8:12 They shall W from sea to sea, and from
Zech 10:2 Therefore the people W like sheep; they are afflicted
2Tim 4:4 to the truth and W into myths.

WANDERED (8)

Gen 21:14 And she departed, and W in the wilderness of
Ps 107:4 Some W in desert wastes, finding no way to
Sir 29:18 exile, and they have W among foreign nations.
Lam 4:14 They W, blind, through the streets, so defiled with
Ezek 34:6 sheep were scattered, they W over all the mountains
Amos 4:8 two or three cities W to one city to
1Tim 1:6 swerving from these have W away into vain
6:10 craving that some have W away from the faith

WANDERER (2)

Gen 4:12 a fugitive and a W on the earth."
4:14 a fugitive and a W on the earth, and

WANDERERS (2)

Lam 4:15 they became fugitives and W; men said among the
Hos 9:17 him; they shall be W among the nations.

WANDERING (11)

Gen 37:15 a man found him W in the fields; and
Deut 26:5 LORD your God, 'A W Aramean was my father;
1Chr 16:20 and sojourners in it, W from nation to nation,
Ps 105:13 and sojourners in it, W from nation to nation,
Eccl 6:9 the eyes than the W of desire; this also
Wis 18:3 journey, and a harmless sun for their glorious W
Hos 8:9 Assyria, a wild ass W alone; Ephraim has hired
Zech 11:16 perishing, or seek the W, or heal the maimed,
2Mac 10:6 booths, they had been W in the mountains and
Heb 11:38 was not worthy—W over deserts and mountains,
Jude 1:13 of their own shame; W stars for whom the

WANDERS (4)

Job 15:23 He W abroad for bread, saying, 'Where is it?'
Prov 21:16 A man who W from the way of understanding
Song 1:7 be like one who W beside the flocks of
Jas 5:19 any one among you W from the truth and

WANDS

2Mac 10:7 Therefore bearing ivy-wreathed W and beautiful

WANED

Judg 19:9 now the day has W toward evening; pray tarry

WANES

Sir 43:7 days, a light that W when it has reached

WANT (78)

Deut 28:48 in nakedness, and in W of all things; and
28:57 eat them secretly, for W of all things, in
Tob 4:13 is loss and great W, because shiftlessness is the
Job 24:8 to the rock for W of shelter.
30:3 Through W and hard hunger they gnaw the dry
Ps 23:1 shepherd, I shall not W;
34:9 saints, for those who fear him have no W
34:10 The young lions suffer W and hunger; but those
Prov 6:11 like a vagabond, and W like an armed man.

11:24 withholds what he should give, and only suffers W
13:25 appetite, but the belly of the wicked suffers W
14:23 is profit, but mere talk tends only to W
21:5 every one who is hasty comes only to W
22:16 gives to the rich, will only come to W
24:34 like a robber, and W like an armed man.
28:22 does not know that W will come upon him.
28:27 the poor will not W, but he who hides
Wis 16:3 thy people, after suffering W a short time, might
16:4 upon those oppressors inexorable W should come,
Sir 4:2 who is hungry, nor anger a man in W
10:25 yourself at a time when you are in W
11:11 on, but is so much the more in W
26:19 me: a warrior in W through poverty, and intelligent
Is 5:13 go into exile for W of knowledge; their honored
Lam 4:9 pined away, stricken by W of the fruits of
Zech 10:2 they are afflicted for W of a shepherd.
Mt 13:28 him, 'Then do you W us to go and
20:21 And he said to her, "What do you W
20:32 saying, "What do you W me to do for
27:17 them, "Whom do you W me to release for
27:21 the two do you W me to release for
Mk 6:25 and asked, saying, "I W you to give me
6:26 guests he did not W to break his word
10:35 to him, "Teacher, we W you to do for
10:36 them, "What do you W me to do for
10:51 him, "What do you W me to do for
15:9 answered them, "Do you W me to release for
Lk 9:54 said, "Lord, do you W us to bid fire
15:14 that country, and he began to be in W
18:41 him, "What do you W me to do for
19:14 saying, 'We do not W this man to reign
19:27 mine, who did not W me to reign over
Jn 5:5 to him, "Do you W to be healed?"
9:27 Why do you W to hear it again?
9:27 Do you too W to become his disciples?"
Acts 7:28 Do you W to kill me as you killed
Rom 1:13 I W you to know, brethren, that I have
7:15 not do what I W, but I do the
7:16 what I do not W, I agree that the
7:19 do the good I W, but the evil I
7:19 evil I do not W is what I do.
7:20 what I do not W, it is no longer
7:21 law that when I W to do right, evil
11:25 your own conceits, I W you to understand this
1Cor 7:32 I W you to be free from anxieties.
10:1 I W you to know, brethren, that our fathers
10:20 I do not W you to be partners with
11:3 But I W you to understand that the head
12:1 brethren, I do not W you to be uninformed.
12:3 Therefore I W you to understand that no one
14:5 Now I W you all to speak in tongues,
16:7 For I do not W to see you now
2Cor 1:8 For we do not W you to be ignorant,
8:1 We W you to know, brethren, about the grace
8:14 time should supply their W, so that their abundance
8:14 abundance may supply your W, that there may be
11:9 you and was in W, I did not burden
Gal 1:7 who trouble you and W to pervert the gospel
4:9 spirits, whose slaves you W to be once more?
4:17 no good purpose; they W to shut you out,
6:12 It is those who W to make a good
Phil 1:12 I W you to know, brethren, that what has
4:11 that I complain of W; for I have learned,
4:12 secret of facing plenty and hunger, abundance and W
Col 2:1 For I W you to know how greatly I
Philem 1:20 Yes, brother, I W some benefit from you in
Jas 2:20 Do you W to be shown, you shallow man,
3Jn 1:10 also stops those who W to welcome them and

WANTED (20)

Neh 6:9 For they all W to frighten us, thinking, "Their
6:14 of the prophets who W to make me afraid.
1Mac 3:34 about all that he W done.
7:5 led by Alcimus, who W to be high priest.
11:45 twenty thousand, and they W to kill the king.
2Mac 13:25 so angry that they W to annul its terms.
Mt 14:5 And though he W to put him to death,
27:15 for the crowd any one prisoner whom they W
Mk 6:19 grudge against him, and W to kill him.
Jn 6:11 so also the fish, as much as they W
7:44 Some of them W to arrest him, but no
16:19 Jesus knew that they W to ask him; so
Acts 5:33 they were enraged and W to kill them.
14:13 to the gates and W to offer sacrifice with
15:36 And Barnabas W to take with them John called
16:3 Paul W Timothy to accompany him; and he took
2Cor 1:15 sure of this, I W to come to you
1:16 a double pleasure; I W to visit you on
1:17 I vacillating when I W to do this?
1Thes 2:18 to face; because we W to come to you–

WANTING

Dan 5:27 the balances and found W;

WANTON (11)

Judg 20:10 Benjamin, for all the W crime which they have
2Sam 13:12 do not do this W folly.
13:13 as one of the W fools in Israel.
Ps 106:14 But they had a W craving in the wilderness,
Prov 9:13 is noisy; she is W and knows no shame.
Jer 50:11 heritage, though you are W as a heifer at
Ezek 6:9 I have broken their W heart which has departed
Zeph 3:4 Her prophets are W, faithless men; her priests
1Tim 5:11 for when they grow W against Christ they desire
Rev 18:7 herself and played the W, so give her a
18:9 committed fornication and were W with her, will

WANTONLY (7)

Num 15:39 eyes, which you are inclined to go after W
2Chr 28:19 for he had dealt W in Judah and had
Ps 25:3 be ashamed who are W treacherous.
Prov 1:11 for blood, let us W ambush the innocent;
Sir 27:13 and their laughter is W sinful.
Is 3:16 with outstretched necks, glancing W with their eyes,
Ezek 6:9 their eyes which turn W after their idols; and

WANTONNESS (3)

Gen 49:6 men, and in their W they hamstring oxen.
Judg 20:6 have committed abomination and W in Israel.
Rev 18:3 have grown rich with the wealth of her W

WANTS (3)

Judg 19:20 care for all your W; only, do not spend
Lk 13:31 from here, for Herod W to kill you."
2Cor 9:12 not only supplies the W of the saints but

WAR (269)

Gen 14:2 Goiim, these kings made W with Bera king of
Ex 1:9 they multiply, and, if W befall us, they join
13:17 repent when they see W, and return to Egypt."
15:3 is a man of W; the LORD is his
17:16 The LORD will have W with Amalek from
32:17 is a noise of W in the camp."
Num 1:3 to go forth to W, you and Aaron shall
1:20 to go forth to W:
1:22 to go forth to W:
1:24 to go forth to W:
1:26 to go forth to W:
1:28 to go forth to W:
1:30 to go forth to W:
1:32 to go forth to W:
1:34 to go forth to W:
1:36 to go forth to W:
1:38 to go forth to W:
1:40 to go forth to W:
1:42 to go forth to W:
1:45 to go forth to W in Israel–
10:9 when you go to W in your land against
26:2 Israel who are able to go forth to W
31:3 among you for the W, that they may go
31:4 each of the tribes of Israel to the W
31:5 from each tribe, twelve thousand armed for W
31:6 sent them to the W, a thousand from each
31:14 hundreds, who had come from service in the W
31:21 to the men of W who had gone to
31:28 from the men of W who went out to
31:32 that the men of W took was: six hundred
31:36 had gone out to W, was in number three
31:42 who had gone to W --
31:49 counted the men of W who are under our
31:53 (The men of W had taken booty, every man
32:6 brethren go to the W while you sit here?
32:20 the LORD for the W,
32:27 who is armed for W, before the LORD to
Deut 1:41 on his weapons of W, and thought it easy
2:14 is, the men of W, had perished from the
2:16 all the men of W had perished and were
4:34 by wonders, and by W, by a mighty hand
20:1 you go forth to W against your enemies, and
20:12 with you, but makes W against you, then you
20:19 a long time, making W against it in order

20:20 the city that makes W with you, until it
21:10 you go forth to W against your enemies, and
Josh 4:13 thousand ready armed for W passed over before the
5:4 all the men of W, had died on the
5:6 nation, the men of W that came forth out
6:3 all the men of W going around the city
10:5 against Gibeon, and made W against it.
10:7 all the people of W with him, and all
10:24 of the men of W who had gone with
11:7 all his people of W, by the waters of
11:18 Joshua made W a long time with all those
11:23 And the land had rest from W
14:11 strength was then, for W, and for going and
14:15 And the land had rest from W
17:1 and Bashan, because he was a man of W
22:12 at Shiloh, to make W against them.
22:33 no more of making W against them, to destroy
Judg 3:1 no experience of any W in Canaan;
3:2 of Israel might know W, that he might teach
3:2 that he might teach W to such at least
3:10 he went out to W, and the LORD gave
5:8 gods were chosen, then W was in the gates.
11:4 time the Ammonites made W against Israel.
11:5 when the Ammonites made W against Israel, the
11:25 he ever go to W with them?
11:27 me wrong by making W on me; the LORD,
18:11 armed with weapons of W, set forth from Zorah
18:16 with their weapons of W, stood by the entrance
18:17 the six hundred men armed with weapons of W
20:17 that drew sword; all these were men of W
1Sam 8:12 make his implements of W and the equipment of
16:18 valor, a man of W, prudent in speech, and
17:20 battle line, shouting the W cry.
17:33 been a man of W from his youth."
18:5 that Saul set him over the men of W
19:8 And there was W again; and David went out
23:8 all the people to W, to go down to
28:1 gathered their forces for W, to fight against Israel.
2Sam 1:27 "and the weapons of W perished!"
3:1 There was a long W between the house of
3:6 While there was W between the house of Saul
8:10 had often been at W with Toi.
11:7 fared, and how the W prospered.
17:8 father is expert in W; he will not spend
21:15 The Philistines had W again with Israel, and David
21:18 this there was again W with the Philistines at
21:19 And there was again W with the Philistines at
21:20 And there was again W at Gath, where there
22:35 trains my hands for W, so that my arms
1Kgs 2:5 had been shed in W, and putting innocent blood
14:30 And there was W between Rehoboam and Jeroboam
15:6 Now there was W between Rehoboam and
15:7 And there was W between Abijam and Jeroboam.
15:16 And there was W between Asa and Baasha king
15:32 And there was W between Asa and Baasha king
20:18 have come out for W, take them alive."
22:1 three years Syria and Israel continued without W
2Kgs 8:28 of Ahab to make W against Hazael king of
13:25 he had taken from Jehoahaz his father in W
16:5 came up to wage W on Jerusalem, and they
18:20 that mere words are strategy and power for W
24:16 thousand, all of them strong and fit for W
25:4 all the men of W fled by night by
25:19 of the men of W, and five men of
1Chr 5:10 of Saul they made W on the Hagrites, who
5:18 the bow, expert in W, forty-four thousand seven
5:19 They made W upon the Hagrites, Jetur, Naphish, and
5:22 fell slain, because the W was of God.
7:4 of the army for W, thirty-six thousand, for they
7:11 thousand and two hundred, ready for service in W
7:40 for service in W, was twenty-six thousand men.
12:1 among the mighty men who helped him in W
12:25 men of valor for W, seven thousand one hundred.
12:33 all the weapons of W, to help David with
12:37 thousand men armed with all the weapons of W
12:38 All these, men of W, arrayed in battle order,
18:10 had often been at W with Tou.
20:4 after this there arose W with the Philistines at
20:5 And there was again W with the Philistines; and
20:6 And there was again W at Gath, where there
2Chr 13:2 Now there was W between Abijah and Jeroboam.
13:3 of valiant men of W, four hundred thousand picked
14:6 He had no W in those years, for the
15:19 there was no more W until the thirty-fifth year
17:10 and they made no W against Jehoshaphat.
17:18 with a hundred and eighty thousand armed for W
18:3 We will be with you in the W
22:5 of Israel to make W against Hazael king of
25:5 picked men, fit for W, able to handle spear
25:8 will be strong for W, God will cast you
26:6 went out and made W against the Philistines, and
26:11 of soldiers, fit for W, in divisions according to
26:13 hundred, who could make W with mighty power, to
28:12 were coming from the W,
35:21 which I am at W; and God has commanded
Jud 1:5 King Nebuchadnezzar made W against King
1:11 join him in the W; for they were not
4:5 food in preparation for W –since their fields had
5:1 Israel had prepared for W and had closed the
5:23 people with no strength or power for making W
6:2 us not to make W against the people of
7:1 hill country and make W on the Israelites.
7:2 force of men of W was one hundred and
Esth 11:7 every nation prepared for W, to fight against the
Job 5:20 from death, and in W from the power of
38:23 of trouble, for the day of battle and W
Ps 18:34 trains my hands for W, so that my arms
27:3 shall not fear; though W arise against me, yet
33:17 The W horse is a vain hope for victory,
55:21 smoother than butter, yet W was in his heart;
68:30 after tribute; scatter the peoples who delight in W
76:3 the shield, the sword, and the weapons of W
76:5 all the men of W were unable to use
120:7 peace; but when I speak, they are for W
144:1 trains my hands for W, and my fingers for
Prov 20:18 established by counsel; by wise guidance wage W
24:6 you can wage your W, and in abundance of
25:18 neighbor is like a W club, or a sword,
Eccl 3:8 hate; a time for W, and a time for
8:8 is no discharge from W, nor will wickedness deliver
9:18 better than weapons of W, but one sinner destroys
Song 3:8 swords and expert in W, each with his sword
Wis 8:15 I shall show myself capable, and courageous in W
Sir 37:11 with a coward about W, with a merchant about
46:1 Nun was mighty in W, and was the successor
46:6 He hurled down W upon that nation, and at
47:5 a man mighty in W, to exalt the power
Is 2:4 neither shall they learn W any more.
7:1 to Jerusalem to wage W against it, but they
36:5 that mere words are strategy and power for W
41:12 find them; those who W against you shall be
42:13 like a man of W he stirs up his
Jer 4:19 the sound of the trumpet, the alarm of W
6:4 "Prepare W against her; up, and let us attack
21:2 of Babylon is making W against us; perhaps the
21:4 back the weapons of W which are in your
21:9 shall have his life as a prize of W
28:8 ancient times prophesied W, famine, and pestilence
38:2 as a prize of W, and live.
39:18 as a prize of W, because you have put
42:14 we shall not see W, or hear the sound
45:5 as a prize of W in all places to
48:14 say, 'We are heroes and mighty men of W
51:20 hammer and weapon of W: with you I break
51:27 prepare the nations for W against her, summon
51:28 Prepare the nations for W against her, the kings
52:7 all the men of W fled and went out
52:25 of the men of W, and seven men of
Bar 3:26 famous of old, great in stature, expert in W
6:15 cannot save itself from W and robbers.
6:48 For when W or calamity comes upon them, the
6:49 cannot save themselves from W or calamity?
Ezek 17:17 not help him in W, when mounds are cast
27:10 as your men of W; they hung the shield
27:14 for your wares horses, W horses, and mules.
27:27 all your men of W who are in you,
32:27 with their weapons of W, whose swords were laid
38:8 that is restored from W, the land where people
Dan 7:21 looked, this horn made W with the saints, and
9:26 end there shall be W; desolations are decreed.
11:10 "His sons shall wage W and assemble a multitude
11:10 again shall carry the W as far as his
11:25 the south shall wage W with an exceedingly great
Hos 1:7 by sword, nor by W, nor by horses, nor
2:18 bow, the sword, and W from the land; and
10:9 Shall not W overtake them in Gibe-ah?
10:14 therefore the tumult of W shall arise among your
Joel 2:4 of horses, and like W horses they run.
3:9 among the nations: Prepare W, stir up the mighty
3:9 all the men of W draw near, let them
Mic 2:8 who pass by trustingly with no thought of W
3:5 to eat, but declare W against him who puts

4:3 neither shall they learn W any more;
Zech 9:10 from Ephraim and the W horse from Jerusalem; and
14:12 the peoples that wage W against Jerusalem: their
1Mac 3:3 on his armor of W and waged battles, protecting
3:14 I will make W on Judas and his companions,
4:7 about it; and these men were trained in W
5:3 But Judas made W on the sons of Esau
5:30 ladders and engines of W to capture the stronghold,
5:56 and of the heroic W they had fought.
5:57 us go and make W on the Gentiles around
6:20 he built siege towers and other engines of W
6:30 and thirty-two elephants accustomed to W
6:31 and built engines of W; but the Jews sallied
6:51 siege towers, engines of W to throw fire and
6:52 also made engines of W to match theirs, and
8:24 If W comes first to Rome or to any
8:26 the enemy who makes W they shall not give
8:27 the same way, if W comes first to the
9:64 it for many days and made machines of W
9:67 city and set fire to the machines of W
11:4 had burned in the W, for they had piled
11:20 built many engines of W to use against it.
12:13 about us have waged W against us.
12:24 than before, to wage W against him.
12:40 so, but might make W on him, so he
12:44 all these people when we are not at W
12:53 therefore let us make W on them and blot
14:1 that he could make W against Trypho.
14:9 the youths donned the glories and garments of W
15:19 their harm or make W against them and their
15:19 alliance with those who W against them.
15:25 and making engines of W; and he shut Trypho
15:39 gates, and to make W on the people; but
2Mac 2:14 on account of the W which had come upon
10:15 from Jerusalem, and endeavored to keep up the W
12:15 battering-rams or engines of W overthrew Jericho in
12:27 and great stores of W engines and missiles were
14:6 Maccabeus, are keeping up W and stirring up
Lk 14:31 encounter another king in W, will not sit down
Rom 7:23 members another law at W with the law of
2Cor 10:3 carrying on a worldly W,
Heb 11:34 weakness, became mighty in W, put foreign armies
Jas 4:1 passions that are at W in your members?
4:2 and cannot obtain; so you fight and wage W
1Pet 2:11 the flesh that wage W against your soul.
Rev 2:16 to you soon and W against them with the
11:7 bottomless pit will make W upon them and conquer
12:7 Now W arose in heaven, Michael and his angels
12:17 went off to make W on the rest of
13:7 was allowed to make W on the saints and
17:14 beast; they will make W on the Lamb, and
19:11 True, and in righteousness he judges and makes W
19:19 armies gathered to make W against him who sits

WARD

2Sam 5:6 and the lame will W you off"—thinking, "David

WARDROBE (4)

2Kgs 10:22 in charge of the W, "Bring out the vestments
22:14 Harhas, keeper of the W (now she dwelt in
2Chr 34:22 Hasrah, keeper of the W (now she dwelt in
Jer 38:11 the king, to a W of the storehouse, and

WARES (14)

Ezra 1:6 beasts, and with costly W, besides all that was
Neh 10:31 the land bring in W or any grain on
13:16 and all kinds of W and sold them on
13:20 of all kinds of W lodged outside Jerusalem once
Ezek 27:9 mariners were in you, to barter for your W
27:12 iron, tin, and lead they exchanged for your W
27:14 Beth-togarmah exchanged for your W horses, war
27:16 they exchanged for your W emeralds, purple,
27:19 they exchanged for your W; wrought iron, cassia, and
27:22 they exchanged for your W the best of all
27:27 Your riches, your W, your merchandise, your
27:33 When your W came from the seas, you satisfied
Jon 1:5 and they threw the W that were in the
Rev 18:15 The merchants of these W, who gained wealth from

WARFARE (4)

1Kgs 5:3 God because of the W with which his enemies
Is 40:2 to her that her W is ended, that her
2Cor 10:4 the weapons of our W are not worldly but
1Tim 1:18 may wage the good W,

WARM (10)

Josh 9:12 bread; it was still W when we took it
1Kgs 1:1 covered him with clothes, he could not get W
1:2 bosom, that my lord the king may be W
2Kgs 4:34 upon him, the flesh of the child became W
Job 30:4 of bushes, and to W themselves the roots of
Eccl 4:11 lie together, they are W; but how can one
4:11 how can one be W alone?
Is 44:16 says, "Aha, I am W, I have seen the
Hos 11:8 me, my compassion grows W and tender.
Hag 1:6 but no one is W; and he who earns

WARMED (4)

Job 31:20 if he was not W with the fleece of
39:14 and lets them be W on the ground,
Wis 16:27 was melted when simply W by a fleeting ray
Jas 2:16 "Go in peace, be W and filled," without giving

WARMING (6)

Is 47:14 No coal for W oneself is this, no fire
Mk 14:54 with the guards, and W himself at the fire.
14:67 came; and seeing Peter W himself, she looked at
Jn 18:18 they were standing and W themselves; Peter also
18:18 with them, standing and W himself.
18:25 Peter was standing and W himself.

WARMLY (2)

Tob 7:8 They received them very W; and they killed a
2Mac 14:24 his presence; he was W attached to the man.

WARMS (2)

Is 44:15 part of it and W himself, he kindles a
44:16 is satisfied; also he W himself and says, "Aha,

WARN (20)

Ex 19:21 Moses, "Go down and W the people, lest they
Deut 8:19 worship them, I solemnly W you this day that
1Sam 8:9 only, you shall solemnly W them, and show them
2Kgs 6:10 Thus he used to W him, so that he
Neh 9:29 And thou didst W them in order to turn
9:30 with them, and didst W them by thy Spirit
Wis 12:2 and dost remind and W them of the things
Jer 4:16 W the nations that he is coming; announce to
Ezek 3:18 warning, nor speak to W the wicked from his
3:19 But if you W the wicked, and he does
3:21 Nevertheless if you W the righteous man not to
33:8 do not speak to W the wicked to turn
33:9 But if you W the wicked to turn from
Lk 12:5 But I will W you whom to fear: fear
16:28 so that he may W them, lest they also
Acts 4:17 the people, let us W them to speak no
2Cor 13:2 the others, and I W them now while absent,
Gal 5:21 I W you, as I warned you before, that
2Thes 3:15 as an enemy, but W him as a brother.
Rev 22:18 I W every one who hears the words of

WARNED (24)

Gen 26:11 So Abimelech W all the people, saying, "Whoever
43:3 him, "The man solemnly W us, saying, 'You shall
Ex 21:29 its owner has been W but has not kept
Judg 2:15 as the LORD had W, and as the LORD
2Kgs 17:13 Yet the LORD W Israel and Judah by every
Neh 9:26 thy prophets, who had W them in order to
13:15 sabbath day; and I W them on the day
13:21 But I W them and said to them, "Why
Ps 2:10 kings, be wise; be W, O rulers of the
19:11 them is thy servant W; in keeping them there
Is 8:11 hand upon me, and W me not to walk
Jer 6:8 Be W, O Jerusalem, lest I be alienated from
11:7 For I solemnly W your fathers when I brought
42:19 certainty that I have W you this day
Ezek 3:20 because you have not W him, he shall die
33:6 the people are not W, and the sword comes,
Mt 2:12 And being W in a dream not to return
2:22 go there, and being W in a dream he
3:7 Who W you to flee from the wrath to
Lk 3:7 Who W you to flee from the wrath to
2Cor 13:2 I W those who sinned before and all the
Gal 5:21 warn you, as I W you before, that those
Heb 11:7 By faith Noah, being W by God concerning events
12:25 they refused him who W them on earth, much

WARNING (22)

Num 26:10 hundred and fifty men; and they became a W
Prov 1:19 Wisdom's W
Wis 11:10 a father does in W, but thou didst examine

12:26 have not heeded the W of light rebukes will
16:6 little while as a W, and received a token
Jer 6:10 I speak and give W, that they may hear?
11:7 the land of Egypt, W them persistently, even to
Ezek 3:17 you shall give them W from me.
3:18 you give him no W, nor speak to warn
3:21 live, because he took W; and you will have
5:15 and a taunt, a W and a horror, to
23:48 all women may take W and not commit lewdness
33:4 trumpet does not take W, and the sword comes
33:5 and did not take W; his blood shall be
33:5 if he had taken W, he would have saved
33:7 you shall give them W from me.
Dan 8:25 Without W he shall destroy many; and he shall
11:21 shall come in without W and obtain the kingdom
11:24 Without W he shall come into the richest parts
2Mac 8:6 Coming without W, he would set fire to towns
1Cor 10:11 to them as a W, but they were written
Col 1:28 Him we proclaim, W every man and teaching every

WARNINGS (4)

2Kgs 17:15 their fathers, and the W which he gave them.
Neh 9:34 thy commandments and thy W which thou didst give
Job 33:16 and terrifies them with W,
1Cor 10:6 Now these things are W for us, not to

WARNS (2)

Ezek 33:3 blows the trumpet and W the people;
Heb 12:25 we reject him who W from heaven.

WARP (9)

Lev 13:48 a linen garment, in W or woof of linen
13:49 the garment, whether in W or woof or in
13:51 in the garment, in W or woof, or in
13:52 garment, whether diseased in W or woof, woolen or
13:53 in the garment in W or woof or in
13:56 the skin or the W or woof;
13:57 in the garment, in W or woof, or in
13:58 But the garment, W or woof, or anything of
13:59 or linen, either in W or woof, or in

WARRED (3)

Num 31:7 They W against Midian, as the LORD commanded
1Kgs 14:19 of Jeroboam, how he W and how he reigned,
22:45 showed, and how he W, are they not written

WARRING (3)

1Sam 28:15 for the Philistines are W against me, and God
2Kgs 6:8 king of Syria was W against Israel, he took
2Mac 10:14 every turn kept on W against the Jews.

WARRIOR (22)

Judg 11:1 Gileadite was a mighty W, but he was the
1Chr 28:3 for you are a W and have shed blood.'
Job 16:14 upon breach; he runs upon me like a W
Ps 33:16 his great army; a W is not delivered by
120:4 A W's sharp arrows, with glowing coals of the
127:4 the hand of a W are the sons of
Wis 18:15 was doomed, a stern W
Sir 26:19 comes over me: a W in want through poverty,
Is 9:5 boot of the tramping W in battle tumult and
43:17 and horse, army and W; they lie down, they
Jer 20:11 me as a dread W; therefore my persecutors will
46:6 flee away, nor the W escape; in the north
46:12 of your cry; for W has stumbled against warrior;
46:12 warrior has stumbled against W; they have both
50:9 are like a skilled W who does not return
Joel 3:10 spears; let the weak say, "I am a W
Zeph 3:17 in your midst, a W who gives victory; he
Zech 9:13 wield you like a W's sword.
10:7 become like a mighty W, and their hearts shall
1Mac 2:66 has been a mighty W from his youth; he
4:30 attack of the mighty W by the hand of
10:19 you are a mighty W and worthy to be

WARRIORS (41)

Num 31:27 two parts, between the W who went out to
1Kgs 12:21 and eighty thousand chosen W, to fight against the
1Chr 5:24 Hodaviah, and Jahdi-el, mighty W, famous men,
7:2 namely of Tola, mighty W of their generations, their
7:5 all eighty-seven thousand mighty W, enrolled by
7:7 of fathers' houses, mighty W; and their enrollment by
7:9 their fathers' houses, mighty W, was twenty thousand
7:11 fathers' houses, mighty W, seventeen thousand and
7:40 fathers' houses, approved, mighty W, chief of the
8:40 men who were mighty W, bowmen, having many sons
12:8 wilderness mighty and experienced W, expert with
28:1 officials, the mighty men, and all the seasoned W
2Chr 11:1 and eighty thousand chosen W, to fight against Israel,
13:3 him with eight hundred thousand picked mighty W
32:21 off all the mighty W and commanders and officers
Jud 7:2 So all their W moved their camp that day;
16:4 with myriads of his W; their multitude blocked up
Song 4:4 a thousand bucklers, all of them shields of W
Is 10:16 sickness among his stout W, and under his glory
Jer 26:21 Jehoiakim, with all his W and all the princes,
46:5 Their W are beaten down, and have fled in
46:9 Let the W go forth: men of Ethiopia and
48:41 The heart of the W of Moab shall be
49:22 the heart of the W of Edom shall be
50:36 A sword upon her W, that they may be
51:30 The W of Babylon have ceased fighting, they remain
51:56 her, upon Babylon; her W are taken, their bows
51:57 her commanders, and her W; they shall sleep a
Ezek 23:6 her lovers the Assyrians, W clothed in purple,
23:12 Assyrians, governors and commanders, W clothed in
23:23 of them, officers and W, all of them riding
39:20 and all kinds of W says the Lord GOD.
Hos 10:13 the multitude of your W,
Joel 2:7 Like W they charge, like soldiers they scale the
3:11 Bring down thy W, O LORD.
Hab 3:14 the head of his W, who came like a
1Mac 2:42 company of Hasideans, mighty W of Israel, every one
9:11 of the army, as did all the chief W
13:10 he assembled all the W and hastened to complete
15:13 and twenty thousand W and eight thousand cavalry.
16:4 the country twenty thousand W and horsemen, and

WARS (26)

Num 21:14 the Book of the W of the LORD, "Waheb
1Chr 22:8 and have waged great W; you shall not build
2Chr 12:15 There were continual W between Rehoboam and
16:9 this; for from now on you will have W
27:7 Jotham, and all his W, and his ways, behold,
Jud 9:7 the Lord who crushest W; the Lord is thy
16:3 the Lord who crushes W; for he has delivered
Ps 46:9 He makes W cease to the end of the
140:2 heart, and stir up W continually.
Sir 46:3 For he waged the W of the Lord.
1Mac 8:2 told him of their W and of the brave
9:22 of Judas, and his W and the brave deeds
12:13 many afflictions and many W have encircled us; the
12:14 and friends with these W,
13:3 you know also the W and the difficulties which
14:29 proclaimed to us: "Since W often occurred in the
16:2 father have fought the W of Israel from our
16:23 of John and his W and the brave deeds
2Mac 2:20 altar, and further the W against Antiochus Epiphanes
10:10 brief summary of the principal calamities of the W
Mt 24:6 you will hear of W and rumors of wars;
24:6 wars and rumors of W; see that you are
Mk 13:7 when you hear of W and rumors of wars,
13:7 wars and rumors of W, do not be alarmed;
Lk 21:9 when you hear of W and tumults, do not
Jas 4:1 What causes W, and what causes fightings among

WARSHIPS

1Mac 15:3 troops and have equipped W,

WARY

Sir 37:8 Be W of a counselor, and learn first what

WASH (77)

Gen 18:4 water be brought, and W your feet, and rest
19:2 spend the night, and W your feet; then you
24:32 camels, and water to W his feet and the
Ex 19:10 tomorrow, and let them W their garments,
29:4 tent of meeting, and W them with water.
29:17 ram into pieces, and W its entrails and its
30:19 and his sons shall W their hands and their
30:20 the LORD, they shall W with water, lest they
30:21 They shall W their hands and their feet, lest
Lev 1:9 its legs he shall W with water.
1:13 the legs he shall W with water.
6:27 a garment, you shall W that on which it
11:25 of their carcass shall W his clothes and be
11:28 carries their carcass shall W his clothes and be
11:40 of its carcass shall W his clothes and be
11:40 carries the carcass shall W his clothes and be
13:6 eruption; and he shall W his clothes, and be
13:34 clean; and he shall W his clothes, and be
13:54 shall command that they W the thing in which

W

49:19 "Surely your W and your desolate places and your
51:3 will comfort all her W places, and will make
52:9 together into singing, you W places of Jerusalem; for
60:12 shall perish; those nations shall be utterly laid W
Jer 2:15 made his land a W; his cities are in
4:7 make your land a W; your cities will be
4:20 hard on disaster, the whole land is laid W
4:23 and lo, it was W and void; and to
7:34 the bride; for the land shall become a W
9:10 because they are laid W so that no one
9:12 land ruined and laid W like a wilderness, so
10:25 him, and have laid W his habitation.
25:11 a ruin and a W, and these nations shall
25:12 says the LORD, making the land an everlasting W
25:18 a desolation and a W, a hissing and a
25:38 land has become a W because of the sword
33:10 say, 'It is a W without man or beast,'
33:12 this place which is W, without man or beast,
44:6 and they became a W and a desolation, as
44:22 a desolation and a W and a curse, without
46:19 Memphis shall become a W, a ruin, without
48:1 Israel: "Woe to Nebo, for it is laid W
48:20 it by the Arnon, that Moab is laid W
49:3 "Wail, O Heshbon, for Ai is laid W
49:13 horror, a taunt, a W, and a curse; and
49:33 of jackals, an everlasting W; no man shall dwell
51:26 shall be a perpetual W, says the LORD.
51:55 LORD is laying Babylon W, and stilling her mighty
Lam 3:4 flesh and my skin W away, and broken my
Ezek 4:17 another in dismay, and W away under their
6:6 your cities shall be W and your high places
6:6 your altars will be W and ruined, your idols
6:14 the land desolate and W, throughout all their
12:20 cities shall be laid W, and the land shall
19:7 their strongholds, and laid W their cities; and the
26:2 that she is laid W
26:19 you a city laid W, like the cities that
29:9 of Egypt shall be a desolation and a W
29:10 of Egypt an utter W and desolation, from Migdol
29:12 desolation forty years among cities that are laid W
30:7 in the midst of cities that are laid W
33:10 upon us, and we W away because of them;
33:24 the inhabitants of these W places in the land
33:27 who are in the W places shall fall by
33:28 a desolation and a W; and her proud might
33:29 a desolation and a W because of all their
35:3 I will make you a desolation and a W
35:4 will lay your cities W, and you shall become
35:7 make Mount Seir a W and a desolation; and
36:10 be inhabited and the W places rebuilt;
36:33 be inhabited, and the W places shall be rebuilt.
36:35 of Eden; and the W and desolate and ruined
36:38 feasts, so shall the W cities be filled with
38:8 had been a continual W; its people were brought
38:12 plunder; to assail the W places which are now
Hos 2:12 And I will lay W her vines and her
Joel 1:7 It has laid W my vines, and splintered my
1:10 The fields are laid W, the ground mourns; because
Amos 4:9 and mildew; I laid W your gardens and your
7:9 Israel shall be laid W, and I will rise
Mic 1:7 idols I will lay W; for from the hire
Nah 1:5 the earth is laid W before him, the world
Zeph 1:13 goods shall be plundered, and their houses laid W
2:9 salt pits, and a W for ever.
2:13 a desolation, a dry W like the desert.
3:6 ruins; I have laid W their streets so that
Zech 11:3 for the jungle of the Jordan is laid W
Mal 1:3 Esau; I have laid W his hill country and
1Mac 2:12 glory have been laid W; the Gentiles have profaned
Mt 12:25 against itself is laid W, and no city or
26:8 saw it, they were indignant, saying, "Why this W
Lk 11:17 against itself is laid W, and a divided household
Rev 18:17 one hour all this wealth has been laid W
18:19 In one hour she has been laid W

WASTED (9)

Num 24:22 set in the rock; nevertheless Kain shall be W
Deut 32:24 them; they shall be W with hunger, and devoured
Judg 6:5 counted; so that they W the land as they
Job 33:21 His flesh is so W away that it cannot
Ps 31:9 distress; my eye is W from grief, my soul
32:3 my sin, my body W away through my groaning
Sir 20:12 his words, but the courtesies of fools are W
Nah 3:7 from you and say, W is Nineveh; who will
Mk 14:4 indignantly, "Why was the ointment thus W

WASTELAND

Wis 10:7 a continually smoking W, plants bearing fruit

WASTES (11)

Job 13:28 Man W away like a rotten thing, like a
14:11 lake, and a river W away and dries up,
Ps 6:7 My eye W away because of grief, it grows
91:6 nor the destruction that W at noonday.
107:4 Some wandered in desert W, finding no way to
107:40 them wander in trackless W;
Sir 31:1 Wakefulness over wealth W away one's flesh, and
38:28 his flesh, and he W away in the heat
Is 10:18 when a sick man W away.
Jer 49:13 curse; and all her cities shall be perpetual W
Ezek 36:4 the valleys, the desolate W and the deserted cities,

WASTING (4)

Ps 106:15 asked, but sent a W disease among them.
Is 10:16 of hosts, will send W sickness among his stout
Lk 16:1 that this man was W his goods.
2Cor 4:16 our outer nature is W away, our inner nature

WATCH (70)

Gen 31:49 he said, "The LORD W between you and me,
Ex 14:24 And in the morning W the LORD in the
Judg 7:19 beginning of the middle W, when they had just
7:19 had just set the W; and they blew the
21:21 in the vineyards, and W; if the daughters of
1Sam 6:9 And W; if it goes up on the way
11:11 camp in the morning W, and cut down the
19:11 to David's house to W him, that he might
26:15 have you not kept W over your lord the
26:16 you have not kept W over your lord, the
2Sam 13:34 man who kept the W lifted up his eyes,
1Chr 26:16 W corresponded to watch.
26:16 Watch corresponded to W
Neh 11:19 their brethren, who kept W at the gates, were
12:24 the man of God, W corresponding to watch.
12:24 David the man of God, watch corresponding to W
Tob 4:14 W yourself, my son, in everything you do, and
Jud 7:13 camp there to keep W that not a man
12:5 Along toward the morning W she arose
Esth 12:1 the king who kept W in the courtyard.
Job 14:16 thou wouldest not keep W over my sin;
21:32 borne to the grave, W is kept over his
Ps 5:3 morning I prepare a sacrifice for thee, and W
10:8 His eyes stealthily W for the hapless,
56:6 together, they lurk, they W my steps.
61:7 steadfast love and faithfulness W over him!
66:7 ever, whose eyes keep W on the nations—
71:10 concerning me, those who W for my life consult
90:4 past, or as a W in the night.
141:3 mouth, O LORD, keep W over the door of
142:4 to the right and W, but there is none
Prov 2:11 your soul; discretion will W over you; understanding
6:22 lie down, they will W over you; and when
15:3 in every place, keeping W on the evil and
22:12 of the LORD keep W over knowledge, but he
24:12 not he who keeps W over your soul know
Sir 1:26 men's sight, and keep W over your lips.
12:11 and goes about cringing, W yourself, and be on
26:10 Keep strict W over a headstrong daughter, lest, when
27:12 Among stupid people W for a chance to leave,
33:16 was the last on W; I was like one
40:6 though he were on W, he is troubled by
42:11 Keep strict W over a headstrong daughter, lest she
Is 29:20 cease, and all who W to do evil shall
Jer 31:28 evil, so I will W over them to build
48:19 by the way and W, O inhabitant of Aroer!
51:12 of Babylon; make the W strong; set up watchmen;
Ezek 34:16 the strong I will W over; I will feed
Nah 2:1 Man the ramparts; W the road; gird your loins;
Hab 2:1 take my stand to W, and station myself on
Mt 14:25 And in the fourth W of the night he
24:42 W therefore, for you do not know on what
25:13 do not know you.' W therefore, for you know
26:38 death; remain here, and W with me."
26:40 "So, could you not W with me one hour?
26:41 W and pray that you may not enter into
27:36 sat down and kept W over him there.
27:54 were with him, keeping W over Jesus, saw the
Mk 6:48 And about the fourth W of the night he
13:33 Take heed, W and pray; for you do not
13:34 and commands the doorkeeper to be on the W
13:35 W therefore—for you do not know when the
13:37 I say to you I say to all: W

14:34 very sorrowful, even to death; remain here, and W
14:37 Could you not W one hour?
14:38 W and pray that you may not enter into
Lk 2:8 in the field, keeping W over their flock by
12:38 comes in the second W, or in the third,
21:36 But W at all times, praying that you may
Heb 13:17 for they are keeping W over your souls, as

WATCHED (14)

Jud 10:10 men of the city W her until she had
Job 29:2 the days when God W over me;
Eccl 5:8 the high official is W by a higher, and
Sir 19:9 has heard you and W you, and when the
46:14 congregation, and the Lord W over Jacob.
Jer 31:28 that as I have W over them to pluck
Lam 4:17 in our watching we W for a nation which
Dan 13:12 And they W eagerly, day after day, to see
2Mac 14:29 oppose the king, he W for an opportunity to
Mt 24:43 coming, he would have W and would not have
Mk 3:2 And they W him, to see whether he would
12:41 opposite the treasury, and W the multitude putting
Lk 6:7 scribes and the Pharisees W him, to see whether
20:20 So they W him, and sent spies, who pretended

WATCHER (3)

Job 7:20 do to thee, thou W of men?
Dan 4:13 bed, and behold, a W, a holy one, came
4:23 the king saw a W, a holy one, coming

WATCHERS

Dan 4:17 the decree of the W, the decision by the

WATCHES (13)

Job 33:11 in the stocks, and W all my paths.'
Ps 37:32 The wicked W the righteous, and seeks to slay
63:6 on thee in the W of the night;
119:148 are awake before the W of the night, that
127:1 Unless the LORD W over the city, the watchman
146:9 The LORD W over the sojourners, he upholds the
Prov 5:21 the LORD, and he W all his paths.
Wis 3:9 his elect, and he W over his holy ones.
4:15 his elect, and he W over his holy ones.
Sir 43:10 stand as ordered, they never relax in their W
Lam 2:19 in the night, at the beginning of the W
Bar 3:34 stars shone in their W, and were glad; he
2Mac 3:39 his dwelling in heaven W over that place himself

WATCHEST

Job 13:27 in the stocks, and W all my paths; thou

WATCHFUL (4)

Sir 13:13 yourself and be very W, for you are walking
1Cor 16:13 Be W, stand firm in your faith, be courageous,
Col 4:2 steadfastly in prayer, being W in it with thanksgiving;
1Pet 5:8 Be sober, be W

WATCHING (24)

Ex 12:42 was a night of W by the LORD, to
12:42 is a night of W kept to the LORD
1Sam 4:13 seat by the road W, for his heart trembled
1Kgs 20:33 Now the men were W for an omen, and
1Chr 9:27 lay the duty of W, and they had charge
Ps 119:82 My eyes fail with W for thy promise; I
119:123 My eyes fail with W for thy salvation, and
Prov 8:34 who listens to me, W daily at my gates,
Jer 1:12 well, for I am W over my word to
5:6 A leopard is W against their cities, every one
20:10 all my familiar friends, W for my fall.
44:27 lives.' Behold, I am W over them for evil
Lam 4:17 Our eyes failed, ever W vainly for help; in
4:17 for help; in our W we watched for a
Bar 6:7 you, and he is W your lives.
Dan 13:15 Once, while they were W for an opportune day,
13:16 hid themselves and were W her.
Zech 11:11 the sheep, who were W me, knew that it
2Mac 7:6 "The Lord God is W over us and in
9:25 to my kingdom keep W for opportunities and waiting
Lk 14:1 the Pharisees, they were W him.
23:34 the people stood by, W; but the rulers scoffed
Acts 9:24 They were W the gates day and night, to
2Cor 6:5 beatings, imprisonments, tumults, labors, W, hunger;

WATCHMAN (20)

2Sam 18:24 two gates; and the W went up to the
18:25 And the W called out and told the king.
18:26 And the W saw another man running; and the
18:26 man running; and the W called to the gate
18:27 And the W said, "I think the running of
2Kgs 9:17 Now the W was standing on the tower in
9:18 And the W reported, saying, "The messenger
9:20 Again the W reported, "He reached them, but he
Job 27:18 a booth which a W makes.
Ps 127:1 over the city, the W stays awake in vain.
Is 21:6 me: "Go, set a W, let him announce what
21:11 to me from Seir, W, what of the night?
21:11 W, what of the night?"
21:12 The W says: "Morning comes, and also the night.
Ezek 3:17 have made you a W for the house of
33:2 and make him their W;
33:6 But if the W sees the sword coming and
33:6 will require at the W's hand.
33:7 I have made a W for the house of
Hos 9:8 The prophet is the W of Ephraim, the people

WATCHMEN (17)

1Sam 14:16 And the W of Saul in Gibe-ah of Benjamin
2Kgs 11:18 And the priest posted W over the house of
2Chr 23:18 And Jehoiada posted W for the house of the
Jud 13:11 from afar to the W at the gates, "Open,
Ps 130:6 the LORD more than W for the morning, more
130:6 the morning, more than W for the morning.
Song 3:3 The W found me, as they went about in
5:7 The W found me, as they went about in
5:7 away my mantle, those W of the walls.
Sir 37:14 better informed than seven W sitting high on a
Is 52:8 Hark, your W lift up their voice, together they
56:10 His W are blind, they are all without knowledge;
62:6 Jerusalem, I have set W; all the day and
Jer 6:17 in it.' I set W over you, saying, 'Give
31:6 be a day when W will call in the
51:12 watch strong; set up W; prepare the ambushes; for
Mic 7:4 The day of their W, of their punishment, has

WATCHTOWER (7)

2Kgs 17:9 all their towns, from W to fortified city;
18:8 and its territory, from W to fortified city.
2Chr 20:24 Judah came to the W of the wilderness, they
Sir 37:14 informed than seven watchmen sitting high on a W
Is 5:2 vines; he built a W in the midst of
21:8 saw cried: "Upon a W I stand, O Lord,
32:14 the hill and the W will become dens for

WATCHWORD (2)

2Mac 8:23 book, and gave the W, "God's help"; then, leading
13:15 gave his men the W, "God's victory," and with

WATER (505)

Gen 2:10 out of Eden to W the garden, and there
16:7 by a spring of W in the wilderness, the
18:4 Let a little W be brought, and wash your
21:14 and a skin of W, and gave it to
21:15 When the W in the skin was gone, she
21:19 saw a well of W; and she went, and
21:19 filled the skin with W, and gave the lad
21:25 about a well of W which Abimelech's servants had
24:11 by the well of W at the time of
24:11 the time when women go out to draw W
24:13 by the spring of W, and the daughters of
24:13 of the city are coming out to draw W
24:14 'Drink, and I will W your camels'—let her
24:15 came out with her W jar upon her shoulder.
24:17 give me a little W to drink from your
24:32 for the camels, and W to wash his feet
24:43 by the spring of W; let the young woman
24:43 give me a little W from your jar to
24:45 came out with her W jar on her shoulder;
26:18 again the wells of W which had been dug
26:19 a well of springing W,
26:20 Isaac's herdsmen, saying, "The W is ours." So he
26:32 dug, and said to him, "We have found W
29:3 of the well, and W the sheep, and put
29:7 to be gathered together; W the sheep, and go,
29:8 the well; then we W the sheep."
37:24 empty, there was no W in it.
43:24 house, and given them W, and they had washed
49:4 Unstable as W, you shall not have pre-eminence
Ex 2:10 said, "Because I drew him out of the W
2:16 they came and drew W, and filled the troughs
2:16 filled the troughs to W their father's flock.
2:19 shepherds, and even drew W for us and watered
4:9 you shall take some W from the Nile and
4:9 dry ground; and the W which you shall take

7:15 going out to the W; wait for him by
7:17 I will strike the W that is in the
7:18 will loathe to drink W from the Nile.'"
7:19 all their pools of W, that they may become
7:20 rod and struck the W that was in the
7:20 Nile, and all the W that was in the
7:21 Egyptians could not drink W from the Nile; and
7:24 about the Nile for W to drink, for they
7:24 could not drink the W of the Nile.
8:20 goes out to the W, and say to him,
12:9 raw or boiled with W, but roasted, its head
14:26 the sea, that the W may come back upon
15:22 three days in the wilderness and found no W
15:23 could not drink the W of Marah because it
15:25 threw it into the W, and the water became
15:25 the water, and the W became sweet.
15:27 were twelve springs of W and seventy palm trees;
15:27 palm trees; and they encamped there by the W
17:1 but there was no W for the people to
17:2 and said, "Give us W to drink." And Moses
17:3 people thirsted there for W, and the people
17:6 strike the rock, and W shall come out of
20:4 that is in the W under the earth;
23:25 your bread and your W; and I will take
29:4 the tent of meeting, and wash them with W
30:18 and you shall put W in it,
30:20 they shall wash with W, lest they die.
32:20 scattered it upon the W, and made the people
34:28 forty nights; he neither ate bread nor drank W
Lev 1:9 entrails and its legs he shall wash with W
1:13 entrails and the legs he shall wash with W
6:28 vessel, that shall be scoured, and rinsed in W
8:6 Aaron and his sons, and washed them with W
8:21 legs were washed with W, Moses burned the whole
11:18 cormorant, the ibis, the W hen, the pelican, the
11:32 must be put into W, and it shall be
11:34 be eaten, upon which W may come, shall be
11:36 or a cistern holding W shall be clean; but
11:38 is clean; but if W is put on the
14:5 the birds in an earthen vessel over running W
14:6 killed over the running W;
14:8 and bathe himself in W, and he shall be
14:9 bathe his body in W, and he shall be
14:50 earthen vessel over running W,
14:51 and in the running W, and sprinkle the house
14:52 and with the running W, and with the living
15:5 and bathe himself in W, and be unclean until
15:6 and bathe himself in W, and be unclean until
15:7 and bathe himself in W, and be unclean until
15:8 and bathe himself in W, and be unclean until
15:10 and bathe himself in W, and be unclean until
15:11 rinsed his hands in W shall wash his clothes,
15:11 and bathe himself in W, and be unclean until
15:12 every vessel of wood shall be rinsed in W
15:13 his body in running W, and shall be clean.
15:16 his whole body in W, and be unclean until
15:17 shall be washed with W, and be unclean until
15:18 shall bathe themselves in W, and be unclean until
15:21 and bathe himself in W, and be unclean until
15:22 and bathe himself in W, and be unclean until
15:27 and bathe himself in W, and be unclean until
16:4 bathe his body in W, and then put them
16:24 bathe his body in W in a holy place,
16:26 bathe his body in W, and afterward he may
16:28 bathe his body in W, and afterward he may
17:15 and bathe himself in W, and be unclean until
22:6 things unless he has bathed his body in W
Num 5:17 priest shall take holy W in an earthen vessel,
5:17 of the tabernacle and put it into the W
5:18 priest shall have the W of bitterness that brings
5:19 be free from this W of bitterness that brings
5:22 body swell; may this W that brings the curse
5:23 them off into the W of bitterness;
5:24 the woman drink the W of bitterness that brings
5:24 the curse, and the W that brings the curse
5:26 and afterward shall make the woman drink the W
5:27 made her drink the W, then, if she has
5:27 against her husband, the W that brings the curse
8:7 cleanse them: sprinkle the W of expiation upon
19:7 bathe his body in W, and afterwards he shall
19:8 wash his clothes in W and bathe his body
19:8 bathe his body in W, and shall be unclean
19:9 of Israel for the W for impurity, for the
19:12 cleanse himself with the W on the third day
19:13 from Israel; because the W for impurity was not
19:17 sin offering, and running W shall be added in

19:18 dip it in the W, and sprinkle it upon
19:19 and bathe himself in W, and at evening he
19:20 the LORD; because the W for impurity has not
19:21 He who sprinkles the W for impurity shall wash
19:21 he who touches the W for impurity shall be
20:2 Now there was no W for the congregation; and
20:5 and there is no W to drink."
20:8 eyes to yield its W; so you shall bring
20:8 so you shall bring W out of the rock
20:10 shall we bring forth W for you out of
20:11 his rod twice; and W came forth abundantly, and
20:17 neither will we drink W from a well; we
20:19 we drink of your W, I and my cattle,
21:5 no food and no W, and we loathe this
21:16 the people together, and I will give them W
21:22 will not drink the W of a well; we
24:7 W shall flow from his buckets, and his seed
31:23 be purified with the W of impurity; and whatever
31:23 stand the fire, you shall pass through the W
33:9 were twelve springs of W and seventy palm trees,
33:14 where there was no W for the people to
Deut 2:6 you shall also buy W of them for money,
2:28 eat, and give me W for money, that I
4:18 that is in the W under the earth.
5:8 that is in the W under the earth;
8:7 land of brooks of W, of fountains and springs,
8:15 where there was no W, who brought you water
8:15 water, who brought you W out of the flinty
9:9 forty nights; I neither ate bread nor drank W
9:18 ate bread nor drank W, because of all the
10:7 Gudgodah to Jotbathah, a land with brooks of W
11:4 how he made the W of the Red Sea
11:11 and valleys, which drinks W by the rain from
12:16 shall pour it out upon the earth like W
12:24 shall pour it out upon the earth like W
14:16 the great owl, the W hen
15:23 shall pour it out on the ground like W
21:4 a valley with running W, which is neither plowed
23:4 with bread and with W on the way, when
23:11 shall bathe himself in W, and when the sun
29:11 he who draws your W,
Josh 2:10 LORD dried up the W of the Red Sea
3:15 the brink of the W (the Jordan overflows all
7:5 hearts of the people melted, and became as W
9:21 wood and drawers of W for all the congregation,
9:23 wood and drawers of W for the house of
9:27 wood and drawers of W for the congregation and
15:19 of the Negeb, give me also springs of W
Judg 1:15 of the Negeb, give me also springs of W
4:19 give me a little W to drink; for I
5:4 and the heavens dropped, yea, the clouds dropped W
5:25 He asked W and she gave him milk, she
6:38 from the fleece to fill a bowl with W
7:4 them down to the W and I will test
7:5 people down to the W; and the LORD said
7:5 one that laps the W with his tongue, as
7:6 rest of the people knelt down to drink W
15:19 Lehi, and there came W from it; and when
1Sam 7:6 at Mizpah, and drew W and poured it out
9:11 coming out to draw W, and said to them,
25:11 my bread and my W and my meat that
26:11 and the jar of W, and let us go."
26:12 and the jar of W from Saul's head; and
26:16 and the jar of W that was at his
30:11 ate, they gave him W to drink,
30:12 eaten bread or drunk W for three days and
2Sam 5:8 him get up the W shaft to attack the
14:14 die, we are like W spilt on the ground,
17:20 them, "They have gone over the brook of W
17:21 go quickly over the W; for thus and so
22:12 him his canopy, thick clouds, a gathering of W
23:15 one would give me W to drink from the
23:16 the Philistines, and drew W out of the well
1Kgs 13:8 eat bread or drink W in this place;
13:9 eat bread, nor drink W, nor return by the
13:16 eat bread nor drink W with you in this
13:17 eat bread nor drink W there, nor return by
13:18 house that he may eat bread and drink W
13:19 and ate bread in his house, and drank W
13:22 eaten bread and drunk W in the place of
13:22 bread, and drink no W; your body shall not
14:15 is shaken in the W, and root up Israel
17:10 "Bring me a little W in a vessel, that
18:4 them with bread and W
18:5 all the springs of W and to all the
18:13 a cave, and fed them with bread and W

18:33 "Fill four jars with W, and pour it on
18:35 And the W ran round about the altar, and
18:35 the altar, and filled the trench also with W
18:38 and licked up the W that was in the
19:6 baked on hot stones and a jar of W
22:27 fare of bread and W, until I come in
2Kgs 2:8 up, and struck the W, and the water was
2:8 the water, and the W was parted to the
2:14 him, and struck the W, saying, "Where is the
2:14 he had struck the W, the water was parted
2:14 struck the water, the W was parted to the
2:19 lord sees; but the W is bad, and the
2:21 to the spring of W and threw salt in
2:21 I have made this W wholesome; henceforth neither
2:22 So the W has been wholesome to this day,
3:9 days, there was no W for the army or
3:11 is here, who poured W on the hands of
3:17 shall be filled with W, so that you shall
3:19 up all springs of W, and ruin every good
3:20 offering the sacrifice, behold, W came from the
3:20 of Edom, till the country was filled with W
3:22 sun shone upon the W, the Moabites saw the
3:22 the Moabites saw the W opposite them as red
3:25 stopped every spring of W, and felled all the
6:5 head fell into the W; and he cried out,
6:22 Set bread and W before them, that they may
8:15 and dipped it in W and spread it over
18:31 you will drink the W of his own cistern;
20:20 the conduit and brought W into the city, are
1Chr 11:17 one would give me W to drink from the
11:18 the Philistines, and drew W out of the well
2Chr 18:26 fare of bread and W, until I return in
32:3 men to stop the W of the springs that
32:4 the kings of Assyria come and find much W
Ezra 10:6 eating bread nor drinking W; for he was mourning
Neh 3:26 a point opposite the W Gate on the east
8:1 the square before the W Gate; and they told
8:3 the square before the W Gate from early morning
8:16 the square at the W Gate and in the
9:15 hunger and bring forth W for them from the
9:20 mouth, and gavest them W for their thirst.
12:37 of David, to the W Gate on the east.
13:2 Israel with bread and W, but hired Balaam against
Jud 2:7 to prepare earth and W, for I am coming
7:7 springs that supplied their W, and seized them and
7:12 of the spring of W that flows from the
7:13 where all the people of Bethulia get their W
7:17 valley and seized the W supply and the springs
7:20 all the vessels of W belonging to every inhabitant
7:21 did not have enough W to drink their fill
8:9 faint for lack of W, and when she heard
10:3 bathed her body with W, and anointed herself with
11:12 is exhausted and their W has almost given out,
Esth 10:6 the sun and abundant W _ the river is
11:10 great river, with abundant W;
Job 3:24 bread, and my groanings are poured out like W
8:11 Can reeds flourish where there is no W
14:9 at the scent of W it will bud and
15:16 and corrupt, a man who drinks iniquity like W
22:7 You have given no W to the weary to
22:11 and a flood of W covers you.
34:7 drinks up scoffing like W,
36:27 up the drops of W, he distils his mist
Ps 1:3 planted by streams of W, that yields its fruit
18:11 around him, his canopy thick clouds dark with W
22:14 am poured out like W, and all my bones
58:7 Let them vanish like W that runs away; like
63:1 weary land where no W is.
65:9 God is full of W; thou providest their grain,
66:12 through fire and through W; yet thou hast brought
72:6 grass, like showers that W the earth!
77:17 The clouds poured out W; the skies gave forth
78:20 the rock so that W gushed out and streams
79:3 out their blood like W round about Jerusalem, and
105:41 opened the rock, and W gushed forth; it flowed
107:33 a desert, springs of W into thirsty ground,
107:35 desert into pools of W, a parched land into
107:35 of water, a parched land into springs of W
109:18 into his body like W, like oil into his
114:8 into a pool of W, the flint into a
114:8 of water, the flint into a spring of W
Prov 5:15 Drink W from your own cistern, flowing water from
5:15 your own cistern, flowing W from your own well.
5:16 scattered abroad, streams of W in the streets?
8:24 forth, when there were no springs abounding with W
9:17 sense she says, Stolen W is sweet, and bread
17:14 is like letting out W; so quit before the
20:5 mind is like deep W, but a man of
21:1 is a stream of W in the hand of
25:21 is thirsty, give him W to drink;
25:25 Like cold W to a thirsty soul, so is
27:19 As in W face answers to face, so the
30:16 earth ever thirsty for W, and the fire which
Eccl 2:6 pools from which to W the forest of growing
Song 4:15 a well of living W, and flowing streams from
5:12 doves beside springs of W, bathed in milk, fitly
Wis 5:10 sails through the billowy W, and when it has
5:22 from a catapult; the W of the sea will
11:4 called upon thee, and W was given them out
11:7 thou gavest them abundant W unexpectedly,
13:2 the stars, or turbulent W, of the luminaries of
16:17 of all--in the W, which quenches all things,
16:19 in the midst of W it burned more intensely
16:29 like wintry frost, and flow away like waste W
17:18 rhythm of violently rushing W,
19:7 dry land emerging where W had stood before, an
19:19 animals were transformed into W creatures, and
19:20 Fire even in W retained its normal power, and
19:20 its normal power, and W forgot its fire-quenching
Sir 3:28 W extinguishes a blazing fire: so almsgiving atones
15:3 and give him the W of wisdom to drink.
15:16 before you fire and W: stretch out your hand
18:9 Like a drop of W from the sea and
24:28 river and like a W channel into a garden.
24:29 I said, "I will W my orchard and drench
25:24 Allow no outlet to W, and no boldness of
26:12 and drinks from any W near him, so will
29:21 essentials for life are W and bread and clothing
31:26 Fire and W prove the temper of steel, so
38:5 Was not W made sweet with a tree in
39:13 by a stream of W;
39:17 and the reservoirs of W at the word of
39:23 as he turns fresh W into salt.
39:26 of man's life are W and fire and iron
40:16 The reeds by any W or river bank will
43:20 ice freezes over the W; it rests upon every
43:20 upon every pool of W, and the water puts
43:20 of water, and the W puts it on like
48:17 his city, and brought W into the midst of
48:17 sheer rock with iron and built pools for W
50:3 days a cistern for W was quarried out, a
50:8 by a spring of W, like a green shoot
Is 1:22 silver has become dross, your wine mixed with W
1:30 whose leaf withers, and like a garden without W
3:1 the whole stay of W;
12:3 joy you will draw W from the wells of
14:23 hedgehog, and pools of W, and I will sweep
19:8 they will languish who spread nets upon the W
21:14 To the thirsty bring W, meet the fugitive with
22:11 two walls for the W of the old pool.
27:3 keeper; every moment I W it.
30:14 or to dip up W out of the cistern."
30:20 of adversity and the W of affliction, yet your
30:25 be brooks running with W, in the day of
32:2 tempest, like streams of W in a dry place,
33:16 be given him, his W will be sure.
35:7 thirsty ground springs of W; the haunt of jackals
36:16 you will drink the W of his own cistern;
41:17 poor and needy seek W, and there is none,
41:18 wilderness a pool of W, and the dry land
41:18 of water, and the dry land springs of W
43:20 ostriches; for I give W in the wilderness, rivers
44:3 For I will pour W on the thirsty land,
44:12 fails, he drinks no W and is faint.
48:21 the deserts; he made W flow for them from
48:21 the rock and the W gushed out.
49:10 and by springs of W will guide them.
50:2 stink for lack of W, and die of thirst.
55:10 return not thither but W the earth, making it
58:11 like a spring of W, whose waters fail not.
64:2 and the fire causes W to boil-- to
Jer 2:13 for themselves, broken cisterns, that can hold no W
6:7 a well keeps its W fresh, so she keeps
8:14 has given us poisoned W to drink, because we
9:15 and give them poisonous W to drink.
9:18 down with tears, and our eyelids gush with W
13:1 your loins, and do not dip it in W
14:3 send their servants for W; they come to the
14:3 cisterns, they find no W, they return with their
17:8 a tree planted by W, that sends out its
17:13 have forsaken the LORD, the fountain of living W
23:15 and give them poisoned W to drink; for from

31:9 walk by brooks of W, in a straight path
38:6 And there was no W in the cistern, but
Lam 2:19 out your heart like W before the presence of
3:54 cast stones on me; W closed over my head;
5:4 must pay for the W we drink, the wood
Ezek 4:11 And W you shall drink by measure, the sixth
4:16 and they shall drink W by measure and in
4:17 may lack bread and W, and look at one
7:17 hands are feeble, and all knees weak as W
12:18 with quaking, and drink W with trembling and with
12:19 with fearfulness, and drink W in dismay, because
16:4 were you washed with W to cleanse you, nor
16:9 I bathed you with W and washed off your
17:7 him that he might W it.
19:10 vineyard transplanted by the W, fruitful and full of
19:10 and full of branches by reason of abundant W
21:7 faint and all knees will be weak as W
24:3 it on, pour in W also;
31:5 branches long, from abundant W in its shoots.
31:14 no trees that drink W may reach up to
31:16 Lebanon, all that drink W, will be comforted in
34:18 to drink of clear W, that you must foul
36:25 I will sprinkle clean W upon you, and you
47:1 the temple; and behold, W was issuing from below
47:1 faced east); and the W was flowing down from
47:2 the east; and the W was coming out on
47:3 led me through the W; and it was ankle-deep.
47:4 led me through the W; and it was knee-deep.
47:4 led me through the W; and it was up
47:5 pass through, for the W had risen; it was
47:8 said to me, "This W flows toward the eastern
47:8 of the sea, the W will become fresh.
47:9 many fish; for this W goes there, that the
47:12 every month, because the W for them flows from
Dan 1:12 vegetables to eat and W to drink.
Hos 2:5 my bread and my W, my wool and my
5:10 them I will pour out my wrath like W
6:3 the spring rains that W the earth."
Joel 1:19 to thee because the W brooks are dried up,
3:18 Judah shall flow with W; and a fountain shall
3:18 of the LORD and W the valley of Shittim.
Amos 4:8 one city to drink W, and were not satisfied;
8:11 nor a thirst for W, but of hearing the
Jon 3:7 not feed, or drink W,
Nah 3:8 by the Nile, with W around her, her rampart
3:8 rampart a sea, and W her wall?
3:14 Draw W for the siege, strengthen your forts; go
1Mac 5:40 to the stream of W, Timothy said to the
5:42 approached the stream of W, he stationed the scribes
9:33 and camped by the W of the pool of
9:45 and behind us; the W of the Jordan is
2Mac 15:39 or, again, to drink W alone, while wine mixed
15:39 while wine mixed with W is sweet and delicious
Mt 3:11 "I baptize you with W for repentance, but he
3:16 up immediately from the W, and behold, the heavens
10:42 a cup of cold W because he is a
14:28 you, bid me come to you on the W
14:29 and walked on the W and came to Jesus;
17:15 falls into the fire, and often into the W
27:24 was beginning, he took W and washed his hands
Mk 1:8 have baptized you with W; but he will baptize
1:10 up out of the W, immediately he saw the
9:22 fire and into the W, to destroy him; but
9:41 you a cup of W to drink because you
14:13 carrying a jar of W will meet you; follow
Lk 3:16 "I baptize you with W; but he who is
7:44 you gave me no W for my feet, but
8:23 they were filling with W, and were in danger.
8:25 commands even wind and W, and they obey him?"
13:15 lead it away to W it?
16:24 of his finger in W and cool my tongue;
22:10 carrying a jar of W will meet you; follow
Jn 1:26 them, "I baptize with W; but among you stands
1:31 I came baptizing with W, that he might be
1:33 me to baptize with W said to me, 'He
2:7 Jesus said to them, "Fill the jars with W
2:9 the feast tasted the W now become wine, and
2:9 who had drawn the W knew), the steward of
3:5 one is born of W and the Spirit, he
3:23 because there was much W there; and people came
4:7 There came a woman of Samaria to draw W
4:10 him, and he would have given you living W
4:11 is deep; where do you get that living W
4:13 who drinks of this W will thirst again,
4:14 whoever drinks of the W that I shall give
4:14 will never thirst; the W that I shall give
4:14 him a spring of W welling up to eternal
4:15 "Sir, give me this W, that I may not
4:28 the woman left her W jar, and went away
4:46 he had made the W wine.
5:6 the pool when the W is troubled, and while
7:38 of his heart shall flow rivers of living W
13:5 Then he poured W into a basin, and began
19:34 and at once there came out blood and W
Acts 1:5 for John baptized with W, but before many days
8:36 they came to some W, and the eunuch said,
8:36 water, and the eunuch said, "See, here is W
8:37 went down into the W, Philip and the eunuch,
8:38 up out of the W, the Spirit of the
10:47 "Can any one forbid W for baptizing these people
11:16 said, 'John baptized with W, but you shall be
Eph 5:26 by the washing of W with the word,
1Tim 5:23 No longer drink only W, but use a little
Heb 9:19 calves and goats, with W and scarlet wool and
10:22 evil conscience and our bodies washed with pure W
Jas 3:11 the same opening fresh W and brackish?
3:12 No more can salt W yield fresh.
1Pet 3:20 few, that is, eight persons, were saved through W
2Pet 3:5 earth formed out of W and by means of
3:5 and by means of W,
3:6 existed was deluged with W and perished.
1Jn 5:6 he who came by W and blood, Jesus Christ,
5:6 Christ, not with the W only but with the
5:6 only but with the W and the blood.
5:8 witnesses, the Spirit, the W, and the blood; and
Rev 7:17 to springs of living W; and God will wipe
8:10 of the rivers and on the fountains of W
8:11 men died of the W, because it was made
12:15 The serpent poured W like a river out of
14:7 and earth, the sea and the fountains of W
16:4 and the fountains of W, and they became blood.
16:5 heard the angel of W say, "Just art thou
16:12 river Euphrates, and its W was dried up, to
21:6 the fountain of the W of life without payment.
22:1 the river of the W of life, bright as
22:17 who desires take the W of life without price.

WATERCOURSES (3)

Ps 126:4 O LORD, like the W in the Negeb!
Ezek 31:12 broken in all the W of the land; and
32:6 flowing blood; and the W will be full of

WATERED (12)

Gen 2:6 from the earth and W the whole face of
13:10 Jordan valley was well W everywhere like the
29:2 for out of that well the flocks were W
29:10 the well's mouth, and W the flock of Laban
Ex 2:17 and helped them, and W their flock.
2:19 water for us and W the flock."
Deut 11:10 sowed your seed and W it with your feet,
Ps 104:16 of the LORD are W abundantly, the cedars of
Prov 11:25 enriched, and one who waters will himself be W
Is 58:11 shall be like a W garden, like a spring
Jer 31:12 shall be like a W garden, and they shall
1Cor 3:6 I planted, Apollos W, but God gave the growth.

WATEREST (3)

Ps 65:9 visitest the earth and W it, thou greatly enrichest
65:10 Thou W its furrows abundantly, settling its ridges,
104:13 thy lofty abode thou W the mountains; the earth

WATERING (2)

Gen 30:38 runnels, that is, the W troughs, where the flocks
Judg 5:11 of musicians at the W places, there they repeat

WATERLESS (5)

Zech 9:11 captives free from the W pit.
Mt 12:43 man, he passes through W places seeking rest, but
Lk 11:24 man, he passes through W places seeking rest; and
2Pet 2:17 These are W springs and mists driven by a
Jude 1:12 together, looking after themselves; W clouds, carried

WATERS (222)

Gen 1:2 God was moving over the face of the W
1:6 the midst of the W, and let it separate
1:6 let it separate the W from the waters."
1:6 and let it separate the waters from the W
1:7 firmament and separated the W which were under
1:7 the firmament from the W which were above the
1:9 God said, "Let the W under the heavens be
1:10 land Earth, and the W that were gathered together
1:20 God said, "Let the W bring forth swarms of

V

1:21 moves, with which the W swarm, according to their
1:22 multiply and fill the W in the seas, and
6:17 bring a flood of W upon the earth, to
7:6 when the flood of W came upon the earth.
7:7 ark, to escape the W of the flood.
7:10 after seven days the W of the flood came
7:17 the earth; and the W increased, and bore up
7:18 The W prevailed and increased greatly upon the
7:18 the ark floated on the face of the W
7:19 And the W prevailed so mightily upon the earth
7:20 heaven were covered; the W prevailed above the
7:24 And the W prevailed upon the earth a hundred
8:1 the earth, and the W subsided;
8:3 was restrained, and the W receded from the earth
8:3 and fifty days the W had abated;
8:5 And the W continued to abate until the tenth
8:7 and fro until the W were dried up from
8:8 to see if the W had subsided from the
8:9 the ark, for the W were still on the
8:11 Noah knew that the W had subsided from the
8:13 of the month, the W were dried from off
9:11 cut off by the W of a flood, and
9:15 all flesh; and the W shall never again become
Ex 7:19 your hand over the W of Egypt, over their
8:6 his hand over the W of Egypt; and the
14:21 dry land, and the W were divided.
14:22 on dry ground, the W being a wall to
14:28 The W returned and covered the chariots and the
14:29 through the sea, the W being a wall to
15:8 of thy nostrils the W piled up, the floods
15:10 them; they sank as lead in the mighty W
15:19 LORD brought back the W of the sea upon
Lev 11:9 may eat, of all that are in the W
11:9 Everything in the W that has fins and scales,
11:10 swarming creatures in the W and of the living
11:10 that are in the W, is an abomination to
11:12 Everything in the W that has not fins and
11:46 that moves through the W and every creature that
Num 20:13 These are the W of Meribah, where the people
20:24 my command at the W of Meribah.
24:6 LORD has planted, like cedar trees beside the W
24:7 shall be in many W, his king shall be
27:14 sanctify me at the W before their eyes." (These
27:14 (These are the W of Meribah of Kadesh in
Deut 14:9 that are in the W you may eat these:
32:51 of Israel at the W of Meri-bath-adesh, in the
33:8 didst strive at the W of Meribah;
Josh 3:8 the brink of the W of the Jordan, you
3:13 shall rest in the W of the Jordan, the
3:13 of the Jordan, the W of the Jordan shall
3:13 from flowing, and the W coming down from above
3:16 time of harvest), the W coming down from above
4:7 tell them that the W of the Jordan were
4:7 over the Jordan, the W of the Jordan were
4:18 on dry ground, the W of the Jordan returned
4:23 God dried up the W of the Jordan for
5:1 had dried up the W of the Jordan for
11:5 encamped together at the W of Merom, to fight
11:7 of war, by the W of Merom, and fell
15:7 passes along to the W of En-shemesh, and ends
15:9 the spring of the W of Nephtoah, and from
16:1 Jericho, east of the W of Jericho, into the
18:15 the spring of the W of Nephtoah;
Judg 5:19 at Taanach, by the W of Megiddo; they got
7:24 Midianites and seize the W against them, as far
7:24 and they seized the W as far as Beth-barah,
2Sam 12:27 Rabbah; moreover, I have taken the city of W
22:17 took me, he drew me out of many W
2Kgs 5:12 better than all the W of Israel?
19:24 wells and drank foreign W, and I dried up
2Chr 32:30 upper outlet of the W of Gihon and directed
Neh 9:11 into the depths, as a stone into mighty W
Jud 9:12 earth, Creator of the W, King of all thy
16:15 their foundations with the W; at thy presence the
Job 5:10 the earth and sends W upon the fields;
11:16 will remember it as W that have passed away.
12:15 If he withholds the W, they dry up; if
14:11 As W fail from a lake, and a river
14:19 from its place; the W wear away the stones;
24:18 the face of the W; their portion is cursed
24:19 snatch away the snow W; so does Sheol those
26:5 shades below tremble, the W and their inhabitants.
26:8 He binds up the W in his thick clouds,
26:10 the face of the W at the boundary between
28:25 and meted out the W by measure;
29:19 spread out to the W, with the dew all
37:10 given, and the broad W are frozen fast.
38:30 The W become hard like stone, and the face
38:34 that a flood of W may cover you?
Ps 18:16 took me, he drew me out of many W
23:2 leads me beside still W;
29:3 LORD is upon the W; the God of glory
29:3 God of glory thunders, the LORD, upon many W
32:6 the rush of great W, they shall not reach
33:7 He gathered the W of the sea as in
46:3 the sea; though its W roar and foam, though
69:1 For the W have come up to my neck.
69:2 have come into deep W, and the flood sweeps
69:14 delivered from my enemies and from the deep W
74:13 break the heads of the dragons on the W
77:16 [Selah] When the W saw thee, O God, when
77:16 O God, when the W saw thee, they were
77:19 path through the great W; yet thy footprints were
78:13 it, and made the W stand like a heap.
78:16 the rock, and caused W to flow down like
81:7 tested you at the W of Meribah.
93:4 the thunders of many W, mightier than the waves
104:3 thy chambers on the W, who makest the clouds
104:6 with a garment; the W stood above the mountains.
105:29 He turned their W into blood, and caused their
106:11 And the W covered their adversaries; not one of
106:32 angered him at the W of Meribah, and it
107:23 business on the great W;
124:5 then over us would have gone the raging W
136:6 the earth upon the W, for his steadfast love
137:1 By the W of Babylon, there we sat down
144:7 me from the many W, from the hand of
147:18 wind blow, and the W flow.
148:4 highest heavens, and you W above the heavens!
Prov 8:29 limit, so that the W might not transgress his
11:25 enriched, and one who W will himself be watered.
18:4 man's mouth are deep W; the fountain of wisdom
30:4 has wrapped up the W in a garment?
Eccl 11:1 your bread upon the W, for you will find
Song 8:7 Many W cannot quench love, neither can floods
Wis 10:18 led them through deep W;
Sir 39:17 At his word the W stood in a heap,
40:11 what is from the W returns to the sea.
Is 8:6 people have refused the W of Shiloah that flow
8:7 up against them the W of the River, mighty
11:9 the LORD as the W cover the sea.
15:6 cry of destruction; the W of Nimrim are a
15:9 For the W of Dibon are full of blood;
17:12 nations, they roar like the roaring of mighty W
17:13 the roaring of many W, but he will rebuke
18:2 the Nile, in vessels of papyrus upon the W
19:5 And the W of the Nile will be dried
22:9 and you collected the W of the lower pool,
23:3 and were on many W; your revenue was the
28:2 storm of mighty, overflowing W, he will cast down
28:17 refuge of lies, and W will overwhelm the shelter."
32:20 who sow beside all W, who let the feet
35:6 For W shall break forth in the wilderness, and
37:25 dug wells and drank W, and I dried up
40:12 Who has measured the W in the hollow of
43:2 you pass through the W I will be with
43:16 path in the mighty W,
44:4 up like grass amid W, like willows by flowing
51:10 up the sea, the W of the great deep;
54:9 I swore that the W of Noah should no
55:1 thirsts, come to the W; and he who has
57:20 cannot rest, and its W toss up mire and
58:11 spring of water, whose W fail not.
63:12 Moses, who divided the W before them to make
Jer 2:13 the fountain of living W, and hewed out cisterns
2:18 Egypt, to drink the W of the Nile?
2:18 Assyria, to drink the W of the Euphrates?
9:1 that my head were W, and my eyes a
10:13 is a tumult of W in the heavens, and
15:18 a deceitful brook, like W that fail?
18:14 Do the mountain W run dry, the cold flowing
46:7 Nile, like rivers whose W surge?
46:8 Nile, like rivers whose W surge.
47:2 says the LORD: Behold, W are rising out of
48:34 For the W of Nimrim also have become desolate.
50:38 A drought upon her W, that they may be
51:13 who dwell by many W, rich in treasures, your
51:16 is a tumult of W in the heavens, and
51:55 waves roar like many W, the noise of their
Ezek 1:24 the sound of many W, like the thunder of
17:5 in fertile soil; he placed it beside abundant W
17:8 good soil by abundant W, that it might bring

26:12 they will cast into the midst of the W
26:19 you, and the great W cover you,
27:34 the depths of the W; your merchandise and all
31:4 The W nourished it, the deep made it grow
31:7 branches; for its roots went down to abundant W
31:14 no trees by the W may grow to lofty
31:15 its rivers, and many W shall be stopped; I
32:2 your rivers, trouble the W with your feet, and
32:13 beasts from beside many W; and no foot of
32:14 I will make their W clear, and cause their
43:2 the sound of many W; and the earth shone
47:8 it enters the stagnant W of the sea, the
47:9 goes there, that the W of the sea may
47:19 as far as the W of Meribath-kadesh, thence along
48:28 from Tamar to the W of Meribath-kadesh, thence
Dan 3:61 Bless the Lord, all W above the heaven, sing
3:80 that move in the W, sing praise to him
12:6 who was above the W of the stream, "How
12:7 who was above the W of the stream, raised
Hos 10:7 like a chip on the face of the W
Amos 5:8 who calls for the W of the sea, and
5:24 justice roll down like W, and righteousness like an
9:6 who calls for the W of the sea, and
Jon 2:5 thy holy temple?' The W closed in over me,
Mic 1:4 before the fire, like W poured down a steep
Nah 2:8 like a pool whose W run away.
Hab 2:14 the LORD, as the W cover the sea.
3:10 and writhed; the raging W swept on; the deep
3:15 sea with thy horses, the surging of mighty W
Zech 14:8 On that day living W shall flow out from
1Mac 11:67 army encamped by the W of Gennesaret.
Mt 8:32 bank into the sea, and perished in the W
1Cor 3:7 plants nor he who W is anything, but only
3:8 plants and he who W are equal, and each
Rev 1:15 the sound of many W;
8:11 A third of the W became wormwood, and many
11:6 have power over the W to turn them into
14:2 the sound of many W and like the sound
17:1 is seated upon many W,
17:15 said to me, "The W that you saw, where
19:6 the sound of many W and like the sound

WATERSKINS
Job 38:37 who can tilt the W of the heavens,

WAVE (36)
Ex 29:24 of his sons, and W them for a wave
29:24 wave them for a W offering before the LORD.
29:26 of Aaron's ordination and W it for a wave
29:26 wave it for a W offering before the LORD;
29:27 the breast of the W offering, and the thigh
Lev 7:30 be waved as a W offering before the LORD.
8:27 waved them as a W offering before the LORD.
8:29 waved it for a W offering before the LORD;
9:21 Aaron waved for a W offering before the LORD;
10:15 of the fat, to W for a wave offering
10:15 to wave for a W offering before the LORD,
14:12 log of oil, and W them for a wave
14:12 wave them for a W offering before the LORD;
14:24 and the priest shall W them for a wave
14:24 wave them for a W offering before the LORD.
23:11 priest; and he shall W the sheaf before the
23:11 sabbath the priest shall W it.
23:12 the day when you W the sheaf, you shall
23:15 the sheaf of the W offering; seven full weeks
23:20 And the priest shall W them with the bread
23:20 first fruits as a W offering before the LORD,
Num 5:25 woman's hand, and shall W the cereal offering
6:20 and the priest shall W them for a wave
6:20 wave them for a W offering before the LORD;
8:11 the LORD as a W offering from the people
8:13 offer them as a W offering to the LORD.
8:15 offered them as a W offering.
8:21 offered them as a W offering before the LORD,
18:11 their gift, all the W offerings of the people
2Kgs 5:11 LORD his God, and W his hand over the
Job 39:13 wings of the ostrich W proudly; but are they
Ps 72:16 the mountains may it W; may its fruit be
Sir 29:18 shaken them like a W of the sea; it
Is 11:15 of Egypt; and will W his hand over the
13:2 cry aloud to them; W the hand for them
Jas 1:6 doubts is like a W of the sea that

WAVED (13)
Ex 29:27 priests' portion, which is W, and which is offered
Lev 7:30 the breast may be W as a wave offering
7:34 the breast that is W and the thigh that
8:27 of his sons, and W them as a wave
8:29 took the breast, and W it for a wave
9:21 the right thigh Aaron W for a wave offering
10:14 the breast that is W and the thigh that
10:15 the breast that is W they shall bring with
14:21 guilt offering to be W, to make atonement for
23:17 of bread to be W, made of two tenths
Num 6:20 the breast that is W and the thigh that
18:18 the breast that is W and as the right
Acts 22:23 they cried out and W their garments and threw

WAVER (3)
Jer 4:1 presence, and do not W,
31:22 How long will you W, O faithless daughter?
Rom 4:20 No distrust made him W concerning the promise of

WAVERING (2)
Ps 26:1 and I have trusted in the LORD without W
Heb 10:23 of our hope without W, for he who promised

WAVES (31)
2Sam 22:5 "For the W of death encompassed me, the torrents
Job 9:8 heavens, and trampled the W of the sea;
38:11 here shall your proud W be stayed?
Ps 42:7 thy cataracts; all thy W and thy billows have
65:7 the roaring of their W, the tumult of the
88:7 and thou dost overwhelm me with all thy W
89:9 the sea; when its W rise, thou stillest them.
93:4 waters, mightier than the W of the sea, the
107:25 which lifted up the W of the sea.
107:29 be still, and the W of the sea were
Wis 5:10 its keel in the W;
14:1 to voyage over raging W calls upon a piece
14:3 safe way through the W,
19:7 out of the raging W,
Sir 24:6 In the W of the sea, in the whole
Is 48:18 your righteousness like the W of the sea;
51:15 sea so that its W roar– the LORD
Jer 5:22 cannot pass; though the W toss, they cannot prevail,
31:35 sea so that its W roar–the LORD of
51:42 on Babylon; she is covered with its tumultuous W
51:55 Their W roar like many waters, the noise of
Ezek 26:3 against you, as the sea brings up its W
Jon 2:3 about me; all thy W and thy billows passed
Zech 10:11 of Egypt, and the W of the sea shall
2Mac 9:8 he could command the W of the sea, in
Mt 8:24 being swamped by the W; but he was asleep.
14:24 land, beaten by the W; for the wind was
Mk 4:37 wind arose, and the W beat into the boat,
Lk 8:24 wind and the raging W; and they ceased, and
21:25 the sea and the W,
Jude 1:13 twice dead, uprooted; wild W of the sea, casting

WAVY
Song 5:11 gold; his locks are W, black as a raven.

WAX (5)
Jud 16:15 rocks shall melt like W, but to those who
Ps 22:14 my heart is like W, it is melted within
68:2 drive them away; as W melts before fire, let
97:5 The mountains melt like W before the LORD, before
Mic 1:4 will be cleft, like W before the fire, like

WAXED (2)
Deut 32:15 "But Jeshurun W fat, and kicked; you waxed fat,
32:15 fat, and kicked; you W fat, you grew thick,

WAY (638)
Gen 3:24 sword which turned every W, to guard the way
3:24 way, to guard the W to the tree of
6:12 flesh had corrupted their W upon the earth.
12:20 set him on the W, with his wife and
14:11 provisions, and went their W;
16:7 the spring on the W to Shur.
18:16 went with them to set them on their W
18:19 him to keep the W of the LORD by
18:33 the LORD went his W, when he had finished
19:2 may rise up early and go on your W
21:16 against him a good W off, about the distance
24:27 led me in the W to the house of
24:40 you and prosper your W; and you shall take
24:42 thou wilt prosper the W which I go,
24:48 me by the right W to take the daughter
24:56 LORD has prospered my W; let me go that
24:61 thus the servant took Rebekah, and went his W

W

	25:34	ate and drank, and rose and went his W
	26:31	set them on their W, and they departed from
	28:20	keep me in this W that I go, and
	31:35	before you, for the W of women is upon
	32:1	Jacob went on his W and the angels of
	33:12	us journey on our W, and I will go
	33:16	that day on his W to Seir.
	33:18	of Canaan, on his W from Paddan-aram; and he
	35:19	was buried on the W to Ephrath (that is,
	37:25	and myrrh, on their W to carry it down
	39:19	him, "This is the W your servant treated me,"
	42:33	the famine of your households, and go your W
	43:7	could we in any W know that he would
	45:24	said to them, "Do not quarrel on the W
	48:7	of Canaan on the W, when there was still
	48:7	her there on the W to Ephrath (that is,
	49:17	a serpent in the W, a viper by the
Ex	2:12	He looked this W and that, and seeing no
	4:24	lodging place on the W the LORD met him
	13:17	not lead them by W of the land of
	13:18	people round by the W of the wilderness toward
	13:21	lead them along the W, and by night in
	18:8	upon them in the W, and how the LORD
	18:20	make them know the W in which they must
	18:27	and he went his W to his own country.
	23:20	guard you on the W and to bring you
	32:8	quickly out of the W which I commanded them;
	33:3	consume you in the W, for you are a
Lev	26:10	the old to make W for the new.
Num	14:25	the wilderness by the W to the Red Sea."
	15:13	these things in this W, in offering an offering
	21:1	was coming by the W of Atharim, he fought
	21:4	set out by the W to the Red Sea,
	21:4	Edom; and the people became impatient on the W
	21:33	went up by the W to Bashan; and Og
	22:22	his stand in the W as his adversary.
	22:26	where there was no W to turn either to
	22:31	LORD standing in the W, with his drawn sword
	22:32	withstand you, because your W is perverse before
	24:25	to his place; and Balak also went his W
	28:24	In the same W you shall offer daily, for
Deut	1:2	from Horeb by the W of Mount Seir to
	1:19	you saw, on the W to the hill country
	1:22	word again of the W by which we must
	1:31	son, in all the W that you went until
	1:33	before you in the W to seek you out
	1:33	show you by what W you should go, and
	3:1	and went up the W to Bashan; and Og
	5:33	walk in all the W which the LORD your
	6:7	you walk by the W, and when you lie
	8:2	shall remember all the W which the LORD your
	9:12	quickly out of the W which I commanded them;
	9:16	aside quickly from the W which the LORD had
	11:19	are walking by the W, and when you lie
	11:28	turn aside from the W which I command you
	13:5	make you leave the W in which the LORD
	14:24	And if the W is too long for you,
	17:16	shall never return that W again.'
	19:6	overtake him, because the W is long, and wound
	22:4	fallen down by the W, and withhold your help
	23:4	with water on the W, when you came forth
	24:9	to Miriam on the W as you came forth
	25:17	to you on the W as you came out
	25:18	attacked you on the W, when you were faint
	28:7	out against you one W, and flee before you
	28:25	shall go out one W against them, and flee
	31:29	turn aside from the W which I have commanded
Josh	1:8	you shall make your W prosperous, and then you
	2:7	after them on the W to the Jordan as
	2:16	have returned; then afterward you may go your W
	2:22	search all along the W and found nothing.
	3:4	you may know the W you shall go, for
	3:4	have not passed this W before.
	5:4	had died on the W in the wilderness after
	5:5	were born on the W in the wilderness after
	5:7	because they had not been circumcised on the W
	8:20	power to flee this W or that, for the
	10:10	chased them by the W of the ascent of
	18:8	men started on their W; and Joshua charged those
	23:14	about to go the W of all the earth,
	24:17	us in all the W that we went, and
Judg	1:24	"Pray, show us the W into the city, and
	1:25	he showed them the W into the city; and
	2:17	turned aside from the W in which their fathers
	2:22	to walk in the W of the LORD as
	5:10	rich carpets and you who walk by the W
	8:8	them in the same W; and the men of
	9:25	by them along that W; and it was told
	18:22	they were a good W from the home of
	18:26	the Danites went their W; and when Micah saw
	19:14	on and went their W; and the sun went
	19:27	to go on his W, behold, there was his
Ruth	1:7	they went on the W to return to the
	1:12	my daughters, go your W, for I am too
1Sam	1:18	the woman went her W and ate, and her
	6:8	send it off, and let it go its W
	6:9	goes up on the W to its own land,
	9:8	the man of God, to tell us our W
	9:14	toward them on his W up to the high
	9:21	then have you spoken to me in this W
	9:26	"Up, that I may send you on your W
	12:23	instruct you in the good and the right W
	15:2	opposing them on the W, when they came up
	17:27	him in the same W, "So shall it be
	17:30	spoke in the same W; and the people answered
	17:52	Philistines fell on the W from Sha-araim as far
	24:3	the sheepfolds by the W, where there was a
	24:7	and left the cave, and went upon his W
	26:25	So David went his W, and Saul returned to
	28:22	may have strength when you go on your W
	30:2	one, but carried them off, and went their W
2Sam	2:24	before Giah on the W to the wilderness of
	3:16	after her all the W to Bahurim.
	4:7	and went by the W of the Arabah all
	13:30	they were on the W, tidings came to David,
	15:2	and stand beside the W of the gate; and
	18:23	Ahima-az ran by the W of the plain, and
	19:36	will go a little W over the Jordan with
	19:40	people of Israel, brought the king on his W
	22:31	This God--his W is perfect; the promise of
	22:33	and has made my W safe.
1Kgs	1:49	trembled, and rose, and each went his own W
	2:2	about to go the W of all the earth.
	2:4	take heed to their W, to walk before me
	8:25	take heed to their W, to walk before me
	8:36	teach them the good W in which they should
	8:44	their enemy, by whatever W thou shalt send them,
	13:9	nor return by the W that you came.'"
	13:10	So he went another W, and did not return
	13:10	not return by the W that he came to
	13:12	said to them, "Which W did he go?" And
	13:12	sons showed him the W which the man of
	13:17	nor return by the W that you came.'"
	13:26	him back from the W heard of it, he
	13:33	turn from his evil W, but made priests for
	15:26	and walked in the W of his father, and
	15:34	and walked in the W of Jeroboam and in
	16:2	have walked in the W of Jeroboam, and have
	16:19	LORD, walking in the W of Jeroboam, and for
	16:26	walked in all the W of Jeroboam the son
	18:7	Obadiah was on the W, behold, Elijah met him;
	19:15	"Go, return on your W to the wilderness of
	20:38	the king by the W, disguising himself with a
	22:43	walked in all the W of Asa his father;
	22:52	and walked in the W of his father, and
	22:52	father, and in the W of his mother, and
	22:52	mother, and in the W of Jeroboam the son
	22:53	to anger in every W that his father had
2Kgs	2:1	Elisha were on their W from Gilgal.
	2:23	going up on the W, some small boys came
	3:8	he said, "By which W shall we march?" Jehoram
	3:8	Jehoram answered, "By the W of the wilderness of
	4:8	whenever he passed that W, he would turn in
	4:9	man of God, who is continually passing our W
	6:19	"This is not the W, and this is not
	7:15	and, lo, all the W was littered with garments
	8:18	he walked in the W of the kings of
	8:27	also walked in the W of the house of
	10:12	On the W, when he was at Beth-eked of
	12:20	of Millo, on the W that goes down to
	16:3	he walked in the W of the kings of
	16:18	And the covered W for the sabbath which had
	19:28	you back on the W by which you came.
	19:33	By the W that he came, by the same
	21:21	walked in all the W in which his father
	21:22	not walk in the W of the LORD.
	22:2	walked in all the W of David his father,
	25:4	by night by the W of the gate between
1Chr	15:13	for it in the W that is ordained."
2Chr	6:16	take heed to their W, to walk in my
	6:27	teach them the good W in which they should
	6:34	their enemies, by whatever W thou shalt send them,

11:17 three years in the W of David and Solomon.
18:23 cheek, and said, "Which W did the Spirit of
20:32 He walked in the W of Asa his father
21:6 he walked in the W of the kings of
21:13 have walked in the W of the kings of
23:19 who was in any W unclean.
25:8 suppose that in this W you will be strong
Ezra 8:21 from him a straight W for ourselves, our children,
8:22 the enemy on our W; since we had told
8:31 of the enemy and from ambushes by the W
Neh 4:17 laden in such a W that each with one
6:4 four times in this W and I answered them
6:5 In the same W Sanballat for the fifth time
6:13 and act in this W and sin, and so
8:10 to them, "Go your W, eat the fat and
8:12 the people went their W to eat and drink
9:12 light for them the W in which they should
9:19 led them in the W did not depart from
9:19 lighted for them the W by which they should
13:18 fathers act in this W, and did not our
Tob 4:15 or let drunkenness go with you on your W
5:6 am familiar with the W, and I have stayed
5:16 heaven will prosper your W, and may his angel
6:1 they proceeded on their W they came at evening
6:5 both continued on their W until they came near
11:1 Tobias went on his W, praising God because he
11:1 he continued on his W until they came near
11:4 So they went their W, and the dog went
Jud 3:4 with them in any W that seems good to
5:14 led them by the W of Sinai and Kadesh-barnea,
5:18 they departed from the W which he had appointed
7:19 and there was no W of escape from them.
10:13 I am on my W to the presence of
10:13 will show him a W by which he can
12:8 Israel to direct her W for the raising up
13:16 protected me in the W I went, it was
Esth 2:13 the king in this W she was given whatever
16:14 thought that in this W he would find us
Job 3:23 to a man whose W is hid, whom God
8:19 the joy of his W; and out of the
11:20 wicked will fail; all W of escape will be
16:22 I shall go the W whence I shall not
17:9 righteous holds to his W, and he that has
19:8 has walled up my W, so that I cannot
21:31 Who declares his W to his face, and who
22:15 keep to the old W which wicked men have
23:10 But he knows the W that I take; when
23:11 I have kept his W and have not turned
28:13 does not know the W to it, and it
28:23 ears.' "God understands the W to it, and he
28:26 the rain, and a W for the lightning of
29:25 I chose their W, and sat as chief, and
31:7 turned aside from the W, and my heart has
33:14 God speaks in one W, and in two, though
36:23 prescribed for him his W, or who can say,
38:19 "Where is the W to the dwelling of light,
38:24 What is the W to the place where the
38:25 of rain, and a W for the thunderbolt,
Ps 1:1 nor stands in the W of sinners, nor sits
1:6 the LORD knows the W of the righteous, but
1:6 the righteous, but the W of the wicked will
2:12 you perish in the W; for his wrath is
5:8 my enemies; make thy W straight before me.
18:30 This God—his W is perfect; the promise of
18:32 strength, and made my W safe.
25:8 the LORD; therefore he instructs sinners in the W
25:9 what is right, and teaches the humble his W
25:12 he instruct in the W that he should choose.
27:11 Teach me thy W, O LORD; and lead me
32:8 and teach you the W you should go; I
35:6 Let their W be dark and slippery, with the
36:4 sets himself in a W that is not good;
37:5 Commit your W to the LORD; trust in him,
37:7 who prospers in his W, over the man who
37:23 establishes him in whose W he delights;
37:34 and keep to his W, and he will exalt
44:18 steps departed from thy W,
50:23 him who orders his W aright I will show
57:6 a pit in my W, but they have fallen
67:2 us, [Selah] that thy W may be known upon
77:13 Thy W, O God, is holy.
77:19 Thy W was through the sea, thy path through
80:12 who pass along the W pluck its fruit?
85:13 go before him, and make his footsteps a W
86:11 Teach me thy W, O LORD, that I may
101:2 give heed to the W that is blameless.
101:6 who walks in the W that is blameless shall
107:4 desert wastes, finding no W to a city to
107:7 them by a straight W, till they reached a
110:7 the brook by the W; therefore he will lift
119:1 Blessed are those whose W is blameless, who walk
119:9 young man keep his W pure?
119:14 In the W of thy testimonies I delight as
119:27 Make me understand the W of thy precepts, and
119:30 I have chosen the W of faithfulness, I set
119:32 will run in the W of thy commandments when
119:33 me, O LORD, the W of thy statutes; and
119:101 feet from every evil W, in order to keep
119:104 I get understanding; therefore I hate every false W
119:128 by all thy precepts; I hate every false W
139:24 there be any wicked W in me, and lead
139:24 lead me in the W everlasting!
142:3 When my spirit is faint, thou knowest my W
143:8 Teach me the W I should go, for to
146:9 the fatherless; but the W of the wicked he
Prov 1:15 not walk in the W with them, hold back
1:31 the fruit of their W and be sated with
2:8 justice and preserving the W of his saints.
2:12 delivering you from the W of evil, from men
2:20 will walk in the W of good men and
3:23 will walk on your W securely and your foot
4:12 have taught you the W of wisdom; I have
4:15 not walk in the W of evil men.
4:20 The W of the wicked is like deep darkness;
5:8 Keep your W far from her, and do not
6:23 of discipline are the W of life,
7:27 Her house is the W to Sheol, going down
8:2 the heights beside the W, in the paths she
8:13 and arrogance and the W of evil and perverted
8:20 I walk in the W of righteousness, in the
9:6 and walk in the W of insight."
9:15 going straight on their W,
10:29 stronghold to him whose W is upright, but
11:5 the blameless keeps his W straight, but the wicked
12:15 The W of a fool is right in his
12:26 from evil, but the W of the wicked leads
12:28 is life, but the W of error leads to
13:6 Righteousness guards him whose W is upright, but
13:15 wins favor, but the W of the faithless is
14:8 is to discern his W, but the folly of
14:12 There is a W which seems right to a
14:12 its end is the W to death.
15:9 The W of the wicked is an abomination to
15:10 him who forsakes the W; he who hates reproof
15:19 The W of a sluggard is overgrown with thorns,
16:9 man's mind plans his W, but the LORD directs
16:17 he who guards his W preserves his life.
16:25 There is a W which seems right to a
16:25 its end is the W to death.
16:29 leads him in a W that is not good.
19:2 who makes haste with his feet misses his W
19:3 man's folly brings his W to ruin, his heart
20:24 the LORD; how then can man understand his W
21:2 Every W of a man is right in his
21:8 The W of the guilty is crooked, but the
21:16 who wanders from the W of understanding will rest
22:5 snares are in the W of the perverse; he
22:6 a child in the W he should go, and
23:19 be wise, and direct your mind in the W
25:26 righteous man who gives W before the wicked.
28:10 upright into an evil W will fall into his
29:27 righteous, but he whose W is straight is an
30:19 do not understand: the W of an eagle in
30:19 in the sky, the W of a serpent on
30:19 on a rock, the W of a ship on
30:19 high seas, and the W of a man with
30:20 This is the W of an adulteress: she eats,
Eccl 8:5 a wise man will know the time and W
8:6 has its time and W, although man's trouble lies
10:15 does not know the W to the city.
12:5 terrors are in the W; the almond tree blossoms,
Wis 5:6 who strayed from the W of truth, and the
5:7 trackless deserts, but the W of the Lord we
10:17 them along a marvelous W, and became a shelter
12:10 inborn, and that their W of thinking would never
14:3 sea, and a safe W through the waves,
18:23 and cut off its W to the living.
19:7 stood before, an unhindered W out of the Red
19:17 tried to find the W through his own door.
Sir 15:11 I left the right W; for he will not
21:10 The W of sinners is smoothly paved with stones,
30:1 may rejoice at the W he turns out.

32:21 overconfident on a smooth W,
33:31 and runs away, which W will you go to
37:9 and tell you, "Your W is good," and then
37:15 he may direct your W in truth.
43:26 his messenger finds the W, and by his word
47:23 Israel to sin and gave Ephraim a sinful W
50:22 all, who in every W does great things; who
Is 8:11 to walk in the W of this people, saying:
9:1 will make glorious the W of the sea, the
16:1 land, from Sela, by W of the desert, to
22:25 sure place will give W; and it will be
26:7 The W of the righteous is level; thou dost
30:11 prophesy illusions, leave the W, turn aside from the
30:21 saying, "This is the W, walk in it," when
35:8 be called the Holy W; the unclean shall not
37:29 you back on the W by which you came.'
37:34 By the W that he came, by the same
40:3 the wilderness prepare the W of the LORD, make
40:14 and showed him the W of understanding?
40:27 speak, O Israel, "My W is hid from the
42:16 the blind in a W that they know not,
43:16 LORD, who makes a W in the sea, a
43:19 I will make a W in the wilderness and
48:15 brought him, and he will prosper in his W
48:17 leads you in the W you should go.
49:11 all my mountains a W, and my highways shall
51:10 of the sea a W for the redeemed to
53:6 one to his own W; and the LORD has
55:7 the wicked forsake his W, and the unrighteous man
56:11 turned to their own W, each to his own
57:10 the length of your W, but you did not
57:14 build up, prepare the W, remove every obstruction
57:14 way, remove every obstruction from my people's W
57:17 on backsliding in the W of his own heart.
59:8 The W of peace they know not, and there
62:10 the gates, prepare the W for the people; build
65:2 who walk in a W that is not good,
Jer 2:17 your God, when he led you in the W
2:23 Look at your W in the valley; know what
2:36 sinned.' How lightly you gad about, changing your W
3:21 they have perverted their W, they have forgotten the
5:4 do not know the W of the LORD, the
5:5 for they know the W of the LORD, the
6:16 paths, where the good W is; and walk in
7:23 walk in all the W that I command you,
10:2 LORD: "Learn not the W of the nations, nor
10:23 O LORD, that the W of man is not
12:1 Why does the W of the wicked prosper?
18:11 one from his evil W, and amend your ways
21:8 set before you the W of life and the
21:8 of life and the W of death.
22:21 This has been your W from your youth, that
23:12 Therefore their W shall be to them like slippery
23:22 them from their evil W, and from the evil
25:5 you, from his evil W and wrong doings, and
26:3 turn from his evil W, that I may repent
28:11 But Jeremiah the prophet went his W
32:39 one heart and one W, that they may fear
35:15 you from his evil W, and amend your doings,
36:3 turn from his evil W, and that I may
36:7 turn from his evil W, for great is the
39:4 city at night by W of the king's garden
42:3 may show us the W we should go, and
48:19 Stand by the W and watch, O inhabitant of
50:5 They shall ask the W to Zion, with faces
52:7 by night by the W of a gate between
Lam 2:15 who pass along the W clap their hands at
3:11 led me off my W and tore me to
Bar 3:13 had walked in the W of God, you would
3:20 have not learned the W to knowledge, nor
3:21 Their sons have strayed far from her W
3:23 have not learned the W to wisdom, nor given
3:27 nor give them the W to knowledge;
3:31 No one knows the W to her, or is
3:36 He found the whole W to knowledge, and gave
6:71 In the same W, their gods of wood, overlaid
Ezek 3:18 wicked from his wicked W, in order to save
3:19 or from his wicked W, he shall die in
7:27 According to their W I will do to them,
13:22 turn from his wicked W to save his life;
18:23 should turn from his W and live?
18:25 "Yet you say, 'The W of the Lord is
18:25 of Israel: Is my W not just?
18:29 of Israel says, 'The W of the Lord is
21:19 the head of the W to a city;
21:20 a city; mark a W for the sword to
21:21 the parting of the W, at the head of
22:31 of my wrath; their W have I requited upon
23:13 she was defiled; they both took the same W
23:31 You have gone the W of your sister; therefore
33:8 to turn from his W, that wicked man shall
33:9 to turn from his W, and he does not
33:9 not turn from his W; he shall die in
33:11 wicked turn from his W and live; turn back,
33:17 your people say, 'The W of the Lord is
33:17 it is their own W that is not just.
33:20 Yet you say, 'The W of the Lord is
44:3 he shall enter by W of the vestibule of
44:3 gate, and shall go out by the same W
44:4 he brought me by W of the north gate
46:8 and he shall go out by the same W
46:9 one shall return by W of the gate by
47:2 brought me out by W of the north gate,
47:15 the Great Sea by W of Hethlon to the
48:1 from the sea by W of Hethlon to the
Dan 3:97 god who is able to deliver in this W
5:6 him; his limbs gave W, and his knees knocked
12:9 He said, "Go your W, Daniel, for the words
12:13 But go your W till the end; and you
Hos 2:6 will hedge up her W with thorns; and I
6:9 they murder on the W to Shechem, yea, they
13:7 like a leopard I will lurk beside the W
Joel 2:7 march each on his W, they do not swerve
Amos 2:7 and turn aside the W of the afflicted; a
8:14 Dan,' and, 'As the W of Beer-sheba lives,' they
Jon 3:8 turn from his evil W and from the violence
3:10 turned from their evil W, God repented of the
Mic 1:11 Pass on your W, inhabitants of Shaphir, in nakedness
Nah 1:3 His W is in whirlwind and storm, and the
Mal 2:8 turned aside from the W; you have caused many
3:1 messenger to prepare the W before me, and the
1Mac 5:29 they went all the W to the stronghold of
5:53 the people all the W till he came to
6:18 were trying in every W to harm them and
8:27 In the same W, if war comes first to
13:20 circled around by the W to Adora.
13:21 come to them by W of the wilderness and
14:5 harbor, and opened a W to the isles of
14:35 He sought in every W to exalt his people.
2Mac 1:17 Blessed in every W be our God, who has
2:6 up to mark the W, but could not find
2:14 In the same W Judas also collected all the
4:10 over to the Greek W of life.
4:34 justice, he immediately put him out of the W
6:14 not deal in this W with us,
6:31 So in this W he died, leaving in his
7:7 had died in this W, they brought forward the
7:13 maltreated and tortured the fourth in the same W
8:17 overthrow of their ancestral W of life.
8:35 uniform and made his W alone like a runaway
9:7 did not in any W stop his insolence, but
9:18 did not in any W abate, for the judgment
9:21 On my W back from the region of Persia
10:36 up in the same W wheeled around against the
11:24 but prefer their own W of living and ask
11:31 be molested in any W for what he may
11:36 we are on our W to Antioch.
12:8 meant in the same W to wipe out the
12:22 were swept on, this W and that, so that
14:3 that there was no W for him to be
14:23 nothing out of the W, but dismissed the flocks
Mt 1:18 birth of Jesus Christ took place in this W
2:9 king they went their W; and lo, the star
2:12 they departed to their own country by another W
3:3 the wilderness: Prepare the W of the Lord, make
7:13 is wide and the W is easy, that leads
7:14 is narrow and the W is hard, that leads
8:28 so fierce that no one could pass that W
11:10 who shall prepare thy W before thee.'
15:32 them away hungry, lest they faint on the W
20:17 aside, and on the W he said to them,
21:32 to you in the W of righteousness, and you
22:16 true, and teach the W of God truthfully, and
27:44 with him also reviled him in the same W
Mk 1:2 who shall prepare thy W;
1:3 the wilderness: Prepare the W of the Lord, make
2:23 as they made their W his disciples began to
7:9 "You have a fine W of rejecting the commandment
7:28 you may go your W; the demon has left
8:3 will faint on the W; and some of them
8:3 and some of them have come a long W
8:27 Philippi; and on the W he asked his disciples,

Job 4:6 the integrity of your W your hope?
13:15 I will defend my W to his face.
21:14 We do not desire the knowledge of thy W
22:3 if you make your W blameless?
22:28 for you, and light will shine on your W
24:13 not acquainted with its W, and do not stay
24:23 are supported; and his eyes are upon their W
26:14 the outskirts of his W; and how small a
30:12 up against me their W of destruction.
31:4 not he see my W, and number all my
34:11 and according to his W he will make it
34:21 eyes are upon the W of a man, and
34:27 for any of his W,
Ps 10:5 His W prosper at all times; thy judgments are
17:4 I have avoided the W of the violent.
18:21 I have kept the W of the LORD, and
25:4 me to know thy W, O LORD; teach me
39:1 "I will guard my W, that I may not
51:13 will teach transgressors thy W, and sinners will
68:21 crown of him who walks in his guilty W
81:13 to me, that Israel would walk in my W
91:11 of you to guard you in all your W
95:10 in heart, and they do not regard my W
103:7 He made known his W to Moses, his acts
107:17 sick through their sinful W, and because of their
119:3 also do no wrong, but walk in his W
119:5 O that my W may be steadfast in keeping
119:15 thy precepts, and fix my eyes on thy W
119:26 I told of my W, thou didst answer me;
119:29 Put false W far from me; and graciously teach
119:37 at vanities; and give me life in thy W
119:59 I think of thy W, I turn my feet
119:168 testimonies, for all my W are before thee.
125:5 aside upon their crooked W the LORD will lead
128:1 who fears the LORD, who walks in his W
138:5 shall sing of the W of the LORD, for
139:3 lying down, and art acquainted with all my W
145:17 just in all his W, and kind in all
Prov 1:19 Such are the W of all who get gain
2:13 to walk in the W of darkness,
2:15 are crooked, and who are devious in their W
3:6 In all your W acknowledge him, and he will
3:17 Her W are ways of pleasantness, and all her
3:17 Her ways are W of pleasantness, and all her
3:31 choose any of his W;
4:27 feet, then all your W will be sure.
5:6 path of life; her W wander, and she does
5:21 For a man's W are before the eyes of
6:6 O sluggard; consider her W, and be wise.
7:25 turn aside to her W, do not stray into
8:32 to me: happy are those who keep my W
10:9 he who perverts his W will be found out.
11:20 but those of blameless W are his delight.
14:2 is devious in his W despises him.
14:14 the fruit of his W, and a good man
16:2 All the W of a man are pure in
16:7 When a man's W please the LORD, he makes
17:23 bosom to pervert the W of justice.
21:29 bold face, but an upright man considers his W
22:25 lest you learn his W and entangle yourself in
23:26 your heart, and let your eyes observe my W
28:6 a rich man who is perverse in his W
28:18 is perverse in his W will fall into a
31:3 strength to women, your W to those who destroy
31:27 looks well to the W of her household, and
Eccl 11:9 youth; walk in the W of your heart and
Wis 2:15 of others, and his W are strange.
2:16 and he avoids our W as unclean; he calls
Sir 2:6 help you; make your W straight, and hope in
2:12 and to the sinner who walks along two W
2:15 and those who love him will keep his W
6:26 soul, and keep her W with all your might.
14:21 his mind on her W will also ponder her
16:18 Who will ponder his W
17:13 Their W are always before him, they will not
17:15 him, and his eyes are continually upon their W
23:19 look upon all the W of men, and perceive
33:11 and appointed their different W;
33:13 for all his W are as he pleases--
39:24 To the holy his W are straight, just as
48:22 held strongly to the W of David his father,
49:9 those who directed their W aright.
Is 2:3 may teach us his W and that we may
42:24 have sinned, in whose W they would not walk,
45:13 make straight all his W; he shall build my
49:9 shall feed along the W, on all bare heights
55:8 thoughts, neither are your W my ways, says the
55:8 are your ways my W, says the LORD.
55:9 earth, so are my W higher than your ways
55:9 ways higher than your W and my thoughts than
57:18 I have seen his W, but I will heal
58:2 delight to know my W, as if they were
58:13 not going your own W, or seeking your own
63:17 us err from thy W and harden our heart,
64:5 righteousness, those that remember thee in thy W
66:3 have chosen their own W, and their soul delights
Jer 2:33 even to wicked women you have taught your W
4:18 Your W and your doings have brought this upon
6:27 people, that you may know and assay their W
7:3 of Israel, Amend your W and your doings, and
7:5 you truly amend your W and your doings, if
12:16 will diligently learn the W of my people, to
15:7 my people; they did not turn from their W
16:17 are upon all their W; they are not hid
17:10 man according to his W, according to the fruit
18:11 way, and amend your W and your doings.'
18:15 have stumbled in their W, in the ancient roads,
26:13 Now therefore amend your W and your doings, and
32:19 open to all the W of men, rewarding every
32:19 man according to his W and according to the
Lam 3:9 he has blocked my W with hewn stones, he
3:40 test and examine our W, and return to the
Bar 2:33 they will remember the W of their fathers, who
4:13 not walk in the W of God's commandments, nor
Ezek 7:3 you according to your W; and I will punish
7:4 punish you for your W, while your abominations are
7:8 you according to your W; and I will punish
7:9 you according to your W, while your abominations
14:22 and you see their W and their doings, you
14:23 when you see their W and their doings; and
16:47 to walk in their W, or do according to
16:47 were more corrupt than they in all your W
16:61 you will remember your W, and be ashamed when
18:25 Is it not your W that are not just?
18:29 of Israel, are my W not just?
18:29 Is it not your W that are not just?
18:30 one according to his W, says the Lord GOD.
20:43 you shall remember your W and all the doings
20:44 according to your evil W, nor according to your
21:19 of man, mark two W for the sword of
21:21 head of the two W, to use divination; he
24:14 repent; according to your W and your doings I
28:15 were blameless in your W from the day you
33:11 back from your evil W; for why will you
33:20 will judge each of you according to his W
36:17 defiled it by their W and their doings; their
36:31 will remember your evil W, and your deeds that
36:32 and confounded for your W, O house of Israel.
Dan 3:27 are true and thy W right, and all thy
4:37 are right and his W are just; and those
5:23 whose are all your W, you have not honored.
Hos 4:9 punish them for their W, and requite them for
9:8 is on all his W, and hatred in the
12:2 Jacob according to his W, and requite him according
14:9 know them; for the W of the LORD are
Obad 1:14 the parting of the W to cut off his
Mic 4:2 may teach us his W and we may walk
Hab 3:6 His W were as of old.
Zech 1:4 Return from your evil W and from your evil
1:6 with us for our W and deeds, so has
3:7 will walk in my W and keep my charge,
Mal 2:9 have not kept my W but have shown partiality
2Mac 4:11 he destroyed the lawful W of living and introduced
4:13 the adoption of foreign W because of the surpassing
4:16 them, and those whose W of living they admired
7:24 would turn from the W of his fathers, and
12:11 and to help his people in all other W
12:12 be useful in many W, agreed to make peace
12:41 they all blessed the W of the Lord, the
Lk 1:76 Lord to prepare his W,
3:5 straight, and the rough W shall be made smooth;
Acts 2:28 known to me the W of life; thou wilt
14:16 walk in their own W;
Rom 11:33 are his judgments and how inscrutable his W
1Cor 4:17 remind you of my W in Christ, as I
13:11 I became a man, I gave up childish W
2Cor 4:2 have renounced disgraceful, underhanded W; we
13:11 Mend your W, heed my appeal, agree with one
2Thes 3:16 give you peace at all times in all W
Heb 1:1 In many and various W God spoke of old
3:10 have not known my W
Jas 1:7 unstable in all his W, will receive anything from

1Pet	1:18	ransomed from the futile W inherited from your
Rev	15:3	and true are thy W, O King of the

WAYSIDE (3)

Gen	38:21	the harlot who was at Enaim by the W
Ps	140:5	a net, by the W they have set snares
Mt	21:19	fig tree by the W he went to it,

WAYSIDES

Jer	3:2	By the W you have sat awaiting lovers like

WAYWARD (3)

Prov	7:11	She is loud and W, her feet do not
Hos	10:10	will come against the W people to chastise them;
Heb	5:2	with the ignorant and W, since he himself is

WEAK (64)

Gen	29:17	Leah's eyes were W, but Rachel was beautiful and
Num	13:18	it are strong or W, whether they are few
Judg	16:7	then I shall become W, and be like any
	16:11	then I shall become W, and be like any
	16:13	then I shall become W, and be like any
	16:17	and I shall become W, and be like any
2Sam	3:39	I am this day W, though anointed king; these
2Chr	14:11	thee to help, between the mighty and the W
	15:7	let your hands be W, for your work shall
Jud	9:11	oppressed, upholder of the W, protector of the
	16:11	shouted for joy; my W people shouted and the
Job	4:3	you have strengthened the W hands.
Ps	6:7	of grief, it grows W because of all my
	35:10	thou who deliverest the W from him who is
	35:10	strong for him, the W and needy from him
	72:13	has pity on the W and the needy, and
	82:3	Give justice to the W and the fatherless; maintain
	82:4	Rescue the W and the needy; deliver them from
	109:24	My knees are W through fasting; my body has
Wis	2:11	right, for what is W proves itself to be
	9:5	a man who is W and short-lived, with little
	13:18	a thing that is W; for life he prays
	17:13	expectation of help, being W, prefers ignorance of
Sir	25:22	Drooping hands and W knees are caused by the
Is	14:10	too have become as W as we!
	35:3	Strengthen the W hands, and make firm the feeble
Bar	6:36	death or rescue the W from the strong.
Ezek	7:17	feeble, and all knees W as water.
	21:7	all knees will be W as water.
	34:4	The W you have not strengthened, the sick you
	34:16	I will strengthen the W, and the fat and
	34:21	thrust at all the W with your horns, till
Joel	3:10	into spears; let the W say, "I am a
Zeph	3:16	fear, O Zion; let not your hands grow W
Mt	26:41	spirit indeed is willing, but the flesh is W
Mk	14:38	spirit indeed is willing, but the flesh is W
Acts	20:35	one must help the W, remembering the words of
Rom	5:6	While we were still W, at the right time
	14:1	the man who is W in faith, welcome him,
	14:2	eat anything, while the W man eats only vegetables.
	15:1	the failings of the W, and not to please
1Cor	1:27	God chose what is W in the world to
	4:10	We are W, but you are strong.
	8:7	and their conscience, being W, is defiled.
	8:9	yours somehow become a stumbling block to the W
	8:10	if his conscience is W, to eat food offered
	8:11	by your knowledge this W man is destroyed, the
	8:12	conscience when it is W, you sin against Christ.
	9:22	To the W I became weak, that I might
	9:22	the weak I became W, that I might win
	9:22	I became weak, that I might win the W
	11:30	many of you are W and ill, and some
2Cor	10:10	his bodily presence is W, and his speech of
	11:21	say, we were too W for that!
	11:29	Who is W, and I am not weak?
	11:29	Who is weak, and I am not W
	12:10	for when I am W, then I am strong.
	13:3	He is not W in dealing with you, but
	13:4	For we are W in him, but in dealing
	13:9	glad when we are W and you are strong.
Gal	4:9	back again to the W and beggarly elemental spirits,
1Thes	5:14	the fainthearted, help the W, be patient with them
2Tim	3:6	households and capture W women, burdened with
Heb	12:12	hands and strengthen your W knees,

WEAKEN

Rom	4:19	He did not W in faith when he considered

WEAKENED

Rom	8:3	done what the law, W by the flesh, could

WEAKENING

Jer	38:4	death, for he is W the hands of the

WEAKER (5)

2Sam	3:1	house of Saul became W and weaker.
	3:1	while the house of Saul became weaker and W
1Mac	6:57	men, "We daily grow W, our food supply is
1Cor	12:22	which seem to be W are indispensable,
1Pet	3:7	the woman as the W sex, since you are

WEAKEST

Judg	6:15	my clan is the W in Manasseh, and I

WEAKLING

Sir	6:20	to the uninstructed; a W will not remain with

WEAKNESS (14)

Gen	42:9	come to see the W of the land."
	42:12	"No, it is the W of the land that
Sir	11:28	spy he observes your W;
Rom	8:26	helps us in our W; for we do not
1Cor	1:25	than men, and the W of God is stronger
	2:3	was with you in W and in much fear
	15:43	It is sown in W, it is raised in
2Cor	11:30	will boast of the things that show my W
	12:9	you, for my power is made perfect in W
	13:4	he was crucified in W, but lives by the
Heb	5:2	and wayward, since he himself is beset with W
	7:18	aside because of its W and uselessness
	7:28	appoints men in their W as high priests, but
	11:34	won strength out of W, became mighty in war,

WEAKNESSES (4)

2Cor	12:5	behalf I will not boast, except of my W
	12:9	gladly boast of my W, that the power of
	12:10	I am content with W, insults, hardships, persecutions,
Heb	4:15	to sympathize with our W, but one who in

WEAL

Is	45:7	create darkness, I make W and create woe, I

WEALTH (96)

Gen	31:1	was our father's he has gained all this W
	34:29	the field; all their W, all their little ones
Deut	8:17	have gotten me this W
	8:18	you power to get W; that he may confirm
Josh	22:8	your homes with much W, and with very many
Judg	18:7	the earth, and possessing W, and how they were
Ruth	2:1	husbands, a man of W, of the family of
1Sam	9:1	Benjaminite, a man of W;
2Chr	1:11	have not asked possessions, W, honor, or the life
Tob	4:21	You have great W if you fear God and
Job	5:5	of thorns; and the thirsty pant after his W
	6:22	Or, 'From your W offer a bribe for me?
	15:29	be rich, and his W will not endure, nor
	20:10	poor, and his hands will give back his W
	27:19	his eyes, and his W is gone.
	31:25	have rejoiced because my W was great, or because
Ps	45:13	richest of the people with all kinds of W
	49:6	who trust in their W and boast of the
	49:10	perish and leave their W to others.
	52:7	of his riches, and sought refuge in his W
	112:3	W and riches are in his house; and his
Prov	8:18	are with me, enduring W and prosperity.
	8:21	of justice, endowing with W those who love me,
	10:15	A rich man's W is his strong city; the
	12:27	prey, but the diligent man will get precious W
	13:7	another pretends to be poor, yet has great W
	13:8	man's life is his W, but a poor man
	13:11	W hastily gotten will dwindle, but he who gathers
	13:22	children, but the sinner's W is laid up for
	18:11	A rich man's W is his strong city, and
	19:4	W brings many new friends, but a poor man
	19:14	House and W are inherited from fathers, but a
	22:16	to increase his own W, or gives to the
	23:4	not toil to acquire W; be wise enough to
	28:8	He who augments his W by interest and increase
	28:22	miserly man hastens after W, and does not know
Eccl	5:10	nor he who loves W, with gain: this also
	5:19	whom God has given W and possessions and power
	6:2	to whom God gives W, possessions, and honor, so
Song	8:7	for love all the W of his house, it
Wis	5:8	good has our boasted W brought us?

W

7:8 thrones, and I accounted W as nothing in comparison
7:11 along with her, and in her hands uncounted W
7:13 do not hide her W,
8:18 of her hands, unfailing W, and in the experience
Sir 5:1 your heart on your W, nor say, "I have
5:8 not depend on dishonest W, for it will not
10:8 nation on account of injustice and insolence and W
10:29 while a rich man is honored for his W
10:30 man honored in poverty, how much more in W
10:30 a man dishonored in W, how much more in
11:14 and death, poverty and W, come from the Lord.
18:24 in the days of W think of poverty and
28:10 in proportion to his W he will heighten his
30:16 There is no W better than health of body,
31:1 Wakefulness over W wastes away one's flesh, and
31:3 man toils as his W accumulates, and when he
37:6 and be not unmindful of him in your W
40:13 The W of the unjust will dry up like
Is 8:4 or 'My mother,' the W of Damascus and the
10:3 for help, and where will you leave your W
10:14 like a nest the W of the peoples; and
45:14 says the LORD: "The W of Egypt and the
60:5 turned to you, the W of the nations shall
60:11 bring to you the W of the nations, with
61:6 you shall eat the W of the nations, and
66:12 a river, and the W of the nations like
Jer 15:13 "Your W and your treasures I will give as
17:3 Your W and all your treasures I will give
20:5 will give all the W of the city, all
Bar 6:35 able to give either W or money; if one
Ezek 7:11 their abundance, nor their W; neither shall there be
27:12 because of your great W of every kind; silver,
27:18 because of your great W of every kind; wine
27:33 peoples; with your abundant W and merchandise you
28:4 understanding you have gotten W for yourself, and
28:5 you have increased your W, and your heart has
28:5 become proud in your W —
29:19 shall carry off its W and despoil it and
30:4 in Egypt, and her W is carried away, and
30:10 an end to the W of Egypt, by the
Hos 12:8 rich, I have gained W for myself": but all
Obad 1:11 strangers carried off his W, and foreigners entered
Mic 4:13 to the LORD, their W to the Lord of
Nah 2:9 end of treasure, or W of every precious thing.
Zech 9:4 possessions and hurl her W into the sea, and
14:14 And the W of all the nations round about
1Mac 6:1 city famed for its W in silver and gold.
Acts 19:25 know that from this business we have our W
2Cor 8:2 have overflowed in a W of liberality on their
Heb 11:26 for the Christ greater W than the treasures of
Rev 5:12 to receive power and W and wisdom and might
18:3 grown rich with the W of her wantonness."
18:15 these wares, who gained W from her, will stand
18:17 one hour all this W has been laid waste."
18:19 had ships at sea grew rich by her W

WEALTHY (4)

Gen 26:13 gained more and more until he became very W
2Sam 19:32 he was a very W man.
2Kgs 4:8 to Shunem, where a W woman lived, who urged
15:20 is, from all the W men, fifty shekels of

WEANED (10)

Gen 21:8 child grew, and was W; and Abraham made a
21:8 great feast on the day that Isaac was W
1Sam 1:22 as the child is W, I will bring him,
1:23 wait until you have W him; only, may the
1:23 her son, until she W him.
1:24 And when she had W him, she took him
1Kgs 11:20 his son, whom Tahpenes W in Pharaoh's house; and
Is 11:8 the asp, and the W child shall put his
28:9 Those who are W from the milk, those taken
Hos 1:8 When she had W Not pitied, she conceived and

WEAPON (10)

Num 35:18 him down with a W of wood in the
2Chr 23:10 every man with his W in his hand, from
Neh 4:17 the work and with the other held his W
4:23 clothes; each kept his W in his hand.
Job 20:24 flee from an iron W; a bronze arrow will
Is 54:16 coals, and produces a W for its purpose.
54:17 ravager to destroy; no W that is fashioned against
Jer 51:20 are my hammer and W of war: with you
Ezek 9:1 each with his destroying W in his hand."
9:2 every man with his W for slaughter in his

WEAPONS (45)

Gen 27:3 Now then, take your W, your quiver and your
49:5 and Levi are brothers; W of violence are their
Deut 1:41 you girded on his W of war, and thought
23:13 a stick with your W; and when you sit
Judg 18:11 of Dan, armed with W of war, set forth
18:16 Danites, armed with their W of war, stood by
18:17 hundred men armed with W of war.
1Sam 20:40 And Jonathan gave his W to his lad, and
21:8 my sword nor my W with me, because the
2Sam 1:27 mighty fallen, and the W of war perished!"
2Kgs 10:2 fortified cities also, and W,
11:8 king, each with his W in his hand; and
11:11 every man with his W in his hand, from
1Chr 12:33 battle with all the W of war, to help
12:37 armed with all the W of war.
2Chr 23:7 king, each with his W in his hand; and
32:5 He also made W and shields in abundance.
Jud 6:12 they caught up their W and ran out of
7:5 man took up his W, and when they had
14:2 valiant man take his W and go out of
14:11 every man took his W, and they went out
Job 39:21 his strength; he goes out to meet the W
Ps 7:13 has prepared his deadly W, making his arrows fiery
76:3 the sword, and the W of war.
Eccl 9:18 Wisdom is better than W of war, but one
Is 13:5 the LORD and the W of his indignation, to
22:8 you looked to the W of the House of
Jer 21:4 will turn back the W of war which are
22:7 you, each with his W; and they shall cut
50:25 and brought out the W of his wrath, for
Ezek 32:27 to Sheol with their W of war, whose swords
39:9 make fires of the W and burn them, shields
39:10 their fires of the W; they will despoil those
Joel 2:8 they burst through the W and are not halted.
1Mac 6:2 golden shields, breastplates, and W left there by
9:39 them with tambourines and musicians and many W
14:42 the country and the W and the strongholds, and
15:7 All the W which you have prepared and the
16:16 rose up, took their W, and rushed in against
2Mac 3:25 to have armor and W of gold.
10:30 their own armor and W, they kept him from
11:8 in white and brandishing W of gold.
Jn 18:3 went there with lanterns and torches and W
2Cor 6:7 of God; with the W of righteousness for the
10:4 worldly war, for the W of our warfare are

WEAR (40)

Gen 28:20 eat and clothing to W,
Ex 18:18 people with you will W yourselves out, for the
29:30 in his place shall W them seven days, when
Lev 13:45 has the disease shall W torn clothes and let
16:4 the linen girdle, and W the linen turban; these
21:10 has been consecrated to W the garments, shall not
Deut 8:4 Your clothing did not W out upon you, and
22:5 "A woman shall not W anything that pertains to
22:11 You shall not W a mingled stuff, wool and
1Sam 2:28 to burn incense, to W an ephod before me;
1Kgs 22:30 into battle, but you W your robes." And the
2Chr 18:29 into battle, but you W your robes." And the
Neh 9:21 their clothes did not W out and their feet
Jud 10:3 which she used to W while her husband Manasseh
Esth 14:16 and I do not W it on the days
Job 14:19 its place; the waters W away the stones; the
27:17 but the just will W it, and the innocent
Ps 102:26 endure; they will all W out like a garment.
Wis 5:18 as a breastplate, and W impartial justice as a
Sir 6:31 You will W her like a glorious robe, and
6:36 early; let your foot W out his doorstep.
27:8 will attain it and W it as a glorious
Is 4:1 our own bread and W our own clothes, only
50:9 all of them will W out like a garment;
51:6 smoke, the earth will W out like a garment,
Bar 6:24 the gold which they W for beauty–they will
6:58 of the robes they W, and go off with
Ezek 44:17 inner court, they shall W linen garments; they shall
Dan 7:25 Most High, and shall W out the saints of
1Mac 11:58 dress in purple and W a gold buckle.
14:43 clothed in purple and W gold.
2Mac 4:12 the young men to W the Greek hat.
12:40 Jamnia, which the law forbids the Jews to W
Mt 6:31 or 'What shall we W
11:8 Behold, those who W soft raiment are in kings'
Mk 6:9 their belts; but to W sandals and not put
Lk 9:12 the day began to W away; and the twelve
18:5 her, or she will W me out by her

W

1Cor 11:6 or shaven, let her W a veil.
11:14 for a man to W long hair is degrading

WEARIED (14)

Gen 19:11 great, so that they W themselves groping for the
Sir 22:11 you will never be W by his madness.
Is 43:23 you with offerings, or W you with frankincense.
43:24 your sins, you have W me with your iniquities.
47:13 You are W with your many counsels; let them
57:10 You were W with the length of your way,
Jer 12:5 foot, and they have W you, how will you
Bar 3:1 in anguish and the W spirit cry out to
Ezek 24:12 In vain I have W myself; its thick rust
Mic 6:3 In what have I W you?
Mal 2:17 You have W the LORD with your words.
2:17 say, "How have we W him?" By saying, "Every
1Mac 12:44 Jonathan, "Why have you W all these people when
Jn 4:6 there, and so Jesus, W as he was with

WEARIES (2)

Eccl 10:15 toil of a fool W him, so that he
Is 16:12 presents himself, when he W himself upon the high

WEARINESS (4)

Judg 4:21 ground, as he was lying fast asleep from W
Eccl 1:8 things are full of W; a man cannot utter
12:12 much study is a W of the flesh.
Mal 1:13 'What a W this is,' you say, and you

WEARING (13)

Lev 16:32 place shall make atonement, W the holy linen
Ruth 3:15 the mantle you are W and hold it out."
1Sam 14:3 the LORD in Shiloh, W an ephod.
2Sam 13:18 Now she was W a long robe with sleeves;
20:8 Now Joab was W a soldier's garment, and over
Jud 9:1 the sackcloth she was W; and at the very
10:3 which she had been W, and took off her
15:13 bearing their arms and W garlands and with songs
Sir 11:4 Do not boast about W fine clothes, nor exalt
2Mac 6:7 in honor of Dionysus, W wreaths of ivy.
Jn 19:5 So Jesus came out, W the crown of thorns
2Tim 2:9 I am suffering and W fetters like a criminal.
1Pet 3:3 decoration of gold, and W of fine clothing,

WEARISOME

Ps 73:16 seemed to me a W task,

WEARS (3)

Prov 26:15 in the dish; it W him out to bring
Sir 40:4 from the man who W purple and a crown
Jas 2:3 to the one who W the fine clothing and

WEARY (46)

Gen 27:46 to Isaac, "I am W of my life because
Ex 17:12 But Moses' hands grew W; so they took a
Deut 25:18 you were faint and W, and cut off at
2Sam 16:14 were with him, arrived W at the Jordan; and
17:2 him while he is W and discouraged, and throw
17:29 people are hungry and W and thirsty in the
21:15 fought against the Philistines; and David grew W
23:10 until his hand was W, and his hand cleaved
Jud 13:1 for they all were W because the banquet had
Job 3:17 troubling, and there the W are at rest.
22:7 no water to the W to drink, and you
Ps 6:6 I am W with my moaning; every night I
63:1 in a dry and W land where no water
69:3 I am W with my crying; my throat is
Prov 3:11 LORD's discipline or be W of his reproof,
25:17 house, lest he become W of you and hate
Sir 16:25 neither hunger nor grow W, and they do not
43:30 and do not grow W, for you cannot praise
Is 1:14 to me, I am W of bearing them.
5:27 None is W, none stumbles, none slumbers or sleeps,
7:13 little for you to W men, that you weary
7:13 weary men, that you W my God also?
28:12 give rest to the W; and this is repose";
32:2 great rock in a W land.
38:14 My eyes are W with looking upward.
40:28 faint or grow W, his understanding is unsearchable.
40:30 shall faint and be W, and young men shall
40:31 run and not be W, they shall walk and
43:22 but you have been W of me, O Israel!
46:1 loaded as burdens on W beasts.
50:4 to sustain with a word him that is W
Jer 2:24 who seek her need W themselves; in her month
6:11 the LORD; I am W of holding it in.
9:5 iniquity and are too W to repent.
15:6 destroyed you;--I am W of relenting.
20:9 bones, and I am W with holding it in,
31:25 I will satisfy the W soul, and every languishing
45:3 my pain; I am W with my groaning, and
51:58 nought, and the nations W themselves only for fire."
Lam 5:5 hard driven; we are W, we are given no
Hab 2:13 for fire, and nations W themselves for nought?
2Mac 12:36 long time and were W, Judas called upon the
Gal 6:9 let us not grow W in well-doing, for in
2Thes 3:13 Brethren, do not be W in well-doing.
Heb 12:3 you may not grow W or fainthearted.
Rev 2:3 my name's sake, and you have not grown W

WEARYING

Ps 77:2 is stretched out without W; my soul refuses to

WEASEL

Lev 11:29 upon the earth: the W, the mouse, the great

WEATHER (2)

Sir 3:15 as frost in fair W, your sins will melt
Mt 16:2 'It will be fair W; for the sky is

WEAVE (4)

Ex 28:39 "And you shall W the coat in checker work
Judg 16:13 to her, "If you W the seven locks of
Is 59:5 hatch adders' eggs, they W the spider's web; he
Mic 7:3 his soul; thus they W it together.

WEAVER (7)

Ex 35:35 linen, or by a W --by any sort of
1Sam 17:7 spear was like a W's beam, and his spear's
2Sam 21:19 spear was like a W's beam.
1Chr 11:23 a spear like a W's beam; but Benaiah went
20:5 spear was like a W's beam.
Job 7:6 are swifter than a W's shuttle, and come to
Is 38:12 shepherd's tent; like a W I have rolled up

WEAVERS

Is 19:9 in despair, and the W of white cotton.

WEB (6)

Judg 16:13 my head with the W and make it tight
16:14 of his head and wove them into the W
16:14 pulled away the pin, the loom, and the W
Job 8:14 in sunder, and his trust is a spider's W
27:18 is like a spider's W, like a booth which
Is 59:5 they weave the spider's W; he who eats their

WEBS

Is 59:6 Their W will not serve as clothing; men will

WEDDING (16)

Tob 8:19 this he gave a W feast for them which
8:20 fourteen days of the W feast were ended,
9:2 bring him to the W feast.
9:6 and came to the W feast.
10:7 fourteen days of the W feast had expired which
Song 3:11 the day of his W, on the day of
1Mac 9:37 are celebrating a great W, and are conducting the
9:41 Thus the W was turned into mourning and the
10:58 marriage, and celebrated her W at Ptolemais with
Mt 9:15 to them, "Can the W guests mourn as long
22:8 to his servants, 'The W is ready, but those
22:10 and good; so the W hall was filled with
22:11 man who had no W garment;
22:12 in here without a W garment?' And he was
Mk 2:19 to them, "Can the W guests fast while the
Lk 5:34 them, "Can you make W guests fast while the

WEDGED

Sir 27:2 stones, so sin is W in between selling and

WEDLOCK

Ezek 16:38 as women who break W and shed blood are

WEEDS (11)

Job 31:40 of wheat, and foul W instead of barley." The
Hos 10:4 springs up like poisonous W in the furrows of
Jon 2:5 was round about me; W were wrapped about my
Mt 13:25 enemy came and sowed W among the wheat, and
13:26 bore grain, then the W appeared also.
13:27 How then has it W
13:29 lest in gathering the W you root up the
13:30 the reapers, Gather the W first and bind them

	13:36	the parable of the W of the field."
	13:38	of the kingdom; the W are the sons of
	13:40	Just as the W are gathered and burned with

WEEK (13)

Gen	29:27	Complete the W of this one, and we will
	29:28	so, and completed her W; then Laban gave him
Dan	9:27	with many for one W; and for half of
	9:27	for half of the W he shall cause sacrifice
Mt	28:1	first day of the W, Mary Magdalene and the
Mk	16:2	first day of the W they went to the
	16:9	first day of the W, he appeared first to
Lk	18:12	I fast twice a W, I give tithes of
	24:1	first day of the W, at early dawn, they
Jn	20:1	first day of the W Mary Magdalene came to
	20:19	first day of the W, the doors being shut
Acts	20:7	first day of the W, when we were gathered
1Cor	16:2	first day of every W, each of you is

WEEKS (21)

Ex	34:22	observe the feast of W, the first fruits of
Lev	12:5	shall be unclean two W, as in her menstruation;
	23:15	wave offering; seven full W shall they be,
	25:8	you shall count seven W of years, seven times
	25:8	time of the seven W of years shall be
Num	28:26	at your feast of W, you shall have a
Deut	16:9	"You shall count seven W; begin to count the
	16:9	to count the seven W from the time you
	16:10	keep the feast of W to the LORD your
	16:16	at the feast of W, and at the feast
2Chr	8:13	bread, the feast of W, and the feast of
Tob	2:1	festival of the seven W, a good dinner was
Jer	5:24	keeps for us the W appointed for the harvest.'
Dan	9:24	"Seventy W of years are decreed concerning your
	9:25	anointed one, a prince, there shall be seven W
	9:25	Then for sixty-two W it shall be built again
	9:26	And after the sixty-two W, an anointed one shall
	10:2	those days I, Daniel, was mourning for three W
	10:3	anoint myself at all, for the full three W
2Mac	12:31	as the feast of W was close at hand.
Acts	17:2	custom, and for three W he argued with them

WEEP (63)

Gen	23:2	for Sarah and to W for her.
	43:30	his brother, and he sought a place to W
Num	11:13	For they W before me and say, 'Give us
1Sam	1:8	husband, said to her, "Hannah, why do you W
	2:33	shall be spared to W out his eyes and
	30:4	wept, until they had no more strength to W
2Sam	1:24	"Ye daughters of Israel, W over Saul, who clothed
2Kgs	8:12	And Hazael said, "Why does my lord W
Neh	8:9	the LORD your God; do not mourn or W
Tob	5:17	his mother, began to W, and said to Tobit,
	7:17	took her there; and the girl began to W
Jud	16:17	their flesh; they shall W in pain for ever.
Job	30:25	Did not I W for him whose day was
	30:31	my pipe to the voice of those who W
Eccl	3:4	up; a time to W, and a time to
Sir	7:34	not fail those who W, but mourn with those
	12:16	pit; an enemy will W with his eyes, but
	22:9	W for the dead, for he lacks the light;
	22:9	lacks the light; and W for the fool, for
	22:9	for he lacks intelligence; W less bitterly for the
Is	15:2	the high places to W; over Nebo and over
	16:9	Therefore I W with the weeping of Jazer for
	22:4	from me, let me W bitter tears; do not
	30:19	at Jerusalem; you shall W no more.
	33:7	the envoys of peace W bitterly.
Jer	9:1	tears, that I might W day and night for
	13:17	listen, my soul will W in secret for your
	13:17	pride; my eyes will W bitterly and run down
	22:10	W not for him who is dead, nor bemoan
	22:10	nor bemoan him; but W bitterly for him who
	48:32	than for Jazer I W for you, O vine
Lam	1:16	"For these things I W; my eyes flow with
Ezek	24:16	shall not mourn or W nor shall your tears
	24:23	shall not mourn or W, but you shall pine
	27:31	with sackcloth, and they W over you in bitterness
Joel	1:5	Awake, you drunkards, and W; and wail, all you
	2:17	ministers of the LORD, W and say, "Spare thy
Mic	1:10	it not in Gath, W not at all; in
Zech	12:10	an only child, and W bitterly over him, as
Mt	8:12	darkness; there men will W and gnash their teeth."
	13:42	fire; there men will W and gnash their teeth.
	13:50	fire; there men will W and gnash their teeth.
	22:13	darkness; there men will W and gnash their teeth.'
	24:51	hypocrites; there men will W and gnash their teeth.
	25:30	darkness; there men will W and gnash their teeth.'
Mk	5:39	them, "Why do you make a tumult and W
Lk	6:21	"Blessed are you that W now, for you shall
	6:25	that laugh now, for you shall mourn and W
	7:13	on her and said to her, "Do not W
	7:32	and you did not W
	8:52	he said, "Do not W; for she is not
	13:28	iniquity!' There you will W and gnash your teeth,
	23:27	of Jerusalem, do not W for me, but weep
	23:27	weep for me, but W for yourselves and for
Jn	11:31	to the tomb to W there.
	16:20	to you, you will W and lament, but the
Rom	12:15	with those who rejoice, W with those who weep.
	12:15	with those who rejoice, weep with those who W
Jas	4:9	Be wretched and mourn and W
	5:1	Come now, you rich, W and howl for the
Rev	5:5	elders said to me, W not; lo, the Lion
	18:9	wanton with her, will W and wail over her
	18:11	merchants of the earth W and mourn for her,

WEEPING (52)

Gen	50:4	when the days of W for him were past,
Num	11:10	Moses heard the people W throughout their families,
	25:6	Israel, while they were W at the door of
Deut	34:8	then the days of W and mourning for Moses
1Sam	11:5	said, "What ails the people, that they are W
2Sam	3:16	husband went with her, W after her all the
	15:30	the Mount of Olives, W as he went, barefoot
	15:30	and they went up, W as they went.
	19:1	"Behold, the king is W and mourning for Absalom."
Ezra	3:13	sound of the people's W, for the people shouted
	10:1	prayed and made confession, W and casting himself
Tob	5:21	So she stopped W
Esth	4:3	Jews, with fasting and W and lamenting, and most
Job	16:16	face is red with W, and on my eyelids
Ps	6:6	with tears; I drench my couch with my W
	6:8	the LORD has heard the sound of my W
	30:5	W may tarry for the night, but joy comes
	126:6	He that goes forth W, bearing the seed for
Sir	38:17	Let your W be bitter and your wailing fervent;
Is	15:5	Luhith they go up W; on the road to
	16:9	I weep with the W of Jazer for the
	22:12	of hosts called to W and mourning, to baldness
	65:19	it the sound of W and the cry of
Jer	3:21	heights is heard, the W and pleading of Israel's
	9:10	"Take up W and wailing for the mountains, and
	31:9	With W they shall come, and with consolations I
	31:15	voice is heard in Ramah, lamentation and bitter W
	31:15	Rachel is W for her children; she refuses to
	31:16	"Keep your voice from W, and your eyes from
	41:6	Mizpah to meet them, W as he came.
	48:5	Luhith they go up W; for at the descent
	50:4	Judah shall come together, W as they come; and
Lam	2:11	eyes are spent with W; my soul is in
Bar	4:11	sent them away with W and sorrow.
	4:23	out with sorrow and W, but God will give
Ezek	8:14	behold, there sat women W for Tammuz.
Dan	13:35	And she, W, looked up toward heaven, for her
Joel	2:12	heart, with fasting, with W, and with mourning;
Mal	2:13	altar with tears, with W and groaning because he
2Mac	13:12	the merciful Lord with W and fasting and lying
Mt	2:18	and loud lamentation, Rachel W for her children; she
Mk	5:38	a tumult, and people W and wailing loudly.
Lk	7:38	him at his feet, W, she began to wet
	8:52	And all were W and bewailing her; but he
Jn	11:33	When Jesus saw her W, and the Jews who
	11:33	came with her also W, he was deeply moved
	20:11	But Mary stood W outside the tomb, and as
	20:13	They said to her, "Woman, why are you W
	20:15	Jesus said to her, "Woman, why are you W
Acts	9:39	widows stood beside him W, and showing tunics and
	21:13	"What are you doing, W and breaking my heart?
Rev	18:15	fear of her torment, W and mourning aloud,

WEEPS (2)

Lam	1:2	She W bitterly in the night, tears on her
Zech	12:10	over him, as one W over a first-born.

WEIGH (8)

Ezra	8:29	keep them until you W them before the chief
Ps	38:4	over my head; they W like a burden too
Sir	6:21	She will W him down like a heavy testing
	26:15	and no balance can W the value of a
Is	46:6	from the purse, and W out silver in the
Zeph	1:11	no more; all who W out silver are cut

2Mac 9:8 imagining that he could W the high mountains in
1Cor 14:29 and let the others W what is said.

WEIGHED (23)

Gen 23:16 with Ephron; and Abraham W out for Ephron the
1Sam 2:3 God of knowledge, and by him actions are W
17:7 and his spear's head W six hundred shekels of
2Sam 14:26 he cut it), he W the hair of his
21:16 the giants, whose spear W three hundred shekels of
2Kgs 12:11 the money that was W out into the hands
1Chr 20:2 he found that it W a talent of gold,
Ezra 8:25 And I W out to them the silver and
8:26 present had offered; I W out into their hand
8:33 and the vessels were W into the hands of
8:34 whole was counted and W, and the weight of
Job 6:2 that my vexation were W, and all my calamity
28:15 and silver cannot be W as its price.
31:6 deceit; (Let me be W in a just balance,
Sir 21:25 the prudent will be W in the balance.
Is 33:18 where is he who W the tribute?
40:12 in a measure and W the mountains in scales
Jer 32:9 Hanamel my cousin, and W out the money to
32:10 it, got witnesses, and W the money on scales.
Dan 5:27 TEKEL, you have been W in the balances and
Zech 11:12 And they W out as my wages thirty shekels
Lk 21:34 lest your hearts be W down with dissipation and
Acts 27:13 obtained their purpose, they W anchor and sailed

WEIGHING (11)

Gen 24:22 took a gold ring W a half-shekel, and two
24:22 bracelets for her arms W ten gold shekels,
Num 7:85 dishes, each silver plate W a hundred and thirty
7:86 dishes, full of incense, W ten shekels apiece
Josh 7:21 a bar of gold W fifty shekels, then I
1Chr 22:3 bronze in quantities beyond W,
22:14 bronze and iron beyond W, for there is so
Eccl 12:9 taught the people knowledge, W and studying and
Ezek 5:1 then take balances for W, and divide the hair.
1Mac 14:24 a large gold shield W a thousand minas, to
15:18 brought a gold shield W a thousand minas.

WEIGHS (6)

Prov 12:25 in a man's heart W him down, but a
16:2 eyes, but the LORD W the spirit.
21:2 eyes, but the LORD W the heart.
24:12 does not he who W the heart perceive it?
Wis 9:15 for a perishable body W down the soul, and
Sir 38:19 of the poor man W down his heart.

WEIGHT (57)

Gen 43:21 our money in full W; so we have brought
Lev 19:35 measures of length or W or quantity.
26:26 your bread again by W; and you shall eat,
Num 7:13 one silver plate whose W was a hundred and
7:19 one silver plate, whose W was a hundred and
7:25 one silver plate, whose W was a hundred and
7:31 one silver plate whose W was a hundred and
7:37 one silver plate, whose W was a hundred and
7:43 one silver plate, whose W was a hundred and
7:49 one silver plate, whose W was a hundred and
7:55 one silver plate, whose W was a hundred and
7:61 one silver plate, whose W was a hundred and
7:67 one silver plate, whose W was a hundred and
7:73 one silver plate, whose W was a hundred and
7:79 one silver plate, whose W was a hundred and
Deut 1:12 I bear alone the W and burden of you
25:15 A full and just W you shall have, a
Judg 8:26 And the W of the golden earrings that he
16:29 and he leaned his W upon them, his right
1Sam 17:5 of mail, and the W of the coat was
2Sam 12:30 from his head; the W of it was a
14:26 his head, two hundred shekels by the king's W
18:12 in my hand the W of a thousand pieces
1Kgs 7:47 many of them; the W of the bronze was
10:14 Now the W of gold that came to Solomon
2Kgs 25:16 the bronze of all these vessels was beyond W
1Chr 21:25 shekels of gold by W for the site.
28:14 of the LORD, the W of gold for all
28:14 for each service, the W of silver vessels for
28:15 for each service, the W of the golden lampstands
28:15 and their lamps, the W of gold for each
28:15 and its lamps, the W of silver for a
28:16 in the service, the W of gold for each
28:17 golden bowls and the W of each; for the
28:17 silver bowls and the W of each;
28:18 refined gold, and its W; also his plan for
2Chr 3:9 The W of the nails was one shekel to
4:18 quantities, so that the W of the bronze was
9:13 Now the W of gold that came to Solomon
Ezra 8:30 Levites took over the W of the silver and
8:34 and weighed, and the W of everything was recorded.
Jud 7:4 the valleys nor the hills will bear their W
Job 28:25 to the wind its W, and meted out the
Prov 11:1 LORD, but a just W is his delight.
Wis 11:20 arranged all things by measure and number and W
Sir 13:2 Do not lift a W beyond your strength, nor
16:23 will impart instruction by W, and declare knowledge
42:7 be by number and W, and make a record
Is 22:24 on him the whole W of his father's house,
Jer 52:20 the bronze of all these things was beyond W
Lam 4:2 of Zion, worth their W in fine gold, how
Ezek 4:10 eat shall be by W, twenty shekels a day;
4:16 shall eat bread by W and with fearfulness; and
Zech 5:8 thrust down the leaden W upon its mouth.
Jn 19:39 of myrrh and aloes, about a hundred pounds' W
2Cor 4:17 for us an eternal W of glory beyond all
Heb 12:1 also lay aside every W, and sin which clings

WEIGHTIER

Mt 23:22 and have neglected the W matters of the law,

WEIGHTS (8)

Gen 23:16 silver, according to the W current among the
Lev 19:36 have just balances, just W, a just ephah, and
Deut 25:13 bag two kinds of W, a large and a
Prov 16:11 the LORDs; all the W in the bag are
20:10 Diverse W and diverse measures are both alike an
20:23 Diverse W are an abomination to the LORD, and
Sir 42:4 accuracy with scales and W, and of acquiring much
Mic 6:11 wicked scales and with a bag of deceitful W

WEIGHTY (2)

Prov 27:3 heavy, and sand is W, but a fool's provocation
2Cor 10:10 say, "His letters are W and strong, but his

WELCOME (15)

Tob 5:13 to him, "You are W, my brother.
11:17 he blessed her, saying, W, daughter!
Sir 15:2 his youth she will W him.
35:20 Mercy is as W when he afflicts them as
41:2 O death, how W is your sentence to one
Mt 25:38 thee a stranger and W thee, or naked and
25:43 and you did not W me, naked and you
Acts 25:13 arrived at Caesarea to W Festus.
Rom 14:1 is weak in faith, W him, but not for
15:7 W one another, therefore, as Christ has welcomed
2Cor 6:17 unclean; then I will W you,
1Thes 1:9 concerning us what a W we had among you,
Heb 11:31 she had given friendly W to the spies.
3Jn 1:10 he refuses himself to W the brethren, and also
1:10 those who want to W them and puts them

WELCOMED (16)

2Kgs 20:13 And Hezekiah W them, and he showed them all
Jud 3:7 the country round about W him with garlands and
Is 39:2 And Hezekiah W them; and he showed them his
1Mac 10:1 They W him, and there he began to reign.
12:8 Onias W the envoy with honor, and received the
2Mac 3:9 and had been kindly W by the high priest
4:22 He was W magnificently by Jason and the city,
Mt 25:35 a stranger and you W me,
Lk 8:40 Jesus returned, the crowd W him, for they were
9:11 followed him; and he W them and spoke to
Jn 4:45 to Galilee, the Galileans W him, having seen all
Acts 15:4 to Jerusalem, they were W by the church and
28:2 kindled a fire and W us all, because it
28:29 his own expense, and W all who came to
Rom 14:3 eats; for God has W him.
15:7 therefore, as Christ has W you, for the glory

WELCOMING

2Mac 6:19 But he, W death with honor rather than life

WELFARE (20)

Gen 43:27 he inquired about their W, and said, "Is your
Ex 18:7 each other of their W, and went into the
Judg 18:15 home of Micah, and asked him of his W
Neh 2:10 come to seek the W of the children of
Esth 10:3 for he sought the W of his people and
Ps 35:27 who delights in the W of his servant!"
Prov 3:2 of life and abundant W will they give you.
Is 38:17 it was for my W that I had great

Jer	14:11	not pray for the W of this people.
	15:5	Who will turn aside to ask about your W
	29:7	But seek the W of the city where I
	29:7	behalf, for in its W you will find your
	29:7	for in its welfare you will find your W
	29:11	the LORD, plans for W and not for evil,
	38:4	is not seeking the W of this people, but
1Mac	12:22	write us concerning your W;
2Mac	4:5	having in view the W, both public and private,
	11:19	endeavor for the future to help promote your W
	13:3	sake of his country's W, but because he thought
Phil	2:20	him, who will be genuinely anxious for your W

WELL (288)

Gen	4:7	If you do W, will you not be accepted?
	4:7	you do not do W, sin is couching at
	12:13	that it may go W with me because of
	12:16	her sake he dealt W with Abram; and he
	13:10	the Jordan valley was W watered everywhere like
	16:14	Therefore the W was called Beer-lahai-roi; it lies
	21:19	and she saw a W of water; and she
	21:25	to Abimelech about a W of water which Abimelech's
	21:30	a witness for me that I dug this W
	24:1	Now Abraham was old, W advanced in years; and
	24:11	the city by the W of water at the
	24:20	ran again to the W to draw, and she
	26:19	and found there a W of springing water,
	26:20	the name of the W Esek, because they contended
	26:21	Then they dug another W, and they quarreled over
	26:22	there and dug another W, and over that they
	26:25	And there Isaac's servants dug a W
	26:32	told him about the W which they had dug,
	29:2	looked, he saw a W in the field, and
	29:2	for out of that W the flocks were watered.
	29:2	The stone on the W's mouth was large,
	29:3	the mouth of the W, and water the sheep,
	29:3	in its place upon the mouth of the W
	29:6	to them, "Is it W with him?" They said,
	29:6	They said, "It is W; and see, Rachel his
	29:8	the mouth of the W; then we water the
	29:10	the stone from the W's mouth, and watered the
	37:14	see if it is W with your brothers, and
	40:14	me, when it is W with you, and do
	43:27	said, "Is your father W, the old man of
	43:28	servant our father is W, he is still alive."
	45:16	it pleased Pharaoh and his servants W
	50:8	land of Egypt, as W as all the household
Ex	1:19	So God dealt W with the midwives; and the
	2:15	of Midian; and he sat down by a W
	4:14	that he can speak W; and behold, he is
Lev	6:21	you shall bring it W mixed, in baked pieces
	7:10	of Aaron, one as W as another.
	7:12	cakes of fine flour W mixed with oil.
	24:16	him; the sojourner as W as the native, when
Num	11:18	For it was W with us in Egypt." Therefore
	13:30	it; for we are W able to overcome it."
	20:17	drink water from a W; we will go along
	21:16	Beer; that is the W of which the LORD
	21:17	song: "Spring up, O W --Sing to it!--
	21:18	to it!-- the W which the princes dug,
	21:22	the water of a W; we will go by
Deut	4:40	that it may go W with you, and with
	5:14	maidservant may rest as W as you.
	5:16	that it may go W with you, in the
	5:29	that it might go W with them and with
	5:33	that it may go W with you, and that
	6:3	that it may go W with you, and that
	6:18	that it may go W with you, and that
	12:25	that all may go W with you and with
	12:28	that it may go W with you and with
	15:16	household, since he fares W with you,
	19:13	that it may be W with you.
	22:7	that it may go W with you, and that
	29:15	us this day as W as with him who
Josh	1:15	to your brethren as W as to you, and
	8:33	all Israel, sojourner as W as homeborn, with their
	22:30	and the Manassites spoke, it pleased them W
	23:1	Joshua was old and W advanced in years,
	23:2	am now old and W advanced in years;
Judg	8:7	And Gideon said, W then, when the LORD has
	9:16	if you have dealt W with Jerubbaal and his
	14:3	"Get her for me; for she pleases me W
	14:7	talked with the woman; and she pleased Samson W
	15:5	the standing grain, as W as the olive orchards.
Ruth	2:22	her daughter-in-law, "It is W, my daughter, that you
	3:1	that it may be W with you?
	3:13	of kin for you, W; let him do it;
1Sam	9:10	said to his servant, W said; come, let us
	12:14	God, it will be W;
	16:16	he will play it, and you will be W
	16:17	man who can play W, and bring him to
	16:23	was refreshed, and was W, and the evil spirit
	18:26	words, it pleased David W to be the king's
	19:4	And Jonathan spoke W of David to Saul his
	19:22	came to the great W that is in Secu;
	20:3	replied, "Your father knows W that I have found
	20:7	'Good!' it will be W with your servant; but
	24:18	how you have dealt W with me, in that
	25:31	the LORD has dealt W with my lord, then
	28:2	said to Achish, "Very W, you shall know what
	28:2	said to David, "Very W, I will make you
2Sam	17:18	Bahurim, who had a W in his courtyard; and
	17:19	a covering over the W's mouth, and scattered grain
	17:21	up out of the W, and went and told
	18:28	Ahima-az cried out to the king, "All is W
	18:29	king said, "Is it W with the young man
	18:32	the Cushite, "Is it W with the young man
	20:9	to Amasa, "Is it W with you, my brother?"
	23:15	to drink from the W of Bethlehem which is
	23:16	water out of the W of Bethlehem which was
1Kgs	2:18	Bathsheba said, "Very W; I will speak for you
	8:18	my name, you did W that it was in
	18:24	people answered, "It is W spoken."
	20:22	strengthen yourself, and consider W what you have to
2Kgs	4:14	Gehazi answered, W, she has no son, and her
	4:23	She said, "It will be W
	4:26	to her, Is it W with you?
	4:26	Is it W with your husband?
	4:26	Is it W with the child?" And she answered,
	4:26	And she answered, "It is W
	5:21	chariot to meet him, and said, "Is all W
	5:22	And he said, "All is W
	9:11	his master, they said to him, "Is all W
	10:30	"Because you have done W in carrying out what
	12:12	and the stonecutters, as W as to buy timber
	22:6	to the masons, as W as for buying timber
	25:24	and it shall be W with you."
1Chr	11:17	to drink from the W of Bethlehem which is
	11:18	water out of the W of Bethlehem which was
	22:3	and for clamps, as W as bronze in quantities
	26:17	four each day, as W as two and two
2Chr	6:8	my name, you did W that it was in
Neh	2:13	Gate to the Jackal's W and to the Dung
Tob	10:6	her, "Be still and stop worrying; he is W
	14:9	that it may be W with you.
Jud	10:16	you have said, and he will treat you W
	11:4	all will treat you W, as they do the
	11:22	her, "God has done W to send you before
	15:10	Israel, and God is W pleased with it.
Esth	16:17	"You will therefore do W not to put in
Job	12:3	I have understanding as W as you; I am
	13:9	Will it be W with you when he searches
Ps	37:10	more; though you look W at his place, he
	48:13	number her towers, consider W her ramparts, go
	49:18	praise when he does W for himself,
	73:2	stumbled, my steps had W nigh slipped.
	75:8	cup, with foaming wine, W mixed; and he will
	78:29	they ate and were W filled, for he gave
	112:5	It is W with the man who deals generously
	119:65	Thou hast dealt W with thy servant, O LORD,
	119:140	Thy promise is W tried, and thy servant loves
	128:2	and it shall be W with you.
	139:14	Thou knowest me right W;
Prov	5:15	your own cistern, flowing water from your own W
	11:10	When it goes W with the righteous, the city
	23:27	a deep pit; an adventures is a narrow W
	27:23	Know W the condition of your flocks, and give
	31:27	She looks W to the ways of her household,
Eccl	4:15	under the sun, as W as that youth, who
	7:14	made the one as W as the other, so
	8:12	that it will be W with those who fear
	8:13	it will not be W with the wicked, neither
Song	4:15	a garden fountain, a W of living water, and
	7:13	choice fruits, new as W as old, which I
Wis	8:1	to the other, and she orders all things W
	8:19	I was by nature W endowed, and a good
Sir	1:11	Lord it will go W at the end; on
	14:11	My son, treat yourself W, according to your means,
	17:23	who is alive and W sings the Lord's praises.
	30:14	poor man who is W and strong in constitution
	38:27	labors by night as W as by day; those
	40:29	who is intelligent and W instructed guards against

Is 3:10 that it shall be W with them, for they
25:6 wine on the lees W refined.
Jer 1:12 me, "You have seen W, for I am watching
2:33 "How W you direct your course to seek lovers!
4:10 saying, 'It shall be W with you'; whereas the
6:7 As a W keeps its water fresh, so she
7:23 that it may be W with you.'
22:15 Then it was W with him.
22:16 of the poor and needy; then it was W
23:17 LORD, 'It shall be W with you'; and to
31:21 yourself guideposts; consider W the highway, the
38:20 and it shall be W with you, and your
39:12 him, look after him W and do him no
40:4 will look after you W; but if it seems
40:9 and it shall be W with you.
42:6 that it may be W with us when we
Ezek 18:4 of the father as W as the soul of
24:10 kindle the fire, boil W the flesh, and empty
33:32 beautiful voice and plays W on an instrument, for
44:5 "Son of man, mark W, see with your eyes,
44:5 its laws; and mark W those who may be
Dan 3:15 which I have made, W and good; but if
3:30 that it might go W with us.
13:55 And Daniel said, "Very W
13:59 And Daniel said to him, "Very W
Jon 4:4 said, "Do you do W to be angry?"
4:9 Jonah, "Do you do W to be angry for
4:9 he said, "I do W to be angry, angry
1Mac 8:15 deliberate concerning the people, to govern them W
8:23 alliance: "May all go W with the Romans and
11:43 then you will do W to send me men
12:45 over to you as W as the other strongholds
2Mac 3:1 the laws were very W observed because of the
9:20 and your children are W and your affairs are
10:18 two very strong towers W equipped to withstand a
10:32 called Gazara, especially W garrisoned, where
11:26 You will do W, therefore, to send word to
11:28 If you are W, it is as we desire.
12:2 son of Gennaeus, as W as Hieronymus and
12:43 this he acted very W and honorably, taking account
14:37 citizens and was very W thought of and for
15:38 If it is W told and to the point,
Mt 3:17 with whom I am W pleased."
5:40 have your cloak as W;
6:33 and all these things shall be yours as W
9:12 said, "Those who are W have no need of
9:21 only touch his garment, I shall be made W
9:22 "Take heart, daughter; your faith has made you W
9:22 And instantly the woman was made W
12:18 whom my soul is W pleased.
14:36 and as many as touched it were made W
15:7 W did Isaiah prophesy of you, when he said:
17:4 Jesus, "Lord, it is W that we are here;
17:5 with whom I am W pleased; listen to him."
25:21 master said to him, W done, good and faithful
25:23 master said to him, W done, good and faithful
Mk 1:11 with thee I am W pleased."
2:17 them, "Those who are W have no need of
5:23 she may be made W, and live."
5:28 touch even his garments, I shall be made W
5:34 faith has made you W; go in peace, and
6:56 and as many as touched it were made W
7:6 he said to them, W did Isaiah prophesy of
7:36 has done all things W; he even makes the
9:5 Jesus, "Master, it is W that we are here;
10:52 "Go your way; your faith has made you W
12:28 that he answered them W, asked him, "Which
Lk 3:22 with thee I am W pleased."
4:22 And all spoke W of him, and wondered at
5:31 them, "Those who are W have no need of
6:26 when all men speak W of you, for so
6:48 because it had been W built.
7:10 returned to the house, they found the slave W
8:48 faith has made you W; go in peace."
8:50 not fear; only believe, and she shall be W
9:33 Jesus, "Master, it is W that we are here;
12:31 kingdom, and these things shall be yours as W
13:9 bears fruit next year, W and good; but if
14:5 has fallen into a W, will not immediately pull
17:19 go your way; your faith has made you W
18:42 "Receive your sight; your faith has made you W
19:17 he said to him, W done, good servant!
20:39 the scribes answered, "Teacher, you have spoken W
Jn 4:6 Jacob's W was there, and so Jesus, wearied as
4:6 was with his journey, sat down beside the W
4:11 draw with, and the W is deep; where do
4:12 who gave us the W, and drank from it
5:13 temple, and said to him, "See, you are W
7:23 the sabbath I made a man's whole body W
Acts 4:10 by him this man is standing before you W
10:22 God-fearing man, who is W spoken of by the
14:9 faith to be made W,
15:29 you keep yourselves from these, you will do W
16:2 He was W spoken of by the brethren at
17:12 of high standing as W as men.
18:24 was an eloquent man, W versed in the scriptures.
22:12 according to the law, W spoken of by all
25:10 have done no wrong, as you know very W
Rom 1:13 harvest among you as W as among the rest
16:2 a helper of many and of myself as W
1Cor 7:1 It is W for a man not to touch
7:8 say that it is W for them to remain
7:26 present distress it is W for a person to
7:37 keep her as his betrothed, he will do W
7:38 marries his betrothed does W; and he who refrains
9:26 W, I do not run aimlessly, I do not
14:17 you may give thanks W enough, but the other
16:18 refreshed my spirit as W as yours.
Gal 5:7 were running W; who hindered you from obeying
Eph 6:3 "that it may be W with you and that
1Thes 5:2 For you yourselves know W that the day of
1Tim 3:4 manage his own household W, keeping his children
3:7 moreover he must be W thought of by outsiders,
3:12 children and their households W;
3:13 for those who serve W as deacons gain a
5:10 and she must be W attested for her good
5:17 the elders who rule W be considered worthy of
2Tim 1:18 that Day—and you W know all the service
Heb 5:3 his own sins as W as for those of
7:12 is necessarily a change in the law as W
11:39 And all these, though W attested by their faith,
13:9 teachings; for it is W that the heart be
Jas 2:8 you do W
2:19 You believe that God is one; you do W
1Pet 5:1 sufferings of Christ as W as a partaker in
2Pet 1:17 with whom I am W pleased,"
1:19 You will do W to pay attention to this
3Jn 1:2 that all may go W with you and that
1:2 know that it is W with your soul.
1:6 You will do W to send them on their

WELL-DISCIPLINED

Sir 31:19 little is for a W man!

WELL-DISPOSED (3)

1Sam 20:12 behold, if he is W toward David, shall I
1Mac 8:1 very strong and were W toward all who made
2Mac 12:31 exhorted them to be W to their race in

WELL-DOING (3)

Rom 2:7 who by patience in W seek for glory and
Gal 6:9 not grow weary in W, for in due season
2Thes 3:13 Brethren, do not be weary in W

WELL-DRAWN

Wis 5:21 target as from a W bow of clouds,

WELL-FED

Jer 5:8 They were W lusty stallions, each neighing for his

WELL-FORTIFIED

Dan 11:15 siegeworks, and take a W city.

WELL-KNOWN (2)

Num 16:2 chosen from the assembly, W men;
2Cor 6:9 as unknown, and yet W; as dying, and behold

WELL-ORDERED (2)

Sir 10:1 the rule of an understanding man will be W
26:16 good wife in her W home.

WELL-SET

Is 3:24 rope; and instead of W hair, baldness; and instead

WELLING

Jn 4:14 a spring of water W up to eternal life."

WELLS (5)

Gen 26:15 with earth all the W which his father's servants
26:18 Isaac dug again the W of water which had
2Kgs 19:24 I dug W and drank foreign waters, and I
Is 12:3 draw water from the W of salvation.

W

W

W

2Mac 11:4 He took no account W of the power of
13:20 in to the garrison W was necessary.
Mt 7:12 So W you wish that men would do to
10:11 And W town or village you enter, find out
14:7 oath to give her W she might ask.
15:17 you not see that W goes into the mouth
16:19 kingdom of heaven, and W you bind on earth
16:19 bound in heaven, and W you loose on earth
17:12 but did to him W they pleased.
18:17 I say to you, W you bind on earth
18:17 bound in heaven, and W you loose on earth
20:4 the vineyard too, and W is right I will
21:22 And W you ask in prayer, you will receive,
23:3 so practice and observe W they tell you, but
Mk 3:28 sons of men, and W blasphemies they utter;
6:22 girl, "Ask me for W you wish, and I
6:23 he vowed to her, W you ask me, I
7:17 you not see that W goes into a man
9:13 they did to him W they pleased, as it
10:35 to do for us W we ask of you."
11:24 Therefore I tell you, W you ask in prayer,
13:11 to say; but say W is given you in
Lk 9:4 And W house you enter, stay there, and from
10:5 W house you enter, first say, 'Peace be to
10:35 care of him; and W more you spend, I
11:8 rise and give him W he needs.
12:3 Therefore W you have said in the dark shall
Jn 2:5 to the servants, "Do W he tells you."
5:18 the Father doing; for W he does, that the
11:22 now I know that W you ask from God,
14:13 W you ask in my name, I will do
15:7 abide in you, ask W you will, and it
15:16 should abide; so that W you ask the Father
16:13 his own authority, but W he hears he will
Acts 3:22 listen to him in W he tells you.
4:28 of Israel, to do W thy hand and thy
28:10 they put on board W we needed.
Rom 3:19 Now we know that W the law says it
14:23 act from faith; for W does not proceed from
15:4 For W was written in former days was written
16:2 and help her in W she may require from
1Cor 7:24 So, brethren, in W state each was called, there
10:25 Eat W is sold in the meat market without
10:27 disposed to go, eat W is set before you
10:31 eat or drink, or W you do, do all
2Cor 11:21 But W any one dares to boast of--I
Gal 6:7 is not mocked, for W a man sows, that
Eph 6:8 to men, knowing that W good any one does,
Phil 3:7 But W gain I had, I counted as loss
4:8 Finally, brethren, W is true, whatever is honorable,
4:8 brethren, whatever is true, W is honorable,
4:8 true, whatever is honorable, W is just, whatever is
4:8 honorable, whatever is just, W is pure, whatever is
4:8 just, whatever is pure, W is lovely, whatever is
4:8 pure, whatever is lovely, W is gracious, if there
4:11 I have learned, in W state I am, to
Col 3:17 And W you do, in word or deed, do
3:23 W your task, work heartily, as serving the Lord
1Tim 1:10 kidnapers, liars, perjurers, and W else is contrary to
2Pet 2:19 slaves of corruption; for W overcomes a man, to
1Jn 3:22 we receive from him W we ask, because we
5:4 For W is born of God overcomes the world;
5:15 he hears us in W we ask, we know
Jude 1:10 But these men revile W they do not understand,

WHEAT (51)

Gen 30:14 In the days of W harvest Reuben went and
Ex 9:32 But the W and the spelt were not ruined,
29:2 make them of fine W flour.
34:22 the first fruits of W harvest, and the feast
Deut 8:8 hills, a land of W and barley, of vines
32:14 the finest of the W --and of the blood
Judg 6:11 Gideon was beating out W in the wine press,
15:1 at the time of W harvest, Samson went to
Ruth 2:23 of the barley and W harvests; and she lived
1Sam 6:13 Beth-shemesh were reaping their W harvest in the
12:17 Is it not W harvest today?
2Sam 4:6 house had been cleaning W, but she grew drowsy
17:28 basins, and earthen vessels, W, barley, meal, parched
1Kgs 5:11 twenty thousand cors of W as food for his
1Chr 21:20 Now Ornan was threshing W; he turned and saw
21:23 the wood, and the W for a cereal offering.
2Chr 2:10 thousand cors of crushed W, twenty thousand cors of
2:15 Now therefore the W and barley, oil and wine,
27:5 ten thousand cors of W and ten thousand of
Ezra 6:9 the God of heaven, W, salt, wine, or oil,
7:22 a hundred cors of W, a hundred baths of
Jud 2:27 of Damascus during the W harvest, and burned all
3:3 land, and all our W fields, and our flocks
Job 31:40 thorns grow instead of W, and foul weeds instead
Ps 81:16 the finest of the W, and with honey from
147:14 he fills you with the finest of the W
Song 7:2 is a heap of W, encircled with lilies.
Sir 39:26 iron and salt and W flour and milk and
Is 28:25 cummin, and put in W in rows and barley
Jer 12:13 They have sown W and have reaped thorns, they
23:28 What has straw in common with W
41:8 we have stores of W, barley, oil, and honey
Ezek 4:9 "And you, take W and barley, beans and lentils,
27:17 exchanged for your merchandise W, olives and early
45:13 from each homer of W, and one sixth of
Joel 1:10 O vinedressers, for the W and the barley; because
Amos 5:11 from him exactions of W, you have built houses
8:5 that we may offer W for sale, that we
8:6 of sandals, and sell the refuse of the W
Mt 3:12 floor and gather his W into the granary, but
13:25 sowed weeds among the W, and went away.
13:29 you root up the W along with them.
13:30 burned, but gather the W into my barn.'"
Lk 3:17 and to gather the W into his granary, but
16:7 'A hundred measures of W He said to him,
22:31 might sift you like W,
Jn 12:24 unless a grain of W falls into the earth
Acts 27:38 ship, throwing out the W into the sea.
1Cor 15:37 bare kernel, perhaps of W or of some other
Rev 6:6 saying, "A quart of W for a denarius, and
18:13 oil, fine flour and W, cattle and sheep, horses

WHEEL (17)

1Kgs 7:32 the height of a W was a cubit and
7:33 made like a chariot W; their axles, their rims,
Prov 20:26 wicked, and drives the W over them.
Eccl 12:6 the fountain, or the W broken at the cistern,
Sir 33:5 is like a cart W, and his thoughts like
38:29 work and turning the W with his feet; he
Is 28:27 nor is a cart W rolled over cummin; but
28:28 he drives his cart W over it with his
Jer 18:3 house, and there he was working at his W
Ezek 1:15 creatures, I saw a W upon the earth beside
1:16 as it were a W within a wheel.
1:16 being as it were a wheel within a W
10:6 he went in and stood beside a W
10:10 likeness, as if a W were within a wheel.
10:10 likeness, as if a wheel were within a W
10:11 whatever direction the front W faced the others
Nah 3:2 whip, and rumble of W, galloping horse and bounding

WHEELED

2Mac 10:36 in the same way W around against the defenders

WHEELS (29)

Ex 14:25 Egyptians, clogging their chariot W so that they
1Kgs 7:30 stand had four bronze W and axles of bronze;
7:32 And the four W were underneath the panels; the
7:32 the axles of the W were of one piece
7:33 The W were made like a chariot wheel; their
Is 5:28 like flint, and their W like the whirlwind.
Jer 47:3 the rumbling of their W, the fathers look not
Ezek 1:16 the appearance of the W and their construction:
1:18 The four W had rims and they had spokes;
1:19 living creatures went, the W went beside them; and
1:19 from the earth, the W rose.
1:20 they went, and the W rose along with them;
1:20 spirit of the living creatures was in the W
1:21 from the earth, the W rose along with them;
1:21 spirit of the living creatures was in the W
3:13 the sound of the W beside them, that sounded
10:2 in among the whirling W underneath the cherubim;
10:6 the whirling W, from between the cherubim,"
10:9 behold, there were four W beside the cherubim, one
10:9 appearance of the W was like sparkling chrysolite.
10:12 their spokes, and the W were full of eyes
10:12 eyes round about--the W that the four of
10:13 As for the W, they were called in my
10:13 they were called in my hearing the whirling W
10:16 the cherubim went, the W went beside them; and
10:16 from the earth, the W did not turn from
10:19 went forth, with the W beside them; and they
11:22 their wings, with the W beside them; and the
Dan 7:9 was fiery flames, its W were burning fire.

W

WHELP (2)
Gen 49:9 Judah is a lion's W; from the prey, my
Deut 33:22 "Dan is a lion's W, that leaps forth from

WHELPS (6)
Job 4:11 of prey, and the W of the lioness are
Jer 51:38 together like lions; they shall growl like lions' W
Ezek 19:2 in the midst of young lions, rearing her W
19:3 up one of her W; he became a young
19:5 took another of her W and made him a
Nah 2:12 tore enough for his W and strangled prey for

WHENCE (22)
Gen 10:14 Lehabim, Naph-tuhim, Pathrusim, Casluhim W came
Judg 13:6 did not ask him W he was, and he
19:17 and W do you come?"
2Kgs 6:27 will not help you, W shall I help you?
20:14 And W did they come to you?" And Hezekiah
1Chr 1:12 Lehabim, Naph-tuhim, Pathrusim, Casluhim W came
Job 1:7 LORD said to Satan, W have you come?" Satan
2:2 LORD said to Satan, W have you come?" Satan
10:21 comfort before I go W I shall not return,
16:22 shall go the way W I shall not return.
28:20 W then comes wisdom?
Ps 121:1 From W does my help come?
Is 39:3 And W did they come to you?" Hezekiah said,
49:21 I was left alone; W then have these come?"
Jon 1:8 And W do you come?
Nah 3:7 W shall I seek comforters for her?
Mt 21:25 The baptism of John, W was it?
Lk 20:7 they did not know W it was.
Jn 3:8 you do not know W it comes or whither
8:14 true, for I know W I have come and
8:14 you do not know W I come or whither
Rev 7:13 in white robes, and W have they come?"

WHENEVER (38)
Gen 30:41 W the stronger of the flock were breeding Jacob
Ex 17:11 W Moses held up his hand, Israel prevailed; and
17:11 hand, Israel prevailed; and W he lowered his hand,
33:8 W Moses went out to the tent, all the
34:34 on his face; but W Moses went in before
Num 9:17 And W the cloud was taken up from over
10:6 is to be blown W they are to set
10:34 over them by day, W they set out from
10:35 And W the ark set out, Moses said, "Arise,
Deut 4:7 God is to us, W we call upon him?
Judg 2:15 W they marched out, the hand of the LORD
2:18 W the LORD raised up judges for them, the
2:19 But W the judge died, they turned back and
6:3 For W the Israelites put in seed the Midianites
1Sam 16:23 And W the evil spirit from God was upon
2Sam 15:5 And W a man came near to do obeisance
1Kgs 8:52 giving ear to them W they call to thee.
2Kgs 4:8 So W he passed that way, he would turn
4:10 a lamp, so that W he comes to us,
12:10 And W they saw that there was much money
1Chr 23:31 likewise at evening, and W burnt offerings are
2Chr 7:6 love endures for ever-- W David offered praises by
19:10 with your whole heart: W a case comes to
24:11 And W the chest was brought to the king's
Wis 12:18 hast power to act W thou dost choose.
Jer 20:8 For W I speak, I cry out, I shout,
48:27 found among thieves, that W you spoke of him
Ezek 3:17 the house of Israel; W you hear a word
13:7 uttered a lying divination, W you have said, 'Says
33:7 the house of Israel; W you hear a word
Mk 3:11 And W the unclean spirits beheld him, they fell
11:25 And W you stand praying, forgive, if you have
14:7 poor with you, and W you will, you can
Lk 10:8 W you enter a town and they receive you,
10:10 near to you.' But W you enter a town
2Cor 3:15 Yes, to this day W Moses is read a
1Jn 3:20 our hearts before him W our hearts condemn us;
Rev 4:9 And W the living creatures give glory and honor

WHEREAS (16)
Deut 9:4 to possess this land'; W it is because of
28:62 W you were as the stars of heaven for
1Sam 24:17 have repaid me good, W I have repaid you
1Kgs 8:18 to David my father, W it was in your
12:11 And now, W my father laid upon you a
2Chr 6:8 to David my father, W it was in your
10:11 And now, W my father laid upon you a
Wis 16:23 the showers of rain; W the fire, in order
Is 60:15 W you have been forsaken and hated, with no
Jer 4:10 be well with you'; W the sword has reached
Dan 4:23 And W the king saw a watcher, a holy
1Mac 15:3 W certain pestilent men have gained control of the
1Tim 1:5 that is in faith; W the aim of our
5:6 prayers night and day; W she who is self-indulgent
Jas 4:14 trade and get gain"; W you do not know
2Pet 2:11 revile the glorious ones, W angels, though greater in

WHEREFORE (6)
Num 21:14 W it is said in the Book of the
Ezek 5:11 W, as I live, says the Lord GOD, surely,
13:20 W thus says the Lord GOD: Behold, I am
16:35 W, O harlot, hear the word of the LORD:
20:30 Bamah to this day.) W say to the house
Acts 26:19 by faith in me.' W, O King Agrippa, I

WHEREIN (6)
Judg 16:5 "Entice him, and see W his great strength lies,
16:6 Samson, "Please tell me W your great strength lies,
16:15 have not told me W your great strength lies."
1Kgs 18:9 And he said, W have I sinned, that you
Job 3:3 "Let the day perish W I was born, and
Wis 12:2 them of the things W they sin, that they

WHEREON
Song 4:4 built for an arsenal, W hang a thousand bucklers,

WHEREVER (54)
Gen 28:15 and will keep you W you go, and will
30:30 LORD has blessed you W I turned.
35:3 has been with me W I have gone."
Ex 5:11 yourselves, get your straw W you can find it;
Num 33:54 give a small inheritance; W the lot falls to
Deut 2:37 the hill country, and W the LORD our God
Josh 1:7 may have good success W you go.
1:9 God is with you W you go."
1:16 we will do, and W you send us we
1Sam 14:47 and against the Philistines; W he turned he put
18:5 out and was successful W Saul sent him; so
23:13 Keilah, and they went W they could go.
2Sam 7:9 have been with you W you went, and have
8:6 gave victory to David W he went.
8:14 gave victory to David W he went.
15:21 lord the king lives, W my lord the king
1Kgs 2:3 that you do and W you turn;
2Kgs 8:1 your household, and sojourn W you can; for the
12:5 them repair the house W any need of repairs
18:7 LORD was with him; W he went forth, he
1Chr 17:8 have been with you W you went, and have
18:6 gave victory to David W he went.
18:13 gave victory to David W he went.
Jud 8:22 heads among the Gentiles, W we serve as slaves;
Esth 4:3 And in every province, W the king's command and
8:17 and in every city, W the king's command and
Prov 17:8 him who gives it; W he turns he prospers.
21:1 LORD; he turns it W he will.
Sir 36:26 no home, and lodges W night finds him?
Jer 40:4 is before you; go W you think it good
40:5 the people; or go W you think it right
Ezek 1:12 each went straight forward; W the spirit would go,
1:20 W the spirit would go, they went, and the
6:6 W you dwell your cities shall be waste and
6:13 under every leafy oak, W they offered pleasing odor
20:28 to give them, then W they saw any high
36:20 came to the nations, W they came, they profaned
47:9 And W the river goes every living creature which
Dan 2:38 hand he has given, W they dwell, the sons
1Mac 5:63 among all the Gentiles, W their name was heard.
6:36 took their position beforehand W the beast was;
6:36 wherever the beast was; W it went they went
Mt 8:19 I will follow you W you go."
24:28 W the body is, there the eagles will be
26:13 I say to you, W this gospel is preached
Mk 6:56 And W he came, in villages, cities, or country,
9:18 a dumb spirit; and W it seizes him, it
14:9 I say to you, W the gospel is preached
14:14 you; follow him, and W he enters, say to
Lk 9:5 And W they do not receive you, when you
9:57 "I will follow you W you go."
1Cor 16:6 me on my journey, W I go.
Jas 3:4 a very small rudder W the will of the
Rev 14:4 who follow the Lamb W he goes; these have

WHEREWITH
1Kgs 8:59 these words of mine, W I have made supplication

WHET (4)

Deut 32:41 for ever, if I W my glittering sword, and
Ps 7:12 not repent, God will W his sword; he has
64:3 scheming of evildoers, who W their tongues like
Eccl 10:10 and one does not W the edge, he must

WHICHEVER (2)

Sir 15:16 out your hand for W you wish.
15:17 life and death, and W he chooses will be

WHIP (6)

Deut 22:18 take the man and W him;
Prov 26:3 A W for the horse, a bridle for the
Sir 28:17 The blow of a W raises a welt, but
30:1 loves his son will W him often, in order
Nah 3:2 The crack of W, and rumble of wheel, galloping
Jn 2:15 And making a W of cords, he drove them

WHIPPED

Job 30:8 brood, they have been W out of the land.

WHIPPING

Sir 42:5 of children, and of W a wicked servant severely.

WHIPS (6)

1Kgs 12:11 father chastised you with W, but I will chastise
12:14 father chastised you with W, but I will chastise
2Chr 10:11 father chastised you with W, but I will chastise
10:14 father chastised you with W, but I will chastise
Sir 23:2 O that W were set over my thoughts, and
2Mac 7:1 king, under torture with W and cords, to partake

WHIRL (2)

Ps 29:9 makes the oaks to W, and strips the forests
Is 22:18 hold on you, and W you round and round,

WHIRLING (7)

Ps 83:13 God, make them like W dust, like chaff before
Is 17:13 before the wind and W dust before the storm.
Jer 23:19 has gone forth, a W tempest; it will burst
30:23 has gone forth, a W tempest; it will burst
Ezek 10:2 "Go in among the W wheels underneath the
10:6 fire from between the W wheels, from between the
10:13 in my hearing the W wheels.

WHIRLWIND (20)

2Kgs 2:1 to heaven by a W, Elijah and Elisha were
2:11 went up by a W into heaven.
Job 27:20 in the night a W carries him off.
37:9 its chamber comes the W, and cold from the
38:1 Job out of the W:
40:6 Job out of the W:
Ps 77:18 thunder was in the W; thy lightnings lighted up
Prov 1:27 calamity comes like a W, when distress and anguish
Sir 43:17 do the tempest from the north and the W
48:9 taken up by a W of fire, in a
48:12 was covered by the W, and Elisha was filled
Is 5:28 seem like flint, and their wheels like the W
29:6 and great noise, with W and tempest, and the
Jer 4:13 his chariots like the W; his horses are swifter
Dan 11:40 upon him like a W, with chariots and horsemen,
Hos 8:7 sow the wind, and they shall reap the W
Amos 1:14 the day of the W;
Nah 1:3 His way is in W and storm, and the
Hab 3:14 who came like a W to scatter me, rejoicing
Zech 7:14 scattered them with a W among all the nations

WHIRLWINDS (2)

Is 21:1 As W in the Negeb sweep on, it comes
Zech 9:14 march forth in the W of the south.

WHIRRING

Is 18:1 Ah, land of W wings which is beyond the

WHISPER (5)

Job 4:12 my ear received the W of it.
26:14 and how small a W do we hear of
Ps 41:7 All who hate me W together about me; they
Sir 12:18 clap his hands, and W much, and change his
Is 29:4 and your speech shall W out of the dust.

WHISPERED (2)

Mt 10:27 and what you hear W, proclaim upon the housetops.
Lk 12:3 and what you have W in private rooms shall

WHISPERER (6)

Prov 16:28 spreads strife, and a W separates close friends.
18:8 The words of a W are like delicious morsels;
26:20 where there is no W, quarreling ceases.
26:22 The words of a W are like delicious morsels;
Sir 21:28 A W defiles his own soul and is hated
28:13 Curse the W and deceiver, for he has destroyed

WHISPERING (3)

2Sam 12:19 that his servants were W together, David perceived
Ps 31:13 Yea, I hear the W of many-- terror
Jer 20:10 For I hear many W

WHISTLE (2)

Is 5:26 nation afar off, and W for it from the
7:18 day the LORD will W for the fly which

WHISTLING (2)

Wis 17:18 Whether there came a W wind, or a melodious
Dan 3:50 furnace like a moist W wind, so that the

WHITE (70)

Gen 30:35 every one that had W on it, and every
30:37 and plane, and peeled W streaks in them, exposing
30:37 in them, exposing the W of the rods.
49:12 wine, and his teeth W with milk.
Ex 4:6 hand was leprous, as W as snow.
16:31 was like coriander seed, W, and the taste of
Lev 13:3 diseased spot has turned W and the disease appears
13:4 if the spot is W in the skin of
13:4 it has not turned W, the priest shall shut
13:10 if there is a W swelling in the skin,
13:10 has turned the hair W, and there is quick
13:13 it has all turned W, and he is clean.
13:16 and is changed to W, then he shall come
13:17 the disease has turned W, then the priest shall
13:19 boil there comes a W swelling or a reddish-white
13:20 its hair has turned W, then the priest shall
13:21 on it is not W and it is not
13:24 a spot, reddish-white or W,
13:25 the spot has turned W and it appears deeper
13:26 the spot is not W and it is no
13:38 skin of the body, W spots,
13:39 are of a dull W, it is tetter that
Num 12:10 Miriam was leprous, as W as snow.
2Kgs 5:27 presence a leper, as W as snow.
Tob 2:10 my open eyes and W films formed on my
3:17 to scale away the W films of Tobit's eyes;
6:8 a man who has W films in his eyes,
11:8 and will cause the W films to fall away,
11:13 rubbed them, and the W films scaled off from
Esth 1:6 There were W cotton curtains and blue hangings
8:15 robes of blue and W, with a great golden
Eccl 9:8 your garments be always W; let not oil be
Is 1:18 they shall be as W as snow; though they
19:9 and the weavers of W cotton.
Ezek 27:18 wine of Helbon, and W wool,
Dan 7:9 seat; his raiment was W as snow, and the
11:35 and to make them W, until the time of
12:10 themselves, and make themselves W, and be refined;
Joel 1:7 and thrown it down; their branches are made W
Zech 1:8 were red, sorrel, and W horses.
6:3 black horses, the third W horses, and the fourth
6:6 the north country, the W ones go toward the
2Mac 11:8 their head, clothed in W and brandishing weapons of
Mt 5:36 cannot make one hair W or black.
17:2 and his garments became W as light.
28:3 lightning, and his raiment W as snow.
Mk 9:3 garments became glistening, intensely W, as no fuller
16:5 side, dressed in a W robe; and they were
Lk 9:29 was altered, and his raiment became dazzling W
Jn 4:35 the fields are already W for harvest.
20:12 saw two angels in W, sitting where the body
Acts 1:10 stood by them in W robes,
Rev 1:14 and his hair were W as white wool, white
1:14 hair were white as W wool, white as snow;
1:14 white as white wool, W as snow; his eyes
2:17 will give him a W stone, with a new
3:4 walk with me in W, for they are worthy.
3:5 be clad thus in W garments, and I will
3:18 may be rich, and W garments to clothe you
4:4 elders, clad in W garments, with golden crowns
6:2 saw, and behold, a W horse, and its rider
6:11 were each given a W robe and told to
7:9 the Lamb, clothed in W robes, with palm branches
7:13 are these, clothed in W robes, and whence have

W

	7:14	robes and made them W in the blood of
	14:14	looked, and lo, a W cloud, and seated on
	19:11	opened, and behold, a W horse!
	19:14	arrayed in fine linen, W and pure, followed him
	19:14	pure, followed him on W horses.
	20:11	I saw a great W throne and him who

WHITENESS

Sir	43:18	the beauty of its W, and the mind is

WHITER (2)

Ps	51:7	and I shall be W than snow.
Lam	4:7	were purer than snow, W than milk; their bodies

WHITEWASH (6)

Job	13:4	As for you, you W with lies; worthless physicians
Ezek	13:10	prophets daub it with W;
	13:11	who daub it with W that it shall fall!
	13:14	you have daubed with W, and bring it down
	13:15	have daubed it with W; and I will say
	22:28	daubed for them with W, seeing false visions and

WHITEWASHED (2)

Mt	23:26	for you are like W tombs, which outwardly appear
Acts	23:3	shall strike you, you W wall!

WHITHER (14)

Ex	34:12	inhabitants of the land W you go, lest it
Deut	1:28	W are we going up?
1Kgs	12:2	was still in Egypt, W he had fled from
	18:10	no nation or kingdom W my lord has not
	18:12	LORD will carry you W I know not; and
2Chr	10:2	he was in Egypt, W he had fled from
Ps	139:7	W shall I go from thy Spirit?
	139:7	Or W shall I flee from thy presence?
Song	6:1	W has your beloved gone, O fairest among women?
	6:1	W has your beloved turned, that we may seek
Ezek	4:13	unclean, among the nations W I will drive them."
Jn	3:8	whence it comes or W it goes; so it
	8:14	I have come and W I am going, but
	8:14	whence I come or W I am going.

WHOEVER (189)

Gen	4:14	on the earth, and W finds me will slay
	9:6	W sheds the blood of man, by man shall
	26:11	all the people, saying, W touches this man or
Ex	19:12	the border of it; W touches the mountain shall
	21:12	W strikes a man so that he dies shall
	21:15	W strikes his father or his mother shall be
	21:16	W steals a man, whether he sells him or
	21:17	W curses his father or his mother shall be
	22:19	W lies with a beast shall be put to
	22:20	W sacrifices to any god, save to the LORD
	24:14	Hur are with you; W has a cause, let
	30:33	W compounds any like it or whoever puts any
	30:33	any like it or W puts any of it
	30:38	W makes any like it to use as perfume
	31:14	be put to death; W does any work on
	31:15	holy to the LORD; W does any work on
	32:33	LORD said to Moses, W has sinned against me,
	35:2	rest to the LORD; W does any work on
	35:5	offering to the LORD; W is of a generous
Lev	6:18	LORD's offerings by fire; W touches them shall
	7:27	W eats any blood, that person shall be cut
	11:24	you shall become unclean; W touches their carcass
	11:25	until the evening, and W carries any part of
	11:27	are unclean to you; W touches their carcass shall
	11:31	among all that swarm; W touches them when they
	15:6	And W sits on anything on which he who
	15:7	And W touches the body of him who has
	15:10	And W touches anything that was under him shall
	15:19	for seven days, and W touches her shall be
	15:21	And W touches her bed shall wash his clothes,
	15:22	And W touches anything upon which she sits shall
	15:27	And W touches these things shall be unclean, and
	17:14	creature is its blood; W eats it shall be
	18:29	For W shall do any of these abominations, the
	22:4	W touches anything that is unclean through contact
	22:5	emission of semen, and W touches a creeping thing
	23:29	For W is not afflicted on this same day
	23:30	And W does any work on this same day,
	24:15	the people of Israel, W curses his God shall
Num	19:13	W touches a dead person, the body of any
	19:16	W in the open field touches one who is
	31:19	the camp seven days; W of you has killed
	31:19	killed any person, and W has touched any slain,
Deut	18:12	For W does these things is an abomination to
	18:19	And W will not give heed to my words
	22:5	a woman's garment; for W does these things is
Josh	1:18	W rebels against your commandment and disobeys
	15:16	And Caleb said, W smites Kiriath-sepher, and takes
Judg	6:31	W contends for him shall be put to death
	7:3	of the people, saying, W is fearful and trembling,
	11:31	into my hand, then W comes forth from the
1Sam	11:7	hand of messengers, saying, W does not come out
2Sam	5:8	said on that day, W would smite the Jebusites,
	17:9	at the first attack, W hears it will say,
	20:11	by Amasa, and said, W favors Joab, and whoever
	20:11	"Whoever favors Joab, and W is for David, let
2Kgs	10:19	to offer to Baal; W is missing shall not
	11:8	in his hand; and W approaches the ranks is
1Chr	11:6	David said, W shall smite the Jebusites first shall
	29:8	And W had precious stones gave them to the
2Chr	13:9	W comes to consecrate himself with a young bull
	15:13	their soul; and that W would not seek the
	23:7	in his hand; and W enters the house shall
	36:23	W is among you of all his people, may
Ezra	1:3	W is among you of all his people, may
	7:26	W will not obey the law of your God
Ps	107:43	W is wise, let him give heed to these
Prov	9:4	places in the town, W is simple, let him
	9:16	straight on their way, W is simple, let him
	12:1	W loves discipline loves knowledge, but he who hates
	20:1	drink a brawler; and W is led astray by
Wis	3:11	against the Lord; for W despises wisdom and
	17:16	And W was there fell down, and thus was
Sir	3:3	W honors his father atones for sins,
	3:4	atones for sins, and W glorifies his mother is
	3:5	W honors his father will be gladdened by his
	3:6	W glorifies his father will have long life, and
	3:6	have long life, and W obeys the Lord will
	3:16	W forsakes his father is like a blasphemer, and
	3:16	like a blasphemer, and W angers his mother is
	3:24	at the end, and W loves danger will perish
	3:29	W requites favors gives thought to the future; at
	4:12	W loves her loves life, and those who seek
	4:13	W holds her fast will obtain glory, and the
	4:15	judge the nations, and W gives heed to her
	6:17	W fears the Lord directs his friendship aright, for
	13:1	W touches pitch will be defiled, and whoever
	13:1	will be defiled, and W associates with a proud
	14:4	W accumulates by depriving himself, accumulates for
	20:7	W uses too many words will be loathed, and
	20:7	will be loathed, and W usurps the right to
	20:27	W cultivates the soil will heap up his harvest,
	20:27	up his harvest, and W pleases great men will
	21:6	W hates reproof walks in the steps of the
	21:11	W keeps the law controls his thoughts, and wisdom
	22:24	me because of him, W hears of it will
	24:21	W obeys me will not be put to shame,
	27:1	for a trifle, and W seeks to get rich
	27:16	W betrays secrets destroys confidence, and he will
	27:21	reconciliation after abuse, but W has betrayed
	27:22	W winks his eye plans evil deeds, and no
	27:25	W throws a stone straight up throws it on
	28:16	W pays heed to slander will not find rest,
	34:21	life of the poor; W deprives them of it
Is	13:15	W is found will be thrust through, and whoever
	13:15	be thrust through, and W is caught will fall
	54:15	is not from me; W stirs up strife with
Dan	3:6	has set up; and W does not fall down
	3:11	the golden image; and W does not fall down
	5:7	wise men of Babylon, W reads this writing, and
	6:7	enforce an interdict, that W makes petition to any
Hos	14:9	W is wise, let him understand these things; whoever
	14:9	him understand these things; W is discerning, let him
Zech	4:10	For W has despised the day of small things
1Mac	1:50	"And W does not obey the command of the
	10:43	And W takes refuge at the temple in Jerusalem,
	14:45	W acts contrary to these decisions or nullifies any
Mt	5:19	W then relaxes one of the least of these
	5:21	shall not kill; and W kills shall be liable
	5:22	be liable to judgment; W insults his brother shall
	5:22	to the council, and W says, 'You fool!' shall
	5:31	"It was also said, W divorces his wife, let
	5:32	her an adulteress; and W marries a divorced woman
	10:33	is in heaven; but W denies me before men,
	10:42	And W gives to one of these little ones
	12:32	And W says a word against the Son of
	12:32	will be forgiven; but W speaks against the Holy
	12:49	For W does the will of my Father in
	16:25	For W would save his life will lose it,

16:25 will lose it, and W loses his life for
18:4 W humbles himself like this child, he is the
18:5 W receives one such child in my name receives
18:6 name receives me; but W causes one of these
19:9 I say to you: W divorces his wife, except
20:26 so among you; but W would be great among
20:27 be your servant, and W would be first among
23:12 shall be your servant; W exalts himself will be
23:12 will be humbled, and W humbles himself will be
Mk 3:29 they utter; but W blasphemes against the Holy
3:35 W does the will of God is my brother,
8:35 For W would save his life will lose it;
8:35 will lose it; and W loses his life for
8:38 For W is ashamed of me and of my
9:37 he said to them, W receives one such child
9:37 name receives me; and W receives me, receives not
9:41 I say to you, W gives you a cup
9:42 W causes one of these little ones who believe
10:11 he said to them, W divorces his wife and
10:15 I say to you, W does not receive the
10:43 so among you; but W would be great among
10:44 be your servant, and W would be first among
11:23 I say to you, W says to this mountain,
Lk 9:24 For W would save his life will lose it;
9:24 will lose it; and W loses his life for
9:26 For W is ashamed of me and of my
9:48 and said to them, W receives this child in
9:48 name receives me, and W receives me receives him
14:27 W does not bear his own cross and come
14:33 So therefore, W of you does not renounce all
17:33 W seeks to gain his life will lose it,
17:33 will lose it, but W loses his life will
18:17 I say to you, W does not receive the
Jn 3:15 be lifted up, that W believes in him may
3:16 his only Son, that W believes in him should
4:14 will thirst again, but W drinks of the water
11:26 shall he live, and W lives and believes in
12:46 into the world, that W believes in me may
16:2 hour is coming when W kills you will think
Acts 2:21 it shall be that W calls on the name
Rom 2:1 no excuse, O man, W you are, when you
1Cor 7:37 But W is firmly established in his heart, being
11:27 W, therefore, eats the bread or drinks the cup
Gal 5:10 will bear his judgment, W he is.
1Thes 4:8 W disregards this, disregards not man but God,
Heb 4:10 people of God; for W enters God's rest also
11:6 For W would draw near to God must believe
Jas 2:10 For W keeps the whole law but fails in
4:4 Therefore W wishes to be a friend of the
4:17 W knows what is right to do and fails
5:20 let him know that W brings back a sinner
1Pet 4:1 the same thought, for W has suffered in the
4:11 of God's varied grace: W speaks, as one who
4:11 utters oracles of God; W renders service, as one
2Pet 1:9 For W lacks these things is blind and shortsighted
1Jn 2:5 not in him; but W keeps his word, in
3:10 children of the devil: W does not do right
4:6 W knows God listens to us, and he who
4:15 W confesses that Jesus is the Son of God,
Rev 14:11 and its image, and W receives the mark of

WHOLE (361)

Gen 2:6 earth and watered the W face of the ground--
2:11 which flows around the W land of Havilah, where
2:13 which flows around the W land of Cush.
7:19 high mountains under the W heaven were covered;
8:9 the face of the W earth.
9:19 and from these the W earth was peopled.
11:1 Now the W earth had one language and few
11:4 the face of the W earth.
13:9 Is not the W land before you?
18:26 I will spare the W place for their sake."
18:28 Wilt thou destroy the W city for lack of
23:17 the field, throughout its W area, was made over
41:1 After two W years, Pharaoh dreamed that he was
Ex 10:14 and settled on the W country of Egypt, such
10:15 the face of the W land, so that the
12:6 month, when the W assembly of the congregation
16:2 And the W congregation of the people of Israel
16:3 wilderness to kill this W assembly with hunger."
16:9 Aaron, "Say to the W congregation of the people
16:10 Aaron spoke to the W congregation of the people
19:18 a kiln, and the W mountain quaked greatly.
25:36 piece with it, the W of it one piece
26:6 the clasps, that the tabernacle may be one W
26:11 the tent together that it may be one W
29:18 head, and burn the W ram upon the altar;
36:13 other with clasps; so the tabernacle was one W
36:18 the tent together that it might be one W
37:22 piece with it; the W of it was one
Lev 1:9 priest shall burn the W on the altar, as
1:13 priest shall offer the W, and burn it on
4:12 and its dung, the W bull he shall carry
4:13 "If the W congregation of Israel commits a sin
6:22 decreed for ever; the W of it shall be
8:21 water, Moses burned the W ram on the altar,
10:6 but your brethren, the W house of Israel, may
15:16 he shall bathe his W body in water, and
25:29 redeem it within a W year after its sale;
Num 1:18 month, they assembled the W congregation together
1:45 So the W number of the people of Israel,
1:46 in Israel-- their W number was six hundred
2:9 The W number of the camp of Judah, by
2:16 The W number of the camp of Reuben, by
2:24 The W number of the camp of Ephraim, by
2:31 The W number of the camp of Dan is
3:7 him and for the W congregation before the tent
4:31 to carry, as the W of their service in
4:33 sons of Merari, the W of their service in
8:9 and assemble the W congregation of the people
11:20 twenty days, but a W month, until it comes
11:21 they may eat a W month!'
14:2 Moses and Aaron; the W congregation said to them,
15:26 among them, because the W population was involved
20:1 people of Israel, the W congregation, came into the
20:22 people of Israel, the W congregation, came to Mount
25:6 the sight of the W congregation of the people
27:21 Israel with him, the W congregation."
27:22 the priest and the W congregation,
Deut 2:25 that are under the W heaven, who shall hear
3:4 them--sixty cities, the W region of Argob, the
3:13 (The W of that Bashan is called the land
4:19 the peoples under the W heaven.
13:16 with fire, as a W burnt offering to the
22:9 of seed, lest the W yield be forfeited to
29:23 it sick-- the W land brimstone and salt,
33:10 incense before thee, and W burnt offering upon thy
Josh 7:3 do not make the W people toil up there,
10:13 down for about a W day.
10:40 So Joshua defeated the W land, the hill country
11:23 So Joshua took the W land, according to all
13:30 through all Bashan, the W kingdom of Og king
18:1 Then the W congregation of the people of Israel
22:12 heard of it, the W assembly of the people
22:16 them, "Thus says the W congregation of the LORD,
22:18 be angry with the W congregation of Israel
Judg 9:1 them and to the W clan of his mother's
18:2 able men from the W number of their tribe,
20:26 people of Israel, the W army, went up and
20:40 them; and behold, the W of the city went
21:13 the W congregation sent word to the Benjaminites
Ruth 1:19 came to Bethlehem, the W town was stirred because
1Sam 5:11 deathly panic throughout the W city.
7:9 offered it as a W burnt offering to the
2Sam 2:29 Jordan, and marching the W forenoon they came to
3:19 that Israel and the W house of Benjamin thought
6:19 all the people, the W multitude of Israel, both
8:9 David had defeated the W army of Hadadezer,
14:7 And now the W family has risen against your
1Kgs 6:10 the structure against the W house, each story five
6:22 And he overlaid the W house with gold, until
6:22 Also the W altar that belonged to the inner
10:24 And the W earth sought the presence of Solomon
11:34 will not take the W kingdom out of his
2Kgs 7:13 will fare like the W multitude of Israel that
9:8 For the W house of Ahab shall perish; and
20:3 faithfulness and with a W heart, and have done
1Chr 18:9 David had defeated the W army of Hadadezer, king
28:9 serve him with a W heart and with a
29:9 willingly, for with a W heart they had offered
29:19 son that with a W heart he may keep
2Chr 15:15 sought him with their W desire, and he was
16:9 and fro throughout the W earth, to show his
19:9 faithfulness, and with your W heart:
26:12 The W number of the heads of fathers' houses
29:28 The W assembly worshiped, and the singers sang,
30:23 Then the W assembly agreed together to keep the
30:25 The W assembly of Judah, and the priests and
30:25 the Levites, and the W assembly that came out
31:18 and their daughters, the W multitude; for they were
Ezra 2:64 The W assembly together was forty-two thousand
4:20 who ruled over the W province Beyond the River,

7:16 shall find in the W province of Babylonia, and
8:34 The W was counted and weighed, and the weight
10:14 officials stand for the W assembly; let all in
Neh 7:66 The W assembly together was forty-two thousand
Tob 1:4 a young man, the W tribe of Naphtali my
Jud 1:9 and Raamses and the W land of Goshen,
1:11 who lived in the W region disregarded the orders
1:12 very angry with this W region, and swore by
1:12 take revenge on the W territory of Cilicia and
1:13 battle, and overthrew the W army of Arphaxad, and
2:1 his revenge on the W region, just as he
2:5 the lord of the W earth: When you leave
2:6 Go and attack the W west country, because they
2:7 and will cover the W face of the earth
2:9 the ends of the W earth.
2:11 and plunder throughout your W region.
2:19 set out with his W army, to go ahead
2:19 and to cover the W face of the earth
2:22 Holofernes took his W army, his infantry, cavalry,
3:10 and remained for a W month in order to
4:8 the senate of the W people of Israel, in
4:15 with favor upon the W house of Israel.
5:12 and he afflicted the W land of Egypt with
5:21 to shame before the W world."
6:4 the lord of the W earth.
7:1 day Holofernes ordered his W army, and all the
7:4 the face of the W land; neither the high
7:18 plain, and covered the W face of the land,
7:20 The W Assyrian army, their infantry, chariots, and
7:27 in and surrender the W city to the army
9:14 And cause thy W nation and every tribe to
10:18 great excitement in the W camp, for her arrival
10:19 able to ensnare the W world!"
11:7 the king of the W earth lives, and as
11:8 is reported throughout the W world that you are
11:8 good man in the W kingdom, thoroughly informed
11:16 that will astonish the W world, as many as
11:18 go out with your W army, and not one
11:23 be renowned throughout the W world."
16:21 her time throughout the W country.
Esth 3:6 Mordecai, throughout the W kingdom of Ahasuerus.
11:9 And the W righteous nation was troubled; they
13:2 and master of the W world, not elated with
16:13 kingdom, together with their W nation.
Job 34:13 laid on him the W world?
37:3 Under the W heaven he lets it go, and
41:11 Whatever is under the W heaven is mine.
Ps 9:1 the LORD with my W heart; I will tell
51:19 in burnt offerings and W burnt offerings; then bulls
72:19 his glory fill the W earth!
86:12 my God, with my W heart, and I will
111:1 the LORD with my W heart, in the company
119:2 seek him with their W heart,
119:10 With my W heart I seek thee; let me
119:34 observe it with my W heart.
119:69 lies, but with my W heart I keep thy
119:145 With my W heart I cry; answer me, O
138:1 O LORD, with my W heart; before the gods
Prov 1:12 swallow them alive and W, like those who go
Eccl 12:13 for this is the W duty of man.
Wis 5:17 his zeal as his W armor, and will arm
5:23 will lay waste the W earth, and evil-doing will
8:21 him, and with my W heart I said:
11:22 Because the W world before thee is like a
17:20 For the W world was illumined with brilliant light,
18:24 his long robe the W world was depicted, and
19:6 For the W creation in its nature was fashioned
Sir 1:15 fruits; she fills their W house with desirable goods,
18:1 for ever created the W universe;
24:6 the sea, in the W earth, and in every
50:13 their hands, before the W congregation of Israel.
50:20 his hands over the W congregation of the sons
Is 1:5 The W head is sick, and the whole heart
1:5 is sick, and the W heart faint.
3:1 stay and staff, the W stay of bread, and
3:1 of bread, and the W stay of water;
4:5 will create over the W site of Mount Zion
6:3 LORD of hosts; the W earth is full of
13:5 indignation, to destroy the W earth.
14:7 The W earth is at rest and quiet; they
14:26 is purposed concerning the W earth; and this is
21:8 post I am stationed W nights.
22:24 hang on him the W weight of his father's
27:6 shoots, and fill the W world with fruit.
28:22 of hosts upon the W land.
38:3 faithfulness and with a W heart, and have done
39:2 the precious oil, his W armory, all that was
53:5 chastisement that made us W, and with his stripes
54:5 the God of the W earth he is called.
Jer 1:18 bronze walls, against the W land, against the kings
3:10 to me with her W heart, but in pretense,
4:20 hard on disaster, the W land is laid waste.
4:27 says the LORD, "The W land shall be a
8:16 of their stallions the W land quakes.
12:11 The W land is made desolate, but no man
13:11 so I made the W house of Israel and
13:11 of Israel and the W house of Judah cling
15:10 and contention to the W land!
24:7 to me with their W heart.
25:11 This W land shall become a ruin and a
31:40 The W valley of the dead bodies and the
35:3 his sons, and the W house of the Rechabites.
37:10 you should defeat the W army of Chaldeans who
40:4 See, the W land is before you; go wherever
45:4 up--that is, the W land.
50:23 the hammer of the W earth is cut down
51:25 LORD, which destroys the W earth; I will stretch
51:41 the praise of the W earth seized!
51:47 images of Babylon; her W land shall be put
Lam 3:3 again and again the W day long.
Bar 2:2 Under the W heaven there has not been done
2:23 the bride, and the W land will be a
3:36 He found the W way to knowledge, and gave
6:62 to go over the W world, they carry out
Ezek 11:15 your fellow exiles, the W house of Israel, all
15:5 Behold, when it was W, it was used for
32:4 the beasts of the W earth with you.
35:14 the rejoicing of the W earth I will make
36:10 men upon you, the W house of Israel, all
37:11 these bones are the W house of Israel.
39:25 have mercy upon the W house of Israel; and
41:19 were carved on the W temple round about;
43:11 its entrances, and its W form; and make known
43:12 of the temple: the W territory round about upon
45:1 be holy throughout its W extent.
45:6 shall belong to the W house of Israel.
48:13 The W length shall be twenty-five thousand cubits
48:20 The W portion which you shall set apart shall
Dan 2:35 mountain and filled the W earth.
2:48 him ruler over the W province of Babylon, and
3:45 God, glorious over the W world."
4:11 the end of the W earth.
4:20 the end of the W earth;
6:1 to be throughout the W kingdom;
6:3 set him over the W kingdom.
7:23 it shall devour the W earth, and trample it
7:27 the kingdoms under the W heaven shall be given
8:5 the face of the W earth, without touching the
9:12 calamity; for under the W heaven there has not
11:17 the strength of his W kingdom, and he shall
14:14 sifted them throughout the W temple in the presence
Amos 1:6 carried into exile a W people to deliver them
1:9 they delivered up a W people to Edom, and
3:1 of Israel, against the W family which I brought
Mic 4:13 the Lord of the W earth.
Zech 4:10 which range through the W earth."
4:14 the Lord of the W earth."
5:3 the face of the W land; for every one
13:8 In the W land, says the LORD, two thirds
14:10 The W land shall be turned into a plain
Mal 3:9 are robbing me; the W nation of you.
1Mac 1:41 king wrote to his W kingdom that all should
1:51 he wrote to his W kingdom.
5:43 them first, and the W army followed him.
8:4 gained control of the W region by their planning
2Mac 2:10 down and consumed the W burnt offerings.
2:21 number they seized the W land and pursued the
2:29 be concerned with the W construction, while the one
3:12 is honored throughout the W world.
3:14 little distress throughout the W city.
3:21 the prostration of the W populace and the anxiety
4:38 led him about the W city to that very
7:38 justly fallen on our W nation."
7:40 his integrity, putting his W trust in the Lord.
8:9 to wipe out the W race of Judea.
8:18 us and even the W world."
9:9 of his stench the W army felt revulsion at
10:8 and vote that the W nation of the Jews
12:7 and root out the W community of Joppa.
14:8 I have mentioned our W nation is now in
15:12 outstretched hands for the W body of the Jews.
Mt 5:29 members than that your W body be thrown into

5:30 members than that your W body go into hell.
6:22 eye is sound, your W body will be full
6:23 is not sound, your W body will be full
8:32 swine; and behold, the W herd rushed down the
12:13 and it was restored, W like the other.
13:2 sat there; and the W crowd stood on the
15:31 dumb speaking, the maimed W, the lame walking,
16:26 if he gains the W world and forfeits his
24:14 be preached throughout the W world, as a testimony
26:13 is preached in the W world, what she has
26:59 chief priests and the W council sought false
27:27 and they gathered the W battalion before him.
Mk 1:33 And the W city was gathered together about the
4:1 the sea; and the W crowd was beside the
5:33 and told him the W truth.
6:55 and ran about the W neighborhood and began to
8:36 man, to gain the W world and forfeit his
12:33 much more than all W burnt offerings and
12:44 everything she had, her W living."
14:9 is preached in the W world, what she has
14:55 chief priests and the W council sought testimony
15:1 and scribes, and the W council held a consultation;
15:16 they called together the W battalion.
15:32 was darkness over the W land until the ninth
16:15 the gospel to the W creation.
Lk 1:10 And the W multitude of the people were praying
7:17 him spread through the W of Judea and all
8:39 proclaiming throughout the W city how much Jesus
9:25 if he gains the W world and loses or
11:34 eye is sound, your W body is full of
11:36 If then your W body is full of light,
19:37 Mount of Olives, the W multitude of the disciples
21:35 the face of the W earth.
23:1 Then the W company of them arose, and brought
23:43 was darkness over the W land until the ninth
Jn 7:23 I made a man's W body well?
11:50 people, and that the W nation should not perish."
Acts 5:11 fear came upon the W church, and upon all
6:5 they said pleased the W multitude, and they chose
10:22 spoken of by the W Jewish nation, was directed
11:26 For a W year they met with the church,
13:6 had gone through the W island as far as
13:44 next sabbath almost the W city gathered together to
15:22 the elders, with the W church, to choose men
20:27 declaring to you the W counsel of God.
22:5 high priest and the W council of elders bear
25:24 man about whom the W Jewish people petitioned
28:29 he lived there two W years at his own
Rom 3:19 be stopped, and the W world may be held
8:22 We know that the W creation has been groaning
11:16 holy, so is the W lump; and if the
16:23 me and to the W church, greets you.
1Cor 5:6 little leaven leavens the W lump?
12:17 If the W body were an eye, where would
12:17 If the W body were an ear, where would
14:23 If, therefore, the W church assembles and all speak
2Cor 1:1 who are in the W of Achaia:
Gal 5:3 bound to keep the W law.
5:9 little leaven leavens the W lump.
5:14 For the W law is fulfilled in one word,
Eph 2:21 cornerstone, in whom the W structure is joined
4:16 Christ, from whom the W body, joined and knit
6:11 Put on the W armor of God, that you
6:13 Therefore take the W armor of God, that you
Phil 1:13 become known throughout the W praetorian guard
Col 1:6 as indeed in the W world it is bearing
2:9 For in him the W fulness of deity dwells
2:19 Head, from whom the W body, nourished and knit
Tit 1:10 since they are upsetting W families by teaching for
Jas 2:10 For whoever keeps the W law but fails in
3:2 able to bridle the W body also.
3:3 us, we guide their W bodies.
3:6 our members, staining the W body, setting on fire
1Jn 2:2 the sins of the W world.
5:19 of God, and the W world is in the
Rev 3:10 is coming on the W world, to try those
12:9 the deceiver of the W world--he was thrown
13:3 was healed, and the W earth followed the beast
16:14 the kings of the W world, to assemble them

WHOLEHEARTED

Ezek 36:5 as a possession with W joy and utter contempt,

WHOLEHEARTEDLY

1Mac 8:25 act as their allies W, as the occasion may

WHOLESOME (4)

2Kgs 2:21 have made this water W; henceforth neither death
2:22 the water has been W to this day, according
Prov 15:31 He whose ear heeds W admonition will abide among
Wis 1:14 of the world are W, and there is no

WHOLLY (29)

Lev 6:23 a priest shall be W burned; it shall not
Num 3:9 his sons; they are W given to him from
8:16 For they are W given to me from among
32:11 because they have not W followed me;
32:12 Nun, for they have W followed the LORD.'
Deut 1:36 trodden, because he has W followed the LORD!'
Josh 3:16 the Salt Sea, were W cut off; and the
14:8 people melt; yet I W followed the LORD my
14:9 ever, because you have W followed the LORD my
14:14 this day, because he W followed the LORD, the
1Kgs 8:61 your heart therefore be W true to the LORD
11:4 his heart was not W true to the LORD
11:6 LORD, and did not W follow the LORD, as
15:3 his heart was not W true to the LORD
15:14 heart of Asa was W true to the LORD
1Chr 28:21 the people will be W at your command."
Job 19:13 and my acquaintances are W estranged from me.
21:23 in full prosperity, being W at ease and secure,
Prov 16:33 but the decision is W from the LORD.
Sir 45:14 His sacrifices shall be W burned twice every day
46:6 the Lord; for he W followed the Mighty One.
Jer 2:21 you a choice vine, W of pure seed.
13:19 is taken into exile, W taken into exile.
Dan 3:40 day, and may we W follow thee, for there
Zech 11:17 Let his arm be W withered, his right eye
2Mac 8:29 merciful Lord to be W reconciled with his servants.
12:42 been committed might be W blotted out.
Lk 11:36 dark, it will be W bright, as when a
1Thes 5:23 peace himself sanctify you W; and may your spirit

WHOMEVER (8)

Gen 44:9 With W of your servants it be found, let
1Sam 28:8 bring up for me W I shall name to
Tob 4:19 his will he humbles W he wishes.
Jer 27:5 I give it to W it seems right to
49:19 will appoint over her W I choose.
50:44 will appoint over her W I choose.
Rom 9:18 he has mercy upon W he wills, and he
9:18 hardens the heart of W he wills.

WICK (3)

Is 42:3 and a dimly burning W he will not quench;
43:17 extinguished, quenched like a W:
Mt 12:20 or quench a smoldering W, till he brings justice

WICKED (343)

Gen 13:13 men of Sodom were W, great sinners against the
18:23 "Wilt thou indeed destroy the righteous with the W
18:25 the righteous with the W, so that the righteous
18:25 wicked, so that the righteous fare as the W
38:7 Er, Judah's first-born, was W in the sight of
Ex 23:1 join hands with a W man, to be a
23:7 and righteous, for I will not acquit the W
Num 14:27 "How long shall this W congregation murmur
14:35 do to all this W congregation that are gathered
16:26 the tents of these W men, and touch nothing
1Sam 2:9 faithful ones; but the W shall be cut off
24:13 says, 'Out of the W comes forth wickedness'; but
30:22 Then all the W and base fellows among the
2Sam 3:34 one falls before the W you have fallen." And
4:11 How much more, when W men have slain a
2Kgs 17:11 And they did W things, provoking the LORD to
21:11 has done things more W than all that the
1Chr 2:3 Er, Judah's first-born, was W in the sight of
2Chr 7:14 and turn from their W ways, then I will
19:2 "Should you help the W and love those who
24:7 sons of Athaliah, that W woman, had broken into
Ezra 4:12 rebuilding that rebellious and W city; they are
Neh 9:35 not turn from their W works.
Jud 8:9 When Judith heard the W words spoken by the
Esth 7:6 This W Haman!" Then Haman was in terror before
9:25 in writing that his W plot which he had
14:15 the splendor of the W and abhor the bed
Job 3:17 There the W cease from troubling, and there the
8:22 the tent of the W will be no more."
9:22 say, he destroys both the blameless and the W
9:24 the hand of the W; he covers the faces
10:3 thy hands and favor the designs of the W
10:15 If I am W, woe to me!

11:20 the eyes of the W will fail; all way
15:20 The W man writhes in pain all his days,
16:11 and casts me into the hands of the W
18:5 the light of the W is put out, and
20:5 the exulting of the W is short, and the
20:29 This is the W man's portion from God, the
21:7 Why do the W live, reach old age, and
21:16 The counsel of the W is far from me.
21:17 the lamp of the W is put out?
21:28 tent in which the W dwelt?'
21:30 their testimony that the W man is spared in
22:15 the old way which W men have trod?
22:18 the counsel of the W is far from me.
24:6 the vineyard of the W man.
24:11 olive rows of the W they make oil; they
27:7 enemy be as the W, and let him that
27:13 the portion of a W man with God, and
34:8 evildoers and walks with W men?
34:18 one,' and to nobles, W man';
34:36 because he answers like W men.
36:6 does not keep the W alive, but gives the
36:17 the judgment on the W; judgment and justice seize
38:13 the earth, and the W be shaken out of
38:15 From the W their light is withheld, and their
40:12 and tread down the W where they stand.
Ps 1:1 the counsel of the W, nor stands in the
1:4 The W are not so, but are like chaff
1:5 Therefore the W will not stand in the judgment,
1:6 the way of the W will perish.
3:7 cheek, thou dost break the teeth of the W
7:9 the evil of the W come to an end,
7:14 Behold, the W man conceives evil, and is pregnant
9:5 thou hast destroyed the W; thou hast blotted out
9:16 has executed judgment; the W are snared in the
9:17 Selah] The W shall depart to Sheol, all the
10:2 In arrogance the W hotly pursue the poor; let
10:3 For the W boasts of the desires of his
10:4 of his countenance the W does not seek him;
10:13 Why does the W renounce God, and say in
10:15 the arm of the W and evildoer; seek out
11:2 mountains; for lo, the W bend the bow, they
11:5 the righteous and the W, and his soul hates
11:6 On the W he will rain coals of fire
12:8 On every side the W prowl, as vileness is
17:9 thy wings, from the W who despoil me, my
17:13 my life from the W by thy sword,
26:5 evildoers, and I will not sit with the W
28:3 not off with the W, with those who are
31:17 on thee; let the W be put to shame,
32:10 the pangs of the W; but steadfast love surrounds
34:21 Evil shall slay the W; and those who hate
36:1 Transgression speaks to the W deep in his heart;
36:11 the hand of the W drive me away.
37:1 yourself because of the W, be not envious of
37:9 For the W shall be cut off; but those
37:10 little while, and the W will be no more;
37:12 The W plots against the righteous, and gnashes his
37:13 LORD laughs at the W, for he sees that
37:14 The W draw the sword and bend their bows,
37:16 the righteous has than the abundance of many W
37:17 the arms of the W shall be broken; but
37:20 But the W perish; the enemies of the LORD
37:21 The W borrows, and cannot pay back, but the
37:28 the children of the W shall be cut off.
37:32 The W watches the righteous, and seeks to slay
37:34 you will look on the destruction of the W
37:35 I have seen a W man overbearing, and towering
37:38 the posterity of the W shall be cut off.
37:40 delivers them from the W, and saves them, because
39:1 so long as the W are in my presence."
50:16 But to the W God says: "What right have
55:3 the enemy, because of the oppression of the W
58:3 The W go astray from the womb, they err
58:10 bathe his feet in the blood of the W
64:2 secret plots of the W, from the scheming of
68:2 before fire, let the W perish before God!
71:4 the hand of the W, from the grasp of
73:3 arrogant, when I saw the prosperity of the W
73:12 Behold, these are the W; always at ease, they
75:4 and to the W, "Do not lift up your
75:8 it, and all the W of the earth shall
75:10 the horns of the W he will cut off,
82:2 you judge unjustly and show partiality to the W
82:4 needy; deliver them from the hand of the W
89:22 not outwit him, the W shall not humble him.
91:8 your eyes and see the recompense of the W
92:7 this: that, though the W sprout like grass and
94:3 how long shall the W, how long shall the
94:3 how long shall the W exult?
94:13 trouble, until a pit is dug for the W
94:16 Who rises up for me against the W
94:20 Can W rulers be allied with thee, who frame
97:10 he delivers them from the hand of the W
101:8 will destroy all the W in the land, cutting
104:35 earth, and let the W be no more!
106:18 in their company; the flame burned up the W
109:2 For W and deceitful mouths are opened against me,
109:6 Appoint a W man against him; let an accuser
112:10 The W man sees it and is angry; he
112:10 the desire of the W man comes to nought.
119:53 me because of the W, who forsake thy law.
119:61 the cords of the W ensnare me, I do
119:95 The W lie in wait to destroy me; but
119:110 The W have laid a snare for me, but
119:119 All the W of the earth thou dost count
119:155 is far from the W, for they do not
129:4 righteous; he has cut the cords of the W
139:19 thou wouldst slay the W, O God, and that
139:24 if there be any W way in me, and
140:4 the hands of the W; preserve me from violent
140:8 the desires of the W; do not further his
141:4 to busy myself with W deeds in company with
141:5 the oil of the W never anoint my head;
141:5 is continually against their W deeds.
141:10 Let the W together fall into their own nets,
145:20 him; but all the W he will destroy.
146:9 the way of the W he brings to ruin.
147:6 downtrodden, he casts the W to the ground.
Prov 2:22 in it; but the W will be cut off
3:25 the ruin of the W, when it comes;
3:33 the house of the W, but he blesses the
4:15 the path of the W, and do not walk
4:20 The way of the W is like deep darkness;
5:22 The iniquities of the W ensnare him, and he
6:12 A worthless person, a W man, goes about with
6:18 a heart that devises W plans, feet that make
9:7 he who reproves a W man incurs injury.
10:3 hungry, but he thwarts the craving of the W
10:6 the mouth of the W conceals violence.
10:7 the name of the W will rot.
10:11 the mouth of the W conceals violence.
10:16 the gain of the W to sin.
10:20 the mind of the W is of little worth.
10:24 What the W dreads will come upon him, but
10:25 the tempest passes, the W is no more, but
10:27 the years of the W will be short.
10:28 the expectation of the W comes to nought.
10:30 be removed, but the W will not dwell in
10:32 the mouth of the W, what is perverse.
11:5 way straight, but the W falls by his own
11:7 When the W dies, his hope perishes, and the
11:8 from trouble, and the W gets into it instead.
11:10 rejoices; and when the W perish there are shouts
11:11 it is overthrown by the mouth of the W
11:18 A W man earns deceptive wages, but one who
11:23 the expectation of the W in wrath.
11:31 how much more the W and the sinner!
12:5 the counsels of the W are treacherous.
12:6 The words of the W lie in wait for
12:7 The W are overthrown and are no more, but
12:10 the mercy of the W is cruel.
12:12 strong tower of the W comes to ruin, but
12:21 the righteous, but the W are filled with trouble.
12:26 the way of the W leads them astray.
13:5 hates falsehood, but a W man acts shamefully and
13:6 whose way is upright, but sin overthrows the W
13:9 the lamp of the W will be put out.
13:25 the belly of the W suffers want.
14:9 God scorns the W, but the upright enjoy his
14:11 The house of the W will be destroyed, but
14:19 before the good, the W at the gates of
14:32 The W is overthrown through his evil-doing, but the
15:6 treasure, but trouble befalls the income of the W
15:8 The sacrifice of the W is an abomination to
15:9 The way of the W is an abomination to
15:26 The thoughts of the W are an abomination to
15:28 the mouth of the W pours out evil things.
15:29 is far from the W, but he hears the
16:4 its purpose, even the W for the day of
17:4 An evildoer listens to W lips; and a liar
17:15 He who justifies the W and he who condemns
17:23 A W man accepts a bribe from the bosom

18:5 be partial to a W man, or to deprive
19:28 the mouth of the W devours iniquity.
20:26 wise king winnows the W, and drives the wheel
21:4 the lamp of the W, are sin.
21:7 The violence of the W will sweep them away,
21:10 The soul of the W desires evil; his neighbor
21:12 the house of the W; the wicked are cast
21:12 of the wicked; the W are cast down to
21:18 The W is a ransom for the righteous, and
21:26 All day long the W covets, but the righteous
21:27 The sacrifice of the W is an abomination; how
21:29 A W man puts on a bold face, but
24:15 in wait as a W man against the dwelling
24:16 rises again; but the W are overthrown by calamity.
24:19 not envious of the W;
24:20 the lamp of the W will be put out.
24:24 who says to the W, "You are innocent," will
24:25 those who rebuke the W will have delight, and
25:5 vessel; take away the W from the presence of
25:26 a righteous man who gives way before the W
28:1 The W flee when no one pursues, but the
28:4 the law praise the W, but those who keep
28:12 glory; but when the W rise, men hide themselves.
28:15 charging bear is a W ruler over a poor
28:28 When the W rise, men hide themselves, but when
29:2 rejoice; but when the W rule, the people groan.
29:7 of the poor; a W man does not understand
29:10 is blameless, and the W seek his life.
29:12 listens to falsehood, all his officials will be W
29:16 When the W are in authority, transgression
29:27 way is straight is an abomination to the W
Eccl 3:17 the righteous and the W, for he has appointed
7:15 and there is a W man who prolongs his
7:17 Be not W overmuch, neither be a fool; why
8:10 Then I saw the W buried; they used to
8:13 be well with the W, neither will he prolong
8:14 the deeds of the W, and there are wicked
8:14 wicked, and there are W men to whom it
9:2 the righteous and the W, to the good and
10:13 of his talk is W madness.
Wis 3:14 who has not devised W things against the Lord;
10:5 the nations in W agreement had been confounded,
11:15 for their foolish and W thoughts, which led them
14:29 lifeless idols they swear W oaths and expect to
19:13 suffered because of their W acts; for they practiced
Sir 20:17 the downfall of the W will occur speedily.
21:9 An assembly of the W is like tow gathered
33:26 neck, and for a W servant there are racks
39:24 straight, just as they are obstacles to the W
40:10 were created for the W, and on their account
42:5 and of whipping a W servant severely.
46:7 sin, and stilled their W murmuring.
49:3 in the days of W men he strengthened godliness.
Is 3:11 Woe to the W
11:4 breath of his lips he shall slay the W
13:11 its evil, and the W for their iniquity; I
14:5 the staff of the W, the scepter of rulers,
26:10 is shown to the W, he does not learn
32:7 are evil; he devises W devices to ruin the
48:22 says the LORD, "for the W
53:9 his grave with the W and with a rich
55:7 is near; let the W forsake his way, and
57:20 But the W are like the tossing sea; for
57:21 is no peace, says my God, for the W
58:4 and to hit with W fist.
Jer 2:33 So that even to W women you have taught
5:26 For W men are found among my people; they
6:29 goes on, for the W are not removed.
12:1 the way of the W prosper?
15:21 the hand of the W, and redeem you from
23:19 it will burst upon the head of the W
25:31 all flesh, and the W he will put to
30:23 it will burst upon the head of the W
Bar 1:21 intent of his own W heart by serving other
2:8 the thoughts of his W heart.
2:33 their stubbornness and their W deeds; for they will
Ezek 3:18 I say to the W, 'You shall surely die,'
3:18 speak to warn the W from his wicked way,
3:18 the wicked from his W way, in order to
3:18 save his life, that W man shall die in
3:19 if you warn the W, and he does not
3:19 wickedness, or from his W way, he shall die
7:21 prey, and to the W of the earth for
11:2 iniquity and who give W counsel in this city;
13:22 you have encouraged the W, that he should not
13:22 not turn from his W way to save his
18:20 the wickedness of the W shall be upon himself.
18:21 "But if a W man turns away from all
18:23 the death of the W, says the Lord GOD,
18:24 abominable things that the W man does, shall he
18:27 Again, when a W man turns away from the
21:3 will cut off from you both righteous and W
21:4 you both righteous and W, therefore my sword shall
21:25 And you, O unhallowed W one, prince of Israel,
21:29 necks of the unhallowed W, whose day has come,
33:8 I say to the W, O wicked man, you
33:8 to the wicked, O W man, you shall surely
33:8 speak to warn the W to turn from his
33:8 from his way, that W man shall die in
33:9 if you warn the W to turn from his
33:11 the death of the W, but that the wicked
33:11 wicked, but that the W turn from his way
33:12 the wickedness of the W, he shall not fall
33:14 I say to the W, 'You shall surely die,'
33:15 and right, if the W restores the pledge, gives
33:19 And when the W turns from his wickedness, and
Dan 3:32 unjust king, the most W in all the world.
12:10 be refined; but the W shall do wickedly; and
12:10 and none of the W shall understand; but those
13:28 came, full of their W plot to have Susanna
13:32 she was veiled, the W men ordered her to
13:52 "You old relic of W days, your sins have
Hos 7:2 is revealed, and the W deeds of Samaria; for
7:13 chastise them for their W deeds.
Mic 6:10 the house of the W, and the scant measure
6:11 acquit the man with W scales and with a
Nah 1:15 never again shall the W come against you, he
Hab 1:4 For the W surround the righteous, so justice goes
1:13 art silent when the W swallows up the man
3:13 the head of the W, laying him bare from
Zeph 1:3 I will overthrow the W; I will cut off
Mal 1:4 they are called the W country, the people with
3:18 the righteous and the W, between one who serves
4:3 shall tread down the W, for they will be
1Mac 7:25 the king and brought W charges against them.
13:46 us according to our W acts but according to
14:14 with every lawless and W man.
2Mac 10:34 terribly and hurled out W words.
Mt 18:31 said to him, 'You W servant!
24:48 But if that W servant says to himself, 'My
25:26 master answered him, 'You W and slothful servant!
Lk 19:22 your own mouth, you W servant!
Acts 17:5 jealous, and taking some W fellows of the rabble,
1Cor 5:13 "Drive out the W person from among you."
2Thes 2:10 wonders, and with all W deception for those who
3:2 may be delivered from W and evil men; for
2Pet 2:7 the licentiousness of the W
2Jn 1:11 greets him shares his W work.

WICKEDLY (24)

Gen 19:7 beg you, my brothers, do not act so W
Judg 19:23 do not act so W; seeing that this man
1Sam 12:25 if you still do W, you shall be swept
2Sam 22:22 LORD, and have not W departed from my God.
24:17 and I have done W; but these sheep, what
1Kgs 8:47 have acted perversely and W;
1Chr 21:17 is I who have sinned and done very W
2Chr 6:37 have acted perversely and W;
20:35 joined with Ahaziah king of Israel, who did W
22:3 for his mother was his counselor in doing W
Neh 9:33 and we have acted W;
Esth 16:7 "What has been W accomplished through the
Job 34:12 God will not do W, and the Almighty will
Ps 18:21 LORD, and have not W departed from my God.
106:6 sinned; we have committed iniquity, we have done W
Wis 14:30 counts: because they thought W of God in devoting
Ezek 5:6 And she has W rebelled against my ordinances more
Dan 9:5 done wrong and acted W and rebelled, turning aside
9:15 this day, we have sinned, we have done W
12:10 the wicked shall do W; and none of the
13:43 things that they have W invented against me!"
13:62 them as they had W planned to do to
1Mac 7:42 that Nicanor has spoken W against the sanctuary,
2Mac 8:16 of Gentiles who were W coming against them, but

WICKEDNESS (134)

Gen 6:5 LORD saw that the W of man was great
39:9 I do this great W, and sin against God?"
Lev 18:17 nakedness; they are your near kinswomen; it is W
19:29 into harlotry and the land become full of W
20:14 mother also, it is W; they shall be burned
20:14 there may be no W among you.

Deut 9:4 is because of the W of these nations that
9:5 but because of the W of these nations the
9:27 this people, or their W, or their sin,
13:11 again do any such W as this among you.
Judg 9:57 also made all the W of the men of
20:3 us, how was this W brought to pass?"
20:12 of Benjamin, saying, "What W is this that has
1Sam 12:17 and see that your W is great, which you
24:13 the wicked comes forth W; but my hand shall
2Sam 3:39 The LORD requite the evildoer according to his W
1Kgs 1:52 the earth; but if W is found in him,
Jud 2:2 own lips, all the W of the region;
Job 11:14 away, and let not W dwell in your tents.
20:12 "Though W is sweet in his mouth, though he
22:5 Is not your W great?
24:20 no longer remembered; so W is broken like a
34:10 that he should do W, and from the Almighty
34:26 strikes them for their W in the sight of
35:8 Your W concerns a man like yourself, and your
Ps 5:4 God who delights in W; evil may not sojourn
10:15 evildoer; seek out his W till thou find none.
17:3 thou wilt find no W in me; my mouth
45:7 scepter of equity; you love righteousness and hate W
84:10 my God than dwell in the tents of W
94:23 them out for their W; the LORD our God
107:34 waste, because of the W of its inhabitants.
107:42 are glad; and all W stops its mouth.
125:3 For the scepter of W shall not rest upon
Prov 4:18 eat the bread of W and drink the wine
8:7 mouth will utter truth; W is an abomination to
10:2 Treasures gained by W do not profit, but
11:5 straight, but the wicked falls by his own W
12:3 is not established by W, but the root of
18:3 When W comes, contempt comes also; and with
26:26 covered with guile, his W will be exposed in
Eccl 3:16 justice, even there was W, and in the place
3:16 in the place of righteousness, even there was W
7:25 and to know the W of folly and the
8:8 from war, nor will W deliver those who are
Wis 2:21 led astray, for their W blinded them,
4:12 For the fascination of W obscures what is good,
4:14 he took him quickly from the midst of W
5:13 virtue to show, but were consumed in our W
10:7 Evidence of their W still remains: a continually
12:2 may be freed from W and put their trust
12:10 was evil and their W inborn, and that their
12:20 to give up their W,
16:14 A man in his W kills another, but he
17:11 For W is a cowardly thing, condemned by its
Sir 3:26 for a plant of W has taken root in
12:10 like the rusting of copper, so is his W
19:5 One who rejoices in W will be condemned,
19:19 But the knowledge of W is not wisdom, nor
25:12 Any W, but not the wickedness of a wife!
25:12 wickedness, but not the W of a wife!
25:16 The W of a wife changes her appearance, and
29:7 Because of such W, therefore, many have refused to
35:3 To keep from W is pleasing to the Lord,
42:13 the moth, and from a woman comes woman's W
42:14 Better is the W of a man than a
46:20 to blot out the W of the people.
47:25 out every sort of W, till vengeance came upon
Is 9:18 For W burns like a fire, it consumes briers
47:10 felt secure in your W, you said, "No one
58:6 loose the bonds of W, to undo the thongs
58:9 the finger, and speaking W,
59:3 your lips have spoken lies, your tongue mutters W
Jer 1:16 them, for all their W in forsaking me; they
2:19 Your W will chasten you, and your apostasy will
4:14 wash your heart from W, that you may be
5:28 bounds in deeds of W; they judge not with
6:7 she keeps fresh her W; violence and destruction are
7:12 to it for the W of my people Israel.
8:6 man repents of his W, saying, 'What have I
12:4 For the W of those who dwell in it
14:16 will pour out their W upon them.
14:20 We acknowledge our W, O LORD, and the iniquity
22:22 be ashamed and confounded because of all your W
23:11 I have found their W, says the LORD.
23:14 one turns from his W; all of them have
33:5 face from this city because of all their W
44:3 them, because of the W which they committed,
44:5 to turn from their W and burn no incense
44:9 Have you forgotten the W of your fathers, the
44:9 of your fathers, the W of the kings of
44:9 kings of Judah, the W of their wives, your
44:9 their wives, your own W, and the wickedness of
44:9 own wickedness, and the W of your wives, which
Bar 2:26 today, because of the W of the house of
Ezek 3:19 not turn from his W, or from his wicked
7:11 into a rod of W; none of them shall
16:23 "And after all your W (woe, woe to you!
16:57 your pride, before your W was uncovered?
18:20 upon himself, and the W of the wicked shall
18:27 turns away from the W he has committed and
31:11 with it as its W deserves.
33:12 and as for the W of the wicked, he
33:12 he turns from his W; and the righteous shall
33:19 wicked turns from his W, and does what is
Dan 13:38 when we saw this W we ran to them.
13:57 a daughter of Judah would not endure your W
Hos 7:4 By their W they make the king glad, and
9:15 Because of the W of their deeds I will
10:15 O house of Israel, because of your great W
Joel 3:13 vats overflow, for their W is great.
Jon 1:2 against it; for their W has come up before
Mic 2:1 to those who devise W and work evil upon
6:10 forget the treasures of W in the house of
Zech 5:8 And he said, "This is W
1Mac 5:4 He also remembered the W of the sons of
7:42 the sanctuary, and judge him according to this W
2Mac 3:1 and his hatred of W,
4:13 because of the surpassing W of Jason, who was
4:50 in office, growing in W, having become the chief
Mt 24:12 And because W is multiplied, most men's love will
Mk 7:21 murder, adultery, coveting, W, deceit, licentiousness,
Lk 11:39 but inside you are full of extortion and W
Acts 1:18 the reward of his W; and falling headlong he
3:26 in turning every one of you from your W
8:22 Repent therefore of this W of yours, and pray
Rom 1:18 against all ungodliness and W of men who by
1:18 men who by their W suppress the truth.
1:29 with all manner of W, evil, covetousness, malice.
2:8 the truth, but obey W, there will be wrath
3:5 But if our W serves to show the justice
6:13 sin as instruments of W, but yield yourselves to
Eph 6:12 the spiritual hosts of W in the heavenly places.
Jas 1:20 and rank growth of W and receive with meekness

WIDE (36)

Ex 25:25 a frame a handbreadth W, and a molding of
37:12 a frame a handbreadth W, and made a molding
Num 16:37 the blaze; then scatter the fire far and W
Deut 15:11 you, You shall open W your hand to your
2Sam 22:37 Thou didst give a W place for my steps
1Kgs 6:2 cubits long, twenty cubits W, and thirty cubits high.
6:20 cubits long, twenty cubits W, and twenty cubits high;
7:27 cubits long, four cubits W, and three cubits high.
2Chr 4:1 long, and twenty cubits W, and ten cubits high.
6:13 cubits long, five cubits W, and three cubits high,
Neh 7:4 The city was W and large, but the people
Jud 1:2 high and fifty cubits W;
1:3 high and sixty cubits W at the foundations;
1:4 high and forty cubits W, so that his armies
4:7 approach was narrow, only W enough for two men
Job 30:14 As through a W breach they come; amid the
Ps 18:36 Thou didst give a W place for my steps
22:13 surround me; they open W their mouths at me,
35:21 They open W their mouths against me; they say,
81:10 Open your mouth W, and I will fill it.
104:25 the sea, great and W, which teems with things
110:6 shatter chiefs over the W earth.
Prov 13:3 life; he who opens W his lips comes to
Wis 8:8 any one longs for W experience, she knows the
Is 22:18 a ball into a W land; there you shall
30:33 pyre made deep and W, with fire and wood
57:4 you open your mouth W and put out your
57:8 you have made it W; and you have made
Ezek 42:4 passage inward, ten cubits W and a hundred cubits
Nah 3:13 of your land are W open to your foes;
Hab 2:5 His greed is as W as Sheol; like death
Zech 14:4 west by a very W valley; so that one
2Mac 12:16 quarter of a mile W, appeared to be running
Mt 7:13 for the gate is W and the way is
1Cor 16:9 until Pentecost, for a W door for effective work
2Cor 6:11 is open to you, Corinthians; our heart is W

WIDE-SPREADING

Wis 17:18 sound of birds in W branches, or the rhythm

WIDELY (3)

Neh 4:19 work is great and W spread, and we are

Bar 6:61 when it flashes, is W seen; and the wind
2Mac 7:5 from the pan spread W, but the brothers and

WIDEN

2Cor 6:13 speak as to children– W your hearts also.

WIDOW (75)

Gen 38:11 his daughter-in-law, "Remain a W in your father's
38:14 she put off her W's garments, and put on
Ex 22:22 shall not afflict any W or orphan.
Lev 21:14 A W, or one divorced, or a woman who
22:13 priest's daughter is a W or divorced, and has
Num 30:9 any vow of a W or of a divorced
Deut 10:18 the fatherless and the W, and loves the sojourner,
14:29 the fatherless, and the W, who are within your
16:11 the fatherless, and the W who are among you,
16:14 the fatherless, and the W who are within your
24:17 fatherless, or take a W's garment in pledge;
24:19 the fatherless, and the W; that the LORD your
24:20 be for the sojourner, the fatherless, and the W
24:21 be for the sojourner, the fatherless, and the W
26:12 the fatherless, and the W, that they may eat
26:13 the fatherless, and the W, according to all thy
27:19 the fatherless, and the W And all the people
Ruth 4:5 Ruth the Moabitess, the W of the dead, in
4:10 Ruth the Moabitess, the W of Mahlon, I have
1Sam 27:3 of Jezreel, and Abigail of Carmel, Nabal's W
30:5 Jezreel, and Abigail the W of Nabal of Carmel.
2Sam 2:2 Jezreel, and Abigail the W of Nabal of Carmel.
3:3 Chile-ab, of Abigail the W of Nabal of Carmel;
14:5 "Alas, I am a W; my husband is dead.
1Kgs 7:14 the son of a W of the tribe of
11:26 name was Zeruah, a W, also lifted up his
17:9 I have commanded a W there to feed you."
17:10 the city, behold, a W was there gathering sticks;
17:20 calamity even upon the W with whom I sojourn,
Jud 8:4 at home as a W for three years and
9:4 O God, my God, hear me also, a W
9:9 give to me, a W, the strength to do
10:3 and took off her W's garments, and bathed her
16:8 she took off her W's mourning to exalt the
16:22 but she remained a W all the days of
Job 24:3 fatherless; they take the W's ox for a pledge.
24:21 childless woman, and do no good to the W
29:13 and I caused the W's heart to sing for
31:16 the eyes of the W to fail,
Ps 94:6 They slay the W and the sojourner, and murder
109:9 his children be fatherless, and his wife a W
146:9 sojourners, he upholds the W and the fatherless; but
Prov 15:25 proud, but maintains the W's boundaries.
Wis 2:10 us not spare the W nor regard the gray
Sir 35:14 the fatherless, nor the W when she pours out
35:15 the tears of the W run down her cheek
Is 1:17 oppression; defend the fatherless, plead for the W
1:23 the fatherless, and the W's cause does not come
47:8 not sit as a W or know the loss
Jer 7:6 the fatherless or the W, or shed innocent blood
22:3 the fatherless, and the W, nor shed innocent blood
Lam 1:1 How like a W has she become, she that
Bar 4:12 rejoice over me, a W and bereaved of many;
4:16 They led away the W's beloved sons, and bereaved
6:38 take pity on a W or do good to
Ezek 22:7 the fatherless and the W are wronged in you.
44:22 shall not marry a W, or a divorced woman,
44:22 of Israel, or a W who is the widow
44:22 widow who is the W of a priest.
Zech 7:10 do not oppress the W, the fatherless, the sojourner,
Mal 3:5 in his wages, the W and the orphan, against
Mt 22:24 brother must marry the W, and raise up children
Mk 12:42 And a poor W came, and put in two
12:43 to you, this poor W has put in more
Lk 2:37 virginity, and as a W till she was eighty-four.
4:26 of Sidon, to a woman who was a W
7:12 and she was a W; and a large crowd
18:3 and there was a W in that city who
18:5 man, yet because this W bothers me, I will
21:2 he saw a poor W put in two copper
21:3 tell you, this poor W has put in more
1Tim 5:4 If a W has children or grandchildren, let them
5:5 who is a real W, and is left all
5:9 Let a W be enrolled if she is not
Rev 18:7 sit, I am no W, mourning I shall never

WIDOWED

Jer 18:21 the sword, let their wives become childless and W

WIDOWHOOD (6)

Gen 38:19 veil she put on the garments of her W
2Sam 20:3 day of their death, living as if in W
Jud 8:5 her loins and wore the garments of her W
8:6 the days of her W, except the day before
Is 47:9 loss of children and W shall come upon you
54:4 the reproach of your W you will remember no

WIDOWS (28)

Ex 22:24 your wives shall become W and your children
Job 22:9 You have sent W away empty, and the arms
27:15 pestilence buries, and their W make no lamentation.
Ps 68:5 fatherless and protector of W is God in his
78:64 the sword, and their W made no lamentation.
Is 9:17 on their fatherless and W; for every one is
10:2 of their right, that W may be their spoil,
Jer 15:8 I have made their W more in number than
49:11 alive; and let your W trust in me."
Lam 5:3 become orphans, fatherless; our mothers are like W
Ezek 22:25 they have made many W in the midst of
2Mac 3:10 some deposits belonging to W and orphans,
8:28 tortured and to the W and orphans, and distributed
8:30 to the orphans and W, and also to the
Mk 12:40 at feasts, who devour W houses and for a
Lk 4:25 you, there were many W in Israel in the
20:47 at feasts, who devour W houses and for a
Acts 6:1 the Hebrews because their W were neglected in the
9:39 All the W stood beside him weeping, and showing
9:41 calling the saints and W he presented her alive.
1Cor 7:8 the unmarried and the W I say that it
1Tim 5:3 Honor W who are real widows.
5:3 Honor widows who are real W
5:11 refuse to enrol younger W; for when they grow
5:14 I would have younger W marry, bear children, rule
5:16 has relatives who are W, let her assist them;
5:16 that it may assist those who are real W
Jas 1:26 to visit orphans and W in their affliction, and

WIDTH (2)

1Kgs 6:3 long, equal to the W of the house, and
2Chr 3:4 long, equal to the W of the house; and

WIELD (5)

Ex 20:25 stones; for if you W your tool upon it
Is 10:15 if a rod should W him who lifts it,
10:26 LORD of hosts will W against them a scourge,
Ezek 30:21 may become strong to W the sword.
Zech 9:13 sons, O Greece, and W you like a warrior's

WIELDED (4)

2Sam 23:8 of the three; he W his spear against eight
23:18 And he W his spear against three hundred men
1Chr 11:11 of the three; he W his spear against three
11:20 And he W his spear against three hundred men

WIELDING (2)

Deut 20:19 destroy its trees by W an axe against them;
Ezek 38:4 with buckler and shield, W swords;

WIELDS

Is 10:15 itself against him who W it?

WIFE (445)

Gen 2:24 and cleaves to his W, and they become one
2:25 the man and his W were both naked, and
3:8 the man and his W hid themselves from the
3:17 the voice of your W, and have eaten of
3:20 The man called his W's name Eve, because she
3:21 Adam and for his W garments of skins, and
4:1 Adam knew Eve his W, and she conceived and
4:17 Cain knew his W, and she conceived and bore
4:25 And Adam knew his W again, and she bore
6:2 and they took to W such of them as
6:18 you, your sons, your W, and your sons' wives
7:7 his sons and his W and his sons' wives
7:13 and Japheth, and Noah's W and the three wives
8:16 ark, you and your W, and your sons and
8:18 his sons and his W and his sons' wives
11:29 the name of Abram's W was Sarai, and the
11:29 the name of Nahor's W, Milcah, the daughter of
11:31 daughter-in-law, his son Abram's W, and they went
12:5 Abram took Sarai his W, and Lot his brother's
12:11 said to Sarai his W, "I know that you
12:12 say, 'This is his W; then they will kill
12:17 with great plagues because of Sarai, Abram's W
12:18 you not tell me that she was your W

12:19 sister,' so that I took her for my W
12:19 then, here is your W, take her, and be
12:20 the way, with his W and all that he
13:1 Egypt, he and his W, and all that he
16:1 Now Sarai, Abram's W, bore him no children.
16:3 of Canaan, Sarai, Abram's W, took Hagar the
16:3 gave her to Abram her husband as a W
17:15 "As for Sarai your W, you shall not call
17:19 "No, but Sarah your W shall bear you a
18:9 They said to him, "Where is Sarah your W
18:10 spring, and Sarah your W shall have a son."
19:15 saying, "Arise, take your W and your two daughters
19:16 seized him and his W and his two daughters
19:26 But Lot's W behind him looked back, and she
20:2 said of Sarah his W, "She is my sister."
20:3 you have taken; for she is a man's W
20:7 then restore the man's W; for he is a
20:11 and they will kill me because of my W
20:12 daughter of my mother; and she became my W
20:14 and restored Sarah his W to him.
20:17 and also healed his W and female slaves so
20:18 house of Abimelech because of Sarah, Abraham's W
21:21 his mother took a W for him from the
23:19 Abraham buried Sarah his W in the cave of
24:3 will not take a W for my son from
24:4 kindred, and take a W for my son Isaac."
24:7 you shall take a W for my son from
24:15 son of Milcah, the W of Nahor, Abraham's brother,
24:36 And Sarah my master's W bore a son to
24:37 shall not take a W for my son from
24:38 kindred, and take a W for my son.'
24:40 you shall take a W for my son from
24:51 let her be the W of your master's son,
24:67 and she became his W; and he loved her.
25:1 Abraham took another W, whose name was Keturah.
25:10 There Abraham was buried, with Sarah his W
25:20 when he took to W Rebekah, the daughter of
25:21 the LORD for his W, because she was barren;
25:21 prayer, and Rebekah his W conceived.
26:7 asked him about his W, he said, "She is
26:7 my sister"; for he feared to say, "My W
26:8 a window and saw Isaac fondling Rebekah his W
26:9 "Behold, she is your W; how then could you
26:10 have lain with your W, and you would have
26:11 this man or his W shall be put to
26:34 old, he took to W Judith the daughter of
28:2 father; and take as W from there one of
28:6 Paddan-aram to take a W from there, and that
28:9 Ishmael and took to W, besides the wives he
29:21 Laban, "Give me my W that I may go
29:28 then Laban gave him his daughter Rachel to W
30:4 maid Bilhah as a W; and Jacob went in
30:9 Zilpah and gave her to Jacob as a W
34:4 Hamor, saying, "Get me this maiden for my W
34:12 only give me the maiden to be my W
36:10 son of Adah the W of Esau, Reuel the
36:10 son of Basemath the W of Esau.
36:12 Eliphaz.) These are the sons of Adah, Esau's W
36:13 These are the sons of Basemath, Esau's W
36:14 son of Zibeon, Esau's W: she bore to Esau
36:17 Edom; they are the sons of Basemath, Esau's W
36:18 sons of Oholibamah, Esau's W: the chiefs Jeush,
36:18 born of Oholibamah the daughter of Anah, Esau's W
36:39 city being Pau; his W's name was Mehetabel, the
38:6 And Judah took a W for Er his first-born,
38:8 in to your brother's W, and perform the duty
38:9 in to his brother's W he spilled the semen
38:12 course of time the W of Judah, Shua's daughter,
39:7 a time his master's W cast her eyes upon
39:8 said to his master's W, "Lo, having me my
39:9 because you are his W; how then can I
39:19 the words which his W spoke to him, "This
44:27 'You know that my W bore me two sons;
46:19 sons of Rachel, Jacob's W: Joseph and Benjamin.
49:31 Abraham and Sarah his W; there they buried Isaac
49:31 Isaac and Rebekah his W; and there I buried

Ex 2:1 went and took to W a daughter of Levi.
4:20 So Moses took his W and his sons and
6:20 Amram took to W Jochebed his father's sister and
6:23 Aaron took to W Elisheba, the daughter of
6:25 Aaron's son, took to W one of the daughters
18:2 had taken Zipporah, Moses' W, after he had sent
18:5 his sons and his W to Moses in the
18:6 to you with your W and her two sons
20:17 not covet your neighbor's W, or his manservant, or
21:3 in married, then his W shall go out with
21:4 master gives him a W and she bears him
21:4 sons or daughters, the W and her children shall
21:5 love my master, my W, and my children; I
21:10 If he takes another W to himself, he shall
22:16 marriage present for her, and make her his W

Lev 18:8 nakedness of your father's W; it is your father's
18:11 nakedness of your father's W's daughter, begotten by
18:14 shall not approach his W; she is your aunt.
18:15 she is your son's W, you shall not uncover
18:16 nakedness of your brother's W; she is your brother's
18:18 woman as a rival W to her sister, uncovering
18:20 carnally with your neighbor's W, and defile yourself
20:10 commits adultery with the W of his neighbor, both
20:11 lies with his father's W has uncovered his father's
20:14 a man takes a W and her mother also,
20:20 lies with his uncle's W, he has uncovered his
20:21 man takes his brother's W, it is impurity; he
21:13 he shall take a W in her virginity.
21:14 he shall take to W a virgin of his

Num 5:12 Israel, If any man's W goes astray and acts
5:14 is jealous of his W who has defiled herself;
5:14 is jealous of his W, though she has not
5:15 man shall bring his W to the priest, and
5:29 of jealousy, when a W, though under her husband's
5:30 is jealous of his W; then he shall set
26:59 The name of Amram's W was Jochebed the daughter
30:16 a man and his W, and between a father
36:8 of Israel shall be W to one of the

Deut 5:21 you covet your neighbor's W; and you shall not
13:6 your daughter, or the W of your bosom, or
20:7 that has betrothed a W and has not taken
21:11 her for yourself as W,
21:13 be her husband, and she shall be your W
22:13 any man takes a W, and goes in to
22:16 to this man to W, and he spurns her;
22:19 she shall be his W; he may not put
22:22 found lying with the W of another man, both
22:24 he violated his neighbor's W; so you shall purge
22:29 she shall be his W, because he has violated
22:30 not take his father's W, nor shall he uncover
24:1 a man takes a W and marries her, if
24:2 and becomes another man's W,
24:3 her to be his W,
24:4 again to be his W, after she has been
24:5 be happy with his W whom he has taken.
25:5 has no son, the W of the dead shall
25:5 take her as his W, and perform the duty
25:7 to take his brother's W, then his brother's wife
25:7 wife, then his brother's W shall go up to
25:9 her,' then his brother's W shall go up to
25:11 one another, and the W of the one draws
27:20 lies with his father's W, because he has uncovered
28:30 You shall betroth a W, and another man shall
28:54 his brother, to the W of his bosom, and

Josh 15:16 him will I give Achsah my daughter as W
15:17 and he gave him Achsah his daughter as W

Judg 1:12 I will give him Achsah my daughter as W
1:13 and he gave him Achsah his daughter as W
4:4 Deborah, a prophetess, the W of Lappidoth, was
4:17 tent of Jael, the W of Heber the Kenite;
4:21 But Jael the W of Heber took a tent
5:24 women be Jael, the W of Heber the Kenite,
11:2 And Gilead's W also bore him sons; and when
11:2 sons; and when his W's sons grew up, they
13:2 was Manoah; and his W was barren and had
13:11 and went after his W, and came to the
13:20 while Manoah and his W looked on; and they
13:21 appeared no more to Manoah and to his W
13:22 Manoah said to his W, "We shall surely die,
13:23 But his W said to him, "If the LORD
14:2 Timnah; now get her for me as my W
14:3 go to take a W from the uncircumcised Philistines?"
14:15 they said to Samson's W, "Entice your husband to
14:16 And Samson's W wept before him, and said, "You
14:20 And Samson's W was given to his companion, who
15:1 went to visit his W with a kid; and
15:1 go in to my W in the chamber." But
15:6 he has taken his W and given her to
21:18 he who gives a W to Benjamin."
21:21 seize each man his W from the daughters of
21:22 man of them his W in battle, neither did

Ruth 1:1 Moab, he and his W and his two sons.
1:2 the name of his W Naomi, and the names
4:10 bought to be my W, to perpetuate the name
4:13 and she became his W; and he went in

1Sam 1:4 portions to Peninnah his W and to all her

1:19 Elkanah knew Hannah his W, and the LORD
2:20 bless Elkanah and his W, and say, "The LORD
4:19 Now his daughter-in-law, the W of Phinehas, was
14:50 the name of Saul's W was Ahino-am the daughter
18:17 to you for a W; only be valiant for
18:19 was given to Adriel the Meholathite for a W
18:27 Saul gave him his daughter Michal for a W
19:11 But Michal, David's W, told him, "If you do
25:3 the name of his W Abigail.
25:14 men told Abigail, Nabal's W, "Behold, David sent
25:37 out of Nabal, his W told him these things,
25:39 sent and wooed Abigail, to make her his W
25:40 you to take you to him as his W
25:42 after the messengers of David, and became his W
25:44 Michal his daughter, David's W, to Palti the son
30:22 may lead away his W and children, and depart."
2Sam 3:5 Abital; and the sixth, Ithre-am, of Eglah, David's W
3:14 saying, "Give me my W Michal, whom I betrothed
11:3 daughter of Eliam, the W of Uriah the Hittite?"
11:11 and to drink, and to lie with my W
11:26 When the W of Uriah heard that Uriah her
11:27 and she became his W, and bore him a
12:9 and have taken his W to be your wife,
12:9 wife to be your W, and have slain him
12:10 and have taken the W of Uriah the Hittite
12:10 Hittite to be your W
12:15 the child that Uriah's W bore to David, and
12:24 Then David comforted his W, Bathsheba, and went in
1Kgs 2:17 to give me Abishag the Shunammite as my W
2:21 be given to Adonijah your brother as his W
4:11 of Solomon as his W;
4:15 of Solomon as his W;
9:16 to his daughter, Solomon's W;
11:19 sister of his own W, the sister of Tahpenes
14:2 Jeroboam said to his W, "Arise, and disguise yourself,
14:2 that you are the W of Jeroboam, and go
14:4 Jeroboam's W did so; she arose, and went to
14:5 to Ahijah, "Behold, the W of Jeroboam is coming
14:6 he said, "Come in, W of Jeroboam; why do
14:17 Then Jeroboam's W arose, and departed, and came
16:31 Nebat, he took for W Jezebel the daughter of
21:5 But Jezebel his W came to him, and said
21:7 And Jezebel his W said to him, "Do you
21:25 Ahab, whom Jezebel his W incited.
2Kgs 4:1 Now the W of one of the sons of
5:2 land of Israel, and she waited on Naaman's W
8:18 done, for the daughter of Ahab was his W
14:9 my son for a W; and a wild beast
22:14 Huldah the prophetess, the W of Shallum the son
1Chr 1:50 was Pai, and his W's name Mehetabel the daughter
2:18 had children by his W Azubah, and by Jerioth;
2:24 in to Ephrathah, the W of Hezron his father,
2:26 Jerahmeel also had another W, whose name was;
2:29 The name of Abishur's W was Abihail, and she
3:3 sixth Ithream, by his W Eglah;
4:18 And his Jewish W bore Jered the father of
4:19 The sons of the W of Hodiah, the sister
7:15 And Machir took a W for Huppim and for
7:16 And Maacah the W of Machir bore a son,
7:23 went in to his W, and she conceived and
8:9 sons by Hodesh his W: Jobab, Zibi-a, Mesha,
8:29 the name of his W was Maacah.
9:35 the name of his W was Maacah,
2Chr 8:11 for he said, "My W shall not live in
11:18 Rehoboam took as W Mahalath the daughter of
21:6 done; for the daughter of Ahab was his W
22:11 of King Jehoram and W of Jehoiada the priest,
25:18 my son for a W; and a wild beast
34:22 Huldah the prophetess, the W of Shallum the son
Ezra 2:61 (who had taken a W from the daughters of
Neh 6:18 of Meshullam the son of Berechiah as his W
7:63 (who had taken a W of the daughters of
Tob 1:20 to me except my W Anna and my son
2:1 arrived home and my W Anna and my son
2:11 Then my W Anna earned money at women's work.
3:8 before he had been with her as his W
3:15 son for whom I should keep myself as W
4:12 of all take a W from among the descendants
4:13 refusing to take a W for yourself from among
6:15 you to take a W from among your own
6:15 she will become your W; and do not worry
7:2 Raguel said to his W Edna, "How much the
7:8 And his W Edna and his daughter Sarah wept.
7:13 Tobias to be his W, saying, "Here she is;
7:14 Next he called his W Edna, and took a
7:16 And Raguel called his W Edna and said to
8:6 gavest him Eve his W as a helper and
8:12 and said to his W Edna, "Send one of
8:21 be his "when my W and I die."
9:6 And Gabael blessed Tobias and his W
10:4 And his W said to him, "The lad has
10:10 and gave him his W Sarah and half of
11:1 blessed Raguel and his W Edna.
11:3 run ahead of your W and prepare the house.
12:3 safely, he cured my W, he obtained the money
14:12 Tobias returned with his W and his sons to
Esth 5:10 his friends and his W Zeresh.
5:14 Then his W Zeresh and all his friends said
6:13 And Haman told his W Zeresh and all his
6:13 wise men and his W Zeresh said to him,
Job 2:9 Then his W said to him, "Do you still
19:17 am repulsive to my W, loathsome to the sons
31:10 door; then let my W grind for another, and
Ps 109:9 be fatherless, and his W a widow!
128:3 Your W will be like a fruitful vine within
Prov 5:18 and rejoice in the W of your youth,
6:29 in to his neighbor's W; none who touches her
12:4 A good W is the crown of her husband,
18:22 He who finds a W finds a good thing,
19:13 his father, and a W's quarreling is a continual
19:14 fathers, but a prudent W is from the LORD.
31:10 A good W who can find?
Eccl 9:9 Enjoy life with the W whom you love, all
Sir 7:19 a wise and good W, for her charm is
7:26 If you have a W who pleases you, do
9:1 be jealous of the W of your bosom, and
9:9 dine with another man's W, nor revel with her
15:2 mother, and like the W of his youth she
25:1 between neighbors, and a W and a husband who
25:8 lives with an intelligent W, and he who has
25:12 Any wickedness, but not the wickedness of a W
25:15 and a dragon than dwell with an evil W
25:16 The wickedness of a W changes her appearance, and
25:18 insignificant compared to a W's iniquity; may a
25:19 such is a garrulous W for a quiet husband.
25:21 great disgrace when a W supports her husband.
25:22 a wounded heart are caused by an evil W
25:22 are caused by the W who does not make
25:24 and no boldness of speech in an evil W
26:1 husband of a good W; the number of his
26:2 A loyal W rejoices her husband, and he will
26:3 A good W is a great blessing; she will
26:6 and sorrow when a W is envious of a
26:7 An evil W is an ox yoke which chafes;
26:8 great anger when a W is drunken; she will
26:9 A W's harlotry shows in her lustful eyes, and
26:13 A W's charm delights her husband, and her skill
26:14 A silent W is a gift of the Lord,
26:15 A modest W adds charm to charm, and no
26:16 beauty of a good W in her well-ordered home.
33:19 To son or W, to brother or friend, do
36:24 He who acquires a W gets his best possession,
36:25 where there is no W, a man will wander
40:19 name, but a blameless W is accounted better than
40:23 one amiss, but a W with her husband is
41:21 gazing at another man's W;
42:6 there is an evil W, a seal is a
Is 54:6 called you like a W forsaken and grieved in
54:6 in spirit, like a W of youth when she
Jer 3:1 a man divorces his W and she goes from
3:1 and becomes another man's W, will he return to
3:20 Surely, as a faithless W leaves her husband, so
5:8 lusty stallions, each neighing for his neighbor's W
6:11 also; both husband and W shall be taken, the
16:2 shall not take a W, nor shall you have
Ezek 16:32 Adulterous W, who receives strangers instead of her
18:6 not defile his neighbor's W or approach a woman
18:11 mountains, defiles his neighbor's W,
18:15 not defile his neighbor's W,
22:11 with his neighbor's W; another lewdly defiles his
24:18 and at evening my W died.
33:26 you defiles his neighbor's W; shall you then possess
Dan 13:2 And he took a W named Susanna, the daughter
13:29 Hilkiah, who is the W of Joakim."
13:63 And Hilkiah and his W praised God for their
Hos 1:2 take to yourself a W of harlotry and have
2:2 she is not my W, and I am not
12:12 did service for a W, and for a wife
12:12 wife, and for a W he herded sheep.)
Amos 7:17 says the LORD: 'Your W shall be a harlot
Mal 2:14 between you and the W of your youth, to
2:14 your companion and your W by covenant.

2:15 be faithless to the W of his youth.
1Mac 10:54 your daughter as my W, and I will become
11:9 daughter who was Alexander's W, and you shall reign
Mt 1:6 of Solomon by the W of Uriah,
1:20 to take Mary your W, for that which is
1:24 him; he took his W,
5:31 said, 'Whoever divorces his W, let him give her
5:32 one who divorces his W, except on the ground
14:3 Herodi-as, his brother Philip's W;
18:24 be sold, with his W and children and all
19:3 lawful to divorce one's W for any cause?"
19:5 be joined to his W, and the two shall
19:9 you: whoever divorces his W, except for unchastity,
19:10 a man with his W, it is not expedient
22:25 no children left his W to his brother.
22:28 to which of the seven will she be W
27:19 the judgment seat, his W sent word to him,
Mk 6:17 Herodi-as, his brother Philip's W; because he had
6:18 not lawful for you to have your brother's W
10:2 it lawful for a man to divorce his W
10:7 be joined to his W,
10:11 them, "Whoever divorces his W and marries another,
12:19 dies and leaves a W, but leaves no child,
12:19 man must take the W, and raise up children
12:20 the first took a W, and when he died
12:23 In the resurrection whose W will she be?
12:23 For the seven had her as W
Lk 1:5 and he had a W of the daughters of
1:13 is heard, and your W Elizabeth will bear you
1:18 old man, and my W is advanced in years."
1:24 After these days his W Elizabeth conceived, and for
3:19 for Herodi-as, his brother's W, and for all the
8:3 out, and Joanna, the W of Chuza, Herod's steward,
14:20 'I have married a W, and therefore I cannot
14:26 father and mother and W and children and brothers
16:18 who divorces his W and marries another commits
17:32 Remember Lot's W
18:29 has left house or W or brothers or parents
20:28 brother dies, having a W but no children, the
20:28 man must take the W and raise up children
20:29 the first took a W, and died without children;
20:33 the resurrection, therefore, whose W will the woman
20:33 For the seven had her as W
Jn 19:25 mother's sister, Mary the W of Clopas, and Mary
Acts 5:1 named Ananias with his W Sapphira sold a piece
5:2 property, and with his W's knowledge he kept back
5:7 about three hours his W came in, not knowing
18:2 from Italy with his W Priscilla, because Claudius had
24:23 Felix came with his W Drusilla, who was a
1Cor 5:1 for a man is living with his father's W
7:2 should have his own W and each woman her
7:3 should give to his W her conjugal rights, and
7:3 rights, and likewise the W to her husband.
7:4 For the W does not rule over her own
7:4 own body, but the W does.
7:10 the Lord, that the W should not separate from
7:11 and that the husband should not divorce his W
7:12 any brother has a W who is an unbeliever,
7:14 is consecrated through his W, and the unbelieving
7:14 wife, and the unbelieving W is consecrated through
7:16 W, how do you know whether you will save
7:16 do you know whether you will save your W
7:27 Are you bound to a W
7:27 Are you free from a W
7:33 how to please his W,
7:39 A W is bound to her husband as long
9:5 be accompanied by a W, as the other apostles
Eph 5:23 the head of the W as Christ is the
5:28 He who loves his W loves himself.
5:31 be joined to his W, and the two shall
5:33 of you love his W as himself, and let
5:33 himself, and let the W see that she respects
1Thes 4:4 how to take a W for himself in holiness
1Tim 3:2 the husband of one W, temperate, sensible, dignified,
3:12 the husband of one W, and let them manage
5:9 age, having been the W of one husband;
Tit 1:5 the husband of one W, and his children are
Rev 21:9 you the Bride, the W of the Lamb."

WILD (80)

Gen 3:1 subtle than any other W creature that the LORD
3:14 cattle, and above all W animals; upon your belly
16:12 He shall be a W ass of a man,
31:39 which was torn by W beasts I did not
37:20 shall say that a W beast has devoured him,
37:33 my son's robe; a W beast has devoured him;
Ex 23:11 what they leave the W beasts may eat.
23:29 become desolate and the W beasts multiply against
Lev 26:22 will let loose the W beasts among you, which
Num 23:22 the horns of the W ox.
24:8 the horns of the W ox, he shall eat
Deut 7:22 at once, lest the W beasts grow too numerous
14:5 gazelle, the roebuck, the W goat, the ibex, the
33:17 the horns of a W ox; with them he
1Sam 17:46 air and to the W beasts of the earth;
2Sam 2:18 of foot as a W gazelle;
2Kgs 4:39 herbs, and found a W vine and gathered from
4:39 his lap full of W gourds, and came and
14:9 a wife'; and a W beast of Lebanon passed
2Chr 25:18 a wife'; and a W beast of Lebanon passed
Neh 8:15 bring branches of olive, W olive, myrtle, palm, and
Job 6:5 Does the W ass bray when he has grass,
11:12 get understanding, when a W ass's colt is born
24:5 Behold, like W asses in the desert they go
39:5 "Who has let the W ass go free?
39:9 "Is the W ox willing to serve you?
39:15 them, and that the W beast may trample them.
40:20 him where all the W beasts play.
Ps 22:21 the horns of the W oxen!
29:6 Sirion like a young W ox.
74:19 thy dove to the W beasts; do not forget
92:10 like that of the W ox; thou hast poured
104:11 of the field; the W asses quench their thirst.
104:18 mountains are for the W goats; the rocks are
Wis 7:20 and the tempers of W beasts, the powers of
12:9 one blow by dread W beasts or thy stern
16:5 the terrible rage of W beasts came upon thy
Sir 10:11 inherit creeping things, and W beasts, and worms.
12:13 any who go near W beasts?
13:18 W asses in the wilderness are the prey of
39:30 vengeance; the teeth of W beasts, and scorpions and
Is 5:2 grapes, but it yielded W grapes.
5:4 why did it yield W grapes?
13:21 But W beasts will lie down there, and its
23:13 They destined Tyre for W beasts.
32:14 ever, a joy of W asses, a pasture of
34:7 W oxen shall fall with them, and young steers
34:14 And W beasts shall meet with hyenas, the satyr
43:20 The W beasts will honor me, the jackals and
Jer 2:21 degenerate and become a W vine?
2:24 interlacing her tracks, a W ass used to the
12:9 Go, assemble all the W beasts; bring them to
14:6 The W asses stand on the bare heights, they
48:6 Be like a W ass in the desert!
50:39 "Therefore W beasts shall dwell with hyenas in
Bar 6:68 The W beasts are better than they are, for
Ezek 5:17 will send famine and W beasts against you, and
14:15 If I cause W beasts to pass through the
34:5 food for all the W beasts.
34:8 food for all the W beasts, since there was
34:25 of peace and banish W beasts from the land,
39:4 sort and to the W beasts to be devoured.
Dan 5:21 dwelling was with the W asses; he was fed
Hos 8:9 up to Assyria, a W ass wandering alone; Ephraim
13:8 a lion, as a W beast would rend them.
Joel 1:19 Even the W beasts cry to thee because the
Zeph 2:15 become, a lair for W beasts!
2Mac 4:25 rage of a savage W beast.
4:41 and threw them in W confusion at Lysimachus and
5:27 in the mountains as W animals do; they continued
5:27 live on what grew W, so that they might
10:6 mountains and caves like W animals.
Mt 3:4 food was locusts and W honey.
Mk 1:6 and ate locusts and W honey.
1:13 he was with the W beasts; and the angels
Rom 11:17 off, and you, a W olive shoot, were grafted
11:24 is by nature a W olive tree, and grafted,
1Pet 4:4 them in the same W profligacy, and they abuse
Jude 1:13 autumn, twice dead, uprooted; W waves of the sea,
Rev 6:8 with pestilence and by W beasts of the earth.

WILDERNESS (296)

Gen 14:6 the border of the W;
16:7 of water in the W, the spring on the
21:14 and wandered in the W of Beer-sheba.
21:20 he lived in the W, and became an expert
21:21 He lived in the W of Paran; and his
36:24 hot springs in the W, as he pastured the
37:22 pit here in the W, but lay no hand
Ex 3:1 west side of the W, and came to Horeb,
3:18 days' journey into the W, that we may sacrifice
4:27 Aaron, "Go into the W to meet Moses." So

W

W

1Thes 3:1 no longer, we were W to be left behind

WILLINGLY (14)

Judg 5:2 the people offered themselves W, bless the LORD!
5:9 Israel who offered themselves W among the people.
8:25 they answered, "We will W give them." And they
1Chr 29:5 Who then will offer W, consecrating himself today to
29:9 because these had given W, for with a whole
29:14 that we should be able thus to offer W
2Chr 35:8 And his princes contributed W to the people, to
Ezra 7:16 and the priests, vowed W for the house of
Neh 11:2 all the men who W offered to live in
Lam 3:33 for he does not W afflict or grieve the
1Mac 2:42 one who offered himself W for the law.
8:27 Jews, the Romans shall W act as their allies,
2Mac 6:28 die a good death W and nobly for the
1Pet 5:2 not by constraint but W, not for shameful gain

WILLOW

Ezek 17:5 set it like a W twig,

WILLOWS (5)

Lev 23:40 of leafy trees, and W of the brook; and
Job 40:22 trees cover him; the W of the brook surround
Ps 137:2 On the W there we hung up our lyres.
Is 15:7 they carry away over the Brook of the W
44:4 grass amid waters, like W by flowing streams.

WILLS (8)

Wis 9:13 Or who can discern what the Lord W
Jn 3:8 wind blows where it W, and you hear the
Acts 18:21 said, "I will return to you if God W
Rom 9:18 mercy upon whomever he W, and he hardens the
9:18 and he hardens the heart of whomever he W
1Cor 4:19 soon, if the Lord W, and I will find
12:11 who apportions to each one individually as he W
Jas 4:15 say, "If the Lord W, we shall live and

WILT (86)

Gen 15:2 "O Lord GOD, what W thou give me, for
18:23 drew near, and said, W thou indeed destroy the
18:24 righteous within the city; W thou then destroy the
18:28 W thou destroy the whole city for lack of
20:4 so he said, "Lord, W thou slay an innocent
24:42 Abraham, if now thou W prosper the way which
Ex 15:17 Thou W bring them in, and plant them on
32:32 But now, if thou W forgive their sin--and
33:12 me know whom thou W send with me.
Num 11:15 If thou W deal thus with me, kill me
16:22 one man sin, and W thou be angry with
21:2 and said, "If thou W indeed give this people
Josh 7:9 the earth; and what W thou do for thy
Judg 6:36 to God, "If thou W deliver Israel by my
6:37 shall know that thou W deliver Israel by my
11:30 and said, "If thou W give the Ammonites into
1Sam 1:11 of hosts, if thou W indeed look on the
1:11 forget thy maidservant, but W give to thy
14:37 W thou give them into the hand of Israel?"
2Sam 5:19 W thou give them into my hand?" And the
1Chr 14:10 W thou give them into my hand?" And the
17:25 thy servant that thou W build a house for
2Chr 20:9 our affliction, and thou W hear and save.'
20:12 O our God, W thou not execute judgment upon
Jud 16:15 who fear thee thou W continue to show mercy.
Job 7:19 How long W thou not look away from me,
7:21 in the earth; thou W seek me, but I
9:28 for I know thou W not hold me innocent.
9:31 with lye, yet thou W plunge me into a
10:9 me of clay; and W thou turn me to
13:25 W thou frighten a driven leaf and pursue dry
17:4 understanding, therefore thou W not let them
30:23 I know that thou W bring me to death,
Ps 10:13 in his heart, "Thou W not call to account"?
10:17 O LORD, thou W hear the desire of the
10:17 of the meek; thou W strengthen their heart, thou
10:17 strengthen their heart, thou W incline thy ear
13:1 W thou forget me for ever?
13:1 How long W thou hide thy face from me?
17:3 thou testest me, thou W find no wickedness in
17:6 upon thee, for thou W answer me, O God;
35:17 How long, O LORD, W thou look on?
38:15 LORD my God, who W answer.
51:17 heart, O God, thou W not despise.
51:19 walls of Jerusalem, then W thou delight in right
55:23 But thou, O God, W cast them down into
71:20 see many sore troubles W revive me again; from
71:20 of the earth thou W bring me up again.
71:21 Thou W increase my honor, and comfort me again.
73:24 counsel, and afterward thou W receive me to glory.
76:10 residue of wrath thou W gird upon thee.
79:5 W thou be angry for ever?
80:4 of hosts, how long W thou be angry with
85:5 W thou be angry with us for ever?
85:5 W thou prolong thy anger to all generations?
85:6 W thou not revive us again, that thy people
89:46 W thou hide thyself for ever?
101:2 Oh when W thou come to me?
102:13 Thou W arise and have pity on Zion; it
119:82 promise; I ask, "When W thou comfort me?"
119:84 When W thou judge those who persecute me?
142:7 surround me; for thou W deal bountifully with me.
Is 26:12 O LORD, thou W ordain peace for us, thou
26:19 of the shades thou W let it fall.
64:12 W thou restrain thyself at these things, O LORD?
64:12 W thou keep silent, and afflict us sorely?
Jer 15:18 W thou be to me like a deceitful brook,
51:62 this place that thou W cut it off, so
Lam 3:64 "Thou W requite them, O LORD, according to the
3:65 Thou W give them dullness of heart; thy curse
3:66 Thou W pursue them in anger and destroy them
Ezek 9:8 W thou destroy all that remains of Israel in
11:13 W thou make a full end of the remnant
Hos 9:14 them, O LORD--what W thou give?
Mic 7:19 Thou W cast all our sins into the depths
7:20 Thou W show faithfulness to Jacob and steadfast
Hab 1:2 for help, and thou W not hear?
1:2 and thou W not save?
Zech 1:12 of hosts, how long W thou have no mercy
Mt 26:39 nevertheless, not as I will, but as thou W
Mk 14:36 yet not what I will, but what thou W
Acts 2:27 For thou W not abandon my soul to Hades,
2:28 ways of life; thou W make me full of
13:35 in another psalm, 'Thou W not let thy Holy
Heb 1:12 like a mantle thou W roll them up, and
Rev 6:10 how long before thou W judge and avenge our

WILY (2)

Job 5:13 the schemes of the W are brought to a
Prov 7:10 dressed as a harlot, W of heart.

WIN (14)

2Chr 32:1 fortified cities, thinking to W them for himself.
Ps 44:3 own sword did they W the land, nor did
Eccl 10:12 a wise man's mouth W him favor, but the
1Mac 3:14 name for myself and W honor in the kingdom.
6:44 his people and to W for himself an everlasting
14:35 he had resolved to W for his nation, and
2Mac 4:45 son of Dorymenes to W over the king.
Rom 15:18 wrought through me to W obedience from the
1Cor 9:19 all, that I might W the more.
9:20 Jew, in order to W Jews; to those under
9:20 law--that I might W those under the law.
9:21 Christ--that I might W those outside the law.
9:22 weak, that I might W the weak.
2Jn 1:8 worked for, but may W a full reward.

WIND (154)

Gen 8:1 And God made a W blow over the earth,
41:6 seven ears, thin and blighted by the east W
41:23 blighted by the east W, sprouted after them,
41:27 blighted by the east W are also seven years
Ex 10:13 LORD brought an east W upon the land all
10:13 was morning the east W had brought the locusts.
10:19 a very strong west W, which lifted the locusts
14:21 by a strong east W all night, and made
15:10 didst blow with thy W, the sea covered them;
Num 11:31 there went forth a W from the LORD, and
2Sam 22:11 he was seen upon the wings of the W
1Kgs 18:45 black with clouds and W, and there was a
19:11 a great and strong W rent the mountains, and
19:11 was not in the W; and after the wind
19:11 wind; and after the W an earthquake, but the
2Kgs 3:17 'You shall not see W or rain, but that
Job 1:19 and behold, a great W came across the wilderness,
6:26 when the speech of a despairing man is W
8:2 the words of your mouth be a great W
15:2 windy knowledge, and fill himself with the east W
15:30 his blossom will be swept away by the W
21:18 like straw before the W, and like chaff that
26:13 By his W the heavens were made fair; his
27:21 The east W lifts him up and he is
28:25 he gave to the W its weight, and meted

W

30:15 pursued as by the W, and my prosperity has
30:22 me up on the W, thou makest me ride
37:17 the earth is still because of the south W
37:21 the skies, when the W has passed and cleared
38:24 or where the east W is scattered upon the
Ps 1:4 like chaff which the W drives away.
11:6 and brimstone; a scorching W shall be the portion
18:10 he came swiftly upon the wings of the W
18:42 as dust before the W; I cast them out
35:5 like chaff before the W, with the angel of
48:7 By the east W thou didst shatter the ships
55:8 shelter from the raging W and tempest."
78:26 He caused the east W to blow in the
78:26 led out the south W;
78:39 were but flesh, a W that passes and comes
83:13 them like whirling dust, like chaff before the W
103:16 the field; for the W passes over it, and
104:3 the wings of the W,
107:25 and raised the stormy W, which lifted up the
135:7 and brings forth the W from his storehouses.
147:18 them; he makes his W blow, and the waters
148:8 snow and frost, stormy W fulfilling his command!
Prov 11:29 his household will inherit W, and the fool will
25:14 Like clouds and W without rain is a man
25:23 The north W brings forth rain; and a backbiting
27:16 is to restrain the W or to grasp oil
30:4 Who has gathered the W in his fists?
Eccl 1:6 The W blows to the south, and goes round
1:6 and round goes the W, and on its circuits
1:6 on its circuits the W returns.
1:14 behold, all is vanity and a striving after W
1:17 that this also is but a striving after W
2:11 and a striving after W, and there was nothing
2:17 for all is vanity and a striving after W
2:26 This also is vanity and a striving after W
4:4 This also is vanity and a striving after W
4:6 hands full of toil and a striving after W
4:16 this also is vanity and a striving after W
5:16 he toiled for the W,
6:9 this also is vanity and a striving after W
11:4 He who observes the W will not sow; and
Song 4:16 Awake, O north W, and come, O south wind!
4:16 Awake, O north wind, and come, O south W
Wis 4:4 be shaken by the W, and by the violence
5:14 chaff carried by the W, and like a light
5:14 like smoke before the W, and it passes like
5:23 overwhelm them; a mighty W will rise against them,
13:2 that either fire or W or swift air, or
17:18 there came a whistling W, or a melodious sound
Sir 5:9 not winnow with every W, nor follow every path:
22:16 stand firm against the W; so a timid heart
34:2 shadow and pursues the W, so is he who
34:16 shelter from the hot W and a shade from
43:16 his will the south W blows.
43:20 The cold north W blows, and ice freezes over
Is 7:2 the trees of the forest shake before the W
11:15 River with his scorching W, and smite it into
17:13 the mountains before the W and whirling dust before
26:18 writhed, we have as it were brought forth W
27:8 fierce blast in the day of the east W
32:2 hiding place from the W, a covert from the
41:16 winnow them and the W shall carry them away,
41:29 works are nothing; their molten images are empty W
49:10 or thirst, neither scorching W nor sun shall smite
57:13 The W will carry them off, a breath will
59:19 rushing stream, which the W of the LORD drives.
64:6 our iniquities, like the W, take us away.
Jer 2:24 to the wilderness, in her heat sniffing the W
4:11 to Jerusalem, "A hot W from the bare heights
4:12 winnow or cleanse, a W too full for this
5:13 The prophets will become W; the word is not
10:13 he brings forth the W from his storehouses.
13:24 chaff driven by the W from the desert.
18:17 Like the east W I will scatter them before
22:22 The W shall shepherd all your shepherds, and your
49:32 will scatter to every W those who cut the
51:16 he brings forth the W from his storehouses.
Bar 6:61 widely seen; and the W likewise blows in every
Ezek 1:4 looked, behold, a stormy W came out of the
5:2 shall scatter to the W, and I will unsheathe
12:14 will scatter toward every W all who are round
13:11 fall, and a stormy W break out;
13:13 will make a stormy W break out in my
17:10 wither when the east W strikes it—wither away
17:21 be scattered to every W; and you shall know
19:12 the ground; the east W dried it up; its
27:26 The east W has wrecked you in the heart
Dan 2:35 threshing floors; and the W carried them away, so
3:50 like a moist whistling W, so that the fire
14:36 rushing sound of the W itself.
Hos 4:19 A W has wrapped them in its wings, and
8:7 For they sow the W, and they shall reap
12:1 Ephraim herds the W, and pursues the east wind
12:1 and pursues the east W all day long; they
13:15 reed plant, the east W, the wind of the
13:15 the east wind, the W of the LORD, shall
Amos 4:13 mountains, and creates the W, and declares to man
Jon 1:4 LORD hurled a great W upon the sea, and
4:8 appointed a sultry east W, and the sun beat
Mic 2:11 go about and utter W and lies, saying, "I
Hab 1:11 sweep by like the W and go on, guilty
Zech 5:9 The W was in their wings; they had wings
Mt 11:7 A reed shaken by the W
14:24 the waves; for the W was against them.
14:30 when he saw the W, he was afraid, and
14:32 into the boat, the W ceased.
Mk 4:37 a great storm of W arose, and the waves
4:39 awoke and rebuked the W, and said to the
4:39 And the W ceased, and there was a great
4:41 is this, that even W and sea obey him?"
6:48 headway painfully, for the W was against them.
6:51 with them and the W ceased.
Lk 7:24 A reed shaken by the W
8:23 And a storm of W came down on the
8:24 awoke and rebuked the W and the raging waves;
8:25 that he commands even W and water, and they
12:55 you see the south W blowing, you say, 'There
Jn 3:8 be born anew.' The W blows where it wills,
6:18 rose because a strong W was blowing.
Acts 2:2 rush of a mighty W, and it filled all
27:7 Cnidus, and as the W did not allow us
27:13 And when the south W blew gently, supposing that
27:14 But soon a tempestuous W, called the northeaster,
27:15 could not face the W, we gave way to
27:40 the foresail to the W they made for the
28:13 one day a south W sprang up, and on
Eph 4:14 carried about with every W of doctrine, by the
Jas 1:6 sea that is driven and tossed by the W
Rev 7:1 the earth, that no W might blow on earth

WINDFALL (3)

Sir 20:8 in adversity, and a W may result in a
29:4 a loan as a W, and cause trouble to
29:6 back half, and will regard that as a W

WINDOW (23)

Gen 8:6 days Noah opened the W of the ark which
26:8 looked out of a W and saw Isaac fondling
Josh 2:15 a rope through the W, for her house was
2:18 scarlet cord in the W through which you let
2:21 and she bound the scarlet cord in the W
Judg 5:28 "Out of the W she peered, the mother of
1Sam 19:12 David down through the W; and he fled away
2Sam 6:16 looked out of the W, and saw King David
1Kgs 7:4 There were W frames in three rows, and window
7:4 in three rows, and W opposite window in three
7:4 rows, and window opposite W in three tiers.
7:5 had square frames, and W was opposite window in
7:5 and window was opposite W in three tiers.
2Kgs 9:30 adorned her head, and looked out of the W
9:32 his face to the W, and said, "Who is
13:17 he said, "Open the W eastward"; and he opened
1Chr 15:29 looked out of the W, and saw King David
Tob 3:11 she prayed by her W and said, "Blessed art
Prov 7:6 For at the W of my house I have
Hos 13:3 the threshing floor or like smoke from a W
Zeph 2:14 shall hoot in the W, the raven croak on
Acts 20:9 young man named Eutychus was sitting in the W
2Cor 11:33 a basket through a W in the wall, and

WINDOWS (29)

Gen 7:11 burst forth, and the W of the heavens were
8:2 the deep and the W of the heavens were
1Kgs 6:4 made for the house W with recessed frames.
7:5 All the doorways and W had square frames, and
2Kgs 7:2 LORD himself should make W in heaven, could this
7:19 LORD himself should make W in heaven, could such
Eccl 12:3 that look through the W are dimmed,
Song 2:9 gazing in at the W, looking through the lattice.
Sir 14:23 who peers through her W will also listen at
Is 24:18 For the W of heaven are opened, and the
60:8 like a cloud, and like doves to their W

W

4:10 is your love than W, and the fragrance of
5:1 honey, I drink my W with my milk.
7:2 is a rounded bowl that never lacks mixed W
7:9 kisses like the best W that goes down smoothly,
8:2 would give you spiced W to drink, the juice
Wis 2:7 our fill of costly W and perfumes, and let
Sir 9:9 revel with her at W; lest your heart turn
9:10 friend is like new W; when it has aged
19:2 W and women lead intelligent men astray, and the
31:25 to be valiant over W, for wine has destroyed
31:25 valiant over wine, for W has destroyed many.
31:26 temper of steel, so W tests hearts in the
31:27 W is like life to men, if you drink
31:27 is life to a man who is without W
31:28 W drunk in season and temperately is rejoicing of
31:29 W drunk to excess is bitterness of soul, with
31:31 at a banquet of W, and do not despise
32:5 a concert of music at a banquet of W
32:6 gold is the melody of music with good W
33:16 grape-gatherer I filled my W press.
40:20 W and music gladden the heart, but the love
49:1 mouth, and like music at a banquet of W
Is 1:22 has become dross, your W mixed with water.
5:2 and hewed out a W vat in it; and
5:11 into the evening till W inflames them!
5:12 timbrel and flute and W at their feasts; but
5:22 are heroes at drinking W, and valiant men in
16:10 no treader treads out W in the presses; the
22:13 oxen and killing sheep, eating flesh and drinking W
24:7 W mourns, the vine languishes, all the merry-hearted
24:9 more do they drink W with singing; strong drink
24:11 streets for lack of W; all joy has reached
25:6 things, a feast of W on the lees, of
25:6 full of marrow, of W on the lees well
28:1 of the rich valley of those overcome with W
28:7 These also reel with W and stagger with strong
28:7 they are confused with W, they stagger with strong
29:9 drunk, but not with W; stagger, but not with
36:17 land of grain and W, a land of bread
49:26 be drunk with their own blood as with W
51:21 drunk, but not with W:
55:1 Come, buy W and milk without money and without
56:12 say, "let us get W, let us fill ourselves
62:8 shall not drink your W for which you have
63:2 that treads in the W press?
63:3 "I have trodden the W press alone, and from
65:8 the LORD: "As the W is found in the
65:11 fill cups of mixed W for Destiny;
Jer 13:12 shall be filled with W And they will say
13:12 will be filled with W
23:9 a man overcome by W, because of the LORD
25:15 this cup of the W of wrath, and make
31:12 over the grain, the W, and the oil, and
35:2 chambers; then offer them W to drink."
35:5 Rechabites pitchers full of W, and cups; and I
35:5 and cups; and I said to them, "Drink W
35:6 "We will drink no W, for Jonadab the son
35:6 'You shall not drink W, neither you nor your
35:8 us, to drink no W all our days, ourselves,
35:14 sons, to drink no W, has been kept; and
40:10 as for you, gather W and summer fruits and
40:12 Mizpah; and they gathered W and summer fruits in
48:33 I have made the W cease from the wine
48:33 wine cease from the W presses; no one treads
51:7 nations drank of her W, therefore the nations went
Lam 1:15 trodden as in a W press the virgin daughter
2:12 cry to their mothers, "Where is bread and W
Ezek 27:18 wealth of every kind; W of Helbon, and white
27:19 and white wool, and W from Uzal they exchanged
44:21 No priest shall drink W, when he enters the
Dan 1:5 ate, and of the W which he drank.
1:8 food, or with the W which he drank; therefore
1:16 rich food and the W they were to drink,
5:1 his lords, and drank W in front of the
5:2 when he tasted the W, commanded that the vessels
5:4 They drank W, and praised the gods of gold
5:23 your concubines have drunk W from them; and you
10:3 delicacies, no meat or W entered my mouth, nor
14:3 flour and forty sheep and fifty gallons of W
14:11 mix and place the W, and shut the door
Hos 2:8 her the grain, the W, and the oil, and
2:9 its time, and my W in its season; and
2:22 answer the grain, the W, and the oil, and
4:11 W and new wine take away the understanding.
4:11 Wine and new W take away the understanding.
7:6 with the heat of W; he stretched out his
7:15 beds; for grain and W they gash themselves, they
9:2 them, and the new W shall fail them.
9:4 not pour libations of W to the LORD; and
14:7 shall be like the W of Lebanon.
Joel 1:5 all you drinkers of W, because of the sweet
1:5 because of the sweet W, for it is cut
1:10 grain is destroyed, the W fails, the oil languishes.
2:19 sending to you grain, W, and oil, and you
2:24 vats shall overflow with W and oil.
3:3 sold a girl for W, and have drunk it.
3:13 in, tread, for the W press is full.
3:18 mountains shall drip sweet W, and the hills shall
Amos 2:8 God they drink the W of those who have
2:12 made the Nazirites drink W, and commanded the
5:11 pleasant vineyards, but you shall not drink their W
6:6 of music; who drink W in bowls, and anoint
9:13 mountains shall drip sweet W, and all the hills
9:14 vineyards and drink their W, and they shall make
Mic 2:11 preach to you of W and strong drink," he
6:15 oil; you shall tread grapes, but not drink W
Hab 2:5 Moreover, W is treacherous; the arrogant man shall
Zeph 1:13 they shall not drink W from them."
Hag 1:11 the grain, the new W, the oil, upon what
2:12 bread, or pottage, or W, or oil, or any
Zech 9:15 drink their blood like W, and be full like
9:17 men flourish, and new W the maidens.
10:7 and their hearts shall be glad as with W
14:10 Hananel to the king's W presses.
2Mac 15:39 is harmful to drink W alone, or, again, to
15:39 drink water alone, while W mixed with water is
Mt 9:17 Neither is new W put into old wineskins; if
9:17 skins burst, and the W is spilled, and the
9:17 are destroyed; but new W is put into fresh
21:33 it, and dug a W press in it, and
27:34 skull), they offered him W to drink, mingled with
Mk 2:22 no one puts new W into old wineskins; if
2:22 if he does, the W will burst the skins,
2:22 the skins, and the W is lost, and so
2:22 the skins; but new W is for fresh skins."
12:1 a pit for the W press, and built a
15:23 And they offered him W mingled with myrrh; but
Lk 1:15 he shall drink no W nor strong drink, and
5:37 no one puts new W into old wineskins; if
5:37 he does, the new W will burst the skins
5:38 But new W must be put into fresh wineskins.
5:39 one after drinking old W desires new; for he
7:33 bread and drinking no W; and you say, 'He
10:34 pouring on oil and W; then he set him
Jn 2:3 When the W failed, the mother of Jesus said
2:3 of Jesus said to him, "They have no W
2:9 the water now become W, and did not know
2:10 man serves the good W first; and when men
2:10 freely, then the poor W; but you have kept
2:10 have kept the good W until now."
4:46 in Galilee, where he had made the water W
Acts 2:13 others mocking said, "They are filled with new W
Rom 14:21 eat meat or drink W or do anything that
Eph 5:18 not get drunk with W, for that is debauchery;
1Tim 3:8 not addicted to much W, not greedy for gain;
5:23 but use a little W for the sake of
Rev 6:6 a denarius; but do not harm oil and W
14:8 all nations drink the W of her impure passion."
14:10 also shall drink the W of God's wrath, poured
14:19 it into the great W press of the wrath
14:20 of God; and the W press was trodden outside
14:20 blood flowed from the W press, as high as
17:2 fornication, and with the W of whose fornication the
18:3 nations have drunk the W of her impure passion,
18:13 spice, incense, myrrh, frankincense, W, oil, fine flour
19:15 he will tread the W press of the fury

WINEBIBBERS

Prov 23:20 Be not among W, or among gluttonous eaters of

WINESKIN

Ps 119:83 have become like a W in the smoke, yet

WINESKINS (8)

Josh 9:4 upon their asses, and W, worn-out and torn and
9:13 dry and moldy; these W were new when we
Job 32:19 no vent; like new W, it is ready to
Mt 9:17 wine put into old W; if it is, the
9:17 is put into fresh W, and so both are
Mk 2:22 new wine into old W; if he does, the
Lk 5:37 new wine into old W; if he does, the
5:38 But new wine must be put into fresh W

W

WINEVAT (2)
Hos 9:2 Threshing floor and W shall not feed them, and
Hag 2:16 one came to the W to draw fifty measures,

WING (19)
1Kgs 6:24 the length of one W of the cherub, and
6:24 length of the other W of the cherub; it
6:24 the tip of one W to the tip of
6:27 out so that a W of one touched the
6:27 one wall, and a W of the other cherub
2Chr 3:11 extended twenty cubits: one W of the one, of
3:11 house, and its other W, of five cubits, touched
3:11 five cubits, touched the W of the other cherub;
3:12 of this cherub, one W, of five cubits, touched
3:12 house, and the other W, also of five cubits,
3:12 was joined to the W of the first cherub.
Is 10:14 none that moved a W, or opened the mouth,
Ezek 1:11 of which touched the W of another, while two
Dan 9:27 cease; and upon the W of abominations shall come
1Mac 9:1 with them the right W of the army.
9:12 Bacchides was on the right W
9:15 they crushed the right W, and he pursued them
9:16 those on the left W saw that the right
9:16 saw that the right W was crushed, they turned

WINGED (9)
Gen 1:21 their kinds, and every W bird according to its
Lev 11:20 "All W insects that go upon all fours are
11:21 Yet among the W insects that go on all
11:23 But all other W insects which have four feet
Deut 4:17 the likeness of any W bird that flies in
14:19 And all W insects are unclean for you; they
14:20 All clean W things you may eat.
Ps 78:27 upon them like dust, W birds like the sand
Eccl 10:20 your voice, or some W creature tell the matter.

WINGS (76)
Ex 19:4 bore you on eagles' W and brought you to
25:20 shall spread out their W above, overshadowing the
25:20 mercy seat with their W, their faces one to
37:9 cherubim spread out their W above, overshadowing
37:9 mercy seat with their W, with their faces one
Lev 1:17 tear it by its W, but shall not divide
Deut 32:11 young, spreading out its W, catching them, bearing
Ruth 2:12 of Israel, under whose W you have come to
2Sam 22:11 was seen upon the W of the wind.
1Kgs 6:27 the house; and the W of the cherubim were
6:27 other wall; their other W touched each other in
8:6 holy place, underneath the W of the cherubim.
8:7 cherubim spread out their W over the place of
1Chr 28:18 cherubim that spread their W and covered the ark
2Chr 3:11 The W of the cherubim together extended twenty
3:13 The W of these cherubim extended twenty cubits;
5:7 holy place, underneath the W of the cherubim.
5:8 cherubim spread out their W over the place of
Job 39:13 "The W of the ostrich wave proudly; but are
39:26 soars, and spreads his W toward the south?
Ps 17:8 the shadow of thy W,
18:10 came swiftly upon the W of the wind.
36:7 men take refuge in the shadow of thy W
55:6 "O that I had W like a dove!
57:1 the shadow of thy W I will take refuge,
61:4 to be safe under the shelter of thy W
63:7 the shadow of thy W I sing for joy.
68:13 the sheepfolds— the W of a dove covered
91:4 pinions, and under his W you will find refuge;
104:3 who ridest on the W of the wind,
139:9 If I take the W of the morning and
Prov 23:5 it takes to itself W, flying like an eagle
Wis 5:11 the movement of its W, and afterward no sign
Sir 34:1 hopes, and dreams give W to fools.
Is 6:2 seraphim; each had six W: with two he covered
8:8 neck; and its outspread W will fill the breadth
18:1 Ah, land of whirring W which is beyond the
40:31 shall mount up with W like eagles, they shall
Jer 48:9 "Give W to Moab, for she would fly away;
48:40 eagle, and spread his W against Moab;
49:22 eagle, and spread his W against Bozrah, and the
Ezek 1:6 four faces, and each of them had four W
1:8 Under their W on their four sides they had
1:8 their faces and their W thus:
1:9 their wings thus: their W touched one another; they
1:11 And their W were spread out above; each creature
1:11 each creature had two W, each of which touched
1:23 under the firmament their W were stretched out
1:23 each creature had two W covering its body.
1:24 the sound of their W like the sound of
1:24 when they stood still, they let down their W
1:25 when they stood still, they let down their W
3:13 the sound of the W of the living creatures
10:5 the sound of the W of the cherubim was
10:8 the form of a human hand under their W
10:16 cherubim lifted up their W to mount up from
10:19 cherubim lifted up their W and mounted up from
10:21 faces, and each four W, and underneath their wings
10:21 and underneath their W the semblance of human
11:22 cherubim lifted up their W, with the wheels beside
17:3 great eagle with great W and long pinions, rich
17:7 great eagle with great W and much plumage; and
Dan 7:4 first was like a lion and had eagles' W
7:4 as I looked its W were plucked off, and
7:6 a leopard, with four W of a bird on
Hos 4:19 wrapped them in its W, and they shall be
Nah 3:16 The locust spreads its W and flies away.
Zech 5:9 wind was in their W; they had wings like
5:9 their wings; they had W like the wings of
5:9 had wings like the W of a stork, and
Mal 4:2 of righteousness shall rise, with healing in its W
Mt 23:36 her brood under her W, and you would not!
Lk 13:34 her brood under her W, and you would not!
Rev 4:8 of them with six W, are full of eyes
9:9 the noise of their W was like the noise
12:14 was given the two W of the great eagle

WINK
Ps 35:19 and let not those W the eye who hate

WINKS (4)
Prov 6:13 about with crooked speech, W with his eyes, scrapes
10:10 He who W the eye causes trouble, but he
16:30 He who W his eyes plans perverse things, he
Sir 27:22 Whoever W his eye plans evil deeds, and no

WINNOW (6)
Wis 5:23 a tempest it will W them away.
Sir 5:9 Do not W with every wind, nor follow every
Is 41:16 like chaff; You shall W them and the wind
Jer 4:11 my people, not to W or cleanse,
51:2 winnowers, and they shall W her, and they shall
Mt 25:24 where you did not W;

WINNOWED (4)
Is 21:10 O my threshed and W one, what I have
30:24 provender, which has been W with shovel and fork.
Jer 15:7 I have W them with a winnowing fork in
Mt 25:26 not sowed, and gather where I have not W

WINNOWERS
Jer 51:2 will send to Babylon W, and they shall winnow

WINNOWING (4)
Ruth 3:2 See, he is W barley tonight at the threshing
Jer 15:7 winnowed them with a W fork in the gates
Mt 3:12 His W fork is in his hand, and he
Lk 3:17 His W fork is in his hand, to clear

WINNOWS (2)
Prov 20:8 the throne of judgment W all evil with his
20:26 A wise king W the wicked, and drives the

WINS
Prov 13:15 Good sense W favor, but the way of the

WINTER (17)
Gen 8:22 and heat, summer and W, day and night, shall
Ps 74:17 of the earth; thou hast made summer and W
Song 2:11 away; for lo, the W is past, the rain
Is 18:6 of the earth will W upon them.
Jer 36:22 was sitting in the W house and there was
Dan 3:68 Bless the Lord, W cold and summer heat, sing
Amos 3:15 I will smite the W house with the summer
Zech 14:8 sea; it shall continue in summer as in W
Mt 24:20 may not be in W or on a sabbath.
Mk 13:18 Pray that it may not happen in W
Jn 10:23 at Jerusalem; it was W, and Jesus was walking
Acts 27:12 was not suitable to W in, the majority advised
27:12 northeast and southeast, and W there.
1Cor 16:6 or even spend the W, so that you may
2Tim 4:21 Do your best to come before W
Tit 3:12 decided to spend the W there.
Rev 6:13 fig tree sheds its W fruit when shaken by

WINTERED

Acts 28:11 a ship which had W in the island, a

WINTRY

Wis 16:29 man will melt like W frost, and flow away

WIPE (14)

2Kgs 21:13 Ahab; and I will W Jerusalem as one wipes
Neh 13:14 God, concerning this, and W not out my good
Ps 83:4 say, "Come, let us W them out as a
94:23 them their iniquity and W them out for their
94:23 LORD our God will W them out.
Sir 36:7 destroy the adversary and W out the enemy.
Is 25:8 the Lord GOD will W away tears from all
1Mac 3:35 force against them to W out and destroy the
2Mac 8:9 of all nations, to W out the whole race
12:8 the same way to W out the Jews who
Lk 10:11 to our feet, we W off against you; nevertheless
Jn 13:5 disciples' feet, and to W them with the towel
Rev 7:17 water; and God will W away every tear from
21:4 with them; he will W away every tear from

WIPED (15)

Josh 10:20 slaughter, until they were W out, and when the
11:21 at that time, and W out the Anakim from
2Kgs 10:17 Samaria, till he had W them out, according to
10:28 Thus Jehu W out Baal from Israel.
Prov 6:33 disgrace will not be W away.
Sir 46:18 mighty sound; and he W out the leaders of
47:7 For he W out his enemies on every side,
48:21 Assyrians, and his angel W them out.
Is 26:14 them with destruction and W out all remembrance of
Bar 6:13 robes, their faces are W because of the dust
Ezek 6:6 down, and your works W out.
Lk 7:38 with her tears, and W them with the hair
7:44 with her tears and W them with her hair.
Jn 11:2 Lord with ointment and W his feet with her
12:3 feet of Jesus and W his feet with her

WIPES (3)

2Kgs 21:13 wipe Jerusalem as one W a dish, wiping it
Prov 30:20 adulteress: she eats, and W her mouth, and says,
Bar 6:24 shine unless some one W off the rust; for

WIPING

2Kgs 21:13 one wipes a dish, W it and turning it

WISDOM (330)

Deut 4:6 that will be your W and your understanding in
34:9 of the spirit of W, for Moses had laid
2Sam 14:20 But my lord has W like the wisdom of
14:20 has wisdom like the W of the angel of
20:22 woman went to all the people in her W
1Kgs 2:6 therefore according to your W, but do not let
3:28 they perceived that the W of God was in
4:29 And God gave Solomon W and understanding beyond
4:30 seashore, so that Solomon's W surpassed the wisdom
4:30 Solomon's wisdom surpassed the W of all the people
4:30 east, and all the W of Egypt.
4:34 peoples to hear the W of Solomon, and from
4:34 of the earth, who had heard of his W
5:12 the LORD gave Solomon W, as he promised him;
7:14 he was full of W, understanding, and skill, for
10:4 had seen all the W of Solomon, the house
10:6 affairs and of your W,
10:7 not told me; your W and prosperity surpass the
10:8 who continually stand before you and hear your W
10:23 kings of the earth in riches and in W
10:24 Solomon to hear his W, which God had put
11:41 he did, and his W, are they not written
2Chr 1:10 Give me now W and knowledge to go out
1:11 life, but have asked W and knowledge for yourself
1:12 have made you king, W and knowledge are granted
9:3 Sheba had seen the W of Solomon, the house
9:5 affairs and of your W,
9:6 the greatness of your W was not told me;
9:7 who continually stand before you and hear your W
9:22 kings of the earth in riches and in W
9:23 Solomon to hear his W, which God had put
Ezra 7:25 Ezra, according to the W of your God which
Jud 8:29 the first time your W has been shown, but
11:8 have heard of your W and skill, and it
11:20 they marveled at her W and said,
11:21 beauty of face or W of speech!"
Job 4:21 die, and that without W
11:6 that he would tell you the secrets of W
12:2 are the people, and W will die with you.
12:12 W is with the aged, and understanding in length
12:13 "With God are W and might; he has counsel
12:16 him are strength and W; the deceived and the
13:5 would keep silent, and it would be your W
15:8 And do you limit W to yourself?
26:3 him who has no W, and plentifully declared sound
28:12 "But where shall W be found?
28:18 crystal; the price of W is above pearls.
28:20 "Whence then comes W
28:28 the Lord, that is W; and to depart from
32:7 and many years teach W
32:13 say, 'We have found W; God may vanquish him,
33:33 me; be silent, and I will teach you W
38:36 Who has put W in the clouds, or given
38:37 Who can number the clouds by W
39:17 has made her forget W, and given her no
39:26 "Is it by your W that the hawk soars,
Ps 37:30 of the righteous utters W, and his tongue speaks
49:3 My mouth shall speak W; the meditation of my
51:6 being; therefore teach me W in my secret heart.
90:12 days that we may get a heart of W
104:24 In W hast thou made them all; the earth
105:22 at his pleasure, and to teach his elders W
111:10 is the beginning of W; a good understanding have
Prov 1:2 That men may know W and instruction, understand
1:7 of knowledge; fools despise W and instruction.
1:19 W's Warning
1:20 Wisdom's Warning W cries aloud in the street; in
2:2 your ear attentive to W and inclining your heart
2:6 For the LORD gives W; from his mouth come
2:7 he stores up sound W for the upright; he
2:10 every good path; for W will come into your
3:12 W's Value
3:13 the man who finds W, and the man who
3:19 The LORD by W founded the earth; by understanding
3:21 My son, keep sound W and discretion; let them
4:1 The Supreme Guidance of W
4:6 and live; "Get W, get understanding!" do not
4:8 The beginning of W is this: Get wisdom, and
4:8 wisdom is this: Get W, and whatever you get,
4:12 you the way of W; I have led you
5:1 be attentive to my W, incline your ear to
7:4 Say to W, "You are my sister," and call
8:1 Does not W call, does not understanding raise her
8:11 than choice gold; for W is better than jewels,
8:12 I, W, dwell in prudence, and I find knowledge
8:14 have counsel and sound W, I have insight, I
9:1 W has built her house, she has set up
9:10 is the beginning of W, and the knowledge of
10:13 him who has understanding W is found, but a
10:31 the righteous brings forth W, but the perverse tongue
11:2 then comes disgrace; but with the humble is W
13:10 strife, but with those who take advice is W
14:1 W builds her house, but folly with her own
14:6 A scoffer seeks W in vain, but knowledge is
14:8 The W of a prudent man is to discern
14:24 the wise is their W, but folly is the
14:33 W abides in the mind of a man of
15:33 LORD is instruction in W, and humility goes before
16:16 To get W is better than gold; to get
16:22 W is a fountain of life to him who
17:16 his hand to buy W, when he has no
17:24 sets his face toward W, but the eyes of
18:4 waters; the fountain of W is a gushing stream.
19:8 He who gets W loves himself; he who keeps
19:20 that you may gain W for the future.
21:30 No W, no understanding, no counsel, can avail
23:9 he will despise the W of your words.
23:23 not sell it; buy W, instruction, and understanding.
24:3 By W a house is built, and by understanding
24:7 W is too high for a fool; in the
24:14 Know that W is such to your soul; if
28:26 he who walks in W will be delivered.
29:3 He who loves W makes his father glad, but
29:15 rod and reproof give W, but a child left
30:3 I have not learned W, nor have I knowledge
31:26 opens her mouth with W, and the teaching of
Eccl 1:13 to search out by W all that is done
1:16 "I have acquired great W, surpassing all who were
1:16 had great experience of W and knowledge."
1:17 my mind to know W and to know madness
1:18 For in much W is much vexation, and he
2:3 still guiding me with W—and how to lay
2:9 in Jerusalem; also my W remained with me.
2:12 I turned to consider W and madness and folly;

2:13 Then I saw that W excels folly as light
2:19 toiled and used my W under the sun.
2:21 who has toiled with W and knowledge and skill
2:26 pleases him God gives W and knowledge and joy;
7:10 it is not from W that you ask this.
7:11 W is good with an inheritance, an advantage to
7:12 For the protection of W is like the protection
7:12 of knowledge is that W preserves the life of
7:19 W gives strength to the wise man more than
7:23 I have tested by W; I said, "I will
7:25 out and to seek W and the sum of
8:1 A man's W makes his face shine, and the
8:16 my mind to know W, and to see the
9:10 thought or knowledge or W in Sheol, to which
9:13 seen this example of W under the sun, and
9:15 and he by his W delivered the city.
9:16 But I say that W is better than might,
9:16 though the poor man's W is despised, and his
9:18 W is better than weapons of war, but one
10:1 a little folly outweighs W and honor.
10:10 forth more strength; but W helps one to succeed.
Wis 1:4 convicts the foolish; because W will not enter a
1:6 For W is a kindly spirit and will not
3:11 Lord; for whoever despises W and instruction is
6:9 that you may learn W and not transgress.
6:12 W is radiant and unfading, and she is easily
6:17 The beginning of W is the most sincere desire
6:20 so the desire for W leads to a kingdom.
6:21 over the peoples, honor W, that you may reign
6:22 will tell you what W is and how she
6:23 sickly envy, for envy does not associate with W
7:7 and the spirit of W came to me.
7:12 in them all, because W leads them; but I
7:15 the guide even of W and the corrector of
7:22 what is manifest, for W, the fashioner of all
7:24 For W is more mobile than any motion; because
7:28 so much as the man who lives with W
7:30 the night, but against W evil does not prevail.
8:5 what is richer than W who effects all things?
8:17 that in kinship with W there is immortality,
8:21 I would not possess W unless God gave her
9:2 word, and by thy W hast formed man, to
9:4 soul, give me the W that sits by thy
9:6 men, yet without the W that comes from thee
9:9 With thee is W, who knows thy works and
9:17 unless thou hast given W and sent thy holy
9:18 taught what pleases thee, and were saved by W
10:1 W protected the first-formed father of the world,
10:4 flooded because of him, W again saved it, steering
10:5 W also, when the nations in wicked agreement had
10:6 W rescued a righteous man when the ungodly were
10:8 For because they passed W by, they not only
10:9 W rescued from troubles those who served her.
10:13 righteous man was sold, W did not desert him,
10:15 and blameless race W delivered from a nation
10:21 thy defending hand, because W opened the mouth of
11:1 W prospered their works by the hand of a
14:2 planned that vessel, and W was the craftsman who
14:5 that works of thy W should not be without
17:7 and their boasted W was scornfully rebuked.
Sir 1:1 All W comes from the Lord
1:3 earth, the abyss, and W—who can search them
1:4 W was created before all things, and prudent
1:5 The root of W—to whom has it been
1:7 The Lord himself created W; he saw her and
1:12 is the beginning of W she is created with
1:14 fear the Lord is W's full measure; she satisfies
1:16 is the crown of W, making peace and perfect
1:18 is the root of W, and her branches are
1:22 In the treasuries of W are wise sayings, but
1:23 If you desire W, keep the commandments, and the
1:24 of the Lord is W and instruction, and he
4:11 W exalts her sons and gives help to those
4:23 the crucial time, and do not hide your W
4:24 For W is known through speech, and education
6:18 until you are old you will keep finding W
6:22 For W is like her name, and is not
6:37 and your desire for W will be granted.
7:5 Lord, nor display your W before the king.
10:25 a display of your W when you do your
11:1 The W of a humble man will lift up
14:20 man who meditates on W and who reasons
14:22 Pursue W like a hunter, and lie in wait
15:1 he who holds to the law will obtain W
15:3 him the water of W to drink.
15:10 should be uttered in W, and the Lord will
15:18 For great is the W of the Lord; he
18:27 Every intelligent man knows W, and he praises the
19:18 All W is the fear of the Lord, and
19:18 Lord, and in all W there is the fulfilment
19:19 of wickedness is not W, nor is there prudence
19:20 but there is a fool who merely lacks W
20:29 Hidden W and unseen treasure, what advantage is
20:30 his folly than the man who hides his W
21:11 controls his thoughts, and W is the fulfilment of
21:18 has vanished, so is W to a fool; and
22:6 chastising and discipline are W at all times.
23:2 and the discipline of W over my mind!
24:1 W will praise herself, and will glory in the
24:23 It fills men with W, like the Pishon, and
25:5 How attractive is W in the aged, and understanding
25:10 How great is he who has gained W
34:8 will be fulfilled, and W is made perfect in
37:21 the Lord, since he is lacking in all W
38:24 The W of the scribe depends on the opportunity
39:1 will seek out the W of all the ancients,
39:6 pour forth words of W and give thanks to
39:10 Nations will declare his W, and the congregation will
40:20 but the love of W is better than both.
41:14 be at peace; hidden W and unseen treasure, what
41:15 his folly than the man who hides his W
42:21 the splendors of his W, and he is from
43:33 things, and to the godly he has granted W
44:16 Peoples will declare their W, and the congregation
45:26 the Lord grant you W in your heart to
50:27 Jerusalem, who out of his heart poured forth W
51:13 my travels, I sought W openly in my prayer.
51:17 to him who gives W I will give glory.
51:18 to live according to W, and I was zealous
51:19 My soul grappled with W, and in my conduct
Is 10:13 it, and by my W, for I have understanding;
11:2 him, the spirit of W and understanding, the spirit
28:29 he is wonderful in counsel, and excellent in W
29:14 and marvelous; and the W of their wise men
33:6 times, abundance of salvation, W, and knowledge;
47:10 one sees me"; your W and your knowledge led
Jer 8:9 the LORD, and what W is in them?
9:23 man glory in his W, let not the mighty
10:12 the world by his W, and by his understanding
49:7 LORD of hosts: "Is W no more in Teman?
49:7 Has their W vanished?
51:15 the world by his W, and by his understanding
Bar 3:9 of life, O Israel; give ear, and learn W
3:12 You have forsaken the fountain of W
3:14 Learn where there is W, where there is strength,
3:23 learned the way to W, nor given thought to
3:28 because they had no W, they perished through their
Ezek 28:4 from you; by your W and your understanding you
28:5 treasuries; by your great W in trade you have
28:7 the beauty of your W and defile your splendor.
28:12 of perfection, full of W and perfect in beauty.
28:17 beauty; you corrupted your W for the sake of
Dan 1:4 and skillful in all W, endowed with knowledge,
1:17 in all letters and W; and Daniel had understanding
1:20 in every matter of W and understanding concerning
2:20 to whom belong W and might.
2:21 up kings; he gives W to the wise and
2:23 thou hast given me W and strength, and hast
2:30 not because of any W that I have more
5:11 light and understanding and W, like the wisdom of
5:11 and wisdom, like the W of the gods, were
5:14 and understanding and excellent W are found in you.
9:22 out to give you W and understanding.
Mic 6:9 and it is sound W to fear thy name:
2Mac 2:9 that being possessed of W Solomon offered sacrifice
Mt 11:19 collectors and sinners!' Yet W is justified by her
12:42 earth to hear the W of Solomon, and behold,
13:54 this man get this W and these mighty works?
Mk 6:2 What is the W given to him?
Lk 1:17 the disobedient to the W of the just, to
2:40 became strong, filled with W; and the favor of
2:52 And Jesus increased in W and in stature, and
7:35 collectors and sinners!' Yet W is justified by all
11:31 earth to hear the W of Solomon, and behold,
11:49 Therefore also the W of God said, 'I will
21:15 you a mouth and W, which none of your
Acts 6:3 the Spirit and of W, whom we may appoint
6:10 could not withstand the W and the Spirit with
7:10 gave him favor and W before Pharaoh, king of
7:22 instructed in all the W of the Egyptians, and
Rom 11:33 of the riches and W and knowledge of God!
1Cor 1:17 and not with eloquent W, lest the cross of

1:19 "I will destroy the W of the wise, and
1:20 God made foolish the W of the world?
1:21 For since, in the W of God, the world
1:21 not know God through W, it pleased God through
1:22 signs and Greeks seek W,
1:24 of God and the W of God.
1:30 whom God made our W, our righteousness and
2:1 the testimony of God in lofty words or W
2:4 in plausible words of W, but in demonstration of
2:5 not rest in the W of men but in
2:6 mature we do impart W, although it is not
2:6 it is not a W of this age or
2:7 a secret and hidden W of God, which God
2:13 not taught by human W but taught by the
3:19 For the W of this world is folly with
12:8 Spirit the utterance of W, and to another the
2Cor 1:12 sincerity, not by earthly W but by the grace
Eph 1:9 to us in all W and insight the mystery
1:17 you a spirit of W and of revelation in
3:10 the church the manifold W of God might now
Col 1:9 will in all spiritual W and understanding,
1:28 every man in all W, that we may present
2:3 all the treasures of W and knowledge.
2:23 indeed an appearance of W in promoting rigor of
3:16 one another in all W, and sing psalms and
Jas 1:5 any of you lacks W, let him ask God,
3:13 him show his works in the meekness of W
3:15 This W is not such as comes down from
3:17 But the W from above is first pure, then
2Pet 3:15 you according to the W given him,
Rev 5:12 power and wealth and W and might and honor
7:12 Blessing and glory and W and thanksgiving and
13:18 This calls for W: let him who has understanding
17:9 for a mind with W: the seven heads are

WISE (228)

Gen 3:6 desired to make one W, she took of its
41:8 Egypt and all its W men; and Pharaoh told
41:33 a man discreet and W, and set him over
41:39 none so discreet and W as you are;
Ex 7:11 Then Pharaoh summoned the W men and the
Deut 1:13 Choose W, understanding, and experienced men,
1:15 heads of your tribes, W and experienced men, and
4:6 great nation is a W and understanding people.'
16:19 the eyes of the W and subverts the cause
32:29 If they were W, they would understand this, they
2Sam 14:2 fetched from there a W woman, and said to
20:16 Then a W woman called from the city, "Hear!
1Kgs 2:9 for you are a W man; you will know
3:12 I give you a W and discerning mind, so
5:7 given to David a W son to be over
2Chr 2:12 given King David a W son, endued with discretion
Tob 4:18 Seek advice from every W man, and do not
Jud 11:23 beautiful in appearance, but W in speech; and if
Esth 1:13 king said to the W men who knew the
6:13 Then his W men and his wife Zeresh said
Job 5:13 He takes the W in their own craftiness; and
9:4 He is W in heart, and mighty in strength
15:2 answered: "Should a W man answer with windy
15:18 I will declare (what W men have told, and
17:10 shall not find a W man among you.
22:2 Surely he who is W is profitable to himself.
32:9 the old that are W, nor the aged that
32:11 I listened for your W sayings, while you searched
34:2 "Hear my words, you W men, and give ear
34:34 to me, and the W man who hears me
37:24 regard any who are W in their own conceit."
Ps 2:10 therefore, O kings, be W; be warned, O rulers
19:7 LORD is sure, making W the simple;
49:10 see that even the W die, the fool and
53:2 are any that are W, that seek after God.
94:8 Fools, when will you be W
107:43 Whoever is W, let him give heed to these
Prov 1:3 , receive instruction in W dealing, righteousness,
1:5 the youth-- the W man also may hear
1:6 the words of the W and their riddles.
3:7 Be not W in your own eyes; fear the
3:35 The W will inherit honor, but fools get disgrace.
6:6 ant, O sluggard; consider her ways, and be W
8:33 Hear instruction and be W, and do not neglect
9:8 hate you; reprove a W man, and he will
9:9 Give instruction to a W man, and he will
9:12 If you are W, you are wise for yourself;
9:12 are wise, you are W for yourself; if you
10:1 A W son makes a glad father, but a
10:8 The W of heart will heed commandments, but a
10:14 W men lay up knowledge, but the babbling of
10:23 to do wrong, but W conduct is pleasure to
11:29 and the fool will be servant to the W
12:15 own eyes, but a W man listens to advice.
12:18 the tongue of the W brings healing.
13:1 A W son hears his father's instruction, but a
13:14 The teaching of the W is a fountain of
13:20 He who walks with W men becomes wise, but
13:20 with wise men becomes W, but the companion of
14:3 the lips of the W will preserve them.
14:16 A W man is cautious and turns away from
14:24 The crown of the W is their wisdom, but
15:2 The tongue of the W dispenses knowledge, but the
15:7 The lips of the W spread knowledge; not so
15:12 be reproved; he will not go to the W
15:20 A W son makes a glad father, but a
15:24 The W man's path leads upward to life, that
15:31 wholesome admonition will abide among the W
16:14 of death, and a W man will appease it.
16:21 The W of heart is called a man of
16:23 The mind of the W makes his speech judicious,
17:28 keeps silent is considered W; when he closes his
18:15 the ear of the W seeks knowledge.
20:1 whoever is led astray by it is not W
20:18 established by counsel; by W guidance wage war.
20:26 A W king winnows the wicked, and drives the
21:11 punished, the simple becomes W; when a wise man
21:11 becomes wise; when a W man is instructed, he
21:20 treasure remains in a W man's dwelling, but a
21:22 A W man scales the city of the mighty
22:17 the words of the W, and apply your mind
23:4 to acquire wealth; be W enough to desist.
23:15 if your heart is W, my heart too will
23:19 my son, and be W, and direct your mind
23:24 he who begets a W son will be glad
24:5 A W man is mightier than a strong man,
24:6 has strength; for by W guidance you can wage
24:23 These also are sayings of the W
25:12 of gold is a W reprover to a listening
26:5 folly, lest he be W in his own eyes.
26:12 a man who is W in his own eyes?
27:11 Be W, my son, and make my heart glad,
28:7 the law is a W son, but a companion
28:11 A rich man is W in his own eyes,
29:8 a city aflame, but W men turn away wrath.
29:9 If a W man has an argument with a
29:11 his anger, but a W man quietly holds it
30:24 but they are exceedingly W:
Eccl 2:14 The W man has his eyes in his head,
2:15 also; why then have I been so very W
2:16 For of the W man as of the fool
2:16 How the W man dies just like the fool!
2:19 he will be a W man or a fool?
4:13 is a poor and W youth than an old
6:8 what advantage has the W man over the fool?
7:4 The heart of the W is in the house
7:5 the rebuke of the W than to hear the
7:7 Surely oppression makes the W man foolish, and a
7:19 gives strength to the W man more than ten
7:23 said, "I will be W; but it was far
8:1 Who is like the W man?
8:5 the mind of a W man will know the
8:17 out; even though a W man claims to know,
9:1 the righteous and the W and their deeds are
9:11 nor bread to the W, nor riches to the
9:15 in it a poor W man, and he by
9:17 The words of the W heard in quiet are
10:2 A W man's heart inclines him toward the right,
10:12 The words of a W man's mouth win him
12:9 Besides being W, the Preacher also taught the
12:11 The sayings of the W are like goads, and
Wis 4:17 the end of the W man, and will not
6:24 A multitude of W men is the salvation of
7:15 even of wisdom and the corrector of the W
Sir 1:6 is One who is W, greatly to be feared,
1:22 treasuries of wisdom are W sayings, but godliness is
3:27 attentive ear is the W man's desire.
6:33 if you incline your ear you will become W
6:34 Who is W
6:35 and do not let W proverbs escape you.
7:19 deprive yourself of a W and good wife, for
9:14 to know your neighbors, and consult with the W
9:17 people's leader is proved W by his words.
10:1 A W magistrate will educate his people, and the
10:24 the service of a W servant, and a man
18:26 A W man is cautious in everything, and in

20:1 is a man who keeps silent but is W
20:4 keeping silent is found W, while another is detested
20:6 A W man will be silent until the right
20:12 The W man makes himself beloved through his
20:28 the eyes of the W; like a muzzle on
21:13 The knowledge of a W man will increase like
21:15 of understanding hears a W saying, he will praise
21:26 but the mouth of W men is in their
27:11 godly man is always W, but the fool changes
33:2 A W man will not hate the law, but
37:22 A man may be W to his own advantage,
37:23 A W man will instruct his own people, and
37:24 A W man will have praise heaped upon him,
37:26 He who is W among his people will inherit
38:24 and he who has little business may become W
38:25 How can he become W who handles the plow,
44:4 learning for the people, W in their words of
47:12 him rose up a W son who fared amply
47:14 How W you became in your youth!
50:28 he who lays them to heart will become W
Is 5:21 to those who are W in their own eyes,
19:11 are utterly foolish; the W counselors of Pharaoh give
19:11 a son of the W, a son of ancient
19:12 Where then are your W men?
29:14 the wisdom of their W men shall perish, and
31:2 And yet he is W and brings disaster, he
44:25 of diviners; who turns W men back, and makes
Jer 8:8 you say, 'We are W, and the law of
8:9 The W men shall be put to shame, they
9:12 is the man so W that he can understand
9:23 LORD: "Let not the W man glory in his
10:7 for among all the W ones of the nations
18:18 nor counsel from the W, nor the word from
50:35 her princes and her W men!
51:57 her princes and her W men, her governors, her
Ezek 28:2 you consider yourself as W as a god--
28:6 you consider yourself as W as a god,
Dan 2:12 commanded that all the W men of Babylon be
2:13 went forth that the W men were to be
2:14 out to slay the W men of Babylon;
2:18 the rest of the W men of Babylon.
2:21 gives wisdom to the W and knowledge to those
2:24 appointed to destroy the W men of Babylon; he
2:24 "Do not destroy the W men of Babylon; bring
2:27 answered the king, "No W men, enchanters,
2:48 prefect over all the W men of Babylon.
4:6 decree that all the W men of Babylon should
4:18 interpretation, because all the W men of my
5:7 king said to the W men of Babylon, "Whoever
5:8 Then all the king's W men came in, but
5:15 Now the W men, the enchanters, have been brought
11:33 the people who are W shall make many understand,
11:35 of those who are W shall fall, to refine
12:3 And those who are W shall shine like the
12:10 but those who are W shall understand.
Hos 14:9 Whoever is W, let him understand these things;
Obad 1:8 the LORD, destroy the W men out of Edom,
Zech 9:2 thereon, Tyre and Sidon, though they are very W
1Mac 2:65 Simeon your brother is W in counsel; always listen
Mt 2:1 Herod the king, behold, W men from the East
2:7 Then Herod summoned the W men secretly and
2:16 been tricked by the W men, was in a
2:16 had ascertained from the W men.
7:24 will be like a W man who built his
10:16 of wolves; so be W as serpents and innocent
11:25 these things from the W and understanding and
23:33 send you prophets and W men and scribes, some
24:45 is the faithful and W servant, whom his master
25:2 Five of them were foolish, and five were W
25:4 with them; but the W took flasks of oil
25:8 foolish said to the W, 'Give us some of
25:9 going out.' But the W replied, 'Perhaps there will
Lk 10:21 these things from the W and understanding and
12:42 is the faithful and W steward, whom his master
Rom 1:14 barbarians, both to the W and to the foolish:
1:22 Claiming to be W, they became fools,
11:25 Lest you be W in your own conceits, I
16:19 I would have you W as to what is
16:26 to the only W God be glory for
1Cor 1:19 the wisdom of the W, and the cleverness of
1:20 Where is the W man?
1:26 many of you were W according to worldly standards,
1:27 world to shame the W, God chose what is
3:18 thinks that he is W in this age, let
3:18 him become a fool that he may become W
3:19 written, "He catches the W in their craftiness,"
3:20 the thoughts of the W are futile."
4:10 sake, but you are W in Christ.
6:5 no man among you W enough to decide between
2Cor 11:19 bear with fools, being W yourselves!
Eph 5:15 unwise men but as W,
Jas 3:13 Who is W and understanding among you?

WISELY (10)

2Chr 11:23 And he dealt W, and distributed some of his
Ps 14:2 are any that act W, that seek after God.
36:3 has ceased to act W and do good.
Prov 14:35 A servant who deals W has the king's favor,
17:2 A slave who deals W will rule over a
Wis 9:11 she will guide me W in my actions and
Sir 20:26 He who speaks W will advance himself, and a
Jer 23:5 as king and deal W, and shall execute justice
Mk 12:34 saw that he answered W, he said to him,
Col 4:5 Conduct yourselves W toward outsiders, making the

WISER (8)

1Kgs 4:31 For he was W than all other men, wiser
4:31 than all other men, W than Ethan the Ezrahite,
Job 35:11 earth, and makes us W than the birds of
Ps 119:98 Thy commandment makes me W than my enemies,
Prov 9:9 he will be still W; teach a righteous man
26:16 The sluggard is W in his own eyes than
Ezek 28:3 you are indeed W than Daniel; no secret
1Cor 1:25 foolishness of God is W than men, and the

WISEST

Judg 5:29 of his chariots?' Her W ladies make answer, nay,

WISH (39)

Lev 27:20 if he does not W to redeem the field,
Num 22:29 I W I had a sword in my hand,
Deut 23:24 as many as you W, but you shall not
25:7 the man does not W to take his brother's
25:8 saying, 'I do not W to take her,'
Josh 15:18 and Caleb said to her, "What do you W
Judg 1:14 and Caleb said to her, "What do you W
1Sam 2:16 first, and then take as much as you W
Neh 6:6 the wall; and you W to become their king,
Job 37:20 Did a man ever W that he would be
Sir 15:16 water: stretch out your hand for whichever you W
23:14 habits; then you will W that you had never
Bar 6:45 but what the craftsmen W them to be.
1Mac 8:13 Those whom they W to help and to make
8:13 and those whom they W they depose; and they
2Mac 2:24 is for those who W to enter upon the
2:25 to please those who W to read, to make
9:20 affairs are as you W, I am glad.
11:29 informed us that you W to return home and
Mt 7:12 So whatever you W that men would do to
12:38 to him, "Teacher, we W to see a sign
17:4 are here; if you W, I will make three
Mk 6:22 me for whatever you W, and I will grant
Lk 6:31 And as you W that men would do to
Jn 4:27 a woman, but none said, "What do you W
6:67 twelve, "Do you also W to go away?"
12:21 to him, "Sir, we W to see Jesus."
21:18 where you do not W to go."
Acts 17:20 to our ears; we W to know therefore what
25:9 to Paul, "Do you W to go up to
Rom 9:3 For I could W that I myself were accursed
1Cor 4:21 What do you W
7:7 I W that all were as I myself am.
2Cor 11:1 I W you would bear with me in a
12:6 Though if I W to boast, I shall not
12:20 you not what I W, and that you may
12:20 me not what you W; that perhaps there may
Gal 4:20 I could W to be present with you now
5:12 I W those who unsettle you would mutilate

WISHED (10)

Job 9:3 If one W to contend with him, one could
Dan 13:15 only two maids, and W to bathe in the
1Mac 5:67 day some priests, who W to do a brave
2Mac 4:16 living they admired and W to imitate completely
12:4 they accepted, because they W to live peaceably and
Mt 18:22 to a king who W to settle accounts with
Acts 18:27 And when he W to cross to Achaia, the
19:30 Paul W to go in among the crowd, but
25:20 I asked whether he W to go to Jerusalem
28:18 had examined me, they W to set me at

WISHES (11)

Lev	27:13	But if he W to redeem it, he shall
	27:15	he who dedicates it W to redeem his house,
	27:19	who dedicates the field W to redeem it, then
	27:31	If a man W to redeem any of his
Num	15:14	your generations, and he W to offer an offering
1Kgs	5:9	you shall meet my W by providing food for
Tob	4:19	according to his will he humbles whomever he W
2Mac	9:19	hearty greetings and good W for their health and
1Cor	7:36	him do as he W: let them marry—it
	7:39	married to whom she W, only in the Lord.
Jas	4:4	Therefore whoever W to be a friend of the

WISHING (8)

Wis	14:19	For he, perhaps W to please his ruler, skilfully
2Mac	12:35	off by main strength, W to take the accursed
	14:39	Nicanor, W to exhibit the enmity which he had
Mk	15:15	So Pilate, W to satisfy the crowd, released for
Acts	19:33	motioned with his hand, W to make a defense
	25:9	But Festus, W to do the Jews a favor,
	27:43	escape; but the centurion, W to save Paul, kept
2Pet	3:9	forbearing toward you, not W that any should perish,

WITCHCRAFT

Lev	19:26	You shall not practice augury or W

WITHDRAW (16)

Num	8:25	fifty years they shall W from the work of
1Sam	14:19	said to the priest, W your hand."
2Sam	20:21	alone, and I will W from the city." And
1Kgs	15:19	Israel, that he may W from me."
2Kgs	18:14	"I have done wrong; W from me; whatever you
2Chr	16:3	Israel, that he may W from me."
Job	13:21	myself from thy face: W thy hand far from
	36:7	He does not W his eyes from the righteous,
Ps	85:3	[Selah] Thou didst W all thy wrath; thou didst
Is	60:20	down, nor your moon W itself; for the LORD
Jer	21:2	and will make him W from us."
Dan	3:35	covenant, and do not W thy mercy from us,
	11:30	shall be afraid and W, and shall turn back
Joel	2:10	darkened, and the stars W their shining.
	3:15	darkened, and the stars W their shining.
Zech	14:4	of the Mount shall W northward, and the other

WITHDRAWAL

2Mac	13:26	the king's attack and W turned out.

WITHDRAWN (10)

Jud	13:14	God, who has not W his mercy from the
Sir	4:31	extended to receive, but W when it is time
Jer	34:21	of Babylon which has W from you.
	37:11	the Chaldean army had W from Jerusalem at the
Lam	2:3	of Israel; he has W from them his right
Hos	5:6	find him; he has W from them.
2Mac	4:33	exposed them, having first W to a place of
Jn	5:12	was, for Jesus had W, as there was a
Acts	15:37	them one who had W from them in Pamphylia,
	26:31	and when they had W, they said to one

WITHDRAWS (2)

2Sam	17:13	If he W into a city, then all Israel
2Mac	6:16	Therefore he never W his mercy from us.

WITHDREW (24)

2Sam	20:2	the men of Israel W from David, and followed
	23:9	there for battle, and the men of Israel W
2Kgs	3:27	upon Israel; and they W from him and returned
Ezra	10:6	Then Ezra W from before the house of God,
Jud	13:1	came, his slaves quickly W, and Bagoas closed the
Job	29:8	men saw me and W, and the aged rose
Jer	37:5	news of them, they W from Jerusalem.
1Mac	9:62	his men, and Simon, W to Bethbasi in the
	12:28	so they kindled fires in their camp and W
2Mac	12:7	gates were closed, he W, intending to come again
	13:16	terror and confusion and W in triumph.
	13:22	gave pledges, received theirs, W, attacked Judas and
Mt	2:22	in a dream he W to the district of
	4:12	had been arrested, he W into Galilee;
	12:15	Jesus, aware of this, W from there.
	14:13	Jesus heard this, he W from there in a
	15:21	away from there and W to the district of
Mk	3:7	Jesus W with his disciples to the sea, and
Lk	5:16	But he W to the wilderness and prayed.
	9:10	he took them and W apart to a city
	22:41	And he W from them about a stone's throw,
Jn	6:15	make him king, Jesus W again to the mountain
Acts	19:9	before the congregation, he W from them, taking the
	22:29	about to examine him W from him instantly; and

WITHER (18)

Job	8:12	not cut down, they W before any other plant.
	18:16	beneath, and his branches W above.
	24:24	then are gone; they W and fade like the
Ps	1:3	in its season, and its leaf does not W
	37:2	like the grass, and W like the green herb.
	58:7	like grass let them be trodden down and W
	102:11	an evening shadow; I W away like grass.
	137:5	forget you, O Jerusalem, let my right hand W
Prov	11:28	in his riches will W, but the righteous will
Wis	2:8	Let us crown ourselves with rosebuds before they W
Is	40:24	upon them, and they W, and the tempest carries
Jer	12:4	land mourn, and the grass of every field W
Ezek	17:9	branches, so that all its fresh sprouting leaves W
	17:10	Will it not utterly W when the east wind
	17:10	east wind strikes it—W away on the bed
	47:12	Their leaves will not W nor their fruit fail,
Nah	1:4	rivers; Bashan and Carmel W, the bloom of Lebanon
Mt	21:20	did the fig tree W at once?"

WITHERED (21)

Gen	41:23	good; and seven ears, W, thin, and blighted by
Ps	102:4	smitten like grass, and W; I forget to eat
Sir	6:3	be left like a W tree.
Is	15:6	desolation; the grass is W, the new growth fails,
Jer	8:13	even the leaves are W, and what I gave
Ezek	19:12	its strong stem was W; the fire consumed it.
Joel	1:11	of the field are W; and gladness fails from
Amos	4:7	it did not rain W;
Jon	4:7	worm which attacked the plant, so that it W
Zech	11:17	his arm be wholly W, his right eye utterly
Mt	12:10	a man with a W hand.
	13:6	had no root they W away.
	21:19	And the fig tree W at once.
Mk	3:1	there who had a W hand.
	3:3	man who had the W hand, "Come here."
	4:6	had no root it W away.
	11:20	saw the fig tree W away to its roots.
	11:21	The fig tree which you cursed has W
Lk	6:6	a man was there whose right hand was W
	6:8	man who had the W hand, "Come and stand
	8:6	it grew up, it W away, because it had

WITHERS (16)

Job	14:2	like a flower, and W; he flees like a
Ps	90:6	is renewed; in the evening it fades and W
	129:6	on the housetops, which W before it grows up,
Sir	14:9	portion, and mean injustice W the soul.
	43:21	up the wilderness, and W the tender grass like
Is	1:30	an oak whose leaf W, and like a garden
	24:4	The earth mourns and W, the world languishes and
	24:4	world languishes and W; the heavens languish
	33:9	Lebanon is confounded and W away; Sharon is like
	40:7	The grass W, the flower fades, when the breath
	40:8	The grass W, the flower fades; but the word
Joel	1:11	The vine W, the fig tree languishes.
Amos	1:2	the shepherds mourn, and the top of Carmel W
Jn	15:6	as a branch and W; and the branches are
Jas	1:10	its scorching heat and W the grass; its flower
1Pet	1:24	The grass W, and the flower falls,

WITHHELD (14)

Gen	22:12	seeing you have not W your son, your only
	22:16	this, and have not W your son, your only
	30:2	of God, who has W from you the fruit
Job	22:7	drink, and you have W bread from the hungry.
	31:16	"If I have W anything that the poor desired,
	38:15	wicked their light is W, and their uplifted arm
Ps	21:2	desire, and hast not W the request of his
Is	63:15	and thy compassion are W from me.
Jer	3:3	the showers have been W, and the spring rain
Ezek	20:22	But I W my hand, and acted for the
Joel	1:12	and drink offering are W from the house of
Amos	4:7	"And I also W the rain from you when
Hag	1:10	heavens above you have W the dew, and the
	1:10	and the earth has W its produce.

WITHHOLD (16)

Gen	23:6	none of us will W from you his sepulchre,
Deut	22:1	sheep go astray, and W your help from them;
	22:3	find; you may not W your help.
	22:4	by the way, and W your help from them;
2Sam	13:13	for he will not W me from you."

W

	10:28	law of God, their W, their sons, their daughters,
Tob	4:12	of old, all took W from among their brethren.
Jud	4:10	They and their W and their children and their
	4:12	as prey and their W as booty, and the
	7:14	They and their W and children will waste away
	7:28	eyes, or see our W and children draw their
	9:4	and thou gavest their W for a prey and
Esth	13:6	shall all, with their W and children, be utterly
Wis	3:12	Their W are foolish, and their children evil;
Is	13:16	be plundered and their W ravished.
Jer	6:12	others, their fields and W together; for I will
	8:10	I will give their W to others and their
	14:16	bury them—them, their W, their sons, and their
	18:21	sword, let their W become childless and widowed.
	29:6	Take W and have sons and daughters; take wives
	29:6	sons and daughters; take W for your sons, and
	29:23	adultery with their neighbors' W, and they have
	35:8	our days, ourselves, our W, our sons, or our
	38:23	from you.' All your W and your sons shall
	44:9	the wickedness of their W, your own wickedness, and
	44:9	the wickedness of your W, which they committed in
	44:15	who knew that their W had offered incense to
	44:25	Israel: You and your W have declared with your
Bar	6:28	money; and likewise their W preserve some with
	6:33	gods to clothe their W and children.
Dan	5:2	and his lords, his W, and his concubines might
	5:3	and his lords, his W, and his concubines drank
	5:23	and your lords, your W, and your concubines have
	6:24	their children, and their W; and before they reached
	14:10	of Bel, besides their W and children.
	14:15	priests came with their W and children, as they
	14:21	the priests and their W and children; and they
Zech	12:12	by itself, and their W by themselves; the family
	12:12	by itself, and their W by themselves;
	12:13	by itself, and their W by themselves; the family
	12:13	by itself, and their W by themselves;
	12:14	by itself, and their W by themselves.
1Mac	2:30	they, their sons, their W, and their cattle, because
	2:38	they died, with their W and children and cattle,
	3:20	destroy us and our W and our children, and
	5:13	enemy have captured their W and children and
	5:23	and Arbatta, with their W and children, and all
	5:45	the great, with their W and children and goods,
	8:10	Romans took captive their W and children; they
	13:6	the sanctuary and your W and children, for all
	13:45	the city, with their W and children, went up
2Mac	12:3	to embark, with their W and children, on boats
	15:18	Their concern for W and children, and also for
Mt	19:8	you to divorce your W, but from the beginning
Acts	21:5	and they all, with W and children, brought us
1Cor	7:29	let those who have W live as though they
Eph	5:22	W, be subject to your husbands, as to the
	5:24	to Christ, so let W also be subject in
	5:25	Husbands, love your W, as Christ loved the church
	5:28	husbands should love their W as their own bodies.
Col	3:18	W, be subject to your husbands, as is fitting
	3:19	Husbands, love your W, and do not be harsh
1Pet	3:1	Likewise you W, be submissive to your husbands, so
	3:1	the behavior of their W,
	3:7	live considerately with your W, bestowing honor on

WIZARD (2)

Lev	20:27	a medium or a W shall be put to
Deut	18:11	a medium, or a W, or a necromancer.

WIZARDS (9)

Lev	19:31	turn to mediums or W; do not seek them
	20:6	turns to mediums and W, playing the harlot after
1Sam	28:3	the mediums and the W out of the land.
	28:9	the mediums and the W from the land.
2Kgs	21:6	and augury, and dealt with mediums and with W
	23:24	the mediums and the W and the teraphim and
2Chr	33:6	and sorcery, and dealt with mediums and with W
Is	8:19	the mediums and the W who chirp and mutter,"
	19:3	the mediums and the W;

WOE (104)

Num	21:29	W to you, O Moab!
1Sam	4:7	And they said, W to us!
	4:8	W to us!
Jud	16:17	W to the nations that rise up against my
Job	10:15	If I am wicked, W to me!
Ps	120:5	W is me, that I sojourn in Meshech, that
Prov	23:29	Who has W
Eccl	4:10	up his fellow; but W to him who is
	10:16	W to you, O land, when your king is
Sir	2:12	W to timid hearts and to slack hands, and
	2:13	W to the faint heart, for it has no
	2:14	W to you who have lost your endurance!
	41:8	W to you, ungodly men, who have forsaken the
Is	3:9	W to them!
	3:11	W to the wicked!
	5:8	W to those who join house to house, who
	5:11	W to those who rise early in the morning,
	5:18	W to those who draw iniquity with cords of
	5:20	W to those who call evil good and good
	5:21	W to those who are wise in their own
	5:22	W to those who are heroes at drinking wine,
	6:5	And I said: W is me!
	10:1	W to those who decree iniquitous decrees, and the
	24:16	W is me!
	28:1	W to the proud crown of the drunkards of
	29:15	W to those who hide deep from the LORD
	30:1	W to the rebellious children," says the LORD, "who
	31:1	W to those who go down to Egypt for
	33:1	W to you, destroyer, who yourself have not been
	45:7	make weal and create W, I am the LORD,
	45:9	W to him who strives with his Maker, an
	45:10	W to him who says to a father, 'What
Jer	4:13	swifter than eagles— W to us, for we
	4:31	stretching out her hands, W is me!
	6:4	W to us, for the day declines, for the
	10:19	W is me because of my hurt!
	13:27	W to you, O Jerusalem!
	15:10	W is me, my mother, that you bore me,
	22:13	W to him who builds his house by unrighteousness,
	23:1	W to the shepherds who destroy and scatter the
	45:3	O Baruch: You said, W is me!
	48:1	the God of Israel: W to Nebo, for it
	48:46	W to you, O Moab!
	50:27	W to them, for their day has come, the
Lam	5:16	fallen from our head; W to us, for we
Ezek	2:10	on it words of lamentation and mourning and W
	13:3	says the Lord GOD, W to the foolish prophets
	13:18	says the Lord GOD: W to the women who
	16:23	after all your wickedness W, woe to you!
	16:23	all your wickedness (woe, W to you!
	24:6	says the Lord GOD: W to the bloody city,
	24:9	says the Lord GOD: W to the bloody city!
Hos	7:14	W to them, for they have strayed from me!
	9:12	W to them when I depart from them!
Amos	5:18	W to you who desire the day of the
	6:1	W to those who are at ease in Zion,
	6:4	W to those who lie upon beds of ivory,
Mic	2:1	W to those who devise wickedness and work evil
	7:1	W is me!
Nah	3:1	W to the bloody city, all full of lies
Hab	2:6	of him, and say, W to him who heaps
	2:9	W to him who gets evil gain for his
	2:12	W to him who builds a town with blood,
	2:15	W to him who makes his neighbors drink of
	2:19	W to him who says to a wooden thing,
Zeph	2:5	W to you inhabitants of the seacoast, you nation
	3:1	W to her that is rebellious and defiled, the
Zech	11:17	W to my worthless shepherd, who deserts the flock!
Mt	11:21	W to you, Chorazin!
	11:21	W to you, Beth-saida!
	18:7	W to the world for temptations to sin!
	18:7	that temptations come, but W to the man by
	23:13	"But W to you, scribes and Pharisees, hypocrites!
	23:14	W to you, scribes and Pharisees, hypocrites!
	23:15	W to you, blind guides, who say, 'If any
	23:22	W to you, scribes and Pharisees, hypocrites!
	23:24	W to you, scribes and Pharisees, hypocrites!
	23:26	W to you, scribes and Pharisees, hypocrites!
	23:28	W to you, scribes and Pharisees, hypocrites!
	26:24	written of him, but W to that man by
Mk	14:21	written of him, but W to that man by
Lk	6:24	"But W to you that are rich, for you
	6:25	W to you that are full now, for you
	6:25	W to you that laugh now, for you shall
	6:26	W to you, when all men speak well of
	10:13	W to you, Chorazin!
	10:13	W to you, Beth-saida!
	11:42	"But W to you Pharisees!
	11:43	W to you Pharisees!
	11:44	W to you!
	11:46	And he said, W to you lawyers also!
	11:47	W to you!
	11:52	W to you lawyers!
	17:1	sure to come; but W to him by whom
	22:22	has been determined; but W to that man by

1Cor 9:16 W to me if I do not preach the
Jude 1:11 W to them!
Rev 8:13 it flew in midheaven, W, woe, woe to those
8:13 flew in midheaven, "Woe, W, woe to those who
8:13 in midheaven, "Woe, woe, W to those who dwell
9:12 The first W has passed; behold, two woes are
11:14 The second W has passed; behold, the third woe
11:14 passed; behold, the third W is soon to come.
12:12 But W to you, O earth and sea, for

WOES

Rev 9:12 has passed; behold, two W are still to come.

WOKE (6)

Mt 1:24 When Joseph W from sleep, he did as the
8:25 And they went and W him, saying, "Save, Lord;
Mk 4:38 the cushion; and they W him and said to
Lk 8:24 And they went and W him, saying, "Master, Master,
Acts 12:7 on the side and W him, saying, "Get up
16:27 When the jailer W and saw that the prison

WOLF (7)

Gen 49:27 Benjamin is a ravenous W, in the morning devouring
Sir 13:16 What fellowship has a W with a lamb?
Is 11:6 The W shall dwell with the lamb, and the
65:25 The W and the lamb shall feed together, the
Jer 5:6 shall slay them, a W from the desert shall
Jn 10:12 are not, sees the W coming and leaves the
10:12 and flees; and the W snatches them and scatters

WOLVES (7)

Ezek 22:27 of her are like W tearing the prey, shedding
Hab 1:8 fierce than the evening W; their horsemen press proudly
Zeph 3:3 her judges are evening W that leave nothing till
Mt 7:15 you in sheep's clothing but inwardly are ravenous W
10:16 in the midst of W; so be wise as
Lk 10:3 you out as lambs in the midst of W
Acts 20:29 after my departure fierce W will come in among

WOMAN (411)

Gen 2:22 he made into a W and brought her to
2:23 she shall be called W, because she was taken
3:1 He said to the W, "Did God say, 'You
3:2 And the W said to the serpent, "We may
3:4 serpent said to the W, "You will not die.
3:6 So when the W saw that the tree was
3:12 The man said, "The W whom thou gavest to
3:13 God said to the W, "What is this that
3:13 The W said, "The serpent beguiled me, and I
3:15 between you and the W, and between your seed
3:16 To the W he said, "I will greatly multiply
12:11 that you are a W beautiful to behold;
12:14 Egyptians saw that the W was very beautiful.
12:15 And the W was taken into Pharaoh's house.
20:3 man, because of the W whom you have taken;
21:10 "Cast out this slave W with her son; for
21:10 son of this slave W shall not be heir
21:12 because of your slave W; whatever Sarah says to
21:13 son of the slave W also, because he is
24:5 to him, "Perhaps the W may not be willing
24:8 But if the W is not willing to follow
24:39 my master, 'Perhaps the W will not follow me.'
24:43 water; let the young W who comes out to
24:44 let her be the W whom the LORD has
38:20 the pledge from the W's hand, he could not
46:10 Zohar, and Shaul, the son of a Canaanitish W
Ex 2:2 The W conceived and bore a son; and when
2:9 So the W took the child and nursed him.
3:22 go empty, but each W shall ask of her
6:15 son of a Canaanite W; these are the families
11:2 his neighbor and every W of her neighbor, jewelry
19:15 the third day; do not go near a W
21:22 together, and hurt a W with child, so that
21:22 fined, according as the W's husband shall lay upon
21:28 a man or a W to death, the ox
21:29 a man or a W, the ox shall be
36:6 "Let neither man nor W do anything more for
Lev 12:2 of Israel, If a W conceives, and bears a
13:29 "When a man or W has a disease on
13:38 a man or a W has spots on the
15:18 man lies with a W and has an emission
15:19 "When a W has a discharge of blood which
15:25 "If a W has a discharge of blood for
15:33 who lies with a W who is unclean.
18:17 the nakedness of a W and of her daughter,
18:18 shall not take a W as a rival wife
18:19 shall not approach a W to uncover her nakedness
18:22 male as with a W; it is an abomination.
18:23 it, neither shall any W give herself to a
19:20 lies carnally with a W who is a slave,
20:13 male as with a W, both of them have
20:16 If a W approaches any beast and lies with
20:16 you shall kill the W and the beast; they
20:18 man lies with a W having her sickness, and
20:27 "A man or a W who is a medium
21:7 a harlot or a W who has been defiled;
21:7 shall they marry a W divorced from her husband;
21:14 one divorced, or a W who has been defiled,
24:10 Now an Israelite W's son, whose father was an
24:10 Israel; and the Israelite W's son and a man
24:11 and the Israelite W's son blasphemed the Name,
Num 5:6 When a man or W commits any of the
5:18 priest shall set the W before the LORD, and
5:18 the hair of the W's head, and place in
5:21 the priest make the W take the oath of
5:21 and say to the W 'the LORD make you
5:22 fall away.' And the W shall say, 'Amen, Amen.'
5:24 he shall make the W drink the water of
5:25 jealousy out of the W's hand, and shall wave
5:26 afterward shall make the W drink the water.
5:27 fall away, and the W shall become an execration
5:28 But if the W has not defiled herself and
5:30 he shall set the W before the LORD, and
5:31 from iniquity, but the W shall bear her iniquity."
6:2 a man or a W makes a special vow,
12:1 because of the Cushite W whom he had married,
12:1 had married a Cushite W;
25:6 and brought a Midianite W to his family, in
25:8 of Israel and the W, through her body.
25:14 slain with the Midianite W, was Zimri the son
25:15 name of the Midianite W who was slain was
30:3 Or when a W vows a vow to the
30:9 or of a divorced W, anything by which she
31:17 ones, and kill every W who has known man
Deut 15:12 man, or a Hebrew W, is sold to you,
17:2 you, a man or W who does what is
17:5 gates that man or W who has done this
17:5 stone that man or W to death with stones.
21:11 the captives a beautiful W, and you have desire
22:5 "A W shall not wear anything that pertains to
22:5 man put on a W's garment; for whoever does
22:14 saying, 'I took this W, and when I came
22:15 father of the young W and her mother shall
22:16 father of the young W shall say to the
22:19 father of the young W, because he has brought
22:20 found in the young W,
22:21 bring out the young W to the door of
22:22 who lay with the W, and the woman; so
22:22 the woman, and the W; so you shall purge
22:24 with stones, the young W because she did not
22:25 man meets a young W who is betrothed, and
22:26 But to the young W you shall do nothing;
22:26 nothing; in the young W there is no offense
22:27 though the betrothed young W cried for help there
22:29 father of the young W fifty shekels of silver,
28:56 tender and delicately bred W among you, who would
29:18 you a man or W or family or tribe,
Josh 2:4 But the W had taken the two men and
6:22 out from it the W, and all who belong
Judg 4:9 will sell Sisera into the hand of a W
9:53 And a certain W threw an upper millstone upon
9:54 say of me, 'A W killed him.'" And his
11:2 house; for you are the son of another W
13:3 LORD appeared to the W and said to her,
13:6 Then the W came and told her husband, "A
13:9 came again to the W as she sat in
13:10 And the W ran in haste and told her
13:11 "Are you the man who spoke to this W
13:13 I said to the W let her beware.
13:24 And the W bore a son, and called his
14:3 "Is there not a W among the daughters of
14:7 and talked with the W; and she pleased Samson
14:10 went down to the W, and Samson made a
16:4 this he loved a W in the valley of
19:26 as morning appeared, the W came and fell down
20:4 the husband of the W who was murdered, answered
21:11 every male and every W that has lain with
Ruth 1:5 died, so that the W was bereft of her
3:8 over, and behold, a W lay at his feet!
3:11 that you are a W of worth.
3:14 be known that the W came to the threshing

W

	4:11	the LORD make the W, who is coming into
	4:12	the LORD will give you by this young W
1Sam	1:13	therefore Eli took her to be a drunken W
	1:15	lord, I am a W sorely troubled; I have
	1:16	maidservant as a base W, for all along I
	1:18	Then the W went her way and ate, and
	1:23	So the W remained and nursed her son, until
	1:26	lord, I am the W who was standing here
	2:20	you children by this W for the loan which
	15:3	kill both man and W, infant and suckling, ox
	20:30	of a perverse, rebellious W, do I not know
	25:3	The W was of good understanding and beautiful, but
	27:9	left neither man nor W alive, but took away
	27:11	saved neither man nor W alive, to bring tidings
	28:7	out for me a W who is a medium,
	28:8	they came to the W by night.
	28:9	The W said to him, "Surely you know what
	28:11	Then the W said, "Whom shall I bring up
	28:12	When the W saw Samuel, she cried out with
	28:12	loud voice; and the W said to Saul, "Why
	28:13	And the W said to Saul, "I see a
	28:21	And the W came to Saul, and when she
	28:23	servants, together with the W, urged him; and he
	28:24	Now the W had a fatted calf in the
2Sam	3:8	charge me today with a fault concerning a W
	11:2	from the roof a W bathing; and the woman
	11:2	woman bathing; and the W was very beautiful.
	11:3	And David sent and inquired about the W
	11:5	And the W conceived; and she sent and told
	11:21	Did not a W cast an upper millstone upon
	13:17	and said, "Put this W out of my presence,
	13:20	Tamar dwelt, a desolate W, in her brother Absalom's
	14:2	from there a wise W, and said to her,
	14:2	but behave like a W who has been mourning
	14:4	When the W of Tekoa came to the king,
	14:8	king said to the W, "Go to your house,
	14:9	And the W of Tekoa said to the king,
	14:12	Then the W said, "Pray let your handmaid speak
	14:13	And the W said, "Why then have you planned
	14:18	the king answered the W, "Do not hide from
	14:18	And the W said, "Let my lord the king
	14:19	The W answered and said, "As surely as you
	14:27	whose name was Tamar; she was a beautiful W
	17:19	And the W took and spread a covering over
	17:20	servants came to the W at the house, they
	17:20	And the W said to them, "They have gone
	20:16	Then a wise W called from the city, "Hear!
	20:17	near her; and the W said, "Are you Joab?"
	20:21	And the W said to Joab, "Behold, his head
	20:22	Then the W went to all the people in
1Kgs	3:17	The one W said, "Oh, my lord, this woman
	3:17	"Oh, my lord, this W and I dwell in
	3:18	I was delivered, this W also gave birth; and
	3:19	And this W's son died in the night, because
	3:22	But the other W said, "No, the living child
	3:26	Then the W whose son was alive said to
	3:27	child to the first W, and by no means
	14:5	When she came, she pretended to be another W
	17:17	the son of the W, the mistress of the
	17:24	And the W said to Elijah, "Now I know
2Kgs	4:8	Shunem, where a wealthy W lived, who urged him
	4:17	But the W conceived, and she bore a son
	6:26	upon the wall, a W cried out to him,
	6:28	She answered, "This W said to me, 'Give your
	6:30	the words of the W he rent his clothes--
	8:1	had said to the W whose son he had
	8:2	So the W arose, and did according to the
	8:3	seven years, when the W returned from the land
	8:5	to life, behold, the W whose son he had
	8:5	king, here is the W, and here is her
	8:6	the king asked the W, she told him.
	9:34	now to this cursed W, and bury her; for
2Chr	2:14	the son of a W of the daughters of
	15:13	to death, whether young or old, man or W
	24:7	of Athaliah, that wicked W, had broken into the
Tob	4:12	not marry a foreign W, who is not of
	6:7	before the man or W, and that person will
Jud	8:31	you are a devout W, and the Lord will
	9:10	crush their arrogance by the hand of a W
	11:1	to her, "Take courage, W, and do not be
	11:21	is not such a W from one end of
	12:11	and persuade the Hebrew W who is in your
	12:12	we let such a W go without enjoying her
	12:15	herself in all her W's finery, and her maid
	13:15	struck him down by the hand of a W
	14:18	One Hebrew W has brought disgrace upon the house
	16:6	has foiled them by the hand of a W
Esth	4:11	if any man or W goes to the king
Job	14:1	is born of a W is of few days,
	15:14	is born of a W, that he can be
	24:21	on the barren childless W, and do no good
	25:4	who is born of W be clean?
	31:9	been enticed to a W, and I have lain
Ps	48:6	anguish as of a W in travail.
	113:9	He gives the barren W a home, making her
Prov	2:16	saved from the loose W, from the adventuress with
	5:3	lips of a loose W drip honey, and her
	5:20	son, with a loose W and embrace the bosom
	6:24	you from the evil W, from the smooth tongue
	7:5	you from the loose W, from the adventuress with
	7:10	And lo, a W meets him, dressed as a
	9:13	A foolish W is noisy; she is wanton and
	11:16	A gracious W gets honor, and violent men get
	11:22	snout is a beautiful W without discretion.
	21:9	than in a house shared with a contentious W
	21:19	desert land than with a contentious and fretful W
	22:14	mouth of a loose W is a deep pit;
	25:24	than in a house shared with a contentious W
	27:15	day and a contentious W are alike;
	30:23	with food; an unloved W when she gets a
	31:30	is vain, but a W who fears the LORD
Eccl	7:26	bitter than death the W whose heart is snares
	7:28	I found, but a W among all these I
	11:5	the womb of a W with child, so you
Wis	3:13	blessed is the barren W who is undefiled, who
Sir	9:2	give yourself to a W so that she gains
	9:3	to meet a loose W, lest you fall into
	9:4	not associate with a W singer, lest you be
	9:8	eyes from a shapely W, and do not look
	9:8	been misled by a W's beauty, and by it
	19:11	suffer pangs like a W in labor with a
	23:22	it is with a W who leaves her husband
	25:20	be ensnared by a W's beauty, and do not
	25:20	do not desire a W for her possessions.
	25:23	From a W sin had its beginning, and because
	34:5	folly, and like a W in travail the mind
	36:21	A W will accept any man, but one daughter
	36:22	A W's beauty gladdens the countenance, and
	37:11	not consult with a W about her rival or
	41:20	of looking at a W who is a harlot,
	42:13	moth, and from a W comes woman's wickedness.
	42:13	from a woman comes W's wickedness.
	42:14	a man than a W who does good; and
	42:14	and it is a W who brings shame and
Is	7:14	Behold, a young W shall conceive and bear a
	13:8	in anguish like a W in travail.
	21:3	the pangs of a W in travail; I am
	26:17	Like a W with child, who writhes and cries
	42:14	cry out like a W in travail, I will
	45:10	begetting?' or to a W, 'With what are you
	49:15	"Can a W forget her sucking child, that she
Jer	4:31	cry as of a W in travail, anguish as
	6:24	pain as of a W in travail.
	13:21	like those of a W in travail?
	22:23	pain as of a W in travail!"
	30:6	his loins like a W in labor?
	31:8	and the lame, the W with child and her
	31:22	on the earth: a W protects a man."
	44:7	from you man and W, infant and child, from
	48:41	the heart of a W in her pangs;
	49:22	the heart of a W in her pangs."
	49:24	her, as of a W in travail.
	50:43	pain as of a W in travail.
	51:22	in pieces man and W; with you I break
Bar	4:16	and bereaved the lonely W of her daughters.
	6:43	with, she derides the W next to her, because
Ezek	18:6	wife or approach a W in her time of
	36:17	the uncleanness of a W in her impurity.
	44:22	widow, or a divorced W, but only a virgin
Dan	13:2	Hilkiah, a very beautiful W and one who feared
	13:31	Now Susanna was a W of great refinement, and
	13:36	the garden alone, this W came in with two
	13:40	So we seized this W and asked her who
	13:46	"I am innocent of the blood of this W
Hos	3:1	"Go again, love a W who is beloved of
Mic	4:9	seized you like a W in travail?
	4:10	of Zion, like a W in travail; for now
Zech	5:7	and there was a W sitting in the ephah!
2Mac	7:21	spirit, she fired her W's reasoning with a man's
Mt	5:28	who looks at a W lustfully has already committed
	5:32	whoever marries a divorced W commits adultery.
	9:20	And behold, a W who had suffered from a

9:22 And instantly the W was made well.
13:33 like leaven which a W took and hid in
15:22 And behold, a Canaanite W from that region came
15:28 Jesus answered her, "O W, great is your faith!
19:9 who marries a divorced W, commits adultery."
22:27 After them all, the W died.
26:7 Simon the leper, a W came up to him
26:10 said to them, "Why do you trouble the W
Mk 5:25 And there was a W who had had a
5:33 But the W, knowing what had been done to
7:24 a W, whose little daughter was possessed
7:25 Now the W was a Greek, a Syrophoenician by
12:22 Last of all the W also died.
14:3 sat at table, a W came with an alabaster
Lk 4:26 of Sidon, to a W who was a widow.
7:37 And behold, a W of the city, who was
7:39 and what sort of W this is who is
7:44 Then turning toward the W he said to Simon,
7:44 he said to Simon, "Do you see this W
7:50 he said to the W, "Your faith has saved
8:43 And a W who had had a flow of
8:47 And when the W saw that she was not
10:38 a village; and a W named Martha received him
11:27 he said this, a W in the crowd raised
13:11 And there was a W who had had a
13:12 and said to her, W, you are freed from
13:16 And ought not this W, a daughter of Abraham
13:21 like leaven which a W took and hid in
15:8 "Or what W, having ten silver coins, if she
16:18 he who marries a W divorced from her husband
20:32 Afterward the W also died.
20:33 whose wife will the W be?
22:55 he denied it, saying, W, I do not know
Jn 2:4 said to her, "O W, what have you to
4:7 There came a W of Samaria to draw water.
4:9 The Samaritan W said to him, "How is it
4:9 drink of me, a W of Samaria?" For Jews
4:11 The W said to him, "Sir, you have nothing
4:15 The W said to him, "Sir, give me this
4:17 The W answered him, "I have no husband." Jesus
4:19 The W said to him, "Sir, I perceive that
4:21 Jesus said to her, W, believe me, the hour
4:25 The W said to him, "I know that Messiah
4:27 was talking with a W, but none said, "What
4:28 So the W left her water jar, and went
4:39 him because of the W's testimony, "He told me
4:42 They said to the W, "It is no longer
8:3 the Pharisees brought a W who had been caught
8:4 to him, "Teacher, this W has been caught in
8:9 left alone with the W standing before him.
8:10 and said to her, W, where are they?
16:21 When a W is in travail she has sorrow,
19:26 said to his mother, W, behold, your son!"
20:13 They said to her, W, why are you weeping?"
20:15 Jesus said to her, W, why are you weeping?
Acts 16:1 son of a Jewish W who was a believer;
16:14 heard us was a W named Lydia, from the
17:34 the Are-opagite and a W named Damaris and others
Rom 7:2 Thus a married W is bound by law to
1Cor 7:1 well for a man not to touch a W
7:2 own wife and each W her own husband.
7:13 If any W has a husband who is an
7:34 And the unmarried W or girl is anxious about
7:34 spirit; but the married W is anxious about worldly
11:3 the head of a W is her husband, and
11:5 his head, but any W who prays or prophesies
11:6 For if a W will not veil herself, then
11:6 is disgraceful for a W to be shorn or
11:7 glory of God; but W is the glory of
11:8 was not made from W, but woman from man.
11:8 made from woman, but W from man.
11:9 was man created for W, but woman for man.)

11:9 created for woman, but W for man.)
11:10 That is why a W ought to have a
11:11 (Nevertheless, in the Lord W is not independent of
11:11 man nor man of W;
11:12 of woman; for as W was made from man,
11:12 from man, so man is now born of W
11:13 it proper for a W to pray to God
11:15 him, but if a W has long hair, it
14:35 is shameful for a W to speak in church.
Gal 4:4 his Son, born of W, born under the law,
4:22 by a slave and one by a free W
4:23 son of the free W through promise.
4:30 not inherit with the son of the free W
4:31 children of the slave but of the free W
1Thes 5:3 travail comes upon a W with child, and there
1Tim 2:11 Let a W learn in silence with all submissiveness.
2:12 I permit no W to teach or to have
2:14 not deceived, but the W was deceived and became
2:15 Yet W will be saved through bearing children, if
5:16 If any believing W has relatives who are widows,
1Pet 3:7 bestowing honor on the W as the weaker sex,
Rev 2:20 that you tolerate the W Jezebel, who calls herself
12:1 appeared in heaven, a W clothed with the sun,
12:4 dragon stood before the W who was about to
12:6 his throne, and the W fled into the wilderness,
12:13 earth, he pursued the W who had borne the
12:14 But the W was given the two wings of
12:15 his mouth after the W, to sweep her away
12:16 the help of the W, and the earth opened
12:17 was angry with the W, and went off to
17:3 and I saw a W sitting on a scarlet
17:4 The W was arrayed in purple and scarlet, and
17:6 And I saw the W, drunk with the blood
17:7 the mystery of the W, and of the beast
17:9 mountains on which the W is seated;
17:18 And the W that you saw is the great

WOMB (71)

Gen 25:23 nations are in your W, and two peoples, born
25:24 were fulfilled, behold, there were twins in her W
29:31 hated, he opened her W; but Rachel was barren.
30:2 has withheld from you the fruit of the W
30:22 and God hearkened to her and opened her W
38:27 her delivery came, there were twins in her W
49:25 beneath, blessings of the breasts and of the W
Ex 13:2 first to open the W among the people of
13:12 to the LORD all that first opens the W
13:15 that first open the W; but all the first-born
34:19 All that opens the W is mine, all your
Num 3:12 first-born that opens the W among the people of
8:16 all that open the W, the first-born of all
12:12 consumed when he comes out of his mother's W
18:15 Everything that opens the W of all flesh, whether
Judg 16:17 been a Nazirite to God from my mother's W
Ruth 1:11 yet sons in my W that they may become
1Sam 1:5 one portion, because the LORD had closed her W
1:6 irritate her, because the LORD had closed her W
Jud 9:2 shame, and polluted her W to disgrace her; for
Job 1:21 came from my mother's W, and naked shall I
3:10 doors of my mother's W, nor hide trouble from
3:11 come forth from the W and expire?
10:18 "Why didst thou bring me forth from the W
10:19 been, carried from the W to the grave.
31:15 made me in the W make him?
31:15 And did not one fashion us in the W
31:18 and from his mother's W I guided him);
38:8 burst forth from the W;
38:29 From whose W did the ice come forth, and
Ps 22:9 took me from the W; thou didst keep me
58:3 go astray from the W, they err from their
71:6 art he who took me from my mother's W
110:3 From the W of the morning like dew your
127:3 the fruit of the W a reward.
139:13 thou didst knit me together in my mother's W
Prov 30:16 "Enough": Sheol, the barren W, the earth ever
31:2 What, son of my W
Eccl 5:15 came from his mother's W he shall go again,
11:5 the bones in the W of a woman with
Wis 7:1 earth; and in the W of a mother I
Sir 1:12 she is created with the faithful in the W
40:1 forth from their mother's W till the day they
49:7 been consecrated in the W as prophet, to pluck
Is 13:18 the fruit of the W; their eyes will not
44:2 formed you from the W and will help you:
44:24 formed you from the W: "I am the LORD,
46:3 birth, carried from the W;
49:1 called me from the W, from the body of
49:5 formed me from the W to be his servant,
49:15 have no compassion on the son of her W
66:9 I, who cause to bring forth, shut the W
Jer 1:5 formed you in the W I knew you, and
20:17 kill me in the W; so my mother would
20:17 my grave, and her W for ever great.
20:18 come forth from the W to see toil and
Hos 9:14 Give them a miscarrying W and dry breasts.
12:3 In the W he took his brother by the
13:13 not present himself at the mouth of the W
2Mac 7:22 know how you came into being in my W
7:27 nine months in my W, and nursed you for
Lk 1:15 with the Holy Spirit, even from his mother's W

1:31 will conceive in your W and bear a son,
1:41 babe leaped in her W; and Elizabeth was filled
1:42 women, and blessed is the fruit of your W
1:44 the babe in my W leaped for joy.
2:21 the angel before he was conceived in the W
2:23 male that opens the W shall be called holy
11:27 him, "Blessed is the W that bore you, and
Jn 3:4 time into his mother's W and be born?"
Rom 4:19 or when he considered the barrenness of Sarah's W

WOMBS (2)

Gen 20:18 had closed all the W of the house of
Lk 23:28 the barren, and the W that never bore, and

WOMEN (229)

Gen 14:16 his goods, and the W and the people.
18:11 to be with Sarah after the manner of W
24:11 evening, the time when W go out to draw
27:46 weary of my life because of the Hittite W
27:46 one of the Hittite W such as these, one
27:46 these, one of the W of the land, what
28:1 "You shall not marry one of the Canaanite W
28:6 "You shall not marry one of the Canaanite W
28:8 saw that the Canaanite W did not please Isaac
30:13 For the W will call me happy"; so she
31:35 for the way of W is upon me." So
33:5 eyes and saw the W and children, he said,
34:1 out to visit the W of the land;
Ex 1:15 midwife to the Hebrew W, and see them upon
1:18 Pharaoh, "Because the Hebrew W are not like the
1:18 not like the Egyptian W; for they are vigorous
2:7 nurse from the Hebrew W to nurse the child
12:37 men on foot, besides W and children.
15:20 hand; and all the W went out after her
35:22 came, both men and W; all who were of
35:25 And all W who had ability spun with their
35:26 twined linen; all the W whose hearts were moved
35:29 All the men and W, the people of Israel,
38:8 mirrors of the ministering W who ministered at the
Lev 26:26 staff of bread, ten W shall bake your bread
Num 31:9 Israel took captive the W of Midian and their
31:15 you let all the W live?
31:35 thousand persons in all, W who had not known
Deut 2:34 destroyed every city, men, W, and children; we left
3:6 destroying every city, men, W, and children.
20:14 the sword, but the W and the little ones,
31:12 Assemble the people, men, W, and little ones, and
Josh 6:21 city, both men and W, young and old, oxen,
8:25 day, both men and W, were twelve thousand, all
8:35 of Israel, and the W, and the little ones,
23:12 that you marry their W and they yours,
Judg 5:24 "Most blessed of W be Jael, the wife of
5:24 the Kenite, of tent-dwelling W most blessed.
9:49 Shechem also died, about a thousand men and W
9:51 all the men and W, and shut themselves in;
16:27 full of men and W; all the lords of
16:27 three thousand men and W, who looked on while
21:10 the sword; also the W and the little ones.
21:14 they gave them the W whom they had saved
21:14 saved alive of the W of Jabesh-gilead; but they
21:16 are left, since the W are destroyed out of
Ruth 1:19 of them; and the W said, "Is this Naomi?"
4:14 Then the W said to Naomi, "Blessed be the
4:17 And the W of the neighborhood gave him a
1Sam 2:22 they lay with the W who served at the
4:20 of her death the W attending her said to
15:33 your sword has made W childless, so shall your
15:33 childless, so shall your mother be childless among W
18:6 slaying the Philistine, the W came out of all
18:7 And the W sang to one another as they
21:4 only the young men have kept themselves from W
21:5 priest, "Of a truth W have been kept from
22:19 sword; both men and W, children and sucklings, oxen,
30:2 and taken captive the W and all who were
2Sam 1:26 to me was wonderful, passing the love of W
6:19 Israel, both men and W, to each a cake
19:35 to the voice of singing men and singing W
1Kgs 11:1 Solomon loved many foreign W: the daughter of
11:1 Edomite, Sidonian, and Hittite W,
2Kgs 8:12 and rip up their W with child."
15:16 ripped up all the W in it who were
23:7 the LORD, where the W wove hangings for the
1Chr 16:3 Israel, both men and W, to each a loaf
2Chr 28:8 thousand of their kinsfolk, W, sons, and daughters;
35:25 singing men and singing W have spoken of Josiah
Ezra 10:1 great assembly of men, W, and children, gathered to
10:2 and have married foreign W from the peoples of
10:10 trespassed and married foreign W, and so increased
10:17 of all the men who had married foreign W
10:18 married foreign W were found Ma-aseiah, Eliezer,
10:44 these had married foreign W, and they put them
Neh 8:2 assembly, both men and W and all who could
8:3 the men and the W and those who could
12:43 with great joy; the W and children also rejoiced.
13:23 Jews who had married W of Ashdod, Ammon, and
13:26 king of Israel sin on account of such W
13:26 all Israel; nevertheless foreign W made even him to
13:27 against our God by marrying foreign W
Tob 2:11 Anna earned money at W's work.
Jud 4:11 all the men and W of Israel, and their
6:16 young men and their W ran to the assembly;
7:23 lost heart, and the W and young men fainted
7:24 the young men, the W, and the children, gathered
7:33 The W and children he sent home.
8:7 silver, and men and W slaves, and cattle, and
10:11 The W went straight on through the valley; and
10:19 these people, who have W like this among them?
13:18 High God above all W on earth; and blessed
15:12 Then all the W of Israel gathered to see
15:12 gave them to the W who were with her;
15:13 dance, leading all the W, while all the men
Esth 1:9 a banquet for the W in the palace which
1:17 made known to all W, causing them to look
1:20 as it is, all W will give honor to
2:3 in charge of the W; let their ointments be
2:8 custody of Hegai who had charge of the W
2:12 the regulations for the W, since this was the
2:12 spices and ointments for W –
2:15 had charge of the W, advised.
2:17 more than all the W, and she found grace
3:13 Jews, young and old, W and children, in one
7:4 as slaves, men and W, I would have held
8:11 with their children and W, and to plunder their
Job 2:10 one of the foolish W would speak.
42:15 land there were no W so fair as Job's
Ps 68:12 The W at home divide the spoil,
Prov 31:3 not your strength to W, your ways to those
31:29 he praises her: "Many W have done excellently, but
Eccl 2:8 singers, both men and W, and many concubines,
Song 1:8 know, O fairest among W, follow in the tracks
5:9 more than another beloved, O fairest among W
6:1 Whither has your beloved gone, O fairest among W
Sir 10:18 men, nor fierce anger for those born of W
19:2 Wine and W lead intelligent men astray, and the
28:15 has driven away courageous W, and deprived them of
42:12 in the midst of W;
47:19 laid your loins beside W, and through your body
48:19 were in anguish, like W in travail.
Is 3:12 are their oppressors, and W rule over them.
4:1 And seven W shall take hold of one man
19:16 Egyptians will be like W, and tremble with fear
27:11 dry, they are broken; W come and make a
32:9 Rise up, you W who are at ease, hear
32:10 will shudder, you complacent W; for the vintage will
32:11 Tremble, you W who are at ease, shudder, you
Jer 2:33 that even to wicked W you have taught your
7:18 kindle fire, and the W knead dough, to make
9:17 call for the mourning W to come; send for
9:17 send for the skilful W to come;
9:20 Hear, O W, the word of the LORD, and
38:22 me: Behold, all the W left in the house
40:7 committed to him men, W, and children, those of
41:16 son of Ahikam–soldiers, W, children, and eunuchs,
43:6 the men, the W, the children, the princesses,
44:15 gods, and all the W who stood by, a
44:19 And the W said, "When we burned incense to
44:20 the people, men and W, all the people who
44:24 people and all the W, "Hear the word of
50:37 troops in her midst, that they may become W
51:30 failed, they have become W; her dwellings are on
Lam 2:20 Should W eat their offspring, the children of their
4:10 The hands of compassionate W have boiled their own
5:11 W are ravished in Zion, virgins in the towns
Bar 6:29 may be touched by W in menstruation or at
6:30 W serve meals for gods of silver and gold
6:43 And the W, with cords about them, sit along
Ezek 8:14 and behold, there sat W weeping for Tammuz.
9:6 maidens, little children and W, but touch no one
13:18 GOD: Woe to the W who sew magic bands
16:34 were different from other W in your harlotries: none
16:38 will judge you as W who break wedlock and
16:41 the sight of many W; I will make you

22:10 in you they humble W who are unclean in
23:2 man, there were two W, the daughters of one
23:10 became a byword among W, when judgment had
23:42 the hands of the W, and beautiful crowns upon
23:45 with the sentence of W that shed blood; because
23:48 the land, that all W may take warning and
30:17 the sword; and the W shall go into captivity.
Dan 11:17 him the daughter of W to destroy the kingdom;
11:37 the one beloved by W; he shall not give
14:20 footsteps of men and W and children."
Hos 13:16 pieces, and their pregnant W ripped open.
Amos 1:13 they have ripped up W with child in Gilead,
Mic 2:9 The W of my people you drive out from
Nah 3:13 Behold, your troops are W in your midst.
Zech 5:9 saw, and behold, two W coming forward!
8:4 Old men and old W shall again sit in
14:2 houses plundered and the W ravished; half of the
1Mac 1:26 faint, the beauty of W faded.
1:32 they took captive the W and children, and seized
1:60 put to death the W who had their children
2Mac 3:19 W, girded with sackcloth under their breasts,
5:13 old, destruction of boys, W, and children, and
5:24 and to sell the W and boys as slaves.
6:4 and had intercourse with W within the sacred
6:10 For example, two W were brought in for having
6:10 These W they publicly paraded about the city, with
12:21 he sent off the W and the children and
Mt 11:11 among those born of W there has risen no
14:21 five thousand men, besides W and children.
15:38 four thousand men, besides W and children.
24:41 Two W will be grinding at the mill; one
27:55 There were also many W there, looking on from
28:5 angel said to the W, "Do not be afraid;
Mk 15:39 There were also W looking on from afar, among
15:40 and also many other W who came up with
Lk 1:42 "Blessed are you among W, and blessed is the
7:28 among those born of W none is greater than
8:2 him, and also some W who had been healed
17:35 There will be two W grinding together; one will
23:26 the people, and of W who bewailed and lamented
23:48 his acquaintances and the W who had followed him
23:54 The W who had come with him from Galilee
24:10 James and the other W with them who told
24:22 Moreover, some W of our company amazed us.
24:24 it just as the W had said; but him
Acts 1:14 prayer, together with the W and Mary the mother
5:14 both of men and W,
8:3 dragged off men and W and committed them to
8:12 Jesus Christ, they were baptized, both men and W
9:2 the Way, men or W, he might bring them
13:50 Jews incited the devout W of high standing and
16:13 and spoke to the W who had come together.
17:4 Greeks and not a few of the leading W
17:12 not a few Greek W of high standing as
22:4 prison both men and W,
Rom 1:26 Their W exchanged natural relations for unnatural,
1:27 up natural relations with W and were consumed with
1Cor 14:34 of the saints, the W should keep silence in
Gal 4:24 is an allegory: these W are two covenants.
Phil 4:3 true yokefellow, help these W, for they have labored
1Tim 2:9 or quarreling; also that W should adorn themselves
2:10 good deeds, as befits W who profess religion.
3:11 The W likewise must be serious, no slanderers, but
5:2 men like brothers, older W like mothers, younger
5:2 women like mothers, younger W like sisters, in all
2Tim 3:6 households and capture weak W, burdened with sins
Tit 2:3 Bid the older W likewise to be reverent in
2:4 so train the young W to love their husbands
Heb 11:35 W received their dead by resurrection.
1Pet 3:5 So once the holy W who hoped in God
Rev 9:8 faces, their hair like W's hair, and their teeth
14:4 not defiled themselves with W, for they are chaste;

WON (14)

2Sam 8:13 And David W a name for himself.
23:18 and slew them, and W a name beside the
23:22 son of Jehoiada, and W a name beside the
1Chr 11:20 and slew them, and W a name beside the
11:24 son of Jehoiada, and W a name beside the
26:27 From spoil W in battles they dedicated gifts for
Jud 8:16 human being, to be W over by pleading.
Esth 2:9 maiden pleased him and W his favor; and he
Ps 78:54 to the mountain which his right hand had W
1Mac 11:24 And he W his favor.
2Mac 12:11 Judas and his men W the victory, by the
15:9 the struggles they had W, he made them the

Heb 11:34 edge of the sword, W strength out of weakness,
1Pet 3:1 the word, may be W without a word by

WONDER (13)

Deut 13:1 a sign or a W,
13:2 and the sign or W which he tells you
28:46 a sign and a W, and upon your descendants
Sir 11:19 Do not W at the works of a sinner,
16:11 it will be a W if he remains unpunished.
26:11 eye, and do not W if she sins against
Hab 1:5 the nations, and see; W and be astounded.
Acts 3:10 they were filled with W and amazement at what
3:12 Israel, why do you W at this, or why
13:41 'Behold, you scoffers, and W, and perish; for I
2Cor 11:14 And no W, for even Satan disguises himself as
1Jn 3:13 Do not W, brethren, that the world hates you.
Rev 13:3 and the whole earth followed the beast with W

WONDERED (12)

Is 59:16 was no man, and W that there was no
Mt 15:31 so that the throng W, when they saw the
27:14 so that the governor W greatly.
Mk 15:5 Jesus made no further answer, so that Pilate W
15:43 And Pilate W if he were already dead; and
Lk 1:21 for Zechariah, and they W at his delay in
2:18 all who heard it W at what the shepherds
4:22 well of him, and W at the gracious words
24:41 disbelieved for joy, and W, he said to them,
Acts 2:7 they were amazed and W, saying, "Are not all
4:13 common men, they W; and they recognized that
7:31 Moses saw it he W at the sight; and

WONDERFUL (38)

Judg 6:13 where are all his W deeds which our fathers
13:18 do you ask my name, seeing it is W
2Sam 1:26 love to me was W, passing the love of
1Chr 16:9 tell of all his W works!
16:12 Remember the W works that he has done, the
2Chr 2:9 I am to build will be great and W
Tob 12:22 confessed the great and W works of God, and
Jud 16:13 are great and glorious, W in strength, invincible.
Esth 13:10 and earth and every W thing under heaven,
15:14 For you are W, my lord, and your countenance
Job 42:3 not understand, things too W for me, which I
Ps 9:1 tell of all thy W deeds.
105:2 tell of all his W works!
105:5 Remember the W works that he has done, his
106:7 did not consider thy W works; they did not
107:8 steadfast love, for his W works to the sons
107:15 steadfast love, for his W works to the sons
107:21 steadfast love, for his W works to the sons
107:31 steadfast love, for his W works to the sons
111:4 He has caused his W works to be remembered;
119:129 Thy testimonies are W; therefore my soul keeps
139:6 Such knowledge is too W for me; it is
139:14 I praise thee, for thou art fearful and W
139:14 W are thy works!
Prov 30:18 Three things are too W for me; four I
Sir 11:4 of the Lord are W, and his works are
31:9 for he has done W things among his people.
Is 9:6 will be called W Counselor, Mighty God, Everlasting
25:1 for thou hast done W things, plans formed of
28:29 of hosts; he is W in counsel, and excellent
29:14 things with this people, W and marvelous; and the
Jer 21:2 according to all his W deeds, and will make
Mt 21:15 the scribes saw the W things that he did,
Mk 13:1 him, "Look, Teacher, what W stones and what
13:1 wonderful stones and what W buildings!"
1Pet 2:9 you may declare the W deeds of him who
Rev 15:1 in heaven, great and W, seven angels with seven
15:3 Lamb, saying, "Great and W are thy deeds, O

WONDERING (2)

Lk 24:12 and he went home W at what had happened"
Acts 5:24 much perplexed about them, W what this would

WONDERS (59)

Ex 3:20 Egypt with all the W which I will do
7:3 multiply my signs and W in the land of
11:9 to you; that my W may be multiplied in
11:10 Aaron did all these W before Pharaoh; and the
15:11 majestic in holiness, terrible in glorious deeds, doing
W
Deut 4:34 trials, by signs, by W, and by war, by
6:22 LORD showed signs and W, great and grievous,
7:19 saw, the signs, the W, the mighty hand, and

26:8 terror, with signs and W;
29:3 signs, and those great W;
34:11 the signs and the W which the LORD sent
Josh 3:5 the LORD will do W among you."
Judg 13:19 rock to the LORD, to him who works W
1Chr 16:12 he has done, the W he wrought, the judgments
Neh 9:10 didst perform signs and W against Pharaoh and all
9:17 not mindful of the W which thou didst perform
Esth 10:9 done great signs and W, which have not occurred
Job 10:16 lion, and again work W against me;
Ps 77:11 I will remember thy W of old.
77:14 the God who workest W, who hast manifested thy
78:4 his might, and the W which he has wrought.
78:32 still sinned; despite his W they did not believe.
88:10 Dost thou work W for the dead?
88:12 Are thy W known in the darkness, or thy
89:5 the heavens praise thy W, O LORD, thy faithfulness
135:9 Egypt, sent signs and W against Pharaoh and all
136:4 who alone does great W, for his steadfast love
Wis 8:8 foreknowledge of signs and W and of the outcome
10:16 withstood dread kings with W and signs.
19:8 through as one nation, after gazing on marvelous W
Sir 18:5 possible to trace the W of the Lord.
36:6 anew, and work further W; make thy hand and
40:7 he wakes up, and W that his fear came
45:19 destroyed; he wrought W against them to consume
48:14 his life he did W, so in death his
Jer 32:20 hast shown signs and W in the land of
32:21 Egypt with signs and W, with a strong hand
Bar 2:11 and with signs and W and with great power
Dan 4:2 show the signs and W that the Most High
4:3 How great are his signs, how mighty his W
6:27 he works signs and W in heaven and on
12:6 shall it be till the end of these W
2Mac 15:21 the Lord who works W; for he knew that
Mt 24:24 show great signs and W, so as to lead
Mk 13:22 and show signs and W, to lead astray, if
Jn 4:48 you see signs and W you will not believe."
Acts 2:19 And I will show W in the heaven above
2:22 with mighty works and W and signs which God
2:43 every soul; and many W and signs were done
4:30 heal, and signs and W are performed through the
5:12 Now many signs and W were done among the
6:8 and power, did great W and signs among the
7:36 them out, having performed W and signs in Egypt
14:3 grace, granting signs and W to be done by
15:12 related what signs and W God had done through
Rom 15:19 power of signs and W, by the power of
2Cor 12:12 patience, with signs and W and mighty works.
2Thes 2:9 with pretended signs and W,
Heb 2:4 witness by signs and W and various miracles and

WONDROUS (15)

Job 37:14 stop and consider the W works of God.
37:16 of the clouds, the W works of him who
Ps 26:7 and telling all thy W deeds.
40:5 LORD my God, thy W deeds and thy thoughts
71:17 I still proclaim thy W deeds.
72:18 Israel, who alone does W things.
75:1 name and recount thy W deeds.
86:10 art great and doest W things, thou alone art
106:22 great things in Egypt, W works in the land
107:24 of the LORD, his W works in the deep.
119:18 that I may behold W things out of thy
119:27 will meditate on thy W works.
145:5 majesty, and on thy W works, I will meditate.
Sir 36:14 the celebration of thy W deeds, and thy temple
48:4 O Elijah, in your W deeds!

WONDROUSLY (4)

Job 37:5 God thunders W with his voice; he does great
Ps 17:7 W show thy steadfast love, O savior of those
31:21 LORD, for he has W shown his steadfast love
Joel 2:26 God, who has dealt W with you.

WONT (4)

2Sam 20:18 she said, "They were W to say in old
Ps 119:132 me, as is thy W toward those who love
Dan 3:19 more than it was W to be heated.
Mk 15:8 do as he was W to do for them.

WONTED

Ex 14:27 sea returned to its W flow when the morning

WOOD (137)

Gen 6:14 an ark of gopher W; make rooms in the
22:3 and he cut the W for the burnt offering,
22:6 And Abraham took the W of the burnt offering,
22:7 the fire and the W; but where is the
22:9 there, and laid the W in order, and bound
22:9 and laid him on the altar, upon the W
Ex 7:19 both in vessels of W and in vessels of
25:5 rams' skins, goatskins, acacia W,
25:10 an ark of acacia W; two cubits and a
25:13 make poles of acacia W, and overlay them with
25:23 a table of acacia W; two cubits shall be
25:28 the poles of acacia W, and overlay them with
26:15 make upright frames for the tabernacle of acacia W
26:26 make bars of acacia W, five for the frames
27:1 the altar of acacia W, five cubits long and
27:6 altar, poles of acacia W, and overlay them with
30:1 incense upon; of acacia W shall you make it.
30:5 the poles of acacia W, and overlay them with
31:5 setting, and in carving W, for work in every
35:7 skins, and goatskins; acacia W,
35:24 whom was found acacia W of any use in
35:33 setting, and in carving W, for work in every
36:20 the upright frames for the tabernacle of acacia W
36:31 made bars of acacia W, five for the frames
37:1 the ark of acacia W; two cubits and a
37:4 made poles of acacia W, and overlaid them with
37:10 the table of acacia W; two cubits was its
37:15 the poles of acacia W to carry the table,
37:25 of incense of acacia W; its length was a
37:28 the poles of acacia W, and overlaid them with
38:1 offering also of acacia W; five cubits was its
38:6 the poles of acacia W, and overlaid them with
Lev 1:7 the altar, and lay W in order upon the
1:8 in order upon the W that is on the
1:12 in order upon the W that is on the
1:17 the altar, upon the W that is on the
3:5 which is upon the W on the fire; it
4:12 on a fire of W; where the ashes are
6:12 the priest shall burn W on it every morning,
11:32 is an article of W or a garment or
15:12 and every vessel of W shall be rinsed in
Num 13:20 and whether there is W in it or not.
31:20 work of goats' hair, and every article of W
35:18 with a weapon of W in the hand, by
Deut 4:28 will serve gods of W and stone, the work
10:1 on the mountain, and make an ark of W
10:3 an ark of acacia W, and hewed two tables
19:5 his neighbor to cut W, and his hand swings
28:36 serve other gods, of W and stone.
28:64 serve other gods, of W and stone, which neither
29:11 he who hews your W and he who draws
29:17 things, their idols of W and stone, of silver
Josh 9:21 they became hewers of W and drawers of water
9:23 be slaves, hewers of W and drawers of water
9:27 that day hewers of W and drawers of water
Judg 6:26 burnt offering with the W of the Asherah which
1Sam 6:14 they split up the W of the cart and
2Sam 24:22 and the yokes of the oxen for the W
1Kgs 6:15 on the inside with W; and he covered the
6:34 two doors of cypress W; the two leaves of
10:11 great amount of almug W and precious stones.
10:12 made of the almug W supports for the house
10:12 singers; no such almug W has come or been
18:23 lay it on the W, but put no fire
18:23 lay it on the W, and put no fire
18:33 And he put the W in order, and cut
18:33 bull in pieces and laid it on the W
18:33 it on the burnt offering, and on the W
18:38 burnt offering, and the W, and the stones, and
2Kgs 19:18 work of men's hands, W and stone; therefore they
1Chr 16:33 the trees of the W sing for joy before
21:23 threshing sledges for the W, and the wheat for
29:2 things of iron, and W for the things of
29:2 for the things of W, besides great quantities of
2Chr 2:14 bronze, iron, stone, and W, and in purple, blue,
3:10 made two cherubim of W and overlaid them with
9:10 from Ophir, brought algum W and precious stones.
9:11 made of the algum W steps for the house
Neh 10:34 the people, for the W offering, to bring it
13:31 I provided for the W offering, at appointed times,
Job 41:27 counts iron as straw, and bronze as rotten W
Ps 74:6 then all its carved W they broke down with
96:12 the trees of the W sing for joy
Prov 26:20 For lack of W the fire goes out; and
26:21 to hot embers and W to fire, so is
Song 2:3 the trees of the W, so is my beloved
3:9 a palanquin from the W of Lebanon.

Wis 10:4 the righteous man by a paltry piece of W
14:1 upon a piece of W more fragile than the
14:5 the smallest piece of W, and passing through the
14:7 For blessed is the W by which righteousness comes.
14:21 objects of stone or W the name that ought
Sir 8:3 a chatterer, nor heap W on his fire.
Is 10:15 a staff should lift him who is not W
30:33 wide, with fire and W in abundance; the breath
37:19 work of men's hands, W and stone; therefore they
40:20 chooses for an offering W that will not rot;
44:19 Shall I fall down before a block of W
60:17 bring silver; instead of W, bronze, instead of stones,
Jer 5:14 fire, and this people W, and the fire shall
7:18 The children gather W, the fathers kindle fire, and
10:8 and foolish; the instruction of idols is but W
Lam 4:8 their bones, it has become as dry as W
5:4 water we drink, the W we get must be
5:13 the mill; and boys stagger under loads of W
Bar 6:4 silver and gold and W, which are carried on
6:11 silver and gold and W,
6:30 silver and gold and W;
6:39 that are made of W and overlaid with gold
6:50 they are made of W and overlaid with gold
6:57 Gods made of W and overlaid with silver and
6:70 are their gods of W, overlaid with gold and
6:71 way, their gods of W, overlaid with gold and
Ezek 15:2 man, how does the W of the vine surpass
15:2 the vine surpass any W, the vine branch which
15:3 Is W taken from it to make anything?
15:6 Lord GOD: Like the W of the vine among
20:32 the countries, and worship W and stone.'
21:10 despised the rod, my son, with everything of W
39:10 not need to take W out of the field
41:16 temple was paneled with W round about, from the
41:22 resembling an altar of W, three cubits high, two
41:22 corners, its base, and its walls were of W
41:25 was a canopy of W in front of the
Dan 5:4 and silver, bronze, iron, W, and stone.
5:23 gold, of bronze, iron, W, and stone, which do
Hos 4:12 of a thing of W, and their staff gives
Hag 1:8 the hills and bring W and build the house,
Zech 12:6 in the midst of W, like a flaming torch
2Mac 1:21 the liquid on the W and what was laid
4:41 stones, some blocks of W, and others took handfuls
Lk 23:30 do this when the W is green, what will
1Cor 3:12 gold, silver, precious stones, W, hay, straw–
2Tim 2:20 silver but also of W and earthenware, and some
Rev 9:20 bronze and stone and W, which cannot either see
18:12 all kinds of scented W, all articles of ivory,
18:12 all articles of costly W, bronze, iron and marble,

WOODCUTTER

Wis 13:11 A skilled W may saw down a tree easy

WOODED (3)

2Chr 27:4 and towers on the W hills.
Jer 26:18 of the house a W height.'
Mic 3:12 of the house a W height.

WOODEN (9)

Neh 8:4 scribe stood on a W pulpit which they had
Ps 74:5 entrance they hacked the W trellis with axes.
Sir 22:14 A W beam firmly bonded into a building will
Is 45:20 who carry about their W idols, and keep on
Jer 28:13 LORD: You have broken W bars, but I will
Bar 6:55 in a temple of W gods overlaid with gold
6:59 gods; better also a W pillar in a palace,
Hab 2:19 who says to a W thing, Awake; to a
1Mac 6:37 upon the elephants were W towers, strong and

WOODS (4)

2Kgs 2:24 came out of the W and tore forty-two of
Bar 5:8 The W and every fragrant tree have shaded Israel
6:63 to consume mountains and W does what it is
Ezek 34:25 securely in the wilderness and sleep in the W

WOODWORK

Hab 2:11 the beam from the W respond.

WOOED

1Sam 25:39 Then David sent and W Abigail, to make her

WOOF (9)

Lev 13:48 garment, in warp or W of linen or wool,
13:49 whether in warp or W or in skin or
13:51 garment, in warp or W, or in the skin,
13:52 diseased in warp or W, woolen or linen, or
13:53 garment in warp or W or in anything of
13:56 or the warp or W;
13:57 garment, in warp or W, or in anything of
13:58 the garment, warp or W, or anything of skin
13:59 either in warp or W, or in anything of

WOOL (17)

Lev 13:48 woof of linen or W, or in a skin
13:59 in a garment of W or linen, either in
Deut 22:11 wear a mingled stuff, W and linen together.
Judg 6:37 laying a fleece of W on the threshing floor;
2Kgs 3:4 thousand lambs, and the W of a hundred thousand
Ps 147:16 He gives snow like W; he scatters hoarfrost like
Prov 31:13 She seeks W and flax, and works with willing
Is 1:18 are red like crimson, they shall become like W
51:8 will eat them like W; but my deliverance will
Ezek 27:18 of Helbon, and white W,
34:3 clothe yourselves with the W, you slaughter the
44:17 shall have nothing of W on them, while they
Dan 7:9 his head like pure W; his throne was fiery
Hos 2:5 and my water, my W and my flax, my
2:9 will take away my W and my flax, which
Heb 9:19 with water and scarlet W and hyssop, and sprinkled
Rev 1:14 were white as white W, white as snow; his

WOOLEN (2)

Lev 13:47 a garment, whether a W or a linen garment,
13:52 in warp or woof, W or linen, or anything

WORD (730)

Gen 15:1 After these things the W of the LORD came
15:4 And behold, the W of the LORD came to
27:8 my son, obey my W as I command you.
27:13 son; only obey my W, and go, fetch them
31:24 you say not a W to Jacob, either good
37:14 flock; and bring me W again." So he sent
38:25 brought out, she sent W to her father-in-law, "By
44:18 pray you, speak a W in my lord's ears,
Ex 8:13 did according to the W of Moses; the frogs
9:20 he who feared the W of the LORD among
9:21 did not regard the W of the LORD left
32:28 did according to the W of Moses; and there
36:6 Moses gave command, and W was proclaimed
Lev 10:7 did according to the W of Moses.
Num 3:16 them according to the W of the LORD, as
3:51 sons, according to the W of the LORD, as
11:23 shall see whether my W will come true for
13:26 Kadesh; they brought back W to them and to
14:20 pardoned, according to your W;
15:31 he has despised the W of the LORD, and
22:8 I will bring back W to you, as the
22:35 men; but only the W which I bid you,
22:38 The W that God puts in my mouth, that
23:5 the LORD put a W in Balaam's mouth, and
23:16 Balaam, and put a W in his mouth, and
24:13 to go beyond the W of the LORD, to
27:14 you rebelled against my W in the wilderness of
27:21 the LORD; at his W they shall go out,
27:21 out, and at his W they shall come in,
30:2 shall not break his W; he shall do according
36:5 Israel according to the W of the LORD, saying,
Deut 1:22 us, and bring us W again of the way
1:25 us, and brought us W again, and said, 'It
1:32 in spite of this W you did not believe
4:2 not add to the W which I command you,
5:5 declare to you the W of the LORD; for
9:5 he may confirm the W which the LORD swore
18:20 presumes to speak a W in my name which
18:21 may we know the W which the LORD has
18:22 the LORD, if the W does not come to
18:22 true, that is a W which the LORD has
21:5 LORD, and by their W every dispute and every
30:14 do it?' But the W is very near you;
33:9 For they observed thy W, and kept thy covenant.
34:5 Moab, according to the W of the LORD,
Josh 1:13 Joshua said, "Remember the W which Moses the
6:10 heard, neither shall any W go out of your
8:27 booty, according to the W of the LORD which
8:35 There was not a W of all that Moses
14:7 and I brought him W again as it was
14:10 the LORD spoke this W to Moses, while Israel
22:32 Israel, and brought back W to them.
Judg 21:13 the whole congregation sent W to the Benjaminites
1Sam 1:23 weaned him; only, may the LORD establish his W
3:1 And the W of the LORD was rare in

W

3:7 the LORD, and the W of the LORD had
3:21 at Shiloh by the W of the LORD.
4:1 And the W of Samuel came to all Israel.
9:27 known to you the W of God."
15:10 The W of the LORD came to Samuel:
15:23 you have rejected the W of the LORD, he
15:26 you have rejected the W of the LORD, and
17:29 Was it not but a W
2Sam 3:11 not answer Abner another W, because he feared him.
7:4 that same night the W of the LORD came
7:7 did I speak a W with any of the
7:25 confirm for ever the W which thou hast spoken
11:6 So David sent W to Joab, "Send me Uriah
12:9 have you despised the W of the LORD, to
14:12 your handmaid speak a W to my lord the
14:17 your handmaid thought, 'The W of my lord the
14:32 Joab, "Behold, I sent W to you, 'Come here,
15:28 of the wilderness, until W comes from you to
19:11 his house, when the W of all Israel has
19:14 so that they sent W to the king, "Return,
23:2 speaks by me, his W is upon my tongue.
24:4 But the king's W prevailed against Joab and the
24:11 in the morning, the W of the LORD came
24:19 went up at Gad's W, as the LORD commanded.
1Kgs 2:4 LORD may establish his W which he spoke
2:23 more also if this W does not cost Adonijah
2:27 LORD, thus fulfilling the W of the LORD which
2:30 Benaiah brought the king W again, saying, "Thus
3:12 right, behold, I now do according to your W
5:2 And Solomon sent W to Hiram,
6:11 Now the W of the LORD came to Solomon,
6:12 I will establish my W with you, which I
8:26 of Israel, let thy W be confirmed, which thou
8:56 he promised; not one W has failed of all
12:15 he might fulfil his W, which the LORD spoke
12:22 But the W of God came to Shemaiah the
12:24 they hearkened to the W of the LORD, and
12:24 again, according to the W of the LORD.
13:1 of Judah by the W of the LORD to
13:2 the altar by the W of the LORD, and
13:5 had given by the W of the LORD.
13:9 commanded me by the W of the LORD, saying,
13:17 to me by the W of the LORD, 'You
13:18 to me by the W of the LORD, saying,
13:20 at the table, the W of the LORD came
13:21 you have disobeyed the W of the LORD, and
13:26 God, who disobeyed the W of the LORD; therefore
13:26 him, according to the W which the LORD spoke
13:32 he cried by the W of the LORD against
14:18 him, according to the W of the LORD, which
15:29 it, according to the W of the LORD which
16:1 And the W of the LORD came to Jehu
16:7 Moreover the W of the LORD came by the
16:12 Baasha, according to the W of the LORD, which
16:34 Segub, according to the W of the LORD, which
17:1 dew nor rain these years, except by my W
17:2 And the W of the LORD came to him,
17:5 did according to the W of the LORD; he
17:8 Then the W of the LORD came to him,
17:16 fail, according to the W of the LORD which
17:24 God, and that the W of the LORD in
18:1 After many days the W of the LORD came
18:21 And the people did not answer him a W
18:31 Jacob, to whom the W of the LORD came,
18:36 I have done all these things at thy W
19:9 there; and behold, the W of the LORD came
20:9 departed and brought him W again.
21:11 as Jezebel had sent W to them.
21:17 Then the W of the LORD came to Elijah
21:28 And the W of the LORD came to Elijah
22:5 "Inquire first for the W of the LORD."
22:13 the king; let your W be like the word
22:13 word be like the W of one of them,
22:19 said, "Therefore hear the W of the LORD: I
22:38 it, according to the W of the LORD which
2Kgs 1:16 to inquire of his W—therefore you shall not
1:17 died according to the W of the LORD which
2:22 day, according to the W which Elisha spoke.
3:7 he went and sent W to Jehoshaphat king of
3:12 And Jehoshaphat said, "The W of the LORD is
4:13 Would you have a W spoken on your behalf
4:44 left, according to the W of the LORD.
5:7 that this man sends W to me to cure
5:14 Jordan, according to the W of the man of
6:9 man of God sent W to the king of
7:1 Elisha said, "Hear the W of the LORD: thus
7:16 shekel, according to the W of the LORD.
8:2 did according to the W of the man of
9:26 in accordance with the W of the LORD."
9:36 said, "This is the W of the LORD, which
10:10 earth nothing of the W of the LORD, which
10:17 out, according to the W of the LORD which
14:9 king of Israel sent W to Amaziah king of
14:25 Arabah, according to the W of the LORD, the
18:28 of Judah: "Hear the W of the great king,
18:36 answered him not a W, for the king's command
19:21 This is the W that the LORD has spoken
20:4 the middle court, the W of the LORD came
20:16 to Hezekiah, "Hear the W of the LORD:
20:19 Hezekiah to Isaiah, "The W of the LORD which
22:20 And they brought back W to the king.
23:16 it, according to the W of the LORD which
24:2 it, according to the W of the LORD which
1Chr 11:3 Israel, according to the W of the LORD by
11:10 king, according to the W of the LORD concerning
12:23 him, according to the W of the LORD.
15:15 commanded according to the W of the LORD.
16:15 for ever, of the W that he commanded, for
17:3 that same night the W of the LORD came
17:6 did I speak a W with any of the
17:23 O LORD, let the W which thou hast spoken
21:4 But the king's W prevailed against Joab.
21:19 went up at Gad's W, which he had spoken
22:8 But the W of the LORD came to me,
2Chr 2:3 And Solomon sent W to Huram the king of
6:17 of Israel, let thy W be confirmed, which thou
10:15 LORD might fulfil his W, which he spoke by
11:2 But the W of the LORD came to Shemaiah
11:4 they hearkened to the W of the LORD, and
12:7 they humbled themselves, the W of the LORD came
18:4 "Inquire first for the W of the LORD."
18:12 the king; let your W be like the word
18:12 word be like the W of one of them,
18:18 said, "Therefore hear the W of the LORD: I
25:18 king of Israel sent W to Amaziah king of
30:12 princes commanded by the W of the LORD.
34:21 have not kept the W of the LORD, to
34:28 And they brought back W to the king.
35:6 do according to the W of the LORD by
36:21 Persia, to fulfil the W of the LORD by
36:22 of Persia, that the W of the LORD by
Ezra 1:1 of Persia, that the W of the LORD by
6:13 Then, according to the W sent by Darius the
Neh 1:8 Remember the W which thou didst command thy
5:8 could not find a W to say.
Jud 5:5 lord now hear a W from the mouth of
7:9 our lord hear a W, lest his army be
11:15 When the W reaches them and they proceed to
14:12 saw them they sent W to their commanders, and
Esth 7:9 prepared for Mordecai, whose W saved the king, is
Job 2:13 no one spoke a W to him, for they
4:2 "If one ventures a W with you, will you
4:12 "Now a W was brought to me stealthily, my
15:11 for you, or the W that deals gently with
29:22 speak again, and my W dropped upon them.
32:15 they have not a W to say.
Ps 17:4 of men, by the W of thy lips I
33:4 For the W of the LORD is upright; and
33:6 By the W of the LORD the heavens were
56:4 In God, whose W I praise, in God I
56:10 In God, whose W I praise, in the LORD,
56:10 in the LORD, whose W I praise,
89:34 covenant, or alter the W that went forth from
103:20 ones who do his W, hearkening to the voice
103:20 his word, hearkening to the voice of his W
105:8 for ever, of the W that he commanded, for
105:19 came to pass the W of the LORD tested
107:20 he sent forth his W, and healed them, and
119:9 By guarding it according to thy W
119:11 have laid up thy W in my heart, that
119:16 in thy statutes; I will not forget thy W
119:17 servant, that I may live and observe thy W
119:25 to the dust; revive me according to thy W
119:28 away for sorrow; strengthen me according to thy W
119:42 who taunt me, for I trust in thy W
119:43 And take not the W of truth utterly out
119:49 Remember thy W to thy servant, in which thou
119:65 with thy servant, O LORD, according to thy W
119:67 I went astray; but now I keep thy W
119:74 and rejoice, because I have hoped in thy W
119:81 languishes for thy salvation; I hope in thy W
119:89 ever, O LORD, thy W is firmly fixed in

119:101 every evil way, in order to keep thy W
119:105 Thy W is a lamp to my feet and
119:107 give me life, O LORD, according to thy W
119:114 place and my shield; I hope in thy W
119:160 The sum of thy W is truth; and every
119:162 I rejoice at thy W like one who finds
119:169 O LORD; give me understanding according to thy W
119:170 come before thee; deliver me according to thy W
119:172 will sing of thy W, for all thy commandments
130:5 waits, and in his W I hope;
138:2 hast exalted above everything thy name and thy W
139:4 Even before a W is on my tongue, lo,
141:6 shall learn that the W of the LORD is
147:15 to the earth; his W runs swiftly.
147:18 He sends forth his W, and melts them; he
147:19 He declares his W to Jacob, his statutes and
Prov 12:25 down, but a good W makes him glad.
13:13 He who despises the W brings destruction on himself,
15:1 wrath, but a harsh W stirs up anger.
15:23 a man, and a W in season, how good
16:20 gives heed to the W will prosper, and happy
19:16 he who despises the W will die.
21:28 will perish, but the W of a man who
25:11 A W fitly spoken is like apples of gold
30:5 Every W of God proves true; he is a
Eccl 5:2 hasty to utter a W before God, for God
8:4 For the W of the king is supreme, and
Wis 1:11 slander; because no secret W is without result, and
9:1 all things by thy W,
12:9 blow by dread wild beasts or thy stern W
16:12 but it was thy W, O Lord, which heals
16:26 man, but that thy W preserves those who trust
18:15 half gone, thy all-powerful W leaped from heaven,
18:22 arms, but by his W he subdued the punisher,
Sir 3:8 Honor your father by W and deed, that a
16:26 another aside, and they will never disobey his W
18:15 So a W is better than a gift.
18:16 Indeed, does not a W surpass a good gift?
19:10 Have you heard a W
19:11 With such a W a fool will suffer pangs
19:12 thigh, so is a W inside a fool.
29:3 Confirm your W and keep faith with him, and
31:31 his merrymaking; speak no W of reproach to him,
39:17 At his W the waters stood in a heap,
39:17 of water at the W of his mouth.
39:31 their times come they will not transgress his W
42:20 him, and not one W is hidden from him.
43:26 way, and by his W all things hold together.
48:1 a fire, and his W burned like a torch.
48:3 By the W of the Lord he shut up
48:5 from Hades, by the W of the Most High;
49:6 desolate, according to the W of Jeremiah.
Is 1:10 Hear the W of the LORD, you rulers of
2:1 The W which Isaiah the son of Amoz saw
2:3 the law, and the W of the LORD from
5:24 and have despised the W of the Holy One
8:10 to nought; speak a W, but it will not
8:20 Surely for this W which they speak there is
9:8 Lord has sent a W against Jacob, and it
16:13 This is the W which the LORD spoke concerning
24:3 utterly despoiled; for the LORD has spoken this W
28:13 Therefore the W of the LORD will be to
28:14 Therefore hear the W of the LORD, you scoffers,
29:21 off, who by a W make a man out
30:12 "Because you despise this W, and trust in oppression
30:21 ears shall hear a W behind you, saying, "This
36:21 answered him not a W, for the king's command
37:22 Assyria, this is the W that the LORD has
38:4 Then the W of the LORD came to Isaiah:
39:5 to Hezekiah, "Hear the W of the LORD of
39:8 Hezekiah to Isaiah, "The W of the LORD which
40:8 flower fades; but the W of our God will
44:26 foolish; who confirms the W of his servant, and
45:23 forth in righteousness a W that shall not return:
50:4 to sustain with a W him that is weary.
55:11 eater, so shall my W be that goes forth
66:2 and contrite in spirit, and trembles at my W
66:5 Hear the W of the LORD, you who tremble
66:5 who tremble at his W: "Your brethren who hate
Jer 1:2 Benjamin, to whom the W of the LORD came
1:4 'Now the W of the LORD came to me
1:11 And the W of the LORD came to me,
1:12 am watching over my W to perform it."
1:13 The W of the LORD came to me a
2:1 The W of the LORD came to me, saying,
2:4 Hear the W of the LORD, O house of
2:31 O generation, heed the W of the LORD.
5:13 will become wind; the W is not in them.
5:14 they have spoken this W, behold, I am making
6:10 cannot listen; behold, the W of the LORD is
7:1 The W that came to Jeremiah from the LORD:
7:2 and proclaim there this W, and say, Hear the
7:2 and say, Hear the W of the LORD, all
8:9 they have rejected the W of the LORD, and
9:20 Hear, O women, the W of the LORD, and
9:20 your ear receive the W of his mouth; teach
10:1 Hear the W which the LORD speaks to you,
11:1 The W that came to Jeremiah from the LORD:
13:2 waistcloth according to the W of the LORD, and
13:3 And the W of the LORD came to me
13:8 Then the W of the LORD came to me:
13:12 speak to them this W: 'Thus says the LORD,
14:1 The W of the LORD which came to Jeremiah
14:17 say to them this W: 'Let my eyes run
16:1 The W of the LORD came to me:
17:15 me, "Where is the W of the LORD?
17:20 and say: 'Hear the W of the LORD, you
18:1 The W that came to Jeremiah from the LORD:
18:5 Then the W of the LORD came to me:
18:18 the wise, nor the W from the prophet.
19:3 shall say, 'Hear the W of the LORD, O
20:8 For the W of the LORD has become for
21:1 This is the W which came to Jeremiah from
21:11 Judah say, 'Hear the W of the LORD,
22:1 and speak there this W,
22:2 and say, 'Hear the W of the LORD, O
22:4 will indeed obey this W, then there shall enter
22:29 land, land, hear the W of the LORD!
23:17 those who despise the W of the LORD, 'It
23:18 and to hear his W, or who has given
23:18 given heed to his W and listened?
23:28 him who has my W speak my word faithfully.
23:28 my word speak my W faithfully.
23:29 Is not my W like fire, says the LORD,
23:36 is every man's own W, and you pervert the
24:4 Then the W of the LORD came to me:
25:1 The W that came to Jeremiah concerning all the
25:3 to this day, the W of the LORD has
26:1 king of Judah, this W came from the LORD,
26:2 speak to them; do not hold back a W
27:1 king of Judah, this W came to Jeremiah from
27:3 Send W to the king of Edom, the king
27:18 prophets, and if the W of the LORD is
28:7 Yet hear now this W which I speak in
28:9 prophesies peace, when the W of that prophet comes
28:12 Jeremiah the prophet, the W of the LORD came
29:20 LORD.– Hear the W of the LORD, all
29:30 Then the W of the LORD came to Jeremiah:
30:1 The W that came to Jeremiah from the LORD:
31:10 "Hear the W of the LORD, O nations, and
32:1 The W that came to Jeremiah from the LORD
32:6 Jeremiah said, "The W of the LORD came to
32:8 in accordance with the W of the LORD, and
32:8 that this was the W of the LORD.
32:26 The W of the LORD came to Jeremiah:
33:1 The W of the LORD came to Jeremiah a
33:19 The W of the LORD came to Jeremiah:
33:23 The W of the LORD came to Jeremiah:
34:1 The W which came to Jeremiah from the LORD,
34:4 Babylon.' Yet hear the W of the LORD, O
34:5 I have spoken the W, says the LORD."
34:8 The W which came to Jeremiah from the LORD,
34:12 The W of the LORD came to Jeremiah from
35:1 The W which came to Jeremiah from the LORD
35:12 Then the W of the LORD came to Jeremiah:
36:1 king of Judah, this W came to Jeremiah from
36:27 at Jeremiah's dictation, the W of the LORD came
37:6 Then the W of the LORD came to Jeremiah
37:17 said, "Is there any W from the LORD?" Jeremiah
39:15 The W of the LORD came to Jeremiah while
40:1 The W that came to Jeremiah from the LORD
42:5 according to all the W with which the LORD
42:7 of ten days the W of the LORD came
42:15 there,' then hear the W of the LORD, O
43:8 Then the W of the LORD came to Jeremiah
44:1 The W that came to Jeremiah concerning all the
44:16 Jeremiah: "As for the W which you have spoken
44:24 the women, "Hear the W of the LORD, all
44:26 Therefore hear the W of the LORD, all you
44:28 live, shall know whose W will stand, mine or
45:1 The W that Jeremiah the prophet spoke to Baruch
46:1 The W of the LORD which came to Jeremiah

46:13 The W which the LORD spoke to Jeremiah the
47:1 The W of the LORD that came to Jeremiah
49:34 The W of the LORD that came to Jeremiah
50:1 The W which the LORD spoke concerning Babylon,
51:59 The W which Jeremiah the prophet commanded
Lam 1:18 have rebelled against his W; but hear, all you
Bar 2:1 the Lord confirmed his W, which he spoke against
4:37 and west, at the W of the Holy One,
5:5 and east, at the W of the Holy One,
Ezek 1:3 of King Jehoiachin), the W of the LORD came
3:16 of seven days, the W of the LORD came
3:17 whenever you hear a W from my mouth, you
6:1 The W of the LORD came to me:
6:3 of Israel, hear the W of the Lord GOD!
7:1 The W of the LORD came to me:
9:11 his side, brought back W, saying, "I have done
11:14 And the W of the LORD came to me:
12:1 The W of the LORD came to me:
12:8 In the morning the W of the LORD came
12:17 Moreover the W of the LORD came to me:
12:21 And the W of the LORD came to me:
12:25 LORD will speak the W which I will speak,
12:25 I will speak the W and perform it, says
12:26 Again the W of the LORD came to me:
12:28 any longer, but the W which I speak will
13:1 The W of the LORD came to me:
13:2 own minds: 'Hear the W of the LORD!'
13:6 and yet they expect him to fulfil their W
14:2 And the W of the LORD came to me:
14:9 deceived and speak a W, I, the LORD, have
14:12 And the W of the LORD came to me:
15:1 And the W of the LORD came to me:
16:1 Again the W of the LORD came to me:
16:35 O harlot, hear the W of the LORD:
17:1 The W of the LORD came to me:
17:11 Then the W of the LORD came to me:
18:1 The W of the LORD came to me again:
20:2 And the W of the LORD came to me:
20:45 And the W of the LORD came to me:
20:47 the Negeb, Hear the W of the LORD: Thus
21:1 The W of the LORD came to me:
21:8 And the W of the LORD came to me:
21:18 The W of the LORD came to me again:
22:1 Moreover the W of the LORD came to me,
22:17 And the W of the LORD came to me:
22:23 And the W of the LORD came to me:
23:1 The W of the LORD came to me:
24:1 of the month, the W of the LORD came
24:15 Also the W of the LORD came to me:
24:20 said to them, "The W of the LORD came
25:1 The W of the LORD came to me:
25:3 the Ammonites, Hear the W of the Lord GOD:
26:1 of the month, the W of the LORD came
27:1 The W of the LORD came to me:
28:1 The W of the LORD came to me:
28:11 Moreover the W of the LORD came to me:
28:20 The W of the LORD came to me:
29:1 of the month, the W of the LORD came
29:17 of the month, the W of the LORD came
30:1 The W of the LORD came to me:
30:20 of the month, the W of the LORD came
31:1 of the month, the W of the LORD came
32:1 of the month, the W of the LORD came
32:17 of the month, the W of the LORD came
33:1 The W of the LORD came to me:
33:7 whenever you hear a W from my mouth, you
33:23 The W of the LORD came to me:
33:30 and hear what the W is that comes forth
34:1 The W of the LORD came to me:
34:7 you shepherds, hear the W of the LORD:
34:9 you shepherds, hear the W of the LORD:
35:1 The W of the LORD came to me:
36:1 of Israel, hear the W of the LORD.
36:4 of Israel, hear the W of the Lord GOD:
36:16 The W of the LORD came to me:
37:4 dry bones, hear the W of the LORD.
37:15 The W of the LORD came to me:
38:1 The W of the LORD came to me:
Dan 2:5 answered the Chaldeans, "The W from me is sure:
2:8 you see that the W from me is sure
4:17 the decision by the W of the holy ones,
4:33 Immediately the W was fulfilled upon
9:2 which, according to the W of the LORD to
9:23 of your supplications a W went forth, and I
9:23 beloved; therefore consider the W and understand
9:25 going forth of the W to restore and build
10:1 king of Persia a W was revealed to Daniel,
10:1 And the W was true, and it was a
10:1 And he understood the W and had understanding of
10:11 he was speaking this W to me, I stood
Hos 1:1 The W of the LORD that
4:1 Hear the W of the LORD, O people of
Joel 1:1 The W of the LORD that
2:11 he that executes his W is powerful.
Amos 3:1 Hear this W that the LORD has spoken against
4:1 "Hear this W, you cows of Bashan, who are
5:1 Hear this W which I take up over you
7:16 "Now therefore hear the W of the LORD.
8:12 fro, to seek the W of the LORD, but
Jon 1:1 Now the W of the LORD came
3:1 Then the W of the LORD came to Jonah
3:3 Nineveh, according to the W of the LORD.
Mic 1:1 The W of the LORD that
4:2 the law, and the W of the LORD from
Zeph 1:1 The W of the LORD which
2:5 The W of the LORD is against you, O
Hag 1:1 of the month, the W of the LORD came
1:3 Then the W of the LORD came by Haggai
2:1 of the month, the W of the LORD came
2:10 year of Darius, the W of the LORD came
2:20 The W of the LORD came a second time
Zech 1:1 year of Darius, the W of the LORD came
1:7 year of Darius, the W of the LORD came
4:6 me, "This is the W of the LORD to
4:8 Moreover the W of the LORD came to me,
6:9 And the W of the LORD came to me:
7:1 of King Darius, the W of the LORD came
7:4 Then the W of the LORD of hosts came
7:8 And the W of the LORD came to Zechariah,
8:1 And the W of the LORD of hosts came
8:18 And the W of the LORD of hosts came
9:1 An Oracle The W of the LORD is against
11:11 that it was the W of the LORD.
12:1 An Oracle The W of the LORD concerning Israel:
Mal 1:1 The oracle of the W of the LORD to
1Mac 7:16 in accordance with the W which was written,
9:55 no longer say a W or give commands concerning
11:53 But he broke his W about all that he
13:19 but Trypho broke his W and did not release
15:35 not answer him a W,
2Mac 8:12 W came to Judas concerning Nicanor's invasion; and
10:21 When W of what had happened came to Maccabeus,
11:6 and his men got W that Lysias was besieging
11:26 well, therefore, to send W to them and give
13:1 hundred and forty-ninth year W came to Judas and
13:23 was defeated he got W that Philip, who had
14:1 Three years later, W came to Judas and his
Mt 2:8 found him bring me W, that I too may
4:4 alone, but by every W that proceeds from the
8:8 but only say the W, and my servant will
8:16 the spirits with a W, and healed all who
11:2 the Christ, he sent W by his disciples
12:32 And whoever says a W against the Son of
12:36 account for every careless W they utter;
13:19 any one hears the W of the kingdom and
13:20 he who hears the W and immediately receives it
13:21 on account of the W, immediately he falls away.
13:22 he who hears the W, but the cares of
13:22 in riches choke the W, and it proves unfruitful.
13:23 he who hears the W and understands it; he
15:6 have made void the W of God.
15:23 But he did not answer her a W
18:15 with you, that every W may be confirmed by
22:46 to answer him a W, nor from that day
27:19 seat, his wife sent W to him, "Have nothing
Mk 2:2 he was preaching the W to them.
4:14 The sower sows the W
4:15 the path, where the W is sown; when they
4:15 and takes away the W which is sown in
4:16 when they hear the W, immediately receive it with
4:17 on account of the W, immediately they fall away.
4:18 those who hear the W,
4:19 in and choke the W, and it proves unfruitful.
4:20 ones who hear the W and accept it and
4:33 parables he spoke the W to them, as they
6:26 want to break his W to her.
7:13 thus making void the W of God through your
Lk 1:2 and ministers of the W,
1:38 let it be to me according to your W
2:29 peace, according to thy W;
3:2 Annas and Caiaphas, the W of God came to
4:32 his teaching, for his W was with authority.

WORDS (627)

	44:7	my lord speak such W as these?
	44:24	we told him the W of my lord.
	45:27	told him all the W of Joseph, which he
Ex	4:15	him and put the W in his mouth; and
	4:28	told Aaron all the W of the LORD with
	4:30	Aaron spoke all the W which the LORD had
	5:9	at it and pay no regard to lying W
	19:6	These are the W which you shall speak to
	19:7	before them all these W which the LORD had
	19:8	And Moses reported the W of the people to
	19:9	Then Moses told the W of the people to
	20:1	God spoke all these W, saying,
	24:3	the people all the W of the LORD and
	24:3	and said, "All the W which the LORD has
	24:4	Moses wrote all the W of the LORD.
	24:8	made with you in accordance with all these W
	34:1	upon the tables the W that were on the
	34:27	to Moses, "Write these W; in accordance with these
	34:27	in accordance with these W I have made a
	34:28	upon the tables the W of the covenant, the
Num	11:24	told the people the W of the LORD; and
	12:6	he said, "Hear my W: If there is a
	14:39	And Moses told these W to all the people
	16:31	finished speaking all these W, the ground under them
	24:4	him who hears the W of God, who sees
	24:16	him who hears the W of God, and knows
Deut	1:1	These are the W that Moses spoke to
	1:34	the LORD heard your W, and was angered, and
	2:26	king of Heshbon, with W of peace, saying,
	4:10	let them hear my W, so that they may
	4:12	heard the sound of W, but saw no form;
	4:36	and you heard his W out of the midst
	5:22	is your neighbors.' "These W the LORD spoke to
	5:28	the LORD heard your W, when you spoke to
	5:28	'I have heard the W of this people, which
	6:6	And these W which I command you this day
	9:10	them were all the W which the LORD had
	10:2	on the tables the W that were on the
	11:18	therefore lay up these W of mine in your
	12:28	to heed all these W which I command you,
	13:3	not listen to the W of that prophet or
	17:19	by keeping all the W of this law and
	18:18	I will put my W in his mouth, and
	18:19	give heed to my W which he shall speak
	27:3	upon them all the W of this law, when
	27:8	the stones all the W of this law very
	27:26	does not confirm the W of this law by
	28:14	from any of the W which I command you
	28:58	to do all the W of this law which
	29:1	These are the W of the covenant which the
	29:9	careful to do the W of this covenant, that
	29:19	when he hears the W of this sworn covenant,
	29:29	may do all the W of this law.
	31:1	continued to speak these W to all Israel.
	31:12	to do all the W of this law,
	31:24	had finished writing the W of this law in
	31:28	I may speak these W in their ears and
	31:30	Then Moses spoke the W of this song until
	32:1	the earth hear the W of my mouth.
	32:44	and recited all the W of this song in
	32:45	finished speaking all these W to all Israel,
	32:46	to heart all the W which I enjoin upon
	32:46	to do all the W of this law.
Josh	1:18	commandment and disobeys your W, whatever you
	2:21	said, "According to your W, so be it." Then
	3:9	hither, and hear the W of the LORD your
	8:34	he read all the W of the law, the
	22:30	with him, heard the W that the Reubenites and
	24:26	And Joshua wrote these W in the book of
	24:27	has heard all the W of the LORD which
Judg	2:4	the LORD spoke these W to all the people
	9:3	kinsmen spoke all these W on his behalf in
	9:30	the city heard the W of Gaal the son
	11:11	Jephthah spoke all his W before the LORD at
	13:12	said, "Now when your W come true, what is
	13:17	so that, when your W come true, we may
	16:16	him hard with her W day after day, and
1Sam	3:19	let none of his W fall to the ground.
	8:10	Samuel told all the W of the LORD to
	8:21	had heard all the W of the people, he
	11:6	when he heard these W, and his anger was
	15:1	therefore hearken to the W of the LORD.
	15:24	the LORD and your W, because I feared the
	17:11	all Israel heard these W of the Philistine, they
	17:23	and spoke the same W as before.
	17:31	When the W which David spoke were heard, they
	18:23	Saul's servants spoke those W in the ears of
	18:26	servants told David these W, it pleased David well
	21:12	And David took these W to heart, and was
	24:7	his men with these W, and did not permit
	24:9	you listen to the W of men who say,
	24:16	had finished speaking these W to Saul, Saul said,
	25:24	ears, and hear the W of your handmaid.
	26:19	the king hear the W of his servant.
	28:20	fear because of the W of Samuel; and there
	28:23	woman, urged him; and he hearkened to their W
2Sam	3:8	very angry over the W of Ish-bosheth, and said,
	7:17	accordance with all these W, and in accordance with
	7:28	art God, and thy W are true, and thou
	14:3	So Joab put the W in her mouth.
	14:19	who put all these W in the mouth of
	19:43	But the W of the men of Judah were
	19:43	were fiercer than the W of the men of
	20:17	him, "Listen to the W of your maidservant." And
	22:1	to the LORD the W of this song on
	23:1	these are the last W of David: The oracle
1Kgs	1:14	will come in after you and confirm your W
	5:7	When Hiram heard the W of Solomon, he rejoiced
	8:59	Let these W of mine, wherewith I have made
	12:7	them, and speak good W to them when you
	13:11	day in Bethel; the W also which he had
	21:27	when Ahab heard those W, he rent his clothes,
	22:13	to him, "Behold, the W of the prophets with
2Kgs	6:12	king of Israel the W that you speak in
	6:30	the king heard the W of the woman he
	18:20	you think that mere W are strategy and power
	18:27	me to speak these W to your master and
	18:37	and told him the W of the Rabshakeh.
	19:4	God heard all the W of the Rabshakeh, whom
	19:4	and will rebuke the W which the LORD your
	19:6	afraid because of the W that you have heard,
	19:16	see; and hear the W of Sennacherib, which he
	22:11	the king heard the W of the book of
	22:13	all Judah, concerning the W of this book that
	22:13	have not obeyed the W of this book, to
	22:16	its inhabitants, all the W of the book which
	22:18	of Israel: Regarding the W which you have heard,
	23:2	their hearing all the W of the book of
	23:3	soul, to perform the W of this covenant that
	23:24	he might establish the W of the law which
1Chr	17:15	accordance with all these W, and in accordance with
	23:27	for by the last W of David these were
2Chr	10:7	them, and speak good W to them, then they
	15:8	When Asa heard these W, the prophecy of Azariah
	18:12	to him, "Behold, the W of the prophets with
	29:15	had commanded, by the W of the LORD, to
	29:30	the LORD with the W of David and of
	32:8	took confidence from the W of Hezekiah king of
	33:18	his God, and the W of the seers who
	34:19	the king heard the W of the law he
	34:21	in Judah, concerning the W of the book that
	34:26	of Israel: Regarding the W which you have heard,
	34:27	when you heard his W against this place and
	34:30	their hearing all the W of the book of
	34:31	soul, to perform the W of the covenant that
	35:22	not listen to the W of Neco from the
	36:16	of God, despising his W, and scoffing at his
Ezra	9:4	who trembled at the W of the God of
Neh	1:1	The W of Nehemiah the son
	1:4	When I heard these W I sat down and
	2:18	and also of the W which the king had
	5:6	angry when I heard their outcry and these W
	6:7	be reported to the king according to these W
	6:19	presence, and reported my W to him.
	8:9	when they heard the W of the law.
	8:12	they had understood the W that were declared to
	8:13	order to study the W of the law.
Tob	6:15	you not remember the W with which your father
	8:2	went he remembered the W of Raphael, and he
	14:1	Here Tobit ended his W of praise.
Jud	6:4	spoken; none of his W shall be in vain.
	6:5	who have said these W on the day of
	6:9	and none of my W shall fail."
	7:16	These W pleased Holofernes and all his servants, and
	8:9	Judith heard the wicked W spoken by the people
	8:28	there is no one who can deny your W
	9:13	Make my deceitful W to be their wound and
	10:1	had ended all these W,
	10:14	the men heard her W, and observed her face—
	11:5	to him, "Accept the W of your servant, and
	11:6	you follow out the W of your maidservant, God
	11:9	we have heard his W, for the men of

W

	11:20	Her W pleased Holofernes and all his servants, and
Esth	3:4	to see whether Mordecai's W would avail; for he
	7:8	As the W left the mouth of the king,
	9:30	kingdom of Ahasuerus, in W of peace and truth,
	15:8	comforted her with soothing W, and said to her,
Job	4:4	Your W have upheld him who was stumbling, and
	6:3	the sea; therefore my W have been rash.
	6:10	have not denied the W of the Holy One.
	6:25	How forceful are honest W
	6:26	that you can reprove W, when the speech of
	8:2	these things, and the W of your mouth be
	8:10	tell you, and utter W out of their understanding?
	9:14	answer him, choosing my W with him?
	11:2	"Should a multitude of W go unanswered, and a
	12:11	not the ear try W as the palate tastes
	13:17	Listen carefully to my W, and let my declaration
	15:3	unprofitable talk, or in W with which he can
	15:13	God, and let such W go out of your
	16:3	Shall windy W have an end?
	16:4	place; I could join W together against you, and
	18:2	Shuhite answered: "How long will you hunt for W
	19:2	torment me, and break me in pieces with W
	19:23	"Oh that my W were written!
	21:2	"Listen carefully to my W, and let this be
	22:22	and lay up his W in your heart.
	23:12	in my bosom the W of his mouth.
	26:4	help have you uttered W, and whose spirit has
	31:40	The W of Job are ended.
	32:11	I waited for your W, I listened for your
	32:12	or that answered his W, among you.
	32:14	has not directed his W against me, and I
	32:18	I am full of W, the spirit within me
	33:1	speech, O Job, and listen to all my W
	33:3	My W declare the uprightness of my heart, and
	33:5	you can; set your W in order before me;
	33:8	and I have heard the sound of your W
	33:13	him, saying, 'He will answer none of my W
	34:2	Elihu said: "Hear my W, you wise men, and
	34:3	for the ear tests W as the palate tastes
	34:35	without knowledge, his W are without insight.'
	34:37	us, and multiplies his W against God."
	35:16	empty talk, he multiplies W without knowledge."
	36:4	For truly my W are not false; one who
	38:2	that darkens counsel by W without knowledge?
	41:3	Will he speak to you soft W
	42:7	LORD had spoken these W to Job, the LORD
Ps	4:2	will you love vain W, and seek after lies?
	5:1	Give ear to my W, O LORD; give heed
	17:6	God; incline thy ear to me, hear my W
	19:3	speech, nor are there W; their voice is not
	19:4	the earth, and their W to the end of
	19:14	Let the W of my mouth and the meditation
	22:1	helping me, from the W of my groaning?
	35:20	the land they conceive W of deceit.
	36:3	The W of his mouth are mischief and deceit;
	41:6	me, he utters empty W, while his heart gathers
	44:16	my face, at the W of the taunters and
	50:17	and you cast my W behind you.
	52:4	[Selah] You love all W that devour, O deceitful
	54:2	give ear to the W of my mouth.
	55:21	in his heart; his W were softer than oil,
	59:12	of their mouths, the W of their lips, let
	64:3	swords, who aim bitter W like arrows,
	78:1	your ears to the W of my mouth!
	94:4	pour out their arrogant W, they boast, all the
	105:28	made the land dark; they rebelled against his W
	106:12	Then they believed his W; they sang his praise.
	106:33	bitter, and he spoke W that were rash.
	107:11	had rebelled against the W of God, and spurned
	109:3	They beset me with W of hate, and attack
	119:57	is my portion; I promise to keep thy W
	119:103	How sweet are thy W to my taste, sweeter
	119:130	The unfolding of thy W gives light; it imparts
	119:139	zeal consumes me, because my foes forget thy W
	119:147	and cry for help; I hope in thy W
	119:161	but my heart stands in awe of thy W
	138:4	they have heard the W of thy mouth;
	145:13	faithful in all his W, and gracious in all
Prov	1:2	wisdom and instruction, understand W of insight,
	1:6	and a figure, the W of the wise and
	1:23	I will make my W known to you.
	2:1	if you receive my W and treasure up my
	2:16	adventuress with her smooth W,
	4:5	heart hold fast my W; keep my commandments, and
	4:6	turn away from the W of my mouth.
	4:11	son, and accept my W, that the years of
	4:21	be attentive to my W; incline your ear to
	5:7	not depart from the W of my mouth.
	6:2	lips, caught in the W of your mouth;
	7:1	My son, keep my W and treasure up my
	7:5	woman, from the adventuress with her smooth W
	7:24	be attentive to the W of my mouth.
	8:8	All the W of my mouth are righteous; there
	10:19	When W are many, transgression is not lacking, but
	12:6	The W of the wicked lie in wait for
	12:14	the fruit of his W a man is satisfied
	12:18	is one whose rash W are like sword thrusts,
	14:7	you do not meet W of knowledge.
	15:26	to the LORD, the W of the pure are
	16:24	Pleasant W are like a honeycomb, sweetness to the
	17:27	He who restrains his W has knowledge, and he
	18:4	The W of a man's mouth are deep waters;
	18:8	The W of a whisperer are like delicious morsels;
	19:7	He pursues them with W, but does not have
	19:27	to stray from the W of knowledge.
	22:12	but he overthrows the W of the faithless.
	22:17	ear, and hear the W of the wise, and
	23:8	which you have eaten, and waste your pleasant W
	23:9	for he will despise the wisdom of your W
	23:12	and your ear to W of knowledge.
	25:27	eat much honey, so be sparing of complimentary W
	26:22	The W of a whisperer are like delicious morsels;
	29:19	By mere W a servant is not disciplined, for
	29:20	see a man who is hasty in his W
	30:1	The W of Agur son of Jakeh of Massa.
	30:6	not add to his W, lest he rebuke you,
	31:1	The W of Lemuel, king of Massa, which his
Eccl	1:1	The W of the Preacher, the
	5:2	earth; therefore let your W be few.
	5:3	much business, and a fool's voice with many W
	5:7	when dreams increase, empty W grow many: but do
	6:11	The more W, the more vanity, and what is
	9:16	is despised, and his W are not heeded.
	9:17	The W of the wise heard in quiet are
	10:12	The W of a wise man's mouth win him
	10:13	The beginning of the W of his mouth is
	10:14	A fool multiplies W, though no man knows what
	12:10	sought to find pleasing W, and uprightly he wrote
	12:10	and uprightly he wrote W of truth.
Wis	1:6	the guilt of his W; because God is witness
	1:9	a report of his W will come to the
	1:16	ungodly men by their W and deeds summoned death;
	2:17	us see if his W are true, and let
	6:9	then, O monarchs, my W are directed, that you
	6:11	your desire on my W; long for them, and
	6:25	be instructed by my W, and you will profit.
	7:16	both we and our W are in his hand,
	8:18	renown in sharing her W, I went about seeking
Sir	1:21	He will hide his W until the right moment,
	2:15	will not disobey his W, and those who love
	4:24	and education through the W of the tongue.
	8:11	fellow, lest he lie in ambush against your W
	9:17	a people's leader is proved wise by his W
	11:8	interrupt a speaker in the midst of his W
	12:12	the truth of my W, and be stung by
	13:11	trust his abundance of W; for he will test
	13:12	who does not keep W to himself; he will
	13:13	Keep W to yourself and be very watchful, for
	13:21	many; he speaks unseemly W, and they justify him.
	16:22	acquire knowledge, and pay close attention to my W
	18:14	cause grief by your W when you present a
	20:7	Whoever uses too many W will be loathed, and
	20:12	himself beloved through his W, but the courtesies of
	21:17	they will ponder his W in their minds.
	21:25	these things, but the W of the prudent will
	23:15	accustomed to use insulting W will never become
	27:23	and he admires your W; but later he will
	27:23	and with your own W he will give offense.
	28:25	and scales for your W, and make a door
	29:5	and will pay in W of unconcern, and will
	29:25	you will hear bitter W:
	31:22	and in the end you will appreciate my W
	32:8	say much in few W; be as one who
	36:19	of game, so an intelligent mind detects false W
	37:20	A man skilled in W may be hated; he
	39:6	he will pour forth W of wisdom and give
	41:16	show respect for my W: For it is good
	41:22	her bed; of abusive W, before friends-- and
	42:15	By the W of the Lord his works are
	43:27	the sum of our W is: "He is the
	44:4	people, wise in their W of instruction;
	45:3	By his W he caused signs to cease; the

46:15 prophet, and by his W he became known as
51:5 unclean tongue and lying W –
Is 29:4 in the dust your W shall come; your voice
29:11 to you like the W of a book that
29:18 deaf shall hear the W of a book, and
31:2 not call back his W, but will arise against
32:7 the poor with lying W, even when the plea
36:5 you think that mere W are strategy and power
36:12 me to speak these W to your master and
36:13 of Judah: "Hear the W of the great king,
36:22 and told him the W of the Rabshakeh.
37:4 your God heard the W of the Rabshakeh, whom
37:4 and will rebuke the W which the LORD your
37:6 afraid because of the W that you have heard,
37:17 and hear all the W of Sennacherib, which he
41:26 it, none who proclaimed, none who heard your W
51:16 I have put my W in your mouth, and
59:13 conceiving and uttering from the heart lying W
59:21 upon you, and my W which I have put
Jer 1:1 The W of Jeremiah, the son
1:9 I have put my W in your mouth.
3:12 Go, and proclaim these W toward the north, and
5:14 I am making my W in your mouth a
6:19 given heed to my W; and as for my
7:4 trust in these deceptive W: 'This is the temple
7:8 you trust in deceptive W to no avail.
7:27 shall speak all these W to them, but they
11:2 the LORD: "Hear the W of this covenant, and
11:3 does not heed the W of this covenant
11:6 me, "Proclaim all these W in the cities of
11:6 of Jerusalem: Hear the W of this covenant and
11:8 upon them all the W of this covenant, which
11:10 refused to hear my W; they have gone after
12:6 though they speak fair W to you."
13:10 refuse to hear my W, who stubbornly follow their
15:16 Thy W were found, and I ate them, and
15:16 ate them, and thy W became to me a
16:10 this people all these W, and they say to
18:2 and there I will let you hear my W
18:18 and let us not heed any of his W
19:2 and proclaim there the W that I tell you.
19:15 have stiffened their neck, refusing to hear my W
22:5 will not heed these W, I swear by myself,
23:9 of the LORD and because of his holy W
23:16 not listen to the W of the prophets who
23:22 would have proclaimed my W to my people, and
23:30 LORD, who steal my W from one another.
23:36 and you pervert the W of the living God,
23:38 you have said these W, "The burden of the
25:8 have not obeyed my W,
25:13 that land all the W which I have uttered
25:30 against them all these W, and say to them:
26:2 the LORD all the W that I command you
26:5 and to heed the W of my servants the
26:7 heard Jeremiah speaking these W in the house of
26:12 this city all the W you have heard.
26:15 to speak all these W in your ears."
26:20 against this land in W like those of Jeremiah.
26:21 the princes, heard his W, the king sought to
27:14 not listen to the W of the prophets who
27:16 not listen to the W of your prophets who
28:6 the LORD make the W which you have prophesied
29:1 These are the W of the letter which Jeremiah
29:19 did not heed my W, says the LORD, which
29:23 in my name lying W which I did not
30:2 a book all the W that I have spoken
30:4 These are the W which the LORD spoke concerning
31:23 they shall use these W in the land of
34:6 prophet spoke all these W to Zedekiah king of
35:13 you not receive instruction and listen to my W
36:2 on it all the W that I have spoken
36:4 of Jeremiah all the W of the LORD which
36:6 you shall read the W of the LORD from
36:8 from the scroll the W of the LORD in
36:10 people, Baruch read the W of Jeremiah from the
36:11 Shaphan, heard all the W of the LORD from
36:13 told them all the W that he had heard,
36:16 they heard all the W, they turned one to
36:16 must report all these W to the king."
36:17 "Tell us, how did you write all these W
36:18 "He dictated all these W to me, while I
36:20 they reported all the W to the king.
36:24 who heard all these W, was afraid, nor did
36:27 the scroll with the W which Baruch wrote at
36:28 it all the former W that were in the
36:32 of Jeremiah all the W of the scroll which
36:32 fire; and many similar W were added to them.
37:2 land listened to the W of the LORD which
38:1 of Malchiah heard the W that Jeremiah was saying
38:4 people, by speaking such W to them.
38:24 one know of these W and you shall not
39:16 I will fulfil my W against this city for
43:1 the people all these W of the LORD their
44:29 may know that my W will surely stand against
45:1 when he wrote these W in a book at
51:60 upon Babylon, all these W that are written
51:61 you read all these W,
51:64 Thus far are the W of Jeremiah.
Bar 1:1 These are the W of the book which
1:3 And Baruch read the W of this book in
1:21 God in all the W of the prophets whom
2:24 thou hast confirmed thy W, which thou didst speak
Ezek 2:6 be afraid of their W, though briers and thorns
2:6 not afraid of their W, nor be dismayed at
2:7 you shall speak my W to them, whether they
2:10 were written on it W of lamentation and mourning
3:4 and speak with my W to them.
3:6 a hard language, whose W you cannot understand.
3:10 of man, all my W that I shall speak
12:28 GOD: None of my W will be delayed any
35:13 mouth, and multiplied your W against me; I heard
Dan 2:9 speak lying and corrupt W before me till the
4:31 While the W were still in the king's mouth,
5:10 queen, because of the W of the king and
6:14 when he heard these W, was much distressed, and
7:11 sound of the great W which the horn was
7:25 He shall speak W against the Most High, and
9:12 He has confirmed his W, which he spoke against
10:6 the sound of his W like the noise of
10:9 the sound of his W; and when I heard
10:9 the sound of his W, I fell on my
10:11 give heed to the W that I speak to
10:12 before your God, your W have been heard, and
10:12 heard, and I have come because of your W
10:15 me according to these W, I turned my face
12:4 Daniel, shut up the W, and seal the book,
12:9 way, Daniel, for the W are shut up and
Hos 6:5 slain them by the W of my mouth, and
10:4 They utter mere W; with empty oaths they make
14:2 Take with you W and return to the LORD;
Amos 1:1 The W of Amos, who was
7:10 land is not able to bear all his W
8:11 but of hearing the W of the LORD.
Mic 2:7 Do not my W do good to him who
Hag 1:12 their God, and the W of Haggai the prophet,
Zech 1:6 But my W and my statutes, which I commanded
1:13 answered gracious and comforting W to the angel
7:7 were not these the W which the LORD proclaimed
7:12 the law and the W which the LORD of
8:9 have been hearing these W from the mouth of
Mal 2:17 You have wearied the LORD with your W
3:13 "Your W have been stout against me, says the
1Mac 1:30 Deceitfully he spoke peaceable W to them, and they
1:51 In such W he wrote to his whole kingdom.
2:22 not obey the king's W by turning aside from
2:23 had finished speaking these W, a Jew came forward
2:62 Do not fear the W of a sinner, for
7:10 and his brothers with peaceable but treacherous W
7:11 no attention to their W, for they saw that
7:15 And he spoke peaceable W to them and swore
10:3 a letter in peaceable W to honor him;
10:17 him, in the following W:
10:24 also will write them W of encouragement and
10:25 them in the following W: "King Demetrius to the
10:46 the people heard these W, they did not believe
10:47 first to speak peaceable W to them, and they
10:74 When Jonathan heard the W of Apollonius, his spirit
11:2 for Syria with peaceable W, and the people of
13:7 when they heard these W,
14:23 a copy of their W in the public archives,
15:32 reported to him the W of the king,
15:36 reported to him these W and the splendor of
2Mac 2:3 And with other similar W he exhorted them that
6:29 ill will, because the W he had uttered were
7:24 appealed to him in W, but promised with oaths
8:21 With these W he filled them with good courage
9:12 stench, he uttered these W: "It is right to
10:34 place, blasphemed terribly and hurled out wicked W
12:25 And when with many W he had confirmed his
14:34 our nation, in these W:
15:11 the inspiration of brave W, and he cheered them
15:17 Encouraged by the W of Judas, so noble and

15:22 upon him in these W: "O Lord, thou didst
15:24 With these W he ended his prayer.
Mt 6:7 that they will be heard for their many W
7:24 then who hears these W of mine and does
7:26 one who hears these W of mine and does
10:14 or listen to your W, shake off the dust
12:37 utter; for by your W you will be justified,
12:37 justified, and by your W you will be condemned."
24:35 pass away, but my W will not pass away.
26:44 prayed for the third time, saying the same W
Mk 8:38 me and of my W in this adulterous and
10:24 And the disciples were amazed at his W
13:31 pass away, but my W will not pass away.
14:39 he went away and prayed, saying the same W
Lk 1:20 did not believe my W, which will be fulfilled
3:4 the book of the W of Isaiah the prophet,
4:22 wondered at the gracious W which proceeded out of
6:47 me and hears my W and does them, I
9:26 me and of my W, of him will the
9:44 his disciples, "Let these W sink into your ears;
19:48 do, for all the people hung upon his W
21:33 pass away, but my W will not pass away.
22:63 they spoke many other W against him, reviling him.
24:8 And they remembered his W,
24:11 the apostles; but these W seemed to them an
24:44 them, "These are my W which I spoke to
Jn 3:34 has sent utters the W of God, for it
4:42 longer because of your W that we believe, for
5:46 believe his writings, how will you believe my W
6:63 of no avail; the W that I have spoken
6:68 You have the W of eternal life;
7:40 When they heard these W, some of the people
8:20 These W he spoke in the treasury, as he
8:47 of God hears the W of God; the reason
10:19 a division among the Jews because of these W
14:10 The W that I say to you I do
14:24 does not keep my W; and the word which
15:7 in me, and my W abide in you, ask
17:1 Jesus had spoken these W, he lifted up his
17:8 have given them the W which thou gavest me,
18:1 Jesus had spoken these W, he went forth with
19:8 When Pilate heard these W, he was the more
19:13 When Pilate heard these W, he brought Jesus out
Acts 2:14 known to you, and give ear to my W
2:22 of Israel, hear these W: Jesus of Nazareth, a
2:40 testified with many other W and exhorted them,
5:5 When Ananias heard these W, he fell down and
5:20 the people all the W of this Life."
5:24 priests heard these W, they were much perplexed
6:11 him speak blasphemous W against Moses and God."
6:13 never ceases to speak W against this holy place
7:22 was mighty in his W and deeds.
14:18 With these W they scarcely restrained the people
15:15 And with this the W of the prophets agree,
15:24 have troubled you with W, unsettling your minds,
15:32 the brethren with many W and strengthened them.
16:36 the jailer reported the W to Paul, saying, "The
16:38 The police reported these W to the magistrates, and
18:15 matter of questions about W and names and your
20:35 the weak, remembering the W of the Lord Jesus,
Rom 3:4 be justified in thy W, and prevail when thou
4:23 But the W, "it was reckoned to him," were
8:26 intercedes for us with sighs too deep for W
10:18 the earth, and their W to the ends of
16:18 by fair and flattering W they deceive the hearts
1Cor 2:1 of God in lofty W or wisdom.
2:4 were not in plausible W of wisdom, but in
2:13 we impart this in W not taught by human
14:19 would rather speak five W with my mind, in
14:19 others, than ten thousand W in a tongue.
Eph 5:6 deceive you with empty W, for it is because
1Thes 2:5 we never used either W of flattery, as you
4:18 Therefore comfort one another with these W
1Tim 4:6 Jesus, nourished on the W of the faith and
6:3 agree with the sound W of our Lord Jesus
6:4 for disputes about W, which produce envy, dissension,
2Tim 1:13 pattern of the sound W which you have heard
2:14 to avoid disputing about W, which does no good,
Heb 4:7 long afterward, in the W already quoted, "Today,
12:19 and a voice whose W made the hearers entreat
2Pet 2:3 exploit you with false W; from of old their
3Jn 1:10 he is doing, prating against me with evil W
Rev 1:3 who reads aloud the W of the prophecy, and
2:1 in Ephesus write: 'The W of him who holds
2:8 in Smyrna write: 'The W of the first and
2:12 in Pergamum write: 'The W of him who has
2:18 in Thyatira write: 'The W of the Son of
3:1 in Sardis write: 'The W of him who has
3:7 in Philadelphia write: 'The W of the holy one,
3:14 in La-odicea write: 'The W of the Amen, the
13:5 uttering haughty and blasphemous W, and it was
17:17 the beast, until the W of God shall be
19:9 me, "These are true W of God."
21:5 "Write this, for these W are trustworthy and true."
22:6 said to me, "These W are trustworthy and true.
22:7 he who keeps the W of the prophecy of
22:9 those who keep the W of this book.
22:10 not seal up the W of the prophecy of
22:18 one who hears the W of the prophecy of
22:19 takes away from the W of the book of

WORE (9)

Gen 37:23 with sleeves that he W;
1Sam 22:18 day eighty-five persons who W the linen ephod.
2Sam 13:19 long robe which she W; and she laid her
2Kgs 1:8 They answered him, "He W a garment of haircloth,
1Chr 15:27 the singers; and David W a linen ephod.
Jud 8:5 about her loins and W the garments of her
Ps 35:13 were sick— I W sackcloth, I afflicted myself
Mt 3:4 Now John W a garment of camel's hair, and
Rev 9:17 my vision: the riders W breastplates the color of

WORK (417)

Gen 2:2 day God finished his W which he had done,
2:2 day from all his W which he had done.
2:3 rested from all his W which he had done
5:29 us relief from our W and from the toil
39:11 house to do his W and none of the
Ex 1:13 in all kinds of W in the field; in
1:13 field; in all their W they made them serve
5:4 do you take the people away from their W
5:9 our God.' Let heavier W be laid upon the
5:11 find it; but your W will not be lessened
5:13 urgent, saying, "Complete your W, your daily task, as
5:18 LORD.' Go now, and W; for no straw shall
12:16 a holy assembly; no W shall be done on
14:13 LORD, which he will W for you today; for
14:31 Israel saw the great W which the LORD did
20:9 and do all your W;
20:10 shall not do any W, you, or your son,
23:12 you shall do your W, but on the seventh
25:18 of gold; of hammered W shall you make them,
25:31 be made of hammered W; its cups, its capitals,
25:36 one piece of hammered W of pure gold.
26:31 twined linen; in skilled W shall it be made,
28:4 a coat of checker W, a turban, and a
28:15 of judgment, in skilled W; like the work of
28:15 skilled work; like the W of the ephod you
28:39 the coat in checker W of fine linen, and
31:4 devise artistic designs, to W in gold, silver, and
31:5 in carving wood, for W in every craft.
31:14 death; whoever does any W on it, that soul
31:15 Six days shall W be done, but the seventh
31:15 LORD; whoever does any W on the sabbath day
32:16 the tables were the W of God, and the
34:10 are shall see the W of the LORD; for
34:21 "Six days you shall W, but on the seventh
35:2 Six days shall W be done, but on the
35:2 LORD; whoever does any W on it shall be
35:24 any use in the W, brought it.
35:29 bring anything for the W which the LORD had
35:32 devise artistic designs, to W in gold and silver
35:33 in carving wood, for W in every skilled craft.
35:35 do every sort of W done by a craftsman
36:1 how to do any W in the construction of
36:1 of the sanctuary shall W in accordance with all
36:2 come to do the W;
36:3 brought for doing the W on the sanctuary.
36:5 enough for doing the W which the LORD has
36:7 to do all the W, and more.
37:17 were made of hammered W; its cups, its capitals,
37:22 one piece of hammered W of pure gold.
38:21 of Moses, for the W of the Levites under
38:24 was used for the W, in all the construction
39:3 cut into threads to W into the blue and
39:8 the breastpiece, in skilled W, like the work of
39:8 skilled work, like the W of the ephod, of
39:32 Thus all the W of the tabernacle of the
39:42 the people of Israel had done all the W
39:43 Moses saw all the W, and behold, they had
Lev 16:29 and shall do no W, either the native or
23:3 Six days shall W be done; but on the

	141:4	company with men who W iniquity; and let me
Prov	8:22	the beginning of his W, the first of his
	12:14	with good, and the W of a man's hand
	16:3	Commit your W to the LORD, and your plans
	16:11	all the weights in the bag are his W
	18:9	is slack in his W is a brother to
	22:29	Do you see a man skillful in his W
	24:12	will he not requite man according to his W
	24:27	Prepare your W outside, get everything ready for
Eccl	2:23	of pain, and his W is a vexation; even
	2:26	sinner he gives the W of gathering and heaping,
	3:17	a time for every matter, and for every W
	3:22	man should enjoy his W, for that is his
	4:4	and all skill in W come from a man's
	5:6	voice, and destroy the W of your hands?
	7:13	Consider the W of God; who can make straight
	8:17	I saw all the W of God, that man
	8:17	cannot find out the W that is done under
	9:10	for there is no W or thought or knowledge
	11:5	do not know the W of God who makes
Song	5:14	His body is ivory W, encrusted with sapphires.
	7:1	are like jewels, the W of a master hand.
Wis	13:10	a useless stone, the W of an ancient hand.
	13:12	castoff pieces of his W to prepare his food,
	13:19	step; for money-making and W and success with his
	14:8	because he did the W, and the perishable thing
	14:20	the charm of his W, now regarded as an
	17:20	was engaged in unhindered W,
Sir	7:15	toilsome labor, or farm W, which were created by
	7:20	servant who performs his W faithfully, or a hired
	9:17	A W will be praised for the skill of
	10:25	when you do your W, nor glorify yourself at
	11:18	attend to it, and grow old in your W
	24:21	shame, and those who W with my help will
	31:22	In all your W be industrious, and no sickness
	33:24	bread and discipline and W for a servant.
	33:25	Set your slave to W, and you will find
	33:27	Put him to W, that he may not be
	33:28	Set him to W, as is fitting for him,
	36:6	Show signs anew, and W further wonders; make thy
	37:11	an idler about any W or with a man
	37:11	year about completing his W, with a lazy servant
	37:16	the beginning of every W, and counsel precedes
	38:25	is occupied with their W, and whose talk is
	38:27	image, and he is careful to finish his W
	38:29	potter sitting at his W and turning the wheel
	38:29	deeply concerned over his W, and all his output
	38:31	hands, and each is skilful in his own W
	42:16	its light, and the W of the Lord is
	43:2	a marvelous instrument, the W of the Most High.
	45:10	blue and purple, the W of an embroiderer; with
	45:11	with twisted scarlet, the W of a craftsman; with
	45:11	setting of gold, the W of a jeweler, for
	45:12	to be prized, the W of an expert, the
	50:16	the trumpets of hammered W, they made a great
	51:8	O Lord, and thy W from of old, that
	51:30	Do your W before the appointed time, and in
Is	1:31	become tow, and his W a spark, and both
	2:8	bow down to the W of their hands, to
	5:12	LORD, or see the W of his hands.
	5:19	let him speed his W that we may see
	10:12	has finished all his W on Mount Zion and
	17:8	for the altars, the W of their hands, and
	19:10	crushed, and all who W for hire will be
	19:25	people, and Assyria the W of my hands, and
	28:21	and to W his work-- alien is his
	28:21	and to work his W -- alien is his
	28:21	to work his work-- alien is his W
	29:23	sees his children, the W of my hands, in
	31:2	helpers of those who W iniquity.
	37:19	no gods, but the W of men's hands, wood
	41:24	are nothing, and your W is nought; an abomination
	43:13	from my hand; I W and who can hinder
	45:9	or 'Your W has no handles?
	45:11	command me concerning the W of my hands?
	60:21	of my planting, the W of my hands, that
	64:8	we are all the W of thy hand.
	65:22	shall long enjoy the W of their hands.
Jer	10:9	They are the W of the craftsman and of
	10:9	they are all the W of skilled men.
	10:15	They are worthless, a W of delusion; at the
	17:22	sabbath or do any W, but keep the sabbath
	17:24	holy and do no W on it,
	25:6	to anger with the W of your hands.
	25:7	to anger with the W of your hands to
	25:14	their deeds and the W of their hands."
	25:29	behold, I begin to W evil at the city
	31:16	from tears; for your W shall be rewarded, says
	32:30	to anger by the W of their hands, says
	48:10	he who does the W of the LORD with
	50:25	of hosts has a W to do in the
	51:10	declare in Zion the W of the LORD our
	51:18	They are worthless, a W of delusion; at the
Lam	3:64	LORD, according to the W of their hands.
	4:2	as earthen pots, the W of a potter's hands!
Bar	6:51	not gods but the W of men's hands, and
	6:51	that there is no W of God in them.
Ezek	27:16	wares emeralds, purple, embroidered W, fine linen,
	27:24	of blue and embroidered W, and in carpets of
Dan	11:28	And he shall W his will, and return to
Hos	13:2	all of them the W of craftsmen.
	14:3	'Our God,' to the W of our hands.
Mic	2:1	who devise wickedness and W evil upon their beds!
	5:13	no more to the W of your hands;
Hab	1:5	I am doing a W in your days that
	3:2	of thee, and thy W, O LORD, do I
Zeph	2:14	threshold; for her cedar W will be laid bare.
Hag	2:4	land, says the LORD; W, for I am with
	2:14	and so with every W of their hands; and
1Mac	2:47	arrogant men, and the W prospered in their hands.
	4:51	they finished all the W they had undertaken.
	9:54	He tore down the W of the prophets!
	9:55	was stricken and his W was hindered; his mouth
	10:11	who were doing the W to build the walls
2Mac	5:25	the Jews not at W, he ordered his men
	15:39	delights the ears of those who read the W
Mt	14:2	these powers are at W in him."
	21:28	said, 'Son, go and W in the vineyard today.'
Mk	6:5	could do no mighty W there, except that he
	6:14	these powers are at W in him."
	9:39	who does a mighty W in my name will
	13:34	each with his W, and commands the doorkeeper
Lk	13:14	six days on which W ought to be done;
Jn	4:34	him who sent me, and to accomplish his W
	6:29	them, "This is the W of God, that you
	6:30	What W do you perform?
	9:4	We must W the works of him who sent
	9:4	is day; night comes, when no one can W
	10:33	not for a good W that we stone you
	17:4	earth, having accomplished the W which thou gavest
	21:7	he was stripped for W, and sprang into the
Acts	13:2	and Saul for the W to which I have
	14:26	of God for the W which they had fulfilled.
	15:37	and had not gone with them to the W
Rom	4:5	one who does not W but trusts him who
	7:5	the law, were at W in our members to
	14:20	of food, destroy the W of God.
	15:17	be proud of my W for God.
	15:23	have any room for W in these regions, and
1Cor	3:13	straw-- each man's W will become manifest; for
	3:13	test what sort of W each one has done.
	3:14	If the W which any man has built on
	3:15	If any man's W is burned up, he will
	12:29	Do all W miracles?
	15:58	always abounding in the W of the Lord, knowing
	16:9	wide door for effective W has opened to me,
	16:10	he is doing the W of the Lord, as
2Cor	1:24	over your faith; we W with you for your
	4:12	So death is at W in us, but life
	8:6	he should also complete among you this gracious W
	8:7	excel in this gracious W also.
	8:19	us in this gracious W which we are carrying
	9:8	and may provide in abundance for every good W
	10:16	you, without boasting of W already done in another's
	11:12	their boasted mission they W on the same terms
Gal	6:4	one test his own W, and then his reason
Eph	2:2	that is now at W in the sons of
	3:20	by the power at W within us is able
	4:12	the saints for the W of ministry, for building
	4:28	him labor, doing honest W with his hands, so
Phil	1:6	who began a good W in you will bring
	2:12	more in my absence, W out your own salvation
	2:13	for God is at W in you, both to
	2:13	to will and to W for his good pleasure.
	2:30	nearly died for the W of Christ, risking his
Col	1:10	fruit in every good W and increasing in the
	3:23	Whatever your task, W heartily, as serving the Lord
1Thes	1:3	God and Father your W of faith and labor
	2:13	God, which is at W in you believers.
	4:11	own affairs, and to W with your hands, as
	5:13	them very highly in love because of their W
2Thes	1:11	every good resolve and W of faith by his

	2:7	lawlessness is already at W; only he who now
	2:17	them in every good W and word.
	3:10	any one will not W, let him not eat.
	3:11	living in idleness, mere busybodies, not doing any W
	3:12	Christ to do their W in quietness and to
2Tim	2:21	master of the house, ready for any good W
	3:17	God may be complete, equipped for every good W
	4:5	endure suffering, do the W of an evangelist, fulfil
Tit	3:1	ready for any honest W,
Heb	1:10	the heavens are the W of thy hands;
	6:10	as to overlook your W and the love which
Jas	1:19	of man does not W the righteousness of God.
2Jn	1:11	for he who greets him shares his wicked W
Rev	13:14	it is allowed to W in the presence of

WORKED (29)

Ex	26:1	stuff; with cherubim skilfully W shall you make them.
	28:6	scarlet stuff, and of fine twined linen, skilfully W
	31:10	base, and the finely W garments, the holy garments
	36:8	purple and scarlet stuff, with cherubim skilfully W
	36:35	linen; with cherubim skilfully W he made it.
	39:41	of meeting; the finely W garments for ministering in
Deut	21:3	which has never been W and which has not
Ruth	2:19	And where have you W
	2:19	with whom she had W, and said, "The man's
	2:19	name with whom I W today is Boaz."
2Kgs	12:11	and the builders who W upon the house of
2Chr	3:14	and fine linen, and W cherubim on it.
Neh	4:16	half of my servants W on construction, and half
Jer	10:3	is cut down, and W with an axe by
Ezek	29:20	he labored, because they W for me, says the
Hag	1:14	and they came and W on the house of
Mt	20:12	householder, saying, 'These last W only one hour, and
Mk	16:20	everywhere, while the Lord W with them and
Acts	18:3	with them, and they W, for by trade they
Rom	16:6	Greet Mary, who has W hard among you.
	16:12	beloved Persis, who has W hard in the Lord.
1Cor	15:10	On the contrary, I W harder than any of
Gal	2:8	circumcised (for he who W through Peter for the
	2:8	mission to the circumcised W through me also for
Col	4:13	witness that he has W hard for you and
1Thes	2:9	and toil, brethren; we W night and day, that
2Thes	3:8	toil and labor we W night and day, that
2Jn	1:8	lose what you have W for, but may win
Rev	19:20	in its presence had W the signs by which

WORKER (12)

1Kgs	7:14	man of Tyre, a W in bronze; and he
Ps	52:2	a sharp razor, you W of treachery.
Prov	16:26	A W's appetite works for him; his mouth urges
Eccl	3:9	What gain has the W from his toil?
Wis	15:7	each of these the W in clay decides.
Sir	40:18	the self-reliant and the W, but he who finds
Rom	16:9	Greet Urbanus, our fellow W in Christ, and my
	16:21	Timothy, my fellow W, greets you; so do Lucius
1Cor	16:16	and to every fellow W and laborer.
2Cor	8:23	my partner and fellow W in your service; and
Phil	2:25	my brother and fellow W and fellow soldier, and
Philem	1:1	Philemon our beloved fellow W

WORKERS (22)

1Chr	4:21	the house of linen W at Beth-ashbea;
2Chr	2:7	be with the skilled W who are with me
	24:12	the LORD, and also W in iron and bronze
Job	31:3	unrighteous, and disaster the W of iniquity?
Ps	6:8	from me, all you W of evil; for the
	28:3	with those who are W of evil, who speak
Wis	15:9	but he competes with W in gold and silver,
	15:9	and silver, and imitates W in copper; and he
Sir	27:10	does sin for the W of iniquity.
Is	19:9	The W in combed flax will be in despair,
	58:3	seek your own pleasure, and oppress all your W
Ezek	48:18	be food for the W of the city.
	48:19	And the W of the city, from all the
Lk	13:27	from me, all you W of iniquity!'
Rom	16:3	and Aquila, my fellow W in Christ Jesus,
	16:12	Greet those W in the Lord, Tryphaena and Tryphosa.
1Cor	3:9	we are God's fellow W; you are God's field,
	12:28	prophets, third teachers, then W of miracles, then
Phil	4:3	rest of my fellow W, whose names are in
Col	4:11	circumcision among my fellow W for the kingdom of
Philem	1:24	Mark, Aristarchus, Demas, and Luke, my fellow W
3Jn	1:8	we may be fellow W in the truth.

WORKEST

Ps	77:14	art the God who W wonders, who hast manifested

WORKING (23)

Ex	7:9	you, 'Prove yourselves by W a miracle,' then you
2Sam	24:16	the angel who was W destruction among the people,
1Chr	22:15	without number, skilled in W
2Chr	34:10	the workmen who were W in the house of
Ps	74:12	is from of old, W salvation in the midst
Wis	7:26	spotless mirror of the W of God, and an
	13:4	at their power and W, let them perceive from
Jer	18:3	and there he was W at his wheel.
Ezek	46:1	shut on the six W days; but on the
Jn	5:16	them, "My Father is W still, and I am
	5:16	"My Father is working still, and I am W
Rom	7:13	It was sin, W death in me through what
1Cor	4:12	homeless, and we labor, W with our own hands.
	9:6	right to refrain from W for a living?
	12:6	there are varieties of W, but it is the
	12:10	Spirit, to another the W of miracles, to another
2Cor	6:1	W together with him, then, we entreat you not
Gal	5:6	any avail, but faith W through love.
Eph	1:19	believe, according to the W of his great might
	3:7	given me by the W of his power.
	4:16	when each part is W properly, makes bodily growth
Col	2:12	through faith in the W of God, who raised
Heb	13:21	may do his will, W in you that which

WORKMAN (9)

Ex	35:35	by any sort of W or skilled designer.
Prov	8:30	him, like a master W; and I was daily
Wis	17:17	a shepherd or a W who toiled in the
Sir	19:1	A W who is a drunkard will not become
	38:27	every craftsman and master W who labors by night
Is	40:19	a W casts it, and a goldsmith overlays it
Hos	8:6	A W made it; it is not God.
Hab	2:18	For the W trusts in his own creation when
2Tim	2:15	as one approved, a W who has no need

WORKMANSHIP (7)

Ex	28:8	be of the same W and materials, of gold,
	39:5	the same materials and W, of gold, blue and
Num	8:4	And this was the W of the lampstand, hammered
1Kgs	7:8	court back of the hall, was of like W
Wis	13:11	and then with pleasing W make a useful vessel
1Cor	9:1	Are not you my W in the Lord?
Eph	2:10	For we are his W, created in Christ Jesus

WORKMEN (15)

Ex	36:8	able men among the W made the tabernacle with
Judg	5:26	right hand to the W's mallet; she struck Sisera
2Kgs	12:11	the hands of the W who had the oversight
	12:14	was given to the W who were repairing the
	12:15	pay out to the W, for they dealt honestly.
	22:5	the hand of the W who have the oversight
	22:5	give it to the W who are at the
	22:9	the hand of the W who have the oversight
1Chr	22:15	abundance of W: stonecutters, masons, carpenters,
2Chr	34:10	delivered it to the W who had the oversight
	34:10	the LORD; and the W who were working in
	34:17	into the hand of the overseers and the W
Ezra	3:9	the oversight of the W in the house of
Acts	19:25	gathered together, with the W of like occupation, and
2Cor	11:13	are false apostles, deceitful W, disguising themselves

WORKS (216)

Ex	23:24	do according to their W, but you shall utterly
Num	16:28	to do all these W, and that it has
Deut	3:24	who can do such W and mighty acts as
Judg	13:19	LORD, to him who W wonders.
1Chr	16:9	praises to him, tell of all his wonderful W
	16:12	Remember the wonderful W that he has done, the
	16:24	the nations, his marvelous W among all the peoples!
2Chr	32:30	And Hezekiah prospered in all his W
	34:25	anger with all the W of their hands, therefore
Neh	9:35	and they did not turn from their wicked W
Tob	3:11	May all thy W praise thee for ever.
	4:14	of any man who W for you, but pay
	12:6	name, worthily declaring the W of God.
	12:7	gloriously to reveal the W of God.
	12:11	gloriously to reveal the W of God.'
	12:22	the great and wonderful W of God, and
Esth	13:8	to remembrance all the W of the Lord.
Job	34:25	Thus, knowing their W, he overturns them in the
	37:14	and consider the wondrous W of God.
	37:16	the clouds, the wondrous W of him who is
	40:19	the first of the W of God; let him
Ps	8:6	him dominion over the W of thy hands; thou
	17:4	With regard to the W of men, by the

W

	28:5	do not regard the W of the LORD, or
	46:8	[Selah] Come, behold the W of the LORD, how
	73:28	refuge, that I may tell of all thy W
	78:7	and not forget the W of God, but keep
	86:8	nor are there any W like thine.
	92:4	thy work; at the W of thy hands I
	92:5	How great are thy W, O LORD!
	96:3	the nations, his marvelous W among all the peoples!
	103:6	The LORD W vindication and justice for all who
	103:22	the LORD, all his W, in all places of
	104:24	O LORD, how manifold are thy W
	104:31	LORD rejoice in his W,
	105:2	praises to him, tell of all his wonderful W
	105:5	Remember the wonderful W that he has done, his
	106:7	not consider thy wonderful W; they did not
	106:13	they soon forgot his W; they did not wait
	106:22	things in Egypt, wondrous W in the land of
	107:8	love, for his wonderful W to the sons of
	107:15	love, for his wonderful W to the sons of
	107:21	love, for his wonderful W to the sons of
	107:24	the LORD, his wondrous W in the deep.
	107:31	love, for his wonderful W to the sons of
	111:2	Great are the W of the LORD, studied by
	111:4	has caused his wonderful W to be remembered; the
	111:6	the power of his W, in giving them the
	111:7	The W of his hands are faithful and just;
	119:27	precepts, and I will meditate on thy wondrous W
	139:14	Wonderful are thy W
	145:4	generation shall laud thy W to another, and shall
	145:5	and on thy wondrous W, I will meditate.
	145:10	All thy W shall give thanks to thee, O
Prov	12:9	of humble standing who W for himself than one
	16:26	A worker's appetite W for him; his mouth urges
	26:28	and a flattering mouth W ruin.
	31:13	wool and flax, and W with willing hands.
	31:31	hands, and let her W praise her in the
Eccl	2:4	I made great W; I built houses and planted
Wis	1:12	on destruction by the W of your hands;
	2:4	one will remember our W; our life will pass
	3:11	are unprofitable, and their W are useless.
	6:3	will search out your W and inquire into your
	8:4	knowledge of God, and an associate in his W
	9:9	wisdom, who knows thy W and was present when
	9:12	Then my W will be acceptable, and I shall
	11:1	Wisdom prospered their W by the hand of a
	12:4	their detestable practices, their W of sorcery and
	12:19	Through such W thou has taught thy people that
	13:1	paying heed to his W;
	13:7	they live among his W they keep searching, and
	13:10	to the W of men's hands, gold and silver
	14:5	is thy will that W of thy wisdom should
Sir	1:7	her, he poured her out upon all his W
	10:26	is a man who W and has an abundance
	11:4	are honored; for the W of the Lord are
	11:4	are wonderful, and his W are concealed from men.
	11:11	is a man who W, and toils, and presses
	11:19	not wonder at the W of a sinner, but
	16:19	so most of his W are concealed.
	16:24	The W of the Lord have existed from the
	16:25	He arranged his W in an eternal order, and
	17:7	hearts to show them the majesty of his W
	17:8	holy name, to proclaim the grandeur of his W
	17:15	All their W are as the sun before him,
	18:3	power to proclaim his W; and who can search
	33:15	Look upon all the W of the Most High;
	35:19	his deeds, and the W of men according to
	38:6	that he might be glorified in his marvelous W
	38:8	His W will never be finished; and from him
	39:14	Lord for all his W;
	39:16	"All things are the W of the Lord, for
	39:19	The W of all flesh are before him, and
	39:33	it in writing: The W of the Lord are
	42:15	call to mind the W of the Lord, and
	42:15	of the Lord his W are done.
	42:17	recount all his marvelous W, which the Lord the
	42:22	desired are all his W, and how sparkling they
	43:4	man tending a furnace W in burning heat, but
	43:25	are strange and marvelous W, all kinds of living
	43:28	For he is greater than all his W
	43:32	for we have seen but few of his W
	47:22	cause any of his W to perish; he will
Is	26:12	us, thou hast wrought for us all our W
	41:29	all a delusion; their W are nothing; their molten
	44:12	ironsmith fashions it and W it over the coals;
	59:6	Their W are works of iniquity, and deeds of
	59:6	Their works are W of iniquity, and deeds of
	64:4	God besides thee, who W for those who wait
	64:5	meetest him that joyfully W righteousness, those that
	66:18	"For I know their W and their thoughts, and
Jer	1:16	gods, and worshiped the W of their own hands.
	44:8	to anger with the W of your hands, burning
Bar	2:9	righteous in all his W which he has commanded
Ezek	6:6	cut down, and your W wiped out.
Dan	3:27	us, and all thy W are true and thy
	3:43	accordance with thy marvelous W, and give glory to
	3:58	"Bless the Lord, all W of the Lord, sing
	4:37	heaven; for all his W are right and his
	6:27	delivers and rescues, he W signs and wonders in
	9:14	righteous in all the W which he has done,
Hos	7:3	not consider that I remember all their evil W
Mic	6:16	Omri, and all the W of the house of
2Mac	15:21	upon the Lord who W wonders; for he knew
Mt	5:16	may see your good W and give glory to
	7:22	and do many mighty W in your name?'
	11:20	most of his mighty W had been done, because
	11:21	for if the mighty W done in you had
	11:23	For if the mighty W done in you had
	13:54	this man get this wisdom and these mighty W
	13:58	not do many mighty W there, because of their
Mk	6:2	What mighty W are wrought by his hands!
Lk	10:13	for if the mighty W done in you had
	19:37	for all the mighty W that they had seen,
Jn	5:19	is doing; and greater W than these will he
	5:35	of John; for the W which the Father has
	5:35	to accomplish, these very W which I am doing,
	6:28	to be doing the W of God?"
	7:3	disciples may see the W you are doing.
	7:4	For no man W in secret if he seeks
	7:7	of it that its W are evil.
	9:3	parents, but that the W of God might be
	9:4	We must work the W of him who sent
	10:25	The W that I do in my Father's name,
	10:32	shown you many good W from the Father; for
	10:37	am not doing the W of my Father, then
	10:38	believe me, believe the W, that you may know
	14:10	the Father who dwells in me does his W
	14:11	the sake of the W themselves.
	14:12	will also do the W that I do; and
	14:12	I do; and greater W than these will he
	15:24	done among them the W which no one else
Acts	2:11	own tongues the mighty W of God."
	2:22	by God with mighty W and wonders and signs
	7:41	and rejoiced in the W of their hands.
	9:36	was full of good W and acts of charity.
Rom	2:6	man according to his W:
	3:20	in his sight by W of the law, since
	3:27	On the principle of W
	3:28	by faith apart from W of law.
	4:2	Abraham was justified by W, he has something to
	4:4	Now to one who W, his wages are not
	4:6	reckons righteousness apart from W:
	8:28	that in everything God W for good with those
	9:11	continue, not because of W but because of his
	9:32	faith, but as if it were based on W
	11:6	on the basis of W; otherwise grace would no
	13:12	then cast off the W of darkness and put
2Cor	12:12	all patience, with signs and wonders and mighty W
Gal	2:16	is not justified by W of the law but
	2:16	Christ, and not by W of the law, because
	2:16	the law, because by W of the law shall
	3:2	receive the Spirit by W of the law, or
	3:5	Spirit to you and W miracles among you do
	3:5	you do so by W of the law, or
	3:10	all who rely on W of the law are
	5:19	Now the W of the flesh are plain: fornication,
Eph	2:9	not because of W, lest any man should
	2:10	Christ Jesus for good W, which God prepared
	5:11	part in the unfruitful W of darkness, but instead
2Tim	1:9	in virtue of our W but in virtue of
Heb	3:9	test and saw my W for forty years.
	4:3	although his W were finished from the foundation of
	4:4	rested on the seventh day from all his W
	6:1	of repentance from dead W and of faith toward
	9:14	your conscience from dead W to serve the living
	10:24	to love and good W,
Jas	2:14	man says he has faith but has not W
	2:17	if it has no W, is dead.
	2:18	will say, "You have faith and I have W
	2:18	faith apart from your W, and I by my
	2:18	and I by my W will show you my
	2:20	that faith apart from W is barren?
	2:21	our father justified by W, when he offered his

W

14:31 me, so that the W may know that I
15:18 "If the W hates you, know that it has
15:19 you were of the W, the world would love
15:19 of the world, the W would love its own;
15:19 are not of the W, but I chose you
15:19 you out of the W, therefore the world hates
15:19 the world, therefore the W hates you.
16:8 will convince the W concerning sin and righteousness
16:11 the ruler of this W is judged.
16:20 and lament, but the W will rejoice; you will
16:21 joy that a child is born into the W
16:28 have come into the W; again, I am leaving
16:28 I am leaving the W and going to the
16:33 In the W you have tribulation; but be of
16:33 be of good cheer, I have overcome the W
17:5 with thee before the W was made.
17:6 me out of the W; thine they were, and
17:9 not praying for the W but for those whom
17:11 no more in the W, but they are in
17:11 they are in the W, and I am coming
17:13 I speak in the W, that they may have
17:14 thy word; and the W has hated them because
17:14 are not of the W, even as I am
17:14 world, even as I am not of the W
17:15 them out of the W, but that thou shouldst
17:16 are not of the W, even as I am
17:16 world, even as I am not of the W
17:18 send me into the W, so I have sent
17:18 world, so I have sent them into the W
17:21 us, so that the W may believe that thou
17:23 one, so that the W may know that thou
17:24 love for me before the foundation of the W
17:25 O righteous Father, the W has not known thee,
18:20 spoken openly to the W; I have always taught
18:36 is not of this W; if my kingship were
18:36 kingship were of this W, my servants would fight,
18:36 Jews; but my kingship is not from the W
18:37 have come into the W, to bear witness to
21:25 I suppose that the W itself could not contain
Acts 11:28 famine over all the W; and this took place
17:6 who have turned the W upside down have come
17:24 God who made the W and everything in it,
17:31 he will judge the W in righteousness by a
19:27 all Asia and the W worship."
24:5 the Jews throughout the W, and a ringleader of
Rom 1:8 because your faith is proclaimed in all the W
1:20 the creation of the W his invisible nature, namely,
3:6 For then how could God judge the W
3:19 stopped, and the whole W may be held accountable
4:13 they should inherit the W, did not come through
5:12 sin came into the W through one man and
5:13 indeed was in the W before the law was
10:18 and their words to the ends of the W
11:12 means riches for the W, and if their failure
11:15 the reconciliation of the W, what will their
12:2 be conformed to this W but be transformed by
1Cor 1:20 not God made foolish the wisdom of the W
1:21 wisdom of God, the W did not know God
1:27 is foolish in the W to shame the wise,
1:27 is weak in the W to shame the strong,
1:28 and despised in the W, even things that are
2:12 the spirit of the W, but the Spirit which
3:19 the wisdom of this W is folly with God.
3:22 or Cephas or the W or life or death
4:9 a spectacle to the W, to angels and to
4:13 the refuse of the W, the offscouring of all
5:10 the immoral of this W, or the greedy and
5:10 you would need to go out of the W
6:2 not know that the saints will judge the W
6:2 And if the W is to be judged by
7:31 who deal with the W as though they had
7:31 the form of this W is passing away.

11:32 we may not be condemned along with the W
14:10 different languages in the W, and none is without
2Cor 1:12 have behaved in the W, and still more toward
4:4 the god of this W has blinded the minds
5:19 God was reconciling the W to himself, not counting
10:3 we live in the W we are not carrying
Gal 6:14 Christ, by which the W has been crucified to
6:14 been crucified to me, and I to the W
Eph 1:4 the foundation of the W, that we should be
2:2 the course of this W, following the prince of
2:12 having no hope and without God in the W
6:12 the powers, against the W rulers of this present
Phil 2:15 as lights in the W,
Col 1:6 indeed in the whole W it is bearing fruit
2:20 live as if you still belonged to the W
1Tim 1:15 Jesus came into the W to save sinners.
3:16 believed on in the W, taken up in glory.
6:7 brought nothing into the W, and we cannot take
6:7 anything out of the W;
6:17 the rich in this W, charge them not to
2Tim 4:10 love with this present W, has deserted me and
Tit 2:12 godly lives in this W,
Heb 1:2 all things, through whom also he created the W
1:6 the first-born into the W, he says, "Let all
2:5 that God subjected the W to come, of which
4:3 works were finished from the foundation of the W
9:26 to suffer repeatedly since the foundation of the W
10:5 Christ came into the W, he said, "Sacrifices and
11:3 we understand that the W was created by the
11:7 this he condemned the W and became an heir
11:38 of whom the W was not worthy--
Jas 1:26 affliction, and to keep oneself unstained from the W
2:5 are poor in the W to be rich in
3:6 tongue is an unrighteous W among our members,
4:4 that friendship with the W is enmity with God?
4:4 a friend of the W makes himself an enemy
1Pet 1:20 the foundation of the W but was made manifest
5:9 is required of your brotherhood throughout the W
2Pet 1:4 that is in the W because of passion, and
2:5 not spare the ancient W, but preserved Noah, a
2:5 a flood upon the W of the ungodly;
2:20 the defilements of the W through the knowledge of
3:6 water, through which the W that then existed was
1Jn 2:2 but also for the sins of the whole W
2:15 Do not love the W or the things in
2:15 love the world or the things in the W
2:15 any one loves the W, love for the Father
2:16 that is in the W, the lust of the
2:16 not of the Father but is of the W
2:17 And the W passes away, and the lust of
3:1 The reason why the W does not know us
3:13 wonder, brethren, that the W hates you.
3:17 any one has the W's goods and sees his
4:1 many false prophets have gone out into the W
4:3 it is in the W already.
4:4 is greater than he who is in the W
4:5 They are of the W, therefore what they say
4:5 say is of the W, and the world listens
4:5 the world, and the W listens to them.
4:9 only Son into the W, so that we might
4:14 sent his Son as the Savior of the W
4:17 as he is so are we in this W
5:4 of God overcomes the W; and this is the
5:4 victory that overcomes the W, our faith.
5:5 it that overcomes the W but he who believes
5:19 God, and the whole W is in the power
2Jn 1:7 gone out into the W, men who will not
Rev 3:10 coming on the whole W, to try those who
11:15 "The kingdom of the W has become the kingdom
12:9 deceiver of the whole W --he was thrown down
13:8 the foundation of the W in the book of
16:14 kings of the whole W, to assemble them for
17:8 the foundation of the W, will marvel to behold

WORLDLY (12)

1Cor 1:26 were wise according to W standards, not many were
7:28 who marry will have W troubles, and I would
7:33 man is anxious about W affairs, how to please
7:34 woman is anxious about W affairs, how to please
2Cor 1:17 my plans like a W man, ready to say
7:10 brings no regret, but W grief produces death.
10:2 us of acting in W fashion.
10:3 not carrying on a W war,
10:4 our warfare are not W but have divine power
11:18 since many boast of W things, I too will
Tit 2:12 to renounce irreligion and W passions, and to live
Jude 1:19 who set up divisions, W people, devoid of the

WORM (9)

Deut 28:39 the grapes; for the W shall eat them.
Job 17:14 father,' and to the W, 'My mother,' or 'My
25:6 and the son of man, who is a W
Ps 22:6 But I am a W, and no man; scorned
Is 41:14 Fear not, you W Jacob, you men of Israel!
51:8 a garment, and the W will eat them like
66:24 against me; for their W shall not die, their
Jon 4:7 day, God appointed a W which attacked the plant,
Mk 9:46 into hell, where their W does not die, and

WORMS (13)

Ex 16:20 morning, and it bred W and became foul; and
16:24 and there were no W in it.
Jud 16:17 of judgment; fire and W he will give to
Job 7:5 flesh is clothed with W and dirt; my skin
21:26 the dust, and the W cover them.
Sir 7:17 the punishment of the ungodly is fire and W
10:11 will inherit creeping things, and wild beasts, and W
19:3 Decay and W will inherit him, and the reckless
Is 14:11 bed beneath you, and W are your covering.
Bar 6:20 hearts have melted, when W from the earth devour
1Mac 2:62 for his splendor will turn into dung and W
2Mac 9:9 man's body swarmed with W, and while he was
Acts 12:23 he was eaten by W and died.

WORMWOOD (9)

Prov 5:4 she is bitter as W, sharp as a two-edged
Jer 9:15 feed this people with W, and give them poisonous
23:15 will feed them with W, and give them poisoned
Lam 3:15 me with bitterness, he has sated me with W
3:19 and my bitterness, the W and the gall!
Amos 5:7 who turn justice to W, and cast down righteousness
6:12 fruit of righteousness into W –
Rev 8:11 The name of the star is W
8:11 of the waters became W, and many men died

WORN (7)

Deut 29:5 your sandals have not W off your feet;
Judg 8:26 and the purple garments W by the kings of
Esth 6:8 which the king has W, and the horse which
Job 16:7 Surely now God has W me out; he has
Sir 11:5 never thought of has W a crown.
1Mac 8:14 on a crown or W purple as a mark
Lk 8:27 long time he had W no clothes, and he

WORN-OUT (7)

Deut 29:5 your clothes have not W upon you, and your
Josh 9:4 ready provisions, and took W sacks upon their asses,
9:4 their asses, and wineskins, W and torn and mended,
9:5 torn and mended, with W, patched sandals on their
9:5 on their feet, and W clothes; and all their
9:13 shoes of ours are W from the very long
Jer 38:11 there old rags and W clothes, which he let

WORRIED

Sir 9:13 you will not be W by the fear of

WORRY (5)

Tob 5:20 to her, "Do not W, my sister; he will
6:15 wife; and do not W about the demon, for
Sir 22:20 your friend, do not W, for reconciliation is possible;
42:9 father secretly wakeful, and W over her robs him
1Mac 6:10 from my eyes and I am downhearted with W

WORRYING

Tob 10:6 "Be still and stop W; he is well."

WORSE (33)

Gen 19:9 Now we will deal W with you than with
Judg 2:19 turned back and behaved W than their fathers, going
1Sam 14:47 wherever he turned he put them to the W
2Sam 19:7 and this will be W for you than all
Ps 39:2 avail; my distress grew W,
Wis 15:18 hateful animals, which are W than all others, when
17:6 they saw to be W than that unseen appearance.
Sir 22:9 of the fool is W than death.
25:14 There is no venom W than a snake's venom,
25:14 venom, and no wrath W than an enemy's wrath.
26:5 accusation–all these are W than death.
39:34 can say, "This is W than that," for all
Jer 7:26 They did W than their fathers.
16:12 because you have done W than your fathers, for
Ezek 23:11 her harlotry, which was W than that of her
2Mac 5:23 over his fellow citizens W than the others did.
7:39 rage, and handled him W than the others, being
13:9 the Jews things far W than those that had
Mt 9:16 the garment, and a W tear is made.
12:45 of that man becomes W than the first.
27:64 last fraud will be W than the first."
Mk 2:21 the old, and a W tear is made.
5:26 had, and was no better but rather grew W
Lk 11:26 of that man becomes W than the first."
13:2 that these Galileans were W sinners than all the
13:4 think that they were W offenders than all the
Jn 5:13 no more, that nothing W befall you."
1Cor 8:8 We are no W off if we do not
11:17 is not for the better but for the W
1Tim 5:8 the faith and is W than an unbeliever.
2Tim 3:13 on from bad to W, deceivers and deceived.
Heb 10:29 How much W punishment do you think will be
2Pet 2:20 last state has become W for them than the

WORSHIP (129)

Gen 22:5 will go yonder and W, and come again to
Ex 24:1 elders of Israel, and W afar off.
33:10 would rise up and W, every man at his
34:14 Asherim (for you shall W no other god, for
Deut 4:19 be drawn away and W them and serve them,
8:19 and serve them and W them, I solemnly warn
11:16 serve other gods and W them,
26:10 LORD your God, and W before the LORD your
30:17 are drawn away to W other gods and serve
Josh 22:25 our children cease to W the LORD.
1Sam 1:3 from his city to W and to sacrifice to
15:25 me, that I may W the LORD."
15:30 me, that I may W the LORD your God."
2Sam 15:8 then I will offer W to the LORD.'"
1Kgs 9:6 serve other gods and W them,
2Kgs 5:18 house of Rimmon to W there, leaning on my
18:22 to Jerusalem, "You shall W before this altar in
1Chr 16:29 W the LORD in holy array;
2Chr 7:19 serve other gods and W them,
32:12 one altar you shall W, and upon it you
Ezra 4:2 with you; for we W your God as you
6:21 of the land to W the LORD, the God
Tob 5:13 to Jerusalem to W and offered the first-born
Jud 3:8 that all nations should W Nebuchadnezzar only, and
Ps 5:7 thy house, I will W toward thy holy temple
22:27 of the nations shall W before him.
29:2 glory of his name; W the LORD in holy
95:6 O come, let us W and bow down, let
96:9 W the LORD in holy array; tremble before him,
99:5 the LORD our God; W at his footstool!
99:9 LORD our God, and W at his holy mountain;
102:22 together, and kingdoms, to W the LORD.
132:7 dwelling place; let us W at his footstool!"
Wis 11:15 led them astray to W irrational serpents and
14:18 did not know the king to intensify their W
14:20 as an object of W the one whom shortly
14:27 For the W of idols not to be named
15:6 make or desire or W them.
15:18 enemies of thy people W even the most hateful
Sir 50:17 upon their faces to W their Lord, the Almighty,
50:19 till the order of W of the Lord was
50:21 they bowed down in W a second time, to
Is 2:20 made for themselves to W, to the moles and
19:21 in that day and W with sacrifice and burnt
19:23 and the Egyptians will W with the Assyrians.
27:13 Egypt will come and W the LORD on the
36:7 to Jerusalem, "You shall W before this altar"?
46:6 into a god; then they fall down and W
66:23 flesh shall come to W before me, says the
Jer 7:2 enter these gates to W the LORD.
13:10 to serve them and W them, shall be like
25:6 gods to serve and W them, or provoke me
26:2 Judah which come to W in the house of
Bar 6:6 "It is thou, O Lord, whom we must W
Ezek 20:32 of the countries, and W wood and stone.'
46:2 offerings, and he shall W at the threshold of
46:3 of the land shall W at the entrance of
46:9 the north gate to W shall go out by
Dan 3:5 to fall down and W the golden image that
3:6 not fall down and W shall immediately be cast
3:10 shall fall down and W the golden image;
3:11 not fall down and W shall be cast into
3:12 serve your gods or W the golden image which
3:14 serve my gods or W the golden image which
3:15 to fall down and W the image which I
3:15 if you do not W, you shall immediately be
3:18 serve your gods or W the golden image which
3:91 Bless him, all who W the Lord, the God
3:96 rather than serve and W any god except their
14:4 went every day to W it.
14:5 "Why do you not W Bel?" He answered, "Because
14:24 a living god; so W him."
14:25 Daniel said, "I will W the Lord my God,
Zech 14:16 year after year to W the King, the LORD
14:17 up to Jerusalem to W the King, the LORD
2Mac 1:3 all a heart to W him and to do
Mt 2:2 and have come to W him."
2:8 too may come and W him."
4:9 will fall down and W me."

4:10 is written, 'You shall W the Lord your God
15:9 in vain do they W me, teaching as doctrines
Mk 7:7 in vain do they W me, teaching as doctrines
Lk 4:7 If you, then, will W me, it shall all
4:8 is written, 'You shall W the Lord your God,
Jn 4:20 Jerusalem is the place where men ought to W
4:21 in Jerusalem will you W the Father.
4:22 You W what you do not know; we worship
4:22 do not know; we W what we know, for
4:23 the true worshipers will W the Father in spirit
4:23 the Father seeks to W him.
4:24 spirit, and those who W him must worship in
4:24 who worship him must W in spirit and truth."
12:20 who went up to W at the feast were
Acts 7:7 shall come out and W me in this place.'
7:42 gave them over to W the host of heaven,
7:43 which you made to W; and I will remove
8:27 come to Jerusalem to W
17:23 the objects of your W, I found also an
17:23 god.' What therefore you W as unknown, this I
18:13 is persuading men to W God contrary to the
19:27 magnificence, she whom all Asia and the world W
24:10 I went up to W at Jerusalem;
24:13 call a sect, I W the God of our
26:7 attain, as they earnestly W night and day.
27:23 belong and whom I W,
Rom 9:4 of the law, the W, and the promises;
12:1 and acceptable to God, which is your spiritual W
1Cor 10:14 my beloved, shun the W of idols.
14:25 his face, he will W God and declare that
Phil 3:3 the true circumcision, who W God in spirit, and
Col 2:18 insisting on self-abasement and W of angels, taking
2Thes 2:4 god or object of W, so that he takes
Heb 1:6 "Let all God's angels W him."
9:1 covenant had regulations for W and an earthly
9:21 the tent and all the vessels used in W
11:21 of Joseph, bowing in W over the head of
12:28 offer to God acceptable W, with reverence and awe;
Rev 4:10 on the throne and W him who lives for
11:1 altar and those who W there,
13:8 dwell on earth will W it, every one whose
13:12 earth and its inhabitants W the first beast, whose
13:15 those who would not W the image of the
14:7 judgment has come; and W him who made heaven
15:4 nations shall come and W thee, for thy judgments
19:10 at his feet to W him, but he said
19:10 W God." For the testimony of Jesus is the
22:3 and his servants shall W him;
22:8 I fell down to W at the feet of
22:9 W God."

WORSHIPED (58)

Gen 24:26 bowed his head and W the LORD,
24:48 bowed my head and W the LORD, and blessed
Ex 4:31 seen their affliction, they bowed their heads and W
12:27 And the people bowed their heads and W
32:8 molten calf, and have W it and sacrificed to
34:8 to bow his head toward the earth, and W
Deut 17:3 served other gods and W them, or the sun
29:26 served other gods and W them, gods whom they
Josh 5:14 to the earth, and W, and said to him,
Judg 7:15 and its interpretation, he W; and he returned to
1Sam 1:19 in the morning and W before the LORD; then
1:28 And they W the LORD there.
15:31 after Saul; and Saul W the LORD.
2Sam 12:20 of the LORD, and W; he then went to
15:32 summit, where God was W, behold, Hushai the
1Kgs 11:33 has forsaken me, and W Ashtoreth the goddess of
16:31 and served Baal, and W him.
22:53 He served Baal and W him, and provoked the
2Kgs 17:16 made an Asherah, and W all the host of
21:3 Israel had done, and W all the host of
21:21 his father served, and W them;
1Chr 29:20 bowed their heads, and W the LORD, and did
2Chr 7:3 on the pavement, and W and gave thanks to
7:22 on other gods, and W them and served them;
25:14 as his gods, and W them, making offerings to
29:28 The whole assembly W, and the singers sang, and
29:29 were present with him bowed themselves and W
29:30 praises with gladness, and they bowed down and W
33:3 and made Asherahs, and W all the host of
Neh 8:6 bowed their heads and W the LORD with their
9:3 they made confession and W the LORD their God.
Jud 5:8 their ancestors, and they W the God of heaven,
6:18 people fell down and W God, and cried out
8:18 city of ours which W gods made with hands,
16:18 arrived at Jerusalem they W God.
Job 1:20 his head, and fell upon the ground, and W
Ps 106:19 calf in Horeb and W a molten image.
Wis 14:16 at the command of monarchs graven images were W
Jer 1:16 to other gods, and W the works of their
8:2 they have sought and W; and they shall not
16:11 and have served and W them, and have forsaken
22:9 LORD their God, and W other gods and served
Dan 3:7 languages fell down and W the golden image which
14:4 But Daniel W his own God.
1Mac 4:55 on their faces and W and blessed Heaven, who
Mt 2:11 they fell down and W him.
Mk 5:6 afar, he ran and W him;
Jn 4:20 Our fathers W on this mountain; and you say
Acts 10:25 at his feet and W him.
Rom 1:25 for a lie and W and served the creature
Rev 5:14 and the elders fell down and W
7:11 before the throne and W God,
11:16 on their faces and W God,
13:4 Men W the dragon, for he had given his
13:4 the beast, and they W the beast, saying, "Who
16:2 of the beast and W its image.
19:4 creatures fell down and W God who is seated
19:20 beast and those who W its image.

WORSHIPER (4)

Jn 9:31 any one is a W of God and does
Acts 16:14 goods, who was a W of God.
18:7 named Titius Justus, a W of God; his house
Heb 9:9 the conscience of the W,

WORSHIPERS (11)

2Kgs 10:19 of Baal, all his W and all his priests;
10:19 order to destroy the W of Baal.
10:21 Israel; and all the W of Baal came, so
10:22 vestments for all the W of Baal." So he
10:23 he said to the W of Baal, "Search, and
10:23 you, but only the W of Baal."
Ps 97:7 All W of images are put to shame, who
Dan 3:33 and disgrace have befallen thy servants and W
Jn 4:23 is, when the true W will worship the Father
Heb 10:2 If the W had once been cleansed, they would
Rev 14:11 day or night, these W of the beast and

WORSHIPING (9)

2Kgs 19:37 And as he was W in the house of
2Chr 20:18 down before the LORD, W the LORD.
Is 37:38 And as he was W in the house of
Bar 6:5 before and behind them W them.
Ezek 8:16 faces toward the east, W the sun toward the
Dan 14:27 And Daniel said, "See what you have been W
Lk 2:37 depart from the temple, W with fasting and prayer
Acts 13:2 While they were W the Lord and fasting, the
Rev 9:20 hands nor give up W demons and idols of

WORSHIPPED (10)

1Kgs 9:9 on other gods, and W them and served them;
Jud 10:8 And she W God.
13:17 and bowed down and W God, and said with
Esth 15:1 in which she had W, and arrayed herself in
Mt 14:33 those in the boat W him, saying, "Truly you
28:9 of his feet and W him.
28:17 they saw him they W him; but some doubted.
Lk 24:52 And they W him, and returned to Jerusalem with
Jn 9:38 I believe"; and he W him.
Rev 20:4 and who had not W the beast or its

WORSHIPPERS

Wis 14:28 For their W either rave in exultation, or prophesy

WORSHIPS (6)

Neh 9:6 the host of heaven W thee.
Ps 66:4 All the earth W thee; they sing praises to
Wis 15:17 than the objects he W, since he has life,
Is 44:15 makes a god and W it, he makes it
44:17 down to it and W it; he prays to
Rev 14:9 voice, "If any one W the beast and its

WORST (2)

Ps 41:7 me; they imagine the W for me.
Ezek 7:24 I will bring the W of the nations to

WORTH (16)

Gen 23:15 a piece of land W four hundred shekels of
Ruth 3:11 townsmen know that you are a woman of W
2Sam 18:3 But you are W ten thousand of us; therefore

W

Ezra 8:26 silver, and silver vessels W a hundred talents, and
8:27 twenty bowls of gold W a thousand darics, and
Prov 10:20 the mind of the wicked is of little W
Wis 15:10 life is of less W than clay,
Sir 7:19 for her charm is W more than gold.
10:27 and ascribe to yourself honor according to your W
Is 7:23 be a thousand vines, W a thousand shekels of
Lam 4:2 precious sons of Zion, W their weight in fine
2Mac 9:15 he had not considered W burying but had planned
Mk 6:37 buy two hundred denarii W of bread, and give
Rom 8:18 present time are not W comparing with the glory
Phil 2:22 But Timothy's W you know, how as a son
3:8 because of the surpassing W of knowing Christ Jesus

WORTHILY (2)

Tob 12:6 to exalt his name, W declaring the works of
13:10 Give thanks W to the Lord, and praise the

WORTHLESS (32)

Num 21:5 and we loathe this W food."
Judg 9:4 with which Abimelech hired W and reckless fellows,
11:3 land of Tob; and W fellows collected round Jephthah,
1Sam 2:12 sons of Eli were W men; they had no
10:27 But some W fellows said, "How can this man
15:9 that was despised and W they utterly destroyed.
2Sam 16:7 man of blood, you W fellow!
20:1 to be there a W fellow, whose name was
2Chr 13:7 his lord; and certain W scoundrels gathered about
Job 11:11 For he knows W men; when he sees iniquity,
13:4 you whitewash with lies; W physicians are you all.
34:18 says to a king, W one,' and to nobles,
Ps 97:7 make their boast in W idols; all gods bow
Prov 6:12 A W person, a wicked man, goes about with
12:11 but he who follows W pursuits has no sense.
16:27 A W man plots evil, and his speech is
19:28 A W witness mocks at justice, and the mouth
28:19 but he who follows W pursuits will have plenty
Wis 9:14 reasoning of mortals is W, and our designs are
11:15 worship irrational serpents and W animals, thou
13:14 makes it like some W animal, giving it a
Is 30:7 For Egypt's help is W and empty, therefore I
Jer 2:5 me, and went after worthlessness, and became W
10:15 They are W, a work of delusion; at the
14:14 you a lying vision, W divination, and the deceit
15:19 and not what is W, you shall be as
16:19 inherited nought but lies, W things in which there
51:18 They are W, a work of delusion; at the
Zech 11:15 the implements of a W shepherd.
11:17 Woe to my W shepherd, who deserts the flock!
Mt 25:30 And cast the W servant into the outer darkness;
Heb 6:8 and thistles, it is W and near to being

WORTHLESSNESS (2)

Jer 2:5 me, and went after W, and became worthless?
Bar 6:26 on men's shoulders, revealing to mankind their W

WORTHY (64)

Gen 32:10 good,' I am not W of the least of
2Sam 22:4 the LORD, who is W to be praised, and
1Kgs 1:42 for you are a W man and bring good
1:52 prove to be a W man, not one of
Ps 18:3 the LORD, who is W to be praised, and
Wis 3:5 them and found them W of himself;
6:16 goes about seeking those W of her, and she
7:15 judgment and have thought W of what I have
9:12 justly, and shall be W of the throne of
12:7 thee might receive a W colony of the servants
Sir 10:19 What race is W of honor?
10:19 What race is W of honor?
10:20 brothers their leader is W of honor, and those
10:20 fear the Lord are W of honor in his
11:29 into evil, and to W actions he will attach
14:11 your means, and present W offerings to the Lord.
Dan 3:26 of our fathers, and W of praise; and thy
1Mac 10:19 a mighty warrior and W to be our friend.
2Mac 6:23 making a high resolve, W of his years and
6:24 "Such pretense is not W of our time of
6:27 I will show myself W of my old age
7:20 was especially admirable and W of honorable
7:29 this butcher, but prove W of your brothers.
9:19 its content: "To his W Jewish citizens, Antiochus
15:11 of vision, which was W of belief.
Mt 3:11 sandals I am not W to carry; he will
8:8 "Lord, I am not W to have you come
10:11 find out who is W in it, and stay
10:13 if the house is W, let your peace come
10:13 if it is not W, let your peace return
10:37 than me is not W of me; and he
10:37 than me is not W of me;
10:38 follow me is not W of me.
22:8 wedding is ready, but those invited were not W
Mk 1:7 sandals I am not W to stoop down and
Lk 3:16 sandals I am not W to untie; he will
7:4 earnestly, saying, "He is W to have you do
7:6 for I am not W to have you come
15:19 I am no longer W to be called your
15:21 I am no longer W to be called your
20:35 those who are accounted W to attain to that
Jn 1:27 sandal I am not W to untie."
Acts 5:41 that they were counted W to suffer dishonor for
13:25 feet I am not W to untie.'
26:20 God and perform deeds W of their repentance.
Eph 4:1 to lead a life W of the calling to
Phil 1:27 manner of life be W of the gospel of
4:8 if there is anything W of praise, think about
Col 1:10 to lead a life W of the Lord, fully
1Thes 2:12 to lead a life W of God, who calls
2Thes 1:5 you may be made W of the kingdom of
1:11 God may make you W of his call, and
1Tim 1:15 saying is sure and W of full acceptance, that
4:9 saying is sure and W of full acceptance.
5:17 rule well be considered W of double honor, especially
6:1 regard their masters as W of all honor, so
Heb 3:3 Jesus has been counted W of as much more
11:38 the world was not W – wandering over deserts
Rev 3:4 walk with me in white, for they are W
4:11 before the throne, singing, W art thou, our Lord
5:2 loud voice, "Who is W to open the scroll
5:4 no one was found W to open the scroll
5:9 a new song, saying, W art thou to take
5:12 with a loud voice, W is the Lamb who

WOULDEST (9)

2Chr 20:10 Mount Seir, whom thou W not let Israel invade
Job 14:13 Oh that thou W hide me in Sheol, that
14:13 in Sheol, that thou W conceal me until thy
14:13 be past, that thou W appoint me a set
14:15 Thou W call, and I would answer thee; thou
14:15 would answer thee; thou W long for the work
14:16 For then thou W number my steps, thou wouldest
14:16 number my steps, thou W not keep watch over
14:17 a bag, and thou W cover over my iniquity.

WOULDST (8)

1Chr 4:10 saying, "Oh that thou W bless me and enlarge
4:10 me, and that thou W keep me from harm
Ezra 9:14 W thou not be angry with us till thou
9:14 with us till thou W consume us, so that
Ps 51:16 a burnt offering, thou W not be pleased.
139:19 O that thou W slay the wicked, O God,
Wis 11:24 hast made, for thou W not have made anything
Is 64:1 O that thou W rend the heavens and come

WOUND (31)

Ex 21:25 foot, burn for burn, W for wound, stripe for
21:25 for burn, wound for W, stripe for stripe.
Deut 19:6 way is long, and W him mortally, though the
32:39 I make alive; I W and I heal; and
1Kgs 22:35 the blood of the W flowed into the bottom
Jud 9:13 words to be their W and stripe, for they
Job 34:6 counted a liar; my W is incurable, though I
Ps 42:10 As with a deadly W in my body, my
Prov 20:30 Blows that W cleanse away evil; strokes make clean
25:20 a cold day, and like vinegar on a W
Sir 21:3 two-edged sword; there is no healing for its W
25:12 Any W, but not a wound of the heart!
25:12 wound, but not a W of the heart!
27:21 For a W may be bandaged, and there is
Jer 6:14 They have healed the W of my people lightly,
8:11 They have healed the W of my people lightly,
8:21 For the W of the daughter of my people
10:19 My W is grievous.
14:17 smitten with a great W, with a very grievous
15:18 my pain unceasing, my W incurable, refusing to be
30:12 is incurable, and your W is grievous.
30:13 no medicine for your W, no healing for you.
Ezek 28:9 hands of those who W you?
Hos 5:13 sickness, and Judah his W, then Ephraim went to
5:13 not able to cure you or heal your W
Mic 1:9 For her W is incurable; and it has come
Nah 3:19 assuaging your hurt, your W is grievous.
Rev 9:19 with heads, and by means of them they W

13:3 to have a mortal W, but its mortal wound
13:3 wound, but its mortal W was healed, and the
13:12 first beast, whose mortal W was healed.

WOUNDED (43)

Judg 9:40 him; and many fell W, up to the entrance
1Sam 17:52 Ekron, so that the W Philistines fell on the
31:3 and he was badly W by the archers.
2Sam 10:18 thousand horsemen, and W Shobach the commander
1Kgs 22:34 me out of the battle, for I am W
2Kgs 8:28 Ramoth-gilead, where the Syrians W Joram.
1Chr 10:3 him; and he was W by the archers.
2Chr 18:33 me out of the battle, for I am W
22:5 And the Syrians W Joram,
24:25 him, leaving him severely W, his servants conspired
35:23 servants, "Take me away, for I am badly W
Jud 2:8 my troops, till their W shall fill their valleys,
6:6 shall fall among their W, when I return.
16:12 them through; they were W like the children of
Job 24:12 the soul of the W cries for help; yet
Ps 64:7 them; they will be W suddenly.
69:26 him whom thou hast W, they afflict still more.
Song 5:7 they beat me, they W me, they took away
Sir 25:22 gloomy face, and a W heart are caused by
Is 53:5 But he was W for our transgressions, he was
Jer 8:21 people is my heart W, I mourn, and dismay
37:10 remained of them only W men, every man in
51:4 of the Chaldeans, and W in her streets.
51:52 all her land the W shall groan.
Lam 2:12 as they faint like W men in the streets
Ezek 26:15 your fall, when the W groan, when slaughter is
30:24 will groan before him like a man mortally W
1Mac 1:18 him, and many were W and fell.
3:11 Many were W and fell, and the rest fled.
8:10 Many of them were W and fell, and the
9:17 on both sides were W and fell.
9:40 Many were W and fell, and the rest fled
16:8 many of them were W and fell; the rest
16:9 brother of John was W, but John pursued them
2Mac 3:16 priest was to be W at heart, for his
4:42 As a result, they W many of them, and
8:24 of the enemy, and W and disabled most of
10:30 armor and weapons, they kept him from being W
11:12 got away stripped and W, and Lysias himself escaped
Mk 12:4 another servant, and they W him in the head,
Lk 20:12 third; this one they W and cast out.
Acts 19:16 they fled out of that house naked and W
Rev 13:14 the beast which was W by the sword and

WOUNDING (3)

Gen 4:23 slain a man for W me, a young man
1Kgs 20:37 struck him, smiting and W him.
1Cor 8:12 against your brethren and W their conscience when

WOUNDS (26)

Deut 19:11 and attacks him, and W him mortally so that
2Kgs 8:29 in Jezreel of the W which the Syrians had
9:15 in Jezreel of the W which the Syrians had
2Chr 22:6 in Jezreel of the W which he had received
Job 5:18 For he W, but he binds up; he smites,
9:17 tempest, and multiplies my W without cause;
Ps 38:5 My W grow foul and fester because of my
147:3 He heals the brokenhearted, and binds up their W
Prov 6:33 W and dishonor will he get, and his disgrace
23:29 Who has W without cause?
26:10 Like an archer who W everybody is he who
27:6 Faithful are the W of a friend; profuse are
Sir 27:25 own head; and a treacherous blow opens up W
30:7 will bind up his W, and his feelings will
31:30 to his injury, reducing his strength and adding W
Is 1:6 and sores and bleeding W; they are not pressed
30:26 people, and heals the W inflicted by his blow.
Jer 6:7 within her; sickness and W are ever before me.
30:17 to you, and your W I will heal, says
50:13 be appalled, and hiss because of all her W
Zech 13:6 him, 'What are these W on your back?' he
13:6 he will say, 'The W I received in the
2Mac 14:45 gushed forth and his W were severe he ran
Lk 10:34 and bound up his W, pouring on oil and
Acts 16:33 night, and washed their W, and he was baptized
1Pet 2:24 By his W you have been healed.

WOVE (2)

Judg 16:14 of his head and W them into the web.
2Kgs 23:7 LORD, where the women W hangings for the

WOVEN (13)

Ex 28:8 And the skilfully W band upon it, to gird
28:27 joining above the skilfully W band of the ephod.
28:28 lie upon the skilfully W band of the ephod,
28:32 the head, with a W binding around the opening,
29:5 him with the skilfully W band of the ephod;
39:5 And the skilfully W band upon it, to gird
39:20 joining above the skilfully W band of the ephod.
39:21 lie upon the skilfully W band of the ephod,
39:22 robe of the ephod W all of blue;
39:27 also made the coats, W of fine linen, for
Lev 8:7 him with the skilfully W band of the ephod,
Jud 10:21 a canopy which was W with purple and gold
Jn 19:23 tunic was without seam, W from top to bottom;

WRANGLE

Mt 12:19 He will not W or cry aloud, nor will

WRANGLING

1Tim 6:5 slander, base suspicions, and W among men who are

WRAP (2)

Is 28:20 covering too narrow to W oneself in it.
Acts 12:8 he said to him, W your mantle around you

WRAPPED (22)

Ex 19:18 And Mount Sinai was W in smoke, because the
Deut 4:11 the heart of heaven, W in darkness, cloud, and
1Sam 21:9 behold, it is here W in a cloth behind
28:14 up; and he is W in a robe." And
1Kgs 19:13 Elijah heard it, he W his face in his
Jud 10:5 fine bread; and she W up all her vessels
Ps 109:29 dishonor; may they be W in their own shame
Prov 30:4 Who has W up the waters in a garment?
Is 59:17 vengeance for clothing, and W himself in fury as
Lam 3:43 "Thou hast W thyself with anger and pursued us,
3:44 without pity; thou hast W thyself with a cloud
Ezek 7:27 mourns, the prince is W in despair, and the
Hos 4:19 A wind has W them in its wings, and
Jon 2:5 about me; weeds were W about my head
Mt 27:59 took the body, and W it in a clean
Mk 15:45 and taking him down, W him in the linen
Lk 2:7 her first-born son and W him in swaddling cloths,
2:12 will find a babe W in swaddling cloths and
23:52 took it down and W it in a linen
Jn 11:44 bandages, and his face W with a cloth.
Acts 5:6 young men rose and W him up and carried
Rev 10:1 coming down from heaven, W in a cloud, with

WRAPPING

Gen 38:14 put on a veil, W herself up, and sat

WRAPS

Ps 109:19 a garment which he W round him, like a

WRATH (263)

Gen 49:7 is fierce; and their W, for it is cruel!
Ex 22:24 their cry; and my W will burn, and I
32:10 me alone, that my W may burn hot against
32:11 LORD, why does thy W burn hot against thy
32:12 Turn from thy fierce W, and repent of this
Lev 10:6 you die, and lest W come upon all the
Num 1:53 there may be no W upon the congregation of
16:46 atonement for them; for W has gone forth from
18:5 altar, that there be W no more upon the
25:11 has turned back my W from the people of
Deut 9:7 LORD your God to W in the wilderness; from
9:8 provoked the LORD to W, and the LORD was
9:22 at Kibroth-hattaavah, you provoked the LORD to W
29:23 in his anger and W –
29:28 and fury and great W, and cast them into
Josh 9:20 let them live, lest W be upon us, because
22:20 the devoted things, and W fell upon all the
1Sam 28:18 carry out his fierce W against Amalek, therefore the
2Kgs 3:27 And there came great W upon Israel; and they
22:13 for great is the W of the LORD that
22:17 their hands, therefore my W will be kindled against
23:26 fierceness of his great W, by which his anger
1Chr 27:24 did not finish; yet W came upon Israel for
2Chr 12:7 some deliverance, and my W shall not be poured
12:12 he humbled himself the W of the LORD turned
19:2 Because of this, W has gone out against you
19:10 before the LORD and W may not come upon
24:18 And W came upon Judah and Jerusalem for this
28:11 taken, for the fierce W of the LORD is
28:13 and there is fierce W against Israel."

WRATH

	29:8	Therefore the W of the LORD came on Judah
	32:25	Therefore W came upon him and Judah and
	32:26	Jerusalem, so that the W of the LORD did
	34:21	for great is the W of the LORD that
	34:25	their hands, therefore my W will be poured out
	36:16	his prophets, till the W of the LORD rose
Ezra	7:23	of heaven, lest his W be against the realm
	8:22	the power of his W is against all that
	10:14	city, till the fierce W of our God over
Neh	13:18	Yet you bring more W upon Israel by profaning
Jud	9:9	pride, and send thy W upon their heads; give
Esth	1:18	will be contempt and W in plenty.
	5:9	he was filled with W against Mordecai.
	7:7	from the feast in W and went into the
	16:24	shall be destroyed in W with spear and fire.
Job	14:13	conceal me until thy W be past, that thou
	16:9	torn me in his W, and hated me; he
	19:11	He has kindled his W against me, and counts
	19:29	of the sword, for W brings the punishment of
	20:28	away, dragged off in the day of God's W
	21:20	them drink of the W of the Almighty.
	21:30	that he is rescued in the day of W
	36:18	Beware lest W entice you into scoffing; and let
	42:7	Eliphaz the Temanite: "My W is kindled against you
Ps	2:5	to them in his W, and terrify them in
	2:12	the way; for his W is quickly kindled.
	6:1	in thy anger, nor chasten me in thy W
	21:9	them up in his W; and fire will consume
	37:8	Refrain from anger, and forsake W
	38:1	in thy anger, nor chasten me in thy W
	56:7	for their crime; in W cast down the peoples,
	59:13	utter, consume them in W, consume them till they
	76:10	[Selah] Surely the W of men shall praise thee;
	76:10	thee; the residue of W thou wilt gird upon
	78:21	he was full of W; a fire was kindled
	78:38	often, and did not stir up all his W
	78:49	them his fierce anger, W, indignation, and distress, a
	78:59	he was full of W, and he utterly rejected
	78:62	sword, and vented his W on his heritage.
	79:5	Will thy jealous W burn like fire?
	85:3	didst withdraw all thy W; thou didst turn from
	88:7	Thy W lies heavy upon me, and thou dost
	88:16	Thy W has swept over me; thy dread assaults
	89:38	thou art full of W against thy anointed.
	89:46	How long will thy W burn like fire?
	90:7	thy anger; by thy W we are overwhelmed.
	90:9	pass away under thy W, our years come to
	90:11	thy anger, and thy W according to the fear
	106:23	to turn away his W from destroying them.
	110:5	will shatter kings on the day of his W
	138:7	thy hand against the W of my enemies, and
Prov	11:4	in the day of W, but righteousness delivers from
	11:23	in good; the expectation of the wicked in W
	14:35	king's favor, but his W falls on one who
	15:1	soft answer turns away W, but a harsh word
	16:14	A king's W is a messenger of death, and
	19:12	A king's W is like the growling of a
	19:19	A man of great W will pay the penalty;
	20:2	The dread W of a king is like the
	21:14	anger; and a bribe in the bosom, strong W
	27:4	W is cruel, anger is overwhelming; but who can
	29:8	a city aflame, but wise men turn away W
	29:22	A man of W stirs up strife, and a
Wis	5:20	shield, and sharpen stern W for a sword, and
	5:22	and hailstones full of W will be hurled as
	10:10	fled from his brother's W, she guided him on
	11:9	how the ungodly were tormented when judged in W
	16:5	of writhing serpents, thy W did not continue to
	18:20	the desert, but the W did not long continue.
	18:22	He conquered the W not by strength of body,
	18:23	and held back the W, and cut off its
	18:25	merely to test the W was enough.
Sir	5:6	for both mercy and W are with him, and
	5:7	day; for suddenly the W of the Lord will
	7:16	of sinners; remember that W does not delay.
	16:6	in a disobedient nation W was kindled.
	16:11	For mercy and W are with the Lord; he
	16:11	is mighty to forgive, and he pours out W
	18:23	Think of his W on the day of death,
	23:16	of men multiply sins, and a third incurs W
	25:14	snake's venom, and no W worse than an enemy's
	25:14	venom, and no wrath worse than an enemy's W
	25:21	There is W and impudence and great disgrace when
	27:30	Anger and W, these also are abominations, and the
	28:5	himself, being flesh, maintains W, who will make
	28:10	proportion to his wealth he will heighten his W
	36:7	and pour out thy W; destroy the adversary and
	36:9	consumed in the fiery W, and may those who
	39:23	nations will incur his W, just as he turns
	44:18	in the time of W he was taken in
	45:18	company of Korah, in W and anger.
	45:19	pleased, and in the W of his anger they
	47:20	so that you brought W upon your children and
	48:10	written, to calm the W of God before it
Is	1:24	I will vent my W on my enemies, and
	9:19	Through the W of the LORD of hosts the
	10:6	the people of my W I command him, to
	13:9	LORD comes, cruel, with W and fierce anger, to
	13:13	its place, at the W of the LORD of
	14:6	smote the peoples in W with unceasing blows, that
	26:20	little while until the W is past.
	27:4	guard it night and day; I have no W
	51:17	the cup of his W, who have drunk to
	51:20	are full of the W of the LORD, the
	51:22	the bowl of my W you shall drink no
	54:8	In overflowing W for a moment I hid my
	59:18	so will he repay, W to his adversaries, requital
	60:10	you; for in my W I smote you, but
	63:3	trampled them in my W; their lifeblood is sprinkled
	63:5	me victory, and my W upheld me.
	63:6	them drunk in my W, and I poured out
Jer	4:4	of Jerusalem; lest my W go forth like fire,
	6:11	am full of the W of the LORD; I
	7:20	my anger and my W will be poured out
	7:29	the generation of his W
	10:10	At his W the earth quakes, and the nations
	10:25	Pour out thy W upon the nations that know
	18:20	to turn away thy W from them.
	21:5	in anger, and in fury, and in great W
	21:12	been robbed, lest my W go forth like fire,
	23:19	W has gone forth, a whirling tempest; it will
	25:15	of the wine of W, and make all the
	30:23	W has gone forth, a whirling tempest; it will
	32:31	aroused my anger and W, from the day it
	32:37	my anger and my W and in great indignation;
	33:5	my anger and my W, for I have hidden
	36:7	is the anger and W that the LORD has
	42:18	my anger and my W were poured out on
	42:18	of Jerusalem, so my W will be poured out
	44:6	Therefore my W and my anger were poured forth
	50:13	Because of the W of the LORD she shall
	50:25	the weapons of his W, for the Lord GOD
Lam	2:2	of Jacob; in his W he has broken down
	3:1	the rod of his W;
	4:11	full vent to his W, he poured out his
Bar	1:13	the Lord and his W have not turned away
	2:20	thy anger and thy W upon us, as thou
	4:9	For she saw the W that came upon you
	4:25	endure with patience the W that has come upon
Ezek	7:8	soon pour out my W upon you, and spend
	7:12	the seller mourn, for W is upon all their
	7:13	For W is upon all their multitude; it shall
	7:14	to battle, for my W is upon all their
	7:19	the day of the W of the LORD; they
	8:18	I will deal in W; my eye will not
	9:8	the outpouring of thy W upon Jerusalem?"
	13:13	break out in my W; and there shall be
	13:13	and great hailstones in W to destroy it.
	13:15	will I spend my W upon the wall, and
	14:19	and pour out my W upon it with blood,
	16:38	you the blood of W and jealousy.
	20:8	would pour out my W upon them and spend
	20:13	would pour out my W upon them in the
	20:21	would pour out my W upon them and spend
	20:33	outstretched arm, and with W poured out, I will
	20:34	outstretched arm, and with W poured out;
	21:31	the fire of my W; and I will deliver
	22:20	anger and in my W, and I will put
	22:21	the fire of my W, and you shall be
	22:22	have poured out my W upon you."
	22:31	the fire of my W; their way have I
	24:8	To rouse my W, to take vengeance, I have
	25:14	and according to my W; and they shall know
	30:15	I will pour my W upon Pelusium, the stronghold
	36:6	speak in my jealous W, because you have suffered
	36:18	I poured out my W upon them for the
	38:18	the Lord GOD, my W will be roused.
	38:19	and in my blazing W I declare, On that
Dan	8:6	and he ran at him in his mighty W
	9:16	thy anger and thy W turn away from thy
Hos	5:10	will pour out my W like water.
	13:11	and I have taken them away in my W

Amos 1:11 and he kept his W for ever.
Mic 5:15 And in anger and W I will execute vengeance
Nah 1:2 his adversaries and keeps W for his enemies.
1:6 His W is poured out like fire, and the
Hab 2:15 the cup of his W, and makes them drunk,
3:2 make it known; in W remember mercy.
3:8 Was thy W against the rivers, O LORD?
Zeph 1:15 A day of W is that day, a day
1:18 the day of the W of the LORD.
1:18 fire of his jealous W, all the earth shall
2:2 the day of the W of the LORD.
2:3 the day of the W of the LORD.
3:8 fire of my jealous W all the earth shall
Zech 7:12 Therefore great W came from the LORD of hosts.
8:2 and I am jealous for her with great W
8:14 fathers provoked me to W, and I did not
1Mac 1:64 And very great W came upon Israel.
2:44 lawless men in their W; the survivors fled to
3:8 thus he turned away W from Israel.
15:36 word, but returned in W to the king and
2Mac 5:20 was forsaken in the W of the Almighty was
7:38 to an end the W of the Almighty which
8:5 withstand him, for the W of the Lord had
Mt 3:7 to flee from the W to come?
Lk 3:7 to flee from the W to come?
4:28 this, all in the synagogue were filled with W
21:23 upon the earth and W upon this people;
Jn 3:36 see life, but the W of God rests upon
Rom 1:18 For the W of God is revealed from heaven
2:5 you are storing up W for yourself on the
2:5 on the day of W when God's righteous judgment
2:8 wickedness, there will be W and fury.
3:5 is unjust to inflict W on us?
4:15 For the law brings W, but where there is
5:9 by him from the W of God.
9:22 desiring to show his W and to make known
9:22 patience the vessels of W made for destruction,
12:19 leave it to the W of God; for it
13:4 God to execute his W on the wrongdoer.
13:5 only to avoid God's W but also for the
Eph 2:3 by nature children of W, like the rest of
4:31 Let all bitterness and W and anger and clamor
5:6 these things that the W of God comes upon
Col 3:6 account of these the W of God is coming.
3:8 them all away: anger, W, malice, slander, and foul
1Thes 1:10 delivers us from the W to come.
2:16 But God's W has come upon them at last!
5:9 not destined us for W, but to obtain salvation
Heb 3:11 I swore in my W, 'They shall never enter
4:3 I swore in my W, 'They shall never enter
Rev 6:16 throne, and from the W of the Lamb;
6:17 great day of their W has come, and who
11:18 nations raged, but thy W came, and the time
12:12 to you in great W, because he knows that
14:10 the wine of God's W, poured unmixed into the
14:19 wine press of the W of God;
15:1 for with them the W of God is ended.
15:7 bowls full of the W of God who lives
16:1 seven bowls of the W of God."
16:19 drain the cup of the fury of his W
19:15 the fury of the W of God the Almighty.

WRATHFUL (4)

Prov 22:24 nor go with a W man,
Sir 8:16 not fight with a W man, and do not
Ezek 25:17 vengeance upon them with W chastisements.
Nah 1:2 LORD is avenging and W; the LORD takes

WREAK

Ps 149:7 in their hands, to W vengeance on the nations

WREATH (2)

Sir 32:2 and receive a W for your excellent leadership.
1Cor 9:25 to receive a perishable W, but we an imperishable.

WREATHS (6)

1Kgs 7:17 of checker work with W of chain work for
7:29 and oxen, there were W of beveled work.
7:30 supports were cast, with W at the side of
7:36 space of each, with W round about.
Jud 15:13 crowned themselves with olive W, she and those who
2Mac 6:7 honor of Dionysus, wearing W of ivy.

WRECKED (4)

1Kgs 22:48 for the ships were W at Ezion-geber.
2Chr 20:37 And the ships were W and were not able
Ezek 27:26 The east wind has W you in the heart
27:34 Now you are W by the seas, in the

WRENCHED

Mk 5:4 but the chains he W apart, and the fetters

WRESTLED (3)

Gen 30:8 mighty wrestlings I have W with my sister, and
32:24 alone; and a man W with him until the
32:25 of joint as he W with him.

WRESTLING

2Mac 4:14 unlawful proceedings in the W arena after the call

WRESTLINGS

Gen 30:8 Rachel said, "With mighty W I have wrestled with

WRETCH (3)

2Mac 7:9 he said, "You accursed W, you dismiss us from
7:34 But you, unholy W, you most defiled of all
15:3 thrice-accursed W asked if there were a sovereign

WRETCHED (6)

Bar 4:31 W will be those who afflicted you and rejoiced
4:32 W will be the cities which your children served
4:32 children served as slaves; W will be the city
Rom 7:24 W man that I am!
Jas 4:9 Be W and mourn and weep.
Rev 3:17 knowing that you are W, pitiable, poor, blind, and

WRETCHEDNESS

Num 11:15 thy sight, that I may not see my W

WRETCHES

Mt 21:41 "He will put those W to a miserable death,

WRING (2)

Lev 1:15 to the altar and W off its head, and
5:8 sin offering; he shall W its head from its

WRINKLE

Eph 5:27 splendor, without spot or W or any such thing,

WRISTS

Ezek 13:18 magic bands upon all W, and make veils for

WRITE (94)

Ex 17:14 LORD said to Moses, W this as a memorial
34:1 first; and I will W upon the tables the
34:27 LORD said to Moses, W these words; in accordance
Num 5:23 "Then the priest shall W these curses in a
17:2 W each man's name upon his rod,
17:3 upon his rod, and W Aaron's name upon the
Deut 6:9 And you shall W them on the doorposts of
10:2 And I will W on the tables the words
11:20 And you shall W them upon the doorposts of
17:18 his kingdom, he shall W for himself in a
27:3 plaster; and you shall W upon them all the
27:8 And you shall W upon the stones all the
31:19 Now therefore W this song, and teach it to
Josh 18:8 those who went to W the description of the
18:8 up and down and W a description of the
Ezra 5:10 information, that we might W down the names of
Neh 9:38 a firm covenant and W it, and our princes,
Tob 12:20 W in a book everything that has happened."
Esth 8:8 And you may W as you please with regard
Prov 3:3 them about your neck, W them on the tablet
7:3 them on your fingers, W them on the tablet
Is 8:1 a large tablet and W upon it in common
10:19 that a child can W them down.
30:8 And now, go, W it before them on a
44:5 Jacob, and another will W on his hand, 'The
Jer 22:30 Thus says the LORD: W this man down as
30:2 the God of Israel: W in a book all
31:33 them, and I will W it upon their hearts;
36:2 "Take a scroll and W on it all the
36:17 us, how did you W all these words?
36:28 "Take another scroll and W on it all the
Bar 2:28 didst command him to W thy law in the
Ezek 24:2 me: "Son of man, W down the name of
37:16 take a stick and W on it, 'For Judah,
37:16 take another stick and W upon it, 'For Joseph
37:20 sticks on which you W are in your hand
43:11 all its laws; and W it down in their
Hos 8:12 Were I to W for him my laws by
Hab 2:2 the LORD answered me: W the vision; make it

1Mac 10:24 I also will W them words of encouragement and
12:22 learned this, please W us concerning your welfare;
12:23 we on our part W to you that your
13:37 with you and to W to our officials to
13:42 the people began to W in their documents and
15:19 therefore have decided to W to the kings and
2Mac 2:16 celebrate the purification, we W to you.
Mk 10:4 allowed a man to W a certificate of divorce,
Lk 1:3 some time past, to W an orderly account for
16:6 sit down quickly and W fifty.'
16:7 'Take your bill, and W eighty.'
Jn 19:21 to Pilate, "Do not W, 'The King of the
Acts 15:20 to God, but should W to them to abstain
25:26 have nothing definite to W to my lord about
25:26 have examined him, I may have something to W
1Cor 4:14 I do not W this to make you ashamed,
16:21 I, Paul, W this greeting with my own hand.
2Cor 1:13 For we W you nothing but what you can
9:1 superfluous for me to W to you about the
13:10 I W this while I am away from you,
Phil 3:1 To W the same things to you is not
Col 4:18 I, Paul, W this greeting with my own hand.
1Thes 4:9 to have any one W to you, for you
2Thes 3:17 I, Paul, W this greeting with my own hand.
3:17 letter of mine; it is the way I W
Philem 1:19 I, Paul, W this with my own hand, I
1:21 of your obedience, I W to you, knowing that
Heb 8:10 into their minds, and W them on their hearts,
10:16 on their hearts, and W them on their minds,"
1Jn 2:13 I W to you, children, because you know the
2:14 I W to you, fathers, because you know him
2:14 I W to you, young men, because you are
2:21 I W to you, not because you do not
2:26 I W this to you about those who would
5:13 I W this to you who believe in the
2Jn 1:12 I have much to W to you, I would
3Jn 1:13 I had much to W to you, but I
1:13 I would rather not W with pen and ink
Jude 1:3 being very eager to W to you of our
1:3 found it necessary to W appealing to you to
Rev 1:11 like a trumpet saying, W what you see in
1:19 Now W what you see, what is and what
2:1 the church in Ephesus W: 'The words of him
2:8 the church in Smyrna W: 'The words of the
2:12 the church in Pergamum W: 'The words of him
2:18 the church in Thyatira W: 'The words of the
3:1 the church in Sardis W: 'The words of him
3:7 the church in Philadelphia W: 'The words of the
3:12 it, and I will W on him the name
3:14 the church in La-odicea W: 'The words of the
10:4 I was about to W, but I heard a
10:4 said, and do not W it down."
14:13 voice from heaven saying, W this: Blessed are the
19:9 angel said to me, W this: Blessed are those
21:5 Also he said, W this, for these words are

WRITER

Rom 16:22 I Tertius, the W of this letter, greet you

WRITERS

Is 10:1 iniquitous decrees, and the W who keep writing

WRITES (4)

Deut 24:1 in her, and he W her a bill of
24:3 husband dislikes her and W her a bill of
Esth 13:1 the governors under them, W thus:
Rom 10:5 Moses W that the man who practices the

WRITEST

Job 13:26 For thou W bitter things against me, and makest

WRITHE (3)

Jer 4:19 I W in pain!
Mic 4:10 W and groan, O daughter of Zion, like a
Zech 9:5 Gaza too, and shall W in anguish; Ekron also,

WRITHED (2)

Is 26:18 were with child, we W, we have as it
Hab 3:10 mountains saw thee, and W; the raging waters swept

WRITHES (3)

Job 15:20 The wicked man W in pain all his days,
Is 26:17 woman with child, who W and cries out in
Jer 51:29 The land trembles and W in pain, for the

WRITHING

Wis 16:5 by the bites of W serpents, thy wrath did

WRITING (43)

Ex 32:16 of God, and the W was the writing of
32:16 the writing was the W of God, graven upon
Deut 10:4 as at the first W, the ten commandments which
31:24 When Moses had finished W the words of this
Josh 18:4 and down the land, W a description of it
1Chr 28:19 made clear by the W from the hand of
2Chr 36:22 also put it in W:
Ezra 1:1 also put it in W:
Esth 8:10 The W was in the name of King Ahasuerus
9:25 he gave orders in W that his wicked plot
9:32 practices of Purim, and it was recorded in W
Sir 39:32 and left it in W:
44:5 set forth verses in W;
Is 10:1 the writers who keep W oppression,
38:9 A W of Hezekiah king of Judah, after he
Ezek 2:10 me; and it had W on the front and
9:2 in linen, with a W case at his side.
9:3 linen, who had the W case at his side.
9:11 in linen, with the W case at his side,
Dan 5:7 Babylon, "Whoever reads this W, and shows me its
5:8 could not read the W or make known to
5:15 me to read this W and make known to
5:16 you can read the W and make known to
5:17 I will read the W to the king and
5:24 was sent, and this W was inscribed.
5:25 And this is the W that was inscribed: MENE,
1Mac 12:21 has been found in W concerning the Spartans and
2Mac 2:4 was also in the W that the prophet, having
11:15 the Jews which Maccabeus delivered to Lysias in W
Lk 1:63 he asked for a W tablet, and wrote, "His
1Cor 9:15 rights, nor am I W this to secure any
14:37 that what I am W to you is a
Gal 1:20 (In what I am W to you, before God,
6:11 large letters I am W to you with my
1Tim 3:14 soon, but I am W these instructions to you
1Jn 1:4 And we are W this that our joy may
2:1 little children, I am W this to you so
2:7 Beloved, I am W you no new commandment, but
2:8 Yet I am W you a new commandment, which
2:12 I am W to you, little children, because your
2:13 I am W to you, fathers, because you know
2:13 I am W to you, young men, because you
2Jn 1:5 as though I were W you a new commandment,

WRITINGS (4)

2Mac 2:13 and prophets, and the W of David, and letters
Jn 5:46 do not believe his W, how will you believe
Rom 16:25 and through the prophetic W is made known to
2Tim 3:15 acquainted with the sacred W which are able to

WRITTEN (263)

Ex 24:12 commandment, which I have W for their instruction."
31:18 testimony, tables of stone, W with the finger of
32:15 hands, tables that were W on both sides; on
32:15 one side and on the other were they W
32:32 thee, out of thy book which thou hast W
Deut 9:10 two tables of stone W with the finger of
28:58 this law which are W in this book, that
29:20 man, and the curses W in this book would
29:21 curses of the covenant W in this book of
29:27 it all the curses W in this book;
30:10 his statutes which are W in this book of
Josh 1:8 to all that is W in it; for then
8:31 Israel, as it is W in the book of
8:32 of the law of Moses, which he had W
8:34 to all that is W in the book of
10:13 Is this not W in the Book of Jashar?
23:6 do all that is W in the book of
2Sam 1:18 Judah; behold, it is W in the Book of
1Kgs 2:3 testimonies, as it is W in the law of
11:41 wisdom, are they not W in the book of
14:19 reigned, behold, they are W in the Book of
14:29 did, are they not W in the Book of
15:7 did, are they not W in the Book of
15:23 built, are they not W in the Book of
15:31 did, are they not W in the Book of
16:5 might, are they not W in the Book of
16:14 did, are they not W in the Book of
16:20 made, are they not W in the Book of
16:27 showed, are they not W in the Book of
21:11 As it was W in the letters which she
22:39 built, are they not W in the Book of

W

3:10 sin, as it is W: "None is righteous, no,
4:17 all, as it is W, "I have made you
4:23 were W not for his sake alone,
7:6 not under the old W code but in the
8:36 As it is W, "For thy sake we are
9:13 As it is W, "Jacob I loved, but Esau
9:33 stone, as it is W, "Behold, I am laying
10:15 As it is W, "How beautiful are the feet
11:8 hardened, as it is W, "God gave them a
11:26 saved; as it is W, "The Deliverer will come
12:19 God; for it is W, "Vengeance is mine, I
14:11 God; for it is W, "As I live, says
15:3 but, as it is W, "The reproaches of those
15:4 For whatever was W in former days was written
15:4 in former days was W for our instruction, that
15:9 As it is W, "Therefore I will praise thee
15:15 some points I have W to you very boldly
15:21 but as it is W, "They shall see who
1Cor 1:19 For it is W, "I will destroy the wisdom
1:31 therefore, as it is W, "Let him who boasts,
2:9 But, as it is W, "What no eye has
3:19 For it is W, "He catches the wise in
4:6 go beyond what is W, that none of you
6:16 For, as it is W, "The two shall become
9:9 For it is W in the law of Moses,
9:10 It was W for our sake, because the plowman
10:7 were; as it is W, "The people sat down
10:11 warning, but they were W down for our instruction,
14:21 the law it is W, "By men of strange
15:45 Thus it is W, "The first man Adam became
15:54 the saying that is W: "Death is swallowed up
2Cor 3:2 our letter of recommendation, W on your hearts, to
3:3 Christ delivered by us, W not with ink but
3:6 covenant, not in a W code but in the
3:6 the Spirit; for the W code kills, but the
8:15 As it is W, "He who gathered much had
9:9 As it is W, "He scatters abroad, he gives
Gal 3:10 curse; for it is W, "Cursed be every one
3:10 abide by all things W in the book of
3:13 us--for it is W, "Cursed be every one
4:22 For it is W that Abraham had two sons,
4:27 For it is W, "Rejoice, O barren one who
Eph 3:3 revelation, as I have W briefly.
1Thes 5:1 need to have anything W to you.
Heb 10:7 God,' as it is W of me in the
13:22 exhortation, for I have W to you briefly.
1Pet 1:16 conduct; since it is W, "You shall be holy,
5:12 regard him, I have W briefly to you, exhorting
2Pet 3:1 letter that I have W to you, beloved, and
3Jn 1:9 I have W something to the church; but Diotrephes,
Rev 1:3 who keep what is W therein; for the time
2:17 with a new name W on the stone which
5:1 the throne a scroll W within and on the
13:8 name has not been W before the foundation of
14:1 and his Father's name W on their foreheads.
17:5 on her forehead was W a name of mystery:
17:8 names have not been W in the book of
20:12 judged by what was W in the books, by
20:15 name was not found W in the book of
21:27 only those who are W in the Lamb's book

WRONG (100)

Gen 16:5 to Abram, "May the W done to me be
44:5 You have done W in so doing.'"
Ex 2:13 man that did the W, "Why do you strike
9:27 and I and my people are in the W
22:21 "You shall not W a stranger or oppress him,
Lev 19:33 in your land, you shall not do him W
19:35 "You shall do no W in judgment, in measures
25:14 neighbor, you shall not W one another.
25:17 You shall not W one another, but you shall
Num 5:7 full restitution for his W, adding a fifth to
5:7 it to him to whom he did the W
5:8 be made for the W, the restitution for wrong
5:8 wrong, the restitution for W shall go to the
Deut 19:15 crime or for any W in connection with any
Judg 11:27 and you do me W by making war on
1Sam 24:11 that there is no W or treason in my
26:21 said, "I have done W; return, my son David,
29:6 I have found nothing W in you from the
2Sam 13:16 my brother; for this W in sending me away
19:19 how your servant did W on the day my
2Kgs 18:14 saying, "I have done W; withdraw from me;
1Chr 12:17 although there is no W in my hands, then
2Chr 26:18 for you have done W, and it will bring
Jud 11:11 God to anger when they do what is W
Esth 1:16 has Queen Vashti done W, but also to all
Job 1:22 Job did not sin or charge God with W
6:29 I pray, let no W be done.
6:30 Is there any W on my tongue?
19:3 you not ashamed to W me?
19:6 put me in the W, and closed his net
21:27 and your schemes to W me.
32:3 they had declared Job to be in the W
34:10 and from the Almighty that he should do W
36:23 way, or who can say, 'Thou hast done W
40:8 Will you even put me in the W
Ps 7:3 this, if there is W in my hands,
119:3 who also do no W, but walk in his
125:3 the righteous put forth their hands to do W
Prov 4:17 unless they have done W; they are robbed of
10:23 a fool to do W, but wise conduct is
15:22 Without counsel plans go W, but with many advisers
17:26 is not good; to flog noble men is W
28:21 a piece of bread a man will do W
30:20 her mouth, and says, "I have done no W
Sir 3:23 led many astray, and W opinion has caused their
7:2 Stay away from W, and it will turn away
13:3 A rich man does W, and he even adds
13:3 a poor man suffers W, and he must add
19:4 one who sins does W to himself.
20:18 story told at the W time, which is continually
22:6 tale told at the W time, but chastising and
28:2 Forgive your neighbor the W he has done, and
Is 61:8 I hate robbery and W; I will faithfully give
Jer 2:5 says the LORD: "What W did your fathers find
22:3 And do no W or violence to the alien,
25:5 his evil way and W doings, and dwell upon
37:18 to King Zedekiah, "What W have I done to
40:4 but if it seems W to you to come
Lam 3:59 Thou hast seen the W done to me, O
Bar 2:12 ungodly, we have done W, O Lord our God,
Ezek 18:16 neighbor's wife, does not W any one, exacts no
Dan 6:22 before you, O king, I have done no W
9:5 have sinned and done W and acted wickedly and
Mic 3:10 who build Zion with blood and Jerusalem with W
Hab 1:13 canst not look on W, why dost thou look
Zeph 3:5 righteous, he does no W; every morning he shows
3:13 they shall do no W and utter no lies,
Mal 2:6 his mouth, and no W was found on his
1Mac 2:67 law, and avenge the W done to your people.
2Mac 3:12 was utterly impossible that W should be done to
10:12 Jews because of the W that had been done
14:28 their agreement when the man had done no W
Mt 20:13 am doing you no W; did you not agree
22:29 answered them, "You are W, because you know
Mk 12:24 this why you are W, that you know neither
12:27 dead, but of the living; you are quite W
Lk 23:40 our deeds; but this man has done nothing W
Jn 18:23 bear witness to the W; but if I have
Acts 7:26 brethren, why do you W each other?'
23:9 contended, "We find nothing W in this man.
25:5 if there is anything W about the man, let
25:10 I have done no W, as you know very
Rom 3:12 together they have gone W; no one does good,
13:4 But if you do W, be afraid, for he
13:10 Love does no W to a neighbor; therefore love
14:20 clean, but it is W for any one to
1Cor 6:7 Why not rather suffer W
6:8 But you yourselves W and defraud, and that even
13:6 does not rejoice at W, but rejoices in the
2Cor 7:12 one who did the W, nor on account of
7:12 one who suffered the W, but in order that
12:13 Forgive me this W
13:7 you may not do W --not that we may
Gal 4:12 You did me no W;
Col 3:25 paid back for the W he has done, and
1Thes 4:6 no man transgress, and W his brother in this
1Pet 2:14 punish those who do W and to praise those
2:20 if when you do W and are beaten for
3:17 that should be God's will, than for doing W
2Pet 2:13 destruction with them, suffering W for their

WRONGDOER (5)

Sir 4:9 the hand of the W; and do not be
Acts 25:11 then I am a W, and have committed anything
Rom 13:4 of God to execute his wrath on the W
Col 3:25 For the W will be paid back for the
1Pet 4:15 a thief, or a W, or a mischief-maker;

WRONGDOERS (2)

Ps 37:1 because of the wicked, be not envious of W

1Pet 2:12 speak against you as W, they may see your

WRONGDOING (10)

Deut 19:16 to accuse him of W,
Tob 4:5 and do not walk in the ways of W
12:8 little with righteousness is better than much with W
Sir 18:26 and in days of sin he guards against W
26:20 can hardly keep from W, and a tradesman will
Acts 18:14 were a matter of W or vicious crime, I
24:19 men themselves say what W they found when I
2Pet 2:13 destruction with them, suffering wrong for their W
2:15 who loved gain from W,
1Jn 5:17 All W is sin, but there is sin which

WRONGDOINGS

Ps 99:8 God to them, but an avenger of their W

WRONGED (8)

Wis 18:2 holy ones, though previously W, were doing them no
Sir 4:9 Deliver him who is W from the hand of
35:13 listen to the prayer of one who is W
Bar 6:54 deliver one who is W, for they have no
Ezek 22:7 and the widow are W in you.
Acts 7:24 one of them being W, he defended the oppressed
2Cor 7:2 to us; we have W no one, we have
Philem 1:18 If he has W you at all, or owes

WRONGFULLY (3)

Ps 35:19 over me who are W my foes, and let
38:19 mighty, and many are those who hate me W
Sir 34:18 from what has been W obtained, the offering is

WRONGING

Acts 7:27 the man who was W his neighbor thrust him

WRONGLY (2)

Jn 18:23 "If I have spoken W, bear witness to the
Jas 4:3 receive, because you ask W, to spend it on

WRONGS (6)

Ps 58:2 your hearts you devise W; your hands deal out
69:5 knowest my folly; the W I have done are
Hab 1:3 thou make me see W and look upon trouble?
1Mac 8:31 "And concerning the W which King Demetrius is
10:5 will remember all the W which we did to
10:46 they remembered the great W which Demetrius had

WROTE (84)

Ex 24:4 And Moses W all the words of the LORD.
34:28 And he W upon the tables the words of
39:30 of pure gold, and W upon it an inscription,
Num 33:2 Moses W down their starting places, stage by stage,
Deut 4:13 ten commandments; and he W them upon two tables
5:22 And he W them upon two tables of stone,
10:4 And he W on the tables, as at the
31:9 And Moses W this law, and gave it to
31:22 So Moses W this song the same day, and
Josh 8:32 people of Israel, he W upon the stones a
24:26 And Joshua W these words in the book of
Judg 8:14 questioned him; and he W down for him the
1Sam 10:25 the kingship; and he W them in a book
2Sam 11:14 In the morning David W a letter to Joab,
11:15 In the letter he W, "Set Uriah in the
1Kgs 21:8 So she W letters in Ahab's name and sealed
21:9 And she W in the letters, "Proclaim a fast,
2Kgs 10:1 So Jehu W letters, and sent them to Samaria,
10:6 Then he W to them a second letter, saying,
17:37 the commandment which he W for you, you shall
2Chr 26:22 last, Isaiah the prophet the son of Amoz W
30:1 Israel and Judah, and W letters also to Ephraim
32:17 And he W letters to cast contempt on the
Ezra 4:6 of his reign, they W an accusation against the
4:7 rest of their associates W to Artaxerxes king of
4:8 Shimshai the scribe W a letter against Jerusalem
4:9 follows– then W Rehum the commander, Shimshai
Tob 7:14 took a scroll and W out the contract; and
13:1 Then Tobit W a prayer of rejoicing, and said:
Jud 4:6 Jerusalem at the time, W to the people of
Esth 8:5 of Hammedatha, which he W to destroy the Jews
12:4 these things, and Mordecai W an account of them.
Eccl 12:10 words, and uprightly he W words of truth.
Jer 36:4 of Neriah, and Baruch W upon a scroll at
36:18 to me, while I W them with ink on
36:27 the words which Baruch W at Jeremiah's dictation,
36:32 son of Neriah, who W on it at the
45:1 of Neriah, when he W these words in a
51:60 Jeremiah W in a book all the evil that
Bar 1:1 Hasadiah, son of Hilkiah, W in Babylon,
Dan 5:5 man's hand appeared and W on the plaster of
5:5 and the king saw the hand as it W
6:25 Then King Darius W to all the peoples, nations,
7:1 Then he W down the dream, and told the
1Mac 1:41 Then the king W to his whole kingdom that
1:51 In such words he W to his whole kingdom.
8:22 the letter which they W in reply, on bronze
10:17 And he W a letter and sent it to
10:56 for you as you W, but meet me at
10:59 Then Alexander the king W to Jonathan to come
11:22 to Ptolemais; and he W Jonathan not to continue
11:29 The king consented, and W a letter to Jonathan
11:31 the letter which we W concerning you to Lasthenes
11:57 Then the young Antiochus W to Jonathan, saying, "I
12:5 the letter which Jonathan W to the Spartans:
13:35 to this request, and W him a letter as
14:18 cities in it they W to him on bronze
14:27 copy of what they W: "On the eighteenth day
15:22 The consul W the same thing to Demetrius the
16:18 Then Ptolemy W a report about these things and
2Mac 1:7 sixty-ninth year, we Jews W to you, in the
8:8 frequent successes, he W to Ptolemy, the governor
9:18 hope for himself and W to the Jews the
14:27 of that depraved man, W to Nicanor, stating that
Mk 10:5 hardness of heart he W you this commandment.
12:19 question, saying, "Teacher, Moses W for us that if
Lk 1:63 a writing tablet, and W, "His name is John."
20:28 question, saying, "Teacher, Moses W for us that if
Jn 1:45 and also the prophets W, Jesus of Nazareth, the
5:45 believe me, for he W of me.
8:6 Jesus bent down and W with his finger on
8:8 he bent down and W with his finger on
19:19 Pilate also W a title and put it on
Acts 18:27 brethren encouraged him, and W to the disciples to
23:25 And he W a letter to this effect:
1Cor 5:9 I W to you in my letter not to
5:11 But rather I W to you not to associate
7:1 Now concerning the matters about which you W
2Cor 2:3 And I W as I did, so that when
2:4 For I W you out of much affliction and
2:9 this is why I W, that I might test
4:13 as he had who W, "I believed, and so
7:12 So although I W to you, it was not
2Pet 3:15 our beloved brother Paul W to you according to

WROTH

Is 28:21 Perazim, he will be W as in the valley

WROUGHT (42)

Gen 34:7 angry, because he had W folly in Israel by
Ex 34:10 as have not been W in all the earth
35:19 their cords; the finely W garments for ministering in
39:1 stuff they made finely W garments, for ministering in
Num 14:11 signs which I have W among them?
14:22 my signs which I W in Egypt and in
23:23 Israel, 'What has God W
31:51 them the gold, all W articles.
Deut 22:21 stones, because she has W folly in Israel by
32:27 the LORD has not W all this.'"
34:12 terrible deeds which Moses W in the sight of
1Sam 11:13 today the LORD has W deliverance in Israel."
14:45 Jonathan die, who has W this great victory in
14:45 ground; for he has W with God this day."
19:5 Philistine, and the LORD W a great victory for
2Sam 7:21 own heart, thou hast W all this greatness, to
23:10 sword; and the LORD W a great victory that
23:12 Philistines; and the LORD W a great victory.
1Chr 16:12 done, the wonders he W, the judgments he uttered,
17:19 own heart, thou hast W all this greatness, in
Ps 22:31 unborn, that he has W it.
31:19 who fear thee, and W for those who take
46:8 LORD, how he has W desolations in the earth.
64:9 tell what God has W, and ponder what he
68:28 God, thou who hast W for us.
78:4 his might, and the wonders which he has W
78:12 of their fathers he W marvels in the land
78:43 the foe; when he W his signs in Egypt,
105:27 They W his signs among them, and miracles in
139:15 made in secret, intricately W in the depths of
143:5 done; I muse on what thy hands have W
Song 3:10 purple; it was lovingly W within by the daughters
Sir 45:19 they were destroyed; he W wonders against them to
Is 26:12 for us, thou hast W for us all our
26:18 We have W no deliverance in the earth, and

W

25:22 sow in the eighth Y, you will be eating
25:22 produce; until the ninth Y, when its produce comes
25:28 bought it until the Y of jubilee; in the
25:29 it within a whole Y after its sale; for
25:29 sale; for a full Y he shall have the
25:30 redeemed within a full Y, then the house that
25:40 with you until the Y of the jubilee;
25:50 bought him from the Y when he sold himself
25:50 to him until the Y of jubilee, and the
25:52 few years until the Y of jubilee, he shall
25:53 As a servant hired Y by year shall he
25:53 servant hired year by Y shall he be with
25:54 be released in the Y of jubilee, he and
27:17 his field from the Y of jubilee, it shall
27:18 that remain until the Y of jubilee, and a
27:23 it up to the Y of jubilee, and the
27:24 In the Y of jubilee the field shall return
Num 1:1 month, in the second Y after they had come
6:12 a male lamb a Y old for a guilt
6:14 one male lamb a Y old without blemish for
6:14 one ewe lamb a Y old without blemish as
7:15 one male lamb a Y old, for a burnt
7:17 five male lambs a Y old.
7:21 one male lamb a Y old, for a burnt
7:23 five male lambs a Y old.
7:27 one male lamb a Y old, for a burnt
7:29 five male lambs a Y old.
7:33 one male lamb a Y old, for a burnt
7:35 five male lambs a Y old.
7:39 one male lamb a Y old, for a burnt
7:41 five male lambs a Y old.
7:45 one male lamb a Y old, for a burnt
7:47 five male lambs a Y old.
7:51 one male lamb a Y old, for a burnt
7:53 five male lambs a Y old.
7:57 one male lamb a Y old, for a burnt
7:59 five male lambs a Y old.
7:63 one male lamb a Y old, for a burnt
7:65 five male lambs a Y old.
7:69 one male lamb a Y old, for a burnt
7:71 five male lambs a Y old.
7:75 one male lamb a Y old, for a burnt
7:77 five male lambs a Y old.
7:81 one male lamb a Y old, for a burnt
7:83 five male lambs a Y old.
7:87 twelve male lambs a Y old, with their cereal
7:88 the male lambs a Y old sixty.
9:1 month of the second Y after they had come
10:11 In the second Y, in the second month, on
14:34 for every day a Y, you shall bear your
15:27 a female goat a Y old for a sin
28:3 two male lambs a Y old without blemish, day
28:9 two male lambs a Y old without blemish, and
28:11 seven male lambs a Y old without blemish;
28:14 of each month throughout the months of the Y
28:19 seven male lambs a Y old; see that they
28:27 seven male lambs a Y old;
29:2 seven male lambs a Y old without blemish;
29:8 seven male lambs a Y old; they shall be
29:13 fourteen male lambs a Y old; they shall be
29:17 fourteen male lambs a Y old without blemish,
29:20 fourteen male lambs a Y old without blemish,
29:23 fourteen male lambs a Y old without blemish,
29:26 fourteen male lambs a Y old without blemish,
29:29 fourteen male lambs a Y old without blemish,
29:32 fourteen male lambs a Y old without blemish,
29:36 seven male lambs a Y old without blemish,
33:38 there, in the fortieth Y after the people of
Deut 1:3 And in the fortieth Y, on the first day
11:12 the beginning of the Y to the end of
11:12 of the year to the end of the Y
14:22 forth from the field Y by year.
14:22 which comes forth from the field year by Y
14:28 produce in the same Y, and lay it up
15:9 you say, 'The seventh Y, the year of release
15:9 'The seventh year, the Y of release is near,'
15:12 and in the seventh Y you shall let him
15:20 the LORD your God Y by year at the
15:20 your God year by Y at the place which
16:16 "Three times a Y all your males shall appear
24:5 free at home one Y, to be happy with
26:12 produce in the third Y, which is the year
26:12 year, which is the Y of tithing, giving it
31:10 set time of the Y of release, at the
Josh 5:12 the fruit of the land of Canaan that Y
Judg 10:8 crushed and oppressed the children of Israel that Y
11:40 daughters of Israel went Y by year to lament
11:40 Israel went year by Y to lament the daughter
11:40 of Jephthah the Gileadite four days in the Y
17:10 pieces of silver a Y, and a suit of
1Sam 1:3 used to go up Y by year from his
1:3 go up year by Y from his city to
1:7 So it went on Y by year; as often
1:7 went on year by Y; as often as she
2:19 it to him each Y, when she went up
7:16 went on a circuit Y by year to Bethel,
7:16 a circuit year by Y to Bethel, Gilgal, and
27:7 the Philistines was a Y and four months.
2Sam 11:1 the spring of the Y, the time when kings
14:26 the end of every Y he used to cut
21:1 David for three years, Y after year; and David
21:1 three years, year after Y; and David sought the
1Kgs 4:7 to make provision for one month in the Y
5:11 gave this to Hiram Y by year.
5:11 Solomon gave this to Hiram year by Y
6:1 four hundred and eightieth Y after the people of
6:1 Egypt, in the fourth Y of Solomon's reign over
6:37 In the fourth Y the foundation of the house
6:38 And in the eleventh Y, in the month of
9:25 Three times a Y Solomon used to offer up
10:14 to Solomon in one Y was six hundred and
10:25 and mules, so much Y by year.
10:25 spices, horses, and mules, so much year by Y
14:25 In the fifth Y of King Rehoboam, Shishak king
15:1 Now in the eighteenth Y of King Jeroboam the
15:9 In the twentieth Y of Jeroboam king of Israel
15:25 Israel in the second Y of Asa king of
15:28 him in the third Y of Asa king of
15:33 In the third Y of Asa king of Judah,
16:8 In the twenty-sixth Y of Asa king of Judah,
16:10 him, in the twenty-seventh Y of Asa king of
16:15 In the twenty-seventh Y of Asa king of Judah,
16:23 In the thirty-first Y of Asa king of Judah,
16:29 In the thirty-eighth Y of Asa king of Judah,
18:1 Elijah, in the third Y, saying, "Go, show yourself
22:2 But in the third Y Jehoshaphat the king of
22:41 Judah in the fourth Y of Ahab king of
22:51 Samaria in the seventeenth Y of Jehoshaphat king of
2Kgs 1:17 stead in the second Y of Jehoram the son
3:1 In the eighteenth Y of Jehoshaphat king of Judah,
8:16 In the fifth Y of Joram the son of
8:25 In the twelfth Y of Joram the son of
8:26 and he reigned one Y in Jerusalem.
9:29 In the eleventh Y of Joram the son of
11:4 But in the seventh Y Jehoiada sent and brought
12:1 In the seventh Y of Jehu Jehoash began to
12:6 But by the twenty-third Y of King Jehoash the
13:1 In the twenty-third Y of Joash the son of
13:10 In the thirty-seventh Y of Joash king of Judah
13:20 invade the land in the spring of the Y
14:1 In the second Y of Joash the son of
14:23 In the fifteenth Y of Amaziah the son of
15:1 In the twenty-seventh Y of Jeroboam king of Israel
15:8 In the thirty-eighth Y of Azariah king of Judah
15:13 reign in the thirty-ninth Y of Uzziah king of
15:17 In the thirty-ninth Y of Azariah king of Judah
15:23 In the fiftieth Y of Azariah king of Judah
15:27 In the fifty-second Y of Azariah king of Judah
15:30 stead, in the twentieth Y of Jotham the son
15:32 In the second Y of Pekah the son of
16:1 In the seventeenth Y of Pekah the son of
17:1 In the twelfth Y of Ahaz king of Judah
17:4 as he had done Y by year; therefore the
17:4 had done year by Y; therefore the king of
17:6 In the ninth Y of Hoshea the king of
18:1 In the third Y of Hoshea son of Elah,
18:9 In the fourth Y of King Hezekiah, which was
18:9 which was the seventh Y of Hoshea son of
18:10 In the sixth Y of Hezekiah, which was the
18:10 which was the ninth Y of Hoshea king of
18:13 the fourteenth Y of King Hezekiah Sennacherib king
19:29 sign for you: this Y you shall eat what
19:29 and in the second Y what springs of the
19:29 then in the third Y sow, and reap, and
22:3 In the eighteenth Y of King Josiah, the king
23:23 but in the eighteenth Y of King Josiah this
24:12 prisoner in the eighth Y of his reign,
25:1 And in the ninth Y of his reign, in
25:2 besieged till the eleventh Y of King Zedekiah.
25:8 which was the nineteenth Y of King Nebuchadnezzar,
25:27 And in the thirty-seventh Y of the exile of
25:27 of Babylon, in the Y that he began to

Y

 YEARS

	45:6	the land these two Y; and there are yet
	45:6	there are yet five Y in which there will
	45:11	there are yet five Y of famine to come;
	47:8	the days of the Y of your life?"
	47:9	"The days of the Y of my sojourning are
	47:9	a hundred and thirty Y; few and evil have
	47:9	the days of the Y of my life, and
	47:9	the days of the Y of the life of
	47:28	land of Egypt seventeen Y; so the days of
	47:28	days of Jacob, the Y of his life, were
	47:28	of his life, were a hundred and forty-seven Y
	50:22	house; and Joseph lived a hundred and ten Y
	50:26	a hundred and ten Y old; and they embalmed
Ex	6:16	Kohath, and Merari, the Y of the life of
	6:16	life of Levi being a hundred and thirty-seven Y
	6:18	Hebron, and Uzziel, the Y of the life of
	6:18	life of Kohath being a hundred and thirty-three Y
	6:20	Aaron and Moses, the Y of the life of
	6:20	life of Amram being one hundred and thirty-seven Y
	7:7	Now Moses was eighty Y old, and Aaron eighty-three
	7:7	old, and Aaron eighty-three Y old, when they spoke
	12:40	dwelt in Egypt was four hundred and thirty Y
	12:41	four hundred and thirty Y, on that very day,
	16:35	ate the manna forty Y, till they came to
	21:2	he shall serve six Y, and in the seventh
	23:10	"For six Y you shall sow your land and
	30:14	the census, from twenty Y old and upward, shall
	38:26	the census, from twenty Y old and upward, for
Lev	19:23	fruit as forbidden; three Y it shall be forbidden
	25:3	Six Y you shall sow your field, and six
	25:3	your field, and six Y you shall prune your
	25:8	count seven weeks of Y, seven times seven years,
	25:8	years, seven times seven Y, so that the time
	25:8	the seven weeks of Y shall be to you
	25:8	weeks of years shall be to you forty-nine Y
	25:15	to the number of Y after the jubilee, you
	25:15	to the number of Y for crops he shall
	25:16	If the Y are many you shall increase the
	25:16	price, and if the Y are few you shall
	25:21	that it will bring forth fruit for three Y
	25:27	let him reckon the Y since he sold it
	25:50	to the number of Y; the time he was
	25:51	there are still many Y, according to them he
	25:52	remain but a few Y until the year of
	25:52	him; according to the Y of service due from
	27:3	a male from twenty Y old up to sixty
	27:3	old up to sixty Y old shall be fifty
	27:5	person is from five Y old up to twenty
	27:5	old up to twenty Y old, your valuation shall
	27:6	old up to five Y old, your valuation shall
	27:7	the person is sixty Y old and upward, then
	27:18	it according to the Y that remain until the
Num	1:3	by head; from twenty Y old and upward, all
	1:18	of names from twenty Y old and upward, head
	1:20	every male from twenty Y old and upward, all
	1:22	every male from twenty Y old and upward, all
	1:24	the names, from twenty Y old and upward, all
	1:26	of names, from twenty Y old and upward, every
	1:28	of names, from twenty Y old and upward, every
	1:30	of names, from twenty Y old and upward, every
	1:32	of names, from twenty Y old and upward, every
	1:34	of names, from twenty Y old and upward, every
	1:36	of names, from twenty Y old and upward, every
	1:38	of names, from twenty Y old and upward, every
	1:40	of names, from twenty Y old and upward, every
	1:42	of names, from twenty Y old and upward, every
	1:45	fathers' houses, from twenty Y old and upward, every
	4:3	fathers' houses, from thirty Y old up to fifty
	4:3	old up to fifty Y old, all who can
	4:23	fathers' houses; from thirty Y old up to fifty
	4:23	old up to fifty Y old, you shall number
	4:30	fathers' houses; from thirty Y old up to fifty
	4:30	old up to fifty Y old, you shall number
	4:35	fathers' houses, from thirty Y old up to fifty
	4:35	old up to fifty Y old, every one that
	4:39	fathers' houses, from thirty Y old up to fifty
	4:39	old up to fifty Y old, every one that
	4:43	fathers' houses, from thirty Y old up to fifty
	4:43	old up to fifty Y old, every one that
	4:47	fathers' houses, from thirty Y old up to fifty
	4:47	old up to fifty Y old, every one that
	8:24	the Levites: from twenty-five Y old and upward they
	8:25	the age of fifty Y they shall withdraw from
	13:22	(Hebron was built seven Y before Zoan in Egypt.)
	14:29	number, numbered from twenty Y old and upward,
	14:33	in the wilderness forty Y, and shall suffer for
	14:34	bear your iniquity, forty Y, and you shall know
	26:2	of Israel, from twenty Y old and upward, by
	26:4	the people, from twenty Y old and upward," as
	32:11	of Egypt, from twenty Y old and upward, shall
	32:13	in the wilderness forty Y, until all the generation
	33:39	a hundred and twenty-three Y old when he died
Deut	2:7	great wilderness; these forty Y the LORD your God
	2:14	brook Zered was thirty-eight Y, until the entire,
	8:2	led you these forty Y in the wilderness, that
	8:4	and your foot did not swell, these forty Y
	14:28	end of every three Y you shall bring forth
	15:1	end of every seven Y you shall grant a
	15:12	shall serve you six Y, and in the seventh
	15:18	a hired servant he has served you six Y
	29:5	have led you forty Y in the wilderness; your
	31:2	a hundred and twenty Y old this day; I
	31:10	end of every seven Y, at the set time
	32:7	of old, consider the Y of many generations; ask
	34:7	a hundred and twenty Y old when he died;
Josh	5:6	of Israel walked forty Y in the wilderness, till
	13:1	old and advanced in Y; and the LORD said
	13:1	old and advanced in Y, and there remains yet
	14:7	I was forty Y old when Moses the servant
	14:10	he said, these forty-five Y since the time that
	14:10	am this day eighty-five Y old.
	23:1	and well advanced in Y,
	23:2	and well advanced in Y;
	24:29	a hundred and ten Y old.
Judg	2:8	at the age of one hundred and ten Y
	3:8	people of Israel served Cushan-rishathaim eight Y
	3:11	So the land had rest forty Y
	3:14	Israel served Eglon the king of Moab eighteen Y
	3:30	And the land had rest for eighty Y
	4:3	oppressed the people of Israel cruelly for twenty Y
	5:31	And the land had rest for forty Y
	6:1	gave them into the hand of Midian seven Y
	6:25	the second bull seven Y old, and pull down
	8:28	land had rest forty Y in the days of
	9:22	Abimelech ruled over Israel three Y
	10:2	And he judged Israel twenty-three Y
	10:3	Jair the Gileadite, who judged Israel twenty-two Y
	10:8	For eighteen Y they oppressed all the people of
	11:26	the Arnon, three hundred Y, why did you not
	12:7	Jephthah judged Israel six Y
	12:9	And he judged Israel seven Y
	12:11	Zebulunite judged Israel; and he judged Israel ten Y
	12:14	on seventy asses; and he judged Israel eight Y
	13:1	into the hand of the Philistines for forty Y
	15:20	Israel in the days of the Philistines twenty Y
	16:31	He had judged Israel twenty Y
Ruth	1:4	lived there about ten Y;
1Sam	4:15	Now Eli was ninety-eight Y old and his eyes
	4:18	He had judged Israel forty Y
	7:2	time passed, some twenty Y, and all the house
	13:1	Y old when he began to reign; and he
	13:1	and two Y over Israel.
	17:12	the man was already old and advanced in Y
	29:3	now for days and Y, and since he deserted
2Sam	2:10	Saul's son, was forty Y old when he began
	2:10	to reign over Israel, and he reigned two Y
	2:11	of Judah was seven Y and six months.
	4:4	He was five Y old when the news about
	5:4	David was thirty Y old when he began to
	5:4	he began to reign, and he reigned forty Y
	5:5	reigned over Judah seven Y and six months; and
	5:5	he reigned over all Israel and Judah thirty-three Y
	13:23	two full Y Absalom had sheepshearers at Baal-hazor,
	13:38	and went to Geshur, and was there three Y
	14:28	Absalom dwelt two full Y in Jerusalem, without
	15:7	the end of four Y Absalom said to the
	19:32	very aged man, eighty Y old; and he had
	19:34	the king, "How many Y have I still to
	19:35	am this day eighty Y old; can I discern
	21:1	of David for three Y, year after year; and
	24:13	to him, "Shall three Y of famine come to
1Kgs	1:1	old and advanced in Y, and although they covered
	2:11	over Israel was forty Y; he reigned seven years
	2:11	years; he reigned seven Y in Hebron, and thirty-three
	2:11	in Hebron, and thirty-three Y in Jerusalem.
	2:39	the end of three Y that two of Shimei's
	6:38	He was seven Y in building it.
	7:1	his own house thirteen Y, and he finished his
	9:10	the end of twenty Y, in which Solomon had
	10:22	Once every three Y the fleet of ships of
	11:42	reigned in Jerusalem over all Israel was forty Y
	14:20	Jeroboam reigned was twenty-two Y; and he slept

14:21 Rehoboam was forty-one Y old when he began to
14:21 and he reigned seventeen Y in Jerusalem, the city
15:2 He reigned for three Y in Jerusalem.
15:10 and he reigned forty-one Y in Jerusalem.
15:25 of Judah; and he reigned over Israel two Y
15:33 over all Israel at Tirzah, and reigned twenty-four Y
16:8 reign over Israel in Tirzah, and reigned two Y
16:23 and reigned for twelve Y; six years he reigned
16:23 for twelve years; six Y he reigned in Tirzah.
16:29 of Omri reigned over Israel in Samaria twenty-two Y
17:1 dew nor rain these Y, except by my word."
22:1 For three Y Syria and Israel continued without war.
22:42 Jehoshaphat was thirty-five Y old when he began to
22:42 and he reigned twenty-five Y in Jerusalem.
22:51 and he reigned two Y over Israel.
2Kgs 3:1 over Israel in Samaria, and he reigned twelve Y
8:1 it will come upon the land for seven Y
8:2 sojourned in the land of the Philistines seven Y
8:3 end of the seven Y, when the woman returned
8:17 He was thirty-two Y old when he became king,
8:17 and he reigned eight Y in Jerusalem.
8:26 Ahaziah was twenty-two Y old when he began to
10:36 reigned over Israel in Samaria was twenty-eight Y
11:3 remained with her six Y, hid in the house
11:21 Jehoash was seven Y old when he began to
12:1 and he reigned forty Y in Jerusalem.
13:1 over Israel in Samaria, and he reigned seventeen Y
13:10 over Israel in Samaria, and he reigned sixteen Y
14:2 He was twenty-five Y old when he began to
14:2 and he reigned twenty-nine Y in Jerusalem.
14:17 of Judah, lived fifteen Y after the death of
14:21 Azariah, who was sixteen Y old, and made him
14:23 to reign in Samaria, and he reigned forty-one Y
15:2 He was sixteen Y old when he began to
15:2 and he reigned fifty-two Y in Jerusalem.
15:17 and he reigned ten Y in Samaria.
15:23 over Israel in Samaria, and he reigned two Y
15:27 reign over Israel in Samaria, and reigned twenty Y
15:33 He was twenty-five Y old when he began to
15:33 and he reigned sixteen Y in Jerusalem.
16:2 Ahaz was twenty Y old when he began to
16:2 and he reigned sixteen Y in Jerusalem.
17:1 in Samaria over Israel, and he reigned nine Y
17:5 Samaria, and for three Y he besieged it.
18:2 He was twenty-five Y old when he began to
18:2 and he reigned twenty-nine Y in Jerusalem.
18:10 the end of three Y he took it.
20:6 I will add fifteen Y to your life.
21:1 Manasseh was twelve Y old when he began to
21:1 and he reigned fifty-five Y in Jerusalem.
21:19 Amon was twenty-two Y old when he began to
21:19 and he reigned two Y in Jerusalem.
22:1 Josiah was eight Y old when he began to
22:1 and he reigned thirty-one Y in Jerusalem.
23:31 Jehoahaz was twenty-three Y old when he began to
23:36 Jehoiakim was twenty-five Y old when he began to
23:36 and he reigned eleven Y in Jerusalem.
24:1 became his servant three Y; then he turned and
24:8 Jehoiachin was eighteen Y old when he became
24:18 Zedekiah was twenty-one Y old when he became
24:18 and he reigned eleven Y in Jerusalem.
1Chr 2:21 when he was sixty Y old; and she bore
3:4 he reigned for seven Y and six months.
3:4 And he reigned thirty-three Y in Jerusalem.
21:12 you will: either three Y of famine; or three
23:3 The Levites, thirty Y old and upward, were
23:24 the individuals from twenty Y old and upward who
23:27 the Levites from twenty Y old and upward--
27:23 number those below twenty Y of age, for the
29:27 over Israel was forty Y; he reigned seven years
29:27 years; he reigned seven Y in Hebron, and thirty-three
29:27 in Hebron, and thirty-three Y in Jerusalem.
2Chr 8:1 the end of twenty Y, in which Solomon had
9:21 Huram; once every three Y the ships of Tarshish
9:30 Solomon reigned in Jerusalem over all Israel forty Y
11:17 Judah, and for three Y they made Rehoboam the
11:17 they walked for three Y in the way of
12:13 Rehoboam was forty-one Y old when he began to
12:13 and he reigned seventeen Y in Jerusalem, the city
13:2 He reigned for three Y in Jerusalem.
14:1 his days the land had rest for ten Y
14:6 no war in those Y, for the LORD gave
18:2 After some Y he went down to Ahab in
20:31 He was thirty-five Y old when he began to
20:31 and he reigned twenty-five Y in Jerusalem.
21:5 Jehoram was thirty-two Y old when he became king,
21:5 and he reigned eight Y in Jerusalem.
21:19 the end of two Y, his bowels came out
21:20 He was thirty-two Y old when he began to
21:20 and he reigned eight Y in Jerusalem; and he
22:2 Ahaziah was forty-two Y old when he began to
22:12 remained with them six Y, hid in the house
24:1 Joash was seven Y old when he began to
24:1 and he reigned forty Y in Jerusalem; his mother's
24:15 a hundred and thirty Y old at his death.
25:1 Amaziah was twenty-five Y old when he began to
25:1 and he reigned twenty-nine Y in Jerusalem.
25:5 He mustered those twenty Y old and upward, and
25:25 of Judah lived fifteen Y after the death of
26:1 Uzziah, who was sixteen Y old, and made him
26:3 Uzziah was sixteen Y old when he began to
26:3 and he reigned fifty-two Y in Jerusalem.
27:1 Jotham was twenty-five Y old when he began to
27:1 and he reigned sixteen Y in Jerusalem.
27:5 same amount in the second and the third Y
27:8 He was twenty-five Y old when he began to
27:8 and he reigned sixteen Y in Jerusalem.
28:1 Ahaz was twenty Y old when he began to
28:1 and he reigned sixteen Y in Jerusalem.
29:1 when he was twenty-five Y old, and he reigned
29:1 and he reigned twenty-nine Y in Jerusalem.
31:16 genealogy, males from three Y old and upwards, all
31:17 the Levites from twenty Y old and upwards was
33:1 Manasseh was twelve Y old when he began to
33:1 and he reigned fifty-five Y in Jerusalem.
33:21 Amon was twenty-two Y old when he began to
33:21 and he reigned two Y in Jerusalem.
34:1 Josiah was eight Y old when he began to
34:1 and he reigned thirty-one Y in Jerusalem.
36:2 Jehoahaz was twenty-three Y old when he began to
36:5 Jehoiakim was twenty-five Y old when he began to
36:5 and he reigned eleven Y in Jerusalem.
36:9 Jehoiachin was eight Y old when he began to
36:11 Zedekiah was twenty-one Y old when he began to
36:11 and he reigned eleven Y in Jerusalem.
36:21 lay desolate it kept sabbath, to fulfil seventy Y
Ezra 3:8 the Levites, from twenty Y old and upward, to
5:11 that was built many Y ago, which a great
Neh 5:14 Artaxerxes the king, twelve Y, neither I nor my
9:21 Forty Y didst thou sustain them in the wilderness,
9:30 Many Y thou didst bear with them, and didst
Tob 14:2 He was fifty-eight Y old when he lost his
14:2 sight, and after eight Y he regained it.
14:11 a hundred and fifty-eight Y old; and Tobias gave
14:14 at the age of a hundred and twenty-seven Y
Jud 8:4 a widow for three Y and four months.
16:23 one hundred and five Y old.
Job 10:5 of man, or thy Y as man's years,
10:5 thy years as man's Y,
15:20 days, through all the Y that are laid up
16:22 For when a few Y have come I shall
32:6 "I am young in Y, and you are aged;
32:7 days speak, and many Y teach wisdom.'
36:11 in prosperity, and their Y in pleasantness.
36:26 the number of his Y is unsearchable.
42:16 a hundred and forty Y, and saw his sons,
Ps 31:10 with sorrow, and my Y with sighing; my strength
61:6 the king; may his Y endure to all generations!
77:5 old, I remember the Y long ago.
78:33 a breath, and their Y in terror.
90:4 For a thousand Y in thy sight are but
90:9 under thy wrath, our Y come to an end
90:10 The Y of our life are threescore and ten,
90:15 us, and as many Y as we have seen
95:10 For forty Y I loathed that generation and said,
102:24 thou whose Y endure throughout all generations!"
102:27 the same, and thy Y have no end.
Prov 3:2 length of days and Y of life and abundant
4:11 my words, that the Y of your life may
5:9 to others and your Y to the merciless;
9:11 will be multiplied, and Y will be added to
10:27 prolongs life, but the Y of the wicked will
Eccl 6:3 children, and lives many Y, so that the days
6:3 the days of his Y are many, but he
6:6 should live a thousand Y twice told, yet enjoy
11:8 a man lives many Y, let him rejoice in
12:1 days come, and the Y draw nigh, when you
Wis 4:8 measured by number of Y;
4:13 time, he fulfilled long Y;
Sir 18:8 days is great if he reaches a hundred Y
18:9 so are a few Y in the day of
26:2 he will complete his Y in peace.

YELLOW (3)

YES (38)

YESTERDAY (9)

Y

Ps 90:4 sight are but as Y when it is past,
Sir 38:22 yours is like it: Y it was mine, and
Jn 4:52 they said to him, Y at the seventh hour
Acts 7:28 you killed the Egyptian Y
Heb 13:8 Christ is the same Y and today and for

YIELD (49)

Gen 4:12 it shall no longer Y to you its strength;
49:20 rich, and he shall Y royal dainties.
Ex 23:10 and gather in its Y;
Lev 19:25 fruit, that they may Y more richly for you:
25:7 your land all its Y shall be for food.
25:19 The land will Y its fruit, and you will
26:4 and the land shall Y its increase, and the
26:4 of the field shall Y their fruit.
26:20 your land shall not Y its increase, and the
26:20 the land shall not Y their fruit.
Num 20:8 before their eyes to Y its water; so you
Deut 11:17 rain, and the land Y no fruit, and you
13:8 other, you shall not Y to him or listen
14:22 shall tithe all the Y of your seed, which
22:9 seed, lest the whole Y be forfeited to the
22:9 have sown and the Y of the vineyard.
33:14 sun, and the rich Y of the months,
2Chr 30:8 your fathers were, but Y yourselves to the LORD,
32:28 storehouses also for the Y of grain, wine, and
Neh 9:37 And its rich Y goes to the kings whom
Jud 2:10 They will Y themselves to you, and you shall
Job 31:39 I have eaten its Y without payment, and caused
40:20 For the mountains Y food for him where all
Ps 85:12 and our land will Y its increase.
107:37 fields, and plant vineyards, and get a fruitful Y
Prov 8:19 fine gold, and my Y than choice silver.
18:20 is satisfied by the Y of his lips.
Is 5:2 looked for it to Y grapes, but it yielded
5:4 looked for it to Y grapes, why did it
5:4 grapes, why did it Y wild grapes?
5:10 acres of vineyard shall Y but one bath, and
5:10 homer of seed shall Y but an ephah."
Ezek 34:27 of the field shall Y their fruit, and the
34:27 and the earth shall Y its increase, and they
36:8 forth your branches, and Y your fruit to my
Hos 8:7 no heads, it shall Y no meal; if it
8:7 if it were to Y, aliens would devour it.
Joel 2:22 the fig tree and vine give their full Y
Hab 3:17 fail and the fields Y no food, the flock
Hag 2:19 the olive tree still Y nothing?
Zech 8:12 peace; the vine shall Y its fruit, and the
Acts 23:21 But do not Y to them; for more than
Rom 6:13 Do not Y your members to sin as instruments
6:13 instruments of wickedness, but Y yourselves to God
6:16 know that if you Y yourselves to any one
6:19 iniquity, so now Y your members to righteousness
Gal 2:5 them we did not Y submission even for a
Jas 3:12 fig tree, my brethren, Y olives, or a grapevine
3:12 more can salt water Y fresh.

YIELDED (9)

Ps 67:6 The earth has Y its increase; God, our God,
Wis 18:25 To these the destroyer Y, these he feared; for
Is 5:2 yield grapes, but it Y wild grapes.
Dan 3:96 the king's command, and Y up their bodies rather
2Mac 13:23 called in the Jews, Y and swore to observe
Mt 27:50 a loud voice and Y up his spirit.
Mk 4:7 choked it, and it Y no grain.
Lk 8:8 soil and grew, and Y a hundredfold." As he
Rom 6:19 just as you once Y your members to impurity

YIELDING (6)

Gen 1:11 put forth vegetation, plants Y seed, and fruit trees
1:12 brought forth vegetation, plants Y seed according to
1:29 given you every plant Y seed which is upon
Song 5:13 like beds of spices, Y fragrance.
Mk 4:8 up and increasing and Y thirtyfold and sixtyfold and
Rev 22:2 twelve kinds of fruit, Y its fruit each month;

YIELDS (6)

Lev 25:12 shall eat what it Y out of the field.
Ps 1:3 streams of water, that Y its fruit in its
Prov 13:23 ground of the poor Y much food, but it
Hos 10:1 a luxuriant vine that Y its fruit.
Mt 13:23 indeed bears fruit, and Y, in one case a
Heb 12:11 than pleasant; later it Y the peaceful fruit of

YIRON

Josh 19:38 Edre-i, En-hazor, Y, Migdal-el, Horem, Beth-anath,

YOKE (69)

Gen 27:40 you shall break his Y from your neck."
Lev 26:13 the bars of your Y and made you walk
Num 19:2 and upon which a Y has never come.
Deut 21:3 worked and which has not pulled in the Y
28:48 he will put a Y of iron upon your
1Sam 6:7 has never come a Y, and yoke the cows
6:7 come a yoke, and Y the cows to the
11:7 He took a Y of oxen, and cut them
1Kgs 12:4 "Your father made our Y heavy.
12:4 father and his heavy Y upon us, and we
12:9 to me, 'Lighten the Y that your father put
12:10 'Your father made our Y heavy, but do you
12:11 upon you a heavy Y, I will add to
12:11 a heavy yoke, I will add to your Y
12:14 "My father made your Y heavy, but I will
12:14 will add to your Y; my father chastised you
19:19 was plowing, with twelve Y of oxen before him,
19:21 him, and took the Y of oxen, and slew
2Chr 10:4 "Your father made our Y heavy.
10:4 father and his heavy Y upon us, and we
10:9 to me, 'Lighten the Y that your father put
10:10 'Your father made our Y heavy, but do you
10:11 upon you a heavy Y, I will add to
10:11 a heavy yoke, I will add to your Y
10:14 "My father made your Y heavy, but I will
Job 1:3 thousand camels, five hundred Y of oxen, and five
42:12 thousand camels, a thousand Y of oxen, and a
Sir 6:30 Her Y is a golden ornament, and her bonds
26:7 wife is an ox Y which chafes; taking hold
28:19 has not borne its Y, and has not been
28:20 its fetters; for its Y is a yoke of
28:20 its yoke is a Y of iron, and its
33:26 Y and thong will bow the neck, and for
40:1 man, and a heavy Y is upon the sons
51:26 your neck under the Y, and let your souls
Is 9:4 For the Y of his burden, and the staff
10:27 your shoulder, and his Y will be destroyed from
14:25 under foot; and his Y shall depart from them,
47:6 aged you made your Y exceedingly heavy.
58:6 the thongs of the Y, to let the oppressed
58:6 the oppressed go free, and to break every Y
58:9 midst of you the Y, the pointing of the
Jer 2:20 ago you broke your Y and burst your bonds;
5:5 alike had broken the Y, they had burst the
27:8 its neck under the Y of the king of
27:11 its neck under the Y of the king of
27:12 your necks under the Y of the king of
28:2 I have broken the Y of the king of
28:4 I will break the Y of the king of
28:11 will I break the Y of Nebuchadnezzar king of
28:14 nations an iron Y of servitude to Nebuchadnezzar
30:8 I will break the Y from off their neck,
Lam 1:14 were bound into a Y; by his hand they
3:27 that he bear the Y in his youth.
5:5 With a Y on our necks we are hard
Ezek 34:27 the bars of their Y, and deliver them from
Hos 10:11 put Ephraim to the Y, Judah must plow, Jacob
11:4 one, who eases the Y on their jaws, and
11:7 are appointed to the Y, and none shall remove
Nah 1:13 I will break his Y from off you and
1Mac 8:18 free themselves from the Y; for they saw that
8:31 have you made your Y heavy upon our friends
13:41 and seventieth year the Y of the Gentiles was
Mt 11:29 Take my Y upon you, and learn from me;
11:30 For my Y is easy, and my burden is
Lk 14:19 'I have bought five Y of oxen, and I
Acts 15:10 God by putting a Y upon the neck of
Gal 5:1 submit again to a Y of slavery.
1Tim 6:1 who are under the Y of slavery regard their

YOKE-BARS (3)

Jer 27:2 "Make yourself thongs and Y, and put them on
28:10 prophet Hananiah took the Y from the neck of
28:12 Hananiah had broken the Y from off the neck

YOKED (3)

Num 25:3 So Israel Y himself to Baal of Peor.
25:5 his men who have Y themselves to Baal of
1Sam 6:10 two milch cows and Y them to the cart,

YOKEFELLOW

Phil 4:3 ask you also, true Y, help these women, for

YOKES (2)

2Sam 24:22 threshing sledges and the Y of the oxen for

Y

1Kgs 19:21 their flesh with the Y of the oxen, and

YON (2)

Judg 5:5 quaked before the LORD, Y Sinai before the LORD,
Ps 68:8 the presence of God; Y Sinai quaked at the

YONDER (11)

Gen 19:20 Behold, Y city is near enough to flee to,
22:5 the lad will go Y and worship, and come
24:65 "Who is the man Y, walking in the field
Num 13:17 up into the Negeb Y, and go up into
23:15 your burnt offering, while I meet the LORD Y
1Sam 14:1 the Philistine garrison on Y side." But he did
20:19 hand, and remain beside Y stone heap.
2Kgs 4:25 Gehazi his servant, "Look, Y is the Shunammite;
23:17 he said, "What is Y monument that I see?"
Ps 104:25 Y is the sea, great and wide, which teems
Mt 26:36 here, while I go Y and pray."

YOUNG (336)

Gen 4:23 for wounding me, a Y man for striking me.
14:24 nothing but what the Y men have eaten, and
15:9 a turtledove, and a Y pigeon."
19:4 men of Sodom, both Y and old, all the
22:3 took two of his Y men with him, and
22:5 Abraham said to his Y men, "Stay here with
22:19 Abraham returned to his Y men, and they arose
24:43 of water; let the Y woman who comes out
34:19 And the Y man did not delay to do
41:12 A Y Hebrew was there with us, a servant
44:20 old man, and a Y brother, the child of
Ex 10:9 will go with our Y and our old; we
23:26 None shall cast her Y or be barren in
24:5 And he sent Y men of the people of
29:1 Take one Y bull and two rams without blemish,
33:11 son of Nun, a Y man, did not depart
Lev 1:14 of turtledoves or of Y pigeons.
4:3 he has committed a Y bull without blemish to
4:14 assembly shall offer a Y bull for a sin
5:7 two turtledoves or two Y pigeons, one for a
5:11 two turtledoves or two Y pigeons, then he shall
12:6 burnt offering, and a Y pigeon or a turtledove
12:8 two turtledoves or two Y pigeons, one for a
14:22 two turtledoves or two Y pigeons, such as he
14:30 of the turtledoves or Y pigeons such as he
15:14 two turtledoves or two Y pigeons, and come before
15:29 two turtledoves or two Y pigeons, and bring them
16:3 holy place: with a Y bull for a sin
22:28 both her and her Y in one day.
23:18 without blemish, and one Y bull, and two rams;
Num 6:10 two turtledoves or two Y pigeons to the priest
7:15 full of incense; one Y bull, one ram, one
7:21 full of incense; one Y bull, one ram, one
7:27 full of incense; one Y bull, one ram, one
7:33 full of incense; one Y bull, one ram, one
7:39 full of incense; one Y bull, one ram, one
7:45 full of incense; one Y bull, one ram, one
7:51 full of incense; one Y bull, one ram, one
7:57 full of incense; one Y bull, one ram, one
7:63 full of incense; one Y bull, one ram, one
7:69 full of incense; one Y bull, one ram, one
7:75 full of incense; one Y bull, one ram, one
7:81 full of incense; one Y bull, one ram, one
8:8 let them take a Y bull and its cereal
8:8 you shall take another Y bull for a sin
11:27 And a Y man ran and told Moses, "Eldad
15:24 congregation shall offer one Y bull for a burnt
28:11 to the LORD: two Y bulls, one ram, seven
28:19 to the LORD: two Y bulls, one ram, and
28:27 to the LORD; two Y bulls, one ram, seven
29:2 to the LORD: one Y bull, one ram, seven
29:8 a pleasing odor: one Y bull, one ram, seven
29:13 to the LORD, thirteen Y bulls, two rams, fourteen
29:17 the second day twelve Y bulls, two rams, fourteen
31:18 But all the Y girls who have not known
Deut 7:13 your cattle and the Y of your flock, in
22:6 on the ground, with Y ones or eggs and
22:6 mother sitting upon the Y or upon the eggs,
22:6 the mother with the Y;
22:7 mother go, but the Y you may take to
22:15 the father of the Y woman and her mother
22:16 the father of the Y woman shall say to
22:19 the father of the Y woman, because he has
22:20 not found in the Y woman,
22:21 shall bring out the Y woman to the door
22:24 death with stones, the Y woman because she did
22:25 a man meets a Y woman who is betrothed,
22:26 But to the Y woman you shall do nothing;
22:26 do nothing; in the Y woman there is no
22:27 and though the betrothed Y woman cried for help
22:29 the father of the Y woman fifty shekels of
28:4 your cattle, and the Y of your flock.
28:18 your cattle, and the Y of your flock.
28:50 show favor to the Y,
28:51 your cattle or the Y of your flock, until
32:11 that flutters over its Y, spreading out its wings,
32:25 be terror, destroying both Y man and virgin, the
Josh 6:21 both men and women, Y and old, oxen, sheep,
6:23 So the Y men who had been spies went
Judg 8:14 And he caught a Y man of Succoth, and
9:54 called hastily to the Y man his armor-bearer, and
9:54 And his Y man thrust him through, and he
14:5 And behold, a Y lion roared against him;
14:10 there; for so the Y men used to do.
17:7 Now there was a Y man of Bethlehem in
17:11 the man; and the Y man became to him
17:12 the Levite, and the Y man became his priest,
18:3 the voice of the Y Levite; and they turned
18:15 the house of the Y Levite, at the home
19:19 your maidservant and the Y man with your servants;
21:12 of Jabesh-gilead four hundred Y virgins who had not
Ruth 2:9 I not charged the Y men not to molest
2:9 and drink what the Y men have drawn."
2:15 glean, Boaz instructed his Y men, saying, "Let her
3:10 have not gone after Y men, whether poor or
4:12 give you by this Y woman."
1Sam 1:24 the LORD at Shiloh; and the child was Y
2:17 the sin of the Y men was very great
5:9 of the city, both Y and old, so that
9:2 was Saul, a handsome Y man.
9:11 the city, they met Y maidens coming out to
14:1 Saul said to the Y man who bore his
14:6 Jonathan said to the Y man who bore his
16:18 One of the Y men answered, "Behold, I have
17:58 "Whose son are you, Y man?" And David answered,
21:2 an appointment with the Y men for such and
21:4 bread; if only the Y men have kept themselves
21:5 the vessels of the Y men are holy, even
25:5 So David sent ten Y men; and David said
25:5 David said to the Y men, "Go up to
25:8 Ask your Y men, and they will tell you.
25:8 Therefore let my Y men find favor in your
25:9 When David's Y men came, they said all this
25:12 So David's Y men turned away, and came back
25:14 But one of the Y men told Abigail, Nabal's
25:19 she said to her Y men, "Go on before
25:25 did not see the Y men of my lord,
25:27 be given to the Y men who follow my
26:22 Let one of the Y men come over and
30:13 said, "I am a Y man of Egypt, servant
30:17 except four hundred Y men, who mounted camels
2Sam 1:5 David said to the Y man who told him,
1:6 And the Y man who told him said, "By
1:13 David said to the Y man who told him,
1:15 called one of the Y men and said, "Go,
2:14 to Joab, "Let the Y men arise and play
2:21 seize one of the Y men, and take his
4:12 And David commanded his Y men, and they killed
9:12 And Mephibosheth had a Y son, whose name was
13:17 He called the Y man who served him and
13:32 have killed all the Y men the king's sons,
13:34 And the Y man who kept the watch lifted
14:21 go, bring back the Y man Absalom."
16:2 summer fruit for the Y men to eat, and
18:5 my sake with the Y man Absalom." And all
18:12 my sake protect the Y man Absalom.'
18:15 Y men, Joab's armor-bearers, surrounded Absalom
18:29 it well with the Y man Absalom?" Ahima-az
18:32 it well with the Y man Absalom?" And the
18:32 evil, be like that Y man."
1Kgs 1:2 to him, "Let a Y maiden be sought for
11:28 Solomon saw that the Y man was industrious he
12:8 took counsel with the Y men who had grown
12:10 And the Y men who had grown up with
12:14 the counsel of the Y men, saying, "My father
2Kgs 5:22 country of Ephraim two Y men of the sons
6:17 the eyes of the Y man, and he saw;
8:12 you will slay their Y men with the sword,
9:4 So the Y man, the prophet, went to Ramoth-gilead.
9:6 the house; and the Y man poured the oil
1Chr 12:28 Zadok, a Y man mighty in valor, and twenty-two
22:5 "Solomon my son is Y and inexperienced, and the

	29:1	God has chosen, is Y and inexperienced, and the
2Chr	10:8	took counsel with the Y men who had grown
	10:10	And the Y men who had grown up with
	10:14	the counsel of the Y men, saying, "My father
	13:7	Solomon, when Rehoboam was Y and irresolute and
	13:9	consecrate himself with a Y bull or seven rams
	15:13	put to death, whether Y or old, man or
	31:15	their brethren, old and Y alike, by divisions,
	36:17	Chaldeans, who slew their Y men with the sword
	36:17	had no compassion on Y man or virgin, old
Ezra	6:9	whatever is needed-- Y bulls, rams, or sheep
Tob	1:4	I was still a Y man, the whole tribe
	5:16	and departed, and the Y man's dog was with
	6:2	Then the Y man went down to wash himself.
	6:2	would have swallowed the Y man;
	6:3	So the Y man seized the fish and threw
	6:5	So the Y man did as the angel told
	6:6	Then the Y man said to the angel, "Brother
	6:10	angel said to the Y man, "Brother, today we
	6:13	Then the Y man said to the angel, "Brother
	7:2	Edna, "How much the Y man resembles my cousin
Jud	2:27	to death all their Y men with the edge
	6:16	city, and all their Y men and their women
	7:23	and the women and Y men fainted from thirst
	7:24	all the people, the Y men, the women, and
	10:9	So they ordered the Y men to open the
	16:5	territory, and kill my Y men with the sword,
	16:7	the hands of the Y men, nor did the
Esth	2:2	him said, "Let beautiful Y virgins be sought out
	2:3	gather all the beautiful Y virgins to the harem
	3:13	to annihilate all Jews, Y and old, women and
Job	1:19	it fell upon the Y people, and they are
	4:10	the teeth of the Y lions, are broken.
	14:9	forth branches like a Y plant.
	19:18	Even Y children despise me; when I rise they
	29:8	in the square, the Y men saw me and
	32:6	Buzite answered: "I am Y in years, and you
	38:39	the appetite of the Y lions,
	38:41	its prey, when its Y ones cry to God,
	39:3	forth their offspring, and are delivered of their Y
	39:4	Their Y ones become strong, they grow up in
	39:16	deals cruelly with her Y, as if they were
	39:30	His Y ones suck up blood; and where the
Ps	17:12	to tear, as a Y lion lurking in ambush.
	29:6	and Sirion like a Y wild ox.
	34:10	The Y lions suffer want and hunger; but those
	37:25	I have been Y, and now am old; yet
	58:6	the fangs of the Y lions, O LORD!
	78:63	Fire devoured their Y men, and their maidens had
	78:71	the ewes that had Y he brought him to
	84:3	she may lay her Y, at thy altars, O
	91:13	and the adder, the Y lion and the serpent
	104:21	The Y lions roar for their prey, seeking their
	105:34	the locusts came, and Y locusts without number;
	119:9	How can a Y man keep his way pure?
	144:14	cattle be heavy with Y, suffering no mischance or
	147:9	food, and to the Y ravens which cry.
	148:12	Y men and maidens together, old men and children!
Prov	7:7	among the youths, a Y man without sense,
	20:29	The glory of Y men is their strength, but
Eccl	11:9	Rejoice, O Y man, in your youth, and let
Song	2:3	is my beloved among Y men.
	2:9	a gazelle, or a Y stag.
	2:17	a gazelle, or a Y stag upon rugged mountains.
	8:14	a gazelle or a Y stag upon the mountains
Wis	3:18	If they die Y, they will have no hope
	8:10	the presence of the elders, though I am Y
Sir	30:12	sides while he is Y, lest he become stubborn
	32:7	Speak, Y man, if there is need of you,
	42:8	or the aged man who quarrels with the Y
	42:9	sleep; when she is Y, lest she do not
	47:3	with lions as with Y goats, and with bears
	50:12	he was like a Y cedar on Lebanon; and
	51:13	While I was still Y, before I went on
Is	5:29	like a lion, like Y lions they roar; they
	7:14	Behold, a Y woman shall conceive and bear a
	7:21	will keep alive a Y cow and two sheep;
	9:17	not rejoice over their Y men, and has no
	11:7	bear shall feed; their Y shall lie down together;
	13:18	bows will slaughter the Y men; they will have
	20:4	Ethiopians exiles, both the Y and the old, naked
	23:4	I have neither reared Y men nor brought up
	31:4	a lion or a Y lion growls over his
	31:8	the sword, and his Y men shall be put
	34:7	fall with them, and Y steers with the mighty
	34:15	hatch and gather her Y in her shadow; yea,
	40:11	bosom, and gently lead those that are with Y
	40:30	and be weary, and Y men shall fall exhausted;
	53:2	before him like a Y plant, and like a
	60:6	shall cover you, the Y camels of Midian and
	62:5	For as a Y man marries a virgin, so
Jer	2:23	have done--a restive Y camel interlacing her tracks,
	6:11	upon the gatherings of Y men, also; both husband
	9:21	the streets and the Y men from the squares.
	11:22	will punish them; the Y men shall die by
	15:8	against the mothers of Y men a destroyer at
	31:12	oil, and over the Y of the flock and
	31:13	the dance, and the Y men and the old
	48:15	the choicest of his Y men have gone down
	49:26	Therefore her Y men shall fall in her squares,
	50:30	Therefore her Y men shall fall in her squares,
	51:3	Spare not her Y men; utterly destroy all her
	51:22	break in pieces the Y man and the maiden;
Lam	1:15	me to crush my Y men; the Lord has
	1:18	my maidens and my Y men have gone into
	2:21	the streets lie the Y and the old; my
	2:21	my maidens and my Y men have fallen by
	4:3	breast and suckle their Y, but the daughter of
	5:13	Y men are compelled to grind at the mill;
	5:14	the city gate, the Y men their music.
Bar	3:20	Y men have seen the light of day, and
Ezek	9:6	slay old men outright, Y men and maidens, little
	17:4	the topmost of its Y twigs and carried it
	17:22	the topmost of its Y twigs a tender one,
	19:2	in the midst of Y lions, rearing her whelps.
	19:3	whelps; he became a Y lion, and he learned
	19:5	and made him a Y lion.
	19:6	lions; he became a Y lion, and he learned
	23:6	all of them desirable Y men, horsemen riding on
	23:12	all of them desirable Y men.
	23:21	bosom and pressed your Y breasts."
	23:23	Assyrians with them, desirable Y men, governors and
	30:17	The Y men of On and of Pibeseth shall
	31:6	field brought forth their Y; and under its shadow
	41:19	the face of a Y lion toward the palm
	45:18	you shall take a Y bull without blemish, and
	45:22	of the land a Y bull for a sin
	45:23	to the LORD seven Y bulls and seven rams
	46:6	he shall offer a Y bull without blemish, and
	46:11	cereal offering with a Y bull shall be an
Dan	13:21	against you that a Y man was with you,
	13:37	Then a Y man, who had been hidden, came
	13:40	asked her who the Y man was, but she
	13:45	holy spirit of a Y lad named Daniel;
Hos	5:14	Ephraim, and like a Y lion to the house
Joel	2:28	dream dreams, and your Y men shall see visions.
Amos	2:11	and some of your Y men for Nazirites.
	3:4	Does a Y lion cry out from his den,
	4:10	Egypt; I slew your Y men with the sword;
	8:13	fair virgins and the Y men shall faint for
Mic	2:9	pleasant houses; from their Y children you take away
	5:8	the forest, like a Y lion among the flocks
Nah	2:11	the cave of the Y lions, where the lion
	2:13	sword shall devour your Y lions; I will cut
Zech	2:4	"Run, say to that Y man, 'Jerusalem shall be
	9:17	Grain shall make the Y men flourish, and new
1Mac	1:26	elders groaned, maidens and Y men became faint,
	11:39	bringing up Antiochus, the Y son of Alexander,
	11:54	and with him the Y boy Antiochus who began
	11:57	Then the Y Antiochus wrote to Jonathan, saying, "I
	13:31	treacherously with the Y king Antiochus; he killed
2Mac	3:26	Two Y men also appeared to him, remarkably strong,
	3:33	of atonement, the same Y men appeared again to
	4:12	the noblest of the Y men to wear the
	5:13	there was killing of Y and old, destruction of
	6:24	"lest many of the Y should suppose that Eleazar
	6:28	and leave to the Y a noble example of
	6:31	not only to the Y but to the great
	7:12	were astonished at the Y man's spirit, for he
	7:25	Since the Y man would not listen to him
	7:30	was still speaking, the Y man said, "What are
	10:35	the fifth day, twenty Y men in the army
	12:27	Stalwart Y men took their stand before the walls
	13:15	force of the bravest Y men, he attacked the
	15:17	the souls of the Y, they determined not to
Mt	19:20	The Y man said to him, "All these I
	19:22	When the Y man heard this he went away
Mk	14:51	And a Y man followed him, with nothing but
	16:5	tomb, they saw a Y man sitting on the
Lk	2:24	of turtledoves, or two Y pigeons."
	7:14	And he said, Y man, I say to you,
Jn	12:14	And Jesus found a Y ass and sat upon

21:18 you, when you were Y, you girded yourself and
Acts 2:17 shall prophesy, and your Y men shall see visions,
5:6 The Y men rose and wrapped him up and
5:10 When the Y men came in they found her
7:58 the feet of a Y man named Saul.
20:9 And a Y man named Eutychus was sitting in
23:17 and said, "Take this Y man to the tribune;
23:18 me to bring this Y man to you, as
23:22 the tribune dismissed the Y man, charging him, "Tell
Tit 2:4 and so train the Y women to love their
1Jn 2:13 am writing to you, Y men, because you have
2:14 I write to you, Y men, because you are

YOUNGER (30)

Gen 19:31 first-born said to the Y, "Our father is old,
19:34 first-born said to the Y, "Behold, I lay last
19:35 night also; and the Y arose, and lay with
19:38 The Y also bore a son, and called his
25:23 than the other, the elder shall serve the Y
27:15 them on Jacob her Y son;
27:42 and called Jacob her Y son, and said to
29:16 the name of the Y was Rachel.
29:18 seven years for your Y daughter Rachel."
29:26 country, to give the Y before the first-born.
48:14 Ephraim, who was the Y, and his left hand
48:19 be great; nevertheless his Y brother shall be greater
Judg 1:13 son of Kenaz, Caleb's Y brother, took it; and
3:9 son of Kenaz, Caleb's Y brother.
15:2 Is not her Y sister fairer than she?
1Sam 14:49 the name of the Y Michal;
1Chr 24:31 father's house and his Y brother alike, cast lots,
Job 30:1 me, men who are Y than I, whose fathers
Ezek 16:46 of you; and your Y sister, who lived to
16:61 your elder and your Y, and give them to
Mk 15:39 mother of James the Y and of Joses, and
Lk 15:12 two sons; and the Y of them said to
15:13 many days later, the Y son gathered all he
Rom 9:12 she was told, "The elder will serve the Y
1Tim 5:1 would a father; treat Y men like brothers,
5:2 older women like mothers, Y women like sisters, in
5:11 But refuse to enrol Y widows; for when they
5:14 So I would have Y widows marry, bear children,
Tit 2:6 Likewise urge the Y men to control themselves.
1Pet 5:5 Likewise you that are Y be subject to the

YOUNGEST (23)

Gen 9:24 and knew what his Y son had done to
42:13 Canaan; and behold, the Y is this day with
42:15 this place unless your Y brother comes here.
42:20 households, and bring your Y brother to me; so
42:32 no more, and the Y is this day with
42:34 Bring your Y brother to me; then I shall
43:29 said, "Is this your Y brother, of whom you
43:33 his birthright and the Y according to his youth;
44:2 the sack of the Y, with his money for
44:12 and ending with the Y; and the cup was
44:23 your servants, 'Unless your Y brother comes down
44:26 If our Y brother goes with us, then we
44:26 man's face unless our Y brother is with us.'
Josh 6:26 the cost of his Y son shall he set
Judg 9:5 stone; but Jotham the Y son of Jerubbaal was
1Sam 16:11 "There remains yet the Y, but behold, he is
17:14 David was the Y; the three eldest followed Saul,
1Kgs 16:34 the cost of his Y son Segub, according to
2Kgs 3:21 on armor, from the Y to the oldest, were
2Chr 21:17 him except Jehoahaz, his Y son.
22:1 Jerusalem made Ahaziah his Y son king in his
2Mac 7:24 The Y brother being still alive, Antiochus not only
Lk 22:26 you become as the Y, and the leader as

YOURSELF (250)

Gen 6:14 Make Y an ark of gopher wood; make rooms
13:9 Separate Y from me.
14:21 me the persons, but take the goods for Y
15:15 As for Y, you shall go to your fathers
30:29 said to him, "You Y know how I have
33:9 enough, my brother; keep what you have for Y
38:29 said, "What a breach you have made for Y
39:9 anything from me except Y, because you are his
Ex 9:17 You are still exalting Y against my people, and
10:3 you refuse to humble Y before me?
10:28 me; take heed to Y; never see my face
20:4 shall not make for Y a graven image, or
34:2 Mount Sinai, and present Y there to me on
34:12 Take heed to Y, lest you make a covenant
34:17 "You shall make for Y no molten gods.

Lev 9:7 and make atonement for Y and for the people;
18:20 neighbor's wife, and defile Y with her.
18:23 any beast and defile Y with it, neither shall
19:18 love your neighbor as Y: I am the LORD.
19:34 shall love him as Y; for you were strangers
25:6 food for you, for Y and for your male
Num 5:20 if you have defiled Y, and some man other
11:17 may not bear it Y alone.
16:13 you must also make Y a prince over us?
Deut 5:8 shall not make for Y a graven image, or
21:11 would take her for Y as wife,
22:7 you may take to Y; that it may go
22:12 "You shall make Y tassels on the four corners
22:12 corners of your cloak with which you cover Y
23:9 then you shall keep Y from every evil thing.
28:40 you shall not anoint Y with the oil; for
Judg 8:21 and Zalmunna said, "Rise Y, and fall upon us;
Ruth 3:3 Wash therefore and anoint Y, and put on your
3:3 but do not make Y known to the man
4:6 my right of redemption Y, for I cannot redeem
4:8 of kin said to Boaz, "Buy it for Y
1Sam 9:27 passed on stop here Y for a while, that
19:2 therefore take heed to Y in the morning, stay
19:2 secret place and hide Y;
20:8 in me, slay me Y; for why should you
20:19 place where you hid Y when the matter was
2Sam 5:24 balsam trees, then bestir Y; for then the LORD
14:2 garments; do not anoint Y with oil, but behave
16:21 that you have made Y odious to your father,
18:13 the king), then you Y would have stood aloof."
20:4 to me within three days, and be here Y
1Kgs 2:2 Be strong, and show Y a man,
2:36 said to him, "Build Y a house in Jerusalem,
3:11 have not asked for Y long life or riches
3:11 but have asked for Y understanding to discern what
11:31 to Jeroboam, "Take for Y ten pieces; for thus
13:7 with me, and refresh Y, and I will give
14:2 wife, "Arise, and disguise Y, that it be not
14:9 gone and made for Y other gods, and molten
17:3 turn eastward, and hide Y by the brook Cherith,
17:13 and afterward make for Y and your son.
18:1 year, saying, "Go, show Y to Ahab; and I
20:22 to him, "Come, strengthen Y, and consider well what
20:34 may establish bazaars for Y in Damascus, as my
20:40 your judgment be; you Y have decided it."
21:20 because you have sold Y to do what is
22:25 you go into an inner chamber to hide Y
2Kgs 2:2 lives, and as you Y live, I will not
2:4 lives, and as you Y live, I will not
2:6 lives, and as you Y live, I will not
4:4 shut the door upon Y and your sons, and
4:30 lives, and as you Y live, I will not
22:19 penitent, and you humbled Y before the LORD, when
2Chr 1:11 wisdom and knowledge for Y that you may rule
18:24 you go into an inner chamber to hide Y
21:13 who were better than Y;
21:15 your possessions, and you Y will have a severe
34:27 penitent and you humbled Y before God when you
34:27 and you have humbled Y before me, and have
Tob 4:9 a good treasure for Y against the day of
4:13 take a wife for Y from among them.
4:14 "Watch Y, my son, in everything you do, and
5:14 day, and expenses for Y as for my son?
Job 15:8 And do you limit wisdom to Y
18:4 You who tear Y in your anger, shall the
22:23 the Almighty and humble Y, if you remove
22:26 then you will delight Y in the Almighty, and
35:8 concerns a man like Y, and your righteousness a
40:10 "Deck Y with majesty and dignity; clothe yourself
40:10 majesty and dignity; clothe Y with glory and splendor.
Ps 37:1 Fret not Y because of the wicked, be not
37:7 for him; fret not Y over him who prospers
37:8 Fret not Y; it tends only to evil.
50:21 silent; you thought that I was one like Y
Prov 5:17 Let them be for Y alone, and not for
6:3 my son, and save Y, for you have come
6:5 eyelids no slumber; save Y like a gazelle from
9:12 you are wise for Y; if you scoff, you
22:25 his ways and entangle Y in a snare.
24:19 Fret not Y because of evildoers, and be not
25:6 Do not put Y forward in the king's presence
26:4 to his folly, lest you be like him Y
30:32 have been foolish, exalting Y, or if you have
Eccl 2:1 I will make a test of pleasure; enjoy Y
7:16 and do not make Y overwise; why should you
7:16 make yourself overwise; why should you destroy Y

7:22 many times you have Y cursed others.
Sir 1:27 Do not exalt Y lest you fall, and thus
1:27 lest you fall, and thus bring dishonor upon Y
2:1 serve the Lord, prepare Y for temptation.
3:10 Do not glorify Y by dishonoring your father, for
3:18 more you must humble Y; so you will find
4:7 Make Y beloved in the congregation; bow your head
4:20 of evil; and do not bring shame on Y
4:27 Do not subject Y to a foolish fellow, nor
6:2 Do not exalt Y through your soul's counsel, lest
6:13 Keep Y far from your enemies, and be on
6:32 and if you apply Y you will become clever.
7:7 and do not disgrace Y among the people.
7:14 the elders, nor repeat Y in your prayer.
7:16 Do not count Y among the crowd of sinners;
7:17 Humble Y greatly, for the punishment of the ungodly
7:19 Do not deprive Y of a wise and good
7:24 and do not show Y too indulgent with them.
7:26 but do not trust Y to one whom you
8:8 the sages, but busy Y with their maxims; because
9:2 Do not give Y to a woman so that
9:6 Do not give Y to harlots lest you lose
10:25 your work, nor glorify Y at a time when
10:27 My son, glorify Y with humility, and ascribe to
10:27 humility, and ascribe to Y honor according to your
11:4 fine clothes, nor exalt Y in the day that
11:10 son, do not busy Y with many matters; if
12:11 goes about cringing, watch Y, and be on your
13:13 Keep words to Y and be very watchful, for
14:11 My son, treat Y well, according to your means,
14:14 Do not deprive Y of a happy day; let
14:16 and take, and beguile Y, because in Hades one
18:19 Before judgment, examine Y, and in the hour of
18:20 Before falling ill, humble Y, and when you are
18:22 making a vow, prepare Y; and do not be
22:11 an unintelligent man; guard Y from him to escape
25:25 not go as you direct, separate her from Y
29:20 but take heed to Y lest you fall.
30:21 Do not give Y over to sorrow, and do
30:21 and do not afflict Y deliberately.
32:1 feast, do not exalt Y; be among them as
32:12 Amuse Y there, and do what you have in
32:23 Guard Y in every act, for this is the
33:19 not give power over Y, as long as you
33:30 let him be as Y, because you have bought
37:29 and do not give Y up to food;
38:21 do the dead no good, and you injure Y
Is 22:16 here a tomb for Y, you who hew a
22:16 carve a habitation for Y in the rock?
33:1 to you, destroyer, who Y have not been destroyed;
51:17 Rouse Y, rouse yourself, stand up, O Jerusalem, you
51:17 Rouse yourself, rouse Y, stand up, O Jerusalem, you
52:2 Shake Y from the dust, arise, O captive Jerusalem;
57:8 made a bargain for Y with them, you have
58:7 and not to hide Y from your own flesh?
58:10 wickedness, if you pour Y out for the hungry
65:5 who say, "Keep to Y, do not come near
Jer 2:17 not brought this upon Y by forsaking the LORD
2:22 Though you wash Y with lye and use much
2:28 where are your gods that you made for Y
4:30 scarlet, that you deck Y with ornaments of gold,
4:30 In vain you beautify Y
13:21 you those whom you Y have taught to be
20:4 you a terror to Y and to all your
27:2 said to me: "Make Y thongs and yoke-bars, and
31:4 Again you shall adorn Y with timbrels, and shall
31:21 "Set up waymarks for Y, make yourself guideposts;
31:21 waymarks for yourself, make Y guideposts; consider
32:8 yours; buy it for Y Then I knew that
38:23 the Chaldeans, and you Y shall not escape from
45:5 And do you seek great things for Y
47:6 Put Y into your scabbard, rest and be still!
Lam 2:18 Give Y no rest, your eyes no respite!
4:21 become drunk and strip Y bare.
Ezek 3:24 to me, "Go, shut Y within your house.
12:3 of man, prepare for Y an exile's baggage, and
12:4 you shall go forth Y at evening in their
16:16 garments, and made for Y gaily decked shrines, and
16:17 you, and made for Y images of men, and
16:24 Lord GOD), you built Y a vaulted chamber, and
16:24 vaulted chamber, and made Y a lofty place in
16:25 prostituted your beauty, offering Y to any passer-by,
23:30 the nations, and polluted Y with their idols.
23:40 For them you bathed Y, painted your eyes, and
23:40 your eyes, and decked Y with ornaments;
28:2 god, though you consider Y as wise as a
28:4 have gotten wealth for Y, and have gathered gold
28:6 GOD: "Because you consider Y as wise as a
32:2 to him: "You consider Y a lion among the
38:14 securely, you will bestir Y
Dan 5:17 your gifts be for Y, and give your rewards
5:23 you have lifted up Y against the Lord of
10:12 to understand and humbled Y before your God, your
14:11 are going outside; you Y, O king, shall set
Hos 1:2 Hosea, "Go, take to Y a wife of harlotry
Amos 7:17 out by line; you Y shall die in an
Hab 2:16 Drink, Y, and stagger!
1Mac 12:45 homes and choose for Y a few men to
2Mac 7:18 said, "Do not deceive Y in vain.
Mt 4:6 Son of God, throw Y down; for it is
8:4 one; but go, show Y to the priest, and
17:26 give it to them for me and for Y
19:19 mother, and, You shall love your neighbor as Y
22:39 like it, You shall love your neighbor as Y
27:4 See to it Y
27:40 temple and build it in three days, save Y
Mk 1:44 one; but go, show Y to the priest, and
12:31 love your neighbor as Y There is no other
15:29 in three days, save Y, and come down from
Lk 4:9 Son of God, throw Y down from here;
4:23 this proverb, 'Physician, heal Y; what we have heard
5:14 but "go and show Y to the priest, and
6:42 your eye,' when you Y do not see the
7:6 "Lord, do not trouble Y, for I am not
10:27 with all your mind; and your neighbor as Y
17:8 for me, and gird Y and serve me, till
23:36 you are the King of the Jews, save Y
23:38 Save Y and us!"
Jn 1:22 What do you say about Y
7:4 do these things, show Y to the world."
8:13 are bearing witness to Y; your testimony is not
10:33 being a man, make Y God."
14:22 that you will manifest Y to us, and not
21:18 were young, you girded Y and walked where you
Acts 12:8 said to him, "Dress Y and put on your
16:28 voice, "Do not harm Y, for we are all
21:24 these men and purify Y along with them and
21:24 you but that you Y live in observance of
24:7 By examining him Y you will be able to
26:1 to Paul, "You have permission to speak for Y
Rom 2:1 upon him you condemn Y, because you, the judge,
2:3 and yet do them Y, you will escape the
2:5 storing up wrath for Y on the day of
2:17 But if you call Y a Jew and rely
2:21 then who teach others, will you not teach Y
13:9 this sentence, "You shall love your neighbor as Y
14:22 you have, keep between Y and God; happy is
1Cor 7:21 gain your freedom, avail Y of the opportunity.
Gal 5:14 one word, "You shall love your neighbor as Y
6:1 Look to Y, lest you too be tempted.
1Tim 4:7 Train Y in godliness;
4:15 Practice these duties, devote Y to them, so that
4:16 Take heed to Y and to your teaching; hold
4:16 you will save both Y and your hearers.
5:22 another man's sins; keep Y pure.
2Tim 2:15 your best to present Y to God as one
4:15 Beware of him Y, for he strongly opposed our
Tit 2:7 Show Y in all respects a model of good
Jas 2:8 the scripture, "You shall love your neighbor as Y

YOURSELVES (230)

Gen 18:4 your feet, and rest Y under the tree,
18:5 that you may refresh Y, and after that you
34:9 daughters to us, and take our daughters for Y
35:2 among you, and purify Y, and change your garments;
45:5 distressed, or angry with Y, because you sold me
47:24 and as food for Y and your households, and
49:1 sons, and said, "Gather Y together, that I may
Ex 5:11 Go Y, get your straw wherever you can find
7:9 says to you, 'Prove Y by working a miracle,'
12:21 them, "Select lambs for Y according to your families,
18:18 with you will wear Y out, for the thing
20:22 'You have seen for Y that I have talked
20:23 shall you make for Y gods of gold.
30:15 give the LORD's offering to make atonement for Y
30:16 the LORD, so as to make atonement for Y
30:37 shall not make for Y; it shall be for
32:29 "Today you have ordained Y for the service of
Lev 11:43 You shall not make Y abominable with any swarming
11:43 you shall not defile Y with them, lest you
11:44 LORD your God; consecrate Y therefore, and be holy,
11:44 You shall not defile Y with any swarming thing

16:29 month, you shall afflict Y, and shall do no
16:31 and you shall afflict Y; it is a statute
18:24 "Do not defile Y by any of these things,
18:30 and never to defile Y by them: I am
19:4 idols or make for Y molten gods: I am
20:7 Consecrate Y therefore, and be holy; for I am
20:25 you shall not make Y abominable by beast or
23:27 and you shall afflict Y and present an offering
23:32 and you shall afflict Y; on the ninth day
26:1 "You shall make for Y no idols and erect
Num 11:18 to the people, 'Consecrate Y for tomorrow, and you
16:3 then do you exalt Y above the assembly of
16:21 Aaron, "Separate Y from among this congregation,
29:7 holy convocation, and afflict Y; you shall do no
31:18 man by lying with him, keep alive for Y
31:19 touched any slain, purify Y and your captives on
Deut 4:15 "Therefore take good heed to Y
4:16 a graven image for Y, in the form of
4:23 Take heed to Y, lest you forget the covenant
4:38 greater and mightier than Y, to bring you in,
7:1 greater and mightier than Y,
7:25 or take it for Y, lest you be ensnared
9:1 greater and mightier than Y, cities great and fortified
9:16 God; you had made Y a molten calf; you
11:23 will dispossess nations greater and mightier than Y
14:1 you shall not cut Y or make any baldness
20:14 take as booty for Y; and you shall enjoy
28:68 there you shall offer Y for sale to your
31:14 call Joshua, and present Y in the tent of
Josh 2:16 meet you; and hide Y there three days, until
3:5 to the people, "Sanctify Y; for tomorrow the LORD
6:18 But you, keep Y from the things devoted to
7:13 people, and say, 'Sanctify Y for tomorrow; for thus
8:2 take as booty for Y; lay an ambush against
8:4 the city, but hold Y all in readiness;
10:19 do not stay there Y, pursue your enemies, fall
17:15 there clear ground for Y in the land of
22:16 the LORD, by building Y an altar this day
22:19 stands, and take for Y a possession among us;
22:19 as rebels by building Y an altar other than
23:7 them, or bow down Y to them,
23:11 Take good heed to Y, therefore, to love the
24:22 "You are witnesses against Y that you have chosen
Judg 15:12 me that you will not fall upon me Y
1Sam 2:29 above me by fattening Y upon the choicest parts
4:9 Take courage, and acquit Y like men, O Philistines,
4:9 been to you; acquit Y like men and fight."
8:18 you have chosen for Y; but the LORD will
10:19 us.' Now therefore present Y before the LORD by
12:17 LORD, in asking for Y a king."
14:34 And Saul said, "Disperse Y among the people, and
16:5 to the LORD; consecrate Y, and come with me
17:8 Choose a man for Y, and let him come
1Kgs 18:25 of Baal, "Choose for Y one bull and prepare
2Kgs 17:35 other gods or bow Y to them or serve
17:36 arm; you shall bow Y to him, and to
1Chr 15:12 of the Levites; sanctify Y, you and your brethren,
2Chr 13:9 and made priests for Y like the peoples of
29:5 Now sanctify Y, and sanctify the house of the
29:31 "You have now consecrated Y to the LORD; come
30:8 fathers were, but yield Y to the LORD, and
35:4 Prepare Y according to your fathers' houses by your
35:6 passover lamb, and sanctify Y, and prepare for your
Ezra 10:11 do his will; separate Y from the peoples of
Neh 13:25 take their daughters for your sons or for Y
Jud 8:12 day, and are setting Y up in the place
Job 19:5 If indeed you magnify Y against me, and make
27:12 you have seen it Y; why then have you
42:8 and offer up for Y a burnt offering; and
Sir 51:25 Get these things for Y without money.
Is 1:16 Wash Y; make yourselves clean; remove the evil of
1:16 Wash yourselves; make Y clean; remove the evil of
8:9 you far countries; gird Y and be dismayed; gird
8:9 and be dismayed; gird Y and be dismayed.
26:20 doors behind you; hide Y for a little while
29:9 Stupefy Y and be in a stupor, blind yourselves
29:9 in a stupor, blind Y and be blind!
32:11 ones; strip, and make Y bare, and gird sackcloth
45:20 "Assemble Y and come, draw near together, you
52:11 midst of her, purify Y, you who bear the
55:2 is good, and delight Y in fatness.
Jer 4:4 Circumcise Y to the LORD, remove the foreskin of
26:15 bring innocent blood upon Y and upon this city
37:9 LORD, Do not deceive Y, saying, "The Chaldeans will
44:7 this great evil against Y, to cut off from
46:19 Prepare Y baggage for exile, O inhabitants of Egypt!
47:5 of the Anakim, how long will you gash Y
48:6 Save Y
49:3 Gird Y with sackcloth, lament, and run to and
49:14 among the nations: "Gather Y together and come
50:14 Set Y in array against Babylon round about, all
Ezek 18:31 against me, and get Y a new heart and
20:7 and do not defile Y with the idols of
20:18 their ordinances, nor defile Y with their idols.
20:30 GOD: Will you defile Y after the manner of
20:31 by fire, you defile Y with all your idols
20:43 which you have polluted Y; and you shall loathe
20:43 and you shall loathe Y for all the evils
34:2 Ho, shepherds of Israel who have been feeding Y
34:3 the fat, you clothe Y with the wool, you
35:13 devour.' And you magnified Y against me with your
36:31 and you will loathe Y for your iniquities and
47:22 as an inheritance for Y and for the aliens
Hos 10:12 Sow for Y righteousness, reap the fruit of steadfast
Joel 3:11 nations round about, gather Y there.
Amos 3:9 Egypt, and say, "Assemble Y upon the mountains of
5:26 which you made for Y;
Mic 1:10 all; in Beth-le-aphrah roll Y in the dust.
1:16 Make Y bald and cut off your hair, for
1:16 of your delight; make Y as bald as the
6:15 olives, but not anoint Y with oil; you shall
Nah 3:15 Multiply Y like the locust, multiply like the
Hag 1:4 a time for you Y to dwell in your
1:6 your fill; you clothe Y, but no one is
1:9 ruins, while you busy Y each with his own
Zech 7:6 you not eat for Y and drink for yourselves?
7:6 you not eat for yourselves and drink for Y
Mal 2:15 So take heed to Y, and let none be
2:16 So take heed to Y and do not be
1Mac 3:58 And Judas said, "Gird Y and be valiant.
13:3 saying to them, "You Y know what great things
2Mac 7:23 since you now forget Y for the sake of
Mt 3:9 presume to say to Y, 'We have Abraham as
6:19 not lay up for Y treasures on earth, where
6:20 but lay up for Y treasures in heaven, where
16:8 do you discuss among Y the fact that you
23:13 for you neither enter Y, nor allow those who
23:14 twice as much a child of hell as Y
23:30 Thus you witness against Y, that you are sons
25:9 dealers and buy for Y
27:24 of this righteous man's blood; see to it Y
Mk 6:31 them, "Come away by Y to a lonely place,
9:48 Have salt in Y, and be at peace with
13:9 "But take heed to Y; for they will deliver
Lk 3:8 begin to say to Y, 'We have Abraham as
11:46 to bear, and you Y do not touch the
11:52 you did not enter Y, and you hindered those
12:33 and give alms; provide Y with purses that do
12:57 you not judge for Y what is right?
13:28 of God and you Y thrust out.
16:9 you, make friends for Y by means of unrighteous
16:15 are those who justify Y before men, but God
17:3 Take heed to Y; if your brother sins, rebuke
17:14 them, "Go and show Y to the priests." And
21:30 leaf, you see for Y and know that the
21:34 "But take heed to Y lest your hearts be
22:17 and divide it among Y;
23:27 me, but weep for Y and for your children.
Jn 3:28 You Y bear me witness, that I said, I
6:43 Jesus answered them, "Do not murmur among Y
7:8 Go to the feast Y; I am not going
16:19 what you are asking Y, what I meant by
18:31 to them, "Take him Y and judge him by
19:6 to them, "Take him Y and crucify him, for
Acts 2:22 your midst, as you Y know—
2:40 exhorted them, saying, "Save Y from this crooked
10:28 said to them, "You Y know how unlawful it
13:46 from you, and judge Y unworthy of eternal life,
15:29 If you keep Y from these, you will do
18:15 law, see to it Y; I refuse to be
20:18 said to them: "You Y know how I lived
20:28 Take heed to Y and to all the flock,
20:34 You Y know that these hands ministered to my
Rom 1:6 all the nations, including Y who are called to
6:11 you also must consider Y dead to sin and
6:13 of wickedness, but yield Y to God as men
6:16 that if you yield Y to any one as
12:19 Beloved, never avenge Y, but leave it to the
15:14 my brethren, that you Y are full of goodness,
1Cor 6:8 But you Y wrong and defraud, and that even
7:5 that you may devote Y to prayer; but then
10:15 sensible men; judge for Y what I say.

11:13 from God.) Judge for Y; is it proper for
14:9 So with Y; if you in a tongue utter
14:12 So with Y; since you are eager for manifestations
2Cor 3:2 You Y are our letter of recommendation, written on
7:11 eagerness to clear Y, what indignation, what alarm,
7:11 point you have proved Y guiltless in the matter.
11:19 For you gladly bear with fools, being wise Y
13:5 Examine Y, to see whether you are holding to
13:5 Test Y
Phil 2:3 conceit, but in humility count others better than Y
2:5 Have this mind among Y, which is yours in
4:15 And you Philippians Y know that in the beginning
Col 1:6 and growing—so among Y, from the day you
4:5 Conduct Y wisely toward outsiders, making the most
4:9 faithful and beloved brother, who is one of Y
4:12 who is one of Y, a servant of Christ
1Thes 2:1 For you Y know, brethren, that our visit to
3:3 You Y know that this is to be our
4:9 to you, for you Y have been taught by
5:2 For you Y know well that the day of
5:13 Be at peace among Y
2Thes 3:7 For you Y know how you ought to imitate
Heb 10:34 you knew that you Y had a better possession
Jas 1:21 of the word, and not hearers only, deceiving Y
2:4 not made distinctions among Y, and become judges
4:7 Submit Y therefore to God.
4:10 Humble Y before the Lord and he will exalt
1Pet 1:15 is holy, be holy Y in all your conduct;
1:17 to his deeds, conduct Y with fear throughout the
2:5 like living stones be Y built into a spiritual
4:1 in the flesh, arm Y with the same thought,
5:5 Clothe Y, all of you, with humility toward one
5:6 Humble Y therefore under the mighty hand of God,
1Jn 5:21 Little children, keep Y from idols.
2Jn 1:8 Look to Y, that you may not lose what
Jude 1:20 But you, beloved, build Y up on your most
1:21 the Holy Spirit; keep Y in the love of

YOUTH (91)

Gen 8:21 is evil from his Y; neither will I ever
43:33 youngest according to his Y; and the men looked
46:34 of cattle from our Y even until now, both
Lev 22:13 house, as in her Y, she may eat of
Num 30:3 father's house, in her Y,
30:16 daughter, while in her Y, within her father's house.
Judg 8:20 But the Y did not draw his sword; for
8:20 he was afraid, because he was still a Y
1Sam 12:2 before you from my Y until this day.
17:33 you are but a Y, and he has been
17:33 has been a man of war from his Y
17:42 he was but a Y, ruddy and comely in
17:55 of the army, "Abner, whose son is this Y
20:22 I say to the Y, 'Look, the arrows are
2Sam 19:7 upon you from your Y until now."
1Kgs 18:12 your servant have revered the LORD from my Y
Job 13:26 and makest me inherit the iniquities of my Y
31:18 it (for from his Y I reared him as
33:25 flesh become fresh with Y; let him return to
36:14 They die in Y, and their life ends in
Ps 25:7 the sins of my Y, or my transgressions; according
71:5 my hope, my trust, O LORD, from my Y
71:17 O God, from my Y thou hast taught me,
88:15 to death from my Y up, I suffer thy
89:45 the days of his Y; thou hast covered him
103:5 live so that your Y is renewed like the
110:3 morning like dew your Y will come to you.
127:4 of a warrior are the sons of one's Y
129:1 "Sorely have they afflicted me from my Y
129:2 afflicted me from my Y, yet they have not
144:12 our sons in their Y be like plants full-grown,
Prov 1:4 and discretion to the Y—
2:17 the companion of her Y and forgets the covenant
5:18 the wife of your Y,
Eccl 4:13 a poor and wise Y than an old and
4:15 as well as that Y, who was to stand
11:9 young man, in your Y, and let your heart
11:9 the days of your Y; walk in the ways
11:10 from your body; for Y and the dawn of
12:1 the days of your Y, before the evil days
Wis 2:6 of the creation to the full as in Y
4:16 who are living, and Y that is quickly perfected
8:2 sought her from my Y, and I desired to
Sir 6:18 My son, from your Y up choose instruction, and
7:23 them, and make them obedient from their Y
15:2 the wife of his Y she will welcome him.
25:3 gathered nothing in your Y; how then can you
30:11 no authority in his Y, and do not ignore
30:12 his neck in his Y, and beat his sides
47:4 In his Y did he not kill a giant,
47:14 How wise you became in your Y
51:15 straight path; from my Y I followed her steps.
Is 3:5 man his neighbor; the Y will be insolent to
47:12 have labored from your Y; perhaps you may be
47:15 with you from your Y; they wander about each
54:4 the shame of your Y, and the reproach of
54:6 like a wife of Y when she is cast
Jer 1:6 how to speak, for I am only a Y
1:7 'I am only a Y; for to all to
2:2 the devotion of your Y, your love as a
3:4 the friend of my Y—
3:24 "But from our Y the shameful thing has devoured
3:25 our fathers, from our Y even to this day;
22:21 your way from your Y, that you have not
31:19 the disgrace of my Y
32:30 my sight from their Y; the sons of Israel
48:11 at ease from his Y and has settled on
51:22 old man and the Y; with you I break
Lam 3:27 man that he bear the yoke in his Y
Ezek 4:14 defiled myself; from my Y up till now I
16:22 the days of your Y, when you were naked
16:43 the days of your Y, but have enraged me
16:60 the days of your Y, and I will establish
23:3 the harlot in their Y; there their breasts were
23:8 Egypt; for in her Y men had lain with
23:19 the days of her Y, when she played the
23:21 the lewdness of your Y, when the Egyptians handled
Hos 2:15 the days of her Y, as at the time
Joel 1:8 girded with sackcloth for the bridegroom of her Y
Zech 13:5 my possession since my Y
Mal 2:14 the wife of your Y, to whom you have
2:15 none be faithless to the wife of his Y
1Mac 1:6 up with him from Y, and divided his kingdom
2:66 mighty warrior from his Y; he shall command the
16:2 of Israel from our Y until this day, and
2Mac 4:9 and a body of Y for it, and to
7:25 her to advise the Y to save himself.
Mk 10:20 "Teacher, all these I have observed from my Y
Lk 18:21 said, "All these I have observed from my Y
Acts 26:4 of life from my Y, spent from the beginning
1Tim 4:12 no one despise your Y, but set the believers

YOUTHFUL (4)

Job 20:11 bones are full of Y vigor, but it will
33:25 the days of his Y vigor';
2Mac 15:30 man who maintained his Y good will toward his
2Tim 2:22 So shun Y passions and aim at righteousness, faith,

YOUTHS (10)

Prov 7:7 have perceived among the Y, a young man without
Is 40:30 Even Y shall faint and be weary, and young
Jer 18:21 death by pestilence, their Y be slain by the
Dan 1:4 and of the nobility, Y without blemish, handsome and
1:10 poorer condition than the Y who are of your
1:13 the appearance of the Y who eat the king's
1:15 flesh than all the Y who ate the king's
1:17 As for these four Y, God gave them learning
1Mac 2:9 in her streets, her Y by the sword of
14:9 good things; and the Y donned the glories and

Z

ZA-ANANNIM (2)

Josh 19:33 from the oak in Z, and Adami-nekeb, and Jabneel,
Judg 4:11 as the oak in Z, which is near Kedesh.

ZAANAN

Mic 1:11 shame; the inhabitants of Z do not come forth;

ZAAVAN (2)

Gen 36:27 sons of Ezer: Bilhan, Z, and Akan.
1Chr 1:42 sons of Ezer: Bilhan, Z, and Jaakan.

ZABAD (8)

1Chr 2:36 was the father of Nathan and Nathan of Z
2:37 Z was the father of Ephlal, and Ephlal of
7:21 son, Tahath his son, Z his son, Shuthelah his
11:41 Ithrite, Uriah the Hittite, Z the son of Ahlai,
2Chr 24:26 conspired against him were Z the son of Shimeath
Ezra 10:27 Eli-o-enai, Eliashib, Mattaniah, Jeremoth, Z, and
10:33 of Hashum: Mattenai, Mattattah, Z, Eliphelet,

10:43 of Nebo: Je-iel, Mattithiah, Z, Zebina, Jaddai, Joel,

ZABADEANS
1Mac 12:31 Arabs who are called Z, and he crushed them

ZABBAI (2)
Ezra 10:28 Bebai were Jehohanan, Hananiah, Z, and Athlai.
Neh 3:20 Baruch the son of Z repaired another section from

ZABDI (6)
Josh 7:1 of Carmi, son of Z, son of Zerah, of
7:17 man by man, and Z was taken;
7:18 of Carmi, son of Z, son of Zerah, of
1Chr 8:19 Jakim, Zichri, Z,
27:27 the wine cellars was Z the Shiphmite.
Neh 11:17 of Mica, son of Z, son of Asaph, who

ZABDIEL (3)
1Chr 27:2 Jashobeam the son of Z was in charge of
Neh 11:14 twenty-eight; their overseer was Z the son of.
1Mac 11:17 And Z the Arab cut off the head of

ZABUD
1Kgs 4:5 was over the officers; Z the son of Nathan

ZACCAI (2)
Ezra 2:9 The sons of Z, seven hundred and sixty.
Neh 7:14 The sons of Z, seven hundred and sixty.

ZACCHAEUS (4)
2Mac 10:19 and Joseph, and also Z and his men, a
Lk 19:2 was a man named Z; he was a chief
19:5 and said to him, Z, make haste and come
19:8 And Z stood and said to the Lord, "Behold,

ZACCUR (10)
Num 13:4 Shammua the son of Z;
1Chr 4:26 Mishma: Hammu-el his son, Z his son, Shimei his
24:27 of Ja-aziah, Beno, Shoham, Z, and Ibri.
25:2 the sons of Asaph: Z, Joseph, Nethaniah, and
25:10 twelve; the third to Z, his sons and his
Ezra 8:14 of Bigvai, Uthai and Z, and with them seventy
Neh 3:2 And next to them Z the son of Imri
10:12 Mica, Rehob, Hashabiah, Z, Sherebiah, Shebaniah,
12:35 of Micaiah, son of Z, son of Asaph;
13:13 Hanan the son of Z, son of Mattaniah, for

ZADOK (55)
2Sam 8:17 Ahilud was recorder; and Z the son of Ahitub
15:24 came up, and lo, Z came also, with all
15:25 the king said to Z, "Carry the ark of
15:27 king also said to Z the priest, "Look, go
15:29 So Z and Abiathar carried the ark of God
15:35 Are not Z and Abiathar the priests with you
15:35 house, tell it to Z and Abiathar the priests.
15:36 there, Ahima-az, Z's son, and Jonathan, Abiathar's
17:15 Then Hushai said to Z and Abiathar the priests,
18:19 Ahima-az the son of Z, "Let me run, and
18:22 Ahima-az the son of Z said again to Joab,
18:27 like the running of Ahima-az the son of Z
19:11 sent this message to Z and Abiathar the priests,
20:25 Sheva was secretary; and Z and Abiathar were
1Kgs 1:8 But Z the priest, and Benaiah the son of
1:26 me, your servant, and Z the priest, and Benaiah
1:32 said, "Call to me Z the priest, Nathan the
1:34 to Gihon; and let Z the priest and Nathan
1:38 So Z the priest, Nathan the prophet, and Benaiah
1:39 There Z the priest took the horn of oil
1:44 has sent with him Z the priest, Nathan the
1:45 the king's mule; and Z the priest and Nathan
2:35 and the king put Z the priest in the
4:2 Azariah the son of Z was the priest;
4:4 command of the army; Z and Abiathar were priests;
2Kgs 15:33 His mother's name was Jerusha the daughter of Z
1Chr 6:8 of Ahitub, Ahitub of Z, Zadok of Ahima-az,
6:8 Ahitub, Ahitub of Zadok, Z of Ahima-az,
6:12 of Ahitub, Ahitub of Z, Zadok of Shallum,
6:12 Ahitub, Ahitub of Zadok, Z of Shallum,
6:53 son, Ahitub his son, Z his son, Ahima-az his
9:11 of Meshullam, son of Z, son of Meraioth, son
12:28 Z, a young man mighty in valor, and twenty-two
15:11 David summoned the priests Z and Abiathar, and the
16:39 And he left Z the priest and his brethren
18:16 Ahilud was recorder; and Z the son of Ahitub
24:3 With the help of Z of the sons of
24:6 and the princes, and Z the priest, and Ahimelech
24:31 presence of King David, Z, Ahimelech, and the heads
27:17 of Kemuel; for Aaron, Z;
29:22 for the LORD, and Z as priest.
2Chr 27:1 His mother's name was Jerushah the daughter of Z
31:10 of the house of Z, answered him, "Since they
Ezra 7:2 of Shallum, son of Z, son of Ahitub,
Neh 3:4 And next to them Z the son of Baana
3:29 After them Z the son of Immer repaired opposite
10:21 Magpiash, Meshullam, Hezir, Meshezabel, Z,
11:11 of Meshullam, son of Z, son of Meraioth, son
13:13 storehouses Shelemiah the priest, Z the scribe, and
Ezek 40:46 are the sons of Z, who alone among the
43:19 of the family of Z, who draw near to
44:15 priests, the sons of Z, who kept the charge
48:11 priests, the sons of Z, who kept my charge,
Mt 1:14 Azor the father of Z, and Zadok the father
1:14 father of Zadok, and Z the father of Achim,

ZAHAM
2Chr 11:19 and she bore him sons, Jeush, Shemariah, and Z

ZAIR
2Kgs 8:21 Joram passed over to Z with all his chariots,

ZALAPH
Neh 3:30 the sixth son of Z repaired another section.

ZALMON (3)
Judg 9:48 went up to Mount Z, he and all the
2Sam 23:28 Mebunnai the Hushathite, Z the Ahohite, Maharai
Ps 68:14 the Almighty scattered kings there, snow fell on Z

ZALMONAH (2)
Num 33:41 set out from Mount Hor, and encamped at Z
33:42 they set out from Z, and encamped at Punon.

ZALMUNNA (12)
Judg 8:5 pursuing after Zebah and Z, the kings of Midian."
8:6 said, "Are Zebah and Z already in your hand,
8:7 has given Zebah and Z into my hand, I
8:10 Now Zebah and Z were in Karkor with their
8:12 And Zebah and Z fled; and he pursued them
8:12 of Midian, Zebah and Z, and he threw all
8:15 said, "Behold Zebah and Z, about whom you taunted
8:15 saying, 'Are Zebah and Z already in your hand,
8:18 said to Zebah and Z, "Where are the men
8:21 Then Zebah and Z said, "Rise yourself, and fall
8:21 and slew Zebah and Z; and he took the
Ps 83:11 princes like Zebah and Z,

ZAMZUMMIM
Deut 2:20 the Ammonites call them Z,

ZANOAH (5)
Josh 15:34 lowland, Eshtaol, Zorah, Ashnah, Z, En-gannim,
15:56 Ziph, Juttah, Jezreel, Jokde-am, Z,
1Chr 4:18 father of Soco, and Jekuthiel the father of Z
Neh 3:13 and the inhabitants of Z repaired the Valley Gate;
11:30 in Zorah, in Jarmuth, Z, Adullam, and their villages,

ZAPHENATH-PANEAH
Gen 41:45 Pharaoh called Joseph's name Z; and he gave him

ZAPHON (2)
Josh 13:27 Beth-haram, Beth-nimrah, Succoth, and Z, the rest
Judg 12:1 and they crossed to Z and said to Jephthah,

ZAREPHATH (4)
1Kgs 17:9 him, "Arise, go to Z, which belongs to Sidon,
17:10 arose and went to Z; and when he came
Obad 1:20 Phoenicia as far as Z; and the exiles of
Lk 4:26 them but only to Z, in the land of

ZARETHAN (3)
Josh 3:16 city that is beside Z, and those flowing down
1Kgs 4:12 Beth-shean which is beside Z below Jezreel, and
7:46 them, in the clay ground between Succoth and Z

ZATTU (5)
Ezra 2:8 The sons of Z, nine hundred and forty-five.
8:5 Of the sons of Z, Shecaniah the son of
10:27 Of the sons of Z: Eli-o-enai, Eliashib, Mattaniah,
Neh 7:13 The sons of Z, eight hundred and forty-five.
10:14 people: Parosh, Pahath-moab, Elam, Z, Bani,

ZAZA

1Chr 2:33 The sons of Jonathan: Peleth and Z

ZEAL (27)

2Sam 21:2 slay them in his Z for the people of
2Kgs 10:16 me, and see my Z for the LORD." So
19:31 The Z of the LORD will do this.
Ps 69:9 For Z for thy house has consumed me, and
119:139 My Z consumes me, because my foes forget thy
Wis 5:17 Lord will take his Z as his whole armor,
14:17 so that by their Z they might flatter the
Sir 48:2 them, and by his Z he made them few
Is 9:7 The Z of the LORD of hosts will do
26:11 Let them see thy Z for thy people, and
37:32 The Z of the LORD of hosts will accomplish
63:15 Where are thy Z and thy might?
Bar 4:28 God, return with tenfold Z to seek him.
1Mac 2:24 it, be burned with Z and his heart was
2:26 Thus he burned with Z for the law, as
2:50 Now, my children, show Z for the law, and
2:58 Elijah because of great Z for the law was
2Mac 14:38 he had with all Z risked body and life.
Jn 2:17 that it was written, Z for thy house will
Rom 10:2 that they have a Z for God, but it
12:8 who gives aid, with Z; he who does acts
12:11 Never flag in Z, be aglow with the Spirit,
2Cor 7:7 longing, your mourning, your Z for me, so that
7:11 alarm, what longing, what Z, what punishment!
7:12 in order that your Z for us might be
9:2 last year; and your Z has stirred up most
Phil 3:6 a Pharisee, as to Z a persecutor of the

ZEALOT (3)

2Mac 4:2 fellow countrymen, and a Z for the laws.
Lk 6:15 who was called the Z,
Acts 1:13 Alphaeus and Simon the Z and Judas the son

ZEALOUS (14)

Jud 9:4 beloved sons, who were Z for thee, and abhorred
Sir 27:3 is not steadfast and Z in the fear of
45:23 glory, for he was Z in the fear of
51:18 wisdom, and I was Z for the good; and
1Mac 2:27 every one who is Z for the law and
2:54 because he was deeply Z, received the covenant of
Acts 21:20 believed; they are all Z for the law,
22:3 of our fathers, being Z for God as you
Gal 1:14 my people, so extremely Z was I for the
Tit 2:14 his own who are Z for good deeds.
1Pet 3:13 you if you are Z for what is right?
2Pet 1:10 brethren, be the more Z to confirm your call
3:14 wait for these, be Z to be found by
Rev 3:19 and chasten; so be Z and repent.

ZEALOUSLY (2)

2Mac 2:21 to those who strove Z on behalf of Judaism,
Mk 7:35 charged them, the more Z they proclaimed it.

ZEBADIAH (9)

1Chr 8:15 Z, Arad, Eder,
8:17 Z, Meshullam, Hizki, Heber,
12:7 Korahites; and Joelah and Z, the sons of Jeroham
26:2 first-born, Jedia-el the second, Z the third, Jathni-el the
27:7 month, and his son Z after him; in his
2Chr 17:8 the Levites, Shemaiah, Nethaniah, Z, Asahel,
19:11 of the LORD; and Z the son of Ishmael,
Ezra 8:8 the sons of Shephatiah, Z the son of Michael,
10:20 Of the sons of Immer: Hanani and Z

ZEBAH (12)

Judg 8:5 I am pursuing after Z and Zalmunna, the kings
8:6 of Succoth said, "Are Z and Zalmunna already in
8:7 the LORD has given Z and Zalmunna into my
8:10 Now Z and Zalmunna were in Karkor with their
8:12 And Z and Zalmunna fled; and he pursued them
8:12 two kings of Midian, Z and Zalmunna, and he
8:15 Succoth, and said, "Behold Z and Zalmunna, about
8:15 taunted me, saying, 'Are Z and Zalmunna already in
8:18 Then he said to Z and Zalmunna, "Where are
8:21 Then Z and Zalmunna said, "Rise yourself, and fall
8:21 Gideon arose and slew Z and Zalmunna; and he
Ps 83:11 all their princes like Z and Zalmunna,

ZEBEDEE (12)

Mt 4:21 James the son of Z and John his brother,
4:21 in the boat with Z their father, mending their
10:2 James the son of Z, and John his brother;
20:20 of the sons of Z came up to him,
26:37 the two sons of Z, he began to be
27:56 Joseph, and the mother of the sons of Z
Mk 1:19 James the son of Z and John his brother,
1:20 they left their father Z in the boat with
3:17 James the son of Z and John the brother
10:35 John, the sons of Z, came forward to him,
Lk 5:10 and John, sons of Z, who were partners with
Jn 21:2 Galilee, the sons of Z, and two others of

ZEBIDAH

2Kgs 23:36 His mother's name was Z the daughter of Pedaiah

ZEBINA

Ezra 10:43 Nebo: Je-iel, Mattithiah, Zabad, Z, Jaddai, Joel, and

ZEBOIIM (5)

Gen 10:19 Sodom, Gomorrah, Admah, and Z, as far as Lasha.
14:2 Admah, Shemeber king of Z, and the king of
14:8 Admah, the king of Z, and the king of
Deut 29:23 and Gomorrah, Admah and Z, which the LORD
Hos 11:8 How can I treat you like Z

ZEBOIM (2)

1Sam 13:18 upon the valley of Z toward the wilderness.
Neh 11:34 Hazor, Ramah, Gittaim, Hadid, Z, Neballat,

ZEBUL (6)

Judg 9:28 son of Jerubbaal and Z his officer serve the
9:30 When Z the ruler of the city heard the
9:36 men, he said to Z, "Look, men are coming
9:36 And Z said to him, "You see the shadow
9:38 Then Z said to him, "Where is your mouth
9:41 dwelt at Arumah; and Z drove out Gaal and

ZEBULUN (48)

Gen 30:20 him six sons"; so she called his name Z
35:23 first-born), Simeon, Levi, Judah, Issachar, and Z
46:14 The sons of Z: Sered, Elon, and Jahleel
49:13 Z shall dwell at the shore of the sea;
Ex 1:3 Levi, and Judah, Issachar, Z, and Benjamin, Dan and
Num 1:9 son of Zuar; from Z, Eliab the son of
1:30 Of the people of Z, their generations, by their
1:31 of the tribe of Z was fifty-seven thousand four
2:7 Then the tribe of Z, the leader of the
2:7 of the people of Z being Eliab the son
7:24 of the men of Z:
10:16 of the men of Z was Eliab the son
13:10 from the tribe of Z, Gaddiel the son of
26:26 The sons of Z, according to their families: of
34:25 of the sons of Z a leader, Eli-zaphan the
Deut 27:13 curse: Reuben, Gad, Asher, Z, Dan, and Naphtali.
33:18 And of Z he said, "Rejoice, Zebulun, in your
33:18 Zebulun he said, "Rejoice, Z, in your going out;
Josh 19:10 for the tribe of Z, according to its families.
19:16 of the tribe of Z, according to its families—
19:27 to Beth-dagon, and touches Z and the valley of
19:34 there to Hukkok, touching Z at the south, and
21:7 and the tribe of Z, twelve cities.
21:34 of the tribe of Z, Jokne-am with its pasture
Judg 1:30 Z did not drive out the inhabitants of Kitron,
4:6 the tribe of Naphtali and the tribe of Z
4:10 And Barak summoned Z and Naphtali to Kedesh;
5:14 the commanders, and from Z those who bear the
5:18 Z is a people that jeoparded their lives to
6:35 sent messengers to Asher, Z, and Naphtali; and they
12:12 was buried at Aijalon in the land of Z
1Chr 2:1 Simeon, Levi, Judah, Issachar, Z,
6:63 out of the tribes of Reuben, Gad, and Z
6:77 out of the tribe of Z: Rimmono with its pasture
12:33 Of Z fifty thousand seasoned troops, equipped for
12:40 far as Issachar and Z and Naphtali, came bringing
27:19 son of Michael; for Z, Ishmaiah the son of
2Chr 30:10 and as far as Z; but they laughed them
30:11 of Manasseh, and of Z humbled themselves and
30:18 Issachar, and Z, had not cleansed themselves,
Ps 68:27 throng, the princes of Z, the princes of Naphtali.
Is 9:1 contempt the land of Z and the land of
Ezek 48:26 side to the west, Z, one portion.
48:27 Adjoining the territory of Z, from the east side
48:33 the gate of Issachar, and the gate of Z
Mt 4:13 in the territory of Z and Naphtali,
4:15 fulfilled: "The land of Z and the land of
Rev 7:8 of the tribe of Z, twelve thousand of the

ZEBULUNITE (2)

Judg 12:11 After him Elon the Z judged Israel; and he
12:12 Then Elon the Z died, and was buried at

ZEBULUNITES

Num 26:27 the families of the Z according to their number,

ZECHARIAH (58)

2Kgs 14:29 kings of Israel, and Z his son reigned in
15:8 Azariah king of Judah Z the son of Jeroboam
15:11 of the deeds of Z, behold, they are written
18:2 His mother's name was Abi the daughter of Z
1Chr 5:7 the chief, Je-iel, and Z,
9:21 Z the son of Meshelemiah was gatekeeper at the
9:37 Ner, Nadab, Gedor, Ahio, Z and Mikloth;
15:18 of the second order, Z, Ja-aziel, Shemiramoth,
15:20 to sound bronze cymbals; Z, Azi-el, Shemiramoth,
15:24 Shebaniah, Joshaphat, Nethanel, Amasai, Z,
16:5 second to him were Z, Je-iel, Shemiramoth, Jehiel,
24:25 of Micah, Isshiah; of the sons of Isshiah, Z
26:2 And Meshelemiah had sons: Z the first-born, Jedia-el
26:11 second, Tebaliah the third, Z the fourth: all the
26:14 also for his son Z, a shrewd counselor, and
27:21 Iddo the son of Z; for Benjamin, Jaasiel the
2Chr 17:7 his princes, Ben-hail, Obadiah, Z, Nethanel, and
20:14 Jahaziel the son of Z, son of Benaiah, son
21:2 of Jehoshaphat: Azariah, Jehiel, Z, Azariah, Michael,
24:20 God took possession of Z the son of Jehoiada
24:22 the kindness which Jehoiada, Z's father, had shown
26:5 in the days of Z, who instructed him in
29:1 His mother's name was Abijah the daughter of Z
29:13 the sons of Asaph, Z and Mattaniah;
34:12 sons of Merari, and Z and Meshullam, of the
35:8 Hilkiah, Z, and Jehiel, the chief officers of the
Ezra 5:1 the prophets, Haggai and Z the son of Iddo,
6:14 Haggai the prophet and Z the son of Iddo.
8:3 the sons of Parosh, Z, with whom were registered
8:11 the sons of Bebai, Z, the son of Bebai,
8:16 Elnathan, Nathan, Z, and Meshullam, leading men,
10:26 sons of Elam: Mattaniah, Z, Jehiel, Abdi, Jeremoth,
Neh 8:4 Malchijah, Hashum, Hash-baddanah, Z, and
11:4 of Uzziah, son of Z, son of Amariah, son
11:5 of Joiarib, son of Z, son of the Shilonite.
11:12 of Amzi, son of Z, son of Pashhur, son
12:16 Meraioth, Helkai; of Iddo, Z; of Ginnethon,
12:35 priests' sons with trumpets: Z the son of Jonathan,
12:41 Ma-aseiah, Miniamin, Micaiah, Eli-o-enai, Z, and
Is 8:2 Uriah the priest and Z the son of Jeberechiah,
Zech 1:1 the LORD came to Z the son of Berechiah,
1:7 the LORD came to Z the son of Berechiah,
1:7 Iddo, the prophet; and Z said,
7:1 the LORD came to Z in the fourth day
7:8 the LORD came to Z, saying,
1Mac 5:18 Joseph, the son of Z, and Azariah, a leader
5:56 Joseph, the son of Z, and Azariah, the commanders
Mt 23:34 to the blood of Z the son of Barachiah,
Lk 1:5 was a priest named Z, of the division of
1:12 And Z was troubled when he saw him, and
1:13 "Do not be afraid, Z, for your prayer is
1:18 And Z said to the angel, "How shall I
1:21 people were waiting for Z, and they wondered at
1:40 entered the house of Z and greeted Elizabeth.
1:59 would have named him Z after his father,
1:67 And his father Z was filled with the Holy
3:2 John the son of Z in the wilderness;
11:51 to the blood of Z, who perished between the

ZECHER

1Chr 8:31 Baal, Nadab, Gedor, Ahio, Z,

ZEDAD

Ezek 47:15 Hamath, and on to Z,

ZEDED

Num 34:8 boundary shall be at Z;

ZEDEKIAH (66)

1Kgs 22:11 And Z the son of Chenaanah made for himself
22:24 Then Z the son of Chenaanah came near and
2Kgs 24:17 in his stead, and changed his name to Z
24:18 Z was twenty-one years old when he became king,
24:20 And Z rebelled against the king of Babylon.
25:2 was besieged till the eleventh year of King Z
25:7 slew the sons of Z before his eyes, and
25:7 out the eyes of Z, and bound him in
1Chr 3:15 second Jehoiakim, the third Z, the fourth Shallum.
3:16 Jehoiakim: Jeconiah his son, Z his son;
2Chr 18:10 And Z the son of Chenaanah made for himself
18:23 Then Z the son of Chenaanah came near and
36:10 and made his brother Z king over Judah and
36:11 Z was twenty-one years old when he began to
Neh 10:1 the son of Hacaliah, Z,
Jer 1:3 the eleventh year of Z, the son of Josiah,
21:1 the LORD, when King Z sent to him Pashhur
21:4 you shall say to Z, 'Thus says the LORD,
21:7 LORD, I will give Z king of Judah, and
24:8 so will I treat Z the king of Judah,
27:1 of the reign of Z the son of Josiah,
27:3 come to Jerusalem to Z king of Judah.
27:12 To Z king of Judah I spoke in like
28:1 of the reign of Z king of Judah, in
29:3 son of Hilkiah, whom Z king of Judah sent
29:21 son of Kolaiah and Z the son of Ma-aseiah,
29:22 LORD make you like Z and Ahab, whom the
32:1 the tenth year of Z king of Judah, which
32:3 For Z king of Judah had imprisoned him, saying,
32:4 he shall take it; Z king of Judah shall
32:5 and he shall take Z to Babylon, and there
34:2 Go and speak to Z king of Judah and
34:4 of the LORD, O Z king of Judah!
34:6 all these words to Z king of Judah, in
34:8 the LORD, after King Z had made a covenant
34:21 And Z king of Judah, and his princes I
36:12 the son of Shaphan, Z the son of Hananiah,
37:1 Z the son of Josiah, whom Nebuchadrezzar king of
37:3 King Z sent Jehucal the son of Shelemiah, and
37:17 there many days, King Z sent for him, and
37:18 also said to King Z, "What wrong have I
37:21 So King Z gave orders, and they committed
38:5 King Z said, "Behold, he is in your hands;
38:14 King Z sent for Jeremiah the prophet and received
38:15 Jeremiah said to Z, "If I tell you, will
38:16 Then King Z swore secretly to Jeremiah, "As the
38:17 Then Jeremiah said to Z, "Thus says the LORD,
38:19 King Z said to Jeremiah, "I am afraid of
38:24 Then Z said to Jeremiah, "Let no one know
39:1 the ninth year of Z king of Judah, in
39:2 the eleventh year of Z, in the fourth month,
39:4 When Z king of Judah and all the soldiers
39:5 pursued them, and overtook Z in the plains of
39:6 slew the sons of Z at Riblah before his
39:7 out the eyes of Z, and bound him in
44:30 life, as I gave Z king of Judah into
49:34 of the reign of Z king of Judah.
51:59 when he went with Z king of Judah to
52:1 Z was twenty-one years old when he became king;
52:3 And Z rebelled against the king of Babylon.
52:5 was besieged till the eleventh year of King Z
52:8 the king, and overtook Z in the plains of
52:10 slew the sons of Z before his eyes, and
52:11 out the eyes of Z, and bound him in
Bar 1:1 of Mahseiah, son of Z, son of Hasadiah, son
1:8 the silver vessels which Z the son of Josiah,

ZEEB (6)

Judg 7:25 of Midian, Oreb and Z; they killed Oreb at
7:25 rock of Oreb, and Z they killed at the
7:25 the wine press of Z, as they pursued Midian;
7:25 heads of Oreb and Z to Gideon beyond the
8:3 of Midian, Oreb and Z; what have I been
Ps 83:11 nobles like Oreb and Z, all their princes like

ZELA (2)

Josh 18:28 Rekem, Irpeel, Taralah, Z, Ha-eleph, Jebus (that is,
2Sam 21:14 land of Benjamin in Z, in the tomb of

ZELEK (2)

2Sam 23:37 Zobah, Bani the Gadite, Z the Ammonite, Naharai of
1Chr 11:39 the son of Hagri, Z the Ammonite, Naharai of

ZELOPHEHAD (11)

Num 26:33 Now Z the son of Hepher had no sons,
26:33 of the daughters of Z were Mahlah, Noah, Hoglah,
27:1 near the daughters of Z the son of Hepher,
27:7 Moses, "The daughters of Z are right; you shall
36:2 give the inheritance of Z our brother to his
36:6 concerning the daughters of Z, 'Let them marry
36:10 The daughters of Z did as the LORD commanded
36:11 Noah, the daughters of Z, were married to sons
Josh 17:3 Now Z the son of Hepher, son of Gilead,
1Chr 7:15 of the second was Z; and Zelophehad had daughters.
7:15 second was Zelophehad; and Z had daughters.

ZELZAH
1Sam 10:2 territory of Benjamin at Z, and they will say

ZEMARAIM (2)
Josh 18:22 Beth-hoglah, Emek-keziz, Beth-arabah, Z, Bethel,
2Chr 13:4 stood up on Mount Z which is in the

ZEMARITES (2)
Gen 10:18 Sinites, the Arvadites, the Z, and the Hamathites.
1Chr 1:16 Sinites, the Arvadites, the Z, and the Hamathites.

ZEMER
Ezek 27:8 rowers; skilled men of Z were in you, they

ZEMIRAH
1Chr 7:8 The sons of Becher: Z, Joash, Eliezer, Eli-o-enai,

ZENAN
Josh 15:37 Z, Hadashah, Migdal-gad,

ZENAS
Tit 3:13 your best to speed Z the lawyer and Apollos

ZEPHANIAH (10)
2Kgs 25:18 the chief priest, and Z the second priest, and
1Chr 6:36 of Azariah, son of Z,
Jer 21:1 son of Malchiah and Z the priest, the son
29:25 in Jerusalem, and to Z the son of Ma-aseiah
29:29 Z the priest read this letter in the hearing
37:3 son of Shelemiah, and Z the priest, the son
52:24 the chief priest, and Z the second priest, and
Zeph 1:1 LORD which came to Z the son of Cushi,
Zech 6:10 to the house of Josiah, the son of Z
6:14 Heldai, Tobijah, Jedaiah, and Josiah the son of Z

ZEPHATH
Judg 1:17 Canaanites who inhabited Z, and utterly destroyed it.

ZEPHATHAH
2Chr 14:10 in the valley of Z at Mareshah.

ZEPHI
1Chr 1:36 of Eliphaz: Teman, Omar, Z, Gatam, Kenaz, Timna,

ZEPHO (2)
Gen 36:11 Eliphaz were Teman, Omar, Z, Gatam, and Kenaz.
36:15 the chiefs Teman, Omar, Z, Kenaz,

ZEPHON
Num 26:15 to their families: of Z, the family of the

ZEPHONITES
Num 26:15 the family of the Z; of Haggi, the family

ZER
Josh 19:35 fortified cities are Ziddim, Z, Hammath, Rakkath,

ZERAH (22)
Gen 36:13 sons of Reuel: Nahath, Z, Shammah, and Mizzah.
36:17 son: the chiefs Nahath, Z, Shammah, and Mizzah;
36:33 Jobab the son of Z of Bozrah reigned in
38:30 upon his hand; and his name was called Z
46:12 Onan, Shelah, Perez, and Z (but Er and Onan
Num 26:13 of the Jachinites; of Z, the family of the
26:20 of the Perezites; of Z, the family of the
Josh 7:1 of Zabdi, son of Z, of the tribe of
7:18 of Zabdi, son of Z, of the tribe of
7:24 Achan the son of Z, and the silver and
22:20 Achan the son of Z break faith in the
1Chr 1:37 sons of Reuel: Nahath, Z, Shammah, and Mizzah.
1:44 Jobab the son of Z of Bozrah reigned in
2:4 daughter-in-law Tamar also bore him Perez and Z
2:6 The sons of Z: Zimri, Ethan, Heman, Calcol, and
4:24 Simeon: Nemuel, Jamin, Jarib, Z, Shaul;
6:21 son, Iddo his son, Z his son, Je-atherai his
6:41 of Ethni, son of Z, son of Adaiah,
9:6 Of the sons of Z: Jeuel and their kinsmen,
2Chr 14:9 Z the Ethiopian came out against them with an
Neh 11:24 of the sons of Z the son of Judah,
Mt 1:3 father of Perez and Z by Tamar, and Perez

ZERAHIAH (5)
1Chr 6:6 of Uzzi, Uzzi of Z, Zerahiah of Meraioth,
6:6 Uzzi, Uzzi of Zerahiah, Z of Meraioth,
6:51 son, Uzzi his son, Z his son,
Ezra 7:4 of Meraioth, son of Z, son of Uzzi, son
8:4 Eli-e-ho-enai the son of Z, and with him two

ZERAHITES (6)
Num 26:13 the family of the Z; of Shaul, the family
26:20 the Perezites; of Zerah, the family of the Z
Josh 7:17 the family of the Z was taken; and he
7:17 the family of the Z man by man, and
1Chr 27:11 the Hushathite, of the Z; in his division were
27:13 of Netophah, of the Z; in his division were

ZERED (4)
Num 21:12 set out, and encamped in the Valley of Z
Deut 2:13 brook Z. So we went over the brook Z
2:14 we crossed the brook Z was thirty-eight years, until

ZEREDAH (2)
1Kgs 11:26 Nebat, an Ephraimite of Z, a servant of Solomon,
2Chr 4:17 them, in the clay ground between Succoth and Z

ZERERAH
Judg 7:22 far as Beth-shittah toward Z, as far as the

ZERESH (4)
Esth 5:10 sent and fetched his friends and his wife Z
5:14 Then his wife Z and all his friends said
6:13 Haman told his wife Z and all his friends
6:13 men and his wife Z said to him, "If

ZERETH
1Chr 4:7 The sons of Helah: Z, Izhar, and Ethnan.

ZERETH-SHAHAR
Josh 13:19 Kiriathaim, and Sibmah, and Z on the hill of

ZERI
1Chr 25:3 sons of Jeduthun: Gedaliah, Z, Jeshaiah, Shimei,

ZEROR
1Sam 9:1 of Abiel, son of Z, son of Becorath, son

ZERUAH
1Kgs 11:26 whose mother's name was Z, a widow, also lifted

ZERUBBABEL (26)
1Chr 3:19 the sons of Pedaiah: Z and Shimei; and the
3:19 and the sons of Z: Meshullam and Hananiah, and
Ezra 2:2 They came with Z, Jeshua, Nehemiah, Seraiah,
3:2 his fellow priests, and Z the son of Shealtiel
3:8 in the second month, Z the son of Shealtiel
4:2 of Israel, they approached Z and the heads of
4:3 But Z, Jeshua, and the rest of the heads
5:2 Then Z the son of Shealtiel and Jeshua the
Neh 7:7 They came with Z, Jeshua, Nehemiah, Azariah,
12:1 who came up with Z the son of Shealtiel,
12:47 in the days of Z and in the days
Sir 49:11 How shall we magnify Z
Hag 1:1 Haggai the prophet to Z the son of Shealtiel,
1:12 Then Z the son of Shealtiel, and Joshua the
1:14 up the spirit of Z the son of Shealtiel,
2:2 prophet, "Speak now to Z the son of Shealtiel,
2:4 now take courage, O Z, says the LORD; take
2:21 the month, "Speak to Z, governor of Judah, saying,
2:23 will take you, O Z my servant, the son
Zech 4:6 of the LORD to Z: Not by might, nor
4:7 Before Z you shall become a plain; and he
4:9 saying, "The hands of Z have laid the foundation
4:10 shall see the plummet in the hand of Z
Mt 1:12 Shealtiel the father of Z,
1:13 father of Zerubbabel, and Z the father of Abiud,
Lk 3:27 Rhesa, the son of Z, the son of Shealtiel,

ZERUIAH (26)
1Sam 26:6 Abishai the son of Z, "Who will go down
2Sam 2:13 Joab the son of Z, and the servants of
2:18 the three sons of Z were there, Joab, Abishai,
3:39 men the sons of Z are too hard for
8:16 Joab the son of Z was over the army;
14:1 Joab the son of Z perceived that the king's
16:9 Abishai the son of Z said to the king,
16:10 I to do with you, you sons of Z
17:25 of Nahash, sister of Z, Joab's mother.
18:2 Abishai the son of Z, Joab's brother, and one
19:21 Abishai the son of Z answered, "Shall not Shimei
19:22 you, you sons of Z, that you should this
21:17 Abishai the son of Z came to his aid,
23:18 Joab, the son of Z, was chief of the

23:37 Joab the son of Z,
1Kgs 1:7 Joab the son of Z and with Abiathar the
2:5 Joab the son of Z did to me, how
2:22 Abiathar the priest and Joab the son of Z
1Chr 2:16 and their sisters were Z and Abigail.
2:16 The sons of Z: Abishai, Joab, and Asahel, three.
11:6 Joab the son of Z went up first, so
11:39 Joab the son of Z,
18:12 Abishai, the son of Z, slew eighteen thousand
18:15 Joab the son of Z was over the army;
26:28 Joab the son of Z had dedicated--all dedicated
27:24 Joab the son of Z began to number, but

ZETHAM (2)
1Chr 23:8 Jehiel the chief, and Z, and Joel, three.
26:22 The sons of Jehieli, Z and Joel his brother,

ZETHAN
1Chr 7:10 Jeush, Benjamin, Ehud, Chenaanah, Z, Tarshish, and

ZETHAR
Esth 1:10 Harbona, Bigtha and Abagtha, Z and Carkas, the

ZEUS (4)
2Mac 6:2 the temple of Olympian Z, and to call the
6:2 Gerizim the temple of Z the Friend of Strangers,
Acts 14:12 Barnabas they called Z, and Paul, because he was
14:13 And the priest of Z, whose temple was in

ZIA
1Chr 5:13 Meshullam, Sheba, Jorai, Jacan, Z, and Eber, seven.

ZIBA (16)
2Sam 9:2 Saul whose name was Z, and they called him
9:2 and the king said to him, "Are you Z
9:3 Z said to the king, "There is still a
9:4 And Z said to the king, "He is in
9:9 Then the king called Z, Saul's servant, and said
9:10 Now Z had fifteen sons and twenty servants.
9:11 Then Z said to the king, "According to all
9:12 all who dwelt in Z's house became Mephibosheth's
16:1 little beyond the summit, Z the servant of
16:2 the king said to Z, "Why have you brought
16:2 Z answered, "The asses are for the king's household
16:3 Z said to the king, "Behold, he remains in
16:4 the king said to Z, "Behold, all that belonged
16:4 And Z said, "I do obeisance; let me ever
19:17 And Z the servant of the house of Saul,
19:29 have decided: you and Z shall divide the land."

ZIBEON (8)
Gen 36:2 Anah the son of Z the Hivite,
36:14 Anah the son of Z, Esau's wife: she bore
36:20 the land: Lotan, Shobal, Z, Anah,
36:24 are the sons of Z: Aiah and Anah; he
36:24 pastured the asses of Z his father.
36:29 the chiefs Lotan, Shobal, Z, Anah,
1Chr 1:38 of Seir: Lotan, Shobal, Z, Anah, Dishon, Ezer, and
1:40 The sons of Z: Aiah and Anah.

ZIBI-A
1Chr 8:9 Hodesh his wife: Jobab, Z, Mesha, Malcam,

ZIBIAH (2)
2Kgs 12:1 His mother's name was Z of Beer-sheba.
2Chr 24:1 his mother's name was Z of Beer-sheba.

ZICHRI (12)
Ex 6:21 The sons of Izhar: Korah, Nepheg, and Z
1Chr 8:19 Jakim, Z, Zabdi,
8:23 Ishpan, Eber, Eliel, Abdon, Z, Hanan,
8:27 Athaliah, Ja-areshiah, Elijah, and Z were the sons of
9:15 of Mica, son of Z, son of Asaph;
26:25 Joram, and his son Z, and his son Shelomoth.
27:16 Eliezer the son of Z was chief officer; for
2Chr 17:16 Amasiah the son of Z, a volunteer for the
23:1 son of Adaiah, and Elishaphat the son of Z
28:7 And Z, a mighty man of Ephraim, slew Ma-aseiah
Neh 11:9 Joel the son of Z was their overseer; and
12:17 Ginnethon, Meshullam; of Abijah, Z; of Miniamin, of

ZIDDIM
Josh 19:35 The fortified cities are Z, Zer, Hammath, Rakkath,

ZIHA (3)
Ezra 2:43 servants: the sons of Z, the sons of Hasupha,
Neh 7:46 servants: the sons of Z, the sons of Hasupha,
11:21 lived on Ophel; and Z and Gishpa were over

ZIKLAG (15)
Josh 15:31 Eltolad, Chesil, Hormah, Z, Madmannah,
19:5 Bethul, Hormah, Z, Beth-marcaboth, Hazar-susah,
1Sam 27:6 day Achish gave him Z; therefore Ziklag has
27:6 gave him Ziklag; therefore Z has belonged to the
30:1 his men came to Z on the third day,
30:1 made a raid upon the Negeb and upon Z
30:1 They had overcome Z, and burned it with fire,
30:14 Caleb; and we burned Z with fire."
30:26 When David came to Z, he sent part of
2Sam 1:1 remained two days in Z;
4:10 and slew him at Z, which was the reward
1Chr 4:30 Ezem, Tolad, Bethuel, Hormah, Z,
12:1 came to David at Z, while he could not
12:20 As he went to Z these men of Manasseh
Neh 11:28 and its villages, in Z, in Meconah and its

ZILLAH (3)
Gen 4:19 was Adah, and the name of the other Z
4:22 Z bore Tubal-cain; he was the forger of all
4:23 his wives: "Adah and Z, hear my voice; you

ZILLETHAI (2)
1Chr 8:20 Jakim, Zichri, Zabdi, Eli-enai, Z, Eliel,
12:20 Michael, Jozabad, Elihu, and Z, chiefs of thousands

ZILPAH (7)
Gen 29:24 (Laban gave his maid Z to his daughter Leah
30:9 she took her maid Z and gave her to
30:10 Then Leah's maid Z bore Jacob a son.
30:12 Leah's maid Z bore Jacob a second son.
35:26 The sons of Z, Leah's maid: Gad and Asher.
37:2 sons of Bilhah and Z, his father's wives; and
46:18 are the sons of Z, whom Laban gave to

ZIMMAH (3)
1Chr 6:20 son, Jahath his son, Z his son,
6:42 of Ethan, son of Z, son of Shimei,
2Chr 29:12 Joah the son of Z, and Eden the son

ZIMRAN (2)
Gen 25:2 She bore him Z, Jokshan, Medan, Midian, Ishbak,
1Chr 1:32 Abraham's concubine: she bore Z, Jokshan, Medan,

ZIMRI (16)
Num 25:14 the Midianite woman, was Z the son of Salu,
1Kgs 16:9 But his servant Z, commander of half his chariots,
16:10 the household in Tirzah, Z came in and struck
16:12 Thus Z destroyed all the house of Baasha, according
16:15 Asa king of Judah, Z reigned seven days in
16:16 encamped heard it said, Z has conspired, and he
16:18 And when Z saw that the city was taken,
16:20 of the acts of Z, and the conspiracy which
2Kgs 9:31 "Is it peace, you Z, murderer of your master?"
1Chr 2:6 The sons of Zerah: Z, Ethan, Heman, Calcol, and
8:36 of Alemeth, Azmaveth, and Z; Zimri was the father
8:36 Alemeth, Azmaveth, and Zimri; Z was the father of
9:42 of Alemeth, Azmaveth, and Z; and Zimri was the
9:42 Azmaveth, and Zimri; and Z was the father of
Jer 25:25 all the kings of Z, all the kings of
1Mac 2:26 as Phinehas did against Z the son of Salu.

ZIN (10)
Num 13:21 from the wilderness of Z to Rehob, near the
20:1 into the wilderness of Z in the first month,
27:14 in the wilderness of Z during the strife of
27:14 in the wilderness of Z
33:36 in the wilderness of Z (that is, Kadesh).
34:3 from the wilderness of Z along the side of
34:4 Akrabbim, and cross to Z, and its end shall
Deut 32:51 in the wilderness of Z; because you did not
Josh 15:1 to the wilderness of Z at the farthest south.
15:3 Akrabbim, passes along to Z, and goes up south

ZINA
1Chr 23:10 sons of Shimei: Jahath, Z, and Jeush, and Beriah.

ZION (178)
2Sam 5:7 took the stronghold of Z, that is, the city
1Kgs 8:1 out of the city of David, which is Z
2Kgs 19:21 the virgin daughter of Z; she wags her head
19:31 and out of Mount Z a band of survivors.
1Chr 11:5 took the stronghold of Z, that is, the city

2Chr	5:2	out of the city of David, which is Z
Jud	9:13	against the top of Z, and against the house
Ps	2:6	set my king on Z, my holy hill."
	9:11	Sing praises to the LORD, who dwells in Z
	9:14	of the daughter of Z I may rejoice in
	14:7	that deliverance for Israel would come out of Z
	20:2	from the sanctuary, and give you support from Z
	48:2	all the earth, Mount Z, in the far north,
	48:11	with victory; let Mount Z be glad!
	48:12	Walk about Z, go round about her, number her
	50:2	Out of Z, the perfection of beauty, God shines
	51:18	Do good to Z in thy good pleasure; rebuild
	53:6	O that deliverance for Israel would come from Z
	65:1	thee, O God, in Z; and to thee shall
	69:35	For God will save Z and rebuild the cities
	74:2	Remember Mount Z, where thou hast dwelt.
	76:2	been established in Salem, his dwelling place in Z
	78:68	tribe of Judah, Mount Z, which he loves.
	84:5	thee, in whose heart are the highways to Z
	84:7	the God of gods will be seen in Z
	87:2	loves the gates of Z more than all the
	87:5	And of Z it shall be said, "This one
	97:8	Z hears and is glad, and the daughters of
	99:2	LORD is great in Z; he is exalted over
	102:13	and have pity on Z; it is the time
	102:16	LORD will build up Z, he will appear in
	102:21	men may declare in Z the name of the
	110:2	LORD sends forth from Z your mighty scepter.
	125:1	LORD are like Mount Z, which cannot be moved,
	126:1	restored the fortunes of Z, we were like those
	128:5	The LORD bless you from Z
	129:5	May all who hate Z be put to shame
	132:13	the LORD has chosen Z; he has desired it
	133:3	of Hermon, which falls on the mountains of Z
	134:3	LORD bless you from Z, he who made heaven
	135:21	be the LORD from Z, he who dwells in
	137:1	we sat down and wept, when we remembered Z
	137:3	saying, "Sing us one of the songs of Z
	146:10	ever, thy God, O Z, to all generations.
	147:12	Praise your God, O Z
	149:2	let the sons of Z rejoice in their King!
Song	3:11	forth, O daughters of Z, and behold King Solomon,
Sir	24:10	before him, and so I was established in Z
	36:14	Fill Z with the celebration of thy wondrous deeds,
	48:18	up his hand against Z and made great boasts
	48:24	last things, and comforted those who mourned in Z
Is	1:8	And the daughter of Z is left like a
	1:27	Z shall be redeemed by justice, and those in
	2:3	For out of Z shall go forth the law,
	3:16	Because the daughters of Z are haughty and walk
	3:17	of the daughters of Z, and the LORD will
	4:3	who is left in Z and remains in Jerusalem
	4:4	of the daughters of Z and cleansed the bloodstains
	4:5	whole site of Mount Z and over her assemblies
	8:18	the LORD of hosts, who dwells on Mount Z
	10:12	his work on Mount Z and on Jerusalem he
	10:24	people, who dwell in Z, be not afraid of
	10:32	of the daughter of Z, the hill of Jerusalem.
	12:6	joy, O inhabitant of Z, for great in your
	14:32	"The LORD has founded Z, and in her the
	16:1	desert, to the mount of the daughter of Z
	18:7	rivers divide, to Mount Z, the place of the
	24:23	will reign on Mount Z and in Jerusalem and
	28:16	I am laying in Z for a foundation a
	29:8	all the nations be that fight against Mount Z
	30:19	Yea, O people in Z who dwell at Jerusalem;
	31:4	to fight upon Mount Z and upon its hill.
	31:9	whose fire is in Z, and whose furnace is
	33:5	high; he will fill Z with justice and righteousness;
	33:14	The sinners in Z are afraid; trembling has seized
	33:20	Look upon Z, the city of our appointed feasts!
	34:8	a year of recompense for the cause of Z
	35:10	return, and come to Z with singing; everlasting joy
	37:22	the virgin daughter of Z; she wags her head
	37:32	and out of Mount Z a band of survivors.
	40:9	a high mountain, O Z, herald of good tidings;
	41:27	have declared it to Z, and I give to
	46:13	will put salvation in Z, for Israel my glory."
	49:14	But Z said, "The LORD has forsaken me, my
	51:3	the LORD will comfort Z; he will comfort all
	51:11	return, and come to Z with singing; everlasting joy
	51:16	earth, and saying to Z, 'You are my people.'"
	52:1	on your strength, O Z; put on your beautiful
	52:2	bonds from your neck, O captive daughter of Z
	52:7	salvation, who says to Z, "Your God reigns."
	52:8	they see the return of the LORD to Z
	59:20	he will come to Z as Redeemer, to those
	60:14	of the LORD, the Z of the Holy One
	61:3	those who mourn in Z – to give them
	62:1	For Z's sake I will not keep silent, and
	62:11	to the daughter of Z, "Behold, your salvation comes;
	64:10	have become a wilderness, Z has become a
	66:8	For as soon as Z was in labor she
Jer	3:14	a family, and I will bring you to Z
	4:6	Raise a standard toward Z, flee for safety, stay
	4:31	of the daughter of Z gasping for breath, stretching
	6:2	delicately bred I will destroy, the daughter of Z
	6:23	man for battle, against you, O daughter of Z
	8:19	of the land: "Is the LORD not in Z
	9:19	wailing is heard from Z: 'How we are ruined!
	14:19	Does thy soul loathe Z
	26:18	the LORD of hosts, Z shall be plowed as
	30:17	an outcast: 'It is Z, for whom no one
	31:6	us go up to Z, to the LORD our
	31:12	on the height of Z, and they shall be
	50:5	ask the way to Z, with faces turned toward
	50:28	Babylon, to declare in Z the vengeance of the
	51:10	let us declare in Z the work of the
	51:24	they have done in Z, says the LORD.
	51:35	let the inhabitant of Z say.
Lam	1:4	The roads to Z mourn, for none come to
	1:6	From the daughter of Z has departed all her
	1:17	Z stretches out her hands, but there is none
	2:1	set the daughter of Z under a cloud!
	2:4	of the daughter of Z; he has poured out
	2:6	to an end in Z appointed feast and sabbath,
	2:8	of the daughter of Z; he marked it off
	2:10	of the daughter of Z sit on the ground
	2:13	I may comfort you, O virgin daughter of Z
	2:18	O daughter of Z
	4:2	The precious sons of Z, worth their weight in
	4:11	kindled a fire in Z, which consumed its foundations.
	4:22	iniquity, O daughter of Z, is accomplished, he will
	5:11	Women are ravished in Z, virgins in the towns
	5:18	grown dim, for Mount Z which lies desolate; jackals
Bar	4:9	"Hearken, you neighbors of Z, God has brought
	4:14	Let the neighbors of Z come; remember the capture
	4:24	as the neighbors of Z have now seen your
Joel	2:1	Blow the trumpet in Z; sound the alarm on
	2:15	Blow the trumpet in Z; sanctify a fast; call
	2:23	glad, O sons of Z, and rejoice in the
	2:32	delivered; for in Mount Z and in Jerusalem there
	3:16	the LORD roars from Z, and utters his voice
	3:17	God, who dwell in Z, my holy mountain.
	3:21	clear the guilty, for the LORD dwells in Z
Amos	1:2	"The LORD roars from Z, and utters his voice
	6:1	are at ease in Z, and to those who
Obad	1:17	But in Mount Z there shall be those that
	1:21	go up to Mount Z to rule Mount Esau;
Mic	1:13	to the daughter of Z, for in you were
	3:10	all equity, who build Z with blood and Jerusalem
	3:12	Therefore because of you Z shall be plowed as
	4:2	For out of Z shall go forth the law,
	4:7	over them in Mount Z from this time forth
	4:8	of the daughter of Z, to you shall it
	4:10	groan, O daughter of Z, like a woman in
	4:11	be profaned, and let our eyes gaze upon Z
	4:13	thresh, O daughter of Z, for I will make
Zeph	3:14	aloud, O daughter of Z; shout, O Israel!
	3:16	"Do not fear, O Z; let not your hands
Zech	1:14	I am exceedingly jealous for Jerusalem and for Z
	1:17	LORD will again comfort Z and again choose
	2:7	Escape to Z, you who dwell with the daughter
	2:10	rejoice, O daughter of Z; for lo, I come
	8:2	I am jealous for Z with great jealousy, and
	8:3	I will return to Z, and will dwell in
	9:9	Rejoice greatly, O daughter of Z
	9:13	brandish your sons, O Z, over your sons, O
1Mac	4:37	army assembled and they went up to Mount Z
	4:60	time they fortified Mount Z with high walls and
	5:54	went up to Mount Z with gladness and joy,
	6:48	the king encamped in Judea and at Mount Z
	6:62	the king entered Mount Z and saw what a
	7:33	After these events Nicanor went up to Mount Z
	10:11	walls and encircle Mount Z with squared stones, for
	14:27	tablets and put it upon pillars on Mount Z
Mt	21:5	"Tell the daughter of Z, Behold, your king is
Jn	12:15	"Fear not, daughter of Z; behold, your king is
Rom	9:33	I am laying in Z a stone that will
	11:26	Deliverer will come from Z, he will banish
Heb	12:22	have come to Mount Z and to the city
1Pet	2:6	I am laying in Z a stone, a cornerstone

Rev 14:1 and lo, on Mount Z stood the Lamb, and

ZIOR

Josh 15:54 (that is, Hebron), and Z: nine cities with their

ZIPH (10)

Josh 15:24 Kedesh, Hazor, Ithnan, Z, Telem, Bealoth,
15:55 Maon, Carmel, Z, Juttah,
1Sam 23:14 in the hill country of the Wilderness of Z
23:15 in the Wilderness of Z at Horesh.
23:24 arose, and went to Z ahead of Saul.
26:2 to the wilderness of Z, with three thousand chosen
26:2 Israel, to seek David in the wilderness of Z
1Chr 2:42 Mareshah his first-born, who was the father of Z
4:16 The sons of Jehallelel: Z, Ziphah, Tiri-a, and Asarel.
2Chr 11:8 Soco, Adullam, Gath, Mareshah, Z,

ZIPHAH

1Chr 4:16 sons of Jehallelel: Ziph, Z, Tiri-a, and Asarel.

ZIPHION

Gen 46:16 The sons of Gad: Z, Haggi, Shuni, Ezbon, Eri,

ZIPHITES (2)

1Sam 23:19 Then the Z went up to Saul at Gibe-ah,
26:1 Then the Z came to Saul at Gibe-ah, saying,

ZIPHRON

Num 34:9 boundary shall extend to Z, and its end shall

ZIPPOR (7)

Num 22:2 Balak the son of Z saw all that Israel
22:4 Balak the son of Z, who was king of
22:10 "Balak the son of Z, king of Moab, has
22:16 Balak the son of Z: 'Let nothing hinder you
23:18 me, O son of Z:
Josh 24:9 Balak the son of Z, king of Moab, arose
Judg 11:25 Balak the son of Z, king of Moab?

ZIPPORAH (3)

Ex 2:21 the man, and he gave Moses his daughter Z
4:25 Then Z took a flint and cut off her
18:2 Moses' father-in-law, had taken Z, Moses' wife, after

ZIV (2)

1Kgs 6:1 in the month of Z, which is the second
6:37 the LORD was laid, in the month of Z

ZIZ

2Chr 20:16 by the ascent of Z; you will find them

ZIZA (2)

1Chr 4:37 Asaiah, Adi-el, Jesimiel, Benaiah, Z the son of
2Chr 11:20 bore him Abijah, Attai, Z, and Shelomith.

ZIZAH

1Chr 23:11 was the chief, and Z the second; but Jeush

ZOAN (7)

Num 13:22 built seven years before Z in Egypt.)
Ps 78:12 the land of Egypt, in the fields of Z
78:43 Egypt, and his miracles in the fields of Z
Is 19:11 The princes of Z are utterly foolish; the wise
19:13 The princes of Z have become fools, and the
30:4 his officials are at Z and his envoys reach
Ezek 30:14 will set fire to Z, and will execute acts

ZOAR (11)

Gen 13:10 in the direction of Z; this was before the
14:2 Zeboiim, and the king of Bela (that is, Z
14:8 of Bela (that is, Z went out, and they
19:22 Therefore the name of the city was called Z
19:23 risen on the earth when Lot came to Z
19:30 went up out of Z, and dwelt in the
19:30 afraid to dwell in Z; so he dwelt in
Deut 34:3 the city of palm trees, as far as Z
Is 15:5 his fugitives flee to Z, to Eglath-shelishiyah.
Jer 48:4 destroyed; a cry is heard as far as Z
48:34 utter their voice, from Z to Horonaim and

ZOBAH (12)

1Sam 14:47 against the kings of Z, and against the Philistines;
2Sam 8:3 of Rehob, king of Z, as he went to
8:5 help Hadadezer king of Z, David slew twenty-two
8:12 of Hadadezer the son of Rehob, king of Z
10:6 and the Syrians of Z, twenty thousand foot soldiers,
10:8 and the Syrians of Z and of Rehob, and
23:36 son of Nathan of Z, Bani the Gadite,
1Kgs 11:23 had fled from his master Hadadezer king of Z
1Chr 18:3 defeated Hadadezer king of Z, toward Hamath, as
18:5 help Hadadezer king of Z, David slew twenty-two
18:9 of Hadadezer, king of Z,
19:6 from Mesopotamia, from Aram-maacah, and from Z

ZOBEBAH

1Chr 4:8 the father of Anub, Z, and the families of

ZOHAR (4)

Gen 23:8 Ephron the son of Z,
25:9 Ephron the son of Z the Hittite, east of
46:10 Jemuel, Jamin, Ohad, Jachin, Z, and Shaul, the son
Ex 6:15 Jemuel, Jamin, Ohad, Jachin, Z, and Shaul, the son

ZOHETH

1Chr 4:20 The sons of Ishi: Z and Ben-zoheth.

ZOPHAH (2)

1Chr 7:35 of Helem his brother: Z, Imna, Shelesh, and Amal.
7:36 The sons of Z: Suah, Harnepher, Shual, Beri, Imrah,

ZOPHAI

1Chr 6:26 Ahimoth, Elkanah his son, Z his son, Nahath his

ZOPHAR (4)

Job 2:11 Bildad the Shuhite, and Z the Naamathite.
11:1 Then Z the Naamathite answered:
20:1 Then Z the Naamathite answered:
42:9 Bildad the Shuhite and Z the Naamathite went and

ZOPHIM

Num 23:14 to the field of Z, to the top of

ZORAH (10)

Josh 15:33 in the lowland, Eshtaol, Z, Ashnah,
19:41 of its inheritance included Z, Eshtaol, Ir-shemesh,
Judg 13:2 a certain man of Z, of th e tribe of
13:25 him in Mahaneh-dan, between Z and Eshtaol.
16:31 and buried him between Z and Eshtaol in the
18:2 of their tribe, from Z and from Eshtaol, to
18:8 to their brethren at Z and Eshtaol, their brethren
18:11 war, set forth from Z and Eshtaol,
2Chr 11:10 Adoraim, Lachish, Azekah, Z, Aijalon, and Hebron,
Neh 11:29 villages, in En-rimmon, in Z, in Jarmuth,

ZORATHITES (2)

1Chr 2:53 from these came the Z and the Eshtaolites.
4:2 These were the families of the Z

ZORITES

1Chr 2:54 Netophathites, Atroth-beth-joab, and half of the

ZUAR (5)

Num 1:8 Nethanel the son of Z;
2:5 Nethanel the son of Z,
7:18 Nethanel the son of Z, the leader of Issachar,
7:23 was the offering of Nethanel the son of Z
10:15 men of Issachar was Nethanel the son of Z

ZUPH (3)

1Sam 1:1 of Tohu, son of Z, an Ephraimite.
9:5 to the land of Z, Saul said to his
1Chr 6:35 of Toah, son of Z, son of Elkanah, son

ZUR (5)

Num 25:15 Cozbi the daughter of Z, who was the head
31:8 their slain, Evi, Rekem, Z, Hur, and Reba, the
Josh 13:21 Evi and Rekem and Z and Hur and Reba,
1Chr 8:30 first-born son: Abdon, then Z, Kish, Baal, Nadab,
9:36 first-born son Abdon, then Z, Kish, Baal, Ner, Nadab,

ZURIEL

Num 3:35 families of Merari was Z the son of Abihail;

ZURISHADDAI (5)

Num 1:6 Shelumi-el the son of Z;
2:12 Shelumi-el the son of Z,
7:36 Shelumi-el the son of Z, the leader of the
7:41 was the offering of Shelumi-el the son of Z
10:19 men of Simeon was Shelumi-el the son of Z

ZUZIM

Gen 14:5 Rephaim in Ashteroth-karnaim, the Z in Ham,

APPENDIX
OF REVISIONS TO THE SECOND EDITION

A

ABANDONED
Neh 9:28 before you, and you A them to the hand

ABODE
Sir 24:12 their inheritance, and my A was in the full

ABRAHAM (2)
Esth 13:8 said: "O God of A, God of Isaac, God
14:3 and said: "God of A, God of Isaac, and

ACCORDANCE
Tob 7:12 she is given to you in accordance with the

ACCORDING (11)
Tob 7:13 to him as wife A to the law of
Ps 110:4 a priest for ever A to the order of
Rom 9:3 my brethren, my kinsmen A to the flesh.
2Cor 5:16 we once regarded Christ A to the flesh, we
5:16 we regard no one A to the flesh; even
Heb 5:6 a priest for ever, A to the order of
5:10 God a high priest A to the order of
6:20 high priest for ever A to the order of
7:11 another priest to arise A to the order of
7:11 rather than one named A to the order of
7:17 a priest for ever, A to the order of

ACCUSING
3Jn 1:10 what he is doing, A me falsely with evil

ACCUSTOMED
Dan 3:19 more than it was A to be heated.

ACKNOWLEDGE (2)
Tob 12:6 with fitting honor to A him.
12:7 with fitting honor to A him.

ACROSS (2)
Rev 1:13 with a golden sash A his chest;
15:6 and with golden sashes A their chests.

ACT
Tob 7:11 and the Lord will A on behalf of you

ADMIRED
Sir 24:2 she is exalted; in holy fulness she is A

ADORNED (2)
Rev 17:4 purple and scarlet, and A with gold and jewels
18:16 in purple and scarlet, A with gold, with jewels,

AFFLICT
Rev 11:6 into blood, and to A the earth with every

AFFLICTED
Ps 44:2 you planted them; you A the peoples, but you

AFFLICTION (2)
Esth 14:14 into gladness and our A into well-being.
Sir 2:11 saves in time of A, and he is the

AFRAID
Tob 2:8 "He is still not A; he has already been

AGES (2)
Tob 11:14 his holy name be blessed throughout all the A
Heb 1:2 all things, through whom also he created the A

AH (2)
Ezek 9:8 my face, and cried, A, Lord GOD!
11:13 loud voice, and said, A, Lord GOD!

AHIKAR
Tob 2:10 sorry for me, and A took care of me

AHITUB
Jud 8:7 Joseph, the son of A, the son of Melchis,

AID
Esth 14:11 God Come to my A, for I am an

ALAS (2)
Judg 11:35 his clothes, and said, A, my daughter!
Mk 13:16 "And A for those who are with child and

ALLOTTED
Neh 9:22 kingdoms and peoples, and A to them every corner;

ALMIGHTY
Sir 17:22 set before you, in prayer to God, the A

ALONE
Esth 14:11 me, who am all A, and have no one

ALREADY (2)
Tob 2:8 not afraid; he has A been hunted down to
6:9 entered Media and was A approaching Ecbatana,

ALWAYS (3)
Ps 119:132 to me, as you A do toward those who
Mk 15:8 to do as he A did for them.
Jn 11:42 I knew that you A hear me, but I

AMEN (2)
Tob 8:8 And they both said, A, amen."
8:8 And they both said, "Amen, A

ANCESTORS
Esth 14:11 the books of my A that you liberate all

ANGELS (4)
Ps 8:5 little less than the A, and you have crowned
82:1 the midst of the A he holds judgment:
97:7 idols; let all his A bow down before him.
138:1 whole heart; before the A I sing your praise;

ANOINT
Ps 23:5 of my enemies; you A my head with oil,

ANOINTED
Acts 4:27 servant Jesus, whom you A, both Herod and Pontius

ANSWERED (4)
Tob 6:10 he A
Ps 99:8 LORD our God, you A them; you were a
119:26 of my ways, you A me; teach me your
138:3 day I called, you A me, my strength of

APART
Is 24:19 the earth is torn A, the earth is violently

APPLIED
Tob 11:12 With this he A the medicine on his eyes.

APPOINT
Lk 22:29 me, so do I A for you

APPOINTED (3)
Ps 104:8 the place which you A for them.
Sir 17:20 failing, and he has A to them the lot
Lk 22:29 trials; as my Father A a kingdom for me,

APPROACHED
Tob 11:7 to Tobias, before they A his father, "I know

APPROACHING
Tob 6:9 Media and was already A Ecbatana,

APRON (2)
Lk 12:37 will put on his A and have them sit
17:8 and put on your A and serve me, till

ARID
Lk 17:23 A they will say to you, Behold, there!

ARIELS (2)
2Sam 23:20 deeds; he struck two A of Moab.
1Chr 11:22 deeds; he struck two A of Moab.

B

40:8 them to me, I B you."
40:14 me the kindness, I B you, to make mention
44:18 let your servant, I B you, speak a word
44:33 let your servant, I B you, remain instead of
45:4 near to me, I B you." And they came
50:4 your eyes, speak, I B you, in the ears
50:5 me go up, I B you, and bury my
50:17 to Joseph, Forgive, I B you, the transgression of
Ex 3:18 us; and now, we B you, let us go
4:18 me go back, I B, to my kinsmen in
5:3 let us go, we B, a three days journey
10:17 forgive my sin, I B you, only this once,
32:32 not, blot me, I B you, out of your
33:13 sight.' Now therefore, I B you, if I have
33:18 Moses said, "I B you, show me your glory."
34:9 let the Lord, I B you, go in the
Num 10:31 not leave us, I B you, for you know
12:13 her, O God, I B you."
14:17 And now, I B you, let the power of
14:19 of this people, I B you, according to the
16:26 the congregation, "Depart, I B you, from the tents
Judg 6:18 depart from here, I B you, until I come
10:15 only deliver us, we B you, this day."
11:17 Let us pass, we B, through your land; but
11:19 Let us pass, we B, through your land to
13:8 said, "O, LORD, I B you, let the man
16:28 GOD, remember me, I B you, and strengthen me,
16:28 and strengthen me, I B you, only this once,
18:5 "Inquire of God, we B you, that we may
1Sam 2:36 say, "Put me, I B you, in one of
15:25 Now therefore, I B, pardon my sin, and return
23:11 God of Israel, I B you, tell your servant."
2Sam 13:13 Now therefore, I B you, speak to the king;
1Kgs 20:35 LORD, "Strike me, I B you." But the man
20:37 said, "Strike me, I B you." And the man
2Kgs 1:13 man of God, I B you, let my life,
2:2 Elisha, "Tarry here, I B you; for the LORD
2:4 "Elisha, tarry here, I B you; for the LORD
2:6 him, "Tarry here, I B you; for the LORD
2:9 And Elisha said, "I B you, let me inherit
5:17 said, "If not, I B you, let there be
6:17 said, "O LORD, I B you, open his eyes
19:19 God, save us, I B you, from his hand,
20:3 now, O LORD, I B you, how I have
Job 6:29 Turn, I B, let no wrong be done.
8:8 For inquire, I B you, of bygone ages, and
Ps 116:4 LORD: "O LORD, I B you, save my life!"
118:25 Save us, we B you, O LORD!
118:25 O LORD, we B you, give us success!
Is 5:3 of Judah, judge, I B you, between me and
Jer 37:20 Now hear, I B you, O my lord the
Amos 7:2 Lord GOD, forgive, I B you!
7:5 Lord GOD, cease, I B you!
Jon 1:14 to the LORD, "We B you, O LORD, let
4:3 life from me, I B you, for it is
2Mac 7:28 I B you, my child, to look at the
9:26 I therefore urge and B you to remember the
Lk 8:28 I B you, do not torment me."
2Cor 5:20 We B you on behalf of Christ, be reconciled
13:7 But we B God that you may not do
Gal 4:12 Brethren, I B you, become as I am, for
1Thes 4:1 Finally, brethren, we B and exhort you in
5:12 But we B you, brethren, to respect those who
1Pet 2:11 Beloved, I B you as aliens and exiles to

BEGGED (23)
Gen 42:21 his soul, when he B us and we would
Ex 32:11 But Moses B the LORD his God, and said,
Deut 3:23 for you.' "And I B the LORD at that
2Mac 1:8 We B the Lord and we were heard, and
8:2 They B the Lord to look upon the people
8:14 at the same time B the Lord to rescue
8:29 made common supplication and B the merciful Lord
10:4 they fell prostrate and B the Lord that they
10:26 before the altar, they B him to be gracious
11:6 with lamentations and tears, B the Lord to send
12:11 The defeated nomads B Judas to grant them pledges
12:24 With great guile he B them to let him
13:12 same petition and had B the merciful Lord with
Mt 14:36 that were sick, and B him that they might
Mk 5:23 at his feet, and B him, saying, "My little
6:56 the market places, and B him that they might
7:31 his speech; and they B him to lay his
Lk 5:12 on his face and B him, "Lord, if you
7:4 came to Jesus, they B him earnestly, saying, "He
8:41 at Jesus feet he B him to come to
Jn 4:31 Meanwhile the disciples B him, saying, "Rabbi, eat."
Acts 16:15 with her household, she B us, saying, "If you
2Cor 12:8 Three times I B the Lord about this, that

BEGGING (4)
2Mac 10:16 making solemn supplication and B God to fight on
12:42 they turned to prayer, B that the sin which
Mt 8:5 came forward to him, B him
Mk 1:40 leper came to him B him, and kneeling said

BEGINNING
Mk 13:18 not been from the B of the creation which

BEGOT
Ps 110:3 of the morning I B you.

BEGOTTEN
1Jn 5:1 parent loves the one B by him.

BEHALF
Tob 7:11 Lord will act on B of you both." But

BEHOLD (117)
Gen 8:11 in the evening, and B, in her mouth a
15:12 fell on Abram; and B, a dread and great
19:28 valley, and beheld, and B, the smoke of the
29:2 in the field, and B, three flocks of sheep
39:8 to his masters wife, B, having me my master
48:11 see your face; and B, God has let me
Ex 2:6 saw the child; and B, the baby was crying.
3:2 and he looked, and B, the bush was burning,
18:6 when one told Moses, B, your father-in-law Jethro is
19:9 LORD said to Moses, B, I am coming to
Num 22:38 Balaam said to Balak, B, I have come to
23:6 returned to him, and B, he and all the
23:9 hills I behold him; B, a people dwelling alone,
23:17 came to him, and, B, he was standing beside
Deut 22:17 he spurns her; and B, he has made shameful
Judg 13:5 eat nothing unclean, for B, you shall conceive and
1Sam 21:14 Achish to his servants, B, you see the man
24:10 B, this day your eyes have seen how the
25:36 came to Nabal; and B, he was holding a
2Sam 1:6 upon his spear; and B, the chariots and the
15:24 Abiathar came up, and B, Zadok came also, with
24:17 the people, and said, B, I have sinned, and
1Kgs 1:51 fears King Solomon; for B, he has laid hold
2Kgs 1:14 B, fire came down from heaven, and consumed the
6:20 and they saw; and B, they were in the
7:15 as the Jordan; and, B, all the way was
13:21 man was being buried, B, a marauding band was
2Chr 29:9 For B, our fathers have fallen by the sword
Jud 9:6 presented themselves and said, B, we are here; for
Job 5:27 B, this we have searched out; it is true.
9:11 B, he passes by me, and I see him
13:1 B, my eye has seen
26:14 B, these are but the outskirts of his ways;
Ps 11:2 to the mountains; for B, the wicked bend the
37:36 I passed by, and, B, he was no more;
40:7 Then I said, B, I come; in the roll
40:9 in the great congregation; B, I have not restrained
48:4 For B, the kings assembled, they came on together.
59:3 For B, they lie in wait for my life;
68:33 heavens, the ancient heavens; B, he sends forth his
73:27 For B, those who are far from you shall
83:2 For B, your enemies are in tumult; those who
92:9 For, B, your enemies, O LORD, for, behold, your
92:9 enemies, O LORD, for, B, your enemies shall perish;
127:3 B, sons are a heritage from the LORD, the
128:4 B, thus shall the man be blessed who fears
132:6 B, we heard of it in Ephrathah, we found
139:4 is on my tongue, B, O LORD, you know
Prov 7:10 And B, a woman meets him, dressed as a
24:31 man without sense; and B, it was all overgrown
Song 2:11 and come away; for B, the winter is past,
Sir 24:29 my garden plot"; and B, my canal became a
Is 5:26 of the earth; and B, swiftly, speedily it comes!
25:9 said on that day, B, this is our God;
38:17 B, it was for my welfare that I had
49:12 B, these shall come from afar, and behold, these
49:12 come from afar, and B, these from the north
Jer 1:15 For, B, I am calling all the tribes of
4:23 on the earth, and B, it was waste and
4:24 on the mountains, and B, they were quaking, and
4:25 I looked, and B, there was no man, and
4:26 I looked, and B, the fruitful land was a
8:9 be dismayed and taken; B, they have rejected the

30:10 dismayed, O Israel; for B, I will save you
46:27 dismayed, O Israel; for B, I will save you
50:12 B, she shall be the last of the nations,
Ezek 3:23 into the plain; and B, the glory of the
8:8 dug in the wall, B, there was a door.
8:17 B, they put the branch to their nose.
9:2 And B, six men came from the direction of
9:11 And B, the man clothed in linen, with the
15:4 B, it is given to the fire for fuel;
23:39 And B, this is what they did in my
23:40 messenger was sent, and B, they came.
30:9 of Egypts doom; for B, it comes!
30:21 king of Egypt; and B, it has not been
33:32 And B, you are to them like one who
Dan 7:6 this I looked, and B, another, like a leopard,
10:20 am through with him, B, the prince of Greece
Amos 4:13 For B, he who forms the mountains, and creates
9:9 "For B, I will command, and shake the house
Hab 1:6 For B, I am rousing the Chaldeans, that bitter
Hag 1:9 looked for much, and B, it came to little;
Zech 2:10 daughter of Zion; for B, I come and I
9:4 But B, the Lord will strip her of her
9:9 B, your king comes to you; triumphant and victorious
11:6 B, I will cause men to fall each into
11:16 For B, I am raising up in the land
12:2 of man within him: B, I am about to
Mt 2:9 went their way; and B, the star which they
3:17 alighting on him; and B, a voice from heaven,
17:5 still speaking, when B, a bright cloud overshadowed
19:27 Peter said in reply, B, we have left everything
24:23 one says to you, B, here is the Christ!
24:25 B, I have told you beforehand.
24:26 they say to you, B, he is in the
24:26 out, if they say, B, he is in the
28:7 B, I have told you."
28:20 have commanded you; and B, I am with you
Mk 10:28 to say to him, B, we have left everything
Lk 13:7 said to the vinedresser, B, these three years I
15:29 he answered his father, B, these many years I
17:21 nor will they say, B, here it is!
17:23 or B, here!
17:23 will say to you, B, there!
18:28 God.' And Peter said, B, we have left our
Jn 19:4 and said to them, B, I am bringing him
Acts 27:24 stand before Caesar; and B, God has granted you
1Cor 15:51 B
Heb 10:7 Then I said, B, I have come to do
10:9 law), then he added, B, I have come to
Rev 4:1 this I looked, and B, in heaven an open
4:2 in the Spirit, and B, a throne stood in
5:5 to me, "Weep not; B, the Lion of the
14:1 Then I looked, and B, on Mount Zion stood
14:14 Then I looked, and B, a white cloud, and
16:15 B, I am coming like a thief!

BELIEVE
Sir 50:24 old, that Israel may B that the God of

BELOVED
Tob 3:10 You only had one B daughter but she hanged

BELT (21)
Ex 28:8 band upon it, to B it on, shall be
29:5 and the breastpiece, and B him with the skilfully
29:9 them, and you shall B them with sashes and
39:5 band upon it, to B it on, was of
1Sam 18:4 even his sword and his bow and his B
25:13 his men, "Every man B on his sword!" And
2Sam 18:11 give you ten pieces of silver and a B
20:8 over it was a B with a sword in
1Kgs 2:5 innocent blood upon the B about my I loins,
2Kgs 1:8 of haircloth, with a B of leather about his
Is 3:24 and instead of a B, a rope; and instead
11:5 Righteousness shall be the B of his waist, and
11:5 waist, and faithfulness the B of his loins.
22:21 and will bind your B on him, and will
Mt 3:4 hair, and a leather B around his waist; and
Mk 1:6 and had a leather B around his waist, and
Jn 21:18 another will fasten your B for you and carry
21:18 you fastened your own B and walked where you
Acts 21:11 us he took Pauls B and bound his own
21:11 man who owns this B and deliver him into
Eph 6:14 therefore, having fastened the B of truth around your

BELTED (11)
Deut 1:41 every man of you B on his weapons of
1Sam 17:39 And David B on his sword over his armor,
25:13 every man of them B on his sword; David
25:13 his sword; David also B on his sword; and
2Sam 6:14 might; and David was B with a linen ephod.
1Kgs 20:32 So they B sackcloth on their loins, and put
Neh 4:18 builders had his sword B at his side while
Jud 8:5 of her house, and B sackcloth about her loins
Song 3:8 men of Israel, all B with swords and expert
Dan 10:5 linen, whose loins were B with gold of Uphaz.
1Mac 3:3 on his breastplate; he B on his armor of

BELTS
1Kgs 20:11 Let not him that B on his armor boast

BESTRODE
Hab 3:12 You B the earth in fury, you trampled the

BETHEL
Tob 2:6 how he said against B, "Your feasts shall be

BETTER
Tob 3:10 It is B for me not to hang myself,

BIND
Ps 76:10 of wrath you will B around you.

BIRDS
Sir 17:4 flesh, and granted them dominion over beasts and B

BIRTH (2)
Is 26:17 writhed, but we gave B only to wind.
26:18 writhed, but we gave B only to wind.

BLACK
Jer 4:28 the heavens above be B, for I have spoken,

BLAMELESSLY
Lk 1:6 all the commandments and ordinances of the Lord B

BLESS (2)
Tob 12:20 And now B the Lord upon the earth and
13:8 B the Lord, all you his chosen ones, all

BLESSED (8)
Gen 30:13 women will call me B; so she called his
30:13 And Leah said, B am I!
Esth 13:8 Isaac, God of Jacob, B are you:
14:3 and God of Jacob, B are you; help me,
Ps 34:8 B is the man who takes refuge in him!
Sir 24:2 the blessed she is B, saying:
24:2 praise, and among the B she is blessed, saying:
Dan 3:52 B are you, O Lord, God of our fathers,

BLEW (2)
Ex 15:10 You B with your wind, the sea covered them;
Tob 11:11 holding him firmly, he B into his eyes, saying,

BLIND
Tob 2:10 by the white films, until I became completely B

BLOOD (3)
Sir 17:27 So flesh and B devise evil.
Lk 22:20 for you is the new covenant in my B
Acts 20:28 the Lord, which he obtained with his own B

BLOODGUILT
Ps 51:14 Deliver me from B, O God, O God of

BODY
1Thes 4:4 to control his own B in holiness and honor,

BOIL
Is 64:2 fire causes water to B to make your name

BOLTS (2)
Job 37:4 does not restrain the B of lightning when his
38:35 Can you send forth B of lightning, that they

BOOK (2)
Tob 7:12 the decree in the B of Moses, and it
7:13 decree written in the B of Moses.

BOOKS
Esth 14:11 have heard from the B of my ancestors that

BORE
Neh 9:30 Many years you B with them, and warned them

BORN (5)
Ps 78:51 struck all the first B in Egypt, the first
105:36 struck all the first B in their land, the
135:8 who struck the first B of Egypt, both of
136:10 who struck the first B of Egypt, for his
1Jn 5:1 the Christ has been B of God, and every

BOTH (3)
Tob 7:11 the Lord will act on behalf of you B
8:8 And they B said, "Amen, amen."
11:13 Next, with B his hands, he peeled off the

BRAVE
Tob 6:12 the girl is sensible, B, and very beautiful, and

BREAD (2)
1Sam 2:36 places, that I may eat a morsel of B
Ps 78:24 and gave them the B of heaven.

BREATHES
Sir 4:11 Wisdom B life into her sons and gives help

BRETHREN (6)
Jn 2:12 his mother and his B and his disciples; and
7:3 So his B said to him, "Leave here and
7:5 For even his B did not believe in him.
7:10 But after his B had gone up to the
Acts 1:14 Mary the mother of Jesus, and with his B
1Cor 9:5 other apostles and the B of the Lord and

BRIGHTER
Sir 17:27 What is B than the sun?

BRIMSTONE (5)
Lk 17:29 from Sodom, fire and B rained from heaven and
Rev 14:10 tormented with fire and B in the presence of
19:20 into the lake of fire that burns with B
20:10 lake of fire and B where the beast and
21:8 burns with fire and B, which is the second

BRING (5)
Tob 7:13 Take her and B her safely to your father.
7:14 and told her to B writing material; and he
Job 39:1 when the mountain goats B forth?
Sir 5:3 or "Who will B me down because of my
Jer 18:22 their houses, when you B the marauder suddenly

BRINGING
Job 39:1 you observe the deer B forth their young?

BROKE
Ps 74:13 by your might; you B the heads of the

BROTHER (6)
Tob 6:10 to the young man, B Tobias!" "Here I am,"
7:1 me straight to our B Raguel." So he took
7:1 Tobias said to him, B Azariah, take me straight
7:9 Tobias said to Raphael, B Azarias, ask Raguel to
7:10 no one except you, B, has the right to
7:12 on you are her B and she is your

BROTHERS
Tob 7:1 "Joyous greetings, B ; welcome and good health!"

BROUGHT (16)
Ex 32:12 With evil intent he B them forth, to slay
Num 14:13 of it, for you B up this people in
Deut 9:29 your heritage, whom you B out by your great
1Kgs 8:51 your heritage, which you B out of Egypt, from
8:53 your servant, when you B our fathers out of
Neh 9:7 who chose Abram and B him forth out of
9:15 for their hunger and B forth water for them
9:23 of heaven, and you B them into the land
Tob 8:1 the young man and B him into the bedroom.
Ps 66:11 You B us into the net; you laid affliction
80:8 You B a vine out of Egypt; you drove
85:1 to your land; you B back the captives of
Jer 32:21 You B your people Israel out of the land
Bar 2:11 God of Israel, who B your people out of
Dan 9:15 Lord our God, who B your people out of
Jon 2:6 for ever; yet you B up my life from

BURNED
Bar 6:55 the gods, will be B in two like beams.

BURY
Tob 2:4 sunset when I might B it.

BYWORD
Tob 3:4 us the talk, the B, and an object of

C

CALF
Jer 31:18 chastened, like an untrained C, bring me back that

CALLED (5)
Tob 2:13 So I C her and said to her, "Where
Wis 18:8 punished our enemies you C us to yourself and
Gal 5:8 not from him who C you,
Eph 4:1 which you have been C
Jas 2:7 blaspheme that honorable name by which you are C

CAME (4)
Neh 9:13 You C down upon Mount Sinai, and spoke with
Tob 11:10 Tobit got up, and C stumbling out through the
Is 64:3 looked not for, you C down, the mountains quaked
Lam 3:57 You C near when I called on you; you

CAMP
Heb 13:13 to him outside the C, bearing abuse for him.

CANNOT (2)
Sir 17:26 For all things C be in men, since a
Hab 1:13 to behold evil and C look on wrong, why

CAPTAINS (2)
Lk 22:4 the chief priests and C how he might betray
22:52 the chief priests and C of the temple and

CAPTIVES
Ps 85:1 you brought back the C of Jacob.

CAPTIVITY
Tob 3:15 the land of my C I am my fathers

CARE
Heb 2:6 of man, that you C for him?

CARRIED
Sir 42:15 his will, justice is C out.

CAT
Ps 102:4 withered; I forget to C my bread.

CEASED
Sir 17:24 not exist, thanksgiving has C; he who is alive

CELEBRATE
Tob 13:8 C days of joy, and give thanks to him.

CHAINED
2Tim 2:9 But the word of God is not C

CHAINS (12)
Sir 6:24 your feet into her C, and your neck into
6:29 Then her C will become for you a strong
21:19 senseless man education is C on his feet, and
28:19 been bound with its C;
28:20 and its chains are C of bronze;
28:20 of iron, and its C are chains of bronze;
33:28 not obey, make his C heavy.
Jer 39:7 and bound him in C to take him to
52:11 and bound him in C, and the king of
Acts 16:26 opened and every ones C were unfastened.
Col 4:18 Remember my C
2Tim 2:9 am suffering and wearing C like a criminal.

CHALICE (17)
Ps 116:13 will lift up the C of salvation and call
Mt 20:22 able to drink the C that I am to
20:23 "You will drink my C, but to sit at
26:27 And he took a C, and when he had
26:39 be possible, let this C pass from me; nevertheless,
Mk 10:38 able to drink the C that I drink, or
10:39 said to them, "The C that I drink you

14:23 And he took a C, and when he had
14:36 to you; remove this C from me; yet not
Lk 22:17 And he took a C, and when he had
22:20 after supper, saying, "This C which is poured out
22:20 And likewise the C after supper, saying, "This chalice
22:42 are willing, remove this C from me; nevertheless not
Jn 18:11 I not drink the C which the Father has
1Cor 11:25 same way also the C, after supper, saying, "This
11:25 after supper, saying, "This C is the new covenant
11:26 bread and drink the C, you proclaim the Lords

CHANCE
1Kgs 22:34 drew his bow by C, and struck the king

CHANGE (2)
Job 14:20 and he passes; you C his countenance, and send
Ps 102:26 You C them like clothing, and they pass away;

CHARGED
Ex 19:23 Sinai; for you yourself C us, saying, Set bounds

CHEEKS
Hos 11:4 an infant to his C, and I bent down

CHEST
Rev 1:13 golden sash across his C;

CHESTS
Rev 15:6 bright linen, and with golden sashes across their C

CHILD (7)
Tob 2:3 And I replied, "Here I am, my C
7:11 for the present, my C, eat and drink, and
7:12 Lord of heaven, my C, guide and prosper you
Mk 2:5 said to the paralytic, C, your sins are forgiven."
13:16 those who are with C and for those who
Lk 1:41 greeting of Mary, the C leaped in her womb;
1:44 to my ears, the C in my womb leaped

CHILDREN
Sir 3:5 gladdened by his own C, and when he prays

CHOSE (3)
Neh 9:7 LORD, the God who C Abram and brought him
1Mac 7:37 wept and said, "You C this house to be
2Mac 1:25 from every evil, who C the fathers and consecrated

CHOSEN (3)
Tob 13:8 Lord, all you his C ones, all of you,
Sir 24:2 the multitude of the C she finds praise, and
24:8 inheritance, and among my C put down your roots.

CHURCH (5)
Mt 16:18 I will build my C, and the gates of
Acts 8:3 Saul laid waste the C, and entering house after
20:28 guardians, to feed the C of the Lord, which
Eph 5:32 to Christ and the C;
3Jn 1:10 welcome them and puts them out of the C

CITY (2)
2Sam 15:24 the people had all passed out of the C
Mic 6:9 name: "Hear, O tribe and assembly of the C

CLAIM
Tob 6:10 other men a hereditary C on her.

CLAIMING
Acts 5:36 these days Theudas arose, C to be somebody, and

CLEAN
Mk 1:40 him, "If you will, you can make me C

CLEARED
Ps 80:9 You C the ground for it; it took deep

CLING (19)
Num 36:7 sons of Israel shall C to the inheritance of
36:9 sons of Israel shall C to its own inheritance."
Deut 10:20 shall serve him and C to him, and by
13:4 shall serve him and C to him.
13:17 the devoted things shall C to your hand; that
28:21 will make the pestilence C to you until he
28:60 of; and they shall C to you.
Josh 22:5 his commandments, and to C to him, and to
23:8 yourselves to them, but C to the LORD your
2Kgs 5:27 leprosy of Naaman shall C to you, and to
Job 19:20 My bones C to my skin and to my
38:38 mass and the clods C tightly together?
41:23 folds of his flesh C together, firmly cast upon
Ps 101:3 away; it shall not C to me.
102:5 loud groaning my bones C to my flesh.
119:31 I C to your testimonies, O LORD; let me
Sir 2:3 Await Gods patience, C to him and do not
6:34 C to him.
Is 14:1 join them and will C to the house of

CLINGING (2)
Deut 11:22 all his ways, and C to him,
30:20 obeying his voice, and C to him; for that

CLINGS (5)
Gen 2:24 and his mother and C to his wife, and
Ps 44:25 the dust; our body C to the ground.
91:14 Because he C to me in love, I will
119:25 My soul C to the dust; revive me according
Lam 4:4 tongue of the infant C to the roof of

CLOAK (5)
Mk 10:50 And throwing off his C he sprang up and
Lk 6:29 who takes away your C do not withhold your
22:36 no sword sell his C and buy one.
Acts 12:8 to him, "Wrap your C around you and follow
Heb 1:12 a garment, like a C you will roll them

CLOTHE (8)
Esth 6:9 noble princes; let him C the man whom the
Sir 15:5 wisdom and understanding, and C him with a robe
Is 45:5 is no God; I C you, though you do
Jer 4:8 For this C yourself with sackcloth, lament and wail;
49:3 C yourselves with sackcloth, lament, and run to and
Ezek 7:18 They C themselves with sackcloth, and horror covers
them;
44:18 loins; they shall not C themselves with anything that
Zeph 1:8 sons and all who C themselves in foreign attire.

CLOTHED (15)
Jud 4:10 purchased slave-they all C themselves with sackcloth.
4:14 Lord, with their loins C with sackcloth, offered the
Esth 15:1 she had worshiped, and C herself in splendid attire.
Job 10:11 You C me with skin and flesh, and knit
Ps 30:11 loosed my sackcloth and C me with gladness,
Joel 1:8 Lament like a virgin C with sackcloth for the
2Mac 3:19 Women, C with sackcloth under their breasts,
Mt 6:29 his glory was not C like one of these.
Lk 12:27 his glory was not C like one of these.
Jn 19:2 on his head, and C him in a purple
1Cor 4:11 thirst, we are poorly C and buffeted and homeless,
Jas 2:15 or sister is poorly C and in lack of
Rev 3:5 who conquers shall be C like them in white
4:4 thrones were twenty-four elders, C in white
17:4 The woman was C in purple and scarlet, and

CLOTHES (2)
Prov 31:17 She C her loins with strength and makes her
Mk 14:63 high priest tore his C, and said, "Why do

CLOTHING (8)
Ps 22:18 them, and for my C they cast lots.
102:26 You change them like C, and they pass away;
Is 63:3 my garments, and I have stained all my C
Ezek 16:13 and silver; and your C was of fine linen,
Dan 7:9 took his seat; his C was white as snow,
Mt 28:3 like lightning, and his C white as snow.
Lk 9:29 was altered, and his C became dazzling white.
23:11 and mocked him; then, C him in gorgeous apparel,

CLUNG (2)
2Sam 23:10 weary, and his hand C to the sword; and
Job 31:7 if any spot has C to my hands;

CO-WORKER
Phil 4:3 who are a true C, help these women, for

COAT (5)
2Kgs 2:8 Then Elijah took his C, and rolled it up,
2:13 he took up the C of Elijah that had
2:14 Then he took the C of Elijah that had
Mt 24:18 the field not turn back to get a C
Mk 13:16 the field not turn back to get a C

COATS
Acts 9:39 weeping, and showing C and garments which Dorcas

COME (3)
Tob 2:2 for you until you C back."
Esth 14:11 O Lord, my God C to my aid, for
Job 28:20 "From where does wisdom C

COMMAND
Num 35:2 the Jordan at Jericho, C the sons of Israel,

COMMANDED (7)
Ezra 9:11 your commandments, which you C by your servants
Neh 1:7 the ordinances which you C your servant Moses.
1:8 the word which you C your servant Moses, saying,
9:14 sabbath and C them commandments and statutes
Jer 32:23 nothing of all you C them to do.
Bar 2:28 the day when you C him to write your
Ezek 9:11 have done as you C me."

COMMANDMENTS
Sir 2:10 ever persevered in his C and was forsaken?

COMMISSION
1Cor 3:10 According to the C of God given to me,

COMMIT
1Jn 3:9 of God does not C sin; for Gods seed

COMPANY
Num 16:40 Korah and as his C as the LORD said

COMPASSION (5)
Ps 25:6 Be mindful of your C, O LORD, and of
40:11 O LORD, withhold your C from me, let your
69:16 according to your abundant C, turn to me.
103:4 you with mercy and C,
119:77 Let your C come to me, that I may

COMPLETELY
Tob 2:10 films, until I became C blind.

CONSECRATE
Ex 13:2 LORD said to Moses, C to me all the

CONSECRATED
2Mac 1:25 chose the fathers and C them,

CONSENT
Judg 11:17 but he would not C, So Israel remained at

CONSIDERED
Wis 15:2 know that we are C yours.

CONTENDED
Is 27:8 measure, by exile you C with them; he removed

CONTRACT
Tob 7:14 copy of the marriage C, to the effect that

CONTROL
1Thes 4:4 you know how to C his own body in

CONVINCED
Wis 16:8 by this also you C our enemies that it

COPY
Tob 7:14 he wrote out a C of the marriage contract,

CORNERSTONE (6)
Ps 118:22 stone which the builders rejected has become the C
Mt 21:42 rejected has become the C; this was the Lords
Mk 12:10 rejected has become the C;
Lk 20:17 stone which the builders rejected has become the C
Acts 4:11 by you builders, but which has become the C
1Pet 2:7 stone which the builders rejected has become the C

COURAGE
Tob 11:11 his eyes, saying, "Take C, Father."

COURT
Ps 45:12 people of Tyre will C your favor with gifts,

COURTYARD (3)
Tob 2:9 I went into my C and slept by the
7:1 Raguel sitting beside the C door.
11:10 stumbling out through the C door.

COVENANT (36)
Ex 16:34 placed it before the C, to be kept.
25:16 into the ark the C which I shall give
25:21 you shall put the C that I shall give
25:22 the ark of the C, I will speak with
26:33 the ark of the C in there within the
26:34 the ark of the C in the most holy
27:21 which is before the C, Aaron and his sons
30:6 the ark of the C, before the mercy seat
30:6 that is over the C, where I will meet
30:26 the ark of the C,
30:36 of it before the C in the tent of
31:7 the ark of the C, and the mercy seat
31:18 two tables of the C, tables of stone, written
32:15 two tables of the C in his hands, tables
34:29 two tables of the C in his hand as
38:21 the tabernacle of the C, as they were counted
39:35 the ark of the C with its poles and
Lev 16:13 which is upon the C, lest he die;
24:3 the veil of the C, in the tent of
Num 1:50 the tabernacle of the C, and over all its
1:53 the tabernacle of the C, that there may be
1:53 shall keep charge of the tabernacle of the C
4:5 the ark of the C with it;
7:89 the ark of the C, from between the two
9:15 the tent of the C; and at evening it
10:11 the tabernacle of the C,
17:4 of meeting before the C, where I meet with
17:7 before the LORD in the tent of the C
17:8 the tent of the C; and behold, the rod
17:10 of Aaron before the C, to be kept as
18:2 with you are before the tent of the C
Josh 4:16 the ark of the C to come up out
2Kgs 11:12 and gave him the C; and they proclaimed him
2Chr 23:11 and gave him the C; and they proclaimed him
24:6 the congregation of Israel for the tent of C
Ps 83:5 you they make a C

COVENANTS (3)
2Kgs 23:3 his commandments and his C and his statutes, with
1Chr 29:19 keep your commandments, your C, and your statutes,
perfo
2Chr 34:31 his commandments and his C and his statutes, with

COVER
Ps 104:2 honor and majesty, who C yourself with light as

COVERED
Ps 104:6 You C it with the deep as with a

CREATED (4)
Sir 17:6 He C in them the knowledge of the spirit;
36:15 to those whom you C in the beginning, and
Mk 13:18 the creation which God C until now, and never
Rev 4:11 and power, for you C all things, and by

CREATION
Mk 13:18 the beginning of the C which God created until

CREATOR
Sir 1:8 who is wise, the C of all, the King

CREATURE
Is 34:14 there shall the night C alight, and find for

CREATURES (2)
Wis 1:14 might exist, and the C of the world are
Sir 24:3 of the Most High, the first-born before all C

CROWN
Ps 65:11 You C the year with your bounty; the tracks

CROWNED
Ps 8:5 angels, and you have C him with glory and

CRUEL
Ps 144:10 your servant from the C sword.

CRUSHED (3)
Ps 74:14 You C the heads of Leviathan, you gave him
89:10 You C Rahab like a carcass, you scattered your
Hab 3:13 You C the head of the wicked, laying him

CRUSHES
Jud 9:7 are the Lord who C wars; the Lord is

C

D

CURIOUS
Sir 3:22 and do not be C about many of his

CUT (2)
Tob 2:12 of Dystrus, when she C off a piece she
Ps 74:15 You C open springs and brooks; you dried up

D

DARKNESS (4)
Mt 22:13 him into the outer D, where there will be
25:30 servant into the outer D, where there will be
2Pet 2:4 to pits of deepest D to be kept until
Jude 1:6 chains in the deepest D until the judgment of

DAUGHTER (3)
Tob 3:10 only had one beloved D but she hanged herself
7:10 right to marry my D Sarah.
Ps 45:13 The D of the king is decked in her

DAUGHTERIN-LAW
Tob 11:16 out to meet his D at the gate of

DAVID
1Kgs 12:16 Look now to your own house, D

DAWNS
Ps 46:5 be moved; God will help her when morning D

DAY (29)
Ex 9:6 And the next D the LORD did this thing;
18:13 The next D Moses sat to judge the people,
32:6 up early the next D, and offered burnt offerings
32:30 The next D Moses said to the people, "You
Lev 19:6 or on the next D; and anything left over
23:11 find acceptance; on the D after the sabbath the
23:16 fifty days to the D after the seventh sabbath;
Num 16:41 But the next D all the congregation of the
17:8 And the next D Moses went into the tent
22:41 And the next D Balak took Balaam and brought
Deut 5:15 to keep the sabbath D
Josh 5:11 And on the next D after the Passover, on
5:12 ceased on the next D, when they ate of
Judg 21:4 And the next D the people rose early, and
1Sam 11:11 And the next D Saul put the people in
20:27 second day, the next D after the new moon,
31:8 On the next D, when the Philistines came to
2Kgs 8:15 But the next D he took the coverlet and
1Chr 10:8 The next D, when the Philistines came to strip
Tob 2:12 One D, the seventh of Dystrus, when she cut
3:10 On that D she was deeply grieved in spirit
Jer 20:3 On the next D, when Pashhur released Jeremiah
Acts 4:3 custody until the next D, for it was already
4:5 On the next D their rulers and elders and
20:7 depart on the next D; and he prolonged his
21:8 The next D we departed and came to Caesarea;
22:30 But the next D, desiring to know the real
23:32 And the next D they returned to the barracks,
25:23 So the next D Agrippa and Bernice came with

DAYS (4)
Tob 13:8 Celebrate D of joy, and give thanks to him.
Sir 3:13 despise him all the D of his life.
Mk 13:16 and for those who are nursing in those D
13:18 For in those D there will be such tribulation

DEAD (3)
Tob 2:9 returned from burying the D, I went into my
3:9 Because your husbands are D
Sir 17:24 From the D, as from one who does not

DEADLY (4)
1Jn 5:16 what is not a D sin, he will ask,
5:16 him life for those whose sin is not D
5:16 is sin which is D; I do not say
5:17 sin, but there is sin which is not D

DEATH (2)
Ps 23:4 of the shadow of D, I fear no evil;
Sir 48:11 but our name, after D, will not be such.

DEBAUCHERY (2)
Tit 1:6 to the charge of D and not being insubordinate.
1Pet 4:4 in the same wild D, and they abuse you;

DEBT (8)
Ex 29:28 sons as a perpetual D from the sons of
Lev 7:34 sons, as a perpetual D from the sons of
7:36 it is a perpetual D throughout their generations."
10:15 with you, as a D for ever; as the
24:9 offerings by fire to the LORD, a perpetual D
Num 18:8 portion, and to your sons as a perpetual D
18:11 you, as a perpetual D; every one who is
18:19 you, as a perpetual D; it is a covenant

DECLARE
Tob 12:11 "I will now D the whole truth to you

DECLARED (4)
1Kgs 8:24 my father what you D to him; yes, you
8:53 your heritage, as you D through Moses, your servant,
2Chr 6:15 my father what you D to him; yes, you
Bar 2:20 upon us, as you D by your servants the

DECREE (2)
Tob 7:12 in accordance with the D in the book of
7:13 the law and the D written in the book

DECREED
Tob 7:12 and it has been D from heaven that she

DECREES (4)
Deut 4:45 Israel; these are the D, the statutes, and the
6:17 your God, and his D, and his statutes, which
6:20 the meaning of the D and the statutes and
Ps 78:56 did not observe his D,

DEEDS (2)
Sir 5:3 "Who will bring me down because of my D
17:8 glory in his wondrous D,

DEEPEST (4)
2Pet 2:4 them to pits of D darkness to be kept
2:17 storm; for them the D gloom of darkness has
Jude 1:6 eternal chains in the D darkness until the judgment
1:13 stars for whom the D darkness has been reserved

DEER (17)
Gen 49:21 Naphtali is a D let loose, that bears comely
Deut 12:15 as of the gazelle and as of the D
12:22 the gazelle or the D is eaten, so you
14:5 sheep, the goat, the D, the gazelle, the roebuck,
15:22 as though it were a gazelle or a D
2Sam 22:34 made my feet like D feet, and set me
1Kgs 4:23 sheep, besides D, gazelles, roebucks, and fatted
Job 39:1 Do you observe the D bringing forth their young?
Ps 18:33 made my feet like D feet, and set me
42:1 As a D longs for flowing streams,
Prov 5:19 your youth, a lovely D, a graceful doe.
Song 2:7 the gazelles or the D of the field, that
3:5 the gazelles or the D of the field, that
Is 35:6 man leap like a D, and the tongue of
Jer 14:5 Even the D in the field forsakes her newborn
Lam 1:6 princes have become like D that find no pasture;
Hab 3:19 makes my feet like D feet, he makes me

DELAY (2)
Ps 40:17 my deliverer; do not D, O my God!
70:5 help and my deliverer; O LORD, do not D

DELICACIES
Rev 18:14 you, and all your D and your splendor are

DELIGHTED
Ps 44:3 your countenance; for you D in them.

DELIVER (3)
Ps 35:10 like you, you who D the weak from him
106:4 help me when you D them;
Wis 16:8 it is you who D from every evil.

DELIVERED (7)
2Sam 22:44 "You D me from strife with the peoples; you
22:49 above my adversaries, you D me from men of
Neh 9:28 and many times you D them according to your
Ps 18:43 You D me from strife with the peoples; I
22:4 they trusted, and you D them.
Wis 19:9 you, O Lord, who D them.
Sir 51:3 were my helper, and D me, in the greatness

DEN (2)
Ps 10:9 a lion in his D; he lurks that he
Jer 25:38 he has left his D, for their land has

DEPEND
Mic 5:7 grass, which do not D upon men nor wait

DEPRIVED
1Thes 2:17 But since we were D of you, brethren, for

DESERTED (2)
Mt 26:56 Then all the disciples D him and fled.
Mk 14:50 And they all D him and fled.

DESIRE
Ps 51:6 Behold, you D truth in the inward being; therefore

DESTROY (3)
2Chr 20:10 avoided and did not D
Job 14:19 the earth; so you D the hope of man.
Ps 5:6 You D those who speak lies; the LORD abhors

DESTROYED (2)
Wis 18:5 their children; and you D them all together by
Sir 48:6 their beds, and easily D their dominion;

DEVISE
Sir 17:27 So flesh and blood D evil.

DEVOUR
Ps 27:2 evildoers assail me, to D my flesh, my adversaries

DIE
Tob 3:10 Lord that I may D and not listen to

DINE
Tob 7:9 and had reclined to D, Tobias said to Raphael,

DIRECT
Sir 36:17 for your people, and D us in the way

DISCERN
Ps 139:2 I rise up; you D my thoughts from afar.

DISCERNING
Jud 8:7 was prudent of heart, D in judgment, and quite

DISCERNMENT (2)
Sir 4:18 him knowledge and the D of what is right.
17:5 thinking, and filled them with the discipline of D

DISCIPLINE
Sir 17:5 filled them with the D of discernment.

DISCRETION
Sir 17:5 He made for them D, with a tongue and

DISGUISE
Sir 4:17 walk with him in D, and at first she

DISPERSED
Tob 3:4 among which you have D us.

DISTRESS (3)
Judg 2:15 sworn to them; and they were in great D
Tob 3:6 be released from my D; release me to go
3:10 daughter but she hanged herself because of her D

DIVIDED (2)
Neh 9:11 And you D the sea before them, so that
Ps 74:13 You D the sea by your might; you broke

DIVISION
Ex 8:23 I will put a D, between my people and

DOINGS
Jer 44:22 longer bear your evil D and the abominations which

DOMINION (3)
Ps 110:3 Yours is D on the day you lead your
Sir 17:4 flesh, and granted them D over beasts and birds.
48:6 and easily destroyed their D;

DONKEY (84)
Gen 16:12 shall be a wild D of a man, his
22:3 the morning, saddled his D, and took two of
22:5 "Stay here with the D; I and the lad
42:27 sack to give his D food at the lodging
44:13 every man loaded his D, and they returned to
49:14 Issachar is a strong D, crouching between the
Ex 4:20 set them on a D, and went back to
13:13 Every firstling of a D you shall redeem with
20:17 his ox, or his D, or anything that is
21:33 an ox or a D falls into it,
22:2 an ox or a D or a sheep, he
22:9 is for ox, for D, for sheep, for clothing,
22:10 to his neighbor a D or an ox or
23:4 enemys ox or his D going astray, you shall
23:5 If you see the D of one who hates
23:12 your ox and your D may have rest, and
34:20 The firstling of a D you shall redeem with
Num 16:15 have not taken one D from them, and I
22:21 morning, and saddled his D, and went with the
22:22 was riding on the D, and his two servants
22:23 And the D saw the angel of the LORD
22:23 his hand; and the D turned aside out of
22:23 and Balaam struck the D, to turn her into
22:25 And when the D saw the angel of the
22:27 When the D saw the angel of the LORD,
22:27 and he struck the D with his staff.
22:28 the mouth of the D, and she said to
22:29 Balaam said to the D, "Because you have made
22:30 And the D said to Balaam, "Am I not
22:30 "Am I not your D, upon which you have
22:32 have you struck your D these three times?
22:33 before me; and the D saw me, and turned
Deut 5:14 your ox, or your D, or any of your
5:21 his ox, or his D, or anything that is
22:3 shall do with his D; so you shall do
22:4 not see your brothers D or his ox fallen
22:10 an ox and a D together.
28:31 eat of it; your D shall be violently taken
Josh 15:18 she alighted from her D, and Caleb said to
Judg 1:14 she alighted from her D, and Caleb said to
6:4 in Israel, and no sheep or ox or D
15:15 fresh jawbone of a D, and put out his
15:16 the jawbone of a D have I slain a
15:16 the jawbone of a D, heaps upon heaps, with
19:28 put her upon the D; and the man rose
1Sam 12:3 Or whose D have I taken?
15:3 infant and suckling, ox and sheep, camel and D
16:20 And Jesse took a D laden with bread, and
25:20 she rode on the D, and came down under
25:23 and alighted from the D, and fell before David
25:42 and mounted on a D, and her five maidens
2Sam 17:23 followed, he saddled his D, and went off home
19:26 to him, Saddle a D for me, that I
1Kgs 2:40 arose and saddled a D, and went to Gath
13:13 So they saddled the D for him and he
13:13 his sons, "Saddle the D for me." So they
13:23 drunk, he saddled the D for the prophet whom
13:24 the road, and the D stood beside it; the
13:27 his sons, "Saddle the D for me." And they
13:28 had not eaten the body or torn the D
13:28 the road, and the D and the lion standing
13:29 laid it upon the D, and brought it back
2Kgs 4:24 Then she saddled the D, and she said to
Job 6:5 Does the wild D bray when he has grass,
24:3 They drive away the D of the fatherless; they
39:5 bonds of the swift D,
39:5 has let the wild D go free?
Prov 26:3 a bridle for the D, and a rod for
Sir 33:24 and burdens for a D; bread and discipline and
Is 1:3 its owner, and the D its masters crib; but
32:20 the ox and the D range free.
Jer 2:24 her tracks, a wild D used to the wilderness,
22:19 the burial of a D he shall be buried,
48:6 Be like a wild D in the desert!
Hos 8:9 to Assyria, a wild D wandering alone; Ephraim has
Zech 9:9 donkey, on a colt the foal of a D
9:9 and riding on a D, on a colt the
Mt 21:2 you will find a D tied, and a colt
21:5 and mounted on a D, and on a colt,
21:5 and on a colt, the foal of a D
21:7 them; they brought the D and the colt, and
Lk 13:15 his ox or his D from the manger, and
Jn 12:14 Jesus found a young D and sat upon it;
2Pet 2:16 transgression; a speechless D spoke with human

DONKEYS (67)
Gen 24:35 gold, menservants and maidservants, camels and D
30:43 maidservants and menservants, and camels and D

32:5 have oxen, D, flocks, menservants, and maidservants;
34:28 and their herds, their D, and whatever was in
36:24 as he pastured the D of Zibeon his father.
42:26 Then they loaded their D with their grain, and
43:18 to make slaves of us and seize our D
43:24 he had given their D food,
44:3 light, the men were sent away with their D
45:23 sent as follows: ten D loaded with the good
47:17 the herds, and the D: and he supplied them
49:11 the vine and his D colt to the choice
Ex 9:3 field, the horses, the D, the camels, the herds,
Num 31:28 oxen and of the D and of the flocks;
31:30 the oxen, of the D, and of the flocks,
31:34 thousand cattle, Sixty-one thousand D,
31:39 The D were thirty thousand five hundred, of which
31:45 thirty thousand five hundred D,
Josh 6:21 old, oxen, sheep, and D, with the edge of
7:24 and his oxen and D and sheep, and his
9:4 worn-out sacks upon their D, and wineskins,
Judg 5:10 who ride on tawny D, you who sit on
10:4 who rode on thirty D; and they had thirty
12:14 who rode on seventy D; and he judged Israel
19:3 with him his servant and a couple of D
19:10 a couple of saddled D, and his concubine was
19:19 and food for our D, with bread and wine
19:21 house, and fed the D; and they washed their
1Sam 8:16 cattle o and your D, and put them to
9:3 Now the D of Kish, Sauls father, were lost.
9:3 you, and arise, go and look for the D
9:5 to care about the D and become anxious about
9:20 As for your D that were lost three days
10:2 say to you, The D which you went to
10:2 to care about the D and is anxious about
10:14 said, "To seek the D; and when we saw
10:16 us plainly that the D had been found." But
22:19 children and sucklings, oxen, D and sheep, he put
25:18 hundred cakes of figs, and laid them on D
27:9 sheep, the oxen, the D, the camels, and the
2Sam 16:1 with a couple of D saddled, bearing two hundred
16:2 Ziba answered, "The D are for the kings household
2Kgs 4:22 and one of the D, that I may quickly
6:25 besieged it, until a D head was sold for
7:7 their horses, and their D, leaving the camp as
7:10 horses tied, and the D tied, and the tents
1Chr 5:21 thousand sheep, two thousand D, and a hundred
12:40 came bringing food on D and on camels and
2Chr 28:15 feeble among them on D, they brought them to
Ezra 2:67 and thirty-five, and their D were six thousand seven
Neh 7:69 and thirty-five, and their D six thousand seven
13:15 and loading them on D; and also wine, grapes,
Jud 2:17 number of camels and D and mules for transport,
Job 1:14 were plowing and the D feeding beside them;
11:12 understanding, when a wild D colt is born a
24:5 themselves, Behold, like wild D in the desert they
Ps 104:11 the field; the wild D quench their thirst.
Sir 13:18 Wild D in the wilderness are the prey of
Is 21:7 in pairs, riders on D, riders on camels, let
30:6 on the backs of D, and their treasures on
30:24 the oxen and the D that till the ground
32:14 a joy of wild D, a pasture of flocks;
Jer 14:6 The wild D stand on the bare heights, they
Ezek 23:20 were like those of D, and whose issue was
Dan 5:21 was with the wild D; he was fed grass
Zech 14:15 mules, the camels, the D, and whatever beasts may
Jn 12:15 coming, sitting on a D colt!"

DOOR (2)
Tob 7:1 and they found Raguel sitting beside the courtyard D
11:10 up, and came stumbling out through the courtyard D

DORCAS
Acts 9:36 named Tabitha, which means D or Gazelle.

DOUBLE
Ps 119:113 I hate D minded men, but I love your

DOUGH (3)
1Cor 5:6 know that a little leaven leavens all the D
5:7 you may be new D, as you really are
Gal 5:9 called you, A little leaven leavens all the D

DOVE
Song 2:10 "Arise, my love, my D, my fair one, and

DOWNFAFL
Esth 14:11 them mock at our D; but turn their plan

DREGS (3)
Jer 48:11 has settled on his D; he has not been
Zeph 1:12 are thickening on their D, those who say in
1Cor 4:13 of the world, the D of all things.

DRESSED
Mt 11:8 To see a man D in soft robes?

DRIED (2)
Ps 74:15 springs and brooks; you D up ever flowing streams.
Is 51:10 it not you who D up the sea, the

DRINK (4)
Gen 24:45 her, Please let me D,
Tob 7:10 said to Tobias, "Eat, D, and be merry; for
7:11 my child, eat and D, and the Lord will
7:15 Then they began to eat and D

DRINKING
Tob 8:1 had finished eating and D, they wanted to retire;

DROVE (2)
Ps 44:2 with your own hand D out the nations, but
80:8 out of Egypt; you D out the nations and

DRY
Is 25:4 like heat in a D place.

DUG
Is 51:1 and to the quarry from which you were D

DULL
Ps 4:2 long will you be D of heart?

DUNG
1Sam 2:8 the needy from the D heap, to make them

DUST
Sir 17:28 but all men are D and ashes.

DYSTRUS
Tob 2:12 day, the seventh of D, when she cut off

E

EAR
Sir 2:2 be steadfast, incline your E, and receive words of

EARS
Sir 17:5 tongue and eyes and E; he gave them a

EARTH (4)
Tob 3:6 the face of the E and become dust.
12:20 the Lord upon the E and give thanks to
Esth 14:3 she lay on the E together with all her
Ps 104:30 created; and you renew the face of the E

EASILY
Sir 48:6 from their beds, and E destroyed their dominion;

EAT (3)
Tob 2:2 Lord, and he shall E together with me.
7:10 and said to Tobias, E, drink, and be merry;
7:15 Then they began to E and drink.

EATING
Tob 8:1 When they had finished E and drinking, they wanted

ECBATANA
Tob 7:1 Now when they reached E, Tobias said to him,

EFFECT
Tob 7:14 marriage contract, to the E that he gave her

EGYPTIANS
Ex 15:26 I put upon the E, for I am the

ELIAB
Jud 8:7 Melchis, the son of E, the son of Nathanael,

EMISSION
Deut 23:10 reason of a nocturnal E, then he shall go

END
Esth 14:11 pleasing to you, O Lord, until the very E

ENDURE
Sir 2:4 brought upon you, and E it in sorrow; in

ENDURED
Is 23:4 saying: "I have neither E labor pains nor given

ENEMIES (4)
2Sam 22:49 me out from my E, you exalted me above
Esth 14:14 the hand of our E; turn our mourning into
Ps 9:6 The E have vanished in everlasting ruins; their cities
Sir 6:5 multiplies friends and softens E, and a gracious

ENLARGE
Ps 119:32 your commandments when you E my understanding!

ENRICH
Ps 65:9 water it, you greatly E it; the river of

ENTERED
Tob 6:9 When he E Media and was already approaching

ESPOUSE (3)
Hos 2:19 And I will E you for ever; I will
2:19 for ever; I will E you in righteousness and
2:20 I will E you in faithfulness; and you shall

ESTABLISHED
2Sam 7:24 And you E for yourself your people Israel to

EVENING (2)
Gen 49:27 the prey, and at E dividing the spoil."
Esth 14:3 maidservants, from morning until E, and said: "God

EVER (3)
Ex 19:9 with you, and may also believe you for E
Tob 7:12 is given to you from today and for E
Ps 74:15 brooks; you dried up E flowing streams.

EVERGIVE
Ps 119:144 testimonies are righteous for E me understanding

EVIL (5)
Sir 15:17 and death, good and E, and whichever he chooses
17:6 with understanding, and showed them good and E
17:27 So flesh and blood devise E
Jer 44:22 no longer bear your E doings and the abominations
Mt 5:37 this comes from the E One.

EXALTED (3)
2Sam 22:49 from my enemies, you E me above my adversaries,
Ps 18:48 my enemies; yes, you E me above my adversaries;
Sir 24:2 her people she is E; in holy fulness she

EXAMINED
Wis 11:10 in warning, but you E the ungodly as a

EXCELLENT (5)
Deut 3:25 beyond the Jordan, that E hill country, and Lebanon.
6:10 you, with great and E cities, which you did
8:12 full, and have built E houses and live in
Prov 28:10 blameless will have an E inheritance.
Jer 11:16 olive tree, fair with E fruit; but with the

EXERCISE
Lev 25:33 the Levites does not E, his right of redemption,

EXILES
Tob 2:2 may find among the E in Nineveh, who is

EXIST
Sir 17:24 one who does not E, thanksgiving has ceased; he

EXODUS
Lk 9:31 and spoke of his E, which he was to

EXPECT
Lk 12:40 is coming at an hour you do not E

EXPLAIN
Tob 7:11 But let me E the true situation to you.

EYES (6)
Tob 11:7 "I know that his E will be opened.
11:8 the fish on his E, and the medicine will
11:12 With this he applied the medicine on his E
11:14 I see my son, the light of my E
Sir 3:22 to see with your E what is hidden.
17:5 with a tongue and E and ears; he gave

F

FACE (2)
Job 2:5 curse you to your F,
Ps 21:6 make him glad with the joy of your F

FAILING
Sir 17:20 those whose endurance is F, and he has appointed

FAILS
Sir 17:27 Yet its light F

FALLEN
Sir 48:11 and those who have F asleep in your love;

FALSELY
3Jn 1:10 is doing, accusing me F with evil words.

FAR (4)
1Kgs 8:46 land of the enemy, F off or near;
Ps 22:19 O LORD, be not F off!
Ezek 43:25 F seven days you shall provide daily a goat
Rev 18:10 burning; they will stand F off, in fear of

FAREWELL
Tob 12:5 all that you two have brought back, and F

FASTEN
Jn 21:18 hands, and another will F your belt for you

FASTENED (2)
Jn 21:18 you were young, you F your own belt and
Eph 6:14 Stand therefore, having F the belt of truth around

FATHER (11)
Tob 2:3 When he came back, he said, F
2:3 on to say, "Look, F, one of our own
3:10 shall they reproach my F, saying to him, You
6:12 very beautiful, and her F is a good man."
7:13 Take her and bring her safely to your F
11:7 before they approached his F, "I know that his
11:8 And your F will regain his sight and see
11:11 he blew into his eyes, saying, "Take courage, F
11:16 he reported to his F the great things that
Sir 3:5 Whoever honors his F will be gladdened by his
Jn 8:41 You do the works of your F

FATHERS (2)
Tob 3:10 gone up to her F upper room, she intended
6:11 you to inherit her F possessions.

FAULT-FINDING
Ex 17:7 Meribah, because of the F of the sons of

FAVOR
Sir 4:12 seek her early will win the Lords good F

FAWN
Jer 14:5 field forsakes her newborn F because there is no

FEAR (4)
Sir 2:1 in justice and in F, and prepare yourself for
2:6 Stay in F of him, and grow old in
17:4 He placed the F of them in all flesh,
17:7 He placed the F of him into their hearts,

FEARSOME
Hab 1:7 Dread and F are they; their justice and dignity

FEAST
Rom 11:9 David says, "Let their F become a snare and

FED
Judg 19:21 into his house, and F the donkeys; and they

FEED
Acts 20:28 made you guardians, to F the Church of the

E
F

FEET (2)
Esth 13:13 the soles of Hamans F to save Israel!
Lk 20:43 I make your enemies a stool for your F

FELLOW
Jas 2:20 be shown, you foolish F, that faith apart from

FESTIVE
Jud 10:3 herself in her most F apparel, which she used

FIELDS
Is 30:23 will graze in open F;

FILL
Sir 15:5 the assembly; she will F him with a spirit

FILLED (2)
Sir 17:5 mind for thinking, and F them with the discipline
17:6 of the spirit; he F their hearts with understanding,

FILMS
Tob 2:10 obscured by the white F, until I became completely

FINDS
Sir 24:2 of the chosen she F praise, and among the

FIRE (2)
Mt 13:42 into the furnace of F, where there will be
13:50 into the furnace of F, where there will be

FIRM
Sir 17:22 of God, and stand F the lot that is

FIRMLY
Tob 11:11 hand, and holding him F, he blew into his

FIRST (3)
Tob 7:1 They greeted him F, and be replied, "Joyous,
Ps 135:8 was who struck the F born of Egypt, both
136:10 him who struck the F born of Egypt, for

FIRST-BORN
Sir 24:3 the Most High, the F before all creatures.

FIRSTBORN (3)
Ex 12:29 LORD struck all the F in the land of
13:13 Every F of man among your sons you shall
Num 8:17 For all the F among the sons of Israel

FISH (2)
Tob 11:8 the gall of the F on his eyes, and
11:11 the gall of the F in his hand, and

FITTING (2)
Tob 12:6 of God, and with F honor to acknowledge him.
12:7 of God, and with F honor to acknowledge him.

FLESH (11)
Ps 27:2 me, to devour my F, my adversaries and foes,
Sir 17:4 of them in all F, and granted them dominion
17:27 So F and blood devise evil.
Mk 10:8 his wife, and the two shall become one F
10:8 So they are no longer two but one F
Rom 9:3 of my brethren, my kinsmen according to the F
1Cor 1:26 wise according to the F, not many were powerful,
1:29 are, so that no F might boast in the
2Cor 5:16 one according to the F; even though we once
5:16 Christ according to the F, we regard him thus
Gal 2:16 the law shall no F be justified.

FLOCK (3)
Tob 7:9 a ram from the F and received them very
Is 30:23 In that day your F will be given pasture,
Jer 31:10 a shepherd keeps his F,

FLOWING
Ps 74:15 you dried up ever F streams.

FOE
Sir 4:19 give him over into the hands of his F

FOES
Ps 56:1 me; all day long F oppress me;

FOLLOWED
Mk 1:36 who were with him F him,

FONDLED
Is 66:12 upon her hip, and F upon her knees.

FOOD (8)
Gen 24:25 have both straw and F enough, and room to
24:32 gave him straw and F for the camels, and
42:27 to give his donkey F at the lodging place,
43:24 had given their donkeys F,
Judg 19:19 We have straw and F for our donkeys, with
Job 36:16 set on your table was full of rich F
Is 30:24 ground will eat salted F, which has been winnowed
55:2 what is good, and delight yourselves in rich F

FOOLISH
Jas 2:20 to be shown, you F fellow, that faith apart

FORBADE
Lam 1:10 those whom you F to enter your congregation.

FORGAVE (2)
Ps 32:5 the LORD"; then you F the guilt of my
85:2 You F the iniquity of your people; you pardoned

FORGIVENESS (2)
Sir 17:25 the Lord, and his F for those who turn
28:5 will he then seek F from God?

FORMED (2)
Ps 104:26 and Leviathan which you F to sport in it.
139:13 For you F my inward parts, you knitted me

FORMER
Rom 6:6 We know that our F man was crucified with

FORTH (16)
Ex 32:27 and go back and F from gate to gate
2Kgs 4:35 walked once back and F in the house, and
2Chr 16:9 LORD move back and F throughout the whole earth,
Job 1:7 "From going back and F on the earth, and
2:2 "From going back and F on the earth, and
28:4 hang afar from men, they swing back and F
39:1 observe the deer bringing F their young?
Jer 4:24 quaking, and all the hills moved back and F
5:1 Run back and F through the streets of
Ezek 1:14 creatures darted back and F, like a flash of
Dan 12:4 shall run back and F, and knowledge shall increase."
Amos 8:12 shall run back and F, to seek the word
Nah 2:4 they rush back and F through the squares; they
Zech 7:14 one went back and F, and the pleasant land
9:8 shall march back and F; no oppressor shall again
Eph 4:14 children, tossed back and F and carried about with

FOUND (2)
Neh 9:8 name Abraham; and you F his heart faithful before
Tob 7:1 of Raguel, and they F Raguel sitting beside the

FOUNDED
Heb 1:10 And, "You, Lord, F the earth in the beginning,

FOUR
Tob 2:10 For F years I remained unable to see, All

FRIENDS
Sir 6:5 A pleasant voice multiplies F and softens enemies,

FULL (2)
Tob 2:12 owners, they paid her F wages and they also
Sir 24:12 abode was in the F assembly of the saints.

FULNESS
Sir 24:2 is exalted; in holy F she is admired.

G

GALL (2)
Tob 11:8 Smear the G of the fish on his eyes,
Ps 69:21 They gave me G for food, and for my

GARMENT (2)
Ruth 3:9 maidservant; spread your G over your maidservant,

Neh 5:13 also shook out my G and said, "So may

GATES
Mt 16:18 my Church, and the G of Hades shall not

GAVE (42)
2Sam 22:37 You G a wide place for my steps under
1Kgs 8:34 the land which you G to their fathers.
8:40 the land which you G to our fathers.
8:48 their land, which you G to their fathers, the
2Chr 6:25 the land which you G to them and to
6:31 the land which you G to our fathers.
6:38 their land, which you G to their fathers, the
Neh 9:7 of the Chaldeans and G him the name Abraham;
9:13 them from heaven and G them right ordinances and
9:15 You G them bread from heaven for their hunger
9:20 from their mouth, and G them water for their
9:20 You G your good Spirit to instruct them, and
9:22 And you G them kingdoms and peoples, and allotted
9:24 land, the Canaanites, and G them into their hands,
9:27 your great mercies you G them saviors who saved
9:27 Therefore you G them into the hand of their
9:30 Therefore you G them into the hand of the
9:34 your warnings which you G them.
9:35 great goodness which you G them, and in the
9:36 the land that you G to our fathers to
Tob 3:4 your commandments, and you G us over to plunder,
7:14 the effect that he G her to him as
8:6 You made Adam and G him Eve his wife
Jud 9:2 Simeon, to whom you G a sword to take
9:3 So you G up their rulers to be slain,
9:4 their thrones; and you G their wives for a
Ps 18:36 You G a wide place for my steps under
21:4 life of you; you G it to him, length
74:14 heads of Leviathan, you G him as food for
Wis 11:7 slay the infants, you G them abundant water
12:10 little by little you G them a chance to
12:21 to whose fathers you G oaths and covenants full
16:20 of these things you G your people the food
Sir 17:5 eyes and ears; he G them a mind for
Is 26:17 we writhed, but we G birth only to wind.
26:18 we writhed, but we G birth only to wind.
Jer 32:22 great terror; and you G them this land, which
Jn 17:4 the work which you G me to do;
17:6 were yours, and you G them to me, and
17:6 the men whom you G me out of the
17:8 the words which you G me, and they have
18:9 "Of those whom you G me I lost not

GAZELLE
Acts 9:36 a disciple named Tabitha, which means Dorcas or G

GENERATIONS
Sir 24:19 and my remembrance lasts throughout all G

GET (2)
Mt 24:18 not turn back to G a coat.
Mk 13:16 not turn back to G a coat.

GIFTS
Sir 3:17 will be loved more than a giver of G

GIRDED (2)
2Sam 22:40 For you G me with strength for the battle;
Ps 18:39 For you G me with strength for the battle;

GIVE (9)
Tob 7:9 Azarias, ask Raguel to G me my kinswoman Sarah."
7:10 not at liberty to G her to any other
Ps 36:8 your house, and you G them drink from the
104:28 When you G to them, they gather it up;
144:10 play to you, who G victory to kings, who
145:15 to you, and you G them their food in
Wis 12:19 good hope, because you G repentance for sins.
Sir 4:19 will forsake him, and G him over into the
51:2 I G thanks to your name, for you have

GIVEN (5)
Tob 7:12 heaven that she be G to you.
7:12 She is G to you from today and for
7:12 She is G to you in accordance with the
Is 30:23 your flock will be G pasture, and the lamb
1Tim 2:6 testimony to which was G at the proper time.

GIVER
Sir 3:17 loved more than a G of gifts.

GLADDENED
Sir 3:5 his father will be G by his own children,

GLADNESS
Esth 14:14 turn our mourning into G and our affliction into

GLORIFIED
Wis 18:8 us to yourself and G us.

GLORIFIES
Sir 3:4 is heard; and whoever G his mother is like

GLORY (4)
Tob 13:8 his chosen ones, all of you, praise his G
Sir 15:5 understanding, and clothe him with a robe of G
17:8 He made them G in his wondrous deeds,
24:2 in the presence of his host she will G

GNASHING (4)
Mt 13:42 will be weeping and G of teeth.
13:50 will be weeping and G of teeth.
22:13 will be weeping and G of teeth.
25:30 will be weeping and G of teeth.

GOD (30)
Gen 17:18 And Abraham said to G "O that Ishmael might
2Sam 7:29 for you, O Lord G, have spoken, and with
1Kgs 8:53 brought our fathers out of Egypt, O Lord G
Tob 7:13 And may the G of heaven prosper your journey
12:6 declaring the works of G, and with fitting honor
12:7 reveal the works of G, and with fitting honor
Esth 13:8 "O God of Abraham, G of Isaac, God of
13:8 Abraham, God of Isaac, G of Jacob, blessed are
13:8 Lord, and said: "O G of Abraham, God of
13:14 to any one but you, O Lord, my G
13:14 above the glory of G ; I will not bow
14:3 until evening, and said: G of Abraham, God of
14:11 you, O Lord, my G Come to my aid,
Ps 29:1 LORD, O sons of G, ascribe to the LORD
109:21 But you, O G my Lord, deal on my
Sir 1:8 feared, sitting upon his throne, and ruling as G
2:6 Trust in G, and he will help you; hope
3:18 humble yourself; so you will find favor with G
5:3 for G will surely punish you.
15:15 if you trust in G, you too shall live.
17:22 and the judgments of G, and stand firm the
17:22 you, in prayer to G, the Almighty.
24:1 and is honored in G, and will glory in
28:5 wrath, will he then seek forgiveness from G
50:24 may believe that the G of mercy is with
Jer 32:25 Yet you, O Lord G, have said to me,
Ezek 27:3 peoples on many islands, thus says the Lord G
Hab 3:19 G, the Lord, is my strength; he makes my
Mk 13:18 of the creation which G created until now, and
Heb 1:8 says, "Your throne, O G is for ever and

GODS (2)
Sir 2:3 Await G patience, cling to him and do not
Bar 6:55 and escape, but the G, will be burned in

GOOD (6)
Tob 6:12 her father is a G man."
7:1 greetings, brothers; welcome and G health!" Then he
Sir 4:12 will win the Lords G favor.
15:17 are life and death, G and evil, and whichever
17:6 understanding, and showed them G and evil.
Mt 12:34 how can you speak G things, when you are

GOT (2)
Neh 9:10 our fathers; and you G yourself a name, as
Tob 11:10 Tobit G up, and came stumbling out through the

GRANT (2)
Tob 7:12 both this night and G you mercy and peace."
8:4 our Lord that he G us mercy and safety."

GRANTED
Sir 17:4 in all flesh, and G them dominion over beasts

GRAVE
Tob 3:10 his old age down in sorrow to the G

GREAT (7)
Judg 2:15 and they were in G distress.
Tob 11:14 and blessed be his G name, and blessed be
11:16 to his father the G things that had happened

Sir 17:25 How G is the mercy of the Lord, and
Eph 5:32 This is a G mystery, and I mean in
Rev 16:17 the air, and a G Voice came out of
21:3 and I heard a G voice from the throne

GREETINGS
Tob 7:1 and be replied, "Joyous G, brothers; welcome and

GRIEVED
Tob 3:10 day she was deeply G in spirit and wept.

GROW
Sir 2:6 fear of him, and G old in him.

GUARDIANS
Acts 20:28 Spirit has made you G to feed the Church

GUM
Num 11:7 appearance like that of G resin.

H

HADES
Mt 16:18 and the gates of H shall not prevail against

HALF
Num 34:13 tribes and to the H tribe;

HAMANS
Esth 13:13 kiss the soles of H feet to save Israel!

HAND (2)
Tob 11:11 the fish in his H, and holding him firmly,
Esth 14:14 save us from the H of our enemies; turn

HANDS (4)
Tob 3:11 same time, with H outstretched toward the window,
11:13 Next, with both his H, he peeled off the
Ps 90:17 upon us, yes, establish the work of our H
Sir 4:19 him over into the H of his foe.

HANG (2)
Tob 3:10 for me not to H myself, but to pray
3:10 room, she intended to H herself.

HANGED
Tob 3:10 beloved daughter but she H herself because of her

HAPPENED (2)
Tob 11:16 great things that had H to him in Media.
12:20 book everything that has H to you."

HARM (3)
Ps 70:2 back and brought to dishonor who desire my H
71:13 disgrace may they be covered who seek my H
71:24 shame and disgraced who sought to do me H

HARPISTS (2)
Rev 14:2 like the sound of H playing on their harps,
18:22 and the sound of H and minstrels, of flute

HASTEN
Song 4:6 shadows flee, I will H to the mountain of

HATE (2)
Ps 5:5 before your eyes; you H all evildoers.
31:6 You H I those who pay regard to vain

HATED
Wis 12:4 your holy land you H for their detestable practices,

HE-DONKEYS (2)
Gen 12:16 he had sheep, oxen, H, menservants, maidservants,
32:15 cows and ten bulls, twenty she-donkeys and ten H

HEAD (2)
1Sam 4:12 with earth upon his H,
Jon 2:6 were wrapped about my H at the roots of

HEAL
Ps 41:3 in his illness you H all his infirmities.

HEALED
Tob 2:10 to physicians to be H, but the more they

HEALTH
Tob 7:1 "Joyous greetings, brothers; welcome and good H

HEAR (6)
1Kgs 8:30 place; and when you H, forgive.
2Kgs 19:16 ear, O LORD, and H, open your eyes, O
2Chr 6:21 place; and when you H, forgive.
Ps 51:8 Make me H I joy and gladness; let the
65:2 Jerusalem, O you who H prayer!
Jn 11:42 knew that you always H me, but I have

HEARD (9)
Neh 9:9 fathers in Egypt and H their cry at the
9:27 to you and you H them from heaven; and
9:28 cried to you, you H from heaven, and many
Esth 14:11 I have H from the books of my ancestors
Ps 31:22 But you H my supplications, when I cried to
Sir 3:5 children, and when he prays he will be H
51:12 My prayer was H, for you saved me from
Lam 3:56 of the pit; you H my plea, Do not
Jon 2:2 I cried, and you H my voice.

HEARING (2)
1Sam 11:4 the matter in the H of the people; and
25:24 handmaid speak in your H, and hear the words

HEART (2)
Jud 8:7 she was prudent of H, discerning in judgment, and
Ps 4:2 men, how long will you be dull of H

HEARTS (3)
Sir 2:9 love him, and your H will be made radiant.
17:6 spirit; he filled their H with understanding, and
17:7 of him into their H, showing them the majesty

HEAT (2)
Tob 2:9 and my face was uncovered because of the H
Is 25:4 against a wall, like H in a dry place.

HEAVEN (7)
Tob 7:12 May the Lord of H, my child, guide and
7:12 has been decreed from H that she be given
7:13 may the God of H prosper your journey with
Ps 85:11 the ground, and righteousness will look down from H
Sir 17:28 of the height of H; but all men are
Jn 1:32 as a dove from H and remain on him.
Rev 15:1 saw another sign in H great and wonderful, seven

HEAVENS (2)
Ps 119:89 firmly fixed in the H,
Sir 24:3 should arise in the H, and I covered the

HEED
2Mac 8:3 the ground, and to H the blood that cried

HEEDED
Rom 10:16 they have not all H the gospel; for Isaiah

HEIGHT
Sir 17:28 the host of the H of heaven; but all

HEIR
Tob 6:10 He has no male H and no daughter except

HELD
Acts 2:42 And they H steadfastly to the apostles teaching and

HELPER
Sir 51:2 by you were my H,

HELPLESS
Rom 5:6 While we were yet H, at the right time

HENCE
Heb 11:19 even from the dead; He did receive him

HERE (18)
Ex 11:1 let you go from H; when he lets you
33:1 "Depart, go up from H, you and the people
Josh 3:9 sons of Israel, "Come H, and hear the words
1Sam 10:22 again of the LORD, "Did the man come H
14:16 the multitude was surging H and there.
14:18 said to Ahijah, "Bring the ark of God H
14:36 "Let us draw near H to God."
14:38 And Saul said, "Come H, all you leaders of
Tob 2:3 And I replied, H I am, my child." And

	6:10	H I am," he answered.
	11:14	he wept and said, H I see my son,
Ps	102:24	not take me from H in the midst of
Is	57:3	you, draw near to H, sons of the sorceress,
Jn	14:31	Rise, let us go from H
	19:5	Pilate said to them, H is the man!"
	19:14	said to the Jews, H is your King!"
Rev	4:1	trumpet, said, "Come up H, and I will show
	11:12	voice from heaven saying to them, "Come up H

HEREDITARY

Tob	6:10	all other men a H claim on her.

HERSELF (2)

Tob	3:10	daughter but she hanged H because of her distress.
Sir	24:1	Wisdom will praise H and is honored in

HID (2)

Job	10:13	Yet these things you H in your heart; I
Ps	30:7	a strong mountain; you H your face, I was

HIDDEN (25)

Job	3:21	it more than for H treasures;
	3:23	man whose way is H, whom God has hedged
	5:21	You shall be H from the scourge of the
	28:11	the thing that is H he brings forth to
	28:21	It is H from the eyes of all living,
Ps	19:6	and there is nothing H from its heat.
	22:24	and he has not H his face from him,
	40:10	I have not H your saving help within my
Sir	17:14	they will not be H from his eyes.
Is	29:14	the discernment of their discerning men shall be H
	40:27	Israel, "My way is H from the LORD, and
	59:2	and your sins have H his face from you
	64:7	you; for you have H your face from us,
	65:16	are forgotten and are H from my eyes.
Jer	16:17	ways; they are not H from me, nor is
Hos	13:14	Compassion is H from my eyes.
Mt	5:14	A city set on a hill cannot be H
Mk	4:22	For there is nothing H, except to be made
	7:23	one know it; yet he could not be H
Lk	8:17	For nothing is H that shall not be made
	18:34	things; this saying was H from them, and they
	19:42	But now they are H from your eyes.
Col	2:3	Christ, in whom are H all the treasures of
	3:3	and your life is H with Christ in God.
Heb	11:23	he was born, was H for three months by

HIDE (3)

Ps	31:20	of your presence you H them from the plots
	104:29	When you H your face, they are dismayed; when
Is	45:15	are a God who H yourself, O God of

HIDING (2)

Job	38:40	in wait in their H places?
	40:21	he lies, in the H place of the reeds

HIGH (2)

Ps	92:1	your name, O Most H,
Sir	5:4	for the Most H is slow to anger.

HILLS (6)

Mt	14:23	went up into the H by himself to pray.
	18:11	the ninety-nine on the H and go in search
Lk	6:12	went out to the H to pray; and all
Jn	6:3	went up into the H, and there sat down
	6:15	withdrew again to the H by himself.
Rev	17:9	seven heads are seven H on which the woman

HIMSELF (2)

2Sam	17:23	in order, and hanged H, and he died, and
Jn	13:4	aside his garments, and tied a towel around H

HITTING

1Kgs	20:37	the man struck him, H and wounding him.

HOLD (2)

Ps	16:5	and my cup; you H my lot.
	31:20	plots of men; you H them safe under your

HOLDING

Tob	11:11	in his hand, and H him firmly, he blew

HOLDS

Sir	4:17	her discipline until he H her in his thoughts,

HOLY (2)

Sir	1:9	created wisdom in the H spirit; he saw her
	24:2	she is exalted; in H fulness she is admired.

HOME

Tob	6:10	this night in the H of Raguel.

HONEYCOMB

Sir	24:19	inheritance sweeter than the H, and my

HONOR (2)

Tob	12:6	God, and with fitting H to acknowledge him.
	12:7	God, and with fitting H to acknowledge him.

HONORED

Sir	24:1	praise herself and is H in God, and will

HONORS

Sir	3:5	Whoever H his father will be gladdened by his

HORMAH

Num	21:3	so the name of the place was called H

HOST

Sir	17:28	He marshals the H of the height of heaven;

HOUR

Lk	12:40	is coming at an H you do not expect."

HOUSE

Sir	3:14	credited to you-a H raised in justice to

HUMBLE (3)

Ps	34:2	the LORD; let the H hear and be glad.
	69:32	and hoofs, Let the H see it and be
	74:21	Let not the H be put to shame; let

HUMILITY

Ps	132:1	in Davids favor, his H;

HUNTED

Tob	2:8	he has already been H down to be put

HUSBAND

Gal	4:27	has more children than she who has a H

HUSBANDS (2)

Tob	3:8	her, "You are the one who kills your H
	3:9	Because your H are dead?

I

IDLE

1Thes	5:14	brethren, admonish the I, encourage the

IMAGE

Sir	17:1	him into his own I;

IMMORAL

Eph	5:5	of this, that no I or impure man, or

IMMORALITY (4)

Gal	5:19	the flesh are plain: I, impurity, licentiousness,
Eph	5:3	But I and all impurity or covetousness must not
Col	3:5	is earthly in you: I, impurity, passion, evil desire,
1Thes	4:3	that you abstain from I;

IMMORTAL

Sir	17:26	men, since a son of man is not I

IMPENDING

1Cor	7:26	in view of the I distress it is well

IMPLORE

Tob	8:4	let us pray and I our Lord that he

IMPLORED

Wis	8:21	to the Lord and I him, and with my

INCIDENT (2)

1Kgs	13:33	After this I Jeroboam did not turn from his
2Kgs	6:11	troubled because of this I; and he called his

INCLINE
Sir 2:2 right and be steadfast, I your ear, and receive

INCREASED
Ps 138:3 you answered me, my strength of soul you I

INFANT (2)
Lam 4:4 The tongue of the I clings to the roof
Hos 11:4 one who raises an I to his cheeks, and

INFANTS (12)
Jud 7:27 the death of our I before our eyes, or
Wis 10:21 made the tongues of I speak clearly.
12:24 enemies despised; they were deceived like foolish I
18:5 resolved to kill the I of your holy ones,
Is 3:4 boys their princes, and I shall rule over them.
1Mac 2:9 Her I have been killed in her streets, her
Mt 11:25 and revealed them to I;
21:16 mouths of babies and I you have brought perfect
Lk 10:21 and revealed them to I; yes, Father, for such
1Cor 3:1 of the flesh, as I in Christ.
14:20 in your thinking; be I in evil, but in
1Pet 2:2 Like newborn I, long for the pure spiritual milk,

INHERIT
Tob 6:11 right for you to I her fathers possessions.

INHERITANCE (3)
Esth 13:15 annihilate us, and they desire to destroy your I
Sir 24:8 in Israel receive your I, and among my chosen
24:12 Lord, who is their I, and my abode was

INSULTS
Tob 3:6 distress in my life and listen to such I

INTEND
Is 55:11 accomplish that which I I, and prosper in the

INTENDED (2)
Tob 3:10 fathers upper room, she I to hang herself.
Jud 9:5 Yes, the things you I came to pass,

INTERIM
Num 27:21 the judgment of the I before the LORD; at

INVITED
Lam 2:22 You I as to the day of an appointed

ISAAC (3)
Esth 13:8 of Abraham, God of I, God of Jacob, blessed
13:15 of Abraham, God of I, and God of Jacob,
14:3 of Abraham, God of I, and God of Jacob,

ISLANDS (21)
Ps 97:1 rejoice; let the many I be glad!
Is 11:11 Hamath, and from the I of the sea.
24:15 the LORD; in the I of the sea, to
41:1 me in silence, O I; let the peoples renew
41:5 The I have seen and are afraid, the ends
42:4 the earth; and the I wait for his law.
42:10 that fills it, the I and their inhabitants.
42:12 the LORD, and declare his praise in the I
49:1 Listen to me, O I, and pay attention, you
51:5 rule the peoples; the I wait for me, and
59:18 his enemies; to the I he will render repayment.
60:9 For the I shall wait for me, the ships
66:19 and Javan, to the I afar off, that have
Jer 25:22 the kings of the I across the sea;
31:10 declare it in the I afar off; say, He
Ezek 26:15 Tyre: Will not the I shake at the sound
27:3 the peoples on many I, thus says the Lord
27:15 traded with you; many I were your own special
27:35 the inhabitants of the I are appalled at you;
39:6 dwell securely in the I; and they shall know
Dan 11:18 his face to the I, and shall take many

ISRAEL (4)
Ex 9:4 of all that belongs to the sons of I
Deut 32:8 according to the number of the sons of I
Sir 50:24 days of old, that I may believe that the
Is 66:20 as the sons of I bring their cereal offering

J

JABESH-GILEAD
Judg 21:10 strike the inhabitants of J with the edge of

JACOB (3)
Esth 13:8 of Isaac, God of J, blessed are you:
13:15 Isaac, and God of J, spare your people; for
14:3 Isaac, and God of J, blessed are you; help

JAR (3)
Mt 26:7 him with an alabaster J of very expensive ointment,
Mk 14:3 came with an alabaster J of ointment of pure
14:3 and she broke the J and poured it over

JERUSALEM
Ps 65:1 vows be performed in J,

JESHUA
Neh 8:17 in the booths; for from the days of J

JOAH
2Kgs 18:26 Hilkiah, and Shebnah, and J said to the Rabshakeh,

JOSEPH
Jud 8:7 Manasseh, the son of J, the son of Ahitub,

JOURNEY
Tob 7:13 of heaven prosper your J with his peace."

JOY
Tob 13:8 Celebrate days of J, and give thanks to him.

JOYOUS
Tob 7:1 first, and be replied, J greetings, brothers; welcome and

JUDGE (4)
Gen 18:25 Shall not the J of all the earth do
Judg 11:27 me; the LORD, the J, decide this day between
Sir 35:17 him, and the just J executes judgment.
Jer 11:20 LORD of hosts, who J righteously, who test the

JUDGED
Job 34:36 Would that Job were J to the end, because

JUDGMENT
Jud 8:7 of heart, discerning in J, and quite virtuous.

JUDGMENTS
Sir 17:22 the justice and the J of God, and stand

JUST (3)
Tob 3:2 all your deeds are J and all your ways
Sir 27:5 so the test of J men is in tribulation.
35:17 visits him, and the J judge executes judgment.

JUSTICE (5)
Sir 2:1 the Lord, remain in J and in fear, and
3:14 a house raised in J to you.
17:11 and showed them his J and his judgments.
17:22 Know the J and the judgments of God, and
42:15 and in his will, J is carried out.

K

KEEP (2)
Neh 9:32 and awesome God, who K covenant and mercy, let
Ps 77:4 [Selah] You K my eyelids from closing; I am

KEEPS
Dan 9:4 and awesome God, who K covenant and merciful love

KEPT (2)
2Sam 22:44 with the peoples; you K me as the head
Ps 22:9 from the womb; you K me safe upon my

KID
Tob 2:12 full wages and they also gave her a K

KILL
Ezek 9:5 city after him, and K; your eye shall not

KILLED (2)
Tob 7:9 Then Raguel K a ram from the flock and
Ezek 9:7 they went forth, and K in the city.

KILLING
Ezek 9:8 And while they were K, and I was left

KILLS
Tob 3:8 are the one who K your husbands!

KIN
Tob 6:10 you, as next of K to her, have before

KINDRED
Tob 2:10 to see, All my K were sorry for me,

KING (3)
Ps 45:13 The daughter of the K is decked in her
Sir 1:8 Creator of all, the K greatly to be feared,
Is 30:33 prepared; yes, for the K, it is made ready,

KINGDOM
Lk 22:29 my Father appointed a K for me, so do

KINGLY
Lk 23:41 you come in your K power."

KINSMEN
Tob 7:11 seven men of our K, and when each came

KINSWOMAN (2)
Tob 7:9 to give me my K Sarah."
7:12 Take your K; from now on you are her

KNEW
Neh 9:10 his land, for you K that they acted insolently

KNITTED
Ps 139:13 my inward parts, you K me together in my

KNOW (29)
2Sam 7:20 For you K your servant, O Lord GOD!
1Kgs 8:39 each whose heart you K, according to all his
8:39 (for you, you only, K the hearts of all
1Chr 17:18 For you K your servant.
2Chr 6:30 each whose heart you K, according to all his
6:30 (for you, you only, K the hearts of the
Tob 3:14 You K, O Lord, that I am innocent of
11:7 approached his father, "I K that his eyes will
Esth 13:12 You K all things;
13:13 know all things; you K, O Lord, that I
14:15 all things; and you K that I hate the
14:16 You K my necessity-that I abhor the sign of
Job 10:7 my sin, although you K that I am not
Ps 40:9 my lips, as you K, O LORD.
69:5 O God, you K my folly; the wrongs I
69:19 You K my reproach, and my shame and my
139:2 You K when I sit down and when I
139:4 behold, O LORD, you K it altogether.
139:14 You K me right well;
142:3 spirit is faint, you K my way!
Sir 17:22 K the justice and the judgments of God, and
Jer 12:3 But you, O LORD, K me; you see me,
15:15 O LORD, you K; remember me and visit me,
17:16 day of disaster, you K; that which came out
18:23 Yet, you, O LORD, K all their plotting to
Ezek 37:3 And I answered, "O Lord GOD, you K
Dan 13:43 come to be, you K that these men have
1Mac 3:52 to destroy us; you K what they plot against
Acts 1:24 and said, "Lord, you K the hearts of all

KNOWLEDGE (2)
Sir 4:18 store up for him K and the discernment of
17:6 created in them the K of the spirit; he

KNOWN
Num 16:2 from the assembly, well K men;

L

LABOR (26)
Gen 35:16 Ephrath, Rachel went into L, and she had hard
Ps 48:6 of a woman with L pains.
Sir 34:5 like a woman with L pains the mind has
48:19 anguish, like women with L pains.
Is 13:8 like a woman with L pains.
21:3 of a woman with L pains; I am bowed
23:4 "I have neither endured L pains nor given birth,
42:14 like a woman with L pains, I will gasp
45:10 what are you suffering L pains?"
54:1 who have not had L pains!
Jer 4:31 of a woman with L pains, anguish as of
6:24 of a woman with L pains.
13:21 of a woman with L pains?
22:23 of a woman with L pains!"
31:8 and her who has L pains, together; a great
48:41 a woman with her L pains;
49:22 a woman with her L pains."
49:24 of a woman with L pains.
50:43 seized him, pain as of a woman in L
Mic 4:9 pangs have seized you like a woman in L
4:10 like a woman with L pains; for now you
5:3 when she who has L pains has brought forth;
Jn 16:21 a woman is in L, she has pain, because
Rom 8:22 has been groaning with L pains together until now;
Gal 4:27 who are not with L pains; for the desolate
1Thes 5:3 come upon them as L pains come upon a

LAID (3)
Ps 66:11 into the net; you L affliction on our backs;
102:25 Of old you L the foundation of the earth,
Acts 8:3 But Saul L waste the Church, and entering house

LAMB (2)
Is 30:23 given pasture, and the L will graze in open
1Cor 5:7 For Christ, our Paschal L, has been sacrificed.

LAND
2Kgs 15:5 the people of the L .

LARGE
Job 41:12 mighty strength, or his L frame.

LAST
Ps 30:5 Weeping may L for the night, but joy comes

LASTS
Sir 24:19 honeycomb, and my remembrance L throughout all

LAW
Tob 7:14 wife according to the L of Moses.

LAY (2)
Esth 14:3 And she L on the earth together with all
Ps 139:5 behind and before, and L your hand upon me.

LAYS
Sir 3:4 is like one who L up treasure.

LEAD
Ps 80:1 of Israel, you who L Joseph like a flock!

LEASE
Mt 21:41 a miserable death, and L the vineyard to other

LEASED (3)
Mt 21:33 built a tower, and L it to tenants, and
Mk 12:1 built a tower, and L it to tenants, and
Lk 20:9 planted a vineyard, and L it to tenants, and

LED (3)
Neh 9:12 pillar of cloud you L them in the day,
Ps 77:20 You L your people like a flock by the
Is 63:14 So you L your people, to make for yourself

LEFT
Wis 12:11 any one that you L them unpunished for their

LEFTHANDED
Judg 3:15 Gera, the Benjaminite, a L man.

LEST
Esth 13:14 did not do this, L I set the glory

LET (7)
Tob 7:11 But L me explain the true situation to you.
Ps 97:7 boast in worthless idols; L all his angels bow
Mt 8:13 centurion Jesus said, "Go; L it be done for
9:29 "According to your faith L it be done to
15:28 L it be done for you as you desire."

Lk 2:29 and said, "Lord, now L your servant depart in
Rev 20:3 that he must be L out for a little

LIBERATE
Esth 14:11 my ancestors that you L all those who are

LIBERTY
Tob 7:10 Likewise, am not at L to give her to

LIES (3)
Gen 49:25 of the deep that L beneath, blessings of the
Deut 33:13 of the deep that L beneath,
Tob 2:3 place, and now he L there strangled."

LIFE (4)
Tob 3:6 much distress in my L and listen to such
Sir 3:13 not despise him all the days of his L
4:11 Wisdom breathes L into her sons and gives help
Rev 21:6 price from the fountain of the water of L

LIFT (2)
Job 30:22 You L me up on the wind, you make
Ps 9:13 me, O you who L me up from the

LIGHT (5)
Tob 11:8 father will regain his sight and see the L
11:14 see my son, the L of my eyes!" Then
Sir 17:27 Yet its L fails.
24:3 ordained that an unfailing L should arise in the
36:1 and show us the L of your mercy;

LIGHTNING (7)
Ex 19:16 there was thunder and L, and a thick cloud
20:18 the thunder and the L and the sound of
Job 37:4 restrain the bolts of L when his voice is
38:35 send forth bolts of L, that they may go
Sir 43:13 snow and speeds the L of his judgment.
Jer 10:13 He makes L for the rain, and he brings
51:16 He makes L for the rain, and he brings

LIKEWISE
Tob 7:10 L, am not at liberty to give her to

LILY
Is 35:1 and blossom; like the L

LINE
Judg 16:9 bowstrings, as a tow L snaps when it touches

LINGER (2)
Is 5:11 after strong drink, who L late into the evening
Jer 14:8 who turns aside to L for a night?

LISTEN (69)
Ex 3:18 honey."' And they will L to your voice; and
15:26 "If you will diligently L to the voice of
23:21 heed to him and L to his voice, do
23:22 "But if you L attentively to his voice and
Lev 26:14 if you will not L to me, and will
26:18 this you will not L to me, then I
26:21 me, and will not L to me, I will
26:27 this you will not L to me, but walk
Deut 1:43 and you would not L; but you rebelled against
1:45 the LORD did not L to your voice or
3:26 account, and would not L to me; and the
7:12 "And because you L to these ordinances, and keep
23:5 your God would not L to Balaam; but the
Josh 5:6 because they did not L to the voice of
1Sam 8:7 LORD said to Samuel, L to the voice of
8:9 Now then, L to their voice; only, you shall
8:22 LORD said to Samuel, L to their voice, and
12:14 and serve him and L to his voice and
12:15 if you will not L to the voice of
15:1 people Israel; now therefore L to the words of
15:22 than sacrifice, and to L than the fat of
28:22 Now therefore, you also L to your handmaid; let
1Kgs 8:29 there, that you may L to the prayer which
11:38 And if you will L to all that I
12:15 the king did not L to the people; for
12:16 the king did not L to them, the people
2Chr 6:20 name, that you may L to the prayer which
6:21 And L to the supplications of your servant and
10:15 the king did not L to the people; for
10:16 the king did not L to them, the people
20:15 And he said, L, all Judah and inhabitants of
Tob 3:6 in my life and L to such insults."
3:10 may die and not L to these reproaches any
Job 36:11 If they L and serve him, they complete their
36:12 if they do not L, they perish by the
37:2 L to the thunder of his voice and the
Ps 5:2 L to the sound of my cry, my King
86:6 LORD, to my prayer; L to my cry of
95:7 that today you would L to his voice!
118:15 L, glad songs of victory in the tents of
Prov 23:22 L to your father who begot you, and do
Sir 33:18 the people, and you leaders of the congregation, L
36:17 L, O Lord, to the prayer of your servants,
Is 10:30 L, O Laishah!
13:4 L, a tumult on the mountains as of a
13:4 L, an uproar of kingdoms, of nations gathering
28:23 and hear my voice; L, and hear my speech.
32:3 and the ears of those who hear will L
46:3 L to me, O house of Jacob, all the
46:12 L to me, you stubborn of heart, you who
48:12 L to me, O Jacob, and Israel, whom I
51:1 L to me, you who
51:7 L to me, you who know righteousness, the people
52:8 L, your watchmen lift up their voice, together they
55:2 L diligently to me, and eat what is good,
66:6 L, an uproar from the city!
Jer 8:19 L, the cry of the daughter of my people
18:19 me, O LORD, and L to my plea.
25:36 L, the cry of the shepherds, and the wail
48:3 L, a cry from Horona'im, 'Desolation
50:28 L! they flee and escape from the land of Babylon
Bar 4:9 God, and she said: L, you neighbors of Zion,
Dan 9:17 therefore, O our God, L to the prayer of
Hos 5:1 L, O house of the king!
Mic 1:2 peoples, all of you; L, O earth, and all
Zech 7:11 But they refused to L, and turned a stubborn
11:3 L, the wail of the shepherds, for their glory
11:3 L, the roar of the lions, for the jungle
Acts 5:9 L, the feet of those that have buried your

LISTENED (25)
Gen 16:2 And Abram L to the voice of Sarai.
Num 21:3 And the LORD L to the voice of Israel,
Deut 9:19 But the LORD L to me that time also.
10:10 nights, and the LORD L to me that time
Josh 10:14 since, when the LORD L to the voice of
1Sam 12:1 Israel, "Behold, I have L to your voice in
19:6 And Saul L to the voice of Jonathan; Saul
25:35 house; see, I have L to your voice, and
28:21 "Behold, your handmaid has L to you; I have
28:21 my hand, and have L to what you have
28:23 urged him; and he L to their words.
1Kgs 12:24 So they L to the word of the LORD,
15:20 And Ben-hadad L to King Asa, and sent the
17:22 And the LORD L to the voice of Elijah;
20:25 And he L to their voice, and did so.
2Kgs 13:4 LORD, and the LORD L to him; for he
16:9 the king of Assyria L to him; the king
2Chr 11:4 So they L to the word of the LORD,
16:4 And Ben-hadad L to King Asa, and sent the
24:17 king; then the king L to them.
Is 48:18 O that you had L to my commandments!
Dan 1:14 So he L to them in this matter, and
Hos 9:17 because they have not L to him; they shall
Acts 8:10 somebody great, They all L to him, from the
8:11 And they L to him, because for a long

LISTENING (2)
1Kgs 8:28 O LORD My God, L to the cry and
2Chr 6:19 O LORD my God, L to the cry and

LIVE (2)
Sir 15:15 if you trust in God, you too shall L
48:11 we also shall surely L, but our name, after

LOATHE
Wis 11:24 that exist, and you L none of the things

LONGER
Is 60:19 The sun shall no L be your light by

LOOK (3)
Tob 2:3 Tobias went out to L for some poor person
2:3 went on to say, L, Father, one of our
Dan 3:55 sit upon cherubim and L upon the deeps, and

LORD (41)
Gen 16:13 the name of the L who spoke to her,

Ex 6:1 But the L said to Moses, "Now
15:1 will sing to the L, for he has triumphed
Judg 5:4 L, when you went forth from Seir, when you
1Sam 7:6 and said there, "We have sinned against the L
7:6 it out before the L, and fasted on that
7:8 to cry to the L our God for us,
7:9 for Israel, and the L answered him.
7:9 burnt offering to the L; and Samuel cried to
7:9 Samuel cried to the L for Israel, and the
2Sam 7:24 ever; and you, O L, became their God.
7:25 And now, O L God, confirm for ever the
7:26 for ever, saying, The L of hosts is God
7:27 For you, O L of hosts, the God of
1Kgs 8:23 heaven; and said, "O L God of Israel, there
14:15 And henceforth the L will strike Israel, as a
2Kgs 9:26 his sons says the L I will repay you
17:8 the nations whom the L drove out before the
19:1 sackcloth, and went into the house of the L
2Chr 34:27 me, I also have heard you, says the L
Tob 3:3 And now, O L, remember me and look favorably
3:6 and do not, O L, turn your face away
3:10 but to pray the L that I may die
3:11 "Blessed are you, O L, merciful God, and blessed
7:11 and drink, and the L will act on behalf
7:12 May the L of heaven, my child, guide and
12:15 into the presence of the glory of the L
12:20 And now bless the L upon the earth and
13:8 Bless the L, all you his chosen ones, all
Esth 13:13 things; you know, O L, that I would have
13:14 one but you, O L, my God.
Ps 6:3 But you, O L how long?
6:4 Turn, O L, save my life; deliver me for
16:2 I say to the L, "You are my Lord;
89:47 Remember, O L, what the measure of life is,
Sir 15:19 The eyes of the L are on those who
17:25 the mercy of the L, and his forgiveness for
Is 25:1 O L you are my God;
Lam 3:59 done to me, O L do judge my cause.
Acts 20:28 the Church of the L, which he obtained with
Rev 14:13 dead who from now on die in the L

LORDS (7)
Ex 12:27 the sacrifice of the L Passover, for he passed
Num 9:7 kept from offering the L offering at its appointed
1Sam 24:10 for he is the L anointed.
Sir 4:12 early will win the L good favor.
17:24 and well sings the L praises.
Jer 51:6 the time of the L vengeance, the repayment he
Zeph 1:8 the day of the L sacrifice—"I will punish

LOT (2)
Sir 17:20 appointed to them the L of truth.
17:22 and stand firm the L that is set before

LOUD (3)
Rev 8:5 were peals of thunder, L noises, flashes of lightning,
11:19 were flashes of lightning, L noises, peals of thunder,
16:18 were flashes of lightning, L noises, peals of thunder,

LOVE (3)
Wis 11:24 For you L all things that exist, and you
11:26 yours, O Lord who L the living.
Sir 2:9 who fear the Lord, L him, and your hearts

LOVED (2)
Ps 88:18 You have caused L one and friend to shun
Wis 16:26 your sons, whom you L, O Lord, might learn

LOWLINESS
Ps 31:7 you have seen my L, you have taken heed

LURKED (3)
Gen 49:9 He stooped down, he L as a lion, and
Num 24:9 He L, he lay down like a lion, and
Ezek 19:2 She L in the midst of young lions, rearing

LURKING
Gen 4:7 do well, sin is L at the door; its

LURKS
Deut 33:20 Gad L like a lion, he tears the arm

M

MADE (20)
2Sam 22:40 for the battle; you M my assailants sink under
22:41 You M my enemies turn their backs to me,
1Chr 17:22 And you M your people Israel to be your
Neh 9:8 faithful before you, and M with him the covenant
9:14 and commandments, and you M known to them your
Tob 3:4 captivity, and death; you M us the talk, the
8:6 You M Adam and gave him Eve his wife
Ps 18:39 for the battle; you M my assailants sink under
18:40 You M my enemies turn their backs to me,
18:43 the peoples; I you M me the head of
139:14 I praise you, for I am wondrously M
Wis 9:9 was present when you M the world, and who
12:12 you for the destruction of nations which you M
Sir 2:9 your hearts will be M radiant.
17:1 out of earth, and M him into his own
17:5 He M for them discretion, with a tongue and
17:8 He M them glory in his wondrous deeds,
Is 51:10 the great deep; who M the depths of the
Acts 4:24 said, "Sovereign Lord, who M the heaven and the
Heb 2:7 You M him for a little while lower than

MAIDSERVANT
Ex 23:12 the son of your M, and the alien, may

MAIDSERVANTS
Esth 14:3 together with all her M, from morning until evening,

MAJESTY
Sir 17:7 hearts, showing them the M of his works.

MAKE (11)
Job 13:26 things against me and M me inherit the iniquities
30:22 on the wind, you M me ride on it,
Ps 4:8 you alone, O LORD, M me dwell in safety.
51:8 M me hear I joy and gladness; let the
65:8 at your signs; you M the outgoings of the
104:3 on the waters, who M the clouds your chariot,
104:4 of the wind, who M the winds your messengers,
104:10 You M springs gush forth in the valleys; they
104:20 You M darkness, and it is night, when all
Ezek 21:29 false visions, while they M up lies for you-
Hab 1:14 For you M men like the fish of the

MAKING
Ezek 22:28 seeing false visions and M up lies for them,

MALE
Tob 6:10 He has no M heir and no daughter except

MAN (12)
Neh 1:11 grant him mercy in the sight of this M
Tob 6:12 very beautiful, and her father is a good M
7:10 her to any other M than yourself, because you
8:1 they took the young M and brought him into
Sir 17:26 since a son of M is not immortal.
Rom 6:6 know that our former M was crucified with him
2Cor 4:16 Though our outer M is wasting away, our inner
4:16 wasting away, our inner M is being renewed every
Eph 4:22 Put off the old M that belongs to your
4:24 put on the new M, created after the likeness
Col 3:9 put off the old M with his practices
3:10 put on the new M, who is being renewed

MANAS
Josh 22:13 and the half-tribe of M seh, in the land

MANASSEH
Jud 8:7 Her husband M, the son of Joseph, the son

MANKIND
Jas 3:7 has been tamed by M,

MANNER (2)
Eph 4:1 to walk in a M worthy of the calling
1Thes 2:12 to walk in a M worthy of God, who

MANY
Sir 3:22 not be curious about M of his works, for

MARCHED (2)
Judg 5:4 from Seir, when you M from the region of
Ps 68:7 your people, when you M through the wilderness,
Selah

MARCHING
Mt 27:32 As they were M out, they came upon a

MARRIAGE
Tob 7:14 a copy of the M contract, to the effect

MARRY
Tob 7:10 has the right to M my daughter Sarah.

MARSHALS
Sir 17:28 He M the host of the height of heaven;

MASTER
Jer 31:32 I showed myself their M, says the LORD.

MASTERS
Sir 3:7 mother; he will serve his parents as his M

MATERIAL
Tob 7:14 her to bring writing M; and he wrote out

MEAL (2)
Mt 13:33 in three measures of M, till it was all
Lk 13:21 in three measures of M, till it was all

MEAN (2)
Rom 14:17 of God does not M food and drink but
Eph 5:32 great mystery, and I M in reference to Christ

MEDIA (2)
Tob 6:9 When he entered M and was already approaching
11:16 great things that had happened to him in M

MEDICINE (2)
Tob 11:8 his eyes, and the M will cause the white
11:12 this he applied the M on his eyes.

MEET
Is 64:5 You M him that joyfully works righteousness, those

MELCHIS
Jud 8:7 Ahitub, the son of M, the son of Eliab,

MEN (7)
Judg 21:10 thousand of their bravest M there, and commanded
Tob 6:10 have before all other M a hereditary claim on
7:11 my daughter to seven M of our kinsmen, and
Sir 17:26 things cannot be in M, since a son of
17:28 of heaven; but all M are dust and ashes.
27:5 the test of just M is in tribulation.
Lk 17:34 there will be two M in one bed; one

MERCIES (2)
Ps 17:7 Wondrously show your M, O savior of those who
89:1 will sing of your M, O LORD, for ever;

MERCIFUL (40)
Ex 15:13 have led in your M love the people whom
34:7 and faithfulness, keeping M love for thousands,
Deut 5:10 hate me, but showing M love to thousands of
7:9 who keeps covenant and M love with those who
7:12 the covenant and the M love which he swore
2Sam 7:15 will not take my M love from him, as
1Kgs 3:6 have shown great and M love to your servant
3:6 him this great and M love, and have given
1Chr 17:13 will not take my M love from him, as
2Chr 1:8 have shown great and M love to David my
6:42 Remember your M love for David your servant."
Ezra 7:28 extended to me his M love before the king
Neh 1:5 who keeps covenant and M love with those who
Tob 3:11 are you, O Lord, M God, and blessed is
Ps 5:7 the abundance of your M love will enter your
6:4 the sake of your M love.
13:5 have trusted in your M love; my heart shall
25:6 LORD, and of your M love, for they have
31:7 be glad for your M love, because you have
31:16 save me in your M love!
31:21 wondrously shown me his M love when I was
33:18 who hope in his M love,
44:26 the sake of your M love!
51:1 God, according to your M love; according to your
63:3 Because your M love is better than life, my
66:20 prayer or removed his M love from me!
69:16 O LORD, for your M love is good; according
85:7 Show us your M love, O LORD, and grant
86:13 For great is your M love toward me; you
89:2 For your M love was established for ever, your
89:28 My M love I will keep for him for
89:33 remove from him my M love, or be false
92:2 High, to declare your M love in the morning,
107:8 the LORD for his M love, for his wonderful
107:31 the LORD for his M love, for his wonderful
109:26 me according to your M love!
143:8 the morning of your M love, for in you
Is 55:3 everlasting covenant, my steadfast, M love for David.
63:7 I will recount the M love of the LORD,
Dan 9:4 who keeps covenant and M love with those who

MERCY (121)
Gen 24:12 beg you, and show M to my master Abraham.
24:14 that you have shown M to my master."
24:27 has not forsaken his M and his faithfulness toward
32:10 least of all the M and all the faithfulness
39:21 Joseph and showed him M, and gave him favor
Ex 20:6 hate me, but showing M to thousands of those
34:6 anger, and abounding in M and faithfulness,
Num 14:18 anger, and abounding in M, forgiving iniquity and
14:19 the greatness of your M, and according as you
2Sam 2:6 may the LORD show M and faithfulness to you!
15:20 the LORD show I M and faithfulness to you."
22:51 his king, and shows M to his anointed, to
1Kgs 8:23 keeping covenant and showing M to your servants
1Chr 16:34 is good; for his M endures for ever!
16:41 the LORD, for his M endures for ever.
2Chr 5:13 is good, for his M endures for ever," the
6:14 keeping covenant and showing M to your servants
7:3 is good, for his M endures for ever."
7:6 the LORD-for his M endures for ever–whenever
20:21 the LORD, for his M endures for ever."
Ezra 3:11 is good, for his M endures for ever toward
9:9 extended to us his M before the kings of
Neh 9:17 anger and abounding in M, and did not forsake
9:32 who keep covenant and M, let not all the
13:22 spare me according to the greatness of your M
Tob 7:12 night and grant you M and peace."
Job 10:12 granted me life and M; and your care has
Ps 6:2 Have M on me, O LORD, for I am
18:50 his king, and shows M to his anointed, to
25:7 transgressions; according to your M remember me,
25:10 of the LORD are M and faithfulness, for those
26:3 For your M is before my eyes, and I
26:11 redeem me, and have M on me.
33:5 is full of the M of the LORD.
33:22 Let your M, O LORD, be upon us, even
36:5 Your M, O LORD, extends to the heavens, your
36:7 How precious is your M, O God!
40:10 have not concealed your M and your faithfulness
48:9 have thought on your M, O God, in the
52:8 I trust in the M of God for ever
56:1 Have M on me, O God,
57:3 will send forth his M and his faithfulness!
57:10 For your M is great to the heavens, your
59:10 My God in his M will meet me; my
59:16 sing aloud of your M in the morning.
59:17 are my fortress, the God who shows me M
69:13 the abundance of your M answer me.
85:10 M and faithfulness will meet; righteousness and
86:3 are my God; have M on me, O Lord,
86:5 and forgiving, abounding in M to all who call
86:15 anger and abounding in M and faithfulness.
88:11 Selah Is your M declared in the grave, or
89:24 My faithfulness and my M shall be with him,
90:14 the morning with your M, that we may rejoice
94:18 your M, O LORD, held me up.
98:3 He has remembered his M and faithfulness to the
100:5 LORD is good; his M endures for ever, and
101:1 I will sing of M and of justice; to
103:4 who crowns you with M and compassion,
103:8 and gracious, slow to anger and abounding in M
103:11 so great is his M toward those who fear
103:17 But the M of the LORD is from everlasting
106:1 is good; for his M endures for ever!
106:7 the abundance of your M, but rebelled against the
106:45 and relented according to the abundance of his M
107:1 is good; for his M endures for ever!
109:21 names sake; because your M is good, deliver me!
115:1 the sake of your M and your faithfulness!
117:2 For great is his M toward us; and the
118:1 he is good; his M endures for ever!
118:2 Let Israel say, "His M endures for ever."
118:3 of Aaron say, "His M endures for ever."
118:4 the LORD say, "His M endures for ever."

118:29 is good; for his M endures for ever!
119:41 Let your M come to me, O LORD, your
119:76 Let your M be ready to comfort me according
119:88 In your M spare my life, that I may
130:7 the LORD there is M, and with him is
136:1 is good, for his M endures for ever.
136:2 of gods, for his M endures for ever.
136:3 of lords, for his M endures for ever;
136:4 great wonders, for his M endures for ever;
136:5 the heavens, for his M endures for ever;
136:6 the waters, for his M endures for ever;
136:7 great lights, for his M endures for ever;
136:8 the day, for his M endures for ever;
136:9 the night, for his M endures for ever;
136:10 of Egypt, for his M endures for ever;
136:11 among them, for his M endures for ever;
136:12 outstretched arm, for his M endures for ever;
136:13 in two, for his M endures for ever;
136:14 of it, for his M endures for ever;
136:15 Red Sea, for his M endures for ever;
136:16 the wilderness, for his M endures for ever;
136:17 great kings, for his M endures for ever;
136:18 famous kings, for his M endures for ever;
136:19 the Amorites, for his M endures for ever;
136:20 of Bashan, for his M endures for ever;
136:21 a heritage, for his M endures for ever;
136:22 his servant, for his M endures for ever.
136:23 low estate, for his M endures for ever;
136:24 our foes, for his M endures for ever;
136:25 all flesh, for his M endures for ever.
136:26 of heaven, for his M endures for ever.
138:2 your name for your M and your faithfulness; for
138:8 purpose for me; your M, O LORD, endures for
144:2 fingers for battle; my M and my fortress, my
145:8 and merciful, slow to anger and abounding in M
Sir 17:25 How great is the M of the Lord, and
36:1 the light of your M;
50:24 that the God of M is with us to
Is 54:8 you, but with everlasting M I will have compassion
54:10 be removed, but my M shall not depart from
63:7 them according to his M, according to the abundance
Jer 32:18 for you, who show M to thousands, but repay
33:11 is good, for his M endures for ever!
Hos 6:6 For I desire M and not sacrifice, the knowledge
10:12 reap the fruit of M; break up your fallow
Jon 4:2 anger, and abounding in M, and that you repent
Mic 7:18 his anger for ever because he delights in M
7:20 faithfulness to Jacob and M to Abraham, as you

MERRY
Tob 7:10 "Eat, drink, and be M; for no one except

MIDST (4)
Ex 34:12 go, lest it become a snare in your M
Lev 15:31 by defiling my tabernacle that is in their M
Sir 24:2 In the M of her people she is exalted;
Lk 17:21 behold, the kingdom of God is in your M

MIGHTY (2)
Ps 89:19 upon one who is M I have exalted one
Rev 19:1 seemed to be the M voice of a great

MIND
Sir 17:5 he gave them a M for thinking, and filled

MINDED
Ps 119:113 I hate double M men, but I love your

MISERLINESS
Sir 31:24 their testimony to his M is accurate.

MISERLY
Sir 31:24 the one who is M with food, and their

MOAN
Nah 3:7 is Nineveh; who will M over her?

MOMENT
Tob 3:16 At that very M the prayer of both was

MORE (4)
Tob 2:10 me with ointments, the M my vision was obscured
2:10 be healed, but the M they treated me with
3:10 die and not listen to these reproaches any M
Sir 3:17 you will be loved M than a giver of

MOREOVER
Tob 6:12 M, the girl is sensible, brave, and very beautiful,

MORNING (2)
Esth 14:3 all her maidservants, from M until evening, and said:
Ps 46:5 will help her when M dawns.

MOSES (3)
Tob 7:12 in the book of M, and it has been
7:13 and the decree written in the book of M
7:14 him as wife according to the law of M

MOST (2)
Jud 10:3 arrayed herself in her M festive apparel, which she
Sir 5:4 for the M High is slow to anger.

MOTHER (2)
Tob 7:14 Then he called her M and told her to
Sir 3:4 and whoever glorifies his M is like one who

MOUNTAIN (2)
Ps 2:6 have set my king on Zion, my holy M
15:1 Who shall dwell on your holy M

MOURNING
Esth 14:14 our enemies; turn our M into gladness and our

MOUTHS (2)
Job 32:5 no answer in the M of these three men,
Mt 21:16 read, Out of the M of babies and infants

MOVE
2Chr 16:9 eyes of the LORD M back and forth throughout

MUCH
Tob 3:6 than to see so M distress in my life

MULTIPLIED
Neh 9:23 You M their descendants as the stars of heaven,

MULTITUDE
Sir 24:2 In the M of the chosen she finds praise,

MURDERED
Tob 2:3 own people has been M and thrown into the

MUST (2)
Tob 6:10 said to him, "We M stay this night in
Eccl 5:7 grow many: but you M fear God.

MUTE (25)
Ex 4:11 Who makes him M, or deaf, or seeing, or
Ps 38:13 not hear, like a M man who does not
39:2 I was M and silent, I held my peace
Prov 31:8 your mouth for the M, for the rights of
Wis 10:21 the mouth of the M, and made the tongues
Is 35:6 the tongue of the M sing for joy.
56:10 knowledge; they are all M dogs, they cannot bark;
Bar 6:41 when they see a M man, who cannot speak,
Ezek 3:26 that you shall be M and unable to reprove
24:27 and you shall speak and be no longer M
33:22 mouth was opened, and I was no longer M
Hab 2:19 thing, Awake; to a M stone, Arise!
Mt 9:32 going away, behold, a M demoniac was brought to
9:33 been cast out, the M man spoke; and the
12:22 Then a blind and M demoniac was brought to
12:22 him, so that the M man spoke and saw.
15:30 maimed, the blind, the M, and many others, and
15:31 when they saw the M speaking, the maimed whole,
Mk 7:36 deaf hear and the M speak."
9:17 for he has a M spirit;
9:25 saying to it, "You M and deaf spirit, I
Lk 1:22 and he made signs to them and remained M
11:14 a demon that was M; when the demon had
11:14 had gone out, the M man spoke, and the
1Cor 12:2 were led astray to M idols, however you may

MYRIADS
Jude 1:14 the Lord came with M of his holy ones,

MYSELF (3)
Tob 3:10 me not to hang M, but to pray the
Jer 31:32 broke, and I showed M their Master, says the
Ezek 16:8 nakedness: yes, I pledged M to you and entered

M

ORDAIN
Ps 44:4 and my God, who O victories for Jacob.

ORDAINED
Sir 24:3 I O that an unfailing light should arise in

ORPHAN
Esth 14:11 Come to my aid, for I am an O

OTHER (2)
Tob 6:10 her, have before all O men a hereditary claim
7:10 give her to any O man than yourself, because

OUTSTRETCHED
Tob 3:11 same time, with hands O toward the window, she

OVERFLOW
Ps 65:11 tracks of your chariot O with richness.

OVERHEARD
Tob 7:10 But Raguel O it and said to Tobias, "Eat,

OVERTHROW
Ex 15:7 of your majesty you O your adversaries; you send

OWN (6)
Tob 2:3 Father, one of our O people has been murdered
Sir 3:5 be gladdened by his O children, and when he
17:1 made him into his O image;
Jn 21:18 young, you fastened your O belt and walked where
Acts 20:28 he obtained with his O blood.
1Thes 4:4 how to control his O body in holiness and

OWNERS (2)
Tob 2:12 sent it to the O, they paid her full
2:12 the product to the O, and they paid her

P

PAIN
Jn 16:21 in labor, she has P, because her hour has

PAINS (22)
Ps 48:6 there, anguish as of a woman with labor P
Sir 34:5 a woman with labor P the mind has fancies.
48:19 they were in anguish, like women with labor P
Is 13:8 be in anguish like a woman with labor P
21:3 a woman with labor P; I am bowed down
23:4 have neither endured labor P nor given birth, I
42:14 a woman with labor P, I will gasp and
45:10 a woman With what are you suffering labor P
54:1 cry aloud, you who have not had labor P
Jer 4:31 a woman with labor P, anguish as of one
6:24 us, pain as of a woman with labor P
13:21 you, like those of a woman with labor P
22:23 you, pain as of a woman with labor P
31:8 her who has labor P, together; a great company,
48:41 woman with her labor P;
49:22 the heart of a woman with her labor P
49:24 of her, as of a woman with labor P
Mic 4:10 a woman with labor P; for now you shall
5:3 she who has labor P has brought forth; then
Rom 8:22 been groaning with labor P together until now;
Gal 4:27 are not with labor P; for the desolate has
1Thes 5:3 upon them as labor P come upon a woman

PARDONED
Ps 85:2 of your people; you P all their sin.

PARENTS
Sir 3:7 he will serve his P as his masters.

PASCHAL
1Cor 5:7 For Christ, our P Lamb, has been sacrificed.

PASSOVER (9)
Ex 12:27 sacrifice of the LORDS P, for he passed over
Num 9:2 of Israel keep the P at its appointed time.
9:4 sons of Israel that they should keep the P
9:5 And they kept the P in the first month,
9:10 shall still keep the P to the LORD.
33:3 the day after the P the sons of Israel
Josh 5:10 Gilgal they kept the P on the fourteenth day
5:11 next day after the P, on that very day,
2Chr 35:17 were present kept the P at that time, and

PASTURE
Is 30:23 flock will be given P, and the lamb will

PATIENCE
Sir 2:3 Await Gods P, cling to him and do not

PAY (3)
Is 49:1 me, O islands, and P attention, you peoples from
Mt 10:8 You received without P, give without pay.
2Tim 4:14 harm; the Lord will P him back for his

PEACE (2)
Tob 7:12 both this night and grant you mercy and P
7:13 God of heaven prosper your journey with his P

PEELED
Tob 11:13 both his hands, he P off the white films

PEOPLE (4)
1Kgs 3:9 to govern this great P of yours?"
Tob 2:3 to look for some poor person of our P
Ps 144:2 refuge, who subdues my P under me.
Sir 24:2 the midst of her P she is exalted; in

PERCEIVED
Sir 3:27 root in them, though it will not be P

PERFORMED (4)
Neh 9:10 the Red Sea, and P signs and wonders against
9:17 the wonders which you P among them; but they
Ps 44:1 us, what deeds you P in their days, in
65:1 you shall vows be P in Jerusalem,

PERSON
Tob 2:3 look for some poor P of our people.

PHYSICIANS
Tob 2:10 I went to P to be healed, but the

PIECE
Tob 2:12 she cut off a P she had woven and

PIERCED (2)
Is 51:9 Rahab in pieces, who P the dragon?
Hab 3:14 Selah You P with your shafts the head of

PITCHER (3)
1Kgs 17:12 little oil in a P; and now, I am
17:14 be spent, and the P of oil shall not
17:16 spent, neither did the P of oil fail, according

PLACE (4)
Tob 2:3 thrown into the market P, and now he lies
Job 40:21 lies, in the hiding P of the reeds and
Ps 90:1 have been our dwelling P, in all generations.
Is 25:4 against a wall, like heat in a dry P

PLACED (2)
Sir 17:4 He P the fear of them in all flesh,
17:7 He P the fear of him into their hearts,

PLACES
Job 38:40 dens, or lie in wait in their hiding P

PLANNED (6)
Is 46:11 to pass; I have P, and I will do
Jer 4:28 have spoken, I have P; I have not relented
Lam 2:17 has done what he P, has carried out his
Bar 4:28 For just as you P to go astray from
Zech 8:14 of hosts: "As I P to do evil to
8:15 so again I have P in these days to

PLANT
Jer 12:2 You P them, and they take root; they grow

PLANTED (2)
Ps 44:2 the nations, but you P them; you afflicted the
80:8 out the nations and P it.

PLEADED (2)
Mt 18:28 servant fell down and P with him, Have patience
18:31 that debt because you P with Me;

O

P

PLEADING
Acts 16:9 of Macedonia was standing P with him and saying,

PLEASE (40)
Gen 24:14 whom I shall say, P let down your jar
24:17 meet her, and said, P give me a little
24:43 whom I shall say, P give me a little
24:45 I said to her, P let me drink.,
Num 22:19 P, now, tarry here this night also, that I
Judg 1:24 they said to him, P, show us the way
4:19 he said to her, P, give me a little
6:13 Gideon said to him, P, sir, if the LORD
6:15 he said to him, P, Lord, how can I
6:39 speak but this once; P, let me make trial
6:39 once with the fleece; P, let it be dry
8:5 the men of Succoth, P, give loaves of bread
13:15 angel of the LORD, P, let us detain you,
15:2 P take her instead."
19:9 has waned toward evening; P tarry all night.
Ruth 2:7 She said, P, let me glean and gather among
1Sam 10:15 And Sauls uncle said, P, tell me what Samuel
22:3 the king of Moab, P let my father and
25:8 P, give whatever you have at hand to your
25:24 lord, be the guilt; P let your handmaid speak
25:28 P forgive the trespass of your handmaid; for the
2Sam 13:6 said to the king, P let my sister Tamar
13:24 your servant has sheepshearers; P let the king and
13:26 Absalom said, "If not, P let my brother Amnon
14:11 Then she said, P let the king invoke the
14:12 Then the woman said, P let your handmaid speak
15:7 said to the king, P let me go and
19:37 P let your servant return, that I may die
1Kgs 2:17 And he said, P ask King Solomon-he will
12:10 our yoke heavy, but P lighten it for us;
20:32 "Your servant Ben-hadad says, P, let me live." And
2Kgs 2:16 servants fifty strong men; P, let them go, and
5:22 sons of the prophets; P, give them a talent
18:26 said to the Rabshakeh, P, speak to your servants
2Chr 10:10 our yoke heavy, but P lighten it for us;
Is 36:11 said to the Rabshakeh, P, speak to your servants
Hag 2:15 P now, consider what will come to pass from
Lk 14:18 out and see it; P, have me excused.
14:19 go to examine them; P, have me excused.
Acts 8:34 eunuch said to Philip, P, about whom does the

PLEASING
Esth 14:11 all those who are P to you, O Lord,

PLEDGED
Ezek 16:8 your nakedness: yes, I P myself to you and

POOR (3)
Tob 2:3 to look for some P person of our people.
Ps 9:12 he does not forget the cry of the P
10:12 God, lift up your hand; forget not the P

POORLY (2)
1Cor 4:11 and thirst, we are P clothed and buffeted and
Jas 2:15 brother or sister is P clothed and in lack

PORTIONS
Gen 4:4 and of their fat P And the LORD had

POSSESSIONS (2)
Tob 6:11 is right for you to inherit her fathers P
Lk 12:44 him over all his P

POSTERIOR (2)
1Kgs 7:25 them, and all their P parts were inward.
2Chr 4:4 them, and all their P parts were inward.

POWER
Lk 23:41 remember me when you come in your kingly P

PRAISE (2)
Tob 13:8 ones, all of you, P his glory.
Sir 24:2 the chosen she finds P, and among the blessed

PRAISES
Sir 17:24 who is alive and well sings the Lords P

PRAY
Tob 3:10 hang myself, but to P the Lord that I

PRAYER (2)
Sir 17:22 set before you, in P to God, the Almighty.
51:12 My P was heard, for you saved me from

PRAYS
Sir 3:5 children, and when he P he will be heard.

PRECEPT
Mt 19:11 men can receive this P, but only those to

PREPARE
Ps 23:5 You P a table before me in the presence

PREPARED (2)
Wis 9:8 holy tent which you P from the beginning.
16:2 your people, and you P quails to eat, a

PRESENT
Tob 7:11 But for the P, my child, eat and drink,

PRESENTED
2Chr 11:13 were in all Israel P themselves to him from

PRESERVE (2)
Neh 9:6 in them; and you P all of them; and
Ps 32:7 place for me, you P me from trouble; you

PREVAIL
Job 14:20 You P for ever against him, and he passes;

PRICE
Rev 21:6 will give water without P from the fountain of

PROMISED (2)
Esth 14:5 that you did for them all that you P
Dan 3:36 one, to whom you P to make their descendants

PRONOUNCED
Ps 76:8 From the heavens you P judgment; the earth feared

PROSPER (2)
Tob 7:12 my child, guide and P you both this night
7:13 the God of heaven P your journey with his

PROVIDE
Ps 65:9 full of water; you P their grain, for so

PROVIDED (2)
Ps 68:10 goodness, O God, you P for the needy.
Wis 18:3 Therefore you P a flaming pillar of fire as

PRUDENCE
Lk 16:8 dishonest steward for his P; for the sons of

PRUDENT
Jud 8:7 lovely face; she was P of heart, discerning in

PRUNING
Song 2:12 earth, the time of P has come, and the

PUBLIC
Esth 14:16 when I appear in P I abhor it like

PUNISHED (3)
Wis 11:8 that time how you P their enemies.
12:20 For if you P with such great care and
18:8 means by which you P our enemies you called

PUT (14)
1Sam 2:36 bread, and shall say, P me, I beg you,
2Sam 3:31 "Tear your clothes, and P on sackcloth, and mourn
2Kgs 4:38 said to his servant, P on the great pot,
Job 13:27 You P my feet in the stocks, and watch
Sir 4:17 at first she will P him to the test;
24:8 and among my chosen P down your roots.
Is 15:3 in the streets they P on sackcloth; on the
32:11 yourselves bare, and P sackcloth upon your loins.
Jer 6:26 daughter of my people, P on sackcloth, and roll
Ezek 27:31 bald for you, and P on sackcloth, and they
Joel 1:13 P on sackcloth and lament, O priests, wail, O
2Mac 10:25 upon their heads and P on sackcloth, in supplication
Lk 12:37 to you, he will P on his apron and
17:8 supper for me, and P on your apron and

PUTTING (2)
Is 3:24 a rich robe, a P on of sackcloth; instead
22:12 mourning, to baldness and P on of sackcloth;

P

Q

QUALIFIED
2Cor 3:6 from God, who has Q us to be ministers

QUITE
Jud 8:7 discerning in judgment, and Q virtuous.

R

RADIANT
Sir 2:9 love him, and your hearts will be made R

RAGUEL (3)
Tob 7:1 Raguel, and they found R sitting beside the courtyard
7:1 "Brother Azariah, take me straight to our brother R
7:10 But R overheard it and said to Tobias, "Eat,

RAIMENT
Lk 7:25 A man clothed in soft R

RAISE
1Chr 21:18 should go up and R an altar to the

RAISED
Sir 3:14 to you-a house R in justice to you.

RAISES
Hos 11:4 them as one who R an infant to his

RAM
Tob 7:9 Then Raguel killed a R from the flock and

RANSOMED
Rev 5:9 by your blood you R men for God from

RAPHAEL (3)
Tob 6:10 was already approaching Ecbatana, R said to the young
6:10 Then R said to him, "We must stay this
7:9 dine, Tobias said to R, "Brother Azarias, ask Raguel

REASON
2Tim 1:6 For this R I remind you to rekindle the

RECEIVE
Sir 2:2 incline your ear, and R words of understanding, and

RECEIVED
Tob 7:9 from the flock and R them very warmly.

RECLINED
Tob 7:9 washed themselves and had R to dine, Tobias said

REDEEMED (3)
1Chr 17:21 your people whom you R from Egypt?
Esth 13:16 your portion, which you R for yourself out of
Ps 77:15 With your arm you R your people, the sons

REFERENCE
Eph 5:32 and I mean in R to Christ and the

REGAIN
Tob 11:8 And your father will R his sight and see

REJOICE (2)
Ps 2:12 with fear, with trembling R, lest he be angry,
2Cor 13:11 Finally, brethren, R

REJOICING
Tob 11:16 his son went in R, and he reported to

RELATIVE
Tob 7:10 man than yourself, because you are my nearest R

RELEASE
Tob 3:6 released from my distress; R me to go to

RELEASED
Rev 20:7 ended, Satan will be R from his prison

RELIEVE
Deut 23:13 weapons; and when you R yourself outside, you shall

REMAIN (3)
Sir 2:1 to serve the Lord, R in justice and in
Jn 1:32 dove from heaven and R on him.
Heb 1:11 will perish, but you R; they will all grow

REMAINED
Tob 2:10 For four years I R unable to see, All

REMAINS
1Jn 3:14 who does not love R in death.

REMEMBER
Tob 3:3 And now, O Lord, R me and look favorably

RENEW
Ps 104:30 are created; and you R the face of the

REPAID (7)
Judg 1:7 done, so God has R me." And they brought
9:56 Thus God R the crime of Abimelech, which he
Job 33:27 and it was not R to me.
Ps 7:4 hands, if I have R my friend with evil
Prov 11:31 If the righteous is R on earth, how much
Ezek 22:31 their way have I R upon their heads, says
23:49 your lewdness shall be R upon you, and you

REPAY (30)
Deut 7:10 hates him, he will R him to his face.
32:6 Do you thus R the LORD, you foolish and
32:41 my adversaries, and will R those who hate me.
Judg 20:10 they come they may R Gibe-ah of Benjamin, for
2Sam 3:39 LORD R the evildoer according to his wickedness!"
2Kgs 9:26 the Lord I will R you on this plot
Job 34:11 a man he will R him, and according to
Ps 28:4 R them according to their work, and according to
28:4 evil of their deeds; R them according to the
35:12 They R me evil for good; my soul is
41:10 up, that I may R them!
54:5 He will R my enemies with evil; in your
62:12 For you R a man according to his work.
103:10 to our sins, nor R us according to our
Prov 24:12 and will he not R man according to his
Sir 17:19 he will arise and R them, and he will
Is 57:18 will lead him and R him with comfort, creating
Jer 32:18 mercy to thousands, but R the guilt of fathers
50:29 R her according to her deeds, do to her
51:24 "I will R Babylon and all the inhabitants of
51:56 is a God of recompense, he will surely R
Lam 3:64 "You will R them, O LORD, according to the
Ezek 9:10 pity, but I will R their deeds upon their
11:21 their abominations, I will R their deeds upon their
16:43 therefore, behold, I will R your deeds upon your
17:19 he broke, I will R upon his head.
Hos 4:9 for their ways, and R them for their deeds.
12:2 to his ways, and R him according to his
Joel 3:4 me back, I will R your deed upon your
3:7 them, and I will R your deed upon your

REPAYING
2Chr 6:23 and judge your servants, R the guilty by bringing

REPAYMENT (4)
Job 34:33 Will he then make R to suit you, because
Is 59:18 wrath to his adversaries, R to his enemies; to
59:18 his enemies; to the islands he will render R
Jer 51:6 the LORDS vengeance, the R he is rendering her.

REPAYS (4)
Deut 7:10 a thousand generations, and R to their face those
Job 21:31 his face, and who R him for what he
Ps 31:23 the faithful, but abundantly R him who acts haughtily.
137:8 shall he be who R you with what you

REPENT
Jon 4:2 mercy, and that you R of evil.

REPENTANCE
2Chr 33:9 Manasseh Restored after R

REPLIED (2)
Tob 2:3 And I R, "Here I am, my child." And
7:1 and he R, "Joyous greetings, brothers; welcome

REPORTED
Tob 11:16 in rejoicing, and he R to his father the

P Q R

REPROACH
Tob 3:10 said, "Never shall they R my father, saying to

REPROACHES
Tob 3:10 not listen to these R any more."

RESCUE
Ps 144:10 victory to kings, who R David your servant from

RESCUED
Sir 51:12 me from destruction and R me from an evil

RESIN
Num 11:7 seed, and its appearance like that of gum R

RESTORED (2)
2Chr 33:9 Manasseh R after Repentance
Ps 68:9 you showered abroad; you R your heritage as it

RETIRE
Tob 8:1 drinking, they wanted to R; so they took the

RICH (2)
Job 36:16 table was full of R food.
Is 55:2 and delight yourselves in R food.

RICHNESS
Ps 65:11 bounty; the tracks of your chariot overflow with R

RIDE
Ps 104:3 clouds your chariot, who R on the wings of

RIGHT (4)
Tob 6:11 Also, it is R for you to inherit her
Sir 4:18 him knowledge and the discernment of what is R
Ezek 47:1 down from below the R side of the threshold
47:2 coming out on the R side.

RIGHTEOUS
Ps 119:137 You are R, O LORD, and right are your

RIGHTEOUSNESS
Sir 36:17 in the way of R, and all who are

RIGHTLY (4)
Sir 39:7 his counsel and knowledge R, and meditate on his
49:9 did good to those who directed their ways R
Is 28:26 For he is instructed R; his God teaches him.
Jer 8:6 they have not spoken R; no man repents of

RISE
Acts 3:6 Jesus Christ of Nazareth, R and walk."

ROBE
Sir 15:5 clothe him with a R of glory.

ROBES (3)
Mt 11:8 To see a man dressed in soft R
11:8 those who wear soft R are in kings houses.
1Pet 3:3 gold, and wearing of R,

RODE
Hab 3:8 the sea, when you R upon your horses, upon

ROOM
Tob 3:10 to her fathers upper R, she intended to hang

ROOTS
Sir 24:8 inheritance, and among my chosen put down your R

ROUTED
Ex 14:27 it, and the LORD R, the Egyptians in the

RULE (3)
1Chr 29:12 from you, and you R over all.
Esth 13:9 Lord, Lord, King who R over all things, for
Wis 12:15 You are righteous and R all things righteously, deeming

RULING
Sir 1:8 upon his throne, and R as God.

S

SAFELY
Tob 7:13 her and bring her S to your father.

SAFETY (2)
Tob 8:4 our Lord that he grant us mercy and S
Ps 37:3 dwell in the land, and be nourished in S

SAINTS
Sir 24:12 abode was in the full assembly of the S

SALTINESS (3)
Mt 5:13 taste, how shall its S be restored?
Mk 9:48 salt has lost its S, how will you season
Lk 14:34 taste, how shall its S be restored?

SAME
Tob 3:11 At that S time, with hands outstretched toward the

SANCTUARY-
Ps 68:24 my King, into the S

SARAH (3)
Tob 6:10 and no daughter except S only, and you, as
7:9 Azarias, ask Raguel to give me my kinswoman S
7:10 brother, has the right to marry my daughter S

SARASADAI
Jud 8:7 Nathanael, the son of S, the son of Simeon,

SASH (6)
Ex 28:4 a turban, and a S; they shall make holy
28:39 you shall make a S embroidered with needlework.
39:29 twined linen, and the S of fine twined linen
Lev 8:7 girded him with the S, and clothed him with
16:4 girded with the linen S, and wear the linen
Rev 1:13 and with a golden S across his chest;

SASHES (5)
Ex 28:40 shall make coats and S and caps; you shall
29:9 shall belt them with S and bind caps on
Lev 8:13 and girded them with S, and bound caps on
Prov 31:24 sells them; she delivers S to the merchant.
Rev 15:6 linen, and with golden S across their chests.

SAT
Lk 7:36 the Pharisees house, and S at table.

SATISFY (4)
Num 11:22 together for them, to S them?"
11:22 slaughtered for them, to S them?
Deut 3:26 to me, Let it S you; speak no more
Ps 145:16 open your hand, you S the desire of every

SAVE (4)
2Sam 22:3 refuge, my savior; you S me from violence.
Ps 36:6 man and beast you S, O LORD.
Sir 15:15 the commandments, they will S you; if you trust
Mt 8:25 and woke him, saying, S us, Lord; we are

SAVED
Sir 51:12 was heard, for you S me from destruction and

SAVIOR (2)
Ps 42:5 again praise him, my S
43:5 again praise him, my S and my God.

SCATTERED
Ps 89:10 like a carcass, you S your enemies with your

SCORN
Nah 3:6 with contempt, and make you an object of S

SCOURGE
Wis 12:22 while chastening us you S our enemies ten thousand

SCOURING
Lam 3:45 have made us off S and refuse among the

SCRIPTURE (3)
Jn 10:35 of God came (and S cannot be nullified),
17:12 of perdition, that the S might be fulfilled.
Acts 8:32 the passage of the S which he was reading

R

S

SCRIPTURES (2)
Mt 21:42 never read in the S: The very stone which
26:56 taken place, that the S of the prophets might

SEARCH
Ps 139:3 You S out my path and my lying down,

SECOND
Heb 10:9 order to establish the S

SEED
1Jn 3:9 commit sin; for Gods S abides in him, and

SEEK (2)
Sir 2:11 shield of all who S him in truth.
28:5 wrath, will he then S forgiveness from God?

SEH
Josh 22:13 the half-tribe of Manas S, in the land of

SELAH (23)
Ps 3:8 your blessing be upon your people. S
21:2 the request of his lips. S
32:4 as by the heat of summer. S
32:5 S Therefore let every one who is godly
32:7 surround me with deliverance. S
39:5 man stands as a mere breath. S
39:11 S "Hear my prayer, O Lord, and give
44:8 give thanks to your name forever. S
57:3 S God will send forth his mercy and his
59:5 S Each evening they come back,
60:4 rally to it from the bow. S
61:4 safe under the shelter of your wings. S
66:4 Sing praises to your name." S
66:15 make an offering of bulls and goats. S
67:1 make his face to shine upon us, S
67:4 S Let the peoples praise you, O God;
68:7 marched through the wilderness, S
77:15 sons of Jacob and Joseph. S
84:4 ever singing your praise! S
85:2 you pardoned all their sin. S
88:7 overwhelm me with all your waves. S
88:10 shades rise up to praise you? S
89:4 your throne for all generations."' S
143:6 thirst for you like a parched land. S

SEND (4)
Ex 15:7 overthrow your adversaries; you S forth your fury, it
Job 14:20 change his countenance, and S him away.
Ps 104:30 When you S forth your Spirit, they are created;
Sir 36:2 light of your mercy; S fear of you upon

SENSIBLE (2)
Tob 6:12 Moreover, the girl is S, brave, and very beautiful,
Sir 26:14 A S and silent wife is a gift of

SENT (10)
Judg 13:8 of God whom you S come again to us,
Tob 2:12 she had woven and S it to the owners,
12:13 the dead, I was S to test you.
Jud 16:14 You S forth your Spirit, and it formed them;
Wis 11:15 and worthless animals, you S upon them a multitude
12:8 were but men, and S wasps as forerunners of
12:25 to thoughtless children, you S your judgment to mock
2Mac 15:22 words: "O Lord, you S your angel in the
Jn 11:42 may believe that you S me."
17:8 have believed that you S me.

SEPARATED
1Kgs 8:53 For you S them from among all the peoples

SERVANT
Ps 144:10 who rescue David your S from the cruel sword.

SERVE
Sir 3:7 his mother; he will S his parents as his

SET (3)
Job 7:12 sea monster, that you S a guard over me?
13:27 all my paths; you S a bound to the
Sir 17:22 the lot that is S before you, in prayer

SEVENTH
Tob 2:12 One day, the S of Dystrus, when she cut

SEWN
Job 16:15 I have S sackcloth upon my skin, and have

SHACKLES (5)
Ps 105:18 feet were hurt with S, his neck was put
1Mac 3:41 in immense amounts, and S, and went to the
Mk 5:4 often been bound with S and chains, but the
5:4 wrenched apart, and the S he broke in pieces;
Lk 8:29 bound with chains and S, but he broke the

SHAKING
Mk 15:28 passed by derided him, S their heads, and saying,

SHALT
Ex 8:23 By tomorrow S this sign be.""

SHARD
Is 30:14 its fragments not a S is found with which

SHARE
2Tim 2:3 Take your S of suffering as a good soldier

SHARPEN
Deut 32:41 for ever, if I S my glittering sword, and

SHATTERED
Ps 48:7 the east wind you S the ships of Tarshish.

SHE-DONKEYS (6)
Gen 12:16 menservants, maidservants, S, and camels.
32:15 and ten bulls, twenty S and ten he-donkeys.
45:23 of Egypt, and ten S loaded with grain, bread,
1Chr 27:30 Ishmaelite; and over the S was Jehdeiah the
Job 1:3 oxen, and five hundred S, and very many servants;
42:12 a thousand yoke of oxen, and a thousand S

SHIELD
Sir 2:11 and he is the S of all who seek

SHOW (3)
Ps 106:4 O LORD, when you S favor to your people;
Sir 36:1 look upon us, and S us the light of
Jer 32:18 hard for you, who S mercy to thousands, but

SHOWBREAD (3)
Mt 12:4 God and ate the S, which it was not
Mk 2:26 priest, and ate the S, which it is not
Lk 6:4 took and ate the S, which it is not

SHOWED (4)
Wis 16:2 of this punishment you S kindness to your people,
Sir 17:6 hearts with understanding, and S them good and evil.
Jer 11:18 I knew; then you S me their evil deeds.
31:32 they broke, and I S myself their Master, says

SHOWERED
Ps 68:9 abundance, O God, you S abroad; you restored your

SHOWING
Sir 17:7 him into their hearts, S them the majesty of

SIDE
Ezek 47:1 from below the right S of the threshold of

SIGHT
Tob 11:8 father will regain his S and see the light."

SIGN (5)
Num 21:8 it up as a S; and every one who
21:9 it up as a S; and if a serpent
Rev 12:1 And a great S appeared in heaven, a
12:3 And another S appeared in heaven; behold, a great
15:1 Then I saw another S in heaven great and

SIGNS
Joel 2:30 "And I will give S in the heavens and

SILENT (4)
Ps 31:18 the lying lips be S, which speak insolently against
39:9 I am S, I do not open my mouth;
Is 53:7 before its shearers is S, so he opened not
Acts 8:32 before its shearer is S, so he opens not

SILVER
Sir 2:5 For gold and S are tested in the fire,

S

SIMEON
Jud 8:7 Sarasadai, the son of S, had left her gold

SIN
1Jn 3:6 in him does not S; any one who sins

SINAI
Judg 5:5 LORD, the One of S, before the LORD, the

SING
Is 54:1 S, O barren one, who

SINGS
Sir 17:24 is alive and well S the Lords praises.

SINNING
Heb 4:15 has been tempted as we are, yet without S

SISTER
Tob 7:12 you are her brother and she is your S

SIT
Dan 3:55 Blessed are you, who S upon cherubim and look

SITTING (2)
Tob 7:1 and they found Raguel S beside the courtyard door.
Lk 7:37 learned that he was S at table in the

SITUATION
Tob 7:11 me explain the true S to you.

SIXTY-ONE
Num 31:34 seventy-two thousand cattle, S thousand donkeys,

SKULL
Ps 7:16 and on his own S his violence descends.

SLANDERED
1Cor 4:13 persecuted, we endure; when S we try to conciliate;

SLEEP
Ps 44:23 Why do you S, O Lord?

SMEAR
Tob 11:8 S the gall of the fish on his eyes,

SODOM
Lk 17:29 Lot went out from S, fire and brimstone rained

SOFTENS
Sir 6:5 voice multiplies friends and S enemies, and a

SOME (2)
Gen 4:4 ground, and Abel brought S of the firstlings of
Tob 2:3 out to look for S poor person of our

SON (12)
Tob 11:14 "Here I see my S, the light of my
11:16 And his S went in rejoicing, and he reported
Jud 8:7 son of Sarasadai, the S of Simeon, had left
8:7 son of Eliab, the S of Nathanael, the son
8:7 son of Ahitub, the S of Melchis, the son
8:7 Her husband Manasseh, the S of Joseph, the son
8:7 son of Nathanael, the S of Sarasadai, the son
8:7 son of Melchis, the S of Eliab, the son
8:7 son of Joseph, the S of Ahitub, the son
Sir 17:26 in men, since a S of man is not
Lk 14:5 of you, having a S or an ox that
Rev 1:13 lampstands one like a S of man, clothed with

SONGS
Tob 2:6 mourning, and all your S into lamentation." And I

SONS (527)
Ex 1:9 his people, "Behold, the S of Israel are too
1:12 in dread of the S of Israel.
1:13 So they made the S of Israel serve with
2:23 And the S of Israel groaned under their bondage,
2:25 And God saw the S of Israel, and God
3:9 the cry of the S of Israel has come
3:13 I come to the S of Israel and say
3:14 "Say this to the S of Israel, I Am
3:15 "Say this to the S of Israel, The LORD,
4:29 the elders of the S of Israel.
4:31 LORD had visited the S of Israel and that
5:14 the foremen of the S of Israel, whom Pharaohs
5:15 the foremen of the S of Israel came and
5:19 The foremen of the S of Israel saw that
6:5 the groaning of the S of Israel whom the
6:6 Say therefore to the S of Israel, I am
6:9 spoke thus to the S of Israel; but they
6:11 Egypt to let the S of Israel go out
6:12 the LORD, "Behold, the S of Israel have not
6:13 Egypt to bring the S of Israel out of
6:13 a charge to the S of Israel and to
6:26 said: "Bring out the S of Israel from the
6:27 about bringing out the S of Israel from Egypt,
7:2 Pharaoh to let the S of Israel go out
7:5 and bring out the S of Israel from among
9:4 that belongs to the S of Israel.""
9:6 the cattle of the S of Israel not one
9:26 of Goshen, where the S of Israel were, there
9:35 did not let the S of Israel go; as
10:23 days; but all the S of Israel had light
11:7 against any of the S of Israel, either man
11:10 did not let the S of Israel go out
12:27 the houses of the S of Israel in Egypt,
12:28 Then the S of Israel went and did so;
12:31 both you and the S of Israel; and go,
12:35 The S of Israel had also done as Moses
12:37 And the S of Israel journeyed from Rameses to
12:40 The time that the S of Israel dwelt in
12:42 LORD by all the S of Israel throughout their
12:50 Thus did all the S of Israel; as the
12:51 the LORD brought the S of Israel out of
13:2 the womb among the S of Israel, both of
13:18 And the S of Israel went up out of
13:19 had solemnly sworn the S of Israel, saying, "God
14:2 to Moses, "Tell the S of Israel to turn
14:3 will say of the S of Israel, They are
14:8 and he pursued the S of Israel as they
14:10 Pharaoh drew near, the S of Israel lifted up
14:10 And the S of Israel cried out to the
14:15 Tell the S of Israel to go forward.
14:16 divide it, that the S of Israel may go
14:22 And the S of Israel went into the midst
14:29 But the S of Israel walked on dry ground
15:1 Then Moses and the S of Israel sang this
15:19 upon them; but the S of Israel walked on
16:1 the congregation of the S of Israel came to
16:2 whole congregation of the S of Israel murmured
16:6 said to all the S of Israel, "At evening
16:9 whole congregation of the S of Israel, Come near
16:10 whole congregation of the S of Israel, they looked
16:12 the murmurings of the S of Israel; say to
16:15 When the S of Israel saw it, they said
16:17 And the S of Israel did so; they gathered,
16:35 And the S of Israel ate the manna forty
17:1 the congregation of the S of Israel moved on
17:7 the fault-finding of the S of Israel, and because
19:1 new moon after the S of Israel had gone
19:3 Jacob, and tell the S of Israel:
24:5 young men of the S of Israel, who offered
24:17 the sight of the S of Israel.
25:2 Moses, "Speak to the S of Israel, that they
25:22 in commandment for the S of Israel.
27:20 you shall command the S of Israel that they
28:30 the judgment of the S of Israel upon his
28:38 holy offering which the S of Israel hallow as
29:43 will meet with the S of Israel, and it
29:45 will dwell among the S of Israel, and will
30:12 the census of the S of Israel, then each
30:16 it may bring the S of Israel to remembrance
30:16 atonement money from the S of Israel, and shall
30:31 shall say to the S of Israel, This shall
31:13 Moses, "Say to the S of Israel, You shall
31:16 Therefore the S of Israel shall keep the sabbath,
31:17 between me and the S of Israel that in
32:20 water, and made the S of Israel drink it.
33:5 Moses, "Say to the S of Israel, You are
33:6 Therefore the S of Israel stripped themselves of
34:30 Aaron and all the S of Israel saw Moses,
34:32 And afterward all the S of Israel came near,
34:34 out, and told the S of Israel what he
34:35 he was commanded, the S of Israel saw the
35:1 the congregation of the S of Israel, and said
35:4 the congregation of the S of Israel, "This is
35:20 the congregation of the S of Israel departed from
35:29 men and women, the S of Israel, whose heart
35:30 Moses said to the S of Israel, "See, the
36:3 freewill offering which the S of Israel had brought
39:32 was finished; and the S of Israel had done

39:42 commanded Moses, so the S of Israel had done
Lev 1:2 saying, Speak to the S of Israel, and say
4:2 Moses, "Say to the S of Israel, If any
7:29 Moses, "Say to the S of Israel, He that
7:34 perpetual debt from the S of Israel.
7:34 have taken from the S of Israel, out of
7:36 given them by the S of Israel, on the
7:38 that he commanded the S of Israel to bring
9:3 And say to the S of Israel, Take a
10:11 are to teach the S of Israel all the
11:2 Aaron, Say to the S of Israel, These are
12:2 Moses, "Say to the S of Israel, If a
15:2 Aaron, "Say to the S of Israel, When any
15:31 you shall keep the S of Israel separate from
16:5 the congregation of the S of Israel two male
16:16 the uncleannesses of the S of Israel, and because
16:19 the uncleannesses of the S of Israel.
16:21 the iniquities of the S of Israel, and all
16:34 be made for the S of Israel once in
17:2 and to all the S of Israel, This is
17:5 the end that the S of Israel may bring
17:12 have said to the S of Israel, No person
17:13 man also of the S of Israel, or of
17:14 have said to the S of Israel, You shall
18:2 Moses, "Say to the S of Israel, I am
19:2 the congregation of the S of Israel, You shall
20:2 Moses, "Say to the S of Israel, Any man
20:2 Any man of the S of Israel, or of
22:3 holy things, which the S of Israel dedicate to
22:15 holy things of the S of Israel, which they
22:32 be hallowed among the S of Israel; I am
23:2 Moses, "Say to the S of Israel, The appointed
23:10 Moses, "Say to the S of Israel, When you
23:24 Moses, "Say to the S of Israel, In the
23:34 Moses, "Say to the S of Israel, On the
23:43 that I made the S of Israel dwell in
23:44 Moses declared to the S of Israel the appointed
24:2 to Moses, "Command the S of Israel to bring
24:8 on behalf of the S of Israel as a
24:10 went out among the S of Israel; and the
24:15 And say to the S of Israel, Whoever curses
24:23 Moses spoke to the S of Israel; and they
24:23 Thus the S of Israel did as the LORD
25:2 Sinai, "Say to the S of Israel, When you
25:33 their possession among the S of Israel.
25:55 For to me the S of Israel are servants,
26:46 between him and the S of Israel on Mount
27:2 Moses, "Say to the S of Israel, When a
27:34 commanded Moses for the S of Israel on Mount
Num 1:2 the congregation of the S of Israel, by families,
1:45 whole number of the S of Israel, by their
1:49 of them among the S of Israel;
1:52 The S of Israel shall pitch their tents by
1:53 the congregation of the S of Israel; and the
1:54 Thus did the S of Israel; they did according
2:2 Moses and Aaron, "The S of Israel shall encamp
2:32 These are the S of Israel as numbered by
2:33 not numbered among the S of Israel, as the
2:34 Thus did the S of Israel.
3:8 the duties for the S of Israel as they
3:9 him from among the S of Israel.
3:12 Levites from among the S of Israel instead of
3:12 the womb among the S of Israel.
3:38 be done for the S of Israel; and any
3:40 first-born males of the S of Israel, from a
3:41 the first-born among the S of Israel, and the
3:41 the cattle of the S of Israel."
3:42 the first-born among the S of Israel, as the
3:45 the first-born among the S of Israel, and the
3:46 the first-born of the S of Israel, over and
3:50 the first-born of the S of Israel he took
5:2 to Moses, "Command the S of Israel that they
5:4 to Moses, so the S of Israel did.
5:4 And the S of Israel did so, and drove
5:6 Moses, "Say to the S of Israel, When a
5:9 holy things of the S of Israel, which they
5:12 Moses, "Say to the S of Israel, If any
6:2 Moses, "Say to the S of Israel, When either
6:23 you shall bless the S of Israel: you shall
6:27 my name upon the S of Israel, and I
8:6 Levites from among the S of Israel, and cleanse
8:9 whole congregation of the S of Israel.
8:10 before the LORD, the S of Israel shall lay
8:11 wave offering from the S of Israel, that it
8:14 Levites from among the S of Israel, and the
8:16 first-born of all the S of Israel, I have
8:16 me from among the S of Israel; instead of
8:17 the firstborn among the S of Israel are mine,
8:18 the first-born among the S of Israel.
8:20 the congregation of the S of Israel to the
8:20 concerning the Levites, the S of Israel did to
9:2 Egypt, saying, "Let the S of Israel keep the
9:4 So Moses told the S of Israel that they
9:5 commanded Moses, so the S of Israel did.
9:7 appointed time among the S of Israel?"
9:10 Moses, "Say to the S of Israel, If any
9:17 tent, after that the S of Israel set out;
9:17 settled down, there the S of Israel encamped.
9:18 of the LORD the S of Israel set out,
9:19 tabernacle many days, the S of Israel kept the
9:22 tabernacle, abiding there, the S of Israel remained
10:12 the covenant, and the S of Israel set out
10:28 of march of the S of Israel according to
13:2 I give to the S of Israel; from each
13:3 were heads of the S of Israel.
13:26 the congregation of the S of Israel in the
13:32 they brought to the S of Israel an evil
14:2 And all the S of Israel murmured against Moses
14:5 the congregation of the S of Israel.
14:7 the congregation of the S of Israel, The land,
14:10 meeting to all the S of Israel.
14:27 the murmurings of the S of Israel, which they
14:39 words to all the S of Israel, and the
15:2 Moses, Say to the S of Israel, When you
15:18 Moses, "Say to the S of Israel, When you
15:25 the congregation of the S of Israel, and they
15:26 the congregation of the S of Israel shall be
15:29 is native among the S of Israel, and for
15:32 While the S of Israel were in the wilderness,
15:38 Moses, "Speak to the S of Israel, and bid
16:2 a number of the S of Israel, two hundred
16:38 a sign to the S of Israel."
16:40 a reminder to the S of Israel, so that
16:41 congregation of the S of Israel murmured against
17:2 Moses, "Speak to the S of Israel, and get
17:5 the murmurings of the S of Israel, which they
17:6 Moses spoke to the S of Israel; and all
17:9 LORD to all the S of Israel; and they
17:12 And the S of Israel said to Moses, "Behold,
18:5 no more upon the S of Israel.
18:6 Levites from among the S of Israel; they are
18:20 your inheritance among the S of Israel.
18:22 And henceforth the S of Israel shall not come
18:23 generations; and among the S of Israel they shall
18:24 no inheritance among the S of Israel."
18:24 the tithe of the S of Israel, which they
18:26 you take from the S of Israel the tithe
18:28 you receive from the S of Israel; and from
18:32 holy things of the S of Israel, lest you
19:2 has commanded: Tell the S of Israel to bring
19:9 the congregation of the S of Israel for the
19:10 shall be to the S of Israel, and to
20:1 And the S of Israel, the whole
20:12 the eyes of the S of Israel, therefore you
20:13 of Meribah, where the S of Israel contended with
20:19 And the S of Israel said to him, "We
20:22 from Kadesh, and the S of Israel, the whole
20:24 have given to the S of Israel, because you
21:6 people, so that many S of Israel died.
21:10 And the S of Israel set out, and encamped
22:1 Then the S of Israel set out,
22:3 with fear of the S of Israel.
25:6 behold, one of the S of Israel came and
25:6 whole congregation of the S of Israel, while they
25:8 was stayed from the S of Israel.
25:11 my wrath from the S of Israel, in that
25:11 did not consume the S of Israel in my
25:13 made atonement for the S of Israel."
26:2 the congregation of the S of Israel, from twenty
26:4 The S of Israel, who came forth out of
26:51 the number of the S of Israel, six hundred
26:62 to them among the S of Israel.
26:62 not numbered among the S of Israel, because there
26:63 priest, who numbered the S of Israel in the
26:64 who had numbered the S of Israel in the
27:8 shall say to the S of Israel, If a
27:11 shall be to the S of Israel a statute
27:12 have given to the S of Israel.
27:20 the congregation of the S of Israel may obey.
27:21 he and all the S of Israel with him,
28:2 to Moses, "Command the S of Israel, and say
29:40 And Moses told the S of Israel everything just

30:1 the tribes of the S of Israel, "This is
31:2 to Moses, "Avenge the S of Israel on the
31:9 And the S of Israel took captive the women
31:12 the congregation of the S of Israel, at the
31:16 Behold, these caused the S of Israel, by the
31:30 And from the S of Israels half you shall
31:42 From the S of Israels half, which Moses separated
31:47 thousand persons from the S of Israels half Moses
31:54 a memorial for the S of Israel before the
32:7 the heart of the S of Israel from going
32:9 the heart of the S of Israel from going
32:17 to go before the S of Israel, until we
32:18 our homes until the S of Israel have inherited
32:28 the tribes of the S of Israel.
33:1 the stages of the S of Israel, when they
33:3 after the Passover the S of Israel went out
33:5 So the S of Israel set out from Rameses,
33:38 fortieth year after the S of Israel had come
33:40 the coming of the S of Israel.
33:51 Jericho, "Say to the S of Israel, When you
34:2 to Moses, "Command the S of Israel, and say
34:13 Moses commanded the S of Israel, saying, "This is
34:29 the inheritance for the S of Israel in the
35:2 at Jericho, "Comand the S of Israel, that they
35:8 the possession of the S of Israel, from the
35:10 Moses, "Say to the S of Israel, When you
35:15 for refuge for the S of Israel, and for
35:34 the midst of the S of Israel."
36:2 by lot to the S of Israel; and my
36:4 the jubilee of the S of Israel comes, then
36:7 every one of the S of Israel shall cling
36:7 The inheritance of the S of Israel shall not
36:8 any tribe of the S of Israel shall be
36:8 every one of the S of Israel may possess
36:9 the tribes of the S of Israel shall cling
36:13 by Moses to the S of Israel in the
Deut 1:3 Moses spoke to the S of Israel according to
3:18 before your brethren the S of Israel.
10:6 "(The S of Israel journeyed from Be-eroth
24:7 of his brethren, the S of Israel, and if
29:1 to make with the S of Israel in the
31:19 for me against the S of Israel.
31:19 teach it to the S of Israel; put it
31:22 taught it to the S of Israel.
32:49 I give to the S of Israel for a
32:51 the midst of the S of Israel at the
32:51 the midst of the S of Israel.
32:52 I give to the S of Israel."
34:8 And the S of Israel wept for Moses in
34:9 upon him; so the S of Israel obeyed him,
Josh 1:2 to them, to the S of Israel.
3:1 Shittim, with all the S of Israel; and they
3:9 Joshua said to the S of Israel, "Come here,
4:4 twelve men from the S of Israel, whom he
4:5 the tribes of the S of Israel,
4:7 shall be to the S of Israel a memorial
4:8 the tribes of the S of Israel, as the
4:21 he said to the S of Israel, "When your
5:1 the Jordan for the S of Israel until they
5:1 them, because of the S of Israel.
5:2 knives and circumcise the S of Israel again the
5:3 knives, and circumcised the S of Israel at
5:6 For the S of Israel walked forty years in
5:10 While the S of Israel were encamped in Gilgal
5:12 the land; and the S of Israel had manna
6:1 without because of the S of Israel; none went
7:1 But the S of Israel broke faith
7:1 LORD burned against the S of Israel.
7:12 Therefore the S of Israel cannot stand before their
7:23 Joshua and all the S of Israel; and they
8:31 LORD had commanded the S of Israel, as it
8:32 the presence of the S of Israel, he wrote
8:33 they should bless the S of Israel.
9:17 And the S of Israel set out and reached
9:18 But the S of Israel did not kill them,
9:26 the hand of the S of Israel; and they
10:4 Joshua and with the S of Israel."
10:21 against any of the S of Israel.
11:14 and the cattle, the S of Israel took for
11:19 made peace with the S of Israel, except the
11:22 the land of the S of Israel; only in
12:1 the land, whom the S of Israel defeated, and
12:6 the LORD, and the S of Israel defeated them;
12:7 whom Joshua and the S of Israel defeated on
13:6 out from before the S of Israel; only allot
13:13 Yet the S of Israel did not drive out
13:22 Beor, the soothsayer, the S of Israel killed with
14:1 the inheritances which the S of Israel received in
14:1 the tribes of the S of Israel distributed to
14:5 The S of Israel did as the LORD commanded
17:13 But when the S of Israel grew strong, they
18:1 whole congregation of the S of Israel assembled at
18:2 There remained among the S of Israel seven tribes
18:3 Joshua said to the S of Israel, "How long
18:10 the land to the S of Israel, to each
19:49 land as inheritances, the S of Israel gave an
19:51 the tribes of the S of Israel distributed by
20:2 Joshua, "Say to the S of Israel, Appoint the
20:9 designated for all the S of Israel, and for
21:1 the tribes of the S of Israel;
21:3 of the LORD the S of Israel gave to
21:8 their pasture lands the S of Israel gave by
21:41 the possession of the S of Israel were in
22:9 home, parting from the S of Israel at Shiloh,
22:11 And the S of Israel heard say, "Behold, the
22:11 that belongs to the S of Israel."
22:12 And when the S of Israel heard of it,
22:12 whole assembly of the S of Israel gathered at
22:13 Then the S of Israel sent to the Reubenites
22:31 you have saved the S of Israel from the
22:32 of Canaan, to the S of Israel, and brought
22:33 the report pleased the S of Israel; and the
22:33 of Israel; and the S of Israel blessed God
Judg 1:1 death of Joshua the S of Israel inquired of
2:4 words to all the S of Israel, the people
2:6 dismissed the people, the S of Israel went each
2:11 And the S of Israel did what was evil
3:2 the generations of the S of Israel might know
3:5 So the S of Israel dwelt among the Canaanites,
3:7 And the S of Israel did what was evil
3:8 of Mesopotamia; and the S of Israel served
3:9 But when the S of Israel cried to the
3:9 a deliverer for the S of Israel, who delivered
3:12 And the S of Israel again did what was
3:14 And the S of Israel served Eglon the king
3:15 But when the S of Israel cried to the
3:15 The S of Israel sent tribute by him to
3:27 of Ephraim; and the S of Israel went down
4:1 And the S of Israel again did
4:3 Then the S of Israel cried to the LORD
4:3 iron, and oppressed the S of Israel cruelly for
4:5 of Ephraim; and the S of Israel came up
4:23 of Canaan before the S of Israel.
4:24 the hand of the S of Israel bore harder
6:1 The S of Israel did what
6:2 because of Midian the S of Israel made for
6:6 of Midian; and the S of Israel cried for
6:7 When the S of Israel cried to the LORD
6:8 a prophet to the S of Israel; and he
8:28 was subdued before the S of Israel, and they
8:33 as Gideon died, the S of Israel turned again
8:34 And the S of Israel did not remember the
10:6 And the S of Israel again did what was
10:8 they oppressed all the S of Israel that were
10:10 And the S of Israel cried to the LORD,
10:11 LORD said to the S of Israel, "Did I
10:15 And the S of Israel said to the LORD,
10:17 in Gilead; and the S of Israel came together,
11:27 this day between the S of Israel and the
11:33 were subdued before the S of Israel.
13:1 And the S of Israel again did
19:12 not belong to the S of Israel; but we
19:30 the day that the S of Israel came up
20:1 Then all the S of Israel came out,
20:3 Benjaminites heard that the S of Israel had gone
20:3 to Mizpah.) And the S of Israel said, "Tell
20:7 Behold, you S of Israel, all of you, give
20:13 of their brethren, the S of Israel.
20:14 to battle against the S of Israel.
20:18 The S of Israel arose and went up to
20:19 Then the S of Israel rose in the morning,
20:23 And the S of Israel went up and wept
20:24 So the S of Israel came near against the
20:25 thousand men of the S of Israel; all these
20:26 Then all the S of Israel, the whole army,
20:27 And the S of Israel inquired of the LORD
20:30 And the S of Israel went up against the
21:5 And the S of Israel said, "Which of all
21:6 And the S of Israel had compassion for Benjamin
21:18 For the S of Israel had sworn, "Cursed be
21:24 And the S of Israel departed from there at
1Sam 2:28 by fire from the S of Israel.

S

7:6 And Samuel judged the S of Israel at Mizpah.
7:7 Philistines heard that the S of Israel had gathered
7:7 And when the S of Israel heard of it
7:8 And the S of Israel said to Samuel, "Do
9:2 a man among the S of Israel more handsome
10:18 he said to the S of Israel, "Thus says
14:18 that time with the S of Israel.
2Sam 7:6 I brought up the S of Israel from Egypt
7:7 moved with all the S of Israel, did I
19:40 and also half the S of Israel, brought the
21:2 his zeal for the S of Israel and Judah.
21:2 were not of the S of Israel, but of
21:2 the Amorites; although the S of Israel had sworn
1Kgs 6:1 eightieth year after the S of Israel came out
8:1 fathers houses of the S of Israel, before King
8:9 a covenant with the S of Israel, when they
8:63 king and all the S of Israel dedicated the
9:20 were not of the S of Israel-
9:21 the land, whom the S of Israel were unable
9:22 But of the S of Israel Solomon made no
11:2 had said to the S of Israel, "You shall
12:17 Rehoboam reigned over the S of Israel who dwelt
12:24 against your kinsmen the S of Israel.
12:33 a feast for the S of Israel, and went
14:24 drove out before the S of Israel.
16:21 Then the S of Israel were divided into two
18:20 sent to all the S of Israel, and gathered
19:10 of hosts; for the S of Israel have forsaken
19:14 of hosts; for the S of Israel have forsaken
20:15 he mustered all the S of Israel, seven thousand.
20:27 And the S of Israel were mustered, and were
20:27 went against them; the S of Israel encamped before
20:29 was joined; and the S of Israel struck a
21:26 cast out before the S of Israel.)
2Kgs 8:12 will do to the S of Israel; you will
9:26 the blood of his S says the Lord I
13:5 the Syrians; and the S of Israel dwelt in
17:7 was so, because the S of Israel had sinned
17:8 drove out before the S of Israel, and in
17:9 And the S of Israel did secretly against the
17:22 The S of Israel walked in all the sins
17:24 Samaria instead of the S of Israel; and they
18:4 until those days the S of Israel had burned
21:9 LORD destroyed before the S of Israel.
1Chr 6:64 So the S of Israel gave the Levites the
2Chr 5:2 fathers houses of the S of Israel, in Jerusalem,
5:10 a covenant with the S of Israel, when they
6:11 he made with the S of Israel."
8:2 him, and settled the S of Israel in them.
8:8 the land, whom the S of Israel had not
8:9 But of the S of Israel Solomon made no
10:17 Rehoboam reigned over the S of Israel who dwelt
10:18 forced labor, and the S of Israel stoned him
30:21 And the S of Israel that were present at
31:1 Then all the S of Israel returned to their
31:5 was spread abroad, the S of Israel gave in
31:6 And the S of Israel and Judah who lived
33:2 drove out before the S of Israel.
33:9 LORD destroyed before the S of Israel.
34:33 that belonged to the S of Israel, and made
35:17 And the S of Israel who were present kept
Ezra 2:2 the men of the S of Israel:
6:16 And the S of Israel, the priests and the
6:21 was eaten by the S of Israel who had
7:7 king, some of the S of Israel, and some
7:13 any one of the S of Israel or their
9:1 me and said, "The S of Israel and the
Neh 1:6 and night for the S of Israel your servants,
1:6 the sins of the S of Israel, which we
7:7 the men of the S of Israel:
8:14 by Moses that the S of Israel should dwell
8:17 to that day the S of Israel had not
9:1 of this month the S of Israel were assembled
Ps 4:2 O S of men, how long will you be
29:1 to the LORD, O S of God, ascribe to
Is 66:20 LORD, just as the S of Israel bring their
Jer 16:14 who brought up the S of Israel out of
16:15 who brought up the S of Israel out of
23:7 who brought up the S of Israel out of
Ezek 2:3 send you to the S of Israel, to a
37:21 I will take the S of Israel from the
43:7 the midst of the S of Israel for ever.
Amos 3:1 spoken against you, O S of Israel, against the
Mic 5:3 shall return to the S of Israel.
Acts 10:36 he sent to the S of Israel, preaching good

SORROW
Sir 2:4 and endure it in S; in changes that humble

SORRY
Tob 2:10 All my kindred were S for me, and Ahikar

SOUL (7)
Gen 2:7 breath of life; and man became a living S
Ps 25:1 To you, O LORD, I lift Up My S
63:8 My S clings to you; your right hand upholds
104:1 Bless the LORD, O My S
119:81 My S languishes for your salvation; I hope in
119:175 Let my S live, that I may praise you,
1Cor 15:45 Adam became a living S; the last Adam became

SOULS (2)
Ps 72:14 violence he redeems their S; and precious is their
74:19 do not forget the S of your poor for

SPARE
Wis 11:26 You S all things, for they are yours, O

SPARED
Wis 12:8 But even these you S, since they were but

SPEAK (3)
Lev 1:2 tent of meeting, saying, S to the sons of
Judg 6:17 it is you who S with me.
Sir 27:7 before you hear him S, for this is the

SPEECHLESS (2)
Dan 10:15 turned my face toward the ground and was S
2Pet 2:16 his own transgression; a S donkey spoke with human

SPIRIT (11)
Tob 3:10 was deeply grieved in S and wept.
Ps 104:29 you take away their S, they die and return
Sir 1:9 wisdom in the holy S; he saw her and
15:5 fill him with a S of wisdom and understanding,
17:6 the knowledge of the S; he filled their hearts
Ezek 37:8 but there was no S in them.
37:9 me, "Prophesy to the S, prophesy, son of man,
37:9 and say to the S, Thus says the Lord
37:9 the four winds, O S, and breathe upon these
37:10 commanded me, and the S came into them, and
Acts 8:16 Holy Spirit; for the S had not yet fallen

SPLENDOR (2)
2Chr 20:21 praise him in holy S, as they went before
Ps 110:3 the day you lead your host in holy S

SPLENID
Esth 15:1 and clothed herself in S attire.

SPLIT
Hab 3:9 Selah You S the earth with rivers.

SPOKE (8)
1Kgs 8:24 to him; yes, you S with your mouth, and
2Chr 6:15 to him; yes, you S with your mouth, and
Neh 9:13 upon Mount Sinai, and S with them from heaven
Jud 16:14 serve you, for you S, and they were made.
Ps 89:19 Of old you S in a vision to your
Jer 32:24 What you S has come to pass, and behold,
Bar 2:24 your words, which you S by your servants the
2:28 great compassion, as you S by your servant Moses

STAND
Sir 17:22 judgments of God, and S firm the lot that

STAY
Sir 2:6 S in fear of him, and grow old in

STEADFASTLY
Acts 2:42 And they held S to the apostles teaching and

STIFFNECKED
Ex 34:9 although it is a S people; and pardon our

STILL (2)
Tob 2:8 and said, "He is S not afraid; he has
Ps 89:9 its waves rise, you S them.

STOOD
Num 22:34 not know that you S in the road against

S

STORE
Sir 4:18 secrets to him, and S up for him knowledge

STRAIGHT (2)
Tob 7:1 "Brother Azariah, take me S to our brother Raguel."
Sir 2:6 in him, and he will make your ways S

STRANGERS (6)
Wis 19:15 hostile reception of the S;
Is 1:7 in your very presence S devour your land; it
1:7 your land; it is desolate, as overthrown by S
14:1 their own land, and S will join them and
25:2 ruin; the palace of S is a city no
25:5 the noise of the S; as heat by the

STRANGLED
Tob 2:3 the market place, and now he lies there S

STREETS
Mt 22:9 Go therefore to the S, and invite to the

STRENGTH
Ps 71:6 from my mothers womb, you have been my S

STRENGTHEN
Sir 4:18 back to him and S him, she will gladden

STRETCH
Acts 4:30 all boldness, while you S out your hand to

STRETCHED
Ex 15:12 You S out your right hand, the earth swallowed

STRIKE (49)
Ex 3:20 out my hand and S Egypt with all the
12:12 night, and I will S all the first-born in
12:13 destroy you, when I S the land of Egypt.
Lev 26:24 and I myself will S you sevenfold for your
Num 25:17 "Harass the Midianites, and S them;
Deut 28:22 The LORD will S you with consumption, and with
28:27 away The LORD Will S you with the boils
28:28 The LORD will S you with madness and blindness
28:35 The LORD Will S you on the knees and
Josh 10:4 me, and let us S Gibeon; for it has
Judg 6:16 you, and you shall S the Midianites as one
20:31 times they began to S and kill some of
20:39 Benjamin had begun to S and kill about thirty
21:10 commanded them, "Go and S the inhabitants of
1Sam 15:3 Now go and S Amalek, and utterly destroy all
20:33 spear at him to S him; so Jonathan knew
26:10 lives, the LORD will S him; or his day
2Sam 2:22 me; why should I S you to the ground?
5:8 that day, "Whoever would S the Jebusites, let him
5:24 out before you to S the army of the
15:14 evil upon us, and S the city with the
1Kgs 14:15 henceforth the Lord will S Israel, as a reed
1Chr 11:6 David said, "Whoever shall S the Jebusites first shall
14:15 out before you to S the army of the
Jud 16:7 sons of the Titans S him, nor did tall
Ps 3:7 For you S all my enemies on the cheek,
121:6 The sun shall not S you by day, nor
Is 3:17 feet; the Lord will S with a scab the
10:24 the Assyrians when they S with the rod and
11:4 earth; and he shall S the earth with the
11:15 his scorching wind, and S it into seven channels
19:22 And the LORD will S Egypt, striking and healing,
49:10 wind nor sun shall S them, for he who
Jer 18:18 Come, let us S him with the tongue, and
21:6 And I will S the inhabitants of this city,
21:7 He shall S them with the edge of the
33:5 men whom I shall S in my anger and
43:11 He shall come and S the land of Egypt,
46:13 king of Babylon to S the land of Egypt:
Ezek 7:9 will know that I am the LORD, who S
21:12 S therefore upon your thigh
32:15 fills it, when I S all who dwell in
Amos 3:15 I will S the winter house with the summer
9:1 altar, and he said: S the capitals until the
Mic 6:13 I have begun to S you, making you desolate
Zech 11:17 May the sword S his arm and his right
14:12 which the LORD will S all the peoples that
Mal 4:6 lest I come and S the land with a
Rev 19:15 sword with which to S the nations, and he

STRIKES (4)
Josh 15:16 And Caleb said, "Whoever S Kiriath-sepher, and
Job 5:18 he binds up; he S, but his hands heal.
Is 30:31 the LORD, when he S with his rod.
Lam 3:30 to the one who S him, and be filled

STRIKING (2)
2Sam 24:17 the angel who was S down the people, and
Is 19:22 LORD will strike Egypt, S and healing, and they

STRIPPED
Hab 3:9 You S the sheath from your bow, and put

STRONGHOLDS
Ps 18:45 lost heart, and came trembling out of their S

STROVE
Deut 33:8 Massah, with whom you S at the waters of

STRUCK (112)
Ex 12:29 At midnight the LORD S all the firstborn in
Lev 26:17 and you shall be S down before your enemies;
Num 11:33 people, and the LORD S the people with a
32:4 land which the LORD S before the congregation of
Deut 3:3 his people; and we S him until no survivor
Josh 8:21 they turned back and S the men of Ai.
8:22 that side; and Israel S them, until there was
8:24 returned to Ai, and S it with the edge
10:10 ascent of Beth-horon, and S them as far as
10:26 And afterward Joshua S them and put them to
10:28 on that day, and S it and its king
10:30 of Israel; and he S it with the edge
10:32 the second day, and S it with the edge
10:33 help Lachish; and Joshua S him and his people,
10:35 on that day, and S it with the edge
10:37 and took it, and S it with the edge
10:39 its towns; and they S them with the edge
11:8 hand of Israel, who S them and chased them
11:8 of Mizpeh; and they S them, until they left
11:10 and took Hazor, and S its king with the
11:12 kings, Joshua took, and S them with the edge
11:14 but every man they S with the edge of
11:17 all their kings, and S them, and put them
Judg 1:8 and took it, and S it with the edge
1:25 the city; and they S the city with the
11:33 And he S them from Aroer to the neighborhood
12:4 the men of Gilead S Ephraim, because they said,
15:8 And he S them hip and thigh with great
18:27 quiet and unsuspecting, and S them with the edge
20:25 the second day, and S down eighteen thousand men
20:37 ambush moved out and S the whole city with
20:39 said, "Surely they are S down before us, as
20:48 against the Benjaminites, and S them with the edge
1Sam 4:8 are the gods who S the Egyptians with every
7:11 pursued the Philistines, and S them, as far as
14:48 he did valiantly, and S the Amalekites, and delivered
17:35 went after him and S him and delivered it
17:35 by his beard, and S him and killed him.
24:5 And afterward Davids heart S him, because he had
25:38 days later the LORD S Nabal; and he died.
27:9 And David S the land, and left neither man
30:17 And David S them from twilight until the evening
2Sam 1:15 And he S him so that he died.
2:23 turn aside; therefore Abner S him in the belly
3:27 privately, and there he S him in the belly,
4:7 in his bedchamber, they S him, and slew him,
5:25 LORD commanded him, and S the Philistines from
6:7 against Uzzah; and God S him there because he
12:9 You have S down Uriah the Hittite with the
23:20 of great deeds; he S two Ariels of Moab.
24:10 But Davids heart S him after he had numbered
1Kgs 20:29 the sons of Israel S a hundred thousand Syrian
2Kgs 8:21 and his chariot commanders S the Edomites who
14:10 You have indeed S down Edom, and your heart
15:5 And the LORD S the king, so that he
18:8 He S the Philistines as far as Gaza and
25:21 the king of Babylon S them, and put them
1Chr 11:22 of great deeds; he S two Ariels of Moab.
13:10 against Uzzah; and he S him because he put
14:16 commanded him, and they S the Philistine army
20:1 And Joab S Rabbah, and overthrew it.
21:7 this thing, and he S Israel.
2Chr 13:20 Abijah; and the LORD S him, and he died.
14:14 And they S all the cities round about Gerar,
14:15 And they S the tents of those who had
21:9 rose by night and S the Edomites who had
21:18 all this the LORD S him in his bowels
25:11 Valley of Salt and S ten thousand men of

	25:19	say, See, I have S Edom, and your heart
	26:20	because the LORD had S him down.
Jud	9:3	with blood, and you S down slaves along with
Esth	9:5	So the Jews S all their enemies with the
Job	26:12	by his understanding he S Rahab.
Ps	69:26	him whom you have S down, and him whom
	78:20	He S the rock so that water gushed out
	78:51	He S all the first born in Egypt, the
	102:4	My heart is S down like grass, and withered;
	105:33	He S their vines and fig trees, and shattered
	105:36	He S all the first born in their land,
	135:8	He it was who S the first born of
	135:10	all his servants; who S many nations and slew
	136:10	ever; to him who S the first born of
	136:17	ever; to him who S great kings, for his
Sir	48:21	The Lord S the camp of the Assyrians, and
Is	1:5	will you still be S down, that you continue
	5:25	hand against them and S them, and the mountains
	9:13	turn to him who S them, nor seek the
	10:20	lean upon him that S them, but will lean
	10:26	scourge, as when he S Midian at the rock
	14:6	scepter of rulers, that S the peoples in wrath
	14:29	that the rod which S you is broken, for
	27:7	he struck those who S them?
	27:7	Has he S them down as he struck those
	27:7	them down as he S those who struck them?
	50:6	back to those who S me, and my cheeks
	53:4	we esteemed him stricken, S down by God, and
	57:17	I was angry, I S him, I hid my
	60:10	in my wrath I S you, but in my
Jer	2:30	In vain have I S down your children, they
	5:3	You have S them down, but they felt no
	14:17	of my people is S down with a great
	14:19	Why have you S us down so that there
	31:19	I was instructed, I S my thigh; I was
	47:1	the Philistines, before Pharaoh S Gaza.
	49:28	of Hazor which Nebuchadrezzar king of Babylon S
	52:27	the king of Babylon S them, and put them
Dan	2:34	human hand, and it S the image on its
Amos	4:9	"I S you with blight and mildew; I laid
	6:11	great house shall be S down into fragments, and
Hag	2:17	I S you and all the products of your
Zech	10:11	the sea shall be S down, and all the
Acts	12:23	angel of the Lord S him, because he did

STUMBLING

Tob	11:10	got up, and came S out through the courtyard

SUBDUED

Neh	9:24	the land, and you S before them the inhabitants

SUCH (3)

Tob	3:6	life and listen to S insults."
Sir	48:11	but our name, after death, will not be S
Mk	13:18	days there will be S tribulation as has not

SUCKLING

1Sam	7:9	So Samuel took a S lamb and offered it

SUFFERING (2)

Neh	9:27	the time of their S, they cried to you
Is	45:10	With what are you S labor pains?"

SUFFERINGS (2)

Mt	24:8	all this is but the beginning of the S
Mk	13:8	famines; this is but the beginning of the S

SUFFICIENCY

2Cor	3:5	coming from us; our S is from God,

SUFFICIENT

2Cor	3:5	Not that we are S of ourselves to claim

SUN

Sir	17:27	What is brighter than the S

SUNSET

Tob	2:4	place of shelter until S when I might bury

SUPPLIED

Wis	16:20	without their toil you S them from heaven with

SURROUND

Ps	32:7	me from trouble; you S me with deliverance.

SURROUNDED (2)

Judg	19:22	the city, base fellows, S the house, beating on
	20:5	rose against me, and S the house by night;

SUSTAINED

Neh	9:21	Forty years you S them in the wilderness, and

SWORD

Ps	144:10	who rescue David your servant from the cruel S

SWORE (5)

Ex	32:13	servants, to whom you S by your own self,
Num	11:12	the land which you S to give their fathers?
Deut	26:15	given us, as you S to our fathers, a
Ps	89:49	by your faithfulness you S to David?
Jer	32:22	this land, which you S to their fathers to

SYMBOL

Heb	11:19	did receive him back and this was a S

SYRIAN

1Kgs	20:29	struck a hundred thousand S foot soldiers in one

T

TAKE (10)

Tob	7:1	to him, "Brother Azariah, T me straight to our
	7:12	T your kinswoman; from now on you are her
	7:13	T her and bring her safely to your father.
	11:11	into his eyes, saying, T courage, Father."
Ps	51:16	For you T no delight in sacrifice; were I
	102:24	I say, "do not T me from here in
	104:29	are dismayed; when you T away their spirit, they
Is	58:3	humbled ourselves, and you T no knowledge of it?
2Tim	1:8	me his prisoner, but T your share of suffering
	2:3	T your share of suffering as a good soldier

TALK (2)

Tob	3:4	you made us the T, the byword, and an
Tit	2:9	they are not to T back,

TEACHING

Sir	24:19	For my T is sweeter than honey, and my

TEAR (8)

Lev	21:10	head hang loose, nor T his clothes;
2Sam	3:31	who were with him, T your clothes, and put
Ps	50:22	forget God, lest I T, and there be none
Eccl	3:7	away; a time to T, and a time to
Is	64:1	O that you would T the heavens and come
Jer	36:24	afraid, nor did they T their garments.
Hos	5:14	I, even I, will T and go away, I
Joel	2:13	and with mourning; and T your hearts and not

TELL

Lk	12:44	Truly I T you, he will set him over

TERRIFYING (3)

Dan	7:7	behold, a fourth beast, T and dreadful and
	7:19	all the rest, exceedingly T, with its teeth of
Zeph	2:11	The LORD will be T against them; yes, he

TEST (10)

Ex	16:4	day, that I may T them, whether they will
	17:2	Why do you put the LORD to the T
	17:7	the LORD to the T by saying, "Is the
	20:20	God has come to T you, and that the
Tob	12:13	I was sent to T you.
Ps	17:3	by night, if you T me, you will find
Sir	4:17	put him to the T; she will bring fear
Jer	11:20	who judge righteously, who T the heart and the
	12:3	you see me, and T my mind toward you.
	20:12	LORD of hosts, who T the righteous, who see

TESTED (3)

Ex	15:25	ordinance and there he T them,
Deut	33:8	godly one, whom you T at Massah, with whom
Wis	11:10	For you T them as a father does in

THANKS

Sir	51:2	I give T to your name, for you have

THANKSGIVING

Sir	17:24	who does not exist, T has ceased; he who

THEMSELVES (2)
2Chr 11:13 in all Israel presented T to him from all
Tob 7:9 had bathed and washed T and had reclined to

THIGH
Ezek 21:12 Strike therefore upon your T

THINGS (3)
Tob 11:16 his father the great T that had happened to
Sir 17:26 For all T cannot be in men, since a
Mt 12:34 can you speak good T, when you are evil?

THINKING
Sir 17:5 them a mind for T, and filled them with

THOUGH (2)
Tob 11:15 T he afflicted me, he has had mercy on
Sir 3:27 taken root in them, T it will not be

THOUGHTS
Sir 4:17 holds her in his T, and she trusts him.

THREE
Num 26:62 of them were twenty T thousand, every male from

THRONE
Sir 1:8 feared, sitting upon his T, and ruling as God.

THUMMIM
Deut 33:8 to Levi O your T, and your Urim to

THUNDER (2)
Ex 19:16 third day there was T and lightning, and a
20:18 the people perceived the T and the lightning and

TIED (2)
Jn 13:4 aside his garments, and T a towel around himself.
13:5 the towel that was T around him.

TIGHTLY
Job 38:38 and the clods cling T together?

TIME
Tob 3:11 At that same T, with hands outstretched toward the

TOBIAS (5)
Tob 2:3 So T went out to look for some poor
6:10 Raphael said to the young man, "Brother T
7:1 they reached Ecbatana, T said to him, "Brother
7:9 had reclined to dine, T said to Raphael, "Brother
7:10 it and said to T, "Eat, drink, and be

TOBIT
Tob 2:9 same night after I, T, returned from burying the

TODAY (2)
1Sam 20:27 Jesse come to the meal, either yesterday or T
Tob 7:12 given to you from T and for ever.

TOGETHER (2)
Tob 2:2 and he shall eat T with me.
Esth 14:3 lay on the earth T with all her maidservants,

TOLD (2)
Neh 9:15 their thirst, and you T them to go in
Tob 7:14 called her mother and T her to bring writing

TOMB (4)
Mt 27:61 the other Mary were there, sitting opposite the T
27:64 again.' Therefore order the T to be made secure
27:66 went and made the T secure by sealing the
28:1 and the other Mary went to see the T

TONGUE
Sir 17:5 them discretion, with a T and eyes and ears;

TOOK (4)
Tob 7:1 So he T him to the house of Raguel,
8:1 to retire; so they T the young man and
Esth 14:5 that you, O Lord, T Israel out of all
Wis 18:5 rescued, in punishment you T away a multitude of

TORE (31)
Gen 37:29 in the pit, he T his clothes
37:34 Then Jacob T his garments, and put sackcloth upon
44:13 Then they T their clothes, and every man loaded
Num 14:6 spied out the land, T their clothes,
Josh 7:6 Then Joshua T his clothes, and fell to the
Judg 11:35 he saw her, he T his clothes, and said,
2Sam 1:11 of his clothes, and T them; and so did
13:19 on her head, and T the long robe which
13:31 the king arose, and T his garments, and lay
13:31 who were standing by t their garments.
1Kgs 19:11 great and strong wind T the mountains, and broke
21:27 heard those words, he T his clothes, and put
2Kgs 2:12 his own clothes and T them in two pieces.
5:7 read the letter, he T his clothes and said,
6:30 of the woman he T his clothes-now he
11:14 And Athaliah T her clothes, and cried, "Treason!
19:1 Hezekiah heard it, he T his clothes, and covered
22:11 of the law, he T his clothes.
2Chr 23:13 And Athaliah T her clothes, and cried, "Treason!
34:19 of the law he T his clothes.
Ezra 9:3 I heard this, I T my garments and my
Jud 14:16 groaned and shouted, and T his garments.
14:19 army heard this, they T their tunics and were
Esth 4:1 had been done, Mordecai T his clothes and put
Job 1:20 Then Job arose, and T his robe, and shaved
2:12 and wept; and they T their robes and sprinkled
Is 37:1 Hezekiah heard it, he T his clothes, and covered
1Mac 2:14 Mattathias and his sons T their clothes, put on
3:47 on their heads, and T their clothes.
4:39 Then they T their clothes, and mourned with great
11:71 Jonathan T his garments and put dust on his

TORMENTED
Wis 12:23 unrighteously you T through their own abominations.

TORN (16)
1Sam 4:12 day, with his clothes T and with earth upon
2Sam 1:2 camp, with his clothes T and earth upon his
15:32 him with his coat T and earth upon his
2Kgs 5:8 king of Israel had T his clothes, he sent
5:8 saying, "Why have you T your clothes?
18:37 Hezekiah with their clothes T, and told him the
22:19 curse, and you have T your clothes and wept
2Chr 34:27 before me, and have T your clothes and wept
Ezra 9:5 garments and my mantle T, and fell upon my
Job 26:8 the cloud is not T under them.
Ps 60:2 to quake, you have T it open; repair its
Is 24:19 broken, the earth is T apart, the earth is
36:22 Hezekiah with their clothes T, and told him the
Bar 6:31 sit with their clothes T, their heads and beards
1Mac 5:14 messengers, with their garments T, came from
13:45 wall with their clothes T, and they cried out

TOSS
Job 30:22 on it, and you T me about in the

TOWEL
Jn 13:4 garments, and tied a T around himself.

TRAMPLED (2)
Hab 3:12 earth in fury, you T the nations in anger.
3:15 You T the sea with your horses, the surging

TREASURE
Sir 3:4 his mother is like one who lays up T

TREATED
Tob 2:10 but the more they T me with ointments, the

TREMBLED
Hab 3:7 affliction; the curtains of the land of Midian T

TRESPASS
Mt 6:12 we forgive those who T against us;

TRESPASSES
Mt 6:12 And forgive us our T, As we forgive those

TRIBE
Num 34:13 and to the half T;

TRIBULATION (2)
Sir 27:5 so the test of just men is in T
Mk 13:18 there will be such T as has not been

TRUE
Tob 7:11 let me explain the T situation to you.

TRULY
Lk 12:44 T I tell you, he will set him over

TRUST
Sir 15:15 save you; if you T in God, you too

TRUTH (4)
Tob 12:11 now declare the whole T to you and I
Sir 2:11 the shield of all who seek him in T
17:20 he has appointed to them the lot of T
Eph 6:14 fastened the belt of T around your waist, and

TRY (3)
1Chr 29:17 my God, that you T the heart, and have
Ps 7:9 the righteous, you who T the minds and hearts,
17:3 If you T my heart, if you visit me

TURN (3)
Esth 14:14 hand of our enemies; T our mourning into gladness
Ps 90:3 You T man back to the dust, and say,
Sir 17:25 forgiveness for those who T to him!

TURNED
Ps 85:3 all your wrath; you T from your hot anger.

TWELVE
Jn 6:67 Jesus said to the T, "Will you also go

TWENTY
Num 26:62 numbered of them were T three thousand, every male

TWO (2)
Tob 2:10 care of me for T years until he went
Ps 136:13 the Red Sea in T, for his mercy endures

U

UNABLE
Tob 2:10 four years I remained U to see, All my

UNCOVER
Is 45:1 nations before him and U the loins of kings,

UNCOVERED
Tob 2:9 and my face was U because of the heat.

UNDERSTANDING (3)
Sir 2:2 and receive words of U, and do not be
15:5 spirit of wisdom and U, and clothe him with
17:6 filled their hearts with U, and showed them good

UNDERSTANDS
Wis 9:9 the world, and who U what is pleasing in

UNFAILING
Sir 24:3 I ordained that an U light should arise in

UNINSTRUCTED
Wis 17:1 hard to describe; therefore U souls have gone astray.

UNKNOWINGLY
2Chr 18:33 drew his bow and U struck the king of

UNLESS
Tob 7:11 will eat nothing here U you make a binding

UPPER
Tob 3:10 up to her fathers U room, she intended to

URGES
2Cor 5:14 the love of Christ U us on, because we

USING
Sir 23:15 A man accustomed to U insulting words will never

USUAL
Ex 14:27 sea returned to its U flow when the morning

UTTERLY-THESE
1Kgs 9:21 were unable to destroy U Solomon made a forced

V

VALIANTLY
Ps 118:15 righteous: "The right hand of the LORD does V

VIRGIN (2)
Is 7:14 Behold, a V shall conceive and bear a son,
1Cor 7:34 the unmarried woman or V is anxious about the

VIRGINITY
Deut 22:17 not find in your daughter the tokens of V

VIRTUOUS
Jud 8:7 prudent of heart, discerning in judgment, and quite V

VISION
Tob 2:10 ointments, the more my V was obscured by the

VISIT (2)
Ps 17:3 my heart, if you V me by night, if
65:9 You V the earth and water it, you greatly

VOW
Judg 11:35 the LORD, and I cannot take back My V

W

WAGES (3)
Tob 2:12 product to the owners, and they paid her W
2:12 they paid her full W and they also gave
12:5 him, "Take for your W half of all that

WAIST
Eph 6:14 of truth around your W, and having put on

WAISTS
Ezek 23:15 with belts around their W, with flowing turbans on

WAIT
Ex 24:14 said to the elders, W here for us, until

WALK (8)
Is 60:3 And nations shall W by your light, and kings
Eph 4:1 Lord, beg you to W in a manner worthy
4:17 walk as the Gentiles W, in the futility of
4:17 you must no longer W as the Gentiles walk,
Phil 3:17 mark those who so W as you have an
3:18 you even with tears, W as enemies of the
1Thes 2:12 and charged you to W in a manner worthy
4:1 how you ought to W and to please God,

WALKED (2)
1Kgs 19:8 ate and drank, and W in the strength of
Jn 6:66 back and no longer W with him.

WALKING (2)
2Thes 3:6 any brother who is W in idleness and not
3:11 some of you are W in idleness, mere busybodies,

WALL
2Kgs 6:30 passing by upon the W and the people looked,

WANTED (2)
Tob 8:1 eating and drinking, they W to retire; so they
Wis 12:6 murder helpless lives, you W to destroy by the

WAR
Num 31:42 who had gone to W

WARMLY
Tob 7:9 ram from the flock and received them very W

WARNED (2)
Neh 9:29 And you W them in order to turn them
9:30 bore with them, and W them by your Spirit

WASHED
Tob 7:9 they had bathed and W themselves and had reclined

WASTE
Acts 8:3 But Saul laid W the Church, and entering house

WATCH
Job 13:27 in the stocks, and W all my paths; you

WATER (3)
Ps 65:9 visit the earth and W it, you greatly enrich
65:10 You W its furrows abundantly, settling its ridges,
104:13 your lofty abode you W the mountains; the earth

WAY (4)
2Chr 6:27 teach them the good W, in which they should
Sir 36:17 direct us in the W of righteousness, and all
Phil 1:7 me to feel this W about you all, because
4:1 stand firm in this W in the Lord, my

WAYS
Sir 2:3 that you may be wise in all your W

WEARIED
Ps 95:10 forty years I was W of that generation and

WEARING (2)
1Kgs 22:10 sitting on their thrones, W their robes, at the
Rev 19:14 the armies of heaven, W fine linen, white and

WEEDS
Jon 2:6 wrapped about my head W were wrapped about my

WEEPING (4)
Mt 13:42 where there will be W and gnashing of teeth.
13:50 where there will be W and gnashing of teeth.
22:13 where there will be W and gnashing of teeth.
25:30 where there will be W and gnashing of teeth.

WELCOME
Tob 7:1 replied, "Joyous greetings, brothers; W and good

WELL (3)
Num 16:2 chosen from the assembly, W known men;
Sir 17:24 who is alive and W sings the Lords praises.
Lk 6:29 your cloak do not withhold your coat as W

WELL-BEING (2)
Esth 14:14 our mourning into gladness and our affliction into W
Is 45:7 create darkness, I make W and create woe, I

WEPT
Tob 3:10 day she was deeply grieved in spirit and W

WHEY
Job 28:4 a valley away from W men live; they are

WHOEVER (2)
Sir 3:4 he is heard; and W glorifies his mother is
3:5 W honors his father will be gladdened by his

WHOLE (2)
Judg 20:37 out and struck the W city with the edge
Tob 12:11 will now declare the W truth to you and

WIFE
Tob 7:13 her to be your W in accordance with the

WILLED
Jud 9:6 and the things you W presented themselves and said,

WIN
Sir 4:12 seek her early will W the Lords good favor.

WIND
Is 26:17 we writhed, but we gave birth only to W

WINDOW
Tob 3:11 hands outstretched toward the W, she prayed and said,

WISDOM (3)
Job 28:20 "From where does W come?
Sir 1:9 The Lord himself created W in the holy spirit;
15:5 with a spirit of W and understanding, and clothe

WISE (2)
Sir 2:3 that you may be W in all your ways.
3:28 the words of the W, and an attentive ear

WISER
Lk 16:8 of this world, are W in their own generation

WITHDREW
Ps 85:3 Selah You W all your wrath; you turned from

WITNESSES
Jer 32:25 for money and get W though the city is given

WOMAN (2)
Num 25:8 of Israel and the W through her body.
Is 45:10 or to a W With what are you suffering

WOMB
Ps 71:6 birth; from my mothers W, you have been my

WONDROUS
Sir 17:8 them glory in his W deeds,

WONDROUSLY
Ps 139:14 you, for I am W made.

WORD (2)
Jn 17:6 them to me, and they have kept your W
2Tim 4:17 strength to proclaim the W fully, that all the

WORDS (2)
Sir 2:2 your ear, and receive W of understanding, and do
3:28 man will ponder the W of the wise, and

WORKS (4)
Ps 77:14 are the God who W wonders, who have manifested
Sir 3:22 about many of his W, for you do not
17:7 their hearts, showing them the majesty of his W
Jn 8:41 You do the W of your father." They said

WORLD
Lk 16:8 the sons of this W, are wiser in their

WORSHIPPED (2)
Jud 13:17 and bowed down and W God, and said with
Esth 15:1 in which she had W, and clothed herself in

WOVEN
Tob 2:12 a piece she had W and sent it to

WRAPPED (2)
Ezek 16:10 you with leather, I W you in fine linen
Jon 2:6 my head weeds were W about my head at

WRITE
Job 13:26 For you W bitter things against me and make

WRITHED
Is 26:17 were with child, we W, but we gave birth

WRITING
Tob 7:14 told her to bring W material; and he wrote

WRITTEN
Tob 7:13 law and the decree W in the book of

Y

YEARS (2)
Tob 2:10 For four Y I remained unable to see, All
2:10 of me for two Y until he went to

YES (83)
Ex 6:1 will send them out, Y, with a strong hand
Deut 29:24 his anger and wrath Y, all the nations would
33:3 Y, he loved his people; I all those consecrated
33:28 of grain and wine; Y, his heavens drop down
Judg 5:4 and the heavens dropped, Y, the clouds dropped
18:10 The land is broad; Y, God has given it
2Sam 22:29 Y, you are my lamp, O LORD, and my
22:30 Y, by you I can crush a troop, and
23:5 Y, does not my house stand so with God?
1Kgs 8:24 you declared to him; Y, you spoke with your
8:30 pray toward this place; Y, hear in heaven your
1Chr 16:30 him, all the earth; Y, the world stands firm,
2Chr 6:15 you declared to him; Y, you spoke with your
6:21 pray toward this place; Y, hear from heaven your
Neh 1:6 Y, I and my fathers house have sinned.
Jud 9:5 Y, the things you intended came to pass,
Job 3:7 Y let that night be barren; let no joyful
18:5 Y, the light of the wicked is put out,
30:23 Y, I know that you will bring me to
Ps 10:14 You see; Y, you note trouble and vexation, that
16:6 me in pleasant places; Y, I have a goodly

Y
Z